Collins

COBUILD
IELTS
Dictionary

HarperCollins Publishers
Westerhill Road
Bishopbriggs
Glasgow
G64 2QT

First edition 2015

10 9 8 7 6 5 4 3 2 1

© HarperCollins Publishers 2015

ISBN 978-0-00-810083-4

Collins® and COBUILD® are registered
trademarks of HarperCollins Publishers Limited

Copyright © HarperCollins Publishers 2015:
Dictionary text, preliminary material,
Writing for IELTS supplement,
Speaking for IELTS supplement

Copyright © HarperCollins Publishers and
New Oriental 2015: Learner features,
including Usage Notes, Vocabulary Builders,
Which Word?, Word Connections, Word
Families, Word Parts and Words in Context
features.

www.collinsdictionary.com/cobuild
www.collinselt.com

A catalogue record for this book is available
from the British Library

Printed in China by South China Printing Co. Ltd

Typeset by Davidson Publishing Solutions,
Glasgow, Scotland

Contents

Publishers and editorial team

For the publisher
Elaine Higgleton
Lisa Sutherland
Celia Wigley

Managing Editor
Penny Hands

Project Managers
Ian Brookes
Mary O'Neill

Contributors
Sandra Anderson
Sarah Chatwin
Rosalind Combley
Andrew Delahunty
Lucy Hollingworth
Virginia Klein
Julie Moore
Kester Newill
Alison Sadler
Chia Suan Chong
Elspeth Summers
Peter Travis
Laura Wedgeworth

Computing Support
Thomas Callan
Krzysztof Siwiec
Agnieszka Urbanowicz

The publishers wish to acknowledge the following sources used for information when writing the sample tasks for the **Writing for IELTS** *guide:*

Household expenditure
Components of Household Expenditure 2008: ONS, Family Spending 2008, © Crown copyright 2010
Adapted from data from the Office for National Statistics licensed under the Open Government Licence v.1.0.

The manufacture of cornflakes
Illustrations based on information taken from How Products Are Made: Volume 3: Cereal
(http://www.madehow.com/Volume-3/Cereal.html) Website administered by Advameg Inc.

The publishers have made every effort to trace copyright holders. Any who have not been acknowledged are invited to contact the publishers so that appropriate acknowledgement may be made in future printings.

About COBUILD dictionaries

When the first COBUILD dictionary was published in 1987, it revolutionized dictionaries for learners. It was the first of a new generation of dictionaries that were based on actual evidence of how English was used, rather than lexicographer intuition.

Collins and the University of Birmingham, led by linguist John Sinclair, developed an electronic corpus in the 1980s called the Collins Birmingham University International Language Database (COBUILD). This corpus, which is also known as the Collins Corpus, became the largest collection of English-language data in the world, and COBUILD dictionary editors use the corpus to analyse the way that people really use the language.

The Collins Corpus contains 4.5 billion words taken from websites, newspapers, magazines, and books published around the world, and from spoken material from radio, TV, and everyday conversations. New data is added to the corpus every month, to help COBUILD editors identify new words and meanings from the moment they are first used.

All COBUILD dictionaries are based on the information our editors find in the Collins Corpus. Because the corpus is so large, our editors can look at lots of examples of how people really use the words. The data tells us how words are used; what they mean; which words are used together; and how often words are used.

This information helps us decide which words to include in COBUILD dictionaries. Did you know, for example, that around 90% of English speech and writing is made up of approximately 3,500 words? The corpus tells us which these words are, and helps us ensure that when you use a COBUILD dictionary, you can be sure that you are learning the words you really need to know.

All of the examples in COBUILD dictionaries are examples of real English, taken from the Collins Corpus. The examples have been carefully chosen to demonstrate typical grammatical patterns, typical vocabulary, and typical contexts for your word.

The corpus lies at the heart of COBUILD and you can be confident that COBUILD will show you what you need to know to be able to communicate easily and accurately in English.

Introduction

Welcome to the **Collins COBUILD IELTS Dictionary**, a brand-new dictionary, specially created for students preparing for the IELTS exam. The content has been carefully selected and compiled to give you all the information you need to prepare for the exam, and to help you achieve the IELTS score you are aiming for.

The Collins Corpus

The **Collins COBUILD IELTS Dictionary**, like all Collins dictionaries, has been created using the Collins Corpus – a huge database of language which contains over 4.5 billion words of contemporary English. The corpus is central to all the information given in Collins dictionaries. It allows us to look in detail at how the language works, so that we can explain meanings, and describe how the language really works with confidence and accuracy.

Content

The Collins Corpus also allows us to see how frequently words occur in the language, and to identify the words that IELTS candidates need to master in order to achieve a high score. You will see that some words in the dictionary are highlighted with a star ✪. These are words that we have identified as being particularly important to IELTS candidates. They are words which regularly appear in discussions of IELTS topics, or which are often used in formal, written contexts. An understanding of the meanings and usage patterns of these words will provide you with a solid grounding in the key words you need when working towards the IELTS exam.

Coverage

In today's globalized world, learners of English need to be aware of the different varieties of English that are spoken around the world. The **Collins COBUILD IELTS Dictionary** clearly shows you which words and phrases are particular to British or American English.

Definitions

One of the most practical and helpful features of the dictionary is the full-sentence definition. Every word is explained in a complete sentence, just as your teacher or a native speaker of English might explain it to you. Definitions formulated in this way use vocabulary and grammatical structures that occur naturally with the word being explained. They give you much more than the meaning of the word that you are looking up, and also contain information on collocates, grammar, context, and usage. The fullness of the definition helps you to understand not only the meaning of the word, but how to use it properly, and how to 'make it your own'.

Examples

All of the examples in this dictionary have been selected from the Collins Corpus. They have been chosen carefully to reflect the style of language used in IELTS texts. Since they are examples of real English, you can be sure that they show the word in use in a natural context.

Additional features

Where relevant, the dictionary provides useful information about grammatical patterns, for example, whether a word is typically followed by a preposition or an infinitive, or whether a noun is typically used with the plural form of a verb. There is a full explanation of the terms and notations used on pages xviii–xxvii.

Many entries give synonyms and antonyms to help you broaden your range of vocabulary and create more variety in your writing style.

You will also find notes giving you additional information about different ways in which the word is used.

Vocabulary enrichment

Another exciting innovation in this dictionary is its 500 vocabulary enrichment features. These eye-catching boxes focus on words that are essential for IELTS. They help you expand your vocabulary and better understand the relationships between words and the contexts in which they appear. They will enable you to use English accurately and confidently when you sit the examination. There is a full explanation of these vocabulary features on pages xv–xvii.

Writing and Speaking guides

While a knowledge of vocabulary and grammatical structures is essential, the ultimate goal is to be able to use the language you have learnt fluently and appropriately in your writing and when speaking. For all the help you need to produce polished written texts and to achieve fluency in your spoken English, turn to the two guides near the end of the book: **Writing for IELTS** and **Speaking for IELTS**.

The **Writing for IELTS** guide gives advice on how to write clearly and effectively in English. It covers general skills, and provides help with writing for academic purposes. The focus is on the writing tasks involved in the IELTS exam.

The **Speaking for IELTS** guide helps you to prepare for the IELTS speaking test. It focuses on the words and structures you need to speak clearly and confidently about yourself and about important topics that typically come up in the IELTS speaking exam. Strategies are given for managing situations such as presenting an argument, giving an opinion, and clarifying what you have just said.

Introduction

Both guides give plenty of examples of real English, and the sample texts fully illustrate the vocabulary and structures being explained. You will also find tips for preparing for the exam: in fact, the guides provide all you need to know to get ready for the test.

Make sure you read these guides as well as consulting the main part of the dictionary. By covering all the bases, you will be ensuring that you are completely prepared to sit the IELTS exam.

We hope you will enjoy preparing for IELTS using the **Collins COBUILD IELTS Dictionary**. Not only will it help you to achieve the IELTS score you are aiming for, but it will also equip you for success in the future.

Guide to the dictionary entries

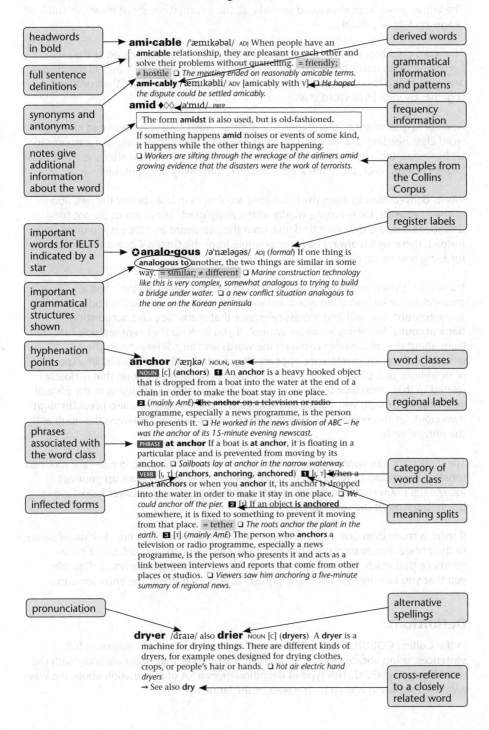

headwords in bold → **ami·cable** /'æmɪkəbəl/ ADJ When people have an amicable relationship, they are pleasant to each other and solve their problems without quarrelling. = friendly; ≠ hostile ❑ *The meeting ended on reasonably amicable terms.*

← **derived words**

full sentence definitions

ami·cably /'æmɪkəbli/ ADV [amicably with v] ❑ *He hoped the dispute could be settled amicably.*

← **grammatical information and patterns**

amid ◆◇◇ /ə'mɪd/ PREP

← **frequency information**

synonyms and antonyms

The form **amidst** is also used, but is old-fashioned.

notes give additional information about the word

If something happens **amid** noises or events of some kind, it happens while the other things are happening. ❑ *Workers are sifting through the wreckage of the airliners amid growing evidence that the disasters were the work of terrorists.*

← **examples from the Collins Corpus**

← **register labels**

important words for IELTS indicated by a star → **✪analo·gous** /ə'næləgəs/ ADJ (*formal*) If one thing is (analogous to) another, the two things are similar in some way. = similar; ≠ different ❑ *Marine construction technology like this is very complex, somewhat analogous to trying to build a bridge under water.* ❑ *a new conflict situation analogous to the one on the Korean peninsula*

important grammatical structures shown

hyphenation points

an·chor /'æŋkə/ NOUN, VERB

← **word classes**

NOUN [c] (**anchors**) **1** An **anchor** is a heavy hooked object that is dropped from a boat into the water at the end of a chain in order to make the boat stay in one place.

2 (*mainly AmE*) The anchor on a television or radio programme, especially a news programme, is the person who presents it. ❑ *He worked in the news division of ABC – he was the anchor of its 15-minute evening newscast.*

← **regional labels**

phrases associated with the word class

PHRASE at anchor If a boat is **at anchor**, it is floating in a particular place and is prevented from moving by its anchor. ❑ *Sailboats lay at anchor in the narrow waterway.*

VERB [I, T] (**anchors, anchoring, anchored**) **1** [I, T] When a boat **anchors** or when you **anchor** it, its anchor is dropped into the water in order to make it stay in one place. ❑ *We could anchor off the pier.* **2** [T] If an object **is anchored** somewhere, it is fixed to something to prevent it moving from that place. = tether ❑ *The roots anchor the plant in the earth.* **3** [T] (*mainly AmE*) The person who **anchors** a television or radio programme, especially a news programme, is the person who presents it and acts as a link between interviews and reports that come from other places or studios. ❑ *Viewers saw him anchoring a five-minute summary of regional news.*

← **category of word class**

inflected forms

← **meaning splits**

pronunciation

← **alternative spellings**

dry·er /draɪə/ also **drier** NOUN [c] (**dryers**) A **dryer** is a machine for drying things. There are different kinds of dryers, for example ones designed for drying clothes, crops, or people's hair or hands. ❑ *hot air electric hand dryers*
→ See also **dry** ◄

← **cross-reference to a closely related word**

ix

Structure of entries

The entries have been structured to make all the information about meaning and usage as clear as possible.

The word class that a word belongs to – noun, verb, etc – is indicated at the beginning of an entry. If a word belongs to more than one word class, all the classes are listed at the beginning of the entry. The senses of the word are then grouped together by individual word class.

Additional grammatical information about these word classes is presented after the word class heading. If a verb can be both transitive and intransitive, or if a noun can be both countable and uncountable, this information is indicated after the word class heading. Then, each sense has a label to show transitivity or countability.

Words derived directly from the headword are shown in bold below the definitions of the headword, for example, **gladly** at the entry **glad**. These words do not have definitions because they directly derive from the headword and are easy to understand. Instead, these words always have an example from the Collins Corpus that makes the meaning and usage clear.

If a word is closely related to another word in the dictionary, you will find a cross-reference to that other word. For example, on a new line at the end of the entry **account**, you will find a cross-reference that reads 'See also **accounting, bank account**' following an arrow symbol. If you look up these entries, you can learn about the relationship between the words and any differences in their meanings. If the cross-reference appears after a number and at the end of a group of definitions of a phrasal verb, then the cross-reference is to a noun that is closely related to that phrasal verb. For example, at the end of the definitions of the phrasal verb **break through**, you will find a cross-reference that reads 'See also **breakthrough**'. If you look up this entry, you can learn about the relationship between the noun and the phrasal verb.

The dictionary also contains a large number of idiomatic phrases. Phrases are grouped together according to word class. So, for example, the idiom **clean up your act** follows the noun senses of the word **act**, and the phrasal verb **answer back** follows the verb senses of the word **answer**.

If there is more than one important word in a phrase, you might find a cross-reference to the phrase. For example, at the end of the entry **length**, you will find a cross-reference that reads 'at arm's length → see arm', following a diamond. This tells you that you can find the idiomatic phrase 'at arm's length' at the entry for **arm**.

Definitions

In the **Collins COBUILD IELTS Dictionary**, all the definitions are written in full sentences, using vocabulary and grammatical structures that occur naturally with the word being explained. This type of definition gives a lot of information about the way a word or meaning is used by speakers of the language.

Information about collocates and structure

For each definition, the word or phrase being defined is printed in bold. In addition, we have highlighted in bold those words which combine with the headword to make a set structure, for example:

> A **band of** people is … (at **band**)
> If you **say** something **to yourself**, you think it … (at **say**)
> If you are **unable to** do something, it is … (at **unable**)

In our definitions, we show the typical collocates of a word: that is, the other words that are commonly used with the word being defined. For example, the definition of the adjective **savoury** reads:

> **sa•voury** /'seɪvəri/ (in AmE, use savory) ADJ **Savoury** food has a salty or spicy flavour rather than a sweet one. □ all

This shows that you use the adjective *savoury* to describe food.

Information about grammar

The definitions also give information about the grammatical structures in which a word is used. For example, meaning 1 of the adjective **candid** reads:

> **can•did** /'kændɪd/ ADJ ■ When you are **candid** about something or with someone, you speak honestly.

This shows that you use **candid** with the preposition *about* before a thing and *with* before a person.

Other definitions show information about transitivity and the type of subject or object that a verb takes. For example, meaning 1 of the verb **soften** reads:

> softened) ■ [I, T] If you **soften** something or if it **softens**, it becomes less hard, stiff, or firm. □ Soften the butter

This shows that the verb can be used both transitively and intransitively. In the transitive use, it takes a human subject and a non-human object. In the intransitive use, it takes a non-human subject.

Finally, the definition of the verb **compel** reads:

> VERB [T] (compels, compelling, compelled) If a situation, a rule, or a person **compels** you **to** do something, they force you to do it. □ the introduction of legislation to compel cyclists

This shows you what types of subject and object to use with **compel**, and it also shows that you typically use the verb in a structure with a to-infinitive.

Information about context and usage

In addition to information about collocation and grammar, definitions also can convey your evaluation of something, for example to express your approval or disapproval. Look at the definition of **unhelpful**:

> **un•help•ful** /ˌʌn'helpfʊl/ ADJ If you say that someone or something is **unhelpful**, you mean that they do not help you or improve a situation, and may even make things worse. □ The criticism is both unfair and unhelpful.

In this definition, the expressions 'if you say that' and 'you mean that' indicate that these words are used subjectively, rather than objectively.

Other kinds of definition

We sometimes explain grammatical words and other function words by paraphrasing the word in context. For example, meaning 3 of the preposition **through** reads:

> flesh but not the bones. **3** To go **through** a town, area, or country means to travel across it or in it. ▢ *Go through*

In many cases, it is impossible to paraphrase the word, and so we explain its function instead. For example, the definition of **unfortunately** reads:

> You can use **unfortunately** to introduce or refer to a statement when you consider that it is sad or disappointing, or when you want to express regret.

Lastly, some full definitions are expressed as if they are cross-references. For example:

> **lab** /læb/ NOUN [c] (labs) A **lab** is the same as a **laboratory**.

If you need to know more about the word **laboratory**, you should look at that entry.

Style and usage

Some words or meanings are used mainly by particular groups of people, or in particular social contexts. In this dictionary, where relevant, entries also give information about the kind of people who are likely to use a word or expression (for example journalists or businesspeople), and the type of social situation in which it is used. This information is shown in italics and within brackets.

In terms of geographical diversity, this dictionary focuses on British and American English using evidence from the Collins Corpus. Where relevant, the American or British form is shown at its equivalent word or meaning.

Geographical labels

BrE (British English): used mainly by speakers and writers in Britain, and in other places where British English is used or taught. Where relevant, the American equivalent is provided.

AmE (American English): used mainly by speakers and writers in the US, and in other places where American English is used or taught. Where relevant, the British equivalent is provided.

Style labels

academic word: from the Academic Word List and often used in academic texts such as essays, e.g. **denote**

business: used mainly when talking about the field of business, e.g. **market share**

computing: used mainly when talking about the field of computing, e.g. **search engine**

formal: used mainly in official situations, or by political and business organizations, or when speaking or writing to people in authority, e.g. **commence**

humorous:	used mainly to indicate that a word or expression is used in a humorous way, e.g. **bite the dust**
informal:	used mainly in informal situations, conversations, and personal letters, e.g. **okay**
journalism:	used mainly in journalism, e.g. **spearhead**
legal:	used mainly in legal documents, in law courts, and by the police in official situations, e.g. **manslaughter**
literary:	used mainly in novels, poetry, and other forms of literature, e.g. **toil**
medical:	used mainly in medical texts, and by doctors in official situations, e.g. **cardiac**
military:	used mainly when talking or writing about military terms, e.g. **mobilize**
offensive:	likely to offend people, or to insult them; words labelled offensive should therefore usually be avoided, e.g. **cripple** (noun)
old-fashioned:	generally considered to be old-fashioned, and no longer in common use, e.g. **spectacles**
spoken:	used mainly in speech rather than in writing, e.g. **pardon**
technical:	used mainly when talking or writing about objects, events, or processes in a specialist subject, such as business, science, or music, e.g. **biotechnology**
trademark:	used to show a designated trademark, e.g. **Biro**
vulgar:	used mainly to describe words which could be considered taboo by some people; words labelled 'vulgar' should therefore usually be avoided, e.g. **damn**
written:	used mainly in writing rather than in speech, e.g. **Dear Sir**

Pragmatics labels

Many uses of words need more than a simple definition to be properly explained. People use words to express their feelings or their attitude, to emphasize what they are saying, and so on. The study and description of the way in which people use language to do these things is called pragmatics.

In the dictionary, we draw attention to certain pragmatic aspects of words and phrases of English. The following labels are used:

approval:	used to show that you approve of the person or thing you are talking about, e.g. **dependable**
disapproval:	used to show that you disapprove of the person or thing you are talking about, e.g. **brute**
emphasis:	used to emphasize the point you are making, e.g. **obviously**
feelings:	used to express your feelings about something, or towards someone, e.g. **unfortunately**

Guide to the dictionary entries

formulae: used in particular situations such as greeting and thanking people, or acknowledging something, e.g. **hello, of course**

politeness: used to express politeness, sometimes even to the point of being euphemistic, e.g. **elderly**

vagueness: used to show how certain you are about the truth or validity of your statements; this is sometimes called 'hedging' or 'modality', e.g. **presumably**

Frequency banding

Information on the frequency of words in this dictionary is given using three frequency bands, shown as diamonds after the headword. The most frequent words have three diamonds, the next most frequent two, and the ones which are less frequent have one diamond. Try to learn these words with one, two, or three diamonds first. They will also help you to understand all the other definitions in the dictionary.

Key words for the IELTS examination

The **Collins COBUILD IELTS Dictionary** highlights with a star ✪ the vocabulary that is especially useful for the IELTS examination.

Focus on academic words

In this dictionary, words that are typically found in academic texts are labelled '(*academic word*)'. This label appears at all entries where the headword can be found in the 'Academic Word List'.

What is the Academic Word List?

The Academic Word List (or 'AWL', as it is commonly known) is a list of the most frequently occurring words in English-language academic texts.

The list was compiled by Averil Coxhead at the Victoria University of Wellington, New Zealand.

The AWL consists of 570 word families, and is divided into 10 sublists, organized by frequency.

The list was compiled based on an analysis of over 3.5 million words of text comprising academic journals, textbooks, course workbooks, lab manuals, and course notes.

Knowing this 'AWL' vocabulary will go a long way towards increasing your IELTS score, and stand you in good stead for studying at an English-speaking university.

Guide to vocabulary features

Usage Note

These notes highlight and explain areas of language that learners of English often have difficulty with. They explain how to use a word, for example by telling you which preposition should be used after it, or whether you should use a to-infinitive or an -ing form after it.

The usage notes often tell you what you should _not_ say, as well as what you should say. Typical usage errors are shown with a line through them, like this:

> Do not say that someone should 'avoid to do something'.
> Say that they should 'avoid doing' it.

Each note contains an example of typical usage taken from the Collins Corpus.

Vocabulary Builder

Vocabulary Builders encourage you to build on what you already know by presenting a range of words that are similar in meaning. A short definition at each word will help you to understand how each word should be used. Information on meaning, level of formality, typical context, and the way the words are used in a sentence helps you to use them with confidence and accuracy.

For example, at the entry for **refer**, the verbs _mention, cite, touch on,_ and _quote_ are presented in the Vocabulary Builder.

Each word in the Vocabulary Builder is followed by an example of typical usage.

VOCABULARY BUILDER
allow VERB
If you **allow** something to happen, you do not prevent it.
❑ _Only one staff member was allowed to enter with her._
permit VERB (formal)
If someone or something **permits** something, they allow it to happen.
❑ _The UN Charter permits the use of force for self-defence._
approve VERB
If someone in a position of authority **approves** a plan or idea, they formally agree to it and say that it can happen.
❑ _MPs approved the Bill by a majority of 97._
consent VERB (formal)
If you **consent to** something, you agree to do it or to allow it to be done, although you may not necessarily be pleased about it.
❑ _He asked if she would consent to a small celebration after the christening._
tolerate VERB
If you **tolerate** a situation, you accept it although you do not particularly like it.
❑ _The police have made it clear that they will not tolerate this type of violent behaviour._

Which Word?

This feature identifies pairs or sets of words that learners often confuse, for example, *admit/acknowledge; between/ among*. The notes explain how these words differ in meaning, and help you to use them accurately and in the correct context.

An example of typical usage is given for each of the words in the pair or set.

WHICH WORD?
arrive or reach?
The verbs **arrive** and **reach** are both used to talk about someone coming to a place at the end of a journey. You usually say that someone **arrives at** a place.
❑ We **arrived at** Victoria station.
However, you say that someone **arrives in** a country or city.
❑ He **arrived in** France on Tuesday.
Reach always takes a direct object. You do not say that someone reaches at a place or reaches to a place.
❑ It was dark by the time I **reached** their house.
Reach can also be used to talk about something getting to a particular point or level. You do not say that something reaches at or reaches to a particular level.
❑ Worldwide, the number of robots is expected to **reach** 873,100 by the end of the decade.

Word Connections

Word Connections boxes show you the strongest and most frequent collocations (words which often go together) of the words that you are most likely to need for the IELTS examination. Most of the Word Connections boxes appear at entries for nouns and verbs, but some appear at adjectives and adverbs.

For each collocation, the headword is repeated, and the collocate (the word that goes with the headword) is given in bold.

WORD CONNECTIONS
VERB + **discussion**
hold a discussion
have a discussion
initiate a discussion
❑ Discussions were held between the police and community representatives.
ADJ + **discussion**
a **detailed** discussion
a **preliminary** discussion
a **frank** discussion
❑ We have had detailed discussions with all relevant parties.
lengthy discussions
further discussions
informal discussions
❑ The majority of problems are resolved by informal discussions outside these meetings.

The boxes are divided first into collocation pattern, e.g. verb + **ability**, and then, within that division, by sense. In some cases, collocations within a single sense can be further divided. For example, within verb + **relationship**, we have *establish, start, form* in one collocate set, and *strengthen, improve* in another.

One word from each group is illustrated with an example from the corpus.

Word Families

Word Families are sets of words that are all related to the headword. For example the words *significant, significantly, significance,* and *insignificant* all appear in the Word Families box at the entry for **significant**.

Each word in the word family is labelled with its part of speech (verb, noun, adjective, etc), followed by an example of use from the corpus, helping you to see how it should be used in a sentence.

WORD FAMILIES	
significant ADJ	The study is too small to show whether this trend is statistically **significant**.
insignificant ADJ	In 1949 Bonn was a small, **insignificant** city.
significance NOUN	People were slow to realize the **significance** of the discovery.
insignificance NOUN	Events that seem very important at the time can later fade into **insignificance**.
significantly ADV	The groups differed **significantly** in two areas.

Word Parts

Word Parts boxes show you how and where to use English prefixes such as *anti-*, *pre-*, and *sub-*. They appear near the beginning of the set of words that begin with this prefix, and a note explains how it affects the meanings of words.

Some of the most common words that take this prefix are then given, followed by a part of speech.

WORD PARTS
The prefix *ante-* often appears in words that have 'before' as part of their meaning: antenatal (ADJ) antecedent (NOUN) anteroom (NOUN)

Words in Context

Words in Context boxes contain texts that demonstrate the use of a vocabulary set relating to a particular topic. All Words in Context texts relate to typical IELTS topics such as technology, the environment, or education.

There are two types of text in Words in Context boxes: mini-essays and semi-authentic materials. Mini-essays replicate the type of discursive essay that you might be required to write for IELTS, and the semi-authentic materials might consist of a report, an email, or a public information leaflet, showing how the words would typically appear in a real-life written context.

WORDS IN CONTEXT: EDUCATION

Remote learning is an ideal choice for people wanting to return to or further their education.

To what extent do you agree or disagree?

Remote or **distance learning** is a very flexible way of studying that enables a student to **study at their own pace** and at a time and place that suits them. It is generally cheaper than the **tuition fees** for a **face-to-face course**, and there are no costly travel expenses. It is particularly useful for people in work who are unable to take time off, allowing them to **top up skills** or to improve their career prospects by **gaining qualifications**. It is also useful for individuals who live a long distance from their local **college** or **university**.

However, in my opinion, distance learning does not suit everyone. Although students often get the chance to meet **tutors** and other students through **residential courses**, the majority of time is spent doing **self-study**. Students therefore need to be **highly motivated** and have the **discipline** to **meet assignment deadlines** and to keep up to date with their **studies**. The courses also tend to be technology-based with access to **online forums** and **virtual learning environments**. This can be daunting for older people who are not confident with technology, and who might have trouble **logging in** and accessing **digital materials**.

List of grammatical notations

Word classes

adjective	ADJ
adverb	ADV
colour word	COLOUR
combining form	COMB
conjunction	CONJ
convention	CONVENTION
determiner	DET
exclamation	EXCLAM
irregular verb, noun, or adjective form	IRREG FORM
noun	NOUN
number	NUM
phrasal verb	PHRASAL VERB
phrase	PHRASE
predeterminer	PREDET
preposition	PREP
pronoun	PRON
quantifier	QUANT
question word	QUEST
verb	VERB

Categories of word class

Noun

countable noun	C
variable noun	C, U
plural noun	PLURAL
singular noun	SING
uncountable noun	U

Verb

auxiliary verb	AUX
intransitive verb	I
intransitive or transitive verb	I, T
link verb	LINK
modal verb	MODAL
passive verb	PASSIVE
reciprocal verb	RECIP
passive reciprocal verb	RECIP-PASSIVE
transitive verb	T

Words and abbreviations used in patterns

adjective group	ADJ
superlative form	ADJ-SUPERL
adverb group	ADV
word or phrase indicating an amount of something	AMOUNT
broad negative	BRD-NEG
clause	CL
comparative form	COMPAR
continuous	CONT
definite noun group	DEF-N
definite noun group with a noun in the plural	DEF-PL-N
determiner	DET
past participle of a verb	-ED
noun group or adjective, adverb, or prepositional phrase	GROUP
infinitive form of a verb	INF
present participle of a verb	-ING
introductory 'it'	'it'
noun or noun group	N
negative word	NEG
proper noun	N-PROPER
number	NUM
uncountable noun, or noun group with an uncountable noun	N-UNCOUNT
often	oft
ordinal	ORD
passive voice	PASSIVE
plural	pl
noun in the plural, plural noun group, or co-ordinated noun group	PL-N
plural number	PL-NUM
possessive	POSS
prepositional phrase or preposition	PREP
pronoun	PRON
indefinite pronoun	PRON-INDEF
reflexive pronoun	PRON-REFL
question word	QUEST
singular	sing
noun in the singular	SING-N
supplementary information accompanying a noun	SUPP
'that'-clause	'that'
the to-infinitive form of a verb	to-INF
usually	usu
verb or verb group	V
link verb	V-LINK
wh-word, clause beginning with a wh-word	WH

Explanation of grammatical notations and terms

The grammar information that is given in this dictionary is of four types:

1. the word class of the word: e.g. **PHRASAL VERB, ADJ, N, QUANT**
2. for nouns and verbs, a further categorization of the word within that class: e.g. **C, AUX**
3. restrictions or extensions to its behaviour, compared to other words of that word class: e.g. **usu passive, also no DET**
4. the patterns that the word most frequently occurs in: e.g. **sense 'of' N**, which means that the word being explained is followed in the sentence by the word *of* and another noun or noun group **(N)**. The order of items in a pattern is the order in which they normally occur in a sentence. Words in inverted commas are words (not word classes) that occur in the pattern. Alternatives are separated by a slash (/), e.g. **shockingly + ADJ/ADV**, which means that the word 'shockingly' is followed in the sentence by an adjective **(ADJ)** or (/) another adverb **(ADV)**.

Word classes and categories

ADJ

An **adjective** can be graded or ungraded, or be in the comparative or the superlative form, e.g. *He has been <u>absent</u> from his desk for two weeks ... the most <u>accurate</u> description of the killer to date ... The <u>eldest</u> child was a daughter called Fatiha.*

ADV

An **adverb** can be graded or ungraded, or be in the comparative or the superlative form, e.g. *Much of our behaviour is <u>biologically</u> determined ... I'll work <u>hard</u> ... Inflation is below 5% and set to fall <u>further</u> ... those areas <u>furthest</u> from the coast.*

COLOUR

A **colour word** refers to a colour. It is like an adjective, e.g. *the <u>blue</u> sky ... The sky was <u>blue</u>,* and also like a noun, e.g. *She was dressed in <u>red</u> ... several shades of <u>yellow</u>.*

COMB

A **combining form** is a word which is joined with another word, usually with a hyphen, to form compounds, e.g. *job-<u>hunting</u>.*

CONJ

A **conjunction** usually links elements of the same grammatical type, such as two words or two clauses, e.g. *She <u>and</u> Simon had already gone ... I sat on the chair to unwrap the package <u>while</u> he stood behind me.*

CONVENTION

A **convention** is a word or a fixed phrase which is used in conversation, for example when greeting someone, apologizing, or replying, e.g. *hello, sorry, no comment.*

DET

A **determiner** is a word that is used at the beginning of a noun group, e.g. *<u>a</u> tray, <u>more</u> time, <u>some</u> books, <u>this</u> amount.* It can also be used to say who or what something belongs or relates to, e.g. *<u>his</u> face, <u>my</u> house,* or to begin a question, e.g. *<u>Whose</u> car were they in?*

Explanation of grammatical notations and terms

EXCLAM

An **exclamation** is a word or phrase which is spoken suddenly, loudly, or emphatically in order to express a strong emotion such as shock or anger. Exclamations are often followed by exclamation marks, e.g. *good heavens! Boo!*

IRREG FORM

Irregular form is used in this dictionary to classify an inflected form of an irregular verb, noun, or adjective, e.g. *drank, children, worse.*

NOUN

A **noun** is a word which is used to refer to a person or thing, e.g. *car, love, Anne.*

Noun categories

C

A **countable noun** has a plural form, usually made by adding -*s*. When it is singular, it must have a determiner in front of it, such as *the, her,* or *such,* e.g. *My <u>cat</u> is getting fatter ... She's a good <u>friend</u>.*

PLURAL

A **plural noun** is always plural, and is used with plural verbs. If a pronoun is used to stand for the noun, it is a plural pronoun such as *they* or *them,* e.g. *These <u>clothes</u> are ready to wear.* Plural nouns which end in -*s* usually lose the -*s* when they come in front of another noun, e.g. *<u>trousers</u>, <u>trouser</u> leg.* If they refer to a single object which has two main parts, such as *jeans* and *glasses,* the expression *a pair of* is sometimes used, e.g. *a pair of jeans.*

SING

A **singular noun** is always singular, and needs a determiner, e.g. *to respect the <u>environment</u> ... Maureen was the <u>epitome</u> of sophistication.* When only *a* or *the* is used, this is indicated: **'a' crawl** or **'the' ground,** e.g. *The traffic slowed to <u>a crawl</u> ... We dropped to <u>the ground</u>.*

U

An **uncountable noun** refers to things that are not normally counted or considered to be individual items. Uncountable nouns do not have a plural form, and are used with a singular verb. They do not need determiners, e.g. *an area of outstanding natural <u>beauty</u>.*

C, U

A **variable noun** typically combines the behaviour of both countable and uncountable nouns in the same sense. Some variable nouns when used like uncountable nouns refer to abstract things like *hardship* and *technology,* and when used like countable nouns refer to individual examples or instances of that thing, e.g. *<u>Technology</u> is changing fast ... They should be allowed to wait for cheaper <u>technologies</u> to be developed.* Others refer to objects which can be mentioned either individually or generally, like *potato* and *salad*: you can talk about *a potato, potatoes,* or *potato.* Other variable nouns refer to substances. They are uncountable when they refer to a mass of the substance, and countable when they refer to types or brands, or to a measure of the substance, e.g. *bread and <u>cheese</u> ... delicious French <u>cheeses</u> ... Would you like <u>some coffee</u>? ... I made a <u>coffee</u>.*

NUM

A **number** is a word such as *three* and *hundred.* Numbers such as *one, two, three* are used like determiners, e.g. *<u>three</u> bears*; like adjectives, e.g. *the <u>four</u> horsemen*; like pronouns, e.g. *She has three cases and I have <u>two</u>*; and like quantifiers, e.g. *<u>Six</u> of the boys stayed behind.* Numbers such as *hundred, thousand, million* always follow a determiner or another number, e.g. *two* *hundred* people, the *thousand* horsemen, She has a *thousand* dollars and I have a *million,* A *hundred* of the boys stayed behind.

PHRASAL VERB
A **phrasal verb** consists of a verb and one or more particles, e.g. *look after, look back, look down on.* Some phrasal verbs are reciprocal, link, or passive verbs.

PHRASE
Phrases are groups of words which are used together with little variation and which have a meaning of their own, e.g. *The emergency services were working against the clock.*

PREDET
A **predeterminer** is used in a noun group before *a, the,* or another determiner, e.g. *What a terrific idea! … both the children … all his life.*

PREP
A **preposition** begins a prepositional phrase and is followed by a noun group or a present participle. Patterns for prepositions are shown in the dictionary only if they are restricted in some way. For example, if a preposition occurs only before a present participle, it is shown as e.g. **in + -ING.**

PRON
Pronouns are used like noun groups, to refer to someone or something that has already been mentioned or whose identity is known, e.g. *They produced their own shampoos and haircare products, all based on herbal recipes … two bedrooms, each with three beds.*

QUANT
A **quantifier** comes before *of* and a noun group, e.g. *most of the house.* If there are any restrictions on the type of noun group, this is indicated: **QUANT 'of' def-n** means that the quantifier occurs before *of* and a definite noun group, e.g. *Most of the kids have never seen the sea.*

QUEST
A **question word** is a wh-word that is used to begin a question, e.g. *Why didn't he stop me?*

VERB
A **verb** is a word that is used to say what someone or something does or what happens to them, or to give information about them, e.g. *sing, feel, die.*

Verb categories
AUX
An **auxiliary verb** is used with another verb to add particular meanings to that verb, for example, to form the continuous aspect or the passive voice, or to form negatives and interrogatives. The verbs *be, do, get,* and *have* have some senses in which they are auxiliary verbs.

I
An **intransitive verb** is one which takes an indirect object or no object, e.g. *The problems generally fall into two categories … As darkness fell outside, they sat down to eat.*

I, T
Some verbs may be **intransitive** or **transitive** depending on how they are used, e.g. *The flower opens to reveal a bee … He opened the window and looked out.*

LINK

A **link verb** connects a subject and a complement. Most link verbs do not occur in the passive voice, e.g. *be, become, feel.*

MODAL

A **modal** is used before the infinitive form of a verb, e.g. *You may go.* In questions, it comes before the subject, e.g. *Must you speak?* In negatives, it comes before the negative word, e.g. *They would not like this.* It does not inflect, for example, it does not take an *-s* in the third person singular, e.g. *She can swim.*

PASSIVE

A **passive verb** occurs in the passive voice only, e.g. *a boy orphaned by the recent disaster.*

RECIP

Reciprocal verbs describe processes in which two or more people, groups, or things interact mutually: they do the same thing to each other, or participate jointly in the same action or event. Reciprocal verbs are used where the subject is both participants, e.g. *Fred and Sally met.* The participants can also be referred to separately, e.g. *Fred met Sally … Fred argued with Sally.* These patterns are reciprocal because they also mean that *Sally met Fred* and *Sally argued with Fred.* Note that many reciprocal verbs can also be used in a way that is not reciprocal. For example, *Fred and Sally kissed* is reciprocal, but *Fred kissed Sally* is not reciprocal (because it does not mean that Sally also kissed Fred).

RECIP-PASSIVE

A **passive reciprocal verb** behaves like both a passive verb and a reciprocal verb, e.g. *He never believed he and Susan would be reconciled.*

T

A **transitive verb** is one which takes a direct object, e.g. *He sent me the contract.*

Grammatical restrictions and patterns

Words used to structure information in patterns

after:

after V, for example, means after a verb. The word is used either immediately after the verb, or after the verb and another word or phrase. For example, the adverb **again**: *He opened his case and then closed it again.*

also:

used with some nouns to show that the word is used in a way that is not typical of that type of noun. For example, **also 'a' panic** means that unlike most uncountable nouns, 'panic' can also be preceded by 'a'.

before:

before V means before a verb. The word is used before the main element in a verb group. For example, the adverb **definitely**: *She had definitely decided that she wanted to continue working.*

no:

used to indicate that a verb is not used in a particular way, for example **no passive**, or that a singular noun is also used without a determiner: **also no DET**.

oft:

used to indicate that a word or phrase often occurs in a particular pattern or behaves in a particular way.

Explanation of grammatical notations and terms

only:

used to indicate that a verb is always used in a particular way, for example **only CONT**.

usu:

used to indicate that a word or phrase usually occurs in a particular pattern or behaves in a particular way.

with:

with is used when the position of a word or phrase is not fixed. This means that the word or phrase sometimes comes before the named word class and sometimes comes after it. For example, **adversely** at **adverse** has the pattern **adversely with V**. It occurs:

before the verb: *Price changes must not <u>adversely</u> affect the living standards of the people.*

after the verb: *people who react <u>adversely</u> to foods*

In addition, **with CL** is used when the word sometimes occurs at the beginning of the clause, sometimes at the end, and sometimes in the middle. For example, **realistically** has the pattern **realistically with CL**. It occurs:

at the beginning of the clause: <u>*Realistically,*</u> *there is never one right answer.*

at the end of the clause: *As an adult, you can assess the situation <u>realistically</u>.*

in the middle of the clause: *What results can you <u>realistically</u> expect?*

Elements used in patterns

ADJ:

stands for **adjective group**. This may be one word, such as 'happy', or a group of words, such as 'very happy' or 'as happy as I have ever been'.

e.g. **ADJ + read**: read NOUN 2 … *Ben Okri's latest novel is a good read.*

ADJ-SUPERL:

stands for **superlative adjective**. It is used to indicate an adjective group with the superlative form of the adjective.

e.g. **second + ADJ-SUPERL**: second ADJ 2 … *The party is still the second strongest in Italy.*

ADV:

stands for **adverb group**. This may be one word, such as 'slowly', or a group of words, such as 'extremely slowly' or 'more slowly than ever'.

e.g. **ADV + else**: else ADV 1 … *I never wanted to live anywhere else.*

AMOUNT:

means **word or phrase indicating an amount of something**, such as 'a lot', 'nothing', 'three percent', 'four hundred pounds', 'more', or 'much'.

e.g. **AMOUNT 'and' above**: above ADV 2 … *Banks have been charging 25 percent and above for unsecured loans.*

BRD-NEG:

indicates a **broad negative**, that is, a clause which is negative in meaning. It may contain a negative element such as 'no one', 'never', or 'hardly', or may show that it is negative in some other way.

e.g. **oft with BRD-NEG**: right ADJ 8 … *It's not right, leaving her like this.*

CL:

indicates a type of **clause**.

e.g. **CL + anyway**: anyway ADV 4 … *What do you want from me, anyway?*

COMPAR:

stands for **comparative form of an adjective or adverb**.

e.g. **even + COMPAR: even** ADV 2 ... *On television he made an even stronger impact as an interviewer.*

CONT:

indicates that a verb is always, usually, or never used in the continuous.

e.g. **no CONT: need** VERB 4 ... *Look, you needn't shout.*

DEF-N:

stands for **definite noun group**. A definite noun group is a noun group that refers to a specific person or thing, or a specific group of people or things, that is known and identified.

e.g. **whole 'of' DEF-N: whole** QUANT ... *I was cold throughout the whole of my body.*

DEF-PL-N:

stands for **definite noun group with a noun in the plural**.

e.g. **many 'of' DEF-PL-N: many** QUANT 1 ... *It seems there are not very many of them left in the sea.*

DET:

stands for **determiner**. A determiner is a word that comes at the beginning of a noun group, such as 'the', 'her', or 'those'.

e.g. **DET + following: following** ADJ 1 ... *We went to dinner the following Monday evening.*

-ED:

stands for **past participle of a verb**, such as 'decided', 'gone', or 'taken'.

e.g. **freshly + -ED: freshly** ... *freshly baked bread.*

GROUP:

stands for **noun group, adjective, adverb, or prepositional phrase**.

e.g. **strictly + GROUP: strictly** 2 ... *He seemed fond of her in a strictly professional way.*

INF:

stands for **infinitive form of a verb**, such as 'decide', 'go', or 'sit'.

e.g. **'can/could' always + INF: always** 4 ... *If you can't find any decent apples, you can always try growing them yourself.*

-ING:

stands for **present participle of a verb**, such as 'deciding', 'going', or 'taking'.

e.g. **before + -ING: before** PREP 2 ... *He spent his early life in Sri Lanka before moving to Canada.*

'it':

means an 'introductory' or 'dummy' it. It does not refer to anything in a previous sentence or in the world; it may refer to what is coming later in the clause or it may refer to things in general.

e.g. **'it' V-LINK + nice + to-INF: nice** 7 ... *It's nice to meet you.*

N:

stands for **noun or noun group**. If the N element occurs in a pattern with something that is part of a noun group, such as an adjective or another noun, it represents a noun. If the N element occurs in a pattern with something that is not part of a noun group, such as a verb or preposition, it represents a noun group. The noun group can be of any kind, including a pronoun.

e.g. **abiding + N: abiding** ... *He has a genuine and abiding love of the craft.*

Explanation of grammatical notations and terms

NEG:

stands for **negative words,** such as 'not' or 'never'.

e.g. **with NEG: need** VERB 4 … *'You needn't bother,' he said gruffly.*

N-PROPER:

stands for proper noun. A proper noun is the name of a particular person or thing.

e.g. **much 'of' N-PROPER/PRON:** much QUANT 2 … *I don't see much of Tony nowadays.*

NUM:

stands for **number.**

e.g. **NUM + odd: odd** ADV … *How many pages was it, 500 odd?*

N-UNCOUNT:

stands for **uncountable noun** or **noun group with an uncountable noun.** An uncountable noun is a noun which has no plural form and which is sometimes used with no determiner.

e.g. **'a' touch 'of' N-UNCOUNT: touch** QUANT … *She thought she just had a touch of flu.*

ORD:

stands for **ordinal,** such as 'first' or 'second'.

e.g. **ORD + generation + N: generation** ADJ … *second generation Jamaicans in New York.*

passive:

stands for **passive voice.** It is used when indicating that a verb usually occurs in the passive voice.

e.g. **usu passive: honour** VERB 1 … *Diego Maradona was honoured with an award.*

pl:

stands for **plural.** It is used when indicating that a noun usually occurs in the plural form.

e.g. **usu pl: amenity** … *The hotel amenities include health clubs, conference facilities, and banqueting rooms.*

PL-N:

stands for **noun in the plural, plural noun group,** or **co-ordinate noun group** (two or more noun groups joined by a co-ordinating conjunction).

e.g. **between + PL-N: between** PREP 2 … *I spent a lot of time in the early Eighties travelling between Waco and El Paso.*

PL-NUM:

stands for **plural number.** A plural number is a number which is used only in the plural.

e.g. **in + POSS PL-NUM: in** PREP 16 … *young people in their twenties.*

POSS:

indicates a **possessive.** Possessives which come before the noun may be a possessive determiner, such as 'my', 'her', or 'their', or a possessive formed from a noun group, such as 'the horse's'. Possessives which come after the noun are of the form 'of N', such as 'of the horse'.

e.g. **usu pl, with POSS: ancestor** 1 … *our daily lives, so different from those of our ancestors.*

PREP:

stands for **prepositional phrase** or **preposition.**

e.g. **PREP + him: him** 1 … *Is Sam there? Let me talk to him.*

PRON:
> stands for **pronoun**. A pronoun is a word such as 'I', 'it', or 'them' which is used like a noun group. It refers to someone or something that has already been mentioned or whose identity is known.
>> e.g. **before + PRON: before** PREP 8 … *Everyone in the room knew it was the single hardest task before them.*

PRON-INDEF:
> stands for **indefinite pronoun**. An indefinite pronoun is a word like *anyone, anything, everyone,* and *something.*
>> e.g. **PRON-INDEF + else: else** ADJ 2 … *I expect everyone else to be truthful.*

PRON-REFL:
> stands for **reflexive pronoun**, such as 'yourself', 'herself', or 'ourselves'.
>> e.g. **among + PRON-REFL: among** 9 … *The girls stood aside, talking among themselves.*

QUEST:
> stands for **question word**. A question word is a wh-word such as 'what', 'how', or 'why' which is used to begin a question.
>> e.g. **QUEST + ever: ever** 6 … *Why ever didn't you tell me?*

sing:
> indicates the word is used in the **singular**.
>> e.g. **usu sing: season** NOUN 7 … *the peak holiday season.*

SING-N:
> stands for **noun in the singular**.
>> e.g. **all + DET SING-N: all** PREDET 2 … *She's worked all her life.*

SUPP:
> stands for **supplementary information accompanying a noun**. Supplementary information that comes before a noun may be given by a determiner, possessive, adjective, or noun modifier. Supplementary information that comes after the noun may be given by a prepositional phrase or a clause.
>> e.g. **SUPP + park: park** NOUN 2 … *a science and technology park.*

'that':
> stands for **'that'-clause**. The clause may begin with the word 'that', but does not necessarily do so.
>> e.g. **usu conviction 'that': conviction** 1 … *It is our conviction that a step forward has been taken.*

to-INF:
> stands for **to-infinitive form of a verb**.
>> e.g. **V-LINK + inclined + to-INF: inclined** 2 … *I am inclined to agree with Alan.*

V:
> stands for **verb** or **verb group**. It is not used to represent a link verb. See also the explanations of **after, before,** and **with**.
>> e.g. **V + her: her** PRON 1 … *I told her I had something to say.*

V-LINK:
> stands for **link verb**. A link verb is a verb such as 'be' which connects a subject and a complement.
>> e.g. **V-LINK + down: down** ADJ 3 … *The computer's down again.*

WH:
> stands for **wh-word**, or **clause beginning with a wh-word**, such as 'what', 'why', 'when', 'how', 'if', or 'whether'.
>> e.g. **here 'be' N/WH: here** ADV 8 … *Now here's what I want you to do.*

Pronunciation

In this dictionary the International Phonetic Alphabet (IPA) is used to show how the words are pronounced. The symbols used in the International Phonetic Alphabet are shown in the table below.

IPA symbols

Vowel sounds		Consonant sounds	
ɑː	calm, ah	b	bed, rub
æ	act, mass	d	done, red
aɪ	dive, cry	f	fit, if
aɪə	fire, buyer	g	good, dog
aʊ	out, down	h	hat, horse
aʊə	flower, sour	j	yellow, you
e	met, lend, pen	k	king, pick
eɪ	day, weight	l	lip, bill
ɛə	bear, where	m	mat, ram
ɪ	fit, win	n	not, tin
iː	feed, me	p	pay, lip
ɪə	fear, mere	r	run, read
ɒ	lot, spot	s	soon, bus
əʊ	note, coat	t	talk, bet
ɔː	claw, maul	v	van, love
ɔɪ	boy, joint	w	win, wool
ʊ	could, stood	x	loch
uː	you, zoo	z	zoo, buzz
ʊə	poor, sure	ʃ	ship, wish
ɜː	burn, learn	ʒ	measure, leisure
ʌ	fund, must	ŋ	sing, working
ə	first vowel in about	tʃ	cheap, witch
i	last vowel in happy	θ	thin, myth
		ð	then, bathe
		dʒ	joy, bridge

Notes

For the majority of words, a single pronunciation is given. Where more than one pronunciation is common, alternative pronunciations are given. The alternative pronunciation may be given by repeating only the syllable or syllables that change:

afternoon /ˌɑːftəˈnuːn, ˌæf-/

Where appropriate, American pronunciations are given immediately after the British English pronunciations, and are preceded by the abbreviation *AmE*.

/æ/ or /ɑː/
A number of words are shown in the dictionary with alternative pronunciations with /ɑː/ and /æ/, such as *path* /pɑːθ, pæθ/. In this case, /pɑːθ/ is the standard British pronunciation. However, in many other accents of English, including standard American English, the pronunciation is /pæθ/.

/r/
Though words like *fire*, *flour*, *fair* and *near* are shown with the pronunciations /faɪə/, /flaʊə/, /fɛə/, and /nɪə/, many speakers pronounce these words /faɪər/, /flaʊər/, /fɛər/, and /nɪər/, with the final 'r' sound.

Length

The symbol : denotes length and is shown together with certain vowel symbols when the vowels are typically long.

Stress

Primary stress is shown by ' immediately before the stressed syllable:

> **result** /rɪˈzʌlt/

Secondary stress is shown by ˌ immediately before the stressed syllable:

> **disappointing** /ˌdɪsəˈpɔɪntɪŋ/

Unstressed syllables

It is an important characteristic of English that vowels in unstressed syllables tend not to be pronounced clearly. Many unstressed syllables contain the vowel /ə/, a neutral vowel which is not found in stressed syllables. The vowels /ɪ/ or /ʊ/, which are relatively neutral in quality, are also common in unstressed syllables.

Single-syllable grammatical words such as 'shall' and 'at' are often pronounced with a weak vowel such as /ə/. However, some of them are pronounced with a more distinct vowel under certain circumstances, for example when they occur at the end of a sentence. This distinct pronunciation is generally referred to as the strong form, and is given in this dictionary after the word STRONG.

> **shall** /ʃəl, STRONG ʃæl/

> **at** /ət, STRONG æt/

Aa

A also **a** /eɪ/ NOUN (**A's, a's**) **A** is the first letter of the English alphabet.

a ♦♦♦ /ə, STRONG eɪ/ or **an** /ən, STRONG æn/ DET

A or an is the indefinite article. It is used at the beginning of noun groups that refer to only one person or thing. The form **an** is used in front of words that begin with vowel sounds.

1 You use **a** or **an** when you are referring to someone or something for the first time or when people may not know which particular person or thing you are talking about. ❑ *A waiter entered with a tray bearing a glass and a bottle of whisky.* ❑ *He started eating an apple.* **2** You use **a** or **an** when you are referring to any person or thing of a particular type and do not want to be specific. ❑ *I suggest you leave it to an expert.* ❑ *Bring a sleeping bag.* **3** You use **a** or **an** in front of an uncount noun when that noun follows an adjective, or when the noun is followed by words that describe it more fully. ❑ *The islanders exhibit a constant happiness with life.* **4** You use **a** or **an** in front of a mass noun when you want to refer to a single type or make of something. ❑ *Bollinger 'RD' is a rare, highly prized wine.* **5** You use **a** in quantifiers such as **a lot, a little**, and **a bit**. ❑ *I spend a lot on expensive jewellery and clothing.* **6** You use **a** or **an** to refer to someone or something as a typical member of a group, class, or type. ❑ *Some parents believe a boy must learn to stand up and fight like a man.* **7** You use **a** or **an** in front of the names of days, months, or festivals when you are referring to one particular instance of that day, month, or festival. ❑ *The interview took place on a Friday afternoon.* **8** You use **a** or **an** when you are saying what someone is or what job they have. ❑ *I explained that I was an artist.* **9** You use **a** or **an** instead of the number 'one', especially with words of measurement such as 'hundred', 'hour', and 'metre', and with fractions such as 'half', 'quarter', and 'third'. ❑ *more than a thousand acres of land* **10** You use **a** or **an** in expressions such as **eight hours a day** to express a rate or ratio. ❑ *Prices start at $13.95 a yard for printed cotton.*

USAGE NOTE

a, an

Remember to use **a** or **an** before a singular countable noun when you are talking about a person or thing for the first time, or when you say what someone's job is. Do not say 'She picked up book' or 'He is architect'.
*She picked up **a** book.*
*He is **an** architect.*

---

aback /ə'bæk/ ADV
PHRASE **be taken aback** If you are **taken aback by** something, you are surprised or shocked by it and you cannot respond at once. ❑ *Roland was taken aback by our strength of feeling.*

✪ aban·don ♦◇◇ /ə'bændən/ VERB, NOUN (*academic word*)
VERB [T] (**abandons, abandoning, abandoned**) **1** If you **abandon** a place, thing, or person, you leave the place, thing, or person permanently or for a long time, especially when you should not do so. = desert, leave ❑ *He claimed that his parents had abandoned him.* **2** If you **abandon** an activity or piece of work, you stop doing it before it is

finished. = give up; ≠ persevere ❑ *The authorities have abandoned any attempt to distribute food in an orderly fashion.* ❑ *The scheme's investors, fearful of bankruptcy, decided to abandon the project.* **3** If you **abandon** an idea or way of thinking, you stop having that idea or thinking in that way. = give up ❑ *Logic had prevailed and he had abandoned the idea.*
PHRASE **abandon ship** If people **abandon ship**, they get off a ship because it is sinking. ❑ *At the captain's order, they abandoned ship.*
NOUN [u] [usu 'with' abandon] (*disapproval*) If you say that someone does something **with abandon**, you mean that they behave in a wild, uncontrolled way and do not think or care about how they should behave. ❑ *He approached life with reckless abandon – I don't think he himself knew what he was going to do next.*
→ See also **abandoned**

aban·doned ♦◇◇ /ə'bændənd/ ADJ An **abandoned** place or building is no longer used or occupied. ❑ *The digging had left a network of abandoned mines and tunnels.*

aban·don·ment /ə'bændənmənt/ NOUN [u] **1** The **abandonment** of a place, thing, or person is the act of leaving it permanently or for a long time, especially when you should not do so. ❑ *memories of her father's complete abandonment of her* **2** The **abandonment** of a piece of work or activity is the act of stopping doing it before it is finished. ❑ *Constant rain forced the abandonment of the next day's competitions.*

ab·bre·vi·ate /ə'briːvieɪt/ VERB [T] (**abbreviates, abbreviating, abbreviated**) If you **abbreviate** something, especially a word or a piece of writing, you make it shorter. = shorten ❑ *The creators of the original X-Men abbreviated the title of its sequel to simply X2.*

ab·bre·via·tion /ə,briːvi'eɪʃən/ NOUN [C] (**abbreviations**) An **abbreviation** is a short form of a word or phrase, made by leaving out some of the letters or by using only the first letter of each word. ❑ *The abbreviation for Kansas is KS.*

ab·do·men /'æbdəmən, AmE æb'doʊ-/ NOUN [C] (**abdomens**) (*formal*) Your **abdomen** is the part of your body below your chest where your stomach and intestines are. ❑ *He went into the hospital to undergo tests for a pain in his abdomen.*

ab·duct /æb'dʌkt/ VERB [T] (**abducts, abducting, abducted**) If someone **is abducted** by another person, he or she is taken away illegally, usually using force. = kidnap ❑ *He was on his way to the airport when his car was held up and he was abducted by four gunmen.*

ab·duc·tion /æb'dʌkʃən/ NOUN [C, u] (**abductions**) ❑ *The UN World Food Programme confirmed the abduction of eight of its workers in northern Darfur.*

abide /ə'baɪd/ VERB
PHRASE **can't abide** If you **can't abide** someone or something, you dislike them very much. ❑ *I can't abide people who can't make up their minds.*
PHRASAL VERB **abide by** (**abides, abiding, abided**) If you **abide by** a law, agreement, or decision, you do what it says you should do. = observe, obey, adhere to; ≠ disobey ❑ *They have got to abide by the rules.*
→ See also **abiding**

A

abid·ing /əˈbaɪdɪŋ/ ADJ [abiding + N] An **abiding** feeling, memory, or interest is one that you have for a very long time. = lasting ❑ He has a genuine and abiding love of the craft.

✪ **abil·ity** ♦♦◇ /əˈbɪlɪti/ NOUN
NOUN [SING, C, U] (**abilities**) **1** [SING] Your **ability to** do something is the fact that you can do it. = capability; ≠ inability ❑ the ability of an individual to work in a team ❑ The public never had faith in his ability to handle the job. **2** [C, U] Your **ability** is the quality or skill that you have which makes it possible for you to do something. ❑ Her drama teacher spotted her ability. ❑ Does the school cater to all abilities?
PHRASE **to the best of your ability** If you do something **to the best of** your **abilities** or **to the best of** your **ability**, you do it as well as you can. ❑ I take care of them to the best of my abilities.

WORD CONNECTIONS
VERB + **ability**
have the ability to …   **possess** the ability to …   **develop** the ability to …   ❑ Some of these young players possess the ability to achieve great things.
lack the ability to …   **lose** the ability to …   ❑ He lacks the ability to communicate his feelings effectively.
demonstrate an ability to …   **show** an ability to …   ❑ Candidates must demonstrate an ability to manage a large team.

ab·ject /ˈæbdʒekt/ ADJ (emphasis) You use **abject** to emphasize that a situation or quality is extremely bad. = total ❑ Both of them died in abject poverty.

able ♦♦♦ /ˈeɪbəl/ ADJ
ADJ (**abler, ablest** /ˈeɪblɪst/) Someone who is **able** is very intelligent or very good at doing something. = capable ❑ one of the brightest and ablest members of the government
PHRASE **be able to 1** If you **are able to** do something, you have skills or qualities which make it possible for you to do it. = can ❑ The older child should be able to prepare a simple meal. ❑ The company says they're able to keep pricing competitive. **2** If you **are able to** do something, you have enough freedom, power, time, or money to do it. = can ❑ You'll be able to read in peace. ❑ Have you been able to have any kind of contact?

able-bodied /ˌeɪbəl ˈbɒdid/ ADJ, NOUN
ADJ An **able-bodied** person is physically strong and healthy, rather than weak or disabled. ❑ The gym can be used by both able-bodied and disabled people.
NOUN [PL] The **able-bodied** are people who are able-bodied. ❑ No doubt such robots would be very useful in the homes of the able-bodied, too.

ably /ˈeɪbli/ ADV [ably with V] **Ably** means skilfully and successfully. ❑ He was ably assisted by a number of members from other branches.

✪ **ab·nor·mal** /æbˈnɔːməl/ ADJ (academic word, formal) Someone or something that is **abnormal** is unusual, especially in a way that is worrying. = aberrant, deviant, irregular, unusual; ≠ normal ❑ Nothing abnormal was detected. ❑ abnormal heart rhythms and high anxiety levels ❑ a child with an abnormal fear of strangers
✪ **ab·nor·mal·ly** /æbˈnɔːməli/ ADV = unusually ≠ normally ❑ abnormally high levels of glucose ❑ This stops the cells from growing abnormally.

ab·nor·mal·ity /ˌæbnɔːˈmælɪti/ NOUN [C, U] (**abnormalities**) (formal) An **abnormality** in something, especially in a person's body or behaviour, is an unusual part or feature of it that may be worrying or dangerous. ❑ Further scans are required to confirm the diagnosis of an abnormality.

aboard /əˈbɔːd/ PREP, ADV
PREP If you are **aboard** a ship or plane, you are on it or in it. ❑ She invited 750 people aboard the luxury yacht, the Savarona.
ADV [aboard after V] If you go **aboard** a ship or plane, you go onto it or into it. ❑ It had taken two hours to load all the people aboard.

✪ **abol·ish** /əˈbɒlɪʃ/ VERB [T] (**abolishes, abolishing, abolished**) If someone in authority **abolishes** a system or practice, they formally put an end to it. = eliminate, end ❑ An Illinois House committee voted on Thursday to abolish the death penalty. ❑ ten years after slavery was formally abolished

✪ **abo·li·tion** /ˌæbəˈlɪʃən/ NOUN [U] The **abolition of** something such as a system or practice is its formal ending. = end ❑ The abolition of slavery in Brazil and the Caribbean closely followed the pattern of the United States. ❑ a book advocating the abolition of capital punishment

abor·tion ♦◇◇ /əˈbɔːʃən/ NOUN [C, U] (**abortions**) If a woman has an **abortion**, she ends her pregnancy deliberately so that the baby is not born alive. ❑ He and his girlfriend had been going out together for a year when they had an abortion.

abound /əˈbaʊnd/ VERB [I] (**abounds, abounding, abounded**) (formal) If things **abound**, or if a place **abounds with** things, there are very large numbers of them. ❑ Stories abound about when he was in charge.

about ♦♦♦ /əˈbaʊt/ PREP, ADV, ADJ

> In addition to the uses shown below, **about** is often used after verbs of movement, such as 'walk' and 'drive', especially in British English, and in phrasal verbs such as 'set about'.

PREP **1** You use **about** to introduce who or what something relates to or concerns. ❑ She knew a lot about food. ❑ He never complains about his wife. **2** When you mention the things that an activity or institution is **about**, you are saying what it involves or what its aims are. ❑ Leadership is about the ability to implement change. **3** You use **about** after some adjectives to indicate the person or thing that a feeling or state of mind relates to. ❑ 'I'm sorry about Patrick,' she said. **4** If you do something **about** a problem, you take action in order to solve it. ❑ Rachel was going to do something about Jacob. **5** When you say that there is a particular quality **about** someone or something, you mean that they have this quality. ❑ There was a warmth and passion about him I never knew existed. **6** (mainly BrE; in AmE, usually use **around**) If you put something **about** a person or thing, you put it around them. = around **7** [V + about + N] (mainly BrE; in AmE, usually use **around**) If you move **about** a place, you keep moving in different directions within that place. = around
ADV **1** [about + NUM] **About** is used in front of a number to show that the number is not exact. = approximately, around ❑ The rate of inflation is running at about 2.7 per cent. **2** [about after V] (mainly BrE; in AmE, usually use **around**) If someone or something moves **about**, they keep moving in different directions. = around
ADJ **1** [V-LINK + about] (mainly BrE; in AmE, usually use **around**) If someone or something is **about**, they are present or available. **2** [V-LINK + about + TO-INF] If you are **about to** do something, you are going to do it very soon. If something is **about to** happen, it will happen very soon. ❑ I think he's about to leave. ❑ Argentina has lifted all restrictions on trade and visas are about to be abolished.
PHRASE **out and about** If someone is **out and about**, they are going out and doing things, especially after they have been unable to for a while. ❑ Despite considerable pain she has been getting out and about almost as normal.
✦ **how about** → see **how**; **what about** → see **what**; **just about** → see **just**

above ♦♦◇ /əˈbʌv/ PREP, ADV, NOUN, ADJ
PREP **1** If one thing is **above** another one, it is directly over it or higher than it. ❑ He lifted his hands above his head. **2** If an amount or measurement is **above** a particular level, it is greater than that level. ❑ The temperature crept

up to just above 40 degrees. ❑ *Victoria Falls has had above average levels of rainfall this year.* ❸ If you hear one sound **above** another, it is louder or clearer than the second one. = over ❑ *Then there was a woman's voice, rising shrilly above the barking.* ❹ If someone is **above** you, they are in a higher social position than you or in a position of authority over you. ❑ *I married above myself.* ❺ If you say that someone thinks they are **above** something, you mean that they act as if they are too good or important for it. ❑ *This was clearly a failure by someone who thought he was above failure.* ❻ [V-LINK + above + N] If someone is **above** criticism or suspicion, they cannot be criticized or suspected because of their good qualities or their position. = beyond ❑ *He was a respected academic and above suspicion.* ❼ If you value one person or thing **above** any other, you value them more or consider that they are more important. ❑ *his tendency to put the team above everything*
ADV ❶ If something happens **above**, it happens directly over you or at a place higher than you. ❑ *A long scream sounded from somewhere above.* ❑ *a picture of the new plane as seen from above* ❷ [AMOUNT 'and' above] You can use **above** to indicate that an amount or measurement is greater than a particular level. ❑ *Banks have been charging 25 per cent and above for unsecured loans.* ❸ ['from' above] If you are given an order or instruction from **above**, you are given an order or instruction from someone in a position of authority over you. ❑ *The policemen admitted beating the student, but said they were acting on orders from above.* ❹ In writing, you use **above** to refer to something that has already been mentioned or discussed. ❑ *Several conclusions could be drawn from the results described above.*
NOUN [SING] In writing, you use **above** to refer to something that has already been mentioned or discussed. ❑ *For additional information, contact any of the above.*
ADJ [above + N] In writing, you use **above** to refer to something that has already been mentioned or discussed. ❑ *For a copy of their brochure, write to the above address.*
✦ over and above → see **over**; above the law → see **law**

abreast /ə'brest/ ADV
ADV If people or things walk or move **abreast**, they are next to each other, side by side, and facing in the same direction. ❑ *The steep pavement was too narrow for them to walk abreast.*
PHRASE **abreast of** If you **keep abreast of** a subject, you know all the most recent facts about it. ❑ *He will be keeping abreast of the news.*

⬥**abroad** ♦◇◇ /ə'brɔːd/ ADV If you go **abroad**, you go to a foreign country, usually one that is separated from the country where you live by an ocean or a sea. = overseas ❑ *I would love to go abroad this year, perhaps to the South of France.* ❑ *He will stand in for Mr. Goh when he is abroad.* ❑ *About 65 per cent of the company's sales come from abroad.*

ab·rupt /ə'brʌpt/ ADJ ❶ An **abrupt** change or action is very sudden, often in a way that is unpleasant. ❑ *Rosie's idyllic world came to an abrupt end when her parents' marriage broke up.* ❷ Someone who is **abrupt** speaks in a rude, unfriendly way. = brusque ❑ *He was abrupt to the point of rudeness.*
ab·rupt·ly /ə'brʌptli/ ADV ❶ [abruptly with V] = suddenly ❑ *He stopped abruptly and looked my way.* ❷ = suddenly ❑ *'Good night, then,' she said abruptly.*

⬥**ab·sence** ♦◇◇ /'æbsəns/ NOUN [C, U, SING] (absences) ❶ [C, U] Someone's **absence** from a place is the fact that they are not there. ❑ *a bundle of letters which had arrived for me in my absence* ❑ *the problem of high sickness absence in the public sector* ❷ [SING] The **absence** of something from a place is the fact that it is not there or does not exist. = lack ❑ *The presence or absence of clouds can have an important impact on temperature.* ❑ *In the absence of a will the courts decide who the guardian is.*

⬥**ab·sent** /'æbsənt/ ADJ ❶ If someone or something is **absent from** a place or situation where they should be or where they usually are, they are not there. ≠ present ❑ *He has been absent from his desk for two weeks.* ❑ *The pictures, too, were absent from the walls.* ❑ *Women are* conspicuously absent from higher management. ❑ *Employees who are absent without a genuine reason should be disciplined.* ❑ *Any soldier failing to report would be considered absent without leave.* ❷ If someone appears **absent**, they are not paying attention because they are thinking about something else. ❑ *'Nothing,' Rosie said in an absent way.* ❸ [absent + N] An **absent** parent does not live with his or her children. ❑ *absent fathers who fail to pay towards the costs of looking after their children*
ab·sent·ly /'æbsəntli/ ADV ❑ *He nodded absently.*

ab·so·lute ♦◇◇ /'æbsəluːt/ ADJ, NOUN
ADJ ❶ **Absolute** means total and complete. = complete ❑ *It's not really suited to absolute beginners.* ❷ [absolute + N] You use **absolute** to emphasize something that you are saying. = complete ❑ *About 12 inches wide is the absolute minimum you should consider.* ❸ [absolute + N] An **absolute** ruler has complete power and authority over his or her country. ❑ *He ruled with absolute power.* ❹ **Absolute** is used to say that something is definite and will not change even if circumstances change. ❑ *John brought the absolute proof that we needed.* ❺ [absolute + N] An amount that is expressed in **absolute** terms is expressed as a fixed amount rather than referring to variable factors such as what you earn or the effects of inflation. ❑ *In absolute terms their wages remain low by national standards.* ❻ **Absolute** rules and principles are believed to be true, right, or relevant in all situations. ❑ *There are no absolute rules.*
NOUN [C] (absolutes) An **absolute** is a rule or principle that is believed to be true, right, or relevant in all situations. ❑ *This is one of the few absolutes in US constitutional law.*

ab·so·lute·ly ♦♦◇ /ˌæbsə'luːtli/ ADV (emphasis) ❶ **Absolutely** means totally and completely. ❑ *Joan is absolutely right.* ❑ *I absolutely refuse to get married.* ❷ [absolutely as reply] Some people say '**absolutely**' as an emphatic way of saying yes or of agreeing with someone. They say '**absolutely not**' as an emphatic way of saying no or of disagreeing with someone. ❑ *'It's worrying that they're doing things without training though, isn't it?'—'Absolutely.'*

ab·sorb /əb'zɔːb/ VERB [T] (absorbs, absorbing, absorbed) ❶ If something **absorbs** a liquid, gas, or other substance, it soaks it up or takes it in. = soak up ❑ *Plants absorb carbon dioxide from the air and moisture from the soil.* ❷ If something **absorbs** light, heat, or another form of energy, it takes it in. ❑ *A household radiator absorbs energy in the form of electric current and releases it in the form of heat.* ❸ If a group **is absorbed into** a larger group, it becomes part of the larger group. ❑ *City schools were absorbed into the countywide school district.* ❹ If something **absorbs** a force or shock, it reduces its effect. ❑ *footwear which does not absorb the impact of the foot striking the ground* ❺ If a system or society **absorbs** changes, effects, or costs, it is able to deal with them. ❑ *The banks would be forced to absorb large losses.* ❻ If something **absorbs** something valuable such as money, space, or time, it uses up a great deal of it. = consume ❑ *It absorbed vast amounts of capital that could have been used for investment.* ❼ If you **absorb** information, you learn and understand it. = digest, assimilate ❑ *Too often he only absorbs half the information in the manual.* ❽ If something **absorbs** you, it interests you a great deal and takes up all your attention and energy. ❑ *a second career which absorbed her more completely than her acting ever had*
→ See also **absorbed, absorbing**

ab·sorbed /əb'zɔːbd/ ADJ [V-LINK + absorbed] If you are **absorbed in** something or someone, you are very interested in them and they take up all your attention and energy. = engrossed ❑ *They were completely absorbed in each other.*

ab·sorb·ing /əb'zɔːbɪŋ/ ADJ An **absorbing** task or activity interests you a great deal and takes up all your attention and energy. ❑ *'Two Sisters' is an absorbing read.*

⬥**ab·stract** /'æbstrækt/ ADJ, NOUN (academic word)
ADJ ❶ An **abstract** idea or way of thinking is based on general ideas rather than on real things and events. = theoretical, conceptual; ≠ actual, concrete ❑ *starting with a few abstract principles* ❑ *It's not a question of some abstract*

A

concept of justice. ❑ *Fractional dimension is an abstract concept that enables mathematicians to measure the complexity of an object.* ❑ *the faculty of abstract reasoning* **2** [abstract + N] In grammar, an **abstract** noun refers to a quality or idea rather than to a physical object. ❑ *abstract words such as glory, honour, and courage* **3** **Abstract** art makes use of shapes and patterns rather than showing people or things. ❑ *A modern abstract painting takes over one complete wall.* ❑ *Pollock's great masterpiece of abstract expressionism* NOUN [c] (**abstracts**) **1** An **abstract** is an abstract work of art. ❑ *His abstracts are held in numerous collections.* **2** An **abstract of** an article, document, or speech is a short piece of writing that gives the main points of it. = summary, précis ❑ *Many scientists only have enough time to read the abstracts of papers.* ❑ *Some indexes also have abstracts or summaries of articles.* ❑ *It might also be necessary to supply an abstract of the review of the literature as well.* PHRASE **in the abstract** When you talk or think about something **in the abstract**, you talk or think about it in a general way, rather than considering particular things or events. ❑ *Money was a commodity she never thought about except in the abstract.*

ab·surd /æbˈsɜːd/ ADJ, NOUN
ADJ (*disapproval*) If you say that something is **absurd**, you are criticizing it because you think that it is ridiculous or that it does not make sense. = ridiculous ❑ *That's absurd.* ❑ *It's absurd to suggest that they knew what was going on but did nothing.* NOUN [SING] ['the' absurd] (*formal*) **The absurd** is something that is absurd. ❑ *Connie had a sharp eye for the absurd.* **ab·surd·ly** /æbˈsɜːdli/ ADV ❑ *Prices were still absurdly low, in his opinion.* **ab·surd·ity** /æbˈsɜːdɪti/ NOUN [C, U] (**absurdities**) ❑ *I find myself growing increasingly angry at the absurdity of the situation.*

abun·dance /əˈbʌndəns/ NOUN [SING] [usu abundance 'of' N, also 'in' abundance] An **abundance of** something is a large quantity of it. = wealth ❑ *This area of Mexico has an abundance of safe beaches and a pleasing climate.*

✪ **abun·dant** /əˈbʌndənt/ ADJ Something that is **abundant** is present in large quantities. = plentiful; ≠ sparse ❑ *There is an abundant supply of cheap labour.* ❑ *Birds are abundant in the tall vegetation.* ❑ *Hydrogen is the most abundant element in the universe.*

✪ **abun·dant·ly** /əˈbʌndəntli/ ADV **1** [abundantly + ADJ] If something is **abundantly** clear, it is extremely obvious. ❑ *He made it abundantly clear that anybody who disagrees with his policies will not last long.* **2** Something that occurs **abundantly** is present in large quantities. = plentifully; ≠ sparsely ❑ *a plant that grows abundantly in the United States* ❑ *All the pages are abundantly illustrated with colour photographs.*

✪ **abuse** ◆◆◇ NOUN, VERB
NOUN /əˈbjuːs/ [U, C] (**abuses**) **1** [U] **Abuse** of someone is cruel and violent treatment of them. = violation, mistreatment ❑ *investigation of alleged child abuse* ❑ *victims of sexual and physical abuse* ❑ *the systematic abuse of prisoners* **2** [U] **Abuse** is extremely rude and insulting things that people say when they are angry. ❑ *I was left shouting abuse as the car sped off.* **3** [C, U] [with SUPP] **Abuse** of something is the use of it in a wrong way or for a bad purpose. = misuse ❑ *What went on here was an abuse of power.* ❑ *liver damage caused by disease, alcohol or drug abuse* VERB /əˈbjuːz/ [T] (**abuses, abusing, abused**) **1** If someone **is abused**, they are treated cruelly and violently. = mistreat, violate ❑ *The report showed that up to one in four girls and one in seven boys are sexually abused.* ❑ *Guards routinely abused prisoners.* ❑ *those who work with abused children* ❑ *Janet had been abused by her father since she was eleven.* ❑ *parents who feel they cannot cope or might abuse their children* **2** You can say that someone **is abused** if extremely rude and insulting things are said to them. = insult ❑ *He alleged that he was verbally abused by other soldiers.* **3** If you **abuse** something, you use it in a wrong way or for a bad purpose. = exploit ❑ *He showed how the rich and powerful can abuse their position.* ❑ *teachers and coaches who abuse the trust they are given*

✪ **abus·er** /əˈbjuːzə/ NOUN [c] (**abusers**) **1** An **abuser** is someone who treats a person cruelly and violently. = molester ❑ *a convicted child abuser* **2** An **abuser** is someone who uses something in a wrong way or for a bad purpose. = alcoholic, addict ❑ *the treatment of alcohol and drug abusers*

abu·sive /əˈbjuːsɪv/ ADJ **1** Someone who is **abusive** behaves in a cruel and violent way towards other people. ❑ *He became violent and abusive towards Ben's mother.* **2** **Abusive** language is extremely rude and insulting. = insulting ❑ *I did not use any foul or abusive language.*

✪ **aca·dem·ic** ◆◇◇ /ˌækəˈdemɪk/ ADJ, NOUN (**academic word**)
ADJ **1** [academic + N] **Academic** is used to describe things that relate to the work done in schools, colleges, and universities, especially work that involves studying and reasoning rather than practical or technical skills. ❑ *Their academic standards are high.* **2** [academic + N] **Academic** is used to describe things that relate to schools, colleges, and universities. ❑ *the start of the last academic year* **3** **Academic** is used to describe work, or a school, college, or university, that places emphasis on studying and reasoning rather than on practical or technical skills. ❑ *The author has settled for a more academic approach.* **4** Someone who is **academic** is good at studying. = scholarly ❑ *The system is failing most disastrously among less academic children.* **5** You can say that a discussion or situation is **academic** if you think it is not important because it has no real effect or cannot happen. = theoretical ❑ *Who wants to hear about contracts and deadlines that are purely academic?* NOUN [c] (**academics**) An **academic** is a member of a university or college who teaches or does research. = scholar ❑ *A group of academics say they can predict house prices through a computer program.*

✪ **aca·dem·ical·ly** /ˌækəˈdemɪkli/ ADV ❑ *He is academically gifted.* ❑ *scholarships for those who excel academically*

an academic **qualification**
an academic **achievement**
❑ *Her academic qualifications are a BSc and PhD in Physics.*

academic **standards**
academic **performance**
❑ *The university is committed to maintaining high academic standards.*

an academic **subject**
❑ *I was always better at practical subjects rather than academic subjects.*

an academic **institution**
academic **staff**
❑ *He has taught at academic institutions including Johns Hopkins University and Sarah Lawrence College.*

acad•emy /əˈkædəmi/ NOUN [C] (**academies**) (*academic word*) **1** **Academy** is sometimes used in the names of schools and colleges, especially those specializing in particular subjects or skills. ❑ *He is an English teacher at the Seattle Academy for Arts and Sciences.* **2** **Academy** appears in the names of some societies formed to improve or maintain standards in a particular field. ❑ *the American Academy of Psychotherapists*

✪ **ac•cel•er•ate** /ækˈseləreɪt/ VERB [I, T] (**accelerates, accelerating, accelerated**) **1** [I, T] If the process or rate of something **accelerates** or if something **accelerates** it, it gets faster and faster. = hasten ❑ *Growth will accelerate to 2.9 per cent next year.* ❑ *The government is to accelerate its privatisation programme.* **2** [I] When a moving vehicle **accelerates**, it goes faster and faster. ≠ decelerate ❑ *Suddenly the car accelerated.* ❑ *Traffic calming often created extra noise as motorists accelerated and braked around traffic islands.* ❑ *A police video showed the patrol car accelerating to 115mph.*

✪ **ac•cel•era•tion** /ækˌseləˈreɪʃən/ NOUN [U] **1** The **acceleration** of a process or change is the fact that it is getting faster and faster. ❑ *He has also called for an acceleration of political reforms.* **2** **Acceleration** is the rate at which a car or other vehicle can increase its speed, often seen in terms of the time that it takes to reach a particular speed. ❑ *Acceleration to 60 mph takes a mere 5.7 seconds.* ❑ *The flexible engine provides smooth acceleration at low speeds.*

ac•cel•era•tor /ækˈseləreɪtə/ NOUN [C] (**accelerators**) The **accelerator** in a car or other vehicle is the pedal that you press with your foot in order to make the vehicle go faster. ❑ *He eased his foot off the accelerator.*

✪ **ac•cent** /ˈæksənt/ NOUN [C] (**accents**) **1** Someone who speaks with a particular **accent** pronounces the words of a language in a distinctive way that shows which country, region, or background they come from. ❑ *He had developed a slight southern accent.* **2** An **accent** is a short line or other mark which is written above certain letters in some languages and which indicates the way those letters are pronounced. ❑ *an acute accent*

✪ **ac•cept** ◆◆◆ /əkˈsept/ VERB [I, T] (**accepts, accepting, accepted**) **1** [I, T] If you **accept** something that you have been offered, you say yes to it or agree to take it. = take, welcome; ≠ refuse ❑ *students who have accepted an offer of a university place* ❑ *Eventually Esteban persuaded her to accept an offer of marriage.* ❑ *All those invited to next week's peace conference have accepted.* **2** [T] If you **accept** an idea, statement, or fact, you believe that it is true or valid. = acknowledge, recognize; ≠ reject, dispute ❑ *It is now accepted as fact that the brain and the immune system communicate.* ❑ *a workforce generally accepted to have the best conditions in Europe* ❑ *I do not accept that there is any kind of crisis in American science.* ❑ *I don't think they would accept that view.* **3** [T] If you **accept** a plan or an intended action, you agree to it and allow it to happen. ❑ *The Council will meet to decide if it should accept his resignation.* **4** [T] If you **accept** an unpleasant fact or situation, you get used to it or recognize that it is necessary or cannot be changed. ❑ *People will accept suffering that can be shown to lead to a greater good.* ❑ *Urban dwellers often accept noise as part of city life.* **5** [T] If a person, company, or organization **accepts** something such as a document, they recognize that it is genuine, correct, or satisfactory and agree to consider it or handle it. ❑ *We took the unusual step of contacting newspapers to advise them not to accept the advertising.* **6** [T] If an organization or person **accepts** you, you are allowed to join the organization or use the services that are offered. ❑ *All-male groups will not be accepted.* **7** [T] If a person or a group of people **accepts** you, they begin to be friendly towards you and are happy with who you are or what you do. ❑ *As far as my grandparents were concerned, they've never had a problem accepting me.* ❑ *Many men still have difficulty accepting a woman as a business partner.* **8** [T] If you **accept** the responsibility or blame for something, you recognize that you are responsible for it. ❑ *The company cannot accept responsibility for loss or damage.* **9** [T] If you **accept** someone's advice or suggestion, you agree to do what they say. ❑ *The army refused to accept orders from the political leadership.* **10** [T] If a machine **accepts** a particular kind of thing, it is designed to take it and deal with it or process it. ❑ *The new parking meters don't accept dollar bills.*
→ See also **accepted**

✪ **ac•cept•able** ◆◇◇ /əkˈseptəbəl/ ADJ **1** **Acceptable** activities and situations are those that most people approve of or consider to be normal. ❑ *It is becoming more acceptable for women to drink.* ❑ *The air pollution exceeds most acceptable levels by 10 times or more.* **2** If something is **acceptable to** someone, they agree to consider it, use it, or allow it to happen. = satisfactory; ≠ unacceptable ❑ *They have thrashed out a compromise formula acceptable to Moscow.* ❑ *They recently failed to negotiate a mutually acceptable new contract.* **3** If you describe something as **acceptable**, you mean that it is good enough or fairly good. ❑ *On the far side of the street was a restaurant that looked acceptable.*
ac•cept•abil•ity /əkˌseptəˈbɪliti/ NOUN [U] ❑ *This assumption played a considerable part in increasing the social acceptability of divorce.*
ac•cept•ably /əkˈseptəbli/ ADV **1** The aim of discipline is to teach children to behave acceptably. **2** *a method that provides an acceptably accurate solution to a problem*

✪ **ac•cept•ance** /əkˈseptəns/ NOUN [C, U] (**acceptances**) **1** [C, U] **Acceptance of** an offer or a proposal is the act of saying yes to it or agreeing to it. ≠ refusal ❑ *The Party is being degraded by its acceptance of secret donations.* ❑ *his acceptance speech for the Nobel Peace Prize* ❑ *a letter of acceptance* **2** [U] If there is **acceptance** of an idea, most people believe or agree that it is true. = agreement; ≠ disagreement ❑ *a theory that is steadily gaining acceptance* ❑ *There was a general acceptance that the defence budget would shrink.* **3** [U] Your **acceptance of** a situation, especially an unpleasant or difficult one, is an attitude or feeling that you cannot change it and that you must get used to it. ❑ *The most impressive thing about him is his calm acceptance of whatever comes his way.* **4** [U] **Acceptance** of someone into a group means beginning to think of them as part of the group and to act in a friendly way towards them. = recognition ❑ *A very determined effort by society will ensure that the disabled achieve real acceptance and integration.*

ac•cept•ed ◆◆◇ /əkˈseptɪd/ ADJ **Accepted** ideas are agreed by most people to be correct or reasonable. ❑ *There is no generally accepted definition of life.*
→ See also **accept**

✪ **ac•cess** ◆◆◇ /ˈækses/ NOUN, VERB (*academic word*)
NOUN [U] **1** If you have **access to** a building or other place, you are able or allowed to go into it. ❑ *The facilities have been adapted to give access to wheelchair users.* ❑ *For logistical and political reasons, scientists have only recently been able to gain access to the area.* **2** If you have **access to** something such as information or equipment, you have the opportunity or right to see it or use it. ❑ *a Code of Practice that would give patients access to their medical records* ❑ *households with internet access* **3** If you have **access to** a person, you have the opportunity or right to see them or meet them. ❑ *He was not allowed access to a lawyer.*
VERB [T] (**accesses, accessing, accessed**) If you **access** something, especially information held on a computer,

you succeed in finding or obtaining it. ❑ *You've illegally accessed and misused confidential security files.* ❑ *a service that allows users to access the internet on their phones*

⭐**ac·ces·si·ble** /æk'sesɪbəl/ ADJ **1** If a place or building is **accessible to** people, it is easy for them to reach it or get into it. If an object is **accessible**, it is easy to reach. ❑ *The centre is easily accessible to the general public.* **2** If something is **accessible** to people, they can easily use it or obtain it. ❑ *The aim of any reform of legal aid should be to make the system accessible to more people.* **3** If you describe a book, painting, or other work of art as **accessible**, you think it is good because it is simple enough for people to understand and appreciate easily. ❑ *Both say they want to write literary books that are accessible to a general audience.*

ac·ces·sibil·ity /æk͵sesɪ'bɪlɪti/ NOUN [U] **1** *the easy accessibility of the area* **2** *growing public concern about the cost, quality and accessibility of health care* **3** *Seminar topics are chosen for their accessibility to a general audience.*

ac·ces·so·ry /æk'sesəri/ NOUN [C] (**accessories**) **1** **Accessories** are items of equipment that are not usually essential, but can be used with or added to something else in order to make it more efficient, useful, or decorative. ❑ *an exclusive range of hand-made bedroom and bathroom accessories* **2** **Accessories** are articles such as belts and scarves which you wear or carry but which are not part of your main clothing. ❑ *It also has a good range of accessories, including sunglasses, handbags and belts.* **3** (*legal*) If someone is guilty of being an **accessory to** a crime, they helped the person who committed it, or knew it was being committed but did not tell the police. = accomplice ❑ *She had been charged with being an accessory to the embezzlement of funds from a co-operative farm.*

ac·ci·dent ◆◇◇ /'æksɪdənt/ NOUN [C, U] (**accidents**) **1** [C] An **accident** happens when a vehicle hits a person, an object, or another vehicle, causing injury or damage. ❑ *She was involved in a serious car accident last week.* **2** [C] If someone has an **accident**, something unpleasant happens to them that was not intended, sometimes causing injury or death. ❑ *5,000 people die every year because of accidents in the home.* **3** [C, U] If something happens **by accident**, it happens completely by chance. = chance ❑ *She discovered the problem by accident during a visit to a nearby school.*

ac·ci·den·tal /͵æksɪ'dentəl/ ADJ An **accidental** event happens by chance or as the result of an accident, and is not intended. ❑ *the tragic accidental shooting of his younger brother*

ac·ci·den·tal·ly /͵æksɪ'dentli/ ADV [accidentally with V] ❑ *A policeman accidentally killed his two best friends with a single bullet.*

ac·claim /ə'kleɪm/ VERB, NOUN
 VERB [T] (**acclaims, acclaiming, acclaimed**) (*formal*) If someone or something **is acclaimed**, they are praised enthusiastically. ❑ *The restaurant has been widely acclaimed for its excellent French cuisine.* ❑ *He was acclaimed as America's greatest film-maker.*
 NOUN [U] (*formal*) **Acclaim** is public praise for someone or something. = praise ❑ *Angela Bassett has won critical acclaim for her excellent performance.*

ac·claimed /ə'kleɪmd/ ADJ ❑ *She has published six highly acclaimed novels.*

⭐**ac·cli·ma·tize** /ə'klaɪmətaɪz/ also **acclimatise** VERB [I, T] (**acclimatizes, acclimatizing, acclimatized**) When you **acclimatize** or are **acclimatized to** a new situation, place, or climate, you become used to it. = adapt, adjust ❑ *The athletes are acclimatizing to the heat by staying in Monte Carlo.* ❑ *Childhood eczema is caused by the body becoming acclimatized to the type of diet that we now eat.* ❑ *This year he has left for St. Louis early to acclimatize himself.*

ac·co·lade /'ækəleɪd/ NOUN [C] (**accolades**) (*formal*) If someone is given an **accolade**, something is done or said about them which shows how much people admire them. = tribute ❑ *The Nobel Prize has become the ultimate accolade in the sciences.* ❑ *He won accolades as one of America's top test pilots.*

ac·com·mo·date /ə'kɒmədeɪt/ VERB [T] (**accommodates, accommodating, accommodated**) (*academic word*) **1** If a building or space can **accommodate** someone or something, it has enough room for them. ❑ *The school was not big enough to accommodate all the children.* **2** To **accommodate** someone means to provide them with a place to live or stay. ❑ *a hotel built to accommodate guests for the wedding of King Alfonso* **3** (*formal*) If something is planned or changed to **accommodate** a particular situation, it is planned or changed so that it takes this situation into account. ❑ *The roads are built to accommodate gradual temperature changes.*

⭐**ac·com·mo·da·tion** /ə͵kɒmə'deɪʃən/ NOUN [U] **Accommodation** is the buildings or rooms where people live or stay. ❑ *The government will provide temporary accommodation for up to three thousand homeless people.*

ac·com·pa·ni·ment /ə'kʌmpnɪmənt/ NOUN
 NOUN [C] (**accompaniments**) **1** The **accompaniment** to a song or tune is the music that is played at the same time as it and forms a background to it. ❑ *He sang 'My Funny Valentine' and 'Wanted' to musical director Jim Steffan's piano accompaniment.* **2** An **accompaniment** is something that goes with another thing. ❑ *This recipe makes a good accompaniment to ice cream.*
 PHRASE **to the accompaniment of something** If one thing happens **to the accompaniment of** another, they happen at the same time.

⭐**ac·com·pa·ny** ◆◇◇ /ə'kʌmpəni/ VERB [T] (**accompanies, accompanying, accompanied**) (*academic word*) **1** (*formal*) If you **accompany** someone, you go somewhere with them. = escort ❑ *Ken agreed to accompany me on a trip to Africa.* ❑ *She was accompanied by her younger brother.* **2** (*formal*) If one thing **accompanies** another, it happens or exists at the same time, or as a result of it. ❑ *This volume of essays was designed to accompany an exhibition in Seattle.* **3** If you **accompany** a singer or a musician, you play one part of a piece of music while they sing or play the main tune. ❑ *On Meredith's new recording, Eddie Higgins accompanies her on all but one song.*

ac·com·plice /ə'kʌmplɪs, AmE ə'kɒm-/ NOUN [C] (**accomplices**) Someone's **accomplice** is a person who helps them to commit a crime. ❑ *Witnesses said the gunman immediately ran to a motorcycle being ridden by an accomplice.*

ac·com·plish /ə'kʌmplɪʃ, AmE ə'ka:m-/ VERB [T] (**accomplishes, accomplishing, accomplished**) If you **accomplish** something, you succeed in doing it. = achieve ❑ *If we'd all work together, I think we could accomplish our goal.*

ac·com·plished /ə'kʌmplɪʃt, AmE ə'ka:m-/ ADJ (*formal*) If someone is **accomplished** at something, they are very good at it. ❑ *She is an accomplished painter and a prolific author of stories for children.*

ac·com·plish·ment /ə'kʌmplɪʃmənt, AmE ə'ka:m-/ NOUN [C] (**accomplishments**) An **accomplishment** is something remarkable that has been done or achieved. = achievement ❑ *For a novelist, that's quite an accomplishment.*

ac·cord ◆◆◇ /ə'kɔ:d/ NOUN, VERB
 NOUN [C] (**accords**) An **accord** between countries or groups of people is a formal agreement; for example, to end a war. ❑ *UNITA was legalized as a political party under the 1991 peace accords.*
 PHRASES **of its own accord** If something happens **of its own accord**, it seems to happen by itself, without anyone making it happen. ❑ *In many cases the disease will clear up of its own accord.*
 of one's own accord If you do something **of your own accord**, you do it because you want to, without being asked or forced. = voluntarily ❑ *He did not quit as France's prime minister of his own accord.*
 VERB [T] (**accords, according, accorded**) (*formal*) If you **are accorded** a particular kind of treatment, people act towards you or treat you in that way. = grant ❑ *His predecessor was accorded an equally tumultuous welcome.* ❑ *On his return home, the government accorded him the rank of Colonel.*

ac·cord·ance /ə'kɔ:dəns/ NOUN
 PHRASE **in accordance with** If something is done **in accordance with** a particular rule or system, it is done in the way that the rule or system says that it should be done. ❑ *Entries which are illegible or otherwise not in accordance with the rules will be disqualified.*

ac·cord·ing·ly /əˈkɔːdɪŋli/ ADV **1** You use **accordingly** to introduce a fact or situation that is a result or consequence of something that you have just referred to. = therefore, consequently ☐ *We have a different background, a different history. Accordingly, we have the right to different futures.* **2** [accordingly after v] If you consider a situation and then act **accordingly**, the way you act depends on the nature of the situation. ☐ *It is a difficult job and they should be paid accordingly.*

✪ **ac·cord·ing to** ♦♦♦

PHRASES **according to** **1** If someone says that something is true **according to** a particular person, book, or other source of information, they are indicating where they got their information. ☐ *The van raced away, according to police reports, and police gave chase.* ☐ *According to current theory, novae are close double stars.* **2** If something is done **according to** a particular set of principles, these principles are used as a basis for the way it is done. = based on ☐ *They both played the game according to the rules.* ☐ *Coal is usually classified according to a scale of hardness and purity.* **3** If something varies **according to** a changing factor, it varies in a way that is determined by this factor. = depending on ☐ *Prices vary according to the quantity ordered.*

according to plan If something happens **according to plan**, it happens in exactly the way that it was intended to happen. ☐ *If all goes according to plan, the first concert will be on Tuesday evening.*

USAGE NOTE

according to

Note that if you want to emphasize that what you are saying is your own opinion, you say 'In my opinion', not 'according to me'.
In my opinion, we are facing a national emergency.

✪ **ac·count** ♦♦♦ /əˈkaʊnt/ NOUN

NOUN [c] (**accounts**) **1** If you have an **account** with a bank or a similar organization, you have an arrangement to leave your money there and take some out when you need it. ☐ *Some banks make it difficult to open an account.* **2** (*business*) In business, a regular customer of a company can be referred to as an **account**, especially when the customer is another company. ☐ *All three Internet agencies boast they've won major accounts.* **3** (*business*) **Accounts** are detailed records of all the money that a person or business receives and spends. ☐ *He kept detailed accounts.* **4** An **account** is a written or spoken report of something that has happened. = report, description ☐ *He gave a detailed account of what happened on the fateful night.* ☐ *According to police accounts, Mr and Mrs Hunt were found dead in their kitchen.*

PHRASES **by all accounts** or **from all accounts** If you say that something is true **by all accounts** or **from all accounts**, you believe it is true because other people say so. ☐ *He is, by all accounts, a superb teacher.*

of no account or **of little account** (*formal*) If you say that something is **of no account** or **of little account**, you mean that it is very unimportant and is not worth considering. ☐ *These obscure groups were of little account in either national or international politics.*

on account If you buy or pay for something **on account**, you pay nothing or only part of the cost at first, and pay the rest later. ☐ *He was ordered to pay the company $500,000 on account pending a final assessment of his liability.*

on account of You use **on account of** to introduce the reason or explanation for something. ☐ *The president declined to deliver the speech himself, on account of a sore throat.*

on someone's account **1** Your feelings **on** someone's **account** are the feelings you have about what they have experienced or might experience, especially when you imagine yourself to be in their situation. ☐ *Mollie told me what she'd done and I was really scared on her account.* **2** (*spoken*) If you tell someone not to do something **on** your **account**, you mean that they should do it only if they want to, and not because they think it will please you. ☐ *Don't leave on my account.*

on no account (*emphasis*) If you say that something should **on no account** be done, you are emphasizing that it should not be done under any circumstances. ☐ *On no account should the mixture come near to boiling.*

on one's own account If you do something **on** your **own account**, you do it because you want to and without being asked, and you take responsibility for your own action. ☐ *I told him if he withdrew it was on his own account.*

take into account or **take account of** If you **take** something **into account**, or **take account of** something, you consider it when you are thinking about a situation or deciding what to do. = consider ☐ *The defendant asked for 21 similar offences to be taken into account.*

be called to account or **be held to account** or **be brought to account** If someone **is called, held**, or **brought to account** for something they have done wrong, they are made to explain why they did it, and are often criticized or punished for it. ☐ *Individuals who repeatedly provide false information should be called to account for their actions.*

give a good account of oneself (*BrE*) If you say that someone **gave a good account of** themselves in a particular situation, you mean that they performed well, although they may not have been completely successful. ☐ *We have been hindered by our lack of preparation, but I'm sure we will give a good account of ourselves.*

PHRASAL VERB **account for** (**accounts, accounting, accounted**) **1** If a particular thing **accounts for** a part or proportion of something, that part or proportion consists of that thing, or is used or produced by it. ☐ *Computers account for 5% of the country's commercial electricity consumption.* ☐ *Pension funds currently account for around a third of all equity investment in Britain.* **2** If something **accounts for** a particular fact or situation, it causes or explains it. = explain ☐ *The gene they discovered today doesn't account for all those cases.* **3** If you can **account for** something, you can explain it or give the necessary information about it. = explain ☐ *How do you account for the company's alarmingly high staff turnover?* **4** If someone has to **account for** an action or policy, they are responsible for it, and may be required to explain it to other people or be punished if it fails. = answer for ☐ *The president and the president alone must account for his government's reforms.* **5** If a sum of money **is accounted for** in a budget, it has been included in that budget for a particular purpose. = budget for ☐ *The really heavy costs have been accounted for.*
→ See also **accounting, bank account**

ac·count·able /əˈkaʊntəbəl/ ADJ If you are **accountable to** someone for something that you do, you are responsible for it and must be prepared to justify your actions to that person. ☐ *Public officials can finally be held accountable for their actions.*
ac·count·abil·ity /əˌkaʊntəˈbɪlɪti/ NOUN [u] ☐ *a drive towards democracy and greater accountability*

ac·count·ant /əˈkaʊntənt/ NOUN [c] (**accountants**) An **accountant** is a person whose job is to keep financial accounts.

ac·count·ing /əˈkaʊntɪŋ/ NOUN [u] **Accounting** is the activity of keeping detailed records of the amounts of money a business or person receives and spends. ☐ *the accounting firm of Leventhal & Horwath*
→ See also **account**

✪ **ac·cu·mu·late** /əˈkjuːmjʊleɪt/ VERB [i, t] (**accumulates, accumulating, accumulated**) (*academic word*) When you **accumulate** things or when they **accumulate**, they collect or are gathered over a period of time. = build up, gather, amass ☐ *Lead can accumulate in the body until toxic levels are reached.* ☐ *Households accumulate wealth across a broad spectrum of assets.*

✪ **ac·cu·mu·la·tion** /əˌkjuːmjʊˈleɪʃən/ NOUN [c, u] (**accumulations**) **1** [c] An **accumulation of** something is a large number of things that have been collected together or acquired over a period of time. ☐ *an accumulation of experience and knowledge* **2** [u] **Accumulation** is the collecting together of things over a period of time. ☐ *the accumulation of capital and the distribution of income*

✪ **ac·cu·ra·cy** /ˈækjʊrəsi/ NOUN [u] **1** The **accuracy of** information or measurements is their quality of being true or correct, even in small details. = exactness, precision, correctness; ≠ inaccuracy, vagueness ❏ *Every care has been taken to ensure the accuracy of all information given in this leaflet.* **2** If someone or something performs a task, for example, hitting a target, **with accuracy**, they do it in an exact way without making a mistake. ❏ *weapons that could fire with accuracy at targets 3,000 yards away*

⧫**ac·cu·rate** ♦◇◇ /ˈækjʊrət/ ADJ (*academic word*)
1 Accurate information, measurements, and statistics are correct to a very detailed level. An **accurate** instrument is able to give you information of this kind. = precise, exact ❏ *Police have stressed that this is the most accurate description of the killer to date.* **2** An **accurate** statement or account gives a true or fair judgment of something. = correct; ≠ incorrect ❏ *Stalin gave an accurate assessment of the utility of nuclear weapons.* **3** You can use **accurate** to describe the results of someone's actions when they do or copy something correctly or exactly. ❏ *We require grammar and spelling to be accurate.* **4** An **accurate** weapon or throw reaches the exact point or target that it was intended to reach. You can also describe a person as **accurate** if they fire a weapon or throw something in this way. ❏ *His throws were long, hard and accurate, as always.*

⧫**ac·cu·rate·ly** /ˈækjʊrətli/ ADV **1** = precisely, exactly, correctly ❏ *The test can accurately predict what a bigger explosion would do.* **2** [accurately with v] = precisely, exactly, correctly ❏ *What many people mean by the word 'power' could be more accurately described as 'control'.* **3** [accurately with v] ≠ inaccurately, incorrectly ❏ *He hit the golf ball powerfully and accurately.*

WORD FAMILIES	
accurate ADJ	The device gives your location *accurate* to within 1 metre.
inaccurate ADJ	Unfortunately the reports were based on *inaccurate* information.
accurately ADV	She ensured that travel times were calculated *accurately*.
inaccurately ADV	He claimed his remarks had been reported *inaccurately*.
accuracy NOUN	Every care has been taken to ensure the *accuracy* of all information given in this leaflet.
inaccuracy NOUN	He was disturbed by the *inaccuracy* of the answers.

VOCABULARY BUILDER

accurately ADV
You use **accurately** to show that great care has been taken to make sure that information or measurements are correct in every respect.
❏ *We want to make sure that we are accurately reflecting contemporary Britain as it is today.*

precisely ADV
You use **precisely** to show that something is correct down to the smallest detail.
❏ *The huge differences between education and wealth in parts of India are precisely matched by the breast cancer rates.*

exactly ADV
You use **exactly** before an amount, number, or position to emphasize that it is no more, no less, or no different from what you are stating.
❏ *The Pakistani prime minister's helicopter landed at exactly 3.45 p.m.*

correctly ADV
You use **correctly** to show that something is being done, or has been done, as it ought to be, without any mistakes.
❏ *It was more than five months before Drew's lump was correctly diagnosed.*

⧫**ac·cu·sa·tion** /ˌækjʊˈzeɪʃən/ NOUN [C, U] (**accusations**)
1 [C, U] If you make an **accusation** against someone, you criticize them or express the belief that they have done something wrong. = charge ❏ *Kim rejects accusations that country music is over-sentimental.* **2** [C] An **accusation** is a statement or claim by a witness or someone in authority that a particular person has committed a crime, although this has not yet been proved. = charge, allegation, complaint ❏ *people who have made public accusations of rape* ❏ *The government denied the accusation that it was involved in the murders.*

⧫**ac·cuse** ♦♦◇ /əˈkjuːz/ VERB
VERB [T] (**accuses, accusing, accused**) **1** If you accuse someone **of** doing something wrong or dishonest, you say or tell them that you believe that they did it. = blame ❏ *My mum was really upset because she was accusing her of having an affair with another man.* **2** If you **are accused of** a crime, a witness or someone in authority states or claims that you did it, and you may be formally charged with it and put on trial. = charge ❏ *Her assistant was accused of theft and fraud by the police.* ❏ *He faced a total of seven charges, all accusing him of lying in his testimony.*
PHRASE **stand accused** If someone **stands accused of** something, they have been accused of it. ❏ *The candidate stands accused of breaking promises even before he's in office.*
→ See also **accused**

ac·cused /əˈkjuːzd/ NOUN [C] (**accused**) (*legal*) You can use **the accused** to refer to a person or a group of people charged with a crime or on trial for it. = defendant ❏ *The accused is alleged to be a member of a right-wing gang.*

ac·cus·tom /əˈkʌstəm/ VERB [T] (**accustoms, accustoming, accustomed**) (*formal*) If you **accustom** yourself or another person **to** something, you make yourself or them become used to it. = familiarize ❏ *She tried to accustom herself to the tight bandages.*
→ See also **accustomed**

ac·cus·tomed /əˈkʌstəmd/ ADJ **1** [V-LINK + accustomed 'to' N/-ING] If you **are accustomed to** something, you know it so well or have experienced it so often that it seems natural, unsurprising, or easy to deal with. = used ❏ *I was accustomed to being the only child at a table full of adults.* **2** [V-LINK + accustomed 'to' N] When your eyes become **accustomed to** darkness or bright light, they adjust so that you start to be able to see things, after not being able to see properly at first. ❏ *My eyes were becoming accustomed to the gloom and I was able to make out a door at one side of the room.*

ace /eɪs/ NOUN, ADJ
NOUN [C] (**aces**) **1** An **ace** is a playing card with a single symbol on it. In most card games, the ace of a particular suit has either the highest or the lowest value of the cards in that suit. ❏ *the ace of hearts* **2** (*journalism*) If you describe someone such as a sports player as an **ace**, you mean that they are very good at what they do. ❏ *Despite the loss of their ace early in the game, Seattle beat the Brewers 6-5.* **3** In tennis, an **ace** is a serve which is so fast that the other player cannot reach the ball. ❏ *Agassi believed he had served an ace at 5-3 (40-30) in the deciding set.*
PHRASE **ace in the hole** [V-LINK + ace in the hole, ace in the hole after V] Something that is an **ace in the hole** is an advantage which you have over an opponent or rival, and which you can use if necessary. ❏ *Our superior technology is our ace in the hole.*
ADJ [ace + N] You can use **ace** to describe someone such as a sports player who is very good at what they do. ❏ *ace horror-film producer Lawrence Woolsey*

ache /eɪk/ VERB, NOUN
VERB [I] (**aches, aching, ached**) If you **ache** or a part of your body **aches**, you feel a steady, fairly strong pain. ❏ *The glands in her neck were swollen, her head was throbbing and she ached all over.* ❏ *My leg is giving me much less pain but still aches when I sit down.*
NOUN [C] (**aches**) An **ache** is a steady, fairly strong pain in a part of your body. ❏ *You feel nausea and aches in your muscles.*
PHRASE **aches and pains** You can use **aches and pains** to refer in a general way to any minor pains that you feel in your body. ❏ *It seems to ease all the aches and pains of a hectic and tiring day.*
→ See also **headache, heartache**

a

⊙ **achieve** ♦♦◇ /əˈtʃiːv/ VERB [T] (**achieves, achieving, achieved**) (*academic word*) If you **achieve** a particular aim or effect, you succeed in doing it or causing it to happen, usually after a lot of effort. = accomplish, manage; ≠ fail ❑ *There are many who will work hard to achieve these goals.* ❑ *We have achieved what we set out to do.*

⊙ **achieve·ment** ♦◇◇ /əˈtʃiːvmənt/ NOUN [C, U] (**achievements**) **1** [C] An **achievement** is something that someone has succeeded in doing, especially after a lot of effort. = accomplishment, success; ≠ failure ❑ *It was a great achievement that a month later a global agreement was reached.* **2** [U] **Achievement** is the process of achieving something. ❑ *It is only the achievement of these goals that will finally bring lasting peace.*

acid ♦◇◇ /ˈæsɪd/ NOUN, ADJ
[NOUN] [C, U] (**acids**) An **acid** is a chemical substance, usually a liquid, which contains hydrogen and can react with other substances to form salts. Some acids burn or dissolve other substances that they come into contact with. ❑ *citric acid*
[ADJ] An **acid** substance contains acid. ❑ *These shrubs must have an acid, lime-free soil.*
acid·ity /æˈsɪdɪti/ NOUN [U] [oft acidity 'of' N] ❑ *the acidity of rainwater*
acid·ic /əˈsɪdɪk/ ADJ **Acidic** substances contain acid. ❑ *Dissolved carbon dioxide makes the water more acidic.*

acid rain NOUN [U] **Acid rain** is rain polluted by acid that has been released into the atmosphere from factories and other industrial processes. Acid rain is harmful to the environment.

⊙ **ac·knowl·edge** ♦◇◇ /əkˈnɒlɪdʒ/ VERB [T] (**acknowledges, acknowledging, acknowledged**) (*academic word*) **1** (*formal*) If you **acknowledge** a fact or a situation, you accept or admit that it is true or that it exists. = recognize, accept, grant ❑ *Naylor acknowledged, in a letter to the judge, that he was a drug addict.* ❑ *It is widely acknowledged that transferring knowledge in a classroom environment is very inefficient.* ❑ *Belatedly, the government has acknowledged the problem.* ❑ *There is an acknowledged risk of lung cancer from radon.* **2** If someone's achievements, status, or qualities **are acknowledged**, they are known about and recognized by a lot of people, or by a particular group of people. = recognize ❑ *He is also acknowledged as an excellent goalkeeper.* ❑ *Some of the clergy refused to acknowledge the new king's legitimacy.* **3** If you **acknowledge** the source of some information in a piece of academic writing, you state clearly where the information came from. ❑ *Every time you borrow the words, facts, or ideas of others, you must acknowledge the source.* **4** If you **acknowledge** a message or letter, you write to the person who sent it in order to say that you have received it. ❑ *The army sent me a postcard acknowledging my request.* **5** If you **acknowledge** someone, for example, by moving your head or smiling, you show that you have seen and recognized them. ❑ *He saw her but refused to even acknowledge her.*

WORD CONNECTIONS
acknowledge + NOUN
acknowledge the **existence** of ...
acknowledge the **importance** of ...
acknowledge the **need** for ...
❑ *The school acknowledges the importance of good communication between teachers and parents.*
acknowledge a **fact**
acknowledge a **mistake**
acknowledge a **risk**
acknowledge **difficulties**
❑ *Dean acknowledged his mistake and apologized.*
ADV + **acknowledge**
publicly acknowledge
readily acknowledge
❑ *The president has publicly acknowledged that he made a mistake.*

widely acknowledged
universally acknowledged
❑ *It was universally acknowledged that the policy had failed.*

⊙ **ac·knowl·edg·ment** /əkˈnɒlɪdʒmənt/ also **acknowledgement** NOUN [SING, PL, U] (**acknowledgments**) **1** [SING] [also no DET] An **acknowledgment** is a statement or action which recognizes that something exists or is true. = recognition ❑ *The president's resignation appears to be an acknowledgment that he has lost all hope of keeping the country together.* ❑ *This is a clear acknowledgement of the need to improve corporate governance.* **2** [PL] The **acknowledgments** in a book are the section in which the author thanks all the people who have helped him or her. ❑ *two whole pages of acknowledgments* ❑ *In the acknowledgements, Weis lists five people who acted as research assistants.* **3** [U] [also 'an' acknowledgment] A gesture of **acknowledgment**, such as a smile, shows someone that you have seen and recognized them. ❑ *Farling smiled in acknowledgment and gave a bow.*

⊙ **acous·tic** /əˈkuːstɪk/ ADJ, NOUN
[ADJ] **1** [acoustic + N] An **acoustic** guitar or other instrument is one whose sound is produced without any electrical equipment. **2** **Acoustic** means relating to sound or hearing. ❑ *acoustic signals* ❑ *acoustic sensors used to detect promising formations for drilling offshore*
[NOUN] [C, U] (**acoustics**) **1** [C] If you refer to the **acoustics** of a space, you are referring to the structural features which determine how well you can hear music or speech in it. ❑ *In this performance, Rattle had the acoustics of the Symphony Hall on his side.* **2** [U] **Acoustics** is the scientific study of sound. ❑ *his work in acoustics*

ac·quaint /əˈkweɪnt/ VERB [T] (**acquaints, acquainting, acquainted**) (*formal*) If you **acquaint** someone with something, you tell them about it so that they know it. If you **acquaint yourself with** something, you learn about it. = familiarize ❑ *Have steps been taken to acquaint breeders with their right to apply for licences?*
→ See also **acquainted**

ac·quaint·ance /əˈkweɪntəns/ NOUN
[NOUN] [C, U] (**acquaintances**) **1** [C] An **acquaintance** is someone who you have met and know slightly, but not well. ❑ *He exchanged a few words with the proprietor, an old acquaintance of his.* **2** [C, U] If you have an **acquaintance** with someone, you have met them and you know them. ❑ *a writer who becomes involved in a real murder mystery through his acquaintance with a police officer*
[PHRASE] **make someone's acquaintance** (*formal*) When you **make** someone's **acquaintance**, you meet them for the first time and get to know them a little. ❑ *I first made his acquaintance in the early 1960s.*

ac·quaint·ed /əˈkweɪntɪd/ ADJ **1** [V-LINK + acquainted 'with' N] (*formal*) If you are **acquainted with** something, you know about it because you have learned it or experienced it. = familiar ❑ *He was well acquainted with the literature of Latin America.* **2** [V-LINK + acquainted] If you get or become **acquainted with** someone that you do not know, you talk to each other or do something together so that you get to know each other. You can also say that two people get or become **acquainted**. ❑ *At first the meetings were a way to get acquainted with each other.*
→ See also **acquaint**

⊙ **ac·quire** ♦◇◇ /əˈkwaɪə/ VERB [T] (**acquires, acquiring, acquired**) (*academic word*) **1** (*formal*) If you **acquire** something, you buy or obtain it for yourself, or someone gives it to you. ≠ lose ❑ *General Motors acquired a 50% stake in Saab for about $400m.* **2** If you **acquire** something such as a skill or a habit, you learn it, or develop it through your daily life or experience. ≠ lose ❑ *I've never acquired a taste for wine.* ❑ *Their sleeping brains were continuing to process the newly acquired information.* **3** If someone or something **acquires** a certain reputation, they start to have that reputation. ❑ *During her film career, she acquired a reputation as a strong-willed, outspoken woman.*

WORD CONNECTIONS

acquire + NOUN

acquire a **stake**
acquire a **share**
❏ *Skywings acquired a 20% stake in the business.*

acquire **land**
acquire **property**
acquire **assets**
acquire **wealth**
❏ *The property was acquired for residential purposes.*

acquire a **skill**
acquire a **habit**
acquire **knowledge**
❏ *The course will help you acquire the skills and knowledge needed to become a nurse.*

acquire a **reputation**
❏ *Ella had acquired a reputation as a troublemaker.*

ADV + **acquire**

newly acquired
recently acquired
❏ *Ahmed's birthday gave me the chance to show off my newly acquired cake making skills.*

✪ **ac·qui·si·tion** ◆◇◇ /ˌækwɪˈzɪʃən/ NOUN [C, U] (**acquisitions**) **1** [C, U] (*business*) If a company or business person makes an **acquisition**, they buy another company or part of a company. = purchase, procurement, achievement, attainment; ≠ sale, loss ❏ *the acquisition of a profitable paper recycling company* ❏ *the number of mergers and acquisitions made by Europe's 1,000 leading firms* **2** [C] If you make an **acquisition**, you buy or obtain something, often to add to things that you already have. = purchase ❏ *How did you go about making this marvelous acquisition then?* **3** [U] The **acquisition** of a skill or a particular type of knowledge is the process of learning it or developing it. ❏ *language acquisition* ❏ *the acquisition of basic skills*

VOCABULARY BUILDER

acquisition NOUN (*formal*)
If you make an **acquisition**, you buy or obtain something.
❏ *Some of the most striking reforms are aimed at making the acquisition of land faster and easier.*

purchase NOUN (*formal*)
The **purchase** of something is the act of buying it.
❏ *Research found that one in five internet users has never made an online purchase.*

procurement NOUN (*formal*)
Procurement is the act of obtaining something such as supplies for an army or other organization.
❏ *Mr Barnett expected to save $180 million by devolving government procurement back to the departments.*

achievement NOUN
Achievement is the process of succeeding in something after a lot of effort.
❏ *The expeditions were considered to be one of the great achievements of the Ming Dynasty.*

attainment NOUN (*formal*)
The **attainment** of an aim is when you succeed in reaching it.
❏ *There are definite links between poor housing, educational attainment, and life chances.*

ac·quit /əˈkwɪt/ VERB [T] (**acquits, acquitting, acquitted**) If someone **is acquitted of** a crime in a court of law, they are formally declared not to have committed the crime. = clear ❏ *Mr Castorina was acquitted of attempted murder.*

ac·quit·tal /əˈkwɪtəl/ NOUN [C, U] (**acquittals**) **Acquittal** is a formal declaration in a court of law that someone who has been accused of a crime is innocent. ❏ *the acquittal of six police officers charged with beating up*

a suspect ❏ *The jury voted 8 to 4 in favour of acquittal.*

✪ **acre** ◆◇◇ /ˈeɪkə/ NOUN [C] (**acres**) An **acre** is an area of land measuring 4,840 square yards or 4,047 square metres. ❏ *The property consists of two acres of land.* ❏ *a 15-acre cattle farm*

across ◆◆◆ /əˈkrɒs, AmE əˈkrɔːs/ PREP, ADV

> In addition to the uses shown below, **across** is used in phrasal verbs such as 'come across', 'get across', and 'put across'.

PREP **1** If someone or something goes **across** a place or a boundary, they go from one side of it to the other. ❏ *She walked across the floor and lay down on the bed.* ❏ *He watched Karl run across the street to Tommy.* **2** If something is situated or stretched **across** something else, it is situated or stretched from one side of it to the other. ❏ *the floating bridge across Lake Washington in Seattle* ❏ *He scrawled his name across the page.* **3** If something is lying **across** an object or place, it is resting on it and partly covering it. = over ❏ *She found her clothes lying across the chair.* **4** Something that is **across** something such as a street, river, or area is on the other side of it. ❏ *Anyone from the houses across the road could see him.* **5** You use **across** to say that a particular expression is shown on someone's face. = over ❏ *An enormous grin spread across his face.* **6** If someone hits you **across** the face or head, they hit you on that part. ❏ *Graham hit him across the face with the gun, then pushed him against the wall.* **7** When something happens **across** a place or organization, it happens equally everywhere within it. ❏ *The film opens across the country on December 11.* **8** When something happens **across** a political, religious, or social barrier, it involves people in different groups. ❏ *parties competing across the political spectrum*

ADV **1** [across after v] If someone or something goes **across**, they go from one side of a place or boundary to the other. ❏ *Richard stood up and walked across to the window.* **2** [across after v] If something is situated or stretched **across**, it is situated or stretched from one side of something to the other. ❏ *Trim toenails straight across using nail clippers.* **3** You can use **across** to talk about being situated on the other side of a street, river, or area. ❏ *They parked across from the Castro Theatre.* **4** If you look **across** at a place, person, or thing, you look towards them. ❏ *He glanced across at his sleeping wife.* ❏ *She rose from the chair and gazed across at him.* **5** [AMOUNT + across] **Across** is used in measurements to show the width of something. ❏ *This hand-decorated plate measures 14 inches across.*
✦ across the board → see **board**

✪ **act** ◆◆◆ /ækt/ VERB, NOUN

VERB [I, T] (**acts, acting, acted**) **1** [I, T] When you **act**, you do something for a particular purpose. ❏ *The deaths occurred when police acted to stop widespread looting and vandalism.* ❏ *the duty of doctors to act in the best interest of patients* **2** [I] If you **act on** advice or information, you do what has been advised or suggested. ❏ *A patient will usually listen to the doctor's advice and act on it.* **3** [I] If someone **acts** in a particular way, they behave in that way. = behave ❏ *a gang of youths who were acting suspiciously* ❏ *He acted as if he hadn't heard any of it.* **4** [I] If someone **acts as** a particular thing, they have that role or function. = function ❏ *Among his other duties, he acted both as the ship's surgeon and as chaplain for the men.* **5** [I] If someone **acts** in a particular way, they pretend to be something that they are not. ❏ *Chris acted astonished as he examined the note.* **6** [I] When professionals such as lawyers **act for** you, or **act on** your **behalf**, they are employed by you to deal with a particular matter. ❏ *Daniel Webster acted for Boston traders while still practising in New Hampshire.* **7** [I] If a force or substance **acts on** someone or something, it has a certain effect on them. ❏ *He's taking a dangerous drug: it acts very fast on the central nervous system.* **8** [I] If you **act** in a play or film, you have a part in it. ❏ *She confessed to her parents her desire to act.*

NOUN [C, SING] (**acts**) **1** [C] (*formal*) An **act** is a single thing that someone does. = action, deed ❏ *Language interpretation is the whole point of the act of reading.* ❏ *He had committed several acts of violence.* **2** [C] An **Act** is a law passed by the government. ❑ *an Act of Congress* **3** [c] [oft act + NUM] An **act** in a play, opera, or ballet is one of the main parts into which it is divided. ❑ *Act II contained one of the funniest scenes I have ever witnessed.* **4** [c] An **act** in a show is a short performance which is one of several in the show. ❑ *This year numerous bands are playing, as well as comedy acts.* **5** [SING] If you say that someone's behaviour is an **act**, you mean that it does not express their real feelings. = pretence ❑ *His anger was real. It wasn't an act.* **PHRASES catch someone in the act** If you **catch** someone **in the act**, you discover them doing something wrong or committing a crime. ❑ *The men were caught in the act of digging up buried explosives.*

clean up your act (*informal*) If someone who has been behaving badly **cleans up** their **act**, they start to behave in a more acceptable or responsible way. ❑ *The nation's advertisers need to clean up their act.*

get in on the act (*informal*) If you **get in on the act**, you take part in or take advantage of something that was started by someone else. ❑ *In the 1970s Kodak, anxious to get in on the act, launched its own instant camera.*

in the act of You say that someone was **in the act of** doing something to indicate what they were doing when they were seen or interrupted. ❑ *Ken was in the act of paying his bill when Neil came up behind him.*

get your act together (*informal*) If you **get** your **act together**, you organize your life or your affairs so that you are able to achieve what you want or to deal with something effectively. ❑ *The government should get its act together.*

✦ act the fool → see fool

VOCABULARY BUILDER

act VERB

If you **act**, you do something in order to deal with a situation.

❑ *We must act swiftly to stop such attacks.*

do something VERB (*fairly informal, mainly spoken*)

If you **do something**, you deal with a situation.

❑ *I realized I had to do something about my weight.*

take action VERB (*mainly journalism*)

If you **take action**, you do something in order to deal with a situation.

❑ *They are taking action to recover the money.*

take steps VERB (*mainly written*)

If you **take steps**, you do a number of things to make sure that something is achieved.

❑ *The government should take steps to improve schools.*

act•ing /ˈæktɪŋ/ NOUN, ADJ

NOUN [U] [oft acting + N] **Acting** is the activity or profession of performing in plays or films. ❑ *She returned to London to pursue her acting career.*

ADJ [acting + N] You use **acting** before the title of a job to indicate that someone is doing that job temporarily. ❑ *The new acting president has a reputation of being someone who is independent.*

✪**ac•tion** ◆◆◆ /ˈækʃən/ NOUN, ADJ, VERB

NOUN [U, c] (**actions**) **1** [U] **Action** is doing something for a particular purpose. ❑ *The government is taking emergency action to deal with a housing crisis.* ❑ *the only possible course of action* **2** [U] The fighting which takes place in a war can be referred to as **action**. ❑ *Our leaders have generally supported military action if it proves necessary.* **3** [c] An **action** is something that you do on a particular occasion. ❑ *As always, Peter had a reason for his action.* ❑ *We are responsible for our own actions.* **4** [c, u] (*legal*) To take legal **action** or to bring a legal **action** against someone means to bring a case against them in a court of law. = suit, case ❑ *Two leading law firms are to prepare legal actions against tobacco companies.*

PHRASES out of action If someone or something is **out of action**, they are injured or damaged and cannot work or be used. ❑ *He's been out of action for 16 months with a serious knee injury.*

a piece of the action or **a slice of the action** If someone wants to have **a piece of the action** or **a slice of the action**, they want to take part in an exciting activity or situation, usually in order to make money or become more important. ❑ *In the late 1990s, investors big and small wanted a piece of the dot.com action.*

put something into action If you **put** an idea or policy **into action**, you begin to use it or cause it to operate. ❑ *They have excelled in learning the lessons of business management theory, and putting them into action.*

ADJ [action + N] An **action** movie is a film in which a lot of dangerous and exciting things happen. An **action** hero is the main character in one of these films.

VERB [T] (**actions, actioning, actioned**) (*business*) If you **action** something that needs to be done, you deal with it. ❑ *Documents can be actioned, or filed immediately.*

✪**ac•ti•vate** /ˈæktɪveɪt/ VERB [T] (**activates, activating, activated**) If a device or process is **activated**, something causes it to start working. = trigger, initiate; ≠ deactivate ❑ *Video cameras with night vision can be activated by movement.* ❑ *a voice-activated computer* ❑ *Heat also destroys enzymes which further destroy vitamins.*

✪**ac•ti•va•tion** /ˌæktɪˈveɪʃən/ NOUN [U] ❑ *A computer controls the activation of an air bag.* ❑ *The activation code must be entered into the computer to print copies.*

✪**ac•tive** ◆◆◇ /ˈæktɪv/ ADJ, NOUN

ADJ **1** Someone who is **active** moves around a lot or does a lot of things. = energetic, mobile; ≠ inactive ❑ *With three active little kids running around, there was plenty to keep me busy.* ❑ *She had a long and active life.* **2** If you have an **active** mind or imagination, you are always thinking of new things. = lively ❑ *the tragedy of an active mind trapped by failing physical health* **3** If someone is **active** in an organization, cause, or campaign, they do things for it rather than just giving it their support. = involved ❑ *We should play an active role in politics, both at the national and local level.* ❑ *He is an active member of his local synagogue.* **4** [active + N] **Active** is used to emphasize that someone is taking action in order to achieve something, rather than just hoping for it or achieving it in an indirect way. = positive ❑ *Companies need to take active steps to increase exports.* **5** If you say that a person or animal is **active** in a particular place or at a particular time, you mean that they are performing their usual activities or performing a particular activity. ❑ *Guerrilla groups are active in the province.* **6** An **active** volcano has erupted recently or is expected to erupt soon. ❑ *molten lava from an active volcano* **7** An **active** substance has a chemical or biological effect on things. ❑ *The active ingredient in some of the mouthwashes was simply detergent.*

NOUN [SING] In grammar, **the active** or **the active voice** means the forms of a verb which are used when the subject refers to a person or thing that does something. For example, in 'I saw her yesterday', the verb is in the active. Compare **passive**.

✪**ac•tive•ly** /ˈæktɪvli/ ADV **1** *They actively campaigned for the vote.* ❑ *people actively seeking work* **2** *They have never been actively encouraged to take such risks.*

✪**ac•tiv•ism** /ˈæktɪvɪzm/ NOUN [U] **Activism** is the process of campaigning in public or working for an organization in order to bring about political or social change. ❑ *He believed in political activism to achieve justice.*

✪**ac•tiv•ist** ◆◇◇ /ˈæktɪvɪst/ NOUN [c] (**activists**) An **activist** is a person who works to bring about political or social changes by campaigning in public or working for an organization. = agitator, protester ❑ *The police say they suspect the attack was carried out by animal rights activists.* ❑ *Dobson blames activist judges for undermining families with favourable gay-marriage rulings.*

✪**ac•tiv•ity** ◆◆◇ /ækˈtɪvɪti/ NOUN [U, c, PL] (**activities**) **1** [U] **Activity** is a situation in which a lot of things are happening or being done. ❑ *Changes in the money supply affect the level of economic activity and the interest rate.* ❑ *Children are supposed to get 60 minutes of physical activity every day.* **2** [c] An **activity** is something that you spend time doing. = pursuit, action, exercise ❑ *For lovers of the great outdoors, activities range from canoeing to bird watching.*

❏ *leisure activities such as watching television* ❏ *ideas for classroom activities* **8** [PL] The **activities** of a group are the things that they do in order to achieve their aims. ❏ *a jail term for terrorist activities*

ac·tor ♦◇◇ /'æktə/ NOUN [C] (**actors**) An **actor** is someone whose job is acting in plays or films. 'Actor' in the singular usually refers to a man, but some women who act prefer to be called 'actors' rather than 'actresses'. ❏ *His father was an actor in the Cantonese Opera Company.*

ac·tress ♦◇◇ /'æktrəs/ NOUN [C] (**actresses**) An **actress** is a woman whose job is acting in plays or films. ❏ *She's not only a great dramatic actress but she's also very funny.*

ac·tual ♦◇◇ /'æktʃuəl/ ADJ (emphasis) **1** [actual + N] You use **actual** to emphasize that you are referring to something real or genuine. = real ❏ *The segments are filmed using either local actors or the actual people involved.* **2** [actual + N] You use **actual** to contrast the important aspect of something with a less important aspect. ❏ *She had compiled pages of notes, but she had not yet got down to doing the actual writing.*

WHICH WORD?

actual, current, or real?

Do not confuse **actual** and **real**. You use **actual** to emphasize that what you are talking about is real or genuine, or to contrast different aspects of something. You use **real** to describe things that exist rather than being imagined or theoretical.

❏ *The predicted results and the actual results are very different.*

❏ *The interpretation bore no relation to the actual words spoken.*

❏ *Robert squealed in mock terror, then in real pain.*

You do not use **actual** to describe something that is happening, being done, or being used at the present time. Instead you use **current** or **present**.

❏ *The store needs more than $100,000 to survive the current crisis.*

---

ac·tu·al·ly ♦♦♦ /'æktʃuəli/ ADV **1** (emphasis) You use **actually** to indicate that a situation exists or happened, or to emphasize that it is true. ❏ *One afternoon, I got bored and actually fell asleep for a few minutes.* **2** [actually with CL] (emphasis) You use **actually** when you are correcting or contradicting someone. ❏ *No, I'm not a student. I'm a doctor, actually.* **8** [actually with CL] You can use **actually** when you are politely expressing an opinion that other people might not have expected from you. ❏ *'Do you think it's a good idea to socialize with one's patients?'—'Actually, I do, I think it's a great idea.'* **4** [actually with CL] You use **actually** to introduce a new topic into a conversation. ❏ *Well actually, John, I called you for some advice.*

acu·punc·ture /'ækjʊpʌŋktʃə/ NOUN [U] **Acupuncture** is the treatment of a person's illness or pain by sticking small needles into their body at certain places. ❏ *I had acupuncture in my lower back.*

❁ **acute** /ə'kjuːt/ ADJ **1** You can use **acute** to indicate that an undesirable situation or feeling is very severe or intense. = severe ❏ *The war has aggravated an acute economic crisis.* ❏ *The report has caused acute embarrassment to the government.* ❏ *The labour shortage is becoming acute.* **2** [acute + N] (medical) An **acute** illness is one that becomes severe very quickly but does not last very long. Compare **chronic**. = severe; ≠ mild ❏ *a patient with acute rheumatoid arthritis* ❏ *an acute case of dysentery* **8** If a person's or animal's sight, hearing, or sense of smell is **acute**, it is sensitive and powerful. = keen ❏ *When she lost her sight, her other senses grew more acute.* **4** [acute + N, N + acute] An **acute** accent is a symbol that is placed over vowels in some languages in order to indicate how that vowel is pronounced or over one letter in a word to indicate where it is stressed. You refer to a letter with this accent as, for example, e **acute**. For example, there is an acute accent over the letter 'e' in the French word 'café'.

acute·ly /ə'kjuːtli/ ADV If you feel or notice something **acutely**, you feel or notice it very strongly. = keenly

❏ *He was acutely aware of the odour of cooking oil.*

AD /ˌeɪ 'diː/ You use **AD** in dates to indicate the number of years or centuries that have passed since the year in which Jesus Christ is believed to have been born. Compare **BC**. ❏ *The original castle was probably built about AD 860.* ❏ *The cathedral was destroyed by the Great Fire of 1136 AD.*

ada·mant /'ædəmənt/ ADJ If someone is **adamant about** something, they are determined not to change their mind about it. ❏ *The president is adamant that he will not resign.*

ada·mant·ly /'ædəməntli/ ADV ❏ *She was adamantly opposed to her husband taking this trip.*

❁ **a·dapt** /ə'dæpt/ VERB [I, T] (**adapts, adapting, adapted**) (academic word) **1** [I, T] If you **adapt to** a new situation or **adapt yourself to** it, you change your ideas or behaviour in order to deal with it successfully. = adjust, acclimatize, become accustomed ❏ *The world will be different, and we will have to be prepared to adapt to the change.* ❏ *They have had to adapt themselves to a war economy.* **2** [T] If you **adapt** something, you change it to make it suitable for a new purpose or situation. = modify ❏ *Shelves were built to adapt the library for use as an office.*

WORD FAMILIES

adapt VERB	*We will have to be prepared to adapt to the change.*
adapted ADJ	*The camel's feet, well adapted for dry sand, are useless on mud.*
adaptation NOUN	*Most living creatures are capable of adaptation when compelled to do so.*
adaptable ADJ	*By making the workforce more adaptable and skilled, he hopes to attract foreign investment.*
adaptability NOUN	*The adaptability of wool is one of its great attractions.*

❁ **adapt·able** /ə'dæptəbəl/ ADJ If you describe a person or animal as **adaptable**, you mean that they are able to change their ideas or behaviour in order to deal with new situations. = flexible; ≠ inflexible, rigid ❏ *By making the workforce more adaptable and skilled, he hopes to attract foreign investment.*

❁ **adapt·abil·ity** /əˌdæptə'bɪlɪti/ NOUN [U] = flexibility; ≠ inflexibility ❏ *The adaptability of wool is one of its great attractions.* ❏ *They are adaptable foragers that learn to survive on a wide range of food sources.*

❁ **ad·ap·ta·tion** /ˌædæp'teɪʃən/ NOUN [C, U] (**adaptations**) **1** [C] An **adaptation** of a book or play is a film or a television programme that is based on it. ❏ *Branagh won two awards for his screen adaptation of Shakespeare's Henry the Fifth.* **2** [U] **Adaptation** is the act of changing something or changing your behaviour to make it suitable for a new purpose or situation. = adjustment, modification ❏ *Most living creatures are capable of adaptation when compelled to do so.*

❁ **add** ♦♦♦ /æd/ VERB

VERB [T, I] (**adds, adding, added**) **1** [T] If you **add** one thing to another, you put it in or on the other thing, to increase, complete, or improve it. ❏ *Add the grated cheese to the sauce.* ❏ *Since 1908, chlorine has been added to drinking water.* **2** [T] If you **add** numbers or amounts **together**, you calculate their total. ❏ *Banks add all the interest and other charges together.* ❏ *Two and three added together are five.* **8** [I] If one thing **adds to** another, it makes the other thing greater in degree or amount. ❏ *This latest incident will add to the pressure on the White House.* **4** [T] To **add** a particular quality **to** something means to cause it to have that quality. ❏ *The generous amount of garlic adds flavour.* **5** [T] If you **add** something when you are speaking, you say something more. ❏ *'You can tell that he is extremely embarrassed,' Mr. Montoya added.*

PHRASAL VERBS **add in** If you **add in** something, you include it as a part of something else. ❏ *Once the vegetables start to cook add in a couple of tablespoons of water.*

add on ◼ If one thing **is added on** to another, it is attached to the other thing, or is made a part of it. ❑ *Holidaymakers can also add on a week in Florida before or after the cruise.* ◼ If you **add on** an extra amount or item to a list or total, you include it. ❑ *Many loan application forms automatically add on insurance.*

add up ◼ If you **add up** numbers or amounts, or if you **add** them **up**, you calculate their total. = total; ≠ subtract ❑ *Add up the total of those six games.* ❑ *We just added all the numbers up and divided one by the other.* ◼ If you can **add up**, you are able to calculate the total of numbers or amounts. ❑ *More than a quarter of seven year-olds cannot add up properly.* ◼ If facts or events do not **add up**, they make you confused about a situation because they do not seem to be consistent. If something that someone has said or done **adds up**, it is reasonable and sensible. ❑ *Police said they arrested Olivia because her statements did not add up.* ◼ If small amounts of something **add up**, they gradually increase. ❑ *Even small savings, 20 pence here or 50 pence there, can add up.*

add up to If amounts **add up to** a particular total, they result in that total when they are put together. = amount to ❑ *For a hit show, profits can add up to millions of dollars.*

✪ **ad·dict** /ˈædɪkt/ NOUN [c] (**addicts**) ◼ An **addict** is someone who takes harmful drugs and cannot stop taking them. ❑ *He's only 24 years old and a drug addict.* ❑ *alcoholics and drug addicts* ◼ If you say that someone is an **addict**, you mean that they like a particular activity very much and spend as much time doing it as they can. ❑ *She is a TV addict and watches as much as she can.*

ad·dict·ed /əˈdɪktɪd/ ADJ ◼ Someone who is **addicted to** a harmful drug cannot stop taking it. = hooked ❑ *Many of the women are addicted to heroin and cocaine.* ◼ If you say that someone is **addicted to** something, you mean that they like it very much and want to spend as much time doing it as possible. ❑ *She had become addicted to golf.*

✪ **ad·dic·tion** /əˈdɪkʃən/ NOUN [c, u] (**addictions**) ◼ **Addiction** is the condition of taking harmful drugs and being unable to stop taking them. = dependence, habit ❑ *She helped him fight his drug addiction.* ❑ *long-term addiction to nicotine* ◼ An **addiction** to something is a very strong desire or need for it. ❑ *He needed money to feed his addiction to gambling.*

✪ **ad·dic·tive** /əˈdɪktɪv/ ADJ ◼ If a drug is **addictive**, people who take it cannot stop taking it. = habit-forming ❑ *Cigarettes are highly addictive.* ❑ *Crack is the most addictive drug on the market.* ◼ Something that is **addictive** is so enjoyable that it makes you want to do it or have it a lot. ❑ *Video movie-making can quickly become addictive.*

✪ **ad·di·tion** ◆◆◇ /əˈdɪʃən/ NOUN
NOUN [c, u] (**additions**) ◼ [c] An **addition to** something is a thing which is added to it. ❑ *This is a fine book; a worthy addition to the series.* ❑ *This plywood addition helps to strengthen the structure.* ◼ [u] The **addition of** something is the fact that it is added to something else. ❑ *It was completely refurbished in 1987, with the addition of a picnic site.* ❑ *the addition of vitamin C to fruit juices* ◼ [u] **Addition** is the process of calculating the total of two or more numbers. ≠ subtraction ❑ *simple addition and subtraction problems using whole numbers*
PHRASE **in addition** You use **in addition** when you want to mention another item connected with the subject you are discussing. = additionally, furthermore ❑ *The website provides regional weather reports, a shipping forecast and gale warnings. In addition, visitors can download satellite images of the US.* ❑ *In addition to the 48 constellations known since ancient times, Bayer showed 12 new constellations.*

✪ **ad·di·tion·al** ◆◇◇ /əˈdɪʃənəl/ ADJ **Additional** things are extra things apart from the ones already present. = supplementary, extra ❑ *The US is sending additional troops to the region.* ❑ *Table 2 gives additional information about participants.* ❑ *The insurer will also have to pay the additional costs of the trial.*

✪ **ad·di·tion·al·ly** /əˈdɪʃənəli/ ADV [additionally with CL] You use **additionally** to introduce something extra such as an extra fact or reason. = further, in addition ❑ *All teachers are qualified to teach their native language.*

Additionally, we select our teachers for their engaging personalities. ❑ *You can pay bills over the Internet. Additionally, you can check your balance or order statements.*

ad·di·tive /ˈædɪtɪv/ NOUN [c] (**additives**) An **additive** is a substance which is added in small amounts to foods or other things in order to improve them or to make them last longer. ❑ *Strict safety tests are carried out on food additives.*

✪ **ad·dress** ◆◆◇ NOUN, VERB /əˈdres, AmE ˈædres/
NOUN [c] (**addresses**) ◼ Your **address** is the number of the house or flat and the name of the street and the town where you live or work. ❑ *The address is 2025 M Street, NW, Washington, DC, 20036.* ◼ The **address** of a website is its location on the Internet, for example, http://www. collinsdictionary.com. ❑ *Full details, including the website address to log on to, are at the bottom of this page.* ◼ An **address** is a speech given to a group of people. ❑ *He had scheduled an address to the American people for the evening of May 27th.*
VERB [T] (**addresses, addressing, addressed**) ◼ If a letter, envelope, or parcel is **addressed** to you, your name and address have been written on it. ❑ *Applications should be addressed to: The business affairs editor.* ◼ If you **address** a group of people, you give a speech to them. ❑ *He is due to address a conference on human rights next week.* ◼ If you **address** a problem or task, you try to understand it or deal with it. ≠ avoid ❑ *Mr King sought to address those fears when he spoke at the meeting.* ❑ *US policy has failed to adequately address this problem.*

adept /əˈdept/ ADJ Someone who is **adept at** something can do it skilfully. ❑ *He's usually very adept at keeping his private life out of the media.*

✪ **ad·equa·cy** /ˈædɪkwəsi/ NOUN [u] **Adequacy** is the quality of being good enough or great enough in amount to be acceptable. = sufficiency; ≠ inadequacy ❑ *There are questions to be raised about the adequacy of the inmates' legal representation.* ❑ *Several studies point to a real cause for concern over the adequacy of the diet eaten by British children.*

✪ **ad·equate** ◆◇◇ /ˈædɪkwət/ ADJ (academic word) If something is **adequate**, there is enough of it or it is good enough to be used or accepted. = sufficient ❑ *One in four people worldwide are without adequate homes.* ❑ *She is prepared to offer me an amount adequate to purchase another house.*

✪ **ad·equate·ly** /ˈædɪkwətli/ ADV [adequately with v] = sufficiently; ≠ inadequately ❑ *Many students are not adequately prepared for higher education.* ❑ *Traditional analysis methods cannot deal adequately with these highly complex systems.*

WORD FAMILIES		
adequate ADJ		Their facilities were not **adequate** to cope with the demand.
inadequate ADJ		Supplies of food and medicines are **inadequate**.
adequately ADV		Many students are not **adequately** prepared for higher education.
inadequately ADV		The programme failed because it was **inadequately** funded.
adequacy NOUN		Several studies point to a real cause for concern over the **adequacy** of the diet eaten by British children.
inadequacy NOUN		The **inadequacy** of the water supply made it difficult to grow crops.

ad·he·sive /ædˈhiːsɪv/ NOUN, ADJ
NOUN [c, u] (**adhesives**) An **adhesive** is a substance such as glue, which is used to make things stick firmly together. ❑ *Glue the mirror in with a strong adhesive.*
ADJ An **adhesive** substance is able to stick firmly to something else. ❑ *adhesive tape*

❂**ad·ja·cent** /ə'dʒeɪsənt/ ADJ (*academic word*) If one thing is **adjacent to** another, the two things are next to each other. = neighbouring, near ❑ *He sat in an adjacent room and waited.* ❑ *The schools were adjacent but there were separate doors.* ❑ *surveys to monitor toxin levels in the areas adjacent to the incinerators*

ad·jec·tive /'ædʒɪktɪv/ NOUN [c] (**adjectives**) An **adjective** is a word such as 'big', 'dead', or 'financial' that describes a person or thing, or gives extra information about them. Adjectives usually come before nouns or after linking verbs.

ad·journ /ə'dʒɜːn/ VERB [I, T] (**adjourns, adjourning, adjourned**) If a meeting or trial **is adjourned** or if it **adjourns**, it is stopped for a short time. ❑ *The proceedings have now been adjourned until next week.*

❂**ad·just** ♦◇◇ /ə'dʒʌst/ VERB [I, T] (**adjusts, adjusting, adjusted**) (*academic word*) **1** [I, T] When you **adjust to** a new situation, you get used to it by changing your behaviour or your ideas. = adapt ❑ *We have been preparing our fighters to adjust themselves to civil society.* ❑ *I felt I had adjusted to the idea of being a mother very well.* **2** [T] If you **adjust** something, you change it so that it is more effective or appropriate. = change ❑ *To attract investors, Panama has adjusted its tax and labour laws.* ❑ *seasonally adjusted figures* **3** [T] If you **adjust** something such as your clothing or a machine, you correct or alter its position or setting. = shift ❑ *Liz adjusted her mirror and then edged the car out of its parking space.* ❑ *The clamp can be adjusted to fit any tyre size.* **4** [I, T] If you **adjust** your vision or if your vision **adjusts**, the muscles of your eye or the pupils alter to cope with changes in light or distance. ❑ *He stopped to try to adjust his vision to the faint starlight.*

WORD CONNECTIONS
adjust + NOUN
adjust **figures**
adjust **rates**
❑ *Figures have been adjusted to take account of the increase.*
adjust + FOR + NOUN
adjust for **inflation**
adjust for **height**
adjust for **age**
❑ *Seats can be adjusted for height.*
ADV + **adjust**
seasonally adjust
periodically adjust
❑ *The seasonally adjusted figures show that unemployment has risen.*
manually adjust
automatically adjust
❑ *This camera is designed to automatically adjust the internal settings to take the best photo in a particular environment.*
adjust + ADV
adjust **accordingly**
❑ *The patient's condition should be monitored, and dosage of the drug should be adjusted accordingly.*

❂**ad·just·ment** /ə'dʒʌstmənt/ NOUN [c] (**adjustments**) **1** An **adjustment** is a small change that is made to something such as a machine or a way of doing something. = adaptation, change ❑ *Compensation could be made by adjustments to taxation.* ❑ *Investment is up by 5.7% after adjustment for inflation.* ❑ *A technician made an adjustment to a smoke machine at the back of the auditorium.* **2** An **adjustment** is a change in a person's behaviour or thinking. ❑ *He will have to make major adjustments to his thinking if he is to survive in office.*

❂**ad·min·is·ter** /æd'mɪnɪstə/ VERB [T] (**administers, administering, administered**) **1** If someone **administers** something such as a country, the law, or a test, they take responsibility for organizing and supervising it. = manage, oversee, supervise ❑ *The plan calls for the UN to administer the country until elections can be held.* ❑ *In some states these*

laws are administered by state agencies, and in others they are administered on a municipal level. **2** (*formal*) If a doctor or a nurse **administers** a drug, they give it to a patient. = dispense ❑ *The doctor may prescribe but not administer the drug.* ❑ *Vitamins are administered orally or by injection into the veins or muscles.*

❂**ad·min·is·tra·tion** ♦♦◇ /æd,mɪnɪ'streɪʃən/ NOUN [U, SING, C] (**administrations**) **1** [U] **Administration** is the range of activities connected with organizing and supervising the way that an organization or institution functions. = management, organization ❑ *Too much time is spent on administration.* ❑ *a master's degree in business administration* **2** [U] The **administration** of something is the process of organizing and supervising it. = organization, regulation ❑ *Standards in the administration of justice have degenerated.* **3** [SING] The **administration** of a company or institution is the group of people who organize and supervise it. = management ❑ *They would like the college administration to exert more control over the students.* **4** [c] You can refer to a country's government as **the administration**; used especially in the United States. ❑ *O'Leary served in federal energy posts in both the Ford and Carter administrations.* ❑ *He urged the administration to come up with a credible package to reduce the budget deficit.*

❂**ad·min·is·tra·tive** /æd'mɪnɪstrətɪv, AmE -streɪt-/ ADJ **Administrative** work involves organizing and supervising an organization or institution. = bureaucratic, organizational, secretarial, clerical ❑ *Other industries have had to sack managers to reduce administrative costs.* ❑ *The project will have an administrative staff of 12.*

ad·min·is·tra·tor /æd'mɪnɪstreɪtə/ NOUN [c] (**administrators**) An **administrator** is a person whose job involves helping to organize and supervise the way that an organization or institution functions. ❑ *On Friday the company's administrators sought permission from a Melbourne court to keep operating.*

ad·mi·rable /'ædmɪrəbəl/ ADJ An **admirable** quality or action is one that deserves to be praised and admired. ❑ *She did an admirable job of holding the audience's attention.* **ad·mi·rably** /'ædmɪrəbli/ ADV ❑ *Peter had dealt admirably with the sudden questions about Keith.*

ad·mi·ra·tion /,ædmɪ'reɪʃən/ NOUN [U] **Admiration** is a feeling of great liking and respect for a person or thing. ❑ *I have always had the greatest admiration for him.*

ad·mire ♦◇◇ /əd'maɪə/ VERB [T] (**admires, admiring, admired**) **1** If you **admire** someone or something, you like and respect them very much. ❑ *I admired her when I first met her and I still think she's marvellous.* ❑ *He admired the way she had coped with life.* **2** If you **admire** someone or something, you look at them with pleasure. ❑ *We took time to stop and admire the view.*

ad·mir·er /əd'maɪərə/ NOUN [c] (**admirers**) If you are an **admirer** of someone, you like and respect them or their work very much. ❑ *He was an admirer of her grandfather's paintings.*

ad·mis·sion /əd'mɪʃən/ NOUN [c, u, PL] (**admissions**) **1** [c, u] **Admission** is permission given to a person to enter a place, or permission given to a country to enter an organization. **Admission** is also the act of entering a place. ❑ *Students apply for admission to a particular college.* **2** [c, u] An **admission** is a statement that something bad, unpleasant, or embarrassing is true. ❑ *By his own admission, he is not playing well.* **3** [PL] **Admissions** to a place such as a school or university are the people who are allowed to enter or join it. ❑ *Each school sets its own admissions policy.* **4** [u] **Admission** at a park, museum, or other place is the amount of money that you pay to enter it. ❑ *Gates open at 10.30 a.m. and admission is free.* ❑ *The admission price is $8 for adults.*

ad·mit ♦♦◇ /æd'mɪt/ VERB [I, T] (**admits, admitting, admitted**) **1** [I, T] If you **admit** that something bad, unpleasant, or embarrassing is true, you agree, often unwillingly, that it is true. = confess ❑ *I am willing to admit that I do make mistakes.* ❑ *Up to two-thirds of 14 to 16 year olds admit to buying alcohol illegally.* ❑ *None of these people will admit responsibility for their actions.* **2** [T] If someone **is**

admitted to a hospital, they are taken into the hospital for treatment and kept there until they are well enough to go home. ❑ *She was admitted to the hospital with a soaring temperature.* **3** [T] If someone **is admitted to** an organization or group, they are allowed to join it. ❑ *He was admitted to the Académie Culinaire de France.* **4** [T] To admit someone **to** a place means to allow them to enter it. ❑ *Embassy security personnel refused to admit him or his wife.*

WHICH WORD?
admit or acknowledge?

These words have similar meanings. If you **admit** something, you agree, often unwillingly, that it is true.
❑ *I **admit** that it was a stupid thing to do.*

If you **acknowledge** something, you accept that it is true or that it exists. **Acknowledge** is more formal than **admit**.
❑ *It is widely **acknowledged** that the policy has failed.*

---

ad·mit·ted·ly /ædˈmɪtɪdli/ ADV [admittedly with CL/GROUP] You use **admittedly** when you are saying something that weakens the importance or force of your statement. ❑ *It's only a theory, admittedly, but the pieces fit together.*

◆**ado·les·cence** /ˌædəˈlesəns/ NOUN [U] **Adolescence** is the period of your life in which you develop from being a child into being an adult. = puberty, youth ❑ *Some young people suddenly become self-conscious and tongue-tied in early adolescence.* ❑ *The need for sleep is even greater during adolescence than at younger ages.* ❑ *When the child reaches adolescence, this bond between mother and child faces its ultimate test.*

◆**ado·les·cent** /ˌædəˈlesənt/ ADJ, NOUN
ADJ **Adolescent** is used to describe young people who are no longer children but who have not yet become adults. It also refers to their behaviour. = teenage ❑ *It is important that an adolescent boy should have an adult in whom he can confide.* ❑ *an area where early marriage and adolescent pregnancy are common*
NOUN [C] (**adolescents**) An **adolescent** is an adolescent boy or girl. = teenager, young adult, youth ❑ *Young adolescents are happiest with small groups of close friends.*

◆**adopt** ◆◆◇ /əˈdɒpt/ VERB [T, I] (**adopts, adopting, adopted**) **1** [T] If you **adopt** a new attitude, plan, or way of behaving, you begin to have it. = embrace, endorse, support, accept ❑ *The United Nations General Assembly has adopted a resolution calling on all parties in the conflict to seek a political settlement.* ❑ *Pupils should be helped to adopt a positive approach to the environment.* **2** [I, T] If you **adopt** someone else's child, you take it into your own family and make it legally your son or daughter. ❑ *There are hundreds of people desperate to adopt a child.*
◆**adop·tion** /əˈdɒpʃən/ (**adoptions**) NOUN [U, C] **1** [U] = acceptance, endorsement ❑ *The group is working to promote the adoption of broadband wireless access over long distances.* ❑ *the widespread adoption of renewable energy* **2** [C, U] ❑ *They gave their babies up for adoption.*

ador·able /əˈdɔːrəbəl/ ADJ (*emphasis*) If you say that someone or something is **adorable**, you are emphasizing that they are very attractive and you feel great affection for them. ❑ *By the time I was 30, we had three adorable children.*

adore /əˈdɔː/ VERB [T] (**adores, adoring, adored**) **1** If you **adore** someone, you feel great love and admiration for them. ❑ *She adored her parents and would do anything to please them.* **2** (*informal*) If you **adore** something, you like it very much. ❑ *My mother adores bananas and eats two a day.*

adrena·lin /əˈdrenəlɪn/ also **adrenaline** NOUN [U] **Adrenalin** is a substance which your body produces when you are angry, scared, or excited. It makes your heart beat faster and gives you more energy. ❑ *That was my first big game in months and the adrenalin was going.*

adrift /əˈdrɪft/ ADJ **1** [V-LINK + adrift, V N + adrift] If a boat is **adrift**, it is floating on the water and is not tied to anything or controlled by anyone. ❑ *They were spotted after three hours adrift in a dinghy.* **2** [V-LINK + adrift, V N + adrift] If someone is **adrift**, they feel alone with no clear

idea of what they should do. ❑ *Amy had the growing sense that she was adrift and isolated.*

◆**adult** ◆◆◇ /ˈædʌlt, AmE əˈdʌlt/ NOUN, ADJ (*academic word*)
NOUN [C] (**adults**) **1** An **adult** is a mature, fully developed person. An adult has reached the age when they are legally responsible for their actions. ❑ *Becoming a father signified that he was now an adult.* ❑ *The course is suitable for teenagers and young adults.* **2** An **adult** is a fully developed animal. ❑ *a pair of adult birds*
ADJ **1** [adult + N] **Adult** means relating to the time when you are an adult, or typical of adult people. ❑ *I've lived most of my adult life in Arizona.* **2** You can describe things such as films or books as **adult** when they deal with sex in a very clear and open way. ❑ *an adult movie*

adul·tery /əˈdʌltəri/ NOUN [U] If a married person commits **adultery**, they have sex with someone that they are not married to. ❑ *She is going to divorce him on the grounds of adultery.*

◆**adult·hood** /ˈædʌlthʊd, AmE əˈdʌlt-/ NOUN [U] **Adulthood** is the state of being an adult. ❑ *Few people nowadays are able to maintain friendships into adulthood.* ❑ *Most people catch the illness before they reach adulthood.*

◆**ad·vance** ◆◆◇ /ədˈvɑːns, -ˈvæns/ VERB, NOUN, ADJ
VERB [I, T] (**advances, advancing, advanced**) **1** [I] To **advance** means to move forward, often in order to attack someone. ❑ *Reports from Chad suggest that rebel forces are advancing on the capital.* ❑ *According to one report, the water is advancing at a rate of between 8 and 10 inches a day.* **2** [I] To **advance** means to make progress, especially in your knowledge of something. = progress, improve ❑ *Medical technology has advanced considerably.* ❑ *Japan has advanced from a rural, feudal society to an urban, industrial power.* **3** [T] If you **advance** someone a sum of money, you lend it to them, or pay it to them earlier than arranged. = lend ❑ *I advanced him some money, which he would repay on our way home.* **4** [T] To **advance** an event, or the time or date of an event, means to bring it forward to an earlier time or date. = bring forward ❑ *Too much protein in the diet may advance the aging process.* **5** [T] If you **advance** a cause, interest, or claim, you support it and help to make it successful. = further ❑ *When not producing art of his own, Oliver was busy advancing the work of others.*
NOUN [C, U, SING] (**advances**) **1** [C] An **advance** is money lent or paid to someone before they would normally receive it. ❑ *She was paid a $100,000 advance for her next two novels.* **2** [C, U] An **advance** is a forward movement of people or vehicles, usually as part of a military operation. ❑ *In an exercise designed to be as real as possible, they simulated an advance on enemy positions.* **3** [C, U] An **advance** in a particular subject or activity is progress in understanding it or in doing it well. = development ❑ *Air safety has not improved since the dramatic advances of the 1970s.* ❑ *Scientific advances have transformed our understanding of DNA.* ❑ *Major advances in microsurgery have been made.* **4** [SING] [usu 'an' advance 'on' N] If something is an **advance on** what was previously available or done, it is better in some way. ❑ *This could be an advance on the present situation.*
PHRASE **in advance** If you do something **in advance**, you do it before a particular date or event. ❑ *The subject of the talk is announced a week in advance.*
ADJ [advance + N] **Advance** booking, notice, or warning is done or given before an event happens. ❑ *They don't normally give any advance notice about which building they're going to inspect.*
→ See also **advanced**

◆**ad·vanced** ◆◇◇ /ədˈvɑːnst, -ˈvænst/ ADJ **1** An **advanced** system, method, or design is modern and has been developed from an earlier version of the same thing. = up-to-date, modern, cutting edge; ≠ basic, elementary, simple ❑ *a superpower equipped with the most advanced military technology in the world* **2** A country that is **advanced** has reached a high level of industrial or technological development. ❑ *Agricultural productivity remained low by comparison with advanced countries like the United States.* **3** An **advanced** student has already learned the basic facts of a subject and is doing more difficult work. An **advanced** course of study is designed for such students. ❑ *The course is suitable for beginners and advanced students.* **4** Something that is at an **advanced** stage or level is at a late stage of development. ❑ *Medicare is available to victims of advanced kidney disease.*

ad·vance·ment /æd'vɑːnsmənt, -'væns-/ NOUN [U, C] (advancements) **1** [U] **Advancement** is progress in your job or in your social position. ❑ *He cared little for social advancement.* **2** [C, U] The **advancement of** something is the process of helping it to progress or the result of its progress. ❑ *Her work for the advancement of the status of women in India was recognized by the whole nation.*

✪ **ad·van·tage** ♦♦◇ /æd'vɑːntɪdʒ, -'væn-/ NOUN
NOUN [C, U] (advantages) **1** [C] An **advantage** is something that puts you in a better position than other people. = aid, edge ❑ *They are breaking the law in order to obtain an advantage over their competitors.* ❑ *A good crowd will be a definite advantage to me and the rest of the team.* ❑ *The great advantage of this technique is the cost.* **2** [C] An **advantage** is a way in which one thing is better than another. = benefit, strength, merit, positive; ≠ drawback, negative ❑ *The great advantage of home-grown oranges is their magnificent flavour.* **3** [U] **Advantage** is the state of being in a better position than others who are competing against you. = dominance, superiority, privilege; ≠ disadvantage ❑ *Men have created a social and economic position of advantage for themselves over women.*
PHRASES **take advantage of something** If you **take advantage of** something, you make good use of it while you can. ❑ *I intend to take full advantage of this trip to buy the things we need.*
take advantage of someone If someone **takes advantage of** you, they treat you unfairly for their own benefit, especially when you are trying to be kind or to help them. ❑ *She took advantage of him even after they were divorced.*
to one's advantage If you use or turn something **to your advantage**, you use it in order to benefit from it, especially when it might be expected to harm or damage you. ❑ *The government has not been able to turn today's demonstration to its advantage.*

WORD CONNECTIONS

VERB + **advantage**

have an advantage
enjoy an advantage
hold an advantage
❑ *You will have an advantage in the job market if you can speak more than one language.*

obtain an advantage
secure an advantage
derive an advantage
❑ *He had obtained an unfair advantage by cheating.*

offer an advantage
provide an advantage
confer an advantage
❑ *Online courses offer several advantages, including the chance to study at a time that suits you.*

ADJ + **advantage**

a competitive advantage
an unfair advantage
a distinct advantage
a huge advantage
❑ *Being young is a huge advantage in many sports.*

advantage + OVER + NOUN

an advantage over **competitors**
an advantage over **rivals**
an advantage over **opponents**
❑ *Businesses need a distinct advantage over their competitors.*

WORD FAMILIES

advantage NOUN	They are breaking the law in order to obtain an **advantage** over their competitors.

---

disadvantage NOUN	His two main rivals suffer the **disadvantage** of having been long-term political exiles.
disadvantaged ADJ	The school has a high proportion of economically and socially **disadvantaged** children.
advantageous ADJ	Free exchange of goods was **advantageous** to all.

VOCABULARY BUILDER

advantage NOUN
An **advantage** is something that puts you in a better position than other people.
❑ *All the games are played simultaneously on the last day of the season to ensure that no club is given an unfair advantage.*

aid NOUN (*written*)
If someone gives you **aid**, they help you in something you are trying to achieve.
❑ *Kenneth ran to give the prisoners aid in their bid for freedom.*

benefit NOUN
The **benefit** of something is the help that you get from it.
❑ *We enjoy the productivity benefit of being in the same time zone as California's Silicon Valley.*

strength NOUN
A person's **strengths** are the qualities and abilities they have which make them successful.
❑ *Intuition and perceptiveness are two of his great strengths on the field.*

merit NOUN
The **merits** of something are its good points.
❑ *Parents are in a prime position to see and value the merits of both orthodox and alternative forms of medicine.*

positive NOUN
The **positive** in a situation is the good and pleasant aspects of it.
❑ *She possessed such confidence and inner strength that she was able to see the positive of any situation.*

✪ **ad·van·taged** /æd'vɑːntɪdʒd, -'væn-/ ADJ A person or place that is **advantaged** is in a better social or financial position than other people or places. = privileged ❑ *Some cities are always going to be more advantaged.*

✪ **ad·van·ta·geous** /ˌædvən'teɪdʒəs/ ADJ If something is **advantageous to** you, it is likely to benefit you. = favourable; ≠ disadvantageous ❑ *Free exchange of goods was advantageous to all.* ❑ *Coca-Cola enjoyed an extraordinarily advantageous market position during the early twentieth century.*

✪ **ad·vent** /'ædvent/ NOUN [U] (*formal*) The **advent of** an important event, invention, or situation is the fact of it starting or coming into existence. = beginning, arrival ❑ *The advent of the computer has brought this sort of task within the bounds of possibility.* ❑ *The advent of war led to a greater austerity.*

ad·ven·ture /æd'ventʃə/ NOUN [C, U] (adventures) **1** [C] If someone has an **adventure**, they become involved in an unusual, exciting, and somewhat dangerous trip or series of events. ❑ *I set off for a new adventure in Alaska on the first day of the new year.* **2** [U] **Adventure** is excitement and willingness to do new, unusual, or somewhat dangerous things. ❑ *Their cultural backgrounds gave them a spirit of adventure.*

ad·ven·tur·ous /æd'ventʃərəs/ ADJ **1** Someone who is **adventurous** is willing to take risks and to try new methods. Something that is **adventurous** involves new things or ideas. = daring ❑ *Warren was an adventurous businessman.* **2** Someone who is **adventurous** is eager to visit new places and have new experiences. ❑ *He had always wanted an adventurous life in the tropics.*

ad•verb /'ædvɜːb/ NOUN [C] (**adverbs**) An **adverb** is a word such as 'slowly', 'now', 'very', 'politically', or 'fortunately' which adds information about the action, event, or situation mentioned in a clause.

⊙ **ad•verse** /'ædvɜːs, AmE æd'vɜːrs/ ADJ **Adverse** decisions, conditions, or effects are unfavourable to you. = negative, unfavourable; ≠ advantageous □ *The police said Mr Hadfield's decision would have no adverse effect on the progress of the investigation.* □ *Despite the adverse conditions, the road was finished in just eight months.*
⊙ **ad•verse•ly** /'ædvɜːsli/ AmE æd'vɜːrsli/ ADV [adversely with v] = negatively, unfavourably; ≠ favourably, advantageously □ *Price changes must not adversely affect the living standards of the people.* □ *people who react adversely to foods*

ad•ver•sity /æd'vɜːsɪti/ NOUN [C, U] (**adversities**) **Adversity** is a very difficult or unfavourable situation. = misfortune □ *He showed courage in adversity.*

ad•vert /'ædvɜːt/ (*BrE*; in *AmE*, use **ad**) NOUN [C] (**adverts**) An **advert** is an announcement in a newspaper, on television, or on a poster about something such as a product, event, or job. = ad, advertisement

⊙ **ad•ver•tise** ◆◇◇ /'ædvətaɪz/ VERB [I, T] (**advertises, advertising, advertised**) **1** [I, T] If you **advertise** something such as a product, an event, or a job, you tell people about it in newspapers, on television, or on posters in order to encourage them to buy the product, go to the event, or apply for the job. = promote, market □ *The company is spending heavily to advertise its strongest brands.* □ *Religious groups are currently not allowed to advertise on television.* □ *In 1991, the house was advertised for sale at $49,000.* **2** [I] If you **advertise for** someone to do something for you, for example, to work for you or share your accommodation, you announce it in a newspaper, on television, or on a noticeboard. □ *We advertised for staff in a local newspaper.* **3** [T] If you do not **advertise** the fact that something is the case, you try not to let other people know about it. □ *There is no need to advertise the fact that you are a single woman.*
→ See also **advertising**

WORD FAMILIES	
advertise VERB	We **advertised** for staff in a local newspaper.
advertising NOUN	The company spends a lot of money on **advertising**.
advertisement NOUN	Miss Parrish recently placed an **advertisement** in the local newspaper.
advertiser NOUN	The publication is having difficulty attracting **advertisers**.

⊙ **ad•ver•tise•ment** /'ædvɜːtɪsmənt, AmE ˌædvəˈtaɪz-/ NOUN [C] (**advertisements**) **1** (*written*) An **advertisement** is an announcement in a newspaper, on television, or on a poster about something such as a product, event, or job. = ad, commercial □ *Miss Parrish recently placed an advertisement in the local newspaper.* □ *a television advertisement for cat food* **2** If you say that an example of something is **an advertisement for** that thing in general, you mean that it shows how good that thing is. □ *The Treviso team was an effective advertisement for the improving state of Italian club rugby.*

ad•ver•tis•er /'ædvətaɪzə/ NOUN [C] (**advertisers**) An **advertiser** is a person or company that pays for a product, event, or job to be advertised in a newspaper, on television, or on a poster. □ *When will advertisers stop bombarding women with images of unattainable beauty?*

⊙ **ad•ver•tis•ing** /'ædvətaɪzɪŋ/ NOUN [U] **Advertising** is the activity of creating advertisements and making sure people see them. □ *I work in advertising.* □ *The company spends a lot of money on advertising.* □ *The actor starred in an advertising campaign for Versace.*

⊙ **ad•vice** ◆◆◇ /ædˈvaɪs/ NOUN [U] If you give someone **advice**, you tell them what you think they should do in a particular situation. = guidance □ *Don't be afraid to ask for advice about ordering the meal.* □ *She has given me some good advice.* □ *Take my advice and stay away from him!* □ *Your doctor can offer advice on health and fitness.*

WORD CONNECTIONS
VERB + **advice**

give advice
offer advice
provide advice
□ *I asked her to give me some advice about buying a guitar.*

ask for advice
seek advice
get advice
receive advice
□ *You should seek medical advice if your symptoms don't improve.*

take advice
follow advice
□ *I decided to take Anne's advice and go to Barcelona.*

ADJ + **advice**

good advice
sound advice
bad advice
□ *The book provides sound advice on choosing a course.*

legal advice
financial advice
medical advice
career advice
□ *I inherited a lot of money and needed some financial advice.*

professional advice
independent advice
expert advice
practical advice
□ *We offer expert advice on planning your wedding.*

WHICH WORD?
advice or advise?

Advice is an uncountable noun. If you give someone **advice**, you tell them what you think they should do in a particular situation.
□ *Lisa, I wonder if you could give me some **advice**?*

Advise is a verb. If you **advise** someone to do something, you tell them that you think they should do it.
□ *She **advised** me to phone the hospital.*
□ *I **advise** you to think carefully before you act.*

ad•vis•able /ædˈvaɪzəbəl/ ADJ [V-LINK + advisable] (*formal*) If you tell someone that it is **advisable to** do something, you are suggesting that they should do it, because it is sensible or is likely to achieve the result they want. = wise □ *Because of the popularity of the region, it is advisable to book hotels or camp sites in advance.*

⊙ **ad•vise** ◆◇◇ /ædˈvaɪz/ VERB [T] (**advises, advising, advised**) **1** If you **advise** someone to do something, you tell them what you think they should do. □ *The minister advised him to leave as soon as possible.* □ *Health experts advise us to eat five portions of fruit and vegetables a day.* □ *I strongly advise you to accept the offer.* □ *I would strongly advise against it.* **2** If an expert **advises** people **on** a particular subject, he or she gives them help and information on that subject. □ *an officer who advises undergraduates from the University on money matters* □ *Your tutor will be able to advise on suitable courses.*

⊙ **ad•vis•er** ◆◇◇ /ædˈvaɪzə/ also **advisor** NOUN [C] (**advisers**) An **adviser** is an expert whose job is to give advice to another person or to a group of people. □ *In Washington, the president and his advisers spent the day in meetings.* □ *a careers adviser*

ad•vi•so•ry /ædˈvaɪzəri/ ADJ (*formal*) An **advisory** group regularly gives suggestions and help to people or organizations, especially about a particular subject or area of activity. ❑ *members of the advisory committee on the safety of nuclear installations*

❂**ad•vo•ca•cy** /ˈædvəkəsi/ NOUN [SING] (*formal*) Someone's **advocacy** of a particular action or plan is their act of recommending it publicly. = support; ≠ opposition ❑ *I support your advocacy of free trade.* ❑ *His advocacy helped persuade the Royal Society to back the project.*

❂**ad•vo•cate** ◆◇◇ VERB, NOUN (*academic word*)
VERB /ˈædvəkeɪt/ [T] (**advocates, advocating, advocated**) (*formal*) If you **advocate** a particular action or plan, you recommend it publicly. = recommend, advance; ≠ oppose ❑ *Mr Williams is a conservative who advocates fewer government controls on business.* ❑ *the tax policy advocated by the Opposition*
NOUN /ˈædvəkət/ [C] (**advocates**) **1** (*formal*) An **advocate** of a particular action or plan is someone who recommends it publicly. = proponent ❑ *He was a strong advocate of free market policies and a multi-party system.* **2** (*legal*) An **advocate** is a lawyer who speaks in favour of someone or defends them in a court of law. = lawyer

aer•ial /ˈeəriəl/ ADJ, NOUN
ADJ [aerial + N] You talk about **aerial** attacks and **aerial** photographs to indicate that people or things on the ground are attacked or photographed by people in aeroplanes. ❑ *Weeks of aerial bombardment had destroyed factories and highways.* ❑ *Patterns that are invisible on the ground can be the most striking part of an aerial photograph.*
NOUN [C] (**aerials**) (*mainly BrE*; in *AmE*, usually use **antenna**) An **aerial** is a device that receives television or radio signals.

aero•bics /eəˈrəʊbɪks/ NOUN [U] [oft aerobics + N] **Aerobics** is a form of exercise which increases the amount of oxygen in your blood, and strengthens your heart and lungs. The verb that follows **aerobics** may be either singular or plural. ❑ *I'd like to join an aerobics class to improve my fitness.*

aero•dy•nam•ic /ˌeərəʊdaɪˈnæmɪk/ ADJ If something such as a car has an **aerodynamic** shape or design, it goes faster and uses less fuel than other cars because the air passes over it more easily. ❑ *The secret of the machine lies in the aerodynamic shape of the one-piece, carbon-fibre frame.*

WORD PARTS

The prefix **aero-** often appears in words for things or activities that are connected with air or with movement through the air:
aerodynamic (ADJ)
aeroplane (NOUN)
aerospace (NOUN)

aero•plane /ˈeərəpleɪn/ (*BrE*; in *AmE*, use **airplane**) NOUN [C] (**aeroplanes**) An **aeroplane** is a vehicle with wings and one or more engines that enable it to fly through the air.

aero•sol /ˈeərəsɒl, *AmE* -sɔːl/ NOUN [C] (**aerosols**) [usu aerosol + N] An **aerosol** can or spray is a small container in which a liquid such as paint or deodorant is kept under pressure. When you press a button, the liquid is forced out as a fine spray or foam. ❑ *an aerosol can of insecticide*

aero•space /ˈeərəʊspeɪs/ NOUN [U] [usu aerospace + N] **Aerospace** companies are involved in developing and making rockets, missiles, space vehicles, and related equipment. ❑ *the US aerospace industry*

❂**aes•thet•ic** /iːsˈθetɪk, *AmE* es-/ (in *AmE*, also use **esthetic**) ADJ, NOUN
ADJ **Aesthetic** is used to talk about beauty or art, and people's appreciation of beautiful things. = artistic, creative ❑ *products chosen for their aesthetic appeal as well as their durability and quality* ❑ *an aesthetic stance towards the reading of literature*
NOUN [SING] The **aesthetic** of a work of art is its aesthetic quality. ❑ *He responded very strongly to the aesthetic of this particular work.*
❂**aes•theti•cal•ly** /iːsˈθetɪkli, *AmE* es-/ ADV = visually, artistically ❑ *A statue which is aesthetically pleasing to one person, however, may be repulsive to another.* ❑ *a country that was aesthetically and intellectually multicultural*

❂**aes•thet•ics** /iːsˈθetɪks, *AmE* es-/ (in *AmE*, also use **esthetics**) NOUN [U] **Aesthetics** is a branch of philosophy concerned with the study of the idea of beauty. ❑ *questions of ethics and aesthetics* ❑ *The fact that there are works of art is a given in aesthetics.*

af•fair ◆◆◇ /əˈfeə/ NOUN [SING, C, PL] (**affairs**) **1** [SING] If an event or a series of events has been mentioned and you want to talk about it again, you can refer to it as **the affair**. = business, matter ❑ *The administration has mishandled the whole affair.* **2** [SING] (*mainly journalism*) You can refer to an important or interesting event or situation as '**the ... affair**'. ❑ *the damage caused to the CIA and FBI in the aftermath of the Watergate affair* **3** [SING] You can describe the main quality of an event by saying that it is a particular kind of **affair**. ❑ *Michael said that his planned 10-day visit would be a purely private affair.* **4** [C] If two people who are not married to each other have an **affair**, they have a sexual relationship. ❑ *Married male supervisors were carrying on affairs with female subordinates in the office.* **5** [PL] You can use **affairs** to refer to all the important facts or activities that are connected with a particular subject. ❑ *He does not want to interfere in the internal affairs of another country.* **6** [PL] Your **affairs** are all the matters connected with your life that you consider to be private and normally deal with yourself. ❑ *The unexpectedness of my father's death meant that his affairs were not entirely in order.* → See also **current affairs**

❂**af•fect** ◆◆◇ /əˈfekt/ VERB [T] (**affects, affecting, affected**) (*academic word*) **1** If something **affects** a person or thing, it influences them or causes them to change in some way. = influence, impact ❑ *Nicotine adversely affects the functioning of the heart and arteries.* ❑ *More than seven million people have been affected by drought.* ❑ *The new law will directly affect thousands of people.* **2** If a disease **affects** someone, it causes them to become ill. = afflict ❑ *Arthritis is a crippling disease which affects people all over the world.* **3** If something or someone **affects** you, they make you feel a strong emotion, especially sadness or pity. ❑ *If Jim had been more independent, the divorce would not have affected him as deeply.*

WHICH WORD?
affect, effect, or influence?

Affect is a verb. To **affect** someone or something means to cause them to change, often in a negative way.
❑ *These problems could affect my work.*
Effect is usually a noun. An **effect** is something that happens or exists because something else has happened.
❑ *They are still feeling the effects of the war.*
❑ *Her words had a strange effect on me.*
Effect is sometimes a verb. If you **effect** something that you are trying to achieve, you succeed in achieving it. This is a formal use.
❑ *We are confident that our knowledge and experience will give us the power to effect change.*
To **influence** a person or situation, or have an **influence** on them, is to have an effect on the person's behaviour or the way that the situation develops.
❑ *Nowadays people are too easily influenced by the media.*
❑ *Van Gogh had a major influence on the development of modern painting.*

af•fec•tion /əˈfekʃən/ NOUN [U, PL] (**affections**) **1** [U] If you regard someone or something with **affection**, you like them and are fond of them. ❑ *She thought of him with affection.* **2** [PL] Your **affections** are your feelings of love or fondness for someone. ❑ *Caroline is the object of his affections.*

af•fec•tion•ate /əˈfekʃənət/ ADJ If you are **affectionate**, you show your love or fondness for another person in the way that you behave towards them. ❑ *They seemed devoted to each other and were openly affectionate.*
af•fec•tion•ate•ly /əˈfekʃənətli/ ADV [affectionately with v] = fondly ❑ *He looked affectionately at his niece.*

af•fili•ate NOUN, VERB
NOUN /əˈfɪliət/ [C] (**affiliates**) (*formal*) An **affiliate** is an

organization which is officially connected with another, larger organization or is a member of it. ❑ *The World Chess Federation has affiliates in around 120 countries.*
VERB /əˈfɪliˌeɪt/ [I] (**affiliates, affiliating, affiliated**) *(formal)* If an organization **affiliates with** another larger organization, it forms a close connection with the larger organization or becomes a member of it. ❑ *He wanted to affiliate with a US firm because he needed expert advice in legal affairs.*

af·fin·i·ty /əˈfɪnɪti/ NOUN [SING] If you have an **affinity** with someone or something, you feel that you are similar to them or that you know and understand them very well. ❑ *He has a close affinity with the landscape and people he knew when he was growing up.*

af·firm /əˈfɜːm/ VERB [T] (**affirms, affirming, affirmed**) *(formal)* **1** If you **affirm** that something is true or that something exists, you state firmly and publicly that it is true or exists. = assert ❑ *The court affirmed that the information can be made public under the Freedom of Information Act.* ❑ *a speech in which he affirmed a commitment to lower taxes* **2** If an event **affirms** something, it shows that it is true or exists. = confirm ❑ *Everything I had accomplished seemed to affirm that opinion.*
af·fir·ma·tion /ˌæfəˈmeɪʃən/ NOUN [C, U] (**affirmations**) **1** [C, U] ❑ *The North Atlantic Treaty begins with the affirmation that its parties 'reaffirm their faith in the purposes and principles of the Charter of the United Nations'.* **2** [U] ❑ *The ruling was a welcome affirmation of the constitutional right to free speech.*

af·flict /əˈflɪkt/ VERB [T] (**afflicts, afflicting, afflicted**) *(formal)* If you **are afflicted by** pain, illness, or disaster, it affects you badly and makes you suffer. = affect ❑ *Italy has been afflicted by political corruption for decades.* ❑ *There are two main problems which afflict people with hearing impairments.*

af·flic·tion /əˈflɪkʃən/ NOUN [C, U] (**afflictions**) *(formal)* An **affliction** is something that causes physical or mental suffering. ❑ *Hay fever is an affliction that arrives at an early age.*

af·flu·ent /ˈæfluənt/ ADJ, NOUN
ADJ If you are **affluent**, you have a lot of money. = prosperous, wealthy ❑ *Cigarette smoking used to be more common among affluent people.*
NOUN [PL] The **affluent** are people who are affluent. ❑ *The diet of the affluent has not changed much over the decades.*

af·ford ♦◇◇ /əˈfɔːd/ VERB [T] (**affords, affording, afforded**) **1** If you **cannot afford** something, you do not have enough money to pay for it. ❑ *My parents can't even afford a new refrigerator.* ❑ *The arts should be available to more people at prices they can afford.* **2** If you say that you **cannot afford to** do something or allow it to happen, you mean that you must not do it or must prevent it from happening because it would be harmful or embarrassing to you. ❑ *We can't afford to wait.*

af·ford·able /əˈfɔːdəbəl/ ADJ If something is **affordable**, most people have enough money to buy it. ❑ *the availability of affordable housing*

af·front /əˈfrʌnt/ VERB, NOUN
VERB [T] (**affronts, affronting, affronted**) *(formal)* If something **affronts** you, you feel insulted and hurt because of it. ❑ *One recent example, which particularly affronted Kasparov, was the European team championship in Hungary.*
NOUN [C] (**affronts**) If something is an **affront to** you, it is an obvious insult to you. = insult ❑ *It's an affront to human dignity to keep someone alive like this.*

afield /əˈfiːld/ ADV
PHRASE further afield or **farther afield** Further afield or farther afield means in places or areas other than the nearest or most obvious one. ❑ *They enjoy participating in a wide variety of activities, both locally and further afield.*

afloat /əˈfləʊt/ ADV **1** If someone or something is **afloat**, they remain partly above the surface of water and do not sink. ❑ *They talked modestly of their valiant efforts to keep the tanker afloat.* **2** *(business)* If a person, business, or country stays **afloat** or is kept **afloat**, they have just enough money to pay their debts and continue operating. = solvent ❑ *A number of efforts were being made to keep the company afloat.*

❖ afore·men·tioned /əˈfɔːmenʃənd/ ADJ [DET + aforementioned, usu 'the' aforementioned + N] *(formal)* If you refer to **the aforementioned** person or subject, you mean the person or subject that has already been mentioned. = aforesaid ❑ *This is the draft of a declaration that will be issued at the end of the aforementioned UN conference.* ❑ *a variation of the aforementioned method*

afraid ♦◇◇ /əˈfreɪd/ ADJ
ADJ 1 [V-LINK + afraid] If you are **afraid of** someone or **afraid to** do something, you are frightened because you think that something very unpleasant is going to happen to you. = frightened ❑ *She did not seem at all afraid.* ❑ *I was afraid of the other boys.* **2** [V-LINK + afraid] If you are **afraid for** someone else, you are worried that something horrible is going to happen to them. ❑ *She's afraid for her family in Somalia.* **3** [V-LINK + afraid] If you are **afraid that** something unpleasant will happen, you are worried that it may happen and you want to avoid it. ❑ *I was afraid that nobody would believe me.*
PHRASE I'm afraid *(spoken, politeness)* If you want to apologize to someone or to disagree with them in a polite way, you can say '**I'm afraid**'. ❑ *We don't have anything like that, I'm afraid.*

WHICH WORD?
afraid or frightened?

If you are **afraid** or **frightened**, you feel fear.
❑ *She was so **afraid** that she ran away.*
❑ *I felt very **frightened** and alone.*
You cannot use **afraid** before a noun. However, you can use **frightened** before a noun.
❑ ***Frightened** residents ran out into the street.*

af·ter ♦♦♦ /ˈɑːftə, ˈæftə/ PREP, CONJ, ADV, CONVENTION

In addition to the uses shown below, **after** is used in phrasal verbs such as 'ask after', 'look after', and 'take after'.

PREP 1 If something happens **after** a particular date or event, it happens during the period of time that follows that date or event. ❑ *After May 19, strikes were occurring on a daily basis.* ❑ *After breakfast Amy took a taxi to the station.* **2** [after + -ING] If you do one thing **after** doing another, you do it during the period of time that follows the other thing. ❑ *After completing and signing it, please return the form to us in the envelope provided.* **3** [N + after + N] You use **after** when you are talking about time. For example, if something is going to happen during **the day after** or **the weekend after** a particular time, it is going to happen during the following day or during the following weekend. ❑ *She's leaving the day after tomorrow.* **4** If you go **after** someone, you follow or chase them. ❑ *Alice said to Gina, 'Why don't you go after him, he's your son.'* **5** If you are **after** something, you are trying to get it. ❑ *They were after the money.* **6** If you call, shout, or stare **after** someone, you call, shout, or stare at them as they move away from you. ❑ *'Come back!' he called after me.* **7** If you tell someone that one place is a particular distance **after** another, you mean that it is situated beyond the other place and further away from you. = past ❑ *a station 134 miles after the train starts its journey* **8** If one thing is written **after** another thing on a page, it is written following it or underneath it. = following ❑ *I wrote my name after Penny's at the bottom of the page.* **9** You use **after** in order to give the most important aspect of something when comparing it with another aspect. ❑ *After Germany, America is Britain's second-biggest customer.* **10** To be named **after** someone means to be given the same name as them. ❑ *He persuaded Virginia to name the baby after him.*
PHRASES one after the other or **one after another** If you do something to several things **one after the other** or **one after another**, you do it to one, then the next, and so on, with no break between your actions. ❑ *a lawyer who wins three cases, one after another*
day after day or **year after year** If something happens **day after day** or **year after year**, it happens every day or

every year, for a long time. ❑ *people who'd been coming here year after year*

CONJ If something happens **after** another thing has happened, it happens during the period of time that follows the first event. ❑ *After Don told me this, he spoke of his mother.*

ADV [after after v] If something happens **after**, it happens during the period of time that follows. ❑ *Tomorrow. Or the day after.*

CONVENTION (*politeness*) If you say '**after you**' to someone, you are being polite and allowing them to go in front of you or through a doorway before you do.

✦ after all → see all

after·math /ˈɑːftəmɑːθ, ˈæftəmæθ/ NOUN [SING] The **aftermath** of an important event, especially a harmful one, is the situation that results from it. ❑ *In the aftermath of the coup, the troops opened fire on the demonstrators.*

after·noon ♦♦◇ /ˌɑːftəˈnuːn, ˌæf-/ NOUN [C, U] (**afternoons**) The **afternoon** is the part of each day that begins at lunchtime and ends at about six o'clock. ❑ *He's arriving in the afternoon.* ❑ *He had stayed in his room all afternoon.*

after·wards ♦◇◇ /ˈɑːftəwədz, ˈæf-/ or **afterward** ADV [afterwards with CL] If you do something or if something happens **afterwards**, you do it or it happens after a particular event or time that has already been mentioned. ❑ *Shortly afterwards, police arrested four suspects.*

again ♦♦♦ /əˈgen, əˈgeɪn/ ADV

ADV 1 You use **again** to indicate that something happens a second time, or after it has already happened before. ❑ *He kissed her again.* ❑ *Again there was a short silence.* **2** [again after v] You use **again** to indicate that something is now in a particular state or place that it used to be in. ❑ *He opened his attaché case, removed a folder, then closed it again.* **3** [again + CL] You can use **again** when you want to point out that there is a similarity between the subject that you are talking about now and a previous subject. ❑ *Again the pregnancy was very similar to my previous two.* **4** [again with CL] You can use **again** in expressions such as **but again**, **then again**, and **there again** when you want to introduce a remark that contrasts with or weakens something that you have just said. ❑ *You may be happy to buy imitation leather, and then again, you may wonder what you're getting for your money.* **5** [CL + again] (*spoken*) You can add **again** to the end of your question when you are asking someone to tell you something that you have forgotten or that they have already told you. ❑ *Sorry, what's your name again?* **6** [AMOUNT + again] (*BrE*) You use **again** in expressions such as **half as much again** when you are indicating how much greater one amount is than another amount that you have just mentioned or are about to mention. ❑ *A similar wine from France would cost you half as much again.*

PHRASE **again and again** or **time and again** (*emphasis*) You can use **again and again** or **time and again** to emphasize that something happens many times. = repeatedly ❑ *He would go over his work again and again until he felt he had it right.*

✦ now and again → see now; once again → see once

against ♦♦♦ /əˈgenst, əˈgeɪnst/ PREP, ADV

In addition to the uses shown below, **against** is used in phrasal verbs such as 'come up against', 'guard against', and 'hold against'.

PREP 1 If one thing is leaning or pressing **against** another, it is touching it. ❑ *She leaned against him.* ❑ *On a table pushed against a wall there were bottles of beer and wine.* **2** If you are **against** something such as a plan, policy, or system, you think it is wrong, bad, or stupid. ❑ *Taxes are unpopular – it is understandable that voters are against them.* ❑ *Joan was very much against commencing drug treatment.* **3** If you compete **against** someone in a game, you try to beat them. ❑ *This is the first of two games against Denver in the next five days.* **4** If you take action **against** someone or something, you try to harm them. ❑ *Security forces are still using violence against opponents of the government.* **5** If you take action **against** a possible future event, you try to

prevent it. ❑ *Experts have been discussing how to improve the fight against crime.* **6** If you do something **against** someone's wishes, advice, or orders, you do not do what they want you to do or tell you to do. ❑ *He discharged himself from the hospital against the advice of doctors.* **7** If you do something in order to protect yourself **against** something unpleasant or harmful, you do something that will make its effects on you less serious if it happens. ❑ *Any business needs insurance against ordinary risks such as fire, flood, and breakages.* **8** If something is **against** the law or **against** the rules, there is a law or a rule which says that you must not do it. ❑ *It is against the law to detain you against your will for any length of time.* **9** If you are moving **against** a current, tide, or wind, you are moving in the opposite direction to it. ❑ *swimming upstream against the current* **10** If something happens or is considered **against** a particular background of events, it is considered in relation to those events, because those events are relevant to it. ❑ *The profits rise was achieved against a backdrop of falling metal prices.* **11** If something is measured or valued **against** something else, it is measured or valued by comparing it with the other thing. ❑ *Our policies have to be judged against a clear test: will it improve the standard of education?* **12** [N + against] The odds **against** something happening are the chances or odds that it will not happen. ❑ *The odds against him surviving are incredible.*

PHRASE **have something against someone** If you **have** something **against** someone or something, you dislike them. ❑ *Have you got something against women, Les?*

ADV 1 [against after v] You use **against** to indicate an action intended to stop something from happening. ❑ *The vote for the suspension of the party was 283 in favour with 29 against.* **2** [N + against] You use **against** to indicate a probability that something will not happen. ❑ *What were the odds against?*

✦ up against → see up; against the clock → see clock

⊕ **age** ♦♦♦ /eɪdʒ/ NOUN, VERB

NOUN [C, U] (**ages**) **1** [C, U] Your **age** is the number of years that you have lived. ❑ *She has a nephew who is just ten years of age.* ❑ *At the age of sixteen he qualified for a place at the University of North Carolina.* **2** [C, U] The **age** of a thing is the number of years since it was made. ❑ *Everything in the room looks in keeping with the age of the building.* **3** [U] **Age** is the state of being old or the process of becoming older. ❑ *Perhaps he has grown wiser with age.* ❑ *This cologne, like wine, improves with age.* **4** [C] An **age** is a period in history. = era ❑ *the age of steam and steel* ❑ *We're living in the digital age.* **5** [C] (*informal*) You can say **an age** or **ages** to mean a very long time. = forever ❑ *He waited what seemed an age.*

VERB [I, T] (**ages**, **aging** or **ageing**, **aged**) When someone **ages**, or when something **ages** them, they seem much older and less strong or less alert. ❑ *He had always looked so young, but he seemed to have aged in the last few months.* ❑ *Worry had aged him.*

→ See also **aged**, **ageing**, **middle age**

WORD CONNECTIONS
ADJ + **age**
a **young** age
an **early** age
❑ *Murray began to play tennis at a very early age.*
middle age
old age
❑ *Loneliness and isolation can be a big problem in old age.*
the **average** age
the **minimum** age
❑ *The average age for a woman to have her first child is 31 in this country.*
VERB + **age**
reach an age
❑ *Children usually leave school when they reach the age of 16 or 18.*

⊕ **aged** ADJ, NOUN

ADJ 1 /eɪdʒd/ You use **aged** followed by a number to say

how old someone is. ❑ *Alan has two children, aged eleven and nine.* **2** /'eɪdʒɪd/ [aged + N] **Aged** means very old. ❑ *She has an aged parent who's capable of being very difficult.* NOUN /'eɪdʒɪd/ [PL] You can refer to all people who are very old as **the aged**. ❑ *The American Society on Aging provides resource services to those dealing with the aged.*
→ See also **middle-aged**

✿**age group** NOUN [c] (**age groups**) An **age group** is the people in a place or organization who were born during a particular period of time, for example, all the people aged between 18 and 25. = generation, peer group ❑ *a style that would appeal to all age groups* ❑ *The research studied the eating habits of people in the 18-25 age group.*

✿**age·ing** /'eɪdʒɪŋ/ also **aging** ADJ, NOUN
ADJ Someone or something that is **ageing** is becoming older and less healthy or efficient. = old, elderly; ≠ young, new ❑ *John lives with his ageing mother.* ❑ *Ageing aircraft need more frequent safety inspections.*
NOUN [u] **Ageing** is the process of becoming old or becoming worn out. ❑ *The only signs of ageing are the flecks of grey that speckle his dark hair.*

agen·cy ♦♦◇ /'eɪdʒənsi/ NOUN [c] (**agencies**) **1** (*business*) An **agency** is a business that provides a service on behalf of other businesses. ❑ *We had to hire maids through an agency.* **2** An **agency** is a government organization responsible for a certain area of administration. ❑ *She is calling for a collaboration of local, state and federal agencies to deal with the problem.*

agen·da ♦◇◇ /ə'dʒendə/ NOUN [c] (**agendas**) **1** You can refer to the political issues that are important at a particular time as an **agenda**. ❑ *Does television set the agenda on foreign policy?* **2** An **agenda** is a list of the items that have to be discussed at a meeting. ❑ *This is sure to be an item on the agenda next week.*

✿**agent** ♦♦◇ /'eɪdʒənt/ NOUN [c] (**agents**) **1** (*business*) An **agent** is a person who looks after someone else's business affairs or does business on their behalf. = representative, rep ❑ *You are buying direct, rather than through an agent.* **2** An **agent** in the arts world is a person who gets work for an actor or musician, or who sells the work of a writer to publishers. ❑ *My literary agent thinks it is not unreasonable to expect $500,000 in total.* **3** An **agent** is a person who works for a country's secret service. ❑ *All these years he's been an agent for the East.* **4** A chemical that has a particular effect or is used for a particular purpose can be referred to as a particular kind of **agent**. ❑ *the bleaching agent in white flour* ❑ *a chemical agent that can produce birth defects*

✿**ag·gra·vate** /'ægrəveɪt/ VERB [T] (**aggravates, aggravating, aggravated**) **1** If someone or something **aggravates** a situation, they make it worse. = exacerbate ❑ *Stress and lack of sleep can aggravate the situation.* ❑ *irritants which cause or aggravate eczema* **2** (*informal*) If someone or something **aggravates** you, they make you annoyed. = annoy ❑ *What aggravates you most about this country?*
ag·gra·vat·ing /'ægrəveɪtɪŋ/ ADJ = annoying ❑ *You don't realize how aggravating you can be.*
ag·gra·va·tion /ˌægrə'veɪʃən/ NOUN [c, u] (**aggravations**) = annoyance ❑ *I just couldn't take the aggravation.*

✿**ag·gre·gate** /'ægrɪgət/ ADJ, NOUN (*academic word*)
ADJ [aggregate + N] An **aggregate** amount or score is made up of several smaller amounts or scores added together. = total, combined; ≠ individual ❑ *The rate of growth of GNP will depend upon the rate of growth of aggregate demand.* ❑ *a total of 57 investments with an aggregate value of $1.47 billion* NOUN [c] (**aggregates**) An **aggregate** is an amount or score made up of several smaller amounts or scores added together. = total, sum ❑ *earlier estimates of the monetary aggregates*

ag·gres·sion /ə'greʃən/ NOUN [u, c] (**aggressions**) **1** [u] **Aggression** is a quality of anger and determination that makes you ready to attack other people. = belligerence ❑ *Aggression is by no means a male-only trait.* **2** [c, u] **Aggression** is violent and attacking behaviour. ❑ *the threat of massive military aggression*

ag·gres·sive ♦◇◇ /ə'gresɪv/ ADJ **1** An **aggressive** person or animal has a quality of anger and determination that makes them ready to attack other people. = belligerent ❑ *Some children are much more aggressive than others.* ❑ *These fish are very aggressive.* **2** People who are **aggressive** in their work or other activities behave in a forceful way because they are very eager to succeed. ❑ *He is respected as a very aggressive and competitive executive.*
ag·gres·sive·ly /ə'gresɪvli/ ADV **1** *They'll react aggressively.* **2** *countries noted for aggressively pursuing energy efficiency*
ag·gres·sor /ə'gresə/ NOUN [c] (**aggressors**) The **aggressor** in a fight or battle is the person, group, or country that starts it. ❑ *They have been the aggressors in this conflict.*

ag·grieved /ə'griːvd/ ADJ If you feel **aggrieved**, you feel upset and angry because of the way in which you have been treated. = resentful, bitter ❑ *I really feel aggrieved at this sort of thing.*

ag·ile /'ædʒaɪl, AmE -dʒəl/ ADJ **1** Someone who is **agile** can move quickly and easily. = nimble ❑ *At 20 years old he was not as strong, as fast, as agile as he is now.* **2** If you have an **agile** mind, you think quickly and intelligently. ❑ *She was quick-witted and had an extraordinarily agile mind.*
agil·ity /ə'dʒɪlɪti/ NOUN [u] **1** *She blinked in surprise at his agility.* **2** *His intellect and mental agility have never been in doubt.*

✿**ag·ing** /'eɪdʒɪŋ/ → See **ageing**

agi·tate /'ædʒɪteɪt/ VERB [T, I] (**agitates, agitating, agitated**) **1** [T] (*formal*) If you **agitate** something, you shake it so that it moves about. ❑ *All you need to do is gently agitate the water with a finger or paintbrush.* **2** [T] If something **agitates** you, it worries you and makes you unable to think clearly or calmly. ❑ *Carl and Martin may inherit their grandmother's possessions when she dies. The thought agitates her.* **3** [I] If people **agitate for** something, they protest or take part in political activity in order to get it. ❑ *The women who worked in these mills had begun to agitate for better conditions.*
agi·tat·ed /'ædʒɪteɪtɪd/ ADJ If someone is **agitated**, they are very worried or upset, and show this in their behaviour, movements, or voice. = upset, distressed ❑ *Susan seemed agitated about something.*
agi·ta·tion /ˌædʒɪ'teɪʃən/ NOUN [u] If someone is in a state of **agitation**, they are very worried or upset, and show this in their behaviour, movements, or voice. = distress ❑ *Danny returned to Father's house in a state of intense agitation.*

ago ♦♦♦ /ə'gəʊ/ ADV You use **ago** when you are referring to past time. For example, if something happened one year **ago**, it is one year since it happened. If it happened a long time **ago**, it is a long time since it happened. ❑ *He was killed a few days ago in a skiing accident.* ❑ *The meeting is the first ever between the two sides since the war there began 14 years ago.*

ago·niz·ing /'ægənaɪzɪŋ/ also **agonising** ADJ **1** Something that is **agonizing** causes you to feel great physical or mental pain. ❑ *He did not wish to die the agonizing death of his mother and brother.* **2** **Agonizing** decisions and choices are very difficult to make. ❑ *He now faced an agonizing decision about his immediate future.*

ago·ny /'ægəni/ NOUN [u] **Agony** is great physical or mental pain. = torment ❑ *A new machine may save thousands of animals from the agony of drug tests.*

✿**agree** ♦♦♦ /ə'griː/ VERB
VERB [RECIP, I, T] (**agrees, agreeing, agreed**) **1** [RECIP] If people **agree with** each other about something, they have the same opinion about it or say that they have the same opinion. = concur ❑ *Both have agreed on the need for the money.* ❑ *So we both agree there's a problem?* ❑ *I agree with you that the open system is by far the best.* ❑ *'It's appalling.'—'It is.' I agree with every word you've just said.* ❑ *Not all scientists agree with this view.* **2** [RECIP] If people **agree on** something, they all decide to accept or do something. ≠ disagree ❑ *The warring sides have agreed on an unconditional ceasefire.* **3** [RECIP] [agree 'with' N, PL-N + agree] In grammar, if a word **agrees with** a noun or pronoun, it

A

has a form that is appropriate to the number or gender of the noun or pronoun. For example, in 'He hates it' the singular verb agrees with the singular pronoun 'he'. **4** [I, T] If you **agree to** do something, you say that you will do it. If you **agree to** a proposal, you accept it. = consent ❏ *He agreed to pay me for the drawings.* **5** [I] If you **agree with** an action or suggestion, you approve of it. ❏ *You didn't want to ask anybody whether they agreed with what you were doing.* **6** [RECIP] If one account of an event or one set of figures **agrees** with another, the two accounts or sets of figures are the same or are consistent with each other. = tally, correspond, match ❏ *His second statement agrees with facts as stated by the other witnesses.* ❏ *The total of columns I and J should agree with the amount shown for income.* [PHRASE] **agree to differ** or **agree to disagree** If two people who are arguing about something **agree to disagree** or **agree to differ**, they decide to stop arguing because neither of them is going to change their opinion. ❏ *You and I are going to have to agree to disagree then.* → See also **agreed**

USAGE NOTE

agree

Remember to use the correct preposition after **agree**. When you **agree with** someone or with something they have said, you have the same opinion as them.

I **agree with** you, Julie.

I **agree with** everything that Mark said.

When you **agree to** something or you **agree to do** something, you say that you accept it or that you will do it.

The company **agreed to** pay my legal fees.

When people **agree on** something, they reach a decision together.

All 25 EU members **agreed on** the need for more aid.

agree•able /əˈgriːəbəl/ ADJ **1** If something is **agreeable**, it is pleasant and you enjoy it. = pleasant ❏ *workers in more agreeable and better paid occupations* **2** If someone is **agreeable**, they are pleasant and try to please people. ❏ *sharing a bottle of wine with an agreeable companion*

agreed /əˈgriːd/ ADJ [V-LINK + agreed] If people are **agreed** on something, they have reached a joint decision on it or have the same opinion about it. ❏ *Okay, so are we agreed on going north?* → See also **agree**

✪ **agree•ment** ♦♦◇ /əˈgriːmənt/ NOUN [NOUN] [c, u] (agreements) **1** [c] An **agreement** is a formal decision about future action that is made by two or more countries, groups, or people. ❏ *It looks as though a compromise agreement has now been reached.* **2** [u] **Agreement on** something is a joint decision that a particular course of action should be taken. ❏ *A spokesman said, however, that the two men had not reached agreement on the issues discussed.* **3** [u] **Agreement** with someone means having the same opinion as they have. ❏ *The judge kept nodding in agreement.* **4** [u] **Agreement** to a course of action means allowing it to happen or giving it your approval. = consent ❏ *The clinic doctor will then write to your doctor to get his agreement.* **5** [u] [oft 'of' agreement] If there is **agreement** between two accounts of an event or two sets of figures, they are the same or are consistent with each other. = concurrence, correspondence ❏ *Many other surveys have produced results essentially in agreement with these figures.* ❏ *There is a measure of agreement between these accounts.* [PHRASE] **in agreement** **1** If you are **in agreement with** someone, you have the same opinion as they have. **2** If you are **in agreement with** a plan or proposal, you approve of it.

✪ **ag•ri•cul•tur•al** ♦◇◇ /ˌægrɪˈkʌltʃərəl/ ADJ **Agricultural** means involving or relating to agriculture. ❏ *Farmers struggling for survival strip the forests for agricultural land.* ❏ *The price of corn and other agricultural products has increased.*

✪ **ag•ri•cul•ture** ♦◇◇ /ˈægrɪkʌltʃə/ NOUN [u] **Agriculture** is farming and the methods that are used to raise and take

care of crops and animals. = farming ❏ *Strong both in industry and agriculture, Ukraine produces much of the grain for the nation.*

aground /əˈgraʊnd/ ADV [aground after v] If a ship runs **aground**, it touches the ground in a shallow part of a river, lake, or the sea, and gets stuck. ❏ *The ship ran aground where there should have been a depth of 35 ft.*

ahead ♦♦◇ /əˈhed/ ADV

In addition to the uses shown below, **ahead** is used in phrasal verbs such as 'get ahead', 'go ahead', and 'press ahead'.

[ADV] **1** Something that is **ahead** is in front of you. If you look **ahead**, you look directly in front of you. ❏ *Brett looked straight ahead.* ❏ *The road ahead was now blocked solid.* **2** [ahead after v] You use **ahead** with verbs such as 'push', 'move', and 'forge' to indicate that a plan, programme, or organization is making fast progress. = forward ❏ *Western countries were moving ahead with plans to send financial aid to all of the former Soviet republics.* **3** If you are **ahead** in your work or achievements, you have made more progress than you expected to and are performing well. ❏ *First half profits have charged ahead from $127.6m to $134.2m.* **4** If a person or a team is **ahead** in a competition, they are winning. ❏ *Australia was ahead throughout the game.* ❏ *The Communists are comfortably ahead in the opinion polls.* **5** **Ahead** also means in the future. ❏ *A much bigger battle is ahead for the president.* **6** [ahead after v] If you prepare or plan something **ahead**, you do it some time before a future event so that everything is ready for that event to take place. ❏ *The government wants figures that help it to administer its policies and plan ahead.* **7** [ahead after v] If you go **ahead**, or if you go on **ahead**, you go in front of someone who is going to the same place so that you arrive there some time before they do. ❏ *I went ahead and waited with Sean.* [PHRASE] **ahead of** **1** If someone is **ahead of** you, they are directly in front of you. If someone is moving **ahead of** you, they are in front of you and moving in the same direction. ❏ *I saw a man in a blue jacket thirty yards ahead of me.* **2** If an event or period of time lies **ahead of** you, it is going to happen or take place soon or in the future. = before ❏ *I tried to think about all the problems that were ahead of me tomorrow.* ❏ *Heather had been awake all night thinking about the future that lay ahead of her.* **3** In a competition, if a person or team does something **ahead of** someone else, they do it before the second person or team. ❏ *Robert Millar finished 1 minute and 35 seconds ahead of the Frenchman.* **4** If something happens **ahead of** schedule or **ahead of** time, it happens earlier than was planned. ❏ *The election was held six months ahead of schedule.* **5** If someone is **ahead of** someone else, they have made more progress and are more advanced in what they are doing. ❏ *Henry generally stayed ahead of the others in the academic subjects.* ✦ one step ahead of → see step; ahead of your time → see time

✪ **aid** ♦♦♦ /eɪd/ NOUN, VERB (academic word) [NOUN] [c, u] (aids) **1** [c, u] **Aid** is money, equipment, or services that are provided for people, countries, or organizations who need them but cannot provide them for themselves. ❏ *regular flights carrying humanitarian aid to Cambodia* ❏ *They have already pledged billions of dollars in aid.* **2** [u] If you perform a task **with the aid of** something, you need or use that thing to perform that task. = help ❏ *He succeeded with the aid of a completely new method he discovered.* **3** [u] (written) **Aid** is help or assistance. = assistance ❏ *He was forced to turn for aid to his former enemy.* **4** [c] An **aid** is an object, device, or technique that makes something easier to do. ❏ *The book is an invaluable aid to teachers of literature.* [PHRASE] **come to someone's aid** or **go to someone's aid** If you **come** or **go** to someone's **aid**, you try to help them when they are in danger or difficulty. ❏ *Dr Fox went to the aid of the dying man despite having been injured in the crash.* [VERB] [I, T] (aids, aiding, aided) **1** [I, T] To **aid** a country, organization, or person means to provide them with money, equipment, or services that they need. ❏ *American*

a

efforts to aid Kurdish refugees ❑ *a charitable organization that has spent millions aiding pharmaceutical research* **2** [T] (*written*) To **aid** someone means to help or assist them. = help, assist ❑ *a software system to aid managers in advanced decision-making* **3** [I, T] If something **aids** a process, it makes it easier or more likely to happen. ❑ *The survey suggests that the export sector will continue to aid the economic recovery.* ❑ *Calcium may aid in the prevention of colon cancer.*
-aided /'eɪdɪd/ COMB ❑ *government-aided research*

aide /eɪd/ NOUN [c] (**aides**) An **aide** is an assistant to someone who has an important job, especially in government or in the armed forces. ❑ *A close aide to the prime minister repeated that Israel would never accept it.*

AIDS ♦♦◊ /eɪdz/ NOUN [u] **AIDS** is a disease that destroys the natural system of protection that the body has against other diseases. **AIDS** is an abbreviation for **acquired immune deficiency syndrome.** ❑ *people suffering from AIDS*

ail·ing /'eɪlɪŋ/ ADJ An **ailing** organization or society is in difficulty and is becoming weaker. ❑ *The rise in overseas sales is good news for the ailing American economy.*

✪ **aim** ♦♦◊ /eɪm/ VERB, NOUN
VERB [I, T] (**aims, aiming, aimed**) **1** [I, T] If you **aim for** something or **aim to** do something, you plan or hope to achieve it. ❑ *He said he would aim for the 100 metre world record at the world championships in August.* ❑ *Businesses will have to aim at long-term growth.* ❑ *The programme aims to educate and prepare students for a challenging career.* **2** [T] If your actions or remarks **are aimed at** a particular person or group, you intend that the person or group should notice them and be influenced by them. ❑ *His message was aimed at the undecided middle ground of Israeli politics.* **3** [I, T] If you **aim** a weapon or object **at** something or someone, you point it towards them before firing or throwing it. ❑ *When he appeared again, he was aiming the rifle at Wade.* ❑ *a missile aimed at the arms factory* **4** [T] If you **aim** a kick or punch at someone, you try to kick or punch them. ❑ *They set on him, punching him in the face and aiming kicks at his shins.* **5** [T] If an action or plan **is aimed at** achieving something, it is intended or planned to achieve it. ❑ *The new measures are aimed at tightening existing sanctions.*
NOUN [c, SING] (**aims**) **1** [c] The **aim** of something that you do is the purpose for which you do it or the result that it is intended to achieve. = objective ❑ *The main aim of the present study was to test Boklage's findings.* ❑ *a research programme that has largely failed to achieve its principal aims* ❑ *The aim of the festival is to increase awareness of Hindu culture and traditions.* **2** [SING] Your **aim** is your skill or action in pointing a weapon or other object at its target. ❑ *He stood with the gun gripped in his right hand and his left hand steadying his aim.*
PHRASE **take aim** When you **take aim**, you point a weapon or object at someone or something, before firing or throwing it. ❑ *She had spotted a man with a shotgun taking aim.*

aim·less /'eɪmləs/ ADJ A person or activity that is **aimless** has no clear purpose or plan. ❑ *After several hours of aimless searching they were getting low on fuel.*
aim·less·ly /'eɪmləsli/ ADV [aimlessly after v] ❑ *I wandered around aimlessly.*

✪ **air** ♦♦♦ /eə/ NOUN, VERB
NOUN [SING, U] **1** [SING, U] **Air** is the mixture of gases that forms the Earth's atmosphere and that we breathe. ❑ *Every living creature needs air to breathe.* ❑ *Draughts help to circulate air.* ❑ *Keith opened the window and leaned out into the cold air.* ❑ *Cars are a major cause of air pollution.* **2** [u] **Air** is used to refer to travel in aircraft. ❑ *Air travel will continue to grow at about 6% per year.* **3** [SING] **The air** is the space around things or above the ground. ❑ *Government troops broke up the protest by firing their guns in the air.*
PHRASES **clear the air** If you do something to **clear the air**, you do it in order to resolve any problems or disagreements that there might be. ❑ *an inquiry just to clear the air and settle the facts of the case*
in the air If something is **in the air** it is felt to be present, but it is not talked about. ❑ *There was great excitement in the air.*

on the air If someone is **on the air**, they are broadcasting on radio or television. If a programme is **on the air**, it is being broadcast on radio or television. If it is **off the air**, it is not being broadcast. ❑ *We go on the air, live, at 11.30 a.m.*
thin air If someone or something disappears **into thin air**, they disappear completely. If someone or something appears **out of thin air**, they appear suddenly and mysteriously. ❑ *He had materialized out of thin air; I had not seen or heard him coming.*
VERB [T] (**airs, airing, aired**) **1** (*mainly AmE*) If a broadcasting company **airs** a television or radio programme, they show it on television or broadcast it on the radio. = broadcast ❑ *Tonight PBS will air a documentary called 'Democracy In Action'.* **2** If you **air** a room or building, you let fresh air into it. ❑ *One day a week her mother cleaned and aired each room.*
air·ing /'eərɪŋ/ NOUN [SING] ❑ *the airing of a new television commercial that attacked the president's war record*

air base also **airbase** NOUN [c] (**air bases**) An **air base** is a centre where military aircraft take off or land and are serviced, and where many of the centre's staff live. ❑ *the largest American air base in Saudi Arabia*

air·borne /'eəbɔːn/ ADJ **1** [V-LINK + airborne] If an aircraft is **airborne**, it is in the air and flying. ❑ *The pilot did manage to get airborne.* **2** [airborne + N] **Airborne** troops use parachutes to get into enemy territory. ❑ *The allies landed thousands of airborne troops.* **3** **Airborne** means in the air or carried in the air. ❑ *Many people are allergic to airborne pollutants such as pollen.*

air-conditioned ADJ If a room or vehicle is **air-conditioned**, the air in it is kept cool and dry by means of a special machine. ❑ *our new air-conditioned trains*

air-condition·ing NOUN [u] **Air-conditioning** is a method of providing buildings and vehicles with cool dry air.

air·craft ♦♦◊ /'eəkrɑːft, -kræft/ NOUN [c] (**aircraft**) An **aircraft** is a vehicle that can fly, for example, an aeroplane or a helicopter. ❑ *The return flight of the aircraft was delayed.*

air·field /'eəfiːld/ NOUN [c] (**airfields**) An **airfield** is an area of ground where aircraft take off and land. It is smaller than an airport.

air force ♦◊◊ NOUN [c] (**air forces**) An **air force** is the part of a country's armed forces that is concerned with fighting in the air. ❑ *the United States Air Force*

air·lift /'eəlɪft/ NOUN, VERB
NOUN [c] (**airlifts**) An **airlift** is an operation to move people, troops, or goods by air, especially in a war or when land routes are closed. ❑ *President Garcia has ordered an airlift of food, medicines and blankets.*
VERB [T] (**airlifts, airlifting, airlifted**) If people, troops, or goods **are airlifted** somewhere, they are carried by air, especially in a war or when land routes are closed. ❑ *The injured were airlifted to a hospital in Dayton.*

air·line ♦♦◊ /'eəlaɪn/ NOUN [c] (**airlines**) An **airline** is a company that provides regular services carrying people or goods in aeroplanes. ❑ *the world's largest discount airline*

air·lin·er /'eəlaɪnə/ NOUN [c] (**airliners**) An **airliner** is a large aeroplane that is used for carrying passengers.

air·man /'eəmæn/ NOUN [c] (**airmen**) An **airman** is a man who flies aircraft, especially one who serves in his country's air force. ❑ *an American airman*

air·port ♦♦◊ /'eəpɔːt/ NOUN [c] (**airports**) An **airport** is a place where aircraft land and take off, and that has buildings and facilities for passengers. ❑ *Heathrow Airport, the busiest international airport in the world*

air raid NOUN [c] (**air raids**) An **air raid** is an attack by military aircraft in which bombs are dropped. ❑ *The war began with overnight air raids on Baghdad and Kuwait.*

air·space /'eəspeɪs/ also **air space** NOUN [u] A country's **airspace** is the part of the sky that is over that country and is considered to belong to it. ❑ *Forty minutes later, they left Colombian airspace.*

air·tight /'eətaɪt/ also **air-tight** ADJ If a container is **airtight**, its lid fits so tightly that no air can get in or out. ❑ *Store the biscuits in an airtight container.*

A

air·way /ˈeəweɪ/ NOUN [C, PL] (**airways**) **1** [C] A person's **airways** are the passages from their nose and mouth down to their lungs, through which air enters and leaves their body. ❑ *an inflammation of the airways* **2** [PL] [usu 'the' airway] The **airways** are all the routes that planes can travel along. ❑ *How does a private pilot get access to the airways?*

aisle /aɪl/ NOUN [C] (**aisles**) An **aisle** is a long narrow gap that people can walk along between rows of seats in a public building such as a church or between rows of shelves in a supermarket. ❑ *the frozen-food aisle*

akin /əˈkɪn/ ADJ [V-LINK + akin 'to' N] (*formal*) If one thing is **akin to** another, it is similar to it in some way. ❑ *Listening to his life story is akin to reading a good adventure novel.*

alarm ♦◇◇ /əˈlɑːm/ NOUN, VERB
NOUN [U, C] (**alarms**) **1** [U] **Alarm** is a feeling of fear or anxiety that something unpleasant or dangerous might happen. ❑ *The news was greeted with alarm by senators.* **2** [C] An **alarm** is an automatic device that warns you of danger, for example, by ringing a bell. ❑ *He heard the alarm go off.*
PHRASES **alarm bells** If you say that something sets **alarm bells** ringing, you mean that it makes people feel worried or concerned about something. ❑ *This has set the alarm bells ringing in Moscow.*
raise the alarm or **sound the alarm** If you **raise the alarm** or **sound the alarm**, you warn people of danger. ❑ *His family raised the alarm when he had not come home by 9 o'clock.*
VERB [T] (**alarms, alarming, alarmed**) If something **alarms** you, it makes you afraid or anxious that something unpleasant or dangerous might happen. = **frighten** ❑ *We could not see what had alarmed him.*
→ See also **alarmed, alarming**

alarmed /əˈlɑːmd/ ADJ If someone is **alarmed**, they feel afraid or anxious that something unpleasant or dangerous might happen. ❑ *They should not be too alarmed by the press reports.*

alarm·ing /əˈlɑːmɪŋ/ ADJ Something that is **alarming** makes you feel afraid or anxious that something unpleasant or dangerous might happen. = **worrying** ❑ *The disease has spread at an alarming rate.*
alarm·ing·ly /əˈlɑːmɪŋli/ ADV ❑ *the alarmingly high rate of heart disease*

✪ **al·be·it** /ɔːlˈbiːɪt/ ADV [albeit with CL/GROUP] (*academic word, formal*) You use **albeit** to introduce a fact or comment that reduces the force or significance of what you have just said. = **although** ❑ *Charles's letter was indeed published, albeit in a somewhat abbreviated form.* ❑ *A growing body of evidence, albeit circumstantial, links aluminium with Alzheimer's disease.*

al·bum ♦♦◇ /ˈælbəm/ NOUN [C] (**albums**) **1** An **album** is a collection of songs that is available on a CD, record, or cassette. ❑ *Chris likes music and has a large collection of albums and cassettes.* ❑ *Oasis release their new album on July 1.* **2** An **album** is a book in which you keep things such as photographs or stamps that you have collected. ❑ *Theresa showed me her photo album.*

al·co·hol ♦◇◇ /ˈælkəhɒl, AmE -hɔːl/ NOUN [U, C] (**alcohols**) **1** [U] Drinks that can make people drunk, such as beer, wine, and whisky, can be referred to as **alcohol**. ❑ *Do either of you smoke cigarettes or drink alcohol?* **2** [C, U] **Alcohol** is a colourless liquid that is found in drinks such as beer, wine, and whisky. It is also used in products such as perfumes and cleaning fluids. ❑ *low-alcohol beer*

al·co·hol·ic /ˌælkəˈhɒlɪk, AmE -ˈhɔːl-/ NOUN, ADJ
NOUN [C] (**alcoholics**) An **alcoholic** is someone who cannot stop drinking large amounts of alcohol, even when this is making them ill. ❑ *He showed great courage by admitting on television that he is an alcoholic.*
ADJ **Alcoholic** drinks are drinks that contain alcohol. ❑ *The serving of alcoholic drinks was forbidden after six o'clock.*

al·co·hol·ism /ˈælkəhɒlɪzəm/ NOUN [U] People who suffer from **alcoholism** cannot stop drinking large quantities of alcohol. ❑ *a doctor who specialized in the problems of alcoholism*

alert ♦◇◇ /əˈlɜːt/ ADJ, NOUN, VERB
ADJ **1** If you are **alert**, you are paying full attention to

things around you and are able to deal with anything that might happen. = **attentive** ❑ *We all have to stay alert.* **2** [V-LINK + alert 'to' N] If you are **alert to** something, you are fully aware of it. ❑ *The bank is alert to the danger.*
NOUN [C] (**alerts**) An **alert** is a situation in which people prepare themselves for something dangerous that might happen soon. ❑ *There has been criticism of how his administration handled last week's terrorism alert.*
PHRASE **on the alert** If you are **on the alert for** something, you are ready to deal with it if it happens. ❑ *They want to be on the alert for similar buying opportunities.*
VERB [T] (**alerts, alerting, alerted**) If you **alert** someone **to** a situation, especially a dangerous or unpleasant situation, you tell them about it. ❑ *He wanted to alert people to the activities of the group.*
alert·ness /əˈlɜːtnəs/ NOUN [U] ❑ *The drug improved mental alertness.*

✪ **al·ge·bra** /ˈældʒɪbrə/ NOUN [U] **Algebra** is a type of mathematics in which letters are used to represent possible quantities. ❑ *a textbook on linear algebra*

al·ien /ˈeɪliən/ ADJ, NOUN
ADJ (*formal*) **1** (*disapproval*) **Alien** means belonging to a different country, race, or group, usually one you do not like or are frightened of. = **foreign** ❑ *He said they were opposed to what he described as the presence of alien forces in the region.* **2** [V-LINK + alien 'to' N] If something is **alien to** you or to your normal feelings or behaviour, it is not the way you would normally feel or behave. = **foreign, unfamiliar** ❑ *Such an attitude is alien to most businessmen.*
NOUN [C] (**aliens**) **1** (*legal*) An **alien** is someone who is not a legal citizen of the country in which they live. = **foreigner** ❑ *Both women had hired illegal aliens for child care.* **2** In science fiction, an **alien** is a creature from outer space. ❑ *aliens from another planet*

al·ien·ate /ˈeɪliəneɪt/ VERB [T] (**alienates, alienating, alienated**) **1** If you **alienate** someone, you make them become unfriendly or unsympathetic towards you. ❑ *The government cannot afford to alienate either group.* **2** To **alienate** a person **from** someone or something that they are normally linked with means to cause them to be emotionally or intellectually separated from them. ❑ *His second wife, Alice, was determined to alienate him from his two boys.*
al·iena·tion /ˌeɪliəˈneɪʃən/ NOUN [U] ❑ *Butler's alienation from the group had been furthered by the experience of travelling around the USA.*

alight /əˈlaɪt/ ADJ, VERB
ADJ **1** [V N + alight, V-LINK + alight] If something is **alight**, it is burning. = **ablaze** ❑ *Several buildings were set alight.* **2** [V-LINK + alight] (*literary*) If someone's eyes are **alight** or if their face is **alight**, the expression in their eyes or on their face shows that they are feeling a strong emotion such as excitement or happiness. ❑ *She paused and turned, her face alight with happiness.*
VERB [I] (**alights, alighting, alighted**) **1** (*literary*) If a bird or insect **alights** somewhere, it lands there. ❑ *A thrush alighted on a branch of the pine tree.* **2** (*formal*) When you **alight** from a train, bus, or other vehicle, you get out of it after a trip. = **get off**

align /əˈlaɪn/ VERB [T] (**aligns, aligning, aligned**) **1** If you **align yourself with** a particular group, you support them because you have the same political aim. ❑ *When war broke out, they aligned themselves with the rebel forces.* **2** If you **align** something, you place it in a certain position in relation to something else, usually parallel to it. ❑ *A tripod will be useful to align and steady the camera.*

✪ **alike** /əˈlaɪk/ ADJ, ADV
ADJ [V-LINK + alike] If two or more things are **alike**, they are similar in some way. = **similar** ❑ *We looked very alike.*
ADV **1** [alike after V] **Alike** means in a similar way. = **similarly** ❑ *They even dressed alike.* ❑ *The article makes the false assumption that all men and women think alike.* **2** You use **alike** after mentioning two or more people, groups, or things in order to emphasize that you are referring to both or all of them. = **equally** ❑ *The techniques are being used almost everywhere by big and small companies alike.*

alive ♦◇◇ /əˈlaɪv/ ADJ
ADJ **1** [V-LINK + alive] If people or animals are **alive**, they

are not dead. ❑ *She does not know if he is alive or dead.* **2** If you say that someone seems **alive**, you mean that they seem to be very lively and to enjoy everything that they do. ❑ *She seemed more alive and looked forward to getting up in the morning.* **3** [V-LINK + alive, 'keep' N + alive] If an activity, organization, or situation is **alive**, it continues to exist or function. ❑ *The big factories are trying to stay alive by cutting costs.* **4** [V-LINK + alive] If a place is **alive with** something, there are a lot of people or things there and it seems busy or exciting. ❑ *The river was alive with birds.* **PHRASE** **come alive** or **bring alive** **1** If people, places, or events **come alive**, they start to be lively again after a quiet period. If someone or something **brings** them **alive**, they cause them to come alive. ❑ *The doctor's voice had come alive and his small eyes shone.* **2** If a story or description **comes alive**, it becomes interesting, lively, or realistic. If someone or something **brings** it **alive**, they make it seem more interesting, lively, or realistic. ❑ *She made history come alive with tales from her own memories.*

all ♦♦♦ /ɔːl/ PREDET, DET, QUANT, PRON, ADV
PREDET **1** You use **all** to indicate that you are referring to the whole of a particular group or thing or to everyone or everything of a particular kind. ❑ *the restaurant that Hugh and all his friends go to* **2** [all + DET SING-N] You use **all** to refer to the whole of a particular period of time. ❑ *She's worked all her life.* **PHRASE** **for all** You use **for all** to indicate that the thing mentioned does not affect or contradict the truth of what you are saying. = despite ❑ *For all its beauty, Prague could soon lose some of the individuality that the communist years helped to preserve.*
DET **1** You use **all** to indicate that you are referring to the whole of a particular group or thing or to everyone or everything of a particular kind. ❑ *There is built-in storage space in all bedrooms.* ❑ *He was passionate about all literature.* **2** You use **all** to refer to the whole of a particular period of time. ❑ *George had to cut grass all afternoon.* **3** (*emphasis*) You use **all** in expressions such as **in all sincerity** and **in all probability** to emphasize that you are being sincere or that something is very likely. ❑ *In all fairness he had to admit that she was neither dishonest nor lazy.*
PHRASES **of all** (*emphasis*) You use **of all** in expressions such as **of all people** or **of all things** when you want to emphasize someone or something surprising. ❑ *One group of women, sitting on the ground, was singing, of all things, 'Greensleeves'.* **of all the X** (*feelings*) You use **of all** in expressions like **of all the nerve** or **of all the luck** to emphasize how angry or surprised you are at what someone else has done or said. ❑ *Of all the lazy, indifferent, unbusinesslike attitudes to have!*
QUANT **1** You use **all** to indicate that you are referring to the whole of a particular group or thing or to everyone or everything of a particular kind. ❑ *He was told to pack up all of his letters and personal belongings.* **2** [all 'of' DEFN-N] You use **all** to refer to the whole of a particular period of time. ❑ *He spent all of that afternoon polishing the silver.* **PHRASE** **all of** (*emphasis*) You use **all of** before a number to emphasize how small or large an amount is. ❑ *It took him all of 41 minutes to score his first goal.*
PRON **1** You use **all** to indicate that you are referring to the whole of a particular group or thing or to everyone or everything. ❑ *The only salon produces its own shampoos and hair-care products, all based on herbal recipes.* **2** [N + all + V] You use **all** to emphasise that you are referring to the whole of a particular group or thing or to everyone or everything of a particular kind. ❑ *Milk, oily fish and eggs all contain vitamin D.* **3** You use **all** to refer to a situation or to life in general. ❑ *All is silent on the island now.* **4** (*emphasis*) You use **all** at the beginning of a clause when you are emphasizing that something is the only thing that is important. ❑ *He said all that remained was to agree to a time and venue.* ❑ *All you ever want to do is go shopping!* **5** You use **all** in expressions such as **seen it all** and **done it all** to emphasize that someone has had a lot of experience of something. ❑ *They've seen it all, so it takes a lot to rattle them.*
PHRASES **all but** All **but** a particular person or thing means everyone or everything except that person or thing. ❑ *The general was an unattractive man to all but his most ardent admirers.* **in all** In **all** means in total. ❑ *There was evidence that thirteen people in all had taken part in planning the murder.*

all in all You use **all in all** to introduce a summary or general statement. ❑ *We both thought that all in all it might not be a bad idea.*
above all (*emphasis*) You say **above all** to indicate that the thing you are mentioning is the most important point. ❑ *Above all, chairs should be comfortable.*
and all (*emphasis*) You use **and all** when you want to emphasize that what you are talking about includes the thing mentioned, especially when this is surprising or unusual. ❑ *He dropped his hot dog on the pavement and someone's dog ate it, mustard and all.*
at all (*emphasis*) You use **at all** at the end of a clause to give emphasis in negative statements, conditional clauses, and questions. ❑ *Robin never really liked him at all.*
for all (*emphasis*) You use **for all** in phrases such as **for all I know**, and **for all he cares**, to emphasize that you do not know something or that someone does not care about something. ❑ *For all we know, he may not even be in this country.*
of all (*emphasis*) You use **of all** to emphasize the words 'first' or 'last', or a superlative adjective or adverb. ❑ *First of all, answer these questions.*
after all **1** You use **after all** when introducing a statement that supports or helps explain something you have just said. ❑ *I thought you might know somebody. After all, you're the man with connections.* **2** You use **after all** when you are saying that something that you thought might not be the case is in fact the case. ❑ *I came out here on the chance of finding you at home after all.*
that's all You can say **that's all** at the end of a sentence when you are explaining something and want to emphasize that nothing more happens or is the case. ❑ *'Why do you want to know that?' he demanded.—'Just curious, that's all.'*
ADV **1** [all + PREP/ADV] (*emphasis*) You use **all** to emphasize that something is completely true, or happens everywhere or always, or on every occasion. ❑ *He loves animals and he knows all about them.* ❑ *He was doing it all by himself.* **2** **All** is used in structures such as **all the more** or **all the better** to mean even more or even better than before. ❑ *The living room is decorated in pale colours that make it all the more airy.* **3** [AMOUNT + all] You use **all** when you are talking about an equal score in a game. For example, if the score is three **all**, both players or teams have three points.
PHRASES **all but** You use **all but** to say that something is almost the case. ❑ *The concrete wall that used to divide this city has now all but gone.*
all that (*spoken, vagueness*) You use **all that** in statements with negative meaning when you want to weaken the force of what you are saying. ❑ *He wasn't all that much older than we were.*
all very well (*disapproval*) You use **all very well** to suggest that you do not really approve of something or you think that it is unreasonable. ❑ *It is all very well to urge people to give more to charity when they have less, but is it really fair?*

WHICH WORD?

after all, at last, or finally?

You use **after all** when you are mentioning an additional point which confirms or supports what you have just said.
❑ *After all, we don't intend to put him on trial.*

You also use **after all** to say that something is the case or may be the case in spite of what had previously been thought.
❑ *Perhaps it isn't such a bad village after all.*

At last is used to indicate that something that you have been waiting for or expecting for a long time has happened.
❑ *At last I've found a girl who really loves me.*

You do not use **after all** or **at last** when you want to introduce a final point, question, or topic. Instead you use **finally**.
❑ *And finally, a word about the winner and runner-up.*

al·le·ga·tion ♦◇◇ /ˌælɪˈɡeɪʃən/ NOUN [c] (**allegations**)
An **allegation** is a statement saying that someone has done something wrong. = claim ❑ *The company has denied the allegations.*

✪ **al•lege** /əˈledʒ/ VERB [T] (**alleges, alleging, alleged**) (formal) If you **allege that** something bad is true, you say it but do not prove it. = claim; ≠ deny ❑ She alleged that there was rampant drug use among the male members of the group. ❑ The accused is alleged to have killed a man.

✪ **al•leged** ♦♦◇ /əˈledʒd/ ADJ [alleged + N] (formal) An **alleged** fact has been stated but has not been proved to be true. = supposed, stated ❑ They have begun a hunger strike in protest at the alleged beating. ❑ a list of alleged war criminals

✪ **al•leg•ed•ly** /əˈledʒɪdli/ ADV = supposedly ❑ His van allegedly struck the two as they were crossing a street.

✪ **al•ler•gic** /əˈlɜːdʒɪk/ ADJ ▪ [V-LINK + allergic 'to' N] If you are **allergic** to something, you become ill or get a rash when you eat it, smell it, or touch it. ❑ I'm allergic to cats. ❑ people with asthma who are allergic to dust mites ▪ [allergic + N] If you have an **allergic** reaction to something, you become ill or get a rash when you eat it, smell it, or touch it. ❑ Soya milk can cause allergic reactions in some children.

✪ **al•ler•gy** /ˈælədʒi/ NOUN [C, U] (**allergies**) If you have a particular **allergy**, you become ill or get a rash when you eat, smell, or touch something that does not normally make people ill. ❑ Food allergies can result in an enormous variety of different symptoms. ❑ Allergy to cats is one of the commonest causes of asthma.

al•le•vi•ate /əˈliːvieɪt/ VERB [T] (**alleviates, alleviating, alleviated**) (formal) If you **alleviate** pain, suffering, or an unpleasant condition, you make it less intense or severe. = ease ❑ Nowadays, a great deal can be done to alleviate back pain.
al•le•via•tion /əˌliːviˈeɪʃən/ NOUN [U] ❑ Their energies were focused on the alleviation of the refugees' misery.

al•ley /ˈæli/ NOUN [C] (**alleys**) An **alley** is a narrow passage or street with buildings or walls on both sides.

al•li•ance ♦◇◇ /əˈlaɪəns/ NOUN [C] (**alliances**) ▪ An **alliance** is a group of countries or political parties that are formally united and working together because they have similar aims. = coalition ❑ The two parties were still too much apart to form an alliance. ▪ [oft alliance 'with/between' N] An **alliance** is a relationship in which two countries, political parties, or organizations work together for some purpose. = partnership ❑ The Socialists' electoral strategy has been based on a tactical alliance with the Communists.

al•lied ♦◇◇ /ˈælaɪd, AmE əˈlaɪd/ ADJ ▪ [allied + N] **Allied** forces or troops are armies from different countries who are fighting on the same side in a war. ❑ the approaching Allied forces ▪ [allied + N, V-LINK + allied 'to' N] **Allied** countries, troops, or political parties are united by a political or military agreement. ❑ forces from three allied nations ▪ [V-LINK + allied 'to/with' N, allied + N] If one thing or group is **allied to** another, it is related to it because the two things have particular qualities or characteristics in common. = associated ❑ lectures on subjects allied to health, beauty, and fitness

✪ **al•lo•cate** /ˈæləkeɪt/ VERB [T] (**allocates, allocating, allocated**) (academic word) If one item or share of something is **allocated to** a particular person or **for** a particular purpose, it is given to that person or used for that purpose. = assign, allot ❑ Tickets are limited and will be allocated to those who apply first. ❑ The 1985 federal budget allocated $7.3 billion for development programmes.

✪ **al•lo•ca•tion** /ˌæləˈkeɪʃən/ NOUN [C, U] (**allocations**) ▪ [C] An **allocation** is an amount of something, especially money, that is given to a particular person or used for a particular purpose. ❑ A State Department spokeswoman said that the aid allocation for Pakistan was still under review. ▪ [U] The **allocation** of something is the decision that it should be given to a particular person or used for a particular purpose. ❑ greater efficiency in the allocation of resources ❑ Town planning and land allocation had to be co-ordinated.

al•lot /əˈlɒt/ VERB [T] (**allots, allotting, allotted**) If something **is allotted** to someone, it is given to them as their share. = assign, allocate ❑ The seats are allotted to the candidates who have won the most votes.

all-out also **all out** ADJ [all-out + N] You use **all-out** to describe actions that are carried out in a very energetic and determined way, using all the resources available. ❑ He launched an all-out attack on his critics.

✪ **al•low** ♦♦♦ /əˈlaʊ/ VERB
VERB [T] (**allows, allowing, allowed**) ▪ If someone is **allowed** to do something, it is all right for them to do it and they will not get into trouble. = permit, let ❑ The children are allowed to watch TV after school. ❑ Smoking will not be allowed. ▪ If you **are allowed** something, you are given permission to have it or are given it. = permit; ≠ ban ❑ Gifts like chocolates or flowers are allowed. ❑ He should be allowed the occasional treat. ▪ If you **allow** something **to** happen, you do not prevent it. = permit, let ❑ He won't allow himself to fail. ❑ If the soil is allowed to dry out the tree could die. ▪ If one thing **allows** another thing **to** happen, the first thing creates the opportunity for the second thing to happen. = permit, let ❑ The compromise will allow him to continue his free-market reforms. ❑ an attempt to allow the Muslim majority a greater share of power ▪ If you **allow** a particular length of time or a particular amount of something **for** a particular purpose, you include it in your planning. ❑ Please allow 28 days for delivery.
PHRASAL VERB **allow for** If you **allow for** certain problems or expenses, you include some extra time or money in your planning so that you can deal with them if they occur. ❑ You have to allow for a certain amount of error.

VOCABULARY BUILDER
allow VERB
If you **allow** something **to** happen, you do not prevent it.
❑ Only one staff member was allowed to enter with her.
permit VERB (formal)
If someone or something **permits** something, they allow it to happen.
❑ The UN Charter permits the use of force for self-defence.
approve VERB
If someone in a position of authority **approves** a plan or idea, they formally agree to it and say that it can happen.
❑ MPs approved the Bill by a majority of 97.
consent VERB (formal)
If you **consent** to something, you agree to do it or to allow it to be done, although you may not necessarily be pleased about it.
❑ He asked if she would consent to a small celebration after the christening.
tolerate VERB
If you **tolerate** a situation, you accept it although you do not particularly like it.
❑ The police have made it clear that they will not tolerate this type of violent behaviour.

al•low•ance /əˈlaʊəns/ NOUN
NOUN [C] (**allowances**) ▪ An **allowance** is money that is given to someone, usually on a regular basis, in order to help them pay for the things that they need. ❑ She gets an allowance for taking care of Amy. ▪ A particular type of **allowance** is an amount of something that you are allowed in particular circumstances. ❑ Most of our flights have a baggage allowance of 44 lbs per passenger. ▪ (BrE; in AmE, use personal exemption) Your tax **allowance** is the amount of money that you are allowed to earn before you have to start paying income tax.
PHRASES **make allowances for something** If you **make allowances for** something, you take it into account in your decisions, plans, or actions. ❑ They'll make allowances for the fact it's affecting our performance. ❑ She tried to make allowances for his age.
make allowances for someone If you **make allowances for** someone, you accept behaviour from them that you would not normally accept, because of a problem that they have. ❑ He's tired so I'll make allowances for him.

all right ♦♦◇ also **alright** ADJ, ADV, CONVENTION
ADJ ▪ [V-LINK + all right] If you say that someone or

something is **all right**, you mean that you find them satisfactory or acceptable. = okay ❑ *I consider you a good friend, and if it's all right with you, I'd like to keep it that way.* ❑ *He's an all right kind of guy really.* **2** [V-LINK + all right] If someone or something is **all right**, they are well or safe. = okay ❑ *All she's worried about is whether he is all right.* **ADV** [all right after v] If you say that something happens or goes **all right**, you mean that it happens in a satisfactory or acceptable manner. = okay ❑ *Things have thankfully worked out all right.*

CONVENTION **1** (*formulae*) You say 'all right' when you are agreeing to something. = okay ❑ *'I think you should go now.'—'All right.'* **2** You say '**all right?**' after you have given an instruction or explanation to someone when you are checking that they have understood what you have just said, or checking that they agree with or accept what you have just said. = okay ❑ *Peter, you get half the fees. All right?* **3** If someone in a position of authority says '**all right**', and suggests talking about or doing something else, they are indicating that they want you to end one activity and start another. ❑ *All right, Bob. You can go now.* **4** You say '**all right**' during a discussion to show that you understand something that someone has just said, and to introduce a statement that relates to it. = okay ❑ *I said there was no room in my mother's house, and he said, 'All right, come to my studio and paint.'* **5** You say **all right** before a statement or question to indicate that you are challenging or threatening someone. = okay ❑ *All right, who are you and what are you doing in my office?*

all-round (*BrE*; in *AmE*, use **all-around**) ADJ **1** [all-round + N] An **all-round** person is good at a lot of different skills, academic subjects, or sports. ❑ *He is a great all-round player.* **2** [all-round + N] **All-round** means doing or relating to all aspects of a job or activity. ❑ *They expect a good level of all-round business competence.*

⚙️**ally** ♦♦◇ NOUN, VERB
NOUN /ˈælaɪ/ [C, PL] (**allies**) **1** [C] A country's **ally** is another country that has an agreement to support it, especially in war. ❑ *Washington would not take such a step without its allies' approval.* ❑ *Russia has since become a key American ally in the fight against terrorism.* **2** [C] If you describe someone as your **ally**, you mean that they help and support you, especially when other people are opposing you. = supporter, friend ❑ *He is a close ally of the president.* ❑ *She will regret losing a close political ally.* **3** [PL] **The Allies** were the armed forces that fought against Germany and Japan in World War II. ❑ *Germany's surrender to the Allies*
VERB /əˈlaɪ/ [T] (**allies, allying, allied**) If you **ally yourself with** someone or something, you give your support to them. ❑ *He will have no choice but to ally himself with the new movement.*
→ See also **allied**

al·mighty /ɔːlˈmaɪti/ ADJ (*informal, emphasis*) **Almighty** means very serious or great in extent. ❑ *I had the most almighty row with the waitress.* ❑ *I heard an almighty bang.*

al·most ♦♦♦ /ˈɔːlməʊst/ ADV You use **almost** to indicate that something is not completely the case but is nearly the case. = nearly ❑ *The couple had been dating for almost three years.* ❑ *The effect is almost impossible to describe.* ❑ *He contracted Spanish flu, which almost killed him.*

WHICH WORD?

almost or nearly?

Almost and **nearly** both mean 'not completely' or 'not quite'. You can use **almost** in front of negative words such as *never*, *no*, and *none*.
❑ *She had **almost** nowhere to go.*
You cannot use **nearly** in front of these negative words.
Almost and **nearly** are used in different ways with *very* and *so*. You can use these words in front of **nearly**.
❑ *We were very **nearly** at the end of our journey.*
You cannot use *very* or *so* in front of **almost**.

---

alone ♦♦◇ /əˈləʊn/ ADJ, ADV
ADJ **1** [V-LINK + alone] When you are **alone**, you are not

with any other people. ❑ *There is nothing so fearful as to be alone in a combat situation.* **2** [V-LINK + alone] If one person is **alone with** another person, or if two or more people are **alone**, they are together, without anyone else present. ❑ *I couldn't imagine why he would want to be alone with me.* **3** [V-LINK + alone] If you say that you are **alone** or feel **alone**, you mean that nobody who is with you, or nobody at all, cares about you. ❑ *Never in her life had she felt so alone, so abandoned.* **4** [V-LINK + alone] If someone is **alone in** doing something, they are the only person doing it, and so are different from other people. = unique ❑ *Am I alone in recognizing that these two statistics have quite different implications?* **ADV** **1** [alone after v] When you do something **alone**, you do it without any other people. ❑ *She has lived alone in this house for almost five years now.* **2** If you **alone** are doing something, you are the only person doing it, and so are different from other people. ❑ *I alone was sane, I thought, in a world of crazy people.* **3** [N + alone] You say that one person or thing **alone** does something when you are emphasizing that only one person or thing is involved. ❑ *You alone should determine what is right for you.* **4** [N + alone] If you say that one person or thing **alone** is responsible for part of an amount, you are emphasizing the size of that part and the size of the total amount. ❑ *CNN alone is sending 300 technicians, directors and commentators.* **5** [alone after v] When someone does something **alone**, they do it without help from other people. ❑ *Bringing up a child alone should give you a sense of achievement.*
PHRASE **go it alone** (*informal*) If you **go it alone**, you do something without any help from other people. ❑ *I missed the stimulation of working with others when I tried to go it alone.*
✦ **leave alone** → see **leave**; **let alone** → see **let**

along ♦♦♦ /əˈlɒŋ, AmE əˈlɔːŋ/ PREP, ADV

> In addition to the uses shown below, **along** is used in phrasal verbs such as 'go along with', 'play along', and 'string along'.

PREP **1** If you move or look **along** something such as a road, you move or look towards one end of it. ❑ *Pedro walked along the street alone.* ❑ *The young man led Mark Ryle along a corridor.* **2** If something is situated **along** a road, river, or corridor, it is situated in it or beside it. ❑ *enormous traffic jams all along the roads*
ADV **1** [along after v] When someone or something moves **along**, they keep moving in a particular direction. ❑ *She skipped and danced along.* ❑ *He raised his voice a little, talking into the wind as they walked along.* **2** [along after v] If you say that something is going **along** in a particular way, you mean that it is progressing in that way. ❑ *the negotiations which have been dragging along interminably* **3** [along after v] If you take someone or something **along** when you go somewhere, you take them with you. ❑ *This is open to women of all ages, so bring along your friends and colleagues.* **4** [along after v] If someone or something is coming **along** or is sent **along**, they are coming or being sent to a particular place. ❑ *She invited everyone she knew to come along.*
PHRASES **along with** You use **along with** to mention someone or something else that is also involved in an action or situation. ❑ *The baby's mother escaped from the fire along with two other children.*
all along If something has been true or been present **all along**, it has been true or been present throughout a period of time. ❑ *I've been fooling myself all along.*
✦ **along the way** → see **way**

along·side ♦◇◇ /əˌlɒŋˈsaɪd, AmE -ˌlɔːŋ-/ PREP, ADV
PREP **1** If one thing is **alongside** another thing, the first thing is next to the second. ❑ *He crossed the street and walked alongside Central Park.* **2** If you work **alongside** other people, you all work together in the same place. ❑ *He had worked alongside Frank and Mark and they had become friends.*
ADV [alongside after v] If something moves **alongside**, it moves so that it is next to another thing. ❑ *He waited several minutes for a car to pull up alongside.*

aloud /əˈlaʊd/ ADV
ADV [aloud after v] When you say something, read, or

A

laugh **aloud**, you speak or laugh so that other people can hear you. ◻ *When we were children, our father read aloud to us.* **PHRASE** **think aloud** If you **think aloud**, you express your thoughts as they occur to you, rather than thinking first and then speaking. ◻ *He really must be careful about thinking aloud. Who knew what he might say?*

✪ **al·pha·bet** /ˈælfəbet/ NOUN [c] (**alphabets**) An **alphabet** is a set of letters usually presented in a fixed order which is used for writing the words of a particular language or group of languages. ◻ *The modern Russian alphabet has 31 letters.*

✪ **al·pha·beti·cal** /ˌælfəˈbetɪkəl/ ADJ [alphabetical + N] **Alphabetical** means arranged according to the normal order of the letters in the alphabet. ◻ *Their herbs and spices are arranged in alphabetical order on narrow open shelves.* ✪ **al·pha·beti·cal·ly** /ˌælfəˈbetɪkli/ ADV ◻ *The catalogue is arranged alphabetically by label name.*

al·ready ◆◆◆ /ɔːlˈredi/ ADV **1** You use **already** to show that something has happened, or that something had happened before the moment you are referring to. Some speakers use **already** with the simple past tense of the verb instead of a perfect tense. ◻ *They had already voted for him at the first ballot.* ◻ *She says she already told the neighbours not to come over for a couple of days.* **2** You use **already** to show that a situation exists at this present moment or that it exists at an earlier time than expected. You use **already** after the verb 'be' or an auxiliary verb, or before a verb if there is no auxiliary. When you want to add emphasis, you can put **already** at the beginning of a sentence. ◻ *The authorities believe those security measures are already paying off.* ◻ *He was already rich.* ◻ *Already, she is thinking ahead.*

al·right /ɔːlˈraɪt/ (*BrE*) → See **all right**

also ◆◆◆ /ˈɔːlsəʊ/ ADV **1** You can use **also** to give more information about a person or thing, or to add another relevant fact. ◻ *The book also includes an appendix with a listing of all US presidents.* ◻ *He is an asthmatic who is also anaemic.* **2** You can use **also** to indicate that something you have just said about one person or thing is true of another person or thing. ◻ *General Geichenko was a survivor. His father, also a top-ranking officer, had perished during the war.* ◻ *This rule has also been applied in the case of a purchase of used tyres and tubes.*

WHICH WORD?

also, too, or as well?

You use **also**, **too**, or **as well** when you want to add information to something you have said. **Also** never comes at the end of a clause or sentence, whereas **too** and **as well** usually come at the end.

◻ *This computer is very modern and fast. **Also**, it's cheap.*

◻ *He was **also** an artist and lived in Cleveland.*

◻ *It's cold outside, and it's raining, **too**.*

◻ *Could I have two coffees, please? And a slice of cake, **as well***.

✪ **al·ter** ◆◇◇ /ˈɔːltə/ VERB [I, T] (**alters, altering, altered**) (*academic word*) If something **alters** or if you **alter** it, it changes. = change, adapt ◻ *Nothing has altered and the deadline still stands.* ◻ *attempts to genetically alter the caffeine content of coffee plants*

✪ **al·tera·tion** /ˌɔːltəˈreɪʃən/ NOUN [c, u] (**alterations**) **1** [c] An **alteration** is a change in or to something. = change ◻ *Making some simple alterations to your diet will make you feel fitter.* ◻ *an alteration in hormone balance which causes blood sugar levels to fall* **2** [u] The **alteration** of something is the process of changing it. ◻ *Her jacket was at the boutique waiting for alteration.*

✪ **al·ter·nate** VERB, ADJ

VERB /ˈɔːltəneɪt/ [RECIP] (**alternates, alternating, alternated**) When you **alternate** two things, you keep using one then the other. When one thing **alternates with** another, the first regularly occurs after the other. ◻ *Her aggressive moods alternated with gentle or more cooperative states.* ◻ *Now you just alternate layers of that mixture and aubergine.*

ADJ /ɔːlˈtɜːnət/ **1** [alternate + N] **Alternate** actions, events, or processes regularly occur after each other. ◻ *They were streaked with alternate bands of colour.* **2** [alternate + N] If something happens on **alternate** days, it happens on one day, then happens on every second day after that. In the same way, something can happen in **alternate** weeks, years, or other periods of time. ◻ *Lesley had agreed to Jim going skiing in alternate years.* **3** [alternate + N] You use **alternate** to describe a plan, idea, or system which is different from the one already in operation and can be used instead of it. = alternative ◻ *His group was forced to turn back and take an alternate route.*

WHICH WORD?

alternate or alternative?

As an adjective, **alternate** is used to talk about things that occur or appear one after the other in a repeated sequence.

◻ *A clear container is filled with **alternate** layers of sand and soil.*

Alternative describes something that is used instead of what is planned, expected, or normal.

◻ *There is no doubt we need **alternative** sources of energy.*

Note that in US English, **alternate** is sometimes also used with this meaning.

◻ *They advised motorists to use an **alternate** route.*

---

al·ter·nate·ly /ɔːlˈtɜːnətli/ ADV ◻ *He could alternately bully and charm people.*

✪ **al·ter·na·tive** ◆◆◇ /ɔːlˈtɜːnətɪv/ NOUN, ADJ (*academic word*)

NOUN [c] (**alternatives**) If one thing is an **alternative to** another, the first can be found, used, or done instead of the second. ◻ *New ways to treat arthritis may provide an alternative to painkillers.* ◻ *This equipment is very expensive and we need to find a cheaper alternative.*

ADJ **1** [alternative + N] An **alternative** plan or offer is different from the one that you already have, and can be done or used instead. = other, alternate, different ◻ *There were alternative methods of travel available.* ◻ *They had a right to seek alternative employment.* **2** [alternative + N] **Alternative** is used to describe something that is different from the usual things of its kind, or the usual ways of doing something, in modern Western society. For example, an **alternative** lifestyle does not follow conventional ways of living and working. ◻ *unconventional parents who embraced the alternative lifestyle of the Sixties* **3** [alternative + N] **Alternative** medicine uses traditional ways of curing people, such as medicines made from plants, massage, and acupuncture. ◻ *alternative health care* **4** [alternative + N] **Alternative** energy uses natural sources of energy such as the sun, wind, or water for power and fuel, rather than oil, coal, or nuclear power.

✪ **al·ter·na·tive·ly** /ɔːlˈtɜːnətɪvli/ ADV [alternatively with CL] You use **alternatively** to introduce a suggestion or to mention something different from what has just been stated. ◻ *Hotels are generally of a good standard and not too expensive. Alternatively you could stay in an apartment.* ◻ *Allow about eight hours for the drive from Calais. Alternatively, you can fly to Brive.*

✪ **al·though** ◆◆◆ /ɔːlˈðəʊ/ CONJ **1** You use **although** to introduce a subordinate clause which contains a statement that contrasts with the statement in the main clause. = even though ◻ *Although he is known to only a few, his reputation among them is very great.* **2** You use **although** to introduce a subordinate clause which contains a statement that makes the main clause of the sentence seem surprising or unexpected. = though, even though ◻ *Although I was only six, I can remember seeing it on TV.* **3** You use **although** to introduce a subordinate clause which gives some information that is relevant to the main clause but modifies the strength of that statement. = though, however ◻ *He was in love with her, although a man seldom puts that name to what he feels.* **4** You use **although** when admitting a fact about something that you regard as less important than a contrasting fact. = even though ◻ *Although they're expensive, they last forever and never go out of style.*

al·ti·tude /ˈæltɪtjuːd, *AmE* -tuːd/ NOUN [c, u] (**altitudes**) If something is at a particular **altitude**, it is at that height above sea level. ❏ *The aircraft had reached its cruising altitude of about 39,000 feet.*

al·to·geth·er ♦◇◇ /ˌɔːltəˈgeðə/ ADV **1** [altogether after v] (*emphasis*) You use **altogether** to emphasize that something has stopped, been done, or finished completely. ❏ *When Artie stopped calling altogether, Julie found a new man.* **2** [altogether + ADJ/ADV] (*emphasis*) You use **altogether** in front of an adjective or adverb to emphasize a quality that someone or something has. ❏ *The choice of language is altogether different.* **3** You use **altogether** to modify a negative statement and make it less forceful. ❏ *We were not altogether sure that the comet would miss the Earth.* **4** [altogether with CL] You can use **altogether** to introduce a summary of what you have been saying. ❏ *Altogether, it was a delightful town garden, peaceful and secluded.* **5** [altogether with AMOUNT] If several amounts add up to a particular amount **altogether**, that amount is their total. ❏ *Brando received eight Oscar nominations altogether.*

al·tru·ism /ˈæltruːɪzəm/ NOUN [U] **Altruism** is unselfish concern for other people's happiness and welfare. ❏ *Fortunately, volunteers are not motivated by self-interest, but by altruism.*

al·tru·is·tic /ˌæltruˈɪstɪk/ ADJ If your behaviour or motives are **altruistic**, you show concern for the happiness and welfare of other people rather than for yourself. = selfless

alu·min·ium /ˌæluːˈmɪniəm/ (*BrE*; in *AmE*, use **aluminum**) NOUN [U] **Aluminium** is a lightweight metal used, for example, for making cooking equipment and aircraft parts. ❏ *aluminium cans*

al·ways ♦♦♦ /ˈɔːlweɪz/ ADV **1** [always before v] If you **always** do something, you do it whenever a particular situation occurs. If you **always** did something, you did it whenever a particular situation occurred. ❏ *She's always late for everything.* ❏ *Always lock your garage.* **2** If something is **always** the case, was **always** the case, or will **always** be the case, it is, was, or will be the case all the time, continuously. ❏ *We will always remember his generous hospitality.* ❏ *He has always been the family solicitor.* **3** [always before -ING] If you say that something is **always** happening, especially something that annoys you, you mean that it happens repeatedly. = forever ❏ *She was always moving things around.* **4** ['can/could' always + INF] You use **always** in expressions such as **can always** or **could always** when you are making suggestions or suggesting an alternative approach or method. ❏ *If you can't find any decent apples, you can always try growing them yourself.* **5** [always before v] You can say that someone **always** was, for example, awkward or lucky to indicate that you are not surprised about what they are doing or have just done. ❏ *She's going to be fine. She always was pretty strong.*

am /əm, STRONG æm/ IRREG FORM **Am** is the first person singular of the present tense of **be**. **Am** is often shortened to **'m** in spoken English. The negative forms are 'I am not' and 'I'm not'. In questions and tags in spoken English, these are usually changed to 'aren't I'.

a.m. /ˌeɪˈem/ also **am** a.m. is used after a number to show that you are referring to a particular time between midnight and noon. Compare **p.m.** ❏ *The programme starts at 9 a.m.*

amass /əˈmæs/ VERB [T] (**amasses, amassing, amassed**) If you **amass** something such as money or information, you gradually get a lot of it. = accumulate, accrue ❏ *How had he amassed his fortune?*

ama·teur ♦◇◇ /ˈæmətə, *AmE* -tʃɜːr/ NOUN, ADJ
 NOUN [c] (**amateurs**) An **amateur** is someone who does something as a hobby and not as a job. ❏ *Jerry is an amateur who dances because he feels like it.*
 ADJ [amateur + N] **Amateur** sports or activities are done by people as a hobby and not as a job. ❏ *professional athletes and amateur runners*

amaze /əˈmeɪz/ VERB [I, T] (**amazes, amazing, amazed**) If something **amazes** you, it surprises you very much. = astonish ❏ *He amazed us by his knowledge of Colorado history.* ❏ *The 'Riverside' restaurant promises a variety of food that never ceases to amaze!*

amazed /əˈmeɪzd/ ADJ = astonished ❏ *Most of the cast was amazed by the play's success.*

amaze·ment /əˈmeɪzmənt/ NOUN [U] [oft 'in' amazement] **Amazement** is the feeling you have when something surprises you very much. = astonishment ❏ *I stared at her in amazement.*

amaz·ing ♦◇◇ /əˈmeɪzɪŋ/ ADJ You say that something is **amazing** when it is very surprising and makes you feel pleasure, approval, or wonder. = astonishing ❏ *It's amazing what we can remember with a little prompting.* **amaz·ing·ly** /əˈmeɪzɪŋli/ ADV ❏ *She was an amazingly good cook.*

am·bas·sa·dor ♦◇◇ /æmˈbæsədə/ NOUN [c] (**ambassadors**) An **ambassador** is an important official who lives in a foreign country and represents his or her own country's interests there. ❏ *the German ambassador to Poland*

✪ **am·bi·gu·ity** /ˌæmbɪˈgjuːɪti/ NOUN [c, u] (**ambiguities**) If you say that there is **ambiguity** in something, you mean that it is unclear or confusing, or it can be understood in more than one way. = vagueness; ≠ clarity ❏ *There is considerable ambiguity about what this part of the agreement actually means.* ❏ *the ambiguities of language*

✪ **am·bigu·ous** /æmˈbɪgjuəs/ ADJ (*academic word*) If you describe something as **ambiguous**, you mean that it is unclear or confusing because it can be understood in more than one way. = vague, unclear, obscure; ≠ clear, unambiguous ❏ *This agreement is very ambiguous and open to various interpretations.* ❏ *The Foreign Secretary's remarks clarify an ambiguous statement issued earlier this week.*
✪ **am·bigu·ous·ly** /æmˈbɪgjuəsli/ ADV = unclearly, uncertainly; ≠ unambiguously ❏ *an ambiguously worded document* ❏ *The national conference on democracy ended ambiguously.*

am·bi·tion ♦◇◇ /æmˈbɪʃən/ NOUN [c, u] (**ambitions**) **1** [c] If you have an **ambition to** do or achieve something, you want very much to do it or achieve it. = goal ❏ *His ambition is to sail around the world.* **2** [u] **Ambition** is the desire to be successful, rich, or powerful. ❏ *Even when I was young I never had any ambition.*

am·bi·tious /æmˈbɪʃəs/ ADJ **1** Someone who is **ambitious** has a strong desire to be successful, rich, or powerful. ❏ *Chris is so ambitious, so determined to do it all.* **2** An **ambitious** idea or plan is on a large scale and needs a lot of work to be carried out successfully. ❏ *The ambitious project was completed in only nine months.*

am·biva·lent /æmˈbɪvələnt/ ADJ If you say that someone is **ambivalent about** something, they seem to be uncertain whether they really want it, or whether they really approve of it. = unsure ❏ *She remained ambivalent about her marriage.*

am·bu·lance /ˈæmbjʊləns/ NOUN [c] (**ambulances**) [also 'by' ambulance] An **ambulance** is a vehicle for taking people to and from a hospital.

am·bush /ˈæmbʊʃ/ VERB, NOUN
 VERB [T] (**ambushes, ambushing, ambushed**) If a group of people **ambush** their enemies, they attack them after hiding and waiting for them. ❏ *The Guatemalan army says rebels ambushed and killed 10 patrolmen.*
 NOUN [c, u] (**ambushes**) An **ambush** is an attack on someone by people who have been hiding and waiting for them. ❏ *Three civilians were killed in guerrilla ambushes.*

✪ **amend** /əˈmend/ VERB, NOUN (*academic word*)
 VERB [T] (**amends, amending, amended**) If you **amend** something that has been written, such as a law, or something that is said, you change it in order to improve it or make it more accurate. = revise ❏ *The president agreed to amend the constitution and allow multi-party elections.* ❏ *the amended version of the Act*
 NOUN
 PHRASE **make amends** If you **make amends** when you have harmed someone, you show that you are sorry by doing something to please them. ❏ *He wanted to make amends for causing their marriage to fail.*

✪ **amend·ment** ♦◇◇ /əˈmendmənt/ NOUN [c, u] (**amendments**) **1** [c, u] An **amendment** is a section that is

A

added to a law or rule in order to change it. ❑ *an amendment to the defence bill* ❑ *In the United States, press freedom is entrenched in the first amendment to the US Constitution.* ❑ *Parliament gained certain rights of amendment.* **2** [c] An **amendment** is a change that is made to a piece of writing. = alteration, change, correction

amen·ity /əˈmiːnɪti, *AmE* -ˈmen-/ NOUN [c] (**amenities**) [usu pl] **Amenities** are things such as shopping centres or sports facilities that are provided for people's convenience, enjoyment, or comfort. = facility ❑ *The hotel amenities include health clubs, conference facilities, and banqueting rooms.*

ami·able /ˈeɪmiəbəl/ ADJ (written) Someone who is **amiable** is friendly and pleasant to be with. = friendly ❑ *She had been surprised at how amiable and polite he had been.*

ami·cable /ˈæmɪkəbəl/ ADJ When people have an **amicable** relationship, they are pleasant to each other and solve their problems without quarrelling. = friendly; ≠ hostile ❑ *The meeting ended on reasonably amicable terms.* **ami·cably** /ˈæmɪkəbli/ ADV [amicably with v] ❑ *He hoped the dispute could be settled amicably.*

amid ♦◇◇ /əˈmɪd/ PREP

> The form **amidst** is also used, but is old-fashioned.

If something happens **amid** noises or events of some kind, it happens while the other things are happening. ❑ *Workers are sifting through the wreckage of the airliners amid growing evidence that the disasters were the work of terrorists.*

amidst /əˈmɪdst/ PREP (old-fashioned) **Amidst** means the same as **amid**.

am·mu·ni·tion /ˌæmjʊˈnɪʃən/ NOUN [u] **1 Ammunition** is bullets and rockets that are made to be fired from weapons. ❑ *He had only seven rounds of ammunition for the revolver.* **2** You can describe information that you can use against someone in an argument or discussion as **ammunition**. ❑ *The improved trade figures have given the government fresh ammunition.*

am·nes·ty /ˈæmnɪsti/ NOUN [c, u] (**amnesties**) **1** [c, u] An **amnesty** is an official pardon granted to a group of prisoners by the state. = pardon ❑ *Activists who were involved in crimes of violence will not automatically be granted amnesty.* **2** [c] An **amnesty** is a period of time during which people can admit to a crime or give up weapons without being punished. ❑ *The government has announced an immediate amnesty for rebel fighters.*

among ♦♦♦ /əˈmʌŋ/ PREP

> The form **amongst** is also used, but is more old-fashioned.

1 Someone or something that is situated or moving **among** a group of things or people is surrounded by them. ❑ *youths in their late teens sitting among adults* ❑ *They walked among the crowds in Red Square.* **2** If you are **among** people of a particular kind, you are with them and having contact with them. ❑ *Things weren't so bad, after all. I was among friends again.* **3** If someone or something is **among** a group, they are a member of that group and share its characteristics. ❑ *A fifteen year old girl was among the injured.* **4** If you want to focus on something that is happening within a particular group of people, you can say that it is happening **among** that group. ❑ *Homicide is the leading cause of death among black men.* **5** If something happens **among** a group of people, it happens within the whole of that group or between the members of that group. ❑ *The calls for reform come as intense debate continues among the leadership over the next five-year economic plan.* **6** If something such as a feeling, opinion, or situation exists **among** a group of people, most of them have it or experience it. ❑ *There was some concern among book and magazine retailers after last Wednesday's news.* **7** If something applies to a particular person or thing **among** others, it also applies to other people or things. ❑ *a news conference attended among others by our foreign affairs correspondent* **8** If something is shared **among** a number of people, some of it is given to all of them. ❑ *Most of the furniture was left to the neighbours or distributed among friends.* **9** [among + PRON-REFL] If people talk, fight, or agree

among themselves, they do it together, without involving anyone else. ❑ *The girls stood aside, talking among themselves, looking over their shoulders at the boys.*

amongst /əˈmʌŋst/ PREP (old-fashioned) **Amongst** means the same as **among**.

✪ amount ♦♦◇ /əˈmaʊnt/ NOUN, VERB
NOUN [c, u] (**amounts**) The **amount of** something is how much there is, or how much you have, need, or get. = number, quantity, volume ❑ *He needs that amount of money to survive.* ❑ *Apricots contain large amounts of vitamin A.* ❑ *A certain amount of land is dedicated to roadways and parks.* ❑ *I still do a certain amount of work for them.*
VERB [i] (**amounts, amounting, amounted**) If something **amounts to** a particular total, all the parts of it add up to that total. ❑ *Consumer spending on sports-related items amounted to $9.75 billion.*
PHRASAL VERB amount to If you say that one thing **amounts to** something else, you consider the first thing to be the same as the second thing. ❑ *The banks have what amounts to a monopoly.*

USAGE NOTE

amount

Do not use 'an amount of' before a countable noun, as in 'an amount of chairs'. Use 'several' or 'a number of' instead.

There were **a number of chairs** in the room.

---

amp /æmp/ NOUN [c] (**amps**) **1** An **amp** is a unit which is used for measuring electric current. Amp is short for ampere. ❑ *Use a 3 amp fuse for equipment up to 720 watts.* **2** (informal) An **amp** is the same as an **amplifier**.

✪ am·phib·ian /æmˈfɪbiən/ NOUN [c] (**amphibians**) **Amphibians** are animals such as frogs and toads that can live both on land and in water. ❑ *Alligators and crocodiles may not have evolved from lizards or amphibians.*

✪ am·phibi·ous /æmˈfɪbiəs/ ADJ **1** [amphibious + N] In an **amphibious** military operation, army and navy forces attack a place from the sea. ❑ *A third brigade is at sea, ready for an amphibious assault.* **2** [amphibious + N] An **amphibious** vehicle is able to move on both land and water. **3 Amphibious** animals are animals such as frogs and toads that can live both on land and in water. ❑ *The area teemed with birdlife and all manner of insects, otters and amphibious creatures.* ❑ *Amphibious creatures feature prominently in ancient legends.*

am·ple /ˈæmpəl/ ADJ (**ampler, amplest**) If there is an **ample** amount of something, there is enough of it and usually some extra. ❑ *There'll be ample opportunity to relax, swim and soak up some sun.* **am·ply** /ˈæmpli/ ADV ❑ *This collection of his essays and journalism amply demonstrates his commitment to democracy.*

am·pli·fi·er /ˈæmplɪfaɪə/ NOUN [c] (**amplifiers**) An **amplifier** is an electronic device in a radio or stereo system that causes sounds or signals to get louder.

am·pu·tate /ˈæmpjʊteɪt/ VERB [T] (**amputates, amputating, amputated**) To **amputate** someone's arm or leg means to cut all or part of it off in an operation because it is diseased or badly damaged. ❑ *To save his life, doctors amputated his legs.* **am·pu·ta·tion** /ˌæmpjʊˈteɪʃən/ NOUN [c, u] (**amputations**) ❑ *He lived only hours after the amputation.*

amuse /əˈmjuːz/ VERB [T] (**amuses, amusing, amused**) **1** If something **amuses** you, it makes you want to laugh or smile. ❑ *The thought seemed to amuse him.* **2** If you **amuse yourself**, you do something in order to pass the time and not become bored. = entertain ❑ *I need distractions. I need to amuse myself so I won't keep thinking about things.*
→ See also **amused, amusing**

amused /əˈmjuːzd/ ADJ If you are **amused by** something, it makes you want to laugh or smile. ❑ *Sara was not amused by Franklin's teasing.*

amuse·ment /əˈmjuːzmənt/ NOUN [u, c, PL] (**amusements**) **1** [u] **Amusement** is the feeling that you have when you think that something is funny or amusing.

He stopped and watched with amusement to see the child so absorbed. **2** [U] **Amusement** is the pleasure that you get from being entertained or from doing something interesting. ▢ I stumbled sideways before landing flat on my back, much to the amusement of the rest of the guys. **3** [C] **Amusements** are ways of passing the time pleasantly. = pastime ▢ People had very few amusements to choose from. There was no radio, or television. **4** [PL] **Amusements** are games, rides, and other things that you can enjoy, for example, at an amusement park or resort. ▢ a place full of swings and amusements

amus·ing /əˈmjuːzɪŋ/ ADJ Someone or something that is **amusing** makes you laugh or smile. = entertaining ▢ He had a terrific sense of humour and could be very amusing. **amus·ing·ly** /əˈmjuːzɪŋli/ ADV ▢ The article must be amusingly written.

an /ən, STRONG æn/ DET **An** is used instead of 'a', the indefinite article, in front of words that begin with vowel sounds.

✪**an·aes·thet·ic** /ˌænɪsˈθetɪk/ (BrE; in AmE, use **anesthetic**) NOUN [C, U] (**anaesthetics**) **Anaesthetic** is a substance that doctors use to stop you feeling pain during an operation, either in the whole of your body when you are unconscious, or in a part of your body when you are awake. ▢ The operation is carried out under a general anaesthetic.

✪**anaes·the·tist** /əˈniːsθətɪst/ (BrE; in AmE, use **anesthesiologist**) NOUN [C] (**anaesthetists**) An **anaesthetist** is a doctor who specializes in giving anaesthetics to patients. ▢ a consultant paediatric anaesthetist ▢ The anaesthetist ordered premedication, which included morphine.

✪**anaes·the·tize** /əˈniːsθətaɪz/ also **anaesthetise** (in AmE, also use **anesthetize**) VERB (**anaesthetizes**, **anaesthetizing**, **anaesthetized**) When a doctor or other trained person **anaesthetizes** a patient, they make the patient unconscious or unable to feel pain by giving them an anaesthetic. ▢ the patient's anaesthetized lung ▢ The operation involves anaesthetising the eye.

✪**analo·gous** /əˈnæləgəs/ ADJ (formal) If one thing is **analogous** to another, the two things are similar in some way. = similar; ≠ different ▢ Marine construction technology like this is very complex, somewhat analogous to trying to build a bridge under water. ▢ a new conflict situation analogous to the one on the Korean peninsula

✪**ana·logue** /ˈænəlɒg, AmE -lɔg/ ADJ **1** **Analogue** technology involves measuring, storing, or recording an infinitely variable amount of information by using physical quantities such as voltage. ≠ digital ▢ The analogue signals from the videotape are converted into digital code. **2** An **analogue** watch or clock shows what it is measuring with a pointer on a dial rather than with a number display. Compare **digital**.

✪**anal·ogy** /əˈnælədʒi/ NOUN [C] (**analogies**) (academic word) If you make or draw an **analogy between** two things, you show that they are similar in some way. = comparison, similarity, resemblance ▢ The analogy between music and fragrance has stuck. ▢ It is probably easier to make an analogy between the courses of the planets and two trains travelling in the same direction. ▢ The term 'social capital' was coined by analogy with the conventional use of the word 'capital' to mean financial assets.

✪**ana·lyse** /ˈænəlaɪz/ (BrE; in AmE, use **analyze**) VERB [T] (**analyses**, **analysing**, **analysed**) (academic word) **1** If you **analyse** something, you consider it carefully or use statistical methods in order to fully understand it. = examine, study, inspect, investigate ▢ McCarthy was asked to analyse the data from the first phase of trials of the vaccine. ▢ This book teaches you how to analyse what is causing the stress in your life. **2** If you **analyse** something, you examine it using scientific methods in order to find out what it consists of. ▢ We haven't had time to analyse those samples yet. ▢ They had their tablets analysed to find out whether they were getting the real drug or not.

✪**analy·sis** ◆◇◇ /əˈnælɪsɪs/ NOUN [C, U] (**analyses**) **1** [C, U] **Analysis** is the process of considering something carefully or using statistical methods in order to

understand it or explain it. ▢ Sporting greatness defies analysis – but we know it when we see it. **2** [C, U] **Analysis** is the scientific process of examining something in order to find out what it consists of. ▢ They collect blood samples for analysis at a national laboratory. **3** [C] An **analysis** is an explanation or description that results from considering something carefully. = examination, study, investigation, inspection ▢ Coming up after the newscast, an analysis of the president's domestic policy. ▢ The main results of the analysis are summarized below.

WORD CONNECTIONS
VERB + **analysis**
undertake an analysis **conduct** an analysis **perform** an analysis
▢ We conducted a statistical analysis of all the data collected.
ADJ + **analysis**
a **detailed** analysis a **thorough** analysis a **comparative** analysis an **objective** analysis
▢ The report contains a detailed analysis of the environmental impact of the project.
chemical analysis **scientific** analysis **statistical** analysis **forensic** analysis **technical** analysis
▢ Chemical analysis was performed to detect the presence of various substances.

✪**ana·lyst** ◆◆◇ /ˈænəlɪst/ NOUN [C] (**analysts**) **1** An **analyst** is a person whose job is to analyse a subject and give opinions about it. ▢ a political analyst ▢ Analysts are predicting total sales for the year to reach 500 million. **2** An **analyst** is someone, usually a doctor, who examines and treats people who have emotional problems. = psychoanalyst ▢ My analyst warned me that I liked married men too much.

ana·lyti·cal /ˌænəˈlɪtɪkəl/ ADJ An **analytical** way of doing something involves the use of logical reasoning. ▢ I have an analytical approach to every survey.

an·ar·chic /æˈnɑːkɪk/ ADJ (disapproval) If you describe someone or something as **anarchic**, you disapprove of them because they do not recognize or obey any rules or laws. ▢ anarchic attitudes and complete disrespect for authority

an·ar·chist /ˈænəkɪst/ NOUN, ADJ
NOUN [C] (**anarchists**) [oft anarchist + N] An **anarchist** is a person who believes that the laws and powers of governments should be replaced by people working together freely. ▢ West Berlin always had a large anarchist community.
ADJ [anarchist + N] If someone has **anarchist** beliefs or views, they believe that the laws and powers of governments should be replaced by people working together freely. ▢ He was apparently quite converted from his anarchist views.

an·ar·chy /ˈænəki/ NOUN [U] (disapproval) If you describe a situation as **anarchy**, you mean that nobody seems to be paying any attention to rules or laws. = chaos ▢ The school's liberal, individualistic traditions were in danger of slipping into anarchy.

✪**ana·tomi·cal** /ˌænəˈtɒmɪkəl/ ADJ **Anatomical** means relating to the structure of the bodies of people and animals. = bodily ▢ minute anatomical differences between insects ▢ the anatomical structure of the heart
✪**ana·tomi·cal·ly** /ˌænəˈtɒmɪkli/ ADV ▢ an anatomically correct drawing ▢ Homo sapiens became anatomically modern in Africa about 100,000 years ago.

✪**anato·my** /əˈnætəmi/ NOUN [U, C] **1** [U] **Anatomy** is the study of the structure of the bodies of people or animals. ▢ a course in anatomy ▢ an anatomy professor at Naples University **2** [C] An animal's **anatomy** is the structure of its body. ▢ It is hard to determine whether an animal's anatomy or physiology has been altered by

A

environmental problems. ❑ *He had worked extensively on the anatomy of living animals.*

✪**an·ces·tor** /'ænsestə/ NOUN [c] (**ancestors**) **1** [usu pl, with POSS] Your **ancestors** are the people from whom you are descended. = forefather ❑ *our daily lives, so different from those of our ancestors* **2** An **ancestor of** something modern is an earlier thing from which it developed. ❑ *The direct ancestor of the modern cat was the Kaffir cat of ancient Egypt.*

an·ces·tral /æn'sestrəl/ ADJ You use **ancestral** to refer to a person's family in former times, especially when the family is important and has property or land that they have had for a long time. ❑ *the family's ancestral home in southern Germany*

✪**an·ces·try** /'ænsestri/ NOUN [c] (**ancestries**) Your **ancestry** is the fact that you are descended from certain people. = heritage, roots ❑ *a family who could trace their ancestry back to the sixteenth century* ❑ *people of Japanese ancestry*

an·chor /'æŋkə/ NOUN, VERB
NOUN [c] (**anchors**) **1** An **anchor** is a heavy hooked object that is dropped from a boat into the water at the end of a chain in order to make the boat stay in one place. **2** *(mainly AmE)* The **anchor** on a television or radio programme, especially a news programme, is the person who presents it. ❑ *He worked in the news division of ABC – he was the anchor of its 15-minute evening newscast.*
PHRASE **at anchor** If a boat is **at anchor**, it is floating in a particular place and is prevented from moving by its anchor. ❑ *Sailboats lay at anchor in the narrow waterway.*
VERB [I, T] (**anchors, anchoring, anchored**) **1** [I, T] When a boat **anchors** or when you **anchor** it, its anchor is dropped into the water in order to make it stay in one place. ❑ *We could anchor off the pier.* **2** [T] If an object **is anchored** somewhere, it is fixed to something to prevent it moving from that place. = tether ❑ *The roots anchor the plant in the earth.* **3** [T] *(mainly AmE)* The person who **anchors** a television or radio programme, especially a news programme, is the person who presents it and acts as a link between interviews and reports that come from other places or studios. ❑ *Viewers saw him anchoring a five-minute summary of regional news.*

✪**an·cient** ◆◇◇ /'eɪnʃənt/ ADJ **1** [ancient + N] **Ancient** means belonging to the distant past, especially to the period in history before the end of the Roman Empire. ≠ modern ❑ *They believed ancient Greece and Rome were vital sources of learning.* **2** **Ancient** means very old, or having existed for a long time. ≠ modern ❑ *ancient Jewish tradition*

and ◆◆◆ /ənd, STRONG ænd/ CONJ **1** You use **and** to link two or more words, groups, or clauses. ❑ *When he returned, she and Simon had already gone.* ❑ *I'm going to write good jokes and become a good comedian.* **2** You use **and** to link two words or phrases that are the same in order to emphasize the degree of something, or to suggest that something continues or increases over a period of time. ❑ *Learning becomes more and more difficult as we get older.* ❑ *We talked for hours and hours.* **3** You use **and** to link two statements about events when one of the events follows the other. = then ❑ *I waved goodbye and went down the stone harbour steps.* **4** You use **and** to link two statements when the second statement continues the point that has been made in the first statement. ❑ *You could only really tell the effects of the disease in the long term, and five years wasn't long enough.* **5** You use **and** to link two clauses when the second clause is a result of the first clause. ❑ *All through yesterday crowds have been arriving and by midnight thousands of people packed the square.* **6** You use **and** to interrupt yourself in order to make a comment on what you are saying. ❑ *Danielle was among the last to find out, and as often happens, too, she learned of it only by chance.* **7** You use **and** at the beginning of a sentence to introduce something else that you want to add to what you have just said. Some people think that starting a sentence with **and** is ungrammatical, but it is now quite common in both spoken and written English. ❑ *Commuter airlines fly to out-of-the-way places. And business travellers are the ones who*

go to those locations. **8** You use **and** to introduce a question that follows logically from what someone has just said. ❑ *'He used to be so handsome.'—'And now?'* **9** **And** is used by broadcasters and people making announcements to change a topic or to start talking about a topic they have just mentioned. ❑ *And now the drought in Sudan.* **10** You use **and** to indicate that two numbers are to be added together. = plus ❑ *What does two and two make?* **11** **And** is used before a fraction that comes after a whole number. ❑ *McCain spent five and a half years in a prisoner-of-war camp in Vietnam.* **12** You use **and** in numbers larger than one hundred, after the words 'hundred' or 'thousand' and before other numbers. ❑ *We printed two hundred and fifty invitations.*

USAGE NOTE
and
And can be used to link adjectives, adverbs, verbs, or clauses, as well as nouns.
*The room was large **and** spacious.*
*They walked up **and** down.*
*She was shouting **and** screaming.*
*I came here in 2005 **and** I've lived here ever since.*

an·ec·dote /'ænɪkdəʊt/ NOUN [c, u] (**anecdotes**) An **anecdote** is a short, amusing account of something that has happened. ❑ *Pete was telling them an anecdote about their mother.*

✪**an·es·thet·ic** /ˌænɪs'θetɪk/ *(AmE)* → See **anaesthetic**

anew /ə'njuː, AmE ə'nuː/ ADV [anew after V] *(written)* If you do something **anew**, you do it again, often in a different way from before. = afresh ❑ *She's ready to start anew.*

an·gel /'eɪndʒəl/ NOUN [c] (**angels**) **1** **Angels** are spiritual beings that some people believe are God's servants in heaven. ❑ *The artist usually painted his angels with multi-coloured wings.* **2** You can call someone you like very much an **angel** in order to show affection, especially when they have been kind to you or done you a favour. ❑ *Thank you a thousand times, you're an angel.* **3** If you describe someone as an **angel**, you mean that they seem to be very kind and good. ❑ *Papa thought her an angel.*

an·ger ◆◇◇ /'æŋgə/ NOUN, VERB
NOUN [u] **Anger** is the strong emotion that you feel when you think that someone has behaved in an unfair, cruel, or unacceptable way. = rage, fury ❑ *He cried with anger and frustration.*
VERB [T] (**angers, angering, angered**) If something **angers** you, it makes you feel angry. = enrage, infuriate ❑ *The decision to allow more offshore oil drilling angered some Californians.*

✪**an·gle** ◆◇◇ /'æŋgəl/ NOUN
NOUN [c] (**angles**) **1** An **angle** is the difference in direction between two lines or surfaces. Angles are measured in degrees. ❑ *The boat is now leaning at a 30 degree angle.* **2** An **angle** is the shape that is created where two lines or surfaces join together. ❑ *the angle of the blade* **3** An **angle** is the direction from which you look at something. ❑ *Thanks to the angle at which he stood, he could just see the sunset.* **4** You can refer to a way of presenting something or thinking about it as a particular **angle**. ❑ *He was considering the idea from all angles.*
PHRASE **at an angle** If something is **at an angle**, it is leaning in a particular direction so that it is not straight, horizontal, or vertical. ❑ *An iron bar stuck out at an angle.*

an·gry ◆◇◇ /'æŋgri/ ADJ (**angrier, angriest**) When you are **angry**, you feel strong dislike or impatience about something. ❑ *Are you angry with me for some reason?* ❑ *I was angry about the rumours.* ❑ *An angry mob gathered outside the courthouse.*

an·gri·ly /'æŋgrɪli/ ADV [angrily with V] ❑ *Officials reacted angrily to those charges.*

an·guish /'æŋgwɪʃ/ NOUN [u] **Anguish** is great mental suffering or physical pain. ❑ *Mark looked at him in anguish.*

an·guished /'æŋgwɪʃt/ ADJ *(written)* **Anguished** means showing or feeling great mental suffering or physical pain. ❑ *She let out an anguished cry.*

a

ani·mal ♦♦◇ /ˈænɪməl/ NOUN, ADJ

NOUN [c] (**animals**) **1** An **animal** is a living creature such as a dog, lion, or rabbit, rather than a bird, fish, insect, or human being. ❑ *He was attacked by wild animals.* **2** Any living creature other than a human being can be referred to as an **animal**. ❑ *Language is something that fundamentally distinguishes humans from animals.* **3** Any living creature, including a human being, can be referred to as an **animal**. ❑ *Watch any young human being, or any other young animal.* **ADJ** **Animal** products come from animals rather than from plants. ❑ *food high in animal fats such as red meat and dairy products*

ani·mat·ed /ˈænɪmeɪtɪd/ ADJ **1** Someone who is **animated** or who is having an **animated** conversation is lively and is showing their feelings. ❑ *She was seen in animated conversation with the singer Yuri Marusin.* **2** [animated + N] An **animated** film is one in which puppets or drawings appear to move. ❑ *Disney has returned to what it does best: making full-length animated feature films.*

ani·ma·tion /ˌænɪˈmeɪʃən/ NOUN [U, c] (**animations**) **1** [U] **Animation** is the process of making films in which drawings or puppets appear to move. ❑ *The films are a mix of animation and full-length features.* **2** [c] An **animation** is a film in which drawings or puppets appear to move. = cartoon ❑ *This film is the first British animation sold to an American network.*

ani·mos·ity /ˌænɪˈmɒsɪti/ NOUN [U] [also animosities] **Animosity** is a strong feeling of dislike and anger. **Animosities** are feelings of this kind. = hostility ❑ *There's a long history of animosity between the two nations.*

an·kle /ˈæŋkəl/ NOUN [c] (**ankles**) Your **ankle** is the joint where your foot joins your leg. ❑ *John twisted his ankle badly.*

an·nex /əˈneks/ VERB [T] (**annexes, annexing, annexed**) If a country **annexes** another country or an area of land, it seizes it and takes control of it. ❑ *Rome annexed the Nabatean kingdom in AD 106.* → See also **annexe**
an·nexa·tion /ˌænekˈseɪʃən/ NOUN [c] (**annexations**) ❑ *Indonesia's annexation of East Timor never won the acceptance of the United Nations.*

an·nexe /ˈæneks/ (BrE; in AmE, use **annex**) NOUN [c] (**annexes**) An **annexe** is a building joined to or next to a larger main building. ❑ *setting up a museum in an annexe to the theatre*

an·ni·hi·late /əˈnaɪɪleɪt/ VERB [T] (**annihilates, annihilating, annihilated**) **1** To **annihilate** something means to destroy it completely. ❑ *There are lots of ways of annihilating the planet.* **2** If you **annihilate** someone in a contest or argument, you totally defeat them. ❑ *The Dutch annihilated the Olympic champions 5–0.*
an·ni·hi·la·tion /əˌnaɪɪˈleɪʃən/ NOUN [U] ❑ *the threat of nuclear war and annihilation of the human race*

an·ni·ver·sa·ry ♦◇◇ /ˌænɪˈvɜːsəri/ NOUN [c] (**anniversaries**) An **anniversary** is a date that is remembered or celebrated because a special event happened on that date in a previous year. ❑ *Vietnam is celebrating the one hundredth anniversary of the birth of Ho Chi Minh.*

⬢an·nounce ♦♦♦ /əˈnaʊns/ VERB [T] (**announces, announcing, announced**) **1** If you **announce** something, you tell people about it publicly or officially. ❑ *He will announce tonight that he is resigning from office.* ❑ *She was planning to announce her engagement to Peter.* ❑ *The company announced plans to sell music over the Internet.* **2** If you **announce** a piece of news or an intention, especially something that people may not like, you say it loudly and clearly, so that everyone you are with can hear it. = declare ❑ *Peter announced that he had no intention of wasting his time at any university.* **3** If an airport or rail employee **announces** something, they tell the public about it by means of a loudspeaker system. ❑ *The loudspeaker announced the arrival of the train.*

⬢an·nounce·ment ♦◇◇ /əˈnaʊnsmənt/ NOUN [c, SING] (**announcements**) **1** [c] An **announcement** is a statement made to the public or to the media that gives information about something that has happened or that will happen.

= declaration, statement ❑ *She made her announcement after talks with the president.* ❑ *There has been no formal announcement by either government.* **2** [c] An **announcement** in a public place, such as a newspaper or the window of a shop, is a short piece of writing telling people about something or asking for something. ❑ *The Seattle Times publishes brief announcements of religious events every Saturday.* **3** [SING] The **announcement of** something that has happened is the act of telling people about it. ❑ *the announcement of their engagement*

an·noy /əˈnɔɪ/ VERB [T] (**annoys, annoying, annoyed**) If someone or something **annoys** you, it makes you fairly angry and impatient. = irritate ❑ *Try making a note of the things that annoy you.* ❑ *It annoyed me that I didn't have time to do more ironing.*
→ See also **annoyed, annoying**

an·noy·ance /əˈnɔɪəns/ NOUN [U, c] (**annoyances**) **1** [U] **Annoyance** is the feeling that you get when someone makes you feel fairly angry or impatient. = irritation ❑ *To her annoyance the stranger did not go away.* **2** [c] An **annoyance** is something that makes you feel angry or impatient. ❑ *Snoring can be more than an annoyance.*

an·noyed /əˈnɔɪd/ ADJ If you are **annoyed**, you are fairly angry about something. = angry ❑ *She is hurt and annoyed that the authorities have banned her from working with children.*
→ See also **annoy**

an·noy·ing /əˈnɔɪɪŋ/ ADJ Someone or something that is **annoying** makes you feel fairly angry and impatient. = irritating ❑ *You must have found my attitude annoying.*

⬢an·nual ♦♦◇ /ˈænjuəl/ ADJ, NOUN (academic word)
ADJ **1** [annual + N] **Annual** events happen once every year. = yearly ❑ *The issues will be voted on at the company's annual meeting on April 21 in Wilmington.* ❑ *the Labour Party's annual conference* ❑ *In its annual report, UNICEF says at least 40,000 children die every day.* **2** [annual + N] **Annual** quantities or rates relate to a period of one year. = yearly ❑ *The electronic and printing unit has annual sales of about $80 million.* ❑ *Annual costs, tuition and fees are £1,600.*
NOUN [c] (**annuals**) **1** An **annual** is a book or magazine that is published once a year. ❑ *The children are reading old Christmas annuals.* **2** An **annual** is a plant that grows and dies within one year. ❑ *Maybe this year I'll sow brilliant annuals everywhere.*
⬢an·nual·ly /ˈænjuəli/ ADV **1** Companies report to their shareholders annually. **2** = yearly ❑ *El Salvador produces 100,000 tons of refined copper annually.*

⬢anony·mous /əˈnɒnɪməs/ ADJ **1** If you remain **anonymous** when you do something, you do not let people know that you were the person who did it. = unknown, unidentified, unnamed; ≠ named, known ❑ *You can remain anonymous if you wish.* ❑ *An anonymous benefactor stepped in to provide the prize money.* **2** Something that is **anonymous** does not reveal who you are. ❑ *Of course, that would have to be by anonymous vote.* ❑ *anonymous phone calls*
⬢ano·nym·ity /ˌænɒˈnɪmɪti/ NOUN [U] **1** = confidentiality ❑ *Both mother and daughter, who have requested anonymity, are doing fine.* ❑ *The system offers participants complete anonymity.* **2** He claims many more people would support him in the anonymity of a voting booth.
anony·mous·ly /əˈnɒnɪməsli/ ADV ❑ *The latest photographs were sent anonymously to the magazine's headquarters.*

ano·rexia /ˌænəˈreksiə/ NOUN [U] **Anorexia** or anorexia nervosa is an illness in which a person has an overwhelming fear of becoming fat, and so refuses to eat enough and becomes thinner and thinner.

ano·rex·ic /ˌænəˈreksɪk/ ADJ, NOUN
ADJ If someone is **anorexic**, they are suffering from anorexia and so are very thin. ❑ *Claire had been anorexic for three years.*
NOUN [c] (**anorexics**) An **anorexic** is someone who is anorexic. ❑ *Not eating makes an anorexic feel in control.*

an·oth·er ♦♦♦ /əˈnʌðə/ DET, PRON
DET **1** **Another** thing or person means an additional thing or person of the same type as one that already exists. ❑ *Divers this morning found the body of another American sailor*

A

drowned during yesterday's ferry disaster. **2** You use **another** when you want to emphasize that an additional thing or person is different from one that already exists. ❑ *I think he's just going to deal with this problem another day.* **3** You use **another** at the beginning of a statement to link it to a previous statement. ❑ *Another time of great excitement for us boys was when war broke out.* **4** You use **another** before a word referring to a distance, length of time, or other amount, to indicate an additional amount. ❑ *Continue down the same road for another 2 miles until you reach the church of Santa Maria.*

PRON **1** You can use **another** to refer to an additional thing or person of the same type as one that already exists. ❑ *The demand generated by one factory required the construction of another.* **2** You can use **another** when you want to emphasize that an additional thing or person is different from one that already exists. ❑ *He didn't really believe that any human being could read another's mind.* **3** [V + another, PREP + another] You use **one another** to indicate that each member of a group does something to or for the other members. ❑ *women learning to help themselves and one another*

PHRASES **one thing after another** If you talk about **one** thing **after another**, you are referring to a series of repeated or continuous events. ❑ *They had faced one difficulty after another with bravery and dedication.*

or another You use **or another** in expressions such as **one kind or another** when you do not want to be precise about which of several alternatives or possibilities you are referring to. ❑ *family members and visiting artists of one kind or another crowding the huge kitchen*

✪**an·swer** ◆◆◆ /ˈɑːnsə, ˈæn-/ VERB, NOUN

VERB [I, T] (**answers, answering, answered**) **1** [I, T] When you **answer** someone who has asked you something, you say something back to them. = reply, respond ❑ *Just answer the question.* ❑ *He paused before answering.* ❑ *Williams answered that he had no specific proposals yet.* **2** [I, T] If you **answer** a letter or advertisement, you write to the person who wrote it. ❑ *Did he answer your letter?* **3** [I, T] When you **answer** the telephone, you pick it up when it rings. When you **answer** the door, you open it when you hear a knock or the bell. ❑ *She answered her phone on the first ring.* **4** [T] When you **answer** a question in a test or quiz, you write or say something in an attempt to give the facts that are asked for. ❑ *Always read an exam all the way through at least once before you start to answer any questions.* **5** [I, T] If someone or something **answers** a particular description or **answers to** it, they have the characteristics described. = fit ❑ *Two men answering the description of the suspects tried to enter Switzerland.*

PHRASAL VERBS **answer back** (BrE) If someone, especially a child, **answers back**, they speak rudely to you when you speak to them. ❑ *My youngest child is eight and she has started answering back too.*

answer for If you have to **answer for** something bad or wrong you have done, you are punished for it. ❑ *He must be made to answer for his terrible crimes.*

PHRASE **have a lot to answer for** ['have' inflects] If you say that someone **has a lot to answer for**, you are saying that their actions have led to problems which you think they are responsible for.

NOUN [c] (**answers**) **1** An **answer** is when someone picks up the telephone when you ring them. An **answer** is also when someone opens the door when you knock on it or ring the bell. ❑ *I knocked at the front door and there was no answer.* **2** [also 'in' answer 'to' N] An **answer** is something that you say when you answer someone. = reply, response ❑ *Without waiting for an answer, he turned and went in through the door.* ❑ *I asked him a question but I didn't get an answer.* **3** [also 'in' answer 'to' N] An **answer** is a letter that you write to someone who has written to you. = reply, response ❑ *I wrote to him but I never had an answer back.* **4** An **answer to** a problem is a solution to it. = solution ❑ *There are no easy answers to the problems facing the economy.* ❑ *Prison is not the answer for most young offenders.* ❑ *Legislation is only part of the answer.* **5** Someone's **answer** to a question in a test or quiz is what they write or say in an attempt to give the facts that are asked for. The **answer** to a question is the fact that was asked for. ❑ *Simply*

marking an answer wrong will not help the student to get future examples correct. **6** [also 'in' answer 'to' N] Your **answer** to something that someone has said or done is what you say or do in response to it or in defence of yourself. = reply, response ❑ *In answer to speculation that she wouldn't finish the race, she boldly declared her intention of winning it.*

PHRASE **not to take no for an answer** If you say that someone will not **take no for an answer**, you mean that they go on trying to make you agree to something even after you have refused. ❑ *She is tough, unwilling to take no for an answer.*

WORD CONNECTIONS

VERB + **answer**

get an answer
give an answer
❑ *Has John given you an answer to your question yet?*

ADJ + **answer**

a **definite** answer
a **straight** answer
an **honest** answer
a **satisfactory** answer
❑ *I was so frustrated because I couldn't get a straight answer from anyone.*

a **simple** answer
an **easy** answer
❑ *There is no easy answer to the problem of unemployment.*

a **possible** answer
❑ *One possible answer would be to take on more staff.*

VOCABULARY BUILDER

answer NOUN
An **answer** is something that you say or write in return when someone asks you a question.
❑ *You asked me a question, and I gave you an honest answer.*

reply NOUN
A **reply** is something that you say or write when you answer someone or answer a letter or advertisement.
❑ *If you email a company from its website and receive no reply, it's the equivalent of being ignored by a shop assistant.*

response NOUN (written)
Your **response** to something that is said or written is what you say or do in return.
❑ *Wendy said the project had received a very positive response from both management and staff.*

solution NOUN
A **solution** to a problem or difficult situation is a way of dealing with it so that the difficulty is removed.
❑ *Russia has denounced the NATO air strikes and called for a peaceful solution of the dispute.*

an·tago·nize /ænˈtæɡənaɪz/ also **antagonise** VERB [T] (**antagonizes, antagonizing, antagonized**) If you **antagonize** someone, you make them feel angry or hostile towards you. ❑ *He didn't want to antagonize her.*

Ant·arc·tic /æntˈɑːktɪk/ NOUN [SING] The Antarctic is the area around the South Pole.

ante·na·tal /ˌæntiˈneɪtəl/ ADJ **Antenatal** means relating to the medical care of women when they are expecting a baby. ≠ postnatal ❑ *antenatal classes*

WORD PARTS

The prefix **ante-** often appears in words that have 'before' as part of their meaning:

antenatal (ADJ)
antecedent (NOUN)
anteroom (NOUN)

an·ten·na /ænˈtenə/ NOUN [c] (**antennae** or **antennas**)
Antennas is the usual plural form for meaning 2.

1 The **antennae** of something such as an insect or crustacean are the two long, thin parts attached to its head that it uses to feel things with. **2** An **antenna** is a device or a piece of wire that sends and receives television or radio signals and is usually attached to a radio, television, car, or building. = aerial

an·them /'ænθəm/ NOUN [C] (**anthems**) An **anthem** is a song that is used to represent a particular nation, society, or group and that is sung on special occasions. ❏ *The band played the Czech anthem.*

◆**an·thro·pol·ogy** /ˌænθrə'pɒlədʒi/ NOUN [U] Anthropology is the scientific study of people, society, and culture. ❏ *a leading scholar of cultural anthropology* ◆**an·thro·polo·gist** /ˌænθrə'pɒlədʒɪst/ NOUN [C] (**anthropologists**) ❏ *an anthropologist who had been in China for three years*

◆**anti·bi·ot·ic** /ˌæntibaɪ'ɒtɪk/ NOUN [C] (**antibiotics**) Antibiotics are medical drugs used to kill bacteria and treat infections. ❏ *Your doctor may prescribe antibiotics.* ❏ *Approximately 60% of antibiotics are prescribed for respiratory infections.* ❏ *A 10-day course of oral antibiotics is the usual treatment mode for cellulitis.*

WORD PARTS

The prefix **anti-** often appears in nouns and adjectives which refer to some sort of opposition:
anti**bi**otic (NOUN)
anti**vi**rus (ADJ)
anti**pa**thy (NOUN)

anti·body /'æntibɒdi/ NOUN [C] (**antibodies**) Antibodies are substances that a person's or an animal's body produces in their blood in order to destroy substances that carry disease. ❏ *Such women carry antibodies which make their blood more likely to clot during pregnancy.*

◆**an·tici·pate** /æn'tɪsɪpeɪt/ VERB [T] (**anticipates, anticipating, anticipated**) (*academic word*) **1** If you **anticipate** an event, you realize in advance that it may happen and you are prepared for it. = expect ❏ *At the time we couldn't have anticipated the result of our campaigning.* ❏ *It is anticipated that the equivalent of 192 full-time jobs will be lost.* ❏ *Surveyors anticipate further price declines over coming months.* ❏ *Officials anticipate that rivalry between leaders of the various drug factions could erupt into full scale war.* **2** If you **anticipate** a question, request, or need, you do what is necessary or required before the question, request, or need occurs. ❏ *What Jeff did was to anticipate my next question.*

◆**an·tici·pa·tion** /ænˌtɪsɪ'peɪʃən/ NOUN
NOUN [U] **Anticipation** is a feeling of excitement about something pleasant or exciting that you know is going to happen. ❏ *There's been an atmosphere of anticipation around here for a few days now.*
PHRASE **in anticipation of something** If something is done **in anticipation of** an event, it is done because people believe that event is going to happen. = in advance of, in expectation of, in preparation for ❏ *Troops in the Philippines have been put on full alert in anticipation of trouble during a planned general strike.* ❏ *the company's ability to constantly renew itself in anticipation of future technology trends*

◆**anti·clock·wise** /ˌænti'klɒkwaɪz/ also **anti-clockwise** (*BrE*; in *AmE*, use **counterclockwise**) ADV, ADJ
ADV If something is moving **anticlockwise**, it is moving in the opposite direction to the direction in which the hands of a clock move. ≠ clockwise ❏ *The cutters are opened by turning the knob anticlockwise.*
ADJ [anticlockwise + N] Something that is **anticlockwise** moves in the opposite direction in which the hands of a clock move. ≠ clockwise ❏ *an anticlockwise route around the coast* ❏ *As seen from above the Sun's north pole, the planets orbit the Sun in an anticlockwise direction.*

an·tics /'æntɪks/ NOUN [PL] **Antics** are funny, silly, or unusual ways of behaving. ❏ *Elizabeth tolerated Sarah's antics.*

anti·dote /'æntidəʊt/ NOUN [C] (**antidotes**) **1** An **antidote** is a chemical substance that stops or controls the effect of a poison. ❏ *When he returned, he noticed their*

sickness and prepared an antidote. **2** Something that is an **antidote to** a difficult or unpleasant situation helps you to overcome the situation. = cure, remedy ❏ *Massage is a wonderful antidote to stress.*

an·tipa·thy /æn'tɪpəθi/ NOUN [U] (*formal*) Antipathy is a strong feeling of dislike or hostility towards someone or something. ❏ *the voting public's antipathy towards the president*

an·tique ◆◇◇ /æn'tiːk/ NOUN [C] (**antiques**) An **antique** is an old object such as a piece of china or furniture that is valuable because of its beauty or rarity. ❏ *a genuine antique*

◆**anti·sep·tic** /ˌænti'septɪk/ NOUN, ADJ
NOUN [C, U] (**antiseptics**) **Antiseptic** is a substance that kills germs and harmful bacteria. = disinfectant ❏ *She bathed the cut with antiseptic.* ❏ *Chlorine is a natural antiseptic.*
ADJ Something that is **antiseptic** kills germs and harmful bacteria. = antibacterial ❏ *These vegetables and herbs have strong antiseptic qualities.* ❏ *the antiseptic properties of eucalyptus*

anti·so·cial /ˌænti'səʊʃəl/ ADJ Someone who is **antisocial** is unwilling to meet and be friendly with other people. ❏ *a generation of teenagers who will become aggressive and antisocial*

anxi·ety ◆◇◇ /æŋ'zaɪɪti/ NOUN [C, U] (**anxieties**) **Anxiety** is a feeling of nervousness or worry. ❏ *Her voice was full of anxiety.*

anx·ious ◆◇◇ /'æŋkʃəs/ ADJ **1** [V-LINK + anxious] If you are **anxious** to do something or **anxious that** something should happen, you very much want to do it or very much want it to happen. = eager, keen ❏ *Both the Americans and the Russians are anxious to avoid conflict in South Asia.* ❏ *He is anxious that there should be no delay.* **2** If you are **anxious**, you are nervous or worried about something. = nervous ❏ *The foreign minister admitted he was still anxious about the situation in the country.*
anx·ious·ly /'æŋkʃəsli/ ADV [anxiously with V] ❏ *They are waiting anxiously to see who will succeed him.*

any ◆◆◆ /'eni/ DET, QUANT, PRON, ADV
DET **1** You use **any** in statements with negative meaning to indicate that no thing or person of a particular type exists, is present, or is involved in a situation. ❏ *I'm not making any promises.* ❏ *We are doing this all without any support from the hospital.* ❏ *It is too early to say what effect, if any, there will be on the workforce.* **2** You use **any** in questions and conditional clauses to ask whether there is some of a particular thing or some of a particular group of people, or to suggest that there might be. ❏ *Do you speak any foreign languages?* **3** You use **any** in positive statements when you are referring to someone or something of a particular kind that might exist, occur, or be involved in a situation, when their exact identity or nature is not important. ❏ *Any actor will tell you that it is easier to perform than to be themselves.*
PHRASE **not just any** If you say that someone or something is **not just any** person or thing, you mean that they are special in some way. ❏ *Finzer is not just any East Coast businessman.*
QUANT **1** You use **any** in statements with negative meaning to refer to no thing or person of a particular type. ❏ *You don't know any of my friends.* **2** You use **any** in questions and conditional clauses to refer to some of a particular thing or some of a particular group of people. ❏ *Introduce foods one at a time and notice if you feel uncomfortable with any of them.* **3** You use **any** in positive statements when you are referring to someone or something of a particular kind that might exist, occur, or be involved in a situation, when their exact identity or nature is not important. ❏ *Nealy disappeared two days ago, several miles away from any of the fighting.*
PRON **1** [any after V] You use **any** in statements with negative meaning to refer to no thing or person of a particular type. ❏ *The children needed new school clothes and Kim couldn't afford any.* **2** [any after V] You use **any** in questions and conditional clauses to refer to some of a particular thing or some of a particular group of people. ❏ *If any bright thoughts occur to you pass them straight to me. Have you got any?* **3** You use **any** in positive statements when you are referring to someone or something of a

A

particular kind that might exist, occur, or be involved in a situation, when their exact identity or nature is not important. ❑ *Clean the mussels and discard any that do not close.*

ADV [any + COMPAR] (*emphasis*) You can also use **any** to emphasize a comparative adjective or adverb in a negative statement. ❑ *I can't see things getting any easier for graduates.*

PHRASE **any longer** or **any more** If something does not happen or is not true **any longer**, it has stopped happening or is no longer true. ❑ *I couldn't keep the tears hidden any longer.*

✦ **in any case** → see **case**; **by any chance** → see **chance**; **in any event** → see **event**; **any old** → see **old**; **at any rate** → see **rate**

any·bod·y ♦◇◇ /'ɛnibɒdi/ PRON **Anybody** means the same as **anyone**.

any·how /'ɛnihaʊ/ ADV **1** **Anyhow** means the same as **anyway**. **2** [anyhow after v] If you do something **anyhow**, you do it in a careless or untidy way. ❑ *Her discarded books were piled up just anyhow.*

any·more ♦◇◇ /ˌɛni'mɔː/ also **any more** ADV [anymore after v] If something does not happen or is not true **anymore**, it has stopped happening or is no longer true. ❑ *I don't ride my motorbike much anymore.* ❑ *I couldn't trust him anymore.*

any·one ♦◇◇ /'ɛniwʌn/ PRON

The form **anybody** is also used.

PRON **1** You use **anyone** or **anybody** in statements with negative meaning to indicate in a general way that nobody is present or involved in an action. ❑ *I won't tell anyone I saw you here.* ❑ *You needn't talk to anyone if you don't want to.* **2** You use **anyone** or **anybody** in questions and conditional clauses to ask or talk about whether someone is present or doing something. ❑ *Why would anyone want that job?* ❑ *How can anyone look sad at an occasion like this?* **3** [anyone + CL/GROUP] You use **anyone** or **anybody** before words that indicate the kind of person you are talking about. ❑ *I always had been the person who achieved things before anyone else at my age.* ❑ *It's not a job for anyone who is slow with numbers.* **4** You use **anyone** or **anybody** to refer to a person when you are emphasizing that it could be any person out of a very large number of people. ❑ *Anyone could be doing what I'm doing.*

PHRASE **anyone who is anyone** or **anybody who is anybody** You use **anyone who is anyone** and **anybody who is anybody** to refer to people who are important or influential. ❑ *It seems anyone who's anyone in business is going to the conference.*

any·thing ♦♦♦ /'ɛniθɪŋ/ PRON

PRON **1** You use **anything** in statements with negative meaning to indicate in a general way that nothing is present or that an action or event does not or cannot happen. ❑ *We can't do anything.* ❑ *She couldn't see or hear anything at all.* **2** You use **anything** in questions and conditional clauses to ask or talk about whether something is present or happening. ❑ *What happened, is anything wrong?* ❑ *Did you find anything?* **3** [anything + CL/GROUP] You can use **anything** before words that indicate the kind of thing you are talking about. ❑ *More than anything else, he wanted to become a teacher.* ❑ *Anything that's cheap this year will be even cheaper next year.* **4** You use **anything** to emphasize a possible thing, event, or situation, when you are saying that it could be any one of a very large number of things. ❑ *He is young, fresh, and ready for anything.* **5** [anything + PREP] You use **anything** in expressions such as **anything near**, **anything close to**, and **anything like** to emphasize a statement that you are making. ❑ *Doctors have decided the only way he can live anything near a normal life is to give him an operation.* **6** [anything 'from' N 'to' N, anything 'between' N 'and' N] When you do not want to be exact, you use **anything** to talk about a particular range of things or quantities. ❑ *Chinese herbs that have cured anything from colds to broken bones.*

PHRASES **anything but** (*emphasis*) You use **anything but** in

expressions such as **anything but quiet** and **anything but attractive** to emphasize that something is not the case. ❑ *There's no evidence that Christopher told anyone to say anything but the truth.*

would not do something for anything or **would not be something for anything** (*informal, spoken, emphasis*) You can say that you **would not** do something **for anything** to emphasize that you definitely would not want to do or be a particular thing. ❑ *I wouldn't want to move for anything in the world.*

if anything You use **if anything**, especially after a negative statement, to introduce a statement that adds to what you have just said. ❑ *I never had to clean up after the lodgers. If anything, they did most of the cleaning.*

or anything (*informal, spoken, vagueness*) You can add **or anything** to the end of a clause or sentence in order to refer vaguely to other things that are or may be similar to what you just mentioned. ❑ *Listen, if you talk to Elizabeth or anything make sure you let everyone know, will you?*

any·time /ˌɛni'taɪm/ ADV You use **anytime** to mean a point in time that is not fixed or set. ❑ *The college admits students anytime during the year.* ❑ *He can leave anytime he wants.*

any·way ♦♦◇ /'ɛniweɪ/ ADV

The form **anyhow** is also used.

1 [anyway with CL] You use **anyway** or **anyhow** to indicate that a statement explains or supports a previous point. = besides ❑ *I'm certain David's told you his business troubles. Anyway, it's no secret that he owes money.* **2** [anyway with CL] You use **anyway** or **anyhow** to suggest that a statement is true or relevant in spite of other things that have been said. ❑ *I don't know why I settled on Miami, but anyway I did.* **3** [CL/GROUP + anyway] You use **anyway** or **anyhow** to correct or modify a statement, for example, to limit it to what you definitely know to be true. ❑ *Mary Ann doesn't want to have children. Not right now, anyway.* **4** [CL + anyway] You use **anyway** or **anyhow** to indicate that you are asking what the real situation is or what the real reason for something is. ❑ *What do you want from me, anyway?* **5** [anyway with CL] You use **anyway** or **anyhow** to indicate that you are leaving out some details in a story and are passing on to the next main point or event. = well ❑ *I was told to go to Denver for this interview. It was a very amusing affair. Anyhow, I got the job.* **6** [anyway + CL] You use **anyway** or **anyhow** to change the topic or return to a previous topic. = well ❑ *'I've got a terrible cold.'—'Have you? Oh dear. Anyway, so you're not going to go away this weekend?'* **7** [anyway + CL] You use **anyway** or **anyhow** to indicate that you want to end the conversation. = well ❑ *'Anyway, I'd better let you have your dinner. Bye.'*

any·where ♦◇◇ /'ɛniweə/ ADV **1** You use **anywhere** in statements with negative meaning to indicate that a place does not exist. ❑ *I haven't got anywhere to live.* **2** You use **anywhere** in questions and conditional clauses to ask or talk about a place without saying exactly where you mean. ❑ *Did you try to get help from anywhere?* **3** [anywhere + CL/GROUP] You use **anywhere** before words that indicate the kind of place you are talking about. ❑ *He'll meet you anywhere you want.* **4** You use **anywhere** to refer to a place when you are emphasizing that it could be any of a large number of places. ❑ *jokes that are so funny they always work anywhere* **5** When you do not want to be exact, you use **anywhere** to refer to a particular range of things. ❑ *His shoes cost anywhere from $200 up.* **6** [anywhere + ADJ/ADV] You use **anywhere** in expressions such as **anywhere near** and **anywhere close to** to emphasize a statement that you are making. ❑ *There weren't anywhere near enough empty boxes.*

apart ♦♦◇ /ə'pɑːt/ ADV, ADJ

In addition to the uses shown below, **apart** is used in phrasal verbs such as 'grow apart' and 'take apart'.

ADV **1** When people or things are **apart**, they are some distance from each other. ❑ *He was standing a bit apart from the rest of us, watching us.* ❑ *Ray and sister Renee lived just 25 miles apart from each other.* **2** [apart after v] If two people or things move **apart** or are pulled **apart**, they move away from each other. ❑ *John and Isabelle moved apart, back into the sun.* **3** If two people are **apart**, they are no longer living together or spending time together, either permanently or just for a short time. ❑ *It was the first time Jane and I had been apart for more than a few days.* **4** [apart after v] If you take something **apart**, you separate it into the pieces that it is made of. If it comes or falls **apart**, its parts separate from each other. ❑ *When the clock stopped he took it apart, found what was wrong, and put the whole thing together again.* **5** [apart after v] If something such as an organization or relationship falls **apart**, or if something tears it **apart**, it can no longer continue because it has serious difficulties. ❑ *Any manager knows that his company will start falling apart if his attention wanders.* **6** If something sets someone or something **apart**, it makes them different from other people or things. ❑ *What really sets Mr Thaksin apart is that he comes not from Southern China, but from northern Thailand.* **7** [N + apart] You use **apart** when you are making an exception to a general statement. = excepted ❑ *This was, New York apart, the first American city I had ever been in where people actually lived downtown.* **PHRASES can't tell apart** If you can't **tell** two people or things **apart**, they look exactly the same to you. ❑ *I can still only tell Mark and Dave apart by the colour of their shoes!* **apart from** You use **apart from** when you are making an exception to a general statement. = except for ❑ *The room was empty apart from one man seated beside the fire.* ❑ *She was the only British competitor apart from Richard Meade.* ADJ [V-LINK AMOUNT + apart, oft apart 'on' N] If people or groups are a long way **apart** on a particular topic or issue, they have completely different views and disagree about it. ❑ *Their concept of a performance and our concept were miles apart.*

apart·heid /əˈpɑːthaɪt/ NOUN [U] Apartheid was a political system in South Africa in which people were divided into racial groups and kept apart by law. ❑ *He praised her role in the struggle against apartheid.*

apart·ment ◆◇◇ /əˈpɑːtmənt/ (*mainly AmE*; in BrE, usually use **flat**) NOUN [C] (**apartments**) An **apartment** is a separate set of rooms for living in, in a house or a building with other apartments. ❑ *Christina has her own apartment, with her own car.*

apa·thet·ic /ˌæpəˈθetɪk/ ADJ (*disapproval*) If you describe someone as **apathetic**, you are criticizing them because they do not seem to be interested in or enthusiastic about doing anything. ❑ *Even the most apathetic students are beginning to sit up and listen.*

apa·thy /ˈæpəθi/ NOUN [U] (*disapproval*) You can use **apathy** to talk about someone's state of mind if you are criticizing them because they do not seem to be interested in or enthusiastic about anything. ❑ *They told me about isolation and public apathy.*

apiece /əˈpiːs/ ADV **1** [AMOUNT + apiece] If people have a particular number of things **apiece**, they have that number each. = each ❑ *He and I had two fish apiece.* **2** [AMOUNT + apiece] If a number of similar things are for sale at a certain price **apiece**, that is the price for each one of them. = each ❑ *Whole roast chickens were sixty cents apiece.*

apolo·get·ic /əˌpɒləˈdʒetɪk/ ADJ If you are **apologetic**, you show or say that you are sorry for causing trouble for someone, for hurting them or for disappointing them. ❑ *The hospital staff were very apologetic but that couldn't really compensate.*
apolo·get·i·cal·ly /əˌpɒləˈdʒetɪkli/ ADV [apologetically with v] ❑ *'It's of no great literary merit,' he said, almost apologetically.*

apolo·gize /əˈpɒlədʒaɪz/ also **apologise** VERB [I] (**apologizes, apologizing, apologized**) When you **apologize** to someone, you say that you are sorry that you have hurt them or caused trouble for them. You can say 'I apologize' as a formal way of saying sorry. ❑ *I apologize for being late but I have just had a message from the hospital.* ❑ *He apologized to the people who had been affected.*

apologize
Remember to use the correct preposition after **apologize**. You **apologize to** someone. You do not say that you 'apologize someone'.
*Afterwards, George **apologized to** me personally.*
You **apologize for** something you have done.
*I **apologized for** being late.*

apol·ogy /əˈpɒlədʒi/ NOUN [C, U, PL] (**apologies**) **1** [C, U] An **apology** is something that you say or write in order to tell someone that you are sorry that you have hurt them or caused trouble for them. ❑ *I didn't get an apology.* ❑ *We received a letter of apology.* **2** [PL] (*formal*) If you offer or make your **apologies**, you apologize. ❑ *When Mary finally appeared, she made her apologies to Mrs Velasquez.*

apos·tro·phe /əˈpɒstrəfi/ NOUN [C] (**apostrophes**) An **apostrophe** is the mark ' when it is written to indicate that one or more letters have been left out of a word, as in 'isn't' and 'we'll'. It is also added to nouns to form possessives, as in 'Mike's car'.

ap·pal /əˈpɔːl/ (*BrE*; in *AmE*, use **appall**) VERB [T] (**appals, appalling, appalled**) If something **appals** you, it disgusts or shocks you because it seems so bad or unpleasant. = horrify ❑ *The new-found strength of local militancy appals many observers.*

ap·palled /əˈpɔːld/ ADJ If you are **appalled** by something, you are shocked or disgusted because it is so bad or unpleasant. ❑ *She said that the Americans are appalled at the statements made at the conference.*

ap·pal·ling /əˈpɔːlɪŋ/ ADJ **1** Something that is **appalling** is so bad or unpleasant that it shocks you. = dreadful ❑ *They have been living under the most appalling conditions for two months.* **2** You can use **appalling** to emphasize that something is very extreme or severe. ❑ *I developed an appalling headache.*
ap·pal·ling·ly /əˈpɔːlɪŋli/ ADV **1** *He says that he understands why they behaved so appallingly.* **2** *It's been an appallingly busy morning.*
→ See also **appal**

⊙ ap·pa·rat·us /ˌæpəˈreɪtəs, -ˈræt-/ NOUN [C, U] (**apparatuses**) **1** **Apparatus** is the equipment, such as tools and machines, which is used to do a particular job or activity. = equipment ❑ *One of the boys had to be rescued by firemen wearing breathing apparatus.* ❑ *a standard piece of laboratory apparatus, the spectrometer* **2** The **apparatus** of an organization or system is its structure and method of operation. ❑ *For many years, the country had been buried under the apparatus of the regime.*

⊙ ap·par·ent ◆◇◇ /əˈpærənt/ ADJ (*academic word*) ADJ **1** [apparent + N] An **apparent** situation, quality, or feeling seems to exist, although you cannot be certain that it does exist. = seeming, supposed; ≠ actual ❑ *I was a bit depressed by our apparent lack of progress.* ❑ *the apparent government lack of concern for the advancement of science* ❑ *There are two reasons for this apparent contradiction.* **2** [V-LINK + apparent] If something is **apparent** to you, it is clear and obvious to you. = clear, obvious; ≠ unclear ❑ *It has been apparent that in other areas standards have held up well.* ❑ *It will be readily apparent from Fig. 108a that there is a link between the monetary side of the economy and the real economy.* ❑ *The shrinkage of the tissue is not immediately apparent from its appearance.*
PHRASE for no apparent reason If you say that something happens **for no apparent reason**, you cannot understand why it happens. ❑ *The person may become dizzy for no apparent reason.*

⊙ ap·par·ent·ly ◆◆◇ /əˈpærəntli/ ADV (*academic word*) **1** (*vagueness*) You use **apparently** to indicate that the information you are giving is something that you have heard, but you are not certain that it is true. = seemingly, ostensibly ❑ *Apparently the girls are not at all amused by the whole business.* **2** You use **apparently** to refer to something that seems to be true, although you are not sure whether it is or not. ❑ *The recent deterioration has been caused by an apparently endless recession.*

A

✪ap·peal ♦♦◇ /əˈpiːl/ VERB, NOUN

VERB [I, T] (appeals, appealing, appealed) **1** [I] If you **appeal to** someone **to** do something, you make a serious and urgent request to them. ◻ He appealed to voters to go to the polls tomorrow. ◻ He will appeal to the state for an extension of unemployment benefits. **2** [I, T] If you **appeal to** someone in authority against a decision, you formally ask them to change it. In British English, you **appeal against** something. In American English, you **appeal** something. ◻ He said they would appeal against the decision. ◻ We intend to appeal the verdict. ◻ Maguire has appealed to the Supreme Court to stop her extradition. **3** [I] If something **appeals to** you, you find it attractive or interesting. ◻ On the other hand, the idea appealed to him.

NOUN [C, U] (appeals) **1** [C] An **appeal** is a serious and urgent request. = petition, request ◻ He has a message from King Fahd, believed to be an appeal for Arab unity. **2** [C] An **appeal** is an attempt to raise money for a charity or for a good cause. ◻ an appeal to save a library containing priceless manuscripts **3** [C, U] An **appeal** is a formal request for a decision to be changed. ◻ They took their appeal to the Supreme Court. ◻ Mr Russell has lodged a formal appeal against his dismissal. ◻ The jury agreed with her, but she lost the case on appeal. **4** [U] The **appeal** of something is a quality that people find attractive or interesting. = attraction ◻ Its new title was meant to give the party greater public appeal.
→ See also **appealing**

ap·peal·ing /əˈpiːlɪŋ/ ADJ

1 Someone or something that is **appealing** is pleasing and attractive. ◻ There was a sense of humour to what he did that I found very appealing. **2** An **appealing** expression or tone of voice indicates to someone that you want help, advice or approval. ◻ She gave him a soft appealing look that would have melted solid ice.
→ See also **appeal**

✪ap·pear ♦♦♦ /əˈpɪə/ VERB [LINK, I] (appears, appearing, appeared)

1 [LINK] (vagueness) If you say that something **appears** to be the way you describe it, you are reporting what you believe or what you have been told, though you cannot be sure it is true. = seem ◻ There appears to be increasing support for the leadership to take a more aggressive stance. ◻ The aircraft appears to have crashed. ◻ There appeared to be a problem with the car. **2** [LINK] If someone or something **appears** to have a particular quality or characteristic, they give the impression of having that quality or characteristic. = seem ◻ She did her best to appear more self-assured than she felt. ◻ He appeared to be depressed. ◻ He is anxious to appear a gentleman. **3** [I] When someone or something **appears**, they move into a position where you can see them. ◻ A woman appeared at the far end of the street. **4** [I] When something new **appears**, it begins to exist or reaches a stage of development where its existence can be noticed. ◻ small white flowers which appear in early summer **5** [I] When something such as a book **appears**, it is published or becomes available for people to buy. ◻ I could hardly wait for 'Boys' Life' to appear each month. **6** [I] When someone **appears in** something such as a play, a show, or a television programme, they take part in it. ◻ Jill Bennett became John Osborne's fourth wife, and appeared in several of his plays. **7** [I] When someone **appears before** a court of law or **before** an official committee, they go there in order to answer charges or to give information as a witness. ◻ The defendants are expected to appear in federal court today.

USAGE NOTE
appear

You often use 'there appeared' to refer to the date or period when something became available. Do not say, for example, ~~'In the 1960s appeared a new type of car'~~.
In the 1960s **there appeared** a new type of car.
The verb 'be' is usually used instead of 'appear' when you are not emphasizing physical appearance. Do not say ~~'There will never appear another person like him'~~.
There will never **be** another person like him.

✪ap·pear·ance ♦♦◇ /əˈpɪərəns/ NOUN

NOUN [C, SING] (appearances) **1** [C] When someone makes an **appearance** at a public event or in a broadcast, they take part in it. ◻ It was the president's second public appearance to date. **2** [SING] Someone's or something's **appearance** is the way that they look. = look ◻ She used to be so fussy about her appearance. ◻ He had the appearance of a college student. ◻ A flat-roofed extension will add nothing to the value or appearance of the house. **3** [SING] The **appearance of** someone or something in a place is their arrival there, especially when it is unexpected. ◻ The sudden appearance of a few bags of rice could start a riot. **4** [SING] The **appearance of** something new is its coming into existence or use. ◻ Flowering plants were making their first appearance, but were still a rarity. **5** [SING] If something has the **appearance of** a quality, it seems to have that quality. ◻ We tried to meet both children's needs without the appearance of favouritism or unfairness.

PHRASE **by all appearances** or **from all appearances** or **to all appearances** If something is true **by all appearances**, **from all appearances**, or **to all appearances**, it seems from what you observe or know about it that it is true. ◻ He was a small and by all appearances an unassuming man.

ap·pease /əˈpiːz/ VERB [T] (appeases, appeasing, appeased)

(disapproval) If you try to **appease** someone, you try to stop them from being angry by giving them what they want. = placate ◻ Gandhi was accused by some of trying to appease both factions of the electorate.

ap·pease·ment /əˈpiːzmənt/ NOUN [U]

(formal, disapproval) **Appeasement** means giving people what they want to prevent them from harming you or being angry with you. ◻ He denied there is a policy of appeasement.

✪ap·pen·dix /əˈpendɪks/ NOUN [C] (appendixes or appendices /əˈpendɪsiːz/) (academic word)

The plural form **appendices** is usually used for meaning 2.

1 Your **appendix** is a small closed tube inside your body that is attached to your digestive system. ◻ a burst appendix **2** An **appendix to** a book is extra information that is placed after the end of the main text. ◻ The survey results are published in full as an appendix to Mr Barton's discussion paper. ◻ An additional 6 per cent was spent in active recreation (see appendix 7.1).

✪ap·pe·tite /ˈæpɪtaɪt/ NOUN [C, U] (appetites)

1 [C, U] Your **appetite** is your desire to eat. = hunger ◻ He has a healthy appetite. ◻ Symptoms are a slight fever, headache and loss of appetite. ◻ stomach hormones that normally increase appetite **2** [C] Someone's **appetite for** something is their strong desire for it. ◻ his appetite for success

ap·plaud /əˈplɔːd/ VERB [I, T] (applauds, applauding, applauded)

1 [I, T] When a group of people **applaud**, they clap their hands in order to show approval, for example when they have enjoyed a play or concert. ◻ The audience laughed and applauded. **2** [T] When an attitude or action is **applauded**, people praise it. ◻ He should be applauded for his courage. ◻ This last move can only be applauded.

ap·plause /əˈplɔːz/ NOUN [U]

Applause is the noise made by a group of people clapping their hands to show approval. ◻ They greeted him with thunderous applause.

ap·ple ♦◇◇ /ˈæpəl/ NOUN [C, U] (apples)

An **apple** is a round fruit with smooth red, yellow or green skin and firm white flesh. ◻ I want an apple. ◻ his ongoing search for the finest varieties of apple

ap·pli·ance /əˈplaɪəns/ NOUN [C] (appliances) (formal)

An **appliance** is a device or machine in your home that you use to do a job such as cleaning or cooking. Appliances are often electrical. ◻ He could also learn to use the vacuum cleaner, the washing machine and other household appliances.

ap·pli·cable /ˈæplɪkəbəl, əˈplɪkə-/ ADJ

Something that is **applicable to** a particular situation is relevant to it or can be applied to it. = relevant ◻ What is a reasonable standard for one family is not applicable for another.

ap·pli·cant /ˈæplɪkənt/ NOUN [C] (applicants)

An **applicant for** something such as a job or a college is someone who makes a formal written request to be considered for it. ❑ *We have had lots of applicants for these positions.*

❍**ap•pli•ca•tion** ♦◇◇ /ˌæplɪˈkeɪʃən/ NOUN [C, U] (**applications**) **1** [C] An **application for** something such as a job or membership of an organization is a formal written request for it. ❑ *His application for membership of the organization was rejected.* ❑ *Turkey's application to join the European Community* ❑ *Applications should be submitted as early as possible.* ❑ *Tickets are available on application.* **2** [C] In computing, an **application** is a piece of software designed to carry out a particular task. ❑ *The service works as a software application that is accessed via the internet.* **3** [C, U] The **application of** a rule or piece of knowledge is the use of it in a particular situation. = use, relevance ❑ *Students learned the practical application of the theory they had learned in the classroom.* ❑ *The book provides a succinct outline of artificial intelligence and its application to robotics.* **4** [U] **Application** is hard work and concentration on what you are doing over a period of time. = diligence ❑ *his immense talent, boundless energy and unremitting application*

WORD CONNECTIONS
VERB + **application**
make an application
submit an application
❑ *Applications for the course must be submitted by 31 December.*
receive an application
accept an application
reject an application
❑ *His job application was rejected on the grounds that he did not have enough experience.*
NOUN + **application**
job application
visa application
passport application
loan application
grant application
❑ *Routine visa applications take about five working days to process.*
application + OF + NOUN
the application of a **rule**
the application of a **theory**
the application of a **principle**
❑ *The company encourages the application of ethical principles to all the professional decisions its managers make.*
the application of **technology**
❑ *The development and application of new technology has allowed us to make significant medical advances.*
ADJ + **application**
practical application
commercial application
clinical application
❑ *Special emphasis was placed on the practical application of scientific knowledge.*

ap•plied /əˈplaɪd/ ADJ [applied + N] An **applied** subject of study has a practical use, rather than being concerned only with theory. ❑ *Applied Physics*

❍**ap•ply** ♦♦◇ /əˈplaɪ/ VERB [I, T] (**applies, applying, applied**) **1** [I, T] If you **apply for** something such as a job or membership of an organization, you write a letter or fill in a form in order to ask formally for it. ❑ *I am continuing to apply for jobs.* ❑ *They may apply to join the organization.* **2** [T] If you **apply yourself to** something or **apply** your mind **to** something, you concentrate hard on doing it or on thinking about it. ❑ *Scymanski has applied himself to this task with considerable energy.* **3** [I] If something such as a rule or a remark **applies to** a person or in a situation, it is relevant to the person or the situation. = pertain, be relevant ❑ *The convention does not apply to us.* ❑ *The rule applies where a person owns stock in a corporation.* **4** [T] If you **apply**

something such as a rule, system, or skill, you use it in a situation or activity. = use ❑ *The government appears to be applying the same principle.* ❑ *His project is concerned with applying the technology to practical business problems.* **5** [T] A name that **is applied to** someone or something is used to refer to them. ❑ *a biological term that cannot be applied to a whole culture* **6** [T] If you **apply** something **to** a surface, you put it on or rub it into the surface. ❑ *The right thing would be to apply direct pressure to the wound.* → See also **applied**

ap•point ♦◇◇ /əˈpɔɪnt/ VERB [T] (**appoints, appointing, appointed**) If you **appoint** someone **to** a job or official position, you formally choose them for it. = assign ❑ *It made sense to appoint a banker to this job.* ❑ *The president has appointed a civilian as defence secretary.*

❍**ap•point•ment** ♦◇◇ /əˈpɔɪntmənt/ NOUN
NOUN [C, U] (**appointments**) **1** [C, U] The **appointment of** a person **to** a particular job is the choice of that person to do it. ❑ *His appointment to the cabinet would please the right wing.* **2** [C] An **appointment** is a job or position of responsibility. = post ❑ *Mr Fay is to take up an appointment as a researcher.* **3** [C] If you have an **appointment with** someone, you have arranged to see them at a particular time, usually in connection with their work or for a serious purpose. ❑ *She has an appointment with her accountant.* ❑ *I made an appointment to see my tutor.* ❑ *a dental appointment*
PHRASE **by appointment** If something can be done **by appointment**, people can arrange in advance to do it at a particular time. ❑ *Viewing is by appointment only.*

ap•prais•al /əˈpreɪzəl/ NOUN [C, U] (**appraisals**) **1** If you make an **appraisal of** something, you consider it carefully and form an opinion about it. = evaluation ❑ *What is needed in such cases is a calm appraisal of the situation.* **2** **Appraisal** is the official or formal assessment of the strengths and weaknesses of someone or something. Appraisal often involves observation or some kind of testing. = evaluation ❑ *One of the most important tools for organizational improvement is the performance appraisal.*

❍**ap•pre•ci•able** /əˈpriːʃəbəl/ ADJ [usu appreciable + N] (*academic word, formal*) An **appreciable** amount or effect is large enough to be important or clearly noticed. = significant; ≠ insignificant ❑ *It contains less than 1 per cent fat, an appreciable amount of protein, and a high content of minerals.* ❑ *This has not had an appreciable effect on production.* ❑ *There was no appreciable difference in test results.*
❍**ap•pre•ci•ably** /əˈpriːʃəbli/ ADV = noticeably, significantly ❑ *The average earnings of women have risen appreciably since the 1970 Equal Pay Act.* ❑ *The calculations would not change appreciably if we included future generations.*

❍**ap•pre•ci•ate** ♦◇◇ /əˈpriːʃieɪt/ VERB [T, I] (**appreciates, appreciating, appreciated**) (*academic word*) **1** [T] If you **appreciate** something, for example, a piece of music or good food, you like it because you recognize its good qualities. ❑ *Anyone can appreciate our music.* **2** [T] If you **appreciate** a situation or problem, you understand it and know what it involves. = acknowledge, recognize ❑ *She never really appreciated the depth and bitterness of the family's conflict.* ❑ *Those arguing the case often do not appreciate the difference between an island nation and a continental one.* ❑ *It is essential to appreciate that addictive behaviour can compromise energy levels.* **3** [T] If you **appreciate** something that someone has done for you or is going to do for you, you are grateful for it. ❑ *Peter stood by me when I most needed it. I'll always appreciate that.* **4** [I] If something that you own **appreciates** over a period of time, its value increases. ❑ *They don't have any confidence that houses will appreciate in value.*

❍**ap•pre•cia•tion** /əˌpriːʃiˈeɪʃən/ NOUN [SING, U]
1 [SING] **Appreciation of** something is the recognition and enjoyment of its good qualities. ❑ *an investigation into children's understanding and appreciation of art* **2** [SING] [also no DET] Your **appreciation for** something that someone does for you is your gratitude for it. = gratitude ❑ *He expressed his appreciation for what he called Saudi Arabia's moderate and realistic oil policies.* **3** [SING] [also no DET] An **appreciation of** a situation or problem is an understanding

of what it involves. = grasp ❑ *They have a stronger appreciation of the importance of economic incentives.* **4** [U] **Appreciation** in the value of something is an increase in its value over a period of time. ❑ *You have to take capital appreciation of the property into account.*

ap·pre·cia·tive /əˈpriːʃətɪv/ ADJ **1** An **appreciative** reaction or comment shows the enjoyment that you are getting from something. ❑ *There is a murmur of appreciative laughter.* **2** If you are **appreciative of** something, you are grateful for it. ❑ *We have been very appreciative of their support.*

ap·pre·hen·sion /ˌæprɪˈhenʃən/ NOUN [C, U] (apprehensions) (formal) **Apprehension** is a feeling of fear that something bad may happen. = worry ❑ *It reflects real anger and apprehension about the future.*

ap·pre·hen·sive /ˌæprɪˈhensɪv/ ADJ Someone who is **apprehensive** is afraid that something bad may happen. ❑ *People are still terribly apprehensive about the future.*

ap·pren·tice /əˈprentɪs/ NOUN, VERB

NOUN [C] (apprentices) An **apprentice** is a young person who works for someone in order to learn their skill. ❑ *I started off as an apprentice and worked my way up.*

VERB [T] (apprentices, apprenticing, apprenticed) If a young person **is apprenticed to** someone, they go to work for them in order to learn their skill. ❑ *I was apprenticed to a plumber when I was fourteen.*

ap·pren·tice·ship /əˈprentɪʃɪp/ NOUN [C, U] (apprenticeships) Someone who has an **apprenticeship** works for a fixed period of time for a person who has a particular skill in order to learn the skill. **Apprenticeship** is the system of learning a skill like this. ❑ *After serving his apprenticeship as a toolmaker, he became a manager.*

✪ **ap·proach** ♦♦◇ /əˈprəʊtʃ/ VERB, NOUN (academic word)

VERB [I, T] (approaches, approaching, approached) **1** [I, T] When you **approach** something, you get closer to it. ❑ *He didn't approach the front door at once.* ❑ *When I approached, they grew silent.* **2** [T] If you **approach** someone **about** something, you speak to them about it for the first time, often making an offer or request. ❑ *When Brown approached me about the job, my first reaction was of disbelief.* ❑ *He approached me to create and design the restaurant.* **3** [T] When you **approach** a task, problem, or situation in a particular way, you deal with it or think about it in that way. = tackle, address ❑ *The Bank has approached the issue in a practical way.* ❑ *Employers are interested in how you approach problems.* **4** [I] As a future time or event **approaches**, it gradually gets nearer as time passes. ❑ *As autumn approached, the plants and colours in the garden changed.* **5** [T] As you **approach** a future time or event, time passes so that you get gradually nearer to it. ❑ *There is a need for understanding and cooperation as we approach the summit.* **6** [T] If something **approaches** a particular level or state, it almost reaches that level or state. ❑ *Oil prices have approached their highest level for almost ten years.*

NOUN [C, SING] (approaches) **1** [C] Someone's **approach** is when they get closer to something. ❑ *At their approach the little boy ran away and hid.* **2** [C] An **approach** is when you speak to someone about something for the first time, often making an offer or request. ❑ *There had already been approaches from buyers interested in the whole of the group.* **3** [SING] The **approach** of an event or time is when it is gradually getting nearer as time passes. ❑ *the festive spirit that permeated the house with the approach of Christmas* **4** [C] An **approach to** a place is a road, path, or other route that leads to it. ❑ *The path serves as an approach to the boathouse.* **5** [C] Your **approach to** a task, problem, or situation is the way you deal with it or think about it. = methodology, procedure, technique ❑ *We will be exploring different approaches to gathering information.* ❑ *The programme adopts a multidisciplinary approach.*

✪ **ap·pro·pri·ate** ♦◇◇ /əˈprəʊpriət/ ADJ (academic word) Something that is **appropriate** is suitable or acceptable for a particular situation. = suitable, acceptable ❑ *It is appropriate that Hispanic names dominate the list.* ❑ *Dress neatly and attractively in an outfit appropriate to the job.* ❑ *The teacher can then take appropriate action.*

✪ **ap·pro·pri·ate·ly** /əˈprəʊpriətli/ ADV = suitably,

acceptably; ≠ inappropriately ❑ *Behave appropriately and ask intelligent questions.* ❑ *It's entitled, appropriately enough, 'Art for the Nation'.*

WORD CONNECTIONS
ADV + **appropriate**
wholly appropriate
entirely appropriate
highly appropriate
perfectly appropriate
❑ *In this situation, anger is healthy, normal, and entirely appropriate.*
appropriate + FOR + NOUN
appropriate for a **purpose**
appropriate for an **occasion**
appropriate for a **task**
❑ *I wanted to wear something appropriate for the occasion.*

✪ **ap·prov·al** ♦◇◇ /əˈpruːvəl/ NOUN [U, C] (approvals) **1** [U] If you win someone's **approval for** something that you ask for or suggest, they agree to it. = sanction, authorization ❑ *efforts to win congressional approval for an aid package for Moscow* ❑ *The chairman has also given his approval for an investigation into the case.* ❑ *The initiative is awaiting the approval of the medical research ethics committee.* **2** [U] If someone or something has your **approval**, you like and admire them. ❑ *His son had an obsessive drive to gain his father's approval.* **3** [C, U] **Approval** is a formal or official statement that something is acceptable. ❑ *The testing and approval of new drugs will be speeded up.*

✪ **ap·prove** ♦♦◇ /əˈpruːv/ VERB [I, T] (approves, approving, approved) **1** [I] If you **approve of** an action, event, or suggestion, you like it or are pleased about it. ❑ *Not everyone approves of the festival.* **2** [I] If you **approve of** someone or something, you like and admire them. ❑ *You've never approved of Henry, have you?* **3** [T] If someone in a position of authority **approves** a plan or idea, they formally agree to it and say that it can happen. = sanction, authorize, allow; ≠ reject, veto ❑ *The Russian Parliament has approved a programme of radical economic reforms.* ❑ *MPs approved the Bill by a majority of 97.*

✪ **ap·proxi·mate** ADJ, VERB (academic word)

ADJ /əˈprɒksɪmət/ **1** [approximate + NUM] An **approximate** number, time, or position is close to the correct number, time, or position, but is not exact. = rough; ≠ exact, precise ❑ *The approximate cost varies from around $150 to $250.* ❑ *The times are approximate only.* **2** An idea or description that is **approximate** is not intended to be precise or accurate, but to give some indication of what something is like. = rough; ≠ exact, precise ❑ *They did not have even an approximate idea what the Germans really wanted.*

VERB /əˈprɒksɪmeɪt/ [T] (approximates, approximating, approximated) If something **approximates** something else or approximates **to** something else, it is similar to it but is not exactly the same. ❑ *The mixture described below will approximate it, but is not exactly the same.* ❑ *Something approximating to a fair outcome will be ensured.* ❑ *By about 6 weeks of age, most babies begin to show something approximating a day/night sleeping pattern.*

✪ **ap·proxi·mate·ly** /əˈprɒksɪmətli/ ADV You use **approximately** before a number, time, or position to say that it is close to the correct one but is not exact. = roughly, about, around; ≠ exactly, precisely ❑ *Approximately $150 million is to be spent on improvements.* ❑ *Each session lasted approximately 30 to 40 minutes.*

apt /æpt/ ADJ **1** An **apt** remark, description or choice is especially suitable. ❑ *The words of this report are as apt today as in 1929.* **2** [V-LINK + apt + to-INF] If someone is **apt to** do something, they often do it and so it is likely that they will do it again. = liable ❑ *She was apt to raise her voice and wave her hands about.* **3** [apt + N] An **apt** student is intelligent and able to understand things easily. ❑ *She had taught him French and he had been an apt student.*

apt·ly /æptli/ ADV ❑ *the beach in the aptly named town of Oceanside*

ap·ti·tude /'æptɪtjuːd, AmE -tuːd/ NOUN [C, U] (**aptitudes**) Someone's **aptitude for** a particular kind of work or activity is their ability to learn it quickly and to do it well. ❑ *He drifted into publishing and discovered an aptitude for working with accounts.*

Arab /'ærəb/ NOUN, ADJ
[NOUN] [C] (**Arabs**) **Arabs** are people who speak Arabic and who come from the Middle East and parts of North Africa. [ADJ] **Arab** means belonging or relating to Arabs or to their countries or customs. ❑ *On the surface, it appears little has changed in the Arab world.*

◆ **ar·bi·trary** /'aːbɪtri, AmE -treri/ ADJ (*academic word, disapproval*) If you describe an action, rule, or decision as **arbitrary**, you think that it is not based on any principle, plan, or system. It often seems unfair because of this. = random, unfounded; ≠ logical, reasonable ❑ *Arbitrary arrests and detention without trial were common.* ❑ *a seemingly arbitrary deadline*
◆ **ar·bi·trari·ly** /ˌaːbɪ'treərɪli/ ADV [arbitrarily with V] = randomly, unreasonably ❑ *The victims were not chosen arbitrarily.* ❑ *It would be wrong arbitrarily to exclude any particular groups of people from consideration.*

ar·bi·tra·tion /ˌaːbɪ'treɪʃən/ NOUN [U] **Arbitration** is the judging of a dispute between people or groups by someone who is not involved. ❑ *The matter is likely to go to arbitration.*

arc /aːk/ NOUN [C] (**arcs**) **1** An **arc** is a smoothly curving line or movement. ❑ *The helicopter made a slow arc, passing over the mound but not stopping.* **2** (*technical*) In geometry, an **arc** is a part of the line that forms the outside of a circle.

arch /aːtʃ/ NOUN, VERB
[NOUN] [C] (**arches**) **1** An **arch** is a structure that is curved at the top and is supported on either side by a pillar, post or wall. ❑ *When she passed under the arch leading out of the park, Mira whooped with delight.* **2** An **arch** is a curved line or movement. = arc ❑ *the arch of the fishing rods* **3** The **arch** of your foot is the curved section at the bottom in the middle. ❑ *'Good girl,' said Frank, winding the bandages around the arch of her foot.*
[VERB] [I, T] (**arches, arching, arched**) If you **arch** a part of your body such as your back or if it **arches**, you bend it so that it forms a curve. ❑ *Don't arch your back, keep your spine straight.*
→ See also **arched**

WORD PARTS
The prefix **arch-** sometimes appears in words to show that someone is the main or most important one: arch-enemy (NOUN) archbishop (NOUN)

◆ **ar·chae·ol·o·gy** /ˌaːki'ɒlədʒi/ also **archeology** NOUN [U] **Archaeology** is the study of the societies and peoples of the past by examining the remains of their buildings, tools, and other objects. ❑ *an archaeology professor at Florida State University*
◆ **ar·chaeo·logi·cal** /ˌaːkiə'lɒdʒɪkəl/ ADJ [archaeological + N] ❑ *one of the region's most important archaeological sites* ❑ *The earliest archaeological evidence for dingoes in Australia is 3500 years old.*
◆ **ar·chae·olo·gist** /ˌaːki'ɒlədʒɪst/ NOUN [C] (**archaeologists**) ❑ *The archaeologists found a house built around 300 BC, with a basement and attic.*

ar·cha·ic /aː'keɪɪk/ ADJ **Archaic** means extremely old or extremely old-fashioned. = antiquated ❑ *archaic laws that are very seldom used*

arched /aːtʃt/ ADJ **1** An **arched** roof, window or doorway is curved at the top. ❑ *From the television room an arched doorway leads into the hall.* **2** An **arched** bridge has arches as part of its structure. ❑ *She led them up some stairs and across a little arched stone bridge.*

◆ **ar·che·ol·o·gy** /ˌaːki'ɒlədʒi/ (*AmE*) → See **archaeology**

ar·che·typ·al /ˌaːkɪ'taɪpəl/ ADJ (*formal*) Someone or something that is **archetypal** has all the most important characteristics of a particular kind of person or thing and is a perfect example of it. ❑ *the archetypal American middle-class family living in the suburbs*

◆ **archi·tect** /'aːkɪtekt/ NOUN [C] (**architects**) **1** An **architect** is a person who designs buildings. **2** [oft architect 'of' N] The **architect of** an idea, event, or institution is the person who invented it or made it happen. ❑ *James Madison was the principal architect of the constitution.*

◆ **archi·tec·tur·al** /ˌaːkɪ'tektʃərəl/ ADJ **Architectural** means relating to the design and construction of buildings. ❑ *Tibet's architectural heritage* ❑ *the unique architectural style of the town*
archi·tec·tur·al·ly /ˌaːkɪ'tektʃərəli/ ADV ❑ *The old city centre is architecturally rich.*

◆ **archi·tec·ture** /'aːkɪtektʃə/ NOUN [U] **1** **Architecture** is the art of planning, designing, and constructing buildings. = design, planning ❑ *He studied classical architecture and design in Rome.* **2** The **architecture** of a building is the style in which it is designed and constructed. ❑ *modern architecture*

◆ **ar·chive** /'aːkaɪv/ NOUN, ADJ, VERB
[NOUN] [C] (**archives**) **Archives** are a collection of documents and records that contain historical information. You can also use **archives** to refer to the place where archives are stored. = collection, library, repository ❑ *the State Library's archives* ❑ *the archives of the Imperial War Museum* ❑ *The state now has an online archive of records, including birth, marriage, death, census and military information.*
[ADJ] [archive + N] **Archive** material is information that comes from archives. ❑ *archive material*
[VERB] [T] (**archives, archiving, archived**) If you **archive** material such as documents or data, you store it in an archive. ❑ *The system will archive the information so agencies can review it in detail.*

◆ **archi·vist** /'aːkɪvɪst/ NOUN [C] (**archivists**) An **archivist** is a person whose job is to collect, sort, and care for historical documents and records. = librarian ❑ *an archivist at the National Library of Medicine*

arc·tic /'aːktɪk/ NOUN, ADJ
[NOUN] [SING] **The Arctic** is the area of the world around the North Pole. It is extremely cold and there is very little light in winter and very little darkness in summer. ❑ *winter in the Arctic*
[ADJ] (*informal, emphasis*) If you describe a place or the weather as **arctic**, you are emphasizing that it is extremely cold. = freezing ❑ *The bathroom, with its spartan pre-war facilities, is positively arctic.*

are /ə, STRONG aː/ IRREG FORM **Are** is the plural and the second person singular of the present tense of the verb **be**. **Are** is often shortened to **-'re** after pronouns in spoken English.

◆ **area** ◆◆◆ /'eəriə/ NOUN [C, U] (**areas**) (*academic word*)
1 [C] An **area** is a particular part of a town, a country, a region, or the world. = region, district ❑ *the large number of community groups in the area* ❑ *The survey was carried out in both urban and rural areas.* ❑ *All the agricultural areas around this town are completely gone.* **2** [C] Your **area** is the part of a town, country, or region where you live. An organization's **area** is the part of a town, country, or region that it is responsible for. ❑ *Local authorities have been responsible for the running of schools in their areas.* **3** [C] A particular **area** is a piece of land or part of a building that is used for a particular activity. ❑ *a picnic area* **4** [C] An **area** is a particular place on a surface or object, for example, on your body. ❑ *You will notice that your baby has two soft areas on the top of his head.* **5** [C] You can use **area** to refer to a particular subject or topic, or to a particular part of a larger, more general situation or activity. = subject, topic, field ❑ *the politically sensitive area of social security* ❑ *Awards were presented to writers in every area of the arts.* **6** [C, U] The **area** of a surface such as a piece of land is the amount of flat space or ground that it covers, measured in square units. = size ❑ *The islands cover a total area of 400 square miles.* ❑ *The house was large in area, but it did not have many rooms.*

a

ADJ + **area**

a **rural** area
a **remote** area
an **urban** area
❑ *Many people left rural areas to work in the new mines.*

the **local** area
the **surrounding** area
❑ *The museum has a large collection of artefacts from the town and the surrounding area.*

a **small** area
a **large** area
❑ *The forest covers a large area, some 16 km by 8 km.*

area + OF + NOUN

an area of **science**
an area of **research**
❑ *Genetic modification is a very important area of research.*

an area of **interest**
an area of **concern**
an area of **disagreement**
❑ *The conference centred on three main areas of concern.*

an area of **expertise**
❑ *Professor McKone's area of expertise is organic chemistry.*

arena /ə'ri:nə/ NOUN [C] (**arenas**) **1** An **arena** is a place where sports, entertainments, and other public events take place. It has seats around it where people sit and watch. = stadium ❑ *the largest indoor sports arena in the world* **2** You can refer to a field of activity, especially one where there is a lot of conflict or action, as an **arena** of a particular kind. ❑ *He made it clear he had no intention of withdrawing from the political arena.*

ar·gu·ably /'ɑ:gjuəbli/ ADV You can use **arguably** when you are stating your opinion or belief, as a way of giving more authority to it. ❑ *They are arguably the most important band since The Rolling Stones.*

✪**ar·gue** ♦♦◇ /'ɑ:gju:/ VERB [RECIP, I, T] (**argues, arguing, argued**) **1** [RECIP] If one person **argues with** another, they speak angrily to each other about something that they disagree about. You can also say that two people **argue**. ❑ *The committee is concerned about players' behaviour, especially arguing with referees.* **2** [RECIP] If you **argue with** someone **about** something, you discuss it with them, with each of you giving your different opinions. ❑ *He was arguing with the king about the need to maintain the cavalry at full strength.* ❑ *They are arguing over foreign policy.* **3** [I] If you tell someone not to **argue with** you, you want them to do or believe what you say without protest or disagreement. ❑ *Don't argue with me.* **4** [T] If you **argue that** something is true, you state it and give the reasons why you think it is true. = claim ❑ *His lawyers are arguing that he is unfit to stand trial.* ❑ *Mawby and Gill argue that there are four areas in which victims' rights need strengthening.* ❑ *It could be argued that incentives should not be necessary.* **5** [I] If you **argue for** something, you say why you agree with it, in order to persuade people that it is right. If you **argue against** something, you say why you disagree with it, in order to persuade people that it is wrong. ❑ *The report argues against tax increases.*

✪**ar·gu·ment** ♦♦◇ /'ɑ:gjumənt/ NOUN [C, U] (**arguments**) **1** [C, U] An **argument** is a statement or set of statements that you use in order to try to convince people that your opinion about something is correct. = statement, case, reasoning ❑ *There's a strong argument for lowering the price.* ❑ *The doctors have set out their arguments against the proposals.* **2** [C, U] An **argument** is a discussion or debate in which a number of people put forward different or opposing opinions. = debate ❑ *The incident has triggered fresh arguments about the role of the extreme right in US politics.* **3** [C] An **argument** is a conversation in which people disagree with each other angrily or noisily. ❑ *Anny described how she got into an argument with one of the marchers.* **4** [U] If you accept something without

argument, you do not question it or disagree with it. = question ❑ *He complied without argument.*

argument NOUN
An **argument** is a statement that you use in order to try to convince people that your opinion about something is correct.
❑ *Which of these arguments is more persuasive?*

statement NOUN
A **statement** is something that you say or write which gives information in a formal or definitive way.
❑ *They called on the government to provide a written statement of maternity rights to every pregnant woman.*

case NOUN
The **case** for or against a plan or idea consists of the facts and reasons to support it or oppose it.
❑ *The case against war remains as strong as it ever was.*

reasoning NOUN
Reasoning is the process by which you reach a conclusion after thinking about all the facts.
❑ *It is important that you should be able to understand the reasoning behind the selection of any particular plan of action.*

✪**arid** /'ærɪd/ ADJ **Arid** land is so dry that very few plants can grow on it. = dry, barren; ≠ lush, fertile ❑ *new strains of crops that can withstand arid conditions* ❑ *the arid zones of the country*

✪**arise** ♦◇◇ /ə'raɪz/ VERB [I] (**arises, arising, arose, arisen**) **1** If a situation or problem **arises**, it begins to exist or people start to become aware of it. = occur ❑ *if a problem arises later in the pregnancy* ❑ *The birds also attack crops when the opportunity arises.* **2** If something **arises from** a particular situation, or **arises out of** it, it is created or caused by the situation. ❑ *This serenity arose in part from Rachel's religious beliefs.*

ar·is·toc·ra·cy /,ærɪ'stɒkrəsi/ NOUN [C] (**aristocracies**) The **aristocracy** is a class of people in some countries who have a high social rank and special titles. = nobility ❑ *a member of the aristocracy*

aris·to·crat /'ærɪstəkræt, ə'rɪst-/ NOUN [C] (**aristocrats**) An **aristocrat** is someone whose family has a high social rank, especially someone who has a title. ❑ *a wealthy southern aristocrat*

aris·to·crat·ic /,ærɪstə'krætɪk/ ADJ **Aristocratic** means belonging to or typical of the aristocracy. ❑ *a wealthy, aristocratic family*

✪**arith·me·tic** /ə'rɪθmɪtɪk/ NOUN [U] **1** **Arithmetic** is the part of mathematics that is concerned with the addition, subtraction, multiplication, and division of numbers. ❑ *teaching the basics of reading, writing and arithmetic* ❑ *an arithmetic test* **2** You can use **arithmetic** to refer to the process of doing a particular sum or calculation. ❑ *4,000 women put in ten rupees each, which if my arithmetic is right adds up to 40,000 rupees.* **3** If you refer to **the arithmetic** of a situation, you are concerned with those aspects of it that can be expressed in numbers, and how they affect the situation. ❑ *The arithmetic was discouraging. In less than two months, they had used up six months' worth of food.*

arm ♦♦♦ /ɑ:m/ NOUN, VERB
NOUN [C, PL] (**arms**) **1** [C] Your **arms** are the two long parts of your body that are attached to your shoulders and that have your hands at the end. ❑ *She stretched her arms out.* **2** [C] The **arm** of a chair is the part on which you rest your arm when you are sitting down. ❑ *Mack gripped the arms of the chair.* **3** [C] An **arm of** an object is a long thin part of it that sticks out from the main part. ❑ *the lever arm of the machine* **4** [C] An **arm of** land or water is a long thin area of it that is joined to a broader area. ❑ *a small area of woodland between two arms of a small stream* **5** [C] An **arm of** an organization is a section of it that operates in a particular country or that deals with a particular activity. = wing ❑ *The agency is the central research and development arm of the Department of Defence.* **6** [C] The **arm** of a piece

of clothing is the part of it that covers your arm. = sleeve ❑ *coats that were short in the arms* **7** [PL] (formal) **Arms** are weapons, especially bombs and guns. ❑ *Soldiers searched their house for illegal arms.*

PHRASES **arm in arm** If two people are walking **arm in arm**, they are walking together with their arms linked. ❑ *He walked from the court arm in arm with his wife.*

at arm's length If you hold something **at arm's length**, you hold it away from your body with your arm straight. ❑ *He struck a match, and held it at arm's length.*

keep someone at arm's length If you **keep** someone **at arm's length**, you avoid becoming too friendly or involved with them. ❑ *She had always kept the family at arm's length.*

with open arms (approval) If you welcome some action or change **with open arms**, you are very pleased about it. If you welcome a person **with open arms**, you are very pleased about their arrival. ❑ *They would no doubt welcome the action with open arms.*

twist someone's arm (informal) If you **twist** someone's **arm**, you persuade them to do something. ❑ *She had twisted his arm to get him to invite her.*

bear arms A person's right to **bear arms** is their right to own and use guns, as a means of defence. ❑ *a country where the right to bear arms is enshrined in the constitution*

take up arms If one group or country **takes up arms against** another, they prepare to attack and fight them. ❑ *They threatened to take up arms against the government if their demands were not met.*

up in arms If people are **up in arms about** something, they are very angry about it and are protesting strongly against it. ❑ *Patient advocates are up in arms over the possible closure of the psychiatric hospital.*

VERB [T] (arms, arming, armed) **1** If you **arm** someone **with** a weapon, you provide them with a weapon. ❑ *She'd been so terrified that she had armed herself with a loaded rifle.* **2** If you **arm** someone **with** something that will be useful in a particular situation, you provide them with it. ❑ *She thought that if she armed herself with all the knowledge she could gather she could handle anything.*
→ See also **armed**

armed ♦♦◇ /ɑːmd/ ADJ **1** Someone who is **armed** is carrying a weapon, usually a gun. ❑ *City police said the man was armed with a revolver.* ❑ *a barbed-wire fence patrolled by armed guards* **2** [armed + N] An **armed** attack or conflict involves people fighting with guns or carrying weapons. ❑ *They had been found guilty of armed robbery.*

✪ armed forces ♦◇◇ NOUN [PL] The **armed forces** of a country are its military forces, usually the army, navy, marines, and air force. = the military ❑ *Every member of the armed forces is a hero.* ❑ *He's a captain in the Russian armed forces.*

✪ army ♦♦♦ /ˈɑːmi/ NOUN [C] (armies) **1** An **army** is a large organized group of people who are armed and trained to fight on land in a war. Most armies are organized and controlled by governments. ❑ *Perkins joined the Army in 2000.* ❑ *The British and American armies invaded Sicily.* ❑ *He's an army officer.* **2** An **army of** people, animals, or things is a large number of them, especially when they are regarded as a force of some kind. ❑ *data collected by an army of volunteers*

arose /əˈrəʊz/ IRREG FORM **Arose** is the past tense of **arise**.

around ♦♦♦ /əˈraʊnd/ PREP, ADV

> **Around** is an adverb and a preposition. In British English, the word 'round' is often used instead. **Around** is often used with verbs of movement, such as 'walk' and 'drive', and also in phrasal verbs such as 'get around' and 'turn around'.

PREP **1** To be positioned **around** a place or object means to surround it or be on all sides of it. To move **around** a place means to go along its edge, back to your starting point. ❑ *She looked at the papers around her.* ❑ *Today she wore her hair down around her shoulders.* **2** If you move **around** a corner or obstacle, you move to the other side of it. If you look **around** a corner or obstacle, you look to see what is on the other side. ❑ *The photographer stopped*

clicking and hurried around the corner.* **3** If you move **around** a place, you travel through it, going to most of its parts. If you look **around** a place, you look at every part of it. ❑ *I've been walking around Moscow and the town is terribly quiet.* **4** If someone moves **around** a place, they move through various parts of that place without having any particular destination. ❑ *These days much of my time is spent weaving my way around cocktail parties.* **5** You use **around** to say that something happens in different parts of a place or area. ❑ *Police in South Africa say ten people have died in scattered violence around the country.* ❑ *Elephants were often to be found in swamp in eastern Kenya around the Tana River.* **6** The people **around** you are the people whom you come into contact with, especially your friends and relatives, and the people you work with. ❑ *We change our behaviour by observing the behaviour of those around us.* **7** If something such as a film, a discussion, or a plan is based **around** something, that thing is its main theme. ❑ *The novel is a political thriller loosely based around current political issues.* **8** When you are giving measurements, you can use **around** to talk about the distance along the edge of something round. ❑ *She was 5 foot 4 inches, 38 around the chest, 28 around the waist and 40 around the hips.* **9** If you hang **around** or sit **around** a place, you spend time there but you do not do anything very important. ❑ *He used to skip lessons and hang around the harbour with some other boys.* **10** If something will happen **around** a particular time, it will happen at approximately that time. ❑ *He expects the elections to be held around November.*

ADV **1** [N + around] **Around** means positioned on all sides of something. ❑ *a village with a rocky river, a ruined castle and hills all around* **2** [around after V] **Around** means in every part of something. ❑ *He backed away from the edge, looking all around at the flat horizon.* **3** [around after V] **Around** means in all directions. ❑ *My mornings are spent rushing around after him.* **4** **Around** means in different parts of a place or area. ❑ *What the hell do you think you're doing following me around?* **5** [around after V] If you turn **around**, you turn so that you are facing in the opposite direction. ❑ *I turned around and wrote the title on the blackboard.* **6** [around after V] If you go **around** to someone's house, you visit them. ❑ *She helped me unpack my things and then we went around to see the other girls.* **7** [around after V] You use **around** in expressions such as **sit around** and **hang around** when you are saying that someone is spending time in a place and not doing anything very important. ❑ *I'm just going to be hanging around twiddling my thumbs.* **8** [around after V] If you move things **around**, you move them so that they are in different places. ❑ *Furniture in the classroom should not be changed around without warning the blind child.* **9** [around after V] If a wheel or object turns around, it turns. ❑ *The boat started to spin around in the water.* **10** If someone or something is **around**, they exist or are present in a place. ❑ *You haven't seen my publisher anywhere around, have you?* **11** You use **around** in expressions such as **this time around** or **to come around** when you are describing something that has happened before or things that happen regularly. ❑ *Senator Bentsen has declined to get involved this time around.* **12** **Around** means approximately. = about ❑ *My salary was around $45,000 plus a car and expenses.*

PHRASE **around about** (spoken) **Around about** means approximately. ❑ *There is an outright separatist party but it only scored around about 10 per cent in the vote.*
✦ **the other way around** → see **way**

arouse /əˈraʊz/ VERB [T] (arouses, arousing, aroused) **1** If something **arouses** a particular reaction or attitude in people, it causes them to have that reaction or attitude. ❑ *His revolutionary work in linguistics has aroused intense scholarly interest.* **2** If something **arouses** a particular feeling or instinct that exists in someone, it causes them to experience that feeling or instinct strongly. ❑ *The smell of frying bacon aroused his hunger.* **3** If you **are aroused** by something, it makes you feel sexually excited. ❑ *Some men are aroused when their partner says erotic words to them.*

❂ar·range ◆◇◇ /əˈreɪndʒ/ VERB [T, I] (**arranges, arranging, arranged**) **1** [T] If you **arrange** an event or meeting, you make plans for it to happen. = organize, plan □ *She arranged an appointment for Friday afternoon at four-fifteen.* □ *It is important that meetings are arranged well in advance.* □ *The Russian leader threw the carefully arranged welcome into chaos.* **2** [I, T] If you **arrange** with someone **to** do something, you make plans with them to do it. □ *I've arranged to see him on Friday morning.* □ *It was arranged that the party would gather for lunch in Grant Park.* □ *The city had arranged for the National Guard to be brought in.* **3** [I, T] If you **arrange** something **for** someone, you make it possible for them to have it or to do it. □ *I will arrange for someone to take you around.* □ *The hotel manager will arrange for a babysitter.* □ *Mr Dambar had arranged a dinner for the three of them.* **4** [T] If you **arrange** things somewhere, you place them in a particular position, usually in order to make them look attractive or neat. □ *When she has a little spare time she enjoys arranging dried flowers.* **5** [T] If a piece of music **is arranged by** someone, it is changed or adapted so that it is suitable for particular instruments or voices, or for a particular performance. □ *The songs were arranged by another well-known bass player, Ron Carter.*

❂ar·range·ment ◆◇◇ /əˈreɪndʒmənt/ NOUN [C] (**arrangements**) **1** **Arrangements** are plans and preparations that you make so that something will happen or be possible. □ *The staff are working frantically on final arrangements for the summit.* □ *She telephoned Ellen, but made no arrangements to see her.* □ *I prefer to make my own travel arrangements.* **2** [also 'by' arrangement] An **arrangement** is an agreement that you make with someone to do something. = agreement □ *The caves can be visited only by prior arrangement.* □ *Her teacher made a special arrangement to discuss her progress once a month.* □ *Our policy is to try and come to an arrangement with the owner.* **3** An **arrangement** of things, for example, flowers or furniture, is a group of them displayed in a particular way. □ *The house was always decorated with imaginative flower arrangements.* **4** If someone makes an **arrangement** of a piece of music, they change it so that it is suitable for particular voices or instruments, or for a particular performance. □ *an arrangement of a well-known piece by Mozart*

ar·ray /əˈreɪ/ NOUN [C] (**arrays**) **1** An **array of** different things or people is a large number or wide range of them. □ *As the deadline approached she experienced a bewildering array of emotions.* **2** An **array** of objects is a collection of them that is displayed or arranged in a particular way. □ *We visited the local markets and saw wonderful arrays of fruit and vegetables.*

❂ar·rest ◆◆◇ /əˈrest/ VERB, NOUN
VERB [T] (**arrests, arresting, arrested**) **1** If the police **arrest** you, they take charge of you and take you to a police station, because they believe you may have committed a crime. = detain □ *Police arrested five young men in connection with one of the attacks.* □ *The police say seven people were arrested for minor offences.* **2** (formal) If something or someone **arrests** a process, they stop it from continuing. = stop, hinder, impede □ *The sufferer may have to make major changes in his or her life to arrest the disease.* □ *The law could arrest the development of good research if applied prematurely.*
NOUN [C, U] (**arrests**) An **arrest** is when the police take charge of someone and take them to a police station because they think the person may have committed a crime. □ *a substantial reward for information leading to the arrest of the bombers* □ *Police chased the fleeing terrorists and later made two arrests.* □ *Murder squad detectives approached the man and placed him under arrest.*

ar·ri·val ◆◇◇ /əˈraɪvəl/ NOUN [C, U, SING] (**arrivals**) **1** [C, U] When a person or vehicle arrives at a place, you can refer to their **arrival**. □ *the day after his arrival in Wichita* □ *He was dead on arrival at the nearby hospital.* **2** [C, U] When someone starts a new job, you can refer to their **arrival** in that job. □ *the power vacuum created by the arrival of a new president* **3** [SING] When something is brought to you or becomes available, you can refer to its **arrival**. □ *I was*
flicking idly through a newspaper while awaiting the arrival of orange juice and coffee. **4** [SING] When a particular time comes or a particular event happens, you can refer to its **arrival**. = coming □ *He celebrated the arrival of the New Year with a bout of drinking that nearly killed him.* **5** [C] You can refer to someone who has just arrived at a place as a new **arrival**. = newcomer □ *A high proportion of the new arrivals are skilled professionals.*

ar·rive ◆◆◇ /əˈraɪv/ VERB [I] (**arrives, arriving, arrived**) **1** When a person or vehicle **arrives** at a place, they come to it from somewhere else. □ *Fresh groups of guests arrived.* □ *a small group of commuters waiting for their train, which arrived on time* **2** When you **arrive** at a place, you come to it for the first time in order to stay, live, or work there. □ *in the old days before the European settlers arrived in the country* **3** When something such as a letter or meal **arrives**, it is brought or delivered to you. □ *Breakfast arrived while he was in the bathroom.* **4** When something such as a new product or invention **arrives**, it becomes available. = appear □ *Several long-awaited movies will finally arrive in the shops this month.* **5** When a particular moment or event **arrives**, it happens, especially after you have been waiting for it or expecting it. □ *The time has arrived when I need to give up smoking.* **6** When you **arrive at** something such as a decision, you decide something after thinking about it or discussing it. □ *if the jury cannot arrive at a unanimous decision*

WHICH WORD?

arrive or reach?

The verbs **arrive** and **reach** are both used to talk about someone coming to a place at the end of a journey.

You usually say that someone **arrives at** a place.

□ *We **arrived at** Victoria station.*

However, you say that someone **arrives in** a country or city.

□ *He **arrived in** France on Tuesday.*

Reach always takes a direct object. You do not say that someone ~~reaches at~~ a place or ~~reaches to~~ a place.

□ *It was dark by the time I **reached** their house.*

Reach can also be used to talk about something getting to a particular point or level. You do not say that something ~~reaches at~~ or ~~reaches to~~ a particular level.

□ *Worldwide, the number of robots is expected to **reach** 873,100 by the end of the decade.*

---

ar·ro·gant /ˈærəgənt/ ADJ (disapproval) Someone who is **arrogant** behaves in a proud, unpleasant way towards other people because they believe that they are more important than others. □ *He was so arrogant.* □ *That sounds arrogant, doesn't it?*

ar·ro·gance /ˈærəgəns/ NOUN [U] □ *At times the arrogance of those in power is quite blatant.*

ar·row /ˈærəʊ/ NOUN [C] (**arrows**) **1** An **arrow** is a long thin weapon that is sharp and pointed at one end and that often has feathers at the other end. An arrow is shot from a bow. □ *Warriors armed with bows and arrows and spears have invaded their villages.* **2** An **arrow** is a written or printed sign that consists of a straight line with another line bent at a sharp angle at one end. This is a printed arrow: →. The arrow points in a particular direction to indicate where something is. □ *A series of arrows points the way to the modest grave of Andrei Sakharov.*

❂art ◆◆◆ /ɑːt/ NOUN, ADJ
NOUN [U, C, PL] (**arts**) **1** [U] **Art** consists of paintings, sculpture, and other pictures or objects that are created for people to look at and admire or think deeply about. □ *the first exhibition of such art in the West* □ *contemporary and modern American art* □ *Whitechapel Art Gallery* **2** [U] **Art** is the activity or educational subject that consists of creating paintings, sculptures, and other pictures or objects for people to look at and admire or think deeply about. □ *a painter, content to be left alone with her all-absorbing art* □ *Savannah College of Art and Design* **3** [C, U] **The arts** are activities such as music, painting, literature, film, and dance, which people can take part in for enjoyment, or to create works that express certain meanings or ideas of beauty.

❑ *Catherine the Great was a patron of the arts and sciences.* ❑ *people working in the arts* ❑ *the art of cinema* **4** [PL] At a university or college, **arts** are subjects such as history, literature, or languages in contrast to scientific subjects. ❑ *arts and social science graduates* ❑ *the Faculty of Arts* **5** [C] If you describe an activity as an **art**, you mean that it requires skill and that people learn to do it by instinct or experience, rather than by learning facts or rules. ❑ *pioneers who transformed clinical medicine from an art to a science* ADJ [art + N] **Arts** and **art** is used to describe theatres or cinemas that show plays or films that are intended to make the audience think deeply about the content, and not simply to entertain them. ❑ *the Cambridge Arts Cinema* → See also state-of-the-art

✪ **ar·te·fact** /'ɑːtɪfækt/ (BrE) also **artifact** NOUN [C] (artefacts) An **artefact** is an ornament, tool, or other object that is made by a human being, especially one that is historically or culturally interesting. ❑ *They also repair broken religious artefacts.* ❑ *The museum holds more than 7000 artefacts collected from the Pandora.* ❑ *illegal traders in ancient artefacts*

✪ **ar·te·rial** /ɑːˈtɪəriəl/ ADJ **1** [arterial + N] **Arterial** means involving or relating to your arteries and the movement of blood through your body. ❑ *people with arterial disease* ❑ *damage in brain cells and arterial walls* **2** [arterial + N] An **arterial** road or railway is a main road or railway within a complex road or rail system.

✪ **ar·tery** /'ɑːtəri/ NOUN [C] (arteries) **1** **Arteries** are the tubes in your body that carry blood from your heart to the rest of your body. Compare **vein**. ❑ *patients suffering from blocked arteries* ❑ *a blood clot which obstructs a coronary artery* **2** You can refer to an important main route within a complex road, railway, or river system as an **artery**. ❑ *Connecticut Ave., one of the main arteries of Washington*

art·ful /'ɑːtfʊl/ ADJ **1** If you describe someone as **artful**, you mean that they are clever and skilful at achieving what they want, especially by deceiving people. = crafty ❑ *Some politicians have realized that there are more artful ways of subduing people than shooting or jailing them.* **2** [usu artful + N] (formal, approval) If you use **artful** to describe the way someone has done or arranged something, you approve of it because it is clever or elegant. ❑ *There is also an artful contrast of shapes.*

ar·thri·tis /ɑːˈθraɪtɪs/ NOUN [U] **Arthritis** is a medical condition in which the joints in someone's body are swollen and painful. ❑ *I have a touch of arthritis in the wrist.*

✪ **ar·ti·cle** ♦♦◇ /'ɑːtɪkəl/ NOUN
NOUN [C] (articles) **1** An **article** is a piece of writing that is published in a newspaper or magazine. = piece ❑ *a newspaper article* ❑ *According to an article in Newsweek the drug could have side effects.* ❑ *The magazine published an article on skin cancer.* **2** You can refer to objects as **articles** of some kind. ❑ *articles of clothing* ❑ *He had stripped the house of all articles of value.* **3** An **article of** a formal agreement or document is a section of it that deals with a particular point. ❑ *The country appears to be violating several articles of the convention.* **4** In grammar, an **article** is a kind of determiner. In English, 'a' and 'an' are called the **indefinite article**, and 'the' is called the **definite article**. PHRASE **the genuine article** (emphasis) If you describe something as **the genuine article**, you are emphasizing that it is genuine, and often that it is very good. ❑ *The vodka was the genuine article.*

ar·ticu·late ADJ, VERB
ADJ /ɑːˈtɪkjʊlət/ (approval) If you describe someone as **articulate**, you mean that they are able to express their thoughts and ideas easily and well. ❑ *She is an articulate young woman.*
VERB /ɑːˈtɪkjʊleɪt/ [T] (articulates, articulating, articulated) **1** (formal) When you **articulate** your ideas or feelings, you express them clearly in words. ❑ *The president has been accused of failing to articulate an overall vision in foreign affairs.* **2** If you **articulate** something, you say it very clearly, so that each word or syllable can be heard. ❑ *He articulated each syllable.*

✪ **ar·ti·fact** /'ɑːtɪfækt/ (AmE) → See artefact

✪ **ar·ti·fi·cial** /ˌɑːtɪˈfɪʃəl/ ADJ **1** **Artificial** objects, materials, or processes do not occur naturally and are created by human beings, often using science or technology. = synthetic, man-made ❑ *The city is dotted with small lakes, natural and artificial.* ❑ *a wholefood diet free from artificial additives, colours and flavours* **2** An **artificial** state or situation exists only because someone has created it, and therefore often seems unnatural or unnecessary. ❑ *Even in the artificial environment of an office, our body rhythms continue to affect us.*

✪ **ar·ti·fi·cial·ly** /ˌɑːtɪˈfɪʃəli/ ADV **1** artificially sweetened lemonade ❑ *drugs which artificially reduce heart rate* ❑ *China is trying to save the endangered species by releasing artificially inseminated giant pandas into the wild.* **2** state subsidies that have kept retail prices artificially low

ar·til·lery /ɑːˈtɪləri/ NOUN [U, SING] **1** [U] **Artillery** consists of large, powerful guns that are transported on wheels and used by an army. ❑ *Using tanks and heavy artillery, they seized the town.* **2** [SING] **The artillery** is the section of an army that is trained to use large, powerful guns. ❑ *From 1935 to 1937 he was in the artillery.*

✪ **art·ist** ♦♦◇ /'ɑːtɪst/ NOUN [C] (artists) **1** An **artist** is someone who draws or paints pictures or creates sculptures as a job or a hobby. = painter ❑ *the studio of a great artist* ❑ *Each poster is signed by the artist.* ❑ *I'm not a good artist.* **2** An **artist** is a person who creates novels, poems, films, or other things which can be considered as works of art. ❑ *His books are enormously easy to read, yet he is a serious artist.* **3** An **artist** is a performer such as a musician, actor, or dancer. ❑ *a popular artist who has sold millions of records*

ar·tis·tic /ɑːˈtɪstɪk/ ADJ **1** Someone who is **artistic** is good at drawing or painting, or arranging things in a beautiful way. ❑ *They encourage boys to be sensitive and artistic.* **2** **Artistic** means relating to art or artists. ❑ *the campaign for artistic freedom* **3** An **artistic** design or arrangement is beautiful. ❑ *an artistic arrangement of stone paving*
ar·tis·ti·cal·ly /ɑːˈtɪstɪkli/ ADV **1** artistically gifted children **2** artistically carved vessels

art·work /'ɑːtwɜːk/ NOUN [U, C] (artworks) **1** [U] **Artwork** is drawings and photographs that are prepared in order to be included in something such as a book or advertisement. ❑ *The artwork for the poster was done by my sister.* **2** [C, U] **Artworks** are paintings or sculptures of high quality. = work of art ❑ *The museum contains 6,000 contemporary and modern artworks.* ❑ *a magnificent collection of priceless artwork*

as ♦♦♦ /əz, STRONG æz/ CONJ, PREP
CONJ **1** If something happens **as** something else happens, it happens at the same time. ❑ *Another policeman has been injured as fighting continued this morning.* ❑ *All the jury's eyes were on him as he continued.* **2** You use **as** to say how something happens or is done, or to indicate that something happens or is done in the same way as something else. ❑ *I'll behave towards them as I would like to be treated.* ❑ *Today, as usual, he was wearing a three-piece suit.* **3** You use **as** to introduce short clauses that comment on the truth of what you are saying. ❑ *As you can see, we're still working.* **4** You can use **as** to mean 'because' when you are giving the reason for something. = since ❑ *Enjoy the first hour of the day. This is important as it sets the mood for the rest of the day.*
PREP **1** You use **as** when you are indicating what someone or something is or is thought to be, or what function they have. ❑ *He has worked as a diplomat in the US, Sudan and Saudi Arabia.* ❑ *The news apparently came as a complete surprise.* **2** If you do something **as** a child or **as** a teenager, for example, you do it when you are a child or a teenager. ❑ *She loved singing as a child and started vocal training at 12.* **3** You use **as** in expressions like **as a result** and **as a consequence** to indicate how two situations or events are related to each other. ❑ *As a result of the growing fears about home security, more people are arranging for someone to stay in their home when they're away.*
PHRASES **as...as** **1** You use the structure **as...as** when you are comparing things. ❑ *I never went through a final exam that was as difficult as that one.* ❑ *Being a mother isn't as bad as I thought at first!* **2** (emphasis) You use **as...as** to emphasize amounts of something. ❑ *She gets as many as eight thousand letters a month.*

as it were (*vagueness*) You say **as it were** in order to make what you are saying sound less definite. ❑ *I'd understood the words, but I didn't, as it were, understand the question.*

as it is or **as it turns out** or **as things stand** You use expressions such as **as it is**, **as it turns out**, and **as things stand** when you are making a contrast between a possible situation and what actually happened or is the case. ❑ *I want to work at home on a Tuesday but as it turns out sometimes it's a Wednesday or a Thursday.*

as for or **as to** You use **as for** and **as to** at the beginning of a sentence in order to introduce a slightly different subject that is still connected to the previous one. ❑ *I don't know why the guy yelled at me. And as for going back there, certainly I would never go back, for fear of receiving further abuse.*

as to You use **as to** to indicate what something refers to. ❑ *They should make decisions as to whether the student needs more help.*

as of If you say that something will happen **as of** a particular date or time, you mean that it will happen from that time on. ❑ *The border, effectively closed since 1981, will be opened as of January the 1st.*

as if or **as though** You use **as if** and **as though** when you are giving a possible explanation for something or saying that something appears to be the case when it is not. ❑ *Anne shrugged, as if she didn't know.*

✦ **as ever** → see **ever**; **as a matter of fact** → see **fact**; **as follows** → see **follow**; **as long as** → see **long**; **as opposed to** → see **opposed**; **as regards** → see **regard**; **as soon as** → see **soon**; **as well** → see **well**; **as well as** → see **well**; **as yet** → see **yet**

as·cer·tain /ˌæsəˈteɪn/ VERB [T] (**ascertains, ascertaining, ascertained**) (*formal*) If you **ascertain** the truth about something, you find out what it is, especially by making a deliberate effort to do so. = establish ❑ *Through doing this, the teacher will be able to ascertain the extent to which the child understands what he is reading.* ❑ *Once they had ascertained that he was not a spy, they agreed to release him.*

as·cribe /əˈskraɪb/ VERB [T] (**ascribes, ascribing, ascribed**) (*formal*) **1** If you **ascribe** an event or condition **to** a particular cause, you say or consider that it was caused by that thing. = attribute ❑ *An autopsy eventually ascribed the baby's death to sudden infant death syndrome.* **2** If you **ascribe** a quality **to** someone, you consider that they possess it. = attribute ❑ *We do not ascribe a superior wisdom to the government or the state.*

ash /æʃ/ NOUN [U, PL, C] (**ashes**) **1** [U; also ashes] **Ash** is the grey or black powdery substance that is left after something is burned. You can also refer to this substance as **ashes**. ❑ *A cloud of volcanic ash is spreading across wide areas of the Philippines.* ❑ *He brushed the cigarette ash from his sleeve.* **2** [PL] A dead person's **ashes** are their remains after their body has been cremated. ❑ *And she asks him to go back there after her death and scatter her ashes on the lake.* **3** [C, U] An **ash** is a tree that has smooth grey bark and loses its leaves in winter. ❑ *The rafters are made from ash.* **4** [U] **Ash** is the wood from this tree.

ashamed /əˈʃeɪmd/ ADJ **1** [V-LINK + ashamed] If someone is **ashamed**, they feel embarrassed or guilty because of something they do or they have done, or because of their appearance. ❑ *I felt incredibly ashamed of myself for getting so angry.* **2** [V-LINK + ashamed 'of' N] If you are **ashamed of** someone, you feel embarrassed to be connected with them, often because of their appearance or because you disapprove of something they have done. ❑ *I've never told this to anyone, but it's true, I was terribly ashamed of my mum.*

WHICH WORD?

ashamed or embarrassed?

If you are **ashamed**, you feel guilty because you have done something you believe is wrong. If you are **embarrassed**, you feel foolish, and you are worried about what other people will think of you, and you often because you have made a mistake.

❑ *She was deeply **ashamed** of what she had done.*

❑ *Girls can get **embarrassed** when they make mistakes in front of boys.*

---

ashore /əˈʃɔː/ ADV Someone or something that comes **ashore** comes from the sea onto the shore. ❑ *Oil has come ashore on a ten-mile stretch to the east of Anchorage.*

Asian ♦♦◇ /ˈeɪʒən/ ADJ, NOUN
ADJ Someone or something that is **Asian** comes from or is associated with Asia. British people use this term especially to refer to India, Pakistan, Sri Lanka and Bangladesh. Americans use this term especially to refer to China, Korea, Thailand, Japan or Vietnam. ❑ *Asian music*
NOUN [C] (**Asians**) An **Asian** is a person who comes from or is associated with a country or region in Asia. ❑ *Many of the shops were run by Asians.*

aside ♦◇◇ /əˈsaɪd/ ADV

In addition to the uses shown below, **aside** is used in phrasal verbs such as 'cast aside', 'stand aside', and 'step aside'.

ADV 1 [aside after v] If you move something **aside**, you move it to one side of you. ❑ *Sarah closed the book and laid it aside.* **2** [aside after v] If you take or draw someone **aside**, you take them a little way away from a group of people in order to talk to them in private. ❑ *Latoya grabbed him by the elbow and took him aside.* **3** [aside after v] If you move **aside**, you get out of someone's way. ❑ *She had been standing in the doorway, but now she stepped aside to let them pass.* **4** [aside after v] If you set something such as time, money or space **aside** for a particular purpose, you save it and do not use it for anything else. ❑ *Many parents are putting money aside for tuition fees.* **5** [aside after v] If you brush or sweep **aside** a feeling or suggestion, you reject it. ❑ *Talk to a friend who will really listen and not brush aside your feelings.* **6** You use **aside** to indicate that you have finished talking about something, or that you are leaving it out of your discussion, and that you are about to talk about something else. = apart ❑ *Leaving aside the tiny minority who are clinically depressed, most people who have bad moods also have very good moods.*
PHRASE aside from 1 You use **aside from** when you are making an exception to a general statement. ❑ *The room was empty aside from one man seated beside the fire.* **2** You use **aside from** to indicate that you are aware of one aspect of a situation, but that you are going to focus on another aspect. ❑ *Quite aside from her tiredness, Amanda seemed unnaturally abstracted.*

ask ♦♦♦ /ɑːsk, æsk/ VERB
VERB [I, T] (**asks, asking, asked**) **1** [I, T] If you **ask** someone something, you say something to them in the form of a question because you want to know the answer. ❑ *'How is Frank?' he asked.* ❑ *I asked him his name.* ❑ *She asked me if I'd enjoyed my dinner.* ❑ *Maybe we should adopt the policy of 'don't ask, don't tell'.* **2** [T] If you **ask** someone **to** do something, you tell them that you want them to do it. ❑ *We had to ask him to leave.* **3** [T] If you **ask to** do something, you tell someone that you want to do it. ❑ *I asked to see the Director.* **4** [I] If you **ask for** something, you say that you would like it. ❑ *I decided to go to the next house and ask for food.* **5** [I] If you **ask for** someone, you say that you would like to speak to them. ❑ *There's a man at the gate asking for you.* **6** [T] If you **ask** someone's permission, opinion, or forgiveness, you try to obtain it by making a request. ❑ *Please ask permission from whoever pays the phone bill before making your call.* **7** [T] If you **ask** someone **to** an event or place, you invite them to go there. ❑ *Couldn't you ask Juan to the party?* **8** [T] If someone **is asking** a particular price **for** something, they are selling it for that price. ❑ *Mr Pantelaras was asking $6,000 for his collection.*
PHRASES if you ask me (*emphasis*) You can say '**if you ask me**' to emphasize that you are stating your personal opinion. ❑ *He was nuts, if you ask me.*
be asking for trouble or **be asking for it** If you say that someone **is asking for trouble** or **is asking for it**, you mean that they are behaving in a way that makes it very likely that they will get into trouble. ❑ *To go ahead with the match after such clear advice had been asking for trouble.*
CONVENTION don't ask me (*feelings*) You reply '**don't ask me**' when you do not know the answer to a question,

usually when you are annoyed or surprised that you have been asked. ❑ *'She's got other things on her mind, wouldn't you think?' 'Don't ask me,' murmured Chris. 'I've never met her.'*

a·sleep /əˈsliːp/ ADJ
▪ [V-LINK + asleep] Someone who is **asleep** is sleeping. ❑ *My four-year-old daughter was asleep on the sofa.*
▪ PHRASE **fall asleep** ◼ When you **fall asleep**, you start sleeping. ❑ *Sam snuggled down in his pillow and fell asleep.* ◼ Someone who is **fast asleep** or **sound asleep** is sleeping deeply. ❑ *They were both fast asleep in their beds.*

✪ **as·pect** ♦♦◊ /ˈæspekt/ NOUN [c] (**aspects**) (*academic word*) ◼ An **aspect** of something is one of the parts of its character or nature. = angle, feature ❑ *Climate and weather affect every aspect of our lives.* ❑ *a framework covering different aspects of telecommunications and information technology* ❑ *He was interested in all aspects of the work here.* ◼ (*formal*) The **aspect** of a building or window is the direction in which it faces. ❑ *The house had a southwest aspect.*

WORD CONNECTIONS

aspect + OF + NOUN

an aspect **of life**
an aspect **of culture**
an aspect **of society**
an aspect **of nature**
❑ *Social media is influencing all aspects of society.*

ADJ + **aspect**

a **positive** aspect
a **negative** aspect
❑ *There are many positive aspects to these changes.*

an **important** aspect
a **key** aspect
❑ *A key aspect of the company's continued success is its excellent customer service.*

a **financial** aspect
a **technical** aspect
a **spiritual** aspect
❑ *Top performers put regular effort into ensuring they are good at the technical aspects of their jobs.*

as·pi·ra·tion /ˌæspɪˈreɪʃən/ NOUN [c, u] (**aspirations**) Someone's **aspirations** are their desire to achieve. ❑ *the needs and aspirations of our pupils* ❑ *He is unlikely to send in the army to quell nationalist aspirations.*

as·pire /əˈspaɪə/ VERB [i] (**aspires, aspiring, aspired**) If you **aspire to** something such as an important job, you have a strong desire to achieve it. ❑ *people who aspire to public office* ❑ *Rice aspired to go to college.*
→ See also **aspiring**

as·pi·rin /ˈæspɪrɪn/ NOUN [c] (**aspirins** or **aspirin**) Aspirin is a mild drug that reduces pain and fever.

as·pir·ing /əˈspaɪərɪŋ/ ADJ [aspiring + N] If you use **aspiring** to describe someone who is starting a particular career, you mean that they are trying to become successful in it. ❑ *Many aspiring young artists are advised to learn by copying the masters.*
→ See also **aspire**

as·sas·sin /əˈsæsɪn/ NOUN [c] (**assassins**) An **assassin** is a person who assassinates someone. ❑ *He saw the shooting and memorized the licence plate of the assassin's car.*

as·sas·si·nate /əˈsæsɪneɪt/ VERB [T] (**assassinates, assassinating, assassinated**) When someone important is **assassinated**, they are murdered as a political act. ❑ *Would the US be radically different today if Kennedy had not been assassinated?*
as·sas·si·na·tion /əˌsæsɪˈneɪʃən/ NOUN [c, u] (**assassinations**) ❑ *She would like an investigation into the assassination of her husband.* ❑ *He lives in constant fear of assassination.*

as·sault ♦◊◊ /əˈsɔːlt/ NOUN, ADJ, VERB
▪ NOUN [c, u] (**assaults**) ◼ [c] An **assault** by an army is a strong attack made on an area held by the enemy. = attack ❑ *The rebels are poised for a new assault on the*

government garrisons. ◼ [c, u] [oft assault 'on/upon' N] An **assault** on a person is a physical attack on them. ❑ *The attack is one of a series of savage sexual assaults on women in the university area.*
▪ ADJ [assault + N] **Assault** weapons such as rifles are intended for soldiers to use in battle rather than for purposes such as hunting.
▪ VERB [T] (**assaults, assaulting, assaulted**) To **assault** someone means to physically attack them. = attack ❑ *The gang assaulted him with iron bars.*

✪ **as·sem·ble** /əˈsembəl/ VERB [i, T] (**assembles, assembling, assembled**) (*academic word*) ◼ [i, T] When people **assemble** or when someone **assembles** them, they come together in a group, usually for a particular purpose such as a meeting. = gather, meet, congregate ❑ *There wasn't even a convenient place for students to assemble between classes.* ❑ *Thousands of people assembled in a stadium in Thokoza.* ❑ *He has assembled a team of experts.* ◼ [T] To **assemble** something means to collect it together or to fit the different parts of it together. ≠ disassemble, dismantle ❑ *Greenpeace managed to assemble a small flotilla of inflatable boats to waylay the ship at sea.* ❑ *He is assembling evidence concerning a murder.* ❑ *a firm which assembles components into a finished product*

✪ **as·sem·bly** ♦◊◊ /əˈsembli/ NOUN [c, u] (**assemblies**) ◼ [c] An **assembly** is a large group of people who meet regularly to make decisions or laws for a particular region or country. ❑ *the campaign for the first free election to the National Assembly* ◼ [c] An **assembly** is a group of people gathered together for a particular purpose. = gathering ❑ *He waited until complete quiet settled on the assembly.* ◼ [u] (*formal*) When you refer to rights of **assembly** or restrictions on **assembly**, you are referring to the legal right that people have to gather together. ❑ *The US Constitution guarantees free speech, freedom of assembly and equal protection.* ◼ [u] The **assembly** of a machine, device, or object is the process of fitting its different parts together. = construction, manufacture ❑ *For the rest of the day, he worked on the assembly of an explosive device.* ❑ *car assembly plants* ◼ [c, u] In a school, an **assembly** is a gathering of all the teachers and students for a particular purpose. ❑ *Recently named the nation's top girls' basketball player, she will be honoured this morning at a school assembly.*

as·sent /əˈsent/ NOUN, VERB
▪ NOUN [u] If someone gives their **assent to** something that has been suggested, they formally agree to it. = agreement, consent ❑ *He gave his assent to the proposed legislation.*
▪ VERB [i] (**assents, assenting, assented**) If you **assent to** something, you agree to it or agree with it. ❑ *I assented to the request of the American publishers to write this book.*

✪ **as·sert** /əˈsɜːt/ VERB [T] (**asserts, asserting, asserted**) ◼ (*formal*) If someone **asserts** a fact or belief, they state it firmly. = declare, state; ≠ deny ❑ *Mr Helm plans to assert that the bill violates the First Amendment.* ❑ *The defendants, who continue to assert their innocence, are expected to appeal.* ❑ *Altman asserted, 'We were making a political statement about western civilization and greed.'* ◼ If you **assert** your authority, you make it clear by your behaviour that you have authority. = establish ❑ *After the war, the army made an attempt to assert its authority in the south of the country.* ◼ If you **assert** your right or claim to something, you insist that you have the right to it. ❑ *The republics began asserting their right to govern themselves.* ◼ If you **assert yourself**, you speak and act in a forceful way, so that people take notice of you. ❑ *He's speaking up and asserting himself and doing things he enjoys.*
✪ **as·ser·tion** /əˈsɜːʃən/ NOUN [c, u] (**assertions**) ◼ [c, u] = statement, argument; ≠ denial ❑ *There is no concrete evidence to support assertions that the recession is truly over.* ❑ *Miedzian (1991) challenges the assertion that participation in organized sports teaches children the importance of teamwork.* ◼ [u] ❑ *The decision is seen as an assertion of his authority within the company.* ◼ [u] ❑ *These institutions have made the assertion of ethnic identity possible.*

as·ser·tive /əˈsɜːtɪv/ ADJ Someone who is **assertive** states their needs and opinions clearly, so that people take notice. ❑ *Women have become more assertive in the past decade.*

as·ser·tive·ness /əˈsɜːtɪvnəs/ NOUN [U] ❑ *Chantelle's assertiveness stirred up his deep-seated sense of inadequacy.*

✿**as·sess** ◆◇◇ /əˈses/ VERB [T] (**assesses, assessing, assessed**) (*academic word*) **1** When you **assess** a person, thing, or situation, you consider them in order to make a judgment about them. = evaluate, judge, test ❑ *The test was to assess aptitude rather than academic achievement.* ❑ *Our correspondent has been assessing the impact of the sanctions.* ❑ *It would be a matter of assessing whether she was well enough to travel.* **2** When you **assess** the amount of money that something is worth or should be paid, you calculate or estimate it. ❑ *Ask them to send you information on how to assess the value of your belongings.*

✿**as·sess·ment** ◆◇◇ /əˈsesmənt/ NOUN [C, U] (**assessments**) **1** An **assessment** is a consideration of someone or something and a judgment about them. = evaluation, test, appraisal ❑ *There is little assessment of the damage to the natural environment.* ❑ *Everything from course learning materials to final assessment is completed via the Web.* ❑ *He was remanded to a mental hospital for assessment by doctors.* **2** An **assessment** of the amount of money that something is worth or that should be paid is a calculation or estimate of the amount. = appraisal ❑ *Tax assessment is all about comparing values of similar properties.*

WORD CONNECTIONS
VERB + **assessment**
undergo an assessment **conduct** an assessment **complete** an assessment ❑ *The department conducted an environmental assessment before approving the genetically engineered corn for planting.*
ADJ + **assessment**
an **objective** assessment an **accurate** assessment a **detailed** assessment ❑ *The company needs to complete a detailed assessment of its business strategy.*
a **frank** assessment a **blunt** assessment a **gloomy** assessment ❑ *The department's survey of households offered an even gloomier assessment of the job market.*
an **initial** assessment a **preliminary** assessment ❑ *After an initial assessment, you may need to be admitted to hospital to receive more in-depth testing.*
a **psychiatric** assessment a **psychological** assessment an **environmental** assessment ❑ *A diagnosis will be made after a complete psychiatric assessment.*

✿**as·set** ◆◆◇ /ˈæset/ NOUN [C, PL] (**assets**) **1** [C] Something or someone that is an **asset** is considered useful or helps a person or organization to be successful. ❑ *Our creativity in the field of technology is our greatest asset.* ❑ *Her leadership qualities were the greatest asset of the Conservative Party.* ❑ *His Republican credentials made him an asset.* **2** [PL] (*business*) The **assets** of a company or a person are all the things that they own. = possessions, property, capital; ≠ liability ❑ *By the end of 1989 the group had assets of $3.5 billion.* ❑ *Some tried to sell assets to pay the debts back.*

✿**as·sign** /əˈsaɪn/ VERB [T] (**assigns, assigning, assigned**) (*academic word*) **1** If you **assign** a piece of work **to** someone, you give them the work to do. = allot, allocate ❑ *When I taught, I would assign a topic to children that they would write about.* ❑ *The task is sometimes jointly assigned to accounting and engineering departments.* ❑ *Workers felt forced to work late because managers assigned them more work than they could complete in a regular shift.* ❑ *When teachers assign homework, students usually feel an obligation to do it.* ❑ *Later*

in the year, she'll assign them research papers. **2** If you **assign** something **to** someone, you say that it is for their use. = allocate ❑ *The selling broker is then required to assign a portion of the commission to the buyer broker.* **3** If someone **is assigned to** a particular place, group, or person, they are sent there, usually in order to work at that place or for that person. ❑ *I was assigned to Troop A of the 10th Cavalry.* ❑ *Did you choose Russia or were you simply assigned there?* **4** If you **assign** a particular function or value **to** someone or something, you say they have it. ❑ *Under the system, each business must assign a value to each job.* ❑ *Assign the letters of the alphabet their numerical values – A equals 1, B equals 2, etc.*

✿**as·sign·ment** ◆◇◇ /əˈsaɪnmənt/ NOUN [C] (**assignments**) (*academic word*) An **assignment** is a task or piece of work that you are given to do, especially as part of your job or studies. = coursework, test, task, job ❑ *The assessment for the course involves written assignments and practical tests.* ❑ *His first overseas assignment was in Ghana.*

✿**as·sist** ◆◇◇ /əˈsɪst/ VERB [T, I] (**assists, assisting, assisted**) (*academic word*) **1** [T] If you **assist** someone, you help them to do a job or task by doing part of the work for them. = help, aid; ≠ hinder ❑ *The family decided to assist me with my chores.* ❑ *Dr Amid was assisted by a young Asian nurse.* **2** [I, T] If you **assist** someone, you give them information, advice, or money. = help, aid, back; ≠ hinder ❑ *The public is urgently requested to assist police in tracing this man.* ❑ *International organizations intensified their activities to locate victims and assist with relief efforts.* ❑ *Foreign Office officials assisted with transport and finance problems.* **3** [I, T] If something **assists in** doing a task, it makes the task easier to do. ❑ *a chemical that assists in the manufacture of proteins* ❑ *Our sales representatives can assist you in selecting suitable investments.* ❑ *an increasing number of techniques to assist people in creating successful strategies* ❑ *Salvage operations have been greatly assisted by the good weather conditions.*

✿**as·sis·tance** ◆◇◇ /əˈsɪstəns/ NOUN
NOUN [U] **1** [oft with POSS] If you give someone **assistance**, you help them do a job or task by doing part of the work for them. = help, aid; ≠ hindrance ❑ *Since 1976 he has been operating the shop with the assistance of volunteers.* ❑ *Employees are being offered assistance in finding new jobs.* **2** If you give someone **assistance**, you give them information or advice. = help, aid ❑ *Any assistance you could give the police will be greatly appreciated.* **3** [oft SUPP + assistance] If someone gives a person or country **assistance**, they help them by giving them money. = help, aid ❑ *a viable programme of economic assistance* **4** If something is done **with the assistance of** a particular thing, that thing is helpful or necessary for doing it. = help, aid ❑ *The translations were carried out with the assistance of a medical dictionary.*
PHRASES **be of assistance** Someone or something that **is of assistance** to you is helpful or useful to you. ❑ *Can I be of any assistance?*
come to someone's assistance If you **come to** someone's **assistance**, you take action to help them. ❑ *They are appealing to the world community to come to Jordan's assistance.*

WORD CONNECTIONS
VERB + **assistance**
provide assistance **offer** assistance **seek** assistance **receive** assistance ❑ *If you experience the following symptoms you should seek immediate medical assistance.*
ADJ + **assistance**
humanitarian assistance **financial** assistance **technical** assistance **medical** assistance ❑ *Japan will provide humanitarian assistance to address problems caused by the drought in the region.*

assistance + WITH + NOUN

assistance with a **matter**
assistance with an **investigation**
assistance with a **case**
❑ *Thank you for your assistance with this matter.*

❖**as·sis·tant** ◆◇◇ /əˈsɪstənt/ ADJ, NOUN (*academic word*)
ADJ [assistant + N] **Assistant** is used in front of titles or jobs to indicate a slightly lower rank. For example, an assistant director is one rank lower than a director in an organization. = deputy, junior ❑ *the assistant secretary of defence* ❑ *a young assistant professor at Harvard* NOUN [C] (**assistants**) **1** Someone's **assistant** is a person who helps them in their work. = aide ❑ *Kalan called his assistant, Hashim, to take over while he went out.* ❑ *She had been accompanied to the meeting by an assistant.* **2** An **assistant** is a person who works in a shop selling things to customers. = sales person ❑ *The assistant took the book and checked the price on the back cover.* ❑ *She got a job as a sales assistant selling handbags.*

as·so·ci·ate ◆◇◇ VERB, NOUN, ADJ
VERB /əˈsəʊsieɪt/ [T, I] (**associates, associating, associated**) **1** [T] If you **associate** someone or something **with** another thing, the two are connected in your mind. ❑ *Through science we've got the idea of associating progress with the future.* **2** [T] If you **are associated with** a particular organization, cause or point of view, or if you **associate** yourself with it, you support it publicly. = affiliate ❑ *I haven't been associated with the project over the last year.* **3** [I] If you say that someone **is associating with** another person or group of people, you mean they are spending a lot of time in the company of people you do not approve of. ❑ *What would they think if they knew that they were associating with a murderer?*
NOUN /əˈsəʊsiət/ [C] (**associates**) Your **associates** are the people you are closely connected with, especially at work. = colleague ❑ *the restaurant owner's business associates*
ADJ /əˈsəʊsiət/ [associate + N] **Associate** is used before a rank or title to indicate a slightly different or lower rank or title. ❑ *Mr Lin is associate director of the Institute.*

❖**as·so·ci·at·ed** ◆◇◇ /əˈsəʊsieɪtɪd/ ADJ **1** If one thing is **associated with** another, the two things are connected with each other. = linked, connected, related; ≠ unrelated ❑ *These symptoms are particularly associated with migraine headaches.* ❑ *Marie Curie's name is still associated with science funding.* **2** [associated + N] **Associated** is used in the name of a company that is made up of a number of smaller companies that have joined together. ❑ *the Associated Press*

❖**as·so·cia·tion** ◆◆◇ /əˌsəʊsiˈeɪʃən/ NOUN
NOUN [C] (**associations**) **1** An **association** is an official group of people who have the same job, aim, or interest. = organization ❑ *the National Basketball Association* ❑ *the British Olympic Association* ❑ *Research associations are often linked to a particular industry.* **2** Your **association with** a person or a thing such as an organization is the connection that you have with them. = affiliation ❑ *the company's six-year association with retailer J.C. Penney Co* **3** If something has particular **associations** for you, it is connected in your mind with a particular memory, idea, or feeling. ❑ *He has a shelf full of things, each of which has associations for him.*
PHRASE **in association with** If you do something **in association with** someone else, you do it together. ❑ *The changes I instigated in association with the board 18 months ago were because I love this company.*

as·sort·ed /əˈsɔːtɪd/ ADJ A group of **assorted** things is a group of similar things that are of different sizes or colours or have different qualities. = various ❑ *It should be a great week, with overnight stops in assorted hotels in the Adirondacks.*

as·sort·ment /əˈsɔːtmənt/ NOUN [C] (**assortments**) An **assortment** is a group of similar things that are of different sizes or colours or have different qualities. ❑ *an assortment of cheese*

❖**as·sume** ◆◆◇ /əˈsjuːm, AmE əˈsuːm/ VERB [T] (**assumes, assuming, assumed**) (*academic word*) **1** If you **assume that** something is true, you imagine it is true, sometimes wrongly. = presume, expect; ≠ doubt ❑ *It is a misconception to assume that the two continents are similar.* ❑ *If mistakes occurred, they were assumed to be the fault of the commander on the spot.* **2** If someone **assumes** power or responsibility, they take power or responsibility. ❑ *Mr Cross will assume the role of CEO with a team of four directors.* **3** If you **assume** a particular expression or way of behaving, you start to look or behave in this way. = adopt ❑ *He managed to assume an air of calm.*

as·sum·ing /əˈsjuːmɪŋ, AmE -ˈsuːm-/ CONJ You use **assuming** or **assuming that** when you are considering a possible situation or event, so that you can think about the consequences. ❑ *'Assuming you're right,' he said, 'there's not much I can do about it, is there?'*

❖**as·sump·tion** ◆◇◇ /əˈsʌmpʃən/ NOUN [C] (**assumptions**) If you make an **assumption that** something is true or will happen, you accept that it is true or will happen, often without any real proof. = presumption, premise, supposition ❑ *You would be making an assumption that's not based on any fact that you could report.* ❑ *Dr Subroto questioned the scientific assumption on which the global warming theory is based.* ❑ *Economists are working on the assumption of an interest rate cut.*

❖**as·sur·ance** ◆◇◇ /əˈʃʊərəns/ NOUN [C, U] (**assurances**) **1** [C, U] If you give someone an **assurance that** something is true or will happen, you say that it is definitely true or will definitely happen, in order to make them feel less worried. = guarantee ❑ *He would like an assurance that other forces will not move into the territory that his forces vacate.* ❑ *He will have been pleased by Marshal Yazov's assurance of the armed forces' loyalty.* **2** [U] If you do something **with assurance**, you do it with a feeling of confidence and certainty. ❑ *Masur led the orchestra with assurance.*

❖**as·sure** /əˈʃʊə/ VERB
VERB [T] (**assures, assuring, assured**) (*academic word*) **1** If you **assure** someone **that** something is true or will happen, you tell them that it is definitely true or will definitely happen, often in order to make them less worried. = reassure ❑ *He hastened to assure me that there was nothing traumatic to report.* ❑ *Assure yourself that the assertion of your paper is both clear and worth supporting.* ❑ *Government officials recently assured Hindus of protection.* ❑ *'Are you sure the raft is safe?' she asked anxiously. 'Couldn't be safer,' Max assured her confidently.* **2** To **assure** someone **of** something means to make certain that they will get it. = guarantee ❑ *His performance yesterday morning assured him of a record eighth medal.* ❑ *Henry VII's Welsh ancestry assured him of the warmest support in Wales.* ❑ *a retraining programme to assure laid-off employees new work* ❑ *A level of self-containment renders us immune to criticism or disapproval, thus assuring our serenity of mind.*
PHRASE **I can assure you** or **let me assure you** (*emphasis*) You use phrases such as **I can assure you** or **let me assure you** to emphasize the truth of what you are saying. ❑ *I can assure you that the animals are well cared for.*
→ See also **assured**

WHICH WORD?

assure, ensure, or insure?

If you **assure** someone that something is true or will happen, you tell them that it is definitely true or will definitely happen, often in order to make them less worried.
❑ *I can **assure** you that you will be perfectly safe.*
To **ensure** that something happens means to make certain that it happens.
❑ ***Ensure** that all equipment is cleaned and stored away safely at the end of each day.*
If you **insure** your property, you pay money to a company so that if the property is lost, stolen, or damaged, the company will pay you a sum of money.
❑ ***Insure** your baggage before you leave home.*

as·sured ◆◇◇ /əˈʃʊəd/ ADJ
ADJ **1** Someone who is **assured** is very confident and relaxed. ❑ *He was infinitely more assured than in his more*

recent concert appearances. **2** [V-LINK + assured] If something is **assured**, it is certain to happen. ▢ *Our victory is assured; nothing can stop us.* **3** [V-LINK + assured 'of' N] If you are **assured of** something, you are certain to get it or achieve it. ▢ *Laura Davies is assured of a place in the Olympic team.*

PHRASE **rest assured** (*emphasis*) If you say that someone **can rest assured that** something is the case, you mean that it is definitely the case, so they do not need to worry about it. ▢ *Their parents can rest assured that their children's safety will be of paramount importance.*

✪**as·ter·isk** /ˈæstərɪsk/ NOUN [c] (**asterisks**) An **asterisk** is the sign *. It is used especially to indicate that there is further information about something in another part of the text. ▢ *An asterisk indicates a title that is the same in both English and French editions.* ▢ *In Table 2, those crops marked with an asterisk are sown or planted out in the summer.*

asth·ma /ˈæsmə, AmE ˈæz-/ NOUN [u] **Asthma** is a lung condition that causes difficulty in breathing.

aston·ish /əˈstɒnɪʃ/ VERB [T] (**astonishes, astonishing, astonished**) If something or someone **astonishes** you, they surprise you very much. = amaze ▢ *My news will astonish you.*

aston·ish·ing /əˈstɒnɪʃɪŋ/ ADJ Something that is **astonishing** is very surprising. = amazing ▢ *an astonishing display of physical strength*

aston·ish·ing·ly /əˈstɒnɪʃɪŋli/ ADV ▢ *Andrea was an astonishingly beautiful young woman.*

aston·ish·ment /əˈstɒnɪʃmənt/ NOUN [u] **Astonishment** is a feeling of great surprise. = amazement ▢ *I spotted a shooting star which, to my astonishment, was bright green in colour.*

astound·ing /əˈstaʊndɪŋ/ ADJ If something is **astounding**, you are shocked or amazed that it could exist or happen. = amazing, astonishing ▢ *The results are quite astounding.*

astray /əˈstreɪ/ ADV
PHRASES **lead someone astray** **1** If you **are led astray** by someone or something, you behave badly or foolishly because of them. ▢ *The judge thought he'd been led astray by older children.* **2** If someone or something **leads** you **astray**, they make you believe something that is not true, causing you to make a wrong decision. = mislead ▢ *The testimony would inflame the jurors and lead them astray from the facts of the case.*

go astray If something **goes astray**, it gets lost while it is being taken or sent somewhere. ▢ *Many items of mail being sent to her have gone astray.*

as·tro·naut /ˈæstrənɔːt/ NOUN [c] (**astronauts**) An **astronaut** is a person who is trained for travelling in a spacecraft.

WORD PARTS

The prefix **astro-** often appears in words for things that relate to stars or outer space:
astronaut (NOUN)
astronomy (NOUN)
astrophysics (NOUN)

✪**as·trono·mer** /əˈstrɒnəmə/ NOUN [c] (**astronomers**) An **astronomer** is a scientist who studies the stars, planets, and other natural objects in space. ▢ *William Herschel, the eminent astronomer who discovered the planet Uranus*

✪**as·tro·nomi·cal** /ˌæstrəˈnɒmɪkəl/ ADJ **1** (*emphasis*) If you describe an amount, especially the cost of something as **astronomical**, you are emphasizing that it is very large. ▢ *Houses in the village are going for astronomical prices.* **2** **Astronomical** means relating to astronomy. ▢ *the American Astronomical Society* ▢ *an alternative method of astronomical observation*

✪**as·trono·my** /əˈstrɒnəmi/ NOUN [u] **Astronomy** is the scientific study of the stars, planets, and other natural objects in space. ▢ *a 10-day astronomy mission*

as·tute /əˈstjuːt, AmE əˈstuːt/ ADJ If you describe someone as **astute**, you think they show an understanding of behaviour and situations, and are skilful at using this

knowledge to their own advantage. = shrewd ▢ *She was politically astute.*

asy·lum /əˈsaɪləm/ NOUN [u, c] (**asylums**) **1** [u] If a government gives a person from another country **asylum**, it allows them to stay, usually because they are unable to return home safely for political reasons. = sanctuary ▢ *He applied for asylum in 1987 after fleeing the police back home.* **2** [c] (*old-fashioned*) An **asylum** is a psychiatric hospital.

asy·lum seek·er NOUN [c] (**asylum seekers**) An **asylum seeker** is a person who is trying to get asylum in a foreign country. ▢ *Fewer than 7% of asylum seekers are accepted as political refugees.*

at ◆◆◆ /ət, STRONG æt/ PREP

> In addition to the uses shown below, **at** is used in phrasal verbs such as 'get at' and 'play at'.

1 You use **at** to indicate the place or event where something happens or is situated. ▢ *He will be at the airport to meet her.* ▢ *I didn't like being alone at home.* ▢ *They agreed to meet at a restaurant in Soho.* **2** If you are **at** something such as a table, a door or someone's side, you are next to it or them. ▢ *At his side was a beautiful young woman.* **3** When you are describing where someone or something is, you can say that they are **at** a certain distance. You can also say that one thing is **at** an angle in relation to another thing. ▢ *The two journalists followed at a discreet distance.* **4** If something happens **at** a particular time, that is the time when it happens or begins to happen. ▢ *The funeral will be carried out this afternoon at 3:00.* **5** If you do something **at** a particular age, you do it when you are that age. ▢ *Zachary started playing violin at age 4.* **6** If someone is **at** a particular school or college, they go there regularly to study. ▢ *Their daughter is a sophomore at Yale.* **7** You use **at** to express a rate, frequency, level or price. ▢ *I drove back down the highway at normal speed.* ▢ *Check the oil at regular intervals and have the car serviced regularly.* **8** [at + AMOUNT] You use **at** before a number or amount to indicate a measurement. ▢ *as unemployment stays pegged at three million* **9** If you look **at** someone or something, you look towards them. If you direct an object or a comment **at** someone, you direct it towards them. ▢ *He looked at Michael and laughed.* **10** [V + at + N] You can use **at** after verbs such as 'smile' or 'wave' and some nouns referring to people to indicate that you have put on an expression or made a gesture that someone is meant to see or understand. ▢ *She opened the door and stood there, frowning at me.* **11** [V + at + N] If you point or gesture **at** something, you move your arm or head in its direction so that it will be noticed by someone you are with. ▢ *He pointed at the empty bottle and the waitress quickly replaced it.* **12** If you are working **at** something, you are dealing with it. If you are aiming **at** something, you are trying to achieve it. ▢ *She has worked hard at her marriage.* **13** [at + N with POSS] If something is done **at** someone's invitation or request, it is done as a result of it. ▢ *She left the light on in the bathroom at his request.* **14** [V-LINK + at + N] You use **at** to say that someone or something is in a particular state or condition. ▢ *I am afraid we are not at liberty to disclose that information.* **15** You use **at** before a possessive pronoun and a superlative adjective to say that someone or something has more of a particular quality than at any other time. ▢ *When I'm on the soccer field, I'm at my happiest.* **16** You use **at** to say how something is being done. ▢ *Three people were killed by shots fired at random from a minibus.* **17** [V + at + N] You use **at** to show that someone is doing something repeatedly. ▢ *She lowered the handkerchief which she had kept dabbing at her eyes.* **18** You use **at** to indicate an activity or task when saying how well someone does it. ▢ *I'm good at my work.* **19** You use **at** to indicate what someone is reacting to. ▢ *Elena was annoyed at having had to wait so long for him.*
✦ **at all** → see all

ate /et, eɪt/ IRREG FORM **Ate** is the past tense of **eat**.

athe·ist /ˈeɪθiɪst/ NOUN [c] (**atheists**) An **atheist** is a person who believes that there is no God.

a

ath·lete ♦◇◇ /'æθliːt/ NOUN [C] (athletes) **1** An **athlete** is a person who does any kind of physical sports, exercise or games, especially in competitions. ◻ *Mark Spitz was a great athlete.* **2** You can refer to someone who is fit and athletic as an **athlete.** ◻ *I was no athlete.*

ath·let·ic /æθ'letɪk/ ADJ **1** [athletic + N] **Athletic** means relating to athletes and athletics. ◻ *They have been given college scholarships purely on athletic ability.* **2** An **athletic** person is fit, and able to perform energetic movements easily. ◻ *Xandra is an athletic 36-year-old with a 21-year-old's body.*

ath·let·ics /æθ'letɪks/ (mainly BrE; in AmE, use **track and field**) NOUN [U] **Athletics** refers to track and field sports such as running, the high jump and the javelin.

✪ **at·mos·phere** ♦◇◇ /'ætməsfɪə/ NOUN [C, SING, U] (atmospheres) **1** [C] A planet's **atmosphere** is the layer of air or other gases around it. ◻ *The shuttle Columbia will re-enter Earth's atmosphere tomorrow morning.* ◻ *There are dangerous levels of pollution in the Earth's atmosphere.* ◻ *The Partial Test-Ban Treaty bans nuclear testing in the atmosphere.* **2** [C] The **atmosphere** of a place is the air that you breathe there. ◻ *These gases pollute the atmosphere of towns and cities.* **3** [SING] The **atmosphere** of a place is the general impression that you get of it. ◻ *There's still an atmosphere of great hostility and tension in the city.* **4** [U] If a place or an event has **atmosphere**, it is interesting. = ambience ◻ *The old harbour is still full of atmosphere and well worth visiting.*

✪ **at·mos·pher·ic** /ˌætməs'ferɪk/ ADJ **1 Atmospheric** is used to describe something that relates to the Earth's atmosphere. ◻ *atmospheric gases* ◻ *atmospheric pressure* **2** If you describe a place or a piece of music as **atmospheric**, you like it because it has a particular quality that is interesting or exciting and makes you feel a particular emotion. ◻ *One of the most atmospheric corners of Prague is the old Jewish ghetto.*

✪ **atom** /'ætəm/ NOUN [C] (atoms) An **atom** is the smallest amount of a substance that can take part in a chemical reaction. ◻ *the news that Einstein's former colleagues Otto Hahn and Fritz Strassmann had split the atom* ◻ *A methane molecule is composed of one carbon atom attached to four hydrogen atoms.*

✪ **atom·ic** /ə'tɒmɪk/ ADJ **1 Atomic** means relating to power that is produced from the energy released by splitting atoms. = nuclear ◻ *atomic energy* ◻ *fears about the spread of atomic weapons* **2** [atomic + N] **Atomic** means relating to the atoms of substances. = molecular ◻ *the atomic number of an element* ◻ *the complex structure of atomic nuclei* ◻ *a device used to study the reactions of atomic particles*

atro·cious /ə'trəʊʃəs/ ADJ **1** (emphasis) If you describe something as **atrocious**, you are emphasizing that its quality is very bad. = appalling, abominable ◻ *I remain to this day fluent in Hebrew, while my Arabic is atrocious.* **2** If you describe someone's behaviour or their actions as **atrocious**, you mean that it is unacceptable because it is extremely violent or cruel. ◻ *The judge said he had committed atrocious crimes against women.*

atroc·ity /ə'trɒsɪti/ NOUN [C, U] (atrocities) An **atrocity** is a very cruel, shocking action. ◻ *The killing was cold-blooded, and those who committed this atrocity should be tried and punished.*

✪ **at·tach** ♦◇◇ /ə'tætʃ/ VERB [T] (attaches, attaching, attached) (academic word) **1** If you **attach** something **to** an object, you join it or fasten it to the object. = connect; ≠ detach ◻ *We attach labels to things before we file them away.* ◻ *The gadget can be attached to any vertical surface.* ◻ *For further information, please contact us on the attached form.* **2** In computing, if you **attach** a file **to** a message that you send to someone, you send it with the message but separate from it. ◻ *It is possible to attach executable program files to e-mail.*
→ See also **attached**
✦ **no strings attached** → see **string**

at·tached /ə'tætʃt/ ADJ **1** [V-LINK + attached 'to' N] If you are **attached to** someone or something, you like them very much. ◻ *She is very attached to her family and friends.* **2** [V-LINK + attached 'to' N] If someone is **attached to** an

organization or group of people, they are working with them, often only for a short time. ◻ *Ford was attached to the 101st Airborne Division.*

✪ **at·tach·ment** /ə'tætʃmənt/ NOUN [C, U] (attachments) **1** [C, U] If you have an **attachment to** someone or something, you are fond of them or loyal to them. ◻ *As a teenager she formed a strong attachment to one of her teachers.* **2** [C] An **attachment** is a device that can be fixed onto a machine in order to enable it to do different jobs. = fixture, fitting, part ◻ *Some models come with attachments for dusting.* **3** [C] In computing, an **attachment** is a file which is attached separately to a message that you send to someone. = appendix, supplement ◻ *When you send an e-mail you can also send a file as an attachment and that file can be a graphic, a program, a sound or whatever.* ◻ *Justice Fitzgerald included a 120-page discussion paper as an attachment to the annual report.*

at·tack ♦♦♦ /ə'tæk/ VERB, NOUN
VERB [I, T] (attacks, attacking, attacked) **1** [I, T] To **attack** a person or place means to try to hurt or damage them using physical violence. ◻ *Fifty civilians in Masawa were killed when government planes attacked the town.* ◻ *He bundled the old lady into her hallway and brutally attacked her.* ◻ *They found the least defended area and attacked.* **2** [T] If you **attack** a person, belief, idea or act, you criticize them strongly. ◻ *He publicly attacked the people who've been calling for secret ballot nominations.* **3** [T] If something such as a disease, a chemical or an insect **attacks** something, it harms or spoils it. ◻ *The virus seems to have attacked his throat.* **4** [T] If you **attack** a job or a problem, you start to deal with it in an energetic way. ◻ *Any attempt to attack the budget problem is going to have to in some way deal with those issues.* **5** [I, T] In games such as soccer, when one team **attacks** the opponent's goal, they try to score a goal. ◻ *Now the US is controlling the ball and attacking the opponent's goal.* ◻ *The goal was just reward for their decision to attack constantly in the second half.*
NOUN [C, U] (attacks) **1** [C, U] An **attack** on a person or place is when you try to hurt or damage them using physical violence. ◻ *a campaign of air attacks on strategic targets* **2** [C, U] [usu with SUPP] An **attack** on a person, belief or act is when you criticize them strongly. ◻ *The role of the state as a prime mover in planning social change has been under attack.* **3** [U] [also attacks] An **attack** is when something such as a disease, a chemical or an insect harms or spoils a person or thing. ◻ *The virus can actually destroy those white blood cells, leaving the body wide open to attack from other infections.* **4** [C] In games such as soccer, an **attack** on the opponent's goal is when one team tries to score a goal. ◻ *Lee was at the hub of some incisive attacks in the second half.* **5** [C] An **attack** of an illness is a short period in which you suffer badly from it. ◻ *It had brought on an attack of asthma.*
→ See also **counterattack, heart attack**

at·tack·er /ə'tækə/ NOUN [C] (attackers) You can refer to a person who attacks someone as their **attacker.** ◻ *There were signs that she struggled with her attacker before she was stabbed.*

✪ **at·tain** /ə'teɪn/ VERB [T] (attains, attaining, attained) (academic word, formal) If you **attain** something, you gain it or achieve it, often after a lot of effort. ◻ *Jim is halfway to attaining his pilot's licence.* ◻ *the best way to attain the objectives of our strategy* ◻ *Business has yet to attain the social status it has in other countries.*

✪ **at·tain·ment** /ə'teɪnmənt/ NOUN [U, C] (attainments) (formal) **1** [U] The **attainment of** an aim is the achieving of it. = achievement ◻ *the attainment of independence* **2** [C] An **attainment** is a skill you have learned or something you have achieved. = achievement, success; ≠ failure ◻ *their educational attainments*

✪ **at·tempt** ♦♦♦ /ə'tempt/ VERB, NOUN
VERB [T] (attempts, attempting, attempted) If you **attempt to** do something, especially something difficult, you try to do it. = try ◻ *The only time that we attempted to do something like that was in the city of Philadelphia.* ◻ *Scientists are attempting to find a cure for the disease.* ◻ *The pilot then attempted an emergency landing.*

NOUN [C] (attempts) **1** If you make an **attempt to** do something, you try to do it, often without success. ❑ *a deliberate attempt to destabilize the defence* ❑ *Her first attempt was unsuccessful.* ❑ *It was one of his rare attempts at humour.* **2** An **attempt on** someone's life is an attempt to kill them. ❑ *an attempt on the life of the former Iranian prime minister*

at·tempt·ed /əˈtɛmptɪd/ ADJ [attempted + N] An **attempted** crime or unlawful action is an unsuccessful effort to commit the crime or action. ❑ *a case of attempted murder*

✪**at·tend** ◆◆◇ /əˈtɛnd/ VERB [I, T] (**attends, attending, attended**) **1** [I, T] If you **attend** a meeting or other event, you are present at it. ≠ miss ❑ *Thousands of people attended the funeral.* ❑ *The meeting will be attended by finance ministers from many countries.* ❑ *The senator was invited but was unable to attend.* **2** [T] If you **attend** an institution such as a school, college, or church, you go there regularly. ❑ *They attended college together at the University of Pennsylvania.* ❑ *Numbers for international students attending FE colleges show an increase of more than 21% over the previous year's figures.* **3** [I] If you **attend to** something, you deal with it. If you **attend to** someone who is hurt or injured, you care for them. ❑ *He took a short leave of absence to attend to personal business.*

WORD CONNECTIONS
attend + NOUN
attend a **meeting**
attend a **conference**
attend a **summit**
attend a **funeral**
❑ *The conference was attended by delegates from 154 nations.*
attend a **school**
attend a **university**
attend a **college**
❑ *My children attend the local school.*
ADV + **attend**
sparsely attended
poorly attended
well attended
❑ *Your event will be poorly attended if you do not send out the invitations early enough.*

✪**at·tend·ance** /əˈtɛndəns/ NOUN [U, C] (**attendances**) **1** [U] Someone's **attendance** at an event or an institution is the fact that they are present at the event or go regularly to the institution. ❑ *Her attendance in school was sporadic.* ❑ *Church attendance continues to decline.* **2** [C, U] The **attendance** at an event is the number of people who are present at it. = presence; ≠ absence ❑ *Rain played a big part in the air show's drop in attendance.* ❑ *Average weekly cinema attendance in February was 2.41 million.* ❑ *This year attendances were 28% lower than forecast.*

at·tend·ant /əˈtɛndənt/ NOUN [C] (**attendants**) **1** An **attendant** is someone whose job is to serve or help people in a place such as a petrol station or a car park. ❑ *Tony Williams was working as a parking lot attendant in Los Angeles.* **2** The **attendants** at a wedding are people such as the bridesmaids and the ushers, who accompany or help the bride and groom. ❑ *If the bride pays, she has the right to decide on the style of dress worn by her attendants.*

✪**at·ten·tion** ◆◆◇ /əˈtɛnʃən/ NOUN

NOUN [U] **1** If you give someone or something your **attention**, you look at them, listen to them, or think about them carefully. ❑ *You have my undivided attention.* ❑ *Later he turned his attention to the desperate state of housing in the city.* **2** **Attention** is great interest that is shown in someone or something, particularly by the general public. = interest ❑ *Volume Two, subtitled 'The Lawyers', will also attract considerable attention.* ❑ *The research attracted international attention.* ❑ *The conference may help to focus attention on the economy.* **3** If someone or something is getting **attention**, they are being dealt with or cared for. ❑ *Each year more than two million household injuries need*

medical **attention**. **4** If you **bring** something **to** someone's **attention** or **draw** their **attention to** it, you tell them about it or make them notice it. ❑ *If we don't keep bringing this to the attention of the people, nothing will be done.*

PHRASES **attract someone's attention** or **catch someone's attention** If someone or something **attracts** your **attention** or **catches** your **attention**, you suddenly notice them. ❑ *A faint aroma of coffee attracted his attention.* **pay attention** If you **pay attention to** someone, you watch them, listen to them, or take notice of them. If you **pay no attention to** someone, you behave as if you are not aware of them or as if they are not important. ❑ *More than ever before, the food industry is paying attention to young consumers.* ❑ *Other people walk along the beach at night, so I didn't pay any attention at first.* **stand to attention** When people **stand to attention**, they stand straight with their feet together and their arms at their sides. ❑ *Soldiers in full combat gear stood to attention.*

at·ten·tive /əˈtɛntɪv/ ADJ **1** If you are **attentive**, you are paying close attention to what is being said or done. ❑ *He wishes the government would be more attentive to detail in their response.* **2** Someone who is **attentive** is helpful and polite. ❑ *At society parties he is attentive to his wife.* **at·ten·tive·ly** /əˈtɛntɪvli/ ADV ❑ *He questioned Chrissie, and listened attentively to what she told him.*

✪**at·ti·tude** ◆◆◇ /ˈætɪtjuːd, AmE -tuːd/ NOUN [C, U] (**attitudes**) (*academic word*) Your **attitude to** something is the way that you think and feel about it, especially when this shows in the way you behave. = outlook, opinion, point of view ❑ *the general change in attitude towards people with disabilities* ❑ *prevailing cultural attitudes* ❑ *Being unemployed produces negative attitudes to work.*

✪**at·tor·ney** ◆◇◇ /əˈtɜːni/ NOUN [C] (**attorneys**) In the United States, an **attorney** or **attorney-at-law** is a lawyer. = lawyer, barrister ❑ *a prosecuting attorney* ❑ *At the hearing, her attorney did not enter a plea.* ❑ *an attorney representing families of 319 victims*

✪**at·tract** ◆◆◇ /əˈtrækt/ VERB [T] (**attracts, attracting, attracted**) **1** If something **attracts** people or animals, it has features that cause them to come to it. ❑ *The Cardiff Bay project is attracting many visitors.* **2** If someone or something **attracts** you, they have particular qualities which cause you to like or admire them. If a particular quality **attracts** you **to** a person or thing, it is the reason why you like them. ❑ *He wasn't sure he'd got it right, although the theory attracted him by its logic.* **3** If you are **attracted to** someone, you are interested in them sexually. ❑ *In spite of her hostility, she was attracted to him.* **4** If something **attracts** support, publicity, or money, it receives support, publicity, or money. ❑ *President Mwinyi said his country would also like to attract investment from private companies.* **5** If one object **attracts** another object, it causes the second object to move towards it. ≠ repel ❑ *Anything with strong gravity attracts other things to it.* ❑ *streams of charged particles which are magnetically attracted to the poles of the earth*

at·tract·ed /əˈtræktɪd/ ADJ [V-LINK + attracted] ❑ *He was nice looking, but I wasn't deeply attracted to him.* ✦ **attract someone's attention** → see **attention**

✪**at·trac·tion** /əˈtrækʃən/ NOUN [U, C] (**attractions**) **1** [U] **Attraction** is a feeling of liking someone, and often of being sexually interested in them. ≠ repulsion ❑ *Our level of attraction to the opposite sex has more to do with our inner confidence than how we look.* **2** [C] An **attraction** is a feature that makes something interesting or desirable. ❑ *the attractions of living on the waterfront* **3** [C] An **attraction** is something that people can go to for interest or enjoyment, for example, a famous building. ❑ *The walled city is an important tourist attraction.* **4** [U] **Attraction** is the force that makes object move towards another. ≠ repulsion ❑ *The Arctic exerts a magnetic attraction even in the Antipodes.* ❑ *Each particle has a strong force of attraction for the particles around it.*

at·trac·tive ◆◆◇ /əˈtræktɪv/ ADJ **1** A person who is **attractive** is pleasant to look at. ❑ *She's a very attractive woman.* ❑ *I thought he was very attractive and obviously very intelligent.* **2** Something that is **attractive** has a pleasant appearance or sound. ❏ *The apartment was small but attractive, if rather shabby.* **3** You can describe something as **attractive** when it seems worth having or doing. = appealing ❏ *Smoking is still attractive to many young people who see it as glamorous.*

at•trac•tive•ness /əˈtræktɪvnəs/ NOUN [U] ❏ *Most of us would maintain that physical attractiveness does not play a major part in how we react to the people we meet.*

❖**at•trib•ute** VERB, NOUN (*academic word*)

  VERB /əˈtrɪbjuːt/ [T] (**attributes, attributing, attributed**) **1** If you **attribute** something **to** an event or situation, you think that it was caused by that event or situation. = ascribe, assign, accredit ❏ *Women tend to attribute their success to external causes such as luck.* ❏ *The rising death toll is attributed largely to the growing number of elderly people, who are especially vulnerable to flu.* **2** If you **attribute** a particular quality or feature **to** someone or something, you think that they have it. = ascribe ❏ *People were beginning to attribute superhuman qualities to him.* ❏ *the tendency to attribute more positive characteristics to physically attractive people* **3** If a piece of writing, a work of art, or a remark **is attributed to** someone, people say that they wrote it, created it, or said it. ❏ *This, and the remaining frescoes, are not attributed to Giotto.* ❏ *The article incorrectly attributed some quotes to evangelist Billy Graham.*

  NOUN /ˈætrɪbjuːt/ [C] (**attributes**) An **attribute** is a quality or feature that someone or something has. = characteristic ❏ *Cruelty is a normal attribute of human behaviour.*

atyp•i•cal /eɪˈtɪpɪkəl/ ADJ Someone or something that is **atypical** is not typical of its kind. ≠ typical ❏ *The economy of the province was atypical because it was particularly small.*

WORD PARTS

The prefix *a-* often appears in adjectives which have 'not', 'without', or 'opposite' in their meaning:

atypical (ADJ)
asexual (ADJ)
atonal (ADJ)

---

auc•tion ◆◇◇ /ˈɔːkʃən/ NOUN, VERB

  NOUN [C, U] (**auctions**) An **auction** is a public sale where items are sold to the person who offers the highest price. ❏ *The painting is expected to fetch up to $400,000 at auction.* VERB [T] (**auctions, auctioning, auctioned**) If something **is auctioned**, it is sold in an auction. ❏ *Eight drawings by French artist Jean Cocteau will be auctioned next week.*

  PHRASAL VERB **auction off** If you **auction off** something, you sell it to the person who offers most for it, often at an auction. ❏ *Any fool could auction off a factory full of engineering machinery.*

auda•cious /ɔːˈdeɪʃəs/ ADJ Someone who is **audacious** takes risks in order to achieve something. = daring ❏ *an audacious plan to win the presidency* ❏ *He was known for risky tactics that ranged from audacious to outrageous.*

audible /ˈɔːdɪbəl/ ADJ A sound that is **audible** is loud enough to be heard. ❏ *The Colonel's voice was barely audible.* **audibly** /ˈɔːdɪbli/ ADV ❏ *Frank sighed audibly.*

❖**audi•ence** ◆◆◇ /ˈɔːdiəns/ NOUN [C] (**audiences**) **1** The **audience** at a play, concert, film, or public meeting is the group of people watching or listening to it. ❏ *The entire audience broke into loud applause.* ❏ *He was speaking to an audience of students at the Institute for International Affairs.* **2** The **audience** for a television or radio programme consists of all the people who watch or listen to it. = viewers ❏ *The concert will be broadcast to a worldwide television audience estimated at one billion.* ❏ *the highest ever audience for a reality game show* **3** The **audience** of a writer or artist is the people who read their books or look at their work. = market ❏ *Say's writings reached a wide audience during his lifetime.*

❖**audio** ◆◆◇ /ˈɔːdiəʊ/ ADJ [audio + N] **Audio** equipment is used for recording and reproducing sound. ❏ *The software was the first to offer access to audio and video files.* ❏ *a digital audio tape*

❖**audit** /ˈɔːdɪt/ VERB, NOUN

  VERB [T] (**audits, auditing, audited**) When an accountant **audits** an organization's accounts, he or she examines the accounts officially in order to make sure that they have been done correctly. = investigate, inspect ❏ *Each year they audit our accounts and certify them as being true and fair.* NOUN [C] (**audits**) An **audit** is an occasion when an accountant officially examines the accounts of an organization. = investigation, inspection ❏ *The bank first learned of the problem when it carried out an internal audit.* ❏ *an independent audit of the organization*

audi•tion /ɔːˈdɪʃən/ NOUN, VERB

  NOUN [C] (**auditions**) An **audition** is a short performance given by an actor, dancer or musician so that a director or conductor can decide if they are good enough to be in a play, film or orchestra. ❏ *an audition for a Broadway musical* VERB [I, T] (**auditions, auditioning, auditioned**) If you **audition** or if someone **auditions** you, you do an audition. ❏ *I was auditioning for the part of a jealous girlfriend.* ❏ *They're auditioning new members for the cast of 'Miss Saigon' today.*

❖**audi•tor** /ˈɔːdɪtə/ NOUN [C] (**auditors**) An **auditor** is an accountant who officially examines the accounts of organizations. ❏ *the company's external auditor* ❏ *The misdirected spending was uncovered by the state auditor.*

aunt ◆◆◇ /ɑːnt, ænt/ NOUN [C] (**aunts**) Someone's **aunt** is the sister of their mother or father, or the wife of their uncle. ❏ *She wrote to her aunt in Alabama.*

❖**aural** /ˈɔːrəl, ˈaʊərəl/ ADJ [usu aural + N] **Aural** means related to the sense of hearing. Compare **acoustic**. ❏ *He became famous as an inventor of astonishing visual and aural effects.*

aus•pices /ˈɔːspɪsɪz/ NOUN

  PHRASE **under the auspices of** or **under someone's auspices** (*formal*) If something is done **under the auspices** of a particular person or organization, or **under** someone's **auspices**, it is done with their support and approval. ❏ *to meet and discuss peace under the auspices of the United Nations*

aus•tere /ɔːˈstɪə/ ADJ **1** (*approval*) If you describe something as **austere**, you approve of its plain and simple appearance. ❏ *a cream linen suit and austere black blouse* **2** If you describe someone as **austere**, you disapprove of them because they are strict and serious. ❏ *I found her a rather austere, distant, somewhat cold person.* **3** An **austere** way of life is one that is simple and without luxuries. = spartan ❏ *The life of the troops was still comparatively austere.* **4** An **austere** economic policy is one that reduces people's living standards sharply. ❏ *a set of very austere economic measures to control inflation*

aus•ter•ity /ɔːˈsterɪti/ NOUN [U] **Austerity** is a situation in which people's living standards are reduced because of economic difficulties. ❏ *the years of austerity which followed the war*

❖**authen•tic** /ɔːˈθentɪk/ ADJ **1** An **authentic** person, object, or emotion is genuine. = genuine, real; ≠ fake, false, imitation, inauthentic ❏ *authentic Italian food* ❏ *She has authentic charm whereas most people simply have nice manners.* **2** If you describe something as **authentic**, you mean that it is such a good imitation that it is almost the same as or as good as the original. ❏ *patterns for making authentic frontier-style clothing* **3** An **authentic** piece of information or account of something is reliable and accurate. ❏ *I had obtained the authentic details about the birth of the organization.*

❖**au•then•tic•ity** /ˌɔːθenˈtɪsɪti/ NOUN [U] ≠ artifice ❏ *There are factors, however, that have cast doubt on the statue's authenticity.* ❏ *efforts to determine the authenticity of the documents*

❖**author** ◆◆◇ /ˈɔːθə/ NOUN [C] (**authors**) (*academic word*) **1** [oft author 'of' N] The **author of** a piece of writing is the person who wrote it. = writer ❏ *Jill Phillips, author of the book 'Give Your Child Music'* **2** An **author** is a person whose job is writing books. = writer, novelist ❏ *Haruki Murakami is Japan's best-selling author.*

authori•tar•ian /ɔːˌθɒrɪˈteəriən, AmE -ˈtɔːr-/ ADJ (*disapproval*) If you describe a person or an organization as **authoritarian**, you are critical of them controlling everything rather than letting people decide things for

A

themselves. = dictatorial ❏ *Senior officers could be considering a coup to restore authoritarian rule.*

authori·ta·tive /ɔːˈθɒrɪtətɪv, AmE əˈθɔːrɪteɪtɪv/ ADJ
1 Someone or something that is **authoritative** gives an impression of power and importance and is likely to be obeyed. ❏ *He has a commanding presence and deep, authoritative voice.* **2** Someone or something that is **authoritative** has a lot of knowledge of a particular subject. ❏ *The first authoritative study of polio was published in 1840.*

✪**author·ity** ◆◆◆ /ɔːˈθɒriti, AmE -ˈθɔːr-/ NOUN [PL, C, U] (**authorities**) (*academic word*) **1** [PL] The **authorities** are the people who have the power to make decisions and to make sure that laws are obeyed. = officials ❏ *This provided a pretext for the authorities to cancel the elections.* ❏ *The prison authorities have been criticised for not acting more quickly.* **2** [C] An **authority** is an official organization or government department that has the power to make decisions. ❏ *the Health Education Authority* **3** [C] Someone who is an **authority on** a particular subject knows a lot about it. = expert ❏ *He's universally recognized as an authority on Russian affairs.* **4** [U] **Authority** is the right to command and control other people. ❏ *A family member in a family business has a position of authority and power.* ❏ *The judge had no authority to order a second trial.* ❏ *The court has no authority over the matter.* **5** [U] If someone has **authority**, they have a quality which makes other people take notice of what they say. ❏ *He had no natural authority and no capacity for imposing his will on others.* **6** [U] **Authority** is official permission to do something. = authorization ❏ *The prison governor has refused to let him go, saying he must first be given authority from his own superiors.*
→ See also **local authority**

author·ize /ˈɔːθəraɪz/ also **authorise** VERB [T] (**authorizes, authorizing, authorized**) If someone in a position of authority **authorizes** something, they give their official permission for it to happen. = sanction ❏ *It would certainly be within his power to authorize a police raid like that.*
authori·za·tion /ˌɔːθəraɪˈzeɪʃən/ NOUN [C, U] (**authorizations**) ❏ *The United Nations will approve his request for authorization to use military force to deliver aid.*

auto·bio·graphi·cal /ˌɔːtəʊbaɪəˈɡræfɪkəl/ ADJ An **autobiographical** piece of writing relates to events in the life of the person who has written it. ❏ *a highly autobiographical novel of a woman's search for identity*

WORD PARTS
The prefix **auto-** often appears in words which refer to someone doing something to, for, or about themselves:
autobiographical (ADJ)
autobiography (NOUN)
autograph (NOUN)
---

auto·bi·og·ra·phy /ˌɔːtəbaɪˈɒɡrəfi/ NOUN [C] (**autobiographies**) Your **autobiography** is an account of your life, which you write yourself. ❏ *He published his autobiography last autumn.*

✪**auto·mate** /ˈɔːtəmeɪt/ VERB [T] (**automates, automating, automated**) (*academic word*) To **automate** a factory, office, or industrial process means to put in machines that can do the work instead of people. = mechanize ❏ *He wanted to use computers to automate the process.*
✪**auto·ma·tion** /ˌɔːtəˈmeɪʃən/ NOUN [U] = mechanization, industrialization ❏ *In the last ten years automation has reduced the work force here by half.* ❏ *the automation of everyday business transactions*

auto·mat·ed /ˈɔːtəmeɪtɪd/ ADJ An **automated** factory, office or industrial process uses machines to do the work instead of people. ❏ *The equipment was made on highly automated production lines.*

✪**auto·mat·ic** ◆◇◇ /ˌɔːtəˈmætɪk/ ADJ, NOUN (*academic word*)
ADJ **1** An **automatic** machine or device is one that has controls that enable it to perform a task without needing to be constantly operated by a person. **Automatic** methods and processes involve the use of such machines.

= automated, mechanical; ≠ manual ❏ *Modern trains have automatic doors.* **2** [automatic + N] An **automatic** weapon is one that keeps firing shots until you stop pulling the trigger. ❏ *Three gunmen with automatic rifles opened fire.* **3** An **automatic** action is one that you do without thinking about it. ❏ *All of the automatic body functions, even breathing, are affected.*
NOUN [C] (**automatics**) **1** An **automatic** is a car in which the gears change automatically as the car's speed increases or decreases. **2** An **automatic** is a weapon that keeps firing until you stop pulling the trigger. ❏ *He drew his automatic and began running in the direction of the sounds.*
✪**auto·mati·cal·ly** /ˌɔːtəˈmætɪkli/ ADV **1** You will automatically wake up after this length of time.

auto·mo·bile /ˈɔːtəməbiːl, AmE ˌɔːtəməʊˈbiːl/ NOUN [C] (**automobiles**) (*mainly AmE*) An **automobile** is a car. ❏ *the automobile industry*

✪**autono·mous** /ɔːˈtɒnəməs/ ADJ **1** An **autonomous** country, organization, or group governs or controls itself rather than being controlled by anyone else. = independent, self-governing, self-determining; ≠ dependent ❏ *They proudly declared themselves part of a new autonomous province.* ❏ *the liberal idea of the autonomous individual* **2** An **autonomous** person makes their own decisions rather than being influenced by someone else. = independent ❏ *He treated us as autonomous individuals who had to learn to make up our own minds about issues.*

✪**autono·my** /ɔːˈtɒnəmi/ NOUN [U] **1** **Autonomy** is the control or government of a country, organization, or group by itself rather than by others. = independence, self-rule, self-determination, self-government; ≠ dependence ❏ *Activists stepped up their demands for local autonomy last month.* **2** (*formal*) **Autonomy** is the ability to make your own decisions about what to do rather than being influenced by someone else or told what to do. = independence, freedom ❏ *Each of the area managers enjoys considerable autonomy in the running of his own area.* ❏ *It is important to respect the autonomy of mature people.*

VOCABULARY BUILDER

autonomy NOUN
Autonomy is the control or government of a country or group by itself rather than by others.
❏ *These men have been fighting for Kurdish autonomy against Iraq and Turkey for decades.*

independence NOUN
If a country has **independence**, it has its own government and is not ruled by any other country.
❏ *Clearly there is more to the question of Scottish independence than tax revenues and public spending.*

self-government NOUN
Self-government is the government of a country or region by its own people rather than by others.
❏ *Many ethnic groups were granted nominal self-government through a complex system of republics and autonomous regions.*

self-rule NOUN
Self-rule is the same as self-government.
❏ *When the French and Spanish established their protectorates in Morocco, Tangier was granted self-rule.*

self-determination NOUN
Self-determination is the right of a country to be independent, instead of being controlled by a foreign country.
❏ *The USA's line on Kashmiri self-determination is more cautious.*
---

autop·sy /ˈɔːtɒpsi/ NOUN [C] (**autopsies**) An **autopsy** is an examination of a dead body by a doctor who cuts it open in order to try to discover the cause of death. = post-mortem ❏ *Macklin had the grim task of carrying out an autopsy on his friend.*

autumn ◆◇◇ /ˈɔːtəm/ (*mainly BrE; in AmE, usually use* **fall**)

NOUN [C, U] (**autumns**) Autumn is the season between summer and winter when the weather becomes cooler and the leaves fall off the trees.

avail /əˈveɪl/ VERB, NOUN

[VERB] [T] (**avails, availing, availed**) (*formal*) If you **avail yourself of** an offer or an opportunity, you accept the offer or make use of the opportunity. ❏ *Guests should feel at liberty to avail themselves of your facilities.*

[NOUN]

[PHRASE] **to no avail** or **to little avail** (*written*) If you do something **to no avail** or **to little avail**, what you do fails to achieve what you want. ❏ *His efforts were to no avail.*

✪ **avail·able** ♦♦♦ /əˈveɪləbəl/ ADJ (*academic word*) **1** If something you want or need is **available**, you can find it or obtain it. ❏ *Since 1978, the amount of money available to buy books has fallen by 17%.* ❏ *The shop has about 500 autographed copies of the book available for purchase.* ❏ *all the available evidence suggests* ❏ *The drug is widely available.* **2** [V-LINK + available] Someone who is **available** is not busy and is therefore free to talk to you or to do a particular task. ❏ *Mr Leach is on holiday and was not available for comment.*

✪ **avail·abil·ity** /əˌveɪləˈbɪlɪti/ NOUN [U] ❏ *the easy availability of guns* ❏ *There is very limited availability of trained and skilled resources.*

WORD CONNECTIONS
ADV + **available**
widely available **freely** available **easily** available **readily** available ❏ *The drug is cheap and readily available.*
currently available **immediately** available ❏ *These packages are currently available for downloading.*
commercially available **publicly** available **generally** available ❏ *The service is expected to be commercially available in November.*

ava·lanche /ˈævəlɑːntʃ, -læntʃ/ NOUN [C] (**avalanches**) An **avalanche** is a large mass of snow that falls down the side of a mountain.

avant-garde /ˌævɒŋ ˈgɑːd/ ADJ **Avant-garde** art, music, theatre and literature is very modern and experimental. ❏ *avant-garde concert music*

avenge /əˈvendʒ/ VERB [T] (**avenges, avenging, avenged**) If you **avenge** a wrong or harmful act, you hurt or punish the person who is responsible for it. ❏ *He has devoted the past five years to avenging his daughter's death.*

av·enue ♦♦◇ /ˈævɪnjuː, AmE -nuː/ NOUN [C] (**avenues**) **1** Avenue is sometimes used in the names of streets. The written abbreviation **Ave** is also used. ❏ *the most expensive apartments on Park Avenue* **2** An **avenue** is a wide, straight road, especially one with trees on either side.

✪ **av·er·age** ♦♦◇ /ˈævərɪdʒ/ NOUN, ADJ, VERB

[NOUN] [C, SING] (**averages**) **1** [C] An **average** is the result that you get when you add two or more numbers together and divide the total by the number of numbers you added together. = mean ❏ *Take the average of those ratios and multiply by a hundred.* ❏ *The school's results are above the national average.* **2** [SING] You use **average** to refer to a number or size that varies but is always approximately the same. ❏ *It takes an average of ten weeks for a house sale to be completed.* **3** [SING] An amount or quality that is **the average** is the normal amount or quality for a particular group of things or people. = norm ❏ *35% of staff time was being spent on repeating work, about the average for a service industry.* ❏ *Most areas suffered more rain than usual, with Northern Ireland getting double the average for the month.* [PHRASE] **on average** You say **on average** to indicate that a number is the average of several numbers. ❏ *Shares rose, on average, by 38%.* [ADJ] **1** [average + N] An **average** price or number is the

result that you get when you add two or more prices or numbers together and divide the total by the number of numbers you added together. = mean ❏ *The average price of goods rose by just 2.2%.* ❏ *The average age for a woman to have her first child was 29.* **2** An **average** amount or quality is the normal amount or quality for a particular group of things or people. ❏ *$2.20 for a beer is average.* ❏ *a woman of average height* **3** [average + N] An **average** person or thing is typical or normal. = typical ❏ *The average adult man burns 1,500 to 2,000 calories per day.* ❏ *Packaging is about a third of what is found in an average British dustbin.* **4** Something that is **average** is neither very good nor very bad, usually when you had hoped it would be better. ❏ *I was only average academically.* [VERB] [T] (**averages, averaging, averaged**) To **average** a particular amount means to do, get, or produce that amount as an average over a period of time. ❏ *We averaged 42 miles per hour.*

aver·sion /əˈvɜːʃən, AmE -ʒən/ NOUN [C, U] (**aversions**) If you have an **aversion to** someone or something, you dislike them very much. ❏ *Many people have a natural and emotional aversion to insects.*

avert /əˈvɜːt/ VERB [T] (**averts, averting, averted**) **1** If you **avert** something unpleasant, you prevent it from happening. ❏ *Talks with the teachers' union over the weekend have averted a strike.* **2** If you **avert** your eyes or gaze **from** someone or something, you look away from them. ❏ *He avoids any eye contact, quickly averting his gaze when anyone approaches.*

avia·tion /ˌeɪviˈeɪʃən/ NOUN [U] **Aviation** is the operation and production of aircraft. ❏ *the aviation industry*

avid /ˈævɪd/ ADJ You use **avid** to describe someone who is very enthusiastic about something that they do. ❏ *He misses not having enough books because he's an avid reader.* **av·id·ly** /ˈævɪdli/ ADV [avidly with V] ❏ *Thank you for a most entertaining magazine, which I read avidly each month.*

✪ **avoid** ♦♦◇ /əˈvɔɪd/ VERB [T] (**avoids, avoiding, avoided**) **1** If you **avoid** something unpleasant that might happen, you take action in order to prevent it from happening. = prevent, stop ❏ *The pilots had to take emergency action to avoid a disaster.* ❏ *Lift the table carefully to avoid damaging it.* **2** If you **avoid** doing something, you choose not to do it, or you put yourself in a situation where you do not have to do it. ❏ *By borrowing from dozens of banks, he managed to avoid giving any of them an overall picture of what he was up to.* **3** If you **avoid** a person or thing, you keep away from them. When talking to someone, if you **avoid** a particular subject, you keep the conversation away from it. ❏ *She eventually had to lock herself in the women's toilets to avoid him.* **4** If a person or vehicle **avoids** someone or something, they change the direction they are moving in, so that they do not hit them. ❏ *The driver had ample time to brake or swerve and avoid the woman.*

USAGE NOTE
avoid
Do not say that someone should 'avoid to do something'. Say that they should 'avoid doing' it. *You must **avoid giving** any unnecessary information.*

avoid·able /əˈvɔɪdəbəl/ ADJ Something that is **avoidable** can be prevented from happening. ❏ *The tragedy was entirely avoidable.*

avoid·ance /əˈvɔɪdəns/ NOUN [U] [usu avoidance 'of' N] **Avoidance** of someone or something is the act of avoiding them. ❏ *the avoidance of stress*

await ♦◇◇ /əˈweɪt/ VERB [T] (**awaits, awaiting, awaited**) (*formal*) **1** If you **await** someone or something, you wait for them. ❏ *Very little was said as we awaited the arrival of the chairman.* **2** Something that **awaits** you is going to happen or come to you in the future. ❏ *A surprise awaited them in Wal-Mart.*

awake /əˈweɪk/ ADJ, VERB

[ADJ] [V-LINK + awake, awake after V] Someone who is **awake** is not sleeping. ❏ *I don't stay awake at night worrying about that.*

[PHRASE] **wide awake** Someone who is **wide awake** is fully

A

awake and unable to sleep. ❑ *I could not relax and still felt wide awake.* VERB (**awakes, awaking, awoke, awoken**) When you **awake** or when something **awakes** you, you wake up. ❑ *At midnight he awoke and listened to the radio for a few minutes.* ❑ *The sound of voices awoke her with a start.*

award ♦♦◇ /əˈwɔːd/ NOUN, VERB
NOUN [c] (**awards**) **1** An **award** is a prize or certificate that a person is given for doing something well. ❑ *The Institute's annual award is presented to organizations that are dedicated to democracy and human rights.* **2** In law, an **award** is a sum of money that a court decides should be given to someone. ❑ *worker's compensation awards* VERB [T] (**awards, awarding, awarded**) **1** If someone **is awarded** something such as a prize or an examination mark, it is given to them. ❑ *She was awarded the prize for both films.* **2** To **award** something **to** someone means to decide that it will be given to that person. ❑ *We have awarded the contract to a New York-based company.*

✪ **aware** ♦♦◇ /əˈweə/ ADJ (*academic word*) **1** [V-LINK + aware] If you are **aware** of something, you know about it. ≠ unaware ❑ *Smokers are well aware of the dangers to their own health.* ❑ *He should have been aware of what his junior officers were doing.* **2** [V-LINK + aware] If you are **aware of** something, you realize that it is present or is happening because you hear it, see it, smell it, or feel it. = conscious ❑ *She was acutely aware of the noise of the city.*
✪ **aware·ness** /əˈweənəs/ NOUN [u] ❑ *The 1980s brought an awareness of green issues.*

WHICH WORD?
awareness, knowledge, or understanding?
Awareness is the fact of knowing that something exists.
❑ *She urged greater public **awareness** of the need for conservation.*
Knowledge is information and understanding about the facts of a subject.
❑ *Her **knowledge** of French and Italian was good.*
If you have an **understanding** of something, you know how it works or what it means.
❑ *There have been huge advances in our **understanding** of how the ear works.*

awash /əˈwɒʃ/ ADJ **1** [V-LINK + awash] If a place is **awash** with something, it contains a large amount of it. ❑ *This is a company that is awash with cash.* **2** [V-LINK + awash] If the ground or a floor is **awash**, it is covered in water, often because of heavy rain or as the result of an accident. ❑ *The bathroom floor was awash.*

away ♦♦♦ /əˈweɪ/ ADV, ADJ

Away is often used with verbs of movement, such as 'go' and 'drive', and also in phrasal verbs such as 'do away with' and 'fade away'.

ADV **1** If someone or something moves or is moved **away** from a place, they move or are moved so that they are no longer there. If you are **away from** a place, you are not in the place where people expect you to be. ❑ *An injured policeman was led away by colleagues.* ❑ *He walked away from his car.* ❑ *Jason was away on a business trip.* **2** If you look or turn **away from** something, you move your head so that you are no longer looking at it. ❑ *She quickly looked away and stared down at her hands.* **3** [away after V] If you put something **away**, you put it where it should be. If you hide someone or something **away**, you put them in a place where nobody can see them or find them. ❑ *I put my journal away and prepared for bed.* ❑ *All her letters were carefully filed away in folders.* **4** ['be' AMOUNT + away] You use **away** to talk about future events. For example, if an event is a week **away**, it will happen after a week. ❑ *the Washington summit, now only just over two weeks away* **5** [away after V] When a sports team plays **away**, it plays on its opponents' playing court or field. ❑ *a sensational 4-3 victory for the team playing away* **6** [away after V] You can use **away** to say that something slowly disappears,

becomes less significant or changes so that it is no longer the same. ❑ *So much snow has already melted away.* ❑ *His voice died away in a whisper.* **7** You use **away** to show that there has been a change or development from one state or situation to another. ❑ *British courts are increasingly moving away from sending young offenders to prison.* **8** [away after V] You can use **away** to emphasize a continuous or repeated action. ❑ *He would often be working away on his word processor late into the night.* **9** [away after V] You use **away** to show that something is removed. ❑ *If you take my work away I can't be happy anymore.*
PHRASE **away from** If something is **away from** a person or place, it is at a distance from that person or place. ❑ *The two women were sitting as far away from each other as possible.*
ADJ [away + N] An **away** game is where a sports team plays on its opponents' playing court or field. ❑ *Pittsburgh is about to play an important away game.*
✦ **right away** → see **right**

WHICH WORD?
away or far?
Do not confuse **away** and **far**. You use **away** to talk about the distance of a particular place from where you are.
❑ *The nearest hospital was 80 kilometres **away**.*
❑ *They live a long way **away**.*
You use **far** in negative sentences and questions about distance.
❑ *Our house is not **far** from the airport.*
❑ *How **far** is it from here?*

awe /ɔː/ NOUN, VERB
NOUN [u] **Awe** is the feeling of respect and amazement that you have when you are faced with something wonderful and often rather frightening. ❑ *She gazed in awe at the great stones.* VERB [T] (**awes, awed**) If you **are awed by** someone or something, they make you feel respectful and amazed, though often rather frightened. ❑ *I am still awed by David's courage.*

awe·some /ˈɔːsəm/ ADJ **1** An **awesome** person or thing is very impressive and often frightening. ❑ *the awesome responsibility of sending men into combat* **2** (*informal, emphasis*) If you describe someone or something as **awesome**, you are emphasizing that you think that they are very impressive or extraordinary. ❑ *Melvill called the flight 'mind-blowing' and 'awesome'.*

aw·ful ♦♦◇ /ˈɔːful/ ADJ **1** If you say that someone or something is **awful**, you dislike that person or thing or you think that they are not very good. = dreadful ❑ *We met and I thought he was awful.* ❑ *an awful smell of paint* **2** If you say that something is **awful**, you mean that it is extremely unpleasant, shocking, or bad. = horrific ❑ *Her injuries were massive. It was awful.* **3** [V-LINK + awful] If you look or feel **awful**, you look or feel ill. = terrible ❑ *I hardly slept at all and felt pretty awful.* **4** [awful + N] You can use **awful** with noun groups that refer to an amount in order to emphasize how large that amount is. = tremendous ❑ *I've got an awful lot of work to do.*
aw·ful·ly /ˈɔːfəli/ ADV = terribly ❑ *The caramel looks awfully good.*

awhile /əˈwaɪl/ ADV **Awhile** means for a short time. ❑ *He worked awhile as a pharmacist in Cincinnati.*

awk·ward /ˈɔːkwəd/ ADJ **1** An **awkward** situation is embarrassing and difficult to deal with. = tricky ❑ *I was the first to ask him awkward questions but there'll be harder ones to come.* **2** Something that is **awkward to** use or carry is difficult to use or carry because of its design. A job that is **awkward** is difficult to do. = tricky ❑ *It was small but heavy enough to make it awkward to carry.* **3** An **awkward** movement or position is uncomfortable or clumsy. ❑ *Amy made an awkward gesture with her hands.* **4** Someone who feels **awkward** behaves in a shy or embarrassed way. = uncomfortable ❑ *Women frequently say that they feel awkward taking the initiative in sex.*
awk·ward·ly /ˈɔːkwədli/ ADV **1** [awkwardly + ADJ/-ED] ❑ *There was an awkwardly long silence.* **2** [awkwardly + -ED]

❑ *The front window switches are awkwardly placed on the dashboard.* **3** [awkwardly with v] ❑ *He fell awkwardly and went down in agony clutching his right knee.* **4** [awkwardly with v] ❑ *'This is Malcolm,' the girl said awkwardly, to fill the silence.*

awoke /əˈwəʊk/ IRREG FORM Awoke is the past tense of **awake**.

awok‧en /əˈwəʊkən/ IRREG FORM Awoken is the past participle of **awake**.

axe /æks/ (*BrE*; in *AmE*, use **ax**) NOUN, VERB

NOUN [c] (**axes**) An **axe** is a tool used for cutting wood. It consists of a heavy metal blade that is sharp at one edge and attached by its other edge to the end of a long handle.

VERB [T] (**axes, axing, axed**) If someone's job or something such as a public service or a television programme **is axed**, it is ended suddenly and without discussion. = cut ❑ *Community projects are being axed by hard-pressed social services departments.*

axes IRREG FORM **1** /ˈæksɪz/ Axes is the plural of **axe**. **2** /ˈæksiːz/ Axes is the plural of **axis**.

○**axis** /ˈæksɪs/ NOUN [c] (**axes**) **1** An **axis** is an imaginary line through the middle of something. = pivot ❑ *the tilt of the Earth's axis* **2** An **axis** of a graph is one of the two lines on which the scales of measurement are marked. ❑ *The level of spiritual achievement is plotted along the Y axis, and the degree of physical health is plotted along the X axis.*

Bb

B also **b** /biː/ NOUN [C, U] (**B's, b's**) B is the second letter of the English alphabet.

baby ♦♦◇ /'beɪbi/ NOUN, ADJ

▪ NOUN [C] (**babies**) **1** A **baby** is a very young child, especially one that cannot yet walk or talk. ☐ *She used to take care of me when I was a baby.* ☐ *My wife has just had a baby.* **2** [usu baby + N] A **baby** animal is a very young animal. ☐ *a baby elephant* **3** If you refer to someone as a **baby**, you mean that they are behaving in a cowardly way or they are being too sensitive about something. ☐ *I know he's an ex-champion boxer, but he can be a big baby sometimes! He hates spiders.* **4** (*informal*) Some people use **baby** as an affectionate way of addressing someone, especially a young woman, or referring to them. ☐ *You have to wake up now, baby.*

▪ ADJ [baby + N] **Baby** vegetables are vegetables picked when they are very small. ☐ *Cook the baby potatoes in their skins.*

baby·sit /'beɪbisɪt/ VERB [I, T] (**babysits, babysitting, babysat**) If you **babysit** for someone or **babysit** their children, you look after their children while they are out. ☐ *I promised to babysit for Mrs Plunkett.* ☐ *She had been babysitting him and his four-year-old sister.*

baby·sitter /'beɪbiˌsɪtə/ NOUN [C] ☐ *It can be difficult to find a good babysitter.*

bach·e·lor /'bætʃələ/ NOUN [C] (**bachelors**) A **bachelor** is a man who has never married. ☐ *America's most eligible bachelor*

◇bach·e·lor's de·gree NOUN [C] (**bachelor's degrees**) A **bachelor's degree** is a first degree awarded by colleges or universities. = **undergraduate degree** ☐ *He received his bachelor's degree in computer science at Brown University in 1976.* ☐ *Lab positions require a bachelor's degree, preferably in biology.*

back ♦♦♦ /bæk/ ADV, NOUN, ADJ, VERB

> In addition to the uses shown below, **back** is also used in phrasal verbs such as 'date back' and 'fall back on'.

▪ ADV **1** If you move **back**, you move in the opposite direction to the one in which you are facing or in which you were moving before. ☐ *She stepped back from the door expectantly.* ☐ *He pushed her away and she fell back on the wooden bench.* **2** If you go **back** somewhere, you return to where you were before. ☐ *I went back to bed.* ☐ *I'll be back as soon as I can.* **3** If someone or something is **back** in a particular state, they were in that state before and are now in it again. ☐ *The rail company said it expected services to get slowly back to normal.* **4** If you give or put something **back**, you return it to the person who had it or to the place where it was before you took it. If you get or take something **back**, you then have it again after not having it for a while. ☐ *She handed the knife back.* ☐ *Put it back in the freezer.* **5** [back after V] If you put a clock or watch **back**, you change the time shown on it so that it shows an earlier time, for example, when the time changes to standard time. ☐ *The clocks go back at 2 o'clock tomorrow morning.* **6** If you write or call **back**, you write to or telephone someone after they have written to or telephoned you. If you look **back** at someone, you look at them after they have started looking at you. ☐ *They wrote back to me and told me I didn't have to do it.* ☐ *If the phone rings, say you'll call back after dinner.* **7** You can say that you

go or come **back to** a particular point in a conversation to show that you are mentioning or discussing it again. ☐ *Can I come back to the question of policing once again?* **8** If something is or comes **back**, it is fashionable again after it has been unfashionable for some time. ☐ *Short skirts are back.* **9** If someone or something is kept or situated **back from** a place, they are at a distance away from it. ☐ *Keep back from the edge of the platform.* ☐ *I'm a few miles back from the border.* **10** [back after V] If something is held or tied **back**, it is held or tied so that it does not hang loosely over something. ☐ *The curtains were held back by tassels.* **11** [back after V] If you lie or sit **back**, you move your body backwards into a relaxed sloping or flat position, with your head and body resting on something. ☐ *She lay back and stared at the ceiling.* **12** If you look or shout **back** at someone or something, you turn to look or shout at them when they are behind you. ☐ *Nick looked back over his shoulder and then stopped, frowning.* **13** You use **back** in expressions like **back in Chicago** or **back at the house** when you are giving an account, to show that you are going to start talking about what happened or was happening in the place you mention. ☐ *Meanwhile, back in Everett, Marc Fulmer is busy raising money to help get the project off the ground.* **14** If you talk about something that happened **back** in the past or several years **back**, you are emphasizing that it happened quite a long time ago. ☐ *The story starts back in 1950, when I was five.* **15** If you think **back to** something that happened in the past, you remember it or try to remember it. ☐ *I thought back to the time in 1975 when my son was desperately ill.*

▪ PHRASE **back and forth** If someone moves **back and forth**, they repeatedly move in one direction and then in the opposite direction. ☐ *He paced back and forth.*

▪ NOUN [C] (**backs**) **1** A person's or animal's **back** is the part of their body between their head and their legs that is on the opposite side to their chest and stomach. ☐ *Her son was lying peacefully on his back.* ☐ *She turned her back to the audience.* **2** The **back of** something is the side or part of it that is towards the rear or farthest from the front. The back of something is normally not used or seen as much as the front. ☐ *a room at the back of the shop* ☐ *She raised her hands to the back of her neck.* **3** The **back** of a chair or sofa is the part that you lean against when you sit on it. ☐ *There was a pink sweater on the back of the chair.* **4** The **back** of something such as a piece of paper or an envelope is the side that is less important. ☐ *Send your answers on the back of a postcard or sealed, empty envelope.* **5** The **back** of a book is the part nearest the end, where you can find the index or the notes, for example. ☐ *The index at the back of the book lists both brand and generic names.*

▪ PHRASES **do something behind someone's back** (*disapproval*) If you say that something was done **behind** someone's **back**, you disapprove of it because it was done without them knowing about it, in an unfair or dishonest way. ☐ *You eat her food, enjoy her hospitality and then criticize her behind her back.*

back to back If two or more things are done **back to back**, one follows immediately after the other without any interruption. ☐ *two half-hour shows, which will be screened back to back*

back to front (*mainly BrE*; *in AmE*, usually use **backward**) If

you are wearing something **back to front**, you are wearing it with the back of it at the front of your body. If you do something **back to front**, you do it the wrong way around, starting with the part that should come last. = **backward** **ADJ** [back + N] **Back** is used to refer to the side or part of something that is towards the rear or farthest from the front. □ *He opened the back door.* □ *Ann could remember sitting in the back seat of their car.* **VERB** [I, T] (**backs, backing, backed**) **1** [I] If a building **backs onto** something, the back of it faces in the direction of that thing or touches the edge of that thing. □ *He lives in a loft that backs onto Friedman's Bar.* **2** [I, T] When you **back** a car or other vehicle somewhere or when it **backs** somewhere, it moves backwards. = **reverse** □ *He backed his car out of the drive.* **3** [T] If you **back** a person or a course of action, you support them, for example, by voting for them or giving them money. = **support** □ *His defence says it has found a new witness to back his claim that he is a victim of mistaken identity.* **4** [T] If you **back** a particular person, team, or horse in a competition, you predict that they will win, and usually you bet money that they will win. □ *She backed the Detroit Lions to beat the Chicago Bears by at least 20-10.* **5** [T] If a singer **is backed by** a band or by other singers, they provide the musical background for the singer. □ *She chose to be backed by a classy trio of acoustic guitar, bass and congas.* **PHRASAL VERBS** **back away** **1** If you **back away from** a commitment that you made or something that you were involved with in the past, you try to show that you are no longer committed to it or involved with it. = **retreat** □ *The company backed away from plans to cut their pay by 15%.* **2** If you **back away**, you walk backwards away from someone or something, often because you are frightened of them. □ *James got to his feet and started to come over, but the girls hastily backed away.*
back down If you **back down**, you withdraw a claim, demand, or commitment that you made earlier, because other people are strongly opposed to it. □ *It's too late to back down now.*
back off **1** If you **back off**, you move away in order to avoid problems or a fight. □ *They backed off in horror.* **2** If you **back off from** a claim, demand, or commitment that you made earlier, or if you **back off** it, you withdraw it. □ *A spokesman says the president has backed off from his threat to boycott the conference.*
back out If you **back out**, or if you **back out of** something, you decide not to do something that you previously agreed to do. = **pull out** □ *The Hungarians backed out of the project in 1989 on environmental grounds.*
back up **1** If someone or something **backs up** a statement, they supply evidence to suggest that it is true. = **support** □ *Radio signals received from the galaxy's centre back up the black hole theory.* **2** (*computing*) If you **back up** a computer file, you make a copy of it that you can use if the original file is damaged or lost. □ *Make a point of backing up your files at regular intervals.* **3** If an idea or intention **is backed up** by action, action is taken to support or confirm it. □ *The secretary general says the declaration must now be backed up by concrete and effective actions.* **4** If you **back** someone **up**, you show your support for them. = **support** □ *His employers backed him up.* **5** If you **back** someone **up**, you help them by confirming that what they are saying is true. □ *The girl denied being there, and the man backed her up.* **6** If you **back up**, the car or other vehicle that you are driving moves back a short distance. = **reverse** □ *Back up, Hans.* **7** If you **back up**, you move backwards a short distance. □ *I backed up carefully until I felt the wall against my back.* **8** → See also **backup**
✦ **take a back seat** → see **seat**; **cast your mind back** → see **mind**

USAGE NOTE
back

Note that you do not use **back** as a verb to mean 'go back' or 'return' to a place. You do not say 'back to a place' or 'return back to a place'.
I **went back** to college last year.

back·bone /ˈbækbəʊn/ NOUN [C, U] (**backbones**) **1** [C] Your **backbone** is the column of small linked bones down the middle of your back. = **spine** **2** [U] [oft with BRD-NEG] If you say that someone has no **backbone**, you think that they do not have the courage to do things which need to be done. □ *You might be taking drastic measures and you've got to have the backbone to do that.*

back·er /ˈbækə/ NOUN [C] (**backers**) A **backer** is someone who helps or supports a project, organization or person, often by giving or lending money. □ *I was looking for a backer to assist me in the attempted buyout.*

back·fire /ˌbækˈfaɪə, AmE -ˈfaɪr/ VERB [I] (**backfires, backfiring, backfired**) **1** If a plan or project **backfires**, it has the opposite result to the one that was intended. □ *The president's tactics could backfire.* **2** When a motor vehicle or its engine **backfires**, it produces an explosion in the exhaust pipe. □ *The car backfired.*

❶ **back·ground** ◆◇◇ /ˈbækgraʊnd/ NOUN [C, SING] (**backgrounds**) **1** [C] Your **background** is the kind of family you come from and the kind of education you have had. It can also refer to such things as your social and racial origins, your financial status, or the type of work experience that you have. □ *The Warners were from a Jewish working-class background.* **2** [C] The **background** to an event or situation consists of the facts that explain what caused it. = **context** □ *The background to the current troubles is provided by the dire state of the country's economy.* □ *The meeting takes place against a background of continuing political violence.* **3** [SING] The **background** is sounds, such as music, that you can hear but that you are not listening to with your full attention. □ *I kept hearing the sound of applause in the background.* **4** [C] You can use **background** to refer to the things in a picture or scene that are less noticeable or important than the main things or people in it. □ *roses patterned on a blue background*

back·ing ◆◇◇ /ˈbækɪŋ/ NOUN [U, C] (**backings**) **1** [U] If someone has the **backing of** an organization or an important person, they receive support or money from that organization or person in order to do something. = **support** □ *He said the president had the full backing of his government to negotiate a deal.* **2** [C, U] A **backing** is a layer of something such as cloth that is put onto the back of something in order to strengthen or protect it. □ *The table mats and coasters have a non-slip, soft green backing.*

back·lash /ˈbæklæʃ/ NOUN [SING] A **backlash against** a tendency or recent development in society or politics is a sudden, strong reaction against it. = **reaction** □ *the male backlash against feminism*

back·log /ˈbæklɒg, AmE -lɔːg/ NOUN [C] (**backlogs**) A **backlog** is a number of things which have not yet been done but which need to be done. □ *There is a backlog of repairs and maintenance in schools.*

back·stage /ˌbækˈsteɪdʒ/ ADV, ADJ
ADV [backstage after V] In a theatre, **backstage** refers to the areas behind the stage. □ *He went backstage and asked for her autograph.*
ADJ [backstage + N] In a theatre, **backstage** refers to the areas behind the stage. □ *a backstage pass*

back·up /ˈbækʌp/ also **back-up** NOUN [C, U] (**backups**) **1** **Backup** consists of extra equipment, resources or people that you can get help or support from if necessary. □ *There is no emergency back-up immediately available.* **2** If you have something such as a second piece of equipment or set of plans as **backup**, you have arranged for them to be available for use in case the first one does not work. □ *Every part of the system has a backup.*

back·ward /ˈbækwəd/ ADJ **1** [backward + N] A **backward** movement or look is in the direction that your back is facing. □ *He unlocked the door of apartment two and disappeared inside after a backward glance at Larry.* **2** If someone takes a **backward** step or a step **backward**, they do something that does not change or improve their situation, but causes them to go back a stage. □ *The current US farm bill, however, is a big step backward.* **3** A **backward** country or society does not have modern industries and machines. □ *We need to accelerate the pace of change in our* backward country. **4** (offensive) A **backward** child has difficulty in learning. ❑ research into teaching techniques to help backward children

back·wards /ˈbækwədz/ ADV (in AmE, use **backward**)
ADV **1** [backwards after V] If you move or look **backwards**, you move or look in the direction that your back is facing. ❑ The diver flipped over backwards into the water. ❑ He took two steps backwards. **2** [backwards after V] If you do something **backwards**, you do it in the opposite way to the usual way. ❑ He works backwards, building a house from the top downwards. **3** You use **backwards** to indicate that something changes or develops in a way that is not an improvement, but is a return to old ideas or methods. ❑ This country is going backwards.
PHRASE **backwards and forwards** If someone or something moves **backwards and forwards**, they move repeatedly first in one direction and then in the opposite direction. ❑ Using a gentle, sawing motion, draw the floss backwards and forwards between the teeth.

back·yard /ˌbækˈjɑːd/ also **back yard** NOUN [C] (**backyards**) **1** A **backyard** is an area of land at the back of a house. **2** If you refer to a country's own **backyard**, you are referring to its own territory or to somewhere that is very close and where that country wants to influence events. ❑ They seem to think that if it isn't happening in their own backyard, it isn't worth worrying about.

ba·con /ˈbeɪkən/ NOUN [U] **Bacon** is salted or smoked meat which comes from the back or sides of a pig. ❑ bacon and eggs

✪**bac·te·ria** /bækˈtɪəriə/ NOUN [PL] **Bacteria** are very small organisms. Some bacteria can cause disease. ❑ Chlorine is added to kill bacteria.

✪**bac·te·rial** /bækˈtɪəriəl/ ADJ [bacterial + N] **Bacterial** is used to describe things that relate to or are caused by bacteria. ❑ Cholera is a bacterial infection.

bad ♦♦♦ /bæd/ ADJ (**worse**, **worst**) **1** Something that is **bad** is unpleasant, harmful or undesirable. ❑ The bad weather conditions prevented the plane from landing. ❑ Divorce is bad for children. **2** You use **bad** to indicate that something unpleasant or undesirable is severe or great in degree. ❑ Glick had a bad accident two years ago and had to give up farming. ❑ The floods are described as the worst in nearly fifty years. **3** A **bad** idea, decision or method is not sensible or not correct. = poor ❑ Giving your address to a man you don't know is a bad idea. ❑ The worst thing you can do is underestimate an opponent. **4** If you describe a piece of news, an action or a sign as **bad**, you mean that it is unlikely to result in benefit or success. ❑ The closure of the project is bad news for her staff. ❑ It was a bad start in my relationship with Warr. **5** Something that is **bad** is of an unacceptably low standard, quality or amount. = poor ❑ Many old people in the United States are living in bad housing. ❑ The schools' main problem is that teachers' pay is so bad. **6** Someone who is **bad** at doing something is not skilful or successful at it. = poor ❑ Howard was so bad at basketball. ❑ He was a bad driver. **7** If you say that it is **bad** that something happens, you mean it is unacceptable, unfortunate or wrong. ❑ Not being able to hear doesn't seem as bad to the rest of us as not being able to see. **8** [with NEG] You can say that something is **not bad** to mean that it is quite good or acceptable, especially when you are rather surprised about this. ❑ 'How much is he paying you?'—'Oh, five thousand.'—'Not bad.' ❑ That's not a bad idea. **9** [usu bad + N] (informal) If you describe someone or something as **bad**, you mean that they are very good. = excellent ❑ the baddest bass music from Miami, featuring Dr Boom & The Dominator **10** A **bad** person has morally unacceptable attitudes and behaviour. = wicked ❑ I was selling drugs, but I didn't think I was a bad person. **11** A **bad** child disobeys rules and instructions or does not behave in a polite and correct way. = naughty ❑ You are a bad boy for repeating what I told you. **12** If you are in a **bad** mood, you are angry and behave unpleasantly to people. ❑ She is in a bit of a bad mood because she's just given up smoking. **13** If you **feel bad about** something, you feel sorry or guilty about it. ❑ You don't have to feel bad about relaxing. ❑ I feel bad that he's doing most of the work. **14** If you have a **bad** back,

heart, leg or eye, it is injured, diseased or weak. ❑ Joe has a bad back so we have a hard bed. **15** Food that has **gone bad** is not suitable to eat because it has started to decay. ❑ They bought so much beef that some went bad. **16** **Bad** language is language that contains offensive words such as swear words. ❑ I don't like to hear bad language in the street.
→ See also **worse**, **worst**
✦ **bad blood** → see **blood**; **get bad press** → see **press**

badge /bædʒ/ NOUN [C] (**badges**) **1** A **badge** is a piece of metal, cloth or plastic which you wear or carry to show that you work for a particular organization, or that you have achieved something. ❑ a police officer's badge **2** (BrE; in AmE, use **button**) A **badge** is a small piece of metal or plastic which you wear in order to show that you support a particular movement, organization or person. You fasten a badge to your clothes with a pin.

bad·ly ♦◇◇ /ˈbædli/ (**worse**, **worst**) ADV **1** [badly with V] If something is done **badly** or goes **badly**, it is not very successful or effective. ❑ I was angry because I played so badly. ❑ The whole project was badly managed. **2** If someone or something is **badly** hurt or **badly** affected, they are severely hurt or affected. = seriously ❑ The bomb destroyed a police station and badly damaged a church. ❑ One man was killed and another badly injured. **3** [badly with V] If you want or need something **badly**, you want or need it very much. = much ❑ Why do you want to go so badly? **4** [badly with V] If someone behaves **badly** or treats other people **badly**, they act in an unkind, unpleasant or unacceptable way. ❑ They have both behaved very badly and I am very hurt. **5** [badly after V] If something reflects **badly** on someone or makes others think **badly** of them, it harms their reputation. ❑ Teachers know that low exam results will reflect badly on them. **6** If a person or their job is **badly** paid, they are not paid very much for what they do. = poorly ❑ You may have to work part-time, in a badly paid job.
→ See also **worse**, **worst**

bad-tempered ADJ Someone who is **bad-tempered** is not very cheerful and gets angry easily. = irritable ❑ When his headaches developed, Nick became bad-tempered and even violent.

baf·fle /ˈbæfəl/ VERB [T] (**baffles**, **baffling**, **baffled**) If something **baffles** you, you cannot understand it or explain it. = puzzle ❑ An apple tree producing square fruit is baffling experts.
baf·fling /ˈbæflɪŋ/ ADJ ❑ I was constantly ill, with a baffling array of symptoms.

bag ♦♦◇ /bæg/ NOUN [C, PL] (**bags**) **1** [C] A **bag** is a container made of thin paper or plastic, for example one that is used in shops to put things in that a customer has bought. **2** [C] A **bag** is a strong container with one or two handles, used to carry things in. ❑ She left the hotel carrying a shopping bag. **3** [C] You can use **bag** to refer to a bag and its contents, or to the contents only. ❑ Mama came in the back door carrying two bags of groceries. **4** [PL] If you have **bags** under your eyes, you have folds of skin there, usually because you have not had enough sleep. ❑ The bags under his eyes have grown darker.

bag·gage /ˈbæɡɪdʒ/ NOUN [U] **1** Your **baggage** consists of the bags that you take with you when you travel. = luggage ❑ The passengers went through immigration control and collected their baggage. **2** You can use **baggage** to refer to someone's emotional problems, fixed ideas or prejudices. ❑ How much emotional baggage is he bringing with him into the relationship?

bag·gy /ˈbægi/ ADJ (baggier, baggiest) If a piece of clothing is **baggy**, it hangs loosely on your body. ❑ *a baggy sweater*

bail /beɪl/ NOUN, VERB

> The spelling **bale** is also used for meaning 2 of the verb, and for meanings 1, 2 and 4 of the phrasal verb.

NOUN [U] **1 Bail** is a sum of money that an arrested person or someone else puts forward as a guarantee that the arrested person will attend their trial in a law court. If the arrested person does not attend it, the money will be lost. ❑ *He was freed on bail pending an appeal.* **2 Bail** is permission for an arrested person to be released after bail has been paid. ❑ *Bilal was held without bail after a court appearance in Detroit.*

PHRASES **make bail** (AmE) If someone who has been arrested **makes bail**, or if another person **makes bail** for them, the arrested person is released on bail. ❑ *Guerrero was ultimately arrested, but he made bail and fled to Colombia.*

jump bail If a prisoner **jumps bail**, he or she does not come back for his or her trial after being released on bail. ❑ *He had jumped bail last year while being tried on drug charges.*

VERB [T, I] (bails, bailing, bailed) **1** [T] If someone is **bailed**, they are released while they are waiting for their trial, after paying an amount of money to the court. ❑ *He was bailed to appear on 26 August.* **2** [I] If you **bail**, you use a container to remove water from a boat or from a place which is flooded. ❑ *We kept her afloat for a couple of hours by bailing frantically.*

PHRASAL VERB **bail out 1 Bail out** means the same as bail VERB 2. ❑ *A crew was sent down the shaft to close it off and bail out all the water.* **2** If you **bail** someone **out**, you help them out of a difficult situation, often by giving them money. ❑ *They will discuss how to bail the economy out of its slump.* **3** If you **bail** someone **out**, you pay bail on their behalf. ❑ *He has been jailed eight times. Each time, friends bailed him out.* **4** If a pilot **bails out** of an aircraft that is crashing, he or she jumps from it, using a parachute to land safely. ❑ *Reid was forced to bail out of the crippled aircraft.*

bait /beɪt/ NOUN, VERB

NOUN [C, U] (baits) **1** [C, U] **Bait** is food which you put on a hook or in a trap in order to catch fish or animals. ❑ *Vivien refuses to put down bait to tempt wildlife to the waterhole.* **2** [U] [also ʻaʼ bait] To use something as **bait** means to use it to trick or persuade someone to do something. ❑ *Television programmes are essentially bait to attract an audience for commercials.*

VERB [T] (baits, baiting, baited) **1** If you **bait** a hook or trap, you put bait on it or in it. ❑ *He baited his hook with pie.* ❑ *The boys dug pits and baited them so that they could spear their prey.* **2** If you **bait** someone, you deliberately try to make them angry by teasing them. = needle ❑ *He delighted in baiting his mother.*

bake ♦◇◇ /beɪk/ VERB [I, T] (bakes, baking, baked) **1** If you **bake**, you spend some time preparing and mixing together ingredients to make bread, cakes, pies or other food which is cooked in the oven. ❑ *How did you learn to bake cakes?* ❑ *I love to bake.* **2** When a cake or bread **bakes** or when you **bake** it, it cooks in the oven without any extra liquid or fat. ❑ *Bake the cake for 35 to 50 minutes.* ❑ *The batter rises as it bakes.*

bak·ing /ˈbeɪkɪŋ/ NOUN, ADJ

NOUN [U] **Baking** is the preparation and mixing together of ingredients to make bread, cakes, pies or other food which is cooked in the oven. ❑ *On a Thursday she used to do all the baking.*

ADJ You can use **baking** to describe weather or a place that is very hot indeed. ❑ *a baking July day* ❑ *The coffins stood in the baking heat surrounded by mourners.*

⊗**bal·ance** ♦♦◇ /ˈbæləns/ VERB, NOUN

VERB [I, T, RECIP] (balances, balancing, balanced) **1** [I, T] If you **balance** something somewhere, or if it **balances** there, it remains steady and does not fall. ❑ *I balanced on the ledge.* **2** [RECIP] If you **balance** one thing with something different, each of the things has the same strength or

importance. ❑ *Balance spicy dishes with mild ones.* ❑ *The government has to find some way to balance these two needs.* ❑ *Supply and demand on the currency market will generally balance.* **3** [T] If you **balance** one thing **against** another, you consider its importance in relation to the other one. ❑ *She carefully tried to balance religious sensitivities against democratic freedom.* **4** [T] If someone **balances** their budget or if a government **balances** the economy of a country, they make sure that the amount of money that is spent is not greater than the amount that is received. ❑ *He balanced his budgets by rigid control over public expenditure.* **5** [I, T] If you **balance** your books or make them **balance**, you prove by calculation that the amount of money you have received is equal to the amount that you have spent. ❑ *teaching them to balance the books*

NOUN [U, SING, C] (balances) **1** [U] **Balance** is the ability to remain steady when you are standing up. ❑ *The medicines you are currently taking could be affecting your balance.* **2** [SING] A **balance** is a situation in which all the different parts are equal in strength or importance. ❑ *the ecological balance of the forest* ❑ *We are for ever trying to achieve a balance between two opposites.* ❑ *a way to ensure that people get the right balance of foods* **3** [SING] If the **balance** tips in your favour, you start winning or succeeding, especially in a conflict or contest. ❑ *a powerful new gun which could tip the balance of the war in their favour* **4** [C] The **balance** in your bank account is the amount of money you have in it. ❑ *I'd like to check the balance in my account please.* **5** [SING] The **balance** of an amount of money is what remains to be paid for something or what remains when part of the amount has been spent. = remainder ❑ *They were due to pay the balance on delivery.*

PHRASES **keep your balance** or **lose your balance** If you **keep** your **balance**, for example, when standing in a moving vehicle, you remain steady and do not fall over. If you **lose** your **balance**, you become unsteady and fall over. ❑ *She was holding onto the rail to keep her balance.*

off balance If you are **off balance**, you are in an unsteady position and about to fall. ❑ *A gust of wind knocked him off balance and he fell face down in the mud.*

on balance You can say **on balance** to indicate that you are stating an opinion after considering all the relevant facts or arguments. ❑ *On balance he agreed with Christine.*
→ See also **bank balance**

bal·anced /ˈbælənst/ ADJ (approval) **1** [usu ADV balanced] If something is **balanced**, each of the different things in it has the same strength or importance. ❑ *This book is a well balanced biography.* **2** A **balanced** report, book or other document takes into account all the different opinions on something and presents information in a fair and reasonable way. ❑ *a fair, balanced, comprehensive report* **3** Something that is **balanced** is pleasing or useful because its different parts or elements are in the correct proportions. ❑ *a balanced diet* **4** Someone who is **balanced** remains calm and thinks clearly, even in a difficult situation. ❑ *I have to prove myself as a respectable, balanced person.*

bal·co·ny /ˈbælkəni/ NOUN [C, SING] (balconies) **1** [C] A **balcony** is a platform on the outside of a building, above ground level, with a wall or railing around it. **2** [SING] The **balcony** in a theatre or cinema is an area of seats above the main seating area.

bald /bɔːld/ ADJ (balder, baldest) **1** Someone who is **bald** has little or no hair on the top of their head. ❑ *The man's bald head was beaded with sweat.* **2** If a tyre is **bald**, its surface has worn down and it is no longer safe to use. **3** [bald + N] A **bald** statement is in plain language and contains no extra explanation or information. = blunt ❑ *The bald truth is he's just not happy.*

bald·ness /ˈbɔːldnəs/ NOUN [U] ❑ *He wears a cap to cover a spot of baldness.*

bald·ly /ˈbɔːldli/ ADV = bluntly ❑ *'The leaders are outdated,' he stated baldly. 'They don't relate to young people.'*

ball ♦♦◇ /bɔːl/ NOUN, VERB

NOUN [C] (balls) **1** A **ball** is a round or oval object that is used in games such as tennis, baseball, football, basketball and soccer. ❑ *a golf ball* **2** A **ball** is something or an amount of something that has a round shape. ❑ *Thomas screwed the letter up into a ball.* ❸ **The ball of** your foot or **the ball of** your thumb is the rounded part where your toes join your foot or where your thumb joins your hand. ❹ A **ball** is a large formal social event at which people dance. ❑ *My Mama and Daddy used to have a grand Christmas ball every year.*

PHRASE **have a ball** (*informal*) If you **are having a ball**, you are having a very enjoyable time. ❑ *Outside the boys were sitting on the ground and, judging by the gales of laughter, they were having a ball.*

VERB [I, T] (**balls, balling, balled**) When you **ball** something or when it **balls**, it becomes round. ❑ *He picked up the sheets of paper and balled them tightly in his fists.*

bal·let /'bæleɪ, AmE bæ'leɪ/ NOUN [U, C] (**ballets**) ❶ [U] [also 'the' ballet, oft ballet + N] **Ballet** is a type of very skilled and artistic dancing with carefully planned movements. ❑ *I trained as a ballet dancer.* ❷ [C] A **ballet** is an artistic work that is performed by ballet dancers. ❑ *The performance will include the premiere of three new ballets.*

bal·loon /bə'luːn/ NOUN, VERB
NOUN [C] (**balloons**) ❶ A **balloon** is a small, thin, rubber bag that you blow air into so that it becomes larger and rounder or longer. Balloons are used as toys or decorations. ❑ *She popped a balloon with her fork.* ❷ A **balloon** is a large, strong bag filled with gas or hot air, which can carry passengers in a container that hangs underneath it. ❑ *They are to attempt to be the first to circle the Earth non-stop by balloon.*
VERB [I] (**balloons, ballooning, ballooned**) When something **balloons**, it increases rapidly in amount. = soar, rocket ❑ *The jail's female and minority populations have both ballooned in recent years.*

bal·lot ♦◇◇ /'bælət/ NOUN, VERB
NOUN [C] (**ballots**) ❶ A **ballot** is a secret vote in which people select a candidate in an election, or express their opinion about something. ❑ *The result of the ballot will not be known for two weeks.* ❷ A **ballot** is a piece of paper on which you indicate your choice or opinion in a secret vote. ❑ *Election boards will count the ballots by hand.*
VERB [T] (**ballots, balloting, balloted**) If you **ballot** a group of people, you find out what they think about a subject by organizing a secret vote. = poll ❑ *The union said they will ballot members on whether to strike.*

bam·boo /bæm'buː/ NOUN [C, U] (**bamboos**) Bamboo is a tall tropical plant with hard, hollow stems. The young shoots of the plant can be eaten and the stems are used to make furniture. ❑ *huts with walls of bamboo*

✪**ban** ♦♦◇ /bæn/ VERB, NOUN
VERB [T] (**bans, banning, banned**) ❶ To **ban** something means to state officially that it must not be done, shown, or used. = prohibit; ≠ permit, legalize ❑ *Canada will ban smoking in all offices later this year.* ❑ *Last year arms sales were banned.* ❷ If you **are banned from** doing something, you are officially prevented from doing it. = bar ❑ *He was banned from driving for three years.*
NOUN [C] (**bans**) A **ban** is an official ruling that something must not be done, shown, or used. = prohibition ❑ *The general lifted the ban on political parties.* ❑ *calls for an outright ban on arms exports*

ba·na·na /bə'naːnə, -'næn-/ NOUN [C, U] (**bananas**) Bananas are long curved fruit with yellow skins. ❑ *a bunch of bananas*

band ♦♦◇ /bænd/ NOUN
NOUN [C] (**bands**) ❶ A **band** is a small group of musicians who play popular music such as jazz, rock or pop. ❑ *He was a drummer in a rock band.* ❷ A **band** is a group of musicians who play brass and percussion instruments. ❑ *Bands played German marches.* ❸ A **band of** people is a group of people who have joined together because they share an interest or belief. ❑ *Bands of government soldiers, rebels and just plain criminals have been roaming some neighborhoods.* ❹ A **band** is a flat, narrow strip of cloth which you wear around your head or wrists, or which forms part of a piece of clothing. ❑ *Almost all hospitals use a wrist-band of some kind with your name and details on it.* ❺ A **band** is a strip of something such as colour, light, land or

cloth that contrasts with the areas on either side of it. ❑ *bands of natural vegetation between strips of crops* ❻ A **band** is a strip or loop of metal or other strong material which strengthens something or which holds several things together. ❑ *Surgeon Geoffrey Horne placed a metal band around the knee cap to help it knit back together.* ❼ A **band** is a range of numbers or values within a system of measurement. ❑ *For an initial service, a 10 megahertz-wide band of frequencies will be needed.*
PHRASAL VERB **band together** (**bands, banding, banded**) If people **band together**, they meet and act as a group in order to try and achieve something. ❑ *Women banded together to protect each other.*

band·age /'bændɪdʒ/ NOUN, VERB
NOUN [C] (**bandages**) A **bandage** is a long strip of cloth that is wrapped around a wounded part of someone's body to protect or support it. ❑ *We put some ointment and a bandage on his knee.*
VERB [T] (**bandages, bandaging, bandaged**) If you **bandage** a wound or part of someone's body, you tie a bandage around it. ❑ *Apply a dressing to the wound and bandage it.*
PHRASAL VERB **bandage up** Bandage up means the same as **bandage** VERB. ❑ *I bandaged the leg up and gave her aspirin for the pain.*

band·wagon /'bændwægən/ NOUN [C] (**bandwagons**) ❶ You can refer to an activity or movement that has suddenly become fashionable or popular as a **bandwagon**. ❑ *the environmental bandwagon* ❷ If someone, especially a politician, jumps or climbs **on the bandwagon**, they become involved in an activity or movement because it is fashionable or likely to succeed and not because they are really interested in it. ❑ *In recent months many conservative politicians have jumped on the anti-immigrant bandwagon.*

band·width /'bændwɪdθ/ NOUN [C, U] (**bandwidths**) A **bandwidth** is the range of frequencies used for a particular telecommunications signal, radio transmission or computer network. ❑ *To cope with this amount of data, the system will need a bandwidth of around 100mhz.*

bang /bæŋ/ NOUN, VERB, ADV
NOUN [C] (**bangs**) ❶ A **bang** is a sudden loud noise such as the noise of an explosion. ❑ *I heard four or five loud bangs.* ❑ *She slammed the door with a bang.* ❷ A **bang** is when you accidentally knock a part of your body against something and hurt yourself. ❑ *a nasty bang on the head*
PHRASE **with a bang** [with a bang after V] If something begins or ends **with a bang**, it begins or ends with a lot of energy, enthusiasm or success. ❑ *Her career began with a bang in 1986.*
VERB [I, T] (**bangs, banging, banged**) ❶ [I] If something **bangs**, it makes a sudden loud noise, once or several times. ❑ *The engine spat and banged.* ❷ [I, T] If you **bang** a door or if it **bangs**, it closes suddenly with a loud noise. = slam ❑ *the sound of doors banging* ❑ *All up and down the street the windows bang shut.* ❸ [I, T] If you **bang on** something or if you **bang** it, you hit it hard, making a loud noise. ❑ *We could bang on the desks and shout till they let us out.* ❹ [T] If you **bang** something on something or if you **bang** it down, you quickly and violently put it on a surface, because you are angry. ❑ *She banged his dinner on the table.* ❺ [T] If you **bang** a part of your body, you accidentally knock it against something and hurt yourself. ❑ *She'd fainted and banged her head.* ❻ [I] If you **bang into** something or someone, you bump or knock them hard, usually because you are not looking where you are going. = bump ❑ *I didn't mean to bang into you.*
ADV [bang + PREP] (*emphasis*) You can use **bang** to emphasize expressions that indicate an exact position or an exact time. = right ❑ *bang in the middle of the track*

ban·ish /'bænɪʃ/ VERB [T] (**banishes, banishing, banished**) ❶ If someone or something **is banished from** a place or area of activity, they are sent away from it and prevented from entering it. = expel ❑ *John was banished from England.* ❑ *I was banished to the small bedroom upstairs.* ❷ If you **banish** something unpleasant, you get rid of it. ❑ *a public investment programme intended to banish the recession*

bank ♦♦♦ /bæŋk/ NOUN, VERB

[NOUN] [c] (**banks**) **1** A **bank** is an institution where people or businesses can keep their money. ❑ *Students should look to see which bank offers them the service that best suits their financial needs.* **2** A **bank** is a building where a bank offers its services. **3** You use **bank** to refer to a store of something. For example, a blood **bank** is a store of blood that is kept ready for use. ❑ *a national data bank of information on hospital employees* **4** The **banks of** a river, canal or lake are the raised areas of ground along its edge. = side ❑ *We pedalled north along the east bank of the river.* **5** A **bank** of ground is a raised area of it with a flat top and one or two sloping sides. ❑ *lounging on the grassy bank* **6** A **bank** of something is a long high mass of it. ❑ *A bank of clouds had built up along the western horizon.* **7** A **bank of** things, especially machines, switches or dials, is a row of them, or a series of rows. ❑ *The typical labourer now sits in front of a bank of dials.*

[VERB] [i] (**banks, banking, banked**) **1** If you **bank with** a particular bank, you have an account with that bank. ❑ *I have banked with Coutts & Co. for years.* **2** When an aircraft **banks**, one of its wings rises higher than the other, usually when it is changing direction. ❑ *A single-engine plane took off and banked above the highway in front of him.*

[PHRASAL VERB] **bank on** If you **bank on** something happening, you expect it to happen and rely on it happening. = count on ❑ *Everyone is banking on an economic rebound to help ease the state's fiscal problems.*

bank ac·count NOUN [c] (**bank accounts**) A **bank account** is an arrangement with a bank which allows you to keep your money in the bank and to take some out when you need it. ❑ *Paul had at least 17 different bank accounts.*

bank bal·ance NOUN [c] (**bank balances**) Your **bank balance** is the amount of money that you have in your bank account at a particular time. ❑ *Do you wish to use the Internet simply to check your bank balance?*

bank card also **bankcard** NOUN [c] (**bank cards**) A **bank card** is a plastic card that your bank gives you so you can get money from your bank account using a cash machine.

bank·er ♦♦◇ /ˈbæŋkə/ NOUN [c] (**bankers**) A **banker** is someone who works in banking at a senior level. ❑ *an investment banker*

bank holi·day (*mainly BrE*; in *AmE*, usually use **national holiday**) NOUN [c] (**bank holidays**) A **bank holiday** is a public holiday. ❑

bank·ing ♦◇◇ /ˈbæŋkɪŋ/ NOUN [u] **Banking** is the business activity of banks and similar institutions. ❑ *the online banking revolution*

⊙**bank·rupt** /ˈbæŋkrʌpt/ ADJ, VERB, NOUN

[ADJ] **1** (*business*) People or organizations that go **bankrupt** do not have enough money to pay their debts. = insolvent; ≠ solvent ❑ *If the firm cannot sell its products, it will go bankrupt.* ❑ *He was declared bankrupt after failing to pay a £114m loan guarantee.* **2** If you say that something is **bankrupt**, you are emphasizing that it lacks any value or worth. ❑ *He really thinks that European civilization is morally bankrupt.*

[VERB] [T] (**bankrupts, bankrupting, bankrupted**) (*business*) To **bankrupt** a person or organization means to make them go bankrupt. ❑ *The move to the market nearly bankrupted the firm and its director.*

[NOUN] [c] (**bankrupts**) A **bankrupt** is a person who has been declared bankrupt by a court of law. ❑ *In total, 80% of bankrupts are men.*

⊙**bank·rupt·cy** /ˈbæŋkrʌptsi/ NOUN [u, c]

(**bankruptcies**) (*business*) **1** [u] **Bankruptcy** is the state of being bankrupt. = insolvency; ≠ solvency ❑ *Pan Am is the second airline in two months to file for bankruptcy.* ❑ *Many established firms were facing bankruptcy.* **2** [c] A **bankruptcy** is an instance of an organization or person going bankrupt. = insolvency ❑ *The number of corporate bankruptcies climbed in August.*

bank state·ment NOUN [c] (**bank statements**) A **bank statement** is a printed document showing all the money paid into and taken out of a bank account. Bank

statements are usually sent by a bank to a customer at regular intervals.

ban·ner /ˈbænə/ NOUN

[NOUN] [c] (**banners**) A **banner** is a long strip of cloth with something written on it. Banners are usually attached to two poles and carried during a protest or rally. ❑ *A large crowd of students followed the coffin, carrying banners and shouting slogans denouncing the government.*

[PHRASE] **under the banner of** If someone does something **under the banner of** a particular cause, idea or belief, they do it saying that they support that cause, idea or belief. ❑ *Russia was the first country to forge a new economic system under the banner of Marxism.*

bar ♦♦◇ /bɑː/ NOUN, VERB, PREP

[NOUN] [c, SING] (**bars**) **1** [c] A **bar** is a place where you can buy and drink alcoholic drinks. ❑ *Devil's Herd, the city's most popular country and western bar* **2** [c] A **bar** is a room in a hotel or other establishment where alcoholic drinks are served. ❑ *Last night in the hotel there was some talk in the bar about drugs.* **3** [c] A **bar** is a counter on which alcoholic drinks are served. ❑ *Michael was standing alone by the bar when Brian rejoined him.* **4** [c] A **bar** is a long, straight, stiff piece of metal. ❑ *a brick building with bars across the ground-floor windows* **5** [c] A **bar of** something is a piece of it which is roughly rectangular. ❑ *What is your favourite chocolate bar?* **6** [c] If something is a **bar to** doing a particular thing, it prevents someone from doing it. ❑ *One of the fundamental bars to communication is the lack of a universally spoken, common language.* **7** [SING] [oft bar + N] (in *BrE*, use **Bar**) **The bar** is used to refer to the profession of any kind of lawyer in the United States, or of a barrister in England. ❑ *Less than a quarter of graduates from the law school pass the bar exam on the first try.* **8** [c] In music, a **bar** is one of the several short parts of the same length into which a piece of music is divided. ❑ *She sat down at the piano and played a few bars of a Chopin Polonaise.*

[PHRASE] **behind bars** If you say that someone is **behind bars**, you mean that they are in prison. ❑ *Fisher was behind bars last night, charged with attempted murder.*

[VERB] [T] (**bars, barring, barred**) **1** If you **bar** a door, you place something in front of it or a piece of wood or metal across it in order to prevent it from being opened. ❑ *For added safety, bar the door to the kitchen.* **2** If you **bar** someone's way, you prevent them from going somewhere or entering a place, by blocking their path. = block ❑ *Harry moved to bar his way.* **3** If someone **is barred from** a place or **from** doing something, they are officially forbidden to go there or to do it. = ban ❑ *Amnesty workers have been barred from the country since 1982.*

[PREP] (*mainly BrE*) You can use **bar** when you mean 'except'. For example, all the work **bar** the laundry means all the work except the laundry. = save ❑ *Bar a plateau in 1989, there has been a rise in inflation ever since the mid-1980s.*

→ See also **barring**

bar·bar·ic /bɑːˈbærɪk/ ADJ (*disapproval*) If you describe someone's behaviour as **barbaric**, you strongly disapprove of it because you think that it is extremely cruel or uncivilized. ❑ *This barbaric treatment of animals has no place in any decent society.*

bar·becue /ˈbɑːbɪkjuː/ also **Bar-B-Q** (in *AmE*, also use **barbeque**) NOUN, VERB

[NOUN] [c] (**barbecues**) **1** A **barbecue** is a piece of equipment which you use for cooking on in the open air. **2** If someone has a **barbecue**, they cook food on a barbecue in the open air. ❑ *On New Year's Eve we had a barbecue on the beach.*

[VERB] [T] (**barbecues, barbecuing, barbecued**) If you **barbecue** food, especially meat, you cook it on a barbecue. ❑ *Tuna can be grilled, fried, or barbecued.* ❑ *Here's a way of barbecuing corn-on-the-cob that I learned from my uncle.*

⊙**bar chart** NOUN [c] (**bar charts**) A **bar chart** is a graph that uses parallel rectangular shapes to represent changes in the size, value, or rate of something or to compare the amount of something relating to a number of different countries or groups. ❑ *They made a bar chart to display the results.* ❑ *The bar chart below shows the huge growth of UK car exports over the past few years.*

bare ♦◊◊ /beə/ ADJ, VERB

[ADJ] (**barer, barest**) **1** If a part of your body is **bare**, it is not covered by any clothing. □ *She was wearing only a thin bathrobe over a flimsy nightgown, and her feet were bare.* **2** A **bare** surface is not covered or decorated with anything. □ *They would have liked bare wooden floors throughout the house.* **3** If a tree or a branch is **bare**, it has no leaves on it. □ *an old, twisted tree, many of its limbs brittle and bare* **4** If a room, cupboard, or shelf is **bare**, it is empty. □ *His fridge was bare apart from three very withered tomatoes.* **5** An area of ground that is **bare** has no plants growing on it. □ *That's probably the most bare, bleak, barren, and inhospitable island I've ever seen.* **6** [DET + bare + N] If someone gives you the **bare** facts or the **barest** details of something, they tell you only the most basic and important things. = plain □ *Newspaper reporters were given nothing but the bare facts by the superintendent in charge of the investigation.* **7** [DET + bare + N] If you talk about the **bare** minimum or the **bare** essentials, you mean the very least that is necessary. = absolute □ *The army would try to hold the western desert with a bare minimum of forces.* **8** ['a' bare + AMOUNT] **Bare** is used in front of an amount to emphasize how small it is. = mere □ *Sales are growing for premium wines, but at a bare 2 per cent a year.* [PHRASE] **with one's bare hands** If someone does something **with** their **bare hands**, they do it without using any weapons or tools. □ *Police believe the killer punched her to death with his bare hands.* [VERB] [T] (**bares, baring, bared**) (*written*) If you **bare** something, you uncover it and show it. □ *Walsh bared his teeth in a grin.*
✦ **bare bones** → see **bone**

bare·ly ♦◊◊ /ˈbeəli/ ADV **1** You use **barely** to say that something is only just true or only just the case. = scarcely □ *Anastasia could barely remember the ride to the hospital.* □ *It was 90 degrees and the air conditioning barely cooled the room.* **2** [barely before V] If you say that one thing **barely** happened when something else happened, you mean that the first event was followed immediately by the second. □ *The water had barely come to a simmer when she cracked four eggs into it.*

bar·gain ♦◊◊ /ˈbɑːgɪn/ NOUN, VERB

[NOUN] [c] (**bargains**) **1** Something that is a **bargain** is good value, usually because it has been sold at a lower price than normal. □ *At this price the wine is a bargain.* **2** A **bargain** is an agreement, especially a formal business agreement, in which two people or groups agree what each of them will do, pay, or receive. = deal □ *I'll make a bargain with you. I'll play hostess if you'll include Matthew in your guest list.* [PHRASE] **into the bargain** or **in the bargain** (*emphasis*) You use **into the bargain** or **in the bargain** when mentioning an additional quantity, feature, fact, or action, to emphasize the fact that it is also involved. □ *This machine is designed to save you effort and keep your work surfaces tidy into the bargain.* [VERB] [I] (**bargains, bargaining, bargained**) When people **bargain** with each other, they discuss what each of them will do, pay, or receive. = negotiate □ *They prefer to bargain with individual clients, for cash.* [PHRASAL VERB] **bargain for** or **bargain on** If you have not **bargained for** or **bargained on** something that happens, you did not expect it to happen and so feel surprised or worried by it. □ *The effects of this policy were more than the government had bargained for.*
bar·gain·ing /ˈbɑːgənɪŋ/ NOUN [u] □ *The government has called for sensible pay bargaining.*

barge /bɑːdʒ/ NOUN, VERB

[NOUN] [c] (**barges**) [also 'by' barge] A **barge** is a long, narrow boat with a flat bottom. Barges are used for carrying heavy loads, especially on rivers and canals. □ *Carrying goods by train costs nearly three times more than carrying them by barge.* [VERB] [I] (**barges, barging, barged**) (*informal*) **1** If you **barge into** a place or **barge through** it, you rush or push into it in a rough and rude way. □ *Students tried to barge into the secretariat buildings.* **2** If you **barge into** someone

or **barge past** them, you bump against them roughly and rudely. □ *He would barge into them and kick them in the shins.* [PHRASAL VERB] **barge in** (*informal*) If you **barge in** or **barge in on** someone, you rudely interrupt what they are doing or saying. □ *I'm sorry to barge in like this, but I have a problem I hope you can solve.*

bark /bɑːk/ VERB, NOUN

[VERB] [I] (**barks, barking, barked**) **1** When a dog **barks**, it makes a short, loud noise, once or several times. □ *Don't let the dogs bark.* **2** If you **bark at** someone, you shout at them aggressively in a loud, rough voice. □ *I didn't mean to bark at you.* [NOUN] [c, u] (**barks**) **1** [c] A **bark** is a short, loud noise made by a dog. □ *The Doberman let out a string of roaring barks.* **2** [u] **Bark** is the tough material that covers the outside of a tree.

barn /bɑːn/ NOUN [c] (**barns**) A **barn** is a building on a farm in which animals, animal food, or crops can be kept.

ba·rom·eter /bəˈrɒmɪtə/ NOUN [c] (**barometers**) **1** A **barometer** is an instrument that measures air pressure and shows when the weather is changing. □ *A man took a barometer reading at half-hour intervals.* **2** If something is a **barometer of** a particular situation, it indicates how things are changing or how things are likely to develop. □ *In past presidential elections, Missouri has been a barometer of the rest of the country.*

bar·racks /ˈbærəks/ NOUN [c] (**barracks**) A **barracks** is a building or group of buildings where soldiers or other members of the armed forces live and work. □ *an army barracks in the north of the city*

bar·rage /ˈbærɑːʒ, AmE bəˈrɑːʒ/ NOUN, VERB

[NOUN] [c] (**barrages**) **1** A **barrage** is continuous firing on an area with large guns and tanks. = bombardment □ *The artillery barrage on the city was the heaviest since the ceasefire.* **2** A **barrage of** something such as criticism or complaints is a large number of them directed at someone, often in an aggressive way. □ *He was faced with a barrage of angry questions from the floor.* **3** /AmE ˈbɑːrɪdʒ/ A **barrage** is a structure that is built across a river to control the level of the water. □ *a hydro-electric tidal barrage* [VERB] [T] (**barrages, barraging, barraged**) If you are **barraged** by people or things, you have to deal with a great number of people or things you would rather avoid. □ *Doctors are complaining about being barraged by drug-company salesmen.*

bar·rel ♦◊◊ /ˈbærəl/ NOUN, VERB

[NOUN] [c] (**barrels**) **1** A **barrel** is a large, round container for liquids or food. □ *The wine is aged for almost a year in oak barrels.* **2** In the oil industry, a **barrel** is a unit of measurement equal to 42 gallons (159 litres). □ *In 1989, Kuwait was exporting 1.5 million barrels of oil a day.* **3** The **barrel** of a gun is the tube through which the bullet moves when the gun is fired. □ *He pushed the barrel of the gun into the other man's open mouth.* [PHRASE] **lock, stock, and barrel** (*emphasis*) If you say, for example, that someone moves or buys something **lock, stock, and barrel**, you are emphasizing that they move or buy every part or item of it. □ *They received a verbal offer to buy the company lock, stock, and barrel.* [VERB] [I] (**barrels, barrelling, barrelled**; in AmE, use **barreling, barreled**) If a vehicle or person is **barrelling** in a particular direction, they are moving very quickly in that direction. = career □ *The car was barrelling down the street at a crazy speed.*

bar·ren ♦◊◊ /ˈbærən/ ADJ **1** A **barren** landscape is dry and bare, and has very few plants and no trees. □ *the Tibetan landscape of high barren mountains* **2 Barren** land consists of soil that is so poor that plants cannot grow in it. = infertile □ *He wants to use the water to irrigate barren desert land.* **3** [oft barren 'of' N] (*written*) If you describe something such as an activity or a period of your life as **barren**, you mean that you achieve no success during it or that it has no useful results. □ *an empty exercise barren of utility* **4** [oft barren 'of' N] (*written, disapproval*) If you describe a room or a place as **barren**, you do not like it because it has almost no furniture or other objects in it.

❑ *The room was austere, nearly barren of furniture or decoration.*

bar·ri·cade /'bærɪkeɪd/ NOUN, VERB

NOUN [c] (**barricades**) A **barricade** is a line of vehicles or other objects placed across a road or open space to stop people from getting past, for example during street fighting or as a protest. = blockade ❑ *Large areas of the city have been closed off by barricades set up by the demonstrators.*

VERB [T] (**barricades, barricading, barricaded**) **1** If you **barricade** something such as a road or an entrance, you place a barricade or barrier across it, usually to stop someone from getting in. ❑ *The rioters barricaded streets with piles of blazing tyres.* **2** If you **barricade** yourself inside a room or building, you place barriers across the door or entrance so that other people cannot get in. ❑ *The students have barricaded themselves into their dormitory building.*

⭕ bar·ri·er ◆◇◇ /'bæriə/ NOUN [C, SING] (**barriers**) **1** [c] A **barrier** is something such as a rule, law, or policy that makes it difficult or impossible for something to happen or be achieved. = obstacle ❑ *Duties and taxes are the most obvious barrier to free trade.* **2** [c] A **barrier** is a problem that prevents two people or groups from agreeing, communicating, or working with each other. = obstacle, divide ❑ *There is no reason why love shouldn't cross the age barrier.* ❑ *She had been waiting for Simon to break down the barrier between them.* **3** [c] A **barrier** is something such as a fence or wall that is put in place to prevent people from moving easily from one area to another. ❑ *The demonstrators broke through heavy police barriers.* **4** [c] A **barrier** is an object or layer that physically prevents something from moving from one place to another. ❑ *A severe storm destroyed a natural barrier between the house and the lake.* **5** [SING] You can refer to a particular number or amount as a **barrier** when you think it is significant, because it is difficult or unusual to go above it. ❑ *They are fearful that unemployment will soon break the barrier of three million.*

bar·ring /'bɑːrɪŋ/ PREP You use **barring** to indicate that the person, thing, or event that you are mentioning is an exception to your statement. ❑ *Barring accidents, I believe they will succeed.*

bar·ris·ter /'bærɪstə/ NOUN [c] (**barristers**) In England and Wales, a **barrister** is a lawyer who represents clients in the higher courts of law. Compare **solicitor**.

⭕ base ◆◆◆ /beɪs/ NOUN, VERB, ADJ

NOUN [c] **1** The **base** of something is its lowest edge or part. = bottom, foot ❑ *There was a bike path running along this side of the wall, right at its base.* **2** The **base** of something is the lowest part of it, where it is attached to something else. ❑ *The surgeon placed catheters through the veins and arteries near the base of the head.* **3** The **base** of an object such as a box or vase is the lower surface of it that touches the surface it rests on. = bottom, underneath ❑ *Remove from the heat and plunge the base of the pan into a bowl of very cold water.* **4** The **base** of an object that has several sections and that rests on a surface is the lower section of it. ❑ *The mattress is best on a solid bed base.* **5** A **base** is a layer of something which will have another layer added to it. ❑ *Mix together the cream cheese, yogurt and honey, and spread over the meringue base.* **6** A position or thing that is a **base** for something is one from which that thing can be developed or achieved. = basis, foundation ❑ *The post will give him a powerful political base from which to challenge the Kremlin.* **7** (business) A company's client **base** or customer **base** is the group of regular clients or customers that the company gets most of its income from. ❑ *The company has been expanding its customer base using trade magazine advertising.* **8** A military **base** is a place that part of the armed forces works from. ❑ *Gunfire was heard at an army base close to the airport.* **9** Your **base** is the main place where you work, stay, or live. ❑ *For most of the spring and early summer her base was her home in Connecticut.* **10** If a place is a **base** for a certain activity, the activity can be carried out at that place or from that place. ❑ *The two hotels are attractive bases from which to explore south-east Tuscany.* **11** The **base** of a substance such as paint or food

is the main ingredient of it, to which other substances can be added. ❑ *Just before cooking, drain off any excess marinade and use it as a base for a sauce.* **12** [also base + NUM] A **base** is a system of counting and expressing numbers. The decimal system uses base 10, and the binary system uses base 2. **13** A **base** in baseball, softball, or rounders is one of the places at each corner of the diamond or square on the pitch. ❑ *The first player to reach second base in the game was John Flaherty.*

VERB [T] If you **base** one thing **on** another thing, the first thing develops from the second thing. ❑ *He based his conclusions on the evidence given by the captured prisoners.* ❑ *Selection decisions are seldom based on test data alone.*

ADJ [base + N] **Base** is used to describe a price or someone's income when this does not include any additional amounts. ❑ *an increase of more than twenty per cent on the base pay of a typical worker*

base·ball ◆◇◇ /'beɪsbɔːl/ NOUN [U, c] (**baseballs**) **1** [u] Baseball is a game played by two teams of nine players. Each player from one team hits a ball with a bat and then tries to run around three bases and get to home plate before the other team can get the ball back. **2** [c] A **baseball** is a small hard ball which is used in the game of baseball.

based ◆◆◆ /beɪst/ ADJ **1** [based + 'on/upon'] If one thing is **based** on another thing, the first thing develops from the second thing. ❑ *Three of the new products are based on traditional herbal medicines.* **2** [V-LINK + based] If you are **based** in a particular place, that is the place where you live or do most of your work. = located ❑ *Both companies are based in Kent.*

base·ment /'beɪsmənt/ NOUN [c] (**basements**) The **basement** of a building is a floor built partly or completely below ground level. ❑ *They bought an old schoolhouse to live in and built a workshop in the basement.*

bases IRREG FORM **1** /'beɪsɪz/ **Bases** is the plural of **base**. **2** /'beɪsiːz/ **Bases** is the plural of **basis**.

bash /bæʃ/ NOUN, VERB

NOUN [c] (**bashes**) (*informal*) A **bash** is a party or celebration, especially a large one held by an official organization or attended by famous people. ❑ *He threw one of the biggest showbiz bashes of the year as a 36th birthday party for Jerry Hall.*

VERB [T] (**bashes, bashing, bashed**) (*informal*) **1** If someone **bashes** you, they attack you by hitting or punching you hard. ❑ *If someone tried to bash my best friend they would have to bash me as well.* ❑ *I bashed him on the head and dumped him in the water.* **2** If you **bash** something, you hit it hard in a rough or careless way. ❑ *Too many golfers try to bash the ball out of sand. That spells disaster.*

⭕ ba·sic ◆◆◇ /'beɪsɪk/ ADJ **1** You use **basic** to describe things, activities, and principles that are very important or necessary, and on which others depend. = fundamental, key; ≠ secondary ❑ *the basic skills of reading, writing and communicating* ❑ *Access to justice is a basic right.* **2** **Basic** goods and services are very simple ones which every human being needs. You can also refer to people's **basic** needs for such goods and services. = essential ❑ *shortages of even the most basic foodstuffs* ❑ *Hospitals lack even basic drugs for surgical operations.* **3** [V-LINK + basic 'to' N] If one thing is **basic to** another, it is absolutely necessary to it, and the second thing cannot exist, succeed, or be imagined without it. = central ❑ *an oily liquid, basic to the manufacture of a host of other chemical substances* **4** [basic + N] You can use **basic** to emphasize that you are referring to what you consider to be the most important aspect of a situation, and that you are not concerned with less important details. = fundamental, main ❑ *There are three basic types of tea.* ❑ *The basic design changed little from that patented by Edison more than 100 years ago.* **5** You can use **basic** to describe something that is very simple in style and has only the most necessary features, without any luxuries. ❑ *We provide two-person tents and basic cooking and camping equipment.* **6** [basic + N] The **basic** rate of income tax is the lowest or most common rate, which applies to people who earn average incomes. ❑ *All this is to be done without big increases in the basic level of taxation.*

B

basic ADJ

You use **basic** to describe things that are very important or necessary and on which other things depend.

❏ *The money will be used for the delivery of basic human needs including food, water, and health care.*

fundamental ADJ

You use **fundamental** to describe things that are very important.

❏ *The choice to marry is a fundamental human right.*

key ADJ

The **key** person or thing in a group is the most important one.

❏ *By 1668 most of the key members of the Oxford group were in London.*

essential ADJ

Something that is **essential** is absolutely necessary to a particular subject, situation, or activity.

❏ *Both oxygen and glucose are essential for life and health.*

main ADJ

The **main** thing is the most important one of several similar things in a particular situation.

❏ *Our main concern is to get the vans back to the depot on time.*

principal ADJ

Principal means the first in order of importance.

❏ *The principal aim of this book is to help amateur gardeners plan and create their ideal garden.*

ba·si·cal·ly ◆◇◇ /ˈbeɪsɪkli/ ADV **1** [basically with CL/GROUP] (*emphasis*) You use **basically** for emphasis when you are stating an opinion, or when you are making an important statement about something. ❏ *This gun is designed for one purpose – it's basically to kill people.* **2** You use **basically** to show that you are describing a situation in a simple, general way, and that you are not concerned with less important details. ❏ *Basically you've got two choices.*

✪ba·sics /ˈbeɪsɪks/ NOUN [PL] **1** The **basics** of something are its simplest, most important elements, ideas, or principles, in contrast to more complicated or detailed ones. = fundamentals ❏ *They will concentrate on teaching the basics of reading, writing and arithmetic.* ❏ *A strong community cannot be built until the basics are in place.* **2** **Basics** are things such as simple food, clothes, or equipment that people need in order to live or to deal with a particular situation. ❏ *supplies of basics such as bread and milk*

ba·sin /ˈbeɪsən/ NOUN [C] (**basins**) **1** A **basin** is a large or deep bowl that you use for holding liquids. ❏ *Water dripped into a basin at the back of the room.* **2** A **basin of** something such as water is an amount of it that is contained in a basin. ❏ *We were given a basin of water to wash our hands in.* **3** A **basin** is a sink. ❏ *a cast-iron bathtub with a matching basin* **4** The **basin** of a large river is the area of land around it from which streams run down into it. ❏ *the Amazon basin* **5** (*technical*) In geography, a **basin** is a particular region of the world where the Earth's surface is lower than in other places. ❏ *countries around the Pacific Basin*

✪ba·sis ◆◆◇ /ˈbeɪsɪs/ NOUN [SING, C] (**bases**) **1** [SING] If something is done **on** a particular **basis**, it is done according to that method, system, or principle. = method, system, footing, principle ❏ *We're going to be meeting there on a regular basis.* ❏ *They want all groups to be treated on an equal basis.* **2** [SING] If you say that you are acting **on** the **basis of** something, you are giving that as the reason for your action. ❏ *McGregor must remain confined, on the basis of the medical reports we have received.* **3** [C] The **basis** of something is its starting point or an important part of it from which it can be further developed. = foundation

❏ *Both factions have broadly agreed that the U.N. plan is a possible basis for negotiation.* **4** [C] The **basis** for something is a fact or argument that you can use to prove or justify it. ❏ *Japan's attempt to secure the legal basis to send troops overseas*

basis NOUN

If something is done on a particular **basis**, it is done according to a particular set of rules and conventions.

❏ *Department heads meet with employees on a regular basis to identify and map out objectives.*

method NOUN

A **method** is a particular way of doing something.

❏ *Previous studies have shown that organic farming methods can benefit the wildlife around farms.*

system NOUN

A **system** is a way of working, organizing, or doing something which follows a fixed plan.

❏ *The new system for bringing criminal cases to court was recommended in early 2000.*

footing NOUN

If something is put on a particular **footing**, it is defined or organized in a particular way, so that people know how it should work.

❏ *It puts the party on a great financial footing heading into an election year.*

principle NOUN

The **principles** of a particular theory are its basic rules.

❏ *The principles of fairness and justice should be applied equally in society.*

bas·ket /ˈbɑːskɪt, ˈbæs-/ NOUN [C] (**baskets**) **1** A **basket** is a stiff container that is used for carrying or storing objects. Baskets are made from thin strips of materials such as straw, plastic, or wire woven together. ❏ *big wicker picnic baskets filled with sandwiches* **2** You can use **basket** to refer to a basket and its contents, or to the contents only. ❏ *a small basket of fruit and snacks* **3** (*business*) In economics, a **basket** of currencies or goods is the average or total value of a number of different currencies or goods. ❏ *The dollar has fallen 6.5 per cent this year against a basket of currencies from its largest trading partners.*

basket·ball ◆◆◇ /ˈbɑːskɪtbɔːl, ˈbæs-/ NOUN [U, C] (**basketballs**) **1** [U] **Basketball** is a game in which two teams of five players each try to score goals by throwing a large ball through a circular net fixed to a metal ring at each end of the court. **2** [C] A **basketball** is a large ball which is used in the game of basketball.

bass ◆◇◇ /beɪs/ NOUN, ADJ

NOUN [C, U] (**basses**) **1** [C] A **bass** is a man with a very deep singing voice. ❏ *the great Russian bass Chaliapin* **2** [C, U] A **bass** is a musical instrument, especially a guitar, that plays low notes. ❏ *Dave Ranson on bass and Kenneth Blevins on drums* **3** [U] On a stereo system or radio, the **bass** is the ability to reproduce the lower musical notes. The **bass** is also the knob that controls this. ❏ *Larger models give more bass.* **4** /bæs/ [C, U] **Bass** are edible fish that are found in rivers and the sea. There are several types of bass. ❏ *They unloaded their catch of cod and bass.* **5** /bæs/ [U] **Bass** is a piece of this fish eaten as food. ❏ *a large fresh fillet of sea bass*

ADJ [bass + N] A **bass** drum, guitar, or other musical instrument is one that produces a very deep sound. ❏ *bass guitarist Dee Murray*

bat ◆◇◇ /bæt/ NOUN, VERB

NOUN [C] (**bats**) **1** A **bat** is a specially shaped piece of wood that is used for hitting the ball in baseball, softball, or cricket. ❏ *a baseball bat* **2** A **bat** is a small flying animal that looks like a mouse with wings made of skin. Bats are active at night.

VERB [I] (**bats**, **batting**, **batted**) When you **bat**, you have a turn at hitting the ball with a bat in baseball, softball, or cricket. ❑ *Pettitte hurt an elbow tendon while batting.*

batch /bætʃ/ NOUN [c] (**batches**) A **batch of** things or people is a group of things or people of the same kind, especially a group that is dealt with at the same time or is sent to a particular place at the same time. ❑ *the current batch of trainee priests* ❑ *She brought a large batch of newspaper clippings.* ❑ *I baked a batch of biscuits.*

bath ◆◇◇ /bɑːθ, bæθ/ NOUN, VERB
NOUN [c] (**baths**) **1** (*BrE*; in *AmE*, use **bathtub**) A **bath** is a container, usually a long rectangular one, which you fill with water and sit in while you wash your body. **2** A **bath** is the process of washing your body in a bath. ❑ *The midwife gave him a warm bath.* **3** When you have or take a **bath**, you sit or lie in a bath filled with water in order to wash your body. ❑ *Have a shower instead of a bath.* **4** A **bath** or a **baths** is a public building containing a swimming pool, and sometimes other facilities that people can use to wash or take a bath. ❑ *a thriving town with houses, government buildings and public baths* **5** A **bath** is a container filled with a particular liquid, such as a dye or an acid, in which particular objects are placed, usually as part of a manufacturing or chemical process. ❑ *a developing photograph placed in a bath of fixer*
VERB [T, I] (**baths, bathing, bathed**) (*BrE*; in *AmE*, use **bathe**) **1** [T] If you **bath** someone, especially a child, you wash them in a bath. = bathe **2** [I] When you **bath**, you take a bath. = bathe

bathe /beɪð/ VERB, NOUN
VERB [I, T] (**bathes, bathing, bathed**) **1** [I] (*mainly AmE*) When you **bathe**, you have a bath. ❑ *At least 60% of us now bathe or shower once a day.* **2** [T] (*mainly AmE*) If you **bathe** someone, especially a child, you wash them in a bath. ❑ *Back home, Shirley plays with, feeds and bathes the baby.* **3** [I] (*mainly BrE, formal*) If you **bathe** in a sea, river, or lake, you swim, play, or wash yourself in it. Birds and animals can also **bathe**. ❑ *The police have warned the city's inhabitants not to bathe in the polluted river.* **4** [T] If you **bathe** a part of your body or a wound, you wash it gently or soak it in a liquid. ❑ *Bathe the infected area in a salt solution.* **5** [T] If a place **is bathed in** light, it is covered with light, especially a gentle, pleasant light. ❑ *The arena was bathed in warm sunshine.* ❑ *I was led to a small room bathed in soft red light.*
NOUN [SING] (*mainly BrE, formal*) A **bathe** in a sea, river, or lake is when you swim, play, or wash yourself in it. ❑ *They took an early morning bathe in the lake.*
bath·ing /beɪðɪŋ/ NOUN [U] ❑ *Bathing is not allowed.*

bath·room ◆◇◇ /bɑːθruːm, bæθ-/ NOUN
NOUN [c] (**bathrooms**) A **bathroom** is a room in a house that contains a bath or shower, a sink, and sometimes a toilet.
PHRASE **go to the bathroom** (*politeness*) People say that they **are going to the bathroom** when they want to say that they are going to use the toilet. ❑ *Although he had been treated with antibiotics, he went to the bathroom repeatedly.*

ba·ton /bætɒn, AmE bəˈtɑːn/ NOUN [c] (**batons**) **1** A **baton** is a light, thin stick used by a conductor to conduct an orchestra or a choir. ❑ *The maestro raises his baton.* **2** In track and field or track events, a **baton** is a short stick that is passed from one runner to another in a relay race. ❑ *their biggest relay outing since dropping the baton in Edmonton last August* **3** (*BrE*; in *AmE*, use **billy**) A **baton** is a short heavy stick which is sometimes used as a weapon by the police.

bat·ter /bætə/ VERB, NOUN
VERB [T] (**batters, battering, battered**) **1** To **batter** someone means to hit them many times, using fists or a heavy object. ❑ *The passengers were battered by flying luggage and cargo as the cabin lost pressure.* ❑ *A karate expert battered a man to death.* **2** If someone **is battered**, they are regularly hit and badly hurt by a member of their family or by their partner. ❑ *evidence that the child was being battered* ❑ *boys who witness fathers battering their mothers* **3** If a place **is battered by** wind, rain, or storms, it is seriously damaged or affected by very bad weather.

= pound ❑ *The country has been battered by winds of between fifty and seventy miles an hour.* **4** If you **batter** something, you hit it many times, using your fists or a heavy object. ❑ *They were battering the door, they were trying to break in.*
NOUN [c, U] (**batters**) **1** [c, U] **Batter** is a mixture of flour, eggs, and milk that is used in cooking. ❑ *pancake batter* **2** [c] In sports such as cricket and baseball, a **batter** is a person who hits the ball with a wooden bat. ❑ *batters and bowlers*

bat·tered /bætəd/ ADJ ❑ *Her battered body was discovered in a field.*
bat·ter·ing /bætərɪŋ/ NOUN [U] ❑ *Leaving the relationship does not mean that the battering will stop.*

bat·tery /bætəri/ NOUN [c] (**batteries**) **1** **Batteries** are small devices that provide the power for electrical items such as radios and children's toys. ❑ *The shavers come complete with batteries.* ❑ *a battery-operated cassette player* **2** A car **battery** is a rectangular box containing acid that is found in a car engine. It provides the electricity needed to start the car. ❑ *a car with a dead battery* **3** A **battery of** equipment such as guns, lights, or computers is a large set of it kept together in one place. ❑ *They stopped beside a battery of abandoned guns.* **4** A **battery of** people or things is a very large number of them. ❑ *a battery of journalists and television cameras*

❖ **bat·tle** ◆◆◇ /bætəl/ NOUN, VERB
NOUN [c, U] (**battles**) **1** [c, U] A **battle** is a violent fight between groups of people, especially one between military forces during a war. = fight, combat ❑ *the victory of King William III at the Battle of the Boyne* ❑ *a gun battle between police and drug traffickers* ❑ *men who die in battle* **2** [c] A **battle** is a conflict in which different people or groups compete in order to achieve success or control. = struggle ❑ *an unfolding political battle over jobs and the economy* ❑ *the eternal battle between good and evil in the world* ❑ *a battle for supremacy* **3** [c] You can use **battle** to refer to someone's efforts to achieve something in spite of very difficult circumstances. = fight, campaign ❑ *the battle against crime* ❑ *She has fought a constant battle with her weight.* ❑ *Greg lost his brave battle against cancer two years ago.*
VERB [RECIP, I, T] (**battles, battling, battled**) **1** [RECIP] To **battle with** an opposing group means to take part in a fight or contest against them. You can also say that one group or person **is battling** another. ❑ *In one town thousands of people battled with police and several were reportedly wounded.* ❑ *The sides must battle again for a quarter-final place on December 16.* **2** [I, T] To **battle** means to try hard to do something in spite of very difficult circumstances. You can also **battle** something, or **battle against** something or **with** something. = fight ❑ *Doctors battled throughout the night to save her life.* ❑ *Firefighters are still battling the two blazes.*
PHRASE **battle it out** If one group or person **battles it out with** another, they take part in a fight or contest against each other until one of them wins or a definite result is reached. You can also say that two groups or two people **battle it out**. ❑ *She will now battle it out with 50 other hopefuls for a place in the last 10.*

WORD CONNECTIONS
ADJ + **battle**
a **fierce** battle a **bitter** battle
❑ *The couple have been involved in a fierce legal battle for custody of their two sons.*
a **continuing** battle an **uphill** battle a **long** battle
❑ *Getting children to eat healthily can be an uphill battle.*
a **legal** battle a **political** battle
❑ *The political battles fought to negotiate and pass the agreement had damaged the president's reputation.*

B

VERB + **battle**

face a battle
fight a battle
win a battle
lose a battle
❏ *The government is winning the battle against inflation.*

---

battle·field /ˈbætəlfiːld/ NOUN [c] (**battlefields**)
1 A **battlefield** is a place where a battle is fought.
= battleground ❏ *the struggle to save America's Civil War battlefields* **2** You can refer to an issue or field of activity over which people disagree or compete as a **battlefield**.
= battleground ❏ *the domestic battlefield of family life*

battle·ship /ˈbætəlʃɪp/ NOUN [c] (**battleships**) A **battleship** is a very large, heavily armed warship.

bay ♦♢♢ /beɪ/ NOUN, ADJ, VERB
NOUN [c] (**bays**) **1** A **bay** is a part of a coast where the land curves inwards. ❏ *a short ferry ride across the bay* ❏ *the Bay of Bengal* **2** A **bay** is a partly enclosed area, inside or outside a building, that is used for a particular purpose. ❏ *The animals are herded into a bay, then butchered.* **3** A **bay** is an area of a room that extends beyond the main walls of a house, especially an area with a large window at the front of a house.
PHRASE **keep at bay** or **hold at bay** If you **keep** something or someone **at bay**, or **hold** them **at bay**, you prevent them from reaching, attacking, or affecting you. ❏ *Eating oranges keeps colds at bay.*
ADJ A **bay** horse is reddish-brown in colour. ❏ *a 10-year-old bay mare*
VERB [i] (**bays, baying, bayed**) **1** If a number of people are **baying for** something, they are demanding something angrily, usually that someone should be punished.
= clamour ❏ *The referee ignored voices baying for a penalty.* ❏ *Opposition politicians have been baying for his blood.* **2** If a dog or wolf **bays**, it makes loud, long cries. ❏ *A dog suddenly howled, baying at the moon.*

BC /ˌbiːˈsiː/ also **B.C.** You use **BC** in dates to indicate a number of years or centuries before the year in which Jesus Christ is believed to have been born. Compare **AD**. ❏ *The brooch dates back to the fourth century BC.*

be ♦♦♦ /bi, STRONG biː/ VERB

In spoken English, forms of **be** are often shortened, for example 'I am' can be shortened to 'I'm'.

VERB [AUX, LINK] (**am, are, is, being, was, were, been**)
1 [AUX] You use **be** with a present participle to form the continuous tenses of verbs. ❏ *This is happening in every school throughout the country.* ❏ *She didn't always think carefully about what she was doing.* **2** [AUX] You use **be** with a past participle to form the passive voice. ❏ *Her husband was killed in a car crash.* ❏ *Similar action is being taken by the US government.* **3** [AUX] You use **be** with an infinitive to indicate that something is planned to happen, that it will definitely happen, or that it must happen. ❏ *The talks are to begin tomorrow.* ❏ *It was to be Johnson's first meeting with the board in nearly a month.* **4** [AUX] You use **be** with an infinitive to say or ask what should happen or be done in a particular situation, how it should happen, or who should do it. ❏ *What am I to do without him?* ❏ *Who is to say which of them had more power?* **5** [AUX] You use **was** and **were** with an infinitive to talk about something that happened later than the time you are discussing, and was not planned or certain at that time. ❏ *He started something that was to change the face of China.* **6** [AUX] You can say that something is **to be** seen, heard, or found in a particular place to mean that people can see it, hear it, or find it in that place. ❏ *Little traffic was to be seen on the streets.* **7** [LINK] You use **be** to introduce more information about the subject, such as its identity, nature, qualities, or position. ❏ *She's my mother.* ❏ *He is a very attractive man.* ❏ *He is fifty and has been through two marriages.* ❏ *The sky was black.* ❏ *His house is next door.* ❏ *He's still alive, isn't he?* **8** [LINK] You use **be**, with 'it' as the subject, in clauses where you are describing something or giving your judgment of a situation. ❏ *It was too chilly for swimming.* ❏ *Sometimes it is necessary to say no.* ❏ *It is likely that investors*

will face losses. ❏ *It's nice having friends to chat to.* **9** [LINK] You use **be** with the impersonal pronoun 'there' in expressions like **there is** and **there are** to say that something exists or happens. ❏ *Clearly there is a problem here.* ❏ *There are very few cars on this street.* **10** [LINK] You use **be** as a link between a subject and a clause and in certain other clause structures, as shown below. ❏ *Our actual problem is convincing them.* ❏ *All she knew was that I'd had a broken marriage.* ❏ *Local residents said it was as if there had been a nuclear explosion.* **11** [LINK] (spoken) You use **be** in expressions like **the thing is** and **the point is** to introduce a clause in which you make a statement or give your opinion. ❏ *The fact is, the players gave everything they had.* **12** [LINK] (formal) The form '**be**' is used occasionally instead of the normal forms of the present tense, especially after 'whether'. ❏ *They should then be able to refer you to the appropriate type of practitioner, whether it be your GP, dentist, or optician.*
PHRASE **if it wasn't for** If you talk about what would happen **if it wasn't for** someone or something, you mean that they are the only thing that is preventing it from happening. ❏ *I could happily move back into an apartment if it wasn't for the fact that I'd miss my garden.*

beach ♦♢♢ /biːtʃ/ NOUN, VERB
NOUN [c] (**beaches**) A **beach** is an area of sand or stones beside the sea. = seashore ❏ *a beautiful sandy beach*
VERB [i, t] (**beaches, beaching, beached**) If something such as a boat **beaches**, or if it **is beached**, it is pulled or forced out of the water and onto land. ❏ *We beached the canoe, running it right up the bank.* ❏ *The boat beached on a mud flat.*

beak /biːk/ NOUN [c] (**beaks**) A bird's **beak** is the hard curved or pointed part of its mouth. = bill ❏ *a black bird with a yellow beak*

beam /biːm/ VERB, NOUN
VERB [i, t] (**beams, beaming, beamed**) **1** [i] (written) If you say that someone **is beaming**, you mean that they have a big smile on their face because they are happy, pleased, or proud about something. ❏ *Frances beamed at her friend with undisguised admiration.* ❏ *'Welcome back,' she beamed.* **2** [t] If radio signals or television pictures **are beamed** somewhere, they are sent there by means of electronic equipment. ❏ *The interview was beamed live across America.* ❏ *The Sci-Fi Channel began beaming into 10 million American homes this week.*
NOUN [c] (**beams**) **1** A **beam** is a line of energy, radiation, or particles sent in a particular direction. ❏ *high-energy laser beams* **2** A **beam of** light is a line of light that shines from an object such as a lamp. ❏ *A beam of light slices through the darkness.* **3** A **beam** is a long thick bar of wood, metal, or concrete, especially one used to support the roof of a building. ❏ *The ceilings are supported by oak beams.*

bean ♦♢♢ /biːn/ NOUN [c] (**beans**) **1** Beans such as green **beans**, French **beans**, or fava **beans** are the seeds of a climbing plant or the long thin cases which contain those seeds. **2** Beans such as soya **beans** and kidney **beans** are the dried seeds of other types of bean plants. **3** Beans such as coffee **beans** or cocoa **beans** are the seeds of plants that are used to produce coffee, cocoa, and chocolate.

bear ♦♦♢ /beə/ VERB, NOUN
VERB [t, i] (**bears, bearing, bore, borne**) **1** [t] (literary) If you **bear** something somewhere, you carry it there or take it there. = carry ❏ *They bore the oblong hardwood box into the kitchen and put it on the table.* **2** [t] (formal) If you **bear** something such as a weapon, you hold it or carry it with you. ❏ *the constitutional right to bear arms* **3** [t] If one thing **bears** the weight of something else, it supports the weight of that thing. = support ❏ *The ice was not thick enough to bear the weight of marching men.* **4** [t] If something **bears** a particular mark or characteristic, it has that mark or characteristic. ❏ *The houses bear the marks of bullet holes and the streets are practically deserted.* ❏ *notepaper bearing the presidential seal* **5** [t] If you **bear** an unpleasant experience, you accept it because you are unable to do anything about it. = endure ❏ *They will have to bear the misery of living in constant fear of war.* **6** [t] If you can't **bear**

someone or something, you dislike them very much. ❑ *I can't bear people who make judgments and label me.* **7** [T] (*old-fashioned*) When a woman **bears** a child, she gives birth to him or her. ❑ *Emma bore a son called Karl.* ❑ *She bore him a daughter, Susanna.* **8** [T] If someone **bears** the cost of something, they pay for it. ❑ *Patients should not have to bear the costs of their own treatment.* **9** [T] If you **bear** the responsibility for something, you accept responsibility for it. = accept ❑ *If a woman makes a decision to have a child alone, she should bear that responsibility alone.* **10** [T] If one thing **bears** no resemblance or no relationship to another thing, they are not at all similar. = have ❑ *Their daily menus bore no resemblance whatsoever to what they were actually fed.* **11** [T] When a plant or tree **bears** flowers, fruit, or leaves, it produces them. = produce ❑ *As the plants grow and start to bear fruit they will need a lot of water.* **12** [T] (*business*) If something such as a bank account or an investment **bears** interest, interest is paid on it. ❑ *The eight-year bond will bear annual interest of 10.5%.* **13** [I] If you **bear** left or **bear** right when you are driving or walking along, you turn and continue in that direction. = veer ❑ *Bear right at the fork up ahead.* **PHRASAL VERBS** **bear out** If someone or something **bears** a person **out** or **bears out** what that person is saying, they support what that person is saying. = confirm, support; ≠ refute, disprove ❑ *Recent studies have borne out claims that certain perfumes can bring about profound psychological changes.* ❑ *Her theories have been borne out by several research studies.*
bear with If you ask someone to **bear with** you, you are asking them to be patient. ❑ *If you'll bear with me, Frank, just let me try to explain.*
NOUN [C] (**bears**) **1** A **bear** is a large, strong wild animal with thick fur and sharp claws. **2** (*business*) In the stock market, **bears** are people who sell shares in expectation of a drop in price, in order to make a profit by buying them back again after a short time. Compare **bull 3**.
→ See also **bore**, **borne**
✦ **bear the brunt of** → see **brunt**; **bear fruit** → see **fruit**; **grin and bear it** → see **grin**; **bear in mind** → see **mind**

beard /bɪəd/ NOUN [C] (**beards**) A man's **beard** is the hair that grows on his chin and cheeks. ❑ *He's decided to grow a beard.*

bear•ing ◆◇◇ /ˈbeərɪŋ/ NOUN
NOUN [SING] (*literary*) Someone's **bearing** is the way in which they move or stand. = manner ❑ *She later wrote warmly of his bearing and behaviour.*
PHRASES **have a bearing on** If something **has a bearing on** a situation or event, it is relevant to it. = influence ❑ *Experts generally agree that diet has an important bearing on your general health.*
get one's bearings or **find one's bearings** or **lose one's bearings** If you **get** your **bearings** or **find** your **bearings**, you find out where you are or what you should do next. If you **lose** your **bearings**, you do not know where you are or what you should do next. ❑ *A sightseeing tour of the city is included to help you get your bearings.*

beat ◆◆◆ /biːt/ VERB, NOUN
VERB [T, I] (**beats**, **beating**, **beat**, **beaten**) **1** [T] If you **beat** someone or something, you hit them very hard. ❑ *My wife tried to stop them and they beat her.* **2** [I] To **beat on**, **at**, or **against** something means to hit it hard, usually several times or continuously for a period of time. = pound ❑ *There was dead silence but for a fly beating against the glass.* ❑ *Nina managed to free herself and began beating at the flames with a pillow.* **3** [I] When your heart or pulse **beats**, it continually makes regular rhythmic movements. ❑ *I felt my heart beating faster.* **4** [I, T] If you **beat** a drum or similar instrument, you hit it in order to make a sound. You can also say that a drum **beats**. ❑ *When you beat the drum, you feel good.* ❑ *drums beating and pipes playing* **5** [T] If you **beat** eggs, cream, or butter, you mix them thoroughly using a fork or beater. ❑ *Beat the eggs and sugar until they start to thicken.* **6** [I, T] When a bird or insect **beats** its wings or when its wings **beat**, its wings move up and down. ❑ *Beating their wings they flew off.* **7** [T] If you **beat** someone in a competition or election, you defeat

them. ❑ *In yesterday's game, Switzerland beat the United States two to one.* **8** [T] If someone **beats** a record or achievement, they do better than it. ❑ *He was as eager as his Captain to beat the record.* **9** [T] If you **beat** something that you are fighting against, for example, an organization, a problem, or a disease, you defeat it. = conquer ❑ *It became clear that the Union was not going to beat the government.* **10** [T] If an attack or an attempt **is beaten off** or **is beaten back**, it is stopped, often temporarily. ❑ *The rescuers were beaten back by strong winds and currents.* **11** [T] (*informal*) If you say that one thing **beats** another, you mean that it is better than it. ❑ *Being boss of a software firm beats selling insurance.* **12** [T] To **beat** a time limit or an event means to achieve something before that time or event. ❑ *They were trying to beat the midnight deadline.*
PHRASE **beat someone to it** If you intend to do something but someone **beats** you **to it**, they do it before you do. ❑ *Don't be too long about it or you'll find someone has beaten you to it.*
PHRASAL VERB **beat up** If someone **beats** a person **up**, they hit or kick the person many times. ❑ *Then they actually beat her up as well.*
NOUN [SING, C] (**beats**) **1** [SING] The **beat** of something is the sound it makes when it hits against something, usually several times or continuously for a period of time. ❑ *the rhythmic beat of the surf* **2** [C] The **beat** of a heart or pulse is the regular rhythmic movement of it. ❑ *He could hear the beat of his heart.* **3** [SING] The **beat** of a drum is the sound that it makes when it is hit. ❑ *the rhythmical beat of the drum* **4** [C] The **beat** of a piece of music is the main rhythm that it has. ❑ *the thumping beat of rock music* **5** [C] In music, a **beat** is a unit of measurement. The number of beats in each bar of a piece of music is indicated by two numbers at the beginning of the piece. ❑ *It's got four beats to a bar.* **6** [C] A police officer's or journalist's **beat** is the area for which he or she is responsible. ❑ *A policeman was patrolling his regular beat, when he saw a group of boys milling about the street.*
✦ **beat someone at their own game** → see **game**

beat•en ◆◇◇ /ˈbiːtən/ IRREG FORM
IRREG FORM **Beaten** is the past participle of **beat**.
PHRASE **off the beaten track** A place that is **off the beaten track** is in an area where not many people live or go. ❑ *Tiny secluded beaches can be found off the beaten track.*

beat•ing ◆◇◇ /ˈbiːtɪŋ/ NOUN [C, SING] **1** [C] If someone is given a **beating**, they are hit hard many times, especially with something such as a stick. ❑ *the investigation into the beating of an alleged car thief* **2** [SING] If something such as a business, a political party, or a team takes **a beating**, it is defeated by a large amount in a competition or an election. ❑ *Our firm has taken a terrible beating in recent years.* **3** [SING] The **beating** of something such as the rain or the wind refers to it striking hard against something, usually several times or continuously for a period of time. ❑ *The silence was broken only by the beating of the rain.* **4** [SING] The **beating** of your heart is its regular rhythmic movement. ❑ *I could hear the beating of my heart.*

beau•ti•ful ◆◆◇ /ˈbjuːtɪfʊl/ ADJ **1** A **beautiful** person is very attractive to look at. ❑ *She was a very beautiful woman.* **2** If you describe something as **beautiful**, you mean that it is very attractive or pleasing. ❑ *New England is beautiful.* ❑ *It was a beautiful morning.* **3** You can describe something that someone does as **beautiful** when they do it very skilfully. ❑ *That's a beautiful shot!*
beau•ti•ful•ly /ˈbjuːtɪfli/ ADV **1** *The children behaved beautifully.* **2** *The Sixers played beautifully.*

beau•ty ◆◇◇ /ˈbjuːti/ NOUN, ADJ
NOUN [U, C] (**beauties**) **1** [U] **Beauty** is the state or quality of being beautiful. ❑ *an area of outstanding natural beauty* **2** [C] (*journalism*) A **beauty** is a beautiful woman. ❑ *She is known as a great beauty.* **3** [C] (*informal*) You can say that something is a **beauty** when you think it is very good. ❑ *It was the one opportunity in the game – the pass was a real beauty but the shot was poor.* **4** [C] (*literary*) The **beauties** of something are its attractive qualities or features. ❑ *He was beginning to enjoy the beauties of nature.* **5** [C] If you say

B

that a particular feature is **the beauty of** something, you mean that this feature is what makes the thing so good. = advantage ❑ *There would be no effect on animals – that's the beauty of such water-based materials.*
ADJ [beauty + N] **Beauty** is used to describe people, products, and activities that are concerned with making women look beautiful. ❑ *Additional beauty treatments can be booked in advance.*

be·came /bɪˈkeɪm/ IRREG FORM **Became** is the past tense of **become**.

be·cause ◆◆◆ /bɪˈkʌz, AmE bɪˈkɔːz/ CONJ
CONJ 1 You use **because** when stating the reason for something. ❑ *He is called Mitch, because his name is Mitchell.* ❑ *Because it is an area of outstanding natural beauty, the number of boats available for hire on the river is limited.* **2** You use **because** when stating the explanation for a statement you have just made. ❑ *Maybe they just didn't want to ask too many questions, because they rented us a room without even asking to see our papers.* ❑ *The president has played a shrewd diplomatic game because from the outset he called for direct talks.*
PHRASE because of If an event or situation occurs **because of** something, that thing is the reason or cause. ❑ *Many families break up because of a lack of money.*

be·come ◆◆◆ /bɪˈkʌm/ VERB
VERB [LINK, T] (**becomes, becoming, became, become**) **1** [LINK] If someone or something **becomes** a particular thing, they start to change and develop into that thing, or start to develop the characteristics mentioned. ❑ *I first became interested in Islam while I was doing my nursing training.* **2** [T] If something **becomes** someone, it makes them look attractive or it seems right for them. = suit ❑ *Does khaki become you?*
PHRASE what has become of If you wonder **what** has **become of** someone or something, you wonder where they are and what has happened to them. ❑ *She thought constantly about her family; she might never know what had become of them.*

bed ◆◆◇ /bed/ NOUN
NOUN [C] (**beds**) **1** [also PREP + bed] A **bed** is a piece of furniture that you lie on when you sleep. ❑ *We finally went to bed at about 4am.* ❑ *By the time we got back from dinner, Nona was already in bed.* **2** If a place such as a hospital or a hotel has a particular number of **beds**, it is able to hold that number of patients or guests. **3** A **bed** in a garden or park is an area of ground that has been specially prepared so that plants can be grown in it. ❑ *beds of strawberries and rhubarb* **4** A **bed** of shellfish or plants is an area in the sea or in a lake where a particular type of shellfish or plant is found in large quantities. ❑ *The whole lake was rimmed with thick beds of reeds.* **5** The sea **bed** or a river **bed** is the ground at the bottom of the sea or of a river. ❑ *For three weeks a big operation went on to recover the wreckage from the sea bed.* **6** A **bed** of rock is a layer of rock that is found within a larger area of rock. ❑ *Between the white limestone and the greyish pink limestone is a thin bed of clay.* **7** If a recipe or a menu says that something is served on a **bed of** a food such as rice or vegetables, it means it is served on a layer of that food. ❑ *Heat the curry thoroughly and serve it on a bed of rice.*
PHRASES go to bed To go to bed with someone means to have sex with them. ❑ *I went to bed with him once, just once.*
make the bed or **make someone's bed** or **make a bed** When you **make** the **bed**, you neatly arrange the sheets and covers of a bed so that it is ready to sleep in. ❑ *He had made the bed after breakfast.*
✦ **bed of roses → see rose**

bed·room ◆◇◇ /ˈbedruːm/ NOUN [C] (**bedrooms**) A **bedroom** is a room used for sleeping in. ❑ *the spare bedroom*

bee /biː/ NOUN [C] (**bees**) A **bee** is an insect with a yellow-and-black striped body that makes a buzzing noise as it flies. Bees make honey and can sting. ❑ *A bee buzzed in the flowers.*

beef /biːf/ NOUN
NOUN [U] **Beef** is the meat of a cow, bull, or ox. ❑ *roast beef* ❑ *beef stew*

PHRASAL VERB beef up (**beefs, beefing, beefed**) If you **beef up** something, you increase, strengthen, or improve it. ❑ *a campaign to beef up security* ❑ *Both sides are still beefing up their military strength.*

been /bɪn, biːn/ IRREG FORM, VERB
IRREG FORM Been is the past participle of **be**.
VERB [I] If you have **been** to a place, you have gone to it or visited it. ❑ *He's already been to Tunisia, and is to go on to Morocco and Mauritania.*

beer ◆◇◇ /bɪə/ NOUN [C, U] (**beers**) **1** [C, U] **Beer** is an alcoholic drink made from grain. ❑ *He sat in the kitchen drinking beer.* **2** [C] A glass, can, or bottle of beer can be referred to as a **beer**. ❑ *Would you like a beer?*

be·fore ◆◆◆ /bɪˈfɔː/ PREP, CONJ, ADV

> In addition to the uses shown below, **before** is used in the phrasal verbs 'go before' and 'lay before'.

PREP 1 If something happens **before** a particular date, time, or event, it happens earlier than that date, time, or event. ❑ *Annie was born a few weeks before Christmas.* ❑ *Before World War II, women were not recruited as intelligence officers.* **2** [before + -ING] If you do one thing **before** doing something else, you do it earlier than the other thing. ❑ *He spent his early life in Sri Lanka before moving to Canada.* **3** [N + before + N] You use **before** when you are talking about an earlier time. ❑ *It's interesting that he sent me the book twenty days before the deadline for my book.* **4** (formal) If someone is **before** something, they are in front of it. ❑ *They drove through a tall iron gate and stopped before a large white villa.* **5** If you tell someone that one place is a certain distance **before** another, you mean that they will come to the first place first. ❑ *The station is on the right, one mile before central Romney.* **6** If you appear or come **before** an official person or group, you go there and answer questions. ❑ *The governor will appear before the committee next Tuesday.* **7** If something happens **before** a particular person or group, it is seen by or happens while this person or this group is present. ❑ *The game followed a colourful opening ceremony before a crowd of seventy-four thousand.* **8** [before + PRON] If you have something such as a trip, a task, or a stage of your life **before** you, you must do it or live through it in the future. = ahead of ❑ *Everyone in the room knew it was the single hardest task before them.* **9** [V + before + N] When you want to say that one person or thing is more important than another, you can say that they come **before** the other person or thing. ❑ *Her husband and her children came before her needs.*
CONJ 1 If something happens **before** a second thing happens, it happens earlier than the second event. ❑ *Stock prices have climbed close to the peak they'd registered before the stock market crashed in 1987.* **2** If you do one thing **before** doing something else, you do it earlier than the other thing. ❑ *He took a cold shower and then towelled off before he put on fresh clothes.* **3** You use **before** when talking about an earlier time. ❑ *Kelman had a book published in the US more than a decade before a British publisher would touch him.* **4** If you do something **before** someone else can do something, you do it when they have not yet done it. ❑ *Before Gallacher could catch up with the ball, Nadlovu had beaten him to it.* **5** If there is a period of time or if several things are done **before** something happens, it takes that amount of time or effort for this thing to happen. = until ❑ *It was some time before the door opened in response to his ring.* **6** If a particular situation has to happen **before** something else happens, this situation must happen or exist in order for the other thing to happen. ❑ *There was additional work to be done before all the troops would be ready.*
ADV 1 [N + before] You use **before** when you are talking about time. For example, if something happened the day **before** a particular date or event, it happened during the previous day. ❑ *The war had ended only a month or so before.* **2** [before after V] If someone has done something **before**, they have done it on a previous occasion. If someone has not done something **before**, they have never done it. ❑ *I've been here before.* ❑ *I had met Professor Lown before.*
✦ **before long → see long**

before·hand /bɪˈfɔːhænd/ ADV If you do something

beforehand, you do it earlier than a particular event. ❑ *How could she tell beforehand that I was going to go out?*

beg /beg/ VERB [I, T] (**begs, begging, begged**) **1** [I, T] If you **beg** someone **to** do something, you ask them very anxiously or eagerly to do it. ❑ *I begged him to come back to New York with me.* ❑ *We are not going to beg for help any more.* **2** [T, I] If someone who is poor **is begging**, they are asking people to give them food or money. ❑ *I was surrounded by people begging for food.* ❑ *homeless people begging on the streets* ❑ *She was living alone, begging food from neighbours.*

be·gan /bɪˈɡæn/ IRREG FORM **Began** is the past tense of **begin**.

be·gin ◆◆◆ /bɪˈɡɪn/ VERB
VERB [T, I] (**begins, beginning, began, begun**) **1** [T] To **begin to** do something means to start doing it. = start ❑ *He stood up and began to move around the room.* ❑ *The weight loss began to look more serious.* **2** [I, T] When something **begins** or when you **begin** it, it takes place from a particular time onwards. = start, commence ❑ *The problems began last November.* ❑ *He has just begun his fourth year in hiding.* **3** [I, T] If you **begin with** something, or **begin by** doing something, this is the first thing you do. = start ❑ *Could I begin with a few formalities?* ❑ *a businessman who began by selling golf shirts from the boot of his car* ❑ *He began his career flipping hamburgers.* **4** [I, T] You use **begin** to mention the first thing that someone says. ❑ *'Professor Theron,' he began, 'I'm very pleased to see you.'* ❑ *He didn't know how to begin.* **5** [I] If one thing **began as** another thing, it first existed as the other thing before it changed into its present form. = start ❑ *What began as a local festival has blossomed into an international event.* **6** [I] If you say that a thing or place **begins** somewhere, you are talking about one of its limits or edges. ❑ *The fate line begins close to the wrist.* **7** [I] If a word **begins with** a particular letter, that is the first letter of that word. = start ❑ *The first word begins with an F.*
PHRASE **to begin with 1** You use **to begin with** when you are talking about the first stage of a situation, event, or process. ❑ *It was great to begin with but now it's difficult.* **2** You use **to begin with** to introduce the first of several things that you want to say. = firstly ❑ *'What do scientists you've spoken with think about that?'—'Well, to begin with, they doubt it's going to work.'*

be·gin·ner /bɪˈɡɪnə/ NOUN [C] (**beginners**) A **beginner** is someone who has just started learning to do something and cannot do it very well yet. ❑ *The course is suitable for both beginners and advanced students.*

be·gin·ning ◆◇◇ /bɪˈɡɪnɪŋ/ NOUN [C, PL, SING] (**beginnings**) **1** [C] The **beginning of** an event or process is the first part of it. = start ❑ *This was also the beginning of her recording career.* **2** [PL] The **beginnings of** something are the signs or events which form the first part of it. ❑ *The discussions were the beginnings of a dialogue with Moscow.* **3** [SING] The **beginning of** a period of time is the time at which it starts. ❑ *The wedding will be at the beginning of March.* **4** [C] The **beginning of** a piece of written material is the first words or sentences of it. ❑ *the question that was raised at the beginning of this chapter* **5** [PL] If you talk about the **beginnings** of a person, company, or group, you are referring to their backgrounds or origins. ❑ *His views come from his own humble beginnings.*

be·gun /bɪˈɡʌn/ IRREG FORM **Begun** is the past participle of **begin**.

○**be·half** ◆◇◇ /bɪˈhɑːf, -ˈhæf/ NOUN (*academic word*)
PHRASE **on someone's behalf** or **on behalf of someone 1** If you do something **on** someone's **behalf**, you do it for that person as their representative. = interest, sake, part ❑ *She made an emotional public appeal on her son's behalf.* ❑ *Secret Service officer Robin Thompson spoke on behalf of his colleagues.* **2** If you feel, for example, embarrassed or angry **on** someone's **behalf**, you feel embarrassed or angry for them. ❑ *'What do you mean?' I asked, offended on Liddie's behalf.*

○**be·have** ◆◇◇ /bɪˈheɪv/ VERB [I, T] (**behaves, behaving, behaved**) **1** [I] The way that you **behave** is the way that you do and say things, and the things that you do and say. = act ❑ *I couldn't believe these people were behaving in this way.* ❑ *He'd behaved badly.* **2** [I, T] If you **behave** or **behave yourself**, you act in the way that people think is correct and proper. ❑ *You have to behave.* **3** [I] In science, the way that something **behaves** is the things that it does. ❑ *Under certain conditions, electrons can behave like waves rather than particles.*

○**be·hav·iour** ◆◆◇ /bɪˈheɪvjə/ (*BrE*; in *AmE*, use **behavior**) NOUN
NOUN [C, U] (**behaviours**) **1** [C, U] People's or animals' **behaviour** is the way that they behave. You can refer to a typical and repeated way of behaving as a **behaviour**. = conduct ❑ *Make sure that good behaviour is rewarded.* ❑ *human sexual behaviour* ❑ *He frequently exhibited violent behaviour.* **2** [U] In science, the **behaviour** of something is the way that it behaves. ❑ *It will be many years before anyone can predict a hurricane's behaviour with much accuracy.* ❑ *the behaviour of sub-atomic particles*
PHRASE **on one's best behaviour** If someone is **on** their **best behaviour**, they are trying very hard to behave well. ❑ *The 1,400 fans were on their best behaviour and filed out peacefully at the end.*

be·hav·iour·al /bɪˈheɪvjərəl/ (*BrE*; in *AmE*, use **behavioral**) ADJ [behavioural + N] **Behavioural** means relating to the behaviour of a person or animal, or to the study of their behaviour. ❑ *emotional and behavioural problems*

be·hind ◆◆◆ /bɪˈhaɪnd/ PREP, ADV, NOUN

> In addition to the uses shown below, **behind** is also used in a few phrasal verbs, such as 'fall behind' and 'lie behind'.

PREP **1** If something is **behind** a thing or person, it is on the other side of them from you, or nearer their back rather than their front. ❑ *I put one of the cushions behind his head.* ❑ *They were parked behind the truck.* **2** If you are walking or travelling **behind** someone or something, you are following them. ❑ *Keith wandered along behind him.* **3** If someone is **behind** a desk, counter, or bar, they are on the other side of it from where you are. ❑ *The colonel was sitting behind a cheap wooden desk.* **4** [behind + PRON] When you shut a door or gate **behind** you, you shut it after you have gone through it. ❑ *I walked out and closed the door behind me.* **5** The people, reason, or events **behind** a situation are the causes of it or are responsible for it. ❑ *It is still not clear who was behind the killing.* **6** [behind + PRON] If something or someone is **behind** you, they support you and help you. ❑ *He had the state's judicial power behind him.* **7** If you refer to what is **behind** someone's outside appearance, you are referring to a characteristic which you cannot immediately see or is not obvious, but which you think is there. ❑ *What lay behind his anger was really the hurt he felt at Grace's refusal.* **8** If you are **behind** someone, you are less successful than them, or have done less or advanced less. ❑ *She finished second behind the American, Ann Cody, in the 800 metres.* **9** [behind + PRON] If an experience is **behind** you, it happened in your past and will not happen again, or no longer affects you. ❑ *Maureen put the nightmare behind her.* **10** ['have/with' N + behind + PRON] If you have a particular achievement **behind** you, you have managed to reach this achievement, and other people consider it to be important or valuable. ❑ *He has 20 years of loyal service to Barclays Bank behind him.* **11** If something is **behind** schedule, it is not as far advanced as people had planned. If someone is **behind** schedule, they are not progressing as quickly at something as they had planned. ❑ *The work is 22 weeks behind schedule.*
ADV **1** If something is **behind**, it is on the other side of a thing or person from you, or nearer their back rather than their front. ❑ *Rising into the hills behind are 800 acres of parkland.* **2** [behind after V] If you are walking or travelling **behind**, you are following someone or something. ❑ *The troopers followed behind, every muscle tensed for the sudden gunfire.* **3** If you are **behind**, you are

less successful than someone, or have done less or advanced less than them. ❑ *The rapid development of technology means that she is now far behind, and will need retraining.* **4** [behind after v] If you stay **behind**, you remain in a place after other people have gone. ❑ *About 1,200 personnel will remain behind to take care of the air base.* **5** [behind after v] If you leave something or someone **behind**, you do not take them with you when you go. ❑ *The rebels fled into the mountains, leaving behind their weapons and supplies.*

NOUN [c] (**behinds**) Your **behind** is the part of your body that you sit on. = bottom

◆ do something **behind someone's back** → see **back**; **behind bars** → see **bar**

be·ing ◆◇◇ /'biːɪŋ/ VERB, NOUN

VERB [LINK] **1** Being is the present participle of **be**. **2** Being is used in nonfinite clauses where you are giving the reason for something. ❑ *It being a Sunday, the old men had the day off.* ❑ *Little boys, being what they are, might decide to play on it.*

NOUN [c, u] (**beings**) **1** [c] You can refer to any real or imaginary creature as a **being**. ❑ *People expect a horse to perform like a car, with no thought for its feelings as a living being.* **2** [u] Being is existence. Something that is **in being** or comes **into being** exists. = existence ❑ *Abraham Maslow described psychology as 'the science of being'.* → See also **human being, well-being**

◆ other things being equal → see **equal**; **for the time being** → see **time**

be·lat·ed /bɪ'leɪtɪd/ ADJ (formal) A **belated** action happens later than it should have. ❑ *the government's belated attempts to alleviate the plight of the poor*

be·lea·guered /bɪ'liːgəd/ ADJ (formal) A **beleaguered** person, organization, or project is experiencing a lot of difficulties, opposition, or criticism. ❑ *There have been seven coup attempts against the beleaguered government.*

be·lie /bɪ'laɪ/ VERB [T] (**belies, belying, belied**) **1** If one thing **belies** another, it hides the true situation and so creates a false idea or image of someone or something. ❑ *Her looks belie her 50 years.* **2** If one thing **belies** another, it proves that the other thing is not true or genuine. = disprove ❑ *The facts of the situation belie his testimony.*

be·lief ◆◇◇ /bɪ'liːf/ NOUN

NOUN [u, PL, SING] (**beliefs**) **1** [u] Belief is a feeling of certainty that something exists, is true, or is good. ❑ *One billion people throughout the world are Muslims, united by belief in one god.* ❑ *a belief in personal liberty* ❑ *stereotyped attitudes and beliefs about men's and women's roles* **2** [PL] Your religious or political **beliefs** are your views on religious or political matters. = faith, ideology, opinion, view ❑ *He refuses to compete on Sundays because of his religious beliefs.* **3** [SING] If it is your **belief** that something is the case, it is your strong opinion that it is the case. ❑ *It is our belief that improvements in health care will lead to a stronger, more prosperous economy.*

PHRASES **beyond belief** (emphasis) You use **beyond belief** to emphasize that something is true to a very great degree or that it happened to a very great degree. ❑ *We are devastated, shocked beyond belief.*

in the belief that If you do one thing in the belief that another thing is true or will happen, you do it because you think, usually wrongly, that it is true or will happen. ❑ *Civilians had broken into the building, apparently in the belief that it contained food.*

be·liev·able /bɪ'liːvəbəl/ ADJ Something that is **believable** makes you think that it could be true or real. = credible ❑ *believable evidence*

be·lieve ◆◆◆ /bɪ'liːv/ VERB [T, I] (**believes, believing, believed**) **1** [T] (formal) If you **believe** that something is true, you think it is true, but you are not sure. = think, consider ❑ *Experts believe that the coming drought will be extensive.* ❑ *We believe them to be hidden here in this apartment.* ❑ *Sleepiness in drivers is widely believed to be an important cause of road traffic injuries.* ❑ *The main problem, I believe, lies elsewhere.* **2** [T] If you **believe** someone or if you **believe** what they say or write, you accept that they are telling the truth. ≠ disbelieve ❑ *He did not sound as if*

he believed her. ❑ *Never believe anything a married man says about his wife.* **3** [I] If you **believe in** fairies, ghosts, or miracles, you are sure that they exist or happen. If you **believe in** a god, you are sure of the existence of that god. ❑ *I don't believe in ghosts.* **4** [I] If you **believe in** a way of life or an idea, you are in favour of it because you think it is good or right. ❑ *He believed in marital fidelity.* **5** [I] If you **believe in** someone or what they are doing, you have confidence in them and think that they will be successful. ❑ *If you believe in yourself you can succeed.*

be·liev·er /bɪ'liːvə/ NOUN [c] (**believers**) **1** If you are a great **believer in** something, you think that it is good, right, or useful. ❑ *Mum was a great believer in herbal medicines.* **2** A **believer** is someone who is sure that God exists or that their religion is true. ❑ *I made no secret of the fact that I was not a believer.*

bell ◆◇◇ /bel/ NOUN

NOUN [c] (**bells**) **1** A **bell** is a device that makes a ringing sound and is used to give a signal or to attract people's attention. ❑ *I had just enough time to finish eating before the bell rang and I was off to my first class.* **2** A **bell** is a hollow metal object shaped like a cup which has a piece hanging inside it that hits the sides and makes a sound. ❑ *My brother, Nick, was born on a Sunday, when all the church bells were ringing.*

PHRASE **ring a bell** (informal) If you say that something **rings a bell**, you mean that it reminds you of something, but you cannot remember exactly what it is. ❑ *The name doesn't ring a bell.*

bel·ly /'beli/ NOUN [c] (**bellies**) The **belly** of a person or animal is their stomach or abdomen. = stomach, tummy ❑ *She laid her hands on her swollen belly.* ❑ *a horse with its belly ripped open*

❂ **be·long** ◆◇◇ /bɪ'lɒŋ, AmE -'lɔːŋ/ VERB [I] (**belongs, belonging, belonged**) **1** If something **belongs to** you, you own it. ❑ *The house had belonged to his family for three or four generations.* **2** You say that something **belongs to** a particular person when you are guessing, discovering, or explaining that it was produced by or is part of that person. ❑ *The handwriting belongs to a male.* **3** If someone **belongs to** a particular group, they are a member of that group. ❑ *I used to belong to a youth club.* **4** If something or someone **belongs in** or **to** a particular category, type, or group, they are of that category, type, or group. ❑ *The judges could not decide which category it belonged in.* **5** If something **belongs to** a particular time, it comes from that time. ❑ *The pictures belong to an era when there was a preoccupation with high society.* **6** If you say that something **belongs to** someone, you mean that person has the right to it. ❑ *but the last word belonged to Rosanne* **7** If you say that a time **belongs to** a particular system or way of doing something, you mean that that time is or will be characterized by it. ❑ *The future belongs to democracy.* **8** If a baby or child **belongs to** a particular adult, that adult is his or her parent or the person who is looking after him or her. ❑ *He deduced that the two children belonged to the couple.* **9** If a person or thing **belongs** in a particular place or situation, that is where they should be. ❑ *You don't belong here.* ❑ *They need to feel they belong.*

be·long·ings /bɪ'lɒŋɪŋz, AmE -'lɔːŋ-/ NOUN [PL] Your **belongings** are the things that you own, especially things that are small enough to be carried. ❑ *I collected my belongings and left.*

be·lov·ed /bɪ'lʌvɪd/ ADJ [beloved + N] A **beloved** person, thing, or place is one that you feel great affection for. ❑ *He lost his beloved wife last year.*

be·low ◆◆◇ /bɪ'ləʊ/ PREP, ADV

PREP **1** If something is **below** something else, it is in a lower position. ❑ *He appeared from the flat directly below Leonard's.* ❑ *The sun had already sunk below the horizon.* **2** If something is **below** a particular amount, rate, or level, it is less than that amount, rate, or level. ❑ *Night temperatures can drop below 15 degrees Celsius.* **3** If someone is **below** you in an organization, they are lower in rank. ❑ *Such people often experience less stress than those in the ranks immediately below them.*

PHRASE **below ground** If something is **below ground** or

below the ground, it is in the ground. ◻ *They have designed a system which pumps up water from nearly 1,000 feet below ground.*

ADV **1** If something is **below**, it is in a lower position than something else. ◻ *We climbed rather perilously down a rope-ladder to the boat below.* ◻ *a view to the street below* **2** You use **below** in a piece of writing to refer to something that is mentioned later. ◻ *Please write to me at the address below.* **3** You use **below** to refer to something that is less than a particular amount, rate, or level. ◻ *temperatures at zero or below*

✦ **below par** → see **par**

belt ◆◇◇ /belt/ NOUN, VERB

NOUN [c] (**belts**) **1** A **belt** is a strip of leather or cloth that you fasten around your waist. ◻ *He wore a belt with a large brass buckle.* **2** A **belt** in a machine is a circular strip of rubber that is used to drive moving parts or to move objects along. ◻ *The turning disk is connected by a drive belt to an electric motor.* **3** A **belt** of land or sea is a long, narrow area of it that has some special feature. = **strip** ◻ *Miners in Zambia's northern copper belt have gone on strike.* **4** If you **give** someone a **belt**, you hit them very hard. If you **give** something a **belt**, you hit it very hard. ◻ *Father would give you a belt over the head with the scrubbing brush.*

PHRASES **below the belt** Something that is **below the belt** is cruel and unfair. ◻ *Do you think it's a bit below the belt what they're doing?*

tighten your belt If you have to **tighten** your **belt**, you have to spend less money and manage without things because you have less money than you used to have. ◻ *Clearly, if you are spending more than your income, you'll need to tighten your belt.*

under your belt If you have something **under** your **belt**, you have already achieved it or done it. ◻ *Clare is now a full-time author with six books, including four novels, under her belt.*

VERB [T, I] (**belts**, **belting**, **belted**) (*informal*) **1** [T] If someone **belts** you, they hit you very hard. If someone **belts** something, they hit it very hard. = **thump** ◻ *'Is it right she belted old George in the gut?' she asked.* ◻ *Torrealba belted the ball up the middle of the field.* **2** [I] If you **belt** somewhere, you move or travel there very fast. = **dash** ◻ *Darren and I belted down the stairs and ran out of the house.*

PHRASAL VERB **belt out** (*informal*) If you **belt out** a song, you sing or play it very loudly. ◻ *He belted out Sinatra and Beatles hits.*

→ See also **seat belt**

bench /bentʃ/ NOUN [c, SING] (**benches**) **1** [c] A **bench** is a long seat of wood or metal that two or more people can sit on. ◻ *He sat down on a park bench.* **2** [c] A **bench** is a long, narrow table in a factory or laboratory. ◻ *the laboratory bench* **3** [SING] In a court of law, **the bench** is the judge or magistrates. ◻ *The chairman of the bench adjourned the case until October 27.*

bench·mark /'bentʃmaːk/ also **bench mark** NOUN [c] (**benchmarks**) A **benchmark** is something whose quality or quantity is known and which can therefore be used as a standard with which other things can be compared. = **yardstick** ◻ *The construction industry is a benchmark for the economy.*

bend ◆◇◇ /bend/ VERB, NOUN

VERB [I, T] (**bends**, **bending**, **bent**) **1** [I] When you **bend**, you move the top part of your body downward and forward. Plants and trees also **bend**. ◻ *I bent over and kissed her cheek.* ◻ *She bent and picked up a plastic bucket.* **2** [T] When you **bend** your head, you move your head forward and downward. ◻ *Rick appeared, bending his head a little to clear the top of the door.* **3** [I, T] When you **bend** a part of your body such as your arm or leg, or when it **bends**, you change its position so that it is no longer straight. ◻ *These cruel devices are designed to stop prisoners from bending their legs.* **4** [T] If you **bend** something that is flat or straight, you use force to make it curved or to put an angle in it. ◻ *Bend the bar into a horseshoe.* **5** [I, T] When a road, beam of light, or other long thin thing **bends**, or when something **bends** it, it changes direction to form a curve or angle. ◻ *The road bent slightly to the right.* **6** [T] If you

bend rules or laws, you interpret them in a way that allows you to do something they would not normally allow you to do. ◻ *A minority of officers were prepared to bend the rules.*

NOUN [c, PL] (**bends**) **1** [c] A **bend** in a road, pipe, or other long thin object is a curve or angle in it. ◻ *The crash occurred on a sharp bend.* **2** [PL] If deep-sea divers suffer from **the bends**, they experience severe pain and difficulty in breathing as a result of coming to the surface of the sea too quickly. ◻ *New evidence suggests that exercise could protect divers from the bends.*

be·neath ◆◇◇ /bɪ'niːθ/ PREP, ADV

PREP **1** Something that is **beneath** another thing is under the other thing. = **under** ◻ *She could see the muscles of his shoulders beneath his T-shirt.* ◻ *Four levels of parking beneath the theatre was not enough.* **2** If you talk about what is **beneath** the surface of something, you are talking about the aspects of it which are hidden or not obvious. = **under** ◻ *emotional strains beneath the surface* ◻ *Somewhere deep beneath the surface lay a caring character.* **3** If you say that someone or something is **beneath** you, you feel that they are not good enough for you or not suitable for you. ◻ *They decided she was marrying beneath her.*

ADV If something is **beneath**, it is under another thing. = **below** ◻ *On a shelf beneath he spotted a photo album.*

ben·efac·tor /'benɪfæktə/ NOUN [c] (**benefactors**) A **benefactor** is someone who helps a person or organization by giving them money. = **patron, sponsor** ◻ *In his old age he became a benefactor of the arts.*

⊕ ben·efi·cial /ˌbenɪ'fɪʃəl/ ADJ Something that is **beneficial** helps people or improves their lives. = **helpful, positive, valuable**; ≠ **detrimental, negative** ◻ *vitamins that are beneficial to our health* ◻ *Using computers has a beneficial effect on children's learning.*

bene·fi·ciary /ˌbenɪ'fɪʃəri, AmE -fieri/ NOUN [c] (**beneficiaries**) **1** Someone who is a **beneficiary of** something is helped by it. = **recipient** ◻ *One of the main beneficiaries of the early election is thought to be the former president.* **2** The **beneficiaries** of a will are legally entitled to receive money or property from someone when that person dies. ◻ *one of the beneficiaries of the will made by the late Mr Steil*

⊕ ben·efit ◆◆◇ /'benɪfɪt/ NOUN, VERB (*academic word*)

NOUN [c, u] (**benefits**) **1** [c, u] The **benefit of** something is the help that you get from it or the advantage that results from it. = **advantage, profit**; ≠ **disadvantage, drawback** ◻ *Each family farms individually and reaps the benefit of its labour.* ◻ *I'm a great believer in the benefits of this form of therapy.* ◻ *For maximum benefit, use your treatment every day.* **2** [u] If something is **to** your **benefit** or is **of benefit to** you, it helps you or improves your life. = **advantage** ◻ *This could now work to Albania's benefit.* ◻ *I hope what I have written will be of benefit to someone else.* **3** [u] If you have the **benefit of** some information, knowledge, or equipment, you are able to use it so that you can achieve something. = **advantage** ◻ *Steve didn't have the benefit of a formal college education.* ◻ *This remarkable achievement took place without the benefit of modern telecommunications.* **4** [c, u] **Benefits** are money or other advantages which come from your job, the government, or an insurance company. ◻ *McCary will receive about $921,000 in retirement benefits.* ◻ *the skyrocketing cost of health care and medical benefits* **5** [c] [oft benefit + N] A **benefit**, or a **benefit** concert or dinner, is an event that is held in order to raise money for a particular charity or person. ◻ *a memorial benefit concert for the Bonhoeffer endowment*

PHRASES **the benefit of the doubt** If you give someone **the benefit of the doubt**, you treat them as if they are telling the truth or as if they have behaved properly, even though you are not sure that this is the case. ◻ *At first I gave him the benefit of the doubt.*

for the benefit of someone If you say that someone is doing something **for the benefit of** a particular person, you mean that they are doing it for that person. ◻ *You need people working for the benefit of the community.*

VERB [I, T] (**benefits**, **benefiting**, **benefited**) If you **benefit**

from something or if it **benefits** you, it helps you or improves your life. = profit, gain, help ☐ *Both sides have benefited from the talks.* ☐ *a variety of government programmes benefiting children*

B

WHICH WORD?

benefit or advantage?

Benefit and **advantage** are both used to talk about the positive aspects of something. They have slightly different meanings, though. An **advantage** is the quality of something that makes it good, helpful, or better than other similar things.

☐ *Running has its **advantages**: it requires minimum equipment, and can be done most places.*

A **benefit** is what people gain as a result of something.

☐ *He spoke about the health **benefits** of regular running.*

WORD CONNECTIONS

VERB + **benefit**

reap the benefit

☐ *In order to reap the benefits of exercise, you have to do it regularly.*

bring benefit
provide benefit

☐ *This contact with parents has brought many benefits to the school.*

ADJ + **benefit**

maximum benefit
potential benefit
additional benefit
added benefit

☐ *Out-of-town shopping centres have the added benefit of free parking.*

economic benefit
financial benefit

☐ *There are enormous economic benefits to the trade links.*

bent /bent/ IRREG FORM, ADJ, NOUN

 IRREG FORM **Bent** is the past tense and past participle of **bend**.

 ADJ **1** When a part of your body is **bent**, its position is changed so that it is no longer straight. ☐ *Keep your knees slightly bent.* **2** If something that was flat or straight is **bent**, it has become curved or has been set at an angle through the use of force. ☐ *a length of bent wire* **3** If an object is **bent**, it is damaged and no longer has its correct shape. ☐ *The trees were all bent and twisted from the wind.* **4** (written) If a person is **bent**, their body has become curved because of old age or disease. ☐ *a bent, frail, old man* **5** [V-LINK + bent 'on/upon' N/-ING] If someone is **bent on** doing something, especially something harmful, they are determined to do it. ☐ *He's bent on suicide.*

 NOUN [SING] **1** If you have a **bent for** something, you have a natural ability to do it or a natural interest in it. = flair ☐ *His bent for natural history directed him towards his first job.* **2** If someone is **of** a particular **bent**, they hold a particular set of beliefs. = persuasion ☐ *economists of a socialist bent*

ber·ry /'beri/ NOUN [C] (berries) Berries are small, round fruit that grow on a bush or a tree. Some berries are edible, for example, blackberries and raspberries.

berth /bɜːθ/ NOUN, VERB

 NOUN [C] (berths) **1** A **berth** is a bed on a ship or train. ☐ *Goldring booked a berth on the first boat he could.* **2** A **berth** is a space in a harbour where a ship stays for a period of time. = mooring ☐ *the slow passage through the docks to the ship's berth*

 PHRASE **give a wide berth** If you give someone or something **a wide berth**, you avoid them because you think they are unpleasant or dangerous, or simply because you do not like them. ☐ *She gives showbiz parties a wide berth.*

 VERB [I] (berths, berthing, berthed) When a ship **berths**, it sails into harbour and stops at the quay. ☐ *As the ship berthed in New York, McClintock was with the first immigration officers aboard.*

be·set /bɪ'set/ VERB [T] (besets, besetting, beset) If someone or something **is beset by** problems or fears, they have many problems or fears which affect them severely. ☐ *The country is beset by severe economic problems.* ☐ *The discussions were beset with difficulties.*

be·side ♦◇◇ /bɪ'saɪd/ PREP

 PREP Something that is **beside** something else is at the side of it or next to it. ☐ *On the table beside an empty plate was a pile of books.*

 PHRASE **beside oneself** If you are **beside yourself with** anger or excitement, you are extremely angry or excited. ☐ *He had shouted down the phone at her, beside himself with anxiety.*

→ See also **besides**

♦ **beside the point** → see **point**

be·sides ♦◇◇ /bɪ'saɪdz/ PREP, ADV

 PREP **Besides** something or **beside** something means in addition to it. ☐ *I think she has many good qualities besides being very beautiful.*

 ADV **1** [CL + besides] **Besides** means in addition to something. ☐ *You get to sample lots of baked things and take home masses of biscuits besides.* **2** **Besides** is used to emphasize an additional point that you are making, especially one that you consider to be important. ☐ *The house was out of our price range and too big anyway. Besides, I'd grown fond of our little rented house.*

be·siege /bɪ'siːdʒ/ VERB [T] (besieges, besieging, besieged) **1** If you **are besieged by** people, many people want something from you and continually bother you. ☐ *She was besieged by the press and the public.* **2** If soldiers **besiege** a place, they surround it and wait for the people in it to stop fighting or resisting. ☐ *The main part of the army moved to Sevastopol to besiege the town.*

best ♦♦♦ /best/ NOUN, ADV **1** **Best** is the superlative of **good**. good ☐ *If you want further information the best thing to do is have a word with the driver as you get on the bus.* **2** **Best** is the superlative of **well**. ☐ *James Fox is best known as the author of 'White Mischief', and he is currently working on a new book.* **3** **Best** is used to form the superlative of compound adjectives beginning with 'good' and 'well'. For example, the superlative of 'well-known' is 'best-known'.

 NOUN [SING] **1** **The best** is used to refer to things of the highest quality or standard. ☐ *We offer only the best to our clients.* **2** Someone's **best** is the greatest effort or highest achievement or standard that they are capable of. ☐ *Miss Blockey was at her best when she played the piano.* **3** If you say that something is **the best** that can be done or hoped for, you think it is the most pleasant, successful, or useful thing that can be done or hoped for. ☐ *A draw seems the best they can hope for.*

 PHRASES **best of all** You use **best of all** to indicate that what you are about to mention is the thing that you prefer or that has most advantages out of all the things you have mentioned. ☐ *It was comfortable and cheap: best of all, most of the rent was being paid by two American friends.*

at best You use **at best** to indicate that even if you describe something as favourably as possible or if it performs as well as it possibly can, it is still not very good. ☐ *This policy, they say, is at best confused and at worst non-existent.*

do your best or **try your best** If you **do** your **best** or **try** your **best to** do something, you try as hard as you can to do it, or do it as well as you can. ☐ *I'll do my best to find out.*

for the best If you say that something is **for the best**, you mean it is the most desirable or helpful thing that could have happened or could be done, considering all the circumstances. ☐ *Whatever the circumstances, parents are supposed to know what to do for the best.*

 ADV If you like something **best** or like it **the best**, you prefer it. = most ☐ *The thing I liked best about the show was the music.* ☐ *Mother liked it best when Daniel got money.*

 PHRASES **as best one can** If someone does something **as best they can**, they do it as well as they can, although it is very difficult. ☐ *Let's leave people to get on with their jobs and do them as best they can.*

know best If you say that a particular person **knows best**, you mean that they have a lot of experience and should therefore be trusted to make decisions for other people. ❏ *He was convinced that doctors and dentists knew best.*

✦ to the best of your ability → see ability; hope for the best → see hope; the best of both worlds → see world

bet ♦◇◇ /bet/ VERB, NOUN

VERB [I, T] (**bets, betting, bet**) **1** If you **bet on** the result of a horse race, football game, or other event, you give someone a sum of money which they give you back with extra money if the result is what you predicted, or which they keep if it is not. ❏ *Jockeys are forbidden to bet on the outcome of races.* ❏ *I bet $20 on a horse called Premonition.* **2** (*journalism*) If someone **is betting** that something will happen, they are hoping or expecting that it will happen. ❏ *The party is betting that the presidential race will turn into a battle for younger voters.* ❏ *People were betting on a further easing of credit conditions.*

PHRASES **I bet** or **I'll bet** or **you can bet** (*informal*) You use expressions such as '**I bet**', '**I'll bet**', and '**you can bet**' to indicate that you are sure something is true. ❏ *I bet you were good at games when you were at school.* ❏ *I'll bet they'll taste out of this world.*

I bet or **I'll bet** **1** (*informal, spoken, feelings*) You use **I bet** or **I'll bet** in reply to a statement to show that you agree with it or that you expected it to be true, usually when you are annoyed or amused by it. ❏ *'I'd like to ask you something,' I said. 'I bet you would,' she grinned.* **2** You say **I bet** or **I'll bet** in reply to a statement to show that you do not believe it or you doubt that it is true. ❏ *'I only kiss girls,' said John. Then he blushed. 'I'll bet,' said Lisa.*

NOUN [c] (**bets**) **1** A **bet** is the act of betting money on the result of a horse race, football game, or other event. ❏ *Do you always have a bet on the Kentucky Derby?* **2** A **bet** is a sum of money which you give to someone when you bet. ❏ *You can put a bet on almost anything these days.*

PHRASES **a good bet** (*informal*) If you tell someone that something is a **good bet**, you are suggesting that it is the thing or course of action that they should choose. ❏ *Your best bet is to choose a guest house.*

a good bet or **a safe bet** (*informal*) If you say that it is **a good bet** or **a safe bet** that something is true or will happen, you are saying that it is extremely likely to be true or to happen. ❏ *It is a safe bet that the current owners will not sell.*

my bet is or **it's my bet that** (*informal*) You can use **my bet is** or **it's my bet** to give your personal opinion about something, when you are fairly sure that you are right. ❏ *My bet is that next year will be different.*

bet·ting /ˈbetɪŋ/ NOUN [u] ❏ *his thousand-dollar fine for illegal betting*

be·tray /bɪˈtreɪ/ VERB [T] (**betrays, betraying, betrayed**) **1** If you **betray** someone who loves or trusts you, your actions hurt and disappoint them. ❏ *When I tell someone I will not betray his confidence I keep my word.* **2** If someone **betrays** their country or their friends, they give information to an enemy, putting their country's security or their friends' safety at risk. ❏ *They offered me money if I would betray my associates.* **3** If you **betray** an ideal or your principles, you say or do something which goes against those beliefs. ❏ *We betray the ideals of our country when we support capital punishment.* **4** If you **betray** a feeling or quality, you show it without intending to. ❏ *She studied his face, but it betrayed nothing.*

be·tray·al /bɪˈtreɪəl/ NOUN [c, u] (**betrayals**) A **betrayal** is an action which betrays someone or something, or the fact of being betrayed. ❏ *She felt that what she had done was a betrayal of Patrick.*

bet·ter ♦♦♦ /ˈbetə/ IRREG FORM, ADJ, ADV, PRON, VERB, NOUN

IRREG FORM **1** Better is the comparative of **good**. **2** Better is the comparative of **well**. **3** Better is used to form the comparative of compound adjectives beginning with 'good' and 'well'. For example, the comparative of 'well-off' is 'better-off'.

ADJ [V-LINK + better] If you are **better** after an illness or injury, you have recovered from it. If you feel **better**, you no longer feel so ill. ❏ *He is much better now, he's fine.*

PHRASES **be better doing something** or **it is better doing something** You can say that someone **is better**

doing one thing than another, or **it is better** doing one thing than another, to advise someone about what they should do. ❏ *Wouldn't it be better putting a time-limit on the task?*

be better off If you say that someone would **be better off** doing something, you are advising them to do it or expressing the opinion that it would benefit them to do it. ❏ *If you've got bags you're better off taking a taxi.*

CONVENTION **that's better** You say '**That's better**' in order to express your approval of what someone has said or done, or to praise or encourage them. ❏ *'I came to ask your advice – no, to ask for your help.'—'That's better. And how can I help you?'*

ADV **1** [better after v] If you like one thing **better than** another, you like it more. ❏ *I like your interpretation better than the one I was taught.* ❏ *They liked it better when it rained.* **2** In spoken English, people sometimes use **better** without 'had' or 'be' before it. It has the same meaning. **hadbe** ❏ *Better not say too much aloud.*

PHRASES **know better** **1** If someone **knows better than** to do something, they are old enough or experienced enough to know it is the wrong thing to do. ❏ *She knew better than to argue with Adeline.* **2** If you **know better than** someone, you have more information, knowledge, or experience than them. ❏ *He thought he knew better than I did, though he was much less experienced.*

think better of it If you intend to do something and then **think better of it**, you decide not to do it because you realize it would not be sensible. ❏ *Alberg opened his mouth, as if to protest. But he thought better of it.*

had better You use **had better** or '**d better** when you are advising, warning, or threatening someone, or expressing an opinion about what should happen. ❏ *It's half past two. I think we had better go home.* ❏ *You'd better run if you're going to get your ticket.*

PRON If you say that you expect or deserve **better**, you mean that you expect or deserve a higher standard of achievement, behaviour, or treatment from people than they have shown you. ❏ *We expect better of you in the future.*

VERB [T] (**betters, bettering, bettered**) **1** If someone **betters** a high achievement or standard, they achieve something higher. ❏ *His throw bettered the American junior record set in 2003.* **2** If you **better** your situation, you improve your social status or the quality of your life. If you **better yourself**, you improve your social status. ❏ *He had dedicated his life to bettering the lot of the oppressed people of South Africa.*

NOUN

PHRASES **change for the better** If something changes **for the better**, it improves. ❏ *He dreams of changing the world for the better.*

get the better of someone **1** If a feeling such as jealousy, curiosity, or anger **gets the better of** you, it becomes too strong for you to hide or control. ❏ *She didn't allow her emotions to get the better of her.* **2** If you **get the better of** someone, you defeat them in a contest, fight, or argument. ❏ *He is used to tough defenders, and he usually gets the better of them.*

so much the better or **all the better** You can say '**so much the better**' or '**all the better**' to indicate that it is desirable that a particular thing is used, done, or available. ❏ *The fog had come in; so much the better when it came to sneaking away.*

✦ be better than nothing → see nothing

be·tween ♦♦♦ /bɪˈtwiːn/ PREP, ADV

In addition to the uses shown below, **between** is used in a few phrasal verbs, such as 'come between'.

PREP **1** If something is **between** two things or is **in between** them, it has one of the things on one side of it and the other thing on the other side. ❏ *She left the table to stand between the two men.* **2** [between + PL-N] If people or things travel **between** two places, they travel regularly from one place to the other and back again. ❏ *I spent a lot of time in the early eighties travelling between Oxford and London.* **3** [between + PL-N] A relationship, discussion, or difference **between** two people, groups, or things is one that involves them both or relates to them both. ❑ *I think the relationship between patients and doctors has got a lot less personal.* ❑ *There have been intensive discussions between the two governments in recent days.* **4** [between + N 'and' N] If something stands **between** you and what you want, it prevents you from having it. ❑ *His sense of duty often stood between him and the enjoyment of life.* **5** [between + NUM 'and' NUM] If something is **between** two amounts or ages, it is greater or older than the first one and smaller or younger than the second one. ❑ *Increase the amount of time you spend exercising by walking between 15 and 20 minutes.* **6** If something happens **between** or **in between** two times or events, it happens after the first time or event and before the second one. ❑ *The canal was built between 1793 and 1797.* **7** [between + PL-N] If you must choose **between** two or more things, you must choose just one of them. ❑ *Students will be able to choose between English, French, and Russian as their first foreign language.* **8** [between + PRON] If people or places have a particular amount of something **between** them, this is the total amount that they have. ❑ *The three sites employ 12,500 people between them.* **9** [between + PL-N] When something is divided or shared **between** people, they each have a share of it. = among ❑ *There is only one bathroom shared between eight bedrooms.* ADV [between with CL/GROUP] If something happens **between** or **in between** two times or events, it happens after one time or event and before another one. **If something or someone is between** or **in between**, they have one thing on one side of them and another on the other. ❑ *My life had been a journey from crisis to crisis with only a brief time in between.*

WHICH WORD?

between or among?

If something is **between** two things, it has one thing on one side and the other thing on the other side. You do not usually say that something is 'between' several things. You say that it is **among** them.

❑ *Janice was standing **between** the two men.*

❑ *There were a few teenagers sitting **among** the adults.*

You do not use **among** when you are talking about differences.

❑ *What is the difference **between** European and American football?*

❑ *There isn't much difference **between** the three parties.*

bev·er·age /ˈbevərɪdʒ/ NOUN [C] (**beverages**) (*written*) **Beverages** are drinks. = drink ❑ *Alcoholic beverages are served in the hotel lounge.* ❑ *artificially sweetened beverages*

be·ware /bɪˈweə/ VERB [I] If you tell someone to **beware** of a person or thing, you are warning them that the person or thing may harm them or be dangerous. ❑ *Beware of being too impatient with others.* ❑ *Motorists were warned to beware of slippery conditions.*

be·wil·der /bɪˈwɪldə/ VERB [T] (**bewilders, bewildering, bewildered**) If something **bewilders** you, it is so confusing or difficult that you cannot understand it. = perplex ❑ *The silence from Alex had hurt and bewildered her.*

be·wil·dered /bɪˈwɪldəd/ ADJ If you are **bewildered**, you are very confused and cannot understand something or decide what you should do. ❑ *Some shoppers looked bewildered by the sheer variety of goods for sale.*

be·wil·der·ing /bɪˈwɪldərɪŋ/ ADJ A **bewildering** thing or situation is very confusing and difficult to understand or to make a decision about. ❑ *A glance along his bookshelves reveals a bewildering array of interests.*

be·yond ♦♦◇ /bɪˈjɒnd/ PREP, ADV PREP **1** If something is **beyond** a place or barrier, it is on the other side of it. ❑ *On his right was a thriving vegetable garden and beyond it a small orchard of apple trees.* **2** If something happens **beyond** a particular time or date, it continues after that time or date has passed. = past ❑ *Few jockeys continue race-riding beyond the age of 40.* **3** If something extends **beyond** a particular thing, it affects or includes other things. ❑ *His interests extended beyond the fine arts to international politics and philosophy.* **4** You use **beyond** to introduce an exception to what you are saying.

❑ *He appears to have almost no personal staff, beyond a secretary who can't make coffee.* **5** If something goes **beyond** a particular point or stage, it progresses or increases so that it passes that point or stage. ❑ *Their five-year relationship was strained beyond breaking point.* **6** If something is, for example, **beyond** understanding or **beyond** belief, it is so extreme in some way that it cannot be understood or believed. ❑ *What Jock had done was beyond my comprehension.* **7** If you say that something is **beyond** someone, or **beyond** their control, you mean that they cannot deal with it. ❑ *The situation was beyond her control.* ADV **1** If something lies **beyond**, it is on the other side of a place or barrier. ❑ *The house had a fabulous view out to the Strait of Georgia and the Rockies beyond.* **2** [CL 'and' beyond] You can use **beyond** to say that something continues after a particular time or date has passed. ❑ *The financing of home ownership will continue through the 1990s and beyond.* ✦ **beyond your wildest dreams** → see **dream**

bi·an·nual /baɪˈænjuəl/ ADJ A **biannual** event happens twice a year. ❑ *You will need to have a routine biannual examination.*

bi·an·nu·al·ly /baɪˈænjuəli/ ADV [biannually after v] ❑ *Only since 1962 has the show been held biannually.*

WORD PARTS

The prefix **bi-** often appears in words that refer to things that happen twice in a period of time, or once in two consecutive periods of time:

biannual (ADJ)

bimonthly (ADJ, ADV)

biweekly (ADJ, ADV)

✪bias /ˈbaɪəs/ NOUN, VERB (*academic word*) NOUN [C, U] (**biases**) **1** **Bias** is a tendency to prefer one person or thing to another, and to favour that person or thing. = prejudice, favour ❑ *his desire to avoid the appearance of bias in favour of one candidate or another* ❑ *Bias against women permeates every level of the judicial system.* ❑ *There were fierce attacks on the BBC for alleged political bias.* **2** **Bias** is a concern with or interest in one thing more than others. ❑ *The department has a strong bias towards neuroscience.* VERB [T] (**biases, biasing, biased**) To **bias** someone means to influence them in favour of a particular choice. ❑ *We mustn't allow it to bias our teaching.*

✪bi·ased /ˈbaɪəst/ ADJ **1** If someone is **biased**, they prefer one group of people to another, and behave unfairly as a result. You can also say that a process or system is **biased**. = prejudiced; ≠ impartial ❑ *He seemed a bit biased against women in my opinion.* ❑ *examples of inaccurate and biased reporting* ❑ *politically biased allegations* **2** [V-LINK + biased 'towards' N] If something is **biased towards** one thing, it is more concerned with it than with other things. ❑ *University funding was tremendously biased towards scientists.*

✪bib·li·og·ra·phy /ˌbɪbliˈɒɡrəfi/ NOUN [C] (**bibliographies**) **1** A **bibliography** is a list of books on a particular subject. ❑ *At the end of this chapter there is a select bibliography of useful books.* **2** A **bibliography** is a list of the books and articles that are referred to in a particular book. ❑ *the full bibliography printed at the end of the second volume*

bi·cy·cle /ˈbaɪsɪkəl/ NOUN [C] (**bicycles**) A **bicycle** is a vehicle with two wheels which you ride by sitting on it and pushing two pedals with your feet. You steer it by turning a bar that is connected to the front wheel. = bike

WORD PARTS

The prefix **bi-** often appears in words that refer to things that have two parts:

bicycle (NOUN)

bilingual (ADJ)

bifocals (NOUN)

bid ♦♦◇ /bɪd/ NOUN, VERB NOUN [C] (**bids**) **1** (*journalism*) A **bid for** something or a **bid to** do something is an attempt to obtain it or do it. = attempt ❑ *Sydney's successful bid for the 2000 Olympic Games* **2** A **bid** is an offer to pay a particular amount of money for something that is being sold. ❑ *Hanson made an agreed takeover bid of $351 million.*

VERB [I, T] (**bids, bidding, bid**) **1** [I, T] If you **bid for** something or **bid to** do something, you try to obtain it or do it. ❑ *Singapore Airlines is rumoured to be bidding for a management contract to run both airports.* **2** [I] If you **bid for** something that is being sold, you offer to pay a particular amount of money for it. ❑ *She wanted to bid for it.* ❑ *The bank announced its intention to bid.*

bid·der /ˈbɪdə/ NOUN [c] (**bidders**) **1** A **bidder** is someone who offers to pay a certain amount of money for something that is being sold. If you sell something to the highest **bidder**, you sell it to the person who offers the most money for it. ❑ *The sale will be made to the highest bidder subject to a reserve price being attained.* **2** A **bidder for** something is someone who is trying to obtain it or do it. ❑ *Vodafone is among successful bidders for two licences to develop mobile phone systems in Greece.*

big ◆◆◆ /bɪg/ ADJ
ADJ (**bigger, biggest**) **1** A **big** person or thing is large in physical size. = large ❑ *Australia's a big country.* ❑ *Her husband was a big man.* **2** Something that is **big** consists of many people or things. = large ❑ *The crowd included a big contingent from Manchester.* **3** If you describe something such as a problem, increase, or change as a **big** one, you mean it is great in degree, extent, or importance. = serious ❑ *Her problem was just too big for her to tackle on her own.* **4** A **big** organization employs many people and has many customers. = large ❑ *one of the biggest companies in Italy* **5** [big + N, V-LINK + big 'in'] (*informal*) If you say that someone is **big in** a particular organization, activity, or place, you mean that they have a lot of influence or authority in it. ❑ *Their father was very big in the army.* **6** [big + N] (*informal, emphasis*) If you call someone a **big** bully or a **big** coward, you are emphasizing your disapproval of them. ❑ *His personality changed. He turned into a big bully.* **7** [big + N] Children often refer to their older brother or sister as their **big** brother or sister. ❑ *She always introduces me as her big sister.* **8** (*informal*) **Big** words are long or rare words which have meanings that are difficult to understand. ❑ *They use a lot of big words.*
PHRASES **make it big** (*informal*) If you **make it big**, you become successful or famous. ❑ *Capone was an underdog hero, a poor boy who made it big.*
think big If you **think big**, you make plans on a large scale, often using a lot of time, effort, or money. ❑ *Maybe we're not thinking big enough.*

WHICH WORD?
big, large, or great?

Big, **large**, and **great** are used to talk about size. They can all be used in front of countable nouns, but only **great** can be used in front of uncountable nouns.

In general, **large** is more formal than **big** and **great** is more formal than **large**.

Use **large** and **great** to describe amounts. You do not usually talk about 'a big amount' or 'a big number'.

❑ *A **large** number of students passed the exam.*

❑ *Young people consume **great** quantities of chips.*

Use **big** or **great** when you are describing a problem or danger. You do not usually talk about 'large problems'.

❑ *Traffic is one of London's **biggest** problems.*

Use **great** when you are describing feelings, reactions, or qualities.

❑ *He has **great** hopes for the future.*

❑ *The book brought back those early days of the war with **great** clarity.*

---

big busi·ness NOUN [u] **1** **Big business** is business which involves very large companies and very large sums of money. ❑ *Big business will never let petty nationalism get in the way of a good deal.* **2** Something that is **big business** is something which people spend a lot of money on, and which has become an important commercial activity. ❑ *Online dating is big business in Britain and the United States.*

big·ot /ˈbɪgət/ NOUN [c] (**bigots**) (*disapproval*) If you describe someone as a **bigot**, you mean they are bigoted. ❑ *Anyone who opposes them is branded a racist, a bigot, or a homophobe.*

big·ot·ed /ˈbɪgətɪd/ ADJ (*disapproval*) Someone who is **bigoted** has strong, unreasonable prejudices or opinions and will not change them, even when they are proved to be wrong. ❑ *He was bigoted and racist.*

big time also **big-time** ADJ, NOUN, ADV
ADJ (*informal*) You can use **big time** to refer to the highest level of an activity or sport where you can achieve the greatest amount of success or importance. If you describe a person as **big time**, you mean they are successful and important. ❑ *He took a long time to settle in to big-time football.*
NOUN [SING] If someone hits **the big time**, they become famous or successful in a particular area of activity. ❑ *He hit the big time with films such as Ghost and Dirty Dancing.*
ADV [big time after V] (*emphasis*) You can use **big time** if you want to emphasize the importance or extent of something that has happened. ❑ *Mike Edwards has tasted success big time.*

bike ◆◇◇ /baɪk/ NOUN, VERB
NOUN [c] (**bikes**) (*informal*) **1** A **bike** is a bicycle. ❑ *When you ride a bike, you exercise all of the leg muscles.* **2** A **bike** is a motorcycle. ❑ *She parked her bike in the alley.*
VERB [I] (**bikes, biking, biked**) To **bike** somewhere means to go there on a bicycle. ❑ *I biked home from the beach.*

bi·lat·er·al /ˌbaɪˈlætərəl/ ADJ [bilateral + N] (*formal*) **Bilateral** negotiations, meetings, or agreements involve only the two groups or countries that are directly concerned. ❑ *bilateral talks between Britain and America*
bi·lat·er·al·ly /ˌbaɪˈlætərəli/ ADV ❑ *The agreement provided for disputes and differences between the two neighbours to be solved bilaterally.*

bi·lin·gual /ˌbaɪˈlɪŋgwəl/ ADJ **1** [bilingual + N] **Bilingual** means involving or using two languages. ❑ *bilingual education* **2** Someone who is **bilingual** can speak two languages equally well, usually because they learned both languages as a child. ❑ *He is bilingual in an Asian language and English.*

bill ◆◆◇ /bɪl/ NOUN, VERB
NOUN [SING, c] (**bills**) **1** [SING, c] A **bill** is a written statement of money that you owe for goods or services. ❑ *They couldn't afford to pay the bills.* ❑ *He paid his bill for the newspapers promptly.* **2** [c] In government, a **bill** is a formal statement of a proposed new law that is discussed and then voted on. ❑ *This is the toughest crime bill that Parliament has passed in a decade.* **3** [SING] The **bill** of a show or concert is a list of the entertainers who will take part in it. ❑ *Bob Dylan topped the bill.* **4** [SING] (*BrE; in AmE, usually use* **check**) The **bill** in a restaurant is a piece of paper on which the price of the meal you have just eaten is written and which you are given before you pay. **5** [c] (*AmE; in BrE, use* **note**) A **bill** is a piece of paper money. ❑ *The case contained a large quantity of US dollar bills.* **6** [c] A bird's **bill** is its beak.
PHRASE **fit the bill** or **fill the bill** If you say that someone or something **fits the bill** or **fills the bill**, you mean that they are suitable for a particular job or purpose. ❑ *If you fit the bill, send a CV to Rebecca Rees.*
VERB [T] (**bills, billing, billed**) **1** If you **bill** someone **for** goods or services you have provided them with, you give or send them a bill stating how much money they owe you for these goods or services. ❑ *Are you going to bill me for this?* **2** If someone **is billed to** appear in a particular show, it has been advertised that they are going to be in it. ❑ *She was billed to play the Wicked Queen in 'Snow White'.* **3** If you **bill** a person or event **as** a particular thing, you advertise them in a way that makes people think they have particular qualities or abilities. ❑ *They bill it as the country's most exciting museum.*
bill·ing /ˈbɪlɪŋ/ NOUN [u] ❑ *their quarrels over star billing*

✪ bil·lion ◆◆◆ /ˈbɪljən/ NUM, QUANT, PRON

The plural form is **billion** after a number, or after a word or expression referring to a number, such as 'several' or 'a few'.

B

NUM (**billions**) A **billion** is a thousand million. ❑ *The Ethiopian foreign debt stands at 3 billion dollars.*

QUANT [billions 'of' PL-N] If you talk about **billions of** people or things, you mean that there is a very large number of them but you do not know or do not want to say exactly how many. ❑ *Biological systems have been doing this for billions of years.*

PRON **Billions** means a very large number or amount of something. ❑ *He thought that it must be worth billions.*
→ See also **trillion**

bil·lion·aire /ˌbɪljəˈneə/ NOUN [c] (**billionaires**) A **billionaire** is an extremely rich person who has money or property worth at least a thousand million pounds or dollars.

bin /bɪn/ NOUN [c] (**bins**) ■ A **bin** is a container that you keep or store things in. ❑ *big steel storage bins* ■ (*BrE; in AmE*, usually use **garbage can, trashcan**) A **bin** is a container that you put rubbish in.

bind /baɪnd/ VERB [T] (**binds, binding, bound**) ■ If something **binds** people **together**, it makes them feel as if they are all part of the same group or have something in common. ❑ *It is the memory and threat of persecution that binds them together.* ❑ *the social and political ties that bind the U.S. to Britain* ■ If you **are bound** by something such as a rule, agreement, or restriction, you are forced or required to act in a certain way. ❑ *All pharmacists are bound by the society's rules of confidentiality.* ❑ *The authorities will be legally bound to arrest any suspects.* ■ If you **bind** something or someone, you tie rope, string, tape, or other material around them so that they are held firmly. ❑ *Bind the ends of the cord together with thread.* ❑ *the red tape which was used to bind the files* ■ When a book **is bound**, the pages are joined together and the cover is put on. ❑ *Each volume is bound in bright-coloured cloth.* ❑ *Their business came from a few big publishers, all of whose books they bound.*

bind·ing /ˈbaɪndɪŋ/ ADJ, NOUN
ADJ A **binding** promise, agreement, or decision must be obeyed or carried out. ❑ *proposals for a legally binding commitment on nations to stabilize emissions of carbon dioxide*
NOUN [c, u] (**bindings**) ■ The **binding** of a book is its cover. ❑ *Its books are noted for the quality of their paper and bindings.* ■ **Binding** is a strip of material that you put around the edge of a piece of cloth or other object in order to protect or decorate it. ❑ *the Regency mahogany dining table with satinwood binding*
→ See also **bind**

binge /bɪndʒ/ NOUN, VERB
NOUN [c] (**binges**) (*informal*) If you go on a **binge**, you do too much of something, such as drinking alcohol, eating, or spending money. ❑ *She went on occasional drinking binges.*
VERB [i] (**binges, bingeing, binged**) If you **binge**, you do too much of something, such as drinking alcohol, eating, or spending money. ❑ *I haven't binged since 1986.*

✪**bio·chemi·cal** /ˌbaɪəʊˈkemɪkəl/ ADJ [biochemical + N] **Biochemical** changes, reactions, and mechanisms relate to the chemical processes that happen in living things. ❑ *Starvation brings biochemical changes in the body.* ❑ *a slight drop in internal heat can slow biochemical reactions*

WORD PARTS

The prefix *bio-* appears in words that refer to life or to the study of living things:
biochemical (ADJ)
biology (NOUN)
biography (NOUN)

✪**bio·chem·ist** /ˌbaɪəʊˈkemɪst/ NOUN [c] (**biochemists**) A **biochemist** is a scientist or student who studies biochemistry. ❑ *the biochemist who discovered p53, the gene that acts as a brake on cancer* ❑ *as a clinical biochemist working in a hospital laboratory*

✪**bio·chem·is·try** /ˌbaɪəʊˈkemɪstri/ NOUN [u]
■ **Biochemistry** is the study of the chemical processes that occur in living things. ❑ *Richard Axel is professor of biochemistry and molecular biophysics at Columbia University.*
■ The **biochemistry** of a living thing is the chemical

processes that occur in it or are involved in it. ❑ *the effects of air pollutants on the biochemistry of plants or animals*

bio·degrad·able /ˌbaɪəʊdɪˈɡreɪdəbəl/ ADJ Something that is **biodegradable** breaks down or decays naturally without any special scientific treatment, and can therefore be thrown away without causing pollution. ❑ *a natural and totally biodegradable plastic*

bi·o·die·sel /ˌbaɪəʊˈdiːzəl/ NOUN [u] **Biodiesel** is fuel made from natural sources such as plant oils, that can be used in diesel engines.

✪**bio·di·ver·sity** /ˌbaɪəʊdaɪˈvɜːsɪti/ NOUN [u] **Biodiversity** is the existence of a wide variety of plant and animal species living in their natural environment. ❑ *The national environment management programme encourages farmers to preserve biodiversity.* ❑ *We must protect the great biodiversity of the oceans.*

bi·o·fu·el /ˌbaɪəʊˈfjuːəl/ NOUN [c, u] A **biofuel** is a gas, liquid, or solid from natural sources such as plants that is used as a fuel. ❑ *Biofuels can be mixed with conventional fuels.*

✪**bio·graphi·cal** /ˌbaɪəˈɡræfɪkəl/ ADJ **Biographical** facts, notes, or details are concerned with the events in someone's life. ❑ *The book contains few biographical details.*

✪**bi·og·ra·phy** /baɪˈɒɡrəfi/ NOUN [c, u] (**biographies**) ■ [c] A **biography** of someone is an account of their life, written by someone else. ❑ *recent biographies of Stalin* ❑ *a very comprehensive and thoroughly researched biography* ■ [u] **Biography** is the branch of literature which deals with accounts of people's lives. ❑ *a volume of biography and criticism*

✪**bio·logi·cal** /ˌbaɪəˈlɒdʒɪkəl/ ADJ ■ **Biological** is used to describe processes and states that occur in the bodies and cells of living things. ❑ *The living organisms somehow concentrated the minerals by biological processes.* ❑ *This is a natural biological response.* ■ [biological + N] **Biological** is used to describe activities concerned with the study of living things. ❑ *all aspects of biological research associated with leprosy* ■ **Biological** weapons and **biological** warfare involve the use of bacteria or other living organisms in order to attack human beings, animals, or plants. ❑ *Such a war could result in the use of chemical and biological weapons.* ■ [biological + N] **Biological** pest control is the use of bacteria or other living organisms in order to destroy other organisms which are harmful to plants or crops. ❑ *a consultant on biological control of agricultural pests* ■ [biological + N] A child's **biological** parents are the man and woman who caused him or her to be born, rather than other adults who look after him or her. = natural ❑ *foster parents for young teenagers whose biological parents have rejected them*
✪**bio·logi·cal·ly** /ˌbaɪəˈlɒdʒɪkli/ ADV ❑ *Much of our behaviour is biologically determined.*

✪**bi·ol·ogy** /baɪˈɒlədʒi/ NOUN [u] ■ **Biology** is the science which is concerned with the study of living things. ❑ *She studied biology at Sydney University.* ■ The **biology** of a living thing is the way in which its body or cells behave. ❑ *The biology of these diseases is terribly complicated.* ❑ *human biology*
✪**bi·ol·o·gist** /baɪˈɒlədʒɪst/ NOUN [c] (**biologists**) ❑ *biologists studying the fruit fly*

✪**bio·tech·nol·ogy** /ˌbaɪəʊtekˈnɒlədʒi/ NOUN [u] (*technical*) **Biotechnology** is the use of living parts such as cells or bacteria in industry and technology. **Biotech** is also used in informal and spoken English. ❑ *the Scottish biotechnology company that developed Dolly the cloned sheep* ❑ *The second generation of agricultural biotechnology will market seeds offering benefits for farmers such as increased yields and drought resistance.*
✪**bio·tech·nolo·gist** /ˌbaɪəʊtekˈnɒlədʒɪst/ NOUN [c] (**biotechnologists**) ❑ *biotechnologists turning proteins into pharmaceuticals* ❑ *a consultant biotechnologist at Cranfield University*

bird ◆◆◇ /bɜːd/ NOUN
NOUN [c] (**birds**) A **bird** is a creature with feathers and wings. Female birds lay eggs. Most birds can fly.
PHRASES **birds of a feather** If you refer to two people as **birds of a feather**, you mean that they have the same

interests or are very similar. ❑ *We're birds of a feather, you and me, Mr Plimpton.*

a bird in the hand A **bird in the hand** is something that you already have and do not want to risk losing by trying to get something else. ❑ *Another temporary discount may not be what you want, but at least it is a bird in the hand.*

little bird If you say that a **little bird** told you about something, you mean that someone has told you about it, but you do not want to say who it was. ❑ *Incidentally, a little bird tells me that your birthday's coming up.*

kill two birds with one stone If you say that doing something will **kill two birds with one stone**, you mean that it will enable you to achieve two things that you want to achieve, rather than just one. ❑ *We can talk about Union Hill while I get this business over with. Kill two birds with one stone, so to speak.*

Biro /ˈbaɪərəʊ/ NOUN [C] (**Biros**) (*BrE, trademark*) A **Biro** is a pen with a very small metal ball at the end which transfers the ink from the pen onto a surface.

birth ♦◇◇ /bɜːθ/ NOUN

  NOUN [C, U] (**births**) **1** [C, U] When a baby is born, you refer to this event as his or her **birth**. ❑ *It was the birth of his grandchildren that gave him greatest pleasure.* ❑ *She weighed 5lb 7oz at birth.* **2** [U] You can refer to the beginning or origin of something as its **birth**. ❑ *the birth of popular democracy* **3** [U] Some people talk about a person's **birth** when they are referring to the social position of the person's family. ❑ *men of low birth*

  PHRASES **by birth** If, for example, you are French **by birth**, you are French because your parents are French, or because you were born in France. ❑ *Sadrudin was an Iranian by birth.*

give birth When a woman **gives birth**, she produces a baby from her body. ❑ *She's just given birth to a baby girl.*

give birth to To **give birth to** something such as an idea means to cause it to start to exist. ❑ *In 1980, strikes at the Lenin shipyards gave birth to the Solidarity trade union.*

of one's birth The country, town, or village **of** your **birth** is the place where you were born. ❑ *He left the town of his birth five years later for Australia.*

→ See also **date of birth**

birth cer·tifi·cate NOUN [C] (**birth certificates**) Your **birth certificate** is an official document that gives details of your birth, such as the date and place of your birth, and the names of your parents.

birth·day ♦◇◇ /ˈbɜːθdeɪ, -di/ NOUN [C] (**birthdays**) Your **birthday** is the anniversary of the date on which you were born. ❑ *On his birthday she sent him presents.*

birth·place /ˈbɜːθpleɪs/ NOUN [C] (**birthplaces**) **1** (*written*) Your **birthplace** is the place where you were born. ❑ *Bob Marley's birthplace in the village of Nine Mile* **2** The **birthplace** of something is the place where it began. ❑ *Athens, the birthplace of the ancient Olympics*

bis·cuit /ˈbɪskɪt/ NOUN

  NOUN [C] (**biscuits**) (*BrE; in AmE, use* **cookie**) A **biscuit** is a small flat cake that is crisp and usually sweet.

  PHRASE **take the biscuit** (*BrE; in AmE, use* **take the cake**; *emphasis*) If someone has done something very stupid, rude, or selfish, you can say that they **take the biscuit** or that what they have done **takes the biscuit**, to emphasize your surprise at their behaviour.

bish·op /ˈbɪʃəp/ NOUN [C] (**bishops**) **1** A **bishop** is a clergyman of high rank in the Roman Catholic, Anglican, and Orthodox churches. **2** In chess a **bishop** is a piece that can be moved diagonally across the board on squares that are the same colour.

bit ♦♦♦ /bɪt/ IRREG FORM, QUANT, NOUN

  IRREG FORM **Bit** is the past tense of **bite**.

  QUANT [ˈa' bit 'of'] N-UNCOUNT] **A bit of** something is a small amount of it. ❑ *All it required was a bit of work.*

  PHRASES **a bit** (*vagueness*) **1** A **bit** means to a small extent or degree. It is sometimes used to make a statement less extreme. = slightly ❑ *This girl was a bit strange.* ❑ *I think people feel a bit more confident.* **2** You use **a bit** before 'more' or 'less' to mean a small amount more or a small amount less. ❑ *I still think I have a bit more to offer.* ❑ *Maybe we'll hear a little bit less noise.*

a bit of a (*vagueness*) You can use **a bit of a** to make a statement less forceful. For example, the statement 'It's a bit of a nuisance' is less forceful than 'It's a nuisance'. ❑ *It's all a bit of a mess.* ❑ *Students have always been portrayed as a bit of a joke.*

quite a bit Quite **a bit** means quite a lot. ❑ *They're worth quite a bit of money.* ❑ *Things have changed quite a bit.*

a bit much (*informal, feelings*) If you say that something is **a bit much**, you are annoyed because you think someone has behaved in an unreasonable way. ❑ *Her stage outfit of hot pants, over-the-knee boots and a tube top was a bit much.*

not a bit (*emphasis*) You use **not a bit** when you want to make a strong negative statement. ❑ *I'm really not a bit surprised.*

  NOUN [C] (**bits**) **1** A **bit of** something is a small part or section of it. = part ❑ *Only a bit of the barley remained.* ❑ *Now comes the really important bit.* **2** A **bit of** something is a small piece of it. = piece ❑ *Only a bit of string looped round a nail in the doorpost held it shut.* **3** You can use **bit** to refer to a particular item or to one of a group or set of things. For example, a **bit of** information is an item of information. ❑ *There was one bit of vital evidence which helped win the case.* **4** In computing, a **bit** is the smallest unit of information that is held in a computer's memory. It is either 1 or 0. Several bits form a byte.

  PHRASES **a bit** or **for a bit** If you do something **a bit** or do something **for a bit**, you do it for a short time. ❑ *Let's wait a bit.* ❑ *I hope there will be time to talk a bit – or at least ask you about one or two things this evening.*

bit by bit If something happens **bit by bit**, it happens in stages. ❑ *Bit by bit I began to understand what they were trying to do.*

do your bit (*BrE; in AmE, use* **do your part**) If you **do** your **bit**, you do something that, to a small or limited extent, helps to achieve something.

every bit as good as (*emphasis*) You say that one thing is **every bit as** good, interesting, or important **as** another to emphasize that the first thing is just as good, interesting, or important as the second. ❑ *My dinner jacket is every bit as good as his.*

bits and pieces (*informal*) You can use **bits and pieces** to refer to a collection of different things. ❑ *The drawers are full of bits and pieces of armour.*

bite ♦♦♦ /baɪt/ VERB, NOUN

  VERB [I, T] (**bites, biting, bit, bitten**) **1** [I, T] If you **bite** something, you use your teeth to cut into it, for example, in order to eat it or break it. If an animal or person **bites** you, they use their teeth to hurt or injure you. ❑ *Both sisters bit their nails as children.* ❑ *He bit into his sandwich.* ❑ *Every year in this country more than 50,000 children are bitten by dogs.* **2** [I, T] If a snake or a small insect **bites** you, or if it **bites**, it makes a mark or hole in your skin, and often causes the surrounding area of your skin to become painful or itchy. ❑ *When an infected mosquito bites a human, spores are injected into the blood.* **3** [I] When an action or policy begins to **bite**, it begins to have a serious or harmful effect. ❑ *As the sanctions begin to bite there will be more political difficulties ahead.* **4** [I] If an object **bites** into a surface, it presses hard against it or cuts into it. ❑ *There may even be some wire or nylon biting into the flesh.* **5** [I] If a fish **bites** when you are fishing, it takes the hook or bait at the end of your fishing line in its mouth. ❑ *After half an hour, the fish stopped biting and we moved on.*

  PHRASES **bite the hand that feeds you** If someone **bites the hand that feeds** them, they behave badly or in an ungrateful way towards someone who they depend on. ❑ *She may be cynical about the film industry, but ultimately she has no intention of biting the hand that feeds her.*

bite your lip or **bite your tongue** If you **bite** your **lip** or your **tongue**, you stop yourself from saying something that you want to say, because it would be the wrong thing to say in the circumstances. ❑ *I must learn to bite my lip.*

  NOUN [C, SING, U] (**bites**) **1** [C] A **bite** of something, especially food, is the action of biting it. ❑ *He took another bite of apple.* **2** [C] A **bite** of food is the amount of food you take into your mouth when you bite it. ❑ *Look forward to eating the food and enjoy every bite.* **3** [SING] (*informal*) If you have **a bite** to eat, you have a small meal or a snack.

B

❑ *It was time to go home for a little rest and a bite to eat.* **4** [c] A **bite** is an injury or a mark on your body where an animal, snake, or small insect has bitten you. ❑ *Any dog bite, no matter how small, needs immediate medical attention.* **5** [u] If you say that a food or drink has **bite**, you like it because it has a strong or sharp taste. ❑ *The olive salad has to have bite and tang.* **6** [c] When you are fishing, a **bite** is when a fish takes the hook or bait at the end of your fishing line in its mouth. ❑ *If I don't get a bite in a few minutes I lift the rod and twitch the bait.*
✦ **bite the bullet** → see **bullet**; **bite the dust** → see **dust**

bit•ten /'bɪtən/ IRREG FORM **Bitten** is the past participle of **bite**.

bit•ter ♦◇◇ /'bɪtə/ ADJ (**bitterest**) **1** In a **bitter** argument or conflict, people argue very angrily or fight very fiercely. ❑ *the scene of bitter fighting during the Second World War* ❑ *a bitter attack on the government's failure to support manufacturing* **2** If someone is **bitter** after a disappointing experience or after being treated unfairly, they continue to feel angry about it. ❑ *She is said to be very bitter about the way she was fired.* **3** A **bitter** taste is sharp, not sweet, and often slightly unpleasant. ❑ *The leaves taste rather bitter.* **4** A **bitter** experience makes you feel very disappointed. You can also use **bitter** to emphasize feelings of disappointment. ❑ *The decision was a bitter blow from which he never quite recovered.* ❑ *A great deal of bitter experience had taught him how to lose gracefully.* **5** **Bitter** weather, or a **bitter** wind, is extremely cold. ❑ *Outside, a bitter east wind was accompanied by flurries of snow.*
bit•ter•ness /'bɪtənəs/ NOUN [u] **1** The rift within the organization reflects the growing bitterness of the dispute. **2** I still feel bitterness and anger towards the person who knocked me down.
✦ **a bitter pill** → see **pill**

bit•ter•ly /'bɪtəli/ ADV **1** If people argue or fight **bitterly**, they argue very angrily or fight very fiercely. ❑ *Any such thing would be bitterly opposed by most of the world's democracies.* **2** If someone speaks or acts **bitterly** after a disappointing experience or after being treated unfairly, they speak or act in way that shows that they are still angry about it. ❑ *'And he sure didn't help us,' Grant said bitterly.* **3** [bitterly + ADJ] If you are **bitterly** disappointed, you are very disappointed. ❑ *I was bitterly disappointed to have lost yet another race so near the finish.* **4** [bitterly + ADJ] If the weather is **bitterly** cold, it is extremely cold. ❑ *It's been bitterly cold here in Moscow.* **5** [bitterly + ADJ] You use **bitterly** when you are describing an attitude which involves strong, unpleasant emotions such as anger or dislike. ❑ *We are bitterly upset at what has happened.*

bi•zarre /bɪ'zɑː/ ADJ Something that is **bizarre** is very odd and strange. = weird ❑ *The game was also notable for the bizarre behaviour of the team's manager.*
bi•zarre•ly /bɪ'zɑːli/ ADV ❑ *She dressed bizarrely.*

black ♦♦♦ /blæk/ COLOUR, ADJ, NOUN
COLOUR Something that is **black** is of the darkest colour that there is, the colour of the sky at night when there is no light at all. ❑ *She was wearing a black coat with a white collar.* ❑ *He had thick black hair.*
ADJ **1** A **black** person belongs to a race of people with dark skins, especially a race originally from Africa. ❑ *He worked for the rights of black people.* ❑ *Sherry is black, tall, slender, and soft-spoken.* **2** [black + N, V N + black] **Black** coffee or tea has no milk or cream added to it. ❑ *A cup of black tea or black coffee contains no calories.* **3** If you describe a situation as **black**, you are emphasizing that it is very bad indeed. ❑ *It was, he said later, one of the blackest days of his political career.* **4** If someone is in a **black** mood, they feel very miserable and depressed. ❑ *In late 1975, she fell into a black depression.*
NOUN [c] (**blacks**) Black people are sometimes referred to as **blacks**. This use could cause offence. ❑ *There are about thirty-one million blacks in the USA.*
PHRASE **be in the black** If a person or an organization is in the **black**, they do not owe anyone any money. ❑ *Remington's operations in Japan are now in the black.*

PHRASAL VERB **black out** (**blacks, blacking, blacked**)
1 If you **black out**, you lose consciousness for a short time. = pass out ❑ *I could feel blood draining from my face. I wondered whether I was about to black out.* **2** If a place **is blacked out**, it is in darkness, usually because it has no electricity supply. ❑ *Large parts of Lima were blacked out after electricity pylons were blown up.* **3** If a film or a piece of writing **is blacked out**, it is prevented from being broadcast or published, usually because it contains information which is secret or offensive. = censor ❑ *TV pictures of the demonstration were blacked out.* **4** If you **black out** a piece of writing, you colour over it in black so that it cannot be seen. = censor ❑ *British government specialists went through each page, blacking out any information a foreign intelligence expert could use.* **5** If you **black out** the memory of something, you try not to remember it because it upsets you. = blot out ❑ *I tried not to think about it. I blacked it out. It was the easiest way of coping.* **6** → See also **blackout**

black and white also **black-and-white** COLOUR, ADJ, NOUN
COLOUR In a **black and white** photograph or film, everything is shown in black, white, and grey. ❑ *old black and white film footage* ❑ *a black-and-white photo of the two of us together*
ADJ **1** A **black and white** television set shows only black and white pictures. **2** A **black and white** issue or situation is one that involves issues that seem simple and therefore easy to make decisions about. = clear-cut ❑ *But this isn't a simple black and white affair, Marianne.*
NOUN
PHRASE **be in black and white** You say that something is in **black and white** when it has been written or printed, and not just said. ❑ *He'd seen the proof in black and white.*

black•board /'blækbɔːd/ (in AmE, also use **chalkboard**) NOUN [c] (**blackboards**) A **blackboard** is a dark-coloured board that you can write on with chalk. Blackboards are often used by teachers in the classroom.

black•en /'blækən/ VERB [i, t] (**blackens, blackening, blackened**) **1** [i, t] To **blacken** something means to make it black or very dark in colour. Something that **blackens** becomes black or very dark in colour. ❑ *The married women of Shitamachi maintained the custom of blackening their teeth.* **2** [t] If someone **blackens** your character, they make other people believe that you are a bad person. ❑ *They're trying to blacken our name.*

black•list /'blæklɪst/ NOUN, VERB
NOUN [c] (**blacklists**) If someone is on a **blacklist**, they are seen by a government or other organization as being one of a number of people who cannot be trusted or who have done something wrong. ❑ *A government official disclosed that they were on a secret blacklist.*
VERB [t] (**blacklists, blacklisting, blacklisted**) If someone **is blacklisted** by a government or organization, they are put on a blacklist. ❑ *He has been blacklisted since being convicted of possessing marijuana in 1969.*

black•mail /'blækmeɪl/ NOUN, VERB
NOUN [u] **1** **Blackmail** is the action of threatening to reveal a secret about someone, unless they do something you tell them to do, such as giving you money. ❑ *It looks like the pictures were being used for blackmail.* **2** If you describe an action as emotional or moral **blackmail**, you disapprove of it because someone is using a person's emotions or moral values to persuade them to do something against their will. ❑ *The tactics employed can range from overt bullying to subtle emotional blackmail.*
VERB [t] (**blackmails, blackmailing, blackmailed**) If one person **blackmails** another person, they use blackmail against them. ❑ *He told her their affair would have to stop, because Jack Smith was blackmailing him.* ❑ *The government insisted that it would not be blackmailed by violence.*
black•mail•er /'blækmeɪlə/ NOUN [c] (**blackmailers**) ❑ *The nasty thing about a blackmailer is that his starting point is usually the truth.*

black mar•ket NOUN [c] (**black markets**) If something is bought or sold **on the black market**, it is bought or sold illegally. ❑ *There is a plentiful supply of arms on the black market.*

black·out /'blækaʊt/ also **black-out** NOUN [C]
(blackouts) **1** A blackout is a period of time during a war in which towns and buildings are made dark so that they cannot be seen by enemy planes. ❑ *blackout curtains* **2** If a blackout is imposed on a particular piece of news, journalists are prevented from broadcasting or publishing it. ❑ *a media blackout imposed by the Imperial Palace* **3** If there is a power blackout, the electricity supply to a place is temporarily cut off. = power cut ❑ *There was an electricity blackout in a large area in the north of the country.* **4** If you have a blackout, you temporarily lose consciousness. ❑ *I suffered a black-out which lasted for several minutes.*

blad·der /'blædə/ NOUN [C] (bladders) Your bladder is the part of your body where urine is stored until it leaves your body. ❑ *an opportunity to empty a full bladder*

blade /bleɪd/ NOUN [C] (blades) **1** The blade of a knife, axe, or saw is the edge, which is used for cutting. ❑ *Many of them will have sharp blades.* **2** The blades of a propeller are the long flat parts that turn around. **3** The blade of an oar is the thin flat part that you put into the water. **4** A blade of grass is a single piece of grass. ❑ *Brian began to tear blades of grass from between the bricks.*

blame ♦♦◇ /bleɪm/ VERB, NOUN
VERB [T] (blames, blaming, blamed) **1** If you blame a person or thing for something bad, or if you blame something bad on somebody, you believe or say that they are responsible for it or that they caused it. ❑ *The commission is expected to blame the army for many of the atrocities.* ❑ *Ms Carey appeared to blame her breakdown on EMI's punishing work schedule.* **2** If you say that you do not blame someone for doing something, you mean that you consider it was a reasonable thing to do in the circumstances. ❑ *I do not blame them for trying to make some money.*
PHRASES **to blame** If someone is to blame for something bad that has happened, they are responsible for causing it. ❑ *If their forces were not involved, then who is to blame?*
have only oneself to blame or **have no one but oneself to blame** If you say that someone has only themselves to blame or has no one but themselves to blame, you mean that they are responsible for something bad that has happened to them and that you have no sympathy for them. ❑ *My life is ruined and I suppose I only have myself to blame.*
NOUN [U] **1** Blame is the feeling that you are responsible for something bad. ❑ *Nothing could relieve my terrible sense of blame.* **2** The blame for something bad that has happened is the responsibility for causing it or letting it happen. ❑ *I'm not going to sit around and take the blame for a mistake he made.*

> ### WHICH WORD?
> **blame or fault?**
>
> Blame and fault are both used to talk about the person who is responsible for something bad. They are used in different ways, though. You can say that someone is 'to blame for' something or that someone 'takes the blame for' something.
> ❑ *Officials decided that Cappellini was **to blame for** the accident.*
> ❑ *The government should **take the blame for** the economic situation.*
> You say that something is 'someone's fault' or that someone is 'at fault'.
> ❑ *It's nobody's **fault**; it's just the way things are.*
> ❑ *I was clearly not **at fault** as my vehicle was stationary at the time.*

bland /blænd/ ADJ (blander, blandest) **1** If you describe someone or something as bland, you mean that they are rather dull and unexciting. ❑ *Serle has a blander personality than Howard.* ❑ *It sounds like a commercial: easy on the ear but bland and forgettable.* **2** Food that is bland has very little flavour. ❑ *It tasted bland and insipid, like warmed cardboard.*

blank /blæŋk/ ADJ, NOUN
ADJ **1** Something that is blank has nothing on it. ❑ *We*

could put some of the pictures over on that blank wall over there. ❑ *He tore a blank page from his notebook.* **2** If you look blank, your face shows no feeling, understanding, or interest. ❑ *Abbot looked blank. 'I don't quite follow, sir.'*
PHRASE **go blank** If your mind goes blank, you are suddenly unable to think of anything appropriate to say, for example in reply to a question.
NOUN [C, SING] (blanks) **1** [C] A blank is a space which is left in a piece of writing or on a printed form for you to fill in particular information. ❑ *Put a word in each blank to complete the sentence.* **2** [SING] If your mind or memory is a blank, you cannot think of anything or remember anything. ❑ *I'm sorry, but my mind is a blank.* **3** [C] Blanks are gun cartridges which contain explosive but do not contain a bullet, so that they cause no harm when the gun is fired. ❑ *a starter pistol which only fires blanks*
blank·ly /'blæŋkli/ ADV [blankly with v] ❑ *She stared at him blankly.*

blank cheque (BrE; in AmE, use **blank check**) NOUN [C]
(blank cheques) **1** If someone is given a blank cheque, they are given the authority to spend as much money as they need or want. ❑ *We are not prepared to write a blank cheque for companies that have run into trouble.* **2** If someone is given a blank cheque, they are given the authority to do what they think is best in a particular situation. = carte blanche ❑ *He has, in a sense, been given a blank cheque to negotiate the new South Africa.*

blan·ket /'blæŋkɪt/ NOUN, VERB, ADJ
NOUN [C] (blankets) **1** A blanket is a large square or rectangular piece of thick cloth, especially one that you put on a bed to keep you warm. **2** A blanket of something such as snow is a continuous layer of it which hides what is below or beyond it. ❑ *The mud disappeared under a blanket of snow.*
VERB [T] (blankets, blanketing, blanketed) If something such as snow blankets an area, it covers it. ❑ *More than a foot of snow blanketed parts of Michigan.*
ADJ [blanket + N] (emphasis) You use blanket to describe something when you want to emphasize that it affects or refers to every person or thing in a group, without any exceptions. = comprehensive ❑ *There's already a blanket ban on foreign unskilled labour in Japan.*

blast ♦◇◇ /blɑːst, blæst/ NOUN, VERB
NOUN [C, SING] (blasts) **1** [C] A blast is a big explosion, especially one caused by a bomb. ❑ *250 people were killed in the blast.* **2** [C] (journalism) A blast is a shot from a gun. ❑ *Anthony died from a shotgun blast to the face.* **3** [C] A blast of water or air is a powerful stream of it that is suddenly sent out. ❑ *Blasts of cold air swept down from the mountains.* **4** [C] A blast from something such as a car horn is a sudden, loud sound. ❑ *The buzzer suddenly responded in a long blast of sound.* **5** [SING] (informal) If you say that something was a blast, you mean that you enjoyed it very much. ❑ *He went sledding with his daughter. 'It was a blast,' he said later.*
PHRASE **full blast** If something such as a radio or a heater is on full blast, or on at full blast, it is producing as much sound or power as it is able to. ❑ *In many of those homes the television is on full blast 24 hours a day.*
VERB [T, I] (blasts, blasting, blasted) **1** [T] If something is blasted into a particular place or state, an explosion causes it to be in that place or state. If a hole is blasted in something, it is created by an explosion. ❑ *There is a risk that toxic chemicals might be blasted into the atmosphere.* ❑ *The explosion which followed blasted out the wall of her apartment.* **2** [T] If workers are blasting rock, they are using explosives to make holes in it or destroy it, for example, so that a road or tunnel can be built. ❑ *Local workmen were blasting the rock face beside the track in order to make it wider.* **3** [T] (journalism) To blast someone means to shoot them with a gun. ❑ *A son blasted his father to death after a lifetime of bullying, a court was told yesterday.* **4** [T] If someone blasts their way somewhere, they get there by shooting at people or causing an explosion. ❑ *The police were reported to have blasted their way into the house using explosives.* **5** [T] If something blasts water or air somewhere, it sends out a sudden, powerful stream of it.

❑ *Blasting cold air over it makes the water evaporate.* **6** [I, T] If you **blast** something such as a car horn, or if it **blasts**, it makes a sudden, loud sound. If something **blasts** music, or music **blasts**, the music is very loud. ❑ *drivers who do not blast their horns*

PHRASAL VERB **blast off** When a space rocket **blasts off**, it leaves the ground at the start of its journey. ❑ *Columbia is set to blast off at 1:20 a.m. Eastern Time tomorrow.*

bla·tant /'bleɪtənt/ ADJ (*emphasis*) You use **blatant** to describe something bad that is done in an open or very obvious way. ❑ *Outsiders will continue to suffer the most blatant discrimination.* ❑ *a blatant attempt to spread the blame for the fiasco*
→ See also **blatantly**

bla·tant·ly /'bleɪtəntli/ ADV **1** You use **blatantly** to indicate that something bad is done in an open or very obvious way. ❑ *a blatantly sexist question* **2** (*emphasis*) **Blatantly** is used to add emphasis when you are describing states or situations that you think are bad. ❑ *It became blatantly obvious to me that the band wasn't going to last.* ❑ *For years, blatantly false assertions have gone unchallenged.*

blaze /bleɪz/ VERB, NOUN
VERB [i] (**blazes, blazing, blazed**) **1** When a fire **blazes**, it burns strongly and brightly. ❑ *Three people died as wreckage blazed, and rescuers fought to release trapped drivers.* ❑ *The log fire was blazing merrily.* **2** (*literary*) If something **blazes with** light or colour, it is extremely bright. ❑ *The gardens blazed with colour.* **3** If guns **blaze**, or **blaze away**, they fire continuously, making a lot of noise. ❑ *Guns were blazing, flares going up and the sky was lit up all around.*
NOUN [C, SING] (**blazes**) **1** [C] (*journalism*) A **blaze** is a large fire which is difficult to control and which destroys a lot of things. ❑ *Some 4,000 firefighters are battling the blaze.* **2** [C] A **blaze** of light or colour is extremely bright. ❑ *I wanted the front garden to be a blaze of colour.* **3** [SING] A **blaze** of publicity or attention is a great amount of it. ❑ *He was arrested in a blaze of publicity.*
✦ **with all guns blazing** → see **gun**

bleak /bliːk/ ADJ (**bleaker, bleakest**) **1** If a situation is **bleak**, it is bad, and seems unlikely to improve. = gloomy ❑ *The immediate outlook remains bleak.* **2** If you describe a place as **bleak**, you mean that it looks cold, empty, and unattractive. ❑ *The island's pretty bleak.* **3** When the weather is **bleak**, it is cold, dull, and unpleasant. ❑ *The weather can be quite bleak on the coast.* **4** If someone looks or sounds **bleak**, they look or sound depressed, as if they have no hope or energy. ❑ *His face was bleak.*
bleak·ness /'bliːknəs/ NOUN [U] ❑ *The continued bleakness of the American job market was blamed.*
bleak·ly /'bliːkli/ ADV ❑ *'There is nothing left,' she says bleakly.*

bleed /bliːd/ VERB [T, I] (**bleeds, bleeding, bled**) **1** [T, I] When you **bleed**, you lose blood from your body as a result of injury or illness. ❑ *His head had struck the sink and was bleeding.* ❑ *He was bleeding profusely.* **2** [i] If the colour of one substance **bleeds into** the colour of another substance that it is touching, it goes into the other thing so that its colour changes in an undesirable way. ❑ *The colouring pigments from the skins are not allowed to bleed into the grape juice.* **3** [T] If someone **is being bled**, money or other resources are gradually being taken away from them. ❑ *We have been gradually bled for twelve years.*
bleed·ing /'bliːdɪŋ/ NOUN [U] ❑ *This results in internal bleeding.*

blem·ish /'blemɪʃ/ NOUN, VERB
NOUN [C] (**blemishes**) **1** A **blemish** is a small mark on something that spoils its appearance. ❑ *Every piece is closely scrutinized, and if there is the slightest blemish on it, it is rejected.* **2** A **blemish on** something is a small fault in it. = imperfection ❑ *This is the one blemish on an otherwise resounding success.*
VERB [T] (**blemishes, blemishing, blemished**) If something **blemishes** someone's character or reputation, it spoils it or makes it seem less good than it was in the past. = tarnish ❑ *He wasn't about to blemish that pristine record.*

blend /blend/ VERB, NOUN
VERB [RECIP, T] (**blends, blending, blended**) **1** [RECIP] If you

---

blend substances together or if they **blend**, you mix them together so that they become one substance. ❑ *Blend the butter with the sugar and beat until light and creamy.* ❑ *Blend the ingredients until you have a smooth cream.* **2** [RECIP] When colours, sounds, or styles **blend**, they come together or are combined in a pleasing way. ❑ *You could paint the walls and ceilings the same colour so they blend together.* **3** [T] If you **blend** ideas, policies, or styles, you use them together in order to achieve something. ❑ *His vision is to blend Christianity with 'the wisdom of all world religions'.*
NOUN [C] (**blends**) A **blend of** things is a mixture or combination of them that is useful or pleasant. ❑ *The public areas offer a subtle blend of traditional charm with modern amenities.* ❑ *a blend of wine and sparkling water*

bless /bles/ VERB, CONVENTION
VERB [T] (**blesses, blessing, blessed**) When someone such as a priest **blesses** people or things, he or she asks for God's favour and protection for them. ❑ *asking for all present to bless this couple and their loving commitment to one another*
CONVENTION (*spoken*) **1** (*informal, feelings*) **Bless** is used in expressions such as 'God bless' or 'bless you' to express affection, thanks, or good wishes. ❑ *'Bless you, Eva,' he whispered.* **2** (*formulae*) You can say **'bless you'** to someone who has just sneezed.
→ See also **blessed, blessing**

bless·ed ADJ **1** /'blesd/ [V-LINK + blessed 'with' N] If someone is **blessed with** a particular good quality or skill, they have that good quality or skill. ❑ *Both are blessed with an uncommon ability to fix things.* **2** /'blesɪd/ [blessed + N] You use **blessed** to describe something that you think is wonderful, and that you are grateful for or relieved about. ❑ *The birth of a live healthy baby is a truly blessed event.*
bless·ed·ly /'blesɪdli/ ADV ❑ *a wall still blessedly warm from the day's sun*
→ See also **bless**

bless·ing /'blesɪŋ/ NOUN [C] (**blessings**) **1** A **blessing** is something good that you are grateful for. ❑ *Rivers are a blessing for an agricultural country.* **2** [with POSS] If something is done with someone's **blessing**, it is done with their approval and support. = approval ❑ *With the blessing of the White House, a group of Democrats in Congress is meeting to find additional budget cuts.* **3** A **blessing** is a prayer asking God to look kindly upon the people who are present or the event that is taking place. ❑ *The Reverend Chris Long led the prayers and pronounced the blessing.*
→ See also **bless**

blew /bluː/ IRREG FORM **Blew** is the past tense of **blow**.

blind ✦◇◇ /blaɪnd/ ADJ, NOUN, VERB
ADJ **1** Someone who is **blind** is unable to see because their eyes are damaged. ❑ *I started helping him run the business when he went blind.* **2** [V-LINK + blind, usu blind 'with' N] If you are **blind with** something such as tears or a bright light, you are unable to see for a short time because of the tears or light. ❑ *Her mother groped for the back of the chair, her eyes blind with tears.* **3** [V-LINK + blind 'to' N] If you say that someone is **blind to** a fact or a situation, you mean that they ignore it or are unaware of it, although you think that they should take notice of it or be aware of it. ❑ *David's good looks and impeccable manners had always made her blind to his faults.* **4** You can describe someone's beliefs or actions as **blind** when you think that they seem to take no notice of important facts or behave in an unreasonable way. ❑ *her blind faith in the wisdom of the church*
PHRASE **turn a blind eye** (*disapproval*) If you say that someone is **turning a blind eye to** something bad or illegal that is happening, you mean that you think they are pretending not to notice that it is happening so that they will not have to do anything about it. ❑ *Teachers are turning a blind eye to pupils smoking at school, a report reveals today.*
NOUN [C, PL] (**blinds**) **1** [C, PL] The **blind** are people who are blind. ❑ *He was a teacher of the blind.* **2** [C] A **blind** is a roll of cloth or paper which you can pull down over a window as a covering. ❑ *Pulling the blinds up, she let some of the bright sunlight in.*
VERB [T] (**blinds, blinding, blinded**) **1** If something **blinds**

you, it makes you unable to see, either for a short time or permanently. ❑ *The sun hit the windshield, momentarily blinding him.* **2** If something **blinds** you **to** the real situation, it prevents you from realizing that it exists or from understanding it properly. ❑ *He never allowed his love of Australia to blind him to his countrymen's faults.*

blind·ness /'blaɪndnəs/ NOUN [U] **1** *blindness in government policy to the very existence of the unemployed* **2** *Early diagnosis and treatment can usually prevent blindness.*

blind·ly /'blaɪndli/ ADV **1** If you move or reach out **blindly**, you act without being able to see what you are doing or where you are going. ❑ *Lettie groped blindly for the glass.* **2** (disapproval) If you say that someone does something **blindly**, you mean that they do it without having enough information, or without thinking about it. ❑ *Don't just blindly follow what the banker says.* ❑ *Without adequate information, many students choose a university almost blindly.*

blink /blɪŋk/ VERB, NOUN
▸ VERB [I, T] (**blinks, blinking, blinked**) **1** [I, T] When you **blink** or when you **blink** your eyes, you shut your eyes and very quickly open them again. ❑ *Kathryn blinked and forced a smile.* ❑ *She was blinking her eyes rapidly.* **2** [I] When a light **blinks**, it flashes on and off. ❑ *Green and yellow lights blinked on the surface of the harbour.* ❑ *The plane was flying normally for about 15 minutes before a warning light blinked on.*
▸ NOUN [C] (**blinks**) A **blink** is the action of shutting your eyes and very quickly opening them again. ❑ *He kept giving quick blinks.*

bliss /blɪs/ NOUN [U] **Bliss** is a state of complete happiness. ❑ *It was a scene of such domestic bliss.*

bliss·ful /'blɪsfʊl/ ADJ **1** A **blissful** situation or period of time is one in which you are extremely happy. ❑ *We spent a blissful week together.* **2** [blissful + N] If someone is in **blissful** ignorance of something unpleasant or serious, they are totally unaware of it. ❑ *Many country towns were still living in blissful ignorance of the post-war crime wave.*
bliss·ful·ly /'blɪsfʊli/ ADV **1** *We're blissfully happy.* **2** At first, he was blissfully unaware of the conspiracy against him.*

blis·ter /'blɪstə/ NOUN, VERB
▸ NOUN [C] (**blisters**) A **blister** is a painful swelling on the surface of your skin. Blisters contain a clear liquid and are usually caused by heat or by something repeatedly rubbing your skin.
▸ VERB [I, T] (**blisters, blistering, blistered**) When your skin **blisters** or when something **blisters** it, blisters appear on it. ❑ *The affected skin turns red and may blister.* ❑ *The sap of this plant blisters the skin.*

blis·ter·ing /'blɪstərɪŋ/ ADJ **1** **Blistering** heat is very great heat. ❑ *a blistering summer day* **2** A **blistering** remark expresses great anger or dislike. ❑ *The president responded to this with a blistering attack on his critics.* **3** [blistering + N] (journalism, emphasis) **Blistering** is used to describe actions in sports to emphasize that they are done with great speed or force. ❑ *Sharon Wild set a blistering pace to take the lead.*

blitz /blɪts/ NOUN, VERB
▸ NOUN [C, SING] (**blitzes**) **1** [C] (informal) If you have a **blitz on** something, you make a big effort to deal with it or to improve it. ❑ *Regional accents are still acceptable but there is to be a blitz on incorrect grammar.* **2** [SING] The heavy bombing of British cities by German aircraft in 1940 and 1941 is referred to as the **Blitz**.
▸ VERB [T] (**blitzes, blitzing, blitzed**) If a city or building is **blitzed** during a war, it is attacked by bombs dropped by enemy aircraft. ❑ *In the autumn of 1940 London was blitzed by an average of two hundred aircraft a night.*

bliz·zard /'blɪzəd/ NOUN [C] (**blizzards**) A **blizzard** is a very bad snowstorm with strong winds.

bloc /blɒk/ NOUN [C] (**blocs**) A **bloc** is a group of countries that have similar political aims and interests and that act together over some issues. ❑ *the former Soviet bloc*

block ♦♦◇ /blɒk/ NOUN, VERB
▸ NOUN [C] (**blocks**) **1** A **block of** a substance is a large rectangular piece of it. ❑ *a block of ice* **2** A **block of** apartments or offices is a large building containing them. ❑ *a white-painted apartment block* **3** A **block** in a town or

city is an area of land with streets on all its sides, or the area or distance between such streets. ❑ *He walked around the block three times.* ❑ *She walked four blocks down High Street.* **4** **Blocks** are wooden or plastic cubes, such as those used as toys by children. **5** [usu block 'of' N] A **block of** something such as tickets or shares is a large quantity of them, especially when they are all sold at the same time and are in a particular sequence or order. ❑ *Those booking a block of seats get them at reduced rates.* **6** If you have a **mental block** or a **block**, you are temporarily unable to do something that you can normally do which involves using, thinking about, or remembering something. ❑ *I cannot do maths. I've got a mental block about it.*
▸ VERB [T] (**blocks, blocking, blocked**) **1** To **block** a road, channel, or pipe means to put an object across it or in it so that nothing can pass through it or along it. ❑ *Some students today blocked a main road that cuts through the centre of the city.* **2** If something **blocks** your view, it prevents you from seeing something because it is between you and that thing. = obstruct ❑ *a row of spruce trees that blocked his view of the long north slope of the mountain* **3** If you **block** someone's way, you prevent them from going somewhere or entering a place by standing in front of them. ❑ *I started to move around him, but he blocked my way.* **4** If you **block** something that is being arranged, you prevent it from being done. ❑ *For years the country has tried to block imports of various cheap foreign products.*
▸ PHRASAL VERB **block out** **1** If someone **blocks out** a thought, they try not to think about it. ❑ *She accuses me of having blocked out the past.* **2** Something that **blocks out** light prevents it from reaching a place. ❑ *He pulled down the blinds, blocking out the bright sunlight.*
→ See also **stumbling block**

block·ade /blɒ'keɪd/ NOUN, VERB
▸ NOUN [C] (**blockades**) A **blockade** of a place is an action that is taken to prevent goods or people from entering or leaving it. ❑ *It's not yet clear who will actually enforce the blockade.*
▸ VERB [T] (**blockades, blockading, blockaded**) If a group of people **blockade** a place, they stop goods or people from reaching that place. If they **blockade** a road or a port, they stop people from using that road or port. ❑ *About 50,000 people are trapped in the town, which has been blockaded for more than 40 days.*

block·age /'blɒkɪdʒ/ NOUN [C] (**blockages**) A **blockage in** a pipe, tube, or tunnel is an object which blocks it, or the state of being blocked. ❑ *The logical treatment is to remove this blockage.*

blog /blɒg, AmE blɔːg/ NOUN [C] (**blogs**) (computing) A **blog** is a website containing a diary or journal on a particular subject. ❑ *When Barbieux started his blog, his aspirations were small; he simply hoped to communicate with a few people.*
blog·ger /'blɒgə, AmE 'blɔːgər/ NOUN [C] (**bloggers**) ❑ *While most bloggers comment on news reported elsewhere, some do their own reporting.*
blog·ging /'blɒgɪŋ, AmE 'blɔːgɪŋ/ NOUN [U] ❑ *the explosion in the popularity of blogging*

blonde /blɒnd/ COLOUR, ADJ, NOUN

The form **blonde** is usually used to refer to women, and **blond** to refer to men.

▸ COLOUR A woman who has **blonde** hair has pale-coloured hair. Blonde hair can be very light brown or light yellow. The form **blond** is used when describing men. ❑ *a little girl with blonde hair*
▸ ADJ (**blonder, blondest**) Someone who is **blonde** has blonde hair. ❑ *He was blonder than his brother.*
▸ NOUN [C] (**blondes**) A **blonde** is a woman who has blonde hair. ❑ *a stunning blonde in her early thirties*

blood ♦♦◇ /blʌd/ NOUN
▸ NOUN [U] **1** **Blood** is the red liquid that flows inside your body, which you can see if you cut yourself. ❑ *His shirt was covered in blood.* **2** You can use **blood** to refer to the race or social class of someone's parents or ancestors. ❑ *There was Greek blood in his veins: his ancestors originally bore the name Karajannis.*
▸ PHRASES **bad blood** If you say that there is **bad blood**

B

between people, you mean that they have argued about something and dislike each other. ❑ *There is, it seems, some bad blood between Mills and the Baldwins.*

in cold blood (*disapproval*) If something violent and cruel is done **in cold blood**, it is done deliberately and in an unemotional way. ❑ *The crime had been committed in cold blood.*

blood on one's hands If you say that someone has a person's **blood** on their **hands**, you mean that they are responsible for that person's death. ❑ *He has my son's blood on his hands. I hope it haunts him for the rest of his days.*

in one's blood If a quality or talent is **in** your **blood**, it is part of your nature, and other members of your family have it too. ❑ *Diplomacy was in his blood: his ancestors had been feudal lords.*

new blood or **fresh blood** or **young blood** You can use the expressions **new blood**, **fresh blood**, or **young blood** to refer to people who are brought into an organization to improve it by thinking of new ideas or new ways of doing things. ❑ *There's been a major reshuffle of the cabinet to bring in new blood.*

✦ **flesh and blood** → see **flesh**; **own flesh and blood** → see **flesh**

⊙**blood pres·sure** NOUN [U] Your **blood pressure** is the amount of force with which your blood flows around your body. ❑ *Your doctor will monitor your blood pressure.* ❑ *Chromium also appears to help prevent and lower high blood pressure.*

blood·shed /'blʌdʃed/ NOUN [U] **Bloodshed** is violence in which people are killed or wounded. ❑ *The government must increase the pace of reforms to avoid further bloodshed.*

blood·stream /'blʌdstriːm/ NOUN [C] (**bloodstreams**) Your **bloodstream** is the blood that flows around your body. ❑ *The disease releases toxins into the bloodstream.*

blood ves·sel NOUN [C] (**blood vessels**) **Blood vessels** are the narrow tubes through which your blood flows.

bloody ♦◇◇ /'blʌdi/ ADJ, VERB

ADJ (**bloodier**, **bloodiest**) **1** If you describe a situation or event as **bloody**, you mean that it is very violent and a lot of people are killed. ❑ *Forty-three demonstrators were killed in bloody clashes.* **2** You can describe someone or something as **bloody** if they are covered in a lot of blood. ❑ *He was arrested last October still carrying a bloody knife.*

VERB [T] (**bloodies**, **bloodying**, **bloodied**) If you have **bloodied** part of your body, there is blood on it, usually because you have had an accident or you have been attacked. ❑ *One of our children fell and bloodied his knee.*

blos·som /'blɒsəm/ NOUN, VERB

NOUN [C, U] (**blossoms**) **Blossom** is the flowers that appear on a tree before the fruit. ❑ *The cherry blossom came out early in Sussex this year.*

VERB [I] (**blossoms**, **blossoming**, **blossomed**) **1** If someone or something **blossoms**, they develop good, attractive, or successful qualities. = **bloom** ❑ *Why do some people take longer than others to blossom?* ❑ *What began as a local festival has blossomed into an international event.* **2** When a tree **blossoms**, it produces blossom. ❑ *Rain begins to fall and peach trees blossom.*

blot /blɒt/ NOUN, VERB

NOUN [C] (**blots**) **1** If something is a **blot on** a person's or thing's reputation, it spoils their reputation. ❑ *a blot on the reputation of the architectural profession* **2** A **blot** is a drop of liquid that has fallen on to a surface and has dried. ❑ *an ink blot*

VERB [T] (**blots**, **blotting**, **blotted**) If you **blot** a surface, you remove liquid from it by pressing a piece of soft paper or cloth onto it. ❑ *Before applying makeup, blot the face with a tissue to remove any excess oils.*

PHRASAL VERB **blot out** **1** If one thing **blots out** another thing, it is in front of the other thing and prevents it from being seen. ❑ *About the time the three climbers were halfway down, clouds blotted out the sun.* ❑ *The victim's face was blotted out by a camera blur.* **2** If you try to **blot out** a memory, you try to forget it. If one thought or memory **blots out** other thoughts or memories, it becomes the only one that you can think about. = **block out** ❑ *Are you saying that she's trying to blot out all memory of the incident?* ❑ *The boy has gaps in his mind about it. He is blotting certain things out.*

blow ♦♦◇ /bləʊ/ VERB, NOUN

VERB [I, T] (**blows**, **blowing**, **blew**, **blown**) **1** [I] When a wind or breeze **blows**, the air moves. ❑ *A chill wind blew at the top of the hill.* **2** [I, T] If the wind **blows** something somewhere or if it **blows** there, the wind moves it there. ❑ *The wind blew her hair back from her forehead.* ❑ *Sand blew in our eyes.* **3** [I] If you **blow**, you send out a stream of air from your mouth. ❑ *Danny rubbed his arms and blew on his fingers to warm them.* **4** [T] If you **blow** something somewhere, you move it by sending out a stream of air from your mouth. ❑ *He picked up his mug and blew off the steam.* **5** [T] If you **blow** bubbles or smoke rings, you make them by blowing air out of your mouth through liquid or smoke. ❑ *He blew a ring of blue smoke.* **6** [I, T] When a whistle or horn **blows** or someone **blows** it, they make a sound by blowing into it. ❑ *The whistle blew and the train slid forward.* **7** [T] When you **blow** your nose, you force air out of it through your nostrils in order to clear it. ❑ *He took out a handkerchief and blew his nose.* **8** [T] To **blow** something **out**, **off**, or **away** means to remove or destroy it violently with an explosion. ❑ *The can exploded, wrecking the kitchen and bathroom and blowing out windows.* **9** [T] (*informal*) If you **blow** a chance or attempt to do something, you make a mistake which wastes the chance or causes the attempt to fail. ❑ *One careless word could blow the whole deal.* ❑ *Oh you fool! You've blown it!* **10** [T] If you say that something **blows** an event, situation, or argument into a particular extreme state, especially an uncertain or unpleasant state, you mean that it causes it to be in that state. ❑ *Someone took an inappropriate use of words on my part and tried to blow it into a major controversy.* **11** [T] (*informal*) If you **blow** a large amount of money, you spend it quickly on luxuries. ❑ *My brother lent me some money and I went and blew it all.*

PHRASAL VERBS **blow away** (*informal*) If you say that you **are blown away** by something, or if it **blows** you **away**, you mean that you are very impressed by it. ❑ *I was blown away by the tone and the quality of the story.* ❑ *Everyone I met overwhelmed me and kind of blew me away.*

blow out If you **blow out** a flame or a candle, you blow at it so that it stops burning. ❑ *I blew out the candle.*

blow over If something such as trouble or an argument **blows over**, it ends without any serious consequences. ❑ *Wait, and it'll all blow over.*

blow up **1** If someone **blows** something **up** or if it **blows up**, it is destroyed by an explosion. ❑ *He was jailed for 45 years for trying to blow up a plane.* **2** If you **blow up** something such as a balloon or a tyre, you fill it with air. ❑ *Other than blowing up a tyre I hadn't done any car maintenance.* **3** If a wind or a storm **blows up**, the weather becomes very windy or stormy. ❑ *A storm blew up over the mountains.* **4** (*informal*) If you **blow up at** someone, you lose your temper and shout at them. = **explode** ❑ *I'm sorry I blew up at you.* **5** If someone **blows** an incident **up** or if it **blows up**, it is made to seem more serious or important than it really is. ❑ *Newspapers blew up the story.* ❑ *The media may be blowing it up out of proportion.* **6** If a photographic image **is blown up**, a large copy is made of it. ❑ *The image is blown up on a large screen.*

NOUN [C] (**blows**) **1** If someone receives a **blow**, they are hit with a fist or weapon. ❑ *He went to the hospital after a blow to the face.* **2** If something that happens is a **blow to** someone or something, it is very upsetting, disappointing, or damaging to them. ❑ *That ruling comes as a blow to environmentalists.*

✦ **blow hot and cold** → see **hot**; **blow the whistle** → see **whistle**

blue ♦♦♦ /bluː/ COLOUR, NOUN, ADJ

COLOUR Something that is **blue** is the colour of the sky on a sunny day. ❑ *There were swallows in the cloudless blue sky.* ❑ *She fixed her pale blue eyes on her father's.*

NOUN [PL] (**blues**) **The blues** is a type of music which was developed by African American musicians in the southern United States. It is characterized by a slow tempo and a strong rhythm. ❑ *Can white girls sing the blues?*

ADJ (**bluer**, **bluest**) [V-LINK + blue] (*informal*) If you are feeling **blue**, you are feeling sad or depressed, often when there is no particular reason. = **down** ❑ *There's no earthly reason for me to feel so blue.*

b

✪**blue-collar** ADJ [blue-collar + N] **Blue-collar** workers work in industry, doing physical work, rather than in offices. ❑ *It wasn't just the blue-collar workers who lost their jobs, it was everyone.* ❑ *Industry analysts are calling for a structural shift away from blue-collar factory jobs to a value-added research and development focus.*

blue·print /ˈbluːprɪnt/ NOUN [C] (**blueprints**) **1** A **blueprint for** something is a plan or set of proposals that shows how it is expected to work. ❑ *The president will offer delegates his blueprint for the country's future.* **2** A **blueprint** of an architect's building plans or a designer's pattern is a photographic print consisting of white lines on a blue background. Blueprints contain all of the information that is needed to build or make something. = design ❑ *a blueprint of the whole picture, complete with heating ducts and wiring* **3** A genetic **blueprint** is a pattern that is contained within all living cells. This pattern decides how the organism develops and what it looks like. ❑ *The offspring contain a mixture of the genetic blueprint of each parent.*

bluff /blʌf/ NOUN, VERB
NOUN [C, U] (**bluffs**) A **bluff** is an attempt to make someone believe that you will do something when you do not really intend to do it. ❑ *The letter was a bluff.* ❑ *It is essential to build up the military option and show that this is not a bluff.*
PHRASE **call someone's bluff** If you **call** someone's **bluff**, you tell them to do what they have been threatening to do, because you are sure that they will not really do it. ❑ *The socialists have decided to call the opposition's bluff.*
VERB [I, T] (**bluffs, bluffing, bluffed**) If you **bluff**, you make someone believe that you will do something when you do not really intend to do it, or that you know something when you do not really know it. ❑ *Either side, or both, could be bluffing.* ❑ *In each case the hijackers bluffed the crew using fake grenades.*

blun·der /ˈblʌndə/ NOUN, VERB
NOUN [C] (**blunders**) A **blunder** is a stupid or careless mistake. ❑ *I think he made a tactical blunder by announcing it so far ahead of time.*
VERB [I] (**blunders, blundering, blundered**) **1** If you **blunder**, you make a stupid or careless mistake. ❑ *No doubt I had blundered again.* **2** If you **blunder into** a dangerous or difficult situation, you get involved in it by mistake. ❑ *People wanted to know how they had blundered into war, and how to avoid it in the future.* **3** If you **blunder** somewhere, you move there in a clumsy and careless way. ❑ *He had blundered into the table, upsetting the flowers.*

blunt /blʌnt/ ADJ, VERB
ADJ (**blunter, bluntest**) **1** If you are **blunt**, you say exactly what you think without trying to be polite. ❑ *She is blunt about her personal life.* **2** [blunt + N] A **blunt** object has a rounded or flat end rather than a sharp one. ❑ *One of them had been struck 13 times over the head with a blunt object.* **3** A **blunt** knife or blade is no longer sharp and does not cut well. ❑ *The edge is as blunt as an old butter knife.*
VERB [T] (**blunts, blunting, blunted**) If something **blunts** an emotion, a feeling, or a need, it weakens it. ❑ *The constant repetition of violence has blunted the human response to it.*
blunt·ly /ˈblʌntli/ ADV [bluntly with V] ❑ *'I don't believe you!' Jeanne said bluntly.*
blunt·ness /ˈblʌntnəs/ NOUN [U] ❑ *His bluntness got him into trouble.*

blur /blɜː/ NOUN, VERB
NOUN [C] (**blurs**) A **blur** is a shape or area which you cannot see clearly because it has no distinct outline or because it is moving very fast. ❑ *Out of the corner of my eye I saw a blur of movement on the other side of the glass.*
VERB [I, T] (**blurs, blurring, blurred**) **1** When a thing **blurs** or when something **blurs** it, you cannot see it clearly because its edges are no longer distinct. ❑ *This creates a spectrum of colours at the edges of objects which blurs the image.* **2** [T] If something **blurs** an idea or a distinction between things, that idea or distinction no longer seems clear. = obscure ❑ *her belief that scientists are trying to blur the distinction between 'how' and 'why' questions* **3** [I, T] If your vision **blurs**, or if something **blurs** it, you cannot see things clearly. ❑ *Her eyes, behind her glasses, began to blur.*

blurred /blɜːd/ ADJ **1** *blurred black and white photographs* **2** *The line between fact and fiction is becoming blurred.* **3** *visual disturbances like eye-strain and blurred vision*

blush /blʌʃ/ VERB, NOUN
VERB [I] (**blushes, blushing, blushed**) When you **blush**, your face becomes redder than usual because you are ashamed or embarrassed. ❑ *'Hello, Maria,' he said, and she blushed again.*
NOUN [C] (**blushes**) A **blush** is an instance of your face becoming redder than usual because you are ashamed or embarrassed. ❑ *'The most important thing is to be honest,' she says, without the trace of a blush.*

board ♦♦◇ /bɔːd/ NOUN, VERB
NOUN [C, U] (**boards**) **1** [C] A **board** is a flat, thin, rectangular piece of wood or plastic which is used for a particular purpose. ❑ *a cutting board* **2** [C] A **board** is a square piece of wood or stiff cardboard that you use for playing games such as chess. ❑ *a draughts board* **3** [C] You can refer to a blackboard or a bulletin board as a **board**. ❑ *He wrote a few more notes on the board.* **4** [C] **Boards** are long flat pieces of wood which are used, for example, to make floors or walls. ❑ *The floor was draughty bare boards.* **5** [C] (business) The **board** of a company or organization is the group of people who control it and direct it. = management ❑ *Arthur has made a recommendation, which he wants her to put before the board at a special meeting scheduled for tomorrow afternoon.* **6** [C] **Board** is used in the names of various organizations which are involved in dealing with a particular kind of activity. ❑ *The Scottish tourist board said 33,000 Japanese visited Scotland last year.* **7** [U] **Board** is the food which is provided when you stay somewhere, for example in a hotel. ❑ *Free room and board are provided for all hotel staff.*
PHRASES **across the board** If a policy or a situation applies **across the board**, it affects everything or everyone in a particular group. ❑ *There are hefty charges across the board for one-way rental.*
go by the board If something **goes by the board**, it is rejected or ignored, or is no longer possible. ❑ *It's a case of not what you know but who you know in this world today and qualifications quite go by the board.*
on board When you are **on board** a train, ship, or aircraft, you are on it or in it. ❑ *All 269 people on board the plane were killed.*
sweep the board If someone **sweeps the board** in a competition or election, they win nearly everything that it is possible to win. ❑ *Spain swept the board in boys' team competitions.*
take on board If you **take on board** an idea or a problem, you begin to accept it or understand it. ❑ *You may have to accept their point of view, but hope that they will take on board some of what you have said.*
VERB [T] (**boards, boarding, boarded**) (formal) When you **board** a train, ship, or aircraft, you get on it in order to travel somewhere. = get on ❑ *I boarded the plane bound for Boston.*
PHRASAL VERB **board up** If you **board up** a door or window, you fix pieces of wood over it so that it is covered up. ❑ *Shopkeepers have boarded up their windows.*

boast /bəʊst/ VERB, NOUN
VERB [I, T] (**boasts, boasting, boasted**) **1** [I, T] (disapproval) If someone **boasts** about something that they have done or that they own, they talk about it very proudly, in a way that other people may find irritating or offensive. ❑ *Witnesses said Furci boasted that he took part in killing them.* ❑ *Carol boasted about her costume.* **2** [T] If someone or something can **boast** a particular achievement or possession, they have achieved or possess that thing. ❑ *The houses will boast the latest energy-saving technology.*
NOUN [C] (**boasts**) A **boast** is the act of talking very proudly about something that you have done or that you own, in a way that other people may find irritating or offensive. ❑ *It is the charity's proud boast that it has never yet turned anyone away.*

boat ♦♦◇ /bəʊt/ NOUN
NOUN [C] (**boats**) **1** [also 'by' boat] A **boat** is something in which people can travel across water. ❑ *One of the best*

B

ways to see the area is in a small boat. **2** You can refer to a passenger ship as a **boat**. ❑ *When the boat reached Cape Town, we said goodbye.*

PHRASE **miss the boat** If you say that someone has **missed the boat**, you mean that they have missed an opportunity and may not get another. ❑ *If you don't want to miss the boat, the auction is scheduled for 2.30 p.m. on June 26.*

bob /bɒb/ VERB [I] (**bobs, bobbing, bobbed**) **1** If something **bobs**, it moves up and down, like something does when it is floating on water. ❑ *Huge balloons bobbed about in the sky above.* **2** If you **bob** somewhere, you move there quickly so that you disappear from view or come into view. ❑ *She handed over a form, then bobbed down behind a typewriter.*

bode /bəʊd/ VERB [I] (**bodes, boding, boded**) (*formal*) If something **bodes** ill, it makes you think that something bad will happen in the future. If something **bodes** well, it makes you think that something good will happen. ❑ *She says the way the bill was passed bodes ill for democracy.*

bodi·ly /ˈbɒdɪli/ ADJ, ADV **ADJ** [bodily + N] Your **bodily** needs and functions are the needs and functions of your body. ❑ *descriptions of natural bodily functions* **ADV** [bodily with V] You use **bodily** to indicate that an action involves the whole of someone's body. ❑ *I was hurled bodily to the deck.*

❂**body** ◆◆◆ /ˈbɒdi/ NOUN [C, SING, U] (**bodies**) **1** [C] Your **body** is all your physical parts, including your head, arms, and legs. ❑ *The largest organ in the body is the liver.* **2** [C] You can also refer to the main part of your body, except for your arms, head, and legs, as your **body**. = torso, trunk ❑ *Lying flat on the floor, twist your body on to one hip and cross your upper leg over your body.* **3** [C] You can refer to a person's dead body as a **body**. = corpse ❑ *Officials said they had found no traces of violence on the body of the politician.* **4** [C] A **body** is an organized group of people who deal with something officially. = organization ❑ *the Chairman of the policemen's representative body, the Police Federation* ❑ *the main trade union body, COSATU, Congress of South African Trade Unions* **5** [C] A **body of** people is a group of people who are together or who are connected in some way. = group ❑ *that large body of people that teaches other people how to teach* **6** [SING] The **body of** something such as a building or a document is the main part of it or the largest part of it. = bulk ❑ *The main body of the church had been turned into a massive television studio.* ❑ *Give an introduction, followed by the body of the material, then a brief summary.* **7** [C] The **body** of a car or aircraft is the main part of it, not including its engine, wheels, or wings. = shell ❑ *The only shade was under the body of the plane.* **8** [C] A **body of** water is a large area of water, such as a lake or sea. ❑ *It is probably the most polluted body of water in the world.* **9** [C] A **body of** information is a large amount of it. = quantity ❑ *An increasing body of evidence suggests that all of us have cancer cells in our bodies at times during our lives.* **10** [U] If you say that an alcoholic drink has **body**, you mean that it has a full and strong flavour. ❑ *a dry wine with good body*

WORD CONNECTIONS
ADJ + **body**
the **ruling** body
the **governing** body
❑ *UEFA is the governing body of European football.*
a **regulatory** body
an **advisory** body
a **professional** body
❑ *Ask if the counsellor is registered with a professional body.*
a **legislative** body
a **statutory** body
a **public** body
an **international** body
an **independent** body
❑ *As it is an independent body it holds unbiased opinions about individual companies.*

body·guard /ˈbɒdiɡɑːd/ NOUN [C] (**bodyguards**) A **bodyguard** is a person or a group of people employed to protect someone. ❑ *Three of his bodyguards were injured in the attack.*

body lan·guage NOUN [U] Your **body language** is the way in which you show your feelings or thoughts to other people by means of the position or movements of your body, rather than with words. ❑ *I can tell by your body language that you're happy with the decision.*

❂**boil** ◆◇◇ /bɔɪl/ VERB, NOUN **VERB** [I, T] (**boils, boiling, boiled**) **1** [I, T] When a hot liquid **boils** or when you **boil** it, bubbles appear in it and it starts to change into steam or vapour. ❑ *I stood in the kitchen, waiting for the water to boil.* ❑ *Gold melts at 1,064 degrees centigrade and boils at 2,808 degrees centigrade.* ❑ *Boil the water in the saucepan and add the sage.* **2** [I, T] When you **boil** a pot or a kettle, or put it on to **boil**, you heat the water inside it until it boils. ❑ *He had nothing to do but boil the kettle and make the tea.* **3** [I] When a pot **is boiling**, the water inside it has reached boiling point. ❑ *The pot was boiling.* **4** [I, T] When you **boil** food, or when it **boils**, it is cooked in boiling water. ❑ *Boil the chick peas, add garlic and lemon juice.* ❑ *I'd peel potatoes and put them on to boil.* **5** [I] If you **are boiling with** anger, you are very angry. ❑ *I used to be all sweetness and light on the outside, but inside I would be boiling with rage.* → See also **boiling**

PHRASAL VERBS **boil down to** If you say that a situation or problem **boils down to** a particular thing or can **be boiled down to** a particular thing, you mean that this is the most important or the most basic aspect of it. = amount to ❑ *What they want boils down to just one thing. It is land.*

boil over **1** When a liquid that is being heated **boils over**, it rises and flows over the edge of the container. ❑ *Heat the liquid in a large, wide container rather than a high narrow one, or it can boil over.* **2** When someone's feelings **boil over**, the person loses their temper or becomes violent. = erupt ❑ *Sometimes frustration and anger can boil over into direct and violent action.*

NOUN [C] (**boils**) A **boil** is a red, painful swelling on your skin that contains a thick yellow liquid called pus. = cyst

PHRASE **bring to the boil** or **come to the boil** When you **bring** a liquid **to the boil**, you heat it until it boils. When it **comes to the boil**, it begins to boil. ❑ *Put water, butter and lard into a saucepan and bring slowly to the boil.*

boil·er /ˈbɔɪlə/ NOUN [C] (**boilers**) A **boiler** is a device that burns gas, oil, electricity, or coal in order to provide hot water, especially for the central heating in a building.

boil·ing /ˈbɔɪlɪŋ/ ADJ **1** Something that is **boiling** or **boiling hot** is very hot. = baking ❑ *'It's boiling in here,'* complained Miriam. **2** [V-LINK + boiling] If you say that you are **boiling** or **boiling hot**, you mean that you feel very hot, usually unpleasantly hot. = sweltering ❑ *When everybody else is boiling hot, I'm freezing!*

bois·ter·ous /ˈbɔɪstərəs/ ADJ Someone who is **boisterous** is noisy, lively, and full of energy. ❑ *a boisterous but good-natured crowd*

bold /bəʊld/ ADJ, NOUN **ADJ** (**bolder, boldest**) **1** Someone who is **bold** is not afraid to do things that involve risk or danger. = brave ❑ *Amrita becomes a bold, daring rebel.* ❑ *In 1960 this was a bold move.* **2** Someone who is **bold** is not shy or embarrassed in the company of other people. = brave ❑ *I don't feel I'm being bold, because it's always been natural for me to just speak out about whatever disturbs me.* **3** A **bold** colour or pattern is very bright and noticeable. ❑ *bold flowers in various shades of red, blue, or white* **4** **Bold** lines or designs are drawn in a clear, strong way. = vivid ❑ *Each picture is shown in colour on one page and as a bold outline on the opposite page.*

NOUN [U] (*technical*) **Bold** is print which is thicker and looks blacker than ordinary printed letters. ❑ *When a candidate is elected his or her name will be highlighted in bold.*

bold·ly /ˈbəʊldli/ ADV **1** [boldly with V] ❑ *You must act boldly and confidently.* **2** *'You should do it,'* the girl said, boldly.

bold·ness /ˈbəʊldnəs/ NOUN [U] ❑ *Don't forget the boldness of his economic programme.*

bol·ster /ˈbəʊlstə/ VERB, NOUN

VERB [T] (**bolsters, bolstering, bolstered**) **1** If you **bolster** something such as someone's confidence or courage, you increase it. = boost ☐ *Hopes of an early cut in interest rates bolstered confidence.* **2** If someone tries to **bolster** their position in a situation, they try to strengthen it. = boost ☐ *The country is free to adopt policies to bolster its economy.*

NOUN [C] (**bolsters**) A **bolster** is a firm pillow shaped like a long tube which is sometimes put across a bed instead of pillows, or under the ordinary pillows.

bolt /bəʊlt/ NOUN, VERB, ADV

NOUN [C] (**bolts**) **1** A **bolt** is a long metal object that screws into a nut and is used to fasten things together. **2** A **bolt** on a door or window is a metal bar that you can slide across in order to fasten the door or window. ☐ *I heard the sound of a bolt being slowly and reluctantly slid open.* **3** A **bolt of** lightning is a flash of lightning that is seen as a white line in the sky. ☐ *Suddenly a bolt of lightning crackled through the sky.*

VERB [T, I] (**bolts, bolting, bolted**) **1** [T] When you **bolt** one thing to another, you fasten them firmly together, using a bolt. ☐ *The safety belt is easy to fit as there's no need to bolt it to seat belt anchorage points.* ☐ *Bolt the components together.* **2** [T] When you **bolt** a door or window, you slide the bolt across to fasten it. ☐ *He reminded her that he would have to lock and bolt the kitchen door after her.* **3** [I] If a person or animal **bolts**, they suddenly start to run very fast, often because something has frightened them. ☐ *The pig rose squealing and bolted.* **4** [T] If you **bolt** your food, you eat it so quickly that you hardly chew it or taste it. ☐ *Being under stress can cause you to miss meals, eat on the move, or bolt your food.*

PHRASAL VERB **bolt down** Bolt down means the same as **bolt** VERB 4. ☐ *I like to think back to secondary school, when I could bolt down three or four burgers and a pile of chips.*

ADV

PHRASE **bolt upright** If someone is sitting or standing **bolt upright**, they are sitting or standing very straight. ☐ *When I pushed his door open, Trevor was sitting bolt upright in bed.*

bomb ♦♦◇ /bɒm/ NOUN, VERB

NOUN [SING, C] (**bombs**) **1** [SING, C] A **bomb** is a device that explodes and damages or destroys a large area. ☐ *Bombs went off at two London train stations.* ☐ *It's not known who planted the bomb.* **2** [SING] Nuclear weapons are sometimes referred to as **the bomb**. ☐ *They are generally thought to have the bomb.*

VERB [T] (**bombs, bombing, bombed**) When people **bomb** a place, they attack it with bombs. ☐ *Air force jets bombed the airport.*

bomb·ing /ˈbɒmɪŋ/ NOUN [C, U] (**bombings**) ☐ *Aerial bombing of rebel positions is continuing.*

bom·bard /bɒmˈbɑːd/ VERB [T] (**bombards, bombarding, bombarded**) **1** If you **bombard** someone **with** something, you make them face a great deal of it. For example, if you **bombard** them **with** questions or criticism, you keep asking them a lot of questions or you keep criticizing them. ☐ *He bombarded Catherine with questions to which he should have known the answers.* **2** When soldiers **bombard** a place, they attack it with continuous heavy gunfire or bombs. ☐ *Rebel artillery units have regularly bombarded the airport.*

bom·bard·ment /bɒmˈbɑːdmənt/ NOUN [C, U] (**bombardments**) **1** A **bombardment** is a strong and continuous attack of gunfire or bombing. = attack ☐ *The city has been flattened by heavy artillery bombardments.* **2** A **bombardment of** ideas, demands, questions, or criticisms is an aggressive and exhausting stream of them. = onslaught ☐ *the constant bombardment of images urging that work was important*

bomb·er /ˈbɒmə/ NOUN [C] (**bombers**) **1** Bombers are people who cause bombs to explode in public places. ☐ *Detectives hunting the bombers will be eager to interview him.* **2** A **bomber** is a military aircraft which drops bombs. ☐ *a high-speed bomber with twin engines*

bomb·shell /ˈbɒmʃel/ NOUN

NOUN [C] (**bombshells**) A **bombshell** is a sudden piece of bad or unexpected news. ☐ *His resignation is a political bombshell.*

PHRASE **drop a bombshell** If someone **drops a bombshell**, they give you a sudden piece of bad or unexpected news.

bo·nan·za /bəˈnænzə/ NOUN [C] (**bonanzas**) You can refer to a sudden great increase in wealth, success, or luck as a **bonanza**. = windfall ☐ *The expected sales bonanza hadn't materialized.*

◆ **bond** ♦♦◇ /bɒnd/ NOUN, VERB (*academic word*)

NOUN [C] (**bonds**) **1** A **bond between** people is a strong feeling of friendship, love, or shared beliefs and experiences that unites them. ☐ *The experience created a very special bond between us.* **2** A **bond between** people or groups is a close connection that they have with each other, for example because they have a special agreement. = tie, connection, link, attachment ☐ *the strong bond between church and nation* ☐ *The republic is breaking its bonds with Moscow.* **3** A **bond between** two things is the way in which they stick to one another or are joined in some way. = attachment ☐ *If you experience difficulty with the superglue not creating a bond with dry wood, moisten the surfaces with water.* ☐ *The molecule contains four carbon atoms arranged in a ring with a triple bond between two of them.* **4** (*business*) When a government or company issues a **bond**, it borrows money from investors. The certificate that is issued to investors who lend money is also called a **bond**. ☐ *Most of it will be financed by government bonds.*

VERB [RECIP] (**bonds, bonding, bonded**) **1** When people **bond with** each other, they form a relationship based on love or shared beliefs and experiences. You can also say that people **bond** or that something **bonds** them. ☐ *Belinda was having difficulty bonding with the baby.* ☐ *They all bonded while writing graffiti together.* **2** When one thing **bonds with** another, it sticks to it or becomes joined to it in some way. You can also say that two things **bond together**, or that something **bonds** them **together**. ☐ *In graphite sheets, carbon atoms bond together in rings.*

bond·age /ˈbɒndɪdʒ/ NOUN [U] **1** Bondage is the condition of being someone's property and having to work for them. = slavery ☐ *Masters sometimes allowed their slaves to buy their way out of bondage.* **2** (*formal*) Bondage is the condition of not being free because you are strongly influenced by something or someone. ☐ *All people, she said, lived their lives in bondage to hunger, pain, and lust.*

◆ **bone** ♦◇◇ /bəʊn/ NOUN, VERB, ADJ

NOUN [C, U] (**bones**) Your **bones** are the hard parts inside your body that together form your skeleton. ☐ *Many passengers suffered broken bones.* ☐ *Stephen fractured a thigh bone.* ☐ *The body is made up primarily of bone, muscle, and fat.*

PHRASES **bare bones** The **bare bones of** something are its most basic parts or details. ☐ *There are not even the bare bones of a garden here – I've got nothing.*

cut something to the bone If something such as costs are cut **to the bone**, they are reduced to the minimum possible. ☐ *It has survived by cutting its costs to the bone.*

VERB [T] (**bones, boning, boned**) If you **bone** a piece of meat or fish, you remove the bones from it before cooking it. ☐ *Make sure that you do not pierce the skin when boning the chicken thighs.*

PHRASAL VERB **bone up on** If you **bone up on** a subject, you try to find out about it or remind yourself what you have already learned about it. ☐ *I had spent the last few months boning up on neurology.*

ADJ [bone + N] A **bone** tool or ornament is made of bone. ☐ *a small, expensive pocketknife with a bone handle*

bon·fire /ˈbɒnfaɪə/ NOUN [C] (**bonfires**) A **bonfire** is a fire that is made outdoors, usually to burn waste. Bonfires are also sometimes lit as part of a celebration. ☐ *With bonfires outlawed in urban areas, gardeners must cart their refuse to a dump.*

bo·nus /ˈbəʊnəs/ NOUN [C] (**bonuses**) **1** A **bonus** is an extra amount of money that is added to someone's pay, usually because they have worked very hard. ☐ *Workers in big firms receive a substantial part of their pay in the form of bonuses and overtime.* ☐ *a $60 bonus* **2** A **bonus** is something good that you get in addition to something else, and which you would not usually expect. = plus

b

❑ *We felt we might finish third. Any better would be a bonus.*

boo /buː/ VERB, NOUN, EXCLAM

VERB [I, T] (**boos, booing, booed**) If you **boo** a speaker or performer, you shout 'boo' or make other loud sounds to indicate that you do not like them, their opinions, or their performance. ❑ *People were booing and throwing things at them.* ❑ *Demonstrators booed and jeered him.*

NOUN [C] (**boos**) A **boo** is a shout of '**Boo!**' or another loud sound to indicate that you do not like a speaker or performer, their opinions, or their performance. ❑ *She was greeted with boos and hisses.*

EXCLAM You say '**Boo!**' loudly and suddenly when you want to surprise someone who does not know that you are there.

boo·ing /'buːɪŋ/ NOUN [U] ❑ *The fans are entitled to their opinion but booing doesn't help anyone.*

book ♦♦♦ /bʊk/ NOUN, VERB

NOUN [C, PL] (**books**) **1** [C] A **book** is a number of pieces of paper, usually with words printed on them, which are fastened together and fixed inside a cover of stronger paper or cardboard. Books contain information, stories, or poetry, for example. ❑ *His eighth book came out earlier this year and was an instant best-seller.* ❑ *the author of a book on politics* ❑ *a new book by Rosella Brown* **2** [C] A **book of** something such as stamps, matches, or tickets is a small number of them fastened together between thin cardboard covers. ❑ *Can I have a book of first class stamps please?* **3** [PL] (*business*) A company's or organization's **books** are its records of money that has been spent and earned or of the names of people who belong to it. ❑ *For the most part he left the books to his managers and accountants.* **4** [C] In a very long written work such as the Bible, a **book** is one of the sections into which it is divided. ❑ *the last book of the Bible*

PHRASE **a closed book** If you say that someone or something is a **closed book**, you mean that you do not know anything about them. ❑ *Frank Spriggs was a very able man but something of a closed book.*

VERB [T] (**books, booking, booked**) **1** When you **book** something such as a hotel room or a ticket, you arrange to have it or use it at a particular time. = reserve ❑ *American officials have booked hotel rooms for the women and children.* ❑ *Laurie booked herself a flight home.* **2** When a police officer **books** someone, he or she officially records their name and the offence that they may be charged with. = charge ❑ *They took him to the station and booked him for assault with a deadly weapon.*

PHRASE **booked up** or **fully booked** or **booked solid** If transport or a hotel, restaurant, or theatre is **booked up**, **fully booked**, or **booked solid**, it has no tickets, rooms, or tables left for a particular time or date. ❑ *The car ferries from the mainland are often fully booked by February.*
→ See also **booking**

book·ing /'bʊkɪŋ/ NOUN [C] (**bookings**) A **booking** is the arrangement that you make when you book something such as a hotel room, a table at a restaurant, or a theatre seat. = reservation ❑ *There was a mistake over his booking.*

book·let /'bʊklət/ NOUN [C] (**booklets**) A **booklet** is a very thin book that has a paper cover and that gives you information about something. = pamphlet ❑ *a 48-page booklet of notes for the completion of the form*

book·mark /'bʊkmɑːk/ NOUN, VERB

NOUN [C] (**bookmarks**) **1** A **bookmark** is a narrow piece of card or leather that you put between the pages of a book so that you can find a particular page easily. **2** (*computing*) In computing, a **bookmark** is the address of an Internet site that you put into a list on your computer so that you can return to it easily. ❑ *This makes it extremely simple to save what you find with an electronic bookmark so you can return to it later.*

VERB [T] (**bookmarks, bookmarking, bookmarked**) (*computing*) In computing, if you **bookmark** the address of an Internet site, you put it into a list on your computer so that you can return to it easily. ❑ *This site is definitely worth bookmarking.*

book·shop /'bʊkʃɒp/ (*mainly BrE; in AmE, usually use* **bookstore**) [C] (**bookshops**) NOUN A **bookshop** is a shop where books are sold.

❂**boom** ♦◇◇ /buːm/ NOUN, VERB

NOUN [C] (**booms**) **1** If there is a **boom** in the economy, there is an increase in economic activity, for example, in the number of things that are being bought and sold. ❑ *An economic boom followed, especially in housing and construction.* ❑ *The 1980s were indeed boom years.* ❑ *the cycle of boom and bust which has damaged us for 40 years* **2** A **boom in** something is an increase in its amount, frequency, or success. ❑ *The boom in the sport's popularity has meant more calls for stricter safety regulations.* ❑ *Public transport has not been able to cope adequately with the travel boom.* ❑ *the collapse of the dotcom boom* **3** A **boom** is a loud, deep sound that lasts for several seconds. ❑ *The stillness of the night was broken by the boom of a cannon.*

VERB [I, T] (**booms, booming, boomed**) **1** If the economy or a business **is booming**, the number of things being bought or sold is increasing. ❑ *By 1988 the economy was booming.* ❑ *Sales are booming.* ❑ *a booming global consumer electronics market* **2** [I, T] When something such as someone's voice, a cannon, or a big drum **booms**, it makes a loud, deep sound that lasts for several seconds. ❑ *'Ladies,' boomed Helena, without a microphone, 'We all know why we're here tonight.'* ❑ *Thunder boomed over Crooked Mountain.*

PHRASAL VERB **boom out** Boom out means the same as **boom** VERB 2. ❑ *Music boomed out from loudspeakers.* ❑ *A megaphone boomed out, 'This is the police.'*

boost ♦◇◇ /buːst/ VERB, NOUN

VERB [T] (**boosts, boosting, boosted**) **1** If one thing **boosts** another, it causes it to increase, improve, or be more successful. ❑ *Lower interest rates can boost the economy by reducing borrowing costs for consumers and businesses.* **2** If something **boosts** your confidence or morale, it improves it. = bolster ❑ *We need a big win to boost our confidence.*

NOUN [C] (**boosts**) **1** A **boost** is something that causes something else to increase, improve, or be more successful. ❑ *It would get the economy going and give us the boost that we need.* **2** A **boost** is something that improves your confidence or morale. ❑ *It did give me a boost to win such a big event.* **3** [usu sing] If you give someone a **boost**, you push or lift them from behind so that they can reach something. ❑ *He cupped his hands and gave her a boost up to the ledge.*

boot ♦◇◇ /buːt/ NOUN, VERB

NOUN [C] (**boots**) **1** Boots are shoes that cover your whole foot and the lower part of your leg. ❑ *He sat in a kitchen chair, reached down and pulled off his boots.* **2** Boots are strong, heavy shoes that cover your ankle and that have thick soles. You wear them to protect your feet, for example, when you are walking or taking part in sports. ❑ *The soldiers' boots resounded in the street.* **3** (*BrE; in AmE, use* **trunk**) The **boot** of a car is a covered space at the back or front in which you put luggage or other things.

PHRASE **get the boot** or **be given the boot** (*informal*) If you **get the boot** or **are given the boot**, you are told that you are not wanted anymore, either in your job or by someone you are having a relationship with. ❑ *She was a disruptive influence, and after a year or two she got the boot.*

VERB [I, T] (**boots, booting, booted**) (*computing*) If a computer **boots** or you **boot** it, it is made ready to use by putting in the instructions it needs in order to start working. ❑ *The computer won't boot.* ❑ *Put the CD into the drive and boot the machine.*

PHRASAL VERB **boot up** Boot up means the same as **boot** VERB. ❑ *Go over to your PC and boot it up.*

❂**bor·der** ♦♦◇ /'bɔːdə/ NOUN, VERB

NOUN [C] (**borders**) **1** The **border** between two countries or regions is the dividing line between them. Sometimes **the border** also refers to the land close to this line. = frontier ❑ *They fled across the border.* ❑ *Soldiers had temporarily closed the border between the two countries.* ❑ *the isolated jungle area near the Panamanian border* ❑ *the Mexican border town of Tijuana* **2** A **border** is a strip or band around the edge of something. ❑ *pillowcases trimmed with a hand-crocheted border* **3** In a garden, a **border** is a long strip of ground planted with flowers, along the edge of a path or lawn. ❑ *a lawn flanked by wide herbaceous borders*

VERB [T] (**borders, bordering, bordered**) **1** A country that **borders** another country, a sea, or a river is next to it. ❑ *the European and Arab countries bordering the Mediterranean* **2** If something **is bordered** by another thing, the other thing forms a line along the edge of it. = flank ❑ *the mile of white sand beach bordered by palm trees and tropical flowers*

PHRASAL VERB **border on** Border on means the same as **border** VERB 1. ❑ *Both republics border on the Black Sea.*

bor•der•line /'bɔːdəlaɪn/ NOUN, ADJ

NOUN [C] (**borderlines**) The **borderline between** two different or opposite things is the division between them. ❑ *a task which involves exploring the borderline between painting and photography* **ADJ** Something that is **borderline** is only just acceptable as a member of a class or group. ❑ *Some were obviously unsuitable and could be ruled out at once. Others were borderline cases.*

bore ♦◇◇ /bɔː/ VERB, NOUN, IRREG FORM

VERB [T] (**bores, boring, bored**) **1** If someone or something **bores** you, you find them dull and uninteresting. ❑ *Dickie bored him all through the meal with stories of the navy.* **2** If you **bore** a hole in something, you make a deep round hole in it using a special tool. ❑ *Get the special drill bit to bore the correct size hole for the job.*

PHRASE **bore to tears** or **bore to death** or **bore stiff** (*informal, emphasis*) If someone or something **bores** you **to tears, bores** you **to death,** or **bores** you **stiff,** they bore you very much. ❑ *Monuments and museums bore him to tears.* **NOUN** [C, SING] (**bores**) **1** [C] You describe someone as a **bore** when you think that they talk in a very uninteresting way. ❑ *There is every reason why I shouldn't enjoy his company – he's a bore and a fool.* **2** [SING] You can describe a situation as **a bore** when you find it annoying. = drag ❑ *It's a bore to be sick, and the novelty of lying in bed all day wears off quickly.*

IRREG FORM **Bore** is the past tense of **bear.** → See also **bored, boring**

bored /bɔːd/ ADJ If you are **bored,** you feel tired and impatient because you have lost interest in something or because you have nothing to do. ❑ *I am getting very bored with this entire business.*

WHICH WORD?
bored or boring?

Do not confuse the adjectives **bored** and **boring.**
If you are **bored,** you feel tired and impatient.
❑ *I remember feeling **bored** and frustrated as a teenager.*
If someone or something is **boring,** it causes you to feel tired and impatient.
❑ *Life in a small town can be rather **boring** for teenagers.*
---

bore•dom /'bɔːdəm/ NOUN [U] **Boredom** is the state of being bored. ❑ *He had given up attending lectures out of sheer boredom.*

bor•ing /'bɔːrɪŋ/ ADJ Someone or something **boring** is so dull and uninteresting that they make people tired and impatient. = dull, tedious ❑ *Not only are mothers not paid but also most of their boring or difficult work is unnoticed.*

born ♦♦◇ /bɔːn/ VERB, ADJ

VERB [PASSIVE] **1** When a baby **is born,** it comes out of its mother's body at the beginning of its life. In formal English, if you say that someone **is born of** someone or to someone, you mean that person is their parent. ❑ *She was born in Milan on April 29, 1923.* ❑ *He was born of German parents and lived most of his life abroad.* **2** If someone **is born with** a particular disease, problem, or characteristic, they have it from the time they are born. ❑ *He was born with only one lung.* ❑ *Some people are born brainy.* **3** (*formal*) You can use **be born** in front of a particular name to show that a person was given this name at birth, although they may be better known by another name. ❑ *She was born Jenny Harvey on June 11, 1946.* **4** (*formal*) When an idea or organization **is born,** it comes into existence. If something **is born of** a particular emotion or activity, it exists as a result of that emotion or activity. ❑ *The idea for the show was born in his hospital room.* ❑ *Congress passed the National Security Act, and the CIA was born.*

ADJ [born + N] You use **born** to describe someone who has a natural ability to do a particular activity or job. For example, if you are a **born** cook, you have a natural ability to cook well. ❑ *Jack was a born teacher.*
→ See also **newborn**

borne /bɔːn/ IRREG FORM **Borne** is the past participle of **bear.**

bor•ough /'bʌrə, AmE 'bɜːrəʊ/ NOUN [C] (**boroughs**) A **borough** is a town or district which has its own council, government, or local services. ❑ *the London borough of Lambeth*

bor•row ♦◇◇ /'bɒrəʊ/ VERB [T, I] (**borrows, borrowing, borrowed**) **1** [T] If you **borrow** something that belongs to someone else, you take it or use it for a period of time, usually with their permission. ❑ *Can I borrow a pen please?* **2** [I, T] If you **borrow** money **from** someone or **from** a bank, they give it to you and you agree to pay it back at some time in the future. ❑ *Morgan borrowed $5,000 from his father to form the company 20 years ago.* ❑ *It's so expensive to borrow from finance companies.* **3** [T] If you **borrow** a book **from** a library, you take it away for a fixed period of time. ❑ *I couldn't afford to buy any, so I borrowed them from the library.* **4** [T] If you **borrow** something such as a word or an idea from another language or from another person's work, you use it in your own language or work. ❑ *I borrowed his words for my book's title.*

WHICH WORD?
borrow or lend?

Do not confuse **borrow** and **lend.**
If you **borrow** something that belongs to someone else, you take it, usually with their permission, intending to return it.
❑ *Could I **borrow** your pen?*
If you **lend** something to someone else, you allow them to have it or use it for a period of time.
❑ *I often **lend** her money.*
❑ *Would you **lend** me your pen?*
---

bor•row•er /'bɒrəʊə/ NOUN [C] (**borrowers**) A **borrower** is a person or organization that borrows money. ❑ *Borrowers with a big mortgage should go for a fixed rate.*

bor•row•ing /'bɒrəʊɪŋ/ NOUN [U] [also borrowings] **Borrowing** is the activity of borrowing money. ❑ *We have allowed spending and borrowing to rise in this recession.*

boss ♦♦◇ /bɒs/ NOUN, VERB

NOUN [C] (**bosses**) **1** Your **boss** is the person in charge of the organization or department where you work. ❑ *He cannot stand his boss.* **2** (*informal*) If you are **the boss** in a group or relationship, you are the person who makes all the decisions. ❑ *He thinks he's the boss.*

VERB [T] (**bosses, bossing, bossed**) If you say that someone **bosses** you, you mean that they keep telling you what to do in a way that is irritating. = order around ❑ *We cannot boss them into doing more.*

PHRASAL VERB **boss around** Boss around means the same as **boss** VERB. ❑ *He started bossing people around.*

bo•tani•cal /bə'tænɪkəl/ ADJ [botanical + N] **Botanical** books, research, and activities relate to the scientific study of plants. ❑ *The area is of great botanical interest.*

bota•nist /'bɒtənɪst/ NOUN [C] (**botanists**) A **botanist** is a scientist who studies plants.

bota•ny /'bɒtəni/ NOUN [U] **Botany** is the scientific study of plants.

both ♦♦♦ /bəʊθ/ DET, QUANT, PRON, PREDET, CONJ

DET You use **both** when you are referring to two people or things and saying that something is true about each of them. ❑ *She cried out in fear and flung both arms up to protect her face.*

QUANT [both 'of' PL-N] **Both of** two people or things means each of them. ❑ *Both of these women have strong memories of the Vietnam War.*

PRON **1** **Both** means each of two people or things. ❑ *Miss Brown and her friend, both from Brooklyn, were arrested on the 8th of June.* **2** [N + both] **Both** is used to emphasize that something is true of each of two people or things. ❑ *He*

b

B

visited the Institute of Neurology in Havana where they both worked.

PREDET [both + DET PL-N] (emphasis) You use **both the** when you are referring to two people or things and saying that something is true about each of them. □ Both the horses were out, tacked up and ready to ride.

CONJ You use the structure **both…and** when you are giving two facts or alternatives and emphasizing that each of them is true or possible. □ Now women work both before and after having their children.

both·er ◆◇◇ /'bɒðə/ VERB, NOUN

VERB [I, T] (**bothers, bothering, bothered**) **1** [I, T] If you do not **bother to** do something or if you do not **bother with** it, you do not do it, consider it, or use it because you think it is unnecessary or because you are too lazy. □ Lots of people don't bother to go through a marriage ceremony these days. □ Nothing I do makes any difference anyway, so why bother? **2** [I, T] If something **bothers** you, or if you **bother** about it, it worries, annoys, or upsets you. □ Is something bothering you? □ It bothered me that boys weren't interested in me. **3** [T] If someone **bothers** you, they talk to you when you want to be left alone or interrupt you when you are busy. □ We are playing a trick on a man who keeps bothering me.

PHRASE can't be bothered If you say that you **can't be bothered to** do something, you mean that you are not going to do it because you think it is unnecessary or because you are too lazy. □ I just can't be bothered to look after the house.

NOUN [U] [also 'a' bother] **Bother** means trouble or difficulty. You can also use **bother** to refer to an activity which causes this, especially when you would prefer not to do it or get involved with it. = trouble □ I usually buy sliced bread – it's less bother. □ The courts take too long and going to the police is a bother.

both·ered /'bɒðəd/ ADJ □ I was bothered about the blister on my hand.

✦ **hot and bothered** → see **hot**

bot·tle ◆◆◇ /'bɒtəl/ NOUN, VERB

NOUN [C] (**bottles**) **1** A **bottle** is a glass or plastic container in which drinks and other liquids are kept. Bottles are usually round with straight sides and a narrow top. □ There were two empty beer bottles on the table. □ He was pulling the cork from a bottle of wine. **2** You can use **bottle** to refer to a bottle and its contents, or to the contents only. □ She had drunk half a bottle of whisky. **3** A **bottle** is a drinking container used by babies. It has a special rubber part at the top through which they can suck their drink. □ Gary was holding a bottle to the baby's lips.

VERB [T] (**bottles, bottling, bottled**) To **bottle** a drink or other liquid means to put it into bottles after it has been made. □ This is a large truck which has equipment to automatically bottle the wine.

bot·tom ◆◆◇ /'bɒtəm/ NOUN, ADJ

NOUN [C, SING] (**bottoms**) **1** [C] **The bottom of** something is the lowest or deepest part of it. □ He sat at the bottom of the stairs. □ Answers can be found at the bottom of page 8. **2** [C] **The bottom of** an object is the flat surface at its lowest point. You can also refer to the inside or outside of this surface as the **bottom**. = base □ Spread the onion slices on the bottom of the dish. **3** [SING] (business, journalism) If you say that **the bottom** has dropped or fallen out of a market or industry, you mean that people have stopped buying the products it sells. □ The bottom had fallen out of the city's property market. **4** [SING] ['the' bottom, oft bottom 'of' N] **The bottom of** an organization or career structure is the lowest level in it, where new employees often start. □ He had worked in the theatre for many years, starting at the bottom. **5** [SING] ['the' bottom, also no DET] If someone is **bottom** or **at the bottom** in a survey, test, or league, their performance is worse than that of all the other people involved. □ He was always bottom of the class. **6** [C] The lower part of a swimsuit, tracksuit, or pair of pyjamas can be referred to as the **bottoms** or the **bottom**. □ She wore blue tracksuit bottoms. **7** [SING] (mainly BrE; in AmE, usually use **end**) **The bottom of** a street or garden is the end farthest away from you or from your house. = end **8** [SING] (mainly BrE; in AmE, usually use **end**) **The bottom of** a table is the end farthest away from where you are sitting. **The bottom of** a bed is the end where you usually rest your feet. = end **9** [C] (mainly BrE; in AmE, usually use **behind**) Your **bottom** is the part of your body that you sit on.

PHRASES at bottom (emphasis) You use **at bottom** to emphasize that you are stating what you think is the real nature of something or the real truth about a situation. □ The two systems are, at bottom, conceptual models.

at the bottom of something If something is **at the bottom of** a problem or an unpleasant situation, it is the real cause of it. □ Often I find that anger and resentment are at the bottom of the problem.

get to the bottom of something If you want to get to **the bottom of** a problem, you want to solve it by finding out its real cause. □ I have to get to the bottom of this.

ADJ [bottom + N] The **bottom** thing or layer in a series of things or layers is the lowest one. □ There's an extra duvet in the bottom drawer of the cupboard.

bought /bɔːt/ IRREG FORM **Bought** is the past tense and past participle of **buy**.

bounce /baʊns/ VERB, NOUN

VERB [I, T] (**bounces, bouncing, bounced**) **1** [I, T] When an object such as a ball **bounces** or when you **bounce** it, it moves upward from a surface or away from it immediately after hitting it. □ My father would burst into the kitchen bouncing a tennis ball. □ a falling pebble, bouncing down the eroded cliff **2** [I, T] If sound or light **bounces off** a surface or **is bounced off** it, it reaches the surface and is reflected back. □ Your arms and legs need protection from light bouncing off glass. **3** [I, T] If something **bounces** or if something **bounces** it, it swings or moves up and down. = bob □ Her long black hair bounced as she walked. □ The car was bouncing up and down as if someone were jumping on it. **4** [I] If you **bounce** on a soft surface, you jump up and down on it repeatedly. □ She lets us do anything, even bounce on our beds. **5** [I] If someone **bounces** somewhere, they move there in an energetic way, because they are feeling happy. □ Moira bounced into the office. **6** [T] If you **bounce** your ideas **off** someone, you tell them to that person, in order to find out what they think about them. □ It was good to bounce ideas off another mind. **7** [I, T] If a cheque **bounces** or if someone **bounces** it, the bank refuses to accept it and pay out the money, because the person who wrote it does not have enough money in their account. □ Our only complaint would be if the cheque bounced. **8** [I] (computing) If an e-mail or other electronic message **bounces**, it is returned to the person who sent it because the address was wrong or because of a problem with one of the computers involved in sending it. □ a message saying that your mail has bounced or was unable to be delivered

PHRASAL VERB bounce back If you **bounce back** after a bad experience, you return very quickly to your previous level of success, enthusiasm, or activity. = recover □ We lost two or three early games but we bounced back. □ He is young enough to bounce back from this disappointment.

NOUN [C] (**bounces**) A **bounce** is an instance of an object such as a ball moving upward from a surface or away from it immediately after being hit. □ The wheelchair tennis player is allowed two bounces of the ball.

bound ◆◇◇ /baʊnd/ IRREG FORM, VERB, ADJ, COMB, NOUN

IRREG FORM Bound is the past tense and past participle of **bind**.

VERB [T, PASSIVE, I] (**bounds, bounding, bounded**) **1** [T] If an area of land **is bounded by** something, that thing is situated around its edge. □ Kirgizia is bounded by Uzbekistan, Kazakhstan and Tajikistan. □ the trees that bounded the parking lot **2** [PASSIVE] If someone's life or situation is **bounded by** certain things, those are its most important aspects and it is limited or restricted by them. □ Our lives are bounded by work, family and television. **3** [I] If a person or animal **bounds** in a particular direction, they move quickly with large steps or jumps. = leap □ He bounded up the steps and pushed the bell of the door. **4** [I] If the quantity or performance of something **bounds** ahead, it increases or improves quickly and suddenly. □ Shares in

the company bounded ahead by almost 3 per cent.
ADJ **1** [bound 'by' N] If you feel **bound** by something such as a rule, agreement, or restriction, you feel forced or required to act in a certain way. ❑ The world of advertising is obviously less bound by convention than the world of banking. **2** [V-LINK + bound 'to' N] If one person, thing, or situation is **bound to** another, they are closely associated with each other, and it is difficult for them to be separated or to escape from each other. ❑ We are as tightly bound to the people we dislike as to the people we love. **3** [V-LINK + bound 'for' N] If a vehicle or person is **bound for** a particular place, they are travelling towards it. ❑ The ship was bound for Italy.
PHRASE **be bound to** **1** If you say that something **is bound to** happen, you mean that you are sure it will happen, because it is a natural consequence of something that is already known or exists. ❑ There are bound to be price increases next year. **2** (spoken) If you say that something **is bound to** be true, you feel confident and certain of it, although you have no definite knowledge or evidence. ❑ I'll show it to Benjamin. He's bound to know.
COMB **Bound** is used in compound adjectives to indicate that a vehicle or person is travelling towards a particular place. ❑ a Texas-bound oil freighter
NOUN [PL, C] (**bounds**) **1** [PL] **Bounds** are limits which normally restrict what can happen or what people can do. ❑ Changes in temperature occur slowly and are constrained within relatively tight bounds. ❑ a forceful personality willing to go beyond the bounds of convention **2** [C] (literary) A **bound** is a long or high jump. ❑ With one bound Jack was free.
PHRASE **out of bounds** **1** If a place is **out of bounds**, people are not allowed to go there. ❑ For the last few days the area has been out of bounds to foreign journalists. **2** If something is **out of bounds**, people are not allowed to do it, use it, see it, or know about it. ❑ American parents may soon be able to rule violent TV programmes out of bounds.
→ See also **bind**

bound·a·ry /ˈbaʊndəri/ NOUN [C] (**boundaries**) **1** The **boundary of** an area of land is an imaginary line that separates it from other areas. = border, frontier ❑ The Bow Brook forms the western boundary of the wood. **2** The **boundaries of** something such as a subject or activity are the limits that people think that it has. ❑ The boundaries between history and storytelling are always being blurred and muddled.

bout /baʊt/ NOUN [C] (**bouts**) **1** If you have a **bout of** an illness or of an unpleasant feeling, you have it for a short period. ❑ He was recovering from a severe bout of flu. **2** A **bout of** something that is unpleasant is a short time during which it occurs a great deal. = spell ❑ The latest bout of violence has claimed twenty four lives. **3** A **bout** is a boxing or wrestling match. ❑ This will be his eighth title bout in 19 months.

bow /baʊ/ VERB, NOUN
VERB [I, T] (**bows, bowing, bowed**) **1** [I] When you **bow to** someone, you briefly bend your body towards them as a formal way of greeting them or showing respect. ❑ They bowed low to Louis and hastened out of his way. **2** [T] If you **bow** your head, you bend it downwards so that you are looking towards the ground, for example, because you want to show respect or because you are thinking deeply about something. = lower ❑ The Colonel bowed his head and whispered a prayer of thanksgiving. **3** [I] If you **bow to** pressure or to someone's wishes, you agree to do what they want you to do. = yield ❑ Some shops are bowing to consumer pressure and stocking organically grown vegetables.
PHRASAL VERB **bow out** If you **bow out of** something, you stop taking part in it. = step down ❑ He had bowed out gracefully when his successor had been appointed.
NOUN [C] (**bows**) **1** A **bow** is when you briefly bend your body towards someone as a formal way of greeting them or showing respect. ❑ I gave a theatrical bow and waved. **2** The front part of a ship is called **the bow** or **the bows**. The plural **bows** can be used to refer either to one or to more than one of these parts. ❑ The waves were about five

feet high now, and the bow of the boat was leaping up and down. **3** /bəʊ/ A **bow** is a knot with two loops and two loose ends that is used in tying shoelaces and ribbons. ❑ Add a length of ribbon tied in a bow. **4** /bəʊ/ A **bow** is a weapon for shooting arrows that consists of a long piece of curved wood with a string attached to both its ends. ❑ Some of the raiders were armed with bows and arrows. **5** /bəʊ/ The **bow** of a violin or other stringed instrument is a long thin piece of wood with fibres stretched along it that you move across the strings of the instrument in order to play it.

bow·el /ˈbaʊəl/ NOUN [C] (**bowels**) Your **bowels** are the tubes in your body through which digested food passes from your stomach to your anus. ❑ Symptoms such as stomach pains and irritable bowels can be signs of bowel cancer.

bowl ◆◇◇ /bəʊl/ NOUN, VERB
NOUN [C] (**bowls**) **1** A **bowl** is a round container with a wide uncovered top. Some kinds of bowl are used, for example, for serving or eating food from, or in cooking, while other larger kinds are used for washing or cleaning. ❑ Put all the ingredients into a large bowl. **2** The contents of a bowl can be referred to as a **bowl of** something. ❑ a bowl of soup **3** You can refer to the hollow rounded part of an object as its **bowl**. ❑ He smacked the bowl of his pipe into his hand.
VERB [T, I] (**bowls, bowling, bowled**) **1** [T] In a sport such as bowling or lawn bowling, when a bowler **bowls** a ball, he or she rolls it down a narrow track or field of grass. ❑ Neither finalist bowled a particularly strong game. **2** [I, T] In a sport such as cricket, when a bowler **bowls** a ball, he or she throws it down the field towards a batsman. ❑ I can't see the point of bowling a ball like that. **3** [I] If you **bowl along** in a car or on a boat, you move along very quickly, especially when you are enjoying yourself. ❑ Veronica looked at him, smiling, as they bowled along.

box ◆◆◇ /bɒks/ NOUN, VERB
NOUN [C, U] (**boxes**) **1** [C] A **box** is a square or rectangular container with hard or stiff sides. Boxes often have lids. ❑ He reached into the cardboard box beside him. ❑ They sat on wooden boxes. **2** [C] You can use **box** to refer to a box and its contents, or to the contents only. ❑ She ate two boxes of chocolates. **3** [C] A **box** is a square or rectangle that is printed or drawn on a piece of paper, a road, or on some other surface. ❑ For more information, just tick the box and send us the form. **4** [C] A **box** is a small separate area in a theatre or at a sports arena or stadium, where a small number of people can sit to watch the performance or game. ❑ Jim watched the game from a private box. **5** [C] **Box** is used before a number as a postal address by people or organizations that rent a post office box. ❑ Country Crafts, Box 111, Landisville **6** [U] [oft box + N] **Box** is a small evergreen tree with dark leaves that is often used to form hedges. ❑ box hedges
VERB [I] (**boxes, boxing, boxed**) To **box** means to fight someone according to the rules of boxing. ❑ At school I boxed and played rugby.
PHRASAL VERB **box in** **1** If you **are boxed in**, you are unable to move from a particular place because you are surrounded by other people or cars. = hem in ❑ The cabs cut in front of them, trying to box them in. **2** If something **boxes** you **in**, it puts you in a situation where you have very little choice about what you can do. ❑ We are not trying to box anybody in, we are trying to find a satisfactory way forward.
→ See also **boxing**

box·er /ˈbɒksə/ NOUN [C] (**boxers**) A **boxer** is someone who takes part in the sport of boxing.

box·ing /ˈbɒksɪŋ/ NOUN [U] **Boxing** is a sport in which two people wearing large padded gloves fight according to special rules.

boy ◆◆◆ /bɔɪ/ NOUN, EXCLAM
NOUN [C] (**boys**) **1** A **boy** is a child who will grow up to be a man. ❑ He was still just a boy. **2** You can refer to a young man as a **boy**, especially when talking about relationships between boys and girls. ❑ the age when girls get interested in boys **3** (informal) Someone's **boy** is their son. ❑ Eric was my cousin Edward's boy. **4** (informal, feelings) You can refer to a

B

man as a **boy**, especially when you are talking about him in an affectionate way. ❑ *the local boy who made president* EXCLAM (*mainly AmE, informal, feelings*) Some people say 'boy' or 'oh boy' in order to express feelings of excitement or admiration. ❑ *Oh boy! what resourceful children I have.*

boy·cott /ˈbɔɪkɒt/ VERB, NOUN
VERB [T] (**boycotts, boycotting, boycotted**) If a country, group, or person **boycotts** a country, organization, or activity, they refuse to be involved with it in any way because they disapprove of it. ❑ *The main opposition parties are boycotting the elections.*
NOUN [C] (**boycotts**) A **boycott** is the refusal of a country, group, or person to be involved in any way with a country, organization, or activity, because they disapprove of it. ❑ *Opposition leaders had called for a boycott of the vote.*

boy·friend /ˈbɔɪfrend/ NOUN [C] (**boyfriends**) Someone's **boyfriend** is a man or boy with whom they are having a romantic or sexual relationship. ❑ *Brenda and her boyfriend Anthony*

brace /breɪs/ VERB, NOUN
VERB [T] (**braces, bracing, braced**) **1** If you **brace yourself for** something unpleasant or difficult, you prepare yourself for it. ❑ *He braced himself for the icy plunge into the black water.* **2** If you **brace yourself against** something or **brace** part of your body **against** it, you press against something in order to steady your body or to avoid falling. ❑ *Elaine braced herself against the dresser and looked in the mirror.* **3** If you **brace** your shoulders or knees, you keep them stiffly in a particular position. ❑ *He braced his shoulders defiantly as another squall of wet snow slashed across his face.* **4** To **brace** something means to strengthen or support it with something else. ❑ *Overhead, the lights showed the old timbers, used to brace the roof.*
NOUN [C, PL] (**braces**) **1** [C] A **brace** is a device attached to a part of a person's body, for example, to a weak leg, in order to strengthen or support it. = support ❑ *He wore leg braces after he had polio in childhood.* **2** [C] (*BrE; in AmE, use* **braces**) A **brace** is a metal device that can be fastened to a person's teeth in order to help them grow straight. ❑ *I used to have to wear a brace.* **3** [PL] (*BrE; in AmE, use* **suspenders**) **Braces** are a pair of straps that pass over your shoulders and fasten to your trousers at the front and back in order to stop them from falling down.

brac·ing /ˈbreɪsɪŋ/ ADJ If you describe something, especially a place, climate, or activity as **bracing**, you mean that it makes you feel fresh and full of energy. = invigorating ❑ *a bracing walk*

⭘**brack·et** /ˈbrækɪt/ NOUN, VERB
NOUN [C] (**brackets**) **1** If you say that someone or something is in a particular **bracket**, you mean that they come within a particular range, for example, a range of incomes, ages, or prices. = range, sector ❑ *a 33% top tax rate on everyone in these high-income brackets* ❑ *Do you fall outside that age bracket?* **2** **Brackets** are pieces of metal, wood, or plastic that are fastened to a wall in order to support something such as a shelf. ❑ *Fix the beam with the brackets and screws.* **3** **Brackets** are pair of marks ( ) that are placed around a series of symbols in a mathematical expression to indicate that those symbols function as one item within the expression. **4** (*BrE; in AmE, use* **parentheses**) **Brackets** are a pair of written marks ( ) that you place around a word, expression, or sentence in order to indicate that you are giving extra information. = parenthesis ❑ *The prices in brackets are special rates for the under 18s.* ❑ *My annotations appear in square brackets.*
VERB [T] (**brackets, bracketing, bracketed**) If two or more people or things **are bracketed together**, they are considered to be similar or related in some way. = categorize ❑ *The Magi, Brahmins, and Druids were bracketed together as men of wisdom.*

brag /bræg/ VERB [I, T] (**brags, bragging, bragged**) (*disapproval*) If you **brag**, you say in a very proud way that you have something or have done something. = boast ❑ *He's always bragging that he's a great martial artist.* ❑ *He'll probably go around bragging to his friends.* ❑ *Winn bragged that he had spies in the department.*

⭘**brain** ◆◆◇ /breɪn/ NOUN [C] (**brains**) **1** Your **brain** is the organ inside your head that controls your body's activities and enables you to think and to feel things such as heat and pain. ❑ *the development of a child's brain* ❑ *Her father died of a brain tumour.* **2** Your **brain** is your mind and the way that you think. = mind, intellect ❑ *Once you stop using your brain you soon go stale.* **3** If someone has **brains** or a good **brain**, they have the ability to learn and understand things quickly, to solve problems, and to make good decisions. ❑ *They were not the only ones to have brains and ambition.* **4** (*informal*) If someone is **the brains** behind an idea or an organization, he or she had that idea or makes the important decisions about how that organization is managed. ❑ *Mr White was the brains behind the scheme.*
✦ rack your brains → see rack

brain·wave /ˈbreɪnweɪv/ (*BrE; in AmE, use* **brainstorm**) NOUN [C] (**brainwaves**) If you have a **brainwave**, you suddenly have a clever idea.

brake /breɪk/ NOUN, VERB
NOUN [C] (**brakes**) **1** **Brakes** are devices in a vehicle that make it go slower or stop. ❑ *A seagull swooped down in front of her car, causing her to slam on the brakes.* **2** You can use **brake** in a number of expressions to indicate that something has slowed down or stopped. ❑ *Illness had put a brake on his progress.*
VERB [I, T] (**brakes, braking, braked**) When a vehicle or its driver **brakes**, or when a driver **brakes** a vehicle, the driver makes it slow down or stop by using the brakes. ❑ *He heard tyres squeal as the car braked to avoid a collision.* ❑ *He braked the car slightly.*

branch ◆◇◇ /brɑːntʃ, bræntʃ/ NOUN
NOUN [C] (**branches**) **1** The **branches** of a tree are the parts that grow out from its trunk and have leaves, flowers, or fruit growing on them. ❑ *the upper branches of a row of pines* **2** A **branch** of a business or other organization is one of the offices, shops, or groups which belong to it and which are located in different places. ❑ *The local branch of Bank of America is handling the accounts.* **3** A **branch of** an organization such as the government or the police force is a department that has a particular function. ❑ *Senate employees could take their employment grievances to another branch of government.* ❑ *He had a fascination for submarines and joined this branch of the service.* **4** A **branch of** a subject is a part or type of it. ❑ *Whole branches of science may not receive any grants.* **5** A **branch of** your family is a group of its members who are descended from one particular person. ❑ *This is one of the branches of the Roosevelt family.*
PHRASAL VERBS **branch off** (**branches, branching, branched**) A road or path that **branches off** from another one starts from it and goes in a slightly different direction. If you **branch off** somewhere, you change the direction in which you are going. ❑ *After a few miles, a small road branched off to the right.*
branch out If a person or an organization **branches out**, they do something that is different from their normal activities or work. ❑ *I continued studying moths, and branched out to other insects.*

⭘**brand** ◆◇◇ /brænd/ NOUN, VERB
NOUN [C] (**brands**) **1** A **brand** of a product is the version of it that is made by one particular manufacturer. = make ❑ *Winston is a brand of cigarette.* ❑ *I bought one of the leading brands.* ❑ *a supermarket's own brand* **2** A **brand of** something such as a way of thinking or behaving is a particular kind of it. = strain ❑ *Joel Hatch brings his own unique brand of humour to the role.* **3** A **brand** is a permanent mark made on an animal's skin in order to show who it belongs to. ❑ *A brand was a mark of ownership burned into the hide of an animal with a hot iron.*
VERB [T] (**brands, branding, branded**) **1** If someone is **branded** as something bad, people think they are that thing. = label ❑ *I was instantly branded as a rebel.* ❑ *The company has been branded racist by some of its own staff.* **2** When you **brand** an animal, you put a permanent mark on its skin in order to show who it belongs to, usually by burning a mark onto its skin. ❑ *The owner couldn't be bothered to brand the cattle.*

WHICH WORD?

brand or make?

Do not confuse **brand** and **make**.

A **brand** is a product that has its own name, and is made by a particular company. You use **brand** to talk about things that you buy in shops, such as food, drink, and clothes.

❑ *There used to be so many different **brands** of tea.*

You use **make** to talk about the names of longer-lasting products such as machines or cars.

❑ *This is a very popular **make** of bicycle.*

---

brand·ed /'brændɪd/ ADJ [branded + N] (*business*) A **branded** product is one that is made by a well-known manufacturer and has the manufacturer's label on it. ❑ *Supermarket lines are often cheaper than branded goods.*

brand-new ADJ A **brand-new** object is completely new. ❑ *Yesterday he went off to buy himself a brand-new car.*

brass /brɑːs, bræs/ NOUN [U, SING] **1** [U] **Brass** is a yellow-coloured metal made from copper and zinc. It is used especially for making ornaments and musical instruments. ❑ *The instrument is beautifully made in brass.* **2** [SING] **The brass** is the section of an orchestra which consists of brass wind instruments such as trumpets and horns. ❑ *Consequently even this vast chorus was occasionally overwhelmed by the brass.*

brave ♦◇◇ /breɪv/ ADJ, VERB **ADJ** (**braver, bravest**) Someone who is **brave** is willing to do things that are dangerous, and does not show fear in difficult or dangerous situations. = courageous ❑ *He was not brave enough to report the loss of the documents.* **VERB** [T] (**braves, braving, braved**) (*written*) If you **brave** unpleasant or dangerous conditions, you deliberately expose yourself to them, usually in order to achieve something. ❑ *Thousands have braved icy rain to demonstrate their support.*

brave·ly /'breɪvli/ ADV ❑ *Our men wiped them out, but the enemy fought bravely and well.*

brav·ery /'breɪvəri/ NOUN [U] **Bravery** is brave behaviour or the quality of being brave. = courage ❑ *He deserves the highest praise for his bravery.*

brawl /brɔːl/ NOUN, VERB **NOUN** [C] (**brawls**) A **brawl** is a rough or violent fight. ❑ *He had been in a drunken street brawl.* **VERB** [RECIP] (**brawls, brawling, brawled**) If someone **brawls**, they fight in a very rough or violent way. ❑ *He was suspended for a year from the university after brawling with police over a speeding ticket.*

breach /briːtʃ/ VERB, NOUN **VERB** [T] (**breaches, breaching, breached**) **1** If you **breach** an agreement, a law, or a promise, you break it. = violate ❑ *The newspaper breached the code of conduct on privacy.* **2** (*formal*) If someone or something **breaches** a barrier, they make an opening in it, usually leaving it weakened or destroyed. = rupture ❑ *The limestone is sufficiently fissured for tree roots to have breached the roof of the cave.* **3** If you **breach** someone's security or their defences, you manage to get through and attack an area that is heavily guarded and protected. ❑ *The bomber had breached security by hurling his dynamite from a roof overlooking the building.* **NOUN** [C, U] (**breaches**) **1** [C, U] A **breach of** an agreement, a law, or a promise is an act of breaking it. = violation ❑ *The congressman was accused of a breach of secrecy rules.* **2** [C] (*formal*) A **breach in** a relationship is a serious disagreement which often results in the relationship ending. = rift, rupture ❑ *Their actions threatened a serious breach in relations between the two countries.* **3** [C] A **breach** of security is an instance of someone gaining access to secret information or to a place that is guarded. ❑ *serious breaches of security at Camp Delta*

bread ♦◇◇ /bred/ NOUN [C, U] (**breads**) **Bread** is a very common food made from flour, water, and usually yeast. ❑ *a loaf of bread* ❑ *bread and butter*

breadth /bretθ, AmE bredθ/ NOUN [U] **1** The **breadth of** something is the distance between its two sides. = width ❑ *The breadth of the whole camp was 400 paces.* **2** The **breadth of** something is its quality of consisting of or involving many different things. = range ❑ *Older people have a tremendous breadth of experience.*

break ♦♦♦ /breɪk/ VERB, NOUN **VERB** [I, T] (**breaks, breaking, broke, broken**) **1** [I, T] When an object **breaks** or when you **break** it, it suddenly separates into two or more pieces, often because it has been hit or dropped. ❑ *He fell through the window, breaking the glass.* ❑ *The plate broke.* ❑ *The plane broke into three pieces.* **2** [I, T] If you **break** a part of your body such as your leg, your arm, or your nose, or if a bone **breaks**, you are injured because a bone cracks or splits. ❑ *She broke a leg in a skiing accident.* ❑ *Old bones break easily.* **3** [I, T] If a surface, cover, or seal **breaks** or if something **breaks** it, a hole or tear is made in it, so that a substance can pass through. ❑ *Once you've broken the seal of a bottle there's no way you can put it back together again.* ❑ *The bandage must be put on when the blister breaks.* **4** [I, T] When a tool or piece of machinery **breaks** or when you **break** it, it is damaged and no longer works. ❑ *When the clutch broke, the car was locked into second gear.* **5** [T] If someone **breaks** something, especially a difficult or unpleasant situation that has existed for some time, they end it or change it. ❑ *We need to break the vicious cycle of violence and counterviolence.* ❑ *New proposals have been put forward to break the deadlock among rival factions.* **6** [T] If someone or something **breaks** a silence, they say something or make a noise after a long period of silence. ❑ *Hugh broke the silence. 'Is she always late?' he asked.* **7** [I, T] If you **break with** a group of people or a traditional way of doing things, or you **break** your connection with them, you stop being involved with that group or stop doing things in that way. ❑ *In 1959, Akihito broke with imperial tradition by marrying a commoner.* ❑ *They were determined to break from precedent.* **8** [T] If you **break** a habit or if someone **breaks** you **of** it, you no longer have that habit. ❑ *If you continue to smoke, keep trying to break the habit.* **9** [I] If someone **breaks for** a short period of time, they rest or change from what they are doing for a short period. ❑ *They broke for lunch.* **10** [T] If you **break** your journey somewhere, you stop there for a short time so that you can have a rest. ❑ *We broke our journey at a small country hotel.* **11** [T] If you **break** a rule, promise, or agreement, you do something that you should not do according to that rule, promise, or agreement. ❑ *We didn't know we were breaking the law.* ❑ *The company has consistently denied it had knowingly broken arms embargoes.* **12** [I] If you **break** free or loose, you free yourself from something or escape from it. ❑ *She broke free by thrusting her elbow into his chest.* **13** [T] To **break** the force of something such as a blow or fall means to weaken its effect, for example, by getting in the way of it. ❑ *He sustained serious neck injuries after he broke someone's fall.* **14** [I] When a piece of news **breaks**, people hear about it from the newspapers, television, or radio. ❑ *The news broke that Montgomery was under investigation.* **15** [T] When you **break** a piece of bad news to someone, you tell it to them, usually in a kind way. ❑ *Then Louise broke the news that she was leaving me.* **16** [T] If you **break** a record, you beat the previous record for a particular achievement. ❑ *Carl Lewis has broken the world record in the 100 metres.* **17** [I] When day or dawn **breaks**, it starts to grow light after the night has ended. ❑ *They continued the search as dawn broke.* **18** [I] When a wave **breaks**, it passes its highest point and turns downward, for example, when it reaches the shore. ❑ *Danny listened to the waves breaking against the shore.* **19** [T] If you **break** a secret code, you work out how to understand it. = crack ❑ *It was feared they could break the Allies' codes.* **20** [I] If someone's voice **breaks** when they are speaking, it changes its sound, for example, because they are sad or afraid. ❑ *Godfrey's voice broke, and halted.* **21** [I] When a boy's voice **breaks**, it becomes deeper and sounds more like a man's voice. ❑ *He sings with the strained discomfort of someone whose voice hasn't quite broken.* **22** [I] If the weather **breaks** or a storm **breaks**, it suddenly becomes rainy or stormy after a period of sunshine. ❑ *I've been waiting for the weather to break.* **PHRASAL VERBS** **break down** **1** If a machine or a vehicle

b

breaks down, it stops working. ❑ *Their car broke down.* **2** If a discussion, relationship, or system **breaks down**, it fails because of a problem or disagreement. ❑ *Talks with business leaders broke down last night.* **3** To **break down** something such as an idea or statement means to separate it into smaller parts in order to make it easier to understand or deal with. ❑ *The report breaks down the results region by region.* **4** When a substance **breaks down** or when something **breaks** it **down**, a biological or chemical process causes it to separate into the substances which make it up. ❑ *Over time, the protein in the eggshell breaks down into its constituent amino acids.* **5** If someone **breaks down**, they lose control of themselves and start crying. ❑ *Because he was being so kind and concerned, I broke down and cried.* **6** If you **break down** a door or barrier, you hit it so hard that it falls to the ground. ❑ *An unruly mob broke down police barricades and stormed the courtroom.* **7** To **break down** barriers or prejudices that separate people or restrict their freedom means to change people's attitudes so that the barriers or prejudices no longer exist. ❑ *Women's sports are breaking down the barriers in previously male-dominated domains.* **8** → See also **breakdown**

break in **1** If someone, usually a thief, **breaks in**, they get into a building by force. ❑ *Masked robbers broke in and made off with $8,000.* **2** If you **break in** on someone's conversation or activity, you interrupt them. = butt in ❑ *O'Leary broke in on his thoughts.* ❑ *Mrs Southern listened keenly, occasionally breaking in with pertinent questions.* **3** If you **break** someone **in**, you get them used to a new job or situation. ❑ *The band is breaking in a new backing vocalist, who sounds great.* **4** If you **break in** something new, you gradually use or wear it for longer and longer periods until it is ready to be used or worn all the time. ❑ *When breaking in an engine, you should refrain from high speeds for the first thousand miles.* **5** → See also **break-in**

break into **1** If someone **breaks into** a building, they get into it by force. ❑ *There was no one nearby who might see him trying to break into the house.* **2** If someone **breaks into** something they suddenly start doing it. For example, if someone **breaks into** a run they suddenly start running, and if they **break into** song they suddenly start singing. ❑ *The moment she was out of sight she broke into a run.* **3** If you **break into** a profession or area of business, especially one that is difficult to succeed in, you manage to have some success in it. ❑ *She finally broke into films after an acclaimed stage career.*

break off **1** If part of something **breaks off** or if you **break** it **off**, it comes off or is removed by force. ❑ *The two wings of the aircraft broke off on impact.* ❑ *Grace broke off a large piece of the clay.* **2** If you **break off** when you are doing or saying something, you suddenly stop doing it or saying it. ❑ *Barry broke off in mid-sentence.* **3** If someone **breaks off** a relationship, they end it. ❑ *The two West African states had broken off relations two years ago.*

break out **1** If something such as war, fighting, or disease **breaks out**, it begins suddenly. ❑ *He was 29 when war broke out.* **2** If a prisoner **breaks out of** a prison, they escape from it. ❑ *The two men broke out of their cells and cut through a perimeter fence.* **3** If you **break out of** a dull situation or routine, you manage to change it or escape from it. ❑ *It's taken a long time to break out of my own conventional training.* **4** If you **break out** in a rash or a sweat, a rash or sweat appears on your skin. ❑ *A person who is allergic to cashews may break out in a rash when he consumes these nuts.*

break through **1** If you **break through** a barrier, you succeed in forcing your way through it. ❑ *Protesters tried to break through a police cordon.* **2** If you **break through**, you achieve success even though there are difficulties and obstacles. ❑ *There is still scope for new writers to break through.* **3** → See also **breakthrough**

break up **1** When something **breaks up** or when you **break** it **up**, it separates or is divided into several smaller parts. ❑ *Civil war could come if the country breaks up.* ❑ *Break up the chocolate and melt it.* **2** If you **break up with** your boyfriend, girlfriend, husband, or wife, your relationship with that person ends. = split up ❑ *My girlfriend has broken up with me.* ❑ *He felt appalled by the idea of marriage*

so we broke up. **3** If a marriage or romantic relationship **breaks up** or if someone **breaks** it **up**, it ends and the partners separate. ❑ *His first marriage broke up.* **4** When a meeting or gathering **breaks up** or when someone **breaks** it **up**, it is brought to an end and the people involved in it leave. = disperse ❑ *A neighbour asked for the music to be turned down and the party broke up.* ❑ *Police used tear gas to break up a demonstration.*

NOUN [c] (**breaks**) **1** A **break** is an injury to the body when a bone cracks or splits. ❑ *It has caused a bad break to Gabriella's leg.* **2** A **break** in a difficult or unpleasant situation is an end or change to it. ❑ *Nothing that might lead to a break in the deadlock has been discussed yet.* **3** A **break** in a tradition is an end to that tradition. A **break** with a group of people is an end to your involvement with that group. ❑ *Making a completely clean break with the past, the couple got rid of all their old furniture.* **4** A **break** is a short period of time when you have a rest or a change from what you are doing, especially if you are working or if you are in a boring or unpleasant situation. ❑ *They may be able to help with childcare so that you can have a break.* ❑ *I thought a 15 minute break from his work would do him good.* **5** A **break** is a short holiday. ❑ *They are currently taking a short break in Spain.* **6** (*informal*) A **break** is a lucky opportunity that someone gets to achieve something. ❑ *Her first break came when she was chosen out of 100 guitarists auditioning for a spot on Michael Jackson's tour.* → See also **broke, broken, heartbreak, outbreak** ♦ **break even** → see **even**; **break new ground** → see **ground**; **break someone's heart** → see **heart**; **all hell breaks loose** → see **hell**; **break the ice** → see **ice**; **break ranks** → see **rank**; **break wind** → see **wind**

break·away /'breɪkəweɪ/ ADJ [breakaway + N] A **breakaway** group is a group of people who have separated from a larger group, for example, because of a disagreement. = splinter ❑ *A breakaway faction of the rebel group has claimed responsibility for the killing.*

break·down /'breɪkdaʊn/ NOUN [c] (**breakdowns**) **1** The **breakdown of** something such as a relationship, plan, or discussion is its failure or ending. = collapse ❑ *the breakdown of talks between the U.S. and E.U. officials* ❑ *the irretrievable breakdown of a marriage* **2** If you have a **breakdown**, you become very depressed, so that you are unable to cope with your life. ❑ *My personal life was terrible. My mother had died, and a couple of years later I had a breakdown.* **3** If a car or a piece of machinery has a **breakdown**, it stops working. ❑ *Her old car was unreliable, so the trip was plagued by breakdowns.* **4** A **breakdown of** something is a list of its separate parts. = analysis ❑ *The organizers were given a breakdown of the costs.*

break·fast ♦◇◇ /'brekfəst/ NOUN, VERB
NOUN [c, u] (**breakfasts**) **Breakfast** is the first meal of the day. It is usually eaten in the early part of the morning. ❑ *What's for breakfast?*
VERB [I] (**breakfasts, breakfasting, breakfasted**) (*formal*) When you **breakfast**, you have breakfast. ❑ *All the ladies breakfasted in their rooms.*

break-in NOUN [c] (**break-ins**) If there has been a **break-in**, someone has got into a building by force. = burglary ❑ *The break-in had occurred just before midnight.*

○break·through /'breɪkθruː/ NOUN [c] (**breakthroughs**) A **breakthrough** is an important development or achievement. = development, achievement, advance; ≠ setback ❑ *The company looks poised to make a significant breakthrough in China.* ❑ *The breakthrough came hours before a U.N. deadline.*

break·up /'breɪkʌp/ NOUN [c] (**breakups**) **1** The **breakup of** a marriage, relationship, or association is the act of it finishing or coming to an end because the people involved decide that it is not working successfully. = collapse ❑ *the acrimonious breakup of the meeting's first session* **2** The **breakup of** an organization or a country is the act of it separating or dividing into several parts. ❑ *The Justice Department advocated a breakup of Microsoft.*

breast ♦◇◇ /brest/ NOUN [c, SING, u] (**breasts**) **1** [c] A woman's **breasts** are the two soft, round parts on her chest that can produce milk to feed a baby. ❑ *She wears a low-cut* dress which reveals her breasts. **2** [c] (literary) A person's **breast** is the upper part of his or her chest. ❑ He struck his breast in a dramatic gesture. **3** [c] A bird's **breast** is the front part of its body. ❑ The cock's breast is tinged with chestnut. **4** [SING] The **breast** of a shirt, jacket, or coat is the part which covers the top part of the chest. **5** [c, u] You can refer to a piece of meat that is cut from the front of a bird or lamb as **breast**. ❑ a chicken breast with vegetables

◆ **breath** ◆◇◇ /breθ/ NOUN

NOUN [c, u] (breaths) **1** Your **breath** is the air that you let out through your mouth when you breathe. If someone has **bad breath**, their breath smells unpleasant. ❑ I could smell the whisky on his breath. **2** When you take a **breath**, you breathe in once. ❑ He took a deep breath, and began to climb the stairs. ❑ Gasping for breath, she leaned against the door.

PHRASES **for a breath of fresh air** or **for a breath of air** If you go outside **for a breath of fresh air** or **for a breath of air**, you go outside because it is unpleasantly warm indoors. ❑ I had to step outside for a breath of fresh air.
be a breath of fresh air (approval) If you describe something new or different as **a breath of fresh air**, you mean that it makes a situation or subject more interesting or exciting. ❑ Her brisk treatment of an almost taboo subject was a breath of fresh air.
get one's breath back When you **get** your **breath back** after doing something energetic, you start breathing normally again. ❑ I reached out a hand to steady myself against the house while I got my breath back.
be out of breath If you are **out of breath**, you are breathing very quickly and with difficulty because you have been doing something energetic. ❑ She was slightly out of breath from running.
in the same breath (disapproval) You can use **in the same breath** or **in the next breath** to indicate that someone says two very different or contradictory things, especially when you are criticizing them. ❑ He hailed this week's arms agreement but in the same breath expressed suspicion about the motivations of the United States.
short of breath If you are **short of breath**, you find it difficult to breathe properly, for example, because you are ill. You can also say that someone suffers from **shortness of breath**. ❑ She felt short of breath and flushed.
under one's breath If you say something **under** your **breath**, you say it in a very quiet voice, often because you do not want other people to hear what you are saying. ❑ Walsh muttered something under his breath.

◆ **breathe** ◆◇◇ /briːð/ VERB

VERB [i, T] (breathes, breathing, breathed) When people or animals **breathe**, they take air into their lungs and let it out again. When they **breathe** smoke or a particular kind of air, they take it into their lungs and let it out again as they breathe. = inhale, exhale ❑ He stood there breathing deeply and evenly. ❑ Breathe through your nose. ❑ No American should have to drive out of town to breathe clean air.
PHRASAL VERBS **breathe in** When you **breathe in**, you take some air into your lungs. When you **breathe** something **in**, you take air or something else into your lungs. = inhale ❑ She breathed in deeply. ❑ A thirteen year old girl is being treated after breathing in smoke.
breathe out When you **breathe out**, you send air out of your lungs through your nose or mouth. = exhale ❑ Breathe out and ease your knees in towards your chest.
breath·ing /briːðɪŋ/ NOUN [u] ❑ Her breathing became slow and heavy.
✦ **be breathing down someone's neck** → see neck; **breathe a sigh of relief** → see sigh

breath·ing space NOUN [c, u] (breathing spaces) A **breathing space** is a short period of time between two activities in which you can recover from the first activity and prepare for the second one. = respite ❑ Firms need a breathing space if they are to recover. ❑ We hope that it will give us some breathing space.

breath·less /breθləs/ ADJ If you are **breathless**, you have difficulty in breathing properly, for example, because you have been running or because you are afraid or

excited. ❑ I was a little breathless and my heartbeat was bumpy and fast.
breath·less·ly /breθləsli/ ADV ❑ 'I'll go in,' he said breathlessly.
breath·less·ness /breθləsnəs/ NOUN [u] ❑ Asthma causes wheezing and breathlessness.

◆ **breath·taking** /breθteɪkɪŋ/ also **breath-taking** ADJ (emphasis) If you say that something is **breathtaking**, you are emphasizing that it is extremely beautiful or amazing. ❑ The house has breathtaking views from every room. ❑ Some of their football was breathtaking, a delight to watch.

◆ **breed** ◆◇◇ /briːd/ NOUN, VERB

NOUN [c] (breeds) A **breed** of a pet animal or farm animal is a particular type of it. For example, terriers are a breed of dog. ❑ rare breeds of cattle ❑ Certain breeds are more dangerous than others.
VERB [T, i] (breeds, breeding, bred) **1** [T] If you **breed** animals or plants, you keep them for the purpose of producing more animals or plants with particular qualities, in a controlled way. ❑ He lived alone, breeding horses and plants. ❑ He used to breed dogs for the police. ❑ These dogs are bred to fight. **2** [i] When animals **breed**, they have babies. ❑ Frogs will usually breed in any convenient pond. **3** [T] If you say that something **breeds** bad feeling or bad behaviour, you mean that it causes bad feeling or bad behaviour to develop. = create ❑ If they are unemployed it's bound to breed resentment.
→ See also breeding

breed·ing /briːdɪŋ/ NOUN [u] **1** The **breeding** of animals or plants is the controlled process of keeping them in order to produce more animals or plants with particular qualities. ❑ There is potential for selective breeding for better yields. **2** **Breeding** is the process by which animals have babies. ❑ During the breeding season the birds come ashore. **3** If someone says that a person has **breeding**, they mean that they think the person is from a good social background and has good manners. ❑ It's a sign of good breeding to know the names of all your staff.

breeze /briːz/ NOUN, VERB

NOUN [c] (breezes) A **breeze** is a gentle wind. ❑ a cool summer breeze
VERB [i] (breezes, breezing, breezed) **1** If you **breeze into** a place or a position, you enter it in a very casual or relaxed manner. ❑ Lopez breezed into the quarter-finals of the tournament. **2** If you **breeze through** something such as a game or test, you cope with it easily. ❑ John seems to breeze effortlessly through his many commitments at work.

brew /bruː/ VERB, NOUN

VERB [T, i] (brews, brewing, brewed) **1** [T] If you **brew** tea or coffee, you make it by pouring hot water over tea leaves or ground coffee. ❑ He brewed a pot of coffee. **2** [T] If a person or company **brews** beer, they make it. ❑ I brew my own beer. **3** [i] If a storm **is brewing**, large clouds are beginning to form and the sky is becoming dark because there is going to be a storm. ❑ We'd seen the storm brewing when we were out in the boat. **4** [i] If an unpleasant or difficult situation **is brewing**, it is starting to develop. ❑ At home a crisis was brewing.
NOUN [c] (brews) A **brew** is a particular kind of tea or coffee. It can also be a particular pot of tea or coffee. ❑ She swallowed a mouthful of the hot strong brew, and wiped her eyes.

bribe /braɪb/ NOUN, VERB

NOUN [c] (bribes) A **bribe** is a sum of money or something valuable that one person offers or gives to another in order to persuade him or her to do something. ❑ He was being investigated for receiving bribes.
VERB [T] (bribes, bribing, bribed) If one person **bribes** another, they give them a bribe. ❑ He was accused of bribing a senior bank official.

brib·ery /braɪbəri/ NOUN [u] **Bribery** is the act of offering someone money or something valuable in order to persuade them to do something for you. ❑ He was jailed on charges of bribery.

brick /brɪk/ NOUN

NOUN [c, u] (bricks) **Bricks** are rectangular blocks of baked

B

clay used for building walls, which are usually red or brown. **Brick** is the material made up of these blocks. ❏ *She built bookshelves out of bricks and planks.*

PHRASE **hit a brick wall** or **come up against a brick wall** (*informal*) If you **hit a brick wall** or **come up against a brick wall**, you are unable to continue or make progress because something stops you. ❏ *After that my career just seemed to hit a brick wall.*

brid·al /ˈbraɪdəl/ ADJ [bridal + N] **Bridal** is used to describe something that belongs or relates to a bride, or to both a bride and her bridegroom. = wedding ❏ *She wore a floor-length bridal gown.*

bride /braɪd/ NOUN [c] (**brides**) A **bride** is a woman who is getting married or who has just got married. ❏ *Guests toasted the bride and groom with champagne.*

bride·groom /ˈbraɪdgruːm/ NOUN [c] (**bridegrooms**) A **bridegroom** is a man who is getting married. = groom

brides·maid /ˈbraɪdzmeɪd/ NOUN [c] (**bridesmaids**) A **bridesmaid** is a woman or a girl who helps and accompanies a bride on her wedding day.

bridge ♦♦◇ /brɪdʒ/ NOUN, VERB

NOUN [c, u] (**bridges**) **1** [c] A **bridge** is a structure that is built over a railway, river, or road so that people or vehicles can cross from one side to the other. ❏ *He walked back over the railway bridge.* **2** [c] A **bridge** between two places is a piece of land that joins or connects them. ❏ *a land bridge linking Serbian territories* **3** [c] If something or someone acts as a **bridge** between two people, groups, or things, they connect them. ❏ *We hope this book will act as a bridge between doctor and patient.* **4** [c] **The bridge** is the place on a ship from which it is steered. ❏ *Captain Ronald Warwick was on the bridge when the wave hit.* **5** [c] The **bridge** of your nose is the thin top part of it, between your eyes. ❏ *On the bridge of his hooked nose was a pair of gold rimless spectacles.* **6** [c] The **bridge** of a pair of glasses is the part that rests on your nose. **7** [c] The **bridge** of a violin, guitar, or other stringed instrument is the small piece of wood under the strings that holds them up. **8** [u] **Bridge** is a card game for four players in which the players begin by declaring how many tricks they expect to win.

VERB [T] (**bridges, bridging, bridged**) **1** To **bridge** the gap between two people or things means to reduce it or get rid of it. = overcome ❏ *It is unlikely that the two sides will be able to bridge their differences.* **2** Something that **bridges** the gap between two very different things has some of the qualities of each of these things. ❏ *the singer who bridged the gap between pop music and opera*

Ⓞbrief ♦♦◇ /briːf/ ADJ, NOUN, VERB (*academic word*)

ADJ (**briefer, briefest**) **1** Something that is **brief** lasts for only a short time. = fleeting ❏ *She once made a brief appearance on television.* **2** A **brief** speech or piece of writing does not contain many words or details. = short, concise ❏ *In a brief statement, he concentrated entirely on international affairs.* **3** [V-LINK + brief] If you are **brief**, you say what you want to say in as few words as possible. = succinct ❏ *Now please be brief – my time is valuable.* **4** You can describe a period of time as **brief** if you want to emphasize that it is very short. ❏ *For a few brief minutes we forgot the anxiety and anguish.*

NOUN [PL, c] (**briefs**) **1** [PL] [also 'a pair of' briefs] Men's or women's underpants can be referred to as **briefs**. ❏ *A bra and a pair of briefs lay on the floor.* **2** [c] A **brief** is a document containing all the information relating to a particular legal case, which is used by a lawyer to defend his or her client in court. ❏ *Griffith's expertise is in writing legal briefs.* **3** [c] (*mainly BrE, formal*) If someone gives you a **brief**, they officially give you responsibility and instructions for dealing with a particular thing. = responsibility ❏ *customs officials with a brief to stop foreign porn coming into Britain*

PHRASE **in brief** You can say **in brief** to indicate that you are about to say something in as few words as possible or to give a summary of what you have just said. ❏ *In brief, take no risks.*

VERB [T] (**briefs, briefing, briefed**) If someone **briefs** you, especially about a piece of work or a serious matter, they give you information that you need before you do it or

consider it. = fill in ❏ *A Defence Department spokesman briefed reporters.*
→ See also **briefing**

brief·case /ˈbriːfkeɪs/ NOUN [c] (**briefcases**) A **briefcase** is a case used for carrying documents in.

brief·ing /ˈbriːfɪŋ/ NOUN [c, u] (**briefings**) A **briefing** is a meeting at which information or instructions are given to people, especially before they do something. ❏ *They're holding a press briefing tomorrow.*
→ See also **brief**

Ⓞbrief·ly /ˈbriːfli/ ADV **1** [briefly with v] Something that happens or is done **briefly** happens or is done for a very short period of time. ❏ *He smiled briefly.* **2** [briefly with v] If you say or write something **briefly**, you use very few words or give very few details. ❏ *There are four basic alternatives; they are described briefly below.* **3** [briefly with CL] You can say **briefly** to indicate that you are about to say something in as few words as possible. ❏ *Briefly, no less than nine of our agents have passed information to us.*

bri·gade /brɪˈɡeɪd/ NOUN [c] (**brigades**) A **brigade** is one of the groups which an army is divided into. ❏ *the soldiers of the 173rd Airborne Brigade*

bright ♦♦◇ /braɪt/ ADJ (**brighter, brightest**) **1** A **bright** colour is strong and noticeable, and not dark. ❏ *a bright red dress* **2** A **bright** light, object, or place is shining strongly or is full of light. ❏ *a bright October day* **3** If you describe someone as **bright**, you mean that they are quick at learning things. = clever ❏ *I was convinced that he was brighter than average.* **4** A **bright** idea is clever and original. = clever ❏ *There are lots of books crammed with bright ideas.* **5** If someone looks or sounds **bright**, they look or sound cheerful and lively. = cheerful, lively ❏ *The boy was so bright and animated.* **6** If the future is **bright**, it is likely to be pleasant or successful. = promising ❏ *Both had successful careers and the future looked bright.*

bright·ly /ˈbraɪtli/ ADV **1** *a display of brightly coloured flowers* **2** [brightly with v] ❏ *a warm, brightly lit room* **3** [brightly with v] ❏ *He smiled brightly as Ben approached.*

bright·ness /ˈbraɪtnəs/ NOUN [u] **1** You'll be impressed with the brightness and the beauty of the colours. **2** An astronomer can determine the brightness of each star.

bright·en /ˈbraɪtən/ VERB

VERB [I, T] (**brightens, brightening, brightened**) **1** [I] If someone **brightens** or their face **brightens**, they suddenly look happier. ❏ *Seeing him, she seemed to brighten a little.* **2** [I] If your eyes **brighten**, you suddenly look interested or excited. ❏ *His eyes brightened and he laughed.* **3** [T] If someone or something **brightens** a place, they make it more colourful and attractive. ❏ *Tubs planted with flowers brightened the area outside the door.* **4** [I, T] If someone or something **brightens** a situation or the situation **brightens**, it becomes more pleasant, enjoyable, or favourable. = improve ❏ *That does not do much to brighten the prospects of kids in the city.* **5** [I, T] When a light **brightens** a place or when a place **brightens**, it becomes brighter or lighter. ❏ *The sky above the ridge of mountains brightened.* **6** [I] If the weather **brightens**, it becomes less cloudy or rainy, and the sun starts to shine. ❏ *By early afternoon the weather had brightened.*

PHRASAL VERB **brighten up 1** Brighten up means the same as **brighten** VERB 1. ❏ *He brightened up a bit.* **2** Brighten up means the same as **brighten** VERB 3. ❏ *David spotted the pink silk lampshade in a shop and thought it would brighten up the room.*

bril·liant ♦◇◇ /ˈbrɪliənt/ ADJ **1** A **brilliant** person, idea, or performance is extremely clever or skilful. ❏ *She had a brilliant mind.* **2** A **brilliant** career or success is very successful. ❏ *He served four years in prison, emerging to find his brilliant career in ruins.* **3** [brilliant + N] A **brilliant** colour is extremely bright. ❏ *The woman had brilliant green eyes.* **4** You describe light, or something that reflects light, as **brilliant** when it shines very brightly. ❏ *The event was held in brilliant sunshine.* **5** (*mainly BrE, informal, spoken*) You can say that something is **brilliant** when you are very pleased about it or think that it is very good. = great ❏ *If you get a chance to see the show, do go – it's brilliant.*

b

bril·liant·ly /ˈbrɪliəntli/ ADV **1** *It is a very high quality production, brilliantly written and acted.* **2** *The strategy worked brilliantly.* **3** *Many of the patterns show brilliantly coloured flowers.* **4** *It's a brilliantly sunny morning.*

bril·liance /ˈbrɪliəns/ NOUN [U] **1** *He was a deeply serious musician who had shown his brilliance very early.* **2** *an iridescent blue butterfly in all its brilliance* **3** *His eyes became accustomed to the dark after the brilliance of the sun outside.*

brim /brɪm/ NOUN, VERB

NOUN [C] (**brims**) The **brim** of a hat is the wide part that sticks outwards at the bottom. □ *Rain dripped from the brim of his baseball cap.*

PHRASE **filled to the brim** or **full to the brim** If something, especially a container, **is filled to the brim** or **full to the brim with** something, it is filled right up to the top. □ *Her glass was filled right up to the brim.*

VERB [I] (**brims**, **brimming**, **brimmed**) **1** If someone or something **is brimming with** a particular quality, they are full of that quality. □ *The team is brimming with confidence after two straight wins in the tournament.* **2** When your eyes **are brimming** with tears, they are full of fluid because you are upset, although you are not actually crying. □ *Michael looked at him imploringly, eyes brimming with tears.*

bring ♦♦♦ /brɪŋ/ VERB

VERB [T] (**brings**, **bringing**, **brought**) **1** If you **bring** someone or something **with** you when you come to a place, they come with you or you have them with you. □ *Remember to bring an apron or an old shirt to protect your clothes.* □ *Someone went upstairs and brought down a huge kettle.* **2** If you **bring** something somewhere, you move it there. □ *Reaching into her pocket, she brought out a cigarette.* **3** If you **bring** something that someone wants or needs, you get it for them or carry it to them. □ *He went and poured a brandy for Dena and brought it to her.* **4** To **bring** something or someone to a place or position means to cause them to come to the place or move into that position. □ *I told you about what brought me here.* □ *The shock of her husband's arrival brought her to her feet.* **5** If you **bring** something new **to** a place or group of people, you introduce it to that place or cause those people to hear or know about it. □ *the drive to bring art to the public* **6** To **bring** someone or something into a particular state or condition means to cause them to be in that state or condition. □ *He brought the car to a stop in front of the square.* □ *They have brought down income taxes.* **7** If something **brings** a particular feeling, situation, or quality, it makes people experience it or have it. □ *He called on the United States to play a more effective role in bringing peace to the region.* □ *Her three children brought her joy.* **8** If a period of time **brings** a particular thing, it happens during that time. □ *For Sandro, the new year brought disaster.* **9** When you are talking, you can say that something **brings** you **to** a particular point in order to indicate that you have now reached that point and are going to talk about a new subject. □ *And that brings us to the end of this special report from Germany.* **10** If you cannot **bring yourself to** do something, you cannot do it because you find it too upsetting, embarrassing, or disgusting. □ *It is all very tragic and I am afraid I just cannot bring myself to talk about it at the moment.*

PHRASAL VERBS **bring about** To **bring** something **about** means to cause it to happen. = cause □ *The only way they can bring about political change is by putting pressure on the country.*

bring along If you **bring** someone or something **along**, you bring them with you when you come to a place. □ *They brought baby Michael along in a carrier.*

bring back **1** Something that **brings back** a memory makes you think about it. □ *Your article brought back sad memories for me.* **2** When people **bring back** a practice or fashion that existed at an earlier time, they introduce it again. = revive □ *Pennsylvania brought back the death penalty in 1978.*

bring down **1** When people or events **bring down** a government or ruler, they cause the government or ruler to lose power. = topple □ *They were threatening to bring down the government by withdrawing from the ruling coalition.* **2** If someone or something **brings down** a person or

aeroplane, they cause them to fall, usually by shooting them. □ *Military historians may never know what brought down the jet.*

bring forward If you **bring forward** a meeting or event, you arrange for it to take place at an earlier date or time than had been planned. = put forward □ *He had to bring forward an 11 o'clock meeting so that he could get to the funeral on time.*

bring in **1** When a government or organization **brings in** a new law or system, they introduce it. = introduce □ *The government brought in a controversial law under which it could take any land it wanted.* **2** Someone or something that **brings in** money makes it or earns it. □ *I have three part-time jobs, which bring in about $24,000 a year.* **3** If you **bring in** someone from outside a team or organization, you invite them to do a job or join in an activity or discussion. = call in □ *The firm decided to bring in a new management team.*

bring out **1** When a person or company **brings out** a new product, especially a new book or CD, they produce it and put it on sale. □ *A journalist all his life, he's now brought out a book.* **2** Something that **brings out** a particular kind of behaviour or feeling in you causes you to show it, especially when it is something you do not normally show. □ *He is totally dedicated and brings out the best in his pupils.*

bring up **1** When someone **brings up** a child, they look after it until it is an adult. If someone has **been brought up** in a certain place or with certain attitudes, they grew up in that place or were taught those attitudes when they were growing up. = raise □ *She brought up four children.* □ *He was brought up in Nebraska.* **2** If you **bring up** a particular subject, you introduce it into a discussion or conversation. = raise □ *He brought up a subject rarely raised during the course of this campaign.*

♦ **bring alive** → see **alive**; **bring the house down** → see **house**; **bring up the rear** → see **rear**

WHICH WORD?
bring, take, or carry?

Do not confuse the verbs **bring**, **take**, and **carry**.

If you **bring** someone or something with you when you come to a place, you have them with you.

□ *Please **bring** your calculator to every lesson.*

If you **take** someone or something with you when you go from a place, you have them with you.

□ *Don't forget to **take** your umbrella.*

If you **carry** something to a place, you hold it in your hands and take it there.

□ *He picked up his suitcase and **carried** it into the bedroom.*

WHICH WORD?
bring up, improve, or lead to?

If something **improves** something else, it makes it get better.

□ *Time won't **improve** the situation.*

If something **leads to** a situation or event, usually an unpleasant one, it begins a process which causes that situation or event to happen.

□ *This drinking spree **led to** his court appearance.*

Do not use **bring up** for either of these meanings.

---

brink /brɪŋk/ NOUN [SING] If you are **on the brink of** something, usually something important, terrible, or exciting, you are just about to do it or experience it. = verge □ *Their economy is teetering on the brink of collapse.*

brisk /brɪsk/ ADJ (**brisker**, **briskest**) **1** A **brisk** activity or action is done quickly and in an energetic way. □ *Taking a brisk walk can often induce a feeling of well-being.* **2** If trade or business is **brisk**, things are being sold very quickly and a lot of money is being made. = good □ *Vendors were doing a brisk trade in souvenirs.* **3** If the weather is **brisk**, it is cold and fresh. = bracing □ *a typically brisk winter's day on the south coast* **4** Someone who is **brisk** behaves in a busy, confident way which shows that they want to get things done quickly. = businesslike ❑ *The Chief summoned me downstairs. He was brisk and businesslike.*

brisk·ly /'brɪskli/ ADV **1** [briskly with V] ❑ *Eve walked briskly down the corridor to her son's room.* **2** [briskly after V] ❑ *A trader said gold sold briskly on the local market.* **3** [briskly with V] ❑ *'Anyhow,' she added briskly, 'it's none of my business.'*

brit·tle /'brɪtl/ ADJ An object or substance that is **brittle** is hard but easily broken. ❑ *Pine is brittle and breaks.*

⊕**broad** ♦♦◊ /brɔːd/ ADJ (**broader, broadest**)
1 Something that is **broad** is wide. ❑ *His shoulders were broad and his waist narrow.* ❑ *The hills rise green and sheer above the broad river.* **2** A **broad** smile is one in which your mouth is stretched very wide because you are very pleased or amused. ❑ *He greeted them with a wave and a broad smile.* **3** You use **broad** to describe something that includes a large number of different things or people. = wide ❑ *A broad range of issues was discussed.* ❑ *a broad coalition of workers, peasants, students and middle-class professionals* **4** You use **broad** to describe a word or meaning which covers or refers to a wide range of different things. = general ❑ *restructuring in the broad sense of the word* **5** [broad + N] You use **broad** to describe a feeling or opinion that is shared by many people, or by people of many different kinds. = widespread ❑ *The agreement won broad support in the US Congress.*
✦ in broad daylight → see daylight

broad·band /'brɔːdbænd/ NOUN [U] [oft broadband + N] (*computing*) **Broadband** is a method of sending many electronic messages at the same time by using a wide range of frequencies. ❑ *A recent study shows many broadband services lack basic security features.*

⊕**broad·cast** ♦◊◊ /'brɔːdkɑːst, -kæst/ NOUN, VERB
NOUN [C] (**broadcasts**) A **broadcast** is a programme, performance, or speech on the radio or on television. = programme, transmission ❑ *In a broadcast on state radio the government announced that it was willing to resume peace negotiations.* ❑ *the first live television broadcast of a presidential news conference*
VERB [I, T] (**broadcasts, broadcasting, broadcast**) To **broadcast** a programme means to send it out by radio waves, wires, or satellites so that it can be heard on the radio or seen on television. = transmit, relay ❑ *The concert will be broadcast live on television and radio.* ❑ *CNN also broadcasts in Europe.*

broad·cast·er /'brɔːdkɑːstə, -kæst-/ NOUN [C] (**broadcasters**) A **broadcaster** is someone who gives talks or takes part in interviews and discussions on radio or television programmes. ❑ *the prominent naturalist and broadcaster, Sir David Attenborough*

broad·cast·ing ♦◊◊ /'brɔːdkɑːstɪŋ, -kæst-/ NOUN [U] **Broadcasting** is the making and sending out of television and radio programmes. ❑ *If this happens it will change the face of religious broadcasting.*

⊕**broad·en** /'brɔːdən/ VERB [I, T] (**broadens, broadening, broadened**) **1** [I] When something **broadens**, it becomes wider. = widen; ≠ narrow ❑ *The trails broadened into roads.* **2** [I, T] When you **broaden** something such as your experience or popularity, or when it **broadens**, the number of things or people that it includes becomes greater. = widen, increase, expand; ≠ narrow, limit ❑ *We must broaden our appeal.* ❑ *I thought you wanted to broaden your horizons.* ❑ *The political spectrum has broadened.*

⊕**broad·ly** /'brɔːdli/ ADV **1** If you smile **broadly**, you smile with your mouth stretched very wide because you are very pleased or amused. ❑ *Charles grinned broadly.* **2** [broadly with V] You can use **broadly** to indicate that something includes a large number of different things or people. ❑ *Such policies will do little to resolve long-standing problems more broadly affecting America's global competitiveness.* **3** [broadly with V] You can use **broadly** to indicate that a word or meaning covers or refers to a wide range of different things. ❑ *We define education very broadly and students can study any aspect of its consequences for society.* **4** [broadly with V] You can use **broadly** to indicate that a feeling or opinion is shared by many people, or by people of many different kinds. ❑ *The new law has been broadly welcomed by road safety organizations.* **5** [broadly

with V] You can use **broadly** to indicate that something is generally true. = largely ❑ *The president broadly got what he wanted out of his meeting.*

bro·chure /'brəʊʃə, AmE brəʊ'ʃʊr/ NOUN [C] (**brochures**) A **brochure** is a thin magazine with pictures that gives you information about a product or service. ❑ *travel brochures*

broke /brəʊk/ IRREG FORM, ADJ
IRREG FORM **Broke** is the past tense of **break**.
ADJ [V-LINK + broke] (*informal*) If you are **broke**, you have no money. ❑ *What do you mean, I've got enough money? I'm as broke as you are.*
PHRASE **go broke** (*informal*) If a company or person **goes broke**, they lose money and are unable to continue in business or to pay their debts. ❑ *Balton went broke twice in his career.*

bro·ken /'brəʊkən/ IRREG FORM, ADJ
IRREG FORM **Broken** is the past participle of **break**.
ADJ **1** [broken + N] A **broken** line is not continuous but has gaps or spaces in it. = dotted ❑ *A broken blue line means the course of a waterless valley.* **2** [broken + N] You can use **broken** to describe a marriage that has ended in divorce, or a home in which the parents of the family are divorced, when you think this is a sad or bad thing. ❑ *She spoke for the first time about the traumas of a broken marriage.* **3** [broken + N] If someone talks in **broken** English, for example, or in **broken** French, they speak slowly and make a lot of mistakes because they do not know the language very well. ❑ *Eric could only respond in broken English.*

bro·ker ♦◊◊ /'brəʊkə/ NOUN, VERB
NOUN [C] (**brokers**) (*business*) A **broker** is a person whose job is to buy and sell securities, foreign money, real estate, or goods for other people.
VERB [T] (**brokers, brokering, brokered**) If a country or government **brokers** an agreement, a ceasefire, or a round of talks, they try to negotiate or arrange it. = negotiate ❑ *The United Nations brokered a peace in Mogadishu at the end of March.*

bronze /brɒnz/ NOUN, COLOUR
NOUN [U] **Bronze** is a yellowish-brown metal which is a mixture of copper and tin. ❑ *a bronze statue of Giorgi Dimitrov*
COLOUR Something that is **bronze** is yellowish-brown in colour. ❑ *Her hair shone bronze and gold.*

broth·er ♦♦♦ /'brʌðə/ NOUN [C] (**brothers**)

The old-fashioned form **brethren** is still sometimes used as the plural for meanings 2 and 3.

1 Your **brother** is a boy or a man who has the same parents as you. ❑ *Oh, so you're Peter's younger brother.* **2** You can describe a man as your **brother** if he belongs to the same race, religion, country, or profession as you, or if he has similar ideas to you. ❑ *He told reporters he'd come to be with his Latvian brothers.* **3** **Brother** is a title given to a man who belongs to a religious community such as a monastery. ❑ *Brother Otto* **4** **Brothers** is used in the names of some companies and shops. ❑ *the film company Warner Brothers*

brother·hood /'brʌðəhʊd/ NOUN [U, C] (**brotherhoods**) **1** [U] **Brotherhood** is the affection and loyalty that you feel for people who you have something in common with. ❑ *People threw flowers into the river between the two countries as a symbolic act of brotherhood.* **2** [C] A **brotherhood** is an organization whose members all have the same political aims and beliefs or the same job or profession. ❑ *the Brotherhood of Locomotive Engineers*

brother-in-law NOUN [C] (**brothers-in-law**) Someone's **brother-in-law** is the brother of their husband or wife, or the man who is married to their sister.

brought /brɔːt/ IRREG FORM **Brought** is the past tense and past participle of **bring**.

brow /braʊ/ NOUN [C] (**brows**) **1** Your **brow** is your forehead. = forehead ❑ *He wiped his brow with the back of his hand.* **2** [usu pl] Your **brows** are your eyebrows. ❑ *He had thick brown hair and shaggy brows.* **3** The **brow** of a hill is the top part of it. ❑ *He was on the lookout just below the brow of the hill.*

brown ♦♦♦ /braʊn/ COLOUR, ADJ, VERB

COLOUR Something that is **brown** is the colour of earth or of wood. ❑ *her deep brown eyes*

ADJ (**browner, brownest**) **1** You can describe a white-skinned person as **brown** when they have been sitting in the sun until their skin has become darker than usual. = tanned **2** **Brown** is used to describe grains that have not had their outer layers removed, and foods made from these grains. ❑ *brown bread* ❑ *spicy tomato sauce served over a bed of brown rice*

VERB [I, T] (**browns, browning, browned**) When food **browns** or when you **brown** food, you cook it, usually for a short time on a high flame. ❑ *Cook for ten minutes until the sugar browns.*

browse /braʊz/ VERB, NOUN

VERB [I] (**browses, browsing, browsed**) **1** If you **browse** in a shop, you look at things in a fairly casual way, in the hope that you might find something you like. ❑ *I stopped in several bookshops to browse.* ❑ *She browsed in an upscale antiques shop.* **2** If you **browse through** a book or magazine, you look through it in a fairly casual way. ❑ *sitting on the sofa browsing through the TV pages of the paper* **3** (*computing*) If you **browse** on a computer, you search for information in computer files or on the Internet, especially on the World Wide Web. ❑ *Try browsing around in the network bulletin boards.*

NOUN [C] (**browses**) If you have a **browse** in a shop, you look at things in a fairly casual way, in the hope that you might find something you like. ❑ *a browse around the shops*

brows•er /ˈbraʊzə/ NOUN [C] (**browsers**) (*computing*) A **browser** is a piece of computer software that you use to search for information on the Internet, especially on the World Wide Web. ❑ *You need an up-to-date Web browser.*

bruise /bruːz/ NOUN, VERB

NOUN [C] (**bruises**) **1** A **bruise** is an injury that appears as a purple mark on your body, although the skin is not broken. ❑ *How did you get that bruise on your cheek?* **2** If a fruit, vegetable, or plant has a **bruise**, it has been damaged by being handled roughly, and has a mark on the skin. ❑ *bruises on the fruit's skin*

VERB [I, T] (**bruises, bruising, bruised**) **1** [I, T] If you **bruise** a part of your body, a bruise appears on it, for example because something hits you. If you **bruise** easily, bruises appear when something hits you only slightly. ❑ *I had only bruised my knee.* **2** [I, T] If a fruit, vegetable, or plant **bruises** or **is bruised**, it is damaged by being handled roughly, making a mark on the skin. ❑ *Choose a warm, dry day to cut them off the plants, being careful not to bruise them.* ❑ *bruised tomatoes and cucumbers* **3** [T] If you **are bruised** by an unpleasant experience, it makes you feel unhappy or upset. ❑ *The government will be severely bruised by yesterday's events.*

bruised /bruːzd/ ADJ ❑ *I escaped with severely bruised legs.*

brunt /brʌnt/ NOUN

PHRASE **bear the brunt of** or **take the brunt of** To bear the brunt or take the brunt of something unpleasant means to suffer the main part or force of it. ❑ *Young people are bearing the brunt of unemployment.*

brush ♦◇◇ /brʌʃ/ NOUN, VERB

NOUN [C, SING, U] (**brushes**) **1** [C] A **brush** is an object that has a large number of bristles or hairs fixed to it. You use brushes for painting, for cleaning things, and for making your hair neat. ❑ *We gave him paint and brushes.* ❑ *Stains are removed with buckets of soapy water and scrubbing brushes.* **2** [SING] If you give something a **brush** you clean it or make it neat using a brush. ❑ *I gave it a quick brush with my hairbrush.* **3** [C] If you have a **brush with** a particular situation, usually an unpleasant one, you almost experience it. = encounter ❑ *the trauma of a brush with death* **4** [U] **Brush** is an area of rough open land covered with small bushes and trees. You also use **brush** to refer to the bushes and trees on this land. = bush ❑ *the brush fire that destroyed nearly 500 acres*

VERB [T, I] (**brushes, brushing, brushed**) **1** [T] If you **brush** something or **brush** something such as dirt off it, you clean it or make it neat using a brush. ❑ *Have you brushed your teeth?* ❑ *She brushed the powder out of her hair.* **2** [T] If you **brush** something **with** a liquid, you apply a layer of that liquid using a brush. ❑ *Brush the dough with beaten egg yolk.* **3** [T] If you **brush** something somewhere, you remove it with quick light movements of your hands. ❑ *He brushed his hair back with both hands.* ❑ *She brushed away tears as she spoke of him.* **4** [I, T] If one thing **brushes against** another or if you **brush** one thing **against** another, the first thing touches the second thing lightly while passing it. ❑ *Something brushed against her leg.* ❑ *I felt her dark brown hair brushing the back of my shoulder.*

PHRASAL VERBS **brush aside** or **brush away** If you **brush aside** or **brush away** an idea, remark, or feeling, you refuse to consider it because you think it is not important or useful, even though it may be. = dismiss ❑ *Perhaps you shouldn't brush the idea aside too hastily.*

brush off If someone **brushes** you **off** when you speak to them, they refuse to talk to you or be nice to you. ❑ *When I tried to talk to her about it she just brushed me off.*

brush up or **brush up on** If you **brush up** something or **brush up on** something, you practise it or improve your knowledge of it. ❑ *I had hoped to brush up my Spanish.*

bru•tal /ˈbruːtəl/ ADJ **1** A **brutal** act or person is cruel and violent. = vicious, savage ❑ *He was the victim of a very brutal murder.* ❑ *the brutal suppression of anti-government protests* **2** If someone expresses something unpleasant with **brutal** honesty or frankness, they express it in a clear and accurate way, without attempting to disguise its unpleasantness. ❑ *It was refreshing to talk about themselves and their feelings with brutal honesty.*

bru•tal•ly /ˈbruːtəli/ ADV **1** Her real parents had been brutally murdered. **2** The talks had been brutally frank.

bru•tal•ity /bruːˈtæliti/ NOUN [C, U] (**brutalities**) **Brutality** is cruel and violent treatment or behaviour. A **brutality** is an instance of cruel and violent treatment or behaviour. ❑ *Her experience of men was of domination and brutality.* ❑ *police brutality*

brute /bruːt/ NOUN [C] (**brutes**) (*disapproval*) If you call someone, usually a man, a **brute**, you mean that they are rough, violent, and insensitive. ❑ *Custer was an idiot and a brute and he deserved his fate.*

bub•ble /ˈbʌbəl/ NOUN, VERB

NOUN [C] (**bubbles**) **1** **Bubbles** are small balls of air or gas in a liquid. ❑ *Ink particles attach themselves to air bubbles and rise to the surface.* **2** A **bubble** is a hollow ball of soapy liquid that is floating in the air or standing on a surface. ❑ *With soap and water, bubbles and boats, children love bathtime.* **3** In a cartoon, a speech **bubble** is the shape which surrounds the words which a character is thinking or saying. ❑ *All that was missing were speech bubbles saying, 'Golly!' and 'Wow!'*

VERB [I] (**bubbles, bubbling, bubbled**) **1** When a liquid **bubbles**, bubbles move in it, for example because it is boiling or moving quickly. ❑ *Heat the seasoned stock until it is bubbling.* ❑ *The fermenting wine has bubbled up and over the top.* **2** A feeling, influence, or activity that **is bubbling** away continues to occur. ❑ *political tensions that have been bubbling away for years*

buck /bʌk/ NOUN, ADJ, VERB

NOUN [C] (**bucks**) **1** (*informal*) A **buck** is a US or Australian dollar. = dollar ❑ *That would probably cost you about fifty bucks.* ❑ *Why can't you spend a few bucks on a coat?* **2** A **buck** is the male of various animals, including the deer, antelope, rabbit, and kangaroo.

PHRASE **pass the buck** (*informal*) If you **pass the buck**, you refuse to accept responsibility for something, and say that someone else is responsible. ❑ *David says the responsibility is Mr Smith's and it's no good trying to pass the buck.*

ADJ [buck + N] If someone has **buck** teeth, their upper front teeth stick forwards out of their mouth.

VERB [I, T] (**bucks, bucking, bucked**) **1** [I] If a horse **bucks**, it kicks both of its back legs wildly into the air, or jumps into the air wildly with all four feet off the ground. ❑ *The stallion bucked as he fought against the reins holding him tightly in.* **2** [T] If you **buck** the trend, you obtain different results from others in the same area. If you **buck** the system, you get what you want by breaking or ignoring the rules.

b

B

□ *While other newspapers are losing circulation, we are bucking the trend.* □ *He wants to be the tough rebel who bucks the system.*

buck·et /'bʌkɪt/ NOUN [c] (**buckets**) **1** A **bucket** is a round metal or plastic container with a handle attached to its sides. Buckets are often used for holding and carrying water. □ *We drew water in a bucket from the well outside the door.* **2** A **bucket of** something such as water is the amount of it that is contained in a bucket. □ *She threw a bucket of water over them.*

bud /bʌd/ NOUN

NOUN [c] (**buds**) A **bud** is a small pointed lump that appears on a tree or plant and develops into a leaf or flower. □ *Rosanna's favourite time is early summer, just before the buds open.*

PHRASE **nip something in the bud** (*informal*) If you **nip** something such as bad behaviour **in the bud**, you stop it before it can develop very far. □ *It is important to recognize jealousy and to nip it in the bud before it gets out of hand.*
→ See also **budding**

Bud·dhism /'bʊdɪzəm/ NOUN [u] **Buddhism** is a religion which teaches that the way to end suffering is by overcoming your desires.

bud·ding /'bʌdɪŋ/ ADJ **1** [budding + N] If you describe someone as, for example, a **budding** businessman or a **budding** artist, you mean that they are starting to succeed or become interested in business or art. □ *The forum is now open to all budding entrepreneurs.* **2** [budding + N] You use **budding** to describe a situation that is just beginning. □ *Our budding romance was over.*

◆budg·et ◆◆◇ /'bʌdʒɪt/ NOUN, VERB, ADJ
NOUN [c] (**budgets**) (*business*) **1** Your **budget** is the amount of money that you have available to spend. The **budget** for something is the amount of money that a person, organization, or country has available to spend on it. □ *This year's budget for AIDS prevention probably won't be much higher.* □ *She will design a fantastic new kitchen for you – and all within your budget.* □ *Someone had furnished the place on a tight budget.* **2** The **budget** of an organization or country is its financial situation, considered as the difference between the money it receives and the money it spends. □ *The hospital obviously needs to balance the budget each year.*

VERB [i, t] (**budgets, budgeting, budgeted**) If you **budget** certain amounts of money for particular things, you decide that you can afford to spend those amounts on those things. □ *The company has budgeted $10 million for advertising.* □ *The movie is only budgeted at $10 million.* □ *I'm learning how to budget.*

PHRASAL VERB **budget for** If you **budget for** something, you take account of it when you are deciding how much you can afford to spend on different things. = allow for □ *The authorities had budgeted for some non-payment.*

ADJ [budget + N] **Budget** is used in advertising to suggest that something is being sold cheaply. = economy □ *Cheap flights are available from budget travel agents from $240.*

budg·et·ing /'bʌdʒətɪŋ/ NOUN [u] □ *We have continued to exercise caution in our budgeting for the current year.*

buff /bʌf/ COLOUR, NOUN

COLOUR Something that is **buff** is pale brown in colour. □ *He took a largish buff envelope from his pocket.*

NOUN [c] (**buffs**) (*informal*) You use **buff** to describe someone who knows a lot about a particular subject. For example, if you describe someone as a film **buff**, you mean that they know a lot about films. = enthusiast □ *Judge Lanier is a real film buff.*

buff·er /'bʌfə/ NOUN, VERB

NOUN [c] (**buffers**) **1** A **buffer** is something that prevents something else from being harmed or that prevents two things from harming each other. □ *Keep savings as a buffer against unexpected cash needs.* **2** (*computing*) A **buffer** is an area in a computer's memory where information can be stored for a short time.

VERB [t] (**buffers, buffering, buffered**) If something is **buffered**, it is protected from harm. □ *The company is buffered by long-term contracts with growers.*

buf·fet NOUN, VERB
NOUN /'bʊfeɪ/ [c] (**buffets**) **1** A **buffet** is a meal of food that is displayed on a long table at a party or public occasion. Guests usually serve themselves. □ *a buffet lunch* **2** A **buffet** is a café, usually in a hotel or station. □ *We sat in the station buffet sipping tea.*

VERB /'bʌfɪt/ [t] (**buffets, buffeting, buffeted**) If something **is buffeted** by strong winds or by stormy seas, it is repeatedly struck or blown around by them. □ *Their plane had been severely buffeted by storms.*

bug /bʌg/ NOUN, VERB
NOUN [c] (**bugs**) **1** (*informal*) A **bug** is an insect or similar small creature. □ *We noticed tiny bugs that were all over the walls.* **2** (*informal*) A **bug** is an illness which is caused by small organisms such as bacteria. □ *I think I've got a bit of a stomach bug.* **3** (*computing*) If there is a **bug** in a computer program, there is a mistake in it. □ *There is a bug in the software.* **4** A **bug** is a tiny hidden microphone that transmits what people are saying. □ *There was a bug on the phone.*

VERB [t] (**bugs, bugging, bugged**) **1** If someone **bugs** a place, they hide tiny microphones in it that transmit what people are saying. □ *He heard that they were planning to bug his office.* **2** (*informal*) If someone or something **bugs** you, they worry or annoy you. □ *I only did it to bug my parents.*

◆build ◆◆◆ /bɪld/ VERB, NOUN
VERB [t, i] (**builds, building, built**) **1** [t] If you **build** something, you make it by joining things together. = construct □ *Developers are now proposing to build a hotel on the site.* □ *The house was built in the early 19th century.* **2** [t] If you **build** something **into** a wall or object, you make it in such a way that it is in the wall or object, or is part of it. □ *If the TV was built into the ceiling, you could lie there while watching your favourite programme.* **3** [t] If people **build** an organization, a society, or a relationship, they gradually form it. = create, establish □ *He and a partner set up on their own and built a successful fashion company.* □ *Their purpose is to build a fair society and a strong economy.* **4** [t] If you **build** an organization, system, or product **on** something, you base it on it. □ *We will then have a firmer foundation of fact on which to build theories.* **5** [t] If you **build** something **into** a policy, system, or product, you make it part of it. = incorporate □ *We have to build computers into the school curriculum.* **6** [t] To **build** someone's confidence or trust means to increase it gradually. □ *Diplomats hope the meetings will build mutual trust.* **7** [i] If you **build on** the success of something, you take advantage of this success in order to make further progress. □ *The new regime has no successful economic reforms on which to build.* **8** [i] If pressure, speed, sound, or excitement **builds**, it gradually becomes greater. □ *Pressure built yesterday for postponement of the ceremony.*

PHRASAL VERB **build up** **1** Build up means the same as build VERB 6. □ *The delegations had begun to build up some trust in one another.* **2** Build up means the same as build VERB 8. □ *We can build up the speed gradually and safely.* **3** If you build up something or if it builds up, it gradually becomes bigger, for example, because more is added to it. □ *The regime built up the largest army in Africa.* □ *The collection has been built up over the last seventeen years.* **4** If you build someone up, you help them to feel stronger or more confident, especially when they have had a bad experience or have been ill. □ *Build her up with kindness and a sympathetic ear.* **5** If you build someone or something up, you make them seem important or exciting, for example, by talking about them a lot. □ *The media will report on it and the tabloids will build it up.* □ *The soccer community built him up as the saviour of the sport.* **6** → See also **build-up, built-up**

NOUN [c, u] (**builds**) Someone's **build** is the shape that their bones and muscles give to their body. □ *He's described as around thirty years old, six feet tall and of medium build.*
→ See also **building, built**

build·er /'bɪldə/ NOUN [c] (**builders**) A **builder** is a person whose job is to build or repair houses and other buildings. □ *The builders have finished the roof.*

build·ing ♦♦♦ /ˈbɪldɪŋ/ NOUN [C, U] (**buildings**) **1** [C] A **building** is a structure that has a roof and walls, for example a house or a factory. ❑ *They were on the upper floor of the building.* **2** [U] **Building** is the act of making something by joining things together. ❑ *In Japan, the building of Kansai airport continues.* **3** [U] The **building** of an organization, a society, or a relationship, is the process by which it is gradually formed. ❑ *the building of the great civilizations of the ancient world*

build-up also **buildup, build up** NOUN [C] (**build-ups**) **1** A **build-up** is a gradual increase in something. ❑ *There has been a build-up of troops on both sides of the border.* **2** The **build-up** to an event is the way that journalists, advertisers, or other people talk about it a lot in the period of time immediately before it, and try to make it seem important and exciting. ❑ *The exams came, almost an anticlimax after the build-up that the students had given them.*

built /bɪlt/ IRREG FORM, ADJ
 IRREG FORM **Built** is the past tense and past participle of **build**.
 ADJ **1** Something that is **built** has been made by joining things together. ❑ *Even newly built houses can need repairs.* ❑ *It's a product built for safety.* **2** If you say that someone is **built** in a particular way, you are describing the kind of body they have. ❑ *a strong, powerfully-built man of 60*

built-in ADJ [built-in + N] **Built-in** devices or features are included in something as a part of it, rather than being separate. = fitted ❑ *modern cameras with built-in flash units*

built-up ADJ A **built-up** area is an area such as a town or city which has a lot of buildings in it. ❑ *A speed limit of 30 mph was introduced in built-up areas.*

bulb /bʌlb/ NOUN [C] (**bulbs**) **1** A **bulb** is the glass part of an electric light or lamp, which gives out light when electricity passes through it. = light bulb ❑ *The stairwell was lit by a single bulb.* **2** A **bulb** is a root shaped like an onion that grows into a flower or plant. ❑ *tulip bulbs*

bulge /bʌldʒ/ VERB, NOUN
 VERB [I] (**bulges, bulging, bulged**) **1** If something such as a person's stomach **bulges**, it sticks out. ❑ *Jiro waddled closer, his belly bulging and distended.* ❑ *He bulges out of his black T-shirt.* **2** If someone's eyes or veins **are bulging**, they seem to stick out a lot, often because the person is making a strong physical effort or is experiencing a strong emotion. = protrude ❑ *He shouted at his brother, his neck veins bulging.* **3** If you say that something **is bulging with** things, you are emphasizing that it is full of them. ❑ *They returned home with the car bulging with boxes.*
 NOUN [C] (**bulges**) **1** **Bulges** are lumps that stick out from a surface which is otherwise flat or smooth. ❑ *Why won't those bulges on your hips and thighs go?* **2** If there is a **bulge** in something, there is a sudden large increase in it. ❑ *a bulge in aircraft sales*

✪ **bulk** /bʌlk/ NOUN, QUANT, PRON (*academic word*)
 NOUN [SING] **1** You can refer to something's **bulk** when you want to emphasize that it is very large. ❑ *The truck pulled out of the lot, its bulk unnerving against the dawn.* **2** You can refer to a large person's body or to their weight or size as their **bulk**. ❑ *Bannol lowered his bulk carefully into the chair.*
 PHRASE **in bulk** If you buy or sell something **in bulk**, you buy or sell it in large quantities. ❑ *Buying in bulk is more economical than shopping for small quantities.*
 QUANT ['the' bulk 'of' DEF-N] The **bulk of** something is most of it. = majority ❑ *The bulk of the text is essentially a review of these original documents.* ❑ *The vast bulk of imports and exports are carried by sea.*
 PRON The **bulk** is most of something. ❑ *They come from all over the world, though the bulk is from the Indian subcontinent.*
 PHRASAL VERB **bulk up** (**bulks, bulking, bulked**) If someone **bulks up** or if they **bulk up** their body, they put on weight in the form of extra muscle. ❑ *They feel I need to bulk up, and to improve my upper body strength.* ❑ *My friend is obsessed with going to the gym and has really bulked up her arms.*

bulky /ˈbʌlki/ ADJ (**bulkier, bulkiest**) Something that is **bulky** is large and heavy. Bulky things are often difficult to move or deal with. ❑ *bulky items like lawn mowers*

bull /bʊl/ NOUN [C, U] (**bulls**) **1** [C] A **bull** is a male animal of the cow family. **2** [C] Some other male animals, including elephants and whales, are called **bulls**. ❑ *Suddenly a massive bull elephant with huge tusks charged us.* **3** [C] (*business*) In the stock market, **bulls** are people who buy shares in expectation of a price rise, in order to make a profit by selling the shares again after a short time. Compare **bear** NOUN 2. ❑ *The bulls argue stock prices are low and there are bargains to be had.* **4** [C] In the Roman Catholic church, a papal **bull** is an official statement on a particular subject that is issued by the pope. = decree **5** [U] (*informal*) If you say that something is **bull** or a load of **bull**, you mean that it is complete nonsense or absolutely untrue. ❑ *I think it's a load of bull.*

bull·doz·er /ˈbʊldəʊzə/ NOUN [C] (**bulldozers**) A **bulldozer** is a large vehicle with a broad metal blade at the front, which is used for knocking down buildings or moving large amounts of earth.

bul·let /ˈbʊlɪt/ NOUN
 NOUN [C] (**bullets**) A **bullet** is a small piece of metal with a pointed or rounded end, which is fired out of a gun. ❑ *Two of the police fired sixteen bullets each.*
 PHRASE **bite the bullet** (*journalism*) If someone **bites the bullet**, they accept that they have to do something unpleasant but necessary. ❑ *Tour operators may be forced to bite the bullet and cut prices.*

bul·letin /ˈbʊlɪtɪn/ NOUN [C] (**bulletins**) **1** A **bulletin** is a short news report on the radio or television. ❑ *the early morning news bulletin* **2** A **bulletin** is a short official announcement made publicly to inform people about an important matter. ❑ *At 3.30 p.m. a bulletin was released announcing that the president was out of immediate danger.* **3** A **bulletin** is a regular newspaper or leaflet that is produced by an organization or group such as a school or church.

bul·letin board NOUN [C] (**bulletin boards**) In computing, a **bulletin board** is a system that enables users to send and receive messages of general interest. ❑ *The Internet is the largest computer bulletin board in the world, and it's growing.*

bullet·proof /ˈbʊlɪtˌpruːf/ also **bullet-proof** ADJ Something that is **bulletproof** is made of a strong material that bullets cannot pass through. ❑ *bulletproof glass*

bul·ly /ˈbʊli/ NOUN, VERB
 NOUN [C] (**bullies**) A **bully** is someone who uses their strength or power to hurt or frighten other people. ❑ *I fell victim to the office bully.*
 VERB [T] (**bullies, bullying, bullied**) **1** If someone **bullies** you, they use their strength or power to hurt or frighten you. ❑ *I wasn't going to let him bully me.* **2** If someone **bullies** you **into** something, they make you do it by using force or threats. ❑ *We think an attempt to bully them into submission would be counterproductive.* ❑ *She used to bully me into doing my schoolwork.*

bul·ly·ing /ˈbʊliɪŋ/ NOUN [U] ❑ *schoolchildren who were victims of bullying*

bump /bʌmp/ VERB, NOUN
 VERB [I, T] (**bumps, bumping, bumped**) **1** [I, T] If you **bump into** something or someone, you accidentally hit them while you are moving. ❑ *They stopped walking and he almost bumped into them.* ❑ *She bumped her head against a low branch.* **2** [I] If a vehicle **bumps over** a surface, it travels in a rough, bouncing way because the surface is very uneven. ❑ *We left the road, and again bumped over the mountainside.*
 PHRASAL VERB **bump into** (*informal*) If you **bump into** someone you know, you meet them unexpectedly. = run into ❑ *I happened to bump into Mervyn Johns in the hallway.*
 NOUN [C] (**bumps**) **1** A **bump** is when you accidentally hit something while you are moving. ❑ *Small children often cry after a minor bump.* **2** A **bump** is the action or the dull sound of two heavy objects hitting each other. ❑ *I felt a little bump and I knew instantly what had happened.* **3** A **bump** is a minor injury or swelling that you get if you bump into something or if something hits you. = lump ❑ *She fell against our coffee table and got a large bump on her*

b

B

forehead. **4** A **bump** on a road is a raised, uneven part. ❑ *The truck hit a bump and bounced.*

bunch ◆◇◇ /bʌntʃ/ NOUN

NOUN [c] (**bunches**) **1** (*informal*) A **bunch of** people is a group of people who share one or more characteristics or who are doing something together. = lot ❑ *My neighbours are a bunch of busybodies.* ❑ *We were a pretty inexperienced bunch of people really.* **2** A **bunch of** flowers is a number of flowers with their stalks held or tied together. ❑ *He had left a huge bunch of flowers in her hotel room.* **3** A **bunch of** bananas or grapes is a group of them growing on the same stem. ❑ *Lili had fallen asleep clutching a fat bunch of grapes.* **4** A **bunch of** keys is a set of keys kept together on a metal ring. ❑ *George took out a bunch of keys and went to work on the complicated lock.*

PHRASAL VERB **bunch up** or **bunch together** (**bunches**, **bunching**, **bunched**) If people or things **bunch up** or **bunch together**, or if you **bunch** them **up** or **together**, they move close to each other so that they form a small tight group. ❑ *They were bunching up, almost stepping on each other's heels.* ❑ *People were bunched up at all the exits.*

bun•dle /'bʌndəl/ NOUN, VERB

NOUN [c, SING] (**bundles**) **1** [c] A **bundle of** things is a number of them that are tied together or wrapped in a cloth or bag so that they can be carried or stored. ❑ *Lance pulled a bundle of papers out of a folder.* ❑ *He gathered the bundles of clothing into his arms.* **2** [SING] If you describe someone as, for example, a **bundle of** fun, you are emphasizing that they are full of fun. If you describe someone as a **bundle of** nerves, you are emphasizing that they are very nervous. ❑ *I remember Mickey as a bundle of fun, great to have around.* ❑ *Life at high school wasn't a bundle of laughs.* VERB [T] (**bundles**, **bundling**, **bundled**) **1** If someone **is bundled** somewhere, someone pushes them there in a rough and hurried way. ❑ *He was bundled into a car and driven 50 miles to a police station.* **2** (*computing*) To **bundle** software means to sell it together with a computer, or with other hardware or software, as part of a set. ❑ *It's cheaper to buy software bundled with a PC than separately.*

bun•ker /'bʌŋkə/ NOUN [c] (**bunkers**) **1** A **bunker** is a place, usually underground, that has been built with strong walls to protect it against heavy gunfire and bombing. ❑ *an extensive network of fortified underground bunkers* **2** A **bunker** is a container for coal or other fuel. **3** On a golf course, a **bunker** is a large area filled with sand that is deliberately put there as an obstacle that golfers must try to avoid. ❑ *He put his second shot in a bunker to the left of the green.*

buoy /bɔɪ, AmE 'buːi/ NOUN, VERB

NOUN [c] (**buoys**) A **buoy** is a floating object that is used to show ships and boats where they can go and to warn them of danger. VERB [T] (**buoys**, **buoying**, **buoyed**) If someone in a difficult situation **is buoyed** by something, it makes them feel more cheerful and optimistic. ❑ *In May they danced in the streets, buoyed by their victory.* PHRASAL VERB **buoy up** Buoy up means the same as **buoy** VERB. ❑ *They are buoyed up by a sense of hope.*

buoy•ant /'bɔɪənt/ ADJ **1** If you are in a **buoyant** mood, you feel cheerful and behave in a lively way. = cheerful ❑ *You will feel more buoyant and optimistic about the future than you have for a long time.* **2** A **buoyant** economy is a successful one in which there is a lot of trade and economic activity. ❑ *We have a buoyant economy and unemployment is considerably lower than the regional average.* **3** A **buoyant** object floats on a liquid. ❑ *While there is still sufficient trapped air within the container to keep it buoyant, it will float.*

❂**bur•den** ◆◇◇ /'bɜːdən/ NOUN, VERB

NOUN [c] (**burdens**) **1** If you describe a problem or a responsibility as a **burden**, you mean that it causes someone a lot of difficulty, worry, or hard work. ❑ *The developing countries bear the burden of an enormous external debt.* ❑ *Its purpose is to ease the burden on accident and emergency departments by filtering out non-emergency calls.* ❑ *Her death will be an impossible burden on Paul.* **2** (*formal*) A

burden is a heavy load that is difficult to carry. ❑ *African women carrying burdens on their heads* VERB [T] (**burdens**, **burdening**, **burdened**) If someone **burdens** you **with** something that is likely to worry you, for example, a problem or a difficult decision, they tell you about it. ❑ *We decided not to burden him with the news.*

USAGE NOTE

burden

To refer to a more challenging problem or responsibility, use 'a greater burden', 'an additional burden', or 'an extra burden'. Do not use '~~more burdens~~'.

*California's cities must bear a **greater burden** in conserving the state's precious water supplies.*

bu•reau /'bjʊərəʊ/ NOUN [c] (**bureaus**) **1** A **bureau** is an office, organization, or government department that collects and distributes information. ❑ *the Federal Bureau of Investigation* **2** (*BrE*) A **bureau** is a writing desk with shelves and drawers and a lid that opens to form the writing surface.

❂**bu•reau•cra•cy** /bjʊˈrɒkrəsi/ NOUN [c, u] (**bureaucracies**) **1** [c] A **bureaucracy** is an administrative system operated by a large number of officials. ❑ *State bureaucracies can tend to stifle enterprise and initiative.* **2** [u] **Bureaucracy** refers to all the rules and procedures followed by government departments and similar organizations, especially when you think that these are complicated and cause long delays. = red tape, regulations, administration ❑ *People usually complain about too much bureaucracy.*

bu•reau•crat /'bjʊərəkræt/ NOUN [c] (**bureaucrats**) (*disapproval*) **Bureaucrats** are officials who work in a large administrative system. You can refer to officials as bureaucrats especially if you disapprove of them because they seem to follow rules and procedures too strictly. ❑ *The economy is still controlled by bureaucrats.*

❂**bu•reau•crat•ic** /ˌbjʊərəˈkrætɪk/ ADJ (*disapproval*) **Bureaucratic** means involving complicated rules and procedures which can cause long delays. ❑ *Bureaucratic delays are inevitable.* ❑ *The department has become a bureaucratic nightmare.*

bur•glar /'bɜːglə/ NOUN [c] (**burglars**) A **burglar** is a thief who enters a house or other building by force. ❑ *Burglars broke into their home.*

bur•gla•ry /'bɜːgləri/ NOUN [c, u] (**burglaries**) If someone commits a **burglary**, they enter a building by force and steal things. **Burglary** is the act of doing this. ❑ *An 11-year-old boy committed a burglary.*

bur•ial /'beriəl/ NOUN [c, u] (**burials**) A **burial** is the act or ceremony of putting a dead body into a grave in the ground. ❑ *The priest prepared the body for burial.*

❂**burn** ◆◆◇ /bɜːn/ VERB, NOUN

VERB [I, T] (**burns**, **burning**, **burned** or **burnt**) **1** [I] If there is a fire or a flame somewhere, you say that there is a fire or flame **burning** there. ❑ *Fires were burning out of control in the centre of the city.* ❑ *There was a fire burning in the fireplace.* **2** [I] If something **is burning**, it is on fire. ❑ *When I arrived one of the vehicles was still burning.* ❑ *The building housed 1,500 refugees and it burned for hours.* **3** [T] If you **burn** something, you destroy or damage it with fire. ❑ *Protesters set cars on fire and burned a building.* ❑ *Incineration plants should be built to burn household waste.* **4** [I, T] If you **burn** a fuel or if it **burns**, it is used to produce heat, light, or energy. ❑ *The power stations burn coal from the Ruhr region.* **5** [I, T] If you **burn** something that you are cooking or if it **burns**, you spoil it by using too much heat or cooking it for too long. ❑ *I burned the toast.* **6** [T] If you **burn** part of your body, **burn yourself**, or **are burned** or **burnt**, you are injured by fire or by something very hot. ❑ *Take care not to burn your fingers.* **7** [T] If someone **is burned** or **burned** to death, they are killed by fire. ❑ *Women were burned as witches in the Middle Ages.* **8** [I] (*literary*) If a light is **burning**, it is shining. ❑ *The building was darkened except for a single light burning in a third-storey window.* **9** [I, T] If you **burn** or get **burned** in the sun, the sun makes your skin become red and sore. ❑ *Build up your tan slowly and don't allow your skin to burn.* **10** [I, T] If a part of your body **burns**

or if something **burns** it, it has a painful hot or stinging feeling. ◻ *My eyes burn from staring at the needle.* ◻ *His face was burning with cold.* **11** [T] (*computing*) To **burn** a CD means to write or copy data onto it. ◻ *You can use this software to burn custom compilations of your favourite tunes.* PHRASAL VERB **burn down** If a building **burns down** or if someone **burns** it **down**, it is completely destroyed by fire. ◻ *Six months after Bud died, the house burned down.* NOUN [C] (**burns**) A **burn** is an injury caused by fire or by something very hot. ◻ *She suffered appalling burns to her back.* → See also **burning, burnt**
✦ **burn something to the ground** → see **ground**; **burn the midnight oil** → see **midnight**; **have money to burn** → see **money**

burned-out or **burnt-out** ADJ **11** Burned-out vehicles or buildings have been so badly damaged by fire that they can no longer be used. ◻ *a burned-out car* **2** (*informal*) If someone is **burned-out**, they exhaust themselves at an early stage in their life or career because they have achieved too much too quickly. ◻ *Everyone I know who kept it up at that intensity is burned-out.*

burn·er /ˈbɜːnə/ NOUN [C] (**burners**) A **burner** is a device which produces heat or a flame, especially as part of a stove or heater. ◻ *He put the frying pan on the gas burner.*

burn·ing /ˈbɜːnɪŋ/ NOUN, ADJ, ADV
NOUN [U] **11** Burning is the state of being on fire. ◻ *When we arrived in our village there was a terrible smell of burning.* **2** The **burning** of something is its destruction or damage by fire. ◻ *The French government has criticized the burning of a US flag outside the American embassy.*
ADJ **11** You use **burning** to describe something that is extremely hot. = scorching ◻ *the burning desert of central Asia* **2** [burning + N] If you have a **burning** interest in something or a **burning** desire to do something, you are extremely interested in it or want to do it very much. = passionate ◻ *I had a burning ambition to become a journalist.* **3** [burning + N] A **burning** issue or question is a very important or urgent one that people feel very strongly about. ◻ *The burning question in this year's debate over the federal budget is: whose taxes should be raised?*
ADV [burning + ADJ] You use **burning** to describe something that is extremely hot. ◻ *He touched the boy's forehead. It was burning hot.*

burnt /bɜːnt/ IRREG FORM, ADJ
IRREG FORM **Burnt** is a past tense and past participle of **burn**. ADJ If something that you are cooking is **burnt**, you have spoiled it by using too much heat or cooking it for too long. ◻ *the smell of burnt toast*

bur·row /ˈbʌrəʊ, AmE ˈbɜː-/ NOUN, VERB
NOUN [C] (**burrows**) A **burrow** is a tunnel or hole in the ground that is dug by an animal such as a rabbit. ◻ *Normally timid, they rarely stray far from their burrows.*
VERB [I] (**burrows, burrowing, burrowed**) **11** If an animal **burrows** into the ground or into a surface, it moves through it by making a tunnel or hole. = tunnel ◻ *The larvae burrow into cracks in the floor.* **2** If you **burrow** in a container or pile of things, you search there for something using your hands. ◻ *the enthusiasm with which he burrowed through old records in search of facts* **3** If you **burrow** into something, you move underneath or press against it, usually in order to feel warmer or safer. ◻ *She turned her face away from him, burrowing into her heap of covers.*

burst ✦◇◇ /bɜːst/ VERB, NOUN
VERB [I, T] (**bursts, bursting, burst**) **11** [I, T] If something **bursts** or if you **burst** it, it suddenly breaks open or splits open and the air or other substance inside it comes out. ◻ *The driver lost control when a tyre burst.* ◻ *It is not a good idea to burst a blister.* **2** [I, T] If a dam **bursts**, or if something **bursts** it, it breaks apart because the force of the river is too great. ◻ *A dam burst and flooded their villages.* **3** [T] If a river **bursts** its banks, the water rises and goes on to the land. ◻ *Monsoons caused the river to burst its banks.* **4** [I] When a door or lid **bursts** open, it opens very suddenly and violently because someone pushes it or there is great pressure behind it. = fly ◻ *The door burst open and an angry young nurse appeared.* **5** [I] To **burst into** or **out** of a place means to enter or leave it suddenly with a

lot of energy or force. = rush ◻ *Gunmen burst into his home and opened fire.* **6** [I] (*journalism*) If you say that something **bursts** onto the scene, you mean that it suddenly starts or becomes active, usually after developing quietly for some time. ◻ *He burst onto the fashion scene in the early 1980s.*
PHRASAL VERBS **burst into 11** If you **burst into** tears, laughter, or song, you suddenly begin to cry, laugh, or sing. ◻ *She burst into tears and ran from the kitchen.* **2** If you say that something **bursts into** a particular situation or state, you mean that it suddenly changes into that situation or state. ◻ *This weekend's fighting is threatening to burst into full-scale war.*
burst out If someone **bursts out** laughing, crying, or making another noise, they suddenly start making that noise. You can also say that a noise **bursts out**. ◻ *The class burst out laughing.* ◻ *Then the applause burst out.*
NOUN [C] (**bursts**) A **burst** of something is a sudden short period of it. ◻ *a burst of machine-gun fire*
✦ **burst into flames** → see **flame**

bury ✦◇◇ /ˈberi/ VERB [T] (**buries, burying, buried**) **11** To **bury** something means to put it into a hole in the ground and cover it up with earth. ◻ *They make the charcoal by burying wood in the ground and then slowly burning it.* ◻ *squirrels who bury nuts and seeds* **2** To **bury** a dead person means to put their body into a grave and cover it with earth. ◻ *Soldiers helped to bury the dead in large communal graves.* ◻ *I was horrified that people would think I was dead and bury me alive.* **3** If someone says they have **buried** one of their relatives, they mean that one of their relatives has died. ◻ *He had buried his wife some two years before he retired.* **4** If you **bury** something under a large quantity of things, you put it there, often in order to hide it. ◻ *She buried it under some leaves.* **5** If something **buries** a place or person, it falls on top of them so that it completely covers them and often harms them in some way. ◻ *Latest reports say that mud slides buried entire villages.* ◻ *Their house was buried by a landslide.* **6** If you **bury** your head or face in something, you press your head or face against it, often because you are unhappy. = hide ◻ *She buried her face in the pillows.* **7** If something **buries itself** somewhere, or if you **bury** it there, it is pushed very deeply in there. ◻ *The missile buried itself deep in the grassy hillside.*

bus ✦◇◇ /bʌs/ NOUN, VERB
NOUN [C] (**buses**) [also 'by' bus] A **bus** is a large motor vehicle that carries passengers from one place to another. Buses drive along particular routes, and you usually have to pay to travel in them. ◻ *He missed his last bus home.*
VERB [I, T] (**buses** or **busses, busing** or **bussing, bused** or **bussed**) When someone is **bused** to a particular place or when they **bus** there, they travel there on a bus. ◻ *On May Day hundreds of thousands used to be bused in to parade through East Berlin.* ◻ *To get our Colombian visas we bused back to Medellin.*

bush /bʊʃ/ NOUN [C, SING] (**bushes**) **11** [C] A **bush** is a large plant which is smaller than a tree and has a lot of branches. = shrub ◻ *Trees and bushes grew down to the water's edge.* **2** [SING] The wild, uncultivated parts of some hot countries are referred to as **the bush**. ◻ *They walked through the dense Mozambican bush for thirty-six hours.*

busi·ly /ˈbɪzɪli/ ADV [busily with V] If you do something **busily**, you do it in a very active way. ◻ *The two saleswomen were busily trying to keep up with the demand.*

◆ **busi·ness** ✦✦✦ /ˈbɪznɪs/ NOUN
NOUN [U, C, SING] (**businesses**) **11** [U] Business is work relating to the production, buying, and selling of goods or services. ◻ *young people seeking a career in business* ◻ *Jennifer has an impressive academic and business background.* ◻ *Harvard Business School* **2** [U] Business is used when talking about how many products or services a company is able to sell. If **business** is good, a lot of products or services are being sold and if **business** is bad, few of them are being sold. ◻ *They worried that German companies would lose business.* **3** [C] A **business** is an organization that produces and sells goods or that provides a service. = company, firm ◻ *The company was a family business.* ◻ *The majority of small businesses fail within the first twenty-four months.* **4** [U]

B

Business is work or some other activity that you do as part of your job and not for pleasure. ❑ *I'm here on business.* ❑ *You can't mix business with pleasure.* **5** [SING] You can use **business** to refer to a particular area of work or activity in which the aim is to make a profit. ❑ *May I ask you what business you're in?* **6** [SING] You can use **business** to refer to something that you are doing or concerning yourself with. ❑ *recording Ben as he goes about his business* **7** [U] You can use **business** to refer to important matters that you have to deal with. ❑ *The most important business was left to the last.* **8** [U] [POSS + business] If you say that something is your **business**, you mean that it concerns you personally and that other people have no right to ask questions about it or disagree with it. = affair, concern ❑ *My sex life is my business.* ❑ *If she doesn't want the police involved, that's her business.* **9** [SING] You can use **business** to refer in a general way to an event, situation, or activity. For example, you can say something is 'a wretched business' or you can refer to 'this assassination business'. = affair ❑ *We have sorted out this wretched business at last.*

PHRASES **do business** If two people or companies **do business** with each other, one sells goods or services to the other. ❑ *I was fascinated by the different people who did business with me.*

have no business If you say that someone **has no business to** be in a place or **to** do something, you mean that they have no right to be there or to do it. ❑ *Really I had no business to be there at all.*

be in business A company that is **in business** is operating and trading. ❑ *You can't stay in business without cash.*

out of business If a shop or company goes **out of business** or is put **out of business**, it has to stop trading because it is not making enough money. ❑ *Thousands of firms could go out of business.*

business as usual In a difficult situation, if you say it is **business as usual**, you mean that people will continue doing what they normally do. ❑ *For the time being it's business as usual for consumers.*

→ See also **big business**

WORD CONNECTIONS

VERB + **business**

conduct business
❑ *A lot of business is conducted using the Internet.*

start a business
run a business
operate a business
own a business
❑ *Ella runs a successful business selling antique dolls.*

grow a business
build a business
❑ *You should always have a strategy for growing your business.*

ADJ + **business**

big business
local business
global business
❑ *Trade rules favour big business.*

a small business
❑ *We offer legal advice to small businesses.*

VOCABULARY BUILDER

business NOUN

A **business** is an organization that produces and sells goods or that provides a service.
❑ *What on earth made him think he had the capacity to run a publishing business?*

company NOUN

A **company** is a business organization that makes money by selling goods or services.
❑ *He now lives in Rome, working as the head of personnel for a pharmaceutical company.*

corporation NOUN

A **corporation** is a large business that has particular rights and responsibilities.
❑ *Multinational corporations are now among the major forces in the world economy.*

firm NOUN

A **firm** is an organization that makes money selling goods or services.
❑ *Siemens is Europe's biggest engineering firm.*

organization NOUN

An **organization** is a group of people working together in a business, although it is not always with the aim of making money.
❑ *He has built affordable housing through Habitat for Humanity, the nonprofit organization he and his wife helped popularize.*

enterprise NOUN (*written*)

An **enterprise** is a company or business, especially one developing new ideas.
❑ *Many of those state-owned enterprises have been privatized since South Africa's first free election in 1994.*

business·like /ˈbɪznəslaɪk/ ADJ If you describe someone as **businesslike**, you mean that they deal with things in an efficient way without wasting time. = efficient ❑ *Mr Penn sounds quite businesslike.*

business·man ♦◇◇ /ˈbɪznɪsmæn/ NOUN [C] (**businessmen**) A **businessman** is a man who works in business. ❑ *a wealthy businessman who owns a printing business in Orlando*

business·person /ˈbɪznɪsˌpɜːsən/ also **business person** NOUN [C] (**businesspeople**) Businesspeople are people who work in business. ❑ *businesspeople who serve or supply the security forces*

business·woman /ˈbɪznɪswʊmən/ NOUN [C] (**businesswomen**) A **businesswoman** is a woman who works in business. ❑ *a successful businesswoman who runs her own international cosmetics company*

bust /bʌst/ VERB, NOUN, ADJ
VERB [T] (**busts, busting, bust** or **busted**) (*informal*) **1** If you **bust** something, you break it or damage it so badly that it cannot be used. ❑ *They will have to bust the door to get him out.* **2** If someone **is busted**, the police arrest them. ❑ *They were busted for possession of cannabis.* **3** If police **bust** a place, they go to it in order to arrest people who are doing something illegal. ❑ *Police busted an underground network of illegal sports gambling.*
NOUN [C] (**busts**) **1** (*informal*) A **bust** is a police raid or arrest. ❑ *Six tons of cocaine were seized last week in Panama's biggest drug bust.* **2** A **bust** is a statue of the head and shoulders of a person. ❑ *a bronze bust of Thomas Jefferson* **3** You can use **bust** to refer to a woman's breasts, especially when you are describing their size. ❑ *Good posture helps your bust look bigger.*
ADJ (*informal*) A company or fund that is **bust** has no money left and has been forced to close down. ❑ *It is taxpayers who will pay most of the bill for bailing out bust banks.*
PHRASE **go bust** (*informal*) If a company **goes bust**, it loses so much money that it is forced to close down. ❑ *a Swiss company which went bust last May*

bus·tle /ˈbʌsəl/ VERB, NOUN
VERB [I] (**bustles, bustling, bustled**) **1** If someone **bustles** somewhere, they move there in a hurried way, often because they are very busy. ❑ *My mother bustled around the kitchen.* **2** A place that **is bustling** or **bustling with** people or activity is full of people who are very busy or lively. ❑ *The pavements are bustling with people.*
NOUN [U] **Bustle** is busy, noisy activity. ❑ *the hustle and bustle of modern life*

busy ♦◇◇ /ˈbɪzi/ ADJ, VERB
ADJ (**busier, busiest**) **1** When you are **busy**, you are working hard or concentrating on a task, so that you are

not free to do anything else. ▫ *What is it? I'm busy.* ▫ *They are busy preparing for a hectic day's activity on Saturday.* **2** A **busy** time is a period of time during which you have a lot of things to do. = hectic ▫ *It'll have to wait. This is our busiest time.* ▫ *Even with her busy schedule she finds time to watch TV.* **3** [V-LINK + busy] If you say that someone is **busy** thinking or worrying about something, you mean that it is taking all their attention, often to such an extent that they are unable to think about anything else. = preoccupied ▫ *Companies are so busy analysing the financial implications that they overlook the effect on workers.* **4** A **busy** place is full of people who are doing things or moving around. ▫ *a busy commercial street* **5** (mainly AmE; in BrE, usually use **engaged**) When a telephone line is **busy**, you cannot make your call because the line is already being used by someone else. = engaged ▫ *I tried to reach him, but the line was busy.*
VERB [T] (**busies, busying, busied**) If you **busy yourself** with something, you occupy yourself by dealing with it. ▫ *He busied himself with the camera.* ▫ *She busied herself getting towels ready.*
→ See also **busily**

but ◆◆◆ /bət, STRONG bʌt/ CONJ, PREP, ADV
CONJ **1** You use **but** to introduce something that contrasts with what you have just said, or to introduce something that adds to what you have just said. ▫ *'You said you'd stay till tomorrow.'—'I know, Bel, but I think I would rather go back.'* ▫ *Place the saucepan over moderate heat until the cider is very hot but not boiling.* **2** You use **but** when you are about to add something further in a discussion or to change the subject. ▫ *After three weeks, they gradually reduced their sleep to about eight hours. But another interesting thing happened.* **3** You use **but** after you have made an excuse or apologized for what you are just about to say. ▫ *Please excuse me, but there is something I must say.* ▫ *I'm sorry, but it's nothing to do with you.* **4** You use **but** to introduce a reply to someone when you want to indicate surprise, disbelief, refusal, or protest. ▫ *'I don't think I should stay in this house.'—'But why?'*
PHRASES **but then** or **but then again** You use **but then** or **but then again** before a remark which slightly contradicts what you have just said. ▫ *My husband spends hours in the bathroom, but then again so do I.*
but then You use **but then** before a remark which suggests that what you have just said should not be regarded as surprising. ▫ *He was a fine young man, but then so had his father been.*
PREP [N + but + N] **But** is used to mean 'except'. ▫ *Europe will be represented in all but two of the seven races.* ▫ *He didn't speak anything but Greek.*
PHRASE **but for** You use **but for** to introduce the only factor that causes a particular thing not to happen or not to be completely true. ▫ *the small square below, empty but for a dirty white van and a clump of palm trees*
ADV (formal) **But** is used to mean 'only'. ▫ *Zach insists that he is but one among many who are fighting for equality.*
✦ **all but** → see **all**; **anything but** → see **anything**

but·ter ◆◇◇ /'bʌtə/ NOUN, VERB
NOUN [C, U] (**butters**) **Butter** is a soft, yellow substance made from cream. You spread it on bread or use it in cooking. ▫ *bread and butter*
VERB [T] (**butters, buttering, buttered**) If you **butter** something such as bread or toast, you spread butter on it. ▫ *She spread pieces of bread on the counter and began buttering them.*

but·ton ◆◇◇ /'bʌtən/ NOUN, VERB
NOUN [C] (**buttons**) **1** **Buttons** are small, hard objects sewn onto shirts, coats, or other pieces of clothing. You fasten the clothing by pushing the buttons through holes called buttonholes. ▫ *a coat with brass buttons* **2** A **button** is a small object on a machine or electrical device that you press in order to operate it. ▫ *He reached for the remote control and pressed the 'play' button.*
VERB [T] (**buttons, buttoning, buttoned**) If you **button** a shirt, coat, or other piece of clothing, you fasten it by pushing its buttons through the buttonholes. ▫ *Ferguson stood up and buttoned his coat.*

PHRASAL VERB **button up** **Button up** means the same as **button** VERB. ▫ *I buttoned up my coat; it was chilly.* ▫ *The young man slipped on the shirt and buttoned it up.*

buy ◆◆◆ /baɪ/ VERB, NOUN
VERB [T] (**buys, buying, bought**) **1** If you **buy** something, you obtain it by paying money for it. ▫ *He could not afford to buy a house.* ▫ *Lizzie bought herself a mountain bike.* **2** If you talk about the quantity or standard of goods an amount of money **buys**, you are referring to the price of the goods or the value of the money. ▫ *About $70,000 buys a habitable house.* **3** If you **buy** something like time, freedom, or victory, you obtain it but only by offering or giving up something in return. ▫ *It was a risky operation, but might buy more time.* **4** [usu passive] If you say that a person can **be bought**, you are criticizing the fact that they will give their help or loyalty to someone in return for money. = bribe ▫ *Any number of our military and government officials can be bought.* **5** (informal) If you **buy** an idea or a theory, you believe and accept it. ▫ *I'm not buying any of that nonsense.*
PHRASAL VERBS **buy into** **1** (business) If you **buy into** a company or an organization, you buy part of it, often in order to gain some control of it. ▫ *Other companies could buy into the firm.* **2** (informal) If you **buy into** an idea or a theory, you believe and accept it. ▫ *I bought into the popular myth that when I got the new car or the next house, I'd finally be happy.*
buy out (business) If you **buy** someone **out**, you buy their share of something such as a company or piece of property that you previously owned together. ▫ *The bank had to pay to buy out most of the 200 former partners.*
buy up If you **buy up** land, property, or a commodity, you buy large amounts of it, or all that is available. ▫ *The mention of price increases sent citizens out to buy up as much as they could.*
NOUN [C] (**buys**) If something is a good **buy**, it is of good quality and not very expensive. = bargain ▫ *This was still a good buy even at the higher price.*

buy·er ◆◇◇ /'baɪə/ NOUN [C] (**buyers**) **1** A **buyer** is a person who is buying something or who intends to buy it. ▫ *Car buyers are more interested in safety and reliability than speed.* **2** A **buyer** is a person who works for a large shop deciding what goods will be bought from manufacturers to be sold in the shop. ▫ *Diana is a buyer for a chain of furniture shops.*

buzz /bʌz/ VERB, NOUN, ADJ
VERB [I, T] (**buzzes, buzzing, buzzed**) **1** [I] If something **buzzes** or **buzzes** somewhere, it makes a long continuous sound, like the noise a bee makes when it is flying. ▫ *The intercom buzzed and he pressed down the appropriate switch.* **2** [I] (written) If people **are buzzing around**, they are moving around quickly and busily. = race ▫ *A few tourists were buzzing around.* **3** [I] If questions or ideas **are buzzing around** your head, or if your head **is buzzing with** questions or ideas, you are thinking about a lot of things, often in a confused way. ▫ *Many more questions were buzzing around in my head.* **4** [I] If a place **is buzzing with** activity or conversation, there is a lot of activity or conversation there, especially because something important or exciting is about to happen. ▫ *The rehearsal studio is buzzing with lunchtime activity.* **5** [T] If an aircraft **buzzes** a place, it flies low over it, usually in a threatening way. ▫ *American fighter planes buzzed the city.*
NOUN [C, SING] (**buzzes**) **1** [C] A **buzz** is a long continuous sound, like the noise a bee makes when it is flying. ▫ *the irritating buzz of an insect* **2** [SING] You can use **buzz** to refer to a long continuous sound, usually caused by lots of people talking at once. ▫ *A buzz of excitement filled the courtroom as the defendant was led in.* **3** [SING] ['a' buzz] If a place or event has **a buzz** around it, it has a lively, interesting, and modern atmosphere. ▫ *There is a real buzz around the place. Everyone is really excited.*
ADJ [buzz + N] You can use **buzz** to refer to a word, idea, or activity which has recently become extremely popular. ▫ *the latest buzz phrase in garden design circles*

buzz·word /'bʌzwɜːd/ also **buzz word** NOUN [C] (**buzzwords**) A **buzzword** is a word or expression that has become fashionable in a particular field and is being used a lot by the media. ❑ *Biodiversity was the buzzword of the Rio Earth Summit.*

by ♦♦♦ /baɪ/ PREP, ADV

PREP **1** If something is done **by** a person or thing, that person or thing does it. ❑ *The feast was served by his mother and sisters.* ❑ *I was amazed by their discourtesy and lack of professionalism.* **2** If you say that something such as a book, a piece of music, or a painting is **by** a particular person, you mean that this person wrote it or created it. ❑ *A painting by Van Gogh has been sold in New York for more than eighty-two million dollars.* **3** If you do something **by** a particular means, you do it using that thing. ❑ *If you're travelling by car, ask whether there are parking facilities nearby.* **4** [by + -ING] If you achieve one thing **by** doing another thing, your action enables you to achieve the first thing. ❑ *Make the sauce by boiling the cream and stock together in a pan.* ❑ *The all-female yacht crew made history by becoming the first to sail around the world.* **5** You use **by** in phrases such as 'by chance' or 'by accident' to indicate whether or not an event was planned. ❑ *I met him by chance out walking yesterday.* ❑ *He opened Ingrid's letter by mistake.* **6** [ADJ/N + by + N] If someone is a particular type of person **by** nature, **by** profession, or **by** birth, they are that type of person because of their nature, their profession, or the family they were born into. ❑ *I am certainly lucky to have a kind wife who is loving by nature.* ❑ *She's a nurse by profession and now runs a counselling service for women.* **7** If something must be done **by** law, it happens according to the law. If something is the case **by** particular standards, it is the case according to the standards. ❑ *Pharmacists are required by law to give the medicine prescribed by the doctor.* **8** If you say what someone means **by** a particular word or expression, you are saying what they intend the word or expression to refer to. ❑ *Stella knew what he meant by 'start again'.* **9** If you hold someone or something **by** a particular part of them, you hold that part. ❑ *He caught her by the shoulder and turned her around.* ❑ *She was led by the arm to a small room at the far end of the corridor.* **10** Someone or something that is **by** something else is beside it and close to it. ❑ *Judith was sitting in a rocking chair by the window.* ❑ *Felicity Maxwell stood by the bar and ordered a glass of wine.* **11** [v + by + N] If a person or vehicle goes **by** you, they move past you without stopping. ❑ *A few cars passed close by me.* **12** If you stop **by** a place, you visit it for a short time. ❑ *We had made arrangements to stop by her house in Pacific Grove.* **13** If something happens **by** a particular time, it happens at or before that time. ❑ *By eight o'clock he had arrived at my hotel.* **14** If you do something **by** day, you do it during the day. If you do it **by** night, you do it during the night. ❑ *By day a woman could safely walk the streets.* **15** [by + NUM] In arithmetic, you use **by** before the second number in a multiplication or division sum. ❑ *an annual rate of 22.8 per cent (1.9 multiplied by 12)* **16** [by + NUM] You use **by** to talk about measurements of area. For example, if a room is

twenty feet **by** fourteen feet, it measures twenty feet in one direction and fourteen feet in the other direction. ❑ *Three prisoners were sharing one small cell 3 metres by 2½ metres.* **17** [by + AMOUNT] If something increases or decreases **by** a particular amount, that amount is gained or lost. ❑ *Violent crime has increased by 10 per cent since last year.* **18** [by 'the' N] Things that are made or sold **by** the million or **by** the dozen are made or sold in those quantities. ❑ *Packages arrived by the dozen from America.* **19** [N + by + N] You use **by** in expressions such as 'minute by minute' and 'drop by drop' to talk about things that happen gradually, not all at once. ❑ *His father began to lose his memory bit by bit, becoming increasingly forgetful.*

PHRASE **by yourself** **1** If you are **by yourself**, you are alone. = alone ❑ *a dark-haired man sitting by himself in a corner* **2** If you do something **by yourself**, you succeed in doing it without anyone helping you. ❑ *I didn't know if I could raise a child by myself.*

ADV **1** [by after V] **By** means in the surrounding area. ❑ *Large numbers of security police stood by.* **2** [by after V] If a person or vehicle moves **by**, they move past you without stopping. ❑ *The bomb went off as a police patrol went by.* **3** [by after V] If someone stops **by**, they visit a place for a short time. ❑ *I'll stop by after dinner and we'll have that talk.*

bye ♦◇◇ /baɪ/ or **bye-bye**

CONVENTION **Bye** and **bye-bye** are informal ways of saying goodbye. ❑ *Bye, Daddy.*

by·pass /'baɪpɑːs, -pæs/ VERB, NOUN

VERB [T] (**bypasses, bypassing, bypassed**) **1** If you **bypass** someone or something that you would normally have to get involved with, you ignore them, often because you want to achieve something more quickly. = sidestep ❑ *A growing number of employers are trying to bypass the unions altogether.* **2** If a road **bypasses** a place, it goes around it rather than through it. ❑ *money for new roads to bypass cities* **3** If you **bypass** a place when you are travelling, you avoid going through it. ❑ *The rebel forces simply bypassed the town on their way further south.*

NOUN [C] (**bypasses**) **1** A **bypass** is a surgical operation performed on or near the heart, in which the flow of blood is redirected so that it does not flow through a part of the heart that is diseased or blocked. ❑ *heart bypass surgery* **2** A **bypass** is a main road that takes traffic around the edge of a town or city rather than through its centre. ❑ *A new bypass around the city is being built.*

by-product NOUN [C] (**by-products**) A **by-product** is something that is produced during the manufacture or processing of another product. ❑ *The raw material for the tyre is a by-product of petrol refining.*

by·stander /'baɪstændə/ NOUN [C] (**bystanders**) A **bystander** is a person who is present when something happens and who sees it but does not take part in it. ❑ *It looks like an innocent bystander was killed instead of you.*

Cc

C also **c** /siː/ NOUN, ABBREVIATION
■ NOUN [c, u] (**C's, c's**) **1** C is the third letter of the English alphabet. **2** In music, **C** is the first note in the scale of C major. **3** If you get a **C** as a mark for a piece of work or in an exam, your work is average. ■ ABBREVIATION **1** **c.** is written in front of a date or number to indicate that it is approximate. **c.** is an abbreviation for 'circa'. □ *the museum's re-creation of a New York dining room (c. 1825–35)* **2** C or c is used as an abbreviation for words beginning with c, such as 'copyright' or 'Celsius'. □ *Heat the oven to 180°C.*

cab /kæb/ NOUN [c] (**cabs**) **1** A **cab** is a taxi. □ *Could I use your phone to call a cab?* **2** The **cab** of a truck or train is the front part in which the driver sits. □ *The van has additional load space over the driver's cab.*

cab·in /'kæbɪn/ NOUN [c] (**cabins**) **1** A **cabin** is a small wooden house, especially one in an area of forests or mountains. □ *a log cabin* **2** A **cabin** is a small room in a ship or boat. □ *He showed her to a small cabin.* **3** A **cabin** is one of the areas inside a plane. □ *He sat quietly in the first-class cabin of the flight looking tired.*

cabi·net ♦♦◊ /'kæbɪnɪt/ NOUN [c] (**cabinets**) **1** A **cabinet** is a cupboard used for storing things such as medicine or alcoholic drinks or for displaying decorative things in. □ *She looked in the medicine cabinet and found some aspirin.* **2** The **cabinet** is a group of the most senior advisers or ministers in a government, who meet regularly to discuss policies. □ *The announcement came after a three-hour cabinet meeting.* □ *a former cabinet minister*

ca·ble ♦◊◊ /'keɪbəl/ NOUN [c, u] (**cables**) **1** [c, u] A **cable** is a kind of very strong, thick rope, made of wires twisted together. □ *The miners rode a conveyance attached to a cable made of braided steel wire.* **2** [c, u] A **cable** is a thick wire, or a group of wires inside a rubber or plastic covering, which is used to carry electricity or electronic signals. □ *overhead power cables* **3** [u] **Cable** is used to refer to television systems in which the signals are sent along underground wires rather than by radio waves. □ *They ran adverts on cable systems across the country.*

café /'kæfeɪ, AmE kæ'feɪ/ also **cafe** NOUN [c] (**cafés**) **1** A **café** is a place where you can buy drinks, simple meals, and snacks. **2** [N + café] A street **café** or a pavement **café** is a café which has tables and chairs on the pavement outside it where people can eat and drink. □ *an Italian street café* □ *pavement cafés and boutiques*

cage /keɪdʒ/ NOUN [c] (**cages**) A **cage** is a structure of wire or metal bars in which birds or animals are kept. □ *I hate to see birds in cages.*

cake ♦◊◊ /keɪk/ NOUN [c, u] (**cakes**) **1** [c, u] A **cake** is a sweet food made by baking a mixture of flour, eggs, sugar, and fat in an oven. Cakes may be large and cut into slices or small and intended for one person only. □ *a piece of cake* □ *Would you like some chocolate cake?* □ *a birthday cake* **2** [c] Food that is formed into flat round shapes before it is cooked can be referred to as **cakes**. □ *fish cakes* **3** [c] A **cake of soap** is a small block of it. □ *a small cake of lime-scented soap*

cal·cium /'kælsiəm/ NOUN [u] **Calcium** is a soft white chemical element which is found in bones and teeth, and also in limestone, chalk, and marble.

✪ cal·cu·late /'kælkjʊleɪt/ VERB [T] (**calculates, calculating, calculated**) **1** If you **calculate** a number or amount, you discover it from information that you already have, by using arithmetic, mathematics, or a special machine. = work out □ *From this you can calculate the total mass in the Galaxy.* □ *We calculate that the average size farm in Lancaster County is 65 acres.* **2** If you **calculate** the effects of something, especially a possible course of action, you think about them in order to form an opinion or decide what to do. □ *I believe I am capable of calculating the political consequences accurately.*

cal·cu·lat·ed /'kælkjʊleɪtɪd/ ADJ **1** [V-LINK + calculated + to-INF] If something is **calculated to** have a particular effect, it is specially done or arranged in order to have that effect. □ *Their movements through the region were calculated to terrify landowners into abandoning their holdings.* **2** [with BRD-NEG, V-LINK + calculated + to-INF] If you say that something is not **calculated to** have a particular effect, you mean that it is unlikely to have that effect. = likely □ *The liberal agenda is not calculated to help minority groups.* **3** You can describe a clever or dishonest action as **calculated** when it is very carefully planned or arranged. □ *Irene's use of the mop had been a calculated attempt to cover up her crime.* **4** [calculated + N] If you take a **calculated risk**, you do something which you think might be successful, although you have fully considered the possible bad consequences of your action. □ *The president took a calculated political risk in throwing his full support behind the rebels.*

✪ cal·cu·la·tion /ˌkælkjʊ'leɪʃən/ NOUN [c, u] (**calculations**) A **calculation** is something that you think about and work out mathematically. **Calculation** is the process of working something out mathematically. = sum □ *Leonard made a rapid calculation: he'd never make it in time.* □ *This calculation is made by subtracting the age of death from 65.* □ *the calculation of their assets* □ *His calculations showed that the price index would go down by half a per cent.*

cal·cu·la·tor /'kælkjʊleɪtə/ NOUN [c] (**calculators**) A **calculator** is a small electronic device that you use for making mathematical calculations. □ *a pocket calculator*

cal·en·dar /'kælɪndə/ NOUN [c] (**calendars**) **1** A **calendar** is a chart or device which displays the date and the day of the week, and often the whole of a particular year divided up into months, weeks, and days. □ *There was a calendar on the wall above, with large squares around the dates.* **2** A **calendar** is a particular system for dividing time into periods such as years, months, and weeks, often starting from a particular point in history. □ *The Christian calendar was originally based on the Julian calendar of the Romans.* **3** You can use **calendar** to refer to a series or list of events and activities which take place on particular dates, and which are important for a particular organization, community, or person. = diary □ *It is one of the hottest tickets on Washington's social calendar.*

cali·bre /'kælɪbə/ (BrE; in AmE, use **caliber**) NOUN [u, c] (**calibres**) **1** [u] The **calibre of** a person is the quality or standard of their ability or intelligence, especially when this is high. □ *I was impressed by the high calibre of the researchers and analysts.* **2** [u] The **calibre** of something is its quality, especially when it is good. □ *The calibre of teaching was very high.* **3** [c] (*technical*) The **calibre** of a gun is the width of the inside of its barrel. ❑ *a small-calibre rifle* **4** [c] (*technical*) The **calibre** of a bullet is its diameter. ❑ *She was hit in the head by a .22-calibre bullet.*

call ♦♦♦ /kɔːl/ VERB, NOUN

VERB [T, I] (**calls, calling, called**) **1** [T] If you **call** someone or something **by** a particular name or title, you give them that name or title. ❑ *I always wanted to call the dog Mufty for some reason.* ❑ *'Doctor…'—'Will you please call me Sarah?'* **2** [T] If you **call** someone or something a particular thing, you suggest they are that thing or describe them as that thing. ❑ *The speech was interrupted by members of the Republican Party, who called him a traitor.* ❑ *She calls me lazy and selfish.* **3** [T] If you **call** something, you say it in a loud voice, because you are trying to attract someone's attention. ❑ *He could hear the others downstairs calling his name.* **4** [T] If you **call** someone, you ask them to come to you by shouting to them. ❑ *She called her young son: 'Here, Stephen, come and look at this!'* **5** [T] If you **call** someone such as a doctor or the police, you ask them to come to you, usually by telephoning them. ❑ *He screamed for his wife to call an ambulance.* **6** [T] If someone in authority **calls** something such as a meeting, rehearsal, or election, they arrange for it to take place at a particular time. ❑ *We're going to call a meeting and discuss how we can work with other groups.* **7** [T] If someone **is called** before a court or committee, they are ordered to appear there, usually to give evidence. = **summon** ❑ *The child waited two hours before she was called to give evidence.* **8** [T] If you **call** someone, you telephone them. = **phone** ❑ *Would you call me as soon as you find out? My number's in the phone book.* ❑ *A friend of mine gave me this number to call.* **9** [I] If you **call** somewhere, you make a short visit there. ❑ *A market researcher called at the house where my uncle was living.* **10** [I] When a train, bus, or ship **calls** somewhere, it stops there for a short time to allow people to get on or off. ❑ *The steamer calls at several palm-fringed ports along the way.*

PHRASAL VERBS **call back** If you **call** someone **back**, you telephone them again or in return for a telephone call that they have made to you. ❑ *If we're not around, she'll take a message and we'll call you back.*
call for **1** If something **calls for** a particular action or quality, it needs it or makes it necessary. = **demand**, **require** ❑ *It's a situation that calls for a blend of delicacy and force.* **2** If you **call for** someone, you go to the building where they are, so that you can both go somewhere. ❑ *I'll call for you at seven o'clock.* **3** If you **call for** something, you demand that it should happen. ❑ *They angrily called for Robinson's resignation.*
call in **1** If you **call** someone **in**, you ask them to come and help you or do something for you. ❑ *Call in an architect or engineer to oversee the work.* **2** If you **call in**, you phone a place, such as the place where you work, or a radio or TV station. ❑ *She reached for the phone to call in sick.* ❑ *24 million viewers called in to cast their final votes last night.* **3** If you **call in** somewhere, you make a short visit there. = **drop in** ❑ *He just calls in occasionally.*
call off If you **call** something **off**, you cancel it. ❑ *He has called off the trip.*
call on or **call upon** **1** If you **call on** someone **to** do something or **call upon** them **to** do it, you say publicly that you want them to do it. ❑ *One of Kenya's leading churchmen has called on the government to resign.* **2** If you **call on** someone or **call upon** someone, you pay them a short visit. ❑ *Sofia was intending to call on Miss Kitts.*
call out **1** **Call out** means the same as **call** VERB **3**. ❑ *The butcher's son called out a greeting.* **2** If you **call** someone **out**, you order or request that they come to help, especially in an emergency. ❑ *Colombia has called out the army and imposed emergency measures.*
call up **1** (*mainly AmE*) If you **call** someone **up**, you telephone them. = **call** ❑ *When I'm in Pittsburgh, I call him up.* ❑ *He called up the museum.* **2** If someone **is called up**, they are ordered to join the army, navy, or air force. = **draft** ❑ *The United States has called up some 150,000 military reservists.*
NOUN [c, u, SING] (**calls**) **1** [c] If there is a **call for** something, someone demands that it should happen. ❑ *There have been calls for a new kind of security arrangement.*

2 [c] The **call** of a particular bird or animal is the characteristic sound that it makes. ❑ *a wide range of animal noises and bird calls* **3** [u] If there is little or no **call for** something, very few people want it to be done or provided. = **demand** ❑ *'Have you got just plain chocolate?'—'No, I'm afraid there's not much call for that.'* **4** [SING] The **call** of something such as a place is the way it attracts or interests you strongly. = **pull, lure** ❑ *But the call of the wild was simply too strong and so he set off once more.* **5** [c] A **call** is a short visit somewhere. ❑ *He decided to pay a call on Tommy Cummings.* **6** [c] When you make a telephone **call**, you telephone someone. ❑ *I made a phone call to the United States to talk to a friend.* ❑ *I've had hundreds of calls from other victims.*
PHRASE **on call** If someone is **on call**, they are ready to go to work at any time if they are needed, especially if there is an emergency. ❑ *In theory I'm on call day and night.*
→ See also **so-called**
✦ **call someone's bluff** → see **bluff**; **call a halt** → see **halt**; **call the tune** → see **tune**; **call it quits** → see **quit**; **call something your own** → see **own**

call cen·tre (*BrE*; in *AmE*, use **call center**) NOUN [c] (**call centres**) A **call centre** is an office where people work answering or making telephone calls for a particular company.

call·er /ˈkɔːlə/ NOUN [c] (**callers**) **1** A **caller** is a person who is making a telephone call. ❑ *An anonymous caller told police what had happened.* **2** A **caller** is a person who comes to see you for a short visit. = **visitor** ❑ *She ushered her callers into a cluttered living room.*

cal·lous /ˈkæləs/ ADJ A **callous** person or action is very cruel and shows no concern for other people or their feelings. ❑ *his callous disregard for human life*
cal·lous·ness /ˈkæləsnəs/ NOUN [u] ❑ *the callousness of Raymond's murder*
cal·lous·ly /ˈkæləsli/ ADV [callously with V] ❑ *He is accused of callously ill-treating his wife.*

calm ♦◇◇ /kɑːm/ ADJ, NOUN, VERB

ADJ **1** A **calm** person does not show or feel any worry, anger, or excitement. ❑ *She is usually a calm and diplomatic woman.* ❑ *Try to keep calm and just tell me what happened.* **2** (*journalism*) If someone says that a place is **calm**, they mean that it is free from fighting or public disorder, when trouble has recently occurred there or had been expected. = **peaceful** ❑ *The city of Sarajevo appears relatively calm today.* **3** If the sea or a lake is **calm**, the water is not moving very much and there are no big waves. = **still** ❑ *the safe, calm waters protected by an offshore reef* **4** **Calm** weather is pleasant weather with little or no wind. ❑ *Tuesday was a fine, clear, and calm day.*
NOUN [u] **1** [also 'a' calm] **Calm** is a feeling or state free from any worry, anger, or excitement. ❑ *He felt a sudden sense of calm, of contentment.* **2** [also 'a' calm] **Calm** is when recent trouble, fighting or public disorder has stopped, or expected trouble has not occurred. ❑ *Community and church leaders have appealed for calm and no retaliation.* **3** **Calm** is used to refer to a quiet, still, or peaceful atmosphere in a place. = **peace** ❑ *The house projects an atmosphere of calm and order.*
VERB [T, I] (**calms, calming, calmed**) **1** [T] If you **calm** someone, you do something to make them feel less angry, worried, or excited. ❑ *The ruling party's veterans know how to calm their critics.* ❑ *She was breathing quickly and tried to calm herself.* **2** [T] To **calm** a situation means to reduce the amount of trouble, violence, or panic there is. ❑ *Officials hoped admitting fewer foreigners would calm the situation.* **3** [I] When the sea **calms**, it becomes still because the wind stops blowing strongly. When the wind **calms**, it stops blowing strongly. ❑ *Dawn came, the sea calmed but the cold was as bitter as ever.*
PHRASAL VERB **calm down** **1** If you **calm down**, or if someone **calms** you **down**, you become less angry, upset, or excited. ❑ *Calm down for a minute and listen to me.* ❑ *I'll try a herbal remedy to calm him down.* **2** If things **calm down**, or someone or something **calms** things **down**, the amount of activity, trouble, or panic is reduced. = **settle down** ❑ *We will go back to normal when things calm down.*

calm·ly /ˈkɑːmli/ ADV ❑ Alan looked at him and said calmly, 'I don't believe you.'

calm·ing /ˈkɑːmɪŋ/ ADJ ❑ a fresh, cool fragrance which produces a very calming effect on the mind

⊙ **calo·rie** /ˈkæləri/ NOUN [c] (**calories**) Calories are units used to measure the energy value of food. People who are on diets try to eat food that does not contain many calories. = energy ❑ Sweetened drinks contain a lot of calories. ❑ calorie controlled diets

came /keɪm/ IRREG FORM Came is the past tense of **come**.

cam·era ♦♦◇ /ˈkæmrə/ NOUN

NOUN [c] (**cameras**) A camera is a piece of equipment that is used for taking photographs, making films, or producing television pictures. ❑ Her grandmother lent her a camera for a school trip to Venice and Egypt.

PHRASES **on camera** If someone or something is on camera, they are being filmed. ❑ Fay was so impressive on camera that a special part was written in for her.

off camera If you do something or if something happens off camera, you do it or it happens when not being filmed. ❑ They were anything but friendly off camera, refusing even to take the same lift.

in camera (formal) If a trial is held in camera, the public and the press are not allowed to attend. ❑ This morning's appeal was held in camera.

camou·flage /ˈkæməflɑːʒ/ NOUN, VERB

NOUN [u] ⓵ [oft camouflage + N] Camouflage consists of things such as leaves, branches, or brown and green paint, which are used to make it difficult for an enemy to see military forces and equipment. ❑ They were dressed in camouflage and carried automatic rifles. ❑ a camouflage jacket ⓶ [also 'a' camouflage] Camouflage is the way in which some animals are coloured and shaped so that they cannot easily be seen in their natural surroundings. ❑ Confident in its camouflage, being the same colour as the rocks, the lizard stands still when it feels danger. ⓷ [also 'a' camouflage] Camouflage is when something such as a feeling or a situation is hidden or made to appear to be something different. ❑ There was much laughter – a perfect camouflage for the anxiety of waiting for the verdict in the trial.

VERB [T] (**camouflages, camouflaging, camouflaged**) ⓵ If military buildings or vehicles are camouflaged, things such as leaves, branches, or brown and green paint are used to make it difficult for an enemy to see them. ❑ The entrance was camouflaged with bricks and dirt. ⓶ If you camouflage something such as a feeling or a situation, you hide it or make it appear to be something different. = conceal ❑ He has never camouflaged his desire to better himself.

camp ♦♦◇ /kæmp/ NOUN, VERB, ADJ

NOUN [c, u] (**camps**) ⓵ [c] A camp is a collection of huts and other buildings that is provided for a particular group of people, such as refugees, prisoners, or soldiers, as a place to live or stay. ❑ a refugee camp ⓶ [c] You can refer to a group of people who all support a particular person, policy, or idea as a particular camp. ❑ The press release provoked furious protests from the Gore camp and other top Democrats. ⓷ [c, u] A camp is an outdoor area with cabins, tents, or caravans where people stay on holiday. ⓸ [c, u] A camp is a collection of tents or caravans where people are living or staying, usually temporarily while they are travelling. ❑ gypsy camps

VERB [I] (**camps, camping, camped**) If you camp somewhere, you stay or live there for a short time in a tent or caravan, or in the open air. ❑ We camped near the beach.

PHRASAL VERB **camp out** Camp out means the same as **camp** VERB. ❑ For six months they camped out in a meadow at the back of the house.

ADJ (informal) If you describe someone's behaviour, performance, or style of dress as camp, you mean that it is exaggerated and amusing, often in a way that is thought to be typical of some male homosexuals. ❑ James Barron turns in a delightfully camp performance.

camp·ing /ˈkæmpɪŋ/ NOUN [u] ❑ They went camping in the wild.

⊙ **cam·paign** ♦♦♦ /kæmˈpeɪn/ NOUN, VERB

NOUN [c] (**campaigns**) ⓵ A campaign is a planned set of activities that people carry out over a period of time in order to achieve something such as social or political change. = protest ❑ During his election campaign he promised to put the economy back on its feet. ❑ a campaign to improve the training of staff ❑ the campaign against public smoking ⓶ In a war, a campaign is a series of planned movements carried out by armed forces. = operation ❑ The allies are intensifying their air campaign.

VERB [I] (**campaigns, campaigning, campaigned**) If someone campaigns for something, they carry out a planned set of activities over a period of time in order to achieve their aim. = lobby, protest, advocate, promote ❑ We are campaigning for law reform. ❑ Mr Burns has actively campaigned against a hostel being set up here. ❑ They have been campaigning to improve the legal status of women.

cam·paign·er /ˌkæmˈpeɪnə/ NOUN [c] (**campaigners**) A campaigner is a person who campaigns for social or political change. ❑ anti-war campaigners

camp·site /ˈkæmpsaɪt/ NOUN [c] (**campsites**) A campsite is a place where people who are on holiday can stay in tents.

⊙ **cam·pus** /ˈkæmpəs/ NOUN [c, u] (**campuses**) [also PREP + campus] A campus is an area of land that contains the main buildings of a university or college. = grounds ❑ during a rally at the campus ❑ Private automobiles are not allowed on campus.

can ♦♦♦ /kən, STRONG kæn/ VERB, NOUN

> Can is a modal verb. It is used with the base form of a verb. The form **cannot** is used in negative statements. The usual spoken form of **cannot** is **can't**, pronounced /kɑːnt/. The inflected forms **cans, canning,** and **canned** are used for meaning 13 of the verb.

VERB [MODAL, T] ⓵ [MODAL] You use can when you are mentioning a quality or fact about something which people may make use of if they want to. ❑ Tickets can be purchased at the Madstone Theatre box office. ❑ A central reservation number can direct you to accommodation that best suits your needs. ⓶ [MODAL] You use can to indicate that someone has the ability or opportunity to do something. ❑ Don't worry yourself about me, I can take care of myself. ❑ I can't give you details because I don't actually have any details. ❑ The United States will do whatever it can to help Greece. ⓷ [MODAL] You use cannot to indicate that someone is not able to do something because circumstances make it impossible for them to do it. ❑ We cannot buy food and clothes and pay for rent and bills on $20 a week. ⓸ [MODAL] You use can to indicate that something is true sometimes or is true in some circumstances. ❑ long-term therapy that can last five years or more ❑ Exercising alone can be boring. ⓹ [MODAL] You use cannot and can't to state that you are certain that something is not the case or will not happen. ❑ From her knowledge of Douglas's habits, she feels sure that that person can't have been Douglas. ❑ Things can't be that bad. ⓺ [MODAL] You use can to indicate that someone is allowed to do something. You use cannot or can't to indicate that someone is not allowed to do something. ❑ Can I really have your jeans when you go? ❑ We can't answer any questions, I'm afraid. ⓻ [MODAL] You use cannot or can't when you think it is very important that something should not happen or that someone should not do something. = mustn't ❑ It is an intolerable situation and it can't be allowed to go on. ⓼ [MODAL] You use can, usually in questions, in order to make suggestions or to offer to do something. ❑ What can I do around here? ❑ This elderly woman was struggling out of the train and I said, 'Oh, can I help you?' ⓽ [MODAL] You use can in questions in order to make polite requests. You use can't in questions in order to request strongly that someone does something. ❑ Can I have a look at that? ❑ Why can't you leave me alone? ⓾ [MODAL] (formal, spoken) You use can as a polite way of interrupting someone or of introducing what you are going to say next. = may ❑ Can I interrupt you just for a minute? ❑ But if I can interrupt, Joe, I don't think anybody here is personally blaming you. ⓫ [MODAL] (informal, spoken, emphasis) You use can with verbs such as 'imagine', 'think', and 'believe' in order to emphasize how you feel about a particular situation. ❑ *You can imagine he was terribly upset.* ❑ *You can't think how glad I was to see them all go.* **12** [MODAL] (spoken, emphasis) You use **can** in questions with 'how' to indicate that you feel strongly about something. ❑ *How can millions of dollars go astray?* ❑ *How can you say such a thing?* **13** /kæn/ [T] When food or drink **is canned**, it is put into a metal container and sealed so that it will remain fresh. ❑ *fruits and vegetables that will be canned, skinned, diced, or otherwise processed*

NOUN /kæn/ [C] (**cans**) **1** A **can** is a metal container in which something such as food, drink, or paint is put. The container is usually sealed to keep the contents fresh. ❑ *Several young men were kicking a tin can along the middle of the road.* ❑ *empty beer cans* **2** You can use **can** to refer to a can and its contents, or to the contents only. ❑ *She grabbed a can of fizzy drink out of the fridge.*

WHICH WORD?
can, could, or be able to?

You use **can** or **be able to** to talk about ability in the present. **Be able to** is more formal than **can**.

❑ *You **can** all read and write.*
❑ *The sheep **are able to** move around in the shed.*

You use **could** or a past form of **be able to** to talk about ability in the past.

❑ *He **could** run faster than anyone else.*
❑ *I **wasn't able to** do these quizzes.*

---

ca·nal /kəˈnæl/ NOUN [C] (**canals**) **1** A **canal** is a long, narrow stretch of water that has been made for boats to travel along or to bring water to a particular area. ❑ *the Grand Union Canal* **2** A **canal** is a narrow tube inside your body for carrying food, air, or other substances. ❑ *delaying its progress through the alimentary canal*

can·cel ♦♦◇◇ /ˈkænsəl/ VERB

VERB [I, T] (**cancels**, **cancelling**, **cancelled**; in *AmE*, use **canceling**, **canceled**) **1** [I, T] If you **cancel** something that has been arranged, you stop it from happening. If you **cancel** an order for goods or services, you tell the person or organization supplying them that you no longer wish to receive them. ❑ *The Russian foreign minister yesterday cancelled his visit to Washington.* ❑ *Many trains have been cancelled and a limited service is operating on other lines.* ❑ *The customer called to cancel.* **2** [T] If someone in authority **cancels** a document, an insurance policy, or a debt, they officially declare that it is no longer valid or no longer legally exists. ❑ *He intends to try to leave the country, in spite of a government order cancelling his passport.* **3** [T] To **cancel** a stamp or a cheque means to mark it to show that it has already been used and cannot be used again. ❑ *The new device can also cancel the cheque after the transaction is complete.*

PHRASAL VERB **cancel out** If one thing **cancels out** another thing, the two things have opposite effects, so that when they are combined no real effect is produced. ❑ *He wonders if the different influences might not cancel each other out.*

can·cel·la·tion /ˌkænsəˈleɪʃən/ NOUN [C, U] (**cancellations**) **1** [C, U] ❑ *Outbursts of violence forced the cancellation of Haiti's first free elections in 1987.* **2** [U] ❑ *a march by groups calling for cancellation of Third World debt*

can·cer ♦♦◇◇ /ˈkænsə/ NOUN [C, U] (**cancers**) **Cancer** is a serious disease in which cells in a person's body increase rapidly in an uncontrolled way, producing abnormal growths. ❑ *Her mother died of breast cancer.* ❑ *Jane was just 25 when she learned she had cancer.*

can·did /ˈkændɪd/ ADJ **1** When you are **candid** about something or with someone, you speak honestly. = frank ❑ *Natalie is candid about the problems she is having with Steve.* ❑ *I haven't been completely candid with him.* **2** [candid + N] A **candid** photograph of someone is one that was taken when the person did not know they were being photographed. ❑ *candid snaps of off-duty film stars*

⊙**can·di·da·cy** /ˈkændɪdəsi/ NOUN [C, U] (**candidacies**) Someone's **candidacy** is their position of being a candidate in an election. = candidature ❑ *Today he is formally announcing his candidacy for president.*

⊙**can·di·date** ♦♦◇ /ˈkændɪdeɪt/ NOUN [C] (**candidates**) **1** A **candidate** is someone who is being considered for a position, for example someone who is standing in an election or applying for a job. = applicant, contender, nominee ❑ *The Democratic candidate is still leading in the polls.* ❑ *He is a candidate for the office of governor.* **2** A **candidate** is a person or thing that is regarded as being suitable for a particular purpose or as being likely to do or be a particular thing. ❑ *Those who are overweight or indulge in high-salt diets are candidates for hypertension.*

WORD CONNECTIONS
candidate + FOR + NOUN

a candidate for the **post**
a candidate for the **leadership**
a candidate for the **seat**
a candidate for the **presidency**
❑ *Romney was the Republican candidate for the presidency.*

ADJ + **candidate**

a **presidential** candidate
a **parliamentary** candidate
a **mayoral** candidate
❑ *Walker was selected as parliamentary candidate for Worcester.*

a **potential** candidate
an **independent** candidate
❑ *His name has been added to the list of potential candidates.*

VERB + **candidate**

elect a candidate
choose a candidate
❑ *A Liberal candidate was elected after decades of Conservative rule.*

support a candidate
favour a candidate
❑ *I am going to support the candidate that has the best chance of getting things done.*

interview a candidate
consider a candidate
❑ *We're interviewing candidates for the job.*

---

can·dle /ˈkændəl/ NOUN [C] (**candles**) A **candle** is a stick of hard wax with a piece of string called a wick through the middle. You light the wick in order to give a steady flame that provides light. ❑ *The bedroom was lit by a single candle.*

can·dour /ˈkændə/ (*BrE*; in *AmE*, use **candor**) NOUN [U] **Candour** is the quality of speaking honestly and openly about things. = frankness ❑ *a brash, forceful man, noted both for his candour and his quick temper*

cane /keɪn/ NOUN [C, U] (**canes**) **1** [C, U] **Cane** is used to refer to the long, hollow, hard stems of plants such as bamboo. Strips of cane are often used to make furniture, and some types of cane can be crushed and processed to make sugar. ❑ *cane furniture* ❑ *cane sugar* **2** [C] A **cane** is a long thin stick with a curved or round top which you can use to support yourself when you are walking, or which in the past was fashionable to carry with you. ❑ *He wore a grey suit and leaned heavily on his cane.*

can·na·bis /ˈkænəbɪs/ NOUN [U] **Cannabis** is the hemp plant when it is used as a drug. = marijuana ❑ *cannabis smokers*

can·non /ˈkænən/ NOUN

NOUN [C] (**cannons**) **1** A **cannon** is a large gun, usually on wheels, which used to be used in battles. ❑ *The cannons boom, the band plays.* **2** A **cannon** is a heavy automatic gun, especially one that is fired from an aircraft. ❑ *Others carried huge cannons plundered from Russian aircraft.*

PHRASE **a loose cannon** If someone is a **loose cannon**, they do whatever they want and nobody can predict what they are going to do. ❑ *Max is a loose cannon politically.*

can·not /ˈkænɒt, kəˈnɒt/ IRREG FORM **Cannot** is the negative form of **can**.

cano•py /ˈkænəpi/ NOUN [c] (**canopies**) **1** A **canopy** is a decorated cover, often made of cloth, which is placed above something such as a bed or a seat. **2** A **canopy** is a layer of something that spreads out and covers an area, for example the branches and leaves that spread out at the top of trees in a forest. ❑ *The trees formed such a dense canopy that all beneath was a deep carpet of pine needles.*

can't /kɑːnt, AmE kænt/ SHORT FORM **Can't** is the usual spoken form of 'cannot'.

can•teen /kænˈtiːn/ NOUN [c] (**canteens**) **1** A **canteen** is a place in a factory or military base where meals or snacks are served to the people who work there. ❑ *Rennie had eaten his supper in the canteen.* **2** A **canteen** is a small metal or plastic bottle for carrying water and other drinks. Canteens are used by soldiers. ❑ *a full canteen of water*

can•vas /ˈkænvəs/ NOUN [u, c] (**canvases**) **1** [u] Canvas is a strong, heavy cloth that is used for making things such as tents, sails, and bags. ❑ *a canvas bag* **2** [c, u] A **canvas** is a piece of canvas or similar material on which an oil painting can be done. **3** [c] A **canvas** is a painting that has been done on canvas. = painting ❑ *The show includes canvases by masters like Carpaccio, Canaletto, and Guardi.*

can•vass /ˈkænvəs/ VERB [i, t] (**canvasses, canvassing, canvassed**) **1** [i] If you **canvass** for a particular person or political party, you go around an area trying to persuade people to vote for that person or party. ❑ *I'm canvassing for the Republican Party.* **2** [t] If you **canvass** public opinion, you find out how people feel about a particular subject. ❑ *Members of Congress are spending the weekend canvassing opinion in their constituencies.*

cap ♦◇◇ /kæp/ NOUN, VERB
NOUN [c] (**caps**) **1** A **cap** is a soft, flat hat with a curved part at the front which is called a visor. ❑ *a dark blue baseball cap* **2** A **cap** is a special hat which is worn as part of a uniform. ❑ *a border guard in olive grey uniform and a cap* **3** The **cap** of a bottle is its lid. ❑ *She unscrewed the cap of her water bottle and gave him a drink.*
VERB [t] (**caps, capping, capped**) (*journalism*) If someone says that a good or bad event **caps** a series of events, they mean it is the final event in the series, and the other events were also good or bad. ❑ *The unrest capped a weekend of right-wing attacks on foreigners.*

✪ **ca•pa•bil•ity** /ˌkeɪpəˈbɪliti/ NOUN [c, u] (**capabilities**) **1** If you have the **capability** or the **capabilities** to do something, you have the ability or the qualities that are necessary to do it. = ability; ≠ inability ❑ *People experience differences in physical and mental capability depending on the time of day.* ❑ *The standards set four years ago in Seoul will be far below the athletes' capabilities now.* **2** A country's military **capability** is its ability to fight in a war. ❑ *Their military capability has gone down because their air force has proved not to be an effective force.*

✪ **ca•pable** ♦◇◇ /ˈkeɪpəbəl/ ADJ (*academic word*) **1** [V-LINK + capable 'of' -ING/N] If a person or thing is **capable of** doing something, they have the ability to do it. ❑ *He appeared hardly capable of conducting a coherent conversation.* ❑ *The kitchen is capable of catering for several hundred people.* ❑ *a man capable of murder* **2** Someone who is **capable** has the skill or qualities necessary to do a particular thing well, or is able to do most things well. = competent, able ❑ *She's a very capable speaker.*
ca•pably /ˈkeɪpəbli/ ADV [capably with V] = competently, ably ❑ *It was all dealt with very capably by the police and security people.*

✪ **ca•pac•ity** ♦◇◇ /kəˈpæsiti/ NOUN, ADJ (*academic word*)
NOUN [c, u, SING] (**capacities**) **1** [c, u] Your **capacity for** something is your ability to do it, or the amount of it that you are able to do. = ability ❑ *Our capacity for giving care, love, and attention is limited.* ❑ *Her mental capacity and temperament are as remarkable as his.* **2** [c, u] The **capacity** of a container is its volume, or the amount of liquid it can hold, measured in units such as pints or gallons. ❑ *containers with a maximum capacity of 200 gallons of water* **3** [u] The **capacity** of something such as a factory, industry, or region is the quantity of things that it can produce or deliver with the equipment or resources that

are available. ❑ *the amount of spare capacity in the economy* ❑ *Bread factories are working at full capacity.* **4** [c] The **capacity** of a piece of equipment is its size or power, often measured in particular units. ❑ *an aircraft with a bomb-carrying capacity of 1000 pounds* ❑ *a feature which gave the vehicles a much greater fuel capacity than other trucks* **5** [c] (*written*) If you do something in a particular **capacity**, you do it as part of a particular job or duty, or because you are representing a particular organization or person. ❑ *Ms Halliwell visited the Philippines in her capacity as a Special Representative of UNICEF.* **6** [SING] [also no DET, oft 'to' capacity] The **capacity** of a building, place, or vehicle is the number of people or things that it can hold. If a place is filled **to capacity**, it is as full as it can possibly be. = size ❑ *Each stadium had a seating capacity of about 50,000.*
ADJ [capacity + N] A **capacity** crowd or audience completely fills a theatre, sports stadium, or other place. ❑ *A capacity crowd of 76,000 people was at the stadium for the event.*

USAGE NOTE

capacity

To refer to someone's ability to do something, use 'capacity for' doing something. Do not use 'capacity of' doing something.
Human beings have a tremendous **capacity for** *learning.*

---

cape /keɪp/ NOUN [c] (**capes**) **1** A **cape** is a large piece of land that sticks out into the sea from the coast. ❑ *Naomi James became the first woman to sail solo around the world via Cape Horn.* **2** A **cape** is a short cloak. ❑ *a woollen cape*

✪ **capi•tal** ♦♦♦ /ˈkæpɪtəl/ NOUN, ADJ
NOUN [u, c] (**capitals**) **1** [u] (*business*) **Capital** is a large sum of money which you use to start a business, or which you invest in order to make more money. ❑ *Companies are having difficulty in raising capital.* **2** [u] (*business*) You can use **capital** to refer to buildings or machinery which are necessary to produce goods or to make companies more efficient, but which do not make money directly. ❑ *capital equipment that could have served to increase production* ❑ *capital investment* **3** [u] (*business*) **Capital** is the part of an amount of money borrowed or invested which does not include interest. ❑ *With a conventional mortgage, the payments consist of both capital and interest.* **4** [c] The **capital** of a country is the city or town where its government meets. ❑ *Kathmandu, the capital of Nepal* **5** [c] If a place is **the capital of** a particular industry or activity, it is the place that is most famous for it, because it happens in that place more than anywhere else. ❑ *Colmar has long been considered the capital of the wine trade.* **6** [c] **Capitals** or **capital letters** are written or printed letters in the form which is used at the beginning of sentences or names. 'T', 'B', and 'F' are capitals. ❑ *The name and address are written in capitals.*
PHRASE **make capital out of something** or **make capital of something** (*formal, disapproval*) If you say that someone **is making capital out of** a situation, you disapprove of the way they are gaining an advantage for themselves through other people's efforts or bad luck. ❑ *He rebuked the president for trying to make political capital out of the hostage situation.*
ADJ [capital + N] A **capital** offence is one that is so serious that the person who commits it can be punished by death. ❑ *Espionage is a capital offence in this country.*

✪ **capi•tal•ism** /ˈkæpɪtəlɪzəm/ NOUN [u] **Capitalism** is an economic and political system in which property, business, and industry are owned by private individuals and not by the state. = private enterprise, free enterprise ❑ *the two fundamentally opposed social systems, capitalism and socialism* ❑ *the return of capitalism to Hungary* ❑ *the headlong rush towards global capitalism*

✪ **capi•tal•ist** /ˈkæpɪtəlɪst/ ADJ, NOUN
ADJ A **capitalist** country or system supports or is based on the principles of capitalism. ❑ *China has pledged to retain Hong Kong's capitalist system for 50 years.* ❑ *capitalist economic theory*
NOUN [c] (**capitalists**) **1** A **capitalist** is someone who believes in and supports the principles of capitalism.

C

❑ *Lenin had hoped to even have a working relationship with the capitalists.* **2** A **capitalist** is someone who owns a business which they run in order to make a profit for themselves. = entrepreneur ❑ *They argue that only private capitalists can remake Poland's economy.* ❑ *relations between capitalists and workers*

capi·tal·ize /'kæpɪtəlaɪz/ also **capitalise** VERB [I, T] (**capitalizes, capitalizing, capitalized**) **1** [I] If you **capitalize on** a situation, you use it to gain some advantage for yourself. ❑ *The rebels seem to be trying to capitalize on the public's discontent with the government.* **2** [T] (*business*) In business, if you **capitalize** something that belongs to you, you sell it in order to make money. ❑ *Our intention is to capitalize the company by any means we can.* **3** [T] If you **capitalize** a letter, you write it as a capital letter. If you **capitalize** a word, you spell it in capital letters, or with the first letter as a capital letter. ❑ *Capitalize all proper nouns but not the articles (a, an) that precede them.*

✪ **capi·tal pun·ish·ment** NOUN [U] **Capital punishment** is punishment which involves the legal killing of a person who has committed a serious crime such as murder. = the death penalty ❑ *A majority of Americans support capital punishment.*

ca·pitu·late /kə'pɪtʃʊleɪt/ VERB [I] (**capitulates, capitulating, capitulated**) If you **capitulate**, you stop resisting and do what someone else wants you to do. = submit, yield ❑ *The club eventually capitulated and now grants equal rights to women.*

cap·size /kæp'saɪz, AmE 'kæpsaɪz/ VERB [I, T] (**capsizes, capsizing, capsized**) If you **capsize** a boat or if it **capsizes**, it turns upside down in the water. = overturn ❑ *The sea got very rough and the boat capsized.*

cap·sule /'kæpsjuːl, AmE 'kæpsəl/ NOUN [C] (**capsules**) **1** A **capsule** is a very small tube containing powdered or liquid medicine, which you swallow. ❑ *cod liver oil capsules* **2** A **capsule** is a small container with a drug or other substance inside it, which is used for medical or scientific purposes. ❑ *They first implanted capsules into the animals' brains.* **3** A space **capsule** is the part of a spacecraft in which people travel, and which often separates from the main rocket. ❑ *A Russian space capsule is currently orbiting the Earth.* **4** A time **capsule** is a container into which people put typical everyday objects from their lives. The container is buried so that people in the future can dig it up, and find out about what life was like in the past. ❑ *Twenty-five years ago they filled a time capsule and buried it.*

cap·tain ♦♦◇ /'kæptɪn/ NOUN, VERB
NOUN [C] (**captains**) **1** In the army, navy, and some other armed forces, a **captain** is an officer of middle rank. ❑ *Captain Mark Phillips* ❑ *a captain in the army* **2** The **captain of** a sports team is the player in charge of it. = skipper ❑ *Mickey Thomas, the captain of the tennis team* **3** The **captain** of a ship is the sailor in charge of it. = skipper ❑ *the captain of an excursion boat* **4** The **captain** of an aeroplane is the pilot in charge of it. **5** In the United States and some other countries, a **captain** is a police officer or firefighter of fairly senior rank. ❑ *a former Honolulu police captain*
VERB [T] (**captains, captaining, captained**) If you **captain** a team or a ship, you are the captain of it. = skipper ❑ *He captained the winning team in 1991.*

cap·tion ♦♦◇ /'kæpʃən/ NOUN [C] (**captions**) A **caption** is the words printed underneath a picture or cartoon which explain what it is about. ❑ *The local paper featured me standing on a stepladder with a caption, 'Wendy climbs the ladder to success'.*

cap·ti·vate /'kæptɪveɪt/ VERB [T] (**captivates, captivating, captivated**) If you **are captivated** by someone or something, you find them fascinating and attractive. ❑ *I was captivated by her brilliant mind.*

cap·tive /'kæptɪv/ ADJ, NOUN
ADJ **1** (*literary*) A **captive** person or animal is being kept imprisoned or enclosed. ❑ *Her heart had begun to pound inside her chest like a captive animal.* **2** [captive + N] A **captive** audience is a group of people who are not free to leave a certain place and so have to watch or listen.

A **captive** market is a group of people who cannot choose whether or where to buy things. ❑ *We all performed action songs, sketches, and dances before a captive audience of parents and patrons.*
PHRASE **take someone captive** or **hold someone captive** If you **take** someone **captive** or **hold** someone **captive**, you take or keep them as a prisoner. ❑ *Richard was finally released on 4 February, one year and six weeks after he'd been taken captive.*
NOUN [C] (**captives**) A **captive** is someone who is captive. = prisoner ❑ *He described the difficulties of surviving for four months as a captive.*

cap·tiv·ity /kæp'tɪvɪti/ NOUN [U] **Captivity** is the state of being kept imprisoned or enclosed. ❑ *The great majority of barn owls are reared in captivity.*

cap·ture ♦◇◇ /'kæptʃə/ VERB, NOUN
VERB [T] (**captures, capturing, captured**) **1** If you **capture** someone or something, you catch them, especially in a war. ❑ *The guerrillas shot down one aeroplane and captured the pilot.* **2** If something or someone **captures** a particular quality, feeling, or atmosphere, they represent or express it successfully. = encapsulate ❑ *Chef Idris Caldora offers an inspired menu that captures the spirit of the Mediterranean.* **3** If something **captures** your attention or imagination, you begin to be interested or excited by it. If someone or something **captures** your heart, you begin to love them or like them very much. ❑ *the great names of the past who usually capture the historian's attention* **4** If an event **is captured** in a photograph or on film, it is photographed or filmed. ❑ *The incident was captured on videotape.* ❑ *The images were captured by TV crews filming outside the base.*
NOUN [U] The **capture** of someone or something is when you catch them, especially in a war. ❑ *the final battles which led to the army's capture of the town*

car ♦♦♦ /kɑː/ NOUN [C] (**cars**) **1** [also 'by' car] A **car** is a motor vehicle with room for a small number of passengers. ❑ *He had left his tickets in his car.* **2** The separate sections of a train are called **cars** when they are used for a particular purpose. ❑ *He made his way into the dining car for breakfast.*

cara·van /'kærəvæn/ NOUN [C] (**caravans**) **1** A **caravan** is a group of people and animals or vehicles who travel together. ❑ *the old caravan routes from Central Asia to China* **2** (*BrE*) A **caravan** is a temporary holiday home that is pulled by a car to each holiday spot.

✪ **car·bo·hy·drate** /ˌkɑːbəʊ'haɪdreɪt/ NOUN [C, U] (**carbohydrates**) **Carbohydrates** are substances, found in certain kinds of food, that provide you with energy. Foods such as sugar and bread that contain these substances can also be referred to as **carbohydrates**. ❑ *carbohydrates such as bread, pasta, or potatoes* ❑ *Food is made up of carbohydrates, proteins and fats.* ❑ *Fibre is automatically present in complex carbohydrates.*

✪ **car·bon** ♦◇◇ /'kɑːbən/ NOUN [U] **Carbon** is a chemical element that diamonds and coal are made up of. ❑ *Carbohydrates contain only carbon, hydrogen and oxygen.*

✪ **car·bon da·ting** NOUN [U] **Carbon dating** is a system of calculating the age of a very old object by measuring the amount of radioactive carbon it contains. ❑ *Carbon dating indicated its age to be around 2500 years.*

✪ **car·bon di·ox·ide** /ˌkɑːbən daɪ'ɒksaɪd/ NOUN [U] **Carbon dioxide** is a gas. It is produced by animals and people breathing out, and by chemical reactions. ❑ *Plants absorb carbon dioxide from the air and moisture from the soil.* ❑ *Scientists say carbon dioxide and other 'greenhouse gases' trap heat in the atmosphere.*

✪ **car·bon foot·print** NOUN [C] [oft POSS + carbon footprint] Your **carbon footprint** is a measure of the amount of carbon dioxide released into the atmosphere by your activities over a particular period. ❑ *We all need to look for ways to reduce our carbon footprint.* ❑ *the carbon footprint of fossil fuelled power plants*

✪ **car·bon neu·tral** ADJ A **carbon neutral** lifestyle, company, or activity does not cause an increase in the overall amount of carbon dioxide in the atmosphere. ❑ *You can make your flights carbon neutral by planting trees to make up for the greenhouse gas emissions.*

car·cass /ˈkɑːkəs/ also **carcase** NOUN [c] (**carcasses**) A **carcass** is the body of a dead animal. ❑ *A cluster of vultures crouched on the carcass of a dead buffalo.*

card ♦♦◊ /kɑːd/ NOUN
NOUN [c, u] (**cards**) **1** [c] A **card** is a piece of stiff paper or thin cardboard on which something is written or printed. ❑ *Check the numbers below against the numbers on your card.* **2** [c] A **card** is a piece of cardboard or plastic, or a small document, which shows information about you and which you carry with you, for example to prove your identity. ❑ *they check my bag and press card* ❑ *her membership card* **3** [c] A **card** is a rectangular piece of plastic, issued by a bank, company, or shop, which you can use to buy things or obtain money. ❑ *He paid the whole bill with an American Express card.* **4** [c] A **card** is a folded piece of stiff paper with a picture and sometimes a message printed on it, which you send to someone on a special occasion. ❑ *She sends me a card on my birthday.* **5** [c] A **card** is the same as a **postcard**. ❑ *Send your details on a card to the following address.* **6** [c] (*business*) A **card** is a piece of thin cardboard carried by someone such as a businessperson in order to give it to other people. A card shows the name, address, telephone number, and other details of the person who carries it. = business card ❑ *Here's my card. You may need me.* **7** [c] **Cards** are thin pieces of cardboard with numbers or pictures printed on them which are used to play various games. = playing card ❑ *a deck of cards* **8** [u] If you are playing **cards**, you are playing a game using cards. ❑ *They enjoy themselves drinking wine, smoking, and playing cards.* **9** [u] **Card** is strong, stiff paper or thin cardboard. ❑ *She put the pieces of card in her pocket.*
PHRASE **on the cards** If you say that something is **on the cards**, you mean that it is very likely to happen. = likely ❑ *Last summer she began telling friends that a New Year marriage was on the cards.*
→ See also **bank card, credit card, debit card**

card·board /ˈkɑːdbɔːd/ NOUN [u] **Cardboard** is thick, stiff paper that is used, for example, to make boxes and models. ❑ *a cardboard box*

car·di·ac /ˈkɑːdiæk/ ADJ [cardiac + N] (*medical*) **Cardiac** means relating to the heart. ❑ *The man was suffering from cardiac weakness.*

car·di·nal /ˈkɑːdnəl/ NOUN, ADJ
NOUN [c] (**cardinals**) A **cardinal** is a high-ranking priest in the Catholic church. ❑ *In 1448, Nicholas was appointed a cardinal.*
ADJ [cardinal + N] (*formal*) A **cardinal** rule or quality is the one that is considered to be the most important. = chief, principal ❑ *As a salesman, your cardinal rule is to do everything you can to satisfy a customer.*

○ **car·dio·vas·cu·lar** /ˌkɑːdiəʊˈvæskjʊlə/ ADJ [cardiovascular + N] **Cardiovascular** means relating to the heart and blood vessels. ❑ *Smoking places you at serious risk of cardiovascular and respiratory disease.* ❑ *Mercury may cause neurological, respiratory, cardiovascular and digestive disorders.* ❑ *exercise contributes to cardiovascular fitness*

care ♦♦♦ /keə/ VERB, NOUN
VERB [I, T] (**cares, caring, cared**) **1** [I, T] If you **care about** something, you feel that it is important and are concerned about it. ❑ *a company that cares about the environment* ❑ *young men who did not care whether they lived or died* **2** [I] If you **care for** someone, you feel a lot of affection for them. ❑ *He wanted me to know that he still cared for me.* **3** [I] If you **care for** someone or something, you look after them and keep them in a good state or condition. ❑ *They hired a nurse to care for her.* ❑ *these distinctive cars, lovingly cared for by private owners* **4** [I, T] You can ask someone if they would **care for** something or if they would **care to** do something as a polite way of asking if they would like to have or do something. = like ❑ *Would you care for some orange juice?*
PHRASES **for all someone cares** (*emphasis*) You can use **for all I care** to emphasize that it does not matter at all to you what someone does. ❑ *You can go right now for all I care.*
couldn't care less (*emphasis*) If you say that you **couldn't care less about** someone or something, you are

emphasizing that you are not interested in them or worried about them. ❑ *I couldn't care less about the woman.*
who cares (*emphasis*) You can say '**Who cares?**' to emphasize that something does not matter to you at all. ❑ *'But we might ruin the stove.'—'Who cares?'*
NOUN [u, c] (**cares**) **1** [u] **Care** is the act of looking after someone or something and keeping them in a good state or condition. ❑ *Most of the staff specialize in the care of children.* ❑ *sensitive teeth which need special care* **2** [u] If you do something **with care**, you give careful attention to it because you do not want to make any mistakes or cause any damage. ❑ *Condoms are an effective method of birth control if used with care.* **3** [c] Your **cares** are your worries, anxieties, or fears. = worry ❑ *Lean back in a hot bath and forget all the cares of the day.*
PHRASES **care of someone** or **in care of someone** If someone sends you a letter or package **care of** or **in care of** a particular person or place, they send it to that person or place, and it is then passed on to you. ❑ *Please write to me care of the publishers.* ❑ *He wrote to me in care of my publisher.*
take care of If you **take care of** someone or something, you look after them and prevent them from being harmed or damaged. = look after ❑ *There was no one else to take care of their children.*
take care to do something If you **take care to** do something, you make sure that you do it. ❑ *Foley followed Albert through the gate, taking care to close the latch.*
take care of something To **take care of** a problem, task, or situation means to deal with it. = deal with ❑ *They leave it to the system to try and take care of the problem.*

○ **ca·reer** ♦♦◊ /kəˈrɪə/ NOUN, ADJ, VERB
NOUN [c] (**careers**) **1** A **career** is the job or profession that someone does for a long period of their life. = profession, work, employment, vocation ❑ *She is now concentrating on a career as a fashion designer.* ❑ *a career in journalism* ❑ *Staff can choose courses based on their career development plans.* **2** Your **career** is the part of your life that you spend working. ❑ *During his career, he wrote more than fifty plays.*
ADJ [career + N] **Career** advice or guidance consists of information about different jobs and help with deciding what kind of job you want to do. ❑ *She received very little career guidance when young.*
VERB [I] (**careers, careering, careered**) If a person or vehicle **careers** somewhere, they move fast and in an uncontrolled way. = hurtle ❑ *His car careered into a river.*

WORD CONNECTIONS
VERB + **career**
have a career
choose a career
pursue a career
❑ *He moved to London to pursue a career in architecture.*
career + IN + NOUN
a career in **politics**
a career in **industry**
a career in **law**
a career in **medicine**
❑ *A career in medicine can be very rewarding.*
career + AS + NOUN
a career as a **writer**
a career as an **actor**
a career as a **teacher**
❑ *Nemes began his career as an actor when he was a teenager.*
ADJ + **career**
a **political** career
a **managerial** career
a **military** career
an **academic** caeer
❑ *Bates had a long and successful military career.*

care·free /ˈkeəfriː/ ADJ A **carefree** person or period of time doesn't have or involve any problems, worries, or responsibilities. ❑ *Chantal remembered carefree summers at the beach.*

C

care·ful ♦♦◇ /'keəfʊl/ ADJ **1** If you are **careful**, you give serious attention to what you are doing, in order to avoid harm, damage, or mistakes. If you are **careful to** do something, you make sure that you do it. □ *Be very careful with this stuff, it can be dangerous if it isn't handled properly.* □ *Careful on those stairs!* **2** **Careful** work, thought, or examination is thorough and shows a concern for details. = painstaking □ *He has decided to prosecute her after careful consideration of all the relevant facts.* **3** [V-LINK + careful 'about/of' -ING] If you tell someone to be **careful about** doing something, you think that what they intend to do is probably wrong, and that they should think seriously before they do it. □ *I think you should be careful about talking of the rebels as heroes.* **4** If you are **careful with** something such as money or resources, you use or spend only what is necessary. = prudent □ *Industries should be more careful with natural resources.*

care·ful·ly /'keəfəli/ ADV **1** [carefully with v] □ *Have a nice time, dear, and drive carefully.* **2** [carefully with v] □ *a vast series of deliberate and carefully planned thefts* **3** [carefully with v] □ *He should think carefully about actions like this which play into the hands of his opponents.*

care·less /'keələs/ ADJ **1** If you are **careless**, you do not pay enough attention to what you are doing, and so you make mistakes, or cause harm or damage. □ *I'm sorry. How careless of me.* □ *Some parents are accused of being careless with their children's health.* **2** If you say that someone is **careless of** something such as their health or appearance, you mean that they do not seem to be concerned about it, or do nothing to keep it in a good condition. □ *He had shown himself careless of personal safety where the life of his colleagues might be at risk.*

care·less·ly /'keələsli/ ADV [carelessly with v] □ *She was fined $200 for driving carelessly.*

care·less·ness /'keələsnəs/ NOUN [U] □ *Errors are sometimes made from simple carelessness.*

car·er /'keərə/ NOUN [C] (carers) (BrE) A **carer** is someone who is responsible for looking after another person, for example a person who is disabled, ill, or very young. □ *His carers labelled him severely disabled.*

care·taker /'keəteɪkə/ NOUN, ADJ
NOUN [C] (caretakers) **1** A **caretaker** is a person whose job it is to take care of a house or property when the owner is not there. □ *Slater remained at the house, acting as his caretaker when the family was not in residence.* **2** (BrE; in AmE, use **janitor**) A **caretaker** is a person whose job it is to take care of a large building such as a school or a block of flats or apartments, and deal with small repairs to it.
ADJ [caretaker + N] A **caretaker** government or leader is in charge temporarily until a new government or leader is appointed. = acting □ *The military intends to hand over power to a caretaker government and hold elections within six months.*

car·go /'kɑːgəʊ/ NOUN [C, U] (cargoes, cargos) The **cargo** of a ship or plane is the goods that it is carrying. = consignment □ *The boat calls at the main port to load its regular cargo of bananas.*

cari·ca·ture /'kærɪkətʃʊə, AmE -tʃər/ NOUN, VERB
NOUN [C] (caricatures) **1** A **caricature of** someone is a drawing or description of them that exaggerates their appearance or behaviour in a humorous or critical way. □ *The poster showed a caricature of Hitler with a devil's horns and tail.* **2** If you describe something as a **caricature of** an event or situation, you mean that it is a very exaggerated account of it. □ *Hall is angry at what he sees as a caricature of the training offered to modern-day social workers.*
VERB [T] (caricatures, caricaturing, caricatured) If you **caricature** someone, you draw or describe them in an exaggerated way in order to be humorous or critical. □ *Her political career has been caricatured in the headlines.*

car·ing ♦◇◇ /'keərɪŋ/ ADJ, NOUN
ADJ **1** If someone is **caring**, they are affectionate, helpful, and sympathetic. □ *He is a lovely boy, very gentle and caring.* **2** [caring + N] The **caring** professions are those such as nursing and social work that are involved with looking after people who are ill or who need help in coping with their lives. □ *The course is also suitable for those in the caring professions.*

NOUN [U] **Caring** is the feeling of great affection for someone. □ *the 'feminine' traits of caring and compassion*

car·ni·val /'kɑːnɪvəl/ NOUN [C] (carnivals) A **carnival** is a public festival during which people play music and sometimes dance in the streets.

❂**car·ni·vore** /'kɑːnɪvɔː/ NOUN [C] (carnivores) **1** (technical) A **carnivore** is an animal that eats meat. □ *The researchers conclude that wide-ranging carnivores should not be kept in captivity.* □ *A herbivore and a carnivore may share the same habitat but their different feeding methods mean that they occupy different niches.* **2** If you describe someone as a **carnivore**, you are saying, especially in a humorous way, that they eat meat. = meat-eater □ *This is a delicious vegetarian dish that even carnivores love.*

❂**car·nivo·rous** /kɑːˈnɪvərəs/ ADJ **1** (technical) Carnivorous animals eat meat. □ *Snakes are carnivorous.* **2** Carnivorous can be used, especially humorously, to describe someone who eats meat. = meat-eating

car park also **carpark** (BrE; in AmE, use **parking lot**) NOUN [C] (car parks) A **car park** is an area or building where people can leave their cars.

car·pet /'kɑːpɪt/ NOUN, VERB
NOUN [C, U] (carpets) A **carpet** is a thick covering of soft material which is laid over a floor or a staircase. □ *They put down wooden boards, and laid new carpets on top.*
VERB [T] (carpets, carpeting, carpeted) If a floor or a room **is carpeted**, a carpet is laid on the floor. □ *The room had been carpeted and the windows glazed with coloured glass.*

car·riage /'kærɪdʒ/ NOUN [C] (carriages) **1** [also 'by' carriage] A **carriage** is an old-fashioned vehicle, usually for a small number of passengers, which is pulled by horses. □ *The president-elect followed in an open carriage drawn by six beautiful grey horses.* **2** (mainly BrE; in AmE, usually use **car**) A **carriage** is one of the separate, long sections of a train that carries passengers. = coach

car·ri·er ♦◇◇ /'kærɪə/ NOUN [C] (carriers) **1** A **carrier** is a vehicle that is used for carrying people, especially soldiers, or things. □ *There were armoured personnel carriers and tanks on the streets.* **2** A **carrier** is a passenger airline. □ *American Airlines is the third-largest carrier at Denver International Airport.* **3** A **carrier** is a company that transports goods from one place to another by truck. □ *The Colorado Motor Carriers Association represents 450 trucking companies across the state.* **4** A **carrier** is a person or an animal that is infected with a disease and so can make other people or animals ill. □ *an AIDS carrier*

car·rot /'kærət/ NOUN [C, U] (carrots) **1** [C, U] **Carrots** are long, thin, orange-coloured vegetables. They grow under the ground, and have green shoots above the ground. **2** [C] Something that is offered to people in order to persuade them to do something can be referred to as a **carrot**. Something that is meant to persuade people not to do something can be referred to in the same sentence as a 'stick'. = incentive □ *Why the new emphasis on sticks instead of diplomatic carrots?*

car·ry ♦♦♦ /'kæri/ VERB
VERB [T, I] (carries, carrying, carried) **1** [T] If you **carry** something, you take it with you, holding it so that it does not touch the ground. □ *He was carrying a briefcase.* □ *She carried her son to the car.* **2** [T] If you **carry** something, you have it with you wherever you go. □ *You have to carry a pager so that they can call you in at any time.* **3** [T] If something **carries** a person or thing somewhere, it takes them there. = transport □ *Flowers are designed to attract insects which then carry the pollen from plant to plant.* □ *The delegation was carrying a message of thanks to President Mubarak.* **4** [T] If a person or animal **is carrying** a disease, they are infected with it and can pass it on to other people or animals. □ *The test could be used to screen healthy people to see if they are carrying the virus.* **5** [T] If an action or situation has a particular quality or consequence, you can say that it **carries** it. □ *Check that any medication you're taking carries no risk for your developing baby.* **6** [T] If a quality or advantage **carries** someone into a particular position or through a difficult situation, it helps them to achieve that position or deal with that situation. □ *He had*

the ruthless streak necessary to carry him into the cabinet. **7** [T] If you **carry** an idea or a method to a particular extent, you use or develop it to that extent. = take ❏ *It's not such a new idea, but I carried it to extremes.* **8** [T] If a newspaper or poster **carries** a picture or a piece of writing, it contains it or displays it. ❏ *Several papers carry the photograph of Mr Anderson.* **9** [T] In a debate, if a proposal or motion **is carried**, a majority of people vote in favour of it. ❏ *A motion backing its economic policy was carried by 322 votes to 296.* **10** [T] If a crime **carries** a particular punishment, a person who is found guilty of that crime will receive that punishment. ❏ *It was a crime of espionage and carried the death penalty.* **11** [I] If a sound **carries**, it can be heard a long way away. ❏ *Even in this stillness Leaphorn doubted if the sound would carry far.* **12** [T] If you **carry yourself** in a particular way, you walk and move in that way. ❏ *They carried themselves with great pride and dignity.* PHRASE **get carried away** or **be carried away** If you **get carried away** or **are carried away**, you are so eager or excited about something that you do something hasty or foolish. ❏ *I got completely carried away and almost cried.*

PHRASAL VERBS **carry off** If you **carry** something **off**, you do it successfully. ❏ *He's got the experience and the authority to carry it off.*

carry on **1** If you **carry on** doing something, you continue to do it. = continue ❏ *The assistant carried on talking.* ❏ *Her bravery has given him the will to carry on with his life and his work.* ❏ *His eldest son Joseph carried on his father's traditions.* **2** If you **carry on** an activity, you do it or take part in it for a period of time. = conduct ❏ *The consulate will carry on a political dialogue with Indonesia.*

carry out If you **carry out** a threat, task, or instruction, you do it or act according to it. ❏ *The Social Democrats could still carry out their threat to leave the government.* ❏ *Police say they believe the attacks were carried out by nationalists.* ❏ *The institute is carrying out research into rural health.*

carry through If you **carry** something **through**, you do it or complete it, often in spite of difficulties. ❏ *We don't have the confidence that the UN will carry through a sustained programme.*

✦ **carry weight** → see **weight**

cart /kɑːt/ NOUN, VERB

NOUN [C] (**carts**) A **cart** is an old-fashioned wooden vehicle that is used for transporting goods or people. Some carts are pulled by animals. = wagon ❏ *a country where horse-drawn carts far outnumber cars*

VERB (**carts, carting, carted**) (*informal*) If you **cart** things or people somewhere, you carry them or transport them there, often with difficulty. ❏ *After their parents died, one of their father's relatives carted off the entire contents of the house.* ❏ *a useful bag for carting around your child's books or toys*

car·tel /kɑːˈtel/ NOUN [C] (**cartels**) (*business*) A **cartel** is an association of similar companies or businesses that have grouped together in order to prevent competition and to control prices. ❏ *a drug cartel*

car·ton /ˈkɑːtən/ NOUN [C] (**cartons**) **1** A **carton** is a plastic or cardboard container in which food or drink is sold. ❏ *A two-pint carton of milk is cheaper than two single pints.* **2** You can use **carton** to refer to the carton and its contents, or to the contents only. ❏ *He went to the shop for a carton of milk.*

car·toon /kɑːˈtuːn/ NOUN [C] (**cartoons**) **1** A **cartoon** is a humorous drawing or series of drawings in a newspaper or magazine. ❏ *Mickey Mouse, Donald Duck, and other Disney cartoon characters gave endless delight to millions of children.* **2** A **cartoon** is a film in which all the characters and scenes are drawn rather than being real people or objects. ❏ *a TV set blares out a cartoon comedy*

car·tridge /ˈkɑːtrɪdʒ/ NOUN [C] (**cartridges**) **1** A **cartridge** is a metal or cardboard tube containing a bullet and an explosive substance. Cartridges are used in guns. ❏ *Only four of the five spent cartridges were recovered by police.* **2** A **cartridge** is part of a machine or device that can be easily removed and replaced when it is worn out or empty. ❏ *Change the filter cartridge as often as instructed by the manufacturer.*

carve /kɑːv/ VERB

VERB [I, T] (**carves, carving, carved**) **1** [I, T] If you **carve** an object, you make it by cutting it out of a substance such as wood or stone. If you **carve** something such as wood or stone into an object, you make the object by cutting it out. = sculpt ❏ *One of the prisoners has carved a beautiful wooden chess set.* ❏ *I picked up a piece of wood and started carving.* **2** [T] If you **carve** writing or a design **on** an object, you cut it into the surface of the object. ❏ *He carved his name on his desk.* **3** [T] If you **carve** a piece of cooked meat, you cut slices from it so that you can eat it. ❏ *Andrew began to carve the chicken.*

PHRASAL VERBS **carve out** If you **carve out** a niche or a career, you succeed in getting the position or the career that you want by your own efforts. ❏ *Vick carved out his niche as the fastest server in tennis.*

carve up (*disapproval*) If you say that someone **carves** something **up**, you disapprove of the way they have divided it into small parts. ❏ *He has set about carving up the company which Hammer created from almost nothing.*

⚙**case** ◆◆◆ /keɪs/ NOUN

NOUN [C] (**cases**) **1** A particular **case** is a particular situation or incident, especially one that you are using as an individual example or instance of something. ❏ *Surgical training takes at least nine years, or 11 in the case of obstetrics.* ❏ *In extreme cases, insurance companies can prosecute for fraud.* ❏ *The Honduran press published reports of eighteen cases of alleged baby snatching.* **2** A **case** is a person or their particular problem that a doctor, social worker, or other professional is dealing with. ❏ *Dr Thomas Bracken describes the case of a 45-year-old Catholic priest much given to prayer whose left knee became painful.* ❏ *Some cases of arthritis respond to a gluten-free diet.* ❏ *the case of a 57-year-old man who had suffered a stroke* ❏ *Child protection workers were meeting to discuss her case.* **3** If you say that someone is a sad **case** or a hopeless **case**, you mean that they are in a sad situation or a hopeless situation. ❏ *I knew I was going to make it – that I wasn't a hopeless case.* **4** A **case** is a crime or mystery that the police are investigating. ❏ *The police have several suspects in the case of five murders committed in Gainesville, Florida.* **5** The **case for** or **against** a plan or idea consists of the facts and reasons used to support it or oppose it. ❏ *He sat there while I made the case for his dismissal.* ❏ *Both these facts strengthen the case against hanging.* **6** In law, a **case** is a trial or other legal inquiry. = trial, action ❏ *It can be difficult for public figures to win a libel case.* ❏ *The case was brought by his family, who say their reputation has been damaged by allegations about him.* **7** A **case** is a container that is specially designed to hold or protect something. ❏ *a black case for his glasses* **8** In the grammar of many languages, the **case** of a group such as a noun group or adjective group is the form it has which shows its relationship to other groups in the sentence.

PHRASES **in any case** (*emphasis*) You say **in any case** when you are adding something which is more important than what you have just said, but which supports or corrects it. = anyway, besides ❏ *The concert was sold out, and in any case, most of the people gathered in the square could not afford the price of a ticket.*

in case or **just in case** If you do something **in case** or **just in case** a particular thing happens, you do it because that thing might happen. ❏ *In case anyone was following me, I made an elaborate detour.*

in case of something If you do something or have something **in case of** a particular thing, you do it or have it because that thing might happen or be true. ❏ *Many shops along the route have been boarded up in case of trouble.*

in case (*feelings*) You use **in case** in expressions like 'in case you didn't know' or 'in case you've forgotten' when you are telling someone in a rather irritated way something that you think is either obvious or none of their business. ❏ *She's nervous about something, in case you didn't notice.*

in that case or **in which case** You say **in that case** or **in which case** to indicate that what you are going to say is true if the possible situation that has just been mentioned actually exists. ❏ *Perhaps you've some doubts about the attack. In that case it may interest you to know that Miss Woods witnessed it.*

C

just in case You can say that you are doing something **just in case** to refer vaguely to the possibility that a thing might happen or be true, without saying exactly what it is. ❑ *I guess we've already talked about this but I'll ask you again just in case.*

a case of If you say that a task or situation is **a case of** a particular thing, you mean that it consists of that thing or can be described as that thing. ❑ *It's not a case of whether anyone would notice or not.*

be the case If you say that something **is the case**, you mean that it is true or correct. ❑ *You'll probably notice her having difficulty swallowing. If this is the case, give her plenty of liquids.*

→ See also **test case, briefcase**

WORD CONNECTIONS

ADJ + **case**

a **particular** case
a **rare** case
an **extreme** case
❑ *In extreme cases the disease can be fatal.*

VERB + **case**

win a case
lose a case
bring a case
continue a case
❑ *He won a case against his employer for unfair dismissal.*

NOUN + **case**

a **murder** case
a **rape** case
a **libel** case
❑ *It is one of the most notorious murder cases in English criminal history.*

a **court** case
❑ *The court case is expected to last for three weeks.*

✪ **case stud·y** NOUN [c] (**case studies**) A **case study** is a written account that gives detailed information about a person, group, or thing and their development over a period of time. ❑ *a large case study of malaria in West African children*

cash ♦♦◇ /kæʃ/ NOUN, VERB
NOUN [u] **1** **Cash** is money in the form of notes and coins rather than cheques. ❑ *two thousand dollars in cash* **2** (*informal*) **Cash** means the same as money, especially money which is immediately available. = money ❑ *a state-owned financial-services group with plenty of cash* **VERB** [T] (**cashes, cashing, cashed**) If you **cash** a cheque, you exchange it at a bank for the amount of money that it is worth. ❑ *There are similar charges if you want to cash a cheque or withdraw money at a branch other than your own.* **PHRASAL VERB** **cash in** **1** (*disapproval*) If you say that someone **cashes in on** a situation, you are criticizing them for using it to gain an advantage, often in an unfair or dishonest way. ❑ *Residents said local gang leaders had cashed in on the violence to seize valuable land.* **2** If you **cash in** something such as an insurance policy, you exchange it for money. ❑ *Avoid cashing in a policy early as you could lose out heavily.*

cash dis·pens·er (*BrE*; in *AmE*, use **ATM**) NOUN [c] (**cash dispensers**) A **cash dispenser** is a machine built into the wall of a bank or other building, which allows people to take out money from their bank account using a special card. = cashpoint

cash·ier /kæˈʃɪə/ NOUN [c] (**cashiers**) A **cashier** is a person who customers pay money to or get money from in places such as shops or banks.

cash·point /ˈkæʃpɔɪnt/ NOUN [c] (**cashpoints**) (*BrE*) A **cashpoint** is the same as a **cash dispenser**.

cash reg·is·ter NOUN [c] (**cash registers**) A **cash register** is a machine in a shop, bar, or restaurant that is used to add up and record how much money people pay, and in which the money is kept. = till

ca·si·no /kəˈsiːnəʊ/ NOUN [c] (**casinos**) A casino is a

building or room where people play gambling games such as roulette.

cast ♦♦◇ /kɑːst, kæst/ NOUN, VERB
NOUN [c] (**casts**) **1** The **cast** of a play or film is all the people who act in it. ❑ *The show is very amusing and the cast is very good.* **2** A **cast** is a model that has been made by pouring a liquid such as plaster or hot metal onto something or into something, so that when it hardens it has the same shape as that thing. ❑ *An orthodontist took a cast of the inside of Billy's mouth to make a dental plate.* **3** A **cast** is a cover made of plaster of Paris which is used to protect a broken bone by keeping a part of the body stiff. **VERB** [T] (**casts, casting, cast**) **1** To **cast** an actor **in** a play or film means to choose them to act a particular role in it. ❑ *The world premiere of Harold Pinter's new play casts Ian Holm in the lead role.* ❑ *He was cast as a college professor.* **2** (*written*) If you **cast** your eyes or **cast** a look in a particular direction, you look quickly in that direction. ❑ *He cast a stern glance at the two men.* ❑ *I cast my eyes down briefly.* **3** (*written*) If something **casts** a light or shadow somewhere, it causes it to appear there. ❑ *The moon cast a bright light over the yard.* **4** To **cast** doubt **on** something means to cause people to be unsure about it. ❑ *Last night a top criminal psychologist cast doubt on the theory.* **5** When you **cast** your vote in an election, you vote. ❑ *About ninety-five per cent of those who cast their votes approve the new constitution.* **6** To **cast** an object means to make it by pouring a liquid such as hot metal into a specially shaped container and leaving it there until it becomes hard. ❑ *Our door knocker is cast in solid brass.* **PHRASAL VERB** **cast aside** If you **cast aside** someone or something, you get rid of them because they are no longer necessary or useful to you. ❑ *We need to cast aside outdated policies.*
✦ **cast your mind back** → see mind

caste /kɑːst, kæst/ NOUN [c, u] (**castes**) **1** [c] A **caste** is one of the traditional social classes into which people are divided in a Hindu society. ❑ *Most of the upper castes worship the goddess Kali.* **2** [u] **Caste** is the system of dividing people in a society into different social classes. ❑ *Caste is defined primarily by social honour attained through personal lifestyle.*

cas·tle ♦◇◇ /ˈkɑːsəl, ˈkæsəl/ NOUN [c] (**castles**) A **castle** is a large building with thick, high walls. Castles were built by important people, such as kings, in former times, especially for protection during wars and battles.

✪ **cas·ual** /ˈkæʒuəl/ ADJ **1** If you are **casual**, you are, or you pretend to be, relaxed and not very concerned about what is happening or what you are doing. ❑ *It's difficult for me to be casual about anything.* **2** [casual + N] A **casual** event or situation happens by chance or without planning. ❑ *What you mean as a casual remark could be misinterpreted.* **3** [casual + N] **Casual** clothes are ones that you normally wear at home or on holiday, and not on formal occasions. ❑ *I also bought some casual clothes for the weekend.* **4** (*mainly BrE*; in *AmE*, use **temporary**) **Casual** work is done for short periods and not on a permanent or regular basis. = temporary; ≠ permanent ❑ *establishments which employ people on a casual basis, such as pubs and restaurants* ❑ *It became increasingly expensive to hire casual workers.*
casu·al·ly /ˈkæʒuəli/ ADV **1** [casually with V] ❑ *'No need to hurry,' Ben said casually.* **2** [casually + -ED, casually after V] ❑ *They were casually dressed.*

casu·al·ty ♦◇◇ /ˈkæʒuəlti/ NOUN [c, u] (**casualties**) **1** [c] A **casualty** is a person who is injured or killed in a war or in an accident. ❑ *Troops fired on the demonstrators causing many casualties.* **2** [c] A **casualty** of a particular event or situation is a person or a thing that has suffered badly as a result of that event or situation. = victim ❑ *The car industry has been one of the greatest casualties of the recession.* **3** [u] (*BrE*; in *AmE*, use **emergency room**) **Casualty** is the part of a hospital where people who have severe injuries or sudden illnesses are taken for emergency treatment.

cat ♦◇◇ /kæt/ NOUN [c] (**cats**) **1** A **cat** is a furry animal that has a long tail and sharp claws. Cats are often kept as pets. **2** **Cats** are lions, tigers, and other wild animals in the same family. ❑ *The lion is perhaps the most famous member of the cat family.*

❖**cata·logue** /ˈkætəlɒg/ (in AmE, use **catalog**) NOUN, VERB

[NOUN] [c] (**catalogues**) ■ A **catalogue** is a list of things such as the goods you can buy from a particular company, the objects in a museum, or the books in a library. = list ❑ *the world's biggest seed catalogue* ■ A **catalogue of** similar things, especially bad things, is a number of them considered or discussed one after another. ❑ *His story is a catalogue of misfortune.*

[VERB] [T] (**catalogues, cataloguing, catalogued**) To **catalogue** things means to make a list of them. = list ❑ *The Royal Greenwich Observatory was founded to observe and catalogue the stars.* ❑ *The report catalogues a long list of extreme weather patterns.*

❖**ca·tas·tro·phe** /kəˈtæstrəfi/ NOUN [C, U] (**catastrophes**) A **catastrophe** is an unexpected event that causes great suffering or damage. = disaster ❑ *From all points of view, war would be a catastrophe.* ❑ *If the world is to avoid environmental catastrophe, advanced economies must undergo a profound transition.*

❖**cata·stroph·ic** /ˌkætəˈstrɒfɪk/ ADJ ■ Something that is **catastrophic** involves or causes a sudden terrible disaster. = disastrous ❑ *A tidal wave caused by the earthquake hit the coast causing catastrophic damage.* ❑ *The water shortage in this country is potentially catastrophic.* ❑ *The minister warned that if war broke out, it would be catastrophic for the whole world.* ■ If you describe something as **catastrophic**, you mean that it is very bad or unsuccessful. = disastrous ❑ *another catastrophic attempt to arrest control from a rival Christian militia*

❖**cata·strophi·cal·ly** /ˌkætəˈstrɒfɪkli/ ADV = disastrously ❑ *The faulty left-hand engine failed catastrophically as the aircraft approached the airport.* ❑ *catastrophically injured people*

catch ◆◆◇ /kætʃ/ VERB, NOUN

[VERB] [T, I, PASSIVE] (**catches, catching, caught**) ■ [T] If you **catch** a person or animal, you capture them after chasing them, or by using a trap, net, or other device. = capture ❑ *Police say they are confident of catching the gunman.* ❑ *Where did you catch the fish?* ■ [T] If you **catch** an object that is moving through the air, you seize it with your hands. ❑ *I jumped up to catch a ball and fell over.* ■ [T] If you **catch** a part of someone's body, you take or seize it with your hand, often in order to stop them from going somewhere. = seize ❑ *Liz caught his arm.* ❑ *He knelt beside her and caught her hand in both of his.* ■ [T] If one thing **catches** another, it hits it accidentally or manages to hit it. ❑ *The stinging slap almost caught his face.* ❑ *I may have caught him with my elbow but it was just an accident.* ■ [I] If something **catches on** or **in** an object, it accidentally becomes attached to the object or stuck in it. ❑ *Her ankle caught on a root, and she almost lost her balance.* ■ [T] When you **catch** a bus, train, or plane, you get on it in order to travel somewhere. = get ❑ *We were in plenty of time for Anthony to catch the ferry.* ■ [T] If you **catch** someone doing something wrong, you see or find them doing it. ❑ *He caught a youth breaking into a car.* ❑ *I don't want to catch you pushing yourself into the picture to get some personal publicity.* ■ [T] If you **catch yourself** doing something, especially something surprising, you suddenly become aware that you are doing it. = find ❑ *I caught myself feeling almost sorry for poor Mr Laurence.* ■ [T] If you **catch** something or **catch** a glimpse of it, you notice it or manage to see it briefly. ❑ *As she turned back she caught the puzzled look on her mother's face.* ■ [T] If you **catch** something that someone has said, you manage to hear it. ❑ *His ears caught a faint cry.* ❑ *I do not believe I caught your name.* ■ [T] If you **catch** a TV or radio programme or an event, you manage to see or listen to it. ❑ *Bill turns on the radio to catch the local news.* ■ [T] If you **catch** someone, you manage to contact or meet them to talk to them, especially when they are just about to go somewhere else. ❑ *I dialled Elizabeth's number thinking I might catch her before she left for work.* ■ [T] If something or someone **catches** you by surprise or at a bad time, you were not expecting them or do not feel

able to deal with them. ❑ *She looked as if the photographer had caught her by surprise.* ❑ *I'm sorry but I just cannot say anything. You've caught me at a bad time.* ■ [T] If something **catches** your attention or your eye, you notice it or become interested in it. ❑ *My shoes caught his attention.* ■ [T] If you **catch** a cold or a disease, you become ill with it. ❑ *The more stress you are under, the more likely you are to catch a cold.* ■ [T] If something **catches** the light or if the light **catches** it, it reflects the light and looks bright or shiny. ❑ *They saw the ship's guns, catching the light of the moon.* ■ [PASSIVE] If you **are caught** in a storm or other unpleasant situation, it happens when you cannot avoid its effects. ❑ *When he was fishing off the island he was caught in a storm and almost drowned.* ■ [PASSIVE] If you **are caught between** two alternatives or two people, you do not know which one to choose or follow. ❑ *The Jordanian leader is caught between both sides in the dispute.*

[PHRASAL VERBS] **catch on** ■ If you **catch on to** something, you understand it, or realize that it is happening. ❑ *He got what he could out of me before I caught on to the kind of person he'd turned into.* ■ If something **catches on**, it becomes popular. ❑ *The idea has been around for ages without catching on.*

catch up ■ If you **catch up with** someone who is in front of you, you reach them by walking faster than they are walking. ❑ *I stopped and waited for her to catch up.* ■ To **catch up with** someone means to reach the same standard, stage, or level that they have reached. ❑ *Most late developers will catch up with their friends.* ❑ *John began the season better than me but I have fought to catch up.* ■ If you **catch up on** an activity that you have not had much time to do recently, you spend time doing it. ❑ *I was catching up on a bit of reading.* ■ If you **catch up** on friends who you have not seen for some time or on their lives, you talk to them and find out what has happened in their lives since you last talked together. ❑ *The ladies spent some time catching up on each other's health and families.* ■ If you **are caught up in** something, you are involved in it, usually unwillingly. ❑ *The people themselves weren't part of the conflict; they were just caught up in it.*

catch up with ■ When people **catch up with** someone who has done something wrong, they succeed in finding them in order to arrest or punish them. ❑ *The law caught up with him yesterday.* ■ If something **catches up with** you, you are forced to deal with something unpleasant that happened or that you did in the past, which you have been able to avoid until now. ❑ *Although he subsequently became a successful businessman, his criminal past caught up with him.*

[NOUN] [c] (**catches**) ■ A **catch** is when you use your hands to seize an object that is moving through the air. ❑ *He missed the catch and the game was lost.* ■ A **catch** on a window, door, or container is a device that fastens it. ❑ *She fiddled with the catch of her bag.* ■ A **catch** is a hidden problem or difficulty in a plan or an offer that seems surprisingly good. = snag ❑ *The catch is that you work for your supper, and the food and accommodations can be very basic.*

✦ **catch sight of** → see **sight**; **catch fire** → see **fire**

❖**cat·ego·rize** /ˈkætɪgəraɪz/ also **categorise** VERB [T] (**categorizes, categorizing, categorized**) If you **categorize** people or things, you divide them into sets or you say which set they belong to. = classify ❑ *Lindsay, like his films, is hard to categorize.* ❑ *new ways of categorizing information* ❑ *Make a list of your child's toys and then categorize them as sociable or antisocial.*

cat·ego·ri·za·tion /ˌkætɪgəraɪˈzeɪʃən/ also **categorisation** NOUN [C, U] (**categorizations**) = classification ❑ *Her first novel defies easy categorization.*

❖**cat·ego·ry** ◆◇◇ /ˈkætɪgri, AmE -gɔːri/ NOUN [c] (**categories**) (*academic word*) If people or things are divided into **categories**, they are divided into groups in such a way that the members of each group are similar to each other in some way. = class, classification ❑ *This book clearly falls into the category of fictionalized autobiography.* ❑ *The tables were organized into six different categories.*

ca·ter /ˈkeɪtə/ VERB [I] (**caters, catering, catered**) ■ To

C

cater for a group of people means to provide all the things that they need or want. ▢ *We cater for an exclusive clientele.* **2** To **cater for** something means to take it into account. ▢ *Exercise classes cater for all levels of fitness.* ▢ *shops that cater for the needs of men* **3** If a person or company **caters for** an occasion such as a wedding or a party, they provide food and drink for all the people there. ▢ *a full-service restaurant equipped to cater for large events*
→ See also **catering**

ca·ter·ing /ˈkeɪtərɪŋ/ NOUN [U] [also 'the' catering, oft catering + N] **Catering** is the activity of providing food and drink for a large number of people, for example at weddings and parties. ▢ *His catering business made him a millionaire at 41.*

ca·the·dral /kəˈθiːdrəl/ NOUN [C] (**cathedrals**) A **cathedral** is a very large and important church which has a bishop in charge of it. ▢ *St Paul's Cathedral*

cat·tle /ˈkætəl/ NOUN [PL] **Cattle** are cows and bulls. ▢ *the finest herd of beef cattle for two hundred miles*

caught /kɔːt/ IRREG FORM **Caught** is the past tense and past participle of **catch**.

✪**cause** ◆◆◆ /kɔːz/ NOUN, VERB
NOUN [C, U] (**causes**) **1** [C] The **cause** of an event, usually a bad event, is the thing that makes it happen. = reason ▢ *Smoking is the biggest preventable cause of death and disease.* **2** [C] A **cause** is an aim or principle which a group of people supports or is fighting for. ▢ *Refusing to have one leader has not helped the cause.* **3** [U] If you have **cause for** a particular feeling or action, you have good reasons for feeling it or doing it. = reason ▢ *Only a few people can find any cause for celebration.*
PHRASE **for a good cause** If you say that something is **for a good cause**, you mean that it is worth doing or giving to because it will help other people, for example by raising money for charity. ▢ *The Raleigh International Bike Ride is open to anyone who wants to raise money for a good cause.*
VERB [T] (**causes, causing, caused**) To **cause** something, usually something bad, means to make it happen. = make, lead to, bring about ▢ *The insecticide used on some weeds can cause health problems.* ▢ *This was a genuine mistake, but it did cause me some worry.* ▢ *a protein that gets into animal cells and attacks other proteins, causing disease to spread*

WORD CONNECTIONS
cause + OF + NOUN
the cause of an **accident** the cause of a **crash** the cause of a **fire** the cause of a **disease** ▢ *Police are investigating the cause of the accident.*
the cause of **death** ▢ *Accidents are the most common cause of death among young people.*
VERB + **cause**
determine the cause **investigate** the cause **identify** the cause **establish** the cause **find** the cause ▢ *Firefighters believe they have identified the cause of the fire.*
ADJ + **cause**
the **root** cause the **underlying** cause ▢ *The underlying cause of many road accidents is driver fatigue.*
a **common** cause a **probable** cause a **major** cause ▢ *Drinking too much alcohol is a major cause of liver disease.*

✪**cau·tion** /ˈkɔːʃən/ NOUN, VERB
NOUN [U] (**cautions**) **1** **Caution** is great care which you take in order to avoid possible danger. = care, prudence

▢ *Extreme caution should be exercised when buying used tyres.* ▢ *The Chancellor is a man of caution.* **2** **Caution** is the act of warning someone about problems or danger. = warning ▢ *There was a note of caution for the treasury in the figures.* VERB [I, T] (**cautions, cautioning, cautioned**) If someone **cautions** you, they warn you about problems or danger. = warn ▢ *Tony cautioned against misrepresenting the situation.* ▢ *The statement clearly was intended to caution Seoul against attempting to block the council's action again.*

✪**cau·tious** ◆◇◇ /ˈkɔːʃəs/ ADJ Someone who is **cautious** acts very carefully in order to avoid possible danger. = careful, circumspect; ≠ rash ▢ *The scientists are cautious about using enzyme therapy on humans.* ▢ *Many Canadians have become overly cautious when it comes to investing.* ▢ *He has been seen as a champion of a more cautious approach to economic reform.* ▢ *There may have been good reasons for this cautious attitude.*
✪**cau·tious·ly** /ˈkɔːʃəsli/ ADV = circumspectly, carefully; ≠ rashly ▢ *David moved cautiously forward and looked over the edge.* ▢ *These borderline differences should be interpreted cautiously given the number of outcomes examined.* ▢ *I am cautiously optimistic that a new government will be concerned and aware about the environment.* ▢ *Rebel sources have so far reacted cautiously to the threat.*

cav·al·ry /ˈkævəlri/ NOUN [SING] **1** The **cavalry** is the part of an army that uses armoured vehicles for fighting. ▢ *The 3rd Cavalry went on the offensive.* **2** The **cavalry** is the group of soldiers in an army who ride horses. ▢ *a young cavalry officer*

cave ◆◇◇ /keɪv/ NOUN
NOUN [C] (**caves**) A **cave** is a large hole in the side of a cliff or hill, or one that is under the ground. ▢ *Outside the cave mouth the blackness of night was like a curtain.*
PHRASAL VERB **cave in** (**caves, caving, caved**) **1** If something such as a roof or a ceiling **caves in**, it collapses inwards. = collapse ▢ *Part of the roof has caved in.* **2** If you **cave in**, you suddenly stop arguing or resisting, especially when people put pressure on you to stop. = give in ▢ *After a ruinous strike, the union caved in.* ▢ *The judge has caved in to political pressure.*

cav·ern /ˈkævən/ NOUN [C] (**caverns**) A **cavern** is a large, deep cave.

CD ◆◇◇ /ˌsiː ˈdiː/ NOUN [C] (**CDs**) **CDs** are small plastic discs on which sound, especially music, is recorded. **CDs** can also be used to store information which can be read by a computer. **CD** is an abbreviation for 'compact disc'. ▢ *The Beatles' Red and Blue compilations are issued on CD for the first time next month.*

CD-ROM /ˌsiː diː ˈrɒm/ NOUN [C] (**CD-ROMs**) (*computing*) A **CD-ROM** is a CD on which a very large amount of information can be stored and then read using a computer. **CD-ROM** is an abbreviation for 'compact disc read-only memory'. ▢ *A single CD-ROM can hold more than 500 megabytes of data.*

✪**cease** ◆◇◇ /siːs/ VERB [I, T] (**ceases, ceasing, ceased**) (*academic word, formal*) **1** [I] If something **ceases**, it stops happening or existing. = halt; ≠ begin ▢ *At one o'clock the rain had ceased.* **2** [T] If you **cease** to do something, you stop doing it. ≠ begin ▢ *He never ceases to amaze me.* ▢ *The secrecy about the president's condition had ceased to matter.* ▢ *A brain deprived of oxygen ceases to function within a few minutes.* **3** [T] If you **cease** something, you stop it happening or working. = stop; ≠ begin ▢ *The Tundra Times, a weekly newspaper in Alaska, ceased publication this week.* ▢ *A small number of firms have ceased trading.*

cease·fire ◆◇◇ /ˈsiːsfaɪə/ NOUN [C] (**ceasefires**) A **ceasefire** is an arrangement in which countries or groups of people that are fighting each other agree to stop fighting. = truce ▢ *They have agreed to a ceasefire after three years of conflict.*

ceil·ing /ˈsiːlɪŋ/ NOUN [C] (**ceilings**) **1** A **ceiling** is the horizontal surface that forms the top part or roof inside a room. ▢ *The rooms were spacious, with tall windows and high ceilings.* **2** A **ceiling on** something such as prices or wages is an official upper limit that cannot be broken. = limit ▢ *an informal agreement to put a ceiling on salaries*

WORDS IN CONTEXT: CELEBRITY

One of the consequences of being a celebrity is being in the public spotlight. However, famous people deserve to be protected from the media when going about their private lives.

To what extent do you agree or disagree?

Being a celebrity often means **seeking publicity** to get **media coverage** for a new project. **TV personalities** might have **to promote** a new programme or book, and **film stars** will **attend movie premieres** and stand on **the red carpet** to **pose for the cameras**.

Equally, the media use **public figures** to sell their newspapers or **glossy magazines**. Large fees are offered to celebrities to encourage them **to sell their story**, or to provide **an exclusive** such as a **photo shoot** of a wedding. This **publicity** also helps the celebrity, as it keeps them **in the media spotlight**, and therefore maintains their **public image**.

However, this type of activity can sometimes go too far. The **tabloids** often print photographs taken by the **paparazzi** of the **private lives** of celebrities. Journalists are encouraged to find out more about the hidden lives of pubic figures. In cases like these, famous people and their families deserve protection. It is not **in the public interest** to learn where someone went on holiday with their children, or whether they have put on weight. In cases like these, there should be a law to protect an individual from **press intrusion**.

cel·e·brate ♦◇◇ /ˈselɪbreɪt/ VERB [I, T] (**celebrates, celebrating, celebrated**) **1** [I, T] If you **celebrate** an occasion or if you **celebrate**, you do something enjoyable because of a special occasion or to mark someone's success. ◻ *I was in a mood to celebrate.* ◻ *Dick celebrated his 60th birthday on Monday.* **2** [T] If an organization or country **is celebrating** an anniversary, it has existed for that length of time and is doing something special because of it. ◻ *The society is celebrating its tenth anniversary this year.* **3** [T] When priests **celebrate** Holy Communion or Mass, they officially perform the actions and ceremonies that are involved. ◻ *Pope John Paul celebrated mass today in a city in central Poland.*

cel·e·brat·ed /ˈselɪbreɪtɪd/ ADJ A **celebrated** person or thing is famous and much admired. = renowned ◻ *He was soon one of the most celebrated young painters in England.*

cel·e·bra·tion ♦◇◇ /ˌselɪˈbreɪʃən/ NOUN [C, SING] (**celebrations**) **1** [C] A **celebration** is a special enjoyable event that people organize because something pleasant has happened or because it is someone's birthday or anniversary. ◻ *I can tell you, there was a celebration in our house that night.* **2** [SING] The **celebration of** something is praise and appreciation which is given to it. ◻ *This was not a memorial service but a celebration of his life.*

✪ ce·leb·ri·ty /sɪˈlebrɪti/ NOUN [C, U] (**celebrities**) **1** [C] A **celebrity** is someone who is famous, especially in areas of entertainment such as films, music, writing, or sport. = star ◻ *In 1944, at the age of 30, Hersey suddenly became a celebrity.* **2** [U] If a person or thing achieves **celebrity**, they become famous, especially in areas of entertainment such as films, music, writing, or sport. ◻ *He achieved celebrity as a sports commentator.*

cel·i·bate /ˈselɪbət/ ADJ, NOUN
ADJ **1** Someone who is **celibate** does not marry or have sex, because of their religious beliefs. ◻ *The Pope bluntly told the world's priests yesterday to stay celibate.* **2** Someone who is **celibate** does not have sex during a particular period of their life. ◻ *I was celibate for two years.*
NOUN [C] (**celibates**) A **celibate** is someone who is celibate. ◻ *the USA's biggest group of celibates*

✪ cell ♦♦◇ /sel/ NOUN [C] (**cells**) **1** A **cell** is the smallest part of an animal or plant that is able to function independently. Every animal or plant is made up of millions of cells. ◻ *Those cells divide and give many other different types of cells.* ◻ *blood cells* ◻ *Soap destroys the cell walls of bacteria.* **2** A **cell** is a small room in which a prisoner is locked. A **cell** is also a small room in which a monk or nun lives. ◻ *Do you recall how many prisoners were placed in each cell?*

cel·lar /ˈselə/ NOUN [C] (**cellars**) **1** A **cellar** is a room underneath a building, which is often used for storing things in. ◻ *The box of papers had been stored in a cellar at the family home.* **2** A person's or restaurant's **cellar** is the collection of different wines that they have. ◻ *Choose a superb wine to complement your meal from our extensive wine cellar.*

cel·lu·lar /ˈseljʊlə/ ADJ **Cellular** means relating to the cells of animals or plants. ◻ *Many toxic effects can be studied at the cellular level.*

✪ Celsius /ˈselsiəs/ ADJ, NOUN
ADJ [N/NUM Celsius] **Celsius** is a scale for measuring temperature, in which water freezes at 0 degrees and boils at 100 degrees. It is represented by the symbol °C. = centigrade ◻ *Highest temperatures 11° Celsius, that's 52° Fahrenheit.* ◻ *an increase of just one degree Celsius in core body temperature*
NOUN [U] The temperature in **Celsius** is measured on a scale in which water freezes at 0 degrees and boils at 100 degrees. = centigrade ◻ *The thermometer shows the temperature in Celsius and Fahrenheit.*

ce·ment /sɪˈment/ NOUN, VERB
NOUN [U] **1 Cement** is a grey powder which is mixed with sand and water in order to make concrete. ◻ *Builders have trouble getting the right amount of cement into their concrete.* **2 Cement** is the same as **concrete**. ◻ *the hard, cold cement floor* **3** Glue that is made for sticking particular substances together is sometimes called **cement**. ◻ *Stick the pieces on with tile cement.*
VERB [T] (**cements, cementing, cemented**) **1** Something that **cements** a relationship or agreement makes it stronger. ◻ *Nothing cements a friendship between countries so much as trade.* **2** If things **are cemented** together, they are stuck or fastened together. ◻ *Most artificial joints are cemented into place.*

cem·e·tery /ˈsemətri, AmE -teri/ NOUN [C] (**cemeteries**) A **cemetery** is a place where dead people's bodies or their ashes are buried. = graveyard

✪ cen·sor /ˈsensə/ VERB, NOUN
VERB [T] (**censors, censoring, censored**) **1** If someone in authority **censors** letters or the media, they officially examine them and cut out any information that is regarded as secret. = cut ◻ *The military-backed government has heavily censored the news.* ◻ *ITV companies tend to censor bad language in feature films.* **2** If someone in authority **censors** a book, play, or film, they officially examine it and cut out any parts that are considered to be immoral or inappropriate. ◻ *The Late Show censored the band's live version of 'Bullet in the Head'.*

C

NOUN [c] (**censors**) **1** A **censor** is a person who has been officially appointed to examine letters or the media and to cut out any parts that are regarded as secret. ❑ *The report was cleared by the American military censors.* **2** A **censor** is a person who has been officially appointed to examine plays, films, and books and to cut out any parts that are considered to be immoral. ❑ *The film had to be cut before the board of censors accepted it.*

✪ **cen·sor·ship** /ˈsensəʃɪp/ NOUN [u] **Censorship** is the censoring of books, plays, films, or reports, especially by government officials, because they are considered immoral or secret in some way. ❑ *The government today announced that press censorship was being lifted.* ❑ *constant battles over censorship and the limits of good taste*

cen·sure /ˈsenʃə/ VERB, NOUN

VERB [T] (**censures, censuring, censured**) (*formal*) If you **censure** someone **for** something that they have done, you tell them that you strongly disapprove of it. = **criticize** ❑ *The ethics committee may take a decision to admonish him or to censure him.*

NOUN [u] An act of **censure** is when you tell someone that you strongly disapprove of something that they have done. ❑ *It is a controversial policy which has attracted international censure.*

✪ **cen·sus** /ˈsensəs/ NOUN [c] (**censuses**) A **census** is an official survey of the population of a country that is carried out in order to find out how many people live there and to obtain details of such things as people's ages and jobs. ❑ *The detailed assessment of the latest census will be ready in three months.* ❑ *Population censuses in India show that the number of girls has been falling steadily for the past 20 years relative to the number of boys.* ❑ *In the new study, Kaplan studied census data collected between 2007 and 2009.*

cent /sent/ NOUN [c] (**cents**) A **cent** is a small unit of money worth one hundredth of some currencies, for example the dollar and the euro. ❑ *A cup of rice which cost thirty cents a few weeks ago is now being sold for up to one dollar.*

✪ **cen·ti·grade** /ˈsentɪɡreɪd/ ADJ, NOUN

ADJ **Centigrade** is a scale for measuring temperature, in which water freezes at 0 degrees and boils at 100 degrees. It is represented by the symbol °C. = **Celsius** ❑ *daytime temperatures of up to forty degrees centigrade*

NOUN [u] The temperature in **centigrade** is measured according to a scale in which water freezes at 0 degrees and boils at 100 degrees. = **Celsius** ❑ *The number at the bottom is the recommended water temperature in centigrade.*

✪ **cen·ti·me·tre** /ˈsentɪmiːtə/ (*BrE*; in *AmE*, use **centimeter**) NOUN (**centimetres**) A **centimetre** is a unit of length in the metric system equal to ten millimetres or one-hundredth of a metre. ❑ *a tiny fossil plant, only a few centimetres high* ❑ *Up to 15 centimetres of snow was expected to fall on mainland Nova Scotia.*

✪ **cen·tral** /ˈsentrəl/ ADJ **1** Something that is **central** is in the middle of a place or area. ❑ *Central America's Caribbean coast* ❑ *The disruption has now spread and is affecting a large part of central Liberia.* **2** A place that is **central** is easy to reach because it is in the centre of a city, town, or particular area. ❑ *a central location in the capital* **3** [central + N] A **central** group or organization makes all the important decisions that are followed throughout a larger organization or a country. ❑ *There is a lack of trust towards the central government in Rome.* **4** The **central** person or thing in a particular situation is the most important one. = **main, chief, key**; ≠ **unimportant** ❑ *Black dance music has been central to mainstream pop since the early '60s.* ❑ *a central part of their culture*

✪ **cen·tral·ly** /ˈsentrəli/ ADV **1** The main cabin has its full-sized double bed placed with plenty of room around it. **2** this centrally located hotel, situated on the banks of the river **3** This is a centrally planned economy.

cen·tral heat·ing NOUN [u] **Central heating** is a heating system for buildings. Air or water is heated in one place and travels around a building through pipes and radiators. ❑ *I am thinking of installing central heating.*

cen·tral·ize /ˈsentrəlaɪz/ also **centralise** VERB [T]

(**centralizes, centralizing, centralized**) To **centralize** a country, state, or organization means to create a system in which one central group of people gives instructions to regional groups. ❑ *In the mass production era, multinational firms tended to centralize their operations.*

cen·trali·za·tion /ˌsentrəlaɪˈzeɪʃən/ NOUN [u] *public hostility to central banks and the centralization of power*

✪ **cen·tre** ♦♦♦ /ˈsentə/ (*BrE*; in *AmE*, use **center**) NOUN, VERB

NOUN [SING, c] (**centres**) **1** [SING, c] The **centre** of something is the middle of it. = **middle**; ≠ **edge** ❑ *A large, wooden table dominates the centre of the room.* ❑ *The pain of a heart attack is generally felt in the centre of the chest.* **2** [c] A **centre** is a building where people have meetings, take part in a particular activity, or get help of some kind. ❑ *She now also does pottery classes at a community centre.* **3** [c] If an area or town is a **centre** for an industry or activity, that industry or activity is very important there. ❑ *New York is also a major international financial centre.* **4** [c] The **centre** of a town or city is the part where there are the most shops and businesses and where a lot of people come from other areas to work or shop. ❑ *the city centre* ❑ *a busy street in the town centre* **5** [c] If something or someone is at the **centre of** a situation, they are the most important thing or person involved. = **heart, middle**; ≠ **edge** ❑ *the man at the centre of the controversy* ❑ *At the centre of the inquiry is real concern for the pensioners involved.* **6** [SING] If someone or something is the **centre of** attention or interest, people are giving them a lot of attention. = **focus** ❑ *The rest of the cast was used to her being the centre of attention.* **7** [SING] In politics, **the centre** refers to groups and their beliefs, when they are considered to be neither left-wing nor right-wing. ❑ *The Democrats have become a party of the centre.*

VERB [I, T] (**centres, centring, centred**) **1** If something **centres** or is **centred on** a particular thing or person, that thing or person is the main subject of attention. ❑ *The improvement was the result of a plan which centred on academic achievement and personal motivation.* ❑ *All his concerns were centred around himself rather than Rachel.* **2** If an industry or event is **centred** in a place, or if it **centres** there, it takes place to the greatest extent there. ❑ *The fighting has been centred around the town of Vucovar.* ❑ *The disturbances have centred around the two main university areas.*

-**centred** /ˈsentəd/ COMB ❑ *a child-centred approach to teaching*

centre·piece /ˈsentəpiːs/ (*BrE*; in *AmE*, use **centerpiece**) NOUN [c] (**centrepieces**) **1** The **centrepiece of** something is the best or most interesting part of it. ❑ *The centrepiece of the plan is the idea of regular referendums, initiated by voters.* **2** A **centrepiece** is an ornament which you put in the middle of something, especially a dinner table. ❑ *He was arranging floral centrepieces in the banquet hall.*

✪ **cen·tu·ry** ♦♦♦ /ˈsentʃəri/ NOUN [c] (**centuries**) **1** A **century** is a period of a hundred years that is used when stating a date. For example, the 19th century was the period from 1801 to 1900. ❑ *The material position of the Church had been declining since the late eighteenth century.* ❑ *a 17th-century merchant's house* **2** A **century** is any period of a hundred years. ❑ *The drought there is the worst in a century.* ❑ *This may be ending centuries of tradition.*

ce·ram·ic /sɪˈræmɪk/ NOUN [c, u] (**ceramics**) **1** [c, u] **Ceramic** is clay that has been heated to a very high temperature so that it becomes hard. ❑ *ceramic tiles* **2** [c] [usu pl] **Ceramics** are ceramic ornaments or objects. ❑ *a collection of Chinese ceramics* **3** [u] **Ceramics** is the art of making artistic objects out of clay. ❑ *a degree in ceramics*

ce·real /ˈsɪəriəl/ NOUN [c, u] (**cereals**) **1** [c, u] **Cereal** or **breakfast cereal** is a food made from grain. It is mixed with milk and eaten for breakfast. ❑ *I have a bowl of cereal every morning.* **2** [c] **Cereals** are plants such as wheat, corn, or rice that produce grain. ❑ *the cereal-growing districts of the Midwest*

cere·bral /ˈserɪbrəl, *AmE* səˈriːbrəl/ ADJ **1** (*formal*) If you describe someone or something as **cerebral**, you mean that they are intellectual rather than emotional. = **intellectual** ❑ *Washington struck me as a precarious place from which to publish such a cerebral newspaper.* **2** [cerebral + N] (*medical*) **Cerebral** means relating to the brain. ❑ *a cerebral haemorrhage*

cer·e·mo·nial /ˌserɪˈməʊniəl/ ADJ **1** [ceremonial + N] Something that is **ceremonial** relates to a ceremony or is used in a ceremony. □ *He represented the nation on ceremonial occasions.* **2** A position, function, or event that is **ceremonial** is considered to be representative of an institution, but has very little authority or influence. □ *Up to now the post of president has been largely ceremonial.*

cer·e·mo·ny ♦◇◇ /ˈserɪməni, AmE -məʊni/ NOUN [C, U] (ceremonies) **1** [c] A **ceremony** is a formal event such as a wedding. □ *his grandmother's funeral, a private ceremony attended only by the family* **2** [U] **Ceremony** consists of the special things that are said and done on very formal occasions. □ *The republic was proclaimed with great ceremony.*

⊙ **cer·tain** ♦◇◇ /ˈsɜːtən/ ADJ, QUANT

ADJ **1** [V-LINK + certain] If you are **certain** about something, you firmly believe it is true and have no doubt about it. If you are not **certain** about something, you do not have definite knowledge about it. = sure; ≠ uncertain □ *She's absolutely certain she's going to make it in the world.* □ *We are not certain whether the appendix had already burst or not.* **2** If you say that something is **certain to** happen, you mean that it will definitely happen. = sure □ *However, the scheme is certain to meet opposition from fishermen's leaders.* □ *It's not certain they'll accept that candidate if he wins.* □ *The prime minister is heading for certain defeat if he forces a vote.* **3** [V-LINK + certain] If you say that something is **certain**, you firmly believe that it is true, or have definite knowledge about it. = definite; ≠ uncertain □ *One thing is certain, both have the utmost respect for each other.* □ *It is certain that stammering becomes more pronounced when the rate of speech is increased.* **4** [DET + certain, certain + N] You use **certain** to indicate that you are referring to one particular thing, person, or group, although you are not saying exactly which it is. = particular, specific □ *There will be certain people who'll say 'I told you so!'* □ *This can create a marked improvement in certain skin conditions.* □ *Leaflets have been air dropped telling people to leave certain areas.* □ *You owe a certain person a sum of money.* **5** You use a **certain** to indicate that something such as a quality or condition exists, and often to suggest that it is not great in amount or degree. □ *That was the very reason why he felt a certain bitterness.*

PHRASES **for certain** If you know something **for certain**, you have no doubt at all about it. □ *She couldn't know what time he'd go, or even for certain that he'd go at all.*

make certain If you **make certain that** something is the way you want or expect it to be, you take action to ensure that it is. □ *Parents should make certain that the children spend enough time doing homework.*

QUANT [certain 'of' DEF-PL-N] (formal) When you refer to **certain** of a group of people or things, you are referring to some particular members of that group. = some □ *They'll have to give up completely on certain of their studies.*

VOCABULARY BUILDER

certain ADJ
If you are **certain** about something, you firmly believe it is true and have no doubt about it.
□ *She was certain that Mary was in the house, but somebody else was in there too.*

definite ADJ
You use **definite** to emphasize the strength of your opinion or belief.
□ *There have been definite improvements in parts of the health service over the past few years.*

known ADJ
If something is **known**, many people are aware of it and acknowledge its existence or accuracy.
□ *There is no known cure for rabies.*

positive ADJ
If you are **positive** about something, you know that it is correct.
□ *US intelligence officials are positive that the meeting took place.*

---

sure ADJ
If you are **sure** about something, you have no doubts that what you think about it is correct.
□ *It was wonderful of you and George to host the dinner, and I'm sure everyone enjoyed it.*

WHICH WORD?
certain or sure?

If you are **certain** or **sure** about something, you have no doubts about it.
□ *He felt certain that she would disapprove.*
□ *I'm sure she's right.*

If it is **certain** that something is true, it is definitely true. If it is **certain** that something will happen, it will definitely happen.
□ *It is certain that they will have some spectacular successes.*
You do not say that it is **sure** that something is true or will happen.

⊙ **cer·tain·ly** ♦♦◇ /ˈsɜːtənli/ ADV **1** [certainly with CL/GROUP] (emphasis) You use **certainly** to emphasize what you are saying when you are making a statement. = undoubtedly, definitely □ *The public is certainly getting tired of hearing about it.* □ *The bombs are almost certainly part of a much bigger conspiracy.* □ *Today's inflation figure is certainly too high.* □ *Certainly, pets can help children develop friendship skills.* **2** [certainly as reply] You use **certainly** when you are agreeing with what someone has said. □ *'In any case you remained friends.'—'Certainly.'* **3** [certainly as reply] (emphasis) You say **certainly not** to say 'no' in a strong way. □ *'Perhaps it would be better if I withdrew altogether.'—'Certainly not!'*

cer·tain·ty /ˈsɜːtənti/ NOUN [U, C] (certainties) **1** [U] **Certainty** is the state of being definite or of having no doubts at all about something. □ *I have told them with absolute certainty there'll be no change of policy.* **2** [U] [also 'a' certainty] **Certainty** is the fact that something is certain to happen. = inevitability □ *A general election became a certainty last week.* □ *the certainty of more violence and bloodshed* **3** [c] [usu pl] **Certainties** are things that nobody has any doubts about. □ *There are no certainties in modern Europe.*

cer·tifi·cate /səˈtɪfɪkət/ NOUN [c] (certificates) **1** A **certificate** is an official document stating that particular facts are true. □ *birth certificates* **2** A **certificate** is an official document that you receive when you have completed a course of study or training. The qualification that you receive is sometimes also called a **certificate**. □ *To the right of the fireplace are various framed certificates.*

cer·ti·fy /ˈsɜːtɪfaɪ/ VERB [T] (certifies, certifying, certified) **1** If someone in an official position **certifies** something, they officially state that it is true. □ *The president certified that the project would receive at least $650m from overseas sources.* □ *The National Election Council is supposed to certify the results of the election.* **2** If someone **is certified as** a particular kind of worker, they are given a certificate stating that they have successfully completed a course of training in their profession. □ *They wanted to get certified as divers.* □ *a certified public accountant*

cer·ti·fi·ca·tion /ˌsɜːtɪfɪˈkeɪʃən/ NOUN [C, U] (certifications) **1** [c, u] □ *An employer can demand written certification that the relative is really ill.* **2** [u] □ *Students would be offered on-the-job training leading to the certification of their skill in a particular field.*

⊙ **cf.** **cf.** is used in writing to introduce something that should be considered in connection with the subject you are discussing. = compare □ *For the more salient remarks on the matter, cf. 'Isis Unveiled', Vol. I.* □ *the beneficial effects of isolation from foreign capital (cf. Taylor, 1975, p.225)*

chain ♦◇◇ /tʃeɪn/ NOUN, VERB
NOUN [C, PL, SING] (chains) **1** [c] A **chain** consists of metal rings connected together in a line. □ *His open shirt revealed a fat gold chain.* **2** [c] A **chain** of things is a group of them existing or arranged in a line. □ *a chain of islands known as the Windward Islands* **3** [c] A **chain of** shops, hotels, or

C

other businesses is a number of them owned by the same person or company. ❑ *a large supermarket chain* **4** [PL] If prisoners are **in chains**, they have thick rings of metal around their wrists or ankles to prevent them from escaping. ❑ *He'd spent four and a half years in windowless cells, much of the time in chains.* **5** [SING] A **chain of** events is a series of them happening one after another. = **series** ❑ *the bizarre chain of events that led to his departure in January 1938*

VERB [T] (**chains, chaining, chained**) If a person or thing **is chained to** something, they are fastened to it with a chain. ❑ *The dogs were chained to a fence.* ❑ *We were sitting together in our cell, chained to the wall.*

PHRASAL VERB **chain up** Chain up means the same as **chain** VERB. ❑ *They kept me chained up every night and released me each day.*

✪ **chain re·ac·tion** NOUN [C] (**chain reactions**) **1** A **chain reaction** is a series of chemical changes, each of which causes the next. ❑ *Chain reactions triggered by bromine oxide are known to destroy ozone.* **2** A **chain reaction** is a series of events, each of which causes the next. ❑ *The powder immediately ignited and set off a chain reaction of explosions.* ❑ *Whenever recession strikes, a chain reaction is set into motion.*

chair ◆◆◇ /tʃeə/ NOUN, VERB

NOUN [C] (**chairs**) **1** A **chair** is a piece of furniture for one person to sit on, with a back and four legs. ❑ *He rose from his chair and walked to the window.* **2** At a university, the **chair** is the position or job of professor. ❑ *He has been appointed to the chair of sociology.* **3** The person who is the **chair of** a committee or meeting is the person in charge of it. = **chairperson** ❑ *She is the chair of the Defence Advisory Committee on Women in the Military.*

VERB [T] (**chairs, chairing, chaired**) If you **chair** a meeting or a committee, you are the person in charge of it. ❑ *He was about to chair a meeting in Venice of EU foreign ministers.*

chair·man ◆◆◇ /tʃeəmən/ NOUN [C] (**chairmen**) **1** The **chairman** of a committee, organization, or company is the head of it. ❑ *Glyn Ford is chairman of the committee which produced the report.* **2** The **chairman** of a meeting or debate is the person in charge, who decides when each person is allowed to speak. ❑ *The chairman declared the meeting open.*

chair·person /tʃeəpɜːsən/ NOUN [C] (**chairpersons**) The **chairperson** of a meeting, committee, or organization is the person in charge of it. ❑ *She's the chairperson of the safety committee.*

chair·woman /tʃeəwʊmən/ NOUN [C] (**chairwomen**) The **chairwoman** of a meeting, committee, or organization is the woman in charge of it. ❑ *Primakov was in Japan meeting with the chairwoman of the Socialist Party there.*

chalk /tʃɔːk/ NOUN, VERB

NOUN [U] (**chalks**) **1** Chalk is a type of soft, white rock. You can use small pieces of it for writing or drawing with. ❑ *white cliffs made of chalk* **2** [also chalks] Chalk is small sticks of chalk, or a substance similar to chalk, used for writing or drawing with. ❑ *somebody writing with a piece of chalk*

VERB [T] (**chalks, chalking, chalked**) If you **chalk** something, you draw or write it using a piece of chalk. ❑ *He chalked the message on the blackboard.*

PHRASAL VERB **chalk up** If you **chalk up** a success, a victory, or a number of points in a game, you achieve it. = **notch up** ❑ *For almost 11 months, the Bosnian army chalked up one victory after another.*

✪ **chal·lenge** ◆◆◇ /tʃælɪndʒ/ NOUN, VERB (*academic word*)

NOUN [C, U] (**challenges**) **1** A **challenge** is something new and difficult which requires great effort and determination. = **test** ❑ *The new government's first challenge is the economy.* ❑ *I like a big challenge and they don't come much bigger than this.* **2** [C, U] A **challenge to** something is a questioning of its truth or value. A **challenge to** someone is a questioning of their authority. ❑ *The demonstrators have now made a direct challenge to the authority of the government.* ❑ *Paranormal dreams pose a challenge to current scientific conceptions.* **3** [C] A **challenge**

is an occasion when someone says they are going to fight or compete with you. ❑ *A third presidential candidate emerged to mount a serious challenge and throw the campaign wide open.*

PHRASE **rise to the challenge** If someone **rises to the challenge**, they act in response to a difficult situation which is new to them and are successful. ❑ *The new Germany must rise to the challenge of its enhanced responsibilities.*

VERB [T] (**challenges, challenging, challenged**) **1** If you **challenge** ideas or people, you question their truth, value, or authority. ❑ *Democratic leaders have challenged the president to sign the bill.* ❑ *I challenged him on the hypocrisy of his political attitudes.* ❑ *The move was immediately challenged by two of the republics.* **2** If you **challenge** someone, you invite them to fight or compete with you in some way. ❑ *Marsyas thought he could play the flute better than Apollo and challenged the god to a contest.* ❑ *He left a note at the scene of the crime, challenging detectives to catch him.*

→ See also **challenging**

chal·leng·er /tʃælɪndʒə/ NOUN [C] (**challengers**) A **challenger** is someone who competes with you for a position or title that you already have, for example being a sports champion or a political leader. ❑ *The strongest challenger, Texas Democrat Martin Frost, has withdrawn from the race.*

chal·leng·ing /tʃælɪndʒɪŋ/ ADJ **1** A **challenging** task or job requires great effort and determination. = **demanding** ❑ *Mike found a challenging job as a computer programmer.* **2** If you do something in a **challenging** way, you seem to be inviting people to argue with you or compete against you in some way. = **defiant** ❑ *Mona gave him a challenging look.*

cham·ber ◆◇◇ /tʃeɪmbə/ NOUN [C] (**chambers**) **1** A **chamber** is a large room, especially one that is used for formal meetings. ❑ *We are going to be in the council chamber every time he speaks.* **2** You can refer to a country's legislature or to one section of it as a **chamber**. = **house** ❑ *More than 80 parties are contesting seats in the two-chamber parliament.* **3** A **chamber** is a room designed and equipped for a particular purpose. ❑ *For many, the dentist's office remains a torture chamber.*

cham·pagne /ʃæmˈpeɪn/ NOUN [C, U] (**champagnes**) Champagne is an expensive French white wine with bubbles in. It is often drunk to celebrate something.

cham·pi·on ◆◆◇ /tʃæmpiən/ NOUN, VERB

NOUN [C] (**champions**) **1** A **champion** is someone who has won the first prize in a competition, contest, or fight. ❑ *a former Olympic champion* ❑ *Kasparov became world champion.* **2** If you are a **champion** of a person, a cause, or a principle, you support or defend them. ❑ *He received acclaim as a champion of the oppressed.*

VERB [T] (**champions, championing, championed**) If you **champion** a person, a cause, or a principle, you support or defend them. ❑ *He passionately championed the poor.*

cham·pi·on·ship ◆◆◇ /tʃæmpiənʃɪp/ NOUN [C, SING] (**championships**) **1** [C] A **championship** is a competition to find the best player or team in a particular sport. ❑ *the world chess championship* **2** [SING] The **championship** refers to the title or status of being a sports champion. ❑ *He went on to take the championship.*

chance ◆◆◆ /tʃɑːns, tʃæns/ NOUN, ADJ, VERB

NOUN [C, U, SING] (**chances**) **1** [C, U] If there is a **chance of** something happening, it is possible that it will happen. ❑ *Do you think they have a chance of beating Australia?* ❑ *There was really very little chance that Ben would ever have led a normal life.* **2** [SING] If you have a **chance to** do something, you have the opportunity to do it. ❑ *The electoral council announced that all eligible people would get a chance to vote.* ❑ *Most refugee doctors never get the chance to practise medicine in our hospitals.* **3** [U] Chance refers to things that are not planned or expected. ❑ *a victim of chance and circumstance*

PHRASES **by chance** Something that happens **by chance** was not planned by anyone. ❑ *He had met Mr Maude by chance.*

by any chance You can use **by any chance** when you are asking questions in order to find out whether something that you think might be true is actually true. = perhaps ❑ *Are they by any chance related?*

stand a chance If you say that someone **stands a chance of** achieving something, you mean that they are likely to achieve it. If you say that someone doesn't **stand a chance of** achieving something, you mean that they cannot possibly achieve it. ❑ *Being very good at science subjects, I stood a good chance of gaining high grades.*

take a chance When you **take a chance**, you try to do something although there is a large risk of danger or failure. ❑ *You take a chance on the weather if you holiday in Maine.* ❑ *Retailers are taking no chances on unknown brands.*

ADJ [chance + N] A **chance** meeting or event is one that is not planned or expected. ❑ *a chance meeting*

VERB [T] (**chances, chancing, chanced**) If you **chance** something, you do it even though there is a risk that you may not succeed or that something bad may happen. = risk ❑ *Andy knew the risks. I cannot believe he would have chanced it.*

chan·cel·lor ♦♦◇ /ˈtʃɑːnslə, ˈtʃæns-/ NOUN [c] (**chancellors**) **Chancellor** is the title of the head of government in Germany and Austria. ❑ *Chancellor Gerhard Schröder of Germany*

change ♦♦♦ /tʃeɪndʒ/ NOUN, VERB
NOUN [c, u, sing] (**changes**) ◼ [c, u] If there is a **change in** something, it becomes different. ❑ *The ambassador appealed for a change in US policy.* ❑ *There are going to have to be some drastic changes.* ◼ [sing] If you say that something is a **change** or **makes** a **change**, you mean that it is enjoyable because it is different from what you are used to. ❑ *It is a complex system, but it certainly makes a change.* ◼ [c] If there is a **change** of something, an existing thing is replaced with something new or different. ❑ *A change of leadership alone will not be enough.* ◼ [c] [change 'of' N] A **change** of clothes is an extra set of clothes that you take with you when you go to stay somewhere or to take part in an activity. ❑ *He stuffed a bag with a few changes of clothing.* ◼ [u] Your **change** is the money that you receive when you pay for something with more money than it costs because you do not have exactly the right amount of money. ❑ *'There's your change.'— 'Thanks very much.'* ◼ [u] **Change** is coins, rather than paper money. ❑ *Thieves ransacked the office, taking a sack of loose change.* ◼ [u] If you have **change for** larger banknotes or coins, you have the same value in smaller banknotes or coins, which you can give to someone in exchange. ❑ *The courier had change for a £10 note.*
PHRASE **for a change** If you say that you are doing something or something is happening **for a change**, you mean that you do not usually do it or it does not usually happen, and you are happy to be doing it or that it is happening. ❑ *Now let me ask you a question, for a change.*
VERB [I, T] (**changes, changing, changed**) ◼ [I] If you **change from** one thing **to** another, you stop using or doing the first one and start using or doing the second. ❑ *His doctor modified the dosage but did not change to a different medication.* ◼ [I, T] When something **changes** or when you **change** it, it becomes different. = alter ❑ *We are trying to detect and understand how the climates change.* ❑ *In the union office, the mood gradually changed from resignation to rage.* ❑ *She has now changed into a happy, self-confident woman.* ❑ *They should change the law to make it illegal to own replica weapons.* ◼ [T] To **change** something means to replace it with something new or different. ❑ *I paid $80 to have my car radio fixed and I bet all they did was change a fuse.* ◼ [I, T] When you **change** your clothes or **change**, you take some or all of your clothes off and put on different ones. ❑ *Ben had merely changed his shirt.* ❑ *They had allowed her to shower and change.* ◼ [T] When you **change** a bed or **change** the sheets, you take off the dirty sheets and put on clean ones. ❑ *After changing the bed, I would fall asleep quickly.* ◼ [T] When you **change** a baby or **change** its nappy, you take off the dirty one and put on a clean one. ❑ *She criticizes me for the way I feed or change him.* ◼ [I, T] When you **change** buses, trains, or planes or **change**, you get off one bus, train, or plane and

get on to another in order to continue your journey. ❑ *At Glasgow I changed trains for Greenock.* ◼ [I, T] (mainly BrE; in AmE, usually use **shift**) When you **change** gear or **change** into another gear, you move the gear lever on a car, bicycle, or other vehicle in order to use a different gear. ◼ [T] When you **change** money, you exchange it for the same amount of money in a different currency, or in smaller notes or coins. ❑ *You can expect to pay the bank a fee of around 1% to 2% every time you change money.*
PHRASAL VERB **change over** If you **change over from** one thing **to** another, you stop doing one thing and start doing the other. ❑ *We are gradually changing over to a completely metric system.*
✦ **change for the better** → see better; **change hands** → see hand; **a change of heart** → see heart; **change your mind** → see mind; **change places** → see place; **change the subject** → see subject; **change your tune** → see tune; **change for the worse** → see worse

⊙ **chan·nel** ♦♦◇ /ˈtʃænəl/ NOUN, VERB (academic word)
NOUN [c] (**channels**) ◼ A **channel** is a television station. = station ❑ *the only serious current affairs programme on either channel* ❑ *the proliferating number of television channels in America* ◼ A **channel** is a band of radio waves on which radio messages can be sent and received. ❑ *The radio channels were filled with the excited, jabbering voices of men going to war.* ◼ If you do something through a particular **channel**, or particular **channels**, that is the system or organization that you use to achieve your aims or to communicate. ❑ *The government will surely use the diplomatic channels available.* ❑ *The Americans recognize that the UN can be the channel for greater diplomatic activity.* ◼ A **channel** is a passage along which water flows. ❑ *Keep the drainage channel clear.* ◼ A **channel** is a route used by boats. ❑ *the busy shipping channels of the harbour*
VERB [T] (**channels, channelling, channelled**; in AmE, use **chaneling, chaneled**) ◼ If you **channel** money or resources into something, you arrange for them to be used for that thing, rather than for a wider range of things. ❑ *Jacques Delors wants a system set up to channel funds to the poor countries.* ◼ If you **channel** your energies or emotions **into** something, you concentrate on or do that one thing, rather than a range of things. ❑ *Stephen is channelling his energies into a novel called 'Blue'.*

chant /tʃɑːnt, tʃænt/ NOUN, VERB
NOUN [c] (**chants**) ◼ A **chant** is a word or group of words that is repeated over and over again. ❑ *He was greeted by the chant of 'Judas! Judas!'* ◼ A **chant** is a religious song or prayer that is sung on only a few notes. ❑ *a Gregorian chant*
VERB [I, T] (**chants, chanting, chanted**) ◼ If you **chant** something or if you **chant**, you repeat the same words over and over again. ❑ *Demonstrators chanted slogans.* ❑ *The crowd chanted 'We are with you'.* ◼ If you **chant** or if you **chant** something, you sing a religious song or prayer. ❑ *Muslims chanted and prayed.*
chant·ing /ˈtʃɑːntɪŋ, tʃæntɪŋ/ NOUN [u] ◼ *A lot of the chanting was in support of the deputy prime minister.* ◼ *The chanting inside the temple stopped.*

cha·os ♦◇◇ /ˈkeɪɒs/ NOUN [u] **Chaos** is a state of complete disorder and confusion. ❑ *The world's first transatlantic balloon race ended in chaos last night.*

cha·ot·ic /keɪˈɒtɪk/ ADJ Something that is **chaotic** is in a state of complete disorder and confusion. ❑ *My own house feels as filthy and chaotic as a bus terminal.*

chap /tʃæp/ NOUN [c] (**chaps**) (mainly BrE, informal) A **chap** is a man or boy. = guy ❑ *'I am a very lucky chap,' he commented. 'The doctors were surprised that I was not paralysed.'*

chap·el /ˈtʃæpəl/ NOUN [c, u] (**chapels**) ◼ [c] A **chapel** is a part of a church which has its own altar and which is used for private prayer. ❑ *the chapel of the Virgin Mary* ◼ [c] A **chapel** is a small church attached to a hospital, school, or prison. ❑ *We married in the college chapel.* ◼ [c, u] A **chapel** is a building used for worship by members of some Christian churches. **Chapel** refers to the religious services that take place there. ❑ *a Methodist chapel*

C

C

✪ **chap·ter** ◆◆◇ /'tʃæptə/ NOUN [c] (**chapters**) (*academic word*) **1** [also chapter + NUM] A **chapter** is one of the parts that a book is divided into. Each chapter has a number, and sometimes a title. ❑ *Chromium supplements were used successfully in the treatment of diabetes (see Chapter 4).* ❑ *the theory proposed in the previous chapter* **2** (*written*) A **chapter** in someone's life or in history is a period of time during which a major event or series of related events takes place. ❑ *This had been a particularly difficult chapter in Lebanon's recent history.*

✪ **char·ac·ter** ◆◆◇ /'kærɪktə/ NOUN [c, SING, u] (**characters**) **1** [c] The **character** of a person or place consists of all the qualities they have that make them distinct from other people or places. = nature ❑ *Perhaps there is a negative side to his character that you haven't seen yet.* ❑ *a series of interviews that look at clients' character traits and circumstances* ❑ *The character of this country has been formed by immigration.* **2** [c] You use **character** to say what kind of person someone is. For example, if you say that someone is a strange **character**, you mean they are strange. ❑ *It's that kind of courage and determination that makes him such a remarkable character.* **3** [c] The **characters** in a film, book, or play are the people that it is about. ❑ *The film is autobiographical and the central character is played by Collard himself.* ❑ *He's made the characters believable.* **4** [c] A **character** is a letter, number, or other symbol that is written or printed. ❑ *a shopping list written in Chinese characters* **5** [SING] [usu SUPP + character, also 'in' character] If something has a particular **character**, it has a particular quality. = nature ❑ *The financial concessions were of a precarious character.* **6** [SING] You can use **character** to refer to the qualities that people from a particular place are believed to have. ❑ *Individuality is a valued and inherent part of the British character.* **7** [c, u] Your **character** is your personality, especially how reliable and honest you are. If someone is of good **character**, they are reliable and honest. If they are of bad **character**, they are unreliable and dishonest. ❑ *He's begun a series of personal attacks on my character.* **8** [u] If you say that someone has **character**, you mean that they have the ability to deal effectively with difficult, unpleasant, or dangerous situations. ❑ *She showed real character in her attempts to win over the crowd.* **9** [u] If you say that a place has **character**, you mean that it has an interesting or unusual quality which makes you notice it and like it. ❑ *A soulless shopping centre stands across from one of the few buildings with character, the town hall.* **10** [c] If you say that someone is a **character**, you mean that they are interesting, unusual, or amusing. ❑ *He's a nut, a real character.*

✪ **char·ac·ter·is·tic** ◆◇◇ /ˌkærɪktə'rɪstɪk/ NOUN, ADJ
NOUN [c] (**characteristics**) The **characteristics** of a person or thing are the qualities or features that belong to them and make them recognizable. = feature, trait ❑ *Genes determine the characteristics of every living thing.* ❑ *their physical characteristics*
ADJ A quality or feature that is **characteristic of** someone or something is one which is often seen in them and seems typical of them. = typical ❑ *the absence of strife between the generations that was so characteristic of such societies* ❑ *Windmills are a characteristic feature of the Mallorcan landscape.* ❑ *Nehru responded with characteristic generosity.* **char·ac·ter·is·ti·cal·ly** /ˌkærɪktə'rɪstɪkli/ ADV ❑ *He replied in characteristically robust style.*

char·ac·teri·za·tion /ˌkærɪktəraɪ'zeɪʃən/ also **characterisation** NOUN [c, u] (**characterizations**) **Characterization** is the way an author or an actor describes or shows what a character is like. ❑ *As a writer, I am interested in characterization.*

char·ac·ter·ize /'kærɪktəraɪz/ also **characterise** VERB [T] (**characterizes, characterizing, characterized**) (*formal*) **1** If something is **characterized by** a particular feature or quality, that feature or quality is an obvious part of it. ❑ *This election campaign has been characterized by violence.* **2** If you **characterize** someone or something **as** a particular thing, you describe them as that thing. = describe ❑ *Both companies have characterized the relationship as friendly.*

✪ **charge** ◆◆◆ /tʃɑːdʒ/ VERB, NOUN
VERB [I, T] (**charges, charging, charged**) **1** [I, T] If you **charge** someone an amount of money, you ask them to pay that amount for something that you have sold to them or done for them. ≠ pay ❑ *Even local nurseries charge $150 a week.* ❑ *Some banks charge if you access your account to determine your balance.* ❑ *The hospitals charge the patients for every aspirin.* ❑ *The architect charged us a fee of seven hundred and fifty dollars.* **2** [T] To **charge** something **to** a person or organization means to tell the people providing it to send the bill to that person or organization. To **charge** something to someone's account means to add it to their account so they can pay for it later. = bill ❑ *Go out and buy a pair of glasses, and charge it to us.* **3** [T] When the police **charge** someone, they formally accuse them of having done something illegal. ❑ *They have the evidence to charge him.* **4** [I] If you **charge** towards someone or something, you move quickly and aggressively towards them. ❑ *He charged through the door to my mother's office.* ❑ *He ordered us to charge.* **5** [T] To **charge** a battery means to pass an electrical current through it in order to make it more powerful or to make it last longer. ❑ *Alex had forgotten to charge the battery.*
PHRASAL VERB **charge up** **Charge up** means the same as **charge** VERB 5. ❑ *There was nothing in the brochure about having to charge it every day to charge up the battery.*
NOUN [c, u] (**charges**) **1** [c] A **charge** is a quick and aggressive move towards someone. ❑ *a bayonet charge* **2** [c] A **charge** is an amount of money that you have to pay for a service. = fee, cost, price, rate ❑ *We can arrange this for a small charge.* ❑ *Customers who arrange overdrafts will face a monthly charge of £5.* **3** [c] A **charge** is a formal accusation that someone has committed a crime. ❑ *He may still face criminal charges.* **4** [c] If you describe someone as your **charge**, they have been given to you to be taken care of and you are responsible for them. ❑ *The coach tried to get his charges motivated.* **5** [c] (*technical*) An electrical **charge** is an amount of electricity that is held in or carried by something. **6** [u] If you take **charge of** someone or something, you make yourself responsible for them and take control over them. If someone or something is in your **charge**, you are responsible for them. ❑ *A few years ago Bacryl took charge of the company.* ❑ *I have been given charge of this class.*
PHRASES **in charge** If you are **in charge** in a particular situation, you are the most senior person and have control over something or someone. ❑ *Who's in charge here?*
free of charge If something is **free of charge**, it does not cost anything. = free ❑ *The leaflet is available free of charge from post offices.*

cha·ris·ma /kə'rɪzmə/ NOUN [u] You say that someone has **charisma** when they can attract, influence, and inspire people by their personal qualities. ❑ *He has neither the policies nor the personal charisma to inspire people.*

char·is·mat·ic /ˌkærɪz'mætɪk/ ADJ A **charismatic** person attracts, influences, and inspires people by their personal qualities. ❑ *With her striking looks and charismatic personality, she was noticed far and wide.*

chari·table /'tʃærɪtəbəl/ ADJ **1** [charitable + N] A **charitable** organization or activity helps and supports people who are ill, disabled, or very poor. ❑ *charitable work for the handicapped* **2** Someone who is **charitable** to people is kind or understanding towards them. ❑ *They were less than charitable towards the referee.*

✪ **char·ity** ◆◇◇ /'tʃærɪti/ NOUN [c, u] (**charities**) **1** [c] A **charity** is an organization which raises money in order to help people who are ill, disabled, or very poor. ❑ *an AIDS charity* ❑ *The National Trust is a registered charity.* ❑ *The event helps raise money for local charities.* **2** [u] If you give money **to charity**, you give it to one or more charitable organizations. If you do something **for charity**, you do it in order to raise money for one or more charitable organizations. ❑ *He made substantial donations to charity.* ❑ *Gooch will be raising money for charity.* **3** [u] People who live on **charity** live on money or goods which other people give them because they are poor. ❑ *Her husband is unemployed and the family depends on charity.*

charm /tʃɑːm/ NOUN, VERB

NOUN [C, U] (**charms**) **1** [C, U] **Charm** is the quality of being pleasant or attractive. ❑ *'Snow White and the Seven Dwarfs', the 1937 Disney classic, has lost none of its original charm.* **2** [U] Someone who has **charm** behaves in a friendly, pleasant way that makes people like them. ❑ *He was a man of great charm and distinction.* **3** [C] A **charm** is a small ornament that is fixed to a bracelet or necklace. ❑ *Inside was a gold charm bracelet, with one charm on it – a star.* **4** [C] A **charm** is an act, saying, or object that is believed to have magic powers. ❑ *They cross their fingers and spit over their shoulders as charms against the evil eye.*

VERB [T] (**charms, charming, charmed**) If you **charm** someone, you please them, especially by using your charm. ❑ *He even charmed Mrs Prichard, carrying her groceries and flirting with her, though she's 83.*

charm·ing /'tʃɑːmɪŋ/ ADJ **1** If you say that something is **charming**, you mean that it is very pleasant or attractive. ❑ *a charming little fishing village* **2** If you describe someone as **charming**, you mean they behave in a friendly, pleasant way that makes people like them. ❑ *a charming young man* ❑ *He found her as smart and beautiful as she is charming.*

charm·ing·ly /'tʃɑːmɪŋli/ ADV **1** = delightfully ❑ *There's something charmingly old-fashioned about his brand of entertainment.* **2** [charmingly after v] ❑ *Calder smiled charmingly and put out his hand. 'A pleasure, Mrs Talbot.'*

✪ **chart** ◆◇◇ /tʃɑːt/ NOUN, VERB (*academic word*)

NOUN [C] (**charts**) **1** A **chart** is a diagram, picture, or graph which is intended to make information easier to understand. = diagram ❑ *Male unemployment was 14.2%, compared with 5.8% for women (see chart on next page).* ❑ *The chart below shows our top 10 choices.* **2** A **chart** is a map of the sea or stars. ❑ *charts of Greek waters*

VERB [T] (**charts, charting, charted**) **1** If you **chart** an area of land, sea, or sky, or a feature in that area, you make a map of the area or show the feature in it. = map ❑ *Ptolemy charted more than 1,000 stars in 48 constellations.* **2** If you **chart** the development or progress of something, you observe it and record or show it. You can also say that a report or graph **charts** the development or progress of something. = record ❑ *One doctor has charted a dramatic rise in local childhood asthma since the road was built.* ❑ *This magnificent show charts his meteoric rise from 'small town' country singer to top international rock idol.*

→ See also **bar chart, flow chart, pie chart**

char·ter ◆◇◇ /'tʃɑːtə/ NOUN, ADJ, VERB

NOUN [C] (**charters**) A **charter** is a formal document describing the rights, aims, or principles of an organization or group of people. ❑ *Article 50 of the United Nations Charter*

ADJ [charter + N] A **charter** plane or boat is one which is rented for use by a particular person or group and which is not part of a regular service. ❑ *the last charter plane carrying out foreign nationals*

VERB [T] (**charters, chartering, chartered**) If a person or organization **charters** a plane, boat, or other vehicle, they rent it for their own use. ❑ *He chartered a jet to fly her home from California to Switzerland.*

char·tered /'tʃɑːtəd/ (*BrE*; in *AmE*, use **certified**) ADJ **Chartered** is used to indicate that someone, such as an accountant or a surveyor, has formally qualified in their profession.

chase ◆◇◇ /tʃeɪs/ VERB, NOUN

VERB [I, T] (**chases, chasing, chased**) **1** [I, T] If you **chase** someone, or **chase after** them, you run after them or follow them quickly in order to catch or reach them. = pursue ❑ *She chased the thief for 100 yards.* **2** [I, T] If you **are chasing** something you want, such as work or money, or are **chasing after** it, you are trying hard to get it. ❑ *In some areas, 14 people are chasing every job.* ❑ *There are too many schools chasing after too few students.* **3** [I, T] If someone **chases** someone that they are attracted to, or **chases after** them, they try hard to persuade them to have a sexual relationship with them. ❑ *Women also have another reason for not chasing men too hard, of course.* **4** [T] If someone **chases** you from a place, they force you to leave by using threats or violence. ❑ *Many farmers will then chase*

you off their land quite aggressively. **5** [T] To **chase** someone **from** a job or a position or **from** power means to force them to leave it. ❑ *In the '70s he had been chased out of his job.* **6** [I] If you **chase** somewhere, you run or rush there. = race, dash ❑ *They chased down the stairs into the narrow, dirty street.*

NOUN [C, SING] (**chases**) **1** [C] A **chase** is when you run after someone or follow them quickly in order to catch or reach them. = pursuit ❑ *He was reluctant to give up the chase.* **2** [SING] [chase 'for' N] A **chase** is when you are trying hard to get something you want, such as work or money. ❑ *They took an invincible lead in the chase for the championship.* **3** [SING] The **chase** is the act of chasing after someone that you are attracted to, trying hard to persuade them to have a sexual relationship with you. ❑ *The chase is always much more exciting than the conquest anyway.*

PHRASE **cut to the chase** If someone **cuts to the chase**, they start talking about or dealing with what is important, instead of less important things. ❑ *Hi everyone, we all know why we are here today, so let's cut to the chase.*

chasm /'kæzəm/ NOUN [C] (**chasms**) **1** A **chasm** is a very deep crack in rock, earth, or ice. ❑ *a yawning fourteen-foot-deep chasm which inexplicably had opened up in the riverbed* **2** If you say that there is a **chasm** between two things or between two groups of people, you mean that there is a very large difference between them. = gulf, gap ❑ *the chasm that divides the worlds of university and industry*

chat ◆◇◇ /tʃæt/ VERB, NOUN

VERB [RECIP] (**chats, chatting, chatted**) When people **chat**, they talk to each other in an informal and friendly way. ❑ *The women were chatting.* ❑ *I was chatting to him the other day.*

NOUN [C] (**chats**) A **chat** is when people talk to each other in an informal and friendly way. ❑ *I had a chat with John.*

chat·ter /'tʃætə/ VERB, NOUN

VERB [I] (**chatters, chattering, chattered**) **1** If you **chatter**, you talk quickly and continuously, usually about things which are not important. ❑ *Everyone's chattering away in different languages.* ❑ *Erica was friendly and chattered about Andrew's children.* **2** If your teeth **chatter**, they keep knocking together because you are very cold or very nervous. ❑ *She was so cold her teeth chattered.* **3** (*literary*) When birds or animals **chatter**, they make high-pitched noises. ❑ *Birds were chattering somewhere, and occasionally he could hear a vehicle pass by.*

NOUN [U] **1** **Chatter** is the act of talking quickly and continuously, usually about things which are not important. ❑ *idle chatter* **2** **Chatter** is when birds or animals make high-pitched noises. ❑ *almond trees vibrating with the chatter of crickets*

chau·vin·ism /'ʃəʊvɪnɪzəm/ NOUN [U] (*disapproval*) **Chauvinism** is a strong, unreasonable belief that your own country, sex, race, or religion is better and more important than any other. ❑ *it may also appeal to the latent chauvinism of many ordinary people*

chau·vin·ist /'ʃəʊvɪnɪst/ NOUN [C] (**chauvinists**) ❑ *He is arrogant and a bit of a chauvinist.*

cheap ◆◆◇ /tʃiːp/ ADJ (**cheaper, cheapest**) **1** Goods or services that are **cheap** cost less money than usual or than you expected. ❑ *I'm going to live off campus if I can find somewhere cheap enough.* ❑ *Operating costs are coming down because of cheaper fuel.* **2** [cheap + N] If you describe goods as **cheap**, you mean they cost less money than similar products but their quality is poor. = shoddy ❑ *Don't resort to cheap imitations; save up for the real thing.* **3** [cheap + N] If you describe someone's remarks or actions as **cheap**, you mean they are unkindly or insincerely using a situation to benefit themselves or to harm someone else. ❑ *These tests will inevitably be used by politicians to make cheap political points.*

cheap·ly /'tʃiːpli/ ADV ❑ *It will produce electricity more cheaply than a nuclear plant.*

cheat /tʃiːt/ VERB, NOUN

VERB [T, I] (**cheats, cheating, cheated**) **1** [T, I] When someone **cheats**, they do not obey a set of rules which they should be obeying, for example in a game or exam. ❑ *Students may be tempted to cheat in order to get into top*

C

schools. **2** [T] If someone **cheats** you **out of** something, they get it from you by behaving dishonestly. ❑ *The company engaged in a deliberate effort to cheat them out of their pensions.*

PHRASAL VERB   **cheat on** (*informal*) If someone **cheats on** their husband, wife, or partner, they have a sexual relationship with another person. ❑ *I'd found Philippe was cheating on me and I was angry and hurt.*

NOUN [C] (**cheats**) Someone who is a **cheat** does not obey a set of rules which they should be obeying. ❑ *Cheats will be disqualified.*

cheat·ing /'tʃiːtɪŋ/ NOUN [U] ❑ *In an election in 1988, he was accused of cheating by his opponent.*

✪**check** ◆◆◇ /tʃek/ VERB, NOUN

VERB [I, T] (**checks**, **checking**, **checked**) **1** [I, T] If you **check** something such as a piece of information or a document, you make sure that it is correct or satisfactory. = inspect, verify ❑ *Check the accuracy of everything in your CV.* ❑ *I think there is an age limit, but I'd have to check.* ❑ *She hadn't checked whether she had a clean, ironed shirt.* ❑ *Check that the soil mixture is moist.* **2** [I] If you **check on** someone or something, you make sure they are in a safe or satisfactory condition. ❑ *Stephen checked on her several times during the night.* **3** [T] To **check** something, usually something bad, means to stop it from spreading or continuing. = curb ❑ *Sex education is also expected to help check the spread of AIDS.*

PHRASAL VERBS   **check in 1** When you **check in** or **check into** a hotel or clinic, or if someone **checks** you **in**, you arrive and go through the necessary procedures before you stay there. = register ❑ *I'll call the hotel. I'll tell them we'll check in tomorrow.* ❑ *He has checked into an alcohol treatment centre.* **2** When you **check in** at an airport, you arrive and show your ticket before going on a flight. ❑ *He had checked in at Amsterdam's Schiphol airport for a flight to Atlanta.* **3** When you **check in** your luggage at an airport, you give it to an official so that it can be taken on to your plane. ❑ *They checked in their luggage and found seats in the departure lounge.*

check off When you **check** things **off**, you check or count them while referring to a list of them, to make sure you have considered all of them. ❑ *Once you've checked off the items you ordered, put this record in your file.* ❑ *I haven't checked them off but I would say that's about the number.*

check out 1 When you **check out of** a hotel or clinic where you have been staying, or if someone **checks** you **out**, you pay the bill and leave. ❑ *They packed and checked out of the hotel.* ❑ *I was disappointed to miss Bryan, who had just checked out.* **2** If you **check out** something or someone, you find out information about them to make sure that everything is correct or satisfactory. = investigate ❑ *Maybe we ought to go down to the library and check it out.* ❑ *We ought to check him out on the computer.* **3** If something **checks out**, it is correct or satisfactory. ❑ *She was in San Diego the weekend Jensen got killed. Her alibi checked out.* **4** If you **check out** a library book, you borrow it for a fixed period of time. ❑ *No books can be checked out after 6 pm tomorrow.* **5** → See also **checkout**

check up 1 If you **check up on** something, you find out information about it. ❑ *It is certainly worth checking up on your benefit entitlements.* **2** If you **check up on** someone, you obtain information about them, usually secretly. ❑ *I'm sure he knew I was checking up on him.* **3** → See also **checkup**

NOUN [C] (**checks**) **1** If you do a **check** on something, you make sure it is in a safe or satisfactory condition. ❑ *He is being constantly monitored with regular checks on his blood pressure.* **2** A pattern of squares, usually of two colours, can be referred to as **checks** or a **check**. ❑ *Styles include stripes and checks.*

PHRASE   **hold something in check** or **keep something in check** If something or someone **is held in check** or **is kept in check**, they are controlled and prevented from becoming too great or powerful. ❑ *Life on Earth will become unsustainable unless population growth is held in check.*

checked /tʃekt/ ADJ Something that is **checked** has a pattern of small squares, usually of two colours. = check ❑ *He was wearing blue jeans and a checked shirt.*

check·list /'tʃeklɪst/ NOUN [C] (**checklists**) A **checklist** is a list of all the things that you need to do, information that you want to find out, or things that you need to take somewhere, which you make in order to ensure that you do not forget anything. = list ❑ *Make a checklist of the tools and materials you will need.*

check·out /'tʃekaʊt/ NOUN [C] (**checkouts**) In a supermarket, a **checkout** is a counter where you pay for things you are buying. ❑ *the supermarket checkout counter*

check·up /'tʃekʌp/ NOUN [C] (**checkups**) A **checkup** is a medical examination by your doctor or dentist to make sure that there is nothing wrong with your health. ❑ *The disease was detected during a routine checkup.*

cheek /tʃiːk/ NOUN [C, SING] (**cheeks**) **1** [C] Your **cheeks** are the sides of your face below your eyes. ❑ *Tears were running down her cheeks.* **2** [SING] [also no DET] (*mainly BrE, informal*) You say that someone has **cheek** when you are annoyed or shocked at something unreasonable that they have done. ❑ *I'm amazed they had the cheek to ask in the first place.*

cheeky /'tʃiːki/ ADJ (**cheekier**, **cheekiest**) (*mainly BrE*) If you describe a person or their behaviour as **cheeky**, you think that they are slightly rude or disrespectful but in a charming or amusing way. ❑ *The boy was cheeky and casual.*

cheer ◆◇◇ /tʃɪə/ VERB, NOUN, CONVENTION

VERB [I, T] (**cheers**, **cheering**, **cheered**) **1** [I, T] When people **cheer**, they shout loudly to show their approval or to encourage someone who is doing something such as taking part in a game. ❑ *The crowd cheered as she went up the steps to the bandstand.* ❑ *Hundreds of thousands of jubilant Americans cheered him on his return.* **2** [T] If you **are cheered** by something, it makes you happier or less worried. = hearten ❑ *Stephen noticed that the people around him looked cheered by his presence.*

PHRASAL VERBS   **cheer on** When you **cheer** someone **on**, you shout loudly in order to encourage them, for example when they are taking part in a game. ❑ *A thousand supporters packed into the stadium to cheer them on.*

cheer up When you **cheer up** or when something **cheers** you **up**, you stop feeling depressed and become more cheerful. ❑ *I think he misses her terribly. You might cheer him up.* ❑ *I wrote that song just to cheer myself up.*

NOUN [C] (**cheers**) A **cheer** is a loud shout, which people use to show their approval or to encourage someone who is doing something such as taking part in a game. ❑ *The colonel was rewarded with a resounding cheer from the men.*

CONVENTION (*mainly BrE*) People sometimes say '**Cheers**' to each other just before they drink an alcoholic drink.

cheer·ing /'tʃɪərɪŋ/ ADJ = heartening ❑ *very cheering news*

cheer·ful /'tʃɪəfʊl/ ADJ **1** Someone who is **cheerful** is happy and shows this in their behaviour. = cheery ❑ *Paddy was always cheerful and jolly.* **2** Something that is **cheerful** is pleasant and makes you feel happy. ❑ *The nursery is bright and cheerful, with plenty of toys.* **3** [usu cheerful + N] If you describe someone's attitude as **cheerful**, you mean they are not worried about something, and you think that they should be. = optimistic ❑ *There is little evidence to support his cheerful assumptions.*

cheer·ful·ly /'tʃɪəfəli/ ADV **1** [cheerfully with V] ❑ *'We've come with good news,' Pat said cheerfully.* **2** ❑ *He cheerfully ignored medical advice which could have prolonged his life.*

cheer·ful·ness /'tʃɪəfəlnəs/ NOUN [U] ❑ *I remember this extraordinary man with particular affection for his unfailing cheerfulness.*

cheese ◆◇◇ /tʃiːz/ NOUN [C, U] (**cheeses**) **Cheese** is a solid food made from milk. It is usually white or yellow. ❑ *bread and cheese* ❑ *delicious French cheeses*

chef /ʃef/ NOUN [C] (**chefs**) A **chef** is a cook in a restaurant or hotel. ❑ *some of Australia's leading chefs*

✪**chemi·cal** ◆◆◇ /'kemɪkəl/ ADJ, NOUN (*academic word*)

ADJ [chemical + N] **Chemical** means involving or resulting from a reaction between two or more substances, or relating to the substances that something consists of. ❑ *chemical reactions that cause ozone destruction* ❑ *the chemical composition of the ocean* ❑ *soldiers exposed to chemical weapons*

NOUN [C] (**chemicals**) **Chemicals** are substances that are used in a chemical process or made by a chemical process. ❑ *The whole food chain is affected by the over-use of chemicals in agriculture.* ❑ *a chemical company* ❑ *a spillage from a chemicals factory*

✪ **chem·i·cal·ly** /ˈkemɪkli/ ADV ❑ *chemically treated foods* ❑ *The medicine chemically affects your physiology.*

✪ **chem·ist** /ˈkemɪst/ NOUN [C] (**chemists**) **1** A **chemist** is a person who does research connected with chemistry or who studies chemistry. ❑ *She worked as a research chemist.* **2** (*BrE*) A **chemist** or a **chemist's** is a shop where drugs and medicines are sold or given out, and where you can buy cosmetics and some household goods. = pharmacy **3** (*BrE*; in *AmE*, use **druggist or pharmacist**) A **chemist** is someone who works in a chemist's shop and is qualified to prepare and sell medicines.

✪ **chem·is·try** /ˈkemɪstri/ NOUN [U] **1** **Chemistry** is the scientific study of the structure of substances and of the way that they react with other substances. ❑ *He studied chemistry at the University of Virginia.* ❑ *a world-class chemistry department* **2** The **chemistry** of an organism or a material is the chemical substances that make it up and the chemical reactions that go on inside it. ❑ *We have literally altered the chemistry of our planet's atmosphere.* **3** If you say that there is **chemistry** between two people, you mean that it is obvious they are attracted to each other or like each other very much. ❑ *the extraordinary chemistry between Ingrid and Bogart*

cheque /tʃek/ (*BrE*; in *AmE*, use **check**) NOUN [C] (**cheques**) A **cheque** is a printed form on which you write an amount of money and who it is to be paid to. Your bank then pays the money to that person from your account. ❑ *He handed me an envelope with a cheque for $1,500.*

cher·ish /ˈtʃerɪʃ/ VERB [T] (**cherishes, cherishing, cherished**) **1** If you **cherish** something such as a hope or a pleasant memory, you keep it in your mind for a long period of time. = treasure ❑ *The president will cherish the memory of this visit to Ohio.* **2** If you **cherish** someone or something, you take good care of them because you love them. ❑ *He genuinely loved and cherished her.* **3** If you **cherish** a right, a privilege, or a principle, you regard it as important and try hard to keep it. ❑ *Chinese people cherish their independence and sovereignty.*

cher·ished /ˈtʃerɪʃt/ ADJ **1** *the cherished dream of a world without wars* **2** *He described the picture as his most cherished possession.* **3** *Freud called into question some deeply cherished beliefs.*

cher·ry /ˈtʃeri/ NOUN [C] (**cherries**) **1** Cherries are small, round fruit with red skins. **2** A **cherry** or a **cherry tree** is a tree that cherries grow on.

chess /tʃes/ NOUN [U] **Chess** is a game for two people, played on a chessboard. Each player has 16 pieces, including a king. Your aim is to move your pieces so that your opponent's king cannot escape being taken. ❑ *He was playing chess with his uncle.*

chest /tʃest/ NOUN [C] (**chests**) **1** Your **chest** is the top part of the front of your body where your ribs, lungs, and heart are. ❑ *He crossed his arms over his chest.* ❑ *He was shot in the chest.* **2** A **chest** is a large, heavy box used for storing things. = trunk ❑ *At the very bottom of the chest were his carving tools.* ❑ *a treasure chest*

chew /tʃuː/ VERB [I, T] (**chews, chewing, chewed**) **1** [I, T] When you **chew** food, you use your teeth to break it up in your mouth so that it becomes easier to swallow. ❑ *Be certain to eat slowly and chew your food extremely well.* ❑ *Daniel leaned back on the sofa, still chewing on his apple.* **2** [T] If you **chew** gum or tobacco, you keep biting it and moving it around your mouth to taste the flavour of it. You do not swallow it. ❑ *One girl was chewing gum.* **3** [T] If you **chew** your lips or your fingernails, you keep biting them because you are nervous. ❑ *He chewed his lower lip nervously.* **4** [I, T] If a person or animal **chews** an object or **chews on** it, they bite it with their teeth. = bite ❑ *They pause and chew their pencils.* ❑ *She chewed through the tape that bound her.*

chick·en ◆◇◇ /ˈtʃɪkɪn/ NOUN, ADJ

NOUN [C, U] (**chickens**) **1** [C] Chickens are birds which are kept on a farm for their eggs and for their meat. = hen ❑ *Lionel built a coop so that they could raise chickens and have a supply of fresh eggs.* **2** [U] **Chicken** is the flesh of this bird eaten as food. ❑ *roast chicken with wild mushrooms* **3** [C] (*informal, disapproval*) If someone calls you a **chicken**, they mean that you are afraid to do something. = coward ❑ *I'm scared of the dark. I'm a big chicken.*

PHRASE **count one's chickens** If you say that someone is **counting** their **chickens**, you mean that they are assuming that they will be successful or get something, when this is not certain. ❑ *I don't want to count my chickens before they are hatched.*

ADJ [V-LINK + chicken] (*informal, disapproval*) If someone calls you **chicken**, they mean that you are afraid to do something. ❑ *Why are you so chicken, Gregory?*

PHRASAL VERB **chicken out** (**chickens, chickening, chickened**) (*informal, disapproval*) If someone **chickens out** of something they were intending to do, they decide not to do it because they are afraid. ❑ *He makes excuses to chicken out of family occasions such as weddings.* ❑ *I had never ridden on a motorcycle before. But it was too late to chicken out.*

✪ **chief** ◆◆◆ /tʃiːf/ NOUN, ADJ

NOUN [C] (**chiefs**) **1** The **chief** of an organization is the person who is in charge of it. ❑ *a commission appointed by the police chief* **2** The **chief** of a tribe is its leader. ❑ *Sitting Bull, chief of the Sioux tribes of the Great Plains*

ADJ **1** [chief + N] **Chief** is used in the job titles of the most senior worker or workers of a particular kind in an organization. = head, senior ❑ *the chief test pilot* ❑ *He rose up through the ranks to become chief engineer.* **2** [chief + N] The **chief** cause, part, or member of something is the most important one. = main, major, key, principal; ≠ minor, unimportant ❑ *Financial stress is well established as a chief reason for divorce.* ❑ *The job went to one of his chief rivals.*

✪ **chief·ly** /ˈtʃiːfli/ ADV You use **chiefly** to indicate that a particular reason, emotion, method, or feature is the main or most important one. = mainly, primarily ❑ *He joined the consular service in China, chiefly because this was one of the few job vacancies.* ❑ *His response to attacks on his work was chiefly bewilderment.*

chief of staff NOUN [C] (**chiefs of staff**) The **chiefs of staff** are the highest-ranking officers of each service of the armed forces.

child ◆◆◆ /tʃaɪld/ NOUN [C] (**children**) **1** A **child** is a human being who is not yet an adult. ❑ *When I was a child I lived in a country village.* ❑ *a child of six* **2** Someone's **children** are their sons and daughters of any age. ❑ *How are the children?* ❑ *His children have left home.*

child·birth /ˈtʃaɪldbɜːθ/ NOUN [U] **Childbirth** is the act of giving birth to a child. = labour ❑ *She died in childbirth.*

child·care /ˈtʃaɪldkeə/ NOUN [U] **Childcare** refers to taking care of children, and to the facilities which help parents to do so. ❑ *Both partners shared childcare.*

✪ **child·hood** ◆◇◇ /ˈtʃaɪldhʊd/ NOUN [C, U] (**childhoods**) A person's **childhood** is the period of their life when they are a child. ❑ *She had a happy childhood.* ❑ *people who experienced poverty in childhood* ❑ *the growing epidemic of childhood obesity* ❑ *He was remembering a story heard in childhood.*

child·ish /ˈtʃaɪldɪʃ/ ADJ **1** **Childish** means relating to or typical of a child. ❑ *childish enthusiasm* **2** If you describe someone, especially an adult, as **childish**, you disapprove of them because they behave in an immature way. = immature ❑ *Penny's selfish and childish behaviour*

child·less /ˈtʃaɪldləs/ ADJ Someone who is **childless** has no children. ❑ *childless couples*

child·like /ˈtʃaɪldlaɪk/ ADJ You describe someone as **childlike** when they seem like a child in their character, appearance, or behaviour. ❑ *His most enduring quality is his childlike innocence.*

chil·dren /ˈtʃɪldrən/ IRREG FORM **Children** is the plural of **child**.

chill /tʃɪl/ VERB, NOUN, ADJ

VERB [I, T] (**chills, chilling, chilled**) **1** [I, T] When you **chill** something or when it **chills**, you lower its temperature so

C

that it becomes colder but does not freeze. ❏ *Chill the fruit salad until serving time.* ❏ *This dough can be rolled out while you wait for the pastry to chill.* **2** [T] When cold weather or something cold **chills** a person or a place, it makes that person or that place feel very cold. ❏ *The marble floor was beginning to chill me.* ❏ *Wade placed his chilled hands on the radiator and warmed them.*

▸ PHRASAL VERB **chill out** (*informal*) To **chill out** means to relax after you have done something tiring or stressful. = relax ❏ *After school, we used to chill out in each others' bedrooms.*

▸ NOUN [C, SING] (**chills**) **1** [C] If something sends a **chill** through you, it gives you a sudden feeling of fear or anxiety. = shiver ❏ *The violence used against the students sent a chill through Indonesia.* **2** [C] A **chill** is a mild illness which can give you a slight fever and headache. ❏ *He caught a chill while performing at a rain-soaked open-air venue.* **3** [SING] A **chill** is when cold weather or something cold makes a person or place feel very cold. ❏ *September is here, bringing with it a chill in the mornings.*

▸ ADJ [chill + N] **Chill** weather is cold and unpleasant. ❏ *chill winds, rain and choppy seas*

chime /tʃaɪm/ VERB, NOUN
▸ VERB [I, T] (**chimes, chiming, chimed**) When a bell or a clock **chimes**, it makes ringing sounds. ❏ *He heard the front doorbell chime.* ❏ *as the town hall clock chimed three o'clock*

▸ PHRASAL VERB **chime in** If you **chime in**, you say something just after someone else has spoken. ❏ *'Why?' Pete asked impatiently. 'Yes, why?' Bob chimed in. 'It seems like a good idea to me.'*

▸ NOUN [C, PL] (**chimes**) **1** [C] A **chime** is a ringing sound made by a bell, especially when it is part of a clock. ❏ *At that moment a chime sounded from the front of the house.* **2** [PL] **Chimes** are a set of small objects which make a ringing sound when they are blown by the wind. ❏ *the haunting sound of the wind chimes*

chin /tʃɪn/ NOUN [C] (**chins**) Your **chin** is the part of your face that is below your mouth and above your neck. ❏ *a double chin*

chip ◆◇◇ /tʃɪp/ NOUN, VERB
▸ NOUN [C] (**chips**) **1** (*BrE*; in *AmE*, use **French fries**) **Chips** are long, thin pieces of potato fried in oil or fat and eaten hot, usually with a meal. **2** A silicon **chip** is a very small piece of silicon with electronic circuits on it which is part of a computer or other piece of machinery. ❏ *an electronic card containing a chip* **3** A **chip** is a small piece of something or a small piece which has been broken off something. ❏ *It contains real chocolate chips.* **4** A **chip** in something such as a piece of china or furniture is where a small piece has been broken off it. ❏ *The cup had a small chip.* **5** **Chips** are plastic counters used in gambling to represent money. ❏ *He put the pile of chips in the centre of the table and drew a card.*

▸ VERB [I, T] (**chips, chipping, chipped**) If you **chip** something or if it **chips**, a small piece is broken off it. ❏ *The blow chipped the woman's tooth.*

▸ PHRASAL VERB **chip in** (*informal*) When a number of people **chip in**, each person gives some money so that they can pay for something together. = contribute ❏ *They chip in for the gas.*

chipped /tʃɪpt/ ADJ ❏ *The wagon's paint was badly chipped on the outside.*

choco·late ◆◇◇ /'tʃɒklət, AmE 'tʃɔːk-/ NOUN, COLOUR
▸ NOUN [C, U] (**chocolates**) **1** [C, U] **Chocolate** is a sweet, hard food made from cacao. It is usually brown in colour and is eaten as a sweet. ❏ *a bar of chocolate* ❏ *Do you want some chocolate?* **2** [U] **Chocolate** or **hot chocolate** is a drink made from a powder containing chocolate. It is usually made with hot milk. ❏ *a small cafeteria where the visitors can buy tea, coffee and chocolate* **3** [C] **Chocolates** are small sweets or nuts covered with a layer of chocolate. They are usually sold in a box. ❏ *a box of chocolates*
▸ COLOUR **Chocolate** is used to describe things that are dark brown in colour. ❏ *The curtains and the bedspread were chocolate velvet.*

✪ choice ◆◆◇ /tʃɔɪs/ NOUN, ADJ
▸ NOUN [C] (**choices**) **1** If there is a **choice of** things, there are several of them and you can choose the one you want.

= selection ❏ *It's available in a choice of colours.* ❏ *At lunchtime, there's a choice between the buffet or the set menu.* ❏ *the choice between rapid growth and a stable economy* ❏ *Graduates have a wide choice of career paths* **2** Your **choice** is someone or something that you choose from a range of things. = selection, option ❏ *Although he was only grumbling, his choice of words made Rodney angry.* ❏ *the information you need to make informed choices about your diet*

▸ PHRASES **have no choice** or **have little choice** If you have **no choice but** to do something or **have little choice but** to do it, you cannot avoid doing it. ❏ *They had little choice but to agree to what he suggested.*

of one's choice The thing or person **of** your **choice** is the one that you choose. ❏ *tickets to see the football team of your choice*

of choice The item **of choice** is the one that most people prefer. ❏ *The drug is set to become the treatment of choice for asthma worldwide.*

▸ ADJ (**choicer, choicest**) [choice + N] (*formal*) **Choice** means of very high quality. = select ❏ *a box of their choicest chocolates*

WORD CONNECTIONS

choice + OF + NOUN

a choice of **colours**
a choice of **subjects**
❏ *The material is available in a wide choice of colours.*

ADJ + **choice**

a **wide** choice
a **limited** choice
❏ *A black couple usually has a limited choice of donors.*

a **wise** choice
an **obvious** choice
an **informed** choice
❏ *Dr Freedman was an obvious choice to speak at the seminar.*

VERB + **choice**

have a choice
be faced with a choice
make a choice
❏ *In Denmark children have a choice between a wide variety of schools.*

---

choir /kwaɪə/ NOUN [C] (**choirs**) A **choir** is a group of people who sing together, for example in a church or school. ❏ *He has been singing in his church choir since he was six.*

choke /tʃəʊk/ VERB, NOUN
▸ VERB [I, T] (**chokes, choking, choked**) **1** [I, T] When you **choke** or when something **chokes** you, you cannot breathe properly or get enough air into your lungs. ❏ *A small child could choke on the doll's hair.* ❏ *Dense smoke swirled and billowed, its rank fumes choking her.* ❏ *The girl choked to death after breathing in smoke.* **2** [T] To **choke** someone means to squeeze their neck until they are dead. = strangle ❏ *The men pushed him into the entrance of a nearby building, where they choked him with his tie.* **3** [T] If a place **is choked with** things or people, it is full of them and they prevent movement in it. ❏ *The village's roads are choked with traffic.*
▸ NOUN [C] (**chokes**) The **choke** in a car, truck, or other vehicle is a device that reduces the amount of air going into the engine and makes it easier to start. ❏ *It is like driving your car with the choke out all the time.*

cho·les·ter·ol /kə'lestərɒl, AmE -rɔːl/ NOUN [U] **Cholesterol** is a substance that exists in the fat, tissues, and blood of all animals. Too much cholesterol in a person's blood can cause heart disease. ❏ *a dangerously high cholesterol level*

✪ choose ◆◆◇ /tʃuːz/ VERB [I, T] (**chooses, choosing, chose, chosen**) **1** If you **choose** someone or something **from** several people or things that are available, you decide which person or thing you want to have. = select, opt; ≠ reject ❏ *They will be able to choose their own leaders in democratic elections.* ❏ *There are several patchwork cushions to choose from.* ❏ *one method chosen from a range of options* ❏ *He did well in his chosen profession.* **2** If you **choose to** do something, you do it because you want to or because you feel that it is right. = opt, decide ❏ *They knew that* discrimination was going on, but chose to ignore it. ❏ *You have the right to remain silent if you choose.* ❏ *We chose to focus on white middle- and working-class families.* ❏ *You can just take out the interest each year, if you choose.*

chop ◆◇◇ /tʃɒp/ VERB, NOUN

VERB [T] (**chops, chopping, chopped**) If you **chop** something, you cut it into pieces with strong, downward movements of a knife or an axe. ❏ *Chop the butter into small pieces.* ❏ *Visitors were set to work chopping wood.*

PHRASAL VERBS **chop down** If you **chop down** a tree, you cut through its trunk with an axe so that it falls to the ground. = cut down ❏ *Sometimes they have to chop down a tree for firewood.*

chop off To **chop off** something such as a part of someone's body means to cut it off. = cut off ❏ *She chopped off her golden, waist-length hair.*

chop up If you **chop** something **up**, you chop it into small pieces. = cut up ❏ *Chop up three firm tomatoes.*

NOUN [C] (**chops**) A **chop** is a small piece of meat cut from the ribs of a sheep or pig. ❏ *grilled lamb chops*

chord /kɔːd/ NOUN

NOUN [C] (**chords**) A **chord** is a number of musical notes played or sung at the same time with a pleasing effect. ❏ *I could play a few chords on the guitar and sing a song.*

PHRASE **strike a chord** If something **strikes a chord with** you, it makes you feel sympathy or enthusiasm. ❏ *Mr Jenkins's arguments for stability struck a chord with Europe's two most powerful politicians.*

chore /tʃɔː/ NOUN [C] (**chores**) A **chore** is a task that you must do but that you find unpleasant or boring. ❏ *She sees exercise primarily as an unavoidable chore.*

cho·rus /'kɔːrəs/ NOUN, VERB

NOUN [C] (**choruses**) **1** A **chorus** is a part of a song which is repeated after each verse. = refrain ❏ *Caroline sang two verses and the chorus of her song.* **2** A **chorus** is a large group of people who sing together. = choir ❏ *The chorus was singing 'The Ode to Joy'.* **3** A **chorus** is a piece of music written to be sung by a large group of people. ❏ *the Hallelujah Chorus* **4** A **chorus** is a group of singers or dancers who perform together in a show, in contrast to the soloists. ❏ *Students played the lesser parts and sang in the chorus.* **5** In drama, a **chorus** is an actor or a group of actors who comment on the action of the play. ❏ *He decides to sort out her life for her, while a pushy Greek chorus dispenses advice from the sidelines.* ❏ *commanding performances from Joe Savino as the chorus and Stephen Brennan as the ghost* **6** When there is a **chorus of** criticism, disapproval, or praise, that attitude is expressed by a lot of people at the same time. ❏ *The government is defending its economic policies against a growing chorus of criticism.*

VERB [T] (**choruses, chorusing, chorused**) (*written*) When people **chorus** something, they say it or sing it together. ❏ *'Hi,' they chorused.*

chose /tʃəʊz/ IRREG FORM **Chose** is the past tense of **choose**.

cho·sen /'tʃəʊzən/ IRREG FORM **Chosen** is the past participle of **choose**.

Christian name /'krɪstʃən ˌneɪm/ NOUN [C] (**Christian names**) Some people refer to their first names as their **Christian names**. ❏ *Despite my attempts to get him to call me by my Christian name, he insisted on addressing me as 'Mr Kennedy'.*

WHICH WORD?

Christian name, first name or forename?

In British English, some people use **Christian name** to refer to the name they were given when they were born. A person's **Christian name** comes before their surname or family name.

❏ *We learn that Mr Kinsky's **Christian name** is Jason.*

In American English, people usually talk about a person's **first name** instead. British people who are not Christians also use **first name**.

❏ *I just realized, I don't know your **first name**.*

Forename is a more formal word that is sometimes used on official forms. It is only used in written English.

Christ·mas ◆◆◇ /'krɪsməs/ NOUN [C, U] (**Christmases**) **1** **Christmas** is a Christian festival when the birth of Jesus Christ is celebrated. Christmas is celebrated on the 25th of December. ❏ *The day after Christmas is generally a busy one for retailers.* **2** **Christmas** is the period of several days around and including Christmas Day. ❏ *During the Christmas holidays there's a tremendous amount of traffic between the Northeast and Florida.*

chron·ic /'krɒnɪk/ ADJ **1** A **chronic** illness or disability lasts for a very long time. Compare **acute**. = long-term ❏ *chronic back pain* ❏ *The condition is often chronic* **2** [chronic + N] You can describe someone's bad habits or behaviour as **chronic** when they have behaved like that for a long time and do not seem to be able to stop themselves. ❏ *a chronic worrier* **3** A **chronic** situation or problem is very severe and unpleasant. = severe ❏ *One cause of the artist's suicide seems to have been chronic poverty.* ❏ *There is a chronic shortage of patrol cars in this police district.*

chron·ic·al·ly /'krɒnɪkli/ ADV **1** [chronically + ADJ/-ED] ❏ *Most of them were chronically ill.* **2** [chronically + ADJ/-ED] = severely ❏ *Research and technology are said to be chronically underfunded.*

chrono·logi·cal /ˌkrɒnə'lɒdʒɪkəl/ ADJ If things are described or shown in **chronological** order, they are described or shown in the order in which they happened. ❏ *I have arranged these stories in chronological order.* ❏ *Such a paper might present a chronological sequence of events.* ❏ *The play is in strict chronological order, and attention is paid to demographic and statistical details.*

chrono·logi·cal·ly /ˌkrɒnə'lɒdʒɪkli/ ADV ❏ *The exhibition is organized chronologically.*

chuck /tʃʌk/ VERB

VERB [T] (**chucks, chucking, chucked**) (*informal*) **1** When you **chuck** something somewhere, you throw it there in a casual or careless way. = throw ❏ *I took a great dislike to the clock, so I chucked it in the trash.* **2** If you **chuck** your job or some other activity, you stop doing it. ❏ *Last summer, he chucked his ten-year career as a stockbroker and headed for the mountains.*

PHRASE **chuck it all in** If someone **chucks it all in**, they stop doing their job, and usually move somewhere else. ❏ *Sometimes I'd like to chuck it all in and go fishing.*

chuck·le /'tʃʌkəl/ VERB, NOUN

VERB [I] (**chuckles, chuckling, chuckled**) When you **chuckle**, you laugh quietly. ❏ *The banker chuckled and said, 'Of course not.'*

NOUN [C] (**chuckles**) A **chuckle** is a quiet laugh. ❏ *He gave a little chuckle.*

chunk /tʃʌŋk/ NOUN [C] (**chunks**) **1** **Chunks of** something are thick, solid pieces of it. = lump ❏ *They had to be careful of floating chunks of ice.* ❏ *a chunk of meat* **2** (*informal*) A **chunk of** something is a large amount or large part of it. ❏ *The company owns a chunk of farmland near the airport.*

church ◆◆◇ /tʃɜːtʃ/ NOUN [C, U] (**churches**) **1** [C, U] A **church** is a building in which Christians worship. You usually refer to this place as **church** when you are talking about the time that people spend there. ❏ *one of the country's most historic churches* ❏ *St Helen's Church* ❏ *The family had gone to church.* **2** [C] A **Church** is one of the groups of people within the Christian religion, for example Catholics or Methodists, that have their own beliefs, clergy, and forms of worship. ❏ *cooperation with the Catholic Church* ❏ *Church leaders said he was welcome to return.*

churn /tʃɜːn/ NOUN, VERB

NOUN [C] (**churns**) A **churn** is a container which is used for making butter.

VERB [T, I] (**churns, churning, churned**) **1** [T] If something **churns** water, mud, or dust, it moves it about violently. ❏ *dirt roads now churned into mud by the annual rains* **2** [I, T] If you say that your stomach **is churning**, you mean that you feel sick. You can also say that something **churns** your stomach. = heave ❏ *My stomach churned as I stood up.*

PHRASAL VERBS **churn out** (*informal*) To **churn out** something means to produce large quantities of it very quickly. ❑ *He began to churn out literary compositions in English.*

churn up Churn up means the same as **churn** VERB **1**. ❑ *The recent rain had churned up the waterfall into a muddy whirlpool.* ❑ *Occasionally dolphins slap the water with their tails or churn it up in play.*

ciga·rette ◆◇◇ /ˌsɪɡəˈret/ NOUN [c] (**cigarettes**) **Cigarettes** are small tubes of paper containing tobacco which people smoke. ❑ *He went out to buy a packet of cigarettes.*

cin·ema ◆◇◇ /ˈsɪnɪmə/ NOUN [u, c, SING] (**cinemas**) **1** [u] **Cinema** is the business and art of making films. = film ❑ *Contemporary African cinema has much to offer.* **2** [c] (*mainly BrE*; *in AmE*, usually use **movie theater**) A **cinema** is a place where people go to watch films for entertainment. **3** [SING] (*mainly BrE*; *in AmE*, usually use **the movies**) You can talk about **the cinema** when you are talking about seeing a film.

✪ **cir·cle** ◆◆◇ /ˈsɜːkəl/ NOUN, VERB
◼NOUN◼ [c] (**circles**) **1** A **circle** is a shape consisting of a curved line completely surrounding an area. Every part of the line is the same distance from the centre of the area. = ring ❑ *The flag was red, with a large white circle in the centre.* ❑ *I wrote down the number 46 and drew a circle around it.* **2** A **circle of** something is a round, flat piece or area of it. = ring ❑ *Cut out 4 circles of pastry.* **3** A **circle of** objects or people is a group of them arranged in the shape of a circle. = ring ❑ *a circle of gigantic stones* **4** You can refer to a group of people as a **circle** when they meet each other regularly because they are friends or because they belong to the same profession or share the same interests. ❑ *He has a small circle of friends.*
◼VERB◼ [I, T] (**circles, circling, circled**) **1** [I, T] If something **circles** an object or a place, or **circles around** it, it forms a circle around it. = encircle ❑ *This is the road that circles the city.* **2** [I, T] If an aircraft or a bird **circles** or **circles** something, it moves around in a circle in the air. ❑ *The plane circled, awaiting permission to land.* ❑ *There were two helicopters circling around.* **3** [T] If you **circle** something on a piece of paper, you draw a circle around it. = ring ❑ *Circle the words on this list that you recognize.*

✪ **cir·cuit** ◆◇◇ /ˈsɜːkɪt/ NOUN [c] (**circuits**) **1** An electrical **circuit** is a complete route which an electric current can flow around. ❑ *Any attempts to cut through the cabling will break the electrical circuit.* ❑ *the thin metal connections that make up the circuits within a microprocessor* **2** A **circuit** is a series of places that are visited regularly by a person or group, especially as a part of their job. ❑ *It's a common problem, the one I'm asked about most when I'm on the lecture circuit.*

✪ **cir·cu·lar** /ˈsɜːkjʊlə/ ADJ, NOUN
◼ADJ◼ **1** Something that is **circular** is shaped like a circle. = round ❑ *a circular hole twelve feet wide and two feet deep* ❑ *Place your hands on your shoulders and move your elbows up, back, and down, in a circular motion.* **2** A **circular** journey or route is one in which you go to a place and return by a different route. ❑ *Both sides of the river can be explored on this circular walk.*
◼NOUN◼ [c] (**circulars**) A **circular** is an official letter or advertisement that is sent to a large number of people at the same time. ❑ *The proposal has been widely publicized in press information circulars sent to 1,800 newspapers.*

✪ **cir·cu·late** /ˈsɜːkjʊleɪt/ VERB [I, T] (**circulates, circulating, circulated**) **1** [I, T] If a piece of writing **circulates** or **is circulated**, copies of it are passed around among a group of people. ❑ *The document was previously circulated in New York at the United Nations.* ❑ *Public employees, teachers and liberals are circulating a petition for his recall.* **2** [I, T] If something such as a rumour **circulates** or **is circulated**, the people in a place tell it to each other. = spread ❑ *Rumours were already beginning to circulate that the project might have to be abandoned.* **3** [I] When something **circulates**, it moves easily and freely within a closed place or system. = flow ❑ *a virus which circulates via the bloodstream and causes ill health in a variety of organs* ❑ *the sound of water circulating through pipes* **4** [I] If you **circulate** at a party, you move among the guests and talk

to different people. ❑ *If you'll excuse me, I really must circulate.*

✪ **cir·cu·la·tion** /ˌsɜːkjʊˈleɪʃən/ NOUN
◼NOUN◼ [u, c] (**circulations**) **1** [u] The **circulation** of a piece of writing is the act of passing round copies of it among a group of people. ❑ *an inquiry into the circulation of 'unacceptable literature'.* **2** [u] The **circulation** of something within a closed place or system is its free and easy movement within the place or system. = flow ❑ *The north pole is warmer than the south and the circulation of air around it is less well contained.* ❑ *the principle of free circulation of goods* **3** [c] The **circulation** of a newspaper or magazine is the number of copies that are sold each time it is produced. ❑ *The Daily News once had the highest circulation of any daily in the country.* **4** [u] Your **circulation** is the movement of blood through your body. ❑ *Anyone with heart, lung, or circulation problems should seek medical advice before flying.*
◼PHRASE◼ **in circulation** or **out of circulation** If something such as money is **in circulation**, it is being used by the public. If something is **out of circulation** or has been **withdrawn from circulation**, it is no longer available for use by the public. ❑ *The supply of money in circulation was drastically reduced overnight.* ❑ *a society like America, with perhaps 180 million guns in circulation*

✪ **cir·cum·fer·ence** /səˈkʌmfrəns/ NOUN [u] **1** The **circumference** of a circle, place, or round object is the distance around its edge. ❑ *a scientist calculating the Earth's circumference* ❑ *The island is 3.5 km in circumference.* **2** The **circumference** of a circle, place, or round object is its edge. ❑ *Cut the salmon into long strips and wrap it round the circumference of the bread.*

WORD PARTS
The prefix *circum-* often appears in words that have 'around' as part of their meaning:
circumference (NOUN)
circumnavigate (VERB)
circumvent (VERB)

cir·cum·stance ◆◇◇ /ˈsɜːkəmstæns/ NOUN (*academic word*)
◼NOUN◼ [c, PL, u] (**circumstances**) **1** [c] The **circumstances** of a particular situation are the conditions which affect what happens. = conditions ❑ *Recent opinion polls show that 60 per cent favour abortion under certain circumstances.* ❑ *The strategy was too dangerous in the explosive circumstances of the times.* **2** [PL] The **circumstances** of an event are the way it happened or the causes of it. ❑ *I'm making enquiries about the circumstances of Mary Dean's murder.* **3** [PL] Your **circumstances** are the conditions of your life, especially the amount of money that you have. = situation ❑ *help and support for the single mother, whatever her circumstances* **4** [u] Events and situations which cannot be controlled are sometimes referred to as **circumstance**. ❑ *There are those, you know, who, by circumstance, end up homeless.*
◼PHRASES◼ **under any circumstances** or **under any circumstance** (*emphasis*) You can emphasize that something must not or will not happen by saying that it must not or will not happen **under any circumstances**. ❑ *Racism is wholly unacceptable under any circumstances.*
in the circumstances or **under the circumstances** You can use **in the circumstances** or **under the circumstances** before or after a statement to indicate that you have considered the conditions affecting the situation before making the statement. ❑ *In the circumstances, Paisley's plans looked highly appropriate.*

cir·cus /ˈsɜːkəs/ NOUN [c, SING] (**circuses**) **1** [c] A **circus** is a group that consists of clowns, acrobats, and animals that travels around to different places and performs shows. ❑ *My real ambition was to work in a circus.* **2** [SING] **The circus** is the show performed by these people. ❑ *My dad took me to the circus.* **3** [SING] If you describe a group of people or an event as a **circus**, you disapprove of them because they attract a lot of attention but do not achieve anything useful. ❑ *It could well turn into some kind of a media circus.*

✪ **cite** ◆◇◇ /saɪt/ VERB [T] (**cites, citing, cited**) (*academic word*)

C

1 (formal) If you **cite** something, you quote it or mention it, especially as an example or proof of what you are saying. = quote, mention ❑ *She cites a favourite poem by George Herbert.* ❑ *The author cites just one example.* ❑ *Domestic interest rates are often cited as a major factor affecting exchange rates.* ❑ *How can we account for the data cited as evidence for that theory?* ❑ *Spain was cited as the most popular holiday destination.* **2** To **cite** a person means to officially name them in a legal case. To **cite** a reason or cause means to state it as the official reason for your case. ❑ *They cited Alex's refusal to return to the marital home.*

citi·zen ♦♦◇ /ˈsɪtɪzən/ NOUN [c] (**citizens**) **1** Someone who is a **citizen** of a particular country is legally accepted as belonging to that country. ❑ *American citizens* **2** The **citizens** of a town or city are the people who live there. ❑ *the citizens of Buenos Aires*

city ♦♦♦ /ˈsɪti/ NOUN [c] (**cities**) A **city** is a large town. ❑ *the city of Bologna*

civ·ic /ˈsɪvɪk/ **1** [civic + N] You use **civic** to describe people or things that have an official status in a town or city. = municipal ❑ *the businessmen and civic leaders of Manchester* **2** [civic + N] You use **civic** to describe the duties or feelings that people have because they belong to a particular community. ❑ *a sense of civic pride*

⊙ **civ·il** ♦♦◇ /ˈsɪvəl/ ADJ (academic word) **1** [civil + N] You use **civil** to describe events that happen within a country and that involve the different groups of people in it. ❑ *civil unrest* **2** You use **civil** to describe people or things in a country that are not connected with its armed forces. ❑ *the US civil aviation industry* **3** [civil + N] You use **civil** to describe things that are connected with the state rather than with a religion. ❑ *They were married on August 9 in a civil ceremony in Venice.* **4** [civil + N] You use **civil** to describe the rights that people have within a society. ❑ *a United Nations covenant on civil and political rights* **5** (formal) Someone who is **civil** is polite in a formal way, but not particularly friendly. = polite ❑ *As visitors, the least we can do is be civil to the people in their own land.*

⊙ **ci·vil·ian** ♦◇◇ /sɪˈvɪliən/ NOUN, ADJ

NOUN [c] (**civilians**) In a military situation, a **civilian** is anyone who is not a member of the armed forces. ≠ soldier ❑ *The safety of civilians caught up in the fighting must be guaranteed.* ❑ *their total disregard for the lives of innocent civilians*

ADJ In a military situation, **civilian** is used to describe people or things that are not military. ≠ military ❑ *the country's civilian population* ❑ *civilian casualties* ❑ *a soldier in civilian clothes*

⊙ **civi·li·za·tion** /ˌsɪvɪlaɪˈzeɪʃən/ also **civilisation** NOUN [c, u] (**civilizations**) **1** [c, u] A **civilization** is a human society with its own social organization and culture. = society ❑ *The ancient civilizations of Central and Latin America were founded upon corn.* ❑ *It seemed to him that western civilization was in grave economic and cultural danger.* **2** [u] **Civilization** is the state of having an advanced level of social organization and a comfortable way of life. ❑ *our advanced state of civilization*

civi·lize /ˈsɪvɪlaɪz/ also **civilise** VERB [t] (**civilizes, civilizing, civilized**) To **civilize** a person or society means to educate them and improve their way of life. ❑ *a comedy about a man who tries to civilize a woman – but she ends up civilizing him*

civi·lized /ˈsɪvɪlaɪzd/ also **civilised** ADJ **1** (approval) If you describe a society as **civilized**, you mean that it is advanced and has established laws and customs. ❑ *I believed that in civilized countries, torture had ended long ago.* **2** If you describe a person or their behaviour as **civilized**, you mean that they are polite and reasonable. ❑ *I wrote to my ex-wife last week. She was very civilized about it.*

⊙ **civ·il rights** NOUN [PL] **Civil rights** are the rights that people have in a society to equal treatment and equal opportunities, whatever their race, sex, or religion. ❑ *the civil rights movement* ❑ *new laws guaranteeing civil rights such as free expression and private business ownership* ❑ *violations of civil rights*

civ·il serv·ant NOUN [c] (**civil servants**) A **civil servant** is a person who works in the civil service in Britain and some other countries, or for the local, state, or federal government in the United States ❑ *two senior civil servants*

civ·il ser·vice NOUN [SING] The **civil service** of a country consists of its government departments and all the people who work in them. In many countries, the departments concerned with military and legal affairs are not part of the civil service. ❑ *a job in the civil service*

civ·il war ♦◇◇ NOUN [c] (**civil wars**) A **civil war** is a war which is fought between different groups of people who live in the same country. ❑ *the American Civil War*

⊙ **claim** ♦♦♦ /kleɪm/ VERB, NOUN

VERB [t, i] (**claims, claiming, claimed**) **1** [t] If you say that someone **claims that** something is true, you mean they say that it is true but you are not sure whether or not they are telling the truth. = maintain, assert, allege ❑ *He claimed that it was all a conspiracy against him.* ❑ *A man claiming to be a journalist threatened to reveal details about her private life.* ❑ *He claims a 70 to 80 per cent success rate.* **2** [t] If you say that someone **claims** responsibility or credit for something, you mean they say that they are responsible for it, but you are not sure whether or not they are telling the truth. ❑ *An underground organization has claimed responsibility for the bomb explosion.* **3** [t] If you **claim** something, you try to get it because you think you have a right to it. ❑ *Now they are returning to claim what was theirs.* **4** [t] (journalism) If someone **claims** a record, title, or prize, they gain or win it. ❑ *Zhuang claimed the record in 54.64 seconds.* **5** [t] If something or someone **claims** your attention, they need you to spend your time and effort on them. ❑ *There is already a long list of people claiming her attention.* **6** [i, t] If you **claim** money from the government, an insurance company, or another organization, you officially apply to them for it, because you think you are entitled to it according to their rules. ❑ *Some 25 per cent of the people who are entitled to claim benefits do not do so.* ❑ *John had taken out insurance but when he tried to claim, the insurance company refused to pay.* **7** [t] If you **claim** money or other benefits from your employers, you demand them because you think you deserve or need them. ❑ *The union claimed a rise worth four times the rate of inflation.* **8** [t] (formal) If you say that a war, disease, or accident **claims** someone's life, you mean that they are killed in it or by it. ❑ *The civil war claimed the life of a UN interpreter yesterday.*

NOUN [c] (**claims**) **1** If you make a **claim**, you officially apply to the government, an insurance company, or other organization for money because you think you are entitled to it according to their rules. ❑ *Last time we made a claim on our insurance, they paid up really quickly.* **2** A **claim** is a demand for money or other benefits from your employers because you think you deserve or need them. ❑ *They are making substantial claims for improved working conditions.* **3** A **claim** is something which someone says which they cannot prove and which may be false. = allegation, assertion ❑ *He repeated his claim that the people of Trinidad and Tobago backed his action.* ❑ *He rejected claims that he had affairs with six women.* **4** A **claim** is a demand for something that you think you have a right to. ❑ *Rival claims to Macedonian territory caused conflict in the Balkans.* **5** If you have a **claim on** someone or their attention, you have the right to demand things from them or to demand their attention. ❑ *She had no claims on him now.*
✦ stake a claim → see stake

clam·our (BrE; in AmE, use **clamor**) VERB [i] (**clamours, clamouring, clamoured**) (journalism) If people are **clamouring for** something, they are demanding it in a noisy or angry way. ❑ *competing parties clamouring for the attention of the voter*

clamp /klæmp/ NOUN, VERB

NOUN [c] (**clamps**) **1** A **clamp** is a device that holds two things firmly together. ❑ *Many openers have a magnet or set of clamps to grip the open lid.* **2** (mainly BrE) A **clamp** is a device fixed to the wheel of a car in order to immobilize it.

VERB [t] (**clamps, clamping, clamped**) **1** When you **clamp** one thing **to** another, you fasten the two things together with a clamp. ❑ *Somebody forgot to bring along the U-bolts to*

C

clamp the microphones to the pole. **2** To **clamp** something in a particular place means to put it or hold it there firmly and tightly. ◻ Simon finished dialling and clamped the phone to his ear. ◻ He clamped his lips together. **3** (BrE) To **clamp** a car is to immobilize it by means of a wheel clamp.

PHRASAL VERB **clamp down** (journalism) To **clamp down on** people or activities means to take strong official action to stop or control them. = crack down ◻ If the government clamps down on the movement, that will only serve to strengthen it in the long run.

clan /klæn/ NOUN [C] (clans) **1** A **clan** is a group which consists of families that are related to each other. ◻ rival clans **2** (informal) You can refer to a group of people with the same interests as a **clan**. ◻ a powerful clan of industrialists from Monterrey

clap /klæp/ VERB, NOUN

VERB [I, T] (claps, clapping, clapped) **1** [I, T] When you **clap**, you hit your hands together to express appreciation or attract attention. ◻ The men danced and the women clapped. ◻ Midge clapped her hands, calling them back to order. **2** [T] If you **clap** your hand or an object onto something, you put it there quickly and firmly. ◻ I clapped a hand over her mouth.

NOUN [C] (claps) A **clap of thunder** is a sudden and loud noise of thunder.

✪ **clari·fy** /ˈklærɪfaɪ/ VERB [T] (clarifies, clarifying, clarified) (academic word, formal) To **clarify** something means to make it easier to understand, usually by explaining it in more detail. ◻ Thank you for writing and allowing me to clarify the present position. ◻ It is important to clarify the distinction between the relativity of values and the relativity of truth. ◻ A bank spokesman was unable to clarify the situation. ◻ You will want to clarify what your objectives are.

✪ **clari·fi·ca·tion** /ˌklærɪfɪˈkeɪʃən/ NOUN [C, U] (clarifications) ◻ The union has written to Detroit asking for clarification of the situation. ◻ Please provide clarification on 'conflict of interest' concerning the awarding of contracts by the board of directors.

✪ **clar·ity** /ˈklærɪti/ NOUN [U] **1** The **clarity** of something such as a book or argument is its quality of being well explained and easy to understand. = lucidity ◻ the ease and clarity with which the author explains difficult technical and scientific subjects ◻ our need as social scientists to strive for clarity of analysis **2** **Clarity** is the ability to think clearly. ◻ In business circles he is noted for his flair and clarity of vision. **3** **Clarity** is the quality of being clear in outline or sound. = precision ◻ This remarkable technology provides far greater clarity than conventional x-rays.

clash ◆◇◇ /klæʃ/ VERB, NOUN

VERB [RECIP, I] (clashes, clashing, clashed) **1** [RECIP] (journalism) When people **clash**, they fight, argue, or disagree with each other. ◻ A group of 400 demonstrators ripped down the front gate and clashed with police. ◻ Behind the scenes, Parsons clashed with almost everyone on the show. **2** [RECIP] Beliefs, ideas, or qualities that **clash with** each other are very different from each other and therefore are opposed. ◻ Don't make any policy decisions which clash with official company thinking. **3** [RECIP] If one colour or style **clashes with** another, the colours or styles look ugly together. You can also say that two colours or styles **clash**. ◻ The red door clashed with the soft, natural tones of the stone walls. **4** [I] (BrE; in AmE, use **conflict**) If one event **clashes with** another, the two events happen at the same time so that you cannot attend both of them.

NOUN [C] (clashes) **1** [oft clash 'between/with' N] (journalism) A **clash** is when people have a fight, argument, or disagreement with each other. ◻ There have been a number of clashes between police in riot gear and demonstrators. **2** A **clash** occurs when someone's beliefs, ideas, or qualities are very different from or opposed to someone else's. ◻ Inside government, there was a clash of views.

clasp /klɑːsp, klæsp/ VERB, NOUN

VERB [T] (clasps, clasping, clasped) If you **clasp** someone or something, you hold them tightly in your hands or arms. ◻ She clasped the children to her.

NOUN [C] (clasps) A **clasp** is a small device that fastens something. ◻ the clasp of her handbag

✪ **class** ◆◆◆ /klɑːs, klæs/ NOUN, VERB

NOUN [C, U, SING] (classes) **1** [C] A **class** is a group of students who are taught together. ◻ He had to spend about six months in a class with younger students. **2** [C] A **class** is a course of teaching in a particular subject. = lesson ◻ He acquired a law degree by taking classes at night. **3** [C] A **class of** things is a group of them with similar characteristics. = type, sort, kind ◻ Harbour staff noticed that measurements given for the same class of boats often varied. ◻ the division of the stars into six classes of brightness **4** [U] If you do something **in class**, you do it during a lesson in school. ◻ There is lots of reading in class. **5** [U] (informal, approval) If you say that someone or something has **class**, you mean that they are elegant and sophisticated. ◻ The most elegant woman I've ever met – she had class in every sense of the word. **6** [SING] The students in a school or college who finish their course in a particular year are often referred to as the **class of** that year. ◻ These two members of Yale's Class of '57 never miss a reunion. **7** [C, U] **Class** refers to the division of people in a society into groups according to their social status. = caste ◻ the relationship between social classes ◻ What it will do is create a whole new ruling class. ◻ the characteristics of the British class structure

VERB [T] (classes, classing, classed) If someone or something **is classed as** a particular thing, they are regarded as belonging to that group of things. = classify, categorize ◻ Since they can and do successfully inter-breed, they cannot be classed as different species. ◻ I class myself as an ordinary working person. ◻ Malaysia wants to send back refugees classed as economic migrants.

→ See also **first-class, middle class, second-class, working class**

WHICH WORD?

class, form, or grade?

A **class** is a group of pupils or students who are taught together.

◻ If **classes** were smaller, children would learn more.

◻ I had forty students in my **class**.

In many British schools and in some American private schools, **form** is used instead of **class**. **Form** is used especially with a number to refer to a particular class or age group.

◻ She's in the fifth **form**.

◻ She's in **form** 5.

A **grade** in an American school is similar to a **form** in a British school. First, second, third, etc. **grade** is sometimes used alone, without 'the' before it.

◻ My brother is in second **grade**.

clas·sic ◆◆◇ /ˈklæsɪk/ ADJ, NOUN (academic word)

ADJ **1** A **classic** example of a thing or situation has all the features which you expect such a thing or situation to have. = typical ◻ The debate in the press has been a classic example of hypocrisy. **2** [classic + N] A **classic** film, piece of writing, or piece of music is of very high quality and has become a standard against which similar things are judged. ◻ the classic children's film 'Huckleberry Finn'

NOUN [C, U] (classics) **1** [C] A **classic** is an example of a thing or situation that has all the features which you expect such a thing or situation to have. ◻ It was a classic of interrogation: first the bully, then the kind one who offers sympathy. **2** [C] A **classic** is a film, piece of writing, or piece of music of very high quality that has become a standard against which similar things are judged. ◻ The record won a gold award and remains one of the classics of modern popular music. **3** [C] A **classic** is a book which is well-known and considered to be of a high literary standard. You can refer to such books generally as **the classics**. ◻ As I grow older, I like to reread the classics regularly. **4** [U] **Classics** is the study of the ancient Greek and Roman civilizations, especially their languages, literature, and philosophy. ◻ a Classics degree

---

WHICH WORD?

classic or classical?

Do not confuse **classic** and **classical**.

A **classic** example of something has all the features or characteristics that you expect something of its kind to have.

❑ *This is a **classic** example of the principle of 'less is more'.*

Classic is also used to describe films or books that are judged to be of outstanding quality.

❑ *It is one of the **classic** works of Hollywood cinema.*

Classical music is music written by composers such as Mozart and Beethoven. Music of this type is often complex in form, and is considered by many people to have lasting value.

❑ *I spend a lot of time listening to **classical** music.*

Classical is also used to refer to things connected with ancient Greek or Roman civilization.

❑ *Truffles have been savoured as a delicacy since **classical** times.*

✪ clas·si·cal ◆◇◇ /'klæsɪkəl/ ADJ (academic word) **1** You use **classical** to describe something that is traditional in form, style, or content. ❑ *Fokine did not change the steps of classical ballet; instead he found new ways of using them.* ❑ *the scientific attitude of Smith and earlier classical economists* **2** **Classical** music is music that is considered to be serious and of lasting value. ❑ *a classical composer like Beethoven* **3** **Classical** is used to describe things which relate to the ancient Greek or Roman civilizations. ❑ *the healers of ancient Egypt and classical Greece* ❑ *It's a technological achievement that is unrivalled in the classical world.* ❑ *classical architecture*

✪ clas·si·fi·ca·tion /ˌklæsɪfɪ'keɪʃən/ NOUN [C, U] (classifications) **1** [C] A **classification** is a division or category in a system which divides things into groups or types. ❑ *The government uses a classification system that includes both race and ethnicity.* **2** [C, U] The **classification** of things is the act of dividing them into groups or types so that things with similar characteristics are in the same group. = categorization ❑ *the arbitrary classification of knowledge into fields of study* ❑ *the British Board of Film Classification*

clas·si·fied /'klæsɪfaɪd/ ADJ **Classified** information or documents are officially secret. ❑ *He has a security clearance that allows him access to classified information.*

✪ clas·si·fy /'klæsɪfaɪ/ VERB [T] (classifies, classifying, classified) To **classify** things means to divide them into groups or types so that things with similar characteristics are in the same group. = categorize, sort ❑ *It is necessary initially to classify the headaches into certain types.* ❑ *Rocks can be classified according to their mode of origin.* ❑ *The coroner immediately classified his death as a suicide.*

class·room /'klɑːsruːm, 'klæs-/ NOUN [C] (classrooms) A **classroom** is a room in a school where lessons take place.

✪ clause /klɔːz/ NOUN [C] (clauses) (academic word) **1** A **clause** is a section of a legal document. ❑ *He has a clause in his contract which entitles him to a percentage of the profits.* ❑ *a complaint alleging a breach of clause 4 of the code* ❑ *a compromise document sprinkled with escape clauses* **2** In grammar, a **clause** is a group of words containing a verb. Sentences contain one or more clauses. ❑ *In both cases it is the subordinate clause which is the governing sentence.* ❑ *A subordinate or dependent clause cannot stand by itself but must be connected to another clause.*

claw /klɔː/ NOUN, VERB

[NOUN] [C] (claws) **1** The **claws** of a bird or animal are the thin, hard, curved nails at the end of its feet. ❑ *The cat tried to cling to the edge by its claws.* **2** The **claws** of a lobster, crab, or scorpion are the two pointed parts at the end of its legs which are used for holding things.

[VERB] [I, T] (claws, clawing, clawed) **1** [I] If an animal **claws** at something, it scratches or damages it with its claws. ❑ *The wolf clawed at the tree and howled the whole night.* **2** [I] To **claw at** something means to try very hard to get

hold of it. ❑ *His fingers clawed at Blake's wrist.* **3** [T] If you **claw** your **way** somewhere, you move there with great difficulty, trying desperately to find things to hold on to. ❑ *From the flooded depths of the ship, some did manage to claw their way up iron ladders to the safety of the upper deck.*

clay /kleɪ/ NOUN [C, U] (clays) **1** [C, U] **Clay** is a kind of earth that is soft when it is wet and hard when it is dry. Clay is shaped and baked to make things such as pots and bricks. ❑ *the heavy clay soils of Georgia* ❑ *As the wheel turned, the potter shaped and squeezed the lump of clay into a graceful shape.* **2** [U] In tennis, matches played on **clay** are played on courts whose surface is covered with finely crushed stones or brick. ❑ *Most tennis is played on hard courts, but a substantial amount is played on clay.*

clean ◆◆◇ /kliːn/ ADJ, VERB, ADV

[ADJ] (cleaner, cleanest) **1** Something that is **clean** is free from dirt or unwanted marks. ❑ *The subway is efficient and spotlessly clean.* ❑ *Tiled kitchen floors are easy to keep clean.* **2** You say that people or animals are **clean** when they keep themselves or their surroundings clean. ❑ *We like pigs, they're very clean.* **3** A **clean** fuel or chemical process does not create many harmful or polluting substances. ❑ *Fans of electric cars say they are clean, quiet, and economical.* **4** If you describe something such as a book, joke, or lifestyle as **clean**, you think that they are not sexually immoral or offensive. ❑ *They're trying to show clean, wholesome, decent movies.* ❑ *Flirting is good clean fun.* **5** If someone has a **clean** reputation or record, they have never done anything illegal or wrong. ❑ *Accusations of tax evasion have tarnished his clean image.* **6** A **clean** game or fight is carried out fairly, according to the rules. = fair ❑ *He called for a clean fight in the election and an end to 'negative campaigning'.* **7** A **clean** sheet of paper has no writing or drawing on it. = blank ❑ *Take a clean sheet of paper and down the left-hand side make a list.*

[VERB] [I, T] (cleans, cleaning, cleaned) **1** If you **clean** something or **clean** dirt off it, you make it free from dirt and unwanted marks, for example by washing or wiping it. If something **cleans** easily, it is easy to clean. ❑ *Her father cleaned his glasses with a paper napkin.* ❑ *It took half an hour to clean the orange powder off the bathtub.* **2** If you **clean** a room or house, you make the inside of it and the furniture in it free from dirt and dust. ❑ *Mary cooked and cleaned for them.*

[PHRASAL VERBS] **clean out** If you **clean out** something such as a cupboard, room, or container, you take everything out of it and clean the inside of it thoroughly. ❑ *Mr Wall asked if I would help him clean out the barrels.*

clean up 1 If you **clean up** a mess or **clean up** a place where there is a mess, you make things neat and free of dirt again. ❑ *Police in the city have been cleaning up the debris left by a day of violent confrontation.* **2** To **clean up** something such as the environment or an industrial process means to make it free from substances or processes that cause pollution. ❑ *Under pressure from the public, many regional governments cleaned up their beaches.* **3** If the police or authorities **clean up** a place or area of activity, they make it free from crime, corruption, and other unacceptable forms of behaviour. ❑ *After years of neglect and decline, the city was cleaning itself up.* **4** If you go and **clean up**, you make yourself clean and neat, especially after doing something that has made you dirty. ❑ *Johnny, go inside and get cleaned up.*

[ADV] (informal, emphasis) **Clean** is used to emphasize that something was done completely. ❑ *It burned clean through the seat of my overalls.* ❑ *The thief got clean away with the money.*

clean·ly /'kliːnli/ ADV ❑ *The game had been cleanly fought.*
clean·ing /'kliːnɪŋ/ NOUN [U] **1** *The windows will have to be given a thorough cleaning.* **2** *I do the cleaning myself.*
✦ **clean up your act** → see **act**; **keep your nose clean** → see **nose**; **a clean slate** → see **slate**; **a clean sweep** → see **sweep**; **clean as a whistle** → see **whistle**

clean·er /'kliːnə/ NOUN [C, U] (cleaners) **1** [C] A **cleaner** is someone who is employed to clean the rooms and furniture inside a building. ❑ *the prison hospital where Sid worked as a cleaner* **2** [C] A **cleaner** is someone whose job

C

is to clean a particular type of thing. ❑ *He was a window cleaner.* **3** [C] A **cleaner** is a device used for cleaning things. ❑ *an air cleaner* **4** [C] A **cleaner** or a **cleaner's** is a shop where things such as clothes are dry-cleaned. ❑ *Did you pick up my suit from the cleaner's?* **5** [C, U] A **cleaner** is a substance used for cleaning things. ❑ *oven cleaner*

clean·li·ness /ˈklɛnlɪnəs/ NOUN [U] **Cleanliness** is the degree to which people keep themselves and their surroundings clean. ❑ *Many of the area's beaches fail to meet minimum standards of cleanliness.*

cleanse /klɛnz/ VERB [T] (**cleanses, cleansing, cleansed**) **1** To **cleanse** a place, person, or organization of something dirty, unpleasant, or evil means to make them free from it. ❑ *Right after your last cigarette, your body will begin to cleanse itself of tobacco toxins.* **2** If you **cleanse** your skin or a wound, you clean it. ❑ *Catherine demonstrated the proper way to cleanse the face.*

✪ **clear** ◆◆◆ /klɪə/ ADJ, VERB, NOUN

 ADJ (**clearer, clearest**) **1** Something that is **clear** is easy to understand, see, or hear. ❑ *The book is clear, readable, and adequately illustrated.* ❑ *The space telescope has taken the clearest pictures ever of Pluto.* ❑ *He repeated his answer, this time in a clear, firm tone of voice.* **2** Something that is **clear** is obvious and impossible to be mistaken about. = obvious; ≠ unclear, ambiguous, uncertain ❑ *It was a clear case of homicide.* ❑ *It became clear that I hadn't been able to convince Mike.* ❑ *A spokesman said the British government's position is perfectly clear.* ❑ *It's not clear whether the incident was an accident or deliberate.* **3** If you are **clear about** something, you understand it completely. ❑ *It is important to be clear about what Chomsky is doing here.* ❑ *He is not entirely clear on how he will go about it.* **4** If your mind or your way of thinking is **clear**, you are able to think sensibly and reasonably, and you are not affected by confusion or by a drug such as alcohol. ❑ *She needed a clear head to carry out her instructions.* **5** A **clear** substance is one which you can see through and which has no colour, like clean water. = transparent ❑ *a clear glass panel* ❑ *a clear gel* **6** If a surface, place, or view is **clear**, it is free of unwanted objects or obstacles. ❑ *The runway is clear – go ahead and land.* ❑ *Caroline prefers her countertops to be clear of clutter.* **7** If it is a **clear** day or if the sky is **clear**, there is no mist, rain, or cloud. ❑ *On a clear day you can see the coast.* **8** **Clear** eyes look healthy, attractive, and shining. ❑ *clear blue eyes* **9** If your skin is **clear**, it is healthy and free from blemishes. ❑ *No amount of cleansing or mineral water consumption can guarantee a clear skin.* **10** If something or someone is **clear of** something else, it is not touching it or is a safe distance away from it. ❑ *As soon as he was clear of the terminal building, he looked around.* **11** If you say that your conscience is **clear**, you mean you do not think you have done anything wrong. ❑ *Mr Garcia said his conscience was clear over the jail incidents.*

 PHRASE **make something clear** If you **make** something **clear**, you say something in a way that makes it impossible for there to be any doubt about your meaning, wishes, or intentions. ❑ *Mr O'Friel made it clear that further insults of this kind would not be tolerated.*

 CONVENTION **is that clear?** or **do I make myself clear?** You can say '**Is that clear?**' or '**Do I make myself clear?**' after you have told someone your wishes or instructions, to make sure that they have understood you, and to emphasize your authority. ❑ *We're only going for half an hour, and you're not going to buy anything. Is that clear?*

 VERB [T, I] (**clears, clearing, cleared**) **1** [T] To **clear** your mind or your head means to free it from confused thoughts or from the effects of a drug such as alcohol. ❑ *He walked up Fifth Avenue to clear his head.* **2** [T] When you **clear** an area or place or **clear** something **from** it, you remove things from it that you do not want to be there. ❑ *To clear the land and harvest the bananas, they decided they needed a male workforce.* ❑ *Workers could not clear the tunnels of smoke.* **3** [I] When fog or mist **clears**, it gradually disappears. ❑ *The early morning mist had cleared.* **4** [I, T] When a bank **clears** a cheque or when a cheque **clears**, the bank agrees to pay the sum of money mentioned on it. ❑ *Banks can still take two or three weeks to clear a cheque.*

5 [T] If something or someone **clears** the way or the path **for** something to happen, they make it possible. ❑ *The prime minister resigned today, clearing the way for the formation of a new government.* **6** [T] If a course of action **is cleared**, people in authority give permission for it to happen. ❑ *Linda Gradstein has this report from Jerusalem, which was cleared by an Israeli censor.* **7** [T] If someone **is cleared**, they are proved to be not guilty of a crime or mistake. ❑ *She was cleared of murder and jailed for just five years for manslaughter.*

 PHRASAL VERBS **clear away** When you **clear** things **away** or **clear away**, you put away the things that you have been using, especially for eating or cooking. ❑ *The waitress had cleared away the plates and brought coffee.*

clear out **1** (*informal, disapproval*) If you tell someone to **clear out of** a place or to **clear out**, you are telling them rather rudely to leave the place. = get out ❑ *She turned to the others in the room. 'The rest of you clear out of here.'* **2** If you **clear out** a container, room, or house, you make it neat and throw away the things in it that you no longer want. ❑ *I took the precaution of clearing out my desk before I left.*

clear up **1** When you **clear up** or **clear** a place **up**, you make things neat and put them away. ❑ *After breakfast they played while I cleared up.* **2** To **clear up** a problem, misunderstanding, or mystery means to settle it or find a satisfactory explanation for it. = sort out ❑ *There should be someone to whom you can turn for any advice or to clear up any problems.* **3** To **clear up** a medical problem, infection, or disease means to cure it or get rid of it. If a medical problem **clears up**, it goes away. ❑ *Antibiotics should be used to clear up the infection.* **4** When the weather **clears up**, it stops raining or being cloudy. ❑ *It all depends on the weather clearing up.*

 NOUN

 PHRASE **in the clear** If someone is **in the clear**, they are not in danger, or are not blamed or suspected of anything. ❑ *It would be stupid to do anything until we know we're in the clear.*

✪ **clear·ly** /ˈklɪəli/ ADV **1** *Whales journey up the coast of California, clearly visible from the beach.* ❑ *It was important for children to learn to express themselves clearly.* **2** [clearly with CL/GROUP] = obviously ❑ *Clearly, the police cannot break the law in order to enforce it.* ❑ *He was clearly unhappy about the decision.* **3** [clearly after V] ❑ *The only time I can think clearly is when I'm alone.*
→ See also **clearing**
✦ **clear the air** → see **air**; **clear your throat** → see **throat**

WORD CONNECTIONS		
ADV + **clear**		
abundantly clear		
perfectly clear		
absolutely clear		
❑ *It soon became abundantly clear that something was very wrong.*		

clear·ance /ˈklɪərəns/ NOUN [C, U] (**clearances**) **1** **Clearance** is the removal of old buildings, trees, or other things that are not wanted from an area. ❑ *a slum clearance operation in Nairobi* ❑ *The UN pledged to help supervise the clearance of mines.* **2** If you get **clearance to** do or have something, you get official approval or permission to do or have it. = authorization ❑ *Thai Airways said the plane had been given clearance to land.*

clear·ing /ˈklɪərɪŋ/ NOUN [C] (**clearings**) A **clearing** is a small area in a forest where there are no trees or bushes. ❑ *A helicopter landed in a clearing in the dense jungle.*

clench /klɛntʃ/ VERB [I, T] (**clenches, clenching, clenched**) **1** [I, T] When you **clench** your fist or your fist **clenches**, you curl your fingers up tightly, usually because you are very angry. ❑ *Alex clenched her fists and gritted her teeth.* ❑ *She pulled at his sleeve and he turned on her, fists clenching again before he saw who it was.* **2** [I, T] When you **clench** your teeth or they **clench**, you squeeze your teeth together firmly, usually because you are angry or upset. = grit ❑ *Patsy had to clench her jaw to suppress her anger.* **3** [T] If you **clench** something in your hand or in your teeth, you

hold it tightly with your hand or your teeth. = grip
❑ *I clenched the arms of my chair.*

cleri·cal /'klerɪkəl/ ADJ **1** [clerical + N] Clerical jobs,
skills, and workers are concerned with routine work that
is done in an office. = administrative ❑ *a strike by
clerical staff in all government departments* **2** [clerical + N]
Clerical means relating to the clergy. ❑ *Iran's clerical
leadership*

clerk /klɑːk, AmE klɜːrk/ NOUN [C] (**clerks**) **1** A clerk is a
person who works in an office, bank, or law court and
whose job is to keep the records or accounts. ❑ *She was
offered a job as a clerk with a travel agency.* **2** (mainly AmE) In
a hotel, office, or hospital, a clerk is the person whose job
is to answer the telephone and deal with people when
they arrive. ❑ *a hotel clerk*

clev·er ◆◇◇ /'klevə/ ADJ (**cleverer, cleverest**) **1** Someone
who is clever is intelligent and able to understand things
easily or plan things well. ❑ *He's a very clever man.* **2** A
clever idea, book, or invention is extremely effective and
shows the skill of the people involved. = ingenious
❑ *It is a clever and gripping novel, yet something is missing
from its heart.*
clev·er·ly /'klevəli/ ADV **1** *She would cleverly pick up on
what I said.* **2** [cleverly + -ED] ❑ *a cleverly designed swimsuit*
clev·er·ness /'klevənəs/ NOUN [U] ❑ *Her cleverness seems to
get in the way of her emotions.*

cli·ché /'kliːʃeɪ, AmE kliːˈʃeɪ/ (in BrE, also use **cliche**) NOUN
[C] (**clichés**) (disapproval) A cliché is an idea or phrase which
has been used so much that it is no longer interesting or
effective or no longer has much meaning. ❑ *I've learned
that the cliché about life not being fair is true.*

click /klɪk/ VERB, NOUN
VERB [I, T] (**clicks, clicking, clicked**) **1** [I, T] If something
clicks or if you click it, it makes a short, sharp sound.
❑ *The applause rose to a crescendo and cameras clicked.*
❑ *He clicked off the radio.* **2** [I, T] (computing) If you click on
an area of a computer screen, you point the cursor at that
area and press one of the buttons on the mouse in order
to make something happen. ❑ *I clicked on a link and recent
reviews of the production came up.* ❑ *Click the link and see
what happens.* **3** [I] (informal) When you suddenly
understand something, you can say that it clicks. ❑ *When
I saw the television report, it all clicked.*
NOUN [C] (**clicks**) **1** A click is a short, sharp sound. ❑ *The
telephone rang three times before I heard a click and then her
recorded voice.* **2** A click on an area of a computer screen is
the act of pointing the cursor at that area and pressing one
of the buttons on the mouse in order to make something
happen. ❑ *You can check your e-mail with a click of your
mouse.*
✦ click into place → see place

✪ **cli·ent** ◆◇◇ /'klaɪənt/ NOUN [C] (**clients**) (business) A
client of a professional person or organization is a person
or company that receives a service from them in return for
payment. = customer ❑ *a lawyer and his client* ❑ *The
company required clients to pay substantial fees in advance.*

cli·en·tele /ˌkliːɒn'tel, ˌklaɪən-/ NOUN [SING] The
clientele of a place or organization is its customers or
clients. ❑ *This pub had a mixed clientele.*

cliff /klɪf/ NOUN [C] (**cliffs**) A cliff is a high area of land
with a very steep side, especially one next to the sea.
❑ *The car rolled over the edge of a cliff.*

✪ **cli·mate** ◆◇◇ /'klaɪmət/ NOUN [C, U] (**climates**) **1** [C, U]
The climate of a place is the general weather conditions
that are typical of it. = weather ❑ *the hot and humid
climate of Florida* ❑ *Herbs tend to grow in temperate climates.*
2 [C] You can use climate to refer to the general
atmosphere or situation somewhere. ❑ *The economic
climate remains uncertain.* ❑ *the existing climate of violence and
intimidation*

cli·max /'klaɪmæks/ NOUN, VERB
NOUN [C] (**climaxes**) The climax of something is the most
exciting or important moment in it, usually near the end.
❑ *For Pritchard, reaching the Olympics was the climax of her
career.* ❑ *It was the climax to 24 hours of growing anxiety.*
VERB [I, T] (**climaxes, climaxing, climaxed**) (journalism) The

event that climaxes a sequence of events is an exciting or
important event that comes at the end. You can also say
that a sequence of events climaxes with a particular event.
❑ *The demonstration climaxed two weeks of strikes.*

climb ◆◇◇ /klaɪm/ VERB, NOUN
VERB [I, T] (**climbs, climbing, climbed**) **1** [I, T] If you climb
something such as a tree, mountain, or ladder, or climb up
it, you move towards the top of it. If you climb down it,
you move towards the bottom of it. ❑ *Climbing the first hill
took half an hour.* ❑ *I told her about him climbing up the
drainpipe.* **2** [I] If you climb somewhere, you move there
carefully, for example because you are moving into a small
space or trying to avoid falling. ❑ *The girls hurried outside,
climbed into the car, and drove off.* ❑ *He must have climbed out
of his bed.* **3** [I] When something such as an aeroplane
climbs, it moves upwards to a higher position. When the
sun climbs, it moves higher in the sky. = rise ❑ *The plane
took off for L.A., lost an engine as it climbed, and crashed just off
the runway.* **4** [I] When something climbs, it increases in
value or amount. ❑ *The nation's unemployment rate has been
climbing steadily since last June.* ❑ *Prices have climbed by 21%
since the beginning of the year.*
NOUN [C] (**climbs**) A climb is the act of moving towards
the top of something such as a tree, mountain, or ladder.
❑ *an hour's leisurely climb through olive groves and vineyards*
→ See also **climbing**
✦ a mountain to climb → see **mountain**

climb·ing /'klaɪmɪŋ/ NOUN [U] Climbing is the activity of
climbing rocks or mountains. ❑ *I had done no skiing, no
climbing, and no hiking.*

clinch /klɪntʃ/ VERB [T] (**clinches, clinching, clinched**) **1** If
you clinch something you are trying to achieve, such as a
business deal or victory in a contest, you succeed in
obtaining it. = secure ❑ *Her second-place finish in the final
race was enough to clinch the overall victory.* **2** The thing
that clinches an uncertain matter settles it or provides a
definite answer. ❑ *Evidently this information clinched the
matter.*

cling /klɪŋ/ VERB [I] (**clings, clinging, clung**) **1** If you cling
to someone or something, you hold onto them tightly.
❑ *Another man was rescued as he clung to the riverbank.* ❑ *She
had to cling onto the door handle until the pain passed.* **2** If
someone clings to a position or a possession they have,
they do everything they can to keep it even though this
may be very difficult. ❑ *Instead, he appears determined to
cling to power.* ❑ *Another congressman clung on with a majority
of only 18.*

✪ **clin·ic** ◆◇◇ /'klɪnɪk/ NOUN [C] (**clinics**) A clinic is a
building where people go to receive medical advice or
treatment. = health centre, medical centre ❑ *a family
planning clinic* ❑ *women who were attending a fertility clinic*
❑ *a clinic offering laser eye surgery*

✪ **clini·cal** /'klɪnɪkəl/ ADJ **1** (medical) Clinical means
involving or relating to the direct medical treatment or
testing of patients. ❑ *The first clinical trials were expected to
begin next year.* ❑ *a clinical psychologist* ❑ *the clinical
after-effects of the accident* **2** You use clinical to describe
thought or behaviour that is very logical and does not
involve any emotion. = impersonal ❑ *All this questioning
is so clinical – it kills romance.*
clini·cal·ly /'klɪnɪkli/ ADV ❑ *She was diagnosed as being
clinically depressed.*

clip /klɪp/ NOUN, VERB
NOUN [C] (**clips**) **1** A clip is a small device, usually made of
metal or plastic, that is specially shaped for holding things
together. ❑ *She took the clip out of her hair.* **2** A clip from a
film or a radio or television programme is a short piece of
it that is broadcast separately. ❑ *an historical film clip of
Lenin speaking*
VERB [I, T] (**clips, clipping, clipped**) **1** [I, T] When you
clip things together or when things clip together, you
fasten them together using a clip or clips. ❑ *He clipped
his safety belt to a fitting on the deck.* **2** [T] If you clip
something, you cut small pieces from it, especially in
order to shape it. ❑ *I saw an old man out clipping his hedge.*
3 [T] If you clip something out of a newspaper or
magazine, you cut it out. ❑ *Kids in his neighbourhood clipped*

his picture from the newspaper and carried it around.
4 [T] If something **clips** something else, it hits it accidentally at an angle before moving off in a different direction. ❑ The lorry clipped the rear of a tanker and then crashed into a second lorry.

cloak /kləʊk/ NOUN [C, SING] (**cloaks**) **1** [C] A **cloak** is a long, loose, sleeveless piece of clothing which people used to wear over their other clothes when they went out. **2** [SING] A **cloak of** something such as mist or snow completely covers and hides something. = blanket ❑ Today most of Wales will be under a cloak of thick mist. **3** [SING] If you refer to something as a **cloak**, you mean that it is intended to hide the truth about something. ❑ Preparations for the wedding were made under a cloak of secrecy.

clock ♦◇◇ /klɒk/ NOUN, VERB
NOUN [C] (**clocks**) **1** A **clock** is an instrument that shows what time of day it is. ❑ He was conscious of a clock ticking. ❑ a digital clock **2** A time **clock** in a factory or office is a device that is used to record the hours that people work. Each worker puts a special card into the device when they arrive and leave, and the times are recorded on the card. ❑ Government workers were made to punch time clocks morning, noon and night.
PHRASES **against the clock** If you are doing something **against the clock**, you are doing it in a great hurry, because there is very little time. ❑ The emergency services were working against the clock as the tide began to rise.
around the clock or **round the clock** If something is done **around the clock** or **round the clock**, it is done all day and all night without stopping. ❑ Rescue services have been working round the clock to free stranded motorists.
VERB [T] (**clocks, clocking, clocked**) **1** To **clock** a particular time or speed in a race means to reach that time or speed. ❑ Elliott clocked the fastest time this year for the 800 metres. **2** If something or someone **is clocked at** a particular time or speed, their time or speed is measured at that level. ❑ He has been clocked at 11 seconds for 100 metres.
PHRASAL VERBS **clock in** When you **clock in** at work, you arrive there or put a special card into a device to show what time you arrived. ❑ I have to clock in by eight.
clock off When you **clock off** at work, you leave work or put a special card into a device to show what time you left. ❑ The night duty officer was ready to clock off.
clock on When workers **clock on** at a factory or office, they put a special card into a device to show what time they arrived. = clock in ❑ They arrived to clock on and found the factory gates locked.
clock out Clock out means the same as **clock off**. ❑ She had clocked out of her bank at 5.02 p.m. using her plastic card.
clock up (BrE; in AmE, use **chalk up**) If you **clock up** a large number or total of things, you reach that number or total. = notch up
→ See also o'clock

✪**clock·wise** /ˈklɒkwaɪz/ ADV, ADJ
ADV [clockwise after v] When something is moving **clockwise**, it is moving in a circle in the same direction as the hands on a clock. ≠ anti-clockwise ❑ He told the children to start moving clockwise around the room.
ADJ [clockwise + N] **Clockwise** means moving in a circle in the same direction as the hands on a clock. ❑ Gently swing your right arm in a clockwise direction.

clock·work /ˈklɒkwɜːk/ ADJ, NOUN
ADJ [clockwork + N] A **clockwork** toy or device has machinery inside it which makes it move or operate when it is wound up with a key. ❑ a clockwork train set
NOUN
PHRASE **like clockwork** If you say that something happens **like clockwork**, you mean that it happens without any problems or delays, or happens regularly. ❑ The president's trip is arranged to go like clockwork, everything pre-planned to the minute.

✪**clone** /kləʊn/ NOUN, VERB, ADJ
NOUN [C] (**clones**) **1** If someone or something is a **clone** of another person or thing, they are so similar to this person or thing that they seem to be exactly the same

as them. ❑ Tom was in some ways a younger clone of his handsome father. **2** A **clone** is an animal or plant that has been produced artificially, for example in a laboratory, from the cells of another animal or plant. A clone is exactly the same as the original animal or plant. ❑ the world's first human clone ❑ Each colony represents a clone of bacterial cells.
VERB [T] (**clones, cloning, cloned**) To **clone** an animal or plant means to produce it as a clone. ❑ The idea of cloning extinct life forms still belongs to science fiction. ❑ highly controversial proposals to clone humans ❑ The scientists will clone embryos from the skin cells of motor neurone disease sufferers.

close ♦♦♦ VERB, ADJ
VERB /kləʊz/ [I, T] (**closes, closing, closed**) **1** [I, T] When you **close** something such as a door or lid or when it **closes**, it moves so that a hole, gap, or opening is covered. = shut ❑ If you are cold, close the window. ❑ Zacharias heard the door close. **2** [T] When you **close** something such as an open book or umbrella, you move the different parts of it together. ❑ Slowly he closed the book. **3** [T] (computing) If you **close** something such as a computer file or window, you give the computer an instruction to remove it from the screen. ❑ To close your document, press CTRL+W on your keyboard. **4** [I, T] When you **close** your eyes or your eyes **close**, your eyelids move downward, so that you can no longer see. ❑ Bess closed her eyes and fell asleep. **5** [I, T] When a place **closes** or **is closed**, work or activity stops there for a short period. = shut ❑ Shops close only on Christmas Day and New Year's Day. ❑ Government troops closed the airport. **6** [I, T] If a place such as a factory, shop, or school **closes**, or if it **is closed**, all work or activity stops there permanently. ❑ Many enterprises will be forced to close. **7** [T] To **close** a road or border means to block it in order to prevent people from using it. ❑ They were cut off from the West in 1948 when their government closed that border crossing. **8** [T] To **close** a conversation, event, or matter means to bring it to an end or to complete it. ❑ Judge Isabel Oliva said last night: 'I have closed the case. There was no foul play.' ❑ The governor is said to now consider the matter closed. **9** [T] If you **close** a bank account, you take all your money out of it and inform the bank that you will no longer be using the account. ❑ He had closed his account with the bank five years earlier. **10** [I] (business) On the stock market or the currency markets, if a share price or a currency **closes** at a particular value, that is its value at the end of the day's business. ❑ The US dollar closed higher in Tokyo today. **11** [I] If you are **closing on** someone or something that you are following, you are getting nearer and nearer to them. ❑ I was within 15 seconds of the guy in second place and closing on him.
PHRASAL VERBS **close down** Close down means the same as **close** VERB 6. ❑ Minford closed down the business and went into politics.
close in If a group of people **close in** on a person or place, they come nearer and nearer to them and gradually surround them. = move in ❑ Hitler himself committed suicide as Soviet forces were closing in on Berlin.
close up If someone **closes up** a building, they shut it completely and securely, often because they are going away. = shut up, lock up ❑ Just close up the shop. ❑ The summer house had been closed up all year. If an opening, gap, or something hollow **closes up**, or if you **close** it **up**, it becomes closed or covered. ❑ Don't use cold water as it shocks the blood vessels into closing up.
ADJ /kləʊs/ (**closer, closest**) **1** If one thing or person is **close to** another, there is only a very small distance between them. = near ❑ Her lips were close to his head and her breath tickled his ear. ❑ The man moved closer, lowering his voice. **2** You say that people are **close to** each other when they like each other very much and know each other very well. ❑ She and Linda became very close. ❑ I shared a house with a close friend from school. **3** [close + N] Your **close** relatives are the members of your family who are most directly related to you, for example your parents and your brothers or sisters. ❑ large changes such as the birth of a child or death of a close relative **4** A **close** ally or partner of someone knows them well and is very involved in their

work. ❑ *He was once regarded as one of Mr Brown's closest political advisers.* **5** [close + N] **Close** contact or co-operation involves seeing or communicating with someone often. ❑ *Both nations are seeking closer links with the West.* **6** If there is a **close** connection or resemblance between two things, they are strongly connected or are very similar. = strong ❑ *There is a close connection between pain and tension.* **7** **Close** inspection or observation of something is careful and thorough. = thorough ❑ *He discovered, on closer inspection, that the rocks contained gold.* **8** A **close** competition or election is won or seems likely to be won by only a small amount. ❑ *It is still a close contest between two leading opposition parties.* **9** [V-LINK + close, usu close 'to' N/-ING] If you are **close** to something or if it is **close**, it is likely to happen or come soon. If you are **close** to doing something, you are likely to do it soon. = near ❑ *She sounded close to tears.* ❑ *A senior White House official said the agreement is close.* **10** [V-LINK + close, usu close 'to' N] If something is **close** or comes **close to** something else, it almost is, does, or experiences that thing. = near ❑ *An airliner came close to disaster while approaching Kennedy Airport.* **11** If the atmosphere somewhere is **close**, it is unpleasantly warm with not enough air.
PHRASES **close by** or **close at hand** Something that is **close by** or **close at hand** is near to you. = nearby ❑ *Did a new hair salon open close by?*
close to or **close on** Close to a particular amount or distance means slightly less than that amount or distance. = almost, nearly ❑ *Sisulu spent close to 30 years in prison.*
close up If you look at something **close up**, you look at it when you are very near to it. ❑ *They always look smaller close up.*
clos·ing /ˈkləʊzɪŋ/ NOUN [SING] = closure ❑ *since the closing of the steel mill in 1984*
close·ly /ˈkləʊsli/ ADV **1** *They crowded more closely around the stretcher.* **2** *Our agencies work closely with local groups in developing countries.* **3** *a pattern closely resembling a cross* **4** [closely with V] ❑ *If you look closely at many of the problems in society, you'll see evidence of racial discrimination.* **5** *This will be a closely fought race.*
close·ness /ˈkləʊsnɪs/ NOUN [U] ❑ *I asked whether her closeness to her mother ever posed any problems.*
→ See also **close-up**
✦ **close your eyes to something** → see **eye**; **close ranks** → see **rank**; **at close quarters** → see **quarter**; **at close range** → see **range**

close-up /ˈkləʊs ʌp/ NOUN
NOUN [c] (**close-ups**) A **close-up** is a photograph or a picture in a film that shows a lot of detail because it is taken very near to the subject. ❑ *a close-up of Harvey's face*
PHRASE **in close-up** If you see something **in close-up**, you see it in great detail in a photograph or piece of film which has been taken very near to the subject.

clo·sure /ˈkləʊʒə/ NOUN [c, u] (**closures**) **1** [c, u] The **closure** of a place such as a business or factory is the permanent ending of the work or activity there. ❑ *the closure of the steel mill* ❑ *protests against the proposed pit closures* **2** [c] The **closure** of a road or border is the blocking of it in order to prevent people from using it. ❑ *Overnight storms left many streets underwater and forced the closure of road tunnels in the city.* **3** [u] (mainly AmE) If someone achieves **closure**, they succeed in accepting something bad that has happened to them. ❑ *I asked McKean if the reunion was meant to achieve closure.*

cloth /klɒθ, AmE klɔːθ/ NOUN [c, u] (**cloths**) **1** [c, u] **Cloth** is fabric which is made by weaving or knitting a substance such as cotton, wool, silk, or nylon. Cloth is used especially for making clothes. = fabric, material ❑ *She began cleaning the wound with a piece of cloth.* **2** [c] A **cloth** is a piece of cloth which you use for a particular purpose, such as cleaning something or covering something. ❑ *Clean the surface with a damp cloth.*

clothes ♦♦◇ /kləʊðz/ NOUN [PL] **Clothes** are the things that people wear, such as shirts, coats, trousers, and dresses. ❑ *Moira walked upstairs to change her clothes.*

WHICH WORD?
clothes, clothing, or cloth?

Do not confuse **clothes**, **clothing**, and **cloth**.
Clothes are things you wear, such as shirts, trousers, dresses, and coats. There is no singular form of this word.
❑ *I need some new clothes.*
Clothing is an uncountable noun. You use it to talk about particular types of clothes, for example *winter clothing* or *warm clothing*.
❑ *Wear protective clothing.*
You do not talk about ~~clothings~~ or ~~a clothing~~. To talk about one thing that you wear, use **an item of clothing**.
❑ *What is the most expensive item of clothing you have ever bought?*
Cloth is fabric such as wool or cotton that is used for making such things as clothes.
❑ *Take three strips of cotton cloth.*
When **cloth** is used like this, it is an uncountable noun.

---

cloth·ing ♦◇◇ /ˈkləʊðɪŋ/ NOUN [u] **Clothing** is the things that people wear. ❑ *Some locals offered food and clothing to the refugees.* ❑ *the clothing industry*

cloud ♦◇◇ /klaʊd/ NOUN, VERB
NOUN [c, u] (**clouds**) **1** [c, u] A **cloud** is a mass of water vapour that floats in the sky. Clouds are usually white or grey in colour. ❑ *the varied shapes of the clouds* ❑ *a black mass of cloud* **2** [c] A **cloud** of something such as smoke or dust is a mass of it floating in the air. ❑ *The hens darted away on all sides, raising a cloud of dust.*
VERB [T, I] (**clouds, clouding, clouded**) **1** [T] If you say that something **clouds** your view of a situation, you mean that it makes you unable to understand the situation or judge it properly. ❑ *Perhaps anger had clouded his vision, perhaps his judgement had been faulty.* **2** [T] If you say that something **clouds** a situation, you mean that it makes it unpleasant. ❑ *The atmosphere has already been clouded by the party's anger at the media.* **3** [I, T] If glass **clouds** or if moisture **clouds** it, tiny drops of water cover the glass, making it difficult to see through. = mist ❑ *The mirror clouded beside her cheek.*

cloudy /ˈklaʊdi/ ADJ (**cloudier, cloudiest**) **1** If it is **cloudy**, there are a lot of clouds in the sky. ❑ *a windy, cloudy day* **2** A **cloudy** liquid is less clear than it should be. ❑ *If the water's cloudy like that, it'll be hard to see anyone underwater.*

club ♦♦♦ /klʌb/ NOUN, VERB
NOUN [c, u] (**clubs**) **1** [c] A **club** is an organization of people interested in a particular activity or subject who usually meet on a regular basis. ❑ *the Young Farmers Club* ❑ *a youth club* **2** [c] A **club** is a place where the members of a club meet. ❑ *I stopped in at the club for a drink.* **3** [c] A **club** is a team which competes in sports competitions. ❑ *The club now has a new manager.* **4** [c] A **club** is the same as a **nightclub**. ❑ *It's a big dance hit in the clubs.* **5** [c] A **club** is a long, thin, metal stick with a piece of wood or metal at one end that you use to hit the ball in golf. = golf club ❑ *a six-iron club* **6** [c] A **club** is a thick heavy stick that can be used as a weapon. ❑ *Men armed with knives and clubs attacked his home.* **7** [u] **Clubs** is one of the four suits in a pack of playing cards. Each card in the suit is marked with one or more black symbols: ♣. ❑ *the ace of clubs* **8** [c] A **club** is a playing card of this suit. ❑ *The next player discarded a club.*
VERB [T] (**clubs, clubbing, clubbed**) To **club** a person or animal means to hit them hard with a thick heavy stick or a similar weapon. ❑ *Two thugs clubbed him with baseball bats.*

clue /kluː/ NOUN
NOUN [c] (**clues**) **1** A **clue to** a problem or mystery is something that helps you to find the answer to it. ❑ *Geneticists in Canada have discovered a clue to the puzzle of why our cells get old and die.* **2** A **clue** is an object or piece of information that helps someone solve a crime. ❑ *The vital clue to the killer's identity was his nickname, Peanuts.* **3** A **clue** in a crossword or game is information which is given

C

to help you to find the answer to a question. □ *Give me a clue. What's it begin with?*

PHRASE **haven't a clue** (*informal*) If you **haven't a clue** about something, you do not know anything about it or you have no idea what to do about it. □ *I haven't a clue what I'll give Carl for his birthday next year.*

clum·sy /'klʌmzi/ ADJ (**clumsier**, **clumsiest**) **1** A clumsy person moves or handles things in a careless, awkward way, often so that things are knocked over or broken. = awkward □ *I'd never seen a clumsier, less coordinated boxer.* **2** A **clumsy** action or statement is not skilful or is likely to upset people. □ *The action seemed a clumsy attempt to topple the government.*
clum·si·ly /'klʌmzɪli/ ADV **1** [clumsily with v] □ *In the sudden pitch darkness, she scrambled clumsily towards the ladder.* **2** *If the matter were handled clumsily, it could cost Miriam her life.*
clum·si·ness /'klʌmzinəs/ NOUN [U] **1** *His clumsiness and ineptitude with the wooden sticks did not embarrass him.* **2** *I was ashamed at my clumsiness and insensitivity.*

clung /klʌŋ/ IRREG FORM **Clung** is the past tense and past participle of **cling**.

clus·ter /'klʌstə/ NOUN, VERB
NOUN [C] (**clusters**) A **cluster of** people or things is a small group of them close together. □ *clusters of men in formal clothes*
VERB [I] (**clusters**, **clustering**, **clustered**) If people **cluster together**, they gather together in a small group. □ *The passengers clustered together in small groups.*

clutch /klʌtʃ/ VERB, NOUN
VERB [I, T] (**clutches**, **clutching**, **clutched**) If you **clutch at** something or **clutch** something, you hold it tightly, usually because you are afraid or anxious. = grasp, grip □ *I staggered and had to clutch at a chair for support.*
NOUN [PL, C] (**clutches**) **1** [PL] If someone is in another person's **clutches**, that person has captured them or has power over them. = grasp □ *Tony fell into the clutches of an attractive American who introduced him to drugs.* **2** [C] In a vehicle, the **clutch** is the pedal that you press before you change gear. □ *Laura let out the clutch and pulled slowly away down the drive.*
✦ **clutch at straws** → see **straw**

clut·ter /'klʌtə/ NOUN, VERB
NOUN [U] **Clutter** is a lot of things in a messy state, especially things that are not useful or necessary. □ *Caroline prefers her worktops to be clear of clutter.*
VERB [T] (**clutters**, **cluttering**, **cluttered**) If things or people **clutter** a place, they fill it in a messy way. □ *Empty soft-drink cans lie everywhere. They clutter the desks and are strewn across the floor.*
PHRASAL VERB **clutter up** **Clutter up** means the same as **clutter** VERB. □ *The vehicles cluttered up the car park.*

cm ABBREVIATION **cm** is the written abbreviation for **centimetre** or **centimetres**. □ *His height had increased by 2.5 cm.*

Co. ♦♦◊ ABBREVIATION (*business*) **Co.** is used as an abbreviation for **company** when it is part of the name of an organization. □ *the Blue Star Amusement Co.*

coach ♦♦◊ /kəʊtʃ/ NOUN, VERB
NOUN [C] (**coaches**) **1** [also 'by' coach] (*BrE*; in *AmE*, use **bus**) A **coach** is a large, comfortable bus that carries passengers on long trips. **2** (*BrE*; in *AmE*, use **car**) A **coach** is one of the separate sections of a train that carries passengers. **3** A **coach** is someone who trains a person or team of people in a particular sport. = trainer □ *Tony Woodcock has joined the team as coach.* **4** A **coach** is someone who gives people special teaching in a particular subject, especially in order to prepare them for an examination. = tutor □ *What you need is a drama coach.* **5** (*mainly AmE*; in *BrE*, usually use **manager**) A **coach** is a person who is in charge of a sports team. **6** A **coach** is an enclosed vehicle with four wheels which is pulled by horses, and in which people used to travel. Coaches are still used for ceremonial events in some countries, such as Britain. □ *a coach pulled by six black horses*
VERB [T] (**coaches**, **coaching**, **coached**) **1** When someone **coaches** a person or a team, they help them to become

better at a particular sport. = train □ *After her pro playing career, she coached a golf team in San Jose.* **2** If you **coach** someone, you give them special teaching in a particular subject, especially in order to prepare them for an examination. □ *He gently coached me in French.*

coal ♦◊◊ /kəʊl/ NOUN [U, PL] (**coals**) **1** [U] **Coal** is a hard, black substance that is extracted from the ground and burned as fuel. □ *Gas is cheaper than coal.* **2** [PL] **Coals** are burning pieces of coal. □ *The iron teakettle was hissing splendidly over live coals.*

coa·li·tion ♦◊◊ /ˌkəʊə'lɪʃən/ NOUN [C] (**coalitions**) **1** A **coalition** is a government consisting of people from two or more political parties. □ *Since June the country has had a coalition government.* **2** A **coalition** is a group consisting of people from different political or social groups who are cooperating to achieve a particular aim. = alliance □ *He had been opposed by a coalition of about 50 civil rights, women's, and Latino organizations.*

coarse /kɔːs/ ADJ (**coarser**, **coarsest**) **1** **Coarse** things have a rough texture because they consist of thick threads or large pieces. = rough □ *a jacket made of very coarse cloth* **2** If you describe someone as **coarse**, you mean that he or she talks and behaves in a rude and offensive way. = vulgar, crude □ *The soldiers did not bother to moderate their coarse humour in her presence.*
coarse·ly /'kɔːsli/ ADV **1** *coarsely ground black pepper* **2** [coarsely with v] □ *The women laughed coarsely at some vulgar joke.*

❂ **coast** ♦♦◊ /kəʊst/ NOUN, VERB
NOUN [C] (**coasts**) The **coast** is an area of land that is next to the sea. □ *Campsites are usually situated along the coast, close to beaches.* □ *the west coast of Scotland*
VERB [I] (**coasts**, **coasting**, **coasted**) If a vehicle **coasts** somewhere, it continues to move there with the engine switched off, or without being pushed or pedalled. □ *He pushed in the clutch and coasted to a halt.*

❂ **coast·al** /'kəʊstəl/ ADJ [coastal + N] **Coastal** is used to refer to things that are in the sea or on the land near a coast. □ *Local radio stations serving coastal areas often broadcast forecasts for yachtsmen.* □ *The fish are on sale from our own coastal waters.*

coast·line /'kəʊstlaɪn/ NOUN [C, U] (**coastlines**) A country's **coastline** is the outline of its coast. □ *This is some of the most exposed coastline in the world.*

coat ♦◊◊ /kəʊt/ NOUN, VERB
NOUN [C] (**coats**) **1** A **coat** is a piece of clothing with long sleeves which you wear over your other clothes when you go outside. □ *He turned off the television, put on his coat, and walked out.* **2** An animal's **coat** is the fur or hair on its body. □ *Vitamin B6 is great for improving the condition of dogs' and horses' coats.* **3** A **coat** of paint or varnish is a thin layer of it on a surface. □ *The front door needs a new coat of paint.*
VERB [T] (**coats**, **coating**, **coated**) If you **coat** something **with** a substance or **in** a substance, you cover it with a thin layer of the substance. □ *Coat the fish with seasoned flour.*

coat·ing /'kəʊtɪŋ/ NOUN [C] (**coatings**) A **coating of** a substance is a thin layer of it spread over a surface. □ *Under the coating of dust and cobwebs, he discovered a fine French Louis XVI clock.*

coax /kəʊks/ VERB [T] (**coaxes**, **coaxing**, **coaxed**) **1** If you **coax** someone **into** doing something, you gently try to persuade them to do it. □ *After lunch, she watched, listened and coaxed Bobby into talking about himself.* **2** If you **coax** something such as information out of someone, you gently persuade them to give it to you. □ *The officer spoke yesterday of her role in trying to coax vital information from the young victim.*

co·caine /kəʊ'keɪn/ NOUN [U] **Cocaine** is a powerful drug which some people take for pleasure, but which they can become addicted to.

cock /kɒk/ (*BrE*; in *AmE*, use **rooster**) NOUN [C] (**cocks**) A **cock** is an adult male chicken.

cock·pit /'kɒkpɪt/ NOUN [C] (**cockpits**) In an aeroplane or racing car, the **cockpit** is the part where the pilot or driver sits.

cock·tail /ˈkɒkteɪl/ NOUN [c] (**cocktails**) **1** A **cocktail** is an alcoholic drink which contains several ingredients. ❏ *On arrival, guests are offered wine or a champagne cocktail.* **2** A **cocktail** is a mixture of a number of different things, especially ones that do not go together well. ❏ *The court was told she had taken a cocktail of drugs and alcohol.*

✪ **code** ♦◇◇ /kəʊd/ NOUN, VERB (*academic word*)
NOUN [c, u] (**codes**) **1** [c] A **code** is a set of rules about how people should behave or about how something must be done. = rules, laws ❏ *Article 159 of the state's penal code* ❏ *Finance ministers agreed to set up a code of conduct on business taxation.* ❏ *local building codes* **2** [c] [also 'in' code] A **code** is a system of replacing the words in a message with other words or symbols, so that nobody can understand it unless they know the system. ❏ *They used elaborate secret codes, as when the names of trees stood for letters.* **3** [c] A **code** is a group of numbers or letters which is used to identify something, such as a postal address or part of a telephone number. ❏ *Callers dialling the wrong area code will not get through.* **4** [c] A **code** is any system of signs or symbols that has a meaning. ❏ *It will need other chips to reconvert the digital code back into normal TV signals.* **5** [c] The genetic **code** of a person, animal, or plant is the information contained in DNA which determines the structure and function of cells, and the inherited characteristics of all living things. ❏ *Scientists provided the key to understanding the genetic code that determines every bodily feature.* **6** [u] (*computing*) Computer **code** is a system or language for expressing information and instructions in a form which can be understood by a computer. ❏ *She began writing software code at the age of nine.*
VERB [T] (**codes, coding, coded**) To **code** something means to give it a code or to mark it with its code. ❏ *He devised a way of coding every statement uniquely.*
→ See also **postcode**

co·erce /kəʊˈɜːs/ VERB [T] (**coerces, coercing, coerced**) (*formal*) If you **coerce** someone **into** doing something, you make them do it, although they do not want to. = pressurize ❏ *Potter had argued that the government coerced him into pleading guilty.*

co·er·cion /kəʊˈɜːʃən/ NOUN [u] **Coercion** is the act or process of persuading someone forcefully to do something that they do not want to do. ❏ *It was vital that the elections should be free of coercion or intimidation.*

cof·fee ♦◇◇ /ˈkɒfi, AmE ˈkɔːfi/ NOUN [u, c] (**coffees**) **1** [u] **Coffee** is a hot drink made with water and ground or powdered coffee beans. ❏ *Would you like some coffee?* **2** [c] A **coffee** is a cup of coffee. ❏ *I made a coffee.* **3** [c, u] **Coffee** is the roasted beans or powder from which the drink is made. ❏ *Brazil harvested 28 million bags of coffee in 1991, the biggest crop for four years.*

cof·fin /ˈkɒfɪn, AmE ˈkɔːfɪn/ NOUN
NOUN [c] (**coffins**) A **coffin** is a box in which a dead body is buried or cremated.
PHRASE **nail in the coffin of something** If you say that one thing is **a nail in the coffin of** another thing, you mean that it will help bring about its end or failure. ❏ *A fine would be the final nail in the coffin of the airline.*

✪ **cog·ni·tive** /ˈkɒgnɪtɪv/ ADJ [cognitive + N] (*formal*) **Cognitive** means relating to the mental process involved in knowing, learning, and understanding things. ❏ *As children grow older, their cognitive processes become sharper.* ❏ *Vygotsky's theory of cognitive development*

✪ **co·her·ence** /kəʊˈhɪərəns/ NOUN [u] **1 Coherence** is a state or situation in which all the parts or ideas fit together well so that they form a united whole. ❏ *The anthology has a surprising sense of coherence.* **2** If something such as a plan or campaign has **coherence**, it is well planned, so that it is clear and sensible and all its parts go well with each other. = cohesion ❏ *The campaign was widely criticized for making tactical mistakes and for a lack of coherence.* ❏ *The three interlocking narratives achieve an overall coherence.* ❏ *The anthology has a surprising sense of coherence.* **3** If someone speaks with **coherence**, they express their thoughts in a clear and calm way, so that other people can

understand what they are saying. ❏ *This was debated eagerly at first, but with diminishing coherence as the champagne took hold.*

✪ **co·her·ent** /kəʊˈhɪərənt/ ADJ (*academic word*) **1** If something is **coherent**, it is well planned, so that it is clear and sensible and all its parts go well with each other. = cohesive; ≠ muddled ❏ *He has failed to work out a coherent strategy for modernizing the service.* ❏ *The President's policy is perfectly coherent.* **2** [V-LINK + coherent] If someone is **coherent**, they express their thoughts in a clear and calm way, so that other people can understand what they are saying. ❏ *He's so calm when he answers questions in interviews. I wish I could be that coherent.*

co·he·sion /kəʊˈhiːʒən/ NOUN [u] If there is **cohesion** within a society, organization, or group, the different members fit together well and form a united whole. ❏ *By 1990, it was clear that the cohesion of the armed forces was rapidly breaking down.*

co·he·sive /kəʊˈhiːsɪv/ ADJ Something that is **cohesive** consists of parts that fit together well and form a united whole. ❏ *'Daring Adventures' from '86 is a far more cohesive and successful album.*

coil /kɔɪl/ NOUN [c] (**coils**) **1** A **coil** of rope or wire is a length of it that has been wound into a series of loops. ❏ *Tod shook his head angrily and slung the coil of rope over his shoulder.* **2** A **coil** is one loop in a series of loops. ❏ *Pythons kill by tightening their coils so that their victim cannot breathe.* **3** A **coil** is a thick spiral of wire through which an electrical current passes.

✪ **coin** /kɔɪn/ NOUN, VERB
NOUN [c] (**coins**) A **coin** is a small piece of metal which is used as money. ❏ *a few loose coins*
PHRASE **the other side of the coin** You use **the other side of the coin** to mention a different aspect of a situation. ❏ *On the other side of the coin, there'll be tax incentives for small businesses.*
VERB [T] (**coins, coining, coined**) If you **coin** a word or a phrase, you are the first person to say it. ❏ *Jaron Lanier coined the term 'virtual reality' and pioneered its early development.* ❏ *Simone de Beauvoir first coined the phrase 'women's liberation' in her book, The Second Sex.*
PHRASE **coin a phrase** You say 'to coin a phrase' to show that you realize you are making a pun or using a cliché. ❏ *Fifty local musicians have, to coin a phrase, banded together to form the Jazz Umbrella.*

✪ **co·in·cide** /ˌkəʊɪnˈsaɪd/ VERB [RECIP] (**coincides, coinciding, coincided**) (*academic word*) **1** If one event **coincides with** another, they happen at the same time. ❏ *The exhibition coincides with the 50th anniversary of his death.* ❏ *Although his mental illness had coincided with his war service it had not been caused by it.* ❏ *The beginning of the solar and lunar years coincided every 13 years.* **2** If the ideas or interests of two or more people **coincide**, they are the same. ❏ *The kids' views on life don't always coincide, but they're not afraid of voicing their opinions.* ❏ *a case in which public and private interests coincide* ❏ *He gave great encouragement to his students, especially if their passions happened to coincide with his own.*

✪ **co·in·ci·dence** /kəʊˈɪnsɪdəns/ NOUN [c, u] (**coincidences**) A **coincidence** is when two or more similar or related events occur at the same time by chance and without any planning. ❏ *Mr Berry said the timing was a coincidence and that his decision was unrelated to Mr Roman's departure.* ❏ *It is, of course, a mere coincidence that the author of this piece is also a pathologist.* ❏ *It is no coincidence that so many of the romantic poets suffered from tuberculosis.*

✪ **co·in·ci·dent·al** /ˌkəʊɪnsɪˈdentəl/ ADJ Something that is **coincidental** is the result of a coincidence and has not been deliberately arranged. ❏ *Any resemblance to actual persons, places, or events is purely coincidental.* ❏ *I think that it is not coincidental that we now have arguably the best bookshops in the world.*

co·in·ci·dent·al·ly /ˌkəʊɪnsɪˈdentli/ ADV You use **coincidentally** when you want to draw attention to a coincidence. ❏ *Coincidentally, I had once found myself in a similar situation.*

C

cold ♦♦◇ /kəʊld/ ADJ, NOUN

ADJ (**colder, coldest**) **1** Something that is **cold** has a very low temperature or a lower temperature than is normal or acceptable. ❑ *Rinse the vegetables under cold running water.* ❑ *He likes his tea neither too hot nor too cold.* **2** If it is **cold**, or if a place is **cold**, the temperature of the air is very low. ❑ *It was bitterly cold.* ❑ *The house is cold because I can't afford to turn the heat on.* **3** If you are **cold**, your body is at an unpleasantly low temperature. ❑ *I was freezing cold.* **4** **Cold** colours or **cold** light give an impression of coldness. ❑ *Generally, warm colours advance in painting and cold colours recede.* **5** A **cold** person does not show much emotion, especially affection, and therefore seems unfriendly and unsympathetic. If someone's voice is **cold**, they speak in an unfriendly, unsympathetic way. ❑ *What a cold, unfeeling woman she was.*

PHRASE **out cold** If someone is **out cold**, they are unconscious or sleeping very heavily. ❑ *She was out cold but still breathing.*

NOUN [c, u] (**colds**) **1** [c, u] [also 'the' cold] Cold weather or low temperatures can be referred to as **the cold**. ❑ *He must have come inside to get out of the cold.* **2** [c] If you have a **cold**, you have a mild, very common illness which makes you sneeze a lot and gives you a sore throat or a cough. ❑ *I had a pretty bad cold.*

PHRASE **catch cold** or **catch a cold** If you **catch cold**, or **catch a cold**, you become ill with a cold. ❑ *Let's dry our hair so we don't catch cold.*

cold·ness /'kəʊldnəs/ NOUN [u] **1** *She complained about the coldness of his hands.* **2** *Within a quarter of an hour, the coldness of the night had gone.* **3** *His coldness angered her.*

cold·ly /'kəʊldli/ ADV ❑ *'I'll see you in the morning,' Hugh said coldly.*

✦ in cold blood → see **blood**; get cold feet → see **foot**; blow hot and cold → see **hot**; pour cold water on something → see **water**

♦**col·lab·o·rate** /kə'læbəreɪt/ VERB [RECIP, I] (**collaborates, collaborating, collaborated**) **1** [RECIP] When one person or group **collaborates with** another, they work together, especially on a book or on some research. ❑ *Much later he collaborated with his son Michael on the English translation of a text on food production.* ❑ *Kodak and Chinon will continue to collaborate on the engineering and development of digital cameras and scanners.* ❑ *He turned his country house into a place where professionals and amateurs collaborated in the making of music.* **2** [I] If someone **collaborates with** an enemy who is occupying their country during a war, they help them. ❑ *He was accused of having collaborated with the Communist secret police.*

WORD PARTS

The prefix *co-* often appears in words that refer to people sharing things or doing things together:

collaborate (VERB)
co-ordinate (VERB)
co-operate (VERB)

♦**col·lab·o·ra·tion** /kə,læbə'reɪʃən/ NOUN [c, u] (**collaborations**) **1** [c, u] **Collaboration** is the act of working together to produce a piece of work, especially a book or some research. ❑ *There is substantial collaboration with neighbouring departments.* ❑ *scientific collaborations* ❑ *Close collaboration between the Bank and the Fund is not merely desirable, it is essential.* ❑ *Drummond was working on a book in collaboration with Zodiac Mindwarp.* **2** [c] A **collaboration** is a piece of work that has been produced as the result of people or groups working together. ❑ *He was also a writer of beautiful stories, some of which are collaborations with his fiancée.* ❑ *one of their collaborations from the second album* **3** [u] **Collaboration** is the act of helping an enemy who is occupying your country during a war. ❑ *rumours of his collaboration with the occupying forces during the war*

♦**col·lab·o·ra·tive** /kə'læbərətɪv, AmE -reɪt-/ ADJ [collaborative + N] (*formal*) A **collaborative** piece of work is done by two or more people or groups working together. ❑ *a collaborative research project* ❑ *This work is a collaborative*

effort with other health care workers, including paediatricians, physiotherapists, and nurses.

col·lab·o·ra·tor /kə'læbəreɪtə/ NOUN [c] (**collaborators**) **1** A **collaborator** is someone that you work with to produce a piece of work, especially a book or some research. ❑ *The Irvine group and their collaborators are testing whether lasers do the job better.* **2** A **collaborator** is someone who helps an enemy who is occupying their country during a war. ❑ *Two alleged collaborators were shot dead by masked activists.*

col·lage /'kɒlɑːʒ, AmE kə'lɑːʒ/ NOUN [c, u] (**collages**) **1** [c] A **collage** is a picture that has been made by sticking pieces of coloured paper and cloth onto paper. ❑ *a collage of words and pictures from magazines* **2** [u] **Collage** is the method of making pictures by sticking pieces of coloured paper and cloth onto paper. ❑ *The illustrations make use of collage, watercolour, and other media.*

♦**col·lapse** ♦♦◇ /kə'læps/ VERB, NOUN (*academic word*)

VERB [i] (**collapses, collapsing, collapsed**) **1** If a building or other structure **collapses**, it falls down very suddenly. ❑ *A section of the Bay Bridge had collapsed.* ❑ *Most of the deaths were caused by landslides and collapsing buildings.* **2** If something, for example a system or institution, **collapses**, it fails or comes to an end completely and suddenly. = fail ❑ *His business empire collapsed under a massive burden of debt.* ❑ *The rural people have been impoverished by a collapsing economy.* **3** If you **collapse**, you suddenly faint or fall down because you are very ill or weak. ❑ *He collapsed following a vigorous exercise session at his home.* **4** If you **collapse** onto something, you sit or lie down suddenly because you are very tired. ❑ *She arrived home exhausted and barely capable of showering before collapsing on her bed.*

NOUN [u] **1** **Collapse** is when a building or other structure falls down very suddenly. ❑ *The governor called for an inquiry into the bridge's collapse.* **2** The **collapse** of something such as a system or institution is when it fails or comes to an end completely and suddenly. ❑ *The coup's collapse has speeded up the drive to independence.* **3** Someone's **collapse** is an occasion when they suddenly faint or fall down because they are very ill or weak. ❑ *A few days after his collapse he was sitting up in bed.*

col·lar /'kɒlə/ NOUN [c] (**collars**) **1** The **collar** of a shirt or coat is the part which fits around the neck and is usually folded over. ❑ *His tie was pulled loose and his collar hung open.* **2** A **collar** is a band of leather or plastic which is put around the neck of a dog or cat.
→ See also **blue-collar, white-collar**

♦**col·late** /kə'leɪt/ VERB [T] (**collates, collating, collated**) **1** When you **collate** pieces of information, you gather them all together and examine them. ❑ *Roberts has spent much of his working life collating the data on which the study was based.* ❑ *They have begun to collate their own statistics on racial abuse.* **2** If someone, or something such as a photocopier, **collates** pieces of paper, they put them together in the correct order. ❑ *They took sheets of paper off piles, collated them and put them into envelopes.*

♦**col·la·tion** /kə'leɪʃən/ NOUN [u] ❑ *Many countries have no laws governing the collation of personal information.* ❑ *The completed surveys are now with Queensland Transport for a more thorough collation and analysis.*

♦**col·league** ♦♦◇ /'kɒliːɡ/ NOUN [c] (**colleagues**) (*academic word*) Your **colleagues** are the people you work with, especially in a professional job. = co-worker ❑ *Without consulting his colleagues, he flew from Los Angeles to Chicago.* ❑ *Female academics are still paid less than their male colleagues.* ❑ *In the corporate world, the best sources of business are your former colleagues.*

♦**col·lect** ♦♦◇ /kə'lekt/ VERB [T, I] (**collects, collecting, collected**) **1** [T] If you **collect** a number of things, you bring them together from several places or from several people. = gather ❑ *Two young girls were collecting firewood.* ❑ *Elizabeth had been collecting snails for a school project.* ❑ *They collected rock samples and fossils.* ❑ *Data were collected by three methods.* ❑ *Fee revenue was collected from four basic sources.* **2** [T] If you **collect** things, such as stamps or books, as a hobby, you get a large number of them over a period of time because they interest you. ❏ *I used to collect stamps.* **3** [I, T] If a substance **collects** somewhere, or if something **collects** it, it keeps arriving over a period of time and is held in that place or thing. ❏ *Methane gas does collect in the mines around here.* **4** [T] If something **collects** light, energy, or heat, it attracts it. ❏ *Like a telescope, it has a curved mirror to collect the sunlight.* **5** [I, T] If you **collect for** a charity or **for** a present for someone, you ask people to give you money for it. ❏ *Are you collecting for charity?* ❏ *The organization has collected $2.5 million for the relief effort.* **6** [T] *(mainly BrE; in AmE, usually use* **pick up***)* When you **collect** someone or something, you go and get them from the place where they are waiting for you or have been left for you.

col·lect·ing /kəˈlektɪŋ/ NOUN [U] ❏ *hobbies like stamp collecting and fishing*

✪ col·lec·tion ♦♦◇ /kəˈlekʃən/ NOUN [C, U] *(collections)* **1** [C] A **collection of** things is a group of similar things that you have deliberately acquired, usually over a period of time. ❏ *Robert's collection of prints and paintings has been bought over the years.* ❏ *The Art Gallery of Ontario has the world's largest collection of sculptures by Henry Moore.* ❏ *a valuable record collection* **2** [C] A **collection of** stories, poems, or articles is a number of them published in one book. ❏ *Two years ago he published a collection of short stories called 'Facing The Music'.* **3** [C] A **collection of** things is a group of things. ❏ *a collection of modern glass office buildings* **4** [C] A fashion designer's new **collection** consists of the new clothes they have designed for the next season. ❏ *Her spring/summer collection for this year deliberately uses both simple and rich fabrics.* **5** [C] If you organize a **collection** for charity, you collect money from people to give to charity. ❏ *I asked my headmaster if he could arrange a collection for a refugee charity.* **6** [C] A **collection** is money that is given by people in church during some Christian services. **7** [U] **Collection** is the act of collecting something from a place or from people. = acquisition ❏ *Money can be sent to any one of 22,000 agents worldwide for collection.* ❏ *computer systems to speed up collection of information* ❏ *new guidelines on online data collection*

col·lec·tive ♦◇◇ /kəˈlektɪv/ ADJ, NOUN

ADJ **1** [collective + N] **Collective** actions, situations, or feelings involve or are shared by every member of a group of people. = joint ❏ *It was a collective decision.* **2** [collective + N] A **collective** amount of something is the total obtained by adding together the amounts that each person or thing in a group has. = combined ❏ *Their collective volume wasn't very large.* **3** [collective + N] The **collective** term for two or more types of thing is a general word or expression which refers to all of them. ❏ *Social science is a collective name, covering a series of individual sciences.*

NOUN [C] *(collectives)* *(business)* A **collective** is a business or farm which is run, and often owned, by a group of people. = cooperative ❏ *He will see that he is participating in all the decisions of the collective.*

col·lec·tive·ly /kəˈlektɪvli/ ADV **1** ❏ *They collectively decided to recognize the changed situation.* **2** ❏ *In 1968 the states collectively spent $2 billion on it.* **3** ❏ *other sorts of cells (known collectively as white corpuscles).*

col·lec·tor /kəˈlektə/ NOUN [C] *(collectors)* **1** A **collector** is a person who collects things of a particular type as a hobby. ❏ *a stamp collector* ❏ *a respected collector of Indian art* **2** You can use **collector** to refer to someone whose job is to take something such as money, tickets, or refuse from people. For example, a rent **collector** collects rent from people. ❏ *He earned his living as a tax collector.*

✪ col·lege ♦♦◇ /ˈkɒlɪdʒ/ NOUN [C, U] *(colleges)* **1** [C, U] A **college** is an institution where students study after they have left school. ❏ *Their daughter is doing business studies at a local college.* ❏ *Stephanie took up making jewellery after leaving art college this summer.* ❏ *business programmes offered to college graduates* **2** [C] A **college** is one of the institutions which some British universities are divided into. ❏ *He was educated at Balliol College, Oxford.* **3** [C] At some universities in the United States, **colleges** are divisions which offer degrees in particular subjects.

❏ *a professor at the University of Florida College of Law*

col·lide /kəˈlaɪd/ VERB [RECIP] *(collides, colliding, collided)* **1** If two or more moving people or objects **collide**, they crash into one another. If a moving person or object **collides with** a person or object that is not moving, they crash into them. ❏ *Two trains collided head-on in Ohio early this morning.* ❏ *Racing up the stairs, he almost collided with Daisy.* **2** If the aims, opinions, or interests of one person or group **collide with** those of another person or group, they are very different from each other and are therefore opposed. = clash ❏ *The aims of the negotiators in New York again seem likely to collide with the aims of the warriors in the field.*

col·li·sion /kəˈlɪʒən/ NOUN [C, U] *(collisions)* **1** [C, U] A **collision** occurs when a moving object crashes into something. = crash ❏ *They were on their way to the airport when their van was involved in a collision with a car.* **2** [C] A **collision** of cultures or ideas occurs when two very different cultures or people meet and conflict. = clash ❏ *The play represents the collision of three generations.*

col·lo·quial /kəˈləʊkwiəl/ ADJ **Colloquial** words and phrases are informal and are used mainly in conversation. ❏ *a colloquial expression*

colo·nel ♦◇◇ /ˈkɜːnəl/ NOUN [C] *(colonels)* A **colonel** is a senior officer in an army, air force, or the marines. ❏ *This particular place was run by an ex-Army colonel.*

✪ co·lo·nial /kəˈləʊniəl/ ADJ [colonial + N] **Colonial** means relating to countries that are colonies, or to colonialism. ❏ *the 31st anniversary of Jamaica's independence from British colonial rule* ❏ *the colonial civil service*

✪ co·lo·ni·al·ism /kəˈləʊniəlɪzəm/ NOUN [U] **Colonialism** is the practice by which a powerful country directly controls less powerful countries and uses their resources to increase its own power and wealth. ❏ *the bitter oppression of slavery and colonialism* ❏ *It is interesting to reflect why European colonialism ended.*

✪ co·lo·ni·al·ist /kəˈləʊniəlɪst/ ADJ, NOUN
ADJ **Colonialist** means relating to colonialism. ❏ *the European colonialist powers* ❏ *Earlier, the Cuban government had accused the Spanish Foreign Minister of colonialist attitudes.* NOUN [C] *(colonialists)* A **colonialist** is a person who believes in colonialism or helps their country to get colonies. ❏ *rulers who were imposed on the people by the colonialists* ❏ *the British colonialists were brutal in the extreme*

✪ colo·nize /ˈkɒlənaɪz/ also **colonise** VERB [T] *(colonizes, colonizing, colonized)* **1** If people **colonize** a foreign country, they go to live there and take control of it. ❏ *The first British attempt to colonize Ireland was in the twelfth century.* ❏ *Liberia was never colonized by the European powers.* **2** When large numbers of animals **colonize** a place, they go to live there and make it their home. ❏ *Toads are colonizing the whole place.* **3** When an area **is colonized by** a type of plant, the plant grows there in large amounts. ❏ *The area was then colonized by scrub.* ❏ *If the bats colonize a new cave, it soon becomes infested with ticks.*

✪ colo·ny /ˈkɒləni/ NOUN [C] *(colonies)* **1** A **colony** is a country which is controlled by a more powerful country. ❏ *In France's former North African colonies, anti-French feeling is growing.* ❏ *Puerto Rico, though it calls itself a Commonwealth, is really a self-governing American colony.* **2** You can refer to a place where a particular group of people lives as a particular kind of **colony**. ❏ *In 1932, he established a school and artists' colony in Stone City, Iowa.* ❏ *a penal colony* **3** A **colony of** birds, insects, or animals is a group of them that live together. ❏ *The islands are famed for their colonies of sea birds.* ❏ *The caterpillars feed in large colonies.*

co·los·sal /kəˈbɒsəl/ ADJ *(emphasis)* If you describe something as **colossal**, you are emphasizing that it is very large. = enormous, immense ❏ *There has been a colossal waste of public money.*

col·our /ˈkʌlə/ *(in AmE, use* **color***)* NOUN, VERB, ADJ
NOUN [C, U, PL] *(colours)* **1** [C] The **colour** of something is the appearance that it has as a result of the way in which it reflects light. Red, blue, and green are colours. ❏ *'What colour is the car?'—'Red.'* ❏ *Judi's favourite colour is pink.* **2** [C] Someone's **colour** is the colour of their skin. People

C

often use **colour** in this way to refer to a person's race. ❑ *I don't care what colour she is.* **3** [C, U] A **colour** is a substance you use to give something a particular colour. Dyes and makeup are sometimes referred to as **colours**. ❑ *It is better to avoid all food colours.* ❑ *Her nail colour was coordinated with her lipstick.* **4** [U] **Colour** is a quality that makes something especially interesting or exciting. ❑ *She had resumed the travel necessary to add depth and colour to her novels.* **5** [PL] A country's national **colours** are the colours of its national flag. ❑ *The Opera House is decorated with the Hungarian national colours: green, red, and white.* **6** [PL] People sometimes refer to the flag of a particular part of an army, navy, or air force, or the flag of a particular country as its **colours**. ❑ *Troops raised the country's colours in a special ceremony.* **7** [PL] A sports team's **colours** are the colours of the clothes they wear when they play. ❑ *I was wearing the team's colours.*

PHRASES **in colour** If a film or television programme is **in colour**, it has been made so that you see the picture in all its colours, and not just in black, white, or grey. ❑ *Was he going to show the film? Was it in colour?*

of colour (*politeness*) People **of colour** are people who belong to a race with dark skins. ❑ *Black communities spoke up to defend the rights of all people of colour.*

VERB [T, I] (**colours, colouring, coloured**) **1** [T] If you **colour** something, you use something such as dyes or paint to change its colour. ❑ *Many women begin colouring their hair in their mid-30s.* ❑ *We'd been making cakes and colouring the posters.* **2** [I] If someone **colours**, their face becomes redder than it normally is, usually because they are embarrassed. = blush ❑ *Andrew couldn't help noticing that she coloured slightly.* **3** [T] If something **colours** your opinion, it affects the way that you think about something. = affect ❑ *All too often it is only the negative images of Ireland that are portrayed, colouring opinions and hiding the true nature of the country.*

PHRASAL VERB **colour in** If you **colour in** a drawing, you give it different colours using crayons or paints. ❑ *Someone had coloured in all the black and white pictures.*

ADJ A **colour** television, photograph, or picture is one that shows things in all their colours, and not just in black, white, and grey. ❑ *In Japan 99 per cent of all households now have a colour television set.*

col·oured /ˈkʌləd/ (in *AmE*, use **colored**) ADJ **1** Something that is **coloured** a particular colour is that colour. ❑ *The illustration shows a cluster of five roses coloured apricot orange.* **2** Something that is **coloured** is a particular colour or combination of colours, rather than being just white, black, or the colour that it is naturally. ❑ *You can often choose between plain white or coloured and patterned scarves.* **3** (*offensive, old-fashioned*) A **coloured** person belongs to a race of people with dark skins.

col·our·ful /ˈkʌləfʊl/ (in *AmE*, use **colorful**) ADJ **1** Something that is **colourful** has bright colours or a lot of different colours. ❑ *The flowers were colourful and the scenery magnificent.* **2** A **colourful** story is full of exciting details. ❑ *The story she told was certainly colourful, and extended over her life in England, Germany, and Spain.* **3** A **colourful** character is a person who behaves in an interesting and amusing way. ❑ *Casey Stengel was probably the most colourful character in baseball.*

col·our·ing /ˈkʌlərɪŋ/ (in *AmE*, use **coloring**) NOUN [U] **1** The **colouring** of something is the colour or colours that it is. ❑ *Other countries vary the colouring of their bank notes as well as their size.* **2** Someone's **colouring** is the colour of their hair, skin, and eyes. ❑ *None of them had their father's dark colouring.* **3** **Colouring** is the act of using dyes or paint to change the colour of something. ❑ *They could not afford to spoil those maps by careless colouring.* **4** **Colouring** is a substance that is used to give colour to food. ❑ *A few drops of green food colouring were added.*

col·our·less /ˈkʌləs/ (in *AmE*, use **colorless**) ADJ **1** Something that is **colourless** has no colour at all. ❑ *a colourless, almost odourless liquid* **2** If someone's face is **colourless**, it is very pale, usually because they are frightened, shocked, or ill. ❑ *Her face was colourless, and she was shaking.* **3** **Colourless** people or places are dull and

uninteresting. ❑ *the much more experienced but colourless general*

col·umn ◆◇◇ /ˈkɒləm/ NOUN [C] (**columns**) **1** A **column** is a tall, often decorated cylinder of stone which is built to honour someone or forms part of a building. = pillar ❑ *Seven massive columns rise up from a marble floor.* **2** A **column** is something that has a tall, narrow shape. ❑ *The explosion sent a column of smoke thousands of feet into the air.* **3** A **column** is a group of people or animals which moves in a long line. ❑ *There were reports of columns of military vehicles appearing on the streets.* **4** On a printed page such as a page of a dictionary, newspaper, or printed chart, a **column** is one of two or more vertical sections which are read downwards. ❑ *We had stupidly been looking at the wrong column of figures.* **5** In a newspaper or magazine, a **column** is a section that is always written by the same person or is always about the same topic. ❑ *His name features frequently in the social columns of the tabloid newspapers.*

col·um·nist /ˈkɒləmɪst/ NOUN [C] (**columnists**) A **columnist** is a journalist who regularly writes a particular kind of article in a newspaper or magazine. ❑ *Clarence Page is a columnist for the Chicago Tribune.*

coma /ˈkəʊmə/ NOUN [C] (**comas**) Someone who is in a **coma** is in a state of deep unconsciousness. ❑ *She was in a coma for seven weeks.*

comb /kəʊm/ NOUN, VERB
NOUN [C] (**combs**) A **comb** is a flat piece of plastic or metal with narrow, pointed teeth along one side, which you use to make your hair neat.
VERB [T, I] (**combs, combing, combed**) **1** [T] When you **comb** your hair, you make it neat using a comb. ❑ *Salvatore combed his hair carefully.* **2** [T] If you **comb** a place, you search everywhere in it in order to find someone or something. ❑ *Officers combed the woods for the murder weapon.* **3** [I] If you **comb through** information, you look at it very carefully in order to find something. ❑ *Eight policemen then spent two years combing through the evidence.*

✪ **com·bat** ◆◇◇ NOUN, VERB
NOUN /ˈkɒmbæt/ [U, C] (**combats**) **1** [U] **Combat** is fighting that takes place in a war. ❑ *Over 16 million men had died in combat.* ❑ *Yesterday saw hand-to-hand combat in the city.* **2** [C] A **combat** is a battle, or a fight between two people. ❑ *It was the end of a long combat.*
VERB /kəmˈbæt/ [T] (**combats, combating** or **combatting, combated** or **combatted**) If people in authority **combat** something, they try to stop it from happening. ❑ *Congress has criticized new government measures to combat crime.* ❑ *drugs used to combat infectious diseases*

com·bat·ant /ˈkɒmbətənt, AmE kəmˈbæt-/ NOUN [C] (**combatants**) A **combatant** is a person, group, or country that takes part in the fighting in a war. ❑ *I have never suggested that U.N. forces could physically separate the combatants in the region.*

com·bat·ive /ˈkɒmbətɪv, AmE kəmˈbætɪv/ ADJ A person who is **combative** is aggressive and eager to fight or argue. ❑ *He conducted the meeting yesterday in his usual combative style, refusing to admit any mistakes.*

✪ **com·bi·na·tion** ◆◇◇ /ˌkɒmbɪˈneɪʃən/ NOUN [C] (**combinations**) A **combination** of things is a mixture of them. = group, mixture, blend ❑ *a fantastic combination of colours* ❑ *A combination of circumstances led to the disaster.* ❑ *a chemical formed by the combination of elements*

✪ **com·bine** ◆◇◇ /kəmˈbaɪn/ VERB [RECIP, T] (**combines, combining, combined**) **1** [RECIP] If you **combine** two or more things or if they **combine**, they exist together. ❑ *The Church has something to say on how to combine freedom with responsibility.* ❑ *Relief workers say it's worse than ever as disease and starvation combine to kill thousands.* ❑ *If improved education is combined with other factors dramatic results can be achieved.* **2** [RECIP] If you **combine** two or more things or if they **combine**, they join together to make a single thing. = join, mix, blend; ≠ separate ❑ *David Jacobs has been given the job of combining the data from these 19 studies into one giant study.* ❑ *Carbon, hydrogen and oxygen combine chemically to* form carbohydrates and fats. ❑ *Combine the flour with 3 tablespoons water to make a paste.* **3** [RECIP] If two or more groups or organizations **combine** or if someone **combines** them, they join to form a single group or organization. = amalgamate ❑ *an announcement by Steetley and Tarmac of a joint venture that would combine their brick, tile, and concrete operations* **4** [T] If someone or something **combines** two qualities or features, they have both those qualities or features at the same time. ❑ *Their system seems to combine the two ideals of strong government and proportional representation.* ❑ *a clever, far-sighted lawyer who combines legal expertise with social concern* **5** [T] If someone **combines** two activities, they do them both at the same time. ❑ *It is possible to combine a career with being a mother.*

com·bined /kəmˈbaɪnd/ ADJ **1** [combined + N] A **combined** effort or attack is made by two or more groups of people at the same time. = joint ❑ *These refugees are taken care of by the combined efforts of the host countries and non-governmental organizations.* **2** [combined + N] The **combined** size or quantity of two or more things is the total of their sizes or quantities added together. = total ❑ *Such a merger would be the largest in U.S. banking history, giving the two banks combined assets of some $146 billion.*

❂**com·bus·tion** /kəmˈbʌstʃən/ NOUN [U] (technical) **Combustion** is the act of burning something or the process of burning. ❑ *The energy is released by combustion on the application of a match.* ❑ *The two principal combustion products are water vapour and carbon dioxide.*

come ♦♦♦ /kʌm/ VERB, PREP

> **Come** is used in a large number of expressions which are explained under other words in this dictionary. For example, the expression 'to come to terms with something' is explained at 'term'.

VERB [I, T, LINK] (**comes, coming, came, come**) **1** [I] When a person or thing **comes** to a particular place, especially to a place where you are, they move there. ❑ *Two police officers came into the hall.* ❑ *Come here, Tom.* ❑ *We heard the train coming.* ❑ *The impact blew out some of the windows and the sea came rushing in.* **2** [T] When someone **comes to** do something, they move to the place where someone else is in order to do it, and they do it. Someone can also **come** do something and **come and** do something. However, you always say that someone **came and** did something. ❑ *Eleanor had come to see her.* ❑ *I want you to come visit me.* **3** [I] When you **come to** a place, you reach it. ❑ *He came to a door that led into a passageway.* **4** [I] If something **comes up to** a particular point or **down to** it, it is tall enough, deep enough, or long enough to reach that point. ❑ *The water came up to my chest.* **5** [I] If something **comes apart** or **comes to pieces**, it breaks into pieces. If something **comes off** or **comes away**, it becomes detached from something else. ❑ *The lid won't come off.* ❑ *The pistol came to pieces, easily and quickly.* **6** [T] If someone **comes to** do something, they do it at the end of a long process or period of time. ❑ *She said it so many times that she came to believe it.* **7** [T] You can ask how something **came to** happen when you want to know what caused it to happen or made it possible. ❑ *How did you come to meet him?* **8** [I] When a particular event or time **comes**, it arrives or happens. ❑ *The announcement came after a meeting at the White House.* ❑ *There will come a time when they will have to negotiate.* **9** [I] If a thought, idea, or memory **comes to** you, you suddenly think of it or remember it. = occur ❑ *He was about to shut the door when an idea came to him.* **10** [I] If money or property is going to **come to** you, you are going to inherit or receive it. ❑ *He did have retirement money coming to him when the factory shut down.* **11** [I] If a case **comes before** a court or tribunal or **comes to** court, it is presented there so that the court or tribunal can examine it. ❑ *The membership application came before the committee in September.* **12** [I] If something **comes to** a particular number or amount, it adds up to it. ❑ *Lunch came to $80.* **13** [I] If someone or something **comes from** a particular place or thing, that place or thing is their origin, source, or starting point. ❑ *Nearly half the students come from overseas.* ❑ *Chocolate comes from the cacao tree.* **14** [I]

Something that **comes from** something else or **comes of** it is the result of it. ❑ *There is a feeling of power that comes from driving fast.* ❑ *Some good might come of all this gloomy business.* **15** [I] If someone or something **comes** first, next, or last, they are first, next, or last in a series, list, or competition. ❑ *The two countries have been unable to agree which step should come next.* ❑ *The alphabet might be more rational if all the vowels came first.* **16** [I] If a type of thing **comes** in a particular range of colours, forms, styles, or sizes, it can have any of those colours, forms, styles, or sizes. ❑ *Bikes come in all shapes and sizes.* **17** [I] The next subject in a discussion that you **come to** is the one that you talk about next. ❑ *Finally, I come to the subject of genetic engineering.* **18** [LINK] You use **come** in expressions such as **come to an end** or **come into operation** to indicate that someone or something enters or reaches a particular state or situation. ❑ *The summer came to an end.* ❑ *Their worst fears may be coming true.*

PHRASES **when it comes down to it** or **when you come down to it** (emphasis) You can use the expression **when it comes down to it** or **when you come down to it** for emphasis, when you are giving a general statement or conclusion. ❑ *When you come down to it, however, the basic problems of life have not changed.*

come to think of it You use the expression **come to think of it** to indicate that you have suddenly realized something, often something obvious. ❑ *He was his distant relative, as was everyone else on the island, come to think of it.*

to come When you refer to a time or an event **to come** or one that is still **to come**, you are referring to a future time or event. ❑ *I hope in years to come he will reflect on his decision.*

where someone is coming from You can use expressions like **I know where you're coming from** or **you can see where she's coming from** to say that you understand someone's attitude or point of view. ❑ *To understand why they are doing it, it is necessary to know where they are coming from.*

PHRASAL VERBS **come about** When you say how or when something **came about**, you say how or when it happened. ❑ *The peace agreement came about through intense pressure by the international community.* ❑ *That came about when we went to New York last year.*

come across **1** If you **come across** something or someone, you find them or meet them by chance. = encounter ❑ *He came across the jawbone of a 4.5 million-year-old marsupial.* **2** If someone or what they are saying **comes across** in a particular way, they make that impression on people who meet them or are listening to them. = come over ❑ *When sober, he can come across as an extremely pleasant and charming young man.*

come along **1** You tell someone to **come along** to encourage them in a friendly way to do something, especially to attend something. = come on ❑ *There's a barbecue tonight and you're very welcome to come along.* **2** When something or someone **comes along**, they occur or arrive by chance. ❑ *I waited a long time until a script came along that I thought was genuinely funny.* **3** If something **is coming along**, it is developing or making progress. ❑ *Pentagon spokesman Williams says those talks are coming along quite well.*

come at If a person or animal **comes at** you, they move towards you in a threatening way and try to attack you. ❑ *He maintained that he was protecting himself from Mr Cox, who came at him with an axe.*

come back **1** If someone **comes back** to a place, they return to it. ❑ *He wanted to come back to Washington.* ❑ *She just wanted to go home and not come back.* **2** If something that you had forgotten **comes back to** you, you remember it. ❑ *I'll think of his name in a moment when it comes back to me.* **3** When something **comes back**, it becomes fashionable again. ❑ *I'm glad hats are coming back.* **4** → See also **comeback**

come between If someone or something **comes between** two people, or **comes between** a person and a thing, they make the relationship or connection between them less close or happy. ❑ *I don't want this misunderstanding to come between us.*

come by To **come by** something means to obtain it or find it. ❏ *How did you come by that cheque?*

come down ■ If the cost, level, or amount of something **comes down**, it becomes less than it was before. ❏ *Interest rates should come down.* ❏ *If you buy three bottles, the bottle price comes down to $10.* ■ If something **comes down**, it falls to the ground. ❏ *The cold rain came down for hours.*

come down on ■ If you **come down on** one side of an argument, you declare that you support that side. ❏ *He clearly and decisively came down on the side of the president.* ■ If you **come down on** someone, you criticize them severely or treat them strictly. ❏ *If Douglas came down hard enough on him, Dale would rebel.*

come down to If a problem, decision, or question **comes down to** a particular thing, that thing is the most important factor involved. ❏ *The problem comes down to money.* ❏ *I think that it comes down to the fact that people do feel very dependent on their cars.*

come down with If you **come down with** an illness, you get it. ❏ *Thomas came down with chickenpox.*

come for If people such as soldiers or police **come for** you, they come to find you, usually in order to harm you or take you away, for example to prison. ❏ *Tanya was getting ready to fight if they came for her.*

come forward If someone **comes forward**, they make themselves known and offer to help. ❏ *A vital witness came forward to say that she saw Tanner wearing the boots.*

come in ■ If information, a report, or a telephone call **comes in**, it is received. ❏ *Reports are now coming in of trouble at yet another jail.* ■ If you have some money **coming in**, you receive it regularly as your income. ❏ *She had no money coming in and no funds.* ■ If someone **comes in on** a discussion, arrangement, or task, they join it. ❏ *Can I come in here too, on both points?* ■ When a new idea, fashion, or product **comes in**, it becomes popular or available. ❏ *It was just when attitudes were really beginning to change and lots of new ideas were coming in.* ■ If you ask where something or someone **comes in**, you are asking what their role is in a particular matter. ❏ *Rose asked again, 'But where do we come in, Henry?'* ■ When the tide **comes in**, the water in the sea gradually moves so that it covers more of the land. ❏ *She became trapped as the tide came in.*

come in for If someone or something **comes in for** criticism or blame, they receive it. ❏ *The plans have already come in for fierce criticism.*

come into ■ If someone **comes into** some money, some property, or a title, they inherit it. = inherit ❏ *My father has just come into a fortune in diamonds.* ■ If someone or something **comes into** a situation, they have a role in it. ❏ *We don't really know where Hortense comes into all this, Inspector.*

come off ■ If something **comes off**, it is successful or effective. ❏ *It was a good try but it didn't really come off.* ■ If someone **comes off** worst in a contest or conflict, they are in the worst position after it. If they **come off** best, they are in the best position. ❏ *Some Democrats still have bitter memories of how they came off worst during the investigation.* ■ You say '**come off it**' to someone to show them that you think what they are saying is untrue or wrong.

come on ■ If you have an illness or a headache **coming on**, you can feel it starting. ❏ *Tiredness and fever are much more likely to be a sign of the flu coming on.* ■ If something or someone **is coming on** well, they are developing well or making good progress. = come along ❏ *Leah is coming on very well now and it's a matter of deciding how to fit her into the team.* ■ When something such as a machine or system **comes on**, it starts working or functioning. ❏ *The central heating was coming on and the ancient wooden boards creaked.* ■ (*spoken*) You say '**Come on**' to someone to encourage them to do something they do not want to do. = come along ❏ *Come on Doreen, let's dance.* ■ (*spoken*) You say '**Come on**' to someone to encourage them to hurry up. = come along ❏ *Come on, darling, we'll be late.*

come on to (*informal*) If someone **comes on to** you, they show that they are interested in starting a sexual relationship with you. ❏ *I met a guy at a party and he came on to me real hard.*

come out ■ When a new product such as a book or CD

comes out, it becomes available to the public. ❏ *The book comes out this week.* ■ If a fact **comes out**, it becomes known to people. ❏ *The truth is beginning to come out about what happened.* ■ When a gay person **comes out**, they let people know that they are gay. ❏ *the few gay men there who dare to come out* ■ To **come out** in a particular way means to be in the position or state described at the end of a process or event. ❏ *In this grim little episode of recent American history, few people come out well.* ❏ *So what makes a good marriage? Faithfulness comes out top of the list.* ■ If you **come out for** something, you declare that you support it. If you **come out against** something, you declare that you do not support it. ❏ *Its members had come out virtually unanimously against the tests.* ■ When the sun, moon, or stars **come out**, they appear in the sky. ❏ *Oh, look! The sun's coming out!* ■ (*BrE*; in *AmE*, use **go on strike**) When a group of workers **comes out** on strike, they go on strike.

come over ■ If a feeling or desire, especially a strange or surprising one, **comes over** you, it affects you strongly. ❏ *As I entered the hallway which led to my room that eerie feeling came over me.* ■ If someone or what they are saying **comes over** in a particular way, they make that impression on people who meet them or are listening to them. = come across ❏ *You come over as a capable and amusing companion.* ■ If someone **comes over to** your house or another place, they visit you there. = follow through ❏ *Maybe I could come over to your house before the party?*

come round (*BrE*; in *AmE*, use **come around**) ■ If someone **comes round to** your house, they come there to see you. = come over ❏ *Beth came round this morning to apologize.* ■ If you **come round to** an idea, you eventually change your mind and accept it or agree with it. ❏ *It looks like they're coming round to our way of thinking.* ■ When something **comes round**, it happens as a regular or predictable event. ❏ *I hope to be fit when the World Championship comes round next year.* ■ When someone who is unconscious **comes round**, they become conscious again. = come to ❏ *When I came round I was on the kitchen floor.*

come through ■ To **come through** a dangerous or difficult situation means to survive it and recover from it. ❏ *The city had faced racial crisis and come through it.* ■ If a feeling or message **comes through**, it is clearly shown in what is said or done. = come across ❏ *The message that comes through is that taxes will have to be raised.* ■ If something **comes through**, it arrives, especially after some procedure has been carried out. ❏ *The father of the baby was waiting for his divorce to come through.* ■ If you **come through** with what is expected or needed from you, you succeed in doing or providing it. ❏ *He puts his administration at risk if he doesn't come through on these promises for reform.*

come to When someone who is unconscious **comes to**, they become conscious. = come round ❏ *When he came to and raised his head, he saw Barney.*

come under ■ If you **come under** attack or pressure, for example, people attack you or put pressure on you. ❏ *The police came under attack from angry crowds.* ■ If something **comes under** a particular authority, it is managed or controlled by that authority. ❏ *They were neglected before because they did not come under NATO.* ■ If something **comes under** a particular heading, it is in the category mentioned. ❏ *Her articles come under the heading of human interest.*

come up ■ If someone **comes up** or **comes up to** you, they approach you until they are standing close to you. ❏ *Her cat came up and rubbed itself against their legs.* ■ If something **comes up** in a conversation or meeting, it is mentioned or discussed. = crop up ❏ *The subject came up at work.* ■ If something **is coming up**, it is about to happen or take place. ❏ *We do have elections coming up.* ■ If something **comes up**, it happens unexpectedly. ❏ *I was delayed – something came up at home.* ■ If a job **comes up** or if something **comes up for** sale, it becomes available. ❏ *A research fellowship came up and I applied for it and got it.* ■ When the sun or moon **comes up**, it rises. ❏ *It will be so great watching the sun come up.* ■ In law, when a case **comes up**, it is heard in a court of law.

❑ *He is one of the reservists who will plead not guilty when their cases come up.*

come up against If you **come up against** a problem or difficulty, you are faced with it and have to deal with it. ❑ *We came up against a great deal of resistance in dealing with the case.*

[PREP] You can use **come** before a date, time, or event to mean when it arrives. For example, you can say **come spring** to mean 'when the spring arrives'. ❑ *Come the election on the 20th of May, we will have to decide.*

WHICH WORD?

come or go?

You use **come** to talk about movement towards the place where you are, or towards a place where you have been or will be.

❑ ***Come*** *and look.*

❑ *Mark* ***came*** *to stay with us.*

When you are talking about movement away from the place where you are, you use **go**, not **come**.

❑ *We often* ***go*** *to France during the summer holidays.*

If you invite someone to accompany you somewhere, you usually use **come**, not **go**.

❑ *Will you* ***come*** *with me to the party?*

USAGE NOTE

come from

Do not use the auxiliary 'be' with 'come from', when you are talking about the place where you were born or where you live. You do not say, for example, ~~'Where are you come from?~~.

Where do you ***come from****?*

---

come·back NOUN [c] (**comebacks**) **1** If someone such as an entertainer or sports personality makes a **comeback**, they return to their profession or sport after a period away. ❑ *Sixties singing star Petula Clark is making a comeback.* **2** If something makes a **comeback**, it becomes fashionable again. ❑ *Tight fitting T-shirts are making a comeback.*

co·median /kəˈmiːdiən/ NOUN [c] (**comedians**) A **comedian** is an entertainer whose job is to make people laugh, by telling jokes or funny stories. = comic ❑ *a stand-up comedian*

com·edy ♦◇◇ /ˈkɒmədi/ NOUN [u, c] (**comedies**) **1** [u] **Comedy** consists of types of entertainment, such as plays and films, or particular scenes in them, that are intended to make people laugh. ❑ *Actor Dom Deluise talks about his career in comedy.* **2** [c] A **comedy** is a play, film, or television programme that is intended to make people laugh. ❑ *The film is a romantic comedy.*

com·fort ♦◇◇ /ˈkʌmfət/ NOUN, VERB

[NOUN] [u, c] (**comforts**) **1** [u] If you are doing something **in comfort**, you are physically relaxed and contented, and are not feeling any pain or other unpleasant sensations. ❑ *This will enable the audience to sit in comfort while watching the shows.* **2** [u] **Comfort** is a style of life in which you have enough money to have everything you need. ❑ *Surely there is some way of ordering our busy lives so that we can live in comfort and find spiritual harmony too.* **3** [u] **Comfort** is what you feel when worries or unhappiness stop. ❑ *He welcomed the truce, but pointed out it was of little comfort to families spending Christmas without a loved one.* ❑ *They will be able to take some comfort from inflation figures due on Friday.* **4** [c] If you refer to a person, thing, or idea as a **comfort**, you mean that it helps you to stop worrying or makes you feel less unhappy. ❑ *It's a comfort talking to you.* **5** [c] **Comforts** are things which make your life easier and more pleasant, such as electrical devices you have in your home. ❑ *She enjoys the material comforts married life has brought her.*

[PHRASE] **too close etc for comfort** If you say that something is **too** close **for comfort**, you mean you are worried because it is closer than you would like it to be. ❑ *The bombs fell in the sea, many too close for comfort.*

[VERB] [T] (**comforts, comforting, comforted**) If you comfort someone, you make them feel less worried, unhappy, or upset, for example by saying kind things to them. = console ❑ *Ned put his arm around her, trying to comfort her.*

com·fort·able ♦◇◇ /ˈkʌmftəbəl/ ADJ **1** If a piece of furniture or an item of clothing is **comfortable**, it makes you feel physically relaxed when you use it, for example because it is soft. ❑ *a comfortable fireside chair* **2** If a building or room is **comfortable**, it makes you feel physically relaxed when you spend time in it, for example because it is warm and has nice furniture. ❑ *A home should be comfortable and friendly.* **3** If you are **comfortable**, you are physically relaxed because of the place or position you are sitting or lying in. ❑ *Lie down on your bed and make yourself comfortable.* **4** If you say that someone is **comfortable**, you mean that they have enough money to be able to live without financial problems. ❑ *'Is he rich?'—'He's comfortable.'* **5** [comfortable + N] In a race, competition, or election, if you have a **comfortable** lead, you are likely to win it easily. If you gain a **comfortable** victory or majority, you win easily. ❑ *By half distance we held a comfortable two-lap lead.* **6** [V-LINK + comfortable] If you feel **comfortable with** a particular situation or person, you feel confident and relaxed with them. ❑ *Nervous politicians might well feel more comfortable with a step-by-step approach.* ❑ *He liked me and I felt comfortable with him.* **7** When a sick or injured person is said to be **comfortable**, they are without pain. ❑ *He was described as comfortable in the hospital last night.*

com·fort·ably /ˈkʌmftəbli/ ADV **1** [usu comfortably + -ED] If a building or room is furnished **comfortably**, it makes you feel physically relaxed when you spend time in it. ❑ *the comfortably furnished living room* **2** [comfortably with V] If you sit or lie **comfortably**, you are physically relaxed because of the place or position you are sitting or lying in. ❑ *Are you sitting comfortably?* **3** If you say that someone lives **comfortably**, you mean that they have enough money to be able to live without financial problems. ❑ *Cayton describes himself as comfortably well-off.* **4** [comfortably with V] In a race, competition, or election, if you lead **comfortably**, you are likely to win easily. If you win **comfortably**, you win easily. ❑ *the Los Angeles Raiders, who comfortably beat the Bears earlier in the season* **5** [comfortably after V] If you behave **comfortably** with a particular situation or person, you behave in a confident and relaxed way with them. ❑ *They talked comfortably of their plans.* **6** [comfortably with V] If you manage to do something **comfortably**, you do it easily. ❑ *Only take upon yourself those things that you know you can manage comfortably.*

com·fort·ing /ˈkʌmfətɪŋ/ ADJ If you say that something is **comforting**, you mean it makes you feel less worried or unhappy. ❑ *My mother had just died and I found the book very comforting.*

com·ic /ˈkɒmɪk/ ADJ, NOUN

[ADJ] **1** If you describe something as **comic**, you mean that it makes you laugh, and is often intended to make you laugh. ❑ *The novel is comic and tragic.* **2** [comic + N] **Comic** is used to describe funny entertainment, and the actors and entertainers who perform it. ❑ *Grodin is a fine comic actor.*

[NOUN] [c] (**comics**) **1** A **comic** is an entertainer who tells jokes in order to make people laugh. = comedian ❑ *the funniest comic in Britain today* **2** (mainly BrE; in AmE, usually use **comic book**) A **comic** is a magazine that contains stories told in pictures. = comic book

comi·cal /ˈkɒmɪkəl/ ADJ If you describe something as **comical**, you mean that it makes you laugh because it is funny or silly. = funny ❑ *Her expression is almost comical.*

com·ing ♦♦♦ /ˈkʌmɪŋ/ NOUN, ADJ

[NOUN] [SING] The **coming** of an event or time is its arrival. ❑ *Most of my patients welcome the coming of summer.*

[ADJ] [coming + N] A **coming** event or time is an event or time that will happen soon. ❑ *This obviously depends on the weather in the coming months.*

com·ma /ˈkɒmə/ NOUN [c] (**commas**) A **comma** is the punctuation mark which is used to separate parts of a sentence or items in a list.

com·mand ♦◇◇ /kəˈmɑːnd, -ˈmænd/ VERB, NOUN

[VERB] [T] (**commands, commanding, commanded**)

1 (*mainly written*) If someone in authority **commands** you to do something, they tell you that you must do it. = instruct, order ❑ *He commanded his troops to attack.* ❑ *'Get in your car and follow me,' she commanded.* **2** If you **command** something such as respect or obedience, you obtain it because you are popular, famous, or important. ❑ *an excellent doctor who commanded the respect of all her colleagues* **3** If an army or country **commands** a place, they have total control over it. = rule ❑ *Yemen commands the strait at the southern end of the Red Sea.* **4** An officer who **commands** part of an army, navy, or air force is responsible for controlling and organizing it. ❑ *the French general who commands the U.N. troops in the region* NOUN [c, u] (**commands**) **1** [c, u] A **command** is an instance of someone telling you that you must do something. = instruction, order ❑ *The tanker failed to respond to a command to stop.* ❑ *I closed my eyes as his command.* **2** [u] If an army or country **has command of** a place, they have total control over it. ❑ *the struggle for command of the air* **3** [u] If part of an army, navy, or air force is **under the command of** an officer, he or she is responsible for controlling and organizing it. = charge ❑ *a small garrison under the command of Major James Craig* **4** [c] In the armed forces, a **command** is a group of officers who are responsible for organizing and controlling part of an army, navy, or air force. ❑ *He had authorization from the military command to retaliate.* **5** [c] In computing, a **command** is an instruction that you give to a computer. ❑ *I entered the command into my navigational computer.* **6** [u] If someone has **command** of a situation, they have control of it because they have, or seem to have, power or authority. ❑ *Mr Baker would take command of the campaign.* **7** [u] Your **command of** something, such as a foreign language, is your knowledge of it and your ability to use this knowledge. ❑ *His command of English was excellent.*

PHRASE **have something at one's command** If you have a particular skill or particular resources **at** your **command**, you have them and can use them fully. ❑ *The country should have the right to defend itself with all legal means at its command.*

com·mand·er ◆◇◇ /kəˈmɑːndə, -ˈmænd-/ NOUN [c] (**commanders**) **1** A **commander** is an officer in charge of a military operation or organization. ❑ *The commander and some of the men had been released.* **2** A **commander** is an officer in the Royal Navy or the U.S. Navy.

com·memo·rate /kəˈmeməreɪt/ VERB [T] (**commemorates, commemorating, commemorated**) To **commemorate** an important event or person means to remember them by means of a special action, ceremony, or specially created object. = celebrate ❑ *One room contained a gallery of paintings commemorating great moments in baseball history.*
com·memo·ra·tion /kəˌmeməˈreɪʃən/ NOUN [c, u] (**commemorations**) ❑ *a march in commemoration of Malcolm X*

✪**com·mence** /kəˈmens/ VERB [i, T] (**commences, commencing, commenced**) (*academic word, formal*) When something **commences** or you **commence** it, it begins. = begin ❑ *The academic year commences at the beginning of October.* ❑ *They commenced a systematic search.* ❑ *The company commenced work on its expansion project in 2011.*

WHICH WORD?
commence, start, emerge, or originate?

There is no difference in meaning between **commence** and **start**, but **commence** is a formal word. You do not use it in conversation.
❑ *What time do classes start in the morning?*
❑ *Course times: Courses commence at 10.00 am.*

Emerge and **originate** are also formal words. You use **emerge** to talk about something becoming known for the first time, especially gradually.
❑ *The virus first emerged in China's Guangdong province in November 2002.*

You use **originate** to talk about where or how something first started.
❑ *The concept originated in Germany in the 1960s.*

com·mend /kəˈmend/ VERB [T] (**commends, commending, commended**) (*formal*) **1** If you **commend** someone or something, you praise them formally. ❑ *I commended her for that action.* ❑ *The reports commend her bravery.* **2** If someone **commends** a person or thing **to** you, they tell you that you will find them good or useful. = recommend ❑ *I can commend it to him as a realistic course of action.*
com·men·da·tion /ˌkɒmenˈdeɪʃən/ NOUN [c] (**commendations**) ❑ *Clare won a commendation for bravery in 1998 after risking his life at the scene of a gas blast.*

com·mend·able /kəˈmendəbəl/ ADJ (*formal, approval*) If you describe someone's behaviour as **commendable**, you approve of it or are praising it. = admirable ❑ *He has acted with commendable speed.*

✪**com·ment** ◆◆◇ /ˈkɒment/ VERB, NOUN (*academic word*) VERB [i, T] (**comments, commenting, commented**) If you **comment on** something, you give your opinion about it or you give an explanation for it. ❑ *So far, Mr Cook has not commented on these reports.* ❑ *You really can't comment until you know the facts.* ❑ *Stratford police refuse to comment on whether anyone has been arrested.* ❑ *'I'm always happy with new developments,' he commented.* ❑ *One student commented that she preferred literature to social science.* NOUN [c, u] (**comments**) A **comment** is something that you say which expresses your opinion of something or which gives an explanation of it. = statement ❑ *He made his comments at a news conference in Amsterdam.* ❑ *There's been no comment so far from police about the allegations.* ❑ *A spokesman declined comment on the matter.* CONVENTION **no comment** People say **'no comment'** as a way of refusing to answer a question, usually when it is asked by a journalist. ❑ *No comment. I don't know anything.*

WHICH WORD?
comment or commentary?

Do not confuse **comment** and **commentary**. A **comment** is something you say which expresses your opinion.
❑ *Florence made a comment about the traffic.*

A **commentary** is a description of an event that is broadcast on radio or television while the event is taking place.
❑ *They listened to the radio commentary of the match.*

WHICH WORD?
comment, mention, or remark?

If you **comment** on a situation, or make a **comment** about it, you give your opinion on it.
❑ *Mr Cook has not commented on these reports.*
❑ *I was wondering whether you had any comments.*

If you **mention** something, you say it, but only briefly, especially when you have not talked about it before.
❑ *He mentioned that he might go to New York.*

If you **remark** on something, or make a **remark** about it, you say what you think or what you have noticed, often in a casual way.
❑ *Visitors often remark on how well the children look.*
❑ *She said that the minister's recent remarks were 'unacceptable'.*

✪**com·men·tary** /ˈkɒməntri, AmE -teri/ NOUN [c, u] (**commentaries**) (*academic word*) **1** [c, u] A **commentary** is a description of an event that is broadcast on radio or television while the event is taking place. ❑ *He gave the listening crowd a running commentary.* **2** [c] A **commentary** is an article or book which explains or discusses something. ❑ *Ms Rich will be writing a twice-weekly commentary on American society and culture.* ❑ *an insightful weekly commentary about life in the United States* **3** [u] [also 'a' commentary, with SUPP] **Commentary** is discussion or criticism of something. = comment ❑ *The show mixed comedy with social commentary.* ❑ *He provides virtually continuous commentary to his passengers.*

✪**com·men·ta·tor** ◆◇◇ /ˈkɒmənteɪtə/ NOUN [c] (**commentators**) **1** A **commentator** is a broadcaster who gives a radio or television commentary on an event. ❑ *a sports commentator* **2** A **commentator** is also someone who often writes or broadcasts about a particular subject. ❑ *a political commentator* ❑ *A. M. Babu was a commentator on African affairs.*

✪ **com·merce** ◆◇◇ /ˈkɒmɜːs/ NOUN [U] **Commerce** is the activities and procedures involved in buying and selling things. = trade ❑ *They have made their fortunes from industry and commerce.* ❑ *The online commerce market is new, rapidly evolving and intensely competitive.*

✪ **com·mer·cial** ◆◆◇ /kəˈmɜːʃəl/ ADJ, NOUN
ADJ **1** **Commercial** means involving or relating to the buying and selling of goods. ❑ *Baltimore in its heyday was a major centre of industrial and commercial activity.* ❑ *Attacks were reported on police, vehicles and commercial premises.* **2** **Commercial** organizations and activities are concerned with making money or profits, rather than, for example, with scientific research or providing a public service. = business ❑ *The company has indeed become more commercial over the past decade.* ❑ *Conservationists in Chile are concerned over the effect of commercial exploitation of forests.* ❑ *Whether the project will be a commercial success is still uncertain.* **3** [commercial + N] A **commercial** product is made to be sold to the public. ❑ *They are the leading manufacturer in both defence and commercial products.* **4** A **commercial** vehicle is a vehicle used for carrying goods, or passengers who pay. ❑ *The route is used every day by many hundreds of commercial vehicles.* **5** **Commercial** television and radio are paid for by the broadcasting of advertisements, rather than by the government. ❑ *There were no commercial radio stations until 1920.* **6** **Commercial** is used to describe something such as a film or a type of music that it is intended to be popular with the public, and is not very original or of high quality. ❑ *There's a feeling among a lot of people that music has become too commercial.*
NOUN [C] (**commercials**) A **commercial** is an advertisement that is broadcast on television or radio. ❑ *Change the channel – there are too many commercials.*
✪ **com·mer·cial·ly** /kəˈmɜːʃəli/ ADV **1** *The plane will be commercially viable if 400 can be sold.* **2** *Designers are becoming more commercially minded.* **3** *It was the first commercially available machine to employ artificial intelligence.* ❑ *Insulin is produced commercially from animals.*

WORD CONNECTIONS

commercially + ADJ

commercially **available**
commercially **viable**
commercially **sensitive**
commercially **successful**

❑ *The exact recipe for the drink is commercially sensitive information.*

---

com·mer·cial·ize /kəˈmɜːʃəlaɪz/ also
commercialise VERB [T] (**commercializes, commercializing, commercialized**) (*disapproval*) If something **is commercialized**, it is used or changed in such a way that it makes money or profits, often in a way that people disapprove of. ❑ *It seems such a pity that a distinguished and honoured name should be commercialized in this way.*
com·mer·cial·ized /kəˈmɜːʃəlaɪzd/ ❑ *Rock'n'roll has become so commercialized and safe since punk.*
com·mer·ci·ali·za·tion /kəˌmɜːʃəlaɪˈzeɪʃən/ NOUN [U] ❑ *the commercialization of Christmas*

✪ **com·mis·sion** ◆◆◇ /kəˈmɪʃən/ VERB, NOUN (*academic word*)
VERB [T] (**commissions, commissioning, commissioned**) If you **commission** something or **commission** someone to do something, you formally arrange for someone to do a piece of work for you. ❑ *The Department of Agriculture commissioned a study into organic farming.* ❑ *You can commission them to paint something especially for you.* ❑ *specially commissioned reports*
NOUN [C, U] (**commissions**) **1** [C, U] **Commission** is a formal arrangement for someone to do a piece of work for you. ❑ *Our china can be bought off the shelf or by commission.* ❑ *He approached John Wexley with a commission to write the*

screenplay of the film. ❑ *Armitage won a commission to design the war memorial.* **2** [C] A **commission** is a piece of work that someone is asked to do and is paid for. ❑ *Just a few days ago, I finished a commission.* **3** [C, U] **Commission** is a sum of money paid to a salesperson for every sale that he or she makes. If a salesperson is paid **on commission**, the amount they receive depends on the amount they sell. ❑ *The salespeople work on commission only.* ❑ *He also got a commission for bringing in new clients.* **4** [U] (*business*) If a bank or other company charges **commission**, they charge a fee for providing a service, for example for exchanging money or issuing an insurance policy. ❑ *Travel agents charge 1 per cent commission on tickets.* ❑ *Sellers pay a fixed commission fee.* **5** [C] A **commission** is a group of people who have been appointed to find out about something or to control something. ❑ *The government has set up a commission to look into those crimes.* ❑ *the Press Complaints Commission* **6** [C] If a member of the armed forces receives a **commission**, he or she becomes an officer. ❑ *He accepted a commission as a naval officer.*

com·mis·sion·er ◆◇◇ /kəˈmɪʃənə/ also
Commissioner NOUN [C] (**commissioners**) A **commissioner** is an important official in a government department or other organization. ❑ *Alaska's commissioner of education*

✪ **com·mit** ◆◆◇ /kəˈmɪt/ VERB [T, I] (**commits, committing, committed**) (*academic word*) **1** [T] If someone **commits** a crime or a sin, they do something illegal or bad. ❑ *I have never committed any crime.* ❑ *This is a man who has committed murder.* **2** [T] If someone **commits** suicide, they deliberately kill themselves. ❑ *There are unconfirmed reports he tried to commit suicide.* **3** [T] If you **commit** money or resources **to** something, you decide to use them for a particular purpose. = give, pledge ❑ *They called on Western nations to commit more money to the poorest nations.* ❑ *The company had committed thousands of dollars for a plan to reduce mercury emissions.* **4** [I, T] If you **commit yourself to** something, you say that you will definitely do it. If you **commit yourself to** someone, you decide that you want to have a long-term relationship with them. = promise ❑ *I would advise people to think very carefully about committing themselves to working Sundays.* ❑ *You don't have to commit to anything over the phone.* ❑ *I'd like a friendship that might lead to something deeper, but I wouldn't want to commit myself too soon.* ❑ *He won't commit.* **5** [T] If you do not want to **commit yourself on** something, you do not want to say what you really think about it or what you are going to do. ❑ *It isn't their diplomatic style to commit themselves on such a delicate issue.* **6** [T] If someone **is committed to** a mental hospital, prison, or other institution, they are officially sent there for a period of time. ❑ *Arthur's drinking caused him to be committed to a psychiatric hospital.* **7** [T] If you **commit** something **to** paper or **to** writing, you record it by writing it down. If you **commit** something **to** memory, you learn it so that you will remember it. ❑ *She had not committed anything to paper about it.*
✪ **com·mit·ted** /kəˈmɪtɪd/ ADJ ❑ *He said the government remained committed to peace.* ❑ *a committed socialist*

✪ **com·mit·ment** ◆◆◇ /kəˈmɪtmənt/ NOUN [U, C] (**commitments**) **1** [U] **Commitment** is a strong belief in an idea or system. ❑ *commitment to the ideals of democracy* **2** [C] A **commitment** is something which regularly takes up some of your time because of an agreement you have made or because of responsibilities that you have. ❑ *I've got a lot of commitments.* **3** [C] If you make a **commitment to** do something, you promise that you will do it. = pledge, promise ❑ *We made a commitment to keep working together.* ❑ *They made a commitment to peace.*

com·mit·tee ◆◆◆ /kəˈmɪti/ NOUN [C] (**committees**) A **committee** is a group of people who meet to make decisions or plans for a larger group or organization that they represent. ❑ *the school yearbook committee*

✪ **com·mod·ity** /kəˈmɒdɪti/ NOUN [C] (**commodities**) (*academic word, business*) A **commodity** is something that is sold for money. ❑ *Prices went up on several basic commodities like bread and meat.* ❑ *Unlike gold, most commodities are not kept solely for investment purposes.*

C

✪ **com·mon** ◆◆◆ /ˈkɒmən/ ADJ, NOUN

ADJ 1 If something is **common**, it is found in large numbers or it happens often. = normal, ordinary; ≠ uncommon, rare ❏ *His name was Hansen, a common name in Norway.* ❏ *Oil pollution is the most common cause of death for seabirds.* ❏ *Earthquakes are not common in this part of the world.* **2** If something is **common to** two or more people or groups, it is done, possessed, or used by them all. ❏ *Moldavians and Romanians share a common language.* **3** [common + N] When there are more animals or plants of a particular species than there are of related species, then the first species is called **common**. ❏ *the common house fly* **4** [common + N] **Common** is used to indicate that someone or something is of the ordinary kind and not special in any way. ❏ *Democracy might elevate the common man to a position of political superiority.* **5** **Common** decency or **common** courtesy is the decency or courtesy which most people have. You usually talk about this when someone has not shown these characteristics in their behaviour to show your disapproval of them. ❏ *It is common decency to give your seat to anyone in greater need.* **6** [common + N] You can use **common** to describe knowledge, an opinion, or a feeling that is shared by people in general. ❏ *It is common knowledge that swimming is one of the best forms of exercise.* **7** (mainly BrE, disapproval) If you describe someone or their behaviour as **common**, you mean that they show a lack of taste, education, and good manners. ❏ *She might be a little common at times, but she was certainly not boring.*

NOUN [c] (**commons**) A **common** is an area of grassy land, usually in or near a village or small town, where the public is allowed to go. ❏ *We are warning women not to go out on to the common alone.*

PHRASE **in common 1** If two or more things have something **in common**, they have the same characteristic or feature. ❏ *The oboe and the clarinet have certain features in common.* **2** If two or more people have something **in common**, they share the same interests or experiences. ❏ *He had very little in common with his sister.*

✪ **com·mon·ly** /ˈkɒmənli/ ADV **1** [commonly with v] = widely; ≠ rarely ❏ *Parsley is one of the most commonly used herbs.* ❏ *Depression occurs most commonly in winter.* **2** *A little adolescent rebellion is commonly believed to be healthy.*

✦ **common ground** → see **ground**

common·place /ˈkɒmənpleɪs/ ADJ If something is **commonplace**, it happens often or is often found, and is therefore not surprising. ❏ *Inter-racial marriages have become commonplace.*

com·mon sense also **commonsense** NOUN [U] Your **common sense** is your natural ability to make good judgments and to behave in a practical and sensible way. ❏ *Use your common sense.* ❏ *She always had a lot of common sense.*

common·wealth /ˈkɒmənwelθ/ NOUN [SING, C] **1** [SING] The **Commonwealth** is an organization consisting of the United Kingdom and most of the countries that were previously under its rule. ❏ *the Asian, Caribbean and African members of the Commonwealth* **2** [c] **Commonwealth** is used in the official names of some countries, groups of countries, or parts of countries. ❏ *the Commonwealth of Australia*

com·mo·tion /kəˈməʊʃən/ NOUN [C, U] (**commotions**) A **commotion** is a lot of noise, confusion, and excitement. ❏ *He heard a commotion outside.*

com·mu·nal /ˈkɒmjʊnəl, AmE kəˈmjuːnəl/ ADJ **1** [communal + N] **Communal** means relating to particular groups in a country or society. ❏ *Communal violence broke out in different parts of the country.* **2** You use **communal** to describe something that is shared by a group of people. ❏ *The inmates ate in a communal dining room.*

com·mune /ˈkɒmjuːn/ NOUN [c] (**communes**) A **commune** is a group of people who live together and share many of their possessions and responsibilities. ❏ *Mack lived in a commune.*

✪ **com·mu·ni·cate** ◆◇◇ /kəˈmjuːnɪkeɪt/ VERB [RECIP, T] (**communicates, communicating, communicated**)

(*academic word*) **1** [RECIP] If you **communicate with** someone, you share or exchange information with them, for example by speaking, writing, or using equipment. You can also say that two people **communicate**. = converse, correspond ❏ *My birth mother has never communicated with me.* ❏ *Officials of the CIA depend heavily on e-mail to communicate with each other.* ❏ *Communicating by text can have disadvantages.* **2** [RECIP] If one person **communicates with** another, they successfully make each other aware of their feelings and ideas. You can also say that two people **communicate**. ❏ *He was never good at communicating with the players.* ❏ *Family therapy showed us how to communicate with each other.* **3** [T] If you **communicate** information, a feeling, or an idea **to** someone, you let them know about it. ❏ *They successfully communicate their knowledge to others.*

✪ **com·mu·ni·ca·tion** ◆◇◇ /kəˌmjuːnɪˈkeɪʃən/ NOUN [U, PL, C] (**communications**) **1** [U] **Communication** is the sharing or exchange of information, for example by speaking, writing, or using equipment. ❏ *Lithuania hasn't had any direct communication with Moscow.* ❏ *use of the radio telephone for communication between controllers and pilots* **2** [U] **Communication** is the act of making other people aware of your feelings and ideas. ❏ *There was a tremendous lack of communication between us.* ❏ *Good communication with people around you could prove difficult.* ❏ *Poor communication skills can be a problem in the workplace.* **3** [PL] **Communications** are the systems and processes that are used to communicate or broadcast information, especially by means of electricity or radio waves. ❏ *a communications satellite* ❏ *advanced communications equipment for emergency workers* **4** [c] (*formal*) A **communication** is a message. ❏ *The ambassador has brought with him a communication from the president.*

com·mu·ni·ca·tive /kəˈmjuːnɪkətɪv/ ADJ **1** Someone who is **communicative** talks to people, for example about their feelings, and tells people things. = open ❏ *She has become a lot more tolerant and communicative.* **2** [usu communicative + N] **Communicative** means relating to the ability to communicate. ❏ *We have a very communicative approach to teaching languages.*

com·mu·ni·qué /kəˈmjuːnɪkeɪ, AmE kəˌmjuːnɪˈkeɪ/ NOUN [c] (**communiqués**) (*formal*) A **communiqué** is an official statement or announcement. ❏ *The communiqué said military targets had been hit.*

✪ **com·mun·ism** /ˈkɒmjʊnɪzəm/ also **Communism** NOUN [U] **Communism** is the political belief that all people are equal, that there should be no private ownership and that workers should control the means of producing things. = socialism; ≠ capitalism ❏ *the ultimate triumph of communism in the world* ❏ *Liberals agree with the assumption that communism is evil and should be fought.*

✪ **com·mun·ist** ◆◆◇ /ˈkɒmjʊnɪst/ also **Communist** NOUN, ADJ

NOUN [c] (**communists**) A **communist** is someone who believes in communism. ❏ *I became a communist out of resistance to fascism.*

ADJ **Communist** means relating to communism. ❏ *the Communist Party* ❏ *the history of the communist leaders in the USSR*

✪ **com·mu·ni·ty** ◆◆◆ /kəˈmjuːnɪti/ NOUN [SING, C, U] (**communities**) (*academic word*) **1** [SING] The **community** is all the people who live in a particular area or place. ❏ *He's well liked by people in the community.* ❏ *The growth of such vigilante gangs has worried community leaders, police and politicians.* **2** [c] A particular **community** is a group of people who are similar in some way. ❏ *The police haven't really done anything for the black community in particular.* ❏ *Friedmann's work received surprisingly little attention from the scientific community.* ❏ *close links to Sao Paulo's business community* **3** [U] **Community** is friendship between different people or groups, and a sense of having something in common. ❏ *Two of our greatest strengths are diversity and community.*

✪ **com·mute** /kəˈmjuːt/ VERB, NOUN

VERB [i] (**commutes, commuting, commuted**) If you **commute**, you travel a long distance every day between

your home and your place of work. = travel ❑ *Mike commutes to Miami every day.* ❑ *McLaren began commuting between Philadelphia and New York.* ❑ *He's going to commute.* NOUN [c] (**commutes**) A **commute** is the journey that you make when you commute. ❑ *The average Los Angeles commute is over 60 miles a day.*
✪ **com·mut·er** /kəˈmjuːtə/ NOUN [c] (**commuters**) ❑ *There are significant numbers of commuters using our streets.* ❑ *The number of commuters to London has dropped by 100,000.* ❑ *The most desirable properties are in the commuter belt with good transport links.*

com·pact /kəmˈpækt/ ADJ ■ (approval) **Compact** things are small or take up very little space. You use this word when you think this is a good quality. ❑ *my compact office in Washington* ■ A **compact** person is small but looks strong. ❑ *He was compact, probably no taller than me.*

com·pact disc also **compact disk** NOUN [c] (**compact discs**) [also 'on' compact disc] **Compact discs** are small shiny discs that contain music or computer information. The abbreviation **CD** is also used.

com·pan·ion /kəmˈpænjən/ NOUN [c] (**companions**) A **companion** is someone who you spend time with or who you are travelling with. ❑ *Fred had been her constant companion for the last six years of her life.*

com·pan·ion·ship /kəmˈpænjənʃɪp/ NOUN [u] **Companionship** is having someone you know and like with you, instead of being on your own. = company ❑ *I depended on his companionship and on his judgment.*

✪ **com·pa·ny** ♦♦♦ /ˈkʌmpəni/ NOUN
NOUN [c, u] (**companies**) ■ [c] A **company** is a business organization that makes money by selling goods or services. = firm, business, corporation, enterprise ❑ *Sheila found some work as a secretary in an insurance company.* ❑ *a successful businessman who owned a company that sold coffee machines* ❑ *the Ford Motor Company* ■ [c] A **company** is a group of opera singers, dancers, or actors who work together. ❑ *the Phoenix Dance Company* ■ [c] A **company** is a group of soldiers that is usually part of a battalion or regiment, and that is divided into two or more platoons. ❑ *The division will consist of two tank companies and one infantry company.* ■ [u] **Company** is having another person or other people with you, usually when this is pleasant or stops you feeling lonely. ❑ *'I won't stay long.'—'No, please. I need the company.'* ❑ *Ross had always enjoyed the company of women.*
PHRASES **have company** If you **have company**, you have a visitor or friend with you. ❑ *He didn't say he had company.*
keep someone company If you **keep** someone **company**, you spend time with them and stop them from feeling lonely or bored. ❑ *Why don't you stay here and keep Emma company?*

com·pa·rable /ˈkɒmpərəbəl/ ADJ ■ Something that is **comparable** to something else is roughly similar, for example in amount or importance. = similar ❑ *paying the same wages to men and women for work of comparable value* ❑ *Farmers were supposed to get an income comparable to that of townspeople.* ■ If two or more things are **comparable**, they are of the same kind or are in the same situation, and so they can reasonably be compared. = equivalent ❑ *In other comparable countries, real wages increased much more rapidly.* ❑ *By contrast, the comparable figure for Canada is 16 per cent.*

✪ **com·para·tive** /kəmˈpærətɪv/ ADJ, NOUN
ADJ ■ [comparative + N] You use **comparative** to show that you are judging something against a previous or different situation. For example, **comparative** calm is a situation which is calmer than before or calmer than the situation in other places. = relative ❑ *The task was accomplished with comparative ease.* ❑ *those who manage to reach comparative safety* ■ [comparative + N] A **comparative** study is a study that involves the comparison of two or more things of the same kind. ❑ *a comparative study of the dietary practices of people from various regions of India* ❑ *a professor of English and comparative literature*
NOUN [c] (**comparatives**) In grammar, a **comparative** is the form of an adjective or adverb which shows that something has more of a quality than something else has.

❑ *The comparative of 'pretty' is 'prettier'.*
✪ **com·para·tive·ly** /kəmˈpærətɪvli/ ADV ❑ *a comparatively small nation* ❑ *children who find it comparatively easy to make and keep friends*

✪ **com·pare** ♦◇◇ /kəmˈpeə/ VERB [T, I] (**compares, comparing, compared**) ■ [T] When you **compare** things, you consider them and discover the differences or similarities between them. ❑ *Compare the two illustrations in Figure 60.* ❑ *Was it fair to compare independent schools with state schools?* ❑ *Note how smooth the skin of the upper arm is, then compare it to the skin on the elbow.* ❑ *Managers analyse their company's data and compare it with data on their competitors.* ■ [T] If you **compare** one person or thing **to** another, you say that they are like the other person or thing. = liken ❑ *Some commentators compared his work to that of James Joyce.* ■ [I] If you say that something does not **compare with** something else, you mean that it is much worse. ❑ *The flowers here do not compare with those at home.* ■ [I] If one thing **compares** favourably **with** another, it is better than the other thing. If it **compares** unfavourably, it is worse than the other thing. ❑ *Our road-safety record compares favourably with that of other countries.*
→ See also **compared**

✪ **com·pared** ♦♦◇ /kəmˈpeəd/ ADJ
PHRASE **compared with something** or **compared to something** ■ If you say, for example, that one thing is large or small **compared with** another or **compared to** another, you mean that it is larger or smaller than the other thing. ❑ *The room was light and lofty compared to the basement.* ❑ *The astronomical unit is large compared with distances on earth.* ❑ *Columbia was a young city compared to venerable Charleston.* ■ You talk about one situation or thing **compared with** another or **compared to** another when contrasting the two situations or things. ❑ *In 1800 Ireland's population was nine million, compared to Britain's 16 million.*

✪ **com·pari·son** ♦◇◇ /kəmˈpærɪsən/ NOUN
NOUN [c, u] (**comparisons**) ■ [c, u] When you make a **comparison**, you consider two or more things and discover the differences between them. ❑ *a comparison of the Mexican and Guatemalan economies* ❑ *Its recommendations are based on detailed comparisons between the public and private sectors.* ❑ *There are no previous statistics for comparison.* ■ [c] When you make a **comparison**, you say that one thing is like another in some way. ❑ *It is demonstrably an unfair comparison.*
PHRASE **in comparison** or **by comparison** If you say, for example, that something is large or small **in comparison with**, **in comparison to**, or **by comparison with** something else, you mean that it is larger or smaller than the other thing. ❑ *The amount of carbon dioxide released by human activities such as burning coal and oil is small in comparison.*

WORD CONNECTIONS
VERB + **comparison**
make a comparison **draw** a comparison ❑ *It is difficult to draw a comparison between the two cultures.*
invite comparison **bear** comparison ❑ *The weapons bear no comparison to the lethal weapons that are available today.*
ADJ + **comparison**
a **difficult** comparison an **unfair** comparison a **valid** comparison ❑ *There is insufficient data to draw valid comparisons between the two periods.*
a **direct** comparison an **inevitable** comparison ❑ *It is possible to make a direct comparison between the constitutional arrangements of the two parties.*

com·part·ment /kəmˈpɑːtmənt/ NOUN [C] (**compartments**) **1** A **compartment** is one of the separate parts of an object that is used for keeping things in. ❑ *The fire started in the baggage compartment.* **2** A **compartment** is one of the separate spaces into which a rail coach is divided. ❑ *On the way home we shared our first class compartment with a group of businessmen.*

com·pass /ˈkʌmpəs/ NOUN [C] (**compasses**) A **compass** is an instrument that you use for finding directions. It has a dial and a magnetic needle that always points to the north. ❑ *We had to rely on a compass and a lot of luck to get here.*

com·pas·sion /kəmˈpæʃən/ NOUN [U] **Compassion** is a feeling of pity, sympathy, and understanding for someone who is suffering. ❑ *Elderly people need time and compassion from their doctors.*

com·pas·sion·ate /kəmˈpæʃənət/ ADJ (*approval*) If you describe someone or something as **compassionate**, you mean that they feel or show pity, sympathy, and understanding for people who are suffering. ❑ *My father was a deeply compassionate man.* ❑ *She has a wise, compassionate face.*

✪**com·pat·ible** /kəmˈpætɪbəl/ ADJ (*academic word*) **1** If things, for example systems, ideas, and beliefs, are **compatible**, they work well together or can exist together successfully. ❑ *Free enterprise, he argued, was compatible with Russian values and traditions.* ❑ *The two aims are not necessarily compatible.* **2** If you say that you are **compatible** with someone, you mean that you have a good relationship with them because you have similar opinions and interests. ❑ *Mildred and I are very compatible. She's interested in the things that interest me.* **3** If one brand of computer or computer equipment is **compatible with** another brand, they can be used together and can use the same software. ≠ **incompatible** ❑ *Fujitsu took over another American firm, Amdal, to help it to make and sell machines compatible with IBM in the United States.* ❑ *Only Windows-based desktop computers less than 4 years old are compatible with the software.*
✪**com·pat·ibil·ity** /kəm-ˌpætɪˈbɪlɪti/ NOUN [U] **1** ≠ **incompatibility** ❑ *National courts can freeze any law while its compatibility with European legislation is being tested.* ❑ *the compatibility between a certain job and a candidate* ❑ *Chapter 13 describes the compatibility of reincarnation with the Christian faith.* **2** ≠ **incompatibility** ❑ *As a result of their compatibility, Haig and Fraser were able to bring about wide-ranging reforms.*

com·pat·ri·ot /kəmˈpætriət, AmE -ˈpeɪt-/ NOUN [C] (**compatriots**) Your **compatriots** are people from your own country. = **countryman** ❑ *Chris Robertson of Australia beat his compatriot Chris Dittmar in the final.*

com·pel /kəmˈpel/ VERB
VERB [T] (**compels, compelling, compelled**) If a situation, a rule, or a person **compels** you **to** do something, they force you to do it. ❑ *the introduction of legislation to compel cyclists to wear a helmet*
PHRASE **feel compelled** If you **feel compelled to** do something, you feel that you must do it, because it is the right thing to do. ❑ *Dickens felt compelled to return to the stage for a final goodbye.*

✪**com·pel·ling** /kəmˈpelɪŋ/ ADJ **1** A **compelling** argument or reason is one that convinces you that something is true or that something should be done. ❑ *Factual and forensic evidence makes a suicide verdict the most compelling answer to the mystery of his death.* ❑ *The evidence was so compelling that the central Government did not have to force this change; it was willingly accepted.* **2** If you describe something such as a film or book, or someone's appearance, as **compelling**, you mean you want to keep looking at it or reading it because you find it so interesting. ❑ *a frighteningly violent yet compelling film*

✪**com·pen·sate** /ˈkɒmpənseɪt/ VERB [T, I] (**compensates, compensating, compensated**) (*academic word*) **1** [T] To **compensate** someone **for** money or things that they have lost, means to pay them money or give them something to replace those things. ❑ *The damages*

are designed to compensate victims for their direct losses.* ❑ *The official promise to compensate people for the price rise clearly hadn't been worked out properly.* ❑ *To ease financial difficulties, farmers could be compensated for their loss of subsidies.* **2** [I] If you **compensate for** a lack of something or **for** something you have done wrong, you do something to make the situation better. ❑ *The company agreed to keep up high levels of output in order to compensate for supplies lost.* **3** [I] Something that **compensates for** something else balances it or reduces its effects. ❑ *Senators say it is crucial that a mechanism is found to compensate for inflation.* ❑ *The drug may compensate for prostaglandin deficiency.* **4** [I] If you try to **compensate for** something that is wrong or missing in your life, you try to do something that removes or reduces the harmful effects. ❑ *Their sense of humour and ability to get along with people are two characteristics that compensate for their lack of experience.*

✪**com·pen·sa·tion** ♦◇◇ /ˌkɒmpənˈseɪʃən/ NOUN [U, C] (**compensations**) **1** [U] **Compensation** is money that someone who has experienced loss or suffering claims from the person or organization responsible, or from the state. ❑ *He received one year's salary as compensation for loss of office.* ❑ *They want $20,000 in compensation for each of about 500 claimants.* ❑ *The Court ordered Dr Williams to pay £300 compensation and £100 costs after admitting assault.* **2** [C, U] If something is some **compensation for** something bad that has happened, it makes you feel better. ❑ *Helen gained some compensation for her earlier defeat by winning the final open class.*

com·pete ♦◇◇ /kəmˈpiːt/ VERB [RECIP, I] (**competes, competing, competed**) **1** [RECIP] When one firm or country **competes with** another, it tries to get people to buy its own goods in preference to those of the other firm or country. You can also say that two firms or countries **compete**. ❑ *The banks have long competed with American Express's credit cards and various store cards.* ❑ *Hardware stores are competing fiercely for business.* **2** [RECIP] If you **compete with** someone **for** something, you try to get it for yourself and stop the other person from getting it. You can also say that two people **compete for** something. ❑ *Kangaroos compete with sheep and cattle for sparse supplies of food and water.* ❑ *Young men compete with each other for membership in these societies and fraternities.* **3** [I] If you **compete** in a contest or a game, you take part in it. ❑ *He will be competing in the 100-metre race.*

com·pe·tence /ˈkɒmpɪtəns/ NOUN [U] **Competence** is the ability to do something well or effectively. ❑ *Many people have testified to his competence.*

com·pe·tent /ˈkɒmpɪtənt/ ADJ **1** Someone who is **competent** is efficient and effective. ❑ *He was a loyal, distinguished, and very competent civil servant.* **2** If you are **competent to** do something, you have the skills, abilities, or experience necessary to do it well. = **qualified** ❑ *Most adults do not feel competent to deal with a medical emergency involving a child.*
com·pe·tent·ly /ˈkɒmpɪtəntli/ ADV ❑ *The government performed competently in the face of multiple challenges.*

✪**com·pe·ti·tion** ♦♦◇ /ˌkɒmpɪˈtɪʃən/ NOUN [U, SING, C] (**competitions**) **1** [U] **Competition** is a situation in which two or more people or groups are trying to get something which not everyone can have. ❑ *There's been some fierce competition for the title.* **2** [U] **Competition** is an activity involving two or more companies, in which each company tries to get people to buy its own goods in preference to the other companies' goods. ❑ *The deal would have reduced competition in the commuter-aircraft market.* ❑ *The farmers have been seeking higher prices as better protection from foreign competition.* ❑ *Clothing stores also face heavy competition from factory outlets.* **3** [U] The **competition** is the goods or services that a rival organization is selling. ❑ *The American aerospace industry has been challenged by some stiff competition.* **4** [SING] The **competition** is the person or people you are competing with. ❑ *I have to change my approach, the competition is too good now.* **5** [C, U] A **competition** is an event in which many people take part in order to find out who is best at a particular activity. ❑ *a surfing competition*

✪ **com·pet·i·tive** ♦◇◇ /kəm'petɪtɪv/ ADJ **1** **Competitive** is used to describe situations or activities in which people or companies compete with each other. ❏ *Only by keeping down costs will America maintain its competitive advantage over other countries.* ❏ *Japan is a highly competitive market system.* **2** A **competitive** person is eager to be more successful than other people. ❏ *He has always been ambitious and fiercely competitive.* **3** Goods or services that are at a **competitive** price or rate are likely to be bought, because they are less expensive than other goods of the same kind. ❏ *Only those homes offered for sale at competitive prices will secure interest from serious purchasers.*

com·pet·i·tive·ly /kəm'petɪtɪvli/ ADV **1** [competitively after V] ❏ *He's now back up on the slopes again, skiing competitively in events for the disabled.* **2** [competitively after V] ❏ *They worked hard together, competitively and under pressure.* **3** *a number of early Martin and Gibson guitars, which were competitively priced*

com·pet·i·tive·ness /kəm'petɪtɪvnəs/ NOUN [U] **1** *I can't stand the pace, I suppose, and the competitiveness, and the unfriendliness.* **2** *It is only on the world market that we can prove the competitiveness and quality of our software.*

com·peti·tor ♦◇◇ /kəm'petɪtə/ NOUN [C] (**competitors**) **1** A company's **competitors** are companies who are trying to sell similar goods or services to the same people. = rival ❏ *The bank isn't performing as well as some of its competitors.* **2** A **competitor** is a person who takes part in a competition or contest. ❏ *One of the oldest competitors won the individual silver medal.*

✪ **com·pi·la·tion** /ˌkɒmpɪ'leɪʃən/ NOUN [C] (**compilations**) A **compilation** is a book, CD, or programme that contains many different items that have been gathered together, usually ones which have already appeared in other places. = collection ❏ *His latest CD is a compilation of his jazz works over the past decade.* ❏ *a compilation of essays and articles on a wide range of topics*

✪ **com·pile** /kəm'paɪl/ VERB [T] (**compiles, compiling, compiled**) (*academic word*) When you **compile** something such as a report, book, or programme, you produce it by collecting and putting together many pieces of information. ❏ *The book took 10 years to compile.* ❏ *The report was compiled by 240 scientists from 96 countries to assess the status of coral reefs worldwide.*

com·pla·cen·cy /kəm'pleɪsənsi/ NOUN [U] (*disapproval*) **Complacency** is being complacent about a situation. ❏ *a worrying level of complacency about the risks of infection from AIDS*

com·pla·cent /kəm'pleɪsənt/ ADJ (*disapproval*) A **complacent** person is very pleased with themselves or feels that they do not need to do anything about a situation, even though the situation may be uncertain or dangerous. ❏ *We cannot afford to be complacent about our health.*

com·plain ♦♦◇ /kəm'pleɪn/ VERB [I, T] (**complains, complaining, complained**) **1** [I, T] If you **complain about** a situation, you say that you are not satisfied with it. ❏ *Miners have complained bitterly that the government did not fulfil their promises.* ❏ *The couple complained about the high cost of visiting New Zealand.* ❏ *I shouldn't complain, I've got a good job to go back to.* ❏ *'I wish someone would do something about it,' he complained.* **2** [I] If you **complain of** pain or illness, you say that you are feeling pain or feeling ill. ❏ *He complained of a headache.*

com·plaint ♦◇◇ /kəm'pleɪnt/ NOUN [C, U] (**complaints**) **1** [C, U] A **complaint** is a statement in which you express your dissatisfaction with a situation. ❏ *There's been a record number of complaints about the standard of service.* ❏ *People have been reluctant to make formal complaints to the police.* **2** [C] A **complaint** is a reason for complaining. ❏ *My main complaint is that we can't go out on the racecourse anymore.* **3** [C] You can refer to an illness as a **complaint**, especially if it is not very serious. = ailment ❏ *Eczema is a common skin complaint which often runs in families.*

✪ **com·ple·ment** VERB, NOUN (*academic word*) **VERB** /'kɒmplɪment/ [T] (**complements, complementing, complemented**) **1** If one thing **complements** another, it goes well with the other thing and makes its good qualities more noticeable. = set off ❏ *Nutmeg, parsley and cider all complement the flavour of these beans well.* **2** If people or things **complement** each other, they are different or do something different, which makes them a good combination. ❏ *There will be a written examination to complement the practical test.* ❏ *Their academic programme is complemented by a wide range of sporting, recreational and cultural activities.*

NOUN /'kɒmplɪmənt/ [C] (**complements**) Something that is a **complement** to something else complements it. ❏ *The green wallpaper is the perfect complement to the old pine of the dresser.*

✪ **com·ple·men·tary** /ˌkɒmplɪ'mentri/ ADJ **1** (*formal*) **Complementary** things are different from each other but make a good combination. ❏ *To improve the quality of life through work, two complementary strategies are necessary.* ❏ *He has done experiments complementary to those of Eigen.* **2** [complementary + N] **Complementary** medicine refers to ways of treating patients which are different from the ones used by most Western doctors, for example acupuncture and homeopathy. = alternative ❏ *combining orthodox treatment with a wide range of complementary therapies*

✪ **com·plete** ♦♦♦ /kəm'pliːt/ ADJ, VERB **ADJ** **1** (*emphasis*) You use **complete** to emphasize that something is as great in extent, degree, or amount as it possibly can be. = total, absolute ❏ *The house is a complete mess.* ❏ *The rebels had taken complete control.* ❏ *The resignation came as a complete surprise.* **2** [complete + N] (*emphasis*) You can use **complete** to emphasize that you are referring to the whole of something and not just part of it. = entire, whole ❏ *A complete apartment complex was burned to the ground.* **3** If something is **complete**, it contains all the parts that it should contain. ❏ *The list may not be complete.* ❏ *a complete dinner service* **4** [complete + N] The **complete** works of a writer are all their books or poems published together in one book or as a set of books. ❏ *the Complete Works of William Shakespeare* **5** [V-LINK + complete] If something is **complete**, it has been finished. ❏ *The work of restoring the farmhouse is complete.*

PHRASE **complete with** If one thing comes **complete with** another, it has that thing as an extra or additional part. ❏ *The diary comes complete with a gold ballpoint pen.*

VERB [T] (**completes, completing, completed**) **1** To **complete** a set or group means to provide the last item that is needed to make it a full set or group. ❏ *Children don't complete their set of 20 baby teeth until they are two to three years old.* **2** If you **complete** something, you finish doing, making, or producing it. ❏ *Peter Mayle has just completed his first novel.* ❏ *the rush to get the stadiums completed on time* **3** If you **complete** something, you do all of it. = finish ❏ *She completed her degree in two years.* ❏ *This book took years to complete.* **4** If you **complete** a form or questionnaire, you write the answers or information asked for in it. = fill in, fill out ❏ *Simply complete part 1 of the application.* ❏ *We ask candidates to complete a psychometric questionnaire.*

com·plete·ly /kəm'pliːtli/ ADV = totally ❏ *Dozens of homes had been completely destroyed.* ❏ *Make sure that you defrost it completely.*

✪ **com·ple·tion** /kəm'pliːʃən/ NOUN [C, U] (**completions**) ❏ *The project is nearing completion.* ❏ *House completions for the year should be up from 1,841 to 2,200.*

✪ **com·plex** ♦♦◇ /'kɒmpleks/ ADJ, NOUN (*academic word*) **ADJ** Something that is **complex** has many different parts, and is therefore often difficult to understand. = complicated, intricate ❏ *in-depth coverage of today's complex issues* ❏ *a complex system of voting* ❏ *complex machines*

NOUN [C] (**complexes**) A **complex** is a group of buildings designed for a particular purpose, or one large building divided into several smaller areas. ❏ *a low-cost apartment complex*

com·plex·ion /kəm'plekʃən/ NOUN [C] (**complexions**) When you refer to someone's **complexion**, you are referring to the natural colour or condition of the skin on their face. ❏ *She had short brown hair and a pale complexion.*

C

com·plex·ity /kəm'pleksɪti/ NOUN [U] **Complexity** is the state of having many different parts connected or related to each other in a complicated way. ❑ *a diplomatic tangle of great complexity*

✪ **com·pli·ance** /kəm'plaɪəns/ NOUN [U] (*formal*) **Compliance with** something, for example a law, treaty, or agreement, means doing what you are required or expected to do. ❑ *Inspectors were sent to visit nuclear sites and verify compliance with the treaty.* ❑ *The company says it is in full compliance with U.S. labor laws.* ❑ *The Security Council aim to ensure compliance by all sides, once an agreement is signed.*

com·pli·cate /'kɒmplɪkeɪt/ VERB [T] (**complicates, complicating, complicated**) To **complicate** something means to make it more difficult to understand or deal with. ❑ *What complicates the issue is the burden of history.* ❑ *The day's events, he said, would only complicate the task of the peacekeeping forces.*

com·pli·cat·ed ◆◇◇ /'kɒmplɪkeɪtɪd/ ADJ If you say that something is **complicated**, you mean it has so many parts or aspects that it is difficult to understand or deal with. = complex ❑ *The situation in Lebanon is very complicated.*

com·pli·ca·tion /ˌkɒmplɪ'keɪʃən/ NOUN [C] (**complications**) **1** A **complication** is a problem or difficulty that makes a situation harder to deal with. ❑ *The age difference was a complication to the relationship.* ❑ *There are too many complications to explain now.* **2** A **complication** is a medical problem that occurs as a result of another illness or disease. ❑ *Blindness is a common complication of diabetes.*

com·pli·ment NOUN, VERB
NOUN /'kɒmplɪmənt/ [C] (**compliments**) A **compliment** is a polite remark that you make to someone to show that you like their appearance, appreciate their qualities, or approve of what they have done. ❑ *You can do no harm by paying a woman compliments.*
VERB /'kɒmplɪment/ [T] (**compliments, complimenting, complimented**) If you **compliment** someone, you give them a compliment. ❑ *They complimented me on the way I looked each time they saw me.*

com·pli·men·tary /ˌkɒmplɪ'mentəri/ ADJ **1** If you are **complimentary** about something, you express admiration for it. = flattering ❑ *The staff have been very complimentary, and so have the customers.* **2** A **complimentary** seat, ticket, or book is given to you free. ❑ *He had complimentary tickets to take his wife to see the movie.*

✪ **com·ply** /kəm'plaɪ/ VERB [I] (**complies, complying, complied**) (*academic word*) If someone or something **complies with** an order or set of rules, they do what is required or expected. ❑ *The commander said that the army would comply with the ceasefire.* ❑ *Some beaches had failed to comply with environmental regulations.*

✪ **com·po·nent** ◆◇◇ /kəm'pəʊnənt/ NOUN, ADJ (*academic word*)
NOUN [C] (**components**) The **components** of something are the parts that it is made of. ❑ *Enriched uranium is a key component of a nuclear weapon.* ❑ *The management plan has four main components.* ❑ *automotive component suppliers to motor manufacturers*
ADJ [component + N] The **component** parts of something are the parts that make it up. ❑ *Gorbachev failed to keep the component parts of the Soviet Union together.*

✪ **com·pose** /kəm'pəʊz/ VERB [T, I] (**composes, composing, composed**) **1** [T] The things that something **is composed of** are its parts or members. The separate things that **compose** something are the parts or members that form it. = make up ❑ *The force would be composed of troops from NATO countries.* ❑ *Protein molecules compose all the complex working parts of living cells.* ❑ *They agreed to form a council composed of leaders of the rival factions.* **2** [I, T] When someone **composes** a piece of music or **composes**, they write music. = write ❑ *Vivaldi composed a large number of very fine concertos.* ❑ *Cale also uses electronic keyboards to compose.* **3** [T] (*formal*) If you **compose**

something such as a letter, poem, or speech, you write it, often using a lot of concentration or skill. ❑ *He started at once to compose a reply to Anna.*

✪ **com·pos·er** /kəm'pəʊzə/ NOUN [C] (**composers**) A **composer** is a person who writes music, especially classical music. ❑ *music by Strauss, Mozart, Beethoven, and other great composers* ❑ *an opera written by the German composer Richard Wagner*

com·po·site /'kɒmpəzɪt, AmE kəm'pɑːzɪt/ ADJ, NOUN
ADJ A **composite** object or item is made up of several different things, parts, or substances. ❑ *Galton devised a method of creating composite pictures in which the features of different faces were superimposed over one another.*
NOUN [C] (**composites**) [usu sing, oft composite 'of' N] A **composite** is made up of several different things, parts, or substances. ❑ *Cuba is a composite of diverse traditions and people.*

✪ **com·po·si·tion** /ˌkɒmpə'zɪʃən/ NOUN [U, C] (**compositions**) **1** [U] When you talk about the **composition** of something, you are referring to the way in which its various parts are put together and arranged. = make-up ❑ *Television has transformed the size and social composition of the audience at great sporting occasions.* ❑ *Forests vary greatly in composition from one part of the country to another.* **2** [C] The **compositions** of a composer, painter, or other artist are the works of art that they have produced. ❑ *Mozart's compositions are undoubtedly among the world's greatest.* **3** [C] A **composition** is a piece of written work that children write at school. ❑ *We had to write a composition on the subject 'My Pet'.*

com·post /'kɒmpɒst, AmE -pəʊst/ NOUN, VERB
NOUN [U, C] (**composts**) **1** [U] **Compost** is a mixture of decayed plants and vegetable waste which is added to the soil to help plants grow. ❑ *a small compost heap* **2** [C, U] **Compost** is specially treated soil that you buy and use to grow seeds and plants in pots. ❑ *a 75-pound bag of compost*
VERB [T] (**composts, composting, composted**) To **compost** things such as unwanted bits of plants means to make them into compost.

com·po·sure /kəm'pəʊʒə/ NOUN [U] (*formal*) **Composure** is the appearance or feeling of calm and the ability to control your feelings. ❑ *She was a little nervous at first but she soon regained her composure.*

✪ **com·pound** NOUN, ADJ, VERB (*academic word*)
NOUN /'kɒmpaʊnd/ [C] (**compounds**) **1** A **compound** is an enclosed area of land that is used for a particular purpose. = enclosure ❑ *They took refuge in the embassy compound.* ❑ *a military compound* **2** In chemistry, a **compound** is a substance that consists of two or more elements. ❑ *Organic compounds contain carbon in their molecules.* **3** (*formal*) If something is a **compound of** different things, it consists of those things. = mixture ❑ *Honey is basically a compound of water, two types of sugar, vitamins and enzymes.*
ADJ /'kɒmpaʊnd/ **1** [compound + N] **Compound** is used to indicate that something consists of two or more parts or things. = composite ❑ *the big compound eyes of dragonflies* **2** [compound + N] In grammar, a **compound** noun, adjective, or verb is one that is made up of two or more words, for example 'fire engine', 'bottle-green', and 'firelight'.
VERB /kəm'paʊnd/ [T] (**compounds, compounding, compounded**) To **compound** a problem, difficulty, or mistake means to make it worse by adding to it. ❑ *Additional loss of life will only compound the tragedy.* ❑ *The problem is compounded by the medical system here.*

✪ **com·pre·hend** /ˌkɒmprɪ'hend/ VERB [I, T] (**comprehends, comprehending, comprehended**) (*formal*) If you cannot **comprehend** something, you cannot understand it. = understand ❑ *I just cannot comprehend your attitude.* ❑ *Patients may not be mentally focused enough to comprehend the full significance of the diagnosis.*

✪ **com·pre·hen·sion** /ˌkɒmprɪ'henʃən/ NOUN [U] (*formal*) **1** **Comprehension** is the ability to understand something. = understanding ❑ *This was utterly beyond her comprehension.* ❑ *a devastating and barbaric act that defies all comprehension* **2** **Comprehension** is full knowledge and understanding of the meaning of something. ❑ *They turned to one another with the same expression of dawning comprehension, surprise, and relief.* ❑ *They have no comprehension of the complexities of law.*

✪ **com·pre·hen·sive** ♦◇◇ /ˌkɒmprɪˈhensɪv/ ADJ (*academic word*) Something that is **comprehensive** includes everything that is needed or relevant. = complete, full, thorough; ≠ partial, limited ❑ *The Rough Guide to Nepal is a comprehensive guide to the region.* ❑ *The first step involves a comprehensive analysis of the job.*

✪ **com·pre·hen·sive·ly** /ˌkɒmprɪˈhensɪvli/ ADV Something that is done **comprehensively** is done thoroughly. = fully, thoroughly, completely; ≠ partially ❑ *She was comprehensively outplayed by Coetzer.* ❑ *This section is not intended to comprehensively cover all possible infectious conditions relating to fatigue.* ❑ *the book is comprehensively illustrated*

com·press /kəmˈpres/ VERB [I, T] (**compresses, compressing, compressed**) **1** [I, T] When you **compress** something or when it **compresses**, it is pressed or squeezed so that it takes up less space. ❑ *Poor posture, sitting or walking slouched over, compresses the body's organs.* **2** [T] If you **compress** something such as a piece of writing or a description, you make it shorter. = condense ❑ *He never understood how to organize or compress large masses of material.* **3** [T] If an event **is compressed** into a short space of time, it is given less time to happen than normal or previously. ❑ *The four debates will be compressed into an eight-day period.*

com·pres·sion /kəmˈpreʃən/ NOUN [U] ❑ *The compression of the wood is easily achieved.*

✪ **com·prise** /kəmˈpraɪz/ VERB [T] (**comprises, comprising, comprised**) (*academic word, formal*) If you say that something **comprises** or **is comprised of** a number of things or people, you mean it has them as its parts or members. ❑ *The special cabinet committee comprises Mr Brown, Mr Mandelson, and Mr Straw.* ❑ *The task force is comprised of congressional leaders, cabinet heads and administration officials.*

WHICH WORD?
comprise, consist, or make up?

You say that something **comprises** particular things when you are mentioning all its parts.
❑ *The village's social facilities **comprised** one cafe and a church hall.*

If you say that one thing **consists of** other things, you mean that those things combine to form it. For example, if a book **consists of** twelve chapters, there are twelve chapters in the book.
❑ *The committee **consists of** scientists and engineers.*

You can also say that something **is made up of** other things. This has the same meaning as **consist of**, but it is slightly less formal.
❑ *All substances **are made up of** molecules.*

✪ **com·pro·mise** ♦◇◇ /ˈkɒmprəmaɪz/ NOUN, VERB
NOUN [C, U] (**compromises**) A **compromise** is a situation in which people accept something slightly different from what they really want, because of circumstances or because they are considering the wishes of other people. = agreement, settlement; ≠ disagreement ❑ *Encourage your child to reach a compromise between what he wants and what you want.* ❑ *Every side makes compromises and concessions in order to reach an agreement.* ❑ *The government's policy of compromise is not universally popular.* **VERB** [RECIP, T] (**compromises, compromising, compromised**) **1** [RECIP] If you **compromise with** someone, you reach an agreement with them in which you both give up something that you originally wanted. You can also say that two people or groups **compromise**. = concede ❑ *The government has compromised with its critics over monetary policies.* ❑ *'Nine,' I said. 'Nine thirty,' he replied. We compromised on 9.15.* **2** [T] If someone **compromises** themselves or **compromises** their beliefs, they do something which damages their reputation for honesty, loyalty, or high moral principles. ❑ *members of the government who*

have compromised themselves by accepting bribes

com·pro·mis·ing /ˈkɒmprəmaɪzɪŋ/ ADJ If you describe information or a situation as **compromising**, you mean that it reveals an embarrassing or guilty secret about someone. ❑ *How had this compromising picture come into the possession of the press?*

com·pul·sion /kəmˈpʌlʃən/ NOUN [C, U] (**compulsions**) **1** [C] A **compulsion** is a strong desire to do something, which you find difficult to control. = urge ❑ *He felt a sudden compulsion to drop the bucket and run.* **2** [U] If someone uses **compulsion** in order to get you to do something, they force you to do it, for example by threatening to punish you if you do not do it. = coercion ❑ *Many universities argued that students learned more when they were in classes out of choice rather than compulsion.*

com·pul·sive /kəmˈpʌlsɪv/ ADJ **1** [compulsive + N] You use **compulsive** to describe people or their behaviour when they cannot stop doing something wrong, harmful, or unnecessary. ❑ *a compulsive liar* ❑ *He was a compulsive gambler and often heavily in debt.* **2** If a book or television programme is **compulsive**, it is so interesting that you do not want to stop reading or watching it. ❑ *Her new series is compulsive viewing.*

✪ **com·pul·so·ry** /kəmˈpʌlsəri/ ADJ If something is **compulsory**, you must do it or accept it, because it is the law or because someone in a position of authority says you must. = mandatory ❑ *In East Germany learning Russian was compulsory.* ❑ *Many companies ask workers to accept voluntary redundancy as opposed to compulsory redundancy.*
✪ **com·pul·so·ri·ly** /kəmˈpʌlsərɪli/ ADV ≠ voluntarily ❑ *Five of the company's senior managers have been made compulsorily redundant.* ❑ *abandon plans to impose the system compulsorily*

✪ **com·put·er** ♦♦◇ /kəmˈpjuːtə/ NOUN [C] (**computers**) (*academic word*) [also 'by/on' computer] A **computer** is an electronic machine that can store and deal with large amounts of information. ❑ *The data are then fed into a computer.* ❑ *The company installed a $650,000 computer system.* ❑ *The car was designed by computer.*
→ See also **personal computer**

WORD CONNECTIONS

VERB + **computer**

use a computer
access a computer
program a computer
❑ *Most students use a computer for homework.*

ADJ + **computer**

a **personal** computer
❑ *Each piece of software is guaranteed to be compatible with every personal computer used in the university.*

NOUN + **computer**

a **laptop** computer
a **desktop** computer
a **notebook** computer
❑ *Laptop computers are a target for thieves because they are easily portable.*

computer + NOUN

computer **software**
computer **hardware**
computer **technology**
❑ *Computer technology has revolutionized the way we work.*

a computer **system**
a computer **network**
a computer **screen**
a computer **game**
a computer **program**
❑ *If you sit at a computer screen all day, you need to find time to exercise.*

---

com·put·er·ize /kəmˈpjuːtəraɪz/ also **computerise** VERB [T] (**computerizes, computerizing, computerized**) To **computerize** a system, process, or type of work means to arrange for a lot of the work to be done by computer. ❑ *I'm trying to make a spreadsheet up to computerize everything that's done by hand at the moment.*

✪com•put•er•ized /kəm'pjuːtəraɪzd/ also **computerised** ADJ **1** A **computerized** system, process, or business is one in which the work is done by computer. ❑ *The National Cancer Institute now has a computerized system that can quickly provide information.* **2 Computerized** information is stored on a computer. ❑ *Computerized databases are proliferating fast.*

✪computer science NOUN [U] **Computer science** is the study of computers and their application. ❑ *a professor of computer science at MIT* ❑ *theoretical work in computer science*

✪computer scientist NOUN [C] (**computer scientists**) ❑ *Computer scientists have devised a simple system to query these databases.* ❑ *a computer scientist at the University of Minnesota*

com•pu•ting /kəm'pjuːtɪŋ/ NOUN, ADJ
NOUN [U] **Computing** is the activity of using a computer and writing programs for it. ❑ *Courses range from cooking to computing.*
ADJ [computing + N] **Computing** means relating to computers and their use. ❑ *Many graduates are employed in the electronics and computing industries.*

con /kɒn/ VERB, NOUN
VERB [T] (**cons, conning, conned**) (*informal*) If someone **cons** you, they persuade you to do something or believe something by telling you things that are not true. = cheat, trick ❑ *He claimed that the businessman had conned him of $10,000.* ❑ *White conned his way into a job as a warehouseman with Dutch airline, KLM.*
NOUN [C] (**cons**) (*informal*) A **con** is a trick in which someone deceives you by telling you something that is not true. ❑ *Snacks that offer miraculous weight loss are a con.*
✦ pros and cons → see pro

con•ceal /kən'siːl/ VERB [T] (**conceals, concealing, concealed**) **1** If you **conceal** something, you cover it or hide it carefully. ❑ *Frances decided to conceal the machine behind a hinged panel.* **2** If you **conceal** a piece of information or a feeling, you do not let other people know about it. ❑ *Robert could not conceal his relief.* **3** If something **conceals** something else, it covers it and prevents it from being seen. ❑ *a pair of carved Indian doors which conceal a built-in cupboard*

con•cede ✦◇◇ /kən'siːd/ VERB [T] (**concedes, conceding, conceded**) **1** If you **concede** something, you admit, often unwillingly, that it is true or correct. ❑ *Bess finally conceded that Nancy was right.* ❑ *'Well,' he conceded, 'I do sometimes mumble a bit.'* **2** If you **concede** something to someone, you allow them to have it as a right or privilege. = cede ❑ *Poland's Communist government conceded the right to establish independent trade unions.* **3** If you **concede** something, you give it to the person who has been trying to get it from you. ❑ *The strike by bank employees ended after employers conceded some of their demands.* **4** If you **concede** a game, contest, or argument, you end it by admitting that you can no longer win. ❑ *Reiner, 56, has all but conceded the race to his rival.* **5** If you **concede** defeat, you accept that you have lost a struggle. = accept ❑ *She has conceded defeat in her bid for the Democratic Party's nomination for governor.*

✪con•ceiv•able /kən'siːvəbəl/ ADJ If something is **conceivable**, you can imagine it or believe it. ❑ *Without their support, the project would not have been conceivable.* ❑ *Through the centuries, flowers have been used for cooking in every conceivable way.*
✪con•ceiv•ably /kən'siːvəbli/ ADV ❑ *The mission could conceivably be accomplished within a week.* ❑ *A series of interest-rate rises might conceivably affect buyers' confidence at the upper end of the market.*

✪con•ceive /kən'siːv/ VERB [I, T] (**conceives, conceiving, conceived**) (*academic word*) **1** [I, T] If you cannot **conceive** of something, you cannot imagine it or believe in it. ❑ *I just can't even conceive of that quantity of money.* ❑ *Western leaders could not conceive of the idea that there might be traitors at high levels in their own governments.* ❑ *We could not*

conceive that he might soon be dead. **2** [I, T] If you **conceive** something **as** a particular thing, you consider it to be that thing. ❑ *The ancients conceived the earth as afloat in water.* ❑ *We conceive of the family as being in a constant state of change.* ❑ *She cannot conceive of herself being anything else but a doctor.* **3** [T] If you **conceive** a plan or idea, you think of it and work out how it can be done. ❑ *She had conceived the idea of a series of novels, each of which would reveal some aspect of Chinese life.* **4** [I, T] When a woman **conceives** a child or **conceives**, she becomes pregnant. ❑ *Women, he says, should give up alcohol before they plan to conceive.*

✪con•cen•trate ✦◇◇ /'kɒnsəntreɪt/ VERB [I, T] (**concentrates, concentrating, concentrated**) (*academic word*) **1** [I, T] If you **concentrate on** something, or **concentrate** your mind on it, you give all your attention to it. ❑ *It was up to him to concentrate on his studies and make something of himself.* ❑ *At work you need to be able to concentrate.* **2** [T] If you **concentrate** something **in** an area or if it **is concentrated** there, it is all in that area rather than being spread around. = gather, collect; ≠ scatter, spread ❑ *Italy's industrial districts are concentrated in its north-central and northeastern regions.* ❑ *The Party should concentrate resources at local rather than national level.*

con•cen•trat•ed /'kɒnsəntreɪtɪd/ ADJ **1** A **concentrated** liquid has been increased in strength by having water removed from it. ❑ *Sweeten dishes sparingly with honey, or concentrated apple or pear juice.* **2** A **concentrated** activity is directed with great intensity in one place. = concerted ❑ *a more concentrated effort to reach out to troubled kids*

✪con•cen•tra•tion ✦◇◇ /ˌkɒnsən'treɪʃən/ NOUN [U, C] (**concentrations**) **1** [U] **Concentration on** something involves giving all your attention to it. ❑ *Neal kept interrupting, breaking my concentration.* **2** [C, U] A **concentration of** something is a large amount of it or large numbers of it in a small area. ❑ *The area has one of the world's greatest concentrations of wildlife.* ❑ *There's been too much concentration of power in the hands of central authorities.* **3** [C, U] The **concentration of** a substance is the proportion of essential ingredients or substances in it. ❑ *pH is a measure of the concentration of free hydrogen atoms in a solution.* ❑ *Global ozone concentrations had dropped over the last decade.*

WORD CONNECTIONS

VERB + **concentration**

lose concentration
require concentration
need concentration
aid concentration

❑ *The job requires concentration, so do it when you are not tired.*

concentration + OF + NOUN

a concentration **of power**
a concentration **of wealth**

❑ *The concentration of wealth is in the south of the country.*

ADJ + **concentration**

a **high** concentration
a **low** concentration
a **dense** concentration
a **heavy** concentration

❑ *It's an area with a high concentration of people on low incomes.*

✪con•cept ✦◇◇ /'kɒnsept/ NOUN [C] (**concepts**) (*academic word*) A **concept** is an idea or abstract principle. = notion ❑ *She added that the concept of arranged marriages is misunderstood in the west.* ❑ *basic legal concepts*

con•cep•tion /kən'sepʃən/ NOUN [C, U] (**conceptions**) **1** A **conception** of something is an idea that you have of it in your mind. = notion ❑ *My conception of a garden was based on gardens I had visited in England.* **2 Conception** is the process in which the egg in a woman is fertilized and she becomes pregnant. ❑ *Six weeks after conception, your baby is the size of your little fingernail.*

✪con·cern ♦♦♦ /kən'sɜːn/ NOUN, VERB

NOUN [U, C, SING] **(concerns)** **1** [U] **Concern** is worry about a situation. ◻ *The group has expressed concern about reports of political violence in Africa.* ◻ *The move follows growing public concern over the spread of the disease.* **2** [C] A **concern** is a fact or situation that worries you. = worry ◻ *His concern was that people would know that he was responsible.* **3** [C] *(formal, business)* You can refer to a company or business as a **concern**, usually when you are describing what type of company or business it is. ◻ *If not a large concern, the Potomac Nursery was at least a successful one.* **4** [C, U] **Concern for** someone is a feeling that you want them to be happy, safe, and well. If you do something out of **concern for** someone, you do it because you want them to be happy, safe, and well. ◻ *Without her care and concern, he had no chance at all.* **5** [SING] If a situation or problem is your **concern**, it is something that you have a duty or responsibility to be involved with. = affair, business ◻ *The technical aspects were the concern of the Army.*

PHRASE going concern *(business)* If a company is a **going concern**, it is actually doing business, rather than having stopped trading or not yet having started trading. ◻ *The receivers will always prefer to sell a business as a going concern.*

VERB [T] **(concerns, concerning, concerned)** **1** If something **concerns** you, it worries you. ◻ *The growing number of people seeking refuge in Thailand is beginning to concern Western aid agencies.* **2** If you **concern yourself with** something, you give it attention because you think that it is important. ◻ *I didn't concern myself with politics.* **3** If something such as a book or a piece of information **concerns** a particular subject, it is about that subject. = cover, relate to ◻ *The bulk of the book concerns Sandy's two middle-aged children.* ◻ *The proceedings concern the fraudulent offer and sale of over $2.1 billion in municipal securities.* **4** If a situation, event, or activity **concerns** you, it affects or involves you. ◻ *It was just a little unfinished business from my past, and it doesn't concern you at all.*

✪con·cerned ♦♦◊ /kən'sɜːnd/ ADJ [V-LINK + concerned + to-INF] If you are **concerned to** do something, you want to do it because you think it is important. ◻ *We are deeply concerned to get out of this problematic situation.*
→ See **concern**

WHICH WORD?
concerned, related, or relevant?

Do not confuse **concerned**, **related**, and **relevant**.

If a book, speech, or piece of information **is concerned** with a subject, it deals with it.
◻ *This chapter **is concerned** with changes that are likely to take place.*

If something is **related** to something else, the two things are connected in some way.
◻ *Physics is closely **related** to mathematics.*

Something that is **relevant**, or **relevant** to a situation or person is important or significant in that situation or to that person.
◻ *Only checks that are strictly **relevant** to the post should be made.*

USAGE NOTE
concerned

The adjective **concerned** is usually used after the verb 'be'. Do not use 'I concerned'.

*He **was concerned** about the level of unemployment.*

✪con·cern·ing /kən'sɜːnɪŋ/ PREP, ADJ

PREP *(formal)* You use **concerning** to indicate what a question or piece of information is about. = about, regarding ◻ *For more information concerning the club, contact Mr Coldwell.* ◻ *a large body of research concerning the relationship between anger and health* ◻ *various questions concerning pollution and the environment*

ADJ [usu 'it' V-LINK + concerning 'that'] If something is **concerning**, it causes you to feel concerned about it. ◻ *It is particularly concerning that he is working for foreign companies while advising on foreign policy.*

con·cert ♦◊◊ /'kɒnsət/ NOUN

NOUN [C] **(concerts)** A **concert** is a performance of music. ◻ *a short concert of piano music* ◻ *I've been to plenty of live rock concerts.*

PHRASE in concert If a musician or group of musicians appears **in concert**, they are giving a live performance. ◻ *I want people to remember Elvis in concert.*

con·cert·ed /kən'sɜːtɪd/ ADJ **1** [concerted + N] A **concerted** action is done by several people or groups working together. ◻ *Martin Parry, author of the report, says it's time for concerted action by world leaders.* **2** [concerted + N] If you make a **concerted** effort to do something, you try very hard to do it. = concentrated ◻ *He made a concerted effort to win me away from my steady, sweet but boring boyfriend.*

WORD PARTS

The prefix **con-** often appears in words that have 'with' or 'together' as part of their meaning:

concerted (ADJ)
connect (VERB)
contain (VERB)

---

con·ces·sion ♦◊◊ /kən'seʃən/ NOUN [C] **(concessions)** **1** If you make a **concession to** someone, you agree to let them do or have something, especially in order to end an argument or conflict. ◻ *We made too many concessions and we got too little in return.* **2** A **concession** is a special right or privilege that is given to someone. ◻ *Farmers were granted concessions from the government to develop the farms.* **3** *(mainly AmE; in BrE, usually use franchise; business)* A **concession** is an arrangement where someone is given the right to sell a product or to run a business, especially in a building belonging to another business. ◻ *the man who ran the catering concession at the Rob Roy Links in Palominas*

con·cili·ation /kənˌsɪli'eɪʃən/ NOUN [U] **Conciliation** is willingness to end a disagreement or the process of ending a disagreement. ◻ *Resolving the dispute will require a mood of conciliation on both sides.*

con·cilia·tory /kən'sɪliətri, AmE -tɔːri/ ADJ When you are **conciliatory** in your actions or behaviour, you show that you are willing to end a disagreement with someone. ◻ *The next time he spoke, he used a more conciliatory tone.*

✪con·cise /kən'saɪs/ ADJ **1** Something that is **concise** says everything that is necessary without using any unnecessary words. = succinct, brief ◻ *Burton's text is concise and informative.* ◻ *Whatever you are writing make sure you are clear, concise, and accurate.* **2** [concise + N] A **concise** edition of a book, especially a dictionary, is shorter than the original edition. ◻ *Sotheby's Concise Encyclopedia of Porcelain* **✪con·cise·ly** /kən'saɪsli/ ADV [concisely with V] ◻ *He'd delivered his report clearly and concisely.*

✪con·clude ♦◊◊ /kən'kluːd/ VERB [T, I] **(concludes, concluding, concluded)** *(academic word)* **1** [T] If you **conclude that** something is true, you decide that it is true using the facts you know as a basis. = decide, judge ◻ *Larry had concluded that he had no choice but to accept Paul's words as the truth.* ◻ *So what can we conclude from this debate?* **2** [I, T] *(formal)* When you **conclude**, you say the last thing that you are going to say. = end, close, finish ◻ *'It's a waste of time,' he concluded.* ◻ *I would like to conclude by saying that I do enjoy your magazine.* **3** [I, T] *(formal)* When something **concludes**, or when you **conclude** it, you end it. = end ◻ *The evening concluded with dinner and speeches.* **4** [T] *(formal)* If one person or group **concludes** an agreement, such as a treaty or business deal, **with** another, they arrange it. You can also say that two people or groups **conclude** an agreement. ◻ *Mexico and the Philippines have both concluded agreements with their commercial bank creditors.*

VOCABULARY BUILDER

conclude VERB *(formal)*

When something **concludes**, or when you **conclude** it, you end it.
◻ *The report concluded that it was impossible to estimate his wealth.*

C

end VERB

When a situation, process, or activity **ends**, or when something or someone **ends** it, it reaches its final point and stops.
❑ *By the time the national anthem ended, tears were streaming down her cheeks.*

close VERB

To **close** a conversation, event, or matter means to bring it to its final point and complete it.
❑ *The gospel choir of 100 singers and full band will close the concert.*

finish VERB

When something **finishes**, or when you **finish** it, it comes to a final point and there is nothing more to do or to happen.
❑ *Interestingly, Kennedy finished the book six months after his son Max was born.*

✪**con·clu·sion** ◆◇◇ /kən'kluːʒən/ NOUN
[NOUN] [C, SING] (conclusions) **1** [C] When you come to a **conclusion**, you decide that something is true after you have thought about it carefully and have considered all the relevant facts. = decision, opinion ❑ *Over the years I've come to the conclusion that she's a very great musician.* ❑ *I have tried to give some idea of how I feel – other people will no doubt draw their own conclusions.* **2** [SING] The **conclusion** of something is its ending. = end ❑ *At the conclusion of the programme, I asked the children if they had any questions they wanted to ask me.* ❑ *The function of the essay's conclusion is to restate the main argument.* ❑ *Your essay lacks only two paragraphs now: the introduction and the conclusion.* **3** [SING] The **conclusion** of a treaty or a business deal is the act of arranging it or agreeing on it. ❑ *the expected conclusion of a free-trade agreement between Mexico and the United States*
[PHRASE] **in conclusion** You say '**in conclusion**' to indicate that what you are about to say is the last thing that you want to say. ❑ *In conclusion, walking is a cheap, safe, enjoyable, and readily available form of exercise.*

✪**con·clu·sive** /kən'kluːsɪv/ ADJ (academic word)
Conclusive evidence shows that something is certainly true. ≠ inconclusive ❑ *Her attorneys claim there is no conclusive evidence that any murders took place.* ❑ *Research on the matter is far from conclusive.*
✪**con·clu·sive·ly** /kən'kluːsɪvli/ ADV ❑ *A new study proved conclusively that smokers die younger than non-smokers.* ❑ *By 1 October they had conclusively established the existence of the antiparticle.*

con·coct /kən'kɒkt/ VERB [T] (concocts, concocting, concocted) **1** If you **concoct** an excuse or explanation, you invent one that is not true. ❑ *Mr Ferguson said the prisoner concocted the story to get a lighter sentence.* **2** If you **concoct** something, especially something unusual, you make it by mixing several things together. ❑ *Eugene was concocting Rossini cocktails from champagne and pureed raspberries.*

con·coc·tion /kən'kɒkʃən/ NOUN [C] (concoctions) A **concoction** is something that has been made out of several things mixed together. ❑ *a concoction of honey, yogurt, oats, and apples*

✪**con·crete** ◆◇◇ /'kɒŋkriːt/ NOUN, VERB, ADJ
[NOUN] [U] **Concrete** is a substance used for building which is made by mixing together cement, sand, small stones, and water. ❑ *The posts have to be set in concrete.* ❑ *We sat on the concrete floor.*
[VERB] [T] (concretes, concreting, concreted) When you **concrete** something such as a path, you cover it with concrete. ❑ *He merely cleared and concreted the floors.*
[ADJ] **1** You use **concrete** to indicate that something is definite and specific. = specific, precise, definite; ≠ vague ❑ *I had no concrete evidence.* ❑ *There were no concrete proposals on the table.* **2** A **concrete** object is a real, physical object. = real, material, actual; ≠ abstract ❑ *using concrete objects to teach addition and subtraction* **3** [concrete + N] A **concrete** noun is a noun that refers to a physical object rather than to a quality or idea.

concrete ADJ
You use **concrete** to indicate that information is definite and specific, and can be trusted.
❑ *Even so, the authorities needed more concrete evidence to prove murder.*

specific ADJ
You use **specific** to refer to a particular exact area, problem, or subject.
❑ *It is a fiction that antidepressant drugs target specific areas of the brain.*

precise ADJ
You use **precise** to emphasize that you are referring to an exact thing, rather than something vague.
❑ *Officials would not give the precise location of the airfield or the number of troops involved.*

definite ADJ
Definite evidence or information is true, rather than being someone's opinion or guess.
❑ *We've no definite proof either way that aliens do or don't exist.*

con·cur /kən'kɜː/ VERB [RECIP] (concurs, concurring, concurred) (formal) If one person **concurs with** another person, the two people agree. You can also say that two people **concur**. = agree ❑ *Local feeling does not necessarily concur with the press.* ❑ *Daniels and Franklin concurred in an investigator's suggestion that the police be commended.*

✪**con·cur·rent** /kən'kʌrənt, AmE -'kɜːr-/ ADJ (academic word) **Concurrent** events or situations happen at the same time. ❑ *Galerie St Etienne is holding three concurrent exhibitions.* ❑ *He will actually be serving three concurrent five-year sentences.* ❑ *free web access concurrent with paper publication*
✪**con·cur·rent·ly** /kən'kʌrəntli, AmE -'kɜːr-/ ADV [concurrently with v] ❑ *He was jailed for 33 months to run concurrently with a sentence he is already serving for burglary.* ❑ *It is unethical for human trials to run concurrently with chronic toxicity tests on animals.*

✪**con·demn** ◆◇◇ /kən'dem/ VERB [T] (condemns, condemning, condemned) **1** If you **condemn** something, you say that it is very bad and unacceptable. = denounce ❑ *Political leaders united yesterday to condemn the latest wave of violence.* ❑ *Graham was right to condemn his players for lack of ability, attitude, and application.* ❑ *a document that condemns sexism as a moral and social evil* **2** If someone **is condemned to** a punishment, they are given this punishment. = sentence ❑ *He was condemned to life imprisonment.* **3** If circumstances **condemn** you **to** an unpleasant situation, they make it certain that you will suffer in that way. = doom ❑ *Their lack of qualifications condemned them to a lifetime of boring, usually poorly-paid work.* **4** If authorities **condemn** a building, they officially decide that it is not safe and must be pulled down or repaired. ❑ *The court's ruling clears the way to condemn buildings in the area.*

✪**con·dem·na·tion** /ˌkɒndem'neɪʃən/ NOUN [C, U] (condemnations) **Condemnation** is the act of saying that something or someone is very bad and unacceptable. ❑ *There was widespread condemnation of Saturday's killings.* ❑ *The raids have drawn a strong condemnation from the United Nations Security Council.*

✪**con·den·sa·tion** /ˌkɒnden'seɪʃən/ NOUN [U] **Condensation** consists of small drops of water which form when warm water vapour or steam touches a cold surface such as a window. ❑ *He used his sleeve to wipe the condensation off the glass.* ❑ *Silicon carbide crystals are formed by the condensation of supersaturated vapour.*

✪**con·dense** /kən'dens/ VERB [T, I] (condenses, condensing, condensed) **1** [T] If you **condense** something, especially a piece of writing or a speech, you make it shorter, usually by including only the most important parts. ❑ *When you summarize, you condense an*

c

extended idea or argument into a sentence or more in your own words. **2** [I, T] When a gas or vapour **condenses**, or **is condensed**, it changes into a liquid. ❏ *Water vapour condenses to form clouds.* ❏ *The compressed gas is cooled and condenses into a liquid.* ❏ *As the air rises it becomes colder and moisture condenses out of it.*

✪ **con·di·tion** ♦♦♦ /kənˈdɪʃən/ NOUN, VERB

▣ NOUN [C, PL, SING] (**conditions**) **1** [C, PL, SING] [also no DET] If you talk about the **condition** of a person or thing, you are talking about the state that they are in, especially how good or bad their physical state is. = state ❏ *He remains in a critical condition in a California hospital.* ❏ *I received several compliments on the condition of my skin.* ❏ *The two-bedroom chalet is in good condition.* ❏ *Poor physical condition leaves you prone to injury.* **2** [PL] The **conditions** under which something is done or happens are all the factors or circumstances which directly affect it. = circumstances, situation ❏ *It's easy to make a wrong turn here even under ideal weather conditions.* ❏ *This change has been timed under laboratory conditions.* ❏ *The mild winter has created the ideal conditions for an ant population explosion.* **3** [PL] The **conditions** in which people live or work are the factors which affect their comfort, safety, or health. ❏ *People are living in appalling conditions.* ❏ *I could not work in these conditions any longer.* **4** [C] A **condition** is something which must happen or be done in order for something else to be possible, especially when this is written into a contract or law. = requirement ❏ *Argentina failed to hit the economic targets set as a condition for loan payments.* ❏ *terms and conditions of employment* ❏ *Egypt had agreed to a summit subject to certain conditions.* **5** [C] If someone has a particular **condition**, they have an illness or other medical problem. = complaint, disorder ❏ *Doctors suspect he may have a heart condition.*

▣ PHRASE **on condition that** When you agree to do something **on condition that** something else happens, you mean that you will only do it if this other thing also happens. ❏ *He agreed to speak to reporters on condition that he was not identified.*

▣ VERB [T] (**conditions, conditioning, conditioned**) If someone **is conditioned** by their experiences or environment, they are influenced by them over a period of time so that they do certain things or think in a particular way. ❏ *We are all conditioned by early impressions and experiences.* ❏ *I just feel women are conditioned into doing housework.*

con·di·tion·ing /kənˈdɪʃənɪŋ/ NOUN [U] ❏ *Because of social conditioning, men don't expect to be managed by women.*

✪ **con·di·tion·al** /kənˈdɪʃənəl/ ADJ **1** If a situation or agreement is **conditional on** something, it will only happen or continue if this thing happens. = dependent, qualified; ≠ unconditional ❏ *Their support is conditional on his proposals meeting their approval.* ❏ *a conditional offer* **2** [conditional + N] In grammar, a **conditional** clause is a subordinate clause which refers to a situation which may exist or happen. Most conditional clauses begin with 'if' or 'unless', for example 'If that happens, we'll be in big trouble.' and 'You don't have to come unless you want to.'

✪ **con·di·tion·al·ly** /kənˈdɪʃənəli/ ADV ≠ unconditionally ❏ *Mr Smith has conditionally agreed to buy a shareholding in the club.* ❏ *Although William conditionally accepted the offer, he disagreed with its principles.*

con·done /kənˈdəʊn/ VERB [T] (**condones, condoning, condoned**) If someone **condones** behaviour that is morally wrong, they accept it and allow it to happen. ❏ *I have never encouraged nor condoned violence.*

con·du·cive /kənˈdjuːsɪv, AmE -ˈduːsɪv/ ADJ If one thing is **conducive** to another thing, it makes the other thing likely to happen. ❏ *Make your bedroom as conducive to sleep as possible.*

✪ **con·duct** ♦♦◊ VERB, NOUN (*academic word*)

▣ VERB /kənˈdʌkt/ [T, I] (**conducts, conducting, conducted**) **1** [T] When you **conduct** an activity or task, you organize it and do it. = carry out, run, direct, manage, organize ❏ *I decided to conduct an experiment.* ❏ *He said they were conducting a campaign against democrats across the country.* **2** [T] If you **conduct** yourself in a particular way, you

behave in that way. ❏ *The way he conducts himself reflects on the family.* **3** [I, T] When someone **conducts** an orchestra or choir, they stand in front of it and direct its performance. ❏ *Dennis had recently begun a successful career conducting opera.* ❏ *Solti continued to conduct here and abroad.* **4** [T] If something **conducts** heat or electricity, it allows heat or electricity to pass through it or along it. ❏ *Water conducts heat faster than air.* ❏ *The molecule did not conduct electricity.*

▣ NOUN /ˈkɒndʌkt/ [SING, U] **1** [SING] The **conduct of** a task or activity is the way in which it is organized and carried out. ❏ *Also up for discussion will be the conduct of free and fair elections.* **2** [U] Someone's **conduct** is the way they behave in particular situations. = behavior ❏ *For Europeans, the law is a statement of basic principles of civilized conduct.*

VOCABULARY BUILDER

conduct VERB
When you **conduct** an activity or task, you organize it and do it.
❏ *The survey was conducted by representatives of local community health councils who visited 180 hospitals.*

carry out VERB
If you **carry out** a threat, task, or instruction, you do it or act according to it.
❏ *The committee said further research should be carried out before a final decision is made.*

run VERB
If you **run** something such as a business or an activity, you are in charge of it.
❏ *I ran a hostel for migrant Hispanic workers.*

direct VERB
When someone **directs** a project or a group of people, they are responsible for organizing the people and the activities that are involved.
❏ *He is currently directing a research project on poverty.*

organize VERB
If you **organize** an event or activity, you make sure that all the necessary arrangements for it are made.
❏ *A few weeks ago, my friend Curtis organized a bowling party for his birthday.*

manage VERB
If you **manage** an organization or system, or the people who work in it, you are responsible for controlling them.
❏ *He certainly had a high opinion of his own intelligence and his ability to manage a department.*

✪ **con·duc·tion** /kənˈdʌkʃən/ NOUN [U] [usu with SUPP] (*technical*) **Conduction** is the process by which heat or electricity passes through or along something.
❏ *Temperature becomes uniform by heat conduction until finally a permanent state is reached.* ❏ *best known for his work on the conduction of electricity by gases*

✪ **con·duc·tive** /kənˈdʌktɪv/ ADJ (*technical*) A **conductive** substance is able to conduct things such as heat and electricity. ❏ *Salt water is much more conductive than fresh water is.* ❏ *electrically conductive polymers*

con·duc·tiv·ity /ˌkɒndʌkˈtɪvɪti/ NOUN [U] ❏ *a device which monitors electrical conductivity*

✪ **con·duc·tor** /kənˈdʌktə/ NOUN [C] (**conductors**) **1** A **conductor** is a person who stands in front of an orchestra or choir and directs its performance. **2** On a tram or a bus, the **conductor** is the person whose job is to sell tickets to the passengers. **3** A **conductor** is a substance that heat or electricity can pass through or along. ❏ *Graphite is a highly efficient conductor of electricity.* ❏ *Because this channel is an electrical conductor, it provides a place for surrounding electrons to go.*

✪ **cone** /kəʊn/ NOUN [C] (**cones**) **1** A **cone** is a shape with a circular base ending in a point at the top. ❏ *orange traffic cones* ❏ *the streetlight's yellow cone of light* ❏ *The steady stream of sand falls to form a cone.* **2** A **cone** is the fruit of a tree such as a pine or fir. ❏ *a bowl of fir cones*

c

con·fed·er·a·tion /kən,fedə'reɪʃən/ NOUN [c] (confederations) A **confederation** is an organization or group consisting of smaller groups or states, especially one that exists for business or political purposes. ❑ *the Confederation of Indian Industry*

con·fer /kən'fɜː/ VERB [RECIP, T] (confers, conferring, conferred) (*academic word*) **1** [RECIP] When you **confer with** someone, you discuss something with them in order to make a decision. You can also say that two people **confer**. ❑ *He conferred with Hill and the others in his office.* **2** [T] (*formal*) To **confer** something such as power or an honour **on** someone means to give it to them. ❑ *The constitution also confers large powers on Brazil's 25 constituent states.*

❍ **con·fer·ence** ◆◆◆ /'kɒnfrəns/ NOUN [c] (conferences) (*academic word*) **1** A **conference** is a meeting, often lasting a few days, which is organized on a particular subject or to bring together people who have a common interest. = meeting ❑ *The president took the unprecedented step of summoning all the state governors to a conference on education.* ❑ *the Alternative Energy conference* ❑ *Last weekend the Roman Catholic Church in Scotland held a conference, attended by 450 delegates.* **2** [also 'in' conference] A **conference** is a meeting at which formal discussions take place. ❑ *They sat down at the dinner table for a conference.*
→ See also **press conference**

con·fess /kən'fes/ VERB [I, T] (confesses, confessing, confessed) **1** If someone **confesses** to doing something wrong, they admit that they did it. = admit ❑ *He had confessed to seventeen murders.* ❑ *I had expected her to confess that she only wrote these books for the money.* ❑ *Ray changed his mind, claiming that he had been forced into confessing.* **2** If someone **confesses** or **confesses** their sins, they tell God or a priest about their sins so that they can be forgiven. ❑ *You just go to the church and confess your sins.*

con·fes·sion /kən'feʃən/ NOUN [c, u] (confessions) **1** [c] A **confession** is a signed statement by someone in which they admit that they have committed a particular crime. ❑ *They forced him to sign a confession.* **2** [c, u] **Confession** is the act of admitting that you have done something that you are ashamed of or embarrassed about. ❑ *I have a confession to make.* ❑ *The diaries are a mixture of confession and observation.* **3** [c, u] If you make a **confession** of your beliefs or feelings, you publicly tell people that this is what you believe or feel. = declaration ❑ *Tatyana's confession of love* **4** [c, u] In the Catholic church and in some other churches, if you go to **confession**, you privately tell a priest about your sins and ask for forgiveness. ❑ *He never went to Father Porter for confession again.*

con·fide /kən'faɪd/ VERB [I, T] (confides, confiding, confided) If you **confide** in someone, you tell them a secret. ❑ *I knew she had some fundamental problems in her marriage because she had confided in me a year earlier.* ❑ *He confided to me that he felt like he was being punished.*

con·fi·dence ◆◆◇ /'kɒnfɪdəns/ NOUN
NOUN [u] **1** If you have **confidence** in someone, you feel that you can trust them. = faith ❑ *I have every confidence in you.* ❑ *This has contributed to the lack of confidence in the FDA.* **2** If you have **confidence**, you feel sure about your abilities, qualities, or ideas. ❑ *The band is in excellent form and brimming with confidence.* **3** If you can say something **with confidence**, you feel certain it is correct. ❑ *I can say with confidence that such rumours were totally groundless.* **4** If you tell someone something **in confidence**, you tell them a secret. ❑ *We told you all these things in confidence.* ❑ *Even telling Lois seemed a betrayal of confidence.*
PHRASE **take someone into one's confidence** If you **take** someone **into** your **confidence**, you tell them a secret.

con·fi·dent ◆◇◇ /'kɒnfɪdənt/ ADJ **1** If you are **confident** about something, you are certain that it will happen in the way you want it to. ❑ *I am confident that everything will come out right in time.* ❑ *Mr Ryan is confident of success.* **2** If a person or their manner is **confident**, they feel sure about their own abilities, qualities, or ideas. = self-assured ❑ *In time he became more confident and*

relaxed. **3** If you are **confident that** something is true, you are sure that it is true. A **confident** statement is one that the speaker is sure is true. ❑ *She is confident that everybody is on her side.*

con·fi·dent·ly /'kɒnfɪdəntli/ ADV **1** [confidently with v] ❑ *I can confidently promise that this year is going to be very different.* **2** She walked confidently across the hall. **3** [confidently with v] ❑ *I can confidently say that none of them were or are racist.*

con·fi·den·tial /,kɒnfɪ'denʃəl/ ADJ **1** Information that is **confidential** is meant to be kept secret or private. ❑ *She accused them of leaking confidential information about her private life.* **2** If you talk to someone in a **confidential** way, you talk to them quietly because what you are saying is secret or private. ❑ *'Look,' he said in a confidential tone, 'I want you to know that me and Joey are cops.'*

con·fi·den·ti·al·ity /,kɒnfɪdenʃi'æliti/ NOUN [u] ❑ *the confidentiality of the client-attorney relationship*

con·figu·ra·tion /kən,fɪgʊ'reɪʃən, AmE -,fɪgjə-/ NOUN [c, u] (configurations) **1** [c] (*formal*) A **configuration** is an arrangement of a group of things. ❑ *Stonehenge, in southwestern England, an ancient configuration of giant stones* **2** [u] (*computing*) The **configuration** of a computer system is the way in which all its parts, such as the hardware and software, are connected together in order for the computer to work. ❑ *Prices range from £399 to £899, depending on the particular configuration.*

con·fine /kən'faɪn/ VERB [T] (confines, confining, confined) (*academic word*) **1** To **confine** something **to** a particular place or group means to prevent it from spreading beyond that place or group. = restrict ❑ *Health officials have successfully confined the epidemic to the Tabatinga area.* **2** If you **confine** somebody or something, you prevent them from leaving or escaping. ❑ *He was confined in an internment camp in Utah.* ❑ *They decided not to let their new dog run loose, confining it to a fenced enclosure during the day.* **3** If you **confine yourself** or your activities **to** something, you do only that thing and are involved with nothing else. = limit, restrict ❑ *He did not confine himself to the one language.*

❍ **con·fined** /kən'faɪnd/ ADJ (*academic word*) **1** [V-LINK + confined 'to' N] If something is **confined to** a particular place, it exists only in that place. If it is **confined to** a particular group, only members of that group have it. = restricted, limited ❑ *The problem is not confined to Georgia.* ❑ *These dangers are not confined to smokers.* **2** A **confined** space or area is small and enclosed by walls. = enclosed ❑ *His long legs bent up in the confined space.* ❑ *The confined area of the crash site made rescue operations difficult* **3** [V-LINK + confined 'to' N] If someone is **confined to** a wheelchair, bed, or house, they have to stay there, because they are disabled or ill. ❑ *He had been confined to a wheelchair since childhood.*

con·fine·ment /kən'faɪnmənt/ NOUN [u] **Confinement** is the state of being forced to stay in a prison or another place which you cannot leave. ❑ *She had been held in solitary confinement for four months.*

❍ **con·firm** ◆◆◇ /kən'fɜːm/ VERB [T] (confirms, confirming, confirmed) (*academic word*) **1** If something **confirms** what you believe, suspect, or fear, it shows that it is definitely true. ❑ *X-rays have confirmed that he has not broken any bones.* ❑ *These new statistics confirm our worst fears about the depth of the recession.* ❑ *This confirms what I suspected all along.* **2** If you **confirm** something that has been stated or suggested, you say that it is true because you know about it. ≠ deny, contradict ❑ *The spokesman confirmed that the area was now in rebel hands.* ❑ *He confirmed what had long been feared.* **3** If you **confirm** an arrangement or appointment, you say that it is definite, usually in a letter or on the telephone. ❑ *You make the reservation, and I'll confirm it in writing.* **4** If someone **is confirmed**, they are formally accepted as a member of a Christian church during a ceremony in which they say they believe what the church teaches. ❑ *He was confirmed as a member of the Methodist Church.* **5** If something **confirms** you **in** your decision, belief, or opinion, it makes you think that you are definitely right. ❑ *It has confirmed* me in my decision not to become a nun. **6** If something **confirms** you **as** something, it shows that you definitely deserve a name, role, or position. ❏ *Her new role could confirm her as one of our leading actors.*

❍ **con·fir·ma·tion** /ˌkɒnfəˈmeɪʃən/ NOUN [U, C] **1** [U] = proof, affirmation ❏ *They took her resignation as confirmation of their suspicions.* **2** [U] ≠ denial ❏ *She glanced over at James for confirmation.* **3** [U] ❏ *Travel arrangements are subject to confirmation by the head office.* **4** [C, U] ❏ *when I was being prepared for Confirmation*

con·fis·cate /ˈkɒnfɪskeɪt/ VERB [T] (**confiscates, confiscating, confiscated**) If you **confiscate** something **from** someone, you take it away from them, usually as a punishment. = seize ❏ *The law has been used to confiscate assets from people who have committed minor offences.*

con·fis·ca·tion /ˌkɒnfɪsˈkeɪʃən/ NOUN [C, U] (**confiscations**) = seizure ❏ *The new laws allow the confiscation of assets purchased with proceeds of the drugs trade.*

❍ **con·flict** ♦♦◇ NOUN, VERB (*academic word*)

NOUN /ˈkɒnflɪkt/ [U, C] (**conflicts**) **1** [U] [oft 'in/into' conflict] **Conflict** is serious disagreement and argument about something important. If two people or groups are **in conflict**, they have had a serious disagreement or argument and have not yet reached agreement. = disagreement; ≠ agreement ❏ *Try to keep any conflict between you and your ex-partner to a minimum.* ❏ *Employees already are in conflict with management over job cuts.* ❏ *The two companies came into conflict.* **2** [U] **Conflict** is a state of mind in which you find it impossible to make a decision. = turmoil ❏ *the anguish of his own inner conflict* **3** [C, U] (*written*) **Conflict** is fighting between countries or groups of people. = hostility, fighting; ≠ peace ❏ *talks aimed at ending four decades of conflict* ❏ *The National Security Council has met to discuss ways of preventing a military conflict.* **4** [C, U] A **conflict** is a serious difference between two or more beliefs, ideas, or interests. If two beliefs, ideas, or interests are **in conflict**, they are very different. ❏ *There is a conflict between what they are doing and what you want.*

VERB /kənˈflɪkt/ [RECIP] (**conflicts, conflicting, conflicted**) If ideas, beliefs, or accounts **conflict**, they are very different from each other and it seems impossible for them to exist together or to each be true. = clash ❏ *Personal ethics and professional ethics sometimes conflict.* ❏ *He held firm opinions which usually conflicted with mine.* ❏ *three powers with conflicting interests*

WORD CONNECTIONS

VERB + conflict

resolve conflict
❏ *Conflict can often be resolved through discussion and negotiation.*

end a conflict
settle a conflict
prevent a conflict
avoid a conflict
❏ *The President agreed to accept an international peacekeeping force as part of a plan to end the conflict.*

ADJ + conflict

a **bloody** conflict
an **armed** conflict
a **violent** conflict
a **bitter** conflict
❏ *If the situation deteriorates into armed conflict, many soldiers and civilians will be killed.*

a **military** conflict
a **civil** conflict
❏ *The weapons are likely to be used in military conflict.*

❍ **con·form** /kənˈfɔːm/ VERB [I] (**conforms, conforming, conformed**) (*academic word*) **1** If something **conforms to** something such as a law or someone's wishes, it is of the required type or quality. ❏ *The lamp has been designed to conform to new safety standards.* ❏ *The meat market can continue only if it is radically overhauled to conform with strict European standards.* **2** If someone or something **conforms**

to a pattern or type, they are very similar to it. ❏ *I am well aware that we all conform to one stereotype or another.* ❏ *Like most 'peacetime wars' it did not conform to preconceived ideas.* **3** If you **conform**, you behave in the way that you are expected or supposed to behave. ❏ *Many children who can't or don't conform are bullied.*

❍ **con·form·ity** /kənˈfɔːmɪti/ NOUN [U] **1** If something happens **in conformity with** something such as a law or someone's wishes, it happens as the law says it should, or as the person wants it to. ❏ *The prime minister is, in conformity with their constitution, chosen by the president.* ❏ *Any action it takes has to be in conformity with international law.* **2** **Conformity** means behaving in the same way as most other people. ❏ *Excessive conformity is usually caused by fear of disapproval.* ❏ *Pressure appears to be mounting for conformity in how people speak English.*

con·found /kənˈfaʊnd/ VERB [T] (**confounds, confounding, confounded**) If someone or something **confounds** you, they make you feel surprised or confused, often by showing you that your opinions or expectations of them were wrong. ❏ *He momentarily confounded his critics by his cool handling of the hostage crisis.*

con·front ♦◇◇ /kənˈfrʌnt/ VERB [T] (**confronts, confronting, confronted**) **1** If you **are confronted with** a problem, task, or difficulty, you have to deal with it. = face ❏ *She was confronted with severe money problems.* **2** If you **confront** a difficult situation or issue, you accept the fact that it exists and try to deal with it. = face ❏ *We are learning how to confront death.* **3** If you **are confronted** by something that you find threatening or difficult to deal with, it is there in front of you. = face ❏ *I was confronted with an array of knobs, levers, and switches.* **4** If you **confront** someone, you stand or sit in front of them, especially when you are going to fight, argue, or compete with them. ❏ *She pushed her way through the mob and confronted him face to face.* ❏ *They don't hesitate to open fire when confronted by police.* **5** If you **confront** someone **with** something, you present facts or evidence to them in order to accuse them of something or force them to deal with a situation. ❏ *She had decided to confront Kathryn with the truth.* ❏ *I could not bring myself to confront him about it.*

con·fron·ta·tion ♦◇◇ /ˌkɒnfrʌnˈteɪʃən/ NOUN [C, U] (**confrontations**) A **confrontation** is a dispute, fight, or battle between two groups of people. ❏ *The commission remains so weak that it will continue to avoid confrontation with governments.*

con·fron·ta·tion·al /ˌkɒnfrʌnˈteɪʃənəl/ ADJ (*disapproval*) If you describe the way that someone behaves as **confrontational**, you are showing your disapproval of the fact that they are aggressive and likely to cause an argument or dispute. ❏ *The committee's confrontational style of campaigning has made it unpopular.*

con·fuse /kənˈfjuːz/ VERB [T] (**confuses, confusing, confused**) **1** If you **confuse** two things, you get them mixed up, so that you think one of them is the other one. ❏ *I always confuse my left with my right.* **2** To **confuse** someone means to make it difficult for them to know exactly what is happening or what to do. ❏ *My words surprised and confused him.* **3** To **confuse** a situation means to make it complicated or difficult to understand. ❏ *To further confuse the issue, there is an enormous variation in the amount of sleep people feel happy with.*

con·fused /kənˈfjuːzd/ ADJ **1** If you are **confused**, you do not know exactly what is happening or what to do. = bewildered ❏ *A survey showed people were confused about what they should eat to stay healthy.* **2** Something that is **confused** does not have any order or pattern and is difficult to understand. ❏ *The situation remains confused as both sides claim success.*

con·fus·ing /kənˈfjuːzɪŋ/ ADJ Something that is **confusing** makes it difficult for people to know exactly what is happening or what to do. ❏ *The statement is really confusing.*

con·fu·sion /kənˈfjuːʒən/ NOUN [C, U] (**confusions**) **1** [C, U] If there is **confusion** about something, it is not clear what the true situation is, especially because people believe different things. ❑ *There's still confusion about the number of students.* **2** [U] **Confusion** is a situation in which everything is in disorder, especially because there are lots of things happening at the same time. ❑ *There was confusion when a man fired shots.* **3** [U] The **confusion** of two things is the act of getting them mixed up, so that you think one of them is the other one. ❑ *Use different colours of felt pen on your sketch to avoid confusion.*

con·gest·ed /kənˈdʒestɪd/ ADJ A **congested** road or area is extremely crowded and blocked with traffic or people. ❑ *He promised to clear the city's congested roads.*

✪ **con·ges·tion** /kənˈdʒestʃən/ NOUN [U] **1** If there is **congestion** in a place, the place is extremely crowded and blocked with traffic or people. = crowding, overcrowding ❑ *The problems of traffic congestion will not disappear in a hurry.* ❑ *Energy consumption, congestion and pollution have increased.* **2 Congestion** in a part of the body is a medical condition in which the part becomes blocked. ❑ *nasal congestion*

con·gratu·late /kənˈgrætʃʊleɪt/ VERB [T] (**congratulates, congratulating, congratulated**) **1** If you **congratulate** someone, you say something to show you are pleased that something nice has happened to them. ❑ *She congratulated him on the birth of his son.* **2** If you **congratulate** someone, you praise them for something good that they have done. ❑ *I really must congratulate the organizers for a well run and enjoyable event.*

con·gratu·la·tion /kənˌgrætʃʊˈleɪʃən/ NOUN [U] ❑ *We have received many letters of congratulation.*

con·gratu·la·tions /kənˌgrætʃʊˈleɪʃənz/ CONVENTION, NOUN

CONVENTION You say '**Congratulations**' to someone in order to congratulate them on something nice that has happened to them or something good that they have done. ❑ *Congratulations, you have a healthy baby girl.* ❑ *Congratulations on your interesting article.*

NOUN [PL] If you offer someone your **congratulations**, you congratulate them on something nice that has happened to them or on something good that they have done. ❑ *The club also offers its congratulations to D. Brown on her appointment as president.*

con·gre·gate /ˈkɒŋgrɪgeɪt/ VERB [I] (**congregates, congregating, congregated**) When people **congregate**, they gather together and form a group. ❑ *Visitors congregated on Sunday afternoons to view public exhibitions.*

✪ **Con·gress** ♦♦◇ NOUN [SING] **Congress** is the elected group of politicians that is responsible for making laws in the United States. It consists of two parts: the House of Representatives and the Senate. ❑ *We want to cooperate with both the administration and Congress.*

con·gress /ˈkɒŋgres/ NOUN [c] (**congresses**) A **congress** is a large meeting that is held to discuss ideas and policies. ❑ *A lot has changed after the party congress.*

✪ **con·gres·sion·al** ♦◇◇ /kənˈgreʃənəl/ also **Congressional** ADJ [congressional + N] A **congressional** policy, action, or person relates to the US Congress. ❑ *The president explained his plans to congressional leaders.* ❑ *a congressional report published on September 5th*

congress·man /ˈkɒŋgrɪsmən/ NOUN [c] (**congressmen**) A **congressman** is a male member of the US Congress, especially of the House of Representatives.

✪ **con·jec·ture** /kənˈdʒektʃə/ NOUN, VERB

NOUN [c, U] (**conjectures**) (*formal*) A **conjecture** is a conclusion that is based on information that is not certain or complete. = surmise ❑ *That was a conjecture, not a fact.* ❑ *There are several conjectures.* ❑ *Ozone creation is a very large-scale natural process and the importance of human-generated CFCs in reducing it is largely a matter of conjecture.*

VERB [I, T] (**conjectures, conjecturing, conjectured**) (*formal*) When you **conjecture**, you form an opinion or reach a conclusion on the basis of information that is not certain or complete. = surmise ❑ *He conjectured that some individuals may be able to detect major calamities.*

con·junc·tion /kənˈdʒʌŋkʃən/ NOUN

NOUN [c] (**conjunctions**) **1** (*formal*) A **conjunction** of two or more things is the occurrence of them at the same time

or place. ❑ *the conjunction of two events* **2** In grammar, a **conjunction** is a word or group of words that joins together words, groups, or clauses. In English, there are coordinating conjunctions such as 'and' and 'but', and subordinating conjunctions such as 'although', 'because', and 'when'.

PHRASE **in conjunction with** [usu in conjunction with + N] If one thing is done **in conjunction with** another, the two things are done or used together. ❑ *Textbooks are designed to be used in conjunction with classroom teaching.*

con·jure /ˈkʌndʒə, AmE ˈkɑːn-/ VERB

VERB [T] (**conjures, conjuring, conjured**) If you **conjure** something out of nothing, you make it appear as if by magic. ❑ *Thirteen years ago she found herself having to conjure a career from thin air.*

PHRASAL VERB **conjure up** **1 Conjure up** means the same as **conjure** VERB. ❑ *Every day a different chef will be conjuring up delicious dishes in the restaurant.* **2** If you **conjure up** a memory, picture, or idea, you create it in your mind. ❑ *When he closed his eyes, he could conjure up in exact colour almost every event of his life.*

✪ **con·nect** /kəˈnekt/ VERB

VERB [RECIP, I, T] (**connects, connecting, connected**) **1** [RECIP] If something or someone **connects** one thing **to** another, or if one thing **connects to** another, or if two things **connect**, the two things are joined together. = attach ❑ *You can connect the speakers to your CD player.* ❑ *I connected the wires for the transformer.* ❑ *Two cables connect to each corner of the plate.* ❑ *a television camera connected to the radio telescope* **2** [RECIP] If two things or places **connect** or if something **connects** them, they are joined and people or things can pass between them. ❑ *the long hallway that connects the rooms* ❑ *A pedestrian bridge now connects the car park with the shopping mall.* **3** [I] If one train or plane, for example, **connects with** another, it arrives at a time which allows passengers to change to the other one in order to continue their journey. = link up ❑ *a train connecting with a ferry to Ireland* **4** [T] If a piece of equipment or a place **is connected to** a source of power or water, it is joined to that source so that it has power or water. ❑ *These appliances should not be connected to power supplies.* ❑ *Ischia was now connected to the mainland water supply.* **5** [T] If you **connect** a person or thing **with** something, you realize that there is a link or relationship between them. = associate ❑ *I hoped he would not connect me with that now-embarrassing review I'd written seven years earlier.* **6** [T] Something that **connects** a person or thing **with** something else shows or provides a link or relationship between them. = link ❑ *A search of Brady's house revealed nothing that could connect him with the robberies.*

PHRASAL VERB **connect up** **Connect up** means the same as **connect** VERB 4. ❑ *The shower is easy to install – it needs only to be connected up to the hot and cold water supply.*

✪ **con·nect·ed** /kəˈnektɪd/ ADJ If one thing is **connected with** another, there is a link or relationship between them. = linked, associated; ≠ unconnected ❑ *Have you ever had any skin problems connected with exposure to the sun?* ❑ *The dispute is not directly connected to the negotiations.*
→ See also **connect**

✪ **con·nec·tion** ♦◇◇ /kəˈnekʃən/ also **connexion** NOUN [c, U] (**connections**) **1** [c, U] A **connection** is a relationship between two things, people, or groups. = association, link, relationship ❑ *There was no evidence of a connection between BSE and the brain diseases recently confirmed in cats.* ❑ *I felt a strong connection between us.* ❑ *The police say he had no connection with the security forces.* ❑ *He has denied any connection to the bombing.* **2** [c] A **connection** is a joint where two wires or pipes are joined together. ❑ *Check all radiators for small leaks, especially round pipework connections.* ❑ *a high-speed internet connection* **3** [c] If a place has good road, rail, or air **connections**, many places can be directly reached from there by car, train, or plane. ❑ *Mexico City has excellent air and rail connections to the rest of the country.* **4** [c] If you get a **connection** at a station or airport, you catch a train, bus, or plane, after getting off another train, bus, or plane, in order to continue your trip. ❑ *My flight was late and I missed the connection.*

con·nois·seur /ˌkɒnəˈsɜː/ NOUN [C] (**connoisseurs**) A **connoisseur** is someone who knows a lot about the arts, food, drink, or some other subject. ❑ *Sarah tells me you're something of an art connoisseur.*

✪ **con·no·ta·tion** /ˌkɒnəˈteɪʃən/ NOUN [C] (**connotations**) The **connotations** of a particular word or name are the ideas or qualities which it makes you think of. = association ❑ *It's just one of those words that's got so many negative connotations.* ❑ *'Urchin', with its connotation of mischievousness, may not be a particularly apt word.*

con·quer /ˈkɒŋkə/ VERB [T] (**conquers, conquering, conquered**) **1** If one country or group of people **conquers** another, they take complete control of their land. ❑ *During 1936, Mussolini conquered Abyssinia.* **2** If you **conquer** something such as a problem, you succeed in ending it or dealing with it successfully. ❑ *I was certain that love was quite enough to conquer our differences.* ❑ *He has never conquered his addiction to smoking.*

con·quer·or /ˈkɒŋkərə/ NOUN [C] (**conquerors**) The **conquerors** of a country or group of people are the people who have taken complete control of that country or group's land. ❑ *The people of an oppressed country obey their conquerors because they want to go on living.*

con·quest /ˈkɒŋkwest/ NOUN [U, SING] (**conquests**) **1** [U] [also conquests, oft conquest 'of' N] **Conquest** is the act of conquering a country or group of people. ❑ *He had led the conquest of southern Poland in 1939.* ❑ *the Spanish conquest of Mexico* **2** [SING] The **conquest** of something such as a problem is success in ending it or dealing with it. = defeat ❑ *The conquest of inflation has been the Government's overriding economic priority for nearly 15 years.*

con·science /ˈkɒnʃəns/ NOUN
NOUN [C, U] (**consciences**) **1** [C] Your **conscience** is the part of your mind that tells you whether what you are doing is right or wrong. If you have a **guilty conscience**, you feel guilty about something because you know it was wrong. If you have a **clear conscience**, you do not feel guilty because you know you have done nothing wrong. ❑ *I have battled with my conscience over whether I should actually send this letter.* ❑ *What if he got a guilty conscience and brought it back?* **2** [U] **Conscience** is doing what you believe is right even though it might be unpopular, difficult, or dangerous. ❑ *He refused for reasons of conscience to eat meat.* **3** [U] **Conscience** is a feeling of guilt because you know you have done something that is wrong. ❑ *I'm so glad he had a pang of conscience.*
PHRASE **on your conscience** If you have something on your **conscience**, you feel guilty because you know you have done something wrong. ❑ *The drunk driver has two deaths on his conscience.*

con·sci·en·tious /ˌkɒnʃiˈenʃəs/ ADJ Someone who is **conscientious** is very careful to do their work properly. ❑ *We are generally very conscientious about our work.*
con·sci·en·tious·ly /ˌkɒnʃiˈenʃəsli/ ADV ❑ *He studied conscientiously and enthusiastically.*

con·scious ◆◇◇ /ˈkɒnʃəs/ ADJ **1** [V-LINK + conscious] If you are **conscious of** something, you notice it or realize that it is happening. = aware ❑ *He was conscious of the faint, musky aroma of aftershave.* ❑ *She was very conscious of Max studying her.* **2** [V-LINK + conscious] If you are **conscious of** something, you think about it a lot, especially because you are unhappy about it or because you think it is important. = aware ❑ *I'm very conscious of my weight.* **3** A **conscious** decision or action is made or done deliberately with you giving your full attention to it. = deliberate ❑ *I don't think we ever made a conscious decision to have a big family.* **4** Someone who is **conscious** is awake rather than asleep or unconscious. ❑ *She was fully conscious throughout the surgery and knew what was going on.* **5** [conscious + N] **Conscious** memories or thoughts are ones that you are aware of. ❑ *He had no conscious memory of his four-week stay in the hospital.*
con·scious·ly /ˈkɒnʃəsli/ ADV **1** [consciously with V] ❑ *Sophie was not consciously seeking a replacement after her*

father died. **2** *Most people cannot consciously remember much before the ages of 3 to 5 years.*

con·scious·ness ◆◇◇ /ˈkɒnʃəsnəs/ NOUN [C, U] (**consciousness**) **1** [C] Your **consciousness** is your mind and your thoughts. = awareness ❑ *That idea has been creeping into our consciousness for some time.* **2** [U] The **consciousness** of a group of people is their set of ideas, attitudes, and beliefs. = mentality ❑ *The Green Party is attempting to shift the American consciousness.* **3** [U] You use **consciousness** to refer to an interest in and knowledge of a particular subject or idea. = awareness ❑ *Her political consciousness sprang from her upbringing when her father's illness left the family short of money.* **4** [U] **Consciousness** is the state of being awake rather than being asleep or unconscious. If someone **loses consciousness**, they become unconscious, and if they **regain consciousness**, they become conscious after being unconscious. ❑ *She banged her head and lost consciousness.*

✪ **con·secu·tive** /kənˈsekjʊtɪv/ ADJ **Consecutive** periods of time or events happen one after the other without interruption. = successive ❑ *The Cup was won for the third consecutive year by the Toronto Maple Leafs.* ❑ *Photographs taken at the same time on two consecutive sunny days can be quite different from one another.*
✪ **con·secu·tive·ly** /kənˈsekjʊtɪvli/ ADV = successively ❑ *The judge decided yesterday that the sentences for the three murders should run consecutively, not concurrently as requested by the prosecution.* ❑ *He will face two further prison sentences, totalling 11 years, to be served consecutively.*

✪ **con·sen·sus** /kənˈsensəs/ NOUN [SING] [also no DET] A **consensus** is general agreement among a group of people. ❑ *The consensus among the world's scientists is that the world is likely to warm up over the next few decades.* ❑ *So far, the Australians have been unable to come to a uniform consensus on the issue.*

✪ **con·sent** /kənˈsent/ NOUN, VERB (academic word)
NOUN [U] (formal) If you give your **consent to** something, you give someone permission to do it. ❑ *At approximately 11:30 p.m., Pollard finally gave his consent to the search.* ❑ *Can my child be medically examined without my consent?*
VERB [I, T] (**consents, consenting, consented**) (formal) If you **consent to** something, you agree to do it or to allow it to be done. = agree ❑ *He finally consented to go.* ❑ *He asked Ginny if she would consent to a small celebration after the christening.* ❑ *Churchill proposed to Stalin a division of influence in the Balkan states. Stalin readily consented.*

✪ **con·se·quence** ◆◇◇ /ˈkɒnsɪkwəns/ NOUN (academic word)
NOUN [C] (**consequences**) The **consequences of** something are the results or effects of it. = result ❑ *Her lawyer said she understood the consequences of her actions and was prepared to go to jail.* ❑ *An economic crisis may have tremendous consequences for our global security.*
PHRASE **in consequence** or **as a consequence** If one thing happens and then another thing happens **in consequence** or **as a consequence**, the second thing happens as a result of the first. ❑ *His death had been totally unexpected and, in consequence, no plans had been made for his replacement.* ❑ *Maternity services were to be reduced as a consequence of falling birth rates.*

WORD CONNECTIONS
consequence + OF + NOUN
the consequences of **war**
the consequences of an **action**
the consequences of **failure**
❑ *The department manager should formally warn the employee of the consequences of a failure to improve his or her attendance.*
consequence + FOR + NOUN
the consequences for the **economy**
the consequences for the **future**
the consequences for the **region**
❑ *What we do today may have consequences for the future of the planet.*

c

VERB + **consequence**

suffer the consequences
face the consequences
accept the consequences
consider the consequences
understand the consequences

❑ *The country was continuing to suffer the consequences of war even five years after the war ended.*

ADJ + **consequence**

a **serious** consequence
a **severe** consequence
a **tragic** consequence

❑ *Unfortunately, some companies ignore health and safety laws, with tragic consequences.*

a **likely** *consequence*
an **unintended** *consequence*

❑ *Some teenagers drink to excess with little regard for the likely consequences.*

con·se·quent /'kɒnsɪkwənt/ ADJ (*academic word, formal*) **Consequent** means happening as a direct result of an event or situation. ❑ *The warming of the Earth and the consequent climatic changes affect us all.*

✪ **con·se·quent·ly** /'kɒnsɪkwəntli/ ADV [consequently with CL] (*formal*) **Consequently** means as a result. = as a result, thus ❑ *Grandfather had sustained a broken back while working in the mines. Consequently, he spent the rest of his life in a wheelchair.* ❑ *They said that Freud had not understood women and consequently belittled them.* ❑ *Apprehension and stress had made him depressed and consequently irritable with his family.*

✪ **con·ser·va·tion** /ˌkɒnsə'veɪʃən/ NOUN [u] **1** **Conservation** is saving and protecting the environment. = ecology; ≠ destruction ❑ *a four-nation regional meeting on elephant conservation* ❑ *tree-planting and other conservation projects* **2** **Conservation** is saving and protecting historical objects or works of art such as paintings, sculptures, or buildings. ❑ *Then he began his most famous work, the conservation and rebinding of the Book of Kells.* **3** The **conservation** of a supply of something is the careful use of it so that it lasts for a long time. ❑ *projects aimed at promoting energy conservation* ❑ *rules concerning the conservation of fishery resources*

✪ **con·serva·tive** ♦♦◇ /kən'sɜːvətɪv/ ADJ, NOUN

The spelling **Conservative** is also used for meaning 2 of the adjective and meaning 2 of the noun.

ADJ **1** Someone who is **conservative** has views that are towards the political right. = right-wing, traditionalist, conventional, reactionary; ≠ left-wing, radical ❑ *counties whose citizens invariably support the most conservative candidate in any election* ❑ *The mood of America is turning back to the conservative views of the Ronald Reagan era* **2** A **Conservative** politician or voter is a member of or votes for the Conservative Party in Britain and in various other countries. = Tory ❑ *Most Conservative MPs appear happy with the government's reassurances.* ❑ *disenchanted Conservative voters* **3** Someone who is **conservative** or has **conservative** ideas is unwilling to accept changes and new ideas. ❑ *People tend to be more liberal when they're young and more conservative as they get older.* ❑ *a narrow conservative approach to child care* **4** If someone dresses in a **conservative** way, their clothes are conventional in style. ❑ *The girl was well dressed, as usual, though in a more conservative style.* **5** A **conservative** estimate or guess is one in which you are cautious and estimate or guess a low amount which is probably less than the real amount. ❑ *The average fan spends $25 – a conservative estimate based on ticket price and souvenirs.*

NOUN [c] (**conservatives**) **1** A **conservative** is someone who has views that are towards the political right. ❑ *The new judge is 50-year-old David Suitor who's regarded as a conservative.* **2** A **Conservative** is a member or supporter of the Conservative Party in Britain and in various other countries. ❑ *In 1951 the Conservatives were returned to power.*

con·ser·va·tive·ly /kən'sɜːvətɪvli/ ADV **1** [conservatively with v] ❑ *She was always very conservatively dressed when we went out.* **2** [conservatively with v] ❑ *The bequest is conservatively estimated at $30 million.*

✪ **con·serve** /kən'sɜːv/ VERB [T] (**conserves, conserving, conserved**) **1** If you **conserve** a supply of something, you use it carefully so that it lasts for a long time. = save; ≠ waste ❑ *The factories have closed for the weekend to conserve energy.* ❑ *We must abandon our wasteful ways and conserve resources.* **2** To **conserve** something means to protect it from harm, loss, or change. = preserve, save, protect ❑ *a big increase in US aid to help developing countries conserve their forests* ❑ *the body responsible for conserving historic buildings*

✪ **con·sid·er** ♦♦♦ /kən'sɪdə/ VERB [T] (**considers, considering, considered**) **1** If you **consider** a person or thing **to** be something, you have the opinion that this is what they are. ❑ *We don't consider our customers to be mere consumers; we consider them to be our friends.* ❑ *I had always considered myself a strong, competent woman.* ❑ *The paper does not explain why foreign ownership should be considered bad.* ❑ *This suggests that we should consider these drugs as addictive.* **2** If you **consider** something, you think about it carefully. ❑ *The administration continues to consider ways to resolve the situation.* ❑ *You do have to consider the feelings of those around you.* **3** If you **are considering** doing something, you intend to do it, but have not yet made a final decision whether to do it. ❑ *I had seriously considered telling the story from the point of view of the wives.*
→ See also **considering**

✪ **con·sid·er·able** ♦♦◇ /kən'sɪdərəbəl/ ADJ (*academic word, formal*) **Considerable** means great in amount or degree. = substantial ❑ *To be without Pearce would be a considerable blow.* ❑ *Doing it properly makes considerable demands on our time.* ❑ *Other studies found considerable evidence to support this finding.*

✪ **con·sid·er·ably** /kən'sɪdərəbli/ ADV = significantly ❑ *Children vary considerably in the rate at which they learn these lessons.* ❑ *In the past ethical standards have often been considerably lower.*

con·sid·er·ate /kən'sɪdərət/ ADJ (*approval*) Someone who is **considerate** pays attention to the needs, wishes, or feelings of other people. ❑ *I think he's the most charming, most considerate man I've ever known.*

con·sid·era·tion ♦◇◇ /kənˌsɪdə'reɪʃən/ NOUN
NOUN [u, c] (**considerations**) **1** [u] **Consideration** is careful thought about something. ❑ *There should be careful consideration about the use of such toxic chemicals.* **2** [u] If something is **under consideration**, it is being discussed. ❑ *Several proposals are under consideration by the state assembly.* **3** [u] If you show **consideration**, you pay attention to the needs, wishes, or feelings of other people. ❑ *Show consideration for your neighbours.* **4** [c] A **consideration** is something that should be thought about, especially when you are planning or deciding something. = factor ❑ *Price has become a more important consideration for shoppers in choosing which store to visit than it was before the recession.*
PHRASE **take something into consideration** If you **take** something **into consideration**, you think about it because it is relevant to what you are doing. ❑ *Safe driving is good driving because it takes into consideration the lives of other people.*

con·sid·er·ing ♦◇◇ /kən'sɪdərɪŋ/ PREP, CONJ, ADV
PREP You use **considering** to indicate that you are thinking about a particular fact when making a judgment or giving an opinion. ❑ *He must be hoping, but considering the situation in June he may be hoping for too much too soon.*
CONJ **considering that** You use **considering that** to indicate that you are thinking about a particular fact when making a judgment or giving an opinion. ❑ *Considering that you are no longer involved with this man, your response is a little extreme.*
ADV [CL + considering] (*spoken*) When you are giving an opinion or making a judgment, you can use **considering** to suggest that you have thought about all the circumstances, and often that something has succeeded in

spite of these circumstances. ❑ *I think you're pretty safe, considering.*

con·sign /kənˈsaɪn/ VERB [T] (**consigns, consigning, consigned**) (*formal*) To **consign** something or someone **to** a place where they will be forgotten about, or **to** an unpleasant situation or place, means to put them there. ❑ *For decades, many of Malevich's works were consigned to the basements of Soviet museums.*

✪ **con·sist** ♦◇◇ /kənˈsɪst/ VERB [i] (**consists, consisting, consisted**) (*academic word*) **1** Something that **consists of** particular things or people is formed from them. = comprise ❑ *My diet consisted almost exclusively of chocolate-covered biscuits and glasses of milk.* ❑ *Her crew consisted of children from Devon and Cornwall.* **2** Something that **consists in** something else has that thing as its main or only part. ❑ *His work as a consultant consisted in advising foreign companies on the siting of new factories.*

✪ **con·sist·en·cy** /kənˈsɪstənsi/ NOUN [U] **1** Consistency is the quality or condition of being consistent. = reliability, agreement; ≠ inconsistency ❑ *She scores goals with remarkable consistency.* ❑ *There's always a lack of consistency in matters of foreign policy.* ❑ *We need to interview them several times to test the consistency of their statements.* **2** The **consistency** of a substance is how thick or smooth it is. ❑ *Dilute the paint with water until it is the consistency of milk.*

✪ **con·sist·ent** ♦◇◇ /kənˈsɪstənt/ ADJ (*academic word*) **1** Someone who is **consistent** always behaves in the same way, has the same attitudes towards people or things, or achieves the same level of success in something. = reliable; ≠ erratic ❑ *Becker was never the most consistent of players anyway.* ❑ *his consistent support of free trade* **2** [V-LINK + consistent, usu consistent 'with' N] If one fact or idea is **consistent with** another, they do not contradict each other. = compatible; ≠ inconsistent, incompatible ❑ *This result is consistent with the findings of Garnett & Tobin.* **3** An argument or set of ideas that is **consistent** is one in which no part contradicts or conflicts with any other part. = coherent ❑ *A theory should be internally consistent.*
✪ **con·sist·ent·ly** /kənˈsɪstəntli/ ADV = constantly; ≠ inconsistently ❑ *It's something I have consistently denied.* ❑ *Jones and Armstrong maintain a consistently high standard.*

con·sole VERB, NOUN
VERB /kənˈsəʊl/ [T] (**consoles, consoling, consoled**) If you **console** someone who is unhappy about something, you try to make them feel more cheerful. = comfort ❑ *'Never mind, Ned,' he consoled me.* ❑ *I can console myself with the fact that I'm not alone.*
NOUN /ˈkɒnsəʊl/ [c] (**consoles**) A **console** is a panel with a number of switches or knobs that is used to operate a machine. ❑ *Several nurses sat before a console of flickering lights and bleeping monitors.*
con·so·la·tion /ˌkɒnsəˈleɪʃən/ NOUN [c, U] (**consolations**) = comfort ❑ *The only consolation for the baseball team is that they look likely to get another chance.*

con·soli·date /kənˈsɒlɪdeɪt/ VERB [T] (**consolidates, consolidating, consolidated**) **1** If you **consolidate** something that you have, for example power or success, you strengthen it so that it becomes more effective or secure. ❑ *The question is: will the junta consolidate its power by force?* **2** To **consolidate** a number of small groups or companies means to make them into one large organization. ❑ *Judge Charles Schwartz is giving the state 60 days to disband and consolidate Louisiana's four higher education boards.*

con·so·nant /ˈkɒnsənənt/ (**consonants**) NOUN [c] A **consonant** is a sound such as 'p', 'f', 'n', or 't' which you pronounce by stopping the air flowing freely through your mouth. Compare **vowel**.

con·sor·tium /kənˈsɔːtiəm/ NOUN [c] (**consortia** or **consortiums**) (*formal*) A **consortium** is a group of people or firms who have agreed to cooperate with each other. ❑ *The consortium includes some of the biggest building contractors in North America.*

con·spicu·ous /kənˈspɪkjuəs/ ADJ If someone or something is **conspicuous**, people can see or notice them

very easily. ❑ *Most people don't want to be too conspicuous.*
con·spicu·ous·ly /kənˈspɪkjuəsli/ ADV ❑ *Britain continues to follow US policy in this and other areas where American policies have most conspicuously failed.*

con·spira·cy /kənˈspɪrəsi/ NOUN [c, U] (**conspiracies**) **1** [c, U] Conspiracy is secret planning by a group of people to do something illegal. ❑ *Seven men, all from North Carolina, admitted conspiracy to commit arson.* **2** [c] A **conspiracy** is an agreement between a group of people which other people think is wrong or is likely to be harmful. ❑ *It's all part of a conspiracy to dispense with the town centre altogether and move everything out to the suburbs.*

con·spire /kənˈspaɪə/ VERB [RECIP, i, T] (**conspires, conspiring, conspired**) **1** [RECIP] If two or more people or groups **conspire to** do something illegal or harmful, they make a secret agreement to do it. = plot ❑ *They'd conspired to overthrow the government.* ❑ *a defendant accused of conspiring with his brother to commit robberies* **2** [i, T] If events **conspire to** produce a particular result, they seem to work together to cause this result. = combine ❑ *History and geography have conspired to bring the country to a moment of decision.*

con·sta·ble /ˈkʌnstəbəl, ˈkɒn-/ NOUN [c] (**constables**) **1** In Britain and some other countries, a **constable** is a police officer of the lowest rank. **2** In the United States, a **constable** is an official who helps keep the peace in a town. They are lower in rank than a sheriff. ❑ *Courts and magistrates may be set up but they cannot function without sheriffs and constables.*

✪ **con·stant** ♦♦◇ /ˈkɒnstənt/ ADJ, NOUN (*academic word*)
ADJ **1** You use **constant** to describe something that happens all the time or is always there. = continual, ongoing; ≠ occasional ❑ *She suggests that women are under constant pressure to behave abnormally thin.* ❑ *Inflation is a constant threat.* **2** If an amount or level is **constant**, it stays the same over a particular period of time. = stable, even; ≠ changeable, uneven ❑ *The body feels hot and the temperature remains more or less constant at the new elevated level.* ❑ *The climate is tropical with a fairly constant temperature at 24°C.*
NOUN (**constants**) A **constant** is a thing or value that always stays the same. ≠ variable ❑ *The constants of nature are certain numbers that enter into the mathematical equations that describe the laws of physics.* ❑ *Two significant constants have been found in a number of research studies.*
✪ **con·stant·ly** /ˈkɒnstəntli/ ADV = always, continually; ≠ sometimes, occasionally ❑ *The direction of the wind is constantly changing.* ❑ *We are constantly being reminded to cut down our fat intake.*

WHICH WORD?
constant, continual, or continuous?

Constant, continual, and continuous have slightly different meanings.

You use **constant** to describe something that happens all the time or never goes away.

❑ *He was in constant pain.*

You use **continual** to talk about a process that does not stop.

❑ *Our sales figures show continual improvement.*

You use **continuous** to talk about an action that happens without stopping.

❑ *The exercise should be one continuous movement.*

---

con·stel·la·tion /ˌkɒnstəˈleɪʃən/ NOUN [c] (**constellations**) A **constellation** is a group of stars which form a pattern and have a name. ❑ *a planet orbiting a star in the constellation of Cepheus*

con·ster·na·tion /ˌkɒnstəˈneɪʃən/ NOUN [U] (*formal*) Consternation is a feeling of anxiety or fear. = dismay ❑ *His decision caused consternation in the art photography community.*

con·stitu·en·cy /kənˈstɪtʃuənsi/ NOUN [c] (**constituencies**) **1** A **constituency** is an area for which someone is elected as the representative in a legislature or government. ❑ *Voters in 17 constituencies are going back to*

C

the polls today. **2** A particular **constituency** is a section of society that may give political support to a particular party or politician. ❑ *In Iowa, farmers are a powerful political constituency.*

✪ **con·stitu·ent** /kən'stɪtʃuənt/ NOUN, ADJ
NOUN [c] (**constituents**) **1** A **constituent** is someone who lives in a particular constituency, especially someone who is able to vote in an election. ❑ *He told his constituents that he would continue to represent them to the best of his ability.* **2** (*formal*) A **constituent** of a mixture, substance, or system is one of the things from which it is formed. = ingredient ❑ *Caffeine is the active constituent of drinks such as tea and coffee.* ❑ *The main constituents were lemon juice and syrup of radish.*
ADJ [constituent + N] (*formal*) The **constituent** parts of something are the things from which it is formed. ❑ *a plan to split the company into its constituent parts and sell them separately*

con·sti·tute /'kɒnstɪtjuːt, AmE -tuːt/ VERB [LINK]
(**constitutes**, **constituting**, **constituted**) (*academic word*) **1** If something **constitutes** a particular thing, it can be regarded as being that thing. ❑ *Testing patients without their consent would constitute a professional and legal offence.* **2** If a number of things or people **constitute** something, they are the parts or members that form it. = comprise ❑ *China's ethnic minorities constitute less than 7 per cent of its total population.*

✪ **con·sti·tu·tion** ♦◇◇ /ˌkɒnstɪ'tjuːʃən, AmE '-tuː-/
NOUN [c] (**constitutions**) (*academic word*) **1** The **constitution** of a country or organization is the system of laws which formally states people's rights and duties. ❑ *The king was forced to adopt a new constitution which reduced his powers.* ❑ *The constitution enshrined religious freedom, civil liberties and the right to form unions.* **2** Your **constitution** is your health. ❑ *He must have an extremely strong constitution.*

WORD CONNECTIONS
VERB + **constitution**
draft a constitution
write a constitution
amend a constitution
ratify a constitution
❑ *The government will amend its constitution to drop its territorial claim to the region.*
uphold a constitution
violate a constitution
suspend a constitution
❑ *Velasco ordered the arrest of his vice president, a move that opened him to charges of violating the constitution.*
ADJ + **constitution**
a **written** constitution
a **permanent** constitution
an **interim** constitution
a **democratic** constitution
❑ *Unlike the USA, the UK is not a federal state with a written constitution.*
the **American** constitution
the **Cuban** constitution
the **Afghan** constitution
❑ *The American constitution enshrines the right to bear arms.*

✪ **con·sti·tu·tion·al** ♦◇◇ /ˌkɒnstɪ'tjuːʃənəl, AmE -'tuː-/ ADJ **Constitutional** means relating to the constitution of a particular country or organization. ❑ *The issue is one of constitutional and civil rights.* ❑ *Political leaders are making no progress in their efforts to resolve the country's constitutional crisis.* ❑ *A Romanian judge has asked for a Constitutional Court ruling on the law.*

✪ **con·strain** /kən'streɪn/ VERB [T] (**constrains**, **constraining**, **constrained**) (*academic word, formal*) To **constrain** someone or something means to limit their development or force them to behave in a particular way. ❑ *Women are too often constrained by family commitments and by low expectations.* ❑ *It's the capacity of those roads which is going to constrain the amount of travel by car that can take place.*

✪ **con·straint** /kən'streɪnt/ NOUN [C, U] (**constraints**) **1** [c] A **constraint** is something that limits or controls what you can do. = limitation ❑ *Their decision to abandon the trip was made because of financial constraints.* ❑ *Water shortages in the area will be the main constraint on development.* **2** [u] **Constraint** is control over the way you behave which prevents you from doing what you want to do. = restraint ❑ *Journalists were given the freedom to visit, investigate, and report without constraint.*

con·strict /kən'strɪkt/ VERB [I, T] (**constricts**, **constricting**, **constricted**) **1** [I, T] If a part of your body, especially your throat, **is constricted** or if it **constricts**, something causes it to become narrower. ❑ *Severe migraines can be treated with a drug that constricts the blood vessels.* **2** [T] If something **constricts** you, it limits your actions so that you cannot do what you want to do. = limit ❑ *She objects to the constant testing because it constricts her teaching style.*

✪ **con·struct** /kən'strʌkt/ VERB [T] (**constructs**, **constructing**, **constructed**) (*academic word*) **1** If you **construct** something such as a building, road, or machine, you build it or make it. = build ❑ *His company recently constructed an office building in downtown Denver.* ❑ *The boxes should be constructed from rough-sawn timber.* **2** If you **construct** something such as an idea, a piece of writing, or a system, you create it by putting different parts together. = create ❑ *He eventually constructed a huge business empire.* ❑ *The novel is constructed from a series of on-the-spot reports.* ❑ *using carefully-constructed tests*

✪ **con·struc·tion** ♦◇◇ /kən'strʌkʃən/ NOUN [U, C] (**constructions**) **1** [u] **Construction** is the building of things such as houses, factories, roads, and bridges. ❑ *He'd already started construction on a hunting lodge.* ❑ *the downturn in the construction industry* ❑ *Jim now works in construction.* ❑ *the only nuclear power station under construction in Britain* **2** [u] The **construction** of something such as a vehicle or machine is the making of it. ❑ *companies who have long experience in the construction of those types of equipment* ❑ *the finest wood for boat construction* **3** [u] The **construction** of something such as a system is the creation of it. = creation ❑ *the construction of a just system of criminal justice* **4** [u] You use **construction** to refer to the structure of something and the way it has been built or made. ❑ *The Shakers believed that furniture should be plain, simple, useful, practical, and of sound construction.* **5** [c] You can refer to an object that has been built or made as a **construction**. = structure ❑ *an impressive steel and glass construction* **6** [c] A grammatical **construction** is a particular arrangement of words in a sentence, clause, or phrase. = structure ❑ *Avoid complex verbal constructions.*

✪ **con·struc·tive** /kən'strʌktɪv/ ADJ A **constructive** discussion, comment, or approach is useful and helpful rather than negative and unhelpful. = positive ❑ *She welcomes constructive criticism.* ❑ *After their meeting, both men described the talks as frank, friendly and constructive.* ❑ *The Prime Minister has promised that Israel will play a constructive role.*

con·strue /kən'struː/ VERB [T] (**construes**, **construing**, **construed**) (*formal*) If something **is construed** in a particular way, its nature or meaning is interpreted in that way. ❑ *What may seem helpful behaviour to you can be construed as interference by others.* ❑ *He may construe the approach as a hostile act.*

✪ **con·sult** ♦◇◇ /kən'sʌlt/ VERB [I, T, RECIP] (**consults**, **consulting**, **consulted**) (*academic word*) **1** [I, T] If you **consult** an expert or someone senior to you or **consult with** them, you ask them for their opinion, advice, or permission. ❑ *Consult your doctor about how much exercise you should get.* ❑ *He needed to consult with a lawyer.* **2** [T] If you **consult** a book or a map, you look in it or look at it in order to find some information. ❑ *Consult the chart on page 44 for the correct cooking times.* **3** [RECIP] If a person or group of people **consults with** other people or **consults** them, or if two people or groups **consult**, they talk and exchange ideas and opinions about what they might decide to do. = confer ❑ *After consulting with her daughter and manager,* she decided to take on the part, on her terms. ❑ *The two countries will have to consult their allies.* ❑ *The umpires consulted quickly.*

con·sul·tan·cy /kən'sʌltənsi/ NOUN [c, u] (**consultancies**) **1** [c] A **consultancy** is a company that gives expert advice on a particular subject. ❑ *A survey of 57 hospitals by Newchurch, a consultancy, reveals striking improvements.* **2** [u] (*mainly BrE*) **Consultancy** is expert advice on a particular subject which a person or group is paid to provide to a company or organization.

✪con·sult·ant ♦◇◇ /kən'sʌltənt/ NOUN [c] (**consultants**) **1** A **consultant** is a person who gives expert advice to a person or organization on a particular subject. = specialist, adviser ❑ *She is a consultant to the government.* ❑ *a team of management consultants sent in to reorganise the department* **2** (*BrE*; in *AmE*, usually use **specialist**) A **consultant** is an experienced doctor with a high position, who specializes in one area of medicine.

✪con·sul·ta·tion /ˌkɒnsəl'teɪʃən/ NOUN [c, u] (**consultations**) **1** A **consultation** is a meeting to discuss something. **Consultation** is discussion about something. = discussion, meeting, deliberation ❑ *Next week he'll be in Florida for consultations with President Vicente Fox.* ❑ *The plans were drawn up in consultation with the World Health Organisation.* **2** A **consultation with** a doctor or other expert is a meeting with them to discuss a particular problem and get their advice. **Consultation** is the process of getting advice from a doctor or other expert. ❑ *A personal diet plan is devised after a consultation with a nutritionist.*

con·sul·ta·tive /kən'sʌltətɪv/ ADJ A **consultative** committee or document gives advice or makes proposals about a particular problem or subject. = advisory ❑ *the consultative committee on local government finance*

✪con·sume /kən'sju:m, AmE -'su:m/ VERB [т] (**consumes**, **consuming**, **consumed**) (*academic word*) **1** (*formal*) If you **consume** something, you eat or drink it. = eat, drink ❑ *Martha would consume nearly a pound of cheese per day.* **2** To **consume** an amount of fuel, energy, or time means to use it up. ❑ *Some of the most efficient refrigerators consume 70 per cent less electricity than traditional models.*
→ See also **consuming**

✪con·sum·er ♦♦◇ /kən'sju:mə, AmE -'su:-/ NOUN [c] (**consumers**) A **consumer** is a person who buys things or uses services. = buyer, user, customer ❑ *claims that tobacco companies failed to warn consumers about the dangers of smoking* ❑ *improving public services and consumer rights*

con·sum·er·ism /kən'sju:mərɪzəm, AmE -'su:-/ NOUN [u] **1** [oft SUPP + consumerism] **Consumerism** is the belief that it is good to buy and use a lot of goods. ❑ *They have clearly embraced Western consumerism.* **2** **Consumerism** is the protection of the rights and interests of consumers.

con·sum·ing /kən'sju:mɪŋ, AmE -'su:-/ ADJ A **consuming** passion or interest is more important to you than anything else. ❑ *He has developed a consuming passion for chess.*
→ See also **consume**, **time-consuming**

con·sum·mate ADJ, VERB
ADJ /'kɒnsəmət/ (*formal*) You use **consummate** to describe someone who is extremely skilful. ❑ *He acted the part with consummate skill.*
VERB /'kɒnsjəmeɪt/ [т] (**consummates**, **consummating**, **consummated**) (*formal*) If two people **consummate** a marriage or relationship, they make it complete by having sex. ❑ *His wife divorced him for failing to consummate their marriage.*

✪con·sump·tion /kən'sʌmpʃən/ NOUN [u] **1** The **consumption** of fuel or natural resources is the act of using them or the amount used. ❑ *The laws have led to a reduction in fuel consumption in the US.* ❑ *a tax on the consumption of non-renewable energy resources* **2** (*formal*) The **consumption** of food or drink is the act of eating or drinking something, or the amount eaten or drunk. ❑ *Most of the wine was unfit for human consumption.* ❑ *The average daily consumption of*

fruit and vegetables is around 200 grams. ❑ *Excessive alcohol consumption is clearly bad.* **3** **Consumption** is the act of buying and using things. ❑ *They were prepared to put people out of work and reduce consumption by strangling the whole economy.* ❑ *the production and consumption of goods and services*

✪con·tact ♦♦◇ /'kɒntækt/ NOUN, ADJ, VERB (*academic word*)
NOUN [u, c] (**contacts**) **1** [u] [also contacts, oft contact 'with/between' N] **Contact** involves meeting or communicating with someone, especially regularly. = communication ❑ *Opposition leaders are denying any contact with the government in Kabul.* ❑ *He forbade contact between directors and executives outside his presence.* **2** [u] If you come **into contact with** someone or something, you meet that person or thing in the course of your work or other activities. ❑ *Doctors I came into contact with voiced their concern.* **3** [u] When people or things are in **contact**, they are touching each other. ❑ *They compared how these organisms behaved when left in contact with different materials.* ❑ *The cry occurs when air is brought into contact with the baby's larynx.* ❑ *There was no physical contact.* **4** [c] A **contact** is someone you know in an organization or profession who helps you or gives you information. ❑ *Their contact at the United States embassy was Phillip Norton.*
PHRASES **in contact (with someone)** If you are **in contact with** someone, you regularly meet them or communicate with them. ❑ *He was in direct contact with the kidnappers.*
make contact (with someone) If you **make contact with** someone, you find out where they are and talk or write to them. ❑ *How did you make contact with the author?*
lose contact If you **lose contact with** someone who you have been friendly with, you no longer see them, speak to them, or write to them. ❑ *Though they all live nearby, I lost contact with them really quickly.*
ADJ [contact + N] Your **contact** details are information such as a telephone number where you can be contacted. ❑ *You must leave your full name and contact details when you phone.*
VERB [т] (**contacts**, **contacting**, **contacted**) If you **contact** someone, you telephone them, write to them, or go to see them in order to tell or ask them something. = communicate with ❑ *Contact the Women's Alliance for further details.* ❑ *His client was on holiday and couldn't be contacted.*

WORD CONNECTIONS
VERB + **contact**
maintain contact
establish contact
❑ *They may not visit each other every day but they maintain contact on a regular basis.*
ADJ + **contact**
direct contact
close contact
regular contact
human contact
social contact
❑ *Since then, Maya has had no direct contact with her mother or husband.*
direct contact
physical contact
sexual contact
❑ *In some cultures physical contact is not acceptable in business situations.*

con·ta·gious /kən'teɪdʒəs/ ADJ **1** A disease that is **contagious** can be caught by touching people or things that are infected with it. Compare **infectious**. ❑ *a highly contagious disease of the lungs* **2** A feeling or attitude that is **contagious** spreads quickly among a group of people. = infectious ❑ *Laughing is contagious.*

✪con·tain ♦♦◇ /kən'teɪn/ VERB [т] (**contains**, **containing**, **contained**) **1** If something such as a box, bag, room, or place **contains** things, those things are inside it. ❑ *The envelope contained a Christmas card.* ❑ *The first two floors of*

C

the building contain retail space and a restaurant. **2** If a substance **contains** something, that thing is a part of it. ❑ *Watermelon contains vitamins and also potassium.* ❑ *Many cars run on petrol which contains lead.* **3** If writing, speech, or film **contains** particular information, ideas, or images, it includes them. ❑ *This sheet contained a list of problems a patient might like to raise with the doctor.* **4** If a group or organization **contains** a certain number of people, those are the people that are in it. ❑ *The committee contains 11 Democrats and nine Republicans.* **5** If you **contain** something, you control it and prevent it from spreading or increasing. ❑ *More than a hundred firemen are still trying to contain the fire at the plant.*
→ See also **self-contained**

✪ **con·tain·er** /kənˈteɪnə/ NOUN [c] (**containers**) **1** A **container** is something such as a box or bottle that is used to hold or store things in. = receptacle, vessel ❑ *the plastic containers in which fish are stored and sold* **2** A **container** is a very large metal or wooden box used for transporting goods so that they can be loaded easily onto ships and trucks. ❑ *The train, carrying loaded containers, was 1.2 miles long.*

con·tain·ment /kənˈteɪnmənt/ NOUN [u] **1** **Containment** is the action or policy of keeping another country's power or area of control within acceptable limits or boundaries. **2** [usu containment 'of' N] The **containment** of something dangerous or unpleasant is the act or process of keeping it under control within a particular area or place. = control ❑ *Fire crews are hoping they can achieve full containment of the fire before the winds pick up.*

✪ **con·tami·nant** /kənˈtæmɪnənt/ NOUN [c] (**contaminants**) [usu pl] (*formal*) A **contaminant** is something that contaminates a substance such as water or food. ❑ *Contaminants found in poultry will also be found in their eggs.* ❑ *We are exposed to an overwhelming number of chemical contaminants every day in our air, water and food.*

✪ **con·tami·nate** /kənˈtæmɪneɪt/ VERB [t] (**contaminates, contaminating, contaminated**) If something **is contaminated by** dirt, chemicals, or radiation, they make it dirty or harmful. ❑ *Have any fish been contaminated in the Arctic Ocean?* ❑ *The water that does run into the park is contaminated by chemicals.*

✪ **con·tami·nat·ed** /kənˈtæmɪneɪtɪd/ ADJ ❑ *Nuclear weapons plants across the country are heavily contaminated with toxic wastes.* ❑ *More than 100,000 people could fall ill after drinking contaminated water.*

✪ **con·tami·na·tion** /kənˌtæmɪˈneɪʃən/ NOUN [u] ❑ *The contamination of the ocean around Puget Sound may be just the beginning.* ❑ *There is a slight danger of bacterial contamination.*

con·tem·plate /ˈkɒntəmpleɪt/ VERB [t] (**contemplates, contemplating, contemplated**) **1** If you **contemplate** an action, you think about whether to do it or not. = consider ❑ *For a time he contemplated a career as an army medical doctor.* **2** If you **contemplate** an idea or subject, you think about it carefully for a long time. ❑ *As he lay in his hospital bed that night, he cried as he contemplated his future.* **3** If you **contemplate** something or someone, you look at them for a long time. ❑ *He contemplated his hands, still frowning.*

con·tem·pla·tion /ˌkɒntəmˈpleɪʃən/ NOUN [u] **1** *It is a place of quiet contemplation.* **2** *He was lost in the contemplation of the landscape for a while.*

✪ **con·tem·po·rary** ◆◇◇ /kənˈtempərəri, AmE -pəreri/ ADJ, NOUN (*academic word*)
ADJ **1** **Contemporary** things are modern and relate to the present time. = modern, present-day, current; ≠ old-fashioned ❑ *She writes a lot of contemporary music for people like Rihanna.* ❑ *one of the finest collections of contemporary art in the country* ❑ *Only the names are ancient; the characters are modern and contemporary.* **2** **Contemporary** people or things were alive or happened at the same time as something else you are talking about. ❑ *drawing upon official records and the reports of contemporary witnesses* ❑ *He was easily recognised from contemporary paintings.*
NOUN [c] (**contemporaries**) Someone's **contemporary** is a

person who is or was alive at the same time as them. ❑ *Like most of my contemporaries, I grew up in a vastly different world.*

con·tempt /kənˈtempt/ NOUN [u] If you have **contempt for** someone or something, you have no respect for them or think that they are unimportant. ❑ *He has contempt for those beyond his immediate family circle.*

✪ **con·tend** /kənˈtend/ VERB [i, t, RECIP] (**contends, contending, contended**) **1** [i] If you have to **contend with** a problem or difficulty, you have to deal with it or overcome it. ❑ *It is time, once again, to contend with racism.* **2** [t] (*formal*) If you **contend that** something is true, you state or argue that it is true. = state, argue ❑ *The government contends that he is fundamentalist.* ❑ *The Government strongly contends that no student should be compelled to pay a fee to support political activism.* **3** [RECIP] If you **contend with** someone **for** something such as power, you compete with them to try to get it. ❑ *the two main groups contending for power* ❑ *Small clubs such as the Kansas City Royals have had trouble contending with richer teams for championships.*

con·tend·er /kənˈtendə/ NOUN [c] (**contenders**) (*journalism*) A **contender** is someone who takes part in a competition. ❑ *Her trainer said yesterday that she would be a strong contender for a place on the Olympic team.*

✪ **con·tent** ◆◇◇ NOUN, ADJ
NOUN /ˈkɒntent/ [PL, u, SING] (**contents**) **1** [PL] The **contents** of a container such as a bottle, box, or room are the things that are inside it. ❑ *Empty the contents of the pan into the sieve.* ❑ *Sandon Hall and its contents will be auctioned by Sotheby's on October 6.* **2** [PL] The **contents** of a book are its different chapters and sections, usually shown in a list at the beginning of the book. = index, chapters ❑ *There is no Table of Contents.* ❑ *I ran my eye down the contents page.* **3** [u] [also contents, usu content 'of' N] If you refer to the **content** or **contents** of something such as a book, television programme, or website, you are referring to the subject that it deals with, the story that it tells, or the ideas that it expresses. ❑ *She is reluctant to discuss the content of the play.* ❑ *Stricter controls were placed on the content of videos.* **4** [u] The **content** of something such as an educational course or a programme of action is the elements that it consists of. ❑ *Previous students have had nothing but praise for the course content and staff.* **5** [SING] You can use **content** to refer to the amount or proportion of something that a substance contains. ❑ *Sunflower margarine has the same fat content as butter.*
ADJ /kənˈtent/ **1** [V-LINK + content] If you are **content with** something, you are willing to accept it, rather than wanting something more or something better. ❑ *I am content to admire the mountains from below.* ❑ *I'm perfectly content with the way the campaign has gone.* **2** [V-LINK + content] If you are **content**, you are fairly happy or satisfied. ❑ *He says his daughter is quite content.*
✦ **to your heart's content** → see **heart**

USAGE NOTE

content

Content is either a plural noun or an uncountable noun. Do not say 'a content'.
*She did not know anything about **the contents** of the report.*
*She did not know anything about **the content** of the report.*

---

con·tent·ed /kənˈtentɪd/ ADJ If you are **contented**, you are satisfied with your life or the situation you are in. ❑ *Whenever he returns to this place, he is happy and contented.*

✪ **con·ten·tion** /kənˈtenʃən/ NOUN [c, u] (**contentions**) **1** [c] Someone's **contention** is the idea or opinion that they are expressing in an argument or discussion. = claim ❑ *It is my contention that death and murder always lurk as potentials in violent relationships.* ❑ *This evidence supports their contention that the outbreak of violence was prearranged.* ❑ *Sufficient research evidence exists to support this contention.* **2** [u] If something is a cause **of contention**, it is a cause of disagreement or argument. ❑ *His case has become a source of contention between civil liberties activists and the government.*

con·ten·tious /kənˈtenʃəs/ ADJ (*formal*) A **contentious**

issue causes a lot of disagreement or arguments. = controversial ❑ *Sanctions are expected to be among the most contentious issues.*

con·tent·ment /kən'tentmənt/ NOUN [U] Contentment is a feeling of quiet happiness and satisfaction. ❑ *I cannot describe the feeling of contentment that was with me at that time.*

con·test ◆◇◇ NOUN, VERB

NOUN /'kɒntest/ [c] (contests) **1** A contest is a competition or game that people try to win. ❑ *Few contests in the recent history of boxing have been as thrilling.* **2** A contest is a struggle to win power or control. ❑ *The state election in November will be the last such ballot before next year's presidential contest.*

VERB /kən'test/ [T] (contests, contesting, contested) **1** If you contest a statement or decision, you object to it formally because you think it is wrong or unreasonable. = dispute ❑ *Your former employer has to reply within 14 days in order to contest the case.* **2** (*BrE*) If someone contests an election or competition, they take part in it and try to win it. ❑ *He quickly won his party's nomination to contest the elections.*

❍**con·text** ◆◆◇ /'kɒntekst/ NOUN (*academic word*) NOUN [c, u] (contexts) **1** The context of an idea or event is the general situation that relates to it, and which helps it to be understood. = circumstances, conditions, situation, background ❑ *We are doing this work in the context of reforms in the economic, social and cultural spheres.* ❑ *It helps to understand the historical context in which Chaucer wrote.* **2** The context of a word, sentence, or text consists of the words, sentences, or text before and after it which help to make its meaning clear. ❑ *Without a context, I would have assumed it was written by a man.* ❑ *a neutral remark which, in the context of the article, sounded condemnatory* PHRASES **in context** If something is seen in context or if it is put into context, it is considered together with all the factors that relate to it. ❑ *Taxation is not popular in principle, merely acceptable in context.* ❑ *It is important that we put Jesus into the context of history.* **out of context** If a statement or remark is quoted out of context, the circumstances in which it was said are not correctly reported, so that it seems to mean something different from the meaning that was intended. ❑ *Thomas says that he has been quoted out of context.*

❍**con·ti·nent** ◆◆◇ /'kɒntɪnənt/ NOUN [c, SING] (continents) **1** [c] A continent is a very large area of land, such as Africa or Asia, that consists of several countries. ❑ *She loved the African continent.* ❑ *Dinosaurs evolved when most continents were joined in a single land mass.* **2** [SING] (*mainly BrE*) People sometimes use the Continent to refer to the continent of Europe except for Britain. ❑ *Its shops are among the most stylish on the Continent.*

❍**con·ti·nen·tal** /ˌkɒntɪ'nentəl/ ADJ **1** Continental is used to refer to something that belongs to or relates to a continent. ❑ *The most ancient parts of the continental crust are 4000 million years old.* **2** [continental + N] (*mainly BrE*) Continental means situated on or belonging to the continent of Europe except for Britain. ❑ *He sees no signs of improvement in the UK and continental economy.*

con·tin·gent /kən'tɪndʒənt/ NOUN [c] (contingents) (*formal*) **1** A contingent of police, soldiers, or military vehicles is a group of them. ❑ *Nigeria provided a large contingent of troops to the West African Peacekeeping Force.* **2** A contingent is a group of people representing a country or organization at a meeting or other event. ❑ *The American contingent will stay overnight in London.*

con·tin·ual /kən'tɪnjuəl/ ADJ **1** [continual + N] A continual process or situation happens or exists without stopping. = continuous ❑ *The school has been in continual use since 1883.* ❑ *They felt continual pressure to perform well.* **2** [continual + N] Continual events happen again and again. ❑ *the government's continual demands for cash to finance its chronic deficit*

con·tinu·al·ly /kən'tɪnjuəli/ ADV **1** If a process or situation happens or exists continually, it happens or exists without stopping. = continuously ❑ *She cried almost continually and threw temper tantrums.* **2** If events

happen continually, they happen again and again. = continuously ❑ *Malcolm was continually changing his mind.*

con·tinu·ation /kənˌtɪnju'eɪʃən/ NOUN [c, u] (continuations) **1** [c, u] The continuation of something is the fact that it continues, instead of stopping. ❑ *It's the coalition forces who are to blame for the continuation of the war.* **2** [c] Something that is a continuation of something else is closely connected with it or forms part of it. ❑ *This chapter is a continuation of Chapter 8.*

con·tinue ◆◆◆ /kən'tɪnjuː/ VERB [I, T] (continues, continuing, continued) **1** [I, T] If someone or something continues to do something, they keep doing it and do not stop. ❑ *I hope they continue to fight for equal justice after I'm gone.* ❑ *Diana and Roy Jarvis are determined to continue working when they reach retirement age.* **2** [I, T] If something continues or if you continue it, it does not stop. ❑ *He insisted that the conflict would continue until conditions were met for a ceasefire.* ❑ *Outside the building people continue their vigil, huddling around bonfires.* **3** [I, T] If you continue something or continue with something, you start doing it again after a break or interruption. = carry on ❑ *I went up to my room to continue with my packing.* ❑ *She looked up for a minute and then continued drawing.* **4** [I, T] If something continues or if you continue it, it starts again after a break or interruption. ❑ *He denies 18 charges. The trial continues today.* **5** [I, T] If you continue, you begin speaking again after a pause or interruption. ❑ *'You have no right to intimidate this man,' Alison continued.* ❑ *Tony drank some coffee before he continued.* **6** [I] If you continue as something or continue in a particular state, you remain in a particular job or state. ❑ *He had hoped to continue as a full-time career officer.* **7** [I] If you continue in a particular direction, you keep walking or travelling in that direction. ❑ *He continued rapidly up the path, not pausing until he neared the Chapter House.*

con·ti·nu·ity /ˌkɒntɪ'njuːɪti, *AmE* -'nuː-/ NOUN [c, u] (continuities) Continuity is the fact that something continues to happen or exist, with no great changes or interruptions. ❑ *a tank designed to ensure continuity of fuel supply during aerobatics*

❍**con·tinu·ous** /kən'tɪnjuəs/ ADJ **1** A continuous process or event continues for a period of time without stopping. = unbroken, constant, uninterrupted; ≠ occasional ❑ *Residents report that they heard continuous gunfire.* ❑ *a record of five years' continuous employment* **2** A continuous line or surface has no gaps or holes in it. ❑ *a continuous line of boats* **3** In English grammar, continuous verb groups are formed using the auxiliary 'be' and the present participle of a verb, as in 'I'm feeling a bit tired' and 'She had been watching them for some time'. Continuous verb groups are used especially when you are focusing on a particular moment. Compare simple. = progressive

❍**con·tinu·ous·ly** /kən'tɪnjuːəsli/ ADV = constantly; ≠ occasionally ❑ *The civil war has raged almost continuously since 1976.* ❑ *It is the oldest continuously-inhabited city in America.*

❍**con·tract** ◆◆◇ NOUN, VERB (*academic word*) NOUN /'kɒntrækt/ [c] (contracts) A contract is a legal agreement, usually between two companies or between an employer and employee, which involves doing work for a stated sum of money. = commission, agreement ❑ *The company won a hefty contract for work on Chicago's tallest building.* ❑ *He was given a seven-year contract with an annual salary of $150,000.* ❑ *Have you read the contract?* PHRASE **under contract** If you are under contract to someone, you have signed a contract agreeing to work for them, and for no one else, during a fixed period of time. ❑ *The director wanted Olivia de Havilland, then under contract to Warner Brothers.*

VERB /kən'trækt/ [T, I] (contracts, contracting, contracted) **1** [T] (*formal*) If you contract with someone to do something, you legally agree to do it for them or for them to do it for you. ❑ *You can contract with us to deliver your cargo.* **2** [I, T] When something contracts or when something contracts it, it becomes smaller or shorter.

C

≠ expand ❑ *Blood is only expelled from the heart when it contracts.* ❑ *New research shows that an excess of meat and salt can contract muscles.* **3** [I] When something such as an economy or market **contracts**, it becomes smaller. ❑ *The manufacturing economy contracted in October for the sixth consecutive month.* **4** [T] (*formal*) If you **contract** a serious illness, you become ill with it. ❑ *He contracted AIDS from a blood transfusion.*

PHRASAL VERB **contract out** (*business*) If a company **contracts out** work, they employ other companies to do it. ❑ *Firms can contract out work to one another.* ❑ *When the bank contracted out its cleaning, the new company was cheaper.*

WORD CONNECTIONS

VERB + **contract**

win a contract
give a contract
award a contract
offer a contract
sign a contract

❑ *The contract for the building work was awarded to a German company.*

ADJ + **contract**

a **one-year** contract
a **long-term** contract
a **new** contract

❑ *New employees are only being offered one-year contracts.*

⊙ **con·trac·tion** /kənˈtrækʃən/ NOUN [C, U] (**contractions**) **1** [C, U] **Contraction** is the process of becoming smaller or shorter. ≠ expansion ❑ *the contraction and expansion of blood vessels* ❑ *Foods and fluids are mixed in the stomach by its muscular contractions.* **2** [C] When a woman who is about to give birth has **contractions**, she experiences a very strong, painful tightening of the muscles of her womb. ❑ *The contractions were getting stronger.* **3** [C] A **contraction** is a shortened form of a word or words. ❑ *'It's' (with an apostrophe) can be used as a contraction for 'it is'.*

con·trac·tor /ˈkɒntræktə, kənˈtræk-/ NOUN [C] (**contractors**) (*business*) A **contractor** is a person or company that does work for other people or organizations. ❑ *We told the building contractor that we wanted a garage big enough for two cars.*

⊙ **contra·dict** /ˌkɒntrəˈdɪkt/ VERB [T] (**contradicts, contradicting, contradicted**) (*academic word*) **1** If you **contradict** someone, you tell them that what they have just said is wrong, or suggest that it is wrong by saying something different. ❑ *She dared not contradict him.* ❑ *His comments appeared to contradict remarks made earlier in the day by the chairman.* **2** If one statement or piece of evidence **contradicts** another, the first one makes the second one appear to be wrong. ❑ *Her version contradicted her daughter's.* ❑ *Often his conclusions flatly contradicted orthodox medical opinion.*

WORD PARTS

The prefix **contra-** often appears in words that have 'opposite' or 'against' as part of their meaning:
contradict (VERB)
contradictory (ADJ)
contravene (VERB)

⊙ **contra·dic·tion** /ˌkɒntrəˈdɪkʃən/ NOUN [C] (**contradictions**) If you describe an aspect of a situation as a **contradiction**, you mean that it is completely different from other aspects, and so makes the situation confused or difficult to understand. = inconsistency, conflict ❑ *The militants see no contradiction in using violence to bring about a religious state.* ❑ *In my opinion, there is no contradiction between the two types of treatment.* ❑ *The performance seemed to me unpardonable, a contradiction of all that the Olympics is supposed to be.* ❑ *There are various contradictions in the evidence.*

⊙ **contra·dic·tory** /ˌkɒntrəˈdɪktəri, AmE -tɔːri/ ADJ If two or more facts, ideas, or statements are **contradictory**, they state or imply that opposite things are true.

= inconsistent, conflicting, incompatible ❑ *Customs officials have made a series of contradictory statements about the equipment.* ❑ *advice that sometimes is contradictory and confusing*

⊙ **con·tra·ry** /ˈkɒntrəri, AmE -treri/ ADJ, NOUN (*academic word*)

ADJ Ideas, attitudes, or reactions that are **contrary to** each other are completely different from each other. ❑ *This view is contrary to the aims of critical social research for a number of reasons.* ❑ *Several of those present had contrary information.* ❑ *people with contrary interests*

PHRASE **contrary to** (*emphasis*) If you say that something is true **contrary to** other people's beliefs or opinions, you are emphasizing that it is true and that they are wrong. ❑ *Contrary to popular belief, moderate exercise actually decreases your appetite.*

NOUN

PHRASES **on the contrary** **1** You use **on the contrary** when you have just said or implied that something is not true and are going to say that the opposite is true. ❑ *It is not an idea around which the community can unite. On the contrary, I see it as one that will divide us.* **2** (*emphasis*) You can use **on the contrary** when you are disagreeing strongly with something that has just been said or implied, or are making a strong negative reply. ❑ *'People just don't do things like that.'—'On the contrary, they do them all the time.'* **to the contrary** When a particular idea is being considered, evidence or statements **to the contrary** suggest that this idea is not true or that the opposite is true. ❑ *He continued to maintain that he did nothing wrong, despite clear evidence to the contrary.*

USAGE NOTE

on the contrary

When you are going to mention a situation that contrasts with one you have just described, use 'on the other hand'. Do not use 'on the contrary'.
It can be dirty and noisy living in the centre of the town. **On the other hand**, *it's useful when you want to buy something.*

⊙ **con·trast** ♦◇◇ NOUN, VERB (*academic word*)

NOUN /ˈkɒntrɑːst/ [C, U] (**contrasts**) **1** [C, U] A **contrast** is a great difference between two or more things which is clear when you compare them. ❑ *the contrast between town and country* ❑ *The two visitors provided a startling contrast in appearance.* **2** [U] **Contrast** is the degree of difference between the darker and lighter parts of a photograph, television picture, or painting. ❑ *a television with brighter colours, better contrast, and digital sound*

PHRASES **by contrast** or **in contrast** or **in contrast to something** You say **by contrast** or **in contrast**, or **in contrast to** something, to show that you are mentioning a very different situation from the one you have just mentioned. ❑ *The private sector, by contrast, has plenty of money to spend.* ❑ *In contrast, the lives of girls in well-to-do families were often very sheltered.*

in contrast If one thing is **in contrast to** another, it is very different from it. ❑ *His public statements have always been in marked contrast to those of his son.*

VERB /kənˈtrɑːst, -ˈtræst/ [T, RECIP] (**contrasts, contrasting, contrasted**) **1** [T] If you **contrast** one thing **with** another, you point out or consider the differences between those things. ❑ *She contrasted the situation then with the present crisis.* ❑ *Contrast that approach with what goes on in most organizations.* ❑ *In this section we contrast four possible broad approaches.* **2** [RECIP] If one thing **contrasts with** another, it is very different from it. = differ ❑ *Johnson's easy charm contrasted sharply with the prickliness of his boss.* ❑ *Paint the wall in a contrasting colour.*

contra·vene /ˌkɒntrəˈviːn/ VERB [T] (**contravenes, contravening, contravened**) (*formal*) To **contravene** a law or rule means to do something that is forbidden by the law or rule. = break ❑ *The board has banned the film on the grounds that it contravenes criminal libel laws.*

contra·ven·tion /ˌkɒntrəˈvenʃən/ NOUN [C, U] (**contraventions**) ❑ *The government has lent millions of dollars to debt-ridden banks in contravention of local banking laws.*

C

♦**con·trib·ute** ♦◇◇ /kən'trɪbjuːt/ VERB [I, T]
(**contributes, contributing, contributed**) (*academic word*) **1** [I] If you **contribute to** something, you say or do things to help to make it successful. ❑ *The three sons also contribute to the family business.* ❑ *I believe that each of us can contribute to the future of the world.* **2** [I, T] To **contribute** money or resources **to** something means to give money or resources to help pay for something or to help achieve a particular purpose. = donate ❑ *The US is contributing $4 billion in loans, credits, and grants.* ❑ *Local businesses have agreed to contribute.* **3** [I] If something **contributes to** an event or situation, it is one of the causes of it. ❑ *The report says design faults in both the vessels contributed to the tragedy.* ❑ *Stress, both human and mechanical, may also be a contributing factor.*

♦**con·tri·bu·tion** ♦◇◇ /ˌkɒntrɪ'bjuːʃən/ NOUN [C]
(**contributions**) **1** If you make a **contribution to** something, you do something to help make it successful or to produce it. ❑ *American economists have made important contributions to the field of financial and corporate economics.* ❑ *He was awarded a prize for his contribution to world peace.* **2** A **contribution** is a sum of money that you give in order to help pay for something. = donation ❑ *This list ranked companies that make charitable contributions of a half million dollars or more.*

con·tribu·tor /kən'trɪbjʊtə/ NOUN [C] (**contributors**) **1** A **contributor** is someone who gives money or resources to help pay for something or to help achieve a particular purpose. ❑ *Candidates for Congress received 53 per cent of their funds from individual contributors.* **2** You can use **contributor** to refer to one of the causes of an event or situation, especially if that event or situation is an unpleasant one. ❑ *Old buses are major contributors to pollution in cities.*

con·trive /kən'traɪv/ VERB [T] (**contrives, contriving, contrived**) (*formal*) If you **contrive** an event or situation, you succeed in making it happen, often by tricking someone. ❑ *The oil companies were accused of contriving a shortage of petrol to justify price increases.*

con·trived /kən'traɪvd/ ADJ (*disapproval*) If you say that something someone says or does is **contrived**, you think it is false and deliberate, rather than natural and not planned. = artificial ❑ *There was nothing contrived about what he said.*

♦**con·trol** ♦♦♦ /kən'trəʊl/ NOUN, VERB
NOUN [U, C] (**controls**) **1** [U] **Control of** an organization, place, or system is the power to make all the important decisions about the way that it is run. = power, command ❑ *The restructuring involves Mr. Ronson giving up control of the company.* ❑ *The first aim of his government would be to establish control over the republic's territory.* **2** [U] [oft control 'of/over' N] If you have **control** of something or someone, you are able to make them do what you want them to do. ❑ *He lost control of his car.* ❑ *Some teachers have more control over pupils than their parents have.* **3** [U] If you show **control**, you prevent yourself behaving in an angry or emotional way. ❑ *He had a terrible temper, and sometimes he would completely lose control.* **4** [C] A **control** is a device such as a switch or lever which you use in order to operate a machine or other piece of equipment. ❑ *I practised operating the controls.* **5** [U] **Control** of prices, wages, or the activity of a particular group is the act by a government of using its power to restrict them. ❑ *Control of inflation remains the government's absolute priority.* **6** [C, U] **Controls** are the methods that a government uses to restrict increases, for example in prices, wages, or weapons. ❑ *Critics question whether price controls would do any good.* **7** [C, U] **Control** is used to refer to a place where your documents or luggage are officially checked when you enter a foreign country. ❑ *He went straight through Passport Control without incident.*
PHRASES **in control** If you are **in control** of something, you have the power to make all the important decisions about the way that it is run. ❑ *Nobody knows who is in control of the club.*
under someone's control If something is **under** your **control**, you have the power to make all the important

decisions about the way that it is run. ❑ *All the newspapers are under government control.*
out of control If something is **out of control**, no one has any power over it. ❑ *The fire is burning out of control.*
under control If something harmful is **under control**, it is being dealt with successfully and is unlikely to cause any more harm. ❑ *The situation is under control.*
VERB [T] (**controls, controlling, controlled**) **1** The people who **control** an organization or place have the power to make all the important decisions about the way that it is run. = manage, direct ❑ *He now controls the largest retail development empire in southern California.* ❑ *Almost all of the countries in Latin America were controlled by dictators.* ❑ *Minebea sold its controlling interest in both firms.* **2** To **control** a piece of equipment, process, or system means to make it work in the way that you want it to work. ❑ *a computerized system to control the gates* ❑ *Scientists would soon be able to manipulate human genes to control the aging process.* **3** When a government **controls** prices, wages, or the activity of a particular group, it uses its power to restrict them. ❑ *The federal government tried to control rising health-care costs.* **4** If you **control** yourself, or if you **control** your feelings, voice, or expression, you make yourself behave calmly even though you are feeling angry, excited, or upset. = restrain ❑ *Jo was advised to learn to control herself.* **5** To **control** something dangerous means to prevent it from becoming worse or from spreading. ❑ *the need to control environmental pollution*
con·trolled /kən'trəʊld/ ADJ **1** *a controlled experiment* **2** *Her manner was quiet and very controlled.*

con·trol·ler /kən'trəʊlə/ NOUN [C] (**controllers**) (*mainly BrE*) A **controller** is a person who has responsibility for a particular organization or for a particular part of an organization. ❑ *the job of controller of BBC1*

♦**con·tro·ver·sial** ♦◇◇ /ˌkɒntrə'vɜːʃəl/ ADJ If you describe something or someone as **controversial**, you mean that they are the subject of intense public argument, disagreement, or disapproval. ❑ *Immigration is a controversial issue in many countries.* ❑ *The changes are bound to be controversial.* ❑ *the controversial 19th century politician Charles Parnell*
♦**con·tro·ver·sial·ly** /ˌkɒntrə'vɜːʃəli/ ADV ❑ *More controversially, he claims that these higher profits cover the cost of finding fresh talent.* ❑ *the issues she controversially espoused*

♦**con·tro·ver·sy** ♦◇◇ /'kɒntrəvɜːsi, kən'trɒvəsi/ NOUN [C, U] (**controversies**) (*academic word*) **Controversy** is a lot of discussion and argument about something, often involving strong feelings of anger or disapproval. = argument, discussion, debate; ≠ agreement ❑ *The proposed cuts have caused considerable controversy.* ❑ *a fierce political controversy over human rights abuses*

con·vene /kən'viːn/ VERB [I, T] (**convenes, convening, convened**) (*academic word, formal*) If someone **convenes** a meeting or conference, they arrange for it to take place. You can also say that people **convene** or that a meeting **convenes**. ❑ *Last August he convened a meeting of his closest advisers at Camp David.*

♦**con·veni·ence** /kən'viːniəns/ NOUN [U, C] (**conveniences**) **1** [U] **Convenience** refers to doing things because they are easy, or very useful or suitable for a particular purpose. ≠ inconvenience ❑ *They may use a credit card for convenience.* ❑ *the convenience of a fast non-stop flight* ❑ *Internet banking offers greater convenience than telephone banking.* **2** [U] If something is done for your **convenience**, it is done in a way that is useful or suitable for you. ❑ *He was happy to make a detour for her convenience.* **3** [C] If you describe something as a **convenience**, you mean that it is very useful. ❑ *Mail order is a convenience for buyers who are too busy to shop.* **4** [C] **Conveniences** are pieces of equipment designed to make your life easier. ❑ *an apartment with all the modern conveniences*

♦**con·veni·ent** /kən'viːniənt/ ADJ **1** If a way of doing something is **convenient**, it is easy, or very useful or suitable for a particular purpose. = handy ❑ *a flexible and convenient way of paying for business expenses* ❑ *Customers find it more convenient to participate online.* **2** If you describe a place as **convenient**, you are pleased because it is near to

C

where you are, or because you can reach another place from there quickly and easily. = handy ❑ *The town is well placed for easy access to Washington DC and convenient for Dulles Airport.* ❑ *the university's convenient city location* **3** A **convenient** time to do something, for example to meet someone, is a time when you are free to do it or would like to do it. ❑ *She will try to arrange a mutually convenient time and place for an interview.*

⚡**con·veni·ent·ly** /kən'viːniəntli/ ADV **1** ≠ inconveniently ❑ *The body spray slips conveniently into your sports bag for freshening up after a game.* ❑ *The region falls conveniently into only four main geological areas.* **2** *It was very conveniently situated just across the road from the City Reference Library.* ❑ *He chose Simi Valley mainly because it was conveniently close to Los Angeles.*

⚡**con·ven·tion** ♦◇◇ /kən'venʃən/ NOUN [C, U] (**conventions**) (*academic word*) **1** [C, U] A **convention** is a way of behaving that is considered to be correct or polite by most people in a society. = custom, tradition, protocol ❑ *It's just a social convention that men don't wear skirts.* ❑ *Despite her wish to defy convention, she had become pregnant and married at 21.* **2** [C] In art, literature, or the theatre, a **convention** is a traditional method or style. ❑ *We go offstage and come back for the convention of the encore.* ❑ *the stylistic conventions of Egyptian art* **3** [C] A **convention** is an official agreement between countries or groups of people. = agreement, treaty ❑ *the UN convention on climate change* **4** [C] A **convention** is a large meeting of an organization or political group. = conference ❑ *the annual convention of the Society of Professional Journalists*

⚡**con·ven·tion·al** ♦◇◇ /kən'venʃənəl/ ADJ **1** Someone who is **conventional** has behaviour or opinions that are ordinary and normal. ❑ *a respectable married woman with conventional opinions* ❑ *this close, fairly conventional English family* **2** A **conventional** method or product is one that is usually used or that has been in use for a long time. = standard, traditional; ≠ unconventional ❑ *the risks and drawbacks of conventional family planning methods* **3** **Conventional** weapons and wars do not involve nuclear explosives. ❑ *We must reduce the danger of war by controlling nuclear, chemical, and conventional arms.*

⚡**con·ven·tion·al·ly** /kən'venʃənəli/ ADV **1** = traditionally ❑ *Men still wore their hair short and dressed conventionally.* **2** (conventionally with v) ❑ *Organically grown produce does not differ greatly in appearance from conventionally grown crops.*

con·verge /kən'vɜːdʒ/ VERB [I] (**converges, converging, converged**) **1** If people or vehicles **converge on** a place, they move towards it from different directions. ❑ *Hundreds of tractors will converge on the capital.* **2** (*formal*) If roads or lines **converge**, they meet or join at a particular place. ❑ *As they flow south, the five rivers converge.*

con·ver·gence /kən'vɜːdʒəns/ NOUN [C, U] (**convergences**) (*formal*) The **convergence** of different ideas, groups, or societies is the process by which they stop being different and become more similar. ❑ *the need to move towards greater economic convergence*

con·ver·sa·tion ♦◇◇ /ˌkɒnvə'seɪʃən/ NOUN [C] (**conversations**) If you have a **conversation with** someone, you talk with them, usually in an informal situation. ❑ *He's a talkative guy, and I struck up a conversation with him.*

con·ver·sa·tion·al /ˌkɒnvə'seɪʃənəl/ ADJ **Conversational** means relating to, or similar to, casual and informal talk. ❑ *What is refreshing is the author's easy, conversational style.*

⚡**con·verse** VERB, NOUN (*academic word*) VERB /kən'vɜːs/ [RECIP] (**converses, conversing, conversed**) (*formal*) If you **converse with** someone, you talk to them. You can also say that two people **converse**. ❑ *Luke sat directly behind the pilot and conversed with him.* NOUN /'kɒnvɜːs/ [SING] (*formal*) The **converse** of a statement is its opposite or reverse. = opposite ❑ *What you do for a living is critical to where you settle and how you live – and the converse is also true.*

⚡**con·verse·ly** /'kɒnvɜːsli, kən'vɜːsli/ ADV [conversely with CL] (*formal*) You say **conversely** to indicate that the situation you are about to describe is the opposite or

reverse of the one you have just described. ❑ *Malaysia and Indonesia rely on open markets for forest and fishery products. Conversely, some Asian countries are highly protectionist.* ❑ *That makes Chinese products even cheaper and, conversely, makes American-made goods more expensive to export.*

⚡**con·ver·sion** /kən'vɜːʃən/ NOUN [C, U] (**conversions**) **1** **Conversion** is the act or process of changing something into a different state or form. = adaptation, modification, alteration, transformation ❑ *the conversion of disused rail lines into cycle routes* ❑ *A loft conversion can add considerably to the value of a house.* **2** If someone changes their religion or beliefs, you can refer to their **conversion to** their new religion or beliefs. ❑ *his conversion to Christianity*

⚡**con·vert** ♦◇◇ VERB, NOUN (*academic word*) VERB /kən'vɜːt/ [I, T] (**converts, converting, converted**) **1** [I, T] If one thing **is converted** or **converts into** another, it is changed into a different form. = change, transform, alter ❑ *The signal will be converted into digital code.* ❑ *naturally occurring substances which the body can convert into vitamins* ❑ *Spreadsheet data is automatically converted to a table.* **2** [T] If someone **converts** a room or building, they alter it in order to use it for a different purpose. ❑ *By converting the attic, they were able to have two extra bedrooms.* ❑ *the entrepreneur who wants to convert County Hall into a hotel* **3** [T] If you **convert** a vehicle or piece of equipment, you change it so that it can use a different fuel. ❑ *Save money by converting your car to run on used vegetable oil.* **4** [T] If you **convert** a quantity **from** one system of measurement **to** another, you calculate what the quantity is in the second system. ❑ *Converting metric measurements to US equivalents is easy.* **5** [I, T] If someone **converts** you, they persuade you to change your religious or political beliefs. You can also say that someone **converts to** a different religion. ❑ *If you try to convert him, you could find he just walks away.* ❑ *He was a major influence in converting Godwin to political radicalism.* NOUN /'kɒnvɜːt/ [C] (**converts**) **1** [oft convert 'to' N] A **convert** is someone who has changed their religious or political beliefs. ❑ *She, too, was a convert to Roman Catholicism.* **2** [usu convert 'to' N] If you describe someone as a **convert to** something, you mean that they have recently become very enthusiastic about it. ❑ *As recent converts to vegetarianism and animal rights, they now live with a menagerie of stray animals.*

con·vert·ible /kən'vɜːtɪbəl/ NOUN, ADJ NOUN [C] (**convertibles**) A **convertible** is a car with a soft roof that can be folded down or removed. ❑ *Her own car is a convertible VW.* ADJ (*business*) In finance, **convertible** investments or money can be easily exchanged for other forms of investments or money. ❑ *the introduction of a convertible currency*

con·vert·ibil·ity /kənˌvɜːtɪ'bɪlɪti/ NOUN [U] ❑ *the convertibility of the peso*

⚡**con·vey** /kən'veɪ/ VERB [T] (**conveys, conveying, conveyed**) To **convey** information or feelings means to cause them to be known or understood by someone. = communicate ❑ *When I returned home, I tried to convey the wonder of this machine to my husband.* ❑ *He also conveyed his views and the views of the bureaucracy.* ❑ *In every one of her pictures she conveys a sense of immediacy.*

⚡**con·vict** ♦◇◇ VERB, NOUN VERB /kən'vɪkt/ [T] (**convicts, convicting, convicted**) If someone **is convicted of** a crime, they are found guilty of that crime in a court of law. ❑ *In 2007 he was convicted of murder and sentenced to life imprisonment.* ❑ *There was insufficient evidence to convict him.* ❑ *a convicted drug dealer* NOUN /'kɒnvɪkt/ [C] (**convicts**) (*journalism*) A **convict** is someone who is in prison. = prisoner ❑ *Neil Jordan's tale of two escaped convicts who get mistaken for priests*

⚡**con·vic·tion** ♦◇◇ /kən'vɪkʃən/ NOUN [C, U] (**convictions**) **1** [C] [usu conviction 'that'] A **conviction** is a strong belief or opinion. = belief ❑ *It is our firm conviction that a step forward has been taken.* **2** [C] If someone has a **conviction**, they have been found guilty of a crime in a court of law. ❑ *He will appeal against his conviction.* ❑ *The man was known to the police because of* previous convictions. **3** [U] If you have **conviction**, you have great confidence in your beliefs or opinions. ❑ *'We shall, sir', said Thorne, with conviction.*

⊙**con·vince** ◆◇◇ /kən'vɪns/ VERB [T] (**convinces, convincing, convinced**) (*academic word*) If someone or something **convinces** you **of** something, they make you believe that it is true or that it exists. ❑ *Although I soon convinced him of my innocence, I think he still has serious doubts about my sanity.* ❑ *We remain to be convinced of the validity of some of the research.* ❑ *The waste disposal industry is finding it difficult to convince the public that its operations are safe.*

WHICH WORD?

convince or persuade?

If you **convince** someone of something, you make them believe it is true.

❑ *It took them a few days to **convince** me that it was possible.*

If you **persuade** someone to do something, you make them do it by talking to them.

❑ *Marsha was trying to **persuade** Katrina to change her mind.*

---

con·vinced ◆◇◇ /kən'vɪnst/ ADJ If you are **convinced that** something is true, you feel sure that it is true. ❑ *He was convinced that I was part of the problem.* ❑ *He became convinced of the need for cheap editions of good quality writing.*

⊙**con·vinc·ing** /kən'vɪnsɪŋ/ ADJ If you describe someone or something as **convincing**, you mean that they make you believe that a particular thing is true, correct, or genuine. ❑ *Scientists say there is no convincing evidence that power lines have anything to do with cancer.* ❑ *The first explanation appears more convincing.*

con·vinc·ing·ly /kən'vɪnsɪŋli/ ADV [usu convincingly with v, also convincingly + ADJ] ❑ *He argued forcefully and convincingly that they were likely to bankrupt the budget.*

con·voy /'kɒnvɔɪ/ NOUN [C] (**convoys**) [also 'in' convoy] A **convoy** is a group of vehicles or ships travelling together. ❑ *a U.N. convoy carrying food and medical supplies* ❑ *humanitarian relief convoys*

con·vul·sion /kən'vʌlʃən/ NOUN [C] (**convulsions**) If someone has **convulsions**, they suffer uncontrollable movements of their muscles. ❑ *Thirteen per cent said they became unconscious at night and 5 per cent suffered convulsions.*

cook ◆◆◇ /kʊk/ VERB, NOUN
▸ VERB [I, T] (**cooks, cooking, cooked**) **1** When you **cook** a meal, you prepare food for eating by heating it. ❑ *I have to go and cook dinner.* ❑ *Chefs at the restaurant once cooked for President Kennedy.* **2** When you **cook** food, or when food **cooks**, it is heated until it is ready to be eaten. ❑ *some basic instructions on how to cook a turkey* ❑ *Let the vegetables cook gently for about 10 minutes.*
▸ PHRASAL VERB **cook up** (*informal*) **1** If someone **cooks up** a dishonest scheme, they plan it. ❑ *He must have cooked up his scheme on the spur of the moment.* **2** If someone **cooks up** an explanation or a story, they make it up. ❑ *She'll cook up a convincing explanation.*
▸ NOUN [C] (**cooks**) **1** A **cook** is a person whose job is to prepare and cook food, especially in someone's home or in an institution. = chef ❑ *They had a butler, a cook, and a maid.* **2** If you say that someone is a good **cook**, you mean they are good at preparing and cooking food. ❑ *I'm a lousy cook.*

cook·er /'kʊkə/ (*BrE; in AmE, use* **stove**) NOUN [C] (**cookers**) A **cooker** is a large metal device for cooking food using gas or electricity. A cooker usually consists of an oven, a grill, and some gas burners or electric rings.

cook·ery /'kʊkəri/ NOUN [U] **Cookery** is the activity of preparing and cooking food. ❑ *The school runs cookery classes throughout the year.*

cook·ing ◆◇◇ /'kʊkɪŋ/ NOUN, ADJ
▸ NOUN [U] **1** **Cooking** is the activity of preparing food by heating it. ❑ *He did the cooking, cleaning, laundry, and home repairs.* **2** **Cooking** is food which has been cooked. ❑ *The menu is based on classic French cooking.*

▸ ADJ [cooking + N] **Cooking** ingredients or equipment are used in cookery. ❑ *Finely slice the cooking apples.*

⊙**cool** ◆◆◇ /ku:l/ ADJ, NOUN, VERB
▸ ADJ (**cooler, coolest**) **1** Something that is **cool** has a temperature which is low but not very low. ❑ *I felt a current of cool air.* ❑ *The water was slightly cooler than a child's bath.* **2** If it is **cool**, or if a place is **cool**, the temperature of the air is low but not very low. ❑ *Thank goodness it's cool in here.* ❑ *Store grains and cereals in a cool, dry place.* **3** Clothing that is **cool** is made of thin material so that you do not become too hot in hot weather. ❑ *In warm weather, you should wear clothing that is cool and comfortable.* **4** [cool + N] **Cool** colours are light colours which give an impression of coolness. ❑ *Choose a cool colour such as cream.* **5** If you say that a person or their behaviour is **cool**, you mean that they are calm and unemotional, especially in a difficult situation. = calm ❑ *He was marvellously cool again, smiling as if nothing had happened.* **6** If you say that a person or their behaviour is **cool**, you mean that they are unfriendly or not enthusiastic. ❑ *I didn't like him at all. I thought he was cool, aloof, and arrogant.* **7** (*informal, approval*) If you say that a person or thing is **cool**, you mean that they are fashionable and attractive. ❑ *He was trying to be really cool and trendy.* ❑ *That's a cool hat.* **8** [V-LINK + cool] (*informal, approval*) If you say that someone is **cool about** something, you mean that they accept it and are not angry or upset about it. ❑ *Bev was really cool about it all.* **9** (*informal*) If you say that something or someone is **cool**, you think they are excellent in some way. = neat ❑ *Kathleen gave me a really cool dress.* ❑ *He's such a cool guy.*
▸ NOUN [SING] The **cool** is a temperature that is low but not very low. ❑ *She walked into the cool of the hallway.*
▸ VERB [I, T] (**cools, cooling, cooled**) **1** When something **cools** or when you **cool** it, it becomes lower in temperature. ≠ warm, heat ❑ *Drain the meat and allow it to cool.* ❑ *Huge fans will have to cool the concrete floor to keep it below 150 degrees.* ❑ *a cooling breeze* **2** When a feeling or emotion **cools**, or when you **cool** it, it becomes less powerful. ❑ *Within a few minutes tempers had cooled.*
▸ PHRASAL VERBS **cool down** **1** To **cool down** means the same as to **cool** VERB 1. ❑ *Avoid putting your car away until the engine has cooled down.* **2** If someone **cools down** or if you **cool them down**, they become less angry than they were. = calm down ❑ *He has had time to cool down and look at what happened more objectively.*
cool off **1** If someone or something **cools off**, or if you **cool them off**, they become cooler after having been hot. ❑ *Maybe he's trying to cool off out there in the rain.* ❑ *She made a fanning motion, pretending to cool herself off.* **2** If someone **cools off**, they become less angry than they were. ❑ *We've got to give him some time to cool off.*
cool·ly /'ku:lli/ ADV **1** *Everyone must think this situation through calmly and coolly.* **2** *'It's your choice, Nina,' David said coolly.*

⊙**co-operate** ◆◇◇ /kəʊ'ɒpəreɪt/ *also* **cooperate** VERB [I, RECIP] (**co-operates, co-operating, co-operated**) (*academic word*) **1** [I, RECIP] If you **co-operate with** someone, you work with them or help them for a particular purpose. You can also say that two people **co-operate**. = collaborate; ≠ conflict ❑ *The UN had been co-operating with the State Department on a plan to find countries willing to take the refugees.* ❑ *It was agreed that the two leaders should co-operate in a joint enterprise.* **2** [I] If you **co-operate**, you do what someone has asked or told you to do. ❑ *He agreed to co-operate with the police investigation.*
⊙**co-operation** /kəʊˌɒpə'reɪʃən/ NOUN [U] **1** = teamwork, collaboration; ≠ opposition ❑ *A deal with Japan could open the door to economic co-operation with East Asia.* **2** *The police underlined the importance of the public's co-operation in the hunt for the bombers.* ❑ *The patient's co-operation is of course essential.*

⊙**co-operative** /kəʊ'ɒpərətɪv/ *also* **cooperative** NOUN, ADJ
▸ NOUN [C] (**co-operatives**) (*business*) A **co-operative** is a business or organization run by the people who work for it, or owned by the people who use it. These people share

C

its benefits and profits. = collective □ *They decided a housing co-operative was the way to regenerate the area.* **ADJ** **1** A **co-operative** activity is done by people working together. □ *He was transferred to FBI custody in a smooth co-operative effort between Egyptian and US authorities.* **2** If you say that someone is **co-operative**, you mean that they do what you ask them to without complaining or arguing. = helpful, obliging, supportive; ≠ unco-operative □ *I made every effort to be co-operative.* □ *friendly and co-operative relations between the two countries* **co-operatively** /kəʊˈɒpərətɪvli/ ADV [co-operatively after v] □ *They agreed to work co-operatively to ease tensions wherever possible.*

✪**co-ordinate** also **coordinate** VERB, NOUN (*academic word*)

VERB /kəʊˈɔːdɪneɪt/ [RECIP, T] (**co-ordinates, co-ordinating, co-ordinated**) **1** [RECIP, T] If you **co-ordinate** an activity, you organize the various people and things involved in it. = organize, synchronize □ *Government officials visited the earthquake zone on Thursday morning to co-ordinate the relief effort.* □ *the setting up of an advisory committee to co-ordinate police work* **2** [T] If you **co-ordinate** the different parts of your body, you make them work together efficiently to perform particular movements. □ *You need to co-ordinate legs, arms, and breathing for the front crawl.* **3** [RECIP] If you **co-ordinate** clothes or furnishings that are used together, or if they **co-ordinate**, they are similar in some way and look nice together. □ *She'll show you how to co-ordinate pattern and colours.* □ *Tie it with fabric bows that co-ordinate with other furnishings.*

NOUN /kəʊˈɔːdɪnət/ [c] (**co-ordinates**) (*technical*) The **co-ordinates** of a point on a map or graph are the two sets of numbers or letters that you need in order to find that point. □ *Can you give me your co-ordinates?*

co-ordinated /kəʊˈɔːdɪneɪtɪd/ ADJ □ *Coalition forces were planning a co-ordinated effort to attack the drug trade.* □ *a well co-ordinated surprise attack*

co-ordinator /kəʊˈɔːdɪneɪtə/ NOUN [c] (**co-ordinators**) □ *the party's campaign co-ordinator, Mr Peter Mandelson*

✪**co-ordination** /kəʊˌɔːdɪˈneɪʃən/ also **coordination** NOUN

NOUN [u] **1** **Co-ordination** means organizing the activities of two or more groups so that they work together efficiently and know what the others are doing. = organization, synchronization □ *the lack of co-ordination between the civilian and military authorities* □ *the co-ordination of economic policy* **2** **Co-ordination** is the ability to use the different parts of your body together efficiently. □ *clumsiness and lack of co-ordination*

PHRASE **in co-ordination with** If you do something **in co-ordination with** someone else, you both organize your activities so that you work together efficiently.

cope ◆◇◇ /kəʊp/ VERB [I] (**copes, coping, coped**) **1** If you **cope with** a problem or task, you deal with it successfully. = manage □ *It was amazing how my mother coped with bringing up three children on less than thirty pounds a week.* **2** If you have to **cope with** an unpleasant situation, you have to accept it or bear it. = contend □ *Never before has the industry had to cope with war and recession at the same time.* **3** If a machine or a system can **cope with** something, it is large enough or complex enough to deal with it satisfactorily. □ *A giant washing machine copes with the mountain of laundry created by their nine boys and five girls.*

copi•er /ˈkɒpiə/ NOUN [c] (**copiers**) **1** A **copier** is a machine which makes exact copies of writing or pictures on paper, usually by a photographic process. = photocopier **2** A **copier** is someone who copies what someone else has done. □ *their reputation as a copier of other countries' designs, patents, and inventions*

cop•per /ˈkɒpə/ NOUN, ADJ

NOUN [u] **Copper** is reddish brown metal that is used to make things such as coins and electrical wires. □ *Chile is the world's largest producer of copper.*

ADJ (*literary*) **Copper** is sometimes used to describe things that are reddish-brown in colour. □ *His hair has reverted back to its original copper hue.*

copy ◆◆◇ /ˈkɒpi/ NOUN, VERB

NOUN [c] (**copies**) **1** If you make a **copy of** something, you produce something that looks like the original thing. = duplicate □ *The reporter apparently obtained a copy of Steve's resignation letter.* **2** A **copy of** a book, newspaper, or CD is one of many that are exactly the same. □ *I bought a copy of 'USA Today' from a street-corner machine.*

VERB [T, I] (**copies, copying, copied**) **1** [T] If you **copy** something, you produce something that looks like the original thing. □ *lawsuits against companies who have unlawfully copied computer programs* □ *He copied the chart from a book.* **2** [I, T] If you **copy**, or **copy** a piece of writing, you write it again exactly. □ *He copied the data into a notebook.* □ *We're copying from textbooks because we don't have enough to go round.* **3** [T] If you **copy** a letter, document, or e-mail to someone, you send them a copy of a letter or document that you have sent to someone else. □ *He fired off a letter and copied it to the president.* **4** [T] If you **copy** someone's answer, you look at what that person has written and write the same thing yourself, in order to cheat in a test or exam. □ *He would allow John slyly to copy his answers to impossibly difficult algebra questions.* **5** [T] If you **copy** a person or what they do, you try to do what they do or try to be like them, usually because you admire them or what they have done. = imitate □ *Children can be seen to copy the behaviour of others whom they admire or identify with.* □ *He can claim to have been defeated by opponents copying his own tactics.*

PHRASAL VERBS **copy in** (*BrE*) If you **copy** someone **in on** something, you send them a copy of something you have written to someone else.

copy out Copy out means the same as **copy** VERB **2**. □ *He wrote the title on the blackboard, then copied out the text, sentence by sentence.*

✪**copy•right** /ˈkɒpiraɪt/ NOUN [c, u] (**copyrights**) If someone has the **copyright** on a piece of writing or music, it is illegal to reproduce or perform it without their permission. □ *Who owns the copyright on this movie?* □ *To order a book one first had to get permission from the monastery that held the copyright.* □ *She threatened legal action against the newspaper for breach of copyright.*

cord /kɔːd/ NOUN [c, u] (**cords**) **1** Cord is strong, thick string. □ *The door had been tied shut with a length of nylon cord.* **2** Cord is wire covered in rubber or plastic which connects electrical equipment to an electricity supply. = cable □ *electrical cord* □ *an extension cord*

✪**core** ◆◇◇ /kɔː/ NOUN, VERB, ADJ (*academic word*)

NOUN [c, SING] (**cores**) **1** [c] The **core** of a fruit is the central part of it that contains seeds. □ *Someone threw an apple core.* **2** [c] [usu with POSS] The **core** of an object, building, or city is the central part of it. = centre □ *the Earth's core* □ *The core of the city is a series of ancient squares.* **3** [SING] The **core** of something such as a problem or an issue is the part of it that has to be understood or accepted before the whole thing can be understood or dealt with. = heart □ *the ability to get straight to the core of a problem* □ *At the core of this ideology was an ethnic nationalism.* **4** [SING] The **core** businesses or the **core** activities of a company or organization are their most important ones. □ *The core activities of social workers were reorganized.* □ *The group plans to concentrate on six core businesses.* □ *However, the main core of the company performed outstandingly.*

VERB [T] (**cores, coring, cored**) If you **core** a fruit, you remove its core. □ *machines for peeling and coring apples*

ADJ **1** A **core** team or a **core** group is a group of people who do the main part of a job or piece of work. Other people may also help, but only for limited periods of time. □ *We already have our core team in place.* **2** In a school or college, **core** subjects are a group of subjects that have to be studied. □ *The core subjects are English, mathematics and science.* □ *I'm not opposed to a core curriculum in principle, but I think requiring a foreign language is unrealistic.*

corn /kɔːn/ NOUN [u] **1** (*BrE; in AmE, use* **grain**) Corn is used to refer to crops such as wheat and barley. It can also be used to refer to the seeds from these plants. **2** (*mainly AmE; in BrE, use* **maize**) Corn is a tall plant which produces long vegetables covered with yellow seeds. It can also be used to refer to the yellow seeds. ❑ *rows of corn in an Iowa field* ❑ *We're having corn-on-the-cob for lunch.*

cor·ner ♦♦◇ /'kɔːnə/ NOUN, VERB

NOUN [c] (**corners**) **1** A **corner** is a point or an area where two or more edges, sides, or surfaces of something join. ❑ *He saw the corner of a magazine sticking out from under the blanket.* **2** The **corner** of a room, box, or similar space is the area inside it where its edges or walls meet. ❑ *a card table in the corner of the living room* ❑ *The ball hurtled into the far corner of the net.* **3** The **corner of** your mouth or eye is the side of it. ❑ *She flicked a crumb off the corner of her mouth.* **4** The **corner** of a street is the place where one of its sides ends as it joins another street. ❑ *She would spend the day hanging around street corners.* ❑ *We can't have police officers on every corner.* **5** A **corner** is a bend in a road. = bend ❑ *a sharp corner* **6** In football, hockey, and some other sports, a **corner** is a free shot or kick taken from the corner of the field. ❑ *McPherson took the corner and James crashed his header off the crossbar and over the line.*

PHRASES **around the corner** or **round the corner** **1** If you say that something is **around the corner**, you mean that it will happen very soon. = imminent ❑ *Economic recovery is just around the corner.* **2** If you say that something is **around the corner**, you mean that it is very near. ❑ *My new place is just around the corner.*

cut corners (*disapproval*) If you **cut corners**, you do something quickly by doing it in a less thorough way than you should. ❑ *Take your time, don't cut corners, and follow instructions to the letter.*

VERB [t, i] (**corners, cornering, cornered**) **1** [t] If you **corner** a person or animal, you force them into a place they cannot escape from. ❑ *A police motorcycle chased his car twelve miles, and cornered him near Gainsborough.* **2** [t] If you **corner** someone, you force them to speak to you when they have been trying to avoid you. ❑ *Thomas managed to corner the young producer-director for an interview.* **3** [t] (*business*) If a company or place **corners** an area of trade, they gain control over it so that no one else can have any success in that area. = monopolize ❑ *Sony has cornered the market in chic-looking MP3 players.* **4** [i] If a car, or the person driving it, **corners** in a particular way, the car goes around bends in roads in this way. ❑ *Peter drove jerkily, cornering too fast and fumbling the gears.*

cor·ner·stone /'kɔːnəstəʊn/ NOUN [c] (**cornerstones**) (*formal*) The **cornerstone of** something is the basic part of it on which its existence, success, or truth depends. = keystone ❑ *Research is the cornerstone of the profession.*

cor·po·ral /'kɔːprəl/ NOUN [c] (**corporals**) A **corporal** is a noncommissioned officer in the army or United States Marines. ❑ *The corporal shouted an order at the men.*

✪**cor·po·rate** ♦◇◇ /'kɔːprət/ ADJ [corporate + N] (*academic word*) **Corporate** means relating to business corporations or to a particular business corporation. ❑ *top US corporate executives* ❑ *a corporate lawyer* ❑ *the UK corporate sector* ❑ *This established a strong corporate image.*

✪**cor·po·ra·tion** ♦◇◇ /ˌkɔːpəˈreɪʃən/ NOUN [c] (**corporations**) (*business*) A **corporation** is a large business or company with special rights and powers. = business, firm, company, organization ❑ *multinational corporations* ❑ *Many voters resented the power of big corporations.* ❑ *the Seiko Corporation*

corps /kɔː/ NOUN [c] (**corps**) **1** A **corps** is a part of the army which has special duties. ❑ *the Army Medical Corps* **2** A **corps** is a small group of people who do a special job. ❑ *the diplomatic corps*

corpse /kɔːps/ NOUN [c] (**corpses**) A **corpse** is a dead body, especially the body of a human being. = body ❑ *Detectives placed the corpse in a body bag.*

✪**cor·rect** ♦♦◇ /kəˈrekt/ ADJ, VERB

ADJ **1** If something is **correct**, it is right and true. = right; ≠ incorrect, wrong, inaccurate ❑ *The correct answers can be found at the bottom of page 8.* ❑ *The following information was correct at time of going to press.* ❑ *Doctors examine their patients thoroughly in order to make a correct diagnosis.* **2** [V-LINK + correct] (*formal*) If someone is **correct**, what they have said or thought is true. = right ❑ *You are absolutely correct. The leaves are from a bay tree.*

3 [correct + N] The **correct** thing or method is the thing or method that is required or is most suitable in a particular situation. = right ❑ *The use of the correct materials was crucial.* ❑ *White was in no doubt the referee made the correct decision.* ❑ *the correct way to produce a crop of tomato plants* **4** [correct with CL] If you say that someone is **correct in** doing something, you approve of their action. = right ❑ *You are perfectly correct in trying to steer your mother towards increased independence.* **5** If a person or their behaviour is **correct**, their behaviour is in accordance with social or other rules. = proper ❑ *He was very polite and very correct.*

VERB [t] (**corrects, correcting, corrected**) **1** If you **correct** a problem, mistake, or fault, you do something which puts it right. = rectify ❑ *He may need surgery to correct the problem.* ❑ *He has criticised the government for inefficiency and delays in correcting past mistakes.* **2** If you **correct** someone, you say something which you think is more accurate or appropriate than what they have just said. ❑ *'Actually, that isn't what happened,' George corrects me.* **3** When someone **corrects** a piece of writing, they look at it and mark the mistakes in it. ❑ *It took an extraordinary effort to focus on preparing his classes or correcting his students' work.*

✪**cor·rect·ly** /kəˈrektli/ ADV **1** [correctly with V] ≠ incorrectly ❑ *Did I pronounce your name correctly?* ❑ *The report correctly identifies the problems.* ❑ *You have to correctly answer each question.* **2** = properly; ≠ incorrectly ❑ *If correctly executed, this shot will give them a better chance of getting the ball close to the hole.* ❑ *The software was not installed correctly.* **3** [correctly with V] ❑ *I think the police commission acted correctly.* **4** *She began speaking politely, even correctly.*

cor·rect·ness /kəˈrektnəs/ NOUN [u] **1** = accuracy ❑ *Ask the investor to check the correctness of what he has written.* **2** *his stiff-legged gait and formal correctness*

VOCABULARY BUILDER

correct ADJ
If something is **correct**, it is right and true.
❑ *Follow the instructions for the correct dosage for your child's age.*

accurate ADJ
Accurate information, measurements, and statistics are correct to a very detailed level.
❑ *Police have stressed that this is the most accurate description of the suspect to date.*

legitimate ADJ
Something that is **legitimate** is acceptable according to the law.
❑ *This is one of the perfectly legitimate ways in which the business has kept its tax bill so low.*

precise ADJ
Something that is **precise** is correct in all its details.
❑ *I seem to remember giving you very precise instructions as to what the scope of your duties were.*

right ADJ
If something is **right**, it contains no mistakes and agrees with the facts.
❑ *I did not know if Mark's answer was right or wrong.*

true ADJ
If something is **true**, it is based on facts rather than being invented or imagined, and is accurate and reliable.
❑ *The judge said that there was no evidence that this popular claim was true.*

✪**cor·rec·tion** /kəˈrekʃən/ NOUN [c, u] (**corrections**) **1** [c, u] The **correction** of a problem, mistake, or fault is the act of doing something which puts it right. ❑ *legislation to require the correction of factual errors* ❑ *We will then make the necessary corrections.* **2** [c] **Corrections** are marks or comments made on a piece of work, especially school work, which indicate where there are mistakes and

C

what are the right answers. ❑ *In a group, compare your corrections to Exercise 2A.*

⊙ **cor·re·late** /ˈkɒrəleɪt, AmE ˈkɔːr-/ VERB [RECIP, T] (**correlates, correlating, correlated**) (*formal*) **1** [RECIP] If one thing **correlates with** another, there is a close similarity or connection between them, often because one thing causes the other. You can also say that two things **correlate**. ❑ *Obesity correlates with increased risk for hypertension and stroke.* ❑ *The political opinions of spouses correlate more closely than their heights.* ❑ *The loss of respect for British science is correlated to reduced funding.* **2** [T] If you **correlate** things, you work out the way in which they are connected or the way they influence each other. ❑ *Attempts to correlate specific language functions with particular parts of the brain have not advanced very far.*

⊙ **cor·re·la·tion** /ˌkɒrəˈleɪʃən, AmE ˌkɔːr-/ NOUN [C] (**correlations**) (*formal*) A **correlation between** things is a connection or link between them. ❑ *the correlation between smoking and disease* ❑ *Studies have shown that there is a direct correlation between poor education and disposition to crime.*

⊙ **cor·re·spond** /ˌkɒrɪˈspɒnd, AmE ˌkɔːr-/ VERB [RECIP] (**corresponds, corresponding, corresponded**) (*academic word*) **1** If one thing **corresponds to** another, there is a close similarity or connection between them. You can also say that two things **correspond**. = match, relate to; ≠ differ ❑ *Racegoers will be given a number which will correspond to a horse running in a race.* ❑ *All buttons and switches were clearly numbered to correspond to the chart on the wall.* ❑ *A 22 per cent increase in car travel corresponds with a 19 per cent drop in cycle mileage per person.* ❑ *The two maps of the Rockies correspond closely.* **2** If you **correspond with** someone, you write letters to them. You can also say that two people **correspond**. ❑ *She still corresponds with friends she met in Majorca nine years ago.*

⊙ **cor·re·spond·ing** /ˌkɒrɪˈspɒndɪŋ, AmE ˌkɔːr-/ ADJ = equivalent, matching, related ❑ *The rise in interest rates was not reflected in a corresponding rise in the dollar.* ❑ *March and April sales this year were up 8 per cent on the corresponding period in 1992.*

cor·re·spond·ence /ˌkɒrɪˈspɒndəns, AmE ˌkɔːr-/ NOUN [U, C] (**correspondences**) **1** [U] [also 'a' correspondence, oft correspondence 'with' N] **Correspondence** is the act of writing letters to someone. ❑ *The judges' decision is final and no correspondence will be entered into.* **2** [U] Someone's **correspondence** is the letters that they receive or send. ❑ *He always replied to his correspondence.* **3** [C] If there is a **correspondence between** two things, there is a close similarity or connection between them. ❑ *In African languages there is a close correspondence between sounds and letters.*

cor·re·spond·ent ♦♦◇ /ˌkɒrɪˈspɒndənt, AmE ˌkɔːr-/ NOUN [C] (**correspondents**) A **correspondent** is a newspaper or television journalist, especially one who specializes in a particular type of news. = reporter ❑ *As our Diplomatic Correspondent Mark Brayne reports, the president was given a sympathetic hearing.*

cor·re·spond·ing·ly /ˌkɒrɪˈspɒndɪŋli, AmE ˌkɔːr-/ ADV You use **correspondingly** when describing a situation which is closely connected with one you have just mentioned or is similar to it. ❑ *As his political stature has shrunk, he has grown correspondingly more dependent on the army.*

cor·ri·dor /ˈkɒrɪdɔː, AmE ˈkɔːrɪdər/ NOUN [C] (**corridors**) **1** (*mainly BrE*) A **corridor** is a long passage in a building, with doors and rooms on one or both sides. ❑ *There were doors on both sides of the corridor.* **2** A **corridor** is a strip of land that connects one country to another or gives it a route to the sea through another country. ❑ *East Prussia and the rest of Germany were separated, in 1919, by the Polish Corridor.* **3** A **corridor** is an area of land between two large cities. ❑ *the Northeast corridor*

cor·rob·o·rate /kəˈrɒbəreɪt/ VERB [T] (**corroborates, corroborating, corroborated**) (*formal*) To **corroborate** something that has been said or reported means to provide evidence or information that supports it. = confirm ❑ *I had access to a wide range of documents which corroborated the story.*

cor·rob·o·ra·tion /kəˌrɒbəˈreɪʃən/ NOUN [U] = confirmation ❑ *He could not get a single witness to establish independent corroboration of his version of the accident.*

⊙ **cor·rupt** /kəˈrʌpt/ ADJ, VERB **ADJ** Someone who is **corrupt** behaves in a way that is morally wrong, especially by doing dishonest or illegal things in return for money or power. = dishonest, unscrupulous; ≠ honest, scrupulous ❑ *to save the nation from corrupt politicians of both parties* ❑ *corrupt police officers* ❑ *He had accused three opposition members of corrupt practices.* **VERB** [I, T] (**corrupts, corrupting, corrupted**) **1** [I, T] If someone **is corrupted by** something, it causes them to become dishonest and unjust and unable to be trusted. ❑ *It is sad to see a man so corrupted by the desire for money and power.* ❑ *Power tends to corrupt.* **2** [T] To **corrupt** someone means to cause them to stop caring about moral standards. ❑ *warning that television will corrupt us all*

⊙ **cor·rup·tion** ♦◇◇ /kəˈrʌpʃən/ NOUN [U] **Corruption** is dishonesty and illegal behaviour by people in positions of authority or power. = dishonesty, fraud ❑ *The president faces 54 charges of corruption and tax evasion.* ❑ *Distribution of food throughout the country is being hampered by inefficiency and corruption.* ❑ *bribery and corruption*

cos·met·ic /kɒzˈmetɪk/ NOUN, ADJ **NOUN** [C] (**cosmetics**) **Cosmetics** are substances such as lipstick or powder, which people put on their face to make themselves look more attractive. ❑ *the cosmetics counter of a department store* **ADJ** (*disapproval*) If you describe measures or changes as **cosmetic**, you mean they improve the appearance of a situation or thing but do not change its basic nature, and you are usually implying that they are inadequate. = superficial ❑ *It is a cosmetic measure which will do nothing to help the situation in the long term.*

cos·met·ic sur·gery NOUN [U] **Cosmetic surgery** is surgery done to make a person look more attractive. ❑ *She is rumoured to have had cosmetic surgery on nine different parts of her body.*

cos·mic /ˈkɒzmɪk/ ADJ **1** **Cosmic** means occurring in, or coming from, the part of space that lies outside Earth and its atmosphere. ❑ *cosmic radiation* **2** **Cosmic** means belonging or relating to the universe. ❑ *the cosmic laws governing our world*

cos·mo·poli·tan /ˌkɒzməˈpɒlɪtən/ ADJ (*approval*) **1** A **cosmopolitan** place is full of people from many different countries and cultures. ❑ *a cosmopolitan city* **2** Someone who is **cosmopolitan** has had a lot of contact with people and things from many different countries and as a result is very open to different ideas and ways of doing things. ❑ *The family is rich, and extremely sophisticated and cosmopolitan.*

⊙ **cost** ♦♦♦ /kɒst, AmE kɔːst/ NOUN, VERB

The form **cost** is used for the past tense and participle of the verb, except for meaning 2, where the form **costed** is used.

NOUN [C, PL, U, SING] (**costs**) **1** [C] The **cost of** something is the amount of money that is needed in order to buy, do, or make it. = price, value ❑ *The cost of a loaf of bread has increased five-fold.* ❑ *In 1989 the price of coffee fell so low that in many countries it did not even cover the cost of production.* ❑ *Badges are also available at a cost of £2.50.* **2** [PL] Your **costs** are the total amount of money that you must spend on running your home or business. = expenses, expenditure; ≠ profit, earnings ❑ *Costs have been cut by 30 to 50 per cent.* ❑ *The company admits its costs are still too high.* **3** [PL] If someone is ordered by a court of law to pay **costs**, they have to pay a sum of money towards the expenses of a court case they are involved in. ❑ *He was jailed for 18 months and ordered to pay $550 costs.* **4** [U] If something is sold **at cost**, it is sold for the same price as it cost the seller to buy it. ❑ *a shop that provided cigarettes and sweets at cost* **5** [SING] The **cost of** something is the loss, damage, or injury that is involved in trying to achieve it. ❑ *In March Mr Salinas shut down the city's oil refinery at a cost of $500 million and 5,000 jobs.*

PHRASES **at all costs** (*emphasis*) If you say that something must be avoided **at all costs**, you are emphasizing that it must not be allowed to happen under any circumstances. ❑ *They told Jacques Delors a disastrous world trade war must be avoided at all costs.*

at any cost (*emphasis*) If you say that something must be done **at any cost**, you are emphasizing that it must be done, even if this requires a lot of effort or money. ❑ *This book is of such importance that it must be published at any cost.* **VERB** [T] (**costs, costing, cost**) **1** If something **costs** a particular amount of money, you can buy, do, or make it for that amount. ❑ *This course is limited to 12 people and costs $150.* ❑ *Painted walls look much more interesting and don't cost much.* ❑ *The project was abandoned because it cost too much.* ❑ *a scheme which cost taxpayers more than £294 million* **2** When something that you plan to do or make **is costed**, the amount of money you need is calculated in advance. ❑ *The building work has not been fully costed but runs into millions of dollars.* **3** If an event or mistake **costs** you something, you lose that thing as the result of it. ❑ *a six-year-old boy whose life was saved by an operation that cost him his sight*

USAGE NOTE

cost

You say that something 'costs time' when you lose time as a result of a mistake. In other contexts, use 'take time'.

*It **cost** us twenty-five minutes to repair the damage.*
*It **takes** seven hours to fly to New York.*

---

cost-effective ADJ Something that is **cost-effective** saves or makes a lot of money in comparison with the costs involved. ❑ *The bank must be run in a cost-effective way.*
cost-effectively ADV ❑ *The management tries to produce the magazine as cost-effectively as possible.*
cost-effectiveness NOUN [U] ❑ *A report has raised doubts about the cost-effectiveness of the proposals.*

cost·ly /'kɒstli, AmE 'kɔːst-/ ADJ (**costlier, costliest**) If you say that something is **costly**, you mean that it costs a lot of money, often more than you would want to pay. = expensive ❑ *Having professionally made curtains can be costly, so why not make your own?*

✪cost of liv·ing NOUN [SING] The **cost of living** is the average amount of money that people in a particular place need in order to be able to afford basic food, housing, and clothing. ❑ *The cost of living has increased dramatically.* ❑ *Companies are moving jobs to towns with a lower cost of living.*

cos·tume /'kɒstjuːm, AmE -tuːm/ NOUN, ADJ
NOUN [C, U] (**costumes**) **1** [C, U] An actor's or performer's **costume** is the set of clothes they wear while they are performing. ❑ *Even from a distance, the effect of his fox costume was stunning.* ❑ *The performers, in costume and makeup, were walking up and down backstage.* **2** [U] The clothes worn by people at a particular time in history, or in a particular country, are referred to as a particular type of **costume**. = dress ❑ *men and women in eighteenth-century costume*
ADJ [costume + N] A **costume** drama is one which is set in the past and in which the actors wear the type of clothes that were worn in that period. ❑ *a lavish costume drama set in Ireland and America in the 1890s*

co·sy /'kəʊzi/ ADJ, NOUN (in AmE, use **cozy**)
ADJ (**cosier, cosiest**) **1** A house or room that is **cosy** is comfortable and warm. = homely ❑ *Downstairs there's a breakfast room and guests can relax in the cosy bar.* **2** [V-LINK + cosy] If you are **cosy**, you are comfortable and warm. ❑ *They like to make sure their guests are comfortable and cosy.* **3** You use **cosy** to describe activities that are pleasant and friendly, and involve people who know each other well. = intimate ❑ *a cosy chat between friends*
NOUN [C] (**cosies**) A **cosy** or a **tea cosy** is a soft knitted or fabric cover which you put over a teapot in order to keep the tea hot. ❑ *a whimsical tea cosy printed with a bright scene of the Tower of London*

cot /kɒt/ (BrE; in AmE, use **crib**) NOUN [C] (**cots**) A **cot** is a bed for a baby.

cot·tage ◆◇◇ /'kɒtɪdʒ/ NOUN [C] (**cottages**) A **cottage** is a small house, usually in the country. ❑ *They used to have a cottage in north-west Scotland.*

cot·ton ◆◇◇ /'kɒtən/ NOUN [C, U] (**cottons**) **1** [C, U] **Cotton** is a type of cloth made from soft fibres from a particular plant. ❑ *a cotton shirt* **2** [U] **Cotton** is a plant which is grown in warm countries and which produces soft fibres used in making cotton cloth. ❑ *a large cotton plantation in Tennessee* **3** [C, U] (BrE; in AmE, use **thread**) **Cotton** is thread that is used for sewing, especially thread that is made from cotton.

couch /kaʊtʃ/ NOUN [C] (**couches**) **1** A **couch** is a long, comfortable seat for two or three people. = sofa, settee **2** A **couch** is a narrow bed which patients lie on while they are being treated by a psychoanalyst. ❑ *Between films he often winds up spending every single morning on his psychiatrist's couch.*

cough ◆◇◇ /kɒf, AmE kɔːf/ VERB, NOUN
VERB [T, I] (**coughs, coughing, coughed**) **1** [T, I] When you **cough**, you force air out of your throat with a sudden, harsh noise. You often cough when you are ill, or when you are nervous or want to attract someone's attention. ❑ *Graham began to cough violently.* **2** [T] If you **cough** blood or mucus, it comes up out of your throat or mouth when you cough. ❑ *I started coughing blood so they transferred me to a hospital.*
PHRASAL VERB **cough up** **1** Cough up means the same as **cough** VERB 2. ❑ *On the chilly seas, Keats became feverish, continually coughing up blood.* **2** (*informal*) If you **cough up** an amount of money, you pay or spend that amount, usually when you would prefer not to. = fork out ❑ *I'll have to cough up £9,000 a year for tuition.*
NOUN [C] (**coughs**) **1** A **cough** is the act of forcing air out of your throat with a sudden, harsh noise. ❑ *Coughs and sneezes spread infections much faster in a warm atmosphere.* **2** A **cough** is an illness in which you cough often and your chest or throat hurts. ❑ *I had a persistent cough for over a month.*
cough·ing /'kɒfɪŋ, AmE 'kɔːfɪŋ/ NOUN [U] ❑ *He was then overcome by a terrible fit of coughing.*

could ◆◆◆ /kəd, STRONG kʊd/ VERB [MODAL]

Could is a modal verb. It is used with the base form of a verb. Could is sometimes considered to be the past form of **can**, but in this dictionary the two words are dealt with separately.

---

1 You use **could** to indicate that someone had the ability to do something. You use **could not** or **couldn't** to say that someone was unable to do something. ❑ *I could see that something was terribly wrong.* ❑ *When I left school at 16, I couldn't read or write.* **2** You use **could** to indicate that something sometimes happened. ❑ *Though he had a temper and could be nasty, it never lasted.* **3** You use **could have** to indicate that something was a possibility in the past, although it did not actually happen. ❑ *He could have made a fortune as a lawyer.* ❑ *You could have been killed!* **4** You use **could** to indicate that something is possibly true, or that it may possibly happen. = might ❑ *Doctors told him the disease could have been caused by years of working in smoky clubs.* ❑ *An improvement in living standards could be years away.* **5** You use **could not** or **couldn't** to indicate that it is not possible that something is true. ❑ *They argued all the time and thought it couldn't be good for the baby.* ❑ *Anne couldn't be expected to understand the situation.* **6** You use **could** to talk about a possibility, ability, or opportunity that depends on other conditions. ❑ *Their hope was that a new and better East Germany could be born.* **7** You use **could** when you are saying that one thing or situation resembles another. ❑ *The charming characters she draws look like they could have walked out of the 1920s.* **8** You use **could**, or **couldn't** in questions, when you are making offers and suggestions. ❑ *I could call the local doctor.* ❑ *You could look for a career abroad where environmental jobs are better paid and more secure.* ❑ *Couldn't we call a special meeting?* **9** You use **could** in questions when you are making a polite request or asking for permission to do something. Speakers sometimes use **couldn't** instead of **could** to show that they realize that their request may be refused. ❑ *Could I stay tonight?* ❑ *He asked if he could have a cup of coffee.* ❑ *Couldn't I watch you do it?* **10** You use **could** to say emphatically that someone ought to do the thing mentioned, especially when you are annoyed because they have not done it. You use **why couldn't** in questions to express your surprise or annoyance that someone has not done something. ❑ *We've come to see you, so you could at least stand and greet us properly.* ❑ *Why couldn't she have said something?* **11** You use **could** when you are expressing strong feelings about something by saying that you feel as if you want to do the thing mentioned, although you do not do it. ❑ *I could kill you! I swear I could!* ❑ *'Welcome back' was all they said. I could have kissed them!* **12** You use **could** after 'if' when talking about something that you do not have the ability or opportunity to do, but which you are imagining in order to consider what the likely consequences might be. **if** ❑ *If I could afford it, I'd have four television sets.* **13** You use **could not** or **couldn't** with comparatives to emphasize that someone or something has as much as is possible of a particular quality. For example, if you say 'I couldn't be happier', you mean that you are extremely happy. ❑ *The rest of the players are great and I couldn't be happier.* **14** You use **how could** in questions to emphasize that you feel strongly about something bad that has happened. ❑ *How could you allow him to do something like that?* ❑ *How could I have been so stupid?*

✦ **could do with** → see **do**

couldn't /ˈkʊdənt/ SHORT FORM **Couldn't** is the usual spoken form of 'could not'.

❍ **coun·cil** ♦♦♦ /ˈkaʊnsəl/ NOUN [c] (**councils**) **1** A **council** is a group of people who are elected to govern a local area such as a city. = local authority ❑ *The city council has voted almost unanimously in favour.* ❑ *Cheshire County Council* ❑ *David Ward, one of just two Liberal Democrats on the council* ❑ *reports of local council meetings* **2** **Council** is used in the names of some organizations. ❑ *the National Council for Civil Liberties* ❑ *the Arts Council* **3** In some organizations, the **council** is the group of people that controls or governs it. ❑ *The permanent council of the Organization of American States meets today here in Washington.* **4** A **council** is a specially organized, formal meeting that is attended by a particular group of people. = conference ❑ *President Najibullah said he would call a grand council of all Afghans.*

❍ **coun·cil·lor** /ˈkaʊnsələ/ (BrE; in AmE, use **councilor**) NOUN [c] (**councillors**) A **councillor** is a member of a local council. ❑ *councillor Michael Poulter* ❑ *the first black New York City councillor, Benjamin Davis Jr*

coun·sel ♦♦◇ /ˈkaʊnsəl/ NOUN, VERB
NOUN [u, c] (**counsels**) **1** [u] (*formal*) **Counsel** is advice. ❑ *He had always been able to count on her wise counsel.* **2** [c] Someone's **counsel** is the lawyer who gives them advice on a legal case and speaks on their behalf in court. ❑ *Singleton's counsel said after the trial that he would appeal.* VERB [T] (**counsels, counselling, counselled**; in AmE, use **counseling, counseled**) **1** (*formal*) If you **counsel** someone to take a course of action, or if you **counsel** a course of action, you advise that course of action. ❑ *My advisers counselled me to do nothing.* **2** If you **counsel** people, you give them advice about their problems. ❑ *a psychologist who counsels people with eating disorders*

coun·sel·lor /ˈkaʊnsələ/ NOUN [c] (**counsellors**) A **counsellor** is a person whose job is to give advice to people who need it, especially advice on their personal problems. ❑ *Children who have suffered like this should see a counsellor experienced in bereavement.*

count ♦♦◇ /kaʊnt/ VERB, NOUN
VERB [I, T] (**counts, counting, counted**) **1** [i] When you **count**, you say all the numbers one after another up to a particular number. ❑ *He was counting slowly under his breath.* **2** [T] If you **count** all the things in a group, you add them up in order to find how many there are. ❑ *I counted the money. It was more than five hundred dollars.* ❑ *I counted 34 wild goats grazing.* **3** [i] If something or someone **counts for** something or **counts**, they are

important or valuable. = matter ❑ *Surely it doesn't matter where charities get their money from: what counts is what they do with it.* **4** [I, T] If something **counts** or is **counted as** a particular thing, it is regarded as being that thing, especially in particular circumstances or under particular rules. ❑ *No one agrees on what counts as a desert.* **5** [T] If you **count** something when you are making a calculation, you include it in that calculation. = include ❑ *It's under 7 per cent only because statistics don't count the people who aren't qualified to be in the work force.*
PHRASAL VERBS **count against** If something **counts against** you, it may cause you to be rejected or punished, or cause people to have a lower opinion of you. ❑ *He is highly regarded, but his youth might count against him.*
count on or **count upon** **1** If you **count on** something or **count upon** it, you expect it to happen and include it in your plans. ❑ *What they did not know was how much support they could count on from Democrats.* **2** If you **count on** someone or **count upon** them, you rely on them to support you or help you. ❑ *Don't count on Lillian.*
count out If you **count out** a sum of money, you count the notes or coins as you put them in a pile one by one. ❑ *Mr Rohmbauer counted out the money and put it in an envelope.*
count up Count up means the same as **count** VERB **2**. ❑ *Couldn't we just count up our ballots and bring them to the courthouse?*
NOUN [c] (**counts**) **1** A **count** is the action of counting or the number that you get when you have counted them. ❑ *The final count in last month's referendum showed 56.7 per cent in favour.* **2** You use **count** when referring to the level or amount of something that someone or something has. ❑ *A glass or two of wine will not significantly add to the calorie count.* **3** In law, a **count** is one of a number of charges brought against someone in court. ❑ *He was indicted by a grand jury on two counts of murder.* **4** A **count** is a European nobleman. ❑ *Her father was a Polish count.*
PHRASE **keep count** or **lose count** If you **keep count of** a number of things, you note or keep a record of how many have occurred. If you **lose count of** a number of things, you cannot remember how many have occurred. ❑ *The authorities say they are not able to keep count of the bodies still being found as bulldozers clear the rubble.*

count·down /ˈkaʊntdaʊn/ NOUN [SING] [also no DET] A **countdown** is the counting aloud of numbers in reverse order before something happens, especially before a spacecraft is launched. ❑ *The countdown has begun for the launch of the space shuttle.*

coun·te·nance /ˈkaʊntɪnəns/ VERB, NOUN
VERB [T] (**countenances, countenancing, countenanced**) (*formal*) If someone will not **countenance** something, they do not agree with it and will not allow it to happen. ❑ *Jake would not countenance Janis's marrying while still a student.* NOUN [c] (*formal*) Someone's **countenance** is their face.

❍ **coun·ter** ♦◇◇ /ˈkaʊntə/ NOUN, VERB
NOUN [c, SING] (**counters**) **1** [c] In a place such as a shop or café, a **counter** is a long narrow table or flat surface at which customers are served. ❑ *those guys we see working behind the counter at our local camera shop* **2** [c] A **counter** is a mechanical or electronic device which keeps a count of something and displays the total. ❑ *The new answering machine has a call counter.* **3** [c] A **counter** is a small, flat, round object used in board games. ❑ *a versatile book which provides boards and counters for fifteen different games* **4** [SING] Something that is **a counter to** something else has an opposite effect to it or makes it less effective. ❑ *NATO's traditional role as a counter to the military might of the Warsaw Pact*
PHRASE **over the counter** **1** If a medicine can be bought **over the counter**, you do not need a prescription to buy it. ❑ *Are you taking any other medicines whether on prescription or bought over the counter?* ❑ *over-the-counter medicines* **2** (*business*) **Over-the-counter** shares are bought and sold directly rather than on a stock exchange. ❑ *In national over-the-counter trading yesterday, Clarcor shares tumbled $6.125 to close at $35.625.*

VERB [I, T] (**counters**, **countering**, **countered**) If you do something to **counter** a particular action or process, you do something which has an opposite effect to it or makes it less effective. ❑ *The leadership discussed a plan of economic measures to counter the effects of such a blockade.* ❑ *It should allow international observers to monitor them, to counter claims that the ballots are rigged.* ❑ *Sears countered by filing an antitrust lawsuit.*

✪ **counter·act** /ˈkaʊntərækt/ VERB [T] (**counteracts**, **counteracting**, **counteracted**) To **counteract** something means to reduce its effect by doing something that produces an opposite effect. ❑ *My husband has to take several pills to counteract high blood pressure.* ❑ *The vitamin counteracts the harmful effect of allergens in the body.*

WORD PARTS

The prefix **counter-** often appears in words for actions or activities that oppose another action or activity:
counteract (VERB)
counterattack (VERB, NOUN)
counterterrorism (NOUN)

counter·at·tack /ˈkaʊntərəˌtæk/ VERB, NOUN
VERB [I] (**counterattacks**, **counterattacking**, **counterattacked**) If you **counterattack**, you attack someone who has attacked you. = retaliate ❑ *The security forces counterattacked the following day and quelled the unrest.*
NOUN [C] (**counterattacks**) A **counterattack** is the act of attacking someone who has attacked you. ❑ *The army began its counterattack this morning.*

counter·feit /ˈkaʊntəfɪt/ ADJ, NOUN, VERB
ADJ **Counterfeit** money, goods, or documents are not genuine, but have been made to look exactly like genuine ones in order to deceive people. = fake ❑ *He admitted possessing and delivering counterfeit currency.*
NOUN [C] (**counterfeits**) A **counterfeit** is a version of something that is not genuine but has been made to look genuine in order to deceive people. = fake ❑ *Levi Strauss says counterfeits of the company's jeans are flooding Europe.*
VERB [T] (**counterfeits**, **counterfeiting**, **counterfeited**) If someone **counterfeits** something, they make a version of it that is not genuine but has been made to look genuine in order to deceive people. ❑ *the coins Davies is alleged to have counterfeited*

✪ **counter·part** ◆◇◇ /ˈkaʊntəpɑːt/ NOUN [C] (**counterparts**) Someone's or something's **counterpart** is another person or thing that has a similar function or position in a different place. ❑ *As soon as he heard what was afoot, he telephoned his German and Italian counterparts to protest.* ❑ *The Finnish organization was very different from that of its counterparts in the rest of the Nordic region.*

counter·pro·duc·tive /ˌkaʊntəprəˈdʌktɪv/ ADJ Something that is **counterproductive** achieves the opposite result from the one that you want to achieve. ❑ *In practice, however, such an attitude is counterproductive.*

coun·ter·ter·ror·ism /ˈkaʊntəˈterərɪzəm/ NOUN [U] **Counterterrorism** consists of activities that are intended to prevent terrorist acts or to get rid of terrorist groups.
coun·ter·ter·ror·ist /ˈkaʊntəˈterərɪst/ ADJ ❑ *There were gaps in their counterterrorist strategy.*

count·less /ˈkaʊntləs/ ADJ [countless + N] **Countless** means very many. = innumerable ❑ *She brought joy to countless people through her music.*

✪ **coun·try** ◆◆◆ /ˈkʌntri/ NOUN [C, SING, U] (**countries**)
1 [C] A **country** is one of the political units which the world is divided into, covering a particular area of land. ❑ *Indonesia is the fifth most populous country in the world.* ❑ *the boundary between the two countries* ❑ *the difficult task of running the country* **2** [SING] The people who live in a particular country can be referred to as **the country**. ❑ *Finally the country got some much-needed good news.* **3** [SING] The **country** consists of places such as farms, open fields, and villages which are away from towns and cities. = countryside ❑ *a healthy life in the country* ❑ *She was cycling along a country road near Compiègne.* **4** [U] A particular kind of **country** is an area of land which has particular characteristics or is connected with a particular

well-known person. ❑ *Varese Ligure is a small town in mountainous country east of Genoa.* **5** [U] **Country** music is popular music from the southern United States. ❑ *For a long time I just wanted to play country music.*

country·man /ˈkʌntrimən/ NOUN [C] (**countrymen**)
1 Your **countrymen** are people from your own country. = compatriot ❑ *He beat his fellow countryman, Rafael Nadal, 6-4, 6-3, 6-2.* **2** A **countryman** is a person who lives in the country rather than in a city or a town. ❑ *He had the red face of a countryman.*

✪ **country·side** ◆◆◇ /ˈkʌntrisaɪd/ NOUN [U] The **countryside** is land which is away from towns and cities. = landscape ❑ *I've always loved the English countryside.* ❑ *Urban areas are often slightly warmer than the surrounding countryside.* ❑ *We are surrounded by lots of beautiful countryside.*

coun·ty ◆◆◇ /ˈkaʊnti/ NOUN [C] (**counties**) A **county** is a region of the US, Britain, or Ireland, which has its own local government. ❑ *He arrived at the Palm Beach County courthouse with his mother.*

✪ **coup** ◆◇◇ /kuː/ NOUN [C] (**coups**) (*academic word*)
1 When there is a **coup**, a group of people seize power in a country. = coup d'état ❑ *a military coup* ❑ *They were sentenced to death for their part in April's coup attempt.* **2** A **coup** is an achievement which is thought to be especially good because it was very difficult. ❑ *The sale is a big coup for the auction house.*

coup d'état /ˈkuː deɪˈtɑː/ NOUN [C] (**coups d'état**) When there is a **coup d'état**, a group of people seize power in a country. = coup

✪ **cou·ple** ◆◆◇ /ˈkʌpəl/ QUANT, PRON, NOUN, VERB (*academic word*)
QUANT ['a' couple 'of' PL-N] If you refer to **a couple of** people or things, you mean two or approximately two of them, although the exact number is not important or you are not sure of it. = a few, several ❑ *Across the street from me there are a couple of police officers standing guard.* ❑ *I think the trouble will clear up in a couple of days.* ❑ *a small town in Massachusetts, a couple of hundred miles from New York City*
PRON A **couple** is two or approximately two when it is clear what you are talking about. ❑ *I've got a couple that don't look too bad.*
NOUN [C] (**couples**) **1** A **couple** is two people who are married, living together, or having a sexual relationship. ❑ *The couple have no children.* ❑ *Burglars ransacked an elderly couple's home.* **2** A **couple** is two people that you see together on a particular occasion or that have some association. ❑ *as the four couples began the opening dance*
VERB [T] (**couples**, **coupling**, **coupled**) If you say that one thing produces a particular effect when it **is coupled with** another, you mean that the two things combine to produce that effect. = combine ❑ *a problem that is coupled with lower demand for the machines themselves*

cou·pon /ˈkuːpɒn/ NOUN [C] (**coupons**) **1** A **coupon** is a piece of printed paper which allows you to pay less money than usual for a product, or to get it free. = voucher ❑ *a money-saving coupon* **2** A **coupon** is a small form, for example, in a newspaper or magazine, which you send off to ask for information, to order something, or to enter a competition. ❑ *Mail this coupon with your cheque or postal order.*

cour·age ◆◆◇ /ˈkʌrɪdʒ, AmE ˈkɜːr-/ NOUN [U] **Courage** is the quality shown by someone who decides to do something difficult or dangerous, even though they may be afraid. = bravery ❑ *General Lewis Mackenzie has impressed everyone with his authority and personal courage.*

cou·ra·geous /kəˈreɪdʒəs/ ADJ Someone who is **courageous** shows courage. = brave ❑ *The children were very courageous.*

cou·ri·er /ˈkʊriə/ NOUN, VERB
NOUN [C] (**couriers**) A **courier** is a person who is paid to take letters and parcels direct from one place to another. ❑ *a motorcycle courier*
VERB [T] (**couriers**, **couriering**, **couriered**) If you **courier** something somewhere, you send it there by courier. ❑ *I couriered it to Darren in New York.*

C

✪ **course** ♦♦♦ /kɔːs/ NOUN, CONVENTION

NOUN [U, C] (**courses**) **1** [U] [also 'a' course] The **course** of a vehicle, especially a ship or aircraft, is the route along which it is travelling. ❏ *Aircraft can avoid each other by altering course to left or right.* **2** [C] A **course of** action is an action or a series of actions that you can do in a particular situation. ❏ *My best course of action was to help Gill by being sympathetic.* **3** [C] A **course** is a series of lessons or lectures on a particular subject. = class, module, degree ❏ *a course in business administration* ❏ *I'm shortly to begin a course on the modern novel.* **4** [C] A **course** of medical treatment is a series of treatments that a doctor gives someone. ❏ *He had a course of antibiotics to kill the bacterium.* **5** [C] A **course** is one part of a meal. ❏ *The lunch was excellent, especially the first course.* **6** [C] In sports, a **course** is an area of land where races are held or golf is played, or the land over which a race takes place. ❏ *Only 12 seconds separated the first three riders on the course.* **7** [C] The **course** of a river is the channel along which it flows. ❏ *Romantic castles overlook the river's twisting course.*

PHRASES **in the course of** If something happens **in the course of** a particular period of time, it happens during that period of time. = during ❏ *In the course of the 1930s steel production approximately doubled.*

as a matter of course If you do something **as a matter of course**, you do it as part of your normal work or way of life. ❏ *If police are carrying arms as a matter of course, then doesn't it encourage criminals to carry them?*

on course or **off course** If a ship or aircraft is **on course**, it is travelling along the correct route. If it is **off course**, it is no longer travelling along the correct route. ❏ *The ship was sent off course into shallow waters.*

on course for If you are **on course for** something, you are likely to achieve it. ❏ *The company is on course for profits of $20m.*

CONVENTION **Course** is often used instead of 'of course' in informal spoken English. See **of course**.

✦ **in due course** → see **due**

course work also **coursework** NOUN [U] **Course work** is work that students do during a course, rather than in exams, especially work that counts towards a student's final mark. ❏ *Some 20 per cent of marks are awarded for coursework.*

✪ **court** ♦♦♦ /kɔːt/ NOUN, VERB

NOUN [C] (**courts**) **1** [oft N + court, court + N, also 'in/at' court] A **court** is a place where legal matters are decided by a judge and jury or by a magistrate. = law court ❏ *At this rate, we could find ourselves in the divorce courts!* ❏ *a county court judge* ❏ *He was deported on a court order following a conviction for armed robbery.* ❏ *The 28-year-old striker was in court last week for breaking a rival player's jaw.* **2** You can refer to the people in a court, especially the judge, jury, or magistrates, as a **court**. ❏ *A court at Tampa, Florida has convicted five officials on charges of handling millions of dollars earned from illegal drug deals.* **3** [usu SUPP + court, also 'on/off' court] A **court** is an area in which you play a game such as tennis, basketball, badminton, or squash. ❏ *The hotel has several tennis and squash courts.* **4** The **court** of a king or queen is the place where he or she lives and carries out ceremonial or administrative duties. ❏ *She came to visit England, where she was presented at the court of James I.*

PHRASES **go to court** or **take sb to court** If you **go to court** or **take** someone **to court**, you take legal action against them. ❏ *They have received at least twenty thousand dollars each but went to court to demand more.*

out of court If a legal matter is decided or settled **out of court**, it is decided without legal action being taken in a court of law. ❏ *The Government is anxious to keep the whole case out of court.*

VERB [T, RECIP] (**courts, courting, courted**) **1** [T] (*journalism*) To **court** a particular person, group, or country means to try to please them or improve your relations with them, often so that they will do something that you want them to do. ❏ *Both Democratic and Republican parties are courting former supporters of Ross Perot.* **2** [T] If you **court** something such as publicity or popularity, you try to attract it. ❏ *Having spent a lifetime avidly courting publicity, Paul has*

suddenly become secretive. **3** [T] If you **court** something unpleasant such as disaster or unpopularity, you act in a way that makes it likely to happen. = invite ❏ *If he thinks he can remain in power by force, he is courting disaster.* **4** [RECIP] (*old-fashioned*) If you **are courting** someone of the opposite sex, you spend a lot of time with them, because you are intending to get married. You can also say that a man and a woman **are courting**. ❏ *I was courting Billy at 19 and married him when I was 21.*

cour·teous /'kɜːtiəs/ ADJ Someone who is **courteous** is polite and respectful to other people. = polite ❏ *He was a kind and courteous man.*

cour·teous·ly /'kɜːtiəsli/ ADV ❏ *Then he nodded courteously to me and walked off to perform his unpleasant duty.*

cour·tesy /'kɜːtɪsi/ NOUN, ADJ

NOUN [U, SING] (*formal*) **1** [U] **Courtesy** is politeness, respect, and consideration for others. = politeness ❏ *a gentleman who behaves with the utmost courtesy towards ladies* **2** [SING] If you refer to **the courtesy** of doing something, you are referring to a polite action. ❏ *By extending the courtesy of a phone call to my clients, I was building a personal relationship with them.*

PHRASE **(by) courtesy of** If something is provided **courtesy of** someone or **by courtesy of** someone, they provide it. You often use this expression in order to thank them. ❏ *The waitress brings over some congratulatory glasses of champagne, courtesy of the restaurant.*

ADJ **1** [courtesy + N] **Courtesy** is used to describe services that are provided free of charge by an organization to its customers, or to the general public. ❏ *A courtesy shuttle bus operates between the hotel and the town.* **2** [courtesy + N] A **courtesy** call or a **courtesy** visit is a formal visit that you pay someone as a way of showing them politeness or respect. ❏ *The president paid a courtesy call on Emperor Akihito.*

court mar·tial also **court-martial** NOUN, VERB

NOUN [C, U] (**court martials** or **courts martial**) A **court martial** is a trial in a military court of a member of the armed forces who is charged with breaking a military law. ❏ *He is due to face a court martial on drugs charges.*

VERB [T] (**court martials, court martialling, court martialled**; in AmE, use **court martialing, court martialed**) If a member of the armed forces **is court martialled**, he or she is tried in a military court. ❏ *I was court martialled and sentenced to six months in a military prison.*

cous·in ♦♦◊ /'kʌzən/ NOUN [C] (**cousins**) Your **cousin** is the child of your uncle or aunt. ❏ *My cousin Mark helped me to bring in the bags.*

cov·er ♦♦♦ /'kʌvə/ VERB, NOUN

VERB [T, I] (**covers, covering, covered**) **1** [T] If you **cover** something, you place something else over it in order to protect it, hide it, or close it. ❏ *Cover the casserole with a tight-fitting lid.* ❏ *He whimpered and covered his face.* **2** [T] If one thing **covers** another, it has been placed over it in order to protect it, hide it, or close it. ❏ *His finger went up to touch the black patch which covered his left eye.* **3** [T] If one thing **covers** another, it forms a layer over its surface. ❏ *The clouds had spread and covered the entire sky.* **4** [T] To **cover** something **with** or **in** something else means to put a layer of the second thing over its surface. ❏ *The desk was covered with papers.* **5** [T] If you **cover** a particular distance, you travel that distance. ❏ *It would not be easy to cover ten miles on that amount of petrol.* **6** [T] An insurance policy that **covers** a person or thing guarantees that money will be paid by the insurance company in relation to that person or thing. ❏ *Their insurer paid the $900 bill, even though the policy did not strictly cover it.* **7** [T] If a law **covers** a particular set of people, things, or situations, it applies to them. ❏ *The law covers four categories of experiments.* **8** [T] If you **cover** a particular topic, you discuss it in a lecture, course, or book. = deal with ❏ *Introduction to Chemistry aims to cover important topics in organic chemistry.* **9** [T] If a sum of money **covers** something, it is enough to pay for it. ❏ *Send it to the address given with $2.50 to cover postage and administration.* **10** [I] If you **cover for** someone who is doing something secret or illegal, you give false information or do not give all the information you have, in order to protect them. ❏ *Why would she cover for someone who was trying to kill her?* **11** [I] If you **cover for** someone who is ill or away, you do their work for them while they are not there. ❏ *She did not have enough nurses to cover for those who were sick.*

PHRASAL VERB **cover up** **1** If you **cover** something or someone **up**, you put something over them in order to protect or hide them. ❏ *He fell asleep in the front room so I covered him up with a duvet.* **2** If you **cover up** something that you do not want people to know about, you hide the truth about it. ❏ *He suspects there's a conspiracy to cover up the crime.* ❏ *They knew they had done something terribly wrong and lied to cover it up.* **3** → See also **cover-up**

NOUN [C, U, PL] (**covers**) **1** [C] A **cover** is something which is put over an object, usually in order to protect it. ❏ *a sofa with washable covers* **2** [C] The **cover** of a book or a magazine is the outside part of it. ❏ *a small book with a green cover* **3** [U] **Cover** is protection from enemy attack that is provided for troops or ships carrying out a particular operation, for example, by aircraft. = protection ❏ *They could not provide adequate air cover for ground operations.* **4** [U] **Cover** is trees, rocks, or other places where you shelter from the weather or from an attack, or hide from someone. = shelter ❏ *Charles lit the fuses and they ran for cover.* **5** [U] Insurance **cover** is a guarantee from an insurance company that money will be paid by them if it is needed. = protection ❏ *Make sure that the firm's insurance cover is adequate.* **6** [C] Something that is a **cover** for secret or illegal activities seems respectable or normal, and is intended to hide the activities. = front ❏ *He ran a construction company as a cover for drug dealing.* **7** [PL] The **covers** on your bed are the things such as sheets and blankets that you have on top of you. = bedclothes ❏ *She set her glass down and slid under the covers.*

PHRASES **take cover** If you **take cover**, you shelter from gunfire, bombs, or the weather. = shelter ❏ *Shoppers took cover behind cars as the gunman fired.*

under cover of If you do something **under cover of** a particular situation, you are able to do it without being noticed because of that situation. ❏ *They move under cover of darkness.*

→ See also **covering**

cov•er•age ◆◇◇ /ˈkʌvərɪdʒ/ NOUN [U] The **coverage** of something in the news is the reporting of it. ❏ *Now a special TV network gives live coverage of most races.*

cov•er•ing /ˈkʌvərɪŋ/ NOUN [C] (**coverings**) A **covering** is a layer of something that protects or hides something else. ❏ *Leave a thin covering of fat.*

cov•er•ing let•ter (*BrE*; in *AmE*, use **cover letter**) NOUN [C] (**covering letters**) A **covering letter** is a letter that you send with a parcel or with another letter in order to provide extra information. ❏ *Your covering letter creates the employer's first impression of you.*

cover-up also **coverup** NOUN [C] (**cover-ups**) A **cover-up** is an attempt to hide a crime or mistake. ❏ *General Schwarzkopf denied there'd been any cover-up.*

cow ◆◇◇ /kaʊ/ NOUN, VERB

NOUN [C] (**cows**) **1** A **cow** is a large female animal that is kept on farms for its milk. People sometimes refer to male and female animals of this species as **cows**. ❏ *He kept a few dairy cows.* ❏ *Dad went out to milk the cows.* **2** Some female animals, including elephants and whales, are called **cows**. ❏ *a cow elephant*

VERB [T] (**cows, cowing, cowed**) (*formal*) If someone **is cowed**, they are made afraid, or made to behave in a particular way because they have been frightened or badly treated. = intimidate ❏ *The government, far from being cowed by these threats, has vowed to continue its policy.* **cowed** /kaʊd/ ADJ ❏ *By this time she was so cowed by the beatings that she meekly obeyed.*

cow•ard /kaʊəd/ NOUN [C] (**cowards**) (*disapproval*) If you call someone a **coward**, you disapprove of them because they are easily frightened and avoid dangerous or difficult situations. ❏ *She accused her husband of being a coward.*

cow•ard•ice /ˈkaʊədɪs/ NOUN [U] **Cowardice** is cowardly behaviour. ❏ *He openly accused his opponents of cowardice.*

cow•ard•ly /ˈkaʊədli/ ADJ (*disapproval*) If you describe someone as **cowardly**, you disapprove of them because they are easily frightened and avoid doing dangerous and difficult things. ❏ *I was too cowardly to complain.*

cow•boy /ˈkaʊbɔɪ/ NOUN [C] (**cowboys**) **1** A **cowboy** is a male character in a western. ❏ *Boys used to play at cowboys and Indians.* **2** A **cowboy** is a man employed to look after cattle in North America, especially in former times. ❏ *In his twenties Roosevelt had sought work as a cowboy on a ranch in the Dakota Territory.*

co-worker NOUN [C] (**co-workers**) Your **co-workers** are the people you work with, especially people on the same job or project as you. = colleague

crack ◆◇◇ /kræk/ VERB, NOUN, ADJ

VERB [I, T] (**cracks, cracking, cracked**) **1** [I, T] If something hard **cracks**, or if you **crack** it, it becomes slightly damaged, with lines appearing on its surface. ❏ *A gas main had cracked under my neighbour's garage and gas had seeped into our homes.* **2** [I, T] If something **cracks**, or if you **crack** it, it makes a sharp sound like the sound of a piece of wood breaking. ❏ *Thunder cracked in the sky.* **3** [T] If you **crack** a hard part of your body, such as your knee or your head, you hurt it by accidentally hitting it hard against something. = bang, bash ❏ *He cracked his head on the pavement and was knocked out cold.* **4** [T] When you **crack** something that has a shell, such as an egg or a nut, you break the shell in order to reach the inside part. = break ❏ *Crack the eggs into a bowl.* **5** [T] If you **crack** a problem or a code, you solve it, especially after a lot of thought. ❏ *He has finally cracked the system after years of painstaking research.* **6** [I] (*informal*) If someone **cracks**, they lose control of their emotions or actions because they are under a lot of pressure. ❏ *She's calm and strong, and she is just not going to crack.* **7** [I] If your voice **cracks** when you are speaking or singing, it changes in pitch because you are feeling a strong emotion. ❏ *Her voice cracked and she began to cry.* **8** [T] If you **crack** a joke, you tell it. ❏ *He drove a Volkswagen, cracked jokes, and talked about beer and girls.*

PHRASAL VERBS **crack down** **1** If people in authority **crack down on** a group of people, they become stricter in making the group obey rules or laws. = clamp down ❏ *The government has cracked down hard on those campaigning for greater democracy.* **2** → See also **crackdown**

crack up (*informal*) **1** If someone **cracks up**, they are under such a lot of emotional strain that they become mentally ill. ❏ *She would have cracked up if she hadn't allowed herself some fun.* **2** If you **crack up** or if someone or something **cracks** you **up**, you laugh a lot. ❏ *She told stories that cracked me up and I swore to write them down so you could enjoy them too.*

NOUN [C, SING, U] (**cracks**) **1** [C] A **crack** is a very narrow gap between two things, or between two parts of a thing. = chink ❏ *Kathryn had seen him through a crack in the curtains.* **2** [C] A **crack** is a line that appears on the surface of something when it is slightly damaged. ❏ *The plate had a crack in it.* **3** [SING] If you open something such as a door, window, or curtain **a crack**, you open it only a small amount. ❏ *He went to the door, opened it a crack, and listened.* **4** [C] A **crack** is a sharp sound, like the sound of a piece of wood breaking. ❏ *Suddenly there was a loud crack and glass flew into the car.* **5** [U] **Crack** is a very pure form of the drug cocaine. **6** [C] A **crack** is a slightly rude or cruel joke. ❏ *Tell Tracy you're sorry for that crack about her weight.*

ADJ [crack + N] A **crack** soldier or sportsman is highly trained and very skilful. ❏ *a crack undercover police officer*

crack•down /ˈkrækdaʊn/ NOUN [C] (**crackdowns**) A **crackdown** is strong official action that is taken to punish people who break laws. ❏ *anti-government unrest that ended with the violent army crackdown*

cra•dle /ˈkreɪdəl/ NOUN, VERB

NOUN [C] (**cradles**) A **cradle** is a baby's bed with high sides. Cradles often have curved bases so that they rock from side to side.

VERB [T] (**cradles, cradling, cradled**) If you **cradle** someone or something **in** your arms or hands, you hold them carefully and gently. ❏ *I cradled her in my arms.*

c

craft ◆◇◇ /krɑːft, kræft/ NOUN, VERB

> **Craft** is both the singular and the plural form for meaning 1 of the noun.

NOUN [C] (**crafts**) **1** You can refer to a boat, a spacecraft, or an aircraft as a **craft**. ❑ *With great difficulty, the fisherman manoeuvred his small craft close to the reef.* **2** A **craft** is an activity such as weaving, carving, or pottery that involves making things skilfully with your hands. ❑ *the arts and crafts of the North American Indians* **3** You can use **craft** to refer to any activity or job that involves doing something skilfully. ❑ *the craft of writing*

VERB [T] (**crafts, crafting, crafted**) If something **is crafted**, it is made skilfully. ❑ *The windows would probably have been crafted in the latter part of the Middle Ages.* ❑ *original, hand-crafted bags at affordable prices*

crafts·man·ship /ˈkrɑːftsmənʃɪp, ˈkræft-/ NOUN [U] **Craftsmanship** is the skill that someone uses when they make beautiful things with their hands. ❑ *It is easy to appreciate the craftsmanship of Armani.*

cramp /kræmp/ NOUN, VERB

NOUN [C, U] [also cramps] A **cramp** is a sudden strong pain caused by a muscle suddenly contracting. You sometimes get cramps in a muscle after you have been making a physical effort over a long period of time. ❑ *Hillsden was complaining of a cramp in his calf muscles.* ❑ *muscle cramps*

VERB (**cramps, cramping, cramped**)

PHRASE **cramp someone's style** (*informal*) If someone or something **cramps** your **style**, their presence or existence restricts your behaviour in some way. ❑ *Like more and more women, she believes wedlock would cramp her style.*

crane /kreɪn/ NOUN, VERB

NOUN [C] (**cranes**) **1** A **crane** is a large machine that moves heavy things by lifting them in the air. ❑ *The little prefabricated hut was lifted away by a huge crane.* **2** A **crane** is a kind of large bird with a long neck and long legs.

VERB [I, T] (**cranes, craning, craned**) If you **crane** your neck or head, you stretch your neck in a particular direction in order to see or hear something better. ❑ *She craned her neck to get a better view.* ❑ *Children craned to get close to him.*

crash ◆◆◇ /kræʃ/ NOUN, VERB

NOUN [C] (**crashes**) **1** A **crash** is an accident in which a moving vehicle hits something and is damaged or destroyed. = accident ❑ *His elder son was killed in a car crash a few years ago.* **2** A **crash** is a sudden, loud noise. ❑ *Two people recalled hearing a loud crash about 1.30 a.m.* **3** If there is a **crash** in a business or financial system, it fails suddenly, often with serious effects. ❑ *He predicted correctly that there was going to be a stock market crash.*

VERB [I, T] (**crashes, crashing, crashed**) **1** [I, T] If a moving vehicle **crashes** or if the driver **crashes** it, it hits something and is damaged or destroyed. ❑ *The plane crashed mysteriously near the island of Ustica.* ❑ *Her car crashed into the rear of a van.* **2** [I] If something **crashes** somewhere, it moves and hits something else violently, making a loud noise. ❑ *The door swung inwards to crash against a chest of drawers behind it.* ❑ *My words were lost as the walls above us crashed down, filling the cellar with brick dust.* **3** [I] (*business*) If a business or financial system **crashes**, it fails suddenly, often with serious effects. ❑ *When the market crashed, they assumed the deal would be cancelled.* **4** [I] If a computer or a computer program **crashes**, it fails suddenly. ❑ *The computer crashed for the second time in 10 days.*

crate /kreɪt/ NOUN, VERB

NOUN [C] (**crates**) **1** A **crate** is a large box used for transporting or storing things. ❑ *a pile of wooden crates* **2** A **crate** is a plastic or wire box divided into sections that is used for carrying bottles. **3** You can use **crate** to refer to a crate and its contents, or to the contents only. ❑ *a crate of oranges*

VERB [T] (**crates, crating, crated**) If something **is crated** or **crated up**, it is packed in a crate so that it can be transported or stored somewhere safely. ❑ *Equipment and office supplies were crated and shipped.*

♦ **cra·ter** /ˈkreɪtə/ NOUN [C] (**craters**) A **crater** is a very large hole in the ground, which has been caused by something hitting it or by an explosion. ❑ *The explosion,* believed to be a car bomb, left a ten-foot crater in the street. ❑ *Experts calculate that a 3km asteroid could gouge a crater 60km across, and destroy an area the size of Mexico.* ❑ *An ancient gigantic volcanic crater provides the perfectly shaped circle of Simpson Harbour.*

crawl /krɔːl/ VERB, NOUN

VERB [I] (**crawls, crawling, crawled**) **1** When you **crawl**, you move forwards on your hands and knees. ❑ *Don't worry if your baby seems a little reluctant to crawl or walk.* ❑ *I began to crawl on my hands and knees towards the door.* **2** When an insect **crawls** somewhere, it moves there quite slowly. ❑ *I watched the moth crawl up the outside of the lampshade.* **3** If someone or something **crawls** somewhere, they move or progress slowly or with great difficulty. ❑ *I crawled out of bed at nine-thirty.* **4** (*informal, emphasis*) If you say that a place **is crawling with** people or animals, you are emphasizing that it is full of them. ❑ *This place is crawling with police.*

NOUN [SING] **1** ['a' crawl] A **crawl** is a very slow rate of movement or progress. ❑ *The traffic on the motorway exit slowed to a crawl.* **2** The **crawl** is a kind of swimming stroke which you do lying on your front, swinging one arm over your head, and then the other arm. ❑ *I expected him to do 50 lengths of the crawl.*

cray·on /ˈkreɪɒn/ NOUN [C] (**crayons**) A **crayon** is a coloured pencil or a rod of coloured wax used for drawing.

craze /kreɪz/ NOUN [C] (**crazes**) If there is a **craze** for something, it is very popular for a short time. = fad ❑ *the craze for Mutant Ninja Turtles*

crazed /kreɪzd/ ADJ (*written*) **Crazed** people are wild and uncontrolled, and perhaps insane. = crazy ❑ *A crazed gunman slaughtered five people last night.*

cra·zy ◆◇◇ /ˈkreɪzi/ ADJ, COMB

ADJ (**crazier, craziest**) (*informal*) **1** (*disapproval*) If you describe someone or something as **crazy**, you think they are very foolish or strange. ❑ *People thought they were all crazy to try to make money from manufacturing.* **2** Someone who is **crazy** is insane. = mad ❑ *If I sat home and worried about all this stuff, I'd go crazy.* **3** [V-LINK + crazy 'about' N] If you are **crazy about** something, you are very enthusiastic about it. If you are **not crazy about** something, you do not like it. = mad ❑ *He's still crazy about both his work and his hobbies.* **4** [V-LINK + crazy 'about' N] If you are **crazy about** someone, you are deeply in love with them. ❑ *We're crazy about each other.*

COMB **Crazy** is also used as a combining form with nouns, when you mean that you are very enthusiastic about something. ❑ *Sports-crazy Coloradans will buy tickets to anything.*

cra·zi·ly /ˈkreɪzɪli/ ADV ❑ *The teenagers shook their long, black hair and gesticulated crazily.*

creak /kriːk/ VERB, NOUN

VERB [I] (**creaks, creaking, creaked**) If something **creaks**, it makes a short, high-pitched sound when it moves. ❑ *The bed-springs creaked.* ❑ *The door creaked open.*

NOUN [C] (**creaks**) A **creak** is a short, high-pitched sound that something makes when it moves. ❑ *The door was pulled open with a creak.*

cream ◆◆◇ /kriːm/ NOUN, COLOUR

NOUN [U, C] (**creams**) **1** [U] **Cream** is a thick yellowish-white liquid taken from milk. You can use it in cooking or put it on fruit or desserts. ❑ *strawberries and cream* **2** [U] [cream 'of' N] **Cream** is used in the names of soups that contain cream or milk. ❑ *cream of mushroom soup* **3** [C, U] A **cream** is a substance that you rub into your skin, for example, to keep it soft or to heal or protect it. ❑ *Gently apply the cream to the affected areas.*

COLOUR Something that is **cream** is yellowish-white in colour. ❑ *cream silk stockings*

PHRASAL VERB **cream off** (**creams, creaming, creamed**) (*disapproval*) **1** To **cream off** part of a group of people means to take them away and treat them in a special way, because they are better than the others. ❑ *The private schools cream off many of the best pupils.* **2** (*informal*) If a person or organization **creams off** a large amount of money, they take it and use it for themselves. ❑ *This means smaller banks can cream off big profits during lending booms.*

→ See also **ice cream**

crease /kriːs/ NOUN, VERB

NOUN [C] (**creases**) **1** Creases are lines that are made in cloth or paper when it is crushed or folded. ❑ *She stood up, frowning at the creases in her silk dress.* ❑ *cream-coloured trousers with sharp creases* **2** Creases in someone's skin are lines which form where their skin folds when they move. = **wrinkle** ❑ *the tiny creases at the corners of his eyes*

VERB [I, T] (**creases, creasing, creased**) If cloth or paper **creases** or if you **crease** it, lines form in it when it is crushed or folded. = **crumple** ❑ *Most outfits crease a bit when you are travelling.*

creased /kriːst/ ADJ **1** *Sweat poured down her deeply creased face.* **2** *His clothes were creased, as if he had slept in them.*

✪ **cre·ate** ♦♦♦ /kriˈeɪt/ VERB [T] (**creates, creating, created**) (*academic word*) **1** To **create** something means to cause it to happen or exist. = **produce** ❑ *We set business free to create more jobs.* ❑ *Changing interest rates can create problems for home owners.* ❑ *She could create a fight out of anything.* **2** When someone **creates** a new product or process, they invent it or design it. ❑ *It is really great for a radio producer to create a show like this.*

✪ **cre·a·tion** /kriˈeɪʃən/ NOUN [U, C] (**creations**) **1** [U] The **creation** of something is the act of causing it to happen or exist. = **production**; ≠ **destruction** ❑ *These businesses stimulate the creation of local jobs.* ❑ *the process of wealth creation* **2** [U] [also 'the' Creation] In many religions, **creation** is the making of the universe, earth, and creatures by God. ❑ *the Creation of the universe as told in Genesis Chapter One* **3** [U] (*literary*) People sometimes refer to the whole universe as **creation**. ❑ *The whole of creation is made up of energy.* **4** [C] You can refer to something that someone has made as a **creation**, especially if it shows skill, imagination, or artistic ability. ❑ *The bathroom is entirely my own creation.*

cre·a·tive ♦◇◇ /kriˈeɪtɪv/ ADJ **1** A **creative** person has the ability to invent and develop original ideas, especially in the arts. ❑ *Like so many creative people, he was never satisfied.* **2** Creative activities involve the inventing and making of new kinds of things. ❑ *creative writing* ❑ *creative arts* **3** If you use something in a **creative** way, you use it in a new way that produces interesting and unusual results. ❑ *his creative use of words*

cre·a·tiv·i·ty /ˌkriːeɪˈtɪvɪti/ NOUN [U] ❑ *American art reached a peak of creativity in the '50s and '60s.*

cre·a·tor /kriˈeɪtə/ NOUN [C, SING] (**creators**) **1** [C] The **creator** of something is the person who made it or invented it. ❑ *Ian Fleming, the creator of James Bond* **2** [SING] God is sometimes referred to as **the Creator**. ❑ *This was the first object placed in the heavens by the Creator.*

✪ **crea·ture** /ˈkriːtʃə/ NOUN [C] (**creatures**) You can refer to any living thing that is not a plant as a **creature**, especially if it is of an unknown or unfamiliar kind. People also refer to imaginary animals and beings as **creatures**. = **being, animal** ❑ *Alaskan Eskimos believe that every living creature possesses a spirit.* ❑ *After more than a century of study, new marine creatures are still being discovered.*

cre·den·tials /krɪˈdenʃəlz/ NOUN [PL] **1** Someone's **credentials** are their previous achievements, training, and general background, which indicate that they are qualified to do something. ❑ *her credentials as a Bach specialist* **2** Someone's **credentials** are a letter or certificate that proves their identity or qualifications. ❑ *The new ambassador to Lebanon has presented his credentials to the president.*

✪ **cred·ibil·ity** /ˌkredɪˈbɪlɪti/ NOUN [U] If someone or something has **credibility**, people believe in them and trust them. ❑ *The police have lost their credibility.* ❑ *He cast doubt on Mr Zimet's credibility as a witness.* ❑ *The president will have to work hard to restore his credibility.*

✪ **cred·ible** /ˈkredɪbəl/ ADJ **1** Credible means able to be trusted or believed. = **plausible** ❑ *Her claims seem credible to many.* ❑ *But in order to maintain a credible threat of intervention, we have to maintain a credible alliance.* **2** A **credible** candidate, policy, or system, for example, is one that appears to have a chance of being successful. ❑ *Mr Robertson would be a credible candidate.*

✪ **cred·it** ♦♦◇ /ˈkredɪt/ NOUN, VERB (*academic word*)

NOUN [U, C, PL, SING] (**credits**) **1** [U] If you are given **credit**, you are allowed to pay for goods or services several weeks or months after you have received them. ❑ *The group can't get credit to buy farming machinery.* ❑ *You can ask a dealer for a discount whether you pay cash or buy on credit.* **2** [U] If you get **the credit** for something good, people praise you because you are responsible for it, or are thought to be responsible for it. ❑ *We don't mind who gets the credit so long as we don't get the blame.* ❑ *It would be wrong for us to take all the credit.* **3** [C] A **credit** is a sum of money which is added to an account. ❑ *The statement of total debits and credits is known as a balance.* **4** [C] A **credit** is an amount of money that is given to someone. = **allowance** ❑ *Senator Bill Bradley outlined his own tax cut, giving families $350 in tax credits per child.* **5** [PL] The list of people who helped to make a film, a CD, or a television programme is called **the credits**. ❑ *It was fantastic seeing my name in the credits.* **6** [C] A **credit** is a successfully completed part of a higher education course, representing about one hour of instruction a week. At universities and colleges you need a certain number of credits to be awarded a degree. ❑ *Through the AP programme students can earn college credits in high school.* **7** [SING] If you say that someone is **a credit to** someone or something, you mean that their qualities or achievements will make people have a good opinion of the person or thing mentioned. ❑ *He is one of the greatest players of recent times and is a credit to his profession.*

PHRASES **give someone credit for something** To give someone **credit for** a good quality means to believe that they have it. ❑ *Bratbakk had more ability than the media gave him credit for.*

to someone's credit If something is **to** someone's **credit**, they deserve praise for it. ❑ *She had managed to pull herself together and, to her credit, continued to look upon life as a positive experience.*

VERB [T] (**credits, crediting, credited**) **1** When a sum of money **is credited to** an account, the bank adds that sum of money to the total in the account. ❑ *She noticed that only $80,000 had been credited to her account.* ❑ *Midland decided to change the way it credited payments to accounts.* **2** If people **credit** someone **with** an achievement or if it **is credited to** them, people say or believe that they were responsible for it. ❑ *The staff are crediting him with having saved Hythe's life.* ❑ *The 74-year-old mayor is credited with helping make Los Angeles the financial capital of the West Coast.*

cred·it·able /ˈkredɪtəbəl/ ADJ **1** A **creditable** performance or achievement is of a reasonably high standard. = **respectable** ❑ *They turned out a quite creditable performance.* **2** If you describe someone's actions or aims as **creditable**, you mean that they are morally good. ❑ *Not a very creditable attitude, I'm afraid.*

cred·it card NOUN [C] (**credit cards**) A **credit card** is a plastic card that you use to buy goods on credit.

✪ **cred·i·tor** /ˈkredɪtə/ NOUN [C] (**creditors**) Your **creditors** are the people who owe you money to. ❑ *The company said it would pay in full all its creditors except Credit Suisse.* ❑ *a consortium of Korean creditor banks*

creed /kriːd/ NOUN [C] (**creeds**) (*formal*) **1** A **creed** is a set of beliefs, principles, or opinions that strongly influence the way people live or work. ❑ *their devotion to their creed of self-help* **2** A **creed** is a religion. = **faith** ❑ *The centre is open to all, no matter what race or creed.*

creep /kriːp/ VERB [I] (**creeps, creeping, crept**) **1** When people or animals **creep** somewhere, they move quietly and slowly. ❑ *Back I go to the hotel and creep up to my room.* **2** If something **creeps** somewhere, it moves very slowly. ❑ *Mist had crept in again from the sea.* **3** If something **creeps** in or **creeps** back, it begins to occur or becomes part of something without people realizing or without them wanting it. ❑ *Insecurity might creep in.* ❑ *An increasing ratio of mistakes, perhaps induced by tiredness, crept into her game.* **4** If a rate or number **creeps up** to a higher level, it gradually reaches that level. ❑ *The inflation rate has been creeping up to 9.5 per cent.*

✦ **make someone's flesh creep** → see **flesh**

cre·mate /krɪˈmeɪt, AmE ˈkriːmeɪt/ VERB [T] (**cremates,**

C

cremating, cremated) When someone **is cremated**, their dead body is burned, usually as part of a funeral service. ❑ *She wants Chris to be cremated.*

cre·ma·tion /krɪ'meɪʃən/ NOUN [C, U] (**cremations**) ❑ *At Miss Garbo's request, there was a cremation after a private ceremony.*

crept /krept/ IRREG FORM **Crept** is the past tense and past participle of **creep**.

cres·cent /'kresənt, 'krez-/ NOUN [C] (**crescents**) **1** A **crescent** is a curved shape that is wider in the middle than at its ends, like the shape of the moon during its first and last quarters. It is the most important symbol of the Islamic faith. ❑ *A glittering Islamic crescent tops the mosque.* ❑ *a narrow crescent of sand dunes* **2** **Crescent** is sometimes used as part of the name of a street or row of houses that is usually built in a curve. ❑ *The address is 44 Colville Crescent.*

crest /krest/ NOUN
NOUN [C] (**crests**) **1** The **crest of** a hill or a wave is the top of it. **2** A bird's **crest** is a group of upright feathers on the top of its head. ❑ *Both birds had a dark blue crest.* **3** A **crest** is a design that is the symbol of a noble family, a town, or an organization. ❑ *On the wall is the family crest.*
PHRASE **on the crest of a wave** If you say that you are **on the crest of a wave**, you mean that you are feeling very happy and confident because things are going well for you. ❑ *The band is riding on the crest of a wave with the worldwide success of their number-one-selling single.*

crew ♦◇◇ /kruː/ NOUN, VERB
NOUN [C] (**crews**) **1** The **crew** of a ship, an aircraft, or a spacecraft is the people who work on and operate it. ❑ *The mission for the crew of the space shuttle is essentially over.* ❑ *Despite their size, these vessels carry small crews, usually of around twenty men.* **2** A **crew** is a group of people with special technical skills who work together on a task or project. ❑ *a two-man film crew making a documentary*
VERB [I, T] (**crews, crewing, crewed**) If you **crew** a boat, you work on it as part of the crew. ❑ *This neighbour crewed on a ferryboat.* ❑ *There were to be five teams of three crewing the boat.*

crick·et ♦◇◇ /'krɪkɪt/ NOUN [U, C] (**crickets**) **1** [U] **Cricket** is an outdoor game played between two teams. Players try to score points, called runs, by hitting a ball with a wooden bat. ❑ *During the summer term we would play cricket at the village ground.* **2** [C] A **cricket** is a small jumping insect that produces short, loud sounds by rubbing its wings together.

✪ **crime** ♦♦◇ /kraɪm/ NOUN [C, U] (**crimes**) **1** [C, U] A **crime** is an illegal action or activity for which a person can be punished by law. = offence, wrongdoing ❑ *He and Lieutenant Cassidy were checking the scene of the crime.* ❑ *Mr Steele has committed no crime and poses no danger to the public.* ❑ *We need a positive programme of crime prevention.* ❑ *the growing problem of organized crime* **2** [C] If you say that doing something is a **crime**, you think it is very wrong or a serious mistake. = sin ❑ *It would be a crime to travel all the way to Australia and not stop in Sydney.*

✪ **crimi·nal** ♦♦◇ /'krɪmɪnəl/ NOUN, ADJ
NOUN [C] (**criminals**) A **criminal** is a person who has committed a crime. = culprit, convict ❑ *A group of gunmen attacked a prison and set free nine criminals.* ❑ *Thousands of criminals are caught every year using DNA technology.*
ADJ **1** **Criminal** means connected with crime. = illegal; ≠ legal, lawful ❑ *Her husband faces various criminal charges.* ❑ *Bribery is a criminal offence.* ❑ *At 17, he had a criminal record for petty theft.* **2** If you describe an action as **criminal**, you think it is very wrong or a serious mistake. ❑ *He said a full-scale dispute involving strikes would be criminal.*

cringe /krɪndʒ/ VERB [I] (**cringes, cringing, cringed**) If you **cringe** at something, you feel embarrassed or disgusted, and perhaps show this feeling in your expression or by making a slight movement. = recoil ❑ *Molly had cringed when Ann started picking up the guitar.* ❑ *Chris had cringed at the thought of using her own family for publicity.*

crip·ple /'krɪpəl/ NOUN, VERB
NOUN [C] (**cripples**) (*offensive*) A person with a physical

disability or a serious permanent injury is sometimes referred to as a **cripple**. ❑ *She has gone from being a healthy, fit, and sporty young woman to being a cripple.*
VERB [T] (**cripples, crippling, crippled**) If someone **is crippled** by an injury, it is so serious that they can never move their body properly again. ❑ *Mr Easton was crippled in an accident and had to leave his job.* ❑ *He had been warned that another bad fall could cripple him for life.*

✪ **cri·sis** ♦♦◇ /'kraɪsɪs/ NOUN [C, U] (**crises**) A **crisis** is a situation in which something or someone is affected by one or more very serious problems. = emergency ❑ *Natural disasters have obviously contributed to the continent's economic crisis.* ❑ *children's illnesses or other family crises* ❑ *someone to turn to in moments of crisis*

crisp /krɪsp/ ADJ, VERB, NOUN
ADJ (**crisper, crispest**) **1** (*approval*) Food that is **crisp** is pleasantly hard, or has a pleasantly hard surface. ❑ *Bake the potatoes for 15 minutes, till they're nice and crisp.* ❑ *crisp bacon* **2** (*approval*) Weather that is pleasantly fresh, cold, and dry can be described as **crisp**. ❑ *a crisp autumn day* **3** **Crisp** cloth or paper is clean and has no creases in it. ❑ *He wore a panama hat and a crisp white suit.* ❑ *I slipped between the crisp clean sheets.*
VERB [I, T] (**crisps, crisping, crisped**) If food **crisps** or if you **crisp** it, it becomes pleasantly hard, for example, because you have heated it at a high temperature. ❑ *Cook the bacon until it begins to crisp.*
NOUN [C] (**crisps**) (*BrE*; in *AmE*, use **chips**) **Crisps** are very thin slices of fried potato that are eaten cold as a snack.

criss-cross /'krɪs krɒs, AmE -krɔːs/ also **crisscross** VERB, ADJ
VERB [T, RECIP] (**criss-crosses, criss-crossing, criss-crossed**) **1** [T] If a person or thing **criss-crosses** an area, they travel from one side to the other and back again many times, following different routes. If a number of things **criss-cross** an area, they cross it, and cross over each other. ❑ *They criss-crossed the country by bus.* **2** [RECIP] If two sets of lines or things **criss-cross**, they cross over each other. ❑ *Wires criss-cross between the tops of the poles, forming a grid.*
ADJ [criss-cross + N] A **criss-cross** pattern or design consists of lines crossing each other. ❑ *Slash the tops of the loaves with a serrated knife in a criss-cross pattern.*

✪ **cri·teri·on** /kraɪ'tɪəriən/ NOUN [C] (**criteria**) (*academic word*) A **criterion** is a factor on which you judge or decide something. = standard, rule ❑ *The most important criterion for entry is that applicants must design and make their own work.* ❑ *British defence policy had to meet three criteria if it was to succeed.*

USAGE NOTE
criteria

The plural noun, **criteria**, is the most common form, because you often talk about several **criteria**.
We have to adhere to strict hygiene criteria.
Remember that the correct singular form is **criterion**.

✪ **crit·ic** ♦♦◇ /'krɪtɪk/ NOUN [C] (**critics**) **1** A **critic** is a person who writes about and expresses opinions about things such as books, films, music, or art. = reviewer ❑ *Mather was a film critic for many years.* ❑ *The New York critics had praised her performance.* **2** Someone who is a **critic** of a person or system disapproves of them and criticizes them publicly. ❑ *The newspaper has been one of the most consistent critics ever of the government.* ❑ *He became a fierce critic of the tobacco industry.* ❑ *Her critics accused her of caring only about success.*

✪ **criti·cal** ♦♦◇ /'krɪtɪkəl/ ADJ **1** A **critical** time, factor, or situation is extremely important. = crucial ❑ *The incident happened at a critical point in the campaign.* ❑ *He says setting priorities is of critical importance.* **2** A **critical** situation is very serious and dangerous. ❑ *The German authorities are considering an airlift if the situation becomes critical.* **3** If a person is **critical** or in a **critical** condition in a hospital, they are seriously ill. ❑ *Ten of the injured are said to be in critical condition.* **4** To be **critical of** someone or something means to criticize them. = disapproving; ≠ complimentary ❑ *His report is highly critical of the trial*

judge. ☐ *He has apologised for critical remarks he made about the referee.* **5** [critical + N] A **critical** approach to something involves examining and judging it carefully. = analytical; ≠ undiscriminating ☐ *We need to become critical text-readers.* ☐ *Marx's work was more than a critical study of capitalist production.* ☐ *the critical analysis of political ideas* **6** [critical + N] If something or someone receives **critical** acclaim, critics say that they are very good. ☐ *The film met with considerable critical and public acclaim.*
○ criti·cal·ly /ˈkrɪtɪkli/ ADV **1** *Economic prosperity depends critically on an open world trading system.* **2** *Moscow is running critically low on food supplies.* **3** *She was critically ill.* **4** *She spoke critically of Lara.* **5** *Wyman watched them critically.*

○ criti·cism ♦♦◇ /ˈkrɪtɪsɪzəm/ NOUN [C, U] (**criticisms**)
1 [C, U] **Criticism** is the action of expressing disapproval of something or someone. A **criticism** is a statement that expresses disapproval. = disapproval; ≠ praise ☐ *This policy had repeatedly come under strong criticism on Capitol Hill.* ☐ *The announcement has drawn criticism from analysts.* ☐ *unfair criticism of his tactics* ☐ *The criticism that the English do not truly care about their children was often voiced.* **2** [U] **Criticism** is a serious examination and judgment of something such as a book or play. ☐ *She has published more than 20 books including novels, poetry and literary criticism.* ☐ *academic film criticism*

○ criti·cize ♦◇◇ /ˈkrɪtɪsaɪz/ also **criticise** VERB [T] (**criticizes, criticizing, criticized**) If you **criticize** someone or something, you express your disapproval of them by saying what you think is wrong with them. ≠ praise, support ☐ *His mother had rarely criticized him or any of her other children.* ☐ *Human rights groups are criticizing the decision.* ☐ *The regime has been harshly criticized for human rights violations.* ☐ *The minister criticised the police for failing to come up with any leads.*

WORD FAMILIES	
criticize VERB	The minister **criticized** the police for failing to come up with any leads.
criticism NOUN	Their imprisonment met with **criticism** from human-rights activitists.
critic NOUN	He became a fierce **critic** of the tobacco industry.
critical ADJ	His report is highly **critical** of the trial judge.
critically ADV	Her supervisor observed her **critically**.

croak /krəʊk/ VERB, NOUN
VERB [I, T] (**croaks, croaking, croaked**) **1** [I] When a frog or bird **croaks**, it makes a harsh, low sound. ☐ *Thousands of frogs croaked in the reeds by the riverbank.* **2** [T] If someone **croaks** something, they say it in a low, rough voice. ☐ *Tiller moaned and managed to croak, 'Help me.'* **3** [I] (*informal*) When someone **croaks**, they die. ☐ *I think the doctors were worried that I was going to croak on their watch.*
NOUN [C] (**croaks**) **1** A **croak** is a harsh, low sound. ☐ *the guttural croak of the frogs* **2** A **croak** is a low, rough voice. ☐ *His voice was just a croak.*

crook /krʊk/ NOUN, VERB
NOUN [C] (**crooks**) **1** (*informal*) A **crook** is a dishonest person or a criminal. ☐ *The man is a crook and a liar.* **2** The **crook** of your arm or leg is the soft inside part where you bend your elbow or knee. ☐ *She hid her face in the crook of her arm.* **3** A **crook** is a long pole with a large hook at the end. A crook is carried by a bishop in religious ceremonies, or by a shepherd.
VERB [T] (**crooks, crooking, crooked**) If you **crook** your arm or finger, you bend it. ☐ *He crooked his finger: 'Come forward,' he said.*

crook·ed /ˈkrʊkɪd/ ADJ **1** If you describe something as **crooked**, especially something that is usually straight, you mean that it is bent or twisted. ☐ *the crooked line of his broken nose* **2** A **crooked** smile is uneven and bigger on one side than the other. = lopsided ☐ *Polly gave her a*

crooked grin. **3** (*informal*) If you describe a person or an activity as **crooked**, you mean that they are dishonest or criminal. = bent ☐ *a crooked cop*

○ crop ♦◇◇ /krɒp/ NOUN, VERB
NOUN [C, SING] (**crops**) **1** [C] **Crops** are plants such as wheat and potatoes that are grown in large quantities for food. ☐ *Rice farmers here still plant and harvest their crops by hand.* ☐ *The main crop is wheat and this is grown even on the very steep slopes.* **2** [C] The plants or fruits that are collected at harvest time are referred to as a **crop**. = harvest ☐ *Each year it produces a fine crop of fruit.* ☐ *The US government says that this year's corn crop should be about 8 per cent more than last year.* **3** [C] A **crop** is a short hairstyle. ☐ *She had her long hair cut into a boyish crop.* **4** [SING] (*informal*) You can refer to a group of people or things that have appeared together as a **crop of** people or things. = batch ☐ *The present crop of books and documentaries about the singer exploit the thirtieth anniversary of her death.*
VERB [I, T] (**crops, cropping, cropped**) **1** [I] When a plant **crops**, it produces fruits or parts which people want. ☐ *Although these vegetables adapt well to our temperate climate, they tend to crop poorly.* **2** [T] To **crop** someone's hair means to cut it short. ☐ *She cropped her hair and dyed it blonde.* **3** [T] If you **crop** a photograph, you cut part of it off, in order to get rid of part of the picture or to be able to frame it. ☐ *I decided to crop the picture just above the water line.*
PHRASAL VERB **crop up** If something **crops up**, it appears or happens, usually unexpectedly. = come up ☐ *His name has cropped up at every selection meeting this season.*

cross ♦♦◇ /krɒs, AmE krɔːs/ VERB, NOUN, ADJ
VERB [I, T, RECIP] (**crosses, crossing, crossed**) **1** [I, T] If you **cross** something such as a room, a road, or an area of land or water, you move or travel to the other side of it. If you **cross to** a place, you move or travel over a room, road, or area of land or water in order to reach that place. ☐ *She was partly to blame for failing to look as she crossed the road.* ☐ *Egan crossed to the drinks cabinet and poured a Scotch.* **2** [T] A road, railway, or bridge that **crosses** an area of land or water passes over it. ☐ *The road crosses the river half a mile outside the town.* **3** [T] If someone or something **crosses** a limit or boundary, for example, the limit of acceptable behaviour, they go beyond it. ☐ *I normally never write in to magazines but Mr Stubbs has finally crossed the line.* **4** [T] (*written*) If an expression **crosses** someone's face, it appears briefly on their face. ☐ *Berg tilts his head and a mischievous look crosses his face.* **5** [T] If you **cross** your arms, legs, or fingers, you put one of them on top of the other. ☐ *Jill crossed her legs and rested her chin on one fist, as if lost in deep thought.* **6** [RECIP] Lines or roads that **cross** meet and go across each other. ☐ *the intersection where Main and Center streets cross*
PHRASAL VERB **cross out** If you **cross out** words on a page, you draw a line through them, because they are wrong or because you want to change them. = delete ☐ *He crossed out 'fellow subjects', and instead inserted 'fellow citizens'.*
NOUN [C, SING] (**crosses**) **1** [C] A **cross** is a shape that consists of a vertical line or piece with a shorter horizontal line or piece across it. It is the most important Christian symbol. ☐ *Around her neck was a cross on a silver chain.* **2** [C] A **cross** is a written mark in the shape of an X. You can use it, for example, to indicate that an answer to a question is wrong, to mark the position of something on a map, or to indicate your vote on a ballot. ☐ *Put a cross next to those activities you like.* **3** [C] In some team sports such as football and hockey, a **cross** is the passing of the ball from the side of the field to a player in the centre, usually in front of the goal. ☐ *Johnson hit an accurate cross to Groves.* **4** [SING] Something that is **a cross between** two things is neither one thing nor the other, but a mixture of both. ☐ *'Ha!' It was a cross between a laugh and a bark.*
ADJ (**crosser, crossest**) Someone who is **cross** is angry or irritated. = annoyed ☐ *The women are cross and bored.* ☐ *I'm terribly cross with him.*
cross·ly /ˈkrɒsli, AmE ˈkrɔːsli/ ADV [crossly with V] ☐ *'No, no, no,' Morris said crossly.*
→ See also **crossing**
✦ **cross your fingers** → see **finger**; **cross my heart** → see

heart; cross your mind → see mind; cross swords → see sword

cross-country NOUN, ADJ, ADV

NOUN [U] **Cross-country** is the sport of running, riding, or skiing across open countryside rather than along roads or around a running track. ❑ *She finished third in the world cross-country championships in Antwerp.*

ADJ [cross-country + N] A **cross-country** journey involves less important roads or railway lines, or takes you from one side of a country to the other. ❑ *cross-country rail services*

ADV [cross-country after v] If you travel **cross-country**, you use less important roads or railway lines, or you travel from one side of a country to the other. ❑ *I drove cross-country in his van.*

○ **cross-examine** VERB [T] (**cross-examines, cross-examining, cross-examined**) When a lawyer **cross-examines** someone during a trial or hearing, he or she questions them about the evidence that they have already given. ❑ *The accused's lawyers will get a chance to cross-examine him.* ❑ *You know you are liable to be cross-examined mercilessly about the assault.*

○ **cross-examination** NOUN [C, U] (**cross-examinations**) ❑ *the cross-examination of a witness in a murder case* ❑ *Under cross-examination, he admitted the state troopers used more destructive ammunition than usual.*

cross•ing /ˈkrɒsɪŋ, AmE ˈkrɔːs-/ NOUN [C] (**crossings**) **1** A **crossing** is a journey by boat or ship to a place on the other side of an ocean, sea, river, or lake. ❑ *He made the crossing from Cape Town to Sydney in just over twenty-six days.* **2** A **crossing** is a place where two roads, paths, or lines cross. ❑ *She sighed and squatted down next to the crossing of the two trails.* **3** A **crossing** is a place where pedestrians can cross the street and where motorists must stop to let them.

○ **cross-section** also **cross section** NOUN [C] (**cross-sections**) **1** If you refer to a **cross-section of** particular things or people, you mean a group of them that you think is typical or representative of all of them. ❑ *I was surprised at the cross-section of people there.* ❑ *For most research projects it is necessary to talk to a cross-section of the public – people from all walks of life and all ages.* ❑ *He also said it was important that the study was done on a broad cross-section of children.* **2** [also 'in' cross-section] A **cross-section** of an object is what you would see if you could cut straight through the middle of it. ❑ *a cross-section of an aeroplane* ❑ *The hall is square in cross-section.*

crouch /kraʊtʃ/ VERB, NOUN

VERB [I] (**crouches, crouching, crouched**) If you **are crouching**, your legs are bent under you so that you are close to the ground and leaning forward slightly. = squat ❑ *We were crouching in the bushes.* ❑ *I crouched on the ground.*

PHRASAL VERB **crouch down** Crouch down means the same as **crouch** VERB. ❑ *He crouched down and reached under the mattress.*

NOUN [SING] A **crouch** is a position in which your legs are bent under you so that you are close to the ground and leaning forward slightly. ❑ *They walked in a crouch, each bent over close to the ground.*

○ **crowd** ◆◆◇ /kraʊd/ NOUN, VERB

NOUN [C] (**crowds**) **1** A **crowd** is a large group of people who have gathered together, for example, to watch or listen to something interesting, or to protest about something. = group, mass, throng; ≠ individual ❑ *A huge crowd gathered in a square outside the Kremlin walls.* ❑ *It took some two hours before the crowd was fully dispersed.* ❑ *The crowd were enormously enthusiastic.* ❑ *The explosions took place in shopping centres as crowds of people were shopping for Mothers' Day.* **2** (*informal*) A particular **crowd** is a group of friends, or a set of people who share the same interests or job. ❑ *All the old crowd have come out for this occasion.*

VERB [I, T] (**crowds, crowding, crowded**) **1** [I] When people **crowd around** someone or something, they gather closely together around them. = cluster ❑ *The hungry refugees crowded around the tractors.* **2** [I, T] If people **crowd**

into a place or **are crowded into** a place, large numbers of them enter it so that it becomes very full. = pack, cram ❑ *Hundreds of thousands of people have crowded into the centre of the Lithuanian capital, Vilnius.* ❑ *One group of journalists were crowded into a minibus.* **3** [T] If a group of people **crowd** a place, there are so many of them there that it is full. = pack ❑ *Thousands of demonstrators crowded the streets shouting slogans.*

○ **crowd•ed** /ˈkraʊdɪd/ ADJ **1** If a place is **crowded**, it is full of people. = busy, congested; ≠ empty, quiet ❑ *He peered slowly around the small crowded room.* ❑ *The street was crowded and noisy.* ❑ *The old town square was crowded with people.* **2** If a place is **crowded**, a lot of people live there. ❑ *a crowded city of 2 million* **3** If your schedule, your life, or your mind is **crowded**, it is full of events, activities, or thoughts. = packed ❑ *Never before has a summit had such a crowded agenda.*

crown ◆◇◇ /kraʊn/ NOUN, VERB

NOUN [C, SING] (**crowns**) **1** [C] A **crown** is a circular ornament, usually made of gold and jewels, which a king or queen wears on their head at official ceremonies. You can also use **crown** to refer to anything circular that is worn on someone's head. ❑ *a crown of flowers* **2** [C] Your **crown** is the top part of your head, at the back. ❑ *He laid his hand gently on the crown of her head.* **3** [C] A **crown** is an artificial top piece fixed over a broken or decayed tooth. ❑ *How long does it take to have crowns fitted?* **4** [SING] The government of a country that has a king or queen is sometimes referred to as **the Crown**. ❑ *She says the sovereignty of the Crown must be preserved.* ❑ *a minister of the Crown*

VERB [T] (**crowns, crowning, crowned**) When a king or queen **is crowned**, a crown is placed on their head as part of a ceremony in which they are officially made king or queen. ❑ *Two days later, Juan Carlos was crowned king.*

○ **cru•cial** ◆◇◇ /ˈkruːʃəl/ ADJ (*academic word*) If you describe something as **crucial**, you mean it is extremely important. = critical ❑ *He had administrators under him but made the crucial decisions himself.* ❑ *the most crucial election campaign for years* ❑ *Improved consumer confidence is crucial to an economic recovery.*

○ **cru•cial•ly** /ˈkruːʃəli/ ADV ❑ *Chewing properly is crucially important.* ❑ *Crucially, though, it failed to secure the backing of the banks.*

crude /kruːd/ ADJ (**cruder, crudest**) **1** A **crude** method or measurement is not exact or detailed, but may be useful or correct in a rough, general way. = rough ❑ *Standard measurements of blood pressure are an important but crude way of assessing the risk of heart disease or strokes.* **2** If you describe an object that someone has made as **crude**, you mean that it has been made in a very simple way or from very simple parts. ❑ *crude wooden boxes* **3** If you describe someone as **crude**, you disapprove of them because they speak or behave in a rude, offensive, or unsophisticated way. = coarse ❑ *Must you be quite so crude?* **4** [crude + N] **Crude** substances are in a natural or unrefined state, and have not yet been used in manufacturing processes. = raw

crude•ly /ˈkruːdli/ ADV **1** *The donors can be split – a little crudely – into two groups.* **2** *a crudely carved wooden form* **3** *He hated it when she spoke so crudely.*

cru•el /ˈkruːəl/ ADJ (**crueller, cruellest; in** AmE, **use crueler, cruelest**) **1** Someone who is **cruel** deliberately causes pain or distress to people or animals. ❑ *Children can be so cruel.* **2** A situation or event that is **cruel** is very harsh and causes people distress. ❑ *struggling to survive in a cruel world with which they cannot cope*

cru•el•ly /ˈkruːəli/ ADV **1** [cruelly with v] ❑ *Douglas was often cruelly tormented by jealous siblings.* **2** *His life has been cruelly shattered by an event not of his own making.*

cru•el•ty /ˈkruːəlti/ NOUN [C, U] (**cruelties**) **Cruelty** is behaviour that deliberately causes pain or distress to people or animals. ❑ *Britain had laws against cruelty to animals but none to protect children.*

cruise ◆◇◇ /kruːz/ NOUN, VERB

NOUN [C] (**cruises**) A **cruise** is a holiday during which you travel on a ship or boat and visit a number of places.

❏ *He and his wife were planning to go on a world cruise.*
VERB [I, T] (**cruises, cruising, cruised**) **1** [I, T] If you **cruise** an ocean, sea, river, or canal, you travel around it or along it on a cruise. ❏ *She wants to cruise the canals of France in a barge.* ❏ *a holiday cruising around the Caribbean* **2** [I] If a car, ship, or aircraft **cruises** somewhere, it moves there at a steady comfortable speed. ❏ *A black and white police car cruised past.*

crumb /krʌm/ NOUN [c] (**crumbs**) **Crumbs** are tiny pieces that fall from bread, biscuits, or cake when you cut it or eat it. ❏ *I stood up, brushing crumbs from my trousers.*

crum•ble /ˈkrʌmbəl/ VERB
VERB [I, T] (**crumbles, crumbling, crumbled**) **1** [I, T] If something **crumbles**, or if you **crumble** it, it breaks into a lot of small pieces. ❏ *Under the pressure, the flint crumbled into fragments.* **2** [I] If an old building or piece of land **is crumbling**, parts of it keep breaking off. = **disintegrate** ❏ *The high- and low-rise blocks of flats built in the 1960s are crumbling.* **3** [I] If something such as a system, relationship, or hope **crumbles**, it comes to an end. ❏ *Their economy crumbled under the weight of United Nations sanctions.*
PHRASAL VERB **crumble away** **1** Crumble away means the same as **crumble** VERB 2. ❏ *Much of the coastline is crumbling away.* **2** Crumble away means the same as **crumble** VERB 3. ❏ *Opposition more or less crumbled away.*

crunch /krʌntʃ/ VERB, NOUN
VERB [I, T] (**crunches, crunching, crunched**) **1** [I, T] If you **crunch** something hard, such as a sweet, or if it **crunches**, you crush it noisily between your teeth. ❏ *She sucked an ice cube into her mouth, and crunched it loudly.* **2** [I, T] If something **crunches** or if you **crunch** it, it makes a breaking or crushing noise, for example, when you step on it. = **scrunch** ❏ *A piece of china crunched under my foot.* **3** [I] If you **crunch** across a surface made of very small stones, you move across it causing it to make a crunching noise. ❏ *I crunched across the gravel.* **4** [T] To **crunch** numbers means to do a lot of calculations using a calculator or computer. ❏ *I pored over the books with great enthusiasm, often crunching the numbers until 1:00 a.m.*
NOUN [c, SING] (**crunches**) **1** [c] A **crunch** is a breaking or crushing noise made when you move across a surface made of very small stones. ❏ *She heard the crunch of tyres on the gravel driveway.* **2** [SING] You can refer to an important time or event, for example, when an important decision has to be made, as **the crunch**. ❏ *He can rely on my support when the crunch comes.* **3** [c] (*business*) A situation in which a business or economy has very little money can be referred to as a **crunch**. = **crisis** ❏ *The U.N. is facing a cash crunch.*

cru•sade /kruːˈseɪd/ NOUN, VERB
NOUN [c] (**crusades**) A **crusade** is a long and determined attempt to achieve something for a cause that you feel strongly about. = **campaign** ❏ *He made it his crusade to teach children to love books.*
VERB [I] (**crusades, crusading, crusaded**) If you **crusade** for a particular cause, you make a long and determined effort to achieve something for it. = **campaign** ❏ *a newspaper that has crusaded against the country's cocaine traffickers*

crush /krʌʃ/ VERB, NOUN
VERB [T] (**crushes, crushing, crushed**) **1** To **crush** something means to press it very hard so that its shape is destroyed or so that it breaks into pieces. ❏ *Andrew crushed his empty can.* ❏ *crushed ice* **2** To **crush** a protest or movement, or a group of opponents, means to defeat it completely, usually by force. ❏ *The military operation was the first step in a plan to crush the uprising.* **3** If you **are crushed** by something, it upsets you a great deal. = **devastate** ❏ *Listen to criticism but don't be crushed by it.* **4** If you **are crushed** against someone or something, you are pushed or pressed against them. ❏ *We were at the front, crushed against the stage.*
NOUN [c] (**crushes**) **1** A **crush** is a crowd of people close together, in which it is difficult to move. ❏ *His thirteen-year-old son somehow got separated in the crush.* **2** (*informal*) If you have a **crush on** someone, you are in love with them but do not have a relationship with them. ❏ *She had a crush on you, you know.*

crush•ing /ˈkrʌʃɪŋ/ NOUN [u] ❏ *the violent crushing of anti-government demonstrations*

crust /krʌst/ NOUN [c] (**crusts**) **1** The **crust** on a loaf of bread is the outside part. ❏ *Cut the crusts off the bread and soak the bread in the milk.* **2** A pie's **crust** is its cooked pastry. ❏ *The Key lime pie was bursting with flavour. Good crust, too.* **3** A **crust** is a hard layer of something, especially on top of a softer or wetter substance. ❏ *As the water evaporates, a crust of salt is left on the surface of the soil.* **4** The Earth's **crust** is its outer layer. ❏ *Earthquakes leave scars in the Earth's crust.*

cry ♦♦◇ /kraɪ/ VERB, NOUN
VERB [T, I] (**cries, crying, cried**) **1** [T, I] When you **cry**, tears come from your eyes, usually because you are unhappy or hurt. ❏ *I hung up the phone and started to cry.* ❏ *He cried with anger and frustration.* **2** [T] If you **cry** something, you shout or say it loudly. ❏ *'Nancy Drew,' she cried, 'you're under arrest!'*
PHRASAL VERBS **cry out** **1** Cry out means the same as **cry** VERB 2. ❏ *'You're wrong, quite wrong!' Henry cried out, suddenly excited.* **2** If you **cry out**, you call out loudly because you are frightened, unhappy, or in pain. ❏ *He was crying out in pain when the ambulance arrived.*
cry out for If you say that something **cries out for** a particular thing or action, you mean that it needs that thing or action very much. ❏ *This is a disgraceful state of affairs and cries out for a thorough investigation.*
NOUN [c, SING] (**cries**) **1** [c, SING] If you have a **cry**, tears come from your eyes, usually because you are unhappy or hurt. ❏ *A nurse patted me on the shoulder and said, 'You have a good cry, dear.'* **2** [c] A **cry** is a loud, high sound that you make when you feel a strong emotion such as fear, pain, or pleasure. ❏ *A cry of horror broke from me.* **3** [c] A **cry** is a shouted word or phrase, usually one that is intended to attract someone's attention. = **shout** ❏ *Thousands of Ukrainians burst into cries of 'bravo'.* **4** [c] (*journalism*) You can refer to a public protest about something or an appeal for something as a **cry** of some kind. ❏ *There have been cries of outrage about this expenditure.* **5** [c] A bird's or an animal's **cry** is the loud, high sound that it makes. = **call** ❏ *the cry of a seagull*

cry•ing /ˈkraɪɪŋ/ NOUN [u] ❏ *She had been unable to sleep for three days because of her 13-week-old son's crying.*
✦ cry your eyes out → see eye; a shoulder to cry on → see shoulder

❂**crys•tal** ♦◇◇ /ˈkrɪstəl/ NOUN [c, u] (**crystals**) (*academic word*) **1** [c] A **crystal** is a small piece of a substance that has formed naturally into a regular symmetrical shape. ❏ *salt crystals* ❏ *ice crystals* ❏ *a single crystal of silicon* **2** [c, u] Crystal is a transparent rock that is used to make jewellery and ornaments. ❏ *She was wearing a strand of crystal beads.* **3** [u] Crystal is a high quality glass, usually with patterns cut into its surface. ❏ *Some of the finest drinking glasses are made from lead crystal.*

❂**cube** /kjuːb/ NOUN, VERB
NOUN [c] (**cubes**) **1** A **cube** is a solid object with six square surfaces which are all the same size. ❏ *cold water with ice cubes in it* ❏ *a box of sugar cubes* **2** The **cube of** a number is another number that is produced by multiplying the first number by itself twice. For example, the cube of 2 is 8. ❏ *The volume of the cell increases proportionally to the cube of its radius*
VERB [T] (**cubes, cubing, cubed**) When you **cube** food, you cut it into cube-shaped pieces. ❏ *Remove the seeds and stones and cube the flesh.*

❂**cu•bic** /ˈkjuːbɪk/ ADJ [cubic + N] **Cubic** is used in front of units of length to form units of volume such as 'cubic metre' and 'cubic foot'. ❏ *3 billion cubic metres of soil*

cud•dle /ˈkʌdəl/ VERB, NOUN
VERB [T] (**cuddles, cuddling, cuddled**) If you **cuddle** someone, you put your arms around them and hold them close as a way of showing your affection. = **hug** ❏ *He cuddled the newborn girl.*
NOUN [c] (**cuddles**) A **cuddle** is the act of putting your arms around someone and holding them close as a way of showing your affection. = **hug** ❏ *It would have been nice to give him a cuddle and a kiss but there wasn't time.*

cue ◆◇◇ /kjuː/ NOUN, VERB

NOUN [c] (**cues**) **1** In the theatre or in a musical performance, a performer's **cue** is something another performer says or does that is a signal for them to begin speaking, playing, or doing something. ❑ *The actors not performing sit at the side of the stage in full view, waiting for their cues.* **2** If you say that something that happens is a **cue for** an action, you mean that people start doing that action when it happens. ❑ *That was the cue for several months of intense bargaining.* **3** A **cue** is a long, thin wooden stick that is used to hit the ball in games such as billiards, pool, and snooker.

VERB [T] (**cues, cueing, cued**) If one performer **cues** another, they say or do something which is a signal for the second performer to begin speaking, playing, or doing something. ❑ *He read the scene, with Seaton cueing him.*

cul·mi·nate /'kʌlmɪneɪt/ VERB [I] (**culminates, culminating, culminated**) If you say that an activity, process, or series of events **culminates in** or **with** a particular event, you mean that event happens at the end of it. = conclude ❑ *They had an argument, which culminated in Tom getting drunk.*

cul·mi·na·tion /ˌkʌlmɪ'neɪʃən/ NOUN [SING] Something, especially something important, that is **the culmination of** an activity, process, or series of events happens at the end of it. ❑ *Their arrest was the culmination of an operation in which 120 other people were detained.*

cul·prit /'kʌlprɪt/ NOUN [c] (**culprits**) **1** When you are talking about a crime or something wrong that has been done, you can refer to the person who did it as **the culprit**. = offender ❑ *All the men being deported even though the real culprits in the fight have not been identified.* **2** When you are talking about a problem or bad situation, you can refer to its cause as **the culprit**. ❑ *About 10% of Japanese teenagers are overweight. Nutritionists say the main culprit is increasing reliance on Western fast food.*

cult /kʌlt/ NOUN, ADJ

NOUN [c, SING] (**cults**) **1** [c] A **cult** is a fairly small religious group, especially one which is considered strange. ❑ *The teenager may have been abducted by a religious cult.* **2** [c] The **cult** of something is a situation in which people regard that thing as very important or special. ❑ *the cult of youth that recently gripped publishing* **3** [SING] Someone or something that is a **cult** has become very popular or fashionable among a particular group of people. ❑ *Violence has become a cult among some young men.*

ADJ [cult + N] **Cult** is used to describe things that are very popular or fashionable among a particular group of people. ❑ *Since her death, she has become a cult figure.*

cul·ti·vate /'kʌltɪveɪt/ VERB [T] (**cultivates, cultivating, cultivated**) **1** If you **cultivate** land or crops, you prepare land and grow crops on it. ❑ *She also cultivated a small garden of her own.* **2** If you **cultivate** an attitude, image, or skill, you try hard to develop it and make it stronger or better. ❑ *He has written eight books and has cultivated the image of an elder statesman.* **3** If you **cultivate** someone or **cultivate** a friendship with them, you try hard to develop a friendship with them. ❑ *Howe carefully cultivated Daniel C. Roper, the Assistant Postmaster General.*

cul·ti·va·tion /ˌkʌltɪ'veɪʃən/ NOUN [U] **1** the cultivation of fruits and vegetables **2** the cultivation of a positive approach to life and health

⚙ **cul·tur·al** ◆◇◇ /'kʌltʃərəl/ ADJ **1** **Cultural** means relating to a particular society and its ideas, customs, and art. ❑ *a deep sense of personal honour which was part of his cultural heritage* ❑ *the Rajiv Gandhi Foundation which promotes cultural and educational exchanges between Britain and India* **2** [cultural + N] **Cultural** means involving or concerning the arts. ❑ *the sponsorship of sports and cultural events by tobacco companies*

cul·tur·al·ly /'kʌltʃərəli/ ADV **1** an informed guide to culturally and historically significant sites **2** one of our better-governed, culturally active regional centres

⚙ **cul·ture** ◆◆◇ /'kʌltʃə/ NOUN [U, c] (**cultures**) (*academic word*) **1** [U] **Culture** consists of activities such as the arts and philosophy, which are considered to be important for the development of civilization and of people's minds. ❑ *There is just not enough fun and frivolity in culture today.* ❑ *aspects of popular culture* ❑ *France's Minister of Culture and Education* **2** [c] A **culture** is a particular society or civilization, especially considered in relation to its beliefs, way of life, or art. = tradition, way of life ❑ *people from different cultures* ❑ *I was brought up in a culture that said you must put back into the society what you have taken out.* **3** [c] The **culture** of a particular organization or group consists of the habits of the people in it and the way they generally behave. ❑ *But social workers say that this has created a culture of dependency, particularly in urban areas.* **4** [c] (*technical*) In science, a **culture** is a group of bacteria or cells which are grown, usually in a laboratory as part of an experiment. ❑ *a culture of human cells*

cum·ber·some /'kʌmbəsəm/ ADJ **1** Something that is **cumbersome** is large and heavy and therefore difficult to carry, wear, or handle. = unwieldy ❑ *Although the machine looks cumbersome, it is actually easy to use.* **2** A **cumbersome** system or process is very complicated and inefficient. = clumsy ❑ *an old and cumbersome computer system*

cun·ning /'kʌnɪŋ/ ADJ, NOUN

ADJ Someone who is **cunning** has the ability to achieve things in a clever way, often by deceiving other people. = crafty ❑ *These disturbed kids can be cunning.*

NOUN [U] **Cunning** is the ability to achieve things in a clever way, often by deceiving other people. ❑ *one more example of the cunning of today's art thieves*

cun·ning·ly /'kʌnɪŋli/ ADV ❑ *They were cunningly disguised in golf clothes.*

cup ◆◆◆ /kʌp/ NOUN, VERB

NOUN [c] (**cups**) **1** A **cup** is a small round container that you drink from. Cups usually have handles and are made from china or plastic. ❑ *cups and saucers* **2** You can use **cup** to refer to the cup and its contents, or to the contents only. ❑ *a cup of coffee* **3** (*mainly AmE*) A **cup** is a unit of measurement used in cooking. It is equal to 16 tablespoons or 8 fluid ounces. ❑ *Gradually add 1 cup of milk, stirring until the liquid is absorbed.* ❑ *half a cup of sugar* **4** Things, or parts of things, that are small, round, and hollow in shape can be referred to as **cups**. ❑ *the brass cups of the small chandelier* **5** A **cup** is a large metal cup with two handles that is given to the winner of a game or competition. = trophy ❑ *The Stars won the Stanley Cup in 1999.* **6** **Cup** is used in the names of some sports competitions in which the prize is a cup. ❑ *Sri Lanka's cricket team will play India in the final of the Asia Cup.*

VERB [T] (**cups, cupping, cupped**) **1** If you **cup** your **hands**, you make them into a curved shape like a cup. ❑ *He cupped his hands around his mouth and called out for Diane.* ❑ *David knelt, cupped his hands and splashed river water on to his face.* **2** If you **cup** something in your hands, you make your hands into a curved dish-like shape and support it or hold it gently. ❑ *He cupped her chin in the palm of his hand.*

cup·board /'kʌbəd/ NOUN [c] (**cupboards**) A **cupboard** is a piece of furniture that has one or two doors, usually contains shelves, and is used to store things. ❑ *The kitchen cupboard was stocked with cans of soup and food.*

cur·able /'kjʊərəbəl/ ADJ If a disease or illness is **curable**, it can be cured. ❑ *Most skin cancers are completely curable if detected in the early stages.*

⚙ **curb** /kɜːb/ VERB, NOUN

VERB [T] (**curbs, curbing, curbed**) **1** If you **curb** something, you control it and keep it within limits. = check, restrain ❑ *advertisements aimed at curbing the spread of AIDS* ❑ *The president will now enact policies to curb greenhouse gas emissions.* ❑ *Inflation needs to be curbed.* **2** If you **curb** an emotion or your behaviour, you keep it under control. = check, restrain ❑ *He curbed his temper.*

NOUN [c] (**curbs**) A **curb** on something is a control and limit on it. ❑ *He called for much stricter curbs on immigration.* ❑ *the government's plans to introduce tough curbs on dangerous dogs*

⚙ **cure** ◆◇◇ /kjʊə/ VERB, NOUN

VERB [T] (**cures, curing, cured**) **1** If doctors or medical treatments **cure** an illness or injury, they cause it to end or disappear. ❑ *An operation finally cured his shin injury.* ❑ *research that could cure diseases such as Alzheimer's* ❑ *Her cancer can only be controlled, not cured.* **2** If doctors or medical treatments **cure** a person, they make the person well again after an illness or injury. = heal ❑ *It is an effective treatment and could cure all the leprosy sufferers worldwide.* ❑ *Almost overnight I was cured.* **3** If someone or something **cures** a problem, they bring it to an end. ❑ *Private firms are willing to make large scale investments to help cure Russia's economic troubles.* **4** When food, tobacco, or animal skin **is cured**, it is dried, smoked, or salted so that it will last for a long time. ❑ *Legs of pork were cured and smoked over the fire.*

NOUN [c] (**cures**) **1** A **cure for** an illness is a medicine or other treatment that cures the illness. = remedy, treatment ❑ *There is still no cure for a cold.* ❑ *There is no known cure for the disease.* ❑ *Doctors hope to find a cure for cancer.* **2** A **cure for** a problem is something that will bring it to an end. = solution ❑ *The magic cure for inflation does not exist.*

cur•few /'kɜːfjuː/ NOUN [c, u] (**curfews**) **1** A **curfew** is a law stating that people must stay inside their houses after a particular time at night, for example, during a war. ❑ *The village was placed under curfew.* **2** **Curfew** or a **curfew** is the time after which a child or student will be punished if they are found outside their home or dormitory. ❑ *They raced back to the dormitory before the nine o'clock curfew.*

cu•ri•os•ity /ˌkjʊəriˈɒsiti/ NOUN [u, c] (**curiosities**) **1** [u] Curiosity is a desire to know about something. ❑ *Ryle accepted more out of curiosity than anything else.* ❑ *enthusiasm and genuine curiosity about the past* **2** [c] A **curiosity** is something that is unusual, interesting, and fairly rare. ❑ *There is much to see in the way of castles, curiosities, and museums.*

cu•ri•ous ♦◇◇ /'kjʊəriəs/ ADJ **1** If you are **curious about** something, you are interested in it and want to know more about it. = inquisitive ❑ *Steve was intensely curious about the world I came from.* **2** If you describe something as **curious**, you mean that it is unusual or difficult to understand. = odd, peculiar ❑ *The pageant promises to be a curious mixture of the ancient and modern.*

cu•ri•ous•ly /'kjʊəriəsli/ ADV **1** [curiously after v] ❑ *The woman in the shop had looked at them curiously.* **2** Harry was curiously silent through all this.

WHICH WORD?

curious, strange, or unusual?

You use **strange** to say that something is unfamiliar or unexpected in a way that makes you puzzled, uneasy, or afraid.

❑ *It was **strange** to hear her voice again.*

❑ *I had a **strange** dream last night.*

If you just want to say that something is not common, you use **unusual**, not **strange**.

❑ *He had an **unusual** name.*

Curious is a slightly formal word. If you describe something as **curious**, you mean that it is unusual and difficult to understand.

❑ *Not long after our arrival, a **curious** thing happened.*

---

curl /kɜːl/ NOUN, VERB
NOUN [c, u] (**curls**) **1** [c] If you have **curls**, your hair is in the form of tight curves and spirals. ❑ *the little girl with blonde curls* **2** [c] A **curl** of something is a piece or quantity of it that is curved or spiral in shape. ❑ *A thin curl of smoke rose from a rusty stove.* **3** [u] If your hair has **curl**, it is full of curls. ❑ *Dry curly hair naturally for maximum curl and shine.*
VERB [i, t] (**curls, curling, curled**) **1** [i, t] If your hair **curls** or if you **curl** it, it is full of curls. ❑ *She has hair that refuses to curl.* ❑ *Maria had curled her hair for the event.* **2** [i, t] If your toes, fingers, or other parts of your body **curl**, or if you **curl** them, they form a curved or round shape. = bend ❑ *His fingers curled gently around her wrist.* ❑ *Raise one foot, curl the toes and point the foot downwards.*

3 [i, t] If something **curls** somewhere, or if you **curl** it there, it moves there in a spiral or curve. ❑ *Smoke was curling up the chimney.* **4** [i] If a person or animal **curls into** a ball, they move into a position in which their body makes a rounded shape. ❑ *He wanted to curl into a tiny ball.* **5** [i] When a leaf, a piece of paper, or another flat object **curls**, its edges bend towards the centre. ❑ *The rose leaves have curled because of an attack by grubs.*

PHRASAL VERB **curl up 1** Curl up means the same as curl VERB **4**. ❑ *In colder weather, your cat will curl up into a tight, heat-conserving ball.* ❑ *She curled up next to him.* **2** Curl up means the same as curl VERB **5**. ❑ *The corners of the rug were curling up.*

curly /'kɜːli/ ADJ (**curlier, curliest**) **1** Curly hair is full of curls. ❑ *I've got naturally curly hair.* **2** Curly is sometimes used to describe things that are curved or spiral in shape. ❑ *cauliflowers with extra-long curly leaves*

✪ **cur•ren•cy** ♦◇◇ /'kʌrənsi, AmE 'kɜːr-/ NOUN [c, u] (**currencies**) (*academic word*) The money used in a particular country is referred to as its **currency**. ❑ *Tourism is the country's top earner of foreign currency.* ❑ *More people favour a single European currency than oppose it.*

✪ **cur•rent** ♦♦♦ /'kʌrənt, AmE 'kɜːr-/ NOUN, ADJ
NOUN [c] (**currents**) **1** A **current** is a steady and continuous flowing movement of some of the water in a river, lake, or sea. ❑ *Under normal conditions, the ocean currents of the tropical Pacific travel from east to west.* ❑ *The couple were swept away by the strong current.* **2** A **current** is a steady flowing movement of air. ❑ *I felt a current of cool air blowing in my face.* ❑ *The spores are very light and can be wafted by the slightest air current* **3** An electric **current** is a flow of electricity through a wire or circuit. ❑ *A powerful electric current is passed through a piece of graphite.* ❑ *the current of electricity from the stun gun* **4** A particular **current** is a particular feeling, idea, or quality that exists within a group of people. ❑ *Each party represents a distinct current of thought.*
ADJ **1** Current means happening, being used, or being done at the present time. = present, present-day; ≠ past, former, future ❑ *The current situation is very different to that in 1990.* ❑ *He plans to repeal a number of current policies.* **2** Ideas and customs that are **current** are generally accepted and used by most people. ❑ *Current thinking suggests that toxins only have a small part to play in the build-up of cellulite.*

✪ **cur•rent•ly** /'kʌrəntli, AmE 'kɜːr-/ ADV [currently before v] = presently, at present ❑ *Twelve potential vaccines are currently being tested on human volunteers.* ❑ *He currently has no strong rivals for power.*

USAGE NOTE

current

To refer to the attitudes of society at the present time, use 'modern society'. Do not use 'current society'.

*He is unhappy with the way consumerism has taken over **modern society**.*

✪ **cur•rent af•fairs** or **current events** NOUN [PL] If you refer to **current affairs**, you are referring to political events and problems in society which are discussed in newspapers, and on television and radio. ❑ *I am ill-informed on current affairs.* ❑ *people who take no interest in politics and current affairs* ❑ *the BBC's current affairs programme 'Panorama'*

✪ **cur•ricu•lum** /kəˈrɪkjʊləm/ NOUN [c] (**curriculums** or **curricula**) **1** A **curriculum** is all the different courses of study that are taught in a school, college, or university. ❑ *Teachers incorporated business skills into the school curriculum.* ❑ *There should be a broader curriculum in schools for post-16-year-old pupils.* ❑ *Russian is the one compulsory foreign language on the school curriculum.* **2** A particular **curriculum** is one particular course of study that is taught in a school, college, or university. = syllabus ❑ *the history curriculum*

cur•ricu•lum vitae /kəˌrɪkjʊləm ˈviːtaɪ, AmE -ti/ (*mainly BrE; in AmE, usually use* **résumé**) NOUN [SING] A **curriculum vitae** is the same as a **CV**.

curse /kɜːs/ VERB, NOUN

VERB [I, T] (curses, cursing, cursed) **1** [I] (written) If you curse, you use very impolite or offensive language, usually because you are angry about something. = swear □ *I cursed and hobbled to my feet.* **2** [T] If you curse someone, you say insulting things to them because you are angry with them. □ *Grandma protested, but he cursed her and rudely pushed her aside.* **3** [T] If you curse something, you complain angrily about it, especially using very impolite language. □ *So we set off again, cursing the delay, towards the west.*

NOUN [C] (curses) **1** A curse is a very impolite, offensive, or insulting word or remark, usually used because you are angry about something or with someone. □ *He shot her an angry look and a curse.* **2** If you say that there is a curse on someone, you mean that there seems to be a supernatural power causing unpleasant things to happen to them. □ *Maybe there is a curse on my family.* **3** You can refer to something that causes a great deal of trouble or harm as a curse. = plague □ *Apathy is the long-standing curse of democracy.*

cur·sor /'kɜːsə/ NOUN [C] (cursors) (computing) On a computer screen, the cursor is a small shape that indicates where anything that is typed by the user will appear. □ *He moves the cursor, clicks the mouse.*

cur·tail /kɜːˈteɪl/ VERB [T] (curtails, curtailing, curtailed) (formal) If you curtail something, you reduce or limit it. = restrict □ *NATO plans to curtail the number of troops being sent to the region.*

cur·tain ♦◇◇ /'kɜːtən/ NOUN [C, SING] (curtains) **1** [C] Curtains are pieces of material which you hang from the top of a window. = drapes □ *Her bedroom curtains were drawn.* **2** [SING] In a theatre, the curtain is the large piece of material that hangs in front of the stage until a performance begins. □ *The curtain rises towards the end of the Prelude.*

✪ curve /kɜːv/ NOUN, VERB

NOUN [C] (curves) **1** A curve is a smooth, gradually bending line, for example, part of the edge of a circle. □ *the curve of his lips* **2** You can refer to a change in something as a particular curve, especially when it is represented on a graph. □ *Youth crime overall is on a slow but steady downward curve.*

VERB [I, T] (curves, curving, curved) **1** [I, T] If something curves, or if someone or something curves it, it has the shape of a curve. □ *Her spine curved.* □ *a knife with a slightly curving blade* □ *The track curved away below him.* □ *A small, unobtrusive smile curved the cook's thin lips.* **2** [I] If something curves, it moves in a curve, for example, through the air. □ *The ball curved strangely in the air.*

✪ curved /kɜːvd/ ADJ A curved object has the shape of a curve or has a smoothly bending surface. = bent □ *the curved lines of the chairs* □ *a small, curved staircase*

cush·ion /'kʊʃən/ NOUN, VERB

NOUN [C] (cushions) **1** A cushion is a fabric case filled with soft material, which you put on a seat to make it more comfortable. □ *a velvet cushion* **2** A cushion is a soft pad or barrier, especially one that protects something. □ *The company provides a polystyrene cushion to protect the tablets during shipping.* **3** Something that is a cushion against something unpleasant reduces its effect. □ *Welfare provides a cushion against hardship.*

VERB [T] (cushions, cushioning, cushioned) **1** Something that cushions an object when it hits something protects it by reducing the force of the impact. □ *There is also a new steering wheel with an energy-absorbing rim to cushion the driver's head in the worst impacts.* **2** To cushion the effect of something unpleasant means to reduce it. □ *They said Western aid was needed to cushion the blows of vital reform.*

cus·to·dy /'kʌstədi/ NOUN

NOUN [U] **1** Custody is the legal right to keep and take care of a child, especially the right given to a child's mother or father when they get divorced. □ *I'm going to go to court to get custody of the children.* □ *Child custody is normally granted to the mother.* **2** If someone is being held in a particular type of custody, they are being kept in a

place that is similar to a prison. □ *The youngster got nine months' youth custody.*

PHRASE in custody Someone who is in custody or has been taken into custody has been arrested and is being kept in prison until they can be tried in a court. □ *Three people appeared in court and two of them were remanded in custody.*

✪ cus·tom /'kʌstəm/ NOUN [C, U, SING] (customs) **1** [C, U] A custom is an activity, a way of behaving, or an event which is usual or traditional in a particular society or in particular circumstances. = tradition, ritual □ *The custom of lighting the Olympic flame goes back centuries.* □ *Chung has tried to adapt to local customs.* **2** [SING] If it is your custom to do something, you usually do it in particular circumstances. □ *It was his custom to approach every problem cautiously.*
→ See also customs

✪ cus·tom·ary /'kʌstəmri, AmE -meri/ ADJ **1** (formal) Customary is used to describe things that people usually do in a particular society or in particular circumstances. = usual, traditional □ *It is customary to offer a drink or a snack to guests.* □ *They interrupted the customary one minute's silence with jeers and shouts.* **2** [customary + N] Customary is used to describe something that a particular person usually does or has. = usual □ *Yvonne took her customary seat behind her desk.*

✪ cus·tom·er ♦♦◇ /'kʌstəmə/ NOUN [C] (customers) A customer is someone who buys goods or services, especially from a shop. = client, consumer, buyer, shopper □ *a satisfied customer* □ *The quality of customer service is extremely important.* □ *Our customers have very tight budgets.* □ *We also improved our customer satisfaction levels.*

WHICH WORD?
customer or client?

A **customer** is someone who buys something, especially from a shop.
□ *She's a regular customer at the flower shop.*

A **client** is a person or company that pays someone for a service.
□ *Many of our clients want advice on how to invest their savings.*

cus·toms /'kʌstəmz/ NOUN, ADJ

NOUN [U] **1** Customs is the official organization responsible for collecting taxes on goods coming into a country and preventing illegal goods from being brought in. □ *What right does Customs have to search my car?* **2** Customs is the place where people arriving from a foreign country have to declare goods that they bring with them. □ *He walked through customs.*

ADJ [customs + N] Customs duties are taxes that people pay for importing and exporting goods. □ *Personal property which is to be re-exported at the end of your visit is not subject to customs duties.*
→ See also custom

✪ cut ♦♦♦ /kʌt/ VERB, NOUN, ADJ, CONVENTION

VERB [I, T] (cuts, cutting, cut) **1** [I, T] If you cut something, you use a knife or a similar tool to divide it into pieces, or to mark it or damage it. If you cut a shape or a hole in something, you make the shape or hole by using a knife or similar tool. □ *Mrs Haines stood nearby, holding scissors to cut a ribbon.* □ *Cut the tomatoes in half vertically.* □ *The thieves cut a hole in the fence.* □ *This little knife cuts really well.* **2** [T] If you cut yourself or cut a part of your body, you accidentally injure yourself on a sharp object so that you bleed. □ *Johnson cut himself shaving.* □ *I started to cry because I cut my finger.* **3** [T] If you cut something such as grass, your hair, or your fingernails, you shorten them using scissors or another tool. □ *The most recent tenants hadn't even cut the grass.* □ *You've had your hair cut, it looks great.* **4** [T] The way that clothes are cut is the way they are designed and made. □ *badly cut blue suits* **5** [T] If you cut something, you reduce it. = reduce; ≠ increase □ *The first priority is to cut costs.* □ *The UN force is to be cut by 90%.* □ *a deal to cut 50 billion dollars from the federal deficit* **6** [T] If you cut a text, broadcast, or performance, you shorten it.

If you **cut** a part of a text, broadcast, or performance, you do not publish, broadcast, or perform that part. ❑ *Branagh has cut the play judiciously.* **7** [I] If you **cut across** or **through** a place, you go through it because it is the shortest route to another place. ❑ *Jesse cut across the car park and strolled through the main entrance.* **8** [I] If you **cut** in front of someone, you move in front of them and take their place. ❑ *Somebody tried to cut in line and a fight broke out.* **9** [T] To **cut** a supply of something means to stop providing it or stop it from being provided. ❑ *Winds have knocked down power lines, cutting electricity to thousands of people.* **10** [T] If you **cut** a deck of playing cards, you divide it into two. ❑ *Place the cards face down on the table and cut them.* **11** [T] (mainly AmE, informal, feelings) If you tell someone to **cut** something, you are telling them in an irritated way to stop it. ❑ *'Cut the euphemisms, Daniel,' Brenda snapped.*

PHRASAL VERBS **cut across** If an issue or problem **cuts across** the division between two or more groups of people, it affects or matters to people in all the groups. ❑ *The problem cuts across all socioeconomic lines and affects all age groups.*
cut back If you **cut back** something such as expenditure or **cut back on** it, you reduce it. ❑ *Customers have cut back spending because of the economic slowdown.* ❑ *The Government has cut back on defence spending.*
cut down **1** If you **cut down on** something or **cut down** something, you use or do less of it. ❑ *He cut down on coffee and cigarettes, and ate a balanced diet.* ❑ *Car owners were asked to cut down travel.* **2** If you **cut down** a tree, you cut through its trunk so that it falls to the ground. = chop down ❑ *A vandal with a chainsaw cut down a tree.*
cut in If you **cut in on** someone, you interrupt them when they are speaking. ❑ *Immediately, Daniel cut in on Joanne's attempts at reassurance.* ❑ *'Not true,' the Duchess cut in.*
cut off **1** If you **cut** something **off**, you remove it with a knife or a similar tool. ❑ *Mrs Johnson cut off a generous piece of the meat.* ❑ *He threatened to cut my hair off.* **2** To **cut** someone or something **off** means to separate them from things that they are normally connected with. = isolate ❑ *One of the goals of the campaign is to cut off the elite Republican Guard from its supplies.* **3** To **cut off** a supply of something means to stop providing it or stop it from being provided. ❑ *The rebels have cut off electricity from the capital.* **4** If you get **cut off** when you are on the telephone, the line is suddenly disconnected and you can no longer speak to the other person. = disconnect ❑ *When you do get through, you've got to speak quickly before you get cut off.* **5** → See also **cutoff**
cut out **1** If you **cut** something **out**, you remove or separate it from what surrounds it using scissors or a knife. ❑ *I cut it out and pinned it to my studio wall.* **2** If you **cut out** a part of a text, you do not print, publish, or broadcast that part, because to include it would make the text too long or unacceptable. = cut, omit ❑ *I listened to the programme and found they'd cut out all the interesting stuff.* **3** To **cut out** something unnecessary or unwanted means to remove it completely from a situation. For example, if you **cut out** a particular type of food, you stop eating it, usually because it is bad for you. = eliminate ❑ *I've simply cut egg yolks out entirely.* **4** If an object **cuts out** the light, it is between you and the light so that you are in the dark. ❑ *The curtains were half drawn to cut out the sunlight.* **5** If an engine **cuts out**, it suddenly stops working. ❑ *The helicopter crash landed when one of its two engines cut out.*
cut up If you **cut** something **up**, you cut it into several pieces. ❑ *Halve the tomatoes, then cut them up coarsely.*
NOUN [C, SING] (cuts) **1** [C] A **cut** is a mark or hole in something made by a knife or similar tool. ❑ *Carefully make a cut in the shell with a small serrated knife.* **2** [C] A **cut** is an injury to your body made by something sharp so that you bleed. ❑ *He had sustained a cut on his left eyebrow.* **3** [SING] A **cut** is the act of shortening something such as hair, grass, or fingernails using scissors or another tool. ❑ *Prices vary from salon to salon, starting at $30 for a cut and blow-dry.* **4** [C] [with SUPP, oft cut 'in' N] A **cut** is a reduction in something. = reduction, cutback; ≠ increase ❑ *The economy needs an immediate 2 per cent cut in interest*

rates. **5** [C] A **cut** to a text, broadcast, or performance is a reduction in its length or the removal of some parts of it. ❑ *It has been found necessary to make some cuts in the text.* **6** [C] [with SUPP, usu cut 'in' N] A **cut** in the supply of something is when the supply is stopped. ❑ *The strike had already led to cuts in electricity and water supplies in many areas.* **7** [C] A **cut** of meat is a piece or type of meat which is cut in a particular way from the animal, or from a particular part of it. ❑ *Use a cheap cut such as spare rib chops.* **8** [SING] (informal) Someone's **cut** of the profits or winnings from something, especially ones that have been obtained dishonestly, is their share. = share ❑ *The agency is expected to take a cut of the money awarded to its client.*
ADJ
PHRASES **cut and dried** If you say that a situation is **cut and dried**, you mean that it is clear and definite. ❑ *Unfortunately, things cannot be as cut and dried as many people would like.*
cut off If you are **cut off** from someone or something you are normally connected with, you are separated from them. ❑ *Without a car we still felt very cut off.*
CONVENTION When a film director says 'cut', they want the actors and the camera crew to stop filming.
→ See also **cutting**
✦ **cut something to the bone** → see **bone**; **cut corners**
→ see **corner**

cute /kjuːt/ ADJ (cuter, cutest) (informal) **1** Something or someone that is **cute** is very pretty or attractive, or is intended to appear pretty or attractive. = sweet ❑ *Oh, look at that dog! He's so cute.* **2** (mainly AmE) If you describe someone as **cute**, you think they are sexually attractive. ❑ *There was this girl, and I thought she was really cute.*

cut·off /ˈkʌtʌf/ NOUN [C] (cutoffs) **1** A **cutoff** or a **cutoff** point is the level or limit at which you decide that something should stop happening. ❑ *The cutoff date for registering is yet to be announced.* **2** The **cutoff** of a supply or service is the complete stopping of the supply or service. ❑ *A total cutoff of supplies would cripple the country's economy.*

cut-throat ADJ (disapproval) If you describe a situation as **cut-throat**, you mean that the people or companies involved all want success and do not care if they harm each other in getting it. = ruthless ❑ *the cut-throat competition in personal computers*

cut·ting ✦◇◇ /ˈkʌtɪŋ/ NOUN, ADJ
NOUN [C] (cuttings) **1** A **cutting** from a plant is a part of the plant that you have cut off so that you can grow a new plant from it. ❑ *Take cuttings from it in July or August.* ❑ *Take cuttings from suitable garden tomatoes in late summer.* **2** (BrE; in AmE, use **clipping**) A **cutting** is a piece of writing which has been cut from a newspaper or magazine.
ADJ A **cutting** remark is unkind and likely to hurt someone's feelings. ❑ *People make cutting remarks to help themselves feel superior or powerful.*

CV /ˌsiː ˈviː/ (mainly BrE; in AmE, usually use **résumé**) NOUN [C] (CVs) Your **CV** is a written account of your personal details, your education, and the jobs you have had. **CV** is an abbreviation for 'curriculum vitae'.

cy·ber·space /ˈsaɪbəspeɪs/ NOUN [U] (computing) In computer technology, **cyberspace** refers to data banks and networks, considered as a place. ❑ *a report circulating in cyberspace*

⊙ **cy·cle** ✦◇◇ /ˈsaɪkəl/ NOUN, VERB (academic word)
NOUN [C] (cycles) **1** A **cycle** is a series of events or processes that is repeated again and again, always in the same order. ❑ *the life cycle of the plant* ❑ *The figures marked the final low point of the present economic cycle.* ❑ *They must break out of the cycle of violence.* **2** A **cycle** is a single complete series of movements in an electrical, electronic, or mechanical process. ❑ *10 cycles per second* **3** A **cycle** is a bicycle. ❑ *We supply the travel ticket for you and your cycle.*
VERB [I] (cycles, cycling, cycled) If you **cycle**, you ride a bicycle. ❑ *He cycled to Ingwold.*

cy·cling /ˈsaɪklɪŋ/ NOUN [U] ❑ *The quiet country roads are ideal for cycling.*

cy·clist /ˈsaɪklɪst/ NOUN [C] (cyclists) A **cyclist** is someone who rides a bicycle, or is riding a bicycle. ❑ *better protection for pedestrians and cyclists*

C

✪ **cy·clone** /ˈsaɪkləʊn/ NOUN [c] (**cyclones**) A **cyclone** is a violent tropical storm in which the air goes around and around. ❑ *The race was called off as a cyclone struck.* ❑ *A cyclone in the Bay of Bengal is threatening the eastern Indian states.* ❑ *The Weather Bureau predicts more cyclones this season, after a relatively quiet five years.*

✪ **cyl·in·der** /ˈsɪlɪndə/ NOUN [c] (**cylinders**) **1** A **cylinder** is an object with flat circular ends and long straight sides. ❑ *It was recorded on a wax cylinder.* **2** A gas **cylinder** is a cylinder-shaped container in which gas is kept under pressure. ❑ *oxygen cylinders* **3** In an engine, a **cylinder** is a cylinder-shaped part in which a piston moves backwards and forwards. ❑ *a four-cylinder engine*

✪ **cy·lin·dri·cal** /sɪˈlɪndrɪkəl/ ADJ Something that is **cylindrical** is in the shape of a cylinder. ❑ *a cylindrical aluminium container* ❑ *It is cylindrical in shape.*

cyn·ic /ˈsɪnɪk/ NOUN [c] (**cynics**) A **cynic** is someone who believes that people always act selfishly. ❑ *I have come to be very much of a cynic in these matters.*

cyni·cal /ˈsɪnɪkəl/ ADJ **1** If you describe someone as **cynical**, you mean they believe that people always act selfishly. ❑ *his cynical view of the world* **2** If you are **cynical about** something, you do not believe that it can be successful or that the people involved are honest. ❑ *It's hard not to be cynical about reform.*

cyni·cal·ly /ˈsɪnɪkli/ ADV [cynically with v] ❑ *The fast-food industry cynically continues to target children.*

cyni·cism /ˈsɪnɪsɪzəm/ NOUN [u] **1** **Cynicism** is the belief that people always act selfishly. ❑ *I found Ben's cynicism wearing at times.* **2** **Cynicism about** something is the belief that it cannot be successful or that the people involved are not honourable. ❑ *In an era of growing cynicism about politicians, Mr Mandela is a model of dignity and integrity.*

Dd

D also **d** /diː/ NOUN [C, U] (**D's, d's**) D is the fourth letter of the English alphabet.

dab·ble /ˈdæbəl/ VERB [I] (**dabbles, dabbling, dabbled**) If you **dabble** in something, you take part in it but not very seriously. ❑ *He dabbled in business.*

❂**dai·ly** ♦♦◇ /ˈdeɪli/ ADV, ADJ
　ADV [daily after v] If something happens **daily**, it happens every day. ❑ *Cathay Pacific flies daily nonstop to Hong Kong.* ❑ *The Visitor Centre is open daily 8.30 a.m.–4.30 p.m.* ❑ *I take aspirin daily to prevent a heart attack.*
　ADJ **1** [daily + N] **Daily** means happening every day. ❑ *They held daily press briefings.* **2** [daily + N] **Daily** quantities or rates relate to a period of one day. ❑ *a diet containing adequate daily amounts of fresh fruit* ❑ *Our average daily turnover is about £300.*
　PHRASE **daily life** Your **daily life** is the things that you do every day as part of your normal life. ❑ *All of us in our daily life react favourably to people who take us and our views seriously.*

dam /dæm/ NOUN [C] (**dams**) A **dam** is a wall that is built across a river in order to stop the water from flowing and to make a lake. ❑ *Before the dam was built, Campbell River used to flood in the spring.*

❂**dam·age** ♦♦◇ /ˈdæmɪdʒ/ VERB, NOUN
　VERB [T] (**damages, damaging, damaged**) **1** To **damage** an object means to break it, spoil it physically, or stop it from working properly. = harm, injure ❑ *He maliciously damaged a car with a baseball bat.* ❑ *The sun can damage your skin.* **2** To **damage** something means to cause it to become less good, pleasant, or successful. = harm ❑ *the electoral chaos that damaged Florida's reputation* ❑ *He warned that the action was damaging the economy.*
　NOUN [U, PL] (**damages**) **1** [U] **Damage** is physical harm that is caused to an object. ❑ *The blast had serious effects with quite extensive damage to the house.* ❑ *Many professional boxers end their careers with brain damage.* **2** [U] **Damage** consists of the unpleasant effects that something has on a person, situation, or type of activity. = harm, injury ❑ *Incidents of this type cause irreparable damage to relations with the community.* ❑ *Adhering to the new rules meant inflicting serious damage on motor racing.* **3** [PL] If a court of law awards **damages** to someone, it orders money to be paid to them by a person who has damaged their reputation or property, or who has injured them. ❑ *She is seeking more than $75,000 in damages.*
　dam·ag·ing /ˈdæmɪdʒɪŋ/ ADJ = harmful ❑ *The weakened currency could have damaging effects for the economy.*

WORD CONNECTIONS

VERB + **damage**

cause damage
do damage
inflict damage
❑ *These birds invade fields and inflict serious damage on crops.*

suffer damage
sustain damage
❑ *Carbon monoxide poisoning kills 50 people a year and many more suffer brain damage.*

assess damage
repair damage
❑ *The cost of repairing the damage is expected to run into thousands of pounds.*

prevent damage
minimize damage
avoid damage
limit damage
❑ *Medical treatments aim to reduce the pressure within the eye and prevent any further damage to vision.*

ADJ + **damage**

serious damage
severe damage
extensive damage
substantial damage
❑ *Storms of this strength can cause severe damage to property.*

permanent damage
irreparable damage
❑ *If we maintain our present waste levels, we risk causing irreparable damage to the environment.*

structural damage
environmental damage
criminal damage
❑ *Devastating winds and torrential rain have brought flooding, travel disruption, and structural damage.*

damn /dæm/ EXCLAM, ADJ, ADV, NOUN, VERB
　EXCLAM (*informal, vulgar, feelings*) **Damn, damn it,** and **dammit** are used by some people to express anger or impatience. ❑ *Don't be flippant, damn it! This is serious.*
　ADJ [damn + N] (*informal, vulgar, emphasis*) **Damn** is used by some people to emphasize what they are saying. ❑ *There's not a damn thing you can do about it now.*
　ADV [damn + ADJ/ADV] (*informal, vulgar, emphasis*) **Damn** is used by some people to emphasize what they are saying. ❑ *As it turned out, I was damn right.*
　NOUN
　PHRASE **not give a damn** (*informal, vulgar, emphasis*) If you say that someone **does not give a damn** about something, you are emphasizing that they do not care about it at all. ❑ *I don't give a damn about the money, Nicole.*
　VERB [T] (**damns, damning, damned**) If you say that a person or a news report **damns** something such as a policy or action, you mean that they are very critical of it. = slam ❑ *a sensational book in which she damns the ultraright party*

damp /dæmp/ ADJ, NOUN
　ADJ (**damper, dampest**) Something that is **damp** is slightly wet. = moist ❑ *Her hair was still damp.* ❑ *the damp, cold air*
　NOUN [U] **Damp** is moisture on the inside walls of a house or in the air. ❑ *There was damp everywhere and the entire building was in need of rewiring.*
　PHRASAL VERB **damp down** (**damps, damping, damped**) To **damp down** something such as a strong emotion, an argument, or a crisis means to make it calmer or less intense. = dampen ❑ *His hand moved to his mouth as he tried to damp down the panic.*

D

damp·en /'dæmpən/ VERB

VERB [T] (**dampens, dampening, dampened**) To **dampen** something such as someone's enthusiasm or excitement means to make it less lively or intense. ❑ *Nothing seems to dampen his perpetual enthusiasm.*

PHRASAL VERB **dampen down** To **dampen** something **down** means the same as to **dampen** it. ❑ *The new penalties were aimed at dampening down consumer spending.*

dance ◆◆◇ /dɑːns, dæns/ VERB, NOUN

VERB [I, T, RECIP] (**dances, dancing, danced**) **1** [I] When you **dance**, you move your body and feet in a way which follows a rhythm, usually in time to music. ❑ *Polly had never learned to dance.* **2** [T] If you **dance** a particular kind of dance, you do it or perform it. ❑ *Then we put the music on, and we all danced the Charleston.* **3** [I] (*literary*) If you **dance** somewhere, you move there lightly and quickly, usually because you are happy or excited. ❑ *He danced off down the road.* **4** [I] (*literary*) If you say that something **dances**, you mean that it moves around, or seems to move around, lightly and quickly. ❑ *Patterns of light, reflected by the river, dance along the base of the cliffs.* **5** [RECIP] When you **dance with** someone, the two of you take part in a dance together, as partners. You can also say that two people **dance**. ❑ *It's a terrible thing when nobody wants to dance with you.* ❑ *Shall we dance?*

NOUN [C, U] (**dances**) **1** [C] A **dance** is a particular series of graceful movements of your body and feet, which you usually do in time to music. ❑ *Sometimes the people doing this dance hold brightly coloured scarves.* **2** [C] A **dance** is a social event where people dance with each other. ❑ *At the school dance he sat and talked to her all evening.* **3** [C] A **dance** is the act of moving your body and feet in a way which follows a rhythm, usually in time to music, or of taking part in a **dance** together with someone else, as partners ❑ *Come and have a dance with me.* **4** [U] **Dance** is the activity of performing dances, as a public entertainment or an art form. ❑ *Their contribution to international dance, drama and music is inestimable.*

danc·er /'dɑːnsə, 'dæns-/ NOUN [C] (**dancers**) **1** A **dancer** is a person who earns money by dancing, or a person who is dancing. ❑ *His girlfriend was a dancer with the New York City Ballet.* **2** If you say that someone is a good **dancer** or a bad **dancer**, you are saying how well or badly they can dance. ❑ *He was the best dancer in LA.*

danc·ing ◆◇◇ /'dɑːnsɪŋ, 'dæns-/ NOUN [U] When people dance for enjoyment or to entertain others, you can refer to this activity as **dancing**. ❑ *All the schools have music and dancing as part of the curriculum.* ❑ *Let's go dancing tonight.*

dan·ger ◆◆◇ /'deɪndʒə/ NOUN

NOUN [U, C, SING] (**dangers**) **1** [U] **Danger** is the possibility that someone may be harmed or killed. ❑ *My friends endured tremendous danger in order to help me.* **2** [C] A **danger** is something or someone that can hurt or harm you. = threat ❑ *the dangers of smoking* **3** [SING] If there is a **danger that** something unpleasant will happen, it is possible that it will happen. ❑ *There is a real danger that some people will no longer be able to afford insurance.* ❑ *There was no danger that any of these groups would be elected to power.*

PHRASE **out of danger** If someone who has been seriously ill is **out of danger**, they are still ill, but they are not expected to die. ❑ *There is some risk of the lung collapsing again, but he is out of danger.*

dan·ger·ous ◆◆◇ /'deɪndʒərəs/ ADJ If something is **dangerous**, it is able or likely to hurt or harm you. = unsafe ❑ *It's a dangerous stretch of road.* ❑ *dangerous drugs*

dan·ger·ous·ly /'deɪndʒərəsli/ ADV ❑ *He is dangerously ill.*

dare ◆◇◇ /deə/ VERB, NOUN

> **Dare** sometimes behaves like an ordinary verb, for example, 'He dared to speak' and 'He doesn't dare to speak' and sometimes like a modal, for example, 'He dare not speak'.

VERB [T, MODAL] (**dares, daring, dared**) **1** [T] If you do not **dare to** do something, you do not have enough courage to do it, or you do not want to do it because you fear the consequences. If you **dare to** do something, you do something which requires a lot of courage. ❑ *Most people hate Harry but they don't dare to say so.* **2** [MODAL] If you **dare** not do something, you do not have enough courage to do it, or you do not want to do it because you fear the consequences. If you **dare** do something, you do something which requires a lot of courage. ❑ *Dare she risk staying where she was?* ❑ *The yen is weakening. But Tokyo dare not raise its interest rates again.* **3** [T] If you **dare** someone **to** do something, you challenge them to prove that they are not frightened of doing it. ❑ *Over coffee, she lit a cigarette, her eyes daring him to comment.*

PHRASES **don't you dare** (*spoken, feelings*) If you say to someone '**don't you dare**' do something, you are telling them not to do it and letting them know that you are angry. ❑ *Allen, don't you dare go anywhere else, you hear?* **how dare you** (*spoken, feelings*) You say '**how dare you**' when you are very shocked and angry about something that someone has done. ❑ *How dare you pick up the phone and listen in on my conversations!* **I daresay** or **I dare say** You can use 'I **daresay**' or 'I **dare say**' before or after a statement to indicate that you believe it is probably true. ❑ *I daresay that the computer would provide a clear answer to that.*

NOUN [C] (**dares**) A **dare** is a challenge which one person gives to another to do something dangerous or frightening. ❑ *Jones broke into a military base on a dare.*

dar·ing /'deərɪŋ/ ADJ, NOUN

ADJ **1** People who are **daring** are willing to do or say things which are new or which might shock or anger other people. = bold ❑ *Bergit was probably more daring than I was.* **2** A **daring** person is willing to do things that might be dangerous. = bold ❑ *His daring rescue saved the lives of the youngsters.*

NOUN [U] **Daring** is the courage to do things which might be dangerous or which might shock or anger other people. = bravery, boldness ❑ *His daring may have cost him his life.*

dark ◆◆◇ /dɑːk/ ADJ, NOUN, COMB

ADJ (**darker, darkest**) **1** When it is **dark**, there is not enough light to see properly, for example, because it is night. ❑ *It was too dark inside to see much.* ❑ *People usually draw the curtains once it gets dark.* **2** If you describe something as **dark**, you mean that it is black in colour, or a shade that is close to black. ❑ *He wore a dark suit and carried a black attaché case.* **3** If someone has **dark** hair, eyes, or skin, they have brown or black hair, eyes, or skin. ❑ *He had dark, curly hair.* **4** A **dark** period of time is unpleasant or frightening. = black ❑ *Once again there's talk of very dark days ahead.* **5** [dark + N] A **dark** place or area is mysterious and not fully known about. ❑ *The spacecraft will enable scientists to study some dark corners of the solar system.* **6** (*literary*) **Dark** thoughts are sad, and show that you are expecting something unpleasant to happen. = gloomy ❑ *Troy's endless happy chatter kept me from thinking dark thoughts.* **7** If you describe something as **dark**, you mean that it is related to things that are serious or unpleasant, rather than lighthearted. ❑ *There's plenty of dark humour in the film.*

NOUN [SING] **The dark** is the lack of light in a place. = darkness ❑ *I've always been afraid of the dark.*

PHRASES **after dark** If you do something **after dark**, you do it when the sun has set and night has begun. ❑ *They avoid going out alone after dark.* **before dark** If you do something **before dark**, you do it before the sun sets and night begins. ❑ *They'll be back well before dark.* **in the dark** If you are **in the dark about** something, you do not know anything about it. ❑ *The investigators admit that they are completely in the dark about the killing.*

COMB When you use **dark** to describe a colour, you are referring to a shade of that colour which is close to black, or seems to have some black in it. ❑ *She was wearing a dark blue dress.*

dark·ness /'dɑːknəs/ NOUN [U] ❑ *The light went out, and the room was plunged into darkness.*

dark·ly /'dɑːkli/ ADV **1** [darkly + -ED] ❑ *In a darkly lit, seedy dance hall, hundreds of men lounge around small tables.* **2** *The freckles on Joanne's face suddenly stood out darkly against her* *pale skin.* **3** [darkly with V] ❑ *She hinted darkly that she might have to resign.* **4** [darkly + ADJ] ❑ *The atmosphere after Wednesday's debut was as darkly comic as the movie itself.*

dark·en /ˈdɑːkən/ VERB [I, T] (**darkens, darkening, darkened**) **1** If something **darkens** or if a person or thing **darkens** it, it becomes darker. ❑ *The sky darkened abruptly.* **2** (*literary*) If someone's mood **darkens** or if something **darkens** their mood, they suddenly become unhappy. ❑ *My sunny mood suddenly darkened.*

dar·ling /ˈdɑːlɪŋ/ NOUN, ADJ
[NOUN] [C] (**darlings**) **1** (*feelings*) You call someone **darling** if you love them or like them very much. ❑ *Thank you, darling.* **2** (*informal*) If you describe someone as a **darling**, you are fond of them and think that they are nice. ❑ *He's such a darling.*
[ADJ] [darling + N] (*informal*) Some people use **darling** to describe someone or something that they love or like very much. ❑ *To have a darling baby boy was the greatest gift I could imagine.*

dart /dɑːt/ VERB, NOUN
[VERB] [I, T] (**darts, darting, darted**) **1** [I] (*written*) If a person or animal **darts** somewhere, they move there suddenly and quickly. ❑ *Ingrid darted across the deserted street.* **2** [I, T] (*literary*) If you **dart** a look **at** someone or something, or if your eyes **dart to** them, you look at them very quickly. ❑ *She darted a sly sideways glance at Bramwell.*
[NOUN] [C, U] (**darts**) **1** [C] A **dart** is a small, narrow object with a sharp point which can be thrown or shot. ❑ *Markov died after being struck by a poison dart.* **2** [U] **Darts** is a game in which you throw darts at a round board which has numbers on it. ❑ *I started playing darts at 15.*

dash /dæʃ/ VERB, NOUN
[VERB] [I, T] (**dashes, dashing, dashed**) **1** [I] If you **dash** somewhere, you run or go there quickly and suddenly. ❑ *Suddenly she dashed down to the cellar.* **2** [I] (*informal*) If you say that you have to **dash**, you mean that you are in a hurry and have to leave immediately. = rush ❑ *Oh, Tim! I'm sorry but I have to dash.* **3** [T] (*literary*) If you **dash** something **against** a wall or other surface, you throw or push it violently, often so hard that it breaks. ❑ *She seized the doll and dashed it against the stone wall with tremendous force.* **4** [T] (*literary, journalism*) If an event or person **dashes** someone's hopes or expectations, it destroys them by making it impossible that the thing that is hoped for or expected will ever happen. ❑ *Renewed fighting has dashed hopes for a United Nations-organized interim government.*
[PHRASAL VERB] **dash off** **1** If you **dash off to** a place, you go there very quickly. ❑ *He dashed off to lunch at the Hard Rock Cafe.* **2** If you **dash off** a piece of writing, you write or compose it very quickly, without thinking about it very much. ❑ *He dashed off a couple of novels.*
[NOUN] [SING, C] (**dashes**) **1** [SING] A **dash** is the act of running or going somewhere quickly and suddenly. ❑ *a 160-mile dash to the hospital* **2** [C] A **dash of** something is a small quantity of it which you add when you are preparing food or mixing a drink. ❑ *Pour over olive oil and a dash of balsamic vinegar to accentuate the sweetness.* **3** [C] A **dash of** a quality is a small amount of it that is found in something and often makes it more interesting or distinctive. ❑ *a story with a dash of mystery thrown in* **4** [C] A **dash** is a straight, horizontal line used in writing, for example, to separate two main clauses whose meanings are closely connected. ❑ *the dash between the birth date and death date*
[PHRASE] **make a dash** If you **make a dash for** a place, you run there very quickly, for example, to escape from someone or something. ❑ *I made a dash for the front door but he got there before me.*

dash·board /ˈdæʃbɔːd/ NOUN [C] (**dashboards**) The **dashboard** in a car is the panel facing the driver's seat where most of the instruments and switches are. ❑ *The clock on the dashboard said it was five to two.*

✪ **da·ta** ◆◆◇ /ˈdeɪtə/ NOUN [U, PL] (*academic word*) **1** [U, PL] You can refer to information as **data**, especially when it is in the form of facts or statistics that you can analyse. ❑ *The study was based on data from 2,100 women.* **2** [U] (*computing*) **Data** is information that can be stored and

used by a computer program. = information, figures, statistics ❑ *This system uses powerful microchips to compress huge amounts of data onto a CD-ROM.*

USAGE NOTE

data

In British English, **data** is usually used as an uncountable noun, so it is followed by a singular verb.
*The new **data shows** that people are consuming less salt.*
In technical or formal writing, **data** is more often used as a plural noun followed by a plural verb.
*The new **data show** that average daily salt consumption has fallen.*
In American English, **data** is usually used as a plural noun.

---

data·base /ˈdeɪtəbeɪs/ also **data base** NOUN [C] (**databases**) A **database** is a collection of data that is stored in a computer and that can easily be used and added to. ❑ *The state maintains a database of names of people allowed to vote.*

✪ **date** ◆◆◇ /deɪt/ NOUN, VERB
[NOUN] [C] (**dates**) **1** A **date** is a specific time that can be named, for example, a particular day or a particular year. ❑ *What's the date today?* ❑ *You will need to give the dates you wish to stay and the number of rooms you require.* ❑ *Closing date for applications is the end of January.* **2** A **date** is an appointment to meet someone or go out with them, especially someone with whom you are having, or may soon have, a romantic relationship. ❑ *I have a date with Bob.* **3** If you have a date with someone with whom you are having, or may soon have, a romantic relationship, you can refer to that person as your **date**. ❑ *He lied to Essie, saying his date was one of the girls in the show.* **4** A **date** is a small, dark-brown, sticky fruit with a stone inside. Dates grow on palm trees in hot countries.
[PHRASE] **to date** To date means up until the present time. ❑ *'Dottie' is by far his best novel to date.*
[VERB] [RECIP, T, I] (**dates, dating, dated**) **1** [RECIP] If you **are dating** someone, you go out with them regularly because you are having, or may soon have, a romantic relationship with them. You can also say that two people **are dating**. ❑ *For a year I dated a woman who was a research assistant.* **2** [T] If you **date** something, you give or discover the date when it was made or when it began. ❑ *I think we can date the decline of Western Civilization quite precisely.* **3** [T] When you **date** something such as a letter or a cheque, you write that day's date on it. ❑ *Once the decision is reached, he can date and sign the sheet.* **4** [I] If something **dates**, it goes out of fashion and becomes unacceptable to modern tastes. ❑ *Blue and white is the classic colour combination for bathrooms. It always looks smart and will never date.*
[PHRASAL VERB] **date back** If something **dates back to** a particular time, it started or was made at that time. ❑ *The issue is not a new one. It dates back to the 1930s at least.* ❑ *a long tradition dating back to the early Greeks*
→ See also **dated, out of date**

dat·ed /ˈdeɪtɪd/ ADJ **Dated** things or ideas seem old-fashioned, although they may once have been fashionable or modern. ❑ *Many of his ideas have value, but some are dated and others are plain wrong.*

date of birth NOUN [C] (**dates of birth**) Your **date of birth** is the exact date on which you were born, including the year. ❑ *The registration form showed his date of birth as August 2, 1979.*

daugh·ter ◆◆◆ /ˈdɔːtə/ NOUN [C] (**daughters**) Someone's **daughter** is their female child. ❑ *Flora and her daughter Catherine* ❑ *the daughter of a university professor*

daughter-in-law NOUN [C] (**daughters-in-law**) Someone's **daughter-in-law** is the wife of their son.

daunt·ing /ˈdɔːntɪŋ/ ADJ Something that is **daunting** makes you feel slightly afraid or worried about dealing with it. = intimidating ❑ *He and his wife Jane were faced with the daunting task of restoring the gardens to their former splendour.*

dawn /dɔːn/ NOUN, VERB
[NOUN] [SING, C, U] (**dawns**) **1** [SING, C, U] **Dawn** is the time of

day when light first appears in the sky, just before the sun rises. ❑ *Nancy woke at dawn.* **2** [SING] (*literary*) **The dawn of** a period of time or a situation is the beginning of it. ❑ *the dawn of the radio age*

VERB [I] (**dawns, dawning, dawned**) (*written*) If something **is dawning**, it is beginning to develop or come into existence. ❑ *A new century was dawning.*

PHRASAL VERB dawn on or **dawn upon** If a fact or idea **dawns on** you, you realize it. = strike ❑ *It gradually dawned on me that I still had talent and ought to run again.*

dawn·ing /'dɔːnɪŋ/ NOUN [SING] ❑ *the dawning of the space age*

day ♦♦♦ /deɪ/ NOUN

NOUN [C, U] (**days**) **1** [C] A **day** is one of the seven twenty-four hour periods of time in a week. ❑ *And it has snowed almost every day for the past week.* **2** [C] You can refer to a particular period in history as a particular **day** or as particular **days**. ❑ *He began to talk about the Ukraine of his uncle's day.* ❑ *his early days of struggle and deep poverty* **3** [C, U] **Day** is the time when it is light, or the time when you are up and doing things. ❑ *Twenty-seven million working days are lost each year due to work accidents and sickness.* ❑ *She gives herself one day a week off, on Thursdays.*

PHRASES day after day If something happens **day after day**, it happens every day without stopping. ❑ *The newspaper job had me doing the same thing day after day.*

day in, day out [V + day in, day out] If you say that something happens **day in, day out** or **day in and day out**, you mean that it happens regularly over a long period of time. ❑ *I used to drink coffee day in, day out.*

in this day and age In this day and age means in modern times. ❑ *Even in this day and age the old attitudes persist.*

have seen better days If you say that something **has seen better days**, you mean that it is old and in poor condition. ❑ *The tweed jacket she wore had seen better days.*

call it a day If you **call it a day**, you decide to stop what you are doing because you are tired of it or because it is not successful. ❑ *Faced with mounting debts, the decision to call it a day was inevitable.*

make someone's day (*informal*) If something **makes** your **day**, it makes you feel very happy. ❑ *Come on, Bill. Send Tom a card and make his day.*

one day or **some day** or **one of these days** One day or some day or one of these days means at some time in the future. ❑ *I too dreamed of living in Dallas one day.* ❑ *I hope some day you will find the woman who will make you happy.*

the other day If you say that something happened **the other day**, you mean that it happened a few days ago. ❑ *I phoned your office the other day.*

save the day If someone or something **saves the day** in a situation which seems likely to fail, they manage to make it successful. ❑ *this story about how he saved the day at his daughter's birthday party*

from day to day If something happens **from day to day** or **day by day**, it happens each day. ❑ *Your needs can differ from day to day.*

to the day If it is a month or a year **to the day** since a particular thing happened, it is exactly a month or a year since it happened. ❑ *It was January 19, a year to the day since he had arrived in Singapore.*

to this day To this day means up until and including the present time. ❑ *The controversy continues to this day.*

all in a day's work If you say that a task is **all in a day's work** for someone, you mean that they do not mind doing it although it may be difficult, because it is part of their job or because they often do it. ❑ *For war reporters, dodging snipers' bullets is all in a day's work.*

✦ **at the end of the day** → see end; **the good old days** → see old

day·light /'deɪlaɪt/ NOUN

NOUN [U] **1** Daylight is the natural light that there is during the day, before it gets dark. ❑ *Lack of daylight can make people feel depressed.* **2** Daylight is the time of day when it begins to get light. ❑ *Quinn returned shortly after daylight yesterday morning.*

PHRASE in broad daylight (*emphasis*) If you say that a crime is committed **in broad daylight**, you are expressing your surprise that it is done during the day when people

can see it, rather than at night. ❑ *A girl was attacked on a train in broad daylight.*

day·time /'deɪtaɪm/ NOUN, ADJ

NOUN [SING] ['the' daytime, also no DET] The daytime is the part of a day between the time when it gets light and the time when it gets dark. ❑ *In the daytime he stayed up in his room, sleeping, or listening to music.*

ADJ [daytime + N] **Daytime** television and radio is broadcast during the morning and afternoon on weekdays. ❑ *She took on the role as host of a daytime TV show.*

day-to-day ADJ [day-to-day + N] **Day-to-day** things or activities exist or happen every day as part of ordinary life. ❑ *I am a vegetarian and use a lot of lentils in my day-to-day cooking.*

daze /deɪz/ NOUN [SING] If someone is **in a daze**, they are feeling confused and unable to think clearly, often because they have had a shock or surprise. ❑ *For an hour I was walking around in a daze.*

dazed /deɪzd/ ADJ If someone is **dazed**, they are confused and unable to think clearly, often because of shock or a blow to the head. = confused ❑ *At the end of the interview I was dazed and exhausted.*

daz·zle /'dæzəl/ VERB, NOUN

VERB [T] (**dazzles, dazzling, dazzled**) **1** If someone or something **dazzles** you, you are extremely impressed by their skill, qualities, or beauty. ❑ *George dazzled her with his knowledge of the world.* **2** If a bright light **dazzles** you, it makes you unable to see properly for a short time. ❑ *The sun, glinting from the pool, dazzled me.*

NOUN [SING] The **dazzle** of something is a quality it has, such as beauty or skill, which is impressive and attractive. ❑ *The dazzle of stardom and status attracts them.*

dead ♦♦◇ /ded/ ADJ, NOUN, ADV

ADJ **1** A person, animal, or plant that is **dead** is no longer living. ❑ *'You're a widow?'—'Yes. My husband's been dead a year now.'* ❑ *The group had shot dead another hostage.* **2** If you describe a place or a period of time as **dead**, you do not like it because there is very little activity taking place in it. ❑ *some dead little town where the liveliest thing is the flies* **3** Something that is **dead** is no longer being used or is finished. ❑ *The dead cigarette was still between his fingers.* **4** If you say that an idea, plan, or subject is **dead**, you mean that people are no longer interested in it or willing to develop it any further. ❑ *It's a dead issue, Baxter.* **5** A telephone or piece of electrical equipment that is **dead** is no longer functioning, for example, because it no longer has any electrical power. ❑ *On another occasion I answered the phone and the line went dead.* **6** [dead + N] **Dead** is used to mean 'complete' or 'absolute', especially before the words 'centre', 'silence', and 'stop'. ❑ *They hurried about in dead silence, with anxious faces.*

PHRASES drop dead or **drop down dead** If you say that a person or animal **dropped dead** or **dropped down dead**, you mean that they died very suddenly and unexpectedly. ❑ *He dropped dead of a heart attack.*

feel (half) dead or **be (half) dead** or **look (half) dead** (*informal, emphasis*) If you say that you **feel dead** or **are half dead**, you mean that you feel very tired or ill and very weak. ❑ *I thought you looked half dead at dinner, and who could blame you after that trip.*

in the dead of night or **at dead of night** or **in the dead of winter** (*literary*) If something happens **in the dead of night**, **at dead of night**, or **in the dead of winter**, it happens in the middle part of the night or the winter, when it is darkest or coldest. ❑ *All three incidents occurred in the dead of night.*

be seen dead or **be caught dead** (*informal, emphasis*) If you say that you wouldn't **be seen dead** or **be caught dead** in particular clothes, places, or situations, you are expressing strong dislike or disapproval of them. ❑ *I wouldn't be seen dead in a straw hat.*

CONVENTION over my dead body (*informal, emphasis*) If you reply '**Over my dead body**' when a plan or action has been suggested, you are emphasizing that you dislike it, and will do everything you can to prevent it. ❑ *'Let's invite her to dinner.'—'Over my dead body!'*

NOUN [PL] The **dead** are people who are dead. ❑ *Two*

American soldiers were among the dead.

ADV (emphasis) [dead + PREP/ADV/ADJ] **Dead** means 'precisely' or 'exactly'. ❑ Mars was visible, dead in the centre of the telescope.

PHRASE **stop dead** or **stop someone dead** To **stop dead** means to suddenly stop happening or moving. To **stop** someone or something **dead** means to cause them to suddenly stop happening or moving. ❑ We all stopped dead and looked at it.

✦ **stop dead in your tracks** → see **track**

dead·line ◆◇◇ /ˈdedlaɪn/ NOUN [C] (**deadlines**) A **deadline** is a time or date before which a particular task must be finished or a particular thing must be done. ❑ We were not able to meet the deadline because of manufacturing delays.

dead·lock /ˈdedlɒk/ NOUN [C, U] (**deadlocks**) If a dispute or series of negotiations reaches **deadlock**, neither side is willing to give in at all and no agreement can be made. ❑ They called for a compromise on all sides to break the deadlock in the world trade talks.

dead·ly /ˈdedli/ ADJ, ADV
ADJ (**deadlier, deadliest**) **1** If something is **deadly**, it is likely or able to cause someone's death, or has already caused someone's death. = lethal, fatal ❑ He was acquitted on charges of assault with a deadly weapon. ❑ a deadly disease currently affecting dolphins **2** If you describe a person or their behaviour as **deadly**, you mean that they will do or say anything to get what they want, without caring about other people. ❑ The Duchess levelled a deadly look at Nikko. **3** A **deadly** situation has unpleasant or dangerous consequences. ❑ the deadly combination of low expectations and low achievement
ADV [deadly + ADJ] (emphasis) You can use **deadly** to emphasize that something has a particular quality, especially an unpleasant or undesirable quality. = deathly ❑ Broadcast news was accurate and reliable but deadly dull.

deaf /def/ ADJ, NOUN
ADJ (**deafer, deafest**) Someone who is **deaf** is unable to hear anything or is unable to hear very well. ❑ She is now profoundly deaf.
NOUN [PL] The **deaf** are people who are deaf. ❑ Many regular TV programmes are captioned for the deaf.
deaf·ness /ˈdefnəs/ NOUN [U] ❑ Because of her deafness she was hard to make conversation with.

✦ **fall on deaf ears** → see **ear**; **turn a deaf ear** → see **ear**

deaf·en /ˈdefən/ VERB [T] (**deafens, deafening, deafened**) **1** If a noise **deafens** you, it is so loud that you cannot hear anything else at the same time. ❑ The noise of the typewriters deafened her. **2** If you **are deafened by** something, you are made deaf by it, or are unable to hear for some time. ❑ He was deafened by the noise from the gun.

deal ◆◇◇ /diːl/ QUANT, ADV, PRON, NOUN, VERB
QUANT (emphasis) If you say that you need or have **a great deal of** or **a good deal of** a particular thing, you are emphasizing that you need or have a lot of it. ❑ a great deal of money
ADV A **deal** means to a great extent or degree. ❑ As a relationship becomes more established, it also becomes a good deal more complex.
PRON A **deal** means a large amount. ❑ Although he had never met Geoffrey Hardcastle, he knew a good deal about him.
NOUN [C] (**deals**) **1** (business) If you **make a deal**, **do a deal**, or **cut a deal**, you complete an agreement or an arrangement with someone, especially in business. ❑ He made a deal to testify against the others and wasn't charged. ❑ Japan will have to do a deal with the US on rice imports. **2** If someone has had a **bad deal**, they have been unfortunate or have been treated unfairly. ❑ The people of Hartford have had a bad deal for many, many years.
VERB [I, T] (**deals, dealing, dealt**) **1** [I] (business) If a person, company, or store **deals in** a particular type of goods, their business involves buying or selling those goods. ❑ They deal in antiques. **2** [T] If someone **deals** illegal drugs, they sell them. ❑ I certainly didn't deal in illicit drugs. **3** [T] If you **deal** playing cards, you give them out to the players in a game of cards. ❑ The croupier dealt each player a card, face down.
PHRASAL VERBS **deal out** **1** **Deal out** means the same as

deal VERB **3**. ❑ Dalton dealt out five cards to each player. **2** (written) If someone **deals out** a punishment or harmful action, they punish or harm someone. = mete out ❑ a failure by the governments of established states to deal out effective punishment to aggressors

deal with **1** When you **deal with** something or someone that needs attention, you give your attention to them, and often solve a problem or make a decision concerning them. = handle, manage, attend to ❑ the way that banks deal with complaints ❑ The President said the agreement would allow other vital problems to be dealt with. **2** If you **deal with** an unpleasant emotion or an emotionally difficult situation, you recognize it, and remain calm and in control of yourself in spite of it. ❑ She saw a psychiatrist who used hypnotism to help her deal with her fear. **3** If a book, speech, or film **deals with** a particular thing, it has that thing as its subject or is concerned with it. ❑ the parts of his book which deal with contemporary Paris **4** If you **deal with** a particular person or organization, you have business relations with them. ❑ When I worked in Florida I dealt with tourists all the time.

→ See also **dealings**

deal·er ◆◇◇ /ˈdiːlə/ NOUN [C] (**dealers**) **1** (business) A **dealer** is a person whose business involves buying and selling things. ❑ an antique dealer **2** A **dealer** is someone who buys and sells illegal drugs. ❑ They will stay on the job for as long as it takes to clear every dealer from the street.

deal·ings /ˈdiːlɪŋz/ NOUN [PL] Someone's **dealings with** a person or organization are the relations that they have with them or the business that they do with them. ❑ He has learned little in his dealings with the international community.

dealt /delt/ IRREG FORM **Dealt** is the past tense and past participle of **deal**.

dear ◆◇◇ /dɪə/ ADJ, CONVENTION, NOUN, EXCLAM
ADJ (**dearer, dearest**) **1** [dear + N] You use **dear** to describe someone or something that you feel affection for. ❑ Mrs Cavendish is a dear friend of mine. **2** [V-LINK + dear 'to' N] If something is **dear to** you or **dear to** your heart, you care deeply about it. ❑ This is a subject very dear to the hearts of academics up and down the country. **3** [dear + N] **Dear** is written at the beginning of a letter, followed by the name or title of the person you are writing to. ❑ Dear Peter, I have been thinking about you so much during the past few days.
CONVENTION (written) You begin formal letters with '**Dear Sir**' or '**Dear Madam**'. You can also begin them with 'Sir' or 'Madam'. ❑ 'Dear Sir,' she began.
NOUN [C] (**dears**) (feelings) You can call someone **dear** as a sign of affection. ❑ You're a lot like me, dear.
EXCLAM (feelings) You can use **dear** in expressions such as '**oh dear**', '**dear me**', and '**dear, dear**' when you are sad, disappointed, or surprised about something. ❑ 'Oh dear, oh dear.' McKinnon sighed. 'You, too.'

dear·ly /ˈdɪəli/ ADV
ADV (formal, emphasis) **1** [dearly with V] If you love someone **dearly**, you love them very much. ❑ She loved her father dearly. **2** [dearly before V] If you would **dearly** like to do or have something, you would very much like to do it or have it. ❑ I would dearly love to marry.
PHRASE **pay dearly** or **cost dearly** (formal) If you **pay dearly** for doing something or if it **costs** you **dearly**, you suffer a lot as a result. ❑ He drank too much and is paying dearly for the pleasure.

death ◆◆◇ /deθ/ NOUN
NOUN [C, U, SING] (**deaths**) **1** [C, U] **Death** is the permanent end of the life of a person or animal. ❑ 1.5 million people are in immediate danger of death from starvation. ❑ the thirtieth anniversary of Judy Garland's death **2** [SING] The **death** of something is the permanent end of it. = end ❑ It meant the death of everything he had ever been or ever hoped to be.
PHRASES **at death's door** (informal) If you say that someone is **at death's door**, you mean they are very ill and likely to die. ❑ He told his boss a tale about his mother being at death's door.

fight to the death (emphasis) If you say that you will

d

D

fight to the death for something, you are emphasizing that you will do anything to achieve or protect it, even if you suffer as a consequence. ❑ *She'd have fought to the death for that child.*

a matter of life and death (*emphasis*) If you say that something is a matter **of life and death**, you are emphasizing that it is extremely important, often because someone may die or suffer great harm if people do not act immediately. ❑ *Well, never mind, John, it's not a matter of life and death.*

put someone to death (*formal*) If someone **is put to death**, they are executed. ❑ *Those put to death by firing squad included three generals.*

to death (*emphasis*) You use **to death** after an adjective or a verb to emphasize the action, state, or feeling mentioned. For example, if you are **frightened to death** or **bored to death**, you are extremely frightened or bored. ❑ *He scares teams to death with his pace and power.*

◆**death pen·al·ty** NOUN [SING] The **death penalty** is the punishment of death used in some countries for people who have committed very serious crimes. = capital punishment, execution ❑ *If convicted for murder, both men could face the death penalty.* ❑ *Prosecutors are seeking the death penalty against him.* ❑ *a special circumstance of double homicide, which could carry the death penalty upon conviction*

death rate NOUN [c] (**death rates**) The **death rate** is the number of people per thousand who die in a particular area during a particular period of time. ❑ *By the turn of the century, Pittsburgh had the highest death rate in the United States.*

death sen·tence NOUN [c] (**death sentences**) A **death sentence** is a punishment of death given by a judge to someone who has been found guilty of a serious crime such as murder. ❑ *His original death sentence was commuted to life in prison.*

de·ba·cle /deɪˈbɑːkəl, AmE dɪ-/ (in BrE, also use **débâcle**) NOUN [c] (**debacles**) A **debacle** is an event or attempt that is a complete failure. = fiasco ❑ *People believed it was a privilege to die for your country, but after the debacle of the war they never felt the same again.*

de·bat·able /dɪˈbeɪtəbəl/ ADJ If you say that something is **debatable**, you mean that it is not certain. ❑ *It is debatable whether or not the shareholders were ever properly compensated.*

◆**de·bate** ◆◆◇ /dɪˈbeɪt/ NOUN, VERB (*academic word*)
NOUN [c, u] (**debates**) **1** [c, u] A **debate** is a discussion about a subject on which people have different views. = discussion, argument ❑ *An intense debate is going on within the Israeli government.* ❑ *There has been a lot of debate among scholars about this.* **2** [c] A **debate** is a formal discussion, for example, in a parliament or institution, in which people express different opinions about a particular subject and then vote on it. ❑ *He is expected to force a debate in Congress on his immigration reform.*
VERB [RECIP, T] (**debates, debating, debated**) **1** [RECIP] If people **debate** a topic, they discuss it fairly formally, putting forward different views. You can also say that one person **debates** a topic **with** another person. = discuss, argue ❑ *The United Nations Security Council will debate the issue today.* ❑ *Scientists were debating whether an asteroid was about to hit the Earth.* **2** [T] If you **debate** whether to do something or what to do, you think or talk about possible courses of action before deciding exactly what you are going to do. ❑ *Taggart debated whether to have yet another double vodka.*

deb·it /ˈdebɪt/ VERB, NOUN
VERB [T] (**debits, debiting, debited**) When your bank **debits** your account, money is taken from it and paid to someone else. ❑ *We will always confirm the revised amount to you in writing before debiting your account.*
NOUN [c] (**debits**) A **debit** is a record of the money taken from your bank account, for example, when you write a cheque. ❑ *The total of debits must balance the total of credits.*

deb·it card NOUN [c] (**debit cards**) A **debit card** is a bank card that you can use to pay for things. When you use it the money is taken out of your bank account immediately.

◆**de·bris** /ˈdeɪbriː, AmE deɪˈbriː/ NOUN [u] **Debris** is pieces from something that has been destroyed or pieces of rubbish or unwanted material that are spread around. = waste, rubbish ❑ *A number of people were killed by flying debris.* ❑ *Rescue workers routed traffic around the debris from the explosions.*

◆**debt** ◆◆◇ /det/ NOUN
NOUN [c, u] (**debts**) **1** [c, u] A **debt** is a sum of money that you owe someone. = deficit; ≠ profit, surplus ❑ *Three years later, he is still paying off his debts.* ❑ *consumers struggling to repay outstanding debts* ❑ *reducing the country's $18 billion foreign debt* **2** [u] **Debt** is the state of owing money. ❑ *a monthly report on the amount of debt owed by consumers* ❑ *Debt is a main reason for stress.* **3** [c] (*formal, feelings*) You use **debt** in expressions such as **I owe you a debt** or **I am in your debt** when you are expressing gratitude for something that someone has done for you. ❑ *He was so good to me that I can never repay the debt I owe him.* ❑ *I owe a debt of thanks to Joyce Thompson, whose careful and able research was of great help.*
PHRASE **in debt** If you are **in debt** or **get into debt**, you owe money. If you are **out of debt** or **get out of debt**, you succeed in paying all the money that you owe. ❑ *He was already deeply in debt through gambling losses.*

debt·or /ˈdetə/ NOUN [c] (**debtors**) A **debtor** is a country, organization, or person who owes money. ❑ *important improvements in the situation of debtor countries*

de·but ◆◇◇ /ˈdeɪbjuː, AmE deɪˈbjuː/ NOUN [c] (**debuts**) The **debut** of a performer or sports player is their first public performance, appearance, or recording. ❑ *She made her debut in a 1937 production of 'Hamlet'.*

◆**dec·ade** ◆◆◇ /ˈdekeɪd/ NOUN [c] (**decades**) (*academic word*) A **decade** is a period of ten years, especially one that begins with a year ending in 0, for example, 1980 to 1989. ❑ *the last decade of the nineteenth century*

deca·dent /ˈdekədənt/ ADJ (*disapproval*) If you say that a person or society is **decadent**, you think that they have low moral standards and are interested mainly in pleasure. ❑ *the excesses and stresses of their decadent rock 'n' roll lifestyles*

deca·dence /ˈdekədəns/ NOUN [u] ❑ *The empire had for years been falling into decadence.*

◆**de·cay** /dɪˈkeɪ/ VERB, NOUN
VERB [I] (**decays, decaying, decayed**) **1** When something such as a dead body, a dead plant, or a tooth **decays**, it is gradually destroyed by a natural process. = rot ❑ *The bodies buried in the fine ash slowly decayed.* **2** If something such as a society, system, or institution **decays**, it gradually becomes weaker or its condition gets worse. ❑ *In practice, the agency system has decayed. Most 'agents' now sell only to themselves or their immediate family.*
NOUN [u] **1 Decay** is the natural process by which something such as a dead body, a dead plant, or a tooth is gradually destroyed. = rot, destruction ❑ *When not removed, plaque causes tooth decay and gum disease.* ❑ *Radon is produced by the radioactive decay of uranium.* **2 Decay** is the process by which something such as a society, system, or institution gradually becomes weaker or its condition gradually gets worse. ≠ improvement ❑ *There are problems of urban decay and gang violence.*

de·cayed /dɪˈkeɪd/ ADJ = rotten ❑ *Even young children have teeth so decayed they need to be pulled.* ❑ *Millipedes enjoy a diet which consists of rotting or partially decayed vegetation.*

de·ceased /dɪˈsiːst/ NOUN, ADJ
NOUN [c] (**deceased**) (*legal*) **The deceased** is used to refer to a particular person or to particular people who have recently died. ❑ *The navy is notifying next of kin now that the identities of the deceased have been determined.*
ADJ (*formal*) A **deceased** person is one who has recently died. ❑ *his recently deceased mother*

de·ceit /dɪˈsiːt/ NOUN [c, u] (**deceits**) **Deceit** is behaviour that is deliberately intended to make people believe something which is not true. = deception ❑ *He was living a secret life of deceit and unfaithfulness.*

de·ceit·ful /dɪˈsiːtfʊl/ ADJ If you say that someone is **deceitful**, you mean that they behave in a dishonest way by making other people believe something that is not true. ❏ *The ambassador called the report deceitful and misleading.*

de•ceive /dɪˈsiːv/ VERB [T] (**deceives, deceiving, deceived**) **1** If you **deceive** someone, you make them believe something that is not true, usually in order to get some advantage for yourself. ❏ *He has deceived and disillusioned us all.* **2** If something **deceives** you, it gives you a wrong impression and makes you believe something that is not true. = mislead ❏ *Do not be deceived by claims on food labels like 'light' or 'low fat'.*

de•cen•cy /ˈdiːsənsi/ NOUN
NOUN [U] **Decency** is the quality of following accepted moral standards. ❏ *His sense of decency forced him to resign.*
PHRASE **have the decency** (*disapproval*) If you say that someone **did not have the decency** to do something, you are criticizing them because there was a particular action which they did not do but which you believe they ought to have done. ❏ *He didn't even have the decency to tell them in person.*

de•cent /ˈdiːsənt/ ADJ **1 Decent** is used to describe something which is considered to be of an acceptable standard or quality. = reasonable ❏ *He didn't get a decent explanation.* **2 Decent** is used to describe something which is morally correct or acceptable. = respectable ❏ *But, after a decent interval, trade relations began to return to normal.* **3 Decent** people are honest and behave in a way that most people approve of. = upright ❏ *The majority of people around here are decent people.*
de•cent•ly /ˈdiːsəntli/ ADV **1** = reasonably ❏ *The allies say they will treat their prisoners decently.* **2** And can't you dress more decently – people will think you're a tramp.

de•cep•tion /dɪˈsepʃən/ NOUN [C, U] (**deceptions**) **Deception** is the act of deceiving someone or the state of being deceived by someone. ❏ *He admitted conspiring to obtain property by deception.*

de•cep•tive /dɪˈseptɪv/ ADJ If something is **deceptive**, it encourages you to believe something which is not true. = misleading ❏ *Johnston isn't tired of Las Vegas yet, it seems, but appearances can be deceptive.*
de•cep•tive•ly /dɪˈseptɪvli/ ADV ❏ *The storyline is deceptively simple.*

⊙ **de•cide** ◆◆◆ /dɪˈsaɪd/ VERB
VERB [I, T] (**decides, deciding, decided**) **1** [I, T] If you **decide** to do something, you choose to do it, usually after you have thought carefully about the other possibilities. ❏ *She decided to take a course in philosophy.* ❏ *Think about it very carefully before you decide.* ❏ *He has decided that he will step down as leader.* **2** [T] If a person or group of people **decides** something, they choose what something should be like or how a particular problem should be solved. ❏ *She was still young, he said, and that would be taken into account when deciding her sentence.* ❏ *This is an issue that should be decided by local and metropolitan government.* **3** [T] If an event or fact **decides** something, it makes it certain that a particular choice will be made or that there will be a particular result. ❏ *What happens next could decide their destiny.* ❏ *The election will decide if either party controls both houses of Congress.* **4** [T] If you **decide** that something is true, you form that opinion about it after considering the facts. ❏ *He decided Franklin must be suffering from a bad cold.* ❏ *The government decided that the company represented a security risk.* ❏ *The committee has to decide whether the applicant is trustworthy.*
PHRASAL VERB **decide on** If you **decide on** something or **decide upon** something, you choose it from two or more possibilities. ❏ *Denikin held a staff meeting to decide on the next strategic objective.*

de•cid•ed•ly /dɪˈsaɪdɪdli/ ADV [decidedly + GROUP] **Decidedly** means to a great extent and in a way that is very obvious. ❏ *He admits there will be moments when he's decidedly uncomfortable at what he sees on the screen.*

⊙ **deci•mal** /ˈdesɪməl/ NOUN, ADJ
ADJ [decimal + N] A **decimal** system involves counting in units of ten. ❏ *The mathematics of ancient Egypt were based on a decimal system.* ❏ *In 1971, the 1p and 2p decimal coins were introduced in Britain.*
NOUN [C] (**decimals**) A **decimal** is a fraction that is written

in the form of a dot followed by one or more numbers which represent tenths, hundredths, and so on: for example, .5, .51, .517. ❏ *simple maths concepts, such as decimals and fractions*

⊙ **deci•mal point** NOUN [C] (**decimal points**) A **decimal point** is the dot in front of a decimal fraction. ❏ *A waiter omitted the decimal point in the $13.09 bill.*

deci•mate /ˈdesɪmeɪt/ VERB [T] (**decimates, decimating, decimated**) **1** To **decimate** something such as a group of people or animals means to destroy a very large number of them. ❏ *The pollution could decimate the river's thriving population of kingfishers.* **2** To **decimate** a system or organization means to reduce its size and effectiveness greatly. ❏ *a recession which decimated the nation's manufacturing industry*

de•ci•pher /dɪˈsaɪfə/ VERB [T] (**deciphers, deciphering, deciphered**) If you **decipher** a piece of writing or a message, you work out what it says, even though it is very difficult to read or understand. ❏ *I'm still no closer to deciphering the code.*

WORD PARTS
The prefix **de-** sometimes appears in verbs to make them have the opposite meaning to the verbs on their own: decipher (VERB) deactivate (VERB) deform (VERB)

⊙ **de•ci•sion** ◆◆◆ /dɪˈsɪʒən/ NOUN [C, U] (**decisions**) **1** [C] When you make a **decision**, you choose what should be done or which is the best of various possible actions. = judgment, conclusion, finding ❏ *I don't want to make the wrong decision and regret it later.* ❏ *A decision was taken to discipline Marshall.* ❏ *A final decision on this issue is long overdue.* **2** [U] **Decision** is the act of deciding something or the need to decide something. ≠ indecision ❏ *The growing pressures of the crisis may mean that the moment of decision can't be too long delayed.* **3** [U] **Decision** is the ability to decide quickly and definitely what to do. = decisiveness ❏ *He is very quick-thinking and very much a man of decision.*

WORD CONNECTIONS
VERB + **decision**
make a decision **reach** a decision **take** a decision ❏ *After some discussion a decision was finally reached.*
ADJ + **decision**
a **tough** decision a **difficult** decision a **hard** decision ❏ *Anja has a sharp mind and is not afraid of making tough decisions.*
a **final** decision a **major** decision an **important** decision ❏ *The director personally considers the applications of each candidate interviewed, before he makes his final decision.*
a **controversial** decision a **unanimous** decision ❏ *The referee's controversial decision to disallow the goal caused outrage among fans.*
the **right** decision the **wrong** decision ❏ *Moving to a new job in Japan was the right decision for me.*

de•ci•sive /dɪˈsaɪsɪv/ ADJ **1** If a fact, action, or event is **decisive**, it makes certain a particular result. ❏ *his decisive victory in the presidential elections* **2** If someone is **decisive**, they have or show an ability to make quick decisions in a difficult or complicated situation. ❏ *He should give way to a younger, more decisive leader.*

D

de·ci·sive·ly /dɪˈsaɪsɪvli/ ADV **1** *The plan was decisively rejected by Congress three weeks ago.* **2** *'I'll call for you at ten,' she said decisively.*

de·ci·sive·ness /dɪˈsaɪsɪvnəs/ NOUN [U] □ *His supporters admire his decisiveness.*

deck ♦◇◇ /dek/ NOUN [C] (**decks**) **1** A **deck** on a vehicle such as a bus or ship is a lower or upper area of it. □ *a luxury liner with five passenger decks* **2** [also 'on' deck] The **deck** of a ship is the top part of it that forms a floor in the open air which you can walk on. □ *She stood on the deck and waved her hand to them as the steamer moved off.* **3** A **deck** is a flat wooden area next to a house, where people can sit and relax or eat. □ *A natural timber deck leads into the main room of the home.* **4** (mainly AmE; in BrE, usually use **pack**) A **deck** of cards is a complete set of playing cards. □ *Matt picked up the cards and shuffled the deck.*

⊕ dec·la·ra·tion ♦◇◇ /ˌdekləˈreɪʃən/ NOUN [C] (**declarations**) **1** A **declaration** is an official announcement or statement. = announcement, pronouncement, statement □ *The opening speeches sounded more like declarations of war than offerings of peace.* □ *They will sign the declaration tomorrow.* □ *the issues arising from their declaration of independence* **2** A **declaration** is a firm, emphatic statement which shows that you have no doubts about what you are saying. □ *declarations of undying love* **3** A **declaration** is a written statement about something which you have signed and which can be used as evidence in a court of law. □ *On the customs declaration, the sender labelled the freight as agricultural machinery.*

⊕ de·clare ♦♦◇ /dɪˈkleə/ VERB [T] (**declares, declaring, declared**) **1** (written) If you **declare** that something is true, you say that it is true in a firm, deliberate way. You can also **declare** an attitude or intention. = announce □ *He declared he would not run for a second term as president.* □ *He declared his intention to become the best golfer in the world.* **2** If you **declare** something, you state officially and formally that it exists or is the case. = assert, state, pronounce □ *The government is ready to declare a permanent ceasefire.* □ *His lawyers are confident that the judges will declare Mr Stevens innocent.* □ *The U.N. has declared it to be a safe zone.* **3** If you **declare** goods that you have bought in another country or money that you have earned, you say how much you have bought or earned so that you can pay tax on it. □ *Declaring the wrong income by mistake will no longer lead to an automatic fine.*

⊕ de·cline ♦♦◇ /dɪˈklaɪn/ VERB, NOUN (academic word) VERB [I, T] (**declines, declining, declined**) **1** [I] If something **declines**, it becomes less in quantity, importance, or strength. □ *The number of staff has declined from 217,000 to 114,000.* □ *Hourly output by workers declined 1.3% in the first quarter.* □ *a declining birth rate* **2** [I, T] (formal) If you **decline** something or **decline to** do something, you politely refuse to accept it or do it. □ *He declined their invitation.* □ *He offered the boys some coffee. They declined politely.* NOUN [C, U] (**declines**) If there is a **decline in** something, it becomes less in quantity, importance, or quality. □ *Official figures show a sharp decline in the number of foreign tourists.* □ *The first signs of economic decline became visible.* PHRASES **in decline** or **on the decline** If something is in **decline** or on the **decline**, it is gradually decreasing in importance, quality, or power. □ *Thankfully the smoking of cigarettes is on the decline.* **into decline** If something **goes** or **falls into decline**, it begins to decrease gradually in importance, quality, or power. □ *Libraries are an investment for the future and they should not be allowed to fall into decline.*

de·com·pose /ˌdiːkəmˈpəʊz/ VERB [I, T] (**decomposes, decomposing, decomposed**) When things such as dead plants or animals **decompose**, or when something **decomposes** them, they change chemically and begin to decay. = rot, decay □ *a dead body found decomposing in the woods* □ *The debris slowly decomposes into compost.*

dec·o·rate ♦◇◇ /ˈdekəreɪt/ VERB [T, I] (**decorates, decorating, decorated**) **1** [T] If you **decorate** something, you make it more attractive by adding things to it. □ *He decorated his room with pictures of all his favourite sports*

figures. **2** [I, T] If you **decorate** a room or the inside of a building, you put new paint or wallpaper on the walls and ceiling, and paint the woodwork. □ *When they came to decorate the rear bedroom, it was Jemma who had the final say.* □ *The boys are planning to decorate when they get the time.*

dec·o·rat·ing /ˈdekəreɪtɪŋ/ NOUN [U] □ *I did a lot of the decorating myself.*

⊕ dec·o·ra·tion /ˌdekəˈreɪʃən/ NOUN [U, C] (**decorations**) **1** [U] The **decoration** of a room is its furniture, wallpaper, and ornaments. = decor □ *The decoration and furnishings had to be practical enough for a family home.* **2** [U] The **decoration** of a room or the inside of a building is the act of putting new paint or wallpaper on the walls and ceiling, and painting the woodwork. □ *The renovation and decoration took four months.* **3** [C, U] **Decorations** are features that are added to something in order to make it look more attractive. □ *The only wall decorations are candles and a single mirror.* **4** [C] **Decorations** are brightly coloured objects such as pieces of paper and balloons, which you put up in a room on special occasions to make it look more attractive. □ *Colourful streamers and paper decorations had been hung from the ceiling.*

dec·o·ra·tive /ˈdekərətɪv/ ADJ Something that is **decorative** is intended to look pretty or attractive. □ *The curtains are for purely decorative purposes and do not open or close.*

de·coy /ˈdiːkɔɪ/ NOUN [C] (**decoys**) If you refer to something or someone as a **decoy**, you mean that they are intended to attract people's attention and deceive them, for example, by leading them into a trap or away from a particular place. □ *A plane was waiting at the airport with its engines running but this was just one of the decoys.*

⊕ de·crease VERB, NOUN VERB /dɪˈkriːs/ [I, T] (**decreases, decreasing, decreased**) When something **decreases** or when you **decrease** it, it becomes less in quantity, size, or intensity. = lower, reduce, fall, drop, decline; ≠ increase, grow, rise, gain □ *Population growth is decreasing by 1.4% each year.* □ *The number of independent firms decreased from 198 to 96.* □ *Since 1945 air forces have decreased in size.* □ *Gradually decrease the amount of vitamin C you are taking.* NOUN /ˈdiːkriːs/ [C] (**decreases**) A **decrease in** the quantity, size, or intensity of something is a reduction in it. = reduction, fall, drop, decline, loss; ≠ increase, growth, rise, gain □ *In Spain and Portugal there has been a decrease in the number of young people out of work.* □ *Bank base rates have fallen from 10 per cent to 6 per cent – a decrease of 40 per cent.*

WHICH WORD?

decrease, fall, or decline?

The verbs **decrease, fall,** and **decline** are all used for talking about things becoming less, but they are used in slightly different contexts.

You use **decrease** in a general way, and in a wide variety of contexts, to talk about things becoming less or smaller.

□ *The amount of swelling has **decreased** somewhat.*

□ *Vegetarian diets **decrease** the risk of cancer and heart disease.*

You use **fall** to talk about a number, rate, or level becoming less.

□ *Prices **fell** to their lowest level in over ten years.*

You use **decline** in a negative way to talk about something such as sales or profits becoming less.

□ *Sales **declined** by 2.4% over the month of September.*

---

de·cree /dɪˈkriː/ NOUN, VERB NOUN [C] (**decrees**) [also 'by' decree] A **decree** is an official order or decision, especially one made by the ruler of a country. □ *In July he issued a decree ordering all unofficial armed groups in the country to disband.* VERB [T] (**decrees, decreeing, decreed**) If someone in authority **decrees** that something must happen, they decide or state this officially. □ *The government decreed that all who wanted to live and work in Kenya must hold Kenyan passports.*

dedi·cate /ˈdedɪkeɪt/ VERB [T] (dedicates, dedicating, dedicated) ■ (approval) If you say that someone has dedicated themselves to something, you approve of the fact that they have decided to give a lot of time and effort to it because they think that it is important. = devote ❑ For the next few years, she dedicated herself to her work. ■ If someone dedicates something such as a book, play, or piece of music to you, they mention your name, for example, in the front of a book or when a piece of music is performed, as a way of showing affection or respect for you. ❑ She dedicated her first album to Woody Allen, who she says understands her obsession.

dedi·cat·ed /ˈdedɪkeɪtɪd/ ADJ ■ You use dedicated to describe someone who enjoys a particular activity very much and spends a lot of time doing it. ❑ Her great-grandfather had clearly been a dedicated and stoical traveller. ■ If you say that someone is dedicated to something, you approve of the fact that they have decided to give a lot of time and effort to it because they think that it is important. ❑ He's quite dedicated to his students. ■ You use dedicated to describe something that is made, built, or designed for one particular purpose or thing. ❑ Such areas should also be served by dedicated cycle routes. ❑ the world's first museum dedicated to ecology

dedi·ca·tion /ˌdedɪˈkeɪʃən/ NOUN [U, C] (dedications) ■ [U] Dedication is the act of giving a lot of time and effort to something because you think that it is important. ❑ We admire her courage, compassion, and dedication to the cause of humanity, justice, and peace. ■ [C] A dedication is a message which is written at the beginning of a book, or a short announcement which is sometimes made before a play or piece of music is performed, as a sign of affection or respect for someone.

de·duce /dɪˈdjuːs, AmE -ˈduːs/ VERB [T] (deduces, deducing, deduced) (academic word) If you deduce something or deduce that something is true, you reach that conclusion because of other things that you know to be true. ❑ Alison cleverly deduced that I was the author of the letter. ❑ The date of the document can be deduced from references to the Civil War. ❑ The researchers have to analyse a huge amount of information in order to deduce any conclusions.

de·duct /dɪˈdʌkt/ VERB [T] (deducts, deducting, deducted) When you deduct an amount from a total, you subtract it from the total. = subtract; ≠ add ❑ The company deducted this payment from his compensation. ❑ Up to 5% of marks in the exams will be deducted for spelling mistakes.

de·duc·tion /dɪˈdʌkʃən/ NOUN [C, U] (deductions) ■ [C] A deduction is an amount that has been subtracted from a total. ≠ addition ❑ Most homeowners can get a federal income tax deduction on interest payments to a home equity loan. ❑ your gross income (before tax and National Insurance deductions) ❑ After deductions for war reparations, the balance would be used to buy food and humanitarian supplies. ■ [C] A deduction is a conclusion that you have reached about something because of other things that you know to be true. = conclusion, inference ❑ It was a pretty astute deduction. ❑ It is a natural instinct rather than a logical deduction. ❑ Children can predict other people's behaviour on the basis of deductions about their beliefs or feelings. ■ [U] Deduction is the process of reaching a conclusion about something because of other things that you know to be true. = reasoning ❑ Miss Allan beamed at him. 'You are clever to guess. I'm sure I don't know how you did it.'— 'Deduction,' James said. ❑ a case that tested his powers of deduction ❑ The assessment was based on rational deduction, not hard evidence.

de·duc·tive /dɪˈdʌktɪv/ ADJ [usu deductive + N] (formal) Deductive reasoning involves drawing conclusions logically from other things that are already known. ≠ inductive ❑ The force of deductive reasoning depends on the reliability of the premises. ❑ The criteria for settling disputes in political theory are partly deductive and partly empirical.

deem /diːm/ VERB [T] (deems, deeming, deemed) (formal) If something is deemed to have a particular quality or to do a particular thing, it is considered to have that quality or do that thing. = judge ❑ French and German were deemed essential. ❑ He says he would support the use of force if the UN deemed it necessary.

deep ♦♦◇ /diːp/ ADJ, ADV, COMB
ADJ (deeper, deepest) ■ If something is deep, it extends a long way down from the ground or from the top surface of something. ❑ The water is very deep and mysterious looking. ❑ Den had dug a deep hole in the centre of the garden. ❑ I found myself in water only three feet deep. ❑ How deep did the snow get? ■ A deep container, such as a cupboard, extends or measures a long distance from front to back. ❑ The wardrobe was very deep. ■ You use deep to emphasize the seriousness, strength, importance, or degree of something. = profound ❑ I had a deep admiration for Sartre. ❑ He wants to express his deep sympathy to the family. ■ [deep + N] If you are in a deep sleep, you are sleeping peacefully and it is difficult to wake you. ❑ Una soon fell into a deep sleep. ■ [V-LINK + deep 'in' N] If you are deep in thought or deep in conversation, you are concentrating very hard on what you are thinking or saying and are not aware of the things that are happening around you. ❑ Before long, we were deep in conversation. ■ [deep + N] A deep breath or sigh uses or fills the whole of your lungs. ❑ Cal took a long, deep breath, struggling to control his own emotions. ■ A deep sound is low in pitch. ❑ His voice was deep and mellow. ■ If you describe something such as a problem or a piece of writing as deep, you mean that it is important, serious, or complicated. ❑ They're written as adventure stories. They're not intended to be deep. ■ Deep colours are strong and fairly dark. ❑ These cushions in traditional deep colours are available in two sizes.
ADV ■ If something goes deep, it goes a long way down from the ground or from the top surface of something. ❑ Gingerly, she put her hand in deeper, to the bottom. ■ Deep in an area means a long way inside it. ❑ Picking up his bag the giant strode off deep into the forest. ■ If you experience or feel something deep inside you or deep down, you feel it very strongly even though you do not necessarily show it. ❑ Deep down, she supported her husband's involvement in the organization. ■ [deep 'in/into' N] If you are deep in debt, you have a lot of debts. ❑ He is so deep in debt and desperate for money that he's apparently willing to say anything.
PHRASE go deep or run deep If you say that something goes deep or runs deep, you mean that it is very serious or strong and is hard to change. ❑ His anger and anguish clearly went deep.
COMB You use deep to describe colours that are strong and fairly dark. ❑ The sky was peach coloured in the east, deep blue and starry in the west.

deep·ly /ˈdiːpli/ ADV ■ = profoundly ❑ He loved his brother deeply. ■ She slept deeply but woke early. ■ She sighed deeply and covered her face with her hands. ■ There isn't time to dig deeply and put in manure or compost. ■ Because of her medical and legal bills, she is now penniless and deeply in debt.
♦ in deep water → see water

deep·en /ˈdiːpən/ VERB [I, T] (deepens, deepening, deepened) ■ [I, T] If a situation or emotion deepens or if something deepens it, it becomes stronger and more intense. ❑ If this is not stopped, the financial crisis will deepen. ■ [T] If you deepen your knowledge or understanding of a subject, you learn more about it and become more interested in it. = broaden ❑ The course is an exciting opportunity for anyone wishing to deepen their understanding of themselves and other people. ■ [I, T] When a sound deepens or is deepened, it becomes lower in tone. ❑ The music room had been made to reflect and deepen sounds. ■ [T] If people deepen something, they increase its depth by digging out its lower surface. ❑ The project would deepen the river from 40 to 45 feet, to allow for larger ships.

deep-seated ADJ A deep-seated problem, feeling, or belief is difficult to change because its causes have been there for a long time. ❑ The country is still suffering from deep-seated economic problems.

deer /dɪə/ NOUN [C] (deer) A deer is a large wild animal that eats grass and leaves. A male deer usually has large, branching horns.

D

⊙ de·fault /dɪˈfɔːlt/ VERB, NOUN, ADJ

VERB [I] (**defaults, defaulting, defaulted**) (*legal*) If a person, company, or country **defaults on** something that they have legally agreed to do, such as paying some money or doing a piece of work before a particular time, they fail to do it. ❏ *The credit card business is down, and more borrowers are defaulting on loans.*

NOUN [U] **1 Default** is the act of failing to do something that you have legally agreed to do, such as paying some money or doing a piece of work before a particular time. ❏ *The corporation may be charged with default on its contract with the government.* **2** (*computing*) In computing, the **default** is a particular set of instructions which the computer always uses unless the person using the computer gives other instructions. ❏ *The default is usually the setting that most users would probably choose.* ❏ *The default setting on Windows Explorer will not show these files.*

PHRASE by default (*formal*) If something happens **by default**, it happens only because something else which might have prevented it or changed it has not happened. ❏ *I would rather pay the individuals than let the money go to the State by default.*

ADJ [default + N] A **default** situation is what exists or happens unless someone or something changes it. = standard ❏ *He appeared unimpressed; but then, unimpressed was his default state.* ❏ *default passwords installed on commercial machines.*

de·feat ♦♦◇ /dɪˈfiːt/ VERB, NOUN

VERB [T] (**defeats, defeating, defeated**) **1** If you **defeat** someone, you win a victory over them in a battle, game, or contest. = beat ❏ *His guerrillas defeated the colonial army in 1954.* **2** If a proposal or motion in a debate **is defeated**, more people vote against it than for it. ❏ *The bill was defeated with support from only two congressmen.* **3** If a task or a problem **defeats** you, it is so difficult that you cannot do it or solve it. ❏ *The book he most wanted to write was the one which nearly defeated him.* **4** To **defeat** an action or plan means to cause it to fail. = thwart ❏ *The navy played a limited but significant role in defeating the rebellion.*

NOUN [C, U] (**defeats**) **Defeat** is the experience of being beaten in a battle, game, or contest, or of failing to achieve what you wanted to. ❏ *The most important thing is not to admit defeat until you really have to.* ❏ *the Sonics' 31-point defeat at Sacramento on Sunday*

de·fect NOUN, VERB

NOUN /ˈdiːfekt/ [C] (**defects**) A **defect** is a fault or imperfection in a person or thing. = imperfection ❏ *He was born with a hearing defect.* ❏ *A report has pointed out the defects of the present system.*

VERB /dɪˈfekt/ [I] (**defects, defecting, defected**) If you **defect**, you leave your country, political party, or other group, and join an opposing country, party, or group. ❏ *a KGB officer who defected in 1963*

de·fec·tion /dɪˈfekʃən/ NOUN [C, U] (**defections**) ❏ *the defection of at least sixteen parliamentary deputies*

de·fec·tive /dɪˈfektɪv/ ADJ If something is **defective**, there is something wrong with it and it does not work properly. ❏ *Retailers can return defective merchandise.*

⊙ de·fence ♦♦◇ /dɪˈfens/ (*BrE*; in *AmE*, use **defense**)
NOUN

NOUN [U, PL, C, SING] (**defences**) **1** [U] **Defence** is action that is taken to protect someone or something against attack. ❏ *The land was flat, giving no scope for defence.* **2** [U] **Defence** is the organization of a country's armies and weapons, and their use to protect the country or its interests. ❏ *Twenty-eight per cent of the federal budget is spent on defence.* ❏ *US defence Secretary Donald Rumsfeld* **3** [PL] The **defences** of a country or region are all its armed forces and weapons. ❏ *He emphasized the need to maintain Britain's defences at a level sufficient to deal with the unexpected.* **4** [C] A **defence** is something that people or animals can use or do to protect themselves. = protection ❏ *Despite anything the science of medicine may have achieved, the immune system is our main defence against disease.* **5** [C] [oft defence 'of' N, also 'in' defence] A **defence** is something that you say or write which supports ideas or actions that have been criticized or questioned. = justification ❏ *Chomsky's*

defence of his approach goes further. **6** [C] In a court of law, an accused person's **defence** is the process of presenting evidence in their favour. **7** [SING] **The defence** is the case that is presented by a lawyer in a trial for the person who has been accused of a crime. You can also refer to this person's lawyers as **the defence**. ≠ prosecution ❏ *The defence was that the records of the interviews were fabricated by the police.* ❏ *The defence pleaded insanity.* **8** [SING] [oft POSS + defence, also 'in' defence] In games such as football or hockey, the **defence** is the group of players in a team who try to stop the opposing players from scoring a goal or a point. ❏ *Their defence, so strong last season, has now conceded 12 goals in six games.*

PHRASE to someone's defence If you come to someone's **defence**, you help them by doing or saying something to protect them. ❏ *He realized none of his schoolmates would come to his defence.*

de·fence·less /dɪˈfensləs/ (*BrE*; in *AmE*, use **defenseless**) ADJ If someone or something is **defenceless**, they are weak and unable to defend themselves properly. = vulnerable ❏ *a savage attack on a defenceless young girl*

⊙ de·fend ♦♦◇ /dɪˈfend/ VERB [T] (**defends, defending, defended**) **1** If you **defend** someone or something, you take action in order to protect them. ❏ *His courage in defending religious and civil rights inspired many outside the church.* **2** If you **defend** someone or something when they have been criticized, you argue in support of them. ❏ *He defended his administration's response to the disaster against critics who charge the federal government is moving too slowly.* **3** When a lawyer **defends** a person who has been accused of something, the lawyer argues on their behalf in a court of law that the charges are not true. ≠ prosecute ❏ *a lawyer who defended political prisoners under the military regime* ❏ *He has hired a lawyer to defend him against the allegation.* **4** (*journalism*) When a sports player plays in the tournament which they won the previous time it was held, you can say that they **are defending** their title. ❏ *Torrence expects to defend her title successfully in the next Olympics.*

⊙ de·fend·ant /dɪˈfendənt/ NOUN [C] (**defendants**) A **defendant** is a person who has been accused of breaking the law and is being tried in court. = accused, suspect ❏ *The defendant pleaded guilty and was fined $500.*

de·fend·er /dɪˈfendə/ NOUN [C] (**defenders**) **1** If someone is a **defender of** a particular thing or person that has been criticized, they argue or act in support of that thing or person. ❏ *the most ardent defenders of conventional family values* **2** A **defender** in a game such as football or hockey is a player whose main task is to try and stop the other side from scoring. ❏ *Graham predicts that the 19-year-old will become one of England's top defenders.*

de·fen·sive /dɪˈfensɪv/ ADJ

ADJ **1** You use **defensive** to describe things that are intended to protect someone or something. ❏ *The Government hastily organized defensive measures, deploying searchlights and anti-aircraft guns around the target cities.* **2** Someone who is **defensive** is behaving in a way that shows they feel unsure or threatened. ❏ *Like their children, parents are often defensive about their private lives.* **3** In sports, **defensive** play is play that is intended to prevent your opponent from scoring points against you. ❏ *I'd always played a defensive game, waiting for my opponent to make a mistake.*

PHRASE on the defensive If someone is **on the defensive**, they are trying to protect themselves or their interests because they feel unsure or threatened. ❏ *The administration has been on the defensive about the war.*

de·fen·sive·ly /dɪˈfensɪvli/ ADV **1** '*Oh, I know, I know,*' said Kate, defensively. **2** [defensively after V] ❏ *We didn't play well defensively in the first half.*

⊙ de·fer /dɪˈfɜː/ VERB [T, I] (**defers, deferring, deferred**) **1** [T] If you **defer** an event or action, you arrange for it to happen at a later date, rather than immediately or at the previously planned time. = postpone, delay ❏ *Customers often defer payment for as long as possible.* ❏ *Sentence was deferred until June 16 for background reports.* ❏ *a system which* will allow approved companies to defer paying VAT on imports **2** [I] If you **defer to** someone, you accept their opinion or do what they want you to do, even when you do not agree with it yourself, because you respect them or their authority. ❑ *Doctors are encouraged to defer to experts.*

de·fi·ance /dɪˈfaɪəns/ NOUN [U] [oft defiance 'of' N] Defiance is behaviour or an attitude which shows that you are not willing to obey someone. ❑ *his courageous defiance of the government*

de·fi·ant /dɪˈfaɪənt/ ADJ If you say that someone is **defiant**, you mean they show aggression or independence by refusing to obey someone. ❑ *The players are in a defiant mood as they prepare for tomorrow's game.*
de·fi·ant·ly /dɪˈfaɪəntli/ ADV ❑ *They defiantly rejected any talk of a compromise.*

⬦ **de·fi·cien·cy** /dɪˈfɪʃənsi/ NOUN [C, U] (deficiencies)
1 **Deficiency in** something, especially something that your body needs, is not having enough of it. = lack, inadequacy; ≠ sufficiency ❑ *They did blood tests on him for signs of vitamin deficiency.* ❑ *Diseases associated with protein and carbohydrate deficiency cause many deaths among young children.* ❑ *brain damage caused by a deficiency of vitamin B12*
2 (formal) A **deficiency** that someone or something has is a weakness or imperfection in them. = weakness, inadequacy ❑ *The most serious deficiency in NATO's air defence is the lack of an identification system to distinguish friend from foe.*

⬦ **de·fi·cient** /dɪˈfɪʃənt/ ADJ (formal) If someone or something is **deficient in** a particular thing, they do not have the full amount of it that they need in order to function normally or work properly. = lacking, inadequate; ≠ sufficient ❑ *a diet deficient in vitamin B* ❑ *The proposal was deficient in several respects.*

⬦ **def·i·cit** ◆◆◇ /ˈdefəsɪt/ NOUN
NOUN [C] (deficits) A **deficit** is the amount by which something is less than what is required or expected, especially the amount by which the total money received is less than the total money spent. = shortage; ≠ surplus ❑ *They're ready to cut the federal budget deficit for the next fiscal year.* ❑ *a deficit of five billion dollars*
PHRASE **in deficit** If an account or organization is **in deficit**, more money has been spent than has been received. ❑ *The current account of the balance of payments is in deficit.*

⬦ **de·fine** ◆◆◇ /dɪˈfaɪn/ VERB [T] (defines, defining, defined) (academic word) If you **define** something, you show, describe, or state clearly what it is and what its limits are, or what it is like. = explain, expound, interpret ❑ *The Convention Against Torture defines torture as any act that inflicts severe pain or suffering, physical or mental.* ❑ *We were unable to define what exactly was wrong with him.* ❑ *a musical era when genres were less narrowly defined*

⬦ **def·i·nite** /ˈdefɪnɪt/ ADJ (academic word) **1** If something such as a decision or an arrangement is **definite**, it is firm and clear, and unlikely to be changed. = certain, definitive, conclusive; ≠ uncertain, inconclusive, inexact ❑ *It's too soon to give a definite answer.* ❑ *She made no definite plans for her future.* **2** **Definite** evidence or information is true, rather than being someone's opinion or guess. ❑ *We didn't have any definite proof.* ❑ *There is no definite conclusion that can be reached from these studies.* ❑ *The police had nothing definite against her.* **3** [definite + N] You use **definite** to emphasize the strength of your opinion or belief. = real ❑ *There has already been a definite improvement.* ❑ *That's a very definite possibility.* **4** Someone who is **definite** behaves or talks in a firm, confident way. ❑ *Mary is very definite about this.*

⬦ **def·i·nite·ly** ◆◇◇ /ˈdefɪnɪtli/ ADV **1** (emphasis) You use **definitely** to emphasize that something is the case, or to emphasize the strength of your intention or opinion. = certainly; ≠ possibly ❑ *I'm definitely going to get in touch with these people.* ❑ *While intra-region trade in Asia has definitely improved, the pace of recovery in individual economies has been uneven.* **2** [definitely before v] If something has been **definitely** decided, the decision will not be changed. ❑ *She had definitely decided that she wanted to continue working with women in prison.*

⬦ **defi·ni·tion** ◆◇◇ /ˌdefɪˈnɪʃən/ NOUN
NOUN [C, U] (definitions) **1** [C] A **definition** is a statement giving the meaning of a word or expression, especially in a dictionary. = explanation, interpretation ❑ *There is no general agreement on a standard definition of intelligence.* **2** [U] **Definition** is the quality of being clear and distinct. ❑ *The first speakers at the conference criticized Professor Johnson's new programme for lack of definition.*
PHRASE **by definition** If you say that something has a particular quality **by definition**, you mean that it has this quality simply because of what it is. ❑ *Human perception is highly imperfect and by definition subjective.*

⬦ **de·fini·tive** /dɪˈfɪnɪtɪv/ ADJ (academic word) **1** Something that is **definitive** provides a firm conclusion that cannot be questioned. = conclusive, absolute, definite; ≠ inconclusive ❑ *No one has come up with a definitive answer as to why this should be so.* ❑ *The study population was too small to reach any definitive conclusions.* **2** A **definitive** book or performance is thought to be the best of its kind that has ever been done or that will ever be done. ❑ *Ian Macdonald's definitive book on The Beatles*
⬦ **de·fini·tive·ly** /dɪˈfɪnɪtɪvli/ ADV = conclusively, absolutely, definitely; ≠ inconclusively ❑ *Law enforcement officials had definitively identified Blanco as a potential suspect.* ❑ *The research also definitively proves that second-hand smoke causes cancer.*

de·flate /dɪˈfleɪt/ VERB [T, I] (deflates, deflating, deflated) **1** [T] If you **deflate** someone or something, you take away their confidence or make them seem less important. ❑ *I hate to deflate your ego, but you seem to have an exaggerated idea of your importance to me.* **2** [I] When something such as a tyre or balloon **deflates**, or when you **deflate** it, all the air comes out of it. ❑ *We drove a few miles until the tyre deflated and we had to stop the car.*
de·flat·ed /dɪˈfleɪtɪd/ ADJ ❑ *When she refused I felt deflated.*

de·flect /dɪˈflekt/ VERB [T] (deflects, deflecting, deflected) **1** If you **deflect** something such as criticism or attention, you act in a way that prevents it from being directed towards you or affecting you. ❑ *Cage changed his name to deflect accusations of nepotism.* **2** To **deflect** someone **from** a course of action means to make them decide not to continue with it by putting pressure on them or by offering them something desirable. ❑ *The war did not deflect him from the path he had long ago taken.* **3** If you **deflect** something that is moving, you make it go in a slightly different direction, for example, by hitting or blocking it. ❑ *My forearm deflected the first punch.*

de·for·est /ˌdiːˈfɒrɪst, AmE -ˈfɔːr-/ VERB [T] (deforests, deforesting, deforested) If an area **is deforested**, all the trees there are cut down or destroyed. ❑ *the 400,000 square kilometres of the Amazon basin that have already been deforested*

de·for·esta·tion /diːˌfɒrɪsˈteɪʃən, AmE -ˈfɔːr-/ NOUN [U] **Deforestation** is the cutting down and destruction of the trees in an area. ❑ *One per cent of Brazil's total forest cover is being lost every year to deforestation.*

de·form /dɪˈfɔːm/ VERB [I, T] (deforms, deforming, deformed) If something **deforms** a person's body or something else, it causes it to have an unnatural shape. In technical English, you can also say that the second thing **deforms** when it changes to an unnatural shape. ❑ *Bad rheumatoid arthritis deforms limbs.*
de·formed /dɪˈfɔːmd/ ADJ ❑ *He was born with a deformed right leg.*

de·fraud /dɪˈfrɔːd/ VERB [T] (defrauds, defrauding, defrauded) If someone **defrauds** you, they take something away from you or stop you from getting what belongs to you by means of tricks and lies. ❑ *He pleaded guilty to charges of conspiracy to defraud the government.*

deft /deft/ ADJ (defter, deftest) (written) A **deft** action is skilful and often quick. ❑ *With a deft flick of his wrist, he extinguished the match.*
deft·ly /ˈdeftli/ ADV ❑ *One of the waiting servants deftly caught him as he fell.*

de·funct /dɪˈfʌŋkt/ ADJ If something is **defunct**, it no longer exists or has stopped functioning or operating.

d

D

❑ *the leader of the now defunct Social Democratic Party*

de·fuse /ˌdiːˈfjuːz/ VERB [T] (**defuses, defusing, defused**) **1** If you **defuse** a dangerous or tense situation, you calm it. ❑ *Police administrators credited the organization with helping defuse potentially violent situations.* **2** If someone **defuses** a bomb, they remove the fuse so that it cannot explode. ❑ *Police have defused a bomb found in a city centre building.*

defy /dɪˈfaɪ/ VERB [T] (**defies, defying, defied**) **1** If you **defy** someone or something that is trying to make you behave in a particular way, you refuse to obey them and behave in that way. ❑ *This was the first (and last) time that I dared to defy my mother.* **2** If you **defy** someone **to do** something, you challenge them to do it when you think that they will be unable to do it or too frightened to do it. = dare ❑ *I defy you to come up with one major accomplishment of the current president.* **3** If something **defies** description or understanding, it is so strange, extreme, or surprising that it is almost impossible to understand or explain. ❑ *It's a devastating and barbaric act that defies all comprehension.*

de·gen·er·ate VERB, ADJ
VERB /dɪˈdʒenəreɪt/ [I] (**degenerates, degenerating, degenerated**) If you say that someone or something **degenerates**, you mean that they become worse in some way, for example, weaker, lower in quality, or more dangerous. = deteriorate ❑ *Inactivity can make your joints stiff, and the bones may begin to degenerate.*
ADJ /dɪˈdʒenərət/ (*disapproval*) If you describe a person or their behaviour as **degenerate**, you disapprove of them because you think they have low standards of behaviour or morality. ❑ *a group of degenerate computer hackers*
de·gen·era·tion /dɪˌdʒenəˈreɪʃən/ NOUN [U] ❑ *various forms of physical and mental degeneration*

deg·ra·da·tion /ˌdegrəˈdeɪʃən/ NOUN [C, U] (**degradations**) **1** [C, U] (*disapproval*) You use **degradation** to refer to a situation, condition, or experience which you consider shameful and disgusting, especially one which involves poverty or immorality. ❑ *They were sickened by the scenes of misery and degradation they found.* **2** [U] **Degradation** is the process of something becoming worse or weaker, or being made worse or weaker. ❑ *air pollution, traffic congestion, and the steady degradation of our quality of life*

de·grade /dɪˈɡreɪd/ VERB [T] (**degrades, degrading, degraded**) **1** Something that **degrades** someone causes people to have less respect for them. ❑ *the notion that pornography degrades women* **2** (*formal*) To **degrade** something means to cause it to get worse. ❑ *the ability to meet human needs indefinitely without degrading the environment*
de·grad·ing /dɪˈɡreɪdɪŋ/ ADJ = humiliating ❑ *Mr Porter was subjected to a degrading strip search.*

✪ **de·gree** ♦♦◇ /dɪˈɡriː/ NOUN
NOUN [C] (**degrees**) **1** You use **degree** to indicate the extent to which something happens or is the case, or the amount which something is felt. = amount, extent ❑ *These man-made barriers will ensure a very high degree of protection for several hundred years.* ❑ *Recent presidents have used television, as well as radio, with varying degrees of success.* **2** A **degree** is a unit of measurement that is used to measure temperatures. It is often written as °, for example, 23°. ❑ *It's over 80 degrees outside.* ❑ *Pure water sometimes does not freeze until it reaches minus 40 degrees Celsius.* **3** A **degree** is a unit of measurement that is used to measure angles, and also longitude and latitude. It is often written as °, for example, 23°. ❑ *It was pointing outward at an angle of 45 degrees.* **4** A **degree** is a title or rank given by a university or college when you have completed a course of study there. It can also be given as an honorary title. ❑ *an engineering degree* ❑ *He took a master's degree in economics at Yale.* ❑ *the first year of a degree course*
PHRASES **a degree of** If something has **a degree of** a particular quality, it has a small but significant amount of that quality.
to some degree or **to a certain degree** (*vagueness*) You use expressions such as **to some degree, to a large degree,**

or **to a certain degree** in order to indicate that something is partly true, but not entirely true. = to some/a certain extent ❑ *These statements are, to some degree, all correct.* ❑ *It is impossible to make these points without generalising to a certain degree.*
to what degree or **to that degree** or **to the degree that** You use expressions such as **to what degree** and **to the degree that** when you are discussing how true a statement is, or in what ways it is true. = to what extent, to the extent that ❑ *To what degree would you say you had control over things that went on?* ❑ *The valves may scar and thicken to the degree that they may fail to open completely or close properly.*

✪ **de·hy·drate** /ˌdiːhaɪˈdreɪt/ VERB [T, I] (**dehydrates, dehydrating, dehydrated**) **1** [T] When something such as food **is dehydrated**, all the water is removed from it, often in order to preserve it. = drain, dry; ≠ hydrate ❑ *Normally specimens have to be dehydrated.* **2** [I, T] If you **dehydrate** or if something **dehydrates** you, you lose too much water from your body so that you feel weak or ill. ❑ *People can dehydrate in weather like this.* ❑ *Alcohol quickly dehydrates your body.*
✪ **de·hy·drat·ed** /ˌdiːhaɪˈdreɪtɪd/ ADJ ≠ hydrated ❑ *Dehydrated meals, soups and sauces contain a lot of salt.* ❑ *During surgery, exposed tissue can become dehydrated.*
✪ **de·hy·dra·tion** /ˌdiːhaɪˈdreɪʃən/ NOUN [U] ❑ *a child who's got diarrhoea and is suffering from dehydration*

de·ity /ˈdeɪɪti, AmE ˈdiː-/ NOUN [C] (**deities**) (*formal*) A **deity** is a god or goddess. ❑ *a deity revered by thousands of Hindus and Buddhists*

✪ **de·lay** ♦♦◇ /dɪˈleɪ/ VERB, NOUN
VERB [I, T] (**delays, delaying, delayed**) **1** [I, T] If you **delay** doing something, you do not do it immediately or at the planned or expected time, but you leave it until later. = postpone ❑ *For sentimental reasons I wanted to delay my departure until June 1980.* ❑ *They had delayed having children, for the usual reason, to establish their careers.* **2** [T] To **delay** someone or something means to make them late or to slow them down. = hold up; ≠ expedite, hasten ❑ *Can you delay him in some way?* ❑ *Various setbacks and problems delayed production.* ❑ *The therapy is known to delay the onset of osteoporosis.* **3** [I] If you **delay**, you deliberately take longer than necessary to do something. ❑ *If he delayed any longer, the sun would be up.*
NOUN [C, U] (**delays**) **1** [C, U] If there is a **delay**, something does not happen until later than planned or expected. = hold-up, setback ❑ *They claimed that such a delay wouldn't hurt anyone.* ❑ *The delay in the implementation of the law has dismayed businesses.* ❑ *Although the tests have caused some delay, flights should be back to normal soon.* **2** [U] **Delay** is a failure to do something immediately or in the required or usual time. ❑ *We'll send you a quote without delay.*

WHICH WORD?

delay, cancel, postpone, or put off?

If you **delay** doing something, you do it at a later time.
❑ *Try and persuade them to delay the launch.*

If a plane, train, ship, or bus **is delayed**, it is prevented from leaving or arriving on time.
❑ *The coach was delayed for about five hours.*

Cancel and **postpone** are used to talk about events that have been arranged in advance. To **cancel** an event means to decide officially that it will not take place.
❑ *The performances were cancelled because the leading man was ill.*

To **postpone** or **put off** an event means to arrange for it to take place at a later time than was originally planned.
❑ *The meeting was postponed until the following week.*
❑ *This is not a decision that can be put off much longer.*

del·egate ♦◇◇ NOUN, VERB
NOUN /ˈdelɪɡət/ [C] (**delegates**) A **delegate** is a person who is chosen to vote or make decisions on behalf of a group of other people, especially at a conference or a meeting. = representative ❑ *The Canadian delegate offered no reply.*

d

VERB /'delɪgeɪt/ [i, t] (**delegates, delegating, delegated**)
1 [i, t] If you **delegate** duties, responsibilities, or power **to** someone, you give them those duties, those responsibilities, or that power so that they can act on your behalf. □ *He talks of travelling less, and delegating more authority to his deputies.* **2** [t] If you **are delegated to** do something, you are given the duty of acting on someone else's behalf by making decisions, voting, or doing some particular work. = appoint □ *Officials have now been delegated to start work on a draft settlement.*

del·e·ga·tion ♦◇◇ /ˌdelɪ'geɪʃən/ NOUN [c, u] (**delegations**)
1 [c] A **delegation** is a group of people who have been sent somewhere to have talks with other people on behalf of a larger group of people. □ *the Chinese delegation to the UN talks in New York* **2** [u] **Delegation** is the act of giving someone duties, responsibilities, or power so that they can act on your behalf. □ *A key factor in running a business is the delegation of responsibility.*

de·lete /dɪ'liːt/ VERB [t] (**deletes, deleting, deleted**) If you **delete** something that has been written down or stored in a computer, you cross it out or remove it. □ *He also deleted files from the computer system.*

◆**de·lib·er·ate** ♦◇◇ ADJ, VERB
ADJ /dɪ'lɪbərət/ **1** If you do something that is **deliberate**, you planned or decided to do it beforehand, and so it happens on purpose rather than by chance. = intentional, conscious; ≠ unintentional, accidental □ *Witnesses say the firing was deliberate and sustained.* **2** If a movement or action is **deliberate**, it is done slowly and carefully. □ *stepping with deliberate slowness up the steep paths*
VERB /dɪ'lɪbəreɪt/ [i, t] (**deliberates, deliberating, deliberated**) If you **deliberate**, you think about something carefully, especially before making a very important decision. = ponder □ *She deliberated over the decision for a good few years before she finally made up her mind.*
◆**de·lib·er·ate·ly** /dɪ'lɪbərətli/ ADV **1** = intentionally, consciously, knowingly; ≠ unintentionally, accidentally, inadvertently □ *It looks as if the blaze was started deliberately.* □ *Mr Christopher's answer was deliberately vague.* **2** [deliberately after v] □ *The Japanese have acted calmly and deliberately.*

de·lib·era·tion /dɪˌlɪbə'reɪʃən/ NOUN [u, pl] (**deliberations**) **1** [u] **Deliberation** is the long and careful consideration of a subject. □ *In this house nothing is there by chance: it is always the result of great deliberation.* **2** [pl] **Deliberations** are formal discussions where an issue is considered carefully. □ *Their deliberations were rather inconclusive.*

deli·ca·cy /'delɪkəsi/ NOUN [u, c] (**delicacies**) **1** [u] **Delicacy** is the quality of being easy to break or harm, and refers especially to people or things that are attractive or graceful. □ *the delicacy of a rose* **2** [u] If you say that a situation or problem is of some **delicacy**, you mean that it is difficult to handle and needs careful and sensitive treatment. □ *There was a matter of some delicacy on which he would be grateful for her advice.* **3** [u] If someone handles a difficult situation **with delicacy**, they handle it very carefully, making sure that nobody is offended. = sensitivity □ *Both countries are behaving with rare delicacy.* **4** [c] A **delicacy** is a rare or expensive food that is considered especially nice to eat. □ *Smoked salmon is considered an expensive delicacy.*

deli·cate /'delɪkət/ ADJ **1** Something that is **delicate** is small and beautifully shaped. = dainty □ *He had delicate hands.* **2** Something that is **delicate** has a colour, taste, or smell which is pleasant and not strong or intense. = subtle □ *Young haricot beans have a tender texture and a delicate, subtle flavour.* **3** If something is **delicate**, it is easy to harm, damage, or break, and needs to be handled or treated carefully. = fragile □ *Although the coral looks hard, it is very delicate.* **4** Someone who is **delicate** is not healthy and strong, and becomes ill easily. = frail □ *She was physically delicate and psychologically unstable.* **5** You use **delicate** to describe a situation, problem, matter, or discussion that needs to be dealt with carefully and sensitively in order to avoid upsetting things or offending people. □ *Ottawa and*

Washington have to find a delicate balance between the free flow of commerce and legitimate security concerns. **6** A **delicate** task, movement, action, or product needs or shows great skill and attention to detail. □ *a long and delicate operation carried out at a hospital in Pittsburgh*
deli·cate·ly /'delɪkətli/ ADV **1** [delicately + -ED/ADJ] = daintily □ *She was a shy, delicately pretty girl with enormous blue eyes.* **2** [delicately + -ED/ADJ] □ *a soup delicately flavoured with nutmeg* **3** [delicately with v] □ *Clearly, the situation remains delicately poised.* **4** [delicately with v] = daintily □ *the delicately embroidered sheets*

de·li·cious /dɪ'lɪʃəs/ ADJ Food that is **delicious** has a very pleasant taste. = tasty □ *There's always a wide selection of delicious meals to choose from.*
de·li·cious·ly /dɪ'lɪʃəsli/ ADV [deliciously + ADJ/-ED] □ *This yogurt has a deliciously creamy flavour.*

de·light ♦◇◇ /dɪ'laɪt/ NOUN, VERB
NOUN [u, c] (**delights**) **1** [u] **Delight** is a feeling of very great pleasure. □ *Throughout the house, the views are a constant source of surprise and delight.* □ *Andrew roared with delight when he heard Rachel's nickname for the baby.* **2** [c] You can refer to someone or something that gives you great pleasure or enjoyment as a **delight**. = joy □ *The aircraft was a delight to fly.*
PHRASE **take delight in** or **take a delight in** If someone **takes delight** or **takes a delight** in something, they get a lot of pleasure from it. □ *Haig took obvious delight in proving his critics wrong.*
VERB [t] (**delights, delighting, delighted**) If something **delights** you, it gives you a lot of pleasure. □ *She has created a style of music that has delighted audiences all over the world.*

de·light·ed ♦◇◇ /dɪ'laɪtɪd/ ADJ **1** If you are **delighted**, you are extremely pleased and excited about something. □ *I know Frank will be delighted to see you.* **2** If someone invites or asks you to do something, you can say that you would be **delighted** to do it, as a way of showing that you are very willing to do it. □ *'You have to come to Todd's graduation party.'—'I'd be delighted.'*
de·light·ed·ly /dɪ'laɪtɪdli/ ADV [delightedly with v] □ *'There!' Jackson exclaimed delightedly.*

de·light·ful /dɪ'laɪtfʊl/ ADJ If you describe something or someone as **delightful**, you mean they are very pleasant. = lovely □ *It was the most delightful garden I had ever seen.*
de·light·ful·ly /dɪ'laɪtfʊli/ ADV [delightfully + ADJ/-ED] □ *This delightfully refreshing cologne can be splashed on liberally.*

de·lin·quent /dɪ'lɪŋkwənt/ ADJ, NOUN
ADJ Someone, usually a young person, who is **delinquent** repeatedly commits minor crimes. □ *homes for delinquent children*
NOUN [c] (**delinquents**) A **delinquent** is someone, usually a young person, who repeatedly commits minor crimes. □ *a nine-year-old delinquent*

de·liri·ous /dɪ'lɪəriəs/ ADJ **1** Someone who is **delirious** is unable to think or speak in a sensible and reasonable way, usually because they are very ill and have a fever. □ *I was delirious and blacked out several times.* **2** Someone who is **delirious** is extremely excited and happy. = ecstatic □ *A raucous crowd of 25,000 delirious fans greeted the team at Grand Central Station.*
de·liri·ous·ly /dɪ'lɪəriəsli/ ADV □ *Dora returned from her honeymoon deliriously happy.*

de·liv·er ♦♦◇ /dɪ'lɪvə/ VERB [t, i] (**delivers, delivering, delivered**) **1** [t] If you **deliver** something somewhere, you take it there. □ *The Canadians plan to deliver more food to southern Somalia.* **2** [i, t] If you **deliver** something that you have promised to do, make, or produce, you do, make, or produce it. □ *They have yet to show that they can really deliver working technologies.* □ *The question is, can he deliver?* **3** [t] (*formal*) If you **deliver** a lecture or speech, you give it in public. □ *The president will deliver a speech about schools.* **4** [t] When someone **delivers** a baby, they help the woman who is giving birth to the baby. □ *Although we'd planned to have our baby at home, we never expected to deliver her ourselves!* **5** [t] (*written*) If someone **delivers** a blow to someone else, they hit them. □ *Those blows to the head could have been delivered by a woman.*

D

de·liv·ery ♦◇◇ /dɪˈlɪvəri/ NOUN, ADJ
NOUN [C, U] (**deliveries**) **1** [C, U] **Delivery** or a **delivery** is the bringing of letters, parcels, or other goods to someone's house or to another place where they want them. □ *Please allow 28 days for delivery.* □ *The uprising is threatening the delivery of humanitarian supplies of food and medicine.* **2** [C, U] **Delivery** is the process of giving birth to a baby. = birth □ *In the end, it was an easy delivery: a fine baby boy.* **3** [C] A **delivery** of something is the goods that are delivered. □ *I got a delivery of fresh eggs this morning.* **4** [U] You talk about someone's **delivery** when you are referring to the way in which they give a speech or lecture. □ *His speeches were magnificently written but his delivery was hopeless.*
ADJ [delivery + N] A **delivery** person or service delivers things to a place. □ *a pizza delivery man*

del·ta /ˈdeltə/ NOUN [C] (**deltas**) A **delta** is an area of low, flat land shaped like a triangle, where a river splits and spreads out into several branches before entering the sea. □ *the Mississippi delta*

del·uge /ˈdeljuːdʒ/ NOUN, VERB
NOUN [C] (**deluges**) A **deluge** of things is a large number of them which arrive or happen at the same time. = flood □ *There was a deluge of requests for interviews and statements.*
VERB [T] (**deluges, deluging, deluged**) If a place or person **is deluged with** things, a large number of them arrive or happen at the same time. □ *During 1933, Papen's office was deluged with complaints.*

de·lu·sion /dɪˈluːʒən/ NOUN [C, U] (**delusions**) **1** [C] A **delusion** is a false idea. □ *I was under the delusion that he intended to marry me.* **2** [U] **Delusion** is the state of believing things that are not true. □ *Insinuations about her mental state, about her capacity for delusion, were being made.*

✪**de·mand** ♦♦♦ /dɪˈmɑːnd, -ˈmænd/ VERB, NOUN
VERB [T] (**demands, demanding, demanded**) **1** If you **demand** something such as information or action, you ask for it in a very forceful way. □ *Human rights groups are demanding an investigation into the shooting.* □ *Russia demanded that UNITA send a delegation to the peace talks.* **2** If one thing **demands** another, the first needs the second in order to happen or be dealt with successfully. = require □ *He said the task of reconstruction would demand much patience, hard work, and sacrifice.*
NOUN [C, U, PL] (**demands**) **1** [C] A **demand** is a firm request for something. □ *There have been demands for services from tenants up there.* **2** [U] If you refer to **demand**, or to the **demand for** something, you are referring to how many people want to have it, do it, or buy it. □ *Another flight would be arranged on Saturday if sufficient demand arose.* □ *Demand for coal is down.* **3** [PL] The **demands of** something or its **demands on** you are the things which it needs or the things which you have to do for it. □ *the demands and challenges of a new job*
PHRASES **in (great) demand** If someone or something is **in demand** or **in great demand**, they are very popular and a lot of people want them. □ *He was much in demand as a lecturer in the US, as well as at universities all over Europe.* **on demand** If something is available or happens **on demand**, you can have it or it happens whenever you want it or ask for it. □ *a new entertainment system that offers 25 movies on demand*

de·mand·ing /dɪˈmɑːndɪŋ, -ˈmænd-/ ADJ **1** A **demanding** job or task requires a lot of your time, energy, or attention. □ *He tried to return to work, but found he could no longer cope with his demanding job.* **2** People who are **demanding** are not easily satisfied or pleased. □ *Ricky was a very demanding child.*

de·mean /dɪˈmiːn/ VERB [T] (**demeans, demeaning, demeaned**) To **demean** someone or something means to make people have less respect for them. = degrade □ *Some groups say that pornography demeans women and incites rape.*

de·mean·ing /dɪˈmiːnɪŋ/ ADJ Something that is **demeaning** makes people have less respect for the person who is treated in that way, or who does that thing. = degrading □ *making demeaning sexist comments*

de·mean·our /dɪˈmiːnə/ (in AmE, use **demeanor**) NOUN [U] (formal) Your **demeanour** is the way you behave, which gives people an impression of your character and feelings. □ *her calm and cheerful demeanour*

de·men·tia /dɪˈmenʃə/ NOUN [C, U] (**dementias**) (medical) **Dementia** is a serious illness of the mind. □ *a treatment for mental conditions such as dementia and Alzheimer's disease*

demi·god /ˈdemiɡɒd/ NOUN [C] (**demigods**) If you describe a famous or important person such as a politician, writer, or musician as a **demigod**, you mean that you disapprove of the way in which people admire them and treat them like a god. □ *Rock gods and political demigods share centre stage.*

de·mise /dɪˈmaɪz/ NOUN [SING] (formal) The **demise** of something or someone is their end or death. □ *the demise of the reform movement*

de·mo·bi·lize /diːˈməʊbɪlaɪz/ also **demobilise** VERB [I, T] (**demobilizes, demobilizing, demobilized**) If a country or armed force **demobilizes** its troops, or if its troops **demobilize**, its troops are released from service and allowed to go home. □ *Dos Santos has demanded that UNITA sign a cease-fire and demobilize its troops.*
de·mo·bi·li·za·tion /diːˌməʊbɪlaɪˈzeɪʃən/ NOUN [U] *The government had previously been opposed to the demobilization of its 100,000 strong army.*

✪**de·moc·ra·cy** ♦♦◇ /dɪˈmɒkrəsi/ NOUN [U, C] (**democracies**) **1** [U] **Democracy** is a system of government in which people choose their rulers by voting for them in elections. □ *The spread of democracy in Eastern Europe appears to have had negative as well as positive consequences.* **2** [C] A **democracy** is a country in which the people choose their government by voting for it. □ *The new democracies face tough challenges.*

✪**demo·crat** ♦♦◇ /ˈdeməkræt/ NOUN [C] (**democrats**) **1** A **democrat** is a person who believes in the ideals of democracy, personal freedom, and equality. □ *This is the time for democrats and not dictators.* **2** A **Democrat** is a member or supporter of a particular political party which has the word 'democrat' or 'democratic' in its title, for example, the Democratic Party in the United States. □ *Murray has joined other Senate Democrats in blocking the legislation.* □ *a senior Christian Democrat* □ *Congressman Tom Downey is a Democrat from New York.*

✪**demo·crat·ic** ♦♦◇ /ˌdeməˈkrætɪk/ ADJ **1** A **democratic** country, government, or political system is governed by representatives who are elected by the people. □ *Bolivia returned to democratic rule in 1982, after a series of military governments.* □ *the country's first democratic elections* **2** Something that is **democratic** is based on the idea that everyone should have equal rights and should be involved in making important decisions. = egalitarian, representative; ≠ totalitarian □ *Education is the basis of a democratic society.*
demo·crati·cal·ly /ˌdeməˈkrætɪkli/ ADV **1** *That June, Yeltsin became Russia's first democratically elected president.* **2** *This committee will enable decisions to be made democratically.*

✪**de·mo·graph·ic** /ˌdeməˈɡræfɪk/ NOUN, ADJ
NOUN [PL, SING] (**demographics**) **1** [PL] The **demographics** of a place or society are the statistics relating to the people who live there. □ *the changing demographics of the United States* **2** [SING] (business) In business, a **demographic** is a group of people in a society, especially people in a particular age group. □ *The station has won more listeners in the 25–39 demographic.* □ *well-read individuals, the target demographic of this newspaper section*
ADJ **Demographic** means relating to or concerning demography. □ *The final impact of industrialization on the family was demographic.* □ *the relationship between economic and demographic change*

✪**de·mog·ra·phy** /dɪˈmɒɡrəfi/ NOUN [U] **Demography** is the study of the changes in numbers of births, deaths, marriages, and cases of disease in a community over a period of time. □ *a major work on the demography of preindustrial societies*
de·mog·ra·pher /dɪˈmɒɡrəfə/ NOUN [C] (**demographers**) □ *a politically astute economist and demographer*

de·mol·ish /dɪ'mɒlɪʃ/ VERB [T] (demolishes, demolishing, demolished) **1** To **demolish** something such as a building means to destroy it completely. ❑ *A storm moved directly over the island, demolishing buildings and flooding streets.* **2** If you **demolish** someone's ideas or arguments, you prove that they are completely wrong or unreasonable. ❑ *Our intention was quite the opposite – to demolish rumours that have surrounded him since he took office.*

demo·li·tion /,demə'lɪʃən/ NOUN [C, U] (demolitions) The **demolition** of a structure, for example, a building, is the act of deliberately destroying it, often in order to build something else in its place. ❑ *The project required the total demolition of the old bridge.*

de·mon /'diːmən/ NOUN [C] (demons) **1** A **demon** is an evil spirit. ❑ *a woman possessed by demons* **2** If you approve of someone because they are very skilled at what they do or because they do it energetically, you can say that they do it like a **demon**. ❑ *She worked like a demon and expected everybody else to do the same.* ❑ *He is a demon organizer.*

✪**dem·on·strate** ♦◇◇ /'demənstreɪt/ VERB [T, I] (demonstrates, demonstrating, demonstrated) (academic word) **1** [T] To **demonstrate** a fact means to make it clear to people. = show, prove; ≠ refute, disprove ❑ *The study also demonstrated a direct link between obesity and mortality.* ❑ *They are anxious to demonstrate to the voters that they have practical policies.* ❑ *His experiments demonstrated that plants alter their shape at night.* **2** [T] If you **demonstrate** a particular skill, quality, or feeling, you show by your actions that you have it. = show, display ❑ *Have they, for example, demonstrated a commitment to democracy?* **3** [I] When people **demonstrate**, they march or gather somewhere to show their opposition to something or their support for something. = protest ❑ *Some 30,000 angry farmers arrived in Brussels yesterday to demonstrate against possible cuts in subsidies.* ❑ *In the cities vast crowds have been demonstrating for change.* **4** [T] If you **demonstrate** something, you show people how it works or how to do it. ❑ *A selection of cosmetic companies will be there to demonstrate their new products.* ❑ *He flew the prototype to West Raynham to demonstrate it to a group of senior officers.*

✪**dem·on·stra·tion** ♦◇◇ /,demən'streɪʃən/ NOUN [C] (demonstrations) **1** A **demonstration** is a march or gathering which people take part in to show their opposition to something or their support for something. ❑ *Riot police used tear gas to break up the demonstration.* **2** A **demonstration** of something is a talk by someone who shows you how to do it or how it works. ❑ *a cooking demonstration* ❑ *demonstrations of new products* **3** A **demonstration of** a fact or situation is a clear proof of it. = explanation, proof ❑ *It was an unprecedented demonstration of people power by the citizens of Moscow.* ❑ *This is a clear demonstration of how technology has changed.* **4** A **demonstration of** a quality or feeling is an expression of it. = display ❑ *There's been no public demonstration of opposition to the president.*

de·mon·stra·tor ♦◇◇ /'demən,streɪtə/ NOUN [C] (demonstrators) **1 Demonstrators** are people who are marching or gathering somewhere to show their opposition to something or their support for something. ❑ *I saw the police using tear gas to try and break up a crowd of demonstrators.* **2** A **demonstrator** is a person who shows people how something works or how to do something. ❑ *a demonstrator in a department store*

de·mor·al·ize /dɪ'mɒrəlaɪz, AmE -'mɔːr-/ also **demoralise** VERB [T] (demoralizes, demoralizing, demoralized) If something **demoralizes** someone, it makes them lose so much confidence in what they are doing that they want to give up. ❑ *Clearly, one of the objectives was to demoralize the enemy troops in any way they can.*

de·mor·al·ized /dɪ'mɒrəlaɪzd, AmE -'mɔːr-/ ADJ ❑ *The Bismarck could now move only at a crawl and her crew were exhausted, hopeless, and utterly demoralized.*

de·mor·al·iz·ing /dɪ'mɒrəlaɪzɪŋ, AmE -'mɔːr-/ also **demoralising** ADJ If something is **demoralizing**, it makes you lose so much confidence in what you are doing that you want to give up. = disheartening ❑ *Losing their star player was another demoralizing blow for the team.*

de·mote /dɪ'məʊt/ VERB [T] (demotes, demoting, demoted) If someone **demotes** you, they give you a lower rank or a less important position than you already have, often as a punishment. ❑ *It's very difficult to demote somebody who has been filling in during maternity leave.*

de·mo·tion /dɪ'məʊʃən/ NOUN [C, U] (demotions) ❑ *He is seeking redress for what he alleges was an unfair demotion.*

den /den/ NOUN [C] (dens) **1** A **den** is the home of certain types of wild animals such as lions or foxes. **2** A **den** is a secret place where people meet, usually for a dishonest purpose. ❑ *I could provide you with the addresses of at least three illegal drinking dens.* **3** If you describe a place as a **den of** a particular type of bad or illegal behaviour, you mean that a lot of that type of behaviour goes on there. ❑ *this den of iniquity called New York City*

✪**de·ni·al** /dɪ'naɪəl/ NOUN [C, U] (denials) **1** [C, U] A **denial** of something is a statement that it is not true, does not exist, or did not happen. ≠ confirmation ❑ *It seems clear that despite official denials, differences of opinion lay behind the ambassador's decision to quit.* ❑ *The archbishop has issued a vigorous denial of these allegations.* **2** [U] (formal) The **denial of** something to someone is the act of refusing to let them have it. ❑ *the denial of visas to international relief workers* **3** [U] In psychology, **denial** is when a person cannot or will not accept an unpleasant truth. ❑ *With major life traumas, like losing a loved one, for instance, the mind's first reaction is denial.*

✪**de·note** /dɪ'nəʊt/ VERB [T] (denotes, denoting, denoted) (academic word, formal) **1** If one thing **denotes** another, it is a sign or indication of it. = indicate ❑ *Red eyes denote strain and fatigue.* ❑ *a sound which denotes that a photograph has been taken* **2** What a symbol **denotes** is what it represents. = represent ❑ *X denotes those not voting.*

de·nounce /dɪ'naʊns/ VERB [T] (denounces, denouncing, denounced) **1** If you **denounce** a person or an action, you criticize them severely and publicly because you feel strongly that they are wrong or evil. ❑ *German leaders all took the opportunity to denounce the attacks and plead for tolerance.* **2** If you **denounce** someone who has broken a rule or law, you report them to the authorities. ❑ *They were at the mercy of informers who might at any moment denounce them.*

✪**dense** /dens/ ADJ (denser, densest) **1** Something that is **dense** contains a lot of things or people in a small area. ❑ *Where Bucharest now stands, there once was a large, dense forest.* ❑ *an area of dense immigrant population* **2 Dense** fog or smoke is difficult to see through because it is very heavy and dark. = thick ❑ *A dense column of smoke rose several miles into the air.* **3** (technical) In science, a **dense** substance is very heavy in relation to its volume. ❑ *a small dense star* ❑ *The densest ocean water is the coldest and most saline.*

dense·ly /'densli/ ADV ❑ *Java is a densely populated island.*

✪**den·sity** /'densɪti/ NOUN [C, U] (densities) **1 Density** is the extent to which something is filled or covered with people or things. ❑ *The region has a very high population density.* ❑ *a law which restricts the density of housing* **2** (technical) In science, the **density** of a substance or object is the relation of its mass or weight to its volume. = mass, hardness ❑ *Jupiter's moon Io, whose density is 3.5 grams per cubic centimetre, is all rock.* ❑ *assessing the temperature, heat capacity, density and hardness of Mercury's surface*

dent /dent/ VERB, NOUN
VERB [T] (dents, denting, dented) **1** If you **dent** the surface of something, you make a hollow area in it by hitting or pressing it. ❑ *Its brass feet dented the carpet's thick pile.* **2** If something **dents** your confidence or your pride, it makes you realize that you are not as good or successful as you thought. ❑ *Record oil prices have dented consumer confidence.*
NOUN [C] (dents) A **dent** is a hollow in the surface of something which has been caused by hitting or pressing it. ❑ *I was convinced there was a dent in the bonnet which hadn't been there before.*

d

D

den·tal /'dentəl/ ADJ [dental + N] Dental is used to describe things that relate to teeth or to the care and treatment of teeth. ❑ *Good oral hygiene and regular dental care are important, whatever your age.*

den·tist /'dentɪst/ NOUN [C, SING] (**dentists**) **1** [C] A **dentist** is a medical practitioner who is qualified to examine and treat people's teeth. ❑ *Visit your dentist twice a year for a checkup.* **2** [SING] The **dentist** or the **dentist's** is used to refer to the surgery or clinic where a dentist works. ❑ *It's worse than being at the dentist's.*

✪**deny** ♦♦◇ /dɪ'naɪ/ VERB [T] (**denies, denying, denied**) (*academic word*) **1** When you **deny** something, you state that it is not true. = refute; ≠ confirm ❑ *She denied both accusations.* ❑ *The government has denied that the authorities have uncovered a plot to assassinate the president.* ❑ *They all denied ever having seen her.* **2** If you **deny** someone something that they need or want, you refuse to let them have it. = refuse ❑ *Two federal courts ruled that the military cannot deny prisoners access to lawyers.*

de·part /dɪ'pɑːt/ VERB [I, T] (**departs, departing, departed**) **1** [I, T] When something or someone **departs from** a place, they leave it and start a trip to another place. You can also say that someone **departs** a place. ❑ *Flight 43 will depart from Denver at 11:45 a.m. and arrive in Honolulu at 4:12 p.m.* ❑ *In the morning Mr McDonald departed for Sydney.* **2** [I] If you **depart from** a traditional, accepted, or agreed way of doing something, you do it in a different or unexpected way. = deviate ❑ *Why is it in this country that we have departed from good educational sense?*

✪**de·part·ment** ♦♦♦ /dɪ'pɑːtmənt/ NOUN [C] (**departments**) A **department** is one of the sections in an organization such as a government, business, or university. A **department** is also one of the sections in a large shop. = section, division ❑ *the US Department of Health and Human Services* ❑ *He moved to the sales department.* ❑ *the geography department of Moscow University*

✪**de·part·men·tal** /ˌdiːpɑːt'mentəl/ ADJ [departmental + N] **Departmental** is used to describe the activities, responsibilities, or possessions of a department in a government, company, or other organization. ❑ *The Secretary of Education is right to seek a bigger departmental budget.*

de·part·ment store NOUN [C] (**department stores**) A **department store** is a large shop which sells many different kinds of goods. ❑ *the dazzling window displays of world-famous department stores such as Macy's and Bloomingdales*

de·par·ture ♦◇◇ /dɪ'pɑːtʃə/ NOUN [C, U] (**departures**) **1** [C, U] **Departure** or a **departure** is the act of going away from somewhere. ❑ *the president's departure for Helsinki* ❑ *They hoped this would lead to the departure of all foreign forces from the country.* **2** [C] If someone does something different or unusual, you can refer to their action as a **departure**. = deviation ❑ *Such a move would have been a startling departure from tradition.*

✪**de·pend** ♦♦◇ /dɪ'pend/ VERB
[VERB] [I] (**depends, depending, depended**) **1** If you say that one thing **depends on** another, you mean that the first thing will be affected or determined by the second. ❑ *The cooking time needed depends on the size of the potato.* ❑ *The value of any tax relief depends upon individual circumstances.* **2** If you **depend on** someone or something, you need them in order to be able to survive physically, financially, or emotionally. = rely ❑ *He depended on his writing for his income.* ❑ *Butterfly survival depends on complex interactions between biological and physical factors in the environment.* **3** If you can **depend on** a person, organization, or law, you know that they will support you or help you when you need them. = rely ❑ *'You can depend on me,' Cross assured him.* **4** You use **depend** in expressions such as **it depends** to indicate that you cannot give a clear answer to a question because the answer will be affected or determined by other factors. ❑ *'But how long can you stay in the house?'—'I don't know. It depends.'*
[PHRASE] **depending on** You use **depending on** when you are saying that something varies according to the circumstances mentioned. ❑ *I tend to have a different answer, depending on the family.* ❑ *Individual vitamin needs vary, depending on size, age and height.*

✪**de·pend·able** /dɪ'pendəbəl/ ADJ (*approval*) If you say that someone or something is **dependable**, you approve of them because you feel that you can be sure that they will always act consistently or sensibly, or do what you need them to do. = reliable ❑ *He was a good friend, a dependable companion.*

✪**de·pend·ence** /dɪ'pendəns/ NOUN [U] **1** Your **dependence** on something or someone is your need for them in order to succeed or be able to survive. = reliance; ≠ independence ❑ *the city's traditional dependence on tourism* ❑ *Nottingham's efforts to encourage cycle use and reduce dependence on the car* **2** If you talk about drug **dependence** or alcohol **dependence**, you are referring to a situation where someone is addicted to drugs or is an alcoholic. = addiction ❑ *French doctors tend to regard dependence as a form of deep-rooted psychological disorder.* **3** You talk about the **dependence** of one thing **on** another when the first thing will be affected or determined by the second. ❑ *the dependence of politicians on rich donors to fund their increasingly expensive campaigns*

de·pend·en·cy /dɪ'pendənsi/ NOUN [C, U] (**dependencies**) **1** [C] A **dependency** is a country which is controlled by another country. ❑ *the tiny British dependency of Montserrat in the eastern Caribbean* **2** [U] You talk about someone's **dependency** when they have a deep emotional, physical, or financial need for a particular person or thing, especially one that you consider excessive or undesirable. ❑ *We saw his dependency on his mother and worried that he might not survive long if anything happened to her.* **3** [C, U] If you talk about alcohol **dependency** or chemical **dependency**, you are referring to a situation where someone is an alcoholic or is addicted to drugs. = addiction ❑ *In 1985, he began to show signs of alcohol and drug dependency.*

✪**de·pend·ent** /dɪ'pendənt/ also **dependant** ADJ, NOUN
[ADJ] **1** To be **dependent on** something or someone means to need them in order to succeed or be able to survive. = reliant; ≠ independent ❑ *The local economy is overwhelmingly dependent on oil and gas extraction.* ❑ *Just 26 per cent of households are married couples with dependent children.* **2** [V-LINK + dependent 'on/upon' N] If one thing is **dependent on** another, the first thing will be affected or determined by the second. = contingent ❑ *companies whose earnings are largely dependent on the performance of the Chinese economy*
[NOUN] [C] (**dependents**) (*formal*) Your **dependents** are the people you support financially, such as your children. ❑ *Companies with 200 or more workers must offer health benefits to employees and their dependents.*

✪**de·pict** /dɪ'pɪkt/ VERB [T] (**depicts, depicting, depicted**) **1** To **depict** someone or something means to show or represent them in a work of art such as a drawing or painting. ❑ *a gallery of pictures depicting Lee's most famous battles* ❑ *St Brigid is often depicted in art with a cow resting at her feet.* **2** To **depict** someone or something means to describe them or give an impression of them in writing. = portray, represent ❑ *Margaret Atwood's novel depicts a gloomy, futuristic America.* ❑ *The character was depicted as a compulsive shoplifter.*

✪**de·pic·tion** /dɪ'pɪkʃən/ NOUN [C, U] (**depictions**) A **depiction** of something is a picture or a written description of it. = portrayal, representation ❑ *The lecture will trace the depiction of horses from earliest times to the present day.* ❑ *the depiction of socialists as Utopian dreamers*

✪**de·plete** /dɪ'pliːt/ VERB [T] (**depletes, depleting, depleted**) (*formal*) To **deplete** a stock or amount of something means to reduce it. = reduce, diminish ❑ *substances that deplete the ozone layer* ❑ *Most native mammal species have been severely depleted.*

de·plet·ed /dɪ'pliːtɪd/ ADJ ❑ *Lee's worn and depleted army*

✪**de·ple·tion** /dɪ'pliːʃən/ NOUN [U] = reduction ❑ *the depletion of underground water supplies* ❑ *the problem of ozone depletion*

de·plor·able /dɪˈplɔːrəbəl/ ADJ (formal) If you say that something is **deplorable**, you think that it is very bad and unacceptable. ❑ Many of them live under deplorable conditions.

de·plore /dɪˈplɔː/ VERB [T] (**deplores, deploring, deplored**) (formal) If you say that you **deplore** something, you think it is very wrong or immoral. ❑ Muslim and Jewish leaders have issued statements deploring the violence and urging the United Nations to take action.

de·ploy /dɪˈplɔɪ/ VERB [T] (**deploys, deploying, deployed**) To **deploy** troops or military resources means to organize or position them so that they are ready to be used. ❑ The president said he had no intention of deploying ground troops.

de·ploy·ment /dɪˈplɔɪmənt/ NOUN [C, U] (**deployments**) The **deployment** of troops, resources, or equipment is the organization and positioning of them so that they are ready for quick action. ❑ the deployment of troops into townships

de·port /dɪˈpɔːt/ VERB [T] (**deports, deporting, deported**) If a government **deports** someone, usually someone who is not a citizen of that country, it sends them out of the country because they have committed a crime or because it believes they do not have the right to be there. ❑ a government decision earlier this month to deport all illegal immigrants
   de·por·ta·tion /ˌdiːpɔːˈteɪʃən/ NOUN [C, U] (**deportations**) ❑ thousands of migrants facing deportation

de·pose /dɪˈpəʊz/ VERB [T] (**deposes, deposing, deposed**) If a ruler or political leader **is deposed**, they are forced to give up their position. = oust ❑ Mr Ben Bella was deposed in a coup in 1965.

❖de·pos·it ◆◇◇ /dɪˈpɒzɪt/ NOUN, VERB
   NOUN [C] (**deposits**) **1** A **deposit** is a sum of money which is part of the full price of something, and which you pay when you agree to buy it. = down payment ❑ A £50 deposit is required when ordering, and the balance is due upon delivery. **2** A **deposit** is a sum of money which is in a bank account or savings account, especially a sum which will be left there for some time. **3** A **deposit** is an amount of a substance that has been left somewhere as a result of a chemical or geological process. = sediment, silt ❑ underground deposits of gold and diamonds **4** [usu sing] A **deposit** is a sum of money which you pay when you start renting something. The money is returned to you if you do not damage what you have rented. = security ❑ I put down a $500 security deposit for another apartment. **5** A **deposit** is a sum of money which you put into a bank account. ≠ withdrawal ❑ She told me I should make a deposit every week and they'd stamp my book. ❑ The initial deposit required to open an account is a minimum 100 dollars.
   VERB [T, PASSIVE] (**deposits, depositing, deposited**) **1** [T] If you **deposit** a sum of money, you put it into a bank account or savings account. ❑ The customer has to deposit a minimum of $100 monthly. **2** [T] To **deposit** someone or something somewhere means to put them or leave them there. = plant ❑ Mr Crenshaw deposited the boys and their suitcases on Mr Peck's lawn. **3** [T] If you **deposit** something somewhere, you put it where it will be safe until it is needed again. ❑ You are advised to deposit valuables in the hotel safe. **4** [PASSIVE] If a substance **is deposited** somewhere, it is left there as a result of a chemical or geological process. ❑ The phosphate was deposited by the decay of marine microorganisms.

de·pot /ˈdepəʊ, AmE ˈdiː-/ NOUN [C] (**depots**) **1** A **depot** is a place where large amounts of raw materials, equipment, arms, or other supplies are kept until they are needed. = warehouse ❑ food depots **2** (BrE) A **depot** is a large building or open area where buses or railway engines are kept when they are not being used.

❖de·press /dɪˈpres/ VERB [T] (**depresses, depressing, depressed**) (academic word) **1** If someone or something **depresses** you, they make you feel sad and disappointed. ❑ I must admit the state of the country depresses me. **2** If something **depresses** prices, wages, or figures, it causes them to become less. = reduce; ≠ increase ❑ The stronger US dollar depressed sales.

❖de·pressed /dɪˈprest/ ADJ **1** If you are **depressed**, you are sad and feel that you cannot enjoy anything, because your situation is so difficult and unpleasant. ❑ She's been very depressed and upset about this whole situation. **2** A **depressed** place or industry does not have enough business or employment to be successful. = run-down; ≠ thriving, booming ❑ Many states already have enterprise zones and legislation that encourage investment in depressed areas. ❑ The construction industry is no longer as depressed as it was.

de·press·ing /dɪˈpresɪŋ/ ADJ Something that is **depressing** makes you feel sad and disappointed. ❑ Yesterday's unemployment figures were as depressing as those of the previous 22 months.
   de·press·ing·ly /dɪˈpresɪŋli/ ADV ❑ It all sounded depressingly familiar to Janet.

❖de·pres·sion ◆◇◇ /dɪˈpreʃən/ NOUN [C, U] (**depressions**) (academic word) **1** [C, U] **Depression** is a mental state in which you are sad and feel that you cannot enjoy anything. = despair, melancholy ❑ Mr Thomas was suffering from depression. ❑ Any prolonged or severe depression should receive professional treatment. **2** [C] A **depression** is a time when there is very little economic activity, which causes a lot of unemployment and poverty. = slump, downturn, recession; ≠ recovery ❑ He never forgot the hardships he witnessed during the Great Depression of the 1930s. **3** [C] A **depression** in a surface is an area which is lower than the parts surrounding it. = hollow ❑ an area pockmarked by rain-filled depressions **4** [C] A **depression** is a mass of air that has a low pressure and that often causes rain. = low ❑ To the northwest lies a depression with clouds and rain.

dep·ri·va·tion /ˌdeprɪˈveɪʃən/ NOUN [C, U] (**deprivations**) If you suffer **deprivation**, you do not have or are prevented from having something that you want or need. ❑ Millions more suffer from serious sleep deprivation caused by long work hours.

de·prive /dɪˈpraɪv/ VERB [T] (**deprives, depriving, deprived**) If you **deprive** someone **of** something that they want or need, you take it away from them, or you prevent them from having it. ❑ They've been deprived of the fuel necessary to heat their homes.

❖de·prived /dɪˈpraɪvd/ ADJ **Deprived** people or people from **deprived** areas do not have the things that people consider to be essential in life, for example, acceptable living conditions or education. = underprivileged, destitute; ≠ privileged ❑ probably the most severely deprived children in the country ❑ the problems associated with life in a deprived inner city area

❖depth ◆◇◇ /depθ/ NOUN
   NOUN [C, U, PL] (**depths**) **1** [C, U] The **depth** of something such as a river or hole is the distance downward from its top surface, or between its upper and lower surfaces. ❑ The depth of the shaft is 520 yards. ❑ The smaller lake ranges from five to fourteen feet in depth. ❑ The depth of a standard straight valance is usually about 12 inches. **2** [C, U] The **depth** of something such as a cupboard or drawer is the distance between its front surface and its back. **3** [C, U] If an emotion is very strongly or intensely felt, you can talk about its **depth**. = strength ❑ I am well aware of the depth of feeling that exists in Ontario. **4** [U] The **depth** of a situation is its extent and seriousness. = severity ❑ The country's leadership had underestimated the depth of the crisis. **5** [U] The **depth** of someone's knowledge is the great amount that they know. ❑ We felt at home with her and were impressed with the depth of her knowledge. **6** [PL] (literary) The **depths** are places that are a long way below the surface of the sea or earth. ❑ Leaves, brown with long immersion, rose to the surface and vanished back into the depths. **7** [PL] If you talk about the **depths** of an area, you mean the parts of it which are very far from the edge. ❑ the depths of the countryside **8** [PL] If you are **in the depths of** an unpleasant emotion, you feel that emotion very strongly. ❑ I was in the depths of despair when the baby was terribly sick every day, and was losing weight.
   PHRASES **in depth** If you deal with a subject **in depth**, you deal with it very thoroughly and consider all the

D

aspects of it. ❑ *We will discuss these three areas in depth.*
out of one's depth ◼ If you say that someone is **out of**
their **depth**, you mean that they are in a situation that is
much too difficult for them to be able to cope with it.
❑ *Mr Gibson is clearly intellectually out of his depth.* ◻ If you
are **out of** your **depth**, you are in water that is deeper than
you are tall, with the result that you cannot stand up with
your head above water. ❑ *Somehow I got out of my depth in
the pool.*

dep•u•ty ◆◆◇ /ˈdepjʊti/ NOUN [C] (**deputies**) ◼ A **deputy**
is the second most important person in an organization
such as a business or government department. Someone's
deputy often acts on their behalf when they are not there.
❑ *Jack Lang, France's minister for culture, and his deputy,
Catherine Tasca* ◻ In some legislatures, the elected
members are called **deputies**. ❑ *The president appealed to
deputies to approve the plan quickly.* ◼ A **deputy** is a person
appointed to act on another person's behalf. ❑ *His brother
was acting as his deputy in America.*

de•ranged /dɪˈreɪndʒd/ ADJ Someone who is **deranged**
behaves in a wild and uncontrolled way, often as a result
of mental illness. ❑ *Three years ago today a deranged man
shot and killed 14 people in the main square.*

de•regu•la•tion /ˌdiːˌregjʊˈleɪʃən/ NOUN [U] (*business*)
Deregulation is the removal of controls and restrictions in
a particular area of business or trade. ❑ *Since deregulation,
banks are permitted to set their own interest rates.*

der•elict /ˈderɪlɪkt/ ADJ, NOUN
ADJ A place or building that is **derelict** is empty and in a
bad state of repair because it has not been used or lived in
for a long time. ❑ *Her body was found dumped in a derelict
warehouse less than a mile from her home.*
NOUN [C] (**derelicts**) (*formal*) A **derelict** is a person who has
no home or job and who has to live on the streets.
= vagrant ❑ *I had never seen so many derelicts in one place.*

de•ride /dɪˈraɪd/ VERB [T] (**derides, deriding, derided**)
(*formal*) If you **deride** someone or something, you say that
they are stupid or have no value. = ridicule ❑ *Critics
derided the move as too little, too late.*

de•ri•sion /dɪˈrɪʒən/ NOUN [U] If you treat someone or
something with **derision**, you express contempt for them.
= disdain ❑ *He tried to calm them, but was greeted with
shouts of derision.*

de•ri•sive /dɪˈraɪsɪv/ ADJ A **derisive** noise, expression, or
remark expresses contempt. = contemptuous ❑ *There
was a short, derisive laugh.*

◐de•riva•tive /dɪˈrɪvətɪv/ NOUN [C] (**derivatives**) A
derivative is something which has been developed or
obtained from something else. = by-product ❑ *a
poppy-seed derivative similar to heroin* ❑ *synthetic derivatives of
male hormones*

◐de•rive /dɪˈraɪv/ VERB [T, I] (**derives, deriving, derived**)
(*academic word*) ◼ [T] (*formal*) If you **derive** something such
as pleasure or benefit **from** a person or from something,
you get it from them. ❑ *Mr Ying is one of those happy people
who derive pleasure from helping others.* ◻ [I, T] If you say
that something such as a word or feeling **derives** or is
derived from something else, you mean that it comes
from that thing. = originate ❑ *The name Anastasia is
derived from a Greek word meaning 'of the resurrection'.*
❑ *Some modern drugs are derived from plant medicines.* ❑ *The
word Easter derives from Eostre, the pagan goddess of spring.*

de•roga•tory /dɪˈrɒgətri, AmE -tɔːri/ ADJ If you make a
derogatory remark or comment about someone or
something, you express your low opinion of them. ❑ *He
refused to withdraw derogatory remarks made about his boss.*

de•scend /dɪˈsend/ VERB [I, T] (**descends, descending,
descended**) ◼ [I, T] (*formal*) If you **descend** or if you
descend a staircase, you move downwards from a higher
to a lower level. = go down ❑ *Things are cooler and more
damp as we descend to the cellar.* ◻ [I] If a large group of
people arrive to see you, especially if their visit is
unexpected or causes you a lot of work, you can say that
they **have descended on** you. ❑ *Some 3,000 city officials will
descend on Capitol Hill on Tuesday to lobby for more money.*
◼ [I] When you want to emphasize that the situation that

someone is entering is very bad, you can say that they **are
descending into** that situation. = fall, slide ❑ *He was
ultimately overthrown and the country descended into chaos.*
◼ [I] If you say that someone **descends to** behaviour
which you consider unacceptable, you are expressing your
disapproval of the fact that they do it. = stoop, sink
❑ *We're not going to descend to such methods.*

de•scend•ant /dɪˈsendənt/ NOUN [C] (**descendants**)
◼ Someone's **descendants** are the people in later
generations who are related to them. ❑ *They are
descendants of the original English and Scottish settlers.*
◻ Something modern which developed from an older
thing can be called a **descendant of** it. ❑ *His design was a
descendant of a 1956 device.*

de•scent /dɪˈsent/ NOUN [C, U, SING] (**descents**) ◼ [C, U] A
descent is a movement from a higher to a lower level or
position. ❑ *Sixteen of the youngsters set off for help, but during
the descent three collapsed in the cold and rain.* ◻ [C] A
descent is a surface that slopes downwards, for example,
the side of a steep hill. ❑ *On the descents, cyclists spin past
cars, freewheeling downhill at tremendous speed.* ◼ [SING]
When you want to emphasize that a situation becomes
very bad, you can talk about someone's or something's
descent into that situation. = decline ❑ *his swift descent
from respected academic to struggling small businessman* ◼ [U]
(*formal*) You use **descent** to talk about a person's family
background, for example, their nationality or social status.
= origin, ancestry ❑ *All the contributors were of African descent.*

◐de•scribe /dɪˈskraɪb/ VERB [T] (**describes,
describing, described**) ◼ If you **describe** a person, object,
event, or situation, you say what they are like or what
happened. = relate, express, depict ❑ *We asked her to
describe what kind of things she did in her spare time.* ❑ *She
read a poem by Carver which describes their life together.* ◻ If
a person **describes** someone or something **as** a particular
thing, he or she believes that they are that thing and says
so. ❑ *He described it as an extraordinarily tangled and
complicated tale.* ❑ *Even his closest allies describe him as
forceful, aggressive, and determined.*

◐de•scrip•tion ◆◇◇ /dɪˈskrɪpʃən/ NOUN [C, U, SING]
(**descriptions**) ◼ [C, U] A **description** of someone or
something is an account which explains what they are or
what they look like. = account, representation, depiction
❑ *Police have issued a description of the man who was aged
between fifty and sixty.* ❑ *The paper provides a detailed
description of how to create human embryos by cloning.*
◻ [SING] If something is **of** a particular **description**, it
belongs to the general class of items that are mentioned.
= kind, type ❑ *Events of this description occurred daily.* ◼ [U]
You can say that something is **beyond description**, or that
it **defies description**, to emphasize that it is very unusual,
impressive, terrible, or extreme. ❑ *His face is weary beyond
description.*

de•scrip•tive /dɪˈskrɪptɪv/ ADJ Descriptive language or
writing indicates what someone or something is like.
❑ *The group adopted the simpler, more descriptive title of Angina
Support Group.*

des•ecrate /ˈdesɪkreɪt/ VERB [T] (**desecrates, desecrating,
desecrated**) If someone **desecrates** something which is
considered to be holy or very special, they deliberately
damage or insult it. ❑ *She shouldn't have desecrated the
picture of a religious leader.*

des•ecra•tion /ˌdesɪˈkreɪʃən/ NOUN [U] ❑ *The whole area has
been shocked by the desecration of the cemetery.*

◐des•ert ◆◇◇ NOUN, VERB
NOUN /ˈdezət/ [C, U] (**deserts**) A **desert** is a large area of
land, usually in a hot region, where there is almost no
water, rain, trees, or plants. ❑ *the Sahara Desert* ❑ *The
vehicles have been modified to suit conditions in the desert.*
PHRASE /dɪˈzɜːts/ **get your just deserts** (*feelings*) If you
say that someone got their **just deserts**, you mean that
they deserved the unpleasant things that happened to
them, because they did something bad. ❑ *At the end of the
book the child's true identity is discovered, and the bad guys get
their just deserts.*
VERB /dɪˈzɜːt/ [T, I] (**deserts, deserting, deserted**) ◼ [T] If
people or animals **desert** a place, they leave it and it

becomes empty. ❑ *Poor farmers are deserting their parched farm fields and coming here looking for jobs.* **2** [T] If someone **deserts** you, they go away and leave you, and no longer help or support you. ❑ *Mrs Roding's husband deserted her years ago.* **3** [I, T] If you **desert** something that you support, use, or are involved with, you stop supporting it, using it, or being involved with it. ❑ *The sport is being written off as boring and predictable and the fans are deserting in droves.* ❑ *He was pained to see many youngsters deserting kibbutz life.* **4** [I, T] If someone **deserts**, or **deserts** a job, especially a job in the armed forces, they leave that job without permission. ❑ *He was a second lieutenant in the army until he deserted.* ❑ *He deserted from army intelligence last month.*

de·sert·ed /dɪˈzɜːtɪd/ ADJ = empty ❑ *She led them into a deserted sidestreet.*

de·ser·tion /dɪˈzɜːʃən/ NOUN [C, U] (**desertions**) **1** *It was a long time since she'd referred to her father's desertion.* **2** *They blamed his proposal for much of the mass desertion by the Republican electorate.*

de·serve ♦◇◇ /dɪˈzɜːv/ VERB [T] (**deserves, deserving, deserved**) If you say that a person or thing **deserves** something, you mean that they should have it or receive it because of their actions or qualities. ❑ *Government officials clearly deserve some of the blame as well.* ❑ *These people deserve to make more than the minimum wage.*

de·serv·ing /dɪˈzɜːvɪŋ/ ADJ If you describe a person, organization, or cause as **deserving**, you mean that you think they should be helped. ❑ *The money saved could be used for more deserving causes.*

✪ **de·sign** ♦♦♦ /dɪˈzaɪn/ VERB, NOUN (*academic word*)
VERB [T, PASSIVE] (**designs, designing, designed**) **1** [T] When someone **designs** a garment, building, machine, or other object, they plan it and make a detailed drawing of it from which it can be built or made. ❑ *They wanted to design a machine that was both attractive and practical.* ❑ *men wearing specially designed boots* **2** [T] When someone **designs** a survey, policy, or system, they plan it and prepare it, and decide on all the details of it. ❑ *We may be able to design a course to suit your particular needs.* ❑ *A number of very well designed studies have been undertaken.* **3** [PASSIVE] If something **is designed** for a particular purpose, it is intended for that purpose. = intend ❑ *This project is designed to help homeless people.* ❑ *It's not designed for anyone under age eighteen.*
NOUN [U, C] (**designs**) **1** [U] **Design** is the process and art of planning and making detailed drawings of something. ❑ *He was a born mechanic with a flair for design.* **2** [U] The **design** of something is the way in which it has been planned and made. ❑ *a new design of clock* **3** [C] A **design** is a drawing which someone produces to show how they would like something to be built or made. = plan ❑ *When Bernardello asked them to build him a home, they drew up the design in a week.* **4** [C] A **design** is a pattern of lines, flowers, or shapes which is used to decorate something. = motif ❑ *Many pictures have been based on simple geometric designs.*

des·ig·nate VERB, ADJ
VERB /ˈdezɪɡneɪt/ [T] (**designates, designating, designated**) **1** When you **designate** someone or something **as** a particular thing, you formally give them that description or name. ❑ *a man interviewed in one of our studies whom we shall designate as E* ❑ *There are efforts under way to designate the bridge a historic landmark.* **2** If something **is designated for** a particular purpose, it is set aside for that purpose. ❑ *Some of the rooms were designated as offices.* **3** When you **designate** someone **as** something, you formally choose them to do that particular job. ❑ *Designate someone as the spokesperson.*
ADJ /ˈdezɪɡnət/ [N + designate] **Designate** is used to describe someone who has been formally chosen to do a particular job, but has not yet started doing it. ❑ *Japan's prime minister-designate is completing his cabinet today.*

de·sign·er ♦◇◇ /dɪˈzaɪnə/ NOUN, ADJ
NOUN [C] (**designers**) A **designer** is a person whose job is to design things by making drawings of them. ❑ *Carolyne is a fashion designer.*
ADJ **1** [designer + N] **Designer** clothes or **designer** labels are expensive, fashionable clothes made by a famous designer, rather than being made in large quantities in a factory. ❑ *He wears designer clothes and drives an antique car.* **2** [designer + N] (*informal*) You can use **designer** to describe things that are worn or bought because they are fashionable. ❑ *She sat up and removed her designer sunglasses.*

de·sir·able /dɪˈzaɪərəbəl/ ADJ **1** Something that is **desirable** is worth having or doing because it is useful, necessary, or popular. ❑ *Prolonged negotiation was not desirable.* **2** Someone who is **desirable** is considered to be sexually attractive. ❑ *the young women of his own age whom his classmates thought most desirable*

de·sir·abil·ity /dɪˌzaɪərəˈbɪlɪti/ NOUN [U] **1** *the desirability of democratic reform* **2** *He had not at all overrated Veronica's desirability.*

de·sire ♦♦◇ /dɪˈzaɪə/ NOUN, VERB
NOUN [C, U] (**desires**) **1** [C] A **desire** is a strong wish to do or have something. ❑ *I had a strong desire to help and care for people.* **2** [U] **Desire** for someone is a strong feeling of wanting to have sex with them. ❑ *It's common to lose your sexual desire when you have your first child.*
VERB [T] (**desires, desiring, desired**) (*formal*) If you **desire** something, you want it. ❑ *She had remarried and desired a child with her new husband.*

de·sired /dɪˈzaɪəd/ ADJ ❑ *You may find that just threatening this course of action will produce the desired effect.*

desk ♦♦◇ /desk/ NOUN [C, SING] (**desks**) **1** [C] A **desk** is a table, often with drawers, which you sit at to write or work. **2** [SING] The place in a hotel, hospital, airport, or other building where you check in or obtain information is referred to as a particular **desk**. ❑ *I told the girl at the reception desk that I was terribly sorry, but I was half an hour late.* **3** [SING] A particular department of a broadcasting company, or of a newspaper or magazine company, can be referred to as a particular **desk**. ❑ *Let our news desk know as quickly as possible.*

desk·top /ˈdesktɒp/ also **desk-top** ADJ, NOUN
ADJ [desktop + N] **Desktop** computers are a convenient size for using on a desk or table, but are not designed to be portable. ❑ *When launched, the Macintosh was the smallest desktop computer ever produced.*
NOUN [C] (**desktops**) **1** A **desktop** is a desktop computer. ❑ *We have stopped making desktops because no one is making money from them.* **2** The **desktop** of a computer is the display of icons that you see on the screen when the computer is ready to use. ❑ *A dramatic full-sized lightning bolt will then fill your screen's desktop.*

deso·late /ˈdesələt/ ADJ **1** A **desolate** place is empty of people and lacking in comfort. = bleak ❑ *a desolate landscape of flat green fields* **2** (*literary*) If someone is **desolate**, they feel very sad, alone, and without hope. ❑ *He was desolate without her.*

deso·la·tion /ˌdesəˈleɪʃən/ NOUN [U] **1** **Desolation** is a feeling of great unhappiness and hopelessness. = misery ❑ *Kozelek expresses his sense of desolation absolutely without self-pity.* **2** If you refer to **desolation** in a place, you mean that it is empty and frightening, for example, because it has been destroyed by a violent force or army. = devastation ❑ *We looked out upon a scene of desolation and ruin.*

des·pair /dɪˈspeə/ NOUN, VERB
NOUN [U] **Despair** is the feeling that everything is wrong and that nothing will improve. ❑ *I looked at my wife in despair.*
VERB [I] (**despairs, despairing, despaired**) **1** If you **despair**, you feel that everything is wrong and that nothing will improve. ❑ *'Oh, I despair sometimes,' he says in mock sorrow.* **2** If you **despair of** something, you feel that there is no hope that it will happen or improve. If you **despair of** someone, you feel that there is no hope that they will improve. ❑ *He wished to earn a living through writing but despaired of doing so.*

des·patch /dɪˈspætʃ/ (*BrE*) → See dispatch

des·per·ate ♦◇◇ /ˈdespərət/ ADJ **1** If you are **desperate**, you are in such a bad situation that you are willing to try

d

D

anything to change it. □ *Troops are needed to help get food into Kosovo where people are in desperate need.* **2** [V-LINK + desperate] If you are **desperate for** something or **desperate to** do something, you want or need it very much indeed. □ *They'd been married nearly four years and June was desperate to start a family.* **3** A **desperate** situation is very difficult, serious, or dangerous. = dire □ *India's United Nations ambassador said the situation is desperate.*

des·per·ate·ly /ˈdespərətli/ ADV **1** [desperately with V] □ *Thousands are desperately trying to leave their battered homes and villages.* **2** *He was a boy who desperately needed affection.*

des·pe·ra·tion /ˌdespəˈreɪʃən/ NOUN [U] **Desperation** is the feeling that you have when you are in such a bad situation that you will try anything to change it. □ *This feeling of desperation and helplessness was common to most of the refugees.*

des·pise /dɪˈspaɪz/ VERB [T] (**despises, despising, despised**) If you **despise** something or someone, you dislike them and have a very low opinion of them. □ *I can never, ever forgive him. I despise him.*

✪**de·spite** ♦♦◇ /dɪˈspaɪt/ PREP (*academic word*) **1** [despite + N/-ING] You use **despite** to introduce a fact which makes the other part of the sentence surprising. = in spite of □ *She has been under house arrest for most of the past decade, despite efforts by the United Nations to have her released.* □ *Despite being the world's richest nation, the USA is also one of the most religious.* **2** You use **despite** to introduce an idea that appears to contradict your main statement, without suggesting that this idea is true or that you believe it. □ *She told friends she will stand by her husband, despite reports that he sent another woman love notes.*

USAGE NOTE

despite

Despite means the same as 'in spite of'. Do not use 'despite of'.

Despite *their different ages, they were close friends.*

---

des·sert /dɪˈzɜːt/ NOUN [C, U] (**desserts**) **Dessert** is something sweet, such as fruit, pastry, or ice cream, that you eat at the end of a meal. □ *She had homemade ice cream for dessert.*

de·sta·bi·lize /diːˈsteɪbəlaɪz/ also **destabilise** VERB [T] (**destabilizes, destabilizing, destabilized**) To **destabilize** something such as a country or government means to create a situation which reduces its power or influence. □ *Their sole aim is to destabilize the Indian government.*

✪**des·ti·na·tion** /ˌdestɪˈneɪʃən/ NOUN [C] (**destinations**) The **destination** of someone or something is the place to which they are going or being sent. ≠ origin □ *Ellis Island has become one of America's most popular tourist destinations.* □ *Only half of the emergency supplies have reached their destination.*

des·tined /ˈdestɪnd/ ADJ **1** If something is **destined to** happen or if someone is **destined to** behave in a particular way, that thing seems certain to happen or be done. □ *Any economic strategy based on a weak dollar is destined to fail.* **2** [V-LINK + destined 'for' N] If someone is **destined for** a particular place, or if goods are **destined for** a particular place, they are travelling towards that place or will be sent to that place. = bound □ *products destined for Saudi Arabia*

des·ti·ny /ˈdestɪni/ NOUN [C, U] (**destinies**) **1** [C] A person's **destiny** is everything that happens to them during their life, including what will happen in the future, especially when it is considered to be controlled by someone or something else. = fate □ *We are masters of our own destiny.* **2** [U] **Destiny** is the force which some people believe controls the things that happen to you in your life. = fate □ *Is it destiny that brings people together, or is it accident?*

des·ti·tute /ˈdestɪtjuːt, AmE -tuːt/ ADJ (*formal*) Someone who is **destitute** has no money or possessions. □ *destitute children who live on the streets*

✪**de·stroy** ♦♦◇ /dɪˈstrɔɪ/ VERB [T] (**destroys, destroying, destroyed**) **1** To **destroy** something means to cause so

much damage to it that it is completely ruined or does not exist any more. = ruin □ *That's a sure recipe for destroying the economy and creating chaos.* □ *No one was injured in the explosion, but the building was completely destroyed.* **2** To **destroy** someone means to ruin their life or to make their situation impossible to bear. □ *If I was younger or more naive, the criticism would have destroyed me.* **3** If an animal **is destroyed**, it is killed, either because it is ill or because it is dangerous. = put down □ *Lindsay was unhurt but the horse had to be destroyed.*

WHICH WORD?

destroy, spoil, or ruin?

If you **destroy** something, you damage it so completely that it can no longer be used.

□ *Several apartment buildings were **destroyed** in the explosion.*

□ *I **destroyed** the letter as soon as I had read it.*

If someone or something prevents an experience from being enjoyable, you do not say that they 'destroy' the experience. You say that they **spoil** it or **ruin** it. **Ruin** is stronger than **spoil**.

□ *I'm sorry if I've **spoiled** your evening.*

□ *The weather had completely **ruined** their day.*

✪**de·struc·tion** ♦◇◇ /dɪˈstrʌkʃən/ NOUN [U] **Destruction** is the act of destroying something, or the state of being destroyed. □ *an international agreement aimed at halting the destruction of the ozone layer* □ *weapons of mass destruction*

de·struc·tive /dɪˈstrʌktɪv/ ADJ Something that is **destructive** causes or is capable of causing great damage, harm, or injury. □ *the awesome destructive power of nuclear weapons*

de·tach /dɪˈtætʃ/ VERB [I, T] (**detaches, detaching, detached**) **1** [I, T] (*formal*) If you **detach** one thing **from** another that it is attached to, you remove it. If one thing **detaches from** another, it becomes separated from it. □ *Detach the white part of the application form and keep it for reference only.* □ *They clambered back under the falls to detach the raft from a jagged rock.* **2** [T] If you **detach yourself from** something, you become less involved in it or less concerned about it than you used to be. □ *It helps them detach themselves from their problems and become more objective.*

de·tached /dɪˈtætʃt/ ADJ **1** Someone who is **detached** is not personally involved in something or has no emotional interest in it. □ *He tries to remain emotionally detached from the prisoners, but fails.* **2** A **detached** building is one that is not joined to any other building. □ *a house on the corner with a detached garage*

✪**de·tail** ♦♦◇ /ˈdiːteɪl/ NOUN, VERB

NOUN [C, PL, U] (**details**) **1** [C] The **details of** something are its individual features or elements. = information, facts, specifics; ≠ generalization □ *The details of the plan are still being worked out.* □ *No details of the discussions have been given.* **2** [C] A **detail** is a minor point or aspect of something, as opposed to the central ones. □ *Only minor details now remain to be settled.* **3** [PL] **Details** about someone or something are facts or pieces of information about them. □ *See the bottom of this page for details of how to apply for this exciting offer.* □ *Full details will be announced soon.* **4** [U] You can refer to the small features of something which are often not noticed as **detail**. □ *We like his attention to detail and his enthusiasm.* **5** [C] [oft detail 'of' N] A **detail** of people such as soldiers or prisoners is a small group of them who have been given a special task to carry out. □ *a sergeant with a detail of four men*

PHRASES **go into detail** If someone does not **go into detail** about a subject, or does not **go into the details**, they mention it without explaining it fully or properly. □ *He doesn't wish to go into detail about all the events of those days.* **in detail** If you examine or discuss something **in detail**, you do it thoroughly and carefully. □ *We examine the wording in detail before deciding on the final text.*

VERB [T] (**details, detailing, detailed**) If you **detail** things, you list them or give information about them. □ *The report detailed the human rights abuses committed during the war.*

de·tailed ♦◇◇ /'diːteɪld, *AmE* dɪ'teɪld/ ADJ A detailed report or plan contains a lot of details. ❑ *Yesterday's letter contains a detailed account of the decisions.*

de·tain /dɪ'teɪn/ VERB [T] (detains, detaining, detained) (*formal*) **1** When people such as the police **detain** someone, they keep them in a place under their control. ❑ *Police have detained two suspects in connection with the attack.* **2** To **detain** someone means to delay them, for example, by talking to them. ❑ *Millson stood up. 'Thank you. We won't detain you any further, Mrs Stebbing.'*

✪**de·tect** /dɪ'tekt/ VERB [T] (detects, detecting, detected) (*academic word*) **1** To **detect** something means to find it or discover that it is present somewhere by using equipment or making an investigation. = discover, reveal; ≠ miss, overlook ❑ *a sensitive piece of equipment used to detect radiation* ❑ *Most skin cancers can be cured if detected and treated early.* **2** If you **detect** something, you notice it or sense it, even though it is not very obvious. = sense ❑ *Arnold could detect a certain sadness in the old man's face.*

✪**de·tec·tion** /dɪ'tekʃən/ NOUN [U] **Detection** is the act of noticing or sensing something. = discovery ❑ *the early detection of breast cancer*

de·tec·tive ♦◇◇ /dɪ'tektɪv/ NOUN, ADJ
NOUN [c] (detectives) A **detective** is someone whose job is to discover what has happened in a crime or other situation and to find the people involved. Some detectives work in the police force and others work privately. ❑ *Now detectives are appealing for witnesses who may have seen anything suspicious last night.*
ADJ [detective + N] A **detective** novel or story is one in which a detective tries to solve a crime. ❑ *Arthur Conan Doyle's classic detective novel*

✪**de·tec·tor** /dɪ'tektə/ NOUN [c] (detectors) A **detector** is an instrument which is used to discover that something is present somewhere, or to measure how much of something there is. ❑ *a metal detector* ❑ *fire alarms and smoke detectors* ❑ *infra-red motion detectors*

de·ten·tion /dɪ'tenʃən/ NOUN [U, c] (detentions) **1** [U] **Detention** is when someone is arrested or put into prison. ❑ *the detention without trial of government critics* **2** [c, U] **Detention** is a punishment for students who misbehave, who are made to stay at school after the other students have gone home. ❑ *The teacher kept the boys in detention after school.*

✪**de·ter** /dɪ'tɜː/ VERB [T] (deters, deterring, deterred) To **deter** someone **from** doing something means to make them not want to do it or continue doing it. = discourage; ≠ encourage ❑ *Supporters of the death penalty argue that it would deter criminals from carrying guns.* ❑ *Arrests and jail sentences have done nothing to deter the protesters.* ❑ *Far from being deterred by the regional financial crisis, the company plans to expand into Asia.*

de·ter·gent /dɪ'tɜːdʒənt/ NOUN [c, U] (detergents) **Detergent** is a chemical substance, usually in the form of a powder or liquid, which is used for washing things such as clothes or dishes. ❑ *a brand of detergent*

✪**de·te·rio·rate** /dɪ'tɪəriəreɪt/ VERB [i] (deteriorates, deteriorating, deteriorated) If something **deteriorates**, it becomes worse in some way. = worsen ❑ *There are fears that the situation might deteriorate into full-scale war.* ❑ *Relations between the two countries steadily deteriorated.* ❑ *Surface transport has become less and less viable with deteriorating road conditions.*

✪**de·te·rio·ra·tion** /dɪˌtɪəriə'reɪʃən/ NOUN [U] = decline, decay, degeneration; ≠ improvement ❑ *concern about the rapid deterioration in relations between the two countries* ❑ *the slow steady deterioration of a patient with Alzheimer's disease*

✪**de·ter·mi·na·tion** /dɪˌtɜːmɪ'neɪʃən/ NOUN [U] **1** **Determination** is the quality that you show when you have decided to do something and you will not let anything stop you. ❑ *Everyone concerned acted with great courage and determination.* **2** (*formal*) The **determination** of the nature of a thing or event is the way that particular factors cause it to be the way it is. ❑ *the gene which is responsible for male sex determination* ❑ *a tool which can be used to help in the determination of a pay structure* **3** [usu sing]

The **determination** of something is the act of deciding about it or settling it. ❑ *We must take into our own hands the determination of our future.*

✪**de·ter·mine** ♦◇◇ /dɪ'tɜːmɪn/ VERB [T] (determines, determining, determined) **1** (*formal*) If a particular factor **determines** the nature of a thing or event, it causes it to be of a particular kind. = dictate, decide ❑ *The size of the chicken pieces will determine the cooking time.* ❑ *What determines whether you are a career success or a failure?* **2** (*formal*) To **determine** a fact means to discover it as a result of investigation. = identify ❑ *The investigation will determine what really happened.* ❑ *Experts say testing needs to be done on each contaminant to determine the long-term effects on humans.* ❑ *Science has determined that the risk is very small.* **3** If you **determine** something, you decide about it or settle it. ❑ *The Baltic people have a right to determine their own future.* **4** (*formal*) If you **determine to** do something, you make a firm decision to do it. ❑ *He determined to rescue his two countrymen.*

de·ter·mined ♦◇◇ /dɪ'tɜːmɪnd/ ADJ If you are **determined to** do something, you have made a firm decision to do it and will not let anything stop you. ❑ *His enemies are determined to ruin him.*
de·ter·mined·ly /dɪ'tɜːmɪndli/ ADV = resolutely ❑ *She shook her head, determinedly.*

✪**de·ter·rent** /dɪ'terənt, *AmE* -'tɜːr-/ NOUN [c] (deterrents) **1** A **deterrent** is something that prevents people from doing something by making them afraid of what will happen to them if they do it. = obstacle; ≠ incentive ❑ *They seriously believe that capital punishment is a deterrent.* ❑ *The tough new law should act as a deterrent.* **2** A **deterrent** is a weapon or set of weapons designed to prevent enemies from attacking by making them afraid to do so. ❑ *The idea of building a nuclear deterrent is completely off the political agenda.*

de·test /dɪ'test/ VERB [T] (detests, detesting, detested) If you **detest** someone or something, you dislike them very much. = loathe ❑ *My mother detested him.*

deto·nate /'detəneɪt/ VERB [i, T] (detonates, detonating, detonated) If someone **detonates** a device such as a bomb, or if it **detonates**, it explodes. ❑ *France is expected to detonate its first nuclear device in the next few days.*

de·tour /'diːtʊə/ NOUN [c] (detours) If you make a **detour** on a trip, you go by a route which is not the shortest way, because you want to avoid something such as a traffic jam, or because there is something you want to do on the way. ❑ *He did not take the direct route to his home, but made a detour around the outskirts of the city.*

de·tract /dɪ'trækt/ VERB [i] (detracts, detracting, detracted) If one thing **detracts from** another, it makes it seem less good or impressive. ❑ *They feared that the publicity surrounding him would detract from their own election campaigns.*

det·ri·ment /'detrɪmənt/ NOUN
PHRASES **to the detriment of** (*formal*) If something happens **to the detriment of** something or **to** a person's **detriment**, it causes harm or damage to them. ❑ *These tests will give too much importance to written exams to the detriment of other skills.*
without detriment to (*formal*) If something happens **without detriment to** a person or thing, it does not harm or damage them. ❑ *These difficulties have been overcome without detriment to performance.*

det·ri·men·tal /ˌdetrɪ'mentəl/ ADJ Something that is **detrimental to** something else has a harmful or damaging effect on it. ❑ *Many foods are suspected of being detrimental to health because of the chemicals and additives they contain.*

de·value /ˌdiː'væljuː/ VERB [T] (devalues, devaluing, devalued) **1** To **devalue** something means to cause it to be thought less impressive or less deserving of respect. ❑ *They spread tales about her in an attempt to devalue her work.* **2** To **devalue** the currency of a country means to reduce its value in relation to other currencies. ❑ *India has devalued the rupee by about eleven per cent.*
de·valu·a·tion /ˌdiːvæljuˈeɪʃən/ NOUN [c, U] (devaluations) ❑ *It will lead to devaluation of a number of currencies.*

d

dev·as·tate /'devəsteɪt/ VERB [T] (**devastates**, **devastating**, **devastated**) If something **devastates** an area or a place, it damages it very badly or destroys it totally. = ravage, wreck ❑ *The tsunami devastated parts of Indonesia and other countries in the region.*

dev·as·tat·ed /'devəsteɪtɪd/ ADJ [V-LINK + devastated] If you are **devastated** by something, you are very shocked and upset by it. ❑ *Teresa was devastated, her dreams shattered.*

dev·as·tat·ing /'devəsteɪtɪŋ/ ADJ (*emphasis*) **1** If you describe something as **devastating**, you are emphasizing that it is very harmful or damaging. ❑ *Affairs do have a devastating effect on marriages.* **2** You can use **devastating** to emphasize that something is very shocking, upsetting, or terrible. ❑ *The diagnosis was devastating. She had cancer.* **3** You can use **devastating** to emphasize that something or someone is very impressive. ❑ *He returned to his best with a devastating display of galloping and jumping.*

dev·as·ta·tion /,devə'steɪʃən/ NOUN [U] **Devastation** is severe and widespread destruction or damage. ❑ *The war brought massive devastation and loss of life to the region.*

✪**de·vel·op** ◆◆◆ /dɪ'veləp/ VERB [I, T] (**develops**, **developing**, **developed**) **1** [I] When something **develops**, it grows or changes over a period of time and usually becomes more advanced, complete, or severe. = establish, progress, improve ❑ *It's hard to say at this stage how the market will develop.* ❑ *These clashes could develop into open warfare.* ❑ *Society begins to have an impact on the developing child.* **2** [I] If a problem or difficulty **develops**, it begins to occur. = arise ❑ *The space agency says a problem has developed with an experiment aboard the space shuttle.* **3** [I] If you say that a country **develops**, you mean that it changes from being a poor agricultural country to being a rich industrial country. ❑ *All countries, it was predicted, would develop and develop fast.* **4** [I, T] (*business*) If you **develop** a business or industry, or if it **develops**, it becomes bigger and more successful. ❑ *An amateur hatmaker has won a scholarship to pursue her dreams of developing her own business.* ❑ *Over the last few years tourism here has developed considerably.* **5** [T] To **develop** land or property means to make it more profitable, by building houses or factories or by improving the existing buildings. ❑ *Local entrepreneurs developed fashionable restaurants, bars and discotheques in the area.* **6** [T] If you **develop** a habit, reputation, or belief, you start to have it and it then becomes stronger or more noticeable. = acquire ❑ *Mr Robinson has developed the reputation of a ruthless cost-cutter.* **7** [I, T] If you **develop** a skill, quality, or relationship, or if it **develops**, it becomes better or stronger. ❑ *Now you have a good opportunity to develop a greater understanding of each other.* **8** [T] If a piece of equipment **develops** a fault, it starts to have the fault. ❑ *The aircraft made an unscheduled landing at Logan after developing an electrical fault.* **9** [T] If someone **develops** a new product, they design it and produce it. ❑ *He claims that several countries have developed nuclear weapons secretly.* **10** [I, T] If you **develop** an idea, theory, story, or theme, or if it **develops**, it gradually becomes more detailed, advanced, or complex. ❑ *I would like to thank them for allowing me to develop their original idea.* ❑ *This point is developed further at the end of this chapter.* **11** [T] To **develop** photographs means to make negatives or prints from a photographic film. ❑ *after developing one roll of film* → See also **developed**, **developing**

WORD CONNECTIONS

develop + ADV

develop **rapidly**
develop **quickly**
❑ *The illness develops very rapidly.*

develop + NOUN

develop a **technique**
develop a **strategy**
develop an **idea**
❑ *The department works closely with surgical colleagues in developing new surgical techniques.*

develop a **business**
develop a **product**
❑ *My work involves designing and developing new products.*

develop **weapons**
develop **technology**
develop **software**
❑ *They are working to save the environment by developing alternative technologies.*

VOCABULARY BUILDER

develop VERB
When something **develops**, it grows or changes over a period of time and usually becomes more advanced or complete.
❑ *The camcorder market is developing so quickly that retailers often discount models which have just been superseded.*

establish VERB
If someone **establishes** something such as an organization or a type of activity, they create in such a way that it is likely to last for a long time.
❑ *The easiest way to cut cleaning is to establish a quick weekly routine that fits into your lifestyle.*

progress VERB
To **progress** means to move over a period of time to a stronger, more advanced, or more desirable state.
❑ *The attraction between the two was so intense that the relationship progressed quickly to a love affair.*

improve VERB
If something **improves**, or if you **improve** it, it gets better.
❑ *Many athletes have seen their careers improve dramatically after giving birth.*

✪**de·vel·oped** /dɪ'veləpt/ ADJ **1** When something is **developed**, it has grown or changed over a period of time and usually becomes more advanced, complete, or severe. ❑ *Their bodies were well developed and super fit.* **2** If you talk about **developed** countries or the **developed** world, you mean the countries or the parts of the world that are wealthy and have many industries. = prosperous, industrialized; ≠ developing, undeveloped ❑ *This scarcity is inevitable in less developed countries.* **3** If land or property is **developed**, it has been made more profitable by the building of houses or factories on it or the improvement of existing buildings. ❑ *Developed land was to grow from 5.3% to 6.9%.* **4** If a habit, reputation, or belief is well **developed**, it has become stronger or more noticeable. ❑ *a highly developed instinct for self-preservation*

de·vel·op·er /dɪ'veləpə/ NOUN [C] (**developers**) **1** (*business*) A **developer** is a person or a company that buys land and builds houses, offices, shops, or factories on it, or buys existing buildings and makes them more modern. ❑ *common land which would have a high commercial value if sold to developers* **2** A **developer** is someone who develops something such as an idea, a design, or a product. ❑ *John Bardeen was also co-developer of the theory of superconductivity.*

✪**de·vel·op·ing** /dɪ'veləpɪŋ/ ADJ [developing + N] If you talk about **developing** countries or the **developing** world, you mean the countries or the parts of the world that are poor and have few industries. = emergent, Third World ❑ *In the developing world cigarette consumption is increasing.* ❑ *Income disparities between industrial and developing countries will continue to grow.*

✪**de·vel·op·ment** ◆◆◆ /dɪ'veləpmənt/ NOUN [U, C] (**developments**) **1** [U] **Development** is the gradual growth or formation of something. ❑ *an ideal system for studying the development of the embryo* ❑ *First he surveys Islam's development.* **2** [U] (*business*) **Development** is the growth of something such as a business or an industry. ❑ *Education is central to a country's economic development.* ❑ *What are your plans for the development of your company?*

3 [U] **Development** is the process of making an area of land or water more useful or profitable. ❑ *The talks will focus on economic development of the region.* **4** [C, U] **Development** is the process or result of making a basic design gradually better and more advanced. ❑ *It is spending $850m on research and development to get to the market place as soon as possible with faster microprocessors.* ❑ *the development of new and innovative telephone services* **5** [C] A **development** is an event or incident which has recently happened and is likely to have an effect on the present situation. ❑ *The police spokesman said: 'We believe there has been a significant development in the case.'* **6** [C] A **development** is an area of houses or buildings which have been built by property developers. ❑ *a 16-house development planned by Everlast Enterprises*

WORD CONNECTIONS
development + OF + NOUN
the development of **technology**
❑ *We invest in the development of low carbon technologies.*
the development of a **product**
the development of a **drug**
the development of a **vaccine**
❑ *Scientists are working on the development of a vaccine against norovirus.*
ADJ + **development**
economic development
technological development
sustainable development
❑ *Resources should be channelled into projects that promote sustainable development.*
commercial development
industrial development
❑ *Is it right that local authorities have the power to sell off green space for commercial development?*
a **technical** development
a **new** development
❑ *We are constantly working to improve the website with new developments happening every day.*

◆**de·vel·op·men·tal** /dɪˌveləpˈmentəl/ ADJ [usu developmental + N] **Developmental** means relating to the development of someone or something. ❑ *the emotional, educational, and developmental needs of the child* ❑ *adults with developmental disabilities*

de·vi·ant /ˈdiːviənt/ ADJ **Deviant** behaviour or thinking is different from what people normally consider to be acceptable. ❑ *the social reactions to deviant and criminal behaviour* • **de·vi·ance** /ˈdiːviəns/ NOUN [U] ❑ *sexual deviance, including the abuse of children*

◆**de·vi·ate** /ˈdiːvieɪt/ VERB [I] (**deviates, deviating, deviated**) (*academic word*) To **deviate from** something means to start doing something different or not planned, especially in a way that causes problems for others. = dependent; ≠ adhere ❑ *They stopped you as soon as you deviated from the script.* ❑ *wage levels that deviate significantly from international norms*

◆**de·vi·a·tion** /ˌdiːviˈeɪʃən/ NOUN [C, U] (**deviations**) **Deviation** means doing something that is different from what people consider to be normal or acceptable. = departure; ≠ adherence ❑ *Deviation from the norm is not tolerated.* ❑ *radical deviations in blood sugar level*

◆**de·vice** ◆◇◇ /dɪˈvaɪs/ NOUN [C] (**devices**) A **device** is an object that has been invented for a particular purpose, for example, for recording or measuring something. = machine, instrument, gadget ❑ *the electronic device that tells the starter when an athlete has moved from his blocks prematurely* ❑ *An explosive device had been left inside a container.*

dev·il /ˈdevəl/ NOUN [SING, C] (**devils**) **1** [SING] In Judaism, Christianity, and Islam, **the Devil** is the most powerful evil spirit. = Satan **2** [C] A **devil** is an evil spirit. = demon ❑ *the idea of angels with wings and devils with horns and hoofs*

de·vi·ous /ˈdiːviəs/ ADJ (*disapproval*) If you describe someone as **devious** you do not like them because you think they are dishonest and like to keep things secret, often in a complicated way. ❑ *Newman was certainly devious, prepared to say one thing in print and something quite different in private.*

de·vise /dɪˈvaɪz/ VERB [T] (**devises, devising, devised**) If you **devise** a plan, system, or machine, you have the idea for it and design it. ❑ *We devised a scheme to help him.*

de·void /dɪˈvɔɪd/ ADJ [V-LINK + devoid 'of' N] (*formal, emphasis*) If you say that someone or something is **devoid of** a quality or something, you are emphasizing that they have none of it. = bereft ❑ *I have never looked on a face that was so devoid of feeling.*

◆**de·vote** /dɪˈvəʊt/ VERB [T] (**devotes, devoting, devoted**) (*academic word*) **1** If you **devote** yourself, your time, or your energy **to** something, you spend all or most of your time or energy on it. = dedicate ❑ *He decided to devote the rest of his life to scientific investigation.* ❑ *Considerable resources have been devoted to proving him a liar.* ❑ *She gave up her part-time job to devote herself entirely to her art.* **2** If you **devote** a particular proportion of a piece of writing or a speech **to** a particular subject, you deal with the subject in that amount of space or time. = dedicate ❑ *He devoted a major section of his massive report to an analysis of US aircraft design.* ❑ *This chapter is devoted to clarifying the nature of risk.*

de·vot·ed /dɪˈvəʊtɪd/ ADJ **1** [devoted + N, V-LINK + devoted 'to' N] Someone who is **devoted to** a person loves that person very much. ❑ *a loving and devoted husband* **2** [V-LINK + devoted 'to' N, devoted + N] If you are **devoted to** something, you care about it a lot and are very enthusiastic about it. ❑ *I have personally been devoted to this cause for many years.* **3** [V-LINK + devoted 'to' N] Something that is **devoted to** a particular thing deals only with that thing or contains only that thing. ❑ *A large part of the Internet is now devoted to weblogs.*

◆**de·vo·tion** /dɪˈvəʊʃən/ NOUN [U] **1** **Devotion** is great love, affection, or admiration for someone. ❑ *At first she was flattered by his devotion.* **2** **Devotion** is commitment to a particular activity. = dedication ❑ *devotion to the cause of the people and to socialism* ❑ *Darwin's devotion to his studies of plants and animals*

de·vout /dɪˈvaʊt/ ADJ, NOUN
ADJ 1 A **devout** person has deep religious beliefs. ❑ *She was a devout Christian.* **2** [devout + N] If you describe someone as a **devout** supporter or a **devout** opponent of something, you mean that they support it enthusiastically or oppose it strongly. ❑ *Devout Marxists believed fascism was the 'last stand of the bourgeoisie'.*
NOUN [PL] **The devout** are people who are devout. ❑ *priests instructing the devout*

dia·be·tes /ˌdaɪəˈbiːtiːz, AmE -tɪs/ NOUN [U] **Diabetes** is a medical condition in which someone has too much sugar in their blood.

dia·bet·ic /ˌdaɪəˈbetɪk/ NOUN, ADJ
NOUN [C] (**diabetics**) A **diabetic** is a person who suffers from diabetes. ❑ *an insulin-dependent diabetic*
ADJ 1 **Diabetic** means suffering from diabetes. ❑ *diabetic patients* **2** [diabetic + N] **Diabetic** means relating to diabetes. ❑ *He found her in a diabetic coma.*

◆**di·ag·nose** /ˈdaɪəgnəʊz, AmE -nəʊs/ VERB [T] (**diagnoses, diagnosing, diagnosed**) If someone or something **is diagnosed as** having a particular illness or problem, their illness or problem is identified. If an illness or problem **is diagnosed**, it is identified. ❑ *The soldiers were diagnosed as having flu.* ❑ *Susan had a mental breakdown and was diagnosed with schizophrenia.* ❑ *In 1894 her illness was diagnosed as cancer.*

◆**di·ag·no·sis** /ˌdaɪəgˈnəʊsɪs/ NOUN [C, U] (**diagnoses**) **Diagnosis** is the discovery and naming of what is wrong with someone who is ill or with something that is not working properly. ❑ *I need to have a second test to confirm the diagnosis.* ❑ *The technique could allow earlier and more accurate diagnosis of conditions ranging from ME to Alzheimer's disease.*

d

D

di·ag·nos·tic /ˌdaɪəgˈnɒstɪk/ ADJ [diagnostic + N]
Diagnostic equipment, methods, or systems are used for discovering what is wrong with people who are ill or with things that do not work properly. ❑ *X-rays and other diagnostic tools*

✪**di·ago·nal** /daɪˈægənəl/ ADJ A **diagonal** line or movement goes in a sloping direction, for example, from one corner of a square across to the opposite corner. ❑ *a pattern of diagonal lines*

✪**di·ago·nal·ly** /daɪˈægənəli/ ADV ❑ *Vaulting the stile, he headed diagonally across the paddock.* ❑ *Tsunamis initiated in South American areas approach the US West Coast diagonally.*

✪**dia·gram** /ˈdaɪəgræm/ NOUN [c] (**diagrams**) A **diagram** is a simple drawing which consists mainly of lines and is used, for example, to explain how a machine works. ❑ *a circuit diagram*

dial /ˈdaɪəl/ NOUN, VERB
NOUN [c] (**dials**) **1** A **dial** is the part of a machine or instrument such as a clock or watch which shows you the time or a measurement that has been recorded. ❑ *The luminous dial on the clock showed five minutes to seven.* **2** A **dial** is a control on a device or piece of equipment which you can move in order to adjust the setting, for example, to select or change the frequency on a radio or the temperature of a heater. ❑ *He turned the dial on the radio.*
VERB [I, T] (**dials, dialling, dialled**; in AmE, use **dialing, dialed**) If you **dial** or if you **dial** a number, you turn the dial or press the buttons on a telephone in order to phone someone. ❑ *He lifted the phone and dialled her number.*

✪**dia·lect** /ˈdaɪəlekt/ NOUN [c] (**dialects**) [also 'in' dialect] A **dialect** is a form of a language that is spoken in a particular area. ❑ *It is often appropriate to use the local dialect to communicate your message.* ❑ *They spoke a dialect of Low German.* ❑ *a selection of short stories written in dialect*

dia·logue ◆◇◇ /ˈdaɪəlɒg, AmE -lɔːg/ (in AmE, use **dialog**) NOUN [c, u] (**dialogues**) **1** **Dialogue** is communication or discussion between people or groups of people such as governments or political parties. ❑ *People of all social standings should be given equal opportunities for dialogue.* **2** A **dialogue** is a conversation between two people in a book, film, or play. ❑ *Although the dialogue is sharp, the actors move too awkwardly around the stage.*

✪**di·am·eter** /daɪˈæmɪtə/ NOUN [c] (**diameters**) [also 'in' diameter] The **diameter** of a round object is the length of a straight line that can be drawn across it, passing through the middle of it. ❑ *a tube less than a fifth of the diameter of a human hair* ❑ *a length of 22-mm diameter steel pipe*

dia·mond /ˈdaɪəmənd/ NOUN [c, u] (**diamonds**) **1** [c, u] A **diamond** is a hard, bright, precious stone which is clear and colourless. Diamonds are used in jewellery and for cutting very hard substances. ❑ *a pair of diamond earrings* **2** [c] A **diamond** is a shape with four straight sides of equal length where the opposite angles are the same, but none of the angles is equal to 90°: ◆. ❑ *forming his hands into the shape of a diamond* **3** [u] **Diamonds** is one of the four suits of cards in a pack of playing cards. Each card in the suit is marked with one or more red symbols in the shape of a diamond. ❑ *He drew the seven of diamonds.* **4** [c] A **diamond** is a playing card of this suit. ❑ *Win the ace of clubs and play a diamond.*

dia·ry ◆◇◇ /ˈdaɪəri/ NOUN [c] (**diaries**) A **diary** is a book which has a separate space for each day of the year. You use a diary to write down things you plan to do, or to record what happens in your life day by day. ❑ *I had earlier read the entry from Harold Nicholson's diary for July 10, 1940.*

dice /daɪs/ NOUN, VERB
NOUN [c] A **dice** is a small cube which has between one and six spots or numbers on its sides, and which is used in games to provide random numbers. In old-fashioned English, 'dice' was used only as a plural form, and the singular was **die**, but now 'dice' is used as both the singular and the plural form. ❑ *I throw both dice and get double 6.*
PHRASE **no dice** If you are trying to achieve something and you say that it's **no dice**, you mean that you are having no success or luck with it. If someone asks you for something and you reply **no dice**, you are refusing to do

what they ask. ❑ *If there'd been a halfway decent house for rent on this island, I would have taken it. But it was no dice.* ❑ *If the Republicans were to say 'no dice', the Democrats would think they have a campaign issue.*
VERB [T] (**dices, dicing, diced**) If you **dice** food, you cut it into small cubes. ❑ *Dice the onion and boil in the water for about fifteen minutes.*

dic·tate VERB, NOUN
VERB /dɪkˈteɪt/ [T, I] (**dictates, dictating, dictated**) **1** [T] If you **dictate** something, you say or read it aloud for someone else to write down. ❑ *Sheldon writes every day of the week, dictating his novels in the morning.* **2** [T, I] If someone **dictates to** someone else, they tell them what they should do or can do. ❑ *What right has one country to dictate the environmental standards of another?* ❑ *What gives them the right to dictate to us what we should eat?* **3** [T] If one thing **dictates** another, the first thing causes or influences the second thing. ❑ *The film's budget dictated a tough schedule.* ❑ *Of course, a number of factors will dictate how long an apple tree can survive.* **4** [T] You say that logic or common sense **dictates that** a particular thing is the case when you believe strongly that it is the case and that logic or common sense will cause other people to agree. ❑ *Logic dictates that our ancestors could not have held a yearly festival until they figured what a year was.*
NOUN /ˈdɪkteɪt/ [c] (**dictates**) **Dictates** are principles or rules which you consider to be extremely important. ❑ *We have followed the dictates of our consciences and have done our duty.*

✪**dic·ta·tor** /dɪkˈteɪtə, AmE ˈdɪkteɪt-/ NOUN [c] (**dictators**) A **dictator** is a ruler who has complete power in a country, especially power which was obtained by force and is used unfairly or cruelly. = despot, tyrant ❑ *The country descended into anarchy when its dictator was overthrown.*

dic·ta·tor·ial /ˌdɪktəˈtɔːriəl/ ADJ (disapproval) If you describe someone's behaviour as **dictatorial**, you do not like the fact that they tell people what to do in a forceful and unfair way. ❑ *his dictatorial management style*

✪**dic·ta·tor·ship** /dɪkˈteɪtəʃɪp/ NOUN [c, u] (**dictatorships**) **1** [c, u] **Dictatorship** is government by a dictator. = tyranny ❑ *a new era of democracy after a long period of military dictatorship in the country* **2** [c] A **dictatorship** is a country which is ruled by a dictator or by a very strict and harsh government. ❑ *Every country in the region was a military dictatorship.*

dic·tion·ary /ˈdɪkʃənri, AmE -neri/ NOUN [c] (**dictionaries**) A **dictionary** is a book in which the words and phrases of a language are listed alphabetically, together with their meanings and their translations in another language. ❑ *a Spanish-English dictionary*

did /dɪd/ IRREG FORM **Did** is the past tense of **do**.

didn't ◆◆◆ /ˈdɪdənt/ SHORT FORM **Didn't** is the usual spoken form of 'did not'.

die ◆◆◆ /daɪ/ VERB
VERB [I, T] (**dies, dying, died**) **1** [I] When people, animals, and plants **die**, they stop living. ❑ *A year later my dog died.* ❑ *Sadly, both he and my mother died of cancer.* ❑ *I would die a very happy person if I could stay in music my whole life.* **2** [I] (informal) If a machine or device **dies**, it stops completely, especially after a period of working more and more slowly or inefficiently. ❑ *Then suddenly, the engine coughed, spluttered, and died.* **3** [I] (informal, emphasis) You can say that you **are dying of** thirst, hunger, boredom, or curiosity to emphasize that you are very thirsty, hungry, bored, or curious. ❑ *Order me a soft drink, I'm dying of thirst.* **4** [I, T] (informal, emphasis) You can say that you **are dying for** something or **are dying to** do something to emphasize that you very much want to have it or do it. ❑ *I'm dying for a breath of fresh air.* **5** [I] (informal, mainly spoken, emphasis) You can use **die** in expressions such as '**I almost died**' or '**I'd die if anything happened**' where you are emphasizing your feelings about a situation, for example, to say that it is very shocking, upsetting, embarrassing, or amusing. ❑ *I nearly died when I read what she'd written about me.* ❑ *I nearly died of shame.* ❑ *I thought I'd die laughing.*
PHRASES **to die for** (informal) If you say that something is **to die for**, you mean that you want it or like it very much. ❑ *It may be that your property has a stunning view, or perhaps*

it has a kitchen or bathroom to die for.

die hard If you say that habits or attitudes **die hard**, you mean that they take a very long time to disappear or change, so that it may not be possible to get rid of them completely. ❑ *Old habits die hard.*

PHRASAL VERB   **die out**   **1** If something **dies out**, it becomes less and less common and eventually disappears completely. ❑ *We used to believe that capitalism would soon die out.* **2** If something such as a fire or wind **dies out**, it gradually stops burning or blowing. ❑ *Once the fire has died out, the salvage team will move in.*
→ See also **dying**

die·sel /'diːzəl/ NOUN [C, U] (**diesels**) **1** [C, U] Diesel or **diesel oil** is the heavy fuel used in a diesel engine. **2** [C] A **diesel** is a vehicle which has a diesel engine. ❑ *I keep hearing that diesels are better now than ever before.*

✪**diet** ♦♦◇ /'daɪət/ NOUN, VERB, ADJ
NOUN [C, U] (**diets**) **1** [C, U] Your **diet** is the type and variety of food that you regularly eat. ❑ *It's never too late to improve your diet.* ❑ *a healthy diet rich in fruit and vegetables* ❑ *Poor diet and excess smoking will seriously damage the health of your hair.* **2** [C, U] If you are on a **diet**, you eat special kinds of food or you eat less food than usual because you are trying to lose weight. ❑ *Have you been on a diet? You've lost a lot of weight.* **3** [C] If a doctor puts someone on a **diet**, he or she makes them eat a special type or variety of foods in order to improve their health. ❑ *Certain chronic conditions, such as diabetes, require special diets that should be monitored by your physician.* **4** [C] If you are fed on a **diet of** something, especially something unpleasant or of poor quality, you receive or experience a very large amount of it. ❑ *The radio had fed him a diet of pop songs.*
VERB [I] (**diets, dieting, dieted**) If you **are dieting**, you eat special kinds of food or you eat less food than usual because you are trying to lose weight. ❑ *I've been dieting ever since the birth of my fourth child.*
ADJ [diet + N] **Diet** drinks or foods have been specially produced so that they do not contain many calories. ❑ *sugar-free diet drinks*

✪**dif·fer** /'dɪfə/ VERB [RECIP] (**differs, differing, differed**) **1** If two or more things **differ**, they are unlike each other in some way. = vary, contrast with ❑ *The story he told police differed from the one he told his mother.* ❑ *Management styles differ.* **2** If people **differ** about something, they do not agree with each other about it. ❑ *The two leaders had differed on the issue of sanctions.* ❑ *That is where we differ.*

WORD FAMILIES	
differ VERB	*The story he told police **differed** from the one he told his mother.*
different ADJ	*We have totally **different** views.*
difference NOUN	*That is the fundamental **difference** between the two societies.*
differently ADV	*Every individual learns **differently**.*

✪**dif·fer·ence** ♦♦◇ /'dɪfrəns/ NOUN
NOUN [C, SING] (**differences**) **1** [C] The **difference** between two things is the way in which they are unlike each other. = contrast, variation, distinction; ≠ similarity ❑ *That is the fundamental difference between the two societies.* ❑ *the vast difference in size* ❑ *There is no difference between the sexes.* **2** [C] If people have their **differences** about something, they disagree about it. ❑ *The two communities are learning how to resolve their differences.* **3** [SING] A **difference** between two quantities is the amount by which one quantity is less than the other. ❑ *The difference is 8532.*
PHRASES   **make a difference** or **make a lot of difference** or **make no difference** If something **makes a difference** or **makes a lot of difference**, it affects you and helps you in what you are doing. If something **makes no difference**, it does not have any effect on what you are doing. ❑ *Where you live can make such a difference to the way you feel.*
difference of opinion If there is a **difference of opinion** between two or more people or groups, they disagree about something. ❑ *Was there a difference of opinion over what to do with the Nobel Prize money?*

WORD CONNECTIONS

VERB + **difference**

tell the difference
notice the difference
❑ *There is a simple way to tell the difference between these two plants.*

ADJ + **difference**

a **significant** difference
a **big** difference
a **huge** difference
a **real** difference
a **fundamental** difference
❑ *There are significant differences in regulations between countries.*

the **main** difference
the **major** difference
the **only** difference
❑ *The only difference between the two products is their size.*

difference + IN + NOUN

a difference **in size**
a difference **in quality**
a difference **in attitude**
a difference **in approach**
❑ *The questionnaire aimed to find the differences in attitudes of the students to both learning and teaching.*

✪**dif·fer·ent** ♦♦♦ /'dɪfrənt/ ADJ **1** If two people or things are **different**, they are not like each other in one or more ways. ❑ *London was different from most European capitals.* ❑ *If he'd attended music school, how might things have been different?* ❑ *We have totally different views.* = contrasting, dissimilar, distinct; ≠ the same, similar, alike, identical **2** [V-LINK + different 'to' N/CL] People sometimes say that one thing is **different to** another. Some people consider this use to be incorrect. ❑ *My approach is totally different to his.* **3** [different + N] You use **different** to indicate that you are talking about two or more separate and distinct things of the same kind. ❑ *Different countries specialized in different products.* **4** [V-LINK + different] You can describe something as **different** when it is unusual and not like others of the same kind. = distinctive ❑ *The result is interesting and different, but do not attempt the recipe if time is short.*
dif·fer·ent·ly /'dɪfrəntli/ ADV ❑ *Every individual learns differently.*
dif·fer·en·tial /ˌdɪfə'renʃəl/ NOUN [C] (**differentials**) In mathematics and economics, a **differential** is a difference between two values in a scale. ❑ *the wage differential between blue-collar and white-collar workers*
✪**dif·fer·en·ti·ate** /ˌdɪfə'renʃieɪt/ VERB [I, T] (**differentiates, differentiating, differentiated**) (*academic word*) **1** [I, T] If you **differentiate between** things or if you **differentiate** one thing **from** another, you recognize or show the difference between them. = distinguish ❑ *A child may not differentiate between his imagination and the real world.* ❑ *At this age your baby cannot differentiate one person from another.* **2** [T] A quality or feature that **differentiates** one thing **from** another makes the two things different. = distinguish ❑ *distinctive policies that differentiate them from the other parties* ❑ *The brand did not have a differentiating factor.*
✪**dif·fer·en·tia·tion** /ˌdɪfərenʃi'eɪʃən/ NOUN [U] = distinction ❑ *For about six or seven weeks after conception, there is no differentiation between male and female.* ❑ *increased product differentiation and customization to niche markets*
✪**dif·fi·cult** ♦♦♦ /'dɪfɪkəlt/ ADJ **1** Something that is **difficult** is not easy to do, understand, or deal with. = challenging, complex, demanding, hard; ≠ easy, simple, straightforward, undemanding, uncomplicated ❑ *The lack of childcare provision made it difficult for single mothers to get jobs.* ❑ *It was a very difficult decision to make.* **2** Someone who is **difficult** behaves in an unreasonable and unhelpful way.

d

= awkward ❑ *I had a feeling you were going to be difficult about this.*

WORD CONNECTIONS

ADV + difficult

extremely difficult
very difficult
increasingly difficult
particularly difficult
❑ *He was 88 and finding it increasingly difficult to cope on his own.*

VOCABULARY BUILDER

difficult ADJ
Something that is **difficult** is not easy to do, understand, or deal with.
❑ *Men with early prostate cancer are faced with a difficult choice about treatments.*

challenging ADJ
A **challenging** job requires great effort and determination, but this is considered to be a good thing.
❑ *We see the market in the west as competitive but we look forward to exciting and challenging projects.*

complex ADJ
Something that is **complex** has many different parts, and is therefore not easy to understand or achieve.
❑ *Extended moon visits were proposed as a stepping stone for the more complex task of reaching Mars.*

demanding ADJ
A **demanding** job or task requires a lot of your time, energy, or attention.
❑ *Nobody realizes how demanding raising a child is until they experience it.*

hard ADJ
Something that is **hard** is not easy to deal with or to do.
❑ *In some respects, exams are harder than they were in the past.*

◆ **dif·fi·cul·ty** ◆◆◇ /ˈdɪfɪkəlti/ NOUN
NOUN [C, U] (**difficulties**) **1** [C] A **difficulty** is a problem. = challenge, problem, obstacle ❑ *the difficulty of getting accurate information* ❑ *The country is facing great economic difficulties* **2** [U] If you have **difficulty** doing something, you are not able to do it easily. = trouble; ≠ ease ❑ *Do you have difficulty getting up?* ❑ *The injured man mounted his horse with difficulty.*
PHRASE **in difficulty** If someone or something is **in difficulty**, they are having a lot of problems. ❑ *The city's film industry is in difficulty.*

WORD CONNECTIONS

VERB + difficulty

face difficulties
experience difficulties
encounter difficulties
❑ *Many companies encounter difficulties in recruiting and retaining good staff.*

cause a difficulty
present a difficulty
create a difficulty
❑ *To split the role might create difficulties.*

overcome a difficulty
❑ *I am sure that you will succeed in overcoming the present difficulties.*

ADJ + difficulty

economic difficulties
financial difficulties
technical difficulties
practical difficulties
❑ *Many households are facing financial difficulties.*

---

great difficulty
considerable difficulty
severe difficulty
little difficulty
❑ *We face considerable difficulties in meeting this challenge.*

dig ◆◇◇ /dɪg/ VERB, NOUN
VERB [I, T] (**digs, digging, dug**) **1** [I, T] If people or animals **dig**, they make a hole in the ground or in a pile of earth, stones, or rubbish. ❑ *I grabbed the spade and started digging.* ❑ *Dig a large hole and drive the stake in first.* **2** [I] If you **dig into** something such as a deep container, you put your hand in it to search for something. = delve ❑ *He dug into his coat pocket for his keys.* **3** [I, T] If you **dig** one thing **into** another or if one thing **digs into** another, the first thing is pushed hard into the second, or presses hard into it. ❑ *She digs the serving spoon into the moussaka.* **4** [I] If you **dig into** a subject or a store of information, you study it very carefully in order to discover or check facts. = probe ❑ *as a special congressional enquiry digs deeper into the alleged financial misdeeds of his government* ❑ *He has been digging into the local archives.* **5** [T] If you **dig yourself out of** a difficult or unpleasant situation, especially one which you caused yourself, you manage to get out of it. ❑ *He's taken these measures to try and dig himself out of a hole.*
PHRASAL VERB **dig out** **1** If you **dig** someone or something **out of** a place, you get them out by digging or by forcing them from the things surrounding them. ❑ *digging minerals out of the earth* **2** (*informal*) If you **dig** something **out**, you find it after it has been stored, hidden, or forgotten for a long time. ❑ *Recently, I dug out Barstow's novel and read it again.*
NOUN [C] (**digs**) **1** If you have a **dig at** someone, you say something which is intended to make fun of them or upset them. = gibe ❑ *She couldn't resist a dig at Dave after his unfortunate performance.* **2** If you give someone a **dig** in a part of their body, you push them with your finger or your elbow, usually as a warning or as a joke. ❑ *Cassandra silenced him with a sharp dig in the small of the back.*
✦ **dig one's heels in →** see **heel**

di·gest VERB, NOUN
VERB /daɪˈdʒest/ [I, T] (**digests, digesting, digested**)
1 [I, T] When food **digests** or when you **digest** it, it passes through your body to your stomach. Your stomach removes the substances that your body needs and gets rid of the rest. ❑ *Do not undertake strenuous exercise for a few hours after a meal to allow food to digest.* ❑ *She couldn't digest food properly.* **2** [T] If you **digest** information, you think about it carefully so that you understand it. ❑ *They learn well but seem to need time to digest information.* **3** [T] If you **digest** some unpleasant news, you think about it until you are able to accept it and know how to deal with it. ❑ *All this has upset me. I need time to digest it all.*
NOUN /ˈdaɪdʒest/ [C] (**digests**) A **digest** is a collection of pieces of writing. They are published together in a shorter form than they were originally published. ❑ *the Middle East Economic Digest*

di·ges·tion /daɪˈdʒestʃən/ NOUN [U, C] (**digestions**)
1 [U] **Digestion** is the process of digesting food. ❑ *No liquids are served with meals because they interfere with digestion.* **2** [C] Your **digestion** is the system in your body which digests your food. ❑ *Keep your digestion working well by eating plenty of fibre.*

di·ges·tive /daɪˈdʒestɪv/ ADJ [digestive + N] You can describe things that are related to the digestion of food as **digestive**. ❑ *digestive juices that normally work on breaking down our food*

◆ **dig·it** /ˈdɪdʒɪt/ NOUN [C] (**digits**) A **digit** is a written symbol for any of the ten numbers from 0 to 9. = number, figure ❑ *Her telephone number differs from mine by one digit.* ❑ *Inflation is still in double digits.*

◆ **digi·tal** ◆◆◇ /ˈdɪdʒɪtəl/ ADJ
ADJ **1** **Digital** systems record or transmit information in the form of thousands of very small signals. ❑ *The new digital technology would allow a rapid expansion in the number of TV channels.* **2** [digital + N] **Digital** devices such as watches or clocks give information by displaying numbers

rather than by having a pointer which moves round a dial. Compare **analogue**. ◻ *a digital display*

PHRASE **digital divide** ['the/a' digital divide] (*mainly journalism*) People sometimes refer to poorer people's lack of access to the latest computer technology as **the digital divide**. ◻ *an attempt to reduce the 'digital divide' between poor students who have no computers and those from well-off families who do*

⊙**dig·it·al·ly** /ˈdɪdʒɪtəli/ ADV ◻ *digitally recorded sound*

dig·ni·fied /ˈdɪɡnɪfaɪd/ ADJ If you say that someone or something is **dignified**, you mean they are calm, impressive, and deserve respect. ◻ *He seemed a very dignified and charming man.*

dig·nity /ˈdɪɡnɪti/ NOUN [U] ◼ If someone behaves or moves with **dignity**, they are calm, controlled, and admirable. = poise ◻ *her extraordinary dignity and composure* ◼ If you talk about the **dignity** of people or their lives or activities, you mean they are valuable and worthy of respect. ◻ *the sense of human dignity* ◼ Your **dignity** is the sense that you have of your own importance and value, and other people's respect for you. = self-respect ◻ *She still has her dignity.*

⊙**di·lem·ma** /daɪˈlemə, AmE dɪl-/ NOUN [C] (**dilemmas**) A **dilemma** is a difficult situation in which you have to choose between two or more alternatives. = difficulty, problem, predicament ◻ *He was faced with the dilemma of whether or not to return to his country.* ◻ *The issue raises a moral dilemma.*

dili·gent /ˈdɪlɪdʒənt/ ADJ Someone who is **diligent** works hard in a careful and thorough way. ◻ *Meyers is a diligent and prolific worker.*

dili·gence /ˈdɪlɪdʒəns/ NOUN [U] ◻ *The police are pursuing their inquiries with great diligence.*

dili·gent·ly /ˈdɪlɪdʒəntli/ ADV [diligently with V] ◻ *The two sides are now working diligently to resolve their differences.*

⊙**di·lute** /daɪˈluːt/ VERB, ADJ
VERB [I, T] (**dilutes, diluting, diluted**) ◼ [I, T] If a liquid **is diluted** or **dilutes**, it is added to or mixes with water or another liquid, and becomes weaker. ≠ concentrate ◻ *If you give your baby juice, dilute it well with cooled, boiled water.* ◻ *The liquid is then diluted.* ◼ [T] If someone or something **dilutes** a belief, quality, or value, they make it weaker and less effective. ◻ *There was a clear intention to dilute black voting power.*
ADJ A **dilute** liquid is very thin and weak, usually because it has had water added to it. ◻ *a dilute solution of bleach*

⊙**di·lu·tion** /daɪˈluːʃən/ NOUN [C, U] (**dilutions**) ◼ [C] A **dilution** is a liquid that has been diluted with water or another liquid, so that it becomes weaker. ◻ *'Aromatherapy oils' are not pure essential oils but dilutions.* ◻ *The synthetic alcohol was mixed in graded dilutions.* ◼ [U] **Dilution** is the process or action of diluting a liquid. ≠ concentration ◻ *readings significantly lower owing to the dilution of the sample*

dim /dɪm/ ADJ, VERB
ADJ (**dimmer, dimmest**) ◼ **Dim** light is not bright. ◻ *She stood waiting in the dim light.* ◼ A **dim** place is rather dark because there is not much light in it. ◻ *The room was dim and cool and quiet.* ◼ A **dim** figure or object is not very easy to see, either because it is in shadow or darkness, or because it is far away. = faint ◻ *Pete's torch picked out the dim figures of Bob and Chang.* ◼ If you have a **dim** memory or understanding of something, it is difficult to remember or is unclear in your mind. = hazy ◻ *It seems that the '60s era of social activism is all but a dim memory.* ◼ If the future of something is **dim**, you have no reason to feel hopeful or positive about it. ◻ *The prospects for a peaceful solution are dim.* ◼ (*informal*) If you describe someone as **dim**, you think that they are stupid. ◻ *Sometimes he thought George was a bit dim.*
VERB [I, T] (**dims, dimming, dimmed**) ◼ If you **dim** a light or if it **dims**, it becomes less bright. ◻ *Dim the lighting – it is unpleasant to lie with a bright light shining in your eyes.* ◼ If your future, hopes, or emotions **dim** or if something **dims** them, they become less good or less strong. ◻ *Their economic prospects have dimmed.* ◼ If your memories **dim** or if something **dims** them, they become less clear in your mind. ◻ *Their memory of what happened has dimmed.*

dim·ly /ˈdɪmli/ ADV ◼ *Two lamps burned dimly.* ◼ *The shoreline could be dimly seen.* ◼ *Christina dimly recalled the procedure.*

⊙**di·men·sion** /daɪˈmenʃən, dɪm-/ NOUN [C, PL] (**dimensions**) (*academic word*) ◼ [C] A particular **dimension** of something is a particular aspect of it. = aspect ◻ *There is a political dimension to the accusations.* ◻ *This adds a new dimension to our work.* ◼ [C] A **dimension** is a measurement such as length, width, or height. If you talk about the **dimensions** of an object or place, you are referring to its size and proportions. = scale, size, extent, measurement ◻ *Drilling will continue on the site to assess the dimensions of the new oilfield.* ◼ [PL] If you talk about the **dimensions** of a situation or problem, you are talking about its extent and size. = scale ◻ *The dimensions of the market collapse, in terms of turnover and price, were certainly not anticipated.*

VOCABULARY BUILDER

dimension NOUN
A **dimension** is a measurement such as length, width, or height.
◻ *Contracts can also stipulate that the developer can vary the property's dimensions and other specifications.*

scale NOUN
If you refer to the **scale** of something, you are referring to its size, especially when it is very big.
◻ *Although the flood waters have receded, the scale of the disaster makes it difficult to assess how many people died.*

size NOUN
The **size** of something is how big or small it is.
◻ *The bump is swollen to the size of a grapefruit.*

extent NOUN
The **extent** of something is its length, area, or size.
◻ *He said it was too early to assess the extent of the oil spill or the environmental damage.*

measurement NOUN
A **measurement** is the number found when you examine something in order to find out how big or small it is.
◻ *Without accurate measurements it is also very difficult to estimate cooking time accurately.*

⊙**di·min·ish** /dɪˈmɪnɪʃ/ VERB [I, T] (**diminishes, diminishing, diminished**) (*academic word*) ◼ [I, T] When something **diminishes**, or when something **diminishes** it, it becomes reduced in size, importance, or intensity. = lessen, decrease ◻ *The threat of nuclear war has diminished.* ◻ *Federalism is intended to diminish the power of the central state.* ◻ *Universities are facing grave problems because of diminishing resources.* ◻ *This could mean diminished public support for the war.* ◼ [T] If you **diminish** someone or something, you talk about them or treat them in a way that makes them appear less important than they really are. ◻ *He never put her down or diminished her.*

dine /daɪn/ VERB [I] (**dines, dining, dined**) (*formal*) When you **dine**, you have dinner. ◻ *He dines alone most nights.*

din·er /ˈdaɪnə/ NOUN [C] (**diners**) The people who are having dinner in a restaurant can be referred to as **diners**. ◻ *They sat in a corner, away from other diners.*

din·ing room NOUN [C] (**dining rooms**) The **dining room** is the room in a house where people have their meals, or a room in a hotel where meals are served.

din·ner ♦♦◇ /ˈdɪnə/ NOUN [C, U] (**dinners**) ◼ [C, U] **Dinner** is the main meal of the day, usually served in the early part of the evening. ◻ *She invited us to her house for dinner.* ◻ *Would you like to stay and have dinner?* ◼ [C, U] Any meal you eat in the middle of the day can be referred to as **dinner**. ◼ [C] A **dinner** is a formal social event at which a meal is served. It is held in the evening. ◻ *a series of official lunches and dinners*

di·no·saur /ˈdaɪnəsɔː/ NOUN [C] (**dinosaurs**) ◼ Dinosaurs were large reptiles which lived in prehistoric times. ◼ If

d

D

you refer to an organization as a **dinosaur**, you mean that it is large, inefficient, and out of date. ❑ *industrial dinosaurs*

✪ **dip** /dɪp/ VERB, NOUN

VERB [T, I] (**dips, dipping, dipped**) **1** [T] If you **dip** something **in** a liquid, you put it into the liquid for a short time, so that only part of it is covered, and take it out again. ❑ *Dip each apple in the syrup until thickly coated.* **2** [I, T] If you **dip** your hand **into** a container or **dip into** the container, you put your hand into it in order to take something out of it. ❑ *She dipped a hand into the jar of sweets and pulled one out.* ❑ *Nancy dipped into the bowl of popcorn that Hannah had made for them.* **3** [I] If something **dips**, it makes a downward movement, usually quickly. ❑ *Blake jumped in expertly; the boat dipped slightly under his weight.* **4** [I] If an area of land, a road, or a path **dips**, it goes down quite suddenly to a lower level. ❑ *The road dipped and rose again as it neared the top of Parker Mountain.* **5** [I] If the amount or level of something **dips**, it becomes smaller or lower, usually only for a short period of time. = fall; ≠ rise ❑ *Unemployment dipped to 6.9 per cent last month.* ❑ *The president became more cautious as his popularity dipped.* **6** [I] If you **dip into** a book, you take a brief look at it without reading or studying it seriously. ❑ *a chance to dip into a wide selection of books on Tibetan Buddhism* **7** [I] If you **dip into** a sum of money that you had intended to save, you use some of it to buy something or pay for something. ❑ *Just when she was ready to dip into her savings, Greg hastened to her rescue.*

NOUN [c] (**dips**) **1** A **dip** is the action of putting something into liquid for a short time, so that only part of it is covered, and taking it out again. ❑ *a quick dip of his toe into the water* **2** A **dip** is a quick downward movement. ❑ *I noticed little things, a dip of the head, a twitch in the shoulder.* **3** A **dip** in an area of land, a road, or a path is a place where it goes down quite suddenly to a lower level. ❑ *Where the road makes a dip, soon after a small vineyard on the right, turn right.* **4** A **dip** is a reduction in the amount or level of something, usually only for a short period of time. ≠ rise ❑ *the current dip in farm spending* **5** If you have or take a **dip**, you go for a quick swim in the ocean, a lake, a river, or a swimming pool. = swim ❑ *She flicked through a romantic paperback between occasional dips in the pool.*

di·plo·ma /dɪ'pləʊmə/ NOUN [c] (**diplomas**) A **diploma** is a document which may be awarded to a student who has completed a course of study by a university or college, or by a high school in the United States. ❑ *a new two-year course leading to a diploma in social work*

di·plo·ma·cy /dɪ'pləʊməsi/ NOUN [u] **1** **Diplomacy** is the activity or profession of managing relations between the governments of different countries. ❑ *Today's Security Council resolution will be a significant success for American diplomacy.* **2** **Diplomacy** is the skill of being careful to say or do things which will not offend people. ❑ *He stormed off in a fury, and it took all Minnelli's powers of diplomacy to get him to return.*

dip·lo·mat ◆◇◇ /'dɪpləmæt/ NOUN [c] (**diplomats**) A **diplomat** is a senior official who discusses affairs with another country on behalf of his or her own country, usually working as a member of an embassy. ❑ *a Western diplomat with long experience in Asia*

dip·lo·mat·ic ◆◇◇ /ˌdɪplə'mætɪk/ ADJ **1** **Diplomatic** means relating to diplomacy and diplomats. ❑ *before the two countries resume full diplomatic relations* **2** Someone who is **diplomatic** is careful to say or do things without offending people. ❑ *She is very direct. I tend to be more diplomatic, I suppose.*

dip·lo·mati·cal·ly /ˌdɪplə'mætɪkli/ ADV **1** *a growing sense of doubt that the conflict can be resolved diplomatically* **2** [diplomatically with v] ❑ *'I really like their sound, although I'm not crazy about their lyrics,' he says, diplomatically.*

dire /daɪə/ ADJ (*emphasis*) **1** **Dire** is used to emphasize how serious or terrible a situation or event is. = awful, desperate ❑ *The government looked as if it would split apart, with dire consequences for domestic peace.* **2** (*informal*) If you describe something as **dire**, you are emphasizing that it is of very low quality. ❑ *a book of children's verse, which ranged from the barely tolerable to the utterly dire*

✪ **di·rect** ◆◆◆ /daɪ'rekt, dɪ-/ ADJ, ADV, VERB

ADJ **1** **Direct** means moving towards a place or object, without changing direction and without stopping, for example, in a journey. ❑ *They'd come on a direct flight from Athens.* ❑ *the direct route from Amman to Bombay* **2** [direct + N] If something is in **direct** heat or light, it is strongly affected by the heat or light, because there is nothing between it and the source of heat or light to protect it. ❑ *All medicines should be stored away from moisture, direct sunlight, and heat.* **3** You use **direct** to describe an experience, activity, or system which only involves the people, actions, or things that are necessary to make it happen. ❑ *He has direct experience of the process of privatization.* ❑ *He seemed to be in direct contact with the Boss.* **4** You use **direct** to emphasize the closeness of a connection between two things. ❑ *They were unable to prove that the unfortunate lady had died as a direct result of his injection.* ❑ *His visit is direct evidence of the improvement in their relationship.* **5** If you describe a person or their behaviour as **direct**, you mean that they are honest and open, and say exactly what they mean. ❑ *He avoided giving a direct answer.*

ADV **1** [direct after V] If you go or travel somewhere **direct**, you go or travel towards it without changing direction and without stopping. ❑ *You can fly direct from Seattle to Europe.* **2** [direct after V] If something is done **direct**, it is done in a way that only involves the people, actions, or things that are necessary to make it happen. ❑ *More farms are selling direct to consumers.* ❑ *I can deal direct with your Inspector Kimble.*

VERB [T, I] (**directs, directing, directed**) **1** [T] If you **direct** something **at** a particular thing, you aim or point it at that thing. = aim ❑ *I reached the cockpit and directed the extinguisher at the fire without effect.* **2** [T] If your attention, emotions, or actions **are directed at** a particular person or thing, you are focusing them on that person or thing. = focus ❑ *The learner's attention needs to be directed to the significant features.* **3** [T] If a remark or look **is directed at** you, someone says something to you or looks at you. ❑ *She could hardly believe the question was directed towards her.* ❑ *The abuse was directed at the TV crews.* **4** [T] If you **direct** someone somewhere, you tell them how to get there. ❑ *Could you direct them to Dr Lamont's office, please?* **5** [T] When someone **directs** a project or a group of people, they are responsible for organizing the people and activities that are involved. ❑ *Christopher will direct day-to-day operations.* **6** [I, T] When someone **directs** a film, play, or television programme, they are responsible for the way in which it is performed and for telling the actors and assistants what to do. ❑ *He directed various TV shows.*

di·rect·ness /daɪ'rektnəs, dɪ-/ NOUN [u] ❑ *Using 'I' ensures clarity and directness, and it adds warmth to a piece of writing.*

✪ **di·rec·tion** ◆◆◇ /daɪ'rekʃən/ NOUN [c, u, pl] (**directions**) **1** [c, u] A **direction** is the general line that someone or something is moving or pointing in. ❑ *St Andrews was ten miles in the opposite direction.* ❑ *He got into Margie's car and swung out onto the road in the direction of Larry's shop.* **2** [c, u] A **direction** is the general way in which something develops or progresses. = course, route ❑ *They threatened to lead a mass walk-out if the party did not sharply change direction.* **3** [PL] **Directions** are instructions that tell you how to get somewhere. ❑ *We downloaded directions to the hotel before leaving the house.* **4** [u] The **direction** of a project or a group of people is the act of organizing the people and activities that are involved. ❑ *Organizations need clear direction, set priorities and performance standards, and clear controls.*

di·rec·tive /daɪ'rektɪv, dɪ-/ NOUN [c] (**directives**) A **directive** is an official instruction that is given by someone in authority. = ruling ❑ *Thanks to a new directive, food labelling will be more specific.*

✪ **di·rect·ly** /daɪ'rektli, dɪ-/ ADV **1** [directly after V] If you go or travel **directly** to somewhere, you go or travel towards there without changing direction and without stopping. ❑ *On arriving in New York, Dylan went directly to Greenwich Village.* ❑ *The jumbo jet is due to fly the hostages* directly back to London. **2** [directly with v] If something is done **directly**, it is done in a way that only involves the people, actions, or things that are necessary to make it happen. ❑ *We cannot measure pain directly. It can only be estimated.* ❑ *The British could do nothing directly to help the Austrians.* **3** [directly + PREP/ADV] If something is **directly** above, below, or in front of something, it is in exactly that position. = right ❑ *The second rainbow will be bigger than the first, and directly above it.* **4** [directly + PREP/ADV] If you do one action **directly after** another, you do the second action as soon as the first one is finished. = immediately ❑ *Most guests left directly after the wake.* **5** [directly after v] If a person speaks or writes **directly**, they are honest and open, and say exactly what they mean. ❑ *At your first meeting, explain simply and directly what you hope to achieve.*

✪ **di·rec·tor** ♦♦♦ /daɪ'rektə, dɪ-/ NOUN [C] (**directors**) **1** The **director** of a play, film, or television programme is the person who decides how it will appear on stage or screen, and who tells the actors and technical staff what to do. ❑ *'Cut!' the director yelled. 'That was perfect.'* **2** In some organizations and public authorities, the person in charge is referred to as **the director**. ❑ *the director of the intensive care unit at Buffalo General Hospital* **3** (*business*) The **directors** of a company are its most senior managers, who meet regularly to make important decisions about how it will be run. = manager, executive, CEO ❑ *He served on the board of directors of a local bank.* ❑ *Karl Uggerholt, the financial director of Braun UK*

di·rec·tory /daɪ'rektəri, dɪ-/ NOUN [C] (**directories**) **1** A **directory** is a book which gives lists of facts, for example, people's names, addresses, and telephone numbers, or the names and addresses of business companies, usually arranged in alphabetical order. ❑ *a telephone directory* **2** (*computing*) A **directory** is an area of a computer disk which contains one or more files or other directories. ❑ *This option lets you search your current directory for files by date, contents, and document summary.*

dirt /dɜːt/ NOUN, ADJ

NOUN [U, SING] **1** [U] If there is **dirt** on something, there is dust, mud, or a stain on it. = grime ❑ *I started to scrub off the dirt.* **2** [U] You can refer to the earth on the ground as **dirt**, especially when it is dusty. = earth ❑ *They all sit on the dirt in the dappled shade of a tree.* **3** [SING] (*informal*) If you say that you have **the dirt on** someone, you mean that you have information that could harm their reputation or career. ❑ *a sleazy reporter assigned to dig up dirt on Jack*

PHRASE **treat someone like dirt** (*disapproval*) If you say that someone **treats** you **like dirt**, you are angry with them because you think that they treat you unfairly and with no respect. ❑ *People think they can treat me like dirt!*

ADJ [dirt + N] A **dirt** road or track is made from hard earth. A **dirt** floor is made from earth without any cement, stone, or wood laid on it. ❑ *I drove along the dirt road.*

dirty ♦◇◇ /'dɜːti/ ADJ, ADV, VERB

ADJ (**dirtier**, **dirtiest**) **1** If something is **dirty**, it is marked or covered with stains, spots, or mud, and needs to be cleaned. = grubby ❑ *She still did not like the woman, who had dirty fingernails.* **2** If you describe an action as **dirty**, you disapprove of it and consider it unfair, immoral, or dishonest. ❑ *The gunman had been hired by a rival Mafia family to do the dirty deed.* **3** If you describe something such as a joke, a book, or someone's language as **dirty**, you mean that it refers to sex in a way that some people find offensive. ❑ *He laughed at their dirty jokes and sang their raucous ballads.*

PHRASES **dirty look** (*informal*) If someone gives you a **dirty look**, they look at you in a way which shows that they are angry with you. ❑ *Jack was being a real pain. Michael gave him a dirty look and walked out.*

do someone's dirty work To do someone's **dirty work** means to do a task for them that is dishonest or unpleasant and which they do not want to do themselves. ❑ *As a member of an elite army hit squad, the army would send us out to do their dirty work for them.*

a dirty word If you say that an expression is **a dirty word** in a particular group of people, you mean it refers to an

idea that they strongly dislike or disagree with. ❑ *Marketing became a dirty word at the company.*

air one's dirty laundry in public (*disapproval*) If you say that someone **airs** their **dirty laundry in public**, you disapprove of their discussing or arguing about unpleasant or private things in front of other people. There are several other forms of this expression, for example **wash** your **dirty linen in public**, or **wash** your **dirty laundry in public**. ❑ *The captain refuses to air the team's dirty laundry in public.*

ADV **1** [dirty after v] **Dirty** means unfairly, immorally, or dishonestly. ❑ *Jim Browne is the kind of fellow who can fight dirty, but make you like it.* **2** [dirty after v] If someone **talks dirty**, they use language that refers to sex. ❑ *I'm often asked whether the men talk dirty to me. The answer is no.*

VERB [T] (**dirties**, **dirtying**, **dirtied**) To **dirty** something means to cause it to become dirty. ❑ *He was afraid the dog's hairs might dirty the seats.*

✪ **dis·abil·ity** /ˌdɪsə'bɪlɪti/ NOUN [C, U] (**disabilities**) **1** [C] A **disability** is a permanent injury, illness, or physical or mental condition that tends to restrict the way that someone can live their life. = handicap, impairment ❑ *Facilities for people with disabilities are still insufficient.* ❑ *athletes who have overcome a physical disability to reach the top of their sport* **2** [U] **Disability** is the state of being disabled. ❑ *Disability can make extra demands on financial resources because the disabled need extra care.*

WORD PARTS
The prefix **dis-** gives some words the opposite meaning:
disability (NOUN)
disagree (VERB)
dishonest (ADJ)

dis·able /dɪ'seɪbəl/ VERB [T] (**disables**, **disabling**, **disabled**) **1** If an injury or illness **disables** someone, it affects them so badly that it restricts the way that they can live their life. = handicap ❑ *She did all this tendon damage and it really disabled her.* **2** If someone or something **disables** a system or mechanism, they stop it from working, usually temporarily. ❑ *if you need to disable a car alarm*

✪ **dis·abled** /dɪ'seɪbəld/ ADJ, NOUN

ADJ Someone who is **disabled** has an illness, injury, or condition that tends to restrict the way that they can live their life, especially by making it difficult for them to move about. = handicapped ❑ *an insight into the practical problems encountered by disabled people in the workplace*

NOUN [PL] People who are disabled are sometimes referred to as **the disabled**. ❑ *There are toilet facilities for the disabled.*

✪ **dis·ad·van·tage** /ˌdɪsəd'vɑːntɪdʒ, -'væn-/ NOUN

NOUN [C] (**disadvantages**) A **disadvantage** is a factor which makes someone or something less useful, acceptable, or successful than other people or things. = drawback, inconvenience, downside; ≠ benefit ❑ *His two main rivals suffer the disadvantage of having been long-term political exiles.* ❑ *the advantages and disadvantages of allowing priests to marry*

PHRASES **at a disadvantage** If you are **at a disadvantage**, you have a problem or difficulty that many other people do not have, which makes it harder for you to be successful. ❑ *The children from poor families were at a distinct disadvantage.*

to someone's disadvantage If something is **to your disadvantage** or works **to your disadvantage**, it creates difficulties for you. ❑ *We need a rethink of the present law which works so greatly to the disadvantage of women.*

dis·ad·van·taged /ˌdɪsəd'vɑːntɪdʒd, -'væn-/ ADJ People who are **disadvantaged** or live in **disadvantaged** areas live in bad conditions and tend not to get a good education or have a reasonable standard of living. ❑ *the educational problems of disadvantaged children*

dis·af·fect·ed /ˌdɪsə'fektɪd/ ADJ **Disaffected** people no longer fully support something such as an organization or political ideal which they previously supported. ❑ *He attracts disaffected voters.*

✪ **dis·agree** /ˌdɪsə'griː/ VERB [RECIP, I] (**disagrees**, **disagreeing**, **disagreed**) **1** [RECIP] If you **disagree with** someone or **disagree with** what they say, you do not accept that what they say is true or correct. You can also say that two people **disagree**. = differ; ≠ concur ❑ *You must continue to see them no matter how much you may disagree with them.* ❑ *They can communicate even when they strongly disagree.* **2** [i] If you **disagree with** a particular action or proposal, you disapprove of it and believe that it is wrong. ❑ *I respect the president but I disagree with his decision.*

✪ **dis·agree·ment** /ˌdɪsəˈgriːmənt/ NOUN [u, c] (**disagreements**) **1** [u] **Disagreement** means objecting to something such as a proposal. = opposition, dissent; ≠ agreement ❑ *Britain and France have expressed some disagreement with the proposal.* **2** [c, u] When there is **disagreement** about something, people disagree or argue about what should be done. = dispute, argument, conflict, dissent; ≠ agreement ❑ *The United States Congress and the president are still locked in disagreement over proposals to reduce the massive budget deficit.* ❑ *My instructor and I had a brief disagreement.*

VOCABULARY BUILDER

disagreement NOUN

When there is **disagreement** about something, people argue about what should be done.

❑ *We do have a fundamental disagreement on the way hospitals ought to be funded.*

dispute NOUN

A **dispute** is a serious argument between groups, organizations, or countries that can last for a long time.

❑ *The two sides in the bus drivers' pay dispute were meeting today in a bid to halt further strike action.*

argument NOUN

An **argument** is a conversation in which people disagree with each other angrily and noisily.

❑ *Everything was going brilliantly until we had a stupid argument during a night out.*

dissent (formal) NOUN

Dissent is strong disagreement with a decision that has been made by people in authority.

❑ *But too often these networks are patriarchal, stifle dissent, and demand loyalty at all cost.*

conflict NOUN

Conflict is serious disagreement about something important.

❑ *Kerry's support of legalized abortion puts him in conflict with Catholic doctrine.*

---

dis·al·low /ˌdɪsəˈlaʊ/ VERB [T] (**disallows, disallowing, disallowed**) If something **is disallowed**, it is not allowed or accepted officially, because it has not been done correctly. ❑ *The goal was disallowed.*

✪ **dis·ap·pear** ◆◇◇ /ˌdɪsəˈpɪə/ VERB [i] (**disappears, disappearing, disappeared**) **1** If you say that someone or something **disappears**, you mean that you can no longer see them, usually because you or they have changed position. = vanish ❑ *The black car drove away from them and disappeared.* **2** If someone or something **disappears**, they go away or are taken away somewhere where nobody can find them. ❑ *a Japanese woman who disappeared thirteen years ago* **3** If something **disappears**, it stops existing or happening. = go, vanish; ≠ appear, emerge ❑ *The immediate threat of the past has disappeared and the security situation in Europe has significantly improved.* ❑ *Symptoms usually disappear gradually.*

✪ **dis·ap·pear·ance** /ˌdɪsəˈpɪərəns/ NOUN [c, u] (**disappearances**) **1** [c, u] If you refer to someone's **disappearance**, you are referring to the fact that nobody knows where they have gone. ≠ appearance, reappearance ❑ *Her disappearance has baffled police.* **2** [c] If you refer to the **disappearance** of an object, you are referring to the fact that it has been lost or stolen. = loss ❑ *Police are investigating the disappearance of key files on the killers.* **3** [u] The **disappearance** of a type of thing, person, or animal is

a process in which it becomes less common and finally no longer exists. = decline ❑ *the virtual disappearance of common dolphins from the western Mediterranean in recent years*

dis·ap·point /ˌdɪsəˈpɔɪnt/ VERB [T] (**disappoints, disappointing, disappointed**) If things or people **disappoint** you, they are not as good as you had hoped, or do not do what you hoped they would do. = let down ❑ *She would do anything she could to please him, but she knew that she was fated to disappoint him.*

dis·ap·point·ed ◆◇◇ /ˌdɪsəˈpɔɪntɪd/ ADJ **1** If you are **disappointed**, you are sad because something has not happened or because something is not as good as you had hoped. ❑ *Adamski says he was very disappointed with the mayor's decision.* ❑ *I was disappointed that John was not there.* **2** [V-LINK + disappointed 'in' N] If you are **disappointed in** someone, you are sad because they have not behaved as well as you expected them to. ❑ *You should have accepted that. I'm disappointed in you.*

dis·ap·point·ing /ˌdɪsəˈpɔɪntɪŋ/ ADJ Something that is **disappointing** is not as good or as large as you hoped it would be. ❑ *The wine was excellent, but the meat was overdone and the vegetables disappointing.*

dis·ap·point·ing·ly /ˌdɪsəˈpɔɪntɪŋli/ ADV ❑ *Progress is disappointingly slow.*

dis·ap·point·ment /ˌdɪsəˈpɔɪntmənt/ NOUN [u, c] (**disappointments**) **1** [u] **Disappointment** is the state of feeling disappointed. ❑ *Despite winning the title, their last campaign ended in great disappointment.* **2** [c] Something or someone that is a **disappointment** is not as good as you had hoped. ❑ *For many, their long-awaited homecoming was a bitter disappointment.*

dis·ap·prov·al /ˌdɪsəˈpruːvəl/ NOUN [u] If you feel or show **disapproval** of something or someone, you feel or show that you do not approve of them. ❑ *His action had been greeted with almost universal disapproval.*

dis·ap·prove /ˌdɪsəˈpruːv/ VERB [i] (**disapproves, disapproving, disapproved**) If you **disapprove of** something or someone, you feel or show that you do not like them or do not approve of them. ❑ *Most people disapprove of such violent tactics.*

dis·ap·prov·ing /ˌdɪsəˈpruːvɪŋ/ ADJ A **disapproving** action or expression shows that you do not approve of something or someone. ❑ *Janet gave him a disapproving look.*

dis·ap·prov·ing·ly /ˌdɪsəˈpruːvɪŋli/ ADV [disapprovingly after V] ❑ *Antonio looked at him disapprovingly.*

dis·ar·ray /ˌdɪsəˈreɪ/ NOUN [u] **1** If people or things are **in disarray**, they are disorganized and confused. = disorder ❑ *The nation is in disarray following rioting led by the military.* **2** If things or places are **in disarray**, they are in a very disorganized state. ❑ *She was left lying on her side and her clothes were in disarray.*

dis·as·ter ◆◇◇ /dɪˈzɑːstə, -ˈzæs-/ NOUN

NOUN [c, u] (**disasters**) **1** [c] A **disaster** is a very bad accident such as an earthquake or a plane crash, especially one in which a lot of people are killed. = tragedy ❑ *It was the second air disaster in the region in less than two months.* **2** [c] If you refer to something as a **disaster**, you are emphasizing that you think it is extremely bad or unacceptable. = catastrophe ❑ *The whole production was just a disaster!* **3** [u] **Disaster** is something which has very bad consequences for you. = catastrophe ❑ *The government brought itself to the brink of fiscal disaster.*

PHRASE **a recipe for disaster** If you say that something is **a recipe for disaster**, you mean that it is very likely to have unpleasant consequences. ❑ *You give them a gun, and it's a recipe for disaster.*

dis·as·trous /dɪˈzɑːstrəs, -ˈzæs-/ ADJ **1** A **disastrous** event has extremely bad consequences and effects. = catastrophic ❑ *the recent, disastrous earthquake* **2** If you describe something as **disastrous**, you mean that it was very unsuccessful. ❑ *after their disastrous performance in the election*

dis·as·trous·ly /dɪˈzɑːstrəsli, -ˈzæs-/ ADV **1** The vegetable harvest is disastrously behind schedule. **2** debts resulting from *the company's disastrously timed venture into property development*

dis·band /dɪs'bænd/ VERB [I, T] (**disbands, disbanding, disbanded**) If someone **disbands** a group of people, or if the group **disbands**, it stops operating as a single unit. ❑ *All the armed groups will be disbanded.*

dis·be·lief /ˌdɪsbɪ'liːf/ NOUN [U] **Disbelief** is not believing that something is true or real. ❑ *She looked at him in disbelief.*

✪ **disc** /dɪsk/ NOUN [C] (**discs**) **1** A **disc** is a flat, circular shape or object. ❑ *Most shredding machines are based on a revolving disc fitted with replaceable blades.* ❑ *a small disc of metal* **2** A **disc** is one of the thin, circular pieces of cartilage which separates the bones in your back. ❑ *I had slipped a disc and was frozen in a spasm of pain.* **3** A disc is the same as a **compact disc**. → See also **disk**

dis·card /dɪs'kɑːd/ VERB [T] (**discards, discarding, discarded**) If you **discard** something, you get rid of it because you no longer want it or need it. = dispose of ❑ *Read the manufacturer's guidelines before discarding the box.*

dis·cern /dɪ'sɜːn/ VERB [T] (**discerns, discerning, discerned**) (formal) **1** If you can **discern** something, you are aware of it and know what it is. ❑ *You need a long series of data to be able to discern such a trend.* **2** If you can **discern** something, you can just see it, but not clearly. ❑ *Below the bridge we could just discern a narrow, weedy ditch.*

dis·cern·ible /dɪ'sɜːnəbəl/ ADJ (formal) If something is **discernible**, you can see it or recognize that it exists. = apparent ❑ *Far away the outline of the island is just discernible.*

dis·cern·ing /dɪ'sɜːnɪŋ/ ADJ (approval) If you describe someone as **discerning**, you mean that they are able to judge what things of a particular kind are good and which are bad. ❑ *Even the most accomplished writers show their work-in-progress to discerning readers.*

dis·charge VERB, NOUN

VERB /dɪs'tʃɑːdʒ/ [T] (**discharges, discharging, discharged**) **1** When someone **is discharged from** a hospital, prison, or one of the armed services, they are officially allowed to leave, or told that they must leave. ❑ *He has a broken nose but may be discharged today.* **2** (formal) If someone **discharges** their duties or responsibilities, they do everything that needs to be done in order to complete them. ❑ *the quiet competence with which he discharged his many duties* **3** (formal) If something **is discharged** from inside a place, it comes out. ❑ *The resulting salty water will be discharged at sea.*

NOUN /'dɪstʃɑːdʒ/ [C, U] (**discharges**) **1** A **discharge** is the release or dismissal of someone from a hospital, prison, or one of the armed services. ❑ *He was given a conditional discharge and ordered to pay Miss Smith $500 compensation.* **2** (formal) When there is a **discharge** of a substance, the substance comes out from inside somewhere. ❑ *They develop a fever and a watery discharge from their eyes.*

dis·ci·ple /dɪ'saɪpəl/ NOUN [C] (**disciples**) If you are someone's **disciple**, you are influenced by their teachings and try to follow their example. = follower ❑ *a major intellectual figure with disciples throughout Europe*

dis·ci·pli·nary /'dɪsɪplɪnəri, AmE -neri/ ADJ [disciplinary + N] **Disciplinary** bodies or actions are concerned with making sure that people obey rules or regulations and that they are punished if they do not. ❑ *He will now face a disciplinary hearing for having an affair.*

✪ **dis·ci·pline** ♦◇◇ /'dɪsɪplɪn/ NOUN, VERB

NOUN [U, C] (**disciplines**) **1** [U] **Discipline** is the practice of making people obey rules or standards of behaviour, and punishing them when they do not. ❑ *Order and discipline have been placed in the hands of governing bodies.* **2** [U] **Discipline** is the quality of being able to behave and work in a controlled way which involves obeying particular rules or standards. = self-control ❑ *It was that image of calm, control, and discipline that appealed to millions of voters.* **3** [C, U] If you refer to an activity or situation as a **discipline**, you mean that, in order to be successful in it, you need to behave in a strictly controlled way and obey particular rules or standards. ❑ *The discipline of studying*

music can help children develop good work habits and improve self-esteem. **4** [C] (formal) A **discipline** is a particular area of study, especially a subject of study in a college or university. = subject, area, speciality ❑ *We're looking for people from a wide range of disciplines.* ❑ *the study of economics as an academic discipline*

VERB [T] (**disciplines, disciplining, disciplined**) **1** If someone **is disciplined** for something that they have done wrong, they are punished for it. ❑ *The workman was disciplined by his company but not dismissed.* **2** If you **discipline yourself** to do something, you train yourself to behave and work in a strictly controlled and regular way. ❑ *Discipline yourself to check your messages once a day or every couple of days.*

dis·ci·plined /'dɪsɪplɪnd/ ADJ Someone who is **disciplined** behaves or works in a controlled way. ❑ *For me it meant being very disciplined about how I run my life.*

dis·close /dɪs'kləʊz/ VERB [T] (**discloses, disclosing, disclosed**) If you **disclose** new or secret information, you tell people about it. = reveal ❑ *Neither side would disclose details of the transaction.*

dis·clo·sure /dɪs'kləʊʒə/ NOUN [C, U] (**disclosures**) **Disclosure** is the act of giving people new or secret information. = revelation ❑ *insufficient disclosure of negative information about the company*

dis·com·fort /dɪs'kʌmfət/ NOUN [U, C] (**discomforts**) **1** [U] **Discomfort** is a painful feeling in part of your body when you have been hurt slightly or when you have been uncomfortable for a long time. ❑ *Steve had some discomfort, but no real pain.* **2** [U] **Discomfort** is a feeling of worry caused by shame or embarrassment. = uneasiness ❑ *She hears the discomfort in his voice.* **3** [C] **Discomforts** are conditions which cause you to feel physically uncomfortable. ❑ *the discomforts of camping*

dis·con·cert·ing /ˌdɪskən'sɜːtɪŋ/ ADJ If you say that something is **disconcerting**, you mean that it makes you feel anxious, confused, or embarrassed. = unsettling ❑ *The reception desk is not at street level, which is a little disconcerting.*
dis·con·cert·ing·ly /ˌdɪskən'sɜːtɪŋli/ ADV ❑ *She looks disconcertingly like a familiar aunt or grandmother.*

dis·con·nect /ˌdɪskə'nekt/ VERB [T] (**disconnects, disconnecting, disconnected**) **1** To **disconnect** a piece of equipment means to separate it from its source of power or to break a connection that it needs in order to work. ❑ *The device automatically disconnects the ignition when the engine is switched off.* **2** If you **are disconnected** by a gas, electricity, water, or telephone company, they turn off the connection to your house, usually because you have not paid the bill. ❑ *You are likely to be given almost three months – until the time of your next bill – before you are disconnected.* **3** If you **disconnect** something **from** something else, you separate the two things. ❑ *He disconnected the IV bottle from the overhead hook and carried it beside the moving trolley.*

dis·con·tent /ˌdɪskən'tent/ NOUN [U] **Discontent** is the feeling that you have that you are not satisfied with your situation. = dissatisfaction ❑ *There are reports of widespread discontent in the capital.*

dis·con·tinue /ˌdɪskən'tɪnjuː/ VERB [T] (**discontinues, discontinuing, discontinued**) **1** (formal) If you **discontinue** something that you have been doing regularly, you stop doing it. ❑ *Do not discontinue the treatment without consulting your doctor.* **2** If a product **is discontinued**, the manufacturer stops making it. ❑ *The Leica M2 was discontinued in 1967.*

dis·count ♦◇◇ NOUN, VERB

NOUN /'dɪskaʊnt/ [C] (**discounts**) A **discount** is a reduction in the usual price of something. ❑ *They are often available at a discount.* ❑ *All full-time staff get a 20 per cent discount.*

VERB /dɪs'kaʊnt/ [T] (**discounts, discounting, discounted**) **1** If a shop or company **discounts** an amount or percentage from something that they are selling, they take the amount or percentage off the usual price. ❑ *This has forced airlines to discount fares heavily in order to spur demand.* **2** If you **discount** an idea, fact, or theory, you consider that it is not true, not important, or not relevant. = disregard ❑ *However, traders tended to discount the rumour.*

dis·cour·age /dɪsˈkʌrɪdʒ, AmE -ˈkɜːr-/ VERB [T] (**discourages, discouraging, discouraged**) **1** If someone or something **discourages** you, they cause you to lose your enthusiasm about your actions. ❑ *It may be difficult to do at first. Don't let this discourage you.* **2** To **discourage** an action or to **discourage** someone from doing it means to make them not want to do it. = deter ❑ *typhoons that discouraged shopping and leisure activities*
dis·cour·aged /dɪsˈkʌrɪdʒd, AmE -ˈkɜːr-/ ADJ ❑ *She was determined not to be too discouraged.*
dis·cour·ag·ing /dɪsˈkʌrɪdʒɪŋ, AmE -ˈkɜːr-/ ADJ ❑ *Today's report is extremely discouraging for the economy.*

dis·cour·age·ment /dɪsˈkʌrɪdʒmənt, AmE -ˈkɜːr-/ NOUN [U] **Discouragement** is the act of trying to make someone not want to do something. ❑ *He persevered in the face of active discouragement from those around him.*

✪**dis·course** /ˈdɪskɔːs/ NOUN [U] (**discourses**) **Discourse** is spoken or written communication between people, especially serious discussion of a particular subject. = communication, dialogue, debate, rhetoric ❑ *a tradition of political discourse* ❑ *public discourse on crime*

✪**dis·cov·er** ♦♦◇ /dɪsˈkʌvə/ VERB [T] (**discovers, discovering, discovered**) **1** If you **discover** something that you did not know about before, you become aware of it or learn of it. = find out, learn ❑ *She discovered that they'd escaped.* ❑ *It was difficult for the inspectors to discover which documents were important and which were not.* **2** If a person or thing **is discovered**, someone finds them, either by accident or because they have been looking for them. = find ❑ *A few days later his badly beaten body was discovered on a roadside outside the city.* **3** When someone **discovers** a new place, substance, scientific fact, or scientific technique, they are the first person to find it or become aware of it. ❑ *the first European to discover America* ❑ *In the 19th century, gold was discovered in California.* ❑ *They discovered how to form the image in a thin layer on the surface.* **4** When an actor, musician, or other performer who is not well known **is discovered**, someone recognizes that they have talent and helps them in their career. ❑ *The Beatles were discovered in the early 1960s.*

WORD CONNECTIONS
discover + NOUN
discover the **truth**
❑ *He was determined to discover the truth about his daughter's death.*
discover a **planet**
discover a **comet**
discover a **tomb**
discover a **species**
discover a **fossil**
❑ *Spanish and German astronomers have discovered three planets about the size of Jupiter.*
discover a **cure** for
❑ *For years scientists have been involved in research to discover a cure for the common cold.*
ADV + **discover**
soon discover
first discover
quickly discover
finally discover
❑ *We soon discovered that we had been tricked.*
newly discovered
recently discovered
❑ *They are examining newly discovered caves.*

✪**dis·cov·ery** ♦◇◇ /dɪsˈkʌvəri/ NOUN [C, U] (**discoveries**) **1** If someone makes a **discovery**, they become aware of something that they did not know about before. ❑ *I felt I'd made an incredible discovery.* **2** If someone makes a

discovery, they are the first person to find or become aware of a place, substance, or scientific fact that no one knew about before. ❑ *In that year, two momentous discoveries were made.* **3** When the **discovery** of people or objects happens, someone finds them, either by accident or as a result of looking for them. ❑ *the discovery and destruction by soldiers of millions of marijuana plants* ❑ *the discovery of the ozone hole over the South Pole*

dis·cred·it /dɪsˈkredɪt/ VERB [T] (**discredits, discrediting, discredited**) To **discredit** someone or something means to cause them to lose people's respect or trust. ❑ *a secret unit within the company that had been set up to discredit its major rival*
dis·cred·it·ed /dɪsˈkredɪtɪd/ ADJ ❑ *The previous government is, by now, thoroughly discredited.*

dis·creet /dɪsˈkriːt/ ADJ **1** If you are **discreet**, you are polite and careful in what you do or say, because you want to avoid embarrassing or offending someone. ❑ *They were gossipy and not always discreet.* **2** If you are **discreet about** something you are doing, you do not tell other people about it, in order to avoid being embarrassed or to gain an advantage. ❑ *We were very discreet about the romance.* **3** If you describe something as **discreet**, you approve of it because it is small in size or degree, or not easily noticed. ❑ *She is wearing a noticeably stylish, feminine dress, plus discreet jewellery.*
dis·creet·ly /dɪsˈkriːtli/ ADV **1** *I took the phone, and she went discreetly into the living room.* **2** *Everyone worked to make him welcome, and, more discreetly, to find out about him.* **3** [discreetly + -ED/ADJ] ❑ *stately houses, discreetly hidden behind great avenues of sturdy trees*

dis·crep·an·cy /dɪsˈkrepənsi/ NOUN [C, U] (**discrepancies**) If there is a **discrepancy between** two things that ought to be the same, there is a noticeable difference between them. = inconsistency ❑ *the discrepancy between press and radio reports*

✪**dis·crete** /dɪsˈkriːt/ ADJ [usu discrete + N] (formal) **Discrete** ideas or things are separate and distinct from each other. = separate, distinct ❑ *instruction manuals that break down jobs into scores of discrete steps* ❑ *Herbal medicine does not treat mind and body as discrete entities, but holistically.*

✪**dis·cre·tion** /dɪsˈkreʃən/ NOUN (academic word) NOUN [U] (formal) **1** **Discretion** is the quality of behaving in a quiet and controlled way without drawing attention to yourself or giving away personal or private information. ❑ *Larsson sometimes joined in the fun, but with more discretion.* **2** If someone in a position of authority uses their **discretion** or has the **discretion** to do something in a particular situation, they have the freedom and authority to decide what to do. ❑ *This committee may want to exercise its discretion to look into those charges.* ❑ *School governors have the discretion to allow parents to withdraw pupils in exceptional circumstances.* PHRASE **at the discretion of someone** (formal) If something happens **at** someone's **discretion**, it can happen only if they decide to do it or give their permission. ❑ *We may vary the limit at our discretion and will notify you of any change.* ❑ *Visits are at the discretion of the owners.*

✪**dis·cre·tion·ary** /dɪsˈkreʃənri, AmE -neri/ ADJ **Discretionary** things are not fixed by rules but are decided on by people in authority, who consider each individual case. ❑ *Magistrates were given wider discretionary powers.* ❑ *The committee decided to pay small discretionary bonuses to reflect the accomplishments of key directors.*

✪**dis·crim·i·nate** /dɪsˈkrɪmɪneɪt/ VERB [I] (**discriminates, discriminating, discriminated**) (academic word) **1** If you can **discriminate between** two things, you can recognize that they are different. ❑ *He is incapable of discriminating between a good idea and a terrible one.* **2** To **discriminate against** a group of people or **in favour of** a group of people means to unfairly treat them worse or better than other groups. ❑ *They believe the law discriminates against women.* ❑ *legislation which would discriminate in favour of racial minorities*

✪**dis·crimi·na·tion** /dɪsˌkrɪmɪˈneɪʃən/ NOUN [U] **1** **Discrimination** is the practice of treating one person or group of people less fairly or less well than other people or groups. = prejudice, bias, unfairness, inequality; ≠ fairness,

equality ❑ *She is exempt from sex discrimination laws.*
❑ *discrimination against immigrants* ❑ *measures to counteract racial discrimination* **2** **Discrimination** is knowing what is good or of high quality. ❑ *They cooked without skill and ate without discrimination.* **3** **Discrimination** is the ability to recognize and understand the differences between two things. = discernment, differentiation ❑ *We will then have an objective measure of how colour discrimination and visual acuity develop at the level of the brain.* ❑ *the system that allows a mother to make the discrimination between her own and alien lambs*

VOCABULARY BUILDER

discrimination NOUN

Discrimination is the practice of treating one person or group of people less fairly or less well than other people or groups.

❑ *Mrs Campbell has accused the company of sex discrimination and unfair dismissal.*

prejudice NOUN

Prejudice is an unreasonable dislike of a particular group of people or things.

❑ *It was difficult for Elizabeth to overcome the established, deep-seated prejudices against female rule.*

bias NOUN

Bias is a tendency to prefer one person or group to another, and to show favour to that person or group.

❑ *Earlier generations of women had to cope with gender bias, hostility, and opposition during their childhood.*

unfairness NOUN

Unfairness is the failure to treat everybody the same and judge everyone by the same standards.

❑ *This government is failing to tackle the fundamental unfairness in our tax system.*

inequality NOUN

Inequality is the difference in social status, wealth, or opportunity between people or groups.

❑ *The funding will help to reduce health inequalities in some of the most disadvantaged areas.*

⭕ **dis·cuss** ♦♦◇ /dɪsˈkʌs/ VERB [T] (**discusses, discussing, discussed**) **1** If people **discuss** something, they talk about it, often in order to reach a decision. ❑ *I will be discussing the situation with colleagues tomorrow.* ❑ *The cabinet met today to discuss how to respond to the ultimatum.* **2** If you **discuss** something, you write or talk about it in detail. = consider, debate, examine ❑ *I will discuss the role of diet in cancer prevention in Chapter 7.*

WORD CONNECTIONS

discuss + NOUN

discuss a **matter**
discuss an **issue**
discuss a **topic**
discuss a **situation**

❑ *Managers are meeting to discuss the issue of pay increases.*

discuss a **proposal**
discuss a **plan**
discuss an **idea**
discuss a **problem**
discuss a **case**

❑ *I'm afraid I can't discuss individual cases.*

discuss the **possibility** of
discuss the **details** of

❑ *We're discussing the possibility of extending our opening hours.*

ADV + discuss

openly discuss
publicly discuss

❑ *Financial advice and support is available so that students can openly discuss any concerns they may have.*

⭕ **dis·cus·sion** ♦♦◇ /dɪsˈkʌʃən/ NOUN, ADJ

NOUN [C, U] (**discussions**) **1** [C, U] If there is **discussion** about something, people talk about it, often in order to reach a decision. = debate, argument, examination, analysis ❑ *There was a lot of discussion about the wording of the report.* ❑ *Board members are due to have informal discussions later on today.* **2** [C] A **discussion of** a subject is a piece of writing or a lecture in which someone talks about it in detail. ❑ *For a discussion of biology and sexual politics, see chapter 4.*

PHRASE **under discussion** If something is **under discussion**, it is still being talked about and a final decision has not yet been reached.

ADJ [discussion + N] A **discussion** document or paper is one that contains information and usually proposals for people to discuss. ❑ *a NASA discussion paper on long-duration ballooning*

WORD CONNECTIONS

VERB + discussion

hold a discussion
have a discussion
initiate a discussion

❑ *Discussions were held between the police and community representatives.*

ADJ + discussion

a **detailed** discussion
a **preliminary** discussion
a **frank** discussion

❑ *We have had detailed discussions with all relevant parties.*

lengthy discussions
further discussions
informal discussions

❑ *The majority of problems are resolved by informal discussions outside these meetings.*

WHICH WORD?

discussion, argument, or debate?

If you have a **discussion** with someone, you have a serious conversation with them.

❑ *After the lecture there was a **discussion**.*

❑ *We had a long **discussion** about our future plans.*

You do not use **discussion** to refer to a disagreement between people, especially one that results in them shouting angrily at each other. This kind of disagreement is usually called an **argument**.

❑ *I said no, and we got into a big **argument** over it.*

A **debate** is a formal discussion about a subject on which people express different views.

❑ *There has been a great deal of **debate** among scholars about this issue.*

---

dis·dain /dɪsˈdeɪn/ NOUN, VERB

NOUN [U] If you feel **disdain for** someone or something, you dislike them because you think that they are inferior or unimportant. = contempt, scorn ❑ *Janet looked at him with disdain.*

VERB [T] (**disdains, disdaining, disdained**) If you **disdain** someone or something, you regard them with disdain. ❑ *Jackie disdained the servants that her millions could buy.*

⭕ **dis·ease** ♦♦◇ /dɪˈziːz/ NOUN [C, U] (**diseases**) A **disease** is an illness which affects people, animals, or plants, for example, one which is caused by bacteria or infection. = illness, infection, disorder, condition, complaint ❑ *the rapid spread of disease in the area* ❑ *illnesses such as heart disease* ❑ *Doctors believe they have cured him of the disease.*

VOCABULARY BUILDER

disease NOUN

A **disease** is an illness which affects people, animals, or plants, for example, one which is caused by bacteria or infection.

❑ *The disease is spreading eastwards from Peru, and more than eighty cases have so far been registered in Brazil.*

D

---

illness NOUN

An **illness** is a particular disease such as measles or pneumonia.
❑ *Over long periods of time, excessive stress increases the risk of illnesses such as heart disease or cancer.*

infection NOUN

An **infection** is a disease caused by germs or bacteria.
❑ *My daughter had repeated ear infections for the first three years of her life.*

condition NOUN

If someone has a particular **condition**, they have a long-lasting illness or medical problem.
❑ *Bliss suffered from a heart condition and was by nature a reserved man.*

disorder NOUN

A **disorder** is a medical problem or illness which affects someone's mind or body.
❑ *I've been diagnosed with an acute form of bipolar disorder, where the mood swings can be hourly.*

complaint NOUN

You can refer to an illness as a **complaint**, especially if it is not very serious.
❑ *Marshall has had a stomach complaint for several months.*

---

dis·eased /dɪˈziːzd/ ADJ Something that is **diseased** is affected by a disease. ❑ *The arteries are diseased and a transplant is the only hope.*

dis·en·chant·ed /ˌdɪsɪnˈtʃɑːntɪd, -ˈtʃænt-/ ADJ If you are **disenchanted with** something, you are disappointed with it and no longer believe that it is good or worthwhile. = disillusioned ❑ *The electorate had grown disenchanted with politics.*

dis·fig·ure /dɪsˈfɪɡə, AmE -ɡjər/ VERB [T] (disfigures, disfiguring, disfigured) If someone **is disfigured**, their appearance is spoiled. ❑ *Many of the wounded had been badly disfigured.*
dis·fig·ured /dɪsˈfɪɡəd, AmE -ɡjərd/ ADJ ❑ *She tried not to look at the scarred, disfigured face.*

dis·grace /dɪsˈɡreɪs/ NOUN, VERB
NOUN [U, SING] (emphasis) **1** [U] If you say that someone is **in disgrace**, you are emphasizing that other people disapprove of them and do not respect them because of something that they have done. ❑ *His vice president also had to resign in disgrace.* **2** [SING] If you say that something is **a disgrace**, you are emphasizing that it is very bad or wrong, and that you find it completely unacceptable. = scandal ❑ *The way the sales were handled was a complete disgrace.* **3** [SING] You say that someone is **a disgrace to** someone else when you want to emphasize that their behaviour causes the other person to feel ashamed. ❑ *Republican leaders called him a disgrace to the party.*
VERB [T] (disgraces, disgracing, disgraced) (emphasis) If you say that someone **disgraces** someone else, you are emphasizing that their behaviour causes the other person to feel ashamed. ❑ *I have disgraced my family's name.*

dis·graced /dɪsˈɡreɪst/ ADJ You use **disgraced** to describe someone whose bad behaviour has caused them to lose the approval and respect of the public or of people in authority. ❑ *the disgraced leader of the coup*

dis·grace·ful /dɪsˈɡreɪsfʊl/ ADJ (disapproval) If you say that something such as behaviour or a situation is **disgraceful**, you disapprove of it strongly, and feel that the person or people responsible should be ashamed of it. = shocking, scandalous ❑ *It's disgraceful that they have detained him for so long.*
dis·grace·ful·ly /dɪsˈɡreɪsfʊli/ ADV ❑ *He felt that his brother had behaved disgracefully.*

dis·grun·tled /dɪsˈɡrʌntəld/ ADJ If you are **disgruntled**, you are angry and dissatisfied because things have not happened the way that you wanted them to happen.
❑ *Disgruntled employees recently called for his resignation.*

dis·guise /dɪsˈɡaɪz/ NOUN, VERB
NOUN [C, U] (disguises) If you are **in disguise**, you are not wearing your usual clothes or you have altered your appearance in other ways, so that people will not recognize you. ❑ *You'll have to travel in disguise.*
VERB [T] (disguises, disguising, disguised) **1** If you **disguise yourself**, you put on clothes which make you look like someone else or alter your appearance in other ways, so that people will not recognize you. ❑ *She disguised herself as a man so she could fight on the battlefield.* **2** To **disguise** something means to hide it or make it appear different so that people will not know about it or will not recognize it. ❑ *He made no attempt to disguise his agitation.*
dis·guised /dɪsˈɡaɪzd/ ADJ **1** *The extremists entered the building disguised as medical workers.* **2** *The proposal is a thinly disguised effort to revive the price controls of the 1970s.*

dis·gust /dɪsˈɡʌst/ NOUN, VERB
NOUN [U] **Disgust** is a feeling of very strong dislike or disapproval. = revulsion ❑ *He spoke of his disgust at the incident.*
VERB [T] (disgusts, disgusting, disgusted) To **disgust** someone means to make them feel a strong sense of dislike and disapproval. ❑ *He disgusted many with his boorish behaviour.*

dis·gust·ed /dɪsˈɡʌstɪd/ ADJ If you are **disgusted**, you feel a strong sense of dislike and disapproval at something. = appalled ❑ *I'm disgusted with the way that he was treated.*
dis·gust·ed·ly /dɪsˈɡʌstɪdli/ ADV [disgustedly with V] ❑ *'It's a little late for that,' Ritter said disgustedly.*

dis·gust·ing /dɪsˈɡʌstɪŋ/ ADJ **1** If you say that something is **disgusting**, you are criticizing it because it is extremely unpleasant. = revolting ❑ *It tasted disgusting.* **2** If you say that something is **disgusting**, you mean that you find it completely unacceptable. = disgraceful ❑ *It's disgusting that all this damage has been caused by mindless vandalism.*

dish ♦◇◇ /dɪʃ/ NOUN
NOUN [C, PL] (dishes) **1** [C] A **dish** is a shallow container with a wide uncovered top. You eat and serve food from dishes and cook food in them. ❑ *plastic bowls and dishes* **2** [C] Food that is prepared in a particular style or combination can be referred to as a **dish**. ❑ *There are plenty of vegetarian dishes to choose from.* **3** [C] You can use **dish** to refer to anything that is round and hollow in shape with a wide uncovered top. ❑ *a dish used to receive satellite broadcasts* **4** [PL] All the objects that have been used to cook, serve, and eat a meal can be referred to as **the dishes**. ❑ *He'd cooked dinner and washed the dishes.*
PHRASE **do the dishes** If you **do the dishes**, you wash the dishes. ❑ *I hate doing the dishes.*
PHRASAL VERBS **dish out** (dishes, dishing, dished) (informal) **1** If you **dish out** something, you distribute it among a number of people. ❑ *Doctors, not pharmacists, are responsible for dishing out drugs.* **2** If someone **dishes out** criticism or punishment, they give it to someone. = dish up ❑ *Do you usually dish out criticism to someone who's doing you a favour?* **3** If you **dish out** food, you serve it to people at the beginning of each course of a meal. ❑ *Here the cooks dish out sweet and sour pork.*
dish up (informal) If you **dish up** food, you serve it. ❑ *They dished up a superb meal.*

di·shev·elled /dɪˈʃevəld/ (BrE; in AmE, also use **disheveled**) ADJ If you describe someone's hair, clothes, or appearance as **dishevelled**, you mean that it is very untidy. ❑ *She arrived flushed and dishevelled.*

dis·hon·est /dɪsˈɒnɪst/ ADJ If you say that a person or their behaviour is **dishonest**, you mean that they are not truthful or honest and that you cannot trust them. ❑ *It would be dishonest to mislead people and not to present the data as fairly as possible.*
dis·hon·est·ly /dɪsˈɒnɪstli/ ADV ❑ *The key issue was whether the four defendants acted dishonestly.*

dis·hon·es·ty /dɪsˈɒnɪsti/ NOUN [U] **Dishonesty** is dishonest behaviour. ❑ *She accused the government of dishonesty and incompetence.*

dis·il·lu·sion /ˌdɪsɪˈluːʒən/ VERB, NOUN
VERB [T] (**disillusions, disillusioning, disillusioned**) If a person or thing **disillusions** you, they make you realize that something is not as good as you thought. ❑ *I'd hate to be the one to disillusion him.*
NOUN [U] **Disillusion** is the disappointment that you feel when you discover that something is not as good as you had expected or thought. ❑ *There is disillusion with established political parties.*

dis·il·lu·sioned /ˌdɪsɪˈluːʒənd/ ADJ If you are **disillusioned with** something, you are disappointed, because it is not as good as you had expected or thought. = disenchanted ❑ *I've become very disillusioned with politics.*

dis·in·te·grate /dɪsˈɪntɪɡreɪt/ VERB [I] (**disintegrates, disintegrating, disintegrated**) **1** If something **disintegrates**, it becomes seriously weakened, and is divided or destroyed. ❑ *During October 1918 the Austro-Hungarian Empire began to disintegrate.* **2** If an object or substance **disintegrates**, it breaks into many small pieces or parts and is destroyed. ❑ *At 420 mph the windshield disintegrated.*
dis·in·te·gra·tion /dɪsˌɪntɪˈɡreɪʃən/ NOUN [U] **1** the violent disintegration of Yugoslavia **2** *The report describes the catastrophic disintegration of the aircraft after the explosion.*

✪**disk** /dɪsk/ also **disc** NOUN [C] (**disks**) In a computer, the **disk** is the part where information is stored. ❑ *The program takes up 2.5 megabytes of disk space and can be run on a standard personal computer.*

dis·like /dɪsˈlaɪk/ VERB, NOUN
VERB [T] (**dislikes, disliking, disliked**) If you **dislike** someone or something, you consider them to be unpleasant and do not like them. ❑ *Liver is a great favourite of his and we don't serve it often because so many people dislike it.*
NOUN [U, C] (**dislikes**) **1** [U] **Dislike** is the feeling that you do not like someone or something. ❑ *My dislike of thunder and even small earthquakes was due to Mother.* **2** [C] Your **dislikes** are the things that you do not like. ❑ *Consider what your likes and dislikes are about your job.*
PHRASE **take a dislike** If you **take a dislike to** someone or something, you decide that you do not like them. ❑ *He may suddenly take a dislike to foods that he's previously enjoyed.*

dis·loy·al /dɪsˈlɔɪəl/ ADJ Someone who is **disloyal** to their friends, family, or country does not support them or does things that could harm them. ❑ *She was so disloyal to her deputy she made his position untenable.*

dis·loy·al·ty /dɪsˈlɔɪəlti/ NOUN [U] **Disloyalty** is disloyal behaviour. ❑ *Charges had already been made against certain officials suspected of disloyalty.*

dis·mal /ˈdɪzməl/ ADJ **1** Something that is **dismal** is bad in a sad or depressing way. ❑ *Israel's dismal record in the Olympics* **2** Something that is **dismal** is sad and depressing, especially in appearance. = dreary ❑ *The main part of the hospital is pretty dismal but the children's ward is really lively.*

dis·man·tle /dɪsˈmæntəl/ VERB [T] (**dismantles, dismantling, dismantled**) **1** If you **dismantle** a machine or structure, you carefully separate it into its different parts. ❑ *He asked for immediate help from the United States to dismantle the warheads.* **2** To **dismantle** an organization or system means to cause it to stop functioning by gradually reducing its power or purpose. ❑ *Public services of all kinds are being dismantled.*

dis·may /dɪsˈmeɪ/ NOUN, VERB
NOUN [U] (*formal*) **Dismay** is a strong feeling of fear, worry, or sadness that is caused by something unpleasant and unexpected. ❑ *Local politicians have reacted with dismay and indignation.*
VERB [T] (**dismays, dismaying, dismayed**) (*formal*) If you **are dismayed** by something, it makes you feel afraid, worried, or sad. ❑ *The committee was dismayed by what it had been told.*
dis·mayed /dɪsˈmeɪd/ ADJ ❑ *He was dismayed at the cynicism of the youngsters.*

dis·miss ♦◇◇ /dɪsˈmɪs/ VERB [T] (**dismisses, dismissing, dismissed**) **1** If you **dismiss** something, you decide or say that it is not important enough for you to think about or consider. = discount ❑ *Mr Wakeham dismissed the reports as speculation.* **2** If you **dismiss** something **from** your mind, you stop thinking about it. = banish ❑ *I dismissed the problem from my mind.* **3** When an employer **dismisses** an employee, the employer tells the employee that they are no longer needed to do the job that they have been doing. = fire ❑ *the power to dismiss civil servants who refuse to work* **4** If you **are dismissed** by someone in authority, they tell you that you can go away from them. ❑ *Two more witnesses were called, heard, and dismissed.* **5** When a judge **dismisses** a case against someone, he or she formally states that there is no need for a trial, usually because there is not enough evidence for the case to continue. ❑ *A federal judge dismissed the charges against the doctor yesterday.*

dis·mis·sal /dɪsˈmɪsəl/ NOUN [C, U] (**dismissals**) **1** [C, U] When an employee is dismissed from their job, you can refer to their **dismissal**. ❑ *Mr Low's dismissal from his post at the head of the commission* **2** [U] **Dismissal of** something means deciding or saying that it is not important. ❑ *bureaucratic indifference to people's rights and needs, and high-handed dismissal of public opinion*

dis·mis·sive /dɪsˈmɪsɪv/ ADJ If you are **dismissive of** someone or something, you say or show that you think they are not important or have no value. ❑ *Mr Jones was dismissive of the report, saying it was riddled with inaccuracies.*
dis·mis·sive·ly /dɪsˈmɪsɪvli/ ADV *'Critical acclaim from people who don't know what they're talking about is meaningless,' he claims dismissively.*

dis·obe·di·ence /ˌdɪsəˈbiːdiəns/ NOUN [U] **Disobedience** is deliberately not doing what someone tells you to do, or what a rule or law says that you should do. ❑ *A single act of rebellion or disobedience was often enough to seal a woman's fate.*

dis·obey /ˌdɪsəˈbeɪ/ VERB [I, T] (**disobeys, disobeying, disobeyed**) When someone **disobeys** a person or an order, they deliberately do not do what they have been told to do. ❑ *a naughty boy who often disobeyed his mother and father*

✪**dis·or·der** /dɪsˈɔːdə/ NOUN [C, U] (**disorders**) **1** [C, U] A **disorder** is a problem or illness which affects someone's mind or body. = complaint, illness ❑ *a rare nerve disorder that can cause paralysis of the arms* **2** [C, U] **Disorder** is violence or rioting in public. = unrest ❑ *Six months ago America's worst civil disorder in more than 100 years erupted in the city of Los Angeles.* **3** [U] **Disorder** is a state of being untidy, badly prepared, or badly organized. = confusion ❑ *The casualty ward was in disorder.*

dis·or·der·ly /dɪsˈɔːdəli/ ADJ (*formal*) **1** If you describe something as **disorderly**, you mean that it is messy, irregular, or disorganized. = chaotic ❑ *There were young men and women working away at tables all over the large and disorderly room.* **2** If you describe someone as **disorderly**, you mean that they are behaving in a noisy, rude, or violent way in public. You can also describe a place or event as **disorderly** if the people there behave in this way. = rowdy ❑ *She was jailed for being drunk and disorderly.*

dis·or·gan·ized /dɪsˈɔːɡənaɪzd/ also
disorganised ADJ **1** Something that is **disorganized** is in a confused state or is badly planned or managed. ❑ *A report by the state prosecutor described the police action as confused and disorganized.* **2** Someone who is **disorganized** is very bad at organizing things in their life. ❑ *My boss is completely disorganized and leaves the most important items until very late.*

dis·ori·ent /dɪsˈɔːrient/ or **disorientate** /dɪsˈɔːriənteɪt/ VERB [T] (**disorients, disorienting, disoriented**) If something **disorients** you, you lose your sense of direction, or you generally feel lost and uncertain, for example because you are in an unfamiliar environment. = confuse ❑ *An overnight stay at a friend's house disorients me.*
dis·ori·ent·ed /dɪsˈɔːrientɪd/ ADJ ❑ *I feel dizzy and disoriented.*
dis·ori·en·ta·tion /dɪsˌɔːriənˈteɪʃən/ NOUN [U] ❑ *Morris was so stunned by this that he experienced a moment of total disorientation.*

d

D

dis·par·ag·ing /ˌdɪsˈpærɪdʒɪŋ/ ADJ If you are **disparaging** about someone or something, or make **disparaging** comments about them, you say things which show that you do not have a good opinion of them. ❑ *He was critical of the people, disparaging of their crude manners.*

dis·patch /dɪsˈpætʃ/ also **despatch** VERB, NOUN
VERB [T] (**dispatches, dispatching, dispatched**) (*formal*) **1** If you **dispatch** someone to a place, you send them there for a particular reason. = send ❑ *He had been continually dispatching scouts ahead.* **2** If you **dispatch** a message, letter, or parcel, you send it to a particular person or destination. = send ❑ *The victory inspired him to dispatch a gleeful telegram to Roosevelt.*
NOUN [U] (**dispatches**) **1** A **dispatch** is the act of sending someone to a place for a particular reason. ❑ *The dispatch of the task force is purely a contingency measure.* **2** A **dispatch** is the act of sending a message, letter, or parcel to a particular person or destination. ❑ *We have 125 cases ready for dispatch.*

dis·pel /dɪsˈpel/ VERB [T] (**dispels, dispelling, dispelled**) To **dispel** an idea or feeling that people have means to stop them having it. = banish ❑ *The president is attempting to dispel the notion that he has neglected the economy.*

dis·pens·er /dɪsˈpensə/ NOUN [C] (**dispensers**) A **dispenser** is a machine or container designed so that you can get an item or quantity of something from it in an easy and convenient way. ❑ *cash dispensers*

⭕**dis·per·sal** /dɪsˈpɜːsəl/ NOUN [U] **1 Dispersal** is the spreading of things over a wide area. = distribution ❑ *Plants have different mechanisms of dispersal for their spores.* ❑ *dispersal of ash during the hurricane season* **2** [oft dispersal 'of' N] The **dispersal** of a crowd involves splitting it up and making the people leave in different directions. ❑ *The police ordered the dispersal of the crowds gathered around the building.*

⭕**dis·perse** /dɪsˈpɜːs/ VERB [I, T] (**disperses, dispersing, dispersed**) **1** When something **disperses** or when you **disperse** it, it spreads over a wide area. = spread, scatter ❑ *The oil appeared to be dispersing.* ❑ *The intense currents disperse the sewage.* ❑ *Because the town sits in a valley, air pollution is not easily dispersed.* **2** When a group of people **disperses** or when someone **disperses** them, the group splits up and the people leave in different directions. = break up ❑ *Police fired shots and used tear gas to disperse the demonstrators.*

⭕**dis·place** /dɪsˈpleɪs/ VERB [T] (**displaces, displacing, displaced**) (*academic word*) **1** If one thing **displaces** another, it forces the other thing out of its place, position, or role, and then occupies that place, position, or role itself. ❑ *These factories have displaced tourism as the country's largest source of foreign exchange.* ❑ *Coal is to be displaced by natural gas and nuclear power.* **2** If a person or group of people **is displaced**, they are forced to move away from the area where they live. ❑ *More than 600,000 people were displaced by the tsunami.* ❑ *In Europe alone thirty million people were displaced.* ❑ *Most of the civilians displaced by the war will be unable to return to their homes.* ❑ *the task of resettling refugees and displaced persons*

⭕**dis·place·ment** /dɪsˈpleɪsmənt/ NOUN [U] **1** (*formal*) **Displacement** is the removal of something from its usual place or position by something which then occupies that place or position. ❑ *the displacement of traditional agriculture by industrial crops* ❑ *too much resistance to the displacement of your reason by your emotions* **2 Displacement** is the forcing of people away from the area or country where they live. ❑ *the gradual displacement of the American Indian*

⭕**dis·play** ♦♦◇ /dɪsˈpleɪ/ VERB, NOUN (*academic word*)
VERB [T] (**displays, displaying, displayed**) **1** If you **display** something that you want people to see, you put it in a particular place, so that people can see it. = exhibit; ≠ hide ❑ *Among the protesters and war veterans proudly displaying their medals was Aubrey Rose.* **2** If you **display** something, you show it to people. = show ❑ *She displayed her wound to the twelve gentlemen of the jury.* **3** If you **display** a characteristic, quality, or emotion, you behave in a way which shows that you have it.

= show ❑ *It was unlike Gordon to display his feelings.* ❑ *Researchers have found that women can display symptoms of a heart attack up to a month in advance.* ❑ *He has displayed remarkable courage in his efforts to reform the party.* **4** When a computer **displays** information, it shows it on a screen. ❑ *They started out by looking at the computer screens which display the images.*
NOUN [U, C] (**displays**) **1** [U] The **display** of something involves putting it in a place where people can see it. ❑ *Most of the other artists whose work is on display were his pupils or colleagues.* **2** [C, U] A **display** of a characteristic, quality, or emotion is the act of behaving in a way which shows that you have it. = show ❑ *Normally, such an outward display of affection is reserved for his mother.* ❑ *a public display of unity* **3** [C] A **display** is an arrangement of things that have been put in a particular place, so that people can see them easily. ❑ *a display of your work* **4** [C] A **display** is a public performance or other event which is intended to entertain people. ❑ *the fireworks display* **5** [C] The **display** on a computer screen is the information that is shown there. The screen itself can also be referred to as the **display**. ❑ *A hard copy of the screen display can also be obtained from a printer.*

dis·pleas·ure /dɪsˈpleʒə/ NOUN [U] Someone's **displeasure** is a feeling of annoyance that they have about something that has happened. ❑ *The population has already begun to show its displeasure at the slow pace of change.*

dis·pos·able /dɪsˈpəʊzəbəl/ ADJ, NOUN
ADJ **1** A **disposable** product is designed to be thrown away after it has been used. ❑ *disposable nappies suitable f or babies up to 8lbs* **2** [disposable + N] Your **disposable** income is the amount of income you have left after you have paid bills and taxes. ❑ *Gerald had little disposable income.*
NOUN [C] (**disposables**) Disposable products can be referred to as **disposables**. ❑ *Currently, disposables account for about 80% to 85% of the $3 billion-plus annual nappy market.*

⭕**dis·pos·al** /dɪsˈpəʊzəl/ NOUN
NOUN [U] **Disposal** is the act of getting rid of something that is no longer wanted or needed. = discarding, dumping ❑ *methods for the permanent disposal of radioactive wastes* ❑ *waste disposal sites*
PHRASE **at one's disposal** If you have something **at** your **disposal**, you are able to use it whenever you want, and for whatever purpose you want. If you say that you are **at** someone's **disposal**, you mean that you are willing to help them in any way you can. ❑ *Do you have this information at your disposal?*

dis·pose /dɪsˈpəʊz/ (*academic word*)
PHRASAL VERB **dispose of** (**disposes, disposing, disposed**) If you **dispose of** something that you no longer want or need, you throw it away. ≠ keep ❑ *the safest means of disposing of nuclear waste* ❑ *Engine oil cannot be disposed of down drains.*

WHICH WORD?

dispose of or get rid of

If you **dispose of** something, you throw it away. Note that you must use **of** after **dispose**. Do not say that someone ‘disposes’ something.

❑ *The cost of disposing of waste is rapidly rising.*

Dispose is a fairly formal word. In conversation, you usually say that someone **gets rid of** something.

❑ *Now let's get rid of all this stuff.*

---

dis·posed /dɪsˈpəʊzd/ ADJ (*formal*) **1** [V-LINK + disposed + to-INF] If you are **disposed to** do something, you are willing or eager to do it. = inclined ❑ *We passed one or two dwellings, but were not disposed to stop.* **2** You can use **disposed** when you are talking about someone's general attitude or opinion. For example, if you are well or favourably **disposed to** or **towards** someone or something, you like them or approve of them. ❑ *I saw that the publishers were well disposed towards my book.*

dis·po·si·tion /ˌdɪspəˈzɪʃən/ NOUN [C] (**dispositions**) Someone's **disposition** is the way that they tend to behave or feel. = nature ❑ *The rides are unsuitable for people of a nervous disposition.*

dis·pro·por·tion·ate /ˌdɪsprəˈpɔːʃənət/ ADJ Something that is **disproportionate** is surprising or unreasonable in amount or size, compared with something else. = excessive ❑ *A disproportionate amount of time was devoted to one topic.*

dis·pro·por·tion·ate·ly /ˌdɪsprəˈpɔːʃəntli/ ADV ❑ *There is a disproportionately high suicide rate among prisoners facing very long sentences.*

✿dis·prove /dɪsˈpruːv/ VERB [T] (**disproves, disproving, disproved, disproven**) To **disprove** an idea, belief, or theory means to show that it is not true. = refute; ≠ prove ❑ *The statistics to prove or disprove his hypothesis will take years to collect.* ❑ *opinion pieces claiming to disprove the global-warming theory*

✿dis·pute ♦♦◇ /dɪsˈpjuːt/ NOUN, VERB

NOUN [C, U] (**disputes**) A **dispute** is an argument or disagreement between people or groups. = argument, disagreement, debate; ≠ agreement ❑ *They have won previous pay disputes with the government.* ❑ *a bitter dispute between the European Community and the United States over subsidies to farmers*

PHRASE **in dispute** ■ If two or more people or groups are **in dispute**, they are arguing or disagreeing about something. ❑ *The two countries are in dispute over the boundaries of their coastal waters.* ❷ If something is **in dispute**, people are questioning it or arguing about it. ❑ *The schedule for the talks has been agreed, but the location is still in dispute.*

VERB [T, RECIP] (**disputes, disputing, disputed**) ■ [T] If you **dispute** a fact, statement, or theory, you say that it is incorrect or untrue. = argue, contest, refute ❑ *He disputed the allegations.* ❑ *Nobody disputed that Davey was clever.* ❑ *No one disputes that vitamin C is of great value in the treatment of scurvy.* ❑ *Some economists disputed whether consumer spending is as strong as the figures suggest.* ❷ [RECIP] When people **dispute** something, they fight for control or ownership of it. You can also say that one group of people **dispute** something with another group. ❑ *Russia and Ukraine have been disputing the ownership of the fleet.*

WORD CONNECTIONS

VERB + **dispute**

settle a dispute
resolve a dispute
solve a dispute
end a dispute
win a dispute

❑ *Our consultancy team will help you avoid legal action, and resolve disputes constructively.*

ADJ + **dispute**

a **bitter** dispute
an **on-going** dispute
a **long-running** dispute

❑ *They have been involved in a long-running dispute with neighbours over car parking.*

dis·quali·fy /dɪsˈkwɒlɪfaɪ/ VERB [T] (**disqualifies, disqualifying, disqualified**) When someone **is disqualified**, they are officially stopped from taking part in a particular event, activity, or competition, usually because they have done something wrong. ❑ *Thomson was disqualified from the 400-metre freestyle.*

dis·quali·fi·ca·tion /ˌdɪsˌkwɒlɪfɪˈkeɪʃən/ NOUN [C, U] (**disqualifications**) ❑ *Livingston faces a four-year disqualification from athletics.*

dis·qui·et /dɪsˈkwaɪət/ NOUN [U] (*formal*) **Disquiet** is a feeling of worry or anxiety. = uneasiness ❑ *There is growing public disquiet about the cost of such policing.*

dis·re·gard /ˌdɪsrɪˈgɑːd/ VERB, NOUN

VERB [T] (**disregards, disregarding, disregarded**) If you **disregard** something, you ignore it or do not take account of it. ❑ *He disregarded the advice of his executives.*

NOUN [U] To show a **disregard** for something means that you ignore it or do not take account of it. ❑ *Whoever*

planted the bomb showed a total disregard for the safety of the public.*

dis·re·pute /ˌdɪsrɪˈpjuːt/ NOUN

PHRASE **into disrepute** or **in disrepute** If something is brought **into disrepute** or falls **into disrepute**, it loses its good reputation, because it is connected with activities that people do not approve of. ❑ *It is a disgrace that such people should bring our profession into disrepute.*

dis·re·spect /ˌdɪsrɪˈspekt/ NOUN [U] If someone shows **disrespect**, they speak or behave in a way that shows lack of respect for a person, law, or custom. ❑ *young people with attitudes and complete disrespect for authority*

dis·re·spect·ful /ˌdɪsrɪˈspektful/ ADJ [oft disrespectful 'to/of' N] If you are **disrespectful**, you show no respect in the way that you speak or behave to someone. ❑ *accusations that he had been disrespectful to a police officer*

dis·re·spect·ful·ly /ˌdɪsrɪˈspektfəli/ ADV ❑ *They get angry if they think they are being treated disrespectfully.*

✿dis·rupt /dɪsˈrʌpt/ VERB [T] (**disrupts, disrupting, disrupted**) If someone or something **disrupts** an event, system, or process, they cause difficulties that prevent it from continuing or operating in a normal way. = interrupt ❑ *Anti-war protesters disrupted the debate.* ❑ *The drought has severely disrupted agricultural production.*

✿dis·rup·tion /dɪsˈrʌpʃən/ NOUN [C, U] (**disruptions**) When there is **disruption** of an event, system, or process, it is prevented from continuing or operating in a normal way. = interruption ❑ *The plan was designed to ensure disruption to business was kept to a minimum.* ❑ *The strike is expected to cause delays and disruption to flights from Britain.* ❑ *A stroke is the result of a disruption in the blood supply to the brain.*

✿dis·rup·tive /dɪsˈrʌptɪv/ ADJ To be **disruptive** means to prevent something from continuing or operating in a normal way. ≠ stabilising, calming ❑ *Alcohol can produce violent, disruptive behaviour.* ❑ *The process of implementing these changes can be very disruptive to a small company.*

dis·sat·is·fac·tion /ˌdɪsˌsætɪsˈfækʃən/ NOUN [C, U] (**dissatisfactions**) If you feel **dissatisfaction with** something, you are not contented or pleased with it. ❑ *She has already expressed her dissatisfaction with this aspect of the policy.*

dis·sat·is·fied /dɪsˈsætɪsfaɪd/ ADJ If you are **dissatisfied with** something, you are not contented or pleased with it. ❑ *Eighty-two per cent of voters are dissatisfied with the way their country is being governed.*

dis·sent /dɪˈsent/ NOUN, VERB

NOUN [U] **Dissent** is strong disagreement or dissatisfaction with a decision or opinion, especially one that is supported by most people or by people in authority. ❑ *He is the toughest military ruler yet and has responded harshly to any dissent.*

VERB [I] (**dissents, dissenting, dissented**) (*formal*) If you **dissent**, you express disagreement with a decision or opinion, especially one that is supported by most people or by people in authority. ❑ *Just one of the 10 members dissented.* ❑ *No one dissents from the decision to unify.*

✿dis·ser·ta·tion /ˌdɪsəˈteɪʃən/ NOUN [C] (**dissertations**) A **dissertation** is a long formal piece of writing on a particular subject, especially for an advanced university degree. = thesis ❑ *He is currently writing a dissertation on the Somali civil war.* ❑ *For his doctoral dissertation he investigated fossil land snails.*

dis·si·dent /ˈdɪsɪdənt/ NOUN, ADJ

NOUN [C] (**dissidents**) **Dissidents** are people who disagree with and criticize their government, especially because it is undemocratic. ❑ *political dissidents*

ADJ [dissident + N] **Dissident** people disagree with or criticize their government or a powerful organization they belong to. ❑ *a dissident Russian novelist*

dis·simi·lar /dɪˈsɪmɪlə/ ADJ If one thing is **dissimilar to** another, or if two things are **dissimilar**, they are very different from each other. ❑ *His methods were not dissimilar to those used by Freud.* ❑ *It would be difficult to find two men who were more dissimilar.*

✿dis·solve /dɪˈzɒlv/ VERB [I, T] (**dissolves, dissolving, dissolved**) ■ [I, T] If a substance **dissolves** in liquid or if

D

you **dissolve** it, it becomes mixed with the liquid and disappears. = melt ☐ *Heat gently until the sugar dissolves.* ☐ *More substances dissolve in water than in any other liquid.* ☐ *Pumping water into an underground salt bed dissolves the salt to make a brine.* ☐ *organic matter that consumes all dissolved oxygen in the water* **2** [T] When an organization or institution **is dissolved**, it is officially ended or broken up. ☐ *The committee has been dissolved.* **3** [T] When a parliament **is dissolved**, it is formally ended, so that elections for a new parliament can be held. ☐ *The present assembly will be dissolved on April 30th.* **4** [T] When a marriage or business arrangement **is dissolved**, it is officially ended. ☐ *The marriage was dissolved in 1976.* **5** [I, T] If something such as a problem or feeling **dissolves** or **is dissolved**, it becomes weaker and disappears. = dissipate ☐ *His new-found optimism dissolved.*

dis·suade /dɪ'sweɪd/ VERB [T] (**dissuades, dissuading, dissuaded**) (*formal*) If you **dissuade** someone **from** doing or believing something, you persuade them not to do or believe it. ☐ *Doctors had tried to dissuade patients from smoking.* ☐ *She steadfastly maintained that her grandsons were innocent, and nothing could dissuade her from that belief.*

⊕**dis·tance** ◆◆◇ /'dɪstəns/ NOUN, ADJ, VERB
NOUN [C, U, SING] (**distances**) **1** [C, U] The **distance between** two points or places is the amount of space between them. = space ☐ *the distance between the island and the nearby shore* ☐ *Everything is within walking distance.* **2** [U] When two things are very far apart, you talk about the **distance** between them. ☐ *The distance wouldn't be a problem.* **3** [U] When you want to emphasize that two people or things do not have a close relationship or are not the same, you can refer to the **distance between** them. ☐ *There was a vast distance between psychological clues and concrete proof.* **4** [U] (*formal*) **Distance** is coolness or unfriendliness in the way that someone behaves towards you. ☐ *There were periods of sulking, of pronounced distance, of coldness.* **5** [SING] ['in/into the' distance] If you can see something **in the distance**, you can see it, far away from you. ☐ *We suddenly saw her in the distance.*
PHRASES **at a distance** or **from a distance** If you are **at a distance** from something, or if you see it or remember it **from a distance**, you are a long way away from it in space or time. ☐ *The only way I can cope with my mother is at a distance.*
keep one's distance If you **keep** your **distance** from someone or something or **keep** them **at a distance**, you do not become involved with them. ☐ *Jay had always tended to keep his girlfriends at a distance.*
ADJ [distance + N] **Distance** learning or **distance** education involves studying at home and sending your work to a college or university, rather than attending the college or university in person. ☐ *The Internet is often used as a resource and as a tool for distance learning.*
VERB [T] (**distances, distancing, distanced**) If you **distance yourself from** a person or thing, or if something **distances** you **from** them, you feel less friendly or positive toward them, or become less involved with them. ☐ *The author distanced himself from some of the comments in his book.*
dis·tanced /'dɪstənst/ ADJ ☐ *Clough felt he'd become too distanced from his fans.*

⊕**dis·tant** /'dɪstənt/ ADJ **1** Distant means very far away. = far off, remote; ≠ nearby, close ☐ *The mountains rolled away to a distant horizon.* ☐ *the war in that distant land* **2** You use **distant** to describe a time or event that is very far away in the future or in the past. = faraway ☐ *There is little doubt, however, that things will improve in the not too distant future.* **3** A **distant** relative is one who you are not closely related to. ☐ *He's a distant relative of the mayor.* **4** [V-LINK + distant] If you describe someone as **distant**, you mean that you find them cold and unfriendly. = aloof ☐ *He found her cold, icelike, and distant.* **5** If you describe someone as **distant**, you mean that they are not concentrating on what they are doing because they are thinking about other things. ☐ *There was a distant look in her eyes from time to time, her thoughts elsewhere.*
dis·tant·ly /'dɪstəntli/ ADV ☐ *The O'Shea girls are distantly related to our family.*

dis·taste /,dɪs'teɪst/ NOUN [U] If you feel **distaste for** someone or something, you dislike them and consider them to be unpleasant, disgusting, or immoral. = aversion ☐ *He professed a violent distaste for everything related to commerce, production, and money.*

dis·taste·ful /,dɪs'teɪstfʊl/ ADJ If something is **distasteful to** you, you think it is unpleasant, disgusting, or immoral. ☐ *He found it distasteful to be offered a cold buffet and drinks before witnessing the execution.*

⊕**dis·tinct** /dɪ'stɪŋkt/ ADJ (*academic word*)
ADJ **1** If something is **distinct from** something else of the same type, it is different or separate from it. = separate, discrete, diverse; ≠ connected ☐ *Engineering and technology are disciplines distinct from one another and from science.* ☐ *This book is divided into two distinct parts.* **2** If something is **distinct**, you can hear, see, or taste it clearly. ☐ *to impart a distinct flavour with a minimum of cooking fat* **3** If an idea, thought, or intention is **distinct**, it is clear and definite. ☐ *Now that Tony was no longer present, there was a distinct change in her attitude.* **4** [distinct + N] You can use **distinct** to emphasize that something is great enough in amount or degree to be noticeable or important. = definite ☐ *Being 6ft 3in tall has some distinct disadvantages!*
PHRASE **as distinct from** If you say that you are talking about one thing **as distinct from** another, you are indicating exactly which thing you mean. ☐ *There's a lot of evidence that oily fish, as distinct from fatty meat, has a beneficial effect.*
dis·tinct·ly /dɪ'stɪŋktli/ ADV **1** [distinctly + ADJ] ☐ *a banking industry with two distinctly different sectors* **2** [distinctly with V] ☐ *I distinctly heard the loudspeaker calling passengers for the Washington-Miami flight.* **3** [distinctly with V] ☐ *I distinctly remember wishing I had not got involved.* **4** [distinctly + ADJ/-ED] ☐ *His government is looking distinctly shaky.*

⊕**dis·tinc·tion** /dɪ'stɪŋkʃən/ NOUN
NOUN [C, U, SING] (**distinctions**) **1** [C] A **distinction between** similar things is a difference. = difference, differentiation, separation ☐ *There are obvious distinctions between the two wine-making areas.* ☐ *The distinction between craft and fine art is more controversial.* ☐ *We have drawn an important distinction between the market value and the intrinsic value of a firm.* **2** [C] A **distinction** is a special award or honour that is given to someone because of their very high level of achievement. ☐ *The award was established in 1902 as a special distinction for eminent men and women.* **3** [U] (*formal*) **Distinction** is the quality of being very good or better than other things of the same type. ☐ *Lewis emerges as a composer of distinction and sensitivity.* **4** [SING] If you say that someone or something has **the distinction of** being something, you are drawing attention to the fact that they have the special quality of being that thing. **Distinction** is normally used to refer to good qualities, but can sometimes also be used to refer to bad qualities. ☐ *He has the distinction of being regarded as the Federal Republic's greatest living writer.*
PHRASE **draw a distinction** or **make a distinction** If you **draw a distinction** or **make a distinction**, you say that two things are different.

⊕**dis·tinc·tive** /dɪ'stɪŋktɪv/ ADJ Something that is **distinctive** has a special quality or feature which makes it easily recognizable and different from other things of the same type. = unique, characteristic, idiosyncratic ☐ *the distinctive odour of chlorine* ☐ *Thompson's distinctive prose style*
⊕**dis·tinc·tive·ly** /dɪ'stɪŋktɪvli/ ADV [distinctively + ADJ/-ED] = uniquely ☐ *the distinctively fragrant taste of elderflowers*

⊕**dis·tin·guish** /dɪ'stɪŋgwɪʃ/ VERB [I, T] (**distinguishes, distinguishing, distinguished**) **1** [I, T] If you can **distinguish** one thing **from** another or **distinguish between** two things, you can see or understand how they are different. = differentiate ☐ *Could he distinguish right from wrong?* ☐ *Research suggests that babies learn to see by distinguishing between areas of light and dark.* ☐ *Asteroids are distinguished from meteorites in terms of their visibility.* **2** [T] A feature or quality that **distinguishes** one thing **from** another causes the two things to be regarded as different,

d

because only the first thing has the feature or quality. ❏ *There is something about music that distinguishes it from all other art forms.* ❑ [T] (*formal*) If you can **distinguish** something, you can see, hear, or taste it although it is very difficult to detect. = discern ❏ *There were cries, calls. He could distinguish voices.* ❹ [T] If you **distinguish yourself**, you do something that makes you famous or important. ❏ *Over the next few years he distinguished himself as a leading constitutional scholar.*

dis·tin·guished /dɪˈstɪŋgwɪʃt/ ADJ ❶ If you describe a person or their work as **distinguished**, you mean that they have been very successful in their career and have a good reputation. = illustrious ❏ *a distinguished academic family* ❷ If you describe someone as **distinguished**, you mean that they look very noble and respectable. ❏ *His suit was immaculately cut and he looked very distinguished.*

✪ **dis·tort** /dɪˈstɔːt/ VERB [T, I] (**distorts, distorting, distorted**) (*academic word*) ❶ [T] If you **distort** a statement, fact, or idea, you report or represent it in an untrue way. = misrepresent ❏ *The media distorts reality; it categorizes people as all good or all bad.* ❏ *allegations that the administration distorted scientific findings to justify political decisions* ❷ [I, T] If something you can see or hear **is distorted** or **distorts**, its appearance or sound is changed so that it seems unclear. ❏ *A painter may exaggerate or distort shapes and forms.* ❏ *the distorting effects of Earth's atmosphere on light passing through it* ❏ *This caused the sound to distort.*
   dis·tort·ed /dɪˈstɔːtɪd/ ADJ ❶ *These figures give a distorted view of the significance for the local economy.* ❷ *Sound was becoming more and more distorted through the use of hearing aids.*

✪ **dis·tor·tion** /dɪˈstɔːʃən/ NOUN [C, U] (**distortions**) ❶ (*disapproval*) **Distortion** is the changing of something into something that is not true or not acceptable. = misrepresentation ❏ *I think it would be a gross distortion of reality to say that they were motivated by self-interest.* ❏ *He later accused reporters of wilful distortion and bias.* ❷ **Distortion** is the changing of the appearance or sound of something in a way that makes it seem strange or unclear. ❏ *He demonstrated how audio signals could be transmitted along cables without distortion.* ❏ *symptoms including some perceptual distortions and hallucinations*

dis·tract /dɪˈstrækt/ VERB [T] (**distracts, distracting, distracted**) If something **distracts** you or your attention **from** something, it takes your attention away from it. ❏ *Tom admits that playing video games sometimes distracts him from his homework.* ❏ *Don't let yourself be distracted by fashionable theories.*

dis·tract·ed /dɪˈstræktɪd/ ADJ If you are **distracted**, you are not concentrating on something because you are worried or are thinking about something else. ❏ *She had seemed curiously distracted.*
   dis·tract·ed·ly /dɪˈstræktɪdli/ ADV [distractedly with v] ❏ *He looked up distractedly. 'Be with you in a second.'*

dis·trac·tion /dɪˈstrækʃən/ NOUN [C, U] (**distractions**) A **distraction** is something that turns your attention away from something you want to concentrate on. ❏ *Total concentration is required with no distractions.*

dis·traught /dɪˈstrɔːt/ ADJ If someone is **distraught**, they are so upset and worried that they cannot think clearly. ❏ *Mr Barker's distraught parents were last night being comforted by relatives.*

dis·tress /dɪˈstres/ NOUN, VERB
   NOUN [U] ❶ **Distress** is a state of extreme sorrow, suffering, or pain. = suffering ❏ *Jealousy causes distress and painful emotions.* ❷ **Distress** is the state of being in extreme danger and needing urgent help. ❏ *He expressed concern that the ship might be in distress.*
   VERB [T] (**distresses, distressing, distressed**) If someone or something **distresses** you, they cause you to be upset or worried. ❏ *The idea of Toni being in danger distresses him enormously.*

dis·tressed /dɪˈstrest/ ADJ If someone is **distressed**, they are upset or worried. ❏ *I feel very alone and distressed about my problem.*

dis·tress·ing /dɪˈstresɪŋ/ ADJ If something is **distressing**, it upsets you or worries you. ❏ *It is very distressing to see your baby attached to tubes and monitors.*
   dis·tress·ing·ly /dɪˈstresɪŋli/ ADV ❏ *A distressingly large number of firms have been breaking the rules.*

✪ **dis·trib·ute** /dɪˈstrɪbjuːt/ VERB [T] (**distributes, distributing, distributed**) (*academic word*) ❶ If you **distribute** things, you hand them or deliver them to a number of people. ❏ *Students shouted slogans and distributed leaflets.* ❏ *Soldiers are working to distribute food to the refugees.* ❏ *Profits are distributed among the policyholders.* ❷ (*business*) When a company **distributes** goods, it supplies them to the shops or businesses that sell them. = disseminate, issue; ≠ collect ❏ *We didn't understand how difficult it was to distribute a national paper.* ❏ *firms that manufacture and distribute DVDs* ❸ (*formal*) To **distribute** a substance **over** something means to scatter it over it. ❏ *Distribute the topping evenly over the fruit.*

✪ **dis·trib·ut·ed** /dɪˈstrɪbjuːtɪd/ ADJ If things are **distributed** throughout an area, object, or group, they exist throughout it. = spread ❏ *These cells are widely distributed throughout the body.* ❏ *Distant galaxies are not as evenly distributed in space as theory predicts.*

✪ **dis·tri·bu·tion** ♦◇◇ /ˌdɪstrɪˈbjuːʃən/ NOUN [U, C] (**distributions**) ❶ [U] The **distribution** of things involves giving or delivering them to a number of people or places. = allocation, dissemination, spread; ≠ collection ❏ *the council which controls the distribution of foreign aid* ❏ *emergency food distribution* ❷ [C, U] The **distribution** of something is how much of it there is in each place or at each time, or how much of it each person has. ❏ *Mr Roh's economic planners sought to achieve a more equitable distribution of wealth.* ❏ *the geographical distribution of parasitic diseases such as malaria*

dis·tribu·tor /dɪˈstrɪbjʊtə/ NOUN [C] (**distributors**) (*business*) A **distributor** is a company that supplies goods to shops or other businesses. ❏ *Spain's largest distributor of petroleum products*

dis·trict ♦♦◇ /ˈdɪstrɪkt/ NOUN [C] (**districts**) A **district** is a particular area of a town or country. ❏ *I drove around the business district.*

dis·trust /ˌdɪsˈtrʌst/ VERB, NOUN
   VERB [T] (**distrusts, distrusting, distrusted**) If you **distrust** someone or something, you think they are not honest, reliable, or safe. = mistrust ❏ *I don't have any particular reason to distrust them.*
   NOUN [U] [also 'a' distrust, oft distrust 'of' N] **Distrust** is the feeling of doubt that you have towards someone or something you distrust. ❏ *What he saw there left him with a profound distrust of all political authority.*

dis·turb /dɪˈstɜːb/ VERB [T] (**disturbs, disturbing, disturbed**) ❶ If you **disturb** someone, you interrupt what they are doing and upset them. ❏ *Did you sleep well? I didn't want to disturb you. You looked so peaceful.* ❷ If something **disturbs** you, it makes you feel upset or worried. = upset ❏ *I dream about him, dreams so vivid that they disturb me for days.* ❸ If something **is disturbed**, its position or shape is changed. ❏ *He'd placed his notes in the brown envelope. They hadn't been disturbed.* ❹ If something **disturbs** a situation or atmosphere, it spoils it or causes trouble. ❏ *What could possibly disturb such tranquility?*

dis·turb·ance /dɪˈstɜːbəns/ NOUN [C, U] (**disturbances**) ❶ [C] A **disturbance** is an incident in which people behave violently in public. ❏ *During the disturbance which followed, three Englishmen were hurt.* ❷ [U] **Disturbance** means upsetting or disorganizing something which was previously in a calm and well-ordered state. ❏ *Successful breeding requires quiet, peaceful conditions with as little disturbance as possible.* ❸ [C, U] You can use **disturbance** to refer to a medical or psychological problem, when someone's body or mind is not working in the normal way. ❏ *Poor educational performance is related to emotional disturbance.*

dis·turbed /dɪˈstɜːbd/ ADJ ❶ A **disturbed** person is very upset emotionally, and often needs special care or treatment. ❏ *working with severely emotionally disturbed* children **2** You can say that someone is **disturbed** when they are very worried or anxious. ❑ *Doctors were disturbed that less than 30 per cent of the patients were women.* **3** If you describe a situation or period of time as **disturbed**, you mean that it is unhappy and full of problems. = troubled ❑ *women from disturbed backgrounds*

dis·turb·ing /dɪˈstɜːbɪŋ/ ADJ Something that is **disturbing** makes you feel worried or upset. ❑ *There was something about him she found disturbing.*
dis·turb·ing·ly /dɪˈstɜːbɪŋli/ ADV ❑ *The government has itself recognized the disturbingly high frequency of racial attacks.*

dis·used /ˌdɪsˈjuːzd/ ADJ A **disused** place or building is empty and is no longer used. ❑ *a disused air field near the village of Ive*

ditch /dɪtʃ/ NOUN, VERB
NOUN [c] (**ditches**) A **ditch** is a long narrow channel cut into the ground at the side of a road or field. ❑ *Both vehicles ended up in a ditch.*
VERB [T, I] (**ditches, ditching, ditched**) **1** [T] (*informal*) If you **ditch** something that you have or are responsible for, you abandon it or get rid of it, because you no longer want it. = dump ❑ *I decided to ditch the sofa bed.*
2 [T] (*informal*) If someone **ditches** someone, they end a relationship with that person. = dump ❑ *I can't bring myself to ditch him and start again.* **3** [I, T] If a pilot **ditches** an aircraft or if it **ditches**, the pilot makes an emergency landing. ❑ *One American pilot was forced to ditch his jet in the Gulf.*

dive /daɪv/ VERB, NOUN
VERB [I] (**dives, diving, dived**) **1** If you **dive into** some water, you jump in head first with your arms held straight above your head. ❑ *He tried to escape by diving into a river.* ❑ *She was standing by a pool, about to dive in.* **2** If you **dive**, you go under the surface of the sea or a lake, using special breathing equipment. ❑ *Bezanik is diving to collect marine organisms.* **3** When birds and animals **dive**, they go quickly downwards, head first, through the air or through water. ❑ *a pelican which had just dived for a fish* **4** If you **dive** in a particular direction or into a particular place, you jump or move there quickly. = leap ❑ *They dived into a taxi.* **5** (*journalism*) If shares, profits, or figures **dive**, their value falls suddenly and by a large amount. ❑ *They feared the stock could dive after its first day of trading.* ❑ *Profits have dived from $7.7m to $7.1m.*
NOUN [c] (**dives**) **1** A **dive** is when you jump head first into some water, with your arms held straight above your head. ❑ *Pat had earlier made a dive of 80 feet from the Chasm Bridge.* **2** A **dive** is when you go under the surface of the sea or a lake, using special breathing equipment. ❑ *This sighting occurred during my dive to a sunken wreck off Sardinia.* **3** A **dive** in a particular direction or into a particular place is when you jump or move there quickly. ❑ *He made a sudden dive for Uncle Jim's legs to try to trip him up.* **4** If shares, profits, or figures take a **dive**, their value falls suddenly and by a large amount. ❑ *Stock prices took a dive.* **5** (*informal, disapproval*) If you describe a bar or club as a **dive**, you mean it is dirty and dark, and not very respectable. ❑ *We've played in all the little clubs and dives around Philadelphia.*

di·verge /daɪˈvɜːdʒ, AmE dɪ-/ VERB [RECIP] (**diverges, diverging, diverged**) **1** If one thing **diverges from** another similar thing, the first thing becomes different from the second or develops differently from it. You can also say that two things **diverge**. ❑ *His interests increasingly diverged from those of his colleagues.* **2** If one opinion or idea **diverges from** another, they contradict each other or are different. You can also say that two opinions or ideas **diverge**. ❑ *The view of the Estonian government does not diverge that far from Lipmaa's thinking.*

✪**di·verse** /daɪˈvɜːs, AmE dɪ-/ ADJ (*academic word*) **1** If a group of things is **diverse**, it is made up of a wide variety of things. = varied; ≠ uniform ❑ *The building houses a wide and diverse variety of antiques.* ❑ *a diverse range of habitats* ❑ *Society is now much more diverse than ever before.* **2** **Diverse** people or things are very different from each other. ❑ *Albert Jones' new style will inevitably put him in touch with a much more diverse and perhaps younger audience.*

❑ *Studies of diverse populations have reached similar conclusions.*

WORD FAMILIES	
diverse ADJ	The island has one of the most biologically **diverse** habitats in the world.
diversity NOUN	She wanted to introduce more choice and **diversity** into the education system.
biodiversity NOUN	The national environment management programme encourages farmers to preserve **biodiversity**.
diversify VERB	The company's troubles started only when it **diversified** into new products.
diversification NOUN	There is a need for more **diversification** of the rural economy to provide jobs outside farming.

✪**di·ver·si·fy** /daɪˈvɜːsɪfaɪ, AmE dɪ-/ VERB [I, T] (**diversifies, diversifying, diversified**) When an organization or person **diversifies** into other things, or **diversifies** their product line, they increase the variety of things that they do or make. = branch out, expand ❑ *The company's troubles started only when it diversified into new products.* ❑ *As demand has increased, so manufacturers have been encouraged to diversify and improve quality.* ❑ *These firms have been given a tough lesson in the need to diversify their markets.*
✪**di·ver·si·fi·ca·tion** /daɪˌvɜːsɪfɪˈkeɪʃən, AmE dɪ-/ NOUN [c, u] (**diversifications**) = expansion ❑ *The seminar was to discuss diversification of agriculture.* ❑ *These strange diversifications could have damaged or even sunk the entire company.*

di·ver·sion /daɪˈvɜːʃən, AmE dɪˈvɜːrʒən/ NOUN [c, u] (**diversions**) **1** [c] A **diversion** is an action or event that attracts your attention away from what you are doing or concentrating on. ❑ *armed robbers who escaped after throwing smoke bombs to create a diversion* **2** [c] (*BrE*; in AmE, use **detour**) A **diversion** is a special route arranged for traffic to follow when the normal route cannot be used. **3** [u] **The diversion of** something involves changing its course or destination. ❑ *the illegal diversion of profits from secret arms sales*

✪**di·ver·si·ty** /daɪˈvɜːsɪti, AmE dɪ-/ NOUN [c, u, SING] (**diversities**) **1** [c, u] The **diversity** of something is the fact that it contains many very different elements. = variety; ≠ uniformity ❑ *the cultural diversity of Latin America* ❑ *to introduce more choice and diversity into the education system* **2** [SING] A **diversity of** things is a range of things which are very different from each other. ❑ *Forslan's object is to gather as great a diversity of genetic material as possible.*

✪**di·vert** /daɪˈvɜːt, AmE dɪ-/ VERB [I, T] (**diverts, diverting, diverted**) **1** [I, T] To **divert** vehicles or travellers means to make them follow a different route or go to a different destination than they originally intended. You can also say that someone or something **diverts from** a particular route or **to** a particular place. ❑ *We diverted a plane to rescue 100 passengers.* ❑ *Abington Memorial Hospital has been diverting trauma patients to other hospitals because it does not have enough surgeons.* ❑ *a project intended to divert water from the north of the country to drought-prone southern and eastern states* ❑ *During the strike, ambulances will be diverted to private hospitals.* ❑ *attempts to divert the lava flow* ❑ *a diverted river* **2** [T] To **divert** money or resources means to cause them to be used for a different purpose. ❑ *A wave of deadly bombings has forced the United States to divert funds from reconstruction to security.* ❑ *The government is trying to divert more public funds from west to east.* ❑ *government departments involved in diverting resources into community care* **3** [T] To **divert** a phone call means to send it to a different number or place from the one that was dialled by the person making the call. ❑ *He instructed the switchboard staff to divert all Laura's calls to him.* **4** [T] If you say that someone **diverts** your attention from something important or serious, you disapprove of them behaving or talking in a way that stops you thinking about it. = distract ❑ *They want to divert the attention of the people from the real issues.*

◐di·vide ◆◇ /dɪˈvaɪd/ VERB, NOUN

VERB [I, T] (**divides, dividing, divided**) **1** [I, T] When people or things **are divided** or **divide into** smaller groups or parts, they become separated into smaller parts. = split, separate, segregate ❑ *The physical benefits of exercise can be divided into three factors.* ❑ *Divide the pastry in half and roll out each piece.* ❑ *It will be easiest if we divide them into groups.* **2** [T] If you **divide** something **among** people or things, you separate it into several parts or quantities which you distribute to the people or things. ❑ *Divide the sauce among 4 bowls.* **3** [T] If you **divide** a larger number **by** a smaller number or **divide** a smaller number **into** a larger number, you calculate how many times the smaller number can fit exactly into the larger number. ❑ *Measure the floor area of the greenhouse and divide it by six.* **4** [T] If a border or line **divides** two areas or **divides** an area into two, it keeps the two areas separate from each other. = separate ❑ *remote border areas dividing Tamil and Muslim settlements* **5** [I, T] If people **divide** over something or if something **divides** them, it causes strong disagreement between them. ❑ *the major issues that divided the country*

PHRASAL VERB **divide up 1** If you **divide** something **up**, you separate it into smaller or more useful groups. = split up ❑ *The idea is to divide up the country into four sectors.* **2** If you **divide** something **up**, you share it out among a number of people or groups in approximately equal parts. ❑ *The aim was to divide up the business, give everyone an equal stake in its future.*

NOUN [C] (**divides**) A **divide** is a significant distinction between two groups, often one that causes conflict. = rift ❑ *a deliberate attempt to create a Hindu–Muslim divide in India*

divi·dend ◆◇ /ˈdɪvɪdend/ NOUN

NOUN [C] (**dividends**) (*business*) A **dividend** is the part of a company's profits which is paid to people who own shares in the company. ❑ *The first quarter dividend has been increased by nearly 4 per cent.*

PHRASE **pay dividends** If something **pays dividends**, it brings advantages at a later date. ❑ *Steps taken now to maximize your health will pay dividends later on.*

di·vine /dɪˈvaɪn/ ADJ **1** You use **divine** to describe something that is provided by or relates to a god or goddess. ❑ *He suggested that the civil war had been a divine punishment.* **2** People use **divine** to express their pleasure or enjoyment of something. ❑ *Her carrot cake is divine.*

di·vine·ly /dɪˈvaɪnli/ ADV ❑ *The law was divinely ordained.*

◐di·vi·sion ◆◆◇ /dɪˈvɪʒən/ NOUN [U, C] (**divisions**) **1** [U] The **division** of a large unit **into** two or more distinct parts is the act of separating it into these parts. = separation, partition ❑ *the unification of Germany, after its division into two states at the end of World War Two* **2** [U] The **division of** something among people or things is its separation into parts which are distributed among the people or things. ❑ *The current division of labour between workers and management will alter.* **3** [U] **Division** is the arithmetical process of dividing one number into another number. ❑ *I taught my daughter how to do division at the age of six.* **4** [C, U] A **division** is a significant distinction or argument between two groups, which causes the two groups to be considered as very different and separate. = divide ❑ *The division between the prosperous west and the impoverished east remains.* **5** [C] In a large organization, a **division** is a group of departments whose work is done in the same place or is connected with similar tasks. ❑ *the bank's Latin American division* **6** [C] A **division** is a group of military units which fight as a single unit. ❑ *Several armoured divisions are being moved from Germany.* **7** [C] In some sports, such as football, baseball, and basketball, a **division** is one of the groups of teams which make up a league. The teams in each division are of the same level, and they all play against each other during the season. ❑ *Chico State reached the NCAA Division II national finals last season.*

di·vorce ◆◇ /dɪˈvɔːs/ NOUN, VERB

NOUN [C, U, SING] (**divorces**) **1** [C, U] A **divorce** is the formal ending of a marriage by law. ❑ *Numerous marriages now end in divorce.* **2** [SING] A **divorce of** one thing **from** another, or a divorce **between** two things is a separation between them which is permanent or is likely to be permanent. ❑ *this divorce of Christian culture from the roots of faith*

VERB [RECIP, T] (**divorces, divorcing, divorced**) **1** [RECIP] If a man and woman **divorce** or if one of them **divorces** the other, their marriage is legally ended. ❑ *He and Lillian had got divorced.* ❑ *I am absolutely furious that he divorced me to marry her.* **2** [T] If you say that one thing cannot **be divorced from** another, you mean that the two things cannot be considered as different and separate things. = dissociate ❑ *Good management in the police cannot be divorced from accountability.* ❑ *Democracy cannot be divorced from social and economic progress.*

di·vorced /dɪˈvɔːst/ ADJ **1** Someone who **is divorced** from their former husband or wife has separated from them and is no longer legally married to them. ❑ *He is divorced, with a young son.* **2** [V-LINK + divorced 'from' N] If you say that one thing **is divorced from** another, you mean that the two things are very different and separate from each other. = unconnected ❑ *speculative theories divorced from political reality*

di·vulge /daɪˈvʌldʒ, AmE dɪ-/ VERB [T] (**divulges, divulging, divulged**) (*formal*) If you **divulge** a piece of secret or private information, you tell it to someone. = reveal, disclose ❑ *Officials refuse to divulge details of the negotiations.*

diz·zy /ˈdɪzi/ ADJ

ADJ (**dizzier, dizziest**) **1** If you feel **dizzy**, you feel that you are losing your balance and are about to fall. ❑ *Her head still hurt, and she felt slightly dizzy and disorientated.* **2** You can use **dizzy** to describe a woman who is careless and forgets things, but is easy to like. ❑ *She is famed for playing dizzy blondes.*

PHRASE **dizzy heights** (*humorous, emphasis*) If you say that someone has reached **the dizzy heights of** something, you are emphasizing that they have reached a very high level by achieving it. ❑ *I escalated to the dizzy heights of director's secretary.*

diz·zi·ness /ˈdɪzinəs/ NOUN [U] ❑ *His head injury causes dizziness and nausea.*

◐DNA /ˌdiː en ˈeɪ/ NOUN [U] **DNA** is an acid in the chromosomes in the centre of the cells of living things. DNA determines the particular structure and functions of every cell and is responsible for characteristics being passed on from parents to their children. **DNA** is an abbreviation for 'deoxyribonucleic acid'. ❑ *A routine DNA sample was taken.* ❑ *DNA profiling matches samples of body fluids left on a victim to the attackers.* ❑ *techniques of extracting DNA from ancient bones*

do ◆◆◆ /də, STRONG duː/ VERB

> **Do** is used as an auxiliary with the simple present tense. **Did** is used as an auxiliary with the simple past tense. In spoken English, negative forms of **do** are often shortened, for example, **do not** is shortened to **don't** and **did not** is shortened to **didn't**.

> **Do** is used in a large number of expressions which are explained under other words in the dictionary. For example, the expression 'easier said than done' is explained at 'easy'.

VERB [AUX, I, T] **1** [AUX] **Do** is used to form the negative of main verbs, by putting 'not' after 'do' and before the main verb in its infinitive form, that is the form without 'to'. ❑ *They don't want to work.* ❑ *I did not know Jamie had a knife.* **2** [AUX] **Do** is used to form questions, by putting the subject after 'do' and before the main verb in its infinitive form, that is the form without 'to'. ❑ *What did he say?* ❑ *Do you like music?* **3** [AUX] **Do** is used in question tags. ❑ *You know about Andy, don't you?* **4** [AUX] You use **do** when you are confirming or contradicting a statement containing 'do', or giving a negative or positive answer to a question. ❑ *'Did he think there was anything suspicious going on?'—'Yes, he did.'* **5** [I, T] **Do** can be used to refer back to another verb group when you are comparing or contrasting two things, or saying that they are the same. ❑ *I make more money than he does.* ❑ *I had fantasies, as do all mothers, about how life would be when my girls were grown.* **6** [T] You use **do** after 'so' and 'nor' to say that the same statement is true for two people or groups. ❑ *You know that's true, and so do I.* **7** [T] When you **do** something, you take some action or perform an activity or task. **Do** is often used instead of a more specific verb, to talk about a common action involving a particular thing. For example you can say 'do your hair' instead of 'brush your hair'. ❑ *I was trying to do some work.* ❑ *After lunch Elizabeth and I did the dishes.* **8** [T] **Do** can be used to stand for any verb group, or to refer back to another verb group, including one that was in a previous sentence. ❑ *What are you doing?* **9** [T] You can use **do** in a clause at the beginning of a sentence after words like 'what' and 'all', to give special emphasis to the information that comes at the end of the sentence. ❑ *All she does is complain.* **10** [T] If you **do** a particular thing **with** something, you use it in that particular way. ❑ *I was allowed to do whatever I wanted with my life.* **11** [T] If you **do** something **about** a problem, you take action to try to solve it. ❑ *They refuse to do anything about the real cause of crime: poverty.* **12** [T] If an action or event **does** a particular thing, such as harm or good, it has that result or effect. ❑ *A few bombs can do a lot of damage.* **13** [T] If you ask someone what they **do**, you want to know what their job or profession is. ❑ *'What does your father do?'—'Well, he's a civil servant.'* **14** [T] If you **are doing** something, you are busy or active in some way, or have planned an activity for some time in the future. ❑ *Are you doing anything tomorrow night?* **15** [I] If you say that someone or something **does** well or badly, you are talking about how successful or unsuccessful they are. ❑ *Connie did well at university and graduated with honours.* **16** [T] You can use **do** when referring to the speed or rate that something or someone achieves or is able to achieve. ❑ *They were doing 70 miles an hour.* **17** [T] If someone **does** drugs, they take illegal drugs. ❑ *I don't do drugs.* **18** [I, T] If you say that something **will do** or **will do** you, you mean that there is enough of it or that it is of good enough quality to meet your requirements or to satisfy you. ❑ *Anything to create a scene and attract attention will do.* **19** [T] (*mainly BrE, spoken*) If you **do** a subject, author, or book, you study them at school or college. ❑ *She planned to do maths at night school.*

PHRASES **could do with** If you say that you **could do with** something, you mean that you need it or would benefit from it. ❑ *I could do with a cup of tea.*

what did you do with You can ask someone **what they did with** something as another way of asking them where they put it. ❑ *What did you do with that notebook?*

what is someone doing here or **what is something doing here** If you ask **what** someone or something **is doing** in a particular place, you are asking why they are there. ❑ *'Dr Campbell,' he said, clearly surprised. 'What are you doing here?'*

have to do with or **be to do with** If you say that one thing **has** something **to do with** or **is** something **to do with** another thing, you mean that the two things are connected or that the first thing is about the second thing. ❑ *Mr Butterfield denies having anything to do with the episode.*

PHRASAL VERBS **do away with** **1** To **do away with** something means to remove it completely or put an end to it. ❑ *The long-range goal must be to do away with nuclear weapons altogether.* **2** (*informal*) If one person **does away with** another, the first murders the second. If you **do away with yourself**, you kill yourself. ❑ *a woman whose husband had made several attempts to do away with her*

do in (*informal*) To **do** someone **in** means to kill them. ❑ *Whoever did him in removed a man who was brave as well as ruthless.*

do up **1** If you **do** something **up**, you fasten it. ❑ *Mari did up the buttons.* **2** If you say that a person or room is **done up** in a particular way, you mean they are dressed or decorated in that way, often a way that is rather ridiculous or extreme. ❑ *a small salon done up in saffron silks and plum velvet cushions*

do without **1** If you **do without** something you need, want, or usually have, you are able to survive, continue, or succeed although you do not have it. ❑ *We can't do without the help of your organization.* **2** (*informal*) If you say that you could **do without** something, you mean that you would prefer not to have it or it is of no benefit to you. ❑ *He could do without her rhetorical questions at five o'clock in the morning.*

dos and don'ts If someone tells you the **dos and don'ts** of a particular situation, they advise you what you should and should not do in that situation. ❑ *Please advise me on the most suitable colour print film and some dos and don'ts.*

dock /dɒk/ NOUN, VERB
  NOUN [C, SING] (**docks**) **1** [c] [also 'in/into' dock] A **dock** is an enclosed area in a harbour where ships go to be loaded, unloaded, and repaired. ❑ *She headed for the docks, thinking that Ricardo might be hiding in one of the boats.* **2** [SING] In a law court, the **dock** is where the person accused of a crime stands or sits. ❑ *What about the odd chance that you do put an innocent man in the dock?*
  VERB [I, T, RECIP] (**docks, docking, docked**) **1** [I, T] When a ship **docks** or **is docked**, it is brought into a dock. ❑ *The crash happened as the ferry attempted to dock on Staten Island.* **2** [T] If you **dock** someone's pay or money, you take some of the money away. ❑ *He threatens to dock her fee.* **3** [T] If you **dock** someone points in a contest, you take away some of the points that they have. **4** [RECIP] When one spacecraft **docks** or **is docked** with another, the two crafts join together in space. ❑ *The space shuttle Atlantis is scheduled to dock with Russia's Mir space station.*

doc·tor ♦♦◇ /'dɒktə/ NOUN, VERB
  NOUN [C] (**doctors**) **1** A **doctor** is someone who has a degree in medicine and treats people who are sick or injured. ❑ *Do not discontinue the treatment without consulting your doctor.* **2** **The doctor's** is used to refer to the office where a doctor works. ❑ *I have an appointment at the doctor's.* **3** A **doctor** is someone who has been awarded the highest academic or honorary degree by a university. ❑ *He is a doctor of philosophy.*
  VERB [T] (**doctors, doctoring, doctored**) If someone **doctors** something, they change it in order to deceive people. ❑ *They doctored the prints, deepening the lines to make her look as awful as possible.*

doc·tor·al /'dɒktərəl/ ADJ [doctoral + N] A **doctoral** thesis or piece of research is written or done in order to obtain a doctorate. = postgraduate ❑ *a doctoral student in mathematics*

doc·tor·ate /'dɒktərət/ NOUN [C] (**doctorates**) A **doctorate** is the highest degree awarded by a university. = PhD, higher degree ❑ *Professor Lanphier obtained his doctorate in social psychology from the University of Michigan.*

doc·trine /'dɒktrɪn/ NOUN [C, U] (**doctrines**) A **doctrine** is a set of principles or beliefs, especially religious ones. ❑ *the Marxist doctrine of perpetual revolution*

docu·ment ♦♦◇ NOUN, VERB (*academic word*)
  NOUN /'dɒkjəmənt/ [C] (**documents**) **1** A **document** is one or more official pieces of paper with writing on them. = paper ❑ *She produces legal documents for a downtown Seattle law firm.* **2** A **document** is a piece of text or graphics, for example, a letter, that is stored as a file on a computer and that you can access in order to read it or change it. ❑ *When you are finished typing, remember to save your document.*
  VERB /'dɒkjəment/ [T] (**documents, documenting, documented**) If you **document** something, you make a detailed record of it in writing or on film or tape. ❑ *He wrote a book documenting his prison experiences.* ❑ *The book represents the first real attempt to accurately document the history of the entire area.* ❑ *The effects of smoking have been well documented.*

docu·men·tary /ˌdɒkjə'mentri/ NOUN, ADJ
  NOUN [C] (**documentaries**) A **documentary** is a television or radio programme, or a film, which shows real events or provides information about a particular subject. ❑ *a TV documentary on homelessness*
  ADJ [documentary + N] **Documentary** evidence consists of things that are written down. ❑ *The government says it has*

documentary evidence that the two countries were planning military action.

docu·men·ta·tion /ˌdɒkjəmen'teɪʃən/ NOUN [U] Documentation consists of documents which provide proof or evidence of something, or are a record of something. ❑ *Passengers must carry proper documentation.*

dodge /dɒdʒ/ VERB, NOUN

  VERB [I, T] (**dodges, dodging, dodged**) **1** [I] If you **dodge**, you move suddenly, often to avoid being hit, caught, or seen. ❑ *I dodged back into the alley and waited a minute.* **2** [T] If you **dodge** something, you avoid it by quickly moving aside or out of reach so that it cannot hit or reach you. = sidestep ❑ *He desperately dodged a speeding car trying to run him down.* **3** [T] If you **dodge** something, you deliberately avoid thinking about it or dealing with it, often by being deceitful. = evade ❑ *He boasts of dodging military service by feigning illness.*
  NOUN [C] (**dodges**) A **dodge** is when you deliberately avoid thinking about something or dealing with it, often by being deceitful. ❑ *This was not just a tax dodge.*

does /dəz, STRONG dʌz/ IRREG FORM **Does** is the third person singular in the present tense of **do**.

doesn't ♦♦♦ /'dʌzənt/ SHORT FORM **Doesn't** is the usual spoken form of 'does not'.

dog ♦♦◇ /dɒg, AmE dɔːg/ NOUN, VERB

  NOUN [C] (**dogs**) A **dog** is a very common four-legged animal that is often kept by people as a pet or to guard or hunt. There are many different breeds of dog. ❑ *The British are renowned as a nation of dog lovers.*
  PHRASES **dog eat dog** (*disapproval*) You use **dog eat dog** to express your disapproval of a situation where everyone wants to succeed and is willing to harm other people in order to do so. = cut-throat ❑ *It is very much dog eat dog out there.*
  go to the dogs (*informal, disapproval*) If you say that something **is going to the dogs**, you mean that it is becoming weaker and worse in quality. ❑ *They sit doing nothing while the country goes to the dogs.*
  VERB [T] (**dogs, dogging, dogged**) If problems or injuries **dog** you, they are with you all the time. ❑ *His career has been dogged by bad luck.*
  → See also **dogged**

dog·ged /'dɒgɪd, AmE 'dɔː-/ ADJ [dogged + N] If you describe someone's actions as **dogged**, you mean that they are determined to continue with something even if it becomes difficult or dangerous. = resolute, persistent ❑ *They have, through sheer dogged determination, slowly gained respect for their efforts.*
  dog·ged·ly /'dɒgɪdli, AmE 'dɔː-/ ADV ❑ *She would fight doggedly for her rights as the children's mother.*
  dog·ged·ness /'dɒgɪdnəs, AmE 'dɔː-/ NOUN [U] ❑ *Most of my accomplishments came as the result of sheer doggedness rather than talent.*

❖**dog·ma** /'dɒgmə, AmE 'dɔːg-/ NOUN [C, U] (**dogmas**) (*disapproval*) If you refer to a belief or a system of beliefs as a **dogma**, you disapprove of it because people are expected to accept that it is true, without questioning it. = ideology, doctrine ❑ *Their political dogma has blinded them to the real needs of the country.* ❑ *He stands for freeing the country from the grip of dogma.*

❖**dog·mat·ic** /dɒg'mætɪk, AmE dɔːg-/ ADJ (*disapproval*) If you say that someone is **dogmatic**, you are critical of them because they are convinced that they are right, and refuse to consider that other opinions might also be justified. = opinionated, intolerant; ≠ tolerant ❑ *Many writers at this time held rigidly dogmatic views.* ❑ *The regime is dogmatic, and no one dares to express personal opinions.*
  ❖**dog·mati·cal·ly** /dɒg'mætɪkli, AmE dɔːg-/ ADV [dogmatically with V] ❑ *Bennett had wanted this list of books to be dogmatically imposed on the nation's universities.* ❑ *He applies the Marxist world view dogmatically to all social phenomena.*

❖**dog·ma·tism** /'dɒgmətɪzəm, AmE 'dɔːg-/ NOUN [U] (*disapproval*) If you refer to an opinion as **dogmatism**, you are criticizing it for being strongly stated without considering all the relevant facts or other people's opinions.

= intolerance; ≠ tolerance ❑ *We cannot allow dogmatism to stand in the way of progress.*

do-it-yourself NOUN [U] **Do-it-yourself** is the activity of making or repairing things yourself, especially in your home. The abbreviation **DIY** is often used.

dole /dəʊl/ NOUN

  NOUN [U] (*mainly BrE*; in *AmE*, usually use **welfare**) **The dole** or **dole** is money that is given regularly by the government to people who are unemployed. = benefit
  PHRASE **on the dole** (*mainly BrE*; in *AmE*, usually use **on welfare**) Someone who is **on the dole** is registered as unemployed and receives money from the government.

doll /dɒl/ NOUN [C] (**dolls**) A **doll** is a child's toy which looks like a small person or baby.

dol·lar ♦♦♦ /'dɒlə/ NOUN [C, SING] (**dollars**) **1** [C] The **dollar** is the unit of money used in the USA, Canada, Australia, and some other countries. It is represented by the symbol $, the dollar sign. A dollar is divided into one hundred smaller units called cents. ❑ *She gets paid seven dollars an hour.* **2** [SING] **The dollar** is also used to refer to the American currency system. ❑ *In early trading in Tokyo, the dollar fell sharply against the yen.*

❖**do·main** /də'meɪn/ NOUN [C] (**domains**) (*academic word*) **1** (*formal*) A **domain** is a particular field of thought, activity, or interest, especially one over which someone has control, influence, or rights. = sphere ❑ *the great experimenters in the domain of art* ❑ *This information should be in the public domain.* **2** On the Internet, a **domain** is a set of addresses that shows, for example, the category or geographical area that an Internet address belongs to. ❑ *An Internet society spokeswoman said .org domain users will not experience any disruptions during the transition.*

dome /dəʊm/ NOUN [C] (**domes**) **1** A **dome** is a round roof. ❑ *the dome of the Capitol* **2** A **dome** is any object that has a similar shape to a dome. ❑ *the dome of the hill*

❖**do·mes·tic** ♦♦◇ /də'mestɪk/ ADJ (*academic word*) **1** **Domestic** political activities, events, and situations happen or exist within one particular country. = internal ❑ *over 100 domestic flights a day to 30 leading US destinations* ❑ *sales in the domestic market* **2** [domestic + N] **Domestic** duties and activities are concerned with the running of a home and family. = household ❑ *a plan for sharing domestic chores* **3** [domestic + N] **Domestic** items and services are intended to be used in people's homes rather than in factories or offices. = household ❑ *domestic appliances* **4** A **domestic** situation or atmosphere is one which involves a family and their home. ❑ *It was a scene of such domestic bliss.* ❑ *victims of domestic violence* **5** A **domestic** animal is one that is not wild and is kept either on a farm to produce food or in someone's home as a pet. ❑ *a domestic cat*
  → See also **gross domestic product**

domi·nance /'dɒmɪnəns/ NOUN [U] The **dominance** of a particular person or thing is the fact that they are more powerful, successful, or important than other people or things. = supremacy ❑ *The latest fighting appears to be an attempt by each group to establish dominance over the other.*

❖**domi·nant** /'dɒmɪnənt/ ADJ Someone or something that is **dominant** is more powerful, successful, influential, or noticeable than other people or things. = pre-eminent, leading, powerful; ≠ inferior, subordinate ❑ *a change which would maintain his party's dominant position in Scotland* ❑ *She was a dominant figure in the French film industry.*

❖**domi·nate** ♦♦◇ /'dɒmɪneɪt/ VERB [I, T] (**dominates, dominating, dominated**) (*academic word*) **1** [I, T] To **dominate** a situation means to be the most powerful or important person or thing in it. = lead, overshadow, govern ❑ *The book is expected to dominate the best-seller lists.* ❑ *countries where life is dominated by war* ❑ *Selling could continue to dominate as investors play it safe.* ❑ *Microsoft's products dominate the global market for computer operating systems.* **2** [T] If one country or person **dominates** another, they have power over them. ❑ *He denied that his country wants to dominate Europe.* ❑ *Women are no longer dominated by the men in their relationships.* **3** [T] If a building, mountain, or other object **dominates** an area,

D

it is so large or impressive that you cannot avoid seeing it. ❑ *It's one of the biggest buildings in this area, and it really dominates this whole place.*

domi·na·tion /ˌdɒmɪˈneɪʃən/ NOUN [U] **1** the domination of the market by a small number of organizations **2** They had five centuries of domination by the Romans.

❍ **do·nate** /dəʊˈneɪt/ VERB [T] (**donates, donating, donated**) **1** If you **donate** something **to** a charity or other organization, you give it to them. ❑ *He frequently donates large sums to charity.* **2** If you **donate** your blood or a part of your body, you allow doctors to use it to help someone who is ill. ❑ *people who are willing to donate their organs for use after death* ❑ *All donated blood is screened for HIV.*

❍ **do·na·tion** /dəʊˈneɪʃən/ NOUN [C, U] (**donations**) **1** [C] A **donation** is something which someone gives to a charity or other organization. ❑ *Employees make regular donations to charity.* **2** [U] The **donation** of something **to** a charity or other organization, is the act of giving it to them. ❑ *the donation of his collection to the art gallery* **3** [U] The **donation** of blood or a part of your body, is the act of allowing doctors to use it to help someone who is ill. ❑ *measures aimed at encouraging organ donation* ❑ *routine screening of blood donations*

done ♦◇◇ /dʌn/ IRREG FORM, ADJ, CONVENTION
   IRREG FORM **Done** is the past participle of **do**.
   ADJ **1** [V-LINK + done] A task or activity that is **done** has been completed successfully. ❑ *When her deal is done, the client emerges with her purchase.* **2** [V-LINK + done] When something that you are cooking is **done**, it has been cooked long enough and is ready. ❑ *As soon as the cake is done, remove it from the oven.*
   CONVENTION (spoken, formulae) You say 'Done' when you are accepting a deal, arrangement, or bet that someone has offered to make with you. ❑ *'You lead and we'll look for it.'—'Done.'*

❍ **do·nor** /ˈdəʊnə/ NOUN, ADJ
   NOUN [C] (**donors**) **1** A **donor** is someone who gives a part of their body or some of their blood to be used by doctors to help a person who is ill. ❑ *Doctors removed the healthy kidney from the donor.* ❑ *trying to find a compatible bone marrow donor* **2** A **donor** is a person or organization who gives something, especially money, to a charity, organization, or country that needs it. ❑ *Donor countries are becoming more choosy about which countries they are prepared to help.*
   ADJ [donor + N] **Donor** organs or parts are organs or parts of the body which people allow doctors to use to help people who are ill. ❑ *the severe shortage of donor organs*

don't /dəʊnt/ SHORT FORM **Don't** is the usual spoken form of 'do not'.

doom /duːm/ NOUN, VERB
   NOUN [U] **1** **Doom** is a terrible future state or event which you cannot prevent. ❑ *his warnings of impending doom* **2** If you have a sense or feeling of **doom**, you feel that things are going very badly and are likely to get even worse. ❑ *Why are people so full of gloom and doom?*
   VERB [T] (**dooms, dooming, doomed**) If a fact or event **dooms** someone or something to a particular fate, it makes certain that they are going to suffer in some way. = condemn ❑ *That argument was the turning point for their marriage, and the one which doomed it to failure.*

doomed /duːmd/ ADJ **1** [V-LINK + doomed] If something **is doomed to** happen, or if you **are doomed to** a particular state, something unpleasant is certain to happen, and you can do nothing to prevent it. ❑ *Their plans seemed doomed to failure.* **2** Someone or something that is **doomed** is certain to fail or be destroyed. ❑ *I used to pour time and energy into projects that were doomed from the start.*

door ♦♦♦ /dɔː/ NOUN
   NOUN [C, PL] (**doors**) **1** [C] A **door** is a piece of wood, glass, or metal, which is moved to open and close the entrance to a building, room, cupboard, or vehicle. ❑ *I was knocking at the front door but there was no answer.* **2** [C] A **door** is the space in a wall when a door is open. = doorway ❑ *She looked through the door of the kitchen. Her daughter was at the stove.* **3** [PL] [AMOUNT + doors 'down/up'] (informal) **Doors** is used in expressions such as **a few doors down** or **three**

doors up to refer to a place that is a particular number of buildings away from where you are. ❑ *Mrs Cade's house was only a few doors down from her daughter's flat.*
   PHRASES **answer the door** When you **answer the door**, you go and open the door because a visitor has knocked on it or rung the bell. ❑ *Carol answered the door as soon as I knocked.*
   by the back door or **through the back door** (disapproval) If you say that someone gets or does something **by the back door** or **through the back door**, you are criticizing them for doing it secretly and unofficially. ❑ *The government would not allow anyone to sneak in by the back door and seize power by force.*
   behind closed doors If people have talks and discussions **behind closed doors**, they have them in private because they want them to be kept secret. ❑ *decisions taken in secret behind closed doors*
   door to door **1** If someone goes **from door to door** or goes **door to door**, they go along a street calling at each house in turn, for example, selling something. ❑ *They are going from door to door collecting money from civilians.* **2** If you talk about a distance or trip **from door to door** or **door to door**, you are talking about the distance from the place where the trip starts to the place where it finishes. ❑ *tickets covering the whole trip from door to door*
   foot in the door If you say that something helps someone to get their **foot in the door**, you mean that it gives them an opportunity to start doing something new, usually in an area that is difficult to succeed in. ❑ *If we can get our foot in the door, that can help us build our market.*
   shut the door in someone's face or **slam the door in someone's face** If someone **shuts the door in** your **face** or **slams the door in** your **face**, they refuse to talk to you or give you any information. ❑ *Did you say anything to him or just shut the door in his face?*
   lay something at someone's door If you **lay** something **at** someone's **door**, you blame them for an unpleasant event or situation. ❑ *Much of the blame for the long delay could be laid at the door of the manufacturer.*
   out of doors When you are **out of doors**, you are not inside a building, but in the open air. = outdoors ❑ *The weather was fine enough for working out of doors.*
   see someone to the door If you **see** someone **to the door**, you go to the door with a visitor when they leave. ❑ *Politely he saw her to the door and opened it for her.*
   show someone the door If someone **shows** you the **door**, they ask you to leave because they are angry with you. ❑ *Would they forgive and forget – or show him the door?*
   → See also **next door**
   ✦ **at death's door** → see **death**

door·way /ˈdɔːweɪ/ NOUN [C] (**doorways**) **1** A **doorway** is a space in a wall where a door opens and closes. ❑ *Hannah looked up to see David and another man standing in the doorway.* **2** A **doorway** is a covered space just outside the door of a building. ❑ *homeless people sleeping in doorways*

❍ **dor·mant** /ˈdɔːmənt/ ADJ Something that is **dormant** is not active, growing, or being used at the present time but is capable of becoming active later on. = inactive; ≠ active ❑ *when the long dormant volcano of Mount St Helens erupted in 1980* ❑ *The virus remains dormant in nerve tissue until activated.* ❑ *The United Nations is resuming a diplomatic effort that has lain dormant for almost two decades.*

❍ **dos·age** /ˈdəʊsɪdʒ/ NOUN [C] (**dosages**) A **dosage** is the amount of a medicine or drug that someone takes or should take. ❑ *He was put on a high dosage of vitamin C.* ❑ *Introduce one supplement at a time and increase the dosage gradually.*

❍ **dose** /dəʊs/ NOUN, VERB
   NOUN [C] (**doses**) A **dose of** medicine or a drug is a measured amount of it which is intended to be taken at one time. ❑ *One dose of penicillin can wipe out the infection.* ❑ *The recommended dose for patients with cardiac arrest is 300 mg.*
   VERB [T] (**doses, dosing, dosed**) If you **dose** a person or animal **with** medicine, you give them an amount of it. ❑ *The doctor fixed the rib, dosed him heavily with drugs, and said he would probably get better.*

PHRASAL VERB **dose up** Dose up means the same as **dose** VERB. □ *I dosed him up with Valium.*

dot /dɒt/ NOUN, VERB

NOUN [c] (**dots**) A **dot** is a very small round mark, for example one that is used as the top part of the letter 'i', as a full stop, or in the addresses of websites. □ *a system of painting using small dots of colour*

PHRASE **on the dot** If you arrive somewhere or do something **on the dot**, you arrive there or do it at exactly the time that you were supposed to. = punctually □ *They appeared on the dot of 9:50 p.m. as always.*

VERB [T] (**dots, dotting, dotted**) When things **dot** a place or an area, they are scattered or spread all over it. □ *Small coastal towns dot the landscape.*

dou·ble ♦♦◇ /ˈdʌbəl/ ADJ, NOUN, PREDET, PRON, VERB

ADJ **1** [double + N] You use **double** to indicate that something includes or is made of two things of the same kind. □ *a pair of double doors into the room from the new entrance hall* **2** [double + N] You use **double** before a singular noun to refer to two things of the same type that occur together, or that are connected in some way. □ *an extremely nasty double murder* **3** You use **double** to describe something which is twice the normal size or can hold twice the normal quantity of something. □ *a double helping of ice cream* **4** A **double** room is a room intended for two people, usually a couple, to stay or live in. □ *bed and breakfast for $180 for two people in a double room* **5** [double + N] A **double** bed is a bed that is wide enough for two people to sleep in. □ *One bedroom had a double bed and the other had single beds for the boys.* **6** [double + N] You use **double** to describe a drink that is twice the normal measure. □ *He was drinking his double whisky too fast and scowling.*

PHRASES **bent double** If you are **bent double**, the top half of your body is bent downward so that your head is close to your knees. □ *I was bent double in agony.*

see double If you **are seeing double**, there is something wrong with your eyes, and you can see two images instead of one. □ *For 35 minutes I was walking around in a daze. I was dizzy, seeing double.*

NOUN [c, u] (**doubles**) **1** [c] A **double** is a room intended for two people, usually a couple, to stay or live in. □ *The Great Western Hotel is ideal, costing around £90 a night for a double.* **2** [c] A **double** is a drink that is twice the normal measure. □ *'Give me a whisky,' Debilly said to Francis. 'Make it a double.'* **3** [c] If you refer to someone as a person's **double**, you mean that they look exactly like them. □ *Your mother sees you as her double.* **4** [u] In tennis or badminton, when people play **doubles**, two teams consisting of two players on each team play against each other on the same court. □ *In the doubles, the pair beat Hungary's Renata Csay and Kornelia Szanda.*

PHRASE **on the double** (*informal*) If you do something on **the double**, you do it very quickly or immediately. □ *I need a copy of the police report on the double.*

PREDET [double 'the' N] If something is **double the** amount or size of another thing, it is twice as large. = twice □ *The offer was to start a new research laboratory at double the salary he was then getting.*

PRON **Double** means twice the amount or size of another thing. □ *On average doctors write just over seven prescriptions each year per patient; in Germany it is double.*

VERB [I, T] (**doubles, doubling, doubled**) **1** [I, T] When something **doubles** or when you **double** it, it becomes twice as great in number, amount, or size. □ *The number of managers must double to 100 within 3 years.* □ *The programme will double the amount of money available to help pay for child care.* **2** [I] If a person or thing **doubles as** someone or something else, they have a second job or purpose as well as their main one. □ *Lots of homes in town double as businesses.*

PHRASAL VERBS **double over** Double over means the same as **double up** PHRASAL VERB 2. □ *Everyone was doubled over in laughter.*

double up **1** Double up means the same as **double** VERB 2. □ *The lids of the casserole dishes are designed to double up as baking dishes.* **2** If something **doubles** you **up**, or if you **double up**, you bend your body quickly or violently, for example, because you are laughing a lot or because you are feeling a lot of pain. □ *a savage blow which doubled him up*

◇doubt ♦♦◇ /daʊt/ NOUN, VERB

NOUN [c, u] (**doubts**) If you have **doubt** or **doubts** about something, you feel uncertain about it and do not know whether it is true or possible. If you say you have **no doubt about** it, you mean that you are certain it is true. = uncertainty, indecision, confusion; ≠ certainty, confidence □ *This raises doubts about the point of advertising.* □ *There is little doubt that man has had an impact on the Earth's climate.* □ *There can be little doubt that he will offend again.*

PHRASES **beyond doubt** (*emphasis*) You say that something is **beyond doubt** or **beyond reasonable doubt** when you are certain that it is true and it cannot be contradicted or disproved. □ *A referendum showed beyond doubt that voters wanted independence.*

in doubt **1** If you are **in doubt** about something, you feel unsure or uncertain about it. □ *He is in no doubt as to what is needed.* **2** If you say that something is **in doubt** or **open to doubt**, you consider it to be uncertain or unreliable. = uncertain □ *The outcome was still in doubt.*

no doubt **1** (*emphasis*) You use **no doubt** to emphasize that something seems certain or very likely to you. = undoubtedly □ *The contract for this will no doubt be widely advertised.* **2** You use **no doubt** to indicate that you accept the truth of a particular point, but that you do not think it is important or contradicts the rest of what you are saying. □ *No doubt many will regard these as harsh words, but regrettably they are true.*

without (a) doubt (*emphasis*) If you say that something is true **without doubt** or **without a doubt**, you are emphasizing that it is definitely true. = undoubtedly □ *This was without doubt the most interesting situation that Amanda had ever found herself in.*

VERB [T] (**doubts, doubting, doubted**) **1** If you **doubt** whether something is true or possible, you believe that it is probably not true or possible. = question □ *Others doubted whether that would happen.* □ *He doubted if he would learn anything new from Marie.* **2** If you **doubt** something, you believe that it might not be true or genuine. □ *No one doubted his ability.* **3** If you **doubt** someone or **doubt** their word, you think that they may not be telling the truth. □ *No one directly involved with the case doubted him.*

CONVENTION **I doubt it** You say **I doubt it** as a response to a question or statement about something that you think is untrue or unlikely. □ *'Somebody would have seen her.'—'I doubt it, not on Monday.'*

✦ a shadow of a doubt → see shadow; the benefit of the doubt → see benefit

WORD CONNECTIONS
VERB + **doubt**
have doubts
express doubts
raise doubts
voice doubts
□ *Some senators began to express doubts about the policy.*
ADJ + **doubt**
grave doubts
serious doubts
considerable doubts
major doubts
□ *I had grave doubts about the accuracy of their claims.*

WORD FAMILIES	
doubt NOUN	There is little **doubt** that man has had an impact on the Earth's climate.
doubtful ADJ	I was still very **doubtful** about the chances for success.
doubtfully ADV	He shook his head **doubtfully**.

D

undoubted ADJ	The event was an **undoubted** success.
undoubtedly ADV	**Undoubtedly**, political and economic factors have played their part.
doubtless ADV	He will **doubtless** try and persuade his colleagues to change their minds.

doubt·ful /'daʊtfʊl/ ADJ **1** If it is doubtful that something will happen, it seems unlikely to happen or you are uncertain whether it will happen. □ *For a time it seemed doubtful that he would move at all.* **2** If you are doubtful about something, you feel unsure or uncertain about it. = dubious □ *I was still very doubtful about the chances for success.* **3** If you say that something is of doubtful quality or value, you mean that it is of low quality or value. = dubious □ *selling something that is overpriced or of doubtful quality* **4** (journalism) If a sports player is doubtful for a match or event, he or she seems unlikely to play, usually because of injury. □ *Forsyth is doubtful for tonight's game with a badly bruised leg.*
doubt·ful·ly /'daʊtfəli/ ADV [doubtfully after v] = dubiously □ *Keeton shook his head doubtfully.*

doubt·less /'daʊtləs/ ADV [doubtless with CL/GROUP] If you say that something is doubtless the case, you mean that you think it is probably or almost certainly the case. □ *He will doubtless try and persuade his colleagues to change their minds.*

down ♦♦♦ /daʊn/ PREP, ADV, VERB, NOUN, ADJ

Down is often used with verbs of movement, such as 'fall' and 'pull', and also in phrasal verbs such as 'bring down' and 'calm down'.

PREP **1** To go down something such as a slope or a pipe means to go towards the ground or to a lower level. □ *We're going down a mountain.* □ *A man came down the stairs to meet them.* **2** [AMOUNT + down + N] If you are a particular distance down something, you are that distance below the top or surface of it. □ *He managed to cling on to a ledge 40 feet down the rock face.* **3** If you go or look down something such as a road or river, you go or look along it. If you are down a road or river, you are somewhere along it. □ *They set off at a jog up one street and down another.*
ADV **1** [down after v] If something is moving down, it is going towards the ground or to a lower level. □ *She went down to the kitchen again.* **2** [AMOUNT + down] If something is a particular distance down, it is that distance below the top or surface of something. □ *At the bottom of the pit, some 1,300 feet down, are huge heaps of ore.* **3** [down after v] You use down to say that you are looking or facing in a direction that is towards the ground or towards a lower level. □ *She was still looking down at her papers.* **4** [down after v] If you put something down, you put it onto a surface. □ *Danny put down his glass.* **5** If an amount of something goes down, it decreases. If an amount of something is down, it has decreased and is at a lower level than it was. □ *Interest rates came down today.* □ *Inflation will be down to three per cent.*
PHRASES **down to** **1** If you are down to a certain amount of something, you have only that amount left. □ *The poor man's down to his last $5.* **2** Down to a particular detail means including everything, even that detail. Down to a particular person means including everyone, even that person. □ *The bedroom was an exact replica of the original, perfect right down to the patterns on the wallpaper and the hairbrushes on the dressing table.*
down for If someone or something is down for a particular thing, it has been arranged that they will do that thing, or that thing will happen. □ *Mark had told me that he was down for an interview.*
down with (spoken, disapproval) If people shout 'down with' something or someone, they are saying that they dislike them and want to get rid of them. □ *Demonstrators chanted 'down with the rebels'.*
VERB [T] (**downs, downing, downed**) **1** If you say that someone downs food or a drink, you mean that they eat or drink it. = consume □ *We downed bottles of local wine.* **2** (journalism) If something or someone is downed, they fall to the ground because they have been hurt or damaged in some way. □ *A couple of jet fighters were downed during the five-week rebellion.*
NOUN [U] **1** Down consists of the small, soft feathers on young birds. Down is used to make bed-covers and pillows. □ *goose down* **2** Down is very fine hair. □ *The whole plant is covered with fine down.*
ADJ **1** [V-LINK + down] (informal) If you are feeling down, you are feeling unhappy or depressed. = low □ *The old man sounded really down.* **2** [V-LINK + down] If something is down on paper, it has been written on the paper. □ *That date wasn't down on our news sheet.* **3** [V-LINK + down] If a piece of equipment, especially a computer system, is down, it is temporarily not working. Compare up ADJECTIVE 3. □ *The computer's down again.*
✦ **up and down** → see up

down·fall /'daʊnfɔːl/ NOUN [C] (**downfalls**) **1** The downfall of a successful or powerful person or institution is their loss of success or power. □ *His lack of experience had led to his downfall.* **2** The thing that was a person's downfall caused them to fail or lose power. = undoing □ *Jeremy's honesty had been his downfall.*

down·grade /ˌdaʊn'grɪd/ VERB [T] (**downgrades, downgrading, downgraded**) **1** If something is downgraded, it is given less importance than it used to have or than you think it should have. □ *The boy's condition has been downgraded from critical to serious.* **2** If someone is downgraded, their job or status is changed so that they become less important or receive less money. = demote □ *There was no criticism of her work until after she was downgraded.*

down·hill /ˌdaʊn'hɪl/ ADV, ADJ
ADV **1** If something or someone is moving downhill or is downhill, they are moving down a slope or are located towards the bottom of a hill. □ *He headed downhill towards the river.* **2** If you say that something is going downhill, you mean that it is becoming worse or less successful. □ *Since I started to work longer hours things have gone steadily downhill.*
ADJ **1** [downhill + N] If something or someone is downhill, they are located down a slope or are heading in the direction of the bottom of a hill. □ *downhill ski runs* **2** [V-LINK + downhill] If you say that a task or situation is downhill after a particular stage or time, you mean that it is easy to deal with after that stage or time. □ *Well, I guess it's all downhill from here.*

down·load /'daʊnləʊd/ VERB [T] (**downloads, downloading, downloaded**) To download data means to transfer it to or from a computer along a line such as a telephone line, a radio link, or a computer network. □ *Users can download their material to a desktop PC back in the office.*

down·right /'daʊnraɪt/ ADV, ADJ
ADV [downright + ADJ] (emphasis) You use downright to emphasize unpleasant or bad qualities or behaviour. = positively □ *ideas that would have been downright dangerous if put into practice*
ADJ [downright + N] You use downright to emphasize something, especially a quality or behaviour that is bad or unpleasant. □ *It was a downright insult.*

down·side /'daʊnsaɪd/ NOUN [SING] The downside of a situation is the aspect of it which is less positive, pleasant, or useful than its other aspects. □ *The downside of this approach is a lack of clear leadership.*

down·stairs /ˌdaʊn'steəz/ ADV, ADJ, NOUN
ADV **1** [downstairs after v] If you go downstairs in a building, you go down a staircase towards the ground floor. □ *Denise went downstairs and made some tea.* **2** If something or someone is downstairs in a building, they are on the ground floor or on a lower floor than you. □ *The telephone was downstairs in the entrance hall.*
ADJ [downstairs + N] Downstairs means situated on the ground floor of a building or on a lower floor than you are. □ *She repainted the downstairs rooms and closed off the second floor.*

NOUN [SING] **The downstairs** of a building is its lower floor or floors. ❑ *The downstairs of the two little houses had been entirely refashioned.*

down·town ◆◇◇ /ˌdaʊnˈtaʊn/ ADJ, ADV, NOUN
ADJ [downtown + N] (*mainly AmE*) **Downtown** places are in or towards the centre of a large town or city, where the shops and places of business are. ❑ *an office in downtown Chicago*
ADV (*mainly AmE*) If you go **downtown**, you go to a place that is in or closer towards the centre of a large town or city. ❑ *By day he worked downtown for American Standard.*
NOUN [U] [oft 'the' downtown] (*mainly AmE*) **Downtown** is the centre of a large town or city, where the shops and places of business are. ❑ *in a large vacant area of the downtown*

down·ward /ˈdaʊnwəd/ ADJ, ADV

The form **downwards** is also used for the adverb.

ADJ **1** [downward + N] A **downward** movement or look is directed towards a lower place or a lower level. ❑ *a firm downward movement of the hands* **2** [downward + N] If you refer to a **downward** trend, you mean that something is decreasing or that a situation is getting worse. ❑ *The downward trend in home ownership is likely to continue.*
ADV **1** If you move or look **downward**, you move or look towards the ground or a lower level. ❑ *Benedict pointed downward again with his stick.* **2** [downward after V] If an amount or rate moves **downward**, it decreases. ❑ *Inflation is moving firmly downwards.* **3** ['from' N + downward] If you want to emphasize that a statement applies to everyone in an organization, you can say that it applies from its leader **downward**. ❑ *from the president downward*

doze /dəʊz/ VERB
VERB [I] (**dozes, dozing, dozed**) When you **doze**, you sleep lightly or for a short period, especially during the daytime. = nap ❑ *For a while she dozed fitfully.*
PHRASAL VERB **doze off** If you **doze off**, you fall into a light sleep, especially during the daytime. = nod off ❑ *I closed my eyes for a minute and must have dozed off.*

doz·en ◆◆◇ /ˈdʌzən/ NUM, QUANT, PRON

The plural form is **dozen** after a number, or after a word or expression referring to a number, such as 'several' or 'a few'.

NUM (**dozens**) **1** If you have **a dozen** things, you have twelve of them. ❑ *You will be able to take ten dozen bottles free of duty through customs.* **2** You can refer to a group of approximately twelve things or people as **a dozen**. You can refer to a group of approximately six things or people as **half a dozen**. ❑ *In half a dozen words, he had explained the bond that linked them.*
QUANT [dozens 'of' PL-N] (*emphasis*) If you refer to **dozens** of things or people, you are emphasizing that there are very many of them. ❑ *a storm which destroyed dozens of homes and buildings*
PRON You can also use **dozens** as a pronoun meaning lots. ❑ *Just as revealing are Mr Johnson's portraits, of which there are dozens.*

Dr ◆◆◇ (**Drs**) ABBREVIATION **Dr** is a written abbreviation for **doctor**. ❑ *Dr John Hardy of St Mary's Medical School*

drab /dræb/ ADJ (**drabber, drabbest**) If you describe something as **drab**, you think that it is dull and boring to look at or experience. = dreary ❑ *his drab little office*
drab·ness /ˈdræbnəs/ NOUN [U] ❑ *the dusty drabness of nearby villages*

✪ **draft** ◆◇◇ /drɑːft, dræft/ NOUN, VERB (*academic word*)
NOUN [C] (**drafts**) **1** A **draft** is an early version of a letter, book, or speech. = version ❑ *I rewrote his rough draft, which was published under my name.* ❑ *I faxed a first draft of this article to him.* ❑ *a final draft of an essay* **2** A **draft** is a written order for payment of money by a bank, especially from one bank to another. ❑ *Payments must be made in US dollars by a bank draft drawn to the order of the United Nations Postal Administration.*
VERB [T] (**drafts, drafting, drafted**) **1** When you **draft** a letter, book, or speech, you write the first version of it. ❑ *He drafted a letter to the editors.* **2** If people **are drafted**

to do something, they are asked to do a particular job. ❑ *She hoped that Fox could be drafted to run the organization.*

drag ◆◇◇ /dræg/ VERB, NOUN
VERB [T, I] (**drags, dragging, dragged**) **1** [T] If you **drag** something, you pull it along the ground, often with difficulty. ❑ *He got up and dragged his chair towards the table.* **2** [T] (*computing*) To **drag** a computer image means to use the mouse to move the position of the image on the screen, or to change its size or shape. ❑ *Use your mouse to drag the pictures to their new size.* **3** [T] If someone **drags** you somewhere, they pull you there, or force you to go there by physically threatening you. ❑ *The vigilantes dragged the men out of the vehicles.* **4** [T] If someone **drags** you somewhere you do not want to go, they make you go there. ❑ *When you can drag him away from his work, he can also be a devoted father.* **5** [T] If you say that you **drag yourself** somewhere, you are emphasizing that you have to make a very great effort to go there. ❑ *I find it really hard to drag myself out and exercise regularly.* **6** [T] If you **drag** your foot or your leg behind you, you walk with great difficulty because your foot or leg is injured in some way. ❑ *He was barely able to drag his poisoned leg behind him.* **7** [T] If the police **drag** a river or lake, they pull nets or hooks across the bottom of it in order to look for something. ❑ *Police are planning to drag the pond later this morning.* **8** [I] If a period of time or an event **drags**, it is very boring and seems to last a long time. ❑ *The minutes dragged past.*
PHRASE **drag your feet** or **drag your heels** If you **drag** your **feet** or **drag** your **heels**, you delay doing something or do it very slowly because you do not want to do it. ❑ *The government was dragging its feet, and this was threatening moves towards peace.*
PHRASAL VERB **drag out 1** If you **drag** something **out**, you make it last for longer than is necessary. = spin out ❑ *a company that was willing and able to drag out the proceedings for years* **2** If you **drag** something **out of** a person, you persuade them to tell you something that they do not want to tell you. ❑ *The families soon discovered that every piece of information had to be dragged out of the authorities.*
NOUN [SING, C, U] (**drags**) **1** [SING] If something is **a drag on** the development or progress of something, it slows it down or makes it more difficult. ❑ *The satellite acts as a drag on the shuttle.* **2** [SING] (*informal, disapproval*) If you say that something is **a drag**, you mean that it is unpleasant or very dull. ❑ *As far as shopping for clothes goes, it's a drag.* **3** [C] (*informal*) If you take a **drag on** a cigarette or pipe that you are smoking, you take in air through it. ❑ *He took a drag on his cigarette, and exhaled the smoke.* **4** [U] **Drag** is the wearing of women's clothes by a male entertainer. ❑ *Drag has been with us since the birth of comedy, because it's funny to see a man pretending to be a woman.*
PHRASE **in drag** If a man is **in drag**, he is wearing women's clothes.

drain ◆◇◇ /dreɪn/ VERB, NOUN
VERB [I, T] (**drains, draining, drained**) **1** [I, T] If you **drain** a liquid from a place or object, you remove the liquid by causing it to flow somewhere else. If a liquid **drains** somewhere, it flows there. ❑ *Miners built the tunnel to drain water out of the mines.* ❑ *Now the focus is on draining the water.* **2** [I, T] If you **drain** a place or object, you dry it by causing water to flow out of it. If a place or object **drains**, water flows out of it until it is dry. ❑ *The authorities have mobilized vast numbers of people to drain flooded land and build or repair dykes.* **3** [I, T] If you **drain** food or if food **drains**, you remove the liquid that it has been in, especially after it has been cooked or soaked in water. ❑ *Drain the pasta well, arrange on four plates and pour over the sauce.* **4** [I, T] (*literary*) If the colour or the blood **drains** or is **drained** from someone's face, they become very pale. You can also say that someone's face **drains** or is **drained** of colour. ❑ *Harry felt the colour drain from his face.* **5** [T] If something **drains** you, it leaves you feeling physically and emotionally exhausted. ❑ *My emotional turmoil had drained me.* **6** [T] If you say that a country's or a company's resources or finances **are drained**, you mean that they are used or spent completely. ❑ *The state's finances have been drained by drought and civil disorder.*
NOUN [C, SING] (**drains**) **1** [C] A **drain** is a pipe that carries

d

water or sewage away from a place, or an opening in a surface that leads to the pipe. ❑ *Tony built his own house and laid his own drains.* **2** [SING] If you say that something is **a drain on** an organization's finances or resources, you mean that it costs the organization a large amount of money, and you do not think that it is worth it. ❑ *an ultramodern printing plant, which has been a big drain on resources*

PHRASE **down the drain** (*informal*) If you say that something is **going down the drain**, you mean that it is being destroyed or wasted. ❑ *They were aware that their public image was rapidly going down the drain.*

drained /dreɪnd/ ADJ ❑ *I began to suffer from headaches, which left me feeling completely drained.*

drain·ing /'dreɪnɪŋ/ ADJ ❑ *This work is physically exhausting and emotionally draining.*

✪ **dra·ma** ◆◇◇ /'drɑːmə/ NOUN [c, u] (**dramas**) (*academic word*) **1** [c] A **drama** is a serious play for the theatre, television, or radio, or a serious film. = **play** ❑ *He acted in radio dramas.* ❑ *The film is a drama about a woman searching for her children.* **2** [u] You use **drama** to refer to plays in general or to work that is connected with plays and the theatre, such as acting or producing. = **theatre** ❑ *He knew nothing of Greek drama.* **3** [c, u] You can refer to a real situation which is exciting or distressing as **drama**. ❑ *There was none of the drama and relief of a hostage release.*

✪ **dra·mat·ic** ◆◆◇ /drə'mætɪk/ ADJ (*academic word*) **1** A **dramatic** change or event happens suddenly and is very noticeable and surprising. = **striking, sudden;** ≠ **gradual** ❑ *A fifth year of drought is expected to have dramatic effects on the California economy.* ❑ *This policy has led to a dramatic increase in our prison populations.* **2** A **dramatic** action, event, or situation is exciting and impressive. ❑ *He witnessed many dramatic escapes as people jumped from as high as the fourth floor.* **3** [dramatic + N] You use **dramatic** to describe things connected with or relating to the theatre, drama, or plays. ❑ *a dramatic arts major in college*

✪ **dra·mati·cal·ly** /drə'mætɪkli/ ADV **1** = **suddenly, strikingly;** ≠ **gradually** ❑ *At speeds above 50 mph, serious injuries dramatically increase.* ❑ *the construction of a dam which will dramatically alter the landscape* **2** *He tipped his head to one side and sighed dramatically.*

✪ **drama·tist** /'dræmətɪst/ NOUN [c] (**dramatists**) A **dramatist** is someone who writes plays. = **playwright** ❑ *Tennessee Williams, the dramatist who wrote A Streetcar Named Desire* ❑ *plays written jointly by several Elizabethan dramatists*

drama·tize /'dræmətaɪz/ also **dramatise** VERB [T] (**dramatizes, dramatizing, dramatized**) **1** If a book or story **is dramatized**, it is written or presented as a play, film, or television drama. ❑ *an incident later dramatized in the film 'The Right Stuff'* **2** If you say that someone **dramatizes** a situation or event, you mean that they try to make it seem more serious, more important, or more exciting than it really is. = **exaggerate** ❑ *They have a tendency to show off, to dramatize almost every situation.*

drama·ti·za·tion /,dræmətaɪ'zeɪʃən/ NOUN [c] (**dramatizations**) ❑ *a dramatization of D H Lawrence's novel, 'Lady Chatterley's Lover'*

drank /dræŋk/ IRREG FORM Drank is the past tense of **drink**.

drape /dreɪp/ VERB [T] (**drapes, draping, draped**) **1** If you **drape** a piece of cloth somewhere, you place it there so that it hangs down in a casual and graceful way. = **hang** ❑ *Natasha took the coat and draped it over her shoulders.* **2** If someone or something **is draped in** a piece of cloth, they are loosely covered by it. ❑ *a casket draped in the Virginia flag*

✪ **dras·tic** /'dræstɪk/ ADJ **1** If you have to take **drastic** action in order to solve a problem, you have to do something extreme to solve it. = **radical, severe, extreme;** ≠ **slight** ❑ *Drastic measures are needed to clean up the profession.* ❑ *He's not going to do anything drastic about economic policy.* **2** A **drastic** change is a very great change. ❑ *Foreign food aid has led to a drastic reduction in the numbers of people dying of starvation.*

✪ **dras·ti·cal·ly** /'dræstɪkli/ ADV [drastically with v] = **radically, severely, extremely;** ≠ **slightly** ❑ *As a result, services have been drastically reduced.*

draught /drɑːft, dræft/ (*BrE; in AmE, use* **draft**) NOUN [c] (**draughts**) A **draught** is a current of air that comes into a place in an undesirable way. ❑ *Block draughts around doors and windows.*

draw ◆◆◆ /drɔː/ VERB, NOUN

VERB [I, T, RECIP] (**draws, drawing, drew, drawn**) **1** [I, T] When you **draw**, or when you **draw** something, you use a pencil or pen to produce a picture, pattern, or diagram. = **sketch** ❑ *She would sit there drawing with the pencil stub.* **2** [I] (*written*) If you **draw** somewhere, you move there slowly. ❑ *She drew away and did not smile.* **3** [T] (*written*) If you **draw** something or someone in a particular direction, you move them in that direction, usually by pulling them gently. = **pull** ❑ *He drew his chair nearer the fire.* ❑ *He put his arm around Caroline's shoulders and drew her close to him.* **4** [T] When you **draw** a curtain or blind, you pull it across a window, either to cover or to uncover it. ❑ *After drawing the curtains, she lit a candle.* **5** [T] If someone **draws** a gun, knife, or other weapon, they pull it out of its container and threaten you with it. = **take out** ❑ *He drew his dagger and turned to face his pursuers.* **6** [I] When a vehicle **draws** somewhere, it moves there smoothly and steadily. ❑ *Claire had seen the taxi drawing away.* **7** [T] If you **draw** a deep breath, you breathe in deeply once. ❑ *He paused, drawing a deep breath.* **8** [I] If you **draw on** a cigarette, you breathe the smoke from it into your mouth or lungs. ❑ *He drew on an American cigarette.* **9** [T] To **draw** something such as water or energy **from** a particular source means to take it from that source. ❑ *Villagers still have to draw their water from wells.* **10** [T] If something that hits or presses part of your body **draws** blood, it cuts your skin so that it bleeds. ❑ *Any practice that draws blood could increase the risk of getting the virus.* **11** [T] If you **draw** money out of a bank account, you get it from the account so that you can use it. ❑ *She was drawing out money from a cash dispenser.* **12** [T] To **draw** something means to choose it or to be given it, as part of a competition, game, or lottery. ❑ *He put the pile of chips in the centre of the table and drew a card.* **13** [T] To **draw** something **from** a particular thing or place means to take or get it from that thing or place. ❑ *I draw strength from this challenge successfully.* **14** [T] If something such as a film or an event **draws** a lot of people, it is so interesting or entertaining that a lot of people go to it. ❑ *The game is currently drawing huge crowds.* **15** [T] If someone or something **draws** you, it attracts you very strongly. ❑ *In no sense did he draw and enthral her as Alex had done.* **16** [T] If you **draw** a particular conclusion, you decide that that conclusion is true. ❑ *He draws two conclusions from this.* **17** [T] If you **draw** a comparison, parallel, or distinction, you compare or contrast two different ideas, systems, or other things. ❑ *literary critics drawing comparisons between George Sand and George Eliot* **18** [T] If you **draw** someone's attention to something, you make them aware of it or make them think about it. ❑ *He was waving his arms to draw their attention.* **19** [T] If someone or something **draws** a particular reaction, people react to it in that way. ❑ *Such a policy would inevitably draw fierce resistance from farmers.* **20** [RECIP] (*mainly BrE; in AmE, usually use* **tie**) In a game or competition, if one person or team **draws with** another one, or if two people or teams **draw**, they have the same number of points or goals at the end of the game. = **tie** ❑ *Holland and the Republic of Ireland drew one-one.* ❑ *We drew with Ireland in the first game.*

PHRASES **draw to a close** or **draw to an end** When an event or period of time **draws to a close** or **draws to an end**, it finishes. ❑ *Another celebration had drawn to its close.*

draw close or **draw near** If an event or period of time **is drawing closer** or **is drawing nearer**, it is approaching. ❑ *Next spring's elections are drawing closer.*

PHRASAL VERBS **draw in** If you **draw** someone **in** or **draw** them **into** something you are involved with, you cause them to become involved with it. ❑ *It won't be easy for you to draw him in.*

draw on If you **draw on** or **draw upon** something such as your skill or experience, you make use of it in order to do something. ❑ *He drew on his experience as a yachtsman to make a documentary programme.*

draw up If you **draw up** a document, list, or plan, you

prepare it and write it out. = formulate ❑ *They agreed to establish a working party to draw up a formal agreement.* NOUN [c] (**draws**) **1** A **draw** is part of a competition, game, or lottery when things are chosen or given out by chance. ❑ *the final draw for all prize winners takes place on March 17* **2** A **draw** is the result of a game or competition when two people or teams have the same number of points or goals.
✦ **draw the line** → see **line**; **draw lots** → see **lot**

◆ draw·back /ˈdrɔːbæk/ NOUN [c] (**drawbacks**) A **drawback** is an aspect of something or someone that makes them less acceptable than they would otherwise be. = disadvantage, difficulty; ≠ benefit, advantage ❑ *He felt the flat's only drawback was that it was too small.*

drawer /ˈdrɔːə/ NOUN [c] (**drawers**) A **drawer** is part of a desk, chest, or other piece of furniture that is shaped like a box and is designed for putting things in. You pull it towards you to open it. ❑ *She opened her desk drawer and took out the manual.*

draw·ing /ˈdrɔːɪŋ/ NOUN [u, c] (**drawings**) **1** [u] Drawing is the activity of using a pencil or pen to produce a picture, pattern, or diagram. ❑ *I like dancing, singing, and drawing.* **2** [c] A **drawing** is a picture made with a pencil or pen. ❑ *She did a drawing of me.*

drawn /drɔːn/ IRREG FORM, ADJ
IRREG FORM **Drawn** is the past participle of **draw**.
ADJ If someone or their face looks **drawn**, their face is thin and they look very tired, ill, worried, or unhappy. ❑ *She looked drawn and tired when she turned towards me.*

dread /dred/ VERB, NOUN
VERB [T] (**dreads**, **dreading**, **dreaded**) If you **dread** something which may happen, you feel very anxious and unhappy about it because you think it will be unpleasant or upsetting. ❑ *I'm dreading Christmas this year.* ❑ *I dreaded coming back, to be honest.*
PHRASE **dread to think** If you say that you **dread to think** what might happen, you mean that you are anxious about it because it is likely to be very unpleasant. ❑ *I dread to think what will happen in the case of a major emergency.*
NOUN [u] **Dread** is a feeling of great anxiety and fear about something that may happen. ❑ *She thought with dread of the cold winters to come.*
→ See also **dreaded**

dread·ed /ˈdredɪd/ ADJ **1** [dreaded + N] **Dreaded** means terrible and greatly feared. ❑ *No one knew how to treat this dreaded disease.* **2** [dreaded + N] (*informal, feelings*) You can use **the dreaded** to describe something that you, or a particular group of people, find annoying, inconvenient, or undesirable. ❑ *She's a victim of the dreaded hay fever.*

dread·ful /ˈdredfʊl/ ADJ **1** If you say that something is **dreadful**, you mean that it is very bad or unpleasant, or very poor in quality. = awful, appalling ❑ *They told us the dreadful news.* **2** [dreadful + N] **Dreadful** is used to emphasize the degree or extent of something bad. = terrible ❑ *We've made a dreadful mistake.*
dread·fully /ˈdredfəli/ ADV **1** [dreadfully with v] ❑ *You behaved dreadfully.* **2** [dreadfully ADJ, dreadfully after v] ❑ *He looks dreadfully ill.*

dream ◆◆◇ /driːm/ NOUN, VERB, ADJ
NOUN [c, SING] (**dreams**) **1** [c] A **dream** is a series of events that you experience only in your mind while you are asleep. ❑ *He had a dream about Claire.* **2** [c] You can refer to a situation or event as a **dream** if you often think about it because you would like it to happen. = ambition ❑ *He had finally accomplished his dream of becoming a pilot.* **3** [c] You can refer to a situation or event that does not seem real as a **dream**, especially if it is very strange or unpleasant. ❑ *When the right woman comes along, this bad dream will be over.* **4** [SING] If you describe something as a particular person's **dream**, you think that it would be ideal for that person and that he or she would like it very much. ❑ *Greece is said to be a botanist's dream.*
PHRASES **like a dream** If you say that someone does something **like a dream**, you think that they do it very well. If you say that something happens **like a dream**, you mean that it happens successfully without any problems. ❑ *She cooked like a dream.*

of your dreams If you describe someone or something as the person or thing **of** your **dreams**, you mean that you consider them to be ideal or perfect. ❑ *This could be the man of my dreams.*
in your wildest dreams (*emphasis*) If you say that you could not imagine a particular thing **in** your **wildest dreams**, you are emphasizing that you think it is extremely strange or unlikely. ❑ *'Never in my wildest dreams did I think I'd ever accomplish this,' said Toni.*
beyond your wildest dreams (*emphasis*) If you describe something as being **beyond** your **wildest dreams**, you are emphasizing that it is better than you could have imagined or hoped for. ❑ *She had already achieved success beyond her wildest dreams.*
VERB [I, T] (**dreams**, **dreaming**, **dreamed** or **dreamt**) **1** [I, T] When you **dream**, you experience events in your mind while you are asleep. ❑ *Ivor dreamed that he was on a bus.* ❑ *She dreamed about her baby.* **2** [I, T] If you often think about something that you would very much like to happen or have, you can say that you **dream of** it. ❑ *As a schoolgirl, she had dreamed of becoming an actress.* ❑ *For most of us, a brand new designer kitchen is something we can only dream about.* ❑ *I dream that my son will go to university.* **3** [I] If you say that you **would not dream of** doing something, you are emphasizing that you would never do it because you think it is wrong or is not possible or suitable for you. ❑ *I wouldn't dream of making fun of you.* **4** [I, T] If you say that you **never dreamed that** something would happen, you are emphasizing that you did not think that it would happen because it seemed very unlikely. ❑ *I never dreamed that I would be able to afford a home here.*
PHRASAL VERB **dream up** If you **dream up** a plan or idea, you work it out or create it in your mind. ❑ *I dreamed up a plan to solve both problems at once.*
ADJ [dream + N] You can use **dream** to describe something that you think is ideal or perfect, especially if it is something that you thought you would never be able to have or experience. ❑ *a dream holiday to Jamaica*

dreary /ˈdrɪəri/ ADJ (**drearier**, **dreariest**) If you describe something as **dreary**, you mean that it is dull and depressing. = dismal ❑ *a dreary little town in the Midwest*

◆ dress ◆◆◇ /dres/ NOUN, VERB
NOUN [c, u] (**dresses**) **1** [c] A **dress** is a piece of clothing worn by a woman or girl. It covers her body and part of her legs. ❑ *She was wearing a black dress.* **2** [u] You can refer to clothes worn by men or women as **dress**. = clothes ❑ *He wore formal evening dress.* ❑ *hundreds of Cambodians in traditional dress*
VERB [I, T] (**dresses**, **dressing**, **dressed**) **1** [I, T] When you **dress** or **dress yourself**, you put on clothes. ❑ *He told Sarah to wait while he dressed.* **2** [T] If you **dress** someone, for example, a child, you put clothes on them. ❑ *She bathed her and dressed her in clean clothes.* **3** [I] If someone **dresses** in a particular way, they wear clothes of a particular style or colour. ❑ *He dresses in a way that lets everyone know he's got authority.* **4** [I] If you **dress for** something, you put on special clothes for it. ❑ *We don't dress for dinner here.* **5** [T] When someone **dresses** a wound, they clean it and cover it. ❑ *The poor child never cried or protested when I was dressing her wounds.*
PHRASAL VERBS **dress down** If you **dress down**, you wear clothes that are less formal than usual. ❑ *She dresses down in dark glasses and baggy clothes to avoid hordes of admirers.*
dress up **1** If you **dress up** or **dress** yourself **up**, you put on different clothes, in order to make yourself look more formal than usual or to disguise yourself. ❑ *You do not need to dress up for dinner.* ❑ *I just love the fun of dressing up in another era's clothing.* **2** If you **dress** someone **up**, you give them special clothes to wear, in order to make them look more formal or to disguise them. ❑ *Mother loved to dress me up.* **3** If you **dress** something **up**, you try to make it seem more attractive, acceptable, or interesting than it really is. ❑ *Politicians are happier to dress up their ruthless ambition as a necessary pursuit of the public good.*
→ See also **dressed**

dressed ◆◇◇ /drest/ ADJ **1** If you are **dressed**, you are wearing clothes rather than being naked or wearing your

D

nightclothes. If you **get dressed**, you put on your clothes. ❑ *He was fully dressed, including shoes.* **2** [V-LINK + dressed] If you are **dressed** in a particular way, you are wearing clothes of a particular colour or kind. ❑ *a tall thin woman dressed in black*

drew /druː/ IRREG FORM Drew is the past tense of **draw**.

drib·ble /'drɪbəl/ VERB [I, T] (dribbles, dribbling, dribbled) **1** [I, T] If a liquid **dribbles** somewhere, or if you **dribble** it, it drops down slowly or flows in a thin stream. = trickle ❑ *Sweat dribbled down Hart's face.* **2** [I, T] When players **dribble** the ball in a game such as basketball or soccer, they keep kicking or tapping it quickly in order to keep it moving. ❑ *He dribbled the ball towards Ferris.* ❑ *He dribbled past four defenders.* **3** [I] If a person **dribbles**, saliva drops slowly from their mouth. = drool ❑ *to protect sheets when the baby dribbles*

dried /draɪd/ ADJ [dried + N] **Dried** food or milk has had all the water removed from it so that it will last for a long time. ❑ *an infusion which may be prepared from the fresh plant or the dried herb*
→ See also **dry**

dri·er /'draɪə/ → See **dry, dryer**

drift ♦◇◇ /drɪft/ VERB, NOUN
VERB [I] (drifts, drifting, drifted) **1** When something **drifts** somewhere, it is carried there by the movement of wind or water. ❑ *We proceeded to drift on up the river.* **2** If someone or something **drifts into** a situation, they get into that situation in a way that is not planned or controlled. ❑ *We need to offer young people drifting into crime an alternative set of values.* **3** If you say that someone **drifts** around, you mean that they travel from place to place without a plan or settled way of life. ❑ *You've been drifting from job to job without any real commitment.* **4** To **drift** somewhere means to move there slowly or gradually. ❑ *As rural factories lay off workers, people drift towards the cities.* **5** If sounds **drift** somewhere, they can be heard but they are not very loud. ❑ *Cool summer dance sounds are drifting from the stereo indoors.* **6** If snow **drifts**, it builds up into piles as a result of the movement of the wind. ❑ *The snow, except where it drifted, was only calf-deep.*
PHRASAL VERB **drift off** If you **drift off** to sleep, you gradually fall asleep. ❑ *It was only when he finally drifted off to sleep that the headaches eased.*
NOUN [C, SING] (drifts) **1** [C] A **drift** is a movement away from somewhere or something, or a movement towards somewhere or something different. ❑ *the drift towards the cities* **2** [C] A **drift** is a mass of snow that has built up into a pile as a result of the movement of wind. ❑ *A nine-year-old boy was trapped in a snow drift.* **3** [SING] The **drift** of an argument or speech is the general point that is being made in it. = gist ❑ *Grace was beginning to get his drift.*

drill /drɪl/ NOUN, VERB
NOUN [C, U] (drills) **1** [C] A **drill** is a tool or machine that you use for making holes. ❑ *a dentist's drill* **2** [C] A **drill** is a routine exercise or activity, in which people practise what they should do in dangerous situations. ❑ *a fire drill* **3** [C, U] A **drill** is repeated training for a group of people, especially soldiers, so that they can do something quickly and efficiently. ❑ *The Marines carried out landing exercises in a drill that includes 18 ships and 90 aircraft.*
VERB [I, T] (drills, drilling, drilled) **1** [I, T] When you **drill** into something or **drill** a hole in something, you make a hole in it using a drill. ❑ *He drilled into the wall of Lili's bedroom.* **2** [I] When people **drill for** oil or water, they search for it by drilling deep holes in the ground or in the bottom of the sea. ❑ *There have been proposals to drill for more oil.*

drink ♦♦◇ /drɪŋk/ VERB, NOUN
VERB [I, T] (drinks, drinking, drank, drunk) **1** [I, T] When you **drink** a liquid, you take it into your mouth and swallow it. ❑ *He drank his cup of tea.* ❑ *He drank thirstily.* **2** [I] To **drink** means to drink alcohol. ❑ *By his own admission, he was smoking and drinking too much.*
PHRASAL VERB **drink to** When people **drink to** someone or something, they wish them success, good luck, or good health before having an alcoholic drink. ❑ *Let's drink to his memory, eh?*

NOUN [U, C] (drinks) **1** [U, C] A **drink** is an amount of a liquid which you drink. ❑ *I'll get you a drink of water.* **2** [C] A **drink** is an alcoholic drink. ❑ *She felt like a drink after a hard day.* **3** [U] (mainly BrE) **Drink** is alcohol, such as beer, wine, or whisky. ❑ *Too much drink is bad for your health.*

drink·ing /'drɪŋkɪŋ/ NOUN [U] ❑ *She had left him because of his drinking.*

drip /drɪp/ VERB, NOUN
VERB [I, T] (drips, dripping, dripped) **1** [I, T] When liquid **drips** somewhere, or you **drip** it somewhere, it falls in individual small drops. ❑ *Blood dripped from the corner of his mouth.* ❑ *Amid the trees the sea mist was dripping and moisture formed on Tom's glasses.* **2** [I] When something **drips**, drops of liquid fall from it. ❑ *A faucet in the kitchen was dripping.* ❑ *Lou was dripping with perspiration.* **3** [I] (literary) If you say that something **is dripping with** a particular thing, you mean that it contains a lot of that thing. ❑ *They were dazed by window displays dripping with diamonds and furs.*
NOUN [C] (drips) **1** A **drip** is a small individual drop of a liquid. ❑ *Drips of water rolled down the trousers of his uniform.* **2** A **drip** is a piece of medical equipment by which a liquid is slowly passed through a tube into a patient's blood. ❑ *He was put on an intravenous drip to treat his dehydration.*

drive ♦♦♦ /draɪv/ VERB, NOUN
VERB [I, T] (drives, driving, drove, driven) **1** [I, T] When you **drive** somewhere, you operate a car or other vehicle and control its movement and direction. ❑ *I drove into town and went to a restaurant for dinner.* ❑ *She never learned to drive.* ❑ *We drove the car down to Richmond for the weekend.* **2** [T] If you **drive** someone somewhere, you take them there in a car or other vehicle. ❑ *His daughter Carly drove him to the train station.* **3** [T] If something **drives** a machine, it supplies the power that makes it work. ❑ *The current flows into electric motors that drive the wheels.* **4** [T] If you **drive** something such as a nail **into** something else, you push it in or hammer it in using a lot of effort. ❑ *I had to use our sledgehammer to drive the pegs into the side of the path.* **5** [I] If the wind, rain, or snow **drives** in a particular direction, it moves with great force in that direction. ❑ *Rain drove against the window.* **6** [T] If you **drive** people or animals somewhere, you make them go to or from that place. ❑ *The last offensive drove thousands of people into Thailand.* **7** [T] To **drive** someone into a particular state or situation means to force them into that state or situation. ❑ *The recession and hospital bills drove them into bankruptcy.* **8** [T] The desire or feeling that **drives** a person **to** do something, especially something extreme, is the desire or feeling that causes them to do it. ❑ *More than once, depression drove him to attempt suicide.* ❑ *Jealousy drives people to murder.*
PHRASAL VERB **drive away** To **drive** people **away** means to make them want to go away or stay away. ❑ *Patrick's rudeness soon drove Monica's friends away.*
NOUN [C, U, SING] (drives) **1** [C] A **drive** is a trip in a car or other vehicle. ❑ *I thought we might go for a drive on Sunday.* **2** [C] A **drive** is a wide piece of hard ground, or sometimes a private road, that leads from the road to a person's house. = driveway ❑ *The boys followed Eleanor up the drive to the house.* **3** [C] You use **drive** to refer to the mechanical part of a computer which reads the data on disks and tapes, or writes data onto them. ❑ *The firm specialized in supplying pieces of equipment, such as terminals, tape drives, or printers.* **4** [C] A **drive** is a very strong need or desire in human beings that makes them act in particular ways. ❑ *compelling, dynamic sex drives* **5** [U] If you say that someone has **drive**, you mean they have energy and determination. ❑ *John will be best remembered for his drive and enthusiasm.* **6** [SING] A **drive** is a special effort made by a group of people for a particular purpose. = campaign ❑ *The ANC is about to launch a nationwide recruitment drive.* **7** [C] **Drive** is used in the names of some streets. ❑ *3091 North Beverly Hills Drive, Beverly Hills, CA*

driv·ing /'draɪvɪŋ/ NOUN [U] ❑ *a qualified driving instructor*

driv·en /'drɪvən/ IRREG FORM Driven is the past participle of **drive**.

driv·er ♦♦◇ /ˈdraɪvə/ NOUN [c] (**drivers**) **1** The **driver** of a vehicle is the person who is driving it. ❑ *The driver got out of his van.* **2** (*computing*) A **driver** is a computer program that controls a device such as a printer. ❑ *Printer driver software includes standard features such as print layout and fit-to-page printing.*

driv·ing li·cence (*BrE*; in *AmE*, use **driver's license**) NOUN [c] (**driving licences**) A **driving licence** is a card showing that you are qualified to drive because you have passed a driving test.

driz·zle /ˈdrɪzəl/ NOUN, VERB

NOUN [U] [also 'a' drizzle] **Drizzle** is light rain falling in fine drops. ❑ *The drizzle had now stopped and the sun was breaking through.*

VERB [I] (**drizzles, drizzling, drizzled**) If it **is drizzling**, it is raining very lightly. ❑ *Clouds had come down and it was starting to drizzle.*

droop /druːp/ VERB, NOUN

VERB [I] (**droops, drooping, drooped**) If something **droops**, it hangs or leans downwards with no strength or firmness. ❑ *Crook's eyelids drooped and he yawned.*

NOUN [SING] A **droop** is when something hangs or leans downwards with no strength or firmness. ❑ *the droop of his shoulders*

✪ drop ♦♦◇ /drɒp/ VERB, NOUN

VERB [I, T] (**drops, dropping, dropped**) **1** [I, T] If a level or amount **drops** or if someone or something **drops** it, it quickly becomes less. = fall, decline; ≠ rise, increase ❑ *Temperatures can drop to freezing at night.* ❑ *His blood pressure had dropped severely.* ❑ *He had dropped the price of his London home by £1.25m.* **2** [T] If you **drop** something, you accidentally let it fall. ❑ *I dropped my glasses and broke them.* **3** [I] If something **drops onto** something else, it falls onto that thing. If something **drops from** somewhere, it falls from that place. ❑ *He felt hot tears dropping onto his fingers.* **4** [I, T] If you **drop** something somewhere or if it **drops** there, you deliberately let it fall there. ❑ *Drop the noodles into the water.* ❑ *television footage of bombs dropping on the city* **5** [I, T] If a person or a part of their body **drops** to a lower position, or if they **drop** a part of their body to a lower position, they move to that position, often in a tired and lifeless way. ❑ *Nancy dropped into a nearby chair.* ❑ *She let her head drop.* **6** [I] To **drop** is used in expressions such as **to be about to drop** and **to dance until you drop** to emphasize that you are exhausted and can no longer continue doing something. ❑ *She looked about to drop.* **7** [I, T] If your voice **drops** or if you **drop** your voice, you speak more quietly. ❑ *Her voice will drop to a dismissive whisper.* **8** [T] If you **drop** someone or something somewhere, you take them somewhere and leave them there, usually in a car or other vehicle. ❑ *He dropped me outside the hotel.* **9** [T] If you **drop** an idea, course of action, or habit, you do not continue with it. ❑ *He was told to drop the idea.* **10** [T] If someone **is dropped** by a sports team or organization, they are no longer included in that team or employed by that organization. ❑ *Alexander has been dropped from his multimillion-dollar-a-year job as spokesman for the company.* **11** [I] If you **drop** to a lower position in a sports competition, you move to that position. ❑ *She has dropped to third in the world ranking.*

PHRASES **drop a hint** If you **drop a hint**, you give a hint or say something in a casual way. ❑ *Jerry dropped hints that he and Julie were talking about getting married.*

drop the subject or **drop it** or **let it drop** If you want someone to **drop the subject**, **drop it**, or **let it drop**, you want them to stop talking about something, often because you are annoyed that they keep talking about it. ❑ *Mary Ann wished he would just drop it.*

PHRASAL VERBS **drop by** If you **drop by**, you visit someone informally. ❑ *She and Danny will drop by later.*

drop in If you **drop in on** someone, you visit them informally, usually without having arranged it. ❑ *Why not drop in for a chat?*

drop off 1 Drop off means the same as **drop** VERB 8. ❑ *Just drop me off at the airport.* **2** (*informal*) If you **drop off** to sleep, you go to sleep. ❑ *I must have dropped off to sleep.* **3** If the level of something **drops off**, it becomes less.

= fall ❑ *Two years later, earnings from the stocks had dropped off by nearly 50%.*

drop out If someone **drops out of** college or a race, for example, they leave it without finishing what they started. ❑ *He'd dropped out of high school at the age of 16.*

NOUN [PL, c] (**drops**) **1** [PL, c] A **drop** in something is an instance of it becoming less or lower. = fall, decline, decrease, reduction; ≠ rise, increase ❑ *He was prepared to take a drop in wages.* ❑ *The poll indicates a drop in support for the Conservatives.* **2** [c] A **drop of** a liquid is a very small amount of it shaped like a little ball. In informal English, you can also use **drop** when you are referring to a very small amount of something such as a drink. ❑ *a drop of blue ink* **3** [c] You use **drop** to talk about vertical distances. For example, a thirty-foot **drop** is a distance of thirty feet between the top of a cliff or wall and the bottom of it. ❑ *There was a sheer drop just outside my window.* **4** [PL] **Drops** are a kind of medicine which you put drop by drop into your ears, eyes, or nose. ❑ *And he had to have these drops in his eyes as well.*

drop·ping /ˈdrɒpɪŋ/ NOUN [U] **1** the dropping of the first atomic bomb **2** This was one of the factors that led to President Suharto's dropping of his previous objections.

♦ **drop dead** → see **dead**; **at the drop of a hat** → see **hat**; **a drop in the ocean** → see **ocean**

WORD CONNECTIONS

ADJ + **drop**

a **big** drop
a **significant** drop
a **sharp** drop
a **steep** drop
a **dramatic** drop

❑ *There has been a significant drop in the number of people who are out of work and looking for a job.*

VERB + **drop**

report a drop
record a drop

❑ *The company reported a 30% drop in sales last year.*

avoid a drop
experience a drop
suffer a drop
show a drop
cause a drop

❑ *Universities have suffered a large drop in student numbers as a result of fee increases.*

drop + IN + NOUN

a drop in **profits**
a drop in **sales**
a drop in **prices**
a drop in **earnings**
a drop in **revenue**

❑ *A drop in household earnings means consumers have less to spend.*

a drop in **temperature**
a drop in **demand**
a drop in **numbers**

❑ *The heat is made bearable by the northerly breeze that leads to a drop in temperature at night.*

✪ drought /draʊt/ NOUN [c, U] (**droughts**) A **drought** is a long period of time during which no rain falls. ❑ *a country where drought and famines have killed up to two million people during the last eighteen years*

drove /drəʊv/ IRREG FORM **Drove** is the past tense of **drive**.

drown /draʊn/ VERB

VERB [I, T] (**drowns, drowning, drowned**) **1** [I, T] When someone **drowns** or **is drowned**, they die because they have gone or been pushed under water and cannot breathe. ❑ *A child can drown in only a few inches of water.* ❑ *Last night a boy was drowned in the river.* **2** [I] If you say that a person or thing **is drowning** in something, you are emphasizing that they have a very large amount of it, or are completely covered in it. ❑ *people who gradually find*

D

themselves *drowning in debt* **3** [T] If something **drowns** a sound, it is so loud that you cannot hear that sound properly. ❑ *Clapping drowned the speaker's words for a moment.*

PHRASE **drown one's sorrows** If you say that someone **is drowning** their **sorrows**, you mean that they are drinking alcohol in order to forget something sad or upsetting that has happened to them. ❑ *Carly drowned her sorrows in vodka cocktails at a South Beach nightclub.*

PHRASAL VERB **drown out** Drown out means the same as **drown** VERB **3**. ❑ *Their cheers drowned out the protests of demonstrators.*

drowsy /'draʊzi/ ADJ (**drowsier, drowsiest**) If you feel **drowsy**, you feel sleepy and cannot think clearly. ❑ *He felt pleasantly drowsy and had to fight off the urge to sleep.*
drowsi·ness /'draʊzinəs/ NOUN [U] ❑ *Big meals during the day cause drowsiness.*

✪ **drug** ◆◆◆ /drʌg/ NOUN, VERB
NOUN [C] (**drugs**) **1** A **drug** is a chemical which is given to people in order to treat or prevent an illness or disease. = medication, medicine, remedy ❑ *The drug will be useful to hundreds of thousands of infected people.* **2 Drugs** are substances that some people take because of their pleasant effects, but which are usually illegal. = narcotic ❑ *His mother was on drugs, on cocaine.* ❑ *She was sure Leo was taking drugs.* ❑ *the problem of drug abuse*
VERB [T] (**drugs, drugging, drugged**) **1** If you **drug** a person or animal, you give them a chemical substance in order to make them sleepy or unconscious. ❑ *She was drugged and robbed.* **2** If food or drink **is drugged**, a chemical substance is added to it in order to make someone sleepy or unconscious when they eat or drink it. ❑ *I wonder now if that drink had been drugged.*

drug ad·dict NOUN [C] (**drug addicts**) A **drug addict** is someone who is addicted to illegal drugs.

drum ◆◇◇ /drʌm/ NOUN, VERB
NOUN [C] (**drums**) **1** A **drum** is a musical instrument consisting of a skin stretched tightly over a round frame. You play a drum by beating it with sticks or with your hands. ❑ *a worker who died after collapsing while beating a drum during a demonstration* **2** A **drum** is a large cylindrical container which is used to store fuel and other substances. ❑ *an oil drum*
VERB [I, T] (**drums, drumming, drummed**) If something **drums on** a surface, or if you **drum** something **on** a surface, it hits it regularly, making a continuous beating sound. ❑ *He drummed his fingers on the leather top of his desk.*
PHRASAL VERBS **drum into** If you **drum** something **into** someone, you keep saying it to them until they understand it or remember it. ❑ *Standard examples were drummed into students' heads.*
drum up If you **drum up** support or business, you try to get it. ❑ *It is to be hoped that he is merely drumming up business.*

drum·mer /'drʌmə/ NOUN [C] (**drummers**) A **drummer** is a person who plays a drum or drums in a band or group. ❑ *He was a drummer in a rock band.*

drunk /drʌŋk/ ADJ, NOUN, IRREG FORM
ADJ Someone who is **drunk** has drunk so much alcohol that they cannot speak clearly or behave sensibly. ❑ *I got drunk and had to be carried home.*
NOUN [C] (**drunks**) A **drunk** is someone who is drunk or frequently gets drunk. ❑ *A drunk lay in the alley.*
IRREG FORM Drunk is the past participle of **drink**.

drunk·en /'drʌŋkən/ ADJ **1** [drunken + N] Drunken is used to describe events and situations that involve people who are drunk. ❑ *The pain roused him from his drunken stupor.* **2** [drunken + N] A **drunken** person is drunk or is frequently drunk. ❑ *Groups of drunken hooligans smashed windows and threw stones.*
drunk·en·ly /'drʌŋkənli/ ADV ❑ *Once Bob stormed drunkenly into her house and smashed some chairs.*
drunk·en·ness /'drʌŋkənnəs/ NOUN [U] ❑ *He was arrested for drunkenness.*

dry ◆◆◇ /draɪ/ ADJ, VERB
ADJ (**drier** or **dryer, driest** or **dryest**) **1** If something is **dry**, there is no water or moisture on it or in it. ❑ *Clean*

the metal with a soft dry cloth. ❑ *Pat it dry with a soft towel.* **2** If you say that your skin or hair is **dry**, you mean that it is less oily than, or not as oily as, normal. ❑ *Nothing looks worse than dry, cracked lips.* **3** If the weather or a period of time is **dry**, there is no rain or there is much less rain than average. ❑ *Exceptionally dry weather over the past year had cut agricultural production.* **4** A **dry** place or climate is one that gets very little rainfall. = arid ❑ *It was one of the driest and dustiest places in Africa.* **5** If a river, lake, or well is **dry**, it is empty of water, usually because of hot weather and lack of rain. ❑ *The aquifer which had once fed the wells was pronounced dry.* **6** If an oil well is **dry**, it is no longer producing any oil. ❑ *To harvest oil and gas profitably from the North Sea, we must focus on the exploitation of small reserves as the big wells run dry.* **7** If your mouth or throat is **dry**, it has little or no saliva in it, and so feels very unpleasant, perhaps because you are tense or ill. ❑ *His mouth was still dry, he would certainly be glad of a drink.* **8** If someone has **dry** eyes, there are no tears in their eyes; often used with negatives or in contexts where you are expressing surprise that they are not crying. ❑ *There were few dry eyes in the house when I finished.* **9 Dry** humour is very amusing, but in a subtle and clever way. = witty ❑ *Though the pressure Fulton is under must be considerable, he has retained his dry humour.* **10** If you describe something such as a book, play, or activity as **dry**, you mean that it is dull and uninteresting. ❑ *My eyelids were drooping over the dry, academic phrases.* **11 Dry** sherry or wine does not have a sweet taste. ❑ *a glass of chilled, dry white wine*
VERB [I, T] (**dries, drying, dried**) **1** [I, T] When something **dries** or when you **dry** it, it becomes dry. ❑ *Let your hair dry naturally whenever possible.* **2** [T] When you **dry** the dishes after a meal, you wipe the water off the plates, cups, cutlery, pans, and other things when they have been washed, using a cloth. = wipe ❑ *Mrs Madrigal picked up a towel and began drying dishes next to her daughter.*
PHRASAL VERBS **dry out** **1** If something **dries out** or is **dried out**, it loses all the moisture that was in it and becomes hard. ❑ *If the soil is allowed to dry out the tree could die.* **2** (informal) If someone **dries out** or is **dried out**, they stop drinking alcohol. ❑ *He checked into Cedars Sinai Hospital to dry out.*
dry up **1** If something **dries up** or if something **dries it up**, it loses all its moisture and becomes completely dry and shrivelled or hard. ❑ *As the day goes on, the pollen dries up and becomes hard.* **2** If a river, lake, or well **dries up**, it becomes empty of water, usually because of hot weather and a lack of rain. ❑ *Reservoirs are drying up and farmers have begun to leave their land in search of water.* **3** If a supply of something **dries up**, it stops. ❑ *The main source of income, tourism, is expected to dry up completely this summer.* **4** If you **dry up** when you are speaking, you stop in the middle of what you were saying, because you cannot think what to say next. ❑ *When he turned around and saw her, his conversation dried up.*
dry·ness /'draɪnəs/ NOUN [U] **1** *the parched dryness of the air* **2** *Dryness of the skin can also be caused by living in centrally heated homes and offices.* **3** *He was advised to spend time in the warmth and dryness of Italy.* **4** *Symptoms included frequent dryness in the mouth.* **5** *It has a wry dryness you won't recognize.*
✦ **high and dry** → see **high**

dry-clean VERB [T] (**dry-cleans, dry-cleaning, dry-cleaned**) When things such as clothes **are dry-cleaned**, they are cleaned with a liquid chemical rather than with water. ❑ *Natural-filled duvets must be dry-cleaned by a professional.*

dry·er /'draɪə/ also **drier** NOUN [C] (**dryers**) A **dryer** is a machine for drying things. There are different kinds of dryers, for example ones designed for drying clothes, crops, or people's hair or hands. ❑ *hot air electric hand dryers*
→ See also **dry**

✪ **dual** /'dju:əl, AmE 'du:-/ ADJ [dual + N] **Dual** means having two parts, functions, or aspects. = twin, double; ≠ single ❑ *his dual role as head of the party and head of state* ❑ *a law allowing dual nationality*

dub /dʌb/ VERB [T] (**dubs, dubbing, dubbed**) **1** (journalism)

If someone or something **is dubbed** a particular thing, they are given that description or name. ❑ *Today's session has been widely dubbed as a 'make or break' meeting.* **2** If a film or soundtrack in a foreign language **is dubbed**, a new soundtrack is added with actors giving a translation. ❑ *It was dubbed into Spanish for Mexican audiences.*

du·bi·ous /'dju:biəs, AmE 'du:-/ ADJ **1** If you describe something as **dubious**, you mean that you do not consider it to be completely honest, safe, or reliable. = questionable ❑ *This claim seems to us to be rather dubious.* **2** [V-LINK + dubious] If you are **dubious about** something, you are not completely sure about it and have not yet made up your mind about it. = doubtful ❑ *My parents were a bit dubious about it all at first but we soon convinced them.*
du·bi·ous·ly /'dju:biəsli, AmE 'du:-/ ADV **1** *Carter was dubiously convicted of shooting three white men in a bar.* **2** *He eyed Coyne dubiously.*

duck /dʌk/ NOUN, VERB
  NOUN   [C, U] (**ducks**) **1** [C, U] A **duck** is a common water bird with short legs, a short neck, and a large flat beak. ❑ *Chickens and ducks scratch around the outbuildings.* **2** [U] **Duck** is the flesh of this bird when it is eaten as food. ❑ *honey roasted duck*
  PHRASES   **like water off a duck's back** (*emphasis*) You say that criticism is **like water off a duck's back** or **water off a duck's back** to emphasize that it is not having any effect on the person being criticized. ❑ *All the criticism is water off a duck's back to me.*
take to something like a duck to water If you **take to** something **like a duck to water**, you discover that you are naturally good at it or that you find it very easy to do. ❑ *Some mothers take to breastfeeding like a duck to water, while others find they need some help to get started.*
  VERB   [I, T] (**ducks, ducking, ducked**) **1** [I] If you **duck**, you move your head or the top half of your body quickly downwards to avoid something that might hit you, to avoid being seen, or to hide the expression on your face. ❑ *He ducked in time to avoid a blow from the poker.* **2** [T] If you **duck** something such as a blow, you avoid it by moving your head or body quickly downwards. = dodge ❑ *Hans deftly ducked their blows.* **3** [T] If you **duck** your head, you move it quickly downwards to hide the expression on your face. ❑ *He ducked his head to hide his admiration.* **4** [T] (*informal, disapproval*) You say that someone **ducks** a duty or responsibility when they disapprove of the fact that they avoid it. ❑ *The defence secretary ducked the question of whether the United States was winning the war.*
  PHRASAL VERB   **duck out** (*informal*) If you **duck out of** something that you are supposed to do, you avoid doing it. = back out ❑ *George ducked out of his forced marriage to a cousin.*

due /dju:, AmE du:/ ADJ
  ADJ   **1** If something is **due** at a particular time, it is expected to happen, be done, or arrive at that time. ❑ *The results are due at the end of the month.* ❑ *Mr Carter is due in Washington on Monday.* **2** [due + N] **Due** attention or consideration is the proper, reasonable, or deserved amount of it under the circumstances. = proper ❑ *After due consideration it was decided to send him away to live with foster parents.* **3** [V-LINK + due] Something that is **due**, or that is **due to** someone, is owed to them, either as a debt or because they have a right to it. ❑ *I was sent a cheque and advised that no further pension was due.* **4** [V-LINK + due 'for' N] If someone is **due for** something, that thing is planned to happen to or be given to them now, or very soon, often after they have been waiting for it for a long time. ❑ *Although not due for release until 2001, he was let out of his low-security prison to spend a weekend with his wife.*
  PHRASES   **due to** **1** If an event is **due to** something, it happens or exists as a direct result of that thing. = because of, caused by ❑ *The country's economic problems are largely due to the weakness of the recovery.* **2** You can say **due to** to introduce the reason for something happening. Some speakers of English believe that it is not correct to use **due to** in this way. ❑ *Due to the large volume of letters he receives Dave regrets he is unable to answer queries personally.*

in due course If you say that something will happen or take place **in due course**, you mean that you cannot make it happen any quicker and it will happen when the time is right for it. ❑ *In due course the baby was born.*
give someone their due You can say '**to give** him his **due**', or '**giving** him his **due**', when you are admitting that there are some good things about someone, even though there are things that you do not like about them. ❑ *To give Linda her due, she had tried to encourage John in his school work.*
with due respect (*politeness*) You can say '**with due respect**' when you are about to disagree politely with someone. ❑ *With all due respect I submit to you that you're asking the wrong question.*

duel /'dju:əl, AmE 'du:-/ NOUN [C] (**duels**) A **duel** is a formal fight between two people in which they use guns or swords in order to settle a quarrel. ❑ *He killed a man in one duel and was himself wounded in another.*

duet /dju:'et, AmE du:-/ NOUN [C] (**duets**) A **duet** is a piece of music sung or played by two people. ❑ *Tonight she sings a duet with first husband Maurice Gibb.*

dug /dʌg/ IRREG FORM **Dug** is the past tense and past participle of **dig**.

dull /dʌl/ ADJ, VERB
  ADJ   (**duller, dullest**) **1** (*disapproval*) If you describe someone or something as **dull**, you mean they are not interesting or exciting. = boring ❑ *I felt she found me boring and dull.* **2** Someone or something that is **dull** is not very lively or energetic. = sluggish ❑ *The body's natural rhythms mean we all feel dull and sleepy between 1 and 3 p.m.* **3** A **dull** colour or light is not bright. ❑ *The stamp was a dark, dull blue colour with a heavy black postmark.* **4** You say the weather is **dull** when it is very cloudy. ❑ *It's always dull and raining.* **5** **Dull** sounds are not very clear or loud. ❑ *The coffin closed with a dull thud.* **6** [dull + N] **Dull** feelings are weak and not intense. ❑ *The pain, usually a dull ache, gets worse with exercise.*
  VERB   [I, T] (**dulls, dulling, dulled**) If something **dulls** or if it **is dulled**, it becomes less intense, bright, or lively. ❑ *Her eyes dulled and she gazed blankly.*
dull·ness /'dʌlnəs/ NOUN [U] **1** *They enjoy anything that breaks the dullness of their routine life.* **2** *Did you notice any unusual depression or dullness of mind?*
dul·ly /'dʌli/ ADV **1** [dully with V] ❑ *His giant face had a rough growth of stubble, his eyes looked dully ahead.* **2** [dully after V] ❑ *The street lamps gleamed dully through the night's mist.* **3** [dully after V] ❑ *He heard his heart thump dully but more quickly.* **4** *His arm throbbed dully.*

duly /'dju:li, AmE 'du:-/ ADV **1** [duly before V] If you say that something **duly** happened or was done, you mean that it was expected to happen or was requested, and it did happen or it was done. ❑ *Westcott appealed to Waite for an apology, which he duly received.* **2** [duly before V] (*formal*) If something is **duly** done, it is done in the correct way. ❑ *He is a duly elected president of the country and we're going to be giving him all the support we can.*

dumb /dʌm/ ADJ
  ADJ   (**dumber, dumbest**) **1** Someone who is **dumb** is completely unable to speak. = mute ❑ *a young deaf and dumb man* **2** [V-LINK + dumb] (*literary*) If someone is **dumb** on a particular occasion, they cannot speak because they are angry, shocked, or surprised. = speechless ❑ *We were all struck dumb for a minute.* **3** (*informal, disapproval*) If you call a person **dumb**, you mean that they are stupid or foolish. ❑ *The questions were set up to make her look dumb.* **4** (*mainly AmE, informal, disapproval*) If you say that something is **dumb**, you think that it is silly and annoying. = stupid ❑ *I came up with this dumb idea.*
  PHRASAL VERB   **dumb down** (**dumbs, dumbing, dumbed**) If you **dumb down** something, you make it easier for people to understand, especially if this spoils it. ❑ *This sounded like a case for dumbing down the magazine, which no one favoured.*

dump /dʌmp/ VERB, NOUN
  VERB   [T] (**dumps, dumping, dumped**) **1** (*informal*) If you **dump** something somewhere, you put it or unload it there quickly and carelessly. ❑ *We dumped our bags at the nearby*

Grand Hotel and hurried towards the market. **2** (*informal*) If something **is dumped** somewhere, it is put or left there because it is no longer wanted or needed. ◻ *The getaway car was dumped near the motorway.* **3** (*informal*) To **dump** something such as an idea, policy, or practice means to stop supporting or using it. = ditch ◻ *The party dumped the policy of nationalization in favour of the free market.* **4** (*business*) If a firm or company **dumps** goods, it sells large quantities of them at prices far below their real value, usually in another country, in order to gain a bigger market share or to keep prices high in the home market. ◻ *It produces more than it needs, then dumps its surplus onto the world market.* **5** (*informal*) If you **dump** someone, you end your relationship with them. = ditch ◻ *My heart sank because I thought he was going to dump me for another girl.* **6** (*computing*) To **dump** computer data or memory means to copy it from one storage system onto another, such as from disk to magnetic tape. ◻ *All the data is then dumped into the main computer.* NOUN [c] (**dumps**) **1** A **dump** is a place where rubbish and waste material are left, for example on open ground outside a town. = landfill ◻ *companies that bring their trash straight to the dump* **2** (*informal, disapproval*) If you say that a place is a **dump**, you think it is ugly and unpleasant to live in or visit. ◻ *'What a dump!' Christabel said, standing in the doorway of the youth hostel.* **3** (*computing*) A **dump** is a list of the data that is stored in a computer's memory at a particular time. **Dumps** are often used by computer programmers to find out what is causing a problem with a program. ◻ *Print it out and it'll do a screen dump of what's there.*

dump·ing /ˈdʌmpɪŋ/ NOUN [u] ◻ *German law forbids the dumping of hazardous waste on German soil.*

dung /dʌŋ/ NOUN [u] **Dung** is faeces from animals, especially from large animals such as cattle and horses. ◻ *Workers at Sydney's harbourside Taronga zoo are refusing to collect animal dung in a protest over wages.*

du·pli·cate VERB, NOUN, ADJ
VERB /ˈdjuːplɪkeɪt, AmE ˈduː-/ [T] (**duplicates, duplicating, duplicated**) **1** If you **duplicate** something that has already been done, you repeat or copy it. ◻ *His task will be to duplicate his success overseas here at home.* **2** To **duplicate** something which has been written, drawn, or recorded onto tape means to make exact copies of it. ◻ *a business which duplicates video tapes for the film-makers* NOUN /ˈdjuːplɪkət, AmE ˈduː-/ [c] (**duplicates**) **1** A **duplicate** is a repeat or copy of something that has already been done. ◻ *The tight race is almost a duplicate of the elections in Georgia and South Dakota last month that pitted a Republican challenger against a Democratic incumbent.* **2** [also 'in' duplicate] A **duplicate** of something which has been written, drawn, or recorded onto tape is an exact copy of it. ◻ *I'm on my way to Switzerland, but I've lost my card. I've got to get a duplicate.* ADJ /ˈdjuːplɪkət, AmE ˈduː-/ [duplicate + N] **Duplicate** is used to describe things that have been made as an exact copy of other things, usually in order to serve the same purpose. ◻ *He let himself in with a duplicate key.*

du·ra·ble /ˈdjʊərəbəl, AmE ˈdʊr-/ ADJ Something that is **durable** is strong and lasts a long time without breaking or becoming weaker. ◻ *Fine bone china is eminently practical, since it is strong and durable.*

du·rabil·ity /ˌdjʊərəˈbɪlɪti, AmE ˌdʊr-/ NOUN [u] ◻ *Airlines recommend hard-sided cases for durability.*

✪ du·ra·tion /djʊˈreɪʃən, AmE dʊ-/ NOUN (*academic word*) NOUN [u] The **duration** of an event or state is the time during which it happens or exists. = extent, period, term ◻ *He was given the task of protecting her for the duration of the trial.* ◻ *The result was an increase in the average duration of prison sentences.* ◻ *Courses are of two years' duration.* PHRASE **for the duration** If you say that something will happen **for the duration**, you mean that it will happen for as long as a particular situation continues. ◻ *His wounds knocked him out of combat for the duration.*

dur·ing ◆◆◆ /ˈdjʊərɪŋ, AmE ˈdʊrɪŋ/ PREP **1** If something happens **during** a period of time or an event, it happens continuously, or happens several times between the

beginning and end of that period or event. ◻ *Sandstorms are common during the Saudi Arabian winter.* **2** If something develops **during** a period of time, it develops gradually from the beginning to the end of that period. ◻ *Wages have fallen by more than twenty per cent during the past two months.* **3** An event that happens **during** a period of time happens at some point or moment in that period. ◻ *During his visit, the Pope will also bless the new hospital.*

WHICH WORD?
during, in, or while?

You use **during** or **in** to talk about an extended or repeated action that happens from the beginning to the end of a specific period of time. Do not use **during** with days of the week, months, or years.

◻ *We often get storms during the winter.*
◻ *This song was popular in 2006.*

Both **during** and **in** can also be used to say that a single event happened at some point in the course of a period of time. Again, do not use **during** with days of the week, months, or years.

◻ *His father died during the night.*
◻ *His father died in the night.*
◻ *Mr Tyrie left Hong Kong in June.*

You use **during** to say that something happens while an activity takes place.

◻ *I fell asleep during the performance.*

If one thing happens **while** another thing is happening, the two things happen at the same time.

◻ *He stayed with me while Dad talked with Dr Leon.*
◻ *I often knit while watching television.*

dusk /dʌsk/ NOUN [u] **Dusk** is the time just before night when the daylight has almost gone but when it is not completely dark. ◻ *We arrived home at dusk.*

dust ◆◇◇ /dʌst/ NOUN, VERB
NOUN [u] **1 Dust** is very small dry particles of earth or sand. ◻ *Tanks raise huge trails of dust when they move.* **2 Dust** is the very small pieces of dirt which you find inside buildings, for example on furniture, floors, or lights. ◻ *I could see a thick layer of dust on the stairs.* **3 Dust** is a fine powder which consists of very small particles of a substance such as gold, wood, or coal. ◻ *The air is so black with diesel fumes and coal dust, I can barely see.* PHRASES **bite the dust** (*humorous, informal, emphasis*) If you say that something **has bitten the dust**, you are emphasizing that it no longer exists or that it has failed. ◻ *In the last 30 years many cherished values have bitten the dust.*
when the dust settles (*informal*) If you say that something will happen when **the dust settles**, you mean that a situation will be clearer after it has calmed down. If you let **the dust settle** before doing something, you let a situation calm down before you try to do anything else. ◻ *Once the dust had settled Beck defended his decision.*
gather dust If you say that something **is gathering dust**, you mean that it has been left somewhere and nobody is using it or doing anything with it. ◻ *Many of the machines are gathering dust in basements.* VERB [I, T] (**dusts, dusting, dusted**) **1** When you **dust** something such as furniture, you remove dust from it, usually using a cloth. ◻ *I vacuumed and dusted and polished the living room.* **2** If you **dust** something with a fine substance such as powder or if you **dust** a fine substance **onto** something, you cover it lightly with that substance. ◻ *Lightly dust the fish with flour.*

dust·bin /ˈdʌstbɪn/ NOUN [c] (**dustbins**) (*BrE*) A **dustbin** is a large container for rubbish, usually used by a household.

dusty /ˈdʌsti/ ADJ (**dustier, dustiest**) **1** If places, roads, or other things outside are **dusty**, they are covered with tiny bits of earth or sand, usually because it has not rained for a long time. ◻ *They started strolling down the dusty road in the moonlight.* **2** If a room, house, or object is **dusty**, it is covered with very small pieces of dirt. ◻ *a dusty attic*

du·ti·ful /ˈdjuːtɪfʊl, AmE ˈduː-/ ADJ If you say that someone is **dutiful**, you mean that they do everything that they are expected to do. ❑ *The days of the dutiful wife, who sacrifices her career for her husband, are over.*

du·ti·ful·ly /'dju:tɪfəli, AmE 'du:-/ ADV [dutifully with V] ❑ *The inspector dutifully recorded the date in a large red book.*

duty ◆◆◇ /'dju:ti, AmE 'du:ti/ NOUN

[NOUN] [U, PL, SING, C] (**duties**) **1** [U] Duty is work that you have to do for your job. ❑ *Staff must report for duty at their normal place of work.* **2** [PL] Your **duties** are tasks which you have to do because they are part of your job. ❑ *I carried out my duties conscientiously.* **3** [SING] If you say that something is your **duty**, you believe that you ought to do it because it is your responsibility. ❑ *I consider it my duty to write to you and thank you.* **4** [C, U] **Duties** are taxes which you pay to the government on goods that you buy. ❑ *Import duties still average 30 per cent.*

[PHRASE] **off duty** or **on duty** If someone such as a police officer or a nurse is **off duty**, they are not working. If someone is **on duty**, they are working. ❑ *I'm off duty.*

DVD /ˌdi: vi: 'di:/ NOUN [C] (**DVDs**) A DVD is a disk on which a film or music is recorded. DVD disks are similar to compact discs but hold a lot more information. **DVD** is an abbreviation for 'digital video disk' or 'digital versatile disk'. ❑ *a DVD player*

dwarf /dwɔ:f/ VERB, ADJ, NOUN

[VERB] [T] (**dwarfs, dwarfing, dwarfed**) If one person or thing **is dwarfed** by another, the second is so much bigger than the first that it makes them look very small. ❑ *His figure is dwarfed by the huge red McDonald's sign.*

[ADJ] [dwarf + N] **Dwarf** is used to describe varieties or species of plants and animals which are much smaller than the usual size for their kind. ❑ *dwarf shrubs*

[NOUN] [C] (**dwarves** or **dwarfs**) **1** In children's stories, a **dwarf** is an imaginary creature that is like a small man. Dwarfs often have magical powers. **2** (*offensive, old-fashioned*) In former times, people who were much smaller than normal were called **dwarves**.

dwell /dwel/ VERB [I] (**dwells, dwelling, dwelt** or **dwelled**) If you **dwell on** something, especially something unpleasant, you think, speak, or write about it a lot or for quite a long time. ❑ *'I'd rather not dwell on the past,' he told me.*
→ See also **dwelling**

dwell·ing /'dwelɪŋ/ NOUN [C] (**dwellings**) (*formal*) A **dwelling** or a **dwelling place** is a place where someone lives. ❑ *Some 3,500 new dwellings are planned for the area.*

dwelt /dwelt/ IRREG FORM **Dwelt** is a past tense and past participle of **dwell**.

⭐**dwin·dle** /'dwɪndəl/ VERB [I] (**dwindles, dwindling, dwindled**) If something **dwindles**, it becomes smaller, weaker, or less in number. = shrink; ≠ expand, grow ❑ *The factory's workforce has dwindled from over 4,000 to a few hundred.* ❑ *a rapidly dwindling population*

dye /daɪ/ VERB, NOUN

[VERB] [T] (**dyes, dyeing, dyed**) If you **dye** something such as hair or cloth, you change its colour by soaking it in a special liquid. ❑ *The women prepared, spun, and dyed the wool.*

[NOUN] [C, U] (**dyes**) **Dye** is a substance made from plants or chemicals which is mixed into a liquid and used to change the colour of something such as cloth or hair. ❑ *bottles of hair dye*

dy·ing /'daɪɪŋ/ IRREG FORM, ADJ, NOUN

[IRREG FORM] **Dying** is the present participle of **die**.

[ADJ] **1** [dying + N] A **dying** person or animal is very ill and likely to die soon. ❑ *a dying man* **2** [dying + N] You use **dying** to describe something which happens at the time when someone dies, or is connected with that time. ❑ *It'll stay in my mind till my dying day.* **3** [dying + N] The **dying** days or **dying** minutes of a state of affairs or an activity are its last days or minutes. = final ❑ *a story of love and war in the dying days of the Ottoman Empire* **4** [dying + N] A **dying** tradition or industry is becoming less important and is likely to disappear completely. ❑ *Shipbuilding is a dying business.*

[NOUN] [PL] The **dying** are people who are dying. ❑ *By the time our officers arrived, the dead and the dying were everywhere.*

⭐**dy·nam·ic** /daɪ'næmɪk/ ADJ, NOUN (*academic word*)

[ADJ] **1** (*approval*) If you describe someone as **dynamic**, you approve of them because they are full of energy or full of new and exciting ideas. ❑ *He seemed a dynamic and energetic leader.* **2** If you describe something as **dynamic**, you approve of it because it is very active and energetic. ❑ *South Asia continues to be the most dynamic economic region in the world.* **3** A **dynamic** process is one that constantly changes and progresses. = active, progressive ❑ *a dynamic, evolving worldwide epidemic* ❑ *Political debate is dynamic.*

[NOUN] [C, PL, U] (**dynamics**) **1** [C] The **dynamic** of a system or process is the force that causes it to change or progress. ❑ *The dynamic of the market demands constant change and adjustment.* ❑ *Politics has its own dynamic.* **2** [PL] The **dynamics** of a situation or group of people are the opposing forces within it that cause it to change. ❑ *What is needed is insight into the dynamics of the social system.* ❑ *The interchange of ideas aids an understanding of family dynamics.* **3** [PL] **Dynamics** are forces which produce power or movement. ❑ *Scientists observe the same dynamics in fluids.* **4** [U] **Dynamics** is the scientific study of motion, energy, and forces. ❑ *His idea was to apply geometry to dynamics.* ❑ *the field of fluid dynamics*

dy·nami·cal·ly /daɪ'næmɪkli/ ADV ❑ *He's one of the most dynamically imaginative jazz pianists of our time.*

Ee

E also **e** /iː/ NOUN [C, U] (**E's, e's**) E is the fifth letter of the English alphabet.

each ♦♦♦ /iːtʃ/ DET, PRON, ADV, QUANT

DET If you refer to **each** thing or **each** person in a group, you are referring to every member of the group and considering them as individuals. ☐ *Each book is beautifully illustrated.* ☐ *Each year, hundreds of animals are killed in this way.*

PHRASE **each and every** (*emphasis*) You can refer to **each and every** member of a group to emphasize that you mean all the members of that group. ☐ *My goal was that each and every person responsible for Yankel's murder be brought to justice.*

PRON **1** Each refers to every member of a group, considering them as individuals. ☐ *two bedrooms, each with three beds* **2** Each is used to emphasize that something applies to every member of a group. ☐ *We each have different needs and interests.* **3** [V + each, PREP + each] You use **each other** when you are saying that each member of a group does something to the others or has a particular connection with the others. ☐ *We looked at each other in silence, each equally shocked.* ☐ *Both sides are willing to make allowances for each other's political sensitivities.*

ADV [AMOUNT + each] If members of a group are given a certain amount **each**, every member of the group is given that amount. ☐ *The children were given one each, handed to them or placed on their plates.*

QUANT **1** [each 'of' DEF-PL-N] Each of a group of people or things means every member of the group. ☐ *He handed each of them a page of photos.* ☐ *Each of these exercises takes one or two minutes to do.* **2** [each 'of' DEF-PL-N] If you refer to **each one of** the members of a group, you are emphasizing that something applies to every one of them. ☐ *He picked up forty of these publications and read each one of them.*

WHICH WORD?

each other or one another?

You can use **each other** or **one another** to talk about two or more people who share an action or a feeling.

☐ *We help **each other** a lot.*

☐ *People tend to mimic **one another** in unconscious ways.*

One another is fairly formal, and some people do not use it at all.

USAGE NOTE

each

You use 'each' in front of the singular form of a countable noun, and 'each of' in front of a definite determiner + plural noun or in front of an object pronoun.

***Each** applicant has five choices.*

***Each of** these phrases has a different meaning.*

***Each of** them had a notebook and a pencil.*

---

eager ♦◇◇ /ˈiːgə/ ADJ **1** If you are **eager** to do or have something, you want to do or have it very much. = keen ☐ *Robert was eager to talk about life in the Army.* ☐ *When my own son was five years old, I became eager for another baby.* **2** If you look or sound **eager**, you look or sound as if you

expect something interesting or enjoyable to happen. = excited ☐ *Arty sneered at the crowd of eager faces around him.*

eager·ness /ˈiːgənəs/ NOUN [U] **1** *an eagerness to learn* **2** *It was the voice of a woman speaking with breathless eagerness.*

eager·ly /ˈiːgəli/ ADV ☐ *'So what do you think will happen?' he asked eagerly.*

ear ♦◇◇ /ɪə/ NOUN

NOUN [C, SING] (**ears**) **1** [C] Your **ears** are the two parts of your body, one on each side of your head, with which you hear sounds. ☐ *He whispered something in her ear.* **2** [SING] If you have **an ear for** music or language, you are able to hear its sounds accurately and to interpret them or reproduce them well. ☐ *Moby certainly has a fine ear for a tune.* **3** [C] **Ear** is often used to refer to people's willingness to listen to what someone is saying. ☐ *What would cause the masses to give him a far more sympathetic ear?* **4** [C] The **ears** of a cereal plant such as corn or barley are the parts at the top of the stem that contain the seeds or grains. ☐ *American farmers use machines to pick the ears of corn from the plants.*

PHRASES **fall on deaf ears** or **turn a deaf ear** If a request **falls on deaf ears** or if the person to whom the request is made **turns a deaf ear to** it, they take no notice of it. ☐ *I hope that our appeals will not fall on deaf ears.*

play by ear If you **play by ear** or **play** a piece of music **by ear**, you play music by relying on your memory rather than by reading printed music. ☐ *Neil sat at the piano and began playing, by ear, the music he'd heard his older sister practising.*

have a tin ear [usu have a tin ear 'for' N] If you say that someone **has a tin ear** for something, you mean that they do not have any natural ability for it and cannot appreciate or understand it fully. ☐ *Worst of all, for a playwright specializing in characters who use the vernacular, he has a tin ear for dialogue.*

♦ **music to your ears** → see **music**

ear·li·er ♦♦◇ /ˈɜːliə/ IRREG FORM, ADV, ADJ

IRREG FORM **Earlier** is the comparative of **early**.

ADV **Earlier** is used to refer to a point or period in time before the present or before the one you are talking about. ☐ *As mentioned earlier, the university supplements this information with an interview.* ☐ *political reforms announced by the president earlier this year*

ADJ [earlier + N] **Earlier** is used to describe something that took place at a point or period in time before the present or before the one you are talking about. ☐ *Earlier reports of gunshots have not been substantiated.*

ear·li·est /ˈɜːliɪst/ IRREG FORM

IRREG FORM **Earliest** is the superlative of **early**.

PHRASE **at the earliest** **At the earliest** means not before the date or time mentioned. ☐ *The first official results are not expected until Tuesday at the earliest.*

ear·ly ♦♦♦ /ˈɜːli/ ADV, ADJ

ADV (**earlier, earliest**) **1** [early after V] **Early** means before the usual time that a particular event or activity happens. ☐ *I knew I had to get up early.* **2** **Early** refers to a time near the beginning of a day, week, year, or other period of time. ☐ *We'll hope to see you some time early next week.* **3** [early after V] **Early** means before the time that was arranged or

expected. ❑ *She arrived early to get a place at the front.*
4 Early refers to a point near the beginning of a period in history, or in the history of something such as the world, a society, or an activity. ❑ *an incident that occurred much earlier in the game* **5** [early with v] **Early** refers to the flowering or cropping of plants before or at the beginning of the main season. ❑ *This early flowering gladiolus is not very hardy.*
PHRASE as early as (*emphasis*) You can use **as early as** to emphasize that a particular time or period is surprisingly early. ❑ *Inflation could fall back into single figures as early as this month.*
ADJ (**earlier, earliest**) **1** [early + N] **Early** refers to something that happens before the usual time that a particular event or activity happens. ❑ *I decided that I was going to take early retirement.* **2** [early + N] **Early** means near the beginning of a day, week, year, or other period of time. ❑ *in the 1970s and the early 1980s* ❑ *She was in her early teens.* **3 Early** means before the time that was arranged or expected. ❑ *I'm always early.* **4** [early + N] **Early** means near the beginning of a period in history, or in the history of something such as the world, a society, or an activity. ❑ *Fassbinder's early films* **5** [early + N] **Early** means near the beginning of something such as a piece of work or a process. ❑ *the book's early chapters* **6** [early + N] **Early** refers to plants that flower or crop before or at the beginning of the main season. ❑ *these early cabbages and cauliflowers* **7** [early + N] (*formal*) **Early** reports or indications of something are the first reports or indications about it. ❑ *The early indications look encouraging.*
PHRASE it is early days If you say about something that might be true that is **early days**, you mean that it is too soon for you to be completely sure about it.

✪ **earn** ♦♦◇ /ɜːn/ [T] (**earns, earning, earned**) **1** If you **earn** money, you receive money in return for work that you do. = receive ❑ *What a lovely way to earn a living.* ❑ *an unskilled worker earning less than £2.50 an hour* ❑ *They moved to Sapa to earn a living in the tourism trade.* ❑ *Executive directors can earn between £70,000 and £90,000.* **2** If something **earns** money, it produces money as profit or interest. ❑ *a bank account that earns little or no interest* **3** If you **earn** something such as praise, you get it because you deserve it. ❑ *Companies must earn a reputation for honesty.*

ear·nest /ˈɜːnɪst/ ADJ
ADJ Earnest people are very serious and sincere in what they say or do, because they think that their actions and beliefs are important. ❑ *Catherine was a pious, earnest woman.*
PHRASE in earnest If something is done or happens **in earnest**, it happens to a much greater extent and more seriously than before. = seriously ❑ *Campaigning will begin in earnest tomorrow.*

✪ **earn·ings** ♦◇◇ /ˈɜːnɪŋz/ NOUN [PL] Your **earnings** are the sums of money that you earn by working. = pay, income ❑ *Average weekly earnings rose by 1.5% in July.* ❑ *He was satisfied with his earnings as an accountant.*

✪ **earth** ♦♦◇ /ɜːθ/ NOUN
NOUN [SING, U] **1** [SING] **Earth** or **the Earth** is the planet on which we live. People usually say **Earth** when they are referring to the planet as part of the universe, and **the Earth** when they are talking about the planet as the place where we live. = world ❑ *The space shuttle Atlantis returned safely to Earth today.* ❑ *a fault in the Earth's crust* **2** [SING] **The earth** is the land surface on which we live and move around. = ground ❑ *The earth shook and swayed and the walls of neighbouring houses fell around them.* **3** [U] **Earth** is the substance on the land surface of the earth, for example clay or sand, in which plants grow. = soil ❑ *The road winds for miles through parched earth, scrub and cactus.* **4** [SING] (*BrE*) The **earth** in an electric plug or piece of electrical equipment is the wire through which electricity passes into the ground and which makes the equipment safe. ❑ *The earth in the lamp was not connected.*
PHRASES on earth (*emphasis*) **1 On earth** is used for emphasis in questions that begin with words such as 'how', 'why', 'what', or 'where'. It is often used to suggest

that there is no obvious or easy answer to the question being asked. ❑ *How on earth did that happen?* **2 On earth** is used for emphasis after some negative noun groups, for example 'no reason'. ❑ *There was no reason on earth why she couldn't have moved in with us.*
down to earth or **back to earth** If you come **down to earth** or **back to earth**, you have to face the reality of everyday life after a period of great excitement. ❑ *When he came down to earth after his win he admitted: 'It was an amazing feeling.'*

✪ **earth·quake** /ˈɜːθkweɪk/ NOUN [C] (**earthquakes**) An **earthquake** is a shaking of the ground caused by movement of the Earth's crust. = tremor ❑ *the San Francisco earthquake of 1906* ❑ *Two powerful earthquakes struck western Japan yesterday.* ❑ *Bhuj was hit by an earthquake measuring 7.9 on the Richter scale.*

✪ **ease** ♦◇◇ /iːz/ NOUN, VERB
NOUN [U] **1** If you talk about the **ease of** a particular activity, you are referring to the way that it has been made easier to do, or to the fact that it is already easy to do. ❑ *For ease of reference, only the relevant extracts of the regulations are included.* **2 Ease** is the state of being very comfortable and able to live as you want, without any worries or problems. = comfort ❑ *She lived a life of ease.*
PHRASES with ease If you do something **with ease**, you do it easily, without difficulty or effort. ❑ *Anne was intelligent and capable of passing her exams with ease.*
at ease If you are **at ease**, you are feeling confident and relaxed, and are able to talk to people without feeling nervous or anxious. If you put someone **at ease**, you make them feel at ease. ❑ *It is essential to feel at ease with your therapist.*
ill at ease If you are **ill at ease**, you feel somewhat uncomfortable, anxious, or worried. ❑ *He appeared embarrassed and ill at ease with the sustained applause that greeted him.*
VERB [I, T] (**eases, easing, eased**) **1** If something unpleasant **eases** or if you **ease** it, it is reduced in degree, speed, or intensity. = reduce, diminish, relax; ≠ increase ❑ *Tensions had eased.* ❑ *I gave him some brandy to ease the pain.* ❑ *editorials calling for the easing of sanctions* **2** If you **ease** your way somewhere or **ease** somewhere, you move there slowly, carefully, and gently. If you **ease** something somewhere, you move it there slowly, carefully, and gently. ❑ *I eased my way towards the door.* ❑ *He eased his foot off the accelerator.*
PHRASAL VERB ease up 1 If something **eases up**, it is reduced in degree, speed, or intensity. ❑ *The rain had eased up.* **2** If you **ease up**, you start to make less effort. ❑ *He told supporters not to ease up even though he's leading in the presidential race.*

eas·i·ly ♦◇◇ /ˈiːzɪli/ ADV **1** [usu easily with v] If you do a job or action **easily**, you do it without difficulty or effort, because it is not complicated and causes no problems. = simply ❑ *Dress your child in layers of clothes you can remove easily.* **2** [easily with v] If you do something **easily**, you do it in a confident, relaxed way. ❑ *They talked amiably and easily about a range of topics.* **3** (*emphasis*) You use **easily** to emphasize that something is very likely to happen, or is very likely to be true. ❑ *It could easily be another year before the economy starts to show some improvement.* **4** [easily after v] You use **easily** to say that something happens more quickly or more often than is usual or normal. ❑ *He had always cried very easily.*

✪ **east** ♦♦♦ /iːst/ also **East** NOUN, ADV, ADJ
NOUN [U, SING] **1** [U] [also 'the' east] **The east** is the direction where the sun rises. ❑ *the vast swamps that lie to the east of the River Nile* ❑ *The canal runs across England from east to west.* **2** [SING] **The east of** a place, country, or region is the part which is in the east. ❑ *a village in the east of the country* **3** [SING] **The East** is used to refer to the southern and eastern part of Asia, including India, China, and Japan. ❑ *Every so often, a new martial art arrives from the East.*
ADV 1 [east after v] If you go **east**, you travel towards the east. ❑ *To drive, go east on Route 9.* **2** Something that is **east of** a place is positioned to the east of it. ❑ *just east of the centre of town*

E

ADJ **1** [east + N] The **east** edge, corner, or part of a place or country is the part toward the east. ❑ *a low line of hills running along the east coast* **2** [east + N] **East** is used in the names of some countries, states, and regions in the east of a larger area. ❑ *He had been on safari in East Africa with his son.* **3** An **east** wind is a wind that blows from the east. ❑ *a bitter east wind*

East·er /ˈiːstə/ NOUN [C, U] (**Easters**) [oft Easter + N] **Easter** is a Christian festival when Jesus Christ's return to life is celebrated. It is celebrated on a Sunday in March or April. ❑ *'Happy Easter,' he yelled.*

✿east·ern ✦✦◇ /ˈiːstən/ **1** [eastern + N] **Eastern** means in or from the east of a region, state, or country. ❑ *Eastern Europe* ❑ *Pakistan's eastern city of Lahore* ❑ *France's eastern border with Germany* **2** [eastern + N] **Eastern** means coming from or associated with the people or countries of the East, such as India, China, or Japan. ❑ *In many Eastern countries massage was and is a part of everyday life.*

east·ward /ˈiːstwəd/ ADV, ADJ

> The form **eastwards** is also used for the adverb.

ADV [eastward after v] **Eastward** or **eastwards** means towards the east. = east ❑ *A powerful snow storm is moving eastward.*
ADJ An **eastward** direction or course is one that goes towards the east. ❑ *the eastward expansion of the city*

easy ✦✦✦ /ˈiːzi/ ADJ

ADJ (**easier, easiest**) **1** If a job or action is **easy**, you can do it without difficulty or effort, because it is not complicated and causes no problems. = simple ❑ *The shower is easy to install.* ❑ *This is not an easy task.* **2** If you describe an action or activity as **easy**, you mean that it is done in a confident, relaxed way. If someone is **easy about** something, they feel relaxed and confident about it. ❑ *He was an easy person to talk to.* **3** If you say that someone has an **easy** life, you mean that they live comfortably without any problems or worries. ❑ *She has not had an easy life.* **4** If you say that someone is **easy** or too **easy**, you are criticizing someone because they have done the most obvious or least difficult thing, and have not considered the situation carefully enough. = simple ❑ *That's easy for you to say.*
PHRASES **go easy on something** (*informal*) If you tell someone to **go easy on** something, you are telling them to use only a small amount of it. ❑ *Go easy on the alcohol.*
go easy on someone or **be easy on someone** (*informal*) If you tell someone to **go easy on**, or **be easy on**, a particular person, you are telling them not to punish or treat that person very severely. ❑ *'Go easy on him,' Sam repeated, opening the door.*
take it easy (*informal*) If someone tells you to **take it easy** or **take things easy**, they mean that you should relax and not do very much at all. ❑ *It is best to take things easy for a week or two.*

easy·going /ˈiːziˌgəʊɪŋ/ ADJ (*approval*) If you describe someone as **easygoing**, you mean that they are not easily annoyed, worried, or upset, and you think this is a good quality. ❑ *He was easygoing and good-natured.*

eat ✦✦◇ /iːt/ VERB

VERB [I, T] (**eats, eating, ate, eaten**) **1** [I, T] When you **eat** something, you put it into your mouth, chew it, and swallow it. ❑ *She was eating a sandwich.* ❑ *I ate slowly and without speaking.* **2** [I] If you **eat** sensibly or healthily, you eat food that is good for you. ❑ *a campaign to persuade people to eat more healthily* **3** [I, T] If you **eat**, you have a meal. ❑ *Let's go out to eat.* ❑ *We ate lunch together every day.* **4** [T] (*informal*) If something is **eating** you, it is annoying or worrying you. ❑ *'What the hell's eating you?' he demanded.*
PHRASAL VERBS **eat away** If one thing **eats away** another or **eats away at** another, it gradually destroys or uses it up. ❑ *Water pours through the roof, encouraging rot to eat away the interior of the house.*
eat into **1** If something **eats into** your time or your resources, it uses them, when they should be used for other things. ❑ *Responsibilities at home and work eat into his time.* **2** If a substance such as acid or rust **eats into**

something, it destroys or damages its surface. ❑ *Ulcers occur when the stomach's natural acids eat into the lining of the stomach.*
✦ dog eat dog → see **dog**

ec·cen·tric /ɪkˈsentrɪk/ ADJ, NOUN

ADJ If you say that someone is **eccentric**, you mean that they behave in a strange way, and have habits or opinions that are different from those of most people. = odd ❑ *He is an eccentric character who likes wearing a beret and dark glasses.*
NOUN [C] (**eccentrics**) An **eccentric** is an eccentric person. ❑ *Askew used several names, and had a reputation as an eccentric.*

echo ✦◇◇ /ˈekəʊ/ NOUN, VERB

NOUN [C] (**echoes**) **1** An **echo** is a sound caused by a noise being reflected off a surface such as a wall. ❑ *He listened and heard nothing but the echoes of his own voice in the cave.* **2** A detail or feature that reminds you of something else can be referred to as an **echo**. ❑ *The accident has echoes of past disasters.*
VERB [I, T] (**echoes, echoing, echoed**) **1** [I] If a sound **echoes**, it is reflected off a surface and can be heard again after the original sound has stopped. = reverberate ❑ *His feet echoed on the hardwood floor.* **2** [I] In a place that **echoes**, a sound is reflected off a surface, and is repeated after the original sound has stopped. ❑ *The room echoed.* ❑ *The corridor echoed with the barking of a dozen dogs.* **3** [T] If you **echo** someone's words, you repeat them or express agreement with their attitude or opinion. ❑ *Their views often echo each other.* **4** [T] If one thing **echoes** another, the first is a copy of a particular detail or feature of the other. = repeat ❑ *Pinks and beiges were chosen to echo the colours of the ceiling.* **5** [I] If something **echoes**, it continues to be discussed and remains important or influential in a particular situation or among a particular group of people. ❑ *The old fable continues to echo down the centuries.*

✿ec·lec·tic /ɪˈklektɪk/ ADJ (*formal*) An **eclectic** collection of objects, ideas, or beliefs is wide-ranging and comes from many different sources. = diverse, wide-ranging ❑ *an eclectic collection of paintings, drawings, and prints* ❑ *These theories tend to be highly eclectic, drawing on several sociological theorists.* ❑ *His musical tastes are eclectic.*

eclipse /ɪˈklɪps/ NOUN, VERB

NOUN [C] (**eclipses**) An **eclipse of** the sun is an occasion when the moon is between the Earth and the sun, so that for a short time you cannot see part or all of the sun. An **eclipse of** the moon is an occasion when the Earth is between the sun and the moon, so that for a short time you cannot see part or all of the moon. ❑ *an eclipse of the sun* ❑ *the solar eclipse on May 21*
VERB [T] (**eclipses, eclipsing, eclipsed**) If one thing is **eclipsed by** a second thing that is bigger, newer, or more important than it, the first thing is no longer noticed because the second thing gets all the attention. = overshadow ❑ *the space programme has been eclipsed by other pressing needs*

✿eco-friendly /ˌiːkəʊˈfrendli/ ADJ **Eco-friendly** products or services are less harmful to the environment than other similar products or services. = environmentally friendly, green ❑ *eco-friendly washing powder* ❑ *Tourism must try to be eco-friendly.*

WORD PARTS

The prefix **eco-** appears in nouns and adjectives that refer to something related to the environment:
eco-friendly (ADJ)
ecosystem (NOUN)
ecotourism (NOUN)

✿eco·logi·cal /ˌiːkəˈlɒdʒɪkəl/ ADJ [ecological + N] **Ecological** means involved with or concerning ecology. = environmental ❑ *Large dams have harmed Siberia's delicate ecological balance.* ❑ *ecological disasters, such as the destruction of rainforest*
✿eco·logi·cal·ly /ˌiːkəˈlɒdʒɪkli/ ADV = environmentally ❑ *It is economical to run and ecologically sound.*

WORD CONNECTIONS

ecological + NOUN

ecological **disaster**
ecological **catastrophe**
ecological **crisis**

❏ *In order to avoid an ecological catastrophe, industrial countries must start putting limits on their use of resources.*

ecological **issue**
ecological **problem**

❏ *In geography, children are learning more about ecological issues like global warming.*

ecological **impact**
ecological **effect**

❏ *There is no doubt that the oil spill has had a massive ecological impact on the area.*

WORD CONNECTIONS

ecologically + ADJ

ecologically **sound**
ecologically **sustainable**
ecologically **friendly**

❏ *Using this method, more energy is produced in an ecologically sustainable manner.*

ecologically **responsible**
ecologically **aware**
ecologically **conscious**

❏ *We want resource development that is sustainable and ecologically responsible.*

ecologically **damaging**
ecologically **unsound**
ecologically **unsustainable**

❏ *Current practices in industry and agriculture are ecologically unsustainable.*

✪ **ecolo·gist** /ɪˈkɒlədʒɪst/ NOUN [c] (**ecologists**) An **ecologist** is a person who studies ecology. ❏ *Ecologists argue that the benefits of treating sewage with disinfectants are doubtful.*

✪ **ecol·ogy** /ɪˈkɒlədʒi/ NOUN [u, c] (**ecologies**) **1** [u] **Ecology** is the study of the relationships between plants, animals, people, and their environment, and the balances between these relationships. ❏ *a professor in ecology* ❏ *a growing interest in conservation and ecology* **2** [c, u] When you talk about the **ecology** of a place, you are referring to the pattern and balance of relationships between plants, animals, people, and the environment in that place. ❏ *the ecology of the rocky Negev desert in Israel*

✪ **eco·nom·ic** ♦♦♦ /ˌiːkəˈnɒmɪk, ˌek-/ ADJ **1** **Economic** means concerned with the organization of the money, industry, and trade of a country, region, or society. = financial, monetary ❏ *Poland's radical economic reforms* ❏ *The pace of economic growth is picking up.* ❏ *the current economic crisis* **2** If something is **economic**, it produces a profit. = profitable ❏ *Critics say that the new system may be more economic but will lead to a decline in programme quality.* **eco·nomi·cal·ly** /ˌiːkəˈnɒmɪkli, ˌek-/ ADV ❏ *an economically depressed area* ❏ *Small English orchards can hardly compete economically with larger French ones.*

WORD CONNECTIONS

economically + ADJ

economically **viable**
economically **feasible**
economically **sustainable**

❏ *Scanners are now relatively inexpensive, and it is usually not economically viable to repair them.*

economically **dependent**
economically **disadvantaged**
economically **depressed**
economically **inefficient**

❏ *In the past women were economically dependent on men.*

✪ **eco·nomi·cal** /ˌiːkəˈnɒmɪkəl, ˌek-/ ADJ **1** Something that is **economical** does not require a lot of money to operate. For example, a car that only uses a small amount of petrol is **economical**. = cost-effective, inexpensive; ≠ uneconomical, expensive, wasteful ❏ *plans to trade in their car for something smaller and more economical* ❏ *the most economical method of extracting essential oils from plant materials* **2** Someone who is **economical** spends money sensibly and does not want to waste it on things that are unnecessary. A way of life that is **economical** does not require a lot of money. ❏ *ideas for economical housekeeping* **3** **Economical** means using the minimum amount of time, effort, or language that is necessary. ❏ *His gestures were economical, his words generally mild.* **eco·nomi·cal·ly** /ˌiːkəˈnɒmɪkli, ˌek-/ ADV [economically after V] ❏ *Services could be operated more efficiently and economically.*

✪ **eco·nom·ics** ♦◇◇ /ˌiːkəˈnɒmɪks, ˌek-/ NOUN [u] **1** **Economics** is the study of the way in which money, industry, and commerce are organized in a society. ❏ *His younger sister is studying economics.* ❏ *He gained a first class Honours degree in economics.* **2** The **economics** of a society or industry is the system of organizing money and trade in it. ❏ *a radical free-market economics policy* ❏ *the economics of the third world*

✪ **econo·mist** ♦♦◇ /ɪˈkɒnəmɪst/ NOUN [c] (**economists**) An **economist** is a person who studies, teaches, or writes about economics. ❏ *the chief economist of the World Bank* ❏ *few economists expect to see a rise this year*

econo·mize /ɪˈkɒnəmaɪz/ also **economise** VERB [I] (**economizes, economizing, economized**) If you **economize**, you save money by spending it very carefully. ❏ *We're going to have to economize from now on.*

✪ **econo·my** ♦♦♦ /ɪˈkɒnəmi/ NOUN, ADJ (*academic word*) NOUN [c, u] (**economies**) **1** [c] An **economy** is the system according to which the money, industry, and commerce of a country or region are organized. ❏ *Zimbabwe boasts Africa's most industrialized economy.* ❏ *the rate at which the US economy grows* ❏ *the region's booming service economy* **2** [c] A country's **economy** is the wealth that it gets from business and industry. ❏ *The Japanese economy grew at an annual rate of more than 10 per cent.* **3** [u] **Economy** is the use of the minimum amount of money, time, or other resources needed to achieve something, so that nothing is wasted. ❏ *improvements in the fuel economy of cars* PHRASE **a false economy** If you describe an attempt to save money as **a false economy**, you mean that you have not saved any money as you will have to spend a lot more later. ❏ *A cheap bed can be a false economy, so spend as much as you can afford.* ADJ **1** [economy + N] **Economy** services such as travel are cheap and have no luxuries or extras. ❏ *the limitations that come with economy travel* **2** [economy + N] **Economy** is used to describe large packs of products that are cheaper than normal sized packs. ❏ *an economy pack containing 150 assorted screws*

WORD CONNECTIONS

ADJ + **economy**

a **booming** economy
a **strong** economy
a **weak** economy

❏ *The booming economy of the past decade has kept unemployment rates down.*

the **global** economy
the **world** economy
the **domestic** economy
the **local** economy

❏ *Businesses must be able to compete in the global economy.*

the **Chinese** economy
the **Japanese** economy
the **American** economy
the **German** economy

❏ *The American economy grew in the second three months of the year.*

E

VERB + **economy**

stimulate the economy
revive the economy
boost the economy

❏ *People working in their home areas spend money locally and stimulate the local economy.*

economy + VERB

the economy grows
the economy shrinks
the economy slows down
the economy recovers

❏ *The world economy is clearly slowing down, with recession in many European countries.*

WORD FAMILIES	
economy NOUN	*The Japanese economy grew at an annual rate of more than 10 per cent.*
economics NOUN	*She is studying politics and economics.*
economist NOUN	*Economists expect to see a rise in interest rates.*
economic ADJ	*Businesses are struggling in the current economic crisis.*
economically ADV	*It is an economically depressed area, with high unemployment.*
economical ADJ	*They plan to trade in their car for something smaller and more economical.*
uneconomical ADJ	*It would be uneconomical to print so many copies.*

◆**eco·sys·tem** /ˈiːkəʊsɪstəm, AmE ˈekə-/ NOUN [C] (**ecosystems**) (*technical*) An **ecosystem** is all the plants and animals that live in a particular area together with the complex relationship that exists between them and their environment. ❏ *the forest ecosystem* ❏ *Madagascar's ecosystems range from rainforest to semi-desert.* ❏ *Human over-fishing has destabilised marine ecosystems.*

ec·sta·sy /ˈekstəsi/ NOUN [C, U] (**ecstasies**) **1** [C, U] **Ecstasy** is a feeling of very great happiness. ❏ *a state of almost religious ecstasy* **2** [U] **Ecstasy** is an illegal drug that makes people feel happy and energetic. ❏ *The teenager died after taking ecstasy on her birthday.*

ec·stat·ic /ekˈstætɪk/ ADJ **1** If you are **ecstatic**, you feel very happy and full of excitement. = delirious ❏ *His wife gave birth to their first child, and he was ecstatic about it.* **2** [ecstatic + N] You can use **ecstatic** to describe reactions that are very enthusiastic and excited. For example, if someone receives an **ecstatic** reception or an **ecstatic** welcome, they are greeted with great enthusiasm and excitement. = rapturous ❏ *They gave an ecstatic reception to the speech.*
ec·stati·cal·ly /ekˈstætɪkəli/ ADV ❏ *We are both ecstatically happy.*

edge ◆◆◇ /edʒ/ NOUN, VERB
NOUN [C, SING] (**edges**) **1** [C] The **edge** of something is the place or line where it stops, or the part of it that is farthest from the middle. ❏ *We were on a hill, right on the edge of town.* ❏ *She was standing at the water's edge.* **2** [C] The **edge** of something sharp such as a knife or an axe is its sharp or narrow side. ❏ *the sharp edge of the sword* **3** [SING] The **edge** of something, especially something bad, is the point at which it may start to happen. = verge, brink ❏ *They have driven the rhino to the edge of extinction.* **4** [SING] If someone or something has an **edge**, they have an advantage that makes them stronger or more likely to be successful than another thing or person. = advantage ❏ *The three days Uruguay have to prepare could give them the edge over Brazil.* **5** [SING] If you say that someone or something has **an edge**, you mean that they have a powerful quality. ❏ *Featuring new bands gives the show*

an **edge**. **6** [SING] If someone's voice has an **edge to** it, it has a sharp, bitter, or emotional quality. ❏ *But underneath the humour is an edge of bitterness.*
PHRASES **on edge** If you or your nerves are **on edge**, you are tense, nervous, and unable to relax. ❏ *My nerves were constantly on edge.*
take the edge off If something **takes the edge off** a situation, it weakens its effect or intensity. ❏ *Poor health took the edge off her performance.*
VERB [I] (**edges, edging, edged**) If someone or something **edges** somewhere, they move very slowly in that direction. ❏ *He edged closer to the telephone, ready to grab it.*
PHRASAL VERB **edge out** If someone **edges out** someone else, they just manage to beat them or get in front of them in a game, race, or contest. ❏ *In the second race, the American competitor edged out the Ethiopian runner by less than a second.*

edged /edʒd/ ADJ, COMB
ADJ [V-LINK + edged 'with/in' N] If something is **edged with** a particular thing, that thing forms a border around it. ❏ *a large lawn edged with flowers and shrubs*
COMB **Edged** is used in compound adjectives to indicate something with a particular type of edge. ❏ *clutching a lace-edged handkerchief*

ed·ible /ˈedɪbəl/ ADJ If something is **edible**, it is safe to eat and not poisonous. ❏ *edible fungi*

◆**edit** ◆◇◇ /ˈedɪt/ VERB [T] (**edits, editing, edited**) (*academic word*) **1** If you **edit** a text such as an article or a book, you correct and adapt it so that it is suitable for publishing. = revise, correct ❏ *The majority of contracts give the publisher the right to edit a book after it's done.* **2** If you **edit** a book or a series of books, you collect several pieces of writing by different authors and prepare them for publishing. ❏ *This collection of essays is edited by Ellen Knight.* ❏ *He edits the literary journal, Murmur.* ❏ *She has edited the media studies quarterly, Screen.* **3** If you **edit** a film or a television or radio programme, you choose some of what has been filmed or recorded and arrange it in a particular order. ❏ *He taught me to edit and splice film.* **4** Someone who **edits** a newspaper, magazine, or journal is in charge of it. ❏ *I used to edit the college paper in the old days.*

◆**edi·tion** ◆◆◇ /ɪˈdɪʃən/ NOUN [C] (**editions**) **1** An **edition** is a particular version of a book, magazine, or newspaper that is printed at one time. ❏ *A paperback edition is now available at bookshops.* ❏ *They brought out a special edition of The Skulker.* **2** An **edition** is the total number of copies of a particular book or newspaper that are printed at one time. ❏ *The second edition was published only in Canada.* **3** An **edition** is a single television or radio programme that is one of a series about a particular subject. = episode ❏ *an interview featured on last week's edition of '60 Minutes'*

◆**edi·tor** ◆◆◇ /ˈedɪtə/ NOUN [C] (**editors**) **1** An **editor** is the person who is in charge of a newspaper or magazine and who decides what will be published in each edition of it. ❏ *Her father was the former editor of the Saturday Review.* **2** An **editor** is a journalist who is responsible for a particular section of a newspaper or magazine. ❏ *Mike later became the sports editor for The Beacon.* **3** An **editor** is a person who checks and corrects texts before they are published. ❏ *Your role as editor is important, for you can look at a piece of writing objectively.* **4** An **editor** is a radio or television journalist who reports on a particular type of news. ❏ *our economics editor, Tom Goldberg* **5** An **editor** is a person who prepares a film, or a radio or television programme, by selecting some of what has been filmed or recorded and putting it in a particular order. ❏ *A few years earlier, she had worked at 20th Century Fox as a film editor.* **6** An **editor** is a person who collects pieces of writing by different authors and prepares them for publication in a book or a series of books. ❏ *Michael Rosen is the editor of the anthology.* ❏ *Editor's Introduction to the British edition* **7** (*computing*) An **editor** is a computer program that enables you to change and correct stored data. ❏ *To edit it, you need to run the built-in Windows Registry editor.*

edi·to·rial ◆◇◇ /ˌedɪˈtɔːriəl/ ADJ, NOUN
ADJ **1** [editorial + N] **Editorial** means involved in preparing a newspaper, magazine, or book for publication.

WORDS IN CONTEXT: EDUCATION

Remote learning is an ideal choice for people wanting to return to or further their education.

To what extent do you agree or disagree?

Remote or **distance learning** is a very flexible way of studying that enables a student to **study at their own pace** and at a time and place that suits them. It is generally cheaper than the **tuition fees** for a **face-to-face course**, and there are no costly travel expenses. It is particularly useful for people in work who are unable to take time off, allowing them to **top up skills** or to improve their career prospects by **gaining qualifications**. It is also useful for individuals who live a long distance from their local **college** or **university**.

However, in my opinion, distance learning does not suit everyone. Although students often get the chance to meet **tutors** and other students through **residential courses**, the majority of time is spent doing **self-study**. Students therefore need to be **highly motivated** and have the **discipline** to **meet assignment deadlines** and to keep up to date with their **studies**. The courses also tend to be technology-based with access to **online forums** and **virtual learning environments**. This can be daunting for older people who are not confident with technology, and who might have trouble **logging in** and accessing **digital materials**.

❏ *I went to the editorial board meetings when I had the time.* **2** [editorial + N] **Editorial** means involving the attitudes, opinions, and contents of something such as a newspaper, magazine, or television programme. ❏ *We are not about to change our editorial policy.*

NOUN [c] (**editorials**) An **editorial** is an article in a newspaper that gives the opinion of the editor or owner on a topic or item of news. ❏ *In an editorial, The New York Times suggests the victory could turn nasty.*

✪ edu•cate /ˈedʒʊkeɪt/ VERB [T] (**educates, educating, educated**) **1** When someone, especially a child, **is educated**, he or she is taught at a school or college. = teach ❏ *He was educated at Yale and Stanford.* **2** To **educate** people means to teach them better ways of doing something or a better way of living. = inform, teach ❏ *World AIDS Day, an event designed to educate people about AIDS*

edu•cat•ed /ˈedʒʊkeɪtɪd/ ADJ Someone who is **educated** has a high standard of learning. = learned ❏ *The new chief executive is an educated, amiable, and decent man.*

✪ edu•ca•tion ♦♦◇ NOUN [c, U] (**educations**) **1** [c, U] **Education** involves teaching people various subjects, usually at a school or college, or being taught. = teaching, learning ❏ *They're cutting funds for education.* ❏ *a long-term plan to improve the education system* ❏ *Paul prolonged his education with six years of advanced study in English.* **2** [U] **Education** of a particular kind involves teaching the public about a particular issue. ❏ *better health education*
→ See also **further education, higher education**

✪ edu•ca•tion•al ♦◇◇ /ˌedʒʊˈkeɪʃənəl/ ADJ **1** **Educational** matters or institutions are concerned with or relate to education. ❏ *the Japanese educational system* ❏ *pupils with special educational needs* ❏ *The educational backgrounds of health workers range from vocational training to Master's degrees.* **2** An **educational** experience teaches you something. = instructive ❏ *The staff should make sure the kids have an enjoyable and educational day.*

✪ ef•fect ♦♦♦ /ɪˈfekt/ NOUN, VERB
NOUN [c, U, PL] (**effects**) **1** [c, U] The **effect of** one thing **on** another is the change that the first thing causes in the second thing. = influence, impact ❏ *Parents worry about the effect of music on their adolescent's behaviour.* ❏ *The internet has had a significant effect on trade.* ❏ *The housing market is feeling the effects of the increase in interest rates.* ❏ *Even minor head injuries can cause long-lasting psychological effects.* **2** [c] An **effect** is an impression that someone creates deliberately, for example in a place or in a piece of writing. = impression ❏ *The whole effect is cool, light, and airy.* **3** [PL] (*formal*) A person's **effects** are the things that

they have with them at a particular time, for example when they are arrested or admitted to a hospital, or the things that they owned when they died. = possessions ❏ *His daughters were collecting his effects.* **4** [PL] The **effects** in a film are the specially created sounds and scenery. ❏ *It's got a gripping story, great acting, superb sets, and stunning effects.*

PHRASES **for effect** If you say that someone is doing something **for effect**, you mean that they are doing it in order to impress people and to draw attention to themselves. ❏ *The southern accent was put on for effect.*
in effect (*vagueness*) You add **in effect** to a statement or opinion that is not precisely accurate, but that you feel is a reasonable description or summary of a particular situation. = effectively ❏ *That deal would create, in effect, the world's biggest airline.*
put something into effect or **bring something into effect** or **carry something into effect** If you put, bring, or carry a plan or idea **into effect**, you cause it to happen in practice. = implement ❏ *These and other such measures ought to have been put into effect in 1985.*
take effect or **come into effect** If a law or policy **takes effect** or **comes into effect** at a particular time, it officially begins to apply or be valid from that time. If it **remains in effect**, it still applies or is still valid. ❏ *the ban on new logging permits which will take effect in July*
take effect You can say that something **takes effect** when it starts to produce the results that are intended. ❏ *The second injection should only have been given once the first drug had taken effect.*
to good effect or **to no effect** You use **effect** in expressions such as **to good effect** and **to no effect** in order to indicate how successful or impressive an action is. ❏ *Mr Morris feels the museum is using advertising to good effect.*
to this effect or **to that effect** You use **to this effect, to that effect**, or **to the effect that** to indicate that you have given or are giving a summary of something that was said or written, and not the actual words used. ❏ *I understand that a circular to this effect will be issued in the next few weeks.*
VERB [T] (**effects, effecting, effected**) (*formal*) If you **effect** something that you are trying to achieve, you succeed in causing it to happen. ❏ *Prospects for effecting real political change seemed to have taken a major step backwards.*
→ See also **greenhouse effect, side-effect**

WORD CONNECTIONS
VERB + **effect**

have an effect
feel the effects
❏ *I was starting to feel the effects of the drug.*

E

ADJ + effect

a **profound** effect
a **dramatic** effect
a **significant** effect
❏ *Bullying can have a profound effect on a child.*

a **negative** effect
a **harmful** effect
an **adverse** effect
a **devastating** effect
❏ *My father's death had a devastating effect on our family.*

a **positive** effect
a **beneficial** effect
the **desired** effect
❏ *The policy is beginning to have the desired effect.*

a **long-term** effect
a **lasting** effect
an **immediate** effect
❏ *Thousands of soldiers suffered lasting effects from the war.*

a **knock-on** effect
❏ *The rise in oil prices has had a knock-on effect on energy prices.*

USAGE NOTE

effect

You say that something 'has an effect' on something else. Do not say that something 'brings an effect' or 'makes an effect' on something.
*Pollution **has a big effect** on people's health.*

⊘**ef·fec·tive** ♦♦◇ /ɪˈfektɪv/ ADJ **1** Something that is **effective** works well and produces the results that were intended. = successful; ≠ ineffective ❏ *The project looks at how we could be more effective in encouraging students to enter teacher training.* ❏ *Simple antibiotics are effective against this organism.* ❏ *an effective public transport system* **2** [effective + N] **Effective** means having a particular role or result in practice, though not officially or in theory. ❏ *They have had effective control of the area since the security forces left.* **3** [V-LINK + effective] When something such as a law or an agreement becomes **effective**, it begins officially to apply or be valid. ❏ *The new rules will become effective in the next few days.*
ef·fec·tive·ness /ɪˈfektɪvnəs/ NOUN [U] ❏ *the effectiveness of computers as an educational tool*

⊘**ef·fec·tive·ly** /ɪˈfektɪvli/ ADV **1** [usu effectively after V, often effectively + -ED] If something works **effectively**, it produces the results that were intended. ❏ *Services need to be organized more effectively than they are at present.* ❏ *the team roles which you believe to be necessary for the team to function effectively* **2** You use **effectively** with a statement or opinion to indicate that it is not accurate in every detail, but that you feel it is a reasonable description or summary of a particular situation. ❏ *The region was effectively independent.*

⊘**ef·fi·cien·cy** /ɪˈfɪʃənsi/ NOUN [U] **Efficiency** is the quality of being able to do a task successfully, without wasting time or energy. ❏ *There are many ways to increase agricultural efficiency in the poorer areas of the world.* ❏ *Refrigerators have improved energy efficiency by a third in 30 years.*

⊘**ef·fi·cient** ♦◇◇ /ɪˈfɪʃənt/ ADJ If something or someone is **efficient**, they are able to do tasks successfully, without wasting time or energy. = systematic, organized ❏ *With today's more efficient contraception women can plan their families and careers.* ❏ *Technological advances allow more efficient use of labour.* ❏ *an efficient way of testing thousands of compounds*
⊘**ef·fi·cient·ly** /ɪˈfɪʃəntli/ ADV ❏ *I work very efficiently and am decisive, and accurate in my judgement.* ❏ *Enzymes work most efficiently within a narrow temperature range.* ❏ *the ability to run a business efficiently*

WORD FAMILIES		
efficient ADJ	Technological advances allow more **efficient** use of labour.	
inefficient ADJ	The old system was **inefficient** and wasteful.	
efficiently ADV	Enzymes work most **efficiently** within a narrow temperature range.	
inefficiently ADV	Energy prices have been kept low, so energy is used **inefficiently**.	
efficiency NOUN	Refrigerators have improved energy **efficiency** by a third in 30 years.	
inefficiency NOUN	Hundreds of hours were wasted due to **inefficiency**.	

⊘**ef·fort** ♦♦♦ /ˈefət/ NOUN
NOUN [C, U, SING] (**efforts**) **1** [C, U] If you make an **effort to** do something, you try very hard to do it. = attempt ❏ *He made no effort to hide his disappointment.* ❏ *Finding a cure requires considerable time and effort.* ❏ *Medical schools must make an effort to enrol promising students from minority ethnic groups.* ❏ *Despite the efforts of the United Nations, the problem of drug traffic continues to grow.* **2** [U] [usu 'with' effort, also 'an' effort] (*written*) If you say that someone did something **with effort** or **with an effort**, you mean it was difficult for them to do it. = difficulty ❏ *She took a deep breath and sat up slowly and with great effort.* **3** [C] An **effort** is a particular series of activities that is organized by a group of people in order to achieve something. ❏ *a famine relief effort in Angola* **4** [SING] If you say that something is **an effort**, you mean that an unusual amount of physical or mental energy is needed to do it. = strain, struggle ❏ *Even carrying the camcorder while hiking in the forest was an effort.*
PHRASE **make the effort** If you **make the effort to** do something, you do it, even though you need extra energy to do it or you do not really want to. ❏ *I don't get lonely now because I make the effort to see people.*

ef·fort·less /ˈefətləs/ ADJ **1** Something that is **effortless** is done easily and well. = easy ❏ *effortless and elegant Italian cooking* **2** You use **effortless** to describe a quality that someone has naturally and does not have to learn. ❏ *She liked him above all for his effortless charm.*
ef·fort·less·ly /ˈefətləsli/ ADV ❏ *Her son Peter adapted effortlessly to his new surroundings.*

⊘**e.g.** /ˌiː ˈdʒiː/ ABBREVIATION **e.g.** is an abbreviation that means 'for example'. It is used before a noun, or to introduce another sentence. = for example, for instance, such as ❏ *We need helpers of all types, e.g., geologists and teachers.* ❏ *Or consider how you can acquire these skills, e.g. by taking extra courses.*

⊘**egg** ♦♦◇ /eg/ NOUN
NOUN [C, U] (**eggs**) **1** [C] An **egg** is an oval object that is produced by a female bird and contains a baby bird. Other animals such as reptiles and fish also lay eggs. ❏ *a baby bird hatching from its egg* ❏ *Sea turtles live in the sea but breathe air and lay eggs on the beach.* ❏ *Sixty per cent of eggs hatched and survived during the breeding season.* **2** [C, U] In many countries, **eggs** often means hen's eggs, eaten as food. ❏ *Break the eggs into a shallow bowl and beat them lightly.* **3** [C] **Egg** is used to refer to an object in the shape of a hen's egg. ❏ *a chocolate egg* **4** [C] An **egg** is a cell that is produced in the bodies of female animals and humans. If it is fertilized by a sperm, a baby develops from it. ❏ *It only takes one sperm to fertilize an egg.*
PHRASES **put all your eggs in one basket** If someone puts **all** their **eggs in one basket**, they put all their effort or resources into doing one thing so that, if it fails, they have no alternatives left. ❏ *The key word here is diversify; don't put all your eggs in one basket.*
have egg on your face or **have egg all over your face** If someone has **egg on** their **face** or has **egg all over** their **face**, they have been made to look foolish. ❏ *If they take this game lightly they could end up with egg on their faces.*

PHRASAL VERB **egg on** (**eggs**, **egging**, **egged**) If you **egg** a person **on**, you encourage them to do something, especially something dangerous or foolish. ❑ *He was lifting up handfuls of leaves and throwing them at her. She was laughing and egging him on.*

ego /ˈiːɡəʊ, ˈeɡəʊ/ NOUN [C, U] (**egos**) Someone's **ego** is their sense of their own worth. For example, if someone has a large **ego**, they think they are very important and valuable. ❑ *He had a massive ego, never would he admit he was wrong.*

eight ◆◆◆ /eɪt/ NUM (**eights**) **Eight** is the number 8. ❑ *So far eight workers have been killed.*

eight·een ◆◆◆ /ˌeɪˈtiːn/ NUM **Eighteen** is the number 18. ❑ *He was employed by them for eighteen years.*

eight·eenth ◆◆◇ /ˌeɪˈtiːnθ/ ADJ The **eighteenth** item in a series is the one that you count as number eighteen. ❑ *The siege is now in its eighteenth day.*

eighth ◆◆◇ /eɪtθ/ ADJ, NOUN
ADJ The **eighth** item in a series is the one that you count as number eight. ❑ *the eighth prime minister of India*
NOUN [C] (**eighths**) An **eighth** is one of eight equal parts of something. ❑ *The Kuban produces an eighth of Russia's grain, meat, and milk.*

eighti·eth ◆◆◇ /ˈeɪtiəθ/ ADJ The **eightieth** item in a series is the one that you count as number eighty. ❑ *Mr Stevens recently celebrated his eightieth birthday.*

eighty ◆◆◆ /ˈeɪti/ NUM, NOUN
NUM **Eighty** is the number 80. ❑ *Eighty horses trotted up.*
NOUN [PL] (**eighties**) **1** When you talk about the **eighties**, you are referring to numbers between 80 and 89. For example, if you are in your **eighties**, you are aged between 80 and 89. If the temperature is **in the eighties**, the temperature is between 80 and 89 degrees. ❑ *He was in his late eighties and had become the country's most respected elder statesman.* **2** The **eighties** is the decade between 1980 and 1989. ❑ *He ran a property development business in the eighties.*

either ◆◆◆ /ˈaɪðə, ˈiːðə/ CONJ, PRON, QUANT, DET, ADV
CONJ **1** You use **either** in front of the first of two or more alternatives, when you are stating the only possibilities or choices that there are. The other alternatives are introduced by 'or'. ❑ *Sightseeing is best done either by tour bus or by bicycles.* ❑ *The former president was demanding that he should be either put on trial or set free.* **2** You use **either** in a negative statement in front of the first of two alternatives to indicate that the negative statement refers to both the alternatives. ❑ *There had been no indication of either breathlessness or any loss of mental faculties right until his death.*
PRON **1** You can use **either** to refer to one of two things, people, or situations, when you want to say that they are both possible and it does not matter which one is chosen or considered. ❑ *There were glasses of iced champagne and cigars. Unfortunately not many of either were consumed.* **2** [with BRD-NEG] You use **either** in a negative statement to refer to each of two things, people, or situations to indicate that the negative statement includes both of them. ❑ *She warned me that I'd never marry or have children. 'I don't want either.'*
QUANT **1** [either 'of' DEF-PL-N] You can talk of **either of** two things, people, or situations, when you want to say that they are both possible and it does not matter which one is chosen or considered. ❑ *Do either of you smoke or drink heavily?* **2** You can use **either of** in a negative statement to refer to each of two things, people, or situations, which are both included in the negative statement. ❑ *There are no simple answers to either of those questions.*
DET **1** **Either** refers to one of two things, people, or situations, when you want to say that they are both possible. ❑ *a special Indian drug police that would have the authority to pursue suspects into either country* **2** In a negative statement, **either** refers to each of two things, people, or situations, which are both included in the negative statement. ❑ *He sometimes couldn't remember either man's name.* **3** You can use **either** to introduce a noun that refers to each of two things when you are talking about both of them. ❑ *The basketball nets hung down from the ceiling at either end of the gymnasium.*

ADV **1** [either after V, with BRD-NEG] You use **either** by itself in negative statements to indicate that there is a similarity or connection with a person or thing that you have just mentioned. ❑ *He did not even say anything to her, and she did not speak to him either.* **2** [either after V] When one negative statement follows another, you can use **either** at the end of the second one to indicate that you are adding an extra piece of information, and to emphasize that both are equally important. ❑ *Don't agree, but don't argue either.*

eject /ɪˈdʒekt/ VERB [I, T] (**ejects**, **ejecting**, **ejected**)
1 [I, T] If you **eject** someone **from** a place, you force them to leave. ❑ *Officials used guard dogs to eject the protesters.* **2** [T] To **eject** something means to remove it or push it out forcefully. = expel ❑ *He aimed his rifle, fired a single shot, then ejected the spent cartridge.* **3** [I] When a pilot **ejects** **from** an aircraft, he or she leaves the aircraft quickly using an ejector seat (a special seat that can throw the pilot from the aircraft), usually because the plane is about to crash. = bail out ❑ *The pilot ejected from the plane and escaped injury.*

ejec·tion /ɪˈdʒekʃən/ NOUN [C, U] (**ejections**) = expulsion ❑ *the ejection and manhandling of hecklers at the meeting*

elabo·rate ADJ, VERB
ADJ /ɪˈlæbərət/ **1** You use **elaborate** to describe something that is very complex because it has a lot of different parts. = complicated ❑ *an elaborate research project* **2** **Elaborate** plans, systems, and procedures are complicated because they have been planned in very great detail, sometimes too much detail. = complicated ❑ *elaborate efforts at the highest level to conceal the problem* **3** **Elaborate** clothing or material is made with a lot of detailed artistic designs. ❑ *He is known for his elaborate costumes.*
VERB /ɪˈlæbəreɪt/ [I, T] (**elaborates**, **elaborating**, **elaborated**) **1** [I, T] If you **elaborate** a plan or theory, you develop it by making it more complicated and more effective. ❑ *His task was to elaborate policies that would make a market economy compatible with a clean environment.* **2** [I] If you **elaborate on** something that has been said, you say more about it, or give more details. ❑ *A spokesman declined to elaborate on a statement released late yesterday.*
elabo·rate·ly /ɪˈlæbərətli/ ADV ❑ *It was clearly an elaborately planned operation.*
elabo·ra·tion /ɪˌlæbəˈreɪʃən/ NOUN [U] ❑ *the elaboration of specific policies and mechanisms*

elapse /ɪˈlæps/ VERB [I] (**elapses**, **elapsing**, **elapsed**) (formal) When time **elapses**, it passes. ❑ *Forty-eight hours have elapsed since his arrest.*

elas·tic /ɪˈlæstɪk/ NOUN, ADJ
NOUN [U] **Elastic** is a rubber material that stretches when you pull it and returns to its original size and shape when you let it go. Elastic is often used in clothes to make them fit tightly, for example around the waist. ❑ *Make a mask with long ears and attach a piece of elastic to go around the back of the head.*
ADJ Something that is **elastic** is able to stretch easily and then returns to its original size and shape. ❑ *Beat it until the dough is slightly elastic.*

elat·ed /ɪˈleɪtɪd/ ADJ If you are **elated**, you are extremely happy and excited because of something that has happened. = euphoric ❑ *I was elated that my recent second bypass had been successful.*

ela·tion /ɪˈleɪʃən/ NOUN [U] **Elation** is a feeling of great happiness and excitement about something that has happened. = euphoria ❑ *His supporters have reacted to the news with elation.*

el·bow /ˈelbəʊ/ NOUN, VERB
NOUN [C] (**elbows**) Your **elbow** is the part of your arm where the upper and lower halves are joined. ❑ *He slipped and fell, badly bruising an elbow.*
VERB [T] (**elbows**, **elbowing**, **elbowed**) **1** If you **elbow** people **aside** or **elbow** your **way** somewhere, you push people with your elbows in order to move somewhere. = jostle ❑ *They also claim that the security team elbowed aside a steward.* **2** If someone or something **elbows** their

way somewhere, or **elbows** other people or things **out of the way**, they achieve success by being aggressive and determined. ❑ *Non-state firms gradually elbow aside the inefficient state-owned ones.*

el·der /'eldə/ ADJ, NOUN

ADJ [elder + N, 'the' elder, 'the' elder 'of' N] **The elder of** two people is the one who was born first. ❑ *his elder brother*

NOUN [c] (**elders**) **1** (*formal*) A person's **elder** is someone who is older than them, especially someone quite a lot older. ❑ *They have no respect for their elders.* **2** In some societies, an **elder** is one of the respected older people who have influence and authority. ❑ *a meeting of political figures and tribal elders*

E

❂ **el·der·ly** ♦◇◇ /'eldəli/ ADJ, NOUN

ADJ (*politeness*) You use **elderly** as a polite way of saying that someone is old. = old; ≠ young ❑ *There was an elderly couple on the terrace.* ❑ *Typical symptoms of pneumonia may be less prominent in elderly patients.* ❑ *Many of those most affected are elderly.*

NOUN [PL] **The elderly** are people who are old. ❑ *The elderly are a formidable force in any election.*

eld·est /'eldɪst/ ADJ The **eldest** person in a group is the one who was born before all the others. ❑ *The eldest child was a daughter called Fatiha.* ❑ *David was the eldest of three boys.*

❂ **elect** ♦♦◇ /ɪ'lekt/ VERB, ADJ

VERB [T] (**elects, electing, elected**) **1** When people **elect** someone, they choose that person to represent them, by voting for them. = choose, vote ❑ *The people of the Philippines have voted to elect a new president.* ❑ *The University of Washington elected him dean in 1956.* ❑ *The country is about to take a radical departure by electing a woman as its new president.* ❑ *Pelton was elected as mayor.* ❑ *the newly elected prime minister* **2** (*formal*) If you **elect to** do something, you choose to do it. ❑ *Those electing to smoke will be seated at the rear.*

ADJ [N + elect] (*formal*) **Elect** is added after words such as 'president' or 'governor' to indicate that a person has been elected to the post but has not officially started to carry out the duties involved. ❑ *the date when the president-elect takes office*

❂ **elec·tion** ♦♦♦ /ɪ'lekʃən/ NOUN [c, u] (**elections**)
1 [c, u] An **election** is a process in which people vote to choose a person or group of people to hold an official position. = vote, poll, ballot ❑ *Poland's first fully free elections for more than fifty years* ❑ *During his election campaign he promised to put the economy back on its feet.* ❑ *The final election results will be announced on Friday.* **2** [u] [usu with POSS] The **election** of a particular person or group of people is their success in winning an election. ❑ *the election of the Democrat candidate last year* ❑ *Vaclav Havel's election as president of Czechoslovakia*

WORD CONNECTIONS
VERB + **election**
hold an election
call an election
❑ *The presidential election was held in November.*
win an election
lose an election
❑ *Obama won the presidential election.*
ADJ + **election**
a **presidential** election
a **parliamentary** election
a **mayoral** election
❑ *Reeves is standing as a candidate in the parliamentary elections next month.*
a **general** election
a **local** election
❑ *The Labour Party won the 1997 general election.*

elec·tor·al ♦◇◇ /ɪ'lektərəl/ ADJ [electoral + N] **Electoral** is used to describe things that are connected with elections.

❑ *The Mongolian Democratic Party is campaigning for electoral reform.*

elec·tor·al·ly /ɪ'lektərəli/ ADV ❑ *He believed that the policies were both wrong and electorally disastrous.*

❂ **elec·tor·ate** /ɪ'lektərət/ NOUN [c] (**electorates**) The **electorate** of a country or area is all the people in it who have the right to vote in an election. = voters ❑ *He has the backing of almost a quarter of the electorate.* ❑ *the Maltese electorate*

❂ **elec·tric** ♦◇◇ /ɪ'lektrɪk/ ADJ **1** An **electric** device or machine works by means of electricity, rather than using some other source of power. ❑ *her electric guitar* ❑ *The tool is powered by an 1100 watt electric motor.* **2** [electric + N] An **electric** current, voltage, or charge is one that is produced by electricity. **3** [electric + N] **Electric** plugs, sockets, or power lines are designed to carry electricity. ❑ *More people are deciding that electric power lines could present a health risk.* **4** [electric + N] (*informal*) **Electric** is used to refer to the supply of electricity. = electricity ❑ *An average electric bill might go up $2 or $3 per month.* **5** If you describe the atmosphere of a place or event as **electric**, you mean that people are in a state of great excitement. ❑ *The mood in the hall was electric.*

WHICH WORD?
electric, electrical, or electronic?

Do not confuse the adjectives **electric, electrical,** and **electronic.**

You use **electric** in front of nouns to talk about machines or devices that use electricity.

❑ *Are **electric** vehicles completely pollution-free?*

You use **electrical** to talk in a more general way about machines, devices, or systems that use electricity.

❑ *They sell **electrical** appliances such as dishwashers and washing machines.*

You use **electronic** to talk about devices or systems that use very small parts such as transistors or silicon chips.

❑ *expensive **electronic** equipment*
❑ ***electronic** surveillance systems*

❂ **elec·tri·cal** /ɪ'lektrɪkəl/ ADJ **1** **Electrical** goods, equipment, or appliances work by means of electricity. ❑ *shipments of electrical equipment* ❑ *The study found that small electrical appliances consume a fifth of the electricity used in a typical American home.* **2** **Electrical** systems or parts supply or use electricity. ❑ *lighting and other electrical systems on the new runway* **3** **Electrical** energy is energy in the form of electricity. ❑ *brief pulses of electrical energy* **4** [electrical + N] **Electrical** industries, engineers, or workers are involved in the production and supply of electricity or electrical products. ❑ *company representatives from the electrical industry*

elec·tri·cal·ly /ɪ'lektrɪkli/ ADV **1** [electrically + -ED] ❑ *electrically powered vehicles* **2** *electrically charged particles*

❂ **elec·tric·ity** ♦◇◇ /ˌɪlek'trɪsɪti, ˌiːlek-/ NOUN [u] **Electricity** is a form of energy that can be carried by wires and is used for heating and lighting, and to provide power for machines. ❑ *We moved into a cabin with electricity but no running water.* ❑ *Approximately 40% of the world's electricity is generated using coal.* ❑ *infrastructure such as water and electricity supplies*

elec·tric shock NOUN [c] (**electric shocks**) If you get an **electric shock**, you get a sudden painful feeling when you touch something connected to a supply of electricity.

elec·tri·fy /ɪ'lektrɪfaɪ/ VERB [T] (**electrifies, electrifying, electrified**) **1** If people **are electrified by** an event or experience, it makes them feel very excited and surprised. = thrill ❑ *The world was electrified by his courage and resistance.* **2** When a railway system or railway line **is electrified**, electric cables are put over the tracks, or electric rails are put beside them, so that the trains can be powered by electricity. ❑ *The line was electrified as long ago as 1974.*

elec·tri·fy·ing /ɪ'lektrɪfaɪɪŋ/ ADJ ❑ *He gave an electrifying performance.*

elec·tro·cute /ɪ'lektrəkjuːt/ VERB [T] (**electrocutes**, electrocuting, electrocuted) **1** If someone **is electrocuted**, they are accidentally killed or badly injured when they touch something connected to a source of electricity. ❏ *Three people were electrocuted by falling power lines.* **2** If a criminal **is electrocuted**, he or she is executed using electricity. ❏ *He was electrocuted for a murder committed when he was 17.*

elec·tro·cu·tion /ɪˌlektrəˈkjuːʃən/ NOUN [C, U] (**electrocutions**) ❏ *The court pronounced him guilty and sentenced him to death by electrocution.*

✪ **elec·trode** /ɪˈlektrəʊd/ NOUN [C] (**electrodes**) An **electrode** is a small piece of metal or other substance that is used to take an electric current to or from a source of power, a piece of equipment, or a living body. ❏ *Two electrodes that measure changes in the body's surface moisture are attached to the palms of your hands.* ❏ *The patient's brain activity is monitored via electrodes taped to the skull.*

✪ **elec·tron** /ɪˈlektrɒn/ NOUN [C] (**electrons**) (*technical*) An **electron** is a tiny particle of matter that is smaller than an atom and has a negative electrical charge. ❏ *Most things are balanced – with equal numbers of electrons and protons.* ❏ *a type of radiation that displaces electrons from atoms* ❏ *an electron microscope capable of viewing single atoms* ❏ *As these electrons are negatively charged they will attempt to repel each other.*

✪ **elec·tron·ic** ◆◇◇ /ɪˌlekˈtrɒnɪk, iːlek-/ ADJ **1** [electronic + N] An **electronic** device has transistors or silicon chips that control and change the electric current passing through the device. ❏ *expensive electronic equipment* ❏ *cameras, mobile phones and other electronic devices* **2** An **electronic** process or activity involves the use of electronic devices. ❏ *electronic music*

elec·troni·cal·ly /ɪˌlekˈtrɒnɪkli, ˌiːlek-/ ADV [electronically with V] ❏ *Data is transmitted electronically.*

elec·tron·ic mail NOUN [SING] **Electronic mail** is the same as **e-mail**.

✪ **elec·tron·ics** /ɪˌlekˈtrɒnɪks/ NOUN [U] **Electronics** is the technology of using transistors and silicon chips, especially in devices such as radios, televisions, and computers. ❏ *Ohio's three main electronics companies* ❏ *cheaper, better consumer electronics*

el·egant ◆◇◇ /ˈelɪgənt/ ADJ **1** If you describe a person or thing as **elegant**, you mean that they are pleasing and graceful in appearance or style. = stylish ❏ *Patricia looked beautiful and elegant as always.* **2** If you describe a piece of writing, an idea, or a plan as **elegant**, you mean that it is simple, clear, and clever. ❏ *The document impressed me with its elegant simplicity.*

el·egance /ˈelɪgəns/ NOUN [U] ❏ *The furniture managed to combine practicality with elegance.*

el·egant·ly /ˈelɪgəntli/ ADV **1** *a tall, elegantly dressed man with a moustache* **2** *an elegantly simple idea*

✪ **el·ement** ◆◆◇ /ˈelɪmənt/ NOUN (*academic word*) NOUN [C, PL] (**elements**) **1** [C] The different **elements** of something are the different parts it contains. = part, constituent, component ❏ *The exchange of prisoners of war was one of the key elements of the UN's peace plan.* ❏ *The plot has all the elements not only of romance but of high drama.* **2** [C] A particular **element** of a situation, activity, or process is an important quality or feature that it has or needs. = factor ❏ *Physical fitness has now become an important element in our lives.* **3** [C] When you talk about **elements** within a society or organization, you are referring to groups of people who have similar aims, beliefs, or habits. ❏ *The government must weed out criminal elements from within the security forces.* **4** [C] If something has an **element of** a particular quality or emotion, it has a certain amount of this quality or emotion. ❏ *These reports clearly contain elements of propaganda.* **5** [C] An **element** is a substance such as gold, oxygen, or carbon that consists of only one type of atom. ❏ *an essential trace element for animals and man* ❏ *the minerals and elements in sea water* **6** [C] The **element** in an electric or water heater is the metal part that changes the electric current into heat. **7** [PL] You can refer to the weather, especially wind and rain, as **the elements**. ❏ *The area where most refugees are waiting is exposed to the elements.*

PHRASE **in one's element** If you say that someone is in their **element**, you mean that they are in a situation they enjoy. ❏ *My stepmother was in her element, organizing everything.*

WORD CONNECTIONS

ADJ + element

a **key** element
an **important** element
an **essential** element
the **main** element
a **vital** element
a **basic** element
a **core** element

❏ *The continuing professional development of teachers is a key element of school improvement.*

certain elements

❏ *Certain elements of the contract are still being discussed.*

element + OF + NOUN

an element of **surprise**
an element of **luck**
an element of **truth**
an element of **danger**
an element of **uncertainty**
an element of **risk**

❏ *There is an element of risk in any operation.*

el·emen·ta·ry /ˌelɪˈmentri/ ADJ Something that is **elementary** is very simple and basic. = basic ❏ *Literacy now includes elementary computer skills.*

el·ephant /ˈelɪfənt/ NOUN [C] (**elephants**) An **elephant** is a very large animal with a long, flexible nose called a trunk, which it uses to pick up things. Elephants live in India and Africa.

el·evate /ˈeliveɪt/ VERB [T] (**elevates, elevating, elevated**) **1** (*formal*) When someone or something achieves a more important rank or status, you can say that they **are elevated to** it. = promote ❏ *He was elevated to the post of president.* **2** If you **elevate** something **to** a higher status, you consider it to be better or more important than it really is. ❏ *Don't elevate your superiors to superstar status.* **3** (*formal*) To **elevate** something means to increase it in amount or intensity. = raise ❏ *Emotional stress can elevate blood pressure.* **4** If you **elevate** something, you raise it higher. ❏ *A few times a day, elevate feet above heart level.* ❏ *I built a platform to elevate the bed.*

elev·en ◆◆◆ /ɪˈlevən/ NUM (**elevens**) **Eleven** is the number 11. ❏ *the Princess and her eleven friends*

elev·enth ◆◆◇ /ɪˈlevənθ/ ADJ The **eleventh** item in a series is the one that you count as number eleven. ❏ *We were working on the eleventh floor.*

✪ **eli·gible** /ˈelɪdʒɪbəl/ ADJ **1** Someone who is **eligible to** do something is qualified or able to do it, for example, because they are old enough. = entitled, qualified; ≠ ineligible ❏ *Almost half the population are eligible to vote in today's election.* ❏ *You could be eligible for a university scholarship.* **2** An **eligible** man or woman is not yet married and is thought by many people to be a suitable partner. ❏ *He's the most eligible bachelor in Japan.*

✪ **eli·gibil·ity** /ˌelɪdʒəˈbɪlɪti/ NOUN [U] ≠ ineligibility ❏ *The rules covering eligibility for benefits changed in the 1980s.* ❏ *Each worker must meet various eligibility requirements.*

✪ **elimi·nate** ◆◇◇ /ɪˈlɪmɪneɪt/ VERB [T, PASSIVE] (**eliminates, eliminating, eliminated**) (*academic word*) **1** [T] (*formal*) To **eliminate** something, especially something you do not want or need, means to remove it completely. = remove, abolish ❏ *Recent measures have not eliminated discrimination in employment.* ❏ *If you think you may be allergic to a food or drink, eliminate it from your diet.* **2** [PASSIVE] When a person or team **is eliminated from** a competition, they are defeated and so stop participating in the competition. = knock out ❏ *I was eliminated from the 400 metres in the semi-finals.* **3** [T] If someone says that they **have eliminated** an enemy, they mean that they have killed them. By using the word 'eliminate,' they are trying to make the action sound more positive than if they used the word 'kill'. ❑ *He declared war on the government and urged right-wingers to eliminate their opponents.*

◆**elimi·na·tion** /ɪˌlɪmɪˈneɪʃən/ NOUN [u] (formal)
❶ The **elimination** of something is its complete removal. = removal, abolition, eradication ❑ *the prohibition and elimination of chemical weapons* ❑ *complete elimination of halitosis is usually possible* ❷ **Elimination** is the process of getting rid of waste products from your body by going to the toilet. ❑ *Breast-feeding is as natural as sex or elimination or any other bodily function.*

◆**elite** /ɪˈliːt, eɪ-/ NOUN, ADJ
NOUN [c] (**elites**) You can refer to the most powerful, rich, or talented people within a particular group, place, or society as the **elite**. ❑ *a government comprised mainly of the elite* ❑ *We have a political elite in this country.* ❑ *the governing elite of the 18th-century Dutch republic*
ADJ [elite + N] **Elite** people or organizations are considered to be the best of their kind. ❑ *the elite troops of the president's bodyguard*

◆**elit·ism** /ɪˈliːtɪzəm, eɪ-/ NOUN [u] **Elitism** is the quality or practice of being elitist. ❑ *It became difficult to promote conventional ideas of excellence without being instantly accused of elitism.* ❑ *the stereotypes of snobbery and elitism associated with the institution*

◆**elit·ist** /ɪˈliːtɪst, eɪ-/ ADJ, NOUN
ADJ (disapproval) **Elitist** systems, practices, or ideas favour the most powerful, rich, or talented people within a group, place, or society. ❑ *He worries about a time when college athletics become even more elitist than they are now.* ❑ *The party leadership denounced the Bill as elitist.* ❑ *The legal profession is starting to be less elitist and more representative.* NOUN [c] (**elitists**) (disapproval) An **elitist** is someone who has elitist ideas or is part of an elite. ❑ *He was an elitist who had no time for the masses.*

◆**el·lipse** /ɪˈlɪps/ NOUN [c] (**ellipses**) An **ellipse** is an oval shape similar to a circle but longer and flatter. ❑ *The Earth orbits in an ellipse.* ❑ *Every known comet orbits the sun, although most of them move in extremely elongated ellipses.*

◆**el·lip·ti·cal** /ɪˈlɪptɪkəl/ ADJ (formal) ❶ Something that is **elliptical** has the shape of an ellipse. ❑ *the moon's elliptical orbit* ❑ *The stadium is elliptical in plan.* ❑ *Spirals can seem to be elliptical in shape when viewed edge-on.*
❷ **Elliptical** references to something are indirect rather than clear. = oblique ❑ *elliptical references to problems best not aired in public*
el·lip·ti·cal·ly /ɪˈlɪptɪkəli/ ADV [elliptically after v]
❑ *He spoke only briefly and elliptically about the mission.*

◆**else** ◆◆◆ /els/ ADJ, ADV
ADJ ❶ You use **else** after words such as 'anywhere', 'someone', and 'what' to refer in a vague way to another person, place, or thing. ❑ *If I can't make a living at painting, at least I can teach someone else to paint.* ❑ *We had nothing else to do on those long trips.* ❷ [PRON-INDEF + else] You use **else** after words such as 'everyone', 'everything', and 'everywhere' to refer in a vague way to all the other people, things, or places except the one you are talking about. ❑ *As I try to be truthful, I expect everyone else to be truthful.*
PHRASES **above all else** (emphasis) Above all else is used to emphasize that a particular thing is more important than other things. ❑ *Above all else I hate the cold.*
if nothing else You can say 'if nothing else' to indicate that what you are mentioning is, in your opinion, the only good thing in a particular situation. ❑ *If nothing else, you'll really enjoy meeting them.*
ADV ❶ [ADV + else] You use **else** after words such as 'anywhere', 'someone', and 'what' to refer in a vague way to another person, place, or thing. ❑ *I never wanted to live anywhere else.* ❷ [ADV + else] You use **else** after words such as 'everyone', 'everything', and 'everywhere' to refer in a vague way to all the other people, things, or places except the one you are talking about. ❑ *Cleveland seems so much dirtier than everywhere else.*
PHRASE **or else** ❶ You use **or else** after stating a logical conclusion, to indicate that what you are about to say is evidence for that conclusion. = otherwise ❑ *Evidently no*

lessons have been learned or else the government would not have handled the problem so badly. ❷ You use **or else** to introduce a statement that indicates the unpleasant results that will occur if someone does or does not do something. = otherwise ❑ *This time we really need to succeed or else people will start giving us funny looks.* ❸ You use **or else** to introduce the second of two possibilities when you do not know which one is true. ❑ *You are either a total genius or else you must be totally crazy.* ❹ (spoken) You say '**or else**' after a command to warn someone that if they do not obey, you will be angry and may harm or punish them. ❑ *Behave, or else!*

◆**else·where** ◆◇◇ /ˌelsˈweə/ ADV **Elsewhere** means in other places or to another place. ❑ *Almost 80 per cent of the state's residents were born elsewhere.* ❑ *They were living well, in comparison with people elsewhere in the world.*

◆**elu·sive** /ɪˈluːsɪv/ ADJ Something or someone that is **elusive** is difficult to find, describe, remember, or achieve. ❑ *In Denver late-night taxis are elusive and far from cheap.*

◆**e-mail** ◆◆◇ also **E-mail, email** NOUN, VERB
NOUN [c, u] (**e-mails**) **E-mail** is a system of sending written messages electronically from one computer to another. **E-mail** is an abbreviation for **electronic mail**. ❑ *You can contact us by e-mail.* ❑ *Do you want to send an E-mail?*
VERB [T] (**e-mails, e-mailing, e-mailed**) If you **e-mail** someone, you send them an e-mail. ❑ *Jamie e-mailed me to say he couldn't come.*

WORD PARTS
The prefix **e-** often appears in words to show that something happens on or uses the internet: e-mail (NOUN)   e-commerce (NOUN)   e-book (NOUN)

◆**em·bar·go** /ɪmˈbɑːgəʊ/ NOUN, VERB
NOUN [c] (**embargoes**) If one country or group of countries imposes an **embargo** against another, it forbids trade with that country. = ban ❑ *The United Nations imposed an arms embargo against the country.*
VERB [T] (**embargoes, embargoing, embargoed**) If goods of a particular kind **are embargoed**, people are not allowed to import them from a particular country or export them to a particular country. = ban ❑ *The fruit was embargoed.* ❑ *They embargoed oil shipments to the US.*

WORD PARTS
The prefix **em-** appears before letters 'b', 'm', and 'p' to make verbs that describe the process of putting someone into a particular state, condition, or place, or to form adjectives and nouns that describe that process or those states and conditions: embargo (NOUN)   empower (VERB)   embed (VERB)

◆**em·bark** /ɪmˈbɑːk/ VERB [i] (**embarks, embarking, embarked**) ❶ If you **embark on** something new, difficult, or exciting, you start doing it. ❑ *He's embarking on a new career as a writer.* ❷ When someone **embarks on** a ship, they go on board before the start of a journey. ❑ *They embarked on a ship bound for Europe.*

◆**em·bar·rass** /ɪmˈbærəs/ VERB [T] (**embarrasses, embarrassing, embarrassed**) ❶ If something or someone **embarrasses** you, they make you feel shy or ashamed. ❑ *His clumsiness embarrassed him.* ❷ If something **embarrasses** a public figure such as a politician or an organization such as a political party, it causes problems for them. ❑ *Aides spoke of disposing of records that would embarrass the governor.*

◆**em·bar·rassed** /ɪmˈbærəst/ ADJ A person who is **embarrassed** feels shy, ashamed, or guilty about something. ❑ *He looked a bit embarrassed.*

◆**em·bar·rass·ing** /ɪmˈbærəsɪŋ/ ADJ ❶ Something that is **embarrassing** makes you feel shy or ashamed. = uncomfortable, awkward ❑ *That was an embarrassing situation for me.* ❷ Something that is **embarrassing to** a

public figure such as a politician or an organization such as a political party causes problems for them. ❏ *He has put the administration in an embarrassing position.*
em·bar·rass·ing·ly /ɪmˈbærəsɪŋli/ ADV ❏ *The lyrics of the song are embarrassingly banal.*

em·bar·rass·ment /ɪmˈbærəsmənt/ NOUN [C, U, SING] (embarrassments) **1** [C, U] **Embarrassment** is the feeling you have when you are embarrassed. ❏ *I think I would have died of embarrassment.* ❏ *We apologize for any embarrassment this may have caused.* **2** [C] An **embarrassment** is an action, event, or situation that causes problems for a politician, political party, government, or other public group. ❏ *The poverty figures were undoubtedly an embarrassment to the president.* **3** [SING] If you refer to a person as **an embarrassment**, you mean that you disapprove of them but cannot avoid your connection with them. ❏ *You have been an embarrassment to us from the day Doug married you.*

em·bas·sy ♦◇◇ /ˈembəsi/ NOUN [C] (embassies) An **embassy** is a group of government officials, headed by an ambassador, who represent their government in a foreign country. The building in which they work is also called an **embassy**. ❏ *The American embassy has already complained.*

em·bed /ɪmˈbed/ VERB [T] (embeds, embedding, embedded) **1** If an object **embeds itself** in a substance or thing, it becomes fixed there firmly and deeply. ❏ *One of the bullets passed through Andrea's chest before embedding itself in a wall.* **2** If something such as an attitude or feeling **is embedded in** a society or system, or in someone's personality, it becomes a permanent and noticeable feature of it. ❏ *This agreement will be embedded in a state treaty to be signed soon.*
em·bed·ded /ɪmˈbedɪd/ ADJ **1** *The fossils at Dinosaur Cove are embedded in hard sandstone.* **2** *I think that hatred of the other is deeply embedded in our society.*

em·bel·lish /ɪmˈbelɪʃ/ VERB [T] (embellishes, embellishing, embellished) **1** If something **is embellished with** decorative features or patterns, it has those features or patterns on it and they make it look more attractive. ❏ *The boat was embellished with carvings in red and blue.* ❏ *Ivy leaves embellish the front of the dresser.* **2** If you **embellish** a story, you make it more interesting by adding details that may be untrue. ❏ *I launched into the parable, embellishing the story with invented dialogue and extra details.*

em·blem /ˈembləm/ NOUN [C] (emblems) **1** An **emblem** is a design representing a country or organization. ❏ *the emblem of the Soviet Union* **2** An **emblem** is something that represents a quality or idea. = symbol ❏ *The eagle was an emblem of strength and courage.*

em·bodi·ment /ɪmˈbɒdimənt/ NOUN [SING] (formal) If you say that someone or something is **the embodiment of** a quality or idea, you mean that that is their most noticeable characteristic or the basis of all they do. ❏ *A baby is the embodiment of vulnerability.*

em·body /ɪmˈbɒdi/ VERB [T] (embodies, embodying, embodied) **1** To **embody** an idea or quality means to be a symbol or expression of that idea or quality. = represent ❏ *Jack Kennedy embodied all the hopes of the 1960s.* ❏ *For twenty-nine years, Checkpoint Charlie embodied the Cold War.* **2** If something **is embodied in** a particular thing, the second thing contains or consists of the first. ❏ *The proposal has been embodied in a draft resolution.*

em·brace /ɪmˈbreɪs/ VERB, NOUN
VERB [RECIP, T] (embraces, embracing, embraced) **1** [RECIP] If you **embrace** someone, you put your arms around them and hold them tightly, usually in order to show your love or affection for them. You can also say that two people **embrace**. = hug ❏ *Penelope came forwards and embraced her sister.* ❏ *At first people were sort of crying for joy and embracing each other.* **2** [T] (formal) If you **embrace** a change, political system, or idea, you accept it and start supporting it or believing in it. ❏ *He embraces the new information age.* **3** [T] (formal) If something **embraces** a group of people, things, or ideas, it includes them in a larger group or category. ❏ *a theory that would embrace the whole field of human endeavour*
NOUN [C, SING] (embraces) **1** [C] An **embrace** is when two

people have their arms around each other, holding tightly, usually in order to show their love or affection. ❏ *a young couple locked in an embrace* **2** [SING] An **embrace** is when someone shows an acceptance of a change, political system, or idea, and starts to support it or believe in it. ❏ *The marriage signalled James's embrace of the Catholic faith.*

✪ **em·bryo** /ˈembriəʊ/ NOUN, ADJ
NOUN [C] (embryos) An **embryo** is an unborn animal or human being in the very early stages of development. ❏ *There are 24,000 frozen embryos in clinics across the country.* ❏ *The embryo lives in the amniotic cavity.* ❏ *the remarkable resilience of very young embryos* ❏ *the cloning of human embryos for stem cell research*
ADJ [embryo + N] An **embryo** idea, system, or organization is in the very early stages of development, but is expected to grow stronger. ❏ *They are an embryo party of government.*

✪ **em·bry·on·ic** /ˌembriˈɒnɪk/ ADJ (formal) An **embryonic** process, idea, organization, or organism is one at a very early stage in its development. ❏ *Romania's embryonic democracy* ❏ *At the time, he was trying to recruit members for his embryonic resistance group.*

✪ **emerge** ♦♦◇ /ɪˈmɜːdʒ/ VERB [I, T] (emerges, emerging, emerged) (academic word) **1** [I] To **emerge** means to come out from an enclosed or dark space such as a room or a vehicle, or from a position where you could not be seen. = appear; ≠ disappear ❏ *Richard was waiting outside the door as she emerged.* ❏ *She then emerged from the courthouse to thank her supporters.* ❏ *like a butterfly emerging from a chrysalis* ❏ *holes made by the emerging adult beetle* **2** [I] If you **emerge from** a difficult or bad experience, you come to the end of it. ❏ *There is growing evidence that the economy is at last emerging from recession.* **3** [I, T] If a fact or result **emerges** from a period of thought, discussion, or investigation, it becomes known as a result of it. ❏ *the growing corruption that has emerged in the past few years* ❏ *It soon emerged that neither the July nor August mortgage payment had been collected.* **4** [I] (journalism) If someone or something **emerges as** a particular thing, they become recognized as that thing. ❏ *Vietnam has emerged as the world's third-biggest rice exporter.* ❏ *New leaders have emerged.* **5** [I] (journalism) When something such as an organization or an industry **emerges**, it comes into existence. ❏ *the new republic that emerged in October 1917*

✪ **emer·gence** /ɪˈmɜːdʒəns/ NOUN [U] The **emergence** of something is the process or event of its coming into existence. = arrival, surfacing, rise, appearance ❏ *the emergence of new democracies in Latin America* ❏ *measures that help to prevent the emergence of future generations of terrorists*

✪ **emer·gen·cy** ♦♦◇ /ɪˈmɜːdʒənsi/ NOUN, ADJ
NOUN [C] (emergencies) An **emergency** is an unexpected and difficult or dangerous situation, especially an accident, that happens suddenly and that requires quick action to deal with it. = crisis ❏ *He deals with emergencies promptly.* ❏ *Staff are trained to handle emergencies.* ❏ *The hospital will cater only for emergencies.*
ADJ **1** [emergency + N] An **emergency** action is one that is done or arranged quickly and not in the normal way, because an emergency has occurred. ❏ *Yesterday, the centre's board held an emergency meeting.* **2** [emergency + N] **Emergency** equipment or supplies are those intended for use in an emergency. ❏ *The plane is carrying emergency supplies for refugees.*

✪ **emer·gen·cy ser·vices** NOUN [PL] The **emergency services** are the public organizations whose job is to take quick action to deal with emergencies when they occur, especially the fire brigade, the police, and the ambulance service. ❏ *members of the emergency services* ❏ *The emergency services launched a rescue helicopter.* ❏ *He called the emergency services and within minutes an ambulance arrived.*

✪ **emi·grant** /ˈemɪɡrənt/ NOUN [C] (emigrants) An **emigrant** is a person who has left their own country to live in another country. Compare **immigrant**. ❏ *Irish emigrants to America*

✪ **emi·grate** /ˈemɪɡreɪt/ VERB [I] (emigrates, emigrating, emigrated) If you **emigrate**, you leave your own country to live in another country. = move, relocate, migrate

e

❑ He emigrated to Belgium. ❑ The family emigrated from England to Canada in 1924. ❑ They planned to emigrate.
✪ **emi‧gra‧tion** /ˌemɪˈɡreɪʃən/ NOUN [U] = departure, migration ❑ the huge emigration of workers to the West ❑ The Spanish Civil War provoked another wave of emigration.

WHICH WORD?

emigration, immigration, or migration?

If you **emigrate**, you leave your own country and go to live permanently in another country. The process by which people leave their own country in order to live somewhere else is called **emigration**.
❑ He had **emigrated** from Germany in the early 1920's.
❑ Famine and **emigration** made it the most depopulated region on the island.

You refer to the process by which people come to live in a country as **immigration**. Do not say that someone immigrates.
❑ She asked for his views on **immigration**.

When people **migrate**, they move to another place for a short period of time in order to find work.
❑ Millions have **migrated** to the cities.

The act of migrating is called **migration**.
❑ Global **migration** brings members of different groups together.

---

emi‧nent /ˈemɪnənt/ ADJ An **eminent** person is well-known and respected, especially because they are good at their profession. ❑ an eminent scientist

emi‧nent‧ly /ˈemɪnəntli/ ADV [eminently + ADJ/-ED] (emphasis) You use **eminently** in front of an adjective describing a positive quality in order to emphasize the quality expressed by that adjective. = highly ❑ His books on diplomatic history were eminently readable.

✪ **emis‧sion** /ɪˈmɪʃən/ NOUN [C, U] (emissions) (formal) An **emission** of something such as gas or radiation is the release of it into the atmosphere. = release, leakage ❑ The emission of gases such as carbon dioxide should be stabilized at their present level. ❑ Sulphur emissions from steel mills become acid rain.

✪ **emit** /ɪˈmɪt/ VERB [T] (emits, emitting, emitted) (formal) **1** If something **emits** heat, light, gas, or a smell, it produces it and sends it out by means of a physical or chemical process. = release ❑ The new device emits a powerful circular column of light. ❑ the amount of carbon dioxide emitted **2** To **emit** a sound or noise means to produce it. ❑ Whitney blinked and emitted a long, low whistle.

✪ **emo‧tion** ◆◇◇ /ɪˈməʊʃən/ NOUN [C, U] (emotions) **1** [C, U] An **emotion** is a feeling such as happiness, love, fear, anger, or hatred, which can be caused by the situation that you are in or the people you are with. = feeling ❑ Happiness was an emotion that Jerry was having to relearn. ❑ the different ways that men and women express emotion ❑ Research has shown that secure children are generally better at dealing with emotions, including sadness and anger. ❑ Her voice trembled with emotion. **2** [U] **Emotion** is the part of a person's character that consists of their feelings, as opposed to their thoughts. ❑ the split between reason and emotion

✪ **emo‧tion‧al** ◆◇◇ /ɪˈməʊʃənəl/ ADJ **1** **Emotional** means concerned with emotions and feelings. = psychological ❑ I needed this man's love, and the emotional support he was giving me. ❑ Victims are left with emotional problems that can last for life. **2** An **emotional** situation or issue is one that causes people to have strong feelings. = emotive ❑ Abortion is a very emotional issue. **3** If someone is or becomes **emotional**, they show their feelings very openly, especially when they are upset. ❑ He is a very emotional man.
✪ **emo‧tion‧al‧ly** /ɪˈməʊʃənəli/ ADV **1** [emotionally + ADJ/-ED] ❑ Are you saying that you're becoming emotionally involved with me? ❑ Play can be used therapeutically with children who are emotionally disturbed. **2** [emotionally + ADJ/-ED] ❑ In an emotionally charged speech, he said he was resigning.

emo‧tive /ɪˈməʊtɪv/ ADJ An **emotive** situation or issue is likely to make people feel strong emotions. = emotional ❑ Embryo research is an emotive issue.

em‧pa‧thy /ˈempəθi/ NOUN [U] **Empathy** is the ability to share another person's feelings and emotions as if they were your own. ❑ Having begun my life in a children's home, I have great empathy with the little ones.

✪ **em‧per‧or** /ˈempərə/ NOUN [C] (emperors) An **emperor** is a man who rules an empire or is the head of state in an empire. ❑ the emperor of Japan ❑ An Indian emperor once proclaimed it a paradise on Earth. ❑ the legendary Aztec emperor, Montezuma ❑ The eighty-three-year-old emperor was deposed in September 1974.

✪ **em‧pha‧sis** ◆◇◇ /ˈemfəsɪs/ NOUN [C, U] (emphases) (academic word) **1** **Emphasis** is special or extra importance that is given to an activity or to a part or aspect of something. = importance, attention, weight, stress ❑ Too much emphasis is placed on research. ❑ Grant puts a special emphasis on weather in his paintings. **2** **Emphasis** is extra force that you put on a syllable, word, or phrase when you are speaking in order to make it seem more important. ❑ The emphasis is on the first syllable of the last word.

✪ **em‧pha‧size** ◆◇◇ /ˈemfəsaɪz/ also **emphasise** VERB [T] (emphasizes, emphasizing, emphasized) To **emphasize** something means to indicate that it is particularly important or true, or to draw special attention to it. = stress ❑ But it's also been emphasized that no major policy changes can be expected to come out of the meeting. ❑ Discuss pollution with your child, emphasizing how nice a clean street, lawn, or park looks.

em‧phat‧ic /ɪmˈfætɪk/ ADJ **1** An **emphatic** response or statement is one made in a forceful way, because the speaker feels very strongly about what they are saying. ❑ His response was immediate and emphatic. **2** [V-LINK + emphatic] If you are **emphatic about** something, you use forceful language that shows you feel very strongly about what you are saying. ❑ The rebels are emphatic that this is not a surrender. **3** An **emphatic** win or victory is one in which the winner has won by a large amount or distance. ❑ Yesterday's emphatic victory was their fifth in succession.

em‧phati‧cal‧ly /ɪmˈfætɪkli/ ADV **1** [emphatically with V] If you say something **emphatically**, you say it in a forceful way that shows you feel very strongly about what you are saying. ❑ 'No fast food,' she said emphatically. **2** [emphatically with CL/GROUP] You use **emphatically** to emphasize the statement you are making. ❑ Making people feel foolish is emphatically not my strategy.

✪ **em‧pire** ◆◇◇ /ˈempaɪə/ NOUN [C] (empires) **1** An **empire** is a number of individual nations that are all controlled by the government or ruler of one particular country. ❑ the Roman Empire ❑ The empire collapsed in 1918. ❑ The French empire had expanded largely through military conquest. **2** You can refer to a group of companies controlled by one person as an **empire**. ❑ the global Murdoch media empire

✪ **em‧piri‧cal** /ɪmˈpɪrɪkəl/ ADJ (academic word) **Empirical** evidence or study relies on practical experience rather than theories. ❑ There is no empirical evidence to support his thesis. ❑ a series of important empirical studies
✪ **em‧piri‧cal‧ly** /ɪmˈpɪrɪkli/ ADV ≠ theoretically ❑ They approached this part of their task empirically. ❑ empirically based research ❑ the empirically confirmed relationship between high service levels and profitability

✪ **em‧ploy** ◆◇◇ /ɪmˈplɔɪ/ VERB [T] (employs, employing, employed) **1** If a person or company **employs** you, they pay you to work for them. = hire, recruit ❑ The company employs 18 workers. ❑ More than 3,000 local workers are employed in the tourism industry. **2** If you **employ** certain methods, materials, or expressions, you use them. = use, utilize ❑ The group will employ a mix of tactics to achieve its aim. ❑ The tactics the police are now to employ are definitely uncompromising. ❑ the language of vulgar speech employed as a political weapon ❑ the approaches and methods employed in the study **3** If your time **is employed in** doing something, you are using the time you have to do that thing. ❑ Your time could be usefully employed in attending night classes.

✪ **em·ploy·ee** ♦♦◇ /ɪmˈplɔiː/ NOUN [C] (**employees**)
An **employee** is a person who is paid to work for an organization or for another person. = worker, staff ❑ He is an employee of Fuji Bank. ❑ Many of its employees are women.

✪ **em·ploy·er** ♦◇◇ /ɪmˈplɔiə/ NOUN [C] (**employers**)
Your **employer** is the person or organization that you work for. ❑ He had been sent to Rome by his employer. ❑ employers who hire illegal workers ❑ The telephone company is the country's largest employer.

✪ **em·ploy·ment** ♦◇◇ /ɪmˈplɔimənt/ NOUN [U]
1 **Employment** is the fact of having a paid job. ❑ She was unable to find employment. ❑ 96% of immigrants are in full-time employment. **2** **Employment** is the fact of employing someone. ❑ the employment of children under nine **3** **Employment** is the work that is available in a country or area. ❑ economic policies designed to secure full employment

em·pow·er /ɪmˈpaʊə/ VERB [T] (**empowers, empowering, empowered**) **1** (formal) If someone **is empowered to** do something, they have the authority or power to do it. = authorize ❑ The army is now empowered to operate on a shoot-to-kill basis. **2** To **empower** someone means to give them the means to achieve something, for example to become stronger or more successful. ❑ You must delegate effectively and empower people to carry out their roles with your full support.

em·pow·er·ment /ɪmˈpaʊəmənt/ NOUN [U] The **empowerment of** a person or group of people is the process of giving them power and status in a particular situation. ❑ This government believes very strongly in the empowerment of women.

emp·ti·ness /ˈemptinəs/ NOUN [U] **1** A feeling of **emptiness** is an unhappy or frightening feeling that nothing is worthwhile, especially when you are very tired or have just experienced something upsetting. ❑ The result later in life may be feelings of emptiness and depression. **2** The **emptiness** of a place is the fact that there is nothing in it. ❑ the emptiness of the desert

emp·ty ♦◇◇ /ˈempti/ ADJ, VERB, NOUN
ADJ (**emptier, emptiest**) **1** An **empty** place, vehicle, or container is one that has no people or things in it. ❑ The room was bare and empty. ❑ empty cans of beer **2** An **empty** gesture, threat, or relationship has no real value or meaning. ❑ His father had threatened disinheritance, but both men had known it was an empty threat. **3** If you describe a person's life or a period of time as **empty**, you mean that nothing interesting or valuable happens in it. ❑ My life was very hectic but empty before I met him. **4** If you feel **empty**, you feel unhappy and have no energy, usually because you are very tired or have just experienced something upsetting. ❑ I feel so empty, my life just doesn't seem worth living any more.
VERB [T, I] (**empties, emptying, emptied**) **1** [T] If you **empty** a container, or **empty** something out of it, you remove its contents, especially by tipping it up. ❑ I emptied the ashtray. ❑ Empty the noodles and liquid into a serving bowl. **2** [I, T] If someone **empties** a room or place, or if it **empties**, everyone in it goes away. ❑ The stadium emptied at the end of the first day of games. **3** [I] A river or canal that **empties into** a lake, river, or sea flows into it. ❑ The Milwaukee River empties into Lake Michigan near that pipe.
NOUN [C] (**empties**) **Empties** are bottles or containers that no longer have anything in them. ❑ After breakfast we'll take the empties down in the sack.

✪ **en·able** ♦◇◇ /ɪnˈeɪbəl/ VERB [T] (**enables, enabling, enabled**) (academic word) **1** If someone or something **enables** you **to** do a particular thing, they give you the opportunity to do it. = help ❑ The new test should enable doctors to detect the disease early. ❑ Hypotheses enable scientists to check the accuracy of their theories. **2** To **enable** something **to** happen means to make it possible for it to happen. = allow; ≠ prevent ❑ The hot sun enables the grapes to reach optimum ripeness. ❑ The working class is still too small to enable a successful socialist revolution. **3** To **enable** someone **to** do something means to give them permission or the right to do it. ❑ legislation which enables young people to do a form of alternative service

en·act /ɪnˈækt/ VERB [T] (**enacts, enacting, enacted**) **1** (technical) When a government or authority **enacts** a proposal, they make it into a law. ❑ The authorities have failed so far to enact a law allowing unrestricted emigration. **2** If people **enact** a story or play, they perform it by acting. ❑ She often enacted the stories told to her by her father. **3** (journalism) If a particular event or situation **is enacted**, it happens; used especially to talk about something that has happened before. ❑ It was a scene enacted month after month for eight years.

en·chant·ing /ɪnˈtʃɑːntɪŋ, -ˈtʃænt-/ ADJ If you describe someone or something as **enchanting**, you mean that they are very attractive or charming. ❑ She's an absolutely enchanting child.

en·cir·cle /ɪnˈsɜːkəl/ VERB [T] (**encircles, encircling, encircled**) To **encircle** something or someone means to surround or enclose them, or to go around them. = surround ❑ A forty-foot-high concrete wall encircles the jail.

en·close /ɪnˈkləʊz/ VERB [T] (**encloses, enclosing, enclosed**) **1** If a place or object **is enclosed** by something, the place or object is inside that thing or completely surrounded by it. ❑ *The rules state that samples must be enclosed in two watertight containers.* ❑ *Enclose the flower in a small muslin bag.* **2** If you **enclose** something with a letter, you put it in the same envelope as the letter. ❑ *I have enclosed a cheque for $100.*

en·clo·sure /ɪnˈkləʊʒə/ NOUN [C] (**enclosures**) An **enclosure** is an area of land that is surrounded by a wall or fence and that is used for a particular purpose. ❑ *This enclosure was so vast that the outermost wall could hardly be seen.*

en·com·pass /ɪnˈkʌmpəs/ VERB [T] (**encompasses, encompassing, encompassed**) **1** If something **encompasses** particular things, it includes them. = embrace ❑ *His repertoire encompassed everything from Bach to Schoenberg.* **2** To **encompass** a place means to surround or cover it completely. ❑ *The map shows the rest of the western region, encompassing nine states.*

❖**en·coun·ter** ◆◇◇ /ɪnˈkaʊntə/ VERB, NOUN (*academic word*)
▪VERB▪ [T] (**encounters, encountering, encountered**) **1** If you **encounter** problems or difficulties, you experience them. = meet, experience, face ❑ *Every day of our lives we encounter major and minor stresses of one kind or another.* ❑ *Environmental problems they found were among the worst they encountered.* **2** (*formal*) If you **encounter** someone, you meet them, usually unexpectedly. = meet ❑ *Did you encounter anyone in the building?*
▪NOUN▪ [C] (**encounters**) **1** An **encounter with** someone is a meeting with them, particularly one that is unexpected or significant. ❑ *The author tells of a remarkable encounter with a group of South Vietnamese soldiers.* **2** An **encounter** is a particular type of experience. ❑ *a sexual encounter*

❖**en·cour·age** ◆◆◇ /ɪnˈkʌrɪdʒ, AmE -ˈkɜːr-/ VERB [T] (**encourages, encouraging, encouraged**) **1** If you **encourage** someone, you give them confidence, for example by letting them know that what they are doing is good and telling them that they should continue to do it. ❑ *When things aren't going well, he encourages me, telling me not to give up.* **2** If someone **is encouraged by** something that happens, it gives them hope or confidence. ≠ discourage ❑ *Investors were encouraged by the news.* **3** If you **encourage** someone **to** do something, you try to persuade them to do it, for example, by telling them that it would be a pleasant thing to do, or by trying to make it easier for them to do it. You can also **encourage** an activity. ≠ discourage ❑ *Herbie Hancock was encouraged by his family to learn music at a young age.* ❑ *Children should be encouraged to participate in at least one sport.* ❑ *Their task is to help encourage private investment in Russia.* **4** If something **encourages** a particular activity or state, it causes it to happen or increase. ≠ discourage ❑ *a natural substance that encourages cell growth* ❑ *Slow music encourages supermarket-shoppers to browse longer but spend more.*
en·cour·aged /ɪnˈkʌrɪdʒd/ ADJ ❑ *We were very encouraged after over 17,000 pictures were submitted.*

en·cour·age·ment /ɪnˈkʌrɪdʒmənt, AmE -ˈkɜːr-/ NOUN [C, U] (**encouragements**) **Encouragement** is the activity of encouraging someone, or something that is said or done in order to encourage them. ❑ *Friends gave me a great deal of encouragement.*

en·cour·ag·ing /ɪnˈkʌrɪdʒɪŋ, AmE -ˈkɜːr-/ ADJ Something that is **encouraging** gives people hope or confidence. ❑ *There are encouraging signs of an artistic revival.* ❑ *The results have been encouraging.*
en·cour·ag·ing·ly /ɪnˈkʌrɪdʒɪŋli, AmE -ˈkɜːr-/ ADV ❑ *The people at the next table watched me eat and smiled encouragingly.*

en·cy·clo·pedia /ɪnˌsaɪkləˈpiːdiə/ also **encyclopaedia** NOUN [C] (**encyclopedias**) An **encyclopedia** is a book or set of books in which facts about many different subjects or about one particular subject are arranged for reference, usually in alphabetical order.

end ◆◆◆ /end/ NOUN, VERB
▪NOUN▪ [SING, C] (**ends**) **1** [SING] **The end of** something such as a period of time, an event, a book, or a film is the last part of it or the final point in it. ❑ *The report is expected by the end of the year.* ❑ *families who settled in the region at the end of the 17th century* **2** [C] An **end to** something or the **end of** it is the act or result of stopping it so that it does not continue any longer. ❑ *The government today called for an end to the violence.* ❑ *I was worried she would walk out or bring the interview to an end.* **3** [C] The two **ends** of something long and narrow are the two points or parts of it that are farthest away from each other. ❑ *The company is planning to place surveillance equipment at both ends of the tunnel.* **4** [C] The **end** of a long, narrow object such as a finger or a pencil is the tip or smallest edge of it, usually the part that is furthest away from you. = tip ❑ *He tapped the ends of his fingers together.* **5** [C] **End** is used to refer to either of the two extreme points of a scale, or of something that you are considering as a scale. ❑ *At the other end of the social scale was the grocer.* **6** [C] The **other end** is one of two places that are connected because people are communicating with each other by telephone or writing, or are travelling from one place to the other. ❑ *When he answered the phone, Fred was at the other end.* **7** [C] (*spoken*) If you refer to a particular **end** of a project or piece of work, you mean a part or aspect of it, such as a part of it that is done by a particular person or in a particular place. ❑ *You take care of your end, kid, I'll take care of mine.* **8** [C] An **end** is the purpose for which something is done or towards which you are working. ❑ *The police force is being manipulated for political ends.*
▪PHRASES▪ **at an end** If something is **at an end**, it has finished and will not continue. ❑ *The recession is definitely at an end.*
come to an end If something **comes to an end**, it stops. ❑ *The cold war came to an end.*
at the end of the day (*informal*) You say **at the end of the day** when you are talking about what happens after a long series of events or what appears to be the case after you have considered the relevant facts. ❑ *At the end of the day it's up to them to decide.*
in the end You say **in the end** when you are saying what is the final result of a series of events, or what is your final conclusion after considering all the relevant facts. ❑ *I toyed with the idea of calling the police, but in the end I didn't.*
make ends meet If you find it difficult to **make ends meet**, you cannot manage very well financially because you hardly have enough money for the things you need. ❑ *With Betty's salary they barely made ends meet.*
no end (*informal*) **No end** means a lot. ❑ *Teachers inform me that Todd's behaviour has improved no end.*
on end **1** When something happens for hours, days, weeks, or years **on end**, it happens continuously and without stopping for the amount of time that is mentioned. ❑ *He is a wonderful companion and we can talk for hours on end.* **2** Something that is **on end** is upright, instead of in its normal or natural position, for example, lying down, flat, or on its longest side. ❑ *Wet books should be placed on end with their pages kept apart.*
put an end to something To put **an end to** something means to cause it to stop. ❑ *Only a political solution could put an end to the violence.*
the end of the road If a process or person has reached **the end of the road**, they are unable to progress any further. ❑ *Given the results of the vote, is this the end of the road for the hardliners in Congress?*
not be the end of the world If you say that something bad is **not the end of the world**, you are trying to stop yourself or someone else being so upset by it, by suggesting that it is not the worst thing that could happen. ❑ *Obviously I'd be disappointed if we don't make it, but it wouldn't be the end of the world.*
▪VERB▪ [I, T] (**ends, ending, ended**) **1** [I, T] When a situation, process, or activity **ends**, or when something or someone **ends** it, it reaches its final point and stops. ❑ *The meeting quickly ended and Steve and I left the room.* **2** [I, T] If you say that someone or something **ends** a period of time in a particular way, you are indicating what the final situation was like. You can also say that a period of time **ends** in a

particular way. ❑ *The markets ended the week on a quiet note.* **3** [I] If a period of time **ends**, it reaches its final point. ❑ *Reports usually come out about three weeks after each month ends.* **4** [I, T] If something such as a book, speech, or performance **ends with** a particular thing or the writer or performer **ends** it **with** that thing, its final part consists of the thing mentioned. ❑ *His statement ended with the words: 'Pray for me.'* ❑ *The book ends on a lengthy description of Hawaii.* **5** [I] If a situation or event **ends** in a particular way, it has that particular result. ❑ *The incident could have ended in tragedy.* ❑ *Our conversations ended with him saying he would try to be more understanding.* **6** [I] If an object **ends with** or **in** a particular thing, it has that thing on its tip or point, or as its last part. ❑ *It has three pairs of legs, each ending in a large claw.* **7** [I] A journey, road, or river that **ends** at a particular place stops there and goes no further. ❑ *The highway ended at an intersection.* **8** [I] If you say that something **ends** at a particular point, you mean that it is applied or exists up to that point, and no further. ❑ *Heather is also 25 and from Boston, but the similarity ends there.* **9** [I] If you **end by** doing something or **end** in a particular state, you do that thing or get into that state even though you did not originally intend to. ❑ *They ended by making themselves miserable.*

PHRASE **end it all** If someone **ends it all**, they kill themselves. ❑ *He grew suicidal, thinking up ways to end it all.*

PHRASAL VERB **end up** **1** If someone or something **ends up** somewhere, they eventually arrive there, usually by accident. = finish up, wind up ❑ *She fled with her children, moving from neighbour to neighbour and ending up in a friend's basement.* **2** If you **end up** doing something or **end up** in a particular state, you do that thing or get into that state even though you did not originally intend to. = finish up ❑ *If you don't know what you want, you might end up getting something you don't want.* ❑ *Every time they went dancing they ended up in a bad mood.*

◆ **make your hair stand on end** → see **hair**; **be on the receiving end** → see **receive**; **get the wrong end of the stick** → see **stick**

⊕ **en·dan·ger** /ɪnˈdeɪndʒə/ VERB [T] (**endangers, endangering, endangered**) To **endanger** something or someone means to put them in a situation where they might be harmed or destroyed completely. = threaten; ≠ protect, conserve ❑ *The debate could endanger the proposed Middle East peace talks.* ❑ *Plastic bags endanger wildlife.* ❑ *endangered species such as the lynx and wolf*

en·dear /ɪnˈdɪə/ VERB [T] (**endears, endearing, endeared**) If something **endears** you to someone or if you **endear yourself** to them, you become popular with them and well liked by them. ❑ *Their taste for gambling has endeared them to Las Vegas casino owners.*

en·dear·ing /ɪnˈdɪərɪŋ/ ADJ [V-LINK + endearing] If you describe someone's behaviour as **endearing**, you mean that it causes you to feel very fond of them. ❑ *She has such an endearing personality.*

en·deav·our /ɪnˈdevə/ (BrE; in AmE, use **endeavor**) VERB, NOUN

VERB [T] (**endeavours, endeavouring, endeavoured**) (*formal*) If you **endeavour to** do something, you try very hard to do it. = strive ❑ *They are endeavouring to protect labour union rights.*

NOUN [C, U] (**endeavours**) (*formal*) An **endeavour** is an attempt to do something, especially something new or original. ❑ *The company's creative endeavours are thriving.* ❑ *Extracting information about the large-scale composition of a planet from a sample weighing a millionth of a gram was a fascinating example of scientific endeavour.*

end·ing /ˈendɪŋ/ NOUN [C, SING] (**endings**) **1** [C] You can refer to the last part of a book, story, play, or film as the **ending**, especially when you are considering the way that the story ends. ❑ *The film has a Hollywood happy ending.* **2** [C] The **ending** of a word is the last part of it. = common word endings, like 'ing' in walking **3** [SING] The **ending** of a situation, process, or activity is the point at which it stops. ❑ *The ending of a marriage by death is different in many ways from an ending caused by divorce.*

end·less /ˈendləs/ ADJ If you say that something is

endless, you mean that it is very large or lasts for a very long time, and it seems as if it will never stop. ❑ *the endless hours I spent on homework*

end·less·ly /ˈendləsli/ ADV ❑ *They talk about it endlessly.*

⊕ **en·dorse** /ɪnˈdɔːs/ VERB [T] (**endorses, endorsing, endorsed**) **1** If you **endorse** someone or something, you say publicly that you support or approve of them. = support, approve ❑ *I can endorse his opinion wholeheartedly.* ❑ *policies agreed by the Labour Party and endorsed by the electorate* **2** If you **endorse** a product or company, you appear in advertisements for it. = promote, advertise ❑ *The twins endorsed a line of household cleaning products.* ❑ *The report also warned people to be wary of diets which are endorsed by celebrities.*

⊕ **en·dorse·ment** /ɪnˈdɔːsmənt/ NOUN [C] (**endorsements**) **1** An **endorsement** is a statement or action that shows you support or approve of something or someone. = approval ❑ *This is a powerful endorsement for his softer style of government.* ❑ *That adds up to an endorsement of the status quo.* **2** An **endorsement for** a product or company involves appearing in advertisements for it or showing support for it. ❑ *His commercial endorsements for everything from running shoes to breakfast cereals will take his earnings to more than ten million dollars a year.* ❑ *Fashion designers still value celebrity endorsements.* ❑ *Bryant has earned millions of dollars in product endorsements.*

en·dow /ɪnˈdaʊ/ VERB [T] (**endows, endowing, endowed**) **1** You say that someone **is endowed with** a particular desirable ability, characteristic, or possession when they have it by chance or by birth. ❑ *You are endowed with wealth, good health and a lively intellect.* **2** If you **endow** something **with** a particular feature or quality, you provide it with that feature or quality. = imbue ❑ *Herbs have been used for centuries to endow a whole range of foods with subtle flavours.* **3** If someone **endows** an institution, scholarship, or project, they provide a large amount of money that will produce the income needed to pay for it. ❑ *The ambassador has endowed a $1 million public-service fellowships programme.*

en·dow·ment /ɪnˈdaʊmənt/ NOUN [C] (**endowments**) An **endowment** is a gift of money that is made to an institution or community in order to provide it with an annual income. ❑ *the National Endowment for the Arts*

en·dur·ance /ɪnˈdjʊərəns, AmE -ˈdʊr-/ NOUN [U] **Endurance** is the ability to continue with an unpleasant or difficult situation, experience, or activity over a long period of time. ❑ *The exercise obviously will improve strength and endurance.*

⊕ **en·dure** /ɪnˈdjʊə, AmE -ˈdʊr/ VERB [T, I] (**endures, enduring, endured**) **1** [T] If you **endure** a painful or difficult situation, you experience it and do not avoid it or give up, usually because you cannot. = undergo ❑ *The company endured heavy financial losses.* ❑ *He endured physical pain and made many sacrifices for the benefit of others.* **2** [I] If something **endures**, it continues to exist without any loss in quality or importance. = persist ❑ *Somehow the language endures and continues to survive.* ❑ *Whether this fragile marriage endures remains to be seen.*

⊕ **en·dur·ing** /ɪnˈdjʊərɪŋ, AmE -ˈdʊr/ ADJ = lasting ❑ *This chance meeting was the start of an enduring friendship.* ❑ *It remained one of his most enduring memories.* ❑ *the enduring legacy of Christianity*

en·emy ♦◇◇ /ˈenəmi/ NOUN [C, SING] (**enemies**) **1** [C] If someone is your **enemy**, they hate you or want to harm you. ❑ *Imagine loving your enemy and doing good to those who hated you.* **2** [C] If someone is your **enemy**, they are opposed to you and to what you think or do. ❑ *Her political enemies were quick to pick up on this series of disasters.* **3** [SING] ['the' enemy, enemy + N] **The enemy** is an army or other force that is opposed to you in a war, or a country with which your country is at war. ❑ *The enemy were pursued for two miles.* **4** [C] (*formal*) If one thing is the **enemy** of another thing, the second thing cannot happen or succeed because of the first thing. ❑ *Reform, as we know, is the enemy of revolution.*

en·er·get·ic /ˌenəˈdʒetɪk/ ADJ **1** If you are **energetic** in what you do, you have a lot of enthusiasm and determination. ❑ *Ibrahim is 59, strong looking, enormously*

E

energetic and accomplished. **2** An **energetic** person is very active and does not feel at all tired. An **energetic** activity involves a lot of physical movement and power. ❑ *Ten-year-olds are incredibly energetic.*

en·er·get·i·cal·ly /ˌenə'dʒetɪkli/ ADV **1** [energetically with v] ❑ *He had worked energetically all day on his new book.* **2** [energetically with v] ❑ *David chewed energetically on the gristly steak.*

✪ **en·er·gy** ◆◆◇ /'enədʒi/ NOUN [U, C] (**energies**) (*academic word*) **1** [U] **Energy** is the ability and strength to do active physical things and the feeling that you are full of physical power and life. ❑ *He was saving his energy for next week's race in Tuscon.* **2** [U] **Energy** is determination and enthusiasm about doing things. ❑ *You have drive and energy for those things you are interested in.* **3** [C] Your **energies** are the efforts and attention that you can direct towards a particular aim. ❑ *She had started to devote her energies to teaching rather than performing.* **4** [U] **Energy** is the power from sources such as electricity and coal that makes machines work or provides heat. = power ❑ *those who favour nuclear energy* ❑ *a scheme for supporting renewable energy in England and Wales* ❑ *Oil shortages have caused an energy crisis.* ❑ *The energy efficiency of public transport could be improved.*

✪ **en·force** /ɪn'fɔːs/ VERB [T] (**enforces, enforcing, enforced**) (*academic word*) **1** If people in authority **enforce** a law or a rule, they make sure that it is obeyed, usually by punishing people who do not obey it. ❑ *Boulder was one of the first cities in the nation to enforce a ban on smoking.* ❑ *Until now, the government has only enforced the ban with regard to American ships.* ❑ *The measures are being enforced by Interior Ministry troops.* ❑ *A strict curfew was enforced.* **2** To **enforce** something means to force or cause it to be done or to happen. ❑ *They struggled to limit the cost by enforcing a low-tech specification.*

✪ **en·force·ment** ◆◆◇ /ɪn'fɔːsmənt/ NOUN [U] If someone carries out the **enforcement of** an act or rule, they enforce it. ❑ *The doctors want stricter enforcement of existing laws.* ❑ *Interpol are liaising with all the major law enforcement agencies around the world.*

en·gage ◆◇◇ /ɪn'geɪdʒ/ VERB [I, T] (**engages, engaging, engaged**) **1** [I] (*formal*) If you **engage in** an activity, you do it or are actively involved with it. ❑ *I have never engaged in drug trafficking.* **2** [T] If something **engages** you or your attention or interest, it keeps you interested in it and thinking about it. ❑ *They never learned skills to engage the attention of the others.* **3** [T] If you **engage** someone **in** conversation, you have a conversation with them. ❑ *They tried to engage him in conversation.* **4** [I] If you **engage with** something or **with** a group of people, you get involved with that thing or group and feel that you are connected with it or have real contact with it. ❑ *She found it hard to engage with office life.* **5** [T] (*formal*) If you **engage** someone to do a particular job, you appoint them to do it. ❑ *We engaged the services of a famous engineer.*
→ See also **engaged, engaging**

en·gaged /ɪn'geɪdʒd/ ADJ **1** [V-LINK + engaged 'in/on' N] (*formal*) Someone who is **engaged in** a particular activity is doing that thing. ❑ *the various projects he was engaged in* **2** When two people are **engaged**, they have agreed to marry each other. ❑ *We got engaged on my eighteenth birthday.* **3** (*BrE*; in *AmE*, use **busy**) If a telephone or a telephone line is **engaged**, it is already being used by someone else so that you are unable to speak to the person you are phoning. **4** (*mainly BrE*; in *AmE*, usually use **occupied**) If a public toilet is **engaged**, it is already being used by someone else.

en·gage·ment /ɪn'geɪdʒmənt/ NOUN [C, U] (**engagements**) **1** [C] (*formal*) An **engagement** is an arrangement that you have made to do something at a particular time. = date ❑ *He had an engagement at a restaurant at eight.* **2** [C] An **engagement** is an agreement that two people have made with each other to get married. ❑ *I've broken off my engagement to Arthur.* **3** [C] You can refer to the period of time during which two people are engaged as their **engagement**. ❑ *We spoke every night during our engagement.* **4** [C, U] A military **engagement** is an armed conflict between two enemies. ❑ *The constitution prohibits them from military engagement on foreign soil.*

5 [U] **Engagement** with something or with a group of people is the act of getting involved with that thing or group and feeling that you are connected with it or have real contact with it. ❑ *the candidate's apparent lack of engagement with younger voters*

en·gag·ing /ɪn'geɪdʒɪŋ/ ADJ An **engaging** person or thing is pleasant, interesting, and entertaining. ❑ *one of her most engaging and least known novels*

✪ **en·gine** ◆◆◇ /'endʒɪn/ NOUN [C] (**engines**) **1** The **engine** of a car or other vehicle is the part that produces the power which makes the vehicle move. = motor ❑ *He got into the driving seat and started the engine.* ❑ *Diesel engines are usually more fuel-efficient than petrol engines.* ❑ *an engine failure that forced a jetliner to crash-land in a field* **2** An **engine** is also the large vehicle that pulls a train. ❑ *In 1941, the train would have been pulled by a steam engine.*

✪ **en·gi·neer** ◆◇◇ /ˌendʒɪ'nɪə/ NOUN, VERB
NOUN [C] (**engineers**) **1** An **engineer** is a person who uses scientific knowledge to design, construct, and maintain engines and machines or structures such as roads, railways, and bridges. ❑ *Structural engineers assessed the damage to the building.* ❑ *one of the engineers who designed the railway* **2** An **engineer** is a person who repairs mechanical or electrical devices. ❑ *They send a service engineer to fix the disk drive.* **3** An **engineer** is a person who is responsible for maintaining the engine of a ship while it is at sea.
VERB [T] (**engineers, engineering, engineered**) **1** When a vehicle, bridge, or building **is engineered**, it is planned and constructed using scientific methods. ❑ *Its spaceship was engineered by Bert Rutan, renowned for designing the Voyager.* **2** If you **engineer** an event or situation, you arrange for it to happen, in a clever or indirect way. ❑ *The takeover was engineered by company directors.*

✪ **en·gi·neer·ing** ◆◇◇ /ˌendʒɪ'nɪərɪŋ/ NOUN [U] **Engineering** is the work involved in designing and constructing engines and machinery or structures such as roads and bridges. **Engineering** is also the subject studied by people who want to do this work. ❑ *graduates with degrees in engineering* ❑ *the design and engineering of aircraft and space vehicles*
→ See also **genetic engineering**

✪ **en·hance** ◆◇◇ /ɪn'hɑːns, -'hæns/ VERB [T] (**enhances, enhancing, enhanced**) (*academic word*) To **enhance** something means to improve its value, quality, or attractiveness. = improve, enrich ❑ *The White House is eager to protect and enhance that reputation.* ❑ *The superb sets are enhanced by Bobby Crossman's marvellous costumes.*

✪ **en·hance·ment** ◆◇◇ /ɪn'hɑːnsmənt, -'hæns-/ NOUN [C, U] (**enhancements**) (*formal*) The **enhancement of** something is the improvement of it in relation to its value, quality, or attractiveness. = improvement ❑ *Music is merely an enhancement to the power of her words.* ❑ *the enhancement of the human condition*

enig·ma /ɪ'nɪgmə/ NOUN [C] (**enigmas**) [usu sing] If you describe something or someone as an **enigma**, you mean they are mysterious or difficult to understand. = mystery ❑ *Iran remains an enigma for the outside world.*

en·joy ◆◆◇ /ɪn'dʒɔɪ/ VERB [T] (**enjoys, enjoying, enjoyed**) **1** If you **enjoy** something, you find pleasure and satisfaction in doing it or experiencing it. ❑ *Ross had always enjoyed the company of women.* ❑ *He was a guy who enjoyed life to the full.* **2** If you **enjoy yourself**, you do something that you like doing or you take pleasure in the situation that you are in. ❑ *I am really enjoying myself at the moment.* **3** (*formal*) If you **enjoy** something such as a right, benefit, or privilege, you have it. ❑ *The average German will enjoy 40 days' paid holiday this year.*

en·joy·able /ɪn'dʒɔɪəbəl/ ADJ Something that is **enjoyable** gives you pleasure. ❑ *It was much more enjoyable than I had expected.*

en·joy·ment /ɪn'dʒɔɪmənt/ NOUN [U] **Enjoyment** is the feeling of pleasure and satisfaction that you have when you do or experience something that you like. ❑ *I apologize if your enjoyment of the film was spoiled.*

✪ **en·large** /ɪn'lɑːdʒ/ VERB [I, T] (**enlarges, enlarging, enlarged**) **1** [I, T] When you **enlarge** something or when it **enlarges**, it becomes bigger. ❑ *The college has announced its intention to enlarge its stadium.* ❑ *The glands in the neck may enlarge.* ❑ *the use of silicone to enlarge the breasts* **2** [i] *(formal)* If you **enlarge on** something that has been mentioned, you give more details about it. = expand ❑ *He didn't enlarge on the form that the interim government and assembly would take.*

⊙ **en·large·ment** /ɪnˈlɑːdʒmənt/ NOUN [u, c] **(enlargements)** **1** [u] The **enlargement of** something is the process or result of making it bigger. ❑ *There is insufficient space for enlargement of the buildings.* ❑ *EU enlargement is a process that is not yet complete.* **2** [c] An **enlargement** is a photograph that has been made bigger. ❑ *Ordering reprints and enlargements is easier than ever.*

en·light·en /ɪnˈlaɪtən/ VERB [T] **(enlightens, enlightening, enlightened)** *(formal)* To **enlighten** someone means to give them more knowledge and greater understanding about something. ❑ *A few dedicated doctors have fought for years to enlighten the profession.*

en·light·en·ing /ɪnˈlaɪtənɪŋ/ ADJ ❑ *an enlightening talk on the work done at the zoo*

en·light·ened /ɪnˈlaɪtənd/ ADJ *(approval)* If you describe someone or their attitudes as **enlightened**, you mean that they have sensible, modern attitudes and ways of dealing with things. ❑ *an enlightened policy*

en·list /ɪnˈlɪst/ VERB [I, T] **(enlists, enlisting, enlisted)** **1** [I, T] If someone **enlists** or is **enlisted**, they join the army, navy, or air force. ❑ *He enlisted in the 82nd Airborne 20 years ago.* ❑ *He enlisted as a private in the Mexican War.* **2** [T] If you **enlist** the help of someone, you persuade them to help or support you in doing something. ❑ *I had to cut down a tree and enlist the help of seven neighbours to get it out of the garden!*

en·liv·en /ɪnˈlaɪvən/ VERB [T] **(enlivens, enlivening, enlivened)** To **enliven** events, situations, or people means to make them more lively or cheerful. ❑ *Even the most boring meeting was enlivened by Dan's presence.*

⊙ **enor·mous** ◆◇◇ /ɪˈnɔːməs/ ADJ *(academic word)* **1** Something that is **enormous** is extremely large in size or amount. = vast, tremendous, huge; ≠ tiny ❑ *The main bedroom is enormous.* ❑ *New technology means that it is possible to send enormous amounts of information at once.* **2** You can use **enormous** to emphasize the great degree or extent of something. = great, significant ❑ *It was an enormous disappointment.* ❑ *This drug holds enormous potential for the treatment of strokes.*

⊙ **enor·mous·ly** /ɪˈnɔːməsli/ ADV = hugely, greatly, incredibly, dramatically, significantly ❑ *This book was enormously influential.* ❑ *Blood levels can vary enormously throughout a 24-hour period.*

VOCABULARY BUILDER

enormous ADJ
Something that is **enormous** is extremely large in size or amount.
❑ *The government last night came under enormous pressure to make concessions over its welfare bill.*

colossal ADJ
If you describe something as **colossal**, you are emphasizing that it is very large. It is used to indicate disapproval.
❑ *In my opinion this inquest was a colossal waste of taxpayers' money.*

huge ADJ
Something or someone that is **huge** is extremely large in size or number.
❑ *There was a huge crowd of reporters waiting to greet him.*

gigantic ADJ
If you describe something as **gigantic**, you are emphasizing that it is extremely large in size. It is mainly used to describe physical objects.
❑ *This gigantic statue of a man stood astride the entrance to the port, welcoming sailors home.*

massive ADJ
Something that is **massive** is very large in size, quantity, or extent.
❑ *These proposals are intended to accommodate a massive increase in air traffic by 2030.*

immense ADJ
If you describe something as **immense**, you mean that it is extremely large or great. It is often used with abstract nouns.
❑ *In the early days, we felt an immense pride in our work.*

tremendous ADJ
You use **tremendous** to emphasize how large an amount is.
❑ *A tremendous amount of research is being made into this aspect of the illness in an attempt to find an answer.*

VOCABULARY BUILDER

enormously ADV
You use **enormously** to emphasize the great degree or extent of something.
❑ *It's one of those operas that was enormously popular in its own day but has since fallen into neglect.*

hugely ADV
You use **hugely** to show the great extent to which something is true.
❑ *Williams is the author of TV and stage plays and several hugely successful novels.*

greatly ADV *(formal, written)*
You use **greatly** to emphasize the degree or extent of something.
❑ *Their humanitarian response will be greatly appreciated in the small community.*

incredibly ADV
You use **incredibly** to emphasize how large, true, or intense something is.
❑ *It is still incredibly difficult to recruit people with the right mix of technical skills and commercial experience.*

dramatically ADV
You use **dramatically** to emphasize how noticeable or surprising something is.
❑ *The message is clear: eating healthily can dramatically reduce your risk of a heart attack.*

significantly ADV
You use **significantly** to indicate that something is large enough to be important or to affect a situation to a noticeable degree.
❑ *The number of applicants increased significantly from 1977 to 1981.*

enough ◆◆◆ /ɪˈnʌf/ DET, ADV, PRON, QUANT, ADJ
DET **1** **Enough** means as much as you need or as much as is necessary. ❑ *They had enough cash for a one-way ticket.* **2** You use **enough** to mean that you do not want something to continue any longer or get any worse. ❑ *Would you shut up, please! I'm having enough trouble with these children!* **ADV** **1** You use **enough** to mean that you have done something as much as you need or as much as is necessary. ❑ *I was old enough to work and earn money.* ❑ *Do you believe that sentences for criminals are tough enough at present?* **2** [ADJ + enough] You can use **enough** to mean that you do not want something to continue any longer or get any worse. ❑ *I'm serious, things are difficult enough as they are.* **3** [ADJ/ADV + enough] You can use **enough** to say that something is the case to a moderate or fairly large degree. ❑ *Winters is a common enough surname.* **4** You use **enough** in expressions such as **strangely enough** and **interestingly enough** to indicate that you think a fact is strange or interesting. ❑ *Strangely enough, the last thing he thought of was his beloved Tanya.*

e

PRON **1** **Enough** means as much as you need or as much as is necessary. ❑ *Although the police say efforts are being made, they are not doing enough.* **2** If you say that something is **enough**, you mean that you do not want it to continue any longer or get any worse. ❑ *I met him only the once, and that was enough.* ❑ *I think I have said enough.* **PHRASE** **have had enough** If you say that you **have had enough**, you mean that you are unhappy with a situation and you want it to stop. ❑ *I had had enough of other people for one night.*

QUANT **1** [enough 'of' DEF-N] **Enough of** something means as much as you need or as much as is necessary. ❑ *All parents worry about whether their child is getting enough of the right foods.* **2** [enough 'of' DEF-N] If you have had **enough** of something, you do not want it to continue any longer or get any worse. ❑ *Ann had heard enough of this.*

ADJ [N + enough] **Enough** means as much as you need or as much as is necessary. ❑ *Her disappearance and death would give proof enough of Charles' guilt.*

✦ **fair enough** → see **fair**; **sure enough** → see **sure**

en·quire /ɪnˈkwaɪə/ → See **inquire**

en·quiry /ɪnˈkwaɪəri/ → See **inquiry**

en·rage /ɪnˈreɪdʒ/ VERB [T] (**enrages, enraging, enraged**) If you **are enraged** by something, it makes you extremely angry. ❑ *Many were enraged by the discriminatory practice.*

en·rich /ɪnˈrɪtʃ/ VERB [T] (**enriches, enriching, enriched**) **1** To **enrich** something means to improve its quality, usually by adding something to it. ❑ *It is important to enrich the soil prior to planting.* **2** To **enrich** someone means to increase the amount of money that they have. ❑ *He will drain, rather than enrich, the country.*

en·rich·ment /ɪnˈrɪtʃmənt/ NOUN [U] **Enrichment** is the act of enriching someone or something or the state of being enriched. ❑ *the enrichment of society*

en·rol /ɪnˈrəʊl/ (*BrE*; in *AmE*, use **enroll**) VERB [I, T] (**enrols, enrolling, enrolled**) If you **enrol** or **are enrolled** at an institution or in a class, you officially join it. ❑ *Cherny was enrolled at the University in 1945.* ❑ *Her mother enrolled her in acting classes.*

en·rol·ment /ɪnˈrəʊlmənt/ (*BrE*; in *AmE*, use **enrollment**) NOUN [U] **1** **Enrolment** is the act of enrolling at an institution or in a class. ❑ *A fee is charged for each year of study and is payable at enrolment.* **2** **Enrolment** is the total number of students enrolled. ❑ *The district's enrolment is expected to stabilize in 2006–07 at 10,200 students.*

❂ **en·sure** ◆◆◇ /ɪnˈʃʊə/ VERB [T] (**ensures, ensuring, ensured**) (*academic word, formal*) To **ensure** something, or to **ensure that** something happens, means to make certain that it happens. = guarantee ❑ *We must ensure that all patients have access to high quality care.* ❑ *Britain's negotiators had ensured that the treaty was a significant change in direction.* ❑ *Ensure that it is written into your contract.*

en·tail /ɪnˈteɪl/ VERB [T] (**entails, entailing, entailed**) (*formal*) If one thing **entails** another, it involves it or causes it. ❑ *Such a decision would entail a huge political risk in the midst of the presidential campaign.*

en·tan·gle /ɪnˈtæŋɡəl/ VERB [T] (**entangles, entangling, entangled**) **1** If one thing **entangles itself with** another, the two things become caught together very tightly. ❑ *The blade of the oar had entangled itself with the strap of her bag.* **2** If something **entangles** you **in** problems or difficulties, it causes you to become involved in problems or difficulties from which it is hard to escape. ❑ *Bureaucracy can entangle applications for months.*

❂ **en·ter** ◆◆◇ /ˈentə/ VERB

VERB [I, T] (**enters, entering, entered**) **1** [I, T] (*formal*) When you **enter** a place such as a room or building, you go into it or come into it. ≠ leave, exit ❑ *He entered the room briskly and stood near the door.* ❑ *Anyone without an ID badge is required to sign in before entering the building.* ❑ *the number of illegal immigrants entering the EU* ❑ *When Spinks entered they all turned to look at him.* **2** [T] If you **enter** an organization or institution, you start to work there or become a member of it. ❑ *He entered the firm as a junior associate.* **3** [T] If something new **enters** your mind, you suddenly think about it. = cross ❑ *Dreadful doubts began*

to enter my mind. **4** [T] If it does not **enter** your head **to** do, think, or say something, you do not think of doing that thing although you should have. ❑ *It never enters his mind that anyone is better than him.* **5** [T] If someone or something **enters** a particular situation or period of time, they start to be in it or part of it. ❑ *The war has entered its second month.* ❑ *A million young people enter the labour market each year.* **6** [T] If you **enter** a competition, race, or examination, you officially state that you will compete or take part in it. ❑ *I run so well I'm planning to enter some races.* ❑ *As a boy soprano he entered many competitions, winning several gold medals.* ❑ *To enter, simply complete the coupon on page 150.* **7** [T] If you **enter** someone **for** a race or competition, you officially state that they will compete or take part in it. ❑ *His wife Marie secretly entered him for the championship.* **8** [T] If you **enter** something in a notebook, register, or financial account, you write it down. ❑ *Each week she meticulously entered in her notebooks all sums received.* **9** [T] To **enter** information **into** a computer or database means to record it there by typing it on a keyboard. = key, input ❑ *When a baby is born, they enter that baby's name into the computer.* ❑ *Postcodes will be entered into the statisticians' computers.* ❑ *A lot less time is now spent entering the data.*

PHRASAL VERB **enter into** (*formal*) If you **enter into** something such as an agreement, discussion, or relationship, you become involved in it. You can also say that two people **enter into** something. ❑ *I have not entered into any financial agreements with them.* ❑ *The United States and Canada may enter into an agreement that would allow easier access to jobs across the border.*

WHICH WORD?
enter or go into?

Enter is a rather formal word, and you do not usually use it in conversation. Instead you say that someone **goes into** (or **comes into**) a room or building.

❑ *He shut the street door behind me as I* **went in**.

You never say that someone 'enters' a car, train, ship, or plane.

USAGE NOTE
enter

You usually say that someone 'starts' school, college, or university. Do not use 'enter school' or 'enter into university'.

We **started school** *together when I was five.*

❂ **en·ter·prise** ◆◇◇ /ˈentəpraɪz/ NOUN [C, U] (**enterprises**) **1** [C] (*business*) An **enterprise** is a company or business, often a small one. = business, company ❑ *There are plenty of small industrial enterprises.* ❑ *one of Japan's most profitable enterprises* **2** [C] An **enterprise** is something new, difficult, or important that you do or try to do. = venture ❑ *Horse breeding is indeed a risky enterprise.* **3** [U] (*business*) **Enterprise** is the activity of managing companies and businesses and starting new ones. ❑ *He is still involved in voluntary work promoting local enterprise.* **4** [U] **Enterprise** is the ability to think of new and effective things to do, together with an eagerness to do them. ❑ *the spirit of enterprise worthy of a free and industrious people*

en·ter·pris·ing /ˈentəpraɪzɪŋ/ ADJ An **enterprising** person is willing to try out new, unusual ways of doing or achieving something. ❑ *Some enterprising members found ways of reducing their expenses or raising their incomes.*

en·ter·tain ◆◇◇ /ˌentəˈteɪn/ VERB [I, T] (**entertains, entertaining, entertained**) **1** [I, T] If a performer, performance, or activity **entertains** you, it amuses you, interests you, or gives you pleasure. ❑ *They were entertained by top singers, dancers and celebrities.* **2** [I, T] If you **entertain**, or **entertain** people, you provide food and drink for them, for example when you have invited them to your house. ❑ *I don't like to entertain guests anymore.* ❑ *He loves to entertain.* **3** [T] (*formal*) If you **entertain** an idea or suggestion, you allow yourself to consider it as possible or as worth thinking about seriously. ❑ *How foolish I am to entertain doubts.*

E

en·ter·tain·ing /ˌentəˈteɪnɪŋ/ ADJ ☐ To generate new money the sport needs to be more entertaining.

◆**en·ter·tain·ment** ◆◇◇ /ˌentəˈteɪnmənt/ NOUN [C, U] (entertainments) **Entertainment** consists of performances of plays and films, and activities such as reading and watching television, that give people pleasure. ☐ the world of entertainment and international stardom ☐ restaurants that provide entertainment as well as food

en·thu·si·asm ◆◇◇ /ɪnˈθjuːziæzəm, AmE -ˈθuː-/ NOUN [C, U] (enthusiasms) **1** [C, U] **Enthusiasm** is great eagerness to be involved in a particular activity that you like and enjoy or that you think is important. ☐ Their skill and enthusiasm has got them on the team. **2** [C] An **enthusiasm** is an activity or subject that interests you very much and that you spend a lot of time on. = interest ☐ Draw him out about his current enthusiasms and future plans.

en·thu·si·ast /ɪnˈθjuːziæst, AmE -ˈθuː-/ NOUN [C] (enthusiasts) An **enthusiast** is a person who is very interested in a particular activity or subject and who spends a lot of time on it. ☐ He is a great sports enthusiast.

en·thu·si·as·tic /ɪnˌθjuːziˈæstɪk, AmE -ˌθuː-/ ADJ If you are **enthusiastic about** something, you show how much you like or enjoy it by the way that you behave and talk. = excited ☐ Tom was very enthusiastic about the place.
en·thu·si·as·ti·cal·ly /ɪnˌθjuːziˈæstɪkli, AmE -ˌθuː-/ ADV ☐ The announcement was greeted enthusiastically.

en·tice /ɪnˈtaɪs/ VERB [T] (entices, enticing, enticed) To **entice** someone **to** go somewhere or **to** do something means to try to persuade them to go to that place or to do that thing. = lure ☐ They'll entice thousands of doctors to move from the cities to the rural areas by paying them better salaries. ☐ Retailers have tried almost everything, from cheap credit to free flights, to entice shoppers through their doors.

en·tic·ing /ɪnˈtaɪsɪŋ/ ADJ Something that is **enticing** is extremely attractive and makes you want to get it or to become involved with it. ☐ A prospective premium of about 30 per cent on their initial investment is enticing.

◆**en·tire** ◆◆◇ /ɪnˈtaɪə/ ADJ [DET + entire] (emphasis) You use **entire** when you want to emphasize that you are referring to the whole of something, for example, the whole of a place, time, or population. = whole, complete, total; ≠ partial, limited ☐ He had spent his entire life in China as a doctor. ☐ There are only 60 swimming pools in the entire country. ☐ The Great Barrier Reef runs almost the entire length of Queensland. ☐ three per cent of the entire Scottish population

◆**en·tire·ly** ◆◇◇ /ɪnˈtaɪəli/ ADV **1** **Entirely** means completely and not just partly. = completely, totally; ≠ partly, partially, slightly ☐ an entirely new approach ☐ Their price depended almost entirely on their scarcity. ☐ The two operations achieve entirely different results. ☐ This administration is not entirely free of suspicion. **2** **Entirely** is also used to emphasize what you are saying. ☐ I agree entirely.

◆**en·ti·tle** ◆◇◇ /ɪnˈtaɪtəl/ VERB [T] (entitles, entitling, entitled) **1** If you **are entitled to** something, you have the right to have it or do it. ☐ If the warranty is limited, the terms may entitle you to a replacement or refund. ☐ They are entitled to first class travel. ☐ There is no document stating we are clearly entitled to vote in this election. ☐ It is a democracy and people are entitled to express their views. **2** If the title of something such as a book, film, or painting is, for example, 'Sunrise', you can say that it **is entitled** 'Sunrise'. ☐ a performance entitled 'United States' ☐ a 1953 article entitled 'A Cognitive Theory of Dreams'

WORD CONNECTIONS
ADV + **entitle**
legally entitle **constitutionally** entitle **fully** entitle ☐ You are legally entitled to a refund or replacement if goods are faulty.
provisionally entitle ☐ She is planning to publish a book provisionally entitled 'A Little Modesty'.

◆**en·ti·tle·ment** /ɪnˈtaɪtəlmənt/ NOUN [C, U] (entitlements) (formal) An **entitlement to** something is the right to have it or do it. ☐ They lose their entitlement to welfare when they start work. ☐ All pupils share the same statutory entitlement to a broad and balanced curriculum.

◆**en·tity** /ˈentɪti/ NOUN [C] (entities) (academic word, formal) An **entity** is something that exists separately from other things and has a clear identity of its own. ☐ The Earth as a living entity ☐ the designation of Kurdistan as a separate federal entity with its own parliament

◆**en·trance** ◆◇◇ NOUN, VERB
NOUN /ˈentrəns/ [C, U, SING] (entrances) **1** [C] The **entrance to** a place is the way into it, for example, a door or gate. = entry; ≠ exit ☐ Beside the entrance to the church, turn right. ☐ He was driven out of a side entrance with his hand covering his face. ☐ A marble entrance hall leads to a sitting room. **2** [C] You can refer to someone's arrival in a place as their **entrance**, especially when you think that they are trying to be noticed and admired. = entry; ≠ exit ☐ If she had noticed her father's entrance, she gave no indication. **3** [C] When a performer makes his or her **entrance** onto the stage, he or she comes onto the stage. = entry; ≠ exit ☐ When he made his entrance on stage there was an uproar. **4** [U] (formal) If you gain **entrance to** a particular place, you manage to get in there. = entry ☐ Hewitt had gained entrance to the Hall by pretending to be a heating engineer. **5** [U] If you gain **entrance to** a particular profession, society, or institution, you are accepted as a member of it. ☐ Many students have insufficient science and mathematics background to gain entrance to engineering school. **6** [SING] If you make an **entrance into** a particular activity or system, you succeed in becoming involved in it. = entry ☐ The acquisition helped BCCI make its initial entrance into the US market.
VERB /ɪnˈtrɑːns, -ˈtræns/ [T] (entrances, entrancing, entranced) If something or someone **entrances** you, they cause you to feel delight and wonder, often so that all your attention is taken up and you cannot think about anything else. = enchant ☐ As soon as I met Dick, he entranced me because he has a lovely voice.
en·tranced /ɪnˈtrɑːnst, -ˈtrænst/ ADJ ☐ He is entranced by the kindness of her smile.

◆**en·tre·pre·neur** /ˌɒntrəprəˈnɜː/ NOUN [C] (entrepreneurs) An **entrepreneur** is a person who sets up businesses and business deals. ☐ The two Sydney-based entrepreneurs founded the company in 1995. ☐ the financial incentives for successful entrepreneurs to innovate and invest

◆**en·tre·pre·neur·ial** /ˌɒntrəprəˈnɜːriəl/ ADJ (business) **Entrepreneurial** means having the qualities that are needed to succeed as an entrepreneur. = business ☐ her prodigious entrepreneurial flair ☐ His initial entrepreneurial venture was setting up Britain's first computer-dating agency. ☐ Germany's entrepreneurial culture is less vigorous than it was.

◆**en·tre·pre·neur·ship** /ˌɒntrəprəˈnɜːʃɪp/ NOUN [U] **Entrepreneurship** is the state of being an entrepreneur, or the activities associated with being an entrepreneur. ☐ When we encourage entrepreneurship, we also encourage risk taking. ☐ measures to encourage innovation and entrepreneurship among small firms

en·trust /ɪnˈtrʌst/ VERB [T] (entrusts, entrusting, entrusted) If you **entrust** something important to someone or **entrust** them **with** it, you make them responsible for looking after it or dealing with it. ☐ He entrusted his cash to a business partner for investment in a series of projects. ☐ They can be entrusted to solve major national problems.

en·try ◆◆◇ /ˈentri/ NOUN
NOUN [U, C, SING] (entries) **1** [U] If you gain **entry to** a particular place, you are able to go in. = entrance ☐ You can gain entry to the club only through a member. ☐ Entry to the museum is free. **2** [C] You can refer to someone's arrival in a place as their **entry**, especially when you think that they are trying to be noticed and admired. = entrance ☐ He made his triumphal entry into Mexico City. **3** [U] Someone's **entry into** a particular society or group is their joining of it. = entrance ☐ China's entry into the World

WORDS IN CONTEXT: ENVIRONMENT

We have enjoyed enormous improvements to our standard of living in recent years. However, if we wish to continue benefiting in this way, we have to accept the damaging impact this will have on the environment.

To what extent do you agree or disagree?

Western societies have witnessed a dramatic improvement in living standards during the past 50–60 years. We travel to countries that were once out of our reach, we commute to and from work in our comfortable cars, and we use our modern kitchen appliances to cook food that has been flown across the world from distant countries.

However, the **environmental impact** of this activity has been very damaging. This growth in air travel and vehicle use, along with the huge increase in industrial and agricultural production, has led to a growth in **greenhouse gas emissions** and damage to the earth's **ozone layer**. This has resulted in significant **climate change** and **global warming**, which some experts believe is causing **natural disasters** such as **floods** and **famines**.

Is it possible to advance economically without causing further environmental harm? **Conservation** has certainly become a key political issue. We are more aware of the consequences of unchecked growth on the earth's **natural resources**, and harnessing **sustainable sources of energy** is a high priority for many. **Environmentalists** campaign around issues such as **deforestation**, the environmental impact of **fossil fuels** and the destruction of the **natural habitat** of many of our **endangered species**. In addition, we all know the importance of **recycling** and **energy efficiency**.

Hopefully, further changes in attitudes and advances in science and technology will allow us to enjoy a comfortable lifestyle without causing harm to our environment.

Trade Organization **4** [C] An **entry** in a diary, account book, computer file, or reference book is a short piece of writing in it. ▢ *Violet's diary entry for 20 April 1917 records Brigit admitting to the affair.* **5** [C] An **entry for** a competition is a piece of work, a story or drawing, or the answers to a set of questions, which you complete in order to take part in the competition. ▢ *The closing date for entries is 31 December.* **6** [SING] Journalists sometimes use **entry** to refer to the total number of people taking part in an event or competition. For example, if a competition has an **entry** of twenty people, twenty people take part in it. ▢ *Our competition has attracted a huge entry.* **7** [U] **Entry** in a competition is the act of taking part in it. ▢ *Entry to this competition is by invitation only.* **8** [C] The **entry to** a place is the way into it, for example a door or gate. = entrance ▢ *the towering marble archway that marked the entry to the Pelican Point development*

PHRASE **no entry** No Entry is used on signs to indicate that you are not allowed to go into a particular area or go through a particular door or gate.

en·vel·op /ɪnˈveləp/ VERB [T] (**envelops, enveloping, enveloped**) If one thing **envelops** another, it covers or surrounds it completely. ▢ *That lovely, rich fragrant smell of the forest enveloped us.*

en·ve·lope /ˈenvələʊp, ˈɒn-/ NOUN
NOUN [C] (**envelopes**) An **envelope** is the rectangular paper cover in which you send a letter to someone through the mail.

PHRASE **push the envelope** If someone **pushes the envelope**, they do something to a greater degree or in a more extreme way than it has ever been done before. ▢ *There's a valuable place for fashion and design that pushes the envelope a bit.*

en·vi·ous /ˈenviəs/ ADJ If you are **envious of** someone, you want something that they have. ▢ *I don't think I'm envious of your success.* ▢ *Do I sound envious? I pity them, actually.*

en·vi·ous·ly /ˈenviəsli/ ADV [enviously with v] ▢ *'You haven't changed,' I am often enviously told.*

✪**en·vi·ron·ment** ♦♦◇ /ɪnˈvaɪərənmənt/ NOUN [C, U, SING] (**environments**) (*academic word*) **1** [C, U] Someone's **environment** is all the circumstances, people, things, and events around them that influence their life. = surroundings, setting, background ▢ *Students in our*

schools are taught in a safe, secure environment. ▢ *The moral characters of men are formed not by heredity but by environment.* **2** [C] Your **environment** consists of the particular natural surroundings in which you live or exist, considered in relation to their physical characteristics or weather conditions. ▢ *a safe environment for marine mammals* **3** [SING] The **environment** is the natural world of land, sea, air, plants, and animals. = the wild, the natural world, the countryside ▢ *persuading people to respect the environment* ▢ *the need to protect the environment* ▢ *Their aim is to increase income from tourism without damaging the environment.*

USAGE NOTE

the environment

Remember that when you use **the environment** to talk about the natural world, you always need to use the definite article 'the'.

*As a shopper you can help to protect **the environment** through your spending decisions.*

WORD CONNECTIONS

ADJ + **environment**

a **safe** environment
a **secure** environment
a **supportive** environment

▢ *Research suggests that prisoners who return to a supportive environment are six times less likely to re-offend than those lacking support.*

the **natural** environment

▢ *People are going to have to be much more restrained in their behaviour if the natural environment is going to survive.*

VERB + **environment**

protect the environment
preserve the environment
conserve the environment

▢ *There should be more laws to protect the environment.*

damage the environment
pollute the environment
harm the environment

▢ *Toxic chemicals in batteries pollute the environment if they are not disposed of properly.*

WORD FAMILIES	
environment NOUN	Oil spills are disastrous for the **environment**.
environmental ADJ	There is concern about the **environmental** impact of new road building.
environmentally ADV	The new homes will be **environmentally** friendly, with low carbon emissions.
environmentalist NOUN	**Environmentalists** fear that the mine will destroy the habitats of grizzly bears.

◆**en·vi·ron·men·tal** ♦♦◇ /ɪnˌvaɪərən'mentəl/ ADJ
1 [environmental + N] **Environmental** means concerned with the protection of the natural world of land, sea, air, plants, and animals. ❏ Environmental groups plan to stage public protests during the conference. **2** [environmental + N] **Environmental** means relating to or caused by the surroundings in which someone lives or something exists. ❏ It protects against environmental hazards such as wind and sun. ❏ the environmental impact of buildings and transport systems

◆**en·vi·ron·men·tal·ly** /ɪnˌvaɪərən'mentəli/ ADV ❏ the high price of environmentally friendly goods ❏ encourage builders to make environmentally sound homes

◆**en·vi·ron·men·tal·ist** /ɪnˌvaɪərən'mentəlɪst/ NOUN [C] (**environmentalists**) An **environmentalist** is a person who is concerned with protecting and preserving the natural environment, for example, by preventing pollution. = conservationist ❏ Environmentalists fear that the mine will destroy the habitats of grizzly bears.

◆**en·vis·age** /ɪn'vɪzɪdʒ/ VERB [T] (**envisages, envisaging, envisaged**) If you **envisage** something, you imagine that it is true, real, or likely to happen. = imagine, envision ❏ He envisages the possibility of establishing direct diplomatic relations in the future. ❏ He had never envisaged spending the whole of his working life in that particular job. ❏ The plan envisaged the creation of an independent state.

en·voy /'envɔɪ/ NOUN [C] (**envoys**) **1** An **envoy** is someone who is sent as a representative from one government or political group to another. ❏ A US envoy is expected in the region this month to collect responses to the proposal. **2** An **envoy** is a diplomat in an embassy who is immediately below the ambassador in rank.

envy /'envi/ NOUN, VERB
NOUN [U, SING] **1** [U] **Envy** is the feeling you have when you wish you could have the same thing or quality that someone else has. ❏ Gradually he began to acknowledge his feelings of envy towards his mother. **2** [SING] If a thing or quality is **the envy of** someone, they wish very much that they could have or achieve it. ❏ Their economy is the envy of the developing world.
VERB [T] (**envies, envying, envied**) If you **envy** someone, you wish that you had the same things or qualities that they have. ❏ I don't envy the young ones who've become TV superstars and know no other world.

en·zyme /'enzaɪm/ NOUN [C] (**enzymes**) (technical) An **enzyme** is a chemical substance found in living creatures that produces changes in other substances without being changed itself.

epic /'epɪk/ NOUN, ADJ
NOUN [C] (**epics**) An **epic** is a long book, poem, or film whose story extends over a long period of time or tells of great events. ❏ the Middle High German epic, 'Nibelungenlied', written about 1200
ADJ **1** **Epic** is used to describe a long book, poem, or film whose story extends over a long period of time or tells of great events. ❏ epic narrative poems **2** Something that is **epic** is very large and impressive. ❏ Columbus's epic voyage of discovery

◆**epi·dem·ic** /ˌepɪ'demɪk/ NOUN [C] (**epidemics**) **1** If there is an **epidemic of** a particular disease somewhere, it affects a very large number of people there and spreads quickly to other areas. ❏ A flu epidemic is sweeping through Moscow. ❏ a killer epidemic of yellow fever ❏ A UN study warns the AIDs epidemic is nowhere near its peak. **2** If an activity that you disapprove of is increasing or spreading rapidly, you can refer to this as an **epidemic of** that activity. ❏ an epidemic of serial killings

epi·lep·sy /'epɪlepsi/ NOUN [U] **Epilepsy** is a brain condition that causes a person to suddenly lose consciousness and sometimes to have seizures. ❏ Shawna suffers from epilepsy.

epi·lep·tic /ˌepɪ'leptɪk/ ADJ, NOUN
ADJ **1** Someone who is **epileptic** suffers from epilepsy. ❏ He was epileptic and refused to take medication for his condition. **2** [epileptic + N] An **epileptic** seizure is caused by epilepsy. ❏ He suffered an epileptic seizure. NOUN [C] (**epileptics**) An **epileptic** is someone who is epileptic. ❏ His wife is an epileptic.

epi·sode /'epɪsəʊd/ NOUN [C] (**episodes**) **1** You can refer to an event or a short period of time as an **episode** if you want to suggest that it is important or unusual, or has some particular quality. ❏ This episode is bound to be a deep embarrassment for Washington. **2** An **episode** of something such as a series on television or a story in a magazine is one of the separate parts in which it is broadcast or published. = instalment ❏ The final episode will be shown next Sunday.

epito·me /ɪ'pɪtəmi/ NOUN [SING] (formal, emphasis) If you say that a person or thing is **the epitome of** something, you are emphasizing that they are the best possible example of it. ❏ Maureen was the epitome of sophistication.

epito·mize /ɪ'pɪtəmaɪz/ also **epitomise** VERB [T] (**epitomizes, epitomizing, epitomized**) If you say that something or someone **epitomizes** a particular thing, you mean that they are a perfect example of it. ❏ Seafood is a regional speciality epitomized by Captain Anderson's Restaurant.

◆**equal** ♦◇◇ /'iːkwəl/ ADJ, NOUN, VERB
ADJ **1** If two things are **equal** or if one thing is **equal** to another, they are the same in size, number, standard, or value. = the same, identical, equivalent; ≠ unequal, differing, contrasting ❏ Investors can borrow an amount equal to the property's purchase price. ❏ in a population having equal numbers of men and women ❏ Research and teaching are of equal importance. **2** If different groups of people have **equal** rights or are given **equal** treatment, they have the same rights or are treated the same as each other, however different they are. ❏ We will be demanding equal rights at work. ❏ the commitment to equal opportunities **3** [V-LINK + equal] If you say that people are **equal**, you mean that they have or should have the same rights and opportunities as each other. ❏ We are equal in every way. ❏ At any gambling game, everyone is equal. **4** [V-LINK + equal 'to' N] If someone is **equal to** a particular job or situation, they have the necessary ability, strength, or courage to deal successfully with it. ❏ She was determined that she would be equal to any test the corporation put to them.
PHRASE **other things being equal** or **all things being equal** If you say 'other things being equal' or 'all things being equal' when talking about a possible situation, you mean if nothing unexpected happens or if there are no other factors that affect the situation. ❏ It appears reasonable to assume that, other things being equal, most hostel tenants would prefer single to shared rooms.
NOUN [C] (**equals**) Someone who is your **equal** has the same ability, status, or rights as you have. ❏ She was one of the boys, their equal.
VERB [LINK, T] (**equals, equalling, equalled**) **1** [LINK] If something **equals** a particular number or amount, it is the same as that amount or the equivalent of that amount. ❏ 9 per cent interest less 7 per cent inflation equals 2 per cent. ❏ The average pay rise equalled 1.41 times inflation. **2** [T] To **equal** something or someone means to be as good or as great as them. ❏ The victory equalled the team's best in history.

WORD FAMILIES	
equal ADJ	Women want **equal** opportunities at work.
equally ADV	All of these techniques are **equally** effective.

e

equality NOUN	Women had not achieved full legal and social **equality** in America by the 1930s.
inequality NOUN	People are concerned about corruption and social **inequality**.

✪**equal·i·ty** /ɪˈkwɒliti/ NOUN [U] **Equality** is the same status, rights, and responsibilities for all the members of a society, group, or family. = fairness, equity; ≠ inequality ❑ equality of the sexes ❑ Women had not achieved full legal and social equality in America by the 1930s.

✪**equal·ly** ◆◇◇ /ˈiːkwəli/ ADV **1** **Equally** means in sections, amounts, or spaces that are the same size as each other. = evenly ❑ Try to get into the habit of eating at least three small meals a day, at equally spaced intervals. ❑ A bank's local market share tends to be divided equally between the local branch and branches located elsewhere. **2** **Equally** means to the same degree or extent. ❑ All these techniques are equally effective. **3** **Equally** is used to introduce another comment on the same topic, that balances or contrasts with the previous comment. ❑ Subscribers should be allowed call-blocking services, but equally, they should be able to choose whether to accept calls from blocked numbers.

equate /ɪˈkweɪt/ VERB [I, T] (**equates, equating, equated**) (academic word) If you **equate** one thing **with** another, or if you say that one thing **equates with** another, you believe that they are strongly connected. ❑ I'm always wary of men wearing suits, as I equate this with power and authority. ❑ The author doesn't equate liberalism and conservatism.

✪**equa·tion** /ɪˈkweɪʒən/ NOUN [C, U] (**equations**) (academic word) **1** [C] An **equation** is a mathematical statement saying that two amounts or values are the same, for example $6x4=12x2$. = formula ❑ He solved complex equations in his head. **2** [C] An **equation** is a situation in which two or more parts have to be considered together so that the whole situation can be understood or explained. ❑ The equation is simple: research breeds new products. ❑ The party fears the equation between higher spending and higher taxes. **3** [U] The **equation** of one thing **with** another is the act of stating that the two things are strongly connected. ❑ The equation of gangsterism with business in general in Coppola's film was intended to be subversive.

✪**equa·tor** /ɪˈkweɪtə/ NOUN [SING] The **equator** is an imaginary line around the middle of the earth at an equal distance from the North Pole and the South Pole. ❑ an orbit 22,000 miles above the Earth's equator ❑ Sarawak straddles the Equator and is hot and humid. ❑ the vernal and autumnal equinox, when the sun crosses the equator travelling north and south

equip /ɪˈkwɪp/ VERB [T] (**equips, equipping, equipped**) (academic word) **1** If you **equip** a person or thing **with** something, you give them the tools or equipment that are needed. ❑ They try to equip their vehicles with gadgets to deal with every possible contingency. ❑ Owners of restaurants have to equip them to admit disabled people. **2** If something **equips** you **for** a particular task or experience, it gives you the skills and attitudes you need for it, especially by educating you in a particular way. ❑ Relative poverty, however, did not prevent Martin from equipping himself with an excellent education.

✪**equip·ment** ◆◆◇ /ɪˈkwɪpmənt/ NOUN [U] (academic word) **Equipment** consists of the things that are used for a particular purpose, such as a hobby or job. = machinery, supplies, tools ❑ computers, electronic equipment and machine tools ❑ a shortage of medical equipment and medicine

USAGE NOTE
equipment
Equipment is an uncountable noun. Do not use 'equipments' or 'an equipment'. You can talk about a single item as a 'piece of equipment'. *This radio is an important **piece of equipment**.*

equi·ty ◆◇◇ /ˈekwɪti/ NOUN [U] (business) In finance, your **equity** is the sum of your assets, for example the value of your house, once your debts have been subtracted from it. ❑ To capture his equity, Murphy must either sell or refinance.

✪**equiva·lence** /ɪˈkwɪvələns/ NOUN [U] If there is **equivalence** between two things, they have the same use, function, size, or value. = equality ❑ the equivalence of science and rationality

✪**equiva·lent** ◆◇◇ /ɪˈkwɪvələnt/ NOUN, ADJ (academic word)

NOUN [SING, C] (**equivalents**) **1** [SING] If one amount or value is **the equivalent of** another, they are the same. ❑ Mr Li's pay is the equivalent of about $80 a month. ❑ The equivalent of two tablespoons of polyunsaturated oils is ample each day. ❑ Even the cheapest car costs the equivalent of 70 years' salary for a government worker. **2** [C] The **equivalent** of someone or something is a person or thing that has the same function in a different place, time, or system. = counterpart ❑ the Red Cross emblem, and its equivalent in Muslim countries, the Red Crescent **3** [SING] You can use **equivalent** to emphasize the great or severe effect of something. ❑ His party has just suffered the equivalent of a near-fatal heart attack.

ADJ **1** **Equivalent** means being the same value or amount as something else. = equal ❑ If they want to change an item in the budget, they will have to propose equivalent cuts elsewhere. **2** **Equivalent** is having the same function in a different place, time, or system. ❑ a decrease of 10% in property investment compared with the equivalent period in 1991

✪**era** ◆◇◇ /ˈɪərə/ NOUN [C] (**eras**) You can refer to a period of history or a long period of time as an **era** when you want to draw attention to a particular feature or quality that it has. = age, time, period ❑ the nuclear era ❑ the Reagan–Bush era ❑ It was an era of austerity.

✪**eradi·cate** /ɪˈrædɪkeɪt/ VERB [T] (**eradicates, eradicating, eradicated**) (formal) To **eradicate** something means to get rid of it completely. = eliminate ❑ They are already battling to eradicate illnesses such as malaria and tetanus. ❑ Vaccination has virtually eradicated anthrax in the developed world. ❑ a campaign that genuinely sought to eradicate poverty

✪**eradi·ca·tion** /ɪˌrædɪˈkeɪʃən/ NOUN [U] = elimination ❑ a significant contribution towards the eradication of corruption ❑ the polio eradication programme ❑ the eradication of child poverty

✪**erase** /ɪˈreɪz, AmE ɪˈreɪs/ VERB [T] (**erases, erasing, erased**) **1** If you **erase** a thought or feeling, you destroy it completely so that you can no longer remember something or no longer feel a particular emotion. ❑ They are desperate to erase the memory of that last defeat. **2** If you **erase** sound that has been recorded on a tape or information which has been stored in a computer, you completely remove or destroy it. = wipe, remove ❑ An intruder broke into the campaign headquarters and managed to erase 17,000 names from computer files. ❑ It appears the names were accidentally erased from computer disks. ❑ software tools that permanently erase single files or entire disks ❑ The job included erasing all email records. **3** If you **erase** something such as writing or a mark, you remove it, usually by rubbing it with a cloth. ❑ It was unfortunate that she had erased the message.

erect /ɪˈrekt/ VERB, ADJ

VERB [T] (**erects, erecting, erected**) **1** (formal) If people **erect** something such as a building, bridge, or barrier, they build it or create it. = construct ❑ Opposition demonstrators have erected barricades in roads leading to the parliament building. ❑ The building was erected in 1900–1901. **2** If you **erect** a system, a theory, or an institution, you create it. ❑ Japanese proprietors are erecting a complex infrastructure of political influence throughout America.

ADJ People or things that are **erect** are straight and upright. ❑ Stand reasonably erect, your arms hanging naturally.

✪**erode** /ɪˈrəʊd/ VERB [I, T] (**erodes, eroding, eroded**) (academic word) **1** If rock or soil **erodes** or **is eroded** by the weather, sea, or wind, it cracks and breaks so that it is gradually destroyed. = disintegrate, crumble, wear away ❑ The storm washed away buildings and roads and eroded beaches. ❑ By 1980, Miami beach had all but totally eroded.

❏ *Once exposed, soil is quickly eroded by wind and rain.*
2 *(formal)* If someone's authority, right, or confidence **erodes** or **is eroded**, it is gradually destroyed or removed. ❏ *His critics say his fumbling on the issue of reform has eroded his authority.* ❏ *America's belief in its own God-ordained uniqueness started to erode.* **3** If the value of something **erodes** or **is eroded** by something such as inflation or age, its value decreases. ❏ *Competition in the financial marketplace has eroded profits.* ❏ *The value of the dollar began to erode rapidly just around this time.*

◆**ero·sion** /ɪˈrəʊʒən/ NOUN [U] **1** Erosion is the gradual destruction and removal of rock or soil in a particular area by rivers, the sea, or the weather. = disintegration, weathering ❏ *erosion of the river valleys* ❏ *As their roots are strong and penetrating, they prevent erosion.* ❏ *soil erosion* **2** The **erosion of** a person's authority, rights, or confidence is the gradual destruction or removal of them. ❏ *the erosion of confidence in world financial markets* ❏ *the widespread erosion of civil liberties* ❏ *the rapid erosion of privacy rights* **3** The **erosion of** support, values, or money is a gradual decrease in its level or standard. ❏ *the erosion of moral standards* ❏ *a dramatic erosion of support for the programme*

erot·ic /ɪˈrɒtɪk/ ADJ If you describe something as **erotic**, you mean that it involves sexual feelings or arouses sexual desire. ❏ *It might sound like a fantasy, but it wasn't an erotic experience at all.*

er·rat·ic /ɪˈrætɪk/ ADJ Something that is **erratic** does not follow a regular pattern, but happens at unexpected times or moves along in an irregular way. = unpredictable ❏ *Argentina's erratic inflation rate threatens to upset the plans.*
er·rati·cal·ly /ɪˈrætɪkli/ ADV ❏ *Police stopped him for driving erratically.*

◆**er·ror** ◆◇◇ /ˈerə/ NOUN *(academic word)*
NOUN [C, U] **(errors)** An **error** is something you have done that is considered to be incorrect or wrong, or that should not have been done. = mistake ❏ *NASA discovered a mathematical error in its calculations.* ❏ *MPs attacked lax management and errors of judgment.* ❏ *the risk of making an error in testing a hypothesis*
PHRASES **in error** If you do something **in error** or if it happens **in error**, you do it or it happens because you have made a mistake, especially in your judgment. ❏ *The plane was shot down in error by a NATO missile.*
see the error of one's ways If someone sees **the error of their ways**, they realize or admit that they have made a mistake or behaved badly. ❏ *I wanted an opportunity to talk some sense into him and try to make him see the error of his ways.*

WORD CONNECTIONS
VERB + **error**
make an error
discover an error
correct an error
❏ *A few changes have been made to the original text to correct a few minor errors.*
ADJ + **error**
a basic error
a common error
❏ *Another common error drivers make is overloading the car.*
a serious error
a grave error
a fatal error
❏ *It would be a grave error to ignore this warning.*
a factual error
a grammatical error
a clerical error
❏ *The article contained several factual errors.*

erupt /ɪˈrʌpt/ VERB [I] **(erupts, erupting, erupted)**
1 When a volcano **erupts**, it throws out a lot of hot, melted rock called lava, as well as ash and steam. ❏ *The volcano erupted in 1980, devastating a large area of Washington state.* **2** *(journalism)* If violence or fighting

erupts, it suddenly begins or gets worse in an unexpected, violent way. = break out ❏ *Heavy fighting erupted there today after a two-day ceasefire.* **3** *(journalism)* When people in a place suddenly become angry or violent, you can say that they **erupt** or that the place **erupts**. ❏ *In Los Angeles, the area known as Watts erupted into riots.* **4** You say that someone **erupts** when they suddenly have a change in mood, usually becoming quite noisy. ❏ *Then, without warning, she erupts into laughter.*

erup·tion /ɪˈrʌpʃən/ NOUN [C, U] **(eruptions)** **1** [C, U] ❏ *the volcanic eruption of Tambora in 1815* **2** [C] ❏ *this sudden eruption of violence* **3** [C] ❏ *an eruption of despair*

es·ca·late /ˈeskəleɪt/ VERB [I, T] **(escalates, escalating, escalated)** *(journalism)* If a bad situation **escalates** or if someone or something **escalates** it, it becomes greater in size, seriousness, or intensity. ❏ *Both unions and management fear the dispute could escalate.* ❏ *The protests escalated into five days of rioting.*
es·ca·la·tion /ˌeskəˈleɪʃən/ NOUN [C, U] **(escalations)** ❏ *The threat of nuclear escalation remains.*

◆**es·cape** ◆◆◇ /ɪˈskeɪp/ VERB, NOUN, ADJ
VERB [I, T] **(escapes, escaping, escaped)** **1** [I] If you **escape from** a place, you succeed in getting away from it. ❏ *A prisoner has escaped from a jail in northern Texas.* ❏ *They are reported to have escaped to the other side of the border.* **2** [I, T] You can say that you **escape** when you survive something such as an accident. ❏ *The two officers were extremely lucky to escape serious injury.* ❏ *The man's girlfriend managed to escape unhurt.* **3** [T] If something **escapes** you or **escapes** your attention, you do not know about it, do not remember it, or do not notice it. ❏ *It was an actor whose name escapes me for the moment.* **4** [I] When gas, liquid, or heat **escapes**, it comes out from a pipe, container, or place. ❏ *Leave a vent open to let some moist air escape.*
NOUN [C] **(escapes)** **1** Someone's **escape** is the act of escaping from a particular place or situation. ❏ *The man made his escape.* **2** An **escape** is the act of surviving something such as an accident. ❏ *I hear you had a very narrow escape on the bridge.* **3** If something is an **escape**, it is a way of avoiding difficulties or responsibilities. ❏ *But for me television is an escape.*
ADJ [escape + N] You can use **escape** to describe things that allow you to avoid difficulties or problems. For example, an **escape route** is an activity or opportunity that lets you improve your situation. An **escape clause** is part of an agreement that allows you to avoid having to do something that you do not want to do. ❏ *We all need the occasional escape route from the boring, routine aspects of our lives.*

es·cort VERB, NOUN
VERB /ɪsˈkɔːt/ [T] **(escorts, escorting, escorted)** If you **escort** someone somewhere, you accompany them there, usually in order to make sure that they leave a place or get to their destination. ❏ *I escorted him to the door.*
NOUN /ˈeskɔːt/ [C] **(escorts)** **1** An **escort** is a person who travels with someone in order to protect or guard them. ❏ *He arrived with a police escort shortly before half past nine.* **2** An **escort** is a person who accompanies another person of the opposite sex to a social event. Sometimes people are paid to be escorts. ❏ *My sister needed an escort for a company dinner.*
PHRASE **under escort** If someone is taken somewhere **under escort**, they are accompanied by guards, either because they have been arrested or because they need to be protected.

◆**es·pe·cial·ly** ◆◆◇ /ɪˈspeʃəli/ ADV *(emphasis)*
1 [especially with CL/GROUP] You use **especially** to emphasize that what you are saying applies more to one person, thing, time, or area than to any others. = particularly ❏ *Millions of wild flowers colour the valleys, especially in April and May.* ❏ *Vitamin A deficiency is one of the most common causes of blindness in poor countries, especially in small children.* ❏ *Regular use of cannabis can damage the respiratory system, especially if it is smoked with tobacco.* **2** [especially + ADJ/ADV] You use **especially** to emphasize a characteristic or quality. = particularly ❏ *Babies lose heat much faster than adults, and are especially vulnerable to the cold in their first month.*

e

E

es·pio·nage /'espɪənɑːʒ/ NOUN [U] (formal) **Espionage** is the activity of finding out the political, military, or industrial secrets of your enemies or rivals by using spies. = spying ❑ *The authorities have arrested several people suspected of espionage.*

es·pouse /ɪ'spaʊz/ VERB [T] (**espouses, espousing, espoused**) (formal) If you **espouse** a particular policy, cause, or belief, you become very interested in it and give your support to it. ❑ *She ran away with him to Mexico and espoused the revolutionary cause.*

❂**es·say** /'eseɪ/ NOUN [C] (**essays**) **1** An **essay** is a short piece of writing on a particular subject written by a student. = assignment ❑ *We asked Jason to write an essay about his home town.* **2** An **essay** is a short piece of writing on a particular subject that is written by a writer for publication. ❑ *Thomas Malthus's essay on population*

es·sence /'esəns/ NOUN
NOUN [U, C] (**essences**) **1** [U] The **essence of** something is its basic and most important characteristic that gives it its individual identity. ❑ *The essence of consultation is to listen to, and take account of, the views of those consulted.* **2** [C, U] **Essence** is a very concentrated liquid that is used for flavouring food or for its smell. ❑ *a few drops of vanilla essence*
PHRASES **in essence** (formal, emphasis) You use **in essence** to emphasize that you are talking about the most important or central aspect of an idea, situation, or event. ❑ *Though complicated in detail, local taxes are in essence simple.* **of the essence** (formal) If you say that something **is of the essence**, you mean that it is absolutely necessary in order for a particular action to be successful. = crucial ❑ *Speed was of the essence in a project of this type.*

❂**es·sen·tial** /ɪ'senʃəl/ ADJ, NOUN
ADJ **1** Something that is **essential** is extremely important or absolutely necessary to a particular subject, situation, or activity. = crucial ❑ *It was absolutely essential to separate crops from the areas that animals used as pasture.* ❑ *As they must also sprint over short distances, speed is essential.* ❑ *Jordan promised to trim the city budget without cutting essential services.* **2** The **essential** aspects of something are its most basic or important aspects. = crucial, vital, fundamental, basic; ≠ inessential, unimportant ❑ *Most authorities agree that play is an essential part of a child's development.* ❑ *Tact and diplomacy are two essential ingredients in international relations.*
NOUN [C, PL] (**essentials**) **1** [C] The **essentials** are the things that are absolutely necessary for the situation you are in or for the task you are doing. ❑ *The apartment contained the basic essentials for bachelor life.* **2** [PL] The **essentials** are the most important principles, ideas, or facts of a particular subject. ❑ *the essentials of everyday life, such as eating and exercise*

es·sen·tial·ly /ɪ'senʃəli/ ADV (formal) **1** [essentially with CL/GROUP] (emphasis) You use **essentially** to emphasize a quality that someone or something has, and to say that it is their most important or basic quality. = fundamentally ❑ *It's been believed for centuries that great writers, composers, and scientists are essentially quite different from ordinary people.* **2** (vagueness) You use **essentially** to indicate that what you are saying is mainly true, although some parts of it are wrong or more complicated than has been stated. ❑ *His analysis of urban use of agricultural land has been proved essentially correct.*

❂**es·tab·lish** /ɪ'stæblɪʃ/ VERB [T, RECIP] (**establishes, establishing, established**) (academic word) **1** [T] If someone **establishes** something such as an organization, a type of activity, or a set of rules, they create it or introduce it in such a way that it is likely to last for a long time. = set up, found ❑ *The UN has established detailed criteria for who should be allowed to vote.* ❑ *The School was established in 1989 by an Italian professor.* **2** [RECIP] (formal) If you **establish** contact with someone, you start to have contact with them. You can also say that two people, groups, or countries **establish** contact. ❑ *We had already established contact with the museum.* **3** [T] (formal) If you **establish that** something is true, you discover facts that show that it is definitely true. = ascertain, prove, confirm ❑ *Medical*

tests established that she was not their own child. ❑ *It will be essential to establish how the money is being spent.* ❑ *An autopsy was being done to establish the cause of death.* **4** [T] If you **establish yourself**, your reputation, or a good quality that you have, you succeed in doing something, and achieve respect or a secure position as a result of this. ❑ *This is going to be the show where up-and-coming comedians will establish themselves.* ❑ *He has established himself as a pivotal figure in state politics.*

es·tab·lished /ɪ'stæblɪʃt/ ADJ **1** An **established** fact or truth is something that has been shown to be definitely true. ❑ *That link is an established medical fact.* **2** If you use **established** to describe something such as an organization, you mean that it is well known because it has existed for a long time. ❑ *These range from established companies to start-ups.*

❂**es·tab·lish·ment** ♦◇◇ /ɪ'stæblɪʃmənt/ NOUN [SING, C] (**establishments**) **1** [SING] (formal) The **establishment of** an organization or system is the act of creating it or beginning it. = creation, formation ❑ *The establishment of the regional government in 1980 did not end terrorism.* ❑ *His ideas influenced the establishment of National Portrait Galleries in London and Edinburgh.* **2** [C] (formal) An **establishment** is a shop, business, or organization occupying a particular building or place. = office, building ❑ *a scientific research establishment* ❑ *shops and other commercial establishments* **3** [SING] You refer to the people who have power and influence in the running of a country, society, or organization as **the establishment**. ❑ *While scientists were once considered the cranks and outsiders to the system, we are now part of the establishment.*

es·tate ♦♦◇ /ɪ'steɪt/ NOUN [C] (**estates**) (academic word) **1** An **estate** is a large area of land in the country which is owned by a person, family, or organization. ❑ *He spent holidays at the 300-acre estate of his aunt and uncle.* **2** (legal) Someone's **estate** is all the money and property that they leave behind when they die. ❑ *His estate was valued at $150,000.*

es·tate agent (BrE; in AmE, use **Realtor**) NOUN [C] (**estate agents**) An **estate agent** is someone who works for a company that sells houses and land for people.

es·teem /ɪ'stiːm/ NOUN [U] (formal) **Esteem** is the admiration and respect that you feel towards another person. ❑ *He is held in high esteem by colleagues in the construction industry.*
→ See also **self-esteem**

❂**es·ti·mate** ♦♦◇ VERB, NOUN (academic word)
VERB /'estɪmeɪt/ [T] (**estimates, estimating, estimated**) If you **estimate** a quantity or value, you make an approximate judgment or calculation of it. = judge, calculate ❑ *Try to estimate how many steps it will take to get to a close object.* ❑ *I estimate that total cost for treatment will go from $9,000 to $12,500.* ❑ *The Academy of Sciences currently estimates that there are approximately one million plant varieties in the world.* ❑ *He estimated the speed of the winds from the degree of damage.*
NOUN /'estɪmət/ [C] (**estimates**) **1** An **estimate** is an approximate calculation of a quantity or value. ❑ *the official estimate of the election result* ❑ *This figure is five times the original estimate.* ❑ *a conservative estimate based on previous findings* **2** An **estimate** is a judgment about a person or situation that you make based on the available evidence. ❑ *I hadn't been far wrong in my estimate of his grandson's capabilities.* **3** An **estimate** from someone who you employ to do a job for you, such as a builder or a plumber, is a written statement of how much the job is likely to cost. ❑ *Quotes and estimates can be prepared by computer on the spot.*

es·ti·mat·ed /'estɪmeɪtɪd/ ADJ ❑ *There are an estimated 90,000 gangsters in the country.*

es·ti·ma·tion /,estɪ'meɪʃən/ NOUN [SING, C] (**estimations**) **1** [SING] (formal) Your **estimation** of a person or situation is the opinion or impression that you have formed about them. ❑ *He has gone down considerably in my estimation.* **2** [C] An **estimation** is an approximate calculation of a quantity or value. = estimate ❑ *estimations of pre-tax profits of 12.25 million*

e

✪**et al.** /ˌet ˈæl/ **et al.** is used after a name or a list of names to indicate that other people are also involved. It is used especially when referring to books or articles that were written by more than two people. ❑ *Blough et al.* ❑ *Second, the analyses of Bollini et al. (1994) suggest that increasing doses does not improve treatment response.*

✪**etc** ◆◇◇ /etˈsetrə/ also **etc.** ABBREVIATION **etc** is used at the end of a list to indicate that you have mentioned only some of the items involved and have not given a full list. **etc** is a written abbreviation for 'et cetera'. ❑ *She knew all about my schoolwork, my hospital work, etc.* ❑ *Each of the twelve major body systems – stomach, lungs, pancreas, etc – is closely related to certain muscles.*

eter·nal /ɪˈtɜːnəl/ ADJ **1** Something that is **eternal** lasts forever. ❑ *the quest for eternal youth* **2** If you describe something as **eternal**, you mean that it seems to last forever, often because you think it is boring or annoying. = interminable, never-ending ❑ *In the background was that eternal hum.*
eter·nal·ly /ɪˈtɜːnəli/ ADV ❑ *She is eternally grateful to her family for their support.*

eter·nity /ɪˈtɜːnɪti/ NOUN [U, SING] **1** [U] **Eternity** is time without an end or a state of existence outside time, especially the state that some people believe they will pass into after they have died. ❑ *I have always found the thought of eternity terrifying.* **2** [SING] If you say that a situation lasted for **an eternity**, you mean that it seemed to last an extremely long time, usually because it was boring or unpleasant. = age ❑ *The war continued for an eternity.*

✪**eth·ic** /ˈeθɪk/ NOUN [PL, U, SING] (**ethics**) (*academic word*) **1** [PL] **Ethics** are moral beliefs and rules about right and wrong. ❑ *Refugee workers said such action was a violation of medical ethics.* ❑ *Its members are bound by a rigid code of ethics which includes confidentiality.* ❑ *the corporate ethics and social responsibility that society expects of business* **2** [PL] Someone's **ethics** are the moral principles about right and wrong behaviour that they believe in. ❑ *He told the police that he had thought honestly about the ethics of what he was doing.* **3** [U] **Ethics** is the study of questions about what is morally right and wrong. ❑ *the teaching of ethics and moral philosophy* ❑ *Lambert, an ethics professor at Wartburg College, concurs.* **4** [SING] An **ethic** of a particular kind is an idea or moral belief that influences the behaviour, attitudes, and philosophy of a group of people. ❑ *the ethic of public service*

✪**ethi·cal** /ˈeθɪkəl/ ADJ **1** **Ethical** means relating to beliefs about right and wrong. ❑ *the medical, nursing and ethical issues surrounding terminally-ill people* ❑ *the moral and ethical standards in the school* ❑ *Indeed, the use of placebos raises a whole range of ethical dilemmas.* **2** If you describe something as **ethical**, you mean that it is morally right or morally acceptable. ❑ *The trade association promotes ethical business practices.* ❑ *ethical investment schemes* ❑ *Does the party think it is ethical to link tax policy with party fund-raising?* ❑ *the ethical treatment of wild animals*
ethi·cal·ly /ˈeθɪkli/ ADV **1** *Attorneys are ethically and legally bound to absolute confidentiality.* **2** [ethically after V] ❑ *Mayors want local companies to behave ethically.*

✪**eth·nic** ◆◇◇ /ˈeθnɪk/ ADJ (*academic word*) **1** **Ethnic** means connected with or relating to different racial or cultural groups of people. ❑ *a survey of Britain's ethnic minorities* ❑ *ethnic tensions* **2** [ethnic + N] You can use **ethnic** to describe people who belong to a particular racial or cultural group but who, usually, do not live in the country where most members of that group live. ❑ *There are still several million ethnic Germans in Russia.* **3** **Ethnic** clothing, music, or food is characteristic of the traditions of a particular ethnic group, and different from what is usually found in modern Western culture. ❑ *a magnificent range of ethnic fabrics*
eth·ni·cal·ly /ˈeθnɪkli/ ADV **1** *a predominantly young, ethnically mixed audience* **2** *a large ethnically Albanian population*

✪**eth·nic·ity** /eθˈnɪsɪti/ NOUN [C, U] (**ethnicities**) **Ethnicity** is the state or fact of belonging to a particular ethnic group. ❑ *He said his ethnicity had not been important to him.* ❑ *a dozen boys of mixed ethnicity*

euphemis·tic /ˌjuːfəˈmɪstɪk/ ADJ [euphemistic with V] **Euphemistic** language uses polite, pleasant, or neutral words and expressions to refer to things that people may find unpleasant, upsetting, or embarrassing to talk about, for example, sex, the human body, or death. ❑ *a euphemistic way of saying that someone has been lying*
euphemis·ti·cal·ly /ˌjuːfəˈmɪstɪkli/ ADV If something is referred to **euphemistically**, it is mentioned using polite, pleasant, or neutral words and expressions to refer to things that people may find unpleasant, upsetting, or embarrassing to talk about. ❑ *political prisons, called euphemistically 're-education camps'*

euro /ˈjʊərəʊ/ NOUN [C] (**euros**) The **euro** is a unit of currency that is used by several member countries of the European Union. ❑ *Millions of words have been written about the introduction of the euro.*

Euro·pean ◆◆◇ /ˌjʊərəˈpiːən/ ADJ, NOUN
ADJ **European** means belonging to, relating to, or coming from Europe. ❑ *in some other European countries*
NOUN [C] (**Europeans**) A **European** is a person who comes from Europe. ❑ *Three-quarters of working-age Americans work, compared with roughly 60% of Europeans.*

eutha·na·sia /ˌjuːθəˈneɪziə, AmE -ʒə/ NOUN [U] **Euthanasia** is the practice of killing someone who is very ill and will never get better in order to end their suffering, usually done at their request or with their consent. ❑ *those in favour of voluntary euthanasia*

evacu·ate /ɪˈvækjueɪt/ VERB [T] (**evacuates, evacuating, evacuated**) **1** To **evacuate** someone means to send them to a place of safety, away from a dangerous building, town, or area. ❑ *They were planning to evacuate the seventy American officials still in the country.* **2** If people **evacuate** a place, they move out of it for a period of time, especially because it is dangerous. ❑ *The fire is threatening about sixty homes, and residents have evacuated the area.*
evacu·ation /ɪˌvækjuˈeɪʃən/ NOUN [C, U] (**evacuations**) **1** *the evacuation of the sick and wounded* ❑ *An evacuation of the city's four million inhabitants is planned for later this week.* **2** *the mass evacuation of the Bosnian town of Srebrenica*

evade /ɪˈveɪd/ VERB [T] (**evades, evading, evaded**) **1** If you **evade** something, you find a way of not doing something that you really ought to do. ❑ *By his own admission, he evaded paying taxes as a Florida real-estate speculator.* **2** If you **evade** a question or a topic, you avoid talking about it or dealing with it. ❑ *Too many companies, she says, are evading the issue.* **3** If you **evade** someone or something, you move so that you can avoid meeting them or avoid being touched or hit. ❑ *She turned and gazed at the river, evading his eyes.*

✪**evalu·ate** /ɪˈvæljueɪt/ VERB [T] (**evaluates, evaluating, evaluated**) (*academic word*) If you **evaluate** something or someone, you consider them in order to make a judgment about them, for example about how good or bad they are. = assess, analyse ❑ *The market situation is difficult to evaluate.* ❑ *They will first send in trained nurses to evaluate the needs of the individual situation.* ❑ *We evaluate how well we do something.*
✪**evalu·ation** /ɪˌvæljuˈeɪʃən/ NOUN [C, U] (**evaluations**) = analysis, appraisal, assessment, review ❑ *the opinions and evaluations of college supervisors* ❑ *Evaluation is standard practice for all training arranged through the school.*
✪**evalu·ative** /ɪˈvæljuətɪv/ ADJ (*formal*) Something that is **evaluative** is based on an assessment of the values, qualities, and significance of a particular person or thing. ❑ *ten years of evaluative research* ❑ *The professor rightly states the need for longer-term evaluative studies.*

✪**evapo·rate** /ɪˈvæpəreɪt/ VERB [I, T] (**evaporates, evaporating, evaporated**) **1** [I, T] When a liquid **evaporates**, or **is evaporated**, it changes from a liquid state to a gas, because its temperature has increased. ❑ *Moisture is drawn to the surface of the fabric so that it evaporates.* ❑ *The water is evaporated by the sun.* ❑ *Hydrocarbons evaporate into the atmosphere.* **2** [I] If a feeling, plan, or activity **evaporates**, it gradually becomes weaker and eventually disappears completely. ❑ *My anger evaporated and I wanted to cry.*

E

✪**evapo·ra·tion** /ɪˌvæpəˈreɪʃən/ NOUN [U] ❑ *The soothing, cooling effect is caused by the evaporation of the sweat on the skin.* ❑ *High temperatures also result in high evaporation from the plants.*

eva·sion /ɪˈveɪʒən/ NOUN [C, U] (**evasions**) **1** **Evasion** means deliberately avoiding something that you are supposed to do or deal with. ❑ *He was arrested for tax evasion.* **2** If you accuse someone of **evasion** when they have been asked a question, you mean that they are deliberately avoiding giving a clear direct answer. ❑ *We want straight answers. No evasions.*

eva·sive /ɪˈveɪsɪv/ ADJ
ADJ If you describe someone as **evasive**, you mean that they deliberately avoid giving clear direct answers to questions. ❑ *He was evasive about the circumstances of his first meeting with Stanley Dean.*
PHRASE **take evasive action** If you **take evasive action**, you deliberately move away from someone or something in order to avoid meeting them or being hit by them. ❑ *At least four high-flying warplanes had to take evasive action.*
eva·sive·ly /ɪˈveɪsɪvli/ ADV [evasively with v] ❑ *'Until I can speak to your husband I can't come to any conclusion about that,' Manuel said evasively.*

eve /iːv/ NOUN [C] (**eves**) **The eve of** a particular event or occasion is the day before it, or the period of time just before it. ❑ *on the eve of his 27th birthday*

✪**even** ◆◆◆ /ˈiːvən/ ADV, ADJ
ADV **1** You use **even** to suggest that what comes just after or just before it in the sentence is rather surprising. ❑ *He kept calling me for years, even after he got married.* ❑ *Even dark-skinned women should use sunscreens.* **2** [even + COMPAR] You use **even** with comparative adjectives and adverbs to emphasize a quality that someone or something has. ❑ *On television he made an even stronger impact as an interviewer.*
PHRASES **even if** or **even though** You use **even if** or **even though** to indicate that a particular fact does not make the rest of your statement untrue. ❑ *Cynthia is not ashamed of what she does, even if she ends up doing something wrong.*
even so (*spoken*) You use **even so** to introduce a surprising fact that relates to what you have just said. = nevertheless ❑ *The bus was only half full. Even so, a young man asked Nina if the seat next to her was taken.*
even then You use **even then** to say that something is the case in spite of what has just been stated or whatever the circumstances may be. ❑ *Peace could come only gradually, in carefully measured steps. Even then, it sounds almost impossible to achieve.*
ADJ **1** An **even** measurement or rate stays at about the same level. = constant ❑ *How important is it to have an even temperature when you're working?* ❑ *The brick-built property keeps the temperature at an even level throughout the year.* **2** An **even** surface is smooth and flat. = level ❑ *The tables are fitted with a glass top to provide an even surface.* **3** If there is an **even** distribution or division of something, each person, group, or area involved has an equal amount. = equal ❑ *Divide the dough into 12 even pieces and shape each piece into a ball.* **4** An **even** contest or competition is equally balanced between the two sides who are taking part. ❑ *It was an even game.* **5** An **even** number can be divided exactly by the number two. ≠ odd ❑ *In each capsule there is an even number of particles coloured black or white.* **6** [even + N] If there is an **even** chance that something will happen, the chances that it will or will not happen are equal. = fifty-fifty ❑ *They have a more than even chance of winning the next election.*
PHRASE **break even** (*business*) When a company or a person running a business **breaks even**, they make neither a profit nor a loss. ❑ *The airline hopes to break even next year and return to profit the following year.*
PHRASAL VERB **even out** (**evens, evening, evened**) If something **evens out**, or if you **even** it **out**, the differences between the different parts of it are reduced. ❑ *The power balance has evened out in the interim government.*
even·ly /ˈiːvənli/ ADV **1** *He looked at Ellen, breathing evenly in her sleep.* **2** *The meat is divided evenly and boiled in a stew.* **3** [evenly + -ED] ❑ *They must choose between two evenly matched candidates for governor.*

eve·ning ◆◆◇ /ˈiːvnɪŋ/ NOUN [C, U] (**evenings**) The **evening** is the part of each day between the end of the afternoon and the time when you go to bed. ❑ *All he did that evening was sit around the house.* ❑ *Supper is from 5:00 to 6:00 in the evening.*

✪**event** ◆◆◆ /ɪˈvent/ NOUN
NOUN [C] (**events**) **1** An **event** is something that happens, especially when it is unusual or important. You can use **events** to describe all the things that are happening in a particular situation. = occurrence, occasion ❑ *A new inquiry into the events of the day was opened in 2002.* ❑ *the events of September 11* ❑ *recent events in Europe* **2** An **event** is a planned and organized occasion, for example a social gathering or a sports tournament. ❑ *major sporting events* **3** An **event** is one of the races or competitions that are part of an organized occasion such as a sports tournament. ❑ *The main events start at 1 p.m.*
PHRASES **in the event of** or **in the event that** or **in that event** You use **in the event of**, **in the event that**, and **in that event** when you are talking about a possible future situation, especially when you are planning what to do if it occurs. ❑ *The bank has agreed to give an immediate refund in the unlikely event of an error being made.*
in any event You say **in any event** after you have been discussing a particular situation, in order to indicate that what you are saying is true or possible, in spite of anything that has happened or may happen. = anyway ❑ *In any event, the bowling alley restaurant proved quite acceptable.*

event·ful /ɪˈventfʊl/ ADJ If you describe an event or a period of time as **eventful**, you mean that a lot of interesting, exciting, or important things have happened during it. ❑ *This has been an eventful year for Tom, both professionally and personally.*

✪**even·tual** /ɪˈventʃuəl/ ADJ [eventual + N] (*academic word*) You use **eventual** to indicate that something happens or is the case at the end of a process or period of time. = ultimate, final ❑ *There are many who believe that civil war will be the eventual outcome of the racial tension in the country.* ❑ *The eventual aim is reunification.*

even·tu·al·i·ty /ɪˌventʃuˈælɪti/ NOUN [C] (**eventualities**) (*formal*) An **eventuality** is a possible future event or result, especially one that is unpleasant or surprising. = contingency ❑ *Every eventuality is covered, from running out of petrol to needing water.*

✪**even·tu·al·ly** ◆◆◇ /ɪˈventʃuəli/ ADV **1** **Eventually** means in the end, especially after a lot of delays, problems, or arguments. = finally ❑ *Eventually, the army caught up with him in Latvia.* ❑ *The flight eventually got away six hours late.* **2** **Eventually** means at the end of a situation or process or as the final result of it. = ultimately ❑ *Eventually your child will leave home to lead her own life as a fully independent adult.* ❑ *Dehydration eventually leads to death.* ❑ *researchers who hope eventually to create insulin-producing cells*

WHICH WORD?
eventually or finally?
Do not confuse **eventually** and **finally**. You use **eventually** to emphasize that something happens after a lot of delays or problems, or at the end of a series of events.
❑ *Eventually, after several setbacks, they reached the hospital.*
You use **finally** when something happens after you have been waiting for it for a long time.
❑ *The taxi finally arrived twenty minutes later.*
You can also use **finally** to show that something is the last in a series or to introduce a final point.
❑ *The fuel has to be mined, processed, transported, then finally burned.*

ever ◆◆◆ /ˈevə/ ADV
Ever is an adverb that you use to add emphasis in negative sentences, commands, questions, and conditional structures.

ADV 1 Ever means at any time. It is used in questions and negative statements. ❑ *I'm not sure I'll ever trust people again.* ❑ *Neither of us had ever skied.* **2** You use **ever** in expressions such as '**did you ever**' and '**have you ever**' to express surprise or shock at something you have just seen, heard, or experienced, especially when you expect people to agree with you. ❑ *Have you ever seen anything like it?* **3** You use **ever** after comparatives and superlatives to emphasize the degree to which something is true or when you are comparing a present situation with the past or the future. ❑ *She's got a great voice and is singing better than ever.* ❑ *Japan is wealthier and more powerful than ever before.* **4** [ever + ADJ/ADV] You use **ever** to say that something happens more all the time. ❑ *They grew ever further apart.* **5** [ever before V] (*informal, emphasis*) You can use **ever** for emphasis after 'never'. ❑ *I can never, ever, forgive myself.* **6** [QUEST + ever] You use **ever** in questions beginning with words such as 'why', 'when', and 'who' when you want to emphasize your surprise or shock. ❑ *Why ever didn't you tell me?*

PHRASES **ever since** If something has been the case **ever since** a particular time, it has been the case all the time from then until now. ❑ *He's been there ever since you left!* ❑ *I simply gave in to him, and I've regretted it ever since.*

all someone ever does (*emphasis*) You use the expression **all** someone **ever does** when you want to emphasize that they do the same thing all the time, and this annoys you. ❑ *All she ever does is complain.*

as ever You say **as ever** in order to indicate that something or someone's behaviour is not unusual because it is like that all the time or very often. ❑ *As ever, the meals are primarily fish-based.*
→ See also **forever**

USAGE NOTE

ever

Use **ever** to mean 'at any time' in negative sentences, questions, and comparisons. Do not use **ever** in positive statements, as in, '~~I ever read an article about that~~'. Use 'once'.
*I **once** read an article about that.*

---

every ◆◆◆ /ˈevri/ DET, ADJ

DET 1 You use **every** to indicate that you are referring to all the members of a group or all the parts of something and not only some of them. ❑ *Every room has a window facing the ocean.* ❑ *Record every expenditure you make.* **2** You use **every** in order to say how often something happens or to indicate that something happens at regular intervals. ❑ *We were made to attend meetings every day.* ❑ *A burglary occurs every three minutes in London.* **3** You use **every** in front of a number when you are saying what proportion of people or things something happens to or applies to. ❑ *Two out of every three people have a mobile phone.* **4** You can use **every** before some nouns, for example 'sign', 'effort', 'reason', and 'intention' in order to emphasize what you are saying. ❑ *The Congressional Budget Office says the federal deficit shows every sign of getting larger.* ❑ *I think that there is every chance that you will succeed.*

PHRASES **every now and then etc** or **every once in a while** or **every so often** You use **every** in the expressions **every now and then**, **every now and again**, **every once in a while**, and **every so often** in order to indicate that something happens occasionally. ❑ *Stir the batter every now and then to keep it from separating.*

every other day or **every second day** If something happens **every other day** or **every second day**, for example, it happens one day, then does not happen the next day, then happens the day after that, and so on. You can also say that something happens **every third week**, **every fourth year**, and so on. ❑ *I went home every other week.*

ADJ 1 [POSS + every + N] You use **every** to indicate that you are referring to all the members of a group or all the parts of something and not only some of them. ❑ *His every utterance will be scrutinized.* **2** [POSS + every + N] If you say that someone's **every** whim, wish, or desire will be satisfied, you are emphasizing that everything they want

will happen or be provided. ❑ *Dozens of servants had catered to his every whim.*
✦ **every bit as good as** → see **bit**

every·body ◆◆◇ /ˈevribɒdi/ PRON Everybody means the same as **everyone**.

○ every·day /ˈevrideɪ/ ADJ You use **everyday** to describe something that happens or is used every day, or forms a regular and basic part of your life, so it is not especially interesting or unusual. = normal, ordinary ❑ *In the course of my everyday life, I had very little contact with teenagers.* ❑ *the everyday problems of living in the city*

WHICH WORD?

everyday or **every day?**

Do not confuse **everyday** and **every day**.

You use the adjective **everyday** to describe something which is normal and not exciting or unusual in any way.
❑ *We talked about the **everyday** problems of living in the city*
❑ *Computers are a central part of **everyday** life.*

Every day has a different meaning. If something happens **every day**, it happens regularly each day.
❑ *Shanti takes the same bus **every day**.*

---

every·one ◆◆◇ /ˈevriwʌn/ PRON

The form **everybody** is also used.

1 You use **everyone** or **everybody** to refer to all the people in a particular group. ❑ *Everyone on the street was shocked when they heard the news.* ❑ *Not everyone thinks that the government is being particularly generous.* **2** You use **everyone** or **everybody** to refer to all people. ❑ *Everyone wrestles with self-doubt and feels like a failure at times.* ❑ *Everyone needs some free time for rest and relaxation.*

WHICH WORD?

everyone or **every one?**

Do not confuse **everyone** and **every one**.

You use **everyone** to refer to all people or to all the people in some group being discussed.
❑ *Everyone has the right to freedom of expression.*
❑ *The police had ordered **everyone** out of the office.*

You use **every one** to emphasize that something is true about each one of the things or people mentioned.
❑ *He read **every one** of my poems.*

---

every·thing ◆◆◆ /ˈevriθɪŋ/ PRON **1** You use **everything** to refer to all the objects, actions, activities, or facts in a particular situation. ❑ *He'd gone to Seattle long after everything else in his life had changed.* **2** You use **everything** to refer to all possible or likely actions, activities, or situations. ❑ *'This should have been decided long before now.'—'We can't think of everything.'* ❑ *Najib and I do everything together.* **3** You use **everything** to refer to a whole situation or to life in general. ❑ *She says everything is going smoothly.* ❑ *Is everything all right?* **4** If you say that someone or something is **everything**, you mean you consider them to be the most important thing in your life, or the most important thing that there is. ❑ *I love him. He is everything to me.* **5** If you say that someone or something has **everything**, you mean they have all the things or qualities that most people consider to be desirable. ❑ *This man had everything. He had the house, the yacht, and a full life with friends and family.*

every·where ◆◇◇ /ˈevriweə/ (in AmE, also use **everyplace**) ADV **1** You use **everywhere** to refer to a whole area or to all the places in a particular area. ❑ *Working people everywhere object to paying taxes.* ❑ *We went everywhere together.* **2** You use **everywhere** to refer to all the places that someone goes to. ❑ *Mary Jo is still accustomed to travelling everywhere in style.* **3** You use **everywhere** to emphasize that you are talking about a large number of places, or all possible places. ❑ *I saw her picture everywhere.* **4** If you say that someone or something is **everywhere**, you mean that they are present in a place in very large numbers. ❑ *There were cartons of cigarettes everywhere.*

e

evict /ɪ'vɪkt/ VERB [T] (**evicts, evicting, evicted**) If someone **is evicted from** the place where they are living, they are forced to leave it, usually because they have broken a law or contract. ◻ *They were evicted from their flat after their mother became addicted to drugs.* ◻ *In the first week, the city police evicted ten families.*

evic·tion /ɪ'vɪkʃən/ NOUN [C, U] (**evictions**) Eviction is the act or process of officially forcing someone to leave a house or piece of land. ◻ *He was facing eviction, along with his wife and family.*

✪ **evi·dence** ♦♦◇ /'evɪdəns/ NOUN (*academic word*)
 NOUN [U] **1** Evidence is anything that you see, experience, read, or are told that causes you to believe that something is true or has really happened. = proof, support ◻ *Ganley said he'd seen no evidence of widespread fraud.* ◻ *a report on the scientific evidence for global warming* ◻ *There is a lot of evidence that stress is partly responsible for disease.* ◻ *To date there is no evidence to support this theory.* **2** Evidence is the information that is used in a court of law to try to prove something. Evidence is obtained from documents, objects, or witnesses. ◻ *The evidence against him was purely circumstantial.*
 PHRASES **give evidence** If you **give evidence** in a court of law or an official inquiry, you officially say what you know about people or events, or describe an occasion at which you were present. = testify ◻ *The forensic scientists who carried out the original tests will be called to give evidence.* **be in evidence** If someone or something **is in evidence**, they are present and can be clearly seen. ◻ *Few soldiers were in evidence.*

WORD CONNECTIONS
VERB + **evidence**
find evidence
gather evidence
collect evidence
◻ *Accident investigation officers examine the scene to gather enough evidence to construct a full picture of what happened.*
present evidence
produce evidence
◻ *He presented new evidence to support his theory.*
ADJ + **evidence**
clear evidence
strong evidence
conclusive evidence
◻ *There is no conclusive evidence that Parkinson's disease is a hereditary condition which can be passed on within families.*
scientific evidence
medical evidence
circumstantial evidence
◻ *Medical evidence shows that there is a link between traffic pollution and the incidence of asthma.*

USAGE NOTE
evidence
Evidence is an uncountable noun. Do not use 'evidences' or 'an evidence'. You can talk about a single item as a 'piece of evidence'.
*This is the latest **piece of evidence** that vaccines will play an important part in the fight against cancer.*

evi·dent /'evɪdənt/ ADJ (*academic word*) **1** If something is evident, you notice it easily and clearly. = noticeable ◻ *His footprints were clearly evident in the heavy dust.* ◻ *The threat of inflation is already evident in bond prices.* **2** You use evident to show that you are certain about a situation or fact and your interpretation of it. = clear ◻ *It was evident that she had once been a beauty.*

evi·dent·ly /'evɪdəntli/ ADV **1** You use evidently to say that something is obviously true, for example, because you have seen evidence of it yourself. = clearly, obviously ◻ *The man wore a bathrobe and had evidently just come from the bathroom.* **2** You use evidently to show that you think

something is true or have been told something is true, but that you are not sure, because you do not have enough information or proof. ◻ *From childhood, he was evidently at once rebellious and precocious.* **3** [evidently with CL] (*formal, emphasis*) You can use evidently to introduce a statement or opinion and to emphasize that you feel that it is true or correct. ◻ *Evidently, it has nothing to do with social background.*

evil ♦◇◇ /'iːvəl/ NOUN, ADJ
 NOUN [U, C] (**evils**) **1** [U] Evil is a powerful force that some people believe to exist, and that causes wicked and bad things to happen. ◻ *There's always a conflict between good and evil in his plays.* **2** [U] Evil is used to refer to all the wicked and bad things that happen in the world. ◻ *He could not, after all, stop all the evil in the world.* **3** [C] If you refer to an evil, you mean a very unpleasant or harmful situation or activity. ◻ *Higher taxes may be a necessary evil.*
 PHRASE **the lesser of two evils** or **the lesser evil** If you have two choices, but think that they are both bad, you can describe the less bad one as **the lesser of two evils**, or **the lesser evil**. ◻ *People voted for him as the lesser of two evils.*
 ADJ **1** If you describe someone as evil, you mean that they are very wicked by nature and take pleasure in doing things that harm other people. ◻ *the country's most evil terrorists* **2** If you describe something as evil, you mean that you think it causes a great deal of harm to people and is morally bad. ◻ *A judge yesterday condemned heroin as evil.* **3** If you describe something as evil, you mean that you think it is influenced by the devil. ◻ *I think this is an evil spirit at work.*

evoca·tive /ɪ'vɒkətɪv/ ADJ (*formal*) If you describe something as evocative, you mean that it is good or interesting because it produces pleasant memories, ideas, emotions, and responses in people. ◻ *Her story is sharply evocative of Italian provincial life.*

✪ **evoke** /ɪ'vəʊk/ VERB [T] (**evokes, evoking, evoked**) (*formal*) To evoke a particular memory, idea, emotion, or response means to cause it to occur. ◻ *the scene evoking memories of those old movies* ◻ *Harriet Walter as Celia marvellously evokes the pathos of the middle-class woman.* ◻ *The entire piece evokes an atmosphere of comfort and quiescence.*

✪ **evo·lu·tion** /ˌiːvə'luːʃən, ˌev-/ NOUN [U, C] (**evolutions**) **1** [U] Evolution is a process of gradual change that takes place over many generations, during which some species of animals, plants, or insects slowly change some of their physical characteristics. ◻ *the evolution of plants and animals* ◻ *the theory of evolution by natural selection* **2** [C, U] (*formal*) Evolution is a process of gradual development in a particular situation or thing over a period of time. = development ◻ *a crucial period in the evolution of modern physics*

evo·lu·tion·ary /ˌiːvə'luːʃənri, AmE -neri/ ADJ Evolutionary means relating to a process of gradual change and development. ◻ *an evolutionary process*

✪ **evolve** /ɪ'vɒlv/ VERB [I, T] (**evolves, evolving, evolved**) (*academic word*) **1** [I] When animals or plants evolve, they gradually change and develop into different forms. ◻ *The bright plumage of many male birds was thought to have evolved to attract females.* ◻ *Birds are widely believed to have evolved from dinosaurs.* ◻ *Maize evolved from a wild grass in Mexico.* ◻ *when amphibians evolved into reptiles* **2** [I, T] If something evolves or you evolve it, it gradually develops over a period of time into something different and usually more advanced. = develop, adapt ◻ *a tiny airline which eventually evolved into Pakistan International Airlines* ◻ *Popular music evolved from folk songs.* ◻ *As medical knowledge evolves, beliefs change.*

✪ **ex·ac·er·bate** /ɪg'zæsəbeɪt/ VERB [T] (**exacerbates, exacerbating, exacerbated**) (*formal*) If something exacerbates a problem or bad situation, it makes it worse. = aggravate ◻ *Longstanding poverty has been exacerbated by racial divisions.* ◻ *Mr Powell-Taylor says that depopulation exacerbates the problem.* ◻ *Stress can also exacerbate the symptoms.*

ex·ac·er·ba·tion /ɪgˌzæsə'beɪʃən/ NOUN [U] ◻ *the exacerbation of global problems*

e

◆**ex·act** ♦♦◇ /ɪgˈzækt/ ADJ, VERB

ADJ **1** Exact means correct in every detail. For example, an **exact** copy is the same in every detail as the thing it is copied from. = precise, accurate; ≠ approximate, inexact, vague, imprecise ❏ *I don't remember the exact words.* ❏ *The exact number of protest calls has not been revealed.* ❏ *an exact copy of the text* ❏ *Predicting earth tremors is not an exact science.* **2** [exact + N] You use **exact** before a noun to emphasize that you are referring to that particular thing and no other, especially something that has a particular significance. ❏ *I hadn't really thought about it until this exact moment.*

PHRASE **to be exact** You say **to be exact** to indicate that you are slightly correcting or giving more detailed information about what you have been saying. ❏ *A small number – five, to be exact – have been bad.*

VERB [T] (**exacts, exacting, exacted**) **1** (*formal*) When someone **exacts** something, they demand and obtain it from another person, especially because they are in a superior or more powerful position. ❏ *Already he has exacted a written apology from the chairman of the commission.* **2** If someone **exacts** revenge **on** a person, they have their revenge on them. ❏ *She uses the media to help her exact a terrible revenge.* **3** If something **exacts** a high price, it has a bad effect on a person or situation. ❏ *The sheer physical effort had exacted a heavy price.*

◆**ex·act·ly** ♦◇◇ /ɪgˈzæktli/ ADV **1** (*emphasis*) You use **exactly** before an amount, number, or position to emphasize that it is no more, no less, or no different from what you are stating. = precisely ❏ *Each corner had a guard tower, each of which was exactly ten metres in height.* **2** Exactly means in precise and correct detail. For example, if something is **exactly** the same as something else it is the same in every detail. = precisely; ≠ approximately ❏ *Try to locate exactly where the smells are entering the room.* ❏ *Both drugs will be exactly the same.* ❏ *No one knows exactly what these substances are.* ❏ *The results were exactly as Bohr and Heisenberg predicted.* **3** [exactly as reply] If you say '**Exactly**', you are agreeing with someone or emphasizing the truth of what they say. If you say '**Not exactly**', you are telling them politely that they are wrong in part of what they are saying. = precisely ❏ *Eve nodded, almost approvingly. 'Exactly.'* **4** (*vagueness*) You use **not exactly** to indicate that a meaning or situation is slightly different from what people think or expect. ❏ *He's not exactly homeless, he just hangs out in this park.* **5** (*emphasis*) You can use **not exactly** to show that you mean the opposite of what you are saying. ❏ *This was not exactly what I wanted to hear.* **6** [exactly with QUEST] (*disapproval*) You use **exactly** with a question to show that you disapprove of what the person you are talking to is doing or saying. = precisely ❏ *What exactly do you mean?* **7** You use **exactly** before a noun to emphasize that you are referring to that particular thing and no other, especially something that has a particular significance. ❏ *These are exactly the people who do not vote.*

ex·ag·ger·ate /ɪgˈzædʒəreɪt/ VERB [I, T] (**exaggerates, exaggerating, exaggerated**) **1** [I, T] If you **exaggerate**, you indicate that something is, for example, worse or more important than it really is. ❏ *He thinks I'm exaggerating.* **2** [T] If something **exaggerates** a situation, quality, or feature, it makes the situation, quality, or feature appear greater, more obvious, or more important than it really is. ❏ *These figures exaggerate the loss of competitiveness.*

ex·ag·ger·a·tion /ɪgˌzædʒəˈreɪʃən/ NOUN [C, U] (**exaggerations**) ❏ *Like many stories about him, it smacks of exaggeration.*

ex·ag·ger·at·ed /ɪgˈzædʒəreɪtɪd/ ADJ Something that is **exaggerated** is or seems larger, better, worse, or more important than it actually needs to be. ❏ *Western fears, he insists, are greatly exaggerated.*

exam /ɪgˈzæm/ NOUN [C] (**exams**) An **exam** is a formal test that you take to show your knowledge or ability in a particular subject, or to obtain a qualification. = examination ❏ *I don't want to take any more exams.*

◆**ex·ami·na·tion** ♦◇◇ /ɪgˌzæmɪˈneɪʃən/ NOUN [C, U] (**examinations**) **1** [C, U] The **examination** of something is the act of looking at it carefully. = inspection ❏ *The navy is to carry out an examination of the wreck tomorrow.* **2** [C] (*formal*) An **examination** is a formal test that you take to show your knowledge or ability in a particular subject, or to obtain a qualification. = exam ❏ *university examination results* **3** [C] If you have a medical **examination**, a doctor looks at your body, feels it, or does simple tests in order to check how healthy you are. ❏ *You must see your doctor for a thorough examination.* **4** [C, U] The **examination** of an idea, proposal, or plan is the act of considering it very carefully. = consideration ❏ *The government said it was studying the implications, which 'required very careful examination and consideration'.*

◆**ex·am·ine** ♦♦◇ /ɪgˈzæmɪn/ VERB [T] (**examines, examining, examined**) **1** If you **examine** something, you look at it carefully. = study, inspect ❏ *He examined her passport and stamped it.* ❏ *Forensic scientists are examining the bombers' car.* **2** If a doctor **examines** you, he or she looks at your body, feels it, or does simple tests in order to check how healthy you are. ❏ *Another doctor examined her and could still find nothing wrong.* **3** If an idea, proposal, or plan **is examined**, it is considered very carefully. = consider, investigate ❏ *The plans will be examined by officials.* ❏ *I have given the matter much thought, examining all the possible alternatives.* ❏ *Psychologists have been examining how we make sense of events.* **4** If you **are examined**, you are given a formal test in order to show your knowledge of a subject. ❏ *learning to cope with the pressures of being judged and examined by our teachers*

ex·am·in·er /ɪgˈzæmɪnə/ NOUN [C] (**examiners**) An **examiner** is a person who conducts an examination. ❏ *FBI senior fingerprint examiner Terry Green*

◆**ex·am·ple** ♦♦♦ /ɪgˈzɑːmpəl, -ˈzæmp-/ NOUN

NOUN [C] (**examples**) **1** An **example of** something is a particular situation, object, or person that shows that what is being claimed is true. ❏ *The doctors gave numerous examples of patients being expelled from the hospital.* ❏ *The following example illustrates the change that took place.* **2** An **example of** a particular class of objects or styles is something that has many of the typical features of such a class or style, and that you consider clearly represents it. = illustration ❏ *Symphonies 103 and 104 stand as perfect* examples of early symphonic construction. **3** If you refer to a person or their behaviour as an **example to** other people, you mean that he or she behaves in a good or correct way that other people should copy. ❑ *He is a model professional and an example to the younger boys.*

PHRASES for example You use **for example** to introduce and emphasize something that shows that something is true. ❑ *Take, for example, the simple sentence: 'The man climbed up the hill.'* ❑ *'educational toys' that are designed to promote the development of, for example, children's spatial ability* ❑ *A few simple precautions can be taken, for example ensuring that desks are the right height.*

follow someone's example If you **follow** someone's **example**, you behave in the same way as they did in the past, or in a similar way, especially because you admire them. ❑ *Following the example set by her father, she has fulfilled her role and done her duty.*

make an example of someone To **make an example of** someone who has done something wrong means to punish them severely as a warning to other people not to do the same thing. ❑ *Let us at least see our courts make an example of these despicable criminals.*

set an example If you **set an example**, you encourage or inspire people by your behaviour to behave or act in a similar way. ❑ *An officer's job was to set an example.*

❂**ex·ca·vate** /'ekskəveɪt/ VERB [T] (**excavates, excavating, excavated**) **1** When archaeologists or other people **excavate** a piece of land, they remove earth carefully from it and look for things such as pots, bones, or buildings that are buried there, in order to discover information about the past. ❑ *A new Danish expedition is again excavating the site in annual summer digs.* ❑ *Archaeologists excavated the skeletal remains in Indonesia.* **2** To **excavate** means to dig a hole in the ground, for example, in order to build there. ❑ *A contractor was hired to drain the reservoir and to excavate soil from one area for replacement with clay.*

❂**ex·ca·va·tion** /,ekskə'veɪʃən/ NOUN [C, U] (**excavations**) **1** *She worked on the excavation of a Mayan archeological site.* ❑ *the excavation of a bronze-age boat* ❑ *In time these new excavations will require conservation.* ❑ *Recent excavations have uncovered sensational evidence.* **2** *the excavation of canals*

❂**ex·ceed** /ɪk'siːd/ VERB [T] (**exceeds, exceeding, exceeded**) (*academic word, formal*) **1** If something **exceeds** a particular amount or number, it is greater or larger than that amount or number. = surpass ❑ *Its research budget exceeds $700 million a year.* ❑ *The demand for places at some schools exceeds the supply.* ❑ *His performance exceeded all expectations.* **2** If you **exceed** a limit or rule, you go beyond it, even though you are not supposed to or it is against the law. ❑ *He accepts that he was exceeding the speed limit.*

WORD FAMILIES	
exceed VERB	*Its research budget **exceeds** $700 million a year.*
excess NOUN	*Large doses of vitamin C are not toxic, since the body will excrete any **excess**.*
excessive ADJ	*They alleged **excessive** use of force by police officers.*
excessively ADV	*Managers are also accused of paying themselves **excessively** high salaries.*

ex·ceed·ing·ly /ɪk'siːdɪŋli/ ADV (*old-fashioned*) **Exceedingly** means very or very much. = extremely ❑ *We had an exceedingly good lunch.*

ex·cel /ɪk'sel/ VERB [I] (**excels, excelling, excelled**) If someone **excels in** something or **excels at** it, they are very good at doing it. ❑ *Mary was a better rider than either of them and she excelled at outdoor sports.* ❑ *Academically he began to excel.*

ex·cel·lence /'eksələns/ NOUN [U] If someone or something has the quality of **excellence**, they are extremely good in some way. ❑ *the top award for excellence in journalism and the arts*

ex·cel·lent ♦♦◇ /'eksələnt/ ADJ, EXCLAM
ADJ Something that is **excellent** is extremely good. ❑ *The recording quality is excellent.*
EXCLAM (*feelings*) Some people say '**Excellent!**' to show that they approve of something. ❑ *'Excellent!' he shouted, yelping happily at the rain. 'Now we'll see how this boat really performs!'*
ex·cel·lent·ly /'eksələntli/ ADV ❑ *They're both playing excellently.*

❂**ex·cept** ♦♦◇ /ɪk'sept/ PREP, CONJ
PREP You use **except** to introduce the only thing or person that a statement does not apply to, or a fact that prevents a statement from being completely true. ❑ *I wouldn't have accepted anything except a job in New York.* ❑ *No illness, except malaria, has caused as much death as smallpox.*
PHRASE except for You use **except** or **except for** to introduce the only thing or person that prevents a statement from being completely true. = apart from, excluding ❑ *He hadn't eaten a thing except for one forkful of salad.* ❑ *Elephant shrews are found over most of Africa, except for the west.*
CONJ You use **except** to introduce a statement that prevents a previous statement from being completely true ❑ *Freddie would tell me nothing about what he was writing, except that it was to be a Christmas play.*

ex·cept·ed /ɪk'septɪd/ ADV [N + excepted] (*formal*) You use **excepted** after you have mentioned a person or thing to show that you do not include them in the statement you are making. ❑ *Jeremy excepted, the men seemed personable.*

ex·cept·ing /ɪk'septɪŋ/ PREP (*formal*) You use **excepting** to introduce the only thing that prevents a statement from being completely true. ❑ *The source of meat for much of this region (excepting Japan) has traditionally been the pig.*

❂**ex·cep·tion** ♦◇◇ /ɪk'sepʃən/ NOUN
NOUN [C] (**exceptions**) An **exception** is a particular thing, person, or situation that is not included in a general statement, judgment, or rule. ❑ *Few guitarists can sing as well as they can play; Eddie, however, is an exception.* ❑ *The law makes no exceptions.*
PHRASES no exception (*emphasis*) If you make a general statement, and then say that something or someone is **no exception**, you are emphasizing that they are included in that statement. ❑ *Marketing is applied to everything these days, and books are no exception.*
take exception to something If you **take exception to** something, you feel offended or annoyed by it, usually with the result that you complain about it. = object ❑ *He also took exception to having been spied on.*
with the exception of You use **with the exception of** to introduce a thing or person that is not included in a general statement that you are making. ❑ *Yesterday was a day off for everybody, with the exception of Lorenzo.* ❑ *The trees there are older than any other trees in the world, with the exception of the Californian redwoods.*
without exception (*emphasis*) You use **without exception** to emphasize that the statement you are making is true in all cases. ❑ *The vehicles are without exception old, rusty and dented.*

ex·cep·tion·al /ɪk'sepʃənəl/ ADJ **1** [exceptional + ADJ/ADV] (*approval*) You use **exceptional** to describe someone or something that has a particular quality, usually a good quality, to an unusually high degree. = extraordinary ❑ *children with exceptional ability* **2** (*formal*) **Exceptional** situations and incidents are unusual and only likely to happen infrequently. = unusual ❑ *A review panel concluded that there were no exceptional circumstances that would warrant a lesser penalty for him.*
ex·cep·tion·al·ly /ɪk'sepʃənəli/ ADV **1** = extremely ❑ *He's an exceptionally talented dancer and needs to practise several hours every day.* **2** [exceptionally with CL] ❑ *Exceptionally, in times of emergency, we may send a team of experts.*

❂**ex·cerpt** ♦◇◇ /'eksɜːpt/ NOUN [C] (**excerpts**) An **excerpt** is a short piece of writing or music taken from a larger piece. = extract, part, section, selection ❑ *an excerpt from Tchaikovsky's Nutcracker* ❑ *He read excerpts from Macbeth and Midsummer Night's Dream.*

e

❂**ex·cess** ♦◇◇ NOUN, ADJ

[NOUN] /ɪk'ses/ [c, u] (**excesses**) An **excess of** something is a larger amount than is needed, allowed, or usual. = surfeit, surplus; ≠ deficiency ❑ *An excess of house plants in a small apartment can be oppressive.* ❑ *Large doses of vitamin C are not toxic, since the body will excrete any excess.*

[PHRASES] **in excess of** (*formal*) **In excess of** means more than a particular amount. ❑ *The value of the company is well in excess of $2 billion.* ❑ *Avoid deposits in excess of £20,000 in any one account.* ❑ *The energy value of dried fruits is considerably in excess of that of fresh items.*

to excess (*disapproval*) If you do something **to excess**, you do it too much. ❑ *I was reasonably fit, played a lot of tennis, and didn't smoke or drink to excess.*

[ADJ] /'ekses/ **1** [excess + N] **Excess** is used to describe amounts that are greater than what is needed, allowed, or usual. = surplus ❑ *After cooking the fish, pour off any excess fat.* **2** [excess + N] (*formal*) **Excess** is used to refer to additional amounts of money that need to be paid for services and activities that were not originally planned or taken into account. ❑ *Make sure that you don't have to pay expensive excess charges.*

❂**ex·ces·sive** /ɪk'sesɪv/ ADJ (*disapproval*) If you describe the amount or level of something as **excessive**, you disapprove of it because it is more or higher than is necessary or reasonable. = inordinate, undue, exorbitant; ≠ insufficient ❑ *Their spending on research is excessive and is slowing developments of new treatments.* ❑ *the alleged use of excessive force by police*

❂**ex·ces·sive·ly** /ɪk'sesɪvli/ ADV ❑ *Managers are also accused of paying themselves excessively high salaries.* ❑ *Some people will resort to smoking excessively, some turn to alcohol.*

❂**ex·change** ♦♦◇ /ɪks'tʃeɪndʒ/ VERB, NOUN

[VERB] [RECIP, T] (**exchanges, exchanging, exchanged**) **1** [RECIP] If two or more people **exchange** things of a particular kind, they give them to each other at the same time. ❑ *We exchanged addresses.* ❑ *The two men exchanged glances.* **2** [T] If you **exchange** something, you replace it with a different thing, especially something that is better or more satisfactory. = change, trade ❑ *the chance to sell back or exchange goods* ❑ *If the car you have leased is clearly unsatisfactory, you can always exchange it for another.*

[NOUN] [c] (**exchanges**) **1** An **exchange** of things of a particular kind happens when two or more people give them to each other at the same time. ❑ *He ruled out any exchange of prisoners with the militants.* **2** (*formal*) An **exchange** is a brief conversation, usually an angry one. ❑ *There've been some bitter exchanges between the two groups.* **3** An **exchange** of fire, for example, is an incident in which people use guns or missiles against each other. ❑ *There was an exchange of fire during which the gunman was wounded.* **4** An **exchange** is an arrangement in which people from two different countries visit each other's country, to strengthen links between them. ❑ *a series of sporting and cultural exchanges with Seoul*

[PHRASE] **in exchange** If you do or give something **in exchange for** something else, you do it or give it in order to get that thing. ❑ *It is illegal for public officials to solicit gifts or money in exchange for favours.*

→ See also **foreign exchange, stock exchange**

ex·change rate ♦◇◇ NOUN [c] (**exchange rates**) The **exchange rate** of a country's unit of currency is the amount of another country's currency that you get in exchange for it. ❑ *a high exchange rate for the Canadian dollar*

ex·cite /ɪk'saɪt/ VERB [T] (**excites, exciting, excited**) **1** If something **excites** you, it makes you feel very happy, eager, or enthusiastic. ❑ *I only take on work that excites me, even if it means turning down lots of money.* **2** If something **excites** a particular feeling, emotion, or reaction in someone, it causes them to experience it. = arouse ❑ *Daniel's early exposure to motor racing did not excite his interest.*

ex·cit·ed /ɪk'saɪtɪd/ ADJ **1** If you are **excited**, you are so happy that you cannot relax, especially because you are thinking about something pleasant that is going to happen to you. ❑ *I was excited about the possibility of playing*

football again. **2** If you are **excited**, you are worried or angry about something, and so you are very alert and cannot relax. = agitated ❑ *I don't think there's any reason to get excited about inflation.*

ex·cit·ed·ly /ɪk'saɪtɪdli/ ADV **1** [excitedly with v] ❑ *'You're coming?' he said excitedly. 'That's fantastic! That's incredible!'* **2** [excitedly with v] ❑ *Larry rose excitedly to the edge of his seat, shook a fist at us and spat.*

ex·cite·ment /ɪk'saɪtmənt/ NOUN [c, u] (**excitements**) You use **excitement** to refer to the state of being excited, or to something that excites you. ❑ *Everyone is in a state of great excitement.*

ex·cit·ing ♦◇◇ /ɪk'saɪtɪŋ/ ADJ If something is **exciting**, it makes you feel very happy or enthusiastic. = thrilling ❑ *The race itself is very exciting.*

ex·claim /ɪks'kleɪm/ VERB [T] (**exclaims, exclaiming, exclaimed**) Writers sometimes use **exclaim** to show that someone is speaking suddenly, loudly, or emphatically, often because they are excited, shocked, or angry. = cry ❑ *'He went back to the lab,' Inez exclaimed impatiently.*

ex·cla·ma·tion /ˌeksklə'meɪʃən/ NOUN [c] (**exclamations**) An **exclamation** is a sound, word, or sentence that is spoken suddenly, loudly, or emphatically and that expresses excitement, admiration, shock, or anger. ❑ *Sue gave an exclamation as we got a clear sight of the house.*

❂**ex·clude** /ɪks'kluːd/ VERB [T] (**excludes, excluding, excluded**) (*academic word*) **1** If you **exclude** someone **from** a place or activity, you prevent them from entering it or taking part in it. ❑ *Many of the youngsters feel excluded.* **2** If you **exclude** something that has some connection with what you are doing, you deliberately do not use it or consider it. = omit, reject; ≠ include ❑ *In some schools, Christmas carols are being modified to exclude any reference to Christ.* ❑ *They eat only plant foods, and take care to exclude animal products from other areas of their lives.* **3** To **exclude** a possibility means to decide or prove that it is wrong and not worth considering. ❑ *I cannot entirely exclude the possibility that some form of pressure was applied to the neck.* **4** To **exclude** something such as the sun's rays or harmful germs means to prevent them physically from reaching or entering a particular place. ❑ *This was intended to exclude the direct rays of the sun.*

❂**ex·clud·ing** /ɪks'kluːdɪŋ/ PREP You use **excluding** before mentioning a person or thing to show that you are not including them in your statement. = except, without; ≠ including ❑ *Excluding water, half of the body's weight is protein.* ❑ *The families questioned, excluding those on income support, have a net income of £200.20 a week.*

❂**ex·clu·sion** /ɪks'kluːʒən/ NOUN

[NOUN] [c, u] (**exclusions**) **1** [c, u] The **exclusion of** something is the act of deliberately not using, allowing, or considering it. ❑ *It calls for the exclusion of all commercial lending institutions from the student loan programme.* ❑ *Certain exclusions and limitations apply.* **2** [u] **Exclusion** is the act of preventing someone from entering a place or taking part in an activity. = ban; ≠ inclusion ❑ *women's exclusion from political power*

[PHRASE] **to the exclusion of** If you do one thing **to the exclusion of** something else, you only do the first thing and do not do the second thing at all. ❑ *Diane had dedicated her life to caring for him to the exclusion of all else.*

ex·clu·sive /ɪks'kluːsɪv/ ADJ, NOUN

[ADJ] **1** If you describe something as **exclusive**, you mean that it is limited to people who have a lot of money or who are privileged, and is therefore not available to everyone. ❑ *It used to be a private, exclusive club, and now it's open to all New Yorkers.* **2** Something that is **exclusive** is used or owned by only one person or group, and not shared with anyone else. ❑ *Our group will have exclusive use of a 60-foot boat.* **3** If a newspaper, magazine, or broadcasting organization describes one of its reports as **exclusive**, they mean it is a special report that does not appear in any other publication or on any other channel. ❑ *He told the magazine in an exclusive interview: 'All my problems stem from drinking.'* **4** If a company states that its prices, goods, or services are **exclusive of** something, that thing is not included in the stated price, although it usually still has to be paid for. ❑ *the average cost of a three-course dinner exclusive of tax, tip and beverage* **PHRASE** **mutually exclusive** If two things are **mutually exclusive**, they are separate and very different from each other, so that it is impossible for them to exist or happen together. ❑ *They both have learned that ambition and successful fatherhood can be mutually exclusive.* **NOUN** [c] (**exclusives**) An **exclusive** is an exclusive article or report. ❑ *Some papers thought they had an exclusive.*

ex·clu·sive·ly /ɪkˈskluːsɪvli/ ADV **Exclusively** is used to refer to situations or activities that involve only the thing or things mentioned, and nothing else. ❑ *an exclusively male domain*

ex·cru·ci·at·ing /ɪkˈskruːʃieɪtɪŋ/ ADJ (*emphasis*) If you describe something as **excruciating**, you are emphasizing that it is extremely painful, either physically or emotionally. = unbearable ❑ *I was in excruciating pain and one leg wouldn't move.*

ex·cur·sion /ɪkˈskɜːʃən, AmE -ʒən/ NOUN [c] (**excursions**) **1** You can refer to a short trip as an **excursion**, especially if it is taken for pleasure or enjoyment. = trip ❑ *In Bermuda, Sam's father took him on an excursion to a coral barrier.* **2** An **excursion** is a trip or visit to an interesting place, especially one that is arranged or recommended by a travel agency or tourist organization. = outing ❑ *Another pleasant excursion is Matamoros, 18 miles away.*

ex·cuse ♦◇◇ NOUN, VERB
NOUN /ɪkˈskjuːs/ [c] (**excuses**) An **excuse** is a reason that you give in order to explain why something has been done or has not been done, or in order to avoid doing something. = justification ❑ *It is easy to find excuses for his indecisiveness.* ❑ *If you stop making excuses and do it you'll wonder what took you so long.* **PHRASE** **no excuse** (*disapproval*) If you say that there is **no excuse for** something, you are emphasizing that it should not happen, or expressing disapproval that it has happened. ❑ *There's no excuse for behaviour like that.* **VERB** /ɪkˈskjuːz/ [T] (**excuses, excusing, excused**) **1** To **excuse** someone or **excuse** their behaviour means to provide reasons for their actions, especially when other people disapprove of these actions. = justify ❑ *He excused himself by saying he was 'forced to rob to maintain my wife and cat'.* **2** If you **excuse** someone for something wrong that they have done, you forgive them for it. = forgive ❑ *Many people might have excused them for shirking some of their responsibilities.* **3** If someone **is excused from** a duty or responsibility, they are told that they do not have to carry it out. ❑ *She is usually excused from her duties during the summer holidays.* **4** If you **excuse yourself**, you use a phrase such as 'Excuse me' as a polite way of saying that you are about to leave. ❑ *He excused himself and went up to his room.* **CONVENTION** **excuse me** **1** (*formulae*) You say **Excuse me** when you want to politely get someone's attention, especially when you are about to ask them a question. ❑ *Excuse me, but are you Mr Honig?* **2** (*formulae*) You use **excuse me** to apologize to someone when you have disturbed or interrupted them. ❑ *Excuse me interrupting, but there's something I need to say.* **3** (*politeness*) You use **excuse me** or a phrase such as **if you'll excuse me** as a polite way of indicating that you are about to leave or that you are about to stop talking to someone. ❑ *'Excuse me,' she said to José, and left the room.* **4** You use **excuse me, but** to indicate that you are about to disagree with someone. ❑ *Excuse me, but I want to know what all this has to do with us.* **5** (*formulae*) You say **Excuse me** to apologize when you have bumped into someone, or when you need to move past someone in a crowd. = sorry ❑ *Saying 'Excuse me', Seaton pushed his way into the crowded living room.* **6** (*formulae*) You say **Excuse me** to apologize when you have done something slightly embarrassing or impolite, such as burping, hiccuping, or sneezing.

✪ex·ecute ♦◇◇ /ˈeksɪkjuːt/ VERB [T] (**executes, executing, executed**) **1** To **execute** someone means to kill them as a punishment for a serious crime. ❑ *He said nobody had been executed as a direct result of the events.*

❑ *One group claimed to have executed the hostage.* **2** (*formal*) If you **execute** a plan, you carry it out. ❑ *We are going to execute our campaign plan to the letter.* ❑ *the expertly executed break-in in which three men overpowered and tied up a detective* **3** If you **execute** a difficult action or movement, you successfully perform it. ❑ *The landing was skilfully executed.*

✪ex·ecu·tion /ˌeksɪˈkjuːʃən/ NOUN [c, u] (**executions**) **1** [c, u] ❑ *Execution by lethal injection is scheduled for July 30th.* **2** [u] ❑ *US forces are fully prepared for the execution of any action once the order is given by the president.* ❑ *the need for top-class customer care and flawless execution*

✪ex·ecu·tive ♦◇◇ /ɪgˈzekjʊtɪv/ NOUN, ADJ
NOUN [c, SING] (**executives**) **1** [c] An **executive** is someone who is employed by a business at a senior level. Executives decide what the business should do, and ensure that it is done. = director, official, manager ❑ *an advertising executive* ❑ *She is a senior bank executive.* **2** [SING] ['the' executive, executive + N] The **executive** committee or board of an organization is a committee within that organization that has the authority to make decisions and ensures that these decisions are carried out. ❑ *They opted to put an executive committee in charge of the project rather than a single person.* **3** [SING] ['the' executive, executive + N] **The executive** is the part of the government of a country that is concerned with carrying out decisions or orders, as opposed to the part that makes laws or the part that deals with criminals. = administration, government ❑ *The government, the executive and the judiciary are supposed to be separate.*
ADJ **1** [executive + N] The **executive** sections and tasks of an organization are concerned with the making of decisions and with ensuring that decisions are carried out. ❑ *A successful job search needs to be as well organised as any other executive task.* **2** [executive + N] **Executive** goods are expensive products designed or intended for executives and other people at a similar social or economic level. ❑ *an executive briefcase*

✪ex·em·pli·fy /ɪgˈzemplɪfaɪ/ VERB [T] (**exemplifies, exemplifying, exemplified**) (*formal*) If a person or thing **exemplifies** something such as a situation, quality, or class of things, they are a typical example of it. ❑ *The room's style exemplifies their ideal of 'beauty and practicality'.* ❑ *the emotional expressiveness of modern dance as exemplified by the work of Martha Graham*

✪ex·empt /ɪgˈzempt/ ADJ, VERB
ADJ If someone or something is **exempt from** a particular rule, duty, or obligation, they do not have to follow it or do it. ❑ *Men in college were exempt from military service.* ❑ *Any income or capital gain received is exempt from tax.*
VERB [T] (**exempts, exempting, exempted**) To **exempt** a person or thing **from** a particular rule, duty, or obligation means to state officially that they are not bound or affected by it. ❑ *South Carolina claimed the power to exempt its citizens from the obligation to obey federal law.*

✪ex·emp·tion /ɪgˈzempʃən/ NOUN [c, u] (**exemptions**) ❑ *the exemption of employer-provided health insurance from taxation* ❑ *new exemptions for students and the low-paid*

ex·er·cise ♦♦◇ /ˈeksəsaɪz/ VERB, NOUN
VERB [T, I] (**exercises, exercising, exercised**) **1** [T] (*formal*) If you **exercise** something such as your authority, your rights, or a good quality, you use it or put it into effect. ❑ *They are merely exercising their right to free speech.* **2** [i] When you **exercise**, you move your body energetically in order to get in shape and to remain healthy. ❑ *She exercises two or three times a week.* **3** [T] If a movement or activity **exercises** a part of your body, it keeps it strong, healthy, or in good condition. ❑ *They call rowing the perfect sport. It exercises every major muscle group.*
NOUN [SING, U, c] (**exercises**) **1** [SING] The **exercise** of something such as your authority, your rights, or a good quality is the act of using or putting into effect your authority, your rights, or a good quality. ❑ *Social structures are maintained through the exercise of political and economic power.* **2** [u] **Exercise** is the activity of moving your body energetically in order to get in shape and to remain healthy. ❑ *Lack of exercise can lead to feelings of depression and exhaustion.* **3** [c] **Exercises** are a series of movements

or actions that you do in order to get in shape, remain healthy, or practise for a particular physical activity. ❑ *I do special neck and shoulder exercises.* ◳ [c] [usu pl, also 'on' exercise] **Exercises** are military activities and operations that are not part of a real war, but that allow the armed forces to practise for a real war. ❑ *General Powell predicted that in the future it might even be possible to stage joint military exercises.* ◳ [c] An **exercise** is a short activity or piece of work that you do, in school for example, which is designed to help you learn a particular skill. ❑ *Try working through the opening exercises in this chapter.*

✪ **ex·ert** /ɪgˈzɜːt/ VERB [T] (**exerts, exerting, exerted**)
◳ (*formal*) If someone or something **exerts** influence, authority, or pressure, they use it in a strong or determined way, especially in order to produce a particular effect. ❑ *He exerted considerable influence on the thinking of the scientific community on these issues.* ❑ *The cyst was causing swelling and exerting pressure on her brain.* ◳ If you **exert yourself**, you make a great physical or mental effort, or work hard to do something. ❑ *Do not exert yourself unnecessarily.*
ex·er·tion /ɪgˈzɜːʃən/ NOUN [u] ❑ *He clearly found the physical exertion exhilarating.*

✪ **ex·hale** /eksˈheɪl/ VERB [I, T] (**exhales, exhaling, exhaled**) (*formal*) When you **exhale**, you breathe out the air that is in your lungs. = breathe out ❑ *Hold your breath for a moment and exhale.* ❑ *The patient should inhale through the nose and exhale through the mouth.* ❑ *The carbon dioxide is exhaled from your lungs.* ❑ *the process of inhaling and exhaling air*
✪ **ex·ha·la·tion** /ˌekshəˈleɪʃən/ (**exhalations**) NOUN ≠ inhalation ❑ *Milton let out his breath in a long exhalation.* ❑ *the quick exhalation of breath through expanded nostrils*

✪ **ex·haust** ♦◇◇ /ɪgˈzɔːst/ VERB, NOUN
VERB [T] (**exhausts, exhausting, exhausted**) ◳ If something **exhausts** you, it makes you so tired, either physically or mentally, that you have no energy left. ❑ *Don't exhaust him.* ◳ If you **exhaust** something such as money or food, you use or finish it all. ❑ *We have exhausted all our material resources.* ❑ *They said that food supplies were almost exhausted.* ❑ *Energy resources were virtually exhausted.* ◳ If you **have exhausted** a subject or topic, you have talked about it so much that there is nothing more to say about it. ❑ *She and Chantal must have exhausted the subject of clothes.*
NOUN [u, c] (**exhausts**) ◳ [u] [also exhausts] **Exhaust** is the gas or steam that is produced when the engine of a vehicle is running. ❑ *the exhaust from a car engine* ❑ *The city's streets are filthy and choked with exhaust fumes.* ❑ *The particles in diesel exhaust can penetrate deeply into the lungs.* ◳ [c] The **exhaust** or the **exhaust pipe** is the pipe which carries the gas out of the engine of a vehicle.
ex·haust·ed /ɪgˈzɔːstɪd/ ADJ = worn out ❑ *She was too exhausted and distressed to talk about the tragedy.*
ex·haust·ing /ɪgˈzɔːstɪŋ/ ADJ = gruelling ❑ *It was an exhausting schedule she had set herself.*

ex·haus·tion /ɪgˈzɔːstʃən/ NOUN [u] **Exhaustion** is the state of being so tired that you have no energy left. ❑ *He is suffering from exhaustion.*

ex·haus·tive /ɪgˈzɔːstɪv/ ADJ If you describe a study, search, or list as **exhaustive**, you mean that it is very thorough and complete. = comprehensive ❑ *This is by no means an exhaustive list but it gives an indication of the many projects taking place.*
ex·haust·ive·ly /ɪgˈzɔːstɪvli/ ADV ❑ *Martin said these costs were scrutinized exhaustively by independent accountants.*

✪ **ex·hib·it** /ɪgˈzɪbɪt/ VERB, NOUN (*academic word*)
VERB [T, I] (**exhibits, exhibiting, exhibited**) ◳ [T] (*formal*) If someone or something shows a particular quality, feeling, or type of behaviour, you can say that they **exhibit** it. = show ❑ *He has exhibited symptoms of anxiety and overwhelming worry.* ❑ *Two cats or more in one house will also exhibit territorial behaviour.* ❑ *The economy continued to exhibit signs of decline in September.* ◳ [T] When a painting, sculpture, or object of interest **is exhibited**, it is put in a public place such as a museum or art gallery so that people can come to look at it. You can also say that animals are

exhibited in a zoo. ❑ *His work was exhibited in the best galleries in America, Europe and Asia.* ◳ [I] When artists **exhibit**, they show their work in public. ❑ *He has also exhibited at galleries and museums in New York and Washington.*
NOUN [c] (**exhibits**) ◳ An **exhibit** is a painting, sculpture, or object of interest that is displayed to the public in a museum or art gallery. ❑ *Shona showed me around the exhibits.* ◳ An **exhibit** is an object that a lawyer shows in court as evidence in a legal case. ❑ *The jury has already asked to see more than 40 exhibits from the trial.*

✪ **ex·hi·bi·tion** ♦◇◇ /ˌeksɪˈbɪʃən/ NOUN [c, sING, u] (**exhibitions**) (*academic word*) ◳ [c] An **exhibition** is a public event at which pictures, sculptures, or other objects of interest are displayed, for example at a museum or art gallery. ❑ *an exhibition of expressionist art* ◳ [sING] An **exhibition of** a particular skilful activity is a display or example of it that people notice or admire. = display ❑ *He responded in champion's style by treating the fans to an exhibition of power and speed.* ◳ [u] The **exhibition** of a painting, sculpture, or object of interest is the act of putting it in a public place such as a museum or art gallery so that people can come to look at it. ❑ *Five large pieces of the wall are currently on exhibition.*

ex·hil·arat·ing /ɪgˈzɪləreɪtɪŋ/ ADJ If you describe an experience or feeling as **exhilarating**, you mean that it makes you feel very happy and excited. ❑ *It was exhilarating to be on the road again and his spirits rose.*

ex·ile ♦◇◇ /ˈeksaɪl, ˈegz-/ NOUN, VERB
NOUN [u, c] (**exiles**) ◳ [u] If someone is living in **exile**, they are living in a foreign country because they cannot live in their own country, usually for political reasons. ❑ *He is now living in exile in Egypt.* ❑ *He returned from exile earlier this year.* ◳ [c] An **exile** is someone who has been exiled. ❑ *He is also an exile, a native of Palestine who has long given up the idea of going home.* ◳ [u] If a person or organization experiences **exile from** a particular place or situation, they have been sent away from it or removed from it against their will. ❑ *the Left's long exile from power from 1958 to 1981*
VERB [T] (**exiles, exiling, exiled**) ◳ If someone **is exiled**, they are living in a foreign country because they cannot live in their own country, usually for political reasons. ❑ *His second wife, Hilary, had been widowed, then exiled from South Africa.* ❑ *They threatened to exile her in southern Spain.* ◳ If you say that someone **has been exiled from** a particular place or situation, you mean that they have been sent away from it or removed from it against their will. = banish ❑ *He served less than a year of a five-year prison sentence, but was permanently exiled from the sport.*

✪ **ex·ist** ♦♦◇ /ɪgˈzɪst/ VERB [I] (**exists, existing, existed**) ◳ If something **exists**, it is present in the world as a real thing. = occur, be found, be present ❑ *He thought that if he couldn't see something, it didn't exist.* ❑ *Research opportunities exist in a wide range of areas.* ❑ *animals that no longer exist* ◳ To **exist** means to live, especially under difficult conditions or with very little food or money. ❑ *I was barely existing.* ❑ *Some people exist on melons or coconuts for weeks at a time.*

USAGE NOTE
exist
When **exist** means 'to be present', you do not use it in a continuous form. You do not say, for example, 'Tendencies towards cruel behaviour are existing in all human beings'. *Tendencies towards cruel behaviour **exist** in all human beings.* The verb 'be' is usually used instead of 'exist' when you are not emphasizing the physical presence of something. Do not say 'There exist numerous reasons for this'. *There **are** numerous reasons for this.*

✪ **ex·ist·ence** ♦◇◇ /ɪgˈzɪstəns/ NOUN [u, c] (**existences**) ◳ [u] The **existence** of something is the fact that it is present in the world as a real thing. = presence, occurrence ❑ *the existence of other galaxies* ❑ *Public worries about accidents are threatening the very existence of the nuclear* power industry. ❑ *The Congress of People's Deputies voted itself out of existence.* **2** [C] You can refer to someone's way of life as an **existence**, especially when they live under difficult conditions. ❑ *You may be stuck with a miserable existence for the rest of your life.*

ex·ist·ing ♦◇◇ /ɪɡˈzɪstɪŋ/ ADJ [existing + N] **Existing** is used to describe something that is now present, available, or in operation, especially when you are contrasting it with something that is planned for the future. ❑ *the need to improve existing products and develop new lines* ❑ *Existing timbers are replaced or renewed.*

exit /ˈeɡzɪt, ˈeksɪt/ NOUN, VERB
NOUN [C, SING] (**exits**) **1** [C] The **exit** is the door through which you can leave a public building. ❑ *He picked up the case and walked towards the exit.* **2** [C] An **exit** on a motorway, major road, or roundabout is a place where traffic can leave it. ❑ *She continued to the next exit, got off the motorway and pulled into a parking area.* **3** [C] (*formal*) If you refer to someone's **exit**, you are referring to the way that they left a room or building, or the fact that they left it. = departure ❑ *I made a hasty exit and managed to open the gate.* **4** [C] (*formal*) If you refer to someone's **exit**, you are referring to the way that they left a situation or activity, or the fact that they left it. = departure ❑ *It's her earliest exit from Wimbledon since going out in the opening round in 1997.* **5** [SING] **Exit** is a command in a computer program or system that stops it running. ❑ *Press Exit to return to your document.*
VERB [I, T] (**exits, exiting, exited**) **1** [I, T] (*formal*) If you **exit** from a room or building, you leave it. ❑ *She exits into the tropical storm.* ❑ *As I exited the final display, I entered a hexagonal room.* **2** [T] (*computing*) If you **exit** a computer program or system, you stop running it. ❑ *I can open other applications without having to exit WordPerfect.*

ex·ot·ic /ɪɡˈzɒtɪk/ ADJ Something that is **exotic** is unusual and interesting, usually because it comes from or is related to a distant country. ❑ *brilliantly coloured, exotic flowers*
ex·oti·cal·ly /ɪɡˈzɒtɪkli/ ADV ❑ *exotically beautiful scenery*

✪**ex·pand** ♦◇◇ /ɪkˈspænd/ VERB (*academic word*)
VERB [I, T] (**expands, expanding, expanded**) **1** If something **expands** or is **expanded**, it becomes larger. ❑ *Engineers noticed that the pipes were not expanding as expected.* ❑ *We have to expand the size of the image.* ❑ *The money supply expanded by 14.6 per cent in the year to September.* ❑ *a rapidly expanding universe* **2** If something such as a business, organization, or service **expands**, or if you **expand** it, it becomes bigger and includes more people, goods, or activities. = increase, grow, enlarge, develop; ≠ contract, shrink ❑ *The popular ceramics industry expanded towards the middle of the 19th century.* ❑ *Health officials are proposing to expand their services by organising counselling.*
PHRASAL VERB **expand on** or **expand upon** If you **expand on** or **expand upon** something, you give more information or details about it when you write or talk about it. = elaborate on, develop, enlarge on ❑ *The president used today's speech to expand on remarks he made last month.*

ex·panse /ɪkˈspæns/ NOUN [C] (**expanses**) An **expanse of** something, usually sea, sky, or land, is a very large amount of it. ❑ *a vast expanse of grassland*

✪**ex·pan·sion** ♦◇◇ /ɪkˈspænʃən/ NOUN [C, U] (**expansions**) **Expansion** is the process of becoming greater in size, number, or amount. = growth, spread, increase, development; ≠ contraction ❑ *the rapid expansion of private health insurance* ❑ *a new period of economic expansion* ❑ *The company has abandoned plans for further expansion.*

ex·pan·sive /ɪkˈspænsɪv/ ADJ If you are **expansive**, you talk a lot, or are friendly or generous, because you are feeling happy and relaxed. ❑ *He was becoming more expansive as he relaxed.*

✪**ex·pect** ♦♦♦ /ɪkˈspekt/ VERB
VERB [T, I] (**expects, expecting, expected**) **1** [T] If you **expect** something to happen, you believe that it will happen. = anticipate ❑ *a workman who expects to lose his job in the next few weeks* ❑ *The talks are expected to continue until tomorrow.* ❑ *They expect a gradual improvement in sales of new cars.* **2** [T] If you **are expecting** something or

someone, you believe that they will be delivered to you or come to you soon, often because this has been arranged earlier. ❑ *I wasn't expecting a visitor.* **3** [T] If you **expect** something, or **expect** a person **to** do something, you believe that it is your right to have that thing, or the person's duty to do it for you. ❑ *He wasn't expecting our hospitality.* ❑ *I do expect to have some time to myself in the evenings.* **4** [T] If you tell someone not to **expect** something, you mean that the thing is unlikely to happen as they have planned or imagined, and they should not hope that it will. ❑ *Don't expect an instant cure.* ❑ *You cannot expect to like all the people you will work with.* **5** [I, T] If you say that a woman **is expecting** a baby, or that she **is expecting**, you mean that she is pregnant. ❑ *She was expecting another baby.*
PHRASE **I expect** (*spoken*) You say '**I expect**' to suggest that a statement is probably correct, or a natural consequence of the present situation, although you have no definite knowledge. ❑ *I expect you can guess what follows.* ❑ *I expect you're tired.*

ex·pec·tan·cy /ɪkˈspektənsi/ NOUN [U] **Expectancy** is the feeling or hope that something exciting, interesting, or good is about to happen. = anticipation ❑ *The supporters had a tremendous air of expectancy.*

ex·pec·tant /ɪkˈspektənt/ ADJ **1** If someone is **expectant**, they are excited because they think something interesting is about to happen. ❑ *An expectant crowd gathered.* **2** [expectant + N] An **expectant** mother or father is someone whose baby is going to be born soon. ❑ *a magazine for expectant mothers*
ex·pect·ant·ly /ɪkˈspektəntli/ ADV [expectantly after V] ❑ *The others waited, looking at him expectantly.*

✪**ex·pec·ta·tion** ♦◇◇ /ˌekspekˈteɪʃən/ NOUN [U, C] (**expectations**) **1** [U] [also expectations] Your **expectations** are your strong hopes or beliefs that something will happen or that you will get something that you want. ❑ *Their hope, and their expectation, was that she was going to be found safe and that she would be returned to her family.* **2** [C] A person's **expectations** are strong beliefs they have about the proper way someone should behave or something should happen. ❑ *Stephen Chase had determined to live up to the expectations of the company.*

ex·pe·di·ent /ɪkˈspiːdiənt/ NOUN, ADJ
NOUN [C] (**expedients**) An **expedient** is an action that achieves a particular purpose, but may not be morally right. ❑ *The curfew regulation is a temporary expedient made necessary by a sudden emergency.*
ADJ If it is **expedient to** do something, it is useful or convenient to do it, even though it may not be morally right. ❑ *Governments frequently ignore human rights abuses in other countries if it is politically expedient to do so.*

ex·pe·di·tion /ˌekspɪˈdɪʃən/ NOUN [C] (**expeditions**) **1** An **expedition** is an organized trip made for a particular purpose such as exploration. ❑ *Byrd's 1928 expedition to Antarctica* **2** You can refer to a group of people who are going on an expedition as an **expedition**. ❑ *Forty-three members of the expedition were killed.* **3** An **expedition** is a short trip that you make for pleasure. = trip ❑ *Officer Goss was on a fishing expedition.*

ex·pel /ɪkˈspel/ VERB [T] (**expels, expelling, expelled**) **1** If someone **is expelled from** a school or organization, they are officially told to leave because they have behaved badly. ❑ *More than five thousand high school students have been expelled for cheating.* **2** If people **are expelled from** a place, they are made to leave it, often by force. ❑ *An American academic was expelled from the country yesterday.* ❑ *They were told that they should expel the refugees.* **3** To **expel** something means to force it out from a container or from your body. ❑ *As the lungs exhale this waste, gas is expelled into the atmosphere.*

✪**ex·pend** /ɪkˈspend/ VERB [T] (**expends, expending, expended**) (*formal*) To **expend** something, especially energy, time, or money, means to use it or spend it. ❑ *Children expend a lot of energy and may need more high-energy food than adults.* ❑ *In fact, health experts have expended a great deal of effort in their search for an acceptable definition.*

✪**ex·pendi·ture** /ɪkˈspendɪtʃə/ NOUN [C, U] (**expenditures**) (*formal*) Expenditure is the spending of money on something, or the money that is spent on something. = spending, costs □ *Policies of tax reduction must lead to reduced public expenditure.* □ *They should cut their expenditure on defence.*

ex·pense ◆◇◇ /ɪkˈspens/ NOUN
NOUN [C, U, PL] (**expenses**) **1** [C, U] Expense is the money that something costs you or that you need to spend in order to do something. □ *He's bought a big TV at vast expense so that everyone can see properly.* **2** [PL] (*business*) Expenses are amounts of money that you spend while doing something in the course of your work, which will be paid back to you afterwards. □ *Her airfare and hotel expenses were paid by the committee.*
PHRASES **at someone's expense** **1** If you do something at someone's **expense**, they provide the money for it. □ *Should architects continue to be trained for five years at public expense?* **2** If someone laughs or makes a joke **at your expense**, they do it to make you seem foolish. □ *I think he's having fun at our expense.*
at the expense of **1** If you achieve something **at the expense of** someone, you do it in a way that might cause them some harm or disadvantage. □ *According to this study, women have made notable gains at the expense of men.* **2** (*disapproval*) If you say that someone does something **at the expense of** another thing, you are expressing concern that they are not doing the second thing, because the first thing uses all their resources. □ *The orchestra has more discipline now, but at the expense of spirit.*
go to the expense of If you **go to the expense of** doing something, you do something that costs a lot of money. If you **go to** great **expense to** do something, you spend a lot of money in order to achieve it. □ *Why go to the expense of buying an electric saw when you can borrow one?*

ex·pen·sive ◆◆◇ /ɪkˈspensɪv/ ADJ If something is **expensive**, it costs a lot of money. = costly □ *Broadband is still more expensive than dial-up services.*
ex·pen·sive·ly /ɪkˈspensɪvli/ ADV □ *She was expensively dressed, with fine furs and jewels.*

✪**ex·peri·ence** ◆◆◆ /ɪkˈspɪəriəns/ NOUN, VERB
NOUN [U, C, SING] (**experiences**) **1** [U] Experience is knowledge or skill in a particular job or activity that you have gained because you have done that job or activity for a long time. ≠ inexperience □ *He has also had managerial experience on every level.* □ *three years of relevant experience in stem-cell research* **2** [U] Experience is used to refer to the past events, knowledge, and feelings that make up someone's life or character. □ *I should not be in any danger here, but experience has taught me caution.* □ *She had learned from experience to take little rests in between her daily routine.* **3** [C] An **experience** is something that you do or that happens to you, especially something important that affects you. = event, incident □ *His only experience of gardening so far proved immensely satisfying.* □ *Many of his clients are very nervous, usually because of a bad experience in the past.* **4** [SING] Experience is the act of experiencing something. □ *the experience of pain*
VERB [T] (**experiences, experiencing, experienced**) **1** If you **experience** a particular situation, you are in that situation or it happens to you. □ *We had never experienced this kind of holiday before and had no idea what to expect.* □ *British business is now experiencing a severe recession.* **2** If you **experience** a feeling, you feel it or are affected by it. □ *Widows seem to experience more distress than widowers.*

USAGE NOTE

experience

When you use **experience** to talk generally about someone's past and the things they have done, it is an uncountable noun. You do not, for example, talk about someone's 'work experiences'.
*You do not need any previous **experience** in studying a language.*
When you use **experience** to talk about a particular event or situation that you go through, it is a countable noun.
*The unique culture and friendly hospitality make this trip an unforgettable **experience**.*

WHICH WORD?
experience or experiment?

Do not confuse **experience** and **experiment**. If you have **experience** of something, you have done it, seen it, or felt it.
□ *I had no military **experience**.*
An **experience** is something that happens to you.
□ *I've also been up in a hot air balloon, which was a wonderful **experience**.*
An **experiment** is a scientific test you do to find out more about something.
□ *Such conclusions are based on laboratory **experiments**.*

WORD CONNECTIONS
VERB + **experience**

have experience
gain experience
lack experience
□ *Work placement programmes allow students to gain experience.*

learn from experience
□ *You need to learn from experience and not make the same mistake again.*

have an experience
enjoy an experience
describe an experience
□ *Enjoy a memorable experience by treating yourself to a weekend at a spa.*

ADJ + **experience**

relevant experience
previous experience
essential experience
valuable experience
□ *Do you have any previous experience of working with children?*

managerial experience
professional experience
□ *We are looking for someone with previous managerial experience.*

past experience
personal experience
first-hand experience
□ *Past experience has taught me to be cautious.*

a good experience
a bad experience
a painful experience
a wonderful experience
□ *Visiting Japan was a wonderful experience.*

the whole experience
□ *The whole experience wasn't nearly as bad as I expected.*

ex·pe·ri·enced /ɪkˈspɪəriənst/ ADJ If you describe someone as **experienced**, you mean that they have been doing a particular job or activity for a long time, and therefore know a lot about it or are very skilful at it. □ *lawyers who are experienced in these matters* □ *It's a team packed with experienced and mature professionals.*

✪**ex·peri·ment** ◆◇◇ NOUN, VERB
NOUN /ɪkˈsperɪmənt/ [C, U] (**experiments**) **1** An **experiment** is a scientific test done in order to discover what happens to something in particular conditions. □ *The astronauts are conducting a series of experiments to learn more about how the body adapts to weightlessness.* □ *a proposed new law on animal experiments* □ *This question can be answered only by experiment.* **2** An **experiment** is the trying out of a new idea or method in order to see what it is like and what effects it has. □ *As an experiment, we bought Ted a watch.*
VERB /ɪkˈsperɪment/ [I] (**experiments, experimenting, experimented**) **1** If you **experiment with** something or

E

experiment on it, you do a scientific test on it in order to discover what happens to it in particular conditions. ❑ *In 1857 Mendel started experimenting with peas in his monastery garden.* ❑ *The scientists have experimented on the tiny neck arteries of rats.* ❑ *The scientists have already experimented at each other's test sites.* **2** To **experiment** means to try out a new idea or method to see what it is like and what effects it has. ❑ *if you like cooking and have the time to experiment*

ex·peri·men·ta·tion /ɪkˌspɛrɪmɛnˈteɪʃən/ NOUN [U] **1** *the ethical aspects of animal experimentation* **2** *Decentralization and experimentation must be encouraged.*

✪**ex·peri·men·tal** /ɪkˌspɛrɪˈmɛntəl/ ADJ **1** Something that is **experimental** is new or uses new ideas or methods, and might be modified later if it is unsuccessful. ❑ *an experimental air-conditioning system* ❑ *The technique is experimental, but the list of its practitioners is growing.* **2** [experimental + N] **Experimental** means using, used in, or resulting from scientific experiments. ❑ *the main techniques of experimental science* ❑ *the use of experimental animals* ❑ *We have experimental and observational evidence concerning things which happened before and after the origin of life.* **3** An **experimental** action is done in order to see what it is like, or what effects it has. ❑ *The senator is ready to argue for an experimental lifting of the ban.*

ex·peri·men·tal·ly /ɪkˌspɛrɪˈmɛntəli/ ADV **1** [experimentally with V] ❑ *an ecology laboratory, where communities of species can be studied experimentally under controlled conditions* **2** [experimentally with V] ❑ *This system is being tried out experimentally at many universities.*

✪**ex·pert** ♦♦◇ /ˈɛkspɜːt/ NOUN, ADJ (academic word) NOUN [C] (**experts**) An **expert** is a person who is very skilled at doing something or who knows a lot about a particular subject. = specialist ❑ *a yoga expert* ❑ *Health experts warn that the issue is a global problem.* ❑ *an expert on trade in that area*

ADJ **1** Someone who is **expert at** doing something is very skilled at it. = skilled ❑ *The Japanese are expert at lowering manufacturing costs.* **2** [expert + N] If you say that someone has **expert** hands or an **expert** eye, you mean that they are very skilful or experienced in using their hands or eyes for a particular purpose. ❑ *Harvey cured the pain with his own expert hands.* **3** [expert + N] **Expert** advice or help is given by someone who has studied a subject thoroughly or who is very skilled at a particular job. ❑ *We'll need an expert opinion.*

ex·pert·ly /ˈɛkspɜːtli/ ADV [expertly with V] ❑ *Shopkeepers expertly rolled spices up in bay leaves.*

✪**ex·per·tise** /ˌɛkspɜːˈtiːz/ NOUN [U] **Expertise** is special skill or knowledge that is acquired by training, study, or practice. ❑ *She was not an accountant and didn't have the expertise to verify all of the financial details.* ❑ *The problem is that most local authorities lack the expertise to deal sensibly in this market.* ❑ *students with expertise in forensics* ❑ *a pooling and sharing of knowledge and expertise*

ex·pire /ɪkˈspaɪə/ VERB [I] (**expires, expiring, expired**) When something such as a contract, deadline, or visa **expires**, it comes to an end or is no longer valid. = run out ❑ *He had lived illegally in the United States for five years after his visitor's visa expired.*

✪**ex·plain** ♦♦◇ /ɪkˈspleɪn/ VERB VERB [I, T] (**explains, explaining, explained**) **1** If you **explain** something, you give details about it or describe it so that it can be understood. = describe ❑ *Not every judge, however, has the ability to explain the law in simple terms.* ❑ *Don't sign anything until your lawyer has explained the contract to you.* ❑ *Professor Griffiths explained how the drug appears to work.* **2** If you **explain**, or **explain** something that has happened, you give people reasons for it, especially in an attempt to justify it. = account for ❑ *'Let me explain, sir.'—'Don't tell me about it. I don't want to know.'* ❑ *Before she ran away, she left a note explaining her actions.* ❑ *Explain why you didn't telephone.* ❑ *The receptionist apologized for the delay, explaining that it had been a hectic day.*

PHRASAL VERB **explain away** If someone **explains away** a mistake or a bad situation they are responsible for, they try to indicate that it is unimportant or that it is not really

their fault. ❑ *He evaded her questions about the war and tried to explain away the atrocities.*

✪**ex·pla·na·tion** ♦◇◇ /ˌɛkspləˈneɪʃən/ NOUN [C] (**explanations**) **1** [also 'of/in' explanation] If you give an **explanation** of something that has happened, you give people reasons for it, especially in an attempt to justify it. = reason, description ❑ *She told the court she would give a full explanation of the prosecution's decision on Monday.* ❑ *The researchers offer two possible explanations of this.* ❑ *an explanation for the different results* **2** If you say there is an **explanation for** something, you mean that there is a reason for it. = reason ❑ *The deputy airport manager said there was no apparent explanation for the crash.* **3** If you give an **explanation of** something, you give details about it or describe it so that it can be understood. ❑ *He has given a very clear explanation of his remarks and the context in which they were made.*

ex·plana·tory /ɪkˈsplænətəri, AmE -tɔːri/ ADJ (formal) **Explanatory** statements or theories are intended to make people understand something by describing it or giving the reasons for it. ❑ *These statements are accompanied by a series of explanatory notes.*

✪**ex·plic·it** /ɪkˈsplɪsɪt/ ADJ (academic word) **1** Something that is **explicit** is expressed or shown clearly and openly, without any attempt to hide anything. = overt ❑ *Sexually explicit scenes in films and books were taboo under the old regime.* ❑ *explicit references to age in recruitment advertising* ❑ *The FBI's instructions were explicit.* **2** [V-LINK + explicit, oft explicit 'about' N] If you are **explicit about** something, you speak about it very openly and clearly. ❑ *He was explicit about his intention to overhaul the party's internal voting system.*

✪**ex·plic·it·ly** /ɪkˈsplɪsɪtli/ ADV **1** = overtly; ≠ implicitly ❑ *The play was the first commercially successful work dealing explicitly with homosexuality.* ❑ *Their intention is not to become involved in explicitly political activities.* **2** *She has been talking very explicitly about AIDS to these groups.*

ex·plode ♦◇◇ /ɪkˈspləʊd/ VERB [I, T] (**explodes, exploding, exploded**) **1** [I, T] If an object such as a bomb **explodes** or if someone or something **explodes** it, it bursts loudly and with great force, often causing damage or injury. ❑ *They were clearing up when the second bomb exploded.* **2** [I] If someone **explodes**, they express strong feelings suddenly and violently. ❑ *Do you fear that you'll burst into tears or explode with anger in front of her?* *'What happened!' I exploded.* **3** [I] If something **explodes**, it increases suddenly and rapidly in number or intensity. ❑ *The population explodes to 40,000 during the tourist season.* **4** [T] If someone **explodes** a theory or myth, they prove that it is wrong or impossible. ❑ *Electricity privatization has exploded the myth of cheap nuclear power.*

✪**ex·ploit** ♦◇◇ VERB, NOUN (academic word) VERB /ɪkˈsplɔɪt/ [T] (**exploits, exploiting, exploited**) **1** If you say that someone **is exploiting** you, you think that they are treating you unfairly by using your work or ideas and giving you very little in return. ❑ *Critics claim he exploited black musicians for personal gain.* ❑ *exploited workers* **2** If you say that someone **is exploiting** a situation, you disapprove of them because they are using it to gain an advantage for themselves, rather than trying to help other people or do what is right. ❑ *The government and its opponents compete to exploit the troubles to their advantage.* **3** If you **exploit** something, you use it well, and achieve something or gain an advantage from it. = use ❑ *You'll need a good antenna to exploit the radio's performance.* ❑ *Cary is hoping to exploit new opportunities in Europe.* ❑ *So you feel that your skills have never been fully appreciated or exploited?* **4** To **exploit** resources or raw materials means to develop them and use them for industry or commercial activities. ❑ *I think we're being very short-sighted in not exploiting our own coal.*

NOUN /ˈɛksplɔɪt/ [C] (**exploits**) If you refer to someone's **exploits**, you mean the brave, interesting, or amusing things that they have done. ❑ *His wartime exploits were later made into a film and a television series.*

✪**ex·ploi·ta·tion** /ˌɛksplɔɪˈteɪʃən/ NOUN [U, SING] **1** [U] ❑ *Extra payments should be made to protect the interests of the staff* and prevent exploitation. **2** [SING] ❏ the exploitation of the famine by local politicians **3** [U] = use ❏ the planned exploitation of its potential oil and natural gas reserves

ex·plor·a·tory /ɪkˈsplɒrətri, AmE -ˈsplɔːrətɔːri/ ADJ Exploratory actions are done in order to discover something or to learn the truth about something. ❏ Exploratory surgery revealed her liver cancer.

✪ **ex·plore** ♦◇◇ /ɪkˈsplɔː/ VERB [I, T] (explores, exploring, explored) **1** [I, T] If you explore, or explore a place, you travel around it to find out what it is like. ❏ I just wanted to explore on my own. ❏ After exploring the old part of town there is a guided tour of the cathedral. ❏ NASA has launched a spacecraft to explore the planet Mars. **2** [T] If you explore an idea or suggestion, you think about it or comment on it in detail, in order to assess it carefully. = investigate ❏ The film is eloquent as it explores the relationship between artist and instrument. ❏ The secretary is expected to explore ideas for post-war reconstruction of the area. **3** [I] If people explore for a substance such as oil or minerals, they study an area and do tests on the land to see whether they can find it. ❏ Central to the operation is a mile-deep well, dug originally to explore for oil. **4** [T] If you explore something with your hands or fingers, you touch it to find out what it feels like. ❏ He explored the wound with his finger, trying to establish its extent.

✪ **ex·plo·ra·tion** /ˌekspləˈreɪʃən/ NOUN [C, U] (explorations) **1** [C, U] ❏ We devote several days to the exploration of the magnificent Maya sites of Copan. **2** [C, U] ❏ I looked forward to the exploration of their theories. ❏ an agonized exploration of the psychology of a criminal intellectual **3** [U] ❏ Oryx is a Dallas-based oil and gas exploration and production concern.

ex·plo·sion ♦◇◇ /ɪkˈspləʊʒən/ NOUN [C, U] (explosions) **1** [C] An explosion is a sudden, violent burst of energy, such as one caused by a bomb. = blast ❏ After the second explosion, all of London's main train and underground stations were shut down. **2** [C, U] Explosion is the act of deliberately causing a bomb or similar device to explode. ❏ Bomb disposal experts blew up the bag in a controlled explosion. **3** [C] An explosion is a large rapid increase in the number or amount of something. ❏ The study also forecast an explosion in the diet soft-drink market. **4** [C] An explosion is a sudden violent expression of someone's feelings, especially anger. = outburst ❏ Every time they met, Myra anticipated an explosion. **5** [C] An explosion is a sudden and serious political protest or violence. ❏ the explosion of protest and violence sparked off by the killing of seven workers

ex·plo·sive /ɪkˈspləʊsɪv/ NOUN, ADJ NOUN [C, U] (explosives) An explosive is a substance or device that can cause an explosion. ❏ one hundred and fifty pounds of Semtex explosive
ADJ **1** Something that is explosive is capable of causing an explosion. ❏ The explosive device was timed to go off at the rush hour. **2** An explosive growth is a sudden, rapid increase in the size or quantity of something. ❏ The explosive growth in casinos is one of the most conspicuous signs of Westernization. **3** An explosive situation is likely to have difficult, serious, or dangerous effects. ❏ He appeared to be treating the potentially explosive situation with some sensitivity. **4** If you describe someone as explosive, you mean that they tend to express sudden violent anger. = fiery ❏ He's inherited his father's explosive temper.

✪ **ex·port** ♦◇◇ VERB, NOUN (academic word) VERB /ɪkˈspɔːt/ [I, T] (exports, exporting, exported) **1** [I, T] To export products or raw materials means to sell them to another country. ❏ The nation also exports beef. ❏ They expect the antibiotic products to be exported to Southeast Asia and Africa. ❏ The company now exports to Japan. ❏ To earn foreign exchange we must export. **2** [T] To export something means to introduce it into another country or make it happen there. ❏ It has exported inflation at times. **3** [T] In computing, if you export files or information from one type of software into another type, you change their format so that they can be used in the new software. ❏ Files can be exported in ASCII or PCX formats. NOUN /ˈekspɔːt/ [C, U] (exports) **1** [C, U] [also exports] Export is the act of selling products or raw materials to another country. ❏ the production and export of cheap casual

wear ❏ A lot of our land is used to grow crops for export. **2** [C] Exports are goods sold to another country and sent there. ❏ He did this to promote American exports. ❏ Ghana's main export is cocoa.
✪ **ex·por·ta·tion** /ˌekspɔːˈteɪʃən/ NOUN [U] (mainly AmE) ≠ importation ❏ an asymmetry between positive and negative exportation

WORD CONNECTIONS

VERB + **export**

halt exports
ban exports
❏ The government has banned exports of live animals.

boost exports
increase exports
❏ They embarked on a programme of economic reform to boost exports and encourage foreign investment.

ADJ + **export**

cheap exports
expensive exports
illegal exports
❏ European firms are having to compete with cheaper exports from Asia.

✪ **ex·pose** ♦◇◇ /ɪkˈspəʊz/ VERB [T] (exposes, exposing, exposed) (academic word) **1** To expose something that is usually hidden means to uncover it so that it can be seen. = uncover, reveal, disclose; ≠ cover, hide ❏ Lowered sea levels exposed the shallow continental shelf beneath the Bering Sea. ❏ a wall with exposed wiring **2** To expose a person or situation means to reveal that they are bad or immoral in some way. ❏ the story of how the press helped expose the truth about the Nixon administration **3** If someone is exposed to something dangerous or unpleasant, they are put in a situation in which it might affect them. = subject ❏ They had not been exposed to most diseases common to urban populations. ❏ A wise mother never exposes her children to the slightest possibility of danger. ❏ people exposed to high levels of radiation **4** If someone is exposed to an idea or feeling, usually a new one, they are given experience of it, or introduced to it. ❏ local people who've not been exposed to glimpses of Western life before

✪ **ex·po·sure** ♦◇◇ /ɪkˈspəʊʒə/ NOUN [U, C] (exposures) **1** [U] Exposure to something dangerous means being in a situation where it might affect you. = subjection, contact, experience ❏ Exposure to lead is known to damage the brains of young children. ❏ the potential exposure of people to nuclear waste **2** [U] Exposure is the harmful effect on your body caused by very cold weather. ❏ He was suffering from exposure and shock but his condition was said to be stable. **3** [U] The exposure of a well-known person is the revealing of the fact that they are bad or immoral in some way. ❏ He undertook increasingly dangerous assignments until his exposure as a spy. **4** [U] Exposure is publicity that a person, company, or product receives. = publicity ❏ All the candidates have been getting an enormous amount of exposure on television and in the press. **5** [C] (technical) In photography, an exposure is a single photograph. ❏ Larger drawings tend to require two or three exposures to cover them.

✪ **ex·press** ♦◇◇ /ɪkˈspres/ VERB, ADJ, ADV, NOUN VERB [T] (expresses, expressing, expressed) **1** When you express an idea or feeling, or express yourself, you show what you think or feel. = communicate, convey ❏ He expressed grave concern at American attitudes. ❏ He expresses himself easily in English. ❏ groping for some way to express what she felt **2** If an idea or feeling expresses itself in some way, it can be clearly seen in someone's actions or in its effects on a situation. = manifest ❏ The anxiety of the separation often expresses itself as anger towards the child for getting lost.
ADJ **1** [express + N] (formal) An express command or order is one that is clearly and deliberately stated. = explicit ❏ This mighty electricity-generating power station was built on the express orders of the president. **2** [express + N] If you refer to an express intention or purpose, you are emphasizing that it is a deliberate and specific one that

E

you have before you do something. = specific ❏ *The express purpose of the flights was to get Americans out of the danger zone.* **3** [express + N] **Express** is used to describe special services provided by companies or organizations such as the Post Office, in which things are sent or done faster than usual for a higher price. ❏ *A special express service is available by fax.*

ADV If you send something or have something done **express**, you use a special and more expensive service so that it is sent or done faster than usual. ❏ *Send it express.*

NOUN [C] (**expresses**) An **express** or an **express** train is a fast train that stops at very few stations. ❏ *Punctually at 7.45, the express to Kuala Lumpur left Singapore station.*

ex·press·ly /ɪkˈspresli/ ADV **1** *He has expressly forbidden her to go out on her own.* **2** *projects expressly designed to support cattle farmers*

❉ **ex·pres·sion** ◆◇◇ /ɪkˈspreʃən/ NOUN [C, U] (**expressions**) **1** [C, U] The **expression** of ideas or feelings is the showing of them through words, actions, or artistic activities. = communication, indication ❏ *Laughter is one of the most infectious expressions of emotion.* ❏ *the rights of the individual to freedom of expression* **2** [C, U] Your **expression** is the way that your face looks at a particular moment. It shows what you are thinking or feeling. ❏ *Levin sat there, an expression of sadness on his face.* **3** [U] **Expression** is the showing of feeling when you are acting, singing, or playing a musical instrument. ❏ *I think I put more expression into my lyrics than a lot of other singers do.* **4** [C] An **expression** is a word or phrase. ❏ *She spoke in a quiet voice but used remarkably coarse expressions.*

ex·pres·sive /ɪkˈspresɪv/ ADJ If you describe a person or their behaviour as **expressive**, you mean that their behaviour clearly indicates their feelings or intentions. ❏ *You can train people to be more expressive.* ❏ *the present fashion for intuitive, expressive painting*

ex·pres·sive·ly /ɪkˈspresɪvli/ ADV [expressively with V] ❏ *He moved his hands expressively.*

ex·pul·sion /ɪkˈspʌlʃən/ NOUN [C, U] (**expulsions**) **1** **Expulsion** is when someone is forced to leave a school, university, or organization. ❏ *Her hatred of authority led to her expulsion from high school.* **2** (formal) **Expulsion** is when someone is forced to leave a place. ❏ *the expulsion of Yemeni workers*

ex·quis·ite /ɪkˈskwɪzɪt, ˈekskwɪzɪt/ ADJ Something that is **exquisite** is extremely beautiful or pleasant, especially in a delicate way. ❏ *The Indians brought in exquisite beadwork to sell.*

ex·quis·ite·ly /ɪkˈskwɪzɪtli, ˈekskwɪzɪtli/ ADV ❏ *exquisitely crafted doll's houses*

ex-serviceman (BrE; in AmE, use veteran) NOUN [C] (**ex-servicemen**) An **ex-serviceman** is a man who used to be in a country's army, navy, or air force. ❏ *a holiday home for ex-servicemen*

WORD PARTS
The prefix *ex-* appears in words to show that someone is no longer a particular thing:
ex-serviceman (NOUN)
ex-wife (NOUN)
ex-soldier (NOUN)

❉ **ex·tend** ◆◆◇ /ɪkˈstend/ VERB [I, T] (**extends, extending, extended**) **1** [I] If you say that something, usually something large, **extends for** a particular distance or **extends from** one place to another, you are indicating its size or position. ❏ *The caves extend for some 12 miles.* ❏ *The main stem will extend to around 12 ft, if left to develop naturally.* **2** [I] If an object **extends from** a surface or place, it sticks out from it. ❏ *A table extended from the front of her desk to create a T-shaped seating arrangement.* **3** [I] If an event or activity **extends over** a period of time, it continues for that time. ❏ *The normal cyclone season extends from December to April.* **4** [I] If something **extends to** a group of people, things, or activities, it includes or affects them. ❏ *The service also extends to wrapping and delivering gifts.* ❏ *The talks will extend to the church, human rights groups, and other social organizations.* **5** [T] If you **extend** something, you make it

longer or bigger. ❏ *This year they have introduced three new products to extend their range.* ❏ *The building was extended in 1500.* **6** [I] If a piece of equipment or furniture **extends**, its length can be increased. ❏ *a table that extends to accommodate extra guests* **7** [I] If you **extend**, you increase the size of a house or other building by constructing one or more extra rooms. ❏ *Investors who cannot afford a larger property now can extend when they have more money.* **8** [T] If you **extend** something, you make it last longer than before or end at a later date. = continue, stretch, lengthen ❏ *They have extended the deadline by twenty-four hours.* ❏ *an extended contract* **9** [T] If you **extend** something to other people or things, you make it include or affect more people or things. ❏ *It might be possible to extend the technique to other crop plants.* **10** [T] If someone **extends** their hand, they stretch out their arm and hand to shake hands with someone. = stretch out ❏ *The man extended his hand: 'I'm Chuck.'*

❉ **ex·ten·sion** /ɪkˈstenʃən/ NOUN [C] (**extensions**) **1** An **extension** is a new room or building that is added to an existing building or group of buildings. ❏ *We are thinking of having an extension built, as we now require an extra bedroom.* **2** An **extension** is a new section of a road or railway that is added to an existing road or railway ❏ *a proposed extension to the No 7 subway line* **3** An **extension** is an extra period of time for which something lasts or is valid, usually as a result of official permission. ❏ *He first entered the country on a six-month visa, and was given a further extension of six months.* ❏ *I was given a two-year extension to my contract.* **4** Something that is an **extension of** something else is a development of it that includes or affects more people, things, or activities. ❏ *Many Filipinos see the bases as an extension of American colonial rule.* **5** [also extension + NUM] An **extension** is a telephone line that is connected to the switchboard of a company or institution, and that has its own number. The written abbreviation **ext** is also used. ❏ *She can get me on extension 308.* **6** An **extension** is a part connected to a piece of equipment in order to make it reach something further away. ❏ *a 30-foot extension lead*

❉ **ex·ten·sive** ◆◇◇ /ɪkˈstensɪv/ ADJ **1** Something that is **extensive** covers or includes a large physical area. ❏ *an extensive tour of Latin America* **2** Something that is **extensive** covers a wide range of details, ideas, or items. ❏ *She recently completed an extensive study of elected officials who began their political careers before the age of 35.* **3** If something is **extensive**, it is very great. ❏ *The security forces have extensive powers of search and arrest.*

ex·ten·sive·ly /ɪkˈstensɪvli/ ADV **1** [extensively after V] ❏ *Mark, however, needs to travel extensively with his varied business interests.* **2** *All these issues have been extensively researched in recent years.* **3** *Hydrogen is used extensively in industry for the production of ammonia.*

❉ **ex·tent** ◆◇◇ /ɪkˈstent/ NOUN

NOUN [SING] **1** If you are talking about how great, important, or serious a difficulty or situation is, you can refer to the **extent of** it. = magnitude, amount, degree, scale ❏ *The government itself has little information on the extent of industrial pollution.* ❏ *The full extent of the losses was disclosed yesterday.* **2** The **extent of** something is its length, area, or size. ❏ *Industry representatives made it clear that their commitment was only to maintain the extent of forests, not their biodiversity.*

PHRASES **to a large extent** or **to some extent** or **to a certain extent** (vagueness) You use expressions such as **to a large extent, to some extent,** or **to a certain extent** in order to indicate that something is partly true, but not entirely true. ❏ *It was and, to a large extent, still is a good show.* ❏ *To some extent this was the truth.* ❏ *To a certain extent it's easier for men to get work.* ❏ *This also endangers American interests in other regions, although to a lesser extent.* **to what extent** or **to that extent** or **to the extent that** (vagueness) You use expressions such as **to what extent, to that extent,** or **to the extent that** when you are discussing how true a statement is, or in what ways it is true. ❏ *It's still not clear to what extent this criticism is originating from within the ruling party.* ❏ *To that extent they helped bring about* their own destruction. ❏ *He could only be sorry to the extent that this affected his grandchildren.* ❏ *We may not be able to do it to the extent that we would like.*

to the extent of or **to the extent that** or **to such an extent that** (*emphasis*) You use expressions such as **to the extent of**, **to the extent that**, or **to such an extent that** in order to emphasize that a situation has reached a difficult, dangerous, or surprising stage. ❏ *Ford kept his suspicions to himself, even to the extent of going to jail for a murder he obviously didn't commit.*

✪**ex·te·ri·or** /ɪkˈstɪəriə/ NOUN, ADJ
NOUN [c] (**exteriors**) **1** The **exterior** of something is its outside surface. = outside; ≠ interior ❏ *The exterior of the building was a masterpiece of architecture, elegant and graceful.* ❏ *Some of the cells on the exterior of the blastula are destined to become eyes or wings.* **2** You can refer to someone's usual appearance or behaviour as their **exterior**, especially when it is very different from their real character. = facade ❏ *According to Mandy, Pat's tough exterior hides a shy and sensitive soul.*
ADJ [exterior + N] You use **exterior** to refer to the outside parts of something or things that are outside something. = outer, outside, external; ≠ interior, inner ❏ *The exterior walls were made of preformed concrete.* ❏ *the oven's exterior surfaces*

ex·ter·mi·nate /ɪkˈstɜːmɪneɪt/ VERB [T] (**exterminates, exterminating, exterminated**) To **exterminate** a group of people or animals means to kill all of them. ❏ *A huge effort was made to exterminate the rats.*
ex·ter·mi·na·tion /ɪkˌstɜːmɪˈneɪʃən/ NOUN [u] ❏ *the extermination of hundreds of thousands of their brethren*

✪**ex·ter·nal** /ɪkˈstɜːnəl/ ADJ (*academic word*) **1** External is used to indicate that something is on the outside of a surface or body, or that it exists, happens, or comes from outside. ❏ *a much reduced heat loss through external walls* ❏ *internal and external allergic reactions* **2** [external + N] External means involving or intended for foreign countries. ❏ *the commissioner for external affairs* ❏ *Jamaica's external debt* **3** [external + N] External means happening or existing in the world in general and affecting you in some way. ❏ *Such events occur only when the external conditions are favourable.*
✪**ex·ter·nal·ly** /ɪkˈstɜːnəli/ ADV **1** ≠ internally ❏ *Vitamins can be applied externally to the skin.* **2** ≠ internally ❏ *protecting the value of the dollar both internally and externally*

✪**ex·tinct** /ɪkˈstɪŋkt/ ADJ **1** A species of animal or plant that is **extinct** no longer has any living members, either in the world or in a particular place. ❏ *At the current rate of decline, many of the rain forest animals could become extinct in less than 10 years.* ❏ *It is 250 years since the wolf became extinct in Britain.* ❏ *the bones of extinct animals* **2** If a particular kind of worker, way of life, or type of activity is **extinct**, it no longer exists, because of changes in society. ❏ *Herbalism had become an all but extinct skill in the Western world.* **3** An **extinct** volcano is one that does not erupt or is not expected to erupt anymore. ❏ *Its tallest volcano, long extinct, is Olympus Mons.*

✪**ex·tinc·tion** /ɪkˈstɪŋkʃən/ NOUN [u] **1** The **extinction** of a species of animal or plant is the death of all its remaining living members. ❏ *An operation is beginning to try to save a species of crocodile from extinction.* ❏ *Many species have been shot to the verge of extinction.* **2** If someone refers to the **extinction** of a way of life or type of activity, they mean that the way of life or activity stops existing. ❏ *The loggers say their jobs are faced with extinction because of declining timber sales.*

ex·tin·guish /ɪkˈstɪŋgwɪʃ/ VERB [T] (**extinguishes, extinguishing, extinguished**) **1** (*formal*) If you **extinguish** a fire or a light, you stop it from burning or shining. = put out ❏ *It took about 50 minutes to extinguish the fire.* **2** If something **extinguishes** a feeling or idea, it destroys it. ❏ *The message extinguished her hopes of Richard's return.*

ex·tra ♦♦◇ /ˈekstrə/ ADJ, PRON, ADV, NOUN
ADJ **1** [extra + N] You use **extra** to describe an amount, person, or thing that is added to others of the same kind, or that can be added to others of the same kind. = additional ❏ *Police warned motorists to allow extra time to get to work.* ❏ *There's an extra blanket in the bottom drawer of the cupboard.* **2** [V-LINK + extra] If something is **extra**, you have to pay more money for it in addition to what you are already paying for something. ❏ *For foreign orders postage is extra.*
PRON You use **extra** to refer to the amount of money you have to pay for something in addition to what you are already paying for it. ❏ *She won't pay any extra.*
ADV **1** If you are charged **extra** for something, you have to pay more money for it in addition to what you are already paying. ❏ *You may be charged 10% extra for this service.* **2** [extra + ADJ/ADV] (*informal, emphasis*) You can use **extra** in front of adjectives and adverbs to emphasize the quality that they are describing. = especially ❏ *I said you'd have to be extra careful.*
NOUN [c] (**extras**) **1** Extras are additional amounts of money that are added to the price that you have to pay for something. ❏ *There are no hidden extras.* **2** Extras are things that are not necessary in a situation, activity, or object, but that make it more comfortable, useful, or enjoyable. ❏ *Optional extras include cooking classes at a top restaurant.* **3** The **extras** in a film are the people who play unimportant parts, for example, as members of a crowd. ❏ *In 1944, Kendall entered films as an extra.*

✪**ex·tract** VERB, NOUN (*academic word*)
VERB /ɪkˈstrækt/ [T, PASSIVE] (**extracts, extracting, extracted**) **1** [T] To **extract** a substance means to obtain it from something else, for example, by using industrial or chemical processes. ❏ *the traditional method of pick and shovel to extract coal* ❏ *Citric acid can be extracted from the juice of oranges, lemons, limes or grapefruit.* ❏ *looking at the differences in the extracted DNA* **2** [T] If you **extract** something **from** a place, you take it out or pull it out. ❏ *He extracted a small notebook from his hip pocket.* **3** [T] When a dentist **extracts** a tooth, they remove it from the patient's mouth. ❏ *A dentist may decide to extract the tooth to prevent recurrent trouble.* **4** [T] If you say that someone **extracts** something, you disapprove of them because they take it for themselves to gain an advantage. ❏ *He sought to extract the maximum political advantage from the cut in interest rates.* **5** [T] If you **extract** information or a response **from** someone, you get it from them with difficulty, because they are unwilling to say or do what you want. ❏ *He made the mistake of trying to extract further information from our director.* **6** [T] If you **extract** a particular piece of information, you obtain it from a larger amount or source of information. ❏ *I've simply extracted a few figures.* ❏ *Britain's trade figures can no longer be extracted from export-and-import documentation at ports.* **7** [PASSIVE] (*journalism*) If part of a book or text **is extracted from** a particular book, it is printed or published. ❏ *This material has been extracted from 'Collins Good Wood Handbook'.*
NOUN /ˈekstrækt/ [c, u] (**extracts**) **1** [c] An **extract from** a book or piece of writing is a small part of it that is printed or published separately. = excerpt, passage ❏ *Read this extract from an information booklet about the work of an airline cabin crew.* **2** [c, u] **Extract** is a very concentrated liquid that is used for flavouring food or for its smell. ❏ *Blend in the vanilla extract, lemon peel, and walnuts.*

✪**ex·trac·tion** /ɪkˈstrækʃən/ NOUN [u, c] **1** [u] The **extraction** of a substance is the act of obtaining it from something else, for example, by using industrial or chemical processes. ❏ *Petroleum engineers plan and manage the extraction of oil.* ❏ *Several mineral extraction companies operate on the lake.* **2** [c, u] The **extraction** of a tooth is the act of removing it from a person's mouth. ❏ *In those days, dentistry was basic. Extractions were carried out without anaesthetic.* **3** [u] [with SUPP] (*formal*) If you say, for example, that someone is **of** French **extraction**, you mean that they or their family originally came from France. = origin, descent ❏ *Her real father was of Italian extraction.*

extra·dite /ˈekstrədaɪt/ VERB [T] (**extradites, extraditing, extradited**) (*formal*) If someone is extradited, they are officially sent back to their own or another country or state to be tried for a crime that they have been accused of. ❏ *A judge agreed to extradite him to Texas.*
extra·di·tion /ˌekstrəˈdɪʃən/ NOUN [c, u] (**extraditions**)

E

❏ *A New York court turned down the British government's request for his extradition.*

extraor·di·nary ♦◇◇ /ɪkˈstrɔːdənri, *AmE* -neri/ ADJ
1 (*approval*) If you describe something or someone as **extraordinary**, you mean that they have some extremely good or special quality. = exceptional, remarkable, amazing ❏ *We've made extraordinary progress as a society in that regard.* ❏ *The task requires extraordinary patience and endurance.* **2** (*emphasis*) If you describe something as **extraordinary**, you mean that it is very unusual or surprising. = remarkable, amazing ❏ *What an extraordinary thing to happen!* **3** [extraordinary + N] (*formal*) An **extraordinary** meeting is arranged to deal with a particular situation or problem, rather than happening regularly. ❏ *The U.S. has called for an extraordinary emergency meeting of the UN Human Rights Commission to examine the crisis.*

extraor·di·nari·ly /ɪkˈstrɔːdənrɪli, *AmE* -nerɪli/ ADV
1 [extraordinarily + ADJ] = exceptionally ❏ *She's extraordinarily disciplined.* **2** *Apart from the hair, he looked extraordinarily unchanged.*

WORD PARTS

The prefix *extra-* often appears in adjectives which refer to something being outside or beyond something else:

extraordinary (ADJ)

extra-marital (ADJ)

extra-curricular (ADJ)

❖**ex·trapo·late** /ɪkˈstræpəleɪt/ VERB [I] (**extrapolates, extrapolating, extrapolated**) (*formal*) If you **extrapolate** from known facts, you use them as a basis for general statements about a situation or about what is likely to happen in the future. ❏ *Extrapolating from his latest findings, he reckons about 80% of these deaths might be attributed to smoking.* ❏ *It is unhelpful to extrapolate general trends from one case.* ❏ *She concedes it will be difficult to extrapolate the data from studies of mice to humans.*
ex·trapo·la·tion /ɪkˌstræpəˈleɪʃən/ NOUN [C, U] (**extrapolations**) ❏ *His estimate of half a million HIV-positive cases was based on an extrapolation of the known incidence of the virus.*

ex·trava·gance /ɪkˈstrævəgəns/ NOUN [U, C] (**extravagances**) **1** [U] **Extravagance** is the spending of more money than is reasonable or than you can afford. ❏ *When the company went under, tales of his extravagance surged through the industry.* **2** [C] An **extravagance** is something that you spend money on but cannot really afford. ❏ *Why waste money on such extravagances?*

ex·trava·gant /ɪkˈstrævəgənt/ ADJ **1** Someone who is **extravagant** spends more money than they can afford or uses more of something than is reasonable. ❏ *We are not extravagant; restaurant meals are a luxury and designer clothes are out.* **2** Something that is **extravagant** costs more money than you can afford or uses more of something than is reasonable. ❏ *Her aunt gave her an uncharacteristically extravagant gift.* ❏ *Baking a whole cheese in pastry may seem extravagant.* **3** **Extravagant** behaviour is extreme behaviour that is often done for a particular effect. ❏ *He was extravagant in his admiration of Hellas.* **4** **Extravagant** claims or ideas are unrealistic or impractical. = wild ❏ *Don't be afraid to consider apparently extravagant ideas.*
ex·trava·gant·ly /ɪkˈstrævəgəntli/ ADV **1** [extravagantly with V] ❏ *The day before they left Jeff had shopped extravagantly for presents for the whole family.* **2** [extravagantly + ADJ/-ED] ❏ *By supercar standards, though, it is not extravagantly priced for a beautifully engineered machine.* **3** *She had on occasion praised him extravagantly.*

❖**ex·treme** ♦◇◇ /ɪkˈstriːm/ ADJ, NOUN
ADJ **1** **Extreme** means very great in degree or intensity. = great ❏ *The girls were afraid of snakes and picked their way along with extreme caution.* ❏ *people living in extreme poverty* ❏ *the author's extreme reluctance to generalise* **2** You use **extreme** to describe situations and behaviour that are much more severe or unusual than you would expect, especially when you disapprove of them because of this.

❏ *The extreme case was Poland, where 29 parties won seats.* ❏ *It is hard to imagine Jesse capable of anything so extreme.* **3** You use **extreme** to describe opinions, beliefs, or political movements that you disapprove of because they are very different from those that most people would accept as reasonable or normal. ❏ *This extreme view hasn't captured popular opinion.* **4** [extreme + N] The **extreme** end or edge of something is its farthest end or edge. = far ❏ *the room at the extreme end of the corridor*
NOUN [C] (**extremes**) You can use **extremes** to refer to situations or types of behaviour that have opposite qualities to each other, especially when each situation or type of behaviour has such a quality to the greatest degree possible. ❏ *a 'middle way' between the extremes of success and failure, wealth and poverty*
PHRASE **go to extremes** or **take something to extremes** or **carry something to extremes** If a person **goes to extremes** or **takes** something **to extremes**, they do or say something in a way that people consider to be unacceptable, unreasonable, or foolish. ❏ *The police went to the extremes of installing the most advanced safety devices in the man's house.*

❖**ex·treme·ly** ♦♦◇ /ɪkˈstriːmli/ ADV [extremely + ADJ/ADV] (*emphasis*) You use **extremely** in front of adjectives and adverbs to emphasize that the specified quality is present to a very great degree. = exceedingly, very, highly, greatly; ≠ moderately ❏ *My mobile phone is extremely useful.* ❏ *Three of them are working extremely well.* ❏ *These headaches are extremely common.*

ex·trem·ism /ɪkˈstriːmɪzəm/ NOUN [U] **Extremism** is the behaviour or beliefs of extremists. ❏ *Greater demands were being placed on the police by growing violence and left- and right-wing extremism.*

ex·trem·ist /ɪkˈstriːmɪst/ NOUN, ADJ
NOUN [C] (**extremists**) (*disapproval*) If you describe someone as an **extremist**, you disapprove of them because they try to bring about political change by using violent or extreme methods. ❏ *He said the country needed a strong intelligence service to counter espionage, terrorism, and foreign extremists.* ❏ *A previously unknown extremist group has said it carried out Friday's bomb attack.*
ADJ (*disapproval*) If you say that someone has **extremist** views, you disapprove of them because they believe in bringing about change by using violent or extreme methods. ❏ *his determination to purge the party of extremist views*

extro·vert /ˈekstrəvɜːt/ ADJ, NOUN
ADJ (*mainly BrE*; in *AmE*, usually use **extroverted**) Someone who is **extrovert** is very active, lively, and friendly. ❏ *His footballing skills and extrovert personality won the hearts of the public.*
NOUN [C] (**extroverts**) An **extrovert** is someone who is extrovert.

exu·ber·ance /ɪɡˈzjuːbərəns, *AmE* -ˈzuː-/ NOUN [U] **Exuberance** is behaviour that is energetic, excited, and cheerful. ❏ *Her burst of exuberance and her brightness overwhelmed me.*

exu·ber·ant /ɪɡˈzjuːbərənt, *AmE* -ˈzuː-/ ADJ If you are **exuberant**, you are full of energy, excitement, and cheerfulness. ❏ *So the exuberant young girl with dark hair and blue eyes decided to become a screen actress.*
exu·ber·ant·ly /ɪɡˈzjuːbərəntli, *AmE* -ˈzuː-/ ADV ❏ *They both laughed exuberantly.*

ex·ude /ɪɡˈzjuːd, *AmE* -ˈzuːd/ VERB [I, T] (**exudes, exuding, exuded**) (*formal*) **1** If someone **exudes** a quality or feeling, or if it **exudes**, they show that they have it to a great extent. = radiate ❏ *The guerrillas exude confidence. Every town, they say, is under their control.* ❏ *She exudes an air of relaxed calm.* **2** If something **exudes** a liquid or smell or if a liquid or smell **exudes from** it, the liquid or smell comes out of it slowly and steadily. ❏ *Nearby was a factory which exuded a pungent smell.*

eye ♦♦♦ /aɪ/ NOUN, VERB
NOUN [C, SING] (**eyes**) **1** [C] Your **eyes** are the parts of your body with which you see. ❏ *I opened my eyes and looked.* ❏ *a tall, thin white-haired lady with piercing dark brown eyes* **2** [C] You use **eye** when you are talking about a person's

ability to judge things or about the way in which they are considering or dealing with things. ❑ *William was a man of discernment, with an eye for quality.* ❑ *He first learned to fish under the watchful eye of his grandmother.* **3** [C] An **eye** is a small metal loop that a hook fits into, as a fastening on a piece of clothing. ❑ *There were lots of hooks and eyes in Victorian costumes!* **4** [C] The **eye** of a needle is the small hole at one end that the thread passes through. ❑ *The only difficult part was threading the cotton through the eye of the needle!* **5** [SING] **The eye** of a storm, tornado, or hurricane is the centre of it. ❑ *The eye of the hurricane hit Florida just south of Miami.*

[PHRASES] **before your eyes** or **in front of your eyes** or **under your eyes** (*emphasis*) If you say that something happens **before your eyes**, **in front of your eyes**, or **under your eyes**, you are emphasizing that it happens where you can see it clearly and often implying that it is surprising or unpleasant. ❑ *A lot of them died in front of our eyes.*

cast your eye or **run your eye** If you **cast your eye** or **run your eye** over something, you look at it or read it quickly. ❑ *I would be grateful if he could cast an expert eye over it and tell me what he thought of it.*

catch someone's eye **1** If something **catches** your **eye**, you suddenly notice it. ❑ *As she turned back, a movement across the lawn caught her eye.* **2** If you **catch** someone's **eye**, you do something to attract their attention, so that you can speak to them. ❑ *He tried to catch Annie's eye as he walked by her seat.*

close your eyes to something or **shut your eyes to something** If you **close** your **eyes** to something bad or if you **shut** your **eyes** to it, you ignore it. ❑ *Most governments must simply be shutting their eyes to the problem.*

cry your eyes out (*informal*) If you **cry** your **eyes out**, you cry very hard. ❑ *He didn't mean to be cruel but I cried my eyes out.*

as far as the eye can see If there is something **as far as the eye can see**, there is a lot of it and you cannot see anything else beyond it. ❑ *There are pine trees as far as the eye can see.*

have an eye for something If you say that someone **has an eye for** something, you mean that they are good at noticing or making judgments about it. ❑ *Susan has a keen eye for detail, so each dress is beautifully finished.*

in someone's eyes or **to someone's eyes** You use expressions such as **in** his **eyes** or **to** her **eyes** to indicate that you are reporting someone's opinion and that other people might think differently. ❑ *The other serious problem in the eyes of the new government is communalism.*

keep your eyes open or **keep an eye out for something** (*informal*) If you **keep** your **eyes open** or **keep an eye out for** someone or something, you watch for them carefully. ❑ *I ask the mounted patrol to keep their eyes open.*

keep your eye on something If you **keep an eye on** something or someone, you watch them carefully, for example to make sure that they are satisfactory or safe, or not causing trouble. ❑ *I went for a run there, keeping*

an eye on the children the whole time.

all eyes are on something (*journalism*) If you say that **all eyes are on** something or that the **eyes of the world are on** something, you mean that everyone is paying careful attention to it and what will happen. ❑ *All eyes will be on tomorrow's vote.*

have your eye on someone If someone **has their eye on** you, they are watching you carefully to see what you do. ❑ *A spokesman for the store said: 'He comes here quite a lot. We've had our eye on him before.'*

have your eye on something (*informal*) If you **have your eye on** something, you want to have it. ❑ *If you're saving up for a new outfit you've had your eye on, cheap dinners for a month might let you buy it.*

with your eyes open If you say that you did something **with your eyes open** or **with your eyes wide open**, you mean that you knew about the problems and difficulties that you were likely to have. ❑ *We want all our members to undertake this trip responsibly, with their eyes open.*

open your eyes If something **opens** your **eyes**, it makes you aware that something is different from the way that you thought it was. ❑ *Watching your child explore the world about her can open your eyes to delights long forgotten.*

see eye to eye If you **see eye to eye with** someone, you agree with them and have the same opinions and views. ❑ *Yuriko saw eye to eye with Yul on almost every aspect of the production.*

take your eyes off something When you **take** your **eyes off** the thing you have been watching or looking at, you stop looking at it. ❑ *She took her eyes off the road to glance at me.*

[VERB] [T] (**eyes, eyeing** or **eying, eyed**) If you **eye** someone or something in a particular way, you look at them carefully in that way. ❑ *Sally eyed Claire with interest.* ❑ *We eyed each other thoughtfully.*
→ See also **eye-catching**
✦ **turn a blind eye** → see **blind**; **feast your eyes** → see **feast**; **in your mind's eye** → see **mind**

eye·brow /ˈaɪbraʊ/ NOUN
[NOUN] [C] (**eyebrows**) Your **eyebrows** are the lines of hair that grow above your eyes.
[PHRASE] **raise an eyebrow** or **raise your eyebrows** If something causes you to **raise an eyebrow** or to **raise** your **eyebrows**, it causes you to feel surprised or disapproving. ❑ *An intriguing item on the news pages caused me to raise an eyebrow over my morning coffee.* ❑ *He raised his eyebrows over some of the suggestions.*

eye-catching ADJ Something that is **eye-catching** is very noticeable. = striking ❑ *a series of eye-catching ads*

eye·sight /ˈaɪsaɪt/ NOUN [U] Your **eyesight** is your ability to see. ❑ *He suffered from poor eyesight and could no longer read properly.*

eye·witness /ˌaɪˈwɪtnəs/ NOUN [C] (**eyewitnesses**) An **eyewitness** is a person who was present at an event and can therefore describe it, for example in a law court. ❑ *Eyewitnesses say the police then opened fire on the crowd.*

e

Ff

F also **f** /ef/ NOUN [C, U] (**F's, f's**) **F** is the sixth letter of the English alphabet.

fab·ric ◆◇◇ /'fæbrɪk/ NOUN [C, U, SING] (**fabrics**) **1** [C, U] **Fabric** is cloth or other material produced by weaving together cotton, nylon, wool, silk, or other threads. Fabrics are used for making things such as clothes, curtains, and sheets. ❑ *small squares of red cotton fabric* **2** [SING] The **fabric** of a society or system is its basic structure, with all the customs and beliefs that make it work successfully. ❑ *The fabric of society has been deeply damaged by the previous regime.*

fab·ri·cate /'fæbrɪkeɪt/ VERB [T] (**fabricates, fabricating, fabricated**) If someone **fabricates** information, they invent it in order to deceive people. ❑ *All four claim that officers fabricated evidence against them.* • **fab·ri·ca·tion** /ˌfæbrɪ'keɪʃən/ NOUN [C, U] (**fabrications**) = invention ❑ *She described the interview as a 'complete fabrication'.*

fabu·lous /'fæbjʊləs/ ADJ (*informal, emphasis*) If you describe something as **fabulous**, you are emphasizing that you like it a lot or think that it is very good. = wonderful ❑ *This is a fabulous album. It's fresh, varied, fun.*

fa·cade /fə'sɑːd/ also **façade** NOUN [C, SING] (**facades**) **1** [C] The **facade** of a building, especially a large one, is its front wall or the wall that faces the street. ❑ *the repairs to the building's facade* **2** [SING] A **facade** is an outward appearance which is deliberately false and gives you a wrong impression about someone or something. = show, semblance ❑ *They hid the troubles plaguing their marriage behind a facade of family togetherness.*

◇face ◆◆◆ /feɪs/ NOUN, VERB

NOUN [C, SING, U] (**faces**) **1** [C] Your **face** is the front part of your head from your chin to the top of your forehead, where your mouth, eyes, nose, and other features are. ❑ *He rolled down his window and stuck his face out.* ❑ *He was going red in the face and breathing with difficulty.* ❑ *She had a beautiful face.* **2** [C] If your **face** is happy, sad, or serious, for example, the expression on your face shows that you are happy, sad, or serious. ❑ *He was walking around with a sad face.* **3** [C] The **face** of a cliff, mountain, or building is a vertical surface or side of it. ❑ *Harrer was one of the first to climb the north face of the Eiger.* **4** [C] The **face** of a clock or watch is the surface with the numbers or hands on it, which shows the time. ❑ *It was too dark to see the face of my watch.* **5** [SING] If you say that **the face of** an area, institution, or field of activity is changing, you mean its appearance or nature is changing. ❑ *the changing face of the countryside* **6** [SING] If you refer to something as **the** particular **face of** an activity, belief, or system, you mean that it is one particular aspect of it, in contrast to other aspects. ❑ *Brothels, she insists, are the acceptable face of prostitution.* **7** [U] If you lose **face**, you do something which makes you appear weak and makes people respect or admire you less. If you do something in order to save **face**, you do it in order to avoid appearing weak and losing people's respect or admiration. ❑ *They don't want a war, but they don't want to lose face.* ❑ *To cancel the airport would mean a loss of face for the present governor.*

PHRASES **face down** or **face up** If someone or something is **face down**, their face or front points downward. If they are **face up**, their face or front points upward. ❑ *All the*

time Stephen was lying face down and unconscious in the bath. **face to face** **1** If you come **face to face** with someone, you meet them and can talk to them or look at them directly. ❑ *We were strolling into the town when we came face to face with Jacques Dubois.* **2** If you come **face to face with** a difficulty or reality, you cannot avoid it and have to deal with it. ❑ *Eventually, he came face to face with discrimination again.*

to fly in the face of If an action or belief **flies in the face of** accepted ideas or rules, it seems to completely oppose or contradict them. ❑ *scientific principles that seem to fly in the face of common sense*

in the face of something If you take a particular action or attitude **in the face of** a problem or difficulty, you respond to that problem or difficulty in that way. ❑ *The president has called for national unity in the face of the violent anti-government protests.*

make a face or **pull a face** If you **make a face**, you show a feeling such as dislike or disgust by putting an exaggerated expression on your face, for example, by sticking out your tongue. ❑ *Opening the door, she made a face at the musty smell.*

on the face of it You say **on the face of it** when you are describing how something seems when it is first considered, in order to suggest that people's opinion may change when they know or think more about the subject. ❑ *On the face of it that seems to make sense. But the figures don't add up.*

show your face If you **show** your **face** somewhere, you go there and see people, although you are not welcome, are somewhat unwilling to go, or have not been there for some time. ❑ *If she shows her face again back in Massachusetts she'll find a warrant for her arrest waiting.*

keep a straight face If you manage to **keep a straight face**, you manage to look serious, although you want to laugh. ❑ *What went through Tom's mind I can't imagine, but he did manage to keep a straight face.*

to someone's face If you say something **to** someone's **face**, you say it openly in their presence. ❑ *Her opponent called her a liar to her face.*

VERB [I, T] (**faces, facing, faced**) **1** [I, T] If someone or something **faces** a particular thing, person, or direction, they are positioned opposite them or are looking in that direction. ❑ *They stood facing each other.* ❑ *Our house faces south.* **2** [T] If you **face** someone or something, you turn so that you are looking at them or it. ❑ *She stood up from the table and faced him.* **3** [T] If you have to **face** a person or group, you have to stand or sit in front of them and talk to them, although it may be difficult and unpleasant. ❑ *Christie looked relaxed and calm as he faced the press.* **4** [T] If you **face** or **are faced** with something difficult or unpleasant, or if it **faces** you, it is going to affect you and you have to deal with it. ❑ *Williams faces life in prison if convicted of attempted murder.* ❑ *The immense difficulties facing European businessmen in Russia were only too evident.* ❑ *We are faced with a serious problem.* **5** [T] If you **face** the truth or **face** the facts, you accept that something is true. If you **face** someone with the truth or with the facts, you try to make them accept that something is true. ❑ *Although your heart is breaking, you must face the truth that a relationship has ended.* ❑ *He accused the Government of refusing to face facts about the economy.* **6** [T] If you **cannot face** something, you do not feel able to do it because it seems so difficult or unpleasant. ❑ *I couldn't face the prospect of spending a Saturday night there, so I decided to press on.* ❑ *My children want me with them for Christmas Day, but I can't face it.*

PHRASAL VERB **face up to** Face up to means the same as **face** VERB 5. ❑ *I have grown up now and I have to face up to my responsibilities.*

PHRASE **let's face it** You use the expression 'let's face it' when you are stating a fact or making a comment about something which you think the person you are talking to may find unpleasant or be unwilling to admit. ❑ *She was always attracted to younger men. But, let's face it, who is not?*
→ See also **face value**

✦ **shut the door in someone's face** → see **door**; **have egg on your face** → see **egg**; **face the music** → see **music**

fac•et /'fæsɪt, -set/ NOUN [c] (facets) **1** A facet of something is a single part or aspect of it. ❑ *The caste system shapes nearly every facet of Indian life.* **2** The **facets** of a diamond or other precious stone are the flat surfaces that have been cut on its outside.

face value NOUN

NOUN [SING] The **face value** of things such as coins, paper money, investment documents, or tickets is the amount of money that they are worth, and that is written on them. ❑ *Tickets were selling at twice their face value.*

PHRASE **at face value** If you take something **at face value**, you accept it and believe it without thinking about it very much, even though it might be untrue. ❑ *Public statements from the various groups involved should not necessarily be taken at face value.*

fa•cial /'feɪʃəl/ ADJ, NOUN

ADJ [facial + N] **Facial** means appearing on or being part of your face. ❑ *Cross didn't answer; his facial expression didn't change.*

NOUN [c] (facials) A **facial** is a sort of beauty treatment in which someone's face is massaged, and creams and other substances are rubbed into it. ❑ *Where's the best place to get a facial in New York City?*

○ **fa•cili•tate** /fə'sɪlɪteɪt/ VERB [T] (facilitates, facilitating, facilitated) (*academic word*) To **facilitate** an action or process, especially one that you would like to happen, means to make it easier or more likely to happen. = aid, assist ❑ *The new airport will facilitate the development of tourism.* ❑ *He argued that the economic recovery had been facilitated by his tough stance.* ❑ *the facilitated diffusion of glucose in red blood cells*

fa•cil•ity ◆◆◇ /fə'sɪlɪti/ NOUN [c] (facilities) (*academic word*) **1** **Facilities** are buildings, pieces of equipment, or services that are provided for a particular purpose. = amenities ❑ *British engineers were disadvantaged by inadequate research facilities.* ❑ *What recreational facilities are now available?* **2** A **facility** is something such as an additional service provided by an organization or an extra feature on a machine which is useful but not essential. ❑ *One of the new models has the facility to reproduce speech as well as text.* **3** [usu sing, usu facility 'for' N, facility + to-INF] If you have a **facility** for something, for example learning a language, you find it easy to do. ❑ *He and Marcia shared a facility for languages.*

WORD CONNECTIONS

VERB + facility

provide facilities
offer facilities
use facilities
❑ *The council provides leisure facilities such as parks and swimming pools.*

improve facilities
upgrade facilities
❑ *The museum plans to expand gallery space and upgrade its visitor facilities.*

NOUN + facility

sports facilities
leisure facilities
❑ *In terms of sports facilities there are a number of golf courses in the area.*

---

training facilities
research facilities
conference facilities
❑ *It is a well-equipped centre with a full range of educational and training facilities.*

ADJ + facility

modern facilities
state-of-the-art facilities
❑ *Many new schools have state-of-the-art facilities.*

recreational facilities
medical facilities
❑ *Access to clean water and medical facilities is vital.*

○ **fact** ◆◆◆ /fækt/ NOUN

NOUN [c, u] (facts) **1** [c] **Facts** are pieces of information that can be discovered. = truth, detail, information; ≠ fiction ❑ *There is so much information you can almost effortlessly find the facts for yourself.* ❑ *His opponent swamped him with facts and figures.* ❑ *The aim of the study was to gather basic facts about the performance of the health service.* **2** [c, u] When you refer to something as a **fact** or as **fact**, you mean that you think it is true or correct. ❑ *a statement of verifiable historical fact* ❑ *It is a simple scientific fact; humans need food.* ❑ *He found it difficult to distinguish between fact and fiction.*

PHRASES **the fact that** **1** You use **the fact that** after some verbs or prepositions, especially in expressions such as **in view of the fact that**, **apart from the fact that**, and **despite the fact that**, to link the verb or preposition with a clause. ❑ *His chances do not seem good in view of the fact that the Chief Prosecutor has already voiced his public disapproval.* ❑ *Despite the fact that the disease is so prevalent, treatment is still far from satisfactory.* **2** You use **the fact that** instead of a simple that-clause either for emphasis or because the clause is the subject of your sentence. ❑ *My family now accepts the fact that I don't eat sugar or bread.*

in fact or **in actual fact** or **in point of fact** **1** You use in **fact**, **in actual fact**, or **in point of fact** to indicate that you are giving more detailed information about what you have just said. ❑ *We've had a pretty bad time while you were away. In fact, we very nearly split up this time.* ❑ *He apologized as soon as he realized what he had done. In actual fact he wrote a nice little note to me.* **2** You use **in fact**, **in actual fact**, or **in point of fact** to introduce or draw attention to a comment that modifies, contradicts, or contrasts with a previous statement. = actually ❑ *That sounds rather simple, but in fact it's very difficult.* ❑ *They complained that they had been trapped inside the police station, but in fact most were seen escaping over the adjacent roofs to safety in nearby buildings.*

as a matter of fact You use **as a matter of fact** to introduce a statement that gives more details about what has just been said, or an explanation of it, or something that contrasts with it. = actually ❑ *The local people saw the suffering to which these deportees were subjected. And, as a matter of fact, the local people helped the victims.*

know something for a fact If you say that you **know** something **for a fact**, you are emphasizing that you are completely certain that it is true. ❑ *I know for a fact that baby corn is very expensive in Europe.*

the fact is You use **the fact is** or **the fact of the matter is** to introduce and draw attention to a summary or statement of the most important point about what you have been saying. ❑ *The fact is blindness hadn't stopped the children from doing many of the things that sighted children enjoy.*

WORD CONNECTIONS

ADJ + fact

the **basic** facts
the **bare** facts
❑ *I only told her the bare facts.*

a **simple** fact
a **plain** fact
❑ *The simple fact is that there is a shortage of engineers in our industry.*

F

a **scientific** fact
a **historical** fact
❑ *There are scientific facts to support that opinion.*

a **well-known** fact
an **interesting** fact
a **fascinating** fact
❑ *It is a well-known fact that the best way to lose weight is to eat a sensible diet and do more exercise.*

VERB + **fact**

establish a fact
consider a fact
ignore a fact
hide a fact
❑ *If you ignore the facts and continue smoking, you are putting yourself at serious risk of disease.*

fac•tion ♦◇◇ /'fækʃən/ NOUN [c] (**factions**) A **faction** is an organized group of people within a larger group, which opposes some of the ideas of the larger group and fights for its own ideas. ❑ *A peace agreement will be signed by the leaders of the country's warring factions.*

✪**fac•tor** ♦♦◇ /'fæktə/ NOUN (academic word)
NOUN [c, SING] (**factors**) ◼ [c] A **factor** is one of the things that affects an event, decision, or situation. = element, point ❑ *Physical activity is an important factor in maintaining fitness.* ❑ *The relatively cheap price of food may be a contributing factor to the increasing number of overweight people.* ◻ [c] If an amount increases by **a factor of** two, for example, or by **a factor of** eight, then it becomes two times bigger or eight times bigger. ❑ *The cost of butter quadrupled and bread prices increased by a factor of five.* ◼ [SING] You can use **factor** to refer to a particular level on a scale of measurement. ❑ *A sunscreen with a protection factor of 30 allows you to stay in the sun without burning.*
PHRASAL VERB **factor in** or **factor into** (**factors, factoring, factored**) If you **factor** a particular cost or element **into** a calculation you are making, or if you **factor** it **in**, you include it. ❑ *You'd better consider this and factor this into your decision making.*

✪**fac•to•ry** ♦♦◇ /'fæktri/ NOUN [c] (**factories**) A **factory** is a large building where machines are used to make large quantities of goods. = plant ❑ *He owned furniture factories in New York State.*

✪**fac•tual** /'fæktʃuəl/ ADJ Something that is **factual** is concerned with facts or contains facts, rather than giving theories or personal interpretations. ❑ *The editorial contained several factual errors.* ❑ *a source of factual information*
✪**fac•tu•al•ly** /'fæktʃuəli/ ADV ❑ *I learned that a number of statements in my talk were factually wrong.* ❑ *She told me coolly and factually the story of her life in prison.*

✪**fac•ul•ty** /'fækəlti/ NOUN [c] (**faculties**) ◼ Your **faculties** are your physical and mental abilities. ❑ *He was drunk and not in control of his faculties.* ◻ (BrE) A **faculty** is a group of related departments in some universities, or the people who work in them. ❑ *the Faculty of Social and Political Sciences.* ❑ *the first staff of Edinburgh's new medical faculty*

fade ♦◇◇ /feɪd/ VERB [i, t] (**fades, fading, faded**) ◼ [i, t] When a coloured object **fades** or when the light **fades** it, it gradually becomes paler. ❑ *All colour fades – especially under the impact of direct sunlight.* ❑ *No matter how soft the light is, it still fades carpets and curtains in every room.* ◻ [i] When light **fades**, it slowly becomes less bright. When a sound **fades**, it slowly becomes less loud. ❑ *Seaton lay on his bed and gazed at the ceiling as the light faded.* ◼ [i] If memories, feelings, or possibilities **fade**, they slowly become less intense or less strong. ❑ *Sympathy for the rebels, the government claims, is beginning to fade.* ❑ *Prospects for peace had already started to fade.*
fad•ed /'feɪdɪd/ ADJ ❑ *a girl in a faded dress*

✪**Fahr•en•heit** /'færənhaɪt/ ADJ, NOUN
ADJ [N/NUM Fahrenheit] **Fahrenheit** is a scale for measuring temperature, in which water freezes at 32 degrees and boils at 212 degrees. It is represented by the symbol °F.

❑ *By mid-morning, the temperature was already above 100 degrees Fahrenheit.* ❑ *choose from degrees centigrade or Fahrenheit*
NOUN [u] **Fahrenheit** is a scale for measuring temperature, in which water freezes at 32 degrees and boils at 212 degrees. It is represented by the symbol °F. ❑ *He was asked for the boiling point of water in Fahrenheit.* ❑ *television weather forecasts given in metric and Fahrenheit*

✪**fail** ♦♦♦ /feɪl/ VERB, NOUN
VERB [i, t] (**fails, failing, failed**) ◼ [i, t] If you **fail** to do something that you were trying to do, you are unable to do it or do not succeed in doing it. ❑ *The party failed to win the election.* ❑ *He narrowly failed to qualify.* ❑ *He failed in his attempt to take control of the company.* ◻ [i] If an activity, attempt, or plan **fails**, it is not successful. ❑ *We tried to develop plans for them to get along, which all failed miserably.* ❑ *He was afraid the revolution they had started would fail.* ❑ *a failed military coup* ◼ [t] (formal) If someone or something **fails** to do a particular thing that they should have done, they do not do it. ❑ *Some schools fail to require any homework.* ❑ *He failed to file tax returns for 1982.* ❑ *The bomb failed to explode.* ◼ [i] If something **fails**, it stops working properly, or does not do what it is supposed to do. ❑ *The lights mysteriously failed, and we stumbled around in complete darkness.* ◻ [i] (business) If a business, organization, or system **fails**, it becomes unable to continue in operation or in existence. ❑ *So far this year, 104 banks have failed.* ❑ *a failed hotel business* ◼ [i] If something such as your health or a physical quality is **failing**, it is becoming gradually weaker or less effective. ❑ *He was 58, and his health was failing rapidly.* ❑ *Here in the hills, the light failed more quickly.* ◼ [t] If someone **fails** you, they do not do what you had expected or trusted them to do. ❑ *We waited twenty-one years, don't fail us now.* ◼ [t] If someone **fails** a test, examination, or course, they perform badly in it and do not reach the standard that is required. ❑ *I lived in fear of failing my final exams.* ◼ [t] If someone **fails** you in a test, examination, or course, they judge that you have not reached a high enough standard in it. ❑ *the two professors who had failed him during his first year of law school*
PHRASE **if all else fails** You say **if all else fails** to suggest what could be done in a certain situation if all the other things you have tried are unsuccessful. ❑ *If all else fails, I could always drive a truck.*
NOUN [c] (**fails**) A **fail** is when someone has judged that you have not reached a high enough standard in a test, examination, or course. ❑ *It's the difference between a pass and a fail.*
PHRASE **without fail** (emphasis) ◼ You use **without fail** to emphasize that something always happens. ❑ *He attended every meeting without fail.* ◻ You use **without fail** to emphasize an order or a promise. ❑ *On the 30th you must without fail hand in some money for Alex.*

fail•ing /'feɪlɪŋ/ NOUN, PREP
NOUN [c] (**failings**) The **failings** of someone or something are their faults or unsatisfactory features. = shortcoming ❑ *Like many in Russia, she blamed the country's failings on futile attempts to catch up with the West.*
PREP
PHRASE **failing that** You say **failing that** to introduce an alternative, in case what you have just said is not possible. ❑ *Find someone who will let you talk things through, or failing that, write down your thoughts.*

✪**fail•ure** ♦♦◇ /'feɪljə/ NOUN [u, c] (**failures**) ◼ [u] **Failure** is a lack of success in doing or achieving something, especially in relation to a particular activity. ❑ *This policy is doomed to failure.* ❑ *Three attempts on the 200-metre record ended in failure.* ❑ *feelings of failure* ◻ [u] Your **failure** to do a particular thing is the fact that you do not do it, even though you were expected to do it. ❑ *They see their failure to produce an heir as a curse from God.* ◼ [c] If something is **a failure**, it is not a success. ❑ *The programme was a complete failure.* ❑ *The marriage was a failure and they both wanted to be free of it.* ◼ [c] If you say that someone is **a failure**, you mean that they have not succeeded in a particular activity, or that they are unsuccessful at everything they do. ❑ *Elgar received many honours and much* acclaim and yet he often considered himself a failure. **5** [C, U] If there is a **failure** of something, for example, a machine or part of the body, it goes wrong and stops working or developing properly. ❑ *There were also several accidents mainly caused by engine failures on take-off.* **6** [C, U] (*business*) If there is a **failure** of a business or bank, it is no longer able to continue operating. = collapse ❑ *Business failures rose 16% last month.*

faint /feɪnt/ ADJ, VERB, NOUN

◾ADJ◾ (**fainter, faintest**) **1** A **faint** sound, colour, mark, feeling, or quality has very little strength or intensity. ❑ *He became aware of the soft, faint sounds of water dripping.* ❑ *There was still the faint hope deep within him that she might never need to know.* **2** [faint + N] A **faint** attempt at something is one that is made without proper effort and with little enthusiasm. ❑ *Caroline made a faint attempt at a laugh.* ❑ *A faint smile crossed the Monsignor's face and faded quickly.* **3** [V-LINK + faint] Someone who is **faint** feels weak and unsteady as if they are about to lose consciousness. ❑ *Other signs of angina are nausea, sweating, feeling faint and shortness of breath.*

◾VERB◾ [I] (**faints, fainting, fainted**) If you **faint**, you lose consciousness for a short time, especially because you are hungry, or because of pain, heat, or shock. = pass out ❑ *She suddenly fell forward on to the table and fainted.*

◾NOUN◾ [C] (**faints**) A **faint** is when you lose consciousness for a short time, especially because you are hungry, or because of pain, heat, or shock. ❑ *She slumped to the ground in a faint.*

faint·ly /ˈfeɪntli/ ADV **1** = slightly ❑ *He was already asleep in the bed, which smelled faintly of mildew.* **2** *John smiled faintly and shook his head.*

✪**fair** ◆◆◇ /feə/ ADJ, COMB, NOUN

◾ADJ◾ (**fairer, fairest**) **1** Something or someone that is **fair** is reasonable, right, and just. = just, reasonable; ≠ unfair ❑ *It didn't seem fair to leave out her father.* ❑ *Do you feel they're paying their fair share?* ❑ *I wanted them to get a fair deal.* ❑ *It wasn't fair to blame him.* ❑ *Independent observers say the campaign's been much fairer than expected.* ❑ *An appeals court had ruled that they could not get a fair trial in Los Angeles.* **2** [fair + N] A **fair** amount, degree, size, or distance is quite a large amount, degree, size, or distance. ❑ *My neighbours across the street travel a fair amount.* **3** [fair + N] A **fair** guess or idea about something is one that is likely to be correct. = reasonable ❑ *It's a fair guess to say that the damage will be extensive.* **4** If you describe someone or something as **fair**, you mean that they are average in standard or quality, neither very good nor very bad. = adequate ❑ *Reimar had a fair command of English.* **5** Someone who is **fair**, or who has **fair** hair, has light-coloured hair. ❑ *Both children were very like Robina, but were much fairer than she was.* **6** **Fair** skin is very pale and usually burns easily. ❑ *It's important to protect my fair skin from the sun.* **7** (*formal*) When the weather is **fair**, it is quite sunny and not raining. = fine ❑ *Weather conditions were fair.*

◾PHRASES◾ **fair enough** (*mainly spoken*) You use **fair enough** when you want to say that a statement, decision, or action seems reasonable to a certain extent, but that perhaps there is more to be said or done. ❑ *If you don't like it, fair enough, but that's hardly a justification to attack the whole thing.*

fair and square If you say that someone won a competition **fair and square**, you mean that they won honestly and without cheating. ❑ *There are no excuses. We were beaten fair and square.*

◾COMB◾ **1** **Fair** combines with -haired and is used for describing someone who has light-coloured hair. ❑ *a tall, fair-haired man* **2** **Fair** combines with -skinned and is used for describing someone who has pale skin and burns easily. ❑ *Fair-skinned people who spend a great deal of time in the sun have the greatest risk of skin cancer.*

◾NOUN◾ [C] (**fairs**) **1** A **fair** is an event where there are, for example, displays of goods and animals, and amusements, games, and competitions. ❑ *Every autumn I go to the county fair.* **2** A **fair** is an event at which people display and sell goods, especially goods of a particular type. ❑ *an antiques fair*

✪**fair·ly** ◆◇◇ /ˈfeəli/ ADV **1** [fairly + ADJ/ADV] **Fairly** means to quite a large degree. For example, if you say that something is **fairly** old, you mean that it is old but not very old. = quite ❑ *We did fairly well, but only fairly well.* **2** [fairly + ADJ/ADV] You use **fairly** instead of 'very' to add emphasis to an adjective or adverb without making it sound too forceful. = pretty ❑ *Were you always fairly bright at school?* ❑ *You've got to be fairly single-minded about it.* **3** If something is done **fairly**, it is done in a way that is reasonable, right, and just. ≠ unfairly ❑ *demonstrating concern for employees and solving their problems quickly and fairly* ❑ *In a society where water was precious, it had to be shared fairly between individuals.*

fair·ness /ˈfeənəs/ NOUN [U] **Fairness** is the quality of being reasonable, right, and just. ❑ *concern about the fairness of the election campaign*

faith ◆◇◇ /feɪθ/ NOUN

◾NOUN◾ [U, C] (**faiths**) **1** [U] If you have **faith in** someone or something, you feel confident about their ability or goodness. = confidence ❑ *People have lost faith in the government.* **2** [U] **Faith** is strong religious belief in a particular god. ❑ *Umberto Eco's loss of his own religious faith is reflected in his novels.* **3** [C] A **faith** is a particular religion, for example, Christianity, Buddhism, or Islam. ❑ *England shifted officially from a Catholic to a Protestant faith in the 16th century.*

◾PHRASE◾ **in good faith** If you do something **in good faith**, you seriously believe that what you are doing is right, honest, or legal, even though this may not be the case. ❑ *This report was published in good faith but we regret any confusion which may have been caused.*

faith·ful /ˈfeɪθfʊl/ ADJ, NOUN

◾ADJ◾ **1** Someone who is **faithful to** a person, organization, idea, or activity remains firm in their belief in them or support for them. ❑ *She had been faithful to her promise to guard this secret.* **2** Someone who is **faithful to** their husband, wife, or lover does not have a sexual relationship with anyone else. ❑ *I'm very faithful when I love someone.* **3** A **faithful** account, translation, or copy of something represents or reproduces the original accurately. ❑ *Colin Welland's screenplay is faithful to the novel.*

◾NOUN◾ [PL] **The faithful** are people who are faithful to someone or something. ❑ *He spends his time making speeches at factories or gatherings of the Party faithful.*

faith·ful·ly /ˈfeɪθfʊli/ ADV, CONVENTION

◾ADV◾ **1** [faithfully with V] If you act **faithfully**, you continue to support a person, organization, idea, or activity for a long time. ❑ *He has since 1965 faithfully followed and supported every twist and turn of government policy.* **2** [faithfully with V] If you translate or copy something **faithfully**, you accurately represent or reproduce the original. ❑ *When I adapt something I translate from one meaning to another as faithfully as I can.*

◾CONVENTION◾ When you start a formal or business letter with 'Dear Sir' or 'Dear Madam', you write **Yours faithfully** before your signature at the end.

fake /feɪk/ ADJ, NOUN, VERB

◾ADJ◾ A **fake** fur or a **fake** painting, for example, is a fur or painting that has been made to look valuable or genuine, usually in order to deceive people. ❑ *The bank manager is said to have issued fake certificates.*

◾NOUN◾ [C] (**fakes**) **1** A **fake** is something that is fake. ❑ *The gallery is filled with famous works of art, and every one of them is a fake.* **2** Someone who is a **fake** is not what they claim to be, for example, because they do not have the qualifications that they claim to have. = fraud ❑ *I think Jack is a good man. He isn't a fake.*

◾VERB◾ [T] (**fakes, faking, faked**) **1** If someone **fakes** something, they try to make it look valuable or genuine, although in fact it is not. ❑ *It's safer to fake a tan with makeup rather than subject your complexion to the harsh rays of the sun.* ❑ *faked evidence* **2** If you **fake** a feeling, emotion, or reaction, you pretend that you are experiencing it when you are not. ❑ *He tried to fake sincerity as he smiled at them.*

✪**fall** ◆◆◆ /fɔːl/ VERB, NOUN

◾VERB◾ [I, LINK] (**falls, falling, fell, fallen**) **1** [I] If someone or something **falls**, they move quickly downwards onto or

F

towards the ground, by accident or because of a natural force. ❑ *He has again fallen from his horse.* ❑ *Bombs fell in the town.* **2** [I] If a person or structure that is standing somewhere **falls**, they move from their upright position, so that they are then lying on the ground. ❑ *The woman gripped the shoulders of her man to stop herself from falling.* ❑ *He lost his balance and fell backwards.* **3** [I] When rain or snow **falls**, it comes down from the sky. ❑ *Winds reached up to 100 mph in some places with an inch of rain falling within 15 minutes.* **4** [I] If you **fall** somewhere, you allow yourself to drop there in a hurried or disorganized way, often because you are very tired. ❑ *Totally exhausted, he tore his clothes off and fell into bed.* **5** [I] If something **falls**, it decreases in amount, value, or strength. = drop, decrease; ≠ rise, increase ❑ *Output will fall by 6%.* ❑ *The rate of convictions has fallen.* ❑ *The unemployment rate fell to 6.2%.* ❑ *Between July and August, oil product prices fell 0.2 per cent.* ❑ *It was a time of falling living standards and emerging mass unemployment.* **6** [I] If a powerful or successful person **falls**, they suddenly lose their power or position. ❑ *Regimes fall, revolutions come and go, but places never really change.* **7** [I] If a place **falls** in a war or election, an enemy army or a different political party takes control of it. ❑ *Croatian army troops retreated from northern Bosnia and the area fell to the Serbs.* **8** [I] If you say that something or someone **falls into** a particular group or category, you mean that they belong in that group or category. ❑ *The problems generally fall into two categories.* **9** [I] If a celebration or other special event **falls on** a particular day or date, it happens to be on that day or date. ❑ *the oddly named Quasimodo Sunday which falls on the first Sunday after Easter* **10** [I] When light or shadow **falls** on something, it covers it. ❑ *Nancy, out of the corner of her eye, saw the shadow that suddenly fell across the doorway.* **11** [I] (*written*) If you say that someone's eyes **fell on** something, you mean they suddenly noticed it. ❑ *As he laid the flowers on the table, his eye fell upon a note in Grace's handwriting.* **12** [I] When night or darkness **falls**, night begins and it becomes dark. ❑ *As darkness fell outside, they sat down to eat at long tables.* **13** [LINK] You can use **fall** to show that someone or something passes into another state. For example, if someone **falls ill**, they become ill, and if something **falls into disrepair**, it is then in a state of disrepair. ❑ *It is almost impossible to visit Florida without falling in love with the state.* ❑ *Almost without exception these women fall victim to exploitation.*

PHRASE **fall to bits** or **fall to pieces** To **fall to bits** or **fall to pieces** means the same as to **fall apart**. ❑ *At that point the radio handset fell to pieces.*

PHRASAL VERBS **fall apart** **1** If something **falls apart**, it breaks into pieces because it is old or badly made. ❑ *The work was never finished and bit by bit the building fell apart.* **2** If an organization or system **falls apart**, it becomes disorganized or unable to work effectively, or breaks up into its different parts. = break down ❑ *Europe's monetary system is falling apart.* **3** (*informal*) If you say that someone **is falling apart**, you mean that they are becoming emotionally disturbed and are unable to think calmly or to deal with the difficult or unpleasant situation that they are in. = crack up ❑ *I was falling apart. I wasn't getting any sleep.*

fall back on If you **fall back on** something, you do it or use it after other things have failed. ❑ *When necessary, instinct is the most reliable resource you can fall back on.*

fall behind **1** If you **fall behind**, you do not make progress or move forward as fast as other people. ❑ *Boris is falling behind all the top players.* **2** If you **fall behind** with something or let it **fall behind**, you do not do it or produce it when you should, according to an agreement or schedule. ❑ *He faces losing his home after falling behind with the payments.* ❑ *Thousands of people could die because the relief effort has fallen so far behind.*

fall down **Fall down** means the same as **fall** VERB **2**. ❑ *I hit him so hard he fell down.*

fall for **1** If you **fall for** someone, you are strongly attracted to them and start loving them. ❑ *He was fantastically handsome – I just fell for him right away.* **2** If you **fall for** a lie or trick, you believe it or are deceived by it. ❑ *It was just a line to get you out here, and you fell for it!*

fall off **1** If something **falls off**, it separates from the thing to which it was attached and moves towards the ground. = drop off ❑ *When your exhaust pipe falls off, you have to replace it.* **2** If the degree, amount, or size of something **falls off**, it decreases. ❑ *Unemployment is rising again and retail buying has fallen off.*

fall out **1** If something such as a person's hair or a tooth **falls out**, it comes out. ❑ *Her hair started falling out as a result of radiation treatment.* **2** If you **fall out** with someone, you have an argument and stop being friendly with them. You can also say that two people **fall out**. ❑ *She fell out with her husband.* **3** → See also **fallout**

fall over If a person or object that is standing **falls over**, they accidentally move from their upright position so that they are then lying on the ground or on the surface supporting them. ❑ *If he drinks more than two glasses of wine he falls over.*

fall through If an arrangement, plan, or deal **falls through**, it fails to happen. ❑ *They wanted to turn the estate into a private golf course and offered $20 million, but the deal fell through.*

fall to If a responsibility, duty, or opportunity **falls to** someone, it becomes their responsibility, duty, or opportunity. ❑ *He's been very unlucky that no chances have fallen to him.*

NOUN [C, SING, PL] (**falls**) **1** [C] A **fall** is an occasion when someone or something moves quickly downwards onto or towards the ground, by accident or because of a natural force. ❑ *The helmets are designed to withstand impacts equivalent to a fall from a bicycle.* **2** [C] A **fall** is when someone or something moves from their upright position and onto the ground. ❑ *She broke her right leg in a bad fall.* **3** [C] A **fall** of rain or snow is when rain or snow comes down from the sky. ❑ *One night there was a heavy fall of snow.* **4** [C] A **fall** is a decrease in the amount, value, or strength of something. = drop, decrease; ≠ rise, increase ❑ *There was a sharp fall in the value of the dollar.* ❑ *October figures show a fall of 11.1%.* **5** [SING] The **fall** of a powerful or successful person is when they suddenly lose their power or position. ❑ *Following the fall of the military dictator in March, the country has had a civilian government.* **6** [SING] The **fall** of a place in a war or election is when an enemy army or different political party takes control of it. ❑ *the fall of Rome* **7** [PL] You can refer to a waterfall as **the falls**. ❑ *The falls have always been an insurmountable obstacle for salmon and sea trout.*

→ See also **rainfall**

✦ **fall foul of** → see **foul**; **fall flat** → see **flat**; **fall into place** → see **place**

fal·la·cy /ˈfæləsi/ NOUN [C, U] (**fallacies**) A **fallacy** is an idea which many people believe to be true, but which is in fact false because it is based on incorrect information or reasoning. ❑ *It's a fallacy that the affluent give relatively more to charity than the less prosperous.*

fall·en /ˈfɔːlən/ IRREG FORM, ADJ

IRREG FORM **Fallen** is the past participle of **fall**.

ADJ If you describe an object as **fallen**, you mean that it has moved from an upright position and is now lying on the ground. ❑ *A number of roads have been blocked by fallen trees.*

fall·out /ˈfɔːlaʊt/ NOUN [U] **1** **Fallout** is the radiation that affects a particular place or area after a nuclear explosion has taken place. ❑ *They were exposed to radioactive fallout during nuclear weapons tests.* **2** If you refer to the **fallout from** something that has happened, you mean the unpleasant consequences that follow it. ❑ *Grundy lost his job in the fallout from the incident.*

false ♦◇◇ /fɔːls/ ADJ **1** If something is **false**, it is incorrect, untrue, or mistaken. ❑ *It was quite clear the president was being given false information by those around him.* ❑ *You do not know whether what you're told is true or false.* **2** You use **false** to describe objects which are artificial but which are intended to look like the real thing or to be used instead of the real thing. = artificial ❑ *a set of false teeth* **3** If you describe a person or their behaviour as **false**, you are criticizing them for being insincere or for hiding their real feelings. ❑ *'Thank you,' she said with false enthusiasm.*

false·ly /ˈfɔːlsli/ ADV **1** [falsely with V] = wrongly

WORDS IN CONTEXT: FAMILY

The family unit has changed over the years as a consequence of social and economic development. However, it should still be the responsibility of the family to look after their elderly relatives.

To what extent do you agree or disagree?

Our parents are our **flesh and blood** who **brought us up** and cared for us as children, so we should be prepared to **provide for** them when they need it. Putting our parents into care, so this argument goes, is simply taking the easy way out: we should not use a **care home** to avoid our responsibilities. Being **cared for** at home by a loving family would help us strengthen **family ties** at a time when we are becoming more isolated from each other.

However, it is often impractical for families to offer the care that their **elderly relatives** require. We no longer enjoy the benefits of the **extended family unit** of the past, where care of the elderly could be shared amongst **family members**. In the modern **nuclear family**, **couples** often wait longer to **begin a family** while they follow a career. As a result, they are under greater pressure to stay in work in order to pay for **childcare** or to support their children's educational needs. Consequently, the costs and the time involved make it very difficult to care for the elderly.

Ideally, a **close-knit family** would be happy and willing to look after their elderly parents until they require full-time professional care. However, when a family is unable to offer the level of support needed, the elderly should be able to look to the state for support.

❑ *a man who is falsely accused of a crime* ◼2◼ *They smiled at one another, somewhat falsely.*

fal·si·fy /ˈfɔːlsɪfaɪ/ VERB [T] (falsifies, falsifying, falsified) If someone **falsifies** something, they change it or add untrue details to it in order to deceive people. ❑ *The charges against him include fraud, bribery, and falsifying business records.*

fal·ter /ˈfɔːltə/ VERB [I] (falters, faltering, faltered) ◼1◼ If something **falters**, it loses power or strength in an uneven way, or no longer makes much progress. ❑ *Normal life is at a standstill, and the economy is faltering.* ◼2◼ If you **falter**, you lose your confidence and stop doing something or start making mistakes. ❑ *I have not faltered in my quest for a new future.*

fame /feɪm/ NOUN [U] If you achieve **fame**, you become very well-known. ❑ *At the height of his fame, his every word was valued.* ❑ *The film earned him international fame.*

fa·mil·iar ◆◇◇ /fəˈmɪliə/ ADJ ◼1◼ If someone or something is **familiar** to you, you recognize them or know them well. ❑ *He talked of other cultures as if they were more familiar to him than his own.* ❑ *They are already familiar faces on our TV screens.* ◼2◼ [V-LINK + familiar 'with' N] If you are **familiar with** something, you know or understand it well. ❑ *Most people are familiar with this figure from Wagner's opera.* ◼3◼ If someone you do not know well behaves in a **familiar** way towards you, they treat you very informally in a way that you might find offensive. ❑ *It isn't appropriate for an officer to be overly familiar with an enlisted man.*

fa·mil·iar·ity /fəˌmɪliˈærɪti/ NOUN [U] ◼1◼ *Tony was unnerved by the uncanny familiarity of her face.* ◼2◼ *The enemy would always have the advantage of familiarity with the rugged terrain.* ◼3◼ *She needed to control her surprise at the easy familiarity with which her host greeted the head waiter.*

fa·mil·iar·ly /fəˈmɪliəli/ ADV ❑ *'Gerald, isn't it?' I began familiarly.*

fa·mil·iar·ize /fəˈmɪliəraɪz/ also **familiarise** VERB [T] (familiarizes, familiarizing, familiarized) If you **familiarize** yourself **with** something, or if someone **familiarizes** you **with** it, you learn about it and start to understand it. ❑ *The goal of the experiment was to familiarize the people with the new laws.*

fam·i·ly ◆◆◆ /ˈfæmɪli/ NOUN, ADJ

NOUN [C] (families) ◼1◼ A **family** is a group of people who are related to each other, especially parents and their children. ❑ *There's room in there for a family of five.* ❑ *Does he have any family?* ◼2◼ When people talk about a **family**,

they sometimes mean children. ❑ *They decided to start a family.* ◼3◼ When people talk about their **family**, they sometimes mean their ancestors. ❑ *Her family came to Los Angeles at the turn of the century.* ◼4◼ A **family** of animals or plants is a group of related species. ❑ *foods in the cabbage family, such as Brussels sprouts*

ADJ ◼1◼ [family + N] You can use **family** to describe things that belong to a particular family. ❑ *He returned to the family home.* ◼2◼ [family + N] You can use **family** to describe things that are designed to be used or enjoyed by both parents and children. ❑ *It had been designed as a family house.*

◐**fam·ine** /ˈfæmɪn/ NOUN [C, U] (famines) **Famine** is a situation in which large numbers of people have little or no food, and many of them die. ❑ *Thousands of refugees are trapped by war, drought and famine.* ❑ *The civil war is obstructing distribution of famine relief by aid agencies.*

fa·mous ◆◆◇ /ˈfeɪməs/ ADJ Someone or something that is **famous** is very well known. ❑ *one of Kentucky's most famous landmarks*

fa·mous·ly /ˈfeɪməsli/ ADV You use **famously** to refer to a fact that is well known, usually because it is remarkable or extreme. ❑ *Authors are famously ignorant about the realities of publishing.*

fan ◆◆◇ /fæn/ NOUN, VERB

NOUN [C] (fans) ◼1◼ If you are a **fan** of someone or something, especially a famous person or a sport, you like them very much and are very interested in them. ❑ *If you're a Billy Crystal fan, you'll love this film.* ❑ *I am a great fan of rave music.* ◼2◼ A **fan** is a piece of electrical or mechanical equipment with blades that go round and round. It keeps a room or machine cool or gets rid of unpleasant smells. ❑ *He cools himself in front of an electric fan.* ◼3◼ A **fan** is a flat object that you hold in your hand and wave in order to move the air and make yourself feel cooler. ❑ *hundreds of dancing girls waving peacock fans*

VERB [T] (fans, fanning, fanned) If you **fan** yourself or your face when you are hot, you wave a fan or other flat object in order to make yourself feel cooler. ❑ *She would have to wait in the truck, fanning herself with a piece of cardboard.*

PHRASAL VERB **fan out** If a group of people or things **fan out**, they move forward away from a particular point in different directions. = spread out ❑ *The main body of British, American, and French troops had fanned out to the west.*

fa·nat·ic /fəˈnætɪk/ NOUN, ADJ

NOUN [C] (fanatics) ◼1◼ (disapproval) If you describe someone as a **fanatic**, you disapprove of them because you

consider their behaviour or opinions to be very extreme, for example, in the way they support particular religious or political ideas. = extremist ❑ *I am not a religious fanatic but I am a Christian.* **2** If you say that someone is a **fanatic**, you mean that they are very enthusiastic about a particular activity, sport, or way of life. = enthusiast ❑ *Both Rod and Phil are football fanatics.*
[ADJ] **Fanatic** means the same as **fanatical**.

fa·nati·cal /fə'nætɪkəl/ ADJ (*disapproval*) If you describe someone as **fanatical**, you disapprove of them because you consider their behaviour or opinions to be very extreme. ❑ *He is a fanatical fan of Mozart.*

fan·ci·ful /'fænsɪfʊl/ ADJ (*disapproval*) If you describe an idea as **fanciful**, you disapprove of it because you think it comes from someone's imagination, and is therefore unrealistic or unlikely to be true. ❑ *fanciful ideas about Martian life*

fan·cy /'fænsi/ ADJ, VERB, EXCLAM, NOUN
[ADJ] (**fancier, fanciest**) **1** If you describe something as **fancy**, you mean that it is special, unusual, or elaborate, for example because it has a lot of decoration. ❑ *The magazine was packaged in a fancy plastic case with attractive graphics.* **2** (*informal*) If you describe something as **fancy**, you mean that it is very expensive or of very high quality, and you often dislike it because of this. ❑ *My parents sent me to a fancy private school.*
[VERB] [T] (**fancies, fancying, fancied**) **1** (*mainly BrE*) If you **fancy yourself as** a particular kind of person or fancy **yourself** doing a particular thing, you like the idea of being that kind of person or doing that thing. ❑ *So you fancy yourself as the boss someday?* **2** If you say that someone **fancies themselves as** a particular kind of person, you mean that they think, often wrongly, that they have the good qualities which that kind of person has. ❑ *She fancies herself a bohemian.* **3** (*mainly BrE, informal*) If you **fancy** something, you want to have it or to do it. ❑ *I just fancied a drink.* **4** (*BrE, informal*) If you **fancy** someone, you feel attracted to them, especially in a sexual way. ❑ *I think he thinks I fancy him.*
[EXCLAM] (*feelings*) You say '**fancy**' or '**fancy that**' when you want to express surprise or disapproval. ❑ *'Fancy that!' smiled Conti.*
[NOUN]
[PHRASES] **take a fancy to** If you **take a fancy to** someone or something, you start liking them, usually for no understandable reason. ❑ *Sylvia took quite a fancy to him.*
take someone's fancy or **tickle someone's fancy** If something **takes** your **fancy** or **tickles** your **fancy**, you like it a lot when you see it or think of it. ❑ *She makes most of her own clothes, copying any fashion which takes her fancy.*

fan·ta·size /'fæntəsaɪz/ also **fantasise** VERB [I, T] (**fantasizes, fantasizing, fantasized**) If you **fantasize** about an event or situation that you would like to happen, you give yourself pleasure by imagining that it is happening, although it is untrue or unlikely to happen. ❑ *I fantasized about writing music.*

fan·tas·tic /fæn'tæstɪk/ ADJ **1** (*informal, emphasis*) If you say that something is **fantastic**, you are emphasizing that you think that it is very good or that you like it a lot. = great ❑ *I have a fantastic social life.* **2** [fantastic + N] A **fantastic** amount or quantity is an extremely large one. ❑ *fantastic amounts of money*
fan·tas·ti·cal·ly /fæn'tæstɪkli/ ADV ❑ *a fantastically expensive restaurant*

fan·ta·sy ◆◇◇ /'fæntəzi/ NOUN, ADJ
[NOUN] [C, U] (**fantasies**) **1** [C] A **fantasy** is a pleasant situation or event that you think about and that you want to happen, especially one that is unlikely to happen. = dream ❑ *fantasies of romance and true love* **2** [C, U] You can refer to a story or situation that someone creates from their imagination and that is not based on reality as **fantasy**. ❑ *The film is more of an ironic fantasy than a horror story.* **3** [U] **Fantasy** is the activity of imagining things. ❑ *a world of imagination, passion, fantasy, reflection*
[ADJ] [fantasy + N] **Fantasy** football, baseball, or another sport is a game in which players choose an imaginary team and score points based on the actual performances of

the members of their team in real games. ❑ *Haskins said he has been playing fantasy baseball for the past five years.*

far ◆◆◆ /fɑː/ ADV, ADJ
[ADV] (**farther** or **further, farthest** or **furthest**) **1** If one place, thing, or person is **far** away from another, there is a great distance between them. ❑ *I know a nice little Italian restaurant not far from here.* ❑ *Both of my sisters moved even farther away from home.* **2** If you ask how **far** a place is, you are asking what distance it is from you or from another place. If you ask **how far** someone went, you are asking what distance they travelled, or what place they reached. ❑ *How far is Pawtucket from Providence?* ❑ *How far is it to Malcy?* ❑ *She followed the tracks as far as the road.* **3** A time or event that is **far** away in the future or the past is a long time from the present or from a particular point in time. ❑ *hidden conflicts whose roots lie far back in time* ❑ *I can't see any farther than the next six months.* **4** You can use **far** to talk about the extent or degree to which something happens or is true. ❑ *How far did the film tell the truth about Barnes Wallis?* **5** You can talk about how **far** someone or something gets to describe the progress that they make. ❑ *Discussions never progressed very far.* ❑ *Think of how far we have come in a little time.* **6** [far with v] You can talk about how **far** a person or action goes to describe the degree to which someone's behaviour or actions are extreme. ❑ *It's still not clear how far the Russian parliament will go to implement its own plans.* ❑ *Competition can be healthy, but if it is pushed too far it can result in bullying.* **7** ['as/so' far 'as'] You can use **far** in expressions like '**as far as I know**' and '**so far as I remember**' to indicate that you are not absolutely sure of the statement you are about to make or have just made, and you may be wrong. ❑ *It only lasted a couple of years, as far as I know.* **8** You can use **far** to mean 'very much' when you are comparing two things and emphasizing the difference between them. For example, you can say that something is **far better** or **far worse** than something else to indicate that it is very much better or worse. You can also say that something is, for example, **far too big** to indicate that it is very much too big. ❑ *Women who eat plenty of fresh vegetables are far less likely to suffer anxiety or depression.* ❑ *The police say the response has been far better than expected.*
[PHRASES] **someone will go far** If you say that someone **will go far**, you mean that they will be very successful in their career. ❑ *I was very impressed with the talent of Michael Ball. He will go far.*
far gone Someone or something that is **far gone** is in such a bad state or condition that not much can be done to help or improve them. ❑ *In his last few days the pain seemed to have stopped, but by then he was so far gone that it was no longer any comfort.*
as far as I can see You can use the expression '**as far as I can see**' when you are about to state your opinion of a situation, or have just stated it, to indicate that it is your personal opinion. ❑ *That's the problem as far as I can see.*
so far **1** If you say that something only goes **so far** or can only go **so far**, you mean that its extent, effect, or influence is limited. ❑ *Their loyalty only went so far.* **2** If you tell or ask someone what has happened **so far**, you are telling or asking them what has happened up until the present point in a situation or story, and often implying that something different might happen later. ❑ *It's been quiet so far.* ❑ *So far, they have met with no success.*
so far so good (*feelings*) You can say **so far so good** to express satisfaction with the way that a situation or activity is progressing, developing, or happening. ❑ *Of course, it's a case of so far, so good, but it's only one step.*
by far (*emphasis*) You use the expression **by far** when you are comparing something or someone with others of the same kind, in order to emphasize how great the difference is between them. For example, you can say that something is **by far the best** or **the best by far** to indicate that it is definitely the best. ❑ *By far the most important issue for them is unemployment.*
far from (*emphasis*) If you say that something is **far from** a particular thing or **far from** being the case, you are emphasizing that it is not that particular thing or not at all the case, especially when people expect or assume that

F

it is. ❑ *It was obvious that much of what they recorded was far from the truth.* ❑ *Far from being relaxed, we both felt so uncomfortable we hardly spoke.*

far from it (*emphasis*) You can use the expression 'far from it' to emphasize a negative statement that you have just made. ❑ *Being dyslexic does not mean that one is unintelligent. Far from it.*

ADJ **1** [far + N] When there are two things of the same kind in a place, **the far** one is the one that is a greater distance from you. ❑ *He had wandered to the far end of the room.* **2** [far + N] You can use **far** to refer to the part of an area or object that is the greatest distance from the centre in a particular direction. For example, **the far north of** a country is the part of it that is the greatest distance to the north. ❑ *A storm was brewing off Port Angeles in the far north of Washington State.* **3** [far + N] You can describe people with extreme left-wing or right-wing political views as the **far** left or the **far** right. = extreme ❑ *The far right is now a greater threat than the extreme left.*

✦ **near and far** → see **near**

far·away /ˌfɑːrəˈweɪ/ ADJ [faraway + N] A **faraway** place is a long distance from you or from a particular place. = distant ❑ *They have just returned from faraway places with wonderful stories to tell.*

farce /fɑːs/ NOUN [C, U, SING] (**farces**) **1** [C] A **farce** is a humorous play in which the characters become involved in complicated and unlikely situations. ❑ *an off-Broadway farce called 'Lucky Stiff'* **2** [U] **Farce** is the style of acting and writing that is typical of farces. ❑ *The plot often borders on farce.* **3** [SING] [also no DET] If you describe a situation or event as a **farce**, you mean that it is so disorganized or ridiculous that you cannot take it seriously. ❑ *The elections have been reduced to a farce.*

fare ◆◇◇ /feə/ NOUN, VERB

NOUN [C] (**fares**) A **fare** is the money that you pay for a trip that you make, for example, in a bus, train, or taxi. ❑ *He could barely afford the fare.*

VERB [I] (**fares, faring, fared**) If you say that someone or something **fares** well or badly, you are referring to the degree of success they achieve in a particular situation or activity. = do ❑ *It is unlikely that the marine industry will fare any better in September.*

far-fetched ADJ (*disapproval*) If you describe a story or idea as **far-fetched**, you are criticizing it because you think it is unlikely to be true or practical. = unrealistic ❑ *The storyline was too far-fetched and none of the actors was particularly good.*

farm ◆◆◇ /fɑːm/ NOUN, VERB

NOUN [C] (**farms**) **1** A **farm** is an area of land, together with the buildings on it, that is used for growing crops or raising animals, usually in order to sell them. ❑ *Farms in France are much smaller than those in the United States or even Britain.* **2** A mink **farm** or a fish **farm**, for example, is a place where a particular kind of animal or fish is bred and kept in large quantities in order to be sold. ❑ *trout fresh from a local trout farm*

VERB [I, T] (**farms, farming, farmed**) If you **farm** an area of land, you grow crops or keep animals on it. ❑ *They farmed some of the best land in the country.* ❑ *Bease has been farming for 30 years.*

PHRASAL VERB **farm out** If you **farm out** something that is your responsibility, you send it to other people for them to deal with or look after. ❑ *Scores of U.S. companies farm out software development.* ❑ *She may have farmed the child out in order to remarry.*

farm·er ◆◆◇ /ˈfɑːmə/ NOUN [C] (**farmers**) A **farmer** is a person who owns or manages a farm.

farm·house /ˈfɑːmhaʊs/ NOUN [C] (**farmhouses**) A **farmhouse** is the main house on a farm, usually where the farmer lives.

farm·ing /ˈfɑːmɪŋ/ NOUN [U] **Farming** is the activity of growing crops or keeping animals on a farm. ❑ *a career in farming*

farm·land /ˈfɑːmlænd/ NOUN [U] [also farmlands] **Farmland** is land which is farmed, or which is suitable for farming. ❑ *It is surrounded by 62 acres of farmland.*

far-reaching ADJ If you describe actions, events, or changes as **far-reaching**, you mean that they have a very great influence and affect a great number of things. = sweeping ❑ *The economy is in danger of collapse unless far-reaching reforms are implemented.*

far·ther /ˈfɑːðə/ IRREG FORM **Farther** is a comparative form of **far**.

far·thest /ˈfɑːðɪst/ IRREG FORM **Farthest** is a superlative form of **far**.

fas·ci·nate /ˈfæsɪneɪt/ VERB [T] (**fascinates, fascinating, fascinated**) If something **fascinates** you, it interests and delights you so much that your thoughts tend to concentrate on it. ❑ *Politics fascinated Franklin's father.*

fas·ci·nat·ed /ˈfæsɪneɪtɪd/ ADJ If you are **fascinated by** something, you find it very interesting and attractive, and your thoughts tend to concentrate on it. ❑ *I sat on the stairs and watched, fascinated.*

fas·ci·nat·ing /ˈfæsɪneɪtɪŋ/ ADJ If you describe something as **fascinating**, you find it very interesting and attractive, and your thoughts tend to concentrate on it. ❑ *Madagascar is the most fascinating place I have ever been to.*

fas·ci·na·tion /ˌfæsɪˈneɪʃən/ NOUN [U] **Fascination** is the state of being greatly interested in or delighted by something. ❑ *I've had a lifelong fascination with the sea and with small boats.*

✪ fas·cism /ˈfæʃɪzəm/ NOUN [U] **Fascism** is a set of right-wing political beliefs that includes strong control of society and the economy by the state, a powerful role for the armed forces, and the stopping of political opposition. ❑ *the rise of fascism in the 1930s* ❑ *Our grandparents came together to fight fascism.* ❑ *She was influenced more by Italian fascism than by Nazism.*

✪ fas·cist /ˈfæʃɪst/ ADJ, NOUN

ADJ You use **fascist** to describe organizations, ideas, or systems which follow the principles of fascism. ❑ *an upsurge of support for extreme rightist, nationalist and fascist organizations* ❑ *the threatening nature of fascist ideology*

NOUN [C] (**fascists**) A **fascist** is someone who has fascist views. ❑ *a reluctant supporter of Mussolini's Fascists*

fash·ion ◆◆◇ /ˈfæʃən/ NOUN

NOUN [U, C, SING] (**fashions**) **1** [U] **Fashion** is the area of activity that involves styles of clothing and appearance. ❑ *There are 20 full-colour pages of fashion for men.* **2** [C] A **fashion** is a style of clothing or a way of behaving that is popular at a particular time. ❑ *In the early seventies I wore false eyelashes, as was the fashion.* ❑ *The demand for perfume resulted in a fashion for fancy scent bottles.* **3** [SING] If you do something in a particular **fashion** or **after** a particular **fashion**, you do it in that way. = manner ❑ *There is another drug called DHE that works in a similar fashion.*

PHRASE **in fashion** or **out of fashion** If something is in fashion, it is popular and approved of at a particular time. If it is **out of fashion**, it is not popular or approved of. ❑ *That sort of house is back in fashion.*

→ See also **old-fashioned**

fash·ion·able /ˈfæʃənəbəl/ ADJ Something or someone that is **fashionable** is popular or approved of at a particular time. ❑ *It became fashionable to eat certain kinds of fish.*

fash·ion·ably /ˈfæʃənəbli/ ADV ❑ *women who are perfectly made up and fashionably dressed*

fast ◆◆◇ /fɑːst, fæst/ ADJ, ADV, VERB, NOUN

ADJ (**faster, fastest**) **1** **Fast** means happening, moving, or doing something at great speed. You also use **fast** in questions or statements about speed. = quick ❑ *fast cars with flashing lights and sirens* ❑ *The only question is how fast the process will be.* **2** [V-LINK + fast] If a watch or clock is **fast**, it is showing a time that is later than the real time. ❑ *That clock's an hour fast.* **3** If colours or dyes are **fast**, they do not come out of the fabrics they are used in when they get wet. ❑ *The fabric was ironed to make the colours fast.* **4** [fast + N] You use **fast** to say that something happens without any delay. = swift ❑ *That would be an astonishingly fast action on the part of the Congress.*

ADV **1** [fast with V] **Fast** means at great speed. = quickly ❑ *They work terrifically fast.* ❑ *It would be nice to go faster and break the world record.* ❑ *How fast would the disease develop?*

F

2 [fast after v] You use **fast** to say that something happens without any delay. = soon, swiftly □ *When you've got a crisis like this you need professional help – fast!* **3** [fast after v] If you hold something **fast**, you hold it tightly and firmly. If something is stuck **fast**, it is stuck very firmly and cannot move. = firmly □ *She climbed the staircase cautiously, holding fast to the rail.* **4** [fast after v] If you hold **fast** to a principle or idea, or if you stand **fast**, you do not change your mind about it, even though people are trying to persuade you to. = firm □ *We can only try to hold fast to the age-old values of honesty, decency and concern for others.*
PHRASE **fast asleep** Someone who is **fast asleep** is completely asleep. □ *When he went upstairs five minutes later, she was fast asleep.*
VERB [I] (**fasts, fasting, fasted**) If you **fast**, you eat no food for a period of time, usually for either religious or medical reasons, or as a protest. □ *I fasted for a day and a half and asked God to help me.*
NOUN [c] (**fasts**) A **fast** is the act of eating no food for a period of time, usually for either religious or medical reasons, or as a protest. □ *The fast is broken at sunset, traditionally with dates and water.*
fast·ing /ˈfɑːstɪŋ, ˈfæstɪŋ/ NOUN [U] □ *the Muslim holy month of fasting and prayer*

fas·ten /ˈfɑːsən, ˈfæs-/ VERB [I, T] (**fastens, fastening, fastened**) **1** [I, T] When you **fasten** something, you close it by means of buttons or a strap, or some other device. If something **fastens** with buttons or straps, you can close it in this way. = do up □ *She got quickly into her Mini and fastened the seat-belt.* □ *Her long fair hair was fastened at the nape of her neck by an elastic band.* **2** [T] If you **fasten** one thing **to** another, you attach the first thing to the second, for example, with a piece of string or tape. = attach □ *There were no instructions on how to fasten the carrying strap to the box.*
→ See also **fastening**

fas·ten·ing /ˈfɑːsənɪŋ, ˈfæs-/ NOUN [c] (**fastenings**) A **fastening** is something such as a clasp or zip that you use to fasten something and keep it shut. □ *The sundress has a neat back zip fastening.*

fat ♦♦◇ /fæt/ ADJ, NOUN
ADJ (**fatter, fattest**) **1** (disapproval) If you say that a person or animal is **fat**, you mean that they have a lot of flesh on their body and that they weigh too much. You usually use the word **fat** when you think that this is a bad thing. = overweight □ *I could eat what I liked without getting fat.* **2** A **fat** object, especially a book, is very thick or wide. = thick □ *'Europe in Figures', a fat book published on September 22nd* **3** [fat + N] (informal) A **fat** profit or fee is a large one. □ *They are set to make a big fat profit.*
PHRASE **fat chance** (informal, mainly spoken, feelings) If you say that there is **fat chance of** something happening, you mean that you do not believe that it will happen. □ *'Would your car be easy to steal?'—'Fat chance. I've got a device that shuts down the petrol and ignition.'*
NOUN [c, U] (**fats**) **1** [c, U] **Fat** is a substance contained in foods such as meat, cheese, and butter which forms an energy store in your body. □ *An easy way to cut the amount of fat in your diet is to avoid eating red meats.* **2** [c, U] **Fat** is a solid or liquid substance obtained from animals or vegetables, which is used in cooking. □ *When you use oil or fat for cooking, use as little as possible.* **3** [U] **Fat** is the extra flesh that animals and humans have under their skin, which is used to store energy and to help keep them warm. □ *Because you're not burning calories, everything you eat turns to fat.*

✪**fa·tal** /ˈfeɪtəl/ ADJ **1** A **fatal** action has very undesirable effects. □ *It would be fatal for the nation to overlook the urgency of the situation.* □ *He made the fatal mistake of compromising early.* **2** A **fatal** accident or illness causes someone's death. □ *the fatal stabbing of a police sergeant* □ *A hospital spokesman said she had suffered a fatal heart attack.* □ *He had taken a massive overdose of pills which had proved fatal.*
✪**fa·tal·ly** /ˈfeɪtəli/ ADV **1** [fatally with v] □ *Failure now could fatally damage his chances in the future.* **2** [The dead soldier is reported to have been fatally wounded in the chest. □ *He was fatally shot two days later.*

✪**fa·tal·ity** /fəˈtæləti/ NOUN [c] (**fatalities**) (formal) A **fatality** is a death caused by an accident or by violence. = death □ *Drunk driving fatalities have declined more than 10 per cent over the past 10 years.* □ *Most fatalities occur in small mines that often lack safety equipment.*

fate ♦♦◇ /feɪt/ NOUN [U, c] (**fates**) **1** [U] [also fates] **Fate** is a power that some people believe controls and decides everything that happens, in a way that cannot be prevented or changed. You can also refer to **the fates**. □ *I see no use arguing with fate.* □ *the fickleness of fate* **2** [c] A person's or thing's **fate** is what happens to them. = destiny □ *The Russian Parliament will hold a special session later this month to decide his fate.* □ *He seems for a moment to be again holding the fate of the country in his hands.*

fa·ther ♦♦♦ /ˈfɑːðə/ NOUN, VERB
NOUN [c] (**fathers**) **1** Your **father** is your male parent. You can also call someone your **father** if he brings you up as if he were this man. □ *His father was a painter.* □ *He would be a good father to my children.* **2** The man who invented or started something is sometimes referred to as the **father of** that thing. □ *Max Dupain, regarded as the father of modern photography*
VERB [T] (**fathers, fathering, fathered**) When a man **fathers** a child, he makes a woman pregnant and their child is born. □ *She claims Mark fathered her child.*

father-in-law NOUN [c] (**fathers-in-law**) Someone's **father-in-law** is the father of their husband or wife.

fa·tigue /fəˈtiːg/ NOUN [U, PL] (**fatigues**) **1** [U] **Fatigue** is a feeling of extreme physical or mental tiredness. □ *She continued to have severe stomach cramps, aches, fatigue, and depression.* **2** [U] You can say that people are suffering from a particular kind of **fatigue** when they have been doing something for a long time and feel they can no longer continue to do it. □ *compassion fatigue caused by endless TV and celebrity appeals* **3** [U] **Fatigue** in metal or wood is a weakness in it that is caused by repeated stress. Fatigue can cause the metal or wood to break. □ *The problem turned out to be metal fatigue in the fuselage.* **4** [PL] **Fatigues** are clothes that soldiers wear when they are fighting or when they are doing routine jobs. □ *He never expected to return home wearing combat fatigues.*

fat·ten /ˈfætən/ VERB
VERB [T] (**fattens, fattening, fattened**) (business, disapproval) If you say that someone **is fattening** something such as a business or its profits, you mean that they are increasing the value of the business or its profits, in a way that you disapprove of. □ *They have kept the price of sugar artificially high and so fattened the company's profits.*
PHRASAL VERB **fatten up** Fatten up means the same as **fatten**. □ *The Government is making the taxpayer pay to fatten up a public sector business for private sale.*

fat·ten·ing /ˈfætənɪŋ/ ADJ Food that is **fattening** is considered to make people fat easily. □ *Some foods are more fattening than others.*

fat·ty /ˈfæti/ ADJ (**fattier, fattiest**) **1** Fatty food contains a lot of fat. □ *Don't eat fatty food or chocolates.* **2** [fatty + N] Fatty acids or fatty tissues, for example, contain or consist of fat. □ *fatty acids*

fault ♦♦◇ /fɔːlt/ NOUN, VERB
NOUN [SING, c] (**faults**) **1** [SING] If a bad or undesirable situation is your **fault**, you caused it or are responsible for it. □ *There was no escaping the fact: it was all his fault.* **2** [c] A **fault** is a mistake in what someone is doing or in what they have done. = error, mistake □ *It is a big fault to think that you can learn how to manage people in business school.* **3** [c] A **fault** in someone or something is a weakness in them or something that is not perfect. = failing, flaw □ *His manners had always made her blind to his faults.* **4** [c] A **fault** is a large crack in the surface of the earth. □ *the San Andreas Fault* **5** [c] A **fault** in tennis is a service that is wrong according to the rules. □ *He caught the ball on his first toss and then served a fault.*
PHRASES **at fault** If someone or something is **at fault**, they are to blame or are responsible for a particular situation that has gone wrong. □ *He could never accept that he had been at fault.*

find fault with If you **find fault with** something or someone, you look for mistakes and complain about them. ❏ *I was disappointed whenever the cook found fault with my work.*

VERB [T] (**faults, faulting, faulted**) If you **cannot fault** someone, you cannot find any reason for criticizing them or the things that they are doing. ❏ *You can't fault them for lack of invention.*

faulty /ˈfɔːlti/ ADJ (**faultier, faultiest**) **1** A **faulty** piece of equipment has something wrong with it and is not working properly. ❏ *The money will be used to repair faulty equipment.* **2** If you describe someone's argument or reasoning as **faulty**, you mean that it is wrong or contains mistakes, usually because they have not been thinking in a logical way. = flawed ❏ *Their interpretation was faulty – they had misinterpreted things.*

✪**fau·na** /ˈfɔːnə/ NOUN [C] (**faunas**) (*technical*) Animals, especially the animals in a particular area, can be referred to as **fauna**. ❏ *the flora and fauna of the African jungle* ❏ *Brackish waters generally support only a small range of faunas.*

✪**fa·vour** ♦♦◇ /ˈfeɪvə/ (*BrE*; in *AmE*, use **favor**) NOUN, VERB

NOUN [U, C] (**favours**) **1** [U] If you regard something or someone with **favour**, you like or support them. ❏ *It remains to be seen if the show will find favour with an audience.* ❏ *No one would look with favour on the continuing military rule.* **2** [C] If you **do** someone **a favour**, you do something for them even though you do not have to. ❏ *I've come to ask you to do me a favour.*

PHRASES in favour of If you are **in favour of** something, you support it and think that it is a good thing. ≠ against ❏ *I wouldn't be in favour of income tax cuts.* ❏ *Yet this is a Government which proclaims that it is all in favour of openness.* ❏ *The vote passed with 111 in favour and 25 against.*

in someone's favour 1 If something is **in** your **favour**, it helps you or gives you an advantage. ❏ *The protection that farmers have enjoyed amounts to a bias in favour of the countryside.* **2** If someone makes a judgment **in** your **favour**, they say that you are right about something. ❏ *The Supreme Court ruled in Fitzgerald's favour.*

in favour of If one thing is rejected **in favour of** another, the second thing is done or chosen instead of the first. ❏ *The policy was rejected in favour of a more cautious approach.*

in favour or **out of favour** If someone or something is **in favour**, people like or support them. If they are **out of favour**, people no longer like or support them. ❏ *Governments and party leaders can only hope to remain in favour with the public for so long.*

VERB [T] (**favours, favouring, favoured**) **1** If you **favour** something, you prefer it to the other choices available. ≠ oppose ❏ *The French say they favour a transition to democracy.* ❏ *Britain and the United States have strongly favoured retaining the sanctions.* **2** If you **favour** someone, you treat them better or in a kinder way than you treat other people. ❏ *The company has no rules about favouring US citizens during layoffs.*

fa·vour·able /ˈfeɪvərəbəl/ (*BrE*; in *AmE*, use **favorable**) ADJ **1** [favourable + N, V-LINK + favourable 'to' N] If your opinion or your reaction is **favourable** to something, you agree with it and approve of it. ❏ *The president's convention speech received favourable reviews.* **2 Favourable** conditions make something more likely to succeed or seem more attractive. ❏ *It's believed the conditions in which the elections are being held are too favourable to the government.* **3** If you make a **favourable** comparison between two things, you say that the first is better than or as good as the second. ❏ *The film bears favourable technical comparison with Hollywood productions costing 10 times as much.*

fa·vour·ite ♦♦◇ /ˈfeɪvərɪt/ (*BrE*; in *AmE*, use **favorite**) ADJ, NOUN

ADJ [favourite + N] Your **favourite** thing or person of a particular type is the one you like most. ❏ *He celebrated by opening a bottle of his favourite champagne.*

NOUN [C] (**favourites**) **1** Your **favourite** of a particular type is the one you like most. ❏ *The Metropole is my favourite. I love those huge, anonymous hotels.* **2** The **favourite** in a race or contest is the competitor that is expected to win.

In a team game, the team that is expected to win is referred to as the **favourites**. ❏ *The U.S. team is considered one of the favourites in next month's games.*

PHRASE old favourite If you refer to something as an **old favourite**, you mean that it has been in existence for a long time and everyone knows it or likes it. ❏ *This recipe is an adaptation of an old favourite.*

fa·vour·it·ism /ˈfeɪvərɪtɪzəm/ (*BrE*; in *AmE*, use **favoritism**) NOUN [U] (*disapproval*) If you accuse someone of **favouritism**, you disapprove of them because they unfairly help or favour one person or group much more than another. = bias ❏ *Maria loved both the children. There was never a hint of favouritism.*

fax /fæks/ NOUN, VERB

NOUN [C] (**faxes**) **1** [also 'by' fax] A **fax** or a **fax machine** is a piece of equipment used to copy documents by sending information electronically along a telephone line, and to receive copies that are sent in this way. ❏ *a modern reception desk with telephone and fax* **2** You can refer to a copy of a document that is transmitted by a fax machine as a **fax**. ❏ *I sent him a long fax, saying I didn't need a maid.*

VERB [T] (**faxes, faxing, faxed**) If you **fax** a document to someone, you send it from one fax machine to another. ❏ *I faxed a copy of the agreement to each of the investors.* ❏ *Did you fax him a reply?*

fear ♦♦♦ /fɪə/ NOUN, VERB

NOUN [C, U] (**fears**) **1 Fear** is the unpleasant feeling you have when you think that you are in danger. = terror, dread ❏ *I was sitting on the floor shivering with fear because a bullet had been fired through a window.* **2** A **fear** is a thought that something unpleasant might happen or might have happened. ❏ *These youngsters are motivated by fear of failure.* ❏ *Then one day his worst fears were confirmed.* **3** If you say that there is a **fear that** something unpleasant and undesirable will happen, you mean that you think it is possible or likely. = risk, chance ❏ *There is a fear that the freeze on bank accounts could prove a lasting deterrent to investors.* **4** If you have **fears for** someone or something, you are very worried because you think that they might be in danger. ❏ *He also spoke of his fears for the future of his country's culture.*

PHRASES in fear of If you are **in fear of** doing or experiencing something unpleasant or undesirable, you are very worried that you might have to do it or experience it. ❏ *The elderly live in fear of assault and murder.*

for fear of If you take a particular course of action **for fear of** something, you take the action in order to prevent that thing happening. ❏ *She was afraid to say anything to them for fear of hurting their feelings.*

VERB [T, I] (**fears, fearing, feared**) **1** [T] If you **fear** someone or something, you are frightened because you think that they will harm you. ❏ *It seems to me that if people fear you they respect you.* **2** [T] If you **fear** something unpleasant or undesirable, you are worried that it might happen or might have happened. ❏ *She had feared she was coming down with pneumonia or bronchitis.* **3** [I] If you **fear for** someone or something, you are very worried because you think that they might be in danger. ❏ *Carla fears for her son.*

fear·ful /ˈfɪəfʊl/ ADJ (*formal*) **1** If you are **fearful of** something, you are afraid of it. ❏ *Bankers were fearful of a world banking crisis.* **2** [fearful + N] (*emphasis*) You use **fearful** to emphasize how serious or bad a situation is. = dreadful ❏ *The region is in a fearful recession.*

fear·less /ˈfɪələs/ ADJ (*approval*) If you say that someone is **fearless**, you mean that they are not afraid at all, and you admire them for this. ❏ *his fearless campaigning for racial justice*

fear·some /ˈfɪəsəm/ ADJ **Fearsome** is used to describe things that are frightening, for example, because of their large size or extreme nature. = formidable ❏ *He had developed a fearsome reputation for intimidating people.*

✪**fea·sible** /ˈfiːzəbəl/ ADJ If something is **feasible**, it can be done, made, or achieved. = practicable, possible; ≠ unfeasible ❏ *She questioned whether it was feasible to stimulate investment in these regions.* ❏ *Supporters argue that the scheme is now technically and economically feasible.*

F

○**fea·sibil·ity** /ˌfiːzəˈbɪlɪti/ NOUN [U] ❑ *The committee will study the feasibility of setting up a national computer network.*

feast /fiːst/ NOUN, VERB

NOUN [C] (**feasts**) **1** A **feast** is a large and special meal. = banquet ❑ *Lunch was a feast of meat and vegetables, cheese, yogurt and fruit, with unlimited wine.* ❑ *The fruit was often served at wedding feasts.* **2** A **feast** is a day or time of the year when a special religious celebration takes place. = festival ❑ *The Jewish feast of Passover began last night.* VERB [I] (**feasts, feasting, feasted**) **1** If you **feast on** a particular food, you eat a large amount of it with great enjoyment. ❑ *They feasted well into the afternoon on mutton and corn stew.* **2** If you **feast**, you take part in a feast. ❑ *Only a few feet away, their captors feasted in the castle's banqueting hall.*

PHRASE **feast your eyes** If you **feast** your **eyes on** something, you look at it for a long time with great attention because you find it very attractive. ❑ *She stood feasting her eyes on the view.*

feast·ing /ˈfiːstɪŋ/ NOUN [U] ❑ *The feasting, drinking, dancing and revelry continued for several days.*

feat /fiːt/ NOUN [C] (**feats**) (approval) If you refer to an action, or the result of an action, as a **feat**, you admire it because it is an impressive and difficult achievement. ❑ *A racing car is an extraordinary feat of engineering.*

feath·er /ˈfeðə/ NOUN [C] (**feathers**) A bird's **feathers** are the soft covering on its body. Each **feather** consists of a lot of smooth hairs on each side of a thin stiff centre. ❑ *a hat that she had made herself from black ostrich feathers*

○**fea·ture** ♦♦◇ /ˈfiːtʃə/ NOUN, VERB (academic word)

NOUN [C, PL] (**features**) **1** [C] A **feature** of something is an interesting or important part or characteristic of it. = characteristic, quality ❑ *Patriotic songs have long been a feature of Kuwaiti life.* ❑ *The spacious gardens are a special feature of this property.* ❑ *The key feature of terrorists is their total disregard for the lives of innocent civilians.* ❑ *Italian democracy's unique feature is that government has not alternated between two parties.* ❑ *The ships have built-in safety features including specially-strengthened hulls.* **2** [C] A **feature** is a special article in a newspaper or magazine, or a special programme on radio or television. ❑ *We are delighted to see the Sunday Times running a long feature on breast cancer.* **3** [C] A **feature** or a **feature** film is a full-length film about a fictional situation, as opposed to a short film or a documentary. ❑ *the first feature-length cartoon, Snow White and the Seven Dwarfs* **4** [C] A geographical **feature** is something noticeable in a particular area of country, for example, a hill, river, or valley. ❑ *one of the area's oddest geographical features – an eight-mile bank of pebbles shelving abruptly into the sea* **5** [PL] Your **features** are your eyes, nose, mouth, and other parts of your face. ❑ *His features seemed to change.*

VERB [T, I] (**features, featuring, featured**) **1** [T] When something such as a film or exhibition **features** a particular person or thing, they are an important part of it. = include ❑ *It's a great movie and it features a Spanish actor who is going to be a world star within a year.* ❑ *The hour-long programme will be updated each week and feature highlights from recent games.* **2** [I] If someone or something **features in** something such as a show, exhibition, or magazine, they are an important part of it. ❑ *Jon featured in one of the show's most thrilling episodes.*

fed /fed/ IRREG FORM **Fed** is the past tense and past participle of **feed**. See also **fed up**.

○**fed·er·al** ♦♦◇ /ˈfedərəl/ ADJ (academic word) **1** [federal + N] A **federal** country or system of government is one in which the different states or provinces of the country have important powers to make their own laws and decisions. ❑ *Five of the six provinces are to become autonomous regions in a new federal system of government.* ❑ *Czechoslovakia would remain a federal state* **2** [federal + N] **Federal** also means belonging or relating to the national government of a federal country rather than to one of the states within it. ❑ *The federal government controls just 6% of the education budget.* ❑ *A federal judge ruled in her favour.*

fed·er·al·ly /ˈfedərəli/ ADV ❑ *residents of public housing and federally subsidized apartments*

○**fed·era·tion** ♦◇◇ /ˌfedəˈreɪʃən/ NOUN [C] (**federations**) **1** A **federation** is a federal country. ❑ *the Russian Federation* **2** A **federation** is a group of societies or other organizations which have joined together, usually because they share a common interest. = association ❑ *the American Federation of Government Employees* ❑ *the British Athletic Federation* ❑ *The organization emerged from a federation of six national agencies.*

fed up ADJ [V-LINK + fed up] (informal) If you are **fed up,** you are unhappy, or bored, or tired of something, especially something that you have been experiencing for a long time. ❑ *I am fed up with reading how women should dress to please men.* ❑ *He had become fed up with city life.*

○**fee** ♦♦◇ /fiː/ NOUN [C] (**fees**) (academic word) **1** A **fee** is a sum of money that you pay to be allowed to do something. = charge ❑ *He paid his licence fee, and walked out with a brand-new driving licence.* ❑ *Expect to pay an entrance fee of 50-60 euros per head.* **2** A **fee** is the amount of money that a person or organization is paid for a particular job or service that they provide. = charge ❑ *Lawyer's fees can be substantial.* ❑ *Find out how much your surveyor's and solicitor's fees will be.*

WORD CONNECTIONS
VERB + **fee**
charge a fee **pay** a fee ❑ *The bank charges a fee for this service.*
ADJ + **fee**
a **monthly** fee an **annual** fee ❑ *You can have unlimited use of the swimming pool and gym for a fixed monthly fee.*
a **high** fee a **low** fee a **small** fee a **nominal** fee a **flat** fee ❑ *We charge a flat fee of £15 for all deliveries.*
NOUN + **fee**
a **membership** fee an **entrance** fee a **licence** fee ❑ *Club members pay an annual membership fee of £200.*
tuition fees **school** fees **university** fees ❑ *Some universiites are charging tuition fees of more than £3000 a year.*

fee·ble /ˈfiːbəl/ ADJ (**feebler, feeblest**) **1** If you describe someone or something as **feeble**, you mean that they are weak. ❑ *He told them he was old and feeble and was not able to walk so far.* **2** If you describe something that someone says as **feeble**, you mean that it is not very good or convincing. = weak ❑ *This is a particularly feeble argument.*

fee·bly /ˈfiːbli/ ADV **1** [feebly with V] ❑ *His left hand moved feebly at his side.* **2** [feebly with V] ❑ *I said 'Sorry', very feebly, feeling rather embarrassed.*

feed ♦♦◇ /fiːd/ VERB, NOUN

VERB [I, T] (**feeds, feeding, fed**) **1** [I, T] If you **feed** a person or animal, you give them food to eat and sometimes actually put it in their mouths. ❑ *We brought along pieces of old bread and fed the birds.* **2** [T] To **feed** a family or a community means to supply food for them. ❑ *Feeding a hungry family can be expensive.* **3** [I] When an animal **feeds**, it eats or drinks something. ❑ *After a few days the caterpillars stopped feeding.* **4** [I, T] When a baby **feeds**, or when you **feed** it, it drinks breast milk or milk from a bottle. ❑ *When a baby is thirsty, it feeds more often.* **5** [T] To **feed** something to a place, means to supply it to that place in a steady flow. ❑ *blood vessels that feed blood to the brain* **6** [T] If you **feed** something **into** a container or piece of equipment, you put it into it. ❑ *He took the compact disc* *from her, then fed it into the player.* **7** [T] If you **feed** a plant, you add substances to it to make it grow well. □ *Feed plants to encourage steady growth.* **8** [I] If one thing **feeds on** another, it becomes stronger as a result of the other thing's existence. □ *The drinking and the guilt fed on each other.* **9** [T] To **feed** information **into** a computer means to gradually put it into it. □ *An automatic weather station feeds information on wind direction to the computer.* **NOUN** [C, U] (**feeds**) [usu N + feed] Animal **feed** is food given to animals, especially farm animals. □ *The grain just rotted and all they could use it for was animal feed.*

feed·ing /ˈfiːdɪŋ/ NOUN [U] □ *The feeding of dairy cows has undergone a revolution.*

✦ **bite the hand that feeds you** → see **bite; mouths to feed** → see **mouth**

feed·back /ˈfiːdbæk/ NOUN [U] **1** If you get **feedback on** your work or progress, someone tells you how well or badly you are doing, and how you could improve. If you get good feedback you have worked or performed well. □ *Continue to ask for feedback on your work.* **2** **Feedback** is the unpleasant high-pitched sound produced by a piece of electrical equipment when part of the signal that comes out goes back into it. □ *The microphone screeched with feedback.*

feel ♦♦♦ /fiːl/ VERB, NOUN

VERB [LINK, I, T] (**feels, feeling, felt**) **1** [LINK] If you **feel** a particular emotion or physical sensation, you experience it. □ *I am feeling very depressed.* □ *Suddenly I felt a sharp pain in my shoulder.* □ *I felt as if all my strength had gone.* □ *I felt like I was being kicked in the teeth every day.* **2** [LINK] If you talk about how an experience or event **feels**, you talk about the emotions and sensations connected with it. □ *It feels good to have finished a piece of work.* □ *The speed at which everything moved felt strange.* □ *Within five minutes of arriving back from holiday, it feels as if I've never been away.* **3** [LINK] If you talk about how an object **feels**, you talk about the physical quality that you notice when you touch or hold it. For example, if something **feels** soft, you notice that it is soft when you touch it. □ *The metal felt smooth and cold.* □ *The ten-foot oars felt heavy and awkward.* **4** [LINK] If you talk about how the weather **feels**, you describe the weather, especially the temperature or whether or not you think it is going to rain or snow. □ *It felt wintry cold that day.* **5** [I, T] If you **feel** an object, you touch it deliberately with your hand, so that you learn what it is like, for example, what shape it is or whether it is rough or smooth. □ *The doctor felt his head.* □ *Feel how soft the skin is in the small of the back.* **6** [T] If you can **feel** something, you are aware of it because it is touching you. □ *Through several layers of clothes I could feel his muscles.* **7** [T] If you **feel** something happening, you become aware of it because of the effect it has on your body. □ *She felt something being pressed into her hands.* □ *He felt something move beside him.* **8** [T] If you **feel yourself** doing something or being in a particular state, you are aware that something is happening to you which you are unable to control. □ *I felt myself blush.* □ *If at any point you feel yourself becoming tense, make a conscious effort to relax.* **9** [T] If you **feel** the presence of someone or something, you become aware of them, even though you cannot see or hear them. = **sense** □ *He felt her eyes on him.* □ *I could feel that a man was watching me very intensely.* **10** [T] If you **feel** that something is the case, you have a strong idea in your mind that it is the case. □ *I feel that not enough is being done to protect the local animal life.* □ *I feel certain that it will all turn out well.* **11** [T] If you **feel** that you should do something, you think that you should do it. □ *I feel I should resign.* □ *You need not feel obliged to contribute.* **12** [I, T] If you talk about how you **feel about** something, you talk about your opinion, attitude, or reaction to it. □ *We'd like to know what you feel about abortion.* □ *She feels guilty about spending less time lately with her two kids.* **13** [I] If you **feel like** doing something or having something, you want to do it or have it because you are in the right mood for it and think you would enjoy it. □ *Neither of them felt like going back to sleep.*

PHRASAL VERB **feel for** **1** If you **feel for** something, for example, in the dark, you try to find it by moving your

hand around until you touch it. □ *I felt for my wallet and papers in my inside pocket.* **2** If you **feel for** someone, you have sympathy for them. □ *She cried on the phone and I really felt for her.*

NOUN [SING] The **feel of** something is how you are aware of it because it is touching you. □ *He remembered the feel of her skin.*

→ See also **feeling, felt**
✦ **feel free** → see **free**

feel·ing ♦♦◇ /ˈfiːlɪŋ/ NOUN

NOUN [C, PL, U, SING] (**feelings**) **1** [C] A **feeling** is an emotion, such as anger or happiness. □ *It gave me a feeling of satisfaction.* □ *He was unable to contain his own destructive feelings.* **2** [C] If you have a **feeling** of hunger, tiredness, or other physical sensation, you experience it. □ *I also had a strange feeling in my neck.* □ *Focus on the feeling of relaxation.* **3** [C] If you have **a feeling that** something is the case or **that** something is going to happen, you think that is probably the case or that it is probably going to happen. □ *I have a feeling that everything will be all right.* **4** [PL] Your **feelings** about something are the things that you think and feel about it, or your attitude towards it. □ *She has strong feelings about the alleged growth in violence against female officers.* □ *I think that sums up the feelings of most discerning and intelligent Indians.* **5** [PL] When you refer to someone's **feelings**, you are talking about the things that might embarrass, offend, or upset them. For example, if you hurt someone's **feelings**, you upset them by something that you say or do. □ *He was afraid of hurting my feelings.* **6** [U] **Feeling** is a way of thinking and reacting to things which is emotional and not planned rather than logical and practical. = **emotion** □ *He was prompted to a rare outburst of feeling.* **7** [U] **Feeling** for someone is love, affection, sympathy, or concern for them. □ *Thomas never lost his feeling for Harriet.* **8** [U] **Feeling** in part of your body is the ability to experience the sense of touch in this part of the body. □ *After the accident he had no feeling in his legs.* **9** [U] **Feeling** is used to refer to a general opinion that a group of people has about something. □ *There is still some feeling in the art world that the market for such works may be declining.* **10** [SING] If you have a **feeling** of being in a particular situation, you feel that you are in that situation. □ *I had the terrible feeling of being left behind to bring up the baby while he had fun.* **11** [SING] If something such as a place or book creates a particular kind of **feeling**, it creates a particular kind of atmosphere. □ *That's what we tried to portray in the book, this feeling of opulence and grandeur.*

PHRASES **bad feeling** or **ill feeling** Bad feeling or ill feeling is bitterness or anger which exists between people, for example, after they have had an argument. □ *There's been some bad feeling between the two families.*

hard feelings Hard feelings are feelings of anger or bitterness towards someone who you have had an argument with or who has upset you. If you say 'no hard feelings', you are making an agreement with someone not to be angry or bitter about something. □ *I don't want any hard feelings between our companies.*

→ See also **feel**

feet /fiːt/ IRREG FORM **Feet** is the plural of **foot**.

feign /feɪn/ VERB [T] (**feigns, feigning, feigned**) (*formal*) If someone **feigns** a particular feeling, attitude, or physical condition, they try to make other people think that they have it or are experiencing it, although this is not true. = **affect** □ *One morning, I didn't want to go to school, and decided to feign illness.*

fell /fel/ IRREG FORM, VERB

IRREG FORM **Fell** is the past tense of **fall**.

VERB [T] (**fells, felling, felled**) If trees **are felled**, they are cut down. □ *Badly infected trees should be felled and burned.*
✦ **in one fell swoop** → see **swoop**

fel·low ♦♦◇ /ˈfeləʊ/ ADJ, NOUN

ADJ [fellow + N] You use **fellow** to describe people who are in the same situation as you, or people you feel you have something in common with. □ *She discovered to her pleasure, a talent for making her fellow guests laugh.*

NOUN [C, PL] (**fellows**) **1** [C] (*informal, old-fashioned*) A **fellow** is a man or boy. □ *By all accounts, Rodger would* appear to be a fine fellow. **2** [c] A **fellow of** an academic or professional association is someone who is a specially elected member of it, usually because of their work or achievements or as a mark of honour. ❑ *the fellows of the Zoological Society* **3** [PL] [POSS + fellow] (formal) Your **fellows** are the people who you work with, do things with, or who are like you in some way. ❑ *He stood out in terms of competence from all his fellows.*

felt /felt/ IRREG FORM, NOUN
IRREG FORM **Felt** is the past tense and past participle of **feel**. NOUN [U] [oft felt + N] **Felt** is a thick cloth made from wool or other fibres packed tightly together. ❑ *She had on an old felt hat.*

✪ **fe·male** ♦♦◇ /ˈfiːmeɪl/ ADJ, NOUN
ADJ **1** Someone who is **female** is a woman or a girl. ❑ *a sixteen-piece dance band with a female singer* ❑ *In 1880, Melbourne University admitted female students for the first time.* ❑ *Only 13 per cent of consultants are female.* ❑ *Female athletes should take extra iron.* **2** [female + N] **Female** matters and things relate to, belong to, or affect women rather than men. ❑ *female infertility* ❑ *Although she works in an engineering company she is in a traditional female role.* **3** A **female** creature can lay eggs or produce babies from its body. ❑ *the scent given off by the female aphid to attract the male*
NOUN [c] (**females**) **1** Women and girls are sometimes referred to as **females** when they are being considered as a type. ❑ *Hay fever affects males more than females.* **2** You can refer to any creature that can lay eggs or produce babies from its body as a **female**. ❑ *Each female will lay just one egg in April or May.*

USAGE NOTE

female

You use **male** and **female** as adjectives to talk about people and animals.

*the number of **female** employees*

*The **male** and **female** birds are different colours.*

You can also use **male** and **female** as nouns, but mostly in scientific writing, especially to refer to animals.

*The adult **female** lays an egg on each fruit.*

✪ **femi·nine** /ˈfemɪnɪn/ ADJ **1** **Feminine** qualities and things relate to or are considered typical of women, in contrast to men. = female ❑ *male leaders worrying about their women abandoning traditional feminine roles* ❑ *a manufactured ideal of feminine beauty* **2** Someone or something that is **feminine** has qualities that are considered typical of women, especially being pretty or gentle. ❑ *I've always been attracted to very feminine women who are not overpowering.* **3** In some languages, a **feminine** noun, pronoun, or adjective has a different form from a masculine or neuter one, or behaves in a different way.

✪ **femi·nism** /ˈfemɪnɪzəm/ NOUN [U] **Feminism** is the belief and aim that women should have the same rights, power, and opportunities as men. ❑ *Barbara Johnson, that champion of radical feminism* ❑ *Feminism may have liberated the feminists, but it has still to change the lives of the majority of women.* ❑ *Proponents of feminism have challenged the traditional views.*

✪ **femi·nist** /ˈfemɪnɪst/ NOUN, ADJ
NOUN [c] (**feminists**) A **feminist** is a person who believes in and supports feminism. ❑ *Only 16 per cent of young women in a 1990 survey considered themselves feminists.* ❑ *radical feminists like Andrea Dworkin*
ADJ [feminist + N] **Feminist** groups, ideas, and activities are involved in feminism. ❑ *the concerns addressed by the feminist movement* ❑ *the reconstruction of history from a feminist perspective*

fence ♦◇◇ /fens/ NOUN, VERB
NOUN [c] (**fences**) **1** A **fence** is a barrier between two areas of land, made of wood or wire supported by posts. ❑ *Villagers say the fence would restrict public access to the hills.* **2** A **fence** in show jumping or horse racing is an obstacle or barrier that horses have to jump over. ❑ *The horse fell at the last fence.*
PHRASE **sit on the fence** If you **sit on the fence**, you avoid supporting a particular side in a discussion or argument. ❑ *They are sitting on the fence and refusing to commit themselves.*
VERB [T] (**fences, fencing, fenced**) If you **fence** an area of land, you surround it with a fence. ❑ *The first task was to fence the wood to exclude sheep.*

fend /fend/ VERB
VERB [I] (**fends, fending, fended**) If you have to **fend for** yourself, you have to look after yourself without relying on help from anyone else. ❑ *The woman and her young baby had been thrown out and left to fend for themselves.*
PHRASAL VERB **fend off** **1** If you **fend off** unwanted questions, problems, or people, you stop them from affecting you or defend yourself from them, but often only for a short time and without dealing with them completely. ❑ *He looked relaxed and determined as he fended off questions from the world's press.* **2** If you **fend off** someone who is attacking you, you use your arms or something such as a stick to defend yourself from their blows. = ward off ❑ *He raised his hand to fend off the blow.*

fe·ro·cious /fəˈrəʊʃəs/ ADJ **1** A **ferocious** animal, person, or action is very fierce and violent. = fierce ❑ *By its very nature a lion is ferocious.* **2** A **ferocious** war, argument, or other form of conflict involves a great deal of anger, bitterness, and determination. ❑ *Fighting has been ferocious.*

fe·roc·ity /fəˈrɒsɪti/ NOUN [U] The **ferocity** of something is its fierce or violent nature. = violence ❑ *The armed forces seem to have been taken by surprise by the ferocity of the attack.*

fer·ry /ˈferi/ NOUN, VERB
NOUN [c] (**ferries**) [also 'by' ferry] A **ferry** is a boat that transports passengers and sometimes also vehicles, usually across short stretches of sea. ❑ *They had recrossed the River Gambia by ferry.*
VERB [T] (**ferries, ferrying, ferried**) If a vehicle **ferries** people or goods, it transports them, usually by means of regular trips between the same two places. = transport ❑ *Every day, a plane arrives to ferry guests to and from Bird Island Lodge.*

fer·tile /ˈfɜːtaɪl, AmE -təl/ ADJ **1** Land or soil that is **fertile** is able to support the growth of a large number of strong healthy plants. = rich ❑ *fertile soil* **2** A **fertile** mind or imagination is able to produce a lot of good, original ideas. ❑ *a product of Flynn's fertile imagination* **3** [fertile + N] A situation or environment that is **fertile** in relation to a particular activity or feeling encourages the activity or feeling. ❑ *a fertile breeding ground for this kind of violent racism* **4** A person or animal that is **fertile** is able to reproduce and have babies or young. ❑ *The operation cannot be reversed to make her fertile again.*

fer·til·ity /fɜːˈtɪlɪti/ NOUN [U] **1** *He was able to bring large sterile acreages back to fertility.* **2** *Doctors will tell you that pregnancy is the only sure test for fertility.*

✪ **fer·ti·lize** /ˈfɜːtɪlaɪz/ also **fertilise** VERB [T] (**fertilizes, fertilizing, fertilized**) **1** When an egg from the ovary of a woman or female animal **is fertilized**, a sperm from the male joins with the egg, causing a baby or young animal to begin forming. A female plant **is fertilized** when its reproductive parts come into contact with pollen from the male plant. = inseminate ❑ *Certain varieties cannot be fertilized with their own pollen.* ❑ *the normal sperm levels needed to fertilize the egg* ❑ *Pregnancy begins when the fertilized egg is implanted in the wall of the uterus.* **2** To **fertilize** land means to improve its quality in order to make plants grow well on it, by spreading solid animal waste or a chemical mixture on it. = enrich ❑ *The faeces contain nitrogen which fertilizes the soil.*

✪ **fer·ti·li·za·tion** /ˌfɜːtɪlaɪˈzeɪʃən/ NOUN [U]
= insemination ❑ *From fertilization until birth is about 266 days.* ❑ *emergency contraception that can prevent fertilization* ❑ *an in vitro fertilization clinic*

fer·ti·liz·er /ˈfɜːtɪlaɪzə/ also **fertiliser** NOUN [c, U] (**fertilizers**) **Fertilizer** is a substance such as solid animal waste or a chemical mixture that you spread on the ground in order to make plants grow more successfully. ❑ *farming without any purchased chemical, fertilizer or pesticide*

fes·ti·val ♦♦◇ /ˈfestɪvəl/ NOUN [C] (**festivals**) **1** A **festival** is an organized series of events such as musical concerts or drama productions. ❑ *Many towns hold their own summer festivals of music, theatre, and dance.* **2** A **festival** is a day or time of the year when people do not go to work or school and celebrate some special event, often a religious event. ❑ *Shavuot is a two-day festival for Orthodox Jews.*

fes·tive /ˈfestɪv/ ADJ **1** Something that is **festive** is special, colourful, or exciting, especially because of a holiday or celebration. ❑ *The town has a festive holiday atmosphere.* **2** [festive + N] **Festive** means relating to a holiday or celebration, especially Christmas. ❑ *With Christmas just around the corner, you should start your festive cooking now.*

fetch /fetʃ/ VERB [T] (**fetches, fetching, fetched**) **1** If you **fetch** something or someone, you go and get them from the place where they are. = get ❑ *Sylvia fetched a towel from the bathroom.* ❑ *Fetch me a glass of water.* **2** If something **fetches** a particular sum of money, it is sold for that amount. = go for ❑ *The painting is expected to fetch between two and three million dollars.*
→ See also **far-fetched**

fe·tus /ˈfiːtəs/ → See **foetus**

feud /fjuːd/ NOUN, VERB
NOUN [C] (**feuds**) A **feud** is a quarrel in which two people or groups remain angry with each other for a long time, although they are not always fighting or arguing. = vendetta ❑ *a long and bitter feud between the state government and the villagers*
VERB [RECIP] (**feuds, feuding, feuded**) If one person or group **feuds** with another, they have a quarrel that lasts a long time. You can also say that two people or groups **feud**. ❑ *He feuded with his ex-wife.*

fe·ver /ˈfiːvə/ NOUN [C, U] (**fevers**) If you have a **fever** when you are ill, your body temperature is higher than usual. ❑ *My Uncle Jim had a high fever.*

few ♦♦♦ /fjuː/ DET, PRON, QUANT, ADJ, NOUN
DET **1** You use **a few** to indicate that you are talking about a small number of people or things. You can also say **a very few**. ❑ *I gave a dinner party for a few close friends.* ❑ *Here are a few more ideas to consider.* **2** You use **few** to indicate that you are talking about a small number of people or things. You can use 'so', 'too', and 'very' in front of **few**. ❑ *She had few friends, and was generally not functioning up to her potential.* ❑ *Few members planned to vote for him.*
PRON **1** **A few** means a small number of people or things. ❑ *Doctors work an average of 90 hours a week, while a few are on call for up to 120 hours.* **2** **Few** means a small number of people or things. ❑ *Few can survive more than a week without water.*
QUANT **1** [few 'of' DEF-PL-N] **A few of** something means a small number of them. ❑ *There are many ways eggs can be prepared; here are a few of them.* **2** [few 'of' DEF-PL-N] **Few of** something means a small number of them. ❑ *Few of the beach houses still had lights on.*
ADJ (**fewer, fewest**) **1** **Few** is used to refer to a small number of people or things. ❑ *spending her few waking hours in front of the TV* **2** [ADJ/DET + few + N] You use **few** after adjectives and determiners to indicate that you are talking about a small number of things or people. ❑ *The past few weeks of her life had been the most pleasant she could remember.* ❑ *in the last few chapters*
PHRASES **as few as** (emphasis) You use **as few as** before a number to suggest that it is surprisingly small. ❑ *One study showed that even as few as ten cigarettes a day can damage fertility.*
few and far between (emphasis) Things that are **few and far between** are very rare or do not happen very often. = rare, uncommon ❑ *Successful women politicians are few and far between.*
no fewer than (emphasis) You use **no fewer than** to emphasize that a number is surprisingly large. ❑ *No fewer than thirteen foreign ministers attended the session.*
NOUN [SING] **The few** means a small set of people considered as separate from the majority, especially because they share a particular opportunity or quality that

the others do not have. ❑ *This should not be an experience for the few.*

WHICH WORD?
few or a few?
Few and **a few** are both used in front of nouns, but they do not have the same meaning. **A few** means 'some' or 'several'. When you use **few** without 'a', you are emphasizing that there are not many people or things of a particular kind. ❑ *A few people left the meeting early.* ❑ *Few people realize how much work is involved in this type of project.*

fi·as·co /fiˈæskəʊ/ NOUN [C] (**fiascos**) (emphasis) If you describe an event or attempt to do something as a **fiasco**, you are emphasizing that it fails completely. = debacle ❑ *The blame for the Charleston fiasco did not lie with him.*

✪**fi·bre** /ˈfaɪbə/ (BrE; in AmE, use **fiber**) NOUN [C, U] (**fibres**) **1** [C] A **fibre** is a thin thread of a natural or artificial substance, especially one that is used to make cloth or rope. ❑ *If you look at the paper under a microscope you will see the fibres.* **2** [C] A **fibre** is a thin piece of flesh like a thread which connects nerve cells in your body or which muscles are made of. ❑ *the nerve fibres* **3** [C, U] A particular **fibre** is a type of cloth or other material that is made from or consists of threads. ❑ *The ball is made of rattan – a natural fibre.* **4** [U] **Fibre** consists of the parts of plants or seeds that your body cannot digest. Fibre is useful because it makes food pass quickly through your body. ❑ *Most vegetables contain fibre.*

fick·le /ˈfɪkəl/ ADJ **1** (disapproval) If you describe someone as **fickle**, you disapprove of them because they keep changing their mind about what they like or want. ❑ *The group has been notoriously fickle in the past.* **2** If you say that something is **fickle**, you mean that it often changes and is unreliable. ❑ *New England's weather can be fickle.*

✪**fic·tion** /ˈfɪkʃən/ NOUN [U, C] (**fictions**) **1** [U] **Fiction** refers to books and stories about imaginary people and events, rather than books about real people or events. = novels, literature; ≠ non-fiction ❑ *Immigrant tales have always been popular themes in fiction.* ❑ *Diana is a writer of historical fiction.* **2** [U] A statement or account that is **fiction** is not true. ❑ *The truth or fiction of this story has never been truly determined.* **3** [C] If something is a **fiction**, it is not true, although people sometimes pretend that it is true. ❑ *Total recycling is a fiction.*

fic·tion·al /ˈfɪkʃənəl/ ADJ **Fictional** characters or events occur only in stories, plays, or films and never actually existed or happened. = fictitious, imaginary ❑ *It is drama featuring fictional characters.*

fic·ti·tious /fɪkˈtɪʃəs/ ADJ **1** **Fictitious** is used to describe something that is false or does not exist, although some people claim that it is true or exists. ❑ *We're interested in the source of these fictitious rumours.* **2** A **fictitious** character, thing, or event occurs in a story, play, or film but never really existed or happened. = fictional, imaginary ❑ *The persons and events portrayed in this production are fictitious.*

fid·dle /ˈfɪdəl/ VERB, NOUN
VERB [I] (**fiddles, fiddling, fiddled**) **1** If you **fiddle with** an object, you keep moving or touching it with your fingers. ❑ *Harriet fiddled with a pen on the desk.* **2** If you **fiddle with** something, you change it in minor ways. ❑ *She told Whistler that his portrait of her was finished and to stop fiddling with it.* **3** If you **fiddle with** a machine, you adjust it. ❑ *He turned on the radio and fiddled with the knob until he got a chat show.*
NOUN [C, U] (**fiddles**) Some people call violins **fiddles**, especially when they are used to play folk music. = violin ❑ *Hardy played the fiddle at local dances.*

✪**field** ♦♦◇ /fiːld/ NOUN, ADJ, VERB
NOUN [C] (**fields**) **1** A **field** is an area of grass, for example, in a park or on a farm. A **field** is also an area of land on which a crop is grown. ❑ *a field of wheat* **2** A sports **field** is an area of grass where sports are played. ❑ *a football field* ❑ *He was the fastest thing I ever saw on a baseball field.* **3** A **field** is an area of land or sea bed under which large

F

amounts of a particular mineral have been found. ❑ *an extensive natural gas field in Alaska* **4** A magnetic, gravitational, or electric **field** is an area in which that particular force is strong enough to have an effect. ❑ *Some people are worried that electromagnetic fields from electric power lines could increase the risk of cancer.* **5** A particular **field** is a particular subject of study or type of activity. = subject, area ❑ *Each of the authors of the tapes is an expert in his field.* ❑ *Exciting artistic breakthroughs have recently occurred in the fields of painting, sculpture and architecture.* **6** (computing) A **field** is an area of a computer's memory or a program where data can be entered, edited, or stored. ❑ *Go to a site like Yahoo! Finance and enter 'AOL' in the Get Quotes field.* **7** Your **field** of vision or your visual **field** is the area that you can see without turning your head. ❑ *Our field of vision is surprisingly wide.* **8** **The field** is a way of referring to all the competitors taking part in a particular race or sports contest. ❑ *Going into the fourth lap, the two most broadly experienced riders led the field.* ▪ PHRASE **in the field** Work or study that is done **in the field** is done in a real, natural environment rather than in a theoretical way or in controlled conditions. ❑ *The zoo is doing major conservation work, both in captivity and in the field.* ❑ *passing on the skills they had learned in the field* ❑ *mutations when studied in the laboratory or in the field* ▪ ADJ [field + N] You use **field** to describe work or study that is done in a real, natural environment rather than in a theoretical way or in controlled conditions. ❑ *I also conducted a field study among the boys about their attitude to relationships.*

▪ VERB [I, T] (**fields, fielding, fielded**) **1** [I] [usu CONT] In a game of baseball or cricket, the team that **is fielding** is trying to catch the ball, while the other team is trying to hit it. ❑ *When we are fielding, the umpires keep looking at the ball.* **2** [T] (journalism) If you say that someone **fields** a question, you mean that they answer it or deal with it, usually successfully. ❑ *He was later shown on television, fielding questions.* **3** [T] If a sports team **fields** a particular number or type of players, the players are chosen to play for the team on a particular occasion. ❑ *We're going to field an exciting and younger team.* **4** [T] (journalism) If a candidate in an election is representing a political party, you can say that the party **is fielding** that candidate. = put up ❑ *There are signs that the new party aims to field candidates in elections scheduled for February next year.* → See also **minefield**

○**field·work** /ˈfiːldwɜːk/ also **field work** NOUN [U] **Fieldwork** is the gathering of information about something in a real, natural environment, rather than in a place of study such as a laboratory or classroom. ❑ *anthropological fieldwork* ❑ *fieldwork conducted among surviving hunting and gathering groups* ❑ *This project, subject to funding, will include extensive fieldwork in both Pakistan and India.*

fierce ♦◇◇ /fɪəs/ ADJ (**fiercer, fiercest**) **1** A **fierce** animal or person is very aggressive or angry. ❑ *They look like the teeth of some fierce animal.* **2** **Fierce** feelings or actions are very intense or enthusiastic, or involve great activity. ❑ *Consumers have a wide array of choices and price competition is fierce.* ❑ *The town was captured after a fierce battle with rebels.* ▪ **fierce·ly** /ˈfɪəsli/ ADV **1** *'I don't know,' she said fiercely.* **2** *He has always been ambitious and fiercely competitive.*

fif·teen ♦♦◇ /fɪfˈtiːn/ NUM (**fifteens**) **Fifteen** is the number 15. ❑ *In India, there are fifteen official languages.*

fif·teenth ♦♦◇ /fɪfˈtiːnθ/ ADJ The **fifteenth** item in a series is the one that you count as number fifteen. ❑ *the invention of the printing press in the fifteenth century*

fifth ♦♦◇ /fɪfθ/ ADJ, NOUN ▪ ADJ The **fifth** item in a series is the one that you count as number five. ❑ *Joe has recently returned from his fifth trip to Australia.* ▪ NOUN [C] (**fifths**) A **fifth** is one of five equal parts of something. ❑ *India spends over a fifth of its budget on defence.*

fif·ti·eth ♦♦◇ /ˈfɪftiəθ/ ADJ The **fiftieth** item in a series is the one that you count as number fifty. ❑ *He retired in 1970, on his fiftieth birthday.*

fif·ty ♦♦♦ /ˈfɪfti/ NUM, NOUN ▪ NUM **Fifty** is the number 50. ▪ NOUN [PL] (**fifties**) **1** When you talk about the **fifties**, you are referring to numbers between 50 and 59. For example, if you are **in** your **fifties**, you are aged between 50 and 59. If the temperature is **in the fifties**, the temperature is between 50 and 59 degrees. ❑ *I probably look as if I'm in my fifties rather than my seventies.* **2** **The fifties** is the decade between 1950 and 1959. ❑ *He began performing in the early fifties, singing and playing guitar.*

fight ♦♦♦ /faɪt/ VERB, NOUN ▪ VERB [RECIP, I, T] (**fights, fighting, fought**) **1** [RECIP, I, T] If you **fight** something unpleasant, you try in a determined way to prevent it or stop it from happening. ❑ *More units to fight forest fires are planned.* ❑ *I've spent a lifetime fighting against racism and prejudice.* **2** [I] If you **fight** for something, you try in a determined way to get it or achieve it. ❑ *Lee had to fight hard for his place on the expedition.* ❑ *I told him how we had fought to hold on to the company.* **3** [I, T] If a person or army **fights** in a battle or a war, they take part in it. ❑ *He fought in the war and was taken prisoner by the Americans.* ❑ *If I were a young man I would sooner go to prison than fight for this country.* **4** [T] If you **fight** your way to a place, you move towards it with great difficulty, for example, because there are a lot of people or obstacles in your way. = battle ❑ *I fought my way into a carriage just before the doors closed.* **5** [I, T] To **fight** means to take part in a boxing match. ❑ *In a few hours' time one of the world's most famous boxers will be fighting here for the first time.* ❑ *I'd like to fight him because he's undefeated and I want to be the first man to beat him.* **6** [T] If you **fight** an election, you are a candidate in the election and try to win it. ❑ *He helped raise almost $40 million to fight the election campaign.* **7** [T] If you **fight** a case or a court action, you make a legal case against someone in a very determined way, or you put forward a defence when a legal case is made against you. ❑ *Watkins sued the Army and fought his case in various courts for 10 years.* **8** [I, T] If you **fight** an emotion or desire, you try very hard not to feel it, show it, or act on it, but do not always succeed. ❑ *I desperately fought the urge to giggle.* ❑ *He fought with the urge to smoke one of the cigars he'd given up a while ago.* **9** [RECIP] If an army or group **fights** a battle with another army or group, they oppose each other with weapons. You can also say that two armies or groups **fight** a battle. ❑ *Police fought a gun battle with a gang which used hand grenades against them.* **10** [RECIP] If one person **fights** with another, or **fights** them, the two people hit or kick each other because they want to hurt each other. You can also say that two people **fight**. ❑ *As a child she fought with her younger sister.* ❑ *I did fight him, I punched him but it was like hitting a wall.* **11** [RECIP] (informal) If one person **fights** with another, or **fights** them, they have an angry disagreement or quarrel. You can also say that two people **fight**. = quarrel, argue ❑ *She was always arguing with him and fighting with him.* ❑ *Gwendolen started fighting her teachers.* ▪ PHRASE **fight for one's life** Someone who **is fighting for** their **life** is making a great effort to stay alive, either when they are being physically attacked or when they are very ill. ❑ *He is still fighting for his life in the hospital.* ▪ PHRASAL VERBS **fight back** **1** If you **fight back** against someone or something that is attacking or harming you, you resist them actively or attack them. ❑ *We should take some comfort from the ability of the judicial system to fight back against corruption.* **2** If you **fight back** an emotion or a desire, you try very hard not to feel it, show it, or act on it. ❑ *She fought back the tears.* ▪ **fight off** **1** If you **fight off** something, for example, an illness or an unpleasant feeling, you succeed in getting rid of it and in not letting it overcome you. = resist ❑ *Unfortunately these drugs are quite toxic and hinder the body's ability to fight off infection.* **2** If you **fight off** someone who has attacked you, you fight with them, and succeed in making them go away or stop attacking you. ❑ *She fought off three armed robbers.* ▪ NOUN [U, C] (**fights**) **1** [U, C] A **fight** is a determined effort to prevent something unpleasant or to stop it from happening. ❑ *the fight against drug addiction* **2** [C] A **fight**

is a determined effort to achieve something. = **battle**
❏ *I too am committing myself to continue the fight for justice.*
3 [c] [oft fight 'with' N] A **fight** is when two people hit or
kick each other because they want to hurt each other.
❏ *He had a fight with Smith and bloodied his nose.* **4** [c] A
fight is an angry disagreement or quarrel. ❏ *We think*
maybe he took off because he had a big fight with his dad the
night before. **5** [c] A **fight** is a boxing match. = **bout**
❏ *The referee stopped the fight.* **6** [c] (*journalism*) You can
use **fight** to refer to a contest such as an election or a
sports competition. = **contest** ❏ *the fight for power*
between the two parties **7** [u] **Fight** is the desire or ability to
keep fighting. ❏ *I thought that we had a lot of fight in us.*
fight·ing /ˈfaɪtɪŋ/ NOUN [u] ❏ *More than nine hundred people*
have died in the fighting.

fight·er ◆◇◇ /ˈfaɪtə/ NOUN [c] (**fighters**) **1** A **fighter** or a
fighter plane is a fast military aircraft that is used for
destroying other aircraft. ❏ *a fighter pilot* **2** If you describe
someone as a **fighter**, you approve of them because they
continue trying to achieve things in spite of great
difficulties or opposition. ❏ *From the start it was clear this*
tiny girl was a real fighter. **3** A **fighter** is a person who
physically fights another person, especially a professional
boxer. ❏ *He was a real street fighter who'd do anything to win.*
→ See also **firefighter**

○**fig·ura·tive** /ˈfɪɡərətɪv, *AmE* -ɡjər-/ ADJ **1** If you use a
word or expression in a **figurative** sense, you use it with a
more abstract or imaginative meaning than its ordinary
literal one. ❏ *an event that will change your route – in both*
the literal and figurative sense ❏ *Most poems are written in*
figurative language. **2** **Figurative** art is a style of art in
which people and things are shown in a realistic way.
❏ *His career spanned some 50 years and encompassed both*
abstract and figurative painting.
○**fig·ura·tive·ly** /ˈfɪɡərətɪvli, *AmE* -ɡjər-/ ADV ❏ *I saw that*
she was, both literally and figuratively, up against a wall.
❏ *Europe, with Germany literally and figuratively at its centre, is*
still at the start of a remarkable transformation. ❏ *This is not an*
artist who, figuratively speaking, climbs into the picture.

○**fig·ure** ◆◆◆ /ˈfɪɡə, *AmE* -ɡjər/ NOUN, VERB
⬛ NOUN [c, PL] (**figures**) **1** [c] A **figure** is a particular amount
expressed as a number, especially a statistic. = **statistic**
❏ *It would be very nice if we had a true figure of how many*
people in this country haven't got a job. ❏ *It will not be long*
before the inflation figure starts to fall. ❏ *Norway is a peaceful*
place with low crime figures. ❏ *Government figures show that*
one in three marriages end in divorce. **2** [c] A **figure** is any of
the ten written symbols from 0 to 9 that are used to
represent a number. = **digit, number** ❏ *the glowing red*
figures on the radio alarm clock which read 4.22 a.m. ❏ *In*
business writing, all numbers over ten are usually written as
figures. **3** [c] You refer to someone that you can see as a
figure when you cannot see them clearly or when you are
describing them. ❏ *Ernie saw the dim figure of Rose in the*
chair. **4** [c] In art, a **figure** is a person in a drawing or a
painting, or a statue of a person. ❏ *a life-size bronze figure of*
a brooding, hooded woman **5** [c] Your **figure** is the shape of
your body. ❏ *Take pride in your health and your figure.* **6** [c]
Someone who is referred to as a **figure** of a particular kind
is a person who is well-known and important in some
way. ❏ *The movement is supported by key figures in the three*
main political parties. **7** [c] If you say that someone is, for
example, a mother **figure** or a hero **figure**, you mean that
other people regard them as the type of person stated or
suggested. ❏ *Daniel Boone, the great hero figure of the frontier*
8 [c] [also figure + NUM] In books and magazines, the
diagrams which help to show or explain information are
referred to as **figures**. ❏ *If you look at a world map (see Figure*
1) you can identify the major wine-producing regions. ❏ *Figure*
1.15 shows which provinces lost populations between 1910 and
1920. **9** [c] (*technical*) In geometry, a **figure** is a shape,
especially a regular shape. ❏ *Draw a pentagon, a regular*
five-sided figure. **10** [PL] An amount or number that is in
single **figures** is between zero and nine. An amount or
number that is in double **figures** is between ten and
ninety-nine. You can also say, for example, that an
amount or number is in three **figures** when it is between

one hundred and nine hundred and ninety-nine.
❏ *Inflation, which has usually been in single figures, is running at*
more than 12%.
⬛ VERB [T, I] (**figures, figuring, figured**) **1** [T] (*informal*) If you
figure that something is the case, you think or guess that
it is the case. ❏ *She figured that both she and Ned had learned*
a lot from the experience. **2** [I] (*informal*) If you say 'That
figures' or 'It figures', you mean that the fact referred to is
not surprising. ❏ *When I finished, he said, 'Yeah. That figures.'*
3 [I] If a person or thing **figures** in something, they appear
in or are included in it. ❏ *Human rights violations figured*
prominently in the report.
⬛ PHRASAL VERB **figure out** (*informal*) If you **figure out** a
solution to a problem or the reason for something, you
succeed in solving it or understanding it. = **work out**
❏ *It took them about one month to figure out how to start the*
equipment. ❏ *They're trying to figure out the politics of this*
whole situation.

WORD CONNECTIONS

VERB + **figure**
publish figures
release figures
❏ *The government has released figures indicating that the*
number of asylum applications has fallen.

ADJ + **figure**
official figures
the **latest** figures
❏ *The latest figures show average spending on food is now*
around 15% of income.

single figures
double figures
❏ *Membership of the group barely reached double figures.*

NOUN + **figure**
government figures
crime figures
unemployment figures
❏ *Unemployment figures have fallen for the third month*
running.

trade figures
profit figures
inflation figures
❏ *The trade figures show that exports of medicines increased.*

figure·head /ˈfɪɡəhed, *AmE* ˈfɪɡjər-/ NOUN [c]
(**figureheads**) **1** If someone is the **figurehead** of an
organization or movement, they are recognized as being
its leader, although they have little real power. ❏ *The*
president will be little more than a figurehead. **2** A **figurehead**
is a large wooden model of a person that was put just
under the pointed front of a sailing ship in former times.

○**file** ◆◆◇ /faɪl/ NOUN, VERB (*academic word*)
⬛ NOUN [c] (**files**) **1** A **file** is a box or a folded piece of heavy
paper or plastic in which letters or documents are kept.
❏ *a file of insurance papers* **2** A **file** is a collection of
information about a particular person or thing. ❏ *We*
already have files on people's tax details. **3** In computing, a
file is a set of related data that has its own name. ❏ *Be sure*
to save the revised version of the file under a new filename.
❏ *Now that you have loaded WordPerfect, it's easy to create a*
file. **4** A **file** is a hand tool which is used for rubbing hard
objects to make them smooth, shape them, or cut through
them.
⬛ PHRASE **in single file** or **single file** A group of people who
are walking or standing **in single file** or **single file** are in a
line, one behind the other. ❏ *We were walking in single file*
to the lake.
⬛ VERB [T, I] (**files, filing, filed**) **1** [T] If you **file** a document,
you put it in the correct file. ❏ *They are all filed*
alphabetically under author. **2** [I, T] If you **file** a formal or
legal accusation, complaint, or request, you make it
officially. ❏ *I filed for divorce on the grounds of adultery a few*
months later. **3** [T] When someone **files** a report or a news
story, they send or give it to their employer. ❏ *He had to*

f

F

rush back to the office and file a housing story before the secretaries went home. **4** [T] If you **file** an object, you smooth it, shape it, or cut it with a file. ❏ *Manicurists are skilled at shaping and filing nails.*

WORD CONNECTIONS
VERB + **file**
create a file
open a file
delete a file
❏ *How can I delete files I no longer need from the web server?*
send a file
share a file
store a file
retrieve a file
❏ *You can send the file as an email attachment.*

fill ◆◆◇ /fɪl/ VERB

VERB [I, T] (**fills, filling, filled**) **1** [I, T] If you **fill** a container or area, or if it **fills**, an amount of something enters it that is enough to make it full. ❏ *She went to the bathroom, filled a glass with water, returned to the bed.* ❏ *The boy's eyes filled with tears.* **2** [T] If something **fills** a space, it is so big, or there are such large quantities of it, that there is very little room left. ❏ *He cast his eyes at the rows of cabinets that filled the enormous work area.* **3** [T] If you **fill** a crack or hole, you put a substance into it in order to make the surface smooth again. ❏ *Fill small holes with wood filler in a matching colour.* **4** [T] If a sound, smell, or light **fills** a space, or the air, it is very strong or noticeable. ❏ *In the school car park, the siren filled the air.* **5** [T] If something **fills** you **with** an emotion, or if an emotion **fills** you, you experience this emotion strongly. ❏ *I admired my father, and his work filled me with awe and curiosity.* **6** [T] If you **fill** a period of time with a particular activity, you spend the time in this way. ❏ *If she wants a routine to fill her day, let her do community work.* **7** [T] If something **fills** a need or a gap, it puts an end to this need or gap by existing or being active. ❏ *She brought him a sense of fun, of gaiety that filled a gap in his life.* **8** [T] If something **fills** a role, position, or function, they have that role or position, or perform that function, often successfully. = perform ❏ *Dena was filling the role of diplomat's wife with the skill she had learned over the years.* **9** [T] If a company or organization **fills** a job vacancy, they choose someone to do the job. If someone **fills** a job vacancy, they accept a job that they have been offered. ❏ *A vacancy has arisen which I intend to fill.* **10** [T] When a dentist **fills** someone's tooth, he or she puts a filling in it. ❏ *Dentists fill teeth and repair broken ones.*

PHRASAL VERBS **fill in** **1** Fill in means the same as fill VERB 3. ❏ *Start by filling in any cracks and gaps between window and door frames and the wall.* **2** If you **fill in** a form or other document requesting information, you write information in the spaces on it. = fill out ❏ *Fill in the coupon and send it first class to the address shown.* **3** If you **fill in** a shape, you cover the area inside the lines with colour or shapes so that none of the background is showing. ❏ *With a lip pencil, outline lips and fill them in.* **4** (*informal*) If you **fill** someone **in**, you give them more details about something that you know about. ❏ *He filled me in on Wilbur Kantor's visit.* **5** If you **fill in** for someone, you do the work or task that they normally do because they are unable to do it. = stand in ❏ *Vice-presidents' wives would fill in for first ladies.* **fill out** **1** (*mainly AmE*) If you **fill out** a form or other document requesting information, you write information in the spaces on it. = fill in ❏ *Fill out the application carefully, and keep copies of it.* **2** If someone or something **fills out**, they become fuller, thicker, or rounder. ❏ *A girl may fill out before she reaches her full height.* **fill up** **1** Fill up means the same as fill VERB 1. ❏ *Warehouses at the frontier between the two countries fill up with sacks of rice and flour.* **2** Fill up means the same as fill VERB 2. ❏ *the complicated machines that fill up today's laboratories* **3** Fill up means the same as fill VERB 6. ❏ *On Thursday night she went to her yoga class, glad to have something to fill up the evening.* **4** If you **fill up** or **fill** yourself **up** with food, you eat so much that you do not feel hungry. ❏ *Fill up on potatoes,*

bread and pasta, which are high in carbohydrate and low in fat. **5** A type of food that **fills** you **up** makes you feel that you have eaten a lot, even though you have only eaten a small amount. ❏ *Potatoes fill us up without overloading us with calories.* **filled** /fɪld/ ADJ ❏ *four museum buildings filled with historical objects*
✦ fill the bill → see bill

fill·ing /'fɪlɪŋ/ NOUN, ADJ

NOUN [C, U] (**fillings**) **1** [C] A **filling** is a small amount of metal or plastic that a dentist puts in a hole in a tooth to prevent further decay. ❏ *The longer your child can go without needing a filling, the better.* **2** [C, U] The **filling** in something such as a cake, pie, or sandwich is a substance or mixture that is put inside it. ❏ *Spread some of the filling over each cold pancake and then either roll or fold.* **3** [C, U] The **filling** in a piece of soft furniture or in a cushion is the soft substance inside it. ❏ *second-hand sofas with old-style foam fillings* **ADJ** Food that is **filling** makes you feel full when you have eaten it. ❏ *Although it is tasty, crab is very filling.*

film ◆◆◆ /fɪlm/ NOUN, VERB

NOUN [C, U] (**films**) **1** [C] A **film** consists of moving pictures that have been recorded so that they can be shown in a cinema or on television. A film tells a story, or shows a real situation. = movie ❏ *Everything about the film was good. Good acting, good story, good fun.* **2** [C] A **film of** powder, liquid, or oil is a very thin layer of it. ❏ *The sea is coated with a film of raw sewage.* **3** [U] **Film** of something is moving pictures of a real event that are shown on television or on a screen. = footage ❏ *He likes to look at film of old-time players.* **4** [U] [also films] The making of films, considered as a form of art or a business, can be referred to as **film** or **films**. ❏ *Film is a business with limited opportunities for actresses.* **5** [U] (*BrE*; in *AmE*, use **plastic wrap**) Plastic **film** is a very thin sheet of plastic used to wrap and cover things. **6** [C, U] A **film** is the narrow roll of plastic that is used in a camera to take photographs. ❏ *The photographers had already shot a dozen rolls of film.* **VERB** [T] (**films, filming, filmed**) If you **film** something, you use a camera to take moving pictures which can be shown on a screen or on television. ❏ *He had filmed her life story.*

film star NOUN [C] (**film stars**) A **film star** is a famous actor who appears in films. = movie star

❍ **fil·ter** /'fɪltə/ VERB, NOUN

VERB [T, I] (**filters, filtering, filtered**) **1** [T] To **filter** a substance means to pass it through a device which is designed to remove certain particles contained in it. ❏ *The best prevention for cholera is to boil or filter water, and eat only well-cooked food.* ❏ *The liver filters toxins from the body.* **2** [I] If light or sound **filters into** a place, it comes in weakly or slowly, either through a partly covered opening, or from a long distance away. ❏ *Light filtered into my kitchen through the soft, green shade of the honey locust tree.* **3** [I] When news or information **filters** through to people, it gradually reaches them. ❏ *It took months before the findings began to filter through to the politicians.* ❏ *News of the attack quickly filtered through the college.*

PHRASAL VERB **filter out** To **filter out** something from a substance or from light means to remove it by passing the substance or light through something acting as a filter. ❏ *Children should have glasses which filter out UV rays.* ❏ *Plants and trees filter carbon dioxide out of the air and produce oxygen.*

NOUN [C] (**filters**) **1** A **filter** is a device through which a substance is passed when it is being filtered. ❏ *a paper coffee filter* ❏ *Sediment from the fuel filters had been stirred up.* **2** A **filter** is a device through which sound or light is passed and which blocks or reduces particular sound or light frequencies. ❏ *You might use a yellow filter to improve the clarity of a hazy horizon.* ❏ *Most filters used in air-conditioning systems are inefficient at removing many of these particles.*

filth /fɪlθ/ NOUN [U] **1** Filth is a disgusting amount of dirt. = muck ❏ *Thousands of tons of filth and sewage pour into the Ganges every day.* **2** People refer to words or pictures, usually ones relating to sex, as **filth** when they think they are very disgusting and rude. ❏ *The dialogue was all filth and innuendo.*

filthy /ˈfɪlθi/ ADJ (**filthier, filthiest**) **1** Something that is filthy is very dirty. = grimy ❑ *He never washed, and always wore a filthy old jacket.* **2** If you describe something as **filthy**, you mean that you think it is morally very unpleasant and disgusting, sometimes in a sexual way. ❑ *Apparently, well known actors were at these filthy parties.*

fin /fɪn/ NOUN [c] (**fins**) **1** A fish's **fins** are the flat parts which stick out of its body and help it to swim and keep its balance. **2** A **fin** on something such as an aeroplane, rocket, or bomb is a flat part which sticks out and which is intended to help control its movement.

❖**fi·nal** ◆◆◆ /ˈfaɪnəl/ ADJ, NOUN (*academic word*)

ADJ **1** [DET + final] In a series of events, things, or people, the **final** one is the last one. = last; ≠ first ❑ *Astronauts will make a final attempt today to rescue a communications satellite from its useless orbit.* ❑ *This is the fifth and probably final day of testimony before the Senate Judiciary Committee.* ❑ *This was the final stage in the process.* **2** [final + N] **Final** means happening at the end of an event or series of events. ❑ *You must have been on stage until the final curtain.* **3** If a decision or someone's authority is **final**, it cannot be changed or questioned. ❑ *The judges' decision is final.*

NOUN [c, PL] (**finals**) **1** [c] The **final** is the last game or contest in a series and decides who is the winner. ❑ *the Gold Cup final* **2** [PL] The **finals** of a sports tournament consist of a smaller tournament that includes only players or teams that have won earlier games. The finals decide the winner of the whole tournament. ❑ *Poland knows it has a chance of qualifying for the World Cup Finals.*
→ See also **quarter-final, semi-final**

fi·nal·ize /ˈfaɪnəlaɪz/ also **finalise** VERB [T] (**finalizes, finalizing, finalized**) If you **finalize** something such as a plan or an agreement, you complete the arrangements for it, especially by discussing it with other people. ❑ *Negotiators from the three countries finalized the agreement in August.* ❑ *We are saying nothing until all the details have been finalized.*

❖**fi·nal·ly** ◆◆◇ /ˈfaɪnəli/ ADV **1** You use **finally** to suggest that something happens after a long period of time, usually later than you wanted or expected it to happen. ❑ *The food finally arrived at the end of last week and distribution began.* **2** [finally with CL/GROUP] You use **finally** to indicate that something is last in a series of actions or events. = lastly; ≠ firstly ❑ *The action slips from comedy to melodrama and finally to tragedy.* **3** You use **finally** in speech or writing to introduce a final point, question, or topic. ❑ *Finally, and perhaps most importantly, Project Challenge has raised awareness of the issue.*

❖**fi·nance** ◆◆◇ /ˈfaɪnæns, fɪˈnæns/ VERB, NOUN (*academic word*)

VERB [T] (**finances, financing, financed**) When someone **finances** something such as a project or a purchase, they provide the money that is needed to pay for them. ❑ *The fund has been used largely to finance the construction of federal prisons.*

NOUN [u] (**finances**) **1** **Finance** is the money provided to pay for something such as a product or purchase. ❑ *A United States delegation is in Japan seeking finance for a major scientific project.* **2** [also finances] **Finance** is the commercial or government activity of managing money, debt, credit, and investment. ❑ *a major player in the world of high finance* ❑ *The report recommends an overhaul of public finances.* ❑ *the principles of corporate finance* ❑ *We looked at three common problems in international finance.* ❑ *A former Finance Minister and five senior civil servants are accused of fraud.* **3** [also finances] You can refer to the amount of money that you have and how well it is organized as your **finances**. ❑ *Be prepared for unexpected news concerning your finances.*

❖**fi·nan·cial** ◆◆◆ /faɪˈnænʃəl, fɪ-/ ADJ **Financial** means relating to or involving money. = monetary, economic ❑ *The company is in financial difficulties.* ❑ *There has been an improvement in the company's financial position.* ❑ *the government's financial advisers*
fi·nan·cial·ly /faɪˈnænʃəli, fɪ-/ ADV ❑ *She would like to be more financially independent.*

❖**find** ◆◆◆ /faɪnd/ VERB, NOUN

VERB [T, PASSIVE] (**finds, finding, found**) **1** [T] If you **find** someone or something, you see them or learn where they are. ❑ *The police also found a pistol.* ❑ *They have spent ages looking at the map and can't find a trace of anywhere called Darrowby.* **2** [T] If you **find** something that you need or want, you succeed in achieving or obtaining it. = get ❑ *Many people here cannot find work.* ❑ *He has to apply for a permit and we have to find him a job.* **3** [T] If you **find** someone or something in a particular situation, they are in that situation when you see them or come into contact with them. ❑ *They found her walking alone and depressed on the beach.* ❑ *She returned to her home to find her back door forced open.* **4** [T] If you **find yourself** doing something, you are doing it without deciding or intending to do it. ❑ *It's not the first time that you've found yourself in this situation.* ❑ *I found myself having more fun than I had had in years.* **5** [T] If you **find** that something is the case, you become aware of it or realize that it is the case. = discover ❑ *The two biologists found, to their surprise, that both groups of birds survived equally well.* ❑ *The study found no link between the age of a mother and the risks of cancer in her children.* ❑ *At my age I would find it hard to get another job.* **6** [T] When a court or jury decides that a person on trial is guilty or innocent, you say that the person **has been found** guilty or not guilty. ❑ *She was found guilty of manslaughter and put on probation for two years.* **7** [T] You can use **find** to express your reaction to someone or something. ❑ *I find most of the young men of my own age so boring.* ❑ *I find it ludicrous that nothing has been done to protect passengers from fire.* **8** [T] If you **find** a feeling such as pleasure or comfort **in** a particular thing or activity, you experience the feeling mentioned as a result of this thing or activity. ❑ *How could anyone find pleasure in hunting and killing this beautiful creature?* **9** [T] If you **find** the time or money **to** do something, you succeed in making or obtaining enough time or money to do it. ❑ *I was just finding more time to write music.* **10** [PASSIVE] If something **is found** in a particular place or thing, it exists in that place. ❑ *Two thousand of France's 4,200 species of flowering plants are found in the park.*

PHRASES **find one's way** If you **find** your **way** somewhere, you successfully get there by choosing the right way to go. ❑ *He was an expert at finding his way, even in strange surroundings.*

finds its way or **finds their way** If something **finds** its **way** somewhere, it comes to that place, especially by chance. ❑ *It is one of the very few Michelangelos that have found their way out of Italy.*

PHRASAL VERB **find out** **1** If you **find** something **out**, you learn something that you did not already know, especially by making a deliberate effort to do so. = discover ❑ *It makes you want to watch the next episode to find out what's going to happen.* ❑ *I was relieved to find out that my problems were due to a genuine disorder.* **2** If you **find** someone **out**, you discover that they have been doing something dishonest. ❑ *Her face was so grave, I wondered for a moment if she'd found me out.*

NOUN [c] (**finds**) If you describe someone or something that has been discovered as a **find**, you mean that they are valuable, interesting, good, or useful. ❑ *Another of his lucky finds was a pair of candleholders.*
→ See also **finding, found**
✦ **find fault with** → see **fault; find one's feet** → see **foot**

❖**find·ing** /ˈfaɪndɪŋ/ NOUN [c] (**findings**) **1** Someone's **findings** are the information they get or the conclusions they come to as the result of an investigation or some research. = results ❑ *One of the main findings of the survey was the confusion about the facilities already in place.* ❑ *These findings suggest that as children grow older, socio-cultural factors become more significant.* ❑ *We hope that manufacturers will take note of the findings and improve their products accordingly.* **2** The **findings** of a court are the decisions that it reaches after a trial or an investigation. ❑ *The government hopes the court will announce its findings before the end of the month.*

❖**fine** ◆◆◇ /faɪn/ ADJ, ADV, CONVENTION, NOUN, VERB
ADJ (**finer, finest**) **1** You use **fine** to describe something

f

F

that you admire and think is very good. ❑ *There is a fine view of the countryside.* ❑ *This is a fine book.* **2** [V-LINK + fine] If you say that you are **fine**, you mean that you are in good health or reasonably happy. ❑ *Lina is fine and sends you her love and best wishes.* **3** If you say that something is **fine**, you mean that it is satisfactory or acceptable. ❑ *The skiing is fine.* ❑ *Everything was going to be just fine.* **4** Something that is **fine** is very delicate, narrow, or small. ❑ *The heat scorched the fine hairs on her arms.* **5** **Fine** objects or clothing are of good quality, delicate, and expensive. ❑ *We waited in our fine clothes.* **6** A **fine** detail or distinction is very delicate, small, or exact. ❑ *Johnson likes the broad outline but is reserving judgment on the fine detail.* **7** A **fine** person is someone you consider good, moral, and worth admiring. ❑ *He was an excellent journalist and a very fine man.* **8** When the weather is **fine**, the sun is shining and it is not raining. = fair ❑ *He might be doing some gardening if the weather is fine.* **ADV** If something is working **fine**, it is working in a satisfactory or acceptable way. ❑ *All the instruments are working fine.* **CONVENTION** (*formulae*) You say '**fine**' or '**that's fine**' to show that you do not object to an arrangement, action, or situation that has been suggested. ❑ *If competition is the best way to achieve it, then, fine.* **NOUN** [c] (**fines**) A **fine** is a punishment in which a person is ordered to pay a sum of money because they have done something illegal or broken a rule. ❑ *You can face a fine of up to £2000 for being drunk on an aircraft.* ❑ *Police can impose heavy fines or tow away vehicles parked illegally.* **VERB** [T] (**fines, fining, fined**) If someone **is fined**, they are punished by being ordered to pay a sum of money because they have done something illegal or broken a rule. ❑ *She was fined $300 and banned from driving for one month.* ❑ *An east London school has set a precedent by fining pupils who break the rules.*

fine•ly /ˈfaɪnli/ ADV **1** [finely + -ED] ❑ *They are finely engineered boats.* **2** [finely with v] ❑ *Chop the ingredients finely and mix them together.* **3** *They had to take the finely balanced decision to let the visit proceed.*

WORD CONNECTIONS

VERB + **fine**

face a fine
pay a fine
impose a fine
❑ *People who drop litter face fines of up to £100.*

ADJ + **fine**

a hefty fine
a heavy fine
a big fine
❑ *Offenders face a hefty fine.*

the **maximum** fine
❑ *The maximum fine for the offence is £200.*

fin•ger ♦♦◇ /ˈfɪŋgə/ NOUN, VERB
NOUN [c] (**fingers**) **1** Your **fingers** are the long thin parts at the end of each hand, sometimes also including the thumb. ❑ *She suddenly held up a small, bony finger and pointed across the room.* ❑ *She ran her fingers through her hair.* **2** The **fingers** of a glove are the parts that a person's fingers fit into. ❑ *He bit the fingers of his right glove and pulled it off.* **3** A **finger** of something such as smoke or land is an amount of it that is shaped rather like a finger. = strip ❑ *a thin finger of land that separates Pakistan from the former Soviet Union* **PHRASES** **cross your fingers** or **keep your fingers crossed** If you **cross** your **fingers**, you put one finger on top of another and hope for good luck. If you say that someone **is keeping their fingers crossed**, you mean they are hoping for good luck. ❑ *He crossed his fingers, asking for luck for the first time in his life.* **lay a finger on** (*emphasis*) If you say that someone did not **lay a finger on** a particular person or thing, you are emphasizing that they did not touch or harm them at all. ❑ *I must make it clear I never laid a finger on her.*

lift a finger or **raise a finger** (*disapproval*) If you say that a person does not **lift a finger** or **raise a finger** to do something, especially to help someone, you are critical of them because they do nothing. ❑ *She never lifted a finger around the house.* **point the finger at someone** or **point an accusing finger at someone** If you **point the finger at** someone or **point an accusing finger at** someone, you blame them or accuse them of doing wrong. ❑ *He said he wasn't pointing an accusing finger at anyone in the government or the army.* **put one's finger on something** If you **put** your **finger on** something, for example, a reason or problem, you see and identify exactly what it is. ❑ *Midge couldn't quite put her finger on the reason.* **VERB** [T] (**fingers, fingering, fingered**) If you **finger** something, you touch or feel it with your fingers. ❑ *He fingered the few coins in his pocket.*

finger•print /ˈfɪŋgəprɪnt/ NOUN, VERB
NOUN [c] (**fingerprints**) **Fingerprints** are marks made by a person's fingers which show the lines on the skin. Everyone's fingerprints are different, so they can be used to identify criminals. ❑ *The detective discovered no fewer than 35 fingerprints.* ❑ *his fingerprint on the murder weapon* **PHRASE** **take someone's fingerprints** If the police **take** someone's **fingerprints**, they make that person press their fingers onto a pad covered with ink, and then onto paper, so that they know what that person's fingerprints look like. **VERB** [T] (**fingerprints, fingerprinting, fingerprinted**) If someone **is fingerprinted**, the police take their fingerprints. ❑ *He took her to jail, where she was fingerprinted and booked.*

fin•ish ♦♦◇ /ˈfɪnɪʃ/ VERB, NOUN
VERB [T, I] (**finishes, finishing, finished**) **1** [T] When you **finish** doing or dealing with something, you do or deal with the last part of it, so that there is no more for you to do or deal with. ❑ *As soon as he'd finished eating, he excused himself.* ❑ *Mr Gould was given a standing ovation and loud cheers when he finished his speech.* **2** [T] When you **finish** something that you are making or producing, you reach the end of making or producing it, so that it is complete. = complete ❑ *The consultants had been working to finish a report this week.* **3** [I, T] When something such as a course, show, or sale **finishes**, especially at a planned time, it ends. = end ❑ *The teaching day finishes at around 4 p.m.* **4** [I, T] You say that someone or something **finishes** a period of time or an event in a particular way to indicate what the final situation was like. You can also say that a period of time or an event **finishes** in a particular way. ❑ *The two of them finished by kissing each other goodbye.* ❑ *The evening finished with the welcoming of three new members.* **5** [I] If someone **finishes** second, for example, in a race or competition, they are in second place at the end of the race or competition. ❑ *He finished second in the championship four years in a row.* **6** [I] To **finish** means to reach the end of saying something. ❑ *Her eyes flashed, but he held up a hand. 'Let me finish.'* **PHRASE** **the finishing touch** If you add **the finishing touches** to something, you add or do the last things that are necessary to complete it. ❑ *Right up until the last minute, workers were still putting the finishing touches on the pavilions.* **PHRASAL VERBS** **Finish off** and **finish up** mean the same as **finish** VERB **2.** ❑ *Now she is busy finishing off a biography of Queen Caroline.* **2** If you **finish off** something that you have been eating or drinking, you eat or drink the last part of it with the result that there is none left. ❑ *Kelly finished off his coffee.* **3** If someone **finishes off** a person or thing that is already badly injured or damaged, they kill or destroy them. ❑ *They meant to finish her off, swiftly and without mercy.* **finish up** **1** (*mainly AmE*) Finish up means the same as **finish** VERB **1.** ❑ *We waited a few minutes outside his office while he finished up his meeting.* **2** If you **finish up** something that you have been eating or drinking, you eat or drink the last part of it. ❑ *Finish up your drinks now, please.* **finish with** If you **finish with** someone or something, you stop dealing with them or being involved with them. ❑ *My boyfriend was threatening to finish with me.*

f

NOUN [SING, C] (finishes) **1** [SING] ['the' finish, with POSS] The **finish** of something is the end of it or the last part of it. = end ❏ I intend to continue it and see the job through to the finish. **2** [c] The **finish** of a race is the end of it. ❏ Win a trip to see the finish of the Tour de France! **3** [c] If the surface of something that has been made has a particular kind of **finish**, it has the appearance or texture mentioned. ❏ The finish and workmanship of the woodwork were excellent.
→ See also **finished**

fin·ished /ˈfɪnɪʃt/ ADJ **1** [V-LINK + finished 'with' N] Someone who is **finished** with something is no longer doing it or dealing with it or is no longer interested in it. ❏ One suspects he will be finished with boxing. **2** [V-LINK + finished] Something that is **finished** no longer exists or is no longer happening. = over ❏ After each game is finished, a message flashes on the screen. **3** [V-LINK + finished] Someone or something that is **finished** is no longer important, powerful, or effective. ❏ Her power over me is finished.

❂ **fi·nite** /ˈfaɪnaɪt/ ADJ (academic word, formal) Something that is **finite** has a definite fixed size or extent. = limited ❏ a finite set of elements ❏ Only a finite number of situations can arise. ❏ Coal and oil are finite resources.

fire ♦♦◇ /faɪə/ NOUN, VERB
NOUN [U, C] (fires) **1** [U] **Fire** is the hot, bright flames produced by things that are burning. ❏ They saw a big flash and a huge ball of fire reaching hundreds of feet into the sky. **2** [c, U] **Fire** or a **fire** is an occurrence of uncontrolled burning which destroys buildings, forests, or other things. ❏ 87 people died in a fire at the Happy Land Social Club. ❏ A forest fire is sweeping across portions of north Maine this evening. **3** [c] A **fire** is a burning pile of wood, coal, or other fuel that you make, for example, to use for heat, light, or cooking. ❏ There was a fire in the grate. **4** [c] (BrE; in AmE, use **heater**) A **fire** is a device that uses electricity or gas to give out heat and warm a room. **5** [U] You can use **fire** to refer to the shots fired from a gun or guns. = gunfire ❏ His car was raked with fire from automatic weapons.
PHRASES **catch fire** If an object or substance **catches fire**, it starts burning. ❏ The blast caused several buildings to catch fire.
on fire If something is **on fire**, it is burning and being damaged or destroyed by an uncontrolled fire. = burning ❏ The captain radioed that the ship was on fire.
set fire to something or **set something on fire** If you **set fire to** something or if you **set** it **on fire**, you start it burning in order to damage or destroy it. ❏ They set fire to vehicles outside that building.
hold your fire If someone **holds** their **fire** or **holds fire**, they stop shooting or they wait before they start shooting. ❏ Devereux ordered his men to hold their fire until the ships got closer.
line of fire If you are in the **line of fire**, you are in a position where someone is aiming their gun at you. If you move into their **line of fire**, you move into a position between them and the thing they were aiming at. ❏ He cheerfully blows away any bad guy stupid enough to get in his line of fire.
open fire If you **open fire on** someone, you start shooting at them. ❏ Then without warning, the troops opened fire on the crowd.
return fire If you **return fire** or you **return** someone's **fire**, you shoot back at someone who has shot at you. ❏ The soldiers returned fire after being attacked.
under fire **1** If you come **under fire** or are **under fire**, someone starts shooting at you. ❏ The Belgians fell back as the infantry came under fire. **2** If you come **under fire from** someone or are **under fire**, they criticize you strongly. ❏ The president's plan first came under fire from critics who said he hadn't included enough spending cuts.
VERB [T, I] (fires, firing, fired) **1** [T] When a pot or clay object is **fired**, it is heated at a high temperature in a special oven, as part of the process of making it. ❏ After the pot is dipped in this mixture, it is fired. **2** [I] When the engine of a motor vehicle **fires**, an electrical spark is produced which causes the fuel to burn and the engine to work. ❏ The engine fired and we moved off. **3** [T] If you **fire**

someone **with** enthusiasm, you make them feel very enthusiastic. If you **fire** someone's imagination, you make them feel interested and excited. ❏ the potential to fire the imagination of an entire generation ❏ It was Allen who fired this rivalry with real passion. **4** [I, T] If someone **fires** a gun or a bullet, or if they **fire**, a bullet is sent from a gun that they are using. ❏ Seven people were wounded when soldiers fired rubber bullets to disperse crowds. **5** [T] If you **fire** an arrow, you send it from a bow. = shoot ❏ He fired an arrow into a clearing in the forest. **6** [T] If you **fire** questions at someone, you ask them a lot of questions very quickly, one after another. ❏ They were bombarded by more than 100 representatives firing questions on pollution. **7** [T] If an employer **fires** you, they dismiss you from your job. = dismiss ❏ If he hadn't been so good at the rest of his job, I probably would have fired him.
PHRASAL VERB **fire up** **1** If you **fire up** a machine, you switch it on. ❏ Fire up your engine and head out. **2** If you **fire** someone **up**, you make them feel very enthusiastic or motivated. ❏ The president knows his task is to fire up the delegates.

fir·ing /ˈfaɪərɪŋ/ NOUN [U, C] **1** [U] ❏ The firing continued even while the protestors were fleeing. **2** [c] ❏ There was yet another round of firings.

✦ **have irons in the fire** → see iron; **like a house on fire** → see house; **where there's smoke there's fire** → see smoke

fire·arm /ˈfaɪəːm/ NOUN [c] (firearms) (formal) **Firearms** are guns. ❏ He was also charged with illegal possession of firearms.

fire·fighter /ˈfaɪəfaɪtə/ NOUN [c] (firefighters) [usu pl] **Firefighters** are people whose job is to put out fires.

fire·wall /ˈfaɪəwɔːl/ NOUN [c] (firewalls) (computing) A **firewall** is a computer system or program that automatically prevents an unauthorized person from gaining access to a computer when it is connected to a network such as the Internet. ❏ New technology should provide a secure firewall against hackers.

❂ **firm** ♦♦♦ /fɜːm/ NOUN, ADJ
NOUN [c] (firms) A **firm** is an organization which sells or produces something or which provides a service which people pay for. = company ❏ The firm's employees were expecting large bonuses. ❏ a legal assistant at a Chicago law firm ❏ a firm of heating engineers
ADJ (firmer, firmest) **1** If something is **firm**, it does not change much in shape when it is pressed but is not completely hard. ❏ Fruit should be firm and in excellent condition. **2** If someone's grip is **firm** or if they perform a physical action in a **firm** way, they do it with quite a lot of force or pressure but also in a controlled way. = strong ❏ The quick handshake was firm and cool. **3** If you describe someone as **firm**, you mean they behave in a way that shows that they are not going to change their mind, or that they are the person who is in control. ❏ She had to be firm with him. 'I don't want to see you again.' **4** A **firm** decision or opinion is definite and unlikely to change. = definite ❏ He made a firm decision to leave Fort Multry by boat. **5** [FIRM + N] **Firm** evidence or information is based on facts and so is likely to be true. = hard, definite ❏ This man may have killed others but unfortunately we have no firm evidence. **6** You use **firm** to describe control or a basis or position when it is strong and unlikely to be ended or removed. = secure ❏ Although the Yakutians are a minority, they have firm control of the territory. **7** If something is **firm**, it does not shake or move when you put weight or pressure on it, because it is strongly made or securely fastened. = secure ❏ If you have to climb up, use a firm platform or a sturdy ladder.
PHRASE **stand firm** If someone **stands firm**, they refuse to change their mind about something. ❏ The council is standing firm against the protest.
PHRASAL VERB **firm up** (firms, firming, firmed) **1** If you **firm up** something or if it **firms up**, it becomes firmer and more solid. ❏ This treatment helps tone the body, firm up muscles and tighten the skin. **2** If you **firm** something **up** or if it **firms up**, it becomes clearer, stronger, or more definite. ❏ We can give you more detail as our plans firm up.

firm·ly /ˈfɜːmli/ ADV **1** [firmly after v] ❏ She held me firmly by the elbow and led me to my aisle seat. **2** [firmly with v] ❑ *'A good night's sleep is what you want,' he said firmly.* **3** *Political values and opinions are firmly held, and can be slow to change.* **4** *This tradition is also firmly rooted in the past.* **5** *The front door is locked and all the windows are firmly shut.*

first ♦♦♦ /fɜːst/ ADJ, PRON, ADV, NOUN

ADJ **1** The **first** thing, person, event, or period of time is the one that happens or comes before all the others of the same kind. ❑ *She lost 16 pounds in the first month of her diet.* ❑ *the first few flakes of snow* **2** When something happens or is done for the **first** time, it has never happened or been done before. ❑ *This is the first time she has experienced disappointment.* **3** The **first** thing, person, or place in a line is the one that is nearest to you or nearest to the front. ❑ *Before him, in the first row, sat the president.* **4** You use **first** to refer to the best or most important thing or person of a particular kind. ❑ *The first duty of any government must be to protect the interests of the taxpayers.* **5** You use **first** to refer to something that happens in the early part of an event or experience, in contrast to what happens later. ❑ *She told him that her first reaction was disgust.*

PHRASES **at first hand** If you learn or experience something **at first hand**, you experience it yourself or learn it directly rather than being told about it by other people. ❑ *He arrived in Natal to see at first hand the effects of the recent heavy fighting.*

not know the first thing about something *(emphasis)* If you say that you **do not know the first thing about** something, you are emphasizing that you know absolutely nothing about it. ❑ *You don't know the first thing about farming.*

PRON **1** The **first** refers to the thing, person, event, or period of time that happens or comes before all the others of the same kind. ❑ *The second paragraph startled me even more than the first.* **2** ['the' first 'that'] The **first** you hear of something or the **first** you know about it is the time when you first become aware of it. ❑ *We heard it on the TV last night – that was the first we heard of it.*

PHRASES **first of all** You use **first of all** to introduce the first of a number of things that you want to say. ❑ *The cut in the interest rates has not had very much impact in California for two reasons. First of all, banks are still afraid to loan.*

at first You use **at first** when you are talking about what happens in the early stages of an event or experience, or just after something else has happened, in contrast to what happens later. = initially ❑ *At first, he seemed surprised by my questions.*

ADV **1** [first with v] If you say that something **first** happened or was done at a particular time, you mean that it had never happened or been done before that time. ❑ *Anne and Steve got engaged two years after they had first started going out.* **2** If you do something **first**, you do it before anyone else does, or before anything else. ❑ *I do not remember who spoke first, but we all expressed the same opinion.* ❑ *First, tell me what you think of my products.* **3** [first before v] You use **first** when you are talking about what happens in the early part of an event or experience, in contrast to what happens later. = initially ❑ *When he first came home he wouldn't say anything about what he'd been doing.* **4** [first after v] In order to emphasize your determination not to do a particular thing, you can say that rather than do it, you would do something else **first**. ❑ *I'll die first, before I let you have all my money!*

PHRASES **come first** If you say that someone or something **comes first** for a particular person, you mean they treat or consider that person or thing as more important than anything else. ❑ *There's no time for boyfriends, my career comes first.*

put someone first or **put something first** If you put someone or something **first**, you treat or consider them as more important than anything else. ❑ *Somebody has to think for the child and put him first.*

NOUN [SING] An event that is described as **a first** has never happened before and is important or exciting. ❑ *It is a first for New York. An outdoor exhibition of Fernando Botero's sculpture on Park Avenue.*

✦ first and foremost → see foremost

WHICH WORD?

first, firstly, or at first?

If an event happens before other events, you say that it happens **first**. Do not use **firstly** to express this meaning.
❑ *Ralph spoke first.*

You can use **first**, **firstly**, or **first of all** to introduce the first thing that you want to say or the first thing in a list.
❑ *First, mix the eggs and flour.*
❑ *There are two reasons why I'm angry. Firstly you're late, and secondly, you've forgotten your homework.*
❑ *First of all, I'd like to thank you all for coming.*

When you are contrasting something at the beginning of an event with something that happened later, you use **at first**.
❑ *At first I thought it was moonlight, but then I realized it was snow.*

first-class also **first class** ADJ, ADV, NOUN
ADJ **1** If you describe something or someone as **first-class**, you mean that they are extremely good and of the highest quality. = first-rate ❑ *The food was first-class.* **2** [first-class + N] You use **first-class** to describe something that is in the group that is considered to be of the highest standard. ❑ *They always stayed in first-class hotels.* **3** [first-class + N] **First-class** accommodation on a train, plane, or ship is the best and most expensive type of accommodation. ❑ *He won himself two first-class tickets to fly to Dublin.* **4** [first-class + N] In Britain, **first-class** postage is the quicker and more expensive form of postage. In the United States, **first-class** postage is the type of postage that is used for sending letters and postcards. ❑ *Two first-class stamps, please.*
ADV [first-class after v] If you travel or fly **first-class**, you travel or fly in the best and most expensive type of accommodation on a train, plane, or ship. ❑ *She had never flown first class before.*
NOUN [u] **First-class** is the first-class accommodation on a train, plane, or ship. ❑ *He paid for and was assigned a cabin in first class.*

first·ly /ˈfɜːstli/ ADV [firstly with CL/GROUP] You use **firstly** in speech or writing when you want to give a reason, make a point, or mention an item that will be followed by others connected with it. ❑ *The programme is now seven years behind schedule as a result, firstly of increased costs, then of technical problems.*

first name NOUN [C] (**first names**) Your **first name** is the first of the names that were given to you when you were born. ❑ *Her first name was Mary. I don't know what her surname was.*

◆fis·cal ♦◇◇ /ˈfɪskəl/ ADJ [fiscal + N] **Fiscal** is used to describe something that relates to government money or public money, especially taxes. = financial ❑ *in 1987, when the government tightened fiscal policy* ❑ *in a climate of increasing fiscal austerity*
◆fis·cal·ly /ˈfɪskəli/ ADV ❑ *The scheme would be fiscally dangerous.* ❑ *Many members are determined to prove they are fiscally responsible.*

fish ♦♦◇ /fɪʃ/ NOUN, VERB
NOUN [C, U] (**fish** or **fishes**) **1** [C] A **fish** is a creature that lives in water and has a tail and fins. There are many different kinds of fish. ❑ *An expert angler was casting his line and catching a fish every time.* **2** [U] **Fish** is the flesh of a fish eaten as food. ❑ *Does dry white wine go best with fish?*
VERB [i] (**fishes, fishing, fished**) **1** If you **fish**, you try to catch fish, either for food or as a form of sport or recreation. ❑ *Brian remembers learning to fish in the Colorado River.* **2** If you say that someone is **fishing for** information or praise, you disapprove of the fact that they are trying to get it from someone in an indirect way. = angle ❑ *He didn't want to create the impression that he was fishing for information.*
→ See also **fishing**

fisher·man /ˈfɪʃəmən/ NOUN [C] (**fishermen**) A **fisherman** is a person who catches fish as a job or for sport. ❑ *The Algarve is a paradise for fishermen, whether river anglers or deep-sea fishermen.*

GET FIT THIS YEAR WITH US!

So, what are your new-year's resolutions? **To lose weight**? **To get fit**? To deal with **stress**?

We can help you tick off all three! Join one of our new **keep-fit** classes and see the benefits over the coming months. We can help you, no matter what your age or **level of fitness** may be.

If you currently have a **less active lifestyle**, start with some **gentle exercise** by joining one of our walking groups.

Feeling a little more **energetic**? **Burn off calories** and **get into shape** with one of our aerobics sessions.

Improve your **flexibility** and **mental health** by signing up for one of our Pilates or yoga sessions.

You'll notice the difference in so many ways. As well as improving your **strength** and **stamina**, exercising will help your **immune system** and improve your **mental health**. **Stress** levels will fall, and you'll enjoy a renewed sense of **well-being**. And you'll meet lots of new people in the process!

Interested? Contact us at the number below for more details.

fish·ery /ˈfɪʃəri/ NOUN [C] (fisheries) **1** Fisheries are areas of the sea where fish are caught in large quantities for commercial purposes. ❑ *the fisheries off Newfoundland* **2** A fishery is a place where fish are bred and reared.

fish·ing ♦◇◇ /ˈfɪʃɪŋ/ NOUN [U] Fishing is the sport, hobby, or business of catching fish. ❑ *Despite the poor weather the fishing has been pretty good.*

fist /fɪst/ NOUN [C] (fists) Your hand is referred to as your fist when you have bent your fingers in towards the palm in order to hit someone, to make an angry gesture, or to hold something. ❑ *Angry protesters with clenched fists shouted their defiance.*

✪ fit ♦♦◇ /fɪt/ VERB, NOUN, ADJ
VERB [I, T] (fits, fitting, fitted or fit) **1** [I, T] If something **fits**, it is the right size and shape to go onto a person's body or onto a particular object. ❑ *The sash, kimono, and other garments were made to fit a child.* ❑ *She has to go to the men's department to find trousers that fit at the waist.* **2** [T] If you **are fitted for** a particular piece of clothing, you try it on so that the person who is making it can see where it needs to be altered. ❑ *She was being fitted for her wedding dress.* **3** [I] If something **fits** somewhere, it can be put there or is designed to be put there. ❑ *a pocket computer which is small enough to fit into your pocket* ❑ *He folded his long legs to fit under the table.* **4** [T] If you **fit** something into a particular space or place, you put it there. ❑ *She fitted her key in the lock.* ❑ *Who could cut the millions of stone blocks and fit them together?* **5** [T] If you **fit** something somewhere, you attach it there, or put it there carefully and securely. ❑ *Fit hinge bolts to give extra support to the door lock.* ❑ *Peter had built the overhead ladders, and the next day he fitted them to the wall.* **6** [I, T] If something **fits** something else or **fits** into it, it goes together well with that thing or is able to be part of it. ❑ *Her daughter doesn't fit the current feminine ideal.* ❑ *Fostering is a full-time job and you should carefully consider how it will fit into your career.* **7** [T] You can say that something **fits** a particular person or thing when it is appropriate or suitable for them or it. = match ❑ *The punishment must always fit the crime.* **8** [T] (formal) If something **fits** someone for a particular task or role, it makes them good enough or suitable for it. ❑ *a man whose past experience fits him for the top job in education*
PHRASAL VERBS **fit in** **1** If you manage to **fit** a person or task in, you manage to find time to deal with them. ❑ *We work long hours both outside and inside the home and we rush around trying to fit everything in.* **2** If you **fit in** as part of a

group, you seem to belong there because you are similar to the other people in it. ❑ *She was great with the children and fitted in beautifully.* **3** If you say that someone or something **fits in**, you understand how they form part of a particular situation or system. ❑ *He knew where I fitted in and what he had to do to get the best out of me.*
fit out or **fit up** If you **fit** someone or something **out**, or you **fit** them **up**, you provide them with equipment and other things that they need. ❑ *We helped to fit him out for a trip to the Baltic.* ❑ *I suggest we fit you up with an office suite.*
NOUN [SING, C] (fits) **1** [SING] If something is a good **fit**, it fits well. ❑ *Eventually he was happy that the sills and doors were a reasonably good fit.* **2** [C] If you have a **fit of** coughing or laughter, you suddenly start coughing or laughing in an uncontrollable way. ❑ *Halfway down the cigarette she had a fit of coughing.* **3** [C] If you do something in a **fit of** anger or panic, you are very angry or afraid when you do it. ❑ *Pattie shot Tom in a fit of jealous rage.* **4** [C] If someone has a **fit** they suddenly lose consciousness and their body makes uncontrollable movements. = seizure ❑ *About two in every five epileptic fits occur during sleep.* **5** [C] (informal) If someone **has** a **fit** or **throws** a **fit**, they suddenly become very agitated because they are angry or worried about something. ❑ *When my landlady said she wanted to keep $380 of my deposit to paint the walls, I threw a fit.* ❑ 'Cathy will have a fit when she finds out you bought all that fishing gear,' Harrington said.
ADJ (fitter, fittest) **1** If something is **fit** for a particular purpose, it is suitable for that purpose. ❑ *Of the seven bicycles we had, only two were fit for the road.* **2** If someone is **fit** to do something, they have the appropriate qualities or skills that will allow them to do it. ❑ *You're not fit to be a mother!* ❑ *In a word, this government isn't fit to rule.* **3** Someone who is **fit** is healthy and physically strong. ❑ *An averagely fit person can master easy ski runs within a few days.* ❑ *Firefighters need to be physically fit.* ❑ *The players are getting fitter all the time.*
PHRASE **see fit** (formal, disapproval) If you say that someone **sees fit to** do something, you mean that they are entitled to do it, but that you disapprove of their decision to do it. ❑ *He's not a friend, you say, yet you saw fit to lend him money.*
✪ fit·ness /ˈfɪtnəs/ NOUN [U] **1** There is a debate about his fitness for the highest office. **2** Squash was once thought to offer all-round fitness. ❑ *Walking lowers blood pressure and improves fitness.* ❑ *Swimming is suitable for people of all ages and fitness levels.*

→ See also **fitted**, **fitting**

✦ **fit like a glove** → see **glove**; **not in a fit state** → see **state**

fit·ted /'fɪtɪd/ ADJ **1** A **fitted** piece of clothing is designed so that it is the same size and shape as your body rather than being loose. ❑ *baggy trousers with fitted jackets* **2** [fitted + N] A **fitted** sheet has the corners sewn so that they fit over the corners of the mattress and do not have to be folded.

fit·ting /'fɪtɪŋ/ NOUN, ADJ

NOUN [C, PL] (**fittings**) **1** [C] A **fitting** is one of the smaller parts on the outside of a piece of equipment or furniture, for example, a handle or a tap. ❑ *brass light fittings* ❑ *industrial fittings for kitchen and bathroom* **2** [C] If someone has a **fitting**, they try on a piece of clothing that is being made for them to see if it fits. ❑ *She lunched and shopped and went for fittings for clothes she didn't need.* **3** [PL] **Fittings** are things such as ovens or heaters, that are fitted inside a building, but can be removed if necessary. ❑ *a detailed list of what fixtures and fittings are included in the purchase price*

ADJ Something that is **fitting** is right or suitable. = appropriate ❑ *A solitary man, it was perhaps fitting that he should have died alone.*

fit·ting·ly /'fɪtɪŋli/ ADV = appropriately ❑ *He closed out his career, fittingly, by hitting a home run.*

five ♦♦♦ /faɪv/ NUM (**fives**) **Five** is the number 5. ❑ *I spent five years there and had a really good time.*

fix ♦◇◇ /fɪks/ VERB, NOUN

VERB [T, I] (**fixes, fixing, fixed**) **1** [T] If you **fix** something which is damaged or which does not work properly, you repair it. = repair ❑ *He cannot fix the electricity.* **2** [T] If you **fix** a problem or a bad situation, you deal with it and make it satisfactory. ❑ *It's not too late to fix the problem, although time is clearly getting short.* **3** [T] If you **fix** some food or a drink for someone, you make it or prepare it for them. ❑ *Sarah fixed some food for us.* ❑ *Let me fix you a drink.* **4** [T] (*informal*) If you **fix** your hair, clothes, or makeup, you arrange or adjust them so you look neat and tidy, showing you have taken care with your appearance. = arrange ❑ *'I've got to fix my hair,' I said and retreated to my bedroom.* **5** [T] If you **fix** something, for example, a date, price, or policy, you decide and say exactly what it will be. = set ❑ *He's going to fix a time when I can see him.* ❑ *The date of the election was fixed.* **6** [T] If you **fix** something for someone, you arrange for it to happen or you organize it for them. ❑ *I've fixed it for you to see Bonnie Lachlan.* ❑ *It's fixed. He's going to meet us at the airport.* ❑ *He vanished after you fixed him with a job.* **7** [T] If something **is fixed** somewhere, it is attached there firmly and securely. = attach ❑ *It is fixed on the wall.* ❑ *Most blinds can be fixed directly to the top of the window-frame.* **8** [I, T] If you **fix** your eyes **on** someone or something or if your eyes **fix on** them, you look at them with complete attention. ❑ *She fixes her steel-blue eyes on an unsuspecting local official.* ❑ *Her soft brown eyes fixed on Kelly.* **9** [T] If someone or something is **fixed in** your mind, you remember them well, for example, because they are very important, interesting, or unusual. ❑ *Leonard was now fixed in his mind.* **10** [T] If someone **fixes** a gun, camera, or radar **on** something, they point it at that thing. ❑ *The U.S. crew fixed its radar on the Turkish ship.* **11** [T] If someone **fixes** a race, election, contest, or other event, they make unfair or illegal arrangements or use deception to affect the result. = rig ❑ *They offered opposing players bribes to fix a decisive game.* **12** [T] (*business, disapproval*) If you accuse someone of **fixing** prices, you accuse them of making unfair arrangements to charge a particular price for something, rather than allowing market forces to decide it. ❑ *a suspected cartel that had fixed the price of steel for the construction market*

PHRASAL VERB **fix up 1** If you **fix** something **up**, you do work that is necessary in order to make it more suitable or attractive. = do up ❑ *I've fixed up Matthew's old room.* **2** If you **fix** someone **up with** something they need, you provide it for them. ❑ *We'll fix him up with a tie.* **3** (*BrE*) If you **fix** something **up**, you arrange it.

NOUN [C, SING] (**fixes**) **1** [C] A **fix** is an unfair or illegal arrangement or the use of deception to affect the result of

a race, election, contest, or other event. ❑ *It's all a fix, a deal they've made.* **2** [C] (*informal*) You can refer to a solution to a problem as a **fix**. ❑ *Many of those changes could just be a temporary fix.* **3** [SING] (*informal*) If you get **a fix on** someone or something, you have a clear idea or understanding of them. ❑ *It's been hard to get a steady fix on what's going on.*

→ See also **fixed**

fixed ♦◇◇ /fɪkst/ ADJ

ADJ **1** You use **fixed** to describe something which stays the same and does not or cannot vary. = set ❑ *They issue a fixed number of shares that trade publicly.* ❑ *Many restaurants offer fixed-price menus.* **2** If you say that someone has **fixed** ideas or opinions, you mean that they do not often change their ideas and opinions, although perhaps they should. ❑ *people who have fixed ideas about things* **3** If someone has a **fixed** smile on their face, they are smiling even though they do not feel happy or pleased. ❑ *I had to go through the rest of the evening with a fixed smile on my face.*

PHRASE **no fixed abode** or **no fixed address** (*formal*) Someone who is of **no fixed abode** or **no fixed address** does not have a permanent place to live. ❑ *They are not able to get a job interview because they have no fixed address.*

→ See also **fix**

fix·ture /'fɪkstʃə/ NOUN [C] (**fixtures**) **Fixtures** are fittings or furniture which belong to a building and are legally part of it, for example, a bath or a toilet. ❑ *a detailed list of what fixtures and fittings are included in the purchase price*

fizz /fɪz/ VERB, NOUN

VERB [I] (**fizzes, fizzing, fizzed**) If a drink **fizzes**, it produces a lot of little bubbles of gas and makes a sound like a long 's'. ❑ *After a while their mother was back, holding a tray of glasses that fizzed.*

NOUN [U] If a drink has **fizz**, it contains a lot of little bubbles of gas and makes a sound like a long 's' when poured. ❑ *I wonder if there's any fizz left in the lemonade.*

flag ♦◇◇ /flæg/ NOUN, VERB

NOUN [C] (**flags**) **1** A **flag** is a piece of cloth which can be attached to a pole and which is used as a sign, signal, or symbol of something, especially of a particular country. ❑ *The Marines climbed to the roof of the embassy building to raise the American flag.* **2** Journalists sometimes refer to the **flag** of a particular country or organization as a way of referring to the country or organization itself and its values or power. ❑ *Every person who serves under the American flag will answer to his or her own superiors and to military law.*

VERB [I] (**flags, flagging, flagged**) If you **flag** or if your spirits **flag**, you begin to lose enthusiasm or energy. ❑ *His enthusiasm was in no way flagging.*

fla·grant /'fleɪɡrənt/ ADJ [flagrant + N] (*disapproval*) You can use **flagrant** to describe an action, situation, or someone's behaviour that you find extremely bad or shocking in a very obvious way. = blatant ❑ *The judge called the decision 'a flagrant violation of international law'.*

flag·ship /'flæɡʃɪp/ NOUN [C] (**flagships**) **1** The **flagship** of a group of things that are owned or produced by a particular organization is the most important one. ❑ *The company plans to open a flagship store in New York this month.* **2** (*mainly BrE*) A **flagship** is the most important ship in a fleet of ships, especially the one on which the commander of the fleet is sailing.

flair /fleə/ NOUN [SING, U] **1** [SING] If you have a **flair for** a particular thing, you have a natural ability to do it well. = talent, gift ❑ *a friend who has a flair for languages* **2** [U] If you have **flair**, you do things in an original, interesting, and stylish way. = style, panache ❑ *Their work has all the usual punch, panache, and flair you'd expect.*

flake /fleɪk/ NOUN, VERB

NOUN [C] (**flakes**) A **flake** is a small thin piece of something, especially one that has broken off a larger piece. ❑ *flakes of paint* ❑ *Large flakes of snow began swiftly to fall.*

VERB [I] (**flakes, flaking, flaked**) If something such as paint **flakes**, small thin pieces of it come off. ❑ *They can see how its colours have faded and where paint has flaked.*

F

f

PHRASAL VERB **flake off** Flake off means the same as **flake** VERB. ❑ *The surface corrosion was worst where the paint had flaked off.*

flam·boy·ant /flæmˈbɔɪənt/ ADJ If you say that someone or something is **flamboyant**, you mean that they are very noticeable, stylish, and exciting. ❑ *Freddie Mercury was a flamboyant star of the hard rock scene.* **flam·boy·ance** /flæmˈbɔɪəns/ NOUN [u] ❑ *Campese was his usual mixture of flamboyance and flair.*

flame /fleɪm/ NOUN, VERB

NOUN [c, u] (**flames**) **1** [c, u] A **flame** is a hot bright stream of burning gas that comes from something that is burning. ❑ *The heat from the flames was so intense that roads melted.* **2** [c] (*informal, computing*) A **flame** is an e-mail message which severely criticizes or attacks someone. ❑ *The best way to respond to a flame is to ignore it.* **PHRASES** **burst into flames** If something **bursts into flames** or **bursts into flame**, it suddenly starts burning strongly. ❑ *She managed to scramble out of the vehicle as it burst into flames.* **in flames** Something that is **in flames** is on fire. ❑ *I woke to a city in flames.* VERB [T] (**flames, flaming, flamed**) If you **flame** someone, you send them an e-mail message which severely criticizes or attacks them. ❑ *Ever been flamed?*

flank /flæŋk/ NOUN, VERB

NOUN [c] (**flanks**) **1** An animal's **flank** is its side, between the ribs and the hip. ❑ *He put his hand on the dog's flank.* **2** A **flank** of an army or navy force is one side of it when it is organized for battle. ❑ *The assault element, led by Captain Ramirez, opened up from their right flank.* **3** The side of anything large can be referred to as its **flank**. ❑ *They continued along the flank of the mountain.* VERB [T] (**flanks, flanking, flanked**) If something **is flanked by** things, it has them on both sides of it, or sometimes on one side of it. ❑ *The altar was flanked by two Christmas trees.*

flap /flæp/ VERB, NOUN

VERB [I, T] (**flaps, flapping, flapped**) **1** [I, T] If something such as a piece of cloth or paper **flaps** or if you **flap** it, it moves quickly up and down or from side to side. = flutter ❑ *Grey sheets flapped on the clothes line.* **2** [I, T] If a bird or insect **flaps** its wings or if its wings **flap**, the wings move quickly up and down. ❑ *The bird flapped its wings furiously.* **3** [T] If you **flap** your arms, you move them quickly up and down as if they were the wings of a bird. ❑ *a kid running and flapping her arms* NOUN [c] (**flaps**) **1** A **flap** of cloth or skin, for example, is a flat piece of it that can move freely up and down or from side to side because it is held or attached by only one edge. ❑ *He drew back the tent flap and strode out into the blizzard.* **2** A **flap** on the wing of an aircraft is an area along the edge of the wing that can be raised or lowered to control the movement of the aircraft. ❑ *the sudden slowing as the flaps were lowered*

flare /fleə/ NOUN, VERB

NOUN [c] (**flares**) A **flare** is a small device that produces a bright flame. Flares are used as signals, for example, on ships. ❑ *a ship which had fired a distress flare* VERB [I] (**flares, flaring, flared**) **1** If a fire **flares**, the flames suddenly become larger. ❑ *Camp fires flared like beacons in the dark.* **2** If something such as trouble, violence, or conflict **flares**, it starts or becomes more violent. ❑ *Even as the president appealed for calm, trouble flared in several American cities.* **3** If people's tempers **flare**, they get angry. ❑ *Tempers flared and harsh words were exchanged.* **PHRASAL VERB** **flare up 1** Flare up means the same as **flare** VERB 1. ❑ *Don't spill too much fat on the barbecue as it could flare up.* **2** Flare up means the same as **flare** VERB 2. ❑ *Dozens of people were injured as fighting flared up.*

flash ♦◇◇ /flæʃ/ NOUN, VERB

NOUN [c, u] (**flashes**) **1** [c] A **flash** is a sudden burst of light or of something shiny or bright. ❑ *A sudden flash of lightning lit everything up for a second.* ❑ *The wire snapped at the wall plug with a blue flash.* **2** [u] **Flash** is the use of special bulbs to give more light when taking a photograph. ❑ *He was one of the first people to use high speed flash in bird photography.*

PHRASES **in a flash** If you say that something happens **in a flash**, you mean that it happens suddenly and lasts only a very short time. ❑ *The answer had come to him in a flash.* **quick as a flash** If you say that someone reacts to something **quick as a flash**, you mean that they react to it extremely quickly. ❑ *Quick as a flash, the man said, 'I have to, don't I?'* VERB [I, T] (**flashes, flashing, flashed**) **1** [I, T] If a light **flashes** or if you **flash** a light, it shines with a sudden bright light, especially as quick, regular flashes of light. ❑ *Lightning flashed among the distant dark clouds.* ❑ *He lost his temper after a driver flashed her headlights as he overtook.* **2** [I] If something **flashes** past or by, it moves past you so fast that you cannot see it properly. ❑ *It was a busy road, cars flashed by every few minutes.* **3** [I] If something **flashes through** or **into** your mind, you suddenly think about it. ❑ *A ludicrous thought flashed through Harry's mind.* **4** [T] (*informal*) If you **flash** something such as an identification card, you show it to people quickly and then put it away again. ❑ *Halim flashed his official card, and managed to get hold of a soldier to guard the Land Rover.* **5** [I, T] If a picture or message **flashes up on** a screen, or if you **flash** it **onto** a screen, it is displayed there briefly or suddenly, and often repeatedly. ❑ *The figures flash up on the scoreboard.* ❑ *The words 'Good Luck' were flashing on the screen.* **6** [T] (*written*) If you **flash** a look or a smile at someone, you suddenly look at them or smile at them. ❑ *I flashed a look at Sue.*

flask /flɑːsk, flæsk/ NOUN [c] (**flasks**) **1** A **flask** is a bottle which you use for carrying drinks around with you. ❑ *He took out a metal flask from a canvas bag.* **2** A **flask** of liquid is the flask and the liquid which it contains. ❑ *There are some sandwiches here and a flask of coffee.* **3** A **flask** is a bottle or other container which is used in science laboratories and industry for holding liquids. ❑ *Flasks for the transport of spent fuel are extremely strong containers made of steel or steel and lead.*

flat ♦♦◇ /flæt/ ADJ, NOUN, ADV

ADJ (**flatter, flattest**) **1** Something that is **flat** is level, smooth, or even, rather than sloping, curved, or uneven. ❑ *Tiles can be fixed to any surface as long as it's flat, firm and dry.* ❑ *windows which a thief can reach from a drainpipe or flat roof* **2** **Flat** means horizontal and not upright. ❑ *Two men near him threw themselves flat.* **3** A **flat** object is not very tall or deep in relation to its length and width. = shallow ❑ *Ellen is walking down the drive with a square flat box balanced on one hand.* **4** **Flat** land is level, with no high hills or other raised parts. ❑ *To the north lie the flat and fertile farmlands of Nebraska.* **5** **Flat** shoes have no heels or very low heels. ❑ *People wear slacks, sweaters, flat shoes, and all manner of casual attire for travel.* **6** A **flat** tyre, ball, or balloon does not have enough air in it. ❑ *One vehicle with a flat tyre can bring the highway to a standstill.* **7** If you have **flat** feet, the arches of your feet are too low. ❑ *The condition of flat feet runs in families.* **8** A drink that is **flat** has lost its fizz. ❑ *Could this really stop the champagne from going flat?* **9** (*BrE; in AmE, use* **dead**) A **flat** battery has lost some or all of its electrical charge. **10** [flat + N] A **flat** rate, price, or percentage is one that is fixed and which applies in every situation. = fixed ❑ *Fees are charged at a flat rate, rather than on a percentage basis.* **11** If trade or business is **flat**, it is slow and inactive, rather than busy and improving or increasing. = sluggish ❑ *During the first eight months of this year, sales of big vans were up 14% while car sales stayed flat.* **12** [N + flat] **Flat** is used after a letter representing a musical note to show that the note should be played or sung half a tone lower than the note which otherwise matches that letter. **Flat** is often represented by the symbol ♭ after the letter. ❑ *Schubert's B flat Piano Trio (Opus 99)* **13** If musical notes are **flat**, they are sung or played slightly lower in pitch than they should be. ❑ *He had been fired because his singing was flat.* **14** [flat + N] A **flat** denial or refusal is definite and firm, and is unlikely to be changed. ❑ *The Foreign Ministry has issued a flat denial of any involvement.* **15** If you describe something as **flat**, you mean that it is dull and not exciting or interesting. ❑ *The past few days have seemed comparatively flat and empty.* NOUN [c] (**flats**) **1** (*BrE; in AmE, use* **apartment**) A **flat** is a set of rooms for living in, usually on one floor and part of a larger building. A flat usually includes a kitchen and bathroom. = apartment **2** You can refer to one of the broad flat surfaces of an object as **the flat of** that object. ❑ He slammed the counter with the flat of his hand. **3** A **flat** is a tyre that does not have enough air in it. ❑ Then, after I finally got back on the main road, I developed a flat. **4** A low flat area of uncultivated land, especially an area where the ground is soft and wet, can be referred to as **flats** or a **flat**. ❑ The salt marshes and mud flats attract large numbers of waterfowl.

ADV **1** [flat after v] If someone sings **flat** or if a musical instrument is **flat**, their singing or the instrument is slightly lower in pitch than it should be. ❑ She had a tendency to sing flat. **2** [NUM N + flat] If you say that something happened, for example, in ten seconds **flat** or ten minutes **flat**, you are emphasizing that it happened surprisingly quickly and only took ten seconds or ten minutes. ❑ You're sitting behind an engine that'll move you from 0 to 60mph in six seconds flat.

PHRASES **fall flat 1** If you **fall flat** on your face, you fall over. ❑ A man walked in off the street and fell flat on his face, unconscious. **2** If an event or attempt **falls flat** or **falls flat on** its **face**, it is unsuccessful. = fail ❑ Liz meant it as a joke but it fell flat.

flat out 1 If you do something **flat out**, you do it as fast or as hard as you can. ❑ Everyone is working flat out to try to trap those responsible. ❑ a flat-out sprint **2** (mainly AmE, informal, emphasis) You use **flat out** to emphasize that something is completely the case. ❑ That allegation is a flat-out lie.

flat·ly /ˈflætli/ ADV ❑ He flatly refused to discuss it.

flat·ten /ˈflætən/ VERB
VERB [I, T] (**flattens, flattening, flattened**) **1** [I, T] If you **flatten** something or if it **flattens**, it becomes flat or flatter. ❑ He carefully flattened the wrappers and put them between the leaves of his book. ❑ The dog's ears flattened slightly as Cook spoke his name. **2** [T] To **flatten** something such as a building, town, or plant means to destroy it by knocking it down or crushing it. ❑ explosives capable of flattening a five-storey building ❑ Bombing raids flattened much of the area. **3** [T] If you **flatten yourself against** something, you press yourself flat against it, for example, to avoid getting in the way or being seen. ❑ He flattened himself against a brick wall as I passed. **4** [T] If you **flatten** someone, you make them fall over by hitting them violently. ❑ 'I've never seen a woman flatten someone like that,' said a crew member. 'She knocked him out cold.'

PHRASAL VERB **flatten out** Flatten out means the same as **flatten** VERB 1. ❑ The hills flattened out just south of the mountain.

flat·ter /ˈflætə/ VERB [T] (**flatters, flattering, flattered**)
1 (disapproval) If someone **flatters** you, they praise you in an exaggerated way that is not sincere, because they want to please you or to persuade you to do something. ❑ I knew she was just flattering me. **2** If you **flatter yourself that** something good is the case, you believe that it is true, although others may disagree. If someone says to you 'you're flattering yourself' or 'don't flatter yourself', they mean that they disagree with your good opinion of yourself. ❑ I flatter myself that this campaign will put an end to the war.

flaunt /flɔːnt/ VERB [T] (**flaunts, flaunting, flaunted**) (disapproval) If you say that someone **flaunts** their possessions, abilities, or qualities, you mean that they display them in a very obvious way, especially in order to try to obtain other people's admiration. = show off ❑ They drove around in Rolls-Royces, openly flaunting their wealth.

fla·vour /ˈfleɪvə/ (BrE; in AmE, use **flavor**) NOUN, VERB
NOUN [C, U] (**flavours**) **1** [C, U] The **flavour** of a food or drink is its taste. ❑ I always add some paprika for extra flavour. **2** [C] If something is orange **flavour** or beef **flavour**, it is made to taste of orange or beef. ❑ It has an orange flavour and smooth texture.
VERB [T] (**flavours, flavouring, flavoured**) If you **flavour** food or drink, you add something to it to give it a particular taste. ❑ Lime preserved in salt is a North African speciality which is used to flavour chicken dishes.

fla·vour·ing /ˈfleɪvərɪŋ/ (BrE; in AmE, use **flavoring**) NOUN [C, U] (**flavourings**) Flavourings are substances that are added to food or drink to give it a particular taste. ❑ lemon flavouring

⚙ **flaw** /flɔː/ NOUN [C] (**flaws**) **1** A **flaw in** something such as a theory or argument is a mistake in it, which causes it to be less effective or valid. = mistake ❑ There were, however, a number of crucial flaws in his monetary theory. ❑ Almost all of these studies have serious flaws. **2** A **flaw in** someone's character is an undesirable quality that they have. = defect, failing ❑ The only flaw in his character seems to be a short temper. **3** A **flaw in** something such as a pattern or material is a fault in it that should not be there. = imperfection ❑ It's like having a flaw in a piece of material – the longer you leave it, the weaker it gets. ❑ lenses containing flaws and imperfections ❑ a special kind of glass that was treasured for its flaws rather than its perfection

⚙ **flawed** /flɔːd/ ADJ Something that is **flawed** has a mark, fault, or mistake in it. ❑ These tests were so seriously flawed as to render the results meaningless. ❑ The problem is the original forecast was based on flawed assumptions. ❑ the unique beauty of a flawed object

flaw·less /ˈflɔːləs/ ADJ If you say that something or someone is **flawless**, you mean that they are extremely good and that there are no faults or problems with them. = perfect ❑ Discovery's takeoff this morning from Cape Canaveral was flawless.
flaw·less·ly /ˈflɔːləsli/ ADV ❑ Each stage of the battle was carried off flawlessly.

fled /fled/ IRREG FORM Fled is the past tense and past participle of **flee**.

flee ◆◇◇ /fliː/ VERB [I, T] (**flees, fleeing, fled**) (written) If you **flee from** something or someone, or **flee** a person or thing, you escape from them. ❑ He slammed the bedroom door behind him and fled. ❑ refugees fleeing persecution or torture

fleet ◆◇◇ /fliːt/ NOUN [C] (**fleets**) **1** A **fleet** is a group of ships organized to do something together, for example, to fight battles or to catch fish. ❑ A fleet sailed for New South Wales to establish the first European settlement in Australia. **2** A **fleet** of vehicles is a group of them, especially when they all belong to a particular organization or business, or when they are all going somewhere together. ❑ With its own fleet of trucks, the company delivers most orders overnight.

flesh /fleʃ/ NOUN
NOUN [U] **1** Flesh is the soft part of a person's or animal's body between the bones and the skin. ❑ the pale pink flesh of trout and salmon **2** You can use **flesh** to refer to human skin and the human body, especially when you are considering it in a sexual way. ❑ the warmth of her flesh **3** The **flesh** of a fruit or vegetable is the soft inside part of it. ❑ Cut the flesh from the olives and discard the stones.
PHRASES **flesh and blood** (emphasis) You use **flesh and blood** to emphasize that someone has human feelings or weaknesses, often when contrasting them with machines. ❑ I'm only flesh and blood, like anyone else.
own flesh and blood (emphasis) If you say that someone is your **own flesh and blood**, you are emphasizing that they are a member of your family. ❑ The kid, after all, was his own flesh and blood. He deserved a second chance.
make someone's flesh creep or **make someone's flesh crawl** If something **makes** your **flesh creep** or **makes** your **flesh crawl**, it makes you feel disgusted, shocked, or frightened. ❑ It makes my flesh creep to think of it.
in the flesh If you meet or see someone **in the flesh**, you actually meet or see them, rather than, for example, seeing them in a film or on television. ❑ The first thing viewers usually say when they see me in the flesh is 'You're smaller than you look on TV.'
PHRASAL VERB **flesh out** (**fleshes, fleshing, fleshed**) If you **flesh out** something such as a story or plan, you add details and more information to it. ❑ Permission for a warehouse development has already been granted and the developers are merely fleshing out the details.

flew /fluː/ IRREG FORM Flew is the past tense of **fly**.

flex /fleks/ VERB, NOUN
VERB [T] (**flexes, flexing, flexed**) If you **flex** your muscles or

parts of your body, you bend, move, or stretch them for a short time in order to exercise them. ❏ *He slowly flexed his muscles and tried to stand.*
NOUN [C, U] (**flexes**) (*mainly BrE*; in *AmE*, use **cord**) A **flex** is an electric cable containing two or more wires that is connected to an electrical appliance.
✦ **flex your muscles** → see **muscle**

✪ flex·i·ble ♦◇◇ /ˈfleksɪbəl/ ADJ (*academic word*) **1** A **flexible** object or material can be bent easily without breaking. = pliable; ≠ inflexible, rigid ❏ *brushes with long, flexible bristles* ❏ *Air is pumped through a flexible tube.* **2** Something or someone that is **flexible** is able to change easily and adapt to different conditions and circumstances as they occur. = adaptable; ≠ inflexible ❏ *flexible working hours* ❏ *more flexible arrangements to allow access to services after normal working hours*
✪ flexi·bil·ity /ˌfleksɪˈbɪlɪti/ NOUN [U] **1** = elasticity ❏ *The flexibility of the lens decreases with age; it is therefore common for our sight to worsen as we get older.* **2** = adaptability; ≠ inflexibility ❏ *The flexibility of distance learning would be particularly suited to busy managers.*

flick /flɪk/ VERB, NOUN
VERB [I, T] (**flicks, flicking, flicked**) **1** [I, T] If something **flicks** in a particular direction, or if someone **flicks** it, it moves with a short, sudden movement. ❏ *His tongue flicked across his lips.* ❏ *He flicked his cigarette out of the window.* **2** [T] If you **flick** something away, or off something else, you remove it with a quick movement of your hand or finger. ❏ *Shirley flicked a piece of lint from the sleeve of her black suit.* **3** [T] If you **flick** something such as a whip or a towel, or **flick** something with it, you hold one end of it and move your hand quickly up and then forwards, so that the other end moves. ❏ *She sighed and flicked a dishcloth at the worktop.* **4** [T] If you **flick** a switch, or **flick** an electrical appliance on or off, you press the switch sharply so that it moves into a different position and works the equipment. ❏ *Sam was flicking a torch on and off.* **5** [I] If you **flick through** a book or magazine, you turn its pages quickly, for example, to get a general idea of its contents or to look for a particular item. If you **flick through** television channels, you continually change channels very quickly, usually using a remote control. ❏ *She was flicking through some magazines on a table.*
NOUN [C, SING] (**flicks**) **1** [C] A **flick** is a short, sudden movement you make with your fingers or with an object held in your hand. ❏ *a flick of a paintbrush* **2** [C] The **flick** of something such as a whip or a towel is a movement you make with it by holding one end of it and moving your hand quickly up and then forwards, so that the other end moves. ❏ *a flick of the whip* **3** [SING] If you **have a flick through** a book or magazine, you turn its pages quickly, for example, to get a general idea of its contents or to look for a particular item. ❏ *I thought I'd have a quick flick through some recent issues.*

flick·er /ˈflɪkə/ VERB, NOUN
VERB [I] (**flickers, flickering, flickered**) If a light or flame **flickers**, it shines unsteadily. ❏ *Fluorescent lights flickered, and then the room was blindingly bright.*
NOUN [C] (**flickers**) The **flicker** of a light or flame is when it shines unsteadily. ❏ *Looking through the window I saw the flicker of flames.*

flight ♦♦◇ /flaɪt/ NOUN [C, U] (**flights**) **1** [C] A **flight** is a trip made by flying, usually in a plane. ❏ *The flight will take four hours.* **2** [C] [also flight + NUM] You can refer to a plane carrying passengers on a particular trip as a particular **flight**. ❏ *BA flight 286 was two hours late.* **3** [C] A **flight of** steps or stairs is a set of steps or stairs that lead from one level to another without changing direction. ❏ *We walked in silence up a flight of stairs and down a long corridor.* **4** [U] **Flight** is the action of flying, or the ability to fly. ❏ *Supersonic flight could become a routine form of travel in the 21st century.* **5** [U] **Flight** is the act of running away from a dangerous or unpleasant situation or place. ❏ *The family was often in flight, hiding out in friends' houses.*

flim·sy /ˈflɪmzi/ ADJ (**flimsier, flimsiest**) **1** A flimsy object is weak because it is made of a weak material, or is badly made. ❏ *a flimsy wooden door* **2** Flimsy cloth or

clothing is thin and does not give much protection. ❏ *a very flimsy pink chiffon nightgown* **3** If you describe something such as evidence or an excuse as **flimsy**, you mean that it is not very good or convincing. = weak, unconvincing ❏ *The charges were based on very flimsy evidence.*

flinch /flɪntʃ/ VERB [I] (**flinches, flinching, flinched**) **1** [usu NEG] If you **flinch**, you make a small sudden movement, especially when something surprises you or hurts you. ❏ *Leo stared back at him without flinching.* **2** If you **flinch from** something unpleasant, you are unwilling to do it or think about it, or you avoid doing it. ❏ *The world community should not flinch in the face of this challenge.*

fling /flɪŋ/ VERB, NOUN
> **Fling** can be used instead of 'throw' in many expressions that usually contain 'throw'.

VERB [T] (**flings, flinging, flung**) **1** If you **fling** something somewhere, you throw it there using a lot of force. ❏ *The woman flung the cup at him.* **2** If you **fling yourself** somewhere, you move or jump there suddenly and with a lot of force. ❏ *He flung himself to the floor.* **3** If you **fling** a part of your body in a particular direction, especially your arms or head, you move it there suddenly. = throw ❏ *She flung her arms around my neck and kissed me.* **4** If you **fling** someone to the ground, you push them very roughly so that they fall over. ❏ *The youth got him by the front of his shirt and flung him to the ground.* **5** If you **fling** something into a particular place or position, you put it there in a quick or angry way. ❏ *Peter flung his shoes into the corner.* **6** If you **fling yourself into** a particular activity, you do it with a lot of enthusiasm and energy. ❏ *She flung herself into her career.*
NOUN [C] (**flings**) (*informal*) If two people have a **fling**, they have a brief sexual relationship. = affair ❏ *She claims she had a brief fling with him 30 years ago.*

flip /flɪp/ VERB [T, I] (**flips, flipping, flipped**) **1** [T] If you **flip** a device on or off, or if you flip a switch, you turn it on or off by pressing the switch quickly. = flick ❏ *He didn't flip on the headlights until he was two blocks away.* ❏ *Then he walked out, flipping the lights off.* **2** [I] If you **flip** through the pages of a book, for example, you quickly turn over the pages in order to find a particular one or to get an idea of the contents. ❏ *He was flipping through a magazine in the living room.* **3** [I, T] If something **flips** over, or if you flip it over or into a different position, it moves or is moved into a different position. ❏ *The plane then flipped over and burst into flames.* **4** [T] If you **flip** something, especially a coin, you use your thumb to make it turn over and over, as it goes through the air. = toss ❏ *I pulled a coin from my pocket and flipped it.*

float ♦◇◇ /fləʊt/ VERB, NOUN
VERB [I, T] (**floats, floating, floated**) **1** [I, T] If something or someone **is floating** in a liquid, they are in the liquid, on or just below the surface, and are being supported by it. You can also **float** something on a liquid. ❏ *They noticed ten and twenty pound notes floating in the water.* ❏ *It's below freezing and small icebergs are floating by.* **2** [I] Something that **floats** lies on or just below the surface of a liquid when it is put in it and does not sink. ❏ *They will also float if you drop them in the water.* **3** [I] Something that **floats** in or through the air hangs in it or moves slowly and gently through it. ❏ *The white cloud of smoke floated away.* **4** [T] If you **float** a project, plan, or idea, you suggest it for others to think about. ❏ *The French had floated the idea of placing the diplomatic work in the hands of the UN.* **5** [T] (*business*) If a company director **floats** their company, they start to sell shares in it to the public. ❏ *He floated his firm on the stock market.* **6** [I, T] (*business*) If a government **floats** its country's currency or allows it to **float**, it allows the currency's value to change freely in relation to other currencies. ❏ *On January 15th Brazil was forced to float its currency.*
NOUN [C] (**floats**) **1** A **float** is a light object that is used to help someone or something float. ❏ *Floats will provide confidence in the water.* **2** A **float** is a small object attached to a fishing line which floats on the water and moves

when a fish has been caught. **3** A **float** is a lorry on which displays and people in special costumes are carried in a parade. ❑ *a procession of makeshift floats bearing loudspeakers and banners*

flock /flɒk/ NOUN, VERB

NOUN [c] (**flocks**) **1** A **flock** of birds, sheep, or goats is a group of them. ❑ *They kept a small flock of sheep.* **2** You can refer to a group of people or things as a **flock** of them to emphasize that there are a lot of them. ❑ *These cases all attracted flocks of famous writers.*

VERB [I] (**flocks, flocking, flocked**) If people **flock to** a particular place or event, a very large number of them go there, usually because it is pleasant or interesting. ❑ *The public has flocked to the show.* ❑ *The criticisms will not stop people flocking to see the film.*

✪ flood ◆◇◇ /flʌd/ NOUN, VERB

NOUN [c, u] (**floods**) **1** [c, u] If there is a **flood**, a large amount of water covers an area which is usually dry, for example, when a river flows over its banks or a pipe bursts. ❑ *More than 70 people were killed in the floods, caused when a dam burst.* ❑ *This is the type of flood dreaded by cavers.* **2** [c] If you say that a **flood** of people or things arrive somewhere, you are emphasizing that a very large number of them arrive there. = tide, torrent ❑ *The administration is trying to stem the flood of refugees out of Haiti and into Florida.*

VERB [I, T] (**floods, flooding, flooded**) **1** [I, T] If something such as a river or a burst pipe **floods** an area that is usually dry or if the area **floods**, it becomes covered with water. ❑ *The kitchen flooded.* **2** [I] If a river **floods**, it overflows, especially after very heavy rain. = overflow ❑ *the relentless rain that caused twenty rivers to flood* **3** [I] If you say that people or things **flood** into a place, you are emphasizing that they arrive there in large numbers. = pour ❑ *Large numbers of immigrants flooded into the area.* ❑ *Inquiries flooded in from all over the world.* **4** [T] If you **flood** a place **with** a particular type of thing, or if a particular type of thing **floods** a place, the place becomes full of so many of them that it cannot hold or deal with any more. = saturate ❑ *Manufacturers are destroying American jobs by flooding the market with cheap imports.*

flood·ing /'flʌdɪŋ/ NOUN [u] If **flooding** occurs, an area of land that is usually dry is covered with water after heavy rain or after a river or lake flows over its banks. ❑ *The flooding, caused by three days of torrential rain, is the worst in sixty-five years.*

floor ◆◆◇ /flɔː/ NOUN, VERB

NOUN [c, SING] (**floors**) **1** [c] The **floor** of a room is the part of it that you walk on. ❑ *Jack's sitting on the floor watching TV.* **2** [c] A **floor** of a building is all the rooms that are on a particular level. = storey ❑ *The café was on the top floor of the hospital.* **3** [c] The ocean **floor** is the ground at the bottom of an ocean. The valley **floor** is the ground at the bottom of a valley. ❑ *They spend hours feeding on the ocean floor.* **4** [c] The place where official debates and discussions are held, especially between members of a legislature, is referred to as the **floor**. ❑ *The issues were debated on the floor of the House.* **5** [SING] In a debate or discussion, the **floor** is the people who are listening to the arguments being put forward but who are not among the main speakers. ❑ *The president is taking questions from the floor.*

PHRASES **have the floor** If someone **has the floor**, they are the person who is speaking in a debate or discussion. ❑ *Since I have the floor for the moment, I want to go back to a previous point.*

take to the floor If you **take to the floor**, you start dancing at a dance or disco. ❑ *The happy couple and their respective parents took to the floor.*

wipe the floor with someone (*informal*) If you **wipe the floor with** someone, you defeat them completely in a competition or discussion. ❑ *He could wipe the floor with the opposition.*

VERB [T] (**floors, flooring, floored**) If you **are floored by** something, you are unable to respond to it because you are so surprised by it. ❑ *He was floored by the announcement.*

flop /flɒp/ VERB, NOUN

VERB [I] (**flops, flopping, flopped**) **1** If you **flop** into a

chair, for example, you sit down suddenly and heavily because you are so tired. = collapse ❑ *Bunbury flopped down upon the bed and rested his tired feet.* **2** If something **flops** onto something else, it falls there heavily or untidily. ❑ *The briefcase flopped onto the desk.* **3** (*informal*) If something **flops**, it is completely unsuccessful. ❑ *The film flopped badly at the box office.*

NOUN [c] (**flops**) (*informal*) If something is a **flop**, it is completely unsuccessful. = failure ❑ *It is the public who decide whether a film is a hit or a flop.*

flop·py /'flɒpi/ ADJ (**floppier, floppiest**) Something that is **floppy** is loose rather than stiff, and tends to hang downwards. ❑ *the girl with the floppy hat and glasses*

✪ flo·ra /'flɔːrə/ NOUN [u] (*formal*) You can refer to plants as **flora**, especially the plants growing in a particular area. ❑ *the variety of food crops and flora which now exists in Dominica* ❑ *The purpose of the expedition was to study the flora and fauna of the heavily wooded island.*

floun·der /'flaʊndə/ VERB [I] (**flounders, floundering, floundered**) **1** If something **is floundering**, it has many problems and may soon fail completely. = founder ❑ *What a pity that his career was left to flounder.* **2** If you say that someone **is floundering**, you are criticizing them for not making decisions or for not knowing what to say or do. = dither ❑ *Right now, you've got a president who's floundering, trying to find some way to get his campaign jump-started.* **3** If you **flounder** in water or mud, you move in an uncontrolled way, trying not to sink. ❑ *Three men were floundering about in the water.*

flour /flaʊə/ NOUN [c, u] (**flours**) **Flour** is a white or brown powder that is made by grinding grain. It is used to make bread, cakes, and pastry.

✪ flour·ish /'flʌrɪʃ, AmE 'flɜːr-/ VERB, NOUN

VERB [I, T] (**flourishes, flourishing, flourished**) **1** [I] If something **flourishes**, it is successful, active, or common, and developing quickly and strongly. = thrive, prosper; ≠ fail ❑ *Business flourished and within six months they were earning 18,000 roubles a day.* ❑ *The Sumerian civilization flourished between 3500 and 2000 BC.* ❑ *the sort of environment in which corruption flourished* **2** [I] If a plant or animal **flourishes**, it grows well or is healthy because the conditions are right for it. = thrive ❑ *The plant flourishes particularly well in slightly harsher climes.* ❑ *bacteria that flourish in damp conditions* ❑ *a long-term management plan that will help wildlife flourish* **3** [T] If you **flourish** an object, you wave it about in a way that makes people notice it. ❑ *He flourished the glass to emphasize the point.*

NOUN [c] (**flourishes**) A **flourish** is the act of waving an object about in a way that makes people notice it. ❑ *He took his cap from under his arm with a flourish and pulled it low over his eyes.*

✪ flour·ish·ing /'flʌrɪʃɪŋ, AmE 'flɜːr-/ ADJ **1** = thriving ❑ *Boston quickly became a flourishing port.* **2** *a flourishing fox population* ❑ *a flourishing career as a freelance writer*

flout /flaʊt/ VERB [T] (**flouts, flouting, flouted**) If you **flout** something such as a law, an order, or an accepted way of behaving, you deliberately do not obey it or follow it. = defy ❑ *illegal campers who persist in flouting the law*

✪ flow ◆◆◇ /floʊ/ VERB, NOUN

VERB [I] (**flows, flowing, flowed**) **1** If a liquid, gas, or electrical current **flows** somewhere, it moves there steadily and continuously. ❑ *A stream flowed gently down into the valley.* ❑ *The current flows into electric motors that drive the wheels.* **2** If a number of people or things **flow** from one place to another, they move there steadily in large groups, usually without stopping. ❑ *Large numbers of refugees continue to flow from the troubled region into the no-man's land.* ❑ *Troops patrol major roads to ensure that traffic flows freely throughout the country.* **3** If information or money **flows** somewhere, it moves freely between people or organizations. ❑ *A lot of this information flowed through other police departments.*

NOUN [c, u] (**flows**) **1** A **flow** is a steady, continuous movement of liquid, gas, or electrical current. ❑ *It works only in the veins, where the blood flow is slower.* ❑ *It should be kept in a darkened room where there is a free flow of warm air.* **2** A **flow** is a steady movement of people or things from one place to another. ❑ *She watched the frantic flow of cars and buses along the street.* **3** If there is a **flow** of information or money, it moves freely between people or organizations. ❑ *the opportunity to control the flow of information*

PHRASE **in full flow** If you say that an activity, or the person who is performing the activity, is **in full flow**, you mean that the activity has started and is being carried out with a great deal of energy and enthusiasm. ❑ *Lunch at Harry's Bar was in full flow when Irene made a splendid entrance.*

✪**flow chart** NOUN [c] (**flow charts**) A **flow chart** or a **flow diagram** is a diagram which represents the sequence of actions in a particular process or activity. ❑ *This flow chart, shown below, summarizes the overall costing process.* ❑ *a flow chart of the process* ❑ *Design a flow chart to explain the registration process.*

flow·er ♦♦◇ /ˈflaʊə/ NOUN, VERB
NOUN [c] (**flowers**) **1** A **flower** is the part of a plant which is often brightly coloured, grows at the end of a stem, and only survives for a short time. ❑ *Each individual flower is tiny.* **2** A **flower** is a stem of a plant that has one or more flowers on it and has been picked, usually with others, for example, to give as a present or to put in a vase. ❑ *a bunch of flowers sent by a new admirer* **3** **Flowers** are small plants that are grown for their flowers as opposed to trees, shrubs, and vegetables. ❑ *a lawned area surrounded by screening plants and flowers*
VERB [i] (**flowers, flowering, flowered**) **1** When a plant or tree **flowers**, its flowers appear and open. ❑ *Their rhododendrons will flower this year for the first time.* **2** When something **flowers**, for example, a political movement or a relationship, it gets stronger and more successful. = blossom ❑ *Their relationship flowered.*

flown /fləʊn/ IRREG FORM **Flown** is the past participle of **fly**.

flu /fluː/ NOUN [u] [also 'the' flu] **Flu** is an illness which is similar to a bad cold but more serious. It often makes you feel very weak and makes your muscles hurt. ❑ *I got the flu.*

✪**fluc·tu·ate** /ˈflʌktʃueɪt/ VERB [i] (**fluctuates, fluctuating, fluctuated**) (*academic word*) If something **fluctuates**, it changes a lot in an irregular way. ❑ *Body temperature can fluctuate if you are ill.* ❑ *Share prices have fluctuated wildly in recent weeks.* ❑ *the fluctuating price of oil*
✪**fluc·tua·tion** /ˌflʌktʃuˈeɪʃən/ NOUN [c, u] (**fluctuations**) ❑ *Don't worry about tiny fluctuations in your weight.* ❑ *Much of the seasonal fluctuation in death rates was caused by cold, the researchers concluded.* ❑ *daily fluctuations in core body temperature*

✪**flu·ent** /ˈfluːənt/ ADJ **1** Someone who is **fluent in** a particular language can speak the language easily and correctly. You can also say that someone speaks **fluent** French, Chinese, or some other language. ❑ *She studied eight foreign languages but is fluent in only six of them.* ❑ *He speaks fluent Russian.* **2** If your speech, reading, or writing is **fluent**, you speak, read, or write easily, smoothly, and clearly with no mistakes. ❑ *He had emerged from being a hesitant and unsure candidate into a fluent debater.*
✪**flu·en·cy** /ˈfluːənsi/ NOUN [u] **1** To work as a translator, you need fluency in at least one foreign language. **2** His son was praised for speeches of remarkable fluency.
✪**flu·ent·ly** /ˈfluːəntli/ ADV **1** He spoke three languages fluently. **2** [fluently with v] ❑ *Alex didn't read fluently till he was nearly seven.*

fluff /flʌf/ NOUN, VERB
NOUN [u] **Fluff** consists of soft threads or fibres in the form of small, light balls or lumps. For example, you can refer to the fur of a small animal as **fluff**. ❑ *The nest contained two chicks: just small grey balls of fluff.*
VERB [T] (**fluffs, fluffing, fluffed**) (*informal*) If you **fluff** something that you are trying to do, you are unsuccessful or you do it badly. ❑ *She fluffed her interview at Harvard.*

✪**flu·id** /ˈfluːɪd/ NOUN, ADJ
NOUN [c, u] (**fluids**) (*formal*) A **fluid** is a liquid. = liquid ❑ *The blood vessels may leak fluid, which distorts vision.* ❑ *Make sure that you drink plenty of fluids.*
ADJ **Fluid** movements or lines or designs are smooth and

graceful. ❑ *His painting became less illustrational and more fluid.*

fluke /fluːk/ NOUN [c] (**flukes**) [usu sing, also 'by' fluke] (*informal*) If you say that something good is a **fluke**, you mean that it happened accidentally rather than by being planned or arranged. ❑ *The discovery was something of a fluke.*

flung /flʌŋ/ IRREG FORM **Flung** is the past tense and past participle of **fling**.

fluo·res·cent /fluəˈresənt/ ADJ **1** A **fluorescent** surface, substance, or colour has a very bright appearance when light is directed onto it, as if it is actually shining itself. ❑ *a piece of fluorescent tape* **2** A **fluorescent** light shines with a very hard, bright light and is usually in the form of a long strip. ❑ *Fluorescent lights flickered, and then the room was brilliantly, blindingly bright.*

flur·ry /ˈflʌri, AmE ˈflɜːri/ NOUN [c] (**flurries**) **1** A **flurry** of something such as activity or excitement is a short intense period of it. ❑ *a flurry of diplomatic activity aimed at ending the war* **2** A **flurry** of something such as snow is a small amount of it that suddenly appears for a short time and moves in a quick, swirling way. ❑ *The Alps expect heavy cloud over the weekend with light snow flurries and strong winds.*

flush /flʌʃ/ VERB, NOUN
VERB [i, T] (**flushes, flushing, flushed**) **1** [i] If you **flush**, your face gets red because you are hot or ill, or because you are feeling a strong emotion such as embarrassment or anger. ❑ *Do you sweat a lot or flush a lot?* **2** [i, T] When someone **flushes** a toilet after using it, they fill the toilet bowl with water in order to clean it, usually by pressing a handle or pulling a chain. You can also say that a toilet **flushes**. ❑ *She flushed the toilet and went back in the bedroom.* **3** [T] If you **flush** something **down** the toilet, you get rid of it by putting it into the toilet bowl and flushing the toilet. ❑ *He was found trying to flush the pills down the toilet.* **4** [T] If you **flush** a part of your body, you clean it or make it healthier by using a large amount of liquid to get rid of dirt or harmful substances. = cleanse ❑ *Flush the eye with clean cold water for at least 15 minutes.* **5** [T] If you **flush** dirt or a harmful substance **out** of a place, you get rid of it by using a large amount of liquid. ❑ *That won't flush out all the sewage, but it should unclog some stinking drains.* **6** [T] If you **flush** people or animals **out** of a place where they are hiding, you find or capture them by forcing them to come out of that place. ❑ *They flushed them out of their hiding places.*
PHRASAL VERB **flush out Flush out** means the same as **flush** VERB 4. ❑ *an 'alternative' therapy that gently flushes out the colon to remove toxins*
NOUN [c] (**flushes**) **1** If a **flush** appears on someone's face, it gets red because they are hot or ill, or because they are feeling a strong emotion such as embarrassment or anger. ❑ *There was a slight flush on his cheeks.* **2** The **flush** of a toilet is when someone fills the toilet bowl with water in order to clean it after using it, usually by pressing a handle or pulling a chain. ❑ *He heard the flush of a toilet.*
flushed /flʌʃt/ ADJ ❑ *Her face was flushed with anger.*

flut·ter /ˈflʌtə/ VERB, NOUN
VERB [i, T] (**flutters, fluttering, fluttered**) **1** [i, T] If something thin or light **flutters**, or if you **flutter** it, it moves up and down or from side to side with a lot of quick, light movements. ❑ *Her chiffon skirt was fluttering in the night breeze.* ❑ *a butterfly fluttering its wings* **2** [i] If something light such as a small bird or a piece of paper **flutters** somewhere, it moves through the air with small quick movements. ❑ *The paper fluttered to the floor.*
NOUN [c] (**flutters**) A **flutter** is the action of something moving up and down or from side to side with a lot of quick, light movements. ❑ *a flutter of white cloth*

flux /flʌks/ NOUN [u] If something is in a state **of flux**, it is constantly changing. ❑ *Education remains in a state of flux which will take some time to settle down.*

fly ♦♦♦ /flaɪ/ NOUN, VERB
NOUN [c] (**flies**) **1** A **fly** is a small insect with two wings. There are many kinds of flies, and the most common are black in colour. ❑ *Flies buzzed at the animals' swishing tails.*

F

2 The front opening on a pair of trousers is referred to as the **flies** or **fly**. It usually consists of a zip or row of buttons behind a band of cloth. ❑ *I'm the kind of person who checks to see if my flies are undone.*

PHRASES **wouldn't hurt a fly** (*emphasis*) If you say that someone wouldn't **hurt a fly** or wouldn't **harm a fly**, you are emphasizing that they are very kind and gentle. ❑ *Ray wouldn't hurt a fly.*

on the fly [V + on the fly] (*mainly AmE*) If you do something **on the fly**, you do it quickly or automatically, without planning it in advance. ❑ *You've got to be able to make decisions on the fly as deadlines loom.*

VERB [T, I] (**flies, flying, flew, flown**) **1** [T, I] When something such as a bird, insect, or aircraft **flies**, it moves through the air. ❑ *The planes flew through the clouds.* **2** [I] If you **fly** somewhere, you travel there in an aircraft. ❑ *He flew to Los Angeles.* ❑ *He flew back to London.* **3** [I, T] When someone **flies** an aircraft, they control its movement in the air. ❑ *Parker had successfully flown both aircraft.* ❑ *He flew a small plane to Cuba.* ❑ *I learned to fly in Vietnam.* **4** [T] To **fly** someone or something somewhere means to take or send them there in an aircraft. ❑ *It may be possible to fly the women and children out on Thursday.* **5** [I] If something such as your hair **is flying** about, it is moving about freely and loosely in the air. ❑ *His long, uncovered hair flew back in the wind.* **6** [I, T] If you **fly** a flag or if it **is flying**, you display it at the top of a pole. ❑ *They flew the flag of the African National Congress.* **7** [I] If you say that someone or something **flies** in a particular direction, you are emphasizing that they move there with a lot of speed or force. ❑ *She flew to their bedsides when they were ill.*

PHRASES **let fly** If you **let fly**, you attack someone, either physically by hitting them, or with words by insulting them. ❑ *A simmering dispute ended with her letting fly with a stream of obscenities.*

send flying or **go flying** If you **send** someone or something **flying** or if they **go flying**, they move through the air and fall down with a lot of force. ❑ *The blow sent the young man flying.*

PHRASAL VERB **fly into** If you **fly into** a bad temper or a panic, you suddenly become very angry or anxious and show this in your behaviour. ❑ *Losing a game would cause him to fly into a rage.*

fly•ing /ˈflaɪɪŋ/ NOUN [U] ❑ *a flying instructor*
✦ **to fly in the face of** → see **face**; **fly off the handle** → see **handle**; **when pigs fly** → see **pig**; **sparks fly** → see **spark**; **time flies** → see **time**

fly•er /ˈflaɪə/ also **flier** NOUN [C] (**flyers**) **1** A **flyer** is a pilot of an aircraft. ❑ *The American flyers sprinted for their planes and got into the cockpit.* **2** You can refer to someone who travels by plane as a **flyer**. ❑ *regular business flyers* **3** A **flyer** is a small printed notice which is used to advertise a particular company, service, or event. ❑ *Thousands of flyers advertising the tour were handed out during the festival.*

foam /fəʊm/ NOUN [U, C] (**foams**) **1** [U] **Foam** consists of a mass of small bubbles that are formed when air and a liquid are mixed together. = froth ❑ *The water curved round the rocks in great bursts of foam.* **2** [C, U] **Foam** is used to refer to various kinds of manufactured products which have a soft, light texture like a thick liquid. = cream ❑ *shaving foam* **3** [C, U] **Foam** or **foam rubber** is soft rubber full of small holes which is used, for example, to make mattresses and cushions. ❑ *modern three-piece suites filled with foam rubber*

fo•cal point /ˈfəʊkəl pɔɪnt/ NOUN [C] (**focal points**) The **focal point** of something is the thing that people concentrate on or pay most attention to. ❑ *The focal point for the town's many visitors is the museum.*

✪ fo•cus ✦✦◇ /ˈfəʊkəs/ VERB, NOUN (*academic word*)
VERB [I, T] (**focuses, focusing** or **focussing, focused** or **focussed**) **1** [I, T] If you **focus on** a particular topic or if your attention is **focused on** it, you concentrate on it and think about it, discuss it, or deal with it, rather than dealing with other topics. = concentrate ❑ *The research effort has focused on tracing the effects of growing levels of five compounds.* ❑ *He is currently focusing on assessment and*

development. ❑ *The company decided to focus exclusively on the home market.* ❑ *Today he was able to focus his message exclusively on the economy.* **2** [I, T] If you **focus** your eyes or if your eyes **focus**, your eyes adjust so that you can clearly see the thing that you want to look at. If you **focus** a camera, telescope, or other instrument, you adjust it so that you can see clearly through it. ❑ *Kelly couldn't focus his eyes well enough to tell if the figure was male or female.* ❑ *His eyes slowly began to focus on what looked like a small dark ball.* **3** [T] If you **focus** rays of light on a particular point, you pass them through a lens or reflect them from a mirror so that they meet at that point. ❑ *Magnetic coils focus the electron beams into fine spots.*

NOUN [C, U] (**focuses**) **1** [C] The **focus** of something is the main topic or main thing that it is concerned with. ❑ *The UN's role in promoting peace is increasingly the focus of international attention.* ❑ *The new system is the focus of controversy.* ❑ *The ethnic problem in the country is crucial but it is not the primary focus of the negotiations.* **2** [C] Your **focus** on something is the special attention that you pay it. ❑ *He said his sudden focus on foreign policy was not motivated by presidential politics.* **3** [U] If you say that something has a **focus**, you mean that you can see a purpose in it. ❑ *Somehow, though, their latest CD has a focus that the others have lacked.* **4** [U] You use **focus** to refer to the fact of adjusting your eyes or a camera, telescope, or other instrument, and to the degree to which you can see clearly. ❑ *His focus switched to the little white ball.*

PHRASES **in focus** **1** If an image or a camera, telescope, or other instrument is **in focus**, the edges of what you see are clear and sharp. ❑ *Pictures should be in focus, with realistic colours and well composed groups.* **2** If something is **in focus**, it is being discussed or its purpose and nature are clear. ❑ *We want to keep the real issues in focus.*

out of focus If an image or a camera, telescope, or other instrument is **out of focus**, the edges of what you see are unclear. ❑ *In some of the pictures the subjects are out of focus while the background is sharp.*

foe•tus /ˈfiːtəs/ also **fetus** NOUN [C] (**foetuses**) A **foetus** is an animal or human being in its later stages of development before it is born. ❑ *Pregnant women who are heavy drinkers risk damaging the unborn foetus.*

fog /fɒg/ NOUN [C, U, SING] (**fogs**) **1** [C, U] When there is **fog**, there are tiny drops of water in the air which form a thick cloud and make it difficult to see things. ❑ *The crash happened in thick fog.* **2** [SING] A **fog** is an unpleasant cloud of something such as smoke inside a building or room. ❑ *a fog of stale cigarette smoke*

foil /fɔɪl/ NOUN, VERB
NOUN [U] **Foil** consists of sheets of metal as thin as paper. It is used to wrap food in. ❑ *Pour cider around the meat and cover with foil.*
VERB [T] (**foils, foiling, foiled**) (*journalism*) If you **foil** someone's plan or attempt to do something, for example, to commit a crime, you succeed in stopping them from doing what they want. = thwart ❑ *A brave police officer foiled an armed robbery by grabbing the raider's shotgun.*

fold ✦◇◇ /fəʊld/ VERB, NOUN
VERB [T, I] (**folds, folding, folded**) **1** [T] If you **fold** something such as a piece of paper or cloth, you bend it so that one part covers another part, often pressing the edge so that it stays in place. ❑ *He folded the paper carefully.* ❑ *Fold the omelette in half.* **2** [I, T] If a piece of furniture or equipment **folds** or if you can **fold** it, you can make it smaller by bending or closing parts of it. ❑ *The back of the bench folds forward to make a table.* ❑ *This portable seat folds flat for easy storage.* **3** [T] If you **fold** your arms or hands, you bring them together and cross or link them, for example, over your chest. ❑ *Meer folded his arms over his chest and turned his head away.*

PHRASAL VERB **fold up** **1** **Fold up** means the same as fold VERB 2. ❑ *When not in use it folds up out of the way.* **2** If you **fold** something **up**, you make it into a smaller, neater shape by folding it, usually several times. ❑ *She folded it up, and tucked it into her purse.*

NOUN [C] (**folds**) **1** A **fold** in a piece of paper or cloth is a bend that you make in it when you put one part of it over another part and press the edge. = crease ❏ *Make another fold and turn the ends together.* **2** The **folds** in a piece of cloth are the curved shapes which are formed when it is not hanging or lying flat. ❏ *The priest fumbled in the folds of his gown.*

fold·er /ˈfəʊldə/ NOUN [C] (**folders**) **1** A **folder** is a thin piece of cardboard in which you can keep loose papers. **2** (*computing*) A **folder** is a group of files that are stored together on a computer.

folk ◆◇◇ /fəʊk/ NOUN, ADJ

> **Folk** can also be used as the plural form for meaning 1 of the noun.

NOUN [PL, U] (**folks**) **1** [PL] You can refer to people as **folk** or **folks**. = people ❏ *Country folk can tell you that there are certain places which animals avoid.* ❏ *These are the folks from the local TV station.* **2** [PL] (*informal*) You can refer to your close family, especially your mother and father, as your **folks**. ❏ *I've been avoiding my folks lately.* **3** [PL] (*informal*) You can use **folks** as a term of address when you are talking to several people. ❏ *'It's a question of money, folks,' I said.* **4** [U] **Folk** is music which is traditional or typical of a particular community or nation. ❏ *a variety of music including classical and folk*

ADJ **1** [folk + N] **Folk** art and customs are traditional or typical of a particular community or nation. ❏ *South American folk art* **2** [folk + N] **Folk** music is music which is traditional or typical of a particular community or nation.

❂fol·low ◆◆◆ /ˈfɒləʊ/ VERB

VERB [I, T] (**follows, following, followed**) **1** [I, T] If you **follow** someone who is going somewhere, you move along behind them because you want to go to the same place. ❏ *We followed him up the steps into a large hall.* ❏ *Please follow me, madam.* ❏ *They took him into a small room and I followed.* **2** [T] If you **follow** someone who is going somewhere, you move along behind them without their knowledge, in order to catch them or find out where they are going. = trail ❏ *She realized that the Mercedes was following her.* **3** [T] If you **follow** someone to a place where they have recently gone and where they are now, you go to join them there. ❏ *He followed Janice to New York, where she was preparing an exhibition.* **4** [I, T] An event, activity, or period of time that **follows** a particular thing happens or comes after that thing, at a later time. ❏ *the rioting and looting that followed the verdict* ❏ *Other problems may follow.* **5** [T] If you **follow** one thing with another, you do or say the second thing after you have done or said the first thing. ❏ *Her first major role was in Martin Scorsese's 'Goodfellas' and she followed this with a part in Spike Lee's 'Jungle Fever'.* **6** [I, T] If it **follows** that a particular thing is the case, that thing is a logical result of something else being true or being the case. ❏ *Just because a bird does not breed one year, it does not follow that it will fail the next.* ❏ *If children acquire self-esteem as a consequence of doing well in school, it does not necessarily follow that raising their self-esteem will improve their academic achievement.* ❏ *If the explanation is right, two things follow.* ❏ *It is easy to see the conclusions described in the text follow from this equation.* **7** [I, T] If you refer to the words that **follow** or **followed**, you are referring to the words that come next or came next in a piece of writing or speech. ❏ *What follows is an eye-witness account.* ❏ *There followed a list of places where Hans intended to visit.* ❏ *General analysis is followed by five case studies.* **8** [T] If you **follow** a path, route, or set of signs, you go somewhere using the path, route, or signs to direct you. ❏ *If they followed the road, they would be certain to reach a village.* ❏ *All we had to do was follow the map.* **9** [T] If something such as a path or river **follows** a particular route or line, it goes along that route or line. ❏ *Our route follows the Pacific coast through densely populated neighbourhoods.* **10** [T] If you **follow** something with your eyes, or if your eyes **follow** it, you watch it as it moves or you look along its route or course. ❏ *Ann's eyes followed a police car as it drove slowly past.* **11** [T] Something that **follows** a particular course of development happens or develops in that way. ❏ *His release turned out to follow the pattern set by that of the other six hostages.* **12** [T] If you **follow** someone in what you do, you do the same thing or

job as they did previously. ❏ *He followed his father and became a surgeon.* **13** [T] If you **follow** advice, an instruction, or a recipe, you act or do something in the way that it indicates. ❏ *Take care to follow the instructions carefully.* **14** [I, T] If you **follow** what someone else has done, you do it too because you think it is a good thing or because you want to copy them. ❏ *His admiration for the athlete did not extend to the point where he would follow his example in taking drugs.* **15** [T] If you **follow** something, you take an interest in it and keep informed about what happens. ❏ *the millions of people who follow football because they genuinely love it* **16** [T] If you **follow** a particular religion or political belief, you have that religion or belief. ❏ *'Do you follow any particular religion?'—'Yes, we're all Hindus.'* **17** [I, T] If you are able to **follow** something such as an explanation or the story of a film, you understand it as it continues and develops. = understand ❏ *Can you follow the plot so far?* ❏ *I'm sorry, I don't follow.*

PHRASES **as follows** You use **as follows** in writing or speech to introduce something such as a list, description, or an explanation. ❏ *The winners are as follows: E. Walker; R. Foster; R. Gates; A. Mackintosh.*

followed by You use **followed by** to say what comes after something else in a list or ordered set of things. ❏ *Potatoes are still the most popular food, followed by white bread.*

PHRASAL VERBS **follow through** If you **follow through** an action, plan, or idea or **follow through** with it, you continue doing or thinking about it until you have done everything possible. = pursue ❏ *The leadership has been unwilling to follow through the implications of these ideas.* ❏ *I was trained to be an actress but I didn't follow it through.*

follow up **1** If you **follow up** one thing with another, you do or say the second thing after you have done or said the first thing. ❏ *The book proved such a success that the authors followed it up with 'The Messianic Legacy'.* **2** If you **follow up** something that has been said, suggested, or discovered, you try to find out more about it or take action about it. = investigate ❏ *State police are following up several leads.* **3** → See also **follow-up**
→ See also **following**

✦ **follow in someone's footsteps** → see **footstep**; **follow your nose** → see **nose**; **follow suit** → see **suit**

fol·low·er /ˈfɒləʊə/ NOUN [C] (**followers**) A **follower** of a particular person, group, or belief is someone who supports or admires this person, group, or belief. = supporter ❏ *followers of the Zulu Inkatha movement*

❂fol·low·ing ◆◆◇ /ˈfɒləʊɪŋ/ PREP, ADJ, PRON, NOUN
PREP **Following** a particular event means after that event. = after ❏ *In the centuries following Christ's death, Christians genuinely believed the world was about to end.* ❏ *Following a day of medical research, the conference focused on educational practices.*

ADJ **1** [DET + following] The **following** day, week, or year is the day, week, or year after the one you have just mentioned. = next ❏ *The following day the picture appeared on the front pages of every newspaper in the world.* ❏ *We went to dinner the following Monday evening.* ❏ *The following year she joined the Royal Opera House.* **2** [DET + following] You use **following** to refer to something that you are about to mention. ❏ *Write down the following information: name of product, type, date purchased and price.* ❏ *The method of helping such patients is explained in the following chapters.*

PRON ['the' following] The **following** refers to the thing or things that you are about to mention. ❏ *The following is a paraphrase of what was said.* ❏ *One serving of any of the following would provide an adult's complete daily requirement of salt.*

NOUN [C] (**followings**) A person or organization that has a **following** has a group of people who support or admire their beliefs or actions. ❏ *Australian rugby league enjoys a huge following in New Zealand.*

follow-up NOUN [C, U] (**follow-ups**) A **follow-up** is something that is done to continue or add to something done previously. ❏ *They are recording a follow-up to their successful 1989 album.*

fol·ly /ˈfɒli/ NOUN [C, U] (**follies**) If you say that a particular

F

WORDS IN CONTEXT: FOOD

There is clear evidence to show that excessive consumption of junk food has a negative effect on our health. Consequently, in order to protect people, the advertising of junk food should be banned.

To what extent do you agree or disagree?

The growth in **fast-food outlets** and the consumption of **ready meals** and **processed food** generally over the past few decades has impacted on the health of people across all generations. Along with an alarming increase in **childhood obesity**, **health experts** have also highlighted the impact on adults of **heart disease**, **high blood pressure**, **food allergies** and **diabetes**.

How to combat this **epidemic** is a challenge facing both **health professionals** and policy makers. Some believe that the advertising of junk food should be regulated or banned in the same way as cigarettes and alcohol.

An additional solution lies in educating people into changing their **eating habits**. This includes simplifying the information about the ingredients on **food packaging** through to formal educational initiatives. Finally, some believe that governments should regulate food production, such as restricting the use of **food additives**.

I believe all three approaches have their merits. Controlling the amount of salt or **E-numbers** permitted in processed food would certainly play its part in making our food healthier. In addition, we could certainly ban the advertising of food generally during TV programmes aimed at young children. However, ultimately, the answer lies in encouraging people to eat a more **balanced diet**. In particular, I think having compulsory cookery lessons at school is a fun introduction to developing **healthy eating habits**. Teaching children how to eat more **nutritious food** by using **fresh ingredients** in simple **recipes** will give them the essential skills that will support them through life.

---

action or way of behaving is **folly** or a **folly**, you mean that it is foolish. ❑ *It's sheer folly to build nuclear power stations in a country that has dozens of earthquakes every year.*

fond /fɒnd/ ADJ (**fonder, fondest**) **1** [V-LINK + fond 'of' N] If you are **fond of** someone, you feel affection for them. ❑ *I am very fond of Michael.* **2** [fond + N] You use **fond** to describe people or their behaviour when they show affection. ❑ *a fond father* **3** [V-LINK + fond 'of' N/-ING] If you are **fond of** something, you like it or you like doing it very much. ❑ *He was fond of marmalade.* **4** [fond + N] If you have **fond** memories of someone or something, you remember them with pleasure. = pleasant ❑ *I have very fond memories of living in our village.* **5** [fond + N] You use **fond** to describe hopes, wishes, or beliefs which you think are foolish because they seem unlikely to be fulfilled. ❑ *My fond hope is that we will be ready by Christmastime.*
fond·ness /ˈfɒndnəs/ NOUN [U] **1** *a great fondness for children* **2** *I've always had a fondness for chocolate cake.*
fond·ly /ˈfɒndli/ ADV **1** *Liz saw their eyes meet fondly across the table.* **2** *My dad took us there when I was about four and I remembered it fondly.* **3** *I fondly imagined that surgery meant a few stitches and an overnight stay in hospital.*

food ♦♦♦ /fuːd/ NOUN
NOUN [C, U] (**foods**) **Food** is what people and animals eat. ❑ *Enjoy your food.* ❑ *frozen foods*
PHRASE **food for thought** If you give someone **food for thought**, you make them think carefully about something. ❑ *Her speech offers much food for thought.*
→ See also **junk food**

✪food chain NOUN [C] (**food chains**) [usu sing] The **food chain** is a series of living things which are linked to each other because each thing feeds on the one next to it in the series. ❑ *The whole food chain is affected by the overuse of chemicals in agriculture.* ❑ *Droppings from seabirds could be introducing radioactive isotopes into the food chain.* ❑ *animals further up the food chain*

fool ♦♢♢ /fuːl/ NOUN, VERB
NOUN [C] (**fools**) (*disapproval*) If you call someone a **fool**, you are indicating that you think they are not at all sensible and show a lack of good judgment. = idiot ❑ *'You fool!' she shouted.*
PHRASES **make a fool of someone** If you **make a fool of** someone, you make them seem silly by telling people about something stupid that they have done, or by

tricking them. ❑ *Your brother is making a fool of you.*
make a fool of yourself If you **make a fool of** yourself, you behave in a way that makes other people think that you are silly or lacking in good judgment. ❑ *He was drinking and making a fool of himself.*

play the fool or **act the fool** If you **play the fool** or **act the fool**, you behave in a playful, childish, and foolish way, usually in order to make other people laugh. ❑ *They used to play the fool together, calling each other silly names and giggling.*
VERB [T, I] (**fools, fooling, fooled**) **1** [T] If someone **fools** you, they deceive or trick you. = trick, con ❑ *Art dealers fool a lot of people.* ❑ *Don't be fooled by his appearance.* **2** [I] If you say that a person **is fooling with** something or someone, you mean that the way they are behaving is likely to cause problems. ❑ *What are you doing fooling with such a staggering sum of money?*
PHRASAL VERB **fool around** If you **fool around**, you behave in a silly, dangerous, or irresponsible way. ❑ *They were fooling around on an Army firing range.*

fool·ish /ˈfuːlɪʃ/ ADJ **1** If someone's behaviour or action is **foolish**, it is not sensible and shows a lack of good judgment. ❑ *It would be foolish to raise hopes unnecessarily.* **2** If you look or feel **foolish**, you look or feel so silly or ridiculous that people are likely to laugh at you. = ridiculous ❑ *I just stood there feeling foolish and watching him.*
fool·ish·ly /ˈfuːlɪʃli/ ADV **1** *He admitted that he had acted foolishly.* **2** [foolishly after V] ❑ *He saw me standing there, grinning foolishly at him.*
fool·ish·ness /ˈfuːlɪʃnəs/ NOUN [U] ❑ *They don't accept any foolishness when it comes to spending money.*

✪foot ♦♦♦ /fʊt/ NOUN, ADJ
NOUN [C, SING] (**feet**) **1** [C] Your **feet** are the parts of your body that are at the ends of your legs, and that you stand on. ❑ *She stamped her foot again.* ❑ *a foot injury* **2** [C] A **foot** is a unit for measuring length, height, or depth, and is equal to 12 inches or 30.48 centimetres. When you are giving measurements, the form 'foot' is often used as the plural instead of the usual plural form 'feet'. ❑ *This beautiful and curiously shaped lake lies at around fifteen thousand feet.* ❑ *He occupies a cell 10 foot long, 6 foot wide and 10 foot high.* ❑ *a shopping and leisure complex of one million square feet* ❑ *He was about six foot tall.* **3** [SING] The

foot of something is the part that is farthest from its top. = bottom ❑ *David called to the children from the foot of the stairs.* ❑ *the foot of the hill* **4** [SING] **The foot** of a bed is the end nearest to the feet of the person lying in it. ❑ *Friends stood at the foot of the bed, looking at her with serious faces.*

PHRASES **get cold feet** If you get **cold feet** about something, you become nervous or frightened about it because you think it will fail. ❑ *The Government is getting cold feet about the reforms.*

find one's feet If you say that someone **is finding** their **feet** in a new situation, you mean that they are starting to feel confident and to deal with things successfully. ❑ *I don't know anyone here but I am sure I will manage when I find my feet.*

have your feet on the ground or **keep your feet on the ground** (*approval*) If you say that someone has their **feet on the ground**, you approve of the fact that they have a sensible and practical attitude towards life, and do not have unrealistic ideas. ❑ *In that respect he needs to keep his feet on the ground and not get carried away.*

on foot If you go somewhere **on foot**, you walk, rather than using any form of transport. ❑ *We rowed ashore, then explored the island on foot for the rest of the day.*

on your feet **1** If you are **on** your **feet**, you are standing up. ❑ *Everyone was on their feet applauding wildly.* **2** If you say that someone or something is **on** their **feet** again after an illness or difficult period, you mean that they have recovered and are back to normal. ❑ *You need someone to take the pressure off and help you get back on your feet.*

land on your feet If you say that someone always **lands** on their **feet**, you mean that they are always successful or lucky, although they do not seem to achieve this by their own efforts. ❑ *He has good looks and charm, and always lands on his feet.*

put your foot down **1** If someone **puts** their **foot down**, they use their authority in order to stop something from happening. ❑ *He had planned to go skiing on his own in March but his wife had decided to put her foot down.* **2** (*BrE*) If someone **puts** their **foot down** when they are driving, they drive as fast as they can.

put your foot in it (*informal*) If someone **puts** their **foot in it** or **puts** their **foot in** their **mouth**, they accidentally do or say something which embarrasses or offends people. ❑ *Our chairman has really put his foot in it, poor man, though he doesn't know it.*

put your feet up If you **put** your **feet up**, you relax or have a rest, especially by sitting or lying with your feet supported off the ground. = rest ❑ *After supper he'd put his feet up and read.*

not put a foot wrong (*mainly BrE*) If you never **put a foot wrong**, you never make any mistakes. ❑ *When he's around, we never put a foot wrong.*

set foot somewhere (*emphasis*) If you say that someone **sets foot** in a place, you mean that they enter it or reach it, and you are emphasizing the significance of their action. If you say that someone **never sets foot** in a place, you are emphasizing that they never go there. ❑ *the day the first man set foot on the moon*

stand on your own two feet If someone has to **stand on** their **own two feet**, they have to be independent and manage their life without help from other people. ❑ *My father didn't mind whom I married, so long as I could stand on my own two feet and wasn't dependent on my husband.*

get off on the wrong foot If someone **gets off on the wrong foot** in a new situation, they make a bad start by doing something in completely the wrong way. ❑ *Even though they called the election and had been preparing for it for some time, they got off on the wrong foot.*

ADJ **1** [foot + N] A **foot** brake or **foot** pump is operated by your foot rather than by your hand. ❑ *I tried to reach the foot brakes but I couldn't.* **2** [foot + N] A **foot** patrol or **foot** soldiers walk rather than travelling in vehicles or on horseback. ❑ *Paratroopers and foot-soldiers entered the building on the government's behalf.*
→ See also **footing**
✦ **foot in the door** → see **door**; **drag your feet** → see **drag**; **vote with your feet** → see **vote**

foot·age /ˈfʊtɪdʒ/ NOUN [u] **Footage** of a particular event

is a film of it or the part of a film which shows this event. ❑ *They are planning to show exclusive footage from this summer's festivals.*

foot·ball ◆◆◇ /ˈfʊtbɔːl/ NOUN [u, c] (**footballs**) **1** [u] (*BrE*; in *AmE*, use **soccer**) Football is a game played by two teams of eleven players using a round ball. Players kick the ball to each other and try to score goals by kicking the ball into a large net. **2** [c] A **football** is a ball that is used for playing football. ❑ *a heavy leather football* **3** [u] (*AmE*; in *BrE*, use **American football**) Football is a game played by two teams of eleven players using an oval ball. Players carry the ball in their hands or throw it to each other as they try to score goals that are called touchdowns. ❑ *Two blocks beyond our school was a field where boys played football.*

foot·ball·er /ˈfʊtbɔːlə/ (*BrE*; in *AmE*, use **soccer player**) NOUN [c] (**footballers**) A **footballer** is a person who plays football (or soccer in American English), especially as a profession.

foot·hold /ˈfʊthəʊld/ NOUN [c] (**footholds**) **1** A **foothold** is a strong or favourable position from which further advances or progress may be made. ❑ *Businesses are investing millions of dollars to gain a foothold in this new market.* **2** A **foothold** is a place such as a small hole or area of rock where you can safely put your foot when climbing. ❑ *He lowered his legs until he felt he had a solid foothold on the rock face beneath him.*

foot·ing /ˈfʊtɪŋ/ NOUN [u] **1** If something is put on a particular **footing**, it is defined, established, or changed in a particular way, often so that it is able to develop or exist successfully. = basis ❑ *The new law will put official corruption on the same legal footing as treason.* **2** If you are **on** a particular kind of **footing** with someone, you have that kind of relationship with them. = basis ❑ *They decided to put their relationship on a more formal footing.* **3** You refer to your **footing** when you are referring to your position and how securely your feet are placed on the ground. For example, if you lose your **footing**, your feet slip and you fall. ❑ *He was cautious of his footing, wary of the edge.*

✪ **foot·note** /ˈfʊtnəʊt/ NOUN [c] (**footnotes**) **1** A **footnote** is a note at the bottom of a page in a book which provides more detailed information about something that is mentioned on that page. ❑ *Chaumette then added a footnote to the document.* ❑ *a footnote in the Byzantine Book of Hours* **2** If you refer to what you are saying as a **footnote**, you mean that you are adding some information that is related to what you have just been mentioning. ❑ *As a footnote, I should add that there was one point on which his bravado was more than justified.* **3** If you describe an event as a **footnote**, you mean that it is fairly unimportant although it will probably be remembered. ❑ *I'm afraid that his name will now become a footnote in history.*

foot·path /ˈfʊtpɑːθ, -pæθ/ NOUN [c] (**footpaths**) A **footpath** is a path for people to walk on, especially in the countryside.

foot·print /ˈfʊtprɪnt/ NOUN [c] (**footprints**) A **footprint** is a mark in the shape of a foot that a person or animal makes in or on a surface. ❑ *His footprints were clearly evident in the heavy dust.*

foot·step /ˈfʊtstep/ NOUN
NOUN [c] (**footsteps**) A **footstep** is the sound or mark that is made by someone walking each time their foot touches the ground. ❑ *I heard footsteps outside.*
PHRASE **follow in someone's footsteps** If you **follow in** someone's **footsteps**, you do the same things as they did earlier. ❑ *My father is extremely proud that I followed in his footsteps and became a doctor.*

for ◆◆◆ /fə, STRONG fɔː/ PREP, ADV
PREP **1** If something is **for** someone, they are intended to have it or benefit from it. ❑ *Isn't that enough for you?* ❑ *a table for two* **2** If you work or do a job **for** someone, you are employed by them. ❑ *I knew he worked for a security firm.* ❑ *Have you had any experience writing for radio?* **3** If you speak or act **for** a particular group or organization, you represent them. ❑ *She appears nightly on the television news,*

F

speaking for the State Department. **4** If someone does something **for** you, they do it so that you do not have to do it. ❑ *If your chemist doesn't stock the product you want, have them order it for you.* ❑ *I hold a door open for an old person.* **5** [ADJ/N + for] If you feel a particular emotion **for** someone, you feel it on their behalf. ❑ *This is the best thing you've ever done – I am so happy for you!* **6** [ADJ/N + for] If you feel a particular emotion **for** someone or something, they are the object of that emotion, and you feel it when you think about them. ❑ *John, I'm sorry for Steve, but I think you've made the right decisions.* **7** You use **for** after words such as 'time', 'space', 'money', or 'energy' when you say how much there is or whether there is enough of it in order to be able to do or use a particular thing. ❑ *Many new trains have space for wheelchair users.* ❑ *a huge room with plenty of room for books* **8** You use **for** when you make a statement about something in order to say how it affects or relates to someone, or what their attitude to it is. ❑ *What matters for most scientists is money and facilities.* ❑ *For her, books were as necessary to life as bread.* **9** [for + N + to-INF] After some adjective, noun, and verb phrases, you use **for** to introduce the subject of the action indicated by the following infinitive verb. ❑ *It might be possible for a single woman to be accepted as a foster parent.* ❑ *I had made arrangements for my affairs to be dealt with by one of my children.* **10** [with NEG] (*informal*) If you say that something is **not for** you, you mean that you do not enjoy it or that it is not suitable for you. ❑ *Wendy decided the sport was not for her.* **11** [for + N + to-INF] If it is **for** you to do something, it is your responsibility or right to do it. ❑ *I wish you would come back to Washington with us, but that's for you to decide.* **12** **For** is the preposition that is used after some nouns, adjectives, or verbs in order to introduce what information or to indicate what a quality, thing, or action relates to. ❑ *Reduced-calorie cheese is a great substitute for cream cheese.* ❑ *Car park owners should be legally responsible for protecting vehicles.* **13** If a word or expression has the same meaning as another word or expression, you can say that the first one is another word or expression **for** the second one. ❑ *The technical term for sunburn is erythema.* **14** You use **for** in a piece of writing when you mention information which will be found somewhere else. ❑ *For further information on the life of William James Sidis, see Amy Wallace, 'The Prodigy'.* **15** **For** is used in conditional sentences, in expressions such as '**if not for**' and '**were it not for**', to introduce the only thing which prevents the main part of the sentence from being true. **if not for** **were it not for** ❑ *If not for John, Brian wouldn't have learned the truth.* ❑ *The earth would be a frozen ball if it were not for the radiant heat of the sun.* **16** [for + N/-ING] You use **for** when you state or explain the purpose of an object, action, or activity. ❑ *drug users who use unsterile equipment for injections of drugs* ❑ *The knife for cutting sausage was sitting in the sink.* **17** [N + for + N/-ING] You use **for** after nouns expressing reason or cause. ❑ *He's soon to make a speech explaining his reasons for going.* ❑ *The local hospital could find no physical cause for Sumner's problems.* **18** If something is **for** sale, hire, or use, it is available to be sold, hired, or used. ❑ *Freshwater fish for sale.* ❑ *a room for rent* **19** If you do something **for** a particular occasion, you do it on that occasion or to celebrate that occasion. ❑ *He asked his daughter what she would like for her birthday.* **20** If you leave **for** a particular place or if you take a bus, train, plane, or boat **for** a place, you are going there. ❑ *They would be leaving for Rio early the next morning.* **21** [for + AMOUNT] You use **for** to say how long something lasts or continues. ❑ *The toaster was on for more than an hour.* ❑ *They talked for a bit.* **22** [for + AMOUNT] You use **for** to say how far something extends. ❑ *We drove on for a few miles.* **23** [for + AMOUNT] If something is bought, sold, or done **for** a particular amount of money, that amount of money is its price. ❑ *We got the bus back to Tange for 30 cents.* ❑ *The Martins sold their house for about 1.4 million dollars.* **24** If something is planned **for** a particular time, it is planned to happen then. ❑ *the Baltimore Boat Show, planned for January 21–29* ❑ *The designer will be unveiling her latest fashions for autumn and winter.* **25** You use **for** when you say that an aspect of something or someone is surprising in relation to

other aspects of them. ❑ *He was tall for an eight-year-old.* **26** You use **for** with 'every' when you are stating a ratio, to introduce one of the things in the ratio. ❑ *For every farm job that is lost, two or three other jobs in the area are put at risk.* **27** [N + for + N] You can use **for** in expressions such as **pound for pound** or **mile for mile** when you are making comparisons between the values or qualities of different things. ❑ *the Antarctic, mile for mile one of the planet's most lifeless areas* **28** If you say that you are **for** a particular activity, you mean that this is what you want or intend to do. ❑ *Right, who's for a toasted sandwich then?* **29** If you are **for** something, you agree with it or support it. ❑ *Are you for or against public transport?* **30** [N/V + for + N] You use **for** after words such as 'argue', 'case', 'evidence', or 'vote' in order to introduce the thing that is being supported or proved. ❑ *Another union has voted for industrial action in support of a pay claim.* ❑ *The case for nuclear power is impressive.* **PHRASES** **for the first time** or **for the last time** You use expressions such as **for the first time** and **for the last time** when you are talking about how often something has happened before. ❑ *He was married for the second time.* **all for** If you say that you are **all for** doing something, you agree or strongly believe that it should be done, but you are also often suggesting that other people disagree with you or that there are practical difficulties. ❑ *He is all for players earning what they can while they are in the game.* **ADV** [for after V] You use **for** after verbs such as 'argue' or 'vote' to say that someone acted in support of something or in agreement with something. ❑ *833 delegates voted for, and only 432 against.* ✦ **as for** → see **as**; **but for** → see **but**; **for all** → see **all**

USAGE NOTE

for

You do not use **for** with an '-ing' form when you are saying when someone does something. You do not say, for example, '~~He went to the city for finding work~~'. You say 'He went to the city **to find** work.'

*He had to hurry **to reach** the next place on his schedule.*

---

for·age /ˈfɒrɪdʒ, AmE ˈfɔːr-/ VERB [I] (**forages**, **foraging**, **foraged**) **1** If someone **forages for** something, they search for it in a busy way. ❑ *They were forced to forage for clothing and fuel.* **2** When animals **forage**, they search for food. ❑ *We disturbed a wild boar that had been foraging by the roadside.*

for·ay /ˈfɒreɪ, AmE ˈfɔːr-/ NOUN [C] (**forays**) **1** If you make a **foray into** a new or unfamiliar type of activity, you start to become involved in it. ❑ *Emporio Armani, the Italian fashion house, has made a discreet foray into furnishings.* **2** You can refer to a short trip that you make as a **foray** if it seems to involve excitement or risk, for example, because it is to an unfamiliar place or because you are looking for a particular thing. ❑ *Most guests make at least one foray into the town.* **3** If a group of soldiers make a **foray into** enemy territory, they make a quick attack there, and then return to their own territory. = raid ❑ *These base camps were used by the PKK guerrillas to make forays into Turkey.*

✪**for·bid** /fəˈbɪd/ VERB [T] (**forbids**, **forbidding**, **forbade**, **forbidden**) **1** If you **forbid** someone **to** do something, or if you **forbid** an activity, you order that it must be not be done. = prohibit, ban; ≠ permit, allow ❑ *They'll forbid you to marry.* ❑ *She was shut away and forbidden to read.* ❑ *Brazil's constitution forbids the military use of nuclear energy.* **2** If something **forbids** a particular course of action or state of affairs, it makes it impossible for the course of action or state of affairs to happen. = prohibit; ≠ permit, allow ❑ *His own pride forbids him to ask Arthur's help.*

✪**for·bid·den** /fəˈbɪdən/ ADJ **1** If something is **forbidden**, you are not allowed to do it or have it. ❑ *Smoking was forbidden everywhere.* ❑ *It is forbidden to drive faster than 20mph.* **2** A **forbidden** place is one that you are not allowed to visit or enter. ❑ *This was a forbidden area for foreigners.* **3** **Forbidden** is used to describe things that people strongly disapprove of or feel guilty about, and that are not often mentioned or talked about. = taboo ❑ *The war was a forbidden subject.* ❑ *Men fantasize as a substitute for acting out forbidden desires.*

force ♦♦♦ /fɔːs/ VERB, NOUN

VERB [T] (**forces, forcing, forced**) **1** If someone **forces** you to do something, they make you do it even though you do not want to, for example, by threatening you. □ *He took two women hostage and forced them to drive away from the area.* □ *He was forced to resign by Russia's conservative parliament.* □ *They were grabbed by three men who appeared to force them into a car.* **2** If a situation or event **forces** you to do something, it makes it necessary for you to do something that you would not otherwise have done. □ *A back injury forced her to withdraw from the competition.* □ *He turned right, down a dirt road that forced him into four-wheel drive.* **3** If someone **forces** something **on** or **upon** you, they make you accept or use it when you would prefer not to. = impose □ *To force this agreement on the nation is wrong.* **4** If you **force** something into a particular position, you use a lot of strength to make it move there. □ *They were forcing her head under the icy waters, drowning her.* **5** If someone **forces** a lock, a door, or a window, they break the lock or fastening in order to get into a building without using a key. □ *That evening police forced the door of the flat and arrested Mr Roberts.* PHRASE **force one's way somewhere** If you **force** your **way through** or **into** somewhere, you have to push or break things that are in your way in order to get there. □ *The miners forced their way through a police cordon.* NOUN [U, C, PL, SING] (**forces**) **1** [U] If someone uses **force** to do something, or if it is done by **force**, strong and violent physical action is taken in order to achieve it. □ *The government decided against using force to break up the demonstrations.* □ *the guerrillas' efforts to seize power by force* **2** [U] **Force** is the power or strength which something has. □ *The force of the explosion shattered the windows of several buildings.* **3** [U] The **force of** something is the powerful effect or quality that it has. □ *He changed our world through the force of his ideas.* **4** [U] **Force** is used before a number to indicate a wind of a particular speed or strength, especially a very strong wind. □ *The airlift was conducted in force ten winds.* **5** [C] If you refer to someone or something as a **force** in a particular type of activity, you mean that they have a strong influence on it. □ *For years the army was the most powerful political force in the country.* □ *The band is still an innovative force in music.* **6** [C] You can use **forces** to refer to processes and events that do not appear to be caused by human beings, and are therefore difficult to understand or control. □ *the protection of mankind against the forces of nature: epidemics, predators, floods, hurricanes* □ *The principle of market forces was applied to some of the country's most revered institutions.* **7** [C, U] In physics, a **force** is the pulling or pushing effect that something has on something else. □ *the Earth's gravitational force* □ *interactions between the forces of gravity and electromagnetism* **8** [C] **Forces** are groups of soldiers or military vehicles that are organized for a particular purpose. □ *the deployment of American forces in the region* **9** [PL] The **forces** means the army, the navy, or the air force, or all three. □ *The more senior you become in the forces, the more likely you are to end up in a desk job.* **10** [SING] The **force** is sometimes used to mean the police force. □ *It was hard for a police officer to make friends outside the force.* PHRASES **force of habit** If you do something **from force of habit**, you do it because you have always done it in the past, rather than because you have thought carefully about it. □ *He looked around from force of habit, but nobody paid any attention to him.* **in force 1** A law, rule, or system that is **in force** exists or is being used. □ *Although the new tax is already in force, you have until November to lodge an appeal.* **2** When people do something **in force**, they do it in large numbers. □ *Voters turned out in force for their first taste of multiparty elections.* **join forces** If you **join forces with** someone, you work together in order to achieve a common aim or purpose. □ *Both groups joined forces to persuade voters to approve a tax break for the industry.* → See also **air force, armed forces, workforce**

force·ful /ˈfɔːsfʊl/ ADJ **1** (*approval*) If you describe someone as **forceful**, you approve of them because they express their opinions and wishes in a strong, emphatic,

and confident way. □ *He was a man of forceful character, with considerable insight and diplomatic skills.* **2** Something that is **forceful** has a very powerful effect and causes you to think or feel something very strongly. = powerful □ *It made a very forceful impression on me.* **3** A **forceful** point or argument in a discussion is one that is good, valid, and convincing. = powerful □ *You may need to be armed with some forceful arguments to persuade a partner into seeing things your way.*

force·ful·ly /ˈfɔːsfʊli/ ADV **1** [forcefully with V] □ *Mrs Dambar was talking very rapidly and somewhat forcefully.* **2** [forcefully with V] □ *Daytime television tended to remind her too forcefully of her own situation.*

for·cible /ˈfɔːsɪbəl/ ADJ **Forcible** action involves physical force or violence. □ *Reports are coming in of the forcible resettlement of villagers from the countryside into towns.*

for·ci·bly /ˈfɔːsɪbli/ ADV If something is done **forcibly**, it is done using physical force or violence. □ *Four protestors had to be forcibly removed by police.*

fore /fɔː/ ADJ, NOUN

ADJ [fore + N] **Fore** is used to refer to parts at the front of an animal, ship, or aircraft. = front □ *There had been no direct damage in the fore part of the ship.* NOUN PHRASE **to the fore** If someone or something comes **to the fore** in a particular situation or group, they become important or popular. □ *A number of low-budget independent films brought new directors and actors to the fore.*

fore·cast ♦♦◇◇ /ˈfɔːkɑːst, -kæst/ NOUN, VERB

NOUN [C] (**forecasts**) A **forecast** is a statement of what is expected to happen in the future, especially in relation to a particular event or situation. □ *a forecast of a 2.25 per cent growth in the economy* □ *He delivered his election forecast.* □ *The weather forecast is better for today.* VERB [T] (**forecasts, forecasting, forecast** or **forecasted**) If you **forecast** future events, you say what you think is going to happen in the future. = predict □ *They forecast a humiliating defeat for the president.* □ *He forecasts that average salary increases will remain around 4 per cent.*

WORD PARTS
The prefix **fore-** appears in words that have 'before' as part of their meaning:
forecast (VERB)
foresee (VERB)
forerunner (NOUN)

fore·cast·er /ˈfɔːkɑːstə, -kæst-/ NOUN [C] (**forecasters**) A **forecaster** is someone who uses detailed knowledge about a particular activity in order to work out what they think will happen in that activity in the future. □ *Some of the nation's top economic forecasters say the economic recovery is picking up speed.*

fore·front /ˈfɔːfrʌnt/ NOUN [SING] **1** If you are **at the forefront of** a campaign or other activity, you have a leading and influential position in it. □ *They have been at the forefront of the campaign for political change.* **2** If something is **at the forefront of** people's minds or attention, they think about it a lot because it is particularly important to them. □ *The pension issue was not at the forefront of his mind in the spring of 1985.*

WORD PARTS
The prefix **fore-** often appears in words that have 'front' or 'in front' as part of their meaning:
forefront (NOUN)
forehead (NOUN)
foreword (NOUN)

fore·go /fɔːˈgəʊ/ also **forgo** VERB [T] (**foregoes, foregoing, forewent, foregone**) (*formal*) If you **forego** something, you decide to do without it, although you would like it. = do without □ *Many skiers are happy to forego a summer vacation to go skiing.*

fore·gone /ˈfɔːgɒn/ IRREG FORM

IRREG FORM **Foregone** is the past participle of **forego**. PHRASE **foregone conclusion** If you say that a particular result is **a foregone conclusion**, you mean you are certain that it will happen. ❑ *Most voters believe the result is a foregone conclusion.*

fore•ground /'fɔːgraʊnd/ NOUN [C, U, SING] (**foregrounds**) ◼ [C, U] The **foreground** of a picture or scene you are looking at is the part or area of it that appears nearest to you. ❑ *He is the bowler-hatted figure in the foreground of Orpen's famous painting.* ◼ [SING] If something or someone is **in the foreground**, or comes **to the foreground**, they receive a lot of attention. ❑ *This is another worry that has come to the foreground in recent years.*

fore•head /'fɔːhed, 'fɒrɪd/ NOUN [C] (**foreheads**) Your **forehead** is the area at the front of your head between your eyebrows and your hair. = brow ❑ *the lines on her forehead*

✪ for•eign ♦♦♦ /'fɒrɪn, AmE 'fɔːr-/ ADJ ◼ Something or someone that is **foreign** comes from or relates to a country that is not your own. = overseas, international; ≠ local ❑ *She was on her first foreign holiday without her parents.* ❑ *a foreign language* ❑ *It is the largest ever foreign investment in the Bolivian mining sector.* ◼ [foreign + N] In politics and journalism, **foreign** is used to describe people, jobs, and activities relating to countries that are not the country of the person or government concerned. = overseas, international; ≠ home, domestic ❑ *the German foreign minister* ❑ *I am the foreign correspondent in Washington of La Tribuna newspaper of Honduras.* ❑ *the effects of US foreign policy* ◼ (*formal*) A **foreign** object is something that has got into something else, usually by accident, and should not be there. ❑ *The patient's immune system would reject the transplanted organ as a foreign object.*

for•eign•er ♦◇◇ /'fɒrɪnə, AmE 'fɔːr-/ NOUN [C] (**foreigners**) A **foreigner** is someone who belongs to a country that is not your own. ❑ *They are discouraged from becoming close friends with foreigners.*

for•eign ex•change NOUN [PL, U, C] (**foreign exchanges**) ◼ [PL] **Foreign exchanges** are the institutions or systems involved with changing one currency into another. ❑ *On the foreign exchanges, the U.S. dollar is up point forty-five.* ◼ [U] **Foreign exchange** is used to refer to foreign currency that is obtained through the foreign exchange system. ❑ *an important source of foreign exchange* ◼ [C] [oft foreign exchange + N] A **foreign exchange** is an arrangement in which people from two different countries visit each other's country, to strengthen links between them. ❑ *He recently hosted a foreign exchange student from Argentina.*

fore•most /'fɔːməʊst/ ADJ, ADV
ADJ The **foremost** thing or person in a group is the most important or best. ❑ *He was one of the world's foremost scholars of ancient Indian culture.*
ADV
PHRASE **first and foremost** (*emphasis*) You use **first and foremost** to emphasize the most important quality of something or someone. ❑ *It is first and foremost a trade agreement.*

✪ fore•run•ner /'fɔːrʌnə/ NOUN [C] (**forerunners**) If you describe a person or thing as the **forerunner** of someone or something similar, you mean they existed before them and either influenced their development or were a sign of what was going to happen. = precursor, predecessor ❑ *a machine which, in some respects, was the forerunner of the modern helicopter* ❑ *The recent exhibition confirms the artist's reputation as a pioneer of Impressionism and forerunner of Monet.* ❑ *the European Economic Community, the forerunner of today's European Union*

✪ fore•see /fɔːˈsiː/ VERB [T] (**foresees, foreseeing, foresaw, foreseen**) If you **foresee** something, you expect and believe that it will happen. = predict, forecast ❑ *He did not foresee any problems.* ❑ *Juveniles may find it harder than adults to foresee the consequences of their actions.* ❑ *a dangerous situation which could have been foreseen* ❑ *He correctly foresaw the importance of nuclear weapons.*

fore•see•able /fɔːˈsiːəbəl/ ADJ
ADJ If a future event is **foreseeable**, you know that it will happen or that it can happen, because it is a natural or obvious consequence of something else that you know. = predictable ❑ *It seems to me that this crime was foreseeable and this death preventable.*
PHRASE **for the foreseeable future** If you say that something will happen **for the foreseeable future**, you think that it will continue to happen for a long time. ❑ *Profit and dividend growth looks above average for the foreseeable future.*

fore•sight /'fɔːsaɪt/ NOUN [U] (*approval*) Someone's **foresight** is their ability to see what is likely to happen in the future and to take appropriate action. ❑ *They had the foresight to invest in new technology.*

✪ for•est ♦◇◇ /'fɒrɪst, AmE 'fɔːr-/ NOUN [C, U] (**forests**) A **forest** is a large area where trees grow close together. ❑ *Parts of the forest are still dense and inaccessible.* ❑ *25 million hectares of forest*

fore•stall /fɔːˈstɔːl/ VERB [T] (**forestalls, forestalling, forestalled**) If you **forestall** someone, you realize what they are likely to do and prevent them from doing it. = stop ❑ *Large numbers of police were in the square to forestall any demonstrations.*

for•est•ry /'fɒrɪstri, AmE 'fɔːr-/ NOUN [U] **Forestry** is the science or skill of growing and taking care of trees in forests, especially in order to obtain wood. ❑ *his great interest in forestry*

for•ever /fəˈrevə/ ADV ◼ [forever with V] If you say that something will happen or continue **forever**, you mean that it will always happen or continue. ❑ *I think that we will live together forever.* ◼ [forever after V] If something has gone or changed **forever**, it has gone or changed completely and permanently. ❑ *The old social order was gone forever.* ◼ [forever after V] (*informal, emphasis*) If you say that something takes **forever** or lasts **forever**, you are emphasizing that it takes or lasts a very long time, or that it seems to. ❑ *The drive seemed to take forever.*

for•feit /'fɔːfɪt/ VERB, NOUN
VERB [T] (**forfeits, forfeiting, forfeited**) ◼ If you **forfeit** something, you lose it or are forced to give it up because you have broken a rule or done something wrong. ❑ *He was ordered to forfeit more than $1.5m.* ◼ If you **forfeit** something, you give it up willingly, especially so that you can achieve something else. ❑ *Do you think that they would forfeit profit in the name of safety?*
NOUN [C] (**forfeits**) A **forfeit** is something that you have to give up because you have done something wrong. = penalty ❑ *That is the forfeit he must pay.*

for•gave /fəˈɡeɪv/ IRREG FORM **Forgave** is the past tense of **forgive**.

forge /fɔːdʒ/ VERB
VERB [RECIP, T] (**forges, forging, forged**) ◼ [RECIP] If one person or institution **forges** an agreement or relationship with another, they create it with a lot of hard work, hoping that it will be strong or lasting. ❑ *The prime minister is determined to forge a good relationship with the country's new leader.* ❑ *They agreed to forge closer economic ties.* ◼ [T] If someone **forges** something such as paper money, a document, or a painting, they copy it or make it so that it looks genuine, in order to deceive people. ❑ *He admitted seven charges including forging passports.* ❑ *They used forged documents to leave the country.*
PHRASAL VERB **forge ahead** If you **forge ahead** with something, you continue with it and make a lot of progress with it. ❑ *He again pledged to forge ahead with his plans for reform.*

forg•er /'fɔːdʒə/ NOUN [C] (**forgers**) ❑ *the most prolific art forger in the country*

for•gery /'fɔːdʒəri/ NOUN [U, C] (**forgeries**) ◼ [U] **Forgery** is the crime of forging money, documents, or paintings.

❏ He was found guilty of forgery. **2** [c] You can refer to a forged document, bill, or painting as a **forgery**. ❏ The letter was a forgery.

for·get ♦♦◊ /fəˈget/ VERB

VERB [T, I] (**forgets, forgetting, forgot, forgotten**) **1** [T] If you **forget** something or **forget** how to do something, you cannot think of it or think how to do it, although you knew it or knew how to do it in the past. ❏ She forgot where she left the car and it took us two days to find it. **2** [I, T] If you **forget** something or **forget** to do it, you fail to think about it or fail to remember to do it, for example, because you are thinking about other things. ❏ She never forgets her daddy's birthday. ❏ She forgot to lock her door one day and two men got in. ❏ When I close my eyes, I forget about everything. **3** [T] If you **forget** something that you had intended to bring with you, you do not bring it because you did not think about it at the right time. ❏ Once when we were going to Paris, I forgot my passport. **4** [I, T] If you **forget** something or someone, you deliberately put them out of your mind and do not think about them any more. ❏ I hope you will forget the bad experience you had today. ❏ I found it very easy to forget about Sumner.

PHRASE **not forgetting** You say **not forgetting** a particular thing or person when you want to include them in something that you have already talked about. ❏ Leave a message, not forgetting your name and address.

CONVENTION **forget it** (spoken, formulae) You say 'Forget it' in reply to someone as a way of telling them not to worry or bother about something, or as an emphatic way of saying no to a suggestion. ❏ 'Sorry, Liz. I think I was a bit rude to you.'—'Forget it, but don't do it again!'

for·get·ful /fəˈgetfʊl/ ADJ Someone who is **forgetful** often forgets things. = absent-minded ❏ My mother has become very forgetful and confused.

for·give /fəˈgɪv/ VERB [T, PASSIVE] (**forgives, forgiving, forgave, forgiven**) **1** [T] If you **forgive** someone who has done something bad or wrong, you stop being angry with them and no longer want to punish them. ❏ Hopefully Jane will understand and forgive you, if she really loves you. ❏ Irene forgave Terry for stealing her money. ❏ He could forgive Petal anything if the children were safe. **2** [T] **Forgive** is used in polite expressions and apologies like 'forgive me' and 'forgive my ignorance' when you are saying or doing something that might seem rude, silly, or complicated. ❏ Forgive me, I don't mean to insult you. ❏ I do hope you'll forgive me but I've got to leave. **3** [PASSIVE] If you say that someone could **be forgiven for** doing something, you mean that they were wrong or mistaken, but not seriously, because many people would have done the same thing in those circumstances. ❏ Looking at the figures, you could be forgiven for thinking the recession is already over.

for·give·ness /fəˈgɪvnəs/ NOUN [U] If you ask for **forgiveness**, you ask to be forgiven for something wrong that you have done. ❏ a spirit of forgiveness and national reconciliation

for·giv·ing /fəˈgɪvɪŋ/ ADJ Someone who is **forgiving** is willing to forgive. ❏ Voters can be remarkably forgiving of presidents who fail to keep their campaign promises.

for·go /fɔːˈgəʊ/ → See forego

for·got /fəˈgɒt/ IRREG FORM **Forgot** is the past tense of **forget**.

for·got·ten /fəˈgɒtən/ IRREG FORM **Forgotten** is the past participle of **forget**.

fork /fɔːk/ NOUN, VERB

NOUN [c] (**forks**) **1** A **fork** is a tool used for eating food which has a row of three or four long metal points at the end. ❏ knives and forks **2** A **fork** in a road, path, or river is a point at which it divides into two parts and forms a 'Y' shape. ❏ We arrived at a fork in the road. ❏ The road divides; you should take the right fork. **3** (mainly BrE; in AmE, usually use **pitchfork**) A garden **fork** is a tool used for breaking up soil which has a row of three or four long metal points at the end.

VERB [T, I] (**forks, forking, forked**) **1** [T] If you **fork** food **into** your mouth or **onto** a plate, you put it there using a fork. ❏ He forked an egg onto a piece of bread and folded it

into a sandwich. **2** [I] If a road, path, or river **forks**, it forms a fork. ❏ Beyond the village the road forked.

PHRASAL VERB **fork out** (informal) If you **fork out for** something, you spend a lot of money on it. = cough up ❏ Visitors to the castle had to fork out for a guidebook.

❍ **form** ♦♦♦ /fɔːm/ NOUN, VERB

NOUN [c, u] (**forms**) **1** [c] A **form** of something is a type or kind of it. = type, kind, sort ❏ He contracted a rare form of cancer. ❏ I am against hunting in any form. ❏ In its present form, the law could lead to new injustices. **2** [c] When something can exist or happen in several possible ways, you can use **form** to refer to one particular way in which it exists or happens. ❏ They received a benefit in the form of a tax reduction. **3** [c] The **form** of something is its shape. = shape ❏ the form of the body **4** [c] You can refer to something that you can see as a **form** if you cannot see it clearly, or if its outline is the clearest or most striking aspect of it. ❏ His form lay still under the blankets. **5** [c] A **form** is a paper with questions on it and spaces marked where you should write the answers. Forms usually ask you to give details about yourself, for example, when you are applying for a job or joining an organization. ❏ You will be asked to fill in a form with details of your birth and occupation. **6** [u] In sports, **form** refers to the ability or success of a person or animal over a period of time. ❏ His form this season has been brilliant.

VERB [I, T] (**forms, forming, formed**) **1** [I, T] When a particular shape **forms** or **is formed**, people or things move or are arranged so that this shape is made. ❏ A line formed to use the bathroom. ❏ They formed a circle and sang 'Auld Lang Syne'. **2** [T] If something is arranged or changed so that it becomes similar to a thing with a particular structure or function, you can say that it **forms** that thing. ❏ These panels folded up to form a screen some five feet tall. **3** [T] If something consists of particular things, people, or features, you can say that they **form** that thing. = constitute ❏ the articles that formed the basis of Randolph's book ❏ Cereals form the staple diet of an enormous number of people around the world. **4** [T] If you **form** an organization, group, or company, you start it. = start, create ❏ They tried to form a study group on human rights. ❏ Threadneedle is a company formed in 1994 with the merger of Allied Dunbar and Eagle Star. **5** [I, T] When something natural **forms** or **is formed**, it begins to exist and develop. = develop ❏ The stars must have formed 10 to 15 billion years ago. ❏ Huge ice sheets were formed. **6** [I, T] If you **form** a relationship, a habit, or an idea, or if it **forms**, it begins to exist and develop. ❏ She had formed the habit of giving herself freely to men. ❏ An idea formed in his mind. **7** [T] If you say that something **forms** a person's character or personality, you mean that it has a strong influence on them and causes them to develop in a particular way. = mould ❏ Anger at injustice formed his character.

❍ **for·mal** ♦♦◊ /ˈfɔːməl/ ADJ **1** Formal speech or behaviour is very correct and serious rather than relaxed and friendly, and is used especially in official situations. ❏ He wrote a very formal letter of apology to Douglas. ❏ Business relationships are necessarily a bit more formal. **2** [formal + N] A **formal** action, statement, or request is an official one. = official; ≠ informal, unofficial ❏ UN officials said a formal request was passed to American authorities. ❏ No formal announcement had been made. **3** Formal occasions are special occasions at which people wear elegant clothes and behave according to a set of accepted rules. ❏ One evening the company arranged a formal dinner after the play. **4** [formal + N] Formal clothes are very elegant clothes that are suitable for formal occasions. ❏ They wore ordinary ties instead of the more formal high collar and cravat. **5** [formal + N] Formal education or training is given officially, usually in a school, college, or university. ❏ Wendy didn't have any formal dance training.

❍ **for·mal·ly** /ˈfɔːməli/ ADV **1** [formally with V] ❏ He took her back to Vincent Square in a taxi, saying goodnight formally on the doorstep. ❏ He spoke formally and politely. **2** = officially; ≠ informally, unofficially ❏ Diplomats haven't formally agreed to Anderson's plan. **3** It was really too warm for her to dress so formally. **4** Usually only formally trained artists from established schools are chosen.

F

⟡for·mal·ity /fɔːˈmælɪti/ NOUN [U, C] (**formalities**)
1 [U] **Formality** is very correct and serious speech or behaviour that is used especially in official situations. ≠ informality □ *Lillith's formality and seriousness amused him.* **2** [C] If you say that an action or procedure is just a **formality**, you mean that it is done only because it is normally done, and that it will not have any real effect on the situation. □ *Some contracts are a mere formality.* **3** [C] **Formalities** are formal actions or procedures that are carried out as part of a particular activity or event. □ *They are whisked through the immigration and customs formalities in a matter of minutes.*

for·mal·ize /ˈfɔːməlaɪz/ also **formalise** VERB [T] (**formalizes, formalizing, formalized**) If you **formalize** a plan, idea, arrangement, or system, you make it formal and official. □ *A recent treaty signed by Russia, Canada, and Japan formalized an agreement to work together to stop the pirates.*

⟡for·mat /ˈfɔːmæt/ NOUN, VERB (*academic word*)
NOUN [C] (**formats**) **1** The **format** of something is the way or order in which it is arranged and presented. = style, form □ *I had met with him to explain the format of the programme and what we had in mind.* □ *He explained the new format and policy of the paper.* □ *You all know the format of the show.* **2** The **format** of a piece of computer software, a film or a musical recording is the type of equipment on which it is designed to be used or played. For example, possible formats for a film are DVD and video cassette. □ *His latest album is available on all formats.*
VERB [T] (**formats, formatting, formatted**) (*computing*) **1** To **format** a computer disk means to run a program so that the disk can be written on. □ *a menu that includes the choice to format a disk* **2** To **format** a piece of computer text or graphics means to arrange the way in which it appears when it is printed or is displayed on a screen. □ *When text is saved from a web page, it is often very badly formatted with many short lines.*

⟡for·ma·tion /fɔːˈmeɪʃən/ NOUN [U, C] (**formations**)
1 [U] The **formation of** something is the starting or creation of it. = creation □ *Time is running out for the formation of a new government.* □ *Lord Harewood announced the formation of English National Opera North.* **2** [U] The **formation of** an idea, habit, relationship, or character is the process of developing and establishing it. = development □ *My profession had an important influence in the formation of my character and temperament.* **3** [C] If people or things are **in formation**, they are arranged in a particular pattern as they move. □ *He was flying in formation with seven other jets.* **4** [C] A rock or cloud **formation** is rock or cloud of a particular shape or structure. □ *a vast rock formation shaped like a pillar* □ *The cloud formations produce rain which falls on a vast territory.*

forma·tive /ˈfɔːmətɪv/ ADJ A **formative** period of time or experience is one that has an important and lasting influence on a person's character and attitudes. □ *She was born in Barbados but spent her formative years growing up in Miami.*

⟡for·mer ♦♦♦ /ˈfɔːmə/ ADJ, PRON
ADJ **1** [former + N] **Former** is used to describe someone who used to have a particular job, position, or role, but no longer has it. = ex- □ *The unemployed executives include former sales managers, directors and accountants.* □ *former president Richard Nixon* □ *He pleaded not guilty to murdering his former wife.* **2** [former + N] **Former** is used to refer to countries which no longer exist or whose boundaries have changed. □ *the former Soviet Union* **3** [former + N] **Former** is used to describe something which used to belong to someone or which used to be a particular thing. □ *the former home of Robert E. Lee* **4** [former + N] (*formal*) **Former** is used to describe a situation or period of time which came before the present one. = previous □ *He would want you to remember him as he was in former years.*
PRON ['the' former] When two people, things, or groups have just been mentioned, you can refer to the first of them as **the former**. □ *They grappled with the problem of connecting the electricity and water supplies. The former proved simple compared with the latter.* □ *He writes about two series of*

works: the Caprichos and the Disparates. □ *The former are a series of etchings done by Goya.* □ *The wife may choose the former and the husband the latter.*

USAGE NOTE

former

When 'the former' is used as a pronoun, it is not followed by 'one'. Do not say 'the former one'.
*The two firms are in direct competition, with **the former** trying to cut costs and increase profits.*

⟡for·mer·ly /ˈfɔːməli/ ADV If something happened or was true **formerly**, it happened or was true in the past. □ *He had formerly been in the navy.* □ *east Germany's formerly state-controlled companies*

⟡for·mi·da·ble /ˈfɔːmɪdəbəl, fəˈmɪ-/ ADJ If you describe something or someone as **formidable**, you mean that you feel slightly frightened by them because they are very great or impressive. □ *We have a formidable task ahead of us.*

⟡for·mu·la ♦◇◇ /ˈfɔːmjʊlə/ NOUN [C, SING] (**formulae** or **formulas**) (*academic word*) **1** [C] A **formula** is a plan that is invented in order to deal with a particular problem. □ *a peace formula* **2** [C] A **formula** is a group of letters, numbers, or other symbols which represents a scientific or mathematical rule. □ *He developed a mathematical formula describing the distances of the planets from the Sun.* □ *using a standard scientific formula* **3** [C] In science, the **formula** for a substance is a list of the amounts of various substances which make up that substance, or an indication of the atoms that it is composed of. □ *Glucose and fructose have the same chemical formula but have very different properties.* □ *Water's chemical formula is H_2O.* □ *NO is the formula for nitric oxide.* **4** [SING] A **formula for** a particular situation, usually a good one, is a course of action or a combination of actions that is certain or likely to result in that situation. = recipe □ *After he was officially pronounced the world's oldest man, he offered this simple formula for a long and happy life.*

⟡for·mu·late /ˈfɔːmjʊleɪt/ VERB [T] (**formulates, formulating, formulated**) **1** If you **formulate** something such as a plan or proposal, you invent it, thinking about the details carefully. = invent, devise □ *Little by little, he formulated his plan for escape.* □ *Detectives tend to formulate one hypothesis and then try to confirm it.* □ *Formulate a strategy for long-term business development.* **2** If you **formulate** a thought, opinion, or idea, you express it or describe it using particular words. = articulate □ *I was impressed by the way he could formulate his ideas.*

for·mu·la·tion /ˌfɔːmjʊˈleɪʃən/ NOUN [C, U] (**formulations**) **1** [C, U] A **formulation** is the way in which you express your thoughts and ideas. □ *This is a far weaker formulation than is in the draft resolution which is being proposed.* **2** [U] The **formulation** of something such as a policy or plan is the process of creating or inventing it. □ *the process of policy formulation and implementation* **3** [C, U] (*mainly BrE*) The **formulation** of something such as a medicine or a beauty product is the way in which different ingredients are combined to make it. You can also say that the finished product is a **formulation**.

fort /fɔːt/ NOUN
NOUN [C] (**forts**) A **fort** is a strong building or a place with a wall or fence around it where soldiers can stay and be safe from the enemy.
PHRASE **hold the fort** If you **hold the fort** for someone, you take care of things for them while they are somewhere else or are busy doing something else. □ *His business partner is holding the fort while he is away.*

⟡forth·com·ing /ˌfɔːθˈkʌmɪŋ/ ADJ (*academic word*)
1 [forthcoming + N] A **forthcoming** event is planned to happen soon. = impending □ *his opponents in the forthcoming elections* □ *the forthcoming meeting, scheduled for January 19* **2** [V-LINK + forthcoming] (*formal*) If something that you want, need, or expect is **forthcoming**, it is given to you or it happens. □ *They promised that the money would be forthcoming.* □ *One source predicts no major shift in policy will be forthcoming at the committee hearings.* **3** If you say that someone is **forthcoming**, you mean that they

willingly give information when you ask them. ❑ *William, sadly, was not very forthcoming about any other names he might have, where he lived or what his phone number was.*

forth·right /'fɔːθraɪt/ ADJ (approval) If you describe someone as **forthright**, you admire them because they show clearly and strongly what they think and feel. = outspoken ❑ *a deeply religious man with forthright opinions*

for·ti·eth ♦♦◇ /'fɔːtiəθ/ ADJ The **fortieth** item in a series is the one that you count as number forty. ❑ *It was the fortieth anniversary of the death of the composer.*

for·ti·fy /'fɔːtɪfaɪ/ VERB [T] (fortifies, fortifying, fortified) **1** To **fortify** a place means to make it stronger and more difficult to attack, often by building a wall or ditch round it. ❑ *soldiers working to fortify an airbase in Bahrain* **2** If food or drink **is fortified**, another substance is added to it to make it healthier or stronger. ❑ *Choose margarine or butter fortified with vitamin D.* ❑ *All sherry is made from wine fortified with brandy.*

fort·night /'fɔːtnaɪt/ NOUN [C] (fortnights) (mainly BrE) A **fortnight** is a period of two weeks. ❑ *I hope to be back in a fortnight.*

for·tress /'fɔːtrɪs/ NOUN [C] (fortresses) A **fortress** is a castle or other large strong building, or a well-protected place, which is intended to be difficult for enemies to enter. ❑ *a 13th-century fortress*

◆for·tu·nate /'fɔːtʃənət/ ADJ If you say that someone or something is **fortunate**, you mean that they are lucky. = lucky; ≠ unfortunate, unlucky ❑ *He was extremely fortunate to survive.* ❑ *She is in the fortunate position of having plenty of choice.* ❑ *It was fortunate that the water was shallow.*

◆for·tu·nate·ly /'fɔːtʃənətli/ ADV **Fortunately** is used to introduce or indicate a statement about an event or situation that is good. = luckily ❑ *Fortunately, the weather that winter was reasonably mild.* ❑ *Bombs hit the building but fortunately no one was hurt.*

for·tune ♦◇◇ /'fɔːtʃuːn/ NOUN
NOUN [C, U, PL] (fortunes) **1** [C] (emphasis) You can refer to a large sum of money as **a fortune** or **a small fortune** to emphasize how large it is. ❑ *He made a small fortune in the property boom.* **2** [C] Someone who has a **fortune** has a very large amount of money. ❑ *He made his fortune in car sales.* **3** [U] **Fortune** or good **fortune** is good luck. Ill **fortune** is bad luck. ❑ *Investors are starting to wonder how long their good fortune can last.* **4** [PL] If you talk about someone's **fortunes** or the **fortunes** of something, you are talking about the extent to which they are doing well or being successful. ❑ *The company had to do something to reverse its sliding fortunes.*
PHRASE **tell your fortune** When someone **tells** your **fortune**, they tell you what they think will happen to you in the future, which they say is shown, for example, by the lines on your hand. ❑ *I was just going to have my fortune told by a gypsy.*

for·ty ♦♦♦ /'fɔːti/ NUM, NOUN
NUM **Forty** is the number 40.
NOUN [PL] (forties) **1** When you talk about the **forties**, you are referring to numbers between 40 and 49. For example, if you are **in** your **forties**, you are aged between 40 and 49. If the temperature is **in the forties**, the temperature is between 40 and 49 degrees. ❑ *He was a big man in his forties, smartly dressed in a suit and tie.* **2** The **forties** is the decade between 1940 and 1949. ❑ *Steel cans were introduced sometime during the forties.*

fo·rum /'fɔːrəm/ NOUN [C] (forums) A **forum** is a place, situation, or group in which people exchange ideas and discuss issues, especially important public issues. ❑ *Members of the council agreed that was an important forum for discussion.*

for·ward ♦♦◇ /'fɔːwəd/ ADV, ADJ, VERB, NOUN
ADV **1** [forward after V] If you move or look **forward**, you move or look in a direction that is in front of you. ❑ *He came forward with his hand out. 'Mr and Mrs Selby?' he said.* ❑ *She fell forward on to her face.* **2 Forward** means in a position near the front of something such as a building or a vehicle. ❑ *The best seats are in the aisle and as far forward*

as possible. **3** If you say that someone looks **forward**, you approve of them because they think about what will happen in the future and plan for it. ❑ *Now the leadership wants to look forward, and to outline a strategy for the rest of the century.* ❑ *People should forget and look forward.* **4** [forward after V] If you move a clock or watch **forward**, you change the time shown on it so that it shows a later time, for example, when the time changes to daylight saving time. ❑ *When we put the clocks forward in March we go into daylight saving time.* **5** ['from' N + forward] When you are referring to a particular time, if you say that something was true **from** that time **forward**, you mean that it became true at that time, and continued to be true afterwards. = on ❑ *Velazquez's work from that time forward was confined largely to portraits of the royal family.* **6** You use **forward** to indicate that something progresses or improves. ❑ *And by boosting economic prosperity in Mexico, Canada, and the United States, it will help us move forward on issues that concern all of us.* ❑ *They just couldn't see any way forward.* **7** [forward after V] If something or someone is put **forward**, or comes **forward**, they are suggested or offered as suitable for a particular purpose. ❑ *Over the years several similar theories have been put forward.* ❑ *Investigations have ground to a standstill because no witnesses have come forward.*
ADJ **1** [forward + N] If something or someone is in a **forward** position they are near the front of something. ❑ *Reinforcements were needed to allow more troops to move into forward positions.* **2** [forward + N] **Forward** thinking or planning thinks about what will happen in the future and plans for it. ❑ *The university system requires more forward planning.*
VERB [T] (forwards, forwarding, forwarded) If a letter or message **is forwarded to** someone, it is sent to the place where they are, after having been sent to a different place earlier. ❑ *When he's out on the road, office calls are forwarded to the mobile phone in his van.*
NOUN [C] (forwards) In football, hockey, or basketball, a **forward** is a player whose usual position is in the opponents' half of the field, and whose usual job is to attack or score goals. ❑ *Junior forward Sam McCracken added 14 points for the home team.*
✦ **backwards and forwards** → see **backwards**

◆fos·sil /'fɒsəl/ NOUN [C] (fossils) A **fossil** is the hard remains of a prehistoric animal or plant that are found inside a rock. ❑ *a newly discovered 425 million-year-old fossil* ❑ *Several enormous prehistoric fossils were found.* ❑ *fossils of dinosaurs and ammonites*

◆fos·sil fuel also **fossil-fuel** NOUN [C, U] (fossil fuels) **Fossil fuel** is fuel such as coal or oil that is formed from the decayed remains of plants or animals. ❑ *Burning fossil fuels uses oxygen and produces carbon dioxide.* ❑ *Gas – the world's cleanest fossil fuel – currently accounts for just over 2% of China's energy consumption.*

fos·ter /'fɒstə, AmE 'fɔːst-/ ADJ, VERB
ADJ [foster + N] **Foster** parents are people who officially take a child into their family for a period of time, without becoming the child's legal parents. The child is referred to as their **foster** child. ❑ *Little Jack was placed with foster parents.*
VERB [T] (fosters, fostering, fostered) **1** If you **foster** a child, you take it into your family for a period of time, without becoming its legal parent. ❑ *She has since gone on to find happiness by fostering more than 100 children.* **2** To **foster** something such as an activity or idea means to help it to develop. ❑ *He said that developed countries had a responsibility to foster global economic growth to help new democracies.*

fought /fɔːt/ IRREG FORM **Fought** is the past tense and past participle of **fight**.

foul /faʊl/ ADJ, VERB, NOUN
ADJ (fouler, foulest) **1** If you describe something as **foul**, you mean that it is dirty and smells or tastes unpleasant. = disgusting ❑ *foul polluted water* **2 Foul** language is offensive and contains swear words or rude words. = filthy ❑ *The teachers had to deal with her foul language, disruptive behaviour, and low academic performance.* **3** If someone has a **foul** temper or is in a **foul** mood, they

become angry or violent very suddenly and easily. = **bad** ❑ *Collins was in a foul mood even before the interviews began.* **4** **Foul** weather is unpleasant, windy, and stormy. ❑ *No amount of foul weather, whether hail, wind, rain, or snow, seems to deter them.* **5** [foul + N] In a game or sport, a **foul** tackle is when a player touches another player or blocks them in a way which is not allowed according to the rules. ❑ *a foul tackle*

PHRASE **fall foul of** If you **fall foul of** someone, you do something which gets you into trouble with them. ❑ *He had fallen foul of the FBI.*

VERB [T] (**fouls, fouling, fouled**) **1** If an animal **fouls** a place, it drops faeces onto the ground. ❑ *It is an offence to let your dog foul a footpath.* **2** In a game or sport, if a player **fouls** another player, they touch them or block them in a way which is not allowed according to the rules. ❑ *Nowitzki fouled Mitchell early in the third quarter.*

PHRASAL VERB **foul up** If someone or something **fouls up**, or if they **foul** something **up**, they make a serious mistake that causes things to go badly wrong. ❑ *A computer software glitch fouled up their presentation.*

NOUN [C] (**fouls**) A **foul** is an act in a game or sport that is not allowed according to the rules. ❑ *Harridge was charged with a flagrant foul and ejected from the game.*

✪**found** ◆◇◇ /faʊnd/ IRREG FORM, VERB (*academic word*)

IRREG FORM **Found** is the past tense and past participle of **find**.

VERB [T] (**founds, founding, founded**) **1** When an institution, company, or organization **is founded** by someone or by a group of people, they get it started, often by providing the necessary money. = **set up, establish** ❑ *The New York Free-Loan Society was founded in 1892.* ❑ *His father founded the American Socialist Party.* ❑ *The Independent Labour Party was founded in 1893.* ❑ *He founded the Centre for Journalism Studies at University College Cardiff.* ❑ *The business, founded by Dawn and Nigel, suffered financial setbacks.* **2** When a town, important building, or other place **is founded** by someone or by a group of people, they cause it to be built. ❑ *The town was founded in 1610.*

found·ing /ˈfaʊndɪŋ/ NOUN [SING] ❑ *The firm has never had an unprofitable year since its founding 65 years ago.*

✪**foun·da·tion** ◆◇◇ /faʊnˈdeɪʃən/ NOUN [C, SING, PL, U] (**foundations**) (*academic word*) **1** [C] The **foundation of** something such as a belief or way of life is the things on which it is based. ❑ *Best friends are the foundation of my life.* ❑ *The issue strikes at the very foundation of our community.* ❑ *This laid the foundations for later modern economic growth.* **2** [SING] The **foundation** of an institution, company, or organization is the act of getting it started, often by providing the necessary money. ❑ *the 150th anniversary of the foundation of Kew Gardens* ❑ *With the foundation of the NHS there was a move away from traditional medicines towards synthetic ones.* **3** [C] A **foundation** is an organization which provides money for a special purpose such as research or charity. = **organization, institute, society** ❑ *the National Foundation for Educational Research* ❑ *Her response was to set about creating a charitable foundation.* **4** [PL] The **foundations** of a building or other structure are the layer of bricks or concrete below the ground that it is built on. **5** [U] If a story, idea, or argument has **no foundation**, there are no facts to prove that it is true. ❑ *The allegations were without foundation.* **6** [C, U] **Foundation** is a skin-coloured cream that you put on your face before putting on the rest of your make-up. ❑ *Use foundation and/or face powder afterwards for an even skin tone.*

✪**found·er** ◆◇◇ /ˈfaʊndə/ NOUN, VERB

NOUN [C] (**founders**) The **founder** of an institution, organization, or building is the person who got it started or caused it to be built, often by providing the necessary money. ❑ *He was one of the founders of the university's medical faculty.* ❑ *the founder of the Zionist movement* ❑ *Hsin Tao, the organization's founder and leader*

VERB [I] (**founders, foundering, foundered**) If something such as a plan or project **founders**, it fails because of a particular point, difficulty, or problem. = **fail** ❑ *The talks have foundered, largely because of the reluctance of some members of the government to do a deal with criminals.*

foun·tain /ˈfaʊntɪn/ NOUN [C] (**fountains**) **1** A **fountain** is an ornamental feature in a pool or lake which consists of a long narrow stream of water that is forced up into the air by a pump. ❑ *the fountains on the 16th Street Mall* **2** (*literary*) A **fountain of** a liquid is an amount of it which is sent up into the air and falls back. = **jet** ❑ *The volcano spewed a fountain of molten rock 650 feet in the air.*

four ◆◆◆ /fɔː/ NUM

NUM (**fours**) **Four** is the number 4. ❑ *Judith is married with four children.*

PHRASE **on all fours** If you are **on all fours**, your knees, feet, and hands are on the ground. ❑ *She crawled on all fours over to the window.*

four·teen ◆◆◆ /ˌfɔːˈtiːn/ NUM (**fourteens**) **Fourteen** is the number 14. ❑ *I'm fourteen years old.*

four·teenth ◆◆◇ /ˌfɔːˈtiːnθ/ ADJ The **fourteenth** item in a series is the one that you count as number fourteen. ❑ *The Festival, now in its fourteenth year, has become a major international jazz event.*

fourth ◆◆◇ /fɔːθ/ ADJ The **fourth** item in a series is the one that you count as number four. ❑ *Last year's winner Greg Lemond of the United States is in fourth place.*

fox /fɒks/ NOUN [C] (**foxes**) A **fox** is a wild animal which looks like a dog and has reddish-brown fur, a pointed face and ears, and a thick tail. Foxes eat smaller animals.

foy·er /ˈfɔɪə, ˈfwaɪeɪ/ NOUN [C] (**foyers**) The **foyer** is the large area where people meet or wait just inside the main doors of a building such as a theatre or hotel. = **lobby** ❑ *I went and waited in the foyer.*

✪**frac·tion** ◆◆◇ /ˈfrækʃən/ NOUN [C] (**fractions**) **1** A **fraction of** something is a tiny amount or proportion of it. = **part, proportion** ❑ *She hesitated for a fraction of a second before responding.* ❑ *Here's how to eat like the stars, at a fraction of the cost.* ❑ *The statistics reflect only a tiny fraction of the problem.* **2** A **fraction** is a number that can be expressed as a proportion of two whole numbers. For example, $\frac{1}{2}$ and $\frac{1}{3}$ are both fractions. ❑ *The students had a grasp of decimals, percentages and fractions.*

frac·ture /ˈfræktʃə/ NOUN, VERB

NOUN [C] (**fractures**) A **fracture** is a crack or break in something, especially a bone. ❑ *At least one third of all women over ninety have sustained a hip fracture.*

VERB [I, T] (**fractures, fracturing, fractured**) **1** If something such as a bone **is fractured** or **fractures**, it gets a crack or break in it. ❑ *You've fractured a rib, maybe more than one.* ❑ *One strut had fractured and been crudely repaired in several places.* **2** (*formal*) If something such as an organization or society **is fractured** or **fractures**, it splits into several parts or stops existing. ❑ *His policy risks fracturing the coalition.*

✪**frag·ile** /ˈfrædʒaɪl, AmE -dʒəl/ ADJ **1** (*journalism*) If you describe a situation as **fragile**, you mean that it is weak or uncertain, and unlikely to be able to resist strong pressure or attack. = **unstable, weak; ≠ strong, stable** ❑ *The fragile economies of several southern African nations could be irreparably damaged.* ❑ *The prime minister's fragile government was on the brink of collapse.* **2** Something that is **fragile** is easily broken or damaged. = **weak; ≠ sturdy, strong** ❑ *He leaned back in his fragile chair.*

fra·gil·i·ty /frəˈdʒɪlɪti/ NOUN [U] **1** By mid-1988 there were clear indications of the extreme fragility of the right-wing coalition. **2** Older drivers are more likely to be seriously injured because of the fragility of their bones.

✪**frag·ment** NOUN, VERB

NOUN /ˈfrægmənt/ [C] (**fragments**) A **fragment of** something is a small piece or part of it. = **piece** ❑ *The only reminder of the shooting is a few fragments of metal in my shoulder.* ❑ *She read everything, digesting every fragment of news.* ❑ *glass fragments*

VERB /frægˈment/ [I, T] (**fragments, fragmenting, fragmented**) If something **fragments** or **is fragmented**, it breaks or separates into small pieces or parts. ❑ *The clouds fragmented and out came the sun.* ❑ *Fierce rivalries have traditionally fragmented the region.* ❑ *By the first century BC, Buddhism was in danger of fragmenting into small sects.*

✪**frag·men·ta·tion** /ˌfrægmenˈteɪʃən/ NOUN [U] ❑ *the extraordinary fragmentation of styles on the music scene*

❑ *This is a time of social fragmentation, when communal and family bonds have eroded.*

✪frag·men·tary /'frægməntəri, AmE -teri/ ADJ Something that is **fragmentary** is made up of small or unconnected pieces. ❑ *Any action on the basis of such fragmentary evidence would be foolish.* ❑ *the fragmentary nature of our knowledge*

fra·grance /'freigrəns/ NOUN [c, u] (**fragrances**) **1** A **fragrance** is a pleasant or sweet smell. ❑ *a shrubby plant with a strong characteristic fragrance* **2** **Fragrance** is a pleasant-smelling liquid which people put on their bodies to make themselves smell nice. = perfume ❑ *The advertisement is for a men's fragrance.*

fra·grant /'freigrənt/ ADJ Something that is **fragrant** has a pleasant, sweet smell. ❑ *fragrant oils and perfumes*

frail /freil/ ADJ (**frailer, frailest**) **1** Someone who is **frail** is not very strong or healthy. = weak ❑ *She lay in bed looking frail.* **2** Something that is **frail** is easily broken or damaged. = fragile ❑ *The frail boat rocked as he clambered in.*

frail·ty /'freilti/ NOUN [c, u] (**frailties**) **1** [c, u] If you refer to the **frailties** or **frailty** of people, you are referring to their weaknesses. ❑ *the frailties of human nature* **2** [u] **Frailty** is the condition of having poor health. ❑ *She died after a long period of increasing frailty.*

frame ♦◇◇ /freim/ NOUN, VERB
NOUN [c] (**frames**) **1** The **frame** of a picture or mirror is the wood, metal, or plastic that is fitted around it, especially when it is displayed or hung on a wall. ❑ *Estelle kept a photograph of her mother in a silver frame on the kitchen mantelpiece.* **2** The **frame** of an object such as a building, chair, or window is the arrangement of wooden, metal, or plastic bars between which other material is fitted, and which give the object its strength and shape. ❑ *He supplied housebuilders with modern timber frames.* ❑ *With difficulty he released the mattress from the metal frame, and groped beneath it.* **3** The **frames** of a pair of glasses are all the metal or plastic parts of it, but not the lenses. ❑ *He was wearing new glasses with gold wire frames.* **4** A **frame** of cine film is one of the many separate photographs that it consists of. ❑ *Standard 8mm projects at 16 frames per second.* **5** You can refer to someone's body as their **frame**, especially when you are describing the general shape of their body. ❑ *Their belts are pulled tight against their bony frames.*
VERB [T] (**frames, framing, framed**) **1** When a picture or photograph **is framed**, it is put in a frame. ❑ *The picture is now ready to be mounted and framed.* **2** If an object **is framed** by a particular thing, it is surrounded by that thing in a way that makes the object more striking or attractive to look at. ❑ *The swimming pool is framed by tropical gardens.* **3** (*informal*) If someone **frames** an innocent person, they make other people think that that person is guilty of a crime, by lying or inventing evidence. ❑ *I need to find out who tried to frame me.*

frame of mind NOUN [c] (**frames of mind**) Your **frame of mind** is the mood that you are in, which causes you to have a particular attitude to something. ❑ *Lewis was not in the right frame of mind to continue.*

✪frame·work /'freimwɜːk/ NOUN [c] (**frameworks**) (*academic word*) **1** A **framework** is a particular set of rules, ideas, or beliefs which you use in order to deal with problems or to decide what to do. ❑ *within the framework of federal regulations* ❑ *The purpose of the chapter is to provide a framework for thinking about why exchange rates change.* ❑ *Doctors need a clear legal framework to be able to deal with difficult clinical decisions.* **2** A **framework** is a structure that forms a support or frame for something. ❑ *wooden shelves on a steel framework*

✪fran·chise /'fræntʃaiz/ NOUN, VERB
NOUN [c, u] (**franchises**) **1** [c] (*business*) A **franchise** is an authority that is given by an organization to someone, allowing them to sell its goods or services or to take part in an activity which the organization controls. ❑ *fast-food franchises* ❑ *the franchise to build and operate the tunnel* ❑ *Talk to other franchise holders and ask them what they think of the parent company.* **2** [u] [also 'the' franchise] **Franchise** is the right to vote in an election. ❑ *the introduction of universal franchise*
VERB [T] (**franchises, franchising, franchised**) (*business*) If a company **franchises** its business, it sells franchises to other companies, allowing them to sell its goods or services. ❑ *She has recently franchised her business.* ❑ *Though the service is available only in California, its founder Michael Cane says he plans to franchise it in other states.* ❑ *It takes hundreds of thousands of dollars to get into the franchised pizza business.*

frank /fræŋk/ ADJ (**franker, frankest**) If someone is **frank**, they state or express things in an open and honest way. = candid ❑ *'It is clear that my client has been less than frank with me,' said his lawyer.*

frank·ly /'fræŋkli/ ADV **1** [frankly with v] If you speak **frankly**, you state or express things in an open and honest way. ❑ *You can talk frankly to me.* **2** (*emphasis*) You use **frankly** when you are expressing an opinion or feeling to emphasize that you mean what you are saying, especially when the person you are speaking to may not like it. ❑ *'You don't give a damn about my feelings, do you.'—'Quite frankly, I don't.'* ❑ *Frankly, Thomas, this question of your loan is beginning to worry me.*

fran·tic /'fræntik/ ADJ **1** If you are **frantic**, you are behaving in a wild and uncontrolled way because you are frightened or worried. = frenzied ❑ *A bird had been locked in and was by now quite frantic.* **2** If an activity is **frantic**, things are done quickly and in an energetic but disorganized way, because there is very little time. ❑ *A busy night in the restaurant can be frantic in the kitchen.*
fran·ti·cal·ly /'fræntikli/ ADV **1** [frantically with v] ❑ *She clutched frantically at Emily's arm.* **2** [frantically with v] ❑ *We have been frantically trying to save her life.*

fra·ter·nity /frə'tɜːniti/ NOUN [c, u] (**fraternities**) **1** [c] You can refer to people who have the same profession or the same interests as a particular **fraternity**. = set ❑ *the spread of stolen guns among the criminal fraternity* **2** [u] (*formal*) **Fraternity** refers to friendship and support between people who feel they are closely linked to each other. ❑ *Bob needs the fraternity of others who share his mission.* **3** [c] In the United States, a **fraternity** is a society of male university or college students. ❑ *He must have been the most popular guy at the most popular fraternity in college.*

✪fraud ♦◇◇ /frɔːd/ NOUN [c, u] (**frauds**) **1** [c, u] **Fraud** is the crime of gaining money or financial benefits by a trick or by lying. ❑ *He was jailed for two years for fraud and deception.* ❑ *Tax frauds are dealt with by the Inland Revenue.* ❑ *officials who are involved in security and fraud prevention* **2** [c] A **fraud** is something or someone that deceives people in a way that is illegal or dishonest. ❑ *He's a fraud and a cheat.*

✪fraudu·lent /'frɔːdʒʊlənt/ ADJ A **fraudulent** activity is deliberately deceitful, dishonest, or untrue. ❑ *fraudulent claims about being a nurse* ❑ *The claim should be met, provided the policyholder has not been fraudulent or deceitful.*
fraudu·lent·ly /'frɔːdʒʊləntli/ ADV [fraudulently with v] ❑ *All 5,000 of the homes were fraudulently obtained.*

fraught /frɔːt/ ADJ **1** [V-LINK + fraught 'with' N] If a situation or action is **fraught with** problems or risks, it is filled with them. ❑ *The earliest operations employing this technique were fraught with dangers.* **2** If you say that a situation or action is **fraught**, you mean that it is worrisome or difficult. ❑ *It has been a somewhat fraught day.*

freak /friːk/ ADJ, NOUN
ADJ [freak + N] A **freak** event or action is one that is a very unusual or extreme example of its type. ❑ *Weir broke his leg in a freak accident playing golf.*
NOUN [c] (**freaks**) **1** (*informal*) If you describe someone as a particular kind of **freak**, you are emphasizing that they are very enthusiastic about a thing or activity, and often seem to think about nothing else. = fanatic ❑ *Diaz is a fitness freak who's trained in martial arts.* **2** People are sometimes referred to as **freaks** when their behaviour or attitude is very different from that of the majority of people. ❑ *Not so long ago, transsexuals were regarded as freaks.*

f

free ♦♦♦ /friː/ ADJ, VERB

ADJ (**freer**, **freest**) **1** If something is **free**, you can have it or use it without paying for it. ❑ *The seminars are free, with lunch provided.* **2** Someone or something that is **free** is not restricted, controlled, or limited, for example, by rules, customs, or other people. ❑ *The government will be free to pursue its economic policies.* ❑ *The elections were free and fair.* **3** Someone who is **free** is no longer a prisoner or a slave. ❑ *He walked from the court house a free man.* **4** [V-LINK + free 'of/from' N] If someone or something is **free of** or **free from** an unpleasant thing, they do not have it or they are not affected by it. ❑ *a future far more free of fear* ❑ *She retains her slim figure and is free of wrinkles.* **5** [V-LINK + free 'of' N] A sum of money or type of goods that is **free of** tax or duty is one that you do not have to pay tax on. ❑ *This benefit is free of tax under current legislation.* **6** If you have a **free** period of time or are **free** at a particular time, you are not working or occupied then. ❑ *She spent her free time shopping.* ❑ *I used to write during my free periods at school.* **7** If something such as a table or seat is **free**, it is not being used or occupied by anyone, or is not reserved for anyone to use. ❑ *There was only one seat free on the train.* **8** If you get something **free** or if it gets **free**, it is no longer trapped by anything or attached to anything. ❑ *He pulled his arm free, and strode for the door.* **9** [free + N] When someone is using one hand or arm to hold or move something, their other hand or arm is referred to as their **free** one. ❑ *He snatched up the receiver and his free hand groped for the switch on the bedside lamp.*

PHRASES **feel free** (*informal, formulae*) You say 'feel free' when you want to give someone permission to do something, in a very willing way. ❑ *If you have any questions at all, please feel free to ask me.*

for free (*informal*) If you do something or get something **for free**, you do it without being paid or get it without having to pay for it. ❑ *I wasn't expecting you to do it for free.*

VERB [T] (**frees**, **freeing**, **freed**) **1** If you **free** someone of something that is unpleasant or restricting, you remove it from them. ❑ *It will free us of a whole lot of debt.* **2** To **free** a prisoner or a slave means to let them go or release them from prison. ❑ *Israel is set to free more Lebanese prisoners.* **3** To **free** someone or something means to make them available for a task or function that they were previously not available for. ❑ *Toolbelts free both hands and lessen the risk of dropping hammers.* ❑ *His deal with Disney will run out shortly, freeing him to pursue his own project.* **4** If you **free** someone or something, you remove them from the place in which they have been trapped or become fixed. ❑ *Rescue workers tried to free him by cutting away part of the car.*

PHRASAL VERB **free up** **1** Free up means the same as free VERB 3. ❑ *It can handle even the most complex graphic jobs, freeing up your computer for other tasks.* **2** (*business*) To **free up** a market, economy, or system means to make it operate with fewer restrictions and controls. ❑ *policies for freeing up markets and extending competition*

free·ly /ˈfriːli/ ADV [freely with V] ❑ *They cast their votes freely and without coercion on election day.*

→ See also **interest-free**

✦ free of charge → see **charge**; **give someone a free hand** → see **hand**; **give someone free rein** → see **rein**

✪ free·dom ♦♦◇ /ˈfriːdəm/ NOUN [U] (**freedoms**) **1** [also freedoms] **Freedom** is the state of being allowed to do what you want to do. **Freedoms** are instances of this. = liberty; ≠ restriction ❑ *freedom of speech* ❑ *The United Nations Secretary-General has spoken of the need for individual freedoms and human rights.* ❑ *They want greater political freedom.* ❑ *Today we have the freedom to decide our own futures.* **2** When prisoners or slaves are set free or escape, they gain their **freedom**. = liberty ❑ *the agreement worked out by the UN, under which all hostages and detainees would gain their freedom* **3** **Freedom from** something you do not want means not being affected by it. ❑ *all the freedom from pain that medicine could provide*

freely /ˈfriːli/ ADV **1** **Freely** means many times or in large quantities. ❑ *We have referred freely to his ideas.* ❑ *George was spending very freely.* **2** [freely after V] If you can talk

freely, you can talk without needing to be careful about what you say. ❑ *She wondered whether he had someone to whom he could talk freely.* **3** [freely with V] If someone gives or does something **freely**, they give or do it willingly, without being ordered or forced to do it. ❑ *Danny shared his knowledge freely with anyone interested.* **4** [freely after V] If something or someone moves **freely**, they move easily and smoothly, without any obstacles or resistance. ❑ *The clay court was slippery and he was unable to move freely.*

→ See also **free**

✪ freeze ♦◇◇ /friːz/ VERB, NOUN

VERB [I, T] (**freezes**, **freezing**, **froze**, **frozen**) **1** [I, T] If a liquid or a substance containing a liquid **freezes**, or if something **freezes**, it becomes solid because of low temperatures. ❑ *If the temperature drops below 0°C, water freezes.* ❑ *The ground froze solid.* ❑ *the discovery of how to freeze water at higher temperatures* **2** [I, T] If you **freeze** something such as food, you preserve it by storing it at a temperature below freezing point. You can also talk about how well food **freezes**. ❑ *You can freeze the soup at this stage.* **3** [I] When **it freezes** outside, the temperature falls below freezing point. ❑ *What if it rained and then froze all through those months?* **4** [I] If you **freeze**, you feel extremely cold. ❑ *The windows didn't fit at the bottom so for a while we froze even in the middle of summer.* **5** [I] (*written*) If someone who is moving **freezes**, they suddenly stop and become completely still and quiet. ❑ *She froze when the beam of the flashlight struck her.* **6** [T] (*business*) If the government or a company **freeze** things such as prices or wages, they state officially that they will not allow them to increase for a fixed period of time. ❑ *They want the government to freeze prices.* **7** [T] (*business*) If someone in authority **freezes** something such as a bank account, fund, or property, they obtain a legal order which states that it cannot be used or sold for a particular period of time. ❑ *The governor's action freezes 300,000 accounts.*

NOUN [C] (**freezes**) **1** A **freeze** is a time when the temperature outside falls below freezing point. ❑ *The trees were damaged by a freeze in December.* **2** If there is a **freeze** on something such as prices or wages, a government or company has stated officially that they will not allow them to increase for a fixed period of time. ❑ *A wage freeze was imposed on all staff earlier this month.* **3** [with SUPP] A **freeze** on something such as a bank account, fund, or property is a legal order which states that it cannot be used or sold for a particular period of time. ❑ *a freeze on private savings*

→ See also **freezing, frozen**

freez·er /ˈfriːzə/ NOUN [C] (**freezers**) A **freezer** is a large container like a refrigerator in which the temperature is kept below freezing point so that you can store food inside it for long periods. = deep freeze

freez·ing /ˈfriːzɪŋ/ ADJ (*emphasis*) **1** If you say that something is **freezing** or **freezing cold**, you are emphasizing that it is very cold. ❑ *The cinema was freezing.* **2** [V-LINK + freezing] If you say that you are **freezing** or **freezing cold**, you are emphasizing that you feel very cold. ❑ *'You must be freezing,' she said.*

→ See also **free**

freight /freɪt/ NOUN [U] **1** **Freight** is the movement of goods by lorries, trains, ships, or planes. ❑ *France derives 16% of revenue from air freight.* **2** **Freight** is goods that are transported by lorries, trains, ships, or planes. ❑ *26 tons of freight*

fre·net·ic /frɪˈnetɪk/ ADJ If you describe an activity as **frenetic**, you mean that it is fast and energetic, but rather uncontrolled. = frantic ❑ *the frenetic pace of life in New York*

fren·zied /ˈfrenzɪd/ ADJ **Frenzied** activities or actions are wild, excited, and uncontrolled. = frantic ❑ *the frenzied activity of the election*

fren·zy /ˈfrenzi/ NOUN [C, U] (**frenzies**) **Frenzy** or a **frenzy** is great excitement or wild behaviour that often results from losing control of your feelings. ❑ *'Get out!' she ordered in a frenzy.*

✪ fre·quen·cy /ˈfriːkwənsi/ NOUN [U, C] (**frequencies**) **1** [U] The **frequency** of an event is the number of times it happens during a particular period. ❏ *The frequency of Kara's phone calls increased rapidly.* ❏ *The tanks broke down with increasing frequency.* **2** [C, U] In physics, the **frequency** of a sound wave or a radio wave is the number of times it vibrates within a specified period of time. ❏ *You can't hear waves of such a high frequency.* ❏ *a frequency of 24 kilohertz*

✪ **fre·quent** ♦♦◇ /ˈfriːkwənt/ ADJ If something is **frequent**, it happens often. = regular; ≠ infrequent, rare ❏ *Bordeaux is on the main Paris–Madrid line so there are frequent trains.* ❏ *He is a frequent visitor to the house.*

✪ **fre·quent·ly** ♦♦◇ /ˈfriːkwəntli/ ADV = often, regularly; ≠ infrequently, rarely ❏ *Iron and folic acid supplements are frequently given to pregnant women.* ❏ *the most frequently asked question*

WORD FAMILIES	
frequent ADJ	Bordeaux is on the main Paris–Madrid line so there are **frequent** trains.
infrequent ADJ	His calls became more and more **infrequent** and eventually stopped.
frequently ADV	Students **frequently** find this point difficult so it is worth repeating.
infrequently ADV	There is a rear gate, but this is used very **infrequently**.
frequency NOUN	He was worried about the **frequency** of her absences.

fresh ♦♦◇ /freʃ/ ADJ (**fresher**, **freshest**) **1** [fresh + N] A **fresh** thing or amount replaces or is added to a previous thing or amount. = new ❏ *He asked the police, who carried out the original investigation, to make fresh inquiries.* **2** Something that is **fresh** has been done, made, or experienced recently. ❏ *There were no fresh car tracks or footprints in the snow.* ❏ *A puppy stepped in the fresh cement.* **3** **Fresh** food has been picked or produced recently, and has not been preserved, by being frozen or put in a can. ❏ *locally caught fresh fish* **4** If you describe something as **fresh**, you like it because it is new and exciting. = original ❏ *These designers are full of fresh ideas.* **5** If you describe something as **fresh**, you mean that it is pleasant, bright, and clean in appearance. ❏ *Gingham fabrics always look fresh and pretty.* **6** If something smells, tastes, or feels **fresh**, it is clean or cool. ❏ *The air was fresh and for a moment she felt revived.* **7** If you feel **fresh**, you feel full of energy and enthusiasm. ❏ *It's vital we are as fresh as possible for those games.* **8** [V-LINK + fresh 'from/out of' N] If you are **fresh from** a particular place or experience, you have just come from that place or you have just had that experience. You can also say that someone is **fresh out of** a place. = straight ❏ *I returned to the office, fresh from the airport.*

fresh·ly /ˈfreʃli/ ADV [freshly + -ED] If something is **freshly** made or done, it has been recently made or done. = recently ❏ *freshly baked bread*

fresh·water /ˈfreʃˌwɔːtə/ ADJ [freshwater + N] A **freshwater** lake contains water that is not salty, usually in contrast to the sea. **Freshwater** creatures live in water that is not salty. ❏ *Lake Balaton, the largest freshwater lake in Europe*

fret /fret/ VERB, NOUN

VERB [I, T] (**frets**, **fretting**, **fretted**) If you **fret** about something, you worry about it. = worry ❏ *I was working all hours and constantly fretting about everyone else's problems.* ❏ *But congressional staffers fret that the project will eventually cost billions more.*

NOUN [C] (**frets**) The **frets** on a musical instrument such as a guitar are the raised lines across its neck.

fric·tion /ˈfrɪkʃən/ NOUN [U] (**frictions**) **1** [also frictions] If there is **friction** between people, there is disagreement and argument between them. = conflict ❏ *Sara sensed that there had been friction between her children.* **2** **Friction** is the force that makes it difficult for things to move freely when they are touching each other. ❏ *The pistons are graphite-coated to reduce friction.*

fridge /frɪdʒ/ NOUN [C] (**fridges**) (*informal*) A **fridge** is the same as a **refrigerator**.

friend ♦♦♦ /frend/ NOUN

NOUN [C, PL] (**friends**) **1** [C] A **friend** is someone who you know well and like, but who is not related to you. ❏ *I had a long talk about this with my best friend.* ❏ *She was never a close friend of mine.* **2** [C] If one country refers to another as a **friend**, they mean that the other country is not an enemy of theirs. = ally ❏ *The president said that Japan is now a friend and international partner.* **3** [PL] If you are **friends with** someone, you are their friend and they are yours. ❏ *I still wanted to be friends with Alison.* ❏ *We remained good friends.* **4** [PL] The **friends of** a country, cause, organization, or a famous politician are the people and organizations who help and support them. ❏ *the friends of Israel*

PHRASE **make friends** If you **make friends with** someone, you begin a friendship with them. You can also say that two people **make friends**. ❏ *He has made friends with the kids on the street.* ❏ *Dennis made friends easily.*

friend·ly ♦◇◇ /ˈfrendli/ ADJ, NOUN

ADJ (**friendlier**, **friendliest**) **1** If someone is **friendly**, they behave in a pleasant, kind way, and like to be with other people. ❏ *Godfrey had been friendly to me.* ❏ *a man with a pleasant, friendly face* **2** [V-LINK + friendly] If you are **friendly with** someone, you like each other and enjoy spending time together. ❏ *I'm friendly with his mother.* **3** You can describe another country or their government as **friendly** when they have good relations with your own country rather than being an enemy. ❏ *a worsening in relations between the two previously friendly countries* **4** (BrE) In sport, a **friendly** game is one which is not part of a competition, and is played for entertainment or practice, often without any serious effort to win.

NOUN [C] (**friendlies**) [friendly + N] (BrE; in AmE, use **exhibition game**) In sport, a **friendly** is a game which is not part of a competition, and is played for entertainment or practice, often without any serious effort to win.

friend·li·ness /ˈfrendlinəs/ NOUN [U] ❏ *She also loves the friendliness of the people.*

friend·ship ♦◇◇ /ˈfrendʃɪp/ NOUN [C, U] (**friendships**) **1** [C, U] A **friendship** is a relationship between two or more friends. ❏ *Giving advice when it's not called for is the quickest way to end a good friendship.* ❏ *She struck up a close friendship with Desiree during the week of rehearsals.* **2** [C, U] **Friendship** is a relationship between two countries in which they help and support each other. = goodwill ❏ *The president set the targets for the future to promote friendship with East Europe.* **3** [U] You use **friendship** to refer in a general way to the state of being friends, or the feelings that friends have for each other. ❏ *a hobby which led to a whole new world of friendship and adventure*

fright /fraɪt/ NOUN [U, C] (**frights**) **1** [U] **Fright** is a sudden feeling of fear, especially the fear that you feel when something unpleasant surprises you. ❏ *The steam pipes rattled suddenly, and Franklin jumped with fright.* ❏ *The birds smashed into the top of their cages in fright.* **2** [C] A **fright** is an experience which makes you suddenly afraid. = scare ❏ *The snake picked up its head and stuck out its tongue which gave everyone a fright.*

fright·en /ˈfraɪtən/ VERB

VERB [T] (**frightens**, **frightening**, **frightened**) If something or someone **frightens** you, they cause you to suddenly feel afraid, anxious, or nervous. = scare ❏ *He knew that Soli was trying to frighten him, so he smiled to hide his fear.*

PHRASE **frighten the life out of someone** or **frighten the wits out of someone** or **frighten someone out of their wits** (*emphasis*) If something frightens the life out of you, **frightens the wits out of** you, or **frightens** you **out of your wits**, it causes you to feel suddenly afraid or gives you a very unpleasant shock. ❏ *Fairground rides are intended to frighten the life out of you.*

PHRASAL VERB **frighten away** or **frighten off** **1** If you **frighten away** a person or animal or **frighten** them **off**, you make them afraid so that they run away or stay some distance away from you. = scare off ❏ *The fishermen said the company's seismic survey was frightening away fish.*

2 To **frighten** someone **away** or **frighten** them **off** means to make them nervous so that they decide not to become involved with a particular person or activity. = scare off □ *Repossessions have frightened buyers off.*

fright·ened /ˈfraɪtənd/ ADJ If you are **frightened**, you are anxious or afraid, often because of something that has just happened or that you think may happen. □ *She was frightened of making a mistake.*

fright·en·ing /ˈfraɪtənɪŋ/ ADJ If something is **frightening**, it makes you feel afraid, anxious, or nervous. = alarming □ *It was a very frightening experience and they were very courageous.*

fright·en·ing·ly /ˈfraɪtənɪŋli/ ADV □ *The country is frighteningly close to possessing nuclear weapons.*

fringe /frɪndʒ/ NOUN, ADJ
NOUN [c] (**fringes**) **1** A **fringe** is a decoration attached to clothes, or other objects such as curtains, consisting of a row of hanging strips or threads. □ *The jacket had leather fringes.* **2** To be **on the fringe** or **the fringes** of a place means to be on the outside edge of it, or to be in one of the parts that are farthest from its centre. □ *black townships located on the fringes of the city* **3** The **fringe** or **the fringes** of an activity or organization are its less important, less typical, or most extreme parts, rather than its main and central part. □ *The party remained on the fringe of the political scene until last year.* **4** (BrE; in AmE, use **bangs**) A **fringe** is hair which is cut so that it hangs over your forehead.
ADJ [fringe + N] **Fringe** groups or events are less important or popular than other related groups or events. □ *The monarchists are a small fringe group who quarrel fiercely among themselves.*

frivo·lous /ˈfrɪvələs/ ADJ **1** If you describe someone as **frivolous**, you mean they behave in a silly or light-hearted way, rather than being serious and sensible. □ *I just decided I was a bit too frivolous to be a doctor.* **2** If you describe an activity as **frivolous**, you disapprove of it because it is not useful and wastes time or money. □ *The group says it wants politicians to stop wasting public money on what it believes are frivolous projects.*

from ♦♦♦ /frəm, STRONG frɒm, AmE frɑːm/ PREP **1** If something comes **from** a particular person or thing, or if you get something **from** them, they give it to you or they are the source of it. □ *He appealed for information from anyone who saw the attackers.* □ *an anniversary present from his wife* **2** Someone who comes **from** a particular place lives in that place or originally lived there. Something that comes **from** a particular place was made in that place. □ *an art dealer from Zurich* □ *Katy Jones is nineteen and comes from Biloxi.* **3** A person **from** a particular organization works for that organization. □ *a representative from the Israeli embassy* **4** If someone or something moves or is moved **from** a place, they leave it or are removed, so that they are no longer there. □ *The guests watched as she fled from the room.* **5** If you take one thing or person **from** another, you move that thing or person so that they are no longer with the other or attached to the other. □ *In many bone transplants, bone can be taken from other parts of the patient's body.* **6** If you take something **from** an amount, you reduce the amount by that much. □ *The $103 is deducted from Mrs Adams' salary.* **7** **From** is used in expressions such as **away from** and **absent from** to say that someone or something is not present in a place where they are usually found. □ *Her husband worked away from home a lot.* **8** If you return **from** a place or an activity, you return after being in that place or doing that activity. □ *My son has just returned from Amsterdam.* **9** If you are back **from** a place or activity, you have left it and have returned to your former place. □ *Elaine was just back from work when he called.* **10** If you see or hear something **from** a particular place, you are in that place when you see it or hear it. □ *Visitors see the painting from behind a plate glass window.* **11** [V + from + N] If something hangs or sticks out **from** an object, it is attached to it or held by it. □ *Hanging from his right wrist is a heavy gold bracelet.* □ *large fans hanging from ceilings* **12** [AMOUNT + from + N] You can use **from** when giving distances. For example, if a place is fifty miles **from** another place, the distance between the two

places is fifty miles. □ *a small park only a few hundred yards from Zurich's main shopping centre* □ *How far is it from here?* **13** If a road or railway line goes **from** one place to another, you can travel along it between the two places. □ *the road from St Petersburg to Tallinn* **14** [V + from + N] **From** is used, especially in the expression **made from**, to say what substance has been used to make something. = out of □ *bread made from white flour* **15** If something changes **from** one thing **to** another, it stops being the first thing and becomes the second thing. □ *The expression on his face changed from sympathy to surprise.* □ *Unemployment has fallen from 7.5 to 7.2%.* **16** [from + N/-ING] You use **from** after some verbs and nouns when mentioning the cause of something. □ *The problem simply resulted from a difference of opinion.* □ *They really do get pleasure from spending money on other people.* **17** You use **from** when you are giving the reason for an opinion. □ *She knew from experience that Dave was about to tell her the truth.* □ *He sensed from the expression on her face that she had something to say.* **18** You can use **from** when you are talking about the beginning of a period of time. □ *She studied painting from 1926 and also worked as a commercial artist.* □ *Breakfast is available to fishermen from 6 a.m.* **19** [from + N/-ING] You say **from** one thing **to** another when you are stating the range of things that are possible, or when saying that the range of things includes everything in a certain category. □ *There are 94 countries represented in Barcelona, from Algeria to Zimbabwe.* **20** **From** is used after verbs with meanings such as 'protect', 'free', 'keep', and 'prevent' to introduce the action that does not happen, or that someone does not want to happen. □ *Such laws could protect the consumer from harmful or dangerous remedies.*

front ♦♦♦ /frʌnt/ NOUN, ADJ
NOUN [c, SING] (**fronts**) **1** [c] The **front of** something is the part of it that faces you, or that faces forward, or that you normally see or use. □ *One man sat in an armchair, and the other sat on the front of the desk.* □ *Stand at the front of the queue.* **2** [c] The **front of** a building is the side or part of it that faces the street. □ *Attached to the front of the house, there was a large veranda.* **3** [c] In a war, the **front** is a line where two opposing armies are facing each other. □ *Sonja's husband is fighting at the front.* **4** [c] If you say that something is happening on a particular **front**, you mean that it is happening with regard to a particular situation or field of activity. □ *research across a wide academic front* **5** [c] If someone puts on a particular kind of **front**, they pretend to have a particular quality. □ *Michael kept up a brave front both to the world and in his home.* **6** [c] An organization or activity that is **a front for** one that is illegal or secret is used to hide it. = cover □ *a firm later identified by the police as a front for crime syndicates* **7** [c] In relation to the weather, a **front** is a line where a mass of cold air meets a mass of warm air. □ *The snow signalled the arrival of a front, and a high-pressure area seemed to be settling in.* **8** [SING] A person's or animal's **front** is the part of their body between their head and their legs that is on the opposite side to their back. □ *When baby is lying on his front, hold something so that he has to raise his head to see it.*
PHRASES **in front 1** If a person or thing is **in front**, they are ahead of others in a moving group, or further forward than someone or something else. □ *Officers will crack down on lunatic motorists who speed or drive too close to the car in front.* **2** Someone who is **in front** in a competition or contest at a particular point is winning at that point. = leading □ *Richard Dunwoody is in front in the jockeys' title race.*

in front of 1 If someone or something is **in front of** a particular thing, they are facing it, ahead of it, or close to the front part of it. □ *She sat down in front of her dressing-table mirror to look at herself.* □ *Something darted out in front of my car, and my car hit it.* **2** If you do or say something **in front of** someone else, you do or say it when they are present. □ *They never argued in front of their children.*
ADJ **1** [front + N] **Front** is used to refer to the side or part of something that is towards the front or nearest to the front. □ *I went out there on the front porch.* □ *She was only*

six and still missing her front teeth. **2** [front + N] The **front page** of a newspaper is the outside of the first page, where the main news stories are printed. □ *The front page carries a photograph of the two foreign ministers.*
→ See also **front line, front-page**

fron·tier /ˈfrʌntɪə, frʌnˈtɪə/ NOUN [c] (**frontiers**) **1** The **frontiers** of something, especially knowledge, are the limits to which it extends. □ *pushing back the frontiers of science* **2** A **frontier** is a border between two countries. □ *It wasn't difficult then to cross the frontier.*

front line also **front-line** NOUN
NOUN [c] (**front lines**) The **front line** is the place where two opposing armies are facing each other and where fighting is going on. □ *a massive concentration of soldiers on the front line*
PHRASE **in the front line** Someone who is **in the front line** has to play a very important part in defending or achieving something. □ *Information officers are in the front line of putting across government policies.*

front-page ADJ [front-page + N] A **front-page** article or picture appears on the front page of a newspaper because it is very important or interesting. □ *a front-page article in last week's paper*

frost /frɒst, AmE frɔːst/ NOUN [c, u] (**frosts**) When there is **frost** or a **frost**, the temperature outside falls below freezing point and the ground becomes covered in ice crystals. □ *There is frost on the ground and snow is forecast.*

froth /frɒθ, AmE frɔːθ/ NOUN, VERB
NOUN [u] **Froth** is a mass of small bubbles on the surface of a liquid. = foam □ *the froth of bubbles on the top of a glass of beer*
VERB [i] (**froths, frothing, frothed**) If a liquid **froths**, small bubbles appear on its surface. □ *The sea froths over my feet.*

frown /fraʊn/ VERB, NOUN
VERB [i] (**frowns, frowning, frowned**) When someone **frowns**, their eyebrows become drawn together, because they are annoyed, worried, or puzzled, or because they are concentrating. □ *Nancy shook her head, frowning.* □ *He frowned at her anxiously.*
PHRASAL VERB **frown upon** or **frown on** If something is **frowned upon** or is **frowned on**, people disapprove of it. □ *This practice is frowned upon as being wasteful.*
NOUN [c] (**frowns**) A **frown** is the facial expression someone has when their eyebrows become drawn together, because they are annoyed, worried, or puzzled, or because they are concentrating. □ *There was a deep frown on the boy's face.*

froze /frəʊz/ IRREG FORM **Froze** is the past tense of **freeze.**

fro·zen /ˈfrəʊzən/ IRREG FORM, ADJ
IRREG FORM **Frozen** is the past participle of **freeze.**
ADJ **1** If the ground is **frozen** it has become very hard because the weather is very cold. □ *It was bitterly cold now and the ground was frozen hard.* **2 Frozen** food has been preserved by being kept at a very low temperature. □ *Frozen fish is a very healthy convenience food.* **3** If you say that you are **frozen**, or a part of your body is **frozen**, you are emphasizing that you feel very cold. □ *He put one hand up to his frozen face.* □ *I'm frozen out here.*
PHRASE **frozen stiff Frozen stiff** means the same as **frozen** ADJ 3.

fru·gal /ˈfruːɡəl/ ADJ **1** People who are **frugal** or who live **frugal** lives do not spend much money on themselves. □ *She lives a frugal life.* **2** A **frugal** meal is small and not expensive. □ *The diet was frugal: cheese and water, rice and beans.*
fru·gal·ity /fruːˈɡælɪti/ NOUN [u] □ *We must practise the strictest frugality and economy.*

fruit ♦♦◇ /fruːt/ NOUN, VERB
NOUN [c, u] (**fruit** or **fruits**) **1** [c, u] **Fruit** or a **fruit** is something which grows on a tree or bush and which contains seeds or a stone covered by a substance that you can eat. □ *Fresh fruit and vegetables provide fibre and vitamins.* □ *bananas and other tropical fruits* **2** [c] The **fruits** or the **fruit of** someone's work or activity are the good things that result from it. □ *The team has really worked hard and Mansell is enjoying the fruits of that labour.*

PHRASE **bear fruit** If the effort that you put into something or a particular way of doing something **bears fruit**, it is successful and produces good results. □ *Eleanor's work among the women will, I trust, bear fruit.*
VERB [i] (**fruits, fruiting, fruited**) If a plant **fruits**, it produces fruit. □ *The scientists will study the variety of trees and observe which are fruiting.*

fruit·ful /ˈfruːtfʊl/ ADJ Something that is **fruitful** produces good and useful results. = productive □ *We had a long, happy, fruitful relationship.*

frui·tion /fruˈɪʃən/ NOUN [u] (formal) If something comes **to fruition**, it starts to succeed and produce the results that were intended or hoped for. □ *These plans take time to come to fruition.*

fruit·less /ˈfruːtləs/ ADJ **Fruitless** actions, events, or efforts do not achieve anything at all. = unproductive □ *It was a fruitless search.*

frus·trate ♦◇◇ /frʌˈstreɪt, AmE ˈfrʌstreɪt/ VERB [t] (**frustrates, frustrating, frustrated**) **1** If something **frustrates** you, it upsets or angers you because you are unable to do anything about the problems it creates. □ *These questions frustrated me.* **2** If someone or something **frustrates** a plan or attempt to do something, they prevent it from succeeding. □ *The government has deliberately frustrated his efforts to gain work permits for his foreign staff.*
frus·trat·ed /frʌˈstreɪtɪd, AmE ˈfrʌstreɪtɪd/ ADJ □ *Roberta felt frustrated and angry.*
frus·tra·tion /frʌˈstreɪʃən/ NOUN [c, u] (**frustrations**) □ *The results show the level of frustration among hospital doctors.*

frus·trat·ing /frʌˈstreɪtɪŋ/ ADJ Something that is **frustrating** annoys you or makes you angry because you cannot do anything about the problems it causes. □ *The current situation is very frustrating for us.*

fry ♦◇◇ /fraɪ/ VERB, NOUN
VERB [t] (**fries, frying, fried**) When you **fry** food, you cook it in a pan that contains hot fat or oil. □ *Fry the breadcrumbs until golden brown.*
NOUN [PL] (**fries**) **Fries** are the same as **chips.**

ft ABBREVIATION **ft** is a written abbreviation for **feet** or **foot.** □ *Flying at 1,000 ft, he heard a peculiar noise from the rotors.*

◊ fuel ♦♦◇ /ˈfjuːəl/ NOUN, VERB
NOUN [c, u] (**fuels**) **Fuel** is a substance such as coal, oil, or petrol that is burned to provide heat or power. □ *They ran out of fuel.* □ *industrial research into cleaner fuels* □ *The country needs to cut its fuel consumption.*
VERB [t] (**fuels, fuelling, fuelled**; in AmE, use **fueling, fueled**) To **fuel** a situation means to make it become worse or more intense. = feed □ *The result will inevitably fuel speculation about the prime minister's future.*

fu·gi·tive /ˈfjuːdʒɪtɪv/ NOUN [c] (**fugitives**) A **fugitive** is someone who is running away or hiding, usually in order to avoid being caught by the police. □ *The rebel leader was a fugitive from justice.*

◊ ful·fil ♦◇◇ /fʊlˈfɪl/ (in AmE, use **fulfill**) VERB [t] (**fulfils, fulfilling, fulfilled**) **1** If you **fulfil** something such as a promise, dream, or hope, you do what you said or hoped you would do. = carry out □ *President Kaunda fulfilled his promise of announcing a date for the referendum.* **2** To **fulfil** a task, role, or requirement means to do or be what is required, necessary, or expected. □ *Without them you will not be able to fulfil the tasks you have hoped for.* **3** If something **fulfils** you, or if you **fulfil yourself**, you feel happy and satisfied with what you are doing or with what you have achieved. = satisfy □ *The war was the biggest thing in her life and nothing after that quite fulfilled her.*
ful·filled /fʊlˈfɪld/ ADJ □ *She has courageously continued to lead a fulfilled life.*
ful·fill·ing /fʊlˈfɪlɪŋ/ ADJ □ *a fulfilling career*

◊ ful·fill ♦◇◇ /fʊlˈfɪl/ (AmE) → See **fulfil**

◊ ful·fil·ment /fʊlˈfɪlmənt/ also **fulfillment** NOUN [u] **1 Fulfilment** is a feeling of satisfaction that you get from doing or achieving something, especially something useful. = satisfaction □ *professional fulfilment* **2** The **fulfilment of** a promise, threat, request, hope, or duty is the event or act of it happening or being made to happen.

f

= realization □ *Visiting Angkor was the fulfilment of a childhood dream.* □ *the fulfilment of an election promise*

full ◆◆◆ /fʊl/ ADJ, ADV

ADJ (**fuller, fullest**) **1** If something is **full**, it contains as much of a substance or as many objects as it can. □ *Once the container is full, it stays shut until you turn it clockwise.* **2** [V-LINK + full 'of' N] If a place or thing is **full of** things or people, it contains a large number of them. = filled □ *The case was full of clothes.* □ *The streets are still full of debris from two nights of rioting.* **3** You say that a place or vehicle is **full** when there is no space left in it for any more people or things. □ *The car park was full when I left at about 10.45.* □ *They stay here a few hours before being sent to refugee camps, which are now almost full.* **4** [V-LINK + full] If your hands or arms are **full**, you are carrying or holding as much as you can carry. □ *Sylvia entered, her arms full of packages.* **5** [V-LINK + full] If you feel **full**, you have eaten or drunk so much that you do not want anything else. □ *It's healthy to eat when I'm hungry and to stop when I'm full.* **6** [V-LINK + full 'of' N] If someone or something **is full of** a particular feeling or quality, they have a lot of it. □ *I feel full of confidence and so open to possibilities.* □ *Mum's face was full of pain.* **7** [full + N] You use **full** before a noun to indicate that you are referring to all the details, things, or people that it can possibly include. = complete □ *Full details will be sent to you once your application has been accepted.* □ *May I have your full name?* **8** [full + N] **Full** is used to describe a sound, light, or physical force which is being produced with the greatest possible power or intensity. □ *From his study came the sound of Mahler, playing at full volume.* □ *Officials say the operation will be carried out in full daylight.* **9** [full + N] You use **full** to emphasize the completeness, intensity, or extent of something. □ *We should conserve oil and gas by making full use of other energy sources.* □ *The lane leading to the farm was in full view of the house windows.* **10** A **full** statement or report contains a lot of information and detail. □ *Mr Primakov gave a full account of his meeting with the president.* **11** If you say that someone has or leads a **full** life, you approve of the fact that they are always busy and do a lot of different things. □ *You will be successful in whatever you do and you will have a very full and interesting life.* **12** [full + N] You use **full** to refer to something which gives you all the rights, status, or importance for a particular position or activity, rather than just some of them. □ *How did the meeting go, did you get your full membership?* **13** [full + N] A **full** flavour is strong and rich. □ *Italian plum tomatoes have a full flavour, and are best for cooking.* **14** If you describe a part of someone's body as **full**, you mean that it is rounded and quite large. □ *The Juno Collection specializes in large sizes for ladies with a fuller figure.* **15** A **full** skirt or sleeve is wide and has been made from a lot of fabric. □ *My wedding dress has a very full skirt so I need to wear a good quality slip.* **16** When there is a **full** moon, the moon appears as a bright, complete circle. □ *those nights when the moon is full*

ADV [full + PREP] (*emphasis*) You use **full** to emphasize the force or directness with which someone or something is hit or looked at. □ *She kissed him full on the mouth.*

PHRASES **know full well** (*emphasis*) If you say that a person **knows full well** that something is true, especially something unpleasant, you are emphasizing that they are definitely aware of it, although they may behave as if they are not. □ *He knew full well he'd be ashamed of himself later.*

in full You say that something has been done or described **in full** when everything that was necessary has been done or described. = fully □ *The medical experts have yet to report in full.*

to the full Something that is done or experienced **to the full** is done to as great an extent as is possible. □ *She probably has a good mind, which should be used to the full.*

full·ness /'fʊlnəs/ NOUN [U] **1** High-fibre diets give the feeling of fullness. **2** The coat has raglan sleeves, and is cut to give fullness at the back.

✦ **in full swing** → see **swing**; **have your hands full** → see **hand**; **full blast** → see **blast**

full-scale ADJ **1** [full-scale + N] **Full-scale** means as complete, intense, or great in extent as possible. □ *the possibility of a full-scale nuclear war* **2** [full-scale + N] A

full-scale drawing or model is the same size as the thing that it represents. □ *working, full-scale prototypes*

full stop (*BrE*; in *AmE*, use **period**) NOUN [C] (**full stops**) A **full stop** is the punctuation mark . which you use at the end of a sentence when it is not a question or exclamation.

⊙**full-time** also **full time** ADJ, ADV

ADJ **Full-time** work or study involves working or studying for the whole of each normal working week rather than for part of it. ≠ part-time □ *a full-time job* □ *full-time staff* ADV [full-time after V] If you work or study **full-time**, you work or study for the whole of each normal working week rather than for part of it. ≠ part-time □ *Deirdre works full-time.*

ful·ly ◆◆◇ /'fʊli/ ADV **1** **Fully** means to the greatest degree or extent possible. = completely □ *She was fully aware of my thoughts.* **2** [fully with V] You use **fully** to say that a process is completely finished. □ *He had still not fully recovered.* **3** [fully with V] If you describe, answer, or deal with something **fully**, you leave out nothing that should be mentioned or dealt with. □ *Fiers promised to testify fully and truthfully.*

fum·ble /'fʌmbəl/ VERB [I] (**fumbles, fumbling, fumbled**) **1** If you **fumble for** something or **fumble with** something, you try to reach for it or hold it in a clumsy way. □ *She crept from the bed and fumbled for her dressing gown.* **2** When you are trying to say something, if you **fumble** for the right words, you speak in a clumsy and unclear way. □ *I fumbled for something to say.*

fume /fjuːm/ NOUN, VERB

NOUN [PL] (**fumes**) **Fumes** are the unpleasant and often unhealthy smoke and gases that are produced by fires or by things such as chemicals, fuel, or cooking. □ *car exhaust fumes*

VERB [I, T] (**fumes, fuming, fumed**) If you **fume** over something, you express annoyance and anger about it. □ *'It's monstrous!' Jackie fumed.*

fun ◆◆◇ /fʌn/ NOUN, ADJ

NOUN [U] **1** You refer to an activity or situation as **fun** if you think it is pleasant and enjoyable and it causes you to feel happy. □ *It's been a learning adventure and it's also been great fun.* □ *It could be fun to watch them.* **2** If you say that someone is **fun**, you mean that you enjoy being with them because they say and do interesting or amusing things. □ *Liz was fun to be with.*

PHRASES **for fun** If you do something **for fun** or **for the fun of it**, you do it in order to enjoy yourself rather than because it is important or necessary. □ *We used to drive too fast, just for fun.*

in fun If you do something **in fun**, you do it as a joke or for amusement, without intending to cause any harm. □ *Don't say such things, even in fun.*

make fun of or **poke fun at** If you **make fun of** someone or something or **poke fun at** them, you laugh at them, tease them, or make jokes about them in a way that causes them to seem ridiculous. □ *Don't make fun of me.*

ADJ [fun + N] (*informal*) If you describe something as a **fun** thing, you mean that you think it is enjoyable. If you describe someone as a **fun** person, you mean that you enjoy being with them. = entertaining □ *It was a fun evening.*

⊙**func·tion** ◆◆◇ /'fʌŋkʃən/ NOUN, VERB (*academic word*)

NOUN [C] (**functions**) **1** The **function** of something or someone is the useful thing that they do or are intended to do. = purpose, role □ *The main function of the investment banks is to raise capital for industry.* □ *This enzyme serves various functions.* **2** A **function** is a large formal dinner or party. □ *a private function hosted by one of his students*

VERB [I] (**functions, functioning, functioned**) **1** If a machine or system **is functioning**, it is working or operating. = operate, work □ *The authorities say the prison is now functioning normally.* □ *Conservation programmes cannot function without local support.* **2** If someone or something **functions as** a particular thing, they do the work or fulfil the purpose of that thing. □ *On weekdays, one third of the room functions as workspace.*

f

✪ **func·tion·al** /ˈfʌŋkʃənəl/ ADJ **1** **Functional** things are useful rather than decorative. ❑ *modern, functional furniture* **2** **Functional** equipment works or operates in the way that it is supposed to. = operational ❑ *We have fully functional smoke alarms on all staircases.*

✪ **fund** ♦♦♦ /fʌnd/ NOUN, VERB *(academic word)*
NOUN [PL, C] (**funds**) **1** [PL] **Funds** are amounts of money that are available to be spent, especially money that is given to an organization or person for a particular purpose. = money, finances ❑ *The concert will raise funds for research into AIDS.* ❑ *Funds are allocated according to regional needs.* **2** [C] A **fund** is an amount of money that is collected or saved for a particular purpose. ❑ *a scholarship fund for undergraduate engineering students*
VERB [T] (**funds, funding, funded**) When a person or organization **funds** something, they provide money for it. = finance ❑ *The Bush Foundation has funded a variety of faculty development programmes.* ❑ *The airport is being privately funded by a construction group.* ❑ *a new privately funded scheme*
→ See also **fund-raising**

✪ **fun·da·men·tal** ♦◇◇ /ˌfʌndəˈmentəl/ ADJ *(academic word)* **1** You use **fundamental** to describe things, activities, and principles that are very important or essential. They affect the basic nature of other things or are the most important element upon which other things depend. = basic ❑ *Our constitution embodies all the fundamental principles of democracy.* ❑ *A fundamental human right is being withheld from these people.* **2** You use **fundamental** to describe something which exists at a deep and basic level, and is therefore likely to continue. = profound ❑ *But on this question, the two leaders have very fundamental differences.* **3** [V-LINK + fundamental 'to' N] If one thing **is fundamental to** another, it is absolutely necessary to it, and the second thing cannot exist, succeed, or be imagined without it. = vital ❑ *He believes better relations with China are fundamental to the well-being of the area.* **4** [fundamental + N] You can use **fundamental** to show that you are referring to what you consider to be the most important aspect of a situation, and that you are not concerned with less important details. = basic ❑ *The fundamental problem lies in their inability to distinguish between reality and invention.*

fun·da·men·tal·ism /ˌfʌndəˈmentəlɪzəm/ NOUN [U] **Fundamentalism** is the belief in the original form of a religion or theory, without accepting any later ideas. ❑ *Religious fundamentalism was spreading in the region.*

fun·da·men·tal·ist /ˌfʌndəˈmentəlɪst/ NOUN [C] (**fundamentalists**) A **fundamentalist** is someone who believes in the original form of a religion or theory, without accepting any later ideas. ❑ *Christian fundamentalists*

✪ **fun·da·men·tal·ly** /ˌfʌndəˈmentəli/ ADV **1** [fundamentally with CL/GROUP] *(emphasis)* You use **fundamentally** for emphasis when you are stating an opinion, or when you are making an important or general statement about something. = basically ❑ *Fundamentally, women like him for his sensitivity and charming vulnerability.* **2** [fundamentally with V] You use **fundamentally** to indicate that something affects or relates to the deep, basic nature of something. = profoundly ❑ *He disagreed fundamentally with the president's judgment.* ❑ *Environmentalists say the treaty is fundamentally flawed.*

✪ **fund·ing** ♦◇◇ /ˈfʌndɪŋ/ NOUN [U] **Funding** is money which a government or organization provides for a particular purpose. = money, finance ❑ *They hope for government funding for the scheme.* ❑ *Many colleges have seen their funding cut.*

WORD CONNECTIONS
VERB + **funding**
seek funding
apply for funding
receive funding
secure funding
❑ *The Poetry Society has secured funding from various sources.*

provide funding
increase funding
cut funding
boost funding
❑ *The University has provided the main funding for the project.*

fund-raising also **fundraising** NOUN [U] **Fund-raising** is the activity of collecting money to support a charity or political campaign or organization. ❑ *Encourage her to get involved in fund-raising for charity.*

fu·ner·al /ˈfjuːnərəl/ NOUN [C] (**funerals**) A **funeral** is the ceremony that is held when the body of someone who has died is buried or cremated. ❑ *The funeral will be held in Joplin, Missouri.*

fun·nel /ˈfʌnəl/ NOUN, VERB
NOUN [C] (**funnels**) **1** A **funnel** is an object with a wide, circular top and a narrow short tube at the bottom. Funnels are used to pour liquids into containers which have a small opening, for example, bottles. ❑ *Rain falls through the funnel into the jar below.* **2** A **funnel** is a metal chimney on a ship or railway engine powered by steam. ❑ *a ship with three masts and two funnels* **3** You can describe as a **funnel** something that is narrow, or narrow at one end, through which a substance flows and is directed. ❑ *Along the road, funnels of dark grey smoke rose from bombed villages.*
VERB [I, T] (**funnels, funnelling, funnelled**; in AmE, use **funneling, funneled**) **1** [I, T] If something **funnels** somewhere or **is funnelled** there, it is directed through a narrow space. ❑ *The winds came from the north, across the plains, funnelling down the valley.* **2** [T] If you **funnel** money, goods, or information from one place or group to another, you cause it to be sent there as it becomes available. = channel ❑ *He secretly funnelled credit-card information to counterfeiters.*

fun·ni·ly /ˈfʌnɪli/ ADV
PHRASE **funnily enough** You use **funnily enough** to indicate that, although something is surprising, it is true or really happened. = oddly ❑ *Funnily enough I can remember what I had for lunch on July 5th, 1956, but I've forgotten what I had for breakfast today.*

fun·ny ♦◇◇ /ˈfʌni/ ADJ (**funnier, funniest**) **1** Someone or something that is **funny** is amusing and likely to make you smile or laugh. = amusing, comical ❑ *I'll tell you a funny story.* **2** If you describe something as **funny**, you think it is strange, surprising, or puzzling. = odd, curious ❑ *Children get some very funny ideas sometimes!* ❑ *There's something funny about him.* **3** *(informal)* If you feel **funny**, you feel slightly ill. ❑ *My head had begun to ache and my stomach felt funny.*

fur /fɜː/ NOUN [C, U] (**furs**) **1** [C, U] **Fur** is the thick and usually soft hair that grows on the bodies of many mammals. ❑ *This creature's fur is short, dense, and silky.* **2** [C, U] **Fur** is an artificial fabric that looks like fur and is used, for example, to make clothing, soft toys, and seat covers. **3** [C, U] **Fur** is the fur-covered skin of an animal that is used to make clothing or small carpets. ❑ *She had on a black coat with a fur collar.* ❑ *the trading of furs from Canada* **4** [C] A **fur** is a coat made from real or artificial fur, or a piece of fur worn around your neck. ❑ *There were women in furs and men in comfortable overcoats.*

fu·ri·ous /ˈfjʊəriəs/ ADJ **1** Someone who is **furious** is extremely angry. ❑ *He is furious at the way his wife has been treated.* **2** **Furious** is also used to describe something that is done with great energy, effort, speed, or violence. ❑ *A furious gun battle ensued.*
fu·ri·ous·ly /ˈfjʊəriəsli/ ADV **1** *He stormed out of the apartment, slamming the door furiously behind him.* **2** *Officials worked furiously to repair the centre court.*

fur·nish /ˈfɜːnɪʃ/ VERB [T] (**furnishes, furnishing, furnished**) **1** If you **furnish** a room or building, you put furniture and furnishings into it. ❑ *Many proprietors try to furnish their hotels with antiques.* **2** *(formal)* If you **furnish** someone **with** something, you provide or supply it. ❑ *They'll be able to furnish you with the rest of the details.*

F

fur·ni·ture ♦◇◇ /'fɜːnɪtʃə/ NOUN [U] **Furniture** consists of large objects such as tables, chairs, or beds that are used in a room for sitting or lying on or for putting things on or in. ❑ *Each piece of furniture in their home suited the style of the house.*

✪fur·ther ♦♦♦ /'fɜːðə/ ADV, ADJ, VERB

ADV **1** [further with v] **Further** means to a greater extent or degree. ❑ *Inflation is below 5% and set to fall further.* ❑ *The rebellion is expected to further damage the country's image.* **2** [further with v] If you go or get **further with** something, or take something **further**, you make some progress. ❑ *They lacked the scientific personnel to develop the technical apparatus much further.* **3** [further after v] If someone goes **further** in a discussion, they make a more extreme statement or deal with a point more thoroughly. ❑ *To have a better comparison, we need to go further and address such issues as repairs and insurance.* **4** [further + ADV/PREP] **Further** means a greater distance than before or than something else. ❑ *People are living further away from their jobs.* ❑ *He came to a halt at a crossroads fifty yards further on.* **5** [further + ADV/PREP] **Further** is used in expressions such as '**further back**' and '**further ahead**' to refer to a point in time that is earlier or later than the time you are talking about. ❑ *Looking still further ahead, by the end of the next century world population is expected to be about ten billion.* ADJ [further + N, PRON-INDEF + further] A **further** thing, number of things, or amount of something is an additional thing, number of things, or amount. = more ❑ *Further evidence of slowing economic growth is likely to emerge this week.* ❑ *They believed there were likely to be further attacks.* VERB [T] (**furthers, furthering, furthered**) If you **further** something, you help it to progress, to be successful, or to be achieved. ❑ *Education needn't only be about furthering your career.*

fur·ther edu·ca·tion (*BrE*; in *AmE*, use **continuing education, adult education**) NOUN [U] **Further education** is the education of people who have left school but who are not at a university or a college of education.

✪further·more /ˌfɜːðə'mɔː/ ADV [furthermore with CL] (*academic word, formal*) **Furthermore** is used to introduce a piece of information or opinion that adds to or supports the previous one. = moreover, in addition ❑ *Furthermore, they claim that any such interference is completely ineffective.* ❑ *Furthermore, even a well-timed therapy intervention may fail.*

fur·thest /'fɜːðɪst/ ADV, ADJ

ADV **1** [furthest with v] **Furthest** means to a greater extent or degree than ever before or than anything or anyone else. ❑ *The south, where prices have fallen furthest, will remain the weakest market.* **2 Furthest** means at a greater distance from a particular point than anyone or anything else, or for a greater distance than anyone or anything else. ❑ *The risk of thunder is greatest in those areas furthest from the coast.* ADJ [furthest + N] The **furthest** point from a particular point is at a greater distance from it than anyone or anything else. ❑ *the furthest point from earth that any controlled spacecraft has ever been*

fury /'fjʊəri/ NOUN [U] **Fury** is violent or very strong anger. = rage ❑ *She screamed, her face distorted with fury and pain.*

fuse /fjuːz/ NOUN, VERB

NOUN [C] (**fuses**) **1** A **fuse** is a safety device in an electric plug or circuit. It contains a piece of wire which melts when there is a fault so that the flow of electricity stops. ❑ *The fuse blew as he pressed the button to start the motor.* **2** A **fuse** is a device on a bomb or firework which delays the explosion so that people can move a safe distance away. ❑ *A bomb was deactivated at the last moment, after the fuse had been lit.*

VERB [RECIP] (**fuses, fusing, fused**) When things **fuse** or are **fused**, they join together physically or chemically, usually to become one thing. You can also say that one thing **fuses** with another. ❑ *The skull bones fuse between the ages of fifteen and twenty-five.* ❑ *Manufactured glass is made by fusing various types of sand.*

fu·selage /'fjuːzɪlɑːʒ/ NOUN [C] (**fuselages**) The **fuselage** is the main body of a plane, missile, or rocket. It is usually cylindrical in shape. ❑ *The force of the impact ripped apart the plane's fuselage.*

fu·sion /'fjuːʒən/ NOUN [C, U] (**fusions**) **1** [C] A **fusion of** different qualities, ideas, or things is something new that is created by joining them together. ❑ *His previous fusions of jazz, pop, and African melodies have proved highly successful.* **2** [C, U] The **fusion** of two or more things involves joining them together to form one thing. ❑ *His final reform was the fusion of regular and reserve forces.* **3** [U] In physics, **fusion** is the process in which atomic particles combine and produce a large amount of nuclear energy. ❑ *research into nuclear fusion*

fuss /fʌs/ NOUN, VERB

NOUN [SING] [also no DET] **Fuss** is anxious or excited behaviour which serves no useful purpose. = bother ❑ *I don't know what all the fuss is about.*

PHRASE **make a fuss** or **kick up a fuss** (*informal*) If you **make a fuss** or **kick up a fuss** about something, you become angry or excited about it and complain. ❑ *I don't know why everybody makes such a fuss about a few mosquitoes.* VERB [I] (**fusses, fussing, fussed**) **1** If you **fuss**, you worry or behave in a nervous, anxious way about unimportant matters or rush around doing unnecessary things. ❑ *Carol fussed about getting me a drink.* ❑ *My wife was fussing over the food and clothing we were going to take.* ❑ *'Stop fussing,' he snapped.* **2** If you **fuss over** someone, you pay them a lot of attention and do things to make them happy or comfortable. ❑ *Auntie Hilda and Uncle Jack couldn't fuss over them enough.*

fussy /'fʌsi/ ADJ (**fussier, fussiest**) (*disapproval*) Someone who is **fussy** is very concerned with unimportant details and is difficult to please. ❑ *She is not fussy about her food.*

fu·tile /'fjuːtaɪl, AmE -təl/ ADJ If you say that something is **futile**, you mean there is no point in doing it, usually because it has no chance of succeeding. = pointless ❑ *He brought his arm up in a futile attempt to ward off the blow.*

✪fu·ture ♦♦♦ /'fjuːtʃə/ NOUN, ADJ

NOUN [SING, C, PL] (**futures**) **1** [SING] **The future** is the period of time that will come after the present, or the things that will happen then. ❑ *The spokesman said no decision on the proposal was likely in the immediate future.* ❑ *He was making plans for the future.* **2** [C] Someone's **future**, or **the future of** something, is what will happen to them or what they will do after the present time. ❑ *His future depends on the outcome of the elections.* ❑ *a proposed national conference on the country's political future* **3** [PL] (*business*) When people trade in **futures**, they buy stocks and shares, commodities such as coffee or oil, or foreign currency at a price that is agreed at the time of purchase for items which are delivered some time in the future. ❑ *This report could spur some buying in corn futures when the market opens today.*

PHRASE **in (the) future** You use **in the future** when saying what will happen from now on, which will be different from what has previously happened. ❑ *I asked her to be more careful in the future.*

ADJ [future + N] **Future** things will happen or exist after the present time. ❑ *She said if the world did not act conclusively now, it would only bequeath the problem to future generations.* ❑ *the future king and queen* ❑ *Meanwhile, the domestic debate on Denmark's future role in Europe rages on.*

Gg

G also **g** /dʒiː/ NOUN [C, U] (**G's, g's**) **G** is the seventh letter of the English alphabet.

gadg·et /'gædʒɪt/ NOUN [C] (**gadgets**) A **gadget** is a small machine or device which does something useful. You sometimes refer to something as a **gadget** when you are suggesting that it is complicated and unnecessary. ❑ *sales of kitchen gadgets including toasters, kettles, and percolators*

gag /gæg/ NOUN, VERB

NOUN [C] (**gags**) **1** A **gag** is something such as a piece of cloth that is tied around or put inside someone's mouth in order to stop them from speaking. ❑ *His captors had put a gag of thick leather in his mouth.* **2** (*informal*) A **gag** is a joke. = joke ❑ *The running gag is that the band never gets to play.*

VERB [T, I] (**gags, gagging, gagged**) **1** [T] If someone **gags** you, they tie a piece of cloth around your mouth in order to stop you from speaking or shouting. ❑ *I gagged him with a towel.* **2** [T] If a person **is gagged** by someone in authority, they are prevented from expressing their opinion or from publishing certain information. ❑ *Judges must not be gagged.* **3** [I] If you **gag**, you cannot swallow and nearly vomit. ❑ *I knelt by the toilet and gagged.*

⊙ **gain** ♦♦◇ /geɪn/ VERB, NOUN

VERB [I, T] (**gains, gaining, gained**) **1** [I, T] If a person or place **gains** something such as an ability or quality, they gradually get more of it. = acquire, attain ❑ *Students can gain valuable experience by working on the campus radio or magazine.* ❑ *His reputation abroad has gained in stature.* ❑ *It wasn't until the 1960s that her ideas first gained wider recognition.* ❑ *While it has lost its tranquillity, the area has gained in liveliness.* **2** [I, T] If you **gain from** something such as an event or situation, you get some advantage or benefit from it. = benefit, profit; ≠ lose ❑ *The company didn't disclose how much it expects to gain from the two deals.* ❑ *It is sad that a major company should try to gain from other people's suffering.* ❑ *There is absolutely nothing to be gained by feeling bitter.* **3** [T] To **gain** something such as weight or speed means to have an increase in that particular thing. = increase; ≠ lose ❑ *Some people do gain weight after they stop smoking.* ❑ *The BMW started coming forward, passing the other cars and gaining speed as it approached.* ❑ *During this time, however, the stock market gained 15% per year.* **4** [T] If you **gain** something, you obtain it, especially after a lot of hard work or effort. = obtain, earn ❑ *To gain a promotion, you might have to work overtime.* ❑ *They realise that passing exams is no longer enough to gain a place at university.* ❑ *Their efforts helped the hostages gain their freedom.*

PHRASE **gain ground** If something such as an idea or an ideal **gains ground**, it gradually becomes more widely known or more popular. ❑ *There are strong signs that his views are gaining ground.*

NOUN [C, U] (**gains**) [usu with SUPP] A **gain** is an increase in something such as weight or speed. = increase, growth; ≠ loss ❑ *News on new home sales is brighter, showing a gain of nearly 8% in June.* ❑ *Excessive weight gain doesn't do you any good.*

WORD CONNECTIONS

gain + NOUN

gain **experience**
gain an **understanding**
❑ *Our overall objective is to gain a greater understanding of the processes involved.*

gain **popularity**
gain **notoriety**
gain **approval**
gain **recognition**
❑ *He gained widespread recognition for his photographs of wildlife.*

gain **weight**
gain **speed**
gain **strength**
gain **value**
❑ *The baby should be feeding well and gaining weight.*

gain **independence**
gain **freedom**
gain **entry**
gain **access**
❑ *The Republic of Zambia gained independence from the UK in 1964.*

gain a **place**
gain a **position**
❑ *His win was enough to gain a place in the record books.*

gain + ADV

gain **financially**
gain **enormously**
gain **considerably**
❑ *He stands to gain financially when his father dies.*

VOCABULARY BUILDER

gain VERB (*formal*)
If you **gain** something, you obtain it, especially after a lot of hard work or effort.
❑ *Eventually the Allies were able to gain control of the German colonies in Africa and the Pacific.*

acquire VERB (*formal*)
If you **acquire** something, you buy it or get it for yourself, or someone gives it to you.
❑ *In 1889 Sir Edmund Loder acquired the property from his wife's parents.*

collect VERB
If you **collect** a number of things, you bring them together from several places or several people.
❑ *Then she tidied herself and was collecting her books when the babysitter arrived.*

obtain VERB (*formal*)
If you **obtain** something, you get it, although it may have been hard to do so, or have taken you a long time.
❑ *The 28-page document, obtained by The Vancouver Sun, will be unveiled at a press conference today.*

USAGE NOTE

gain
You do not say that someone 'gains wages' or 'gains a salary'. Use 'earn'.
*The number of Canadians **earning** big salaries soared in the 1990s.*

✪ **gal·axy** /ˈgæləksi/ also **Galaxy** NOUN [C, SING] (**galaxies**) **1** [C] A **galaxy** is an extremely large group of stars and planets that extends over many billions of light years. ❑ *Astronomers have discovered a distant galaxy.* ❑ *At some later point, galaxies of stars started to form.* **2** [SING] **The Galaxy** is the extremely large group of stars and planets to which the Earth and the solar system belong. ❑ *The Galaxy consists of 100 billion stars.* ❑ *The more distant stars in the Galaxy crowd together in a hazy band called the Milky Way.*

gale /geɪl/ NOUN [C] (**gales**) **1** A **gale** is a very strong wind. ❑ *forecasts of fierce gales over the next few days* **2** (*written*) You can refer to the loud noise made by a lot of people all laughing at the same time as a **gale of** laughter or **gales of** laughter. ❑ *This was greeted with gales of laughter from the audience.*

✪ **gal·lery** ♦◇◇ /ˈgæləri/ NOUN [C] (**galleries**) **1** A **gallery** is a place that has permanent exhibitions of works of art in it. ❑ *an art gallery* ❑ *Check with staff before using a camera in museums or art galleries.* ❑ *the National Gallery* **2** A **gallery** is a privately owned building or room where people can look at and buy works of art. ❑ *The painting is in the gallery upstairs.* **3** A **gallery** is an area high above the ground at the back or at the sides of a large room or hall. ❑ *A crowd already filled the gallery.* **4** **The gallery** in a theatre or concert hall is an area high above the ground that usually contains the cheapest seats. ❑ *They had been forced to find cheap tickets in the gallery.*

PHRASE **play to the gallery** If you **play to the gallery**, you do something in public in a way which you hope will impress people. ❑ *but I must tell you that in my opinion you're both now playing to the gallery*

✪ **gal·lon** /ˈgælən/ NOUN [C] (**gallons**) A **gallon** is a unit of measurement for liquids that is equal to eight pints. In Britain, it is equal to 4.564 litres. In America, it is equal to 3.785 litres. ❑ *80 million gallons of water a day* ❑ *thousands of gallons of fuel*

gal·lop /ˈgæləp/ VERB, NOUN
VERB [I, T] (**gallops, galloping, galloped**) **1** [I, T] When a horse **gallops**, it runs very fast so that all four legs are off the ground at the same time. If you **gallop** a horse, you make it gallop. ❑ *The horses galloped away.* **2** [I] If you **gallop**, you ride a horse that is galloping. ❑ *Major Winston galloped into the distance.* **3** [I] If something such as a process **gallops**, it develops very quickly and is often difficult to control. ❑ *China's economy galloped ahead.*
NOUN [SING] A **gallop** is a ride on a horse that is galloping. ❑ *I was forced to attempt a gallop.*
PHRASE **at a gallop** If you do something **at a gallop**, you do it very quickly. ❑ *I read the book at a gallop.*

ga·lore /gəˈlɔː/ ADJ [N + galore] (*informal, written, emphasis*) You use **galore** to emphasize that something you like exists in very large quantities. ❑ *You'll be able to win prizes galore.*

gal·va·nize /ˈgælvənaɪz/ also **galvanise** VERB [T] (**galvanizes, galvanizing, galvanized**) To **galvanize** someone means to cause them to take action, for example by making them feel very excited, afraid, or angry. = stir ❑ *The aid appeal has galvanized the country's business community.*

gam·ble /ˈgæmbəl/ NOUN, VERB
NOUN [C] (**gambles**) A **gamble** is a risky action or decision that you take in the hope of gaining money, success, or an advantage over other people. = risk ❑ *Yesterday, he named his cabinet and took a big gamble in the process.*
VERB [I, T] (**gambles, gambling, gambled**) **1** If you **gamble on** something, you take a risky action or decision in the hope of gaining money, success, or an advantage over other people. ❑ *Few firms will be willing to gamble on new products.* ❑ *They are not prepared to gamble their careers on this matter.* **2** If you **gamble** an amount of money, you bet it in a game such as cards or on the result of a race or competition. People who **gamble** usually do it frequently. ❑ *Most people visit Las Vegas to gamble their hard-earned money.* ❑ *John gambled heavily on the horses.*

gam·bling /ˈgæmblɪŋ/ NOUN [U] **Gambling** is the act or activity of betting money, for example in card games or on horse racing. ❑ *Gambling is a form of entertainment.*

game ♦♦♦ /geɪm/ NOUN, ADJ
NOUN [C, PL, U] (**games**) **1** [C] A **game** is an activity or sport usually involving skill, knowledge, or chance, in which you follow fixed rules and try to win against an opponent or to solve a puzzle. ❑ *the wonderful game of football* ❑ *a playful game of hide-and-seek* **2** [C] A **game** is one particular occasion on which a game is played. = match ❑ *It was the first game of the season.* ❑ *He regularly watched our games from the stands.* **3** [C] A **game** is a part of a match, for example in tennis or bridge, consisting of a fixed number of points. ❑ *She won six games to love in the second set.* **4** [PL] **Games** are an organized event in which competitions in several sports take place. ❑ *the 1996 Olympic Games at Atlanta* **5** [C] You can use **game** to describe a way of behaving in which a person uses a particular plan, usually in order to gain an advantage for himself or herself. ❑ *Until now, the Americans have been playing a very delicate political game.* **6** [U] Wild animals or birds that are hunted for sport and sometimes cooked and eaten are referred to as **game**. ❑ *As men who shot game for food, they were natural marksmen.*

PHRASES **give the game away** If someone or something **gives the game away**, they reveal a secret or reveal their feelings, and this puts them at a disadvantage. ❑ *The faces of the two conspirators gave the game away!*

new to a game If you are **new to** a particular **game**, you have not done a particular activity or been in a particular situation before. ❑ *Don't forget that she's new to this game and will take a while to complete the task.*

beat someone at their own game If you beat someone at their **own game**, you use the same methods that they have used, but more successfully, so that you gain an advantage over them. ❑ *He must anticipate the manoeuvres of the other lawyers and beat them at their own game.*

playing games (*disapproval*) If you say that someone is **playing games** or **playing silly games**, you mean that they are not treating a situation seriously and you are annoyed with them. ❑ *This seemed to annoy Professor Steiner. 'Don't play games with me,' he thundered.*

ADJ [V-LINK + game] If you are **game for** something, you are willing to do something new, unusual, or risky. ❑ *He said he's game for a similar challenge next year.*

gam·ing /ˈgeɪmɪŋ/ NOUN [U] **Gaming** means the same as **gambling**. ❑ *offences connected with vice, gaming, and drugs*

gang ♦◇◇ /gæŋ/ NOUN
NOUN [C, SING] (**gangs**) **1** [C] A **gang** is a group of people, especially young people, who go around together and often deliberately cause trouble. ❑ *During the fight with a rival gang he lashed out with his flick knife.* ❑ *Gang members were behind a lot of the violence.* **2** [C] A **gang** is a group of criminals who work together to commit crimes. ❑ *Police were hunting for a gang that had allegedly stolen fifty-five cars.* ❑ *an underworld gang* **3** [SING] (*informal*) **The gang** is a group of friends who frequently meet. ❑ *Come on over, we've got lots of the old gang here.* **4** [C] A **gang** is a group of workers who do physical work together. ❑ *a gang of labourers*

PHRASAL VERB **gang up** (**gangs, ganging, ganged**) (*informal*) If people **gang up on** someone, they unite against them for a particular reason, for example in a fight or argument. ❑ *Harrison complained that his colleagues ganged up on him.* ❑ *All the other parties ganged up to keep them out of power.*

gang·ster /ˈgæŋstə/ NOUN [C] (**gangsters**) A **gangster** is a member of an organized group of violent criminals. ❑ *a gangster movie*

✪ **gap** ♦◇◇ /gæp/ NOUN [C] (**gaps**) **1** A **gap** is a space between two things or a hole in the middle of something solid. ❑ *He pulled the thick curtains together, leaving just a narrow gap.* **2** A **gap** is a period of time when you are not busy or when you stop doing something that you normally do. = break ❑ *There followed a gap of four years, during which William joined the Army.* **3** If there is something missing from a situation that prevents it from being complete or satisfactory, you can say that there is a gap. ❑ *The manifesto calls for a greater effort to recruit young scientists to fill the gap left by a wave of retirements expected over the next decade.* **4** A **gap between** two groups of people, things, or sets of ideas is a big difference between them. = difference ❑ *the gap between rich and poor* ❑ *The overall pay gap between men and women narrowed slightly.* ❑ *America's trade gap widened.*

gape /geɪp/ VERB [I] (**gapes, gaping, gaped**) **1** If you **gape**, you look at someone or something in surprise, usually with an open mouth. ❑ *His secretary stopped taking notes to gape at me.* ❑ *He was not the type to wander around gaping at everything like a tourist.* **2** If you say that something such as a hole or a wound **gapes**, you are emphasizing that it is big or wide. ❑ *The front door was missing. A hole gaped in the roof.*

gap·ing /ˈgeɪpɪŋ/ ADJ ❑ *The aircraft took off with a gaping hole in its fuselage.*

gar·age /ˈgærɑːʒ, ˈgærɪdʒ, AmE gəˈrɑːʒ/ NOUN [C] (**garages**) **1** A **garage** is a building in which you keep a car. A garage is often built next to or as part of a house. ❑ *They have turned the garage into a study.* **2** A **garage** is a place where you can get your car repaired. ❑ *Nancy took her car to a local garage for a check-up.*

gar·den ♦♦◇ /ˈgɑːdən/ NOUN, VERB
[NOUN] [C, PL] (**gardens**) **1** [C] (*BrE*) A **garden** is a piece of land next to someone's house, with grass and plants growing in it. ❑ *the most beautiful garden on Earth* **2** [PL] **Gardens** are places like a park that have areas of plants, trees, and grass, and that people can visit and walk around. ❑ *The Gardens are open from 5:00 a.m. until 5:00 p.m.* **3** [C] **Gardens** is sometimes used as part of the name of a street. ❑ *He lives at 9 Acacia Gardens.*
[VERB] [I] (**gardens, gardening, gardened**) If you **garden**, you do work in your garden such as weeding or planting. ❑ *Jim gardened at the homes of friends on weekends.*

gar·den·ing /ˈgɑːdənɪŋ/ NOUN [U] ❑ *I have taken up gardening again.*
→ See also **yard**

gar·den·er /ˈgɑːdənə/ NOUN [C] (**gardeners**) **1** A **gardener** is a person who is paid to work in someone else's garden. ❑ *She employed a gardener.* **2** A **gardener** is someone who enjoys working in their own garden growing flowers or vegetables. ❑ *The majority of sweet peas are still bred by enthusiastic amateur gardeners.*

gar·ment /ˈgɑːmənt/ NOUN [C] (**garments**) A **garment** is a piece of clothing; used especially in contexts where you are talking about the manufacture or sale of clothes. ❑ *Many of the garments have the customers' name tags sewn into the linings.*

❍gas ♦♦◇ /gæs/ NOUN, VERB

Gases is the plural form of the noun and **gasses** is the third person singular of the present tense of the verb.

[NOUN] [U, C] (**gases**) **1** [U] **Gas** is a substance like air that is neither liquid nor solid and burns easily. It is used as a fuel for cooking and heating. ❑ *Coal is actually cheaper than gas.* ❑ *Shell signed a contract to develop oil and gas reserves near Archangel.* **2** [C, U] A **gas** is any substance that is neither liquid nor solid, for example oxygen or hydrogen. ❑ *Helium is a very light gas.* ❑ *a huge cloud of gas and dust from the volcanic eruption* **3** [C, U] **Gas** is a poisonous gas that can be used as a weapon. ❑ *The problem was that the exhaust gases contain many toxins.*
[VERB] [T] (**gasses, gassing, gassed**) To **gas** a person or animal means to kill them by making them breathe poisonous gas. ❑ *Her husband ran a pipe from her car exhaust to the bedroom in an attempt to gas her.*
→ See also **greenhouse gas**

gasp /gɑːsp, gæsp/ NOUN, VERB
[NOUN] [C] (**gasps**) A **gasp** is a short, quick breath of air that you take in through your mouth, especially when you are surprised, shocked, or in pain. ❑ *An audible gasp went around the court as the jury announced the verdict.*
[PHRASE] **last gasp** (*emphasis*) You describe something as **the last gasp** to emphasize that it is the final part of something or happens at the last possible moment. ❑ *the last gasp of a dying system of censorship*

[VERB] [I] (**gasps, gasping, gasped**) When you **gasp**, you take a short, quick breath through your mouth, especially when you are surprised, shocked, or in pain. ❑ *She gasped for air and drew in a lungful of water.*

gate ♦◇◇ /geɪt/ NOUN [C, U] (**gates**) **1** [C] A **gate** is a structure like a door which is used at the entrance to a field, a garden, or the grounds of a building. ❑ *He opened the gate and started walking up to the house.* **2** [C] In an airport, a **gate** is a place where passengers leave the airport and get on their plane. ❑ *Passengers with hand luggage can go straight to the departure gate to check in there.* **3** [U] The **gate** is the total amount of money that is paid by the people who go to a sports match or other event.

❍gath·er ♦♦◇ /ˈgæðə/ VERB
[VERB] [I, T] (**gathers, gathering, gathered**) **1** [I, T] If people **gather** somewhere, or if someone **gathers** people somewhere, they come together in a group. = assemble, collect ❑ *In the evenings, we gathered around the fireplace and talked.* **2** [T] If you **gather** things, you collect them together so that you can use them. = collect ❑ *I suggest we gather enough firewood to last the night.* ❑ *The expedition gathered samples of animal and plant life.* ❑ *Search teams spent weeks gathering thousands of pieces of wreckage.* **3** [T] If you **gather** information or evidence, you collect it, especially over a period of time and after a lot of hard work. = collect, amass ❑ *a private detective using a hidden tape recorder to gather information* ❑ *The organization gathers information on the dangers of smoking.* ❑ *The commission began to gather evidence for the forthcoming trial.* ❑ *The book gathers together all the short stories in a single volume.* **4** [T] If something **gathers** speed, momentum, or force, it gradually becomes faster or more powerful. = gain ❑ *Demands for his dismissal have gathered momentum in recent weeks.* **5** [T] When you **gather** something such as your strength, courage, or thoughts, you make an effort to prepare yourself to do something. = muster ❑ *You must gather your strength for the journey.* **6** [T] You use **gather** in expressions such as '**I gather**' and '**as far as I can gather**' to introduce information that you have found out, especially when you have found it out in an indirect way. ❑ *I gather his report is highly critical of the trial judge.* ❑ *'He speaks English,' she said to Graham. 'I gathered that.'*
[PHRASAL VERB] **gather up** **1** Gather up means the same as **gather** VERB 2. ❑ *When Steinberg had gathered up his papers, he went out.* **2** Gather up means the same as **gather** VERB 5. ❑ *She was gathering up her courage to approach him when he called to her.*
✦ **gather dust** → see **dust**

gath·er·ing /ˈgæðərɪŋ/ NOUN, ADJ
[NOUN] [C] (**gatherings**) A **gathering** is a group of people meeting together for a particular purpose. ❑ *the twenty-second annual gathering of the South Pacific Forum*
[ADJ] [gathering + N] If there is **gathering** darkness, the light is gradually decreasing, usually because it is nearly night. ❑ *The lighthouse beam was quite distinct in the gathering dusk.*
→ See also **gather**

❍gauge /geɪdʒ/ VERB, NOUN
[VERB] [T] (**gauges, gauging, gauged**) **1** If you **gauge** the speed or strength of something, or if you gauge an amount, you measure or calculate it, often by using a device of some kind. = measure ❑ *He gauged the wind at over thirty knots.* ❑ *Distance is gauged by journey time rather than miles.* **2** If you **gauge** people's actions, feelings, or intentions in a particular situation, you carefully consider and judge them. = assess ❑ *His mood can be gauged by his reaction to the most trivial of incidents.*
[NOUN] [C, SING] (**gauges**) **1** [C] [oft N + gauge] A **gauge** is a device that measures the amount or quantity of something and shows the amount measured. ❑ *temperature gauges* ❑ *The unit keeps track of usage and, like a fuel gauge on a car, warns when the card is getting close to empty.* ❑ *The pilot reads the altitude gauge, of course; but there are other people watching.* **2** [SING] A **gauge of** someone's feelings or a situation is a fact or event that can be used to judge them. = measure ❑ *The index is the government's chief gauge of future economic activity.*

gave /geɪv/ IRREG FORM **Gave** is the past tense of **give**.

G

gay ♦♦◇ /geɪ/ ADJ, NOUN

ADJ A **gay** person is homosexual. ❑ *The quality of life for gay men has improved over the last two decades.*
NOUN [PL] (**gays**) **Gays** are homosexual people, especially homosexual men. ❑ *More importantly, gays have proved themselves to be style leaders.*
gay·ness /ˈgeɪnəs/ NOUN [U] ❑ *Mike's admission of his gayness*

gaze /geɪz/ VERB, NOUN

VERB [I] (**gazes, gazing, gazed**) If you **gaze at** someone or something, you look steadily at them for a long time, for example because you find them attractive or interesting, or because you are thinking about something else. ❑ *gazing at herself in the mirror* ❑ *Sitting in his wicker chair, he gazed reflectively at the fire.*
NOUN [C] (**gazes**) *(written)* You can talk about someone's **gaze** as a way of describing how they are looking at something, especially when they are looking steadily at it. ❑ *The Monsignor turned his gaze from the flames to meet the Colonel's.* ❑ *She felt increasingly uncomfortable under the woman's steady gaze.*
PHRASE **public gaze** If someone or something is **in the public gaze**, they are receiving a lot of attention from the general public. ❑ *You won't find a couple more in the public gaze than Michael and Lizzie.*

●GDP /ˌdʒiː diː ˈpiː/ NOUN [C, U] (**GDPs**) In economics, a country's **GDP** is the total value of goods and services produced within a country in a year, not including its income from investments in other countries. **GDP** is an abbreviation for **gross domestic product**. ❑ *That is 2.6 per cent of total UK GDP.* ❑ *Per capita GDP has increased, at today's rates, from 12,637 to 17,096.*

gear ♦◇◇ /gɪə/ NOUN, VERB

NOUN [C, U] (**gears**) **1** [C] The **gears** on a machine or vehicle are a device for changing the rate at which energy is changed into motion. ❑ *On hills, he must use low gears.* ❑ *The car was in fourth gear.* **2** [U] The **gear** involved in a particular activity is the equipment or special clothing that you use. ❑ *About 100 officers in riot gear were needed to break up the fight.* **3** [U] *(informal)* **Gear** means clothing. ❑ *I used to wear trendy gear but it just looked ridiculous.*
VERB [PASSIVE] (**gears, gearing, geared**) If someone or something **is geared to** or **towards** a particular purpose, they are organized or designed in order to achieve that purpose. ❑ *Colleges are not always geared to the needs of mature students.* ❑ *My training was geared towards winning gold.*
PHRASAL VERB **gear up** If someone **is gearing up for** a particular activity, they are preparing to do it. If they **are geared up to** do a particular activity, they are prepared to do it. ❑ *another indication that the country is gearing up for an election*

gel /dʒel/ VERB, NOUN

> The spelling **jell** is sometimes used for meanings 1 and 2 of the verb.

VERB [RECIP, I] (**gels, gelling, gelled**) **1** [RECIP] If people **gel** with each other, or if two groups of people **gel**, they work well together because their skills and personalities fit together well. ❑ *They have gelled very well with the rest of the side.* ❑ *Their partnership gelled, and scriptwriting for television followed.* **2** [I] If a vague shape, thought, or creation **gels**, it becomes clearer or more definite. ❑ *Even if her interpretation has not yet gelled into a satisfying whole, she displays real musicianship.*
NOUN [C, U] (**gels**) **Gel** is a thick, jelly-like substance, especially one used to keep your hair in a particular style.

●gen·der /ˈdʒendə/ NOUN [C, U] (**genders**) *(academic word)* **1** [C, U] A person's **gender** is the fact that they are male or female. = sex ❑ *Women are sometimes denied opportunities solely because of their gender.* ❑ *groups that are traditionally discriminated against on grounds of gender, colour, race, or age* **2** [C] You can refer to all male people or all female people as a particular **gender**. = sex ❑ *While her observations may be true about some men, they could hardly apply to the entire gender.* **3** [C, U] In grammar, the **gender** of a noun, pronoun, or adjective is whether it is

masculine, feminine, or neuter. A word's gender can affect its form and behaviour. In English, only personal pronouns such as 'she', reflexive pronouns such as 'itself', and possessive determiners such as 'his' have gender. ❑ *In both Welsh and Irish the word for 'moon' is of feminine gender.*

●gene ♦◇◇ /dʒiːn/ NOUN [C] (**genes**) A **gene** is the part of a cell in a living thing which controls its physical characteristics, growth, and development. ❑ *The gene for asthma has been identified.* ❑ *a change in a single DNA letter that appears in 70 per cent of defective genes* ❑ *Molecular genetics is enabling scientists to identify individual genes involved in the control of sleep.*

●gen·er·al ♦♦♦ /ˈdʒenərəl/ NOUN, ADJ

NOUN [C] (**generals**) A **general** is a high-ranking officer in the armed forces, usually in the army. ❑ *The General's visit to Sarajevo is part of preparations for the deployment of extra troops.*
PHRASE **in general 1** You use **in general** to indicate that you are talking about something as a whole, rather than about part of it. ❑ *I think we need to improve our educational system in general.* **2** You say **in general** to indicate that you are referring to most people or things in a particular group. ❑ *People in general will support us.*
ADJ 1 [general + N] If you talk about the **general** situation somewhere or talk about something in **general** terms, you are describing the situation as a whole rather than considering its details or exceptions. ❑ *The figures represent a general decline in employment.* ❑ *a general deterioration in the quality of life* **2** [general + N] You use **general** to describe several items or activities when there are too many of them or when they are not important enough to mention separately. ❑ *$2,500 for software is soon swallowed up in general costs.* **3** [general + N] You use **general** to describe something that involves or affects most people, or most people in a particular group. = common, widespread; ≠ specific ❑ *The project should raise general awareness about bullying.* ❑ *There was a general feeling of satisfaction.* ❑ *a general awareness of the problem* **4** [general + N] If you describe something as **general**, you mean that it is not restricted to any one thing or area. ❑ *a general ache radiating from the back of the neck* ❑ *a general sense of well-being* **5** [general + N] *(business)* **General** is used to describe a person's job, usually as part of their title, to indicate that they have complete responsibility for the administration of an organization or business. ❑ *He joined Sanders Roe, moving on later to become general manager.*
PHRASE **in general terms** If you describe something **in general terms**, you describe it without giving details. ❑ *Newton explained his theory in general terms.*
→ See also **generally**

WORD CONNECTIONS
general + NOUN
a general **decline** a general **improvement** a general **trend** ❑ *The general trend is essentially upwards.*
the general **nature** the general **state** the general **idea** the general **impression** ❑ *The general impression I get is that the organization is very well run.*
a general **feeling** a general **sense** a general **awareness** ❑ *There seems to be a general awareness that things need to change.*
a general **consensus** a general **agreement** a general **observation** ❑ *The general consensus among the fans I talked to was that the new manager was doing a good job.*

gen·er·al elec·tion ♦◇◇ NOUN [C] (**general elections**) In Britian, a **general election** is an election in which all the people in a country who can vote elect people to represent them in Parliament.

gen·er·al·i·za·tion /ˌdʒenərəlaɪˈzeɪʃən/ also **generalisation** NOUN [C, U] (**generalizations**) A generalization is a statement that seems to be true in most situations or for most people, but that may not be completely true in all cases. ❑ *He is making sweeping generalizations to get his point across.* ❑ *It's dangerous to make generalizations about education.*

gen·er·al·ize /ˈdʒenərəlaɪz/ also **generalise** VERB [I, T] (**generalizes, generalizing, generalized**) **1** [I] If you generalize, you say something that seems to be true in most situations or for most people, but that may not be completely true in all cases. = stereotype, hypothesize ❑ *Critics love to generalize, to formulate trends into which all new work must be fitted, however contradictory.* ❑ *'In my day, children were a lot better behaved.'—'It's not true, you're generalizing.'* ❑ *It is still possible to generalize about regional styles.* **2** [T] If you generalize something such as an idea, you apply it more widely than its original context, as if it was true in many other situations. ❑ *A child first labels the household pet cat as a 'cat' and then generalizes this label to other animals that look like it.*

gen·er·al·ly ♦♦◇ /ˈdʒenərəli/ ADV **1** You use generally to give a summary of a situation, activity, or idea without referring to the particular details of it. = mainly ❑ *University teachers generally have admitted a lack of enthusiasm about their subjects.* ❑ *Generally speaking, standards have improved.* ❑ *a generally positive economic outlook* **2** You use generally to say that something happens or is used on most occasions but not on every occasion. = usually, normally, mostly, commonly ❑ *As women we generally say and feel too much about these things.* ❑ *In the diet, it is generally true that the darker the fruit the higher its iron content.* ❑ *Blood pressure less than 120 over 80 is generally considered ideal.*

VOCABULARY BUILDER

generally ADV
You use generally to say that something happens or is used on most occasions but not on every occasion.
❑ *Arriving in Denpasar, she immediately boards a bus to Ubud, generally acknowledged as the hub of Balinese culture.*

normally ADV
If you say that you normally do a particular thing, you mean that it is what you tend to do in a particular situation.
❑ *These are not words that scientists normally use to describe the work of other researchers.*

commonly ADV
You use commonly to show that something happens very often or is very often true.
❑ *Two other groups of drugs are commonly used to treat high blood pressure.*

mostly ADV
You use mostly to show that a statement is true about the majority of a group of things or people or true for most of the time.
❑ *The duo, both 63, delighted a mostly middle-aged audience in London's Hyde Park.*

typically ADV
You use typically to say that something almost always happens in the way that you are describing.
❑ *A cup of fresh coffee typically contains between 80 and 100 milligrams of caffeine.*

characteristically ADV
You use characteristically to say that a quality or feature is very often found in a person or thing.
❑ *His argument was characteristically direct and unsentimental.*

gen·er·ate ♦◇◇ /ˈdʒenəreɪt/ VERB [T] (**generates, generating, generated**) (academic word) **1** To generate something means to cause it to begin and develop. = create, cause ❑ *The Employment Minister said the reforms would generate new jobs.* ❑ *the excitement generated by the changes in Eastern Europe* **2** To generate a form of energy or power means to produce it. = produce ❑ *The company, New England Electric, burns coal to generate power.*

gen·era·tion ♦♦◇ /ˌdʒenəˈreɪʃən/ NOUN, ADJ (academic word)
NOUN [C, U] (**generations**) **1** [C] A generation is all the people in a group or country who are of a similar age, especially when they are considered as having the same experiences or attitudes. ❑ *the younger generation of party members* ❑ *the problems of previous generations* ❑ *David Mamet has long been considered the leading American playwright of his generation.* ❑ *future generations of schoolchildren* **2** [C] A generation is the period of time, usually considered to be about thirty years, that it takes for children to grow up and become adults and have children of their own. ❑ *Within a generation, flight has become the method used by many travellers.* **3** [C] [generation 'of' N] You can use generation to refer to a stage of development in the design and manufacture of machines or equipment. ❑ *a new generation of Apple computers* **4** [U] Generation is the production of energy or power from fuel or another source of power, such as water. = production ❑ *Japan has announced plans for a sharp rise in its nuclear power generation.*
ADJ [ORD + generation + N] Generation is used to indicate how long members of your family have had a particular nationality. For example, second generation means that you were born in the country you live in, but your parents were not. ❑ *second-generation Jamaicans in New York*

gen·era·tor /ˈdʒenəreɪtə/ NOUN [C] (**generators**) **1** A generator is a machine which produces electricity. ❑ *The house is far from water mains and electricity and relies on its own generators.* **2** A generator of something is a person, organization, product, or situation which produces it or causes it to happen. ❑ *The company has been a very good cash generator.*

ge·ner·ic /dʒɪˈnerɪk/ ADJ, NOUN
ADJ **1** You use generic to describe something that refers or relates to a whole class of similar things. ❑ *Parmesan is a generic term used to describe a family of hard Italian cheeses.* **2** A generic drug or other product is one that does not have a trademark and that is known by a general name, rather than the manufacturer's name. ❑ *Doctors sometimes prescribe cheaper generic drugs instead of more expensive brand names.*
NOUN [C] (**generics**) A generic is a drug or other product that does not have a trademark and that is known by a general name, rather than the manufacturer's name. ❑ *The programme saved £5 million in 1988 by substituting generics for brand-name drugs.*

gen·er·os·ity /ˌdʒenəˈrɒsɪti/ NOUN [U] If you refer to someone's generosity, you mean that they are generous, especially in doing or giving more than is usual or expected. ❑ *There are stories about his generosity, the massive amounts of money he gave to charities.*

gen·er·ous ♦◇◇ /ˈdʒenərəs/ ADJ **1** A generous person gives more of something, especially money, than is usual or expected. ❑ *Dietler is generous with his time and money.* **2** A generous person is friendly, helpful, and willing to see the good qualities in someone or something. ❑ *He was always generous in sharing his enormous knowledge.* **3** A generous amount of something is much larger than is usual or necessary. ❑ *He should be able to keep his room tidy with the generous amount of storage space.*
gen·er·ous·ly /ˈdʒenərəsli/ **1** [generously with V] ❑ *We would like to thank all the judges who gave so generously of their time.* **2** [generously with V] ❑ *The students generously gave them instruction in social responsibility.* **3** Season the steaks generously with salt and pepper.

ge·net·ic /dʒɪˈnetɪk/ ADJ You use genetic to describe something that is concerned with genetics or with genes. ❑ *Cystic fibrosis is the most common fatal genetic disease in the United States.* ❑ *The causes of prostate cancer are unknown, but environmental and genetic factors are suspected.*
ge·neti·cal·ly /dʒɪˈnetɪkli/ ADV ❑ *Some people are*

g

genetically predisposed to diabetes. ❑ *foetuses that are genetically abnormal*

ge·neti·cal·ly modi·fied ADJ Genetically modified plants and animals have had one or more genes changed, for example so that they resist pests and diseases better. **Genetically modified** food contains ingredients made from genetically modified plants or animals. The abbreviation **GM** is often used. ❑ *Top supermarkets are to ban many genetically modified foods.*

ge·net·ic en·gi·neer·ing NOUN [U] Genetic engineering is the science or activity of changing the genetic structure of an animal, plant, or other organism in order to make it stronger or more suitable for a particular purpose. ❑ *Scientists have used genetic engineering to protect tomatoes against the effects of freezing.*

✿**ge·neti·cist** /dʒɪˈnetɪsɪst/ NOUN [C] (**geneticists**) A **geneticist** is a person who studies or specializes in genetics. ❑ *Some geneticists want to identify genes that encode for hearing.*

✿**ge·net·ics** /dʒɪˈnetɪks/ NOUN [U] Genetics is the study of heredity and how qualities and characteristics are passed on from one generation to another by means of genes. ❑ *Genetics is also bringing about dramatic changes in our understanding of cancer.* ❑ *There is a plethora of government advisory committees dealing with different aspects of human molecular genetics.* ❑ *Psychology, biology and genetics teach us that emotions should be broadly the same worldwide in every period.*

ge·ni·us /ˈdʒiːniəs/ NOUN [U, C] (**geniuses**) **1** [U] Genius is very great ability or skill in a particular subject or activity. ❑ *This is the mark of her real genius as a designer.* ❑ *The man had genius and had made his mark in the aviation world.* **2** [C] A **genius** is a highly talented, creative, or intelligent person. ❑ *Chaplin was not just a genius, he was among the most influential figures in film history.*

geno·cide /ˈdʒenəsaɪd/ NOUN [U] Genocide is the deliberate murder of a whole community or race. ❑ *They have alleged that acts of genocide and torture were carried out.*

✿**gen·re** /ˈʒɑːnrə/ NOUN [C] (**genres**) (*formal*) A **genre** is a particular type of literature, painting, music, film, or other art form which people consider as a class because it has special characteristics. ❑ *his love of films and novels in the horror genre.* ❑ *Genre films have a role in Scottish filmmaking whether or not it is to an individual's personal taste.*

gen·tle ◆◇◇ /ˈdʒentəl/ ADJ (**gentler, gentlest**) **1** Someone who is **gentle** is kind, mild, and calm. ❑ *My son was a quiet and gentle man who liked sports and enjoyed life.* **2** Gentle actions or movements are performed in a calm and controlled manner, with little force. ❑ *a gentle game of tennis* **3** A **gentle** slope or curve is not steep or severe. ❑ *gentle, rolling meadows* **4** A **gentle** heat is a fairly low heat. ❑ *Cook for 30 minutes over a gentle heat.*
gen·tly /ˈdʒentli/ ADV **1** [gently with v] ❑ *She smiled gently at him.* **2** Patrick took her gently by the arm and led her to a chair. **3** With its gently rolling hills it looks like Tuscany. **4** [gently with v] ❑ *Add the onion and cook gently for about 5 minutes.*
gen·tle·ness /ˈdʒentəlnəs/ NOUN [U] ❑ *the gentleness with which she treated her pregnant mother*

gentle·man ◆◇◇ /ˈdʒentəlmən/ NOUN [C] (**gentlemen**) **1** If you say that a man is a **gentleman**, you mean he is polite and educated, and can be trusted. ❑ *He was always such a gentleman.* **2** A **gentleman** is a man who comes from a family of high social standing. ❑ *this wonderful portrait of English gentleman Joseph Greenway* **3** You can address men as **gentlemen**, or refer politely to them as **gentlemen**. ❑ *This way, please, ladies and gentlemen.* ❑ *It seems this gentleman was waiting for the doctor.*

genu·ine ◆◇◇ /ˈdʒenjuɪn/ ADJ **1** Genuine is used to describe people and things that are exactly what they appear to be, and are not false or an imitation. ❑ *There was a risk of genuine refugees being returned to Vietnam.* ❑ *genuine leather* **2** Genuine refers to things such as emotions that are real and not pretended. = sincere ❑ *If this offer is genuine, I will gladly accept it.* **3** If you describe a person as **genuine**, you approve of them because they are

honest, truthful, and sincere in the way they live and in their relationships with other people. ❑ *She is very caring and very genuine.*
genu·ine·ly /ˈdʒenjuɪnli/ ADV ❑ *He was genuinely surprised.*

✿**ge·og·ra·pher** /dʒiˈɒɡrəfə/ NOUN [C] (**geographers**) A **geographer** is a person who studies geography or is an expert in it.

WORD PARTS

The prefix **geo-** appears in words that refer to the whole of the world or to the Earth's surface:
geographer (NOUN)
geology (NOUN)
geothermal (ADJ)

✿**geo·graphi·cal** /ˌdʒiːəˈɡræfɪkəl/ ADJ

The form **geographic** /ˌdʒiːəˈɡræfɪk/ is also used.

Geographical or geographic means concerned with or relating to geography. ❑ *Its geographical location stimulated overseas mercantile enterprise.* ❑ *a vast geographical area*
✿**geo·graphi·cal·ly** /ˌdʒiːəˈɡræfɪkli/ ADV ❑ *It is geographically more diverse than any other continent.*

✿**ge·og·ra·phy** /dʒiˈɒɡrəfi/ NOUN [U] **1** Geography is the study of the countries of the world and of such things as the land, seas, climate, towns, and population. ❑ *She studied geography at Cambridge University.* ❑ *He teaches geography and history.* **2** The **geography** of a place is the way that features such as rivers, mountains, towns, or streets are arranged within it. ❑ *policemen who knew the local geography*

✿**geo·logi·cal** /ˌdʒiːəˈlɒdʒɪkəl/ ADJ Geological means relating to geology. ❑ *With geological maps, books, and atlases you can find out all the proven sites of precious minerals.* ❑ *a lengthy geological survey*

✿**ge·ol·ogy** /dʒiˈɒlədʒi/ NOUN [U] **1** Geology is the study of the Earth's structure, surface, and origins. ❑ *He was visiting professor of geology at the University of Georgia.* **2** The **geology** of an area is the structure of its land, together with the types of rocks and minerals that exist within it. ❑ *the geology of Asia*
✿**ge·olo·gist** /dʒiˈɒlədʒɪst/ NOUN [C] (**geologists**) ❑ *Geologists have studied the way that heat flows from the earth.*

geo·met·ric /ˌdʒiːəˈmetrɪk/ ADJ

The form **geometrical** /ˌdʒiːəˈmetrɪkəl/ is also used.

1 Geometric or geometrical patterns or shapes consist of regular shapes or lines. ❑ *Geometric designs were popular wall decorations in the 14th century.* **2** Geometric or geometrical means relating to or involving the principles of geometry. ❑ *Euclid was trying to convey his idea of a geometrical point.*

✿**ge·om·etry** /dʒiˈɒmɪtri/ NOUN [U] **1** Geometry is the branch of mathematics concerned with the properties and relationships of lines, angles, curves, and shapes. ❑ *the very ordered way in which mathematics and geometry describe nature* **2** The **geometry** of an object is its shape or the relationship of its parts to each other. ❑ *the geometry of the curved roof*

geri·at·ric /ˌdʒeriˈætrɪk/ ADJ, NOUN
ADJ [geriatric + N] (*medical*) Geriatric is used to describe things relating to the illnesses and medical care of old people. ❑ *There is a question mark over the future of geriatric care.*
NOUN [C] (**geriatrics**) (*disapproval*) If you describe someone as a **geriatric**, you are implying that they are old and that their mental or physical condition is poor. This use could cause offence. ❑ *He will complain about having to spend time with such a boring bunch of geriatrics.*

✿**germ** /dʒɜːm/ NOUN [C, SING] (**germs**) **1** [C] A **germ** is a very small organism that causes disease. = bacteria ❑ *Chlorine is widely used to kill germs.* ❑ *a germ that destroyed hundreds of millions of lives* **2** [SING] The **germ of** something such as an idea is something which developed or might develop into that thing. ❑ *This was the germ of a book.*

✿**ger·mi·nate** /ˈdʒɜːmɪneɪt/ VERB [I, T] (**germinates,**

germinating, germinated) **1** [I, T] If a seed **germinates** or if it **is germinated**, it starts to grow. ❑ *Some seed varieties germinate fast, so check every day or so.* ❑ *First, the researchers germinated the seeds.* **2** [I] If an idea, plan, or feeling **germinates**, it comes into existence and begins to develop. ❑ *a big book that was germinating in his mind*

✪ger‧mi‧na‧tion /ˌdʒɜːmɪˈneɪʃən/ NOUN [U] ❑ *The poor germination of your seed could be because the soil was too cold.* ❑ *Some small seeds need light and alternating temperatures to trigger germination.*

✪ges‧ture ◆◇◇ /ˈdʒestʃə/ NOUN, VERB

NOUN [C] (**gestures**) **1** A **gesture** is a movement that you make with a part of your body, especially your hands, to express emotion or information. = movement, motion ❑ *Sarah made a menacing gesture with her fist.* ❑ *He throws his hands open in a gesture.* **2** A **gesture** is something that you say or do in order to express your attitude or intentions, often something that you know will not have much effect. ❑ *He questioned the government's commitment to peace and called on it to make a gesture of goodwill.*

VERB [I] (**gestures, gesturing, gestured**) If you **gesture**, you use movements of your hands or head in order to tell someone something or draw their attention to something. ❑ *I gestured towards the boathouse, and he looked inside.*

get ◆◆◆ /get/ VERB

> In most of its uses **get** is a fairly informal word.

VERB [LINK, T, I, AUX] (**gets, getting, got**) **1** [LINK] You use **get** with adjectives to mean 'become'. For example, if someone **gets cold**, they become cold, and if they **get angry**, they become angry. ❑ *The boys were getting bored.* ❑ *From here on, it can only get better.* **2** [LINK] **Get** is used with expressions referring to states or situations. For example, to **get into trouble** means to start being in trouble. ❑ *Half the pleasure of an evening out is getting ready.* ❑ *Perhaps I shouldn't say that – I might get into trouble.* **3** [T] To **get** someone or something into a particular state or situation means to cause them to be in it. ❑ *I don't know if I can get it clean.* ❑ *Brian will get them out of trouble.* **4** [T] If you **get** someone **to** do something, you cause them to do it by asking, persuading, or telling them to form passives. = persuade ❑ *a long campaign to get US politicians to take the AIDS epidemic more seriously* **5** [T] If you **get** something done, you cause it to be done. ❑ *I might benefit from getting my teeth fixed.* **6** [I] To **get** somewhere means to move there. ❑ *I got off the bed and opened the door.* ❑ *How can I get past her without her seeing me?* **7** [I] When you **get** to a place, you arrive there. ❑ *Generally I get to work at 9.30 a.m.* **8** [T] To **get** something or someone into a place or position means to cause them to move there. ❑ *Mack got his wallet out.* ❑ *Go and get your coat on.* **9** [AUX] **Get** is often used in place of 'be' as an auxiliary verb to form passives. **be** ❑ *A pane of glass got broken.* **10** [T] If you **get to** do something, you eventually or gradually reach a stage at which you do it. ❑ *No one could figure out how he got to be so wealthy.* **11** [T] If you **get to** do something, you manage to do it or have the opportunity to do it. ❑ *How do these people get to be the bosses of major companies?* ❑ *Do you get to see him often?* **12** [T] You can use **get** in expressions like **get moving, get going,** and **get working** when you want to tell people to begin moving, going, or working quickly. ❑ *I aim to be at the lake before dawn, so let's get moving.* **13** [I] If you **get to** a particular stage in your life or in something you are doing, you reach that stage. ❑ *We haven't got to the stage of a full-scale military conflict.* ❑ *It got to the point where I was so ill I was waiting to die.* **14** [I, T] You can use **get** to talk about the progress that you are making. For example, if you say that you **are getting somewhere**, you mean that you are making progress, and if you say that something **won't get you anywhere**, you mean it will not help you to progress at all. ❑ *Radical factions say the talks are getting nowhere and they want to withdraw.* ❑ *This bout of self-pity was getting me nowhere.* **15** [LINK] When **it gets to be** a particular time, it is that time. If **it is getting towards** a particular time, it is approaching that time. ❑ *It got to be after 1 a.m. and I was exhausted.* ❑ *It was getting towards evening when we got back.* **16** [I] If something that has continued for some time **gets to** you, it starts causing

you to suffer. ❑ *That's the first time I lost my cool in 20 years in this job. This whole thing's getting to me.* **17** [T] If you **get** something that you want or need, you obtain it. ❑ *I got a job at the sawmill.* **18** [T] If you **get** something, you receive it or are given it. ❑ *I'm getting a bike for my birthday.* ❑ *He gets a lot of letters from women.* **19** [T] If you **get** someone or something, you go and bring them to a particular place. ❑ *I came down this morning to get the newspaper.* ❑ *Go and get me a large brandy.* **20** [T] If you **get** a particular result, you obtain it from some action that you take, or from a calculation or experiment. ❑ *What do you get if you multiply six by nine?* **21** [T] If you **get** a particular price **for** something that you sell, you obtain that amount of money by selling it. ❑ *He can't get a good price for his crops.* **22** [T] If you **get** the time or opportunity to do something, you have the time or opportunity to do it. ❑ *You get time to think in prison.* **23** [T] If you **get** an idea, impression, or feeling, you begin to have that idea, impression, or feeling as you learn or understand more about something. ❑ *I get the feeling that you're an honest man.* **24** [T] If you **get** a feeling or benefit from an activity or experience, the activity or experience gives you that feeling or benefit. ❑ *Charles got a shock when he saw him.* ❑ *She gets enormous pleasure out of working freelance.* **25** [T] If you **get** a look, view, or glimpse of something, you manage to see it. = obtain ❑ *Young men climbed on buses and fences to get a better view.* **26** [T] If you **get** a joke or **get** the point of something that is said, you understand it. ❑ *Did you get that joke, Ann? I'll explain later.* **27** [T] If you **get** an illness or disease, you become ill with it. ❑ *When I was five I got measles.* **28** [T] When you **get** a train, bus, plane, or boat, you leave a place on a particular train, bus, plane, or boat. ❑ *It'll be a dollar to get the bus.*

PHRASES **as good as you can get** You can say that something is, for example, **as good as you can get** to mean that it is as good as it is possible for that thing to be. ❑ *Consort has a population of 714 and is about as rural and isolated as you can get.* ❑ *the diet that is as near to perfect as you can get*

you can't get away from or **there's no getting away from** (*informal, emphasis*) If you say **you can't get away from** something or **there is no getting away from** something, you are emphasizing that it is true, even though people might prefer it not to be true. ❑ *There is no getting away from the fact that he is on the left of the party.*

get away from it all If you **get away from it all**, you have a holiday in a place that is very different from where you normally live and work. ❑ *the ravishing island of Ischia, where rich Italians get away from it all*

you get (*spoken*) You can use **you get** instead of 'there is' or 'there are' to say that something exists, happens, or can be experienced. ❑ *That's where you get some differences of opinion.*

PHRASAL VERBS **get across** When an idea **gets across** or when you **get** it **across**, you succeed in making other people understand it. = get over ❑ *Officers felt their point of view was not getting across to the generals.*

get along If you **get along with** someone, you have a friendly relationship with them. You can also say that two people **get along**. = get on ❑ *It's impossible to get along with him.*

get around **1** To **get around** a problem or difficulty means to overcome it. = get over ❑ *None of these countries has found a way yet to get around the problem of the polarization of wealth.* **2** If you **get around** a rule or law, you find a way of doing something that the rule or law is intended to prevent, without actually breaking it. = evade ❑ *Although tobacco ads are prohibited, companies get around the ban by sponsoring music shows.* **3** If news **gets around**, it becomes well known as a result of being told to lots of people. ❑ *They threw him out because word got around that he was taking drugs.* **4** If you **get around** someone, you persuade them to allow you to do or have something by pleasing them or flattering them. ❑ *Max could always get around her.* **5** If you **get around**, you visit a lot of different places as part of your way of life. ❑ *He claimed to be a journalist, and he got around.* **6** The way that someone **gets around** is the way that they walk or go from one place to another. ❑ *It is difficult for Gail to get around since she broke her leg.*

get around to When you **get around to** doing something that you have delayed doing or have been too busy to do, you finally do it. ❑ *I said I would write to you, but as usual I never got around to it.*

get at ◼ To **get at** something means to succeed in reaching it. ❑ *A goat was standing up against a tree on its hind legs, trying to get at the leaves.* ◼ If you **get at** the truth about something, you succeed in discovering it. = find out ❑ *We want to get at the truth. Who killed him? And why?* ◼ If you ask someone what they **are getting at**, you are asking them to explain what they mean, usually because you think that they are being unpleasant or are suggesting something that is untrue. ❑ *'What are you getting at now?' demanded Rick.*

get away ◼ If you **get away**, you succeed in leaving a place or a person's company. = escape ❑ *She'd gladly have gone anywhere to get away from the city.* ◼ If you **get away**, you go away for a period of time in order to have a holiday. ❑ *He is too busy to get away.* ◼ When someone or something **gets away**, or when you **get** them **away**, they escape. ❑ *Dr Dunn was apparently trying to get away when he was shot.*

get away with If you **get away with** doing something wrong or risky, you do not suffer any punishment or other bad consequences because of it. ❑ *The criminals know how to play the system and get away with it.*

get back ◼ If someone or something **gets back to** a state they were in before, they are then in that state again. ❑ *Then life started to get back to normal.* ◼ If you **get back to** a subject that you were talking about before, you start talking about it again. = return ❑ *It wasn't until we sat down to eat that we got back to the subject of Tom Halliday.* ◼ If you **get** something **back** after you have lost it or after it has been taken from you, you then have it again. ❑ *You have 14 days in which you can cancel the contract and get your money back.*

get back to ◼ If you **get back to** an activity, you start doing it again after you have stopped doing it. ❑ *I think I ought to get back to work.* ◼ If you **get back to** someone, you contact them again after a short period of time, often by telephone. ❑ *We'll get back to you as soon as possible.*

get by If you can **get by** with what you have, you can manage to live or do things in a satisfactory way. = survive, manage ❑ *I'm a survivor. I'll get by.*

get down ◼ If something **gets** you **down**, it makes you unhappy. ❑ *At times when my work gets me down, I like to fantasize about being a farmer.* ◼ If you **get down**, you lower your body until you are sitting, kneeling, or lying on the ground. ❑ *'Get down!' she yelled. 'Somebody's shooting!'*

get down to If you **get down to** something, especially something that requires a lot of attention, you begin doing it. ❑ *With the election out of the way, the government can get down to business.*

get in ◼ If a political party or a politician **gets in**, they are elected. ❑ *If the Republicans got in they might decide to change it.* ◼ If you **get** something **in**, you manage to do it at a time when you are very busy doing other things. ❑ *I plan to get a few lessons in.* ◼ When a train, bus, or plane **gets in**, it arrives. ❑ *We would have come straight here, except our flight got in too late.*

get into ◼ If you **get into** a particular kind of work or activity, you become involved in it. ❑ *He was eager to get into politics.* ◼ If you **get into** a school, college, or university, you are accepted there as a student. ❑ *I was working hard to get into Yale.*

get off ◼ If someone who has broken a law or rule **gets off**, they are not punished, or are given only a very small punishment. ❑ *He is likely to get off with a small fine.* ◼ If you tell someone to **get off** a piece of land or a property, you are telling them to leave, because they have no right to be there and you do not want them there. ❑ *I told you. Get off the farm.* ◼ You can tell someone to **get off** when they are touching something and you do not want them to. ❑ *I kept telling him to get off.*

get on If you **get on with** something, you continue doing it or start doing it. ❑ *Jane got on with her work.*

get on to If you **get on to** a topic when you are speaking, you start talking about it. ❑ *We got on to the subject of relationships.*

get out ◼ If you **get out**, you leave a place because you want to escape from it, or because you are made to leave it. ❑ *They probably wanted to get out of the country.* ◼ If you **get out**, you go to places and meet people, usually in order to have a more enjoyable life. = go out ❑ *Get out and enjoy yourself, make new friends.* ◼ If you **get out of** an organization or a commitment, you withdraw from it. ❑ *I wanted to get out of the group, but they wouldn't let me.* ◼ If news or information **gets out**, it becomes known. ❑ *If word got out now, a scandal could be disastrous.*

get out of If you **get out of** doing something that you do not want to do, you succeed in avoiding doing it. = wriggle out of ❑ *It's amazing what people will do to get out of paying taxes.*

get over ◼ If you **get over** an unpleasant or unhappy experience or an illness, you recover from it. ❑ *It took me a very long time to get over the shock of her death.* ◼ If you **get over** a problem or difficulty, you overcome it. = get around ❑ *'How would they get over that problem?' he wondered.*

get through ◼ If you **get through** a task or an amount of work, especially when it is difficult, you complete it. ❑ *I think you can get through the first two chapters.* ◼ If you **get through** a difficult or unpleasant period of time, you manage to live through it. = survive ❑ *It is hard to see how people will get through the winter.* ◼ If you **get through** to someone, you succeed in making them understand something that you are trying to tell them. ❑ *An old friend might well be able to get through to her and help her.* ◼ If you **get through to** someone, you succeed in contacting them on the telephone. ❑ *Look, I can't get through to this number.* ◼ If a law or proposal **gets through**, it is officially approved by something such as a parliament or committee. = go through ❑ *Such a radical proposal would never get through Congress.*

get together ◼ When people **get together**, they meet in order to discuss something or to spend time together. ❑ *A whole range of people from all backgrounds can get together and enjoy themselves.* ◼ If you **get** something **together**, you organize it. ❑ *Paul and I were getting a band together, and we needed a new record deal.* ◼ If you **get** an amount of money **together**, you succeed in getting all the money that you need in order to pay for something. = scrape together ❑ *Now you've finally got enough money together to put a down payment on your dream home.*

get up ◼ When someone who is sitting or lying down **gets up**, they rise to a standing position. = stand up ❑ *I got up and walked over to where he was.* ◼ When you **get up**, you get out of bed. ❑ *They have to get up early in the morning.*

→ See also **got**

get·ting /ˈgetɪŋ/ IRREG FORM **Getting** is the present participle of **get**.

ghet·to /ˈgetəʊ/ NOUN [c] (**ghettos** or **ghettoes**) A ghetto is a part of a city in which many poor people or many people of a particular race, religion, or nationality live separately from everyone else. ❑ *the black ghettos of New York and Los Angeles*

ghost /gəʊst/ NOUN [c] (**ghosts**) ◼ A ghost is the spirit of a dead person that someone believes they can see or feel. ❑ *the ghost of Marie Antoinette* ◼ The **ghost of** something, especially of something bad that has happened, is the memory of it. ❑ *the ghost of anti-Americanism*

gi·ant ◆◇◇ /ˈdʒaɪənt/ ADJ, NOUN

ADJ [giant + N] Something that is described as **giant** is much larger or more important than most others of its kind. = huge ❑ *America's giant car maker, General Motors* ❑ *a giant oak table*

NOUN [c] (**giants**) ◼ (*journalism*) **Giant** is often used to refer to any large, successful business organization or country. ❑ *Japanese electronics giant, Sony* ◼ A **giant** is an imaginary person who is very big and strong, especially one mentioned in old stories. ❏ *a Nordic saga of giants*

gift ♦◊◊ /gɪft/ NOUN [c] (**gifts**) **1** A **gift** is something that you give someone as a present. ❏ *a gift of $50.00* **2** They believed the unborn child was a gift from God. **2** If someone has a **gift for** doing something, they have a natural ability for doing it. ❏ *As a youth he discovered a gift for teaching.*

gift·ed /'gɪftɪd/ ADJ **1** Someone who is **gifted** has a natural ability to do something well. = **talented** ❏ *one of the most gifted players in the world* **2** A **gifted** child is much more intelligent or talented than average. ❏ *a national programme for gifted children*

gi·gan·tic /dʒaɪ'gæntɪk/ ADJ (*emphasis*) If you describe something as **gigantic**, you are emphasizing that it is extremely large in size, amount, or degree. = **colossal** ❏ *In Red Rock Valley the road is bordered by gigantic rocks.*

gig·gle /'gɪgəl/ VERB, NOUN
VERB [I, T] (**giggles, giggling, giggled**) If someone **giggles**, they laugh in a childlike way, because they are amused, nervous, or embarrassed. ❏ *Both girls began to giggle.* ❏ *'I beg your pardon?' she giggled.*
NOUN [C, PL] (**giggles**) **1** A **giggle** is a childlike laugh that someone gives because they are amused, nervous, or embarrassed. ❏ *She gave a little giggle.* **2** [PL] If you say that someone has **the giggles**, you mean they cannot stop giggling. ❏ *I was so nervous I got the giggles.*

gim·mick /'gɪmɪk/ NOUN [c] (**gimmicks**) (*disapproval*) A **gimmick** is an unusual and unnecessary feature or action whose purpose is to attract attention or publicity. ❏ *It is just a public relations gimmick.*

gip·sy /'dʒɪpsi/ (*BrE*) → See **gypsy**

girl ♦♦♦ /gɜːl/ NOUN [c] (**girls**) **1** A **girl** is a female child. ❏ *an eleven-year-old girl* **2** You can refer to someone's daughter as a **girl**. ❏ *We had a little girl.* **3** Young women are often referred to as **girls**. This use could cause offence. ❏ *a pretty twenty-year-old girl* **4** (*informal*) Some people refer to a man's girlfriend as his **girl**. ❏ *I've been with my girl for nine years.*

girl·friend /'gɜːlfrend/ NOUN [c] (**girlfriends**)
1 Someone's **girlfriend** is a girl or woman with whom they are having a romantic or sexual relationship. ❏ *He had been going out with his girlfriend for seven months.* **2** A **girlfriend** is a female friend. ❏ *I met a girlfriend for lunch.*

give ♦♦♦ /gɪv/ VERB, NOUN
VERB [T, I, PASSIVE] (**gives, giving, gave, given**) **1** [T] You can use **give** with nouns that refer to physical actions. The whole expression refers to the performing of the action. For example, **She gave a smile** means almost the same as 'She smiled'. ❏ *She stretched her arms out and gave a great yawn.* ❏ *He gave her a fond smile.* **2** [T] You use **give** to say that a person does something for another person. For example, if you **give** someone a lift, you take them somewhere in your car. ❏ *I gave her a lift back to her house.* ❏ *He was given mouth-to-mouth resuscitation.* **3** [T] You use **give** with nouns that refer to information, opinions, or greetings to indicate that something is communicated. For example, if you **give** someone some news, you tell it to them. ❏ *He gave no details.* ❏ *Would you like to give me your name?* **4** [T] You use **give** to say how long you think something will last or how much you think something will be. ❏ *A recent poll gave Campbell a 68 per cent support rating.* **5** [T] (*informal, feelings*) People use **give** in expressions such as **I don't give a damn** to show that they do not care about something. ❏ *They don't give a damn about the country.* **6** [T] If someone or something **gives** you a particular idea or impression, it causes you to have that idea or impression. ❏ *They gave me the impression that they were doing exactly what they wanted in life.* **7** [T] If someone or something **gives** you a particular physical or emotional feeling, it makes you experience it. ❏ *He gave me a shock.* **8** [T] If you **give** a performance or speech, you perform or speak in public. ❏ *Kotto gives a stupendous performance.* **9** [T] If you **give** something thought or attention, you think about it, concentrate on it, or deal with it. ❏ *I've been giving it some thought.* **10** [T] If you **give** a party or other social event, you organize it. = **have** ❏ *That evening, I gave a dinner party for a few close friends.* **11** [I, T] If

you **give** someone something that you own or have bought, you provide them with it, so that they have it or can use it. ❏ *They gave us T-shirts and stickers.* ❏ *He gave money to the World Health Organization to help defeat smallpox.* ❏ *Americans are still giving to charity despite hard times.* **12** [T] If you **give** someone something that you are holding or that is near you, you pass it to them, so that they are then holding it. ❏ *Give me that pencil.* **13** [T] To **give** someone or something a particular power or right means to allow them to have it. = **grant** ❏ *The new law would give the president the power to appoint the central bank's chairman.* **14** [I] If something **gives**, it collapses or breaks under pressure. ❏ *My knees gave under me.* **15** [PASSIVE] (*formal, vagueness*) You say that you **are given to** understand or believe that something is the case when you do not want to say how you found out about it, or who told you. ❏ *We were given to understand that he was ill.*

PHRASES **give me** You use **give me** to say that you would rather have one thing than another, especially when you have just mentioned the thing that you do not want. ❏ *'I hate Sundays,' he said. 'They're endless. Give me a Saturday night any day.'*

give or take **Give or take** is used to indicate that an amount is approximate. For example, if you say that something has fifty years old, **give or take** a few years, you mean that it is approximately fifty years old. ❏ *They grow to a height of 12 inches – give or take a couple of inches.*

give it up for (*informal*) If an audience is asked to **give it up for** a performer, they are being asked to applaud. ❏ *Ladies and gentlemen, give it up for Fred Durst.*

PHRASAL VERBS **give away** **1** If you **give away** something that you own, you give it to someone, rather than selling it, often because you no longer want it. ❏ *He was giving his collection away for free.* **2** If someone **gives away** an advantage, they accidentally cause their opponent or enemy to have that advantage. = **throw away** ❏ *Military advantages should not be given away.* **3** If you **give away** information that should be kept secret, you reveal it to other people. ❏ *She would give nothing away.* **4** To **give** someone or something **away** means to show their true nature or identity, which is not obvious. ❏ *Although they are pretending hard to be young, grey hair and cellulite give them away.*

give back If you **give** something **back**, you return it to the person who gave it to you. ❏ *You gave me back the projector.*

give in **1** If you **give in**, you admit that you are defeated or that you cannot do something. ❏ *'I wasn't going to give in. I wasn't going to fail. I was going to fight like hell.'* **2** If you **give in**, you agree to do something that you do not want to do. ❏ *I pressed my parents until they finally gave in and registered me for skating classes.*

give off or **give out** If something **gives off** or **gives out** a gas, heat, or a smell, it produces it and sends it out into the air. ❏ *natural gas, which gives off less carbon dioxide than coal*

give out **1** If you **give out** a number of things, you distribute them among a group of people. = **hand out** ❏ *There were people at the entrance giving out leaflets.* **2** If you **give out** information, you make it known to people. ❏ *He wouldn't give out any information.*

give over to or **give up to** If something **is given over** or **given up to** a particular use, it is used entirely for that purpose. ❏ *Much of the garden was given over to vegetables.*

give up **1** If you **give up** something, you stop doing it or having it. ❏ *The Coast Guard had given up all hope of finding the two divers alive.* **2** If you **give up**, you decide that you cannot do something and stop trying to do it. ❏ *After a fruitless morning sitting at his desk he had given up.* **3** If you **give up** your job, you resign from it. ❏ *She gave up her job to join her husband's campaign.* **4** If you **give up** something that you have or that you are entitled to, you allow someone else to have it. ❏ *One of the men with him gave up his place on the bench.* **5** If you **give yourself up**, you let the police or other people know where you are, after you have been hiding from them. ❏ *A 28-year-old man later gave himself up and will appear in court today.*

give up on If you **give up on** something or someone, you decide that you will never succeed in doing what you want to with them, and you stop trying. ❑ *He urged them not to give up on peace efforts.*

NOUN

PHRASE **give and take** If you say that something requires **give-and-take**, you mean that people must compromise or cooperate for it to be successful. ❑ *a happy relationship where there's a lot of give-and-take*
→ See also **given**

✦ **give the game away** → see **game**; **give notice** → see **notice**; **give rise to** → see **rise**; **give way** → see **way**

giv•en ◆◇◇ /'gɪvən/ IRREG FORM, ADJ, PREP
IRREG FORM **Given** is the past participle of **give**.
ADJ [DET + given] If you talk about, for example, any **given** position or a **given** time, you mean the particular position or time that you are discussing. = **particular** ❑ *In chess there are typically about 36 legal moves from any given board position.*
PREP **1** **Given** is used when indicating a possible situation in which someone has the opportunity or ability to do something. For example, **given the chance** means 'if I had the chance'. ❑ *Write down the sort of thing you would like to do, given the opportunity.* **2** If you say **given** something, you mean taking that thing into account. ❑ *Given the uncertainty over Leigh's future I was left with little other choice.*
PHRASE **given that** If you say **given that** something is the case, you mean taking that fact into account. = **considering** ❑ *Usually, I am sensible with money, as I have to be, given that I don't earn that much.*

❂ **gla•ci•er** /'glæsiə, AmE 'gleɪʃə/ NOUN [c] (**glaciers**) A **glacier** is an extremely large mass of ice which moves very slowly, often down a mountain valley. ❑ *University of Alaska scientists report that the state's glaciers are melting faster than expected.* ❑ *Twenty thousand years ago, the last great ice age buried the northern half of Europe under a massive glacier.*

glad ◆◇◇ /glæd/ ADJ **1** [V-LINK + glad] If you are **glad** about something, you are happy and pleased about it. ❑ *The people seem genuinely glad to see you.* ❑ *I'd be glad if the boys slept a little longer so I could do some ironing.* **2** [V-LINK + glad + to-INF] If you say that you will be **glad to** do something, usually for someone else, you mean that you are willing and eager to do it. = **happy** ❑ *I'll be glad to show you everything.*
glad•ly /'glædli/ ADV **1** *Malcolm gladly accepted the invitation.* ❑ *They will gladly baby-sit if you need to go out.*

glam•or•ous /'glæmərəs/ ADJ If you describe someone or something as **glamorous**, you mean that they are more attractive, exciting, or interesting than ordinary people or things. ❑ *some of the world's most beautiful and glamorous women*

glam•our /'glæmə/ (in AmE, use **glamor**) NOUN [u]
Glamour is the quality of being more attractive, exciting, or interesting than ordinary people or things. ❑ *the glamour of show biz*

glance ◆◇◇ /glɑːns, glæns/ VERB, NOUN
VERB [i] (**glances, glancing, glanced**) **1** If you **glance at** something or someone, you look at them very quickly and then look away again immediately. ❑ *He glanced at his watch.* **2** If you **glance through** or **at** a newspaper, report, or book, you spend a short time looking at it without reading it very carefully. ❑ *I picked up the phone book and glanced through it.*
NOUN [c] (**glances**) A **glance** is a quick look at someone or something. ❑ *Trevor and I exchanged a glance.*
PHRASES **at a glance** If you see something **at a glance**, you see or recognize it immediately, and without having to think or look carefully. ❑ *One could tell at a glance that she was a compassionate person.*
at first glance If you say that something is true or seems to be true **at first glance**, you mean that it seems to be true when you first see it or think about it, but that your first impression may be wrong. ❑ *At first glance, organic farming looks much more expensive for the farmer.*

gland /glænd/ NOUN [c] (**glands**) [usu SUPP + gland] A **gland** is an organ in the body which produces chemical substances for the body to use or get rid of. ❑ *the hormones secreted by our endocrine glands*

glare /gleə/ VERB, NOUN
VERB [i] (**glares, glaring, glared**) **1** If you **glare at** someone, you look at them with an angry expression on your face. ❑ *The old woman glared at him.* **2** If the sun or a light **glares**, it shines with a very bright light which is difficult to look at. ❑ *The sunlight glared.*
NOUN [c, u, sing] (**glares**) **1** [c] A **glare** is an angry, hard, and unfriendly look. ❑ *His glasses magnified his irritable glare.* **2** [u] **Glare** is very bright light that is difficult to look at. ❑ *the glare of a car's headlights* **3** [sing] If someone is in **the glare of** publicity or public attention, they are constantly being watched and talked about by a lot of people. ❑ *Norma is said to dislike the glare of publicity.*

glar•ing /'gleərɪŋ/ ADJ (emphasis) If you describe something bad as **glaring**, you are emphasizing that it is very obvious and easily seen or noticed. = **blatant** ❑ *I never saw such a glaring example of misrepresentation.*
glar•ing•ly /'gleərɪŋli/ ADV ❑ *It was glaringly obvious.*
→ See also **glare**

glass ◆◆◇ /glɑːs, glæs/ NOUN [u, c, PL] (**glasses**) **1** [u] **Glass** is a hard, transparent substance that is used to make things such as windows and bottles. ❑ *a pane of glass* **2** [c] A **glass** is a container made from glass, which you can drink from and which does not have a handle. ❑ *Grossman raised the glass to his lips.* **3** [c] The contents of a glass can be referred to as a **glass of** something. ❑ *a glass of milk* **4** [u] **Glass** is used to mean objects made of glass, for example drinking containers and bowls. ❑ *There's a glittering array of glass to choose from at markets.* **5** [PL] **Glasses** are two lenses in a frame that some people wear in front of their eyes in order to help them see better. ❑ *He took off his glasses.*

gleam /gliːm/ VERB, NOUN
VERB [i] (**gleams, gleaming, gleamed**) If an object or a surface **gleams**, it reflects light because it is shiny and clean. = **glimmer, glint** ❑ *His black hair gleamed in the sun.*
NOUN [c] (**gleams**) A **gleam of** something is a faint sign of it. = **glimmer** ❑ *There was a gleam of hope for a peaceful settlement.*

glide /glaɪd/ VERB [i] (**glides, gliding, glided**) **1** If you **glide** somewhere, you move silently and in a smooth and effortless way. ❑ *Waiters glide between tightly packed tables bearing trays of pasta.* **2** When birds or planes **glide**, they float on air currents. ❑ *Our only companion is the wandering albatross, which glides effortlessly and gracefully behind the yacht.*

glim•mer /'glɪmə/ VERB, NOUN
VERB [i] (**glimmers, glimmering, glimmered**) If something **glimmers**, it produces or reflects a faint, gentle, often unsteady light. ❑ *The moon glimmered faintly through the mists.*
NOUN [c] (**glimmers**) **1** A **glimmer** is a faint, gentle, often unsteady light. = **flicker** ❑ *In the east there is the slightest glimmer of light.* **2** A **glimmer of** something is a faint sign of it. = **gleam** ❑ *Despite an occasional glimmer of hope, this campaign has not produced any results.*

glimpse /glɪmps/ NOUN, VERB
NOUN [c] (**glimpses**) **1** If you get a **glimpse of** someone or something, you see them very briefly and not very well. ❑ *Some of the fans had waited 24 hours outside the hotel to catch a glimpse of their heroine.* **2** A **glimpse of** something is a brief experience of it or an idea about it that helps you understand or appreciate it better. ❑ *As university campuses become increasingly multiethnic, they offer a glimpse of the conflicts society will face tomorrow.*
VERB [T] (**glimpses, glimpsing, glimpsed**) If you **glimpse** someone or something, you see them very briefly and not very well. ❑ *She glimpsed a group of people standing on the bank of a river.*

glit•ter /'glɪtə/ VERB, NOUN
VERB [i] (**glitters, glittering, glittered**) If something **glitters**, light comes from or is reflected off different parts of it. = **sparkle** ❑ *The bay glittered in the sunshine.*
NOUN [u] **1** **Glitter** consists of tiny, shining pieces of

G

metal. It is glued to things for decoration. □ *Cut out a piece of sandpaper and sprinkle it with glitter.* **2** You can use **glitter** to refer to superficial attractiveness or to the excitement connected with something. □ *She was blinded by the glitter and the glamour of her own life.*

✪ **glob·al** ◆◇◇ /'gləʊbəl/ ADJ **1** You can use **global** to describe something that happens in all parts of the world or affects all parts of the world. = worldwide, international; ≠ local □ *a global ban on nuclear testing* □ *On a global scale, AIDS may well become the leading cause of infant death.* **2** A **global** view or vision of a situation is one in which all the different aspects of it are considered. □ *a global vision of contemporary societies*

✪ **glob·al·ly** /'gləʊbəli/ ADV = worldwide, internationally □ *a globally familiar trade name* □ *Indian companies that compete globally*

WORD CONNECTIONS
global + NOUN
the global **economy** the global **marketplace** □ *Businesses need to be able to compete in the global economy.*
a global **recession** a global **downturn** a global **recovery** □ *The risk is that a global recession will jeopardise any chances of economic growth in developing countries.*
global **trade** global **growth** global **poverty** global **terrorism** □ *Aid alone is not the answer to global poverty.*
a global **brand** a global **trend** □ *Understanding global trends in today's world economy is crucial for corporate success.*
ADV + **global**
increasingly global □ *Our universities operate in an increasingly global market place.*

glob·al·i·za·tion /ˌgləʊbəlaɪˈzeɪʃən/ also **globalisation** NOUN [U] (*business*) **Globalization** is the linking of companies from different countries so that they can do business with each other. □ *Trends towards the globalization of industry have dramatically affected food production in California.* □ *a period of rapid economic globalization*

✪ **glob·al·ize** /'gləʊbəlaɪz/ also **globalise** VERB [I, T] (**globalizes, globalizing, globalized**) (*business*) When industry **globalizes** or is **globalized**, companies from one country link with companies from another country in order to do business with them. □ *One way to lower costs will be to forge alliances with foreign companies or to expand internationally through appropriate takeovers – in short, to "globalize."*

✪ **glob·al warm·ing** NOUN [U] **Global warming** is the gradual rise in the Earth's temperature caused by high levels of carbon dioxide and other gases in the atmosphere. = greenhouse effect, climate change □ *The threat of global warming will eventually force the US to slow down its energy consumption.* □ *the impact of global warming* □ *It may be too late to reverse the effects of global warming.*

✪ **globe** /gləʊb/ NOUN [SING, C] (**globes**) (*academic word*) **1** [SING] You can refer to the world as **the globe** when you are emphasizing how big it is or that something happens in many different parts of it. = planet, earth, world □ *bottles of beer from every corner of the globe* □ *anticapitalism protests spanning the globe from Seattle to Genoa* □ *70% of our globe's surface is water.* **2** [C] A **globe** is a ball-shaped object with a map of the world on it. It is usually fixed on a stand. □ *Three large globes stand on the floor.* **3** [C] Any

ball-shaped object can be referred to as a **globe**. = sphere □ *The overhead light was covered now with a white globe.*

WORD FAMILIES	
globe NOUN	The brand is now well-known across the entire **globe**.
global ADJ	They proposed a **global** ban on nuclear testing.
globalize VERB	In today's **globalized** business world, communication is more important than ever.
globalization NOUN	Trends towards the **globalization** of industry have dramatically affected food production in California.

gloom /gluːm/ NOUN [SING, U] **1** [SING] The **gloom** is a state of near darkness. □ *the gloom of a foggy November morning* **2** [U] **Gloom** is a feeling of sadness and lack of hope. □ *the deepening gloom over the economy*

gloomy /'gluːmi/ ADJ (**gloomier, gloomiest**) **1** If a place is **gloomy**, it is almost dark so that you cannot see very well. □ *Inside it's gloomy after all that sunshine.* **2** If people are **gloomy**, they are unhappy and have no hope. = despondent □ *Miller is gloomy about the fate of the serious playwright in America.* **3** If a situation is **gloomy**, it does not give you much hope of success or happiness. = grim □ *a gloomy picture of an economy sliding into recession* □ *Officials say the outlook for next year is gloomy.* **gloomi·ly** /'gluːmɪli/ ADV [gloomily with V] □ *He tells me gloomily that he has been called up for army service.*

glo·ri·fy /'glɔːrɪfaɪ/ VERB [T] (**glorifies, glorifying, glorified**) To **glorify** something means to praise it or make it seem good or special, usually when it is not. □ *This magazine in no way glorifies gangs.* **glo·ri·fi·ca·tion** /ˌglɔːrɪfɪˈkeɪʃən/ NOUN [U] □ *the glorification of violence*

glo·ri·ous /'glɔːriəs/ ADJ **1** Something that is **glorious** is very beautiful and impressive. = magnificent □ *a glorious rainbow in the air* □ *She had missed the glorious blooms of the desert spring.* **2** If you describe something as **glorious**, you are emphasizing that it is wonderful and it makes you feel very happy. = wonderful □ *The win revived glorious memories of his championship-winning days.* **3** A **glorious** career, victory, or occasion involves great fame or success. □ *Harrison had a glorious career spanning more than six decades.* **glo·ri·ous·ly** /'glɔːriəsli/ ADV **1** *A tree, gloriously lit by autumn, pressed against the windowpane.* **2** *her gloriously happy love life* **3** *But the mission was successful, gloriously successful.*

glo·ry /'glɔːri/ NOUN [U, PL] (**glories**) **1** [U] **Glory** is the fame and admiration that you gain by doing something impressive. □ *Walsham had his moment of glory when he won a 20km race.* **2** [PL] A person's **glories** are the occasions when they have done something people greatly admire which makes them famous. □ *The album sees them re-living past glories but not really breaking any new ground.*

gloss /glɒs, AmE glɔːs/ NOUN, VERB

NOUN [SING, U] (**glosses**) **1** [SING] A **gloss** is a bright shine on the surface of something. = sheen □ *Sheets of rain were falling and produced a black gloss on the asphalt.* **2** [U] **Gloss** is an appearance of attractiveness or good quality which sometimes hides less attractive features or poor quality. □ *Television commercials might seem more professional, but beware of mistaking the gloss for the content.* **3** [SING] If you put **a gloss on** a bad situation, you try to make it seem more attractive or acceptable by giving people a false explanation or interpretation of it. □ *He used his diary to put a fine gloss on the horrors the regime perpetrated.*

VERB [T] (**glosses, glossing, glossed**) If you **gloss** a difficult word or idea, you provide an explanation of it. □ *'Aventure' is often glossed as simply good or bad 'fortune' or 'chance'.*

PHRASAL VERB **gloss over** If you **gloss over** a problem, a mistake, or an embarrassing moment, you try to make it seem unimportant by ignoring it or by dealing with it very quickly. ❑ *Some foreign governments gloss over human rights abuses.*

✪ **glos·sa·ry** /ˈglɒsəri, AmE ˈglɔːs-/ NOUN [C] (**glossaries**) A **glossary** of special, unusual, or technical words or expressions is an alphabetical list of them giving their meanings, for example at the end of a book on a particular subject. ❑ *A glossary of terms is included for the reader's convenience.* ❑ *a glossary of commonly used Japanese business terms*

glossy /ˈglɒsi, AmE ˈglɔːsi/ ADJ (**glossier**, **glossiest**)
1 Glossy means smooth and shiny. ❑ *glossy black hair*
2 You can describe something as **glossy** if you think that it has been designed to look attractive but has little practical value or may have hidden faults. ❑ *a glossy new office* **3** [glossy + N] Glossy magazines, leaflets, books, and photographs are produced on expensive, shiny paper. ❑ *a glossy magazine*

G

glove /glʌv/ NOUN
NOUN [C] (**gloves**) **Gloves** are pieces of clothing which cover your hands and wrists and have individual sections for each finger. You wear gloves to keep your hands warm or dry or to protect them. ❑ *He stuck his gloves in his pocket.*
PHRASE **fit like a glove** (*emphasis*) If you say that something **fits like a glove**, you are emphasizing that it fits exactly. ❑ *I gave one of the bikinis to my sister Sara and it fit like a glove.*

glow /gləʊ/ NOUN, VERB
NOUN [C, SING] (**glows**) **1** [C] A **glow** is a dull, steady light, for example the light produced by a fire when there are no flames. ❑ *The cigarette's red glow danced about in the darkness.* **2** [SING] A **glow** is a pink colour on a person's face, usually because they are healthy or have been exercising. ❑ *The moisturizer gave my face a healthy glow that lasted all day.* **3** [SING] If you feel a **glow of** satisfaction or achievement, you have a strong feeling of pleasure because of something that you have done or that has happened. ❑ *Exercise will give you a glow of satisfaction at having achieved something.*
VERB [I] (**glows**, **glowing**, **glowed**) **1** If something **glows**, it produces a dull, steady light. ❑ *The night lantern glowed softly in the darkness.* **2** If someone's skin **glows**, it looks pink because they are healthy or excited, or have been doing physical exercise. ❑ *Her freckled skin glowed with health again.* **3** If someone **glows with** an emotion such as pride or pleasure, the expression on their face shows how they feel. ❑ *The expectant mothers that Amy had encountered positively glowed with pride.*
→ See also **glowing**

glow·ing /ˈgləʊɪŋ/ ADJ A **glowing** description or opinion about someone or something praises them highly or supports them strongly. ❑ *The media has been speaking in glowing terms of the relationship between the two countries.*
→ See also **glow**

glue /gluː/ NOUN, VERB
NOUN [C, U] (**glues**) **Glue** is a sticky substance used for joining things together, often for repairing broken things. ❑ *a tube of glue*
VERB [T, PASSIVE] (**glues**, **glueing** or **gluing**, **glued**) **1** [T] If you glue one object to another, you stick them together using glue. ❑ *Glue the fabric around the window.* ❑ *The material is cut and glued in place.* **2** [PASSIVE] If you say that someone **is glued to** something, you mean that they are giving it all their attention. ❑ *They are all glued to the Olympic Games.*

glut /glʌt/ NOUN, VERB
NOUN [C] (**gluts**) [usu sing, usu with SUPP] If there is a **glut** of something, there is so much of it that it cannot all be sold or used. = surplus ❑ *Exports have become increasingly important to wineries as they battle a global wine glut.*
VERB [T] (**gluts**, **glutting**, **glutted**) (*business*) If a market **is glutted with** something, there is a glut of that thing. ❑ *The region is glutted with hospitals.*

go ◆◆◆ /gəʊ/ VERB, NOUN
VERB [I, T, LINK, RECIP] (**goes**, **going**, **went**, **gone**) **1** [I, T] When you **go** somewhere, you move or travel there.

❑ *We went to Rome.* ❑ *I went home for the weekend.* ❑ *It took us an hour to go three miles.* **2** [I] When you **go**, you leave the place where you are. ❑ *Let's go.* **3** [I, T] You use **go** to say that someone leaves the place where they are and does an activity, often a leisure activity. ❑ *We went swimming very early.* ❑ *Maybe they've just gone shopping.* ❑ *He went for a walk.* **4** [I, T] When you **go and** do something, you move to a place in order to do it and you do it. ❑ *I have to go and see the doctor.* ❑ *I finished my beer, then went and got another.* **5** [I] If you **go to** school, work, or church, you attend is regularly as part of your normal life. ❑ *She will have to go to school.* **6** [I] When you say where a road or path **goes**, you are saying where it begins or ends, or what places it is in. = lead ❑ *There's a mountain road that goes from Blairstown to Millbrook Village.* **7** [I] You can use **go** with words like 'further' and 'beyond' to show the degree or extent of something. ❑ *The governor went further by agreeing that all policy announcements should be made first in the House.* **8** [I] If you say that a period of time **goes** quickly or slowly, you mean that it seems to pass quickly or slowly. = pass ❑ *The weeks go so quickly!* **9** [I] If you say where money **goes**, you are saying what it is spent on. ❑ *Most of my money goes towards paying the bills.* **10** [I] If you say that something **goes to** someone, you mean that it is given to them. ❑ *A lot of credit must go to the chairman and his father.* **11** [I] If someone **goes** on television or radio, they take part in a television or radio programme. ❑ *The president has gone on television to defend stringent new security measures.* **12** [I] If something **goes**, someone gets rid of it. ❑ *Exactly how many jobs will go remains unclear.* **13** [I] If someone **goes**, they leave their job, usually because they are forced to. ❑ *He had made a humiliating tactical error and he had to go.* **14** [I] If something **goes into** something else, it is put in it as one of the parts or elements that form it. ❑ *the really interesting ingredients that go into the dishes that we all love to eat* **15** [I] If something **goes** in a particular place, it belongs there or should be put there, because that is where you normally keep it. ❑ *The shoes go on the shoe shelf.* **16** [I] If you say that one number **goes into** another a particular number of times, you are dividing the second number by the first. ❑ *Six goes into thirty five times.* **17** [I] (*informal*) If one of a person's senses, such as their sight or hearing, **is going**, it is getting weak and they may soon lose it completely. = fail ❑ *His eyes are going; he says he has glaucoma.* **18** [I] If something such as a light bulb or a part of an engine **is going**, it is no longer working properly and will soon need to be replaced. ❑ *I thought it looked as though the battery was going.* **19** [LINK] You can use **go** to say that a person or thing changes to another state or condition. For example, if someone **goes crazy**, they become crazy, and if something **goes bad**, it deteriorates. ❑ *I'm going bald.* ❑ *Sometimes food goes bad, but people don't know it, so they eat it anyway and then they get ill.* **20** [I] You use **go** to talk about the way something happens. For example, if an event or situation **goes well**, it is successful. ❑ *She says everything is going smoothly.* **21** [I] If a machine or device **is going**, it is working. ❑ *What about my copier? Can you get it going again?* **22** [RECIP] If something **goes with** something else, or if two things **go together**, they look or taste good together. ❑ *I was searching for a pair of grey gloves to go with my new gown.* ❑ *I can see that some colours go together and some don't.* **23** [I, T] You use **go** to introduce something you are quoting. For example, you say **the story goes** or **the argument goes** just before you quote all or part of it. ❑ *The story goes that she went home with him that night.* ❑ *The story goes like this.* **24** [T] You use **go** when indicating that something makes or produces a sound. For example, if you say that something **goes 'bang'**, you mean it produces the sound 'bang'. ❑ *She stopped in front of a painting of a dog and she started going 'woof woof'.* **25** [T] (*informal*) You can use **go** instead of 'say' when you are quoting what someone has said or what you think they will say. ❑ *He goes to me: 'Oh, what do you want?'*
PHRASES **as you go along** If you do something **as you go along**, you do it while you are doing another thing, without preparing it beforehand. ❑ *Learning how to become a parent takes time. It's a skill you learn as you go along.*
to go 1 If you say that there are a particular number of

things **to go**, you mean that they still remain to be dealt with. ❑ *I still had another five operations to go.* **2** If you say that there is a certain amount of time **to go**, you mean that there is that amount of time left before something happens or ends. ❑ *There is a week to go until the elections.* **3** (*mainly AmE*; in *BrE*, use **to take away**) If you are in a café or restaurant and ask for an item of food **to go**, you mean that you want to take it with you and not eat it there. ❑ *large fries to go*

my heart goes out to someone or **my sympathy goes out to someone** or **my thoughts go out to someone** (*feelings*) You can say '**My heart goes out to him**' or '**My sympathy goes out to her**' to express the strong sympathy you have for someone in a difficult or unpleasant situation. ❑ *My heart goes out to Mrs Adams and her fatherless children.*

CONVENTION **where do we go from here?** If someone says '**Where do we go from here?**' they are asking what should be done next, usually because a problem has not been solved in a satisfactory way.

PHRASAL VERBS **go about** **1** The way you **go about** a task or problem is the way you approach it and deal with it. ❑ *I want him back, but I just don't know how to go about it.* **2** When you **are going about** your normal activities, you are doing them. ❑ *We were simply going about our business when we were pounced upon by these police officers.*

go after If you **go after** something, you try to get it, catch it, or hit it. ❑ *We're not going after civilian targets.*

go against **1** If a person or their behaviour **goes against** your wishes, beliefs, or expectations, their behaviour is the opposite of what you want, believe in, or expect. ❑ *Changes are being made here which go against my principles and I cannot agree with them.* **2** If a decision, vote, or result **goes against** you, you do not get the decision, vote, or result that you wanted. ❑ *The mayor will resign if the vote goes against him.*

go ahead **1** If someone **goes ahead with** something, they begin to do it or make it, especially after planning, promising, or asking permission to do it. ❑ *The board will vote today on whether to go ahead with the plan.* **2** If a process or an organized event **goes ahead**, it takes place or is carried out. ❑ *The event will go ahead as planned in Chicago next summer.*

go along with **1** If you **go along with** a rule, decision, or policy, you accept it and obey it. ❑ *Whatever the majority decided I was prepared to go along with.* **2** If you **go along with** a person or an idea, you agree with them. ❑ *'I don't think a government has properly done it for about the past twenty-five years.'—'I'd go along with that.'*

go around **1** If you **go around** to someone's house, you go to visit them at their house. ❑ *I asked them to go around to the house to see if they were there.* **2** If you **go around** in a particular way, you behave or dress in that way, often as part of your normal life. = go about ❑ *I got in the habit of going around with bare feet.* **3** If a piece of news or a joke is **going around**, it is being told by many people in the same period of time. ❑ *There's a nasty sort of rumour going around about it.* **4** If there is enough of something **to go around**, there is enough of it to be shared among a group of people, or to do all the things for which it is needed. ❑ *Eventually we will not have enough water to go around.*

go away **1** If you **go away**, you leave a place or a person's company. ❑ *I think we need to go away and think about this.* **2** If you **go away**, you leave a place and spend a period of time somewhere else, especially as a holiday. ❑ *Why don't you and I go away this weekend?*

go back on If you **go back on** a promise or agreement, you do not do what you promised or agreed to do. ❑ *The budget crisis has forced the president to go back on his word.*

go back to **1** If you **go back to** a task or activity, you start doing it again after you have stopped doing it for a period of time. ❑ *I now look forward to going back to work as soon as possible.* **2** If you **go back to** a particular point in a lecture, discussion, or book, you start to consider or discuss it again. ❑ *Let me just go back to the point I was making.*

go before **1** Something that **has gone before** has happened or been discussed at an earlier time. ❑ *This is a*

rejection of most of what has gone before. **2** To **go before** a judge, tribunal, or court of law means to be present there as part of an official or legal process. ❑ *The case went before Justice Henry on December 23 and was adjourned.*

go by **1** If you say that time **goes by**, you mean that it passes. = go on ❑ *My grandmother was becoming more and more sad and frail as the years went by.* **2** If you **go by** something, you use it as a basis for a judgment or action. ❑ *If they prove that I was wrong, then I'll go by what they say.*

go down **1** If a price, level, or amount **goes down**, it becomes lower or less than it was. = fall ❑ *Income from taxation went down.* ❑ *Crime has gone down 70 per cent.* **2** If you **go down on** your knees or **on** all fours, you lower your body until it is supported by your knees, or by your hands and knees. = get down ❑ *I went down on my knees and prayed for guidance.* **3** If you say that a remark, idea, or type of behaviour **goes down** in a particular way, you mean that it gets a particular kind of reaction from a person or group of people. ❑ *Lawyers advised their clients that a neat appearance went down well with the judges.* **4** When the sun **goes down**, it goes below the horizon. = set ❑ *the glow left in the sky after the sun has gone down* **5** If a ship **goes down**, it sinks. If a plane **goes down**, it crashes out of the sky. ❑ *Their aircraft went down during a training exercise.* **6** If a computer **goes down**, it stops functioning temporarily. ❑ *The main computers went down for 30 minutes.* **7** (*informal*) Something that **is going down** is happening. = go on ❑ *The patrol can detect if something is going down or is about to go down.*

go for **1** If you **go for** a particular thing or way of doing something, you choose it. ❑ *People tried to persuade him to go for a more gradual reform programme.* **2** If you **go for** someone, you attack them. ❑ *Pantieri went for him, gripping him by the throat.* **3** If you say that a statement you have made about one person or thing also **goes for** another person or thing, you mean that the statement is also true of this other person or thing. ❑ *It is illegal to dishonour reservations; that goes for restaurants as well as customers.* **4** If something **goes for** a particular price, it is sold for that amount. = fetch ❑ *Some old machines go for as much as 35,000 dollars.*

go in If the sun **goes in**, a cloud comes in front of it and it can no longer be seen. ❑ *The sun went in, and the breeze became cold.*

go in for If you **go in for** a particular activity, you decide to do it as a hobby or interest. ❑ *They go in for tennis and bowling.*

go into **1** If you **go into** something, you describe or examine it fully or in detail. ❑ *It was a private conversation and I don't want to go into details about what was said.* **2** If you **go into** something, you decide to do it as your job or career. ❑ *Mr Pok has now gone into the tourism business.* **3** If an amount of time, effort, or money **goes into** something, it is spent or used to do it, get it, or make it. ❑ *Is there a lot of effort and money going into this sort of research?*

go off **1** If an explosive device or a gun **goes off**, it explodes or fires. ❑ *A few minutes later the bomb went off, destroying the vehicle.* **2** If an alarm bell **goes off**, it makes a sudden loud noise. ❑ *Then the fire alarm went off. I just grabbed my clothes and ran out.* **3** If an electrical device **goes off**, it stops operating. ❑ *As the water came in the windows, all the lights went off.*

go off with **1** If someone **goes off with** another person, they leave their husband, wife, or lover and have a relationship with that person. ❑ *I suppose Carolyn went off with some man she'd fallen in love with.* **2** If someone **goes off with** something that belongs to another person, they leave and take it with them. ❑ *He's gone off with my passport.*

go on **1** If you **go on** doing something, or **go on with** an activity, you continue to do it. = carry on ❑ *Unemployment is likely to go on rising this year.* ❑ *I'm all right here. Go on with your work.* **2** If something **is going on**, it is happening. = happen ❑ *While this conversation was going on, I was listening with earnest attention.* **3** If a process or institution **goes on**, it continues to happen or exist. ❑ *The population failed to understand the necessity for the war to go on.* **4** If you say that a period of time **goes on**, you mean that it passes. = go by ❏ *Renewable energy will become progressively more important as time goes on.* **5** If you **go on to** do something, you do it after you have done something else. ❏ *Alliss retired from golf in 1969 and went on to become a successful broadcaster.* **6** If you **go on to** a place, you go to it from the place that you have reached. ❏ *He goes on to New Orleans tomorrow.* **7** If you **go on**, you continue saying something or talking about something. ❏ *Meer cleared his throat several times before he went on.* **8** (*informal*) If you **go on about** something, you continue talking about the same thing, often in an annoying way. ❏ *He's always going on about his son and daughter.* **9** (*informal*) You say '**Go on**' to someone to persuade or encourage them to do something. ❏ *Go on, it's fun.* **10** If you talk about the information you have **to go on**, you mean the information you have available to base an opinion or judgment on. ❏ *But you have to go on the facts.* **11** If an electrical device **goes on**, it begins operating. = come on ❏ *A light went on at seven every evening.*

go out **1** If you **go out**, you leave your home in order to do something enjoyable, for example to go to a party, a bar, or the cinema. ❏ *I'm going out tonight.* **2** If you **go out with** someone, the two of you spend time together socially, and have a romantic or sexual relationship. ❏ *I once went out with a French man.* **3** If you **go out to** do something, you make a deliberate effort to do it. ❏ *You do not go out to injure opponents.* **4** If a light **goes out**, it stops shining. ❏ *The bedroom light went out after a moment.* **5** If something that is burning **goes out**, it stops burning. ❏ *The fire seemed to be going out.* **6** If a message **goes out**, it is announced, published, or sent out to people. ❏ *Word went out that a column of tanks was on its way.* **7** When the tide **goes out**, the water in the sea gradually moves back to a lower level. ❏ *The tide was going out.*

go over If you **go over** a document, incident, or problem, you examine, discuss, or think about it very carefully. ❏ *I won't know how successful it is until an accountant has gone over the books.*

go through **1** (*BrE*) If you **go through** an experience or a period of time, especially an unpleasant or difficult one, you experience it. ❏ *He was going through a very difficult time.* **2** If you **go through** a lot of things such as papers or clothes, you look at them, usually in order to sort them into groups or to search for a particular item. ❏ *It was evident that someone had gone through my possessions.* **3** If you **go through** a list, story, or plan, you read or check it from beginning to end. ❏ *Going through his list of customers is a massive job.* **4** If a law, agreement, or official decision **goes through**, it is approved by a legislature or committee. = get through ❏ *The bill might have gone through if the economy was growing.*

go through with If you **go through with** an action you have decided on, you do it, even though it may be very unpleasant or difficult for you. ❏ *Richard pleaded for Belinda to reconsider and not to go through with the divorce.*

go under (*business*) If a business or project **goes under**, it becomes unable to continue in operation or in existence. = collapse ❏ *If one firm goes under it could provoke a cascade of bankruptcies.*

go up **1** If a price, amount, or level **goes up**, it becomes higher or greater than it was. = rise, increase ❏ *Interest rates went up.* ❏ *The cost has gone up to $1.95 a minute.* **2** When a building, wall, or other structure **goes up**, it is built or fixed in place. ❏ *He noticed a new building going up near Whitaker Park.* **3** If something **goes up**, it explodes or starts to burn, usually suddenly and with great intensity. ❏ *The hotel went up in flames.* **4** If a shout or cheer **goes up**, it is made by a lot of people together. ❏ *A cheer went up from the other passengers.*

go with **1** If one thing **goes with** another thing, the two things officially belong together, so that if you get one, you also get the other. = accompany ❏ *the lucrative $250,000 salary that goes with the job* **2** If one thing **goes with** another thing, it is usually found or experienced together with the other thing. ❏ *For many women, the status which goes with being a wife is important.*

go without If you **go without** something that you need

or usually have or do, you do not get it or do it. ❏ *I have known what it is like to go without food for days.*

NOUN [c] (**goes**) **1** A **go** is an attempt at doing something. ❏ *I always wanted to have a go at football.* ❏ *She won on her first go.* **2** [POSS + go] If it is your **go** in a game, it is your turn to do something, for example to play a card or move a piece. = turn ❏ *Now whose go is it?*

PHRASES **make a go of something** If you say that someone **is making a go of** something such as a business or relationship, you mean that they are having some success with it. ❏ *I knew we could make a go of it and be happy.*

on the go (*informal*) If you say that someone is always **on the go**, you mean that they are always busy and active. ❏ *I got a new job this year where I am on the go all the time.*
→ See also **going, gone**

goad /gəʊd/ VERB, NOUN
VERB [T] (**goads, goading, goaded**) If you **goad** someone, you deliberately make them feel angry or irritated, often causing them to react by doing something. ❏ *Charles was always goading me.*
NOUN [c] (**goads**) A **goad** is something someone does deliberately which makes you feel angry or irritated, often causing you to react by doing something. ❏ *Her presence was just one more goad to Joanna's unravelling nerves.*

go-ahead NOUN, ADJ
NOUN [SING] If you give someone or something the **go-ahead**, you give them permission to start doing something. ❏ *Chuck gave Pellman the go-ahead to speak publicly about the injury he sustained.*
ADJ [go-ahead + N] A **go-ahead** person or organization tries hard to succeed, often by using new methods. ❏ *Fairview Estate is one of the oldest and the most go-ahead wine producers in South Africa.*

✪ **goal** ♦♦◇ /gəʊl/ NOUN [c] (**goals**) (*academic word*) **1** In games such as football or hockey, the **goal** is the space into which the players try to get the ball in order to score a point for their team. ❏ *He was back in the goal after breaking a knuckle.* **2** In games such as football or hockey, a **goal** is when a player gets the ball into the goal, or the point that is scored by doing this. ❏ *They scored five goals in the first half of the match.* **3** Something that is your **goal** is something that you hope to achieve, especially when much time and effort will be needed. = aim, objective, ambition ❏ *It's a matter of setting your own goals and following them.* ❏ *Their goals are ambitious: to nearly double federal money for Down syndrome research.* ❏ *the Nationalist goal of independence*

go-between NOUN [c] (**go-betweens**) A **go-between** is a person who takes messages between people who are unable or unwilling to meet each other. = intermediary ❏ *He will act as a go-between to try and work out an agenda.*

god ♦♦◇ /gɒd/ NOUN, CONVENTION
NOUN [SING, c] (**gods**) **1** [SING] The name **God** is given to the spirit or being who is worshipped as the creator and ruler of the world, especially by Jews, Christians, and Muslims. ❏ *He believes in God.* **2** [c] In many religions, a **god** is one of the spirits or beings that are believed to have power over a particular part of the world or nature. ❏ *Zeus, king of the gods* **3** [c] Someone who is admired very much by a person or group of people, and who influences them a lot, can be referred to as a **god**. ❏ *To his followers he was a god.*

PHRASES **God knows** or **God only knows** or **God alone knows** (*emphasis*) You can say **God knows**, **God only knows**, or **God alone knows** to emphasize that you do not know something. ❏ *God alone knows what she thinks.*

God knows (*emphasis*) If someone says **God knows** in reply to a question, they mean that they do not know the answer. ❏ *'Where is he now?'—'God knows.'*

in God's name (*informal, emphasis*) If someone uses expressions such as **what in God's name**, **why in God's name**, or **how in God's name**, they are emphasizing how angry, annoyed, or surprised they are. ❏ *What in God's name do you expect me to do?*

God's gift (*informal*) If a person thinks they are **God's gift** to someone or something, they think they are perfect or extremely good. ❑ *Are men God's gift to women? Some of them think they are.*

play God (*disapproval*) If someone **plays God**, they act as if they have unlimited power and can do anything they want. ❑ *You have no right to play God in my life!*

to God (*emphasis*) You can use **God** in expressions such as **I hope to God**, or **I wish to God**, or **I swear to God**, in order to emphasize what you are saying. ❑ *I hope to God they are paying you well.*

God willing If you say **God willing**, you are saying that something will happen if all goes well. ❑ *God willing, there will be a breakthrough.*

CONVENTION (*emphasis*) People sometimes use **God** in exclamations to emphasize something that they are saying, or to express surprise, fear, or excitement. This use could cause offence. ❑ *Oh my God, he's shot somebody.* ❑ *Good God, it's Mr Harper!*

✦ **honest to God** → see **honest**; **for God's sake** → see **sake**; **thank God** → see **thank**

god·dess /ˈɡɒdes/ NOUN [C] (**goddesses**) In many religions, a **goddess** is a female spirit or being that is believed to have power over a particular part of the world or nature. ❑ *Diana, the goddess of war*

going ♦♦♦ /ˈɡəʊɪŋ/ NOUN, ADJ, VERB

NOUN [U] You use **the going** to talk about how easy or difficult it is to do something. You can also say that something is, for example, **hard going** or **tough going**. ❑ *He has her support to fall back on when the going gets tough.*

PHRASE **while the going is good** If you say that someone should do something **while the going is good**, you are advising them to do it while things are going well and they still have the opportunity, because you think it will become much more difficult to do. ❑ *People are leaving in the thousands while the going is good.*

ADJ [going + N] The **going** rate or the **going** salary is the usual amount of money that you expect to pay or receive for something. ❑ *That's about half the going price on world oil markets.*

VERB

PHRASES **be going to** ■ If you say that something **is going to** happen, you mean that it will happen in the future, usually quite soon. ❑ *I think it's going to be successful.* ❑ *You're going to enjoy this.* ■ You say that you **are going to** do something to express your intention or determination to do it. ❑ *I'm going to go to bed.* ❑ *He announced that he's going to resign.*

have a lot going for you or **have something going for you** If someone or something **has** a lot **going for** them, they have a lot of advantages. ❑ *This area has a lot going for it.*

get going When you **get going**, you start doing something or start a journey, especially after a delay. ❑ *Now what about that shopping list? I've got to get going.*

keep going If you **keep going**, you continue doing things or doing a particular thing. ❑ *I like to keep going. I hate to sit still.*

→ See also **go**

✦ **going concern** → see **concern**

goings-on NOUN [PL] If you describe activities or events as **goings-on**, you mean that they are strange, interesting, amusing, or dishonest. ❑ *The Mexican girl had found out about the goings-on in the factory.*

gold ♦♦◇ /ɡəʊld/ NOUN, COLOUR

NOUN [U, C] (**golds**) ■ [U] **Gold** is a valuable, yellow-coloured metal that is used for making jewellery and ornaments, and as an international currency. ❑ *a sapphire set in gold* ❑ *The price of gold was going up.* ■ [U] **Gold** is jewellery and other things that are made of gold. ❑ *We handed over all our gold and money.* ■ [C, U] (*informal*) A **gold** is the same as a **gold medal**. ❑ *His ambition was to win gold at the Atlanta Games in 1996.*

PHRASES **good as gold** (*emphasis*) If you say that a child is being **as good as gold**, you are emphasizing that they are behaving very well and are not causing you any problems. ❑ *The boys were as good as gold on our walk.*

a heart of gold (*emphasis*) If you say that someone has **a heart of gold**, you are emphasizing that they are very

good and kind to other people. ❑ *They are all good boys with hearts of gold. They would never steal.*

COLOUR Something that is **gold** is a bright yellow colour, and is often shiny. ❑ *I'd been wearing Michel's black and gold shirt.*

gold·en ♦◇◇ /ˈɡəʊldən/ ADJ

ADJ ■ Something that is **golden** is bright yellow in colour. ❑ *She combed and arranged her golden hair.* ■ **Golden** things are made of gold. ❑ *a golden chain with a golden locket* ■ [golden + N] If you describe something as **golden**, you mean it is wonderful because it is likely to be successful and rewarding, or because it is the best of its kind. ❑ *He says there's a golden opportunity for peace which must be seized.*

PHRASE **golden boy** or **golden girl** If you refer to a man as a **golden boy** or a woman as a **golden girl**, you mean that they are especially popular and successful. ❑ *When the film came out the critics went wild, hailing Tarantino as the golden boy of the 1990s.*

gold med·al NOUN [C] (**gold medals**) A **gold medal** is a medal made of gold which is awarded as first prize in a contest or competition. ❑ *her ambition to win a gold medal at the Winter Olympics*

golf ♦◇◇ /ɡɒlf/ NOUN [U] **Golf** is a game in which you use long sticks called clubs to hit a small, hard ball into holes that are spread out over a large area of grassy land. ❑ *'Do you play golf?' he asked me suddenly.*

gone ♦♦◇ /ɡɒn, AmE ɡɑːn/ IRREG FORM, ADJ

IRREG FORM **Gone** is the past participle of **go**.

ADJ [V-LINK + gone] When someone is **gone**, they have left the place where you are and are no longer there. When something is **gone**, it is no longer present or no longer exists. ❑ *He knows how hard it was for her while he was gone.* ❑ *He's already been gone four hours!*

good ♦♦♦ /ɡʊd/ ADJ, CONVENTION, NOUN

ADJ (**better, best**) ■ **Good** means pleasant or enjoyable. ❑ *We had a really good time together.* ❑ *I know they would have a better life here.* ■ **Good** means of a high quality, standard, or level. ❑ *Exercise is just as important to health as good food.* ❑ *His parents wanted Raymond to have the best possible education.* ■ If you are **good at** something, you are skilful and successful at doing it. ❑ *He was very good at his work.* ❑ *I'm not very good at singing.* ■ If you describe a piece of news, an action, or an effect as **good**, you mean that it is likely to result in benefit or success. ❑ *On balance, biotechnology should be good news for developing countries.* ❑ *I think the response was good.* ■ A **good** idea, reason, method, or decision is a sensible or valid one. ❑ *They thought it was a good idea to make some offenders do community service.* ❑ *There is good reason to doubt this.* ■ If you say that **it is good that** something should happen or **good to** do something, you mean it is desirable, acceptable, or right. ❑ *I think it's good that some people are going.* ■ A **good** estimate or indication of something is an accurate one. ❑ *We have a fairly good idea of what's going on.* ❑ *This is a much better indication of what a school is really like.* ■ If you get a **good** deal or a **good** price when you buy or sell something, you receive a lot in exchange for what you give. ❑ *Whether such properties are a good deal will depend on individual situations.* ■ Someone who is in a **good** mood is cheerful and pleasant to be with. ❑ *People were in a pretty good mood.* ❑ *He exudes natural charm and good humour.* ■ [good + N] If people are **good** friends, they get along well together and are very close. ❑ *She and Gavin are good friends.* ■ ['a' good + N] You use **good** to emphasize the great extent or degree of something. ❑ *We waited a good fifteen minutes.* ■ [V-LINK + good 'for' N] If something is **good for** a person or organization, it benefits them. = beneficial ❑ *Rain water was once considered to be good for the complexion.* ■ Someone who is **good** is morally correct in their attitudes and behaviour. ❑ *The president is a good man.* ■ Someone, especially a child, who is **good** obeys rules and instructions and behaves in a socially correct way. ❑ *The children were very good.* ❑ *I'm going to be a good boy now.* ■ Someone who is **good** is kind and thoughtful. ❑ *You are good to me.* ❑ *Her good intentions were thwarted almost immediately.*

G

PHRASES **it's a good thing** or **it's a good job** If you say **it's a good thing** that something is the case, you mean that it is fortunate. □ *It's a good thing you aren't married.*

as good as new If you say that something or someone is **as good as new**, you mean that they are in a very good condition or state, especially after they have been damaged or ill. □ *I only use that on special occasions, s o it's as good as new.*

good old (*feelings*) You use **good old** before the name of a person, place, or thing when you are referring to them in an affectionate way. □ *Good old Harry. Reliable to the end.*

as good as As good as can be used to mean 'almost'. = practically □ *His career is as good as over.*

make good (*mainly AmE*) If someone **makes good** a threat or promise or **makes good on** it, they do what they have threatened or promised to do. □ *He was confident the allies would make good on their pledges.*

CONVENTION You say '**Good**' or '**Very good**' to express pleasure, satisfaction, or agreement with something that has been said or done, especially when you are in a position of authority. □ *'Are you all right?'—'I'm fine.'—'Good. So am I.'* □ *Oh good, Tom's just come in.*

NOUN [U, SING] **1** [U] [with BRD-NEG] If someone or something is **no good** or is **not any good**, they are not satisfactory or are of a low standard. □ *If the weather's no good then I won't take any pictures.* **2** [SING] [with POSS] If something is done for **the good** of a person or organization, it is done in order to benefit them. = benefit □ *The president urged him to resign for the good of the country.* □ *Victims want to see justice done not just for themselves, but for the greater good of society.* **3** [U] If you say that doing something is **no good** or does **not do any good**, you mean that doing it is not of any use or will not bring any success. □ *It's no good worrying about it now.* □ *We gave them water and kept them warm, but it didn't do any good.* **4** [U] **Good** is what is considered to be right according to moral standards or religious beliefs. □ *Good and evil may co-exist within one family.*

PHRASES **do someone good** If you say that something will **do someone good**, you mean that it will benefit them or improve them. □ *The outing will do me good.* □ *It's probably done you good to get away for a few hours.*

for good If something changes or disappears **for good**, it never changes back or comes back as it was before. □ *Some of the nation's manufacturing jobs may be gone for good.*
→ See also **best, goods**

✦ **in good faith** → see **faith**; **so far so good** → see **far**; the **good old days** → see **old**; **in good shape** → see **shape**; **in good time** → see **time**; **too good to be true** → see **true**; **good as gold** → see **gold**

good·bye /gʊdˈbaɪ/ also **good-bye, good-by**
CONVENTION, NOUN

CONVENTION (*formulae*) You say '**Goodbye**' to someone when you or they are leaving, or at the end of a telephone conversation.

PHRASE **say goodbye to something** or **wave goodbye to something** If you **say goodbye** or **wave goodbye** to something that you want or usually have, you accept that you are not going to have it. □ *He has probably said goodbye to his last chance of Olympic gold.*

NOUN [C] (**goodbyes**) When you say your **goodbyes**, you say something such as 'Goodbye' when you leave. □ *He said his goodbyes knowing that a long time would pass before he would see his child again.* □ *Perry and I exchanged goodbyes.*
✦ **kiss something goodbye** → see **kiss**

good-looking ADJ (**better-looking, best-looking**) Someone who is **good-looking** has an attractive face. □ *Cassandra noticed him because he was good-looking.*

good·ness /ˈgʊdnəs/ EXCLAM, NOUN

EXCLAM (*feelings*) People sometimes say '**goodness**' or '**my goodness**' to express surprise. □ *Goodness, I wonder if he knows.*

NOUN [U] **Goodness** is the quality of being kind, helpful, and honest. □ *He retains a faith in human goodness.*
✦ **for goodness' sake** → see **sake**; **thank goodness**
→ see **thank**

○ **goods** ◆◆◇ /gʊdz/ NOUN [PL] **1 Goods** are things that are made to be sold. = merchandise, products □ *Money can be exchanged for goods or services.* □ *China is now producing high-quality goods at low cost.* □ *a wide range of consumer goods* **2** Your **goods** are the things that you own and that can be moved. □ *You can give your unwanted goods to charity.*

good·will /gʊdˈwɪl/ NOUN [U] **1 Goodwill** is a friendly or helpful attitude towards other people, countries, or organizations. □ *I invited them to dinner, a gesture of goodwill.* **2** (*business*) The **goodwill** of a business is something such as its good reputation, which increases the value of the business. □ *We do not want to lose the goodwill built up over 175 years.*

gore /gɔː/ VERB, NOUN

VERB [T] (**gores, goring, gored**) If someone **is gored** by an animal, they are badly wounded by its horns or tusks. □ *Carruthers had been gored by a rhinoceros.*

NOUN [U] **Gore** is blood from a wound that has become thick. □ *There were pools of blood and gore on the pavement.*

gor·geous /ˈgɔːdʒəs/ ADJ (*informal*) **1** If you say that something is **gorgeous**, you mean that it gives you a lot of pleasure or is very attractive. = beautiful □ *gorgeous mountain scenery* □ *It's a gorgeous day.* **2** If you describe someone as **gorgeous**, you mean that you find them very sexually attractive. □ *The cosmetics industry uses gorgeous women to sell their skincare products.*

gos·pel /ˈgɒspəl/ NOUN [C, SING, U] (**gospels**) **1** [C] In the New Testament of the Bible, the **Gospels** are the four books which describe the life and teachings of Jesus Christ. □ *the parable in St Matthew's Gospel* **2** [SING] In the Christian religion, the **gospel** refers to the message and teachings of Jesus Christ, as explained in the New Testament. □ *I didn't shirk my duties. I visited the sick and I preached the gospel.* **3** [U] **Gospel** or **gospel music** is a style of religious music that uses strong rhythms and vocal harmony. It is especially popular among black Christians in the southern United States. □ *I had to go to church, so I grew up singing gospel.* **4** [U] If you say something as **gospel**, or it is **the gospel truth**, you believe that it is completely true. □ *He wouldn't say this if it weren't the gospel truth.*

gos·sip /ˈgɒsɪp/ NOUN, VERB

NOUN [U, C] (**gossips**) **1** [U] [also 'a' gossip] **Gossip** is informal conversation, often about other people's private affairs. □ *He spent the first hour talking gossip.* □ *There has been much gossip about the possible reasons for his absence.* **2** [C] (*disapproval*) If you describe someone as a **gossip**, you mean that they enjoy talking informally to people about the private affairs of others. □ *He was a vicious gossip.*

VERB [RECIP] (**gossips, gossiping, gossiped**) If you **gossip** with someone, you talk informally, especially about other people or local events. You can also say that two people **gossip**. □ *We spoke, debated, gossiped into the night.* □ *Eva gossiped with Sarah.*

got ◆◆◆ /gɒt/ IRREG FORM

IRREG FORM **Got** is the past tense and sometimes the past participle of **get**.

PHRASES **have got something** (*spoken*) You use **have got** to say that someone has a particular thing, or to mention a quality or characteristic that someone or something has. In informal American English, people sometimes just use 'got'. = have □ *I've got a coat just like this.* □ *After a pause he asked, 'You got any identification?'*

have got to do something (*spoken*) **1** You use **have got to** when you are saying that something is necessary or must happen in the way stated. In informal American English, the 'have' is sometimes omitted. = must □ *I'm not happy with the situation, but I've just got to accept it.* □ *You got to come clean about things.* **2** (*emphasis*) People sometimes use **have got to** in order to emphasize that they are certain that something is true, because of the facts or circumstances involved. In informal American English, the 'have' is sometimes omitted. = must □ *'You've got to be joking!' he wisely replied.*

USAGE NOTE

have got

Do not use **have got** when you are talking about an event or action. Do not say, for example, 'I've got a bath every morning'. Say 'I have a bath every morning.'

---

gov·ern ♦◇◇ /ˈɡʌvən/ VERB [T] (**governs, governing, governed**) **1** To **govern** a place such as a country, or its people, means to be officially in charge of the place, and to have responsibility for making laws, managing the economy, and controlling public services. = rule ❑ *They go to the polls on Friday to choose the people they want to govern their country.* **2** If a situation or activity **is governed by** a particular factor, rule, or force, it is controlled by that factor, rule, or force. ❑ *Marine insurance is governed by a strict series of rules and regulations.*

✪ gov·ern·ment ♦♦♦ /ˈɡʌvənmənt/ NOUN [C, U] (**governments**) **1** [C] The **government** of a country is the group of people who are responsible for governing it. ❑ *The Government has insisted that confidence is needed before the economy can improve.* ❑ *democratic governments in countries like Britain and the US* ❑ *the governments of 12 European countries* ❑ *the government's foreign policy* **2** [U] **Government** consists of the activities, methods, and principles involved in governing a country or other political unit. ❑ *The first four years of government were completely disastrous.*

gov·ern·men·tal /ˌɡʌvənˈmentəl/ ADJ [governmental + N] **Governmental** means relating to a particular government, or to the practice of governing a country. ❑ *a governmental agency for providing financial aid to developing countries*

gov·er·nor ♦♦◇ /ˈɡʌvənə/ NOUN [C] (**governors**) **1** In some systems of government, a **governor** is a person who is in charge of the political administration of a state, colony, or region. ❑ *He was governor of Iowa in the late 1970s.* **2** A **governor** is a member of a committee which controls an organization such as a university or a hospital. ❑ *Wayne Hansen was added to the board of governors at City University, Bellevue.*

gown /ɡaʊn/ NOUN [C] (**gowns**) **1** A **gown** is a dress, usually a long dress, which women wear on formal occasions. ❑ *The new ball gown was a great success.* **2** A **gown** is a loose black garment worn on formal occasions by people such as lawyers and academics. ❑ *an old headmaster in a flowing black gown*

grab ♦◇◇ /ɡræb/ VERB, NOUN

VERB [T, I] (**grabs, grabbing, grabbed**) **1** [T] If you **grab** something, you take it or pick it up suddenly and roughly. ❑ *I managed to grab her hand.* **2** [I] If you **grab at** something, you try to grab it. ❑ *He was clumsily trying to grab at Alfred's arms.* **3** [T] (*informal*) If you **grab** someone who is walking past, you succeed in getting their attention. ❑ *Grab that waiter, Mary Ann.* **4** [T] If you **grab** someone's attention, you do something in order to make them notice you. ❑ *I jumped on the wall to grab the attention of the crowd.* **5** [T] (*informal*) If you **grab** something such as food, drink, or sleep, you manage to get some quickly. ❑ *Grab a beer.*

NOUN [C] (**grabs**) [usu sing, grab 'for/at' N] If you **make a grab for** or **at** something, you try to take it or pick it up suddenly. ❑ *I made a grab for the knife.*

PHRASE **up for grabs** (*informal*) If something is **up for grabs**, it is available to anyone who is interested. ❑ *The famous Ritz hotel is up for grabs for $100 million.*

grace /ɡreɪs/ NOUN, VERB

NOUN [U, PL, C] (**graces**) **1** [U] If someone moves with **grace**, they move in a smooth, controlled, and attractive way. ❑ *He moved with the grace of a trained boxer.* **2** [PL] The **graces** are the ways of behaving and doing things which are considered polite and well-mannered. ❑ *She didn't fit in and she had few social graces.* **3** [U] In Christianity and some other religions, **grace** is the kindness that God shows to people because He loves them. ❑ *It was only by the grace of God that no one died.* **4** [C, U] When someone says **grace** before or after a meal, they say a prayer in

which they thank God for the food and ask Him to bless it. ❑ *Leo, will you say grace?*

VERB [T] (**graces, gracing, graced**) (*formal*) If you say that something **graces** a place or a person, you mean that it makes them more attractive. ❑ *He went to the beautiful old Shaker dresser that graced this homely room.*

grace·ful /ˈɡreɪsfʊl/ ADJ **1** Someone or something that is **graceful** moves in a smooth and controlled way that is attractive to watch. ❑ *His movements were so graceful they seemed effortless.* **2** Something that is **graceful** is attractive because it has a pleasing shape or style. ❑ *His handwriting, from earliest young manhood, was flowing and graceful.*

grace·ful·ly /ˈɡreɪsfʊli/ ADV **1** [gracefully with V] ❑ *She stepped gracefully onto the stage.* **2** [gracefully + ADJ/-ED] ❑ *She loved the gracefully high ceiling, with its white-painted cornice.*

gra·cious /ˈɡreɪʃəs/ ADJ, EXCLAM

ADJ **1** (*formal*) If you describe someone as **gracious**, you mean that they are very well-mannered and pleasant. = courteous ❑ *She is a lovely and gracious woman.* **2** (*formal*) If you describe the behaviour of someone in a position of authority or high social standing as **gracious**, you mean that they behave in a polite and considerate way. ❑ *She closed with a gracious speech of thanks.* **3** You use **gracious** to describe the comfortable way of life of wealthy people. ❑ *He drove through the gracious suburbs with the swimming pools and tennis courts.*

EXCLAM (*feelings*) Some people say '**good gracious**' or '**goodness gracious**' in order to express surprise or annoyance. ❑ *Good gracious, look at that specimen, will you?*

gra·cious·ly /ˈɡreɪʃəsli/ ADV [graciously with V] ❑ *Hospitality at the presidential guest house was graciously declined.*

✪ grade ♦◇◇ /ɡreɪd/ VERB, NOUN, COMB (*academic word*)

VERB [T] (**grades, grading, graded**) If something **is graded**, its quality is judged, and it is often given a number or a name that indicates how good or bad it is. = mark, categorize ❑ *Dust masks are graded according to the protection they offer.* ❑ *Hampshire College does not grade the students' work.*

NOUN [C] (**grades**) **1** The **grade** of a product is its quality, especially when this has been officially judged. ❑ *a good grade of plywood* **2** Your **grade** in an examination or piece of written work is the mark you get, usually in the form of a letter or number, that indicates your level of achievement. = mark, score ❑ *What grade are you hoping to get?* ❑ *Results show a 0.8 percentage point increase in candidates achieving a grade A.* **3** Your **grade** in a company or organization is your level of importance or your rank. ❑ *Staff turnover is particularly high among junior grades.* **4** In the United States, a **grade** is a group of classes in which all the children are of a similar age. When you are six years old you go into the first grade and you leave school after the twelfth grade. ❑ *Mr. White teaches first grade in south Georgia.*

PHRASE **make the grade** If someone **makes the grade**, they succeed, especially by reaching a particular standard. ❑ *She had a strong desire to be a dancer but failed to make the grade.*

COMB **Grade** is combined with some nouns and adjectives to describe the quality of something. ❑ *weapons-grade plutonium*

✪ grad·ual /ˈɡrædʒuəl/ ADJ A **gradual** change or process occurs in small stages over a long period of time, rather than suddenly. = slow; ≠ sudden ❑ *Losing weight is a slow, gradual process.* ❑ *You can expect her progress at school to be gradual rather than brilliant.*

✪ grad·ual·ly ♦◇◇ /ˈɡrædʒuəli/ ADV [gradually with V] If something changes or is done **gradually**, it changes or is done in small stages over a long period of time, rather than suddenly. = slowly, gently, steadily; ≠ suddenly, sharply ❑ *Electricity lines to 30,000 homes were gradually being restored yesterday.* ❑ *The slope gradually decreased.* ❑ *Start slowly and gradually increase the number of steps.* ❑ *Gradually we learned to cope.*

✪ grad·u·ate ♦◇◇ NOUN, VERB

NOUN /ˈɡrædʒʊət/ [C] (**graduates**) **1** [usu graduate 'of' N]

In Britain, a **graduate** is a person who has successfully completed a degree at a university or college and has received a certificate that shows this. ❑ *In 1973, the first Open University graduates received their degrees.* ❑ *an Economics graduate from Leeds University* **2** In the United States, a **graduate** is a student who has successfully completed a course at a high school, college, or university. ❑ *The top one-third of all high school graduates are entitled to an education at California State University.*

VERB /ˈɡrædʒʊeɪt/ [I] (**graduates, graduating, graduated**) **1** In Britain, when a student **graduates** from university, they have successfully completed a degree course. ❑ *She graduated in English and Drama from Manchester University.* **2** In the United States, when a student **graduates**, they complete their studies successfully and leave their school or university. You can also say that a school or university **graduates** a student or students. ❑ *When the boys graduated from high school, Ann moved to a small town in Vermont.* ❑ *Last year American universities graduated a record number of students with degrees in computer science.* **3** If you **graduate from** one thing **to** another, you go from a less important job or position to a more important one. = progress ❑ *Bruce graduated to chef at the Bear Hotel.*

✪ **gradua·tion** /ˌɡrædʒuˈeɪʃən/ NOUN [U, c] (**graduations**) **1** [U] Graduation is the successful completion of a course of study at a university, college, or school, for which you receive a degree or diploma. ❑ *They asked what his plans were after graduation.* **2** [c] A graduation is a special ceremony at a university, college, or school, at which degrees and diplomas are given to students who have successfully completed their studies. ❑ *the graduation ceremony at Yale*

graf·fi·ti /ɡrəˈfiːti/ NOUN [U] Graffiti is words or pictures that are written or drawn in public places, for example on walls or posters. ❑ *Buildings old and new are thickly covered with graffiti.*

graft /ɡrɑːft, ɡræft/ NOUN, VERB
NOUN [c] (**grafts**) A **graft** is a piece of healthy skin or bone, or a healthy organ, which is attached to a damaged part of your body by a medical operation in order to replace it. ❑ *I am having a skin graft on my arm soon.*
VERB [T] (**grafts, grafting, grafted**) **1** If a piece of healthy skin or bone or a healthy organ **is grafted onto** a damaged part of your body, it is attached to that part of your body by a medical operation. ❑ *The top layer of skin has to be grafted onto the burns.* **2** If a part of one plant or tree **is grafted** onto another plant or tree, they are joined together so that they will become one plant or tree, often in order to produce a new variety. ❑ *Pear trees are grafted on quince rootstocks.*

grain ◆◇◇ /ɡreɪn/ NOUN
NOUN [c, U, SING] (**grains**) **1** [c] A **grain of** wheat, rice, or other cereal crop is a seed from it. ❑ *a grain of wheat* **2** [c, U] Grain is a cereal crop, especially wheat or corn, that has been harvested and is used for food or in trade. ❑ *a bag of grain* **3** [c] A **grain of** something such as sand or salt is a tiny, hard piece of it. ❑ *a grain of sand* **4** [SING] [grain 'of' N] A **grain of** a quality is a very small amount of it. ❑ *There's more than a grain of truth in that.* **5** [SING] The **grain** of a piece of wood is the direction of its fibres. You can also refer to the pattern of lines on the surface of the wood as the **grain**. ❑ *Brush the paint generously over the wood in the direction of the grain.*
PHRASE **go against the grain** If you say that an idea or action **goes against the grain**, you mean that it is very difficult for you to accept it or do it, because it conflicts with your previous ideas, beliefs, or principles. ❑ *Privatization goes against the grain of their principle of opposition to private ownership of industry.*
◆ **take something with a grain of salt** → see **salt**

✪ **gram** /ɡræm/ (in *BrE*, also use **gramme**) NOUN [c] (**grams**) A **gram** is a unit of weight. One thousand grams are equal to one kilogram. ❑ *A football weighs about 400 grams.* ❑ *A single cinnamon roll contains 27 grams of fat.*

✪ **gram·mar** /ˈɡræmə/ NOUN [U] **1** Grammar is the ways that words can be put together in order to make sentences. ❑ *He doesn't have mastery of the basic rules of grammar.* ❑ *the*

difference between Sanskrit and English grammar **2** Someone's **grammar** is the way in which they obey or do not obey the rules of grammar when they write or speak. ❑ *His vocabulary was sound and his grammar excellent.*

✪ **gram·mati·cal** /ɡrəˈmætɪkəl/ ADJ **1** [grammatical + N] **Grammatical** is used to indicate that something relates to grammar. ❑ *Should the teacher present grammatical rules to students?* ❑ *grammatical errors* **2** If someone's language is **grammatical**, it is considered correct because it obeys the rules of grammar. ❑ *a new test to determine whether students can write grammatical English*

gramme /ɡræm/ (**grammes**) (*BrE*) → See **gram**

grand ◆◆◇ /ɡrænd/ ADJ, NOUN
ADJ (**grander, grandest**) **1** If you describe a building or a piece of scenery as **grand**, you mean that its size or appearance is very impressive. = majestic ❑ *This grand building in the centre of town used to be the hub of the capital's social life.* **2** **Grand** plans or actions are intended to achieve important results. ❑ *Hamilton revealed his grand design for the economic future of the United States.* **3** People who are **grand** think they are important or socially superior. ❑ *He is grander and even richer than the Prince of Wales.* **4** [grand + N] A **grand** total is one that is the final amount or the final result of a calculation. ❑ *It came to a grand total of $220,329.* **5** [grand + N] **Grand** is often used in the names of buildings such as hotels, especially when they are very large. ❑ *They stayed at The Grand Hotel, Budapest.*
NOUN [c] (**grand**) (*informal*) A **grand** is a thousand pounds or a thousand dollars. ❑ *They're paying you ten grand now for those adaptations of old plays.*

grand·child /ˈɡræntʃaɪld/ NOUN [c] (**grandchildren**) Someone's **grandchild** is the child of their son or daughter. ❑ *Mary loves her grandchildren.*

grand·daughter /ˈɡrændˌdɔːtə/ NOUN [c] (**granddaughters**) Someone's **granddaughter** is the daughter of their son or daughter. ❑ *a drawing of my granddaughter Amelia*

grand·father /ˈɡrændˌfɑːðə/ NOUN [c] (**grandfathers**) Your **grandfather** is the father of your father or mother. ❑ *His grandfather was a professor.*

grand·mother /ˈɡrænˌmʌðə/ NOUN [c] (**grandmothers**) Your **grandmother** is the mother of your father or mother. ❑ *My grandmothers are both widows.*

grand·parent /ˈɡrænˌpeərənt/ NOUN [c] (**grandparents**) Your **grandparents** are the parents of your father or mother. ❑ *Tammy was raised by her grandparents.*

grand·son /ˈɡrænsʌn/ NOUN [c] (**grandsons**) Someone's **grandson** is the son of their son or daughter. ❑ *My grandson's birthday was on Tuesday.*

✪ **grant** ◆◆◇ /ɡrɑːnt, ɡrænt/ NOUN, VERB (*academic word*)
NOUN [c] (**grants**) A **grant** is an amount of money that a government or other institution gives to an individual or to an organization for a particular purpose such as education or home improvements. ❑ *They'd got a special grant to encourage research.* ❑ *Unfortunately, my application for a grant was rejected.*
VERB [T] (**grants, granting, granted**) **1** (*formal*) If someone in authority **grants** you something, or if something **is granted to** you, you are allowed to have it. = give, allow, award; ≠ refuse ❑ *France has agreed to grant him political asylum.* ❑ *Single parents tend to grant more independence to their children than other parents do.* ❑ *It was a Labour government which granted independence to India and Pakistan.* ❑ *Permission was granted a few weeks ago.* **2** If you **grant that** something is true, you accept that it is true, even though your opinion about it does not change. ❑ *The magistrates granted that the charity was justified in bringing the action.*
PHRASES **take someone for granted** If you say that someone **takes** you **for granted**, you are complaining that they benefit from your help, efforts, or presence without showing that they are grateful. ❑ *What right has the family to take me for granted, Martin?*
take something for granted If you **take** something **for granted**, you believe that it is true or accept it as normal

without thinking about it. ❑ *I was amazed that virtually all the things I took for granted up north just didn't happen in Savannah.*

take it for granted If you **take it for granted** that something is the case, you believe that it is true or you accept it as normal without thinking about it. ❑ *He seemed to take it for granted that he should speak as a representative.*

grant·ed /'grɑːntɪd, 'græntɪd/ CONJ, ADV

■ CONJ You use **granted** or **granted that** at the beginning of a clause to say that something is true, before you make a comment on it. ❑ *Granted that the firm has not broken the law, is the law what it should be?*

■ ADV [granted with CL] You use **granted** at the beginning of a clause to say that something is true, before you make a comment on it. ❑ *Granted, he doesn't look too bad for his age, but I don't care for him.*

grape /greɪp/ NOUN

■ NOUN [c] (**grapes**) **Grapes** are small green or purple fruit which grow in bunches. Grapes can be eaten raw, used for making wine, or dried. ❑ *a bunch of grapes*

■ PHRASE **sour grapes** If you describe someone's attitude as **sour grapes**, you mean that they say something is worthless or undesirable because they want it themselves but cannot have it. ❑ *These accusations have been going on for some time now, but it is just sour grapes.*

❖**graph** /grɑːf, græf/ NOUN [c] (**graphs**) A **graph** is a mathematical diagram which shows the relationship between two or more sets of numbers or measurements. ❑ *a graph showing that breast cancer deaths rose about 20 per cent from 1960 to 1985* ❑ *The bar graph opposite shows this.* ❑ *As the graph below illustrates, savings peaked at 15.8 per cent in September 2008 and have been falling steadily ever since.*

graph·ic /'græfɪk/ ADJ, NOUN

■ ADJ (*emphasis*) If you say that a description or account of something unpleasant is **graphic**, you are emphasizing that it is clear and detailed. = explicit ❑ *The descriptions of sexual abuse are graphic.* ■ [graphic + N] **Graphic** means concerned with drawing or pictures, especially in publishing, industry, or computing. ❑ *fine and graphic arts*

■ NOUN [U, c] (**graphics**) ■ [U] **Graphics** is the activity of drawing or making pictures, especially in publishing, industry, or computing. ❑ *a computer manufacturer that specializes in graphics* ■ [c] **Graphics** are drawings and pictures that are composed using simple lines and sometimes strong colours. ❑ *The Agriculture Department today released a new graphic to replace the old symbol.*

graphi·cal·ly /'græfɪkəli/ ADV [graphically with v] ❑ *Here, graphically displayed, was confirmation of the entire story.*

grasp /grɑːsp, græsp/ VERB, NOUN

■ VERB [T] (**grasps, grasping, grasped**) ■ If you **grasp** something, you take it in your hand and hold it very firmly. ❑ *He grasped both my hands.* ■ If you **grasp** something that is complicated or difficult to understand, you understand it. ❑ *The government has not yet grasped the seriousness of the crisis.*

■ NOUN [SING] ■ A **grasp** is a very firm hold or grip. ❑ *His hand was taken in a warm, firm grasp.* ■ If you say that something is **in** someone's **grasp**, you disapprove of the fact that they possess or control it. If something slips **from** your **grasp**, you lose it or lose control of it. ❑ *The people in your grasp are not guests, they are hostages.* ❑ *She allowed victory to slip from her grasp.* ■ A **grasp of** something is an understanding of it. ❑ *They have a good grasp of foreign languages.*

■ PHRASE **within someone's grasp** If you say that something is **within** someone's **grasp**, you mean that it is very likely that they will achieve it. ❑ *Peace is now within our grasp.*

grass ♦◊◊ /grɑːs, græs/ NOUN

■ NOUN [c, U] (**grasses**) **Grass** is a very common plant consisting of large numbers of thin, spiky, green leaves that cover the surface of the ground. ❑ *Small things stirred in the grass around the tent.*

■ PHRASE **the grass is greener** If you say **the grass is greener** somewhere else, you mean that other people's situations always seem better or more attractive than your own, but may not really be so. ❑ *He was very happy with us but wanted to see if the grass was greener elsewhere.*

grate /greɪt/ NOUN, VERB

■ NOUN [c] (**grates**) A **grate** is a framework of metal bars in a fireplace, which holds the wood or coal. ❑ *A wood fire burned in the grate.*

■ VERB [T, I] (**grates, grating, grated**) ■ [T] If you **grate** food such as cheese or carrots, you rub it over a metal tool called a grater so that the food is cut into very small pieces. ❑ *Grate the cheese into a mixing bowl.* ■ [I] When something **grates**, it rubs against something else, making a harsh, unpleasant sound. ❑ *His chair grated as he got to his feet.* ■ [I] If something such as someone's behaviour **grates on** you or **grates**, it makes you feel annoyed. ❑ *His manner always grated on me.*

grate·ful /'greɪtfʊl/ ADJ If you are **grateful for** something that someone has given you or done for you, you have warm, friendly feelings towards them and wish to thank them. ❑ *She was grateful to him for being so good to her.*

grate·ful·ly /'greɪtfəli/ ADV [gratefully with v] ❑ *'That's kind of you, Sally,' Claire said gratefully.*

grati·fy /'grætɪfaɪ/ VERB [T] (**gratifies, gratifying, gratified**) (*formal*) ■ If you **are gratified** by something, it gives you pleasure or satisfaction. ❑ *Mr Dambar was gratified by his response.* ■ If you **gratify** your own or another person's desire, you do what is necessary to please yourself or them. = satisfy ❑ *We gratified our friend's curiosity.*

grati·fy·ing /'grætɪfaɪɪŋ/ ADJ ❑ *We took a chance and we've won. It's very gratifying.*

grati·fi·ca·tion /ˌgrætɪfɪ'keɪʃən/ NOUN [U] ■ He is waiting for them to recognize him and eventually they do, much to his gratification. ■ *sexual gratification*

grati·tude /'grætɪtjuːd, AmE -tuːd/ NOUN [U] **Gratitude** is the state of feeling grateful. ❑ *I wish to express my gratitude to Kathy Davis for her immense practical help.*

grave ♦◊◊ NOUN, ADJ /greɪv/

■ NOUN [c] (**graves**) A **grave** is a place where a dead person is buried. ❑ *They used to visit her grave twice a year.*

■ PHRASE **turn in their grave** If you say that someone who is dead would **turn** or **turn over** in their **grave at** something that is happening now, you mean that they would be very shocked or upset by it, if they were alive. ❑ *Darwin must be turning in his grave at the thought of what is being perpetrated in his name.*

■ ADJ (**graver, gravest**) ■ A **grave** event or situation is very serious, important, and worrying. ❑ *He said that the situation in his country is very grave.* ■ A **grave** person is quiet and serious in their appearance or behaviour. ❑ *Anxiously, she examined his unusually grave face.* ■ /grɑːv/ [grave + N] In some languages, such as French, a **grave** accent is a symbol that is placed over a vowel in a word to show how the vowel is pronounced. For example, the word 'mère' has a grave accent over the first 'e'.

grave·ly /'greɪvli/ ADV ■ *They had gravely impaired the credibility of the government.* ■ *'I think I've covered that business more than adequately,' he said gravely.*

❖**grav·ity** /'grævɪti/ NOUN [U] ■ **Gravity** is the force that causes things to drop to the ground. ❑ *Arrows would continue to fly forward forever in a straight line were it not for gravity, which brings them down to earth.* ■ The **gravity of** a situation or event is its extreme importance or seriousness. ❑ *The president said those who grab power through violence deserve punishment which matches the gravity of their crime.* ■ The **gravity** of someone's behaviour or speech is the extremely serious way in which they behave or speak. ❑ *There was an appealing gravity to everything she said.*

graze /greɪz/ VERB, NOUN

■ VERB [I, T] (**grazes, grazing, grazed**) ■ [I, T] When animals **graze** or **are grazed**, they eat the grass or other plants that are growing in a particular place. You can also say that a field **is grazed** by animals. ❑ *Five cows graze serenely around a massive oak.* ❑ *Several horses grazed the meadowland.* ■ [T] If you **graze** a part of your body, you injure your skin by scraping against something. ❑ *I had grazed my knees a little.* ■ [T] If something **grazes** another thing, it touches that thing lightly as it passes by. ❑ *A bullet had grazed his arm.*

G

NOUN [C] **(grazes)** A **graze** is a small wound caused by scraping against something. ❑ *Although cuts and grazes are not usually very serious, they can be quite painful.*

grease /griːs/ NOUN, VERB
NOUN [U] **1** **Grease** is a thick, oily substance which is put on the moving parts of cars and other machines in order to make them work smoothly. = oil ❑ *grease-stained hands* **2** **Grease** is an oily substance that is produced by your skin. ❑ *His hair is thick with grease.* **3** **Grease** is animal fat that is produced by cooking meat. You can use **grease** for cooking. ❑ *He could smell the bacon grease.*
VERB [T] **(greases, greasing, greased)** **1** If you **grease** a part of a car, machine, or device, you put grease on it in order to make it work smoothly. = oil ❑ *I greased the front and rear hubs and adjusted the brakes.* **2** If you **grease** a dish, you put a small amount of fat or oil around the inside of it in order to prevent food from sticking to it during cooking. ❑ *Grease two sturdy baking sheets and heat the oven to 200 degrees.*

great ♦♦♦ /greɪt/ ADJ, NOUN, EXCLAM
ADJ **(greater, greatest)** **1** [great + N] You use **great** to describe something that is very large. **Great** is more formal than **big**. ❑ *The room had a great bay window.* **2** **Great** means large in amount or degree. ❑ *Benjamin Britten did not live to a great age.* **3** You use **great** to describe something that is important, famous, or exciting. ❑ *the great cultural achievements of the past* **4** You can describe someone who is successful and famous for their actions, knowledge, or skill as **great**. ❑ *He has the potential to be a great player.* **5** *(informal, approval)* If you describe someone or something as **great**, you approve of them or admire them. ❑ *Arturo has this great place in Cozumel.* ❑ *They're a great bunch of guys.* **6** ['feel' great] If you **feel great**, you feel very healthy, energetic, and enthusiastic. ❑ *I feel just great.* **7** You use **great** in order to emphasize the size or degree of a characteristic or quality. ❑ *a great big Italian wedding* NOUN [PL] **(greats)** *(journalism)* The **greats** in a particular subject or field of activity are the people who have been most successful or famous in it. ❑ *all the greats of Hollywood* EXCLAM *(feelings)* You say **great** in order to emphasize that you are pleased or enthusiastic about something. ❑ *Oh great! That'll be good for Fred.*
great·ness /'greɪtnəs/ NOUN [U] **1** *A nation must take certain risks to achieve greatness.* **2** *Abraham Lincoln achieved greatness.*

great·ly /'greɪtli/ ADV *(formal, emphasis)* You use **greatly** to emphasize the degree or extent of something. ❑ *People would benefit greatly from a pollution-free vehicle.*

greed /griːd/ NOUN [U] **Greed** is the desire to have more of something, such as food or money, than is necessary or fair. ❑ *an insatiable greed for personal power*

greedy /'griːdi/ ADJ **(greedier, greediest)** If you describe someone as **greedy**, you mean that they want to have more of something such as food or money than is necessary or fair. ❑ *He attacked greedy bosses for awarding themselves big raises.*
greedi·ly /'griːdɪli/ ADV [greedily with V] ❑ *Laurie ate the pastries greedily and with huge enjoyment.*

green ♦♦♦ /griːn/ COLOUR, ADJ, NOUN
COLOUR **Green** is the colour of grass or leaves. ❑ *Yellow and green together make a pale green.*
ADJ **(greener, greenest)** **1** A place that is **green** is covered with grass, plants, and trees and not with houses or factories. ❑ *Every street and bit of park or bit of green space.* **2** [green + N] **Green** issues and political movements relate to or are concerned with the protection of the environment. ❑ *The power of the Green movement in Germany has made that country a leader in the drive to recycle more waste materials.* **3** If you say that someone or something is **green**, you mean they harm the environment as little as possible. ❑ *trying to persuade governments to adopt greener policies* **4** If you say that someone is **green**, you mean that they have had very little experience of life or a particular job. ❑ *He was a young fellow, very green, very immature.*
PHRASE **green fingers** *(BrE; in AmE, use **a green thumb**)* If someone has **green fingers**, they are very good at

gardening and their plants grow well. ❑ *She has unbelievably green fingers, she can grow anything.*
NOUN [C] **(greens)** **1** **Greens** are members of green political movements. ❑ *The Greens see themselves as a radical alternative to the two major political parties.* **2** A **green** is a smooth, flat area of grass around a hole on a golf course. ❑ *the 18th green* **3** A **green** is an area of land covered with grass, especially in a town or in the middle of a village. ❑ *the village green*
green·ness /'griːnnəs/ NOUN [U] **1** *the lush greenness of the river valleys* **2** *If you'd like to recognize the greenness of an individual or organization, why not nominate them for an Environmental Achievement Award.*
✦ **give someone a green light** → see **light**

green·house /'griːnhaʊs/ NOUN, ADJ
NOUN [C] **(greenhouses)** A **greenhouse** is a glass building in which you grow plants that need to be protected from bad weather.
ADJ [greenhouse + N] **Greenhouse** means relating to or causing the greenhouse effect. ❑ *controls on greenhouse emissions*

✪ **green·house ef·fect** NOUN [SING] The **greenhouse effect** is the problem caused by increased quantities of gases such as carbon dioxide in the air. These gases trap the heat from the sun, and cause a gradual rise in the temperature of the Earth's atmosphere. = global warming ❑ *gases that contribute to the greenhouse effect* ❑ *the fight against the greenhouse effect*

✪ **green·house gas** NOUN [C, U] **(greenhouse gases)** **Greenhouse gases** are the gases which are responsible for causing the greenhouse effect. The main greenhouse gas is carbon dioxide. ❑ *Methane is a powerful greenhouse gas.* ❑ *carbon dioxide, water vapour and other greenhouse gases*

greet /griːt/ VERB [T] **(greets, greeting, greeted)** **1** When you **greet** someone, you say 'Hello' or shake hands with them. ❑ *She liked to be home to greet Steve when he came in from school.* **2** If something **is greeted** in a particular way, people react to it in that way. ❑ *His research was greeted with scepticism by advocates for children, who thought it was based on faulty data.*

greet·ing /'griːtɪŋ/ NOUN [C, U] **(greetings)** A **greeting** is something friendly that you say or do when you meet someone. ❑ *His greeting was familiar and friendly.* ❑ *They exchanged greetings.*

gre·nade /grɪ'neɪd/ NOUN [C] **(grenades)** A **grenade** or a **hand grenade** is a small bomb that can be thrown by hand. ❑ *A hand grenade was thrown at an army patrol.*

grew /gruː/ IRREG FORM **Grew** is the past tense of **grow**.

grey /greɪ/ *(BrE; in AmE, use **gray**)* COLOUR, ADJ
COLOUR **Grey** is the colour of ashes or of clouds on a rainy day. ❑ *a grey suit*
ADJ **(greyer, greyest)** **1** If the weather is **grey**, there are many clouds in the sky and the light is dull. ❑ *It was a grey, wet, April Sunday.* **2** If you describe a situation as **grey**, you mean that it is dull, unpleasant, or difficult. = bleak ❑ *Brazilians look gloomily forward to a New Year that even the president admits will be grey and cheerless.* **3** If you describe someone or something as **grey**, you think that they are boring and unattractive, and very similar to other things or other people. ❑ *Miles is one of those little grey men you find in every company.*

grid /grɪd/ NOUN [C] **(grids)** **1** A **grid** is something which is in a pattern of straight lines that cross over each other, forming squares. On maps, the grid is used to help you find a particular thing or place. ❑ *a grid of ironwork* ❑ *a grid of narrow streets* **2** A **grid** is a network of wires and cables by which sources of power, such as electricity, are distributed throughout a country or area. ❑ *breakdowns in communications and electric-power grids* **3** The **grid** or the **starting grid** is the starting line on a car-racing track. ❑ *The Ferrari driver was starting second on the grid.*

grief /griːf/ NOUN, EXCLAM
NOUN [C, U] **(griefs)** **Grief** is a feeling of extreme sadness. ❑ *a huge outpouring of national grief for the victims of the shootings*
PHRASE **come to grief** If something **comes to grief**, it

fails. If someone **comes to grief**, they fail in something they are doing, and may be hurt. ❑ *So many marriages have come to grief over lack of money.*
[EXCLAM] *(feelings)* Some people say '**Good grief**' when they are surprised or shocked. ❑ *'He's been arrested for theft and burglary.'—'Good grief!'*

griev·ance /ˈgriːvəns/ NOUN [C, U] (**grievances**) If you have a **grievance** about something that has happened or been done, you believe that it was unfair. ❑ *They had a legitimate grievance.* ❑ *The main grievance of the drivers is the imposition of higher fees for driving licences.*

grieve /griːv/ VERB [I] (**grieves, grieving, grieved**) If you **grieve over** something, especially someone's death, you feel very sad about it. ❑ *He's grieving over his dead wife and son.* ❑ *I didn't have any time to grieve.*

grill /grɪl/ NOUN, VERB
[NOUN] [C] (**grills**) **1** A **grill** is a flat frame of metal bars on which food can be cooked over a fire. ❑ *Jerry forced scrap wood through the vents in the grill to stoke the fire.* **2** *(BrE; in AmE, use* **broiler**) A **grill** is a part of a stove which produces strong direct heat to cook food that has been placed underneath it. **3** A **grill** is a restaurant that serves grilled food. ❑ *patrons of the Savoy Grill*
[VERB] [I, T] (**grills, grilling, grilled**) **1** [I, T] When you **grill** food, or when it **grills**, you cook it on metal bars above a fire or barbecue. ❑ *Grill the steaks over a wood or charcoal fire that is quite hot.* **2** [I, T] *(BrE; in AmE, use* **broil**) When you **grill** food, or when it **grills**, you cook it in a stove using very strong heat directly above it. ❑ *Grill the meat for 20 minutes on each side.* ❑ *Apart from peppers and aubergine, many other vegetables grill well.* **3** [T] *(informal)* If you **grill** someone **about** something, you ask them a lot of questions for a long period of time. ❑ *Grill your travel agent about the facilities for families with children.*
grill·ing /ˈgrɪlɪŋ/ NOUN [U, C] **1** [U] ❑ *The breast can be cut into portions for grilling.* **2** [C] ❑ *He faced a hostile grilling from the committee's Republicans.*

grim /grɪm/ ADJ (**grimmer, grimmest**) **1** A situation or piece of information that is **grim** is unpleasant, depressing, and difficult to accept. ❑ *They painted a grim picture of growing crime.* ❑ *There was further grim economic news yesterday.* **2** A place that is **grim** is unattractive and depressing in appearance. ❑ *The city might be grim at first, but there is a vibrancy and excitement.*

grin /grɪn/ VERB, NOUN
[VERB] [I] (**grins, grinning, grinned**) When you **grin**, you smile broadly. ❑ *He grins, delighted at the memory.* ❑ *Sarah tried several times to catch Philip's eye, but he just grinned at her.*
[PHRASE] **grin and bear it** If you **grin and bear it**, you accept a difficult or unpleasant situation without complaining because you know there is nothing you can do to make things better. ❑ *They cannot stand the sight of each other, but they will just have to grin and bear it.*
[NOUN] [C] (**grins**) A **grin** is a broad smile. ❑ *a big grin on her face*

grind /graɪnd/ VERB, NOUN
[VERB] [T, I] (**grinds, grinding, ground**) **1** [T] If you **grind** a substance such as corn, you crush it between two hard surfaces or with a machine until it becomes a fine powder. ❑ *Store the peppercorns in an airtight container and grind the pepper as you need it.* **2** [T] If you **grind** something **into** a surface, you press and rub it hard into the surface using small circular or sideways movements. ❑ *'Well,' I said, grinding my cigarette nervously into the granite step.* **3** [T] If you **grind** something, you make it smooth or sharp by rubbing it against a hard surface. ❑ *It was beyond my ability to grind a blade this broad.* **4** [I] If a vehicle **grinds** somewhere, it moves there very slowly and noisily. ❑ *Tanks had crossed the border at five fifteen and were grinding south.*
[PHRASES] **grind your teeth** If you **grind** your **teeth**, you rub your upper and lower teeth together as though you are chewing something.
grind to a halt **1** If a country's economy or something such as a process **grinds to a halt**, it gradually becomes slower or less active until it stops. ❑ *The peace process has*

ground to a halt while Israel struggles to form a new government. **2** If a vehicle **grinds to a halt**, it stops slowly and noisily. ❑ *The tanks ground to a halt after a hundred yards because the fuel had been siphoned out.*
[PHRASAL VERBS] **grind down** If you say that someone **grinds** you **down**, you mean that they treat you very harshly and cruelly, reducing your confidence or your will to resist them. ❑ *'You see,' said Hughes, 'there's people who want to humiliate you and grind you down.'*
grind up Grind up means the same as **grind** VERB 1. ❑ *He makes his own paint, grinding up the pigment with a little oil.*
[NOUN] [SING] **1** The **grind of** a machine is the harsh, scraping noise that it makes, usually because it is old or is working too hard. ❑ *The grind of heavy machines could get on their nerves.* **2** *(informal, disapproval)* If you refer to routine tasks or activities as **the grind**, you mean they are boring and take up a lot of time and effort. ❑ *Life continues to be a terrible grind for the ordinary person.*

grip ◆◇◇ /grɪp/ VERB, NOUN
[VERB] [T] (**grips, gripping, gripped**) **1** If you **grip** something, you take hold of it with your hand and continue to hold it firmly. ❑ *She gripped the rope.* **2** If something **grips** you, it affects you very strongly. ❑ *The entire community has been gripped by fear.* **3** If you are **gripped** by something such as a story or a series of events, your attention is concentrated on it and held by it. ❑ *The nation is gripped by the dramatic story.*
[NOUN] [C, SING, U] (**grips**) **1** [C] A **grip** is a firm, strong hold on something. ❑ *His strong hand eased the bag from her grip.* **2** [SING] Someone's **grip on** something is the power and control they have over it. ❑ *The president maintains an iron grip on his country.* **3** [U] If things such as shoes or car tyres have **grip**, they do not slip. ❑ *a new way of reinforcing rubber which gives car tyres a better grip*
[PHRASES] **come to grips with** If you **come to grips with** a problem, you consider it seriously, and start taking action to deal with it. ❑ *The administration's first task is to come to grips with the economy.*
get a grip If you **get a grip** on yourself, you make an effort to control or improve your behaviour or work. ❑ *Part of me was very frightened and I consciously had to get a grip on myself.*
in the grip of something If a person, group, or place is **in the grip of** something, they are being severely affected by it.
lose your grip If you **lose** your **grip**, you become less efficient and less confident, and less able to deal with things. ❑ *He wondered if perhaps he was getting old and losing his grip.*
a grip on reality If you say that someone has a **grip on reality**, you mean they recognize the true situation and do not have mistaken ideas about it. ❑ *Shakur loses his fragile grip on reality and starts blasting away at friends and foes alike.*
grip·ping /ˈgrɪpɪŋ/ ADJ = riveting ❑ *The film turned out to be a gripping thriller.*

groan /grəʊn/ VERB, NOUN
[VERB] [I, T] (**groans, groaning, groaned**) **1** [I] If you **groan**, you make a long, low sound because you are in pain, or because you are upset or unhappy about something. = moan ❑ *Slowly, he opened his eyes. As he did so, he began to groan with pain.* ❑ *They glanced at the man on the floor, who began to groan.* **2** [T] If you **groan** something, you say it in a low, unhappy voice. ❑ *'My leg – I think it's broken,' Eric groaned.* **3** [I] If you **groan about** something, you complain about it. ❑ *His parents were beginning to groan about the price of university tuition fees.* **4** [I] If wood or something made of wood **groans**, it makes a loud sound when it moves. ❑ *The timbers groan and creak and the floorboards shift.* **5** [I] If you say that something such as a table **groans under** the weight of food, you are emphasizing that there is a lot of food on it. ❑ *The bar counter groans under the weight of huge plates of the freshest fish.* **6** [I] If you say that someone or something **is groaning under** the weight of something, you think there is too much of that thing. ❑ *Consumers were groaning under the weight of high interest rates.*
[NOUN] [C] (**groans**) **1** A **groan** is a long, low sound made by someone who is in pain, upset, or unhappy about

g

something. = moan ❏ *She heard him let out a pitiful, muffled groan.* **2** A **groan** is a complaint about something. ❏ *Listen sympathetically to your child's moans and groans about what she can't do.*

groom /gruːm/ NOUN, VERB

NOUN [C] (**grooms**) **1** A **groom** is the same as a **bridegroom**. ❏ *the bride and groom* **2** A **groom** is someone whose job is to look after the horses in a stable and to keep them clean.

VERB [T] (**grooms**, **grooming**, **groomed**) **1** If you **groom** an animal, you clean its fur, usually by brushing it. ❏ *The horses were exercised and groomed with special care.* **2** If you **are groomed for** a special job, someone prepares you for it by teaching you the skills you will need. ❏ *George was already being groomed for the top job.*

groove /gruːv/ NOUN [C] (**grooves**) A **groove** is a deep line cut into a surface. ❏ *Prior to assembly, grooves were made in the shelf, base, and sides to accommodate the back panel.*

grope /grəʊp/ VERB [I, T] (**gropes**, **groping**, **groped**) **1** [I] If you **grope for** something that you cannot see, you try to find it by moving your hands around in order to feel it. = fumble ❏ *With his left hand he groped for the knob, turned it, and pulled the door open.* **2** [T] If you **grope** your **way** to a place, you move there, holding your hands in front of you and feeling the way because you cannot see anything. = feel ❏ *I didn't turn on the light, but groped my way across the room.* **3** [I] If you **grope for** something, for example the solution to a problem, you try to think of it, when you have no real idea what it could be. ❏ *He groped for solutions to his problems.*

✪ **gross** ◆◇◇ /grəʊs/ ADJ, ADV, VERB, NUM

ADJ (**grosser**, **grossest**) **1** [gross + N] You use **gross** to describe something unacceptable or unpleasant to a very great amount, degree, or intensity. ❏ *The company was guilty of gross negligence.* **2** If you say that someone's speech or behaviour is **gross**, you think it is very coarse, vulgar, or unacceptable. ❏ *He abused the Admiral in the grossest terms.* **3** (informal, disapproval) If you describe something as **gross**, you think it is very unpleasant. ❏ *They had a commercial on the other night for Drug Free America that was so gross I thought Dad was going to faint.* **4** [V-LINK + gross] If you describe someone as **gross**, you mean that they are extremely fat and unattractive. ❏ *I only resist things like chocolate if I feel really gross.* **5** [gross + N] **Gross** means the total amount of something, especially money, before any has been taken away. ❏ *a fixed rate account guaranteeing 10.4% gross interest or 7.8% net until October* ❏ *a recorded gross profit before tax of £4.8 million* **6** [gross + N] **Gross** means the total amount of something, after all the relevant amounts have been added together. = total ❏ *Gross sales reached nearly $2 million a year.* ❏ *gross proceeds of about $20.4 million.*

ADV [gross after V] **Gross** means in total before anything is taken away. ❏ *Interest is paid gross, rather than having tax deducted.* ❏ *a father earning £20,000 gross a year*

VERB [T] (**grosses**, **grossing**, **grossed**) (*business*) If a person or a business **grosses** a particular amount of money, they earn that amount of money before tax has been taken away. ❏ *The company grossed $16.8 million last year.* ❏ *a factory worker who grossed £9,900 last year* ❏ *So far the films have grossed more than £590 million.*

NUM (**gross**) **Gross** is a group of 144 things. ❏ *In all honesty he could not have justified ordering more than twelve gross of the disks.*

gross·ly /'grəʊsli/ ADV ❏ *Funding of education had been grossly inadequate for years.*

gross do·mes·tic prod·uct NOUN [C, U] (**gross domestic products**) (*business*) A country's **gross domestic product** is the total value of all the goods it has produced and the services it has provided in a particular year, not including its income from investments in other countries. = GDP

gro·tesque /grəʊˈtesk/ ADJ, NOUN

ADJ **1** You say that something is **grotesque** when it is so unnatural, unpleasant, and exaggerated that it upsets or shocks you. ❏ *the grotesque disparities between the wealthy*

few and nearly everyone else **2** If someone or something is **grotesque**, they are very ugly. = hideous ❏ *They tried to avoid looking at his grotesque face and his crippled body.*

NOUN [C] (**grotesques**) A **grotesque** is a person who is very ugly in a strange or unnatural way, especially one in a novel or painting. ❏ *Grass's novels are peopled with outlandish characters: grotesques, clowns, scarecrows, dwarfs.*

gro·tesque·ly /grəʊˈteskli/ ADV **1** *He called it the most grotesquely tragic experience he's ever had.* **2** [grotesquely + ADJ/-ED] ❏ *grotesquely deformed beggars*

ground ◆◆◆ /graʊnd/ NOUN, IRREG FORM, VERB, ADJ

NOUN [SING, U, C, PL] (**grounds**) **1** [SING] ['the' ground] The **ground** is the surface of the earth. ❏ *Forty or fifty women were sitting cross-legged on the ground.* ❏ *We slid down the roof and dropped to the ground.* **2** [SING] If you say that something takes place **on the ground**, you mean it takes place on the surface of the earth and not in the air. ❏ *Co-ordinating airline traffic on the ground is as complicated as managing the traffic in the air.* **3** [SING] The **ground** is the soil and rock on the earth's surface. ❏ *The ground had eroded.* **4** [U] You can refer to land as **ground**, especially when it has very few buildings or when it is considered to be special in some way. ❏ *a stretch of waste ground* **5** [C] You can use **ground** to refer to an area of land, sea, or air which is used for a particular activity. ❏ *The best fishing grounds are around the islands.* **6** [PL] The **grounds** of a large or important building are the garden or area of land which surrounds it. ❏ *the palace grounds* **7** [C, U] You can use **ground** to refer to a place or situation in which particular methods or ideas can develop and be successful. ❏ *The company has maintained its reputation as the developing ground for new techniques.* **8** [U] You can use **ground** in expressions such as **on shaky ground** and **the same ground** to refer to a particular subject, area of experience, or basis for an argument. ❏ *Sensing she was on shaky ground, Marie changed the subject.* ❏ *This is the most solid ground for optimism.* **9** [U] (*journalism*) **Ground** is used in expressions such as **gain ground**, **lose ground**, and **give ground** in order to indicate that someone gets or loses an advantage. ❏ *There are signs that the party is gaining ground in the latest polls.* **10** [C, U] If something is **grounds for** a feeling or action, it is a reason for it. If you do something **on the grounds** of a particular thing, that thing is the reason for your action. ❏ *In the interview he gave some grounds for optimism.* ❏ *The court overturned that decision on the grounds that the prosecution had withheld crucial evidence.*

PHRASES **below ground** or **above ground** Something that is **below ground** is under the Earth's surface or under a building. Something that is **above ground** is on top of the earth's surface.

break new ground (*approval*) If you **break new ground**, you do something completely different or you do something in a completely different way. ❏ *Gellhorn may have broken new ground when she filed her first report on the Spanish Civil War.*

burn something to the ground or **raze something to the ground** (*emphasis*) If you say that a town or building **is burned to the ground** or **is razed to the ground**, you are emphasizing that it has been completely destroyed by fire. ❏ *The town was razed to the ground after the French Revolution.*

common ground If two people or groups find **common ground**, they agree about something, especially when they do not agree about other things. ❏ *The participants seem unable to find common ground on the issue of agriculture.*

middle ground The **middle ground** between two groups, ideas, or plans involves things which do not belong to either of these groups, ideas, or plans but have elements of each, often in a less extreme form. ❏ *The sooner we find a middle ground between freedom of speech and protection of the young, the better for everyone.*

off the ground If something such as a project gets **off the ground**, it begins or starts functioning. ❏ *We help small companies to get off the ground.*

prepare the ground If you **prepare the ground for** a future event, course of action, or development, you make it easier for it to happen. ❏ *a political initiative which would prepare the ground for war*

shift one's ground or **change one's ground** If you **shift** your **ground** or **change** your **ground**, you change the basis on which you are arguing. □ *Robert considered this, then shifted his ground slightly in line with a new thought.*

stand your ground or **hold your ground** If you **stand** your **ground** or **hold** your **ground**, you do not run away from a situation, but face it bravely. □ *She had to force herself to stand her ground when she heard someone approaching.*

IRREG FORM **Ground** is the past tense and past participle of **grind**.

VERB [T, I] (**grounds, grounding, grounded**) **1** [T] If an argument, belief, or opinion **is grounded** in something, that thing is used to justify it. = base □ *Her argument was grounded in fact.* **2** [T] If an aircraft or its passengers **are grounded**, they are made to stay on the ground and are not allowed to take off. □ *The civil aviation minister ordered all the planes to be grounded.* **3** [T] When parents **ground** a child, they forbid them to go out and enjoy themselves for a period of time, as a punishment. □ *They grounded him for a month, and banned television.* **4** [I, T] If a ship or boat **is grounded** or if it **grounds**, it touches the bottom of the sea, lake, or river it is on, and is unable to move off. □ *Residents have been told to stay away from the region where the ship was grounded.* □ *The boat finally grounded on a soft, underwater bank.* **5** [T] If something **grounds** you, it causes you to have a sensible and practical attitude towards life and not to have unrealistic ideas. □ *These things have grounded me and made me who I am.*

ADJ (*mainly AmE; in BrE, usually use* **minced**) **Ground** meat has been cut into very small pieces in a machine. □ *The sausages are made of coarsely ground pork*

ground•ed /'graʊndɪd/ ADJ □ *She seems very grounded and down-to-earth.*

♦**ground•break•ing** /'graʊnd,breɪkɪŋ/ ADJ [usu groundbreaking + N] You use **groundbreaking** to describe things which you think are significant because they provide new and positive ideas, and influence the way people think about things. = original, innovative □ *his groundbreaking novel on homosexuality* □ *groundbreaking research*

ground•work /'graʊndwɜːk/ NOUN [SING] The **groundwork for** something is the early work on it which forms the basis for further work. □ *Yesterday's meeting was to lay the groundwork for the task ahead.*

♦**group** ♦♦♦ /gruːp/ NOUN, VERB
NOUN [C] (**groups**) **1** A **group of** people or things is a number of people or things that are together in one place at one time. □ *The trouble involved a small group of football fans.* **2** A **group** is a set of people who have the same interests or aims, and who organize themselves to work or act together. □ *Members of an environmental group are staging a protest inside a chemical plant.* **3** A **group** is a set of people, organizations, or things which are considered together because they have something in common. □ *She is among the most promising players in her age group.* □ *As a group, today's old people are still relatively deprived.* □ *the most vulnerable groups in society* **4** (*business*) A **group** is a number of separate commercial or industrial firms that all have the same owner. □ *The group made a pre-tax profit of $1.05 million.* **5** A **group** is a number of musicians who perform together, especially ones who play popular music. = band □ *At school he played bass in a pop group called The Urge.*

VERB [I, T] (**groups, grouping, grouped**) If a number of things or people **are grouped together** or **group together**, they are together in one place or within one organization or system. □ *Plants are grouped into botanical 'families' that have certain characteristics in common.* □ *The Species Survival Network groups together 80 international environmental organizations.*

→ See also **pressure group**

grove /graʊv/ NOUN [C] (**groves**) [usu with SUPP] A **grove** is a group of trees that are close together. □ *an olive grove*

♦**grow** ♦♦♦ /graʊ/ VERB
VERB [I, T, LINK] (**grows, growing, grew, grown**) **1** [I] When people, animals, and plants **grow**, they increase in size

and change physically over a period of time. □ *We stop growing at maturity.* **2** [I] If a plant or tree **grows** in a particular place, it is alive there. □ *The station had roses growing at each end of the platform.* **3** [T] If you **grow** a particular type of plant, you put seeds or young plants in the ground and take care of them as they develop. □ *Lettuce was grown by the ancient Romans.* **4** [I] When someone's hair **grows**, it gradually becomes longer. Your nails also **grow**. □ *Then the hair began to grow again and I felt terrific.* **5** [T] If someone **grows** their hair, or **grows** a beard or moustache, they stop cutting their hair or shaving so that their hair becomes longer. You can also **grow** your nails. □ *I'd better start growing my hair.* **6** [I] If someone **grows** mentally, they change and develop in character or attitude. □ *They began to grow as individuals.* **7** [LINK] You use **grow** to say that someone or something gradually changes until they have a new quality, feeling, or attitude. □ *I grew a little afraid of the guy next door.* □ *He's growing old.* **8** [I] If an amount, feeling, or problem **grows**, it becomes greater or more intense. = increase, intensify, strengthen, heighten; ≠ decrease, lessen, reduce, diminish □ *From 2000 to 2002, the number of uninsured grew by almost 4 million.* □ *Opposition grew and the government agreed to negotiate.* □ *The number of unemployed people in Poland has grown by more than a quarter in the last month.* □ *Productivity grew at an annual rate of more than 3 per cent.* □ *a growing number of immigrants* **9** [I] If one thing **grows into** another, it develops or changes until it becomes that thing. □ *The boys grew into men.* **10** [I] If something such as an idea or a plan **grows out of** something else, it develops from it. □ *The idea for this book grew out of conversations with Philippa Brewster.* **11** [I] (*business*) If the economy or a business **grows**, it increases in wealth, size, or importance. □ *The economy continues to grow.* **12** [T] (*business*) If someone **grows** a business, they take actions that will cause it to increase in wealth, size, or importance. □ *To grow the business, he needs to develop management expertise and innovation across his team.*

PHRASAL VERBS **grow apart** If people who have a close relationship **grow apart**, they gradually start to have different interests and opinions from each other, and their relationship starts to fail. □ *He and his wife grew apart.*
grow into When a child **grows into** an item of clothing, they become taller or bigger so that it fits them properly. □ *It's a little big, but she'll soon grow into it.*
grow on If someone or something **grows on** you, you start to like them more and more. □ *Slowly and strangely, the place began to grow on me.*
grow out of 1 If you **grow out of** a type of behaviour or an interest, you stop behaving in that way or having that interest, as you develop or change. = outgrow □ *Most children who stammer grow out of it.* **2** When a child **grows out of** an item of clothing, they become so tall or big that it no longer fits them properly. = outgrow □ *You've grown out of your shoes again.*
grow up 1 When someone **grows up**, they gradually change from being a child into being an adult. □ *She grew up in Tokyo.* **2** (*informal, disapproval*) If you tell someone to **grow up**, you are telling them to stop behaving in a silly or childish way. □ *It's time you grew up.* **3** If something **grows up**, it starts to exist and become larger or more important. □ *A variety of heavy industries grew up alongside the port.* **4** → See also **grown-up**
→ See also **grown**

grow•er /'graʊə/ NOUN [C] (**growers**) A **grower** is a person who grows large quantities of a particular plant or crop in order to sell them. □ *The state's apple growers are fighting an uphill battle against foreign competition.*

growl /graʊl/ VERB, NOUN
VERB [I, T] (**growls, growling, growled**) **1** [I] When a dog or other animal **growls**, it makes a low noise in its throat, usually because it is angry. □ *The dog was biting, growling, and wagging its tail.* **2** [T] (*written*) If someone **growls** something, they say something in a low, rough, and angry voice. □ *His fury was so great he could hardly speak. He growled some unintelligible words at Pete.*

NOUN [C] (**growls**) **1** A **growl** is a low noise that a dog or other animal makes in its throat, usually because it is angry. ❏ *Their noise modulated to a concerted menacing growl punctuated by sharp yaps.* **2** A **growl** is a low, rough, and angry voice. ❏ *with an angry growl of contempt for her own weakness*

grown /ɡrəʊn/ ADJ [grown + N] A **grown** man or woman is one who is fully developed and mature, both physically and mentally. ❏ *Few women can understand a grown man's love of sports.*

grown-up NOUN, ADJ

> The spelling **grownup** is also used. The syllable **up** is not stressed when it is a noun.

NOUN [C] (**grown-ups**) A **grown-up** is an adult. = adult ❏ *Jan was almost a grown-up.*
ADJ **1** Someone who is **grown-up** is physically and mentally mature and no longer depends on their parents or another adult. ❏ *I seem to have everything anyone could want – a good husband, a lovely home, grown-up children who're doing well.* **2** If you say that someone is **grown-up**, you mean that they behave in an adult way, often when they are in fact still a child. ❏ *She's very grown-up.* **3** (*informal*) **Grown-up** things seem suitable for or typical of adults. = adult ❏ *Her songs tackle grown-up subjects.*

⭐**growth** ♦♦◇ /ɡrəʊθ/ NOUN, ADJ
NOUN [U, C] (**growths**) **1** [U] The **growth of** something such as an industry, organization, or idea is its development in size, wealth, or importance. ❏ *the growth of nationalism* ❏ *Japan's enormous economic growth* **2** [U] [also 'a' growth] The **growth** in something is the increase in it. = increase, intensification; ≠ decrease, reduction ❏ *A steady growth in the popularity of two smaller parties may upset the polls.* ❏ *The area has seen a rapid population growth.* **3** [U] Someone's **growth** is the development and progress of their character. ❏ *the child's emotional and intellectual growth* **4** [U] **Growth** in a person, animal, or plant is the process of increasing in physical size and development. ❏ *hormones which control fertility and body growth* **5** [C, U] You can use **growth** to refer to plants that have recently developed or that developed at the same time. ❏ *This helps to ripen new growth and makes it flower profusely.* **6** [C] A **growth** is a lump that grows inside or on a person, animal, or plant, and that is caused by a disease. ❏ *This type of surgery could even be used to extract cancerous growths.*
ADJ [growth + N] (*business*) A **growth** industry, area, or market is one that is increasing in size or activity. ❏ *Computers and electronics are growth industries and need skilled technicians.*

grudge /ɡrʌdʒ/ NOUN [C] (**grudges**) If you have or bear a **grudge against** someone, you have unfriendly feelings towards them because of something they did in the past. ❏ *He appears to have a grudge against certain players.*

grudg·ing /'ɡrʌdʒɪŋ/ ADJ A **grudging** feeling or action is felt or done very unwillingly. = reluctant ❏ *He even earned his opponents' grudging respect.*
grudg·ing·ly /'ɡrʌdʒɪŋli/ ADV [grudgingly with V] = reluctantly ❏ *The film studio grudgingly agreed to allow him to continue working.*

grue·some /'ɡruːsəm/ ADJ Something that is **gruesome** is extremely unpleasant and shocking. = grisly ❏ *There has been a series of gruesome murders in the capital.*

grum·ble /'ɡrʌmbəl/ VERB, NOUN
VERB [I, T] (**grumbles, grumbling, grumbled**) **1** [I, T] If someone **grumbles**, they complain about something in a bad-tempered way. = moan ❏ *They grumble about how hard they have to work.* ❏ *Taft grumbled that the law so favoured the criminal that trials seemed like a game of chance.* **2** [I] (*literary*) If something **grumbles**, it makes a low continuous sound. ❏ *It was quiet now, the thunder had grumbled away to the west.*
NOUN [C, SING] (**grumbles**) **1** [C] A **grumble** is a complaint. ❏ *My only grumble is that there isn't a non-smoking section.* **2** [SING] [usu grumble 'of' N] A **grumble** is a low, continuous sound. ❏ *One could often hear, far to the east, the grumble of guns.*

⭐**guar·an·tee** ♦♦◇ /ˌɡærən'tiː/ VERB, NOUN (*academic word*)
VERB [T] (**guarantees, guaranteeing, guaranteed**) **1** If one

thing **guarantees** another, the first is certain to cause the second thing to happen. ❏ *Surplus resources alone do not guarantee growth.* ❏ *one of the few ways to virtually guarantee that a fraudster cannot open an account in your name* **2** If you **guarantee** something, you promise that it will definitely happen, or that you will do or provide it for someone. = ensure, promise ❏ *Most states guarantee the right to free and adequate education.* ❏ *We guarantee that you will find a community with which to socialize.* ❏ *All students are guaranteed campus accommodation.* **3** If a company **guarantees** its product or work, they provide a guarantee for it. ❏ *Some builders guarantee their work.* ❏ *All Dreamland's electric blankets are guaranteed for three years.*
NOUN [C] (**guarantees**) **1** Something that is a **guarantee of** something else makes it certain that it will happen or that it is true. ❏ *A famous old name on a firm is not necessarily a guarantee of quality.* **2** A **guarantee** is a promise that something will definitely happen or that you will do or provide it for someone. = promise, pledge ❏ *The editors can give no guarantee that they will fulfil their obligations.* ❏ *California's state Constitution includes a guarantee of privacy.* **3** [also 'under' guarantee] A **guarantee** is a written promise by a company to replace or repair a product free of charge if it has any faults within a particular time. ❏ *Whatever a guarantee says, when something goes wrong, you can still claim your rights from the store.* **4** A **guarantee** is money or something valuable that you give to someone to show that you will do what you have promised. ❏ *Males between 18 and 20 had to leave a deposit as a guarantee of returning to do their military service.*

guard ♦♦◇ /ɡɑːd/ VERB, NOUN
VERB [T] (**guards, guarding, guarded**) **1** If you **guard** a place, person, or object, you stand near them in order to watch and protect them. ❏ *Gunmen guarded homes near the cemetery with shotguns.* **2** If you **guard** someone, you watch them and keep them in a particular place to stop them from escaping. ❏ *Marines with rifles guarded them.* **3** If you **guard** some information or advantage that you have, you try to protect it or keep it for yourself. ❏ *He closely guarded her identity.*
PHRASAL VERB **guard against** If you **guard against** something, you are careful to prevent it from happening, or to avoid being affected by it. ❏ *The armed forces were on high alert to guard against any retaliation.*
NOUN [C, SING] (**guards**) **1** [C] A **guard** is someone such as a soldier, police officer, or prison officer who is guarding a particular place or person. ❏ *The prisoners overpowered their guards and locked them in a cell.* **2** [SING] A **guard** is a specially organized group of people, such as soldiers or police officers, who protect or watch someone or something. ❏ *We have a security guard around the whole area.* **3** [C] [usu with SUPP] A **guard** is a protective device which covers a part of someone's body or a dangerous part of a piece of equipment. ❏ *the chin guard of my helmet* **4** [C] (*BrE*; in *AmE*, use **conductor**) On a train, a **guard** is a person whose job is to travel on the train in order to help passengers, check tickets, and make sure that the train travels safely and on time.
PHRASES **catch someone off guard** If someone **catches** you **off guard**, they surprise you by doing something you do not expect. If something **catches** you **off guard**, it surprises you by happening when you are not expecting it. ❏ *Charm the audience and catch them off guard.*
lower your guard or **let your guard down**, or **drop your guard** If you **lower** your **guard**, **let** your **guard down**, or **drop** your **guard**, you relax when you should be careful and alert, often with unpleasant consequences. ❏ *The ANC could not afford to lower its guard until everything had been carried out.* ❏ *You can't let your guard down.*
on your guard If you are **on** your **guard** or **on guard**, you are being very careful because you think a situation might become difficult or dangerous. ❏ *The police have questioned him thoroughly, and he'll be on his guard.*
on guard If someone is **on guard**, they are on duty and responsible for guarding a particular place or person. ❏ *Police were on guard at Barnet town hall.*
stand guard If you **stand guard**, you stand near a particular person or place because you are responsible for

watching or protecting them. ❑ *One young policeman stood guard outside the locked embassy gates.*

under guard If someone is **under guard**, they are being guarded. ❑ *Three men were arrested and one was under guard in a hospital.*

→ See also **bodyguard**

guard·ian /'gɑːdiən/ NOUN [c] (**guardians**) **1** A guardian is someone who has been legally appointed to take charge of the affairs of another person, for example a child or someone who is mentally ill. ❑ *Destiny's legal guardian was her grandmother.* **2** The **guardian** of something is someone who defends and protects it. ❑ *an institution acting as the guardian of democracy in Europe*

guer·ril·la ◆◇◇ /gə'rɪlə/ also **guerilla** NOUN [c] (**guerrillas**) A guerrilla is someone who fights as part of an unofficial army, usually against an official army or police force. ❑ *The guerrillas threatened to kill their hostages.*

guess ◆◆◇ /ges/ VERB, NOUN

  VERB [i, т] (**guesses, guessing, guessed**) **1** [i, т] If you **guess** something, you give an answer or provide an opinion which may not be true because you do not have definite knowledge about the matter concerned. ❑ *Yvonne guessed that he was a very successful publisher or a banker.* ❑ *You can only guess at what mental suffering they endure.* ❑ *Guess what I did for the whole of the first week.* **2** [т] If you **guess that** something is the case, you correctly form the opinion that it is the case, although you do not have definite knowledge about it. ❑ *By now you will have guessed that I'm back in Ohio.* ❑ *He should have guessed what would happen.*

  PHRASES **I guess** (*mainly AmE, informal, vagueness*) You say **I guess** to show that you are slightly uncertain or reluctant about what you are saying. ❑ *I guess he's right.* ❑ *'I think you're being paranoid.'—'Yeah. I guess so.'*

keep someone guessing If someone **keeps** you **guessing**, they do not tell you what you want to know. ❑ *The author's intention is to keep everyone guessing until the bitter end.*

  CONVENTION **guess what** (*informal*) You say **guess what** to draw attention to something exciting, surprising, or interesting that you are about to say. ❑ *Guess what, I just got my first part in a film.*

  NOUN [c] (**guesses**) A guess is an attempt to give an answer or provide an opinion which may not be true because you do not have definite knowledge about the matter concerned. ❑ *My guess is that the chance that these vaccines will work is zero.* ❑ *He'd taken her pulse and made a guess at her blood pressure.*

  PHRASES **anyone's guess** or **anybody's guess** (*informal*) If you say that something is **anyone's guess** or **anybody's guess**, you mean that no one can be certain about what is really true. ❑ *Just when this will happen is anyone's guess.*

at a guess (*mainly BrE, vagueness*) You say **at a guess** to indicate that what you are saying is only an estimate or what you believe to be true, rather than being a definite fact. ❑ *At a guess he's been dead for two days.*

guest ◆◆◇ /gest/ NOUN

  NOUN [c] (**guests**) **1** A guest is someone who is visiting you or is at an event because you have invited them. ❑ *She was a guest at the wedding.* **2** A guest is someone who visits a place or organization or appears on a radio or television show because they have been invited to do so. ❑ *a frequent chat show guest* ❑ *Dr Gerald Jeffers is the guest speaker.* **3** A guest is someone who is staying in a hotel. ❑ *I was the only hotel guest.*

  CONVENTION **be my guest** If you say **be my guest** to someone, you are giving them permission to do something. ❑ *If anybody wants to work on this, be my guest.*

❖**guid·ance** /'gaɪdəns/ NOUN [u] Guidance is help and advice. = advice ❑ *an opportunity for young people to improve their performance under the guidance of professional coaches* ❑ *The nation looks to them for guidance.*

guide ◆◆◇ /gaɪd/ NOUN, VERB

  NOUN [c] (**guides**) **1** A guide is a book that gives you information or instructions to help you do or understand something. = guidebook ❑ *Our 10-page guide will help you to change your life for the better.* **2** A guide is a book that gives tourists information about a town, area, or country.

= guidebook ❑ *The Rough Guide to Paris lists accommodation for as little as $35 a night.* **3** A **guide** is someone who shows tourists around places such as museums or cities. ❑ *We've arranged a walking tour of the city with your guide.* **4** A **guide** is someone who shows people the way to a place in a difficult or dangerous region. ❑ *The mountain people say that, with guides, the journey can be done in fourteen days.* **5** A **guide** is something that can be used to help you plan your actions or to form an opinion about something. ❑ *As a rough guide, a horse needs 2.5 per cent of its body weight in food every day.*

  VERB [т] (**guides, guiding, guided**) **1** If you **guide** someone around a city, museum, or building, you show it to them and explain points of interest. ❑ *a young Egyptologist who guided us through tombs and temples with enthusiasm* **2** If you **guide** someone somewhere, you go there with them in order to show them the way. = lead ❑ *He took the bewildered Elliott by the arm and guided him out.* **3** If you **guide** a vehicle somewhere, you control it carefully to make sure that it goes in the right direction. ❑ *Captain Shelton guided his plane down the runway and took off.* **4** If something **guides** you somewhere, it gives you the information you need in order to go in the right direction. ❑ *They sailed across the Caribbean with only a compass to guide them.* **5** If something or someone **guides** you, they influence your actions or decisions. ❑ *He should have let his instinct guide him.* ❑ *Development has been guided by a concern for the ecology of the area.* **6** If you **guide** someone through something that is difficult to understand or to achieve, you help them to understand it or to achieve success in it. ❑ *Gym owner David Barton will guide them through a workout.*

guide·book /'gaɪdbʊk/ also **guide book** NOUN [c] (**guidebooks**) A guidebook is a book that gives tourists information about a town, area, or country. = guide

❖**guide·line** /'gaɪdlaɪn/ NOUN [c] (**guidelines**) (*academic word*) **1** If an organization issues **guidelines on** something, it issues official advice about how to do it. = rule, procedure, recommendation, principle ❑ *The government should issue clear guidelines on the content of religious education.* ❑ *The accord also lays down guidelines for the conduct of American drug enforcement agents.* **2** A **guideline** is something that can be used to help you plan your actions or to form an opinion about something. ❑ *A written IQ test is merely a guideline.*

guild /gɪld/ NOUN [c] (**guilds**) A guild is an organization of people who do the same job. ❑ *the Writers' Guild of America*

guilt /gɪlt/ NOUN [u] **1** Guilt is an unhappy feeling that you have because you think or know that you have done something wrong or think that you have done something wrong. ❑ *Her emotions had ranged from anger to guilt in the space of a few seconds.* **2** Guilt is the fact that you have done something wrong or illegal. ❑ *The trial is concerned only with the determination of guilt according to criminal law.*

❖**guilty** ◆◇◇ /'gɪlti/ ADJ (**guiltier, guiltiest**) **1** If you feel **guilty**, you feel unhappy because you think that you have done something wrong or have failed to do something which you should have done. ❑ *I feel so guilty, leaving all this to you.* **2** [guilty + N] **Guilty** is used of an action or fact that you feel guilty about. ❑ *Many may be keeping it a guilty secret.* **3** If someone is **guilty of** a crime or offence, they have committed that crime or offence. ≠ innocent, not guilty ❑ *They were found guilty of murder.* ❑ *He pleaded guilty to causing actual bodily harm.* **4** If someone is **guilty of** doing something wrong, they have done that thing. ❑ *He claimed Mr Brooke had been guilty of a 'gross error of judgment'.*

guilti·ly /'gɪltɪli/ ADV [guiltily with V] ❑ *He glanced guiltily over his shoulder.*

guise /gaɪz/ NOUN [c] (**guises**) You use **guise** to refer to the outward appearance or form of someone or something, which is often temporary or different from their real nature. ❑ *He turned up at an Easter party in the guise of a white rabbit.*

gui·tar ◆◇◇ /gɪ'tɑː/ NOUN [c, u] (**guitars**) A guitar is a musical instrument with six strings and a long neck. You play the guitar by plucking or strumming the strings.

gui·tar·ist /gɪˈtɑːrɪst/ NOUN [c] (guitarists) A guitarist is someone who plays the guitar.

gulf /gʌlf/ NOUN [c] (gulfs) **1** A gulf is an important or significant difference between two people, things, or groups. ❑ *Within society, there is a growing gulf between rich and poor.* **2** A gulf is a large area of sea which extends a long way into the surrounding land. ❑ *Hurricane Andrew was last night heading into the Gulf of Mexico.*

gum /gʌm/ NOUN [c, u] (gums) **1** [c, u] Gum is a substance, usually tasting of mint, which you chew for a long time but do not swallow. ❑ *I do not chew gum in public.* **2** [c] Your gums are the areas of firm, pink flesh inside your mouth, which your teeth grow out of. ❑ *The toothbrush gently removes plaque without damaging the gums or causing bleeding.*

gun ♦♦◇ /gʌn/ NOUN, VERB

NOUN [c] (guns) **1** A gun is a weapon from which bullets or other things are fired. ❑ *He fled, pointing the gun at officers as they chased him.* ❑ *He just seemed like a normal military guy who liked guns.* **2** A gun or a starting gun is an object like a gun that is used to make a noise to signal the start of a race. ❑ *The starting gun blasted and they were off.*

PHRASES **with guns blazing** or **with all guns blazing** If you come out with guns blazing or with all guns blazing, you put all your effort and energy into trying to achieve something. ❑ *The company came out with guns blazing.*

jump the gun (informal) If you jump the gun, you do something before everyone else or before the proper or right time. ❑ *It wasn't due to be released until September 10, but some booksellers have jumped the gun and decided to sell it early.*

stick to your guns (informal) If you stick to your guns, you continue to have your own opinion about something even though other people are trying to tell you that you are wrong. ❑ *He should have stuck to his guns and refused to meet her.*

VERB [T] (guns, gunning, gunned) (mainly AmE) To gun an engine or a vehicle means to make it start or go faster by pressing on the accelerator pedal. ❑ *He gunned his engine and drove off.*

PHRASAL VERB **gun down** (journalism) If someone is gunned down, they are shot and severely injured or killed. ❑ *He had been gunned down and killed at point-blank range.*

gun·fire /ˈgʌnfaɪə/ NOUN [u] Gunfire is the repeated shooting of guns. ❑ *The sound of gunfire and explosions grew closer.*

gun·man /ˈgʌnmən/ NOUN [c] (gunmen) (journalism) A gunman is a man who uses a gun to commit a crime such as murder or robbery. ❑ *Two policemen were killed when gunmen opened fire on their patrol vehicle.*

gun·point /ˈgʌnpɔɪnt/ NOUN

PHRASE **at gunpoint** If you are held at gunpoint, someone is threatening to shoot and kill you if you do not obey them. ❑ *She and her two daughters were held at gunpoint by a gang who burst into their home.*

gun·shot /ˈgʌnʃɒt/ NOUN [u, c] (gunshots) **1** [u] Gunshot is used to refer to bullets that are fired from a gun. ❑ *They had died of gunshot wounds.* **2** [c] A gunshot is the firing of a gun or the sound of a gun being fired. ❑ *They heard thousands of gunshots.*

gush /gʌʃ/ VERB, NOUN

VERB [i, T] (gushes, gushing, gushed) **1** When liquid gushes out of something, or when something gushes a liquid, the liquid flows out very quickly and in large quantities. ❑ *Piping-hot water gushed out.* **2** If someone gushes, they express their admiration or pleasure in an exaggerated way. ❑ *'Oh, it was brilliant,' he gushes.*

NOUN [SING] [usu gush 'of' N] A gush of liquid is a sudden, rapid flow of liquid, or a quantity of it that suddenly flows out. ❑ *I heard a gush of water.*

gush·ing /ˈgʌʃɪŋ/ ADJ ❑ *He delivered a gushing speech.*

gust /gʌst/ NOUN, VERB

NOUN [c] (gusts) **1** A gust is a short, strong, sudden rush of wind. ❑ *A gust of wind drove down the valley.* **2** [gust 'of' N] If you feel a gust of emotion, you feel the emotion suddenly and intensely. ❑ *a small gust of pleasure*

VERB [i] (gusts, gusting, gusted) When the wind gusts, it blows with short, strong, sudden rushes. ❑ *The wind gusted again.*

gut /gʌt/ NOUN, VERB, ADJ

NOUN [PL, SING, u, c] (guts) **1** [PL] A person's or animal's guts are all the organs inside them. ❑ *By the time they finish, the crewmen are standing ankle-deep in fish guts.* **2** [SING] ['the'/POSS gut] The gut is the tube inside the body of a person or animal through which food passes while it is being digested. ❑ *Toxins can leak from the gut into the bloodstream.* **3** [u] (informal) Guts is the will and courage to do something that is difficult or unpleasant, or which might have unpleasant results. ❑ *The new governor has the guts to push through unpopular tax increases.* **4** [c] (informal) You can refer to someone's stomach as their gut, especially when it is very large and sticks out. ❑ *His gut sagged out over his belt.* **5** [u] Gut is string made from part of the stomach of an animal. Traditionally, it is used to make the strings of sports rackets or musical instruments such as violins. ❑ *Gerald's violin strings are made of gut rather than steel.*

PHRASES **hate someone's guts** (informal, emphasis) If you hate someone's guts, you dislike them very much. ❑ *We hate each other's guts.*

work your guts out (informal, emphasis) If you say that you are working your guts out, you are emphasizing that you are working as hard as you can. ❑ *Most have worked their guts out and made sacrifices.*

VERB [T] (guts, gutting, gutted) **1** When someone guts a dead animal or fish, they prepare it for cooking by removing all the organs from inside it. ❑ *It is not always necessary to gut the fish prior to freezing.* **2** To gut a building means to destroy the inside of it so that only its outside walls remain. ❑ *Over the weekend, a firebomb gutted a building where 60 people lived.*

ADJ A gut feeling is based on instinct or emotion rather than reason. ❑ *Let's have your gut reaction to the facts as we know them.*

guy ♦♦◇ /gaɪ/ NOUN [c, PL] (guys) (informal) **1** [c] A guy is a man. ❑ *I was working with a guy from Milwaukee.* **2** [PL] ['you' guys] People sometimes address a group of people, whether they are male or female, as guys or you guys. ❑ *Hi, guys. How are you doing?*

gym /dʒɪm/ NOUN [c, u] (gyms) **1** [c] A gym is a club, building, or large room, usually containing special equipment, where people go to do physical exercise and get fit. ❑ *While the boys are golfing, I work out in the gym.* **2** [u] Gym is the activity of doing physical exercises in a gym, especially at school. ❑ *gym classes*

gym·nas·tics /dʒɪmˈnæstɪks/ NOUN [u]

The form **gymnastic** is used as a modifier.

Gymnastics consists of physical exercises that develop your strength, coordination, and ease of movement. ❑ *She competes in gymnastics, with hopes of making it to the Olympics.*

gyp·sy /ˈdʒɪpsi/ also **gipsy** NOUN, ADJ

NOUN [c] (gypsies) A gypsy is a member of a race of people who travel from place to place, usually in caravans, rather than living in one place. Some people find this word offensive. ❑ *I'm proud of being brought up by gypsies.*

ADJ Someone or something that is gypsy comes from or is associated with a race of people who travel from place to place, usually in caravans, rather than living in one place. Some people find this word offensive. ❑ *the largest gypsy community of any country*

Hh

H also **h** /eɪtʃ/ (**H's, h's** /ˈeɪtʃɪz/) H is the eighth letter of the English alphabet.

◊hab·it ◆◇◇ /ˈhæbɪt/ NOUN

[NOUN] [c, u] (**habits**) **1** [c, u] A **habit** is something that you do often or regularly. = practice □ *He has an endearing habit of licking his lips when he's nervous.* □ *Many people add salt to their food out of habit, without even tasting it first.* □ *Good exercise habits should be developed when you are young.* □ *a survey on eating habits in the UK* **2** [c] A **habit** is an action considered bad that someone does repeatedly and finds it difficult to stop doing. □ *A good way to break the habit of eating too quickly is to put your knife and fork down after each mouthful.* □ *an estimated 32 million Americans are trying to kick the habit of smoking* **3** [c] A drug **habit** is an addiction to a drug such as heroin or cocaine. □ *She became a prostitute in order to pay for her cocaine habit.*

[PHRASES] **creature of habit** If you say that someone is **a creature of habit,** you mean that they usually do the same thing at the same time each day, rather than doing new and different things. □ *Jesse is a creature of habit and always eats breakfast.*

in the habit of or **into the habit of** If you are **in the habit of** doing something, you do it regularly or often. If you **get into the habit of** doing something, you begin to do it regularly or often. □ *They were in the habit of giving two or three dinner parties a month.*

make a habit of If you **make a habit of** doing something, you do it regularly or often. □ *You can phone me at work as long as you don't make a habit of it.*

◊hab·i·tat /ˈhæbɪtæt/ NOUN [c, u] (**habitats**) The **habitat** of an animal or plant is the natural environment in which it normally lives or grows. = territory □ *In its natural habitat, the hibiscus will grow up to 25 ft.* □ *It is essential that we protect wildlife habitats.* □ *an ideal habitat for birds*

ha·bit·u·al /həˈbɪtʃuəl/ ADJ **1** A **habitual** action, state, or way of behaving is one that someone usually does or has, especially one that is considered to be typical or characteristic of them. □ *If bad posture becomes habitual, you risk long-term effects.* **2** [habitual + N] You use **habitual** to describe someone who usually or often does a particular thing. □ *Three out of four of them would become habitual criminals if actually sent to jail.*

ha·bit·u·al·ly /həˈbɪtʃuəli/ ADV □ *His mother had a patient who habitually flew into rages.*

hack /hæk/ VERB, NOUN

[VERB] [i, t] (**hacks, hacking, hacked**) **1** [i, t] If you **hack** something or **hack** at it, you cut it with strong, rough strokes using a sharp tool such as an axe or a knife. □ *An armed gang barged onto the train and began hacking and shooting anyone in sight.* □ *Matthew desperately hacked through the leather.* **2** [i] If someone **hacks into** a computer system, they break into the system, especially in order to get secret information. □ *The saboteurs had demanded money in return for revealing how they hacked into the systems.*

[PHRASE] **can't hack it** (*informal*) If you say that someone **can't hack it** or **couldn't hack it,** you mean that they do not or did not have the qualities needed to do a task or cope with a situation. □ *You have to be strong and confident, and never give the slightest impression that you can't hack it.*

[NOUN] [c] (**hacks**) (*disapproval*) **1** If you refer to a politician as a **hack,** you disapprove of them because they are too loyal to their party and perhaps do not deserve the position they have. □ *Far too many party hacks from the old days still hold influential jobs.* **2** If you refer to a professional writer, such as a journalist, as a **hack,** you disapprove of them because they write for money without worrying very much about the quality of their writing. □ *tabloid hacks, always eager to find victims in order to sell newspapers*

hack·ing /ˈhækɪŋ/ NOUN [u] □ *the common and often illegal art of computer hacking*

hack·er /ˈhækə/ NOUN [c] (**hackers**) **1** A computer **hacker** is someone who tries to break into computer systems, especially in order to get secret information. □ *a hacker who steals credit card numbers* **2** A computer **hacker** is someone who uses a computer a lot, especially so much that they have no time to do anything else.

had IRREG FORM, VERB /həd, STRONG hæd/

[IRREG FORM] **Had** is the past tense and past participle of **have.**

[VERB] [AUX] **Had** is sometimes used instead of 'if' to begin a clause which refers to a situation that might have happened but did not. For example, the clause 'had he been elected' means the same as 'if he had been elected'. **if** □ *Had he succeeded, he would have acquired a monopoly.*

[PHRASES] **be had** (*informal*) If you **have been had,** someone has tricked you, for example by selling you something at too high a price. □ *If your customer thinks he's been had, you have to make him happy.*

have had it (*informal*) **1** If you say that someone **has had it,** you mean they are in very serious trouble or have no hope of succeeding. □ *Unless she loses some weight, she's had it.* **2** If you say that you **have had it,** you mean that you are very tired of something or very annoyed about it, and do not want to continue doing it or it to continue happening. □ *I've had it. Let's call it a day.*

hail /heɪl/ VERB, NOUN

[VERB] [t, i] (**hails, hailing, hailed**) **1** [t] If a person, event, or achievement **is hailed as** important or successful, they are praised publicly. □ *Faulkner has been hailed as the greatest American novelist of his generation.* **2** [i] When it **hails,** hail falls like rain from the sky. □ *It started to hail, huge great stones.* **3** [i] (*formal*) Someone who **hails from** a particular place was born there or lives there. □ *He hails from Memphis.* **4** [t] If you **hail** a taxi, you wave at it in order to stop it because you want the driver to take you somewhere. □ *I hurried away to hail a taxi.*

[NOUN] [u, sing] **1** [u] **Hail** consists of small balls of ice that fall like rain from the sky. □ *a sharp short-lived storm with heavy hail* **2** [sing] A **hail** of things, usually small objects, is a large number of them that hit you at the same time and with great force. □ *The victim was hit by a hail of bullets.*

hair ◆◆◇ /heə/ NOUN

[NOUN] [c, u] (**hairs**) **1** Your **hair** is the fine threads that grow in a mass on your head. □ *I wash my hair every night.* □ *I get some grey hairs but I pull them out.* **2** **Hair** is the short, fine threads that grow on different parts of your body. □ *The majority of men have hair on their chest.* **3** **Hair** is the threads that cover the body of an animal such as a dog, or make up a horse's mane and tail. □ *I am allergic to cat hair.*

[PHRASES] **let your hair down** If you **let** your **hair down,** you relax completely and enjoy yourself. □ *the* *world-famous Oktoberfest, a time when everyone in Munich really lets their hair down*

make your hair stand on end Something that **makes** your **hair stand on end** shocks or frightens you very much. ❏ *This was the kind of smile that made your hair stand on end.*

not a hair out of place (*emphasis*) If you say that someone has **not a hair out of place**, you are emphasizing that they are extremely neat and well dressed. ❏ *She had a lot of makeup on and not a hair out of place.*

split hairs If you say that someone **is splitting hairs**, you mean that they are making unnecessary distinctions between things when the differences between them are so small they are not important. = quibble ❏ *Don't split hairs. You know what I'm getting at.*

hair·cut /'heəkʌt/ NOUN [c] (**haircuts**) **1** If you get a **haircut**, someone cuts your hair for you. ❏ *Your hair is all right; it's just that you need a haircut.* **2** A **haircut** is the style in which your hair has been cut. ❏ *Who's that guy with the funny haircut?*

hair·style /'heəstaɪl/ NOUN [c] (**hairstyles**) Your **hairstyle** is the style in which your hair has been cut or arranged. ❏ *I think her new short hairstyle looks simply great.*

hairy /'heəri/ ADJ (**hairier, hairiest**) **1** Someone or something that is **hairy** is covered with hairs. ❏ *He was wearing shorts which showed his long, muscular, hairy legs.* **2** (*informal*) If you describe a situation as **hairy**, you mean that it is exciting, worrying, and somewhat frightening. ❏ *His driving was a bit hairy.*

✪half ◆◆◆ /hɑːf, AmE hæf/ NOUN, PREDET, ADJ, ADV

NOUN [c] (**halves**) **1** Half of a number, an amount, or an object is one of two equal parts that together make up the whole number, amount, or object. ❏ *She wore a diamond ring worth half a million dollars.* ❏ *More than half of all US households are heated with natural gas.* ❏ *They need an extra two and a half thousand pounds to complete the project.* ❏ *More than half of all households have incomes above £35,000.* ❏ *The bridge was re-built in two halves.* ❏ *400 jobs were cut in the first half of this year.* **2** In games such as football, rugby, and basketball, games are divided into two equal periods of time which are called **halves**. ❏ *The only goal was scored by Jakobsen early in the second half.*

PHRASES **half past** You use **half past** to refer to a time that is thirty minutes after a particular hour. ❏ *'What time were you planning lunch?'—'Half past twelve, if that's convenient.'*
go halves If two people **go halves**, they divide the cost of something equally between them. ❏ *She went halves on petrol.*

PREDET **1** You use **half** to indicate that you are referring to one of two equal parts of a particular group or thing. ❏ *We just sat and talked for half an hour or so.* ❏ *They had only received half the money promised.* ❏ *She's half his age.* **2** Half can also be used in this way with a noun referring to a long period of time or a large quantity. ❏ *I thought about you half the night.*

ADJ [half + N] A **half** amount or object is one of two equal parts of that amount or object. ❏ *a half measure of fresh lemon juice* ❏ *Steve did not say anything during the first half hour.*

ADV **1** You use **half** to say that something is only partly the case or happens to only a limited extent. ❏ *His eyes were half closed.* ❏ *His refrigerator frequently looked half empty.* **2** [half + ADJ] You use **half** to say that someone has parents of different nationalities. For example, if you are **half** German, one of your parents is German but the other is not. ❏ *She was half Italian and half English.* **3** [half + ADJ] (*informal, emphasis*) You can use **half** before an adjective describing an extreme quality, as a way of emphasizing and exaggerating something. ❏ *He felt half dead with tiredness.* **4** You use **'not half'** to emphasize a negative quality that someone has. ❏ *You're not half the man you think you are.*

half·way /ˌhɑːf'weɪ, AmE ˌhæf-/ ADV, ADJ

ADV **1** Halfway means in the middle of a place or between two points, at an equal distance from each of them. ❏ *He was halfway up the ladder.* **2** [halfway + PREP/ADV] Halfway means in the middle of a period of time or of an event. ❏ *By then, it was October and we were more than halfway*

through our tour. **3** [halfway + ADJ] (*informal*) **Halfway** means fairly or reasonably. ❏ *You need hard currency to get anything halfway decent.*

PHRASE **meet someone halfway** If you **meet** someone **halfway**, you accept some of the points they are making so that you can come to an agreement with them. ❏ *The Democrats are willing to meet the president halfway.*

ADJ [halfway + N] The **halfway** stage or point of a period of time or of an event means the middle of that period of time or event. ❏ *Cleveland held a 12-point advantage at the halfway point.*

hall ◆◇◇ /hɔːl/ NOUN [c] (**halls**) **1** The **hall** in a house or flat is the area just inside the front door, into which some of the other rooms open. ❏ *The lights were on in the hall and in the bedroom.* **2** A **hall** is a large room or building which is used for public events such as concerts, exhibitions, and meetings. ❏ *We picked up our conference materials and filed into the lecture hall.*

hall·mark /'hɔːlmɑːk/ NOUN [c] (**hallmarks**) **1** The **hallmark** of something or someone is their most typical quality or feature. ❏ *It's a technique that has become the hallmark of Amber Films.* **2** A **hallmark** is an official mark put on things made of gold, silver, or platinum that indicates the quality of the metal, where the object was made, and who made it. ❏ *Early pieces of Scottish silver carry the hallmarks of individual silversmiths.*

hal·lu·ci·nate /hə'luːsɪneɪt/ VERB [I] (**hallucinates, hallucinating, hallucinated**) If you **hallucinate**, you see things that are not really there, either because you are ill or because you have taken a drug. ❏ *Hunger made him hallucinate.*

hal·lu·ci·na·tion /həˌluːsɪ'neɪʃən/ NOUN [c, u] (**hallucinations**) A **hallucination** is the experience of seeing something that is not really there because you are ill or have taken a drug. ❏ *The drug induces hallucinations at high doses.*

halt ◆◇◇ /hɔːlt/ VERB, NOUN

VERB [I, T] (**halts, halting, halted**) **1** When a person or a vehicle **halts** or when something **halts** them, they stop moving in the direction they were going and stand still. ❏ *They halted at a short distance from the house.* **2** When something such as growth, development, or activity **halts** or when you **halt** it, it stops completely. ❏ *Striking workers halted production at the car factory yesterday.*

NOUN

PHRASES **call a halt** If someone **calls a halt to** something such as an activity, they decide not to continue with it or to end it immediately. ❏ *The Russian government had called a halt to the construction of a new project in the Rostov region.*
to a halt **1** If someone or something comes **to a halt**, they stop moving. ❏ *The lift creaked to a halt at the ground floor.* **2** If something such as growth, development, or activity **comes** or **grinds to a halt** or **is brought to a halt**, it stops completely. ❏ *Her political career came to a halt in December 1988.*

✪halve ◆◇◇ /hɑːv, AmE hæv/ VERB, IRREG FORM

VERB [I, T] (**halves, halving, halved**) **1** [I, T] When you **halve** something or when it **halves**, it is reduced to half its previous size or amount. ❏ *Dr Lee believes that men who exercise can halve their risk of colon cancer.* ❏ *The workforce has been halved in two years.* ❏ *Sales of vinyl records halved in 1992 to just 6.7m.* **2** [T] If you **halve** something, you divide it into two equal parts. ❏ *Halve the pineapple and scoop out the inside.*

IRREG FORM **Halves** is the plural of **half**.

ham /hæm/ NOUN [c, u] (**hams**) Ham is meat from the top of the back leg of a pig, specially treated so that it can be kept for a long period of time. ❏ *ham sandwiches*

ham·mer /'hæmə/ NOUN, VERB

NOUN [c, SING] (**hammers**) **1** [c] A **hammer** is a tool that consists of a heavy piece of metal at the end of a handle. It is used, for example, to hit nails into a piece of wood or a wall, or to break things into pieces. ❏ *He used a hammer and chisel to chip away at the wall.* **2** [c] In athletics, a **hammer** is a heavy weight on a piece of wire, which the athlete throws as far as possible. **3** [SING] The **hammer** also refers to the sport of throwing the hammer. ❏ *Events like* *the hammer and the discus are not traditional crowd-pleasers in the West.*

PHRASE **hammer and tongs** If you say that someone **was going at** something **hammer and tongs**, you mean that they were doing it with great enthusiasm or energy. □ *He loved gardening. He went at it hammer and tongs as soon as he got back from work.*

VERB [T, I] **(hammers, hammering, hammered)** ◼ [T] If you **hammer** an object such as a nail, you hit it with a hammer. □ *To avoid damaging the tree, hammer a wooden peg into the hole.* ◻ [I] If you **hammer on** a surface, you hit it several times in order to make a noise, or to emphasize something you are saying when you are angry. = **pound** □ *We had to hammer and shout before they would open up.* □ *A crowd of reporters was hammering on the door.* ◼ [I, T] If you **hammer** something such as an idea **into** someone or you **hammer at** it, you keep repeating it forcefully so that it will have an effect on them. □ *He hammered it into me that I had not suddenly become a rotten goalkeeper.* ◼ [T] *(informal)* If you say that someone **hammers** another person, you mean that they attack, criticize, or punish the other person severely. □ *Democrats insisted they will continue to hammer Bush on his tax plan.* ◼ [T] *(informal)* In sport, if you say that one player or team **hammered** another, you mean that the first player or team defeated the second completely and easily. = **thrash** □ *He hammered the young left-hander in three straight sets.*

PHRASAL VERB **hammer out** If people **hammer out** an agreement or treaty, they succeed in producing it after a long or difficult discussion. □ *I think we can hammer out a solution.*

ham·per /ˈhæmpə/ VERB, NOUN

VERB [T] **(hampers, hampering, hampered)** If someone or something **hampers** you, they make it difficult for you to do what you are trying to do. □ *The bad weather hampered rescue operations.*

NOUN [C] **(hampers)** ◼ A **hamper** is a basket containing food of various kinds that is given to people as a present. □ *a luxury food hamper* ◼ A **hamper** is a large basket with a lid, used especially for carrying food. □ *a picnic hamper* ◼ A **hamper** is a storage container for soiled laundry. □ *He tossed his damp towel into the laundry hamper.*

hand ♦♦♦ /hænd/ NOUN, VERB

NOUN [C, SING, PL] **(hands)** ◼ [C] Your **hands** are the parts of your body at the end of your arms. Each hand has four fingers and a thumb. □ *I put my hand into my pocket and pulled out the letter.* ◼ [SING] The **hand** of someone or something is their influence in an event or situation. □ *The hand of the military authorities can be seen in the entire electoral process.* ◼ [PL] If you say that something is **in** a particular person's **hands**, you mean that they are taking care of it, own it, or are responsible for it. □ *I feel that possibly the majority of these dogs are in the wrong hands.* □ *We're in safe hands.* ◼ [SING] If you ask someone for **a hand** with something, you are asking them to help you in what you are doing. □ *Come and give me a hand in the garden.* ◼ [SING] If someone asks an audience to give someone **a hand**, they are asking the audience to clap loudly, usually before or after that person performs. □ *Let's give 'em a big hand.* ◼ [C] In a game of cards, your **hand** is the set of cards that you are holding in your hand at a particular time or the cards that are dealt to you at the beginning of the game. □ *He carefully inspected his hand.* ◼ [C] The **hands** of a clock or watch are the thin pieces of metal or plastic that indicate what time it is. □ *The hands of the clock on the wall moved with a slight click. Half past ten.*

PHRASES **at hand** If something is **at hand**, **near at hand**, or **close at hand**, it is very near in place or time. □ *Having the right equipment at hand will be enormously helpful.*

at the hands of If someone experiences a particular kind of treatment, especially unpleasant treatment, **at the hands of** a person or organization, they receive it from them. □ *The civilian population was suffering greatly at the hands of the security forces.*

by hand If you do something **by hand**, you do it using your hands rather than a machine. = **manually** □ *Each pleat was stitched in place by hand.*

change hands When something **changes hands**, its

ownership changes, usually because it is sold to someone else. □ *The firm has changed hands many times over the years.*

have your hands full If you **have** your **hands full** with something, you are very busy because of it. □ *She had her hands full with new arrivals.*

give someone a free hand If someone **gives** you **a free hand**, they give you the freedom to use your own judgment and to do exactly as you wish. □ *He gave Stephanie a free hand in the decoration.*

get your hands on something or **lay your hands on something** *(informal)* If you **get** your **hands on** something or **lay** your **hands on** something, you manage to find it or obtain it, usually after some difficulty. □ *Patty began reading everything she could get her hands on.*

hand in hand ◼ If two people are **hand in hand**, they are holding each other's nearest hand, usually while they are walking or sitting together. People often do this to show their affection for each other. □ *I saw them making their way, hand in hand, down the path.* ◼ If two things **go hand in hand**, they are closely connected and cannot be considered separately from each other. □ *For us, research and teaching go hand in hand.*

have a hand in something If you **have a hand in** something such as an event or activity, you are involved in it. □ *He thanked all who had a hand in his release.*

hold hands If two people **are holding hands**, they are holding each other's nearest hand, usually while they are walking or sitting together. People often do this to show their affection for each other. □ *She approached a young couple holding hands on a bench.*

in hand ◼ The job or problem **in hand** is the job or problem that you are dealing with at the moment. □ *The business in hand was approaching some kind of climax.* ◼ If a situation is **in hand**, it is under control. □ *The Olympic organizers say that matters are well in hand.*

lend a hand If you **lend** someone **a hand**, you help them. □ *I'd be glad to lend a hand.*

live hand to mouth If someone **lives hand to mouth** or **lives from hand to mouth**, they have hardly enough food or money to live on. □ *I have a wife and two children and we live from hand to mouth on what I earn.*

keep one's hands off something or **take one's hands off something** If you tell someone to **keep** their **hands off** something or to **take** their **hands off** it, you are telling them in a slightly aggressive way not to touch it or interfere with it. □ *Keep your hands off my milk.*

off hand *(spoken)* If you do not know something **off hand**, you do not know it without having to ask someone else or look it up in a book. □ *I can't think of any off hand.*

on one's hands or **off one's hands** If you have a problem or responsibility **on** your **hands**, you have to deal with it. If it is **off** your **hands**, you no longer have to deal with it. □ *They now have yet another drug problem on their hands.*

on hand If someone or something is **on hand**, they are near and able to be used if they are needed. = **available** □ *There are experts on hand to give you all the help and advice you need.*

on the one hand You use **on the one hand** to introduce the first of two contrasting points, facts, or ways of looking at something. It is always followed later by 'on the other hand' or 'on the other'. □ *On the one hand, if the body doesn't have enough cholesterol, we would not be able to survive. On the other hand, if the body has too much cholesterol, the excess begins to line the arteries.*

on the other hand You use **on the other hand** to introduce the second of two contrasting points, facts, or ways of looking at something. □ *The movie lost money; reviews, on the other hand, were by and large favourable.*

out of hand ◼ If a person or a situation gets **out of hand**, you are no longer able to control them. □ *His drinking got out of hand.* ◼ If you dismiss or reject something **out of hand**, you do so immediately and do not consider believing or accepting it. □ *I initially dismissed the idea out of hand.*

take in hand If you **take** something or someone **in hand**, you take control or responsibility over them, especially in order to improve them. □ *She took the twins in hand, encouraging them to turn their thoughts to the future.*

your hands are tied If you say that your **hands are tied**,

h

H

you mean that something is preventing you from acting in the way that you want to. □ *Politicians are always saying that they want to help us but their hands are tied.*

try your hand If you **try** your **hand** at an activity, you attempt to do it, usually for the first time. □ *He tried his hand at fishing, but he wasn't really very good at it.*

turn one's hand to something If you **turn** your **hand to** something such as a practical activity, you learn about it and do it for the first time. □ *a person who can turn his hand to anything*

wash your hands of If you **wash** your **hands of** someone or something, you refuse to be involved with them any more or to take responsibility for them. □ *He seems to have washed his hands of the job.*

win hands down If you **win hands down**, you win very easily. □ *We have been beaten in some games which we should have won hands down.*

VERB [T] (**hands, handing, handed**) If you **hand** something to someone, you pass it to them. □ *He handed me a little rectangle of white paper.*

PHRASAL VERBS **hand back** If you **hand back** something that you have borrowed or taken from someone, you return it to them. □ *He handed the book back.*

hand down If you **hand down** something such as knowledge, a possession, or a skill, you give or leave it to people who belong to a younger generation. = pass on □ *The idea of handing down his knowledge from generation to generation is important to McLean.*

hand in **1** If you **hand in** something such as homework or something that you have found, you give it to a teacher, police officer, or other person in authority. □ *I'm supposed to have handed in a first draft of my dissertation.* **2** If you **hand in** your notice or resignation, you tell your employer, in speech or in writing, that you no longer wish to work there. □ *I handed my notice in on Saturday.*

hand on If you **hand** something **on**, you give it or transfer it to another person, often someone who replaces you. = pass on □ *Natural resources should be handed on to the next generation intact.*

hand out **1** If you **hand** things **out** to people, you give one or more to each person in a group. = give out □ *One of my jobs was to hand out the prizes.* **2** When people in authority **hand out** something such as advice or permission to do something, they give it. □ *I listened to a lot of people handing out a lot of advice.*

hand over **1** If you **hand** something **over** to someone, you give them the responsibility for dealing with a particular situation or problem. □ *I wouldn't dare hand this project over to anyone else.* **2** If you **hand over to** someone or **hand** something **over to** them, you give them the responsibility for dealing with a particular situation or problem. □ *The present leaders have to decide whether to hand over to a younger generation.*

✦ **with one's bare hands** → see **bare**; **shake someone's hand** → see **shake**; **shake hands** → see **shake**

hand·ful /ˈhændfʊl/ NOUN [SING, C] (**handfuls**) **1** [SING] A **handful of** people or things is a small number of them. □ *He surveyed the handful of customers at the bar.* **2** [C] A **handful of** something is the amount of it that you can hold in your hand. □ *She scooped up a handful of sand and let it trickle through her fingers.* **3** [SING] (*informal*) If you say that someone, especially a child, is a **handful**, you mean that they are difficult to control. □ *Zara can be a handful sometimes.*

handi·cap /ˈhændikæp/ NOUN, VERB
NOUN [C] (**handicaps**) **1** A **handicap** is a physical or mental disability. □ *He lost his leg when he was ten, but learned to overcome his handicap.* **2** A **handicap** is an event or situation that places you at a disadvantage and makes it harder for you to do something. □ *Being a foreigner was not a handicap.* **3** In golf, a **handicap** is an advantage given to someone who is not a good player, in order to make the players more equal. As you improve, your handicap gets lower. □ *I see your handicap is down from 16 to 12.* **4** In horse racing, a **handicap** is a race in which some competitors are given a disadvantage of extra weight in an attempt to give everyone an equal chance of winning. □ *the Melbourne Cup, a two-mile handicap*

VERB [T] (**handicaps, handicapping, handicapped**) If an event or a situation **handicaps** someone or something, it places them at a disadvantage. □ *Greater levels of stress may seriously handicap some students.*

handi·capped /ˈhændikæpt/ ADJ, NOUN
ADJ Someone who is **handicapped** has a physical or mental disability that prevents them from living a totally normal life. □ *I'm going to work two days a week teaching handicapped kids to fish.*
NOUN [PL] You can refer to people who are handicapped as **the handicapped**. □ *measures to prevent discrimination against the handicapped*

hand·ker·chief /ˈhæŋkətʃɪf/ NOUN [C] (**handkerchiefs**) A **handkerchief** is a small square piece of fabric which you use for blowing your nose.

✪**han·dle** ♦♦◇ /ˈhændəl/ NOUN, VERB
NOUN [C] (**handles**) **1** A **handle** is a small round object or a lever that is attached to a door and is used for opening and closing it. □ *I turned the handle and found the door was open.* **2** A **handle** is the part of an object such as a tool, bag, or cup that you hold in order to be able to pick up and use the object. □ *a broom handle*
PHRASE **fly off the handle** (*informal*) If you **fly off the handle**, you suddenly and completely lose your temper. □ *He flew off the handle at the slightest thing.*
VERB [T] (**handles, handling, handled**) **1** If you say that someone can **handle** a problem or situation, you mean that they have the ability to deal with it successfully. = deal with, manage, cope with; ≠ mishandle □ *To tell the truth, I don't know if I can handle the job.* □ *She cannot handle pressure.* **2** If you talk about the way that someone **handles** a problem or situation, you mention whether or not they are successful in achieving the result they want. □ *I think I would handle a meeting with Mr Siegel very badly.* □ *Pavane might have handled the situation better.* □ *The government was criticised for the way it handled the crisis.* **3** If you **handle** a particular area of work, you have responsibility for it. □ *She handled travel arrangements for the press corps during the presidential campaign.* **4** When you **handle** something, you hold it or move it with your hands. □ *Wear rubber gloves when handling cat litter.*
han·dling /ˈhændlɪŋ/ NOUN [U] □ *The family has criticized the military's handling of Robert's death.*

hand·made /ˌhændˈmeɪd/ also **hand-made** ADJ **Handmade** objects have been made by someone using their hands or using tools rather than by machines. □ *Because they're handmade, each one varies slightly.*

hand·over /ˈhændəʊvə/ NOUN [C] (**handovers**) [usu sing, oft handover 'of' N] The **handover of** something is when possession or control of it is given by one person or group of people to another. □ *The handover is expected to be completed in the next ten years.*

hand·shake /ˈhændʃeɪk/ NOUN [C] (**handshakes**) If you give someone a **handshake**, you take their right hand with your own right hand and hold it firmly or move it up and down, as a sign of greeting or to show that you have agreed about something such as a business deal. □ *He has a strong handshake.*

hand·some /ˈhænsəm/ ADJ **1** A **handsome** man has an attractive face with regular features. = good-looking □ *a tall, dark, handsome sheep farmer* **2** [handsome + N] (*formal*) A **handsome** sum of money is a large or generous amount. □ *They will make a handsome profit on the property.*

handy /ˈhændi/ ADJ
ADJ (**handier, handiest**) **1** Something that is **handy** is useful. □ *The book gives handy hints on looking after indoor plants.* **2** A thing or place that is **handy** is nearby and therefore easy to get at or reach. □ *It would be good to have a pencil and paper handy.*
PHRASE **come in handy** If something **comes in handy**, it is useful in a particular situation. □ *The £20 cheque came in very handy.*

hang ♦♦◇ /hæŋ/ VERB, NOUN

The form **hanged** is used as the past tense and past participle for meaning 5 of the verb.

VERB [I, T] (**hangs, hanging, hung** or **hanged**) **1** [I, T] If something **hangs** in a high place or position, or if you **hang** it there, it is attached there so it does not touch the ground. □ *Notices painted on sheets hang at every entrance.* □ *small hanging lanterns* **2** [I] If a piece of clothing or fabric **hangs** in a particular way or position, that is how it is worn or arranged. □ *a ragged fur coat that hung down to her calves* **3** [I] If something **hangs** loose or **hangs** open, it is partly fixed in position, but is not firmly held, supported, or controlled, often in such a way that it moves freely. □ *her long golden hair which hung loose about her shoulders* **4** [T] If something such as a wall **is hung with** pictures or other objects, they are attached to it. □ *The walls were hung with huge modern paintings.* **5** [I, T] If someone **is hanged** or if they **hang**, they are killed, usually as a punishment, by having a rope tied around their neck and the support taken away from under their feet. □ *The five were expected to be hanged at 7 a.m. on Tuesday.* □ *He hanged himself two hours after arriving at a mental hospital.* **6** [I] If something such as someone's breath or smoke **hangs** in the air, it remains there without appearing to move or change position. □ *His breath was hanging in the air before him.* **7** [I] If a possibility **hangs over** you, it worries you and makes your life unpleasant or difficult because you think it might happen. □ *A constant threat of unemployment hangs over thousands of university researchers.*

PHRASE **hang in there** or **hang on in there** (*informal*) If you tell someone to **hang in there** or to **hang on in there**, you are encouraging them to keep trying to do something and not to give up even though it might be difficult. □ *Hang in there and you never know what is achievable.*

PHRASAL VERBS **hang back** **1** If you **hang back**, you move or stay slightly behind a person or group, usually because you are shy or nervous about something. □ *I saw him step forward momentarily but then hang back, nervously massaging his hands.* **2** If a person or organization **hangs back**, they do not do something immediately. □ *They will then hang back on closing the deal.*

hang on **1** (*informal*) If you ask someone to **hang on**, you ask them to wait or stop what they are doing or saying for a moment. = hold on □ *Can you hang on for a minute?* **2** If you **hang on**, you manage to survive, achieve success, or avoid failure in spite of great difficulties or opposition. □ *He hung on to finish second.* **3** If you **hang on to** or **hang onto** something that gives you an advantage, you succeed in keeping it for yourself, and prevent it from being taken away or given to someone else. □ *The driver was unable to hang on to his lead.* **4** If you **hang on to** or **hang onto** something, you hold it very tightly, for example to stop it from falling or to support yourself. = cling □ *She was conscious of a second man hanging on to the rail.* □ *a flight attendant who helped save the life of a pilot by hanging onto his legs* **5** (*informal*) If you **hang on to** or **hang onto** something, you keep it for a longer time than you would normally expect. □ *You could, alternatively, hang onto it in the hope that it will be worth millions in 10 years time.* **6** If one thing **hangs on** another, it depends on it in order to be successful. = depend □ *Much hangs on the success of the collaboration between the Group of Seven governments and Brazil.*

hang out **1** If you **hang out** clothes that you have washed, you hang them on a clothes line to dry. □ *I was worried I wouldn't be able to hang my laundry out.* **2** (*informal*) If you **hang out** in a particular place or area, you go and stay there for no particular reason, or spend a lot of time there. □ *I often used to hang out in supermarkets.*

hang up **1** Hang up means the same as **hang** VERB 1. □ *I found his jacket, which was hanging up in the hallway.* **2** If you **hang up** or you **hang up** the phone, you end a phone call. If you **hang up on** someone you are speaking to on the phone, you end the phone call suddenly and unexpectedly, usually because you are angry or upset with the person you are speaking to. □ *Mum hung up the phone.* □ *Don't hang up!*

NOUN
PHRASE **get the hang of something** (*informal*) If you **get the hang of** something such as a skill or activity, you begin to understand or realize how to do it. □ *It's a bit*

tricky at first till you get the hang of it.
→ See also **hung**

hap·haz·ard /ˌhæpˈhæzəd/ ADJ (*disapproval*) If you describe something as **haphazard**, you are critical of it because it is not at all organized or is not arranged according to a plan. □ *The investigation does seem haphazard.*
hap·haz·ard·ly /ˌhæpˈhæzədli/ ADV □ *She looked at the books jammed haphazardly in the shelves.*

hap·pen ♦♦♦ /ˈhæpən/ VERB
VERB [I, T] (**happens, happening, happened**) **1** [I] Something that **happens** occurs or is done without being planned. □ *We cannot say for sure what will happen.* **2** [I] If something **happens**, it occurs as a result of a situation or course of action. □ *She wondered what would happen if her parents found her.* **3** [I] When something, especially something unpleasant, **happens to** you, it takes place and affects you. □ *If we had been spotted at that point, I don't know what would have happened to us.* **4** [T] If you **happen to do** something, you do it by chance. If **it happens that** something is the case, it occurs by chance. □ *We happened to discover we had a friend in common.*
PHRASE **as it happens** You use **as it happens** in order to introduce a statement, especially one that is rather surprising. □ *He called Amy to see if she knew where his son was. As it happened, Amy did know.*

WHICH WORD?
happen, occur, or take place?

Happen is usually used after vague words like 'something', 'thing', 'what', or 'this'. After words with a more precise meaning, you usually use **occur**.
□ *There'll be an investigation into what **happened**.*
□ *Accidents often **occur** in confused circumstances.*
You do not say that a planned event 'happens' or 'occurs'. You say that it **takes place**.
□ *The election **took place** in June.*

USAGE NOTE
happen

Happen does not have a passive form. You do not say, for example, that something 'was happened'.

---

hap·pi·ly /ˈhæpɪli/ ADV **1** If you do something **happily**, you do it with feelings of pleasure. □ *Albert leaned back happily and lit a cigarette.* **2** If you say that you will **happily** do something, you mean that you are very willing to do it. □ *If I've caused any offence over something I have written, I will happily apologize.* **3** [happily with CL] You can add **happily** to a statement to indicate that you are glad that something happened. = fortunately □ *Happily, his neck injuries were not serious.*

hap·py ♦♦◇ /ˈhæpi/ ADJ (**happier, happiest**) **1** Someone who is **happy** has feelings of pleasure, usually because something nice has happened or because they feel satisfied with their life. □ *Marina was a confident, happy child.* **2** A **happy** time, place, or relationship is full of happy feelings and pleasant experiences, or has an atmosphere in which people feel happy. □ *Except for her illnesses, she had a particularly happy childhood.* □ *It had always been a happy place.* **3** [V-LINK + happy] If you are **happy about** a situation or arrangement, you are satisfied with it, for example, because you think that something is being done in the right way. □ *If you are not happy about a repair, go back and complain.* □ *He's happy that I deal with it myself.* **4** [V-LINK + happy] If you say you are **happy to** do something, you mean that you are very willing to do it. □ *I'll be happy to answer questions if there are any.* **5** [happy + N] **Happy** is used in greetings and other conventional expressions to say that you hope someone will enjoy a special occasion. □ *Happy birthday!*
hap·pi·ness /ˈhæpinəs/ NOUN [U] □ *I think mostly she was looking for happiness.*

har·ass /ˈhærəs, həˈræs/ VERB [T] (**harasses, harassing, harassed**) If someone **harasses** you, they trouble or annoy you, for example by attacking you repeatedly or by causing you as many problems as they can. ❏ *A woman reporter complained one of them sexually harassed her in the locker room.*

har·assed /ˈhærəst, həˈræst/ ADJ If you are **harassed**, you are anxious and tense because you have too much to do or too many problems to cope with. ❏ *This morning, looking harassed and drawn, Lewis tendered his resignation.*

har·ass·ment /ˈhærəsmənt, həˈræs-/ NOUN [U] **Harassment** is behaviour which is intended to trouble or annoy someone, for example repeated attacks on them or attempts to cause them problems. ❏ *Another survey found that 51 per cent of women had experienced some form of sexual harassment in their working lives.*

har·bour /ˈhɑːbə/ NOUN, VERB (*BrE*; in *AmE*, use **harbor**)
[NOUN] [c] (**harbours**) A **harbour** is an area of the sea at the coast which is partly enclosed by land or strong walls, so that boats can be left there safely. ❏ *She led us to a room with a balcony overlooking the harbour.*
[VERB] [T] (**harbours, harbouring, harboured**) **1** If you **harbour** an emotion, thought, or secret, you have it in your mind over a long period of time. ❏ *He might have been murdered by a former client or someone harbouring a grudge.* **2** If a person or country **harbours** someone who is wanted by the police, they let them stay in their house or country and offer them protection. ❏ *Accusations of harbouring suspects were raised against the former Hungarian leadership.*

hard ◆◆◆ /hɑːd/ ADJ, ADV
[ADJ] (**harder, hardest**) **1** Something that is **hard** is very firm and stiff to touch and is not easily bent, cut, or broken. ❏ *He shuffled his feet on the hard wooden floor.* **2** Something that is **hard** is very difficult to do or deal with. = difficult ❏ *It's hard to tell what effect this latest move will have.* ❏ *That's a very hard question.* **3** [hard + N] A **hard** worker works intensely, with a lot of effort. ❏ *I admired him as a true scientist and hard worker.* **4** **Hard** work involves a lot of activity and effort. ❏ *Coping with three babies is very hard work.* ❏ *a hard day's work* **5** If you take a **hard** look at something, you do it carefully and with a great deal of attention. ❏ *It might be worth taking a long hard look at your frustrations and resentments.* **6** [hard + N] If you give something or someone a **hard** push or kick, you push or kick them with a lot of force. ❏ *He gave her a hard push which toppled her backwards into an armchair.* **7** If a person or their expression is **hard**, they show no kindness or sympathy. ❏ *His father was a hard man.* **8** [V-LINK + hard 'on' N] If you are **hard on** someone, you treat them severely or unkindly. ❏ *Don't be so hard on him.* **9** [V-LINK + hard 'on' N] If you say that something is **hard on** a person or thing, you mean it affects them in a way that is likely to cause them damage or suffering. ❏ *The grey light was hard on the eyes.* **10** If you have a **hard** life or a **hard** period of time, your life or that period is difficult and unpleasant for you. = tough ❏ *It had been a hard life for her.* **11** [hard + N] **Hard** evidence or facts are definitely true and do not need to be questioned. ❏ *He wanted more hard evidence.* **12** [hard + N] **Hard** drugs are very strong illegal drugs such as heroin or cocaine. ❏ *He then graduated from soft drugs to hard ones.*
[PHRASES] **be hard going** If you say that something is **hard going**, you mean it is difficult and requires a lot of effort. ❏ *The talks had been hard going at the start.*
play hard to get If someone **plays hard to get**, they pretend not to be interested in another person or in what someone is trying to persuade them to do. ❏ *I wanted her and she was playing hard to get.*
[ADV] **1** [hard after V] If you work **hard** doing something, you are very active or work intensely, with a lot of effort. ❏ *I'll work hard. I don't want to let him down.* **2** [hard after V] If you look, listen, or think **hard**, you do it carefully and with a great deal of attention. ❏ *He looked at me hard.* **3** [hard after V] If you strike or take hold of something **hard**, you strike or take hold of it with a lot of force. ❏ *I kicked a dustbin very hard and broke my toe.* **4** [hard after V] You can use **hard** to indicate that something happens intensely and for a long time. ❏ *I've never seen Terry laugh so hard.* **5** [hard after V] If you come down or crack down

hard on someone, you treat them severely or unkindly. ❏ *He said the security forces would continue to crack down hard on the protesters.*
[PHRASE] **be hard hit** To be **hard hit by** something means to be affected very severely by it. ❏ *California's been particularly hard hit by the recession.*

hard·ness /ˈhɑːdnəs/ NOUN [U] **1** *He felt the hardness of the iron railing press against his spine.* **2** *In America, people don't normally admit to the hardness of life.*

hard·back /ˈhɑːdbæk/ NOUN [c] (**hardbacks**) [also 'in' hardback] A **hardback** is a book which has a stiff, hard cover. Compare **paperback**. = hardcover ❏ *The book was published in hardback last October.*

hard·en /ˈhɑːdən/ VERB [I, T] (**hardens, hardening, hardened**) **1** [I, T] When something **hardens** or when you **harden** it, it becomes stiff or firm. ❏ *Mould the mixture into shape while hot, before it hardens.* **2** [I, T] When an attitude or opinion **hardens** or **is hardened**, it becomes harsher, stronger, or fixed. ❏ *Their action can only serve to harden the attitude of landowners.* **3** [I, T] When events **harden** people or when people **harden**, they become less easily affected emotionally and less sympathetic and gentle than they were before. ❏ *Her years of drunken bickering hardened my heart.* **4** [I] If you say that someone's face or eyes **harden**, you mean that they suddenly look serious or angry. ❏ *His smile died and the look in his face hardened.*

hard·en·ing /ˈhɑːdənɪŋ/ NOUN [SING] ❏ *a hardening of the government's attitude towards rebellious parts of the army*

hard-line also **hardline** ADJ If you describe someone's policy or attitude as **hard-line**, you mean that it is strict or extreme, and that they refuse to change it. ❏ *The United States has taken a lot of criticism for its hard-line stance.*

hard·ly ◆◆◇ /ˈhɑːdli/ ADV, CONVENTION
[ADV] **1** (*emphasis*) You use **hardly** to modify a statement when you want to emphasize that it is only a small amount or detail which makes it true, and that therefore it is best to consider the opposite statement as being true. = scarcely, barely ❏ *I hardly know you.* ❏ *I've hardly slept in three days.* **2** [hardly 'ever/any'] You use **hardly** in expressions such as **hardly ever**, **hardly any**, and **hardly anyone** to mean almost never, almost none, or almost no one. ❏ *We hardly ever eat fish.* ❏ *Most of the others were so young they had hardly any experience.* **3** [hardly + N] (*emphasis*) You use **hardly** before a negative statement in order to emphasize that something is usually true or usually happens. = scarcely ❏ *Hardly a day goes by without a visit from someone.* **4** ['can/could' hardly + INF] (*emphasis*) When you say you can **hardly** do something, you are emphasizing that it is very difficult for you to do it. ❏ *My garden was covered with so many butterflies that I could hardly see the flowers.* **5** You use **hardly** to mean 'not' when you want to suggest that you are expecting your listener or reader to agree with your comment. ❏ *We have not seen the letter, so we can hardly comment on it.*
[CONVENTION] (*spoken*) You use **hardly** to mean 'no', especially when you want to express surprise or annoyance at a statement that you disagree with. ❏ *'They all thought you were marvelous!'—'Well, hardly.'*

USAGE NOTE

hardly

Hardly is an adverb that has a totally different meaning from 'hard'. If you work with a lot of effort, you 'work hard'. Do not use 'work hardly' in this sense.
*They all worked **hard**, and finished the job to schedule.*

✪ hard·ship /ˈhɑːdʃɪp/ NOUN [c, U] (**hardships**) **Hardship** is a situation in which your life is difficult or unpleasant, often because you do not have enough money. = privation, suffering, adversity ❏ *Many people are suffering economic hardship.* ❏ *The publicity surrounding the case had caused the family considerable hardship.*

✪ hard·ware /ˈhɑːdweə/ NOUN [U] **1** In computer systems, **hardware** refers to the machines themselves as opposed to the programs which tell the machines what to do. Compare **software**. ❏ *To be totally secure, you need a piece of hardware that costs about $200.* ❏ *The price of* computer hardware has fallen. **2** Military **hardware** is the machinery and equipment that is used by the armed forces, such as tanks, aircraft, and missiles. ❏ the billions which are spent on military hardware **3** **Hardware** refers to tools and equipment that are used in the home and garden, for example nuts and bolts, screwdrivers, and hinges. ❏ a shop from which an uncle had sold hardware and timber

hard·working /ˈhɑːdˌwɜːkɪŋ/ also **hard-working** ADJ If you describe someone as **hardworking**, you mean that they work very hard. ❏ He was hardworking and energetic.

har·dy /ˈhɑːdi/ ADJ (**hardier, hardiest**) Plants that are **hardy** are able to survive cold weather. ❏ The silver-leaved varieties of cyclamen are not quite as hardy.

✪ **harm** ◆◇◇ /hɑːm/ VERB, NOUN
　VERB [T] (**harms, harming, harmed**) **1** To **harm** a person or animal means to cause them physical injury, usually on purpose. = injure, hurt ❏ The hijackers seemed anxious not to harm anyone. **2** To **harm** a thing, or sometimes a person, means to damage them or make them less effective or successful than they were. = damage, ruin ❏ a warning that the product may harm the environment ❏ Low-priced imports will harm the industry.
　NOUN [U] **1** **Harm** is physical injury to a person or an animal which is usually caused on purpose. = injury ❏ All dogs are capable of doing harm to human beings. ❏ High levels of nitrate in the water may cause harm to humans. **2** **Harm** is the damage to something which is caused by a particular course of action. = damage ❏ The abuse of your powers does harm to all other officers who do their job properly. ❏ To cut taxes would probably do the economy more harm than good. ❏ These metals are doing harm to the soil.
　PHRASES **do no harm** or **no harm in doing** If you say it **does no harm** to do something or **there is no harm in** doing something, you mean that it might be worth doing, and you will not be blamed for doing it. ❏ They are not always willing to take on untrained workers, but there's no harm in asking.
　out of harm's way If someone or something is **out of harm's way**, they are in a safe place away from danger or from the possibility of being damaged. ❏ For parents, it is an easy way of keeping their children entertained, or simply out of harm's way.
　no harm done If you say that there is **no harm done**, you are telling someone not to worry about something that has happened because it has not caused any serious injury or damage. ❏ There, now, you're all right. No harm done.
　someone will come to no harm or **no harm will come to someone** If you say that someone or something **will come to no harm** or that **no harm will come to** them, you mean that they will not be hurt or damaged in any way. ❏ There is always a lifeguard to ensure that no one comes to any harm.

WORD CONNECTIONS
ADV + **harm**
physically harm
seriously harm
❏ He shouts at the children but would never physically harm them.
irreparably harm
seriously harm
❏ An incident like this could irreparably harm their business.
deliberately harm
intentionally harm
❏ He was admitted to hospital after deliberately harming himself.
harm + NOUN
harm the **environment**
harm **relations**
❏ Waste should be disposed of in a way that does not harm the environment.

VERB + **harm**
do harm
cause harm
❏ The harm caused by drug misuse can affect whole families.
ADJ + **harm**
serious harm
physical harm
❏ Violence and threats of physical harm will not be tolerated.
real harm
irreparable harm
❏ This policy could cause irreparable harm to national security.

✪ **harm·ful** /ˈhɑːmfʊl/ ADJ Something that is **harmful** has a bad effect on something else, especially on a person's health. = damaging; ≠ safe ❏ the harmful effects of smoking ❏ The chemical is potentially harmful to fish.

✪ **harm·less** /ˈhɑːmləs/ ADJ **1** Something that is **harmless** does not have any bad effects, especially on people's health. = safe ❏ This experiment was harmless to the animals. ❏ Scientists are trying to develop harmless substitutes for these gases. **2** If you describe someone or something as **harmless**, you mean that they are not important and therefore unlikely to annoy other people or cause trouble. ❏ He seemed harmless enough.

har·mo·ni·ous /hɑːˈməʊniəs/ ADJ A **harmonious** relationship, agreement, or discussion is friendly and peaceful. = amicable ❏ Their harmonious relationship resulted in part from their similar goals.
har·mo·ni·ous·ly /hɑːˈməʊniəsli/ ADV [harmoniously after V] ❏ To live together harmoniously as men and women is an achievement.

har·mo·ny /ˈhɑːməni/ NOUN [U, C] (**harmonies**) **1** [U] If people are living **in harmony with** each other, they are living together peacefully rather than fighting or arguing. ❏ the notion that man should dominate nature rather than live in harmony with it **2** [C, U] **Harmony** is the pleasant combination of different notes of music played at the same time. ❏ singing in harmony **3** [U] The **harmony** of something is the way in which its parts are combined into a pleasant arrangement. ❏ the ordered harmony of the universe

✪ **har·ness** /ˈhɑːnɪs/ VERB, NOUN
　VERB [T] (**harnesses, harnessing, harnessed**) **1** If you **harness** something such as an emotion or natural source of energy, you bring it under your control and use it. = exploit, utilize ❏ Turkey plans to harness the waters of the Tigris and Euphrates rivers for big hydro-electric power projects. ❏ chemical reactors that destroy dangerous chemicals by harnessing the power of the sun **2** If a horse or other animal **is harnessed**, a harness is put on it, especially so that it can pull a carriage, cart, or plough. ❏ On Sunday the horses were harnessed to a heavy wagon for a day-long ride over the border.
　NOUN [C] (**harnesses**) **1** A **harness** is a set of straps which fit under a person's arms and fasten around their body in order to keep a piece of equipment in place or to prevent the person moving from a place. **2** A **harness** is a set of leather straps and metal links fastened around a horse's head or body so that the horse can have a carriage, cart, or plough fastened to it.

har·row·ing /ˈhærəʊɪŋ/ ADJ A **harrowing** experience is extremely upsetting or disturbing. ❏ You've had a harrowing time this past month.

✪ **harsh** /hɑːʃ/ ADJ (**harsher, harshest**) **1** **Harsh** climates or conditions are very difficult for people, animals, and plants to live in. = severe ❏ the harsh desert environment ❏ The climate is too harsh for grape growing. ❏ after the harsh experience of the war **2** **Harsh** actions or speech are unkind and show no understanding or sympathy. = cruel, brutal, severe, stern; ≠ kind, lenient ❏ He said many harsh and unkind things about his opponents. ❏ Immediate and harsh punishments could have a deterrent effect on others. ❏ In 1994, a riot at Kingston prison brought about harsh criticism of the facility. **3** Something that is **harsh** is so hard, bright, or

h

rough that it seems unpleasant or harmful. ❑ *Tropical colours may look rather harsh in our dull northern light.* **4** **Harsh** voices and sounds are ones that are rough and unpleasant to listen to. ❑ *It's a pity she has such a loud harsh voice.* **5** If you talk about **harsh** realities or facts, or the **harsh** truth, you are emphasizing that they are true or real, although they are unpleasant and people try to avoid thinking about them. = bitter ❑ *The harsh truth is that luck plays a big part in who will live or die.* ⬦**harsh•ness** /ˈhɑːʃnəs/ NOUN [U] **1** = severity, cruelty; ≠ mildness, leniency ❑ *the harshness of their living conditions* **2** *treating him with great harshness* ❑ *Police officers expressed surprise at the harshness of the seven year sentence.* **3** *As the wine ages, it loses its bitter harshness.* **4** *Then in a tone of abrupt harshness, he added, 'Open these trunks!'* **harsh•ly** /ˈhɑːʃli/ ADV **1** [harshly with v] ❑ *She's been told that her husband is being harshly treated in prison.* **2** [harshly with v] ❑ *Chris laughed harshly.*

har•vest /ˈhɑːvɪst/ NOUN, VERB
NOUN [SING, C] (**harvests**) **1** [SING] The **harvest** is the gathering in of a crop. ❑ *There was about 300 million tons of grain in the fields at the start of the harvest.* **2** [C] A **harvest** is the crop that is gathered in. ❑ *Millions of people are threatened with starvation as a result of drought and poor harvests.*
VERB [T] (**harvests, harvesting, harvested**) When you **harvest** a crop, you gather it in. ❑ *Rice farmers here still plant and harvest their crops by hand.*

has /həz, STRONG hæz/ IRREG FORM **Has** is the third person singular of the present tense of **have**.

haste /heɪst/ NOUN
NOUN [U] **Haste** is the quality of doing something quickly, sometimes too quickly so that you are careless and make mistakes. ❑ *In their haste to escape the rising water, they dropped some expensive equipment.*
PHRASE **in haste** If you do something **in haste**, you do it quickly and hurriedly, and sometimes carelessly. ❑ *Don't act in haste or be hot-headed.*

has•ten /ˈheɪsən/ VERB [T] (**hastens, hastening, hastened**) **1** If you **hasten** an event or process, often an unpleasant one, you make it happen faster or sooner. = speed up ❑ *But if he does this, he may hasten the collapse of his own country.* **2** If you **hasten to** do something, you are quick to do it. ❑ *She more than anyone had hastened to sign the contract.*

has•ty /ˈheɪsti/ ADJ (**hastier, hastiest**) **1** A **hasty** movement, action, or statement is sudden, and often done in reaction to something that has just happened. = swift, quick ❑ *Donald had overturned a chair in his hasty departure.* **2** If you describe a person or their behaviour as **hasty**, you mean that they are acting too quickly, without thinking carefully, for example because they are angry. = rash ❑ *A number of the United States' allies had urged him not to make a hasty decision.*
hast•i•ly /ˈheɪstɪli/ ADV **1** [hastily with v] = swiftly ❑ *The council was hastily called on a rather father said he was resigning.* **2** [hastily with v] ❑ *I decided that nothing should be done hastily, that things had to be sorted out carefully.*

hat ♦◇◇ /hæt/ NOUN
NOUN [C] (**hats**) **1** A **hat** is a head covering, often with a brim around it, which is usually worn outdoors to give protection from the weather. ❑ *a plump woman in a red hat* **2** If you say that someone is wearing a particular **hat**, you mean that they are performing a particular role at that time. If you say that they wear several **hats**, you mean that they have several roles or jobs. ❑ *Now I'll take off my 'friend hat' and put on my 'therapist hat'.*
PHRASES **at the drop of a hat** If you say that you are ready to do something **at the drop of a hat**, you mean that you are willing to do it immediately, without hesitating. ❑ *India is one part of the world I would go to at the drop of a hat.*
keep something under your hat If you tell someone to **keep** a piece of information **under** their **hat**, you are asking them not to tell anyone else about it. ❑ *Look, if I tell you something, will you promise to keep it under your hat?*
take your hat off to someone (approval) If you say that

you **take** your **hat off to** someone, you mean that you admire them for something that they have done. ❑ *I take my hat off to Mr Clarke for taking this action.*
pull something out of a hat To pull something **out of a hat** means to do something unexpected which helps you to succeed, often when you are failing. ❑ *There are expectations that he'll pull a ceasefire out of a hat.*
draw something out of a hat or **pick something out of a hat** or **pull something out of a hat** In competitions, if you say that the winners will be **drawn** or **picked out of a hat**, you mean that they will be chosen randomly, so everyone has an equal chance of winning. ❑ *The first 10 correct entries drawn out of the hat will win a pair of tickets, worth $30 each.*

hatch /hætʃ/ VERB, NOUN
VERB [I, T] (**hatches, hatching, hatched**) **1** [I, T] When a baby bird, insect, or other animal **hatches**, or when it is **hatched**, it comes out of its egg by breaking the shell. ❑ *The young disappeared soon after they were hatched.* **2** [I, T] When an egg **hatches** or when a bird, insect, or other animal **hatches** an egg, the egg breaks open and a baby comes out. ❑ *The eggs hatch after a week or ten days.* **3** [T] If you **hatch** a plot or a scheme, you think of it and work it out. ❑ *He has accused opposition parties of hatching a plot to assassinate the Pope.*
NOUN [C] (**hatches**) A **hatch** is an opening in the deck of a ship, through which people or cargo can go. You can also refer to the door of this opening as a **hatch**. ❑ *He stuck his head up through the hatch.*

hate ♦◇◇ /heɪt/ VERB, NOUN
VERB [T] (**hates, hating, hated**) **1** If you **hate** someone or something, you have an extremely strong feeling of dislike for them. = detest, loathe ❑ *Most people hate him, but they don't dare to say so, because he still rules the country.* **2** If you say that you **hate** something such as a particular activity, you mean that you find it very unpleasant. = dislike ❑ *Ted hated parties, even gatherings of people he liked individually.* ❑ *He hates to be interrupted during training.* ❑ *He hated coming home to the empty house.* **3** You can use **hate** in expressions such as '**I hate to trouble you**' or '**I hate to bother you**' when you are apologizing to someone for interrupting them or asking them to do something. ❑ *I hate to rush you but I have another appointment later on.* **4** You can use **hate** in expressions such as '**I hate to say it**' or '**I hate to tell you**' when you want to express regret about what you are about to say, because you think it is unpleasant or should not be the case. ❑ *I hate to tell you this, but tomorrow's your last day.* **5** You can use **hate** in expressions such as '**I hate to see**' or '**I hate to think**' when you are emphasizing that you find a situation or an idea unpleasant. ❑ *I just hate to see you doing this to yourself.* **6** You can use **hate** in expressions such as '**I'd hate to think**' when you hope that something is not true or that something will not happen. ❑ *I'd hate to think my job would not be secure if I left it temporarily.*
NOUN [U] **Hate** is an extremely strong feeling of dislike for someone or something. = hatred ❑ *I was 17 and filled with a lot of hate.*
✦ **hate someone's guts** → see gut

ha•tred /ˈheɪtrɪd/ NOUN [U] **Hatred** is an extremely strong feeling of dislike for someone or something. = hate ❑ *Her hatred of them would never lead her to murder.*

haul /hɔːl/ VERB, NOUN
VERB [T] (**hauls, hauling, hauled**) **1** If you **haul** something which is heavy or difficult to move, you move it using a lot of effort. ❑ *A crane had to be used to haul the car out of the stream.* **2** If someone **is hauled before** a court or someone in authority, they are made to appear before them because they are accused of having done something wrong. ❑ *He was hauled before the managing director and fired.*
PHRASAL VERB **haul up** Haul up means the same as **haul** VERB 2. ❑ *He was hauled up before the board of trustees.*
NOUN [C] (**hauls**) A **haul** is a quantity of things that are stolen, or a quantity of stolen or illegal goods found by police or customs. ❑ *The size of the drug haul shows that the international trade in heroin is still flourishing.*

PHRASE **long haul** If you say that a task or a journey is a **long haul**, you mean that it takes a long time and a lot of effort. ▢ *Revitalizing the Romanian economy will be a long haul.*

haunt /hɔːnt/ VERB, NOUN

VERB [T] (**haunts, haunting, haunted**) **1** If something unpleasant **haunts** you, you keep thinking or worrying about it over a long period of time. ▢ *He would always be haunted by that scene in Well Park.* **2** Something that **haunts** a person or organization regularly causes them problems over a long period of time. ▢ *The stigma of being a bankrupt is likely to haunt him for the rest of his life.* **3** A ghost or spirit that **haunts** a place or a person regularly appears in the place, or is seen by the person and frightens them. ▢ *His ghost is said to haunt some of the rooms, banging a toy drum.*

NOUN [C] (**haunts**) A place that is the **haunt** of a particular person is one which they often visit because they enjoy going there. ▢ *The islands are a favourite summer haunt for yachtsmen.*

have ♦♦♦ /həv, STRONG hæv/ VERB

In spoken English, forms of **have** are often shortened, for example **I have** is shortened to **I've** and **has not** is shortened to **hasn't**.

Have is used in combination with a wide range of nouns, where the meaning of the combination is mostly given by the noun.

VERB [AUX, T] (**has, having, had**) **1** [AUX] You use the forms **have** and **has** with a past participle to form the present perfect tense of verbs. ▢ *Alex has already gone.* ▢ *What have you found so far?* ▢ *Frankie hasn't been feeling well for a long time.* **2** [AUX] You use the form **had** with a past participle to form the past perfect tense of verbs. ▢ *When I met her, she had just returned from a job interview.* **3** [AUX] **Have** is used in question tags. ▢ *You haven't sent her away, have you?* **4** [AUX] You use **have** when you are confirming or contradicting a statement containing 'have', 'has', or 'had', or answering a question. ▢ *'You'd never seen the Marilyn Monroe film?'—'No I hadn't.'* **5** [AUX] The form **having** with a past participle can be used to introduce a clause in which you mention an action which had already happened before another action began. ▢ *He arrived in San Francisco, having left New Jersey on January 19th.* **6** [T] You can use **have** followed by a noun to talk about an action or event, when it would be possible to use the same word as a verb. For example, you can say **'I had a look at the photos'** instead of 'I looked at the photos'. ▢ *I went out and had a walk around.* ▢ *We had a laugh over that one.* **7** [T] In normal spoken or written English, people use **have** with a wide range of nouns to talk about actions and events, often instead of a more specific verb. For example people are more likely to say **'we had ice cream'** or **'he's had a shock'** than 'we ate ice cream' or 'he's suffered a shock'. ▢ *Come and have a meal with us tonight.* ▢ *We will be having a meeting to decide what to do.* **8** [T] You use **have** to say that someone or something owns a particular thing, or when you are mentioning one of their qualities or characteristics. ▢ *Oscar had a new bicycle.* ▢ *I want to have my own business.* ▢ *She had no job and no money.* ▢ *You have beautiful eyes.* ▢ *Do you have any brothers and sisters?* **9** [T] If you have **something** to do, you are responsible for doing it or must do it. ▢ *He had plenty of work to do.* **10** [T] You can use **have** instead of 'there is' to say that something exists or happens. For example, you can say **'you have no alternative'** instead of 'there is no alternative', or **'he had a good view from his window'** instead of 'there was a good view from his window'. ▢ *He had two tenants living with him.* **11** [T] If you **have** something such as a part of your body in a particular position or state, it is in that position or state. ▢ *Mary had her eyes closed.* ▢ *They had the curtains open.* **12** [T] If you **have** something done, someone does it for you or you arrange for it to be done. ▢ *We had your rooms cleaned and aired.* ▢ *They had him killed.* **13** [T] If someone **has** something unpleasant happen to them, it happens to them. ▢ *We had our money stolen.* **14** [T] If you **have** someone do something, you persuade, cause, or order them to do it. ▢ *The bridge is not as impressive as some*

guides would have you believe. **15** [T] If someone **has** you **by** a part of your body, they are holding you there and they are trying to hurt you or force you to go somewhere. ▢ *He had her by the arm and he was screaming at her.* **16** [T] If you **have** something from someone, they give it to you. ▢ *You can have my ticket.* ▢ *Can I have your name please?* **17** [T] If you **have** an illness or disability, you suffer from it. ▢ *I had a headache.* **18** [T] If a woman **has** a baby, she gives birth to it. If she **is having** a baby, she is pregnant. ▢ *My wife has just had a baby boy.* **19** [T] You can use **have** in expressions such as **'I won't have it'** or **'I'm not having that'** to mean that you will not allow or put up with something. ▢ *I'm not having any of that nonsense.*

PHRASES **rumour has it** or **legend has it** (*vagueness*) You can use **has it** in expressions such as **'rumour has it that'** or **'as legend has it'** when you are quoting something that you have heard, but you do not necessarily think it is true. ▢ *Rumour has it that tickets were being sold for $300.*
have it in for someone (*informal*) If someone **has it in for** you, they do not like you and they want to make life difficult for you. ▢ *He's always had it in for the Dawkins family.*
have it in you If you **have it in** you, you have abilities and skills which you do not usually use and which only show themselves in a difficult situation. ▢ *'You were brilliant!' he said. 'I didn't know you had it in you.'*
have it out If you **have it out** or **have things out with** someone, you discuss a problem or disagreement very openly with them, even if it means having an argument, because you think this is the best way to solve the problem. ▢ *Why not have it out with your critic, discuss the whole thing face to face?*
have to /hæv, hæf/ [AUX, T] **1** You use **have to** when you are saying that something is necessary or required, or must happen. If you do not **have to** do something, it is not necessary or required. = must ▢ *He had to go to Germany.* ▢ *You have to be careful what you say on TV.* **2** You can use **have to** in order to say that you feel certain that something is true or will happen. = must ▢ *There has to be some kind of way out.*
✦ **be had** → see **had**

ha·ven /ˈheɪvən/ NOUN [C] (**havens**) A **haven** is a place where people or animals feel safe, secure, and happy. = refuge ▢ *Lake Baringo, a freshwater haven for a mixed variety of birds*

hav·oc /ˈhævək/ NOUN
NOUN [U] **Havoc** is great disorder and confusion. ▢ *Rioters caused havoc in the centre of the town.*
PHRASE **play havoc** or **wreak havoc** If one thing **plays havoc with** another or **wreaks havoc on** it, it prevents it from continuing or functioning as normal, or damages it. ▢ *The weather played havoc with airline schedules.*

hawk /hɔːk/ NOUN
NOUN [C] (**hawks**) **1** A **hawk** is a large bird with a short, hooked beak, sharp claws, and very good eyesight. Hawks catch and eat small birds and animals. **2** In politics, if you refer to someone as a **hawk**, you mean that they believe in using force and violence to achieve something, rather than using more peaceful or diplomatic methods. ▢ *Both hawks and doves have expanded their conditions for ending the war.*
PHRASE **watch someone like a hawk** If you **watch** someone **like a hawk**, you observe them very carefully, usually to make sure that they do not make a mistake or do something you do not want them to do. ▢ *If we hadn't watched him like a hawk, he would have escaped.*

hay /heɪ/ NOUN
NOUN [U] **Hay** is grass which has been cut and dried so that it can be used to feed animals. ▢ *bales of hay*
PHRASE **make hay** or **make hay while the sun shines** If you say that someone **is making hay** or **is making hay while the sun shines**, you mean that they are taking advantage of a situation that is favourable to them while they have the chance to. ▢ *We knew war was coming, and were determined to make hay while we could.*

haz·ard /ˈhæzəd/ NOUN, VERB
NOUN [C] (**hazards**) A **hazard** is something which could be

dangerous to you, your health or safety, or your plans or reputation. ❑ *A new report suggests that chewing gum may be a health hazard.*

VERB [T] (**hazards, hazarding, hazarded**) If you **hazard** a **guess**, you make a suggestion about something which is only a guess and which you know might be wrong. ❑ *I would hazard a guess that they'll do fairly well in the next election.*

haz·ard·ous /ˈhæzədəs/ ADJ Something that is **hazardous** is dangerous, especially to people's health or safety. = dangerous ❑ *They have no way to dispose of the hazardous waste they produce.*

he ◆◆◆ /hi, STRONG hiː/ PRON

> **He** is a third person singular pronoun. **He** is used as the subject of a verb.

1 You use **he** to refer to a man, boy, or male animal. ❑ *He could never quite remember all our names.* **2** In written English, **he** is sometimes used to refer to a person without saying whether that person is a man or a woman. Some people dislike this use and prefer to use 'he or she' or 'they'. ❑ *The teacher should encourage the child to proceed as far as he can, and when he is stuck, ask for help.*

head ◆◆◆ /hed/ NOUN, VERB, ADV

NOUN [C, SING] (**heads**) **1** [C] Your **head** is the top part of your body, which has your eyes, mouth, and brain in it. ❑ *She turned her head away from him.* **2** [C] You can use **head** to refer to your mind and your mental abilities. ❑ *an exceptional analyst who could do complex maths in his head* **3** [SING] The **head** of a queue of people or vehicles is the front of it, or the first person or vehicle in the queue. ❑ *He made his way to the head of the queue.* **4** [C] The **head** of a company or organization is the person in charge of it and in charge of the people in it. ❑ *Heads of government from more than 100 countries gather in Geneva tomorrow.* **5** [C] The **head** of something long and thin is the end which is wider than or a different shape from the rest, and which is often considered to be the most important part. ❑ *There should be no exposed screw heads.*

PHRASES **a head** or **per head** You use **a head** or **per head** after stating a cost or amount in order to indicate that that cost or amount is for each person in a particular group. ❑ *This simple chicken dish costs less than $3 a head.*

a head for something If you a have **a head for** something, you can deal with it easily. For example, if you have **a head for figures**, you can do arithmetic easily, and if you have **a head for heights**, you can climb to a great height without feeling afraid. ❑ *I don't have a head for business.*

get something into one's head **1** If you **get** a fact or idea **into** your **head**, you suddenly realize or think that it is true and you usually do not change your opinion about it. ❑ *Once you get an idea into their heads, they never give up.* **2** If you say that someone has **got** something **into** their **head**, you mean that they have finally understood or accepted it, and you are usually criticizing them because it has taken them a long time to do this. ❑ *Managers have at last got it into their heads that they can no longer rest content with inefficient operations.*

go to one's head **1** If alcoholic drink **goes to** your **head**, it makes you feel drunk. ❑ *That wine was strong, it went to your head.* **2** (*disapproval*) If you say that something such as praise or success **goes to** someone's **head**, you are criticizing them because you think that it makes them too proud or confident. ❑ *Ford is definitely not a man to let a little success go to his head.*

head over heels or **head over heels in love** If you are **head over heels** or **head over heels in love**, you are very much in love. ❑ *I was very attracted to men and fell head over heels many times.*

keep your head or **lose your head** If you **keep** your **head**, you remain calm in a difficult situation. If you **lose** your **head**, you panic or do not remain calm in a difficult situation. ❑ *She was able to keep her head and not panic.*

laugh one's head off (*emphasis*) Phrases such as **laugh** your **head off** and **scream** your **head off** can be used to emphasize that someone is laughing or screaming a lot or

very loudly. ❑ *He carried on telling a joke, laughing his head off.*

be over someone's head If something such as an idea, joke, or comment goes **over** someone's **head**, it is too difficult for them to understand. ❑ *I admit that a lot of the ideas went way over my head.*

over someone's head If someone does something **over** another person's **head**, they do it without asking them or discussing it with them, especially when they should do so because the other person is in a position of authority. ❑ *He was reprimanded for trying to go over the heads of senior officers.*

rear its ugly head or **raise its ugly head** If you say that something unpleasant or embarrassing **rears its ugly head** or **raises its ugly head**, you mean that it occurs, often after not occurring for some time. ❑ *There was a problem which reared its ugly head about a week after she moved back in.*

stand on one's head If you **stand on** your **head**, you balance upside down with the top of your head and your hands on the ground. ❑ *He was photographed standing on his head doing yoga.*

cannot make head nor tail of something or **cannot make heads or tails of something** (*informal*) If you say that you cannot **make head nor tail of** something or you cannot **make heads or tails of** it, you are emphasizing that you cannot understand it at all. ❑ *I couldn't make head nor tail of the damn film.*

take it into one's head If somebody **takes it into** their **head** to do something, especially something strange or foolish, they suddenly decide to do it. ❑ *He suddenly took it into his head to go out to Australia to stay with his son.*

come to a head or **bring something to a head** If a problem or disagreement **comes to a head** or **is brought to a head**, it becomes so bad that something must be done about it. ❑ *These problems came to a head in September when five of the station's journalists were fired.*

put one's heads together If two or more people **put** their **heads together**, they talk about a problem they have and try to solve it. ❑ *So everyone put their heads together and eventually an amicable arrangement was reached.*

keep one's head above water If you **keep** your **head above water**, you just avoid getting into difficulties; used especially to talk about business. ❑ *We are keeping our head above water, but our cash flow position is not too good.*

heads will roll If you say that **heads will roll** as a result of something bad that has happened, you mean that people will be punished for it, especially by losing their jobs. ❑ *The group's problems have led to speculation that heads will roll.*

VERB [T, I] (**heads, heading, headed**) **1** [T] If someone or something **heads** a queue or procession, they are at the front of it. ❑ *The parson, heading the procession, had just turned right towards the churchyard.* **2** [T] If something **heads** a list or group, it is at the top of it. ❑ *Running a business heads the list of ambitions among the 1,000 people interviewed by Good Housekeeping magazine.* **3** [T] If you **head** a department, company, or organization, you are the person in charge of it. ❑ *Michael Williams, who heads the department's Office of Civil Rights* **4** [I, T] If you **are heading** or **are headed** for a particular place, you are going towards that place. ❑ *He was headed for the bus stop.* ❑ *It is not clear how many of them will be heading back to Saudi Arabia tomorrow.* **5** [I, T] If something or someone **is heading for** or **is headed for** a particular result, the situation they are in is developing in a way that makes that result very likely. ❑ *The latest talks aimed at ending the civil war appear to be heading for deadlock.* **6** [T] If a piece of writing **is headed** a particular title, it has that title written at the beginning of it. ❑ *One chapter is headed, 'Beating the Test'.* **7** [T] If you **head** a ball in football, you hit it with your head in order to make it go in a particular direction. ❑ *He headed the ball across the face of the goal.*

ADV If you toss a coin and it comes down **heads**, you can see the side of the coin which has a picture of a head on it. ❑ *'We might flip a coin for it,' suggested Ted. 'If it's heads, then we'll talk.'*

→ See also **heading**

head·ache /ˈhedeɪk/ NOUN [C] (**headaches**) **1** If you have a **headache**, you have a pain in your head. ❑ *I have*

H

had a terrible headache for the last two days. **2** If you say that something is a **headache**, you mean that it causes you difficulty or worry. = problem □ *The airline's biggest headache is the increase in the price of aviation fuel.*

head·ing /'hedɪŋ/ NOUN [C] (**headings**) A **heading** is the title of a piece of writing, which is written or printed at the top of the page. = title □ *helpful chapter headings* □ *Use headings to make information easy to find.*

head·light /'hedlaɪt/ NOUN [C] (**headlights**) A vehicle's **headlights** are the large powerful lights at the front. □ *Motorists were forced to turn on their headlights at midday.*

head·line ◆◇◇ /'hedlaɪn/ NOUN, VERB
NOUN [C, PL] (**headlines**) **1** [C] A **headline** is the title of a newspaper story, printed in large letters at the top of the story, especially on the front page. □ *The Sydney Morning Herald carried the headline: 'Sorry Ma'am, Most Australians Want a Republic.'* **2** [PL] The **headlines** are the main points of the news which are read on radio or television. □ *I'm Claudia Polley with the news headlines.*
PHRASE **hit the headlines** or **grab the headlines** Someone or something that **hits the headlines** or **grabs the headlines** gets a lot of publicity from the media. □ *El Salvador first hit the world headlines at the beginning of the 1980s.*
VERB [T] (**headlines, headlining, headlined**) If a newspaper or magazine article **is headlined** a particular thing, that is the headline that introduces it. □ *The article was headlined 'Tell us the truth.'*

head·long /'hedlɒŋ, AmE -lɔŋ/ ADV, ADJ
ADV **1** [headlong after V] If you move **headlong** in a particular direction, you move there very quickly. □ *He ran headlong for the open door.* **2** [headlong after V] If you fall or move **headlong**, you fall or move with your head furthest forward. □ *She missed her footing and fell headlong down the stairs.* **3** [headlong after V] If you rush **headlong** into something, you do it quickly without thinking carefully about it. □ *Do not leap headlong into decisions.*
ADJ [headlong + N] If you describe a rush or dash as **headlong** you mean that it is very quick. □ *the headlong rush to independence*

head·master /ˌhed'mɑːstə, -'mæst-/ NOUN [C] (**headmasters**) A **headmaster** is the head teacher of a private school.

head of state NOUN [C] (**heads of state**) A **head of state** is the leader of a country, for example a president, king, or queen. □ *The Algerian authorities have still not named a new head of state.*

head-on ADV, ADJ
ADV **1** [head-on after V] If two vehicles hit each other **head-on**, they hit each other with their fronts pointing towards each other. □ *The car collided head-on with a van.* **2** [head-on after V] If you approach or confront an issue **head-on**, you approach or confront it directly, without any attempt to compromise or avoid the issue. □ *Once again, I chose to confront the issue head-on.*
ADJ **1** [head-on + N] A **head-on** collision is when two vehicles hit each other with their fronts pointing towards each other. □ *Their car was in a head-on collision with a truck.* **2** [head-on + N] A **head-on** conflict or approach is direct, without any attempt to compromise or avoid the issue. □ *The only victors in a head-on clash between the president and the assembly would be the hardliners on both sides.*

head·phones /'hedfəʊnz/ NOUN [PL] [also 'a pair of' headphones] **Headphones** are a pair of padded speakers which you wear over your ears in order to listen to a radio, CD player, or tape recorder without other people hearing it. □ *while out cycling one evening and listening to your programme on headphones*

head·quarters ◆◇◇ /'hedkwɔːtəz/ NOUN [SING] The **headquarters** of an organization are its main offices. = HQ □ *fraud squad officers from Chicago's police headquarters*

head·way /'hedweɪ/ NOUN
PHRASE **make headway** If you **make headway**, you progress towards achieving something. = progress □ *There was concern in the city that police* were making little headway in the investigation.

heal ◆◇◇ /hiːl/ VERB [I, T] (**heals, healing, healed**) **1** When a broken bone or other injury **heals**, or if someone or something **heals** it, it becomes healthy and normal again. □ *Within six weeks the bruising had gone, but it was six months before it all healed.* **2** If you **heal** something such as a rift or a wound, or if it **heals**, the situation is put right so that people are friendly or happy again. □ *We have begun to heal the wounds of war in our society.*

health ◆◆◆ /helθ/ NOUN [U] **1** A person's **health** is the condition of their body and the extent to which it is free from illness or is able to resist illness. = well-being □ *Tea contains caffeine. It's bad for your health.* □ *He was 88 and in poor health.* □ *The clinic aimed to improve the health of the local population.* □ *the effects of pesticides on human health* **2** **Health** is a state in which a person is not suffering from any illness and is feeling well. □ *In the hospital they nursed me back to health.* **3** The **health** of something such as an organization or a system is its success and the fact that it is working well. = prosperity □ *There's no way to predict the future health of the banking industry.*

health care ◆◆◇ also **healthcare** NOUN [U] [oft health care + N] **Health care** is the various services for the prevention or treatment of illness and injuries. □ *Nobody wants to pay more for health care.* □ *the nation's health care system*

healthy ◆◇◇ /'helθi/ ADJ (**healthier, healthiest**) **1** Someone who is **healthy** is well and is not suffering from any illness. ≠ ill, unhealthy □ *Most of us need to lead more balanced lives to be healthy and happy.* □ *the glow of healthy skin* **2** Something that is **healthy** is good for your health. □ *a healthy diet* **3** A **healthy** organization or system is successful. □ *an economically healthy socialist state* **4** A **healthy** amount of something is a large amount that shows success. = substantial □ *He predicts a continuation of healthy profits in the current financial year.* **5** If you have a **healthy** attitude about something, you show good sense. □ *She has a refreshingly healthy attitude to work.*
health·i·ly /'helθɪli/ ADV □ *What I really want is to live healthily for as long as possible.* □ *You should try to eat healthily.*

USAGE NOTE

healthy

Note that **healthy** is an adjective and not a noun. The related noun is 'health'.
*Fish is considered a **healthy** food.*
*Fish is good for your **health**.*

---

heap /hiːp/ NOUN, VERB, QUANT
NOUN [C] (**heaps**) A **heap of** things is a pile of them, especially a pile arranged in a rather messy way. □ *a heap of bricks*
VERB [T] (**heaps, heaping, heaped**) **1** If you **heap** things in a pile, you arrange them in a large pile. □ *Mrs Madrigal heaped more carrots onto Michael's plate.* **2** If you **heap** praise or criticism on someone or something, you give them a lot of praise or criticism. □ *The head of the navy heaped scorn on both the methods and motives of the conspirators.*
PHRASAL VERB **heap up** Heap up means the same as heap VERB 1. □ *Off to one side, the militia was heaping up wood for a bonfire.*
QUANT (informal) **Heaps of** something or a **heap of** something is a large quantity of it. = load □ *You have heaps of time.*

hear ◆◆◆ /hɪə/ VERB
VERB [I, T] (**hears, hearing, heard**) **1** [I, T] When you **hear** a sound, you become aware of it through your ears. □ *She heard no further sounds.* □ *They heard the protesters shout: 'No more fascism!'* □ *He doesn't hear very well.* **2** [T] If you **hear** something such as a lecture or a piece of music, you listen to it. □ *You can hear commentary on the game at half time.* □ *I don't think you've ever heard Doris talking about her emotional life before.* **3** [T] (formal) When a judge or a court of law **hears** a case, or evidence in a case, they listen to it officially in order to make a decision about it. □ *The jury*

has heard evidence from defence witnesses. **4** [I] If you **hear from** someone, you receive a letter or telephone call from them. ❑ *Drop us a line, it's always great to hear from you.* **5** [I, T] If you **hear** some news or information about something, you find out about it by someone telling you, or from the radio or television. ❑ *My mother heard of this school through Leslie.* ❑ *He had heard that the trophy had been sold.* **6** [I] If you **have heard of** something or someone, you know about them, but not in great detail. ❑ *Many people haven't heard of reflexology.*

PHRASES **have heard something before** If you say that you **have heard** something **before**, you mean that you are not interested in it, or do not believe it, or are not surprised about it, because you already know about it or have experienced it. ❑ *Frank shrugs wearily. He has heard it all before.*

you can't hear yourself think (*informal, emphasis*) If you say that you **can't hear yourself think**, you are complaining and emphasizing that there is a lot of noise, and that it is disturbing you or preventing you from doing something. ❑ *those noisy late-night clubs where you can't even hear yourself think*

won't hear of something If you say that you **won't hear** of someone doing something, you mean that you refuse to let them do it. ❑ *I've always wanted to be an actor but Dad wouldn't hear of it.*

hear·ing ♦◇◇ /ˈhɪərɪŋ/ NOUN

NOUN [U, C] (**hearings**) **1** [U] A person's or animal's **hearing** is the sense which makes it possible for them to be aware of sounds. ❑ *His mind still seemed clear and his hearing was excellent.* **2** [C] A **hearing** is an official meeting which is held in order to collect facts about an incident or problem. ❑ *After more than two hours of pandemonium, the judge adjourned the hearing until next Tuesday.*

PHRASES **a fair hearing** If someone gives you **a fair hearing** or **a hearing**, they listen to you when you give your opinion about something. ❑ *Weber gave a fair hearing to anyone who held a different opinion.*

in someone's hearing or **within someone's hearing** If someone says something in your **hearing** or **within** your **hearing**, you can hear what they say because they are with you or near you. ❑ *No one spoke disparagingly of her father in her hearing.*

♦heart ♦♦◇ /hɑːt/ NOUN

NOUN [C, U, SING] (**hearts**) **1** [C] Your **heart** is the organ in your chest that pumps the blood around your body. People also use **heart** to refer to the area of their chest that is closest to their heart. ❑ *The bullet had passed less than an inch from Andrea's heart.* ❑ *His heart was beating very fast.* ❑ *The baby was born with a heart condition.* **2** [C] (*literary*) You can refer to someone's **heart** when you are talking about their deep feelings and beliefs. ❑ *Alik's words filled her heart with pride.* **3** [C, U] You use **heart** when you are talking about someone's character and attitude towards other people, especially when they are kind and generous. ❑ *She loved his brilliance and his generous heart.* **4** [SING] The **heart of** something is the most central and important part of it. = crux ❑ *The heart of the problem is supply and demand.* **5** [SING] The **heart of** a place is its centre. ❑ *a busy dentists' practice in the heart of the city* **6** [C] A **heart** is a shape that is used as a symbol of love: ♥. ❑ *heart-shaped chocolates* **7** [U] **Hearts** is one of the four suits in a pack of playing cards. Each card in the suit is marked with one or more symbols in the shape of a heart. **8** [C] A **heart** is a playing card of this suit. ❑ *West had to decide whether to play a heart.*

PHRASES **with all one's heart** (*emphasis*) If you feel or believe something **with all** your **heart**, you feel or believe it very strongly. ❑ *My own family I loved with all my heart.*

at heart If you say that someone is a particular kind of person **at heart**, you mean that that is what they are really like, even though they may seem very different. ❑ *He was a very gentle boy at heart.*

have someone's interests at heart If you say that someone has your interests or your welfare **at heart**, you mean that they are concerned about you and that is why they are doing something. ❑ *She told me she only had my interests at heart.*

break someone's heart **1** (*literary*) If someone **breaks** your **heart**, they make you very sad and unhappy, usually because they end a love affair or close relationship with you. ❑ *I fell in love on holiday but the girl broke my heart.* **2** If something **breaks** your **heart**, it makes you feel very sad and depressed, especially because people are suffering but you can do nothing to help them. ❑ *It really breaks my heart to see them this way.*

by heart If you know something such as a poem **by heart**, you have learned it so well that you can remember it without having to read it. ❑ *Mack knew this passage by heart.*

a change of heart If someone has a **change of heart**, their attitude towards something changes. ❑ *Several brokers have had a change of heart about prospects for the company.*

close to one's heart or **near to one's heart** If something such as a subject or project is **close to** your **heart** or **near** to your **heart**, it is very important to you and you are very interested in it and concerned about it. ❑ *This is a subject very close to my heart.*

to your heart's content If you can do something **to** your **heart's content**, you can do it as much as you want. ❑ *I was delighted to be able to eat my favourite dishes to my heart's content.*

from the heart or **from the bottom of one's heart** If you say something **from the heart** or **from the bottom of** your **heart**, you sincerely mean what you say. = sincerely ❑ *He spoke with confidence, from the heart.*

not have the heart If you want to do something but do **not have the heart to** do it, you do not do it because you know it will make someone unhappy or disappointed. ❑ *We knew all along but didn't have the heart to tell her.*

in your heart of hearts If you believe or know something **in your heart of hearts**, that is what you really believe or think, even though it may sometimes seem that you do not. ❑ *I know in my heart of hearts that I am the right man for that mission.*

your heart is not in something If your **heart isn't in** the thing you are doing, you have very little enthusiasm for it, usually because you are depressed or are thinking about something else. ❑ *I tried to learn some lines but my heart wasn't really in it.*

lose heart If you **lose heart**, you become sad and depressed and are no longer interested in something, especially because it is not progressing as you would like. ❑ *He appealed to his countrymen not to lose heart.*

heart in your mouth If your **heart is in** your **mouth**, you feel very excited, worried, or frightened. ❑ *My heart was in my mouth when I walked into her office.*

open your heart or **pour out your heart** If you **open** your **heart** or **pour out** your **heart** to someone, you tell them your most private thoughts and feelings. ❑ *She opened her heart to millions yesterday and told how she came close to suicide.*

heart in the right place If you say that someone's **heart is in the right place**, you mean that they are kind, considerate, and generous, although you may disapprove of other aspects of their character. ❑ *He's rich, handsome, funny, and his heart is in the right place.*

set your heart on something If you have **set** your **heart on** something, you want it very much or want to do it very much. ❑ *He had always set his heart on a career in the fine arts.*

take heart If you **take heart from** something, you are encouraged and made to feel optimistic by it. ❑ *Investors and dealers also took heart from the better than expected industrial production figures.*

take something to heart If you **take** something **to heart**, for example someone's behaviour, you are deeply affected and upset by it. ❑ *If someone says something critical I take it to heart.*

CONVENTION **cross my heart** (*spoken*) You can say '**cross my heart**' when you want someone to believe that you are telling the truth. You can also ask '**cross your heart?**' when you are asking someone if they are really telling the truth. ❑ *And I won't tell any of the other girls anything you tell me about it. I promise, cross my heart.*

H

heart·ache /'hɑːteɪk/ NOUN [C, U] (**heartaches**)
Heartache is very great sadness and emotional suffering.
❑ *after suffering the heartache of her divorce from her first
husband*

⊙ **heart at·tack** NOUN [C] (**heart attacks**) If someone
has a **heart attack**, their heart begins to beat very
irregularly or stops completely. = cardiac arrest ❑ *He died
of a heart attack brought on by overwork.* ❑ *My grandfather
had a heart attack.*

heart·beat /'hɑːtbiːt/ NOUN [SING] Your **heartbeat** is the
regular movement of your heart as it pumps blood around
your body. ❑ *Your baby's heartbeat will be monitored
continuously.*

heart·break /'hɑːtbreɪk/ NOUN [C, U] (**heartbreaks**)
Heartbreak is very great sadness and emotional suffering,
especially after the end of a love affair or close
relationship. ❑ *suffering and heartbreak for those close to the
victims*

heart·en /'hɑːtən/ VERB [T] (**heartens, heartening,
heartened**) If someone **is heartened by** something, it
encourages them and makes them cheerful. = cheer
❑ *The news heartened everybody.*
   heart·ened /'hɑːtənd/ ADJ [V-LINK + heartened] ❑ *I feel
heartened by her progress.*
   heart·en·ing /'hɑːtənɪŋ/ ADJ ❑ *This is heartening news.*

heart·felt /'hɑːtfelt/ ADJ **Heartfelt** is used to describe a
deep or sincere feeling or wish. = sincere ❑ *My heartfelt
sympathy goes out to all the relatives.*

heart·land /'hɑːtlænd/ NOUN [C] (**heartlands**)
❶ Journalists use **heartland** or **heartlands** to refer to the
area or region where a particular set of activities or beliefs
is most significant. ❑ *his six-day bus tour around the
industrial heartland of America* ❷ (*written*) The most central
area of a country or continent can be referred to as its
heartland or **heartlands**. ❑ *For many, the essence of French
living is to be found in the rural heartlands.*

hearty /'hɑːti/ ADJ (**heartier, heartiest**) ❶ **Hearty** people
or actions are loud, cheerful, and energetic. ❑ *Wade was a
hearty, athletic sort of guy.* ❷ **Hearty** feelings or opinions are
strongly felt or strongly held. ❑ *With the last sentiment,
Arnold was in hearty agreement.* ❸ A **hearty** meal is large
and very satisfying. ❑ *The men ate a hearty breakfast.*
   heart·i·ly /'hɑːtɪli/ ADV ❶ [heartily after v] ❑ *He laughed
heartily.* ❷ [Most Afghans are heartily sick of war.] ❸ [heartily
after v] ❑ *He ate heartily but would drink only beer.*

⊙ **heat** ◆◆◇ /hiːt/ VERB, NOUN
   VERB [T] (**heats, heating, heated**) When you **heat**
something, you raise its temperature, for example, by
using a flame or a special piece of equipment. ≠ cool
❑ *Meanwhile, heat the tomatoes and oil in a pan.* ❑ *heated
swimming pools*
   PHRASAL VERB **heat up** ❶ When you **heat** something **up**,
especially food which has already been cooked and
allowed to go cold, you make it hot. = warm up
❑ *Freda heated up a pie for me but I couldn't eat it.* ❷ When
a situation **heats up**, things start to happen much more
quickly and with increased interest and excitement
among the people involved. = hot up ❑ *Then in the last
couple of years, the movement for democracy began to heat up.*
❸ When something **heats up**, it gradually becomes hotter.
❑ *In the summer her home heats up like an oven.*
   NOUN [U, SING, C] (**heats**) ❶ [U] Heat is warmth or the
quality of being hot. = warmth ❑ *The seas store heat and
release it gradually during cold periods.* ❑ *Its leaves drooped a
little in the fierce heat of the sun.* ❷ [U] [also 'the' heat] The
heat is very hot weather. ❑ *As an asthmatic, he cannot cope
with the heat and humidity.* ❸ [U] The **heat** of something is
the temperature of something that is warm or that is being
heated. ❑ *Adjust the heat of the barbecue by opening and
closing the air vents.* ❹ [SING] You use **heat** to refer to a
source of heat, for example a ring on a hob or the heating
system of a house. ❑ *Immediately remove the pan from the
heat.* ❺ [U] You use **heat** to refer to a state of strong
emotion, especially of anger or excitement. ❑ *It was all
done in the heat of the moment and I have certainly learned
from my mistake.* ❻ [SING] The **heat of** a particular activity is

the point when there is the greatest activity or excitement.
❑ *People say all kinds of things in the heat of an argument.*
❼ [C] A **heat** is one of a series of races or competitions. The
winners of a heat take part in another race or competition,
against the winners of other heats. ❑ *the heats of the men's
100 metre breaststroke*

heat·ed /'hiːtɪd/ ADJ ❶ A **heated** discussion or quarrel
is one where the people involved are angry and excited.
❑ *It was a very heated argument and they were shouting at
each other.* ❷ [V-LINK + heated 'about/over' N] If someone
gets **heated about** something, they get angry and excited
about it. ❑ *You will understand that people get a bit heated
about issues such as these.*
   heat·ed·ly /'hiːtɪdli/ ADV ❑ *The crowd continued to argue
heatedly about the best way to tackle the problem.*

heat·er /'hiːtə/ NOUN [C] (**heaters**) A **heater** is a piece of
equipment or a machine which is used to raise the
temperature of something, especially of the air inside a
room or a car. ❑ *There's an electric heater in the bedroom.*

heat·ing /'hiːtɪŋ/ NOUN [U] ❶ Heating is the process of
heating a building or room, considered especially from the
point of view of how much this costs. ❑ *We wanted to
reduce the cost of heating and air-conditioning.* ❷ Heating is
the system and equipment that is used to heat a building.
❑ *I wish I knew how to turn on the heating.*
→ See also **central heating**

heave /hiːv/ VERB, NOUN
   VERB [T, I] (**heaves, heaving, heaved**) ❶ [T] If you **heave**
something heavy or difficult to move somewhere, you
push, pull, or lift it using a lot of effort. ❑ *It took five strong
men to heave it up a ramp and lower it into place.* ❷ [I] If
something **heaves**, it moves up and down with large
regular movements. ❑ *His chest heaved, and he took a deep
breath.* ❸ [I] If you **heave**, or if your stomach **heaves**, you
vomit or feel as if you are about to vomit. ❑ *He gasped and
heaved again.* ❑ *The greasy food made her stomach heave.*
❹ [T] If you **heave** a sigh, you give a big sigh. ❑ *Mr Collier
heaved a sigh and got to his feet.* ❺ [I] (*mainly BrE, informal*) If
a place **is heaving** or if it **is heaving with** people, it is full
of people. ❑ *The Happy Bunny club was heaving.* ❑ *Father
Auberon's Academy Club positively heaved with dashing young
men.*
   NOUN [C] (**heaves**) A **heave** is a pushing, pulling, or lifting
movement that uses a lot of effort to move something
heavy or difficult to move. ❑ *It took only one heave to hurl
him into the river.*
   ✦ **heave a sigh of relief** → see **sigh**

heav·en ◆◇◇ /'hevən/ NOUN, EXCLAM
   NOUN [U] (**heavens**) ❶ In some religions, **heaven** is said to
be the place where God lives, where good people go when
they die, and where everyone is always happy. It is usually
imagined as being high up in the sky. = paradise
❑ *I believed that when I died I would go to heaven and see God.*
❷ (*informal*) You can use **heaven** to refer to a place or
situation that you like very much. = paradise ❑ *I would
go to films in the afternoon and football matches in the evening.
It was heaven.*
   PHRASES **heaven help someone** (*spoken, disapproval*) You
say '**Heaven help** someone' when you are worried that
something bad is going to happen to them, often because
you disapprove of what they are doing or the way they are
behaving. ❑ *If this makes sense to our leaders, then heaven
help us all.*
   heaven knows (*spoken, emphasis*) ❶ You can say '**Heaven
knows**' to emphasize that you do not know something, or
that you find something very surprising. ❑ *Heaven knows
what they put in it.* ❷ You can say '**Heaven knows**' to
emphasize something that you feel or believe very
strongly. ❑ *Heaven knows they have enough money.*
   the heavens open If **the heavens open**, it suddenly starts
raining very heavily. ❑ *The match had just begun when the
heavens open and play was suspended.*
   EXCLAM (*spoken, feelings*) You say '**Good heavens!**' or
'**Heavens!**' to express surprise or to emphasize that you
agree or disagree with someone. ❑ *Good Heavens! That
explains a lot!*
   ✦ **for heaven's sake** → see **sake**; **thank heavens** → see **thank**

H

heavy ♦♦◇ /'hevi/ ADJ, NOUN

ADJ (**heavier, heaviest**) **1** Something that is **heavy** weighs a lot. ❑ *These scissors are awfully heavy.* **2** You use **heavy** to ask or talk about how much someone or something weighs. ❑ *How heavy are you?* **3** **Heavy** means great in amount, degree, or intensity. ❑ *Heavy fighting has been going on.* ❑ *He worried about her heavy drinking.* **4** A **heavy** meal is large in amount and often difficult to digest. = filling ❑ *He had been feeling drowsy, the effect of an unusually heavy meal.* **5** [V-LINK + heavy 'with' N] (*literary*) Something that is **heavy with** things is full of them or loaded with them. = laden ❑ *The air is heavy with moisture.* **6** If a person's breathing is **heavy**, it is very loud and deep. ❑ *Her breathing became slow and heavy.* **7** [heavy + N] A **heavy** movement or action is done with a lot of force or pressure. ❑ *a heavy blow on the back of the skull* **8** [heavy + N] A **heavy** machine or piece of military equipment is very large and very powerful. ❑ *government militia backed by tanks and heavy artillery* **9** If you describe a period of time or a schedule as **heavy**, you mean it involves a lot of work. = busy ❑ *It's been a heavy day and I'm tired.* **10** **Heavy** work requires a lot of strength or energy. ❑ *The business is thriving and Philippa employs two full-timers for the heavy work.* **11** [V-LINK + heavy 'on' N] If you say that something is **heavy on** another thing, you mean that it uses a lot of that thing or too much of that thing. ❑ *Tanks are heavy on fuel, destructive to roads and difficult to park.* **12** Air or weather that is **heavy** is unpleasantly still, hot, and damp. = oppressive ❑ *The outside air was heavy and moist and sultry.* **13** (*informal*) A situation that is **heavy** is serious and difficult to cope with. = serious ❑ *I don't want any more of that heavy stuff.*

NOUN [c] (**heavies**) (*informal*) A **heavy** is a large strong man who is employed to protect a person or place, often by using violence. You can also use **heavy** to refer to a male character who represents such a man in a film or play. ❑ *They had employed heavies to evict squatters from neighbouring sites.* ❑ *In 1943, he received his first role as a heavy in 'Double Indemnity'.*

heavi·ness /'hevinəs/ NOUN [u] **1** *a sensation of warmth and heaviness in the muscles* **2** *the heaviness of the blood loss*

heavi·ly /'hevɪli/ ADV **1** *It has been raining heavily all day.* **2** [heavily after V] ❑ *She sank back on the pillow and closed her eyes, breathing heavily as if asleep.* **3** [heavily after V] ❑ *I sat down heavily on the ground beside the road.*

heavy·weight /'heviweɪt/ NOUN [c] (**heavyweights**) **1** A **heavyweight** is a boxer weighing more than 175 pounds and therefore in the heaviest class. **2** If you refer to a person or organization as a **heavyweight**, you mean that they have a lot of influence, experience, and importance in a particular field, subject, or activity. ❑ *He was a political heavyweight.*

⊙**hec·tare** /'hekteə/ NOUN [c] (**hectares**) A **hectare** is a measurement of an area of land which is equal to 10,000 square metres, or 2.471 acres. ❑ *hundreds of hectares of farmland* ❑ *a small strip of twelve hectares stretching from the road to the shore*

hec·tic /'hektɪk/ ADJ A **hectic** situation is one that is very busy and involves a lot of rushed activity. = busy ❑ *Despite his hectic work schedule, Benny has rarely suffered poor health.*

hedge /hedʒ/ NOUN, VERB

NOUN [c] (**hedges**) **1** A **hedge** is a row of bushes or small trees, usually along the edge of a lawn, garden, field, or road. **2** Something that is a **hedge against** something unpleasant will protect you from its effects. ❑ *Gold is traditionally a hedge against inflation.*

VERB [i] (**hedges, hedging, hedged**) If you **hedge against** something unpleasant or unwanted that might affect you, especially losing money, you do something which will protect you from it. ❑ *You can hedge against illness with insurance.*

PHRASE **hedge one's bets** If you **hedge** your **bets**, you reduce the risk of losing a lot by supporting more than one person or thing in a situation where they are opposed to each other. ❑ *The company tried to hedge its bets by diversifying into other fields.*

heed /hi:d/ VERB, NOUN

VERB [T] (**heeds, heeding, heeded**) (*formal*) If you **heed** someone's advice or warning, you pay attention to it and do what they suggest. ❑ *But few at the conference in London last week heeded his warning.*

NOUN

PHRASE **take heed** or **pay heed** (*formal*) If you **take heed** of what someone says or if you **pay heed** to them, you pay attention to them and consider carefully what they say. ❑ *But what if the government takes no heed?*

heel /hi:l/ NOUN

NOUN [c, PL] (**heels**) **1** [c] Your **heel** is the back part of your foot, just below your ankle. ❑ *He had an operation on his heel last week.* **2** [c] The **heel** of a shoe is the raised part on the bottom at the back. ❑ *the shoes with the high heels* **3** [PL] **Heels** are women's shoes that are raised very high at the back. ❑ *She was dressed in heels and a clingy dress.*

PHRASES **dig one's heels in** If you **dig** your **heels in** or **dig in** your **heels**, you refuse to do something such as change your opinions or plans, especially when someone is trying very hard to make you do so. ❑ *It was really the British who, by digging their heels in, prevented any last-minute deal.*

hard on the heels of or **hot on the heels of** If you say that one event follows **hard on the heels of** another or **hot on the heels of** another, you mean that one happens very quickly or immediately after another. ❑ *Unfortunately, bad news has come hard on the heels of good.*

hot on someone's heels (*emphasis*) If you say that someone is **hot on** your **heels**, you are emphasizing that they are chasing you and are not very far behind you. ❑ *They sped through the southwest with the law hot on their heels.*

✦ **drag your heels** → see **drag**; **head over heels** → see **head**

⊙**height** ♦◇◇ /haɪt/ NOUN [c, u, SING, PL] (**heights**) **1** [c, u] The **height** of a person or thing is their size or length from the bottom to the top. ❑ *Her weight is about normal for her height.* ❑ *I am 5'6" in height.* ❑ *The tree can grow to a height of 7 metres.* ❑ *He was a man of medium height.* **2** [u] **Height** is the quality of being tall. ❑ *She admits that her height is intimidating for some men.* **3** [c, u] A particular **height** is the distance that something is above the ground or above something else mentioned. ❑ *At the speed and height at which he was moving, he was never more than half a second from disaster.* **4** [c] A **height** is a high position or place above the ground. ❑ *I'm not afraid of heights.* **5** [SING] When an activity, situation, or organization is at its **height**, it is at its most successful, powerful, or intense. = peak ❑ *At its height, the antiwar movement drew supporters from nearly every political camp.* **6** [SING] If you say that something is the **height of** a particular quality, you are emphasizing that it has that quality to the greatest degree possible. ❑ *The hip-hugging black and white polka-dot dress was the height of fashion.* **7** [PL] If something reaches great **heights**, it becomes very extreme or intense. ❑ *the mid-1980s, when prices rose to absurd heights*

height·en /'haɪtən/ VERB [i, T] (**heightens, heightening, heightened**) If something **heightens** a feeling or if the feeling **heightens**, the feeling increases in degree or intensity. = intensify ❑ *The move has heightened tension in the state.* ❑ *Cross's interest heightened.*

heir /eə/ NOUN [c] (**heirs**) An **heir** is someone who has the right to inherit a person's money, property, or title when that person dies. ❑ *the heir to the throne*

held /held/ IRREG FORM **Held** is the past tense and past participle of **hold**.

heli·cop·ter ♦◇◇ /'helikɒptə/ NOUN [c] (**helicopters**) A **helicopter** is an aircraft with long blades on top that go around very fast. It is able to stay still in the air and to move straight upwards or downwards.

hell ♦◇◇ /hel/ NOUN, EXCLAM

NOUN [c, u] (**hells**) **1** [c] In some religions, **hell** is the place where the Devil lives, and where wicked people are sent to be punished when they die. Hell is usually imagined as being under the ground and full of flames. ❑ *I've never believed. Not in heaven or hell or God or Satan until now.* **2** [c, u] If you say that a particular situation or place is

hell, you are emphasizing that it is extremely unpleasant. = misery □ *the hell of the Siberian labour camps*

PHRASES **as hell** (*informal, emphasis*) You can use **as hell** after adjectives or some adverbs to emphasize the adjective or adverb. □ *The men might be armed, but they sure as hell weren't trained.*

for the hell of it (*informal*) If someone does something **for the hell of it**, or **just for the hell of it**, they do it for fun or for no particular reason. □ *I started shouting in German, just for the hell of it.*

from hell (*informal, emphasis*) You can use **from hell** after a noun when you are emphasizing that something or someone is extremely unpleasant or evil. □ *He's a child from hell.*

go to hell 1 (*informal, vulgar, feelings*) If you tell someone to **go to hell**, you are angrily telling them to go away and leave you alone. □ *'Well, you can go to hell!' He swept out of the room.* 2 (*informal, vulgar, emphasis*) If you say that someone can **go to hell**, you are emphasizing angrily that you do not care about them and that they will not stop you doing what you want. □ *Peter can go to hell. It's my money and I'll leave it to who I want.*

hell for leather (*informal, emphasis*) If you say that someone **is going hell for leather**, you are emphasizing that they are doing something or are moving very quickly and perhaps carelessly. □ *The first horse often goes hell for leather, hits a few fences but gets away with it.*

like hell (*informal, emphasis*) 1 Some people say **like hell** to emphasize that they strongly disagree with you or are strongly opposed to what you say. □ *'I'll go myself.'—'Like hell you will!'* 2 Some people use **like hell** to emphasize how strong an action or quality is. □ *It hurts like hell.*

all hell breaks loose (*informal, emphasis*) If you say that **all hell breaks loose**, you are emphasizing that a lot of arguing or fighting suddenly starts. □ *He had an affair, I found out and then all hell broke loose.*

a hell of a lot or **one hell of a lot** (*informal, emphasis*) 1 If you talk about **a hell of a lot** of something, or **one hell of a lot** of something, you mean that there is a large amount of it. □ *The manager took a hell of a lot of money out of the club.* 2 Some people use **a hell of** or **one hell of** to emphasize that something is very good, very bad, or very big. □ *Whatever the outcome, it's going to be one hell of a fight.*

the hell out of (*informal, emphasis*) Some people use **the hell out of** for emphasis after verbs such as 'scare', 'irritate', and 'beat'. □ *I patted the top of her head in the condescending way I knew irritated the hell out of her.*

there'll be hell to pay (*informal, emphasis*) If you say **there'll be hell to pay**, you are emphasizing that there will be serious trouble. □ *There would be hell to pay when Ferguson and Tony found out about it.*

play hell (*informal*) To **play hell with** something means to have a bad effect on it or cause great confusion. □ *The rain had played hell with business.*

the hell (*informal, vulgar, emphasis*) People sometimes use **the hell** for emphasis in questions, after words such as 'what', 'where', and 'why', often in order to express anger. □ *Where the hell have you been?*

go through hell (*informal*) If you **go through hell**, or if someone **puts** you **through hell**, you have a very difficult or unpleasant time. □ *All of you seem to have gone through hell making this record.*

hope to hell or **wish to hell** (*informal, emphasis*) If you say you **hope to hell** or **wish to hell that** something is true, you are emphasizing that you strongly hope or wish it is true. □ *I hope to hell you're right.*

what the hell (*informal, feelings*) You can say '**what the hell**' when you decide to do something in spite of the doubts that you have about it. □ *What the hell, I thought, at least it will give the lazy old man some exercise.*

to hell with (*informal, emphasis*) If you say '**to hell with**' something, you are emphasizing that you do not care about something and that it will not stop you from doing what you want to do. □ *To hell with this, I'm getting out of here.*

EXCLAM (*emphasis*) **Hell** is used by some people when they are angry or excited, or when they want to emphasize

what they are saying. This use could cause offence. □ *'Hell, no!' the doctor snapped.*

hel‧lo ♦♦◊ /heˈləʊ/ also **hallo, hullo**, CONVENTION, NOUN
CONVENTION 1 (*formulae*) You say '**Hello**' to someone when you meet them. □ *Hello, Trish. I won't shake hands, because I'm filthy.* 2 (*formulae*) You say '**Hello**' to someone at the beginning of a telephone conversation, either when you answer the phone or before you give your name or say why you are phoning. □ *A moment later, Cohen picked up the phone. 'Hello?'* 3 You can call '**Hello**' to attract someone's attention. □ *Very softly, she called out: 'Hello? Who's there?'* NOUN [c] (**hellos**) A **hello** is a greeting you use when meeting someone. □ *The salesperson greeted me with a warm hello.*

hel‧met /ˈhelmɪt/ NOUN [c] (**helmets**) A **helmet** is a hat made of a strong material which you wear to protect your head.

help ♦♦♦ /help/ VERB, NOUN
VERB [i, t] (**helps, helping, helped**) 1 [i, t] If you **help** someone, you make it easier for them to do something, for example by doing part of the work for them or by giving them advice or money. □ *He has helped to raise a lot of money.* □ *You can of course help by giving them a donation directly.* 2 [i, t] If you say that something **helps**, you mean that it makes something easier to do or get, or that it improves a situation to some extent. □ *The right style of swimsuit can help to hide, minimize, or emphasize what you want it to.* □ *Building more bypasses will help the environment by reducing pollution and traffic jams in towns and cities.* □ *If it would help, I'd be happy to take photographs.* 3 [t] If you **help** someone go somewhere or move in some way, you give them support so that they can move more easily. □ *Martin helped Tanya over the rail.* 4 [t] If you **help yourself to** something, you serve yourself or you take it for yourself. If someone tells you to **help yourself**, they are telling you politely to serve yourself anything you want or to take anything you want. □ *There's bread on the table. Help yourself.* 5 [t] (*informal*) If someone **helps themselves to** something, they steal it. □ *Two men forced the clerks to flee before helping themselves to the cash register.*

PHRASES **can't help something** If you **can't help** the way you feel or behave, you cannot control it or stop it from happening. You can also say that you **can't help yourself**. □ *I can't help feeling sorry for the poor man.*

can't help (*vagueness*) If you say you **can't help** thinking something, you are expressing your opinion in an indirect way, often because you think it seems rude. □ *I can't help feeling that this may just be another of her schemes.*

PHRASAL VERB **help out** If you **help** someone **out**, you help them by doing some work for them or by lending them some money. □ *I help out with the secretarial work.* □ *All these presents came to more money than I had, and my mother had to help me out.*

NOUN [u, SING] 1 [u] **Help** is something you do to make it easier for someone to do something, for example by doing part of the work for them or by giving them advice or money. = assistance □ *Thanks very much for your help.* 2 [SING] ['a' help, also no DET] If you say that someone or something has been a **help** or has been **some help**, you mean that they have helped you to solve a problem. □ *Thank you. You've been a great help already.* 3 [u] **Help** is action taken to rescue a person who is in danger. You shout '**Help!**' when you are in danger in order to attract someone's attention so that they can come and rescue you. □ *He was screaming for help.* 4 [u] (*computing*) In computing, **help**, or the **help** menu, is a file that gives you information and advice, for example about how to use a particular program. □ *If you get stuck, click on Help.*

PHRASE **be of help** If someone or something **is of help**, they make a situation easier or better. □ *Can I be of help to you?*

help‧er /ˈhelpə/ NOUN [c] (**helpers**) A **helper** is a person who helps another person or group with a job they are doing. = assistant □ *Phyllis and her helpers provided us with refreshment.*

help‧ful /ˈhelpfʊl/ ADJ 1 If you describe someone as

helpful, you mean that they help you in some way, such as doing part of your job for you or by giving you advice or information. ◻ *The staff in the branch office are helpful but only have limited information.* **2** If you describe information or advice as **helpful**, you mean that it is useful for you. ◻ *The catalogue includes helpful information on the different bike models available.* **3** Something that is **helpful** makes a situation more pleasant or more easy to tolerate. ◻ *It is often helpful to have your spouse in the room when major news is expected.*

help·ful·ly /ˈhelpfəli/ ADV [helpfully with v] ◻ *They had helpfully provided us with instructions on how to find the house.*

help·less /ˈhelpləs/ ADJ If you are **helpless**, you do not have the strength or power to do anything useful or to control or protect yourself. ◻ *Parents often feel helpless, knowing that all the hugs in the world won't stop the tears.*

help·less·ly /ˈhelpləsli/ ADV ◻ *Their son watched helplessly as they vanished beneath the waves.*

help·less·ness /ˈhelpləsnəs/ NOUN [u] ◻ *I remember my feelings of helplessness.*

❂**hemi·sphere** /ˈhemɪsfɪə/ NOUN [c] (**hemispheres**) **1** A **hemisphere** is one half of the earth. ◻ *the depletion of the ozone layer in the northern hemisphere* ◻ *In the southern hemisphere with its reversed patterns of seasons, these festivals are usually held at different times.* ◻ *In the northern hemisphere the sun rises in the east and sets in the west at the spring and autumn equinoxes.* **2** A **hemisphere** is one half of the brain. ◻ *In most people, the left hemisphere is bigger than the right.* ◻ *the right hemisphere, which governs creativity, spatial perception, musical and visual appreciation, and intuition*

hen /hen/ NOUN [c] (**hens**) A **hen** is a female chicken. People often keep hens in order to eat or sell their eggs.

❂**hence** /hens/ ADV (*academic word, formal*) **1** [hence CL/GROUP] You use **hence** to indicate that the statement you are about to make is a consequence of what you have just said. = therefore, thus ◻ *The trade imbalance is likely to rise again in 2007. Hence a new set of policy actions will be required soon.* ◻ *European music happens to use a scale of eight notes, hence the use of the term octave.* **2** [AMOUNT + hence] You use **hence** in expressions such as '**several years hence**' or '**six months hence**' to refer to a time in the future, especially a long time into the future. ◻ *The gases that may be warming the planet will have their main effect many years hence.*

her ◆◆◆ /hə, STRONG hɜː/ PRON, DET

> **Her** is a third person singular pronoun. **Her** is used as the object of a verb or a preposition. **Her** is also a possessive determiner.

PRON **1** [V + her, PREP + her] You use **her** to refer to a woman, girl, or female animal. ◻ *I went in the room and told her I had something to say to her.* **2** [V + her, PREP + her] In written English, **her** is sometimes used to refer to a person without saying whether that person is a man or a woman. Some people dislike this use and prefer to use 'him or her' or 'them'. ◻ *Talk to your baby, play games, and show her how much you enjoy her company.* **3** [V + her, PREP + her] (*formal, written*) **Her** is sometimes used to refer to a country or nation. **4** [V + her, PREP + her] People sometimes use **her** to refer to a car, machine, or ship. ◻ *Kemp got out of his truck. 'Just fill her up, thanks.'*

DET **1** **Her** means belonging or relating to a woman, girl, or female animal. ◻ *Liz travelled around the world for a year with her boyfriend James.* **2** In written English, **her** is sometimes used to refer to things belonging or relating to a person without saying whether that person is a man or a woman. Some people dislike this use and prefer to use 'his or her' or 'their'. ◻ *The non-drinking, non-smoking model should do nothing to risk her reputation.* **3** **Her** is sometimes used to mean belonging or relating to a country or nation. ◻ *America and her partners are helping to rebuild roads and bridges and buildings.* **4** People sometimes use **her** when referring to things relating to a car, machine, or ship. ◻ *This dramatic photograph was taken from Carpathia's deck by one of her passengers.*

her·ald /ˈherəld/ VERB, NOUN

VERB [T] (**heralds**, **heralding**, **heralded**) (*formal*)

1 Something that **heralds** a future event or situation is a sign that it is going to happen or appear. ◻ *the sultry evening that heralded the end of the baking hot summer* **2** If an important event or action **is heralded by** people, announcements are made about it so that it is publicly known and expected. ◻ *Janet Jackson's new album has been heralded by a massive media campaign.*

NOUN [c] (**heralds**) (*formal*) Something that is a **herald of** a future event or situation is a sign that it is going to happen or appear. ◻ *I welcome the report as a herald of more freedom.*

herb /hɜːb, AmE ɜːb/ NOUN [c] (**herbs**) A **herb** is a plant whose leaves are used in cooking to add flavour to food, or as a medicine. ◻ *beautiful, fragrant herbs such as basil and coriander*

herb·al /ˈhɜːbəl, AmE ˈɜːb-/ ADJ [herbal + N] **Herbal** means made from or using herbs. ◻ *herbal remedies for colds*

❂**her·bi·vore** /ˈhɜːbɪvɔː, AmE ˈɜːb-/ NOUN [c] (**herbivores**) (*technical*) A **herbivore** is an animal that only eats plants. ◻ *These are found in both herbivores and omnivores.* ◻ *In herbivores the stomach has several chambers.*

❂**herbivorous** /hɜːˈbɪvərəs/ ADJ (*technical*) **Herbivorous** animals only eat plants. ◻ *Mammoths were herbivorous mammals.* ◻ *It comes from a group of long-necked herbivorous dinosaurs, the sauropods.*

herd /hɜːd/ NOUN, VERB

NOUN [c, SING] (**herds**) **1** [c] A **herd** is a large group of animals of one kind that live together. ◻ *Chobe is also renowned for its large herds of elephant and buffalo.* **2** [SING] If you say that someone has joined **the herd** or follows **the herd**, you are criticizing them because you think that they behave just like everyone else and do not think for themselves. = pack ◻ *They are individuals; they will not follow the herd.*

VERB [T] (**herds**, **herding**, **herded**) **1** If you **herd** people somewhere, you make them move there in a group. ◻ *He began to herd the prisoners out.* **2** If you **herd** animals, you make them move along as a group. ◻ *Stefano used a motorcycle to herd the sheep.*

here ◆◆◆ /hɪə/ ADV

ADV **1** You use **here** when you are referring to the place where you are. ◻ *I'm here all by myself and I know I'm going to get lost.* ◻ *Well, I can't stand here chatting all day.* **2** You use **here** when you are pointing towards a place that is near you, in order to draw someone else's attention to it. ◻ *if you will just sign here* **3** You use **here** in order to indicate that the person or thing that you are talking about is near you or is being held by you. ◻ *My friend here writes for radio.* **4** ['be' here + to-INF] If you say that you are **here to** do something, that is your role or function. ◻ *I'm here to help you.* **5** You use **here** in order to draw attention to something or someone who has just arrived in the place where you are, or to draw attention to the place you have just arrived at. ◻ *'Here's the taxi,' she said politely.* **6** You use **here** to refer to a particular point or stage of a situation or subject that you have come to or that you are dealing with. ◻ *It's here that we come up against the difference of approach.* **7** You use **here** to refer to a period of time, a situation, or an event that is present or happening now. ◻ *Economic recovery is here.* **8** [here 'be' N/WH] You use **here** at the beginning of a sentence in order to draw attention to something or to introduce something. ◻ *Now here's what I want you to do.* **9** [here 'be' N] You use **here** when you are offering or giving something to someone. ◻ *Here's your coffee, just the way you like it.* ◻ *Here are some letters I want you to sign.*

PHRASES **here we go again** (*informal*) You use expressions such as '**Here we go**' and '**Here we go**' in order to indicate that something is happening again in the way that you expected, especially something unpleasant. ◻ *'Police! Open up!'—'Oh well,' I thought, 'here we go.'*

here and now (*emphasis*) You use **here and now** to emphasize that something is happening at the present time, rather than in the future or past, or that you would like it to happen at the present time. ◻ *I'm a practising GP trying to help people here and now.*

here and there If something happens **here and there**, it happens in several different places. ❏ *I do a bit of teaching here and there.*

CONVENTIONS **here we are** You say 'Here we are' when you have just found something that you have been looking for. ❏ *I rummaged through the drawers and came up with Amanda's folder. 'Here we are.'*

here goes You say 'Here goes' when you are about to do or say something difficult or unpleasant. ❏ *Dr Culver nervously muttered 'Here goes', and gave the little girl an injection.*

here's to something You use expressions such as 'Here's to us' and 'Here's to your new job' before drinking a toast in order to wish someone success or happiness. ❏ *He raised his glass. 'Here's to neighbours.'*

✪**he·red·i·tary** /hɪˈredɪtri/ ADJ **1** A hereditary characteristic or illness is passed on to a child from its parents before it is born. = genetic, inherited ❏ *Cystic fibrosis is the commonest fatal hereditary disease.* ❏ *In men, hair loss is hereditary.* **2** A title or position in society that is **hereditary** is one that is passed on as a right from parent to child. ❏ *The position of the head of state is hereditary.*

✪**he·red·i·ty** /hɪˈredɪti/ NOUN [U] **Heredity** is the process by which features and characteristics are passed on from parents to their children before the children are born. = genetics ❏ *Heredity is not a factor in causing the cancer.* ❏ *the view that heredity determines intelligence*

✪**her·it·age** /ˈherɪtɪdʒ/ NOUN [C, U] (**heritages**) A country's **heritage** is all the qualities, traditions, or features of life there that have continued over many years and have been passed on from one generation to another. ❏ *The historic building is as much part of our heritage as the paintings.* ❏ *the rich heritage of Russian folk music*

hero ♦◇◇ /ˈhɪərəʊ/ NOUN [C] (**heroes**) **1** The **hero** of a book, play, film, or story is the main male character, who usually has good qualities. = protagonist ❏ *The hero of Doctor Zhivago dies in 1929.* **2** A **hero** is someone, especially a man, who has done something brave, new, or good, and who is therefore greatly admired by a lot of people. ❏ *He called Mr Mandela a hero who had inspired millions.* **3** If you describe someone as your **hero**, you mean that you admire them a great deal, usually because of a particular quality or skill that they have. = idol ❏ *My boyhood hero was Kit Carson.*

he·ro·ic /hɪˈrəʊɪk/ ADJ, NOUN
ADJ **1** If you describe a person or their actions as **heroic**, you admire them because they show extreme bravery. = courageous ❏ *His heroic deeds were celebrated in every corner of India.* **2** If you describe an action or event as **heroic**, you admire it because it involves great effort or determination to succeed. ❏ *The company has made heroic efforts at cost reduction.* **3** **Heroic** means being or relating to the hero or heroine of a story. ❏ *the book's central, heroic figure*
NOUN [PL] (**heroics**) **1** **Heroics** are actions involving bravery, courage, or determination. ❏ *the man whose aerial heroics helped save the helicopter pilot* **2** (spoken, disapproval) If you describe someone's actions or plans as **heroics**, you think that they are foolish or dangerous because they are too difficult or brave for the situation in which they occur. ❏ *He said his advice was: 'No heroics, stay within the law.'*
he·roi·cal·ly /hɪˈrəʊɪkli/ ADV **1** [heroically with v] ❏ *He had acted heroically during the liner's evacuation.* **2** *Single parents cope heroically in doing the job of two people.*

hero·in /ˈherəʊɪn/ NOUN [U] **Heroin** is a powerful drug which some people take for pleasure, but which they can become addicted to.

hero·ine /ˈherəʊɪn/ NOUN [C] (**heroines**) **1** The **heroine** of a book, play, film, or story is the main female character, who usually has good qualities. = protagonist ❏ *The heroine is a senior TV executive.* **2** A **heroine** is a woman who has done something brave, new, or good, and who is therefore greatly admired by a lot of people. ❏ *The national heroine of the day was Xing Fen, winner of the first gold medal of the Games.* **3** If you describe a woman as your **heroine**, you mean that you admire her greatly, usually because of a particular quality or skill that she has. = idol ❏ *My heroine was Elizabeth Taylor.*

hero·ism /ˈherəʊɪzəm/ NOUN [U] **Heroism** is great courage and bravery. ❏ *individual acts of heroism*

hers /hɜːz/ PRON

> **Hers** is a third person possessive pronoun.

1 You use **hers** to indicate that something belongs or relates to a woman, girl, or female animal. ❏ *His hand as it shook hers was warm and firm.* ❏ *Professor Camm was a great friend of hers.* **2** In written English, **hers** is sometimes used to refer to a person without saying whether that person is a man or a woman. Some people dislike this use and prefer to use 'his or hers' or 'theirs'. ❏ *The author can report other people's results which more or less agree with hers.*

her·self ♦♦♦ /həˈself/ PRON

> **Herself** is a third person singular reflexive pronoun. **Herself** is used when the object of a verb or preposition refers to the same person as the subject of the verb, except in meaning 3.

1 [V + herself, PREP + herself] You use **herself** to refer to a woman, girl, or female animal. ❏ *She let herself out of the room.* ❏ *Jennifer believes she will move out on her own when she is financially able to support herself.* **2** In written English, **herself** is sometimes used to refer to a person without saying whether that person is a man or a woman. Some people dislike this use and prefer to use 'himself or herself' or 'themselves'. ❏ *How can anyone believe stories for which she feels herself to be in no way responsible?* **3** You use **herself** to emphasize the person or thing that you are referring to. **Herself** is sometimes used instead of 'her' as the object of a verb or preposition. ❏ *She herself was not a keen gardener.*

hesi·tant /ˈhezɪtənt/ ADJ If you are **hesitant about** doing something, you do not do it quickly or immediately, usually because you are uncertain, embarrassed, or worried. ❏ *She was hesitant about coming forward with her story.*
hesi·tan·cy /ˈhezɪtənsi/ NOUN [U] = reluctance ❏ *A trace of hesitancy showed in Dr Stockton's eyes.*
hesi·tant·ly /ˈhezɪtəntli/ ADV [hesitantly with v] ❏ *'Would you do me a favour?' she asked hesitantly.*

✪**hesi·tate** /ˈhezɪteɪt/ VERB [I, T] (**hesitates**, **hesitating**, **hesitated**) **1** [I] If you **hesitate**, you do not speak or act for a short time, usually because you are uncertain, embarrassed, or worried about what you are going to say or do. ❏ *The telephone rang. Catherine hesitated, debating whether to answer it.* ❏ *She hesitated for a while and then she said 'Yes'.* **2** [T] If you **hesitate to** do something, you delay doing it or are unwilling to do it, usually because you are not certain it would be right. If you do not **hesitate to** do something, you do it immediately. ❏ *Some parents hesitate to take these steps because they suspect that their child is exaggerating.* ❏ *I hesitate to criticize the referee because I thought he was generally good.* ❏ *I wouldn't hesitate to talk to them.* **3** [T] You can use **hesitate** in expressions such as **'don't hesitate to call me'** or **'don't hesitate to contact us'** when you are telling someone that they should do something as soon as it needs to be done and should not worry about disturbing other people. ❏ *In the event of difficulties, please do not hesitate to contact our Customer Service Department.*

✪**hesi·ta·tion** /ˌhezɪˈteɪʃən/ NOUN
NOUN [C, U] (**hesitations**) **1** **Hesitation** is a failure to speak or act for a short time, usually because you are uncertain, embarrassed, or worried about what you are going to say or do. = pause ❏ *Asked if he would go back, Mr Searle said after some hesitation, 'I'll have to think about that.'* ❏ *Despite some hesitations, members voted 15-0 to accept the resolution.* ❏ *Mirella approached him and, after a brief hesitation, shook his hand.* **2** **Hesitation** is an unwillingness to do something, or a delay in doing it, because you are uncertain, worried, or embarrassed about it. ❏ *He promised there would be no more hesitations in pursuing reforms.*
PHRASES **have no hesitation** (emphasis) If you say that you **have no hesitation in** doing something, you are emphasizing that you will do it immediately or willingly because you are certain that it is the right thing to do.

h

❏ *The board said it had no hesitation in unanimously rejecting the offer.*

without hesitation (*emphasis*) If you say that someone does something **without hesitation**, you are emphasizing that they do it immediately and willingly. ❏ *The great majority of players would, of course, sign the contract without hesitation.*

hetero·sex·ual /ˌhetərəʊˈsekʃʊəl/ ADJ, NOUN
ADJ **1** A **heterosexual** relationship is a sexual relationship between a man and a woman. ❏ *An increasing number of people are becoming infected with HIV through heterosexual sex.* **2** Someone who is **heterosexual** is sexually attracted to people of the opposite sex. ❏ *It doesn't matter whether people are heterosexual or homosexual.*
NOUN [c] (**heterosexuals**) A **heterosexual** is a person who is sexually attracted to people of the opposite sex. ❏ *In Denmark the age of consent is fifteen for both heterosexuals and homosexuals.*
hetero·sexu·al·ity /ˌhetərəʊsekʃuˈælɪti/ NOUN [u] ❏ *a challenge to the assumption that heterosexuality was 'normal'*

❖**hexa·gon** /ˈheksəgən, AmE -gɒn/ NOUN [c] (**hexagons**) A **hexagon** is a shape that has six straight sides. ❏ *The symmetry of the crystal is explained by the shape of water molecules, which link to form hexagons.* ❏ *As a matter of fact there are twelve pentagons and twenty hexagons.*

❖**hex·ago·nal** /hekˈsægənəl/ ADJ A **hexagonal** object or shape has six straight sides. ❏ *Each column was about half a metre in diameter, with a hexagonal or pentagonal outline.* ❏ *With triangular, square, or hexagonal tiles, it is easy to cover a floor completely.*

hey·day /ˈheɪdeɪ/ NOUN [SING] Someone's **heyday** is the time when they are most powerful, successful, or popular. ❏ *In its heyday, the studio's boast was that it had more stars than there are in heaven.*

❖**hi·ber·nate** /ˈhaɪbəneɪt/ VERB [i] (**hibernates, hibernating, hibernated**) Animals that **hibernate** spend the winter in a state like a deep sleep. ❏ *Dormice hibernate from October to May.* ❏ *Hibernating insects begin to move.*
❖**hibernation** /ˌhaɪbəˈneɪʃən/ NOUN [u] ❏ *The animals consume three times more calories to prepare for hibernation.* ❏ *The young are less likely to survive the winter hibernation.*

hid /hɪd/ IRREG FORM Hid is the past tense of **hide**.

hid·den /ˈhɪdən/ IRREG FORM, ADJ
IRREG FORM Hidden is the past participle of **hide**.
ADJ **1** Hidden facts, feelings, activities, or problems are not easy to notice or discover. ❏ *Under all the innocent fun, there are hidden dangers, especially for children.* **2** A **hidden** place is difficult to find. ❏ *As you descend, suddenly you see at last the hidden waterfall.*

hide ♦◇◇ /haɪd/ VERB, NOUN
VERB [T, i] (**hides, hiding, hid, hidden**) **1** [T] If you **hide** something or someone, you put them in a place where they cannot easily be seen or found. = conceal ❏ *He hid the bicycle in the hawthorn hedge.* **2** [i, T] If you **hide** or if you **hide yourself**, you go somewhere where you cannot easily be seen or found. ❏ *At their approach the little boy scurried and hid.* **3** [T] If you **hide** your face, you press your face against something or cover your face with something, so that people cannot see it. ❏ *She hid her face under the collar of his jacket and started to cry.* **4** [T] If you **hide** what you feel or know, you keep it a secret, so that no one knows about it. ❏ *Lee tried to hide his excitement.* **5** [T] If something **hides** an object, it covers it and prevents it from being seen. ❏ *The man's heavy moustache hid his upper lip completely.*
NOUN [c, u] (**hides**) A **hide** is the skin of a large animal such as a cow, horse, or elephant, which can be used for making leather. = skin ❏ *the process of tanning animal hides*
→ See also **hidden, hiding**

hid·eous /ˈhɪdiəs/ ADJ **1** If you say that someone or something is **hideous**, you mean that they are very ugly or unattractive. = monstrous, horrible ❏ *She saw a hideous face at the window and screamed.* **2** You can describe an event, experience, or action as **hideous** when you mean that it is very unpleasant, painful, or difficult to bear.

= horrendous ❏ *His family was subjected to a hideous attack by the gang.*

hid·ing /ˈhaɪdɪŋ/ NOUN [u] If someone is **in hiding**, they have secretly gone somewhere where they cannot be seen or found. ❏ *Gray is thought to be in hiding near the France/Italy border.*

❖**hi·er·ar·chi·cal** /haɪəˈrɑːkɪkəl/ ADJ A **hierarchical** system or organization is one in which people have different ranks or positions, depending on how important they are. ❏ *the traditional hierarchical system of military organization* ❏ *a rigidly hierarchical command structure*

❖**hi·er·ar·chy** /ˈhaɪərɑːki/ NOUN [c, u] (**hierarchies**) (*academic word*) **1** [c, u] A **hierarchy** is a system of organizing people into different ranks or levels of importance, for example in society or in a company. ❏ *Like most other American companies with a rigid hierarchy, workers and managers had strictly defined duties.* ❏ *She rose up the Tory hierarchy by the local government route.* ❏ *Even in the desert there was a kind of social hierarchy.* **2** [c] The **hierarchy** of an organization is the group of people who manage and control it. ❏ *The church hierarchy today feels the church should reflect the social and political realities of the country.*

high ♦♦♦ /haɪ/ ADJ, ADV, NOUN
ADJ (**higher, highest**) **1** Something that is **high** extends a long way from the bottom to the top when it is upright. You do not use **high** to describe people, animals, or plants. ❏ *a house with a high wall all around it* ❏ *Mount Marcy is the highest mountain in the Adirondacks.* **2** You use **high** to talk or ask about how much something upright measures from the bottom to the top. ❏ *an elegant bronze horse only nine inches high* ❏ *The grass in the yard was a foot high.* **3** If something is **high**, it is a long way above the ground, above sea level, or above a person or thing. ❏ *I looked down from the high window.* ❏ *The sun was high in the sky, blazing down on us.* **4** You can use **high** to indicate that something is great in amount, degree, or intensity. ❏ *The European country with the highest birth rate is Ireland.* ❏ *Official reports said casualties were high.* **5** [V-LINK + high 'in' N] If a food or other substance is **high in** a particular ingredient, it contains a large amount of that ingredient. ❏ *Don't indulge in rich sauces, fried food, and thick pastry as these are high in fat.* **6** If you say that something is a **high** priority or is **high on** your list, you mean that you consider it to be one of the most important things you have to do or deal with. ❏ *The party has not made the issue a high priority.* **7** [V-LINK + high 'in' N, high + N] Someone who is **high in** a particular profession or society, or has a **high** position, has a very important position and has great authority and influence. ❏ *Was there anyone particularly high in the administration who was an advocate of a different policy?* ❏ *corruption in high places* **8** If someone has a **high** reputation, or people have a **high** opinion of them, people think they are very good in some way, for example at their work. ❏ *People have such high expectations of you.* **9** If the quality or standard of something is **high**, it is extremely good. ❏ *This is high quality stuff.* **10** A **high** sound or voice is close to the top of a particular range of notes. ❏ *Her high voice really irritated Maria.* **11** If your spirits are **high**, you feel happy and excited. ❏ *Her spirits were high with the hope of seeing Nick in minutes rather than hours.* **12** [V-LINK + high] (*informal*) If someone is **high on** alcohol or drugs, they are affected by the alcoholic drink or drugs they have taken. ❏ *He was too high on drugs and alcohol to remember them.*
PHRASES **high up 1** If something is **high up**, it is a long way above the ground, above sea level, or above a person or thing. ❏ *His farm was high up in the hills.* **2** Someone who is **high up in** a profession or society has a very important position. ❏ *His cousin is somebody quite high up in the navy.*
the high 70s or **the high 80s** or **the high 90s** You can use phrases such as 'in the high 80s' to indicate that a number or level is, for example, more than 85 but not as much as 90.

high and dry (*emphasis*) If you say that you were left **high and dry**, you are emphasizing that you were left in a difficult situation and were unable to do anything about it. ❏ *Schools with better reputations will be flooded with*

applications while poorer schools will be left high and dry.
ADV (**higher, highest**) **1** [high after v] If something is piled or stacked **high**, it forms an upright shape that extends a long way from the bottom to the top. □ *wagons packed high with bureaus, bedding, and cooking pots* **2** [high after v] If something moves up **high**, it moves a long way above the ground, above sea level, or above a person or thing. □ *being able to run faster or jump higher than other people* **3** [high after v] You can use **high** to indicate a great increase in amount, degree, or intensity. □ *He expects the unemployment figures to rise even higher in coming months.* **4** [high after v] If you aim **high**, you try to obtain or to achieve the best that you can. □ *You should not be afraid to aim high in the quest for an improvement in your income.*
PHRASE **look high and low** (*emphasis*) If you say that you **looked high and low** for something, you are emphasizing that you looked for it in every place that you could think of. □ *I rambled around the apartment looking high and low for an aspirin or painkiller.*
NOUN [c] (**highs**) **1** [oft high 'of' AMOUNT] If something reaches a **high of** a particular amount or degree, that is the greatest it has ever been. □ *Traffic from Jordan to Iraq is down to a dozen loaded trucks a day, compared with a high of 200 a day.* **2** (*informal*) A **high** is a feeling or mood of great excitement or happiness. □ *'I'm still on a high,' she said after the show.*
PHRASES **on high** If you say that something came from **on high**, you mean that it came from a person or place of great authority. □ *Orders had come from on high that extra care was to be taken during this week.*
highs and lows If you refer to the **highs and lows** of someone's life or career, you are referring to both the successful or happy times, and the unsuccessful or bad times. □ *Here, she talks about the highs and lows of her life.*

◆**high·er edu·ca·tion** NOUN [U] **Higher education** is education at universities and colleges. □ *students in higher education* □ *The government wants more young people to go into higher education.* □ *There has been a cut in higher education funding.*

◆**high·light** ◆◇◇ /ˈhaɪlaɪt/ VERB, NOUN (*academic word*)
VERB [T] (**highlights, highlighting, highlighted**) **1** If someone or something **highlights** a point or problem, they emphasize it or make you think about it. = emphasize, draw attention to, illustrate, expose □ *Last year Collins wrote a moving ballad which highlighted the plight of the homeless.* □ *This incident highlights the care needed when disposing of unwanted plants.* □ *Once again, the 'Free Press' prefers not to highlight these facts.* **2** To **highlight** a piece of text means to mark it in a different colour, either with a special type of pen or on a computer screen. □ *Highlight the chosen area by clicking and holding down the left mouse button.*
NOUN [c] (**highlights**) The **highlights of** an event, activity, or period of time are the most interesting or exciting parts of it. □ *a match that is likely to prove one of the highlights of the tournament*

◆**high·ly** ◆◆◇ /ˈhaɪli/ ADV **1** [highly + ADJ] **Highly** is used before some adjectives to mean 'very'. = extremely, very □ *Mr Singh was a highly successful salesman.* □ *It seems highly unlikely that she ever existed.* □ *the highly controversial nuclear energy programme* **2** [highly + -ED] You use **highly** to indicate that someone has an important position in an organization or set of people. □ *a highly placed government advisor* **3** [highly + -ED] If someone is **highly** paid, they receive a large salary. □ *the 30 most highly paid athletes in the world* **4** If you think **highly** of something or someone, you think they are extremely good. □ *Daphne and Michael thought highly of the school.*

◆**high school** ◆◆◆ NOUN [C, U] (**high schools**)
1 In Britain, a **high school** is a school for children aged between eleven and eighteen. = secondary school □ *Sunderland High School* □ *My sister's going to high school next year.* **2** In the United States, a **high school** is a school for children usually aged between fourteen and eighteen. □ *an 18-year-old inner-city kid who dropped out of high school* □ *the high school football team*

> **WHICH WORD?**
> ### high school or secondary school?
> In the United States, a **high school** is a school for older pupils up to the age of 18. In Britain, the general term for a school of this type is **secondary school**.

high-speed ADJ **1** [high-speed + N] A **high-speed** vehicle or piece of equipment moves or operates very quickly. □ *Japan's high-speed trains travel a long way in a short time.* **2** [high-speed + N] A **high-speed** accident happens when the vehicles involved are travelling very fast. □ *They were killed in a high-speed crash in a tunnel in Paris.* **3** [high-speed + N] A **high-speed** Internet connection allows users to access websites very quickly. □ *Most of our customers have now upgraded to a high-speed broadband connection.*

high street (*mainly BrE; in AmE, use* **main street**) NOUN [c] (**high streets**) The **high street** of a town is the main street where most of the stores and banks are.

◆**high-tech** also **high tech, hi tech** ADJ **High-tech** activities or equipment use the most modern technology. = state-of-the-art, cutting edge; ≠ low-tech □ *such high-tech industries as computers or telecommunications* □ *New high-tech equipment allows doctors to magnify a section of your skin and project it on to a computer screen.*

high·way ◆◆◇ /ˈhaɪweɪ/ NOUN [c] (**highways**) (*mainly AmE*) A **highway** is a main road, especially one that connects towns or cities. □ *I crossed the highway, dodging the traffic.*

hi·jack /ˈhaɪdʒæk/ VERB, NOUN
VERB [T] (**hijacks, hijacking, hijacked**) **1** If someone **hijacks** a plane or other vehicle, they illegally take control of it by force while it is travelling from one place to another. □ *Two men tried to hijack a plane on a flight from Riga to Murmansk.* **2** If you say that someone **has hijacked** something, you disapprove of the way in which they have taken control of it when they had no right to do so. □ *A peaceful demonstration had been hijacked by anarchists intent on causing trouble.*
NOUN [c] (**hijacks**) A **hijack** is the act of illegally taking control of a plane or other vehicle by force while it is travelling from one place to another. □ *Every minute during the hijack seemed like a week.*
hi·jack·ing /ˈhaɪdʒækɪŋ/ NOUN [c] (**hijackings**) □ *Car hijackings are running at a rate of nearly 50 a day.*

hi·jack·er /ˈhaɪdʒækə/ NOUN [c] (**hijackers**) A **hijacker** is a person who hijacks a plane or other vehicle.

hike /haɪk/ NOUN, VERB
NOUN [c] (**hikes**) **1** A **hike** is a long walk in the country, especially one that you go on for pleasure. = walk □ *The site is reached by a 30-minute hike through dense forest.* **2** (*informal*) A **hike** is a sudden or large increase in prices, rates, taxes, or quantities. = rise, increase □ *a sudden 1.75 per cent hike in interest rates*
VERB [T, I] (**hikes, hiking, hiked**) **1** [T, I] If you **hike**, you go for a long walk in the country. □ *You could hike through the Fish River Canyon – it's entirely up to you.* **2** [T] (*informal*) To **hike** prices, rates, taxes, or quantities means to increase them suddenly or by a large amount. = raise □ *It has now been forced to hike its rates by 5.25 percent.*
PHRASAL VERB **hike up** Hike up means the same as hike VERB 2. □ *The insurers have started hiking up premiums by huge amounts.*
hik·ing /ˈhaɪkɪŋ/ NOUN [U] □ *some harder, more strenuous hiking on cliff pathways*

hi·lari·ous /hɪˈleəriəs/ ADJ If something is **hilarious**, it is extremely funny and makes you laugh a lot. □ *We thought it was hilarious when we first heard about it.*
hi·lari·ous·ly /hɪˈleəriəsli/ ADV □ *She found it hilariously funny.*

hill ◆◇◇ /hɪl/ NOUN
NOUN [c] (**hills**) A **hill** is an area of land that is higher than the land that surrounds it. □ *the shady street that led up the hill to the office building*
PHRASE **over the hill** (*informal, disapproval*) If you say that someone is **over the hill**, you are saying rudely that they are old and no longer fit, attractive, or capable of doing

useful work. ❑ *He doesn't take kindly to suggestions that he is over the hill.*

hilly /ˈhɪli/ ADJ (**hillier, hilliest**) A **hilly** area has many hills. ❑ *The areas where the fighting is taking place are hilly and densely wooded.*

him ♦♦♦ /hɪm/ PRON

> **Him** is a third person singular pronoun. **Him** is used as the object of a verb or a preposition.

1 [V + him, PREP + him] You use **him** to refer to a man, boy, or male animal. ❑ *John's aunt died suddenly and left him a surprisingly large sum.* ❑ *Is Sam there? Let me talk to him.* **2** [V + him, PREP + him] In written English, **him** is sometimes used to refer to a person without saying whether that person is a man or a woman. Some people dislike this use and prefer to use 'him or her' or 'them'. ❑ *If the child encounters 'hear', we should show him that this is the base word in 'hearing' and 'hears'.*

him·self ♦♦♦ /hɪmˈself/ PRON

> **Himself** is a third person singular reflexive pronoun. **Himself** is used when the object of a verb or preposition refers to the same person as the subject of the verb, except in meaning 3.

1 [V + himself, PREP + himself] You use **himself** to refer to a man, boy, or male animal. ❑ *He poured himself a whisky and sat down in the chair.* ❑ *William went away muttering to himself.* **2** [V + himself, PREP + himself] In written English, **himself** is sometimes used to refer to a person without saying whether that person is a man or a woman. Some people dislike this use and prefer to use 'himself or herself' or 'themselves'. ❑ *There is nothing more dangerous than someone who thinks of himself as a victim.* **3** You use **himself** to emphasize the person or thing that you are referring to. **Himself** is sometimes used instead of 'him' as the object of a verb or preposition. ❑ *The president himself is on a visit to Beijing.*

hin·der /ˈhɪndə/ VERB [T] (**hinders, hindering, hindered**) **1** If something **hinders** you, it makes it more difficult for you to do something or make progress. ❑ *Further investigation was hindered by the loss of all documentation on the case.* **2** If something **hinders** your movement, it makes it difficult for you to move forward or move around. ❑ *A thigh injury increasingly hindered her mobility.*

✪hind·sight /ˈhaɪndsaɪt/ NOUN [U] **Hindsight** is the ability to understand and realize something about an event after it has happened, although you did not understand or realize it at the time. ❑ *With hindsight, we'd all do things differently.* ❑ *With hindsight it can be seen as an important first stage in the controlled evolution of democracy.* ❑ *In hindsight, the benefits of Internet advertising were grossly exaggerated.*

hinge /hɪndʒ/ NOUN
NOUN [C] (**hinges**) A **hinge** is a piece of metal, wood, or plastic that is used to join a door to its frame or to join two things together so that one of them can swing freely. ❑ *The top swung open on well-oiled hinges.*
PHRASAL VERB **hinge on** (**hinges, hinging, hinged**) Something that **hinges on** one thing or event depends entirely on it. ❑ *The plan hinges on a deal being struck with a new company.*

hint ♦♢♢ /hɪnt/ NOUN, VERB
NOUN [C, SING] (**hints**) **1** [C] A **hint** is a suggestion about something that is made in an indirect way. ❑ *I'd dropped a hint about having an exhibition of his work up here.* **2** [C] A **hint** is a helpful piece of advice, usually about how to do something. = tip ❑ *Here are some helpful hints to make your journey easier.* **3** [SING] A **hint** of something is a very small amount of it. = trace ❑ *She added only a hint of vermouth to the gin.*
PHRASE **take a hint** If you **take a hint**, you understand something that is suggested to you indirectly. ❑ *'I think I hear the telephone ringing.'—'Okay, I can take a hint.'*
VERB [I] (**hints, hinting, hinted**) If you **hint at** something, you suggest it in an indirect way. ❑ *She hinted at the possibility of a treat of some sort.*

hip ♦♢♢ /hɪp/ NOUN, ADJ, EXCLAM
NOUN [C] (**hips**) **1** Your **hips** are the two areas at the sides

of your body between the tops of your legs and your waist. ❑ *Tracey put her hands on her hips and sighed.* **2** You refer to the bones between the tops of your legs and your waist as your **hips**. ❑ *Eventually, surgeons replaced both hips and both shoulders.*
PHRASE **shoot from the hip** If you say that someone **shoots from the hip**, you mean that they react to situations or give their opinion very quickly, without stopping to think. ❑ *Judges don't have to shoot from the hip. They have the leisure to think, to decide.*
ADJ (*informal*) If you say that someone is **hip**, you mean that they are very modern and follow all the latest fashions, for example in clothes and ideas. = trendy, cool ❑ *a hip young character with tight-cropped blond hair and stylish glasses*
EXCLAM If a large group of people want to show their appreciation or approval of someone, one of them says '**Hip hip**' and they all shout '**hooray**'.

hire ♦♢♢ /haɪə/ VERB, NOUN
VERB [I, T] (**hires, hiring, hired**) **1** [I, T] If you **hire** someone, you employ them or pay them to do a particular job for you. ❑ *Sixteen of the contestants have hired lawyers and are suing the organizers.* ❑ *He will be in charge of all hiring and firing at PHA.* **2** [T] (*mainly BrE; in AmE, usually use* **rent**) If you **hire** something, you pay money to the owner so that you can use it for a period of time.
PHRASAL VERB **hire out** If you **hire out** a person's services, you allow them to be used in return for payment. ❑ *employment agencies which hire out personnel to foreign companies*
NOUN [U] (*mainly BrE; in AmE, usually use* **rental**) You use **hire** to refer to the activity or business of hiring something.
PHRASE **for hire** (*mainly BrE; in AmE, usually use* **for rent**) If something is **for hire**, it is available for you to hire.

WHICH WORD?
hire, rent, or let?

Do not confuse **hire**, **rent**, and **let**.

If you pay to use something for a short period of time, you can say that you **hire** it or **rent** it. **Hire** is more common in British English and **rent** is more common in American English.

❑ We **hired** a car and drove across the island.

❑ He **rented** a car for the weekend.

If you pay regularly in order to use something such as a house for a long period, you say that you **rent** it.

❑ She **rents** the house with three other women.

If someone allows you to live in a house that they own in return for money, you say that the person who owns it **lets** it to you or **lets** it out to you. This usage is more common in British English. In American English, you use **rent** and **rent out**.

❑ The cottage was **let** to an actress from London.

❑ I couldn't sell the London flat, so I **let** it out.

❑ The house was **rented out** to a farmer.

his ♦♦♦ /hɪz/ DET, PRON

> **His** is a third person singular possessive determiner. **His** is also a possessive pronoun.

DET You use **his** to indicate that something belongs or relates to a man, boy, or male animal. ❑ *Brian splashed water on his face, then brushed his teeth.* ❑ *He spent a large part of his career in Hollywood.*
PRON You use **his** to indicate that something belongs or relates to a man, boy, or male animal. ❑ *Staff say the decision was his.*

hiss /hɪs/ VERB, NOUN
VERB [I] (**hisses, hissing, hissed**) **1** To **hiss** means to make a sound like a long 's'. ❑ *The tyres of Lenny's bike hissed over the wet road as he slowed down.* ❑ *My cat hissed when I stepped on its tail.* **2** If people **hiss at** someone such as a performer or a person making a speech, they express their disapproval or dislike of that person by making long loud 's' sounds. ❑ *One had to listen hard to catch the words of the*

president's speech as the delegates booed and hissed.
NOUN [c] (**hisses**) **1** A **hiss** is a sound like a long 's'. ❑ *the hiss of water running into the burned pan* **2** A **hiss** is a long loud 's' sound made by people expressing their disapproval or dislike of someone such as a performer or a person making a speech. = hissing ❑ *She was greeted with boos and hisses.*

hiss·ing /ˈhɪsɪŋ/ NOUN [u] ❑ *a silence broken only by a steady hissing from above my head*

✪ **his·to·rian** /hɪˈstɔːriən/ NOUN [c] (**historians**) A **historian** is a person who specializes in the study of history, and who writes books and articles about it. ❑ *Some historians believe the famine continued until 1851.*

✪ **his·tor·ic** ◆◇◇ /hɪˈstɒrɪk, AmE -ˈtɔːr-/ ADJ Something that is **historic** is important in history, or likely to be considered important at some time in the future. ❑ *the historic changes in Eastern Europe* ❑ *The opening of the Scottish Parliament was a historic moment.* ❑ *a fourth historic election victory*

✪ **his·tori·cal** ◆◇◇ /hɪˈstɒrɪkəl, AmE -ˈtɔːr-/ ADJ **1** [historical + N] **Historical** people, situations, or things existed in the past and are considered to be a part of history. = ancient ❑ *an important historical figure* ❑ *the historical impact of Western capitalism on the world* ❑ *In Buda, several historical monuments can be seen.* **2** [historical + N] **Historical** books, films, or pictures describe or represent people, situations, or things that existed in the past. ❑ *He is writing a historical novel about nineteenth-century France.* **3** [historical + N] **Historical** information, research, and discussion is related to the study of history. ❑ *historical records* ❑ *modern historical research*

his·tori·cal·ly /hɪˈstɒrɪkli, AmE -ˈtɔːr-/ ADV ❑ *Historically, royal marriages have been cold, calculating affairs.*

✪ **his·to·ry** ◆◆◆ /ˈhɪstəri/ NOUN **NOUN** [u, c] (**histories**) **1** [u] You can refer to the events of the past as **history**. You can also refer to the past events which concern a particular topic or place as its **history**. ❑ *The Catholic Church has played a prominent role throughout Polish history.* ❑ *the most evil mass killer in history* ❑ *religious history* **2** [u] **History** is a subject studied in schools, colleges, and universities that deals with events that have happened in the past. ❑ *a lecturer in history at Birmingham University* **3** [c] A **history** is an account of events that have happened in the past. ❑ *his magnificent history of broadcasting in Canada* **4** [c] If a person or a place has **a history of** something, it has been very common or has happened frequently in their past. ❑ *He had a history of drinking problems.* **5** [c] Someone's **history** is the set of facts that are known about their past. ❑ *He couldn't get a new job because of his medical history.*

PHRASES **make history** Someone who **makes history** does something that is considered to be important and significant in the development of the world or of a particular society. ❑ *Willy Brandt made history by visiting East Germany in 1970.*

go down in history If someone or something **goes down in history**, people in the future remember them because of particular actions that they have done or because of particular events that have happened. ❑ *Bradley will go down in history as Los Angeles' longest serving mayor.*

the rest is history If you are telling someone about an event and say **the rest is history**, you mean that you do not need to tell them what happened next because everyone knows about it already. ❑ *We met in college, the rest is history.*

hit ◆◆◆ /hɪt/ VERB, NOUN **VERB** [T] (**hits, hitting, hit**) **1** If you **hit** someone or something, you deliberately touch them with a lot of force, with your hand or an object held in your hand. = strike ❑ *Find the exact grip that allows you to hit the ball hard.* **2** When one thing **hits** another, it touches it with a lot of force. = strike ❑ *The car had apparently hit a traffic sign before skidding out of control.* **3** If a bomb or missile **hits** its target, it reaches it. ❑ *multiple-warhead missiles that could hit many targets at a time* **4** (journalism) If something **hits** a person, place, or thing, it affects them very badly. ❑ *The plan to charge motorists to use the freeway is going to hit*

me hard. ❑ *About two hundred people died in the earthquake which hit northern Peru.* **5** When a feeling or an idea **hits** you, it suddenly affects you or comes into your mind. ❑ *It hit me that I had a choice.* **6** (journalism) If you **hit** a particular high or low point on a scale of something such as success or health, you reach it. ❑ *He admits to having hit the lowest point in his life.*

PHRASE **hit it off** (informal) If two people **hit it off**, they like each other and become friendly as soon as they meet. ❑ *Dad and Walter hit it off straight away.*

PHRASAL VERB **hit on** or **hit upon** **1** If you **hit on** an idea or a solution to a problem, or **hit upon** it, you think of it. = stumble on ❑ *After running through the numbers in every possible combination, we finally hit on a solution.* **2** (informal) If someone **hits on** you, they speak or behave in a way that shows they want to have a sexual relationship with you. ❑ *She was hitting on me and I was surprised and flattered.*

NOUN [c] (**hits**) **1** A **hit** is when a bomb or missile reaches its target. ❑ *First a house took a direct hit and then the rocket exploded.* **2** If a recording, film, or play is a **hit**, it is very popular and successful. ❑ *The song became a massive hit in 1945.* **3** (computing) A **hit** is a single visit to a website. ❑ *Our small company has had 78,000 hits on its Internet pages.* **4** If someone who is searching for information on the Internet gets a **hit**, they find a website where there is that information.

✦ hit the headlines → see headline; hit home → see home; hit the nail on the head → see nail; hit the roof → see roof

hitch /hɪtʃ/ NOUN, VERB **NOUN** [c] (**hitches**) A **hitch** is a slight problem or difficulty which causes a short delay. = snag ❑ *After some technical hitches the show finally got under way.*

VERB [I, T] (**hitches, hitching, hitched**) **1** [I, T] (informal) If you **hitch**, **hitch** a lift, or **hitch** a ride, you hitchhike. ❑ *There was no garage in sight, so I hitched a lift into town.* **2** [T] If you **hitch** something **to** something else, you hook it or fasten it there. ❑ *Last night we hitched the horse to the cart and moved here.*

hitch·hike /ˈhɪtʃhaɪk/ VERB [I] (**hitchhikes, hitchhiking, hitchhiked**) If you **hitchhike**, you travel by getting lifts from passing vehicles without paying. ❑ *Neff hitchhiked to Newcastle during his Christmas holiday.*

hitch·hiker /ˈhɪtʃhaɪkə/ NOUN [c] (**hitchhikers**) ❑ *On my way to Vancouver one Friday night I picked up a hitchhiker.*

✪ **hi tech** → See high-tech

HIV ◆◇◇ /ˌeɪtʃ aɪ ˈviː/ NOUN **NOUN** [u] **HIV** is a virus which reduces people's resistance to illness and can cause AIDS. **HIV** is an abbreviation for 'human immunodeficiency virus'.

PHRASE **HIV positive** or **HIV negative** If someone is **HIV positive**, they are infected with the HIV virus, and may develop AIDS. If someone is **HIV negative**, they are not infected with the virus.

hive /haɪv/ NOUN [c] (**hives**) **1** A **hive** is a structure in which bees are kept, which is designed so that the beekeeper can collect the honey that they produce. **2** If you describe a place as a **hive of** activity, you approve of the fact that there is a lot of activity there or that people are busy working there. ❑ *In the morning the house was a hive of activity.*

hoax /həʊks/ NOUN [c] (**hoaxes**) A **hoax** is a trick in which someone tells people a lie, for example that there is a bomb somewhere when there is not, or that a picture is genuine when it is not. ❑ *He denied making the hoax call but was convicted after a short trial.*

hob·by /ˈhɒbi/ NOUN [c] (**hobbies**) A **hobby** is an activity that you enjoy doing in your spare time. = pastime ❑ *My hobbies are letter writing, music, photography, and tennis.*

hock·ey /ˈhɒki/ NOUN [u] **1** (mainly BrE; in AmE, usually use **field hockey**) **Hockey** is an outdoor game played between two teams of 11 players who use long curved sticks to hit a small ball and try to score goals. **2** (mainly AmE; in BrE, usually use **ice hockey**) **Hockey** is a game played on ice between two teams of 11 players who use long curved sticks to hit a small rubber disc, called a puck, and try to score goals. ❑ *a new hockey arena*

h

hoist /hɔɪst/ VERB, NOUN

- VERB [T] (**hoists, hoisting, hoisted**) **1** If you **hoist** something heavy somewhere, you lift it or pull it up there. ❑ *Hoisting my suitcase on to my shoulder, I turned and headed towards my hotel.* **2** If something heavy **is hoisted** somewhere, it is lifted there using a machine such as a crane. ❑ *A twenty-foot steel pyramid is to be hoisted into position on top of the tower.* **3** If you **hoist** a flag or a sail, you pull it up to its correct position by using ropes. ❑ *A group forced their way through police cordons and hoisted their flag on top of the disputed monument.*
- NOUN [C] (**hoists**) A **hoist** is a machine for lifting heavy things. ❑ *He uses a hydraulic hoist to unload two empty barrels.*

hold ♦♦♦ /həʊld/ VERB, NOUN

> **Hold** is often used to indicate that someone or something has the particular thing, characteristic, or attitude that is mentioned. Therefore it takes most of its meaning from the word that follows it.

VERB [T, RECIP, I] (**holds, holding, held**) **1** [T] When you **hold** something, you carry or support it, using your hands or your arms. ❑ *Hold the knife at an angle.* **2** [T] When you **hold** someone, you put your arms around them, usually because you want to show them how much you like them or because you want to comfort them. ❑ *If only he would hold her close to him.* **3** [T] If you **hold** someone in a particular position, you use force to keep them in that position and stop them from moving. ❑ *He then held the man in an armlock until police arrived.* **4** [T] When you **hold** a part of your body, you put your hand on or against it, often because it hurts. ❑ *Soon she was crying bitterly about the pain and was holding her throat.* **5** [T] When you **hold** a part of your body in a particular position, you put it into that position and keep it there. ❑ *Hold your hands in front of your face.* **6** [T] If one thing **holds** another in a particular position, it keeps it in that position. ❑ *the wooden wedge which held the heavy door open* **7** [T] If one thing is used to **hold** another, it is used to store it. = store ❑ *Two knife racks hold her favourite knives.* **8** [T] If a place **holds** something, it keeps it available for reference or for future use. ❑ *The Better Business Bureau holds an enormous amount of information on any business problem.* **9** [T] If something **holds** a particular amount of something, it can contain that amount. ❑ *One CD-ROM disk can hold over 100,000 pages of text.* **10** [T] **Hold** is used with words and expressions indicating an opinion or belief, to show that someone has a particular opinion or believes that something is true. ❑ *He held firm opinions which usually conflicted with my own.* ❑ *Current thinking holds that obesity is more a medical than a psychological problem.* **11** [T] **Hold** is used with words such as 'fear' or 'mystery' to indicate someone's feelings towards something, as if those feelings were a characteristic of the thing itself. ❑ *Death doesn't hold any fear for me.* **12** [T] **Hold** is used with nouns such as 'office', 'power', and 'responsibility' to indicate that someone has a particular position of power or authority. ❑ *She has never held an elected office.* **13** [T] **Hold** is used with nouns such as 'permit', 'degree', or 'ticket' to indicate that someone has a particular document that allows them to do something. ❑ *Applicants should normally hold a good degree.* ❑ *He did not hold a firearms licence.* **14** [T] **Hold** is used with nouns such as 'party', 'meeting', 'talks', 'election', and 'trial' to indicate that people are organizing a particular activity. ❑ *The country will hold democratic elections within a year.* **15** [RECIP] **Hold** is used with nouns such as 'conversation', 'interview', and 'talks' to indicate that two or more people meet and discuss something. ❑ *The prime minister is holding consultations with his colleagues to finalize the deal.* ❑ *The engineer and his son held frequent meetings concerning technical problems.* **16** [T] **Hold** is used with nouns such as 'shares' to indicate that someone owns a particular proportion of a business. ❑ *The group said it continues to hold 1,774,687 shares in the company.* **17** [T] **Hold** is used with nouns such as 'attention' or 'interest' to indicate that what you do or say keeps someone interested or listening to you. = keep ❑ *If you want to hold someone's attention, look them directly in the eye but don't stare.* **18** If

you **hold** someone responsible, liable, or accountable for something, you will blame them if anything goes wrong. ❑ *It's impossible to hold any individual responsible.* **19** [T] If someone **holds** you in a place, they keep you there as a prisoner and do not allow you to leave. ❑ *The inside of a van was as good a place as any to hold a kidnap victim.* ❑ *Somebody is holding your wife hostage.* **20** [T] If people such as an army or a violent crowd **hold** a place, they control it by using force. ❑ *Demonstrators have been holding the square since Sunday.* **21** [I, T] If you ask someone to **hold**, or to **hold the line**, when you are answering a telephone call, you are asking them to wait for a short time, for example so that you can find the person they want to speak to. = hold on ❑ *Could you hold the line and I'll just get my pen.* **22** [T] If you **hold** telephone calls for someone, you do not allow people who phone to speak to that person, but take messages instead. ❑ *He tells his secretary to hold his calls.* **23** [I, T] If something **holds** at a particular value or level, or **is held** there, it is kept at that value or level. ❑ *OPEC production is holding at around 21.5 million barrels a day.* **24** [T] If you **hold** a sound or musical note, you continue making it. ❑ *a voice which hit and held every note with perfect ease and clarity* **25** [T] If you **hold** something such as a train or a lift, you delay it. ❑ *A spokesman defended the decision to hold the train until police arrived.* **26** [I] If an offer or invitation still **holds**, it is still available for you to accept. ❑ *Does your offer still hold?* **27** [I] If a good situation **holds**, it continues and does not get worse or fail. ❑ *Our luck couldn't hold forever.* **28** [I] If an argument or theory **holds**, it is true or valid, even after close examination. ❑ *Today, most people think that argument no longer holds.* **29** [I] If part of a structure **holds**, it does not fall or break although there is a lot of force or pressure on it. ❑ *How long would the roof hold?* **30** [I] If laws or rules **hold**, they exist and remain in force. ❑ *These laws also hold for universities.* **31** [I] (formal) If you **hold to** a promise or to high standards of behaviour, you keep that promise or continue to behave according to those standards. = stick to ❑ *Will the president be able to hold to this commitment?* **32** [T] If someone or something **holds** you **to** a promise or **to** high standards of behaviour, they make you keep that promise or those standards. ❑ *'I won't make you marry him.'—'I'll hold you to that.'*

PHRASES **hold forth** If you **hold forth on** a subject, you speak confidently and for a long time about it, especially to a group of people. ❑ *Barry was holding forth on something.*

hold your own 1 If you **hold** your **own**, you are able to resist someone who is attacking or opposing you. ❑ *The Frenchman held his own against the challenger.* **2** If you can do something well enough to **hold** your **own**, you do not appear foolish when you are compared with someone who is generally thought to be very good at it. ❑ *She can hold her own against almost any player.*

hold still If you **hold still**, you do not move. ❑ *Can't you hold still for a second?*

hold tight 1 If you **hold tight**, you put your hand around or against something in order to prevent yourself from falling over. A bus driver might say '**Hold tight!**' to you if you are standing on a bus when it is about to move. = hang on ❑ *He held tight to the rope.* **2** If you **hold tight**, you do not immediately start a course of action that you have been planning or thinking about. ❑ *The advice for individual investors is to hold tight.*

CONVENTION **hold it** If you say '**Hold it**', you are telling someone to stop what they are doing and to wait. = stop ❑ *Hold it! Don't move!*

PHRASAL VERBS **hold against** If you **hold** something **against** someone, you let their actions in the past influence your present attitude towards them and cause you to deal severely or unfairly with them. ❑ *Bernstein lost the case, but never held it against Grundy.*

hold back 1 If you **hold back** or if something **holds** you **back**, you hesitate before you do something because you are not sure whether it is the right thing to do. ❑ *The Bush administration had several reasons for holding back.* **2** To **hold** someone or something **back** means to prevent someone from doing something, or to prevent something from happening. = inhibit ❑ *Stagnation in home sales is holding back economic recovery.* **3** If you **hold** something **back**, you

H

keep it in reserve to use later. ❑ *Farmers apparently hold back produce in the hope that prices will rise.* **4** If you **hold** something **back**, you do not include it in the information you are giving about something. ❑ *You seem to be holding something back.* **5** If you **hold back** something such as tears or laughter, or if you **hold back**, you make an effort to stop yourself from showing how you feel. ❑ *She kept trying to hold back her tears.*

hold down **1** If you **hold down** a job or a place on a team, you manage to keep it. ❑ *He never could hold down a job.* **2** If you **hold** someone **down**, you keep them under control and do not allow them to have much freedom or power or many rights. ❑ *Everyone thinks there is some vast conspiracy wanting to hold down the younger generation.*

hold off **1** If you **hold off** doing something, you delay doing it or delay making a decision about it. ❑ *The hospital staff held off taking Rosenbaum in for an X-ray.* **2** If you **hold off** a challenge in a race or competition, you do not allow someone to pass you. ❑ *Between 1987 and 1990, Steffi Graf largely held off Navratilova's challenge for the crown.*

hold on or **hold onto** **1** If you **hold on**, or **hold onto** something, you keep your hand on it or around it, for example to prevent the thing from falling or to support yourself. ❑ *His right arm was extended up beside his head, still holding on to a coffee cup.* ❑ *He was struggling to hold onto a rock on the face of the cliff.* **2** If you **hold on**, you manage to achieve success or avoid failure in spite of great difficulties or opposition. ❑ *The Danes held on to defeat the Swedish side.* **3** (*spoken*) If you ask someone to **hold on**, you are asking them to wait for a short time. = hang on ❑ *The manager asked him to hold on while he investigated.*

hold out **1** If you **hold out** your hand or something you have in your hand, you move your hand away from your body, for example to shake hands with someone. ❑ *'I'm Nancy Drew,' she said, holding out her hand.* **2** If you **hold out for** something, you refuse to accept something which you do not think is good enough or large enough, and you continue to demand more. ❑ *I should have held out for a better deal.* **3** (*informal*) If you say that someone **is holding out on** you, you think that they are refusing to give you information that you want. ❑ *He had always believed that kids could sense it when you held out on them.* **4** If you **hold out**, you manage to resist an enemy or opponent in difficult circumstances and refuse to give in. ❑ *One prisoner was still holding out on the roof of the jail.* **5** If you **hold out** hope of something happening, you hope that in the future something will happen as you want it to. ❑ *He still holds out hope that they could be a family again.*

hold up **1** If you **hold up** your hand or something you have in your hand, you move it upward into a particular position and keep it there. ❑ *She held up her hand stiffly.* **2** If one thing **holds up** another, it is placed under the other thing in order to support it and prevent it from falling. ❑ *Mills have iron pillars all over the place holding up the roof.* **3** To **hold up** a person or process means to make them late or delay them. = delay ❑ *Why were you holding everyone up?* **4** **Hold up** means the same as **hold** VERB **28**. ❑ *Democrats say arguments against the bill won't hold up.* **5** If someone **holds up** a place such as a bank or a shop, they point a weapon at someone there to make them give them money or valuable goods. = rob ❑ *When his money was gone he held up a filling station with a toy gun.* **6** If you **hold up** something such as someone's behaviour, you make it known to other people, so that they can criticize or praise it. ❑ *He had always been held up as an example to the younger ones.* **7** If something such as a type of business **holds up** in difficult conditions, it stays in a reasonably good state. ❑ *Children's wear is one area that is holding up well in the recession.* **8** If an argument or theory **holds up**, it is true or valid, even after close examination. = stand up ❑ *I'm not sure if the argument holds up, but it's stimulating.*

NOUN [C, U, SING] (**holds**) **1** [C] If you have a **hold** on something, you carry or support it, using your hands or your arms. ❑ *He released his hold on the camera.* **2** [U] **Hold** is used in expressions such as **grab hold of**, **catch hold of**, and **get hold of**, to indicate that you close your hand tightly around something, for example to stop something moving or falling. ❑ *I was woken up by someone grabbing*

hold of my sleeping bag. ❑ *A doctor and a nurse caught hold of his arms.* **3** [C] A **hold** is a particular way of keeping someone in a position using your own hands, arms, or legs. ❑ *The man wrestled the Indian to the ground, locked in a hold he couldn't escape.* **4** [C] In a ship or aeroplane, a **hold** is a place where cargo or luggage is stored. ❑ *A fire had been reported in the cargo hold.* **5** [SING] If you have a **hold over** someone, you have power or control over them, for example because you know something about them you can use to threaten them or because you are in a position of authority. ❑ *He had ordered his officers to keep an exceptionally firm hold over their men.*

PHRASES **get hold of something** If you **get hold of** an object or information, you obtain it, usually after some difficulty. ❑ *It is hard to get hold of guns in this country.*

get hold of someone If you **get hold of** someone, you manage to contact them. ❑ *The only electrician we could get hold of was miles away.*

on hold If you put something **on hold**, you decide not to do it, deal with it, or change it now, but to leave it until later. ❑ *He put his retirement on hold to work 16 hours a day, seven days a week to find a solution.*

take hold If something **takes hold**, it gains complete control or influence over a person or thing. ❑ *She felt a strange excitement taking hold of her.*

✦ hold at bay → see bay; hold something in check → see check; hold the fort → see fort; hold your ground → see ground; hold someone to ransom → see ransom; hold sway → see sway

hold·er ♦♦◇ /ˈhəʊldə/ NOUN [C] (**holders**) **1** A **holder** is someone who owns or has something. ❑ *This season the club has had 73,500 season-ticket holders.* **2** A **holder** is a container in which you put an object, usually in order to protect it or to keep it in place. ❑ *a toothbrush holder*

hold·ing /ˈhəʊldɪŋ/ NOUN [U, C] (**holdings**) **1** [U] The **holding** of an activity such as a party, meeting, or election is the act of organizing it. ❑ *They also called for the holding of multi-party general elections.* **2** [C] (*business*) If you have a **holding** in a company, you own shares in it. = investment ❑ *That would increase Olympia & York's holding to 35%.*

hole ♦♦◇ /həʊl/ NOUN

NOUN [C] (**holes**) **1** A **hole** is a hollow space in something solid, with an opening on one side. ❑ *He took a shovel, dug a hole, and buried his once-prized possessions.* **2** A **hole** is an opening in something that goes right through it. ❑ *kids with holes in the knees of their jeans* **3** A **hole** is the home or hiding place of a small animal, rabbit, or other small animal. ❑ *a rabbit hole* **4** A **hole in** a law, theory, or argument is a fault or weakness that it has. ❑ *There were some holes in that theory, some unanswered questions.* **5** A **hole** is also one of the nine or eighteen sections of a golf course. ❑ *I played nine holes with Gary Carter today.*

PHRASES **in a hole** (*informal*) If you say that you are **in a hole**, you mean that you are in a difficult or embarrassing situation. ❑ *We were in a hole, but I was proud with the way we came back.*

a hole in one If you get **a hole in one** in golf, you get the golf ball into the hole with a single stroke. ❑ *All they ever dream about is getting a hole in one.*

pick holes in something (*informal*) If you **pick holes in** an argument or theory, you find weak points in it so that it is no longer valid. ❑ *He then goes on to pick holes in the article before reaching his conclusion.*

holi·day ♦♦◇ /ˈhɒlɪdeɪ/ NOUN, VERB

NOUN [C, PL, U] (**holidays**) **1** [C] (*BrE*; in *AmE*, use **vacation**) A **holiday** is a period of time during which you relax and enjoy yourself away from home. People sometimes refer to their holiday as their **holidays**. **2** [C] A **holiday** is a day when people do not go to work or school because of a religious or national celebration. ❑ *New Year's Day is a public holiday.* **3** [PL] (*BrE*; in *AmE*, use **vacation**) The **holidays** are the time when children do not have to go to school. **4** [U] (*BrE*; in *AmE*, use **vacation**) If you have a particular number of days' or weeks' **holiday**, you do not have to go to work for that number of days or weeks.

VERB [I] (**holidays, holidaying, holidayed**) (*BrE*; in *AmE*, use

vacation) If you **are holidaying** in a place away from home, you are on holiday there.
→ See also **bank holiday**

USAGE NOTE
holiday

Note that you usually use a determiner or a possessive form in front of 'holiday' or 'holidays'. Do not say, for example, 'I went to India for holidays'.
I went to India for **a holiday**.
I went to India for **my holidays**.

---

hol·low /ˈhɒləʊ/ ADJ, NOUN, VERB
ADJ 1 Something that is **hollow** has a space inside it, as opposed to being solid all the way through. ❑ *a hollow tree* **2** A surface that is **hollow** curves inwards. ❑ *He looked young, dark and sharp-featured, with hollow cheeks.* **3** If you describe a statement, situation, or person as **hollow**, you mean they have no real value, worth, or effectiveness. ❑ *Any threat to bring in the police is a hollow one.* **4** [hollow + N] If someone gives a **hollow** laugh, they laugh in a way that shows that they do not really find something amusing. ❑ *Murray Pick's hollow laugh had no mirth in it.* **5** [hollow + N] A **hollow** sound is dull and echoing. ❑ *the hollow sound of a gunshot*
NOUN [C] (**hollows**) A **hollow** is an area that is lower than the surrounding surface. ❑ *Below him the town lay warm in the hollow of the hill.*
VERB [T] (**hollows**, **hollowing**, **hollowed**) If something **is hollowed**, its surface is made to curve inwards or downwards. ❑ *The mule's back was hollowed by the weight of its burden.*
hol·low·ness /ˈhɒləʊnəs/ NOUN [U] ❑ *One month before the deadline we see the hollowness of these promises.*

holy ♦◇◇ /ˈhəʊli/ ADJ (**holier**, **holiest**) If you describe something as **holy**, you mean that it is considered to be special because it is connected with God or a particular religion. ❑ *To them, as to all Popes, this is a holy place.*

home ♦♦♦ /həʊm/ NOUN, ADV, ADJ
NOUN [C, U, SING] (**homes**) **1** [C] [oft POSS + home, also 'at' home] Someone's **home** is the house or flat where they live. ❑ *Last night they stayed at home and watched TV.* ❑ *The general divided his time between his shabby offices and his home in Hampstead.* **2** [U] You can use **home** to refer in a general way to the house, town, or country where someone lives now or where they were born, often to emphasize that they feel they belong in that place. ❑ *She gives frequent performances of her work, both at home and abroad.* ❑ *His father worked away from home for much of Jim's first five years.* **3** [C] A **home** is a large house or institution where a number of people live and are cared for, instead of living in their own houses or flats. They usually live there because they are too old or ill to take care of themselves or for their families to care for them. ❑ *It's going to be a home for disabled children.* **4** [C] You can refer to a family unit as a **home**. ❑ *She had, at any rate, provided a peaceful and loving home for Harriet.* **5** [SING] If you refer to the **home of** something, you mean the place where it began or where it is most typically found. ❑ *This southwest region of France is the home of claret.* **6** [C] If you find a **home for** something, you find a place where it can be kept. ❑ *The equipment itself is getting smaller, neater and easier to find a home for.* **7** [U] When a sports team plays **at home**, they play a game on their own field, rather than on the opposing team's field. ❑ *I scored in both games; we drew at home and beat them away.*
PHRASES at home If you feel **at home**, you feel comfortable in the place or situation that you are in. ❑ *He spoke very good English and appeared pleased to see us, and we soon felt quite at home.*
a home away from home (*approval*) You can say **a home away from home** to refer to a place in which you are as comfortable as in your own home. ❑ *The café seems to be her home away from home these days.*
CONVENTION make yourself at home (*politeness*) If you say to a guest '**Make yourself at home**', you are making them feel welcome and inviting them to behave in an informal, relaxed way. ❑ *Take off your jacket and make yourself at home.*

ADV 1 Home means to or at the place where you live. ❑ *His wife wasn't feeling too well and she wanted to go home.* ❑ *I'll call you as soon as I get home.* **2** [home after V] If you press, drive, or hammer something **home**, you explain it to people as forcefully as possible. ❑ *It is now up to all of us to debate this issue and press home the argument.*
PHRASES bring something home To **bring** something **home to** someone means to make them understand how important or serious it is. ❑ *Their sobering conversation brought home to everyone present the serious and worthwhile work the Red Cross does.*
hit home or **strike home** If a situation or what someone says **hits home** or **strikes home**, people accept that it is real or true, even though it may be painful for them to realize. ❑ *Did the reality of war finally hit home?*
nothing to write home about (*informal*) If you say that something is **nothing to write home about**, you mean that it is not very interesting or exciting. ❑ *I see growth slightly up, but nothing to write home about.*
strike home (*written*) If something that is thrown or fired **strikes home**, it reaches its target. ❑ *Only two torpedoes struck home.*
ADJ 1 [home + N] **Home** means made or done in the place where you live. ❑ *cheap but healthy home cooking* **2** [home + N] **Home** means relating to your own country as opposed to foreign countries. = domestic ❑ *Europe's software companies still have a growing home market.* **3** [home + N] In sport, **home** refers to a team's own field, rather than the opposing team's field. ❑ *All three are fans, and attend all home games together.*
PHRASE home and dry or **home free** If you say that someone is **home free** you mean that they have been successful or that they are certain to be successful. ❑ *Just when she thought she was home free, her father spoke from behind her.*
PHRASAL VERB home in (**homes**, **homing**, **homed**) **1** If you **home in on** one particular aspect of something, you give all your attention to it. ❑ *The critics immediately homed in on the group's essential members.* **2** If something such as a missile **homes in on** something else, it is aimed at that thing and moves towards it. ❑ *Two rockets homed in on it from behind without a sound.*

home·land /ˈhəʊmlænd/ NOUN [C] (**homelands**)
1 (*mainly written*) Your **homeland** is your native country. ❑ *Many are planning to return to their homeland.* **2** The **homelands** were regions within South Africa in which black South Africans had a limited form of self-government.

home·less ♦◇◇ /ˈhəʊmləs/ ADJ, NOUN
ADJ Homeless people have nowhere to live. ❑ *the growing number of homeless families*
NOUN [PL] **The homeless** are people who are homeless. ❑ *shelters for the homeless*
home·less·ness /ˈhəʊmləsnəs/ NOUN [U] ❑ *The only way to solve homelessness is to provide more homes.*

home·sick /ˈhəʊmsɪk/ ADJ If you are **homesick**, you feel unhappy because you are away from home and are missing your family, friends, and home very much. ❑ *She's feeling a little homesick.*
home·sick·ness /ˈhəʊmsɪknəs/ NOUN [U] ❑ *There were inevitable bouts of homesickness.*

home·work /ˈhəʊmwɜːk/ NOUN [U] **1 Homework** is schoolwork that teachers give to students to do at home in the evening or at the weekend. ❑ *Have you done your homework, Gemma?* **2** If you **do** your **homework**, you find out what you need to know in preparation for something. ❑ *Before you go near a stockbroker, do your homework.*

homi·cide /ˈhɒmɪsaɪd/ NOUN [C, U] (**homicides**) (*mainly AmE*) **Homicide** is the illegal killing of a person. ❑ *The police arrived at the scene of the homicide.*

homoeo·path·ic /ˌhəʊmiəʊˈpæθɪk/ also **homeopathic** ADJ **Homoeopathic** means relating to or used in homoeopathy. ❑ *homoeopathic remedies*

homoeopa·thy /ˌhəʊmiˈɒpəθi/ also **homeopathy** NOUN [U] **Homoeopathy** is a way of treating an illness in which the patient is given very small amounts of a drug that produces signs of the illness in healthy people.

H

homo·geneous /ˌhɒməˌdʒiːniəs, ˈhəʊ-/ also
homogenous ADJ (formal) Homogeneous is used to
describe a group or thing which has members or parts that
are all the same. ❑ The unemployed are not a homogeneous
group.

homo·sex·ual ◆◇◇ /ˌhɒməʊˈsekʃuəl, AmE ˌhəʊ-/ ADJ,
NOUN
ADJ **1** A homosexual relationship is a sexual relationship
between people of the same sex. ❑ partners in a homosexual
relationship **2** Someone who is homosexual is sexually
attracted to people of the same sex. ❑ a fraud trial involving
two homosexual lawyers
NOUN [C] (homosexuals) A homosexual is a person who is
sexually attracted to people of the same sex. ❑ The judge
said that discrimination against homosexuals is deplorable.
homo·sex·ual·ity /ˌhɒməʊsekʃuˈæliti, AmE ˌhəʊm-/
NOUN [U] ❑ a place where gays could openly discuss
homosexuality

hon·est ◆◇◇ /ˈɒnɪst/ ADJ, ADV
ADJ **1** If you describe someone as honest, you mean that
they always tell the truth, and do not try to deceive people
or break the law. ❑ I know she's honest and reliable. **2** If
you are honest in a particular situation, you tell the
complete truth or give your sincere opinion, even if this is
not very pleasant. = frank ❑ I was honest about what I was
doing. ❑ He had been honest with her and she had tricked him!
PHRASE **to be honest** (feelings) You can say 'to be honest'
before or after a statement to indicate that you are telling
the truth about your own opinions or feelings, especially if
you think these will disappoint the person you are talking
to. ❑ To be honest the house is not quite our style.
ADV [honest with CL] (informal, emphasis) You say 'honest'
before or after a statement to emphasize that you are
telling the truth and that you want people to believe you.
❑ I'm not sure, honest.
PHRASE **honest to God** (informal, emphasis) Some people
say 'honest to God' to emphasize their feelings or to
emphasize that something is really true. ❑ I wish we
weren't doing this, Lillian, honest to God, I really do.

hon·est·ly /ˈɒnɪstli/ ADV **1** [honestly after v] If you
behave honestly, you always tell the truth and do not try
to deceive people or break the law. ❑ She fought honestly for
a just cause and for freedom. **2** [honestly with v] If you
speak or write honestly, you tell the complete truth or give
your sincere opinion, even if this is not very pleasant. ❑ It
came as a shock to hear an old friend speak so honestly about
Ted. **3** [honestly before v] (emphasis) You use honestly to
emphasize that you are referring to your, or someone
else's, true beliefs or feelings. ❑ But did you honestly think we
wouldn't notice? **4** [honestly with CL] (spoken, emphasis)
You use honestly to emphasize that you are telling the
truth and that you want people to believe you. ❑ Honestly,
I don't know anything about it. **5** [honestly with CL] (spoken,
feelings) You use honestly to indicate that you are annoyed
or impatient. = really ❑ Honestly, Nev! Must you be so
crude!

hon·es·ty /ˈɒnɪsti/ NOUN
NOUN [U] Honesty is the quality of being honest. ❑ They
said the greatest virtues in a politician were integrity, correctness,
and honesty.
PHRASE **in all honesty** (emphasis) You say in all honesty
when you are saying something that might be
disappointing or upsetting, and you want to soften its
effect by emphasizing your sincerity.

hon·ey /ˈhʌni/ NOUN [C, U] (honeys) **1** [C, U] Honey is a
sweet, sticky, yellowish substance that is made by bees.
2 [C] (mainly AmE) You call someone honey as a sign of
affection. ❑ Honey, I don't really think that's a good idea.

hon·or·ary /ˈɒnərəri, AmE ˈɒnəreri/ ADJ **1** [honorary
+ N] An honorary title or membership of a group is given
to someone without their needing to have the necessary
qualifications, usually because of their public
achievements. ❑ Harvard awarded him an honorary degree.
2 [honorary + N] Honorary is used to describe an official
job that is done without payment. ❑ the honorary secretary
of the Beekeepers' Association

hon·our /ˈɒnə/ (BrE; in AmE, use **honor**) NOUN, VERB
NOUN [U, C, SING] (honours) **1** [U] Honour means doing
what you believe to be right and being confident that you
have done what is right. ❑ The officers died faithful to the
honour of a soldier. **2** [C] An honour is a special award that
is given to someone, usually because they have done
something good or because they are greatly respected.
❑ He was showered with honours – among them an Oscar.
3 [SING] If you describe doing or experiencing something
as an honour, you mean you think it is something special
and desirable. ❑ Five other cities had been competing for the
honour of staging the Games. **4** [C] [POSS + honour] Judges
and mayors are sometimes called Your Honour or referred
to as His Honour or Her Honour. ❑ I bring this up, Your
Honour, because I think it is important to understand the
background of the defendant.
PHRASES **in honour of** If something is arranged in honour
of a particular event, it is arranged in order to celebrate
that event. ❑ The Foundation is holding a dinner at the
Museum of American Art in honour of the opening of its new
show.
in someone's honour If something is arranged or
happens in someone's honour, it is done specially to show
appreciation of them. ❑ Mr Mandela will attend an outdoor
concert in his honour.
VERB [T, PASSIVE] (honours, honouring, honoured)
1 [T] [usu passive] If someone is honoured, they are given
public praise or an award for something they have done.
❑ Diego Maradona was honoured with an award presented by
Argentina's soccer association. **2** [PASSIVE] If you say that you
would be honoured to do something, you are saying very
politely and formally that you would be pleased to do it.
If you say that you are honoured by something, you are
saying that you are grateful for it and pleased about it.
❑ Ms Payne said she was honoured to accept the appointment
and looked forward to its challenges. **3** [T] To honour
someone means to treat them or regard them with special
attention and respect. ❑ They honoured me with a seat at the
head of the table. **4** [T] If you honour an arrangement or
promise, you do what you said you would do. ❑ The two
sides agreed to honour a new ceasefire.

hon·our·able /ˈɒnrəbəl/ (BrE; in AmE, use **honorable**)
ADJ If you describe people or actions as honourable, you
mean that they are good and deserve to be respected and
admired. ❑ He argued that the only honourable course of
action was death.
hon·our·ably /ˈɒnrəbli/ ADV ❑ He also felt she had not
behaved honourably in the leadership election.

hood /hʊd/ NOUN [C] (hoods) A hood is a part of a coat
which you can pull up to cover your head. It is in the
shape of a triangular bag attached to the neck of the coat
at the back. ❑ She threw back the hood of her cloak.

hook ◆◇◇ /hʊk/ NOUN, VERB
NOUN [C] (hooks) **1** A hook is a bent piece of metal or
plastic that is used for catching or holding things, or for
hanging things up. ❑ One of his jackets hung from a hook.
2 A hook is a short sharp blow with your fist that you
make with your elbow bent, usually in a boxing match.
❑ Lewis desperately needs to keep clear of Ruddock's big left
hook.
PHRASES **let someone off the hook** (informal) If someone
gets off the hook or is let off the hook, they manage to get
out of the awkward or unpleasant situation that they are
in. ❑ Officials accused of bribery and corruption get off the hook
with monotonous regularity.
off the hook If you take a phone off the hook, you take
the receiver off the part that it normally rests on, so that
the phone will not ring. ❑ I'd taken my phone off the hook in
order to get some sleep.
VERB [I, T] (hooks, hooking, hooked) **1** [I, T] If you hook
one thing to another, you attach it there using a hook.
If something hooks somewhere, it can be hooked there.
❑ Paul hooked his tractor to the car and pulled it to safety.
2 [T] If you hook your arm, leg, or foot round an object,
you place it like a hook round the object in order to move
it or hold it. ❑ She latched on to his arm, hooking her other
arm around a tree. **3** [T] If you hook a fish, you catch

h

it with a hook on the end of a line. ❑ *At the first cast I hooked a huge fish, probably a tench.*

PHRASAL VERB **hook up** **1** (*informal*) If someone **hooks up with** another person, they begin a sexual or romantic relationship with that person. You can also say that two people **hook up**. ❑ *I could be about to hook up with this incredibly intelligent, beautiful girl.* ❑ *We haven't exactly hooked up yet.* **2** (*mainly AmE, informal*) If you **hook up with** someone, you meet them and spend time with them. You can also say that two people **hook up**. ❑ *He hooked up with fellow cycling enthusiasts and joined several clubs.* ❑ *This afternoon Iz and Jude and Chris hooked up.* **3** When someone **hooks up** a computer or other electronic machine, they connect it to other similar machines or to a central power supply. ❑ *technicians who hook up computer systems and networks* ❑ *He brought it down, hooked it up, and we got the generator going.*

hooked /hʊkt/ ADJ **1** If you describe something as **hooked**, you mean that it is shaped like a hook. ❑ *He was thin and tall, with a hooked nose.* **2** [V-LINK + hooked] (*informal*) If you enjoy something so much that it takes up a lot of your interest and attention. ❑ *Many of the leaders have become hooked on power and money.* **3** [V-LINK + hooked] (*informal*) If you are **hooked on** a drug, you are addicted to it. ❑ *He spent a number of years hooked on cocaine, heroin, and alcohol.*

hoo·li·gan /ˈhuːlɪɡən/ NOUN [c] (**hooligans**) (*disapproval*) If you describe people, especially young people, as **hooligans**, you are critical of them because they behave in a noisy and violent way in a public place. ❑ *the problem of football hooligans*

hoo·li·gan·ism /ˈhuːlɪɡənɪzəm/ NOUN [u] **Hooliganism** is the behaviour and actions of hooligans. ❑ *Officials dismiss these incidents as simple hooliganism.*

hop /hɒp/ VERB, NOUN

VERB [i] (**hops, hopping, hopped**) **1** If you **hop**, you move along by jumping on one foot. ❑ *I hopped down three steps.* **2** When birds and some small animals **hop**, they move along by jumping on both or all four feet. ❑ *A small brown fawn hopped across the trail in front of them.* **3** (*informal*) If you **hop** somewhere, you move there quickly or suddenly. = jump ❑ *My wife and I were the first to arrive and hopped on board.*

NOUN [c] (**hops**) **1** A **hop** is a jump on one foot. ❑ *'This really is a catching rhythm, eh?' he added, with a few little hops.* **2** A **hop** is a jump on both or all four feet that birds and some small animals make. ❑ *The rabbit got up, took four hops and turned around.* **3** (*informal*) A **hop** is a short, quick trip, usually by plane. ❑ *It is a three-hour drive but can be reached by a 20-minute hop in a private helicopter.* **4** **Hops** are flowers that are dried and used for making beer.

hope ◆◆◆ /həʊp/ VERB, NOUN

VERB [i, t] (**hopes, hoping, hoped**) **1** If you **hope** that something is true, or if you **hope** for something, you want it to be true or to happen, and you usually believe that it is possible or likely. ❑ *She had decided she must go on as usual, follow her normal routine, and hope and pray.* ❑ *He hesitates before leaving, almost as though he had been hoping for conversation.* **2** If you say that you cannot **hope for** something, or if you talk about the only thing that you can **hope to** get, you mean that you are in a bad situation, and there is very little chance of improving it. ❑ *Things aren't ideal, but that's the best you can hope for.*

PHRASES **hope for the best** If you are in a difficult situation and do something and **hope for the best**, you hope that everything will happen in the way you want, although you know that it may not. ❑ *Some companies are cutting costs and hoping for the best.*

hope against hope If you **hope against hope** that something will happen, you hope that it will happen, although it seems impossible. ❑ *She glanced about the hall, hoping against hope that Richard would be waiting for her.*

I hope **1** (*politeness*) You use '**I hope**' in expressions such as '**I hope you don't mind**' and '**I hope I'm not disturbing you**', when you are being polite and want to make sure that you have not offended someone or disturbed them. ❑ *I hope you don't mind me coming to see you.* **2** You say

'**I hope**' when you want to warn someone not to do something foolish or dangerous. ❑ *You're not trying to see him, I hope?*

NOUN [c, u] (**hopes**) **1** [c, u] Your **hope** is something that you want to be true or to happen, and that you believe to be possible or likely. ❑ *The only hope for underdeveloped countries is to become, as far as possible, self-reliant.* **2** [u] **Hope** is a feeling of desire and expectation that things will go well in the future. ❑ *Now that he has become president, many people once again have hope for genuine changes in the system.* ❑ *But Kevin hasn't given up hope of getting in shape.* **3** [c] If someone wants something to happen, and considers it likely or possible, you can refer to their **hopes of** that thing, or to their **hope that** it will happen. ❑ *They have hopes of increasing trade between the two regions.* ❑ *My hope is that, in the future, I will go over there and marry her.* **4** [c] If you think that the help or success of a particular person or thing will cause you to be successful or to get what you want, you can refer to them as your **hope**. ❑ *Roemer represented the best hope for a businesslike climate in Louisiana.*

PHRASES **get your hopes up** or **build your hopes up** If you tell someone not to **get** their **hopes up**, or not to **build** their **hopes up**, you are warning them that they should not become too confident of progress or success. ❑ *There is no reason for people to get their hopes up over this mission.*

not a hope in hell (*informal, emphasis*) If you say that someone has **not** got **a hope in hell of** doing something, you are emphasizing that they will not be able to do it. ❑ *Everybody knows they haven't got a hope in hell of forming a government anyway.*

high hopes or **great hopes** If you have **high hopes** or **great hopes that** something will happen, you are confident that it will happen. ❑ *I had high hopes that Derek Randall might play an important part.*

in the hope of or **in the hope that** If you do one thing **in the hope of** another thing happening, you do it because you think it might cause or help the other thing to happen, which is what you want. ❑ *He was studying in the hope of being admitted to an engineering course.*

live in hope If you **live in hope** that something will happen, you continue to hope that it will happen, although it seems unlikely, and you realize that you are being foolish. ❑ *I just live in hope that one day she'll talk to me.*

hope·ful /ˈhəʊpfʊl/ ADJ, NOUN

ADJ **1** If you are **hopeful**, you are fairly confident that something that you want to happen will happen. ❑ *I am hopeful this misunderstanding will be rectified very quickly.* **2** If something such as a sign or event is **hopeful**, it makes you feel that what you want to happen will happen. ❑ *The result of the election is yet another hopeful sign that peace could come to the Middle East.* **3** [hopeful + N] A **hopeful** action is one that you do in the hope that you will get what you want to get. ❑ *We've chartered the aircraft in the hopeful anticipation that the government will allow them to leave.*

NOUN [c] (**hopefuls**) If you refer to someone as a **hopeful**, you mean that they are hoping and trying to achieve success in a particular career, election, or competition. ❑ *His skills continue to be put to good use in his job as coach to young hopefuls.*

hope·ful·ly /ˈhəʊpfʊli/ ADV **1** [hopefully with CL/GROUP] You say **hopefully** when mentioning something that you hope will happen. Some careful speakers of English think that this use of **hopefully** is not correct, but it is very frequently used. ❑ *Hopefully, you won't have any problems after reading this.* **2** [hopefully with v] If you do something **hopefully**, you do it in the belief that something that you want to happen will happen. ❑ *'Am I welcome?' He smiled hopefully, leaning on the door.*

hope·less /ˈhəʊpləs/ ADJ **1** If you feel **hopeless**, you feel very unhappy because there seems to be no possibility of a better situation or success. ❑ *He had not heard her cry before in this uncontrolled, hopeless way.* **2** Someone or something that is **hopeless** is certain to fail or be unsuccessful. ❑ *I don't believe your situation is as hopeless as you think. If you* *love each other, you'll work it out.* **3** *(informal)* If someone is **hopeless at** something, they are very bad at it. ▫ *I'd be hopeless at working for somebody else.* **4** You use **hopeless** to emphasize how bad or inadequate something or someone is. ▫ *Argentina's economic policies were a hopeless mess.*

hope·less·ly /ˈhəʊpləsli/ ADV **1** *I looked around hopelessly.* **2** *Harry was hopelessly lost.*

hope·less·ness /ˈhəʊpləsnəs/ NOUN [U] ▫ *She had a feeling of hopelessness about the future.*

ho·ri·zon /həˈraɪzən/ NOUN
NOUN [SING, C] (**horizons**) **1** [SING] The **horizon** is the line in the far distance where the sky seems to meet the land or the sea. ▫ *In the distance, the dot of a boat appeared on the horizon.* **2** [C] Your **horizons** are the limits of what you want to do or of what you are interested or involved in. ▫ *As your horizons expand, these new ideas can give a whole new meaning to life.*
PHRASE **on the horizon** If something is **on the horizon**, it is almost certainly going to happen or be done quite soon. ▫ *With breast cancer, as with many common diseases, there is no obvious breakthrough on the horizon.*

✪ hori·zon·tal /ˌhɒrɪˈzɒntəl, AmE ˌhɔːrɪ-/ ADJ, NOUN
ADJ Something that is **horizontal** is flat and level with the ground, rather than at an angle to it. ▫ *The board consists of vertical and horizontal lines.* ▫ *The horizontal axis in both figures shows unexpected changes in exchange rates.*
NOUN [SING] A **horizontal** or the **horizontal** is a flat and level line or surface. ▫ *Do not raise your left arm above the horizontal.*
✪ hori·zon·tal·ly /ˌhɒrɪˈzɒntəli, AmE ˌhɔːrɪ-/ ADV ▫ *The wind was cold and drove the snow at him almost horizontally.* ▫ *The wings are designed to provide uplift when the plane is flying horizontally.* ▫ *a fence placed horizontally across the painting*

hor·mone /ˈhɔːməʊn/ NOUN [C] (**hormones**) A **hormone** is a chemical, usually occurring naturally in your body, that makes an organ of your body do something. ▫ *the male sex hormone testosterone*

horn /hɔːn/ NOUN
NOUN [C] (**horns**) **1** On a vehicle such as a car, the **horn** is the device that makes a loud noise as a signal or warning. ▫ *He sounded the car horn.* **2** The **horns** of an animal such as a cow or deer are the hard pointed things that grow from its head. ▫ *A mature cow has horns.* **3** A **horn** is a musical instrument of the brass family. It is a long circular metal tube, wide at one end, which you play by blowing. ▫ *He started playing the horn when he was eight.* **4** A **horn** is a simple musical instrument consisting of a metal tube that is wide at one end and narrow at the other. You play it by blowing into it. ▫ *a hunting horn*
PHRASE **lock horns** If two people **lock horns**, they argue about something. ▫ *During his six years in office, Seidman has often locked horns with lawmakers.*

hor·ri·ble /ˈhɒrɪbəl, AmE ˈhɔːr-/ ADJ **1** *(informal)* If you describe something or someone as **horrible**, you do not like them at all. ▫ *Her voice sounds horrible.* **2** You can call something **horrible** when it causes you to feel great shock, fear, and disgust. = **terrible** ▫ *Still the horrible shrieking came out of his mouth.* **3** [horrible + N] **Horrible** is used to emphasize how bad something is. = **awful** ▫ *That seems like a horrible mess that will drag on for years.*
hor·ri·bly /ˈhɒrɪbli, AmE ˈhɔːr-/ ADV **1** [horribly with V] ▫ *When trouble comes they behave selfishly and horribly.* **2** [horribly with V] ▫ *A two-year-old boy was horribly murdered.* **3** *Our plans have gone horribly wrong.*

hor·rid /ˈhɒrɪd, AmE ˈhɔːr-/ ADJ *(informal)* **1** If you describe something as **horrid**, you mean that it is extremely unpleasant. = **horrible** ▫ *What a horrid smell!* **2** If you describe someone as **horrid**, you mean that they behave in a very unpleasant way towards other people. = **horrible** ▫ *I must have been a horrid little girl.*

hor·rif·ic /həˈrɪfɪk, AmE hɔːˈr-/ ADJ **1** If you describe a physical attack, accident, or injury as **horrific**, you mean that it is very bad, so that people are shocked when they see it or think about it. = **horrendous** ▫ *I have never seen such horrific injuries.* **2** If you describe something as **horrific**, you mean that it is so big that it is extremely

unpleasant. = **horrendous** ▫ *piling up horrific extra amounts of money on top of your original debt*
hor·rifi·cal·ly /həˈrɪfɪkli, AmE hɔːˈr-/ **1** *He had been horrifically assaulted before he died.* **2** [horrifically + ADJ] ▫ *Opera productions are horrifically expensive.*

hor·ri·fy /ˈhɒrɪfaɪ, AmE ˈhɔːr-/ VERB [T] (**horrifies, horrifying, horrified**) If someone **is horrified**, they feel shocked or disgusted, usually because of something that they have seen or heard. = **appal** ▫ *His family was horrified by the change.*

hor·ri·fy·ing /ˈhɒrɪfaɪɪŋ/ ADJ If you describe something as **horrifying**, you mean that it is shocking or disgusting. = **appalling** ▫ *These were horrifying experiences.*

hor·ror ♦◇◇ /ˈhɒrə, AmE ˈhɔːr-/ NOUN, ADJ
NOUN [U, SING, C] (**horrors**) **1** [U] **Horror** is a feeling of great shock, fear, and worry caused by something extremely unpleasant. = **terror** ▫ *I felt numb with horror.* **2** [SING] If you have a **horror of** something, you are afraid of it or dislike it very much. ▫ *his horror of death* **3** [SING] The **horror of** something, especially something that hurts people, is its very great unpleasantness. ▫ *the horror of this most bloody of civil wars* **4** [C] You can refer to extremely unpleasant or frightening experiences as **horrors**. ▫ *Can you possibly imagine all the horrors we have undergone since I last wrote to you?*
ADJ **1** [horror + N] A **horror** film or story is intended to be very frightening. ▫ *a psychological horror film* **2** [horror + N] You can refer to an account of a very unpleasant experience or event as a **horror** story. ▫ *a horror story about lost luggage while flying*

horse ♦♦◇ /hɔːs/ NOUN
NOUN [C] (**horses**) A **horse** is a large animal which people can ride. Some horses are used for pulling ploughs and carts. ▫ *A small man on a grey horse had appeared.*
PHRASE **from the horse's mouth** If you hear something **from the horse's mouth**, you hear it from someone who knows that it is definitely true. ▫ *He has got to hear it from the horse's mouth. Then he can make a judgment as to whether his policy is correct or not.*
PHRASAL VERB **horse around** (**horses, horsing, horsed**) *(informal)* If you **horse around**, you play roughly and carelessly, so that you could hurt someone or damage something. ▫ *My friends and I would horse around and try to push each other.*

hos·pi·table /hɒˈspɪtəbəl, ˈhɒspɪt-/ ADJ **1** A **hospitable** person is friendly, generous, and welcoming to guests or people they have just met. ▫ *The locals are hospitable and welcoming.* **2** A **hospitable** climate or environment is one that encourages the existence or development of particular people or things. ▫ *Even in summer this place did not look exactly hospitable; in winter, conditions must have been exceedingly harsh.*

hos·pi·tal ♦♦♦ /ˈhɒspɪtəl/ NOUN [C, U] (**hospitals**) A **hospital** is a place where people who are ill are cared for by nurses and doctors. ▫ *a children's hospital with 120 beds*

hos·pi·tal·ity /ˌhɒspɪˈtælɪti/ NOUN [U] **1 Hospitality** is friendly, welcoming behaviour towards guests or people you have just met. ▫ *Every visitor to Georgia is overwhelmed by the kindness, charm, and hospitality of the people.* **2 Hospitality** is the food, drink, and other privileges which some companies provide for their visitors or clients at major sports events or other public events. ▫ *corporate hospitality tents*

✪ host ♦♦♦ /həʊst/ NOUN, VERB, QUANT
NOUN [C] (**hosts**) **1** The **host** at a party is the person who has invited the guests and provides the food, drink, or entertainment. ▫ *Apart from my host, I didn't know a single person there.* **2** A country, city, or organization that is the **host** of an event provides the facilities for that event to take place. ▫ *Atlanta was chosen to be host of the 1996 Olympic games.* **3** The **host** of a radio or television programme is the person who introduces it and talks to the people who appear in it. = **presenter** ▫ *I am host of a live radio programme.* **4** A **host** or a **host computer** is the main computer in a network of computers, which controls the most important files and programs. ▫ *Subscribers dial directly from their computers into the BBS host computer.*

5 The **host** of a parasite is the plant or animal which it lives on or inside and from which it gets its food. ❏ *When the eggs hatch the larvae eat the living flesh of the host.* ❏ *Farmed fish are perfect hosts for parasites.*
PHRASE **play host** If a person or country **plays host to** an event or an important visitor, they host the event or the visit. ❏ *Bush played host to Russian President Vladimir Putin.*
VERB [T] (**hosts, hosting, hosted**) **1** If someone **hosts** a party, dinner, or other function, they have invited the guests and provide the food, drink, or entertainment. ❏ *Tonight she hosts a ball for 300 guests.* **2** If a country, city, or organization **hosts** an event, they provide the facilities for the event to take place. ❏ *New Bedford hosts a number of lively festivals throughout the summer months.* **3** The person who **hosts** a radio or television programme introduces it and talks to the people who appear in it. ❏ *She also hosts a show on St Petersburg Radio.*
QUANT A **host of** things is a lot of them. = multitude ❏ *A host of problems may delay the opening of the new bridge.*

hos·tage ◆◆◇ /ˈhɒstɪdʒ/ NOUN
NOUN [C, U] (**hostages**) **1** [C] A **hostage** is someone who has been captured by a person or organization and who may be killed or injured if people do not do what that person or organization demands. ❏ *It is hopeful that two hostages will be freed in the next few days.* **2** If you say you are **hostage to** something, you mean that your freedom to take action is restricted by things that you cannot control. ❏ *Wine growers say they've been held hostage to the interests of cereal farmers.*
PHRASE **take someone hostage** or **hold someone hostage** If someone **is taken hostage** or **is held hostage**, they are captured and kept as a hostage. ❏ *He was taken hostage while on his first foreign assignment as a television journalist.*

◆**hos·tile** /ˈhɒstaɪl, AmE -təl/ ADJ **1** If you are **hostile to** another person or an idea, you disagree with them or disapprove of them, often showing this in your behaviour. ❏ *Many people felt he would be hostile to the idea of foreign intervention.* ❏ *The West has gradually relaxed its hostile attitude to this influential state.* **2** Someone who is **hostile** is unfriendly and aggressive. = aggressive ❏ *Drinking may make a person feel relaxed and happy, or it may make her hostile, violent, or depressed.* **3** **Hostile** situations and conditions make it difficult for you to achieve something. = unfavourable, difficult; ≠ favourable ❏ *some of the most hostile climatic conditions in the world* ❏ *If this round of talks fails, the world's trading environment is likely to become increasingly hostile.* **4** (*business*) A **hostile** takeover bid is one that is opposed by the company that is being bid for. ❏ *Soon after he arrived, Kingfisher launched a hostile bid for Dixons.* **5** [hostile + N] In a war, you use **hostile** to describe your enemy's forces, organizations, weapons, land, and activities. = enemy ❏ *The city is encircled by a hostile army.*

hos·til·ities /hɒˈstɪlɪtiz/ NOUN [PL] (*formal*) You can refer to fighting between two countries or groups who are at war as **hostilities**. ❏ *The authorities have urged people to stock up on fuel in case hostilities break out.*

hos·til·ity /hɒˈstɪlɪti/ NOUN [U] **1** **Hostility** is unfriendly or aggressive behaviour towards people or ideas. ❏ *The last decade has witnessed a serious rise in the levels of racism and hostility to black and ethnic groups.* **2** Your **hostility to** something you do not approve of is your opposition to it. ❏ *There is hostility among traditionalists to this method of teaching history.*

hot ◆◆◇ /hɒt/ ADJ, NOUN
ADJ (**hotter, hottest**) **1** Something that is **hot** has a high temperature. ❏ *When the oil is hot, add the sliced onion.* ❏ *What he needed was a hot bath and a good sleep.* **2** **Hot** is used to describe the weather or the air in a room or building when the temperature is high. ❏ *It was too hot even for a gentle stroll.* **3** If you are **hot**, you feel as if your body is at an unpleasantly high temperature. ❏ *I was too hot and tired to eat more than a few mouthfuls.* **4** You can say that food is **hot** when it has a strong, burning taste caused by chillies, pepper, or other spices. = spicy ❏ *hot curries* **5** (*journalism*) A **hot** issue or topic is one that is very important at the present time and is receiving a lot of

publicity. ❏ *The role of women in war has been a hot topic of debate since the Gulf conflict.* **6** (*informal*) **Hot** news is new, recent, and fresh. ❏ *eight pages of the latest movies, video releases, and the hot news from Tinseltown* **7** (*informal*) You can use **hot** to describe something that is very exciting and that many people want to see, use, obtain, or become involved with. ❏ *When I was in Chicago in 1990 a friend got me a ticket for the hottest show in town: the Monet Exhibition at the Art Institute.* **8** (*informal*) A **hot** contest is one that is intense and involves a great deal of activity and determination. = fierce ❏ *It took hot competition from abroad, however, to show us just how good our product really is.* **9** [hot + N] If a person or team is the **hot** favourite, people think that they are the one most likely to win a race or competition. ❏ *Atlantic City is the hot favourite to stage the fight.* **10** Someone who has a **hot** temper gets angry very quickly and easily. ❏ *His hot temper was making it increasingly difficult for others to work with him.* **11** (*informal*) If you describe someone as **hot**, you mean that they are sexually attractive or sexually desirable. ❏ *'He's great,' Caroline said, 'hot.'* ❏ *If a hot chick comes on to you, smile and walk away.*
PHRASES **blow hot and cold** If someone **blows hot and cold**, they keep changing their attitude towards something, sometimes being very enthusiastic and at other times expressing no interest at all. ❏ *The media, meanwhile, has blown hot and cold over the affair.*
hot and bothered If you are **hot and bothered**, you are so worried and anxious that you cannot think clearly or behave sensibly. ❏ *Ray was getting very hot and bothered about the idea.*
NOUN
PHRASE **have the hots for** or **get the hots for** (*informal*) If you say that one person **has the hots for** another, you mean that they feel a strong sexual attraction to that person. ❏ *I've had the hots for him ever since he arrived.*

ho·tel ◆◆◇ /ˌhəʊˈtel/ NOUN [C] (**hotels**) A **hotel** is a building where people stay, for example on holiday, paying for their rooms and meals.

hound /haʊnd/ NOUN, VERB
NOUN [C] (**hounds**) A **hound** is a type of dog that is often used for hunting or racing. ❏ *Rainey's chief interest in life is hunting with hounds.*
VERB [T] (**hounds, hounding, hounded**) **1** If someone **hounds** you, they constantly disturb or speak to you in an annoying or upsetting way. ❏ *Newcomers are constantly hounding them for advice.* **2** If someone **is hounded out of** a job or place, they are forced to leave it, often because other people are constantly criticizing them. ❏ *There is a general view around that he has been hounded out of office by the press.*

hour ◆◆◆ /aʊə/ NOUN
NOUN [C, PL, SING] (**hours**) **1** [C] An **hour** is a period of sixty minutes. ❏ *They waited for about two hours.* ❏ *I only slept about half an hour that night.* **2** [PL] People say that something takes or lasts **hours** to emphasize that it takes or lasts a very long time, or what seems like a very long time. ❏ *Getting there would take hours.* **3** [SING] A clock that strikes **the hour** strikes when it is exactly one o'clock, two o'clock, and so on. ❏ *She'd heard a clock somewhere strike the hour as she'd slipped from her room.* **4** [SING] (*literary*) You can refer to a particular time or moment as a particular **hour**. = time ❏ *the hour of his execution* **5** [C] (*literary*) If you refer, for example, to someone's **hour of** need or **hour of** happiness, you are referring to the time in their life when they are or were experiencing that condition or feeling. ❏ *He recalled her devotion to her husband during his hour of need.* **6** [PL] You can refer to the period of time during which something happens or operates each day as the **hours** during which it happens or operates. ❏ *the hours of darkness* ❏ *Phone us on this number during office hours.* **7** [PL] If you refer to the **hours** involved in a job, you are talking about how long you spend each week doing it and when you do it. ❏ *I worked quite irregular hours.*
PHRASES **after hours** If you do something **after hours**, you do it outside normal business hours or the time when you are usually at work. ❏ *a local restaurant where steel workers unwind after hours*

at all hours (*disapproval*) If you say that something happens **at all hours of** the day or night, you disapprove of it happening at the time that it does or as often as it does. ❑ *She didn't want her fourteen-year-old daughter coming home at all hours of the morning.*

the early hours or **the small hours** or **the wee hours** If something happens **in the early hours, in the small hours,** or **in the wee hours,** it happens in the early morning after midnight. ❑ *Gibbs was arrested in the early hours of yesterday morning.*

on the hour If something happens **on the hour,** it happens every hour at, for example, nine o'clock, ten o'clock, and so on, and not at any number of minutes past an hour. ❑ *During this war in the Persian Gulf, NPR will have newscasts every hour on the hour.*

hour·ly /ˈaʊəli/ ADJ, ADV

■ [hourly + N] An **hourly** event happens once every hour. ❑ *He flipped on the radio to get the hourly news broadcast.* ■ [hourly + N] Your **hourly** earnings are the money that you earn in one hour. ❑ *They have little prospect of finding new jobs with the same hourly pay.* ADV [hourly after V] If an event happens **hourly,** it happens once every hour. ❑ *The hospital issued press releases hourly.*

house ♦♦♦ NOUN, VERB, ADJ

NOUN /haʊs/ [C, SING] (**houses**) ■ [C] A **house** is a building in which people live, usually the people belonging to one family. ❑ *She has moved to a small house and is living off her meagre savings.* ■ [SING] You can refer to all the people who live together in a house as **the house.** = household ❑ *If he set his alarm clock for midnight, it would wake the whole house.* ■ [C] **House** is used in the names of types of places where people go to eat and drink. ❑ *a steak house* ■ [C] **House** is used in the names of types of companies, especially ones which publish books, lend money, or design clothes. ❑ *Many of the clothes come from the world's top fashion houses.* ■ [C] You can refer to one of the two bodies of the US Congress as a **House.** The House of Representatives is sometimes referred to as **the House.** ❑ *Some members of the House and Senate worked all day yesterday.*

PHRASES **bring the house down** (*informal*) If a person or their performance or speech **brings the house down,** the audience claps, laughs, or shouts loudly because the performance or speech is very impressive or amusing. ❑ *It's really an amazing dance. It just always brings the house down.*

like a house on fire (*informal*) If two people **get on like a house on fire,** they quickly become close friends, for example because they have many interests in common. ❑ *I went over and struck up a conversation, and we got on like a house on fire.*

on the house If you are given something in a restaurant or bar **on the house,** you do not have to pay for it. ❑ *The owner knew about the engagement and brought them glasses of champagne on the house.*

get your house in order or **put your house in order** or **set your house in order** If someone **gets** their **house in order, puts** their **house in order,** or **sets** their **house in order,** they arrange their affairs and solve their problems. ❑ *He's got his house in order and made some tremendous decisions.*

VERB /haʊz/ [T] (**houses, housing, housed**) ■ To **house** someone means to provide a house or apartment for them to live in. ❑ *homes that house up to nine people* ■ A building or container that **houses** something is the place where it is located or from where it operates. ❑ *The building is open to the public and houses a museum of motorcycles and cars.* ■ If you say that a building **houses** a number of people, you mean that is the place where they live or where they are staying. = accommodate ❑ *The building will house twelve boys and eight girls.*

ADJ /haʊs/ [house + N] A restaurant's **house** wine is the cheapest wine it sells, which is not listed by name on the wine list. ❑ *Tweed ordered a carafe of the house wine.*

⊙ **house·hold** ♦◇◇ /ˈhaʊshəʊld/ NOUN, ADJ

NOUN [C, SING] (**households**) ■ [C] A **household** is all the people in a family or group who live together in a house. ❑ *growing up in a male-only household* ❑ *Many poor households are experiencing real hardship.* ■ [SING] The **household** is your home and everything that is connected with taking care of it. ❑ *household chores* ADJ [household + N] Someone or something that is a **household** name or word is very well known. ❑ *Today, fashion designers are household names.*

house·holder /ˈhaʊshəʊldə/ NOUN [C] (**householders**) The **householder** is the person who owns or rents a particular house. ❑ *Officials appealed to householders to open their homes to the thousands of persons made homeless by the storm.*

house·keeping /ˈhaʊskiːpɪŋ/ NOUN [U] Housekeeping is the work and organization involved in running a home, including the shopping and cleaning. ❑ *I thought that cooking and housekeeping were unimportant, easy tasks.*

house·wife /ˈhaʊswaɪf/ NOUN [C] (**housewives**) A **housewife** is a married woman who does not have a paid job, but instead takes care of her home and children. ❑ *Married at nineteen, she was a traditional housewife and mother of four children.*

house·work /ˈhaʊswɜːk/ NOUN [U] Housework is the work such as cleaning, washing, and ironing that you do in your home. ❑ *Men are doing more housework nowadays.*

⊙ **hous·ing** ♦♦◇ /ˈhaʊzɪŋ/ NOUN [U] You refer to the buildings in which people live as **housing** when you are talking about their standard, price, or availability. = accommodation ❑ *a shortage of affordable housing* ❑ *Poor housing can affect physical and mental health.*

hov·er /ˈhɒvə, AmE ˈhʌv-/ VERB [I] (**hovers, hovering, hovered**) ■ To **hover** means to stay in the same position in the air without moving forwards or backwards. Many birds and insects can hover by moving their wings very quickly. ❑ *Beautiful butterflies hovered above the wild flowers.* ■ If you **hover,** you stay in one place and move slightly in a nervous way, for example because you cannot decide what to do. ❑ *Judith was hovering in the doorway.* ■ If you **hover,** you are in an uncertain situation or state of mind. ❑ *She hovered on the brink of death for three months as doctors battled to save her.* ■ If something such as a price, value, or score **hovers** around a particular level, it stays at more or less that level and does not change much. ❑ *In September 1989 the exchange rate hovered around 140 yen to the dollar.*

how ♦♦♦ /haʊ/ QUEST, CONVENTION, CONJ, ADV

QUEST ■ You use **how** to ask about the way in which something happens or is done. ❑ *How do I make payments into my account?* ❑ *How do you manage to keep the place so neat?* ■ You use **how** to ask questions about the quantity or degree of something. ❑ *How much money are we talking about?* ❑ *How many full-time staff have we got?* ❑ *How long will you be staying?* ❑ *How old is your son now?* ■ You use **how** when you are asking someone whether something was successful or enjoyable. ❑ *How was your trip down to Orlando?* ❑ *How did your date go?* ■ You use **how** to ask about someone's health or to find out someone's news. ❑ *Hi! How are you doing?* ❑ *How's Rosie?* ■ [how 'can/could'] You use **how** in expressions such as '**How can you...**' and '**How could you...**' to indicate that you disapprove of what someone has done or that you find it hard to believe. ❑ *How can you drink so much beer, Luke?* ■ You use **how** in expressions such as '**How about...**' or '**How would you like...**' when you are making an offer or a suggestion. ❑ *How about a cup of coffee?*

PHRASES **how come** or **how so** (*informal*) You ask '**How come?**' or '**How so?**' when you are surprised by something and are asking why it happened or was said. ❑ *'They don't say a single word to each other.'—'How come?'*

how about You use **how about** to introduce a new subject which you think is relevant to the conversation you have been having. ❑ *Are your products and services competitive? How about marketing?*

CONVENTION If you ask someone '**How about you?**', you are asking them what they think or want. ❑ *Well, I enjoyed that. How about you two?*

CONJ **1** You use **how** to describe the way in which something happens or is done. □ *I don't want to know how he died.* **2** You use **how** after certain adjectives and verbs to introduce a statement or fact, often something that you remember or expect other people to know about. □ *It's amazing how people collect so much stuff over the years.* □ *It's funny how I never seem to get a thing done on my day off.* **ADV** (*emphasis*) **1** [how + ADJ/ADV] You use **how** to emphasize the degree to which something is true. □ *I didn't realize how heavy that bag was going to be.* **2** [how + ADJ/ADV/CL] You use **how** in exclamations to emphasize an adjective, adverb, or statement. □ *How strange that something so simple as a walk on the beach could suddenly mean so much.*

◊how·ev·er ♦♦♦ /haʊˈevə/ ADV, CONJ, QUEST
ADV **1** [however with CL] You use **however** when you are adding a comment which is surprising or which contrasts with what has just been said. □ *This was not an easy decision. It is, however, a decision that we feel is dictated by our duty.* □ *Some of the food crops failed. However, the cotton did quite well.* □ *Higher sales have not helped profits, however.* **2** You use **however** before an adjective or adverb to emphasize that the degree or extent of something cannot change a situation. = no matter how □ *You should always strive to achieve more, however well you have done before.* □ *However hard she tried, nothing seemed to work.* □ *However much it hurt, he could do it.* **3** You use **however** in expressions such as **or however long it takes** and **or however many there were** to indicate that the figure you have just mentioned may not be accurate. □ *Wait 30 to 60 minutes or however long it takes.*
CONJ You use **however** when you want to say that it makes no difference how something is done. □ *However we adopt healthcare reform, it isn't going to save major amounts of money.*
QUEST (*emphasis*) You can use **however** to ask in an emphatic way how something has happened which you are very surprised about. Some speakers of English think that this form is incorrect and prefer to use 'how ever'. = how □ *However did you find this place in such weather?*

USAGE NOTE
however
Note that when **however** expresses contrast, it is followed by a comma.
*Western societies have witnessed a dramatic improvement in living standards in the past five decades. **However**, the environmental impact has been very damaging.*
When **however** acts as a conjunction, it is not followed by a comma.
*We may never be able to repair the damage, **however** hard we try.*

howl /haʊl/ VERB, NOUN
VERB [I, T] (**howls, howling, howled**) **1** [I] If an animal such as a wolf or a dog **howls**, it makes a long, loud, crying sound. □ *Somewhere a dog suddenly howled, baying at the moon.* **2** [I] If a person **howls**, they make a long, loud cry expressing pain, anger, or unhappiness. □ *He howled like a wounded animal as blood spurted from the gash.* **3** [I] When the wind **howls**, it blows hard and makes a loud noise. □ *The wind howled all night, but I slept a little.* **4** [T] (*informal*) If you **howl** something, you say it in a very loud voice. □ *'Get away, get away, get away,' he howled.* **5** [I] (*informal*) If you **howl with** laughter, you laugh very loudly. □ *Joe, Pink, and Booker howled with delight.*
NOUN [C] (**howls**) **1** A **howl** is a long, loud, crying sound by an animal such as a wolf or a dog. □ *The dog let out a savage howl and, wheeling round, flew at him.* **2** A **howl** is a long, loud cry by a person expressing pain, anger, or unhappiness. □ *With a howl of rage, he grabbed the neck of a broken bottle and advanced.* **3** A **howl** of laughter is a very loud laugh. □ *His stories caused howls of laughter.*

HR /eɪtʃ ˈɑːr/ NOUN [U] (*business*) In a company or other organization, the **HR** department is the department with responsibility for the recruiting, training, and welfare of the staff. **HR** is an abbreviation for **human resources**.

hub /hʌb/ NOUN [C] (**hubs**) **1** You can describe a place as a **hub of** an activity when it is a very important centre for that activity. = centre □ *The island's social hub is the Cafe Sport.* **2** The **hub** of a wheel is the part at the centre. **3** A **hub** or a **hub airport** is a large airport from which you can travel to many other airports. □ *a campaign to secure Heathrow's place as Europe's main international hub* **4** (*computing*) A **hub** is a device for connecting computers in a network.

hug /hʌg/ VERB, NOUN
VERB [RECIP, T] (**hugs, hugging, hugged**) **1** [RECIP] When you **hug** someone, you put your arms around them and hold them tightly, for example because you like them or are pleased to see them. You can also say that two people **hug** each other or that they **hug**. = embrace □ *She had hugged him exuberantly and invited him to dinner the next day.* **2** [T] If you **hug** something, you hold it close to your body with your arms tightly around it. □ *Shaerl trudged towards them, hugging a large box.* **3** [T] (*written*) Something that **hugs** the ground or a stretch of land or water stays very close to it. □ *The road hugs the coast for hundreds of miles.*
NOUN [C] (**hugs**) If you give someone a **hug** you put your arms around them and hold them tightly, for example because you like them or are pleased to see them. □ *She leapt out of the back seat, and gave him a hug.*

huge ♦♦◊ /hjuːdʒ/ ADJ (**huger, hugest**) **1** Something or someone that is **huge** is extremely large in size. = massive □ *a tiny little woman with huge black glasses* **2** Something that is **huge** is extremely large in amount or degree. = enormous □ *I have a huge number of ties because I never throw them away.* **3** Something that is **huge** exists or happens on a very large scale, and involves a lot of different people or things. = enormous □ *Another team is looking at the huge problem of debts between companies.*
huge·ly /ˈhjuːdʒli/ ADV = enormously □ *In summer this hotel is a hugely popular venue for wedding receptions.*

hull /hʌl/ NOUN [C] (**hulls**) The **hull** of a boat or tank is the main body of it. □ *The hull had suffered extensive damage to the starboard side.*

hum /hʌm/ VERB, NOUN
VERB [I, T] (**hums, humming, hummed**) **1** [I] If something **hums**, it makes a low continuous noise. □ *The birds sang, the bees hummed.* **2** [I, T] When you **hum**, or **hum** a tune, you sing a tune with your lips closed. □ *She was humming a merry little tune.* **3** [I] If you say that a place **hums**, you mean that it is full of activity. □ *The place is really beginning to hum.*
NOUN [SING] A **hum** is a low continuous noise. □ *the hum of traffic*

◊hu·man ♦♦♦ /ˈhjuːmən/ ADJ, NOUN
ADJ **1** [human + N] **Human** means relating to or concerning people. □ *the human body* □ *It was one of the worst disasters in human history.* **2** **Human** feelings, weaknesses, or errors are ones that are typical of humans rather than machines. □ *an ever-growing risk of human error*
NOUN [C] (**humans**) You can refer to people as **humans**, especially when you are comparing them with animals or machines. = person, human being □ *Like humans, cats and dogs are omnivores.* □ *The drug was tested on animals before it was tested on humans.*

hu·man be·ing NOUN [C] (**human beings**) A **human being** is a man, woman, or child. □ *The treatment will be tried out on human beings only after it has been shown to be safe and foolproof in animals.*

hu·mane /hjuːˈmeɪn/ ADJ **1** **Humane** people act in a kind, sympathetic way towards other people and animals, and try to do them as little harm as possible. □ *In the mid-nineteenth century, Dorothea Dix began to campaign for humane treatment of the mentally ill.* **2** **Humane** values and societies encourage people to act in a kind and sympathetic way towards others, even towards people they do not agree with or like. □ *the humane values of socialism*
hu·mane·ly /hjuːˈmeɪnli/ ADV [humanely with V] □ *Suffering animals should be humanely euthanized on the farm.*

❂**hu·man·i·tar·ian** /hjuːˌmænɪˈteəriən/ ADJ If a person or society has **humanitarian** ideas or behaviour, they try to avoid making people suffer or they help people who are suffering. ❑ *Air bombardment raised criticism on the humanitarian grounds that innocent civilians might suffer.* ❑ *The UN also orchestrated humanitarian aid though there was much criticism at the lack of competence revealed that winter.*

❂**hu·man·i·ty** /hjuːˈmænɪti/ NOUN [U, PL] (**humanities**)
1 [U] All the people in the world can be referred to as **humanity**. ❑ *They face charges of committing crimes against humanity.* ❑ *a young lawyer full of illusions and love of humanity* **2** [U] (*formal*) A person's **humanity** is their state of being a human being, rather than an animal or an object. ❑ *He was under discussion and it made him feel deprived of his humanity.* ❑ *Only in dialogue with those who are different from ourselves do we enrich understanding of our shared humanity.* **3** [U] **Humanity** is the quality of being kind, thoughtful, and sympathetic towards others. ❑ *Her speech showed great maturity and humanity.* ❑ *a man who's almost lost his humanity in his bitter hatred of his rivals* **4** [PL] The **humanities** are the subjects such as history, philosophy, and literature which are concerned with human ideas and behaviour. = arts ❑ *Job seeking can be difficult for many humanities graduates.* ❑ *The number of students majoring in the humanities has declined by about half.*

hu·man rights ◆◇◇ NOUN [PL] **Human rights** are basic rights which many societies believe that all people should have. ❑ *In the treaty both sides pledge to respect human rights.*

hum·ble /ˈhʌmbəl/ ADJ, VERB
ADJ (**humbler, humblest**) **1** A **humble** person is not proud and does not believe that they are better than other people. ❑ *He gave a great performance, but he was very humble.* **2** People with low social status are sometimes described as **humble**. = lowly ❑ *Spyros Latsis started his career as a humble fisherman in the Aegean.* **3** A **humble** place or thing is ordinary and not special in any way. ❑ *There are restaurants, both humble and expensive, that specialize in noodles.* **4** People use **humble** in a phrase such as **in my humble opinion** as a polite way of emphasizing what they think, even though they do not feel humble about it. = modest ❑ *It is, in my humble opinion, perhaps the best steak restaurant in the city.*
PHRASE **eat humble pie** If you **eat humble pie**, you speak or behave in a way which tells people that you admit you were wrong about something. ❑ *Anson was forced to eat humble pie and publicly apologize to her.*
VERB [T] (**humbles, humbling, humbled**) **1** If you **humble** someone who is more important or powerful than you, you defeat them easily. ❑ *Honda won fame in the 1980s as the little car company that humbled the industry giants.* **2** If something or someone **humbles** you, they make you realize that you are not as important or good as you thought you were. ❑ *Ted's words humbled him.*
hum·bly /ˈhʌmbli/ ADV **1** [humbly with v] ❑ *'I'm a lucky man, undeservedly lucky,' he said humbly.* **2** [humbly before v] ❑ *So may I humbly suggest we all do something next time.*
hum·bling /ˈhʌmblɪŋ/ ADJ ❑ *Giving up an addiction is a humbling experience.*

hu·mid /ˈhjuːmɪd/ ADJ You use **humid** to describe an atmosphere or climate that is very damp, and usually very hot. = sticky, heavy ❑ *Visitors can expect hot and humid conditions.*

hu·mid·i·ty /hjuːˈmɪdɪti/ NOUN [U] **1** You say there is **humidity** when the air feels very heavy and damp. ❑ *The heat and humidity were insufferable.* **2** **Humidity** is the amount of water in the air. ❑ *The humidity is relatively low.*

hu·mil·i·ate /hjuːˈmɪlieɪt/ VERB [T] (**humiliates, humiliating, humiliated**) To **humiliate** someone means to say or do something which makes them feel ashamed or stupid. ❑ *She had been beaten and humiliated by her husband.*
hu·mil·i·at·ed /hjuːˈmɪlieɪtɪd/ ADJ ❑ *I have never felt so humiliated in my life.*

hu·mil·i·at·ing /hjuːˈmɪlieɪtɪŋ/ ADJ If something is **humiliating**, it embarrasses you and makes you feel ashamed and stupid. = crushing ❑ *The Democrats have suffered a humiliating defeat.*

hu·mil·i·a·tion /hjuːˌmɪliˈeɪʃən/ NOUN [U, C]
(**humiliations**) **1** [U] **Humiliation** is the embarrassment and shame you feel when someone makes you appear stupid, or when you make a mistake in public. ❑ *She faced the humiliation of discussing her husband's affair.* **2** [C] A **humiliation** is an occasion or a situation in which you feel embarrassed and ashamed. ❑ *The result is a humiliation for the president.*

hu·mil·i·ty /hjuːˈmɪlɪti/ NOUN [U] Someone who has **humility** is not proud and does not believe that they are better than other people. ❑ *a deep sense of humility*

hu·mor·ous /ˈhjuːmərəs/ ADJ If someone or something is **humorous**, they are amusing, especially in a clever or witty way. ❑ *He was quite humorous, and I liked that about him.*
hu·mor·ous·ly /ˈhjuːmərəsli/ ADV ❑ *He looked at me humorously as he wrestled with the door.*

hu·mour /ˈhjuːmə/ (*BrE*; in *AmE*, use **humor**) NOUN, VERB
NOUN [U, C] (**humours**) **1** [U] You can refer to the amusing things that people say as their **humour**. ❑ *Her humour and determination were a source of inspiration to others.* **2** [U] **Humour** is a quality in something that makes you laugh, for example in a situation, in someone's words or actions, or in a book or movie. ❑ *She felt sorry for the man but couldn't ignore the humour of the situation.* **3** [C, U] If you are **in a good humour**, you feel cheerful and happy, and are pleasant to people. If you are **in a bad humour**, you feel bad tempered and unhappy, and are unpleasant to people. = temper ❑ *Christina was still not clear why he had been in such ill humour.* **4** [U] If you do something with good **humour**, you do it cheerfully and pleasantly. ❑ *Hugo bore his illness with great courage and good humour.*
VERB [T] (**humours, humouring, humoured**) If you **humour** someone who is behaving strangely, you try to please them or pretend to agree with them, so that they will not become upset. ❑ *She disliked Dido but was prepared to tolerate her for a weekend in order to humour her husband.*

hump /hʌmp/ NOUN
NOUN [C] (**humps**) **1** A **hump** is a small hill or raised area. = mound ❑ *The path goes over a large hump by a tree before running near a road.* **2** A camel's **hump** is the large lump on its back. ❑ *Camels rebuild fat stores in their hump.*
PHRASE **over the hump** [V-LINK + over the hump] If you are **over the hump** in an unpleasant or difficult situation, you are past the worst part of it. ❑ *It has been a traumatic week, but they are over the hump.*

hun·dred ◆◆◆ /ˈhʌndrəd/ NUM, QUANT, PRON

> The plural form is **hundred** after a number, or after a word or expression referring to a number, such as 'several' or 'a few'.

NUM (**hundreds**) A **hundred** or **one hundred** is the number 100. ❑ *According to one official more than a hundred people have been arrested.*
PHRASE **a hundred per cent** or **one hundred per cent** (*informal, emphasis*) You can use **a hundred per cent** or **one hundred per cent** to emphasize that you agree completely with something or that it is completely right or wrong. = absolutely ❑ *Are you a hundred per cent sure it's your neighbour?*
QUANT [hundreds 'of' PL-N] (*emphasis*) If you refer to **hundreds of** things or people, you are emphasizing that there are very many of them. ❑ *Hundreds of tree species face extinction.*
PRON If you use **hundreds** to refer to things or people, you are emphasizing that there are very many of them. ❑ *Hundreds have been killed in the fighting and thousands made homeless.*

hun·dredth ◆◆◇ /ˈhʌndrədθ/ ADJ, NOUN
ADJ The **hundredth** item in a series is the one that you count as number one hundred. ❑ *The bank celebrates its hundredth anniversary in December.*
NOUN [C] (**hundredths**) A **hundredth of** something is one of a hundred equal parts of it. ❑ *Mitchell beat Lewis by three-hundredths of a second.*

hung /hʌŋ/ IRREG FORM, ADJ
IRREG FORM **Hung** is the past tense and past participle of most of the senses of **hang**.

ADJ A **hung** jury is the situation that occurs when a jury is unable to reach a decision because there is not a clear majority of its members in favour of any one decision. ❑ *His first trial ended in a hung jury.*

hun·ger /'hʌŋgə/ NOUN, VERB

NOUN [U, SING] **1** [U] **Hunger** is the feeling of weakness or discomfort that you get when you need something to eat. ❑ *Hunger is the body's signal that levels of blood sugar are too low.* **2** [U] **Hunger** is a severe lack of food which causes suffering or death. = starvation ❑ *Three hundred people in this town are dying of hunger every day.* **3** [SING] [also no DET] (*written*) If you have a **hunger for** something, you want or need it very much. = craving ❑ *Geffen has a hunger for success that seems bottomless.*

VERB [I] (**hungers, hungering, hungered**) (*formal, emphasis*) If you say that someone **hungers for** something or **hungers after** it, you are emphasizing that they want it very much. ❑ *But Jules was not eager for classroom learning, he hungered for adventure.*

hun·gry /'hʌŋgri/ ADJ, COMB

ADJ (**hungrier, hungriest**) **1** When you are **hungry**, you want some food because you have not eaten for some time and have an uncomfortable or painful feeling in your stomach. ❑ *My friend was hungry, so we drove to a shopping centre to get some food.* **2** (*literary, emphasis*) If you say that someone is **hungry** for something, you are emphasizing that they want it very much. = eager ❑ *I was hungry to be heard by my contemporaries.*

PHRASE **go hungry** If people **go hungry**, they do not have enough food to eat. ❑ *They brought her meat so that she never went hungry.*

COMB Hungry is also used in compound adjectives to indicate someone who wants a particular thing very much. ❑ *power-hungry politicians*

hun·gri·ly /'hʌŋgrɪli/ ADV **1** [hungrily with V] ❑ *James ate hungrily.* **2** [hungrily with V] ❑ *He looked at her hungrily. What eyes! What skin!*

hunt ♦◇◇ /hʌnt/ VERB, NOUN

VERB [I, T] (**hunts, hunting, hunted**) **1** [I] If you **hunt for** something or someone, you try to find them by searching carefully or thoroughly. = search ❑ *A forensic team was hunting for clues.* **2** [T] If you **hunt** a criminal or an enemy, you search for them in order to catch or harm them. ❑ *Detectives have been hunting him for seven months.* **3** [I, T] When people or animals **hunt**, or **hunt** something, they chase and sometimes kill wild animals for food or as a sport. ❑ *As a child I learned to hunt and fish.*

PHRASAL VERB **hunt down** If you **hunt down** a criminal or an enemy, you find them after searching for them. ❑ *Last December they hunted down and killed one of the gangsters.*

NOUN [C] (**hunts**) **1** A **hunt for** something or someone is when you try to find them by searching carefully or thoroughly. = search ❑ *The couple had helped in the hunt for the toddlers.* **2** A **hunt** for a criminal or an enemy is a search for them in order to catch or harm them. ❑ *Despite a nationwide hunt for the kidnap gang, not a trace of them was found.* **3** A **hunt** is when people or animals chase and sometimes kill wild animals for food or as a sport. ❑ *He set off for a nineteen-day moose hunt in Nova Scotia.*

PHRASE **in the hunt** (*informal*) If a team or competitor is **in the hunt for** something, they still have a chance of winning it. ❑ *Six teams were still in the hunt for the team title.*

hunt·er ♦◇◇ /'hʌntə/ NOUN [C] (**hunters**) **1** A **hunter** is a person who hunts wild animals for food or as a sport. ❑ *The hunters stalked their prey.* **2** People who are searching for things of a particular kind are often referred to as **hunters**. = seeker ❑ *job-hunters*

hunt·ing /'hʌntɪŋ/ NOUN, COMB

NOUN [U] **1 Hunting** is the chasing and usually the killing of wild animals by people or other animals, angry for food or as a sport. ❑ *He'd gone deer hunting with his cousins.* **2 Hunting** is the activity of searching for a particular thing. ❑ *Job hunting should be approached as a job in itself.*

COMB Hunting is used in compound nouns that refer to the search for a particular thing. ❑ *Make job-hunting a full-time job until you find one.*

hur·dle /'hɜːdəl/ NOUN, VERB

NOUN [C] (**hurdles**) **1** A **hurdle** is a problem, difficulty, or part of a process that may prevent you from achieving something. = obstacle ❑ *Two-thirds of candidates fail at this first hurdle and are sent home.* **2 Hurdles** is a race in which people have to jump over a number of obstacles that are also called hurdles. You can use **hurdles** to refer to one or more races. ❑ *Davis won the 400-metre hurdles in a new Olympic time of 49.3 sec.*

VERB [I, T] (**hurdles, hurdling, hurdled**) If you **hurdle**, you jump over something while you are running. ❑ *He crossed the lawn and hurdled the short fence.*

hurl /hɜːl/ VERB [T] (**hurls, hurling, hurled**) **1** If you **hurl** something, you throw it violently and with a lot of force. ❑ *Groups of angry youths hurled stones at police.* ❑ *Simon caught the grenade and hurled it back.* **2** If you **hurl** abuse or insults **at** someone, you shout insults at them aggressively. ❑ *How would you handle being locked in the back of a cab while the driver hurled abuse at you?*

❖hur·ri·cane /'hʌrɪkən, AmE 'hɜːrɪkeɪn/ NOUN [C] (**hurricanes**) A **hurricane** is an extremely violent storm that begins over ocean water. ❑ *In September 1813, a major hurricane destroyed US gunboats and ships that were defending St Mary's, Georgia, from the British.* ❑ *Around eight hurricanes are predicted to strike America this year.*

hur·ry /'hʌri, AmE 'hɜːri/ VERB, NOUN

VERB [I, T] (**hurries, hurrying, hurried**) **1** [I] If you **hurry** somewhere, you go there as quickly as you can. ❑ *Claire hurried along the road.* **2** [T] If you **hurry to** do something, you start doing it as soon as you can, or try to do it quickly. ❑ *Mrs Hardie hurried to make up for her tactlessness by asking her guest about his holiday.* **3** [T] To **hurry** something means the same as to **hurry up** something. ❑ *the president's attempt to hurry the process of independence* **4** [T] If you **hurry** someone to a place or into a situation, you try to make them go to that place or get into that situation quickly. = rush ❑ *They say they are not going to be hurried into any decision.*

PHRASAL VERB **hurry up** **1** If you tell someone to **hurry up**, you are telling them to do something more quickly than they were doing it. ❑ *Franklin told Howe to hurry up and take his bath; otherwise, they'd miss their train.* **2** If you **hurry** something **up** or **hurry** it **along**, you make it happen faster or sooner than it would otherwise have done. = speed up ❑ *if you're not a traditionalist and you want to hurry up the process*

NOUN [SING] If you are **in a hurry to** do something, you need or want to do something quickly. If you do something **in a hurry**, you do it quickly or suddenly. ❑ *Kate was in a hurry to grow up, eager for knowledge and experience.*

PHRASES **there's no hurry** If you say to someone 'There's no hurry' or 'I'm in no hurry', you are telling them that there is no need for them to do something immediately. ❑ *I'll need to talk with you, but there's no hurry.*

in no hurry If you are **in no hurry to** do something, you are very unwilling to do it. ❑ *I love it here so I'm in no hurry to go anywhere.*

hurt ♦♦◇ /hɜːt/ VERB, ADJ, NOUN

VERB [T, I] (**hurts, hurting, hurt**) **1** [T] If you **hurt yourself** or **hurt** a part of your body, you feel pain because you have injured yourself. ❑ *Yasin had seriously hurt himself while trying to escape from the police.* **2** [I] If a part of your body **hurts**, you feel pain there. ❑ *His collar bone only hurt when he lifted his arm.* **3** [I, T] If you **hurt** someone, you cause them to feel pain. ❑ *I didn't mean to hurt her, only to keep her still.* ❑ *That hurts!* **4** [I, T] If someone **hurts** you, they say or do something that makes you unhappy. ❑ *He is afraid of hurting Bessy's feelings.* ❑ *What hurts most is the betrayal.* **5** [I] If you say that you **are hurting**, you mean that you are experiencing emotional pain. ❑ *I am lonely and I am hurting.* **6** [T] To **hurt** someone or something means to have a bad effect on them or prevent them from succeeding. = damage ❑ *The combination of hot weather and decreased water supplies is hurting many industries.*

PHRASE **it won't hurt** or **it never hurts** (*informal*) If you say 'It **won't hurt to** do something' or 'It **never hurts to** do something', you are recommending an action which you think is helpful or useful. ❑ *It never hurts to ask.*

ADJ **1** If you are **hurt**, you have been injured. ❑ *His comrades asked him if he was hurt.* **2** If you are **hurt**, you are upset because of something that someone has said or done. ❑ *She was deeply hurt and shocked by what Smith had said.*

NOUN [c, u] (**hurts**) A feeling of **hurt** is a feeling that you have when you think that you have been treated badly or judged unfairly. = pain ❑ *I was full of jealousy and hurt.*

hurt·ful /ˈhɜːtfʊl/ ADJ If you say that someone's comments or actions are **hurtful**, you mean that they are unkind and upsetting. = upsetting ❑ *Her comments can only be very hurtful to Mrs Green's family.*

hus·band ♦♦♦ /ˈhʌzbənd/ NOUN [c] (**husbands**) A woman's **husband** is the man she is married to. ❑ *Eva married her husband Jack in 1957.*

hus·tle /ˈhʌsəl/ VERB, NOUN
VERB [T, I] (**hustles**, **hustling**, **hustled**) **1** [T] If you **hustle** someone, you try to make them go somewhere or do something quickly, for example by pulling or pushing them along. ❑ *The guards hustled Harry out of the car.* **2** [I] If you **hustle**, you go somewhere or do something as quickly as you can. ❑ *You'll have to hustle if you're to get home for supper.* **3** [I] (*mainly AmE*) If someone **hustles**, they try hard to earn money or to gain an advantage from a situation. ❑ *I like it here. It forces you to hustle and you can earn money.* ❑ *Hustling for social contacts isn't something that just happens. You have to make it happen.* **4** [T] (*mainly AmE*) If someone **hustles** you, or if they **hustle** something, they try hard to get something, often by using dishonest or illegal means. ❑ *Two teenage boys asked us for money, saying they were forming a baseball team. Anna said they were hustling us.* ❑ *He hustled several daytime jobs and finished his education at night.*

NOUN [u] **Hustle** is busy, noisy activity. = bustle ❑ *the hustle and bustle of New York*

hut /hʌt/ NOUN [c] (**huts**) **1** A **hut** is a small house with only one or two rooms, especially one which is made of wood, mud, grass, or stones. **2** (*BrE*; in *AmE*, use **shed**) A **hut** is a small wooden building in someone's garden, or a temporary building used by builders or repair workers.

⊕hy·brid /ˈhaɪbrɪd/ NOUN, ADJ
NOUN [c] (**hybrids**) **1** (*technical*) A **hybrid** is an animal or plant that has been bred from two different species of animal or plant. ❑ *All these brightly coloured hybrids are so lovely in the garden.* ❑ *a hybrid between water mint and spearmint* **2** A **hybrid** is a car that can be powered by either petrol or electricity. ❑ *Hybrids, unlike pure electric cars, never need to be plugged in.* **3** You can use **hybrid** to refer to anything that is a mixture of other things, especially two other things. ❑ *a hybrid of solid and liquid fuel* ❑ *a hybrid of psychological thriller and sci-fi mystery*

ADJ **1** [hybrid + N] A **hybrid** animal or plant is one that has been bred from two different species of animal or plant. ❑ *the hybrid corn seed* ❑ *You can cheat by buying a disease-resistant hybrid tea rose.* **2** A **hybrid car** is one that can be powered by either petrol or electricity. ❑ *Hybrid cars can go almost 600 miles between refuelling.* **3** [hybrid + N] A **hybrid** system or object is a mixture of other things, especially two other things. ❑ *a hybrid system* ❑ *incredible, strange, hybrid nonfiction*

⊕hy·drau·lic /haɪˈdrɒlɪk, AmE -ˈdrɔːl-/ ADJ [hydraulic + N] **Hydraulic** equipment or machinery involves or is operated by a fluid that is under pressure, such as water or oil. ❑ *The boat has no fewer than five hydraulic pumps.* ❑ *Below 400–500m, depth does not appear to be related to hydraulic conductivity.*

⊕hy·drau·li·cal·ly /haɪˈdrɒlɪkli/ ADV ❑ *hydraulically operated pistons for raising and lowering the blade* ❑ *a giant hydraulically powered cargo lift*

⊕hy·drau·lics /haɪˈdrɒlɪks, AmE -ˈdrɔːl-/ NOUN [u] **Hydraulics** is the study and use of systems that work using hydraulic pressure. ❑ *So for simple propulsion situations, hydraulics clearly aren't cost effective.*

⊕hydro·elec·tric /ˌhaɪdrəʊɪˈlektrɪk/ also **hydro-electric** ADJ [hydroelectric + N] **Hydroelectric** means

relating to or involving electricity made from the energy of running water. ❑ *Engineers say the river has huge potential for developing hydroelectric power.* ❑ *a vast impoverished region containing a hydroelectric dam and fertilizer factories*

⊕hydro·elec·tric·ity /ˌhaɪdrəʊɪlekˈtrɪsɪti/ NOUN [u] **Hydroelectricity** is electricity made from the energy of running water. ❑ *The greater benefit in Manitoba is because renewable hydroelectricity is used to run ethanol plants.* ❑ *Hydroelectricity is most efficiently generated in rugged topography.*

⊕hydro·gen /ˈhaɪdrədʒən/ NOUN [u] **Hydrogen** is a colourless gas that is the lightest and commonest element in the universe. ❑ *a ball of liquid and gaseous hydrogen* ❑ *Pure hydrogen is an explosive gas and difficult to store.*

⊕hy·giene /ˈhaɪdʒiːn/ NOUN [u] **Hygiene** is the practice of keeping yourself and your surroundings clean, especially in order to prevent illness or the spread of diseases. = cleanliness, sanitation ❑ *Be extra careful about personal hygiene.* ❑ *It was difficult to ensure hygiene when doctors were conducting numerous operations in quick succession.*

⊕hy·gien·ic /haɪˈdʒiːnɪk, AmE ˌhaɪdʒiˈenɪk/ ADJ Something that is **hygienic** is clean and unlikely to cause illness. = clean, sanitary; ≠ unhygienic ❑ *a white, clinical-looking kitchen that was easy to keep clean and hygienic* ❑ *Young people are generally less scrupulous in following hygienic food practices.* ❑ *Hospitals should be clean and hygienic.*

hype /haɪp/ (*disapproval*) NOUN, VERB
NOUN [u] (*disapproval*) **Hype** is the use of a lot of publicity and advertising to make people interested in something such as a product. ❑ *We are certainly seeing a lot of hype by some companies.*
VERB [T] (**hypes**, **hyping**, **hyped**) (*disapproval*) To **hype** a product means to advertise or praise it a lot. ❑ *We had to hype the film to attract the financiers.*
PHRASAL VERB **hype up** (*disapproval*) **Hype up** means the same as **hype** VERB. ❑ *The media seems obsessed with hyping up individuals or groups.*

hyper·link /ˈhaɪpəlɪŋk/ NOUN, VERB (*computing*)
NOUN [c] (**hyperlinks**) In an HTML document, a **hyperlink** is a link to another part of the document or to another document. Hyperlinks are shown as words with a line under them. ❑ *Web pages full of hyperlinks*
VERB [T] (**hyperlinks**, **hyperlinking**, **hyperlinked**) If a document or file is **hyperlinked**, it contains hyperlinks. ❑ *The database is fully hyperlinked both within the database and to thousands of external links.*

hy·phen /ˈhaɪfən/ NOUN [c] (**hyphens**) A **hyphen** is the punctuation sign used to join words together to make a compound, as in 'left-handed'. People also use a hyphen to show that the rest of a word is on the next line.

hyp·no·tism /ˈhɪpnətɪzəm/ NOUN [u] **Hypnotism** is the practice of hypnotizing people. = hypnosis ❑ *Dulcy also saw a psychiatrist who used hypnotism to help her deal with her fear.*

hyp·no·tist /ˈhɪpnətɪst/ NOUN [c] (**hypnotists**) A **hypnotist** is someone who hypnotizes people. ❑ *He was put into a trance by a police hypnotist.*

hyp·no·tize /ˈhɪpnətaɪz/ also **hypnotise** VERB [T] (**hypnotizes**, **hypnotizing**, **hypnotized**) **1** If someone **hypnotizes** you, they put you into a state in which you seem to be asleep but can still see, hear, or respond to things said to you. ❑ *A hypnotherapist will hypnotize you and will stop you from smoking.* **2** If you **are hypnotized by** someone or something, you are so fascinated by them that you cannot think of anything else. = mesmerize ❑ *He's hypnotized by that black hair and that white face.*

hy·poc·ri·sy /hɪˈpɒkrɪsi/ NOUN [c, u] (**hypocrisies**) (*disapproval*) If you accuse someone of **hypocrisy**, you mean that they pretend to have qualities, beliefs, or feelings that they do not really have. ❑ *He accused newspapers of hypocrisy in their treatment of the story.*

hypo·crite /ˈhɪpəkrɪt/ NOUN [c] (**hypocrites**) (*disapproval*) If you accuse someone of being a **hypocrite**, you mean that they pretend to have qualities, beliefs, or feelings that they do not really have. ❑ *The magazine wrongly suggested he was a liar and a hypocrite.*

hypo‧criti‧cal /ˌhɪpəˈkrɪtɪkəl/ ADJ (disapproval) If you accuse someone of being **hypocritical**, you mean that they pretend to have qualities, beliefs, or feelings that they do not really have. ❑ *It would be hypocritical to say I travel at 70 mph simply because that is the law.*

✪**hy‧poth‧esis** /haɪˈpɒθɪsɪs/ NOUN [C, U] (**hypotheses**) (academic word, formal) A **hypothesis** is an idea which is suggested as a possible explanation for a particular situation or condition, but which has not yet been proved to be correct. = theory, proposal ❑ *Work will now begin to test the hypothesis in rats.* ❑ *Different hypotheses have been put forward to explain why these foods are more likely to cause problems.*

✪**hy‧poth‧esize** /haɪˈpɒθɪsaɪz/ VERB [T] (**hypothesizes, hypothesizing, hypothesized**) (formal) If you **hypothesize that** something will happen, you say that you think that thing will happen because of various facts you have considered. ❑ *To explain this, they hypothesize that galaxies must contain a great deal of missing matter which cannot be detected.* ❑ *I have long hypothesized a connection between these factors.* ❑ *Hypothesizing other time dimensions does not in practice progress our understanding of precognition.*

✪**hypo‧theti‧cal** /ˌhaɪpəˈθetɪkəl/ ADJ If something is **hypothetical**, it is based on possible ideas or situations rather than actual ones. = theoretical ❑ *Let's look at a*

hypothetical situation in which Carol, a recovering alcoholic, gets invited to a party. ❑ *Candidates are required to describe what they would do in a variety of hypothetical situations.* ❑ *a purely hypothetical question*

✪**hypo‧theti‧cal‧ly** /ˌhaɪpəˈθetɪkli/ ADV = theoretically ❑ *He was invariably willing to discuss the possibilities hypothetically.* ❑ *It bases its figures on what it might, hypothetically, be earning on past investment.*

hys‧te‧ria /hɪˈstɪəriə, AmE -ˈster-/ NOUN [U] **Hysteria** among a group of people is a state of uncontrolled excitement, anger, or panic. ❑ *No one could help getting carried away by the hysteria.*

hys‧teri‧cal /hɪˈsterɪkəl/ ADJ **1** Someone who is **hysterical** is in a state of uncontrolled excitement, anger, or panic. ❑ *Police and bodyguards had to form a human shield around him as the almost hysterical crowds struggled to approach him.* **2** (informal) **Hysterical** laughter is loud and uncontrolled. ❑ *The young woman burst into hysterical laughter.* **3** (informal) If you describe something or someone as **hysterical**, you think that they are very funny and they make you laugh a lot. ❑ *Paul Mazursky was Master of Ceremonies, and he was pretty hysterical.*

hys‧teri‧cal‧ly /hɪˈsterɪkli/ ADV **1** [hysterically with V] ❑ *I don't think we can go around screaming hysterically: 'Ban these dogs. Muzzle all dogs.'* **2** She says she hasn't laughed as hysterically since she was 13. **3** [hysterically + ADJ] ❑ *It wasn't supposed to be a comedy but I found it hysterically funny.*

H

I i

I ◆◆◆ PRON, NOUN

[PRON] [I + v] A speaker or writer uses **I** to refer to himself or herself. **I** is a first person singular pronoun. **I** is used as the subject of a verb. ❑ *Jim and I are getting married.*

[NOUN] (also **i**) [C, U] (**I's, i's**) **I** is the ninth letter of the English alphabet.

○ **ibid.** /ˈɪbɪd/

[CONVENTION] **Ibid.** is used in books and journals to indicate that a piece of text taken from somewhere else is from the same source as the previous piece of text. ❑ *Edwin A Lane, Letter to the Editor, ibid., p 950.* ❑ *'to be able to obliterate or rather to unite the names of federalists and republicans' (quoted ibid., p155)*

○ **ice** ◆◆◇ /aɪs/ NOUN, VERB

[NOUN] [U] **Ice** is frozen water. ❑ *Glaciers are moving rivers of ice.* ❑ *The ice is melting.*

[PHRASES] **break the ice** If you **break the ice** at a party or meeting, or in a new situation, you say or do something to make people feel relaxed and comfortable. ❑ *That sort of approach should go a long way towards breaking the ice.*

cuts no ice If you say that something **cuts no ice** with you, you mean that you are not impressed or influenced by it. ❑ *That sort of romantic attitude cuts no ice with moneymen.*

on ice If someone puts a plan or project **on ice**, they delay doing it. ❑ *There would be a three-month delay while the deal would be put on ice.*

on thin ice If you say that someone is **on thin ice** or is **skating on thin ice**, you mean that they are doing something risky that may have serious or unpleasant consequences. ❑ *I had skated on thin ice on many assignments and somehow had got away with it.*

[VERB] [T] (**ices, icing, iced**) If you **ice** a cake, you cover it with icing. = frost ❑ *I've made the cake. I've iced and decorated it.*

ice cream also **ice-cream** NOUN [C, U] (**ice creams**)
1 [C, U] **Ice cream** is a very cold sweet food made from frozen cream or a substance like cream and has a flavour such as vanilla, chocolate, or strawberry. ❑ *I'll get you some ice cream.* **2** [C] An **ice cream** is an amount of ice cream sold in a small container or a cone made of a thin biscuit. ❑ *Do you want an ice cream?*

○ **icon** /ˈaɪkɒn/ also **ikon** NOUN [C] (**icons**) **1** If you describe something or someone as an **icon**, you mean that they are important as a symbol of a particular thing. = legend ❑ *only Marilyn has proved as enduring a fashion icon* ❑ *Mondale's icon status was on display on Wednesday night as nearly 1,000 Democrats nominated him for a return engagement in the Senate.* **2** An **icon** is a picture of Christ, his mother, or a saint painted on a wooden panel. ❑ *a painter of religious icons* **3** (computing) An **icon** is a picture on a computer screen representing a particular computer function. If you want to use it, you move the cursor onto the icon using a mouse. ❑ *Kate clicked on the mail icon on her computer screen.* ❑ *By default, you have just three icons on the desktop.*

○ **icon•ic** /aɪˈkɒnɪk/ ADJ An **iconic** image or thing is important or impressive because it seems to be a symbol of something. ❑ *The ads helped Nike to achieve iconic status.* ❑ *Doreen Lawrence is an iconic figure to many in the black community.*

icy /ˈaɪsi/ ADJ (**icier, iciest**) **1** If you describe something as **icy** or **icy cold**, you mean that it is extremely cold. ❑ *An icy wind blew hard across the open spaces.* **2** An **icy** road has ice on it. ❑ *The roads were icy.* **3** If you describe a person or their behaviour as **icy**, you mean that they are not affectionate or friendly, and they show their dislike or anger in a quiet, controlled way. = cold, frosty ❑ *His response was icy.*

ID /ˌaɪ ˈdiː/ NOUN [C, U] (**IDs**) If you have **ID** or an **ID**, you are carrying a document such as an identity card or driving licence that tells who you are. = identification ❑ *I had no ID on me so the police couldn't establish that I was the owner of the car.*

○ **idea** ◆◆◆ /aɪˈdiːə/ NOUN [C, SING] (**ideas**) **1** [C] An **idea** is a plan, suggestion, or possible course of action. ❑ *It's a good idea to have your blood pressure checked regularly.* ❑ *I really like the idea of helping people.* ❑ *She told me she'd had a brilliant idea.* **2** [C] An **idea** is an opinion or belief about what something is like or should be like. = notion, concept ❑ *Some of his ideas about democracy are entirely his own.* ❑ *the idea that reading too many books ruins your eyes* **3** [SING] If someone gives you an **idea of** something, they give you information about it without being very exact or giving a lot of detail. ❑ *This table will give you some idea of how levels of ability in a foreign language can be measured.* **4** [SING] If you have an **idea** of something, you know about it to some extent. ❑ *No one has any real idea how much the company will make next year.* ❑ *We had no idea what was happening.* **5** [SING] If you have an **idea that** something is the case, you think that it may be the case, although you are not certain. ❑ *I had an idea that he joined the army later, after college, but I may be wrong.* **6** [SING] The **idea** of an action or activity is its aim or purpose. = objective ❑ *The idea is to get industry to be more efficient in the way it uses energy.* **7** [C] If you have the **idea of** doing something, you intend to do it. = intention ❑ *He sent for a number of books he admired with the idea of rereading them.*

WORD CONNECTIONS
VERB + **idea**
have an idea
get an idea
❑ *If you have any ideas where we could go, let me know.*
ADJ + **idea**
a **good** idea
a **bright** idea
a **brilliant** idea
a **great** idea
an **interesting** idea
❑ *It's a good idea to fit smoke alarms throughout the house.*
a **bad** idea
a **crazy** idea
❑ *I had the crazy idea that I could give up my job and live on a small island.*
a **new** idea
an **original** idea
❑ *The book is full of original ideas for decorating your home.*

the **whole** idea
the **main** idea
❏ *The whole idea was to make some money.*

⊕**ideal** ♦◇◇ /aɪˈdiːəl/ NOUN, ADJ
NOUN [C, SING] (**ideals**) **1** [C] An **ideal** is a principle, idea, or standard that seems very good and worth trying to achieve. = principle, belief, value ❏ *Walt Disney stayed true to his ideals.* ❏ *The party has drifted too far from its socialist ideals.* ❏ *Republics embody the ideal of equality among citizens in political affairs.* **2** [SING] Your **ideal of** something is the person or thing that seems to you to be the best possible example of it. ❏ *Her features were almost the opposite of the Japanese ideal of beauty in those days.*
ADJ **1** The **ideal** person or thing for a particular task or purpose is the best possible person or thing for it. = perfect ❏ *She decided that I was the ideal person to take over the job.* ❏ *I see this as an ideal place to start my managerial career.* ❏ *ideal conditions for growth* **2** [ideal + N] An **ideal** society or world is the best possible one that you can imagine. ❏ *We do not live in an ideal world.*

⊕**ideal·ism** /aɪˈdiːəlɪzəm/ NOUN [U] **Idealism** is the beliefs and behaviour of someone who has ideals and who tries to base their behaviour on these ideals. = optimism; ≠ realism, pessimism, cynicism ❏ *She never lost her respect for the idealism of the 1960s.* ❏ *This experience has tempered their idealism.*
ideal·ist /aɪˈdiːəlɪst/ NOUN [C] (**idealists**) ❏ *He is not such an idealist that he cannot see the problems.*

⊕**ideal·is·tic** /ˌaɪdiəˈlɪstɪk/ ADJ If you describe someone as **idealistic**, you mean that they have ideals, and base their behaviour on these ideals, even though this may be impractical. = optimistic, impractical; ≠ realistic, pessimistic, cynical ❏ *Idealistic young people died for the cause.* ❏ *an over-simplistic and idealistic vision of family dynamics*

ideal·ize /aɪˈdiːəlaɪz/ also **idealise** VERB [T] (**idealizes, idealizing, idealized**) If you **idealize** something or someone, you think of them, or represent them to other people, as being perfect or much better than they really are. ❏ *People idealize the past.*

⊕**ideal·ly** /aɪˈdiːəli/ ADV **1** [ideally with CL/GROUP] If you say that **ideally** a particular thing should happen or be done, you mean that this is what you would like to happen or be done, but you know that this may not be possible or practical. = preferably ❏ *People should, ideally, be persuaded to eat a diet with much less fat or oil.* ❏ *The restructuring ideally needs to be completed this year.* **2** If you say that someone or something is **ideally** suited, **ideally** located, or **ideally** qualified, you mean that they are as well suited, located, or qualified as they could possibly be. = perfectly ❏ *They were an extremely happy couple, ideally suited.* ❏ *The hotel is ideally situated for country walks.*

⊕**iden·ti·cal** /aɪˈdentɪkəl/ ADJ (*academic word*) Things that are **identical** are exactly the same. = the same, indistinguishable; ≠ different ❏ *The three bombs were virtually identical.* ❏ *The new buildings look identical to those built 200 years ago.* ❏ *The two parties fought the last election on almost identical manifestos.*
⊕**iden·ti·cal·ly** /aɪˈdentɪkli/ ADV ≠ differently ❏ *nine identically dressed female dancers* ❏ *two separate but identically worded statements* ❏ *Not all people respond identically to the same diet.*

iden·ti·fi·able /aɪˌdentɪˈfaɪəbəl/ ADJ Something or someone that is **identifiable** can be recognized. = recognizable ❏ *In the corridor were four dirty, ragged bundles, just identifiable as human beings.*

⊕**iden·ti·fi·ca·tion** /aɪˌdentɪfɪˈkeɪʃən/ NOUN [C, U] (**identifications**) **1** [C, U] The **identification** of something is the recognition that it exists, is important, or is true. = recognition ❏ *Early identification of a disease can prevent death and illness.* ❏ *the identification of training needs* **2** [C, U] The **identification** of a particular person or thing is the ability to name them because you know them or recognize them. ❏ *Officials are awaiting positive identification before charging the men with war crimes.* **3** [U] If someone asks you for some **identification**, they want to see something such

as a driving licence, that proves who you are. = ID ❏ *He did not have any identification when he arrived at the hospital.* **4** [C, U] The **identification of** one person or thing **with** another is the close association of one with the other. = association ❏ *the identification of Spain with Catholicism* **5** [U] **Identification with** someone or something is the feeling of sympathy and support for them. = empathy ❏ *Marilyn had an intense identification with animals.*

⊕**iden·ti·fy** ♦♦◇ /aɪˈdentɪfaɪ/ VERB [T, I] (**identifies, identifying, identified**) (*academic word*) **1** [T] If you can **identify** someone or something, you are able to recognize them or distinguish them from others. = recognize, distinguish ❏ *There are a number of distinguishing characteristics by which you can identify a Hollywood epic.* **2** [T] If you **identify** someone or something, you name them or say who or what they are. = name ❏ *Police have already identified 10 murder suspects.* **3** [T] If you **identify** something, you discover or notice its existence. = discover ❏ *Scientists claim to have identified chemicals produced by certain plants which have powerful cancer-fighting properties.* ❏ *It was not until the twentieth century that mosquitoes were identified as the carriers of malaria.* **4** [T] If a particular thing **identifies** someone or something, it makes them easy to recognize, by making them different in some way. = distinguish ❏ *She wore a little nurse's hat on her head to identify her.* **5** [I] If you **identify with** someone or something, you feel that you understand them or their feelings and ideas. ❏ *She would only play a role if she could identify with the character.* **6** [T] If you **identify** one person or thing **with** another, you think that they are closely associated or involved in some way. = associate ❏ *Moore really hates to play the sweet, passive women that audiences have identified her with.*

⊕**iden·tity** ♦◇◇ /aɪˈdentɪti/ NOUN [C, U] (**identities**) **1** [C] Your **identity** is who you are. ❏ *Abu is not his real name, but it's one he uses to disguise his identity.* ❏ *The identities of the victims were announced.* ❏ *the growing problem of identity theft* **2** [C, U] The **identity** of a person or place is the characteristics that distinguish them from others. ❏ *I wanted a sense of my own identity.*

WORD CONNECTIONS
VERB + **identity**
reveal an identity
disclose an identity
establish an identity
confirm an identity
❏ *Police haven't yet disclosed the identity of the victim.*
steal an identity
protect an identity
❏ *If a thief gets hold of your personal details, they can steal your identity, and apply for loans in your name.*
ADJ + **identity**
mistaken identity
false identity
true identity
❏ *A man was shot in what is believed to be a case of mistaken identity.*

⊕**ideo·logi·cal** /ˌaɪdiəˈlɒdʒɪkəl/ ADJ **Ideological** means relating to principles or beliefs. ❏ *Others left the party for ideological reasons.* ❏ *The ideological divisions between the parties aren't always obvious.* ❏ *a world divided along ideological lines*
ideo·logi·cal·ly /ˌaɪdiəˈlɒdʒɪkli/ ADV ❏ *an ideologically sound organization*

⊕**ideol·ogy** /ˌaɪdiˈɒlədʒi/ NOUN [C, U] (**ideologies**) (*academic word*) An **ideology** is a set of beliefs, especially the political beliefs on which people, parties, or countries base their actions. = values, beliefs, doctrine ❏ *capitalist ideology* ❏ *North Carolina, more than any other southern state, is the home of two disparate, yet equally powerful, political ideologies.* ❏ *Fifteen years after the president embraced the ideology of privatization, the people were worse off than ever.*

idio·syn·crat·ic /ˌɪdiəʊsɪŋˈkrætɪk/ ADJ If you describe

someone's actions or characteristics as **idiosyncratic,** you mean that they are somewhat unusual. = eccentric □ *a highly idiosyncratic personality*

id·i·ot /'ɪdiət/ NOUN [c] (**idiots**) (*disapproval*) If you call someone an **idiot,** you are showing that you think they are very stupid or have done something very stupid. = fool □ *I knew I'd been an idiot to stay there.*

idle /'aɪdəl/ ADJ, VERB

ADJ **1** [V-LINK + idle] If people who were working are **idle,** they have no jobs or work. □ *4,000 workers have been idle for 12 of the first 27 weeks of this year.* **2** [V-LINK + idle] If machines or factories are **idle,** they are not working or being used. □ *Now the machine is lying idle.* **3** If you say that someone is **idle,** you disapprove of them because they are not doing anything and you think they should be. □ *idle bureaucrats who spent the day reading newspapers* **4** [idle + N] **Idle** is used to describe something that you do for no particular reason, often because you have nothing better to do. □ *Brian kept up the idle chatter for another five minutes.* **5** [idle + N] You refer to an **idle** threat or boast when you do not think the person making it will or can do what they say. = empty □ *It was more of an idle threat than anything.*

VERB [i] (**idles, idling, idled**) If an engine or vehicle is **idling,** the engine is running slowly and quietly because it is not in gear, and the vehicle is not moving. □ *Beyond a stand of trees a small plane idled.*

idly /'aɪdli/ ADV **1** [idly with V] □ *We were not idly sitting around.* **2** *We talked idly about magazines and baseball.*

✪ **i.e.** /,aɪ 'iː/ **i.e.** is used to introduce a word or sentence that makes what you have just said clearer or gives details. = that is, in other words □ *an artificial intelligence system, i.e. a computer program* □ *strategic points – i.e. airports or military bases* □ *concerns that the vitamin might be carcinogenic (i.e. cancer inducing)*

if ♦♦♦ /ɪf/ CONJ

CONJ **1** You use **if** in conditional sentences to introduce the circumstances in which an event or situation might happen, might be happening, or might have happened. □ *She gets very upset if I exclude her from anything.* □ *You can go if you want.* **2** You use **if** in indirect questions where the answer is either 'yes' or 'no'. = whether □ *He asked if I had left with you, and I said no.* **3** You use **if** to suggest that something might be slightly different from what you are stating in the main part of the sentence, for example, that there might be slightly more or less of a particular quality. □ *Sometimes that standard is quite difficult, if not impossible, to achieve.* **4** You use **if,** usually with 'can', 'could', 'may', or 'might', in a conversation when you are politely trying to make a point, change the subject, or interrupt another speaker. □ *If I could just make another small point about the weightlifters in the Olympics.* **5** You use **if** at or near the beginning of a clause when politely asking someone to do something. □ *I wonder if you'd be kind enough to give us some information, please?* **6** You use **if** to introduce a subordinate clause in which you admit a fact that you regard as less important than the statement in the main clause. □ *If there was any disappointment it was probably temporary.*

PHRASES **if not** You use **if not** in front of a word or phrase to indicate that your statement does not apply to that word or phrase, but to something closely related to it that you also mention. □ *She understood his meaning, if not his words, and took his advice.*

if ever (*emphasis*) You use **if ever** with past tenses when you are introducing a description of a person or thing, to emphasize how appropriate it is. □ *I became a distraught, worried mother, a useless role if ever there was one.*

if only 1 You use **if only** with past tenses to introduce what you think is a fairly good reason for doing something, although you realize it may not be a very good one. □ *She always writes me once a month, if only to scold me because I haven't answered her last letter yet.* **2** (*feelings*) You use **if only** to express a wish or desire, especially one that cannot be fulfilled. □ *If only you had told me that some time ago.*

as if 1 You use **as if** when you are making a judgment about something that you see or notice. Your belief or impression might be correct, or it might be wrong. □ *It looked as if she had forgotten how to breathe.* **2** You use **as if** to describe something or someone by comparing them with another thing or person. □ *He points two fingers at his head, as if he were holding a gun.* **3** (*spoken, emphasis*) You use **as if** to emphasize that something is not true. □ *Getting my work done! My God! As if it mattered.*

ig·no·rance /'ɪgnərəns/ NOUN [u] **Ignorance of** something is lack of knowledge about it. □ *I am beginning to feel embarrassed by my complete ignorance of world history.*

ig·no·rant /'ɪgnərənt/ ADJ (*academic word*) **1** If you describe someone as **ignorant,** you mean that they do not know things they should know. If they are **ignorant of** a fact, they do not know it. □ *People don't like to ask questions for fear of appearing ignorant.* **2** People are sometimes described as **ignorant** when they do something that is not polite or kind. □ *I met some ignorant people who called me all kinds of names.*

✪ **ig·nore** ♦♦◇ /ɪg'nɔː/ VERB [T] (**ignores, ignoring, ignored**) (*academic word*) **1** If you **ignore** someone or something, you pay no attention to them. □ *She said her husband ignored her.* □ *They had ignored the warning signs.* □ *She ignored legal advice to drop the case.* **2** If you say that an argument or theory **ignores** an important aspect of a situation, you are criticizing it because it fails to consider that aspect or to take it into account. = overlook; ≠ notice □ *Such arguments ignore the question of where ultimate responsibility lay.* □ *His article ignores the fact that the environment can exaggerate small genetic differences.*

ill ♦♦◇ /ɪl/ ADJ, NOUN, ADV

ADJ **1** Someone who is **ill** is suffering from a disease or a health problem. □ *In November 1941 Payne was seriously ill with pneumonia.* **2** [ill + N] (*formal*) You can use **ill** in front of some nouns to indicate that you are referring to something harmful or unpleasant. = bad □ *She had brought ill luck into her family.*

PHRASE **fall ill** or **be taken ill** If you **fall ill** or **are taken ill,** you suddenly become ill. □ *Shortly before Christmas, he was mysteriously taken ill.*

NOUN [PL, c, u] (**ills**) **1** [PL] People who are ill in some way can be referred to as, for example, **the mentally ill.** □ *The hospice provides care for the terminally ill.* **2** [c] (*formal*) Difficulties and problems are sometimes referred to as **ills.** □ *His critics maintain that he's responsible for many of Algeria's ills.* **3** [u] (*literary*) **Ill** is evil or harm. □ *They say they mean you no ill.*

ADV [ill with V] (*formal*) **Ill** means the same as 'badly'. □ *The company's conservative instincts sit ill with competition.*

PHRASE **can ill afford** (*formal*) If you say that someone **can ill afford to** do something, or **can ill afford** something, you mean that they must prevent it from happening because it would be harmful or embarrassing to them. □ *It's possible he won't play but I can ill afford to lose him.*

✦ **speak ill of someone** → see **speak**

✪ **il·legal** ♦◇◇ /ɪ'liːgəl/ ADJ, NOUN (*academic word*)

ADJ **1** If something is **illegal,** the law says that it is not allowed. = unlawful; ≠ legal □ *It is illegal to intercept radio messages.* □ *illegal drugs* □ *Birth control was illegal there until 1978.* **2** [illegal + N] **Illegal** immigrants or workers have travelled into a country or are working without official permission.

NOUN [c] (**illegals**) Illegal immigrants or workers are sometimes referred to as **illegals.** □ *a clothing factory where many other illegals also worked*

✪ **il·legal·ly** /ɪ'liːgəli/ ADV [illegally with V] ≠ legally □ *He was convicted of illegally using a handgun.* □ *The previous government had acted illegally.*

WORD PARTS
The prefix **il-** often gives a word the opposite meaning:
illegal (ADJ)
illogical (ADJ)
illiterate (ADJ)

il·legiti·mate /,ɪlɪ'dʒɪtɪmət/ ADJ **1** A person who is **illegitimate** was born of parents who were not married to each other. □ *They discovered he had an illegitimate child.*

2 Illegitimate is used to describe activities and institutions that are not in accordance with the law or with accepted standards of what is right. ❏ *He realized that, otherwise, the election would have been dismissed as illegitimate by the international community.*

il·lic·it /ɪˈlɪsɪt/ ADJ An **illicit** activity or substance is not allowed by law or the social customs of a country. ❏ *Dante clearly condemns illicit love.*

✪ il·lit·er·ate /ɪˈlɪtərət/ ADJ, NOUN
ADJ Someone who is **illiterate** does not know how to read or write. ≠ literate ❏ *A large percentage of the population is illiterate.* ❏ *Seven out of ten prisoners are functionally illiterate.* ❏ *India's neglected and largely illiterate tribal populations*
NOUN [c] (**illiterates**) An **illiterate** is someone who is illiterate. ❏ *a subclass of illiterates*

ill·ness ◆◇◇ /ˈɪlnəs/ NOUN [U, C] (**illnesses**) **1** [U] **Illness** is the fact or experience of being ill. ❏ *If your child shows any signs of illness, take her to the doctor.* **2** [c] An **illness** is a particular disease such as measles or pneumonia. ❏ *She returned to her family home to recover from an illness.*

WHICH WORD?
illness or disease?

If you have an **illness**, there is something wrong with your health, so that you cannot work or live normally. An **illness** can affect several parts of your body. It can last for a long time or a short time, and its effects can be serious or not serious.

❏ *The doctor believed that Stephen's **illness** was due to overwork.*
❏ *He died at the age of 66 after a long **illness**.*

A **disease** is a particular kind of illness, often caused by bacteria or an infection. It is usually fairly serious, and affects the organs.

❏ *I have a rare eye **disease**.*
❏ *Whooping cough is a dangerous **disease** for babies.*

✪ il·log·i·cal /ɪˈlɒdʒɪkəl/ ADJ (academic word, disapproval) If you describe an action, feeling, or belief as **illogical**, you are critical of it because you think that it does not result from a logical and ordered way of thinking. = irrational, unreasonable; ≠ logical, rational, reasonable ❏ *It was absurd and illogical to go out into such a storm.* ❏ *It is illogical to oppose the repatriation of economic migrants.* ❏ *But, however hard it is, you have to accept that bombing is just the illogical conclusion of everyday prejudice.*

il·lu·mi·nate /ɪˈluːmɪneɪt/ VERB [T] (**illuminates, illuminating, illuminated**) (formal) **1** To **illuminate** something means to shine light on it and to make it brighter and more visible. ❏ *No streetlights illuminated the street.* **2** If you **illuminate** something that is unclear or difficult to understand, you make it clearer by explaining it carefully or giving information about it. ❏ *Instead of formulas and charts, the two instructors use games and drawings to illuminate their subject.*
il·lu·mi·nat·ing /ɪˈluːmɪneɪtɪŋ/ ADJ ❏ *It would be illuminating to hear the views of the club vice-chairman.*

il·lu·mi·na·tion /ɪˌluːmɪˈneɪʃən/ NOUN [U] (formal) **Illumination** is the lighting that a place has. ❏ *The only illumination came from a small window high in the opposite wall.*

il·lu·sion /ɪˈluːʒən/ NOUN [C, U] (**illusions**) **1** [c, u] An **illusion** is a false idea or belief. = delusion ❏ *No one really has any illusions about winning the war.* **2** [c] An **illusion** is something that appears to exist or be a particular thing but does not actually exist or is in reality something else. ❏ *Floor-to-ceiling windows can look stunning, giving the illusion of extra height.*

✪ il·lus·trate ◆◇◇ /ˈɪləstreɪt/ VERB [T] (**illustrates, illustrating, illustrated**) (academic word) **1** If you say that something **illustrates** a situation that you are drawing attention to, you mean that it shows that the situation exists. = demonstrate ❏ *The example of the United States illustrates this point.* ❏ *The situation illustrates how vulnerable the president is.* ❏ *The incident graphically illustrates how parlous their position is.* ❏ *The case also illustrates that some*

women are now trying to fight back. **2** If you use an example, story, or diagram to **illustrate** a point, you use it to show that what you are saying is true or to make your meaning clearer. = demonstrate, exemplify ❏ *Let me give another example to illustrate this difficult point.* ❏ *To illustrate this point, Wolf gives an example from the car production sector in America.* ❏ *Throughout, she illustrates her analysis with excerpts from discussions.* **3** If you **illustrate** a book, you put pictures, photographs, or diagrams into it. ❏ *She went on to art school and is now illustrating a book.*

✪ il·lus·tra·tion ◆◇◇ /ˌɪləˈstreɪʃən/ NOUN [C, U] (**illustrations**) **1** [c] An **illustration** is an example or a story that is used to make a point clear. ❏ *An illustration of China's dynamism is that a new company is formed in Shanghai every 11 seconds.* **2** [u] **Illustration** is the use of examples, stories, or diagrams to show that what you are saying is true or to make your meaning clearer. = demonstration, example ❏ *Here, by way of illustration, are some extracts from our new catalogue.* ❏ *a perfect illustration of the way Britain absorbs and adapts external influences* ❏ *This can best be described by way of illustration.* **3** [c] An **illustration** in a book is a picture, design, or diagram. ❏ *She looked like a princess in a nineteenth-century illustration.* **4** [u] **Illustration** is the act of creating pictures, photographs, or diagrams for a book. ❏ *the world of children's book illustration*

✪ im·age ◆◆◇ /ˈɪmɪdʒ/ NOUN (academic word)
NOUN [c] (**images**) **1** If you have an **image** of something or someone, you have a picture or idea of them in your mind. ❏ *The image of art theft as a gentleman's crime is outdated.* **2** The **image** of a person, group, or organization is the way that they appear to other people. = impression, reputation ❏ *the government's negative public image* ❏ *He has cultivated the image of an elder statesman.* ❏ *The tobacco industry has been trying to improve its image.* **3** (formal) An **image** is a picture of someone or something. = picture ❏ *photographic images of young children* ❏ *A computer in the machine creates an image on the screen.* **4** (formal) An **image** is a poetic description of something. ❏ *The natural images in the poem are meant to be suggestive of realities beyond themselves.*
PHRASE **be the image of someone** If you **are the image** of someone else, you look very much like them. ❏ *Marianne's son was the image of his father.*
✦ spitting image → see spit

✪ im·age·ry /ˈɪmɪdʒri/ NOUN [U] (academic word, formal) **1** You can refer to the descriptions in something such as a poem or song, and the pictures they create in your mind, as its **imagery**. ❏ *the nature imagery of the ballad* ❏ *Her prose was poetic and subtly energized by her use of visual imagery.* **2** You can refer to pictures and representations of things as **imagery**, especially when they act as symbols. ❏ *This is an ambitious and intriguing film, full of striking imagery.* ❏ *Sexual imagery in advertising is hardly anything new.*

im·agi·nable /ɪˈmædʒɪnəbəl/ ADJ (emphasis) **1** You use **imaginable** after a superlative such as 'best' or 'worst' to emphasize that something is extreme in some way. = conceivable ❏ *their imprisonment under some of the most horrible circumstances imaginable* **2** [imaginable + N, N + imaginable] You use **imaginable** after a word like 'every' or 'all' to emphasize that you are talking about all the possible examples of something. You use **imaginable** after 'no' to emphasize that something does not have the quality mentioned. = possible ❏ *Parents encourage every activity imaginable.* ❏ *a place of no imaginable strategic value*

im·agi·nary /ɪˈmædʒɪnəri, AmE -neri/ ADJ An **imaginary** person, place, or thing exists only in your mind or in a story, and not in real life. ❏ *Lots of children have imaginary friends.*

im·agi·na·tion ◆◇◇ /ɪˌmædʒɪˈneɪʃən/ NOUN
NOUN [c, u] (**imaginations**) **1** [c, u] Your **imagination** is the ability that you have to form pictures or ideas in your mind of things that are new and exciting, or things that you have not experienced. ❏ *Latanya is a woman with a vivid imagination.* **2** [c] Your **imagination** is the part of your mind that allows you to form pictures or ideas of things that do not necessarily exist in real life. ❏ *Long before I ever went there, Africa was alive in my imagination.*

PHRASE **capture someone's imagination** or **catch someone's imagination** If you say that someone or something **captured** your **imagination**, you mean that you thought they were interesting or exciting when you saw them or heard them for the first time. ❑ *Their music continues to capture the imagination of the American public.*
✦ **not by any stretch of the imagination** → see **stretch**

im·agi·na·tive /ɪˈmædʒɪnətɪv/ ADJ *(approval)* If you describe someone or their ideas as **imaginative**, you are praising them because they are easily able to think of or create new or exciting things. = inventive ❑ *an imaginative writer*
im·agi·na·tive·ly /ɪˈmædʒɪnətɪvli/ ADV [imaginatively with V] ❑ *The hotel is decorated imaginatively and attractively.*

im·ag·ine ◆◆◇ /ɪˈmædʒɪn/ VERB [T] **(imagines, imagining, imagined)** **1** If you **imagine** something, you think about it and your mind forms a picture or idea of it. ❑ *He could not imagine a more peaceful scene.* **2** If you **imagine** that something is the case, you think that it is the case. = suppose ❑ *I imagine you're referring to Jean-Paul Sartre.* **3** If you **imagine** something, you think that you have seen, heard, or experienced that thing, although actually you have not. = dream ❑ *Looking back on it now, I realized that I must have imagined the whole thing.*

im·bal·ance /ɪmˈbæləns/ NOUN [C, U] **(imbalances)** If there is an **imbalance** in a situation, the things involved are not the same size, or are not the right size in proportion to each other. ❑ *the imbalance between the two sides in this war*

⊕**imi·tate** /ˈɪmɪteɪt/ VERB [T] **(imitates, imitating, imitated)** **1** If you **imitate** someone, you copy what they do or produce. = copy, recreate ❑ *a genuine German musical that does not try to imitate the American model* ❑ *an American style of architecture that has been widely imitated in Europe* **2** If you **imitate** a person or animal, you copy the way they speak or behave, usually because you are trying to be funny. = mimic ❑ *Clarence screws up his face and imitates the Colonel again.*

⊕**imi·ta·tion** /ˌɪmɪˈteɪʃən/ NOUN, ADJ
NOUN [C, U] **(imitations)** **1** [C] An **imitation** of something is a copy of it. = copy, replica ❑ *the most accurate imitation of Chinese architecture in Europe* ❑ *Then the British invasion of Spanish beaches created the Euro-pub, albeit a pale imitation of the real thing.* **2** [U] **Imitation** means copying someone else's actions. ❑ *They discussed important issues in imitation of their elders.* **3** [C] If someone does an **imitation** of another person, they copy the way they speak or behave, sometimes in order to be funny. = impersonation ❑ *One boy did an imitation of a soldier with a loudspeaker.*
ADJ [imitation + N] **Imitation** things are not genuine but are made to look as if they are. ❑ *a complete set of Dickens bound in imitation leather*

im·macu·late /ɪˈmækjʊlət/ ADJ **1** If you describe something as **immaculate**, you mean that it is extremely clean, tidy, or neat. = pristine ❑ *Her kitchen was kept immaculate.* **2** If you say that something is **immaculate**, you are emphasizing that it is perfect, without any mistakes or bad parts at all. = flawless ❑ *The goalie's performance was immaculate.*
im·macu·late·ly /ɪˈmækjʊlətli/ ADV **1** As always he was immaculately dressed. **2** [immaculately with V] ❑ *The orchestra plays immaculately.*

im·ma·ture /ˌɪməˈtjʊə, AmE -ˈtʊr/ ADJ **1** Something or someone that is **immature** is not yet completely grown or fully developed. ❑ *She is emotionally immature.* **2** *(disapproval)* If you describe someone as **immature**, you are being critical of them because they do not behave in a sensible or responsible way. ❑ *She's just being childish and immature.*

WORD PARTS
The prefix **im-** often gives a word the opposite meaning:
immature (ADJ)
impossible (ADJ)
impractical (ADJ)
---

im·ma·tur·ity /ˌɪməˈtjʊərɪti, AmE -ˈtʊr-/ NOUN [U] **1** **Immaturity** is the state of being not yet completely

grown or fully developed. ❑ *Photographs of the boy showed his physical immaturity.* **2** *(disapproval)* **Immaturity** is a lack of the qualities and behaviour that you would expect from a sensible adult. ❑ *I am disgusted by the immaturity and stupidity presented in this column.*

im·medi·ate ◆◇◇ /ɪˈmiːdiət/ ADJ **1** An **immediate** result, action, or reaction happens or is done without any delay. = instant ❑ *These tragic incidents have had an immediate effect.* **2** **Immediate** needs and concerns exist at the present time and must be dealt with quickly. = pressing ❑ *Relief agencies say the immediate problem is not a lack of food, but transportation.* **3** [immediate + N] The **immediate** person or thing comes just before or just after another person or thing in a sequence. ❑ *In the immediate aftermath of the riots, a mood of hope and reconciliation sprang up.* **4** [immediate + N] You use **immediate** to describe an area or position that is next to or very near a particular place or person. ❑ *Only a handful had returned to work in the immediate vicinity.* **5** [immediate + N] Your **immediate** family are the members of your family who are most closely related to you, such as your parents, children, brothers, and sisters. ❑ *The presence of his immediate family is obviously having a calming effect on him.*

im·medi·ate·ly ◆◆◇ /ɪˈmiːdiətli/ ADV **1** [immediately with V] If something happens **immediately**, it happens without any delay. ❑ *He immediately flung himself to the floor.* **2** [immediately + ADJ] If something is **immediately** obvious, it can be seen or understood without any delay. = instantly ❑ *The cause of the accident was not immediately apparent.* **3** [immediately + ADJ/-ED] **Immediately** is used to indicate that someone or something is closely and directly involved in a situation. ❑ *The man immediately responsible for this misery is the province's governor.* **4** [immediately + PREP/ADJ] **Immediately** is used to emphasize that something comes next, or is next to something else. = directly ❑ *They wish to begin immediately after dinner.*

im·mense /ɪˈmens/ ADJ If you describe something as **immense**, you mean that it is extremely large or great. = enormous ❑ *an immense cloud of smoke*
im·mense·ly /ɪˈmensli/ ADV *(emphasis)* You use **immensely** to emphasize the degree or extent of a quality, feeling, or process. = enormously ❑ *I enjoyed this movie immensely.*

⊕**im·mi·grant** ◆◇◇ /ˈɪmɪɡrənt/ NOUN [C] **(immigrants)** An **immigrant** is a person who has come to live in a country from some other country. Compare **emigrant**. ❑ *illegal immigrants* ❑ *Portugal, Spain and Italy all have large immigrant populations from Africa.*

⊕**im·mi·grate** /ˈɪmɪɡreɪt/ VERB [I] **(immigrates, immigrating, immigrated)** *(academic word)* If someone **immigrates** to a particular country, they come to live or work in that country, after leaving the country where they were born. ❑ *a Russian-born professor who had immigrated to the United States* ❑ *He immigrated from India at the age of 18.* ❑ *10,000 people are expected to immigrate in the next two years.*

⊕**im·mi·gra·tion** ◆◇◇ /ˌɪmɪˈɡreɪʃən/ NOUN [U] **1** **Immigration** is the coming of people into a country in order to live and work there. ❑ *The government has decided to tighten its immigration policy.* ❑ *immigration into Europe* ❑ *measures aimed at curbing illegal immigration* **2** **Immigration** or **immigration control** is the place at a port, airport, or international border where officials check the passports of people who wish to come into the country. ❑ *First, you have to go through immigration and customs.*

⊕**im·mi·nent** /ˈɪmɪnənt/ ADJ If you say that something is **imminent**, especially something unpleasant, you mean it is almost certain to happen very soon. = impending ❑ *There appeared no imminent danger.* ❑ *They warned that an attack was imminent.* ❑ *He had no direct involvement in any alleged crimes and was not viewed as an imminent threat to security.*

im·mor·al /ɪˈmɒrəl, AmE -ˈmɔːr-/ ADJ *(disapproval)* If you describe someone or their behaviour as **immoral**, you believe that their behaviour is morally wrong. ❑ *those who think that birth control and abortion are immoral*

i

⊙im·mune ♦◇◇ /ɪˈmjuːn/ ADJ **1** [V-LINK + immune] If you are **immune to** a particular disease, you cannot be affected by it. ❑ *About 93 per cent of US residents are immune to measles either because they were vaccinated or they had the disease as a child.* ❑ *This blood test will show whether or not you're immune to the disease.* ❑ *Most adults are immune to rubella.* **2** [V-LINK + immune] If you are **immune to** something that happens or is done, you are not affected by it. = unaffected ❑ *Higher education is no longer immune to state budget cuts.* ❑ *Whilst Marc did gradually harden himself to the poverty, he did not become immune to the sight of death.* ❑ *Football is not immune to economic recession.* **3** [V-LINK + immune] Someone or something that is **immune from** a particular process or situation is able to escape it. ❑ *People with diplomatic passports are immune from criminal prosecution.*

⊙im·mun·ity /ɪˈmjuːnɪti/ NOUN [U] **1** = resistance ❑ *Birds in outside cages develop immunity to airborne bacteria.* ❑ *The disease develops mostly in children since they have less natural immunity than adults.* **2** *The police are offering immunity to witnesses who help identify the murderers.*

⊙im·mune sys·tem NOUN [C] (**immune systems**) Your **immune system** consists of all the organs and processes in your body that protect you from illness and infection. ❑ *His immune system completely broke down and he became very ill.* ❑ *People who exercise have stronger immune systems, so they're less likely to need time off due to illness.* ❑ *Boost your immune system and prolong longevity.*

⊙im·mun·ize /ˈɪmjuːnaɪz/ also **immunise** VERB [T] (**immunizes, immunizing, immunized**) If people or animals **are immunized**, they are made immune to a particular disease, often by being given an injection. = inoculate, vaccinate ❑ *We should require that every student is immunized against hepatitis B.* ❑ *The monkeys used in those experiments had previously been immunized with a vaccine made from killed infected cells.* ❑ *All parents should have their children immunized.*

⊙im·mun·iza·tion /ˌɪmjʊnaɪˈzeɪʃən/ also **immunisation** NOUN [C, U] (**immunizations**) = inoculation, vaccination ❑ *universal immunization against childhood diseases* ❑ *Only half of America's children get the full range of immunizations.*

⊙im·pact ♦♦◇ NOUN, VERB (*academic word*)
NOUN /ˈɪmpækt/ [C, U] (**impacts**) **1** [C] The **impact** that something has **on** a situation, process, or person is a sudden and powerful effect that it has on them. = effect, mark, impression ❑ *They say they expect the meeting to have a marked impact on the future of the country.* ❑ *the mining industry's devastating impact on the environment* ❑ *an area where technology can make a real impact* **2** [C, U] An **impact** is the action of one object hitting another, or the force with which one object hits another. ❑ *The plane is destroyed, a complete wreck: the pilot must have died on impact.*
VERB /ɪmˈpækt/ [I, T] (**impacts, impacting, impacted**) **1** To **impact** a situation, process, or person means to affect them. = affect ❑ *Such schemes mean little unless they impact people.* ❑ *That would require that women impact on inflation and competition.* ❑ *the potential for women to impact the political process* **2** (*formal*) If one object **impacts on** another, it hits it with great force. ❑ *the sharp tinkle of metal impacting on stone*

WORD CONNECTIONS
ADJ + **impact**

a **significant** impact
a **major** impact
an **important** impact
a **profound** impact
❑ *Car use has a significant impact on the environment.*

a **negative** impact
an **adverse** impact
a **positive** impact
❑ *Smoking has a negative impact on health.*

a **lasting** impact
an **immediate** impact
❑ *Job losses have an immediate impact on people's lives.*

an **economic** impact
an **environmental** impact
❑ *The expansion of the airport will have an environmental impact.*

im·pair /ɪmˈpeə/ VERB [T] (**impairs, impairing, impaired**) (*formal*) If something **impairs** something such as an ability or the way something works, it damages it or makes it worse. ❑ *Consumption of alcohol impairs your ability to drive a car or operate machinery.*
im·paired /ɪmˈpeəd/ ADJ ❑ *The blast left him with permanently impaired hearing.*

im·part /ɪmˈpɑːt/ VERB [T] (**imparts, imparting, imparted**) (*formal*) **1** If you **impart** information **to** people, you tell it to them. = convey ❑ *The ability to impart knowledge and command respect is the essential qualification for teachers.* **2** To **impart** a particular quality to something means to give it that quality. ❑ *She managed to impart great elegance to the unpretentious dress she was wearing.*

⊙im·par·tial /ɪmˈpɑːʃəl/ ADJ Someone who is **impartial** is not directly involved in a particular situation, and is therefore able to give a fair opinion or decision about it. = unbiased, neutral, objective, disinterested ❑ *Careers advisers offer impartial advice, guidance and information to all pupils.* ❑ *Citizens have the right to a speedy and public trial before an impartial jury.*
⊙im·par·tial·ity /ɪmˌpɑːʃiˈælɪti/ NOUN [U] = neutrality, objectivity; ≠ partiality, bias ❑ *a justice system lacking impartiality by democratic standards*
⊙im·par·tial·ly /ɪmˈpɑːʃəli/ ADV [impartially with v] = neutrally, objectively ❑ *He has vowed to oversee the elections impartially.* ❑ *an impartially conducted study*

im·passe /ˈæmpæs, ˈɪm-/ NOUN [SING] If people are in a difficult position in which it is impossible to make any progress, you can refer to the situation as an **impasse**. = deadlock ❑ *The company says it has reached an impasse in negotiations with the union.*

im·pa·tient /ɪmˈpeɪʃənt/ ADJ **1** [V-LINK + impatient] If you are **impatient**, you are annoyed because you have to wait too long for something. ❑ *Investors are growing impatient with promises of improved earnings.* **2** If you are **impatient**, you are easily irritated by things. ❑ *Beware of being too impatient with others.* **3** [V-LINK + impatient] If you are **impatient to** do something or **impatient for** something to happen, you are eager to do it or for it to happen and do not want to wait. ❑ *He didn't want to tell Mr Morrisson why he was impatient to get home.*
im·pa·tient·ly /ɪmˈpeɪʃəntli/ ADV **1** *People have been waiting impatiently for a chance to improve the situation.* **2** [impatiently with v] ❑ *'Come on, David,' Harry said impatiently.*
im·pa·tience /ɪmˈpeɪʃəns/ NOUN [U] **1** *There is considerable impatience with the slow pace of political change.* **2** *There was a hint of impatience in his tone.* **3** *She showed impatience to continue the climb.*

im·per·fect /ɪmˈpɜːfɪkt/ ADJ (*formal*) Something that is **imperfect** has faults and is not exactly as you would like it to be. ❑ *We live in an imperfect world.*

im·per·fec·tion /ˌɪmpəˈfekʃən/ NOUN [C, U] (**imperfections**) **1** [C, U] An **imperfection in** someone or something is a fault, weakness, or undesirable feature that they have. = flaw, failing ❑ *He concedes that there are imperfections in the program.* **2** [C] An **imperfection in** something is a small mark or damaged area that may spoil its appearance. = flaw, blemish ❑ *Optical scanners ensure that imperfections in the cloth are located and removed.*

im·perial /ɪmˈpɪəriəl/ ADJ **1** [imperial + N] **Imperial** is used to refer to things or people that are or were connected with an empire. ❑ *the Imperial Palace in Tokyo* **2** [imperial + N] The **imperial** system of measurement uses inches, feet, yards, and miles to measure length, and ounces and pounds to measure weight, and pints, quarts, and gallons to measure volume.

im·per·son·al /ɪmˈpɜːsənəl/ ADJ **1** (*disapproval*) If you describe a place, organization, or activity as **impersonal**, you mean that it is not very friendly and makes you feel unimportant because it involves or is used by a large number of people. ❑ *Before then many children were cared for in large impersonal orphanages.* **2** If you describe someone's behaviour as **impersonal**, you mean that they do not show any emotion about the person they are dealing with. ❑ *We must be as impersonal as a surgeon with his knife.* **3** An **impersonal** room or statistic does not give any information about the character of the person to whom it belongs or relates. ❑ *The rest of the room was neat and impersonal.*

im·per·son·ate /ɪmˈpɜːsəneɪt/ VERB [T] (**impersonates, impersonating, impersonated**) If someone **impersonates** a person, they pretend to be that person, either to deceive people or to make people laugh. ❑ *He was returned to prison in 1977 for impersonating a police officer.* ◆**im·per·son·a·tion** /ɪmˌpɜːsəˈneɪʃən/ NOUN [C] (**impersonations**) ❑ *She excelled at impersonations of his teachers, which provided great amusement for him.*

im·petus /ˈɪmpɪtəs/ NOUN [U] [also 'an' impetus, oft impetus 'for'] Something that gives a process **impetus** or an **impetus** makes it happen or progress more quickly. = stimulus ❑ *The impetus for change came from lawyers.*

◆**im·ple·ment** ◆◇◇ VERB, NOUN (*academic word*) VERB /ˈɪmplɪment/ [T] (**implements, implementing, implemented**) If you **implement** something such as a plan, you ensure that what has been planned is done. = carry out ❑ *The government promised to implement a new system to control financial loan institutions.* ❑ *The report sets out strict inspection procedures to ensure that the recommendations are properly implemented.* NOUN /ˈɪmplɪmənt/ [C] (**implements**) (*formal*) An **implement** is a tool or other piece of equipment. ❑ *writing implements* ◆**im·ple·men·ta·tion** /ˌɪmplɪmənˈteɪʃən/ NOUN [U] ❑ *Very little has been achieved in the implementation of the peace agreement signed last January.* ❑ *Full implementation of the ban was deferred until 2012.*

im·pli·cate /ˈɪmplɪkeɪt/ VERB [T] (**implicates, implicating, implicated**) (*academic word*) To **implicate** someone means to show or claim that they were involved in something wrong or criminal. ❑ *He was obliged to resign when one of his own aides was implicated in a financial scandal.*

◆**im·pli·ca·tion** ◆◇◇ /ˌɪmplɪˈkeɪʃən/ NOUN (*academic word*) NOUN [C, U] (**implications**) **1** [C] The **implications of** something are the things that are likely to happen as a result. = consequence, effect, ramifications ❑ *The Attorney General was aware of the political implications of his decision to prosecute.* ❑ *The low level of investment has serious implications for future economic growth.* **2** [C] The **implication** of a statement, event, or situation is what it implies or suggests is the case. ❑ *The implication was obvious: vote for us or it will be very embarrassing for you.* **3** [U] The **implication** of someone in something wrong or criminal is the act of showing or claiming that they were involved in it. ❑ *Implication in a murder finally brought him to the gallows.* PHRASE **by implication** If you say that something is the case **by implication**, you mean that a statement, event, or situation implies that it is the case. ❑ *Now his authority and, by implication, that of the whole management team are under threat as never before.*

◆**im·plic·it** /ɪmˈplɪsɪt/ ADJ (*academic word*) **1** Something that is **implicit** is expressed in an indirect way. = indirect ❑ *an implicit warning to the Moroccans not to continue or repeat the military actions they began a week ago* ❑ *There has been an implicit assumption in much of the thinking that quality can only improve if productivity declines.* **2** [V-LINK + implicit 'in' N] (*formal*) If a quality or element is **implicit in** something, it is involved in it or is shown by it. ❑ *Trust is implicit in the system.* **3** If you say that someone has an **implicit** belief or faith in something, you mean that they have complete faith in it and no doubts at all. = absolute ❑ *He had implicit faith in the noble intentions of the Emperor.* ◆**im·plic·it·ly** /ɪmˈplɪsɪtli/ ADV **1** [implicitly with V] = indirectly ❑ *The jury implicitly criticized the government by their verdict.* ❑ *The prime minister implicitly acknowledged the government's failure to enthuse the country.*

2 [implicitly after V] ❑ *I trust him implicitly.*

◆**im·ply** ◆◇◇ /ɪmˈplaɪ/ VERB [T] (**implies, implying, implied**) (*academic word*) **1** If you **imply that** something is the case, you say something that indicates that it is the case in an indirect way. = suggest ❑ *'Are you implying that I have something to do with those attacks?' she asked coldly.* **2** If an event or situation **implies** that something is the case, it makes you think that it is the case. = suggest, indicate, point to ❑ *Exports in June rose 1.5%, implying that the economy was stronger than many investors had realized.* ❑ *A 'frontier-free' Europe implies a greatly increased market for all economic operators.*

im·po·lite /ˌɪmpəˈlaɪt/ ADJ If you say that someone is **impolite**, you mean that they are rather rude and do not have good manners. ❑ *The Count acknowledged the two newcomers as briefly as was possible without being impolite.*

◆**im·port** ◆◆◇ VERB, NOUN VERB /ɪmˈpɔːt/ [I, T] (**imports, importing, imported**) **1** [I, T] To **import** products or raw materials means to buy them from another country for use in your own country. ❑ *Rich countries benefited from importing Indonesia's timber.* ❑ *To import from Russia, a Ukrainian firm needs Russian roubles.* ❑ *Britain spent nearly £5000 million more on importing food than selling abroad.* ❑ *imported goods from Mexico* **2** [T] (*computing*) If you **import** files or information into one type of software from another type, you open them in a format that can be used in the new software. ❑ *Users can import files made in other packages.* NOUN /ˈɪmpɔːt/ [C, U] (**imports**) **1** [C, U] [also imports] **Import** is the act of buying products or raw materials from another country for use in your own country. ≠ export ❑ *Germany, however, insists on restrictions on the import of Polish coal.* ❑ *import duties on cars* **2** [C] **Imports** are products or raw materials bought from another country for use in your own country. ❑ *cheap imports from other countries* ❑ *Exports fell 3 per cent while imports rose 1 per cent.* **3** [U] (*formal*) The **import** of something is its importance. = consequence ❑ *Such arguments are of little import.* ◆**im·por·ta·tion** /ˌɪmpɔːˈteɪʃən/ NOUN [U] ≠ exportation ❑ *restrictions concerning the importation of birds*

WORD CONNECTIONS
VERB + **import**
ban imports
restrict imports
allow imports
❑ *The UK has banned the import of birds and poultry from affected areas.*

ADJ + **import**
cheap imports
expensive imports
illegal imports
❑ *The textile industry could not compete with cheap imports from abroad.*

◆**im·por·tance** ◆◇◇ /ɪmˈpɔːtəns/ NOUN [U] **1** The **importance** of something is its quality of being significant, valued, or necessary in a particular situation. = significance; ≠ insignificance ❑ *China has been stressing the importance of its ties with third world countries.* ❑ *Safety is of paramount importance.* ❑ *Institutions place great importance on symbols of corporate identity.* **2** **Importance** means having influence, power, or status. ❑ *Obviously a man of his importance is going to be missed.*

WORD CONNECTIONS
VERB + **importance**
recognize the importance of ...
stress the importance of ...
emphasize the importance of ...
❑ *He stressed the importance of a balanced diet for athletes.*
understand the importance of ...
know the importance of ...
❑ *People working in restaurants need to understand the importance of good hygiene.*

ADJ + **importance**
great importance
critical importance
enormous importance
growing importance
increasing importance
❏ *The issue of graduate employability is of increasing importance in higher education policy.*

✪ **im·por·tant** ◆◆◆ /ɪmˈpɔːtənt/ ADJ **1** Something that is **important** is very significant, is highly valued, or is necessary. = significant, critical, essential; ≠ unimportant, insignificant ❏ *The most important thing in my life was my career.* ❏ *It's important to answer her questions as honestly as you can.* ❏ *The planned general strike represents an important economic challenge to the government.* **2** Someone who is **important** has influence or power within a society or a particular group. ❏ *an important figure in the media world* ✪ **im·por·tant·ly** /ɪmˈpɔːtəntli/ ADV ❏ *I was hungry, and, more importantly, my children were hungry.* ❏ *Finally, and perhaps most importantly, the early warning system provides a means of monitoring performance.*

USAGE NOTE
important
You do not use **important** to say that an amount or quantity is very large. You don't, for example, talk about 'an important sum of money'. Instead, you use an adjective such as **large**, **considerable** or **significant**.
*Staff spend **significant amounts** of time in admin-related tasks.*

WORD FAMILIES

important ADJ	The most **important** thing in my life was my career.
unimportant ADJ	When they had married, six years before, the difference in their ages had seemed **unimportant**.
importantly ADV	This procedure is costly and, more **importantly**, can be dangerous.
importance NOUN	Safety is of paramount **importance**.

✪ **im·pose** ◆◆◇ /ɪmˈpəʊz/ VERB [T, I] (imposes, imposing, imposed) (*academic word*) **1** [T] If you **impose** something on people, you use your authority to force them to accept it. = dictate, enforce ❏ *Fines are imposed on retailers who sell tobacco to minors.* ❏ *A third of companies reviewing pay since last August have imposed a pay freeze of up to a year.* **2** [T] If you **impose** your opinions or beliefs on other people, you try and make people accept them as a rule or as a model to copy. ❏ *Parents should beware of imposing their own tastes on their children.* **3** [T] If something **imposes** strain, pressure, or suffering **on** someone, it causes them to experience it. = inflict ❏ *The filming imposed an additional strain on her.* **4** [I] If someone **imposes on** you, they unreasonably expect you to do something for them which you do not want to do. ❏ *I was afraid you'd feel we were imposing on you.* **5** [T] If someone **imposes themselves on** you, they force you to accept their company although you may not want to. ❏ *I didn't want to impose myself on my married friends.*

✪ **im·po·si·tion** /ˌɪmpəˈzɪʃən/ NOUN [U, C] **1** [U] = enforcement ❏ *the imposition of sanctions against Pakistan* ❏ *The key factor is that there is no imposition of locally unpopular development.* **2** [C] ❏ *I know this is an imposition. But please hear me out.*

im·pos·ing /ɪmˈpəʊzɪŋ/ ADJ If you describe someone or something as **imposing**, you mean that they have an impressive appearance or manner. ❏ *He was an imposing man.*

im·pos·sible ◆◆◇ /ɪmˈpɒsɪbəl/ ADJ, NOUN
ADJ **1** Something that is **impossible** cannot be done or cannot happen. ❏ *It was impossible for anyone to get in because no one knew the password.* ❏ *He thinks the tax is*

impossible to administer. **2** [impossible + N] An **impossible** situation or an **impossible** position is one that is very difficult to deal with. = hopeless ❏ *I think he was in an impossible position.* **3** If you describe someone as **impossible**, you are annoyed that their bad behaviour or strong views make them difficult to deal with. = intolerable ❏ *The woman is impossible, thought Francesca.*
NOUN [SING] [impossible + ADJ] **The impossible** is something that is impossible. ❏ *They were expected to do the impossible.*
im·pos·sibly /ɪmˈpɒsɪbli/ ADV ❏ *Mathematical physics is an almost impossibly difficult subject.*
im·pos·sibil·ity /ɪmˌpɒsɪˈbɪlɪti/ NOUN [C, U] (impossibilities) ❏ *the impossibility of knowing absolute truth*

im·prac·ti·cal /ɪmˈpræktɪkəl/ ADJ **1** If you describe an object, idea, or course of action as **impractical**, you mean that it is not sensible or realistic, and does not work well in practice. ❏ *Once there were regularly scheduled airlines, it became impractical to make a business trip by boat.* **2** If you describe someone as **impractical**, you mean that they do not have the abilities or skills to do practical work such as making, repairing, or organizing things. ❏ *Geniuses are supposed to be difficult, eccentric and hopelessly impractical.*

im·pre·cise /ˌɪmprɪˈsaɪs/ ADJ Something that is **imprecise** is not clear, accurate, or precise. ❏ *The charges were vague and imprecise.*

im·press ◆◇◇ /ɪmˈpres/ VERB [I, T] (impresses, impressing, impressed) **1** [I, T] If something **impresses** you, you feel great admiration for it. ❏ *What impressed him most was their speed.* **2** [T] If you **impress** something **on** someone, you make them understand its importance or degree. ❏ *I had always impressed upon the children that if they worked hard they would succeed in life.* ❏ *I've impressed upon them the need for more professionalism.* **3** [T] If something **impresses itself on** your mind, you notice and remember it. ❏ *But this change has not yet impressed itself on the minds of the public.* **4** [T] If someone or something **impresses** you **as** a particular thing, usually a good one, they give you the impression of being that thing. ❏ *It didn't impress me as a good place to live.*
im·pressed /ɪmˈprest/ ADJ ❏ *I was very impressed by one young man at my lectures.*

im·pres·sion ◆◇◇ /ɪmˈpreʃən/ NOUN
NOUN [C, SING] (impressions) **1** [C] Your **impression** of a person or thing is what you think they are like, usually after having seen or heard them. Your **impression** of a situation is what you think is going on. ❏ *What were your first impressions of college?* ❏ *My impression is that they are totally out of control.* **2** [SING] If someone gives you a particular **impression**, they cause you to believe that something is the case, often when it is not. ❏ *I don't want to give the impression that I'm running away from the charges.* **3** [C] An **impression** is an amusing imitation of someone's behaviour or way of talking, usually someone well-known. = impersonation ❏ *I did an impression of daddy saying 'Do as I say, not as I do'.* **4** [C] An **impression** of an object is a mark or outline that it has left after being pressed hard onto a surface. ❏ *the world's oldest fossil impressions of plant life*
PHRASES **make an impression** If someone or something **makes an impression**, they have a strong effect on people or a situation. ❏ *The type of aid coming in makes no immediate impression on the horrific death rates.*
under the impression If you are **under the impression** that something is the case, you believe that it is the case, usually when it is not actually the case. ❏ *He had apparently been under the impression that a military coup was in progress.*

im·pres·sive ◆◇◇ /ɪmˈpresɪv/ ADJ Something that is **impressive** impresses you, for example because it is great in size or degree, or is done with a lot of skill. ❏ *It is an impressive achievement.*
im·pres·sive·ly /ɪmˈpresɪvli/ ADV ❏ *an impressively bright and energetic woman called Cathie Gould*

✪ **im·pris·on** /ɪmˈprɪzən/ VERB [T] (imprisons, imprisoning, imprisoned) If someone **is imprisoned**, they are locked up or kept somewhere, usually in prison, as a punishment for a crime or for political opposition.

= jail, detain, incarcerate; ≠ free, release ❑ *He was imprisoned for 18 months on charges of theft.* ❑ *Dutch colonial authorities imprisoned him for his part in the independence movement.* ❑ *A Canadian civilian claims he was falsely imprisoned.*

◑**im·pris·on·ment** /ɪmˈprɪzənmənt/ NOUN [U] **Imprisonment** is the state of being imprisoned. = custody, detention, incarceration, captivity ❑ *She was sentenced to seven years' imprisonment.* ❑ *Many others face indefinite imprisonment without trial.*

im·prob·able /ɪmˈprɒbəbəl/ ADJ **1** Something that is **improbable** is unlikely to be true or to happen. = unlikely ❑ *Ordered arrangements of large groups of atoms and molecules are highly improbable.* **2** If you describe something as **improbable**, you mean it is strange, unusual, or ridiculous. = unlikely ❑ *On the face of it, their marriage seems an improbable alliance.*
  im·prob·abil·ity /ˌɪmˌprɒbəˈbɪlɪti/ NOUN [C, U] (**improbabilities**) ❑ *the improbability of such an outcome*
  im·prob·ably /ɪmˈprɒbəbli/ ADV ❑ *The sea is an improbably pale turquoise.*

im·prop·er /ˌɪmˈprɒpə/ ADJ **1** (formal) **Improper** activities are illegal or dishonest. ❑ *25 officers were investigated following allegations of improper conduct.* **2** [improper + N] (formal) **Improper** conditions or methods of treatment are not suitable or good enough for a particular purpose. = inappropriate ❑ *The improper use of medicine could lead to severe adverse reactions.* **3** If you describe someone's behaviour as **improper**, you mean it is rude or shocking or in some way socially unacceptable. ❑ *Such improper behaviour and language from a young lady left me momentarily incapable of speech.*
  im·prop·er·ly /ˌɪmˈprɒpəli/ ADV **1** [improperly with V] ❑ *I acted neither fraudulently nor improperly.* **2** The study confirmed many reports that doctors were improperly trained. **3** [improperly with V] ❑ *The company turns down people who show up at job interviews improperly dressed.*

◑**im·prove** ♦♦◇ /ɪmˈpruːv/ VERB [I, T] (**improves, improving, improved**) **1** [I, T] If something **improves** or if you **improve** it, it gets better. ≠ deteriorate ❑ *Within a month, both the texture and condition of your hair should improve.* ❑ *Time won't improve the situation.* **2** [I, T] If a skill you have **improves** or you **improve** a skill, you get better at it. ❑ *Their French has improved enormously.* **3** [I] If you **improve** after an illness or an injury, your health gets better or you get stronger. = recover ❑ *He had improved so much the doctor had cut his dosage.* **4** [I] If you **improve on** a previous achievement of your own or of someone else, you achieve a better standard or result. ❑ *We need to improve on our performance against Nabisco.*

◑**im·prove·ment** ♦◇◇ /ɪmˈpruːvmənt/ NOUN [C, U] (**improvements**) **1** [C, U] If there is an **improvement in** something, it becomes better. If you make **improvements** to something, you make it better. ≠ deterioration ❑ *the dramatic improvements in organ transplantation in recent years* ❑ *There is considerable room for improvement in state facilities for treating the mentally handicapped.* **2** [C] If you say that something is an **improvement on** a previous thing or situation, you mean that it is better than that thing. ❑ *The new governor is an improvement on his predecessor.*

WORD CONNECTIONS

VERB + **improvement**

show an improvement
see an improvement
make an improvement
❑ *I've seen a huge improvement in Josh's work over the year.*

ADJ + **improvement**

a **big** improvement
a **dramatic** improvement
a **marked** improvement
a **significant** improvement
❑ *There has been a marked improvement in educational standards.*

---

a **gradual** improvement
a **slight** improvement
❑ *You won't see any changes overnight, but you should begin to see a gradual improvement in your physical fitness.*

improvement + IN + NOUN

an improvement in **quality**
an improvement in **performance**
an improvement in **relations**
❑ *There needs to be a significant improvement in the quality of care for older people.*

---

im·pro·vise /ˈɪmprəvaɪz/ VERB [I, T] (**improvises, improvising, improvised**) **1** If you **improvise**, you make or do something using whatever you have or without having planned it in advance. ❑ *You need a wok with a steaming rack for this; if you don't have one, improvise.* ❑ *The vet had improvised a harness.* **2** When performers **improvise**, they invent music or words as they play, sing, or speak. ❑ *I asked her what the piece was and she said, 'Oh, I'm just improvising.'* ❑ *Uncle Richard read a chapter from the Bible and improvised a prayer.*

im·pu·dent /ˈɪmpjʊdənt/ ADJ (formal, disapproval) If you describe someone as **impudent**, you mean they are rude or disrespectful, or do something they have no right to do. = brazen ❑ *Some of them spoke pleasantly and were well behaved, while others were impudent and insulting.*

im·pulse /ˈɪmpʌls/ NOUN, ADJ ◾NOUN◾ [C, U] (**impulses**) **1** [C, U] An **impulse** is a sudden desire to do something. ❑ *Unable to resist the impulse, he glanced at the sea again.* **2** [C] An **impulse** is a short electrical signal that is sent along a wire or nerve or through the air, usually as one of a series. ❑ *It works by sending a series of electrical impulses which are picked up by hi-tech sensors.* ◾PHRASE◾ **on impulse** If you do something **on impulse**, you suddenly decide to do it, without planning it. ❑ *Sean's a fast thinker, and he acts on impulse.* ◾ADJ◾ [impulse + N] An **impulse** buy or **impulse** purchase is something that you decide to buy when you see it, although you had not planned to buy it. ❑ *The curtains were an impulse buy.*

im·pul·sive /ɪmˈpʌlsɪv/ ADJ If you describe someone as **impulsive**, you mean that they do things suddenly without thinking about them carefully first. ❑ *He is too impulsive to be a responsible mayor.*
  im·pul·sive·ly /ɪmˈpʌlsɪvli/ ADV [impulsively with V] ❑ *He studied her face for a moment, then said impulsively: 'Let's get married.'*

im·pure /ɪmˈpjʊə/ ADJ A substance that is **impure** is not of good quality because it has other substances mixed with it. ❑ *diarrhoea, dysentery and other diseases borne by impure water*

im·pu·rity /ɪmˈpjʊərɪti/ NOUN [C] (**impurities**) **Impurities** are substances that are present in small quantities in another substance and make it dirty or of an unacceptable quality. ❑ *The air in the factory is filtered to remove impurities.*

in ♦♦♦ /ɪn/ PREP, ADV, ADJ, NOUN

In addition to the uses shown below, **in** is used with verbs of movement such as 'walk' and 'push', and in phrasal verbs such as 'give in' and 'dig in'.

◾PREP◾ **1** Someone or something that is **in** something else is enclosed by it or surrounded by it. If you put something **in** a container, you move it so that it is enclosed by the container. ❑ *He was in his car.* **2** If something happens **in** a place, it happens there. ❑ *spending a few days in a hotel* **3** Something that is **in** a window, especially a shop window, is just behind the window so that you can see it from outside. ❑ *There was a camera for sale in the window.* **4** When you see something **in** a mirror, the mirror shows an image of it. ❑ *I couldn't bear to see my reflection in the mirror.* **5** If you are dressed **in** a piece of clothing, you are wearing it. ❑ *He was a big man, dressed in a suit and tie.* **6** Something that is covered or wrapped **in** something else has that thing over or around its surface. ❑ *His legs were covered in mud.* **7** If there is something such as a crack or

hole **in** something, there is a crack or hole on its surface. ❑ *There was a deep crack in the ceiling above him.* **8** If something is **in** a book, film, play, or picture, you can read it or see it there. ❑ *Don't stick too precisely to what it says in the book.* **9** If you are **in** something such as a play or a race, you are one of the people taking part. ❑ *Alfredo offered her a part in the play he was directing.* **10** Something that is **in** a group or collection is a member of it or part of it. ❑ *The New England team is the worst in the league.* **11** You use **in** to specify a general subject or field of activity. ❑ *those working in the defence industry* **12** If something happens **in** a particular year, month, or other period of time, it happens during that time. ❑ *that early spring day in April 1949* ❑ *Export orders improved in the last month.* **13** If something happens **in** a particular situation, it happens while that situation is going on. ❑ *His father had been badly wounded in the last war.* **14** [in + AMOUNT] If you do something **in** a particular period of time, that is how long it takes you to do it. ❑ *He walked two hundred and sixty miles in eight days.* **15** [in + AMOUNT] If something will happen **in** a particular length of time, it will happen after that length of time. ❑ *I'll have some breakfast ready in a few minutes.* **16** [in + POSS PL-NUM] You use **in** to indicate roughly how old someone is. For example, if someone is **in** their fifties, they are between 50 and 59 years old. ❑ *young people in their twenties* **17** You use **in** to indicate roughly how many people or things do something. ❑ *men who came there in droves* **18** [NUM + in + NUM] You use **in** to express a ratio, proportion, or probability. ❑ *One in three marriages end in divorce.* **19** [V-LINK + in + N] If something or someone is **in** a particular state or situation, that is their present state or situation. ❑ *The economy was in trouble.* ❑ *Dave was in a hurry to get back to work.* **20** You use **in** to indicate the feeling or desire that someone has when they do something, or which causes them to do it. ❑ *Simpson looked at them in surprise.* **21** If a particular quality or ability is **in** you, you naturally have it. ❑ *Violence is not in his nature.* **22** You use **in** when saying that someone or something has a particular quality. ❑ *He had all the qualities I was looking for in a partner.* **23** You use **in** to indicate how someone is expressing something. ❑ *Information is given to the patient verbally and in writing.* **24** You use **in** in expressions such as **in a row** or **in a ball** to describe the arrangement or shape of something. ❑ *The cards need to be laid out in two rows.* **25** If something is **in** a particular colour, it has that colour. ❑ *white flowers edged in pink* **26** You use **in** to specify which feature or aspect of something you are talking about. ❑ *The film is nearly two hours in length.* ❑ *There is a big difference in the amounts that banks charge.* **27** [in + -ING] You use **in** with a present participle to indicate that when you do something, something else happens as a result. ❑ *He shifted uncomfortably on his feet. In doing so he knocked over Steven's briefcase.* ■ PHRASE ■ **in that** You use **in that** to introduce an explanation of a statement you have just made. ❑ *I'm lucky in that I've got four sisters.* ■ ADV ■ **1** ['be' in] If you **are in**, you are present at your home or place of work. ❑ *My roommate was in at the time.* **2** [in after v] When someone comes **in**, they enter a room or building. ❑ *She looked up anxiously as he came in.* **3** If a train, boat, or plane has come **in** or is **in**, it has arrived at a station, port, or airport. ❑ *every plane coming in from Melbourne* **4** When the sea or tide comes **in**, the sea moves towards the shore rather than away from it. ❑ *She thought of the tide rushing in, covering the wet sand.* ■ PHRASES ■ **be in for** If you say that someone **is in for** a shock or a surprise, you mean that they are going to experience it. ❑ *You might be in for a shock at the sheer hard work involved.*
have it in for someone (*informal*) If someone **has it in for** you, they dislike you and try to cause problems for you. ❑ *The other kids had it in for me.*
■ ADJ ■ (*informal*) If you say that something is **in**, or is the **in** thing, you mean that it is fashionable or popular. ❑ *A few years ago jogging was the in thing.*
■ PHRASES ■ **in on** If you are **in on** something, you are involved in it or know about it. ❑ *I don't know. I wasn't in on that particular argument.*

be in with (*informal*) If you **are in with** a person or group, they like you and accept you, and are likely to help you.
■ NOUN ■
■ PHRASE ■ **ins and outs** The **ins and outs** of a situation are all the detailed points and facts about it. ❑ *the ins and outs of high finance*

in·abil·ity /ˌɪnəˈbɪlɪti/ NOUN [u] If you refer to someone's **inability** to do something, you are referring to the fact that they are unable to do it. ❑ *Her inability to concentrate could cause an accident.*

WORD PARTS
The prefix **in-** often gives a word the opposite meaning:
inability (NOUN)
ineffective (ADJ)
inaccuracy (NOUN)

✪ **in·ac·cu·ra·cy** /ɪnˈækjʊrəsi/ NOUN [c, u] (**inaccuracies**) The **inaccuracy** of a statement or measurement is the fact that it is not accurate or correct. = incorrectness, mistakes ❑ *He was disturbed by the inaccuracy of the answers.* ❑ *The report contains serious factual inaccuracies.*

✪ **in·ac·cu·rate** /ɪnˈækjʊrət/ ADJ If a statement or measurement is **inaccurate**, it is not accurate or correct. = wrong, incorrect; ≠ correct ❑ *The book is both inaccurate and exaggerated.* ❑ *The reports were based on inaccurate information.*
✪ **in·ac·cu·rate·ly** /ɪnˈækjʊrətli/ ADV = wrongly, incorrectly; ≠ accurately, correctly ❑ *He claimed his remarks had been reported inaccurately.* ❑ *Your story inaccurately cites a Waikato University study.*

in·ac·tion /ɪnˈækʃən/ NOUN [u] (*disapproval*) If you refer to someone's **inaction**, you disapprove of the fact that they are doing nothing. ❑ *He is bitter about the inaction of the other political parties.*

in·ac·tive /ɪnˈæktɪv/ ADJ Someone or something that is **inactive** is not doing anything or is not working. ❑ *He certainly was not politically inactive.*
in·ac·tiv·ity /ˌɪnækˈtɪvɪti/ NOUN [u] ❑ *The players have comparatively long periods of inactivity.*

in·ad·equa·cy /ɪnˈædɪkwəsi/ NOUN [c, u] (**inadequacies**) **1** [c, u] The **inadequacy** of something is the fact that there is not enough of it, or that it is not good enough. = deficiency ❑ *the inadequacy of the water supply* **2** [u] If someone has feelings of **inadequacy**, they feel that they do not have the qualities and abilities necessary to do something or to cope with life in general. ❑ *his deep-seated sense of inadequacy*

✪ **in·ad·equate** /ɪnˈædɪkwət/ ADJ **1** If something is **inadequate**, there is not enough of it or it is not good enough. = deficient ❑ *Supplies of food and medicines are inadequate.* ❑ *The problem goes far beyond inadequate staffing.* **2** If someone feels **inadequate**, they feel that they do not have the qualities and abilities necessary to do something or to cope with life in general. = deficient; ≠ adequate ❑ *I still feel inadequate, useless and mixed up.*
✪ **in·ad·equate·ly** /ɪnˈædɪkwətli/ ADV [inadequately with v] = deficiently; ≠ adequately ❑ *The projects were inadequately funded.* ❑ *inadequately trained staff*

in·ap·pro·pri·ate /ˌɪnəˈprəʊpriət/ ADJ **1** Something that is **inappropriate** is not useful or suitable for a particular situation or purpose. ❑ *There is no suggestion that clients have been sold inappropriate policies.* **2** If you say that someone's speech or behaviour in a particular situation is **inappropriate**, you are criticizing it because you think it is not suitable for that situation. ❑ *I feel the remark was inappropriate for such a serious issue.*
in·ap·pro·pri·ate·ly /ˌɪnəˈprəʊpriətli/ ADV **1** *No evidence is given that products are used inappropriately.* **2** *The report's authors accused him of acting inappropriately.*

in·box /ˈɪnˌbɒks/ also **in-box** NOUN [c] (**inboxes**) On a computer, your **inbox** is the part of your mailbox which stores e-mails that have arrived for you. ❑ *I returned home and checked my inbox.*

in·ca·pable /ɪnˈkeɪpəbəl/ ADJ **1** [V-LINK + incapable 'of' -ING/N] Someone who is **incapable of** doing something is unable to do it. ❑ *She seemed incapable of making the decision.* **2** An **incapable** person is weak or stupid. ❑ *He lost his job for allegedly being incapable.*

✪ **in·cen·tive** /ɪnˈsɛntɪv/ NOUN [C, U] (**incentives**) (*academic word*) If something is an **incentive to** do something, it encourages you to do it. = inducement, enticement; ≠ disincentive ❑ *There is little or no incentive to adopt such measures.* ❑ *Many companies in Britain are keen on the idea of tax incentives for R&D.*

✪ **inch** ♦◇◇ /ɪntʃ/ NOUN, VERB

NOUN [C] (**inches**) An **inch** is an imperial unit of length, approximately equal to 2.54 centimetres. There are twelve inches in a foot. ❑ *18 inches below the surface* ❑ *white paper no larger than 8 x 11 inches in size*

PHRASE **every inch** (*emphasis*) If you say that someone looks **every inch** a certain type of person, you are emphasizing that they look exactly like that kind of person. ❑ *He looks every inch the businessman, with his grey suit, dark blue shirt and blue tie.*

VERB [I, T] (**inches, inching, inched**) To **inch** somewhere means to move there very slowly and carefully, or to make something do this. ❑ *a climber inching up a vertical wall of rock* ❑ *He inched the van forward.*

✪ **in·ci·dence** /ˈɪnsɪdəns/ NOUN [C, U] (**incidences**) (*academic word*) **The incidence of** something, especially something bad such as a disease, is the frequency with which it occurs, or the occasions when it occurs. ❑ *The incidence of breast cancer increases with age.* ❑ *Excess fat is thought to be responsible for the high incidence of heart disease in Western countries.* ❑ *It is time for action to prevent increasing incidences of HIV infection in prisons.*

✪ **in·ci·dent** ♦♦◇ /ˈɪnsɪdənt/ NOUN [C] (**incidents**) [also 'without' incident] (*academic word, formal*) An **incident** is something that happens, often something that is unpleasant. ❑ *These incidents were the latest in a series of disputes between the two nations.* ❑ *The attack on Liquica was the worst in a series of violent incidents in East Timor.* ❑ *The voting went ahead without incident.*

in·ci·den·tal /ˌɪnsɪˈdɛntəl/ ADJ If one thing is **incidental** to another, it is less important than the other thing or is not a major part of it. ❑ *The playing of music proved to be incidental to the main business of the evening.*

in·ci·den·tal·ly /ˌɪnsɪˈdɛntli/ ADV **1** [incidentally with CL] You use **incidentally** to introduce a point that is not directly relevant to what you are saying, often a question or extra information that you have just thought of. ❑ *'I didn't ask you to come. Incidentally, why have you come?'* **2** [incidentally with V] If something occurs only **incidentally**, it is less important than another thing or is not a major part of it. ❑ *The letter mentioned my great aunt and uncle only incidentally.*

in·cite /ɪnˈsaɪt/ VERB [T] (**incites, inciting, incited**) If someone **incites** people **to** behave in a violent or illegal way, they encourage people to behave in that way, usually by making them excited or angry. ❑ *He incited his fellow citizens to take their revenge.* ❑ *The party agreed not to incite its supporters to violence.*

✪ **in·cli·na·tion** /ˌɪnklɪˈneɪʃən/ NOUN [C, U] (**inclinations**) An **inclination** is a feeling that makes you want to act in a particular way. = desire ❑ *He had neither the time nor the inclination to think of other things.* ❑ *She showed no inclination to go.* ❑ *His natural inclination in such a dilemma was to do nothing and watch.*

in·cline VERB, NOUN (*academic word*)

VERB /ɪnˈklaɪn/ [T] (**inclines, inclining, inclined**) **1** (*written*) If you **incline** your head, you bend your neck so that your head is leaning forwards. ❑ *Jack inclined his head very slightly.* **2** (*formal*) If you **incline to** think or act in a particular way, or if something **inclines** you **to** it, you are likely to think or act in that way. ❑ *the factors that incline us towards particular beliefs* ❑ *Those who fail incline to blame the world for their failure.*

NOUN /ˈɪnklaɪn/ [C] (**inclines**) (*formal*) An **incline** is land that slopes at an angle. = slope ❑ *He came to a halt at the edge of a steep incline.*

✪ **in·clined** /ɪnˈklaɪnd/ ADJ (*academic word*) **1** [V-LINK + inclined] If you are **inclined to** behave in a particular way, you often behave in that way, or you want to do so. = disposed ❑ *Nobody felt inclined to argue with Smith.* ❑ *He was inclined to self-pity.* ❑ *If you are so inclined, you can watch TV.* **2** [V-LINK + inclined + to-INF] If you say that you are **inclined to** have a particular opinion, you mean that you hold this opinion but you are not expressing it strongly. ❑ *I am inclined to agree with Alan.* **3** [ADV + inclined] Someone who is mathematically **inclined** or artistically **inclined**, for example, has a natural talent for mathematics or art. ❑ *the needs of academically inclined pupils*
→ See also **incline**

✪ **in·clude** ♦♦♦ /ɪnˈkluːd/ VERB [T] (**includes, including, included**) **1** If one thing **includes** another thing, it has the other thing as one of its parts. ≠ exclude ❑ *The trip has been extended to include a few other events.* **2** If someone or something **is included in** a large group, system, or area, they become a part of it or are considered a part of it. ≠ exclude ❑ *I had worked hard to be included in a project like this.* ❑ *The President is expected to include this idea in his education plan.*

in·clud·ed ♦♦◇ /ɪnˈkluːdɪd/ ADJ [N + included, V-LINK + included] (*emphasis*) You use **included** to emphasize that a person or thing is part of the group of people or things that you are talking about. ❑ *Many runners, myself included, are loners.*

✪ **in·clud·ing** ♦♦♦ /ɪnˈkluːdɪŋ/ PREP [including + N/-ING] You use **including** to introduce examples of people or things that are part of the group of people or things that you are talking about. ❑ *Thousands were killed, including many women and children.* ❑ *The drug will have anything up to a hundred side effects, including death.* ❑ *Preparation time (not including chilling): 5 minutes.*

✪ **in·clu·sion** /ɪnˈkluːʒən/ NOUN [C, U] (**inclusions**) **Inclusion** is the act of making a person or thing part of a group or collection. ≠ exclusion ❑ *a confident performance that justified his inclusion in the team* ❑ *the inclusion of the term 'couplehood' in a Dictionary of New Words*

in·clu·sive /ɪnˈkluːsɪv/ ADJ, ADV

ADJ **1** If you describe a group or organization as **inclusive**, you mean that it allows all kinds of people to belong to it, rather than just one kind of person. ❑ *The academy is far more inclusive now than it used to be.* **2** [N + inclusive] After stating the first and last item in a set of things, you can add **inclusive** to make it clear that the items stated are included in the set. ❑ *You are also invited to join us on our prayer days (this year, 6 June to 14 June inclusive).* **3** If a price is **inclusive**, it includes all the charges connected with the goods or services offered. If a price is **inclusive of** postage and packaging, it includes the charge for this. ❑ *All prices are inclusive of delivery.*

ADV [AMOUNT + inclusive] You can use **inclusive** after a price to mean that all charges for the goods and services offered are included in the price. ❑ *The outpatient programme costs $105 per day, all inclusive.*

✪ **in·co·her·ent** /ˌɪnkəʊˈhɪərənt/ ADJ **1** If someone is **incoherent**, they are talking in a confused and unclear way. = unintelligible ❑ *The man was almost incoherent with fear.* ❑ *As the evening progressed, he became increasingly incoherent.* ❑ *She dissolved into incoherent sobs.* **2** If you say that something such as a policy is **incoherent**, you are criticizing it because the different parts of it do not fit together properly. = disjointed ❑ *an incoherent set of objectives* ❑ *This is a vote against bad pension reform and a contradictory, incoherent pension policy.*
✪ **in·co·her·ence** /ˌɪnkəʊˈhɪərəns/ NOUN [U] ≠ coherence ❑ *Beth's incoherence told Amy that something was terribly wrong.* ❑ *the general incoherence of government policy.*
✪ **in·co·her·ent·ly** /ˌɪnkəʊˈhɪərəntli/ ADV ≠ coherently ❑ *He collapsed on the floor, mumbling incoherently.* ❑ *Outside jail he lived on VP wine and babbled incoherently.*

✪ **in·come** ♦♦◇ /ˈɪnkʌm/ NOUN [C, U] (**incomes**) (*academic word, business*) A person's or organization's **income** is the money that they earn or receive, as opposed to the money that they have to spend or pay out. = earnings, salary, revenue; ≠ costs, expenses ❑ *Many families on low incomes will be unable to afford to buy their own home.* ❑ *To*

i

cover its costs, the company will need an annual income of £15 million.

WORD CONNECTIONS
VERB + **income**
earn an income
supplement an income
❑ *Many of the villagers earn an income from fishing.*
ADJ + **income**
a **high** income
a **large** income
a **low** income
a **small** income
❑ *People on low incomes are struggling to heat their homes.*
an **annual** income
a **fixed** income
a **steady** income
an **average** income
❑ *In some of the world's poorest countries annual income is barely $100 per person.*
net income
gross income
❑ *Gross income is the full amount of money earned before any deductions.*

in·come tax NOUN [c, u] (**income taxes**) (*business*) Income tax is a part of your income that you have to pay regularly to the government. ❑ *You pay income tax on all your earnings, not just your salary.*

in·com·ing /ˈɪnkʌmɪŋ/ ADJ **1** [incoming + N] An **incoming** message or phone call is one that you receive. ❑ *We keep a tape of incoming calls.* **2** [incoming + N] An **incoming** plane or passenger is one that is arriving at a place. ❑ *The airport was closed for incoming flights.* **3** [incoming + N] An **incoming** official or government is one that has just been appointed or elected. ❑ *the problems confronting the incoming government*

◆**in·com·pat·ible** /ˌɪnkəmˈpætɪbəl/ ADJ (*academic word*) **1** If one thing or person is **incompatible with** another, they are very different in important ways, and do not suit each other or agree with each other. = mismatched, unsuited ❑ *They feel strongly that their religion is incompatible with the political system.* ❑ *His behaviour has been incompatible with his role as head of state.* ❑ *We were totally incompatible.* **2** If one type of computer or computer system is **incompatible with** another, they cannot use the same programs or be linked up. ❑ *This made its mini-computers incompatible with its mainframes.*

◆**in·com·pat·ibil·ity** /ˌɪnkəmpætɪˈbɪlɪti/ NOUN [u] ≠ compatibility ❑ *Incompatibility between the mother's and the baby's blood groups may cause jaundice.* ❑ *Their sexual incompatibility eventually separated them.*

in·com·pe·tence /ɪnˈkɒmpɪtəns/ NOUN [u] (*disapproval*) If you refer to someone's **incompetence**, you are criticizing them because they are unable to do their job or a task properly. ❑ *The incompetence of government officials is appalling.*

in·com·pe·tent /ɪnˈkɒmpɪtənt/ ADJ, NOUN ADJ (*disapproval*) If you describe someone as **incompetent**, you are criticizing them because they are unable to do their job or a task properly. ❑ *He wants the power to fire incompetent employees.* NOUN [c] (**incompetents**) An **incompetent** is someone who is incompetent. ❑ *The president turned furiously on his staff. 'I'm surrounded by incompetents!'*

in·com·plete /ˌɪnkəmˈpliːt/ ADJ Something that is **incomplete** is not yet finished, or does not have all the parts or details that it needs. ❑ *The clearing of rubbish and drains is still incomplete.*

in·con·ceiv·able /ˌɪnkənˈsiːvəbəl/ ADJ If you describe something as **inconceivable**, you think it is very unlikely to happen or be true. = unthinkable ❑ *It was inconceivable to me that Toby could have been my attacker.*

◆**in·con·clu·sive** /ˌɪnkənˈkluːsɪv/ ADJ (*academic word*)

1 If research or evidence is **inconclusive**, it has not proved anything. ❑ *Research has so far proved inconclusive.* ❑ *The judge ruled that the medical evidence was inconclusive.* **2** If a contest or conflict is **inconclusive**, it is not clear who has won or who is winning. ❑ *The past two elections were inconclusive.*

in·con·gru·ous /ɪnˈkɒŋgruəs/ ADJ (*formal*) Someone or something that is **incongruous** seems strange when considered together with other aspects of a situation. ❑ *She was small and fragile and looked incongruous in an army uniform.*

in·con·gru·ous·ly /ɪnˈkɒŋgruəsli/ ADV ❑ *a town of Western-style buildings perched incongruously in a high green valley*

◆**in·con·sist·en·cy** /ˌɪnkənˈsɪstənsi/ NOUN [u, c] (**inconsistencies**) **1** [u] (*disapproval*) If you refer to someone's **inconsistency**, you are criticizing them for not behaving in the same way every time a similar situation occurs. ❑ *His worst fault was his inconsistency.* **2** [c, u] If there are **inconsistencies** between two statements, one cannot be true if the other is true. = contradiction; ≠ consistency ❑ *We were asked to investigate the alleged inconsistencies in his evidence.* ❑ *the glaring inconsistency between the two statements*

◆**in·con·sist·ent** /ˌɪnkənˈsɪstənt/ ADJ **1** (*disapproval*) If you describe someone as **inconsistent**, you are criticizing them for not behaving in the same way every time a similar situation occurs. ❑ *You are inconsistent and unpredictable.* **2** Someone or something that is **inconsistent** does not stay the same, being sometimes good and sometimes bad. ❑ *We had a terrific start to the season, but recently we've been inconsistent.* **3** If two statements are **inconsistent**, one cannot possibly be true if the other is true. = contradictory, conflicting, incompatible ❑ *The evidence given in court was inconsistent with what he had previously told them.* ❑ *The report is internally inconsistent and conflicts directly with previous reports by the Academy.* **4** [V-LINK + inconsistent 'with' N] If something is **inconsistent with** a set of ideas or values, it does not fit in well with them or match them. = contradictory, conflicting, incompatible ❑ *This legislation is inconsistent with what they call Free Trade.* ❑ *The details of that meeting are by no means inconsistent with other evidence.*

VOCABULARY BUILDER
inconsistent ADJ
If two statements are **inconsistent**, one cannot possibly be true if the other is true.
❑ *Mr Willox complains that small businesses are given inconsistent messages from the government.*
contradictory ADJ
If two or more facts, ideas, or statements are **contradictory**, they state or imply that opposite things are true.
❑ *And which, then, of two contradictory statements do the public accept?*
conflicting ADJ
Conflicting stories or statements say completely different things from each other.
❑ *The situation is still confused, and there are conflicting reports regarding the number of terrorists involved.*
incompatible ADJ
If one thing or person is **incompatible** with another, they are very different in important ways, and do not agree with each other.
❑ *The church's 70 million worldwide adherents hold a huge range of sometimes mutually incompatible beliefs.*

in·con·ven·ience /ˌɪnkənˈviːniəns/ NOUN, VERB NOUN [c, u] (**inconveniences**) If someone or something causes **inconvenience**, they cause problems or difficulties. ❑ *We apologize for any inconvenience caused during the repairs.* VERB [T] (**inconveniences, inconveniencing, inconvenienced**)

If someone **inconveniences** you, they cause problems or difficulties for you. ❑ *He promised to be quick so as not to inconvenience them any further.*

in·con·ven·ient /ˌɪnkənˈviːniənt/ ADJ Something that is **inconvenient** causes problems or difficulties for someone. ❑ *Can you come at 10:30? I know it's inconvenient, but I have to see you.*

✪**in·cor·po·rate** /ɪnˈkɔːpəreɪt/ VERB [T] (**incorporates, incorporating, incorporated**) (*academic word, formal*) **1** If one thing **incorporates** another thing, it includes the other thing. = include, contain; ≠ omit ❑ *The new cars will incorporate a number of major improvements.* ❑ *Many sports garments now incorporate technology which helps to carry any sweat away from the body.* **2** If someone or something **is incorporated into** a large group, system, or area, they become a part of it. ≠ exclude ❑ *The agreement would allow the rebels to be incorporated into a new national police force.* ❑ *The party vowed to incorporate environmental considerations into all its policies.*

✪**In·cor·po·rated** /ɪnˈkɔːpəreɪtɪd/ ADJ [N + Incorporated] (*academic word, business*) **Incorporated** is used after a company's name to show that it is a legally established company in the United States. ❑ *MCA Incorporated*

✪**in·cor·rect** /ˌɪnkəˈrekt/ ADJ **1** Something that is **incorrect** is wrong and untrue. = wrong, inaccurate; ≠ correct, accurate ❑ *He denied that his evidence about the telephone call was incorrect.* ❑ *People often have incorrect information about food.* **2** Something that is **incorrect** is not the thing that is required or is most suitable in a particular situation. = inappropriate, bad; ≠ correct, appropriate ❑ *injuries caused by incorrect posture* ❑ *incorrect diet*

✪**in·cor·rect·ly** /ˌɪnkəˈrektli/ ADV **1** [incorrectly with V] = wrongly, inaccurately; ≠ correctly ❑ *The magazine suggested, incorrectly, that he was planning to announce his retirement.* **2** [incorrectly with V] ❑ *He was told that the doors had been installed incorrectly.* ❑ *These substances can, if taken incorrectly, be harmful.*

✪**in·crease** ♦♦♦ VERB, NOUN
VERB /ɪnˈkriːs/ [I, T] (**increases, increasing, increased**) If something **increases** or you **increase** it, it becomes greater in number, level, or amount. = rise, raise; ≠ reduce ❑ *The population continues to increase.* ❑ *Japan's industrial output increased by 2%.*
NOUN /ˈɪnkriːs/ [C] (**increases**) If there is an **increase in** the number, level, or amount of something, it becomes greater. = rise; ≠ reduction ❑ *a sharp increase in productivity* ❑ *He called for an increase of 1p on income tax.*
PHRASE **on the increase** If something is **on the increase**, it is happening more often or becoming greater in number or intensity. ❑ *Crime is on the increase.*

WORD CONNECTIONS
ADJ + increase
a **big** increase
a **marked** increase
a **sharp** increase
❑ *There has been a sharp increase in oil prices.*
increase + IN + NOUN
an increase in **crime**
an increase in **demand**
an increase in **spending**
❑ *If a business faces an increase in demand for its products, it may have to order in more stock and it needs the funds available to be able to do that.*
an increase in **size**
an increase in **temperature**
an increase in **value**
❑ *Wood expands as a result of an increase in temperature.*

✪**in·creas·ing·ly** ♦♦◇ /ɪnˈkriːsɪŋli/ ADV You can use **increasingly** to indicate that a situation or quality is becoming greater in intensity or more common. = more ❑ *He was finding it increasingly difficult to make decisions.*

❑ *The US has increasingly relied on Japanese capital.*

in·cred·ible ♦◇◇ /ɪnˈkredɪbəl/ ADJ **1** (*approval*) If you describe something or someone as **incredible**, you like them very much or are impressed by them, because they are extremely or unusually good. = fantastic ❑ *The wildflowers will be incredible after this rain.* **2** If you say that something is **incredible**, you mean that it is very unusual or surprising, and you cannot believe it is really true, although it may be. ❑ *It seemed incredible that people would still want to play football during a war.* **3** (*emphasis*) You use **incredible** to emphasize the degree, amount, or intensity of something. = amazing ❑ *I work an incredible amount of hours.*
in·cred·ibly /ɪnˈkredɪbli/ ADV **1** [incredibly + ADJ/ADV] ❑ *Their father was incredibly good-looking.* **2** Incredibly, some people don't like the name. **3** [incredibly + ADJ/ADV] ❑ *It was incredibly hard work.*

in·cum·bent /ɪnˈkʌmbənt/ NOUN, ADJ
NOUN [C] (**incumbents**) (*formal*) An **incumbent** is someone who holds an official post at a particular time. ❑ *In general, incumbents have a 94 per cent chance of being re-elected.*
ADJ **1** [incumbent + N] An **incumbent** official is someone who holds an official post at a particular time. ❑ *the only candidate who defeated an incumbent senator* **2** (*formal*) If it is **incumbent on** or **upon** you to do something, it is your duty or responsibility to do it. ❑ *She felt it was incumbent on herself to act immediately.*

✪**in·cur** /ɪnˈkɜː/ VERB [T] (**incurs, incurring, incurred**) (*written*) If you **incur** something unpleasant, it happens to you because of something you have done. = sustain ❑ *The government had also incurred huge debts.* ❑ *the terrible damage incurred during the past decade*

in·cur·able /ɪnˈkjʊərəbəl/ ADJ **1** If someone has an **incurable** disease, they cannot be cured of it. ❑ *He is suffering from an incurable skin disease.* **2** [incurable + N] You can use **incurable** to indicate that someone has a particular quality or attitude and will not change. ❑ *Poor old Willy is an incurable romantic.*
in·cur·ably /ɪnˈkjʊərəbli/ ADV **1** [incurably + ADJ] ❑ *youngsters who are disabled, or incurably ill* **2** *I know you think I'm incurably nosy, but the truth is I'm concerned about you.*

in·debt·ed /ɪnˈdetɪd/ ADJ **1** [V-LINK + indebted 'to' N] If you say that you are **indebted** to someone for something, you mean that you are very grateful to them for something. ❑ *I am deeply indebted to him for his help.* **2** **Indebted** countries, organizations, or people are ones that owe money to other countries, organizations, or people. ❑ *The treasury secretary identified the most heavily indebted countries.*

in·de·cen·cy /ɪnˈdiːsənsi/ NOUN [U, C] (**indecencies**) **1** [U] If you talk about the **indecency** of something or someone, you are indicating that you find them morally or sexually offensive. ❑ *the indecency of their language* **2** [C] In law, an **indecency** is an illegal sexual act. ❑ *sexual indecencies*

in·de·cent /ɪnˈdiːsənt/ ADJ **1** If you describe something as **indecent**, you mean that it is shocking and offensive, usually because it relates to sex or nakedness. = obscene ❑ *He accused Mrs Moore of making an indecent suggestion.* **2** If you describe the speed or amount of something as **indecent**, you are indicating, often in a humorous way, that it is much quicker or larger than is usual or desirable. ❑ *She finished her first glass of wine with indecent haste.*
in·de·cent·ly /ɪnˈdiːsəntli/ ADV **1** *an indecently short skirt* **2** *an indecently large office*

in·de·ci·sive /ˌɪndɪˈsaɪsɪv/ ADJ **1** If you say that someone is **indecisive**, you mean that they find it very difficult to make decisions. ❑ *He was criticized as a weak and indecisive leader.* **2** An **indecisive** result in a contest or election is one that is not clear or definite. = inconclusive ❑ *The outcome of the battle was indecisive.*

in·deed ♦♦◇ /ɪnˈdiːd/ ADV (*emphasis*) **1** You use **indeed** to confirm or agree with something that has just been said. ❑ *Later, he admitted that the payments had indeed been made.* ❑ '*Did you know him?'—'I did indeed.'* **2** [indeed with CL]

i

You use **indeed** to introduce a further comment or statement that strengthens the point you have already made. ❏ *We have nothing against diversity; indeed, we want more of it.* **3** [ADJ + indeed] You use **indeed** at the end of a clause to give extra force to the word 'very', or to emphasize a particular word. ❏ *The results are often strange indeed.*

✪**in·defi·nite** /ɪnˈdefɪnɪt/ ADJ (*academic word*) **1** If you describe a situation or period as **indefinite**, you mean that people have not decided when it will end. ≠ finite ❏ *The trial was adjourned for an indefinite period.* ❏ *an indefinite strike by government workers* **2** Something that is **indefinite** is not exact or clear. ❏ *at some indefinite time in the future*

✪**in·defi·nite·ly** /ɪnˈdefɪnɪtli/ ADV [indefinitely with V] If a situation will continue **indefinitely**, it will continue forever or until someone decides to change it or end it. ❏ *The visit has now been postponed indefinitely.* ❏ *The school has been closed indefinitely.*

✪**in·de·pend·ence** ♦♦◇ /ˌɪndɪˈpendəns/ NOUN [U] **1** If a country has or gains **independence**, it has its own government and is not ruled by any other country. ❏ *In 1816, Argentina declared its independence from Spain.* ❏ *the country's first elections since independence in 1962* **2** Someone's **independence** is the fact that they do not rely on other people. = freedom, liberty; ≠ dependence ❏ *He was afraid of losing his independence.*

✪**in·de·pend·ent** ♦♦♦ /ˌɪndɪˈpendənt/ ADJ, NOUN
ADJ **1** If one thing or person is **independent of** another, they are separate and not connected, so the first one is not affected or influenced by the second. ❏ *Your questions should be independent of each other.* ❏ *We're going independent from the university and setting up our own group.* ❏ *Two independent studies have been carried out.* **2** If someone is **independent**, they do not need help or money from anyone else. = self-reliant, self-supporting ❏ *Phil was now much more independent of his parents.* ❏ *She would like to be financially independent.* **3** **Independent** countries and states are not ruled by other countries but have their own government. = liberated, self-governing; ≠ dependent ❏ *Papua New Guinea became independent from Australia in 1975.* ❏ *a fully independent state* **4** [independent + N] An **independent** organization or other body is one that controls its own finances and operations, rather than being controlled by someone else. ❏ *an independent television station* **5** [independent + N] An **independent** inquiry or opinion is one that involves people who are not connected with a particular situation, and should therefore be fair. ❏ *There were calls in Congress for an independent inquiry.* **6** An **independent** politician is one who does not represent any political party. ❏ *There's been a late surge of support for an independent candidate.*
NOUN [C] (**independents**) An **independent** is an independent politician. ❏ *Mr Vassiliou, standing as an independent, succeeded in convincing a significant number of voters of his argument.*
✪**in·de·pen·dent·ly** /ˌɪndɪˈpendəntli/ ADV **1** = separately, autonomously ❏ *several people working independently in different areas of the world* ❏ *The commission will operate independently of ministers.* **2** *helping disabled students to live and study as independently as possible*

✪**in·dex** ♦◇◇ /ˈɪndeks/ NOUN, VERB (*academic word*)

The usual plural of the noun is **indexes**, but the form **indices** can be used for meaning 1.

NOUN [C] (**indices** or **indexes**) **1** An **index** is a system by which changes in the value of something and the rate at which it changes can be recorded, measured, or interpreted. ❏ *the consumer price index* **2** An **index** is an alphabetical list that is printed at the back of a book and tells you on which pages important topics are referred to. ❏ *There's even a special subject index.*
VERB [T] (**indexes**, **indexing**, **indexed**) **1** If you **index** a book or a collection of information, you make an alphabetical list of the items in it. ❏ *A quarter of this vast archive has been indexed and made accessible to researchers.* **2** If a quantity or value **is indexed to** another, a system is arranged so that it increases or decreases whenever the

other one increases or decreases. ❏ *Minimum benefits and wages are to be indexed to inflation.*

✪**in·di·cate** ♦♦◇ /ˈɪndɪkeɪt/ VERB [T, I] (**indicates**, **indicating**, **indicated**) (*academic word*) **1** [T] If one thing **indicates** another, the first thing shows that the second is true or exists. = demonstrate, show ❏ *A survey of retired people has indicated that most are independent and enjoying life.* ❏ *Our vote today indicates a change in United States policy.* ❏ *This indicates whether remedies are suitable for children.* **2** [T] If you **indicate** an opinion, an intention, or a fact, you mention it in an indirect way. ❏ *Mr Rivers has indicated that he may resign.* **3** [T] (*formal*) If you **indicate** something to someone, you show them where it is, especially by pointing to it. ❏ *He indicated a chair. 'Sit down.'* **4** [T] If one thing **indicates** something else, it is a sign of that thing. ❏ *Dreams can help indicate your true feelings.* **5** [T] If a technical instrument **indicates** something, it shows a measurement or reading. = show ❏ *an instrument used to indicate wind direction* ❏ *The needles that indicate your height are at the top right-hand corner.* ❏ *The temperature gauge indicated that it was boiling.* **6** [I, T] (*BrE*; in *AmE*, use **signal**) When drivers **indicate**, they make lights flash on one side of their vehicle to show that they are going to turn in that direction. = signal

---
WHICH WORD?
indicate or show?

Indicate and **show** are not always used in the same way when they have a person as their subject.
If someone **indicates** an object, they show someone else where it is, usually by pointing or nodding towards it.
❏ *He indicated to him the inside of the hut.*
If you **show** an object to someone, you hold it up or give or take it to them, so that they can see it and examine it.
❏ *I showed William what I had written.*

✪**in·di·ca·tion** ♦◇◇ /ˌɪndɪˈkeɪʃən/ NOUN [C, U] (**indications**) An **indication** is a sign that suggests, for example, what people are thinking or feeling. = sign ❏ *He gave no indication that he was ready to compromise.* ❏ *All the indications are that we are going to receive reasonable support from abroad.* ❏ *These numbers give an indication of the extent of the disease.*

✪**in·di·ca·tor** /ˈɪndɪkeɪtə/ NOUN [C] (**indicators**) **1** An **indicator** is a measurement or value that gives you an idea of what something is like. ❏ *vital economic indicators, such as inflation, growth and the trade gap* ❏ *The number of wells is a fair indicator of the demand for water.* **2** (*mainly BrE*; in *AmE*, use **turn signals**) A car's **indicators** are the flashing lights that tell you when it is going to turn left or right.

in·di·ces /ˈɪndɪsiːz/ IRREG FORM **Indices** is a plural form of **index**.

in·dict·ment /ɪnˈdaɪtmənt/ NOUN [C] (**indictments**) If you say that one thing is **an indictment of** another thing, you mean that it shows how bad the other thing is. ❏ *The film is an indictment of Hollywood.*

✪**in·dig·enous** /ɪnˈdɪdʒɪnəs/ ADJ (*formal*) **Indigenous** people or things belong to the country in which they are found, rather than coming there or being brought there from another country. = native; ≠ non-indigenous, foreign ❏ *the country's indigenous population* ❏ *animals that are indigenous to Asia* ❏ *It offers the opportunity of travel to places where Buddhism forms a part of the indigenous culture – Nepal, India, Japan, Thailand.*

✪**in·di·rect** /ˌɪndaɪˈrekt, -dɪˈrekt/ ADJ **1** An **indirect** result or effect is not caused immediately and obviously by a thing or person, but happens because of something else that they have done. ❏ *Businesses are feeling the indirect effects from the recession that's going on elsewhere.* ❏ *Millions could die of hunger as an indirect result of the war.* **2** An **indirect** route or journey does not use the shortest or easiest way between two places. ❏ *He took an indirect route back home.* **3** **Indirect** remarks and information suggest something or refer to it, without actually mentioning it or stating it clearly. ❏ *His remarks amounted to an indirect appeal for economic aid.*

✪in·di·rect·ly /ˌɪndaɪˈrektli, -dɪˈrektli/ ADV **1** ≠ directly ❑ *Drugs are indirectly responsible for the violence.* ❑ *The depletion of atmospheric ozone may indirectly affect our use of the coastal zone.* **2** [indirectly with V] ❑ *He referred indirectly to the territorial dispute.*

in·dis·pen·sable /ˌɪndɪˈspensəbəl/ ADJ If you say that someone or something is **indispensable**, you mean that they are absolutely essential and other people or things cannot function without them. = essential ❑ *She was becoming indispensable to him.*

✪in·di·vid·ual ♦♦◇ /ˌɪndɪˈvɪdʒuəl/ ADJ, NOUN (*academic word*)
[ADJ] **1** [individual + N] **Individual** means relating to one person or thing, rather than to a large group. = single; ≠ collective, joint ❑ *waiting for the group to decide rather than making individual decisions* ❑ *Aid to individual countries is linked to progress towards democracy.* **2** If you describe someone or something as **individual**, you mean that you admire them because they are very unusual and do not try to imitate other people or things. ❑ *It was really all part of her very individual personality.*
[NOUN] [C] (**individuals**) An **individual** is a person. = human being, person ❑ *anonymous individuals who are doing good things within our community* ❑ *the rights and responsibilities of the individual*

✪in·di·vid·ual·ly /ˌɪndɪˈvɪdʒuəli/ ADV = singly; ≠ collectively, jointly ❑ *individually crafted tiles* ❑ *There are 96 pieces and they are worth, individually and collectively, a lot of money.* ❑ *Individually they're weak, but as a group they can be devastating.*

in·di·vidu·al·ity /ˌɪndɪvɪdʒuˈæliti/ NOUN [U] The **individuality** of a person or thing consists of the qualities that make them different from other people or things. ❑ *People should be free to express their individuality.*

in·door /ˈɪndɔː/ ADJ [indoor + N] **Indoor** activities or things are ones that happen or are used inside a building and not outside. ❑ *No smoking in any indoor facilities.*

in·doors /ˌɪnˈdɔːz/ ADV If something happens **indoors**, it happens inside a building. ❑ *I think perhaps we should go indoors.*

✪in·duce /ɪnˈdjuːs, AmE -ˈduːs-/ VERB [T] (**induces, inducing, induced**) (*academic word*) **1** To **induce** a state or condition means to cause it. = cause, trigger, precipitate ❑ *Doctors said surgery could induce a heart attack.* ❑ *an economic crisis induced by high oil prices* **2** If you **induce** someone to do something, you persuade or influence them to do it. = persuade ❑ *More than 4,000 teachers were induced to take early retirement.*

in·duc·tion /ɪnˈdʌkʃən/ NOUN [C, U] (**inductions**) **Induction** is a procedure or ceremony for introducing someone to a new job, organization, or way of life. ❑ *his induction as president*

in·dulge /ɪnˈdʌldʒ/ VERB [I, T] (**indulges, indulging, indulged**) **1** [I, T] If you **indulge in** something or if you **indulge** yourself, you allow yourself to have or do something that you know you will enjoy. ❑ *Only rarely will she indulge in a glass of wine.* ❑ *He returned to Ohio so that he could indulge his passion for football.* **2** [T] If you **indulge** someone, you let them have or do what they want, even if this is not good for them. = spoil ❑ *He did not agree with indulging children.*

in·dul·gence /ɪnˈdʌldʒəns/ NOUN [C, U] (**indulgences**) **Indulgence** means treating someone with special kindness, often when it is not a good thing. ❑ *The king's indulgence towards his sons angered the business community.*

in·dul·gent /ɪnˈdʌldʒənt/ ADJ If you are **indulgent**, you treat a person with special kindness, often in a way that is not good for them. ❑ *His indulgent mother was willing to let him do anything he wanted.*

in·dul·gent·ly /ɪnˈdʌldʒəntli/ ADV ❑ *Najib smiled at him indulgently and said, 'Come on over when you feel like it.'*

✪in·dus·trial ♦♦◇ /ɪnˈdʌstriəl/ ADJ **1** You use **industrial** to describe things that relate to or are used in industry. ❑ *industrial machinery and equipment* ❑ *a link between industrial chemicals and cancer* **2** An **industrial** city or country is one in which industry is important or highly

developed. = industrialized, developed ❑ *leading western industrial countries*

in·dus·trial·ly /ɪnˈdʌstriəli/ ADV ❑ *Stalin turned Russia into an industrially powerful nation.*

✪in·dus·tri·al·ize /ɪnˈdʌstriəlaɪz/ also **industrialise** VERB [I, T] (**industrializes, industrializing, industrialized**) When a country **industrializes** or is **industrialized**, it develops a lot of industries. ❑ *Energy consumption rises as countries industrialize.*

in·dus·tri·ali·za·tion /ɪnˌdʌstriəlaɪˈzeɪʃən/ NOUN [U] ❑ *Industrialization began early in Spain.*

in·dus·trial re·la·tions NOUN [PL] (*business*) **Industrial relations** refers to the relationship between employers and employees in industry, and the political decisions and laws that affect it. ❑ *The offer is seen as an attempt to improve industrial relations.*

✪in·dus·try ♦♦♦ /ˈɪndəstri/ NOUN [U, C] (**industries**) **1** [U] **Industry** is the work and processes involved in collecting raw materials, and making them into products in factories. ❑ *Our industry suffers through insufficient investment in research.* ❑ *The changes will boost jobs and benefit Australian industry.* ❑ *in countries where industry is developing rapidly* **2** [C] A particular **industry** consists of all the people and activities involved in making a particular product or providing a particular service. = business ❑ *the motor vehicle and textile industries* ❑ *the Scottish tourist industry* **3** [C] If you refer to a social or political activity as an **industry**, you are criticizing it because you think it involves a lot of people in unnecessary or useless work. ❑ *the industry of western capitalism* **4** [U] (*formal*) **Industry** is the fact of working very hard. ❑ *No one doubted his ability, his industry or his integrity.*

in·ed·ible /ɪnˈedɪbəl/ ADJ If you say that something is **inedible**, you mean that you cannot eat it, for example because it tastes bad or is poisonous. ❑ *Detainees complained of being given inedible food.*

in·ef·fec·tive /ˌɪnɪˈfektɪv/ ADJ If you say that something is **ineffective**, you mean that it has no effect on a process or situation. ❑ *Economic reform will continue to be painful and ineffective.*

in·ef·fi·cient /ˌɪnɪˈfɪʃənt/ ADJ **Inefficient** people, organizations, systems, or machines do not use time, energy, or other resources in the best way. ❑ *Their communication systems are inefficient in the extreme.*

in·ef·fi·cien·cy /ˌɪnɪˈfɪʃənsi/ NOUN [C, U] (**inefficiencies**) ❑ *The inefficiency of the distribution system has led to the loss of millions of tonnes of food.*

in·ef·fi·cient·ly /ˌɪnɪˈfɪʃəntli/ ADV [inefficiently with V] ❑ *Energy prices have been kept low, so energy is used inefficiently.*

in·ept /ɪnˈept/ ADJ (*disapproval*) If you say that someone is **inept**, you are criticizing them because they do something with a complete lack of skill. ❑ *He was inept and lacked the intelligence to govern.*

✪in·equal·ity /ˌɪnɪˈkwɒliti/ NOUN [C, U] (**inequalities**) **Inequality** is the difference in social status, wealth, or opportunity between people or groups. = injustice, inequity ❑ *People are concerned about corruption and social inequality.* ❑ *In addition to bearing down hard on unemployment, they would seek to reduce inequalities in wealth.* ❑ *inequality between the sexes*

✪in·evi·tabil·ity /ɪnˌevɪtəˈbɪlɪti/ NOUN [C, U] (**inevitabilities**) The **inevitability** of something is the fact that it is certain to happen and cannot be prevented or avoided. ❑ *We are all bound by the inevitability of death.* ❑ *a statement which appeared to accept the inevitability of war*

✪in·evi·table ♦◇◇ /ɪnˈevɪtəbəl/ ADJ, NOUN (*academic word*)
[ADJ] If something is **inevitable**, it is certain to happen and cannot be prevented or avoided. = unavoidable, certain; ≠ avoidable ❑ *If the case succeeds, it is inevitable that other trials will follow.* ❑ *The defeat had inevitable consequences for British policy.*
[NOUN] [SING] **The inevitable** is something that is inevitable. ❑ *'It's just delaying the inevitable', he said.*

✪in·evi·tably /ɪnˈevɪtəbli/ ADV If something will

inevitably happen, it is certain to happen and cannot be prevented or avoided. = unavoidably, certainly ❑ *Technological changes will inevitably lead to unemployment.* ❑ *Inevitably, the proposal is running into difficulties.*

✪ **in·exo·rable** /ɪnˈeksərəbəl/ ADJ (*formal*) You use **inexorable** to describe a process that cannot be prevented from continuing or progressing. = relentless ❑ *the seemingly inexorable rise in unemployment* ❑ *He is acutely aware of the inexorable march of time.*
　✪ **in·exo·rably** /ɪnˈeksərəbli/ ADV [inexorably with v] = relentlessly ❑ *Spending on health is growing inexorably.* ❑ *The crisis is moving inexorably towards war.*

in·ex·pen·sive /ˌɪnɪkˈspensɪv/ ADJ Something that is **inexpensive** does not cost very much. = cheap ❑ *There is a large variety of good, inexpensive restaurants.*

in·ex·pe·ri·ence /ˌɪnɪkˈspɪəriəns/ NOUN [U] If you refer to someone's **inexperience**, you mean that they have little knowledge or experience of a particular situation or activity. ❑ *Critics attacked the youth and inexperience of his staff.*

in·ex·pe·ri·enced /ˌɪnɪkˈspɪəriənst/ ADJ If you are **inexperienced**, you have little knowledge or experience of a particular situation or activity. ❑ *Routine tasks are often delegated to inexperienced young doctors.*

✪ **in·fan·cy** /ˈɪnfənsi/ NOUN [U] **1** **Infancy** is the period of your life when you are a very young child. = childhood ❑ *the development of the mind from infancy onwards* ❑ *Only 50% of Afghan babies survive infancy.* **2** If something is **in its infancy**, it is new and has not developed very much. ❑ *Computing science was still in its infancy.*

✪ **in·fant** /ˈɪnfənt/ NOUN, ADJ
　NOUN [c] (**infants**) (*formal*) An **infant** is a baby or very young child. = baby, child ❑ *holding the infant in his arms* ❑ *They are saying that he is tiring of playing daddy to their infant son.* ❑ *vaccinations of newborn infants* ❑ *the infant mortality rate in Britain*
　ADJ **1** [infant + N] (*BrE*; in *AmE*, use **baby**) **Infant** means designed especially for very young children. **2** [infant + N] An **infant** organization or system is new and has not developed very much. ❑ *The infant company was based in Nebraska.*

✪ **in·fect** ◆◇◇ /ɪnˈfekt/ VERB [T] (**infects, infecting, infected**) **1** To **infect** people, animals, or plants means to cause them to have a disease or illness. ❑ *A single mosquito can infect a large number of people.* ❑ *objects used by an infected person* ❑ *people infected with HIV* **2** To **infect** a substance or area means to cause it to contain harmful germs or bacteria. = contaminate ❑ *The birds infect the milk.* **3** When people, places, or things **are infected** by a feeling or influence, it spreads to them. ❑ *For an instant I was infected by her fear.* ❑ *He thought they might infect others with their bourgeois ideas.* **4** (*computing*) If a virus **infects** a computer, it damages or destroys files or programs. ❑ *This virus infected thousands of computers across the U.S. and Europe within days.*

✪ **in·fec·tion** ◆◇◇ /ɪnˈfekʃən/ NOUN [U, c] (**infections**) **1** [U] The **infection** of people, animals, or plants is the process of causing them to have a disease or illness. ❑ *plants that are resistant to infection* **2** [c] An **infection** is a disease caused by germs or bacteria. = disease, illness, virus ❑ *Ear infections are common in preschool children.* ❑ *Exactly which bacteria cause the infection is still unknown.*

✪ **in·fec·tious** /ɪnˈfekʃəs/ ADJ **1** A disease that is **infectious** can be caught by being near a person who has it. Compare **contagious**. ❑ *infectious diseases such as measles* ❑ *These viruses are highly infectious.* **2** If a feeling is **infectious**, it spreads to other people. ❑ *She radiates an infectious enthusiasm for everything she does.*

✪ **in·fer** /ɪnˈfɜː/ VERB [T] (**infers, inferring, inferred**) (*academic word*) **1** If you **infer** that something is the case, you decide that it is true on the basis of information that you already have. = deduce ❑ *I inferred from what she said that you have not been well.* ❑ *By measuring the motion of the galaxies in a cluster, astronomers can infer the cluster's mass.* **2** Some people use **infer** to mean 'imply', but this use is incorrect. ❑ *The police inferred, though they didn't exactly*

say it, that they found her behaviour rather suspicious.

✪ **in·fer·ence** /ˈɪnfərəns/ NOUN [c, u] (**inferences**) **1** [c] An **inference** is a conclusion that you draw about something by using information that you already know about it. = conclusion ❑ *There were two inferences to be drawn from her letter.* ❑ *A more reasonable inference is that his evidence flows from a desire for self-preservation.* **2** [U] **Inference** is the act of drawing conclusions about something on the basis of information that you already have. = deduction ❑ *It had an extremely tiny head and, by inference, a tiny brain.*

✪ **in·fe·ri·or** /ɪnˈfɪəriə/ ADJ, NOUN
　ADJ **1** Something that is **inferior** is not as good as something else. = worse; ≠ better ❑ *The cassettes were of inferior quality.* ❑ *This resulted in overpriced and often inferior products.* **2** If one person is regarded as **inferior to** another, they are regarded as less important because they have less status or ability. ❑ *He preferred the company of those who were intellectually inferior to himself.* ❑ *If children were made to feel inferior to other children their confidence declined.*
　NOUN [c] (**inferiors**) A person's **inferior** is someone who is regarded as less important because they have less status or ability. ❑ *It was a gentleman's duty always to be civil, even to his inferiors.*

in·fe·ri·or·ity /ɪnfɪəriˈɒrɪti, AmE -ˈɔːr-/ NOUN [U] ❑ *I found it difficult to shake off a sense of social inferiority.*

in·fil·trate /ˈɪnfɪltreɪt/ VERB [I, T] (**infiltrates, infiltrating, infiltrated**) **1** [I, T] If people **infiltrate** a place or organization, or **infiltrate into** it, they enter it secretly in order to spy on it or influence it. ❑ *Activists had infiltrated the student movement.* **2** [T] To **infiltrate** people **into** a place or organization means to get them into it secretly in order to spy on it or influence it. ❑ *He claimed that some countries have been trying to infiltrate their agents into the republic.*

in·fil·tra·tion /ˌɪnfɪlˈtreɪʃən/ NOUN [c, u] (**infiltrations**) ❑ *an inquiry into alleged infiltration by the far left group*

✪ **in·fi·nite** /ˈɪnfɪnɪt/ ADJ **1** (*emphasis*) If you describe something as **infinite**, you are emphasizing that it is extremely great in amount or degree. ❑ *an infinite variety of landscapes* ❑ *With infinite care, John shifted position.* **2** Something that is **infinite** has no limit, end, or edge. = boundless, limitless; ≠ finite ❑ *an infinite number of atoms* ❑ *Obviously, no company has infinite resources.*

in·fi·nite·ly /ˈɪnfɪnɪtli/ ADV **1** [infinitely + ADJ/ADV] ❑ *His design was infinitely better than anything I could have done.* **2** [infinitely with v] ❑ *A centimetre can be infinitely divided into smaller units.*

✪ **in·fin·ity** /ɪnˈfɪnɪti/ NOUN [U] **1** [also 'an' infinity 'of' N] **Infinity** is a number that is larger than any other number and can never be given an exact value. ❑ *These permutations multiply toward infinity.* ❑ *There is always an infinity of numbers between any two numbers.* **2** **Infinity** is a point that is further away than any other point and can never be reached. ❑ *the darkness of a starless night stretching to infinity*

in·flame /ɪnˈfleɪm/ VERB [T] (**inflames, inflaming, inflamed**) (*journalism*) If something **inflames** a situation or **inflames** people's feelings, it makes people feel even more strongly about something. ❑ *They are responsible for inflaming the situation.*

✪ **in·flate** /ɪnˈfleɪt/ VERB [I, T] (**inflates, inflating, inflated**) **1** [I, T] If you **inflate** something such as a balloon or tyre, or if it **inflates**, it becomes bigger as it is filled with air or a gas. ≠ deflate ❑ *Stuart jumped into the sea and inflated the liferaft.* ❑ *Don's life jacket had failed to inflate.* **2** [I, T] If you say that someone **inflates** the price of something, or that the price **inflates**, you mean that the price increases. = increase ❑ *The promotion of a big release can inflate a film's final cost.* **3** [T] If someone **inflates** the amount or effect of something, they say it is bigger, better, or more important than it really is, usually so that they can profit from it. ❑ *They inflated their clients' medical injuries and treatment to defraud insurance companies.*

in·flat·ed /ɪnˈfleɪtɪd/ ADJ ❑ *They had to buy everything at inflated prices at the ranch store.*

✪in·fla·tion ♦♦◇ /ɪnˈfleɪʃən/ NOUN [U] (*business*)
Inflation is a general increase in the prices of goods and services in a country. ≠ deflation □ *rising unemployment and high inflation* □ *an inflation rate of only 2.2%*

in·flex·ible /ɪnˈfleksɪbəl/ ADJ **1** Something that is **inflexible** cannot be altered in any way, even if the situation changes. = rigid □ *Workers insisted the new system was too inflexible.* **2** If you say that someone is **inflexible**, you are criticizing them because they refuse to change their mind or alter their way of doing things. □ *His opponents viewed him as stubborn, dogmatic, and inflexible.* **in·flex·ibil·ity** /ˌɪnˌfleksɪˈbɪlɪti/ NOUN [U] **1** *The system's inflexibility was highlighted by several recent failures.* □ *Marvin's father was exceptional for the inflexibility of his rules.* **2** *Joyce was irritated by the inflexibility of her colleagues.*

in·flict /ɪnˈflɪkt/ VERB [T] (**inflicts, inflicting, inflicted**) To **inflict** harm or damage **on** someone or something means to make them suffer it. □ *the damage being inflicted on industries by the recession*

✪in·flu·ence ♦♦◇ /ˈɪnfluəns/ NOUN, VERB
▸ NOUN [U, c] (**influences**) **1** [U] **Influence** is the power to make other people agree with your opinions or do what you want. □ *He used his influence to get his son into medical school.* □ *He denies exerting any political influence over them.* **2** [c] To have an **influence on** people or situations means to affect what they do or what happens. = effect □ *Van Gogh had a major influence on the development of modern painting.* □ *Many other medications have an influence on cholesterol levels.* **3** [c] Someone or something that is a good or bad **influence** on people has a good or bad effect on them. □ *I thought Sonny would be a good influence on you.* ▸ PHRASE **under the influence of** If you are **under the influence of** someone or something, you are being affected or controlled by them. □ *He was arrested on suspicion of driving under the influence of alcohol.*
▸ VERB [T] (**influences, influencing, influenced**) **1** If you **influence** someone, you use your power to make them agree with you or do what you want. □ *He is trying to improperly influence a witness.* **2** If someone or something **influences** a person or situation, they have an effect on that person's behaviour or that situation. = affect □ *We became the best of friends and he influenced me deeply.* □ *What you eat may influence your risk of getting cancer.* □ *Leadership means influencing the organization to follow the leader's vision.*

WORD CONNECTIONS
VERB + **influence**
have an influence
exert an influence
□ *These events clearly had a major influence on much of Mahler's work.*
ADJ + **influence**
a **considerable** influence
a **powerful** influence
a **strong** influence
a **major** influence
an **important** influence
□ *The media has a strong influence on how people view disabilities.*
a **good** influence
a **positive** influence
a **bad** influence
□ *There is evidence that attractively designed buildings with green open spaces have a positive influence on mental health.*
political influence
□ *He used his political influence to block the plans.*

✪in·flu·en·tial /ˌɪnfluˈenʃəl/ ADJ Someone or something that is **influential** has a lot of influence over people or events. = effective, powerful; ≠ ineffective □ *It helps to have influential friends.* □ *He had been influential in shaping economic policy.* □ *one of the most influential books ever written*

in·flux /ˈɪnflʌks/ NOUN [c] (**influxes**) An **influx of** people or things into a place is their arrival there in large numbers. □ *problems caused by the influx of refugees*

✪in·form ♦◇◇ /ɪnˈfɔːm/ VERB [T, I] (**informs, informing, informed**) **1** [T] If you **inform** someone **of** something, you tell them about it. ≠ conceal □ *They would inform him of any progress they had made.* □ *My daughter informed me that she was pregnant.* □ *contracts that inform customers that their details will be passed to a third party* **2** [i] If someone **informs on** a person, they give information about the person to the police or another authority, which causes the person to be suspected or proved guilty of doing something bad. □ *Thousands of American citizens have informed on these organized crime syndicates.* **3** [T] (*formal*) If a situation or activity **is informed** by an idea or a quality, that idea or quality is very noticeable in it. □ *All great songs are informed by a certain sadness and tension.*

✪in·for·mal /ɪnˈfɔːməl/ ADJ **1** **Informal** speech or behaviour is relaxed and friendly rather than serious, very correct, or official. = relaxed, casual □ *She is refreshingly informal.* **2** An **informal** situation is one that is relaxed and friendly and not very serious or official. = relaxed □ *The house has an informal atmosphere.* □ *This door leads to the informal living area.* **3** **Informal** clothes are casual and suitable for wearing when you are relaxing, but not on formal occasions. = casual □ *For lunch, dress is informal.* **4** You use **informal** to describe something that is done unofficially or casually without planning. = unofficial; ≠ formal □ *The two leaders will retire to Camp David for informal discussions.* □ *This was an informal, unofficial investigation.*
✪in·for·mal·ly /ɪnˈfɔːməli/ ADV **1** [informally after v] □ *She was always there at half past eight, chatting informally to the children.* **2** *Everyone dressed informally in shorts or faded jeans, and baggy sweatshirts.* **3** = unofficially; ≠ formally □ *He began informally to handle Ted's tax affairs for him.* □ *All meetings were held informally, and off the record.*
✪in·for·mal·ity /ˌɪnfɔːˈmælɪti/ NOUN [U] **1** ≠ formality □ *He was overwhelmed by their friendly informality.* □ *a sign that more informality is gradually coming into the language* **2** ≠ formality □ *She enjoyed the relative informality of island life.* □ *the informality of the communication process*

in·form·ant /ɪnˈfɔːmənt/ NOUN [c] (**informants**) **1** (*formal*) An **informant** is someone who gives another person a piece of information. □ *On the basis of data furnished by her informants, Mead concluded that adolescents in Samoa had complete sexual freedom.* **2** An **informant** is the same as an **informer**.

✪in·for·ma·tion ♦♦♦ /ˌɪnfəˈmeɪʃən/ NOUN [U]
1 **Information** about someone or something consists of facts about them. = facts, data, details □ *Pat refused to give her any information about Sarah.* □ *Each centre would provide information on technology and training.* □ *For further information contact the number below.* □ *an important piece of information* **2** (*computing*) **Information** consists of the facts and figures that are stored and used by a computer program. = data □ *Pictures are scanned into a form of digital information that computers can recognize.*

USAGE NOTE
information
Remember that **information** is an uncountable noun. You do not use 'an' in front of it, and you do not talk about 'informations'.
*You'll find all the background **information** you need in the file.*
However, you can talk about a **piece of information**.
*Each **piece of information** is entered into a separate box.*

WHICH WORD?
information or news?
Information consists of facts that you obtain about something.
□ *I'd like some **information** about trains to London.*
You do not use 'information' to refer to descriptions of recent events, especially in newspapers, on television, etc. The word you use is **news**.
□ ***News** of the deaths spread quickly.*
□ *He's recently been in the **news**.*

i

⊙in·for·ma·tion tech·nol·ogy NOUN [U]
Information technology is the theory and practice of using computers to store and analyse information. The abbreviation **IT** is often used. ❑ *the information technology industry* ❑ *The rapid growth of information technology has transformed the working environment.*

in·forma·tive /ɪnˈfɔːmətɪv/ ADJ Something that is **informative** gives you useful information. ❑ *Both men termed the meeting friendly and informative.*

in·form·er /ɪnˈfɔːmə/ NOUN [C] (**informers**) An **informer** is a person who tells the police that someone has done something illegal. ❑ *two men suspected of being police informers*

⊙in·fra·struc·ture /ˈɪnfrəstrʌktʃə/ NOUN [C, U] (**infrastructures**) (*academic word*) The **infrastructure** of a country, society, or organization consists of the basic facilities such as transport, communications, power supplies, and buildings, which enable it to function. ❑ *improvements in the country's infrastructure* ❑ *investment in infrastructure projects* ❑ *a focus on improving existing infrastructure*

in·fre·quent /ɪnˈfriːkwənt/ ADJ If something is **infrequent**, it does not happen often. = rare ❑ *John's infrequent visits to Topeka*
• **in·fre·quent·ly** /ɪnˈfriːkwəntli/ ADV [usu infrequently with V, also infrequently with CL/GROUP] ❑ *The bridge is used infrequently.*

in·furi·ate /ɪnˈfjʊərieɪt/ VERB [T] (**infuriates, infuriating, infuriated**) If something or someone **infuriates** you, they make you extremely angry. = madden ❑ *His manner infuriated him.*

in·genu·ity /ˌɪndʒəˈnjuːɪti, AmE -ˈnuː-/ NOUN [U]
Ingenuity is skill at working out how to achieve things or skill at inventing new things. ❑ *Inspecting the nest can be difficult and may require some ingenuity.*

⊙in·gre·di·ent ♦◇◇ /ɪnˈɡriːdiənt/ NOUN [C] (**ingredients**) ❶ **Ingredients** are the things that are used to make something, especially all the different foods you use when you are cooking a particular dish. ❑ *Mix in the remaining ingredients.* ❑ *They found that the original active ingredient or solute changes the water or solvent.* ❷ An **ingredient** of a situation is one of the essential parts of it. = part, element ❑ *The meeting had all the ingredients of high political drama.* ❑ *What then are the common ingredients of most of our programmes?*

⊙in·hab·it /ɪnˈhæbɪt/ VERB [T] (**inhabits, inhabiting, inhabited**) If a place or region **is inhabited** by a group of people or a species of animal, those people or animals live there. ❑ *The valley is inhabited by the Dani tribe.* ❑ *the people who inhabit these islands*

⊙in·hab·it·ant /ɪnˈhæbɪtənt/ NOUN [C] (**inhabitants**) The **inhabitants** of a place are the people who live there. = resident, citizen ❑ *the inhabitants of Boise* ❑ *Jamaica's original inhabitants were the Arawak Indians.*

⊙in·ha·la·tion /ˌɪnhəˈleɪʃən/ NOUN [C, U] (**inhalations**) ❶ [C, U] (*formal*) **Inhalation** is the process or act of breathing in, taking air and sometimes other substances into your lungs. ❑ *They were taken to the hospital suffering from smoke inhalation.* ❑ *Take several deep inhalations.* ❑ *a complete cycle of inhalation and exhalation* ❷ [C] An **inhalation** is a treatment for colds and other illnesses in which you dissolve substances in hot water and breathe in the vapour. ❑ *Inhalations can soothe and control the cough.*

⊙in·hale /ɪnˈheɪl/ VERB [I, T] (**inhales, inhaling, inhaled**) When you **inhale**, you breathe in. When you **inhale** something such as smoke, you take it into your lungs when you breathe in. = breathe in ❑ *He took a long slow breath, inhaling deeply.* ❑ *He was treated for the effects of inhaling smoke.*

⊙in·her·ent /ɪnˈherənt, -ˈhɪər-/ ADJ (*academic word*) The **inherent** qualities of something are the necessary and natural parts of it. = intrinsic, integral ❑ *Stress is an inherent part of dieting.* ❑ *There are inherent risks to operating any business, whether it is a franchise or not.* ❑ *I doubt whether he realized the inherent contradiction in his own argument.* ❑ *the dangers inherent in an outbreak of war*

⊙in·her·ent·ly /ɪnˈherəntli, -ˈhɪər-/ ADV = intrinsically ❑ *Man is not inherently violent.* ❑ *Aeroplanes are not inherently dangerous.* ❑ *There is nothing inherently wrong with pleasure.*

⊙in·her·it /ɪnˈherɪt/ VERB [T] (**inherits, inheriting, inherited**) ❶ If you **inherit** money or property, you receive it from someone who has died. ❑ *He has no son to inherit his land.* ❑ *paintings that he inherited from his father* ❷ If you **inherit** something such as a task, problem, or attitude, you get it from the people who used to have it, for example, because you have taken over their job or been influenced by them. ❑ *The Endara government inherited an impossibly difficult situation from its predecessors.* ❸ If you **inherit** a characteristic or quality, you are born with it, because your parents or ancestors also had it. ❑ *We inherit from our parents many of our physical characteristics.* ❑ *Her children have inherited her love of sports.* ❑ *All sufferers from asthma have inherited a gene that makes them susceptible to the disease.* ❑ *Stammering is probably an inherited defect.*

in·her·it·ance /ɪnˈherɪtəns/ NOUN [C, U, SING] (**inheritances**) ❶ [C, U] An **inheritance** is money or property that you receive from someone who has died. ❑ *She feared losing her inheritance to her stepmother.* ❷ [C] If you get something such as a job, problem, or attitude from someone who used to have it, you can refer to this as an **inheritance**. ❑ *starvation and disease over much of Europe and Asia, which was Truman's inheritance as president* ❸ [SING] Your **inheritance** is the particular characteristics or qualities that your family or ancestors had and that you are born with. ❑ *Eye colour shows more than your genetic inheritance.*

⊙in·hib·it /ɪnˈhɪbɪt/ VERB [T] (**inhibits, inhibiting, inhibited**) (*academic word*) ❶ If something **inhibits** an event or process, it prevents it or slows it down. = hamper, hinder, interfere with; ≠ encourage, aid ❑ *The high cost of borrowing is inhibiting investment by industry in new equipment.* ❑ *Excessive trace elements, such as copper, in the soil will inhibit plant growth.* ❷ To **inhibit** someone **from** doing something means to prevent them from doing it, although they want to do it or should be able to do it. ❑ *Officers will be inhibited from doing their duty.*

in·hib·it·ed /ɪnˈhɪbɪtɪd/ ADJ (*disapproval*) If you say that someone is **inhibited**, you mean that they find it difficult to behave naturally and show their feelings, and that you think this is a bad thing. ❑ *Men are more inhibited about touching each other than women are.*

⊙in·hi·bi·tion /ˌɪnɪˈbɪʃən/ NOUN [C, U] (**inhibitions**) ❶ [C, U] **Inhibitions** are feelings of or embarrassment that make it difficult for you to behave naturally. ❑ *The whole point about dancing is to stop thinking and lose all your inhibitions.* ❷ [U] the fact or process of preventing something or slowing it down ❑ *Nicotine's many actions include both stimulation and inhibition of the nervous system, depending on dosage.* ❑ *The study of enzyme inhibition has had practical benefits.*

in·hu·man /ˌɪnˈhjuːmən/ ADJ ❶ If you describe treatment or an action as **inhuman**, you mean that it is extremely cruel. ❑ *The detainees are often held in cruel and inhuman conditions.* ❷ If you describe someone or something as **inhuman**, you mean that they are strange or bad because they do not seem human in some way. ❑ *inhuman screams and moans*

in·hu·mane /ˌɪnhjuːˈmeɪn/ ADJ If you describe something as **inhumane**, you mean that it is extremely cruel. ❑ *He was kept under inhumane conditions.*

⊙ini·tial ♦◇◇ /ɪˈnɪʃəl/ ADJ, NOUN, VERB (*academic word*)
ADJ [initial + N] You use **initial** to describe something that happens at the beginning of a process. = first, preliminary; ≠ last ❑ *The initial reaction has been excellent.* ❑ *The aim of this initial meeting is to clarify the issues.*
NOUN [C] (**initials**) **Initials** are the capital letters that begin each word of a name. For example, if your full name is Michael Dennis Stocks, your initials are M.D.S. ❑ *a silver Porsche with her initials JB on the side*
VERB [T] (**initials, initialling, initialled**; in AmE, use **initialing, initialed**) If someone **initials** an official document, they write their initials on it, to show that they have seen it or that they accept or agree with it. ❑ *Would you mind initialling this voucher?*

✪**ini·tial·ly** ◆◇◇ /ɪˈnɪʃəli/ ADV **Initially** means soon after the beginning of a process or situation, rather than in the middle or at the end of it. = originally; ≠ finally ❑ *Forecasters say the storms may not be as bad as they initially predicted.*

✪**ini·ti·ate** /ɪˈnɪʃieɪt/ VERB [T] (**initiates, initiating, initiated**) (*academic word*) **1** If you **initiate** something, you start it or cause it to happen. = instigate, set in motion ❑ *They wanted to initiate a discussion on economics.* ❑ *A peace process was initiated by the Indian prime minister in April.* **2** If you **initiate** someone **into** something, you introduce them to a particular skill or type of knowledge and teach them about it. ❑ *He initiated her into the study of other cultures.* **3** If someone **is initiated into** something such as a religion, secret society, or social group, they become a member of it by taking part in special ceremonies. ❑ *In many societies, young people are formally initiated into their adult roles.*

✪**ini·tia·tion** /ɪˌnɪʃiˈeɪʃən/ NOUN [U, C] (**initiations**) **1** [U] The **initiation** of something is the starting of it. = instigation, launch ❑ *the initiation of a rural development scheme* ❑ *Hypertension is perhaps the most common reason for initiation of lifelong drug treatment.* **2** [C, U] Someone's **initiation into** a particular group is the act or process by which they officially become a member, often involving special ceremonies. ❑ *This was my initiation into the peace movement.*

✪**ini·tia·tive** ◆◇◇ /ɪˈnɪʃətɪv/ NOUN (*academic word*)
NOUN [C, SING, U] (**initiatives**) **1** [C] An **initiative** is an important act or statement that is intended to solve a problem. ❑ *Local initiatives to help young people have been inadequate.* ❑ *There's talk of a new peace initiative.* **2** [SING] In a fight or contest, if you have **the initiative**, you are in a better position than your opponents to decide what to do next. ❑ *We have the initiative; we intend to keep it.* **3** [U] If you have **initiative**, you have the ability to decide what to do next and to do it, without needing other people to tell you what to do. ❑ *She was disappointed by his lack of initiative.*
PHRASE **take the initiative** If you **take the initiative** in a situation, you are the first person to act, and are therefore able to control the situation. ❑ *We are the only power willing to take the initiative in the long struggle to end the war.*

WORD CONNECTIONS
VERB + **initiative**
announce an initiative
launch an initiative
introduce an initiative
❑ *The government has launched a major new initiative to address energy efficiency and climate change.*
welcome an initiative
support an initiative
back an initiative
❑ *Environmental experts have welcomed the initiative.*
ADJ + **initiative**
a **new** initiative
a **major** initiative
a **bold** initiative
❑ *It was a bold initiative and the achievements were new and exciting.*

in·ject /ɪnˈdʒekt/ VERB [T] (**injects, injecting, injected**) **1** To **inject** a substance such as a medicine into someone means to put it into their body using a device with a needle called a syringe. ❑ *His son was injected with strong drugs.* ❑ *The technique consists of injecting healthy cells into the weakened muscles.* **2** If you **inject** a new, exciting, or interesting quality **into** a situation, you add it. ❑ *She kept trying to inject a little fun into their relationship.* **3** (*business*) If you **inject** money or resources **into** a business or organization, you provide more money or resources for it. ❑ *The insurance fund would inject $750 into the banks.*

✪**in·jec·tion** /ɪnˈdʒekʃən/ NOUN [C] (**injections**) **1** [also 'by' injection] If you have an **injection**, a doctor or nurse puts a medicine into your body using a device with a needle called a syringe. = shot ❑ *They gave me an injection to help me sleep.* ❑ *It has to be given by injection, usually twice daily.* **2** (*business*) An **injection of** money or resources into an organization is the act of providing it with more money or resources, to help it become more efficient or profitable. ❑ *An injection of cash is needed to fund some of these projects.*

✪**in·jure** /ˈɪndʒə/ VERB [T] (**injures, injuring, injured**) (*academic word*) If you **injure** a person or animal, you damage some part of their body. ❑ *A number of bombs have exploded, seriously injuring at least five people.* ❑ *stiff penalties for motorists who kill, maim, and injure*

✪**in·jured** ◆◇◇ /ˈɪndʒəd/ ADJ, NOUN
ADJ **1** An **injured** person or animal has physical damage to part of their body, usually as a result of an accident or fighting. = maimed, wounded ❑ *The other injured man had a superficial stomach wound.* ❑ *Many of them will have died because they were so badly injured.* **2** If you have **injured** feelings, you feel upset because you believe someone has been unfair or unkind to you. = hurt ❑ *a look of injured pride*
NOUN [PL] **The injured** are people who are injured. ❑ *Army helicopters tried to evacuate the injured.*

✪**in·ju·ry** ◆◆◇ /ˈɪndʒəri/ NOUN [C, U] (**injuries**) **1** An **injury** is damage done to a person's or an animal's body. = wound ❑ *Four police officers sustained serious injuries in the explosion.* ❑ *The two other passengers escaped serious injury.* ❑ *a serious injury to his left leg* **2** (*legal*) If someone suffers **injury to** their feelings, they are badly upset by something. If they suffer **injury to** their reputation, their reputation is seriously harmed. ❑ *She was awarded $3,500 for injury to her feelings.*
✦ add insult to injury → see **insult**

in·jus·tice /ɪnˈdʒʌstɪs/ NOUN [C, U] (**injustices**) **1** [C, U] **Injustice** is a lack of fairness in a situation. ❑ *They'll continue to fight injustice.* **2** [C] An **injustice** is an action or statement in which someone judges you or treats you unfairly. ❑ *Calling them a bunch of capricious kids with half-formed ideas does them an injustice.*

ink /ɪŋk/ NOUN [C, U] (**inks**) **Ink** is the coloured liquid used for writing or printing. ❑ *The letter was handwritten in black ink.*

in·land ADV, ADJ
ADV /ɪnˈlænd/ If something is situated **inland**, it is away from the coast, towards or near the middle of a country. If you go **inland**, you go away from the coast, towards the middle of a country. ❑ *The vast majority live further inland.* ❑ *It's about 15 minutes' drive inland from Pensacola.*
ADJ /ˈɪnlænd/ [inland + N] **Inland** areas, lakes, and places are not on the coast, but in or near the middle of a country. ❑ *a rather quiet inland town*

in·mate /ˈɪnmeɪt/ NOUN [C] (**inmates**) The **inmates** of a prison or mental hospital are the prisoners or patients who are living there. ❑ *education for prison inmates*

in·nate /ɪˈneɪt/ ADJ An **innate** quality or ability is one that a person is born with. = natural ❑ *Americans have an innate sense of fairness.*
in·nate·ly /ɪˈneɪtli/ ADV [innately + ADJ] ❑ *I believe everyone is innately psychic.*

✪**in·ner** ◆◇◇ /ˈɪnə/ ADJ **1** [inner + N] The **inner** parts of something are the parts contained or enclosed inside the other parts, closest to the centre. ❑ *She got up and went into an inner office.* ❑ *inhabitants of the inner city* ❑ *Wade stepped inside and closed the inner door behind him.* **2** [inner + N] Your **inner** feelings are feelings that you have but do not show to other people. ❑ *Loving relationships that a child makes will give him an inner sense of security.*

in·ner city NOUN [C] (**inner cities**) You use **inner city** to refer to the areas in or near the centre of a large city where people live and where there are often social and economic problems. ❑ *No one could deny that problems of crime in the inner city exist.*

in·no·cence /ˈɪnəsəns/ NOUN [U] **1 Innocence** is the quality of having no experience or knowledge of the more complex or unpleasant aspects of life. ❑ *the sweet*

i

innocence of youth **2** If someone proves their **innocence**, they prove that they are not guilty of a crime. ❑ *He claims he has evidence which could prove his innocence.*

◆**in·no·cent**◆◇◇ /'ɪnəsənt/ ADJ, NOUN

ADJ **1** If someone is **innocent**, they did not commit a crime that they have been accused of. ❑ *He was sure that the man was innocent of any crime.* ❑ *She has pleaded innocent to the charge.* **2** If someone is **innocent**, they have no experience or knowledge of the more complex or unpleasant aspects of life. = naive ❑ *They seemed so young and innocent.* **3 Innocent** people are those who are not involved in a crime or conflict, but are injured or killed as a result of it. ❑ *All those wounded were innocent victims.* **4** An **innocent** question, remark, or comment is not intended to offend or upset people, even if it does so. = harmless ❑ *It was probably an innocent question, but Michael got flustered anyway.*
NOUN [c] (**innocents**) An **innocent** is someone who is innocent. ❑ *She had always regarded Greg as a hopeless innocent where women were concerned.*
in·no·cent·ly /'ɪnəsəntli/ ADV ❑ *The baby gurgled innocently on the bed.*

in·no·vate /'ɪnəveɪt/ VERB [i] (**innovates, innovating, innovated**) (*academic word*) To **innovate** means to introduce changes and new ideas in the way something is done or made. ❑ *What sets Rice apart from most engineers is his constant desire to innovate and experiment.*

◆**in·no·va·tion** /ˌɪnə'veɪʃən/ NOUN [c, u] (**innovations**) **1** [c] An **innovation** is a new thing or a new method of doing something. ❑ *They produced the first vegetarian beanburger – an innovation which was rapidly exported.* ❑ *the transformation wrought by the technological innovations of the industrial age* **2** [u] **Innovation** is the introduction of new ideas, methods, or things. = novelty, creativity; ≠ tradition ❑ *We must promote originality, inspire creativity and encourage innovation.*

◆**in·no·va·tive** /'ɪnəveɪtɪv/ ADJ **1** Something that is **innovative** is new and original. = new, original, state-of-the-art, creative; ≠ traditional ❑ *products which are cheaper, more innovative and more reliable than those of their competitors* **2** An **innovative** person introduces changes and new ideas. ❑ *He was one of the most creative and innovative engineers of his generation.*

◆**in·put** /'ɪnpʊt/ NOUN, VERB (*academic word*)
NOUN [c, u] (**inputs**) **1** [c, u] **Input** consists of information or resources that a group or project receives. ❑ *It's up to the teacher to provide a variety of types of input in the classroom.* **2** [u] (*computing*) **Input** is information that is put into a computer. ❑ *The x-ray detectors feed the input into computer programs.* ❑ *an error in data input* **3** [c] (*computing*) An **input** is a connection where information enters a computer or other device. ≠ output ❑ *an amplifier with an input socket*
VERB [T] (**inputs, inputting, input**) (*computing*) If you **input** information into a computer, you feed it in, for example, by typing it on a keyboard. = type, enter ❑ *The computer acts as a word processor where the text of a speech can be input at any time.* ❑ *All this information had to be input onto the computer.*

in·quire /ɪn'kwaɪə/ also **enquire** VERB [i, T] (**inquires, inquiring, inquired**) **1** [i, T] (*formal*) If you **inquire** about something, you ask for information about it. ❑ *'What are you doing there?' she inquired.* ❑ *He called them several times to inquire about job possibilities.* **2** [i] If you **inquire into** something, you investigate it carefully. ❑ *Inspectors were appointed to inquire into the affairs of the company.*

◆**in·quiry** ◆◇◇ /ɪn'kwaɪəri/ also **enquiry** NOUN [c, u] (**inquiries**) **1** [c] An **inquiry** is a question you ask in order to get some information. = question ❑ *He made some inquiries and discovered she had gone to Connecticut.* ❑ *Having made further inquiries, we can confirm that a relationship did take place.* **2** [c] An **inquiry** is an official investigation. = investigation ❑ *a shocking murder inquiry* ❑ *The Democratic Party has called for an independent inquiry into the incident.* **3** [u] **Inquiry** is the process of asking about or investigating something in order to find out more about it. ❑ *The investigation has suddenly switched to a new line of inquiry.*

WORD CONNECTIONS

VERB + **inquiry**

make an inquiry
❑ *I'll make some inquiries and see what I can find out.*

conduct an inquiry
hold an inquiry
launch an inquiry
order an inquiry
❑ *The government has ordered an immediate inquiry into the tragedy.*

adjourn an inquiry
reopen an inquiry
❑ *New evidence prompted police to reopen the murder inquiry.*

ADJ + **inquiry**

further inquiries
❑ *He decided to make some further inquiries.*

a **judicial** inquiry
a **public** inquiry
an **independent** inquiry
❑ *The family called for a public inquiry into their daughter's death.*

inquiry + INTO + NOUN

an inquiry into a **murder**
an inquiry into a **death**
an inquiry into an **affair**
an inquiry into an **incident**
❑ *The firm which runs the airport has launched an inquiry into the incident.*

---

in·sane /ɪn'seɪn/ ADJ **1** Someone who is **insane** is severely mentally ill. = mad ❑ *Some people simply can't take it and they just go insane.* **2** If you describe a decision or action as **insane**, you think it is very foolish or excessive. ❑ *He asked me what I thought and I said, 'Listen, this is completely insane.'*
in·sane·ly /ɪn'seɪnli/ ADV ❑ *I would be insanely jealous if Bill left me for another woman.*

in·san·ity /ɪn'sænɪti/ NOUN [u] **1 Insanity** is the state of being insane. = madness ❑ *a psychiatrist who specialized in diagnosing insanity* **2** If you describe a decision or an action as **insanity**, you think it is very foolish. ❑ *the final financial insanity of the 1980s*

◆**in·sect** /'ɪnsekt/ NOUN [c] (**insects**) An **insect** is a small animal that has six legs. Most insects have wings. Ants, flies, butterflies, and beetles are all insects. ❑ *These bears eat insects, rodents and other small animals.* ❑ *blood poisoning from insect bites*

in·secure /ˌɪnsɪ'kjʊə/ ADJ **1** If you are **insecure**, you lack confidence because you think that you are not good enough or are not loved. ❑ *Most mothers are insecure about their performance as mothers.* **2** Something that is **insecure** is not safe or protected. ❑ *low-paid, insecure jobs*
in·secu·rity /ˌɪnsɪ'kjʊərɪti/ NOUN [c, u] (**insecurities**) **1** [c, u] ❑ *She is always assailed by self-doubt and emotional insecurity.* **2** [u] ❑ *the increase in crime, which has created feelings of insecurity in the population*

in·sen·si·tive /ɪn'sensɪtɪv/ ADJ **1** (*disapproval*) If you describe someone as **insensitive**, you are criticizing them for being unaware of or unsympathetic to other people's feelings. ❑ *I feel my husband is very insensitive about my problem.* **2** Someone who is **insensitive to** a situation or to a need does not think or care about it. ❑ *women's and Latino organizations that say he is insensitive to civil rights* **3** Someone who is **insensitive to** a physical sensation is unable to feel it. ❑ *He had become insensitive to cold.*
in·sen·si·tiv·ity /ɪnˌsensɪ'tɪvɪti/ NOUN [u] **1** *I was ashamed and appalled at my clumsiness and insensitivity towards her.* **2** *insensitivity to the environmental consequences*

◆**in·sert** VERB, NOUN (*academic word*)
VERB /ɪn'sɜːt/ [T] (**inserts, inserting, inserted**) **1** If you **insert** an object **into** something, you put the object inside it.

❑ *He took a small key from his pocket and slowly inserted it into the lock.* ❑ *tubes that are inserted into diseased arteries* **2** If you **insert** a comment into a piece of writing or a speech, you add it. ❑ *They joined with the monarchists to insert a clause calling for a popular vote on the issue.* NOUN /'ɪnsɜːt/ [c] (**inserts**) An **insert** is something that is inserted somewhere, especially an advertisement on a piece of paper that is placed between the pages of a book or magazine. ❑ *Sunday is the preferred day for advertising inserts in newspapers.*

in·ser·tion /ɪn'sɜːʃən/ NOUN [c, u] (**insertions**) **1** the first experiment involving the insertion of a new gene into a human being **2** an item for insertion in the programme

in·side ◆◆◇ PREP, ADV, ADJ, NOUN

> The form **inside of** can also be used as a preposition in American English.

PREP /ɪn'saɪd/ **1** Something or someone that is **inside** a place, container, or object is in it or is surrounded by it. ❑ *Inside the passport was a folded slip of paper.* **2** If you are **inside** an organization, you belong to it. ❑ *75 per cent of chief executives come from inside the company.* **3** If you say that a feeling is **inside** someone, you mean that they have the feeling but have not expressed it. ❑ *He felt a great weight of sorrow inside him.* **4** [inside + AMOUNT] If you do something **inside** a particular time, you do it before the end of that time. = within ❑ *They should have everything working inside an hour.*

ADV /ɪn'saɪd/ **1** You can say that someone or something is **inside** if it is contained within a place, container, or object. ❑ *The couple chatted briefly on the doorstep before going inside.* **2** [ADJ + inside] **Inside** refers to the part or area of something that its sides surround or contain. ❑ *The potato cakes can be shallow or deep-fried until crisp outside and meltingly soft inside.* **3** (*informal*) You can say that someone is **inside** when they are in prison. ❑ *They've both done prison time – he's been inside three times.* **4** If you say that someone has a feeling **inside**, you mean that they have it but have not expressed it. ❑ *There is nothing left inside – no words, no anger, no tears.*

ADJ /'ɪnsaɪd/ **1** [inside + N] If you describe something or someone as **inside**, it is found within the area or part of a place or object that is contained or surrounded by its sides. ❑ *an inside wall* **2** [inside + N] If you describe someone or something as **inside**, it is contained within a place or object. ❑ *The popular papers all have photo features on their inside pages.* **3** [inside + N] **Inside** information is obtained from someone who is involved in a situation and therefore knows a lot about it. ❑ *Sloane used inside diplomatic information to make himself rich.* ❑ *I cannot claim any inside knowledge of government policies.* **4** [inside + N] If you describe something or someone as **inside**, it means that it belongs to an organization or group. ❑ *a recent book about the inside world of pro football*

NOUN /'ɪnsaɪd/ [c, SING, PL] (**insides**) **1** [c] The **inside** of something is the part or area that its sides surround or contain. ❑ *The doors were locked from the inside.* **2** [SING] You can talk about the people who belong within an organization or group as **the inside**. ❑ *McAvoy was convinced he could control things from the inside but he lost control.* **3** /ˌɪn'saɪdz/ [PL] (*informal*) Your **insides** are your internal organs, especially your stomach. ❑ *Every pill made my insides turn upside down.* **4** [SING] You can use the **inside** to refer to important feelings that you have but have not expressed. ❑ *What is needed is a change from the inside, a real change in outlook and attitude.*

PHRASE **inside out 1** If something such as a piece of clothing is **inside out**, the part that is normally inside now faces outwards. ❑ *Her umbrella blew inside out.* **2** (*emphasis*) If you say that you know something or someone **inside out**, you are emphasizing that you know them extremely well. ❑ *He knew the game inside out.*

in·sid·er /ˌɪn'saɪdə/ NOUN [c] (**insiders**) An **insider** is someone who is involved in a situation and who knows more about it than other people. ❑ *An insider said, 'Katharine has told friends it is time to end her career.'*

✪ in·sight /'ɪnsaɪt/ NOUN [c, u] (**insights**) (*academic word*)

1 [c, u] If you gain **insight** or an **insight into** a complex situation or problem, you gain an accurate and deep understanding of it. = awareness, understanding; ≠ ignorance ❑ *The project would give scientists new insights into what is happening to the Earth's atmosphere.* **2** [u] If someone has **insight**, they are able to understand complex situations. ❑ *He was a man of forceful character, with considerable insight and diplomatic skills.*

in·sig·nifi·cance /ˌɪnsɪg'nɪfɪkəns/ NOUN [u] Insignificance is the quality of being insignificant. ❑ *These prices pale into insignificance when compared with what was paid for two major works by the late Alfred Stieglitz.*

✪ in·sig·nifi·cant /ˌɪnsɪg'nɪfɪkənt/ ADJ Something that is **insignificant** is unimportant, especially because it is very small. = unimportant ❑ *In 1949 Bonn was a small, insignificant city.* ❑ *The data were based on statistically insignificant samples.*

in·sin·cere /ˌɪnsɪn'sɪə/ ADJ (*disapproval*) If you say that someone is **insincere**, you are being critical of them because they say things they do not really mean, usually pleasant, admiring, or encouraging things. ❑ *Some people are so terribly insincere you can never tell if they are telling the truth.*

in·sist ◆◆◇ /ɪn'sɪst/ VERB [i, T] (**insists, insisting, insisted**) **1** If you **insist that** something should be done, you say so very firmly and refuse to give in about it. If you **insist on** something, you say firmly that it must be done or provided. ❑ *My family insisted that I should not give in, but stay and fight.* ❑ *She insisted on being present at all the interviews.* **2** If you **insist** that something is the case, you say so very firmly and refuse to say otherwise, even though other people do not believe it. ❑ *The president insisted that he was acting out of compassion, not political opportunism.* ❑ *'It's not that difficult,' she insists.* ❑ *He insisted on his innocence.*

USAGE NOTE

insist

Note that you do not say that someone 'insists to do' something. You say that they 'insist on doing' something. *He insisted on paying for the repairs.*

---

in·sist·ence /ɪn'sɪstəns/ NOUN [u] Someone's **insistence** on something is the fact that they insist that it should be done or insist that it is the case. ❑ *her insistence on personal privacy*

in·sist·ent /ɪn'sɪstənt/ ADJ **1** Someone who is **insistent** keeps insisting that a particular thing should be done or is the case. ❑ *Stalin was insistent that the war would be won and lost in the machine shops.* **2** An **insistent** noise or rhythm keeps going on for a long time and holds your attention. = unrelenting ❑ *the insistent rhythms of the Caribbean and Latin America*
in·sist·ent·ly /ɪn'sɪstəntli/ ADV [insistently with V] ❑ *'What is it?' his wife asked again, gently but insistently.*

✪ in·sol·uble /ɪn'sɒljʊbəl/ ADJ **1** An insoluble problem is so difficult that it is impossible to solve. ❑ *I pushed the problem aside; at present it was insoluble.* **2** If a substance is **insoluble**, it does not dissolve in a liquid. ❑ *Carotenes are insoluble in water and soluble in oils and fats.* ❑ *A mask of pure insoluble collagen fibre is placed over the skin.*

in·som·nia /ɪn'sɒmniə/ NOUN [u] Someone who suffers from insomnia finds it difficult to sleep.

✪ in·spect ◆◇◇ /ɪn'spekt/ VERB [T] (**inspects, inspecting, inspected**) (*academic word*) **1** If you **inspect** something, you look at every part of it carefully in order to find out about it or check that it is all right. = examine ❑ *Elaine went outside to inspect the playing field.* ❑ *Safety engineers will periodically inspect the boiler and other machinery for structural defects.* **2** When an official **inspects** a place or a group of people, they visit it and check it carefully, for example, in order to find out whether regulations are being obeyed. = examine, check ❑ *The Public Utilities Commission inspects us once a year.* ❑ *Each hotel is inspected and, if it fulfils certain criteria, is recommended.* ❑ *UN nuclear officials inspected four suspected nuclear weapons sites.*

✪ in·spec·tion /ɪn'spekʃən/ NOUN [c, u] (**inspections**)

1 = examination, check, inquiry □ *'Excellent work', he said when he had completed his inspection of the painted doors.* **2** *Officers making a routine inspection of the vessel found fifty kilograms of cocaine.* □ *demands for weapons inspections*

WORD CONNECTIONS

VERB + **inspection**

conduct an inspection
carry out an inspection
resume an inspection
□ *Officials conduct cleanliness inspections of all hospitals.*

pass an inspection
fail an inspection
□ *More than 50 restaurants in the city failed a food hygiene inspection last year.*

ADJ + **inspection**

a **routine** inspection
a **close** inspection
□ *The faults were discovered during a routine inspection of the aircraft.*

---

in·spec·tor ♦◇◇ /ɪnˈspektə/ NOUN [c] (**inspectors**) **1** An **inspector** is a person, usually employed by a government agency, whose job is to find out whether people are obeying safety regulations. □ *The mill was finally shut down by state safety inspectors.* **2** In the United States, an **inspector** is an officer in the police who is next in rank to a superintendent or police chief. □ *San Francisco police inspector Tony Camileri*

in·spi·ra·tion /ˌɪnspɪˈreɪʃən/ NOUN [u, SING, c] (**inspirations**) **1** [u] **Inspiration** is a feeling of enthusiasm you get from someone or something, that gives you new and creative ideas. □ *My inspiration comes from poets like Baudelaire and Jacques Prévert.* **2** [SING] If you describe someone or something good as **an inspiration**, you mean that they make you or other people want to do or achieve something. □ *Powell's unusual journey to high office is an inspiration to millions.* **3** [SING] If something or someone is **the inspiration for** a particular book, work of art, or action, they are the source of the ideas in it or act as a model for it. □ *India's myths and songs are the inspiration for her books.* **4** [c] If you suddenly have an **inspiration**, you suddenly think of an idea of what to do or say. □ *She had an inspiration, 'Could we take Janice?'*

in·spi·ra·tion·al /ˌɪnspɪˈreɪʃənəl/ ADJ (approval) Something that is **inspirational** provides you with inspiration. □ *Gandhi was an inspirational figure.*

in·spire /ɪnˈspaɪə/ VERB [T] (**inspires, inspiring, inspired**) **1** If someone or something **inspires** you to do something new or unusual, they make you want to do it. □ *Our challenge is to motivate those voters and inspire them to join our cause.* **2** If someone or something **inspires** you, they give you new ideas and a strong feeling of enthusiasm. □ *In the 1960s, the electric guitar virtuosity of Jimi Hendrix inspired a generation.* **3** If a book, work of art, or action **is inspired by** something, that thing is the source of the idea for it. □ *The book was inspired by a real person, namely Tamara de Treaux.* **4** Someone or something that **inspires** a particular emotion or reaction in people makes them feel that emotion or reaction. □ *The car's performance is effortless and its handling is precise and quickly inspires confidence.*
-inspired /ɪnˈspaɪəd/ COMB □ *Mediterranean-inspired ceramics in bright yellow and blue*

in·stabil·ity /ˌɪnstəˈbɪlɪti/ NOUN [u] **Instability** is the quality of being unstable. □ *unpopular policies, which resulted in social discontent and political instability*

in·stall ♦◇◇ /ɪnˈstɔːl/ also **instal** VERB [T] (**installs** or **instals, installing, installed**) **1** If you **install** a piece of equipment, you put it somewhere so that it is ready to be used. □ *They had installed a new phone line in the apartment.* **2** If someone **is installed** in a new job or important position, they are officially given the job or position, often in a special ceremony. □ *A temporary government was installed.* □ *Professor Sawyer was formally installed as president last Thursday.* **3** (formal) If you **install yourself** in a particular place, you settle there and make yourself

comfortable. □ *Before her husband's death she had installed herself in a modern villa.*

in·stal·la·tion /ˌɪnstəˈleɪʃən/ NOUN [u, c] (**installations**) **1** [u] The **installation** of a piece of equipment is the act of putting it somewhere so that it is ready to be used. □ *Hundreds of lives could be saved if the installation of alarms was more widespread.* **2** [u] The **installation** of a person in a new job or important position is a special ceremony where they are officially given the job or position. □ *He sent a letter inviting Naomi to attend his installation as chief of his tribe.* **3** [c] An **installation** is a place that contains equipment and machinery that are being used for a particular purpose. □ *The building was turned into a secret military installation.*

in·stal·ment /ɪnˈstɔːlmənt/ (BrE; in AmE, use **installment**) NOUN [c] (**instalments**) **1** If you pay for something in **instalments**, you pay small sums of money at regular intervals over a period of time, rather than paying the whole amount at once. □ *Upper-bracket taxpayers who elected to pay their tax increase in instalments must pay the third instalment by 15 April.* **2** An **instalment** of a story or plan is one of its parts that are published or carried out separately one after the other. = **part** □ *The next instalment of this four-part series deals with the impact of the war on the continent of Africa.*

◆**in·stance** ♦◆◇ /ˈɪnstəns/ NOUN (academic word)
NOUN [c] (**instances**) An **instance** is a particular example or occurrence of something. = **example, case, occurrence** □ *an investigation into a serious instance of corruption* □ *The committee reported numerous instances where key information was not shared.*
PHRASES **for instance** You use **for instance** to introduce a particular event, situation, or person that is an example of what you are talking about. = **for example** □ *In sub-Saharan Africa today, for instance, gross investment accounts for roughly 15% of national income.* □ *There are a number of improvements; for instance, both mouse buttons can now be used.* □ *TB is an infinitely bigger problem than, for instance, AIDS.*
in the first instance (informal) You say **in the first instance** to mention something that is the first step in a series of actions. □ *In the first instance your child will be seen by an ear, nose and throat specialist.*

in·stant ♦◆◇ /ˈɪnstənt/ NOUN, ADJ
NOUN [c, SING] (**instants**) **1** [c] An **instant** is an extremely short period of time. = **moment** □ *For an instant, Barney was tempted to flee.* **2** [SING] If you say that something happens **at** a particular **instant**, you mean that it happens at exactly the time you have been referring to, and you are usually suggesting that it happens quickly or immediately. = **moment** □ *At that instant the museum was plunged into total darkness.*
PHRASE **the instant** (emphasis) To do something **the instant** something else happens means to do it immediately. □ *I bolted the door the instant I saw the bat.*
ADJ **1** You use **instant** to describe something that happens immediately. = **immediate** □ *Mr Porter's book was an instant hit.* **2** [instant + N] **Instant** food is food that you can prepare very quickly, for example by just adding water. □ *He stirred instant coffee into a mug of hot water.*
in·stant·ly /ˈɪnstəntli/ ADV □ *The man was killed instantly.*

in·stead ♦◆◇ /ɪnˈsted/ ADV
ADV [instead with CL] If you do not do something, but do something else instead, you do the second thing and not the first thing, as the result of a choice or a change of behaviour. □ *My husband asked why I couldn't just forget about dieting and eat normally instead.*
PHRASE **instead of** If you do one thing **instead of** another, you do the first thing and not the second thing, as the result of a choice or a change of behaviour. □ *They raised prices and cut production, instead of cutting costs.*

in·sti·gate /ˈɪnstɪɡeɪt/ VERB [T] (**instigates, instigating, instigated**) Someone who **instigates** an event causes it to happen. = **initiate** □ *He did not instigate the coup or even know of it beforehand.*
in·sti·ga·tion /ˌɪnstɪˈɡeɪʃən/ NOUN [u] □ *The talks are taking place at the instigation of Germany.*

✪ **in·stinct** /ˈɪnstɪŋkt/ NOUN [C, U] (**instincts**) **1** [C, U] **Instinct** is the natural tendency that a person or animal has to behave or react in a particular way. = intuition, sense ❑ *I didn't have as strong a maternal instinct as some other mothers.* ❑ *He always knew what time it was, as if by instinct.* **2** [C] If you have an **instinct for** something, you are naturally good at it or able to do it. = aptitude ❑ *He seems to have an instinct for smart advertising and marketing.* **3** [C, U] If it is your **instinct to** do something, you feel that it is right to do it. ❑ *I should've gone with my first instinct, which was not to do the interview.* **4** [C, U] **Instinct** is a feeling, rather than an opinion or idea based on facts, that something is the case. = intuition ❑ *There is scientific evidence to support our instinct that being surrounded by plants is good for health.*

✪ **in·stinc·tive** /ɪnˈstɪŋktɪv/ ADJ An **instinctive** feeling, idea, or action is one that you have or do without thinking or reasoning. = natural, intuitive ❑ *It's an instinctive reaction – if a child falls you pick it up.* ❑ *Ms Senatorova showed an instinctive feel for market economics.*
     in·stinc·tive·ly /ɪnˈstɪŋktɪvli/ ADV [instinctively with V] ❑ *Jane instinctively knew all was not well with her 10-month old son.*

✪ **in·sti·tute** ♦♦◇ /ˈɪnstɪtjuːt, AmE -tuːt/ NOUN, VERB (*academic word*)
   NOUN [C] (**institutes**) An **institute** is an organization set up to do a particular type of work, especially research or teaching. You can also use **institute** to refer to the building the organization occupies. = organization, foundation ❑ *the National Cancer Institute* ❑ *an elite research institute devoted to computer software*
   VERB [T] (**institutes, instituting, instituted**) (*formal*) If you **institute** a system, rule, or course of action, you start it. ❑ *We will institute a number of measures to better safeguard the public.*

✪ **in·sti·tu·tion** ♦♦◇ /ˌɪnstɪˈtjuːʃən, AmE -ˈtuː-/ NOUN [C, U] (**institutions**) (*academic word*) **1** [C] An **institution** is a large important organization such as a university, church, or bank. = organization, establishment ❑ *financial institutions* ❑ *the Institution of Civil Engineers* ❑ *Class size varies from one type of institution to another.* **2** [C] An **institution** is a building where certain people are cared for, such as people who are mentally ill or children who have no parents. ❑ *Larry has been in an institution since he was four.* **3** [C] An **institution** is a custom or system that is considered an important or typical feature of a particular society or group, usually because it has existed for a long time. ❑ *I believe in the institution of marriage.* **4** [U] The **institution** of a new system is the act of starting it or bringing it in. ❑ *There was never an official institution of censorship in Albania.*

in·sti·tu·tion·al /ˌɪnstɪˈtjuːʃənəl, AmE -ˈtuː-/ ADJ **1** [institutional + N] **Institutional** means relating to a large organization, such as a university, bank, or church. ❑ *NATO remains the United States' chief institutional anchor in Europe.* **2** [institutional + N] **Institutional** means relating to a building where people are cared for or held. ❑ *Outside the protected environment of institutional care he could not survive.* **3** [institutional + N] An **institutional** value or quality is considered an important and typical feature of a particular society or group, usually because it has existed for a long time. ❑ *social and institutional values* **4** [usu institutional + N] If someone accuses an organization of **institutional** racism or sexism, they mean that the organization is deeply racist or sexist and has been so for a long time. ❑ *The report accused the police department of institutional racism.*
     in·sti·tu·tion·al·ly /ˌɪnstɪˈtjuːʃənəli, AmE -ˈtuː-/ ADV ❑ *The government's policy still appeared to be institutionally racist.*

in·sti·tu·tion·al·ize /ˌɪnstɪˈtjuːʃənəlaɪz, AmE -ˈtuː-/ also **institutionalise** VERB [T] (**institutionalizes, institutionalizing, institutionalized**) **1** If someone such as a sick, mentally ill, or old person **is institutionalized**, they are sent to stay in a special hospital or home, usually for a long period. ❑ *She became seriously ill and had to be institutionalized for a lengthy period.* **2** To **institutionalize**

something means to establish it as part of a culture, social system, or organization. ❑ *The goal is to institutionalize family planning into community life.*

✪ **in·struct** /ɪnˈstrʌkt/ VERB [T] (**instructs, instructing, instructed**) (*academic word*) **1** (*formal*) If you **instruct** someone to do something, you formally tell them to do it. ❑ *A doctor will often instruct patients to exercise.* ❑ *'Go and have a word with her, Ken,' Wojtowicz instructed.* **2** Someone who **instructs** people in a subject or skill teaches it to them. ❑ *He instructed family members in nursing techniques.*

✪ **in·struc·tion** ♦◇◇ /ɪnˈstrʌkʃən/ NOUN [C, U, PL] (**instructions**) (*academic word*) **1** [C] An **instruction** is something that someone tells you to do. ❑ *Two lawyers were told not to leave the building but no reason for this instruction was given.* **2** [U] (*formal*) If someone gives you **instruction** in a subject or skill, they teach it to you. ❑ *Each candidate is given instruction in safety.* **3** [PL] **Instructions** are clear and detailed information on how to do something. = directions ❑ *This book gives instructions for making a wide range of skin and hand creams.* ❑ *Always read the instructions before you start taking the medicine.* ❑ *an instruction manual for a camera*

✪ **in·struc·tor** /ɪnˈstrʌktə/ NOUN [C] (**instructors**) An **instructor** is someone who teaches a skill such as driving or skiing. ❑ *a fitness instructor*

✪ **in·stru·ment** ♦◇◇ /ˈɪnstrəmənt/ NOUN [C] (**instruments**) **1** An **instrument** is a tool or device that is used to do a particular task, especially a scientific task. = tool, device, mechanism ❑ *instruments for cleaning and polishing teeth* ❑ *The environment will be measured by about 60 scientific instruments.* **2** A musical **instrument** is an object such as a piano, guitar, or flute, which you play in order to produce music. ❑ *Learning a musical instrument introduces a child to an understanding of music.* **3** An **instrument** is a device that is used for making measurements of something such as speed, height, or sound, for example, on a ship or plane or in a car. ❑ *The design of crucial instruments on the control panel will have to be improved.* **4** Something that is an **instrument** for achieving a particular aim is used by people to achieve that aim. ❑ *The veto has been a traditional instrument of diplomacy for centuries.*

in·stru·men·tal /ˌɪnstrəˈmentəl/ ADJ, NOUN
   ADJ **1** Someone or something that is **instrumental** in a process or event helps to make it happen. ❑ *In his first years as chairman he was instrumental in raising the company's wider profile.* **2** [instrumental + N] **Instrumental** music is performed by instruments and not by voices. ❑ *a CD of vocal and instrumental music*
   NOUN [C] (**instrumentals**) **Instrumentals** are pieces of instrumental music. ❑ *After a couple of brief instrumentals, he puts his guitar down.*

✪ **in·suf·fi·cient** ♦◇◇ /ˌɪnsəˈfɪʃənt/ ADJ (*academic word, formal*) Something that is **insufficient** is not large enough in amount or degree for a particular purpose. = inadequate; ≠ sufficient, enough, adequate ❑ *He decided there was insufficient evidence to justify criminal proceedings.* ❑ *These efforts were insufficient to contain the burgeoning crisis.* ❑ *The income was proving insufficient to clear her debts.*
✪ **in·suf·fi·cien·cy** /ˌɪnsəˈfɪʃənsi/ NOUN [U] = inadequacy; ≠ sufficiency ❑ *Late miscarriages are usually not due to hormonal insufficiency.*
✪ **in·suf·fi·cient·ly** /ˌɪnsəˈfɪʃəntli/ ADV [insufficiently + ADJ/-ED] = inadequately; ≠ sufficiently, enough, adequately ❑ *Food that is insufficiently cooked can lead to food poisoning.* ❑ *The president has described the recovery as insufficiently robust.*

in·sult VERB, NOUN
   VERB /ɪnˈsʌlt/ [T] (**insults, insulting, insulted**) If someone **insults** you, they say or do something that is rude or offensive. ❑ *I did not mean to insult you.*
   NOUN /ˈɪnsʌlt/ [C] (**insults**) An **insult** is a rude remark, or something a person says or does which insults you. ❑ *Their behaviour was an insult to the people they represent.*
   PHRASE **add insult to injury** You say **to add insult to injury** when mentioning an action or fact that makes an unfair or unacceptable situation even worse. ❑ *It is the*

victim who is often put on trial and, to add insult to injury, she is presumed guilty until proven innocent of provoking the rape.

in·sult·ed /ɪnˈsʌltɪd/ ADJ □ *I mean, I was a bit insulted that they thought I needed bribing to shut up.*

✪ in·sur·ance ♦♦◇ /ɪnˈʃʊərəns/ NOUN [C, U] (**insurances**) **1** Insurance is an arrangement in which you pay money to a company, and they pay you if something unpleasant happens to you, for example, if your property is stolen or damaged, or if you get a serious illness. = cover □ *The house was a total loss and the insurance company promptly paid us the policy limit.* □ *We recommend that you take out travel insurance on all holidays.* □ *regulation of the insurance industry* **2** If you do something as **insurance against** something unpleasant happening, you do it to protect yourself in case the unpleasant thing happens. □ *Attentive proofreading is the only insurance against the kind of omissions described in this section.*

in·sure /ɪnˈʃʊə/ VERB [I, T] (**insures**, **insuring**, **insured**) **1** [I, T] If you **insure** yourself or your property, you pay money to an insurance company so that, if you become ill or if your property is damaged or stolen, the company will pay you a sum of money. □ *For protection against unforeseen emergencies, you insure your house, your furnishings, and your car.* □ *While many people insure against death, far fewer take precautions against long-term loss of income because of sickness.* **2** [T] If you **insure yourself against** something unpleasant that might happen in the future, you do something to protect yourself in case it happens, or to prevent it from happening. □ *All the electronics in the world cannot insure people against accidents, though.*

in·sur·er /ɪnˈʃʊərə/ NOUN [C] (**insurers**) (*business*) An **insurer** is a company that sells insurance.

in·tact /ɪnˈtækt/ ADJ Something that is **intact** is complete and has not been damaged or changed. □ *Customs men put dynamite in the water to destroy the cargo, but most of it was left intact.*

✪ in·take /ˈɪnteɪk/ NOUN [SING, C] (**intakes**) **1** [SING] Your **intake** of a particular kind of food, drink, or air is the amount that you eat, drink, or breathe in. = consumption □ *Your intake of alcohol should not exceed two units per day.* □ *Reduce your salt intake.* **2** [C] (*BrE*) The people who are accepted into an organization or place at a particular time are referred to as a particular **intake**. □ *one of this year's intake of students*

✪ in·te·ger /ˈɪntɪdʒə/ NOUN [C] (**integers**) (*technical*) In mathematics, an **integer** is an exact whole number such as 1, 7, or 24 as opposed to a number with fractions or decimals. = whole number □ *Prime numbers are positive integers that can only be divided by themselves and one.* □ *They asked patients to score the degree of discomfort or distress caused by their diagnostic test on an 0-6 integer scale.*

✪ in·te·gral /ˈɪntɪgrəl/ ADJ (*academic word*) Something that is an **integral** part of something is an essential part of that thing. = basic, fundamental, intrinsic □ *Rituals, celebrations, and festivals form an integral part of every human society.* □ *The municipal park plays an integral role in urban Chinese life.* □ *Anxiety is integral to the human condition.*

✪ in·te·grate ♦◇◇ /ˈɪntɪgreɪt/ VERB [RECIP, I, T] (**integrates**, **integrating**, **integrated**) (*academic word*) **1** [RECIP, I, T] If someone **integrates** into a social group, or **is integrated** into it, they behave in such a way that they become part of the group or are accepted into it. □ *He didn't integrate successfully into the Italian way of life.* □ *Integrating the kids with the community is essential.* **2** [RECIP] If you **integrate** one thing **with** another, or one thing **integrates with** another, the two things become closely linked or form part of a whole idea or system. You can also say that two things **integrate**. = fuse, incorporate, merge, assimilate, combine; ≠ separate, divide □ *Writing about a topic helps you integrate new knowledge with what you already know.* □ *historic landmarks that integrate with the community* □ *Little attempt was made to integrate the parts into a coherent whole.*

✪ in·te·gra·tion /ˌɪntɪˈgreɪʃən/ NOUN [U] **1** = fusion, incorporation, assimilation; ≠ separation, division □ *Americans overwhelmingly support the integration of disabled people into mainstream society.* **2** □ *With Germany, France has been the prime mover behind closer European integration.*

integrate VERB
If you **intergrate** one thing **with** another, or one thing **integrates with** another, the two things become closely linked or form part of a whole idea or system.
□ *Nothing integrates newcomers better than sharing a classroom or extracurricular activities with their classmates.*

fuse VERB
When things **fuse** or **are fused**, they join together physically or chemically, usually to become one thing.
□ *'Overnight, his toes fused together and had to be cut apart,' said Mrs Young.*

assimilate VERB
When a thing or a group **assimilates into** a larger thing or group, or when that larger thing or group **assimilates** them, it becomes accepted as part of the larger thing or group.
□ *Italian immigrants were determined to assimilate into American culture.*

merge VERB
If one thing **merges with** another, or **is merged with** another, they come together to make one whole thing.
□ *The software developer moved from California to Florida after his employer merged with another company.*

combine VERB
If you **combine** two or more things, or if they **combine**, they join together to make a single thing.
□ *In a small bowl, combine the sugar, salt, vinegar, egg, and water.*

incorporate VERB (*formal*)
If one thing **incorporates** another thing, it includes the other thing.
□ *He is passionate about incorporating elements of Asian design into his works.*

in·te·grat·ed /ˈɪntɪgreɪtɪd/ ADJ **1** If a social group is **integrated**, different people have been accepted into it. □ *He thinks we are living in a fully integrated, supportive society.* **2** If several things are **integrated**, they become closely linked or form part of a whole idea or system. □ *There is, he said, a lack of an integrated national transport policy.* **3** An **integrated** institution is intended for use by all races or religious groups. □ *We believe that students of integrated schools will have more tolerant attitudes.*

✪ in·teg·rity /ɪnˈtegrɪti/ NOUN [U] (*academic word*) **1** If you have **integrity**, you are honest and firm in your moral principles. □ *I have always regarded him as a man of integrity.* □ *The game relies on the integrity of the individual to show consideration for other players and to abide by the rules.* **2** (*formal*) The **integrity** of something such as a group of people or a text is its state of being a united whole. = unity □ *Separatist movements are a threat to the integrity of the nation.* □ *Kerensky declared that he would maintain Russia's territorial integrity.*

in·tel·lect /ˈɪntɪlekt/ NOUN [C, U] (**intellects**) **1** Intellect is the ability to understand or deal with ideas and information. □ *Do the emotions develop in parallel with the intellect?* **2** Intellect is the quality of being intelligent. □ *She is famed for her intellect.*

in·tel·lec·tual ♦◇◇ /ˌɪntɪˈlektʃuəl/ ADJ, NOUN
ADJ **1** [intellectual + N] **Intellectual** means involving a person's ability to think and to understand ideas and information. □ *High levels of lead could damage the intellectual development of children.* **2** If you describe someone as **intellectual** you mean that they spend a lot of time studying and thinking about complicated ideas. □ *They were very intellectual and witty.*
NOUN [C] (**intellectuals**) An **intellectual** is someone who spends a lot of time studying and thinking about complicated ideas. □ *Teachers, artists and other intellectuals urged political parties to launch a united movement against the government.*

in·tel·lec·tual·ly /ˌɪntɪˈlɛktʃuəli/ ADV ❑ *intellectually satisfying work*

✪ **in·tel·li·gence** ♦◇◇ /ɪnˈtɛlɪdʒəns/ NOUN [U]
1 **Intelligence** is the quality of being intelligent or clever. = intellect; ≠ stupidity, ignorance ❑ *She's a woman of exceptional intelligence.* **2** **Intelligence** is the ability to think, reason, and understand instead of doing things automatically or by instinct. ❑ *Nerve cells, after all, do not have intelligence of their own.* **3** **Intelligence** is information that is gathered by the government or the army about their country's enemies and their activities. ❑ *Why was military intelligence so lacking?*

✪ **in·tel·li·gent** ♦◇◇ /ɪnˈtɛlɪdʒənt/ ADJ (*academic word*)
1 A person or animal that is **intelligent** has the ability to think, understand, and learn things quickly and well. ≠ stupid, unintelligent ❑ *Susan's a very bright and intelligent woman who knows her own mind.* ❑ *lively and intelligent conversation* ❑ *the opinion that whales are as intelligent as human beings* **2** Something that is **intelligent** can think and understand instead of doing things automatically or by instinct. ❑ *Intelligent computers will soon be an indispensable diagnostic tool for every doctor.*

✪ **in·tel·li·gent·ly** /ɪnˈtɛlɪdʒəntli/ ADV = cleverly; ≠ stupidly ❑ *They are incapable of thinking intelligently about politics.* ❑ *voting systems that are intelligently designed*

✪ **in·tend** ♦♦◇ /ɪnˈtɛnd/ VERB [T] (**intends, intending, intended**) **1** If you **intend** to do something, you have decided or planned to do it. = mean, plan ❑ *Maybe he intends to leave her.* ❑ *What do you intend doing when you get to this place?* ❑ *We had always intended that the new series would be live.* **2** If something **is intended** for a particular purpose, it has been planned to fulfill that purpose. If something **is intended** for a particular person, it has been planned to be used by that person or to affect them in some way. ❑ *This money is intended for the development of the tourist industry.* ❑ *Columns are usually intended in architecture to add grandeur and status.* ❑ *Originally, Hatfield had been intended as a leisure complex.* **3** If you **intend** a particular idea or feeling in something that you say or do, you want to express it or want it to be understood. = mean ❑ *He didn't intend any sarcasm.* ❑ *Barzun's response seemed a little patronizing, though he undoubtedly hadn't intended it that way.*

✪ **in·tense** ♦◇◇ /ɪnˈtɛns/ ADJ (*academic word*) **1** **Intense** is used to describe something that is very great or extreme in strength or degree. = extreme, acute ❑ *He was sweating from the intense heat.* ❑ *Stevens's murder was the result of a deep-seated and intense hatred.* **2** If you describe an activity as **intense**, you mean that it is very serious and concentrated, and often involves doing a lot in a short time. ❑ *The battle for third place was intense.* **3** If you describe the way someone looks at you as **intense**, you mean that they look at you very directly and seem to know what you are thinking or feeling. = piercing ❑ *I felt so self-conscious under Luke's mother's intense gaze.* **4** If you describe a person as **intense**, you mean that they appear to concentrate very hard on everything that they do, and they feel their emotions very strongly. ❑ *I know he's an intense player, but he does enjoy what he's doing.*

✪ **in·tense·ly** /ɪnˈtɛnsli/ ADV **1** = acutely, extremely; ≠ mildly ❑ *The fast-food business is intensely competitive.* **2** [intensely with V] ❑ *He sipped his drink, staring intensely at me.*

✪ **in·ten·si·ty** /ɪnˈtɛnsɪti/ NOUN [C, U] (**intensities**) **1** [C, U] = acuteness, extremity; ≠ mildness ❑ *The attack was anticipated but its intensity came as a shock.* ❑ *A detector measured the intensity of the light.* **2** [U] ❑ *His intensity and the ferocity of his feelings alarmed me.*

✪ **in·ten·si·fy** /ɪnˈtɛnsɪfaɪ/ VERB [I, T] (**intensifies, intensifying, intensified**) If you **intensify** something or if it **intensifies**, it becomes greater in strength, amount, or degree. = increase ❑ *I jump, intensifying the pain in all my muscles.* ❑ *Britain is intensifying its efforts to secure the release of the hostages.* ❑ *The conflict is almost bound to intensify.* ❑ *Groups of refugees are on the move following intensified fighting in the region.*

✪ **in·ten·si·fi·ca·tion** /ɪnˌtɛnsɪfɪˈkeɪʃən/ NOUN [U] = increase; ≠ decrease ❑ *The country was on the verge of*

collapse because of the intensification of violent rebel attacks. ❑ *A further intensification of violence seems certain.*

✪ **in·ten·sive** /ɪnˈtɛnsɪv/ ADJ **1** **Intensive** activity involves concentrating a lot of effort or people on one particular task in order to try to achieve a lot in a short time. ❑ *after several days and nights of intensive negotiations* **2** **Intensive** farming involves producing as many crops or animals as possible from your land, usually with the aid of chemicals. ❑ *intensive methods of rearing poultry*

in·ten·sive·ly /ɪnˈtɛnsɪvli/ ADV **1** [intensively with V] ❑ *Caitlin's parents opted to educate her intensively at home.* **2** [intensively with V] ❑ *Will they farm the rest of their land less intensively?*

✪ **in·tent** /ɪnˈtɛnt/ ADJ, NOUN
ADJ **1** [V-LINK + intent 'on/upon' -ING/N] If you are **intent on** doing something, you are eager and determined to do it. ❑ *The rebels are obviously intent on keeping up the pressure.* **2** (*written*) If someone does something in an **intent** way, they pay great attention to what they are doing. ❑ *She looked from one intent face to another.*
NOUN [C, U] (**intents**) (*formal*) A person's **intent** is their intention to do something. ❑ *The timing of this strong statement of intent on arms control is crucial.*
PHRASE **to all intents and purposes** or **to all intents** You say **to all intents and purposes** to suggest that a situation is not exactly as you describe it but the effect is the same as if it were. ❑ *To all intents and purposes he was my father.*

in·tent·ly /ɪnˈtɛntli/ ADV [intently after V] ❑ *He listened intently, then slammed down the phone.*

✪ **in·ten·tion** ♦◇◇ /ɪnˈtɛnʃən/ NOUN
NOUN [C, U] (**intentions**) An **intention** is an idea or plan of what you are going to do. = goal, objective, plan, purpose ❑ *The company has every intention of keeping the share price high.* ❑ *Beveridge announced his intention of standing for parliament.* ❑ *The book achieved in the end the precise opposite of its stated intention.* ❑ *It is my intention to remain in my position until a successor is elected.*
PHRASE **have no intention** or **have every intention** (*emphasis*) If you say that you **have no intention of** doing something, you are emphasizing that you are not going to do it. If you say that you **have every intention of** doing something, you are emphasizing that you intend to do it. ❑ *I have no intention of allowing you to continue living here alone.*

✪ **in·ten·tion·al** /ɪnˈtɛnʃənəl/ ADJ Something that is **intentional** is deliberate. = deliberate, planned; ≠ unintentional ❑ *Women who are the victims of intentional discrimination will be able to get compensation.*

in·ten·tion·al·ly /ɪnˈtɛnʃənəli/ ADV ❑ *I've never intentionally hurt anyone.*

✪ **inter·act** /ˌɪntəˈrækt/ VERB [I, RECIP] (**interacts, interacting, interacted**) (*academic word*) **1** [I, RECIP] When people **interact with** each other or **interact**, they communicate as they work or spend time together. = communicate ❑ *While the other children interacted and played together, Ted ignored them.* ❑ *rhymes and songs to help parents interact with their babies* **2** [I] When people **interact with** computers, or when computers **interact with** other machines, information or instructions are exchanged. ❑ *new, simplified ways of interacting with a computer* ❑ *There will be a true global village in which telephones, computers and televisions interact.* **3** [RECIP] When one thing **interacts with** another or two things **interact**, the two things affect each other's behaviour or condition. ❑ *You have to understand how cells interact.* ❑ *Atoms within the fluid interact with the minerals that form the grains.*

✪ **inter·ac·tion** /ˌɪntəˈrækʃən/ NOUN [C, U] (**interactions**) **1** = communication ❑ *superficial interactions with other people* ❑ *our experience of informal social interaction among adults* **2** *experts on human-computer interaction* **3** *the interaction between physical and emotional illness*

✪ **inter·ac·tive** /ˌɪntəˈræktɪv/ ADJ **1** An **interactive** computer program or electronic device is one that allows direct communication between the user and the machine. ❑ *This will make computer games more interactive than ever.* ❑ *high speed Internet services and interactive television*

i

2 If you describe a group of people or their activities as **interactive**, you mean that the people communicate with each other. ❑ *There is little evidence that this encouraged flexible, interactive teaching in the classroom.*
inter·ac·tiv·ity /ˌɪntəræk'tɪvɪti/ NOUN [U] ❑ *digital television, with more channels and interactivity*

WORD PARTS
The prefix *inter-* often appears in adjectives that refer to things that move, exist, or happen between two or more people or things:
interactive (ADJ)
international (ADJ)
interconnect (VERB)

inter·cept /ˌɪntə'sept/ VERB [T] **(intercepts, intercepting, intercepted)** If you **intercept** someone or something that is travelling from one place to another, you stop them before they get to their destination. ❑ *Gunmen intercepted him on his way to the airport.*
inter·cep·tion /ˌɪntə'sepʃən/ NOUN [C, U] **(interceptions)** ❑ *the interception of a ship off the coast of Oregon*

◆**inter·con·nect** /ˌɪntəkə'nekt/ VERB [RECIP] **(interconnects, interconnecting, interconnected)** Things that **interconnect** or **are interconnected** are connected to or with each other. You can also say that one thing **interconnects with** another. = link, interrelate
❑ *The causes are many and may interconnect.* ❑ *Their lives interconnect with those of celebrated figures of the late eighteenth-century.* ❑ *a dense network of nerve fibres that interconnects neurons in the brain*

◆**inter·con·nec·tion** /ˌɪntəkə'nekʃən/ NOUN [C, U] **(interconnections)** *(formal)* If you say that there is an **interconnection** between two or more things, you mean that they are very closely connected. = link, connection, interrelation ❑ *the alarming interconnection of drug abuse and AIDS infection* ❑ *Global population and industrial, urban, and environmental systems form complex interconnections.*

inter·con·ti·nen·tal /ˌɪntəkɒntɪ'nentəl/ ADJ [intercontinental + N] **Intercontinental** is used to describe something that exists or happens between continents. ❑ *intercontinental flights*

◆**inter·de·pend·ence** /ˌɪntədɪ'pendəns/ NOUN [U] **Interdependence** is the condition of a group of people or things that all depend on each other. ❑ *the interdependence of nations* ❑ *economic interdependence*

◆**inter·de·pend·ent** /ˌɪntədɪ'pendənt/ ADJ People or things that are **interdependent** all depend on each other. ❑ *We live in an increasingly interdependent world.* ❑ *the universe as a complex web of interdependent relationships*

◆**in·ter·est** ◆◆◆ /'ɪntrəst, -tərəst/ NOUN, VERB
NOUN [U, C] **(interests)** **1** [U] [also 'an' interest] If you have an **interest** in something, you think it is important and want to learn or hear more about it. ❑ *There has been a lively interest in the elections in the last two weeks.* ❑ *She'd liked him at first, but soon lost interest.* ❑ *material which was of immense interest to the press* **2** [C] Your **interests** are the things that you enjoy doing. ❑ *Encourage your child in her interests and hobbies.* **3** [C] If something is in the **interests** of a particular person or group, it will benefit them in some way. ❑ *Did those directors act in the best interests of their club?* ❑ *The media were required to act in the public interest.* **4** [C] You can use **interests** to refer to groups of people who you think use their power or money to benefit themselves. ❑ *The government accused unnamed 'foreign interests' of inciting the trouble.* **5** [C] *(business)* A person or organization that has an **interest** in an area, a company, a property or in a particular type of business owns shares in it. ❑ *My father had many business interests in Vietnam.* **6** [C] If a person, country, or organization has an **interest** in a possible event or situation, they want that event or situation to happen because they are likely to benefit from it. ❑ *The West has an interest in promoting democratic forces in Eastern Europe.* **7** [U] **Interest** is extra money that you receive if you have invested a sum of money. **Interest** is also the extra money that you pay if you have borrowed money or are buying something on credit. ❑ *Does your current account pay interest?*

❑ *This is an important step towards lower interest rates.*
PHRASE **in the interests of** or **in the interest of** If you do something **in the interests of** a particular result or situation, you do it in order to achieve that result or maintain that situation. ❑ *a call for all businessmen to work together in the interests of national stability*
VERB [T] **(interests, interesting, interested)** **1** If something **interests** you, it attracts your attention so that you want to learn or hear more about it or continue doing it. ❑ *Your financial problems do not interest me.* ❑ *It may interest you to know that Miss Woods, the housekeeper, witnessed the attack.* **2** If you are trying to persuade someone to buy or do something, you can say that you are trying to **interest** them **in** it. ❑ *Can I interest you in a new car?*
→ See also **interested, interesting**
✦ **have someone's interests at heart** → see **heart**

WORD FAMILIES	
interest NOUN	There has been a lively **interest** in the elections in the last two weeks.
interesting ADJ	The research has yielded some **interesting** findings.
interested ADJ	Medical researchers will be very **interested** in the outcome of the study.
uninteresting ADJ	If the students find the topic **uninteresting**, they will not pay attention.
uninterested ADJ	He was **uninterested** in art and never visited museums.
disinterested ADJ	The final decision should be made by a **disinterested** third party.
interestingly ADV	**Interestingly** and perhaps surprisingly, the two results were very different.

◆**in·ter·est·ed** ◆◆◇ /'ɪntrəstɪd/ ADJ **1** If you are **interested** in something, you think it is important and want to learn more about it or spend time doing it. = curious ❑ *I thought she might be interested in Paula's proposal.* ❑ *I'd be interested to meet her.* **2** [interested + N] An **interested** party or group of people is affected by or involved in a particular event or situation. = involved; ≠ disinterested ❑ *The success was only possible because all the interested parties eventually agreed to the idea.* **3** [usu V-LINK + interested 'in' N] If you say that one person is **interested in** another person, you mean that the first person would like to have a romantic or sexual relationship with the other person. ❑ *I heard there are a lot of guys interested in her.*

WHICH WORD?
interested or interesting?

Do not confuse the adjectives **interested** and **interesting**.
If you want to know more about something, you can say that you are **interested** in it.
❑ *I am very interested in politics.*
If you say that someone or something is **interesting**, you mean that you like them and you want to know more about them.
❑ *I've met some very interesting people.*

interest-free ADJ, ADV
ADJ An **interest-free** loan has no interest charged on it. ❑ *He was offered a $10,000 interest-free loan.*
ADV [interest-free after V] If someone buys something **interest-free**, there is no interest charged on the purchase. ❑ *Customers allowed the banks to use their money interest-free.*

◆**in·ter·est·ing** ◆◇◇ /'ɪntrɪstɪŋ/ ADJ If you find something **interesting**, it attracts your attention, for example, because you think it is exciting or unusual. = fascinating; ≠ boring ❑ *It was interesting to be in a* different environment. ❑ *The research has yielded some interesting findings.*

in·ter·est·ing·ly /ˈɪntrɪstɪŋli/ ADV [interestingly with CL] You use **interestingly** to introduce a piece of information that you think is interesting or unexpected. ❑ *Interestingly enough, a few weeks later, Benjamin remarried.*

in·ter·est rate NOUN [C] (**interest rates**) (*business*) The **interest rate** is the amount of interest that must be paid. It is expressed as a percentage of the amount that is borrowed or gained as profit. ❑ *The Federal Reserve lowered interest rates by half a point.*

⊘**inter·face** /ˈɪntəfeɪs/ NOUN, VERB
NOUN [C] (**interfaces**) **1** The **interface** between two subjects or systems is the area in which they affect each other or have links with each other. ❑ *a witty exploration of that interface between bureaucracy and the working world* ❑ *the new interface between capitalism and chaos in the old Soviet Union* **2** (*computing*) The user **interface** of a particular piece of computer software is its presentation on the screen and how easy it is to operate. ❑ *the development of better user interfaces* ❑ *The software features a more user-friendly interface.*
VERB [RECIP] (**interfaces, interfacing, interfaced**) (*formal*) If one thing **interfaces with** another, or if two things **interface**, they have connections with each other. If you **interface** one thing with another, you connect the two things. ❑ *the way we interface with the environment* ❑ *He had interfaced all this machinery with a master computer.* ❑ *The different components all have to interface smoothly.*

⊘**inter·fere** /ˌɪntəˈfɪə/ VERB [I] (**interferes, interfering, interfered**) **1** (*disapproval*) If you say that someone **interferes in** a situation, you mean they get involved in it although it does not concern them and their involvement is not wanted. = intervene ❑ *I wish everyone would stop interfering and just leave me alone.* ❑ *The UN cannot interfere in the internal affairs of any country.* **2** Something that **interferes with** a situation, activity, or process has a damaging effect on it. = disrupt, affect, inhibit, obstruct ❑ *Smoking and drinking interfere with your body's ability to process oxygen.*

VOCABULARY BUILDER

interfere VERB
Something that **interferes with** a situation, activity, or process has a damaging effect on it.
❑ *Scott believed the council had to be careful not to interfere with press freedom.*

disrupt VERB
If someone or something **disrupts** an event, system, or process, they cause difficulties that prevent it from continuing or operating in the normal way.
❑ *Oil prices have surged in recent weeks as fears of terrorist attacks disrupting oil supplies have grown.*

affect VERB
If something **affects** a person or thing, it influences them or causes them to change in some way.
❑ *Any form of concentrated sugar affects blood sugar balance.*

inhibit VERB
If something **inhibits** an event or process, it prevents it or slows it down.
❑ *Exposure to tobacco smoke inhibits the body's ability to fight off infection.*

obstruct VERB
To **obstruct** progress or a process means to prevent it from happening properly.
❑ *Even now, he's trying to obstruct the resumption of the peace process.*

⊘**inter·fer·ence** /ˌɪntəˈfɪərəns/ NOUN [U]
1 (*disapproval*) **Interference** by a person or group is their unwanted or unnecessary involvement in something. = meddling, intervention ❑ *Airlines will be able to set*

cheap fares without further interference from the government. ❑ *The parliament described the decree as interference in the republic's internal affairs.* **2** When there is **interference**, a radio signal is affected by other radio waves or electrical activity so that it cannot be received properly. ❑ *electrical interference*

⊘**in·ter·im** ♦◇◇ /ˈɪntərɪm/ ADJ, NOUN
ADJ [interim + N] **Interim** is used to describe something that is intended to be used until something permanent is done or established. ❑ *She was sworn in as head of an interim government in March.* ❑ *These interim reports provide an outline of the problem and a general idea of the work being carried out.*
NOUN
PHRASE **in the interim** (*formal*) **In the interim** means until a particular thing happens or until a particular thing happened. = in the meantime, meanwhile ❑ *But, in the interim, we obviously have a duty to maintain law and order.*

⊘**in·te·ri·or** ♦◇◇ /ɪnˈtɪəriə/ NOUN, ADJ
NOUN [C, SING] (**interiors**) **1** [C] The **interior** of something is the inside part of it. = inside; ≠ exterior ❑ *The interior of the house was furnished with heavy, old-fashioned pieces.* ❑ *the boat's interior* **2** [SING] The **interior** of a country or continent is the central area of it. ❑ *The Yangtze River would give access to much of China's interior.*
ADJ **1** [interior + N] You use **interior** to describe something that is inside a building or vehicle. ❑ *The interior walls were painted green.* **2** [interior + N] An **interior** minister, ministry, or department in some countries deals with affairs within that country, such as law and order. ❑ *The French Interior Minister has intervened in a scandal over the role of a secret police force.*

inter·medi·ary /ˌɪntəˈmiːdiəri/ NOUN [C]
(**intermediaries**) An **intermediary** is a person who passes messages or proposals between two people or groups. = go-between ❑ *She wanted him to act as an intermediary in the dispute with Moscow.*

⊘**inter·medi·ate** /ˌɪntəˈmiːdiət/ ADJ, NOUN (*academic word*)
ADJ **1** An **intermediate** stage, level, or position is one that occurs between two other stages, levels, or positions. = middle; ≠ initial, final ❑ *Do you make any intermediate stops between your home and work?* ❑ *hourly trains to Perugia, Assisi, and intermediate stations* **2** **Intermediate** learners of something have some knowledge or skill but are not yet advanced. ❑ *Students are categorized as novice, intermediate, or advanced.*
NOUN [C] (**intermediates**) An **intermediate** is an intermediate learner. ❑ *The ski school coaches beginners, intermediates, and advanced skiers.*

in·ter·mi·nable /ɪnˈtɜːmɪnəbəl/ ADJ (*emphasis*) If you describe something as **interminable**, you are emphasizing that it continues for a very long time and indicating that you wish it was shorter or would stop. = endless ❑ *an interminable meeting*
in·ter·mi·nably /ɪnˈtɜːmɪnəbli/ ADV ❑ *He talked to me interminably about his first wife.*

⊘**inter·mit·tent** /ˌɪntəˈmɪtənt/ ADJ Something that is **intermittent** happens occasionally rather than continuously. = sporadic ❑ *After three hours of intermittent rain, the game was abandoned.* ❑ *The constant movement of cables can easily damage the fragile wires inside, causing intermittent problems that are hard to detect.*
⊘**inter·mit·tent·ly** /ˌɪntəˈmɪtəntli/ ADV = sporadically; ≠ constantly, continuously ❑ *The talks went on intermittently for three years.*

in·tern VERB, NOUN /ɪnˈtɜːn/ /ˈɪntɜːn/
VERB [usu passive] [T] (**interns, interning, interned**) If someone **is interned**, they are put in prison or in a prison camp for political reasons. ❑ *He was interned as an enemy alien at the outbreak of the Second World War.*
NOUN [C] (**interns**) (*mainly AmE*) An **intern** is an advanced student or a recent graduate, especially in medicine, who is being given practical training under supervision. ❑ *a medical intern*

⊘**in·ter·nal** ♦◇◇ /ɪnˈtɜːnəl/ ADJ (*academic word*)
1 [internal + N] **Internal** is used to describe things that

exist or happen inside a country or organization.
= domestic; ≠ external, foreign ❑ *The country stepped up internal security.* ❑ *Russia's Ministry of Internal Affairs* ❑ *We now have a Europe without internal borders.* **2** [internal + N] **Internal** is used to describe things that exist or happen inside a particular person, object, or place. ≠ external ❑ *The doctor said the internal bleeding had been massive.* ❑ *disorders which affected the skin and internal organs alike*
✪in·ter·nal·ly /ɪnˈtɜːnəli/ ADV **1** ≠ externally ❑ *The state is not a unified and internally coherent entity.* **2** *Evening primrose oil is used on the skin as well as taken internally.*

✪inter·na·tion·al ♦♦♦ /ˌɪntəˈnæʃənəl/ ADJ
International means between or involving different countries. ≠ domestic ❑ *an international agreement against exporting arms to that country* ❑ *emergency aid from the international community*
✪inter·na·tion·al·ly /ˌɪntəˈnæʃənəli/ ADV ❑ *internationally agreed-upon rules* ❑ *There are only two internationally recognized certificates in Teaching English as a Foreign Language.* ❑ *I am one of the few young women who has made it as a writer financially and internationally.*

In·ter·net ♦♦♦ /ˈɪntənet/ also **internet** NOUN [SING]
The **Internet** is the network that allows computer users to connect with computers all over the world, and that carries e-mail.

in·tern·ship /ˈɪntɜːnʃɪp/ NOUN [C] (**internships**) (*mainly AmE*) An **internship** is the position held by an intern, or the period of time when someone is an intern. ❑ *an internship in surgery in New York*

inter·per·son·al /ˌɪntəˈpɜːsənəl/ ADJ [interpersonal + N] **Interpersonal** means relating to relationships between people. ❑ *Training in interpersonal skills is essential.*

✪in·ter·pret /ɪnˈtɜːprɪt/ VERB [T, I] (**interprets, interpreting, interpreted**) (*academic word*) **1** [T] If you **interpret** something in a particular way, you decide that this is its meaning or significance. = understand ❑ *The fact that they had decided to come was interpreted as a positive sign.* ❑ *The judge quite rightly says that he has to interpret the law as it's been passed.* ❑ *methods of gathering and interpreting data* **2** [I, T] If you **interpret** what someone is saying, you translate it immediately into another language. ❑ *The chambermaid spoke little English, so her husband came with her to interpret.*

✪in·ter·pre·ta·tion /ɪnˌtɜːprɪˈteɪʃən/ NOUN [C, U] (**interpretations**) **1** [C, U] An **interpretation** of something is an opinion about what it means. = understanding, reading ❑ *Professor Wolfgang gives the data a very different interpretation.* **2** [C] A performer's **interpretation** of something such as a piece of music or a role in a play is the particular way in which they choose to perform it. ❑ *a pianist celebrated for his interpretation of Chopin*

in·ter·pret·er /ɪnˈtɜːprɪtə/ NOUN [C] (**interpreters**)
An **interpreter** is a person whose job is to translate what someone is saying into another language. ❑ *Speaking through an interpreter, Aristide said that Haitians had hoped coups were behind them.*

✪inter·re·late /ˌɪntərɪˈleɪt/ VERB [RECIP] (**interrelates, interrelating, interrelated**) If two or more things **interrelate**, there is a connection between them and they have an effect on each other. = interconnect ❑ *The body and the mind interrelate.* ❑ *Each of these cells have their specific jobs to do, but they also interrelate with each other.* ❑ *the way in which we communicate and interrelate with others* ❑ *All things are interrelated.*

in·ter·ro·gate /ɪnˈterəgeɪt/ VERB [T] (**interrogates, interrogating, interrogated**) If someone, especially a police officer, **interrogates** someone, they question them thoroughly for a long time in order to get some information from them. = question ❑ *I interrogated everyone even slightly involved.*

in·ter·ro·ga·tion /ɪnˌterəˈgeɪʃən/ NOUN [C, U] (**interrogations**) An **interrogation** is the act of interrogating someone. ❑ *the right to silence in police interrogations*

in·ter·rupt /ˌɪntəˈrʌpt/ VERB [I, T] (**interrupts, interrupting, interrupted**) **1** [I, T] If you interrupt

someone who is speaking, you say or do something that causes them to stop. ❑ *Turkin tapped him on the shoulder. 'Sorry to interrupt, Colonel.'* **2** [T] If someone or something **interrupts** a process or activity, they stop it for a period of time. ❑ *People kept nosing around the place, interrupting my work.* **3** [T] If something **interrupts** a line, surface, or view, it stops it from being continuous or makes it look irregular. ❑ *Taller plants interrupt the views from the house.*

in·ter·rup·tion /ˌɪntəˈrʌpʃən/ NOUN [C, U] (**interruptions**) **1** *The sudden interruption stopped Justin in mid-sentence.* **2** *interruptions in the supply of food and fuel*

✪inter·sect /ˌɪntəˈsekt/ VERB [RECIP] (**intersects, intersecting, intersected**) **1** If two or more lines or roads **intersect**, they meet or cross each other. You can also say that one line or road **intersects** another. = cross ❑ *The orbit of this comet intersects the orbit of the Earth.* ❑ *The circles will intersect in two places.* **2** If one thing **intersects with** another or if two things **intersect**, the two things cross at a particular point. = overlap, connect ❑ *the ways in which historical events intersect with individual lives* ❑ *Their histories intersect.*

✪inter·sec·tion /ˌɪntəˈsekʃən/ NOUN [C] (**intersections**) An **intersection** is a place where roads or other lines meet or cross. = junction ❑ *We crossed at a busy intersection.* ❑ *at the intersection of two main canals*

✪in·ter·val /ˈɪntəvəl/ NOUN (*academic word*)
NOUN [C] (**intervals**) **1** An **interval** between two events or dates is the period of time between them. = gap ❑ *The process is repeated after a short interval of time.* ❑ *The ferry service has restarted after an interval of 12 years.* **2** (*mainly BrE*; in *AmE*, usually use intermission) An **interval** during a concert, show, movie, or game is a short break between two of the parts.
PHRASE at intervals **1** If something happens **at intervals**, it happens several times with gaps or pauses in between. = regularly, periodically ❑ *She woke him for his medicines at intervals throughout the night.* **2** If things are placed **at** particular **intervals**, there are spaces of a particular size between them. ❑ *Several red and white barriers marked the road at intervals of about a mile.*

✪inter·vene /ˌɪntəˈviːn/ VERB [I] (**intervenes, intervening, intervened**) (*academic word*) **1** If you **intervene in** a situation, you become involved in it and try to change it. = step in ❑ *The situation calmed down when police intervened.* ❑ *The Government is doing nothing to intervene in the crisis.* **2** If you **intervene**, you interrupt a conversation in order to add something to it. ❑ *Hernandez intervened and told me to stop it.* **3** If an event **intervenes**, it happens suddenly in a way that stops, delays, or prevents something from happening. ❑ *The mailboat arrived on Friday mornings unless bad weather intervened.*

✪inter·ven·tion ♦♦◇ /ˌɪntəˈvenʃən/ NOUN [C, U] (**interventions**) **Intervention** is the act of intervening in a situation. ❑ *the role of the United States and its intervention in the internal affairs of many countries* ❑ *The impact of American military intervention in Europe was not felt for a year.*

✪inter·view ♦♦◇ /ˈɪntəvjuː/ NOUN, VERB
NOUN [C, U] (**interviews**) **1** [C, U] An **interview** is a formal meeting at which someone is asked questions in order to find out information about them, such as whether they are suitable for a job. ❑ *The interview went well.* ❑ *Not everyone who writes in can be invited for interview.* ❑ *The three-year study is based on interviews with judges, solicitors, parents, counsellors and written judgements.* **2** [C] An **interview** is a conversation in which a journalist puts questions to someone such as a famous person or politician. ❑ *The trouble began when Allan gave an interview to the Chicago Tribune last month.*
VERB [T] (**interviews, interviewing, interviewed**) **1** If you **are interviewed**, someone asks you questions about yourself to find out information about you, such as whether you are suitable for a job. ❑ *When Wardell was interviewed, he was impressive, and on that basis, he was hired.* ❑ *He was among the three candidates interviewed for the job.* ❑ *The junior doctor interviewed her and prepared a case history.* **2** When a journalist **interviews** someone such as a famous person, they ask them a series of questions. ❑ *I'd interviewed*

him often in the past. **3** When the police **interview** someone, they ask them questions about a crime that has been committed. = question ❑ *The police interviewed the driver, but had no evidence to go on.*

in·ter·viewee /ˌɪntəvjuːˈiː/ NOUN [C] (**interviewees**) An **interviewee** is a person who is being interviewed. ❑ *Is there any interviewee who stands out as memorable?*

in·ti·ma·cy /ˈɪntɪməsi/ NOUN [U] **1** **Intimacy** between two people is a very close personal relationship between them. ❑ *a means of achieving intimacy with another person* **2** You sometimes use **intimacy** to refer to sex or a sexual relationship. ❑ *He did not feel like intimacy with any woman.*

in·ti·mate ADJ, VERB
ADJ /ˈɪntɪmət/ **1** If you have an **intimate** friendship with someone, you know them very well and like them a lot. ❑ *I discussed with my intimate friends whether I would immediately have a baby.* **2** If two people are in an **intimate** relationship, they are involved with each other in a loving or sexual way. ❑ *their intimate moments with their boyfriends* **3** An **intimate** conversation or detail, for example, is very personal and private. = private ❑ *He wrote about the intimate details of his family life.* **4** If you use **intimate** to describe an occasion or the atmosphere of a place, you like it because it is quiet and pleasant, and seems suitable for close conversations between friends. ❑ *an intimate candlelit dinner for two* **5** An **intimate** connection between ideas or organizations, for example, is a very strong link between them. ❑ *an intimate connection between madness and wisdom* **6** An **intimate** knowledge of something is a deep and detailed knowledge of it. = thorough ❑ *He surprised me with his intimate knowledge of Kierkegaard and Schopenhauer.*
VERB /ˈɪntɪmeɪt/ [T] (**intimates, intimating, intimated**) (*formal*) If you **intimate** something, you say it in an indirect way. = hint ❑ *He went on to intimate that he was indeed contemplating a shake-up of the company.*

in·ti·mate·ly /ˈɪntɪmətli/ ADV **1** *He did not feel he had gotten to know them intimately.* **2** [intimately after V] ❑ *You have to be willing to get to know yourself and your partner intimately.* **3** [intimately after V] ❑ *It was the first time they had attempted to talk intimately.* **4** [intimately after V] ❑ *Scientific research and conservation are intimately connected.* **5** *a golden age of musicians whose work she knew intimately*

in·timi·date /ɪnˈtɪmɪdeɪt/ VERB [T] (**intimidates, intimidating, intimidated**) If you **intimidate** someone, you deliberately make them frightened enough to do what you want them to do. ❑ *Jones had set out to intimidate and dominate Paul.*

in·timi·da·tion /ɪnˌtɪmɪˈdeɪʃən/ NOUN [U] ❑ *an inquiry into allegations of intimidation during last week's vote*

in·timi·dat·ing /ɪnˈtɪmɪdeɪtɪŋ/ ADJ If you describe someone or something as **intimidating**, you mean that they are frightening and make people lose confidence. ❑ *He was a huge, intimidating figure.*

into ♦♦♦ /ˈɪntuː/ PREP

In addition to the uses shown below, **into** is used with verbs of movement, such as 'walk' and 'push', and in phrasal verbs such as 'enter into' and 'talk into'.

1 If you put one thing **into** another, you put the first thing inside the second. = in ❑ *Combine the remaining ingredients and put them into a dish.* **2** If you go **into** a place or vehicle, you move from being outside it to being inside it. ❑ *I have no idea how he got into Iraq.* **3** If one thing goes **into** another, the first thing moves from the outside to the inside of the second thing, by breaking or damaging the surface of it. ❑ *The blade missed his kidney, but went into his bowel.* **4** If one thing gets **into** another, the first thing enters the second and becomes part of it. ❑ *Poisonous chemicals got into the water supply.* **5** If you are walking or driving a vehicle and you bump **into** something or crash **into** something, you hit it accidentally. ❑ *A train from New Jersey ploughed into the barrier at the end of the track.* **6** When you get **into** a piece of clothing, you put it on. ❑ *She could change into a different outfit in two minutes.* **7** [V + into + N, N + into + N] If someone or something gets **into** a particular state, they start being in that state. ❑ *I slid into a depression.* **8** [V N + into + N/-ING] If you talk someone

into doing something, you persuade them to do it. ❑ *They sweet-talked him into selling the farm.* **9** If something changes **into** something else, it then has a new form, shape, or nature. ❑ *to turn a nasty episode into a joke* **10** If something is cut or split **into** a number of pieces or sections, it is divided so that it becomes several smaller pieces or sections. ❑ *Sixteen teams are taking part, divided into four groups.* **11** [N + into + N] An investigation **into** a subject or event is concerned with that subject or event. ❑ *It would provide hundreds of millions of dollars for research into alternative energy sources.* **12** If you move or go **into** a particular career or business, you start working in it. ❑ *In the early 1980s, it was easy to get into the rental business.* **13** If something continues **into** a period of time, it continues until after that period of time has begun. ❑ *He had three children, and lived on into his sixties.* **14** /ˈɪntuː/ [V-LINK + into + N] (*informal*) If you are very interested in something and like it very much, you can say that you are **into** it. ❑ *I'm into electronics myself.*

in·tol·er·ant /ɪnˈtɒlərənt/ ADJ (*disapproval*) If you describe someone as **intolerant**, you mean that they do not accept behaviour and opinions that are different from their own. ❑ *intolerant attitudes towards non-Catholics*

in·tra·net /ˈɪntrənet/ NOUN [C] (**intranets**) An **intranet** is a network of computers, similar to the Internet, within a particular company or organization. ❑ *The materials are available to pupils through the school intranet.*

WORD PARTS

The prefix **intra-** often appears in words to show that something exists or happens inside or within something:

intranet (NOUN)

intravenous (ADJ)

intramural (ADJ)

in·tri·cate /ˈɪntrɪkət/ ADJ You use **intricate** to describe something that has many small parts or details. ❑ *the production of carpets with highly intricate patterns*

in·tri·cate·ly /ˈɪntrɪkətli/ ADV ❑ *intricately carved sculptures*

in·trigue NOUN, VERB
NOUN /ˈɪntriːg/ [C, U] (**intrigues**) **Intrigue** is the making of secret plans to harm or deceive people. ❑ *political intrigue*
VERB /ɪnˈtriːg/ [T] (**intrigues, intriguing, intrigued**) If something, especially something strange, **intrigues** you, it interests you and you want to know more about it. = fascinate ❑ *The novelty of the situation intrigued him.*

in·trigued /ɪnˈtriːgd/ ADJ If you are **intrigued by** something, especially something strange, it interests you and you want to know more about it. ❑ *I would be intrigued to hear others' views.*

in·tri·guing /ɪnˈtriːgɪŋ/ ADJ If you describe something as **intriguing**, you mean that it is interesting or strange. = fascinating ❑ *This intriguing book is both thoughtful and informative.*

in·tri·guing·ly /ɪnˈtriːgɪŋli/ ADV ❑ *the intriguingly named newspaper Le Canard enchainé (The Chained Duck)*

⊕**in·trin·sic** /ɪnˈtrɪnsɪk/ ADJ [intrinsic + N] (*academic word, formal*) If something has **intrinsic** value or **intrinsic** interest, it is valuable or interesting because of its basic nature or character, and not because of its connection with other things. = basic, fundamental, inherent ❑ *Diamonds have little intrinsic value and their price depends almost entirely on their scarcity.*

⊕**in·trin·si·cal·ly** /ɪnˈtrɪnsɪkli/ ADV = basically, fundamentally, inherently ❑ *Sometimes I wonder if people are intrinsically evil.* ❑ *There is nothing intrinsically wrong with a voluntary approach but there is a great concern that it will not work.*

⊕**intro·duce** ♦♦◊ /ˌɪntrəˈdjuːs, AmE -ˈduːs/ VERB [T] (**introduces, introducing, introduced**) **1** To **introduce** something means to cause it to enter a place or exist in a system for the first time. = establish, launch ❑ *MGM introduced a new system for hiring writers.* ❑ *The word 'Pagoda' was introduced to Europe by the 17th-century Portuguese.* **2** If you **introduce** one person to another, or you **introduce** two people, you tell them each other's names, so that they can get to know each other. If you **introduce yourself** to someone, you tell them your name. ❑ *Tim, may I introduce you to my uncle's secretary, Mary Waller?* ❑ *We haven't been introduced. My name is Nero Wolfe.* ❸ If you **introduce** someone **to** something, you cause them to learn about it or experience it for the first time. ❑ *He introduced us to the delights of natural food.* ❹ The person who **introduces** a television or radio programme speaks at the beginning of it, and often between the different items in it, in order to explain what the programme or the items are about. = present ❑ *talk shows introduced by women*

✪ **intro·duc·tion** /ˌɪntrəˈdʌkʃən/ NOUN [C, U, SING] (**introductions**) ❶ [C, U] The **introduction** of something is the act of causing it to enter a place or exist in a system for the first time. = establishment, launch ❑ *What he is better remembered for is the introduction of the moving assembly-line in Detroit in 1913.* ❑ *the introduction of a privacy bill* ❷ [SING] A person's **introduction to** something is when they learn about it or experience it for the first time. ❑ *His introduction to fieldwork was a series of expeditions.* ❸ [C] The **introduction to** a book or talk is the part that comes at the beginning and tells you what the rest of the book or talk is about. = preface; ≠ conclusion ❑ *Ellen Malos, in her introduction to 'The Politics of Housework', provides a summary of the debates.* ❑ *An essay's introduction usually indicates what the topic and thesis are and why the topic is of some importance.* ❹ [C] If you refer to a book as an **introduction to** a particular subject, you mean that it explains the basic facts about that subject. ❑ *The book is a friendly, down-to-earth introduction to physics.* ❺ [C] You can refer to a new product as an **introduction** when it becomes available in a place for the first time. ❑ *There are two among their most recent introductions that have greatly impressed me.* ❻ [C, U] You can say that you make an **introduction** when you tell two people each other's names, so that they can get to know each other. ❑ *With considerable shyness, Elaine performed the introductions.*

intro·duc·tory /ˌɪntrəˈdʌktəri/ ADJ ❶ [introductory + N] An **introductory** remark, talk, or part of a book gives a small amount of general information about a particular subject, often before a more detailed explanation. ❑ *an introductory course in religion and theology* ❷ [introductory + N] (*business*) An **introductory** offer or price on a new product is something such as a free gift or a low price that is meant to attract new customers. ❑ *a special introductory offer*

in·trud·er /ɪnˈtruːdə/ NOUN [C] (**intruders**) An **intruder** is a person who goes into a place where they are not supposed to be. ❑ *He owned a gun for scaring off intruders.*

✪ **in·tui·tion** /ˌɪntjuˈɪʃən, AmE -tuː-/ NOUN [C, U] (**intuitions**) Your **intuition** or your **intuitions** are unexplained feelings that something is true even when you have no evidence or proof of it. = instinct, gut feeling ❑ *Her intuition was telling her that something was wrong.* ❑ *He'd have to rely on his own intuitions.*

✪ **in·tui·tive** /ɪnˈtjuːətɪv, AmE -ˈtuː-/ ADJ If you have an **intuitive** idea or feeling about something, you feel that it is true although you have no evidence or proof of it. = instinctive ❑ *A positive pregnancy test soon confirmed her intuitive feelings.* ❑ *He had a deep knowledge and intuitive understanding of cricket.*

✪ **in·tui·tive·ly** /ɪnˈtjuːətɪvli, AmE -ˈtuː-/ ADV = instinctively ❑ *He seemed to know intuitively that I must be missing my mother.* ❑ *Most children reading this sentence would probably fill in the blank with a noun, because they intuitively know how language works.*

in·vade /ɪnˈveɪd/ VERB [I, T] (**invades, invading, invaded**) ❶ [I, T] To **invade** a country means to enter it by force with an army. ❑ *In autumn 1944 the Allies invaded the Italian mainland at Anzio and Salerno.* ❷ [T] If you say that people or animals **invade** a place, you mean that they enter it in large numbers, often in a way that is unpleasant or difficult to deal with. ❑ *People invaded the streets in victory processions almost throughout the day.*

✪ **in·va·lid** NOUN, ADJ
NOUN /ˈɪnvəlɪd/ [C] (**invalids**) An **invalid** is someone who needs to be cared for because they have an illness or disability. ❑ *I hate being treated as an invalid.*

ADJ /ɪnˈvælɪd/ ❶ If an action, procedure, or document is **invalid**, it cannot be accepted, because it breaks the law or some official rule. = null, false; ≠ valid ❑ *The trial was stopped and the results declared invalid.* ❑ *He tried to leave for the Philippines on an invalid passport.* ❷ An **invalid** argument or conclusion is wrong because it is based on a mistake. ❑ *We think that those arguments are rendered invalid by the facts.* ❑ *The paper lacked a coherent method and was statistically invalid.*

✪ **in·vali·date** /ɪnˈvælɪdeɪt/ VERB [T] (**invalidates, invalidating, invalidated**) ❶ If something **invalidates** something such as a law, contract, or election, it causes it to be considered illegal. = nullify, falsify; ≠ validate ❑ *An official decree invalidated the vote in the capital.* ❑ *A contract signed now might be invalidated at some future date.* ❷ To **invalidate** something such as an argument, conclusion, or result means to prove that it is wrong or cause it to be wrong. ❑ *Any form of physical activity will invalidate the results.* ❑ *Some of the other criticisms were invalidated years ago.*

in·valu·able /ɪnˈvæljəbəl/ ADJ If you describe something as **invaluable**, you mean that it is extremely useful. ❑ *I was able to gain invaluable experience over that year.*

in·vari·ably /ɪnˈveəriəbli/ ADV If something **invariably** happens or is **invariably** true, it always happens or is always true. ❑ *They almost invariably get it wrong.*

in·va·sion ♦◇◇ /ɪnˈveɪʒən/ NOUN [C, U] (**invasions**) ❶ If there is an **invasion** of a country, a foreign army enters it by force. ❑ *seven years after the Roman invasion of Britain* ❷ If you refer to the arrival of a large number of people or things as an **invasion**, you are emphasizing that they are unpleasant or difficult to deal with. ❑ *this year's annual invasion of flies, wasps and ants* ❸ If you describe an action as an **invasion**, you disapprove of it because it affects someone or something in a way that is not wanted. ❑ *Is reading a child's diary always a gross invasion of privacy?*

✪ **in·vent** /ɪnˈvent/ VERB [T] (**invents, inventing, invented**) ❶ If you **invent** something such as a machine or process, you are the first person to think of it or make it. = come up with, devise ❑ *He invented the first electric clock.* ❑ *Writing had not been invented then.* ❷ If you **invent** a story or excuse, you try to make other people believe that it is true when in fact it is not. ❑ *I stood still, trying to invent a plausible excuse.*

✪ **in·ven·tion** /ɪnˈvenʃən/ NOUN [C, U] (**inventions**) ❶ [C] An **invention** is a machine, device, or system that has been invented by someone. ❑ *The spinning wheel was a Chinese invention.* ❷ [U] **Invention** is the act of inventing something that has never been made or used before. ❑ *the invention of the telephone* ❸ [C, U] If you refer to someone's account of something as an **invention**, you think that it is untrue and that they have made it up. = fabrication ❑ *The story was certainly a favourite one, but it was undoubtedly pure invention.* ❹ [U] **Invention** is the ability to invent things or to have clever and original ideas. = creativity ❑ *Perhaps, with such powers of invention and mathematical ability, he will be offered a job in computers.*

in·ven·tive /ɪnˈventɪv/ ADJ An **inventive** person is good at inventing things or has clever and original ideas. = creative ❑ *It inspired me to be more inventive with my own cooking.*

in·ven·tive·ness /ɪnˈventɪvnəs/ NOUN [U] ❑ *He has surprised us before with his inventiveness.*

in·ven·tor /ɪnˈventə/ NOUN [C] (**inventors**) An **inventor** is a person who has invented something, or whose job is to invent things. ❑ *Alexander Graham Bell, the inventor of the telephone*

in·ven·tory /ˈɪnvəntri, AmE -tɔːri/ NOUN [C] (**inventories**) An **inventory** is a written list of all the objects in a particular place such as all the merchandise in a store. ❑ *Before starting, he made an inventory of everything that was to stay.*

✪ **in·vest** ♦◇◇ /ɪnˈvest/ VERB [I, T] (**invests, investing, invested**) (*academic word*) ❶ [I, T] If you **invest in** something, or if you **invest** a sum of money, you use your money in a way that you hope will increase its value, for example, by putting it in a bank, or buying securities or property. ❑ *Many people don't like to invest in shares.* ❑ *I'm tired of watching you invest our money in insane projects.* **2** [I, T] If you **invest in** something useful, you buy it, because it will help you to do something more efficiently or more cheaply. ❑ *The company has invested a six-figure sum in an electronic order-control system which is used to keep shops stocked.* **3** [I, T] When a government or organization **invests** in something, it gives or lends money for a purpose that it considers useful or profitable. ❑ *the need to invest in new technology* ❑ *Government agencies must invest more funds in training and development programmes.* **4** [T] If you **invest** time or energy **in** something, you spend a lot of time or energy on it because you think it will be useful or successful. ❑ *I would rather invest time in my children than in the kitchen.* **5** [T] (*formal*) To **invest** someone **with** rights or responsibilities means to give them those rights or responsibilities legally or officially. ❑ *The constitution invested him with certain powers.*

◆ **in·ves·ti·gate** ◆◆◇ /ɪnˈvestɪgeɪt/ VERB [I, T] (**investigates, investigating, investigated**) (*academic word*) If someone, especially an official, **investigates** an event, situation, or claim, they try to find out what happened or what is the truth. = examine, explore, study, analyse ❑ *They're still investigating the accident.* ❑ *Research in Oxford is now investigating a possible link between endometriosis and the immune system.*

◆ **in·ves·ti·ga·tion** /ɪnˌvestɪˈgeɪʃən/ NOUN [C, U] (**investigations**) = examination, study, analysis ❑ *He ordered an investigation into the affair.* ❑ *Brain functions are measurable and open to scientific investigation.*

in·ves·ti·ga·tive /ɪnˈvestɪgətɪv, AmE -geɪt-/ ADJ **Investigative** work, especially journalism, involves investigating things. ❑ *an investigative reporter*

in·ves·ti·ga·tor /ɪnˈvestɪgeɪtə/ NOUN [C] (**investigators**) An **investigator** is someone who carries out investigations, especially as part of their job. ❑ *an undercover investigator*

◆ **in·vest·ment** ◆◆◇ /ɪnˈvesmənt/ NOUN [U, C] (**investments**) **1** [U] **Investment** is the activity of investing money. ❑ *He said the government must introduce tax incentives to encourage investment.* **2** [C, U] An **investment** is an amount of money that you invest, or the thing that you invest it in. ❑ *an investment of twenty-eight million dollars* ❑ *Total foreign investment in America still constitutes only about 5% of U.S. assets.* **3** [C] If you describe something you buy as an **investment**, you mean that it will be useful, especially because it will help you to do a task more cheaply or efficiently. ❑ *When selecting boots, fine, quality leather will be a wise investment.* **4** [U] **Investment** of time or effort is the spending of time or effort on something in order to make it a success. ❑ *I worry about this big investment of time not working.*

◆ **in·ves·tor** ◆◆◇ /ɪnˈvestə/ NOUN [C] (**investors**) An **investor** is a person or organization that buys stocks and shares or property in order to receive a profit. = banker, lender ❑ *The main investor in the project is the French bank Credit National.*

in·vin·cible /ɪnˈvɪnsɪbəl/ ADJ **1** If you describe an army or sports team as **invincible**, you believe that they cannot be defeated. = unbeatable ❑ *You couldn't help feeling the military's fire power was invincible.* **2** If someone has an **invincible** belief or attitude, it cannot be changed. ❑ *He also had an invincible faith in the medicinal virtues of garlic.*

in·vis·ible /ɪnˈvɪzɪbəl/ ADJ **1** If you describe something as **invisible**, you mean that it cannot be seen, for example because it is transparent, hidden, or very small. ❑ *The lines were so finely etched as to be invisible from a distance.* **2** [invisible + N] You can use **invisible** when you are talking about something that cannot be seen but has a definite effect. In this sense, **invisible** is often used before a noun that refers to something visible. ❑ *All the time you are in doubt about the cause of your illness, you are fighting against an invisible enemy.* **3** If you say that you feel **invisible**, you are complaining that you are being ignored by other people. If you say that a particular problem or situation is **invisible**, you are complaining that it is not being

considered or dealt with. ❑ *It was strange, how invisible a clerk could feel.* **4** In stories, **invisible** people or things have a magic quality that makes people unable to see them. ❑ *The Invisible Man* **5** [invisible + N] (*business*) In economics, **invisible** earnings are the money that a country makes as a result of services such as banking and tourism, rather than by producing goods. ❑ *The revenue from tourism is the biggest single item in the country's invisible earnings.*

in·vis·ibly /ɪnˈvɪzɪbli/ ADV **1** [invisibly with V] ❑ *A thin coil of smoke rose almost invisibly into the sharp, bright sky.* **2** *the tradition that invisibly shapes things in the present*

in·vis·ibil·ity /ɪnˌvɪzɪˈbɪlɪti/ NOUN [U] ❑ *She takes up the issue of the invisibility of women and women's concerns in society.*

◆ **in·vi·ta·tion** ◆◇◇ /ˌɪnvɪˈteɪʃən/ NOUN [C, SING] (**invitations**) **1** [C] An **invitation** is a written or spoken request to come to an event such as a party, a meal, or a meeting. ❑ *an invitation to lunch* ❑ *The Syrians have not yet accepted an invitation to attend.* **2** [C] An **invitation** is the card or paper on which an invitation is written or printed. ❑ *Hundreds of invitations are being sent out this week.* **3** [SING] If you believe that someone's action is likely to have a particular result, especially a bad one, you can refer to the action as an **invitation** to that result. ❑ *Don't leave your shopping on the back seat of your car – it's an open invitation to a thief.*

in·vite ◆◆◇ /ɪnˈvaɪt/ VERB, NOUN
VERB /ɪnˈvaɪt/ [T] (**invites, inviting, invited**) **1** If you **invite** someone to something such as a party or a meal, you ask them to come to it. ❑ *She invited him to her 26th birthday party in New Jersey.* ❑ *Barron invited her to accompany him to the races.* **2** If you **are invited to** do something, you are formally asked or given permission to do it. ❑ *At a future date, managers will be invited to apply for a management buy-out.* ❑ *He invited me to go into partnership with him.* **3** If something you say or do **invites** trouble or criticism, it makes trouble or criticism more likely. ❑ *Their refusal to compromise will inevitably invite more criticism from the UN.*
NOUN /ˈɪnvaɪt/ [C] (**invites**) (*informal*) An **invite** is an invitation to something such as a party or a meal. ❑ *She tried to wangle an invite to the party.*

in·vit·ing /ɪnˈvaɪtɪŋ/ ADJ If you say that something is **inviting**, you mean that it has good qualities that attract you or make you want to experience it. ❑ *The February air was soft, cool, and inviting.*

in·vit·ing·ly /ɪnˈvaɪtɪŋli/ ADV ❑ *The waters of the tropics are invitingly clear.*
→ See also **invite**

in·voice /ˈɪnvɔɪs/ NOUN, VERB
NOUN [C] (**invoices**) An **invoice** is a document that lists goods that have been supplied or services that have been done, and says how much money you owe for them. = bill ❑ *We will then send you an invoice for the total course fees.*
VERB [T] (**invoices, invoicing, invoiced**) If you **invoice** someone, you send them a bill for goods or services you have provided them with. = bill ❑ *The agency invoices the client who then pays the full amount to the agency.*

◆ **in·voke** /ɪnˈvəʊk/ VERB [T] (**invokes, invoking, invoked**) (*academic word*) **1** If you **invoke** a law, you state that you are taking a particular action because that law allows or tells you to. ❑ *The judge invoked an international law that protects refugees.* ❑ *The 18 Nato ambassadors invoked the mutual defence clause.* **2** If you **invoke** something such as a principle, a saying, or a famous person, you refer to them in order to support your argument. ❑ *economists who invoke the principle of 'consumer sovereignty' to support their arguments* **3** If something such as a piece of music **invokes** a feeling or an image, it causes someone to have the feeling or to see the image. Many people consider this use to be incorrect and that the word **evoke** should be used. = evoke, conjure up ❑ *'Appalachian Spring' by Aaron Copland invoked the atmosphere of the wide open spaces of the prairies.*

◆ **in·volve** ◆◆◇ /ɪnˈvɒlv/ VERB [T] (**involves, involving, involved**) (*academic word*) **1** If a situation or activity involves something, that thing is a necessary part or consequence of it. = entail ❑ *Running a kitchen involves lots of discipline and speed.* ❑ *Nicky's job as a public relations director involves spending quite a lot of time with other people.* ❑ *the risks involved in the procedure* **2** If a situation or activity **involves** someone, they are taking part in it. = include ❑ *If there was a cover-up, it involved people at the very highest levels of government.* ❑ *a riot involving a hundred inmates* **3** If you say that someone **involves** themselves **in** something, you mean that they take part in it, often in a way that is unnecessary or unwanted. ❑ *I seem to have involved myself in something I don't understand.* **4** If you **involve** someone **in** something, you get them to take part in it. ❑ *Nasser and I do everything together, he involves me in everything.* **5** If one thing **involves** you **in** another thing, especially something unpleasant or inconvenient, the first thing causes you to do or deal with the second. ❑ *I don't want to do anything that will involve me in a long-term commitment.*

in·volved ♦♦◇ /ɪnˈvɒlvd/ ADJ **1** [V-LINK + involved] If you are **involved in** a situation or activity, you are taking part in it or have a strong connection with it. ❑ *If she were involved in business, she would make a strong chief executive.* **2** [V-LINK + involved] If you are **involved in** something, you give a lot of time, effort, or attention to it. ❑ *The family was deeply involved in Jewish culture.* **3** [V-LINK + involved] The things **involved in** something such as a job or system are the necessary parts or consequences of it. ❑ *We believe the time and hard work involved in completing such an assignment are worthwhile.* **4** If a situation or activity is **involved**, it has a lot of different parts or aspects, often making it difficult to understand, explain, or do. = complicated, complex ❑ *The operations can be quite involved, requiring many procedures in order to restructure the anatomy.* **5** If one person is **involved with** another, especially someone they are not married to, they are having a sexual or romantic relationship. ❑ *During a visit to Kenya in 1928 he became romantically involved with a married woman.*

✪ in·volve·ment ♦♦◇ /ɪnˈvɒlvmənt/ NOUN [U, C] (**involvements**) **1** [U] Your **involvement in** or **with** something is the fact that you are taking part in it. ❑ *She disliked his involvement with the group and disliked his friends.* ❑ *There was a strong popular feeling for human involvement in space travel.* **2** [U] **Involvement** is the enthusiasm that you feel when you care deeply about something. ❑ *Ben has always felt a deep involvement with animals.* **3** [C, U] An **involvement** is a close relationship between two people, especially if they are not married to each other. ❑ *They were very good friends but there was no romantic involvement.*

in·ward /ˈɪnwəd/ ADJ, ADV

The form **inwards** can also be used for the adverb.

ADJ **1** [inward + N] Your **inward** thoughts or feelings are the ones that you do not express or show to other people. = inner ❑ *I sighed with inward relief.* **2** [inward + N] An **inward** movement is one towards the inside or centre of something. ❑ *a sharp, inward breath like a gasp* **ADV** [inward after V] If something moves or faces **inward** or **inwards**, it moves or faces towards the inside or centre of something. ❑ *He pushed open the front door, which swung inwards with a groan.*

in·ward·ly /ˈɪnwədli/ ADV ❑ *Sara was inwardly furious.*

IQ /ˌaɪ ˈkjuː/ NOUN [C, U] (**IQs**) Your **IQ** is your level of intelligence, as indicated by a special test that you do. **IQ** is an abbreviation for 'intelligence quotient'. ❑ *His IQ is above average.*

iron ♦◇◇ /ˈaɪən/ NOUN, VERB, ADJ **NOUN** [C, U] (**irons**) **1** [C, U] **Iron** is an element that usually takes the form of a hard, dark grey metal. It is used to make steel, and also forms part of many tools, buildings, and vehicles. Very small amounts of iron occur in your blood and in food. ❑ *The huge, iron gate was locked.* ❑ *the highest grade iron ore deposits in the world* **2** [C] An **iron** is an electrical device with a flat metal base. You heat it until the base is hot, then rub it over clothes to remove creases. **PHRASE** **have irons in the fire** If someone has a lot of

irons in the fire, they are involved in several different activities or have several different plans. ❑ *Too many irons in the fire can sap your energy and prevent you from seeing which path to take.* **VERB** [T] (**irons, ironing, ironed**) If you **iron** clothes, you remove the creases from them using an iron. ❑ *She used to iron his shirts.* **PHRASAL VERB** **iron out** If you **iron out** difficulties, you resolve them and bring them to an end. = smooth out ❑ *'It was in the beginning, when we were still ironing out problems,' a company spokesman said.* **ADJ** **1** [iron + N] You can use **iron** to describe the character or behaviour of someone who is very firm in their decisions and actions, or who can control their feelings well. ❑ *a man of icy nerve and iron will* **2** [iron + N] **Iron** is used in expressions such as **an iron hand** and **iron discipline** to describe strong, harsh, or unfair methods of control that do not allow people much freedom. ❑ *He died in 1985 after ruling Albania with an iron fist for 40 years.*

iron·ing /ˈaɪənɪŋ/ NOUN [U] ❑ *I managed to get all the ironing done this morning.*

iron·ic /aɪˈrɒnɪk/ or **ironical** /aɪˈrɒnɪkəl/ ADJ **1** When you make an **ironic** remark, you say the opposite of what you really mean, as a joke. ❑ *At the most solemn moments he will flash a mocking smile or make an ironic remark.* **2** If you say that something is **ironic** that something happens, you mean that it is odd or amusing because it involves a contrast. ❑ *It is ironic that so many women are anti-feminist.*

ironi·cal·ly /aɪˈrɒnɪkli/ ADV **1** [ironically with CL] You use **ironically** to draw attention to a situation that is odd or amusing because it involves a contrast. ❑ *Ironically, for a man who hated war, he would have made a superb war cameraman.* **2** [ironically with V] If you say something **ironically**, you say the opposite of what you really mean, as a joke. ❑ *Classmates at West Point had ironically dubbed him Beauty.*

iro·ny /ˈaɪrəni/ NOUN [U, C] (**ironies**) **1** [U] **Irony** is a subtle form of humour that involves saying things that are the opposite of what you really mean. ❑ *His tone was tinged with irony.* **2** [C, U] If you talk about the **irony** of a situation, you mean that it is odd or amusing because it involves a contrast. ❑ *The irony is that many officials in Washington agree in private that their policy is inconsistent.*

ir·ra·tion·al /ɪˈræʃənəl/ ADJ If you describe someone's feelings and behaviour as **irrational**, you mean they are not based on logical reasons or clear thinking. = unreasonable ❑ *an irrational fear of science*

ir·ra·tion·al·ly /ɪˈræʃənəli/ ADV ❑ *My husband is irrationally jealous over my past loves.*

ir·ra·tion·al·ity /ɪˌræʃəˈnælɪti/ NOUN [U] ❑ *the irrationality of his behaviour*

WORD PARTS
The prefix **ir-** often gives a word the opposite meaning: irrational (ADJ) irregular (ADJ) irresponsible (ADJ)

✪ ir·regu·lar /ɪˈregjʊlə/ ADJ **1** If events or actions occur at **irregular** intervals, the periods of time between them are of different lengths. = variable ❑ *Cars passed at irregular intervals.* ❑ *She was taken to a hospital suffering from an irregular heartbeat.* ❑ *He worked irregular hours.* **2** Something that is **irregular** is not smooth or straight, or does not form a regular pattern. = uneven; ≠ even ❑ *He had bad teeth, irregular and discoloured.* ❑ *Irregular shapes were a feature of the design.* **3** **Irregular** behaviour is dishonest or not in accordance with the normal rules. ❑ *irregular business practices* **4** An **irregular** verb, noun, or adjective has different forms from most other verbs, nouns, or adjectives in the language. For example, 'break' is an irregular verb because its past form is 'broke', not 'breaked'.

ir·regu·lar·ly /ɪˈregjʊləli/ ADV **1** [irregularly with V] ❑ *He was eating irregularly, steadily losing weight.* **2** Located off-centre in the irregularly shaped lake was a fountain.

ir·regu·lar·ity /ɪˌregjʊˈlærɪti/ NOUN [C, U] (**irregularities**)

1 a dangerous irregularity in her heartbeat **2** treatment of abnormalities or irregularities of the teeth **3** He faced charges arising from alleged financial irregularities.

ir·rel·evance /ɪˈreləvəns/ NOUN [U, C] (**irrelevances**)
1 [U] If you talk about the **irrelevance of** something, you mean that it is irrelevant. □ the utter irrelevance of the debate **2** [C] If you describe something as an **irrelevance**, you have a low opinion of it because it is not important in a situation. □ The Patriotic Front has been a political irrelevance since it was abandoned by its foreign backers.

◆**ir·rel·evant** /ɪˈreləvənt/ ADJ (academic word) **1** If you describe something such as a fact or remark as **irrelevant**, you mean that it is not connected with what you are discussing or dealing with. = beside the point, unrelated, unimportant; ≠ pertinent □ irrelevant details □ The government decided that their testimony would be irrelevant to the case. **2** If you say that something is **irrelevant**, you mean that it is not important in a situation. □ The choice of subject matter is irrelevant.

◆**ir·repa·rable** /ɪˈrepərəbəl/ ADJ (formal) **Irreparable** damage or harm is so bad that it cannot be repaired or corrected. = irreversible; ≠ reversible □ The move would cause irreparable harm to the organization. □ He had broken the trust between them and done irreparable damage.
◆**ir·repa·rably** /ɪˈrepərəbli/ ADV [irreparably with V, irreparably + -ED] = irreversibly □ Her heart was irreparably damaged by a virus. □ Commercial netting has already irreparably harmed many salmon stocks.

ir·re·sist·ible /ˌɪrɪˈzɪstɪbəl/ ADJ **1** If you describe something such as a desire or force as **irresistible**, you mean that it is so powerful that it makes you act in a certain way, and there is nothing you can do to prevent this. = overwhelming □ It proved an irresistible temptation to Bob to go back. **2** (informal) If you describe something or someone as **irresistible**, you mean that they are so good or attractive that you cannot stop yourself from liking them or wanting them. □ The music is irresistible.
ir·re·sist·ibly /ˌɪrɪˈzɪstɪbli/ ADV **1** [irresistibly with V] □ I found myself irresistibly drawn to Steve's world.
2 [irresistibly + ADJ] □ She had a charm that men found irresistibly attractive.

ir·re·spec·tive /ˌɪrɪˈspektɪv/ ADV
PHRASE **irrespective** (of formal) If you say that something happens or should happen **irrespective of** a particular thing, you mean that it is not affected or should not be affected by that thing. □ their commitment to a society based on equality for all citizens irrespective of ethnic origin

ir·re·spon·sible /ˌɪrɪˈspɒnsɪbəl/ ADJ (disapproval) If you describe someone as **irresponsible**, you are criticizing them because they do things without properly considering their possible consequences. □ I felt that it was irresponsible to advocate the legalization of drugs.
ir·re·spon·sibly /ˌɪrɪˈspɒnsɪbli/ ADV □ They resent the implication that they have behaved irresponsibly.
ir·re·spon·sibil·ity /ˌɪrɪˌspɒnsɪˈbɪlti/ NOUN [U] □ I can only wonder at the irresponsibility of people who advocate such destruction to our environment.

ir·revo·cable /ɪˈrevəkəbəl/ ADJ (formal) If a decision, action, or change is **irrevocable**, it cannot be changed or reversed. □ He said the decision was irrevocable.
ir·revo·cably /ɪˈrevəkəbli/ ADV □ My relationships with friends have been irrevocably altered by their reactions to my illness.

ir·ri·table /ˈɪrɪtəbəl/ ADJ If you are **irritable**, you are easily annoyed. □ He had been waiting for over an hour and was beginning to feel irritable.
ir·ri·tably /ˈɪrɪtəbli/ ADV [irritably with V] □ 'Why are you whispering?' he asked irritably.
ir·ri·tabil·ity /ˌɪrɪtəˈbɪlɪti/ NOUN [U] □ Patients usually suffer from memory loss, personality changes, and increased irritability.

ir·ri·tate /ˈɪrɪteɪt/ VERB [T] (**irritates, irritating, irritated**)
1 If something **irritates** you, it keeps annoying you. = annoy □ Their attitude irritates me. **2** If something **irritates** a part of your body, it causes it to itch or become sore. □ Wear rubber gloves while chopping chillis as they can irritate the skin.

ir·ri·tat·ed /ˈɪrɪteɪtɪd/ ADJ □ Not surprisingly, her teacher is getting irritated with her.

ir·ri·ta·tion /ˌɪrɪˈteɪʃən/ NOUN [U, C] (**irritations**)
1 [U] **Irritation** is a feeling of annoyance, especially when something is happening that you cannot easily stop or control. = annoyance □ He tried not to let his irritation show as he blinked in the glare of the television lights.
2 [C] An **irritation** is something that keeps annoying you. = annoyance □ Don't allow a minor irritation in the workplace to mar your ambitions. **3** [C, U] **Irritation** in a part of your body is a feeling of slight pain and discomfort there. □ These oils may cause irritation to sensitive skins.

is /ɪz/ IRREG FORM **Is** is the third person singular of the present tense of **be**. **Is** is often added to other words and shortened to -'s.

is·land ◆◆◇ /ˈaɪlənd/ NOUN [C] (**islands**) An **island** is a piece of land that is completely surrounded by water. □ the Canary Islands

isle /aɪl/ NOUN [C] (**isles**) An **isle** is an island; often used as part of an island's name, or in literary English. □ the Isle of Pines

isn't /ˈɪzənt/ SHORT FORM **Isn't** is the usual spoken form of 'is not'.

◆**iso·late** /ˈaɪsəleɪt/ VERB [T] (**isolates, isolating, isolated**)
(academic word) **1** To **isolate** a person or organization means to cause them to lose their friends or supporters. □ This policy could isolate the country from the other permanent members of the United Nations Security Council. **2** If you **isolate yourself**, or if something **isolates** you, you become physically or socially separated from other people. = cut off □ She seemed determined to isolate herself from everyone, even him. □ His radicalism and refusal to compromise isolated him. **3** If you **isolate** something such as an idea or a problem, you separate it from others that it is connected with, so that you can concentrate on it or consider it on its own. ≠ integrate □ Our anxieties can also be controlled by isolating thoughts, feelings and memories. □ attempts to isolate a single factor as the cause of the decline of Britain **4** (technical) To **isolate** a substance means to obtain it by separating it from other substances using scientific processes. = separate □ We can use genetic engineering techniques to isolate the gene that is responsible. □ Researchers have isolated a new protein from the seeds of poppies. **5** To **isolate** a sick person or animal means to keep them apart from other people or animals, so that their illness does not spread. □ Patients will be isolated from other people for between three days and one month after treatment.

◆**iso·lat·ed** /ˈaɪsəleɪtɪd/ ADJ **1** An **isolated** place is a long way away from large towns and is difficult to reach. = remote □ Many of the refugee villages are in isolated areas. **2** If you feel **isolated**, you feel lonely and without friends or help. = cut off □ Some patients may become very isolated and depressed. **3** If a person or organization is **isolated**, they lose their friends or supporters. □ They are finding themselves increasingly isolated within the teaching profession. **4** [isolated + N] An **isolated** example is an example of something that is not very common. = rare □ They said the allegations related to an isolated case of cheating.

◆**iso·la·tion** /ˌaɪsəˈleɪʃən/ NOUN
NOUN [U] **1** **Isolation** is the state of feeling alone and without friends or help. □ Many deaf people have feelings of isolation and loneliness. **2** The **isolation** of a person or organization is the loss of their friends or supporters. □ Diplomatic isolation could lead to economic disaster. **3** **Isolation** is physical or social separation from other people. □ Hayley contracted tuberculosis and had to be put in an isolation ward. □ The epidemic finally stopped in mid-2003, due to stringent isolation of cases.
PHRASE **in isolation** **1** If something is considered **in isolation from** other things that it is connected with, it is considered separately, and those other things are not considered. = separately □ Punishment cannot, therefore, be discussed in isolation from social and political theory. **2** If someone does something **in isolation**, they do it without other people present or without their help. = alone □ Malcolm, for instance, works in isolation but I have no doubts about his abilities.

i

I

⊙**is·sue** ♦♦♦ /ˈɪsjuː, ˈɪʃuː/ NOUN, VERB (*academic word*)

NOUN [C, SING, U] (**issues**) **1** [C] An **issue** is an important subject that people are arguing about or discussing. = subject, matter ❏ *Agents will raise the issue of prize-money for next year's world championships.* ❏ *A key issue for higher education is the need for greater diversity of courses.* ❏ *Is it right for the Church to express a view on political issues?* **2** [SING] If something is **the issue**, it is the thing you consider to be the most important part of a situation or discussion. ❏ *I was earning a lot of money, but that was not the issue.* ❏ *Do not draw it on the chart, however, as this will confuse the issue.* **3** [C] An **issue** of something such as a magazine or newspaper is the version of it that is published, for example, in a particular month or on a particular day. = edition ❏ *The growing problem is underlined in the latest issue of the Scientific American.* **4** [U] **Issue** is the act of officially giving something to someone. ❏ *a standard army issue rifle*

PHRASES **at issue** The question or point **at issue** is the question or point that is being argued about or discussed. ❏ *The problems of immigration were not the question at issue.* **make an issue of** If you **make an issue of** something, you try to make other people think about it or discuss it, because you are concerned or annoyed about it. ❏ *It seemed the Colonel had no desire to make an issue of the affair.* **take issue** with If you **take issue with** someone or something they said, you disagree with them, and start arguing about it. = argue ❏ *I will not take issue with the fact that we have a recession.* **have issues** [oft have issues 'with/about' N] If someone **has issues with** a particular aspect of their life, they have problems connected with it. ❏ *Once you have issues with food, you're going to have them for the rest of your life.*

VERB [T] (**issues, issuing, issued**) **1** If you **issue** a statement or a warning, you make it known formally or publicly. = put out ❏ *Last night he issued a statement denying the allegations.* ❏ *The government issued a warning that the strikers should end their action or face dismissal.* **2** If you **are issued with** something, it is officially given to you. ❏ *On your appointment you will be issued with a written statement of particulars of employment.*

WORD CONNECTIONS

VERB + **issue**

become an issue
❏ *Immigration has become an issue for many voters.*

debate an issue
discuss an issue
raise an issue
address an issue
❏ *It is clear that a lot of work will need to be done to address the issues raised at the conference.*

resolve an issue
❏ *The service helps people resolve consumer issues by providing information and advice.*

ADJ + **issue**

a **complicated** issue
a **controversial** issue
a **sensitive** issue
a **difficult** issue
❏ *We need a long-term solution to this controversial issue.*

a **key** issue
an **important** issue
a **serious** issue
a **critical** issue
❏ *Security is a key issue for banks.*

a **legal** issue
a **political** issue
an **environmental** issue
❏ *There is a growing awareness of environmental issues.*

an **unresolved** issue
❏ *Pay is still a crucial unresolved issue.*

IT ♦♦♦ /ˌaɪ ˈtiː/ ABBREVIATION **IT** is an abbreviation for **information technology**. ❏ *people with IT skills*

it ♦♦♦ /ɪt/ PRON

It is a third person singular pronoun. **It** is used as the subject or object of a verb, or as the object of a preposition.

PRON **1** You use **it** to refer to an object, animal, or other thing that has already been mentioned. ❏ *It's a wonderful city, really. I'll show it to you if you want.* ❏ *My wife has become crippled by arthritis. She is embarrassed to ask the doctor about it.* **2** You use **it** to refer to a child or baby whose sex you do not know or whose sex is not relevant to what you are saying. ❏ *She could compel him to support the child after it was born.* **3** You use **it** to refer in a general way to a situation that you have just described. ❏ *He was through with sports, not because he had to be but because he wanted it that way.* **4** You use **it** before certain nouns, adjectives, and verbs to introduce your feelings or point of view about a situation. ❏ *It was nice to see Steve again.* ❏ *It's a pity you never got married, Sarah.* **5** You use **it** in passive clauses that report a situation or event. ❏ *It has been said that stress causes cancer.* **6** You use **it** with some verbs that need a subject or object, although there is no noun that 'it' refers to. ❏ *Of course, as it turned out, three-fourths of the people in the group were psychiatrists.* **7** You use **it** as the subject of 'be' to say what the time, day, or date is. **be** ❏ *It's three o'clock in the morning.* ❏ *It was a Monday, so she was at home.* **8** You use **it** as the subject of a linking verb to describe the weather, the light, or the temperature. ❏ *It was very wet and windy the day I drove over the hill to Del Norte.* **9** You use **it** when you are telling someone who you are, or asking them who they are, especially at the beginning of a phone call. You also use **it** in statements and questions about the identity of other people. ❏ *'Who is it?' he called.—'It's your neighbour.'* **10** When you are emphasizing or drawing attention to something, you can put that thing immediately after **it** and a form of the verb 'be'. ❏ *It's really the poor countries that don't have an economic base that have the worst environmental records.*

PHRASE **it's not that** or **it's not just that** You use **it** in expressions such as **it's not that** or **it's not just that** when you are giving a reason for something and are suggesting that there are several other reasons. ❏ *It's not that I didn't want to be with my family.*

✦ **if it wasn't for** → see **be**

ital·ic /ɪˈtælɪk/ NOUN, ADJ

NOUN [PL] (**italics**) **Italics** are letters that slope to the right. Italics are often used to emphasize a particular word or sentence. The examples in this dictionary are printed in italics. ❏ *The title is printed in italics.*

ADJ [italic + N] **Italic** letters slope to the right. ❏ *She addressed them by hand in her beautiful italic script.*

itch /ɪtʃ/ VERB, NOUN

VERB [T, I] (**itches, itching, itched**) **1** [T, I] When a part of your body **itches**, you have an unpleasant feeling on your skin that makes you want to scratch. ❏ *When someone has hay fever, the eyes and nose will stream and itch.* **2** [I, T] (*informal*) If you **are itching** to do something, you are very eager or impatient to do it. ❏ *I was itching to get involved.*

NOUN [SING, C] (**itches**) **1** [SING, C] When you have an **itch** on a part of your body, you have an unpleasant feeling on your skin that makes you want to scratch. ❏ *Scratch my back – I've got an itch.* **2** [SING] If you have an **itch** to do something, you are very eager or impatient to do it. ❏ *cable TV viewers with an insatiable itch to switch from channel to channel*

itch·ing /ˈɪtʃɪŋ/ NOUN [U] ❏ *It may be that the itching is caused by contact with irritant material.*

itchy /ˈɪtʃi/ ADJ

ADJ (*informal*) If a part of your body or something you are wearing is **itchy**, you have an unpleasant feeling on your skin that makes you want to scratch. ❏ *itchy, sore eyes*

PHRASE **itchy feet** (*informal*) If you have **itchy feet**, you have a strong desire to leave a place and to travel.

❑ *The thought gave me really itchy feet so within a couple of months I decided to leave.*

✪**item** ♦♦◇ /'aɪtəm/ NOUN [C, SING] (**items**) (*academic word*) **1** [C] An **item** is one of a collection or list of objects. ❑ *The most valuable item on show will be a Picasso drawing.* ❑ *Only one item of hand luggage is permitted.* **2** [C] An **item** is one of a list of things for someone to do, deal with, or talk about. = matter, topic ❑ *The other item on the agenda is the tour.* **3** [C] An **item** is a report or article in a newspaper or magazine, or on television or radio. ❑ *There was an item in the paper about him.* ❑ *a recent news item in a magazine* **4** [SING] (*informal*) If you say that two people are an **item**, you mean that they are having a romantic or sexual relationship. ❑ *She and Gino were an item.*

WORD CONNECTIONS
item + OF + NOUN
an item of **clothing**
an item of **equipment**
an item of **furniture**
❑ *The suitcase contained items of clothing.*
an item of **interest**
an item of **value**
❑ *Guests should leave items of value in the hotel safe.*

USAGE NOTE
item
Don't use **item** to refer to things that are not part of a list, as in '~~Soccer is one item where teamwork is important~~'.
*Soccer is one **game** where teamwork is important.*

itin·er·ary /aɪ'tɪnərəri, *AmE* -eri/ NOUN [C] (**itineraries**) An **itinerary** is a plan of a trip, including the route and the places that you will visit. ❑ *The next place on our itinerary was Sedona.*

it's /ɪts/ SHORT FORM **1** It's is the usual spoken form of 'it is'. ❑ *It's the best news I've heard in a long time.* **2** It's is the usual spoken form of 'it has', especially when 'has' is an auxiliary verb. **it has** ❑ *It's been such a long time since I played.*

its ♦♦♦ /ɪts/ DET

Its is a third person singular possessive determiner.

You use **its** to indicate that something belongs or relates to a thing, place, or animal that has just been mentioned or whose identity is known. You can use **its** to indicate that something belongs or relates to a child or baby. ❑ *He held the knife by its blade.*

it·self ♦♦♦ /ɪt'self/ PRON **1** [V + itself, PREP + itself] Itself is used as the object of a verb or preposition when it refers to something that is the same thing as the subject of the verb. ❑ *Scientists have discovered remarkable new evidence showing how the body rebuilds itself while we sleep.* **2** You use **itself** to emphasize the thing you are referring to. ❑ *I think life itself is a learning process.* **3** [N + itself] If you say that someone is, for example, politeness **itself** or kindness **itself**, you are emphasizing that they are extremely polite or extremely kind. ❑ *He is rarely satisfied with anything less than perfection itself.*

I've /aɪv/ SHORT FORM **I've** is the usual spoken form of 'I have', especially when 'have' is an auxiliary verb. ❑ *I've been invited to meet with the ambassador.*

ivo·ry /'aɪvəri/ NOUN, COLOUR
NOUN [U] **Ivory** is a hard cream-coloured substance that forms the tusks of elephants and some other animals. It is valuable and can be used for making carved ornaments. ❑ *the international ban on the sale of ivory*
COLOUR **Ivory** is a creamy-white colour. ❑ *small ivory flowers*

i

Jj

J also **j** /dʒeɪ/ NOUN [c, u] (**J's, j's**) J is the tenth letter of the English alphabet.

jack /dʒæk/ NOUN [c] (**jacks**) **1** A **jack** is a device for lifting a heavy object, such as a car, off the ground. **2** A **jack** is a playing card whose value is between a ten and a queen. A jack is usually represented by a picture of a young man. ❑ *the jack of spades*

jack·et ◆◇◇ /'dʒækɪt/ NOUN [c] (**jackets**) **1** A **jacket** is a short coat with long sleeves. ❑ *a black leather jacket* **2** (mainly AmE) The **jacket** of a book is the paper cover that protects the book. ❑ *A beautiful girl gazes from the jacket of this book.*

jail ◆◇◇ /dʒeɪl/ also **gaol** NOUN, VERB
NOUN [c, u] (**jails**) A **jail** is a place where criminals are kept in order to punish them, or where people waiting to be tried are kept. = prison ❑ *Three prisoners escaped from a jail.*
VERB [T] (**jails, jailing, jailed**) If someone **is jailed**, they are put into jail. ❑ *He was jailed for twenty years.*

jam /dʒæm/ VERB, NOUN
VERB [I, T] (**jams, jamming, jammed**) **1** [I, T] If you **jam** something somewhere, you push or put it there roughly. ❑ *Pete jammed his hands into his pockets.* **2** [I, T] If something such as a part of a machine **jams**, or if something **jams** it, the part becomes fixed in position and is unable to move freely or work properly. ❑ *The second time he fired his gun jammed.* ❑ *A rope jammed the boat's propeller.* **3** [T] If vehicles **jam** a road, there are so many of them that they cannot move. ❑ *Hundreds of departing motorists jammed roads that had been closed during the height of the storm.* **4** [I, T] If a lot of people **jam** a place, or **jam into** a place, they are pressed tightly together so that they can hardly move. = cram ❑ *Hundreds of people jammed the boardwalk to watch.* **5** [T] To **jam** a radio or electronic signal means to interfere with it and prevent it from being received or heard clearly. ❑ *They will try to jam the transmissions electronically.* **6** [T] If callers **are jamming** telephone lines, there are so many callers that the people answering the telephones find it difficult to deal with them all. ❑ *Hundreds of callers jammed the switchboard for more than an hour.*
NOUN [c, u] (**jams**) **1** [c, u] (mainly BrE; in AmE, use **jelly**) **Jam** is a sweet food consisting of pieces of fruit cooked with a large amount of sugar until it is thickened. Jam is usually spread on bread. **2** [c] If vehicles are in a **jam** on a road, there are so many of them that they cannot move. ❑ *400 trucks may sit in a jam for ten hours waiting to cross the limited number of bridges.*

jammed /dʒæmd/ ADJ **1** = packed ❑ *The stadium was jammed and they had to turn away hundreds of disappointed fans.* **2** Nearby roads and the dirt track to the beach were jammed with cars.

jam·ming /'dʒæmɪŋ/ NOUN [u] ❑ *The plane is used for electronic jamming and radar detection.*

jar /dʒɑː/ NOUN, VERB
NOUN [c] (**jars**) **1** A **jar** is a glass container with a lid that is used for storing food. ❑ *cucumbers in glass jars* **2** You can use **jar** to refer to a jar and its contents, or to the contents only. ❑ *She opened up a jar of plums.*
VERB [I, T] (**jars, jarring, jarred**) **1** If something **jars**, or **jars** you, you find it unpleasant, disturbing, or shocking. ❑ *televised congressional hearings that jarred the nation's faith in the presidency* **2** If an object **jars**, or if something **jars** it, the object moves with a fairly hard shaking movement. ❑ *The ship jarred a little.* ❑ *The sudden movement jarred the box and it fell off the table.*

jar·ring /'dʒɑːrɪŋ/ ADJ ❑ *In the context of this chapter, Dore's comments strike a jarring note.*

jaw /dʒɔː/ NOUN [c, PL] (**jaws**) **1** [c] Your **jaw** is the lower part of your face below your mouth. The movement of your jaw is sometimes considered to express a particular emotion. For example, if your **jaw drops**, you are very surprised. ❑ *He thought for a moment, stroking his well-defined jaw.* **2** [c] A person's or animal's **jaws** are the two bones in their head that their teeth are attached to. ❑ *a forest rodent with powerful jaws* **3** [PL] If you talk about the **jaws of** something unpleasant such as death or hell, you are referring to a dangerous or unpleasant situation. ❑ *A family dog rescued a newborn boy from the jaws of death.*

jazz ◆◇◇ /dʒæz/ NOUN [u] **Jazz** is a style of music that was invented by African-American musicians in the early part of the twentieth century. Jazz music has very strong rhythms and often involves improvisation. ❑ *The club has live jazz on Sundays.*

jeal·ous /'dʒeləs/ ADJ **1** If someone is **jealous**, they feel angry or bitter because they think that another person is trying to take a lover or friend, or a possession, away from them. ❑ *She got insanely jealous and there was a terrible fight.* **2** If you are **jealous of** another person's possessions or qualities, you feel angry or bitter because you do not have them. ❑ *She was jealous of his wealth.*

jeal·ous·ly /'dʒeləsli/ ADV **1** [jealously after v] ❑ *The formula is jealously guarded.* **2** [jealously after v] ❑ *Gloria eyed them jealously.*

jeal·ousy /'dʒeləsi/ NOUN [u] **1** **Jealousy** is the feeling of anger or bitterness that someone has when they think that another person is trying to take a lover or friend, or a possession, away from them. ❑ *At first his jealousy only showed in small ways – he didn't mind me talking to other guys.* **2** **Jealousy** is the feeling of anger or bitterness that someone has when they wish that they could have the qualities or possessions that another person has. ❑ *Her beauty causes envy and jealousy.*

jeans /dʒiːnz/ NOUN [PL] [also 'a pair of' jeans] **Jeans** are casual trousers that are usually made of strong cotton cloth called denim. ❑ *a young man in jeans and a worn T-shirt*

jeer /dʒɪə/ VERB, NOUN
VERB [I, T] (**jeers, jeering, jeered**) To **jeer at** someone means to say or shout rude and insulting things to them to show that you do not like or respect them. ❑ *Marchers jeered at white passers-by, but there was no violence, nor any arrests.* ❑ *Demonstrators jeered the mayor as he arrived for a week-long visit.*
NOUN [c] (**jeers**) **Jeers** are rude and insulting things that people shout to show they do not like or respect someone. ❑ *the heckling and jeers of his audience*

jeer·ing /'dʒɪərɪŋ/ NOUN [u] ❑ *There was constant jeering and interruption from the floor.*

jeop·ard·ize /'dʒepədaɪz/ also **jeopardise** VERB [T] (**jeopardizes, jeopardizing, jeopardized**) To **jeopardize** a situation or activity means to do something that may destroy it or cause it to fail. = threaten, endanger ❑ *He has jeopardized his future career.*

jeop•ardy /'dʒepədi/ NOUN

PHRASE **in jeopardy** If someone or something is **in jeopardy**, they are in a dangerous situation where they might fail, be lost, or be destroyed. ❑ *A series of setbacks have put the whole project in jeopardy.*

jerk /dʒɜːk/ VERB, NOUN

VERB [I, T] (jerks, jerking, jerked) If you **jerk** something or someone in a particular direction, or they **jerk** in a particular direction, they move a short distance very suddenly and quickly. ❑ *Mr Griffin jerked forward in his chair.* ❑ *'This is Brady Coyne', said Sam, jerking his head in my direction.*

NOUN [c] (jerks) **1** A **jerk** is a sudden, quick movement. ❑ *He indicated the bedroom with a jerk of his head.* **2** (informal, offensive, disapproval) If you call someone a **jerk**, you are insulting them because you think they are stupid or you do not like them. ❑ *The guy is such a jerk! He only cares about himself.*

jet ◆◇◇ /dʒet/ NOUN, VERB

NOUN [c] (jets) **1** [also 'by' jet] A **jet** is an aircraft that is powered by jet engines. ❑ *Her private jet landed in the republic on the way to Japan.* ❑ *He had arrived from Key West by jet.* **2** A **jet** of liquid or gas is a strong, fast, thin stream of it. ❑ *A jet of water poured through the windows.*

VERB [I] (jets, jetting, jetted) If you **jet** somewhere, you travel there in a fast plane. ❑ *The president will be jetting off to Germany today.*

jet en•gine NOUN [c] (jet engines) A **jet engine** is an engine in which hot air and gases are forced out at the back. Jet engines are used for most modern aircraft.

jew•el /'dʒuːəl/ NOUN

NOUN [c] (jewels) **1** A **jewel** is a precious stone used to decorate valuable things that you wear, such as rings or necklaces. ❑ *a golden box containing precious jewels* **2** If you describe something or someone as a **jewel**, you mean that they are better, more beautiful, or more special than other similar things or than other people. = gem ❑ *a small jewel of a theatre*

PHRASE **jewel in someone's crown** If you refer to an achievement or thing as the **jewel** in someone's **crown**, you mean that it is considered to be their greatest achievement or the thing they can be most proud of. ❑ *His achievement is astonishing and this book is the jewel in his crown.*

jew•el•lery /'dʒuːəlri/ (BrE; in AmE, use **jewelry**) NOUN [U] **Jewellery** is ornaments that people wear, such as rings, bracelets, and necklaces. It is often made of a valuable metal such as gold, and sometimes decorated with precious stones. ❑ *Discover a full selection of fine watches and jewellery at these two Upper Manhattan stores.*

jin•gle /'dʒɪŋgəl/ VERB, NOUN

VERB [I, T] (jingles, jingling, jingled) When something **jingles** or when you **jingle** it, it makes a gentle ringing noise, like small bells. ❑ *Brian put his hands in his pockets and jingled some change.*

NOUN [SING, c] (jingles) **1** [SING] The **jingle** of something is the gentle ringing noise it makes, like small bells. ❑ *the jingle of money in a man's pocket* **2** [c] A **jingle** is a short, simple tune, often with words, that is used to advertise a product or programme on radio or television. ❑ *advertising jingles*

✪job ◆◆◆ /dʒɒb/ NOUN (academic word)

NOUN [c, SING] (jobs) **1** [c] A **job** is the work that someone does to earn money. = work, employment, occupation, position, post ❑ *Once I'm in Miami I can get a job.* ❑ *Thousands have lost their jobs.* ❑ *overseas job vacancies* **2** [c] A **job** is a particular task. = task, assignment ❑ *He said he hoped that the job of putting together a coalition wouldn't take too much time.* ❑ *Save major painting jobs for the spring or summer.* **3** [c] The **job** of a particular person or thing is their duty or function. ❑ *Their main job is to preserve health rather than treat illness.* ❑ *His first job will be to try and get talks going between the two sides.* **4** [SING] If you say that someone is doing a good **job**, you mean that they

are doing something well. ❑ *We could do a far better job of managing it than they have.* **5** [SING] If you say that you have **a job** doing something, you are emphasizing how difficult it is. ❑ *He may have a hard job selling that argument to investors.*

PHRASE **on the job** If someone is **on the job**, they are actually doing a particular job or task. ❑ *The top pay scale after five years on the job would reach $5.00 an hour.*

WORD CONNECTIONS
VERB + **job**
get a job **find** a job **have** a job **lose** a job ❑ *It can be difficult for young people to find a job.*
create jobs **cut** jobs ❑ *The opening of a new supermarket is expected to create over a hundred jobs.*
do a job **start** a job **finish** a job ❑ *Make sure you have the right tools before you start the job.*
ADJ + **job**
a **full-time** job a **part-time** job a **permanent** job a **temporary** job ❑ *I'm hoping to get a part-time job.*
a **good** job a **top** job a **well-paid** job ❑ *Vanya has it all – a well-paid job, and a luxurious apartment.*
a **new** job ❑ *He's looking for a new job.*

VOCABULARY BUILDER
job NOUN A **job** is the work that someone does to earn money. ❑ *Her social life was ruined, and she had already lost two jobs from taking so much time off.*
work NOUN Your **work** consists of the things you are paid or required to do in your job. ❑ *A lot of my work involves speaking to journalists and editors on the phone.*
employment NOUN **Employment** is the fact of having a paid job. ❑ *Overseas students are unlikely to find employment in this area except as trainee chartered accountants.*
position NOUN (formal) A **position** is a job within a company or organization. ❑ *By that Christmas he had made such an impression that he was offered a permanent position with the magazine.*
post NOUN (formal) A **post** in a company or organization is a job in it, usually one that involves responsibility. ❑ *After the war, Matthews obtained a post as head of department at St Dunstan's College.*
occupation NOUN (written) Your **occupation** is your job or profession. ❑ *The survey of 373 people in a variety of occupations showed that 222 had experienced bullying.*

job de•scrip•tion NOUN [c] (job descriptions) A **job description** is a written account of all the duties and responsibilities involved in a particular job or position. ❑ *the job description for the position of division general manager*

job·less /'dʒɒbləs/ ADJ, NOUN

ADJ Someone who is **jobless** does not have a job, although they would like one. = unemployed ❑ *He has turned his back on millions of jobless Americans.*

NOUN [PL] **The jobless** are people who are jobless. ❑ *They joined the ranks of the jobless.*

job share VERB [I] (**job shares, job sharing, job shared**) If two people **job share**, they share the same job by working part-time, for example, one person working in the mornings and the other in the afternoons. ❑ *They both want to job share.*

join ♦♦♦ /dʒɔɪn/ VERB, NOUN

VERB [T, I, RECIP] (**joins, joining, joined**) **1** [T] If one person **joins** another, they move or go to the same place, for example, so that both of them can do something together. ❑ *His wife and children moved to join him in their new home.* **2** [T] If you **join** an organization, you become a member of it or start work as an employee of it. ❑ *He joined the Army five years ago.* **3** [I, T] If you **join** an activity that other people are doing, you take part in it or become involved with it. ❑ *The United States joined the war in April 1917.* ❑ *The pastor requested the women present to join him in prayer.* ❑ *Nine Republicans joined in supporting the measure.* **4** [T] If you **join** a queue, you stand at the end of it so that you are part of it. ❑ *It is advised that fans seeking autographs join the queue before practice starts.* **5** [T] To **join** two things means to attach or fasten them together. ❑ *The opened link is used to join the two ends of the chain.* ❑ *the conjunctiva, the skin which joins the eye to the lid* **6** [T] If something such as a line or path **joins** two things, it connects them. ❑ *a global highway of cables joining all the continents together* **7** [RECIP] If two roads or rivers **join**, they meet or come together at a particular point. ❑ *Do you know the highway to Tulsa? The airport road joins it.*

PHRASAL VERBS **join in** If you **join in** an activity, you take part in it or become involved in it. ❑ *I hope everyone will join in the fun.*

join up **1** If someone **joins up**, they become a member of the army, the navy, or the air force. = enlist ❑ *When hostilities broke out he joined up.* **2** If one person or organization **joins up with** another, they start doing something together. = get together, link up ❑ *Dwight decided to withdraw from the committee and join up with the opposition.*

NOUN [C] (**joins**) A **join** is a place where two things are fastened or fixed together.

♦ join forces → see force

joint ♦♦◇ /dʒɔɪnt/ ADJ, NOUN

ADJ [joint + N] **Joint** means shared by or belonging to two or more people. = shared, collective; ≠ separate ❑ *She and Frank had never got round to opening a joint account.* ❑ *a commercial joint venture between the BBC and Flextech* ❑ *The two leaders issued a joint statement.*

NOUN [C] (**joints**) **1** A **joint** is a part of your body such as your elbow or knee where two bones meet and are able to move together. ❑ *Her joints ache if she exercises.* **2** A **joint** is the place where two things are fastened or joined together. ❑ *the joint between the inner and outer panels*

PHRASE **put someone's nose out of joint** (*informal*) If something puts someone's **nose out of joint**, it upsets or offends them because it makes them feel less important or less valued. ❑ *Barry had his nose put out of joint by Lucy's aloof sophistication.*

joint·ly /'dʒɔɪntli/ ADV = together; ≠ separately, singly ❑ *The Port Authority is an agency jointly run by New York and New Jersey.* ❑ *federal and state governments which jointly fund public hospitals*

joke ♦◇◇ /dʒəʊk/ NOUN, VERB

NOUN [C, SING] (**jokes**) **1** [C] A **joke** is something that is said or done to make you laugh, such as a funny story. ❑ *No one told worse jokes than Claus.* **2** [C] A **joke** is something untrue that you tell another person in order to amuse yourself. ❑ *It was probably just a joke to them, but it wasn't funny to me.* **3** [SING] (*informal, disapproval*) If you say that something or someone is **a joke**, you think they are

ridiculous and do not deserve respect. ❑ *It's ridiculous, it's pathetic, it's a joke.*

PHRASES **make a joke of** If you **make a joke of** something, you laugh at it even though it is in fact serious or sad. ❑ *I wish I had your courage, Michael, to make a joke of it like that.*

no joke (*informal, emphasis*) If you describe a situation as **no joke**, you are emphasizing that it is very difficult or unpleasant. ❑ *Eight hours on a bus is no joke, is it.*

the joke is on someone If you say that **the joke is on** a particular person, you mean that they have been made to look very foolish by something. ❑ *'For once,' he said, 'the joke's on me. And it's not very funny.'*

VERB [I] (**jokes, joking, joked**) **1** If you **joke**, you tell funny stories or say amusing things. ❑ *She would joke about her appearance.* ❑ *Luanne was laughing and joking with Tritt.* **2** If you **joke**, you tell someone something that is not true in order to amuse yourself. ❑ *Don't get defensive, Charlie. I was only joking.*

CONVENTION **you're joking** or **you must be joking** or **you've got to be joking** (*spoken, feelings*) You say **you're joking** or **you must be joking** to someone when they have just told you something that is so surprising or unreasonable that you find it difficult to believe. ❑ *You're joking. Are you serious?*

jol·ly /'dʒɒli/ ADJ (**jollier, jolliest**) **1** Someone who is **jolly** is happy and cheerful in their appearance or behaviour. ❑ *She was a jolly, kindhearted woman.* **2** A **jolly** event is lively and enjoyable. ❑ *She had a very jolly time in Korea.*

○jour·nal ♦♦◇ /'dʒɜːnəl/ NOUN [C] (**journals**) (*academic word*) **1** A **journal** is a magazine, especially one that deals with a specialized subject. ❑ *All our results are published in scientific journals.* **2** A **journal** is a daily or weekly newspaper. The word journal is often used in the name of the paper. ❑ *ads in The New York Times, the Wall Street Journal and other publications* **3** A **journal** is an account that you write of your daily activities. = diary ❑ *Sara confided to her journal.*

○jour·nal·ism /'dʒɜːnəlɪzəm/ NOUN [U] **Journalism** is the job of collecting news and writing about it for newspapers, magazines, television, or radio. = reporting, the press ❑ *He began a career in journalism, working for the Rocky Mountain News.* ❑ *It was an accomplished piece of investigative journalism.*

○jour·nal·ist ♦♦◇ /'dʒɜːnəlɪst/ NOUN [C] (**journalists**) A **journalist** is a person whose job is to collect news and write about it for newspapers, magazines, television, or radio. = reporter, correspondent ❑ *Journalists reported that residents were in shock.*

jour·ney ♦◇◇ /'dʒɜːni/ NOUN, VERB

NOUN [C] (**journeys**) **1** When you make a **journey**, you travel from one place to another. = trip ❑ *There is an express service from Paris that completes the journey to Bordeaux in under 4 hours.* **2** You can refer to a person's experience of changing or developing from one state of mind to another as a **journey**. ❑ *My films try to describe a journey of discovery, both for myself and the viewer.*

VERB [I] (**journeys, journeying, journeyed**) (*formal*) If you **journey** somewhere, you travel there. = travel ❑ *In February 1935, Naomi journeyed to the United States for the first time.*

WHICH WORD?

journey, trip, or travel?

A **journey** is an occasion when someone travels from one place to another by land, air, or sea.

❑ *They were tired from the long car journey.*

A **trip** is an occasion when someone travels from one place to another, stays there, usually for a short time, and comes back again.

❑ *They met during a business trip to Milan.*

The noun **travel** is used to talk about the general activity of travelling. It is either uncountable or plural. You cannot say 'a travel'.

❑ *First-class rail travel to Paris or Brussels is included.*

❑ *Marsha told us all about her travels.*

joy ◆◇◇ /dʒɔɪ/ NOUN

NOUN [U, C] (joys) **1** [U] **Joy** is a feeling of great happiness. ❑ *Salter shouted with joy.* **2** [C] A **joy** is something or someone that makes you feel happy or gives you great pleasure. = delight ❑ *Spending evenings outside is one of the joys of summer.*

PHRASE **jump for joy** If you say that someone **is jumping for joy**, you mean that they are very pleased or happy about something. ❑ *He jumped for joy on being told the news.*

joy·ful /ˈdʒɔɪfʊl/ ADJ (formal) **1** Something that is **joyful** causes happiness and pleasure. ❑ *A wedding is a joyful celebration of love.* **2** Someone who is **joyful** is extremely happy. ❑ *We're a very joyful people; we're very musical people and we love music.*

joy·ful·ly /ˈdʒɔɪfəli/ ADV ❑ *They greeted him joyfully.*

✪ **judge** ◆◆◇ /dʒʌdʒ/ NOUN, VERB

NOUN [C] (judges) **1** A **judge** is the person in a court of law who decides how the law should be applied, for example how criminals should be punished. ❑ *The judge adjourned the hearing until next Tuesday.* ❑ *Judge Mr Justice Schiemann jailed him for life.* **2** A **judge** is a person who decides who will be the winner of a competition. ❑ *A panel of judges is now selecting the finalists.* **3** If someone is a good **judge** of something, they understand it and can make sensible decisions about it. If someone is a bad **judge** of something, they cannot do this. ❑ *I'm a pretty good judge of character.*

VERB [T] (judges, judging, judged) **1** If you **judge** something such as a competition, you decide who or what is the winner. ❑ *He was asked to judge a literary competition.* **2** If you **judge** something or someone, you form an opinion about them after you have examined the evidence or thought carefully about them. ❑ *It will take a few more years to judge the impact of these ideas.* ❑ *I am ready to judge any book on its merits.* ❑ *It's for other people to judge how much I have improved.* **3** If you **judge** something, you guess its amount, size, or value or you guess what it is. = estimate ❑ *It is important to judge the weight of your washing load correctly.* ❑ *I judged him to be about forty.*

PHRASE **judging by** or **judging from** or **to judge from** You use **judging by**, **judging from**, or **to judge from** to introduce the reasons why you believe or think something. ❑ *Judging by the opinion polls, he seems to be succeeding.* ❑ *Judging from the way he laughed as he told it, it was meant to be humorous.*

judge·ment /ˈdʒʌdʒmənt/ → See judgment

judg·ment ◆◇◇ /ˈdʒʌdʒmənt/ also **judgement** NOUN

NOUN [C, U] (judgments) **1** [C, U] A **judgment** is an opinion that you have or express after thinking carefully about something. ❑ *In your judgment, what has changed over the past few years?* **2** [U] **Judgment** is the ability to make sensible guesses about a situation or sensible decisions about what to do. ❑ *I respect his judgment and I'll follow any advice he gives me.* **3** [C, U] A **judgment** is a decision made by a judge or by a court of law. = verdict, ruling ❑ *We are awaiting a judgment from the Supreme Court.*

PHRASES **against your better judgment** If something is **against** your **better judgment**, you believe that it would be more sensible or better not to do it. ❑ *Against our better judgment, we buy the products of manufacturers whose claims seem too good to be true.*

pass judgment If you **pass judgment** on someone or something, you give your opinion about it, especially if you are making a criticism. ❑ *They won't pass judgment on their friends or family.*

reserve judgment If you **reserve judgment on** something, you refuse to give an opinion about it until you know more about it. ❑ *I think I'd have to reserve judgment on whether it'll make any difference until I see some of those key details.*

ju·di·cial /dʒuːˈdɪʃəl/ ADJ [judicial + N] **Judicial** means relating to the legal system and to judgments made in a court of law. ❑ *an independent judicial system* ❑ *efforts to manipulate the judicial process*

ju·di·cial·ly /dʒuːˈdɪʃəli/ ADV ❑ *Even if the amendment is passed it can be defeated judicially.*

ju·di·ci·ary /dʒuːˈdɪʃəri, AmE -ʃieri/ NOUN [SING] (formal) The **judiciary** is the branch of authority in a country that is concerned with law and the legal system. ❑ *The judiciary must think very hard before jailing nonviolent offenders.*

juice ◆◇◇ /dʒuːs/ NOUN [C, U, PL] (juices) **1** [C, U] **Juice** is the liquid that can be obtained from a fruit or vegetable. ❑ *fresh orange juice* **2** [PL] The **juices** of a piece of meat are the liquid that comes out of it when you cook it. ❑ *When cooked, drain off the juices and put the meat in a processor.*

juicy /ˈdʒuːsi/ ADJ (juicier, juiciest) **1** If food is **juicy**, it has a lot of juice in it and is very enjoyable to eat. ❑ *a thick, juicy steak* **2** (informal) **Juicy** gossip or stories contain details about people's lives, especially details that are normally kept private. ❑ *It provided some juicy gossip for a few days.*

jump ◆◆◇ /dʒʌmp/ VERB, NOUN

VERB [I, T] (jumps, jumping, jumped) **1** [I, T] If you **jump**, you bend your knees, push against the ground with your feet, and move quickly upward into the air. ❑ *I jumped over the fence.* ❑ *I'd jumped seventeen feet six in the long jump, which was a school record.* **2** [I, T] If you **jump** from something above the ground, you deliberately push yourself into the air so that you drop towards the ground. = leap ❑ *I jumped the last six feet down to the deck.* ❑ *He jumped out of a third-floor window.* **3** [T] If you **jump** something such as a fence, you move quickly up and through the air over or across it. ❑ *He jumped the first fence beautifully.* **4** [I] If you **jump** somewhere, you move there quickly and suddenly. ❑ *Adam jumped from his seat at the girl's cry.* **5** [I] If something **makes** you **jump**, it makes you make a sudden movement because you are frightened or surprised. ❑ *The phone shrilled, making her jump.* **6** [I, T] If an amount or level **jumps**, it suddenly increases or rises by a large amount in a short time. ❑ *Sales jumped from $94 million to over $101 million.* ❑ *The number of crimes jumped by ten per cent last year.* ❑ *Squibb shares jumped $2.50.* **7** [I] If you **jump at** an offer or opportunity, you accept it quickly and eagerly. ❑ *Members of the public would jump at the chance to become part owners of the corporation.* **8** [I] If someone **jumps on** you, they quickly criticize you for doing something that they do not approve of. ❑ *A lot of people jumped on me about that, you know.* **9** [T] (mainly AmE, informal) If someone **jumps** you, they attack you suddenly or unexpectedly. ❑ *Half a dozen sailors jumped him.*

NOUN [C] (jumps) **1** A **jump** is an act of jumping. ❑ *The longest jumps by a man and a woman were witnessed in Sestriere, Italy, yesterday.* **2** A **jump** in an amount or level is a sudden increase or rise by a large amount in a short time. ❑ *A big jump in energy conservation could be achieved without much disruption of anyone's standard of living.*

✦ **jump bail** → see bail; **jump the gun** → see gun; **jump for joy** → see joy

jump·er /ˈdʒʌmpə/ NOUN [C] (jumpers) **1** If you refer to a person or a horse as a particular kind of **jumper**, you are describing how good they are at jumping or the way that they jump. ❑ *He is a terrific athlete and a brilliant jumper.* **2** (BrE; in AmE, use **sweater**) A **jumper** is a warm knitted piece of clothing that covers the upper part of your body and your arms. = sweater, pullover

junc·tion /ˈdʒʌŋkʃən/ (BrE; in AmE, usually use **intersection**) NOUN [C] (junctions) A **junction** is a place where roads or railway lines join.

jun·gle /ˈdʒʌŋɡəl/ NOUN [C, U, SING] (jungles) **1** [C, U] A **jungle** is a forest in a tropical country where large numbers of tall trees and plants grow very close together. ❑ *the mountains and jungles of Papua New Guinea* **2** [SING] If you describe a place as a **jungle**, you are emphasizing that it is full of lots of things and very messy. ❑ *a jungle of stuffed sofas, stuffed birds, knick-knacks, potted plants* **3** [SING] If you describe a situation as a **jungle**, you dislike it because it is complicated and difficult to get what you want from it. ❑ *Social Security law and procedure remain a jungle of complex rules.*

jun·ior ◆◇◇ /ˈdʒuːniə/ ADJ, NOUN

ADJ A **junior** official or employee holds a low-ranking position in an organization or profession. ❑ *A handful of junior officers were made to bear responsibility for the incident.*

NOUN [C, SING] (**juniors**) **1** [C] A **junior** is an official or employee who holds a low-ranking position in an organization or profession. ❑ *He has said legal aid work is for juniors when they start out in the law.* **2** [SING] If you are someone's **junior**, you are younger than they are. ❑ *She now lives with actor Denis Lawson, 10 years her junior.*

junk /dʒʌŋk/ NOUN, VERB
NOUN [U] **Junk** is old and used things that have little value and that you do not want any more. ❑ *Rose finds her furniture in junk shops.*
VERB [T] (**junks, junking, junked**) (*informal*) If you **junk** something, you get rid of it or stop using it. = ditch, jettison ❑ *Consumers will not have to junk their old cassettes to use the new format.*

junk food NOUN [C, U] (**junk foods**) If you refer to food as **junk food**, you mean that it is quick and easy to prepare but is not good for your health. ❑ *Sharon fears that her love of junk food may have contributed to her cancer.*

❍ **ju·ris·dic·tion** /ˌdʒʊərɪsˈdɪkʃən/ NOUN [U, C] (**jurisdictions**) **1** [U] (*formal*) **Jurisdiction** is the power that a court of law or an official has to carry out legal judgments or to enforce laws. = authority, power, influence ❑ *The British police have no jurisdiction over foreign bank accounts.* ❑ *US courts must assert jurisdiction to review detention of enemy combatants.* **2** [C] (*legal*) A **jurisdiction** is a country, state or other area in which a particular court and system of laws has authority. ❑ *In the UK, unlike in most other European jurisdictions, there is no right to strike.*

❍ **jury** ◆◇◇ /ˈdʒʊəri/ NOUN
NOUN [C] (**juries**) **1** [also 'by' jury] In a court of law, the **jury** is the group of people who have been chosen from the general public to listen to the facts about a crime and to decide whether the person accused is guilty or not. ❑ *The jury convicted Mr Hampson of all offences.* ❑ *the tradition of trial by jury* **2** A **jury** is a group of people who choose the winner of a competition. = panel ❑ *I am not surprised that the jury chose to award this novel the prize.*
PHRASE **the jury is out** If you say that **the jury is out** or that **the jury is still out** on a particular subject, you mean that people in general have still not made a decision or formed an opinion about that subject. ❑ *The jury is out on whether or not this is true.*

just ◆◆◆ /dʒʌst/ ADV, ADJ
ADV **1** [just before v] You use **just** to say that something happened a very short time ago, or is starting to happen at the present time. For example, if you say that someone **just arrived** or **has just arrived**, you mean that they arrived a very short time ago. ❑ *I've just bought a new house.* ❑ *I just had the most awful dream.* **2** If you say that you are **just** doing something, you mean that you are doing it now and will finish it very soon. If you say that you are **just about to** do something, or **just going to** do it, you mean that you will do it very soon. ❑ *I'm just making the sauce for the cauliflower.* ❑ *I'm just going to go post a letter.* **3** You can use **just** to emphasize that something is happening at exactly the moment of speaking or at exactly the moment that you are talking about. ❑ *Randall would just now be getting the Sunday paper.* ❑ *Just then the phone rang.* **4** [just + GROUP/CL] You use **just** to indicate that something is no more important, interesting, or difficult, for example, than you say it is, especially when you want to correct a wrong idea that someone may get or has already got. = simply ❑ *It's just a suggestion.* ❑ *It's not just a financial matter.* **5** [just + N] You use **just** to emphasize that you are talking about a small part, not the whole of an amount. = only, merely ❑ *That's just one example of the kind of experiments you can do.* **6** [just + AMOUNT] You use **just** to emphasize how small an amount is or how short a length of time is. = only ❑ *Stephanie and David redecorated a room in just three days.* **7** [just before v] You can use **just** in front of a verb to indicate that the result of something is unfortunate or undesirable and is likely to make the situation worse rather than better. = only ❑ *By doing what they did, they just hurt the people in their community.* **8** You use **just** to indicate that what you are saying is the case, but only by a very small degree or amount. ❑ *Her hand was just visible in the dimly lit room.* ❑ *I arrived just in*

time for my flight to London. **9** [just with MODAL] You use **just** with 'might', 'may', and 'could', when you mean that there is a small chance of something happening, even though it is not very likely. ❑ *It's an old trick but it just might work.* **10** You use **just** to emphasize the following word or phrase, in order to express feelings such as annoyance, admiration, or certainty. ❑ *She just won't relax.* **11** [just + N] (*spoken*) You use **just** in expressions such as **just a minute** and **just a moment** to ask someone to wait for a short time. = hold on ❑ *'Let me in, Di.' – 'Okay. Just a minute.'* **12** [just + N] (*spoken*) You can use **just** in expressions such as **just a second** and **just a moment** to interrupt someone, for example, in order to disagree with them, explain something, or calm them down. ❑ *Well, now just a second, I don't altogether agree.* **13** [just before v] If you say that you can **just** see or hear something, you mean that it is easy for you to imagine seeing or hearing it. = almost ❑ *I can just hear her telling her friends, 'Well, I blame his mother!'* **14** You use **just** in expressions such as **just like**, **just as...as**, and **just the same** when you are emphasizing the similarity between two things or two people. ❑ *Behind the facade they are just like the rest of us.* ❑ *He worked just as hard as anyone.*
PHRASE **just about 1** You use **just about** to indicate that what you are talking about is so close to being the case that it can be regarded as being the case. = practically ❑ *There are those who believe that Nick Price is just about the best golfer in the world.* **2** You use **just about** to indicate that what you are talking about is in fact the case, but only by a very small degree or amount. ❑ *I can just about tolerate it at the moment.*
ADJ (*formal*) If you describe a situation, action, or idea as **just**, you mean that it is right or acceptable according to particular moral principles, such as respect for all human beings. ❑ *They believe that they are fighting a just war.*
✦ **it just goes to show** → see **show**

❍ **jus·tice** ◆◆◇ /ˈdʒʌstɪs/ NOUN
NOUN [U, C] (**justices**) **1** [U] **Justice** is fairness in the way that people are treated. = fairness, equality, law, legality; ≠ injustice, unfairness ❑ *He has a good overall sense of justice and fairness.* ❑ *He only wants freedom, justice and equality.* **2** [U] The **justice of** a cause, claim, or argument is its quality of being reasonable, fair, or right. = legitimacy ❑ *We are a minority and must convince people of the justice of our cause.* **3** [U] **Justice** is the legal system that a country uses in order to deal with people who break the law. ❑ *Many in Toronto's black community feel that the justice system does not treat them fairly.* ❑ *A lawyer is part of the machinery of justice.* **4** [C] **Justice** is used before the names of judges. ❑ *A preliminary hearing was due to start today before Justice Hutchison, but was adjourned.*
PHRASES **bring someone to justice** If a criminal is **brought to justice**, he or she is punished for a crime by being arrested and tried in a court of law. ❑ *They demanded that those responsible be brought to justice.*
do justice 1 To **do justice** to a person or thing means to reproduce them accurately and show how good they are. ❑ *The photograph I had seen didn't do her justice.* **2** If you **do justice** to someone or something, you deal with them properly and completely. ❑ *No one article can ever do justice to the topic of fraud.*
do oneself justice If you **do yourself justice**, you do something as well as you are capable of doing it. ❑ *I don't think he did himself justice in the game today.*

VOCABULARY BUILDER

justice NOUN
Justice is fairness in the way that people are treated.
❑ *They're demanding justice for the people who died fighting the old regime.*

fairness NOUN
Fairness is the quality of treating everybody the same and judging everyone by the same standards.
❑ *To ensure fairness at the interview disabled applicants should receive treatment on a par with non-disabled applicants.*

equality NOUN

If there is **equality** in a society, all its members have the same status, rights, and responsibilities.
❏ *Their pressure for racial equality has transformed public policy.*

law NOUN

The **law** is a set of rules that has been developed to deal with crime.
❏ *Juveniles who break the law have been dealt with by separate courts since 1908.*

legality NOUN

When you talk about the **legality** of something, you are talking about whether or not it is allowed by law.
❏ *There were doubts about the legality of the war.*

jus·ti·fi·able /ˈdʒʌstɪˈfaɪəbəl/ ADJ An action, situation, emotion, or idea that is **justifiable** is acceptable or correct because there is a good reason for it. = legitimate ❏ *The violence of the revolutionary years was justifiable on the grounds of political necessity.*
jus·ti·fi·ably /ˈdʒʌstɪˈfaɪəbli/ ADV ❏ *He was justifiably proud of his achievements.*

✪**jus·ti·fi·ca·tion** /ˌdʒʌstɪfɪˈkeɪʃən/ NOUN [c, u] (**justifications**) A **justification for** something is an acceptable reason or explanation for it. = explanation, reason, excuse ❏ *To me the only justification for a zoo is educational.* ❏ *Most believed that the war lacked justification.*

jus·ti·fied /ˈdʒʌstɪfaɪd/ ADJ **1** If you describe a decision,

action, or idea as **justified**, you think it is reasonable and acceptable. ❏ *In my opinion, the decision was wholly justified.* **2** [V-LINK + justified 'in' -ING] If you think that someone is **justified in** doing something, you think that their reasons for doing it are good and valid. ❏ *He's absolutely justified in resigning. He was treated shamefully.*

✪**jus·ti·fy** ♦◇◇ /ˈdʒʌstɪfaɪ/ VERB [T] (**justifies, justifying, justified**) (*academic word*) **1** To **justify** a decision, action, or idea means to show or prove that it is reasonable or necessary. = rationalize, explain, legitimize ❏ *No argument can justify a war.* ❏ *Ministers agreed that this decision was fully justified by economic conditions.* **2** To **justify** printed text means to adjust the spaces between the words so that each line of type is exactly the same length. ❏ *Click on this icon to align or justify text at both the left and right margins.*

just·ly /ˈdʒʌstli/ ADV **1** [justly with V] If you act **justly**, you act in a way that is right or acceptable according to particular moral principles, such as respect for all human beings. = fairly ❏ *They were not treated justly in the past.* **2** (*approval*) You use **justly** to show that you approve of someone's attitude towards something, because it seems to be based on truth or reality. = justifiably ❏ *Australians are justly proud of their native wildlife.*

ju·ve·nile /ˈdʒuːvənaɪl/ NOUN, ADJ
NOUN [c] (**juveniles**) (*formal*) A **juvenile** is a child or young person who is not yet old enough to be regarded as an adult. ❏ *The number of juveniles in the general population has fallen by a fifth in the past 10 years.*
ADJ [juvenile + N] **Juvenile** activity or behaviour involves young people who are not yet adults. ❏ *Juvenile crime is increasing at a terrifying rate.*

j

Kk

K also **k** /keɪ/ NOUN [C, U] (**K's**, **k's**) **K** is the eleventh letter of the English alphabet.

keen ♦◇◇ /kiːn/ ADJ (**keener**, **keenest**) **1** [keen + N] If you say that someone has a **keen** mind, you mean that they are very clever and aware of what is happening around them. ❑ *They described him as a man of keen intellect.* **2** If you have a **keen** eye or ear, you are able to notice things that are difficult to detect. = sharp ❑ *an amateur artist with a keen eye for detail* **3** (mainly BrE) A **keen** interest or emotion is one that is very intense. ❑ *He had retained a keen interest in the progress of the work.* **4** [V-LINK + keen] If you are **keen on** doing something, you very much want to do it. ❑ *You're not keen on going, are you?* **5** [V-LINK + keen 'on' N] If you are **keen on** something, you like it a lot and are very enthusiastic about it. ❑ *I wasn't too keen on physics and chemistry.* **6** You use **keen** to indicate that someone has a lot of enthusiasm for a particular activity and spends a lot of time doing it. ❑ *She was a keen amateur photographer.* **7** (mainly BrE) A **keen** fight or competition is one in which the competitors are all trying very hard to win, and it is not easy to predict who will win.

keen·ly /'kiːnli/ ADV **1** *They're keenly aware that whatever they decide will set a precedent.* **2** [keenly with V] ❑ *Charles listened keenly.* **3** *She remained keenly interested in international affairs.* **4** *The contest should be very keenly fought.*

keen·ness /'kiːnnəs/ NOUN [U] = enthusiasm ❑ *Doyle's keenness to please*

keep ♦♦♦ /kiːp/ VERB, NOUN
VERB [LINK, I, T] (**keeps**, **keeping**, **kept**) **1** [LINK] If someone **keeps** or **is kept** in a particular state, they remain in it. ❑ *The noise kept him awake.* ❑ *People had to burn these trees to keep warm during harsh winters.* **2** [I, T] If you **keep** or you **are kept** in a particular position or place, you remain in it. ❑ *He kept his head down, hiding his features.* **3** [I] If you **keep off** something or **keep away from** it, you avoid it. If you **keep out of** something, you avoid getting involved in it. ❑ *I managed to stick to the diet and keep off sweet foods.* ❑ *Keep away from the doors while the train is moving.* **4** [T] If you **keep** doing something, you do it repeatedly or continue to do it. ❑ *I keep forgetting it's December.* **5** [T] **Keep** is used with some nouns to indicate that someone does something for a period of time or continues to do it. For example, if you **keep a grip** on something, you continue to hold or control it. ❑ *Until last year, the regime kept a tight grip on the country.* **6** [T] If you **keep** something, you continue to have it in your possession and do not throw it away, give it away, or sell it. ❑ *We must decide what to keep and what to give away.* **7** [T] If you **keep** something in a particular place, you always have it or store it in that place so that you can use it whenever you need it. ❑ *She kept her money under the mattress.* **8** [T] When you **keep** something such as a promise or an appointment, you do what you said you would do. ❑ *I'm hoping you'll keep your promise to come for a long visit.* **9** [T] If you **keep** a record of a series of events, you write down details of it so that they can be referred to later. ❑ *Eleanor began to keep a diary.* **10** [I] If food **keeps** for a certain length of time, it stays fresh and suitable to eat for that time. ❑ *Whatever is left over may be put into the refrigerator, where it will keep for 2-3 weeks.* **11** [I] You can say

or ask how someone **is keeping** as a way of saying or asking whether they are well. ❑ *She hasn't been keeping too well lately.* **12** [T] If someone or something **keeps** you **from** a particular action, they prevent you from doing it. = stop ❑ *Embarrassment has kept me from doing all sorts of things.* **13** [T] If someone or something **keeps** you, they delay you and make you late. ❑ *Sorry to keep you, Jack.* **14** [T] If you **keep** something **from** someone, you do not tell them about it. ❑ *She knew that Gabriel was keeping something from her.* **15** [T] If you **keep** animals, you own them and take care of them. ❑ *I've brought you some eggs. We keep chickens.* **16** [T] (mainly BrE) If you **keep** yourself or **keep** someone else, you support yourself or the other person by earning enough money to provide food, clothing, money, and other necessary things. ❑ *She could just about afford to keep her five kids.* ❑ *I just cannot afford to keep myself.*

PHRASES keep at it If you **keep at it**, you continue doing something that you have started, even if you are tired and would prefer to stop. ❑ *It may take a number of attempts, but it is worth keeping at it.*

keep going If you **keep going**, you continue moving along or doing something that you have started, even if you are tired and would prefer to stop. ❑ *She forced herself to keep going.*

in keeping or **out of keeping** If one thing is **in keeping** with another, it is suitable in relation to that thing. If one thing is **out of keeping with** another, you mean that it is not suitable in relation to that thing. ❑ *This is not in keeping with our objective of representing the community.*

keep it up If you **keep it up**, you continue working or trying as hard as you have been in the past. ❑ *There are fears that he will not be able to keep it up when he gets to the particularly demanding third year.*

keep something to yourself If you **keep** something **to yourself**, you do not tell anyone else about it. ❑ *I have to tell someone. I can't keep it to myself.*

keep to yourself If you **keep to yourself**, you stay on your own most of the time and do not mix socially with other people. ❑ *He was a quiet man who always kept to himself.*

PHRASAL VERBS keep down 1 If you **keep** the number, size, or amount of something **down**, you do not let it get bigger or go higher. ❑ *The prime aim is to keep inflation down.* **2** If someone **keeps** a group of people **down**, they prevent them from getting power and status and being completely free. = hold down ❑ *No matter what a woman tries to do to improve her situation, there is some barrier or attitude to keep her down.* **3** If you **keep** food or drink **down**, you manage to swallow it properly and not vomit, even though you feel sick. ❑ *I tried to give her something to drink but she couldn't keep it down.*

keep on 1 Keep on means the same as **keep** VERB 4. ❑ *Did he give up or keep on trying?* **2** If you **keep** someone **on**, you continue to employ them, for example after other employees have lost their jobs. ❑ *They concluded that firing him would be more damaging than keeping him on.*

keep to 1 If you **keep to** a rule, plan, or agreement, you do exactly what you are expected or supposed to do. = stick to ❑ *You've got to keep to the speed limit.* **2** If you **keep to** something such as a path or river, you do not move away from it as you go somewhere. = stick to ❑ *Please keep to the paths.* **3** If you **keep to** a particular subject, you talk only about that subject, and do not talk about anything else. = stick to ❑ *Let's keep to the subject, or you'll get me too confused.* **4** If you **keep** something **to** a particular number or quantity, you limit it to that number or quantity. ❑ *Keep costs to a minimum.*

keep up **1** If you **keep up with** someone or something that is moving near you, you move at the same speed. ❑ *He lengthened his stride to keep up with his father.* **2** To **keep up with** something that is changing means to be able to cope with the change, usually by changing at the same rate. ❑ *The union called the strike to press for wage increases which keep up with inflation.* **3** If you **keep up with** your work or **with** other people, you manage to do or understand all your work, or to do or understand it as well as other people. ❑ *Penny tended to work through her lunch hour in an effort to keep up with her work.* **4** If you **keep up with** what is happening, you make sure that you know about it. ❑ *She did not bother to keep up with the news.* **5** If you **keep** something **up**, you continue to do it or provide it. ❑ *I was so hungry all the time that I could not keep the diet up for longer than a month.* **6** If you **keep** something **up**, you prevent it from growing less in amount, level, or degree. ❑ *The riders had to keep their pace up.*

NOUN [SING, C] (**keeps**) **1** [SING] Someone's **keep** is the cost of food and other things that they need in their daily life. ❑ *Ray will earn his keep on local farms while studying.* **2** [C] A **keep** is the main tower of a medieval castle, in which people lived. ❑ *the first stone-built castle keep in Britain*

✦ **keep someone company** → see **company**; **keep a straight face** → see **face**; **keep your head** → see **head**; **keep pace** → see **pace**; **keep the peace** → see **peace**; **keep a secret** → see **secret**; **keep track** → see **track**

USAGE NOTE

keep

Do not say that someone 'keeps to do' something. You should say that they 'keep doing' it.
*The government **keeps making** the same mistakes.*

---

keep·er /ˈkiːpə/ NOUN [C] (**keepers**) A **keeper** at a zoo is a person who takes care of the animals.

kept /kept/ IRREG FORM **Kept** is the past tense and past participle of **keep**.

kerb /kɜːb/ (*BrE*; in *AmE*, use **curb**) NOUN [C] (**kerbs**) The **kerb** is the raised edge of a pavement which separates it from the road. ❑ *I pulled over to the kerb.*

❂ **key** ♦♦◇ /kiː/ NOUN, ADJ

NOUN [C, U] (**keys**) **1** [C] A **key** is a specially shaped piece of metal that you place in a lock and turn in order to open or lock a door, or to start or stop the engine of a vehicle. ❑ *They put the key in the door and entered.* **2** [C] The **keys** on a computer keyboard or typewriter are the buttons that you press in order to operate it. ❑ *Finally, press the Delete key.* **3** [C] The **keys** of a piano or organ are the long narrow pieces of wood or plastic that you press in order to play it. ❑ *the black and white keys on a piano keyboard* **4** [C, U] In music, a **key** is a scale of musical notes that starts on one specific note. ❑ *the key of A minor* **5** [C] The **key** on a map or diagram or in a technical book is a list of the symbols or abbreviations used and their meanings. = legend ❑ *You will find a key at the front of the book.* **6** [C] The **key to** a desirable situation or result is the way in which it can be achieved. ❑ *The key to success is to be ready from the start.*

ADJ [key + N] The **key** person or thing in a group is the most important one. = essential, vital, crucial; ≠ minor, unimportant ❑ *He is expected to be the key witness at the trial.* ❑ *Education is likely to be a key issue in the next election.* ❑ *an area of the brain that plays a key role in voluntary movement*

PHRASAL VERB **key in** (**keys, keying, keyed**) If you **key** something **in**, you put information into a computer or you give the computer a particular instruction by typing the information or instruction on the keyboard. = type in ❑ *Brian keyed in his personal code.*

key·board /ˈkiːbɔːd/ NOUN [C] (**keyboards**) **1** The **keyboard** of a typewriter or computer is the set of keys that you press in order to operate it. ❑ *He was in his office, battering the keyboard of his computer as if it were an old manual typewriter.* **2** The **keyboard** of a piano or organ is the set of black and white keys that you press in order to play it. ❑ *Tanya's hands rippled over the keyboard.* **3** People sometimes refer to musical instruments that have a keyboard as **keyboards**. ❑ *Sean O'Hagan on keyboards*

kg ABBREVIATION **kg** is a written abbreviation for **kilogram** or **kilograms**.

kick ♦♦◇ /kɪk/ VERB, NOUN

VERB [I, T] (**kicks, kicking, kicked**) **1** [I, T] If you **kick** someone or something, you hit them forcefully with your foot. ❑ *He kicked the door hard.* ❑ *He threw me to the ground and started to kick.* **2** [T] When you **kick** a ball or other object, you hit it with your foot so that it moves through the air. ❑ *I went to kick the ball and I completely missed it.* ❑ *He kicked the ball away.* **3** [I, T] If you **kick** or if you **kick** your legs, you move your legs with very quick, small, and forceful movements, once or repeatedly. ❑ *They were dragged away struggling and kicking.* ❑ *First he kicked the left leg, then he kicked the right.* **4** [T] If you **kick** your legs, you lift your legs up very high one after the other, for example when you are dancing. ❑ *kicking his legs like a cancan dancer* **5** [T] (*informal*) If you **kick** a habit, you stop doing something that is bad for you and that you find difficult to stop doing. ❑ *She's kicked her drug habit and learned that her life has value.*

PHRASES **kick you when you are down** If you say that someone **kicks** you **when** you **are down**, you think they are behaving unfairly because they are attacking you when you are in a weak position. ❑ *In the end I just couldn't kick Jimmy when he was down.*

kicking and screaming (*emphasis*) If you say that someone is dragged **kicking and screaming into** a particular course of action, you are emphasizing that they are very unwilling to do what they are being made to do. ❑ *He had to be dragged kicking and screaming into action.*

PHRASAL VERBS **kick around** If you **kick around** ideas or suggestions, you discuss them informally. ❑ *We kicked a few ideas around.* ❑ *They started to kick around the idea of going to Brazil next month.*

kick off **1** In soccer or football, when the players **kick off**, they start a game by kicking the ball. ❑ *They kicked off an hour ago.* **2** In football, when the players **kick off**, they resume a game by kicking the ball. **3** If an event, game, series, or discussion **kicks off**, or **is kicked off**, it begins. ❑ *The shows kick off on October 24th.* ❑ *The mayor kicked off the party.* **4** If you **kick off** your shoes, you shake your feet so that your shoes come off. ❑ *She stretched out on the sofa and kicked off her shoes.* **5** (*informal*) To **kick** someone **off** an area of land means to force them to leave it. ❑ *We can't kick them off the island.*

kick out **1** Kick out means the same as **kick** VERB 3. ❑ *As its rider tried to free it, the horse kicked out and rolled over, crushing her.* **2** (*informal*) To **kick** someone **out of** a place or an organization means to force them to leave it. = throw out ❑ *The country's leaders kicked five foreign journalists out of the country.*

NOUN [C, SING] (**kicks**) **1** [C] A **kick** is a forceful hit made with the foot. ❑ *He suffered a kick to the knee.* **2** [C] A **kick** is when you hit a ball or other object with your foot so that it moves through the air. ❑ *He missed an easy kick.* **3** [SING] (*informal*) If something gives you **a kick**, it makes you feel very excited or very happy for a short period of time. ❑ *I got a kick out of seeing my name in print.*

PHRASES **for kicks** (*informal*) If you say that someone does something **for kicks**, you mean that they do it because they think it will be exciting. ❑ *They made a few small bets for kicks.*

kick in the teeth (*informal, emphasis*) If you describe an event as **a kick in the teeth**, you are emphasizing that it is very disappointing and upsetting. = setback ❑ *We've been struggling for years and it's a real kick in the teeth to see a new band make it ahead of us.*

✦ **kick up a fuss** → see **fuss**

k

kid ♦♦◇ /kɪd/ NOUN, VERB

NOUN [c] (**kids**) **1** (*informal*) You can refer to a child as a **kid**. ❏ *They've got three kids.* **2** A **kid** is a young goat.

VERB [I, T] (**kids, kidding, kidded**) **1** [I] (*informal*) If you **are kidding**, you are saying something that is not really true, as a joke. ❏ *I'm not kidding, Frank. There's a cow out there, just standing around.* ❏ *I'm just kidding.* **2** [T] If you **kid** someone, you tease them. ❏ *He liked to kid Ingrid a lot.* **3** [T] If people **kid themselves**, they allow themselves to believe something that is not true because they wish that it was true. = **fool** ❏ *We're kidding ourselves, Bill. We're not winning, we're not even doing well.*

PHRASE **you've got to be kidding** or **you must be kidding** (*informal, feelings*) You can say '**you've got to be kidding**' or '**you must be kidding**' to someone if they have said something that you think is ridiculous or completely untrue. ❏ *You've got to be kidding! I can't live here!*

kid·nap /ˈkɪdnæp/ VERB, NOUN

VERB [I, T] (**kidnaps, kidnapping, kidnapped**) To **kidnap** someone is to take them away illegally and by force, and usually to hold them prisoner in order to demand something from their family, employer, or government. ❏ *Police in Brazil uncovered a plot to kidnap him.* ❏ *They were middle-class university students, intelligent and educated, yet they chose to kidnap and kill.*

NOUN [c, u] (**kidnaps**) **Kidnap** or a **kidnap** is the crime of taking someone away by force. = **abduction** ❏ *Stewart denies attempted murder and kidnap.*

kid·nap·per /ˈkɪdnæpə/ NOUN [c] (**kidnappers**) ❏ *His kidnappers have threatened that they will kill him unless three militants are released from prison.*

kid·nap·ping /ˈkɪdnæpɪŋ/ NOUN [c, u] (**kidnappings**) ❏ *Two youngsters have been arrested and charged with kidnapping.*

kid·ney /ˈkɪdni/ NOUN [c, u] (**kidneys**) **1** [c] Your **kidneys** are the organs in your body that take waste matter from your blood and send it out of your body as urine. ❏ *a kidney transplant* **2** [c, u] **Kidneys** are the kidneys of an animal, for example a lamb, calf, or pig, that are eaten as meat. ❏ *lambs' kidneys*

kill ♦♦♦ /kɪl/ VERB, NOUN

VERB [I, T] (**kills, killing, killed**) **1** [I, T] If a person, animal, or other living thing **is killed**, something or someone causes them to die. ❏ *More than 1,000 people have been killed by the armed forces.* ❏ *He had attempted to kill himself on several occasions.* ❏ *Drugs can kill.* **2** [T] If someone or something **kills** a project, activity, or idea, they completely destroy or end it. ❏ *His objective was to kill the space station project altogether.* **3** [T] If something **kills** pain, it weakens it so that it is no longer as strong as it was. ❏ *He was forced to take opium to kill the pain.* **4** [T] (*informal*) If you say that something **is killing** you, you mean that it is causing you physical or emotional pain. ❏ *My feet are killing me.* **5** [T] (*informal, emphasis*) If you say that you **kill yourself** to do something, you are emphasizing that you make a great effort to do it, even though it causes you a lot of trouble or suffering. ❏ *I'm killing myself to get my work done.* **6** [T] If you say that you will **kill** someone for something they have done, you are emphasizing that you are extremely angry with them. ❏ *Tell Richard I'm going to kill him when I get hold of him.* **7** [T] (*informal*) If you say that something will not **kill** you, you mean that it is not really as difficult or unpleasant as it might seem. ❏ *Three or four more weeks won't kill me!* **8** [T] If you **are killing** time, you are doing something because you have some time available, not because you really want to do it. ❏ *I'm just killing time until I can talk to the other witnesses.*

PHRASES **if it kills me** (*emphasis*) If you say that you will do something **if it kills you**, you are emphasizing that you are determined to do it even though it is extremely difficult or painful. ❏ *I'll make this marriage work if it kills me.*

kill yourself laughing (*informal, emphasis*) If you say that you **killed yourself laughing**, you are emphasizing that you laughed a lot because you thought something was extremely funny. ❏ *I eventually got to the top about an hour after everyone else, and they were all killing themselves laughing.*

PHRASAL VERB **kill off** **1** Kill off means the same as kill VERB 2.

❏ *He would soon launch a second offensive, killing off the peace process.* **2** If you say that a group or an amount of something **has been killed off**, you mean that all of them or all of it have been killed or destroyed. ❏ *Their natural predators have been killed off.* ❏ *It is an effective treatment for the bacteria and does kill it off.*

NOUN [c] (**kills**) The act of killing an animal after hunting it is referred to as **the kill**. ❏ *After the kill the men and old women collect in an open space and eat a meal of whale meat.*

PHRASE **move in for the kill** or **close in for the kill** If you **move in for the kill** or if you **close in for the kill**, you take advantage of a changed situation in order to do something that you have been preparing to do. ❏ *Seeing his chance, Dennis moved in for the kill.*

✦ be killed outright → see **outright**

kill·er ♦◇◇ /ˈkɪlə/ NOUN [c] (**killers**) **1** A **killer** is a person who has killed someone, or who intends to kill someone. = **murderer** ❏ *The police are searching for his killers.* **2** You can refer to something that causes death or is likely to cause death as a **killer**. ❏ *Heart disease is the biggest killer of men in developed countries.*

kill·ing ♦◇◇ /ˈkɪlɪŋ/ NOUN

NOUN [u, c] (**killings**) **1** [u] **Killing** is the act of causing a person, animal, or other living thing to die. ❏ *There is tension in the region following the killing of seven civilians.* **2** [c] A **killing** is an act of deliberately killing a person. = **murder** ❏ *This is a brutal killing.*

PHRASE **make a killing** (*informal*) If you **make a killing**, you make a large profit very quickly and easily. ❏ *They have made a killing on the deal.*

kilo /ˈkiːləʊ/ NOUN [c] (**kilos**) A **kilo** is the same as a **kilogram**. ❏ *He'd lost ten kilos in weight.*

kilo·byte /ˈkɪləbaɪt/ NOUN [c] (**kilobytes**) In computing, a **kilobyte** is one thousand bytes of data.

WORD PARTS
The prefix **kilo-** often appears in words for things that have one thousand parts: **kilo**byte (NOUN) **kilo**gram (NOUN) **kilo**metre (NOUN)

✪ **kilo·gram** /ˈkɪləgræm/ (*in BrE, also use* **kilogramme**) NOUN [c] (**kilograms**) A **kilogram** is a metric unit of weight. One kilogram is a thousand grams, or a thousandth of a metric ton, and is equal to 2.2 pounds. = **kilo** ❏ *a parcel weighing around 4.5 kilograms* ❏ *a kilogram of butter*

✪ **kilo·gramme** /ˈkɪləgræm/ (*BrE*) → See **kilogram**

✪ **kilo·metre** /ˈkɪləˌmiːtə, kɪˈlɒmɪtə/ (*BrE; in AmE, use* **kilometer**) NOUN [c] (**kilometres**) A **kilometre** is a metric unit of distance or length. One kilometre is a thousand metres and is equal to 0.62 miles. ❏ *only one kilometre from the border* ❏ *The fire destroyed some 40,000 square kilometres of forest.* ❏ *vehicles travelling at up to 300 kilometres per hour*

✪ **kind** ♦♦♦ /kaɪnd/ NOUN, ADJ

NOUN [c] (**kinds**) **1** If you talk about a particular **kind of** thing, you are talking about one of the types or sorts of that thing. = **sort, type** ❏ *The party needs a different kind of leadership.* ❏ *Had Jamie ever been in any kind of trouble?* ❏ *the kind of person who takes advice well* ❏ *This is the biggest project of its kind in the world.* ❏ *Ear pain of any kind must never be ignored.* **2** If you refer to someone's **kind**, you are referring to all the other people that are like them or that belong to the same class or set. = **sort, type** ❏ *I can take care of your kind.*

PHRASES **all kinds of** (*emphasis*) You can use **all kinds of** to emphasize that there are a great number and variety of particular things or people. ❏ *Adoption can fail for all kinds of reasons.*

kind of (*spoken, vagueness*) You use **kind of** when you want to say that something or someone can be roughly described in a particular way. ❏ *It was kind of sad, really.*

one of a kind (*approval*) If you refer to someone or something as **one of a kind**, you mean that there is nobody or nothing else like them. ❏ *She's a very unusual woman, one of a kind.*

two of a kind or **three of a kind** or **four of a kind** If you refer, for example, to **two**, **three**, or **four of a kind**, you mean two, three, or four similar people or things that seem to go well or belong together. ❑ *They were two of a kind, from the same sort of background.*

in kind ◼ If you respond **in kind**, you react to something that someone has done to you by doing the same thing to them. ❑ *They hurled defiant taunts at the riot police, who responded in kind.* ◼ If you pay a debt **in kind**, you pay it in the form of goods or services and not money. ❑ *benefits in kind*

of a kind (*mainly BrE*) You can use **of a kind** to indicate that something is not as good as it might be expected to be, but that it seems to be the best that is possible or available. ❑ *She finds solace of a kind in alcohol.*

ADJ (**kinder**, **kindest**) ◼ Someone who is **kind** behaves in a gentle, caring, and helpful way towards other people. ❑ *I must thank you for being so kind to me.* ◼ [V-LINK + kind] You can use **kind** in expressions such as **please be so kind as to** and **would you be kind enough to** in order to ask someone to do something in a firm but polite way. ❑ *Please be so kind as to see to it that all the alterations are made at once!*

→ See also **kindly**, **kindness**

kin·der·gar·ten /ˈkɪndəɡɑːtən/ (*mainly AmE; in BrE, usually use* **nursery**) NOUN [c] (**kindergartens**) [also 'in/to/ at' kindergarten] A **kindergarten** is a school or class for children aged 4 to 6 years old. ❑ *She's in kindergarten now.*

kind·ly /ˈkaɪndli/ ADJ, ADV

ADJ A **kindly** person is kind, caring, and sympathetic. ❑ *He was a stern critic but an extremely kindly man.*

ADV ◼ [kindly after v] If you behave **kindly**, you behave in a gentle, caring, and helpful way towards other people. ❑ *'You seem tired this morning, Jenny,' she said kindly.* ◼ [kindly before v] If someone **kindly** does something for you, they act in a thoughtful and helpful way. ❑ *She kindly offered to go and fetch him some beer.* ◼ [kindly before v] (*formal*) If someone asks you to **kindly** do something, they are asking you in a way which shows that they have authority over you, or that they are angry with you. ❑ *Will you kindly obey the instructions I am about to give?*

kind·ness /ˈkaɪndnəs/ NOUN [u] **Kindness** is the quality of being gentle, caring, and helpful. ❑ *We have been treated with such kindness by everybody.*

✪ **ki·net·ic** /kɪˈnetɪk/ ADJ [usu kinetic + N] (*technical*) In physics, **kinetic** is used to describe something that is concerned with movement. ❑ *Kinetic energy is shown in body movements including growth and physical activities.* ❑ *Kinetic cues come from either your own motion or the motion of some object.*

king ◆◆◇ /kɪŋ/ NOUN [c] (**kings**) ◼ A **king** is a man who is the most important member of the royal family of his country, and who is considered to be the head of state of that country. ❑ *the king and queen of Spain* ◼ If you describe a man as **the king of** something, you mean that he is the most important person doing that thing or he is the best at doing it. ❑ *He was the king of the cowboys.* ◼ A **king** is a playing card with a picture of a king on it. ❑ *the king of diamonds* ◼ In chess, the **king** is the most important piece. When you are in a position to capture your opponent's king, you win the game.

king·dom /ˈkɪŋdəm/ NOUN [c, SING] (**kingdoms**) ◼ [c] A **kingdom** is a country or region that is ruled by a king or queen. ❑ *The kingdom's power declined.* ◼ [SING] All the animals, birds, and insects in the world can be referred to together as the animal **kingdom**. All the plants can be referred to as the plant **kingdom**. ❑ *The animal kingdom is full of fine and glorious creatures.*

kiss ◆◇◇ /kɪs/ VERB, NOUN

VERB [RECIP, T] (**kisses**, **kissing**, **kissed**) ◼ [RECIP] If you **kiss** someone, you touch them with your lips to show affection or sexual desire, or to greet them or say goodbye. ❑ *She leaned up and kissed him on the cheek.* ❑ *Her parents kissed her goodbye as she set off from their home.* ◼ [T] If you say that something **kisses** another thing, you mean that it touches that thing very gently. ❑ *The wheels of the aircraft kissed the runway.*

PHRASE **kiss something goodbye** (*informal*) If you say

that you **kiss** something **goodbye** or **kiss goodbye to** something, you accept the fact that you are going to lose it, although you do not want to. ❑ *I felt sure I'd have to kiss my dancing career goodbye.*

NOUN [c] (**kisses**) If you give someone a **kiss**, you touch them with your lips to show affection or sexual desire, or to greet them or say goodbye. ❑ *I put my arms around her and gave her a kiss.*

PHRASE **blow a kiss** or **blow someone a kiss** If you **blow** someone **a kiss** or **blow a kiss**, you touch the palm of your hand lightly with your lips, and then blow across your hand towards the person, in order to show them your affection. ❑ *Maria blew him a kiss.*

kit /kɪt/ NOUN [c, u] ◼ [c] A **kit** is a group of items that are kept together, often in the same container, because they are all used for similar purposes. ❑ *Make sure you keep a well-stocked first aid kit ready to deal with any emergency.* ◼ [c] A **kit** is a set of parts that can be put together in order to make something. ❑ *Her popular potholder is also available in do-it-yourself kits.* ◼ [u] (*mainly BrE; in AmE, usually use* **gear**) **Kit** is special clothing and equipment that you use when you take part in a particular activity, especially a sport.

kitch·en ◆◆◇ /ˈkɪtʃɪn/ NOUN [c] (**kitchens**) A **kitchen** is a room that is used for cooking and for household jobs such as washing dishes.

km (**kms**) ABBREVIATION **km** is a written abbreviation for kilometre.

knack /næk/ NOUN [c] (**knacks**) A **knack** is a particularly clever or skilful way of doing something successfully, especially something which most people find difficult. ❑ *He's got the knack of getting people to listen.*

knee ◆◇◇ /niː/ NOUN, VERB

NOUN [c, PL] (**knees**) ◼ [c] Your **knee** is the place where your leg bends. ❑ *He will receive physical therapy on his damaged left knee.* ◼ [c] If something or someone is **on** your **knee** or **on** your **knees**, they are resting or sitting on the upper part of your legs when you are sitting down. = lap ❑ *He sat with the package on his knees.* ◼ [PL] If you are **on** your **knees**, your legs are bent and your knees are on the ground. ❑ *She fell to the ground on her knees and prayed.*

PHRASE **bring to its knees** If a country or organization **is brought to its knees**, it is almost completely destroyed by someone or something. ❑ *The country was being brought to its knees by the loss of 2.4 million manufacturing jobs.*

VERB [T] (**knees**, **kneeing**, **kneed**) If you **knee** someone, you hit them using your knee. ❑ *Ian kneed him in the groin.*

kneel /niːl/ VERB

VERB [I] (**kneels**, **kneeling**, **kneeled** or **knelt**) When you **kneel**, you bend your legs so that your knees are touching the ground. ❑ *She knelt by the bed and prayed.* ❑ *Other people were kneeling, but she just sat.*

PHRASAL VERB **kneel down** Kneel down means the same as **kneel** VERB. ❑ *She kneeled down beside him.*

knew /njuː, AmE nuː/ IRREG FORM **Knew** is the past tense of **know**.

knife ◆◇◇ /naɪf/ NOUN, VERB

Knives is the plural form of the noun and **knifes** is the third person singular of the present tense of the verb.

NOUN [c] (**knives**) A **knife** is a tool for cutting or a weapon and consists of a flat piece of metal with a sharp edge on the end of a handle. ❑ *a knife and fork*

PHRASE **twist the knife** If you **twist the knife** or **twist the knife in someone's wound**, you do or say something to make an unpleasant situation they are in even more unpleasant. ❑ *Hearing his own plans was like having a knife twisted in his wound.*

VERB [T] (**knifes**, **knifing**, **knifed**) To **knife** someone means to attack and injure them with a knife. ❑ *Dawson takes revenge on the man by knifing him to death.*

knit /nɪt/ VERB, COMB

VERB [I, T] (**knits**, **knitting**, **knitted**) ◼ [I, T] If you **knit** something, especially an article of clothing, you make it from wool or a similar thread by using two knitting needles or a machine. ❑ *I had endless hours to knit and sew.* ❑ *I have already started knitting baby clothes.* **2** [T] If someone or something **knits** things or people **together**, they make them fit or work together closely and successfully. ❑ *The best thing about sports is that they knit the whole family close together.* **3** [I] When broken bones **knit**, the broken pieces grow together again. ❑ *The bone hasn't knitted together properly.*

COMB **1** [ADJ + knit + N] **Knit** is used in compound adjectives to describe the way an article of clothing is knitted. ❑ *Ferris wore a heavy knit sweater.* **2** **Knit** is also used in compound adjectives to describe the way that a group of people work together. ❑ *a closer-knit family*

knives /naɪvz/ IRREG FORM **Knives** is the plural of **knife**.

knob /nɒb/ NOUN [C] (**knobs**) **1** A **knob** is a round handle on a door or drawer which you use in order to open or close it. ❑ *He turned the knob and pushed against the door.* **2** A **knob** is a round switch on a piece of machinery or equipment. ❑ *the volume knob*

knock ♦◇◇ /nɒk/ VERB, NOUN

VERB [T, I] (**knocks, knocking, knocked**) **1** [T, I] If you **knock on** something such as a door or window, you hit it, usually several times, to attract someone's attention. ❑ *She went directly to Simon's flat and knocked on the door.* **2** [T] If you **knock** something, you touch or hit it roughly, especially so that it falls or moves. ❑ *She accidentally knocked the glass off the shelf.* **3** [T] To **knock** someone into a particular position or condition means to hit them very hard so that they fall over or become unconscious. ❑ *The third wave was so strong it knocked me backwards.* **4** [T] To **knock** a particular quality or characteristic **out of** someone means to make them lose it. ❑ *The school system is designed to knock passion out of people.* **5** [T] (informal) If you **knock** something or someone, you criticize them and say unpleasant things about them. ❑ *I'm not knocking them: if they want to do it, it's up to them.*

PHRASAL VERBS **knock around** (in BrE, also use **knock about**) **1** If someone **knocks around** somewhere, they spend time there, experiencing different situations or just passing time. ❑ *reporters who knock around in troubled parts of the world* ❑ *They knock around on weekends in grubby sweaters and trousers.* **2** (informal) If someone **knocks** you **around**, they hit or kick you several times. ❑ *He lied to me constantly and started knocking me around.*

knock down **1** To **knock down** a building or part of a building means to demolish it. = pull down ❑ *Why doesn't he just knock the wall down?* **2** (mainly AmE; in BrE, usually use **bring down**) To **knock down** a price or amount means to decrease it. ❑ *First-quarter revenue forecasts were knocked down from £23.9million to £23.7million.* **3** (mainly BrE; in AmE, usually use **hit**) If someone **is knocked down** or **is knocked over** by a vehicle or its driver, they are hit by a car and fall to the ground, and are often injured or killed. = run over ❑ *He died after being knocked down by a car.* ❑ *A drunk driver knocked down and killed two girls.* ❑ *A car knocked him over.*

knock off **1** To **knock off** an amount from a price, time, or level means to reduce it by that amount. ❑ *We have knocked 10% off admission prices.* **2** (informal) When you **knock off**, you finish work at the end of the day or before a break. ❑ *If I get this report finished I'll knock off early.*

knock out **1** To **knock** someone **out** means to cause them to become unconscious or to go to sleep. ❑ *The three drinks knocked him out.* **2** If a person or team **is knocked out** of a competition, they are defeated in a game, so that they take no more part in the competition. ❑ *He got knocked out in the first round.* **3** If something **is knocked out** by enemy action or bad weather, it is destroyed or stops functioning because of it. ❑ *Our bombers have knocked out the mobile launchers.* **4** → See also **knockout**

knock up (informal) **1** (BrE) If you **knock** something **up**, you make it or build it very quickly, using whatever materials are available. = knock together **2** (vulgar) If a woman **is knocked up** by a man, she is made pregnant by him. ❑ *When I got knocked up, the whole town knew it.*

NOUN [C] (**knocks**) **1** A **knock** is when someone hits a door or window to attract someone's attention. ❑ *They*

heard a knock at the front door.* **2** A **knock** is a firm touch that causes something to fall or move. ❑ *The bags have tough exterior materials to protect against knocks, rain, and dust.* **3** If someone receives a **knock**, they have an unpleasant experience which prevents them from achieving something or which causes them to change their attitudes or plans. = blow

knock·ing /ˈnɒkɪŋ/ NOUN [SING] [also no DET] ❑ *They were awakened by a loud knocking at the door.*

✦ **knock into shape** → see **shape**

knock·out /ˈnɒkaʊt/ also **knock-out** NOUN, ADJ

NOUN [C, SING] (**knockouts**) **1** [C] [also 'by' knockout] In boxing, a **knockout** is a situation in which a boxer wins the fight by making their opponent fall to the ground and be unable to stand up before the referee has counted to ten. ❑ *Lennox Lewis ended the scheduled 12-round fight with a knockout in the eighth round.* **2** [SING] (informal, approval) If you describe someone as a **knockout**, you think that they are extremely attractive or impressive. ❑ *Jill was a knockout with her biker leathers and t-shirt.*

ADJ **1** [knockout + N] A **knockout** blow is an action or event that completely defeats an opponent. ❑ *He delivered a knockout blow to all of his rivals.* **2** [knockout + N] (mainly BrE; in AmE, use **elimination**) A **knockout** competition is one in which the players or teams that win continue playing until there is only one winner left.

knot /nɒt/ NOUN, VERB

NOUN [C] (**knots**) **1** If you tie a **knot** in a piece of string, rope, cloth, or other material, you pass one end or part of it through a loop and pull it tight. ❑ *One lace had broken and been tied in a knot.* **2** If you feel a **knot** in your stomach, you get an uncomfortable tight feeling in your stomach, usually because you are afraid or excited. ❑ *There was a knot of tension in his stomach.* **3** A **knot** in a piece of wood is a small hard area where a branch grew. ❑ *A carpenter often rejects half his wood because of knots or cracks.* **4** A **knot** is a unit of speed. The speed of ships, aircraft, and wind is measured in knots. ❑ *They travel at speeds of up to 30 knots.*

VERB [T, I] (**knots, knotting, knotted**) **1** [T] If you **knot** a piece of string, rope, cloth, or other material, you pass one end or part of it through a loop and pull it tight. ❑ *He knotted the laces securely together.* ❑ *He knotted the bandanna around his neck.* **2** [I, T] If your stomach **knots** or if something **knots** it, it feels tight because you are afraid or excited. ❑ *I felt my stomach knot with apprehension.* **3** [I] If part of your face or your muscles **knot**, they become tense, usually because you are worried or angry. ❑ *His forehead knotted in a frown.*

know ♦♦♦ /nəʊ/ VERB

VERB [I, T] (**knows, knowing, knew, known**) **1** [I, T] If you **know** a fact, a piece of information, or an answer, you have it correctly in your mind. ❑ *I don't know the name of the place.* ❑ *'People like doing things for nothing.'—'I know they do.'* ❑ *I don't know what happened to her husband.* ❑ *'How did he meet your mother?'—'I don't know.'* **2** [T] If you **know** someone, you are familiar with them because you have met them and talked to them before. ❑ *Gifford was a friend. I'd known him for nine years.* **3** [I] If you say that you **know of** something, you mean that you have heard about it but you do not necessarily have a lot of information about it. ❑ *We know of the incident but have no further details.* ❑ *The president admitted that he did not know of any rebels having surrendered so far.* **4** [I] If you **know about** a subject, you have studied it or taken an interest in it, and understand part or all of it. ❑ *Hire someone with experience, someone who knows about property.* ❑ *She didn't know anything about music.* **5** [T] If you **know** a language, you have learned it and can understand it. ❑ *It helps to know French and Creole if you want to understand some of the lyrics.* **6** [T] If you **know** something such as a place, a work of art, or an idea, you have visited it, seen it, read it, or heard about it, and so you are familiar with it. ❑ *No matter how well you know this city, it is easy to get lost.* **7** [T] If you **know how to** do something, you have the necessary skills and knowledge to do it. ❑ *The health authorities now know how to deal with the disease.* **8** [T] You can say that someone **knows that** something is happening when they become aware of it. ❑ *Then I saw a gun under the hall table so I knew that something was wrong.* **9** [T] If you **know** something or someone, you recognize them when you see them or hear them. ❑ *Would she know you if she saw you on the street?* **10** [T] If someone or something **is known as** a particular name, they are called by that name. ❑ *The disease is more commonly known as Mad Cow Disease.* ❑ *Peter and his wife Antonella (also known as Tony)* **11** [T] If you **know** someone or something **as** a person or thing that has particular qualities, you consider that they have those qualities. ❑ *Lots of people know her as a very kind woman.*

PHRASES **as we know it** If you talk about a thing or system **as we know it**, you are referring to the form in which it exists now and which is familiar to most people. ❑ *He planned to end the welfare system as we know it.*

get to know someone If you **get to know** someone, you find out what they are like by spending time with them. ❑ *The new neighbours were getting to know each other.*

goodness knows or **Heaven knows** or **God knows** (*informal*) People use expressions such as **goodness knows**, **Heaven knows**, and **God knows** when they do not know something and want to suggest that nobody could possibly know it. ❑ *'Who's he?'—'God knows.'*

I don't know (about that) You can use **I don't know** to indicate that you do not completely agree with something or do not really think that it is true. ❑ *'He should quite simply resign.'—'I don't know about that.'*

I don't know about you You can say **'I don't know about you'** to indicate that you are going to give your own opinion about something and you want to find out if someone else feels the same. ❑ *I don't know about the rest of you, but I'm hungry.*

I don't know how or **I don't know what** (*disapproval*) You use **I don't know** in expressions which indicate criticism of someone's behaviour. For example, if you say that you **do not know how** someone can do something, you mean that you cannot understand or accept them doing it. ❑ *I don't know how he could do this to his own daughter.*

in the know If you are **in the know** about something, especially something that is not known about or understood by many people, you have information about it. ❑ *It was gratifying to be in the know about important people.*

you don't know (*spoken, emphasis*) You can say **'You don't know'** in order to emphasize how strongly you feel about the remark you are going to make. ❑ *You don't know how good it is to speak to somebody from home.*

CONVENTIONS **I know** You say **'I know'** to show that you agree with what has just been said. ❑ *'This country is so awful.'—'I know, I know.'*

you know what I mean (*spoken*) You can use expressions such as **you know what I mean** and **if you know what I mean** to suggest that the person listening to you understands what you are trying to say, and so you do not have to explain any more. ❑ *None of us stayed long. I mean, the atmosphere wasn't – well, you know what I mean.*

you never know You say **'You never know'** or **'One never knows'** to indicate that it is not definite or certain what will happen in the future, and to suggest that there is some hope that things will turn out well. ❑ *You never know, I might get lucky.*

not that I know of You say **'Not that I know of'** when someone has asked you whether or not something is true and you think the answer is 'no' but you cannot be sure because you do not know all the facts. ❑ *'Is he married?'—'Not that I know of.'*

you know (*spoken, emphasis*) You use **you know** to emphasize or to draw attention to what you are saying. ❑ *The conditions in there are awful, you know.*
→ See also **known**

✦ **know best** → see **best**; **know something for a fact** → see **fact**; **not know the first thing about something** → see **first**; **know full well** → see **full**; **let someone know** → see **let**; **know your own mind** → see **mind**; **know the ropes** → see **rope**

USAGE NOTE

get to know

You do not use 'know' without 'get to' when you are talking about developing a relationship with someone. Do not say, '~~I look forward to knowing you.~~'
*I look forward to **getting to know** you.*

---

know-how ♦◇◇ NOUN [U] (*informal*) **Know-how** is knowledge of the methods or techniques of doing something, especially something technical or practical. = expertise ❑ *He hasn't got the know-how to run a farm.*

know·ing·ly /ˈnəʊɪŋli/ ADV [knowingly before V] If you **knowingly** do something wrong, you do it even though you know it is wrong. ❑ *He repeated that he had never knowingly taken illegal drugs.*

❶ **knowl·edge** ♦♦◇ /ˈnɒlɪdʒ/ NOUN
NOUN [U] **Knowledge** is information and understanding about a subject which a person has, or which all people have. = awareness, understanding, expertise; ≠ ignorance ❑ *She disclaims any knowledge of her husband's business concerns.* ❑ *Our ancestors had a detailed knowledge of wildlife.* ❑ *the quest for scientific knowledge*
PHRASE **to the best of your knowledge** or **to (the best of) sb's knowledge** If you say that something is true to your **knowledge** or **to the best of** your **knowledge**, you mean that you believe it to be true but it is possible that you do not know all the facts. ❑ *Alec never carried a gun to my knowledge.*

USAGE NOTE

knowledge

You 'gain knowledge' or 'acquire knowledge'. Do not use '~~learn knowledge~~'.
*Children **acquire knowledge** about reading by writing.*
Knowledge is an uncountable noun. Do not use '~~a knowledge~~' or '~~knowledges~~'.

---

knowl·edge·able /ˈnɒlɪdʒəbəl/ also **knowledgable** ADJ Someone who is **knowledgeable** has or shows a clear understanding of many different facts about the world or about a particular subject. = well-informed ❑ *Do you think you are more knowledgeable about life than your parents were at your age?*

known /nəʊn/ IRREG FORM, ADJ
IRREG FORM **Known** is the past participle of **know**.
ADJ **1** You use **known** to describe someone or something that is clearly recognized by or familiar to all people or to a particular group of people. ❑ *He was a known drug dealer*
2 [V-LINK + known 'for' N/-ING] If someone or something is **known for** a particular achievement or feature, they are familiar to many people because of that achievement or feature. ❑ *He is better known for his film and TV work.*
PHRASE **let it be known** If you **let it be known that** something is the case, or you **let** something **be known**, you make sure that people know it or can find out about it. ❑ *The president has let it be known that he is against it.*

k

L l

L also **l** /el/ NOUN [C, U] (**L's, l's**) **L** is the twelfth letter of the English alphabet.

lab /læb/ NOUN [C] (**labs**) A **lab** is the same as a **laboratory**.

◆**la·bel** ◆◇◇ /'leɪbəl/ NOUN, VERB (*academic word*)
　NOUN [C] (**labels**) **1** A **label** is a piece of paper or plastic that is attached to an object in order to give information about it. ❏ *He peered at the label on the bottle.* **2** A **label** on a diagram, chart, or picture is a piece of writing that says what a part is or represents. ❏ *The pattern is obvious as we look at all of the pictures and their labels in Figure 7.3.*
　VERB [T] (**labels, labelling, labelled**; in *AmE*, use **labeling, labeled**) **1** If you **label** a diagram, chart, picture, etc, you write information saying what each part is or what each part represents. ❏ *You could be asked to label diagrams.* ❏ *There is a map, with key targets circled in red and clearly labelled.* **2** If something is **labelled**, a label is attached to it giving information about it. ❏ *It requires foreign frozen-food imports to be clearly labelled.* ❏ *The produce was labelled 'Made in China'.* **3** If you say that someone or something **is labelled as** a particular thing, you mean that people generally describe them that way, and often that you think this is unfair. = brand ❏ *It won't be labelled in any way as a military expedition.* ❏ *It does not matter whether these duties are labelled 'duties' or 'tasks'.*

◆**la·bora·tory** ◆◇◇ /lə'bɒrətri, *AmE* 'læbrətɔːri/ NOUN [C] (**laboratories**) **1** A **laboratory** is a building or a room where scientific experiments, analyses, and research are carried out. **Lab** is also used in informal and spoken English. ❏ *a brain research laboratory at Columbia University* ❏ *The two scientists tested the idea in laboratory experiments.* **2** A **laboratory** in a school, college, or university is a room containing scientific equipment where students are taught science subjects such as chemistry. ❏ *my old school chemistry laboratory*

◆**la·bour** /'leɪbə/ (*BrE*; in *AmE*, use **labor**) NOUN, VERB (*academic word*)
　NOUN [U] **1** [also **labours**] **Labour** is very hard work, usually physical work. ❏ *the labour of hauling the rocks away* **2** **Labour** is used to refer to the workers of a country or industry, considered as a group. ❏ *We have a problem of skilled labour.* ❏ *Employers want cheap labour and consumers want cheap houses.* ❏ *Immigrants arrived in the 1950s to deal with Britain's postwar labour shortages.* **3** The work done by a group of workers or by a particular worker is referred to as their **labour**. ❏ *He exhibits a profound humility in the low rates he pays himself for his labour.* **4** **Labour** is the last stage of pregnancy, in which the baby is gradually pushed out of the womb by the mother. ❏ *Her labour had lasted ten hours before the doctor arranged a Cesarean section.*
　VERB [I, T] (**labours, labouring, laboured**) **1** [I] Someone who **labours** works hard using their hands. ❏ *He will be labouring 14 hundred metres below ground.* **2** [I, T] If you **labour to** do something, you do it with difficulty. = struggle ❏ *Scientists laboured for months to unravel the mysteries of Neptune and still remain baffled.* ❏ *We're labouring under an unfair disadvantage.*

la·bour·er /'leɪbərə/ (*BrE*; in *AmE*, use **laborer**) NOUN [C] (**labourers**) A **labourer** is a person who does a job which involves a lot of hard physical work. ❏ *She still lives on the farm where he worked as a labourer.*

lace /leɪs/ NOUN, VERB
　NOUN [U, C] (**laces**) **1** [U] **Lace** is a very delicate cloth which is made with a lot of holes in it. It is made by twisting together very fine threads of cotton to form decorative patterns. ❏ *She finally found the perfect gown, a beautiful creation trimmed with lace.* **2** [C] **Laces** are thin pieces of material that are put through special holes in some types of clothing, especially shoes. The laces are tied together in order to tighten the clothing. ❏ *Barry was sitting on the bed, tying the laces of an old pair of running shoes.*
　VERB [T] (**laces, lacing, laced**) **1** If you **lace** something such as a pair of shoes, you tighten the shoes by pulling the laces through the holes, and usually tying them together. = tie ❏ *I have a good pair of skates, but no matter how tightly I lace them, my ankles wobble.* **2** To **lace** food or drink with a substance such as alcohol or a drug means to put a small amount of the substance into the food or drink. ❏ *She laced his food with sleeping pills.*
　PHRASAL VERB **lace up** Lace up means the same as **lace** VERB 1. ❏ *He sat on the steps, and laced up his boots.*

◆**lack** ◆◆◇ /læk/ NOUN, VERB
　NOUN [U] [also 'a' lack, usu lack 'of' N] If there is a **lack of** something, there is not enough of it or it does not exist at all. = shortage, absence, deficiency; ≠ abundance ❏ *Despite his lack of experience, he got the job.* ❏ *The charges were dropped due to lack of evidence.*
　PHRASE **no lack of something** (*emphasis*) If you say there is **no lack of** something, you are emphasizing that there is a great deal of it. ❏ *He said there was no lack of things for them to talk about.*
　VERB [I, T] (**lacks, lacking, lacked**) If you say that someone or something **lacks** a particular quality or that a particular quality **is lacking** in them, you mean that they do not have any or enough of it. ❏ *It lacked the power of the Italian cars.* ❏ *He lacked the judgment and political acumen for the post of chairman.* ❏ *Certain vital information is lacking in the report.*

WORD CONNECTIONS

lack + OF + NOUN

| a lack **of** experience |
| a lack **of** knowledge |
| a lack **of** interest |
| ❏ *The course was cancelled due to a lack of interest.* |

| a lack **of** resources |
| a lack **of** support |
| a lack **of** evidence |
| a lack **of** progress |
| ❏ *He was disappointed by the lack of progress.* |

| a lack **of** sleep |
| a lack **of** confidence |
| ❏ *Most parents of young babies suffer from lack of sleep.* |

ADJ + **lack**

| a complete lack |
| a total lack |
| a distinct lack |
| ❏ *There is a distinct lack of sports facilities in the area.* |

a **relative** lack
an **apparent** lack
a **perceived** lack
❏ *The major advantage of this new type of treatment is the relative lack of side effects.*

VERB + **lack**

show a lack
cite a lack
❏ *Their response showed a complete lack of understanding.*

USAGE NOTE

lack

Note that you do not say that someone or something 'lacks-of' a quality.
*The government's growth strategy **lacks** detail.*

lack·ing /ˈlækɪŋ/ ADJ [V-LINK + lacking] If something or someone **is lacking in** a particular quality, they do not have any of it or enough of it. ❏ *if your hair is lacking in lustre and feeling dry* ❏ *She felt nervous, increasingly lacking in confidence about herself.*

lack·lustre /ˈlæklʌstə/ (BrE; in AmE, use **lackluster**) ADJ If you describe something or someone as **lacklustre**, you mean that they are not exciting or energetic. ❏ *He has already been blamed for his party's lacklustre performance during the election campaign.*

lad·der /ˈlædə/ NOUN [C, SING] (ladders) **1** [C] A **ladder** is a piece of equipment used for climbing up something or down from something. It consists of two long pieces of wood, metal, or rope with steps fixed between them. ❏ *He climbed the ladder to the next deck.* **2** [SING] You can use the **ladder** to refer to something such as a society, organization, or system which has different levels that people can progress up or drop down. ❏ *If they want to climb the ladder of success they should be given that opportunity.* **3** [C] (BrE; in AmE, use **run**) A **ladder** is a hole or torn part in a woman's stocking or tights, where some of the vertical threads have broken, leaving only the horizontal threads.

lady ♦♦◊ /ˈleɪdi/ NOUN [C] (ladies) **1** You can use **lady** when you are referring to a woman, especially when you are showing politeness or respect. ❏ *She's a very sweet old lady.* ❏ *a cream-coloured lady's shoe* **2** In Britain, **Lady** is a title in front of the names of some female members of the nobility, or the wives of knights.

lag /læg/ VERB, NOUN
VERB [I] (lags, lagging, lagged) If one thing or person **lags behind** another thing or person, their progress is slower than that of the other thing or person. ❏ *Western banks still lag behind financial institutions in most other regions of the country.* ❏ *The restructuring of the pattern of consumption also lagged behind.*
NOUN [C] (lags) A time **lag** or a **lag** of a particular length of time is a period of time between one event and another related event. ❏ *There's a time lag between infection with HIV and developing AIDS.*

laid /leɪd/ IRREG FORM **Laid** is the past tense and past participle of **lay**.

lain /leɪn/ IRREG FORM **Lain** is the past participle of **lie**.

lake ♦◊◊ /leɪk/ NOUN [C] (lakes) A **lake** is a large area of fresh water, surrounded by land. ❏ *They can go fishing in the lake.*

lamb /læm/ NOUN [C, U] (lambs) **1** [C] A **lamb** is a young sheep. **2** [U] **Lamb** is the flesh of a lamb eaten as food. ❏ *Laura was basting the leg of lamb.*

lamp /læmp/ NOUN [C] (lamps) A **lamp** is a light that works by using electricity or by burning oil or gas. ❏ *She switched on the bedside lamp.*

❶**land** ♦♦♦ /lænd/ NOUN, VERB
NOUN [U, C, SING] (lands) **1** [U] **Land** is an area of ground, especially one that is used for a particular purpose such as farming or building. ❏ *Good agricultural land is in short supply.* ❏ *160 acres of land* ❏ *a small piece of grazing land* **2** [C] You can refer to an area of land which someone

owns as their **land** or their **lands**. ❏ *Their home is on his father's land.* **3** [SING] If you talk about **the land**, you mean farming and the way of life in farming areas, in contrast to life in the cities. ❏ *Living off the land was hard enough at the best of times.* **4** [U] [also 'the' land] **Land** is the part of the world that consists of ground, rather than sea or air. ❏ *It isn't clear whether the plane went down over land or sea.* ❏ *a stretch of sandy beach that was almost inaccessible from the land* **5** [C] (literary) You can use **land** to refer to a country in a poetic or emotional way. ❏ *America, land of opportunity*
VERB [I, T] (lands, landing, landed) **1** [I] When someone or something **lands**, they come down to the ground after moving through the air or falling. ❏ *He was sent flying into the air and landed 20 feet away.* **2** [I, T] When someone **lands** a plane, ship, or spacecraft, or when it **lands**, it arrives somewhere after a journey. ❏ *The jet landed after a flight of just under three hours.* ❏ *He landed his troops on the western shore.* **3** [I, T] (informal) If you **land** in an unpleasant situation or place or if something **lands** you **in** it, something causes you to be in it. ❏ *He landed in a psychiatric ward.* **4** [I] (informal) If something **lands** somewhere, it arrives there unexpectedly, often causing problems. = **arrive** ❏ *Two days later the book had already landed on his desk.*
✦ **land on your feet** → see **foot**

❶**land·fill** /ˈlændfɪl/ NOUN [U] (landfills) **1** [U] **Landfill** is a method of getting rid of very large amounts of rubbish by burying it in a large deep hole. ❏ *the environmental costs of landfill* ❏ *There are serious scientific issues involved in the debate over landfill sites and global warming.* **2** [C] A **landfill** is a large deep hole in which very large amounts of rubbish are buried. ❏ *The rubbish in modern landfills does not rot.*

land·ing /ˈlændɪŋ/ NOUN [C, U] (landings) **1** [C] In a house or other building, the **landing** is the area at the top of the staircase which has rooms leading off it. ❏ *I ran out onto the landing.* **2** [C, U] A **landing** is an act of bringing an aircraft or spacecraft down to the ground. ❏ *I had to make a controlled landing into the sea.* **3** [C] When a **landing** takes place, troops are unloaded from boats or aircraft at the beginning of a military invasion or other operation. ❏ *American forces have begun a big landing.*

land·lord /ˈlændlɔːd/ NOUN [C] (landlords) Someone's **landlord** is the man who allows them to live or work in a building which he owns, in return for rent. ❏ *His landlord doubled the rent.*

❶**land·mark** /ˈlændmɑːk/ NOUN [C] (landmarks) **1** A **landmark** is a building or feature which is easily noticed and can be used to judge your position or the position of other buildings or features. ❏ *The Menger Hotel is a San Antonio landmark.* ❏ *The building, designated a historic landmark by the city, now houses apartments and a laundry business.* **2** You can refer to an important stage in the development of something as a **landmark**. = **milestone, watershed** ❏ *a landmark arms control treaty* ❏ *In a landmark decision, the council of the Law Society voted to dismantle its present governing body.*

❶**land·scape** ♦◊◊ /ˈlændskeɪp/ NOUN, VERB
NOUN [U, C] (landscapes) **1** [U, C] The **landscape** is everything you can see when you look across an area of land, including hills, rivers, buildings, trees, and plants. = **scenery** ❏ *Arizona's desert landscape* ❏ *We moved to Northamptonshire and a new landscape of hedges and fields.* **2** [C] A **landscape** is all the features that are important in a particular situation. ❏ *June's events completely altered the political landscape.* **3** [C] A **landscape** is a painting which shows a scene in the countryside. ❏ *Kenna's latest series of landscapes is on show at the Zelda Cheatle Gallery.* **4** [U] [oft landscape + N] If a sheet of paper is in **landscape** format or mode, the longer edge of the paper is horizontal and the shorter edge is vertical. ❏ *Most powerpoint presentations are prepared for screens in landscape format.*
VERB [T] (landscapes, landscaping, landscaped) If an area of land **is landscaped**, it is changed to make it more attractive, for example, by adding streams or ponds and planting trees and bushes. ❏ *The gravel pits have been landscaped and planted to make them attractive to wildfowl.*

❏ *They had landscaped their property with trees, shrubs, and lawns.*

land·scap·ing /ˈlændskeɪpɪŋ/ NOUN [U] ❏ *The landowner insisted on a high standard of landscaping.*

lane ◆◇◇ /leɪn/ NOUN [C] (**lanes**) **1** A **lane** is a narrow road, especially in the country. ❏ *a quiet country lane* **2** **Lane** is also used in the names of roads, either in cities or in the country. ❏ *They had a house on Spring Park Lane in East Hampton.* **3** A **lane** is a part of a main road which is marked by the edge of the road and a painted line, or by two painted lines. ❏ *The lorry was travelling at 20 mph in the slow lane.* **4** At a swimming pool, athletics track, or bowling alley, a **lane** is a long narrow section which is separated from other sections, for example by lines or ropes. ❏ *after being disqualified for running out of his lane in the 200 metres* **5** A **lane** is a route that is frequently used by aircraft or ships. ❏ *The collision took place in one of the busiest shipping lanes in the world.*

❖**lan·guage** ◆◆◇ /ˈlæŋgwɪdʒ/ NOUN [C, U] (**languages**) **1** [C] A **language** is a system of communication which consists of a set of sounds and written symbols which are used by the people of a particular country or region for talking or writing. ❏ *the English language* ❏ *Students are expected to master a second language.* **2** [U] **Language** is the use of a system of communication which consists of a set of sounds or written symbols. ❏ *Students examined how children acquire language.* **3** [U] You can refer to the words used in connection with a particular subject as **the language of** that subject. ❏ *the language of business* **4** [U] You can refer to someone's use of rude words or swearing as **bad language** when you find it offensive. ❏ *Television companies tend to censor bad language in feature films.* **5** [U] The **language** of a piece of writing or speech is the style in which it is written or spoken. ❏ *a booklet summarizing it in plain language* ❏ *The tone of his language was diplomatic and polite.* **6** [C, U] You can use **language** to refer to various means of communication involving recognizable symbols, non-verbal sounds, or actions. ❏ *Some sign languages are very sophisticated means of communication.* ❏ *the digital language of computers*

lap ◆◇◇ /læp/ NOUN, VERB
NOUN [C] (**laps**) **1** If you have something on your **lap** when you are sitting down, it is on top of your legs and near to your body. ❏ *She waited quietly with her hands in her lap.* **2** In a race, a competitor completes a **lap** when they have gone around a course once. ❏ *that last lap of the race* **3** A **lap** of a long journey is one part of it, between two points where you stop. = leg ❏ *I had thought we might travel as far as Oak Valley, but we only managed the first lap of the journey.*
VERB [I, T] (**laps, lapping, lapped**) **1** [I, T] In a race, if you **lap** another competitor, you go past them while they are still on the previous lap. ❏ *He then built a 10-bike lead before lapping his first rider on lap 14.* **2** [I] (*written*) When water **laps** against something such as the shore or the side of a boat, it touches it gently and makes a soft sound. ❏ *the water that lapped against the pillars of the boathouse* ❏ *With a rising tide the water was lapping at his chin before rescuers arrived.* **3** [T] When an animal **laps** a drink, it uses short quick movements of its tongue to take liquid up into its mouth. ❏ *It lapped milk from a dish.*
PHRASAL VERB **lap up** **1** Lap up means the same as lap VERB 3. ❏ *She poured some water into a plastic bowl. Faust, her Great Dane, lapped it up with relish.* **2** If you say that someone **laps up** something such as information or attention, you mean that they accept it eagerly, usually when you think they are being foolish for believing that it is sincere. ❏ *Their audience will lap up whatever they throw at them.*

lap·ping /ˈlæpɪŋ/ NOUN [U] ❏ *The only sound was the lapping of the waves.*

lapse /læps/ NOUN, VERB
NOUN [C, SING] (**lapses**) **1** [C] A **lapse** is a moment or instance of bad behaviour by someone who usually behaves well. ❏ *On Friday he showed neither decency nor dignity. It was an uncommon lapse.* **2** [C] A **lapse of** something such as concentration or judgment is a

temporary lack of that thing, which can often cause you to make a mistake. ❏ *I had a little lapse of concentration in the middle of the race.* ❏ *He was a genius and because of it you could accept lapses of taste.* **3** [C] A **lapse** into a particular way of speaking or behaving happens when someone starts speaking or behaving in that way, usually for a short period. ❏ *Her lapse into German didn't seem peculiar. After all, it was her native tongue.* **4** [SING] A **lapse of** time is a period that is long enough for a situation to change or for people to have a different opinion about it. ❏ *the restoration of diplomatic relations after a lapse of 24 years*
VERB [I] (**lapses, lapsing, lapsed**) **1** If you **lapse into** a quiet or inactive state, you stop talking or being active. ❏ *She muttered something unintelligible and lapsed into silence.* **2** If someone **lapses into** a particular way of speaking or behaving, they start speaking or behaving in that way, usually for a short period. = slip ❏ *She lapsed into a little girl voice to deliver a nursery rhyme.* **3** If a period of time **lapses**, it passes. ❏ *New products and production processes are transferred to the developing countries only after a substantial amount of time has lapsed.* **4** If a situation or legal contract **lapses**, it is allowed to end rather than being continued, renewed, or extended. ❏ *The terms of the treaty lapsed in 1987.* **5** If a member of a particular religion **lapses**, they stop believing in it or stop following its rules and practices. ❏ *I lapsed in my 20s, returned to it, then lapsed again, while writing the life of historical Jesus.*

lap·top /ˈlæptɒp/ NOUN [C] (**laptops**) A **laptop** or a **laptop computer** is a small portable computer. ❏ *She used to work at her laptop until four in the morning.*

large ◆◆◆ /lɑːdʒ/ ADJ
ADJ (**larger, largest**) **1** A **large** thing or person is greater in size than usual or average. = big ❏ *The pike lives mainly in large rivers and lakes.* ❏ *In the largest room about a dozen children and seven adults are sitting on the carpet.* **2** A **large** amount or number of people or things is more than the average amount or number. ❏ *The gang finally fled with a large amount of cash and jewellery.* ❏ *There are a large number of centres where you can take full-time courses.* **3** **Large** is used to indicate that a problem or issue which is being discussed is very important or serious. = serious ❏ *the already large problem of under-age drinking*
PHRASE **at large** **1** You use **at large** to indicate that you are talking in a general way about most of the people mentioned. ❏ *I think the chances of getting reforms accepted by the community at large remain extremely remote.* **2** If you say that a dangerous person, thing, or animal is **at large**, you mean that they have not been captured or made safe. = free ❏ *The man who tried to have her killed is still at large.*
✦ **to a large extent** → see extent

❖**large·ly** ◆◆◇ /ˈlɑːdʒli/ ADV **1** You use **largely** to say that a statement is not completely true but is mostly true. = mainly ❏ *The fund is largely financed through government borrowing.* ❏ *I largely work with people who already are motivated.* **2** [largely + PREP] **Largely** is used to introduce the main reason for a particular event or situation. = mainly, mostly ❏ *Retail sales dipped 6/10ths of a per cent last month, largely because Americans were buying fewer cars.* ❏ *The French empire had expanded, largely through military conquest.*

large-scale also **large scale** ADJ **1** [large-scale + N] A **large-scale** action or event happens over a very wide area or involves a lot of people or things. ❏ *a large scale military operation* **2** [large-scale + N] A **large-scale** map or diagram represents a small area of land or a building or machine on a scale that is large enough for small details to be shown. ❏ *a large-scale map of the county*

❖**lar·va** /ˈlɑːvə/ NOUN [C] (**larvae**) A **larva** is an insect at the stage of its life after it has developed from an egg and before it changes into its adult form. ❏ *The eggs quickly hatch into larvae.* ❏ *Moth larvae spin a thread and use wind currents to float from tree to tree.*

❖**la·ser** /ˈleɪzə/ NOUN [C] (**lasers**) A **laser** is a narrow beam of concentrated light produced by a special machine. It is used for cutting very hard materials, and in many technical fields such as surgery and telecommunications. ❏ *new laser technology* ❏ *Therapies currently under*

L

investigation include laser surgery and bone-marrow transplants. ❑ Researchers realized that a tunable laser beam might be useful in surgery.

lash /læʃ/ NOUN, VERB

NOUN [c] (**lashes**) **1** Your **lashes** are the hairs that grow on the edge of your upper and lower eyelids. = eyelash ❑ sombre grey eyes, with unusually long lashes **2** A **lash** is a blow with a whip, especially a blow on someone's back as a punishment. ❑ The villagers sentenced one man to five lashes for stealing a ham from his neighbour.

VERB [T, I] (**lashes, lashing, lashed**) **1** [T] If you **lash** two or more things together, you tie one of them firmly to the other. = tie ❑ Secure the anchor by lashing it to the rail. ❑ The shelter is built by lashing poles together to form a small dome. **2** [I, T] (written) If wind, rain, or water **lashes** someone or something, it hits them violently. ❑ The worst winter storms of the century lashed the east coast of North America. **3** [I, T] If someone **lashes** you or **lashes into** you, they speak very angrily to you, criticizing you or saying you have done something wrong. ❑ She went quiet for a moment while she summoned up the words to lash him.

PHRASAL VERB **lash out** **1** If you **lash out**, you attempt to hit someone quickly and violently with a weapon or with your hands or feet. ❑ Riot police fired in the air and lashed out with clubs to disperse hundreds of demonstrators. **2** If you **lash out** at someone or something, you speak to them or about them very angrily or critically. ❑ As a politician Jefferson frequently lashed out at the press.

last ♦♦♦ /lɑːst, læst/ DET, ADJ, PRON, ADV, NOUN, VERB

DET You use **last** in expressions such as **last Friday, last night**, and **last year** to refer, for example, to the most recent Friday, night, or year. ❑ I got married last July. ❑ He never made it home at all last night.

ADJ **1** [DET + last] The **last** event, person, thing, or period of time is the most recent one. ❑ Much has changed since my last visit. ❑ I split up with my last boyfriend three years ago. **2** [DET + last] **Last** is used to refer to the only thing, person, or part of something that remains. ❑ Jed nodded, finishing off the last piece of pizza. **3** [DET + last] You can use **last** to indicate that something is extremely undesirable or unlikely. ❑ The last thing I wanted to do was teach. **4** The **last** thing, person, event, or period of time is the one that happens or comes after all the others of the same kind. ❑ the last three pages of the chapter

PRON **1** The **last** is the most recent event, person, thing, or period of time. ❑ The next tide, it was announced, would be even higher than the last. **2** The **last** refers to the thing, person, event, or period of time that happens or comes after all the others of the same kind. ❑ It wasn't the first time that this particular difference had divided them and it wouldn't be the last. **3** [last + to-INF] If you are the **last to** do or know something, everyone else does or knows it before you. ❑ She was the last to go to bed. **4** [last + to-INF] You can use **the last** to indicate that something is extremely undesirable or unlikely. ❑ I would be the last to say that science has explained everything. **5** ['the' last 'that'] **The last** you see of someone or **the last** you hear of them is the final time that you see them or talk to them. ❑ She disappeared shouting, 'To the river, to the river!' And that was the last we saw of her.

ADV **1** [last with V] If something **last** happened on a particular occasion, that is the most recent occasion on which it happened. ❑ When were you there last? ❑ The house is a little more dilapidated than when I last saw it. **2** [last after V] If you do something **last**, you do it after everyone else does, or after you do everything else. ❑ I testified last. ❑ I was always picked last for the football team at school.

PHRASE **leave something until last** If you **leave** something or someone **until last**, you delay using, choosing, or dealing with them until you have used, chosen, or dealt with all the others. ❑ I have left my best wine until last.

NOUN [SING] The **last of** something is only person or part of it that remains. ❑ He finished off the last of the wine.

PHRASES **at last** or **at long last** If you say that something has happened **at last** or **at long last** you mean it has happened after you have been hoping for it for a long

time. = finally ❑ I'm so glad that we've found you at last! ❑ Here, at long last, was the moment he had waited for.

the something before last You use expressions such as **the night before last, the election before last**, and **the leader before last** to refer to the period of time, event, or person that came immediately before the most recent one in a series. ❑ It was the dog he'd heard the night before last.

the last someone heard You can use expressions such as **the last I heard** and **the last she heard** to introduce a piece of information that is the most recent that you have on a particular subject. ❑ The last I heard, Joe and Irene were still happily married.

VERB [I, T] (**lasts, lasting, lasted**) **1** If an event, situation, or problem **lasts** for a particular length of time, it continues to exist or happen for that length of time. ❑ The marriage had lasted for less than two years. ❑ The games lasted only half the normal time. **2** If something **lasts** for a particular length of time, it continues to be able to be used for that time, for example, because there is some of it left or because it is in good enough condition. ❑ You only need a very small blob of glue, so one tube lasts for ages. ❑ The repaired sail lasted less than 24 hours.

→ See also **lasting**
✦ **the last straw** → see straw; **last thing** → see thing

last·ing /'lɑːstɪŋ, 'læst-/ ADJ You can use **lasting** to describe a situation, result, or agreement that continues to exist or have an effect for a very long time. ❑ We are well on our way to a lasting peace.

→ See also **last**

last·ly /'lɑːstli, 'læst-/ ADV **1** [lastly with CL/GROUP] You use **lastly** when you want to make a final point, ask a final question, or mention a final item that is connected with the other ones you have already asked or mentioned. = finally ❑ Lastly, I would like to ask about your future plans. **2** [lastly + CL] You use **lastly** when you are saying what happens after everything else in a series of actions or events. = finally ❑ They wash their hands, arms and faces, and lastly, they wash their feet.

last-minute → See minute

late ♦♦♦ /leɪt/ ADV, ADJ

ADV (**later, latest**) **1** **Late** means near the end of a day, week, year, or other period of time. ❑ It was late in the afternoon. ❑ His autobiography was written late in life. **2** **Late** means after the time that was arranged or expected. ❑ Steve arrived late. ❑ The talks began some fifteen minutes late. **3** [late after V] **Late** means after the usual time that a particular event or activity happens. ❑ We went to bed very late.

PHRASE **too late** If an action or event is **too late**, it is useless or ineffective because it occurs after the best time for it. ❑ It was too late to turn back.

ADJ (**later, latest**) **1** [late + N] **Late** means near the end of a day, week, year, or other period of time. ❑ The talks eventually broke down in late spring. ❑ He was in his late 20s. **2** [V-LINK + late] If it is **late**, it is near the end of the day or it is past the time that you feel something should have been done. ❑ It was very late and the streets were deserted. **3** **Late** means after the time that was arranged or expected. ❑ His campaign got off to a late start. ❑ The train was 40 minutes late. **4** [late + N] **Late** means after the usual time that a particular event or activity happens. ❑ They had a late lunch in a café. **5** [DET + late] You use **late** when you are talking about someone who is dead, especially someone who has died recently. ❑ my late husband

late·ness /'leɪtnəs/ NOUN [U] **1** A large crowd had gathered despite the lateness of the hour. **2** He apologized for his lateness.

→ See also **later, latest**
✦ **a late night** → see night

late·ly /'leɪtli/ ADV You use **lately** to describe events in the recent past, or situations that started a short time ago. = recently ❑ Dad's health hasn't been too good lately. ❑ 'Have you talked to her lately?' – 'Not lately, really.'

lat·er ♦♦♦ /'leɪtə/ ADV, ADJ

ADV **1** **Later** is the comparative of **late**. **2** You use **later** to refer to a time or situation that is after the one that you have been talking about or after the present one. ❑ He resigned ten years later.

PHRASE **later on** You use **later on** to refer to a time or situation that is after the one that you have been talking about or after the present one. ❑ *Later on I'll be speaking to Patty Davis.*

ADJ **1** **Later** is the comparative of **late**. **2** [later + N, 'the' later, 'the' later 'of' N] You use **later** to refer to an event, period of time, or other thing which comes after the one that you have been talking about or after the present one. ❑ *At a later news conference, he said differences should not be dramatized.* ❑ *The competition should have been re-scheduled for a later date.* **3** You use **later** to refer to the last part of someone's life or career or the last part of a period of history. ❑ *He found happiness in later life.* ❑ *the later part of the 20th century*
→ See also **late**

lat•er•al /ˈlætərəl/ ADJ Lateral means relating to the sides of something, or moving in a sideways direction. ❑ *McKinnon estimated the lateral movement of the bridge to be between four and six inches.*

lat•est ◆◇ /ˈleɪtɪst/ ADJ
ADJ **1** **Latest** is the superlative of **late**. **2** You use **latest** to describe something that is the most recent thing of its kind. ❑ *her latest book* **3** You can use **latest** to describe something that is very new and modern and is better than older things of a similar kind. ❑ *Crooks are using the latest laser photocopiers to produce millions of fake banknotes.* ❑ *I got to drive the latest model.*

PHRASE **at the latest** (*emphasis*) You use **at the latest** in order to indicate that something must happen at or before a particular time and not after that time. ❑ *She should be back by ten o'clock at the latest.*
→ See also **late**

Lat•in ◆◇◇ /ˈlætɪn/ NOUN, ADJ
NOUN [U] **Latin** is the language which the ancient Romans used to speak.
ADJ **Latin** countries are countries where Spanish, or perhaps Portuguese, Italian, or French, is spoken. You can also use **Latin** to refer to things and people that come from these countries. ❑ *Cuba was one of the least Catholic of the Latin countries.*

❖**lati•tude** /ˈlætɪtjuːd, AmE -tuːd/ NOUN, ADJ
NOUN [C, U] (**latitudes**) **1** [C, U] The **latitude** of a place is its distance from the equator. Compare **longitude**. ❑ *In the middle to high latitudes rainfall has risen steadily over the last 20-30 years.* ❑ *Vitamin D deficiency is widespread in the country, not just at northern latitudes.* **2** [U] (*formal*) **Latitude** is freedom to choose the way in which you do something. ❑ *He would be given every latitude in forming a new government.*
ADJ **Latitude** describes the distance of a place from the equator. ❑ *The army must cease military operations above 36° latitude north.*

❖**lat•ter** ◆◇◇ /ˈlætə/ PRON, ADJ
PRON ['the' latter] When two people, things, or groups have just been mentioned, you can refer to the second of them as **the latter**. ❑ *He tracked down his cousin and uncle. The latter was sick.* ❑ *At school, he enjoyed football and boxing; the latter remained a lifelong habit.* ❑ *without hesitation they chose the latter*
ADJ **1** [latter + N] You use **latter** to describe the second of two people, things, or groups that have just been mentioned. ≠ **former** ❑ *There are the people who speak after they think and the people who think while they're speaking. Mike definitely belongs in the latter category.* ❑ *Private share holdings exist in the UK, Italy and Portugal and plans are underway to increase the level of private investment in the latter two countries.* ❑ *Adrienne heard nothing of the latter part of this speech.* **2** [latter + N] You use **latter** to describe the later part of a period of time or event. = **later** ❑ *He is getting into the latter years of his career.*

USAGE NOTE

latter

When 'the latter' is used as a pronoun, it is not followed by 'one'. Do not say ~~the latter one~~.
*She used both systems but felt that **the latter** was more suitable.*

laugh ◆◆◆ /lɑːf, læf/ VERB, NOUN
VERB [I, T] (**laughs, laughing, laughed**) **1** [I, T] When you **laugh**, you make a sound with your throat while smiling and show that you are happy or amused. People also sometimes laugh when they feel nervous or are being unfriendly. ❑ *He was about to offer an explanation, but she was beginning to laugh.* ❑ *I just couldn't laugh at his jokes the way I used to.* ❑ *'We could do with some help from our friends,' he laughed.* **2** [I] If people **laugh at** someone or something, they mock them or make jokes about them. ❑ *I thought they were laughing at me because I was ugly.*
PHRASAL VERB **laugh off** If you **laugh off** a difficult or serious situation, you try to suggest that it is amusing and unimportant, for example, by making a joke about it. ❑ *Frank tried to laugh off his aunt's worry.*
NOUN [C] (**laughs**) A **laugh** is the act or sound of laughing. ❑ *Lysenko gave a deep rumbling laugh at his own joke.*
PHRASES **for a laugh** or **for laughs** If you do something **for a laugh** or **for laughs**, you do it as a joke or for fun. ❑ *They were persuaded onstage for a laugh.*
a laugh or **a good laugh** or **a bit of a laugh** (*informal*) If you describe a situation as **a laugh** or **a good laugh**, you think that it is fun and do not take it too seriously. ❑ *Working there's great. It's a good laugh.*

laugh•ter ◆◇◇ /ˈlɑːftə, ˈlæf-/ NOUN [U] **Laughter** is the sound of people laughing, for example, because they are amused or happy. ❑ *Their laughter filled the corridor.* ❑ *He delivered the line perfectly, and everybody roared with laughter.*

❖**launch** ◆◆◇ /lɔːntʃ/ VERB, NOUN
VERB [T] (**launches, launching, launched**) **1** To **launch** a rocket, missile, or satellite means to send it into the air or into space. ❑ *NASA plans to launch a satellite to study cosmic rays.* **2** To **launch** a ship or a boat means to put it into water, often for the first time after it has been built. ❑ *There was no time to launch the lifeboats because the ferry capsized with such alarming speed.* **3** To **launch** a large and important activity, for example, a military attack, means to start it. ❑ *A group of 80 attackers launched an all-out assault just before dawn.* ❑ *The police have launched an investigation into the incident.* **4** If a company **launches** a new product, it makes it available to the public. = **unveil** ❑ *powerful allies to help the company launch a low-cost network computer* ❑ *Crabtree & Evelyn has just launched a new jam, Worcesterberry Preserve.* ❑ *Marks & Spencer hired model Linda Evangelista to launch its new range.*
PHRASAL VERB **launch into** If you **launch into** something such as a speech, task, or fight, you enthusiastically start it. ❑ *Horrigan launched into a speech about the importance of new projects.*
NOUN [C, U] (**launches**) **1** [C, U] The **launch** of a rocket, missile, or satellite is the act of sending it into the air or into space. ❑ *This morning's launch of the space shuttle Columbia has been delayed.* **2** [C] The **launch** of a ship or a boat is the act of putting it into water, often for the first time after it has been built. ❑ *The launch of a ship was a big occasion.* **3** [C] The **launch** of a large and important activity, for example a military attack, is the act of starting it. ❑ *the launch of a campaign to restore law and order* **4** [C] The **launch** of a new product is the time when a company starts to make it available to the public. ❑ *The company's spending has also risen following the launch of a new Sunday magazine.* ❑ *legal wrangling threatens to delay the launch of the product*

USAGE NOTE

launch

Don't use **launch** to talk about starting up a new organization or system. Use 'form' or 'establish'.
*The seven airlines **formed** a consortium.*
*They **established** the current system in the 1970s.*

laun•dry /ˈlɔːndri/ NOUN [U, C] (**laundries**) **1** [U] **Laundry** is used to refer to clothes, sheets, and towels that are about to be washed, are being washed, or have just been washed. = **washing** ❑ *I'll do your laundry.* ❑ *the room where I hang the laundry* **2** [C] A **laundry** is a business that washes and irons clothes, sheets, and towels for people. ❑ *We had to*

WORDS IN CONTEXT: LAW

Although a prison sentence is a punishment for committing a crime, the aim should principally be to rehabilitate the offender.

To what extent do you agree or disagree?

It is an unfortunate fact of life that a significant minority of people in any society will end up being **sent to prison** as a result of being **convicted of a criminal offence**. It is the duty of our **legal system** to protect us all in **the fight against crime**. As well as **acting as a deterrent**, a **custodial sentence** is seen by most people as a justifiable way of punishing those who **break the law**: if you **commit a crime**, you should be prepared to **face the consequences** of your actions.

However, the majority of those facing **imprisonment** will receive a short **sentence**. Having been **released**, they will be back on the streets, free to **commit further offences**, unless they can be persuaded to **change their ways**. Consequently, prison cannot simply be a form of **punishment**, but it must also give an **offender** the chance to be **rehabilitated** into society. The time spent **in custody** should be a period when they can reflect on their actions and the impact they have on others.

In conclusion, it is important that the **victims** of crime see that offenders are **prosecuted** and punished. However, those with a **criminal record** and a lifetime ahead of them deserve **a second chance**. Society does not benefit from having people **arrested** again and again, and the long-term aim must be to try to make them **law-abiding citizens**.

---

have the washing done at the laundry. **3** [C] A **laundry** or a **laundry room** is a room in a house, hotel, or institution where clothes, sheets, and towels are washed. ❑ *He worked in the laundry at Oxford prison.*

lav·ish /ˈlævɪʃ/ ADJ, VERB

ADJ **1** If you describe something as **lavish**, you mean that it is very elaborate and impressive and a lot of money has been spent on it. ❑ *a lavish party to celebrate Bryan's fiftieth birthday* ❑ *He staged the most lavish productions of Mozart.* **2** If you say that spending, praise, or the use of something is **lavish**, you mean that someone spends a lot or that something is praised or used a lot. = extravagant ❑ *Critics attack his lavish spending and flamboyant style.* **3** If you say that someone is **lavish** in the way they behave, you mean that they give, spend, or use a lot of something. ❑ *Reviewers are lavish in their praise of this book.*

VERB [T] (**lavishes, lavishing, lavished**) If you **lavish** money, affection, or praise **on** someone or something, you spend a lot of money on them or give them a lot of affection or praise. ❑ *He lavished praise on his opponents.*

lav·ish·ly /ˈlævɪʃli/ ADV **1** [lavishly with V] ❑ *The apartment building was lavishly decorated.* **2** [lavishly with V] ❑ *Entertaining in style needn't mean spending lavishly.*

◆ **law** ♦♦♦ /lɔː/ NOUN

NOUN [SING, U, C, PL] (**laws**) **1** [SING] **The law** is a system of rules that a society or government develops in order to deal with crime, business agreements, and social relationships. You can also use **the law** to refer to the people who work in this system. ❑ *Obscene and threatening phone calls are against the law.* ❑ *They are beginning criminal proceedings against him for breaking the law on financing political parties.* ❑ *The book analyses why women kill and how the law treats them.* **2** [U] **Law** is used to refer to a particular branch of the law, such as **criminal law** or **business law**. ❑ *He was a professor of criminal law at Harvard University law school.* ❑ *Under international law, diplomats living in foreign countries are exempt from criminal prosecution.* **3** [C] A **law** is one of the rules in a system of law which deals with a particular type of agreement, relationship, or crime. = rule, regulation ❑ *the country's liberal political asylum law* ❑ *The law was passed on a second vote.* **4** [PL] **The laws of** an organization or activity are its rules, which are used to organize and control it. = rule ❑ *the laws of the Catholic Church* **5** [C] A **law** is a rule or set of rules for good behaviour which is considered right and important by the majority of people for moral, religious, or emotional reasons. = code ❑ *inflexible moral laws* **6** [C] A **law** is a natural process in which a particular event or thing always leads

to a particular result. ❑ *The laws of nature are absolute.* **7** [C] A **law** is a scientific rule that someone has invented to explain a particular natural process. = principle ❑ *the law of gravity* ❑ *Newton's laws of motion* ❑ *the laws of physics* **8** [U] **Law** or **the law** is all the professions which deal with advising people about the law, representing people in court, or giving decisions and punishments. ❑ *A career in law is becoming increasingly attractive to young people.* **9** [U] **Law** is the study of systems of law and how laws work. ❑ *He studied law.* ❑ *He holds a law degree from Bristol University.*

PHRASES **above the law** (*disapproval*) If you accuse someone of thinking they are **above the law**, you criticize them for thinking that they are so clever or important that they do not need to obey the law. ❑ *He accuses the government of wanting to be above the law.*

by law If you have to do something **by law** or if you are not allowed to do something **by law**, the law states that you have to do it or that you are not allowed to do it. ❑ *By law all restaurants must display their prices outside.*

law and or·der NOUN [U] When there is **law and order** in a country, the laws are generally accepted and obeyed, so that society there functions normally. ❑ *If there were a breakdown of law and order, the army might be tempted to intervene.*

lawn /lɔːn/ NOUN [C, U] (**lawns**) A **lawn** is an area of grass that is kept cut short and is usually part of someone's garden, or part of a park. ❑ *They were sitting on the lawn under a large beech tree.*

◆ **law·suit** ♦♦◇ /ˈlɔːsuːt/ NOUN [C] (**lawsuits**) (*formal*) A **lawsuit** is a case in a court of law which concerns a dispute between two people or organizations. = case, action, litigation ❑ *The dispute culminated last week in a lawsuit against the government.* ❑ *a lawsuit brought by Barclays Bank*

◆ **law·yer** ♦♦◇ /ˈlɔɪə/ NOUN [C] (**lawyers**) A **lawyer** is a person who is qualified to advise people about the law and represent them in court. = attorney, barrister ❑ *Prosecution and defence lawyers are expected to deliver closing arguments next week.*

lax /læks/ ADJ (**laxer, laxest**) If you say that a person's behaviour or a system is **lax**, you mean they are not careful or strict about maintaining high standards. ❑ *One of the problem areas is lax security for airport personnel.* ❑ *There have been allegations from survivors that safety standards had been lax.*

lax·ity /ˈlæksɪti/ NOUN [U] ❑ *The laxity of export control authorities has made a significant contribution to the problem.*

lay ♦♦◇ /leɪ/ VERB, ADJ

VERB [T, I] (**lays, laying, laid**) **1** [T] If you **lay** something somewhere, you put it there in a careful, gentle, or neat way. ❑ *Lay a sheet of newspaper on the floor.* ❑ *Mothers routinely lay babies on their backs to sleep.* **2** [T] If you **lay** something such as carpets, cables, or foundations, you put them into their permanent position. ❑ *A man came to lay the carpet.* **3** [I, T] When a female bird **lays**, or **lays** an egg, it produces an egg by pushing it out of its body. ❑ *My canary has laid an egg.* **4** [T] **Lay** is used with some nouns to talk about making official preparations for something. For example, if you **lay the basis** for something or **lay plans** for it, you prepare it carefully. ❑ *Diplomats meeting in Chile have laid the groundwork for far-reaching environmental regulations.* **5** [T] **Lay** is used with some nouns in expressions about accusing or blaming someone. For example, if you **lay the blame** for a mistake on someone, you say it is their fault, or if the police **lay charges** against someone, they officially accuse that person of a crime. ❑ *She refused to lay the blame on any one party.* **6** [T] (*old-fashioned*) If you **lay** the table or **lay** the places at a table, you arrange the knives, forks, and other things that people need on the table before a meal. ❑ *The butler always laid the table.*

PHRASAL VERBS **lay aside** **1** If you **lay aside** a feeling or belief, you reject it or give it up in order to progress with something. = put aside ❑ *Perhaps the opposed parties will lay aside their sectional interests and rise to this challenge.* **2** (*BrE*) If you **lay** something **aside**, you put it down, usually because you have finished using it or want to save it to use later. ❑ *He finished the tea and laid the cup aside.*
lay down **1** If you **lay** something **down**, you put it down, usually because you have finished using it. ❑ *Daniel finished the article and laid the newspaper down on his desk.* **2** If rules or people in authority **lay down** what people should do or must do, they officially state what they should or must do. = set down ❑ *Not all companies lay down written guidelines and rules.* **3** If someone **lays down** their weapons, they stop fighting a battle or war and make peace. ❑ *The drug-traffickers have offered to lay down their arms.*
lay off (*business*) If workers **are laid off**, they are told by their employers to leave their job, usually because there is no more work for them to do. ❑ *100,000 federal workers will be laid off to reduce the deficit.*
lay on (*mainly BrE*) If you **lay on** something such as food, entertainment, or a service, you provide or supply it, especially in a generous or grand way. ❑ *They laid on a superb evening.*
lay out **1** If you **lay out** a group of things, you spread them out and arrange them neatly, for example, so that they can all be seen clearly. ❑ *Grace laid out the knives and forks on the table.* **2** To **lay out** ideas, principles, or plans means to explain or present them clearly, for example, in a document or a meeting. ❑ *Maxwell listened closely as Johnson laid out his plan.* **3** → See also **layout**
lay up (*informal*) If someone **is laid up with** an illness, the illness makes it necessary for them to stay in bed. ❑ *She was in the hospital for a week and laid up for a month after that.* ❑ *Powell ruptured a disc in his back and was laid up for a year.*

ADJ **1** [lay + N] You use **lay** to describe people who are involved with a Christian church but are not members of the clergy or are not monks or nuns. ❑ *Edwards is a Methodist lay preacher and social worker.* **2** [lay + N] You use **lay** to describe people who are not experts or professionals in a particular subject or activity. ❑ *It is difficult for a lay person to gain access to medical libraries.*
✦ **lay something at someone's door** → see **door**; **lay a finger on** → see **finger**; **lay your hands on something** → see **hand**; **lay siege to something** → see **siege**

❍ **lay·er** ◆◇◇ /ˈleɪə/ NOUN, VERB (*academic word*)
NOUN [c] (**layers**) **1** A **layer** of a material or substance is a quantity or piece of it that covers a surface or that is between two other things. ❑ *the depletion of the ozone layer* ❑ *The eyelids are protective layers of skin.* **2** If something such as a system or an idea has many **layers**, it has many different levels or parts. ❑ *Critics and the public puzzle out the layers of meaning in his photos.*
VERB [T] (**layers, layering, layered**) If you **layer** something, you arrange it in layers. ❑ *Layer half the onion slices on top of the potatoes.*

lay·out /ˈleɪaʊt/ NOUN [c] (**layouts**) The **layout** of a park, building, or piece of writing is the way in which the parts of it are arranged. ❑ *He tried to recall the layout of the farmhouse.*

lazy /ˈleɪzi/ ADJ (**lazier, laziest**) **1** If someone is **lazy**, they do not want to work or make any effort to do anything. = idle ❑ *Lazy and incompetent police officers are letting the public down.* **2** [lazy + N] You can use **lazy** to describe an activity or event in which you are very relaxed and which you do or take part in without making much effort. = relaxed ❑ *Her latest novel is perfect for a lazy summer's afternoon's reading.*
la·zi·ness /ˈleɪzinəs/ NOUN [u] ❑ *Current employment laws will be changed to reward effort and punish laziness.*
la·zi·ly /ˈleɪzɪli/ ADV ❑ *Liz went back into the kitchen, stretching lazily.*

lb (lbs) ABBREVIATION **lb** is a written abbreviation for **pound**, when it refers to weight. ❑ *The baby was born three months early at 3 lbs 5 oz.*

❍ **lead** ◆◆◆ /liːd/ VERB, NOUN
VERB [T, I] (**leads, leading, led**) **1** [T] If you **lead** a group of people, you walk or ride in front of them. ❑ *The president and vice president led the mourners.* ❑ *He walks with a stick but still leads his soldiers into battle.* **2** [T] If you **lead** someone to a particular place or thing, you take them there. ❑ *He took Dickon by the hand to lead him into the house.* ❑ *She confessed to the killing and led police to his remains.* **3** [I] If a road, gate, or door **leads** somewhere, you can get there by following the road or going through the gate or door. ❑ *the door that led to the yard* ❑ *a hallway leading to the living room* **4** [I] If you **are leading** at a particular point in a race or competition, you are winning at that point. ❑ *He's leading in the presidential race.* ❑ *So far Fischer leads by five wins to two.* **5** [T] If one company or country **leads** others in a particular activity such as scientific research or business, it is more successful or advanced than they are in that activity. ❑ *In 1920, the United States led the world in iron and steel manufacturing.* **6** [T] If you **lead** a group of people, an organization, or an activity, you are in control or in charge of the people or the activity. = control, manage, direct ❑ *He led the country between 1949 and 1984.* ❑ *Mr Mendes was leading a campaign to save Brazil's rainforest from exploitation.* **7** [T] You can use **lead** when you are saying what kind of life someone has. For example, if you **lead** a busy life, your life is busy. ❑ *She led a normal, happy life with her sister and brother.* **8** [I] If something **leads to** a situation or event, usually an unpleasant one, it begins a process which causes that situation or event to happen. = result in, bring about, give rise to, prompt ❑ *Ethnic tensions among the republics could lead to civil war.* **9** [T] If something **leads** you **to** do something, it influences or affects you in such a way that you do it. ❑ *His abhorrence of racism led him to write 'The Algiers Motel Incident'.* **10** [T] You can say that one point or topic in a discussion or piece of writing **leads** you **to** another in order to introduce a new point or topic that is linked with the previous one. = bring ❑ *Well, I think that leads me to the real point.*
PHRASAL VERB **lead up to** **1** The events that **led up to** a particular event happened one after the other until that event occurred. ❑ *Alan Tomlinson has reconstructed the events that led up to the deaths.* **2** If someone **leads up to** a particular subject, they gradually guide a conversation to a point where they can introduce it. ❑ *I'm leading up to something quite important.*
NOUN [SING, C, U] (**leads**) **1** [SING] If you have **the lead** or are **in the lead** in a race or competition, you are winning. ❑ *Harvard took the lead and remained unperturbed by the repeated challenges.* **2** [c] If you take **the lead**, you do something new or develop new ideas or methods that other people consider to be a good example or model to follow. ❑ *The American and Japanese navies took the lead in the development of naval aviation.* **3** [c] A **lead** is a piece of information or an idea which may help people to discover the facts in a situation where many facts are not known, for example, in the investigation of a crime or in a scientific experiment. ❑ *The inquiry team is also following up possible leads after receiving 400 calls from the public.*

4 [c] (*BrE*; in *AmE*, use **leash**) A dog's **lead** is a long, thin chain or piece of leather which you attach to the dog's collar so that you can control the dog. = **leash** **5** [c] A **lead** in a piece of equipment is a piece of wire covered in plastic which supplies electricity to the equipment or carries it from one part of the equipment to another. ◻ *a lead that plugs into a socket on the camcorder* **6** [c] **The lead** in a play, film, or show is the most important part in it. The person who plays this part can also be called the **lead**. ◻ *Nina Ananiashvili and Alexei Fadeyechev from the Bolshoi Ballet dance the leads.* ◻ *Neve Campbell is the lead, playing one of the dancers.* **7** /led/ [u] **Lead** is a soft, grey, heavy metal. ◻ *drinking water supplied by old-fashioned lead pipes* **8** /led/ [c] The **lead** in a pencil is the centre part of it which makes a mark on paper. ◻ *He grabbed a pencil, and the lead immediately broke.*
→ See also **leading**
✦ **lead someone astray** → see **astray**; **lead the way** → see **way**

⊕ **lead·er** ◆◆◆ /'liːdə/ NOUN [c] (**leaders**) **1** The **leader** of a group of people or an organization is the person who is in control of it or in charge of it. = **head** ◻ *We now need a new leader of the party and a new style of leadership.* ◻ *We are going to hold a rally next month to elect a new leader.* **2** The **leader** at a particular point in a race or competition is the person who is winning at that point. ◻ *The leaders came in two minutes clear of the field.*

⊕ **lead·er·ship** ◆◆◇ /'liːdəʃɪp/ NOUN [c, u] (**leaderships**) **1** [c] You refer to people who are in control of a group or organization as the **leadership**. ◻ *He is expected to hold talks with both the Croatian and Slovenian leaderships.* ◻ *the Labour leadership of Haringey council in north London* **2** [u] Someone's **leadership** is their position or state of being in control of a group of people. ◻ *He praised her leadership during the crisis.*

⊕ **lead·ing** ◆◆◇ /'liːdɪŋ/ ADJ **1** [leading + N] The **leading** person or thing in a particular area is the one which is most important or successful. = **prominent, foremost** ◻ *a leading member of the city's Sikh community* ◻ *Britain's future as a leading industrial nation depends on investment.* **2** [leading + N] The **leading** role in a play or film is the main role. A **leading** lady or man is an actor who plays this role. ◻ *an offer to play the leading role in an Arthur Miller play* **3** [leading + N] The **leading** group, vehicle, or person in a race or procession is the one that is at the front. ◻ *The leading car came to a halt.*

⊕ **leaf** ◆◇◇ /liːf/ NOUN
NOUN [c] (**leaves**) **1** [usu pl, also 'in/into' leaf] The **leaves** of a tree or plant are the parts that are flat, thin, and usually green. Many trees and plants lose their leaves in the winter and grow new leaves in the spring. ◻ *In the garden, the leaves of the horse chestnut had already fallen.* ◻ *The Japanese maple that stands across the drive had just come into leaf.* **2** A **leaf** is one of the pieces of paper of which a book is made. = **page** ◻ *He flattened the wrappers and put them between the leaves of his book.*
PHRASE **turn over a new leaf** If you say that you are going to **turn over a new leaf**, you mean that you are going to start to behave in a better or more acceptable way. ◻ *He realized he was in the wrong and promised to turn over a new leaf.*
PHRASAL VERB **leaf through** (**leafs, leafing, leafed**) If you **leaf through** something such as a book or magazine, you turn the pages without reading or looking at them very carefully. ◻ *Most patients derive enjoyment from leafing through old picture albums.*

leaf·let /'liːflət/ NOUN [c] (**leaflets**) A **leaflet** is a little book or a piece of paper containing information about a particular subject. ◻ *Campaigners handed out leaflets on passive smoking.*

league ◆◆◇ /liːg/ NOUN
NOUN [c] (**leagues**) **1** A **league** is a group of people, clubs, or countries that have joined together for a particular purpose, or because they share a common interest. ◻ *the League of Nations* **2** A **league** is a group of teams that play the same sport or activity against each other. ◻ *the American League series between the Boston Red Sox and World*

Champion Oakland Athletics **3** You use **league** to make comparisons between different people or things, especially in terms of their quality. ◻ *Her success has taken her out of my league.*
PHRASE **in league** If you say that someone is **in league with** another person to do something bad, you mean that they are working together to do that thing. ◻ *There is no evidence that the broker was in league with the fraudulent vendor.*

leak ◆◇◇ /liːk/ VERB, NOUN
VERB [i, t] (**leaks, leaking, leaked**) **1** If a container **leaks**, there is a hole or crack in it which lets a substance such as liquid or gas escape. You can also say that a container **leaks** a substance such as liquid or gas. ◻ *The roof leaked.* ◻ *The pool's fibreglass sides had cracked and the water had leaked out.* **2** If a secret document or piece of information **leaks** or **is leaked**, someone lets the public know about it. ◻ *Mr Ashton accused police of leaking information to the press.* ◻ *We don't know how the transcript leaked.*
PHRASAL VERB **leak out** Leak out means the same as **leak** VERB **2**. ◻ *More details are now beginning to leak out.*
NOUN [c] (**leaks**) **1** A **leak** is an amount of a liquid or gas that escapes through a hole or crack in something. ◻ *It's thought a gas leak may have caused the blast.* **2** A **leak** is a crack, hole, or other gap that a substance such as a liquid or gas can pass through. ◻ *a leak in the radiator* **3** A **leak** is an act of letting the public know about a secret document or piece of information. ◻ *More serious leaks, possibly involving national security, are likely to be investigated by the police.*

lean ◆◇◇ /liːn/ VERB, ADJ
VERB [i, t] (**leans, leaning, leaned** or **leant**) **1** [i] When you **lean** in a particular direction, you bend your body in that direction. ◻ *Eileen leaned across and opened the passenger door.* **2** [i, t] If you **lean on** or **against** someone or something, you rest against them so that they partly support your weight. If you **lean** an object **on** or **against** something, you place the object so that it is partly supported by that thing. ◻ *She was feeling tired and was glad to lean against him.* ◻ *Lean the plants against a wall and cover the roots with peat.*
PHRASAL VERB **lean on** or **lean upon** If you **lean on** someone or **lean upon** them, you depend on them for support and encouragement. ◻ *She leaned on him to help her to solve her problems.*
ADJ (**leaner, leanest**) **1** (*approval*) If you describe someone as **lean**, you mean that they are thin but look strong and healthy. ◻ *Like most athletes, she was lean and muscular.* **2** If meat is **lean**, it does not have very much fat. ◻ *It is a beautiful meat, very lean and tender.* **3** If you describe an organization as **lean**, you mean that it has become more efficient and less wasteful by getting rid of staff, or by dropping projects which were unprofitable. ◻ *reforms which turned us into a lean and competitive nation* **4** If you describe periods of time as **lean**, you mean that people have less of something such as money or are less successful than they used to be. ◻ *My parents lived through the lean years of the 1930s.*

leant /lent/ IRREG FORM **Leant** is a past tense and past participle of **lean**.

leap ◆◇◇ /liːp/ VERB, NOUN
VERB [i, t] (**leaps, leaping, leaped** or **leapt**) **1** [i, t] If you **leap**, you jump high in the air or jump a long distance. = **jump** ◻ *He leaped in the air and waved his fists to the fans as he ran out of the stadium.* ◻ *Frederick leaped 22 feet, 7¼ inches on his second attempt.* **2** [i] If you **leap** somewhere, you move there suddenly and quickly. ◻ *The two men leapt into the jeep and roared off.* **3** [i] If a vehicle **leaps** somewhere, it moves there in a short sudden movement. ◻ *The car leapt forward.* **4** [i] If you **leap to** a particular place or position, you make a large and important change, increase, or advance. ◻ *Bush's approval rating leapt to an astounding 88 per cent.*
NOUN [c] (**leaps**) **1** A **leap** is a high or long jump. ◻ *The suspect took a leap out of a third-story window.* **2** (*journalism*) A **leap** is a large and important change, increase, or advance. ◻ *The result has been a giant leap in productivity.*

I

❏ *the leap in the unemployed from 35,000 to 75,000*

leapt /lept/ IRREG FORM **Leapt** is a past tense and past participle of **leap**.

leap year NOUN [C] (**leap years**) A **leap year** is a year which has 366 days. The extra day is February 29th. There is a leap year every four years.

◆learn ◆◆◆ /lɜːn/ VERB [I, T] (**learns, learning, learned** or **learnt**) **1** [I, T] If you **learn** something, you obtain knowledge or a skill through studying or training. = master, grasp ❏ *Their children were going to learn English.* ❏ *He is learning to play the piano.* ❏ *It's going to be tough, but these guys learn quickly.* ❏ *learning how to use new computer systems* **2** [I, T] If you **learn** of something, you find out about it. = find out, discover ❏ *It was only after his death that she learned of his affair with Betty.* ❏ *It didn't come as a shock to learn that the fuel and cooling systems are the most common causes of breakdown.* ❏ *The zoological world learned of two new species of lizard.* **3** [T] If people **learn to** behave or react in a particular way, they gradually start to behave in that way as a result of a change in attitudes. ❏ *You have to learn to face your problem.* **4** [I, T] If you **learn from** an unpleasant experience, you change the way you behave so that it does not happen again or so that, if it happens again, you can deal with it better. ❏ *I am convinced that he has learned from his mistakes.* ❏ *I just hope we all learn some lessons from this.* **5** [T] If you **learn** something such as a poem or a role in a play, you study or repeat the words so that you can remember them. ❏ *He learned this song as an inmate at a Texas prison.*
✦ **learn the ropes →** see **rope**

learn·er /ˈlɜːnə/ NOUN [C] (**learners**) A **learner** is someone who is learning about a particular subject or how to do something. ❏ *Clinton proved to be a quick learner and soon settled into serious struggles over cutting the budget.*

learn·ing /ˈlɜːnɪŋ/ NOUN [U] **Learning** is the process of gaining knowledge through studying. ❏ *The brochure described the library as the focal point of learning on the campus.*

lease ◆◇◇ /liːs/ NOUN, VERB
NOUN [C] (**leases**) A **lease** is a legal agreement by which the owner of a building, a piece of land, or something such as a car allows someone else to use it for a period of time in return for money. ❏ *He took up a 10-year lease on the house.*
VERB [T] (**leases, leasing, leased**) If you **lease** property or something such as a car from someone or if they **lease** it **to** you, they allow you to use it in return for regular payments of money. ❏ *He went to Toronto, where he leased an apartment.* ❏ *She hopes to lease the building to students.*

least ◆◆◆ /liːst/ ADJ, PRON, ADV
ADJ **1** ['the' least + N] You use **the least** to mean a smaller amount than anyone or anything else, or the smallest amount possible. ❏ *I try to offend the least amount of people possible.* **2** ['the' least + N] You use **the least** to emphasize the smallness of something, especially when it hardly exists at all. ❏ *I don't have the least idea of what you're talking about.* **3** [least 'of' DEF-N] You use **least** in structures where you are emphasizing that a particular situation or event is much less important or serious than other possible or actual ones. ❏ *Having to get up at three o'clock every morning was the least of her worries.*
PRON **1** ['the' least] You use **the least** to mean a smaller amount than anyone or anything else, or the smallest amount possible. ❏ *On education funding, Japan performs best but spends the least per student.* **2** ['the' least + CL] You use **the least** in structures where you are stating the minimum that should be done in a situation, and suggesting that more should really be done. ❏ *Well, the least you can do, if you won't help me myself, is to tell me where to go instead.*
ADV **1** ['the' least after V] You use **the least** to mean a smaller amount than anyone or anything else, or the smallest amount possible. ❏ *Damming the river may end up benefiting those who need it the least.* **2** [least + ADJ/ADV] You use **least** to indicate that someone or something has less of a particular quality than most other things of its kind. ❏ *He was one of the least warm human beings I had ever met.*

3 [least with V] You use **least** to indicate that something is true or happens to a smaller degree or extent than anything else or at any other time. ❏ *He had a way of throwing Helen off guard with his charm when she least expected it.*
PHRASE **at least 1** You use **at least** to say that a number or amount is the smallest that is possible or likely and that the actual number or amount may be greater. The forms **at the least** and **at the very least** are also used. ❏ *Aim to have at least half a pint of milk each day.* ❏ *About two-thirds of adults consult their doctor at least once a year.* **2** You use **at least** to say that something is the minimum that is true or possible. The forms **at the least** and **at the very least** are also used. ❏ *She could take a nice vacation at least.* ❏ *His possession of classified documents in his home was, at the very least, a violation of navy security regulations.* **3** You use **at least** to indicate an advantage that exists in spite of the disadvantage or bad situation that has just been mentioned. ❏ *We've no idea what his state of health is but at least we know he is still alive.* **4** You use **at least** to indicate that you are correcting or changing something that you have just said. ❏ *It's not difficult to get money for research or at least it's not always difficult.*

leath·er ◆◇◇ /ˈleðə/ NOUN [C, U] (**leathers**) **Leather** is treated animal skin, usually from cows, which is used for making shoes, clothes, bags, and furniture. ❏ *He wore a leather jacket and dark trousers.*

leave ◆◆◆ /liːv/ VERB, NOUN
VERB [I, T] (**leaves, leaving, left**) **1** [I, T] If you **leave** a place or person, you go away from that place or person. ❏ *He would not be allowed to leave the country.* ❏ *My flight leaves in less than an hour.* **2** [I, T] If you **leave** an institution, group, or job, you permanently stop attending that institution, being a member of that group, or doing that job. ❏ *He left school with no qualifications.* ❏ *I am leaving to concentrate on writing fiction.* **3** [I, T] If you **leave** your husband, wife, or some other person with whom you have had a close relationship, you stop living with them or you end the relationship. ❏ *He'll never leave you. You needn't worry.* **4** [T] If you **leave** something or someone in a particular place, you let them remain there when you go away. If you **leave** something or someone with a person, you let them remain with that person so they are safe while you are away. ❏ *I left my bags in the car.* ❏ *From the moment that Philippe had left her in the bedroom at the hotel, she had heard nothing of him.* **5** [T] If you **leave** a message or an answer, you write it, record it, or give it to someone so that it can be found or passed on. ❏ *You can leave a message on our answering machine.* ❏ *I left my phone number with several people.* **6** [T] If you **leave** someone doing something, they are doing that thing when you go away from them. ❏ *Salter drove off, leaving Callendar surveying the scene.* **7** [T] If you **leave** someone **to** do something, you go away from them so that they do it on their own. If you **leave** someone **to** himself or herself, you go away from them and allow them to be alone. ❏ *I'll leave you to get to know each other.* ❏ *Diana took the hint and left them to it.* **8** [T] To **leave** an amount of something means to keep it available after the rest has been used or taken away. ❏ *He always left a little food for the next day.* **9** [T] To **leave** someone **with** something, especially when that thing is unpleasant or difficult to deal with, means to make them have it or make them deal with it. ❏ *a crash which left him with a broken collar-bone* **10** [T] If an event **leaves** people or things in a particular state, they are in that state when the event has finished. ❏ *violent disturbances which have left at least ten people dead* **11** [T] If you **leave** food or drink, you do not eat or drink it, often because you do not like it. ❏ *If you don't like the cocktail you ordered, just leave it and try a different one.* **12** [T] If something **leaves** a mark, effect, or sign, it causes that mark, effect, or sign to remain as a result. ❏ *A muscle tear will leave a scar after healing.* **13** [T] If you **leave** something in a particular state, position, or condition, you let it remain in that state, position, or condition. ❏ *He left the album open on the table.* ❏ *I've left the car lights on.* **14** [T] If you **leave** a space or gap in something, you deliberately make that space or gap. ❏ *Leave a gap at the top and bottom so air can circulate.*

L

15 [T] If you **leave** a job, decision, or choice **to** someone, you give them the responsibility for dealing with it or making it. ❑ *Affix the blue airmail label and leave the rest to us.* ❑ *The judge should not have left it to the jury to decide.* **16** [T] To **leave** someone **with** a particular course of action or the opportunity to do something means to let it be available to them, while restricting them in other ways. ❑ *He was left with no option but to resign.* **17** [T] If you **leave** something **until** a particular time, you delay doing it or dealing with it until then. ❑ *Don't leave it all until the last minute.* **18** [T] If you **leave** a particular subject, you stop talking about it and start discussing something else. ❑ *I think we'd better leave the subject of nationalism.* **19** [T] If you **leave** property or money **to** someone, you arrange for it to be given to them after you have died. ❑ *He died two and a half years later, leaving everything to his wife.* **20** [T] If you **leave** something somewhere, you forget to bring it with you. ❑ *I left my purse back there on the gas pump.*
PHRASES **leave something too late** If you **leave** something **too late**, you delay doing it so that when you eventually do it, it is useless or ineffective.
leave alone or **leave be** If you **leave** someone or something **alone**, or if you **leave** them **be**, you do not pay them any attention or bother them. ❑ *Some people need to confront a traumatic past; others find it better to leave it alone.*
where you left off If something continues **from where** it **left off**, it starts happening again at the point where it had previously stopped. ❑ *As soon as the police disappear the violence will take up from where it left off.*
PHRASAL VERBS **leave behind** **1** If you **leave** someone or something **behind**, you go away permanently from them. ❑ *'I'd go and live there and leave England,' says Brown.* **2** If you **leave behind** an object or a situation, it remains after you have left a place. ❑ *I don't want to leave anything behind.* **3** If a person, country, or organization **is left behind**, they remain at a lower level than others because they are not as quick at understanding things or developing. ❑ *We're going to be left behind by the rest of the world.* ❑ *People are concerned about getting left behind right now.*
leave off If someone or something **is left off** a list, they are not included on that list. ❑ *She has been deliberately left off the guest list.*
leave out If you **leave** someone or something **out** of an activity, collection, discussion, or group, you do not include them in it. ❑ *Some would question the wisdom of leaving her out of the team.* ❑ *If you prefer mild flavours reduce or leave out the chilli.*
NOUN [U] **Leave** is a period of time when you are not working at your job, because you are on vacation, or for some other reason. If you are **on leave**, you are not working at your job. ❑ *Why don't you take a few days' leave?* ❑ *maternity leave*
✦ **take it or leave it** → see **take**

leaves /liːvz/ IRREG FORM **Leaves** is the plural form of **leaf**, and the third person singular form of **leave**.

⊙**lec·ture** ◆◇◇ /ˈlektʃə/ NOUN, VERB (*academic word*)
NOUN [C] (**lectures**) **1** A **lecture** is a talk someone gives in order to teach people about a particular subject, usually at a university or college. = **talk** ❑ *a series of lectures by Professor Eric Robinson* ❑ *He gave a three-hour lecture on Goethe.* **2** A **lecture** is a talk that someone gives you to criticize you or tell you how you should behave. ❑ *Our captain gave us a stern lecture on safety.*
VERB [I, T] (**lectures, lecturing, lectured**) **1** [I] If you **lecture on** a particular subject, you give a lecture or a series of lectures about it. ❑ *She then invited him to Atlanta to lecture on the history of art.* **2** [T] If someone **lectures** you about something, they criticize you or tell you what they think you should behave. ❑ *He used to lecture me about getting too much sun.* ❑ *Chuck would lecture me, telling me to get a haircut.*

⊙**lec·tur·er** /ˈlektʃərə/ NOUN [C] (**lecturers**) **1** A **lecturer** is a teacher at a university or college. ❑ *a lecturer in law* ❑ *there was an opening for a senior lecturer* **2** A **lecturer** is a person who gives lectures.

led /led/ IRREG FORM **Led** is the past tense and past participle of **lead**.

left ◆◇◇ /left/ IRREG FORM, ADJ, NOUN, ADV

The spelling **Left** is also used for meanings 2 and 3 of the noun.

IRREG FORM **Left** is the past tense and past participle of **leave**.
ADJ **1** [V-LINK + left, V N + left] If there is a certain amount of something **left**, or if you have a certain amount of it **left**, it remains when the rest has gone or been used. ❑ *Is there any gin left?* ❑ *They still have six games left to play.* **2** [left + N] Your **left** arm, leg, or ear, for example, is the one which is on the left side of your body. Your **left** shoe or glove is the one which is intended to be worn on your left foot or hand. ❑ *Ferdinand landed awkwardly on top of Delgado's right boot and twisted his left leg.*
PHRASE **left over** If there is a certain amount of something **left over**, or if you have it **left over**, it remains when the rest has gone or been used. ❑ *So much income is devoted to monthly mortgage payments that nothing is left over.*
NOUN [SING] **1** The **left** is one of two opposite directions, sides, or positions. If you are facing north and you turn to the left, you will be facing west. In the word 'to', the 't' is to the left of the 'o'. ❑ *Go back to the last fork in the road and take a left.* ❑ *the brick wall to the left of the conservatory* **2** The **left** refers to people who support the ideas of socialism. ❑ *the traditional parties of the Left* **3** If you say that a person or political party has moved **to the left**, you mean that their political beliefs have become more left-wing. ❑ *After 1979, the party moved sharply to the left.*
ADV [left after V] If something goes or is situated **left**, it goes to the left or is situated to the left side of something. ❑ *Turn left at the crossroads into Clay Lane.*

left-hand ADJ [left-hand + N] If something is on the **left-hand** side of something, it is positioned on the left of it. ❑ *The Japanese drive on the left-hand side of the road.*

left-handed ADJ Someone who is **left-handed** uses their left hand rather than their right hand for activities such as writing and sports and for picking things up. ❑ *There is a shop in town that supplies practically everything for left-handed people.*

⊙**left-wing** also **left wing** ADJ, NOUN
ADJ **Left-wing** people support the ideas of the political left. ❑ *They said they would not be voting for him because he was too left-wing.* ❑ *left-wing guerrillas*
NOUN [SING] The **left wing** of a group of people, especially a political party, consists of the members of it whose beliefs are closer to those of the political left than are those of its other members. ❑ *She belongs on the left wing of the Democratic Party.*

leg ◆◆◇ /leg/ NOUN
NOUN [C] (**legs**) **1** A person's or animal's **legs** are the long parts of their body that they use to stand on. ❑ *He was tapping his walking stick against his leg.* **2** The **legs** of a pair of trousers are the parts that cover your legs. ❑ *He moved on through wet grass that soaked the legs of his trousers.* **3** A **leg** of lamb, pork, chicken, or other meat is a piece of meat that consists of the animal's or bird's leg, especially the thigh. ❑ *a chicken leg* **4** The **legs** of a table, chair, or other piece of furniture are the parts that rest on the floor and support the furniture's weight. ❑ *His ankles were tied to the legs of the chair.* **5** A **leg** of a long journey is one part of it, usually between two points where you stop. ❑ *The first leg of the journey was by boat to Lake Naivasha in Kenya.* **6** (*mainly BrE*) A **leg** of a sports competition is one of a series of games that are played to find an overall winner.
PHRASE **pull someone's leg** (*informal*) If you **are pulling** someone's **leg**, you are teasing them by telling them something shocking or worrying as a joke. ❑ *Of course I won't tell them; I was only pulling your leg.*

leg·a·cy /ˈlegəsi/ NOUN [C] (**legacies**) **1** A **legacy** is money or property which someone leaves to you when they die. ❑ *You could make a real difference to someone's life by leaving them a generous legacy.* **2** A **legacy of** an event or period of history is something which is a direct result of it and which continues to exist after it is over. ❑ *a programme to overcome the legacy of inequality and injustice created by Apartheid*

◆le·gal ♦♦◇ /ˈliːgəl/ ADJ (academic word) **1** [legal + N]
Legal is used to describe things that relate to the law. ❑ *He
vowed to take legal action.* ❑ *the British legal system* ❑ *I sought
legal advice on this.* **2** An action or situation that is **legal** is
allowed or required by law. ❑ *What I did was perfectly legal.*
❑ *drivers who have more than the legal limit of alcohol*
◆le·gal·ly /ˈliːgəli/ ADV ≠ illegally, unlawfully ❑ *It could
be a bit problematic, legally speaking.* ❑ *A lorry driver can
legally work eighty-two hours a week.*

WORD CONNECTIONS
legal + NOUN
legal **action**
legal **proceedings**
❑ *He began legal proceedings against the company.*
the legal **profession**
the legal **system**
❑ *The Scottish legal system is different from the English one.*
legal **costs**
legal **fees**
❑ *The company spent over £10,000 in legal fees.*
legal **rights**
legal **advice**
❑ *It might be a good idea to get some legal advice.*
a legal **expert**
a legal **adviser**
❑ *Some legal experts had expected Zimmerman to face a lesser count of manslaughter.*
a legal **requirement**
the legal **limit**
❑ *It's a legal requirement to wear a seatbelt.*
ADV + **legal**
perfectly legal
entirely legal
❑ *It is perfectly legal for people to use whatever name they want.*

le·gal·ity /liːˈgæliti/ NOUN [U] If you talk about the
legality of an action or situation, you are talking about
whether it is legal or not. ❑ *The auditor has questioned the
legality of the contracts.*

le·gal·ize /ˈliːgəlaɪz/ also **legalise** VERB [T] (legalizes,
legalizing, legalized) If something is **legalized**, a law is
passed that makes it legal. ❑ *Divorce was legalized in 1981.*
le·gal·iza·tion also **legalisation** /ˌliːgəlaɪzˈeɪʃən/ NOUN [U]
❑ *Legalization of drugs would drive the drug-dealing business off
the streets.*

leg·end /ˈledʒənd/ NOUN [C, U] (legends) **1** [C, U] A
legend is a very old and popular story that may be true.
❑ *the legends of ancient Greece* **2** [C] If you refer to
someone as a **legend**, you mean that they are very famous
and admired by a lot of people. ❑ *blues legends John Lee
Hooker and B. B. King*

leg·end·ary /ˈledʒəndri, AmE -deri/ ADJ **1** If you
describe someone or something as **legendary**, you mean
that they are very famous and that many stories are told
about them. ❑ *the legendary jazz singer Adelaide Hall*
2 A **legendary** person, place, or event is mentioned or
described in an old legend. ❑ *The hill is supposed to be the
resting place of the legendary King Lud.*

◆leg·is·late /ˈledʒɪsleɪt/ VERB [I, T] (legislates,
legislating, legislated) (academic word, formal) When a
government or state **legislates**, it passes a new law. ❑ *Most
member countries have already legislated against excessive
overtime.* ❑ *You cannot legislate to change attitudes.*

◆leg·is·la·tion ♦◇◇ /ˌledʒɪsˈleɪʃən/ NOUN [U] (formal)
Legislation consists of a law or laws passed by a
government. ❑ *a letter calling for legislation to protect
women's rights* ❑ *European legislation on copyright*

◆leg·is·la·tive /ˈledʒɪslətɪv, AmE -leɪ-/ ADJ [legislative
+ N] (formal) **Legislative** means involving or relating to the
process of making and passing laws. ❑ *Today's hearing was
just the first step in the legislative process.* ❑ *the country's
highest legislative body*

leg·is·la·tor /ˈledʒɪsleɪtə/ NOUN [C] (legislators) (formal)
A **legislator** is a person who is involved in making or passing
laws. ❑ *an attempt to get US legislators to change the system*

◆leg·is·la·ture /ˈledʒɪslətʃə, AmE -leɪ-/ NOUN [C]
(legislatures) (academic word, formal) The **legislature** of a
particular state or country is the group of people in it who
have the power to make and pass laws. ❑ *The proposals
before the legislature include the creation of two special courts to
deal exclusively with violent crimes.* ❑ *The legislature passed a
bill that would permit referendums on constitutional and
sovereignty issues.*

◆le·giti·mate /lɪˈdʒɪtɪmət/ ADJ **1** [legitimate with V]
Something that is **legitimate** is acceptable according to the
law. = legal, authentic, valid; ≠ illegitimate ❑ *The French
government has condemned the coup in Haiti and has demanded
the restoration of the legitimate government.* ❑ *The government
will not seek to disrupt the legitimate business activities of the
defendant.* **2** If you say that something such as a feeling
or claim is **legitimate**, you think that it is reasonable and
justified. = reasonable, justified ❑ *That's a perfectly
legitimate fear.* ❑ *The New York Times has a legitimate claim to
be a national newspaper.*
◆le·giti·ma·cy /lɪˈdʒɪtɪmɪsi/ NOUN [U] **1** = authenticity,
validity; ≠ illegitimacy ❑ *The opposition parties do not
recognize the political legitimacy of his government.* **2** *Sampras
beat Carl-Uwe Steeb by 6-1, 6-2, 6-1 to underline the legitimacy
of his challenge for the title.* ❑ *As if to prove the legitimacy of
these fears, the Cabinet of Franz von Papen collapsed on
December 2.*
◆le·giti·mate·ly /lɪˈdʒɪtɪmətli/ ADV **1** The government has
been **legitimately** elected by the people. **2** [legitimately with V]
❑ *They could quarrel quite legitimately with some of my choices.*

◆lei·sure /ˈleʒə, AmE ˈliːʒ-/ NOUN
NOUN [U] **Leisure** is the time when you are not working
and you can relax and do things that you enjoy.
= recreation, free time; ≠ work ❑ *a relaxing way to fill my
leisure time* ❑ *one of Britain's most popular leisure activities*
PHRASE **at leisure** or **at someone's leisure** If someone
does something **at leisure** or **at** their leisure, they enjoy
themselves by doing it when they want to, without
hurrying. ❑ *You will be able to stroll at leisure through the
gardens.*

lei·sure·ly /ˈleʒəli, AmE ˈliːʒ-/ ADJ, ADV
ADJ A **leisurely** action is done in a relaxed and unhurried
way. ❑ *Lunch was a leisurely affair.*
ADV [leisurely with V] If you do something **leisurely**, you
do it in a relaxed and unhurried way. ❑ *We walked leisurely
into the hotel.*

lem·on /ˈlemən/ NOUN [C, U] (lemons) A **lemon** is a bright
yellow fruit with very sour juice. Lemons grow on trees in
warm countries. ❑ *a slice of lemon* ❑ *oranges, lemons and
other citrus fruits*

◆lend ♦◇◇ /lend/ VERB [I, T] (lends, lending, lent)
1 [I, T] When people or organizations such as banks **lend**
you money, they give it to you and you agree to pay it
back at a future date, often with an extra amount as
interest. = loan, advance; ≠ borrow ❑ *The bank is
reassessing its criteria for lending money.* ❑ *The government will
lend you money at incredible rates, between zero per cent and 3
per cent.* ❑ *financial de-regulation that led to institutions being
more willing to lend* ❑ *the bank's policy on lending money to
political parties* **2** [T] If you **lend** something that you own,
you allow someone to have it or use it for a period of time.
❑ *Will you lend me your jacket for a little while?* **3** [T] If you
lend your support **to** someone or something, you help
them with what they are doing or with a problem that
they have. = give ❑ *He was approached by the organizers to
lend support to a benefit concert.* **4** [T] If something **lends
itself** to a particular activity or result, it is easy for it to be
used for that activity or to achieve that result. ❑ *The room
lends itself well to summer eating with its light, airy atmosphere.*
lend·ing /ˈlendɪŋ/ NOUN [U] ❑ *a financial institution that
specializes in the lending of money*
→ See also **lent**
✦ **lend a hand** → see **hand**

L

lend·er /'lendə/ NOUN [c] (**lenders**) (*business*) A **lender** is a person or an institution that lends money to people. ◻ *the six leading mortgage lenders*

⊙ **length** ♦♦◇ /leŋθ/ NOUN [c, u] (**lengths**) ◼ [c, u] The **length** of something is the amount that it measures from one end to the other along the longest side. ◻ *It is about a metre in length.* ◻ *the length of the fish* ◻ *the length of the field* ◻ *The plane had a wing span of 34ft and a length of 22ft.* ◼ [c, u] The **length** of something such as a piece of writing is the amount of writing that is contained in it. ◻ *a book of at least 100 pages in length* ◻ *The length of a paragraph depends on the information it conveys.* ◼ [c, u] The **length** of an event, activity, or situation is the period of time from beginning to end for which something lasts or during which something happens. ◻ *The exact length of each period may vary.* ◻ *His film, over two hours in length, is a subtle study of family life.* ◼ [c] A **length** of rope, cloth, wood, or other material is a piece of it that is intended to be used for a particular purpose or that exists in a particular situation. ◻ *a 30 feet length of rope* ◼ [u] The **length of** something is its quality of being long. ◻ *Many have been surprised at the length of time it has taken him to make up his mind.*
✦ **at arm's length** → see **arm**

WORD CONNECTIONS
VERB + **length**
have a length of …
◻ *The missile had a length of 6.3 metres.*
walk the length of …
run the length of …
travel the length of …
◻ *You can travel the length of Britain's coastlines, stopping at seaside towns.*
ADJ + **length**
the **entire** length
the **full** length
the **whole** length
the **total** length
the **overall** length
◻ *One road ran almost the entire length of the South American Pacific coast.*
a **considerable** length
the **exact** length
the **average** length
a **short** length
the **maximum** length
◻ *Its shorter length makes it ideal for small rooms.*

length·en /'leŋθən/ VERB [i, t] (**lengthens, lengthening, lengthened**) ◼ When something **lengthens** or when you **lengthen** it, it increases in length. ◻ *The evening shadows were lengthening.* ◼ When something **lengthens** or when you **lengthen** it, it lasts for a longer time than it did previously. ◻ *Holidays have lengthened and the working week has shortened.*

lengthy /'leŋθi/ ADJ (**lengthier, lengthiest**) ◼ You use **lengthy** to describe an event or process which lasts for a long time. ◻ *The board members held a lengthy meeting to decide future policy.* ◼ A **lengthy** report, article, book, or document contains a lot of speech, writing, or other material. ◻ *Friedman's lengthy report quoted an unnamed source.*

le·ni·ent /'li:niənt/ ADJ When someone in authority is **lenient**, they are not as strict or severe as expected. ◻ *He believes the government already is lenient with drug traffickers.* **le·ni·ent·ly** /'li:niəntli/ ADV [leniently after v] ◻ *Many people believe reckless drivers are treated too leniently.*

⊙ **lens** ♦◇◇ /lenz/ NOUN [c] (**lenses**) ◼ A **lens** is a thin curved piece of glass or plastic used in things such as cameras, telescopes, and pairs of glasses. You look through a lens in order to make things look larger, smaller, or clearer. ◻ *a camera lens* ◻ *a seven-megapixel camera with an optical zoom lens* ◼ In your eye, the **lens** is the part behind the pupil that focuses light and helps you to see clearly. ◻ *degenerative changes in the lens of the eye*

lent /lent/ IRREG FORM **Lent** is the past tense and past participle of **lend**.

les·bian ♦◇◇ /'lezbiən/ ADJ, NOUN
ADJ **Lesbian** is used to describe homosexual women. ◻ *a woman who had contacts in the homosexual and lesbian community*
NOUN [c] (**lesbians**) A **lesbian** is a woman who is lesbian. ◻ *a youth group for lesbians, gays and bisexuals*

less ♦♦♦ /les/ DET, PRON, QUANT, ADV, PREP
DET You use **less** to indicate that there is a smaller amount of something than before or than average. You can use 'a little', 'a lot', 'a bit', 'far', and 'much' in front of **less**. ◻ *People should eat less fat to reduce the risk of heart disease.* ◻ *a dishwasher that uses less water and electricity than older machines*
PRON **Less** means a smaller amount of something than before or than average. ◻ *Borrowers are striving to ease their financial position by spending less and saving more.*
QUANT **Less of** something means a smaller amount of it than before or than average. ◻ *Last year less of the money went into high-technology companies.*
ADV ◼ You use **less** to indicate that something or someone has a smaller amount of a quality than they used to or than is average or usual. ◻ *I often think about those less fortunate than me.* ◻ *Other amenities, less commonly available, include a library and exercise room.* ◼ If you say that something is **less** one thing **than** another, you mean that it is like the second thing rather than the first. ◻ *At first sight it looked less like a capital city than a mining camp.* ◼ [less with v] If you do something **less** than before or **less** than someone else, you do it to a smaller extent or not as often. ◻ *We are eating more and exercising less.*
PHRASE **less than** ◼ You use **less than** before a number or amount to say that the actual number or amount is smaller than this. ◻ *a country whose entire population is less than 12 million* ◼ (*emphasis*) You use **less than** to say that something does not have a particular quality. For example, if you describe something as **less than** perfect, you mean that it is not perfect at all. ◻ *Her greeting was less than enthusiastic.*
PREP When you are referring to amounts, you use **less** in front of a number or quantity to indicate that it is to be subtracted from another number or quantity already mentioned. = **minus** ◻ *You will pay between ten and twenty-five per cent, less tax.*
✦ **couldn't care less** → see **care**; **more or less** → see **more**

USAGE NOTE
less
Do not use **less** in front of the comparative form of an adjective. You do not say, for example, ~~'People are less healthier than they used to be'~~.
People are **less healthy** than they used to be.

less·en /'lesən/ VERB [i, t] (**lessens, lessening, lessened**) If something **lessens** or you **lessen** it, it becomes smaller in size, amount, degree, or importance. ◻ *He is used to a lot of attention from his wife, which will inevitably lessen when the baby is born.* **less·en·ing** /'lesənɪŋ/ NOUN [u] ◻ *increased trade and a lessening of tension on the border*

less·er /'lesə/ ADJ, ADV
ADJ ◼ [lesser + N, 'the' lesser 'of' N] You use **lesser** in order to indicate that something is smaller in extent, degree, or amount than another thing that has been mentioned. ◻ *No medication works in isolation but is affected to a greater or lesser extent by many other factors.* ◼ [lesser + N, 'the' lesser 'of' N] You can use **lesser** to refer to something or someone that is less important than other things or people of the same type. ◻ *They pleaded guilty to lesser charges of criminal damage.*
ADV [lesser + -ED] You use **lesser** to indicate that someone or something has less of a particular quality than other people or things of the same type. ◻ *lesser known works by famous artists*
✦ **the lesser of two evils** → see **evil**

les·son ♦◇◇ /'lesən/ NOUN
NOUN [c] (**lessons**) ◼ A **lesson** is a fixed period of time

when people are taught about a particular subject or taught how to do something. ❑ *It would be his last French lesson for months.* **2** You use **lesson** to refer to an experience which acts as a warning to you or an example from which you should learn. ❑ *There's still one lesson to be learned from the crisis – we all need to better understand the thinking of the other side.*

PHRASE **teach someone a lesson** If you say that you are going to **teach** someone **a lesson**, you mean that you are going to punish them for something that they have done so that they do not do it again.

lest /lest/ CONJ (*formal*) If you do something **lest** something unpleasant should happen, you do it to try to prevent the unpleasant thing from happening. = in case ❑ *I was afraid to open the door lest he should follow me.* ❑ *And, lest we forget, Einstein wrote his most influential papers while working as a clerk.*

let ♦♦♦ /let/

VERB [T] (**lets, letting, let**) **1** If you **let** something happen, you allow it to happen without doing anything to stop or prevent it. ❑ *People said we were interfering with nature, and that we should just let the animals die.* ❑ *I can't let myself be distracted by those things.* **2** If you **let** someone do something, you give them your permission to do it. ❑ *I love sweets but Mum doesn't let me have them very often.* **3** If you **let** someone into, out of, or through a place, you allow them to enter, leave, or go through it, for example, by opening a door or making room for them. ❑ *I had to let them into the building because they had lost their keys.* **4** You use **let me** when you are introducing something you want to say. ❑ *Let me tell you what I saw last night.* ❑ *Let me explain why.* **5** You use **let me** when you are offering politely to do something. ❑ *Let me take your coat.* **6** You say **let's** or, in more formal English, **let us**, to direct the attention of the people you are talking to towards the subject that you want to consider next. ❑ *Let us look at these views in more detail.* **7** You say **let's** or, in formal English, **let us**, when you are making a suggestion that involves both you and the person you are talking to, or when you are agreeing to a suggestion of this kind. ❑ *I'm bored. Let's go home.* **8** Someone in authority, such as a teacher, can use **let's** or, in more formal English, **let us**, in order to give a polite instruction to another person or group of people. ❑ *Let's have some quiet, please.* **9** You can use **let** when you are saying what you think someone should do, usually when they are behaving in a way that you think is unreasonable or wrong. ❑ *Let him get his own cup of tea.* **10** (*mainly BrE; in AmE, use* rent) If you **let** your house or land **to** someone, you allow them to use it in exchange for money that they pay you regularly. = rent

PHRASES **let alone** (*emphasis*) **Let alone** is used after a statement, usually a negative one, to indicate that the statement is even more true of the person, thing, or situation that you are going to mention next. ❑ *It is incredible that the 12-year-old managed to even reach the pedals, let alone drive the car.*

let go of If you **let go of** someone or something, you stop holding them. ❑ *She let go of Mona's hand and took a sip of her drink.*

let down If you are **let down** by someone or something, you are disappointed because they did not do something that they said they would do or that you expected them to do. ❑ *The company now has a large number of workers who feel badly let down.*

let someone go **1** If you **let** someone or something **go**, you allow them to leave or escape. ❑ *They held him for three hours and they let him go.* **2** (*business*) When someone leaves a job, either because they are told to or because they want to, the employer sometimes says that they are **letting** that person **go**. ❑ *I've assured him I have no plans to let him go.*

let oneself in for If you say that you did not know what you were **letting yourself in for** when you decided to do something, you mean you did not realize how difficult, unpleasant, or expensive it was going to be. ❑ *He got the impression that Miss Hawes had no idea of what she was letting herself in for.*

let someone know If you **let** someone **know** something,

you tell them about it or make sure that they know about it. ❑ *They want to let them know that they are safe.*

PHRASAL VERBS **let down** **1** If you **let** someone **down**, you disappoint them, by not doing something that you have said you will do or that they expected you to do. ❑ *Don't worry, Xiao, I won't let you down.* **2** If something **lets** you **down**, it is the reason you are not as successful as you could have been. ❑ *Many believe it was his shyness and insecurity which let him down.*

let in If an object **lets in** something such as air, light, or water, it allows air, light, or water to get into it, for example, because the object has a hole in it. ❑ *balconies shaded with lattice-work which lets in air but not light*

let off **1** If someone in authority **lets** you **off** a task or duty, they give you permission not to do it. ❑ *I realized that having a new baby lets you off going to boring dinner parties.* **2** If you **let** someone **off**, you give them a lighter punishment than they expect or no punishment at all. ❑ *Because he was a Christian, the judge let him off.* **3** If you **let off** an explosive or a gun, you explode or fire it. ❑ *A resident of his neighbourhood had let off fireworks to celebrate the revolution.*

let out **1** **Let out** means the same as **let** VERB **10**. ❑ *I couldn't sell the flat, so I let it out.* **2** If something or someone **lets** water, air, or breath **out**, they allow it to flow out or escape. ❑ *It lets sunlight in but doesn't let heat out.* **3** (*written*) If you **let out** a particular sound, you make that sound. = give out ❑ *When she saw him, she let out a cry of horror.* **4** If you **let out** a dress or pair of trousers, you make it larger by undoing the seams and sewing closer to the edge of the material. ❑ *I'll have to let this dress out a bit before the wedding next week.*

let up If an unpleasant, continuous process **lets up**, it stops or becomes less intense. ❑ *The traffic in this city never lets up, even at night.*

✦ **let fly** → see **fly**; **let your hair down** → see **hair**; **let someone off the hook** → see **hook**; **let it be known** → see **known**

WHICH WORD?

let or make?

Do not confuse **let** and **make**.

If you **let** someone do something, you allow them to do it or give them your permission to do it.

❑ *The farmer lets me live in a caravan behind his barn.*

If you **make** someone do something, you force them to do it.

❑ *Mama made him clean up the plate.*

---

le·thal /ˈliːθəl/ ADJ **1** A substance that is **lethal** can kill people or animals. ❑ *a lethal dose of sleeping pills* **2** If you describe something as **lethal**, you mean that it is capable of causing a lot of damage. ❑ *Amorality and intelligence is probably the most lethal combination to be found within one personality.*

let's ♦♦◇ /lets/ SHORT FORM **Let's** is the usual spoken form of 'let us'.

let·ter ♦♦♦ /ˈletə/ NOUN [C] (**letters**) **1** [also 'by' letter] If you write a **letter** to someone, you write a message on paper and send it to them, usually by post. ❑ *I had received a letter from a very close friend.* ❑ *a letter of resignation* **2** **Letters** are written symbols which represent one of the sounds in a language. ❑ *the letters of the alphabet* → See also **covering letter**

let·ter·box /ˈletəbɒks/ also **letter box** NOUN, ADJ **NOUN** [C] (**letterboxes**) (*mainly BrE; in AmE, usually use* mailbox) A **letterbox** is a rectangular hole in a door or a small box at the entrance to a building into which letters and small packages are delivered. **ADJ** If something is displayed on a television or computer screen in **letterbox** format, it is displayed across the middle of the screen with dark bands at the top and bottom of the screen.

let·ter·ing /ˈletərɪŋ/ NOUN [U] **Lettering** is writing, especially when you are describing the type of letters used. ❑ *a small blue sign with white lettering*

❂ **lev·el** ♦♦♦ /ˈlevəl/ NOUN, ADJ, ADV, VERB **NOUN** [C, SING] (**levels**) **1** [C] A **level** is a point on a scale, for example, a scale of amount, quality, or difficulty. = position, degree, stage ❑ *If you don't know your cholesterol level, it's a good idea to have it checked.* ❑ *We do have the lowest level of inflation for some years.* **2** [SING] The **level** of a river, lake, or sea or the **level** of liquid in a container is the height of its surface. ❑ *The water level of the Mississippi River is already 6.5 feet below normal.* **3** [SING] If something is at a particular **level**, it is at that height. ❑ *Liz sank down until the water came up to her chin and the bubbles were at eye level.* **4** [c] A **level** of a building is one of its different storeys, which is situated above or below other storeys. ❑ *Thurlow and Brown's rooms were on the second level, to the rear of the building.* **ADJ** **1** [V-LINK + level] If one thing is **level with** another thing, it is at the same height as it. ❑ *He leaned over the counter so his face was almost level with the boy's.* **2** When something is **level**, it is completely flat with no part higher than any other. ❑ *The floor was level, but the ceiling sloped towards his head.* **3** [V-LINK + level] If you are **level** with someone or something, you are by their side. ❑ *He waited until they were level with the door before he pivoted around sharply and punched Graham hard.* **ADV** [level after v] If you draw **level** with someone or something, you get closer to them until you are by their side. ❑ *Just before we drew level with the gates, he slipped out of the jeep and disappeared.* **VERB** [T] (**levels, levelling, levelled**; in AmE, use **leveling, leveled**) **1** If someone or something such as a violent storm **levels** a building or area of land, they destroy it completely or make it completely flat. ❑ *The storm was the most powerful to hit Hawaii this century. It levelled sugar plantations and destroyed homes.* **2** If an accusation or criticism **is levelled at** someone, they are accused of doing wrong or they are criticized for something they have done. ❑ *Allegations of corruption were levelled at him and his family.* **PHRASAL VERB** **level off** or **level out** **1** If a changing number or amount **levels off** or **levels out**, it stops increasing or decreasing at such a fast speed. ❑ *The figures show evidence that murders in the nation's capital are beginning to level off.* **2** If an aircraft **levels off** or **levels out**, it travels horizontally after having been travelling in an upwards or downwards direction. ❑ *The aircraft levelled out at about 30,000 feet.*

WORD CONNECTIONS
VERB + **level**
reduce a level
lower a level
increase a level
raise a level
❑ *Regular exercise can help to reduce stress levels.*
reach a level
maintain a level
achieve a level
❑ *Unemployment has reached its highest level for six years.*
ADJ + **level**
a **high** level
a **low** level
a **minimum** level
an **average** level
a **normal** level
❑ *Water is scarce due to low rainfall levels.*
a **record** level
❑ *Gas prices have risen to record levels.*

lev·er /ˈliːvə, AmE ˈlevˈ-/ NOUN, VERB
NOUN [c] (**levers**) **1** A **lever** is a handle or bar that is attached to a piece of machinery and which you push or pull in order to operate the machinery. ❑ *Push the tiny lever on the lock and let the door lock itself.* **2** A **lever** is a long bar, one end of which is placed under a heavy object so that when you press down on the other end you can move the object. ❑ *He examined the machine, worked a lever that lifted the lid.*
VERB [T] (**levers, levering, levered**) If you **lever** something

in a particular direction, you move it there, especially by using a lot of effort. ❑ *Neighbours eventually levered open the door with a crowbar.*

lev·er·age /ˈliːvərɪdʒ, AmE ˈlevˈ-/ NOUN, VERB
NOUN [u] **Leverage** is the ability to influence situations or people so that you can control what happens. ❑ *His position as mayor gives him leverage to get things done.*
VERB [T] (**leverages, leveraging, leveraged**) (business) To **leverage** a company or investment means to use borrowed money in order to buy it or pay for it. ❑ *He might feel that leveraging the company at a time when he sees tremendous growth opportunities would be a mistake.*

✪**levy** /ˈlevi/ NOUN, VERB (academic word)
NOUN [c] (**levies**) A **levy** is a sum of money that you have to pay, for example, as a tax to the government. = tax, charge ❑ *an annual levy on all drivers* ❑ *plans to impose a flat-rate levy on all businesses involved with the sale of food*
VERB [T] (**levies, levying, levied**) If a government or organization **levies** a tax or other sum of money, it demands it from people or organizations. = tax, charge ❑ *They levied religious taxes on Christian commercial transactions.* ❑ *Taxes should not be levied without the authority of Parliament.*

✪**lia·bil·ity** /ˌlaɪəˈbɪlɪti/ NOUN [c, u] (**liabilities**) **1** [c] If you say that someone or something is **a liability**, you mean that they cause a lot of problems or embarrassment. ❑ *As the president's prestige continues to fall, they're clearly beginning to consider him a liability.* **2** [u] **Liability for** something such as a debt is a legal responsibility for it. = responsibility ❑ *The company does not accept liability for fragile, valuable or perishable articles.* ❑ *He is claiming damages from London Underground, which has admitted liability but disputes the amount of his claim.* ❑ *This covers your legal liability for injury or damage which you may cause to others and their property.* **3** [c] (business, legal) A company's or organization's **liabilities** are the sums of money which it owes. ❑ *The company had assets of $138 million and liabilities of $120.5 million.*

✪**lia·ble** /ˈlaɪəbəl/ ADJ
ADJ **1** [V-LINK + liable 'to' N] If people or things are **liable to** something unpleasant, they are likely to experience it or do it. = prone ❑ *She will grow into a woman particularly liable to depression.* ❑ *This makes the muscles of the airways liable to constriction.* **2** [V-LINK + liable] If you are **liable for** something such as a debt, you are legally responsible for it. = legally responsible ❑ *The airline's insurer is liable for damages to the victims' families.* ❑ *As the killings took place outside British jurisdiction, the Ministry of Defence could not be held liable.*
PHRASE **be liable to** When something **is liable to** happen, it is very likely to happen. = likely to ❑ *Only a small minority of the mentally ill are liable to harm themselves or others.* ❑ *He is liable to change his mind quite rapidly.*

li·aise /liˈeɪz/ VERB [RECIP] (**liaises, liaising, liaised**) (mainly BrE) When organizations or people **liaise**, or when one organization **liaises with** another, they work together and keep each other informed about what is happening. ❑ *Detectives are liaising with police following the bomb explosion early today.*

liai·son /liˈeɪzɒn, AmE ˈliːəzɑːn/ NOUN [u, SING] **1** [u] **Liaison** is cooperation and the exchange of information between different organizations or between different sections of an organization. ❑ *Liaison between police forces and the art world is vital to combat art crime.* **2** [u, SING] [also 'a' liaison, oft liaison 'with' N] If someone acts as **liaison** with a particular group, or **between** two or more groups, their job is to encourage co-operation and the exchange of information. ❑ *He is acting as liaison with the film crew.* ❑ *She acts as a liaison between patients and staff.*

liar /ˈlaɪə/ NOUN [c] (**liars**) If you say that someone is a **liar**, you mean that they tell lies. ❑ *He was a liar and a cheat.*

li·bel /ˈlaɪbəl/ NOUN, VERB
NOUN [c, u] (**libels**) (legal) **Libel** is a written statement which wrongly accuses someone of something, and which is therefore against the law. Compare **slander**. ❑ *Warren sued him for libel over the remarks.*
VERB [T] (**libels, libelling, libelled**; in AmE, use **libeling, libeled**)

(legal) To **libel** someone means to write or print something in a book, newspaper, or magazine which wrongly damages that person's reputation and is therefore against the law. ❑ *The newspaper which libelled him had already offered compensation.*

✪ **lib·er·al** ◆◆◇ /'lɪbərəl/ ADJ, NOUN *(academic word)*
ADJ **1** Someone who has **liberal** views believes people should have a lot of freedom in deciding how to behave and think. ❑ *She is known to have liberal views on divorce and contraception.* ❑ *Traditional values were challenged in the 1960s by a more liberal attitude.* **2** A **liberal** system allows people or organizations a lot of political or economic freedom. ❑ *a liberal democracy with a multiparty political system* ❑ *They favour liberal free-market policies.* **3** [liberal + N] A **Liberal** politician or voter is a member of a Liberal Party or votes for a Liberal Party. ❑ *She withdrew because she did not wish to split the Liberal vote.* **4** **Liberal** means giving, using, or taking a lot of something, or existing in large quantities. ❑ *As always he is liberal with his jokes.*
NOUN [c] **(liberals)** **1** A **liberal** is someone who believes that people should have a lot of freedom in deciding how to behave and think. ❑ *a nation of free-thinking liberals* **2** A **liberal** is someone who believes in a political and economic system that gives people and organizations freedom to act as they choose. ❑ *These kinds of price controls go against all the financial principles of the free-market liberals.* ❑ *Even the bleeding-heart liberals must surely realise that in a war zone occasionally innocents get killed.* **3** A **Liberal** is someone who votes for or is a member of a Liberal Party. ❑ *The Liberals hold twenty-three seats.*
lib·er·al·ly /'lɪbərəli/ ADV [liberally with v] ❑ *Chemical products were used liberally over agricultural land.*

✪ **lib·er·al·ize** /'lɪbrəlaɪz/ also **liberalise** VERB [I, T] **(liberalizes, liberalizing, liberalized)** When a country or government **liberalizes**, or **liberalizes** its laws or its attitudes, it becomes less strict and allows people more freedom in their actions. = relax, ease, moderate ❑ *authoritarian states that have only now begun to liberalize* ❑ *the decision to liberalize travel restrictions*
✪ **lib·er·al·iza·tion** /ˌlɪbrə·laɪˈzeɪʃən/ NOUN [u] = relaxation, easing, moderation ❑ *the liberalization of divorce laws in the late 1960s*

✪ **lib·er·ate** ◆◇◇ /'lɪbəreɪt/ VERB [T] **(liberates, liberating, liberated)** **1** To **liberate** a place or the people in it means to free them from the political or military control of another country, area, or group of people. ❑ *They planned to march on and liberate the city.* ❑ *They made a triumphal march into their liberated city.* **2** To **liberate** someone from something means to help them escape from it or overcome it, and lead a better way of life. = free ❑ *He asked how committed the leadership was to liberating its people from poverty.*
✪ **lib·era·tion** /ˌlɪbəˈreɪʃən/ NOUN [u] **1** = freedom ❑ *a mass liberation movement* **2** *the women's liberation movement*
lib·er·at·ing /'lɪbəreɪtɪŋ/ ADJ ❑ *If you have the chance to spill your problems out to a therapist it can be a very liberating experience.* ❑ *Knowledge can be both empowering, liberating and a source of economic well being.*

✪ **lib·er·ty** ◆◇◇ /'lɪbəti/ NOUN
NOUN [c, u] **(liberties)** **1** [c, u] **Liberty** is the freedom to live your life in the way that you want, without interference from other people or the authorities. = freedom ❑ *the ideal of equality and the appreciation of liberty* ❑ *Wit Wolzek claimed the legislation could impinge on privacy, self determination and respect for religious liberty.* ❑ *Such a system would be a fundamental blow to the rights and liberties of the English people.* **2** [u] **Liberty** is the freedom to go wherever you want, which you lose when you are a prisoner. ❑ *Why not say that three convictions before court for stealing cars means three months' loss of liberty.*
PHRASE **at liberty to do** If someone is **at liberty to do** something, they have been given permission to do it. = able ❑ *The island's in the Pacific Ocean; I'm not at liberty to say exactly where, because we're still negotiating for its purchase.*

li·brar·ian /laɪˈbreəriən/ NOUN [c] **(librarians)** A **librarian** is a person who is in charge of a library or who has been specially trained to work in a library. ❑ *The new librarian is a friend of mine.*

✪ **li·brary** ◆◇◇ /'laɪbrəri, AmE -breri/ NOUN [c] **(libraries)** **1** A public **library** is a building where things such as books, newspapers, videos, and music are kept for people to read, use, or borrow. ❑ *the local library* ❑ *She issued them library cards.* **2** A private **library** is a collection of things such as books or music, that is normally only used with the permission of the owner. ❑ *The company owns a very diverse library of Arabic music.* **3** A **library** is a building or a room, for example in a school or hospital, where things such as books, newspapers, videos, and music are kept for people to read, use, or borrow. ❑ *a manuscript held in the university library* **4** In some large houses the **library** is the room where most of the books are kept. ❑ *Guests were rarely entertained in the library.*

✪ **li·cence** ◆◇◇ /'laɪsəns/ **(BrE; in AmE, use license) (licences)** NOUN [c, u] *(academic word)* **1** [c] A **licence** is an official document which gives you permission to do, use, or own something. = permit ❑ *The judge fined the man and suspended his licence.* ❑ *The company has applied to the FDA for a licence to sell the drug.* ❑ *Payne lost his driving licence a year ago for drink-driving.* ❑ *It gained a licence to operate as a bank in 1981.* **2** [u] [also 'a' licence, licence + to-INF] If you say that something gives someone **licence** or **a licence to** act in a particular way, you mean that it gives them an excuse to behave in an irresponsible or excessive way. ❑ *Partition would give licence to other aggressors in other conflicts.*

WORD CONNECTIONS
VERB + **licence**
issue a licence **grant** a licence ❑ *The Driver and Vehicle Licensing Agency may issue a driving licence that is valid for a limited period.*
suspend a licence **revoke** a licence ❑ *Gun owners who develop mental health problems are likely to have have their licences revoked.*
ADJ + **licence**
a **valid** licence ❑ *Driving without a valid licence is a criminal offence.*
NOUN + **licence**
a **driving** licence a **fishing** licence a **gun** licence a **marriage** licence ❑ *It is illegal to fish in this river without a fishing licence.*
a **software** licence an **entertainment** licence a **television** licence a **gaming** licence ❑ *People over the age of 75 are entitled to free television licences in Britain.*

✪ **li·cense** ◆◇◇ /'laɪsəns/ VERB [T] **(licenses, licensing, licensed)** To **license** a person or activity means to give official permission for the person to do something or for the activity to take place. ❑ *a proposal that would require the state to license guns the way it does cars* ❑ *Under the agreement, the council can license a US company to produce the drug.*

lick /lɪk/ VERB, NOUN
VERB [T] **(licks, licking, licked)** When people or animals **lick** something, they move their tongue across its surface. ❑ *She folded up her letter, licking the envelope flap with relish.*
NOUN [c] **(licks)** **1** When people or animals have a **lick** of something, they move their tongue across its surface. ❑ *It's incredible how long a cat can go without more than a lick of milk or water.* **2** [usu lick 'of' N] *(informal)* A **lick** of something is a small amount of it. ❑ *It could do with a lick of paint to brighten up its premises.*
✦ **lick into shape** → see **shape**

lid /lɪd/ NOUN [c] (**lids**) A **lid** is the top of a box or other container which can be removed or raised when you want to open the container. = **top** □ *She lifted the lid of the box and displayed the contents.*

lie ♦♦◇ /laɪ/ VERB, NOUN

The form **lied** is used as the past tense and past participle for meaning 8 of the verb.

VERB [I, LINK, T] (**lies, lying, lay, lain**) **1** [I] If you **are lying** somewhere, you are in a horizontal position and are not standing or sitting. □ *There was a child lying on the ground.* **2** [I] If an object **lies** in a particular place, it is in a flat position in that place. □ *a newspaper lying on a nearby couch* **3** [I] If you say that a place **lies** in a particular position or direction, you mean that it is situated there. = **sit** □ *The islands lie at the southern end of the Kurile chain.* **4** [LINK] You can use **lie** to say that something is or remains in a particular state or condition. For example, if something **lies forgotten**, it has been and remains forgotten. □ *The picture lay hidden in the archives for over 40 years.* **5** [I] You can talk about where something such as a problem, solution, or fault **lies** to say what you think it consists of, involves, or is caused by. □ *The problem lay with the family and the school system rather than with television.* **6** [I] You use **lie** in expressions such as **lie ahead, lie in store**, and **lie in wait** when you are talking about what someone is going to experience in the future, especially when it is something unpleasant or difficult. □ *She'd need all her strength and bravery to cope with what lay in store.* **7** [I, T] (*BrE*) You can use **lie** to say what position a competitor or team is in during a competition. □ *I was going well and was lying fourth.* **8** [I] If someone **is lying**, they are saying something which they know is not true. □ *I know he's lying.*

PHRASAL VERBS **lie around** (in *BrE*, also use **lie about**) If things are left **lying around** or **lying about**, they are not put away but left casually somewhere where they can be seen. □ *People should be careful about their possessions and not leave them lying around.*
lie behind If you refer to what **lies behind** a situation or event, you are referring to the reason the situation exists or the event happened. □ *It seems that what lay behind the clashes was disagreement over the list of candidates.*
lie down When you **lie down**, you move into a horizontal position, usually in order to rest or sleep. □ *Why don't you go upstairs and lie down for a bit?*
NOUN [c] (**lies**) A **lie** is something that someone says or writes which they know is untrue. □ *'Who else do you work for?'—'No one.'—'That's a lie.'* □ *I've had enough of your lies.*
✦ **lie in state** → see **state; take something lying down** → see **take**

lieu /ljuː, *AmE* luː/ NOUN
PHRASES **in lieu of** (*formal*) If you do, get, or give one thing **in lieu of** another, you do, get, or give it instead of the other thing, because the two things are considered to have the same value or importance. □ *He left what little furniture he owned to his landlord in lieu of rent.*
in lieu (*formal*) If you do, get, or give something **in lieu**, you do, get, or give it instead of something else, because the two things are considered to have the same value or importance. □ *an increased salary or time off in lieu*

life ♦♦♦ /laɪf/ NOUN
NOUN [U, c] (**lives**) **1** [U] **Life** is the quality which people, animals, and plants have when they are not dead, and which objects and substances do not have. □ *a baby's first minutes of life* □ *Amnesty International opposes the death penalty as a violation of the right to life.* **2** [U] You can use **life** to refer to things or groups of things which are alive. □ *Is there life on Mars?* **3** [c] If you refer to someone's **life**, you mean their state of being alive, especially when there is a risk or danger of them dying. □ *Your life is in danger.* □ *A nurse began to try to save his life.* **4** [c] Someone's **life** is the period of time during which they are alive. □ *He spent the last fourteen years of his life in retirement.* **5** [c] You can use **life** to refer to a period of someone's life when they are in a particular situation or job. □ *Interior designers spend their working lives keeping up to date with the latest trends.*

6 [c] You can use **life** to refer to particular activities which people regularly do during their lives. □ *My personal life has had to take second place to my career.* **7** [U] You can use **life** to refer to the things that people do and experience that are characteristic of a particular place, group, or activity. □ *How did you adjust to college life?* □ *He abhors the wheeling-and-dealing associated with conventional political life.* **8** [U] A person, place, book, or film that is full of **life** gives an impression of excitement, energy, or cheerfulness. □ *The town itself was full of life and character.* **9** [U] (*informal*) If someone is sentenced to **life**, they are sentenced to stay in prison for the rest of their life or for a very long time. □ *He could get life in prison, if convicted.* **10** [c] The **life** of something such as a machine, organization, or project is the period of time that it lasts for. □ *The repairs did not increase the value or the life of the equipment.*
PHRASES **bring something to life** or **come to life** If you **bring** something **to life** or if it **comes to life**, it becomes interesting or exciting. □ *The cold, hard cruelty of two young men is vividly brought to life in this true story.*
come to life or **spring to life** or **roar into life** (*literary*) You can use expressions such as **to come to life, to spring to life**, and **to roar into life** to indicate that a machine or vehicle suddenly starts working or moving. □ *To his great relief the engine came to life.*
fight for one's life (*journalism*) If you say that someone **is fighting for** their **life**, you mean that they are in a very serious condition and may die as a result of an accident or illness. □ *a horrifying robbery that left a man fighting for his life*
for life For **life** means for the rest of a person's life. □ *He was jailed for life in 1966 for the murder of three policemen.* □ *She may have been scarred for life.*
take someone's life (*formal*) If someone **takes** another person's **life**, they kill them. If someone **takes** their own **life**, they kill themselves. □ *Before execution, he admitted to taking the lives of at least 35 more women.*
✦ **a matter of life and death** → see **death**

◆**life ex·pec·tan·cy** NOUN [c, u] (**life expectancies**) The **life expectancy** of a person, animal, or plant is the length of time that they are normally likely to live. □ *The average life expectancy was 40.* □ *a dramatic increase in Western average life expectancy* □ *They had longer life expectancies than their parents.*

life·line /ˈlaɪflaɪn/ NOUN [c] (**lifelines**) A **lifeline** is something that enables an organization or group to survive or to continue with an activity. □ *Information about the job market can be a lifeline for those who are out of work.*

life·long /ˈlaɪflɒŋ, *AmE* -lɔːŋ/ ADJ [lifelong + N] **Lifelong** means existing or happening for the whole of a person's life. □ *her lifelong friendship with Naomi*

life·span /ˈlaɪfspæn/ also **life span** NOUN [c, u] (**lifespans**) **1** [c, u] The **lifespan** of a person, animal, or plant is the period of time for which they live or are normally expected to live. □ *A 15-year lifespan is not uncommon for a dog.* **2** [c] The **lifespan** of a product, organization, or idea is the period of time for which it is expected to work properly or to last. □ *Most boilers have a lifespan of 15 to 20 years.*

◆**life·style** /ˈlaɪfstaɪl/ also **life-style, life style** NOUN, ADJ
NOUN [c, u] (**lifestyles**) The **lifestyle** of a particular person or group of people is the living conditions, behaviour, and habits that are typical of them or are chosen by them. = **way of life** □ *They enjoyed an income and lifestyle that many people would envy.* □ *the change of lifestyle occasioned by the baby's arrival*
ADJ **1** [lifestyle + N] **Lifestyle** magazines, television programmes, and products are aimed at people who wish to be associated with glamorous and successful lifestyles. □ *This year people are going for luxury and buying lifestyle products.* **2** [lifestyle + N] **Lifestyle** drugs are drugs that are intended to improve people's quality of life rather than to treat particular medical disorders. □ *'I see anti-depressants as a lifestyle drug,' says Dr Charlton.*

◆**life·time** /ˈlaɪftaɪm/ NOUN [c] (**lifetimes**) A **lifetime** is the length of time that someone is alive. ❑ *During my lifetime I haven't got around to much travelling.* ❑ *a trust fund to be administered throughout his wife's lifetime* ❑ *an extraordinary lifetime of achievement*

lift ◆◆◇ /lɪft/ VERB, NOUN

VERB [T, I] (**lifts, lifting, lifted**) **1** [T] If you **lift** something, you move it to another position, especially upward. ❑ *The colonel lifted the phone and dialled his superior.* **2** [T] If you **lift** your eyes or your head, you look up, for example, when you have been reading and someone comes into the room. = raise ❑ *When he finished he lifted his eyes and looked out the window.* **3** [T] If people in authority **lift** a law or rule that prevents people from doing something, they end it. ❑ *The European Commission has urged France to lift its ban on imports of British beef.* **4** [I, T] If something **lifts** your spirits or your mood, or if they **lift**, you start feeling more cheerful. ❑ *He used his incredible sense of humour to lift my spirits.* **5** [T] If a government or organization **lifts** people or goods in or out of an area, it transports them there by aircraft, especially when there is a war. = fly ❑ *The army lifted people off rooftops where they had climbed to escape the flooding.* **6** [T] (*BrE*) To **lift** something means to increase its amount or to increase the level or the rate at which it happens. = increase

PHRASAL VERB **lift up** Lift **up** means the same as **lift** VERB **1**. ❑ *She put her arms around him and lifted him up.*

NOUN [C, U] (**lifts**) **1** [C] (*BrE*; in *AmE*, use **elevator**) A **lift** is a device that carries people or goods up and down inside tall buildings. **2** [C] If you give someone a **lift** somewhere, you take them there in your car as a favour to them. = ride ❑ *He had a car and often gave me a lift home.* **3** [U] **Lift** is the force that makes an aircraft leave the ground and stay in the air. ❑ *A plane has to reach a certain speed before there is enough lift to get it off the ground.*

✦ **lift a finger** → see **finger**

light ◆◆◇ /laɪt/ NOUN, VERB, ADJ, COMB

NOUN [PL, C, U] (**lights**) **1** [PL, C, U] [also 'the' light] **Light** is the brightness that lets you see things. Light comes from sources such as the sun, moon, lamps, and fire. ❑ *Cracks of light filtered through the shutters.* ❑ *ultraviolet light* **2** [C] A **light** is something such as an electric lamp which produces light. ❑ *The janitor comes around to turn the lights out.* **3** [PL] You can use **lights** to refer to a set of traffic lights. ❑ *the heavy city traffic with its endless delays at lights and crosswalks* **4** [C] If something is presented in a particular **light**, it is presented so that you think about it in a particular way or so that it appears to be of a particular nature. ❑ *He has worked hard in recent months to portray New York in a better light.*

PHRASES **come to light** or **bring something to light** If something **comes to light** or is **brought to light**, it becomes obvious or is made known to a lot of people. ❑ *Nothing about this sum has come to light.*

give someone a green light or **give someone the green light** If someone in authority gives you **a green light**, they give you permission to do something. ❑ *The food industry was given a green light to extend the use of these chemicals.*

in the light of something If something is possible **in the light of** particular information, it is only possible because you have this information. ❑ *In the light of this information it is now possible to identify a number of key issues.*

shed light on something or **throw light on something** or **cast light on something** To **shed light on**, **throw light on**, or **cast light on** something means to make it easier to understand, because more information is known about it. = clarify ❑ *A new approach offers an answer, and may shed light on an even bigger question.*

set light to something (*mainly BrE*; in *AmE*, usually use **set fire to**) If you **set light to** something, you make it start burning.

VERB [T, I] (**lights, lighting, lit** or **lighted**) **1** [T] If a place or object **is lit** by something, it has light shining on it. ❑ *It was dark and a giant moon lit the road so brightly you could see the landscape clearly.* ❑ *The room was lit by only the one light.* **2** [I, T] If you **light** something such as a cigarette or fire, or if it **lights**, it starts burning. ❑ *Stephen hunched down to light a cigarette.* ❑ *If the charcoal does fail to light,*

use a special liquid spray and light it with a long taper.

PHRASAL VERB **light up** **1** If you **light** something **up** or if it **lights up**, it becomes bright, usually when you shine light on it. ❑ *a keypad that lights up when you pick up the handset* **2** If your face or your eyes **light up**, you suddenly look very surprised or happy. ❑ *Sue's face lit up with surprise.*

ADJ (**lighter, lightest**) **1** If it is **light**, the sun is providing light at the beginning or end of the day. ❑ *It was still light when we arrived at Lalong Creek.* **2** If a room or building is **light**, it has a lot of natural light in it, for example, because it has large windows. = bright ❑ *It is a light room with tall windows.* **3** [usu with SUPP] Something that is **light** does not weigh very much, or weighs less than you would expect it to. ❑ *Modern tennis rackets are now apparently 20 per cent lighter.* ❑ *weight training with light weights* **4** Something that is **light** is not very great in amount, degree, or intensity. ❑ *It's a Sunday like any other with the usual light traffic in the city.* ❑ *Trading was very light ahead of yesterday's auction.* **5** Something that is **light** is very pale in colour. ❑ *He is light haired with grey eyes.* **6** [light + N] A **light** sleep is one that is easily disturbed and in which you are often aware of the things around you. If you are a **light** sleeper, you are easily woken when you are asleep. ❑ *She had drifted into a light sleep.* **7** A **light** meal consists of food that is easy to digest. ❑ *a light, healthy lunch* **8** **Light** work does not involve much physical effort. ❑ *He was on the training field for some light work yesterday.* **9** If you describe the result of an action or a punishment as **light**, you mean that it is less serious or severe than you expected. = lenient ❑ *She confessed her astonishment at her light sentence when her father visited her at the jail.* **10** Movements and actions that are **light** are graceful or gentle and are done with very little force or effort. = gentle ❑ *Use a light touch when applying cream or makeup.* **11** **Light** is used to describe foods or drinks that contain few calories or low amounts of sugar, fat, or alcohol. ❑ *There's been a flood of low-fat and light ice creams on the market.* ❑ *They refreshed themselves with cans of light beer.* **12** If you describe things such as books, music, and films as **light**, you mean that they entertain you without making you think very deeply. ❑ *He doesn't like me reading light novels.* ❑ *light classical music* **13** If you say something in a **light** way, you sound as if you think that something is not important or serious. ❑ *Talk to him in a friendly, light way about the relationship.*

PHRASE **make light of something** If you **make light of** something, you treat it as though it is not serious or important, when in fact it is. = play down ❑ *Roberts attempted to make light of his discomfort.*

COMB **Light** is used before a colour to describe something that is a pale shade of that colour. ❑ *We know he has a light green van.*

light-ness /ˈlaɪtnəs/ NOUN [U] **1** *The dark green spare bedroom is in total contrast to the lightness of the large main bedroom.* **2** *The toughness, lightness, strength, and elasticity of whalebone gave it a wide variety of uses.* **3** *She danced with a grace and lightness that were breathtaking.* **4** *'I'm not an authority on them,' Jessica said with forced lightness.*

light·ly /ˈlaɪtli/ ADV **1** *Put the onions in the pan and cook until lightly browned.* **2** *He was dozing lightly in his chair.* **3** [lightly after V] ❑ *She found it impossible to eat lightly.* **4** [lightly after V] ❑ *One of the accused got off lightly in exchange for pleading guilty to withholding information from Congress.* **5** [lightly after V] ❑ *He kissed her lightly on the mouth.* **6** [lightly after V] ❑ *'Once a detective, always a detective,' he said lightly.*

→ See also **lighter, lighting**

✦ **all sweetness and light** → see **sweetness**

light·en /ˈlaɪtən/ VERB [I, T] (**lightens, lightening, lightened**) **1** [I, T] When something **lightens** or when you **lighten** it, it becomes less dark in colour. ❑ *The sky began to lighten.* **2** [T] If someone **lightens** a situation, they make it less serious or less boring. ❑ *Anthony felt the need to lighten the atmosphere.* **3** [I, T] If your attitude or mood **lightens**, or if something or someone **lightens** it, they make you feel more cheerful, happy, and relaxed. ❑ *As they approached the outskirts of the city, Ella's mood visibly lightened.*

light·er /ˈlaɪtə/ NOUN [C] (**lighters**) A **lighter** is a small device that produces a flame which you can use to light cigarettes, cigars, and pipes.

light·hearted /'laɪt'hɑːtɪd/ also **light-hearted** ADJ **1** Someone who is **lighthearted** is cheerful and happy. ❑ *I was amazingly lighthearted and peaceful.* **2** Something that is **lighthearted** is intended to be entertaining or amusing, and not at all serious. ❑ *There have been many attempts, both lighthearted and serious, to locate the Loch Ness Monster.*

light·ing /'laɪtɪŋ/ NOUN [U] The **lighting** in a place is the way that it is lit, for example, by electric lights, by candles, or by windows, or the quality of the light in it. ❑ *the bright fluorescent lighting of the laboratory* ❑ *The whole room is bathed in soft lighting.*

light·ning /'laɪtnɪŋ/ NOUN, ADJ
NOUN [U] **Lightning** is the very bright flashes of light in the sky that happen during thunderstorms. ❑ *One man died when he was struck by lightning.* ❑ *Another flash of lightning lit up the cave.*
ADJ [lightning + N] **Lightning** describes things that happen very quickly or last for only a short time. ❑ *Driving today demands lightning reflexes.*

light·weight /'laɪtweɪt/ also **light-weight** ADJ, NOUN
ADJ **1** Something that is **lightweight** weighs less than most other things of the same type. ❑ *lightweight denim* **2** If you describe someone or something as **lightweight**, you mean that they are not very important or impressive. ❑ *Some of the discussion in the book is lightweight and unconvincing.*
NOUN [U, C] (**lightweights**) **1** [U] **Lightweight** is a category in some sports, such as boxing, judo, or rowing, based on the weight of the athlete. ❑ *By the age of sixteen he was the junior lightweight champion of Poland.* **2** [C] If you describe someone as a **lightweight**, you are critical of them because you think that they are not very important or skilful in a particular area of activity. ❑ *Brian considered Sam a lightweight, a real amateur.*

lik·able /'laɪkəbəl/ also **likeable** ADJ Someone or something that is **likable** is pleasant and easy to like. = pleasant ❑ *He was a bright guy, a likable guy.*

like ◆◆◆ /laɪk/ PREP, CONJ, VERB, NOUN
PREP **1** If you say that one person or thing is **like** another, you mean that they share some of the same qualities or features. ❑ *He looks like Father Christmas.* ❑ *It's a bit like going to the dentist; it's never as bad as you fear.* ❑ *It's nothing like what happened in the mid-Seventies.* **2** If you talk about what something or someone is **like**, you are talking about their qualities or features. ❑ *What was Bulgaria like?* ❑ *What did she look like?* **3** [N + like + N/-ING] You can use **like** to introduce an example of the set of things or people that you have just mentioned. ❑ *The neglect that large cities like New York have received over the past 12 years is tremendous.* **4** You can use **like** to say that someone or something is in the same situation as another person or thing. ❑ *It also moved those who, like me, are too young to have lived through the war.* **5** [V + like + N] If you say that someone is behaving **like** something or someone else, you mean that they are behaving in a way that is typical of that kind of thing or person. **Like** is used in this way in many fixed expressions, for example, **to cry like a baby** and **to watch someone like a hawk**. ❑ *I was shaking all over, trembling like a leaf.* **6** [with NEG] You can use **like** in negative expressions such as **nothing like it** and **no place like it** to emphasize that there is nothing as good as the situation, thing, or person mentioned. ❑ *There's nothing like candlelight for creating a romantic mood.* **7** [with NEG] You can use **like** in expressions such as **nothing like** to make an emphatic negative statement. ❑ *Three hundred million dollars will be nothing like enough.*
PHRASES **like this** or **like that** or **like so** You say **like this**, **like that**, or **like so** when you are showing someone how something is done. ❑ *It opens and closes, like this.*
like this or **like that** You use **like this** or **like that** when you are drawing attention to something that you are doing or that someone else is doing. ❑ *I'm sorry to intrude on you like this.*

something like You use the expression **something like** with an amount, number, or description to indicate that it is approximately accurate. = about ❑ *They can get something like $3,000 a year.*
CONJ **1** **Like** is sometimes used as a conjunction in order to say that something appears to be the case when it is not. Some people consider this use to be incorrect. ❑ *His arms look like they might snap under the weight of his gloves.* **2** **Like** is sometimes used as a conjunction in order to indicate that something happens or is done in the same way as something else. Some people consider this use to be incorrect. ❑ *People are strolling, buying ice cream for their children, just like they do every Sunday.* ❑ *He spoke exactly like I did.*
VERB [T] (**likes**, **liking**, **liked**) **1** If you **like** something or someone, you think they are interesting, enjoyable, or attractive. ❑ *He likes baseball.* ❑ *I just didn't like being in crowds.* ❑ *Do you like to go swimming?* **2** If you ask someone how they **like** something, you are asking them for their opinion of it and whether they enjoy it or find it pleasant. ❑ *How do you like America?* **3** If you say that you **like to** do something or that you **like** something to be done, you mean that you prefer to do it or prefer it to be done as part of your normal life or routine. ❑ *I like to get to airports in good time.* **4** If you say that you **would like** something or **would like** to do something, you are indicating a wish or desire that you have. ❑ *I'd like a bath.* **5** If you ask someone if they **would like** something or **would like** to do something, you are making a polite offer or invitation. ❑ *Here's your change. Would you like a bag?* ❑ *Perhaps while you wait you would like a drink at the bar.* **6** If you say to someone that you **would like** something or you **would like** them to do something, or ask them if they **would like** to do it, you are politely telling them what you want or what you want them to do. ❑ *I'd like an explanation.* ❑ *We'd like you to look around and tell us if anything is missing.*
PHRASE **if you like** You say **if you like** when you are making or agreeing to an offer or suggestion in a casual way. ❑ *You can stay here if you like.*
NOUN [U, PL] (**likes**) **1** [U] You can use **like** in expressions such as **like attracts like**, when you are referring to two or more people or things that have the same or similar characteristics. ❑ *You have to make sure you're comparing like with like.* **2** [PL] Someone's **likes** are the things that they enjoy or find pleasant. ❑ *I thought that I knew everything about Jemma: her likes and dislikes, her political viewpoints.*
→ See also **liking**

USAGE NOTE
would like You use **would like** followed by a 'to'-infinitive to talk about a wish or a desire, or, in the form of a question, to invite someone politely. *I'd like to see him again.* **Would you like to come** for dinner? You do not use an '-ing' form after **would like**. You do not say, for example, '~~Would you like coming for dinner?~~'

like·able /'laɪkəbəl/ → See **likable**

✪ **like·li·hood** /'laɪklihʊd/ NOUN [U, SING] **1** [U] The **likelihood of** something happening is how likely it is to happen. = probability, possibility, chance ❑ *The likelihood of infection is minimal.* ❑ *concerns that these changes would increase the likelihood of wrongful conviction* **2** [SING] If something is a **likelihood**, it is likely to happen. = probability, possibility ❑ *But the likelihood is that people would be willing to pay if they were certain that their money was going to a good cause.*

VOCABULARY BUILDER
likelihood NOUN (*fairly formal*) The **likelihood of** something happening is how likely it is to happen. ❑ *In this snow, there was little likelihood that the tour would depart on schedule.*

I

probability NOUN

The **probability** of something happening is how likely it is to happen, sometimes expressed as a fraction or a percentage.

❑ *Without a transfusion, the victim's probability of dying was 100%.*

possibility NOUN

If you say there is a **possibility** that something is the case or that something will happen, you mean that it might be the case or it might happen.

❑ *Tax on food has become a very real possibility.*

chance NOUN (*mainly spoken*)

If there is a **chance** of something happening, it is possible that it will happen.

❑ *Do you think they have a chance of beating Australia?*

○**like·ly** ♦♦♦ /'laɪkli/ ADJ, ADV

ADJ (**likelier, likeliest**) **1** You use **likely** to indicate that something is probably the case or will probably happen in a particular situation. = probable, apt, expected, liable, anticipated; ≠ unlikely ❑ *Experts say a 'yes' vote is still the likely outcome.* ❑ *If this is your first baby, it's far more likely that you'll get to the hospital too early.* **2** [V-LINK + likely + to-INF] If someone or something is **likely to** do a particular thing, they will very probably do it. ❑ *In the meantime the war of nerves seems likely to continue.* ❑ *Once people have seen that something actually works, they are much more likely to accept change.*

ADV [likely with CL/GROUP] If something will **likely** happen, it will probably happen. = probably ❑ *Profit will most likely have risen by about $25 million.*

VOCABULARY BUILDER

likely ADJ
You use **likely** to indicate that something is probably the case or will probably happen in a particular situation.
❑ *Inflation is likely to rise in the coming months.*

probable ADJ
If you say that something is **probable**, you mean that you expect it to be true or to happen.
❑ *It is probable that the medication will suppress the symptoms.*

apt ADJ
If someone is **apt** to do something, they often do it and so it is likely that they will do it again.
❑ *She was apt to raise her voice and wave her hands about.*

expected ADJ (*fairly formal*)
If something is **expected**, you believe that it will happen.
❑ *The talks are expected to continue until tomorrow.*

liable ADJ
When something is **liable** to happen, it is very likely to happen.
❑ *He is liable to change his mind quite suddenly.*

anticipated ADJ (*mainly formal*)
If something is **anticipated**, you realize that it may happen and you prepare for it in advance.
❑ *Slightly less than half of the anticipated investment actually occurred.*

like-minded ADJ Like-minded people have similar opinions, ideas, attitudes, or interests. ❑ *the opportunity to mix with hundreds of like-minded people*

lik·en /'laɪkən/ VERB [T] (**likens, likening, likened**) If you **liken** one thing or person **to** another thing or person, you say that they are similar. = compare ❑ *She likens marriage to slavery.*

like·ness /'laɪknəs/ NOUN [SING, C] (**likenesses**) **1** [SING] If two things or people have a **likeness to** each other, they are similar to each other. = similarity ❑ *These myths have*

a startling **likeness** to one another. **2** [C] A **likeness of** someone is a picture or sculpture of them. ❑ *The museum displays wax likenesses of every US president.* **3** [C] If you say that a picture of someone is a good **likeness**, you mean that it looks just like them. ❑ *She says the artist's impression is an excellent likeness of her abductor.*

○**like·wise** /'laɪkwaɪz/ ADV (*academic word*) **1** You use **likewise** when you are comparing two methods, states, or situations and saying that they are similar. = similarly ❑ *What is fair for homeowners likewise should be fair to businesses.* ❑ *All attempts by the Socialists to woo him back were spurned. Similar overtures from the right have likewise been rejected.* ❑ *The V2 was not an ordinary weapon: it could only be used against cities. Likewise the atom bomb.* **2** [likewise after v] If you do something and someone else does **likewise**, they do the same or a similar thing. ❑ *He lent money, made donations and encouraged others to do likewise.*

lik·ing /'laɪkɪŋ/ NOUN

NOUN [SING] If you have a **liking for** something or someone, you like them. ❑ *She had a liking for good clothes.* ❑ *He bought me CDs to encourage my liking for music.*

PHRASES **for someone's liking** If something is, for example, too fast **for** your **liking**, you would prefer it to be slower. If it is not fast enough **for** your **liking**, you would prefer it to be faster. ❑ *He had become too powerful for their liking.*

to someone's liking If something is **to** your **liking**, it suits your interests, tastes, or wishes. ❑ *London was more to his liking than Rome.*

lily /'lɪli/ NOUN [C, U] (**lilies**) A **lily** is a plant with large flowers that are often white.

limb /lɪm/ NOUN

NOUN [C] (**limbs**) Your **limbs** are your arms and legs. ❑ *She would be able to stretch out her cramped limbs and rest for a few hours.*

PHRASE **out on a limb** If someone goes **out on a limb**, they do something they strongly believe in even though it is risky or extreme, and is likely to fail or be criticized by other people. ❑ *They can see themselves going out on a limb, voting for a very controversial energy bill.*

lime /laɪm/ NOUN [C, U] (**limes**) **1** [C, U] A **lime** is a green fruit that tastes like a lemon. Limes grow on trees in tropical countries. ❑ *peeled slices of lime* **2** [U] **Lime** is a substance containing calcium. It is found in soil and water. ❑ *If your soil is very acidic, add lime.*

lime·light /'laɪmlaɪt/ NOUN [U] If someone is in the **limelight**, a lot of attention is being paid to them, because they are famous or because they have done something very unusual or exciting. ❑ *Tony has now been thrust into the limelight, with a high-profile job.*

○**lim·it** ♦♦◇ /'lɪmɪt/ NOUN, VERB

NOUN [C, PL] (**limits**) **1** [C] A **limit** is the greatest amount, extent, or degree of something that is possible. = utmost ❑ *Her love for him was being tested to its limits.* ❑ *There is no limit to how much fresh fruit you can eat in a day.* ❑ *warnings that hospitals are being stretched to the limit* **2** [C] A **limit** of a particular kind is the largest or smallest amount of something such as time or money that is allowed because of a rule, law, or decision. = restriction ❑ *The three month time limit will be up in mid-June.* ❑ *The economic affairs minister announced limits on petrol sales.* **3** [C] The **limit** of an area is its boundary or edge. ❑ *the city limits of Baghdad* **4** [PL] The **limits of** a situation are the facts involved in it which make only some actions or results possible. ❑ *She has to work within the limits of a fairly tight budget.*

PHRASE **off limits** If an area or a place is **off limits**, you are not allowed to go there. ❑ *A one-mile area around the wreck is still off limits.*

VERB [T] (**limits, limiting, limited**) **1** If you **limit** something, you prevent it from becoming greater than a particular amount or degree. = restrict ❑ *He limited payments on the country's foreign debt.* ❑ *The view was that the economy would grow by 2.25 per cent. This would limit unemployment to around 2.5 million.* **2** If you **limit yourself** to something, or if someone or something **limits** you, the number of things that you have or do is reduced. ❑ *Please limit letters to 125 words or less.* **3** If something **is limited to**

a particular place or group of people, it exists only in that place, or is had or done only by that group. ☐ *The protests were not limited to New York.*

lim·it·ing /ˈlɪmɪtɪŋ/ ADJ ☐ *The conditions laid down to me were not too limiting.*

→ See also **limited**

WORD CONNECTIONS
VERB + **limit**
impose a limit
set a limit
place a limit
☐ *Most providers impose a limit on how much data you can download.*
reach a limit
exceed a limit
☐ *Should manufacturers make cars that can exceed the speed limit by a substantial amount?*
raise a limit
reduce a limit
☐ *The government is considering raising the age limit for buying knives from 16 to 18.*
ADJ + **limit**
a strict limit
a legal limit
a daily limit
a reasonable limit
an absolute limit
☐ *There are strict limits on what you may legally copy, to protect the rights of both author and publisher.*
a maximum limit
an upper limit
a minimum limit
a lower limit
☐ *There is no upper age limit for membership.*
NOUN + **limit**
a speed limit
a time limit
an age limit
a credit limit
☐ *I slowed down to keep inside the speed limit.*

limi·ta·tion /ˌlɪmɪˈteɪʃən/ NOUN [U, C, PL] (**limitations**) **1** [U] The **limitation** of something is the act or process of controlling or reducing it. ☐ *All the talk had been about the limitation of nuclear weapons.* **2** [C, U] A **limitation on** something is a rule or decision which prevents that thing from growing or extending beyond certain limits. ☐ *a limitation on the tax deductions for people who make more than $100,000 a year* **3** [PL] If you talk about the **limitations** of someone or something, you mean that they can only do some things and not others, or cannot do something very well. ☐ *I realized how possible it was to overcome your limitations, to achieve well beyond what you believe yourself capable of.* **4** [C, U] A **limitation** is a fact or situation that allows only some actions and makes others impossible. ☐ *This drug has one important limitation. Its effects only last six hours.*

lim·it·ed ◆◇◇ /ˈlɪmɪtɪd/ ADJ **1** Something that is **limited** is not very great in amount, range, or degree. = small ☐ *They may only have a limited amount of time to get their points across.* **2** (BrE; in AmE, use **incorporated**; *business*) A **limited** company is one whose owners are legally responsible for only a part of any money that it may owe if it goes bankrupt.

lim·it·less /ˈlɪmɪtləs/ ADJ If you describe something as **limitless**, you mean that there is or appears to be so much of it that it will never be exhausted. = endless ☐ *a cheap and potentially limitless supply of energy*

limp /lɪmp/ VERB, NOUN, ADJ
VERB [I] (**limps, limping, limped**) **1** If a person or animal **limps**, they walk with difficulty or in an uneven way because one of their legs or feet is hurt. ☐ *I wasn't badly*

hurt, but I injured my thigh and had to limp. **2** If you say that something such as an organization, process, or vehicle **limps along**, you mean that it continues slowly or with difficulty, for example because it has been weakened or damaged. ☐ *In recent years the newspaper had been limping along on limited resources.*

NOUN [C] (**limps**) If a person or animal has a **limp**, they walk with difficulty or in an uneven way because one of their legs or feet is hurt. ☐ *A stiff knee following surgery forced her to walk with a limp.*

ADJ (**limper, limpest**) **1** If you describe something as **limp**, you mean that it is soft or weak when it should be firm or strong. ☐ *She was told to reject applicants with limp handshakes.* **2** If someone is **limp**, their body has no strength and is not moving, for example, because they are asleep or unconscious. ☐ *He carried her limp body into the room and laid her on the bed.*

limp·ly /ˈlɪmpli/ ADV [limply with V] ☐ *Flags and bunting hung limply in the still, warm air.*

line ◆◆◆ /laɪn/ NOUN, VERB
NOUN [C, U, PL] (**lines**) **1** [C] A **line** is a long thin mark which is drawn or painted on a surface. ☐ *Draw a line down that page's centre.* ☐ *a dotted line* **2** [C] The **lines** on someone's skin, especially on their face, are long thin marks that appear there as they grow older. = wrinkle ☐ *He has a large, generous face with deep lines.* **3** [C] A **line** of people or things is a number of them arranged one behind the other or side by side. = row ☐ *The sparse line of spectators noticed nothing unusual.* **4** [C] A **line** of a piece of writing is one of the rows of words, numbers, or other symbols in it. ☐ *The next line should read: Five days, 23.5 hours.* **5** [C] A **line** of a poem, song, or play is a group of words that are spoken or sung together. If an actor **learns** his or her **lines** for a play or film, they learn what they have to say. ☐ *a line from Shakespeare's Othello: 'one that loved not wisely but too well'* ☐ *Every time I sing that line, I have to compete with that darn trombone!* **6** [C, U] You can refer to a long piece of wire, string, or cable as a **line** when it is used for a particular purpose. ☐ *She put her washing on the line.* ☐ *a piece of fishing-line* **7** [C] A **line** is a connection which makes it possible for two people to speak to each other on the telephone. ☐ *The telephone lines went dead.* ☐ *It's not a very good line. Shall we call you back Susan?* **8** [C] You can use **line** to refer to a telephone number which you can call in order to get information or advice. ☐ *the 24-hour information line* **9** [C] A **line** is a route, especially a dangerous or secret one, along which people move or send messages or supplies. ☐ *The North American continent's geography severely limited the lines of attack.* ☐ *Negotiators say they're keeping communication lines open.* **10** [C] The **line** in which something or someone moves is the particular route that they take, especially when they keep moving straight ahead. ☐ *Walk in a straight line.* **11** [C] A **line** is a particular route, involving the same stations, roads, or stops along which a train or bus service regularly operates. ☐ *They've got to ride all the way to the end of the line.* **12** [C] A railway **line** consists of the pieces of metal and wood which form the track that the trains travel along. = track ☐ *Floods washed out much of the railway line.* **13** [C] (*business*) A shipping, air, or bus **line** is a company which provides services for transporting people or goods by sea, air, or bus. = company ☐ *The Cunard shipping line came up with a clever slogan: 'Getting there is half the fun…'* **14** [C] You can use **lines** to refer to the set of physical defences or the soldiers that have been established along the boundary of an area occupied by an army. ☐ *Their unit was shelling the German lines only seven miles away.* **15** [C] The particular **line** that a person has towards a problem is the attitude that they have towards it. For example, if someone takes a **hard line** on something, they have a firm strict policy which they refuse to change. ☐ *Forty members of the governing Conservative party rebelled, voting against the government line.* **16** [C] You can use **line** to refer to the way in which someone's thoughts or activities develop, particularly if it is logical. ☐ *Our discussion in the previous chapter continues this line of thinking.* **17** [PL] If you say that something happens **along** particular **lines**, or **on** particular **lines**, you are giving a general summary or approximate account of

what happens, which may not be correct in every detail. ❑ *There followed an assortment of praise for the coffee along the lines of 'Hey, this coffee is fantastic!'* ❑ *He'd said something on those lines already.* **18** [PL] If something is organized **on** particular **lines**, or **along** particular **lines**, it is organized according to that method or principle. ❑ *so-called autonomous republics based on ethnic lines* **19** [C] (business) Your **line of** business or work is the kind of work that you do. ❑ *So what was your father's line of business?* **20** [C] In a factory, a **line** is an arrangement of workers or machines where a product passes from one worker to another until it is finished. ❑ *a production line capable of producing three different products* **21** [C] You can use **line** when you are referring to a number of people who are ranked according to status. ❑ *Nicholas Paul Patrick was seventh in the line of succession to the throne.* **22** [C] A particular **line of** people or things is a series of them that has existed over a period of time, when they have all been similar in some way, or done similar things. ❑ *We were part of a long line of artists.*

PHRASES **cross the line** or **step over the line** If you say that someone has **crossed the line** or has **stepped over the line**, you mean that they have behaved in a way that is considered unacceptable. ❑ *He has crossed the line, and it must stop.* ❑ *Sometimes, I think the administration steps over the line when they make these kinds of accusations.*

draw the line If you **draw the line at** a particular activity, you refuse to do it, because you disapprove of it or because it is more extreme than what you normally do. ❑ *Letters have come from prisoners, declaring that they would draw the line at hitting an old lady.*

in the line of duty If you do something or if it happens to you **in the line of duty**, you do it or it happens as part of your regular work or as a result of it. ❑ *More than 3,000 police officers were wounded in the line of duty last year.*

the first line of If you refer to a method as the **first line of**, for example, defence or treatment, you mean that it is the first or most important method to be used in dealing with a problem. ❑ *Residents have the responsibility of being the first line of defence against wildfires.*

in line or **into line** **1** If one object is **in line with** others, or moves **into line with** others, they are arranged in a line. You can also say that a number of objects are **in line** or move **into line**. ❑ *The device itself was right under the vehicle, almost in line with the gear lever.* **2** If one thing is **in line with** another, or is brought **into line with** it, the first thing is, or becomes, similar to the second, especially in a way that has been planned or expected. ❑ *The structure of our schools is now broadly in line with the major countries of the world.* ❑ *This brings the law into line with most medical opinion.* **3** If you **keep** someone **in line** or **bring** them **into line**, you make them obey you, or you make them behave in the way you want them to. ❑ *All this was just designed to frighten me and keep me in line.*

on line or **off line** If a machine or piece of equipment comes **on line**, it starts operating. If it is **off line**, it is not operating. ❑ *The new machine will go on line in June 2006.*

VERB [T] (**lines, lining, lined**) **1** If people or things **line** a road, room, or other place, they are present in large numbers along its edges or sides. ❑ *Thousands of local people lined the streets and clapped as the procession went by.* **2** If you **line** a wall, container, or other object, you put a layer of something such as leaves or paper on the inside surface of it in order to make it stronger, warmer, or cleaner. ❑ *Line the basket with a bright checked cloth just before adding the biscuits.*

PHRASAL VERB **line up** **1** If people **line up** or if you **line** them **up**, they move so that they are standing in a line. ❑ *The senior leaders lined up behind him in orderly rows.* ❑ *The gym teachers lined us up against the cement walls.* **2** If you **line** things **up**, you move them into a straight row. ❑ *I would line up my toys on this windowsill and play.* **3** If you **line** one thing **up** with another, or one thing **lines up with** another, the first thing is moved into its correct position in relation to the second. You can also say that two things **line up**, or **are lined up**. ❑ *You have to line the car up with the ones beside you.* ❑ *The plane circled twice, trying in vain to line up with the runway.* **4** If you **line up** an event or activity, you arrange for it to happen. If you **line** someone

up for an event or activity, you arrange for them to be available for that event or activity. ❑ *She lined up executives, politicians and educators to serve on the board of directors.* **5** → See also **lineup**
→ See also **front line, online, lining, picket line**

lin·en /ˈlɪnɪn/ NOUN [C, U] (**linens**) **1** [C, U] **Linen** is a kind of cloth that is made from a plant called flax. It is used for making clothes and things such as tablecloths and sheets. ❑ *a white linen suit* **2** [U] [also linens] **Linen** is tablecloths, sheets, pillowcases, and similar things made of cloth that are used in the home. ❑ *embroidered bed linen*

lin·er /ˈlaɪnə/ NOUN [C] (**liners**) A **liner** is a large ship in which people travel long distances, especially on holiday. ❑ *luxury ocean liners*

line·up /ˈlaɪnˌʌp/ NOUN [C] (**lineups**) **1** A **lineup** is a group of people or a series of things that have been gathered together to be part of a particular event. ❑ *One player sure to be in the lineup is star midfielder Landon Donovan.* **2** At a **lineup**, a witness to a crime tries to identify the criminal from among a line of people. = identity parade ❑ *He failed to identify Graham from photographs, but later picked him out of a police lineup.*

lin·ger /ˈlɪŋɡə/ VERB [I] (**lingers, lingering, lingered**) **1** When something such as an idea, feeling, or illness **lingers**, it continues to exist for a long time, often much longer than expected. ❑ *The scent of her perfume lingered on in the room.* ❑ *He was ashamed. That feeling lingered, and he was never comfortable in church after that.* **2** If you **linger** somewhere, you stay there for a longer time than is necessary, for example, because you are enjoying yourself. ❑ *Customers are welcome to linger over coffee until around midnight.*

✪**lin·guist** /ˈlɪŋɡwɪst/ NOUN [C] (**linguists**) **1** A **linguist** is someone who is good at speaking or learning foreign languages. ❑ *He had a scholarly air and was an accomplished linguist.* **2** A **linguist** is someone who studies or teaches linguistics. ❑ *Many linguists have looked at language in this way.*

✪**lin·guis·tic** /lɪŋˈɡwɪstɪk/ ADJ, NOUN
ADJ **Linguistic** abilities or ideas relate to language or linguistics. ❑ *linguistic skills* ❑ *linguistic theory*
NOUN [U] (**linguistics**) **Linguistics** is the study of the way in which language works. ❑ *Modern linguistics emerged as a distinct field in the nineteenth century.*
✪**lin·guis·ti·cal·ly** /lɪŋˈɡwɪstɪkli/ ADV ❑ *Somalia is an ethnically and linguistically homogeneous nation.* ❑ *those from culturally and linguistically diverse backgrounds*

lin·ing /ˈlaɪnɪŋ/ NOUN [C, U] (**linings**) **1** [C, U] The **lining** of something such as a piece of clothing or a curtain is a layer of cloth attached to the inside of it in order to make it thicker or warmer, or in order to make it hang better. ❑ *a padded satin jacket with quilted lining* **2** [C] The **lining** of your stomach or other organ is a layer of tissue on the inside of it. ❑ *a bacterium that attacks the lining of the stomach*

✪**link** ♦♦◇ /lɪŋk/ NOUN, VERB (*academic word*)
NOUN [C] (**links**) **1** If there is a **link between** two things or situations, there is a relationship between them, for example, because one thing causes or affects the other. = connection, relationship, association ❑ *the link between smoking and lung cancer* ❑ *Police are investigating potential links with the bombing of a car on Monday.* **2** A **link between** two things or places is a physical connection between them. ❑ *the rail link between Boston and New York* ❑ *Drivers ran into a field of weeds at the state border, where no link with the neighbouring state had yet been planned.* **3** A **link** between two people, organizations, or places is a friendly or business connection between them. ❑ *Kiev hopes to cement close links with Bonn.* ❑ *In 1984 the long link between AC Cars and the Hurlock family was severed.* **4** A **link** to another person or organization is something that allows you to communicate with them or have contact with them. ❑ *She was my only link with the past.* ❑ *The Red Cross was created to provide a link between soldiers in battle and their families at home.* **5** In computing, a **link** is a connection between different documents, or between different parts of the same document, using hypertext. ❑ *Available in*

English, French, German and Italian, it has links to other relevant tourism sites. **6** A **link** is one of the rings in a chain. □ *a chain of heavy gold links*

VERB [T] (**links, linking, linked**) **1** If someone or something **links** two things or situations, there is a relationship between them, for example, because one thing causes or affects the other. □ *The UN Security Council has linked any lifting of sanctions to compliance with the ceasefire terms.* □ *The study further strengthens the evidence linking smoking with early death.* □ *The detention raised two distinct but closely linked questions.* **2** If two places or objects **are linked** or something **links** them, there is a physical connection between them. □ *the Rama Road, which links the capital, Managua, with the Caribbean coast* □ *Seven miles of track were installed to link the hotel to the golf course.* **3** If you **link** one person or thing to another, you claim that there is a relationship or connection between them. □ *Criminologist Dr Ann Jones has linked the crime to social circumstances.* □ *They've linked her with various men, including magnate Donald Trump.* **4** In computing, to **link** different documents or different parts of the same document is to connect them using hypertext. □ *Certainly, Andreessen didn't think up using hypertext to link Internet documents.* **5** If you **link** one thing with another, you join them by putting one thing through the other. □ *She linked her arm through his.*

PHRASE **link arms** If two or more people **link arms**, or if one person **links arms** with another, they stand next to each other, and each person puts their arm around the arm of the person next to them. □ *It was so slippery that some of the walkers linked arms and proceeded very carefully.*

PHRASAL VERB **link up 1** If you **link up with** someone, you join them for a particular purpose. = **join up** □ *They linked up with a series of local anti-nuclear and anti-apartheid groups.* **2** If one thing **is linked up to** another, the two things are connected to each other. = **connect** □ *The television screens of the next century will be linked up to an emerging world telecommunications grid.*

lion /ˈlaɪən/ NOUN [C] (**lions**) A **lion** is a large wild member of the cat family that is found in Africa. Lions have yellowish fur, and male lions have long hair on their head and neck.

lip ♦◇◇ /lɪp/ NOUN [C] (**lips**) Your **lips** are the two outer parts of the edge of your mouth. □ *Wade stuck the cigarette between his lips.*

lip·stick /ˈlɪpstɪk/ NOUN [C, U] (**lipsticks**) **Lipstick** is a coloured substance in the form of a stick which women put on their lips. □ *She was wearing red lipstick.*

⧫liq·uid /ˈlɪkwɪd/ NOUN, ADJ

NOUN [C, U] (**liquids**) A **liquid** is a substance which is not solid but which flows and can be poured, for example, water. = **fluid; ≠ solid** □ *Drink plenty of liquid.* □ *Boil for 20 minutes until the liquid has reduced by half.* □ *a container filled with a flammable liquid*

ADJ 1 A **liquid** substance is in the form of a liquid rather than being solid or a gas. **≠ solid** □ *Wash in warm water with liquid detergent.* □ *The tanker was carrying liquid nitrogen.* □ *Fats are solid at room temperature, and oil is liquid at room temperature.* **2** (*business*) **Liquid** assets are the things that a person or company owns which can be quickly turned into cash if necessary. □ *The bank had sufficient liquid assets to continue operations.*

⧫liq·ui·date /ˈlɪkwɪdeɪt/ VERB [T] (**liquidates, liquidating, liquidated**) (*business*) **1** To **liquidate** a company is to close it down and sell all its assets, usually because it is in debt. = **sell, close down** □ *A unanimous vote was taken to liquidate the company.* □ *The High Court has appointed an official receiver to liquidate a bankrupt travel company.* **2** If a company **liquidates** its assets, its property such as buildings or machinery is sold in order to get money. = **sell** □ *The company closed down operations and began liquidating its assets in January.*

⧫liq·ui·da·tion /ˌlɪkwɪˈdeɪʃən/ NOUN [C, U] (**liquidations**) □ *The company went into liquidation.* □ *The number of company liquidations rose 11 per cent.*

⧫list ♦♦♦ /lɪst/ NOUN, VERB

NOUN [C] (**lists**) **1** A **list** of things such as names or addresses is a set of them which all belong to a particular category, written down one below the other. □ *We are making a list of the top ten men we would not want to be married to.* □ *There were six names on the list.* **2** A **list** of things is a set of them that you think of as being in a particular order. □ *High on the list of public demands is to end military control of broadcasting.* □ *I would have thought if they were looking for redundancies I would be last on the list.* □ *The criminal judicial system always comes up at the top of the list of voters' concerns in focus groups.*

VERB [T, I] (**lists, listing, listed**) **1** To **list** several things such as reasons or names means to write or say them one after another, usually in a particular order. = **itemize, record** □ *The pupils were asked to list the sports they loved most and hated most.* □ *Manufacturers must list ingredients in order of the amount used.* □ *Results are listed alphabetically.* **2** [T] To **list** something in a particular way means to include it in that way in a list or report. □ *A medical examiner has listed the deaths as homicides.* **3** [I, T] (*business*) If a company **is listed**, or if it **lists**, on a stock exchange, it obtains an official quotation for its shares so that people can buy and sell them. □ *a basket of blue chip stocks listed on the American Exchange*
→ See also **waiting list**

lis·ten ♦♦◇ /ˈlɪsən/ VERB, CONVENTION

VERB [I] (**listens, listening, listened**) **1** If you **listen to** someone who is talking or **to** a sound, you give your attention to them or it. □ *He spent his time listening to the radio.* **2** If you **listen for** a sound, you keep alert and are ready to hear it if it occurs. □ *We listen for footsteps approaching.* **3** If you **listen to** someone, you do what they advise you to do, or you believe them. □ *Anne, you need to listen to me this time.*

CONVENTION You say **listen** when you want someone to pay attention to you because you are going to say something important. = **look** □ *Listen, I finish at one.*

PHRASAL VERB **listen in** If you **listen in** to a private conversation, you secretly listen to it. = **eavesdrop** □ *He assigned federal agents to listen in on Martin Luther King's phone calls.*

lis·ten·er /ˈlɪsnə/ NOUN [C] (**listeners**) **1** A **listener** is someone who gives their attention to a person who is talking or to a sound. □ *One or two listeners had fallen asleep while the president was speaking.* **2** A **listener** is a person who listens to the radio or to a particular radio programme. □ *I'm a regular listener to her show.* **3** If you describe someone as a good **listener**, you mean that they listen carefully and sympathetically to you when you talk, for example, about your problems. □ *Dr Brian was a good listener.*

lit /lɪt/ IRREG FORM **Lit** is a past tense and past participle of **light**.

⧫lit·era·cy /ˈlɪtərəsi/ NOUN [U] **Literacy** is the ability to read and write. □ *Many adults have problems with literacy and numeracy.* □ *The literacy rate there is the highest in Central America.*

⧫lit·er·al /ˈlɪtərəl/ ADJ **1** The **literal** sense of a word or phrase is its most basic sense. □ *In many cases, the people there are fighting, in a literal sense, for their homes.* □ *The concert ended with a bang in the most literal sense.* □ *the literal definition of reaping what you sow* **2** A **literal** translation is one in which you translate each word of the original work rather than giving the meaning of each expression or sentence using words that sound natural. = **exact** □ *A literal translation of the name Tapies is 'walls'.* □ *'Ethnic cleansing' is a literal translation of the Serbo-Croatian phrase 'etnicko ciscenje'.*

⧫lit·er·al·ly /ˈlɪtərəli/ ADV **1** (*emphasis*) You can use **literally** to emphasize an exaggeration. Some careful speakers of English think that this use is incorrect. □ *We've got to get the economy under control or it will literally eat us up.* **2** (*emphasis*) You use **literally** to emphasize that what you are saying is true, even though it seems exaggerated or surprising. □ *Putting on an opera is a tremendous enterprise involving literally hundreds of people.* **3** If a word or expression is translated **literally**, its most simple or basic meaning is translated. □ *The word 'volk'* translates literally as 'folk'. ❑ A stanza is, literally, a room.

lit·er·ary ♦◇◇ /'lɪtərəri, AmE -reri/ ADJ **1** **Literary** means concerned with or connected with the writing, study, or appreciation of literature. ❑ Her literary criticism focuses on the way great literature suggests ideas. ❑ She's the literary editor of the 'Sunday Review'. **2** **Literary** words and expressions are often unusual in some way and are used to create a special effect in a piece of writing such as a poem, speech, or novel. ❑ archaic, literary words from the Tang dynasty

◇**lit·er·ate** /'lɪtərət/ ADJ **1** Someone who is **literate** is able to read and write. ❑ Over one-quarter of the adult population are not fully literate. ❑ Around one third of the prison population was literate and numerate. ❑ He had left school barely literate and with little ambition or self-esteem. **2** If you describe someone as **literate** in a particular subject, especially one that many people do not know anything about, you mean that they have a good knowledge and understanding of that subject. ❑ Head teachers need to be financially literate. ❑ We want to have more scientifically literate people running our television stations.

◇**lit·era·ture** ♦◇◇ /'lɪtrətʃə, AmE -tərətʃʊr/ NOUN [C, U] (literatures) **1** [C, U] Novels, plays, and poetry are referred to as **literature**, especially when they are considered to be good or important. ❑ classic works of literature ❑ I have spent my life getting to know diverse literatures of different epochs. ❑ a Professor of English Literature **2** [U] The **literature** on a particular subject of study is all the books and articles that have been published about it. ❑ the literature on immigration policy ❑ This work is documented in the scientific literature. **3** [U] **Literature** is written information produced by people who want to sell you something or give you advice. ❑ I am sending you literature from two other companies that provide a similar service.

◇**liti·gate** /'lɪtɪgeɪt/ VERB [I, T] (litigates, litigating, litigated) To **litigate** means to take legal action. ❑ the cost of litigating personal injury claims in the county court ❑ If we have to litigate, we will. ❑ The prospect of similar cases being successfully litigated in Britain seems unlikely.

◇**liti·ga·tion** /,lɪtɪ'geɪʃən/ NOUN [U] **Litigation** is the process of fighting or defending a case in a civil court of law. ❑ The settlement ends more than four years of litigation on behalf of the residents. ❑ The company does not comment on pending litigation.

◇**li·tre** /'li:tə/ (BrE; in AmE, use **liter**) NOUN [C] (litres) A **litre** is a metric unit of volume that is a thousand cubic centimetres. It is equal to 1.76 British pints. ❑ a 13-thousand-litre water tank ❑ It is sold to the public at eight cents a litre. ❑ 15 litres of water ❑ This tax would raise petrol prices by about 3.5p per litre. ❑ a Ford Escort with a 1.9-litre engine

lit·ter /'lɪtə/ NOUN, VERB, ADJ
   NOUN [U, C] (litters) **1** [U] **Litter** is small pieces of rubbish, such as paper and cans, that are left lying around outside. ❑ If you see litter in the corridor, pick it up. **2** [C] A **litter** is a group of animals born to the same mother at the same time. ❑ a litter of pups
   VERB [T] (litters, littering, littered) If a number of things **litter** a place, they are scattered around it or over it. ❑ Glass from broken bottles litters the pavement.
   ADJ [V-LINK + litter 'with' N] If something is **littered with** things, it contains many examples of it. ❑ History is littered with men and women spurred into achievement by a father's disregard.
   lit·tered /'lɪtəd/ ADJ ❑ The entrance hall is littered with toys.

lit·tle ♦♦♦ /'lɪtəl/ DET, QUANT, PRON, ADV, ADJ
   DET **1** You use **little** to indicate that there is only a very small amount of something. You can use 'so', 'too', and 'very' in front of **little**. ❑ I had little money and little free time. ❑ I find that I need very little sleep these days. **2** A **little** of something is a small amount of it, but not very much. You can also say a **very little**. ❑ Mrs Caan needs a little help getting her groceries home. ❑ A little food would do us all some good.
   QUANT **1** [little 'of' DEF-N] **Little** of something means only a very small amount of it. ❑ Little of the existing housing is of good enough quality. **2** A **little** of something means a small

amount of it, but not very much. ❑ Pour a little of the sauce over the chicken.
   PRON **1** **Little** means only a small amount of something. ❑ He ate little, and drank less. ❑ In general, employers do little to help the single working mother. **2** A **little** means a small amount of something. ❑ They get paid for it. Not much. Just a little.
   ADV **1** [little with V] **Little** means not very often or to only a small extent. ❑ On their way back to Marseille they spoke very little. **2** [little after V] If you do something **a little**, you do it for a short time. ❑ He walked a little by himself in the garden. **3** A **little** or a **little bit** means to a small extent or degree. ❑ He complained a little of a nagging pain between his shoulder blades. ❑ He was a little bit afraid of his father's reaction.
   ADJ **1** **Little** things are small in size. **Little** is slightly more informal than **small**. = small ❑ We sat around a little table, eating and drinking wine. **2** [little + N] You use **little** to indicate that someone or something is small, in a pleasant and attractive way. ❑ She's got the nicest little house not far from the library. ❑ a little old lady **3** [little + N] Your **little** sister or brother is younger than you are. ❑ Whenever Daniel's little sister was asked to do something she always had a naughty reply. **4** [little + N] A **little** distance, period of time, or event is short in length. ❑ Just go down the road a little way, turn left, and cross the bridge. ❑ Why don't we just wait a little while and see what happens. **5** [little + N] A **little** sound or gesture is quick. ❑ I had a little laugh to myself. **6** [little + N] You use **little** to indicate that something is not serious or important. ❑ irritating little habits

─────────────────────────
USAGE NOTE

little

Do not use 'little' or 'a little' with a countable noun to refer to a small number of people or things. You do not say, for example, ~~'They are having a little problems'~~. They are having **a few** problems.
─────────────────────────

live ♦♦♦ VERB, ADJ, ADV
   VERB /lɪv/ [I, T] (lives, living, lived) **1** [I] If someone **lives** in a particular place or with a particular person, their home is in that place or with that person. ❑ She has lived here for 10 years. ❑ Where do you live? **2** [I, T] If you say that someone **lives** in particular circumstances or that they **live** a particular kind of life, you mean that they are in those circumstances or that they have that kind of life. ❑ We lived quite grandly. ❑ Compared to people living only a few generations ago, we have greater opportunities to have a good time. **3** [I] If you say that someone **lives for** a particular thing, you mean that it is the most important thing in their life. ❑ He lived for his work. **4** [I, T] To **live** means to be alive. If someone **lives to** a particular age, they stay alive until they are that age. ❑ He's got a terrible disease and will not live long. ❑ He lived to be 103. **5** [I] If people **live by** doing a particular activity, they get the money, food, or clothing they need by doing that activity. ❑ the last indigenous people to live by hunting
   PHRASE **live it up** (informal) If you **live it up**, you have a very enjoyable and exciting time, for example by going to lots of parties or going out drinking with friends. ❑ There is no reason why you couldn't live it up once in a while.
   PHRASAL VERBS **live down** If you are unable to **live down** a mistake, failure, or bad reputation, you are unable to make people forget about it. ❑ It was unable to live down its reputation as the party of high taxes.
   live off If you **live off** another person, you rely on them to provide you with money. ❑ a man who all his life had lived off his father
   live on or **live off** **1** If you **live on** or **live off** a particular amount of money, you have that amount of money to buy things. ❑ people trying to live on $100 a week **2** If you **live on** or **live off** a particular source of income, that is where you get the money that you need. ❑ The proportion of people living on state benefits rose. **3** If an animal **lives on** or **lives off** a particular food, this is the kind of food that it eats. ❑ The fish live on the plankton.
   live on If someone **lives on**, they continue to be alive for a long time after a particular point in time or after a particular

event. ❑ *I know my life has been cut short by this terrible virus but Daniel will live on after me.*

live up to If someone or something **lives up to** what they were expected to be, they are as good as they were expected to be. ❑ *Sales have not lived up to expectations this year.*

ADJ /laɪv/ **1** [live + N] **Live** animals or plants are alive, rather than being dead or artificial. ❑ *a protest against the company's tests on live animals* **2** A **live** television or radio programme is one in which an event or performance is broadcast at exactly the same time as it happens, rather than being recorded first. ❑ *Murray was a guest on a live radio show.* ❑ *They watch all the live matches.* **3** A **live** performance is given in front of an audience, rather than being recorded and then broadcast or shown in a film. ❑ *The Rainbow has not hosted live music since the end of 1981.* ❑ *A live audience will pose the questions.* **4** A **live** wire or piece of electrical equipment is directly connected to a source of electricity. ❑ *The plug broke, exposing live wires.* **5 Live** bullets are made of metal, rather than rubber or plastic, and are intended to kill people rather than injure them. ❑ *They trained in the jungle using live ammunition.*

ADV /laɪv/ **1** [live after V] If a television or radio programme is broadcast **live**, it is broadcast at exactly the same time as it happens, rather than being recorded first. ❑ *It was broadcast live in 50 countries.* **2** [live after V] If a play or a piece of music is performed **live**, it is performed in front of an audience, rather than being recorded and then broadcast or shown in a film. ❑ *Kat Bjelland has been playing live with her new band.*
→ See also **living**
✦ **live hand to mouth** → see **hand**

live-in ◆◇◇ /ˌlɪv ˈɪn/ ADJ **1** [live-in + N] A **live-in** partner is someone who lives in the same house as the person they are having a sexual relationship with, but is not married to them. ❑ *She shared the apartment with her live-in partner.* **2** [live-in + N] A **live-in** servant or other domestic worker sleeps and eats in the house where they work. ❑ *I have a live-in nanny for my youngest daughter.*

live·li·hood /ˈlaɪvlihʊd/ NOUN [C, U] (**livelihoods**) Your **livelihood** is the job or other source of income that gives you the money to buy the things you need. ❑ *fishermen who depend on the seas for their livelihood*

live·ly /ˈlaɪvli/ ADJ (**livelier, liveliest**) **1** You can describe someone as **lively** when they behave in an enthusiastic and cheerful way. ❑ *She had a sweet, lively personality.* **2** A **lively** event or a **lively** discussion, for example, has lots of interesting and exciting things happening or being said in it. ❑ *It turned out to be a very interesting session with a lively debate.* **3** Someone who has a **lively** mind is intelligent and interested in a lot of different things. ❑ *She was a very well educated girl with a lively mind, a girl with ambition.*
live·li·ness /ˈlaɪvlinəs/ NOUN [U] **1** *Amy could sense his liveliness even from where she stood.* **2** *Some may enjoy the liveliness of such a restaurant for a few hours a day or week.*

liv·en /ˈlaɪvən/
PHRASAL VERB **liven up** (**livens, livening, livened**) **1** If a place or event **livens up**, or if something **livens** it **up**, it becomes more interesting and exciting. ❑ *How could we decorate the room to liven it up?* ❑ *The multicoloured rag rug was chosen to liven up the grey carpet.* **2** If people **liven up**, or if something **livens** them **up**, they become more cheerful and energetic. = **perk up** ❑ *Talking about her daughters livens her up.*

liv·er /ˈlɪvə/ NOUN [C, U] (**livers**) **1** [C] Your **liver** is a large organ in your body which processes your blood and helps to clean unwanted substances out of it. ❑ *Three weeks ago, it was discovered the cancer had spread to his liver.* **2** [C, U] **Liver** is the liver of some animals, especially lambs, pigs, and cows, which is cooked and eaten. ❑ *grilled calves' liver*

lives IRREG FORM **1** /laɪvz/ **Lives** is the plural of **life**. **2** /lɪvz/ **Lives** is the third person singular form of **live**.

live·stock /ˈlaɪvstɒk/ NOUN [U] Animals such as cattle and sheep which are kept on a farm are referred to as **livestock**. ❑ *The heavy rains and flooding killed scores of livestock.*

liv·ing ◆◇◇ /ˈlɪvɪŋ/ NOUN, ADJ
NOUN [C, U] (**livings**) **1** [C] The work that you do for a

living is the work that you do in order to earn the money that you need. ❑ *Father never talked about what he did for a living.* **2** [U] You use **living** when you are talking about the quality of people's daily lives. ❑ *Olivia has always been a model of healthy living.*
ADJ [living + N] You use **living** to talk about the places where people relax when they are not working. ❑ *The spacious living quarters were on the second floor.*

liv·ing room also **living-room** NOUN [C] (**living rooms**) The **living room** in a house is the room where people sit and relax. = **sitting-room, lounge** ❑ *We were sitting on the couch in the living room watching TV.*

liz·ard /ˈlɪzəd/ NOUN [C] (**lizards**) A **lizard** is a reptile with short legs and a long tail.

load ◆◇◇ /ləʊd/ VERB, NOUN, QUANT
VERB [T] (**loads, loading, loaded**) **1** If you **load** a vehicle or a container, you put a large quantity of things into it. ❑ *The three men seemed to have finished loading the truck.* ❑ *Mr Dambar had loaded his plate with lasagne.* **2** When someone **loads** a weapon such as a gun, they put a bullet or missile in it so that it is ready to use. ❑ *I knew how to load and handle a gun.* ❑ *He carried a loaded gun.* **3** To **load** a camera or other piece of equipment means to put film, tape, or data into it so that it is ready to use. ❑ *A photographer from the newspaper was loading his camera with film.*
PHRASAL VERBS **load down** If you **load** someone **down** with things, especially heavy things, you give them a large number of them or put a large number of them on them. ❑ *She loaded me down with around a dozen cassettes.* ❑ *They had come up from London loaded down with six suitcases.*
load up Load up means the same as **load** VERB 1. ❑ *I've just loaded my lorry up.* ❑ *The giggling couple loaded up their red sports car and drove off.*
NOUN [C, SING] (**loads**) **1** [C] A **load** is something, usually a large quantity or heavy object, which is being carried. ❑ *He drove by with a big load of hay.* **2** [C] You can refer to the amount of work you have to do as a **load**. ❑ *She's taking some of the load off the secretaries.* **3** [C] The **load** of a system or piece of equipment, especially a system supplying electricity or a computer, is the extent to which it is being used at a particular time. ❑ *An efficient bulb may lighten the load of power stations.* **4** [SING] The **load on** something is the amount of weight that is pressing down on it or the amount of strain that it is under. ❑ *Some of these chairs have flattened feet which spread the load on the ground.*
QUANT (*informal, emphasis*) If you refer to **a load of** people or things or **loads of** them, you are emphasizing that there are a lot of them. ❑ *I've got loads of money.* ❑ *a load of kids*
→ See also **loaded**
✦ **a load off your mind** → see **mind**

load·ed /ˈləʊdɪd/ ADJ **1** A **loaded** question or word has more meaning or purpose than it appears to have, because the person who uses it hopes it will cause people to respond in a particular way. ❑ *That's a loaded question.* **2** If something is **loaded with** a particular characteristic, it has that characteristic to a very great degree. ❑ *The president's visit is loaded with symbolic significance.* **3** If a place or object is **loaded with** things, it has very many of them in it or it is full of them. ❑ *a tray loaded with cups* ❑ *The second store you enter is loaded with jewellery.* **4** If you say that something is **loaded in favour of** someone, you mean it works unfairly to their advantage. If you say it is **loaded against** them, you mean it works unfairly to their disadvantage. = **biased** ❑ *The press is loaded in favour of this present government.*

loaf /ləʊf/ NOUN, VERB
NOUN [C] (**loaves**) A **loaf** of bread is bread which has been shaped and baked in one piece. It is usually large enough for more than one person and can be cut into slices. ❑ *a loaf of crusty bread*
VERB [I] (**loafs, loafing, loafed**) If you **loaf**, you spend time in a lazy way, doing nothing in particular, especially when you should be working. ❑ *There were always a lot of men loafing in the shop.*

◉ **loan** ◆◆◇ /ləʊn/ NOUN, VERB
NOUN [C, SING] (**loans**) **1** [C] A **loan** is a sum of money that

you borrow. = advance, credit □ *The country has no access to foreign loans or financial aid.* □ *The president wants to make it easier for small businesses to get bank loans.* □ *loan repayments* **2** [SING] If someone gives you a **loan of** something, you borrow it from them. □ *I am in need of a loan of a bike for a few weeks.*

PHRASE **on loan** If something is **on loan**, it has been borrowed. □ *impressionist paintings on loan from the National Gallery*

VERB [T] **(loans, loaning, loaned)** If you **loan** something to someone, you lend it to them. = lend □ *He had kindly offered to loan us all the plants required for the exhibit.*

PHRASAL VERB **loan out** Loan out means the same as **loan** VERB. □ *It is common practice for clubs to loan out players to sides in the lower divisions.*

loathe /ləʊð/ VERB [T] **(loathes, loathing, loathed)** If you **loathe** something or someone, you dislike them very much. = detest □ *The two men loathe each other.*

loath·ing /ˈləʊðɪŋ/ NOUN [U] **Loathing** is a feeling of great dislike and disgust. = hatred □ *She looked at him with loathing.*

loaves /ləʊvz/ IRREG FORM **Loaves** is the plural of **loaf**.

lob·by ◆◇◇ /ˈlɒbi/ VERB, NOUN

VERB [I, T] **(lobbies, lobbying, lobbied)** If you **lobby** someone such as a member of a government or council, you try to persuade them that a particular law should be changed or that a particular thing should be done. □ *The Wilderness Society lobbied Congress to authorize the Endangered Species Act.*

NOUN [C] **(lobbies)** **1** A **lobby** is a group of people who represent a particular organization or campaign, and try to persuade a government or council to help or support them. □ *Agricultural interests are some of the most powerful lobbies in Washington.* **2** In a hotel or other large building, the **lobby** is the area near the entrance that usually has corridors and staircases leading off it. □ *I met her in the lobby of the museum.*

lo·cal ◆◆◆ /ˈləʊkəl/ ADJ, NOUN

ADJ **1** [local + N] **Local** means existing in or belonging to the area where you live, or to the area that you are talking about. = regional, provincial; ≠ national, international, foreign □ *We'd better check on the game in the local paper.* □ *Some local residents joined the students' protest.* □ *encouraging children to use the local library* **2** **Local** government is elected by people in one area of a country and controls aspects such as education, housing, and transport within that area. □ *Education comprises two-thirds of all local government spending.* **3** (*medical*) A **local** anaesthetic or condition affects only a small area of your body. □ *The procedure was done under local anesthetic in the physician's office.*

NOUN [C] **(locals)** The **locals** are local people. □ *Camping is a great way to meet the locals as the Portuguese themselves are enthusiastic campers.*

◆**lo·cal·ly** /ˈləʊkəli/ ADV = regionally; ≠ nationally, internationally □ *We've got cards which are drawn and printed and designed by someone locally.* □ *the importance of buying locally produced food*

lo·cal author·ity ◆◇◇ NOUN [C] **(local authorities)** A **local authority** is an organization that is officially responsible for all the public services and facilities in a particular area.

lo·cal gov·ern·ment NOUN [U] **Local government** is the system of electing representatives to be responsible for the administration of public services and facilities in a particular area. □ *careers in local government*

lo·cate /ləʊˈkeɪt, AmE ˈləʊkeɪt/ VERB [T] **(locates, locating, located)** (*academic word, formal*) **1** If you **locate** something or someone, you find out where they are. = find □ *The scientists want to locate the position of the gene on a chromosome.* **2** If you **locate** something in a particular place, you put it there or build it there. □ *Atlanta was voted the best city in which to locate a business by more than 400 chief executives.*

◆**lo·cat·ed** /ləʊˈkeɪtɪd, AmE ˈləʊkeɪt-/ ADJ [V-LINK + located + PREP, ADV + located] (*academic word, formal*) If

something is **located** in a particular place, it is present or has been built there. = situated □ *A boutique and beauty salon are conveniently located within the grounds.* □ *The restaurant is located near the cathedral.*

◆**lo·ca·tion** ◆◇◇ /ləʊˈkeɪʃən/ NOUN [C, U] **(locations)** **1** [C] A **location** is the place where something happens or is situated. = setting, place, situation □ *The first thing he looked at was his office's location.* □ *Macau's newest small luxury hotel has a beautiful location.* **2** [C] The **location** of someone or something is their exact position. = position □ *She knew the exact location of The Eagle's headquarters.* **3** [C, U] A **location** is a place away from a studio where a film or part of a film is made. □ *an art movie with dozens of exotic locations*

WORD CONNECTIONS
VERB + **location**
reveal a location
identify a location
pinpoint a location
determine a location
□ *Church registers should help you identify the location of the grave.*
ADJ + **location**
a **secret** location
an **undisclosed** location
□ *The man will remain in detention at an undisclosed location.*
a **prime** location
an **ideal** location
a **central** location
□ *The hotel is in a prime location on the lakeside.*
an **exotic** location
a **remote** location
□ *This course involves field-based work sometimes in rugged and remote locations.*
a **specific** location
the **exact** location
the **precise** location
□ *The exact location of this battle has been disputed for centuries.*

lock ◆◇◇ /lɒk/ VERB, NOUN

VERB [T, I] **(locks, locking, locked)** **1** [T] When you **lock** something such as a door, drawer, or case, you fasten it, usually with a key, so that other people cannot open it. □ *Are you sure you locked the front door?* **2** [T] If you **lock** something or someone in a place, room, or container, you put them there and fasten the lock. □ *Her maid locked the case in the safe.* **3** [I, T] If you **lock** something in a particular position, or if it **locks** there, it is held or fitted firmly in that position. □ *He leaned back in the swivel chair and locked his fingers behind his head.*

PHRASAL VERBS **lock away** **1** If you **lock** something **away** in a place or container, you put or hide it there and fasten the lock. □ *She meticulously cleaned the gun and locked it away in its case.* **2** To **lock** someone **away** means to put them in prison or a secure mental hospital. □ *Locking them away is not sufficient, you have to give them treatment.*

lock out **1** If someone **locks** you **out** of a place, they prevent you entering it by locking the doors. □ *His wife locked him out of his bedroom after the argument.* **2** (*business*) In an industrial dispute, if a company **locks** its workers **out**, it closes the factory or office in order to prevent the employees coming to work. □ *The company locked out the workers, and then the rest of the work force went on strike.*

lock up **1** If you **lock** something **up** in a place or container, you put or hide it there and fasten the lock. □ *Give away any food you have on hand, or lock it up and give the key to the neighbours.* **2** To **lock** someone **up** means to put them in prison or a secure psychiatric hospital. □ *Mr Milner persuaded the federal prosecutors not to lock up his client.* **3** When you **lock up** a building or car or **lock up**, you make sure that all the doors and windows are locked so

L

that nobody can get in. □ *Don't forget to lock up.*
NOUN [c] (**locks**) **1** The **lock** on something such as a door or a drawer is the device which is used to keep it shut and prevent other people from opening it. Locks are opened with a key. □ *At that moment he heard Gill's key turning in the lock of the door.* **2** On a canal or river, a **lock** is a place where walls have been built with gates at each end so that boats can move to a higher or lower section of the canal or river, by gradually changing the water level inside the gates. □ *As the lock filled, the ducklings rejoined their mother to wait for another vessel to go through.* **3** A **lock** of hair is a small bunch of hairs on your head that grow together and curl or curve in the same direction. □ *She brushed a lock of hair off his forehead.*

lo·co·mo·tive /ˈləʊkəməʊtɪv/ NOUN [c] (**locomotives**) (*formal*) A **locomotive** is a large vehicle that pulls a train.

lodge /lɒdʒ/ NOUN, VERB
NOUN [c] (**lodges**) **1** A **lodge** is a house or hotel in the country or in the mountains where people stay on holiday, especially when they want to hunt or fish. □ *a Victorian hunting lodge* **2** A **lodge** is a small house at the entrance to the grounds of a large house. □ *I drove out of the gates, past the keeper's lodge.*
VERB [T, I] (**lodges, lodging, lodged**) **1** [T] If you **lodge** a complaint, protest, accusation, or claim, you officially make it. = **make** □ *He has four weeks in which to lodge an appeal.* **2** [I, T] If you **lodge** somewhere, such as in someone else's house or if you **are lodged** there, you live there, usually paying rent. □ *the story of the farming family she lodged with as a young teacher* **3** [I] If an object **lodges** somewhere, it becomes stuck there. □ *The bullet lodged in the sergeant's leg, shattering his thigh bone.*

lofty /ˈlɒfti, AmE ˈlɔːf-/ ADJ (**loftier, loftiest**) **1** A **lofty** ideal or ambition is noble, important, and admirable. □ *It was a bank that started out with grand ideas and lofty ideals.* **2** (*formal*) A **lofty** building or room is very high. □ *a light, lofty apartment in the suburbs of Salzburg* **3** If you say that someone behaves in a **lofty** way, you are critical of them for behaving in a proud and rather overbearing way, as if they think they are very important. □ *the lofty disdain he often expresses for his profession*

log /lɒg, AmE lɔːg/ NOUN, VERB
NOUN [c] (**logs**) **1** A **log** is a piece of a thick branch or of the trunk of a tree that has been cut so that it can be used for fuel or for making things. □ *He dumped the logs on the big stone hearth.* **2** A **log** is an official written account of what happens each day, for example, on board a ship. □ *The family made an official complaint to a ship's officer, which was recorded in the log.*
VERB [T] (**logs, logging, logged**) If you **log** an event or fact, you record it officially in writing or on a computer. = **record** □ *They log everyone and everything that comes in and out of here.*
PHRASAL VERBS log in or **log on** When someone **logs in** or **logs on**, or **logs into** a computer system, they start using the system, usually by typing their name or identity code and a password. □ *Customers pay to log on and gossip with other users.*
log out or **log off** When someone who is using a computer system **logs out** or **logs off**, they finish using the system by typing a particular command. □ *If a computer user fails to log off, the system is accessible to all.*

✪log·ic /ˈlɒdʒɪk/ NOUN [u] (*academic word*) **1** Logic is a method of reasoning that involves a series of statements, each of which must be true if the statement before it is true. □ *Apart from criminal investigation techniques, students learn forensic medicine, philosophy and logic.* □ *to prove God's existence by means of deductive logic* **2** The **logic** of a conclusion or an argument is its quality of being correct and reasonable. □ *I don't follow the logic of your argument.* **3** A particular kind of **logic** is the way of thinking and reasoning about things that is characteristic of a particular type of person or particular field of activity. □ *The plan was based on sound commercial logic.*

✪logi·cal /ˈlɒdʒɪkəl/ ADJ **1** In a **logical** argument or method of reasoning, each step must be true if the step before it is true. □ *Only when each logical step has been*

checked by other mathematicians will the proof be accepted. **2** The **logical** conclusion or result of a series of facts or events is the only one which can come from it, according to the rules of logic. □ *If the climate gets drier, then the logical conclusion is that even more drought will occur.* □ *a society that dismisses God as a logical impossibility* **3** Something that is **logical** seems reasonable or sensible in the circumstances. = **reasonable** □ *Connie suddenly struck her as a logical candidate.* □ *There was a logical explanation.*
✪logi·cal·ly /ˈlɒdʒɪkli/ ADV **1** *My professional training has taught me to look at things logically.* **2** [logically with V] □ *From that it followed logically that he would not be meeting Hildegarde.* **3** *This was the one possibility I hadn't taken into consideration, though logically I should have.*

✪logo /ˈləʊgəʊ/ NOUN [c] (**logos**) The **logo** of a company or organization is the special design or way of writing its name that it puts on all its products, stationery, or advertisements. = **emblem** □ *the famous MGM logo of the roaring lion* □ *Staff should wear uniforms, and vehicles should bear company logos.* □ *a red T-shirt with a logo on the front*

lone /ləʊn/ ADJ [lone + N] If you talk about a **lone** person or thing, you mean that they are alone. □ *A lone woman motorist waited for six hours for help yesterday because of a name mix-up.*

lone·li·ness /ˈləʊnlinəs/ NOUN [u] **Loneliness** is the unhappiness that is felt by someone because they do not have any friends or do not have anyone to talk to. □ *I have so many friends, but deep down, underneath, I have a fear of loneliness.*

lone·ly /ˈləʊnli/ ADJ (**lonelier, loneliest**) **1** Someone who is **lonely** is unhappy because they are alone or do not have anyone they can talk to. □ *lonely people who just want to talk* **2** A **lonely** situation or period of time is one in which you feel unhappy because you are alone or do not have anyone to talk to. □ *I desperately needed something to occupy me during those long, lonely nights.* **3** A **lonely** place is one where very few people come. □ *It felt like the loneliest place in the world.*

✪long ♦♦♦ /lɒŋ, AmE lɔːŋ/ ADV, ADJ, COMB, VERB
ADV (**longer, longest** /ˈlɒŋgɪst/) **1 Long** means a great amount of time or for a great amount of time. □ *Repairs to the cable did not take too long.* □ *Have you known her parents long?* □ *I learned long ago to avoid these invitations.* **2** You use **long** to ask or talk about amounts of time. □ *How long have you lived around here?* □ *He has been on a diet for as long as any of his friends can remember.* **3** [N + long] **Long** is used in expressions such as **all year long, the whole day long,** and **your whole life long** to say and emphasize that something happens for the whole of a particular period of time. □ *We played that CD all night long.*
PHRASES for long The expression **for long** is used to mean 'for a great amount of time'. □ *'Did you live there?'—'Not for long.'*
as long as or **so long as** If you say that something is the case **as long as** or **so long as** something else is the case, you mean that it is only the case if the second thing is the case. □ *He said he would still support them, as long as they didn't break the rules.*
won't be long If you say that someone **won't be long,** you mean that you think they will arrive or be back soon. If you say that it **won't be long** before something happens, you mean that you think it will happen soon. □ *'What's happened to her?'—'I'm sure she won't be long.'*
before long If you say that something will happen or happened **before long,** you mean that it will happen or it happened soon. □ *German interest rates will come down before long.*
no longer or **any longer** Something that is **no longer** the case used to be the case but is not the case now. You can also say that something is not the case **any longer.** □ *Food shortages are no longer a problem.* □ *She could no longer afford to keep him at school.*
so long You can say **so long** as an informal way of saying goodbye. □ *Well, so long, pal, see you around.*
ADJ (**longer, longest**) **1** A **long** event or period of time lasts for a great amount of time or takes a great amount of

time. ❑ *We had a long meeting with the attorney general.* ❑ *She is planning a long holiday in Europe.* ❑ *Camels can survive for long periods without drinking.* **2** ['how' long, AMOUNT + long] **Long** is also used to ask or talk about amounts of time. ❑ *So how long is your commute?* **3** A **long** speech, book, film, or list contains a lot of information or a lot of items and takes a lot of time to listen to, read, watch, or deal with. ❑ *He was making quite a long speech.* **4** If you describe a period of time or work as **long**, you mean it lasts for more hours or days than is usual, or seems to last for more time than it actually does. ❑ *Go to sleep. I've got a long day tomorrow.* ❑ *She was a TV reporter and worked long hours.* **5** If someone has a **long** memory, they are able to remember things that happened far back in the past. ❑ *Mr. Assad, who has a long memory, will not have forgotten that meeting.* **6** Something that is **long** measures a great distance from one end to the other. ❑ *a long table* ❑ *Lucy was 27, with long dark hair.* **7** A **long** distance is a great distance. A **long** journey or route covers a great distance. ❑ *These people were a long way from home.* ❑ *The long journey tired him.* **8** [long + N] A **long** piece of clothing covers the whole of someone's legs or more of their legs than usual. Clothes with **long** sleeves cover the whole of someone's arms. ❑ *She is wearing a long black dress.* **9** You use **long** to talk or ask about the distance something measures from one end to the other. ❑ *An eight-week-old embryo is only an inch long.* ❑ *How long is the tunnel?* ❑ *In the roots of the olives, you could find centipedes as long as a pencil.*
COMB **Long** combines with a number to describe the distance that something measures from one end to the other. ❑ *a three-foot-long gash in the tanker's side*
VERB [I, T] (**longs**, **longing**, **longed**) If you **long for** something, you want it very much. ❑ *Steve longed for the good old days.* ❑ *I'm longing to meet her.*
→ See also **longing**
✦ **at long last** → see **last**; **in the long run** → see **run**; **a long shot** → see **shot**; **in the long term** → see **term**; **go a long way** → see **way**

long-distance ADJ **1** [long-distance + N] **Long-distance** is used to describe travel between places that are far apart. ❑ *Trains are reliable, cheap and best for long-distance travel.* **2** **Long-distance** is used to describe communication that takes place between people who are far apart. ❑ *He received a long-distance phone call from his girlfriend in Colorado.*

lon·gev·i·ty /lɒn'dʒevɪti/ NOUN [U] (formal) **Longevity** is long life. ❑ *Human longevity runs in families.* ❑ *The main characteristic of the strike has been its longevity.*

long·ing /'lɒŋɪŋ, AmE 'lɔ:ŋ-/ NOUN [C, U] (**longings**) If you feel **longing** or a **longing for** something, you have a rather sad feeling because you want it very much. ❑ *He felt a longing for the familiar.*

❂**lon·gi·tude** /'lɒndʒɪtju:d, AmE -tu:d/ NOUN, ADJ
NOUN [C, U] (**longitudes**) The **longitude** of a place is its distance to the west or east of a line passing through Greenwich, England. Compare **latitude**. ❑ *He noted the latitude and longitude, then made a mark on the admiralty chart.* ❑ *Determining longitude exactly was a problem of vital importance for the safety of commercial shipping.*
ADJ **Longitude** describes a place's distance to the west or east of a line passing through Greenwich, England. ❑ *A similar feature is found at 13 degrees north between 230 degrees and 250 degrees longitude.*

long-lost ADJ [long-lost + N] You use **long-lost** to describe someone or something that you have not seen for a long time. ❑ *For me it was like meeting a long-lost sister. We talked, and talked, and talked.*

long-range ADJ **1** A **long-range** piece of military equipment or vehicle is able to hit or detect a target a long way away or to travel a long way in order to do something. ❑ *He is eager to reach agreement with the US on reducing long-range nuclear missiles.* **2** A **long-range** plan or prediction relates to a period extending a long time into the future. ❑ *Eisenhower was intensely aware of the need for long-range planning.*

long-standing ADJ A **long-standing** situation has existed for a long time. ❑ *They are on the brink of resolving their long-standing dispute over money.*

❂**long-term** ◆◆◇ ADJ, NOUN
ADJ (**longer-term**) Something that is **long-term** has continued for a long time or will continue for a long time in the future. ❑ *They want their parents to have access to affordable long-term care.* ❑ *a new training scheme to help the long-term unemployed* ❑ *a long-term solution to credit card fraud*
NOUN [SING] When you talk about what happens in the **long term**, you are talking about what happens over a long period of time, either in the future or after a particular event. ≠ **the short term** ❑ *In the long term the company hopes to open in Moscow and other major cities.* ❑ *Over the long term, such measures may only make the underlying situation worse.*

long-time ◆◇◇ ADJ [long-time + N] You use **long-time** to describe something that has existed or been a particular thing for a long time. ❑ *Newcomers had to pay far more in taxes than long-time land owners.*

look ◆◆◆ /lʊk/ VERB, CONVENTION, NOUN
VERB [I, T, LINK] (**looks**, **looking**, **looked**) **1** [I] If you **look** in a particular direction, you direct your eyes in that direction, especially so that you can see what is there or see what something is like. ❑ *I looked down the hallway to room number nine.* ❑ *If you look, you'll see what was a lake.* **2** [I] If you **look at** a book, newspaper, or magazine, you read it fairly quickly or read part of it. ❑ *You've just got to look at the last bit of Act Three.* **3** [I] If you **look at** someone in a particular way, you look at them with your expression showing what you are feeling or thinking. ❑ *She looked at him earnestly. 'You don't mind?'* **4** [I] If you **look for** something, for example, something that you have lost, you try to find it. ❑ *I'm looking for a child. I believe your husband can help me find her.* ❑ *I looked everywhere for ideas.* **5** [I] If you are **looking for** something such as the solution to a problem or a new method, you want it and are trying to obtain it or think of it. = **seek** ❑ *The working group will be looking for practical solutions to the problems faced by doctors.* **6** [I] If you **look at** a subject, problem, or situation, you think about it or study it, so that you know all about it and can perhaps consider what should be done in relation to it. = **examine**, **consider** ❑ *Next term we'll be looking at the Second World War period.* ❑ *Anne Holker looks at the pros and cons of making changes to your property.* **7** [I] If you **look at** a person, situation, or subject from a particular point of view, you judge them or consider them from that point of view. ❑ *Brian had learned to look at her with new respect.* **8** [I, T] You can use **look** to draw attention to a particular situation, person, or thing, for example because you find it very surprising, significant, or annoying. ❑ *Hey, look at the time! We'll talk about it tonight. All right?* ❑ *I mean, look at how many people watch television and how few read books.* ❑ *Look what you've done!* **9** [I] If something such as a building or window **looks** somewhere, it has a view of a particular place. ❑ *The castle looks over private parkland.* **10** [LINK] You use **look** when describing the appearance of a person or thing or the impression that they give. ❑ *Sheila was looking miserable.* ❑ *They look like stars to the naked eye.* ❑ *He looked as if he was going to smile.* **11** [LINK] You use **look** when indicating what you think will happen in the future or how a situation seems to you. ❑ *He had lots of time to think about the future, and it didn't look good.* ❑ *So far it looks like Warner Brothers' gamble is paying off.* ❑ *The Europeans had hoped to win, and, indeed, had looked like they would win.*
CONVENTION You say **look** when you want someone to pay attention to you because you are going to say something important. ❑ *Look, I'm sorry. I didn't mean it.*
PHRASE **what someone looks like** or **what something looks like** If you ask **what** someone or something **looks like**, you are asking for a description of them.
PHRASAL VERBS **look after** **1** If you **look after** someone or something, you do what is necessary to keep them healthy, safe, or in good condition. = **take care of** ❑ *I love looking after the children.* **2** If you **look after** something, you are responsible for it and deal with it or make sure it is all right, especially because it is your job to do so. ❑ *the*

farm manager who looks after the day-to-day organization

look around If you **look around** or **look round** a building or place, you walk round it and look at the different parts of it. ❏ *She left Annie and Cooper looking around the store and headed back onto the street.*

look back If you **look back**, you think about things that happened in the past. ❏ *Looking back, I am staggered how easily it was all arranged.*

look down on To **look down on** someone means to consider that person to be inferior or unimportant, usually when this is not true. ❏ *I wasn't successful, so they looked down on me.*

look forward to **1** If you **look forward to** something that is going to happen, you want it to happen because you think you will enjoy it. ❏ *He was looking forward to working with the new manager.* **2** If you say that someone **is looking forward** to something useful or positive, you mean they expect it to happen. ❏ *He now says that he's looking forward to increased trade after the war.*

look in If you **look in on** a person, you visit that person for a short time to check on their health or safety. ❏ *Could I look in on Sam?* ❏ *I think I'll look in on my parents on the way home from work.*

look into If a person or organization **is looking into** a possible course of action, a problem, or a situation, they are finding out about it and examining the facts relating to it. = investigate ❏ *He had once looked into buying his own island off Nova Scotia.*

look on If you **look on** while something happens, you watch it happening without taking part yourself. = watch ❏ *About 150 local people looked on in silence as the two coffins were taken into the church.*

look on or **look upon** If you **look on** or **look upon** someone or something in a particular way, you think of them in that way. = consider ❏ *A lot of people looked on him as a healer.* ❏ *A lot of people look on it like that.*

look out **1** If you **look out for** something, you pay attention to things so that you notice it if or when it occurs. = watch for ❏ *Look out for special deals.* **2** If you say or shout '**look out!**' to someone, you are warning them that they are in danger. ❏ *'Look out!' somebody shouted, as the lorry started to roll towards the sea.* **3 Look out** means the same as look VERB 9. ❏ *Nine windows looked out over the sculpture gardens.*

look over If you **look** something **over**, you examine it in order to get an idea of what it is like. ❏ *They presented their draft to the president, who looked it over and signed it.*

look through **1** If you **look through** a group of things, you examine each one so that you can find or choose the one that you want. = go through ❏ *Peter starts looking through the mail as soon as the door shuts.* **2** If you **look through** something that has been written or printed, you read it. ❏ *He happened to be looking through the medical book 'Gray's Anatomy' at the time.*

look to **1** If you **look to** someone or something for a particular thing that you want, you expect or hope that they will provide it. ❏ *He runs the team because he commands their respect. The kids really look to him.* **2** If you **look to** something that will happen in the future, you think about it. ❏ *Looking to the future, though, we asked him what the prospects are for a vaccine to prevent infection in the first place.*

look up **1** If you **look up** a fact or a piece of information, you find it out by looking in something such as a reference book or a list. = research ❏ *I looked your address up in the personnel file.* ❏ *Many people have to look up the meaning of this word in the dictionary.* **2** If you **look** someone **up**, you visit them after not having seen them for a long time. = visit ❏ *I'll try to look him up, ask him a few questions.*

look up to If you **look up to** someone, especially someone older than you, you respect and admire them. = admire ❏ *You're a popular girl, Grace, and a lot of the younger ones look up to you.*

NOUN [SING, C, PL] (**looks**) **1** [SING] If you take a **look** in a particular direction, you direct your eyes in that direction, especially so that you can see what is there or see what something is like. ❏ *Lucille took a last look in the mirror.*

2 [SING] A **look** at a newspaper or magazine is a quick attempt to read part of it. ❏ *A quick look at Monday's newspapers shows that there's plenty of interest in foreign news.* **3** [C] A **look** is an expression that shows what you are feeling or thinking. ❏ *He gave her a blank look, as if he had no idea who she was.* **4** [SING] If you have a **look** for something that you have lost, you try to find it. ❏ *Go and have another look.* **5** [SING] A **look** at a subject, problem, or situation is an attempt to learn about it so that you can consider what should be done in relation to it. ❏ *A close look at the statistics reveals a troubling picture.* **6** [SING] If someone or something has a particular **look**, they have a particular appearance or expression. ❏ *She had the look of someone deserted and betrayed.* ❏ *When he came to decorate the kitchen, Kenneth opted for a friendly rustic look.* **7** [PL] When you refer to someone's **looks**, you are referring to how beautiful or ugly they are, especially how beautiful they are. ❏ *I never chose people just because of their looks.* **PHRASES** **by the look of** or **by the looks of** You use expressions such as **by the look of him** and **by the looks of it** when you want to indicate that you are giving an opinion based on the appearance of someone or something. ❏ *He was not a well man by the look of him.*

not like the look of If you **don't like the look of** something or someone, you feel that they may be dangerous or cause problems. ❏ *I don't like the look of those clouds.*

✦ **look down your nose at someone** → see nose

look forward to

You can use **look forward to** followed by a noun.
*I am **looking forward to the party**.*
You can also use an '-ing' form after **look forward to**.
*I **look forward to seeing** you in Washington.*
Do not use an infinitive after 'look forward to'. Do not say, for example, 'He's looking forward to go home'.

look for or find?

Do not confuse **look for** and **find**.
If you **look for** something, you do not know where it is and spend time trying to see it or learn where it is.
❏ *He **looked for** his shoes under the bed.*
If you **find** something you have been looking for, you see it or learn where it is.
❏ *The police searched the house and **found** a gun.*
❏ *I eventually **found** what I was **looking for**.*

look·out /ˈlʊkaʊt/ NOUN

NOUN [C] (**lookouts**) **1** A **lookout** is a place from which you can see clearly in all directions. ❏ *Troops tried to set up a lookout post inside a refugee camp.* **2** A **lookout** is someone who is watching for danger in order to warn other people about it. ❏ *One of them, Bayer's girlfriend, helped plan the botched burglary and acted as a lookout.* **PHRASE** **keep a lookout** If someone **keeps a lookout** they look around all the time in order to make sure there is no danger. ❏ *He denied that he'd failed to keep a proper lookout that night.*

loom /luːm/ VERB, NOUN

VERB [I] (**looms, looming, loomed**) **1** If something **looms over** you, it appears as a large or unclear shape, often in a frightening way. ❏ *Vincent loomed over me, as pale and grey as a tombstone.* **2** (journalism) If a worrying or threatening situation or event **is looming**, it seems likely to happen soon. ❏ *Another government spending crisis is looming in the United States.* ❏ *The threat of renewed civil war looms ahead.* **NOUN** [C] (**looms**) A **loom** is a machine that is used for weaving thread into cloth.

loop /luːp/ NOUN, VERB

NOUN [C] (**loops**) A **loop** is a curved or circular shape in something long, for example, in a piece of string. ❏ *Mrs Morrell reached for a loop of garden hose.* **VERB** [T, I] (**loops, looping, looped**) **1** [T] If you **loop** something such as a piece of rope around an object, you tie a length of it in a loop around the object, for example, in order to fasten it to the object. ❏ *He looped the rope over the wood.* **2** [I] If something **loops** somewhere, it goes there in a circular direction that makes the shape of a loop. ❏ *The enemy was looping around the south side.*

loop·hole /'luːphəʊl/ NOUN [c] (**loopholes**) A **loophole** in the law is a small mistake which allows people to do something that would otherwise be illegal. ❏ *It is estimated that 60,000 businesses are exploiting a loophole in the law to avoid prosecution.*

loose ♦◇◇ /luːs/ ADJ
ADJ (**looser, loosest**) **1** Something that is **loose** is not firmly held or fixed in place. ❏ *If a tooth feels very loose, your dentist may recommend that it's taken out.* ❏ *Two wooden beams had come loose from the ceiling.* **2** Something that is **loose** is not attached to anything, or held or contained in anything. ❏ *Frank emptied a handful of loose change on the table.* **3** If people or animals break **loose** or are set **loose**, they are no longer held, tied, or kept somewhere and can move around freely. ❏ *She broke loose from his embrace and crossed to the window.* **4** Clothes that are **loose** are rather large and do not fit closely. = baggy ❏ *A pistol wasn't that hard to hide under a loose shirt.* **5** If your hair is **loose**, it hangs freely around your shoulders and is not tied back. ❏ *She was still in her nightgown, with her hair hanging loose over her shoulders.* **6** A **loose** grouping, arrangement, or organization is flexible rather than strictly controlled or organized. ❏ *Murray and Alison came to some sort of loose arrangement before he went home.*
PHRASE **on the loose** If a person or an animal is **on the loose**, they are free because they have escaped from a person or place. ❏ *Up to a thousand prisoners may be on the loose inside the jail.*

loose·ly /'luːsli/ ADV **1** [loosely with v] ❏ *Tim clasped his hands together and held them loosely in front of his belly.* **2** His shirt hung loosely over his thin shoulders. **3** [loosely with v] ❏ *The investigation had aimed at a loosely organized group of criminals.*
✦ **a loose cannon** → see **cannon**; **all hell breaks loose** → see **hell**

loos·en /'luːsən/ VERB
VERB [T, I] (**loosens, loosening, loosened**) **1** [T] If someone **loosens** restrictions or laws, for example, they make them less strict or severe. ❏ *Many business groups have been pressing the Federal Reserve to loosen interest rates.* **2** [I, T] If someone or something **loosens** the ties between people or groups of people, or if the ties **loosen**, they become weaker. ❏ *The Federal Republic must loosen its ties with the United States.* ❏ *The deputy leader is cautious about loosening the links with the unions.* **3** [T] If you **loosen** your clothing or something that is tied or fastened, you undo it slightly so that it is less tight or less firmly held in place. ❏ *He reached up to loosen the scarf around his neck.* ❏ *Loosen the bolt so the bars can be turned.* **4** [I, T] If you **loosen** your grip on something, or if your grip **loosens**, you hold it less tightly. ❏ *Harry loosened his grip momentarily and Anna wriggled free.* **5** [I, T] If a government or organization **loosens** its grip on a group of people or an activity, or if its grip **loosens**, it begins to have less control over it. = relax ❏ *There is no sign that the party will loosen its grip on the country.*
PHRASAL VERB **loosen up** **1** If a person or situation **loosens up**, they become more relaxed and less tense. ❏ *Relax; smile; loosen up in mind and body.* ❏ *Things loosened up, in politics and the economy.* **2** If you **loosen up** your body, or if it **loosens up**, you do simple exercises to get your muscles ready for a difficult physical activity, such as running or playing sports. ❏ *Squeeze the foot with both hands to loosen up tight muscles.*

loos·en·ing /'luːsənɪŋ/ NOUN [SING] ❏ *Domestic conditions did not justify a loosening of monetary policy.*

loot /luːt/ VERB [I, T] (**loots, looting, looted**) **1** [I, T] If people **loot**, or **loot** stores or houses, they steal things from them, for example, during a war or riot. ❏ *The trouble began when gangs began breaking windows and looting shops.* **2** [T] If someone **loots** things, they steal them, for example, during a war or riot. ❏ *The town has been plagued by armed thugs who have looted food supplies and terrorized the population.*

loot·ing /'luːtɪŋ/ NOUN [U] ❏ *In the country's largest cities there has been rioting and looting.*

lord ♦◆◇ /lɔːd/ NOUN, EXCLAM
NOUN [c, SING] (**lords**) **1** [c] A **lord** is a man who has a high rank in the nobility, for example, an earl, a viscount, or a marquis. ❏ *She married a lord and lives in this huge house in the Cotswolds.* **2** [SING] [usu 'the' LORD; Lord] In the Christian church, people refer to God and to Jesus Christ as the **Lord**. ❏ *I know the Lord will look after him.* ❏ *She prayed now. 'Lord, help me to find courage.'*
EXCLAM (*feelings*) **Lord** is used in exclamations such as '**good Lord!**' and '**oh Lord!**' to express surprise, shock, frustration, or annoyance about something. ❏ *'Good lord, that's what he is: he's a policeman.'*

lor·ry /'lɒri, AmE 'lɔːri/ (BrE; in AmE, use **truck**) NOUN [c] (**lorries**) A **lorry** is a vehicle with a large area in the back for carrying things with low sides to make it easy to load and unload.

❍ **lose** ♦♦♦ /luːz/ VERB
VERB [I, T] (**loses, losing, lost**) **1** [I, T] If you **lose** a contest, a fight, or an argument, you do not succeed because someone does better than you and defeats you. ❏ *The Golden Bears have lost three games this season.* ❏ *The government lost the argument over the pace of reform.* ❏ *No one likes to lose.* **2** [T] If you **lose** something, you do not know where it is, for example, because you have forgotten where you put it. ❏ *I lost my keys.* **3** [T] You say that you **lose** something when you no longer have it because it has been taken away from you or destroyed. ❏ *I lost my job when the company moved to another state.* ❏ *He lost his licence for six months.* ❏ *She was terrified they'd lose their home.* **4** [T] If someone **loses** a quality, characteristic, attitude, or belief, they no longer have it. ❏ *He lost all sense of reason.* ❏ *The government had lost all credibility.* **5** [T] If you **lose** an ability, you stop having that ability because of something such as an accident. ❏ *They lost their ability to hear.* **6** [T] If someone or something **loses** heat, their temperature becomes lower. ❏ *Babies lose heat much faster than adults.* **7** [T] If you **lose** blood or fluid from your body, it leaves your body so that you have less of it. ❏ *The victim suffered a dreadful injury and lost a lot of blood.* **8** [T] If you **lose** weight, you become less heavy, and usually look thinner. ❏ *I have lost a lot of weight.* **9** [T] If someone **loses** their life, they die. ❏ *the ferry disaster in 1987, in which 192 people lost their lives* **10** [T] If you **lose** a close relative or friend, they die. ❏ *My Grandma lost her brother in the war.* **11** [T] If things **are lost**, they are destroyed in a disaster. ❏ *the famous Nankin pottery that was lost in a shipwreck off the coast of China* **12** [T] If you **lose** time, something slows you down so that you do not make as much progress as you hoped. ❏ *They claim that police lost valuable time in the early part of the investigation.* **13** [T] If you **lose** an opportunity, you do not take advantage of it. ❏ *If you don't do it soon you're going to lose the opportunity.* ❏ *They did not lose the opportunity to say what they thought of events.* **14** [T] If you **lose yourself in** something or if you **are lost in** it, you give a lot of attention to it and do not think about anything else. = absorb ❏ *Michael held on to her arm, losing himself in the music.* **15** [T] (*business*) If a business **loses** money, it earns less money than it spends, and is therefore in debt. ≠ gain, make ❏ *His stores stand to lose millions of dollars.* ❏ *$1 billion a year may be lost.* **16** [T] If something **loses** you a contest or **loses** you something that you had, it causes you to fail or to no longer have what you had. ❏ *My own stupidity lost me the match.*
PHRASE **lose one's way** If you **lose** your **way**, you become lost when you are trying to go somewhere. ❏ *The men lost their way in a sandstorm.*
PHRASAL VERB **lose out** If you **lose out**, you suffer a loss or disadvantage because you have not succeeded in what you were doing. = miss out ❏ *We both lost out.* ❏ *Laura lost out to Tom.*
→ See also **lost**
✦ **lose your balance** → see **balance**; **lose contact** → see **contact**; **lose your grip** → see **grip**; **lose your head** → see **head**; **lose heart** → see **heart**; **lose your mind** → see **mind**; **lose your nerve** → see **nerve**; **lose sight of** → see **sight**; **lose

your temper → see **temper**; lose touch → see **touch**; lose track of → see **track**

los•er /ˈluːzə/ NOUN

NOUN [c] (**losers**) **1** The **losers** of a game, contest, or struggle are the people who are defeated or beaten. ❑ *the Dallas Cowboys and Buffalo Bills, the winners and losers of this year's Super Bowl* **2** (informal, disapproval) If you refer to someone as a **loser**, you have a low opinion of them because you think they are always unsuccessful. = **failure** ❑ *They've only been trained to compete with other men, so a successful woman can make them feel like a real loser.* **3** People who are **losers** as the result of an action or event are in a worse situation because of it or do not benefit from it. ❑ *Some of the top business successes of the 1980s became the country's greatest losers in the recession.* PHRASE **good loser** or **bad loser** If someone is a **good loser**, they accept that they have lost a game or contest without complaining. If someone is a **bad loser**, they hate losing and complain about it. ❑ *I'm a great winner and I try to be a good loser.*

⊙loss ♦♦◇ /lɒs, AmE lɔːs/ NOUN

NOUN [c, u] (**losses**) **1** [c, u] **Loss** is the fact of no longer having something or having less of it than before. ❑ *loss of sight* ❑ *hair loss* ❑ *Wildlife is under threat from hunting, pollution and loss of habitat.* ❑ *The job losses will reduce the total workforce to 7,000.* **2** [c, u] **Loss** of life occurs when people die. ❑ *a terrible loss of human life* **3** [u] The **loss** of a relative or friend is their death. = **death** ❑ *They took the time to talk about the loss of Thomas and how their grief was affecting them.* **4** [u] **Loss** is the feeling of sadness you experience when someone or something you like is taken away from you. ❑ *Talk to others about your feelings of loss and grief.* **5** [c] A **loss** is the disadvantage you suffer when a valuable and useful person or thing leaves or is taken away. ❑ *She said his death was a great loss to herself.* **6** [u] The **loss** of something such as heat, blood, or fluid is the gradual reduction of it or of its level in a system or in someone's body. ❑ *blood loss* ❑ *a rapid loss of heat from the body* **7** [c, u] If a business makes a **loss**, it earns less than it spends. ❑ *In 1986 Rover made a loss of nine hundred million dollars.* ❑ *The company said it will stop producing fertilizer in 1990 because of continued losses.* ❑ *Both firms reported pre-tax losses in the first half.*

PHRASES **at a loss** (business) If a business produces something **at a loss**, they sell it at a price which is less than it cost them to produce it or buy it. ❑ *Timber owners have often produced lumber at a loss and survived these down cycles in demand.*

be at a loss If you say that you are **at a loss**, you mean that you do not know what to do in a particular situation. ❑ *I was at a loss for what to do next.*

WORD CONNECTIONS
VERB + **loss**
make a loss
incur a loss
❑ *Patients are often reluctant to stay off work because of the financial loss they incur.*
post a loss
report a loss
❑ *The firm reported a loss of $19.4 million for the quarter.*
suffer a loss
sustain a loss
❑ *No company could continue to sustain such huge losses and survive.*
cause a loss
❑ *Between 1970 and 2000, economic losses caused by natural disasters doubled.*
ADJ + **loss**
a **heavy** loss
a **significant** loss
a **huge** loss
❑ *The state owned companies were making significant losses.*

a **financial** loss
❑ *The attacks can result in huge financial losses for individuals and business.*

lost ♦◇◇ /lɒst, AmE lɔːst/ IRREG FORM, ADJ

IRREG FORM **Lost** is the past tense and past participle of **lose**. ADJ **1** If you are **lost** or if you get **lost**, you do not know where you are or are unable to find your way. ❑ *Barely had I set foot in the street when I realized I was lost.* **2** If something is **lost**, or gets **lost**, you cannot find it, for example, because you have forgotten where you put it. ❑ *a lost book* ❑ *He was scrabbling for his pen, which had got lost somewhere under the sheets of paper.* **3** If you feel **lost**, you feel very uncomfortable because you are in an unfamiliar situation. ❑ *Of the funeral he remembered only the cold, the waiting, and feeling very lost.* **4** If you describe something as **lost**, you mean that you no longer have it or it no longer exists. ❑ *their lost homeland* ❑ *The sense of community is lost.* **5** [lost + N] You use **lost** to refer to a period or state of affairs that existed in the past and no longer exists. ❑ *He seemed to pine for his lost youth.* ❑ *They are links to a lost age.* **6** If something is **lost**, it is not used properly and is considered wasted. ❑ *Smith is not bitter about the lost opportunity to compete in the games.*

lot ♦♦♦ /lɒt/ QUANT, PRON, ADV, NOUN

QUANT [lot 'of' N] **A lot of** something or **lots of** it is a large amount of it. **A lot of** people or things, or **lots of** them, is a large number of them. ❑ *A lot of our land is used to grow crops for export.* ❑ *He drank lots of milk.* PRON You use **a lot** or **lots** to refer to a large amount or a large number of something. ❑ *I personally prefer to be in a town where there's lots going on.* ❑ *I learned a lot from him about how to run a band.* ADV **1** **A lot** means to a great extent or degree. ❑ *Matthew's out quite a lot doing his research.* ❑ *I like you, a lot.* **2** [lot after v] If you do something **a lot**, you do it often or for a long time. ❑ *They went out a lot, to restaurants and bars.* NOUN [c, sing] (**lots**) **1** [c] You can use **lot** to refer to a set or group of things or people. ❑ *He bought two lots of 1,000 shares in the company during August and September.* **2** [sing] (informal) You can refer to a specific group of people as a particular **lot**. = **bunch** ❑ *Future generations are going to think that we were a pretty boring lot.* **3** [sing] (informal) You can use **the lot** to refer to the whole of an amount that you have just mentioned. ❑ *This may turn out to be the best football game of the lot.* **4** [sing] Your **lot** is the kind of life you have or the things that you have or experience. ❑ *She tried to accept her marriage as her lot in life but could not.* **5** [c] A **lot** in an auction is one of the objects or groups of objects that are being sold. ❑ *The receivers are keen to sell the stores as one lot.* PHRASE **draw lots** If people **draw lots** to decide who will do something, they each take a piece of paper from a container. One or more pieces of paper is marked, and the people who take marked pieces are chosen. ❑ *For the first time in the World Cup finals, lots had to be drawn to decide who would finish second and third.*

USAGE NOTE
lot
The phrase 'lots of' is only used in informal contexts. In writing, you should use 'a lot of'.
They are offering the farmers a lot of money.

loud ♦◇◇ /laʊd/ ADJ, ADV

ADJ (**louder, loudest**) **1** If a noise is **loud**, the level of sound is very high and it can be easily heard. Someone or something that is **loud** produces a lot of noise. ❑ *Suddenly there was a loud bang.* ❑ *His voice became harsh and loud.* **2** If you describe something, especially a piece of clothing, as **loud**, you dislike it because it has very bright colours or very large, bold patterns which look unpleasant. = **garish** ❑ *He liked to shock with his gold chains and loud clothes.* ADV [loud after v] If you, for example, play music **loud** or speak **loud**, you do it so that the level of sound is very high and it can be easily heard. ❑ *She wonders whether Paul's hearing is OK because he turns the television up very loud.*

L

PHRASE **out loud** If you say or read something **out loud**, you say it or read it so that it can be heard, rather than just thinking it. □ *Even Ford, who seldom smiled, laughed out loud a few times.*
loud·ly /'laʊdli/ ADV □ *His footsteps echoed loudly in the tiled hall.*

lounge /laʊndʒ/ NOUN, VERB
NOUN [C] (**lounges**) **1** (*BrE*; in *AmE*, use **family room**) In a house, a **lounge** is a room where people sit and relax. **2** In a hotel, club, or other public place, a **lounge** is a room where people can sit and relax. □ *I spoke to her in the lounge of a big Johannesburg hotel where she was attending a union meeting.* **3** In an airport, a **lounge** is a very large room where people can sit and wait for aircraft to arrive or leave. □ *Instead of taking me to the departure lounge they took me right to my seat on the plane.*
VERB [I] (**lounges**, **lounging**, **lounged**) If you **lounge** somewhere or something that you are in a relaxed or lazy way. □ *They ate and drank and lounged in the shade.*

lout /laʊt/ NOUN [C] (**louts**) (*disapproval*) If you describe a man or boy as a **lout**, you are critical of them because they behave in an impolite or aggressive way. □ *a drunken lout*

lov·able /'lʌvəbəl/ ADJ If you describe someone as **lovable**, you mean that they have attractive qualities, and are easy to like. = endearing □ *His vulnerability makes him even more lovable.*

love ♦♦♦ /lʌv/ VERB, NOUN, NUM, CONVENTION
VERB [T] (**loves**, **loving**, **loved**) **1** If you **love** someone, you feel romantically or sexually attracted to them, and they are very important to you. □ *Oh, Amy, I love you.* **2** You say that you **love** someone when their happiness is very important to you, so that you behave in a kind and caring way towards them. □ *You'll never love anyone the way you love your baby.* **3** If you **love** something, you like it very much. □ *We loved the food so much, especially the fish dishes.* □ *one of these people that loves to be in the outdoors* **4** You can say that you **love** something when you consider that it is important and want to protect or support it. □ *I love my country as you love yours.* **5** If you **would love to** have or do something, you very much want to have it or do it. □ *I would love to play for England again.* □ *I would love a hot bath and clean clothes.*
NOUN [U, C] (**loves**) **1** [U] **Love** is a very strong feeling of affection towards someone who you are romantically or sexually attracted to. □ *Our love for each other has been increased by what we've been through together.* □ *an old fashioned love story* **2** [U] **Love** is the feeling that a person's happiness is very important to you, and the way you show this feeling in your behaviour towards them. □ *My love for all my children is unconditional.* **3** [U] **Love** is a strong liking for something, or a belief that it is important. □ *This is no way to encourage a love of literature.* **4** [C] Your **love** is someone or something that you love. □ *'She is the love of my life,' he said.* **5** [U] If you send someone your **love**, you ask another person, who will soon be speaking or writing to them, to tell them that you are thinking about them with affection. □ *Please give her my love.*
PHRASES **fall in love** **1** If you **fall in love with** someone, you start to be in love with them. □ *I fell in love with him because of his kind nature.* **2** If you **fall in love with** something, you start to like it very much. □ *I fell in love with the movies.*
be in love **1** If you **are in love with** someone, you feel romantically or sexually attracted to them, and they are very important to you. □ *Laura had never before been in love.* **2** If you **are in love with** something, you like it very much. □ *He had always been in love with the enchanted landscape of the West.*
make love When two people **make love**, they have sex. □ *Have you ever made love to a girl before?*
NUM In tennis, **love** is a score of zero. □ *He beat Thomas Muster of Austria three sets to love.*
CONVENTION You can use expressions such as **love**, **love from**, and **all my love**, followed by your name, as an informal way of ending a letter to a friend or relative. □ *with love from Grandma and Grandpa*
→ See also **loving**

love·ly ♦◇◇ /'lʌvli/ ADJ (**lovelier**, **loveliest**) **1** If you describe someone or something as **lovely**, you mean that they are very beautiful and therefore pleasing to look at or listen to. □ *You look lovely, Marcia.* □ *He had a lovely voice.* **2** (*mainly spoken*) If you describe something as **lovely**, you mean that it gives you pleasure. = wonderful □ *Mary! How lovely to see you!* □ *It's a lovely day.*
love·li·ness /'lʌvlinəs/ NOUN [U] = beauty □ *You are a vision of loveliness.*

lov·er ♦◇◇ /'lʌvə/ NOUN [C] (**lovers**) **1** Someone's **lover** is someone who they are having a sexual relationship with but are not married to. □ *Every Thursday she would meet her lover Leon.* **2** If you are a **lover** of something such as animals or the arts, you enjoy them very much and take great pleasure in them. □ *She is a great lover of horses and horse racing.*

lov·ing /'lʌvɪŋ/ ADJ **1** Someone who is **loving** feels or shows love to other people. = affectionate □ *Jim was a most loving husband and father.* **2** **Loving** actions are done with great enjoyment and care. □ *The house has been restored with loving care.*
lov·ing·ly /'lʌvɪŋli/ ADV **1** □ *Brian gazed lovingly at Mary Ann.* **2** □ *I lifted the box and ran my fingers lovingly over the top.*

low ♦♦♦ /ləʊ/ ADJ, NOUN, COMB
ADJ (**lower**, **lowest**) **1** Something that is **low** measures only a short distance from the bottom to the top, or from the ground to the top. □ *the low garden wall that separated the front garden from next door* □ *The country, with its low, rolling hills was beautiful.* **2** If something is **low**, it is close to the ground, to sea level, or to the bottom of something. □ *He bumped his head on the low beams.* □ *It was late afternoon and the sun was low in the sky.* **3** When a river is **low**, it contains less water than usual. □ *pumps that guarantee a constant depth of water even when the supplying river is low* **4** You can use **low** to indicate that something is small in amount or that it is at the bottom of a particular scale. You can use phrases such as **in the low 80s** to indicate that a number or level is less than 85 but not as little as 80. □ *Casualties remained remarkably low.* □ *They are still having to live on very low incomes.* **5** **Low** is used to describe people who are not considered to be very important because they are near the bottom of a particular scale or system. □ *She refused to promote Colin above the low rank of 'legal adviser'.* **6** If the quality or standard of something is **low**, it is very poor. = poor □ *A school would not accept work of a low quality from any student.* □ *The inquiry team criticizes staff at the psychiatric hospital for the low standard of care.* **7** [V-LINK + low 'in' N] If a food or other substance is **low in** a particular ingredient, it contains only a small amount of that ingredient. □ *They look for foods that are low in calories.* **8** If you have a **low** opinion of someone or something, you disapprove of them or dislike them. □ *The majority of sex offenders have a low opinion of themselves.* **9** You can use **low** to describe negative feelings and attitudes. □ *We are all very tired and morale is low.* **10** If a sound or noise is **low**, it is deep. = deep □ *Then suddenly she gave a low, choking moan and began to tremble violently.* **11** If someone's voice is **low**, it is quiet or soft. □ *Her voice was so low he had to strain to catch it.* **12** A light that is **low** is not bright or strong. = dim □ *Their eyesight is poor in low light.* **13** If a radio, oven, or light is on **low**, it has been adjusted so that only a small amount of sound, heat, or light is produced. □ *She turned her little kitchen radio on low.* □ *Buy a dimmer switch and keep the light on low, or switch it off altogether.* **14** [V-LINK + low] If you are **low on** something or if a supply of it is **low**, there is not much of it left. □ *We're a bit low on bed linen.* **15** (*informal*) If you are **low**, you are depressed. = down □ *'I didn't ask for this job, you know,' he tells friends when he is low.*
NOUN [C] (**lows**) If something reaches a **low** of a particular amount or degree, that is the smallest it has ever been. □ *Prices dropped to a low of about $1.12 in December.*
COMB **Low** is also used in combination with nouns, for example income or alcohol, to indicate that something is small in amount or that it contains only a small amount of a particular ingredient. □ *low-sodium tomato sauce*
→ See also **lower**

✦ **look high and low** → see **high**; **low profile** → see **profile**;
be running low → see **run**

✪ low•er ◆◇◇ /'ləʊə/ ADJ, VERB

ADJ **1** [lower + N, 'the' lower, 'the' lower 'of'] You can use **lower** to refer to the bottom one of a pair of things. ❑ *She bit her lower lip.* ❑ *the lower of the two holes* ❑ *the lower deck of the bus* **2** [lower + N] You can use **lower** to refer to the bottom part of something. ❑ *Use a small cushion to help give support to the lower back.* ❑ *fires which started in the lower part of a tower block* **3** [lower + N, 'the' lower] You can use **lower** to refer to people or things that are less important than similar people or things. ❑ *Already the awards are causing resentment in the lower ranks of council officers.* ❑ *The nation's highest court reversed the lower court's decision.* VERB [T, I] (**lowers, lowering, lowered**) **1** [T] If you **lower** something, you move it slowly downwards. ❑ *Two reporters had to help lower the coffin into the grave.* ❑ *Sokolowski lowered himself into the black leather chair.* **2** [T] If you **lower** something, you make it less in amount, degree, value, or quality. = drop, reduce, decrease, lessen, diminish; ≠ raise ❑ *The Central Bank has lowered interest rates by 2 per cent.* ❑ *This drug lowers cholesterol levels by binding fats in the intestine.* **3** [T] If someone **lowers** their head or eyes, they look downward, for example, because they are sad or embarrassed. ❑ *She lowered her head and brushed past photographers as she went back inside.* **4** [T] If you say that you would not **lower yourself** by doing something, you mean that you would not behave in a way that would make you or other people respect you less. ❑ *Don't lower yourself, don't be the way they are.* **5** [I, T] If you **lower** your voice or if your voice **lowers**, you speak more quietly. ❑ *The man moved closer, lowering his voice.*

low•er•ing /'ləʊərɪŋ/ NOUN [U] **1** the extinguishing of the Olympic flame and the lowering of the flag **2** a package of social measures which included the lowering of the retirement age
→ See also **low**

VOCABULARY BUILDER

lower VERB
If you **lower** something, you make it less in amount, degree, value, or quality.
❑ *Some doctors feared that insulin would lower blood-sugar levels too much.*

drop VERB (*mainly spoken*)
If a level or amount **drops** or if someone **drops** it, it quickly becomes less.
❑ *He had dropped the price of his London home by £1.25m.*

reduce VERB (*fairly formal*)
If you **reduce** something, you make it smaller in size or amount, or less in degree.
❑ *It reduces the risks of heart disease.*

decrease VERB
When something **decreases** or when you **decrease** it, it becomes less in quantity, size, or intensity.
❑ *Population growth is decreasing by 1.4% each year.*

lessen VERB (*fairly formal*)
If something **lessens**, it becomes smaller in size, amount, degree, or importance.
❑ *The attention he gets from his wife will inevitably lessen when the baby is born.*

diminish VERB (*formal*)
When something **diminishes**, or when something **diminishes** it, it becomes reduced in size, importance, or intensity.
❑ *The threat of nuclear war has diminished.*

---

low•ly /'ləʊli/ ADJ (**lowlier, lowliest**) If you describe someone or something as **lowly**, you mean that they are low in rank, status, or importance. ❑ *lowly bureaucrats pretending to be senators*

loy•al /'lɔɪəl/ ADJ (*approval*) Someone who is **loyal** remains firm in their friendship or support for a person or thing. = faithful ❑ *They had remained loyal to the president.*

loy•al•ly /'lɔɪəli/ ADV [loyally with V] ❑ *They have loyally supported their party and their leader.*

loy•al•ty /'lɔɪəlti/ NOUN [U, C] (**loyalties**) **1** [U] **Loyalty** is the quality of staying firm in your friendship or support for someone or something. ❑ *I have sworn an oath of loyalty to the monarchy.* **2** [C] **Loyalties** are feelings of friendship, support, or duty towards someone or something. ❑ *She had developed strong loyalties to the Manet family.*

luck ◆◇◇ /lʌk/ NOUN

NOUN [U] **1** **Luck** or **good luck** is success or good things that happen to you, that do not come from your own abilities or efforts. ❑ *I knew I needed a bit of luck to win.* ❑ *The Sri Lankans have been having no luck with the weather.* **2** **Bad luck** is lack of success or bad things that happen to you, that have not been caused by yourself or other people. ❑ *I had a lot of bad luck during the first half of this season.*

PHRASES **be in luck** You can say someone **is in luck** when they are in a situation where they can have what they want or need. ❑ *You're in luck. The doctor's still in.*

be out of luck If you say that someone **is out of luck**, you mean that they cannot have something which they can normally have. ❑ *'What do you want, Roy? If it's money, you're out of luck.'*

CONVENTIONS **any luck** (*informal*) If you ask someone the question '**Any luck?**' or '**No luck?**', you want to know if they have been successful in something they were trying to do. ❑ *'Any luck?'—'No.'*

bad luck or **hard luck** (*informal, formulae*) You can say '**Bad luck**' or '**Hard luck**' to someone when you want to express sympathy to them. ❑ *Bad luck, man, just bad luck.*

good luck or **best of luck** (*informal, formulae*) If you say '**Good luck**' or '**Best of luck**' to someone, you are telling them that you hope they will be successful in something they are trying to do. ❑ *He kissed her on the cheek. 'Best of luck!'*

luck•i•ly /'lʌkɪli/ ADV [luckily with CL] You add **luckily** to a statement to indicate that it is good that a particular thing happened or is the case because otherwise the situation would have been difficult or unpleasant. = fortunately ❑ *Luckily, we both love football.*

lucky ◆◇◇ /'lʌki/ ADJ

ADJ (**luckier, luckiest**) **1** You say that someone is **lucky** when they have something that is very desirable or when they are in a very desirable situation. = fortunate ❑ *I am luckier than most. I have a job.* ❑ *He is incredibly lucky to be alive.* **2** Someone who is **lucky** seems to always have good luck. ❑ *Some people are born lucky, aren't they?* **3** If you describe an action or experience as **lucky**, you mean that it was good or successful, and that it happened by chance and not as a result of planning or preparation. ❑ *They admit they are now desperate for a lucky break.* **4** A **lucky** object is something that people believe helps them to be successful. ❑ *He did not have on his other lucky charm, a pair of green socks.*

PHRASE **someone will be lucky** If you say that someone **will be lucky** to do or get something, you mean that they are very unlikely to do or get it, and will definitely not do or get any more than that. ❑ *You'll be lucky if you get any breakfast.* ❑ *Those remaining in work will be lucky to get the smallest of pay increases.*

lu•cra•tive /'lu:krətɪv/ ADJ A **lucrative** activity, job, or business deal is very profitable. ❑ *Thousands of ex-army officers have found lucrative jobs in private security firms.*

lug•gage /'lʌgɪdʒ/ NOUN [U] **Luggage** is the suitcases and bags that you take with you when you travel. ❑ *Leave your luggage in the hotel.*

luke•warm /ˌluːk'wɔːm/ ADJ **1** Something, especially a liquid, that is **lukewarm** is only slightly warm. = tepid ❑ *Wash your face with lukewarm water.* **2** If you describe a person or their attitude as **lukewarm**, you mean that they are not showing much enthusiasm or interest. ❑ *Economists have never been more than lukewarm towards him.*

lump /lʌmp/ NOUN

NOUN [C] (**lumps**) **1** A **lump of** something is a solid piece of it. ❑ *The potter shaped and squeezed the lump of clay into a graceful shape.* ❑ *a lump of wood* **2** A **lump** on or in someone's body is a small, hard swelling that has been caused by an injury or an illness. ❑ *I've got a lump on my shoulder.* **3** A **lump** of sugar is a small cube of it. ❑ *a nugget of rough gold about the size of a lump of sugar*

PHRASE **a lump in your throat** If you say that you have a **lump in** your throat, you mean that you have a tight feeling in your throat because of a strong emotion such as sorrow or gratitude. ❑ *I stood there with a lump in my throat and tried to fight back tears.*

PHRASAL VERB **lump together** (lumps, lumping, lumped) If a number of different people or things **are lumped together**, they are considered as a group rather than separately. ❑ *Policemen and prostitutes, bankers and butchers are all lumped together in the service sector.*

❍**lu·nar** /'luːnə/ ADJ [lunar + N] **Lunar** means relating to the moon. ❑ *The vast volcanic slope was eerily reminiscent of a lunar landscape.* ❑ *a magazine article celebrating the anniversary of man's first lunar landing*

lunch ♦♦◇ /lʌntʃ/ NOUN, VERB

NOUN [C, U] (lunches) **Lunch** is the meal that you have in the middle of the day. ❑ *Shall we meet somewhere for lunch?* ❑ *He did not enjoy business lunches.*

VERB [I] (lunches, lunching, lunched) (*formal*) When you **lunch**, you have lunch, especially at a restaurant. ❑ *Only the extremely rich could afford to lunch at the Mirabelle.*

lunch·time /'lʌntʃtaɪm/ also **lunch time** NOUN [C, U] (lunchtimes) **Lunchtime** is the period of the day when people have their lunch. ❑ *Could we meet at lunchtime?*

❍**lung** /lʌŋ/ NOUN [C] (lungs) Your **lungs** are the two organs inside your chest which fill with air when you breathe in. ❑ *a smoker who died of lung cancer* ❑ *a patient suffering from a collapsed lung* ❑ *X-rays indicated that her lungs were filled with fluid.*

lure /ljʊə, AmE lʊr/ VERB, NOUN

VERB [T] (lures, luring, lured) To **lure** someone means to trick them into a particular place or to trick them into doing something that they should not do. = entice ❑ *He lured her to his home and shot her with his father's gun.* ❑ *They did not realize that they were being lured into a trap.*

NOUN [C] (lures) **1** A **lure** is an object which is used to attract animals, especially fish, so that they can be caught. **2** A **lure** is an attractive quality that something has, or something that you find attractive. ❑ *The excitement of hunting big game in Africa has been a lure to Europeans for 200 years.*

luxu·ri·ous /lʌg'ʒʊəriəs/ ADJ **1** If you describe something as **luxurious**, you mean that it is very comfortable and expensive. ❑ *Our honeymoon was two days in Las Vegas at a luxurious hotel called Le Mirage.* **2** **Luxurious** means feeling or expressing great pleasure and comfort. ❑ *Amy tilted her wine in her glass with a luxurious sigh.*

luxu·ri·ous·ly /lʌg'ʒʊəriəsli/ ADV **1** *The dining-room is luxuriously furnished and carpeted.* **2** [luxuriously after V] ❑ *Liz laughed, stretching luxuriously.*

luxu·ry ♦◇◇ /'lʌkʃəri/ NOUN, ADJ

NOUN [U, C, SING] (luxuries) **1** [U] **Luxury** is very great comfort, especially among beautiful and expensive surroundings. = extravagance ❑ *By all accounts he leads a life of considerable luxury.* **2** [C] A **luxury** is something expensive which is not necessary but which gives you pleasure. = extravagance ❑ *A week by the sea is a luxury they can no longer afford.* **3** [SING] A **luxury** is a pleasure which you do not often have the opportunity to enjoy. ❑ *Hot baths are my favourite luxury.*

ADJ [luxury + N] A **luxury** item is something expensive which is not necessary but which gives you pleasure. ❑ *He could not afford luxury food on his pay.*

ly·ing /'laɪɪŋ/ IRREG FORM, NOUN

IRREG FORM **Lying** is the present participle of **lie**.

NOUN [U] **Lying** is the act of saying something which you know is not true. ❑ *Lying is something that I will not tolerate.*

lynch /lɪntʃ/ VERB [T] (lynches, lynching, lynched) If an angry crowd of people **lynch** someone, they kill that person by hanging them, without letting them have a trial, because they believe that that person has committed a crime. ❑ *They were about to lynch him when reinforcements from the army burst into the room and rescued him.*

lynch·ing /'lɪntʃɪŋ/ NOUN [C, U] (lynchings) ❑ *Some towns found that lynching was the only way to drive away bands of outlaws.*

L

Mm

M also **m** /em/ NOUN [C, U] (**M's, m's**) M is the thirteenth letter of the English alphabet.

✪ **ma·chine** ♦♦◇ /məˈʃiːn/ NOUN, VERB

NOUN [C] (**machines**) **1** [also 'by' machine] A **machine** is a piece of equipment that uses electricity or an engine in order to do a particular kind of work. = device, gadget, appliance ❑ *I put the coin in the machine and pulled the lever.* ❑ *The machine can be remotely operated and monitored.* ❑ *machines designed to detect hazardous gases* ❑ *an electrically operated machine* **2** You can use **machine** to refer to a large and well-controlled system or organization. ❑ *Nazi Germany's military machine*
VERB [T] (**machines, machining, machined**) If you **machine** something, you make it or work on it using a machine. ❑ *The material is machined in a factory.* ❑ *machined brass zinc alloy gears*

WORD CONNECTIONS
VERB + **machine**
design a machine
invent a machine
build a machine
❑ *Babbage designed a machine that could perform different operations.*
operate a machine
use a machine
❑ *Sadly, he did not know how to operate a washing machine.*
ADJ + **machine**
a powerful machine
a reliable machine
an efficient machine
a modern machine
❑ *Modern sewing machines produce much better results than older ones.*
a faulty machine
an unreliable machine
a defective machine
❑ *A faulty machine caused one employee to lose a hand.*

ma·chine gun NOUN [C] (**machine guns**) A **machine gun** is a gun which fires a lot of bullets one after the other very quickly. ❑ *Attackers fired machine guns at the convoy.*

✪ **ma·chin·ery** /məˈʃiːnəri/ NOUN [U, SING] **1** [U] You can use **machinery** to refer to machines in general, or machines that are used in a factory or on a farm. = equipment, hardware, technology ❑ *quality tools and machinery* ❑ *hi-tech packaging machinery* **2** [SING] The **machinery** of a government or organization is the system and all the procedures that it uses to deal with things. ❑ *The machinery of democracy could be created quickly.*

USAGE NOTE
machinery
Machinery is an uncountable noun. Do not use 'machineries' or 'a machinery'. Note that when you refer to machines in general, you should use 'machinery' rather than 'machines'.
*Farmers import most of their **machinery**.*

✪ **ma·cro·ec·o·nom·ic** /ˌmækrəʊˌekəˈnɒmɪk/ also **macro-economic** ADJ [usu macroeconomic + N] **Macroeconomic** means concerned with the major, general features of a country's economy, such as the level of inflation, unemployment, or interest rates. ❑ *the attempt to substitute low inflation for full employment as a goal of macro-economic policy* ❑ *Greater macroeconomic stability is a prize well worth having.*

WORD PARTS
The prefix **macro-** often appears in technical words that refer to things which are large or involve the whole of something:
macroeconomic (ADJ)
macroeconomics (NOUN)
macrocosm (NOUN)

✪ **macro·eco·nom·ics** /ˌmækrəʊˌiːkəˈnɒmɪks/ also **macro-economics** NOUN [U] (*business*) **Macroeconomics** is the branch of economics that is concerned with the major, general features of a country's economy, such as the level of inflation, unemployment, or interest rates. ❑ *Too many politicians forget the importance of macroeconomics.* ❑ *The UK macroeconomics show that there will not be enough people to fulfil the work that needs to be done.*

mad ♦◇◇ /mæd/ ADJ, COMB

ADJ (**madder, maddest**) **1** Someone who is **mad** has a mind that does not work in a normal way, with the result that their behaviour is very strange. = insane ❑ *She was afraid of going mad.* **2** You use **mad** to describe people or things that you think are very foolish. = crazy ❑ *You'd be mad to work with him again.* **3** (*informal*) If you say that someone is **mad**, you mean that they are very angry. ❑ *You're just mad at me because I don't want to go.* **4** [V-LINK + mad 'about/on' N] (*informal*) If you are **mad about** something or someone, you like them very much. ❑ *She's not as mad about sports as I am.* ❑ *He's mad about you.* **5** **Mad** behaviour is wild and uncontrolled. ❑ *You only have an hour to complete the game so it's a mad dash against the clock.*
PHRASES **drive someone mad** (*informal*) If you say that someone or something **drives** you **mad**, you mean that you find them extremely annoying. ❑ *There are certain things he does that drive me mad.*
like mad (*informal*) If you do something **like mad**, you do it very energetically or enthusiastically. ❑ *He was weight training like mad.*
COMB (*mainly BrE*) **Mad** is also used in combination with nouns to indicate that you like something very much. ❑ *his football-mad son*

mad·ness /ˈmædnəs/ NOUN [U] **1** *It is political madness.* **2** *He was driven to the brink of madness.*

mad·am /ˈmædəm/ also **Madam** NOUN [C] (*politeness*) People sometimes say **Madam** as a very formal and polite way of addressing a woman whose name they do not know. For example, a shop assistant might address a woman customer as **Madam**. ❑ *Try them on, madam.*

mad·den /ˈmædən/ VERB [T] (**maddens, maddening, maddened**) To **madden** a person or animal means to make them very angry. = infuriate ❑ *The deer were maddening farmers by eating their crops.*

mad·den·ing /ˈmædənɪŋ/ ADJ If you describe something as **maddening**, you mean that it makes you feel angry, irritated, or frustrated. = infuriating ❏ *Shopping during sales can be maddening.*
mad·den·ing·ly /ˈmædənɪŋli/ ADV ❏ *The service is maddeningly slow.*

made /meɪd/ IRREG FORM, ADJ
IRREG FORM **Made** is the past tense and past participle of **make**.
ADJ [V-LINK + made 'of/out of' N] If something is **made of** or **made out of** a particular substance, that substance was used to build it. ❏ *The top of the table is made of glass.*
PHRASE **have it made** (*informal*) If you say that someone **has it made** or **has got it made**, you mean that they are certain to be rich or successful. ❏ *When I was at school, I thought I had it made.*

made-up ♦◇◇ also **made up** ADJ ❶ [V-LINK + made-up] If you are **made-up**, you are wearing makeup such as powder or eye shadow. ❏ *She was beautifully made up, beautifully groomed.* ❷ A **made-up** word, name, or story is invented, rather than really existing or being true. ❏ *It looks like a made-up word.*

mad·ly /ˈmædli/ ADV ❶ [madly with v] If you do something **madly**, you do it in a wild and uncontrolled manner. ❏ *Down in the streets people were waving madly.* ❷ You can use **madly** to indicate that one person loves another a great deal. ❏ *She has fallen madly in love with him.*

maga·zine ♦♦◇ /ˌmægəˈziːn, AmE ˈmægəziːn/ NOUN [c] (**magazines**) ❶ A **magazine** is a publication with a paper cover which is issued regularly, usually every week or every month, and which contains articles, stories, photographs, and advertisements. ❏ *Her face is on the cover of a dozen or more magazines.* ❷ In an automatic gun, the **magazine** is the part that contains the bullets. ❏ *The corporal ignored him, sliding the empty magazine from his weapon and replacing it with a fresh one.*

mag·ic ♦◇◇ /ˈmædʒɪk/ NOUN, ADJ
NOUN [u] ❶ **Magic** is the power to use supernatural forces to make impossible things happen, such as making people disappear or controlling events in nature. ❏ *They believe in magic.* ❏ *the use of magic to combat any adverse powers or influences* ❷ You can use **magic** when you are referring to an event that is so wonderful, strange, or unexpected that it seems as if supernatural powers have caused it. You can also say that something happens **as if by magic** or **like magic**. ❏ *All this was supposed to work like magic.* ❸ **Magic** is the art and skill of performing mysterious tricks to entertain people, for example by making things appear and disappear. ❏ *His secret hobby was performing magic tricks.* ❹ If you refer to **the magic** of something, you mean that it has a special mysterious quality which makes it seem wonderful and exciting to you and which makes you feel happy. ❏ *It infected them with some of the magic of a lost age.* ❺ If you refer to a person's **magic**, you mean a special talent or ability that they have, which you admire or consider very impressive. ❏ *The 32-year-old Jamaican-born fighter believes he can still regain some of his old magic.*
ADJ ❶ [magic + N] You use **magic** to describe something that does things, or appears to do things, by magic. ❏ *So it's a magic potion?* ❷ You can say that a moment or time is **magic** when it has a special mysterious quality that makes it seem wonderful and exciting. ❏ *Then came those magic moments in the rose garden.* ❸ ['the' magic + N] You can use expressions such as **the magic number** and **the magic word** to indicate that a number or word is the one which is significant or desirable in a particular situation. ❏ *their quest to gain the magic number of 270 electoral votes on election day* ❹ [magic + N, with NEG] **Magic** is used in expressions such as **there is no magic formula** and **there is no magic solution** to say that someone will have to make an effort to solve a problem, because it will not solve itself. ❏ *There is no magic formula for producing winning products.*

magi·cal /ˈmædʒɪkəl/ ADJ ❶ Something that is **magical** seems to use magic or to be able to produce magic. ❏ *the story of Sin-Sin, a little boy who has magical powers* ❷ You can say that a place or object is **magical** when it has a special mysterious quality that makes it seem wonderful

and exciting. ❏ *The beautiful island of Bermuda is a magical place to get married.*
magi·cal·ly /ˈmædʒɪkli/ ADV [magically with v] ❏ *During December the town is magically transformed into a Christmas wonderland.*

mag·is·trate /ˈmædʒɪstreɪt/ NOUN [c] (**magistrates**) A **magistrate** is an official who acts as a judge in law courts which deal with minor crimes or disputes. ❏ *She will face a local magistrate on Tuesday.*

✪ **mag·net** /ˈmægnɪt/ NOUN [c] (**magnets**) ❶ If you say that something is a **magnet** or is like a **magnet**, you mean that people are very attracted by it and want to go to it or look at it. ❏ *Prospect Park, with its vast lake, is a magnet for all health freaks.* ❷ A **magnet** is a piece of iron or other material which attracts iron towards it. ❏ *It's possible to hang a nail from a magnet and then use that nail to pick up another nail.* ❏ *about a hundred times more powerful than a fridge magnet* ❏ *superconductors are now used in power cables and to make powerful magnets*

✪ **mag·net·ic** /mægˈnetɪk/ ADJ ❶ If something metal is **magnetic**, it acts like a magnet. ❏ *magnetic particles* ❷ You use **magnetic** to describe something that is caused by or relates to the force of magnetism. ❏ *The electrically charged gas particles are affected by magnetic forces.* ❏ *The moon exerts a magnetic pull on the Earth's water levels.* ❸ You use **magnetic** to describe tapes and other objects which have a coating of a magnetic substance and contain coded information that can be read by computers or other machines. ❏ *her magnetic-strip ID card* ❹ If you describe something as **magnetic**, you mean that it is very attractive to people because it has unusual, powerful, and exciting qualities. ❏ *the magnetic effect of the prosperous American economy on would-be immigrants*

mag·net·ism /ˈmægnɪtɪzəm/ NOUN [u] ❶ Someone or something that has **magnetism** has unusual, powerful, and exciting qualities which attract people to them. ❏ *There was no doubting the animal magnetism of the man.* ❷ **Magnetism** is the natural power of some objects and substances, especially iron, to attract other objects towards them. ❏ *his research in electricity and magnetism*

✪ **mag·ni·fi·ca·tion** /ˌmægnɪfɪˈkeɪʃən/ NOUN [u, c] (**magnifications**) ❶ [u] **Magnification** is the act or process of magnifying something. ❏ *The man was tall, his figure shortened by the magnification of Lenny's binoculars.* ❏ *Pores are visible without magnification.* ❏ *the magnification of minute sounds through a computer* ❷ [c, u] **Magnification** is the degree to which a lens, mirror, or other device can magnify an object, or the degree to which the object is magnified. ❏ *The electron microscope uses a beam of electrons to produce images at high magnifications.* ❏ *The magnification is 833,333 times the original size.*

mag·nifi·cent /mægˈnɪfɪsənt/ ADJ If you say that something or someone is **magnificent**, you mean that you think they are extremely good, beautiful, or impressive. = splendid ❏ *a magnificent country house in wooded grounds*
mag·nifi·cence /mægˈnɪfɪsəns/ NOUN [u] = splendour ❏ *I shall never forget the magnificence of the Swiss mountains and the beauty of the lakes.*
mag·nifi·cent·ly /mægˈnɪfɪsəntli/ ADV = splendidly ❏ *The team played magnificently throughout the competition.*

✪ **mag·ni·fy** /ˈmægnɪfaɪ/ VERB [T] (**magnifies, magnifying, magnified**) ❶ To **magnify** an object means to make it appear larger than it really is, by means of a special lens or mirror. = enlarge ❏ *This version of the Digges telescope magnifies images 11 times.* ❏ *A lens would magnify the picture so it would be like looking at a large TV screen.* ❏ *magnifying lenses* ❷ To **magnify** something means to increase its effect, size, loudness, or intensity. ❏ *Poverty and human folly magnify natural disasters.* ❸ If you **magnify** something, you make it seem more important or serious than it really is. = exaggerate ❏ *They do not grasp the broad situation and spend their time magnifying ridiculous details.*

✪ **mag·ni·tude** /ˈmægnɪtjuːd, AmE -tuːd/ NOUN
NOUN [u] If you talk about the **magnitude** of something, you are talking about its great size, scale, or importance. = immensity, extent, enormity; ≠ smallness ❏ *An*

M

operation of this magnitude is going to be difficult. ❑ These are issues of great magnitude. ❑ No one seems to realise the magnitude of this problem.

PHRASE **order of magnitude** You can use **order of magnitude** when you are giving an approximate idea of the amount or importance of something. = scale ❑ America and Russia do not face a problem of the same order of magnitude as Japan.

maid /meɪd/ NOUN [C] (**maids**) A **maid** is a woman who works as a servant in a hotel or private house. ❑ A maid brought me breakfast at nine o'clock.

maid·en name NOUN [C] (**maiden names**) A married woman's **maiden name** is her parents' surname, which she used before she got married and started using her husband's surname. ❑ The marriage broke up in 1997 and she took back her maiden name of Boreman.

mail ♦◇◇ /meɪl/ NOUN, VERB
NOUN [SING, U, C] **1** [SING] ['the' mail, also 'by' mail] The **mail** is the public service or system by which letters and parcels are collected and delivered. ❑ Your cheque is in the mail. **2** [U] [also 'the' mail] You can refer to letters and parcels that are delivered to you as **mail**. ❑ There was no mail except the usual junk addressed to the occupant. **3** [C] A **mail** is an e-mail. ❑ If you have any problems then send me a mail.
VERB [T] (**mails, mailing, mailed**) **1** (mainly AmE; in BrE, usually use **post**) If you **mail** a letter or parcel to someone, you send it to them by putting it in a postbox or taking it to a post office. ❑ Last year, he mailed the documents to French journalists. ❑ He mailed me the contract. **2** To **mail** a message to someone means to send it to them by means of e-mail or a computer network.
→ See also **electronic mail, e-mail**

mail or·der NOUN [U] **Mail order** is a system of buying and selling goods. You choose the goods you want from a company by looking at their catalogue, and the company sends them to you through the post. ❑ The toys are available by mail order from Opi Toys.

✪**main** ♦♦♦ /meɪn/ ADJ, NOUN
ADJ [DET + main] The **main** thing is the most important one of several similar things in a particular situation. = primary, principal, major, chief ❑ one of the main tourist areas of San Francisco ❑ My main concern now is to protect the children. ❑ Our main objective was to improve safety. ❑ What are the main differences and similarities between them?
NOUN [C] (**mains**) The **mains** are the pipes which supply gas or water to buildings, or which take sewage away from them. ❑ the water supply from the mains
PHRASE **in the main** If you say that something is true **in the main**, you mean that it is generally true, although there may be exceptions. ❑ Tourists are, in the main, sympathetic people.

main·land /ˈmeɪnlænd/ NOUN [SING] You can refer to the largest part of a country or continent as **the mainland** when contrasting it with the islands around it. ❑ She was going to Nanaimo to catch the ferry to the mainland.

✪**main·ly** ♦♦◇ /ˈmeɪnli/ ADV **1** You use **mainly** when mentioning the main reason or thing involved in something. = primarily, principally, chiefly, largely ❑ I don't play golf, mainly because I'm no good at it. ❑ The birds live mainly on nectar. ❑ The stock market scandal is refusing to go away, mainly because there's still no consensus over how it should be dealt with. **2** [mainly with GROUP] You use **mainly** when you are referring to a group and stating something that is true of most of it. = mostly, predominantly ❑ The African half of the audience was mainly from Senegal or Mali. ❑ The staff were mainly Russian. ❑ the mainly Muslim country ❑ a mainly elderly population

---
VOCABULARY BUILDER

mainly ADV
You use **mainly** when mentioning the main reason or thing involved in something.
❑ I could see he was in terrible pain, mainly from the left side of his chest.
---

primarily ADV (often formal)
You use **primarily** to talk about the most important reason for something.
❑ Public order is primarily an urban problem.

principally ADV (formal)
Principally means more than anything else.
❑ Embryonic development seems to be controlled principally by a very small number of master genes.

chiefly ADV (mainly written)
You use **chiefly** to indicate that a particular reason, emotion, method, or feature is the main or most important one.
❑ His response to attacks on his work was chiefly bewilderment.

largely ADV (fairly formal)
Largely is used to introduce the main reason for a particular event or situation.
❑ The French empire had expanded, largely through military conquest.

✪**main·stream** /ˈmeɪnstriːm/ NOUN [C] (**mainstreams**) People, activities, or ideas that are part of the **mainstream** are regarded as the most typical, normal, and conventional because they belong to the same group or system as most others of their kind. = typical, average ❑ people outside the economic mainstream ❑ This was the company's first step into the mainstream of scientific and commercial computing. ❑ The show wanted to attract a mainstream audience.

✪**main·tain** ♦♦◇ /meɪnˈteɪn/ VERB [T] (**maintains, maintaining, maintained**) (academic word) **1** If you **maintain** something, you continue to have it, and do not let it stop or grow weaker. ❑ Such extrovert characters try to maintain relationships no matter how damaging these relationships may be. ❑ emergency powers to try to maintain law and order **2** If you say that someone **maintains that** something is true, you mean that they have stated their opinion strongly but not everyone agrees with them or believes them. = claim ❑ He has maintained that the money was donated for international purposes. ❑ 'Not all feminism has to be like this,' Jo maintains. **3** If you **maintain** something **at** a particular rate or level, you keep it at that rate or level. ❑ The government was right to maintain interest rates at a high level. ❑ Action is required to ensure standards are maintained at as high a level as possible. **4** If you **maintain** a road, building, vehicle, or machine, you keep it in good condition by regularly checking it and repairing it when necessary. = look after ❑ The house costs a fortune to maintain. **5** If you **maintain** someone, you provide them with money and other things that they need. = provide for, support ❑ the basic costs of maintaining a child

✪**main·te·nance** /ˈmeɪntɪnəns/ NOUN [U] **1** The **maintenance** of a building, vehicle, road, or machine is the process of keeping it in good condition by regularly checking it and repairing it when necessary. = upkeep ❑ maintenance work on government buildings ❑ The window had been replaced last week during routine maintenance. **2 Maintenance** is money that someone gives regularly to another person to pay for the things that the person needs. ❑ the government's plan to make absent fathers pay maintenance for their children **3** If you ensure the **maintenance of** a state or process, you make sure that it continues. = continuation ❑ the maintenance of peace and stability in Asia ❑ the importance of natural food to the maintenance of health

ma·jes·tic /məˈdʒestɪk/ ADJ If you describe something or someone as **majestic**, you think they are very beautiful, dignified, and impressive. = grand ❑ a majestic country home that once belonged to the Astor family
ma·jes·ti·cal·ly /məˈdʒestɪkli/ ADV ❑ She rose majestically to her feet.

maj·es·ty /ˈmædʒɪsti/ NOUN [C, U] (**majesties**) **1** [C] [POSS + majesty] (politeness) You use majesty in expressions such

m

as **Your Majesty** or **Her Majesty** when you are addressing or referring to a king or queen. ❑ *His Majesty requests your presence in the royal chambers.* **2** [u] **Majesty** is the quality of being beautiful, dignified, and impressive. ❑ *the majesty of the mainland mountains*

✪ **ma·jor** ♦♦♦ /'meɪdʒə/ ADJ, NOUN, VERB (*academic word*)

ADJ **1** [major + N] You use **major** when you want to describe something that is more important, serious, or significant than other things in a group or situation. = key, crucial, central, primary; ≠ minor ❑ *The major factor in the decision to stay or to leave was usually professional.* ❑ *Drug abuse has long been a major problem for the authorities there.* ❑ *Exercise has a major part to play in preventing disease.* **2** [N + major, major + N] In music, a **major** scale is one in which the third note is two tones higher than the first. ❑ *The orchestra played Mozart's Symphony No. 35 in D Major.*

NOUN [c] (**majors**) **1** A **major** is an officer who is one rank above captain in the British army and in United States Army, Air Force, or Marines. ❑ *I was a major in the war, you know.* **2** A **major** is an important sports competition, especially in golf or tennis. ❑ *Sarazen became the first golfer to win all four majors.*

VERB [i] (**majors, majoring, majored**) (*mainly AmE*) If a student at a university or college **majors in** a particular subject, that subject is the main one they study. ❑ *He majored in finance at Claremont Men's College in California.*

✪ **ma·jor·ity** ♦♦◇ /mə'dʒɒrɪti, AmE -'dʒɔːr-/ NOUN, ADJ (*academic word*)

NOUN [SING, c, u] (**majorities**) **1** [SING] The **majority** of people or things in a group is more than half of them. ❑ *The majority of my patients come to me from out of town.* ❑ *Before the war a majority opposed invasion, yet 51% now think it was justified.* ❑ *The vast majority of our cheeses are made with pasteurised milk.* **2** [c] A **majority** is the difference between the number of votes or seats that the winner gets in an election, and the number of votes or seats that the next person or party gets. ❑ *Members of parliament approved the move by a majority of ninety-nine.* **3** [u] **Majority** is the state of legally being an adult. In Britain and most states in the United States, people reach their majority at the age of eighteen. ❑ *a citizen of Russia who has reached the age of majority*

PHRASE **in a majority** or **in the majority** If a group is **in a majority** or **in the majority**, they form more than half of a larger group. ❑ *Surveys indicate that supporters of the treaty are still in the majority.*

ADJ [majority + N] **Majority** is used to describe opinions, decisions, and systems of government that are supported by more than half the people involved. ❑ *her continuing disagreement with the majority view*

USAGE NOTE
majority
Do not use 'the majority' when you are talking about an amount of something or part of something. You do not say, for example, '~~The majority of the forest has been cut down~~'. Use 'most of' instead. ***Most of** the forest has been cut down.*

make ♦♦♦ /meɪk/ VERB, NOUN

Make is used in a large number of expressions which are explained under other words in this dictionary. For example, the expression 'to make sense' is explained at 'sense'.

VERB [T, I, LINK] (**makes, making, made**) **1** [T] You can use **make** with a wide range of nouns to indicate that someone performs an action or says something. For example, if you **make** a suggestion, you suggest something. ❑ *I'd just like to make a comment.* ❑ *I made a few phone calls.* **2** [T] You can use **make** with certain nouns to indicate that someone does something well or badly. For example, if you **make** a success of something, you do it successfully, and if you **make** a mess of something, you do it very badly. ❑ *Apparently he made a mess of his audition.* **3** [I, T] (*written*) If you **make as if to** do something or **make to** do something, you behave in a way that makes it seem that

you are just about to do it. ❑ *Mary made as if to protest, then hesitated.* **4** [T] If something **makes** you do something, it causes you to do it. ❑ *Dirt from the road made him cough.* ❑ *The white tips of his shirt collar made him look like a choirboy.* **5** [T] If you **make** someone do something, you force them to do it. ❑ *You can't make me do anything.* **6** [T] You use **make** to talk about causing someone or something to be a particular thing or to have a particular quality. For example, to **make** someone a star means to cause them to become a star, and to **make** someone angry means to cause them to become angry. ❑ *James Bond, the role that made him a star* ❑ *She made life very difficult for me.* **7** [T] If you say that one thing or person **makes** another seem, for example, small, stupid, or good, you mean that they cause them to seem small, stupid, or good in comparison, even though they are not. ❑ *They live in fantasy worlds which make Disneyland seem uninventive.* **8** [T] If you **make yourself** understood, heard, or known, you succeed in getting people to understand you, hear you, or know that you are there. ❑ *He learned enough Spanish to make himself understood.* **9** [T] If you **make** someone something, you appoint them to a particular job, role, or position. ❑ *He made her a director in his numerous companies.* **10** [T] If you **make** something **into** something else, you change it in some way so that it becomes that other thing. ❑ *We made it into a beautiful home.* **11** [T] To **make** a total or score a particular amount means to increase it to that amount. ❑ *This makes the total cost of the bulb and energy $27.* **12** [T] When someone **makes** a friend or an enemy, someone becomes their friend or their enemy, often because of a particular thing they have done. ❑ *Lorenzo was a natural leader who made friends easily.* **13** [T] To **make** something means to produce, construct, or create it. ❑ *She made her own bread.* ❑ *Having curtains made professionally can be costly.* **14** [T] If you **make** a note or list, you write something down in that form. = write ❑ *Mr Perry made a note in his book.* **15** [T] If you **make** rules or laws, you decide what these should be. ❑ *The police don't make the laws, they merely enforce them.* **16** [T] If you **make** money, you get it by working for it, by selling something, or by winning it. ❑ *I think every business's goal is to make money.* **17** [T] If you **make** a case **for** something, you try to establish or prove that it is the best thing to do. ❑ *You could certainly make a case for this point of view.* **18** [LINK] You can use **make** to say that someone or something has the right qualities for a particular task or role. For example, if you say that someone will **make** a good politician, you mean that they have the right qualities to be a good politician. ❑ *She'll make a good actress, if she gets the right training.* ❑ *You've a very good idea there. It will make a good book.* **19** [LINK] If people **make** a particular pattern such as a line or a circle, they arrange themselves in this way. = form ❑ *A group of people made a circle around the Pentagon.* **20** [LINK] You can use **make** to say what two numbers add up to. ❑ *Four twos make eight.* **21** [T] If someone **makes** a particular team or **makes** a particular high position, they do so well that they are put in that team or get that position. ❑ *The athletes are just happy to make the team.* **22** [T] If you **make** a place in or by a particular time, you get there in or by that time, often with some difficulty. ❑ *The engine is gulping two tons of fuel an hour in order to make New Orleans by nightfall.* **23** [T] You use **make it** when saying what you calculate or guess an amount to be. ❑ *'How many shots has she got left?'—'I make it two.'* **24** [T] You use **make it** when saying what time your watch says it is. ❑ *I make it nearly nine o'clock.*

PHRASES **make do** If you **make do** with something, you use or have it instead of something else that you do not have, although it is not as good. ❑ *Why make do with a copy if you can afford the genuine article?*

make it 1 If you **make it** somewhere, you succeed in getting there, especially in time to do something. ❑ *So you did make it to America, after all.* ❑ *the hostages who never made it home* **2** If you **make it**, you are successful in achieving something difficult, or in surviving through a very difficult period. ❑ *I believe I have the talent to make it.* **3** If you cannot **make it**, you are unable to attend an event that you have been invited to. ❑ *He hadn't been able to make it to our dinner.*

PHRASAL VERBS **make for** **1** If you **make for** a place, you move towards it. ❑ *He rose from his seat and made for the door.* **2** (informal) If something **makes for** another thing, it causes or helps to cause that thing to happen or exist. ❑ *A happy parent makes for a happy child.*

make of If you ask a person what they **make of** something, you want to know what their impression, opinion, or understanding of it is. ❑ *Nancy wasn't sure what to make of Mick's apology.*

make off If you **make off**, you leave somewhere as quickly as possible, often in order to escape. ❑ *They broke free and made off in a stolen car.*

make off with If you **make off with** something, you steal it and take it away with you. ❑ *Otto made off with the last of the brandy.*

make out **1** If you **make** something **out**, you manage with difficulty to see or hear it. ❑ *I could just make out a tall, pale, shadowy figure tramping through the undergrowth.* ❑ *She thought she heard a name. She couldn't make it out, though.* **2** If you try to **make** something **out**, you try to understand it or decide whether or not it is true. = understand ❑ *I couldn't make it out at all.* ❑ *It is hard to make out what criteria are used.* **3** If you **make out that** something is the case or **make** something **out to** be the case, you try to cause people to believe that it is the case. ❑ *They were trying to make out that I'd actually done it.* ❑ *I don't think it was as glorious as everybody made it out to be.* **4** When you **make out** a cheque, receipt, or order form, you write all the necessary information on it. ❑ *I'll make the cheque out to you and put it in the post this afternoon.*

make up **1** The people or things that **make up** something are the members or parts that form that thing. = form, constitute ❑ *The Chinese make up the largest single ethnic group in the city's public classrooms.* ❑ *Women officers make up 13 per cent of the police force.* **2** If you **make up** something such as a story or excuse, you invent it, sometimes in order to deceive people. ❑ *I think it's very unkind of you to make up stories about him.* **3** If you **make up** an amount, you add something to it so that it is as large as it should be. ❑ *Less than half of the money that students receive is in the form of grants, and loans have made up the difference.* **4** If you **make up** time or hours, you work some extra hours because you have previously taken some time off work. ❑ *They'll have to make up time lost during the strike.* **5** If two people **make up** after a quarrel or disagreement, they become friends again. ❑ *She came back and they made up.* **6** If you **make up** something such as food or medicine, you prepare it by mixing or putting different things together. ❑ *Prepare the soufflé dish before making up the soufflé mixture.* **7** If you **make up** a bed, you put sheets and blankets on it so that someone can sleep there. ❑ *Her mother made up a bed in her old room.* **NOUN** [c] (**makes**) The **make** of something such as a car or radio is the name of the company that made it. = brand ❑ *The only car parked outside is a black Saab – a different make.* ✦ **make friends** → see **friend**

mak•er ♦♦◇ /ˈmeɪkə/ NOUN [c] (**makers**) **1** The **maker** of a product is the company that manufactures it. = manufacturer ❑ *Japan's two largest car makers* **2** You can refer to the person who makes something as its **maker**. ❑ *the makers of news and current affairs programmes*

make•shift /ˈmeɪkʃɪft/ ADJ Makeshift things are temporary and usually of poor quality, but they are used because there is nothing better available. ❑ *the cardboard boxes and makeshift shelters of the homeless*

make•up ♦◇◇ /ˈmeɪkˌʌp/ NOUN [u] **1** Makeup consists of things such as lipstick, eye shadow, and powder which some women put on their faces to make themselves look more attractive or which actors use to change or improve their appearance. ❑ *Normally she wore little makeup, but this evening was clearly an exception.* **2** Someone's **makeup** is their nature and the various qualities in their character. = personality ❑ *There was some fatal flaw in his makeup, and as time went on he lapsed into long silences or became off-hand.* **3** The **makeup** of something consists of its different parts and the way these parts are arranged. ❑ *The ideological makeup of the unions was now radically different from what it had been.*

mak•ing /ˈmeɪkɪŋ/ NOUN **NOUN** [u] (**makings**) The **making** of something is the act or process of producing or creating it. ❑ *Salamon's book about the making of this film* **PHRASES** **in the making** If you describe a person or thing as something **in the making**, you mean that they are going to become known or recognized as that thing. ❑ *Her drama teacher is confident Julie is a star in the making.* **be the making of** If something **is the making of** a person or thing, it is the reason that they become successful or become very much better than they used to be. ❑ *This discovery may yet be the making of him.* **have the makings of something** If you say that a person or thing **has the makings of** something, you mean it seems possible or likely that they will become that thing, as they have the necessary qualities. ❑ *Godfrey had the makings of a successful journalist.* **of your own making** If you say that something such as a problem you have is **of** your **own making**, you mean you have caused or created it yourself. ❑ *Some of the university's financial troubles are of its own making.*

✪**male** ♦♦◇ /meɪl/ ADJ, NOUN **ADJ** **1** Someone who is **male** is a man or a boy. ❑ *Many women achievers appear to pose a threat to their male colleagues.* ❑ *The company has engaged two male dancers from the Bolshoi.* ❑ *Most of the demonstrators were white and male.* **2** [male + N] **Male** means relating to, belonging to, or affecting men rather than women. ❑ *Massive male unemployment has diminished the status of men in the family.* ❑ *male violence* ❑ *a deep male voice* **3** **Male** means belonging to the sex that cannot lay eggs or have babies. ❑ *After mating, the male wasps tunnel through the sides of their nursery.* **NOUN** [c] (**males**) **1** Men and boys are sometimes referred to as **males** when they are being considered as a type. = man ❑ *the remains of a Caucasian male, aged 65-70* **2** You can refer to any creature that belongs to the sex that cannot lay eggs or have babies as a **male**. ❑ *Males and females take turns brooding the eggs.*

mal•ice /ˈmælɪs/ NOUN [u] **Malice** is behaviour that is intended to harm people or their reputations, or cause them embarrassment and upset. ❑ *There was a strong current of malice in many of his portraits.*

WORD PARTS

The prefix **mal-** often appears in words that refer to things that are bad or unpleasant, or that are unsuccessful or imperfect:

malice (NOUN)

malnutrition (NOUN)

malfunction (VERB)

ma•li•cious /məˈlɪʃəs/ ADJ If you describe someone's words or actions as **malicious**, you mean that they are intended to harm people or their reputation, or cause them embarrassment and upset. ❑ *That might merely have been malicious gossip.* **ma•li•cious•ly** /məˈlɪʃəsli/ ADV ❑ *his maliciously accurate imitation of Hubert de Burgh*

mall /mɔːl, mæl/ NOUN [c] (**malls**) (mainly AmE) A **mall** is a very large, enclosed shopping area.

mal•nu•tri•tion /ˌmælnjuːˈtrɪʃən, AmE -nuː-/ NOUN [u] If someone is suffering from **malnutrition**, they are physically weak and extremely thin because they have not eaten enough food. ❑ *Infections are more likely in those suffering from malnutrition.*

m

M

✪**mam·mal** /'mæməl/ NOUN [C] (mammals) Mammals are animals such as humans, dogs, lions, and whales. In general, female mammals give birth to babies rather than laying eggs, and feed their young with milk. ❑ *This is the best place on the west coast of Scotland for seeing large marine mammals.*

man ♦♦♦ /mæn/ NOUN, VERB
NOUN [C, U, SING] (men) **1** [C] A **man** is an adult male human being. ❑ *He had not expected the young man to reappear before evening.* ❑ *I have always regarded him as a man of integrity.* **2** [C, U] **Man** and **men** are sometimes used to refer to all human beings, including both males and females. Some people dislike this use. ❑ *The chick initially has no fear of man.* **3** [C] If you say that a man is, for example, a **gambling man** or an **outdoors man**, you mean that he likes gambling or outdoor activities. ❑ *Are you a gambling man, Mr Graham?* **4** [C] If you say that a man is, for example, a **Cambridge man** or a **Labour man**, you mean that he went to that university or that his political sympathies lie with the Labour Party. ❑ *Stewart, a Yale man, was invited to stay on and write the script.* **5** [C] (journalism) If you refer to a particular company's or organization's **man**, you mean a man who works for or represents that company or organization. ❑ *the Chicago Tribune's man in Abu Dhabi* **6** [SING] (informal) Some people refer to a woman's husband, lover, or boyfriend as her **man**. ❑ *if they see your man cuddle you in the kitchen or living room* **7** [C] In very informal social situations, **man** is sometimes used as a greeting or form of address to a man. ❑ *Hey wow, man! Where d'you get those boots?*
PHRASES **man enough to** or **man enough for** If you say that a man is **man enough** to do something, you mean that he has the necessary courage or ability to do it. ❑ *I told him that he should be man enough to admit he had done wrong.*
a man's man If you describe a man as **a man's man**, you mean that he has qualities which make him popular with other men rather than with women. ❑ *Very much a man's man, he enjoyed drinking and jesting with his cronies.*
own man (approval) If you say that a man **is** his **own man**, you approve of the fact that he makes his decisions and his plans himself, and does not depend on other people. ❑ *Be your own man. Make up your own mind.*
to a man (emphasis) If you say that a group of men are, do, or think something **to a man**, you are emphasizing that every one of them is, does, or thinks that thing. ❑ *To a man, the survivors blamed the government.*
VERB [T] (mans, manning, manned) If you **man** something such as a place or machine, you operate it or are in charge of it. ❑ *French soldiers manned roadblocks in the capital city.* ❑ *the person manning the phone in the complaints department* → See also **manned**

✪**man·age** ♦♦◇ /'mænɪdʒ/ VERB
VERB [T, I] (manages, managing, managed) **1** [T] If you **manage** an organization, business, or system, or the people who work in it, you are responsible for controlling them. = organize, run, direct ❑ *Within two years he was managing the store.* ❑ *There is a lack of confidence in the government's ability to manage the economy.* ❑ *The factory was badly managed.* **2** [T] If you **manage** time, money, or other resources, you deal with them carefully and do not waste them. ≠ mismanage, waste ❑ *In a busy world, managing your time is increasingly important.* ❑ *We are trying to manage water resources effectively.* **3** [T] If you **manage** to do something, especially something difficult, you succeed in doing it. ❑ *Somehow, he'd managed to persuade Kay to buy one for him.* ❑ *I managed to pull myself up onto a wet, sloping ledge.* **4** [I] If you **manage**, you succeed in coping with a difficult situation. = cope ❑ *She had managed perfectly well without medication for three years.* **5** [T] If you say that you can **manage** an amount of time or money for something, you mean that you can afford to spend that time or money on it. = spare ❑ *I try to manage about five hours a week on my bike.* **6** [T] If you say that someone **managed** a particular response, such as a laugh or a greeting, you mean that it was difficult for them to do it because they were feeling sad or upset. ❑ *He looked dazed*

as he spoke to reporters, managing only a weak smile.
CONVENTION **I will manage** or **I can manage** You say 'I can manage' or 'I'll manage' as a way of refusing someone's offer of help and insisting on doing something by yourself. ❑ *I know you mean well, but I can manage by myself.*

man·age·able /'mænɪdʒəbəl/ ADJ Something that is **manageable** is of a size, quantity, or level of difficulty that people are able to deal with. ❑ *He will now try to cut down the task to a manageable size.*

✪**man·age·ment** ♦♦◇ /'mænɪdʒmənt/ NOUN [U, C] (managements) **1** [U] **Management** is the control and organizing of a business or other organization. = organization, control, directorship ❑ *The zoo needed better management rather than more money.* ❑ *The dispute is about wages, working conditions, and the management of the mining industry.* ❑ *the responsibility for its day-to-day management* **2** [C, U] (business) You can refer to the people who control and organize a business or other organization as the **management**. = staff ❑ *The management is doing its best to improve the situation.* ❑ *We need to get more women into top management.* **3** [U] **Management** is the way people control different parts of their lives. ❑ *her management of her professional life*

✪**man·ag·er** ♦♦◇ /'mænɪdʒə/ NOUN [C] (managers) **1** A **manager** is a person who is responsible for running part of or the whole of a business organization. = director, head, executive, leader ❑ *The chef, staff, and managers are all Chinese.* ❑ *a retired bank manager* **2** The **manager** of a pop star or other entertainer is the person who takes care of their business interests. ❑ *the star's manager and agent, Anne Chudleigh* **3** The **manager** of a sports team is the person responsible for training the players and organizing the way they play. In American English, manager is only used for baseball; in other sports **coach** is used instead. ❑ *The team expects to have a new manager before spring training.*

mana·gerial /ˌmænɪ'dʒɪəriəl/ ADJ **Managerial** means relating to the work of a manager. ❑ *his managerial skills* ❑ *a managerial career*

man·ag·ing di·rec·tor NOUN [C] (managing directors) (mainly BrE, business) The **managing director** of a company is the most important working director, and is in charge of the way the company is managed.

man·date /'mændeɪt/ NOUN, VERB
NOUN [C] (mandates) **1** If a government or other elected body has a **mandate** to carry out a particular policy or task, they have the authority to carry it out as a result of winning an election or vote. ❑ *The president and his supporters are almost certain to read this vote as a mandate for continued economic reform.* **2** If someone is given a **mandate** to carry out a particular policy or task, they are given the official authority to do it. ❑ *How much longer does the independent prosecutor have a mandate to pursue this investigation?* **3** (formal) You can refer to the fixed length of time that a country's leader or government remains in office as their **mandate**. ❑ *his intention to leave politics once his mandate ends*
VERB [T] (mandates, mandating, mandated) (formal) When someone **is mandated to** carry out a particular policy or task, they are given the official authority to do it. ❑ *He'd been mandated by the West African Economic Community to go in and to enforce a ceasefire.*

ma·ni·ac /'meɪniæk/ NOUN, ADJ
NOUN [C] (maniacs) **1** A **maniac** is a crazy person who is violent and dangerous. ❑ *The cabin looked as if a maniac had been let loose there.* **2** (disapproval) If you call someone, for example, a religious **maniac** or a sports **maniac**, you are critical of them because they have such a strong interest in religion or sports. = fanatic ❑ *My mum is turning into a religious maniac.*
ADJ [maniac + N] (emphasis) If you describe someone's behaviour as **maniac**, you are emphasizing that it is extremely foolish and uncontrolled. = lunatic ❑ *He could not maintain his maniac speed for much longer.*

mani·fest /'mænɪfest/ ADJ, VERB
ADJ (formal) **1** If you say that something is **manifest**, you

mean that it is clearly true and that nobody would disagree with it if they saw it or considered it. = patent ❑ *the manifest failure of the policies* **2** If a particular quality, feeling, or illness is **manifest**, it is visible or obvious. ❑ *The same alarm is manifest everywhere.*

VERB [T] (**manifests, manifesting, manifested**) (*formal*) If you **manifest** a particular quality, feeling, or illness, or if it **manifests itself**, it becomes visible or obvious. = show ❑ *He manifested a pleasing personality on stage.* ❑ *The virus needs two weeks to manifest itself.*

mani·fest·ly /ˈmænɪfestli/ ADV = patently ❑ *She manifestly failed to last the mile-and-a-half of the race.*

mani·fes·to /ˌmænɪˈfestəʊ/ NOUN [C] (**manifestos** or **manifestoes**) A **manifesto** is a statement published by a person or group of people, especially a political party or a government, in which they say what their aims and policies are. ❑ *The Republicans are currently drawing up their election manifesto.*

✪**ma·nipu·late** /məˈnɪpjʊleɪt/ VERB [T] (**manipulates, manipulating, manipulated**) (*academic word*) **1** (*disapproval*) If you say that someone **manipulates** people, you disapprove of them because they skilfully force or persuade people to do what they want. ❑ *She's always borrowing my clothes and manipulating me to give her vast sums of money.* **2** (*disapproval*) If you say that someone **manipulates** an event or situation, you disapprove of them because they use or control it for their own benefit, or cause it to develop in the way they want. ❑ *She was unable, for once, to control and manipulate events.* ❑ *He said that the state television was trying to manipulate the election outcome.* ❑ *They felt he had been cowardly in manipulating the system to avoid the draft.* **3** If you **manipulate** something that requires a skill, such as a complicated piece of equipment or a difficult idea, you operate it or process it. = work, handle ❑ *The technology uses a pen to manipulate a computer.* ❑ *The puppets are expertly manipulated by Liz Walker.* ❑ *His mind moves in quantum leaps, manipulating ideas and jumping on to new ones as soon as he can.* **4** If someone **manipulates** your bones or muscles, they skilfully move and press them with their hands in order to push the bones into their correct position or make the muscles less stiff. ❑ *The way he can manipulate my leg has helped my arthritis so much.*

✪**ma·nipu·la·tion** /məˌnɪpjʊˈleɪʃən/ NOUN [C, U] (**manipulations**) **1** *repeated criticism or manipulation of our minds* **2** *accusations of political manipulation* **3** *science that requires only the simplest of mathematical manipulations* **4** *A permanent cure will only be effected by acupuncture, chiropractic, or manipulation.*

man·kind /ˌmænˈkaɪnd/ NOUN [U] You can refer to all human beings as **mankind** when considering them as a group. Some people dislike this use. ❑ *the evolution of mankind*

man·ly /ˈmænli/ ADJ (**manlier, manliest**) (*approval*) If you describe a man's behaviour or appearance as **manly**, you approve of it because it shows qualities that are considered typical of a man, such as strength or courage. ❑ *He set himself manly tasks and expected others to follow his example.* **man·li·ness** /ˈmænlinəs/ NOUN [U] ❑ *He has no doubts about his manliness.*

✪**man-made** also **manmade** ADJ Man-made things are created or caused by people, rather than occurring naturally. = artificial, synthetic; ≠ natural ❑ *Man-made and natural disasters have disrupted the government's economic plans.* ❑ *man-made lakes* ❑ *a variety of materials, both natural and man-made*

manned /mænd/ ADJ A **manned** vehicle such as a spacecraft has people in it who are operating its controls. ❑ *In thirty years from now the United States should have a manned spacecraft on Mars.*
→ See also man VERB

man·ner ◆◇◇ /ˈmænə/ NOUN [PL, SING] (**manners**) **1** [PL, SING] The **manner** in which you do something is the way that you do it. ❑ *She smiled again in a friendly manner.* ❑ *I'm a professional and I have to conduct myself in a professional manner.* **2** [SING] Someone's **manner** is the way in which they behave and talk when they are with other

people, for example whether they are polite, confident, or bad-tempered. ❑ *His manner was self-assured and brusque.* **3** [PL] If someone has **good manners**, they are polite and observe social customs. If someone has **bad manners**, they are impolite and do not observe these customs. ❑ *He dressed well and had impeccable manners.* ❑ *The manners of many doctors were appalling.*
-mannered /ˈmænəd/ COMB ❑ *Forrest was normally mild-mannered, affable, and untalkative.*

ma·noeu·vre /məˈnuːvə/ (*BrE*; in *AmE*, use **maneuver**) VERB, NOUN
VERB [I, T] (**manoeuvres, manoeuvring, manoeuvred**) **1** If you **manoeuvre** something into or out of an awkward position, you skilfully move it there. ❑ *That will allow them to manoeuvre the satellite into the shuttle's cargo bay.* ❑ *I manoeuvred my way among the tables to the back corner of the place.* **2** If you **manoeuvre** a situation, you change it in a clever and skilful way so that you can benefit from it. ❑ *The president has tried to manoeuvre the campaign away from himself.*
NOUN [C, U, PL] (**manoeuvres**) **1** [C, U] A **manoeuvre** is a movement or action requiring dexterity and skill. ❑ *The chopper shot upwards in a manoeuvre matched by the other pilot.* **2** [C] A **manoeuvre** is a clever and skilful plan or action designed to change a situation, possibly in a deceptive way. ❑ *The company announced a series of manoeuvres to raise cash and reduce debt.* **3** [PL] Military **manoeuvres** are training exercises which involve the movement of soldiers and equipment over a large area. ❑ *Allied troops begin manoeuvres tomorrow to show how quickly forces could be mobilized in case of a new invasion.*

man·power /ˈmænpaʊə/ NOUN [U] Workers are sometimes referred to as **manpower** when they are being considered as a part of the process of producing goods or providing services. ❑ *the shortage of skilled manpower in the industry*

man·sion /ˈmænʃən/ NOUN [C] (**mansions**) A **mansion** is a very large house. ❑ *an eighteenth-century mansion in New Hampshire*

man·slaugh·ter /ˈmænslɔːtə/ NOUN [U] (*legal*) **Manslaughter** is the illegal killing of a person by someone who did not intend to kill them. ❑ *A judge accepted her plea that she was guilty of manslaughter, not murder.*

✪**manu·al** /ˈmænjuəl/ ADJ, NOUN (*academic word*) **ADJ** **1** **Manual** work is work in which you use your hands or your physical strength rather than your mind. = blue-collar, physical; ≠ clerical, white-collar ❑ *skilled manual workers* ❑ *They work in factory or manual jobs.* **2** [manual + N] (*formal*) **Manual** is used to talk about movements which are made by someone's hands. ❑ *toys designed to help develop manual dexterity* **3** [manual + N] **Manual** means operated by hand, rather than by electricity or a motor. ❑ *There is a manual pump to get rid of the water.*
NOUN [C] (**manuals**) A **manual** is a book which tells you how to do something or how a piece of machinery works. ❑ *the instruction manual*
manu·al·ly /ˈmænjuəli/ ADV ❑ *The device is manually operated, using a simple handle.*

✪**manu·fac·ture** ◆◇◇ /ˌmænjʊˈfæktʃə/ VERB, NOUN
VERB [T] (**manufactures, manufacturing, manufactured**) **1** (*business*) To **manufacture** something means to make it in a factory, usually in large quantities. = produce ❑ *They manufacture the class of plastics known as thermoplastic materials.* ❑ *The first three models are being manufactured at the factory in Dayton.* ❑ *The company imports foreign manufactured goods.* **2** (*disapproval*) If you say that someone **manufactures** information, you are criticizing them because they invent information that is not true. = fabricate ❑ *According to the prosecution, the officers manufactured an elaborate story.*
NOUN [U, C] (**manufactures**) (*business*) **1** [U] **Manufacture** is the process or fact of making something in a factory, usually in large quantities. ❑ *the manufacture of nuclear weapons* **2** [C] In economics, **manufactures** are goods or products which have been made in a factory. ❑ *a long-term rise in the share of manufactures in non-oil exports*
✪**manu·fac·tur·ing** /ˌmænjʊˈfæktʃərɪŋ/ NOUN [U]

m

❏ *management headquarters for manufacturing in China*
❏ *the manufacturing of a luxury type automobile*

○manu·fac·tur·er ◆◇◇ /ˌmænjʊˈfæktʃərə/ NOUN [c]
(**manufacturers**) (*business*) A **manufacturer** is a business or
company which makes goods in large quantities to sell.
= producer ❏ *the world's largest doll manufacturer* ❏ *major
manufacturers and retailers of woodworking tools*

○manu·script /ˈmænjʊskrɪpt/ NOUN [c] (**manuscripts**)
[also 'in' manuscript] A **manuscript** is a handwritten or
typed document, especially a writer's first version of a book
before it is published. ❏ *He had seen a manuscript of the
book.* ❏ *discovering an original manuscript of the song in Paris*

many ◆◆◆ /ˈmeni/ DET, PRON, QUANT, ADJ, ADV, PREDET, NOUN
DET ■ You use **many** to indicate that you are talking
about a large number of people or things. ❏ *I don't think
many people would argue with that.* ❏ *Not many films are
made in Finland.* ■ You use **many** after 'how' to ask
questions about numbers or quantities. You use **many** after
'how' in reported clauses to talk about numbers or
quantities. ❏ *How many years have you been here?* ■ You
use **many** with 'as' when you are comparing numbers of
things or people. ❏ *I've always entered as many photo
competitions as I can.*
PRON ■ **Many** means a large number of people or things.
❏ *We stood up, thinking through the possibilities. There weren't
many.* ■ ['how' many] You use **many** after 'how' to ask
questions about numbers or quantities. You use **many** after
'how' in reported clauses to talk about numbers or
quantities. ❏ *How many do you smoke a day?* ■ ['as' many]
You use **many** with 'as' when you are comparing numbers
of things or people. ❏ *Let the child try on as many as she
likes.* ■ You use **many** to mean 'many people'. ❏ *Iris
Murdoch was regarded by many as a supremely good and
serious writer.*
QUANT [many 'of' DEF-PL-N] **Many of** a group of people or
things is a large number of that group. ❏ *So, once we have
cohabited, why do many of us feel the need to get married?*
❏ *It seems there are not very many of them left in the sea.*
ADJ You use **many** to indicate that you are talking about a
large number of people or things. ❏ *Among his many
hobbies was the breeding of fine horses.*
ADV [many as reply] You use **many** in expressions such as
'not many', 'not very many', and 'too many' when
replying to questions about numbers of things or people.
❏ *'How many of the songs that dealt with this theme became hit
songs?'—'Not very many.'*
PHRASE **as many as** (*emphasis*) You use **as many as** before a
number to suggest that it is surprisingly large. ❏ *As many
as 4 million people watched today's parade.*
PREDET (*emphasis*) You use **many** followed by 'a' and a
noun to emphasize that there are a lot of people or things
involved in something. ❏ *Many a mother tries to act out her
unrealized dreams through her daughter.*
NOUN [SING] **The many** means a large group of people,
especially the ordinary people in society, considered as
separate from a particular small group. ❏ *The printing press
gave power to a few to change the world for the many.*

USAGE NOTE
many

You use **many** immediately in front of a plural noun, but
'many of' in front of a plural pronoun. Do not say, for
example, '~~many of people~~'.
Many people *have moved to the cities from the countryside.*

---

map ◆◇◇ /mæp/ NOUN, VERB
NOUN [c] (**maps**) A **map** is a drawing of a particular area
such as a city, a country, or a continent, showing its main
features as they would appear if you looked at them from
above. ❏ *He unfolded the map and set it on the floor.*
VERB [T] (**maps, mapping, mapped**) To **map** an area means
to make a map of it. ❏ *a spacecraft which is using radar to
map the surface of Venus*
PHRASAL VERB **map out** If you **map out** something that
you are intending to do, you work out in detail how you
will do it. ❏ *I went home and mapped out my strategy.*
❏ *I cannot conceive of anybody writing a play by sitting
down and mapping it out.*

mar /mɑː/ VERB [T] (**mars, marring, marred**) To **mar**
something means to spoil or damage it. ❏ *A number of
problems marred the smooth running of this event.*

mara·thon /ˈmærəθən, AmE -θɒn/ NOUN, ADJ
NOUN [c] (**marathons**) A **marathon** is a race in which
people run a distance of 26 miles, which is about 42 km.
❏ *running in his first marathon*
ADJ [marathon + N] (*emphasis*) If you use **marathon** to
describe an event or task, you are emphasizing that it takes
a long time and is very tiring. ❏ *People make marathon
journeys to buy glass here.*

mar·ble /ˈmɑːbəl/ NOUN [U, c] (**marbles**) ■ [U] **Marble** is a
type of very hard rock which feels cold when you touch it
and which shines when it is cut and polished. Statues and
parts of buildings are sometimes made of marble. ❏ *The
house has a superb staircase made from oak and marble.*
■ [c] **Marbles** are sculptures made of marble. ❏ *marbles
and bronzes from the Golden Age of Athens* ■ [U] **Marbles** is a
children's game played with small balls, usually made of
coloured glass. You roll a ball along the ground and try to
hit an opponent's ball with it. ❏ *On the far side of the street,
two boys were playing marbles.* ■ [c] A **marble** is one of the
small balls used in the game of marbles. ❏ *a glass marble*

march ◆◇◇ /mɑːtʃ/ VERB, NOUN
VERB [I, T] (**marches, marching, marched**) ■ [I, T] When
soldiers **march** somewhere, or when a commanding officer
marches them somewhere, they walk there with very
regular steps, as a group. ❏ *A US infantry battalion was
marching down the street.* ❏ *Captain Ramirez called them to
attention and marched them off to the main camp.* ■ [I] When
a large group of people **march** for a cause, they walk
somewhere together in order to express their ideas or to
protest about something. ❏ *The demonstrators then marched
through the capital chanting slogans and demanding free
elections.* ■ [I] If you say that someone **marches**
somewhere, you mean that walk there quickly and in a
determined way, for example because they are angry. ❏ *He
marched into the kitchen without knocking.* ■ [T] If you **march**
someone somewhere, you force them to walk there with
you, for example by holding their arm tightly. ❏ *They were
marched through a crocodile-infested area and, if they slowed
down, were beaten with sticks.*
NOUN [SING, c] (**marches**) ■ [SING, c] A **march** is when
soldiers walk somewhere with very regular steps, as a
group. ❏ *After a short march, the column entered the village.*
■ [c] A **march** is when a large group of people walk
somewhere together in order to express their ideas or to
protest about something. ❏ *Organizers expect up to 300,000
protesters to join the march.* ■ [SING] **The march of**
something is its steady development or progress. ❏ *It is
easy to feel trampled by the relentless march of technology.*
■ [c] A **march** is a piece of music with a regular rhythm
that you can march to. ❏ *A military band played Russian
marches and folk tunes at the parade last Sunday.*
march·er /ˈmɑːtʃə/ NOUN [c] (**marchers**) ❏ *Fights between
police and marchers lasted for three hours.*

mare /meə/ NOUN [c] (**mares**) A **mare** is an adult female
horse.

○mar·gin ◆◇◇ /ˈmɑːdʒɪn/ NOUN [c, u, PL] (**margins**)
(*academic word*) ■ [c] A **margin** is the difference between
two amounts, especially the difference in the number of
votes or points between the winner and the loser in an
election or other contest. ❏ *They could end up with a
50-point winning margin.* ❏ *The Sunday Times remains the
brand leader by a huge margin.* ❏ *The margin in favour was
280 to 153.* ■ [c] The **margin** of a written or printed page
is the empty space at the side of the page. ❏ *She added her
comments in the margin.* ❏ *The wood-eating insects also don't
like the taste of ink and prefer the binding and the margin of the
pages.* ■ [c, u] If there is a **margin** for something in a
situation, there is some freedom to choose what to do or
decide how to do it. ❏ *The money is collected in a
straightforward way with little margin for error.* ■ [c] The
margin of a place or area is the extreme edge of it. = edge,
periphery ❏ *the low coastal plain along the western margin*
❏ *These islands are on the margins of human habitation.* ■ [PL]
To be **on the margins** of a society, group, or activity means

to be among the least typical or least important parts of it. ☐ *Students have played an important role in the past, but for the moment, they're on the margins.*

❖**mar·gin·al** /ˈmɑːdʒɪnəl/ ADJ **1** If you describe something as **marginal**, you mean that it is small or not very important. ☐ *This is a marginal improvement on October.* ☐ *The role of the opposition party proved marginal.* **2** If you describe people as **marginal**, you mean that they are not involved in the main events or developments in society because they are poor or have no power. ☐ *The tribunals were established for the well-integrated members of society and not for marginal individuals.* ☐ *I don't want to call him marginal, but he's not a major character.* **3** (*business*) **Marginal** activities, costs, or taxes are not the main part of a business or an economic system, but often make the difference between its success or failure, and are therefore important to control. ☐ *The analysts applaud the cuts in marginal businesses, but insist the company must make deeper sacrifices.*

❖**mar·gin·al·ly** /ˈmɑːdʒɪnəli/ ADV **Marginally** means to only a small extent. = slightly ☐ *Sales last year were marginally higher than in 2011.* ☐ *The Christian Democrats did marginally worse than expected.* ☐ *These cameras have increased only marginally in value over the past decade.*

ma·ri·jua·na /ˌmærɪˈwɑːnə/ NOUN [U] **Marijuana** is a drug which is made from the dried leaves and flowers of the hemp plant, and which can be smoked.

❖**ma·rine** ♦◇◇ /məˈriːn/ NOUN, ADJ
NOUN [C] (**marines**) A **marine** is a member of an armed force, for example the US Marine Corps or the Royal Marines, who is specially trained for military duties at sea as well as on land. ☐ *A small number of Marines were wounded.*
ADJ **1** [marine + N] **Marine** is used to describe things relating to the sea or to the animals and plants that live in the sea. ☐ *breeding grounds for marine life* ☐ *research in marine biology* ☐ *By encouraging wider awareness of the marine environment, Sea Life Centres have a vital role to play in the conservation of our sea.* **2** [marine + N] **Marine** is used to describe things relating to ships and their movement at sea. = maritime ☐ *a lawyer specializing in marine law*

mari·tal /ˈmærɪtəl/ ADJ [marital + N] **Marital** is used to describe things relating to marriage. ☐ *Caroline was hoping to make her marital home in Pittsburgh to be near her family.*

❖**mari·tal sta·tus** NOUN [U] (*formal*) Your **marital status** is whether you are married, single, or divorced. ☐ *How well off you are in old age is largely determined by race, sex, and marital status.*

❖**mari·time** /ˈmærɪtaɪm/ ADJ [maritime + N] **Maritime** is used to describe things relating to the sea and to ships. ☐ *the largest maritime museum of its kind* ☐ *It was one of Africa's worst maritime disasters.*

mark ♦♦◇ /mɑːk/ NOUN, VERB
NOUN [C, PL, SING] (**marks**) **1** [C] A **mark** is a small area of something such as dirt that has accidentally got onto a surface or piece of clothing. ☐ *The dogs are always rubbing against the wall and making dirty marks.* **2** [C] A **mark** is a written or printed symbol, for example a letter of the alphabet. ☐ *He made marks with a pencil.* **3** [C] A **mark** is a point that is given for a correct answer or for doing something well in an exam or competition. A **mark** can also be a written symbol such as a letter that indicates how good a student's or competitor's work or performance is. ☐ *a simple scoring device of marks out of 10, where '1' equates to 'Very poor performance'.* **4** [PL] If someone gets good or high **marks** for doing something, they have done it well. If they get poor or low **marks**, they have done it badly. ☐ *You have to give her top marks for moral guts.* **5** [C] A particular **mark** is a particular number, point, or stage which has been reached or might be reached, especially a significant one. ☐ *Unemployment is rapidly approaching the one million mark.* **6** [C] The **mark** of something is the characteristic feature that enables you to recognize it. = sign ☐ *The mark of a civilized society is that it looks after its weakest members.* **7** [SING] If you say that a type of behaviour or an event is **a mark of** a particular quality, feeling, or situation, you mean it shows that that quality, feeling, or situation exists.

= indication, sign ☐ *It was a mark of his unfamiliarity with Hollywood that he didn't understand that an agent was paid out of his client's share.*
PHRASES **leave your mark** or **leave a mark** If someone or something **leaves** their **mark** or **leaves a mark**, they have a lasting effect on another person or thing. ☐ *Years of conditioning had left their mark on her, and she never felt inclined to talk to strange men.*
make your mark or **make a mark** If you **make** your **mark** or **make a mark**, you become noticed or famous by doing something impressive or unusual. ☐ *She made her mark in the film industry in the 1960s.*
wide of the mark If something such as a claim or estimate is **wide of the mark**, it is incorrect or inaccurate. ☐ *That comparison isn't as wide of the mark as it seems.*
VERB [I, T] (**marks, marking, marked**) **1** [I, T] If something **marks** a surface, or if the surface **marks**, the surface is damaged by marks or a mark. ☐ *Leather overshoes were put on the horses' hooves to stop them from marking the turf.* **2** [T] If you **mark** something with a particular word or symbol, you write that word or symbol on it. ☐ *The bank marks the cheque 'certified'.* ☐ *Mark them with a symbol.* **3** [T] When a teacher **marks** a student's work, the teacher decides how good it is and writes a number or letter on it to indicate this opinion. ☐ *He was marking essays in his small study.* **4** [T] If something **marks** a place or position, it shows where something else is or where it used to be. ☐ *A huge crater marks the spot where the explosion happened.* **5** [T] An event that **marks** a particular stage or point is a sign that something different is about to happen. ☐ *The announcement marks the end of an extraordinary period in European history.* **6** [T] If you do something to **mark** an event or occasion, you do it to show that you are aware of the importance of the event or occasion. ☐ *Hundreds of thousands of people took to the streets to mark the occasion.* **7** [T] Something that **marks** someone **as** a particular type of person indicates that they are that type of person. ☐ *Her opposition to abortion and feminism marks her as a convinced traditionalist.*
PHRASAL VERBS **mark down** **1** To **mark** an item **down** or **mark** its price **down** means to reduce its price. = reduce ☐ *A toyshop has marked down the latest computer games.* **2** If you **mark** something **down**, you write it down. ☐ *I tend to forget things unless I mark them down.*
mark off If you **mark off** a piece or length of something, you make it separate, for example by putting a line on it or around it. ☐ *He used a rope to mark off the circle.*
mark up If you **mark** something **up**, you increase its price. = increase ☐ *You can sell it to them at a set wholesale price, allowing them to mark it up for retail.*
→ See also **marked, marking, punctuation mark, question mark**

❖**marked** ♦◇◇ /mɑːkt/ ADJ A **marked** change or difference is very obvious and easily noticed. ☐ *There has been a marked increase in crimes against property.* ☐ *He was a man of austere habits, in marked contrast to his more flamboyant wife.* ☐ *The trends since the 1950s have become even more marked.*

❖**mark·ed·ly** /ˈmɑːkɪdli/ ADV ☐ *The current economic downturn is markedly different from previous recessions.* ☐ *The quality of their relationship improved markedly.*

mark·er /ˈmɑːkə/ NOUN [C] (**markers**) **1** A **marker** is an object which is used to show the position of something, or is used to help someone remember something. ☐ *He put a marker in his book and followed her out.* **2** A **marker** or a **marker pen** is a pen with a thick tip made of felt, which is used for drawing and for colouring things. ☐ *Draw your child's outline with a heavy black marker or crayon.*

❖**mar·ket** ♦♦♦ /ˈmɑːkɪt/ NOUN, ADJ, VERB
NOUN [C, SING] (**markets**) **1** [C] A **market** is a place where goods are bought and sold, usually outdoors. ☐ *He sold boots at a market stall.* **2** [C] (*business*) The **market** for a particular type of thing is the number of people who want to buy it, or the area of the world in which it is sold. ☐ *The foreign market was increasingly crucial.* ☐ *the markets targeted by global chains* ☐ *the Russian market for personal computers* ☐ *There is no youth market in cars.* **3** [SING]

m

M

(business) The **market** refers to the total amount of a product that is sold each year, especially when you are talking about the competition between the companies who sell that product. ❑ *The two big companies control 72% of the market.* **4** [SING] (business) **The job market** or **the labour market** refers to the people who are looking for work and the jobs available for them to do. ❑ *Every year, 250,000 people enter the job market.* **5** [SING] (business) The stock market is sometimes referred to as **the market**. ❑ *The market collapsed last October.*

PHRASES **a buyer's market** or **a seller's market** (business) If you say that it is **a buyer's market**, you mean that it is a good time to buy a particular thing, because there is a lot of it available, so its price is low. If you say that it is **a seller's market**, you mean that very little of it is available, so its price is high. ❑ *Don't be afraid to haggle: for the moment, it's a buyer's market.*

in the market for something If you are **in the market for** something, you are interested in buying it. ❑ *If you're in the market for a new radio, you'll see that the latest models are very different.*

on the market (business) If something is **on the market**, it is available for people to buy. If it comes **onto the market**, it becomes available for people to buy. ❑ *putting more empty offices on the market*

price yourself out of the market (business) If you **price** yourself **out of the market**, you try to sell goods or services at a higher price than other people, with the result that no one buys them from you. ❑ *At $250,000 for a season, he really is pricing himself out of the market.*

ADJ [market + N] (business) If you talk about a **market** economy, or the **market** price of something, you are referring to an economic system in which the prices of things depend on how many are available and how many people want to buy them, rather than prices being fixed by governments. ❑ *Their ultimate aim was a market economy for Hungary.* ❑ *He must sell the house for the current market value.*

VERB [T] (**markets, marketing, marketed**) (business) To **market** a product means to organize its sale, by deciding on its price, where it should be sold, and how it should be advertised. = advertise, promote, sell ❑ *if you marketed our music the way we market pop music* ❑ *the company that markets the drug* ❑ *The devices are being marketed in America this year.* ❑ *The soap is marketed as an anti-acne product.*
→ See also **black market**

✪mar·ket·ing ◆◇◇ /ˈmɑːkɪtɪŋ/ NOUN [U] (business) **Marketing** is the organization of the sale of a product, for example, deciding on its price, the areas it should be supplied to, and how it should be advertised. = advertising, promotion ❑ *expert advice on production and marketing* ❑ *a marketing campaign* ❑ *their sales and marketing director*

market·place /ˈmɑːkɪtpleɪs/ NOUN [C] (**marketplaces**) **1** (business) The **marketplace** refers to the activity of buying and selling products. ❑ *It's our hope that we will play an increasingly greater role in the marketplace and, therefore, supply more jobs.* **2** A **marketplace** is a small area in a town or city where goods are bought and sold, often outdoors. ❑ *The marketplace was jammed with a noisy crowd of buyers and sellers.*

mar·ket share NOUN [C, U] (**market shares**) (business) A company's **market share** in a product is the proportion of the total sales of that product that is produced by that company. ❑ *Ford has been gaining market share this year at the expense of GM and some Japanese car manufacturers.*

mark·ing /ˈmɑːkɪŋ/ NOUN [C, U] (**markings**) **1** [C] **Markings** are coloured lines, shapes, or patterns on the surface of something, which help to identify it. ❑ *A plane with Danish markings was over-flying his vessel.* **2** [U] The **marking** of a student's work is the act of deciding how good it is and writing a number or letter on it to indicate this opinion. ❑ *For the rest of the lunch break I do my marking.*

mar·riage ◆◆◇ /ˈmærɪdʒ/ NOUN [C, U] (**marriages**) **1** [C] A **marriage** is the relationship between a husband and wife. ❑ *In a good marriage, both husband and wife work hard to solve any problems that arise.* ❑ *When I was 35 my*

marriage broke up. **2** [C, U] A **marriage** is the act of marrying someone, or the ceremony at which this is done. ❑ *I opposed her marriage to Darryl.*

mar·ried ◆◇◇ /ˈmærɪd/ ADJ **1** If you are **married**, you have a husband or wife. ❑ *We have been married for 14 years.* ❑ *She is married to an Englishman.* **2** [married + N] **Married** means relating to marriage or to people who are married. ❑ *For the first ten years of our married life we lived in a farmhouse.* **3** [V-LINK + married 'to' N] If you say that someone is **married to** their work or another activity, you mean that they are very involved with it and have little interest in anything else. ❑ *'Sam was married to his job,' McWhorter said.*

WHICH WORD?

married or marry?

If you are **married to** someone, they are your husband or wife.

❑ *Her daughter was **married to** a Frenchman.*

When you **marry** someone, you become their husband or wife during a special ceremony.

❑ *I wanted to **marry** him.*

When two people **get married** or **marry**, they become husband and wife. **Get married** is less formal and more commonly used than **marry**.

❑ *I'm **getting married** next month.*

❑ *They **married** last year.*

---

mar·ry ◆◆◇ /ˈmæri/ VERB [RECIP, T] (**marries, marrying, married**) **1** [RECIP] When two people **get married** or **marry**, they legally become husband and wife in a special ceremony. **Get married** is less formal and more commonly used than **marry**. ❑ *I thought he would change after we got married.* ❑ *They married a month after they met.* ❑ *He wants to marry her.* **2** [T] When a priest or official **marries** two people, he or she conducts the ceremony in which the two people legally become husband and wife. ❑ *The minister has agreed to marry us in the college chapel.*

marsh /mɑːʃ/ NOUN [C, U] (**marshes**) A **marsh** is a wet, muddy area of land. = bog

mar·shal /ˈmɑːʃəl/ VERB, NOUN
VERB [T] (**marshals, marshalling, marshalled**; in AmE, use **marshaling, marshaled**) If you **marshal** people or things, you gather them together and arrange them for a particular purpose. = organize ❑ *The company turned its attention to marshalling its creditors' approval.*
NOUN [C] (**marshals**) **1** A **marshal** is an official who helps to supervise a public event, especially a sports event. ❑ *The grand prix is controlled by well-trained marshals.* **2** In the United States and some other countries, a **marshal** is a police officer, often one who is responsible for a particular area. ❑ *A federal marshal was killed in a shoot-out.*

mar·tial /ˈmɑːʃəl/ ADJ (formal) **Martial** is used to describe things relating to soldiers or war. ❑ *The paper was actually twice banned under the martial regime.*
→ See also **court martial**

mar·tial law NOUN [U] **Martial law** is control of an area by soldiers, not the police. ❑ *The military leadership has lifted martial law in several more towns.*

mar·vel /ˈmɑːvəl/ VERB, NOUN
VERB [I] (**marvels, marvelling, marvelled**; in AmE, use **marveling, marveled**) If you **marvel** at something, you express your great surprise, wonder, or admiration. ❑ *Her fellow members marvelled at her seemingly infinite energy.* ❑ *Sara and I read the story and marvelled.*
NOUN [C] (**marvels**) You can describe something or someone as a **marvel** to indicate that you think that they are wonderful. = wonder ❑ *The whale, like the dolphin, has become a symbol of the marvels of creation.*

mar·vel·lous /ˈmɑːvələs/ ADJ (BrE; in AmE, use **marvelous**) If you describe someone or something as **marvellous**, you are emphasizing that they are very good. = wonderful ❑ *It's the most marvellous piece of music.*
mar·vel·lous·ly /ˈmɑːvələsli/ ADV ❑ *We want people to think he's doing marvellously.*

mas·cu·line /ˈmæskjʊlɪn/ ADJ **1 Masculine** qualities

and things relate to or are considered typical of men, in contrast to women. = male ❑ *masculine characteristics like a husky voice and facial hair* **2** If you say that someone or something is **masculine**, you mean that they have qualities such as strength or confidence which are considered typical of men. ❑ *her aggressive, masculine image* **3** In some languages, a **masculine** noun, pronoun, or adjective has a different form from a feminine or neuter one, or behaves in a different way.

mask ♦◇◇ /maːsk, mæsk/ NOUN, VERB

NOUN [c] (**masks**) **1** A **mask** is a piece of cloth or other material, which you wear over your face so that people cannot see who you are, or so that you look like someone or something else. ❑ *The gunman, whose mask had slipped, fled.* **2** A **mask** is a piece of cloth or other material that you wear over all or part of your face to protect you from germs or harmful substances. ❑ *You must wear goggles and a mask that will protect you against the fumes.* **3** If you describe someone's behaviour as a **mask**, you mean that they do not show their real feelings or character. ❑ *His mask of detachment cracked, and she saw for an instant an angry and violent man.* **4** A **mask** is a thick cream or paste made of various substances, which you spread over your face and leave for some time in order to improve your skin. ❑ *This mask leaves your complexion feeling soft and supple.*

VERB [T] (**masks, masking, masked**) **1** If you **mask** your feelings, you deliberately do not show them in your behaviour, so that people cannot know what you really feel. = conceal, hide ❑ *Dina lit a cigarette, trying to mask her agitation.* **2** If one thing **masks** another, it prevents people from noticing or recognizing the other thing. ❑ *He was squinting through the smoke that masked the enemy.*

✪ **mass** ♦◇◇ /mæs/ NOUN, QUANT, ADJ, VERB

NOUN [SING, C, PL, U] (**masses**) **1** [SING] A **mass of** things is a large number of them grouped together. ❑ *On his desk is a mass of books and papers.* **2** [SING] A **mass of** something is a large amount of it. ❑ *She had a mass of auburn hair.* **3** [c] A **mass of** a solid substance, a liquid, or a gas is an amount of it, especially a large amount which has no definite shape. ❑ *before it cools and sets into a solid mass* ❑ *The fourteenth century cathedral was reduced to a mass of rubble.* ❑ *the strong temperature difference between the two masses of air* **4** [PL] If you talk about **the masses**, you mean the ordinary people in society, in contrast to the leaders or the highly educated people. ❑ *His music is commercial. It is aimed at the masses.* **5** [SING] **The mass of** people are most of the people in a country, society, or group. = bulk, majority ❑ *The 1939-45 world war involved the mass of the population.* **6** [SING] If you say that something is **a mass of** things, you mean that it is covered with them or full of them. ❑ *His body was a mass of sores.* **7** [c, u] (*technical*) In physics, the **mass** of an object is the amount of physical matter that it has. ❑ *Astronomers know that Pluto and Triton have nearly the same size, mass, and density.* ❑ *the relative atomic mass of each atom within the molecule* **8** [c, u] **Mass** is a Christian church ceremony, especially in a Roman Catholic or Orthodox church, during which people eat bread and drink wine in order to remember the last meal of Jesus Christ. ❑ *She attended a convent school and went to Mass each day.*

QUANT (*informal*) **Masses of** something means a great deal of it. ❑ *There's masses of work for her to do.*

ADJ [mass + N] **Mass** is used to describe something which involves or affects a very large number of people. ❑ *ideas on combating mass unemployment* ❑ *All the lights went off, and mass hysteria broke out.* ❑ *weapons of mass destruction* ❑ *the harm caused by mass tourism*

VERB [I, T] (**masses, massing, massed**) When people or things **mass**, or when you **mass** them, they gather together into a large crowd or group. = gather ❑ *Shortly after the workers went on strike, police began to mass at the shipyard.*

→ See also **massed**

mas·sa·cre /ˈmæsəkə/ NOUN, VERB

NOUN [c, u] (**massacres**) A **massacre** is the killing of a large number of people at the same time in a violent and cruel way. ❑ *Maria lost her 62-year-old mother in the massacre.*

VERB [T] (**massacres, massacring, massacred**) If people **are massacred**, a large number of them are attacked and killed in a violent and cruel way. ❑ *300 civilians are believed to have been massacred by the rebels.*

mas·sage /ˈmæsaːʒ, AmE məˈsɑːʒ/ NOUN, VERB

NOUN [c, u] (**massages**) **Massage** is the action of squeezing and rubbing someone's body, as a way of making them relax or reducing their pain. ❑ *Alex asked me if I wanted a massage.*

VERB [T] (**massages, massaging, massaged**) **1** If you **massage** someone or a part of their body, you squeeze and rub their body, in order to make them relax or reduce their pain. ❑ *She continued massaging her right foot, which was bruised and aching.* **2** If you say that someone **massages** statistics, figures, or evidence, you are criticizing them for changing or presenting the facts in a way that misleads people. ❑ *Their governments have no reason to massage the statistics.*

massed /mæst/ ADJ [massed + N] **Massed** is used to describe a large number of people who have been brought together for a particular purpose. ❑ *He could not escape the massed ranks of newsmen who spotted him crossing the lawn.*

mas·sive ♦◇◇ /ˈmæsɪv/ ADJ **1** (*emphasis*) Something that is **massive** is very large in size, quantity, or extent. = huge ❑ *There was evidence of massive fraud.* ❑ *massive air attacks* **2** [massive + N] If you describe a medical condition as **massive**, you mean that it is extremely serious. ❑ *He died six weeks later of a massive heart attack.*

mas·sive·ly /ˈmæsɪvli/ ADV ❑ *a massively popular game*

mass pro·duc·tion NOUN [u] (*business*) **Mass production** is the production of something in large quantities, especially by machine. ❑ *equipment that would allow the mass production of baby food*

mas·ter ♦◇◇ /ˈmɑːstə, ˈmæs-/ NOUN, ADJ, VERB

NOUN [c, u, SING] (**masters**) **1** [c] A servant's **master** is the man that he or she works for. ❑ *My master ordered me not to deliver the message except in private.* **2** [c] If you say that someone is a **master** of a particular activity, you mean that they are extremely skilled at it. ❑ *She was a master of the English language.* **3** [c, u] If you are **master** of a situation, you have complete control over it. ❑ *Jackson remained calm and always master of his passions.* **4** [c] A famous male painter of the past is often called a **master**. ❑ *a portrait by the Dutch master, Vincent Van Gogh* **5** [SING] A **master's degree** can be referred to as a **master's**. ❑ *I've got a master's in economics.*

ADJ **1** [master + N] If you say that someone is a **master craftsman** you mean that they are extremely skilled at that activity. If you say that someone is, for example, a **master builder** or a **master carpenter**, you mean that they are fully qualified to practise their trade and to train others in it. ❑ *a master craftsman* **2** [master + N] A **master** copy of something, such as a film or a tape recording, is an original copy that can be used to produce other copies. ❑ *Keep one as a master copy for your own reference and circulate the others.*

VERB [T] (**masters, mastering, mastered**) **1** If you **master** something, you learn how to do it properly or you succeed in understanding it completely. ❑ *Duff soon mastered the skills of radio production.* **2** If you **master** a difficult situation, you succeed in controlling it. ❑ *When you have mastered one situation you have to go on to the next.*

→ See also **headmaster**

master·piece /ˈmɑːstəpiːs, ˈmæs-/ NOUN [c] (**masterpieces**) **1** A **masterpiece** is an extremely good painting, novel, film, or other work of art. ❑ *His book, I must add, is a masterpiece.* **2** An artist's, writer's, or composer's **masterpiece** is the best work that they have ever produced. ❑ *'Man's Fate', translated into sixteen languages, is probably his masterpiece.* **3** A **masterpiece** is an extremely clever or skilful example of something. ❑ *The whole thing was a masterpiece of crowd management.*

✪ **mas·ter's de·gree** also **Master's degree** NOUN [c] (**master's degrees**) A **master's degree** is a university degree such as an MA or an MSc which is of a higher level than a bachelor's degree and usually takes one or two years to complete. ❑ *a Master's degree in Art Education*

❑ *She then took a master's degree at Oxford University.*

mas·tery /ˈmɑːstəri, ˈmæs-/ NOUN [U] If you show **mastery** of a particular skill or language, you show that you have learned or understood it completely and have no difficulty using it. ❑ *He doesn't have mastery of the basic rules of grammar.*

match ◆◆◆ /mætʃ/ NOUN, VERB

NOUN [C, SING] (**matches**) **1** [C] A **match** is an organized game of tennis, football, cricket, or some other sport. = game ❑ *He was watching a football match.* **2** [C] A **match** is a small wooden stick with a substance on one end that produces a flame when you rub it along the rough side of a box of matches. ❑ *a packet of cigarettes and a book of matches* **3** [SING] If a combination of things or people is a good **match**, they have a pleasing effect when placed or used together. ❑ *Helen's choice of lipstick was a good match for her skin tone.*

VERB [RECIP, T] (**matches, matching, matched**) **1** [RECIP] If something of a particular colour or design **matches** another thing, they have the same colour or design, or have a pleasing appearance when they are used together. ❑ *'The shoes are too tight.'—'Well, they do match your dress.'* ❑ *All the chairs matched.* **2** [RECIP] If something such as an amount or a quality **matches with** another amount or quality, they are both the same or equal. If you **match** two things, you make them the same or equal. ❑ *Their strengths in memory and spatial skills matched.* ❑ *Our value system does not match with their value system.* **3** [RECIP] If one thing **matches** another, they are connected or suit each other in some way. ❑ *The students are asked to match the books with the authors.* ❑ *It can take time and effort to match buyers and sellers.* **4** [T] If you **match** something, you are as good as it or equal to it, for example in speed, size, or quality. ❑ *They played some fine offensive football, but I think we matched them in every department.*

PHRASAL VERB **match up 1 Match up** means the same as **match** VERB 1. ❑ *The pillow cover can match up with the sheets.* **2 Match up** means the same as **match** VERB 3. ❑ *The consultant seeks to match up jobless professionals with small companies in need of expertise.* ❑ *They compared the fat intake of groups of vegetarians and meat eaters, and matched their diets up with levels of harmful blood fats.* → See also **matching**

match·ing /ˈmætʃɪŋ/ ADJ [matching + N] **Matching** is used to describe things that are of the same colour or design. ❑ *a coat and a matching handbag*

◒**mate** ◆◇◇ /meɪt/ NOUN, VERB

NOUN [C] (**mates**) **1** Someone's wife, husband, or sexual partner can be referred to as their **mate**. = partner ❑ *He has found his ideal mate.* **2** An animal's **mate** is its sexual partner. ❑ *The males guard their mates zealously.* ❑ *Male nightingales sing to attract a mate and establish their territory.*

VERB [RECIP] (**mates, mating, mated**) When animals **mate**, a male and a female have sex in order to produce young. ❑ *This allows the pair to mate properly and stops the hen from staying in the nest.* ❑ *They want the males to mate with wild females.* ❑ *It is easy to tell when a female is ready to mate.* ❑ *the mating season*

◒**ma·terial** ◆◆◇ /məˈtɪəriəl/ NOUN, ADJ

NOUN [C, U, PL] (**materials**) **1** [C, U] A **material** is a solid substance. = substance ❑ *electrons in a conducting material such as a metal* ❑ *the design of new absorbent materials* ❑ *recycling of all materials* **2** [C, U] **Material** is cloth. ❑ *the thick material of her skirt* **3** [PL] **Materials** are the things that you need for a particular activity. = supplies ❑ *The builders ran out of materials.* ❑ *sewing materials* **4** [U] Ideas or information that are used as a basis for a book, play, or film can be referred to as **material**. ❑ *In my version of the story, I added some new material.*

ADJ **1 Material** things are related to possessions or money, rather than to more abstract things such as ideas or values. ❑ *Every room must have been stuffed with material things.* ❑ *his descriptions of their poor material conditions* **2** [material + N] (formal) **Material** evidence or information is directly relevant and important in a legal or academic argument. ❑ *The nature and availability of material evidence was not to be discussed.*

◒**ma·teri·al·ly** /məˈtɪəriəli/ ADV ❑ *He has tried to help this child materially and spiritually.* ❑ *They believe that a tough, materially poor childhood is character-building.* ❑ *The object has no real value, materially or emotionally.*

ma·teri·al·ism /məˈtɪəriəlɪzəm/ NOUN [U] **1 Materialism** is the attitude of someone who attaches a lot of importance to money and wants to possess a lot of material things. ❑ *the rising consumer materialism in society at large* **2 Materialism** is the belief that only physical matter exists, and that there is no spiritual world. ❑ *Scientific materialism thus triumphed over ignorance and superstition.*

ma·teri·al·is·tic /mə,tɪəriə'lɪstɪk/ ADJ (disapproval) If you describe a person or society as **materialistic**, you are critical of them because they attach too much importance to money and material possessions. ❑ *During the 1980s the US became a very materialistic society.*

ma·teri·al·ize /məˈtɪəriəlaɪz/ also **materialise** VERB [I] (**materializes, materializing, materialized**) **1** If a possible or expected event does not **materialize**, it does not happen. ❑ *A rebellion by radicals failed to materialize.* **2** If a person or thing **materializes**, they suddenly appear, after they have been invisible or in another place. = appear ❑ *A moment later Jane materialized, coming in the front door.*

◒**ma·ter·nal** /məˈtɜːnəl/ ADJ **1 Maternal** is used to describe feelings or actions which are typical of those of a kind mother towards her child. ❑ *She had little maternal instinct.* ❑ *Her feelings towards him were almost maternal.* **2** [maternal + N] **Maternal** is used to describe things that relate to the mother of a baby. ❑ *Maternal smoking can damage the unborn child.* ❑ *Likewise the incidence of maternal morbidity is now so low that it makes the papers rather than popular novels.* **3** [maternal + N] A **maternal** relative is one who is related through a person's mother rather than their father. ❑ *Her maternal grandfather was mayor of Karachi.* ❑ *If, for example, your mother, maternal aunt and sister had breast cancer, you would be in an extremely high-risk category.*

◒**ma·ter·nity** /məˈtɜːnɪti/ ADJ [maternity + N] **Maternity** is used to describe things relating to the help and medical care given to a woman when she is pregnant and when she gives birth. ❑ *Your job will be kept open for your return after maternity leave.* ❑ *The boy was born in the city's maternity hospital.*

◒**math·emati·cal** /ˌmæθəˈmætɪkəl/ ADJ **1** [mathematical + N] Something that is **mathematical** involves numbers and calculations. ❑ *mathematical calculations* **2** If you have **mathematical** abilities or a **mathematical** mind, you are good at doing calculations or understanding problems that involve numbers. ❑ *a mathematical genius*

math·emati·cal·ly /ˌmæθəˈmætɪkli/ ADV **1** *a mathematically complicated formula* **2** [mathematically + -ED/ADJ] ❑ *Anyone can be an astrologer as long as they are mathematically minded.*

math·ema·ti·cian /ˌmæθəməˈtɪʃən/ NOUN [C] (**mathematicians**) **1** A **mathematician** is a person who is trained in the study of numbers and calculations. ❑ *The risks can be so complex that banks hire mathematicians to assess them.* **2** A **mathematician** is a person who is good at doing calculations and using numbers. ❑ *I'm not a very good mathematician.*

◒**math·emat·ics** /ˌmæθəˈmætɪks/ NOUN [U] **1 Mathematics** is the study of numbers, quantities, or shapes. = arithmetic ❑ *a professor of mathematics at Boston College* ❑ *Elizabeth studied mathematics and classics.* **2 The mathematics of** a problem is the calculations that are involved in it. ❑ *Once you understand the mathematics of debt you can work your way out of it.*

maths /mæθs/ NOUN [U] (BrE) **Maths** is the same as **mathematics**.

◒**mat·ter** ◆◆◆ /ˈmætə/ NOUN, VERB

NOUN [C, PL, SING, U] (**matters**) **1** [C] A **matter** is a task, situation, or event which you have to deal with or think about, especially one that involves problems. = affair, issue, concern ❑ *It was clear that she wanted to discuss some private matter.* ❑ *Business matters drew him to Louisville.*

M

❏ *Until the matter is resolved the athletes will be unable to compete.* ❏ *Don't you think this is now a matter for the police?* **2** [PL] [NO DET] You use **matters** to refer to the situation you are talking about, especially when something is affecting the situation in some way. ❏ *We have no objection to this change, but doubt that it will significantly improve matters.* ❏ *If it would facilitate matters, I would be happy to come to New York.* **3** [SING] If you say that a situation is **a matter of** a particular thing, you mean that that is the most important thing to be done or considered when you are involved in the situation or explaining it. = question ❏ *History is always a matter of interpretation.* ❏ *Observance of the law is a matter of principle for us.* ❏ *Jack had attended these meetings as a matter of routine for years.* **4** [U] Printed **matter** consists of books, newspapers, and other texts that are printed. Reading **matter** consists of things that are suitable for reading, such as books and newspapers. ❏ *the government's plans to place a tax on printed matter* **5** [U] **Matter** is the physical part of the universe consisting of solids, liquids, and gases. ❏ *A proton is an elementary particle of matter that possesses a positive charge.* ❏ *He has spent his career studying how matter behaves at the fine edge between order and disorder.* **6** [U] You use **matter** to refer to a particular type of substance. = substance ❏ *waste matter from industries* ❏ *They feed mostly on decaying vegetable matter.* **7** [SING] You use **matter** in expressions such as **'What's the matter?'** or **'Is anything the matter?'** when you think that someone has a problem and you want to know what it is. ❏ *Carole, what's the matter? You don't seem happy.* **8** [SING] You use **matter** in expressions such as **'a matter of weeks'** when you are emphasizing how small an amount is or how short a period of time is. ❏ *Within a matter of days she was back at work.*

PHRASES **another matter** or **a different matter** If you say that something is **another matter** or **a different matter**, you mean that it is very different from the situation that you have just discussed. ❏ *Being responsible for one's own health is one thing, but being responsible for another person's health is quite a different matter.*

as a matter of If you are going to do something **as a matter of** urgency or priority, you are going to do it as soon as possible, because it is important. ❏ *Your doctors can help a great deal and you need to talk about it with them as a matter of urgency.*

no easy matter If something is **no easy matter**, it is difficult to do it. ❏ *Choosing the colour for the living-room walls was no easy matter.*

that's the end of the matter or **that's an end to the matter** If someone says **that's the end of the matter** or **that's an end to the matter**, they mean that a decision that has been taken must not be changed or discussed any more. ❏ *'He's moving in here,' Maria said. 'So that's the end of the matter.'*

the fact of the matter or **the truth of the matter** You use **the fact of the matter is** or **the truth of the matter is** to introduce a fact which supports what you are saying or which is not widely known, for example because it is a secret. ❏ *The fact of the matter is that most people consume far more protein than they actually need.*

make matters worse If you say that something **makes matters worse**, you mean that it makes a difficult situation even more difficult. ❏ *Don't let yourself despair; this will only make matters worse.*

no matter You use **no matter** in expressions such as **'no matter how'** and **'no matter what'** to say that something is true or happens in all circumstances. ❏ *No matter what your age, you can lose weight by following this programme.* **VERB** [I, T] (**matters**, **mattering**, **mattered**) If you say that something does not **matter**, you mean that it is not important to you because it does not have an effect on you or on a particular situation. ❏ *A lot of the food goes on the floor but that doesn't matter.* ❏ *As long as staff members are well-groomed, it does not matter how long their hair is.* **CONVENTION** **it doesn't matter** You say **'it doesn't matter'** to tell someone who is apologizing to you that you are not angry or upset, and that they should not worry. ❏ *'Did I wake you?'—'Yes, but it doesn't matter.'*

✦ **a matter of life and death** → see **death**; **as a matter of course** → see **course**; **as a matter of fact** → see **fact**

VOCABULARY BUILDER

matter NOUN
A **matter** is a task, situation, or event which you have to deal with or think about, especially one that involves problems.
❏ *I couldn't think of anything else to say on the matter, so I let it drop.*

affair NOUN
If an event or a series of events has been mentioned and you want to talk about it again, you can refer to it as the **affair**.
❏ *The administration has mishandled the whole affair.*

issue NOUN (*fairly formal*)
An **issue** is an important subject that people are arguing about or discussing.
❏ *A key issue for higher education is the need for greater diversity of courses.*

concern NOUN (*mainly formal*)
If a situation or problem is your **concern**, it is something that you have a duty or responsibility to be involved with.
❏ *The technical aspects were the concern of the Army.*

ma·ture /məˈtjʊə/ VERB, ADJ (*academic word*) **VERB** [I, T] (**matures**, **maturing**, **matured**) **1** [I] When a child or young animal **matures**, it becomes an adult. = grow up, develop ❏ *You will learn what to expect as your child matures physically.* ❏ *Children are maturing earlier physically, and are more exposed to, and targeted by, the media.* ❏ *The eggs hatched and the chicks matured.* **2** [I] When something **matures**, it reaches a state of complete development. = develop ❏ *When the trees matured they were cut.* ❏ *Their songwriting has matured.* **3** [I] If someone **matures**, they become more fully developed in their personality and emotional behaviour. = grow up ❏ *They have matured way beyond their age.* ❏ *Many colleges actually recommend a year off before starting classes as a means to mature emotionally.* ❏ *You can see how he has matured as a person over the last 12 months.* **4** [I, T] If something such as wine or cheese **matures** or **is matured**, it is left for a time to allow its full flavour or strength to develop. ❏ *Unlike wine, brandy matures only in wood, not glass.* **5** [I] (*business*) When an investment such as an insurance policy or bond **matures**, it reaches the stage when the company pays you back the money you have saved, and the interest your money has earned. ❏ *These bonuses will be paid when your savings plan matures in ten years' time.* **ADJ** (**maturer**, **maturest**) **1** (*approval*) If you describe someone as **mature**, you think that they are fully developed and balanced in their personality and emotional behaviour. ❏ *They are emotionally mature and should behave responsibly.* **2** **Mature** cheese or wine has been left for a time to allow its full flavour or strength to develop. ❏ *Grate some mature cheddar cheese.* **3** (*politeness*) If you say that someone is **mature** or of **mature** years, you are saying politely that they are middle-aged or old. ❏ *a man of mature years who had been in the job for longer than most of the members could remember*

ma·tur·ity /məˈtjʊərɪti/ NOUN [U] **1** **Maturity** is the state of being fully developed or adult. ❏ *Humans experience a delayed maturity; we arrive at all stages of life later than other mammals.* **2** Someone's **maturity** is their quality of being fully developed in their personality and emotional behaviour. ❏ *Her speech showed great maturity and humanity.* **3** (*business*) When an investment such as an insurance policy or bond reaches **maturity**, it reaches the stage when the company pays you back the money you have saved, and the interest your money has earned. ❏ *Customers are told what their policies will be worth on maturity, not what they are worth today.*

max·im·ize /ˈmæksɪmaɪz/ also **maximise** VERB [T] (**maximizes**, **maximizing**, **maximized**) (*academic word*) **1** If you **maximize** something, you make it as great in amount or importance as you can. ❑ *In order to maximize profit, the firm would seek to maximize output.* ❑ *They were looking for suitable ways of maximising their electoral support.* **2** If you **maximize** a window on a computer screen, you make it as large as possible. ❑ *Click on the square icon to maximize the window.*

❖**maxi‧mi‧za‧tion** also **maximisation** /ˌmæksɪmaɪˈzeɪʃən/ NOUN [U] ≠ minimization ❑ *a pricing policy that was aimed at profit maximisation* ❑ *Craftsmanship was conceived as a means of human fulfilment which could not survive where the maximization of profits was the primary end.*

❖**maxi‧mum** ♦◇◇ /ˈmæksɪməm/ ADJ, NOUN, ADV (*academic word*)

ADJ **1** [maximum + N] You use **maximum** to describe an amount which is the largest that is possible, allowed, or required. ❑ *Under planning law the maximum height for a fence or hedge is 6 feet.* ❑ *The maximum sentence for supplying illegal drugs is life imprisonment.* ❑ *China headed the table with maximum points.* **2** [maximum + N] You use **maximum** to indicate how great an amount is. ❑ *I need the maximum amount of information you can give me.* ❑ *It was achieved with minimum fuss and maximum efficiency.* ❑ *a maximum security prison*

NOUN [SING] **Maximum** is the largest that is possible, allowed, or required. ❑ *The law provides for a maximum of two years in prison.* ❑ *Twelve hours is the minimum, sixty hours the maximum.*

ADV [AMOUNT + maximum] If you say that something is a particular amount **maximum**, you mean that this is the greatest amount it should be or could possibly be, although a smaller amount is acceptable or very possible. ❑ *We need an extra 6 grams a day maximum.*

may ♦♦♦ /meɪ/ VERB [MODAL]

May is a modal verb. It is used with the base form of a verb.

1 (*vagueness*) You use **may** to indicate that something will possibly happen or be true in the future, but you cannot be certain. = might ❑ *We may have some rain today.* ❑ *I may be back next year.* **2** (*vagueness*) You use **may** to indicate that there is a possibility that something is true, but you cannot be certain. = might ❑ *Civil rights officials say there may be hundreds of other cases of racial violence.* **3** (*vagueness*) You use **may** to indicate that something is sometimes true or is true in some circumstances. = might ❑ *A vegetarian diet may not provide enough calories for a child's normal growth.* **4** You use **may have** with a past participle when suggesting that it is possible that something happened or was true, or when giving a possible explanation for something. ❑ *He may have been to some of those places.* **5** You use **may** in statements where you are accepting the truth of a situation, but contrasting it with something that is more important. ❑ *I may be almost 50, but there's not much I've forgotten.* **6** You use **may** when you are mentioning a quality or fact about something that people can make use of if they want to. = can ❑ *The bag has narrow straps, so it may be worn over the shoulder or carried in the hand.* **7** You use **may** to indicate that someone is allowed to do something, usually because of a rule or law. You use **may not** to indicate that someone is not allowed to do something. ❑ *In the US, any two persons may marry provided that both persons are at least 16 years of age on the day of their marriage.* **8** (*formal*) You use **may** when you are giving permission to someone to do something, or when asking for permission. = can ❑ *Mr Hobbs? May we come in?* **9** (*formal, politeness*) You use **may** when you are making polite requests. = can ❑ *I'd like the use of your living room, if I may.* **10** You use **may** when you are mentioning the reaction or attitude that you think someone is likely to have to something you are about to say. ❑ *You know, Brian, whatever you may think, I work hard for a living.* **11** If you do something so that a particular thing **may** happen, you do it so that there is an opportunity for that thing to happen. = can ❑ *the need for an increase in the numbers of surgeons so that patients may be treated as soon as possible*

♦ **may as well** → see **well**

may‧be ♦♦◇ /ˈmeɪbi/ ADV **1** [maybe with CL/GROUP] (*vagueness*) You use **maybe** to express uncertainty, for example when you do not know that something is definitely true, or when you are mentioning something that may possibly happen in the future in the way you describe. = perhaps ❑ *Maybe she is in love.* ❑ *I do think about having children, maybe when I'm 40.* **2** [maybe with CL/GROUP] (*politeness*) You use **maybe** when you are making suggestions or giving advice. **Maybe** is also used to introduce polite requests. = perhaps ❑ *Maybe we can go to the cinema or something.* ❑ *Maybe you'd better tell me what this is all about.* **3** [maybe + CL] You use **maybe** to indicate that, although a comment is partly true, there is also another point of view that should be considered. = perhaps ❑ *Maybe there is jealousy, but I think the envy is more powerful.* **4** [maybe as reply] You can say **maybe** as a response to a question or remark, when you do not want to agree or disagree. = perhaps ❑ *'Is she coming back?'—'Maybe. No one hears from her.'* **5** [maybe + AMOUNT] You use **maybe** when you are making a rough guess at a number, quantity, or value, rather than stating it exactly. = about ❑ *The men were maybe a hundred feet away and coming closer.* **6** [maybe with CL/GROUP] People use **maybe** to mean 'sometimes', particularly in a series of general statements about what someone does, or about something that regularly happens. ❑ *They'll come to the bar for a year, or maybe even two, then they'll find another favourite spot.*

mayor ♦◇◇ /meə, meɪə/ NOUN [C] (**mayors**) The **mayor** of a town or city is the person who has been elected for a fixed period of time to run its government. ❑ *the new mayor of New York*

maze /meɪz/ NOUN [C] (**mazes**) **1** A **maze** is a complex system of passages or paths between walls or hedges that is designed to confuse people who try to find their way through it, often as a form of amusement. ❑ *The palace has extensive gardens, a maze, and tennis courts.* **2** A **maze** of streets, rooms, or tunnels is a large number of them that are connected in a complicated way, so that it is difficult to find your way through them. = labyrinth ❑ *The children lead me through the maze of alleys to the edge of the city.* **3** You can refer to a set of ideas, topics, or rules as a **maze** when a large number of them are related to each other in a complicated way that makes them difficult to understand. ❑ *The book tries to steer you through the maze of alternative therapies.*

me ♦♦♦ /mi, STRONG miː/ PRON [V + me, PREP + me] A speaker or writer uses **me** to refer to himself or herself. **Me** is a first person singular pronoun. **Me** is used as the object of a verb or a preposition. ❑ *I had to make important decisions that would affect me for the rest of my life.* ❑ *He asked me to go to California with him.*

mea‧gre /ˈmiːgə/ (*BrE*; in *AmE*, use **meager**) ADJ (*disapproval*) If you describe an amount or quantity of something as **meagre**, you are critical of it because it is very small or not enough. ❑ *The rations that they gave us were meagre and inadequate.*

meal ♦◇◇ /miːl/ NOUN

NOUN [C] (**meals**) **1** A **meal** is an occasion when people sit down and eat, usually at a regular time. ❑ *She sat next to him throughout the meal.* **2** A **meal** is the food you eat during a meal. ❑ *The waiter offered him red wine or white wine with his meal.*

PHRASE **a square meal** If you have a **square meal**, you have a large, healthy meal. ❑ *The troops are very tired. They haven't had a square meal for four or five days.*

❖**mean** ♦♦♦ /miːn/ VERB, ADJ, NOUN

VERB [T] (**means**, **meaning**, **meant**) **1** If you want to know what a word, code, signal, or gesture **means**, you want to know what it refers to or what its message is. ❑ *'Credible' means 'believable'.* ❑ *What does 'evidence' mean?* ❑ *In modern Welsh, 'glas' means 'blue'.* ❑ *The red signal means you have to stop.* ❑ *What do you think he means by that?* **2** If you ask someone what they **mean**, you are asking them to explain exactly what or who they are referring to or what they are intending to say. ❑ *Do you mean me?* ❑ *Let me illustrate what I mean with an old story.* **3** If something **means** something **to** you, it is important to you in some way.

❏ *The idea that she witnessed this shameful incident meant nothing to him.* **4** If one thing **means** another, it shows that the second thing exists or is true. ❏ *An enlarged prostate does not necessarily mean cancer.* ❏ *If they didn't see him it doesn't necessarily mean he wasn't there.* **5** If one thing **means** another, the first thing leads to the second thing happening. = signify, denote, lead to ❏ *It would almost certainly mean the end of NATO.* ❏ *Trade and product discounts can also mean big savings.* ❏ *The change will mean that the country no longer has full diplomatic relations with other states.* **6** If doing one thing **means** doing another, it involves doing the second thing. ❏ *Children universally prefer to live in peace and security, even if that means living with only one parent.* **7** If you say that you **mean** what you are saying, you are telling someone that you are serious about it and are not joking, exaggerating, or just being polite. ❏ *He says you're fired if you're not back at work on Friday. And I think he meant it.* **8** If you say that someone **meant** to do something, you are saying that they did it deliberately. = intend ❏ *I didn't mean to hurt you.* ❏ *If that sounds harsh, it is meant to.* **9** If you say that someone **did not mean any** harm, offence, or disrespect, you are saying that they did not intend to upset or offend people or to cause problems, even though they may in fact have done so. = intend ❏ *I'm sure he didn't mean any harm.* **10** If you **mean to** do something, you intend or plan to do it. = intend ❏ *Summer is the perfect time to catch up on the new books you meant to read.* **11** If you say that something **was meant to** happen, you believe that it was made to happen by God or fate, and did not just happen by chance. ❏ *John was constantly reassuring me that we were meant to be together.*

PHRASES I mean (*spoken*) **1** You say '**I mean**' when making clearer something that you have just said. ❏ *It was his idea. Gordon's, I mean.* **2** You can use '**I mean**' to introduce a statement, especially one that justifies something that you have just said. ❏ *I'm sure he wouldn't mind. I mean, I was the one who asked him.* **3** You say '**I mean**' when correcting something that you have just said. ❏ *It was law or classics – I mean English or classics.*

know what it means to do something or **know what something means** If you know what it means to do something, you know everything that is involved in a particular activity or experience, especially the effect that it has on you. ❏ *I know what it means to lose a child under such tragic circumstances.*

mean something to someone If a name, word, or phrase **means something to** you, you have heard it before and you know what it refers to. ❏ *'Oh, Gairdner,' he said, as if that meant something to him.*

you mean You use '**you mean**' in a question to check that you have understood what someone has said. ❏ *What accident? You mean Christina's?*

ADJ (**meaner, meanest**) **1** If someone is being **mean**, they are being unkind to another person, for example by not allowing them to do something. ❏ *The little girls had locked themselves in the room because Mack had been mean to them.* **2** (*mainly AmE*) If you describe a person or animal as **mean**, you are saying that they are very bad-tempered and cruel. ❏ *The state's former commissioner of prisons once called Leonard the meanest man he'd ever seen.* **3** (*BrE; in AmE, use* **cheap**; *disapproval*) If you describe someone as **mean**, you are being critical of them because they are unwilling to spend much money or to use very much of a particular thing. = stingy

NOUN [SING] The **mean** is a number that is the average of a set of numbers. = average ❏ *Take a hundred and twenty values and calculate the mean.* ❏ *the mean score for 26-year-olds*

→ See also **meaning, means, meant**

❂**mean·ing** ♦◇◇ /ˈmiːnɪŋ/ NOUN [C, U] (**meanings**)
1 [C, U] The **meaning** of a word, expression, or gesture is the thing or idea that it refers to or represents and which can be explained using other words. = significance, sense ❏ *I hadn't a clue as to the meaning of 'activism'.* ❏ *They should look up the meaning of the word in the dictionary.* ❏ *I became more aware of the symbols and their meanings.* **2** [C, U] The **meaning** of what someone says or of something such as a book or film is the thoughts or ideas that are intended to

be expressed by it. = significance ❏ *Unsure of the meaning of this remark, Ryle chose to remain silent.* **3** [U] If an activity or action has **meaning**, it has a purpose and is worthwhile. ❏ *Art has real meaning when it helps people to understand themselves.*

mean·ing·ful /ˈmiːnɪŋfʊl/ ADJ **1** If you describe something as **meaningful**, you mean that it is serious, important, or useful in some way. ❏ *She believes these talks will be the start of a constructive and meaningful dialogue.* **2** [meaningful + N] A **meaningful** look or gesture is one that is intended to express something, usually to a particular person, without anything being said. ❏ *Upon the utterance of this word, Dan and Harry exchanged a quick, meaningful look.*

mean·ing·ful·ly /ˈmiːnɪŋfəli/ ADV ❏ *He glanced meaningfully at the other policeman, then he went up the stairs.*

mean·ing·less /ˈmiːnɪŋləs/ ADJ **1** If something that someone says or writes is **meaningless**, it has no meaning, or appears to have no meaning. ❏ *The sentence 'kicked the ball the man' is meaningless.* **2** Something that is **meaningless** in a particular situation is not important or relevant. ❏ *Fines are meaningless to guys earning millions.* **3** If something that you do is **meaningless**, it has no purpose and is not at all worthwhile. = futile ❏ *They seek strong sensations to dull their sense of a meaningless existence.*

❂**means** ♦♦◇ /miːnz/ NOUN
NOUN [C, PL] **1** [C] A **means** of doing something is a method, instrument, or process which can be used to do it. **Means** is both the singular and the plural form for this use. = way, method ❏ *The move is a means to fight crime.* ❏ *The army had perfected the use of terror as a means of controlling the population.* ❏ *They didn't provide me with any means of transport.* ❏ *Mobile phones have overtaken landline phones as the primary means of voice communication.* **2** [PL] (*formal*) You can refer to the money that someone has as their **means**. ❏ *a person of means*

PHRASE by means of If you do something **by means of** a particular method, instrument, or process, you do it using that method, instrument, or process. ❏ *This is a two-year course taught by means of lectures and seminars.*

CONVENTION by all means (*formulae*) You can say '**by all means**' to tell someone that you are very willing to allow them to do something. ❏ *'Can I come and have a look at your house?'—'Yes, by all means.'*

meant /ment/ IRREG FORM, ADJ
IRREG FORM Meant is the past tense and past participle of **mean**.
ADJ **1** [V-LINK + meant + to-INF] You use **meant to** to say that something or someone was intended to be or do a particular thing, especially when they have failed to be or do it. ❏ *I can't say any more, it's meant to be a big secret.* ❏ *Everything is meant to be businesslike.* **2** [V-LINK + meant 'for' N] If something **is meant for** particular people or for a particular situation, it is intended for those people or for that situation. ❏ *Fairy tales weren't just meant for children.* ❏ *The seeds were not meant for human consumption.*

PHRASE be meant to **1** If you say that something **is meant to** happen, you mean that it is expected to happen or that it ought to happen. ❏ *The peculiar thing about getting engaged is that you're meant to announce it to everyone.* **2** If you say that something **is meant to** have a particular quality or characteristic, you mean that it has a reputation for being like that. ❏ *Spurs are meant to be one of the top teams in the league.*

mean·time /ˈmiːntaɪm/
PHRASES (in the) meantime In the meantime or meantime means in the period of time between two events. = meanwhile ❏ *Eventually your child will leave home to lead her own life, but in the meantime she relies on your support.*
for the meantime For the meantime means for a period of time from now until something else happens. ❏ *Some of her stuff is stored for the meantime with her children.*

mean·while ♦♦◇ /ˈmiːnwaɪl/ ADV **1** [meanwhile with CL] **Meanwhile** means while a particular thing is happening. ❏ *Brush the aubergine with oil, add salt and pepper, and bake till soft. Meanwhile, heat the remaining oil in a*

m

heavy pan. **2** [meanwhile with CL] **Meanwhile** means in the period of time between two events. ❑ *You needn't worry; I'll be ready to greet them. Meanwhile, I'm off to discuss the Fowlers' party with Felix.* **3** [meanwhile with CL] You use **meanwhile** to introduce a different aspect of a particular situation, especially one that is completely opposite to the one previously mentioned. ❑ *He had always found his wife's mother a bit annoying. The mother-daughter relationship, meanwhile, was close.*

meas·ur·able /ˈmeʒərəbəl/ ADJ **1** *(formal)* If you describe something as **measurable**, you mean that it is large enough to be noticed or to be significant. ❑ *Both leaders seemed to expect measurable progress.* **2** Something that is **measurable** can be measured. ❑ *Economists emphasize measurable quantities – the number of jobs, the per capita income.*

✪ **meas·ure** ♦♦◇ /ˈmeʒə/ VERB, NOUN
VERB [T] (**measures, measuring, measured**) **1** If you **measure** the quality, value, or effect of something, you discover or judge how great it is. ❑ *I continued to measure his progress against the charts in the doctor's office.* ❑ *The college measures student progress against national standards.* ❑ *The school's success was measured in terms of the number of pupils who got into university.* ❑ *It was difficult to measure the impact of the war.* **2** If you **measure** a quantity that can be expressed in numbers, such as the length of something, you discover it using a particular instrument or device, for example a ruler. ❑ *Measure the length and width of the gap.* ❑ *He measured the speed at which ultrasonic waves travel along the bone.* **3** If something **measures** a particular length, width, or amount, that is its size or intensity, expressed in numbers. = be ❑ *It measures 20 yards from side to side.* ❑ *The house is twenty metres long and measures six metres in width.* ❑ *This dinner plate measures 30cm across.*
PHRASAL VERB **measure up** If you do not **measure up to** a standard or to someone's expectations, you are not good enough to achieve the standard or fulfil the person's expectations. ❑ *It was fatiguing sometimes to try to measure up to her standard of perfection.*
NOUN [SING, C] (**measures**) **1** [SING] *(formal)* A **measure of** a particular quality, feeling, or activity is a fairly large amount of it. ❑ *With the exception of Juan, each attained a measure of success.* **2** [SING] If you say that one aspect of a situation is **a measure of** that situation, you mean that it shows that the situation is very serious or has developed to a very great extent. ❑ *That is a measure of how bad things have become at the bank.* **3** [C] *(formal)* When someone, usually a government or other authority, takes **measures** to do something, they carry out particular actions in order to achieve a particular result. = actions ❑ *The government warned that police would take tougher measures to contain the trouble.* ❑ *He said stern measures would be taken against the killers.* **4** [C] *(BrE)* A **measure of** a strong alcoholic drink such as brandy or whisky is an amount of it in a glass. In bars, a **measure** is an official standard amount. ❑ *He poured himself another generous measure of whisky.*
PHRASE **beyond measure** *(emphasis)* If you say that something has changed or that it has affected you **beyond measure**, you are emphasizing that it has done this to a great extent. ❑ *Mankind's knowledge of the universe has increased beyond measure.*

✪ **meas·ure·ment** /ˈmeʒəmənt/ NOUN [C, U, PL] (**measurements**) **1** [C] A **measurement** is a result, usually expressed in numbers, that you obtain by measuring something. ❑ *We took lots of measurements.* ❑ *The measurements are very accurate.* **2** [C, U] **Measurement** of something is the process of measuring it in order to obtain a result expressed in numbers. ❑ *Tests include measurement of height, weight, and blood pressure.* ❑ *Measurement of blood pressure can be undertaken by nurses.* ❑ *the measurement of output in the non-market sector* **3** [C, U] The **measurement** of the quality, value, or effect of something is the activity of deciding how great it is. ❑ *The measurement of intelligence has been the greatest achievement of twentieth-century scientific psychology.* **4** [PL] Your **measurements** are the size of your waist, chest, hips, and other parts of your body, which you need to know when you are buying

clothes. ❑ *I know all her measurements and find it easy to buy stuff she likes.*

meat ♦◇◇ /miːt/ NOUN [C, U] (**meats**) **Meat** is flesh taken from a dead animal that people cook and eat. ❑ *Meat and fish are relatively expensive.* ❑ *imported meat products*

me·chan·ic /mɪˈkænɪk/ NOUN [C, PL, U] (**mechanics**) **1** [C] A **mechanic** is someone whose job is to repair and maintain machines and engines, especially car engines. ❑ *If you smell something unusual (gas fumes or burning, for instance), take the car to your mechanic.* **2** [PL] The **mechanics of** a process, system, or activity are the way in which it works or the way in which it is done. ❑ *What are the mechanics of this new process?* **3** [U] **Mechanics** is the part of physics that deals with the natural forces that act on moving or stationary objects. ❑ *He has not studied mechanics or engineering.* ❑ *the theory of quantum mechanics*

✪ **me·chan·i·cal** /mɪˈkænɪkəl/ ADJ **1** A **mechanical** device has parts that move when it is working, often using power from an engine or from electricity. ❑ *a small mechanical device that taps out the numbers* ❑ *This is the oldest working mechanical clock in the world.* **2** [mechanical + N] **Mechanical** means relating to machines and engines and the way they work. ❑ *mechanical engineering* ❑ *The train had stopped due to a mechanical problem.* **3** If you describe a person as **mechanical**, you mean they are naturally good at understanding how machines work. ❑ *He was a very mechanical person, who knew a lot about sound.* **4** If you describe someone's action as **mechanical**, you mean that they do it automatically, without thinking about it. ❑ *It is real prayer, and not mechanical repetition.*
✪ **me·chani·cal·ly** /mɪˈkænɪkli/ ADV **1** [mechanically with V] ❑ *The air was circulated mechanically.* **2** The car was mechanically sound, he decided. **3** [mechanically + -ED] ❑ *I'm not mechanically minded.* **4** [mechanically with V] ❑ *He nodded mechanically, his eyes fixed on the girl.*

✪ **mecha·nism** ♦◇◇ /ˈmekənɪzəm/ NOUN [C] (**mechanisms**) *(academic word)* **1** In a machine or piece of equipment, a **mechanism** is a part, often consisting of a set of smaller parts, which performs a particular function. = device ❑ *the locking mechanism* ❑ *A bomb has been detonated by a special mechanism.* **2** A **mechanism** is a special way of getting something done within a particular system. ❑ *There's no mechanism for punishing arms exporters who break the rules.* **3** A **mechanism** is a part of your behaviour that is automatic and that helps you to survive or to cope with a difficult situation. ❑ *a survival mechanism, a means of coping with intolerable stress*

med·al ♦◇◇ /ˈmedəl/ NOUN [C] (**medals**) A **medal** is a small metal disc which is given as an award for bravery or as a prize in a sports event. ❑ *Dufour was awarded his country's highest medal for bravery.*

✪ **me·dia** ♦♦◇ /ˈmiːdiə/ NOUN [SING, PL] *(academic word)* **1** [SING] You can refer to television, radio, newspapers, and magazines as **the media**. = press ❑ *It is hard work and not a glamorous job as portrayed by the media.* ❑ *They are wondering whether bias in the news media contributed to the president's defeat.* ❑ *the intensive media coverage of the issue* **2** [PL] **Media** is a plural of **medium**.

M

the **mass media**
the **mainstream** media
the **news** media
❑ *Our values are influenced by the mass media.*

✪ **me·dian** /ˈmiːdiən/ ADJ [median + N] (*technical*) The **median** value of a set of values is the middle one when they are arranged in order. For example, if a group of five students take a test and their scores are 5, 7, 7, 8, and 10, the median score is 7. ❑ *The median sentence for hard drugs offences increased by 60 per cent from 150 in 1982 to 240 days in 1986.* ❑ *Pessimists point out that the median price for new homes has slipped.*

✪ **me·di·ate** /ˈmiːdieɪt/ VERB [I, T] (**mediates, mediating, mediated**) (*academic word*) **1** [I, T] If someone **mediates between** two groups of people, or **mediates** an agreement **between** them, they try to settle an argument between them by talking to both groups and trying to find things that they can both agree to. = **arbitrate** ❑ *My mum was the one who mediated between Zelda and her mum.* ❑ *United Nations officials have mediated a series of peace meetings between the two sides.* ❑ *The Vatican successfully mediated in a territorial dispute between Argentina and Chile in 1984.* ❑ *UN peacekeepers mediated a new cease-fire.* **2** [T] (*formal*) If something **mediates** a particular process or event, it allows that process or event to happen and influences the way in which it happens. ❑ *the thymus, the organ which mediates the response of the white blood cells* ❑ *People's responses to us have been mediated by their past experience of life.* = **influence**

✪ **me·di·a·tion** /ˌmiːdiˈeɪʃən/ NOUN [U] **1** = **arbitration** ❑ *The agreement provides for United Nations mediation between the two sides.* ❑ *There is still a possibility the two sides could reach a compromise through the mediation of a third party.* **2** *This works through the mediation of the central nervous system.*

me·di·a·tor /ˈmiːdieɪtə/ NOUN [C] (**mediators**) ❑ *An archbishop has been acting as mediator between the rebels and the authorities.*

✪ **medi·cal** ♦♦◇ /ˈmedɪkəl/ ADJ, NOUN (*academic word*) ADJ [medical + N] **Medical** means relating to illness and injuries and to their treatment or prevention. ❑ *Several police officers received medical treatment for cuts and bruises.* ❑ *the medical profession*
NOUN [C] (**medicals**) (*mainly BrE; in AmE, use* **physical**) A **medical** is a thorough examination of your body by a doctor, for example before you start a new job.
✪ **medi·cal·ly** /ˈmedɪkli/ ADV ❑ *Therapists cannot prescribe drugs as they are not necessarily medically qualified.* ❑ *She was deemed medically fit to travel.*

medi·ca·tion /ˌmedɪˈkeɪʃən/ NOUN [C, U] (**medications**) **Medication** is medicine that is used to treat and cure illness. ❑ *When somebody comes for treatment I always ask them if they are on any medication.*

me·dici·nal /meˈdɪsənəl/ ADJ **Medicinal** substances or substances with **medicinal** effects can be used to treat and cure illnesses. ❑ *medicinal plants*

✪ **medi·cine** ♦♦◇ /ˈmedsən, AmE ˈmedɪsɪn/ NOUN [U, C] (**medicines**) (*academic word*) **1** [U] **Medicine** is the treatment of illness and injuries by doctors and nurses. = **health care** ❑ *He pursued a career in medicine.* ❑ *I was interested in alternative medicine and becoming an aromatherapist.* ❑ *Psychiatry is an accepted branch of medicine.* **2** [C, U] **Medicine** is a substance that you drink or swallow in order to cure an illness. ❑ *People in hospitals are dying because of shortages of medicine.*

✪ **me·di·eval** /ˌmediˈiːvəl, AmE ˌmiːd-/ (*in BrE, also use* **mediaeval**) ADJ Something that is **medieval** relates to or was made in the period of European history between the end of the Roman Empire in AD 476 and about AD 1500. ❑ *a medieval castle* ❑ *It goes back to a medieval knight's sense of personal honour.*

me·dio·cre /ˌmiːdiˈəʊkə/ ADJ (*disapproval*) If you describe something as **mediocre**, you mean that it is of average quality but you think it should be better. ❑ *His school record was mediocre.*

medi·ta·tion /ˌmedɪˈteɪʃən/ NOUN [U] **Meditation** is the act of remaining in a silent and calm state for a period of time, as part of a religious training, or so that you are more able to deal with the problems of everyday life. ❑ *Many busy executives have begun to practise yoga and meditation.*

Medi·ter·ra·nean /ˌmedɪtəˈreɪniən/ NOUN [SING] **1** **The Mediterranean** is the sea between southern Europe and North Africa. ❑ *You have the choice of night fishing in the Mediterranean, or windsurfing on a lake in Switzerland.* **2** **The Mediterranean** refers to the southern part of Europe, which is next to the Mediterranean Sea. ❑ *Barcelona has become one of the most dynamic and prosperous cities in the Mediterranean.*

✪ **me·dium** ♦◇◇ /ˈmiːdiəm/ ADJ, ADV, COMB, NOUN (*academic word*)

> The plural of the noun can be either **mediums** or **media** for meanings 1 and 2. The form **mediums** is the plural for meaning 3.

ADJ **1** If something is of **medium** size, it is neither large nor small, but approximately halfway between the two. ❑ *A medium dose produces severe nausea within hours.* **2** You use **medium** to describe something that is average in degree or amount, or approximately halfway along a scale between two extremes. ❑ *Foods that contain only medium levels of sodium are bread, cakes, milk, butter, and margarine.*
ADV [medium + ADJ] **Medium** means halfway along a scale between two extremes. ❑ *Toast by stirring in a medium-hot skillet for a few minutes.*
COMB If something is of a **medium** colour, it is neither light nor dark, but approximately halfway between the two. ❑ *Andrea has medium brown hair, grey eyes, and very pale skin.*
NOUN [C] (**mediums** or **media**) **1** A **medium** is a way or means of expressing your ideas or of communicating with people. = **means** ❑ *In Sierra Leone, English is used as the medium of instruction for all primary education.* ❑ *But Artaud was increasingly dissatisfied with film as a medium.* **2** A **medium** is a substance or material which is used for a particular purpose or in order to produce a particular effect. = **material, substance** ❑ *Blood is the medium in which oxygen is carried to all parts of the body.* ❑ *Hyatt has found a way of creating these qualities using the more permanent medium of oil paint.* **3** A **medium** is a person who claims to be able to contact and speak to people who are dead, and to pass messages between them and people who are still alive. ❑ *Bruce Willis says he has been talking to his dead brother through a medium.*
→ See also **media**

✪ **medium-sized** also **medium size** ADJ [usu medium-sized + N] **Medium-sized** means neither large nor small, but approximately halfway between the two. = **average-sized, middle-sized, mid-sized** ❑ *a medium-sized saucepan* ❑ *medium-sized accountancy firms* ❑ *small and medium-sized businesses*

meet ♦♦♦ /miːt/ VERB
VERB [RECIP, T, I] (**meets, meeting, met**) **1** [RECIP] If you **meet** someone, you happen to be in the same place as them and start talking to them. You may know the other person, but be surprised to see them, or you may not know them at all. ❑ *I have just met the man I want to spend the rest of my life with.* ❑ *He's the kindest and sincerest person I've ever met.* **2** [RECIP] If two or more people **meet**, they go to the same place, which they have earlier arranged to do, so that they can talk or do something together. ❑ *We could meet for a drink after work.* **3** [T] If you **meet** someone, you are introduced to them and begin talking to them and getting to know them. ❑ *Hey, Terry, come and meet my Dad.* **4** [T] You use **meet** in expressions such as '**Pleased to meet you**' and '**Nice to have met you**' when you want to politely say hello or goodbye to someone you have just met for the first time. ❑ *'Jennifer,' Miss Mallory said, 'this is Leigh Taylor.'—'Pleased to meet you,' Jennifer said.* **5** [T] If you **meet** someone at or off their train, plane, or bus, you go to the station, airport, or bus stop in order to be there when they arrive. ❑ *Mum met me at the station.* ❑ *Lili and*

m

my father met me off the boat. **6** [I] When a group of people such as a committee **meet**, they gather together for a particular purpose. ❑ *Officials from the two countries will meet again soon to resume negotiations.* **7** [I] (*mainly AmE*) If you **meet** with someone, you have a meeting with them. ❑ *Most of the lawmakers who met with the president yesterday said they backed the mission.* **8** [I, T] If something such as a suggestion, proposal, or new book **meets with** or **is met with** a particular reaction, it gets that reaction from people. ❑ *The idea met with a cool response from various quarters.* ❑ *We hope today's offer will meet with your approval too.* **9** [T] If something **meets** a need, requirement, or condition, it is good enough to do what is required. = satisfy ❑ *He suggested that the current arrangements for the care of severely mentally ill people are inadequate to meet their needs.* **10** [T] If you **meet** something such as a problem or challenge, you deal with it satisfactorily or do what is required. ❑ *Manufacturing failed to meet the crisis of the 1970s.* **11** [T] If you **meet** the cost of something, you provide the money that is needed for it. ❑ *The government said it will help meet some of the cost of the damage.* **12** [T] If you **meet** a situation, attitude, or problem, you experience it or become aware of it. = come across, encounter ❑ *I honestly don't know how I will react the next time I meet a potentially dangerous situation.* **13** [I] You can say that someone **meets with** success or failure when they are successful or unsuccessful. ❑ *Attempts to find civilian volunteers have met with embarrassing failure.* **14** [RECIP] When a moving object **meets** another object, it hits or touches it. ❑ *He held the lighter so it met the tip of his cigarette.* **15** [RECIP] (*written*) If your eyes **meet** someone else's, you both look at each other at the same time. ❑ *Nina's eyes met her sister's across the table.* **16** [RECIP] If two areas **meet**, especially two areas of land or sea, they are next to one another. ❑ *It is one of the rare places in the world where the desert meets the sea.* **17** [RECIP] The place where two lines **meet** is the place where they join together. ❑ *Parallel lines will never meet no matter how far extended.*

PHRASAL VERB **meet up** **1** Meet up means the same as **meet** VERB 1. ❑ *Last night, when he was parking my car, he met up with a pal he had at Stanford.* **2** Meet up means the same as **meet** VERB 2. ❑ *We tend to meet up for lunch once a week.*

✦ **make ends meet** → see **end**; **meet someone halfway** → see **halfway**

meet·ing ♦♦♦ /ˈmiːtɪŋ/ NOUN [C, SING] (**meetings**) **1** [C] A **meeting** is an event in which a group of people come together to discuss things or make decisions. ❑ *Can we have a meeting to discuss that?* **2** [SING] You can also refer to the people at a meeting as **the meeting**. ❑ *The meeting decided that further efforts were needed.* **3** [C] When you meet someone, either by chance or by arrangement, you can refer to this event as a **meeting**. = encounter ❑ *In January, 37 years after our first meeting, I was back in the studio with Dennis.*

mega·byte /ˈmegəbaɪt/ NOUN [C] (**megabytes**) (*computing*) In computing, a **megabyte** is one million bytes of data. ❑ *256 megabytes of memory*

WORD PARTS

The prefix *mega-* appears in words for units that are a million times bigger:

megabyte (NOUN)
megawatt (NOUN)
megahertz (NOUN)

---

melo·dy /ˈmelədi/ NOUN [C] (**melodies**) (*formal*) A **melody** is a tune. ❑ *I whistle melodies from Beethoven and Vivaldi and the more popular classical composers.*

✪**melt** /melt/ VERB

VERB [I, T] (**melts, melting, melted**) **1** [I, T] When a solid substance **melts** or when you **melt** it, it changes to a liquid, usually because it has been heated. = dissolve; ≠ freeze, solidify ❑ *The snow had melted, but the lake was still frozen solid.* ❑ *Meanwhile, melt the white chocolate in a bowl suspended over simmering water.* ❑ *The world's glaciers are melting away.* ❑ *Add the melted butter.* **2** [I] (*literary*) If something such as your feelings **melt**, they suddenly

disappear and you no longer feel them. = dissolve ❑ *His anxiety about the outcome melted, only to return later.* **3** [I] (*literary*) If a person or thing **melts into** something such as darkness or a crowd of people, they become difficult to see, for example because they are moving away from you or are the same colour as the background. = disappear ❑ *The youths dispersed and melted into the darkness.*

PHRASAL VERB **melt away** Melt away means the same as **melt** VERB 2. ❑ *When he heard these words, Scot felt his inner doubts melt away.*

✪**mem·ber** ♦♦♦ /ˈmembə/ NOUN, ADJ

NOUN [C] (**members**) **1** A **member** of a group is one of the people, animals, or things belonging to that group. ❑ *He refused to name the members of staff involved.* ❑ *a sunflower or a similar member of the daisy family* ❑ *the brightest members of a dense cluster of stars* **2** A **member** of an organization such as a club or a political party is a person who has officially joined the organization. ❑ *The support of our members is of great importance to the association.* ❑ *Britain is a full member of NATO.* **3** A **member** or **Member** is a person who has been elected to a legislature or parliament. ❑ *He was elected to Parliament as the Member for Leeds.*

ADJ [member + N] A **member country** or **member state** is one of the countries that has joined an international organization or group. ❑ *the member countries of the North American Free Trade Association*

Mem·ber of Par·lia·ment NOUN [C] (**Members of Parliament**) A **Member of Parliament** is a person who has been elected by the people in a particular area to represent them in a country's parliament. The abbreviation **MP** is often used. = MP ❑ *the Member of Parliament for Torbay*

✪**mem·ber·ship** ♦◊◊ /ˈmembəʃɪp/ NOUN [U, C] (**memberships**) **1** [U] **Membership** of an organization is the state of being a member of it. ❑ *his membership in the Communist Party* ❑ *The country has been granted membership of the World Trade Organisation.* ❑ *He sent me a membership form.* **2** [C, U] The **membership** of an organization is the people who belong to it, or the number of people who belong to it. ❑ *By 1890 the organization had a membership of 409,000.*

mem·oirs /ˈmemwɑːz/ NOUN [PL] [usu with POSS] A person's **memoirs** are a written account of the people who they have known and events that they remember. ❑ *In retirement he published his memoirs.*

memo·rable /ˈmemərəbəl/ ADJ Something that is **memorable** is worth remembering or likely to be remembered, because it is special or very enjoyable. ❑ *the perfect setting for a nostalgic memorable day*

me·mo·rial /mɪˈmɔːriəl/ NOUN, ADJ

NOUN [C] (**memorials**) **1** A **memorial** is a structure built in order to remind people of a famous person or event. ❑ *Building a memorial to Columbus has been his lifelong dream.* **2** If you say that something will be a **memorial to** someone who has died, you mean that it will continue to exist and remind people of them. ❑ *The museum will serve as a memorial to the millions who passed through Ellis Island.*

ADJ [memorial + N] A **memorial** event, object, or prize is in honour of someone who has died, so that they will be remembered. ❑ *A memorial service is being held for her at St Paul's Church.*

memo·rize /ˈmeməraɪz/ also **memorise** VERB [T] (**memorizes, memorizing, memorized**) If you **memorize** something, you learn it so that you can remember it exactly. ❑ *He studied his map, trying to memorize the way to Rose's street.*

✪**memo·ry** ♦♦◊ /ˈmeməri/ NOUN

NOUN [C, U, SING] (**memories**) **1** [C, U] Your **memory** is your ability to remember things. = recollection ❑ *All the details of the meeting are fresh in my memory.* ❑ *But locals with long memories thought this was fair revenge for the injustice of 1961.* ❑ *He had a good memory for faces.* ❑ *He suffers from poor memory and concentration.* **2** [C] A **memory** is something that you remember from the past. = recollection ❑ *She cannot bear to watch the film because of the bad memories it brings back.* ❑ *Her earliest memory is of singing at the age of four to wounded soldiers.* **3** [C] (*computing*) A computer's

memory is the part of the computer where information is stored, especially for a short time before it is transferred to disks or magnetic tapes. ❑ *The data are stored in the computer's memory.* ❑ *The device has 32GB of built-in memory.* ❑ *Flash memory is used in digital cameras.* ❑ *You can upgrade your computer's memory.* **4** [SING] If you talk about the **memory** of someone who has died, especially someone who was loved or respected, you are referring to the thoughts, actions, and ceremonies by which they are remembered. ❑ *She remained devoted to his memory.*
PHRASES **down memory lane** (*informal*) If you say that someone is taking a walk or trip **down memory lane**, you mean that they are talking, writing, or thinking about something that happened to them a long time ago. ❑ *His 1998 memoir is a delightful trip down memory lane.*
from memory If you do something **from memory**, for example speak the words of a poem or play a piece of music, you do it without looking at it, because you know it very well. ❑ *Many members of the church sang from memory.*
in living memory (*emphasis*) If you say that something is, for example, the best, worst, or first thing of its kind **in living memory**, you are emphasizing that it is the only thing of that kind that people can remember. ❑ *The floods are the worst in living memory.*
lose your memory If you **lose your memory**, you forget things that you used to know. ❑ *His illness caused him to lose his memory.*

mem·o·ry card NOUN [C] (**memory cards**) (*computing*) A **memory card** is a type of card containing computer memory that is used in digital cameras and other devices.

men /men/ IRREG FORM **Men** is the plural of **man**.

men·ace /ˈmenɪs/ NOUN, VERB
NOUN [C, U] (**menaces**) **1** [C] If you say that someone or something is a **menace** to other people or things, you mean that person or thing is likely to cause serious harm. ❑ *In my view, you are a menace to the public.* **2** [C] (*informal*) You can refer to someone or something as a **menace** when you want to say that they cause you trouble or annoyance. = nuisance ❑ *You're a menace to my privacy, Kenton.* **3** [U] **Menace** is a quality or atmosphere that gives you the feeling that you are in danger or that someone wants to harm you. ❑ *There is a pervading sense of menace.*
VERB [T] (**menaces, menacing, menaced**) If you say that one thing **menaces** another, you mean that the first thing is likely to cause the second thing serious harm. = threaten ❑ *They seem determined to menace the United States and its allies.*

men·ac·ing /ˈmenɪsɪŋ/ ADJ If someone or something looks **menacing**, they give you a feeling that they are likely to cause you harm or put you in danger. ❑ *The strong, dark eyebrows give his face an oddly menacing look.*
men·ac·ing·ly /ˈmenɪsɪŋli/ ADV ❑ *A group of men suddenly emerged from a doorway and moved menacingly forward to block her way.*

mend /mend/ VERB, NOUN
VERB [T, I] (**mends, mending, mended**) **1** [T] (*mainly BrE*) If you **mend** something that is broken or not working, you repair it, so that it works properly or can be used. = repair, fix ❑ *They took a long time to mend the roof.* **2** [T] If you **mend** a tear or a hole in a piece of clothing, you repair it by sewing it. ❑ *Men say that we are only good for cooking their meals and mending their socks.* **3** [I, T] If a person or a part of their body **mends** or **is mended**, they get better after they have been ill or have had an injury. ❑ *I'm feeling a lot better. The cut aches, but it's mending.* **4** [T] If you try to **mend** divisions between people, you try to end the disagreements or quarrels between them. = heal ❑ *He sent Evans as his personal envoy to discuss ways to mend relations between the two countries.*
PHRASE **mend one's ways** If someone who has been behaving badly **mends** their **ways**, they begin to behave well. ❑ *He has promised drastic disciplinary action if they do not mend their ways.*
NOUN
PHRASE **on the mend** (*informal*) **1** If a relationship or situation is **on the mend** after a difficult or unsuccessful period, it is improving. ❑ *More evidence that the economy*

was on the mend was needed. **2** If you are **on the mend** after an illness or injury, you are recovering from it. ❑ *The baby had been ill but seemed to be on the mend.*

❂ **men·tal** ◆◇◇ /ˈmentəl/ ADJ (*academic word*) **1** [mental + N] **Mental** means relating to the process of thinking. ❑ *The intellectual environment has a significant influence on the mental development of the children.* ❑ *intensive mental effort* **2** [mental + N] **Mental** means relating to the state or the health of a person's mind. ❑ *The mental state that had created her psychosis was no longer present.* ❑ *mental health problems* **3** [mental + N] A **mental** act is one that involves only thinking and not physical action. ❑ *Practise mental arithmetic when you go out shopping.*
❂ **men·tal·ly** /ˈmentəli/ ADV **1** I think you are mentally tired. ❑ *the way the person functions physically, emotionally and mentally at work* **2** *an inmate who is mentally disturbed* ❑ *the needs of the mentally ill* **3** *This technique will help people mentally organize information.*

men·tal·ity /menˈtæləti/ NOUN [C] (**mentalities**) Your **mentality** is your attitudes and your way of thinking. ❑ *a criminal mentality*

❂ **men·tion** ◆◆◇ /ˈmenʃən/ VERB, NOUN
VERB [T] (**mentions, mentioning, mentioned**) **1** If you **mention** something, you say something about it, usually briefly. ❑ *She did not mention her mother's absence.* ❑ *I may not have mentioned it to her.* ❑ *I had mentioned that I didn't really like contemporary music.* ❑ *For example, Sydney University's Professor of Medicine did not even mention insulin when lecturing on diabetes in 1923.* **2** If someone **is mentioned** in writing, a reference is made to them by name, often to criticize or praise something that they have done. ❑ *I was absolutely outraged that I could be even mentioned in an article of this kind.*
CONVENTION **don't mention it** (*formulae*) People sometimes say '**don't mention it**' as a polite reply to someone who has just thanked them for doing something. ❑ *'Thank you very much.' — 'Don't mention it.'*
NOUN [C, U] (**mentions**) **1** A **mention** is a reference to something or someone. ❑ *The statement made no mention of government casualties.* **2** A special or honourable **mention** is formal praise that is given for an achievement that is very good, although not usually the best of its kind. = commendation ❑ *Two of the losers deserve special mention: Caroline Swaithes, of Kingston, and Maria Pons, of Valley Stream.*

men·tor /ˈmentɔː/ NOUN, VERB
NOUN [C] (**mentors**) A person's **mentor** is someone who gives them help and advice over a period of time, especially help and advice related to their job. ❑ *Leon Sullivan was my mentor and my friend.*
VERB [T] (**mentors, mentoring, mentored**) To **mentor** someone means to give them help and advice over a period of time, especially help and advice related to their job. ❑ *He had mentored scores of younger doctors.*

menu /ˈmenjuː/ NOUN [C] (**menus**) **1** In a restaurant or café or at a formal meal, the **menu** is a list of the meals and drinks that are available. ❑ *A waiter offered him the menu.* **2** A **menu** is the food that you serve at a meal. ❑ *Try out the menu on a few friends.* **3** (*computing*) On a computer screen, a **menu** is a list of choices. Each choice represents something that you can do using the computer. ❑ *Hold down the shift key and press F7 to display the print menu.*

mer·chan·dise /ˈmɜːtʃəndaɪz, -daɪs/ NOUN [U] (*formal*) **Merchandise** is products that are bought, sold, or traded. ❑ *a mail-order company that provides merchandise for people suffering from allergies*

mer·chan·dis·ing /ˈmɜːtʃəndaɪzɪŋ/ NOUN [U] **1** (*business*) **Merchandising** is used to refer to the way stores and businesses organize the sale of their products, for example the way they are displayed and the prices that are chosen. ❑ *Company executives say revamped merchandising should help Macy's earnings to grow.* **2** **Merchandising** consists of goods such as toys and clothes that are linked with something such as a film, sports team, or pop group. ❑ *We are selling the full range of World Cup merchandising.*

m

mer·chant ♦◇◇ /'mɜːtʃənt/ NOUN, ADJ

[NOUN] [C] (**merchants**) A **merchant** is a person who buys or sells goods in large quantities, especially who imports and exports them. ◻ *Any knowledgeable wine merchant would be able to advise you.*

[ADJ] [merchant + N] **Merchant** seamen or ships are involved in carrying goods for trade. ◻ *There's been a big reduction in the size of the merchant fleet in recent years.*

mer·ci·less /'mɜːsɪləs/ ADJ If you describe someone as **merciless**, you mean that they are very cruel or determined and do not show any concern for the effect their actions have on other people. = ruthless ◻ *the merciless efficiency of a modern police state*

mer·ci·less·ly /'mɜːsɪləsli/ ADV ◻ *We teased him mercilessly.*

mer·cy /'mɜːsi/ NOUN, ADJ

[NOUN] [U, C] (**mercies**) **1** [U] If someone in authority shows **mercy**, they choose not to harm someone they have power over, or they forgive someone they have the right to punish. ◻ *Neither side took prisoners or showed any mercy.* **2** [C] If you refer to an event or a situation as **a mercy**, you mean that it makes you feel happy or relieved, usually because it stops something unpleasant from happening. ◻ *It really was a mercy that he'd gone so rapidly at the end.*

[PHRASE] **at the mercy of someone** If one person or thing is **at the mercy of** another, the first person or thing is in a situation where they cannot prevent themselves from being harmed or affected by the second. ◻ *Buildings are left to decay at the mercy of vandals and the weather.*

[ADJ] [mercy + N] (*journalism*) **Mercy** is used to describe a special journey to help someone in great need, such as people who are sick or made homeless by war. ◻ *She vanished nine months ago while on a mercy mission to West Africa.*

mere ♦◇◇ /mɪə/ ADJ

Mere does not have a comparative form. The superlative form **merest** is used to emphasize how small something is, rather than in comparisons.

(**merest**) **1** [mere + N] (*emphasis*) You use **mere** to emphasize how unimportant or inadequate something is, in comparison to the general situation you are describing. ◻ *successful exhibitions which go beyond mere success* ◻ *There is more to good health than the mere absence of disease.* **2** [mere + N] You use **mere** to indicate that a quality or action that is usually unimportant has a very important or strong effect. ◻ *The mere mention of food had triggered off hunger pangs.* **3** ['a' mere + AMOUNT] (*emphasis*) You use **mere** to emphasize how small a particular amount or number is. ◻ *Sixty per cent of teachers are women, but a mere five per cent of head teachers are women.*

mere·ly ♦◇◇ /'mɪəli/ ADV

[ADV] (*emphasis*) **1** You use **merely** to emphasize that something is only what you say and not better, more important, or more exciting. = just, simply ◻ *Michael is now merely a good friend.* ◻ *Francis Watson was far from being merely a furniture expert.* **2** [merely + AMOUNT] You use **merely** to emphasize that a particular amount or quantity is very small. = only ◻ *The brain accounts for merely three per cent of body weight.*

[PHRASE] **not merely** (*emphasis*) You use **not merely** before the less important of two contrasting statements, as a way of emphasizing the more important statement. ◻ *The team needs players who want to play for Canada, not merely any country that will have them.*

✪**merge** /mɜːdʒ/ VERB [RECIP] (**merges, merging, merged**) **1** If one thing **merges with** another, or **is merged with** another, they combine or come together to make one whole thing. You can also say that two things **merge**, or **are merged**. = join; ≠ separate, split ◻ *Bank of America merged with a rival bank.* ◻ *The rivers merge just north of a vital irrigation system.* ◻ *The two countries merged into one.* **2** If one sound, colour, or object **merges** into another, the first changes so gradually into the second that you do not notice the change. ◻ *Like a chameleon, he could merge unobtrusively into the background.* ◻ *His features merged with the darkness.*

✪**mer·ger** ♦◇◇ /'mɜːdʒə/ NOUN [C] (**mergers**) (*business*) A **merger** is the joining together of two separate companies or organizations so that they become one. = union, amalgamation ◻ *a merger between two of America's biggest trade unions* ◻ *the proposed merger of two Japanese banks*

mer·it /'merɪt/ NOUN, VERB

[NOUN] [U, PL] (**merits**) **1** [U] If something has **merit**, it has good or worthwhile qualities. ◻ *The argument seemed to have considerable merit.* **2** [PL] The **merits** of something are its advantages or other good points. ◻ *They have been persuaded of the merits of peace.*

[VERB] [T] (**merits, meriting, merited**) (*formal*) If someone or something **merits** a particular action or treatment, they deserve it. = deserve ◻ *He said he had done nothing wrong to merit a criminal investigation.*

mer·ry /'meri/ ADJ

[ADJ] (**merrier, merriest**) (*old-fashioned*) If you describe someone's character or behaviour as **merry**, you mean that they are happy and cheerful. = jolly ◻ *From the house come bursts of merry laughter.*

[CONVENTION] **Merry Christmas** (*formulae*) Just before Christmas and on Christmas Day, people say '**Merry Christmas**' to other people to express the hope that they will have a happy time. ◻ *Merry Christmas, everyone.*

mesh /meʃ/ NOUN, VERB

[NOUN] [C, U] (**meshes**) **Mesh** is material like a net made from wire, thread, or plastic. ◻ *The ground-floor windows are obscured by wire mesh.*

[VERB] [RECIP] (**meshes, meshing, meshed**) If two things or ideas **mesh** or **are meshed**, they go together well or fit together closely. ◻ *Their senses of humour meshed perfectly.* ◻ *This of course meshes with the economic philosophy of those on the right.*

mes·mer·ize /'mezməraɪz/ also **mesmerise** VERB [T] (**mesmerizes, mesmerizing, mesmerized**) If you are **mesmerized** by something, you are so interested in it or so attracted to it that you cannot think about anything else. ◻ *He was absolutely mesmerized by Pavarotti on television.*

mess ♦◇◇ /mes/ NOUN

[NOUN] [SING, C, U] (**messes**) **1** [SING] [also no DET] If you say that something is **a mess** or **in a mess**, you think that it is not neat. ◻ *The house is a mess.* **2** [C, U] If you say that a situation is **a mess**, you mean that it is full of trouble or problems. You can also say that something is **in a mess**. ◻ *I've made such a mess of my life.* ◻ *the many reasons why the economy is in such a mess* **3** [C, U] A **mess** is something liquid or sticky that has been accidentally dropped on something. ◻ *I'll clear up the mess later.* **4** [C] The **mess** at a military base or military barracks is the building in which members of the armed forces can eat or relax. ◻ *a party at the officers' mess*

[PHRASAL VERBS] **mess around** (**messes, messing, messed**) **1** If you **mess around**, you spend time doing things without any particular purpose or without achieving anything. ◻ *We were just messing around playing with paint.* **2** If you say that someone **is messing around with** something, you mean that they are interfering with it in a harmful way. ◻ *'Don't be stupid,' Max snapped. 'You don't want to go messing around with bears.'* **3** If someone **is messing around**, they are behaving in a joking or silly way. = fool around ◻ *I thought she was messing around.* **mess up** (*informal*) **1** If you **mess** something **up** or if you **mess up**, you cause something to fail or be spoiled. ◻ *When politicians mess things up, it is the people who pay the price.* ◻ *He had messed up one career.* **2** If you **mess up** a place or a thing, you make it dirty or not neat. ◻ *I hope they haven't messed up the living room.* **mess with** If you tell someone not to **mess with** a person or thing, you are warning them not to get involved with that person or thing. ◻ *You are messing with people's religion and they don't like that.*

✪**mes·sage** ♦♦◇ /'mesɪdʒ/ NOUN, VERB

[NOUN] [C] **1** A **message** is a piece of information or a request that you send to someone or leave for them when you cannot speak to them directly. ◻ *I got a message you were trying to reach me.* **2** The **message** that someone is trying to communicate, for example in a book or play, is the idea or point that they are trying to communicate.

= idea, point ❑ *The report's message was unequivocal.*
❑ *I no longer want to be friends with her but I don't know how to get the message across.* ❑ *The film has a very powerful anti-war message.* ❑ *The clear message from this research is that children do not benefit from this.*
VERB [I, T] (**messages, messaging, messaged**) If you **message** someone, you send them a message electronically using a computer or another device such as a mobile phone. ❑ *People who message a lot feel unpopular if they don't get many back.*

mes·sen·ger /ˈmesɪndʒə/ NOUN [c] (**messengers**) [also 'by' messenger] A **messenger** takes a message to someone, or takes messages regularly as their job. ❑ *There will be a messenger at the airport to collect the photographs from our courier.*

messy /ˈmesi/ ADJ (**messier, messiest**) **1** A **messy** person or activity makes things dirty or not neat. ❑ *She was a good, if messy, cook.* **2** Something that is **messy** is dirty or not neat. ❑ *Don't worry if this first coat of paint looks messy.* **3** If you describe a situation as **messy**, you are emphasizing that it is confused or complicated, and therefore unsatisfactory. ❑ *John had been through a messy divorce himself.*

met /met/ IRREG FORM **Met** is the past tense and past participle of **meet**.

✪ **met·al** ♦◇◇ /ˈmetəl/ NOUN [c, u] (**metals**) **Metal** is a hard substance such as iron, steel, gold, or lead. ❑ *pieces of furniture in wood, metal, and glass* ❑ *The roof is made of corrugated sheet metal.* ❑ *deposits of precious metals*

✪ **me·tal·lic** /məˈtælɪk/ ADJ **1** A **metallic** sound is like the sound of one piece of metal hitting another. ❑ *There was a metallic click and the gates swung open.* **2** **Metallic** paint or colours shine like metal. ❑ *He had painted all the wood with metallic silver paint.* **3** Something that tastes **metallic** has a bitter, unpleasant taste. ❑ *There was a metallic taste at the back of his throat.* **4** **Metallic** means consisting entirely or partly of metal. = metal ❑ *Even the smallest metallic object, whether a nail file or cigarette lighter, is immediately confiscated.*

✪ **meta·phor** /ˈmetəfɔː/ NOUN
NOUN [c, u] (**metaphors**) **1** A **metaphor** is an imaginative way of describing something by referring to something else which is the same in a particular way. For example, if you want to say that someone is very shy and frightened of things, you might say that they are a mouse. ❑ *the avoidance of violent expressions and metaphors like 'kill two birds with one stone'* ❑ *the writer's use of metaphor* **2** If one thing is a **metaphor for** another, it is intended or regarded as a symbol of it. ❑ *The divided family remains a powerful metaphor for a society that continued to tear itself apart.*
PHRASE **mix your metaphors** If you **mix your metaphors**, you use two conflicting metaphors. People do this accidentally, or sometimes deliberately as a joke. ❑ *To mix yet more metaphors, you were trying to run before you could walk, and I've clipped your wings.*

✪ **meta·phori·cal** /ˌmetəˈfɒrɪkəl, AmE -ˈfɔːr-/ ADJ You use the word **metaphorical** to indicate that you are not using words with their ordinary meaning, but are describing something by means of an image or symbol. ≠ literal ❑ *It turns out Levy is talking in metaphorical terms.* ❑ *The ship may be heading for the metaphorical rocks unless a buyer can be found.*
✪ **meta·phori·cal·ly** /ˌmetəˈfɒrɪkli, AmE -ˈfɔːr-/ ADV ≠ literally ❑ *You're speaking metaphorically, I hope.* ❑ *Her camel journey across the Western Australian desert was one of shedding burdens both literally and metaphorically.* ❑ *If, metaphorically speaking, Derrida is reason, there was no choice about the matter.*

✪ **me·teoro·logi·cal** /ˌmiːtiərəˈlɒdʒɪkəl/ ADJ [meteorology + N] **Meteorological** means relating to meteorology. ❑ *adverse meteorological conditions* ❑ *The science of this meteorological phenomenon is well explained.*

✪ **me·teor·olo·gist** /ˌmiːtiəˈrɒlədʒɪst/ NOUN [c] (**meteorologists**) A **meteorologist** is a person who studies the processes in the Earth's atmosphere that cause particular weather conditions, especially in order to

predict the weather. ❑ *Meteorologists have predicted mild rains for the next few days.* ❑ *A senior meteorologist with the National Climate Centre said the weather was linked to a major shift of climate.*

✪ **me·teor·ol·ogy** /ˌmiːtiəˈrɒlədʒi/ NOUN [u] **Meteorology** is the study of the processes in the Earth's atmosphere that cause particular weather conditions, especially in order to predict the weather. ❑ *Meteorology is science in action, and it happens in close to real time.* ❑ *some interesting and important research in meteorology and evolutionary biology*

✪ **me·ter** /ˈmiːtə/ NOUN, VERB
NOUN [c] (**meters**) A **meter** is a device that measures and records something such as the amount of gas or electricity that you have used. ❑ *He was there to read the electricity meter.* ❑ *Light in the ocean can be measured by light meters.* ❑ *The meter shows the amount of carbon dioxide released in the emissions.*
VERB [T] (**meters, metering, metered**) To **meter** something such as gas or electricity means to use a meter to measure how much of it people use, usually in order to calculate how much they have to pay. ❑ *Only a third of these households thought it reasonable to meter water.*

✪ **meth·od** ♦♦◇ /ˈmeθəd/ NOUN [c] (**methods**) (*academic word*) A **method** is a particular way of doing something. = manner, procedure, mode ❑ *The pill is the most efficient method of birth control.* ❑ *new teaching methods* ❑ *Child psychologists have devised many ingenious methods of investigating this.* ❑ *Experts will use a variety of scientific methods to measure fatigue levels.*

WORD CONNECTIONS
VERB + **method**
develop a method
use a method
❑ *Scientists have developed a new method of collecting the samples.*
ADJ + **method**
the **best** method
the **preferred** method
an **effective** method
❑ *The doctor then decides on the best method of treating the disease.*
an **alternative** method
a **new** method
❑ *If this does not work, an alternative method is used.*
a **traditional** method
❑ *Traditional methods of construction take a very long time.*

WHICH WORD?
method or manner?
Do not confuse **method** and **manner**.
A **method** is a particular way of doing something.
❑ *She has studied the latest teaching methods.*
The **manner** in which you do something is the particular way that you do it, for example the way that you behave with other people.
❑ *She dealt with the customer in a professional manner.*

me·thodi·cal /məˈθɒdɪkəl/ ADJ If you describe someone as **methodical**, you mean that they do things carefully, thoroughly, and in order. ❑ *Da Vinci was methodical in his research, carefully recording his observations and theories.*
me·thodi·cal·ly /məˈθɒdɪkli/ ADV [methodically with V] ❑ *She methodically put the things into her suitcase.*

✪ **meth·od·ol·ogy** /ˌmeθəˈdɒlədʒi/ NOUN [c, u] (**methodologies**) (*formal*) A **methodology** is a system of methods and principles for doing something, for example for teaching or for carrying out research. ❑ *Teaching methodologies vary according to the topic.* ❑ *In their own work they may have favoured the use of methodology different from mine.*
meth·odo·logi·cal /ˌmeθədəˈlɒdʒɪkəl/ ADJ ❑ *theoretical*

m

and methodological issues raised by the study of literary texts

✪**me·tre** ◆◇◇ /ˈmiːtə/ (*BrE*; in *AmE*, use **meter**) NOUN [C] (**metres**) A **metre** is a metric unit of length equal to 100 centimetres. ❑ *She's running the 1,500 metres here.* ❑ *He won the 400 metres freestyle.* ❑ *The tunnel is 10 metres wide and 600 metres long.* → See also **meter**

✪**met·ric sys·tem** NOUN [SING] [ˈthe' metric system] The **metric system** is the system of measurement that uses metres, grams, and litres. ≠ imperial system ❑ *The country has adopted the metric system.*

met·ro·poli·tan /ˌmetrəˈpɒlɪtən/ ADJ [metropolitan + N] **Metropolitan** means belonging to or typical of a large, busy city. ❑ *the metropolitan district of Miami* ❑ *a dozen major metropolitan hospitals*

mice /maɪs/ IRREG FORM **Mice** is the plural of **mouse**.

✪**micro·bio·logi·cal** /ˌmaɪkrəʊbaɪəˈlɒdʒɪkəl/ ADJ [microbiological + N] **Microbiological** refers to studies or tests relating to very small living things such as bacteria and their effects on people. ❑ *microbiological testing* ❑ *There was no evidence of a public health risk and to date there have been no adverse microbiological or chemical results.*

WORD PARTS

The prefix ***micro-*** appears in words which have 'small' as part of their meaning:

microbiological (ADJ)

microscope (NOUN)

microchip (NOUN)

✪**micro·bi·ol·ogy** /ˌmaɪkrəʊbaɪˈɒlədʒi/ NOUN [U] **Microbiology** is the branch of biology which is concerned with very small living things such as bacteria and their effects on people. ❑ *a professor of microbiology and immunology* ❑ *The Centre provides a valuable base for research into the immunology and microbiology of marine mammals.* ✪**micro·bi·olo·gist** /ˌmaɪkrəʊbaɪˈɒlədʒɪst/ NOUN [C] (**microbiologists**) ❑ *a microbiologist at Columbia University* ❑ *Microbiologists have discovered that a bacteria-eating virus holds the ability to both detect and defeat anthrax.*

micro·chip /ˈmaɪkrəʊtʃɪp/ NOUN [C] (**microchips**) (*computing*) A **microchip** is a very small piece of silicon inside a computer. It has electronic circuits on it and can hold large quantities of information or perform mathematical and logical operations.

✪**micro·eco·nom·ic** /ˌmaɪkrəʊiːkəˈnɒmɪk/ ADJ [usu microeconomic + N] **Microeconomic** means concerned with individual areas of economic activity, such as those within a particular company or relating to a particular market. ❑ *an important flaw in microeconomic theory* ❑ *It is possible to have a microeconomic success and a macroeconomic failure, as Britain did in the late eighties.* ❑ *a textbook on microeconomic theory* ❑ *The integration of markets for manufactures has also changed the microeconomic environment.*

✪**micro·ec·o·nom·ics** /ˌmaɪkrəʊiːkəˈnɒmɪks/ also **micro-economics** NOUN [U] (*business*) **Microeconomics** is the branch of economics that is concerned with individual areas of economic activity, such as those within a particular company or relating to a particular market. ❑ *He has 250 students in his microeconomics module.* ❑ *Microeconomics is concerned with the efficient supply of particular products.*

micro·phone /ˈmaɪkrəfəʊn/ NOUN [C] (**microphones**) A **microphone** is a device that is used to make sounds louder or to record them on a tape recorder.

micro·proc·es·sor /ˌmaɪkrəʊˈprəʊsesə/ NOUN [C] (**microprocessors**) (*computing*) In a computer, the **microprocessor** is the main microchip, which controls its most important functions.

✪**micro·scope** /ˈmaɪkrəskəʊp/ NOUN [C] (**microscopes**) A **microscope** is a scientific instrument which makes very small objects look bigger so that more detail can be seen. ❑ *Dr. Maler can take thin sections of fish brain and use a microscope to study neurons at work.* ❑ *They examined the remains under a powerful microscope.*

✪**micro·scop·ic** /ˌmaɪkrəˈskɒpɪk/ ADJ **1** **Microscopic** objects are extremely small, and usually can be seen only

through a microscope. ❑ *Microscopic fibres of protein were visible.* ❑ *Clouds of smoke contain microscopic particles that, when inhaled, penetrate deep into the lungs.* **2** [microscopic + N] A **microscopic** examination is done using a microscope. ≠ macroscopic ❑ *Microscopic examination of a cell's chromosomes can reveal the sex of the foetus.* ❑ *Finally, the cells were examined by microscopic autoradiography.*

micro·wave /ˈmaɪkrəweɪv/ NOUN, VERB NOUN [C] (**microwaves**) A **microwave** or a **microwave oven** is an oven which cooks food very quickly by electromagnetic radiation rather than by heat. VERB [T] (**microwaves, microwaving, microwaved**) To **microwave** food or drink means to cook or heat it in a microwave oven. ❑ *Steam or microwave the vegetables until tender.*

mid-air NOUN [U] If something happens in **mid-air**, it happens in the air, rather than on the ground. ❑ *The bird stopped and hovered in mid-air.*

WORD PARTS

The prefix ***mid-*** appears in nouns and adjectives which refer to the middle part of a particular period of time, or the middle part of a particular place:

mid-air (NOUN)

midnight (NOUN)

the **Mid**west (NOUN)

---

mid·day /ˌmɪdˈdeɪ/ NOUN [U] **1** **Midday** is twelve o'clock in the middle of the day. ❑ *At midday everyone would go down to Reg's Café.* **2** **Midday** is the middle part of the day, from late morning to early afternoon. ❑ *People were beginning to tire in the midday heat.*

mid·dle ◆◆◆ /ˈmɪdəl/ NOUN, ADJ NOUN [C, SING] (**middles**) **1** The **middle of** something is the part of it that is farthest from its edges, ends, or outside surface. ❑ *Howard stood in the middle of the room sipping a cup of coffee.* ❑ *They had a volleyball court in the middle of the courtyard.* **2** [SING] The **middle of** an event or period of time is the part that comes after the first part and before the last part. ❑ *I woke up in the middle of the night and could hear a tapping on the window.* PHRASE **in the middle of** If you are **in the middle of** doing something, you are busy doing it. ❑ *It's a bit hectic. I'm in the middle of cooking for nine people.* ADJ **1** [middle + N] The **middle** object in a row of objects is the one that has an equal number of objects on each side. ❑ *The middle button of his uniform jacket was strained over his belly.* **2** [middle + N] **Middle** is used to describe the part of a period of time that comes after the first part and before the last part. ❑ *Many classical violinists and pianists become conductors in their middle years.* ✦ **the middle of nowhere** → see **nowhere**

✪**mid·dle age** NOUN [U] **Middle age** is the period in your life when you are no longer young but have not yet become old. Middle age is usually considered to take place between the ages of 40 and 60. = midlife; ≠ youth, old age ❑ *Men tend to put on weight in middle age.* ❑ *When we reach middle age we often need more sleep.*

✪**middle-aged** ADJ **1** If you describe someone as **middle-aged**, you mean that they are neither young nor old. People between the ages of 40 and 60 are considered to be middle-aged. ≠ young, elderly ❑ *middle-aged, married businessmen* ❑ *More and more middle-aged adults have to care for older parents.* ❑ *She was middle-aged and single.* **2** If you describe someone's activities or interests as **middle-aged**, you are critical of them because you think they are typical of a middle-aged person, for example by being conventional or old-fashioned. ❑ *Her novels are middle-aged and boring.*

✪**Mid·dle Ages** NOUN [PL] [ˈthe' Middle Ages] In European history, **the Middle Ages** was the period between the end of the Roman Empire in AD 476 and about AD 1500, especially the later part of this period. ❑ *In the Middle Ages theories about madness were concerned with possession by the Devil and damnation by God.* ❑ *Up until the Middle Ages, however, the low-lying lands surrounding the Tor were indeed regularly flooded.*

M

mid·dle class ◆◇◇ NOUN, ADJ

The adjective is usually spelled **middle-class**.

NOUN [c] (**middle classes**) The **middle class** or **middle classes** are the people in a society who are not working class or upper class. Business people, managers, doctors, lawyers, and teachers are usually regarded as middle class. ◻ *the expansion of the middle class in the late 19th century*

ADJ A **middle-class** person is someone who is not working class or upper class. Business people, managers, doctors, lawyers, and teachers are usually regarded as middle class. ◻ *He is rapidly losing the support of blue-collar voters and of middle-class conservatives.*

middle-of-the-road ADJ **1** If you describe someone's opinions or policies as **middle-of-the-road**, you mean that they are neither left wing nor right wing, and not at all extreme. ◻ *Consensus need not be weak, nor need it result in middle-of-the-road policies.* **2** If you describe something or someone as **middle-of-the-road**, you mean that they are ordinary or unexciting. ◻ *I actually don't want to be a middle-of-the-road person, married with a mortgage.*

mid·night ◆◇◇ /'mɪdnaɪt/ NOUN, ADJ

NOUN [U] **Midnight** is twelve o'clock in the middle of the night. ◻ *It was well after midnight by the time Anne returned to her apartment.*

ADJ [midnight + N] **Midnight** is used to describe something that happens or appears at midnight or in the middle of the night. ◻ *It is totally out of the question to postpone the midnight deadline.*

PHRASE **burn the midnight oil** If someone **is burning the midnight oil**, they are staying up very late in order to study or do some other work. ◻ *Chris is asleep after burning the midnight oil trying to finish his article.*

midst /mɪdst/ NOUN

PHRASE **in the midst of** **1** If you are **in the midst of** doing something, you are doing it at the moment. ◻ *We are in the midst of one of the worst recessions for many, many years.* **2** If something happens **in the midst of** an event, it happens during it. ◻ *Eleanor arrived in the midst of a blizzard.* **3** If someone or something is **in the midst of** a group of people or things, they are among them or surrounded by them. = amid, among ◻ *Many were surprised to see him exposed like this in the midst of a large crowd.*

mid·way /ˌmɪd'weɪ/ ADV, ADJ

ADV **1** [midway + PREP] If something is **midway between** two places, it is between them and the same distance from each of them. = halfway ◻ *The studio is midway between his aunt's old home and his cottage.* **2** If something happens **midway through** a period of time, it happens during the middle part of it. ◻ *He crashed midway through the race.*

ADJ **1** [midway + N] The **midway** point between two places is between them and the same distance from each of them. = halfway ◻ *Fresno is close to the midway point between LA and San Francisco.* **2** [midway + N] The **midway** point in a period of time is during the middle part of it. ◻ *They were denied an obvious penalty before the midway point of the first half.*

might ◆◆◆ /maɪt/ VERB, NOUN

Might is a modal verb. It is used with the base form of a verb.

VERB [MODAL] **1** (vagueness) You use **might** to indicate that something will possibly happen or be true in the future, but you cannot be certain. = may ◻ *There's a report today that smoking might be banned in most buildings.* ◻ *I might well regret it later.* **2** (vagueness) You use **might** to indicate that there is a possibility that something is true, but you cannot be certain. = may ◻ *She and Robert's father had not given up hope that he might be alive.* ◻ *You might be right.* **3** (vagueness) You use **might** to indicate that something could happen or be true in particular circumstances. = could ◻ *America might sell more cars to the islands if they*

were made with the steering wheel on the right. **4** You use **might have** with a past participle to indicate that it is possible that something happened or was true, or when giving a possible explanation for something. ◻ *I heard what might have been an explosion.* **5** You use **might have** with a past participle to indicate that something was a possibility in the past, although it did not actually happen. ◻ *If she had had to give up riding she might have taken up sailing competitively.* **6** You use **might** in statements where you are accepting the truth of a situation, but contrasting it with something that is more important. = may ◻ *They might not have two pennies to rub together, but at least they have a kind of lifestyle that is different.* **7** (emphasis) You use **might** when you are saying emphatically that someone ought to do the thing mentioned, especially when you are annoyed because they have not done it. = could ◻ *You might have told me that before!* **8** (politeness) You use **might** to make a suggestion or to give advice in a very polite way. ◻ *They might be wise to stop advertising on television.* **9** (formal, spoken, politeness) You use **might** as a polite way of interrupting someone, asking a question, making a request, or introducing what you are going to say next. = could ◻ *Might I make a suggestion?* ◻ *Might I ask what you're doing here?* **10** You use **might** in expressions such as **I might have known** and **I might have guessed** to indicate that you are not surprised at a disappointing event or fact. = should ◻ *I might have known I'd find you with some little slut.*

NOUN [U] (formal) **Might** is power or strength. = strength ◻ *The might of the army could prove a decisive factor.*

PHRASE **with all one's might** If you do something **with all your might**, you do it using all your strength and energy. ◻ *She swung the hammer at his head with all her might.*

✦ might as well → see well

mighty /'maɪti/ ADJ, ADV

ADJ (**mightier, mightiest**) (literary) **Mighty** is used to describe something that is very large or powerful. ◻ *There was a flash and a mighty bang.*

ADV [mighty + ADJ/ADV] (mainly AmE, informal, emphasis) **Mighty** is used in front of adjectives and adverbs to emphasize the quality that they are describing. ◻ *It's something you'll be mighty proud of.*

mi·grant /'maɪɡrənt/ NOUN [c] (migrants) **1** A **migrant** is a person who moves from one place to another, especially in order to find work. ◻ *The government divides asylum seekers into economic migrants and genuine refugees.* **2** **Migrants** are birds, fish, or animals that migrate from one part of the world to another. ◻ *Migrant birds shelter in the reeds.*

✪ mi·grate /maɪ'ɡreɪt, AmE 'maɪɡreɪt/ VERB [I] (migrates, migrating, migrated) (academic word) **1** If people **migrate**, they move from one place to another, especially in order to find work or to live somewhere for a short time. = move ◻ *People migrate to cities like Jakarta in search of work.* ◻ *Farmers have learned that they have to migrate if they want to survive.* **2** When birds, fish, or animals **migrate**, they move at a particular season from one part of the world or from one part of a country to another, usually in order to breed or to find new feeding grounds. ◻ *Most birds have to fly long distances to migrate.* ◻ *a dam system that kills the fish as they migrate from streams to the ocean*

✪ mi·gra·tion /maɪ'ɡreɪʃən/ NOUN [c, U] (migrations) **1** = movement, shift ◻ *the migration of Soviet Jews to Israel* **2** *the migration of animals in the Serengeti*

WORD FAMILIES	
migrate VERB	People **migrate** to cities like Jakarta in search of work.
emigrate VERB	The family **emigrated** from England to Canada in 1924.
immigrate VERB	She was a baby when her family **immigrated** to the UK from India.
migration NOUN	The book is about the **migration** of Soviet Jews to Israel.

m

emigration NOUN	The Spanish Civil War provoked another wave of **emigration**.
immigration NOUN	The government introduced measures aimed at curbing illegal **immigration**.
migrant NOUN	The government divides asylum seekers into economic **migrants** and genuine refugees.
emigrant NOUN	Thousands of Irish **emigrants** set sail for America.
immigrant NOUN	He was born in New York, the son of German **immigrants**.

mild ◆◇◇ /maɪld/ ADJ (**milder, mildest**) **1** Mild is used to describe something such as a feeling, attitude, or illness that is not very strong or severe. ❑ Teddy turned to Mona with a look of mild confusion. **2** A **mild** person is gentle and does not get angry easily. ❑ He is a mild man, who is reasonable almost to the point of blandness. **3** Mild weather is pleasant because it is neither extremely hot nor extremely cold. ❑ The area is famous for its very mild winter climate. **4** You describe food as **mild** when it does not taste or smell strong, sharp, or bitter, especially when you like it because of this. ❑ This cheese has a soft, mild flavour.

mild·ly /ˈmaɪldli/ ADV
ADV 1 If you experience something such as a feeling, attitude, or illness **mildly**, you are not strongly or severely affected by it. ❑ Josephine must have had the disease very mildly as she showed no symptoms. **2** [mildly after v] If you behave **mildly**, you behave gently and do not get angry. ❑ 'I'm not meddling,' Ken said mildly, 'I'm just curious.'
PHRASE put it mildly You use **to put it mildly** to indicate that you are describing something in language that is much less strong, direct, or critical than what you really think. ❑ But not all the money, to put it mildly, has been used wisely.

✪ mile ◆◆◇ /maɪl/ NOUN [C, PL] (**miles**) **1** [C] A **mile** is a unit of distance equal to 1760 yards or approximately 1.6 kilometres. ❑ They drove 600 miles across the desert. ❑ She lives just half a mile away. ❑ The hurricane is moving at about 18 miles per hour. ❑ The lake is about ten miles long. ❑ a 50-mile bike ride **2** [PL] **Miles** is used, especially in the expression **miles away**, to refer to a long distance. ❑ If you enrol at a gym that's miles away, you won't be visiting it as often as you should. **3** [C] (informal, emphasis) **Miles** or **a mile** is used with the meaning 'very much' in order to emphasize the difference between two things or qualities, or the difference between what you aimed to do and what you actually achieved. ❑ You're miles better than most of the performers we see nowadays. ❑ With a Democratic candidate in place they won by a mile.

✪ mile·stone /ˈmaɪlstəʊn/ NOUN [C] (**milestones**) A **milestone** is an important event in the history or development of something or someone. ❑ He said the launch of the party represented a milestone in Zambian history. ❑ Starting school is a milestone for both children and parents.

mili·tant ◆◇◇ /ˈmɪlɪtənt/ ADJ, NOUN
ADJ You use **militant** to describe people who believe in something very strongly and are active in trying to bring about political or social change, often in extreme ways that other people find unacceptable. ❑ Militant mine workers in the Ukraine have voted for a one-day stoppage next month.
NOUN [C] (**militants**) A **militant** is a person who believes in something very strongly and is active in trying to bring about political or social change, often in extreme ways that other people find unacceptable. ❑ Even now we could not be sure that the militants would not find some new excuse to call a strike the following winter.

mili·tan·cy /ˈmɪlɪtənsi/ NOUN [U] ❑ the rise of trade union militancy

✪ mili·tary ◆◆◆ /ˈmɪlɪtri, AmE -teri/ ADJ, NOUN (academic word)
ADJ 1 Military means relating to the armed forces of a country. = armed forces, army; ≠ civilian ❑ Military action

may become necessary. ❑ The president is sending in almost 20,000 military personnel to help with the relief efforts. ❑ last year's military coup **2** Military means well organized, controlled, or neat, in a way that is typical of a soldier. ❑ Your working day will need to be organized with military precision.
NOUN [C] (**militaries**) **The military** are the armed forces of a country, especially officers of high rank. = army ❑ The bombing has been far more widespread than the military will admit. ❑ The military has overthrown the government. ❑ Did you serve in the military?

mili·tari·ly /ˌmɪlɪˈteərɪli/ ADV ❑ They remain unwilling to intervene militarily in what could be an unending war.

WORD CONNECTIONS

VERB + **military**

serve in the military
❑ At that time, women could not serve in the military.

involve the military
deploy the military
❑ The government is reluctant to involve the military in the crisis.

equip the military
❑ The president made promises to better equip the military.

---

mi·li·tia /mɪˈlɪʃə/ NOUN [C] (**militias**) A **militia** is an organization that operates like an army but whose members are not professional soldiers. ❑ The troops will not attempt to disarm the warring militias.

milk ◆◇◇ /mɪlk/ NOUN, VERB
NOUN [U, C] (**milks**) **1** [U] **Milk** is the white liquid produced by cows, goats, and some other animals, which people drink and use to make butter, cheese, and yogurt. ❑ He stepped out to buy a pint of milk. **2** [U] **Milk** is the white liquid produced by women to feed their babies. ❑ Milk from the mother's breast is a perfect food for the human baby. **3** [C, U] Liquid products for cleaning your skin or making it softer are sometimes referred to as **milks**. = lotion ❑ Sales of cleansing milks, creams, and gels have doubled over the past decade.
VERB [T] (**milks, milking, milked**) **1** If someone **milks** a cow or goat, they get milk from it, using either their hands or a machine. ❑ Farm workers milked cows by hand. **2** If you say that someone **milks** something, you mean that they get as much benefit or profit as they can from it, without caring about the effects this has on other people. ❑ A few people tried to milk the insurance companies.

mill ◆◇◇ /mɪl/ NOUN, VERB
NOUN [C] (**mills**) **1** A **mill** is a building in which grain is crushed to make flour. ❑ There was an old mill that really did grind corn. **2** A **mill** is a small device used for grinding something such as coffee beans or pepper into powder. = grinder ❑ a pepper mill **3** A **mill** is a factory used for making and processing materials such as steel, wool, or cotton. ❑ a steel mill
VERB [T] (**mills, milling, milled**) To **mill** something such as wheat or pepper means to grind it in a mill. ❑ They do not have the capacity to mill the grain.
PHRASAL VERB mill around When a crowd of people **mill around**, they move around within a particular place or area, so that the movement of the whole crowd looks very confused. ❑ Quite a few people were milling around, but nothing was happening.

✪ mil·len·nium /mɪˈleniəm/ NOUN [C, SING] (**millenniums** or **millennia**) **1** [C] (formal) A **millennium** is a period of one thousand years, especially one which begins and ends with a year ending in '000', for example the period from the year 1000 to the year 2000. ❑ the dawn of a new millennium **2** [SING] Many people refer to the year 2000 as **the Millennium**. ❑ the eve of the Millennium ❑ France begins celebrating the millennium an hour before Britain, and Eurotunnel wants to make sure supplies are maintained.

✪ mil·li·metre /ˈmɪlɪmiːtə/ (BrE; in AmE, use **millimeter**) NOUN [C] (**millimetres**) A **millimetre** is a metric unit of length that is equal to a tenth of a centimetre or a thousandth of a metre. ❏ *The creature is a tiny centipede, just 10 millimetres long.* ❏ *It measures just one millimetre in diameter.*

WORD PARTS

The prefix **milli-** appears in words for units that are a thousand times smaller:

millimetre (NOUN)

millilitre (NOUN)

milligram (NOUN)

✪ mil·lion ◆◆◆ /'mɪljən/ NUM, QUANT

The plural form is **million** after a number, or after a word or expression referring to a number, such as 'several' or 'a few'.

NUM (millions) A **million** or one **million** is the number 1,000,000. ❏ *Up to five million people a year visit the county.* ❏ *Profits for 2012 topped £100 million.*

QUANT [millions 'of' PL-N] If you talk about **millions of** people or things, you mean that there is a very large number of them but you do not know or do not want to say exactly how many. = a lot of, many ❏ *The programme was viewed on television in millions of homes.* ❏ *The rain forest is millions of years old.*

mil·lion·aire /,mɪljə'neə/ NOUN [C] **(millionaires)**
A **millionaire** is a very rich person who has money or property worth at least a million pounds. ❏ *By the time he died, he was a millionaire.*

mil·lionth ◆◆◇ /'mɪljənθ/ ADJ, NOUN

ADJ The **millionth** item in a series is the one you count as number one million. ❏ *Last year the millionth truck rolled off the assembly line.*

NOUN [C] **(millionths)** A **millionth** of something is one of a million equal parts of it. ❏ *The bomb must explode within less than a millionth of a second.*

mim·ic /'mɪmɪk/ VERB, NOUN

VERB [T] **(mimics, mimicking, mimicked)** **1** If you **mimic** the actions or voice of a person or animal, you imitate them, usually in a way that is meant to be amusing or entertaining. = imitate ❏ *He could mimic anybody, and he often reduced Isabel to helpless laughter.* **2** If someone or something **mimics** another person or thing, they try to be like them. = imitate ❏ *The computer doesn't mimic human thought; it reaches the same ends by different means.*

NOUN [C] **(mimics)** A **mimic** is a person who is able to mimic people or animals. ❏ *At school I was a good mimic.*

✪ mind ◆◆◆ /maɪnd/ NOUN, VERB

NOUN [C] **(minds)** **1** You refer to someone's **mind** when talking about their thoughts. For example, if you say that something is **in your mind**, you mean that you are thinking about it, and if you say that something is **at the back of your mind**, you mean that you are aware of it, although you are not thinking about it very much. = head, brain; ≠ body ❏ *I'm trying to clear my mind of all this.* ❏ *There was no doubt in his mind that the man was serious.* **2** Your **mind** is your ability to think and reason. = intellect, head, brain ❏ *You have a good mind.* ❏ *Studying stretched my mind and got me thinking about things.* **3** If you have a particular type of **mind**, you have a particular way of thinking which is part of your character, or a result of your education or professional training. = brain ❏ *Andrew, you have a very suspicious mind.* ❏ *The key to his success is his logical mind.* **4** You can refer to someone as a particular kind of **mind** as a way of saying that they are clever, intelligent, or imaginative. = intellect ❏ *She moved to New York, meeting some of the best minds of her time.*

PHRASES bear in mind or **keep in mind** If you tell someone to **bear** something **in mind** or to **keep** something **in mind**, you are reminding or warning them about something important which they should remember. ❏ *Bear in mind that petrol stations are scarce in the more remote areas.*

cast your mind back If you **cast** your **mind back** to a time in the past, you think about what happened then. ❏ *Cast your mind back to 1978, when Forest won the title.*

change your mind If you **change** your **mind**, or if someone or something **changes** your **mind**, you change a decision you have made or an opinion that you had. ❏ *I was going to vote for him, but I changed my mind and voted for Reagan.*

come to mind or **spring to mind** If something **comes to mind** or **springs to mind**, you think of it without making any effort. ❏ *Integrity and honesty are words that spring to mind when talking of the man.*

cross your mind If you say that an idea or possibility never **crossed** your **mind**, you mean that you did not think of it. ❏ *It had never crossed his mind that there might be a problem.*

in your mind's eye If you see something **in** your **mind's eye**, you imagine it and have a clear picture of it in your mind. ❏ *In his mind's eye, he can imagine the effect he's having.*

have a good mind to do or **have half a mind to do** If you say that you **have a good mind to** do something or **have half a mind to** do it, you are threatening or announcing that you have a strong desire to do it, although you probably will not do it. ❏ *He raged on about how he had a good mind to resign.*

have something in mind If you ask someone what they **have in mind**, you want to know in more detail about an idea or wish they have. ❏ *'Maybe we could celebrate tonight.'—'What did you have in mind?'*

with something in mind If you do something **with** a particular thing **in mind**, you do it with that thing as your aim or as the reason or basis for your action. ❏ *These families need support. With this in mind a group of 35 specialists met last weekend.*

all in the mind If you say that something such as an illness is **all in the mind**, you mean that it relates to someone's feelings or attitude, rather than having any physical cause. ❏ *It could be a virus, or it could be all in the mind.*

know your own mind If you **know** your **own mind**, you are sure about your opinions, and are not easily influenced by other people. ❏ *She knows her own mind and won't let anyone talk her into something she doesn't want to do.*

lose your mind If you say that someone is **losing** their **mind**, you mean that they are becoming mad. ❏ *Sometimes I feel like I'm losing my mind.*

make up your mind If you **make up** your **mind** or **make your mind up**, you decide which of a number of possible things you will have or do. = decide ❏ *Once he made up his mind to do something, there was no stopping him.*

of one mind or **of like mind** or **of the same mind** If a number of people are **of one mind**, **of like mind**, or **of the same mind**, they all agree about something. ❏ *Contact with other disabled yachtsmen of like mind would be helpful.*

a load off your mind or **a weight off your mind** If you say that something that happens is **a load off** your **mind** or **a weight off** your **mind**, you mean that it causes you to stop worrying, for example because it solves a problem that you had. ❏ *Knowing that she had medical insurance took a great load off her mind.*

on your mind If something is **on** your **mind**, you are worried or concerned about it and think about it a lot. ❏ *This game has been on my mind all week.*

your mind is on something or **have your mind on something** If your **mind is on** something or you **have** your **mind on** something, you are thinking about that thing. ❏ *At school I was always in trouble – my mind was never on my work.*

an open mind If you have **an open mind**, you avoid forming an opinion or making a decision until you know all the facts. ❏ *It's hard to see it any other way, though I'm trying to keep an open mind.*

open your mind If something **opens** your **mind to** new ideas or experiences, it makes you more willing to accept them or try them. ❏ *She also stimulated his curiosity and opened his mind to other cultures.*

out of your mind (informal, disapproval) If you say that someone is **out of their mind**, you mean that they are mad or very foolish. = crazy ❏ *What are you doing? Are you out of your mind?*

m

be out of your mind with something or **go out of your mind with something** (*informal, emphasis*) If you say that someone is **out of their mind** with a feeling such as worry or fear, you are emphasizing that they are extremely worried or afraid. ❑ *I was out of my mind with fear. I didn't know what to do.*

bored out of your mind or **scared out of your mind** or **stoned out of your mind** (*informal, emphasis*) If you say that someone is, for example, **bored out of** their **mind**, **scared out of** their **mind**, or **stoned out of** their **mind**, you are emphasizing that they are extremely bored, scared, or affected by drugs. ❑ *That was one of the most depressing experiences of my life. I was bored out of my mind after five minutes.*

put your mind to something If you **put your mind to** something, you start making an effort to do it. ❑ *You could do fine in the world if you put your mind to it.*

read someone's mind If you can **read someone's mind**, you know what they are thinking without them saying anything. ❑ *Don't expect others to read your mind.*

put someone's mind at rest or **set someone's mind at rest** To **put** someone's **mind at rest** or **set** their **mind at rest** means to stop them from worrying about something. ❑ *It may be advisable to have a blood test to put your mind at rest.*

nobody in their right mind (*emphasis*) If you say that nobody **in** their **right mind** would do a particular thing, you are emphasizing that it is an irrational thing to do and you would be surprised if anyone did it. ❑ *No one in her right mind would make such a major purchase without asking questions.*

set your mind on something or **have your mind set on something** If you **set your mind on** something or **have your mind set on** it, you are determined to do it or obtain it. ❑ *When my wife sets her mind on something, she invariably finds a way to achieve it.*

slip your mind If something **slips** your **mind**, you forget it. ❑ *I was going to mention it, but it slipped my mind.*

speak your mind If you **speak your mind**, you say firmly and honestly what you think about a situation, even if this may offend or upset people. ❑ *Martina Navratilova has never been afraid to speak her mind.*

stick in your mind If something **sticks in** your **mind**, it remains firmly in your memory. ❑ *I've always been fond of poetry and one piece has always stuck in my mind.*

take your mind off If something **takes** your **mind off** a problem or unpleasant situation, it helps you to forget about it for a while. ❑ *'How about a game of tennis?' suggested Alan. 'That'll take your mind off things.'*

to my mind You say or write **to my mind** to indicate that the statement you are making is your own opinion. ❑ *There are scenes in this play which, to my mind, are incredibly violent.*

of two minds If you are **of two minds**, you are uncertain about what to do, especially when you have to choose between two courses of action. = unsure, undecided ❑ *He was of two minds about this plan.*

VERB [I, T] (**minds, minding, minded**) **1** [I, T] If you do not **mind** something, you are not annoyed or bothered by it. ❑ *I don't mind the noise during the day.* ❑ *I hope you don't mind me calling in like this, without an appointment.* ❑ *I lit a cigarette and nobody seemed to mind.* **2** [I, T] You use **mind** in the expressions '**do you mind?**' and '**would you mind?**' as a polite way of asking permission or asking someone to do something. ❑ *Do you mind if I ask you one more thing?* ❑ *Would you mind waiting outside for a moment?* **3** [T] If someone does not **mind** what happens or what something is like, they do not have a strong preference for any particular thing. ❑ *I don't mind what we play, really.* **4** [T] If you **mind** a child or something such as a shop or luggage, you take care of it, usually while the person who owns it or is usually responsible for it is somewhere else. ❑ *Jim Coulters will mind the store while I'm away.* **5** [T] (*mainly BrE; in AmE, usually use* **watch**) If you tell someone to **mind** something, you are warning them to be careful not to hurt themselves or other people, or damage something. = watch **6** [T] (*mainly BrE; in AmE, usually use* **make sure**) You use **mind** when you are reminding someone to do

something or telling them to be careful not to do something. = watch

PHRASES **if you don't mind** (*feelings*) People use the expression **if you don't mind** when they are rejecting an offer or saying that they do not want to do something, especially when they are annoyed. ❑ *'Sit down.'—'I prefer standing for a while, if you don't mind.'*

mind you (*emphasis*) You use **mind you** to emphasize a piece of information that you are adding, especially when the new information explains what you have said or contrasts with it. Some people use **mind** in a similar way. ❑ *They pay full rates. Mind you, they can afford it.*

never mind You use **never mind** to tell someone that they need not do something or worry about something, because it is not important or because you will do it yourself. ❑ *'Was his name David?'—'No I don't think it was, but never mind, go on.'* ❑ *Dorothy, come on. Never mind your shoes. They'll soon dry off.*

never mind something (*emphasis*) You use **never mind** after a statement, often a negative one, to indicate that the statement is even more true of the person, thing, or situation that you are going to mention next. ❑ *I'm not going to believe it myself, never mind convince anyone else.*

someone wouldn't mind something or **someone wouldn't mind doing something** If you say that you **wouldn't mind** something, you mean that you would quite like it. ❑ *I wouldn't mind a coffee.*

CONVENTION **never mind** (*emphasis*) You say **never mind** when you are emphasizing that something is not serious or important, especially when someone is upset about it or is saying they are sorry. ❑ *Her voice trembled. 'Oh, Sylvia, I'm so sorry.'—'Never mind.'*

→ See also **frame of mind**

✦ **give someone a piece of your mind** → see **piece**

mind·ful /ˈmaɪndfʊl/ ADJ [V-LINK + mindful] (*formal*) If you are **mindful of** something, you think about it and consider it when taking action. = aware ❑ *We must be mindful of the consequences of selfishness.*

mind·less /ˈmaɪndləs/ ADJ (*disapproval*) **1** If you describe a violent action as **mindless**, you mean that it is done without thought and will achieve nothing. = senseless ❑ *a plot that mixes blackmail, extortion, and mindless violence* **2** If you describe a person or group as **mindless**, you mean that they are stupid or do not think about what they are doing. ❑ *She wasn't at all the mindless little wife so many people perceived her to be.* **3** If you describe an activity as **mindless**, you mean that it is so dull that people do it or take part in it without thinking. ❑ *the mindless repetitiveness of some tasks*

mind·less·ly /ˈmaɪndləsli/ ADV **1** [mindlessly with V] ❑ *I was annoyed with myself for having so quickly and mindlessly lost thirty dollars.* **2** [mindlessly with V] ❑ *I spent many hours mindlessly banging a tennis ball against the wall.*

mine ♦♦♦ /maɪn/ PRON, NOUN, VERB

PRON **Mine** is the first person singular possessive pronoun. A speaker or writer uses **mine** to refer to something that belongs or relates to himself or herself. ❑ *Her right hand is inches from mine.* ❑ *That wasn't his fault, it was mine.*

NOUN [C] (**mines**) **1** A **mine** is a place where deep holes and tunnels are dug under the ground in order to obtain a mineral such as coal, diamonds, or gold. ❑ *coal mines* **2** A **mine** is a bomb which is hidden in the ground or in water and which explodes when people or things touch it. **VERB** [T] (**mines, mining, mined**) **1** When a mineral such as coal, diamonds, or gold **is mined**, it is obtained from the ground by digging deep holes and tunnels. ❑ *The pit is being shut down because it no longer has enough coal that can be mined economically.* **2** If an area of land or water is **mined**, mines are placed there which will explode when people or things touch them. ❑ *The approaches to the garrison have been heavily mined.*

→ See also **mining**

mine·field /ˈmaɪnfiːld/ NOUN [C] (**minefields**) **1** A **minefield** is an area of land or water where explosive mines have been hidden. **2** If you describe a situation as a **minefield**, you are emphasizing that there are a lot of hidden dangers or problems, and people need to behave with care because things could easily go wrong. ❑ *The whole subject is a political minefield.*

min·er ◆◇◇ /ˈmaɪnə/ NOUN [C] (**miners**) A **miner** is a person who works underground in mines in order to obtain minerals such as coal, diamonds, or gold.

✪min·er·al /ˈmɪnərəl/ NOUN [C] (**minerals**) A **mineral** is a substance such as tin, salt, or sulphur that is formed naturally in rocks and in the earth. Minerals are also found in small quantities in food and drink. ❑ *Warring factions obtained arms from international backers in exchange for money or precious minerals.* ❑ *vitamin and mineral supplements*

min·gle /ˈmɪŋɡəl/ VERB [RECIP] (**mingles, mingling, mingled**) **1** If things such as sounds, smells, or feelings **mingle**, they become mixed together but are usually still recognizable. ❑ *Now the cheers and applause mingled in a single sustained roar.* **2** At a party, if you **mingle with** the other people there, you move around and talk to them. ❑ *Go out of your way to mingle with others at the wedding.* ❑ *Guests ate and mingled.*

minia·ture /ˈmɪnɪtʃə, AmE ˈmɪniətʃʊr/ ADJ, NOUN
▪ADJ▪ [miniature + N] **Miniature** is used to describe something that is very small, especially a smaller version of something which is normally much bigger. ❑ *Rosehill Farm has been selling miniature roses since 1979.*
▪NOUN▪ [C] (**miniatures**) A **miniature** is a very small, detailed painting, often of a person.
▪PHRASE▪ **in miniature** If you describe one thing as another thing **in miniature**, you mean that it is much smaller in size or scale than the other thing, but is otherwise exactly the same. ❑ *Ecuador provides a perfect introduction to South America; it's a continent in miniature.*

WORD PARTS

The prefix *mini-* often appears in words for things which are a smaller version of something else:

miniature (ADJ)
minibus (NOUN)
miniseries (NOUN)

---

mini·bus /ˈmɪnɪbʌs/ also **mini-bus** NOUN [C] (**minibuses**) [also 'by' minibus] A **minibus** is a large van which has seats in the back for passengers, and windows along its sides. ❑ *He was then taken by minibus to the military base.*

✪mini·mal /ˈmɪnɪməl/ ADJ (*academic word*) Something that is **minimal** is very small in quantity, value, or degree. ≠ maximal ❑ *The cooperation between the two is minimal.* ❑ *One aim of these reforms is effective defence with minimal expenditure.*
✪mini·mal·ly /ˈmɪnɪməli/ ADV ❑ *He was paid, but only minimally.* ❑ *minimally invasive techniques*

✪mini·mize /ˈmɪnɪmaɪz/ also **minimise** VERB [T] (**minimizes, minimizing, minimized**) (*academic word*)
1 If you **minimize** a risk, problem, or unpleasant situation, you reduce it to the lowest possible level, or prevent it from increasing beyond that level. ❑ *Concerned people want to minimize the risk of developing cancer.* ❑ *Many of these problems can be minimised by sensible planning.*
2 If you **minimize** something, you make it seem smaller or less significant than it really is. = play down ❑ *Some have minimized the importance of ideological factors.* **3** If you **minimize** a window on a computer screen, you make it very small, because you do not want to use it. ❑ *Click the square icon again to minimize the window.*

✪mini·mum ◆◇◇ /ˈmɪnɪməm/ ADJ, NOUN, ADV (*academic word*)
▪ADJ▪ **1** [minimum + N] You use **minimum** to describe an amount which is the smallest that is possible, allowed, or required. ❑ *He was only five feet nine, the minimum height for a policeman.* ❑ *If found guilty, she faces a minimum sentence of ten years and 30 lashes.* ❑ *a rise in the minimum wage* **2** [minimum + N] You use **minimum** to state how small an amount is. ❑ *The basic needs of life are available with minimum effort.*
▪NOUN▪ [SING] **1** The **minimum** is the smallest amount that is possible, allowed, or required. ❑ *This will take a minimum of*

one hour. ❑ *To provide welfare at a level greater than this bare minimum discourages self-reliance.* **2** A **minimum** of something is a very small amount of it. ❑ *With a minimum of fuss, she produced the grandson he had so desperately wished for.*
▪ADV▪ [AMOUNT + minimum] If you say that something is a particular amount **minimum**, you mean that this is the smallest amount it should be or could possibly be, although a larger amount is acceptable or very possible. ❑ *You're talking over a thousand dollars minimum for one course.*

min·ing /ˈmaɪnɪŋ/ NOUN [U] **Mining** is the industry and activities connected with getting valuable or useful minerals from the ground, for example coal, diamonds, or gold. ❑ *traditional industries such as coal mining and steel making*

min·is·ter ◆◆◆ /ˈmɪnɪstə/ NOUN [C] (**ministers**) **1** A **minister** is a member of the clergy, especially in Protestant churches. ❑ *His father was a Baptist minister.* **2** In some countries, a **minister** is a person who is in charge of a particular government department. ❑ *When the government came to power, he was named minister of culture.*

min·is·te·rial /ˌmɪnɪˈstɪəriəl/ ADJ [ministerial + N] You use **ministerial** to refer to people, events, or jobs that are connected with government ministers. ❑ *The prime minister's initial ministerial appointments haven't pleased all his supporters.*

✪min·is·try ◆◆◇ /ˈmɪnɪstri/ NOUN [C] (**ministries**) (*academic word*) In many countries, a **ministry** is a government department which deals with a particular thing or area of activity, for example trade, defence, or transport. ❑ *the Ministry of Justice* ❑ *a spokesman for the Agriculture Ministry*

✪mi·nor ◆◇◇ /ˈmaɪnə/ ADJ, NOUN (*academic word*)
▪ADJ▪ **1** You use **minor** when you want to describe something that is less important, serious, or significant than other things in a group or situation. = unimportant, small; ≠ major, important ❑ *She is known in Italy for a number of minor roles in films.* ❑ *Officials say the problem is minor, and should be quickly overcome.* **2** A **minor** illness or operation is not likely to be dangerous to someone's life or health. ❑ *Sarah had been plagued continually by a series of minor illnesses since her mid teens.* **3** A **minor** scale is one in which the third note is three semitones higher than the first. ❑ *the unfinished sonata movement in F minor*
▪NOUN▪ [C] (**minors**) A **minor** is a person who is still legally a child. In Britain and in most states in the United States, people are minors until they reach the age of eighteen. ❑ *The approach has virtually ended cigarette sales to minors.*

✪mi·nor·ity ◆◆◇ /mɪˈnɒrɪti, AmE -ˈnɔːr-/ NOUN (*academic word*)
▪NOUN▪ [SING, C] (**minorities**) **1** [SING] If you talk about a **minority** of people or things in a larger group, you are referring to a number of them that forms less than half of the larger group, usually much less than half. ❑ *Local authority child-care provision covers only a tiny minority of working mothers.* ❑ *These children are only a small minority.* **2** [C] A **minority** is a group of people of the same race, culture, or religion who live in a place where most of the people around them are of a different race, culture, or religion. ❑ *the region's ethnic minorities* ❑ *Students have called for greater numbers of women and minorities on the faculty.*
▪PHRASE▪ **in a minority** or **in the minority** If people are **in a minority** or **in the minority**, they belong to a group of people or things that form less than half of a larger group. ❑ *Even in the 1960s, politically active students and academics were in a minority.*

WORD CONNECTIONS

ADJ + **minority**

a **small** minority
a **tiny** minority
a **sizable** minority
a **significant** minority
❑ *A small minority of football fans are badly behaved.*

---

m

an **ethnic** minority
a **racial** minority
a **religious** minority
❑ There should be more equality for women and ethnic minorities.

minority + OF + NOUN

the minority of the **population**
the minority of **voters**
the minority of **individuals**
❑ The minority of voters are prepared to change their vote.

mint /mɪnt/ NOUN, VERB
NOUN [U, C] (**mints**) **1** [U] Mint is a herb with fresh-tasting leaves. ❑ Garnish with mint sprigs. **2** [C] A **mint** is a sweet with a peppermint flavour. Some people suck mints in order to make their breath smell fresher. ❑ She popped a mint into her mouth. **3** [C] The mint is the place where the official coins of a country are made. ❑ In 1965 the mint stopped putting silver in dimes. VERB [T] (**mints, minting, minted**) To **mint** coins or medals means to make them in a mint. ❑ the right to mint coins

⚙**mi·nus** /'maɪnəs/ CONJ, ADJ, PREP, NOUN
CONJ You use **minus** to show that one number or quantity is being subtracted from another. = less ❑ One minus one is zero.
ADJ **1** [minus + AMOUNT] Minus before a number or quantity means that the number or quantity is less than zero. ❑ The aircraft was subjected to temperatures of minus 65 degrees and plus 120 degrees. ❑ What's the square root of minus 1? **2** Teachers use **minus** in marking work in schools and colleges. 'B minus' is not as good as 'B', but is a better grade than 'C'. ❑ I'm giving him a B minus.
PREP To be **minus** something means not to have that thing. = without ❑ The film company collapsed, leaving Chris jobless and minus his life savings.
NOUN [C] (**minuses**) (informal) A **minus** is a disadvantage. = drawback ❑ The minuses far outweigh that possible gain.

mi·nus·cule /'mɪnɪskjuːl/ ADJ If you describe something as **minuscule**, you mean that it is very small. = minute ❑ The film was shot in 17 days, a minuscule amount of time.

mi·nute ◆◆◆ NOUN, VERB, ADJ
NOUN /'mɪnɪt/ [C, PL] (**minutes**) **1** [C] A **minute** is one of the sixty parts that an hour is divided into. People often say 'a minute' or 'minutes' when they mean a short length of time. ❑ The pizza will then take about twenty minutes to cook. ❑ Bye Mum, see you in a minute. **2** [PL] The **minutes** of a meeting are the written records of the things that are discussed or decided at it. ❑ He'd been reading the minutes of the last meeting.
PHRASES **(at) any minute (now)** (emphasis) If you say that something will or may happen **at any minute** or **any minute now**, you are emphasizing that it is likely to happen very soon. ❑ It looked as though it might rain at any minute.
last minute A **last-minute** action is one that is done at the latest time possible. ❑ He will probably wait until the last minute.
the minute (emphasis) If you say that something happens **the minute** something else happens, you are emphasizing that it happens immediately after the other thing. ❑ The minute you do this, you'll lose control.
CONVENTION **wait a minute** People often use expressions such as **wait a minute** or **just a minute** when they want to stop you doing or saying something. = hang on ❑ Wait a minute, folks, something is wrong here.
VERB /'mɪnɪt/ [T] (**minutes, minuting, minuted**) When someone **minutes** something that is discussed or decided at a meeting, they make a written record of it. ❑ You don't need to minute that.
ADJ /maɪ'njuːt, AmE -'nuːt/ (**minutest**) If you say that something is **minute**, you mean that it is very small. = tiny ❑ Only a minute amount is needed.

mira·cle /'mɪrəkəl/ NOUN, ADJ
NOUN [C] (**miracles**) **1** If you say that a good event is a **miracle**, you mean that it is very surprising and

unexpected. ❑ It is a miracle no one was killed. **2** A **miracle** is a wonderful and surprising event that is believed to be caused by God. ❑ Jesus's ability to perform miracles
ADJ [miracle + N] (journalism) A **miracle** drug or product does something that was thought almost impossible. ❑ the miracle drugs that keep his 94-year-old mother healthy

mi·racu·lous /mɪ'rækjʊləs/ ADJ **1** If you describe a good event as **miraculous**, you mean that it is very surprising and unexpected. ❑ The horse made a miraculous recovery to finish a close third. **2** If someone describes a wonderful event as **miraculous**, they believe that the event was caused by God. ❑ miraculous healing
mi·racu·lous·ly /mɪ'rækjʊləsli/ ADV ❑ Miraculously, the guards escaped death or serious injury.

⚙**mir·ror** ◆◇◇ /'mɪrə/ NOUN, VERB
NOUN [C] (**mirrors**) A **mirror** is a flat piece of glass which reflects light, so that when you look at it you can see yourself reflected in it. ❑ He went into the bathroom absent-mindedly and looked at himself in the mirror.
VERB [T] (**mirrors, mirroring, mirrored**) **1** If something **mirrors** something else, it has similar features to it, and therefore seems like a copy or representation of it. = reflect ❑ Despite the fact that I have tried to be objective, the book inevitably mirrors my own interests and experiences. ❑ It touched off a row which mirrored exactly the ideological struggles taking place over diversity. **2** (literary) If you see something reflected in water, you can say that the water **mirrors** it. = reflect ❑ the sudden glitter where a newly flooded field mirrors the sky

mis·be·have /ˌmɪsbɪ'heɪv/ VERB [I] (**misbehaves, misbehaving, misbehaved**) If someone, especially a child, **misbehaves**, they behave in a way that is not acceptable to other people. ❑ When the children misbehaved she was unable to cope.

WORD PARTS
The prefix **mis-** often appears in nouns and verbs that refer to something being done badly or wrongly:
misbehave (VERB)
misunderstand (VERB)
mismanagement (NOUN)

mis·car·riage /ˌmɪs'kærɪdʒ/ NOUN [C, U] (**miscarriages**) If a pregnant woman has a **miscarriage**, her baby dies and she gives birth to it before it is properly formed. ❑ No one had any idea she had had a miscarriage.

mis·cel·la·neous /ˌmɪsə'leɪniəs/ ADJ [miscellaneous + N] A **miscellaneous** group consists of many different kinds of things or people that are difficult to put into a particular category. ❑ a hoard of miscellaneous junk

mis·chief /'mɪstʃɪf/ NOUN [U] **1** Mischief is playing harmless tricks on people or doing things you are not supposed to do. It can also refer to the desire to do this. ❑ The little boy was a real handful. He was always up to mischief. **2** Mischief is behaviour that is intended to cause trouble for people. It can also refer to the trouble that is caused. ❑ The more sinister explanation is that he is about to make mischief in the Middle East again.

mis·chie·vous /'mɪstʃɪvəs/ ADJ **1** A **mischievous** person likes to have fun by playing harmless tricks on people or doing things they are not supposed to do. ❑ She rocks back and forth on her chair like a mischievous child. **2** A **mischievous** act or suggestion is intended to cause trouble. = malicious ❑ 'I have a few mischievous plans,' says Zevon.
mis·chie·vous·ly /'mɪstʃɪvəsli/ ADV **1** Kathryn winked mischievously. **2** That does not require 'massive' military intervention, as some have mischievously claimed.

mis·con·cep·tion /ˌmɪskən'sepʃən/ NOUN [C] (**misconceptions**) A **misconception** is an idea that is not correct. ❑ It is a misconception that Peggy was fabulously wealthy.

mis·con·duct /ˌmɪs'kɒndʌkt/ NOUN [U] Misconduct is bad or unacceptable behaviour, especially by a professional person. ❑ A psychologist was found guilty of serious professional misconduct yesterday.

mis·de·mean·our /ˌmɪsdɪ'miːnə/ (in AmE, use

misdemeanor) NOUN [c] (**misdemeanours**) **1** (formal) A **misdemeanour** is an act that some people consider to be wrong or unacceptable. ❑ Paul appeared before the faculty to account for his various misdemeanours. **2** (legal) In the United States and other countries where the legal system distinguishes between very serious crimes and less serious ones, a **misdemeanour** is a less serious crime. ❑ Under state law, it is a misdemeanour to possess a firearm on school premises.

mis·er·able /ˈmɪzərəbəl/ ADJ **1** If you are **miserable**, you are very unhappy. ❑ I took a series of badly paid secretarial jobs which made me really miserable. **2** If you describe a place or situation as **miserable**, you mean that it makes you feel unhappy or depressed. = depressing ❑ There was nothing at all in this miserable place to distract him. **3** If you describe the weather as **miserable**, you mean that it makes you feel depressed, because it is raining or dull. ❑ On a grey, wet, miserable day our teams congregated in Port Townsend. **4** [miserable + N] If you describe someone as **miserable**, you mean that you do not like them because they are bad-tempered or unfriendly. ❑ He always was a miserable man. He never spoke to me nor anybody else, not even to pass the time of day. **5** You can describe a quantity or quality as **miserable** when you think that it is much smaller or worse than it ought to be. ❑ Our speed over the ground was a miserable 2.2 knots. **6** [miserable + N] A **miserable** failure is a very great one. ❑ The film was a miserable commercial failure both in Italy and in the United States.

mis·er·ably /ˈmɪzərəbli/ ADV **1** He looked miserably down at his plate. **2** [miserably + ADJ] ❑ the miserably inadequate supply of books now provided for schools **3** Some manage it. Some fail miserably.

mis·ery /ˈmɪzəri/ NOUN

NOUN [c, u] (**miseries**) **1** [c, u] **Misery** is great unhappiness. ❑ All that money brought nothing but sadness and misery and tragedy. **2** [u] **Misery** is the way of life and unpleasant living conditions of people who are very poor. ❑ A tiny, educated elite profited from the misery of their two million fellow countrymen.

PHRASES **make someone's life a misery** If someone **makes** your **life a misery**, they behave in an unpleasant way towards you over a period of time and make you very unhappy. ❑ I would really like living here if it wasn't for the gangs of kids who make our lives a misery.

put someone out of their misery (informal) If you **put** someone **out of** their **misery**, you tell them something that they are very anxious to know. ❑ Please put me out of my misery. How do you do it?

put something out of its misery If you **put** an animal **out of** its **misery**, you kill it because it is sick or injured and cannot be cured or healed. = put down ❑ He notes grimly that the Watsons have called the vet to put their dog out of its misery.

mis·fit /ˈmɪsfɪt/ NOUN [c] (**misfits**) A **misfit** is a person who is not easily accepted by other people, often because their behaviour is very different from that of everyone else. ❑ I have been made to feel a social and psychological misfit for not wanting children.

mis·for·tune /ˌmɪsˈfɔːtʃuːn/ NOUN [c, u] (**misfortunes**) A **misfortune** is something unpleasant or unlucky that happens to someone. ❑ She seemed to enjoy the misfortunes of others.

mis·giv·ing /ˌmɪsˈɡɪvɪŋ/ NOUN [c, u] (**misgivings**) If you have **misgivings** about something that is being suggested or done, you feel that it is not quite right, and are worried that it may have unwanted results. ❑ She had some misgivings about what she was about to do.

mis·guid·ed /ˌmɪsˈɡaɪdɪd/ ADJ (disapproval) If you describe an opinion or plan as **misguided**, you are critical of it because you think it is based on an incorrect idea. You can also describe people as misguided. ❑ In a misguided attempt to be funny, he manages only offensiveness.

mis·han·dle /ˌmɪsˈhændəl/ VERB [T] (**mishandles, mishandling, mishandled**) (disapproval) If you say that someone has **mishandled** something, you are critical of them because you think they have dealt with it badly.

= mismanage ❑ She completely mishandled an important project purely through lack of attention.

mis·han·dling /ˌmɪsˈhændlɪŋ/ NOUN [u] ❑ the government's mishandling of the economy

mis·hap /ˈmɪshæp/ NOUN [c, u] (**mishaps**) A **mishap** is an unfortunate but not very serious event that happens to someone. ❑ After a number of mishaps she did manage to get back to Germany.

✪ **mis·in·ter·pret** /ˌmɪsɪnˈtɜːprɪt/ VERB [T] (**misinterprets, misinterpreting, misinterpreted**) (academic word) If you **misinterpret** something, you understand it wrongly. = misread ❑ He was amazed that he'd misinterpreted the situation so completely. ❑ The Prince's words had been misinterpreted. ❑ people who deliberately misinterpret behaviour in order to sell papers

✪ **mis·in·ter·pre·ta·tion** /ˌmɪsɪnˌtɜːprɪˈteɪʃən/ NOUN [c, u] (**misinterpretations**) ❑ a misinterpretation of the aims and ends of socialism ❑ The message left no room for misinterpretation.

mis·judge /ˌmɪsˈdʒʌdʒ/ VERB [T] (**misjudges, misjudging, misjudged**) If you say that someone **has misjudged** a person or situation, you mean that they have formed an incorrect idea or opinion about them, and often that they have made a wrong decision as a result of this. ❑ Perhaps I had misjudged him, and he was not so predictable after all.

mis·lead /ˌmɪsˈliːd/ VERB [T] (**misleads, misleading, misled**) If you say that someone or something **has misled** you, you mean that they have made you believe something that is not true, either by telling you a lie or by giving you a wrong idea or impression. ❑ It's this legend which has misled scholars.

mis·lead·ing /ˌmɪsˈliːdɪŋ/ ADJ If you describe something as **misleading**, you mean that it gives you a wrong idea or impression. ❑ It would be misleading to say that we were friends.

mis·lead·ing·ly /ˌmɪsˈliːdɪŋli/ ADV ❑ The data had been presented misleadingly.

mis·led /ˌmɪsˈled/ IRREG FORM **Misled** is the past tense and past participle of **mislead**.

mis·man·age·ment /ˌmɪsˈmænɪdʒmənt/ NOUN [u] Someone's **mismanagement** of a system or organization is the bad way they have dealt with it or organized it. = mishandling ❑ His gross mismanagement left the company desperately in need of restructuring.

mis·placed /ˌmɪsˈpleɪst/ ADJ (disapproval) If you describe a feeling or action as **misplaced**, you are critical of it because you think it is inappropriate, or directed towards the wrong thing or person. ❑ A telling sign of misplaced priorities is the concentration on health, not environmental issues.

mis·read /ˌmɪsˈriːd/ VERB [T] (**misreads, misreading, misread** /ˌmɪsˈred/) **1** If you **misread** a situation or someone's behaviour, you do not understand it properly. = misinterpret ❑ The administration largely misread the mood of the electorate. **2** If you **misread** something that has been written or printed, you look at it and think that it says something that it does not say. ❑ His chauffeur misread his route and took a wrong turn.

mis·read·ing /ˌmɪsˈriːdɪŋ/ NOUN [c] (**misreadings**) ❑ a misreading of opinion in France

mis·rep·re·sent /ˌmɪsreprɪˈzent/ VERB [T] (**misrepresents, misrepresenting, misrepresented**) If someone **misrepresents** a person or situation, they give a wrong or inaccurate account of what the person or situation is like. ❑ He said that the press had misrepresented him as arrogant and bullying. ❑ Hollywood films misrepresented us as drunks, maniacs, and murderers.

mis·rep·re·sen·ta·tion /ˌmɪsˌreprɪzenˈteɪʃən/ NOUN [c, u] (**misrepresentations**) ❑ I wish to point out your misrepresentation of the facts.

Miss ◆◆◆ /mɪs/ NOUN [c] (**Misses**) (formal) You use **Miss** in front of the name of a girl or unmarried woman when you are speaking to her or referring to her. ❑ It was nice talking to you, Miss Ellis.

miss ◆◆◆ /mɪs/ VERB, NOUN

VERB [I, T] (**misses, missing, missed**) **1** [I, T] If you **miss**

m

something, you fail to hit it, for example when you have thrown something at it or you have shot a bullet at it. ❑ *She hurled the ashtray across the room, narrowly missing my head.* ❑ *When I'd missed a few times, he suggested I rest the rifle on a rock to steady it.* **2** [I, T] In sports, if you **miss** a shot, you fail to get the ball in the goal, net, or hole. ❑ *He scored four of the baskets but missed a free throw.* ❑ *He dived for the ball and missed.* **3** [T] If you **miss** something, you fail to notice it. ❑ *From this vantage point he watched, his searching eye never missing a detail.* **4** [T] If you **miss** the meaning or importance of something, you fail to understand or appreciate it. ❑ *One ABC correspondent had totally missed the point of the question.* **5** [T] If you **miss** a chance or opportunity, you fail to take advantage of it. ❑ *It was too good an opportunity to miss.* **6** [T] If you **miss** someone who is no longer with you or who has died, you feel sad and wish that they were still with you. ❑ *Your mum and I are going to miss you at Christmas.* **7** [T] If you **miss** something, you feel sad because you no longer have it or are no longer doing or experiencing it. ❑ *I could happily move back into a flat if it wasn't for the fact that I'd miss my garden.* **8** [T] If you **miss** something such as a plane or train, you arrive too late to catch it. ❑ *He missed the last bus home and had to stay with a friend.* **9** [T] If you **miss** something such as a meeting or an activity, you do not go to it or take part in it. ❑ *It's a pity Martha and I had to miss our class last week.* ❑ *You won't be missing much on TV tonight apart from the usual repeats.*
PHRASAL VERB **miss out** **1** If you **miss out on** something that would be enjoyable or useful to you, you are not involved in it or do not take part in it. = lose out ❑ *We're missing out on a tremendous opportunity.* **2** (BrE; in AmE, use **leave out**) If you **miss out** something or someone, you fail to include them. = leave out
NOUN [C] (**misses**) **1** A **miss** is when you fail to hit something, for example when you have thrown something at it or you have shot a bullet at it. ❑ *After more misses, they finally put two arrows into the lion's chest.* **2** In sports, a **miss** is when you take a shot and fail to get the ball in the goal, net, or hole. ❑ *Snow made his first basket of the game after eight misses.*
→ See also **missing**
✦ **miss the boat** → see **boat**

mis·sile ◆◇◇ /'mɪsaɪl, AmE -səl/ NOUN [C] (**missiles**) **1** A **missile** is a tube-shaped weapon that travels long distances through the air and explodes when it reaches its target. ❑ *The authorities offered to stop firing missiles if the rebels agreed to stop attacking civilian targets.* **2** Anything that is thrown as a weapon can be called a **missile**. ❑ *The football fans began throwing missiles, one of which hit the referee.*

miss·ing ◆◇◇ /'mɪsɪŋ/ ADJ
ADJ **1** If something is **missing** or has **gone missing**, it is not in its usual place, and you cannot find it. ❑ *It was only an hour or so later that I discovered that my gun was missing.* **2** If a part of something is **missing**, it has been removed or has come off, and has not been replaced. ❑ *Three buttons were missing from his shirt.* **3** If you say that something is **missing**, you mean that it has not been included, and you think that it should have been. ❑ *She had given me an incomplete list. One name was missing from it.* **4** Someone who is **missing** cannot be found, and it is not known whether they are alive or dead. ❑ *Five people died in the explosion and more than one thousand were injured. One person is still missing.*
PHRASE **missing in action** If a member of the armed forces is **missing in action**, they have not returned from a battle, their body has not been found, and they are not thought to have been captured.

mis·sion ◆◆◇ /'mɪʃən/ NOUN [C, SING] (**missions**) **1** [C] A **mission** is an important task that people are given to do, especially one that involves travelling to another country. ❑ *Salisbury sent him on a diplomatic mission to North America.* **2** [C] A **mission** is a group of people who have been sent to a foreign country to carry out an official task. = delegation ❑ *a senior member of a diplomatic mission* **3** [C] A **mission** is a special journey made by a military plane or spacecraft. ❑ *a bomber that crashed during a*

training mission in the west Texas mountains **4** [SING] If you say that you have a **mission**, you mean that you have a strong commitment and sense of duty to do or achieve something. = vocation ❑ *He viewed his mission in life as protecting the weak from the evil.* **5** [C] A **mission** is the activities of a group of Christians who have been sent to a place to teach people about Christianity. ❑ *They say God spoke to them and told them to go on a mission to the poorest country in the Western Hemisphere.*

mist /mɪst/ NOUN, VERB
NOUN [C, U] (**mists**) **Mist** consists of a large number of tiny drops of water in the air, which make it difficult to see very far. ❑ *Thick mist made flying impossible.*
VERB [I, T] (**mists, misting, misted**) If a piece of glass **mists** or **is misted**, it becomes covered with tiny drops of moisture, so that you cannot see through it easily. ❑ *The windows misted, blurring the stark streetlight.*
PHRASAL VERB **mist over** **Mist over** means the same as **mist** VERB. ❑ *The front windscreen was misting over.*

mis·take ◆◆◇ /mɪ'steɪk/ NOUN, VERB
NOUN [C] (**mistakes**) **1** [oft mistake 'of' -ING, also 'by' mistake] If you make a **mistake**, you do something which you did not intend to do, or which produces a result that you do not want. ❑ *They made the big mistake of thinking they could seize its border with a relatively small force.* ❑ *There must be some mistake.* **2** A **mistake** is something or part of something that is incorrect or not right. = error ❑ *Her mother sighed and rubbed out another mistake in the crossword puzzle.*
VERB [T] (**mistakes, mistaking, mistook, mistaken**) **1** If you **mistake** one person or thing **for** another, you wrongly think that they are the other person or thing. ❑ *When hay fever first occurs it is often mistaken for a summer cold.* **2** If you **mistake** something, you fail to recognize or understand it. = misjudge ❑ *The administration completely mistook the feeling of the country.*
PHRASE **there's no mistaking** (emphasis) You can say **there is no mistaking** something when you are emphasizing that you cannot fail to recognize or understand it. ❑ *There's no mistaking the eastern flavour of the food.*

mis·tak·en /mɪ'steɪkən/ ADJ
ADJ **1** [V-LINK + mistaken] If you are **mistaken about** something, you are wrong about it. = wrong ❑ *I see I was mistaken about you.* **2** [mistaken + N] A **mistaken** belief or opinion is incorrect. ❑ *I had a mistaken view of what was happening.*
PHRASE **if I'm not mistaken** (emphasis) You use expressions such as **if I'm not mistaken** and **unless I'm very much mistaken** as a polite way of emphasizing the statement you are making, especially when you are confident that it is correct. ❑ *I think Alfred wanted to marry Jennifer, if I am not mistaken.*

mis·tak·en·ly /mɪ'steɪkənli/ ADV ❑ *He says they mistakenly believed the standard licences they held were sufficient.*

mis·took /mɪ'stʊk/ IRREG FORM **Mistook** is the past tense of **mistake**.

mis·trust /ˌmɪs'trʌst/ NOUN, VERB
NOUN [U] **Mistrust** is the feeling that you have towards someone who you do not trust. = distrust ❑ *There was mutual mistrust between the two men.*
VERB [T] (**mistrusts, mistrusting, mistrusted**) If you **mistrust** someone or something, you do not trust them. = distrust ❑ *It frequently appears that Bell mistrusts all journalists.*

mis·under·stand /ˌmɪsʌndə'stænd/ VERB
VERB [I, T] (**misunderstands, misunderstanding, misunderstood**) If you **misunderstand** someone or something, you do not understand them properly. ❑ *I misunderstood you.* ❑ *They have simply misunderstood what rock and roll is.*
CONVENTION **don't misunderstand me** You can say **don't misunderstand me** when you want to correct a wrong impression that you think someone may have got about what you are saying.
→ See also **misunderstood**

mis·under·stand·ing /ˌmɪsʌndə'stændɪŋ/ NOUN [C, U]

(misunderstandings) ◼ [c, u] A **misunderstanding** is a failure to understand something properly, for example a situation or a person's remarks. ❑ *There has been some misunderstanding of our publishing aims.* ◼ [c] *(formal)* You can refer to a disagreement or slight quarrel as a **misunderstanding**. ❑ *There was a little misunderstanding with the police and he was arrested.*

mis·under·stood /ˌmɪsʌndəˈstʊd/ IRREG FORM, ADJ

IRREG FORM **Misunderstood** is the past tense and past participle of **misunderstand**.

ADJ If you describe someone or something as **misunderstood**, you mean that people do not understand them and have a wrong impression or idea of them. ❑ *Eric is very badly misunderstood.*

mis·use NOUN, VERB

NOUN /ˌmɪsˈjuːs/ [c, u] **(misuses)** The **misuse** of something is incorrect, careless, or dishonest use of it. ❑ *the misuse of power and privilege*

VERB /ˌmɪsˈjuːz/ [t] **(misuses, misusing, misused)** If someone **misuses** something, they use it incorrectly, carelessly, or dishonestly. ❑ *She misused her position in the appointment of 26,000 party supporters to government jobs.* ❑ *Tess would like a pound for every time she had heard that word misused by television journalists.*

miti·gate /ˈmɪtɪgeɪt/ VERB [t] **(mitigates, mitigating, mitigated)** *(formal)* To **mitigate** something means to make it less unpleasant, serious, or painful. = alleviate ❑ *ways of mitigating the effects of an explosion*

mix ♦♦◇ /mɪks/ VERB, NOUN

VERB [RECIP, t] **(mixes, mixing, mixed)** ◼ [RECIP] If two substances **mix** or if you **mix** one substance **with** another, you stir or shake them together, or combine them in some other way, so that they become a single substance. ❑ *Oil and water don't mix.* ❑ *A quick stir will mix them thoroughly.* ❑ *Mix the cinnamon with the rest of the sugar.* ◼ [t] If you **mix** something, you prepare it by mixing other things together. ❑ *He had spent several hours mixing cement.* ◼ [RECIP] If two things or activities do not **mix**, it is not a good idea to have them or do them together, because the result would be unpleasant or dangerous. ❑ *Politics and sport don't mix.* ❑ *Some of these pills don't mix with drink.* ◼ [RECIP] If you **mix** with other people, you meet them and talk to them. You can also say that people **mix**. = socialize ❑ *I ventured the idea that the secret of staying young was to mix with older people.* ❑ *People are supposed to mix, do you understand?*

PHRASAL VERB **mix up** ◼ If you **mix up** two things or people, you confuse them, so that you think that one of them is the other one. ❑ *People often mix me up with other actors.* ❑ *Depressed people may mix up their words.* ◼ If you **mix up** a number of things, you put things of different kinds together or place things so that they are not in order. ❑ *I like to mix up designer clothes.* ❑ *Take the cards and mix them up.*

NOUN [c, u] **(mixes)** ◼ [c, u] A **mix** is a powder containing all the substances that you need in order to make something such as a cake or a sauce. When you want to use it, you add liquid. ❑ *For speed we used packets of pizza dough mix.* ◼ [c] A **mix of** different things or people is two or more of them together. ❑ *The story is a magical mix of fantasy and reality.*
→ See also **mixed**
✦ **mix your metaphors** → see **metaphor**

mixed ♦♦◇ /mɪkst/ ADJ ◼ If you have **mixed** feelings about something or someone, you feel uncertain about them because you can see both good and bad points about them. ❑ *I came home from the meeting with mixed feelings.* ◼ A **mixed** group of people consists of people of many different types. ❑ *I found a very mixed group of individuals, some of whom I could relate to and others with whom I had very little in common.* ◼ **Mixed** is used to describe something that involves people from two or more different races. ❑ *Sally had attended a racially mixed school.* ◼ **Mixed** education or accommodation are intended for both males and females. ❑ *Girls who have always been at a mixed school know how to stand up for themselves.* ◼ [mixed + N] **Mixed** is used to describe something which includes or consists of

different things of the same general kind. ❑ *a teaspoon of mixed herbs*

mix·er /ˈmɪksə/ NOUN [c] **(mixers)** ◼ A **mixer** is a machine used for mixing things together. ❑ *an electric mixer* ◼ A **mixer** is a nonalcoholic drink such as fruit juice or soda that you mix with strong alcohol such as gin. ❑ *At the Tropicana you order ice and mixers from the waiters at the table.* ◼ If you say that someone is a good **mixer**, you mean that they are good at talking to people and making friends. ❑ *Cooper was a good mixer, he was popular.* ◼ A **mixer** is a piece of equipment that is used to make changes to recorded music or film. ❑ *a three-channel audio mixer*

mix·ture ♦◇◇ /ˈmɪkstʃə/ NOUN [SING, c] **(mixtures)** ◼ [SING] A **mixture of** things consists of several different things together. ❑ *They looked at him with a mixture of horror, envy, and awe.* ◼ [c] A **mixture** is a substance that consists of other substances which have been stirred or shaken together. ❑ *a mixture of water and sugar and salt*

mm ♦◇◇ ABBREVIATION **mm** is a written abbreviation for **millimetre** or **millimetres**. ❑ *a 135mm lens*

moan /məʊn/ VERB, NOUN

VERB [i, t] **(moans, moaning, moaned)** ◼ [i, t] If you **moan**, you make a low sound, usually because you are unhappy or in pain. = groan ❑ *Tony moaned in his sleep and then turned over on his side.* ◼ [i] To **moan** means to complain or speak in a way which shows that you are very unhappy. ❑ *I used to moan if I didn't get at least six hours' sleep at night.* ❑ *moaning about the weather*

NOUN [c] **(moans)** ◼ A **moan** is a low sound you make, usually because you are unhappy or in pain. ❑ *Suddenly she gave a low, choking moan and began to tremble violently.* ◼ *(informal)* A **moan** is a complaint. ❑ *They have been listening to people's moans and praise.*

mob /mɒb/ NOUN, VERB

NOUN [c, SING] **(mobs)** ◼ [c] A **mob** is a large, disorganized, and often violent crowd of people. ❑ *The inspectors watched a growing mob of demonstrators gathering.* ◼ [SING] *(mainly BrE, disapproval)* People sometimes use **the mob** to refer in a disapproving way to the majority of people in a country or place, especially when these people are behaving in a violent or uncontrolled way. ❑ *If they continue like this there is a danger of the mob taking over.* ◼ [SING] *(informal)* You can refer to the people involved in organized crime as **the Mob**. ❑ *He makes ends meet by working as a forger for the Mob.*

VERB [t] **(mobs, mobbing, mobbed)** If you say that someone **is being mobbed by** a crowd of people, you mean that the people are trying to talk to them or get near them in an enthusiastic or threatening way. ❑ *Her car was mobbed by the media.*

mo·bile ♦◇◇ /ˈməʊbaɪl, AmE -bəl/ ADJ, NOUN

ADJ ◼ You use **mobile** to describe something large that can be moved easily from place to place. ❑ *the four-hundred seat mobile theatre* ◼ If you are **mobile**, you can move or travel easily from place to place, for example because you are not physically disabled or because you have your own transport. ❑ *I'm still very mobile.* ◼ In a **mobile** society, people move easily from one job, home, or social class to another. ❑ *We are a very mobile society and can't resist trying to take everything with us.*

NOUN [c] **(mobiles)** ◼ A **mobile** is a decoration that you hang from a ceiling. It usually consists of several small objects which move as the air around them moves. ◼ *(mainly BrE)* A **mobile** is the same as a **mobile phone**.

mo·bil·ity /məʊˈbɪlɪti/ NOUN [u] ◼ *Two cars gave them the freedom and mobility to go their separate ways.* ◼ *Prior to the nineteenth century, there were almost no channels of social mobility.*

mo·bile phone NOUN [c] **(mobile phones)** *(BrE; in AmE, use* **cellphone***)* A **mobile phone** is a telephone that you carry with you and use to make or receive calls wherever you are.

mo·bi·lize /ˈməʊbɪlaɪz/ also **mobilise** VERB [i, t] **(mobilizes, mobilizing, mobilized)** ◼ [i, t] If you **mobilize** support or **mobilize** people to do something, you succeed in encouraging people to take action, especially political

m

action. If people **mobilize**, they prepare to take action. ❑ *The best hope is that we will mobilize international support and get down to action.* **2** [T] If you **mobilize** resources, you start to use them or make them available for use. ❑ *If you could mobilize the resources, you could get it done.* **3** [I, T] (*journalism, military*) If a country **mobilizes**, or **mobilizes** its armed forces, or if its armed forces **mobilize**, they are given orders to prepare for a conflict. ❑ *Sudan even threatened to mobilize in response to the ultimatums.*

mo·bi·li·za·tion /ˌməʊbɪlaɪˈzeɪʃən/ NOUN [U] **1** *the rapid mobilization of international opinion in support of the revolution* **2** *the mobilization of resources for education* **3** *a demand for full-scale mobilization to defend the republic*

mock /mɒk/ VERB, ADJ

VERB [T] (**mocks, mocking, mocked**) If someone **mocks** you, they show or pretend that they think you are foolish or inferior, for example by saying something funny about you, or by imitating your behaviour. ❑ *I thought you were mocking me.*

ADJ [mock + N] You use **mock** to describe something which is not real or genuine, but which is intended to be very similar to the real thing. ❑ *'It's tragic!' swoons Jeffrey in mock horror.*

mock·ery /ˈmɒkəri/ NOUN [U, SING] **1** [U] If someone **mocks** you, you can refer to their behaviour or attitude as **mockery**. ❑ *Was there a glint of mockery in his eyes?* **2** [SING] If something makes **a mockery of** something, it makes it appear worthless and foolish. ❑ *This action makes a mockery of the administration's continuing protestations of concern.*

✪**mode** /məʊd/ NOUN [C] (**modes**) (*academic word*) **1** (*formal*) A **mode** of life or behaviour is a particular way of living or behaving. ❑ *the capitalist mode of production* ❑ *He switched automatically into interview mode.* **2** A **mode** is a particular style in art, literature, or dress. ❑ *a slightly more elegant and formal mode of dress* **3** On some cameras or electronic devices, the different **modes** available are the different programs or settings that you can choose when you use them. ❑ *when the camera is in manual mode* ❑ *In automatic mode, shutter priority and aperture priority are selected by the mere touch of a button next to the control dial.*

✪**mod·el** ♦♦◇ /ˈmɒdəl/ NOUN, ADJ, VERB

NOUN [C] (**models**) **1** A **model** of an object is a physical representation that shows what it looks like or how it works. The model is often smaller than the object it represents. ❑ *an architect's model of a wooden house* ❑ *I made a model out of paper and glue.* **2** (*formal*) A **model** is a system that is being used and that people might want to copy in order to achieve similar results. ❑ *the Chinese model of economic reform* ❑ *We believe that this is a general model of managerial activity.* ❑ *the European model of social responsibility* **3** (*formal*) A **model** of a system or process is a theoretical description that can help you understand how the system or process works, or how it might work. = **theory** ❑ *Darwin eventually put forward a model of biological evolution.* **4** If you say that someone or something is **a model of** a particular quality, you are showing approval of them because they have that quality to a large degree. ❑ *A model of good manners, he has conquered any inward fury.* **5** A particular **model** of a machine is a particular version of it. ❑ *To keep the cost down, opt for a basic model.* **6** An artist's **model** is a person who stays still in a particular position so that the artist can make a picture or sculpture of them. ❑ *the model for his portrait of Mary Magdalene, the Marchesa Attavanti* **7** A fashion **model** is a person whose job is to display clothes by wearing them. ❑ *Paris's top fashion model*

ADJ **1** [model + N] A **model** structure is a physical representation of something that shows what it looks like or how it works. It is often smaller than the object it represents. ❑ *a model railway* **2** [model + N] You use **model** to express approval of someone when you think that they perform their role or duties extremely well. = **exemplary** ❑ *As a girl she had been a model student.*

VERB [I, T] (**models, modelling, modelled**; in AmE, use **modeling, modeled**) **1** [T] (*formal*) If someone such as a scientist **models** a system or process, they make an accurate theoretical description of it in order to

understand or explain how it works. ❑ *I have moved from trying to model and understand the distribution and evolution of water vapour.* ❑ *The mathematics needed to model a nonlinear system like an atmosphere* ❑ *It is no surprise that we find such processes hard to model mathematically.* **2** [T] If one thing **is modelled on** another, the first thing is made so that it is like the second thing in some way. ❑ *The quota system was modelled on those operated in America and continental Europe.* **3** [T] If you **model** yourself **on** someone, you copy the way that they do things, because you admire them and want to be like them. ❑ *You have been modelling yourself on others all your life.* **4** [I] If someone **models** for an artist, they stay still in a particular position so that the artist can make a picture or sculpture of them. ❑ *Tullio has been modelling for Sandra for eleven years.* **5** [I, T] If someone **models** clothes, they display them by wearing them. ❑ *She began modelling in Paris at age 15.* **6** [I, T] If you **model** shapes or figures, you make them out of a substance such as clay or wood. ❑ *There she began to model in clay.*

mod·el·ling /ˈmɒdəlɪŋ/ (*BrE*; in AmE, use **modeling**) NOUN [U] ❑ *She was being offered a modelling contract.*

✪**mod·er·ate** ♦◇◇ ADJ, NOUN, VERB

ADJ /ˈmɒdərət/ **1** **Moderate** political opinions or policies are not extreme. ❑ *He was an easygoing man of very moderate views.* **2** You use **moderate** to describe people or groups who have moderate political opinions or policies. ❑ *a moderate Democrat* **3** You use **moderate** to describe something that is neither large nor small in amount or degree. = **reasonable** ❑ *While a moderate amount of stress can be beneficial, too much stress can exhaust you.* ❑ *Heavy drinkers die earlier than moderate drinkers.* **4** A **moderate** change in something is a change that is not great. = **slight** ❑ *Most drugs offer either no real improvement or, at best, only moderate improvements.*

NOUN /ˈmɒdərət/ [C] (**moderates**) A **moderate** is someone with moderate political opinions. ❑ *If he presents himself as a radical he risks scaring off the moderates whose votes he so desperately needs.*

VERB /ˈmɒdəreɪt/ [I, T] (**moderates, moderating, moderated**) If you **moderate** something or if it **moderates**, it becomes less extreme or violent and easier to deal with or accept. ❑ *They are hoping that once in office he can be persuaded to moderate his views.*

✪**mod·er·ate·ly** /ˈmɒdərətli/ ADV **1** = **reasonably**; ≠ **excessively** ❑ *Both are moderately large insects, with a wingspan of around four centimetres.* **2** [moderately after V] = **slightly** ❑ *Share prices on the Tokyo Exchange declined moderately.*

mod·era·tion /ˌmɒdəˈreɪʃən/ NOUN

NOUN [U] (*approval*) If you say that someone's behaviour shows **moderation**, you approve of them because they act in a way that you think is reasonable and not extreme. = **restraint** ❑ *The United Nations Secretary General called on all parties to show moderation.*

PHRASE **in moderation** If you say that someone does something such as eat, drink, or smoke **in moderation**, you mean that they do not eat, drink, or smoke too much or more than is reasonable.

✪**mod·ern** ♦♦◇ /ˈmɒdən/ ADJ **1** [modern + N] **Modern** means relating to the present time, for example the present decade or present century. = **contemporary, current, present** ❑ *We had a long talk about the problem of materialism in modern society.* ❑ *the alienation of the modern world* **2** Something that is **modern** is new and involves the latest ideas or equipment. = **advanced, up-to-date, state-of-the-art**; ≠ **old-fashioned, ancient, primitive, out-of-date, outdated** ❑ *In many ways, it was a very modern school for its time.* ❑ *Modern technology has opened our eyes to many things.* **3** People are sometimes described as **modern** when they have opinions or ways of behaving that have not yet been accepted by most people in a society. = **progressive**; ≠ **old-fashioned, out-of-date** ❑ *She is very modern in outlook.* **4** [modern + N] **Modern** is used to describe styles of art, dance, music, and architecture that have developed in recent times, in contrast to classical styles. = **contemporary**; ≠ **traditional** ❑ *She'd been a dancer with a modern dance company in New York.*

M

VOCABULARY BUILDER

modern ADJ
Modern means relating to the present time, for example the present decade or present century.
❑ He says that football managers have become the gladiators of modern times.

contemporary ADJ
Contemporary things relate to the present time.
❑ one of the finest collections of contemporary art in the country

current ADJ (fairly formal)
Current means happening, being used, or being done at the present time.
❑ The current situation is very different from that in 1990.

present ADJ
You use present to describe things and people that exist now, rather than those that existed in the past or those that may exist in the future.
❑ the government's present economic difficulties

up-to-date ADJ
If something is up-to-date, it is the newest thing of its kind.
❑ the most up-to-date information available on foods today

state-of-the-art ADJ (mainly spoken)
If you describe something as state-of-the-art, you mean that it is the best available because it has been made using the most modern techniques and technology.
❑ the production of state-of-the-art military equipment

⬦**mod•ern•ize** /'mɒdənaɪz/ also **modernise** VERB [T] (modernizes, modernizing, modernized) To modernize something such as a system or a factory means to change it by replacing old equipment or methods with new ones. = update ❑ plans to modernize the refinery ❑ We need to modernise our electoral system. ❑ the cost of modernizing the economy ⬦**mod•ern•i•za•tion** /,mɒdənaɪ'zeɪʃən/ NOUN [U] ❑ a five-year modernization programme ❑ the modernization of the region

mod•est ◆◇◇ /'mɒdɪst/ ADJ **1** A modest house or other building is not large or expensive. ❑ They had spent the night at a modest hotel. **2** You use modest to describe something such as an amount, rate, or improvement which is fairly small. ❑ Unemployment rose to the still modest rate of 0.7%. **3** If you say that someone is modest, you approve of them because they do not talk much about their abilities or achievements. ❑ He's modest, as well as being a great player. **mod•est•ly** /'mɒdɪstli/ ADV **1** The nation's balance of payments improved modestly last month. **2** [modestly in v] ❑ 'You really must be very good at what you do.'—'I suppose I am,' Kate said modestly.

mod•es•ty /'mɒdɪsti/ NOUN [U] **1** (approval) Someone who shows modesty does not talk much about their abilities or achievements. ❑ His modesty does him credit, for the food he produces speaks for itself. **2** You can refer to the modesty of something such as a place or amount when it is fairly small. ❑ The modesty of the town itself comes as something of a surprise. **3** If someone, especially a woman, shows modesty, they are cautious about the way they dress and behave because they are aware that other people may view them in a sexual way. ❑ There were shrieks of embarrassment, mingled with giggles, from some of the girls as they struggled to protect their modesty.

⬦**mod•i•fy** /'mɒdɪfaɪ/ VERB [T] (modifies, modifying, modified) (academic word) If you modify something, you change it slightly, usually in order to improve it. = alter ❑ The club members did agree to modify their recruitment policy. ❑ The plane was a modified version of the C-130. ⬦**modi•fi•ca•tion** /,mɒdɪfɪ'keɪʃən/ NOUN [C, U] (modifications) = alteration, change ❑ Relatively minor

modifications were required. ❑ behaviour modification techniques

mod•ule /'mɒdʒuːl/ NOUN [C] (modules) **1** A module is a part of a machine, especially a computer, which performs a particular function. **2** A module is a part of a spacecraft which can operate by itself, often away from the rest of the spacecraft. ❑ A rescue plan could be achieved by sending an unmanned module to the space station.

moist /mɔɪst/ ADJ (moister, moistest) Something that is moist is slightly wet. ❑ The soil is reasonably moist after the September rain.

mois•ture /'mɔɪstʃə/ NOUN [U] Moisture is tiny drops of water in the air, on a surface, or in the ground. ❑ When the soil is dry, more moisture is lost from the plant.

⬦**mo•lecu•lar** /mə'lekjʊlə/ ADJ [molecular + N] Molecular means relating to or involving molecules. ❑ the molecular structure of fuel ❑ This coincided with the rise of molecular biology.

⬦**mol•ecule** /'mɒlɪkjuːl/ NOUN [C] (molecules) A molecule is the smallest amount of a chemical substance which can exist by itself. ❑ the hydrogen bonds between water molecules

mo•lest /mə'lest/ VERB [T] (molests, molesting, molested) A person who molests someone, especially a woman or a child, interferes with them in a sexual way against their will. ❑ He was accused of sexually molesting a female colleague.

mol•ten /'məʊltən/ ADJ Molten rock, metal, or glass has been heated to a very high temperature and has become a hot, thick liquid. ❑ The molten metal is poured into the mould.

mo•ment ◆◆◆ /'məʊmənt/ NOUN
NOUN [C] (moments) **1** You can refer to a very short period of time, for example a few seconds, as a moment or moments. = minute, second ❑ In a moment he was gone. ❑ In moments, I was asleep once more. **2** A particular moment is the point in time at which something happens. ❑ At this moment a car stopped at the house.
PHRASES (at) any moment (now) (emphasis) If you say that something will or may happen at any moment or any moment now, you are emphasizing that it is likely to happen very soon. ❑ He'll be here to see you any moment now.
at the moment or at this moment or at the present moment You use expressions such as at the moment, at this moment, and at the present moment to indicate that a particular situation exists at the time when you are speaking. = now, currently ❑ At the moment, no one is talking to me. ❑ He's touring South America at this moment in time.
for the moment You use for the moment to indicate that something is true now, even if it will not be true in the future. ❑ For the moment, a potential crisis appears to have been averted.
have one's moments If you say that someone or something has their moments, you are indicating that there are times when they are successful or interesting, but that this does not happen very often. ❑ The film has its moments.
the last moment If someone does something at the last moment, they do it at the latest time possible. ❑ They changed their minds at the last moment and refused to go.
the next moment (emphasis) You use the expression the next moment, or expressions such as 'one moment he was there, the next he was gone', to emphasize that something happens suddenly, especially when it is very different from what was happening before. ❑ He is unpredictable, weeping one moment, laughing the next.
of the moment You use of the moment to describe someone or something that is or was especially popular at a particular time, especially when you want to suggest that their popularity is unlikely to last long or did not last long. ❑ He's the man of the moment, isn't he?
the moment (emphasis) If you say that something happens the moment something else happens, you are emphasizing that it happens immediately after the other thing. ❑ The moment I closed my eyes, I fell asleep.
✦ spur of the moment → see **spur**

m

mo·men·tari·ly /ˌməʊmənˈteərɪli/ ADV **Momentarily** means for a short time. = briefly ❑ *She paused momentarily when she saw them.*

mo·men·tary /ˈməʊməntəri, AmE -teri/ ADJ Something that is **momentary** lasts for a very short period of time, for example for a few seconds or less. = brief ❑ *a momentary lapse of concentration*

mo·men·tous /məʊˈmentəs/ ADJ If you refer to a decision, event, or change as **momentous**, you mean that it is very important, often because of the effects that it will have in the future. ❑ *the momentous decision to send in the troops*

✪ **mo·men·tum** /məʊˈmentəm/ NOUN [U] **1** If a process or movement gains **momentum**, it keeps developing or happening more quickly and keeps becoming less likely to stop. = impetus ❑ *This campaign is really gaining momentum.* ❑ *They are each anxious to maintain the momentum of the search for a solution.* **2** (technical) In physics, **momentum** is the mass of a moving object multiplied by its speed in a particular direction. ❑ *The position, energy, and momentum of particles vary over time in an unpredictable manner.* ❑ *The planet's gravity can rob the comet of some of its orbital momentum.*

✪ **mon·arch** /ˈmɒnək/ NOUN [C] (monarchs) The **monarch** of a country is the king, queen, emperor, or empress. ❑ *His attempts to act as an absolute monarch eventually provoked a successful rebellion.* ❑ *Australia is an effectively independent member of the Commonwealth, with the British monarch as Head of State.*

✪ **mon·ar·chy** /ˈmɒnəki/ NOUN [C, U] (monarchies) **1** [C, U] A **monarchy** is a system in which a country has a monarch. ❑ *a serious debate on the future of the monarchy* ❑ *In a few years we may no longer have a monarchy.* **2** [C] A **monarchy** is a country that has a monarch. ❑ *Britain is a constitutional monarchy.* **3** [C] The **monarchy** is used to refer to the monarch and his or her family. = royal family ❑ *The monarchy has to create a balance between its public and private lives.* ❑ *the tendency for the monarchy and aristocracy to ally for their own purposes against the people*

mon·etary ♦◇◇ /ˈmʌnɪtri, AmE ˈmɑːnɪteri/ ADJ [monetary + N] (business) **Monetary** means relating to money, especially the total amount of money in a country. ❑ *Some countries tighten monetary policy to avoid inflation.*

mon·ey ♦♦♦ /ˈmʌni/ NOUN

NOUN [U, PL] (monies or moneys) **1** [U] **Money** is the coins or bank notes that you use to buy things, or the sum that you have in a bank account. ❑ *A lot of the money that you pay at the cinema goes back to the film distributors.* ❑ *Players should be allowed to earn money from advertising.* **2** [PL] (formal) **Monies** is used to refer to several separate sums of money that form part of a larger amount that is received or spent. ❑ *We drew up a schedule of payments for the rest of the monies owed.*

PHRASES **have money to burn** If you say that someone **has money to burn**, you mean that they have more money than they need, or that they spend their money on things that you think are unnecessary. ❑ *He was a high-earning stockbroker with money to burn.*

in the money (informal) If you are **in the money**, you have a lot of money to spend. ❑ *If you are one of the lucky callers chosen to play, you could be in the money.*

make money If you **make money**, you obtain money by earning it or by making a profit. ❑ *the only part of the firm that consistently made money*

put your money where your mouth is If you say that you want someone to **put** their **money where** their **mouth is**, you want them to spend money to improve a bad situation, instead of just talking about improving it. ❑ *The government might be obliged to put its money where its mouth is to prove its commitment.*

the smart money (journalism) If you say that **the smart money** is on a particular person or thing, you mean that people who know a lot about it think that this person will be successful, or this thing will happen. ❑ *With Japan not playing, the smart money was on the Canadians.*

money talks If you say that **money talks**, you mean that if

someone has a lot of money, they also have a lot of power. ❑ *The formula in Hollywood is simple – money talks.*

throw money at something (disapproval) If you say that someone is **throwing money at** a problem, you are critical of them for trying to improve it by spending money on it, instead of doing more thoughtful and practical things to improve it. ❑ *The governor's answer to the problem has been to throw money at it.*

(get your) money's worth If you **get** your **money's worth**, you get something which is worth the money that it costs or the effort you have put in. ❑ *The fans get their money's worth.*

✦ give someone a run for their money → see run

✪ **moni·tor** ♦◇◇ /ˈmɒnɪtə/ VERB, NOUN

VERB [T] (monitors, monitoring, monitored) (academic word) **1** If you **monitor** something, you regularly check its development or progress, and sometimes comment on it. = observe, oversee ❑ *Officials had not been allowed to monitor the voting.* ❑ *Senior managers can then use the budget as a control document to monitor progress against the agreed actions.* **2** If someone **monitors** radio broadcasts from other countries, they record them or listen carefully to them in order to obtain information. ❑ *Peter Murray is in Washington and has been monitoring reports out of Monrovia.* NOUN [C] (monitors) **1** A **monitor** is a machine that is used to check or record things, for example processes or substances inside a person's body. ❑ *The heart monitor shows low levels of consciousness.* ❑ *A blood glucose monitor at a local drug store costs around $25.* **2** A **monitor** is a screen which is used to display certain kinds of information, for example on a computer, in airports, or in television studios. = screen ❑ *He was watching a game of tennis on a television monitor.* **3** You can refer to a person who checks that something is done correctly, or that it is fair, as a **monitor**. ❑ *Government monitors will continue to accompany reporters.*

monk /mʌŋk/ NOUN [C] (monks) A **monk** is a member of a male religious community that is usually separated from the outside world. ❑ *saffron-robed Buddhist monks*

mon·key /ˈmʌŋki/ NOUN [C] (monkeys) **1** A **monkey** is an animal with a long tail which lives in hot countries and climbs trees. **2** If you refer to a child as a **monkey**, you are saying in an affectionate way that he or she is very lively and naughty. ❑ *She's such a little monkey.*

mo·noga·my /məˈnɒɡəmi/ NOUN [U] **Monogamy** is used to refer to the state or custom of being married to only one person or having a sexual relationship with only one partner. ❑ *In many non-Western societies, however, monogamy has never dominated.*

WORD PARTS

The prefix **mono-** appears in words that have 'one' or 'single' as part of their meaning:
monogamy (NOUN)
monologue (NOUN)
monolingual (ADJ)

---

mono·lin·gual /ˌmɒnəʊˈlɪŋɡwəl/ ADJ [usu monolingual + N] **Monolingual** means involving, using, or speaking one language. ❑ *a largely monolingual country such as Great Britain*

✪ **mono·logue** /ˈmɒnəlɒɡ, AmE -lɔːɡ/ NOUN [C, U] (monologues) **1** If you refer to a long speech by one person during a conversation as a **monologue**, you mean it prevents other people from talking or expressing their opinions. = speech ❑ *Morris ignored the question and continued his monologue.* ❑ *the communication characteristics of both monologue and dialogue* **2** A **monologue** is a long speech which is spoken by one person as an entertainment, or as part of an entertainment such as a play. = speech ❑ *a monologue based on the writing of Quentin Crisp* ❑ *her brilliant series of dramatic monologues*

✪ **mo·nopo·lize** /məˈnɒpəlaɪz/ also **monopolise** VERB [T] (monopolizes, monopolizing, monopolized) **1** If you say that someone **monopolizes** something, you mean that they have a very large share of it and prevent other people from having a share. = control, dominate ❑ *They*

are controlling so much cocoa that they are virtually monopolizing the market. ❑ *He himself is pushing quite aggressively to try to monopolize power in the government.* **2** If something or someone **monopolizes** you, they demand a lot of your time and attention, so that there is very little time left for anything or anyone else. ❑ *He would monopolize her totally, to the exclusion of her brothers and sisters.*
mo·nopo·li·za·tion /məˌnɒpəlaɪˈzeɪʃən/ NOUN [U] ❑ *the monopolization of a market by a single supplier*

✪**mo·nopo·ly** /məˈnɒpəli/ NOUN [C, U, SING] (**monopolies**) (*business*) **1** [C, U] If a company, person, or state has a **monopoly on** something such as an industry, they have complete control over it, so that it is impossible for others to become involved in it. ❑ *Russian moves to end a state monopoly on land ownership* ❑ *the governing party's monopoly over the media* **2** [C] A **monopoly** is a company which is the only one providing a particular product or service. ❑ *a state-owned monopoly* ❑ *The television industry continues to rake in the profits as a protected, regulated monopoly.* **3** [SING] If you say that someone does not have a **monopoly on** something, you mean that they are not the only person who has that thing. ❑ *Women do not have a monopoly on feelings of betrayal.*

✪**mo·noto·nous** /məˈnɒtənəs/ ADJ Something that is **monotonous** is very boring because it has a regular, repeated pattern which never changes. = repetitive ❑ *It's monotonous work, like most factory jobs.* ❑ *The food may get a bit monotonous, but there'll be enough of it.* ✪**mo·noto·nous·ly** /məˈnɒtənəsli/ ADV ❑ *The rain dripped monotonously from the trees.* ❑ *It's almost impossible to say such sentences monotonously.*

✪**mo·noto·ny** /məˈnɒtəni/ NOUN [U] [oft monotony 'of' N] The **monotony** of something is the fact that it never changes and is boring. ❑ *A night on the town may help to break the monotony of the week.* ❑ *a life of secure monotony*

✪**mon·soon** /mɒnˈsuːn/ NOUN [C, PL] (**monsoons**) **1** [C] The **monsoon** is the season in Southern Asia when there is a lot of very heavy rain. ❑ *the end of the monsoon* ❑ *Light monsoon rain falls from June to September.* **2** [PL] Monsoon rains are sometimes referred to as **the monsoons**. ❑ *In Bangladesh, the monsoons have started.*

mon·ster /ˈmɒnstə/ NOUN, ADJ
NOUN [C] (**monsters**) **1** A **monster** is a large imaginary creature that looks very ugly and frightening. ❑ *Both films are about a monster in the bedroom closet.* **2** A **monster** is something which is extremely large, especially something that is difficult to manage or which is unpleasant. ❑ *the monster which is now the London marathon* **3** If you describe someone as a **monster**, you mean that they are cruel, frightening, or evil. ❑ *Galbraith said that her husband was a depraved monster who threatened and humiliated her.*
ADJ [monster + N] (*informal, emphasis*) **Monster** means extremely and surprisingly large. = giant ❑ *a monster weapon*

mon·strous /ˈmɒnstrəs/ ADJ **1** If you describe a situation or event as **monstrous**, you mean that it is extremely shocking or unfair. = atrocious ❑ *She endured the monstrous behaviour for years.* **2** If you describe an unpleasant thing as **monstrous**, you mean that it is extremely large in size or extent. ❑ *A group of men are erecting a monstrous copper edifice.* **3** If you describe something as **monstrous**, you mean that it is extremely frightening because it appears unnatural or ugly. = hideous ❑ *the film's monstrous fantasy figure* **mon·strous·ly** /ˈmɒnstrəsli/ ADV **1** [monstrously after V] ❑ *Your husband's family has behaved monstrously.* **2** [monstrously + ADJ/-ED] ❑ *It would be monstrously unfair.*

month ♦♦♦ /mʌnθ/ NOUN [C] (**months**) **1** A **month** is one of the twelve periods of time that a year is divided into, for example January or February. ❑ *The trial is due to begin next month.* ❑ *an exhibition which opens this month at the Guggenheim Museum* **2** A **month** is a period of about four weeks. ❑ *She was here for a month.* ❑ *Over the next several months I met most of her family.*

month·ly ♦♦◇ /ˈmʌnθli/ ADJ, ADV, NOUN
ADJ **1** [monthly + N] A **monthly** event or publication

happens or appears every month. ❑ *Many people are now having trouble making their monthly house payments.* ❑ *Kidscape runs monthly workshops for teachers.* **2** [monthly + N] **Monthly** quantities or rates relate to a period of one month. ❑ *Consumers are charged a monthly fee above their basic cable costs.*
ADV [monthly after V] If an event happens or a publication appears **monthly**, it happens or appears every month. ❑ *In some areas the property price can rise monthly.*
NOUN [C] (**monthlies**) You can refer to a publication that is published monthly as a **monthly**. ❑ *a satirical monthly*

monu·ment /ˈmɒnjʊmənt/ NOUN [C] (**monuments**) **1** A **monument** is a large structure, usually made of stone, which is built to remind people of an event in history or of a famous person. ❑ *a newly restored monument commemorating a 119-year-old tragedy* **2** A **monument** is something such as a castle or bridge that was built a very long time ago and is regarded as an important part of a country's history. ❑ *the ancient monuments of Mexico and Peru* **3** If you describe something as a **monument to** someone's qualities, you mean that it is a very good example of the results or effects of those qualities. ❑ *By his international achievements he leaves a fitting monument to his beliefs.*

monu·men·tal /ˌmɒnjʊˈmentəl/ ADJ **1** (*emphasis*) You can use **monumental** to emphasize the large size or extent of something. = huge, massive ❑ *It had been a monumental blunder to give him the assignment.* **2** (*emphasis*) If you describe a book or musical work as **monumental**, you are emphasizing that it is very large and impressive, and is likely to be important for a long time. ❑ *his monumental work on Chinese astronomy* **3** [monumental + N] A **monumental** building or sculpture is very large and impressive. ❑ *I take no real interest in monumental sculpture.*

mood ♦◇◇ /muːd/ NOUN
NOUN [C, SING] (**moods**) **1** [C] Your **mood** is the way you are feeling at a particular time. If you are in a good **mood**, you feel cheerful. If you are in a bad **mood**, you feel angry and impatient. ❑ *He is clearly in a good mood today.* ❑ *Lily was in one of her aggressive moods.* **2** [C] If someone is **in a mood**, the way they are behaving shows that they are feeling angry and impatient. = temper ❑ *She was obviously in a mood.* **3** [SING] The **mood** of a group of people is the way that they think and feel about an idea, event, or question at a particular time. ❑ *The government seemed to be in tune with the popular mood.* **4** [C] The **mood** of a place is the general impression that you get of it. = atmosphere ❑ *First set the mood with music.*
PHRASE **in the mood for** or **in the mood to** If you say that you are **in the mood for** something, you mean that you want to do it or have it. If you say that you are **in no mood to** do something, you mean that you do not want to do it or have it. ❑ *After a day of air and activity, you should be in the mood for a good meal.*

moody /ˈmuːdi/ ADJ (**moodier, moodiest**) **1** If you describe someone as **moody**, you mean that their feelings and behaviour change frequently, and in particular that they often become depressed or angry without any warning. ❑ *David's mother was unstable and moody.* **2** If you describe a picture, film, or piece of music as **moody**, you mean that it suggests particular emotions, especially sad ones. = atmospheric ❑ *moody black and white photographs* **moodi·ly** /ˈmuːdɪli/ ADV ❑ *He sat and stared moodily out of the window.*
moodi·ness /ˈmuːdinəs/ NOUN [U] ❑ *His moodiness may have been caused by his poor health.*

✪**moon** ♦◇◇ /muːn/ NOUN [SING, C] (**moons**) **1** [SING] [usu 'the' moon, also 'full/new' moon] The **moon** is the object that you can often see in the sky at night. It goes around the earth once every four weeks, and as it does so its appearance changes from a circle to part of a circle. ❑ *the first man on the moon* ❑ *the light of a full moon* ❑ *The moon orbits the earth approximately once each month.* **2** [C] A **moon** is an object similar to a small planet that travels around a planet. ❑ *Neptune's large moon*

moor /mʊə/ NOUN, VERB
NOUN [C, U] (**moors**) **1** [C, U] (*mainly BrE*) A **moor** is an area

of open and usually high land with poor soil that is covered mainly with grass and heather. ❑ *Colliford is higher, right up on the moors.* **2** [c] The **Moors** were a Muslim people who established a civilization in North Africa and Spain between the 8th and the 15th centuries AD.
VERB [I, T] (**moors, mooring, moored**) If you **moor**, or **moor** a boat somewhere, you stop and tie it to the land with a rope or chain so that it cannot move away. = tie up ❑ *She had moored her barge on the right bank of the river.* ❑ *I decided to moor near some tourist boats.*

✪ **mor·al** ◆◇◇ /'mɒrəl, AmE 'mɔːr-/ NOUN, ADJ
NOUN [PL, C] (**morals**) **1** [PL] **Morals** are principles and beliefs concerning right and wrong behaviour. ❑ *Western ideas and morals* **2** [c] The **moral** of a story or event is what you learn from it about how you should or should not behave. = message ❑ *I think the moral of the story is let the buyer beware.*
ADJ **1** [moral + N] **Moral** means relating to beliefs about what is right or wrong. = ethical ❑ *She describes her own moral dilemma in making the film.* ❑ *matters of church doctrine and moral teaching* ❑ *the moral issues involved in 'playing God'* **2** [moral + N] **Moral** courage or duty is based on what you believe is right or acceptable, rather than on what the law says should be done. ❑ *The government had a moral, if not a legal, duty to pay compensation.* **3** A **moral** person behaves in a way that is believed by most people to be good and right. = ethical ❑ *The people who will be on the committee are moral, cultured, competent people.* **4** [moral + N] If you give someone **moral** support, you encourage them in what they are doing by expressing approval. ❑ *Moral as well as financial support is what the West should provide.*
✪ **mor·al·ly** /'mɒrəli, AmE 'mɔːr-/ ADV **1** = ethically ❑ *When, if ever, is it morally justifiable to allow a patient to die?* ❑ *Is there really morally any difference between slaughtering a cow for food and a horse for food?* **2** [morally with V] ❑ *Art is not there to improve you morally.*
✦ **moral victory** → see **victory**

mo·rale /mə'rɑːl, -'ræl/ NOUN [U] **Morale** is the amount of confidence and cheerfulness that a group of people have. ❑ *Many pilots are suffering from low morale.*

mo·ral·ity /mə'ræliti/ NOUN [U, C] (**moralities**) **1** [U] **Morality** is the belief that some behaviour is right and acceptable and that other behaviour is wrong. ❑ *standards of morality and justice in society* **2** [C] A **morality** is a system of principles and values concerning people's behaviour, which is generally accepted by a society or by a particular group of people. = ethic ❑ *a morality that is sexist* **3** [U] The **morality of** something is how right or acceptable it is. ❑ *the arguments about the morality of blood sports*

more ◆◆◆ /mɔː/ DET, PRON, QUANT, ADV, ADJ
DET **1** You use **more** to indicate that there is a greater amount of something than before or than average, or than something else. You can use 'a little', 'a lot', 'a bit', 'far', and 'much' in front of **more**. ❑ *More and more people are surviving heart attacks.* ❑ *He spent more time perfecting his dance moves instead of gym work.* **2** You use **more** to refer to an additional thing or amount. You can use 'a little', 'a lot', 'a bit', 'far', and 'much' in front of **more**. ❑ *They needed more time to consider whether to hold an inquiry.*
PRON **1** **More** is a greater amount of something than before or than average, or than something else. You can use 'a little', 'a lot', 'a bit', 'far', and 'much' in front of **more**. ❑ *As the level of work increased from light to heavy, workers ate more.* **2** **More** means an additional thing or amount. You can use 'a little', 'a lot', 'a bit', 'far', and 'much' in front of **more**. ❑ *Oxfam has appealed to western nations to do more to help the refugees.*
PHRASES **what's more** (*emphasis*) You can use **what is more** or **what's more** to introduce an extra piece of information which supports or emphasizes the point you are making. = moreover, furthermore ❑ *Many more institutions, especially banks, were allowed to lend money for mortgages, and what was more, banks could lend out more money than they actually held.*
some more You can use **some more** to indicate that something continues to happen for a further period of time.

QUANT [more 'of' DEF-N] You use **more of** to indicate that there is a greater amount of something than before or than average, or than something else. You can use 'a little', 'a lot', 'a bit', 'far', and 'much' in front of **more of**. ❑ *Employees may face increasing pressure to take on more of their own medical costs in retirement.*
ADV **1** [more + ADJ/ADV] You use **more** to indicate that something or someone has a greater amount of a quality than they used to or than is average or usual. ❑ *Prison conditions have become more brutal.* **2** If you say that something is **more** one thing **than** another, you mean that it is like the first thing rather than the second. ❑ *He's more like a film star than a lifeguard, really.* ❑ *Sue screamed, not loudly, more in surprise than terror.* **3** [more with V] If you do something **more** than before or **more** than someone else, you do it to a greater extent or more often. ❑ *When we are tired, tense, depressed, or unwell, we feel pain much more.* **4** [more after V] You can use **more** to indicate that something continues to happen for a further period of time. ❑ *Things might have been different if I'd talked a bit more.* **5** You use **more** to indicate that something is repeated. For example, if you do something 'once more', you do it again once. ❑ *This train would stop twice more in the suburbs before rolling southeast towards Baltimore.* **6** [more + ADV/ADJ] You use **more** in conversations when you want to draw someone's attention to something interesting or important that you are about to say. ❑ *More seriously for him, there are members who say he is wrong on this issue.*
PHRASES **more than** **1** You use **more than** before a number or amount to say that the actual number or amount is even greater. = over ❑ *The Afghan authorities say the airport had been closed for more than a year.* **2** If something is **more than** a particular thing, it has greater value or importance than this thing. ❑ *He's more than a coach, he's a friend.* **3** You use **more than** to say that something is true to a greater degree than is necessary or than average. ❑ *The company has more than enough cash available to refinance the loan.*
more and more You can use **more and more** to indicate that something is becoming greater in amount, extent, or degree all the time. ❑ *Her life was heading more and more where she wanted it to go.*
more or less (*vagueness*) If something is **more or less** true, it is true in a general way, but is not completely true. ❑ *The conference is more or less over.*
ADJ [more + N] You use **more** to refer to an additional thing or amount. ❑ *We stayed in Danville two more days.*

✪ **more·over** ◆◇◇ /mɔː'rəʊvə/ ADV (*formal*) You use **moreover** to introduce a piece of information that adds to or supports the previous statement. = furthermore, in addition ❑ *She saw that there was indeed a man immediately behind her. Moreover, he was observing her strangely.* ❑ *The young find everything so simple. The young, moreover, see it as their duty to be happy and do their best to be so.* ❑ *A new species, it was unique to Bali – moreover, it is this island's only endemic bird.*

morn·ing ◆◆◆ /'mɔːnɪŋ/ NOUN
NOUN [C, U, SING] (**mornings**) **1** [C, U] The **morning** is the part of each day between the time that people usually wake up and 12 o'clock noon or lunchtime. ❑ *During the morning your guide will take you around the city.* ❑ *On Sunday morning Bill was woken by the telephone.* **2** [SING] If you refer to a particular time in **the morning**, you mean a time between 12 o'clock midnight and 12 o'clock noon. ❑ *I often stayed up until two or three in the morning.*
PHRASES **in the morning** If you say that something will happen **in the morning**, you mean that it will happen during the morning of the following day. ❑ *I'll fly it to St Louis in the morning.*
morning, noon and night If you say that something happens **morning, noon and night**, you mean that it happens all the time. ❑ *You get fit by playing the game, day in, day out, morning, noon and night.*

mor·tal /'mɔːtəl/ ADJ, NOUN
ADJ **1** If you refer to the fact that people are **mortal**, you mean that they have to die and cannot live forever.

❏ *A man is deliberately designed to be mortal. He grows, he ages, and he dies.* **2** [mortal + N] You can use **mortal** to show that something is very serious or may cause death. ❏ *The police were defending themselves and others against mortal danger.* **3** [mortal + N] You can use **mortal** to emphasize that a feeling is extremely great or severe. ❏ *When self-esteem is high, we lose our mortal fear of jealousy.* NOUN [c] (**mortals**) You can describe someone as a **mortal** when you want to say that they are an ordinary person. = human ❏ *Tickets seem unobtainable to the ordinary mortal.*

mor·tal·ly /ˈmɔːtəli/ ADV **1** *He falls, mortally wounded.* **2** *Candace admits to having been 'mortally embarrassed'.*

mor·tal·ity /mɔːˈtælɪti/ NOUN [u] **1 Mortality** refers to the fact that people have to die and cannot live forever. ❏ *She has suddenly come face to face with her own mortality.* **2** The **mortality** in a particular place or situation is the number of people who die. = death rate ❏ *The nation's infant mortality rate has reached a record low.*

mor·tar /ˈmɔːtə/ NOUN [c, u] (**mortars**) **1** [c] A **mortar** is a big gun that fires missiles high into the air over a short distance. ❏ *The two sides exchanged fire with mortars and small arms.* **2** [u] **Mortar** is a mixture of sand, water, and cement or lime which is put between bricks to hold them together. ❏ *the mortar between the bricks* **3** [c] A **mortar** is a bowl in which you can crush things such as herbs, spices, or grain using a rod called a pestle. ❏ *Use a mortar and pestle to crush the shells and claws.*

✪ **mort·gage** ◆◆◇ /ˈmɔːgɪdʒ/ NOUN, VERB
NOUN [c] (**mortgages**) A **mortgage** is a loan of money which you get from a bank or building society in order to buy a house. ❏ *an increase in mortgage rates* ❏ *The borrower was free to repay the mortgage at any time.*
VERB [T] (**mortgages, mortgaging, mortgaged**) If you **mortgage** your house or land, you use it as a guarantee to a company in order to borrow money from them. ❏ *They had to mortgage their home to pay the bills.*

mosque /mɒsk/ NOUN [c] (**mosques**) A **mosque** is a building where Muslims go to worship.

most ◆◆◆ /məʊst/ QUANT, DET, PRON, ADJ, ADV
QUANT [most 'of' DEF-N] You use **most of** to refer to the majority of a group of things or people or the largest part of something. ❏ *Most of the houses in the capital don't have indoor plumbing.* ❏ *By stopping smoking you are undoing most of the damage smoking has caused.*
PHRASE **most of all** You use **most of all** to indicate that something happens or is true to a greater extent than anything else.
DET You use **most** to refer to the majority of a group of things or people or the largest part of something. ❏ *Most people think the queen has done a good job over the last 60 years.*
PRON **1 Most** means the majority of a group of things or people or the largest part of something. ❏ *Seventeen civilians were hurt. Most are students who had been attending a twenty-first birthday party.* **2** The **most** means a larger amount than anyone or anything else, or the largest amount possible. ❏ *The most they earn in a day is fifty roubles.*
PHRASES **at most** or **at the most** You use **at most** or **at the most** to say that a number or amount is the maximum that is possible and that the actual number or amount may be smaller. ❏ *Poach the pears in apple juice or water and sugar for ten minutes at most.*
make the most of something If you **make the most of** something, you get the maximum use or advantage from it. ❏ *Happiness is the ability to make the most of what you have.*
ADJ ['the' most + N] You use **the most** to mean a larger amount than anyone or anything else, or the largest amount possible. ❏ *The president himself won the most votes.*
ADV **1** [most with v] You use **most** to indicate that something is true or happens to a greater degree or extent than anything else. ❏ *What she feared most was becoming like her mother.* ❏ *Professor Morris, the person he most hated* **2** [most + ADJ/ADV] You use **most** to indicate that someone or something has a greater amount of a particular quality than most other things of its kind. ❏ *Her children had the*

best, most elaborate birthday parties in the neighbourhood. ❏ *He was one of the most influential performers of modern jazz.* **3** ['the' most after v] If you do something **the most**, you do it to the greatest extent possible or with the greatest frequency. ❏ *What question are you asked the most?* **4** [most + ADV/ADJ] You use **most** in conversations when you want to draw someone's attention to something very interesting or important that you are about to say. ❏ *Most surprisingly, quite a few said they don't intend to vote at all.*

most·ly ◆◇◇ /ˈməʊstli/ ADV [mostly with CL/GROUP] You use **mostly** to indicate that a statement is generally true, for example true about the majority of a group of things or people, true most of the time, or true in most respects. = mainly ❏ *I am working with mostly highly motivated people.* ❏ *Cars are mostly metal.*

moth·er ◆◆◆ /ˈmʌðə/ NOUN, VERB
NOUN [c] (**mothers**) Your **mother** is the woman who gave birth to you. You can also call someone your **mother** if she brings you up as if she was this woman. ❏ *She sat on the edge of her mother's bed.* ❏ *She's an English teacher and a mother of two children.*
VERB [T] (**mothers, mothering, mothered**) **1** If a woman **mothers** a child, she takes care of it and brings it up, usually because she is its mother. ❏ *Colleen had dreamed of mothering a large family.* **2** If you **mother** someone, you treat them with great care and affection, as if they were a small child. ❏ *Stop mothering me.*

moth·er·hood /ˈmʌðəhʊd/ NOUN [u] **Motherhood** is the state of being a mother. ❏ *women who try to combine work and motherhood*

mother-in-law NOUN [c] (**mothers-in-law**) Someone's **mother-in-law** is the mother of their husband or wife.

✪ **moth·er tongue** NOUN [c] (**mother tongues**) [oft POSS + mother tongue] Your **mother tongue** is the language that you learn when you are a baby. = native tongue, first language ❏ *The islanders speak English, but their mother tongue is Gaelic.* ❏ *A truly bilingual person has not one mother tongue, but two.*

✪ **mo·tion** ◆◇◇ /ˈməʊʃən/ NOUN, VERB (*academic word*)
NOUN [u, c] (**motions**) **1** [u] **Motion** is the activity or process of continually changing position or moving from one place to another. = movement ❏ *the laws governing light, sound, and motion* ❏ *One group of muscles sets the next group in motion.* **2** [c] A **motion** is an action, gesture, or movement. = movement ❏ *He made a neat chopping motion with his hand.* **3** [c] A **motion** is a formal proposal or statement in a meeting, debate, or trial, which is discussed and then voted on or decided on. ❏ *The conference is now debating the motion and will vote on it shortly.* ❏ *Opposition parties are likely to bring a no-confidence motion against the government.*
PHRASES **go through the motions** If you say that someone **is going through the motions**, you think they are only saying or doing something because it is expected of them without being interested, enthusiastic, or sympathetic. ❏ *'You really don't care, do you?' she said quietly. 'You're just going through the motions.'* ❏ *The startled players went through the motions of the rest of the script.* ❏ *The Home Office is 'merely going through the motions so that they can come back with a compulsory scheme,' he said.*
in motion If a process or event is **in motion**, it is happening. If it is set **in motion**, it is happening or beginning to happen. ❏ *The current chain of events was set in motion by that kidnapping.*
set the wheels in motion If someone **sets the wheels in motion**, they take the necessary action to make something start happening. ❏ *I have set the wheels in motion to sell their Arizona ranch.*
VERB [i, T] (**motions, motioning, motioned**) If you **motion** to someone, you move your hand or head as a way of telling them to do something or telling them where to go. = signal, gesture ❏ *She motioned for the locked front doors to be opened.* ❏ *He stood aside and motioned Don to the door.*

✪ **mo·ti·vate** ◆◇◇ /ˈməʊtɪveɪt/ VERB [T] (**motivates, motivating, motivated**) (*academic word*) **1** If you **are motivated** by something, especially an emotion, it causes you to behave in a particular way. ❏ *They are motivated by*

m

a need to achieve. ❑ *The crime was not politically motivated.*
2 If someone **motivates** you to do something, they make
you feel determined to do it. = inspire ❑ *How do you
motivate people to work hard and efficiently?* ❑ *Never let it be
said that the manager doesn't know how to motivate his players.*
mo·ti·vat·ed /ˈməʊtɪveɪtɪd/ ADJ ❑ *highly motivated
employees*

✪ **mo·ti·va·tion** /ˌməʊtɪˈveɪʃən/ NOUN [u, c]
(**motivations**) **1** [u] **Motivation** is an emotion that causes
you to behave in a particular way. = inspiration,
determination ❑ *His poor performance may be attributed to
lack of motivation rather than to reading difficulties.* **2** [u]
Motivation is the act of making someone feel determined
to achieve something. = inspiration ❑ *Given parental
motivation, we are optimistic about the ability of people to
change.* **3** [c] Your **motivation** for doing something is
what causes you to want to do it. ❑ *Money is my motivation.*

✪ **mo·tive** /ˈməʊtɪv/ NOUN [c] (**motives**) (*academic word*)
Your **motive** for doing something is your reason for doing
it. = reason, grounds, motivation ❑ *Police have ruled out
robbery as a motive for the killing.* ❑ *the motives and objectives
of British foreign policy* ❑ *The doctor's motive was to bring an
end to his patient's suffering.*

mo·tor ♦♦◇ /ˈməʊtə/ NOUN, ADJ
NOUN [c] (**motors**) The **motor** in a machine, vehicle, or
boat is the part that uses electricity or fuel to produce
movement, so that the machine, vehicle, or boat can
work. = engine ❑ *She got in and started the motor.*
ADJ **1** [motor + N] **Motor** vehicles and boats have a petrol
or diesel engine. ❑ *Theft of motor vehicles is up by 15.9%.*
2 (*mainly BrE; in AmE, usually use* **automotive**) **Motor** is
used to describe activities relating to vehicles such as cars
and buses.
→ See also **motoring**

motor·bike /ˈməʊtəbaɪk/ NOUN [c] (**motorbikes**) (*BrE*)
A **motorbike** is the same as a **motorcycle**.

motor·cycle /ˈməʊtəsaɪkəl/ NOUN [c] (**motorcycles**)
A **motorcycle** is a vehicle with two wheels and an engine.
= motorbike

motor·cyclist /ˈməʊtəsaɪklɪst/ NOUN [c]
(**motorcyclists**) A **motorcyclist** is a person who rides a
motorcycle.

mo·tor·ing /ˈməʊtərɪŋ/ ADJ (*mainly BrE; in AmE, usually
use* **driving**) **Motoring** means relating to cars and driving.

✪ **mo·tor·ist** /ˈməʊtərɪst/ NOUN [c] (**motorists**)
A **motorist** is a person who drives a car. = driver;
≠ pedestrian ❑ *Police urged motorists to take extra care on the
roads.* ❑ *Two-thirds (66.3%) of motorists were driving at, or
above, the speed limit.* ❑ *a scene witnessed by a passing
motorist*

motor·way /ˈməʊtəweɪ/ NOUN [c, u] (**motorways**) (*BrE;
in AmE, usually use* **freeway**) A **motorway** is a major road
that has been specially built for fast travel over long
distances. Motorways have several lanes and special places
where traffic gets on and leaves.

mot·to /ˈmɒtəʊ/ NOUN [c] (**mottoes** or **mottos**) A **motto**
is a short sentence or phrase that expresses a rule for
sensible behaviour, especially a way of behaving in a
particular situation. ❑ *'Stay true to yourself' has always been
his motto.*

mould /məʊld/ NOUN, VERB (in AmE, use **mold**)
NOUN [c, u] (**moulds**) **1** [c] A **mould** is a hollow container
that you pour liquid into. When the liquid becomes solid,
it takes the same shape as the mould. ❑ *He makes plastic
reusable moulds.* **2** [c] If a person fits into or is cast in a
mould of a particular kind, they have the characteristics,
attitudes, behaviour, or lifestyle that are typical of that
type of person. ❑ *He could never be accused of fitting the
mould.* **3** [c, u] **Mould** is a soft grey, green, or blue
substance that sometimes forms in spots on old food or on
damp walls or clothes. ❑ *She discovered black and green
mould growing in her hall cupboard.*
PHRASE **break the mould** If you say that someone **breaks
the mould**, you mean that they do completely different
things from what has been done before or from what is
usually done.

VERB [T, I] (**moulds, moulding, moulded**) **1** [T] If you
mould a soft substance such as plastic or clay, you make it
into a particular shape or into an object. ❑ *He would
dampen the clay and begin to mould it into an entirely different
shape.* **2** [T] To **mould** someone or something means to
change or influence them over a period of time so that
they develop in a particular way. = form, shape ❑ *It was
a very safe, long childhood with Diane, and she really moulded
my ideas a lot.* **3** [I, T] When something **moulds** to an
object or when you **mould** it there, it fits around the
object tightly so that the shape of the object can still be
seen. ❑ *It looked as though the plastic wrap was moulded to
the fruit.*

mound /maʊnd/ NOUN [c] (**mounds**) **1** A **mound** of
something is a large, rounded pile of it. ❑ *The bulldozers
piled up huge mounds of earth.* **2** In baseball, the **mound** is
the raised area where the pitcher stands when he or she
throws the ball. ❑ *He went to the mound to talk with a
struggling pitcher who spoke only Spanish.*

mount ♦◇◇ /maʊnt/ VERB, NOUN
VERB [I, T] (**mounts, mounting, mounted**) **1** [I, T] If you
mount a campaign or event, you organize it and make it
take place. = organize ❑ *The ANC announced it was
mounting a major campaign of mass political protests.* **2** [I] If
something **mounts**, it increases in intensity. = rise ❑ *For
several hours, tension mounted.* **3** [I] If something **mounts**, it
increases in quantity. ❑ *The uncollected rubbish mounts in
city streets.* **4** [T] (*formal*) If you **mount** the stairs or a
platform, you go up the stairs or go up onto the platform.
❑ *Larry was mounting the stairs up into the attic.* **5** [T] If you
mount a horse or motorcycle, you climb on to it so that
you can ride it. = get on ❑ *A man in a crash helmet was
mounting a motorcycle.* **6** [T] If you **mount** an object on
something, you fix it there firmly. ❑ *Her husband mounts
the work on velour paper and makes the frame.* **7** [T] If you
mount an exhibition or display, you organize and present
it. = put on, stage ❑ *The gallery has mounted an exhibition
of art by Irish women painters.*
PHRASAL VERB **mount up** To **mount up** means the same as
to **mount 3**. ❑ *Her medical bills mounted up.*
NOUN [c] (**mounts**) **Mount** is used as part of the name of a
mountain. ❑ *Mount Everest*
-mounted /ˈmaʊntɪd/ COMB ❑ *She installed a wall-mounted
electric fan.*
→ See also **mounted**

✪ **moun·tain** ♦♦◇ /ˈmaʊntɪn, AmE -tən/ NOUN, QUANT
NOUN [c] (**mountains**) A **mountain** is a very high area of
land with steep sides. ❑ *Mount McKinley, in Alaska, is the
highest mountain in North America.* ❑ *the rugged mountains of
Wales*
PHRASE **a mountain to climb** (*journalism*) If you say that
someone has **a mountain to climb**, you mean that it will
be difficult for them to achieve what they want to achieve.
❑ *'We had a mountain to climb after the second goal went in,'
said Crosby.*
QUANT (*informal, emphasis*) If you talk about a **mountain** of
something, or **mountains** of something, you are
emphasizing that there is a large amount of it. ❑ *They are
faced with a mountain of bureaucracy.*

✪ **moun·tain·ous** /ˈmaʊntɪnəs/ ADJ **1** A **mountainous**
place has a lot of mountains. = hilly; ≠ flat ❑ *the
mountainous region of New Mexico* ❑ *the more mountainous
terrain of New Hampshire* **2** [mountainous + N] You use
mountainous to emphasize that something is great in size,
quantity, or degree. = huge ❑ *The plan is designed to
reduce some of the company's mountainous debt.*

moun·tain·side /ˈmaʊntɪnsaɪd/ NOUN [c]
(**mountainsides**) A **mountainside** is one of the steep sides
of a mountain. ❑ *The couple trudged up the dark
mountainside.*

mount·ed /ˈmaʊntɪd/ ADJ [mounted + N] **Mounted**
police or soldiers ride horses when they are on duty.
❑ *A dozen mounted police rode into the square.*
→ See also **mount**

mourn /mɔːn/ VERB [I, T] (**mourns, mourning, mourned**)
1 If you **mourn** someone who has died or **mourn for**
them, you are very sad that they have died and show your

M

sorrow in the way that you behave. ❑ *Joan still mourns her father.* ❑ *He mourned for his valiant men.* **2** If you **mourn** something or **mourn for** it, you regret that you no longer have it and show your regret in the way that you behave. ❑ *We mourned the loss of our cities.*

mouse /maʊs/ NOUN [C] (**mice**) **1** A **mouse** is a small, furry animal with a long tail. ❑ *a mouse running in a wheel in its cage* **2** (computing) A **mouse** is a device that is connected to a computer. By moving it over a flat surface and pressing its buttons, you can move the cursor around the screen and do things without using the keyboard. ❑ *Her message had been written; all she had to do was click the mouse.*

mouth ♦♦◇ NOUN, VERB

NOUN /maʊθ/ [C] (**mouths** /maʊðz/) **1** Your **mouth** is the area of your face where your lips are, or the space behind your lips where your teeth and tongue are. ❑ *She clamped her hand against her mouth.* **2** You can say that someone has a particular kind of **mouth** to indicate that they speak in a particular kind of way or that they say particular kinds of things. ❑ *I've always had a loud mouth, I refuse to be silenced.* **3** The **mouth** of a cave, hole, or bottle is its entrance or opening. = entrance ❑ *By the mouth of the tunnel he bent to retie his shoelace.* **4** The **mouth** of a river is the place where it flows into the sea. ❑ *the town at the mouth of the River Fox*

PHRASES **mouths to feed** If you have a number of **mouths to feed**, you have the responsibility of earning enough money to feed and take care of that number of people. ❑ *He had to feed his family on the equivalent of seven hundred dollars a month and, with five mouths to feed, he found this very hard.*

open your mouth (*emphasis*) If you say that someone does not **open** their **mouth**, you are emphasizing that they never say anything at all. ❑ *Sometimes I hardly dare open my mouth.*

keep your mouth shut If you **keep** your **mouth shut** about something, you do not talk about it, especially because it is a secret. ❑ *You wouldn't be here now if she'd kept her mouth shut.*

VERB /maʊð/ [T] (**mouths, mouthing, mouthed**) If you **mouth** something, you form words with your lips without making any sound. ❑ *I mouthed a goodbye and hurried in behind Mummy.*

-mouthed /-maʊðd/ COMB **1** *He straightened up and looked at me, open-mouthed.* **2** *Sam, their smart-mouthed teenage son* **3** *He put the flowers in a wide-mouthed blue vase.*

✦ **live hand to mouth** → see **hand**; **heart in your mouth** → see **heart**; **from the horse's mouth** → see **horse**; **put your money where your mouth is** → see **money**; **word of mouth** → see **word**

❍**move** ♦♦♦ /muːv/ VERB, NOUN

VERB [I, T] (**moves, moving, moved**) **1** [I, T] When you **move** something or when it **moves**, its position changes and it does not remain still. ❑ *She moved the sheaf of papers into position.* ❑ *You can move the camera both vertically and horizontally.* ❑ *A traffic policeman asked him to move his car.* ❑ *The train began to move.* ❑ *I could see the branches of the trees moving back and forth.* **2** [I] When you **move**, you change your position or go to a different place. = shift, go, proceed; ≠ stop, halt, remain still ❑ *She waited for him to get up, but he didn't move.* ❑ *He moved around the room, putting his possessions together.* ❑ *She moved away from the window.* **3** [I] If you **move**, you act or you begin to do something. = act ❑ *Industrialists must move fast to take advantage of new opportunities in Eastern Europe.* **4** [I] If a person or company **moves**, they leave the building where they have been living or working, and they go to live or work in a different place, taking their possessions with them. ❑ *Two people in love are at home wherever they are, no matter how often they move.* ❑ *She had often considered moving to Seattle.* **5** [T] If people in authority **move** someone, they make that person go from one place or job to another one. = transfer ❑ *His superiors moved him to another parish.* **6** [I] If you **move from** one job or interest to another, you change to it. ❑ *He moved from being a part-time tutor to being a lecturer in social history.* **7** [I] If you **move to** a new topic in a conversation, you start talking

about something different. ❑ *Let's move to another subject, Dan.* **8** [T] If you **move** an event or the date of an event, you change the time at which it happens. ❑ *The club has moved its meeting to Saturday, January 22nd.* **9** [I] If you **move** towards a particular state, activity, or opinion, you start to be in that state, do that activity, or have that opinion. ❑ *The Labour Party has moved to the right and become like your Democratic Party.* **10** [I] If a situation or process **is moving**, it is developing or progressing, rather than staying still. ❑ *Events are moving fast.* **11** [T] If you say that you will not **be moved**, you mean that you have come to a decision and nothing will change your mind. = budge ❑ *Everyone thought I was crazy to go back, but I wouldn't be moved.* **12** [T] If something **moves** you to do something, it influences you and causes you to do it. ❑ *It was punk that first moved him to join a band seriously.* **13** [T] If something **moves** you, it has an effect on your emotions and causes you to feel sadness or sympathy for another person. ❑ *These stories surprised and moved me.* **14** [I] If you say that someone **moves in** a particular society, circle, or world, you mean that they know people in a particular social class or group and spend most of their time with them. ❑ *She moves in high-society circles in Palm Beach.* **15** [I, T] At a meeting, if you **move for** something or **move that** something should happen, you formally suggest it so that everyone present can vote on it. = put forward, propose ❑ *Somebody needs to move for an adjournment.*

PHRASAL VERBS **move in** **1** When you **move in** somewhere, you begin to live there as your home. ❑ *Her house was in perfect order when she moved in.* ❑ *Her husband had moved in with a younger woman.* **2** If police, soldiers, or attackers **move in**, they go towards a place or person in order to deal with or attack them. ❑ *There were violent and chaotic scenes when police moved in to disperse the crowd.* **3** If someone **moves in on** an area of activity which was previously only done by a particular group of people, they start becoming involved with it for the first time. ❑ *I don't want another guy moving in on my territory, you know?*

move off When you **move off**, you start moving away from a place. = set off ❑ *Gil waved his hand and the car moved off.*

move on **1** When you **move on** somewhere, you leave the place where you have been staying or waiting and go there. ❑ *Mr Brooke moved on from LA to Phoenix.* **2** If someone such as a police officer **moves** you **on**, they order you to stop standing in a particular place and to go somewhere else. ❑ *Eventually the police were called to move them on.* **3** If you **move on**, you finish or stop one activity and start doing something different. ❑ *She ran this shop for ten years before deciding to move on to fresh challenges.*

move out If you **move out**, you stop living in a particular house or place and go to live somewhere else. ❑ *The harassment had become too much to tolerate and he decided to move out.*

move over **1** If you **move over to** a new system or way of doing something, you change to it. = change ❑ *The government is having to introduce some difficult changes, particularly in moving over to a market economy.* **2** If someone **moves over**, they leave their job or position in order to let someone else have it. ❑ *Mr Jenkins should make balanced programmes or move over and let someone else who can.* **3** If you **move over**, you change your position in order to make room for someone else. ❑ *Move over and let me drive.*

move up **1** If you **move up**, you change your position, especially in order to be nearer someone or to make room for someone else. ❑ *Move up, John, and let the lady sit down.* **2** If someone or something **moves up**, they go to a higher level, grade, or class. = go up ❑ *Share prices moved up.*

NOUN [C] (**moves**) **1** When someone makes a **move**, they change their position or go to a different place. = movement, motion, shift ❑ *The doctor made a move towards the door.* ❑ *Daniel's eyes followed her every move.* **2** A **move** is an action that you take in order to achieve something. ❑ *The one-point cut in interest rates was a wise move.* ❑ *It may also be a good move to suggest she talks things over.* **3** A **move** is an occasion when a person or company leaves the building where they have been living or working, and they go to live or work in a different place, taking their possessions with them. ❑ *Modigliani announced his move to Montparnasse in 1909.* **4** A **move** from one job or interest to another is a change to it. ❑ *His move to the chairmanship means he will take a less active role in day-to-day management.* **5** A **move** towards a particular state, activity, or opinion is the act of starting to be in that state, do that activity, or have that opinion. = shift ❑ *His move to the left was not a sudden leap but a natural working out of ideas.* **6** A **move** is an act of putting a chess piece or other counter in a different position on a board when it is your turn to do so in a game. ❑ *With no idea of what to do for my next move, my hand hovered over the board.*

PHRASES **one false move** or **a false move** If you say that one **false move** will cause a disaster, you mean that you or someone else must not make any mistakes because the situation is so difficult or dangerous. ❑ *He knew one false move would end in death.*

make a move **1** If you **make a move**, you prepare or begin to leave one place and go somewhere else. ❑ *He glanced at his wristwatch. 'I suppose we'd better make a move'.* **2** If you **make a move**, you take a course of action. ❑ *The week before the deal was supposed to close, fifteen Japanese banks made a move to pull out.*

on the move If you are **on the move**, you are going from one place to another. ❑ *Jack never wanted to stay in one place for very long, so they were always on the move.*

moved /muːvd/ ADJ ❑ *Those who listened to him were deeply moved.*

✦ **move a muscle** → see **muscle**

⚙ **move·ment** ♦♦◇ /ˈmuːvmənt/ NOUN [C, U, PL]
(**movements**) **1** [C] A **movement** is a group of people who share the same beliefs, ideas, or aims. ❑ *It's part of a broader nationalist movement that's gaining strength throughout the country.* ❑ *the women's movement* **2** [C, U] **Movement** involves changing position or going from one place to another. = motion ❑ *They actually monitor the movement of the fish going up river.* ❑ *There was movement behind the window in the back door.* ❑ *the movements of a large removal van* ❑ *Her hand movements are becoming more animated.* **3** [C, U] A **movement** is a planned change in position that an army makes during a battle or military exercise. ❑ *There are reports of fresh troop movements across the border.* **4** [C, U] **Movement** is a gradual development or change of an attitude, opinion, or policy. = shift, change, development, progress ❑ *the movement towards democracy in Latin America* ❑ *Participants at the peace talks believed movement forward was possible.* **5** [PL] Your **movements** are everything that you do or plan to do during a period of time. ❑ *I want a full account of your movements the night Mr Gower was killed.*

VOCABULARY BUILDER

movement NOUN (formal)
Movement is a gradual development or change of an attitude, opinion, or policy.
❑ *Lawyers from both sides say there has been no movement toward a negotiated settlement .*

shift NOUN
A **shift** is a slight change in someone's opinion, a situation, or a policy.
❑ *a shift in government policy*

change NOUN
If there is a **change** in something, it becomes different.
❑ *The ambassador appealed for a change in US policy.*

development NOUN
Development is the gradual growth of something.
❑ *First he surveys Islam's development.*

progress NOUN
Progress is the process of gradually improving or getting nearer to achieving or completing something.
❑ *The two sides made little if any progress towards agreement.*

---

movie ♦♦◇ /ˈmuːvi/ NOUN [C, PL] (**movies**) **1** [C] A **movie** is a series of moving pictures that have been recorded so that they can be shown in a cinema or on television. A movie tells a story, or shows a real situation. ❑ *In the first movie Tony Curtis ever made he played a shop assistant in a grocer's.* **2** [PL] (mainly AmE; in BrE, usually use **the cinema**) You can talk about the **movies** when you are talking about seeing a film in a cinema. ❑ *He took her to the movies.*

mov·ing /ˈmuːvɪŋ/ ADJ **1** If something is **moving**, it makes you feel an emotion such as sadness, pity, or sympathy very strongly. = touching ❑ *It is very moving to see how much strangers can care for each other.* **2** [moving + N] A **moving** model or part of a machine moves or is able to move. ❑ *It also means there are no moving parts to break down.* **mov·ing·ly** /ˈmuːvɪŋli/ ADV [movingly with V] ❑ *You write very movingly of your sister Amy's suicide.*

Mr ♦♦♦ /ˈmɪstə/ NOUN **1 Mr** is used before a man's name when you are speaking or referring to him. ❑ *Mr Grant* ❑ *Mr Bob Price* **2 Mr** is sometimes used in front of words such as 'president' and 'chairman' to address the man who holds the position mentioned. ❑ *Mr President, you're aware of the system.*

Mrs ♦♦♦ /ˈmɪsɪz/ NOUN **Mrs** is used before the name of a married woman when you are speaking or referring to her. ❑ *Hello, Mrs Miles.* ❑ *Mrs Anne Pritchard*

Ms ♦♦♦ /məz, mɪz/ NOUN **Ms** is used, especially in written English, before a woman's name when you are speaking to her or referring to her. If you use **Ms**, you are not specifying if the woman is married or not. ❑ *Ms Brown*

much ♦♦♦ /mʌtʃ/ ADV, DET, PRON, QUANT
ADV **1** [much after V] You use **much** to indicate the great intensity, extent, or degree of something such as an action, feeling, or change. **Much** is usually used with 'so', 'too', and 'very', and in negative clauses with this meaning. ❑ *She laughs too much.* ❑ *Thank you very much.* **2** If something does not happen **much**, it does not happen very often. = often ❑ *He said that his father never talked much about the war.* ❑ *Gwen had not seen her dad all that much, because he mostly worked on the ships.* **3** You use **much** in front of 'too' or comparative adjectives and adverbs in order to emphasize that there is a large amount of a particular quality. = far ❑ *The skin is much too delicate.* **4** If one thing is **much** the same as another thing, it is very similar to it. ❑ *The day ended much as it began.* **5** [much as reply] You use **much** in expressions such as **not much**, **not very much**, and **too much** when replying to questions about amounts. ❑ *'Can you hear it where you live?' He shook his head. 'Not much.'* **6** You use **much** in the expression **how much** to give information about the amount or degree of something. ❑ *She knows how much this upsets me but she persists in doing it.*

PHRASES **much as** You use **much as** to introduce a fact which makes something else you have just said or will say rather surprising. ❑ *Much as they hope to go home tomorrow, they're resigned to staying on until the end of the year.*

as much You use **as much** in expressions such as **'I thought as much'** and **'I guessed as much'** after you have just been told something and you want to say that you already believed or expected it to be true. ❑ *You're waiting for a woman – I thought as much.*

as much as (emphasis) You use **as much as** before an amount to suggest that it is surprisingly large. ❑ *The organizers hope to raise as much as $6M for charity.*

much less You use **much less** after a statement, often a negative one, to indicate that the statement is more true of the person, thing, or situation that you are going to mention next. ❑ *They are always short of water to drink, much less to bathe in.*

not so much If you say that something is not **so much** one thing **as** another, you mean that it is more like the second thing than the first. ❑ *I don't really think of her as a daughter so much as a very good friend.*

so much so You use **so much so** to indicate that your previous statement is true to a very great extent, and therefore it has the result mentioned. ❑ *He himself believed in freedom, so much so that he would rather die than live without it.*

M

very much (*emphasis*) You use **very much** to emphasize that someone or something has a lot of a particular quality, or that the description you are about to give is particularly accurate. ❑ *a man very much in charge of himself* **DET** **1** You use **much** to indicate that you are referring to a large amount of a substance or thing. ❑ *They are grown on the hillsides in full sun, without much water.* ❑ *Japan has been reluctant to offer much aid to Russia.* **2** You use **much** in the expression **how much** to ask questions about amounts or degrees, and also in reported clauses and statements to give information about the amount or degree of something. ❑ *How much money can I afford?* **3** You use **much** in the expression **as much** when you are comparing amounts. ❑ *I shall try, with as much patience as is possible, to explain yet again.* ❑ *Their aim will be to produce as much milk as possible.*
PRON **1** **Much** refers to a large amount of a substance or thing. ❑ *eating too much and drinking too much* **2** ['how' much] You use **much** in the expression **how much** to ask questions about amounts or degrees, and also in reported clauses and statements to give information about the amount or degree of something. ❑ *How much do you earn?*
PHRASE **too much** If a situation or action is **too much for** you, it is so difficult, tiring, or upsetting that you cannot cope with it. ❑ *His inability to stay at one job for long had finally proved too much for her.*
QUANT **1** **Much of** a substance or thing is a large amount of that substance or thing. ❑ *Much of the time we do not notice that we are solving problems.* **2** [with BRD-NEG, much 'of' N-PROPER/PRON] If you do not see **much of** someone, you do not see them very often. ❑ *I don't see much of Tony nowadays.*
✦ **a bit much** → see **bit**

USAGE NOTE
much
Use **much** as a determiner only in front of an uncountable noun. Do not say, for example, 'much benefits'.
*The new dam will bring **many benefits** to the region.*
Use 'how much is' only when you are asking about the price of something. Do not use it to ask about other amounts of money or other units of measurement. Do not say, for example, 'How much is his income?' or 'How much is the temperature outside?'. Use 'What is...?' instead.
***What is** his income?*
***What is** the temperature outside?*

mud /mʌd/ NOUN [U] **Mud** is a sticky mixture of earth and water. ❑ *His uniform was crumpled, untidy, splashed with mud.*

mud·dle /ˈmʌdəl/ NOUN, VERB
NOUN [c, u] (**muddles**) If people or things are **in a muddle**, they are in a state of confusion or disorder. = mess ❑ *My thoughts are all in a muddle.* ❑ *We are going to get into a hopeless muddle.*
VERB [t] (**muddles, muddling, muddled**) If you **muddle** things or people, you get them mixed up, so that you do not know which is which. = mix up, confuse ❑ *Already, one or two critics have begun to muddle the two names.*
PHRASAL VERBS **muddle through** If you **muddle through**, you manage to do something even though you do not have the proper equipment or do not really know how to do it. ❑ *We will muddle through and just play it day by day.* ❑ *They may be able to muddle through the next five years like this.*
muddle up **Muddle up** means the same as **muddle** VERB. ❑ *The question muddles up three separate issues.*
mud·dled up /ˌmʌdəld ˈʌp/ ADJ ❑ *I know that I am getting my words muddled up.*

mug /mʌg/ NOUN, VERB
NOUN [c] (**mugs**) **1** A **mug** is a large, deep cup with straight sides and a handle, used for hot drinks. ❑ *He spooned instant coffee into two of the mugs.* **2** You can use **mug** to refer to the mug and its contents, or to the contents only. ❑ *He had been drinking mugs of coffee to keep himself awake.* **3** (*informal*) Someone's **mug** is their face. ❑ *He managed to get his ugly mug on TV.*
VERB [t] (**mugs, mugging, mugged**) If someone **mugs** you,

they attack you in order to steal your money. ❑ *I was walking out to my car when this guy tried to mug me.*
mug·ging /ˈmʌgɪŋ/ NOUN [c, u] (**muggings**) ❑ *Bank robberies, burglaries, and muggings are reported almost daily in the press.*

✪ **multi·cul·tur·al** /ˌmʌltiˈkʌltʃərəl/ ADJ **Multicultural** means consisting of or relating to people of many different nationalities and cultures. ❑ *children growing up in a multicultural society* ❑ *The school has been attempting to bring a multicultural perspective to its curriculum.*

WORD PARTS
The prefix ***multi-*** often appears in words which refer to something that consists of many things of a particular kind:
multicultural (ADJ)
multinational (ADJ, NOUN)
multicoloured (ADJ)

✪ **multi·cul·tur·al·ism** /ˌmʌltiˈkʌltʃərəlɪzəm/ NOUN [U] **Multiculturalism** is a situation in which all the different cultural or racial groups in a society have equal rights and opportunities, and none is ignored or regarded as unimportant. ❑ *Malik's attempt to start a debate about multiculturalism is commendable.* ❑ *the latest troubled liberal to criticize multiculturalism*

✪ **multi·na·tion·al** /ˌmʌltiˈnæʃənəl/ ADJ, NOUN
ADJ **1** A **multinational** company has branches or owns companies in many different countries. = international ❑ *The multinational company is increasingly becoming a world-wide phenomenon.* ❑ *Not a single multinational firm operates in that country.* **2** **Multinational** armies, organizations, or other groups involve people from several different countries. = international ❑ *The US troops would be part of a multinational force.* **3** **Multinational** countries or regions have a population that is made up of people of several different nationalities. ❑ *We live in a multinational country.*
NOUN [c] (**multinationals**) A **multinational** is a company that has branches or owns companies in many different countries. ❑ *multinationals such as Ford and IBM* ❑ *Large multinationals are also realising that they can become more efficient.*

✪ **multi·ple** /ˈmʌltɪpəl/ ADJ, NOUN
ADJ You use **multiple** to describe things that consist of many parts, involve many people, or have many uses. ❑ *He died of multiple injuries.* ❑ *The most common multiple births are twins, two babies born at the same time.*
NOUN [c] (**multiples**) If one number is a **multiple of** a smaller number, it can be exactly divided by that smaller number. ❑ *Their numerical system, derived from the Babylonians, was based on multiples of the number six.*

✪ **multi·pli·ca·tion** /ˌmʌltɪplɪˈkeɪʃən/ NOUN [U] **1** **Multiplication** is the process of calculating the total of one number multiplied by another. ❑ *There will be simple tests in addition, subtraction, multiplication, and division.* ❑ *formulas that help children learn multiplication tables* **2** The **multiplication** of things of a particular kind is the process or fact of them increasing in number or amount. ❑ *Increasing gravity is known to speed up the multiplication of cells.*

✪ **multi·ply** /ˈmʌltɪplaɪ/ VERB [i, t] (**multiplies, multiplying, multiplied**) **1** [i, t] When something **multiplies** or when you **multiply** it, it increases greatly in number or amount. ❑ *Such disputes multiplied in the eighteenth and nineteenth centuries.* **2** [i] When animals and insects **multiply**, they increase in number by giving birth to large numbers of young. ❑ *These creatures can multiply quickly.* **3** [t] If you **multiply** one number by another, you add the first number to itself as many times as is indicated by the second number. For example 2 multiplied by 3 is equal to 6. ❑ *What do you get if you multiply six by nine?* ❑ *The frequency was multiplied by the distance to find the speed of sound at each temperature.*

multi·tude /ˈmʌltɪtjuːd, AmE -tuːd/ QUANT, NOUN
QUANT ['a' multitude 'of' PL-N] A **multitude of** things or people is a very large number of them. ❑ *There are a*

m

multitude of small, quiet roads to cycle along. ❑ Addiction to drugs can bring a multitude of other problems.
PHRASE **a multitude of sins** If you say that something covers or hides **a multitude of sins**, you mean that it hides something unattractive or does not reveal the true nature of something.
NOUN [C] (multitudes) **1** (written) You can refer to a very large number of people as a **multitude**. = crowd ❑ surrounded by a noisy multitude **2** You can refer to the great majority of people in a particular country or situation as **the multitude** or **the multitudes**. ❑ The hideous truth was hidden from the multitude.

mun·dane /ˌmʌnˈdeɪn/ ADJ, NOUN
ADJ Something that is **mundane** is very ordinary and not at all interesting or unusual. = boring ❑ Be willing to do mundane tasks with good grace.
NOUN [SING] You can refer to mundane things as the **mundane**. ❑ It's an attitude that turns the mundane into something more interesting and exciting.

mu·nici·pal /mjuːˈnɪsɪpəl/ ADJ [municipal + N] **Municipal** means associated with or belonging to a city or town that has its own local government. ❑ The municipal authorities gave the go-ahead for the march. ❑ next month's municipal elections

mur·der ♦♦◇ /ˈmɜːdə/ NOUN, VERB
NOUN [C, U] (murders) **Murder** is the deliberate and illegal killing of a person. ❑ The three accused, aged between 19 and 20, are charged with attempted murder. ❑ She refused to testify, unless the murder charge against her was dropped.
PHRASE **get away with murder** (informal, disapproval) If you say that someone **gets away with murder**, you are complaining that they can do whatever they like without anyone trying to control them or punish them. ❑ His charm and the fact that he is so likeable often allows him to get away with murder.
VERB [T] (murders, murdering, murdered) To **murder** someone means to commit the crime of killing them deliberately. ❑ a thriller about two men who murder a third to see if they can get away with it

mur·der·er /ˈmɜːdərə/ NOUN [C] (murderers) A **murderer** is a person who has murdered someone. ❑ One of these men may have been the murderer.

mur·mur /ˈmɜːmə/ VERB, NOUN
VERB [T] (murmurs, murmuring, murmured) If you **murmur** something, you say it very quietly, so that not many people can hear what you are saying. ❑ He turned and murmured something to the professor. ❑ 'How lovely,' she murmured.
NOUN [C, SING] (murmurs) **1** [C] A **murmur** is something that is said but can hardly be heard. ❑ They spoke in low murmurs. **2** [SING] A **murmur** is a continuous low sound, like the noise of a river or of voices far away. = hum ❑ The piano music mixes with the murmur of conversation. **3** [C] A **murmur of** a particular emotion is a quiet expression of it. ❑ The promise of some basic working rights draws murmurs of approval. **4** [C] A **murmur** is an abnormal sound which is made by the heart and which shows that there is probably something wrong with it. ❑ The doctor said James had now developed a heart murmur.
PHRASE **without a murmur** If someone does something **without a murmur**, they do it without complaining. ❑ Then came the bill and my friend paid up without a murmur.

✪mus·cle ♦◇◇ /ˈmʌsəl/ NOUN
NOUN [C, U] (muscles) **1** [C, U] A **muscle** is a piece of tissue inside your body that connects two bones and which you use when you make a movement. ❑ Keeping your muscles strong and in tone helps you to avoid back problems. ❑ He is suffering from a strained thigh muscle. ❑ There are three types of muscle in the body. **2** [U] If you say that someone has **muscle**, you mean that they have power and influence, which enables them to do difficult things. = clout ❑ Eisenhower used his muscle to persuade Congress to change the law.
PHRASES **flex your muscles** If a group, organization, or country **flexes its muscles**, it does something to impress or frighten people, in order to show them that it has power

and is considering using it. ❑ The Fair Trade Commission has of late been flexing its muscles, cracking down on cases of corruption.
move a muscle If you say that someone did not **move a muscle**, you mean that they stayed absolutely still. ❑ He stood without moving a muscle, unable to believe what his eyes saw so plainly.
PHRASAL VERB **muscle in** (muscles, muscling, muscled) (disapproval) If someone **muscles in** on something, they force their way into a situation where they have no right to be and where they are not welcome, in order to gain some advantage for themselves. ❑ Cohen complained that Kravis was muscling in on his deal.

mus·cu·lar /ˈmʌskjʊlə/ ADJ **1** [muscular + N] **Muscular** means involving or affecting your muscles. ❑ As a general rule, all muscular effort is enhanced by breathing in as the effort is made. **2** If a person or their body is **muscular**, they are very fit and strong, and have firm muscles which are not covered with a lot of fat. ❑ Like most female athletes, she was lean and muscular.

muse /mjuːz/ VERB [I, T] (muses, musing, mused) (written) If you **muse** on something, you think about it, usually saying or writing what you are thinking at the same time. ❑ Many of the papers muse on the fate of the president. ❑ 'As a whole,' she muses, 'the "organized church" turns me off.'
mus·ing /ˈmjuːzɪŋ/ NOUN [C] (musings) ❑ His musings were interrupted by Montagu who came and sat down next to him.

mu·seum ♦♦◇ /mjuːˈziːəm/ NOUN [C] (museums) A **museum** is a building where a large number of interesting and valuable objects, such as works of art or historical items, are kept, studied, and displayed to the public. ❑ For months Malcolm had wanted to visit the New York art museums.

mush·room /ˈmʌʃruːm/ NOUN, VERB
NOUN [C, U] (mushrooms) **Mushrooms** are fungi that you can eat. They have short stems and round tops. ❑ There are many types of wild mushrooms.
VERB [I] (mushrooms, mushrooming, mushroomed) If something such as an industry or a place **mushrooms**, it grows or comes into existence very quickly. ❑ The media training industry has mushroomed over the past decade.

✪mu·sic ♦♦♦ /ˈmjuːzɪk/ NOUN
NOUN [U] **1** **Music** is the pattern of sounds produced by people singing or playing instruments. ❑ classical music ❑ the music of George Gershwin **2** **Music** is the art of creating or performing music. ❑ He went on to study music, specializing in the clarinet. ❑ a music lesson **3** **Music** is the symbols written on paper which represent musical sounds. ❑ He's never been able to read music.
PHRASES **music to your ears** (feelings) If something that you hear is **music to your ears**, it makes you feel very happy. ❑ Popular support – it's music to the ears of any politician.
face the music If you **face the music**, you put yourself in a position where you will be criticized or punished for something you have done. ❑ Sooner or later, I'm going to have to face the music.

✪mu·si·cal ♦◇◇ /ˈmjuːzɪkəl/ ADJ, NOUN
ADJ **1** [musical + N] You use **musical** to indicate that something is connected with playing or studying music. ❑ We have a wealth of musical talent in this region. ❑ Stan Getz's musical career spanned five decades. **2** Someone who is **musical** has a natural ability and interest in music. ❑ I came from a musical family. **3** Sounds that are **musical** are light and pleasant to hear. ❑ He had a soft, almost musical voice.
NOUN [C] (musicals) A **musical** is a play or film that uses singing and dancing in the story. ❑ the smash hit musical, Miss Saigon
mu·si·cal·ly /ˈmjuːzɪkli/ ADV ❑ Musically there is a lot to enjoy.

✪mu·si·cian ♦◇◇ /mjuːˈzɪʃən/ NOUN [C] (musicians) A **musician** is a person who plays a musical instrument as their job or hobby. ❑ He was a brilliant musician. ❑ one of Britain's best known rock musicians

must ◆◆◆ VERB, NOUN

> **Must** is a modal verb. It is followed by the base form of a verb.

VERB /məst, STRONG mʌst/ [MODAL] **1** You use **must** to indicate that you think it is very important or necessary for something to happen. You use **must not** or **mustn't** to indicate that you think it is very important or necessary for something not to happen. ▢ *What you wear should be stylish and clean, and must definitely fit well.* ▢ *You are going to have to take a certain amount of criticism, but you must cope with it.* **2** You use **must** to indicate that it is necessary for something to happen, usually because of a rule or law. ▢ *Candidates must satisfy the general conditions for admission.* ▢ *Mr Allen must pay Mr Farnham's legal costs.* **3** You use **must** to indicate that you are fairly sure that something is the case. ▢ *At 29, Russell must be one of the youngest ever international referees.* ▢ *Claire's car wasn't there so she must have gone to her mother's.* **4** You use **must**, or **must have** with a past participle, to indicate that you believe that something is the case, because of the available evidence. ▢ *'You must be Emma,' said the visitor.* ▢ *Miss Holloway had a weak heart. She must have had a heart attack.* **5** If you say that one thing **must have** happened in order for something else to happen, you mean that it is necessary for the first thing to have happened before the second thing can happen. ▢ *In order to take that job, you must have left another job.* **6** You use **must** to express your intention to do something. ▢ *I must be getting back.* ▢ *I must telephone my parents.* **7** You use **must** to make suggestions or invitations very forcefully. ▢ *You must see a doctor, Frederick.* **8** You use **must** in remarks and comments where you are expressing sympathy. ▢ *This must be a very difficult job for you.* **9** You use **must** in conversation in expressions such as '**I must say**' and '**I must admit**' in order to emphasize a point that you are making. ▢ *This came as a surprise, I must say.* ▢ *I must admit I like looking feminine.* **10** You use **must** in expressions such as '**it must be noted**' and '**it must be remembered**' in order to draw the reader's or listener's attention to what you are about to say. ▢ *It must be noted, however, that not all British and American officers carried out orders.* **11** You use **must** in questions to express your anger or irritation about something that someone has done, usually because you do not understand their behaviour. ▢ *Why must he interrupt?* **12** You use **must** in exclamations to express surprise or shock. ▢ *'Go! Please go.'—'You must be joking!'* ▢ *I really must be quite mad!*

PHRASES **if you must** You say '**if you must**' when you know that you cannot stop someone doing something that you think is wrong or stupid. ▢ *If you must be in the sunlight, use the strongest sunscreen you can get.*

if you must know You say '**if you must know**' when you tell someone something that you did not want them to know and you want to suggest that you think they were wrong to ask you about it. ▢ *It scared the hell out of her, if you must know. And me, too.*

NOUN /mʌst/ [c] (**musts**) (*informal*) If you refer to something as a **must**, you mean that it is absolutely necessary. ▢ *Taking out travel insurance may seem an unnecessary expense, but it is a must.*

mute /mjuːt/ ADJ, VERB

ADJ **1** Someone who is **mute** is silent for a particular reason and does not speak. ▢ *He was mute, distant, and indifferent.* **2** Someone who is **mute** is unable to speak. ▢ *Marianna, the duke's daughter, became mute after a shock.*

VERB [T] (**mutes, muting, muted**) **1** If someone **mutes** something such as their feelings or their activities, they reduce the strength or intensity of them. ▢ *The corruption does not seem to have muted the country's prolonged economic boom.* **2** If you **mute** a noise or sound, you lower its volume or make it less distinct. ▢ *They begin to mute their voices, not be as assertive.*

mut•ed /'mjuːtɪd/ ADJ **1** *The threat contrasted starkly with his administration's previous muted criticism.* **2** *'Yes,' he muttered, his voice so muted I hardly heard his reply.*

mut•ter /'mʌtə/ VERB, NOUN

VERB [I, T] (**mutters, muttering, muttered**) If you **mutter** or if you **mutter** something, you speak very quietly so that you cannot easily be heard, often because you are complaining about something. ▢ *'God knows,' she muttered, 'what's happening in that madman's mind.'* ▢ *She can hear the old woman muttering about consideration.*

NOUN [c] (**mutters**) A **mutter** is an utterance, often expressing complaint, that is so quiet that it cannot easily be heard. ▢ *They make no more than a mutter of protest.*

mut•ter•ing /'mʌtərɪŋ/ NOUN [c, u] (**mutterings**) ▢ *He heard muttering from the front of the crowd.*

✪ mu•tu•al ◆◇◇ /'mjuːtʃuəl/ ADJ (*academic word*) **1** You use **mutual** to describe a situation, feeling, or action that is experienced, felt, or done by both of two people mentioned. = shared, reciprocal ▢ *The East and the West can work together for their mutual benefit and progress.* **2** You use **mutual** to describe something such as an interest which two or more people share. ▢ *They do, however, share a mutual interest in design.*

✪ mu•tu•al•ly /'mjuːtʃuəli/ ADV ▢ *Attempts to reach a mutually agreed solution had been fruitless.* ▢ *A meeting would take place at a mutually convenient time.*

✦ mutually exclusive → see **exclusive**

my ◆◆◆ /maɪ/ DET

> **My** is the first person singular possessive determiner.

1 A speaker or writer uses **my** to indicate that something belongs or relates to himself or herself. ▢ *I invited him back to my flat for coffee.* **2** In conversations or in letters, **my** is used in front of a word like 'dear' or 'darling' to show affection. ▢ *My sweet Freda.* **3** (*spoken, feelings*) **My** is used in phrases such as '**My God**' and '**My goodness**' to express surprise or shock. ▢ *My God, I've never seen you so nervous.*

my•self ◆◆◇ /maɪ'self/ PRON

> **Myself** is the first person singular reflexive pronoun.

1 [V + myself, PREP + myself] A speaker or writer uses **myself** to refer to himself or herself. **Myself** is used as the object of a verb or preposition when the subject refers to the same person. ▢ *I asked myself what I would have done in such a situation.* **2** You use **myself** to emphasize a first person singular subject. In more formal English, **myself** is sometimes used instead of 'me' as the object of a verb or preposition, for emphasis. ▢ *I myself enjoy films, poetry, eating out, and long walks.* **3** If you say something such as 'I did it **myself**', you are emphasizing that you did it, rather than anyone else. ▢ *'Where did you get that embroidery?'—'I made it myself.'*

mys•teri•ous /mɪ'stɪəriəs/ ADJ **1** Someone or something that is **mysterious** is strange and is not known about or understood. ▢ *He died in mysterious circumstances.* ▢ *A mysterious illness confined him to bed for over a month.* **2** [V-LINK + mysterious] If someone is **mysterious** about something, they deliberately do not talk much about it, sometimes because they want to make people more interested in it. ▢ *As for his job – well, he was very mysterious about it.*

mys•teri•ous•ly /mɪ'stɪəriəsli/ ADV **1** *A couple of messages had mysteriously disappeared.* **2** *Asked what she meant, she said mysteriously: 'Work it out for yourself.'*

mys•tery ◆◇◇ /'mɪstəri/ NOUN, ADJ

NOUN [c, u] (**mysteries**) **1** [c] A **mystery** is something that is not understood or known about. ▢ *The source of the gunshots still remains a mystery.* **2** [u] If you talk about the **mystery** of someone or something, you are talking about how difficult they are to understand or know about, especially when this gives them a rather strange or magical quality. ▢ *She's a lady of mystery.* **3** [c] A **mystery** is a story in which strange things happen that are not explained until the end. ▢ *His fourth novel is a murder mystery set in London.*

ADJ [mystery + N] A **mystery** person or thing is one whose identity or nature is not known. ▢ *The mystery hero*

m

immediately alerted police after spotting a bomb.

mys·ti·fy /ˈmɪstɪfaɪ/ VERB [T] (**mystifies, mystifying, mystified**) If you **are mystified** by something, you find it impossible to explain or understand. = baffle ❑ *The audience must have been totally mystified by the plot.*

mys·ti·fy·ing /ˈmɪstɪfaɪɪŋ/ ADJ = puzzling ❑ *I find your attitude a little mystifying, Marilyn.*

myth ♦◇◇ /mɪθ/ NOUN [C, U] (**myths**) **1** A **myth** is a well-known story which was made up in the past to explain natural events or to justify religious beliefs or social customs. ❑ *There is a famous Greek myth in which Icarus flew too near to the Sun.* **2** If you describe a belief or explanation as a **myth**, you mean that many people believe it but it is actually untrue. = fallacy ❑ *Contrary to the popular myth, women are not reckless spendthrifts.*

Nn

N also **n** /en/ NOUN [c, u] (**N's, n's**) N is the fourteenth letter of the English alphabet.

nail /neɪl/ NOUN, VERB

NOUN [c] (**nails**) **1** A **nail** is a thin piece of metal with one pointed end and one flat end. You hit the flat end with a hammer in order to push the nail into something such as a wall. ❑ *A mirror hung on a nail above the sink.* **2** Your **nails** are the thin hard parts that grow at the ends of your fingers and toes. ❑ *Keep your nails short and your hands clean.*

PHRASE **hit the nail on the head** If you say that someone **has hit the nail on the head**, you think they are exactly right about something. ❑ *'I think it would civilize people a bit more if they had decent conditions.'—'I think you've hit the nail on the head.'*

VERB [T] (**nails, nailing, nailed**) **1** If you **nail** something somewhere, you fasten it there using one or more nails. ❑ *Frank put the first plank down and nailed it in place.* ❑ *They nail shut the front door.* **2** (*informal*) To **nail** someone means to catch them and prove that they have been breaking the law. ❑ *The prosecution still managed to nail him for robberies at the homes of leading industrialists.*

PHRASAL VERB **nail down 1** If you **nail down** something unknown or uncertain, you find out exactly what it is. = pin down ❑ *It would be useful if you could nail down the source of this tension.* **2** If you **nail down** an agreement, you manage to reach a firm agreement with a definite result. ❑ *The Secretary of State and his Russian counterpart met to try to nail down the elusive accord.*

na·ive /naɪˈiːv, AmE naːˈ-/ also **naïve** ADJ If you describe someone as **naive**, you think they lack experience and so expect things to be easy or people to be honest or kind. = unrealistic ❑ *It's naive to think that teachers are always tolerant.* ❑ *Their view was that he had been politically naive.*

na·ive·ly /naɪˈiːvli, AmE naːˈ-/ ADV ❑ *naively applying Western solutions to Eastern problems*

na·ive·ty /naɪˈiːviti/ NOUN [u] ❑ *I was alarmed by his naivety and ignorance of international affairs.*

na·ked /ˈneɪkɪd/ ADJ **1** Someone who is **naked** is not wearing any clothes. ❑ *Her naked body was found wrapped in a sheet in a field.* ❑ *They stripped me naked.* **2** If an animal or part of an animal is **naked**, it has no fur or feathers on it. ❑ *The nest contained eight little mice that were naked and blind.* **3** You can describe an object as **naked** when it does not have its normal covering. ❑ *a naked bulb dangling in a bare room* **4** [naked + N] (*journalism*) You can use **naked** to describe unpleasant or violent actions and behaviour which are not disguised or hidden in any way. = blatant ❑ *Naked aggression and an attempt to change frontiers by force could not go unchallenged.* ❑ *violence and the naked pursuit of power*

na·ked·ness /ˈneɪkɪdnəs/ NOUN [u] ❑ *He had pulled the blanket over his body to hide his nakedness.*

name ♦♦♦ /neɪm/ NOUN, VERB

NOUN [c] (**names**) **1** The **name** of a person, place, or thing is the word or group of words that is used to identify them. ❑ *'What's his name?'—'Peter.'* ❑ *I don't even know if Sullivan's his real name.* **2** You can refer to the reputation of a person or thing as their **name**. = reputation ❑ *He had a name for good judgement.* **3** (*journalism*) You can refer to someone as, for example, a famous **name** or a great

name when they are well known. = star ❑ *some of the most famous names in modelling and show business*

PHRASES **in someone's name** or **in the name of someone 1** If something is in someone's **name**, it officially belongs to them or is reserved for them. ❑ *The house is in my husband's name.* **2** If someone does something **in the name of** a group of people, they do it as the representative of that group. ❑ *In the United States the majority governs in the name of the people.*

in the name of something If you do something **in the name of** an ideal or an abstract thing, you do it in order to preserve or promote that thing. ❑ *one of those rare occasions in history when a political leader risked his own power in the name of the greater public good*

by name When you mention someone or something **by name**, or address someone **by name**, you use their name. ❑ *When he walks down 131st Street, he greets most people he sees by name.*

by name or **by the name of something** (*formal*) You can use **by name** or **by the name of** when you are saying what someone is called. ❑ *In 1911 he met up with a young Australian by the name of Harry Busteed.*

call someone names If someone **calls** you **names**, they insult you by saying unpleasant things to you or about you. ❑ *At my last school they called me names because I was so slow.*

make a name for oneself or **make one's name** If you **make a name for yourself** or **make** your **name** as something, you become well known for that thing. ❑ *She was beginning to make a name for herself as a portrait photographer.*

VERB [T] (**names, naming, named**) **1** When you **name** someone or something, you give them a name, usually at the beginning of their life. ❑ *My mother insisted on naming me Horace.* ❑ *a man named John T. Benson* **2** If you **name** someone or something **after** another person or thing, you give them the same name as that person or thing. ❑ *Why haven't you named any of your sons after yourself?* **3** If you **name** someone, you identify them by stating their name. ❑ *It's nearly thirty years since a journalist was jailed for refusing to name a source.* **4** If you **name** something such as a price, time, or place, you say what you want it to be. = state ❑ *Call Marty, tell him to name his price.* **5** If you **name** the person for a particular job, you say who you want to have the job. ❑ *The chief executive has named a finance director.* ❑ *When the chairman of Campbell's retired, McGovern was named as his successor.*

→ See also **Christian name, first name, maiden name**

⊘**name·ly** /ˈneɪmli/ ADV You use **namely** to introduce detailed information about the subject you are discussing, or a particular aspect of it. = that is (to say), specifically ❑ *A district should serve its clientele, namely students, staff, and parents.* ❑ *One group of people seems to be forgotten, namely pensioners.* ❑ *They were hardly aware of the challenge facing them, namely, to re-establish prosperity.*

nan·ny /ˈnæni/ NOUN [c] (**nannies**) A **nanny** is a woman who is paid by parents to take care of their child or children.

nar·cot·ic /naːˈkɒtɪk/ NOUN, ADJ

NOUN [c] (**narcotics**) **Narcotics** are drugs such as opium or heroin which make you sleepy and stop you from feeling pain. You can also use **narcotics** to mean any kind of illegal drugs. ❑ *He was charged with dealing in narcotics.* [ADJ] If something, especially a drug, has a **narcotic** effect, it makes the person who uses it feel sleepy. ❑ *hormones that have a narcotic effect on the immune system*

❍ **nar·rate** /nəˈreɪt, AmE ˈnæreɪt/ VERB [T] (**narrates, narrating, narrated**) **1** (*formal*) If you **narrate** a story, you tell it from your own point of view. = tell, recount, relate ❑ *The three of them narrate the same events from three perspectives.* ❑ *The book is narrated by Richard Papen, a Californian boy.* **2** The person who **narrates** a film or programme speaks the words which accompany the pictures, but does not appear in it. ❑ *She also narrated a documentary about the Kirov Ballet School.*

nar·ra·tion /nəˈreɪʃən/ NOUN [U] **1** *Its story-within-a-story method of narration is confusing.* **2** *As soon as the crew gets back from lunch, we can put your narration on it right away.*

❍ **nar·ra·tor** /nəˈreɪtə, AmE -ˈreɪt-/ NOUN [C] (**narrators**) **1** *Jules, the story's narrator, is an actress in her late thirties.* **2** *the narrator of the documentary*

❍ **nar·ra·tive** /ˈnærətɪv/ NOUN [C, U] (**narratives**) **1** [C] A **narrative** is a story or an account of a series of events. = account, story ❑ *a fast-moving narrative* ❑ *Sloan began his narrative with the day of the murder.* **2** [U] **Narrative** is the description of a series of events, usually in a novel. = description ❑ *Neither author was very strong on narrative.* ❑ *Nye's simple narrative style*

❍ **nar·row** ◆◆◇ /ˈnærəʊ/ ADJ, VERB
[ADJ] (**narrower, narrowest**) **1** Something that is **narrow** measures a very small distance from one side to the other, especially compared to its length or height. = thin, slender; ≠ wide, broad ❑ *through the town's narrow streets* ❑ *She had long, narrow feet.* ❑ *the narrow strip of land joining the peninsula to the rest of the island* **2** If you describe someone's ideas, attitudes, or beliefs as **narrow**, you disapprove of them because they are restricted in some way, and often ignore the more important aspects of an argument or situation. = limited ❑ *a narrow and outdated view of family life* **3** If you have a **narrow** victory, you succeed in winning but only by a small amount. ❑ *Voters approved the plan by a narrow majority.* **4** [narrow + N] If you have a **narrow** escape, something unpleasant nearly happens to you. ❑ *Two police officers had a narrow escape when rioters attacked their vehicles.*
[VERB] [T, I] (**narrows, narrowing, narrowed**) **1** [T, I] If something **narrows**, it becomes less wide. = constrict, contract; ≠ open, widen ❑ *The wide track narrows before crossing another stream.* ❑ *Narrowed blood vessels prevent blood from flowing to the heart.* **2** [I, T] (*written*) If your eyes **narrow** or if you **narrow** your eyes, you almost close them, for example because you are angry or because you are trying to concentrate on something. ❑ *Coggins' eyes narrowed angrily. 'You think I'd tell you?'* **3** [I, T] If something **narrows** or if you **narrow** it, its extent or range becomes smaller. ❑ *Most recent opinion polls suggest that the gap between the two main parties has narrowed.*
[PHRASAL VERB] **narrow down** If you **narrow down** a range of things, you reduce the number of things included in it. ❑ *What's happened is that the new results narrow down the possibilities.*

nar·row·ness /ˈnærəʊnəs/ NOUN [U] **1** *the narrowness of the river mouth* **2** *the narrowness of their mental and spiritual outlook* **3** *The narrowness of the victory reflected deep division within the party.*

nar·row·ly /ˈnærəʊli/ ADV **1** *They may define their contribution too narrowly.* **2** *She narrowly failed to win enough votes.* **3** *Five firemen narrowly escaped death when a staircase collapsed beneath their feet.*

nar·row·ing /ˈnærəʊɪŋ/ NOUN [SING] ❑ *a narrowing of the gap between rich members and poor*

narrow-minded ADJ (*disapproval*) If you describe someone as **narrow-minded**, you are criticizing them because they are unwilling to consider new ideas or other people's opinions. ❑ *a narrow-minded bigot*

nas·ty /ˈnɑːsti, ˈnæsti/ ADJ (**nastier, nastiest**)
1 Something that is **nasty** is very unpleasant to see, experience, or feel. = horrible ❑ *an extremely nasty murder*

2 If you describe a person or their behaviour as **nasty**, you mean that they behave in an unkind and unpleasant way. = horrid ❑ *What nasty little snobs you all are.* ❑ *The guards looked really nasty.* **3** If you describe something as **nasty**, you mean it is unattractive, undesirable, or in bad taste. = horrid ❑ *They should put warning labels on those nasty little devices.* **4** A **nasty** problem or situation is very worrisome and difficult to deal with. ❑ *A spokesman said this firm action had defused a very nasty situation.* **5** If you describe an injury or a disease as **nasty**, you mean that it is serious or looks unpleasant. ❑ *My little granddaughter caught her heel in the spokes of her bicycle – it was a very nasty wound.*

nas·ti·ness /ˈnɑːstinəs, ˈnæstinəs/ NOUN [U] **1** *the nastiness of war* **2** *As the years went by his nastiness began to annoy his readers.*

nas·ti·ly /ˈnɑːstɪli, ˈnæstɪli/ ADV [nastily after V] ❑ *She took the money and eyed me nastily.*

❍ **na·tion** ◆◆◆ /ˈneɪʃən/ NOUN [C, SING] (**nations**) **1** [C] A **nation** is an individual country considered together with its social and political structures. = country ❑ *Such policies would require unprecedented cooperation between nations.* ❑ *The Arab nations agreed to meet in Baghdad.* **2** [SING] (*journalism*) **The nation** is sometimes used to refer to all the people who live in a particular country, or all the people who belong to a particular ethnic group. ❑ *It was a story that touched the nation's heart.* ❑ *the former chief of the Cherokee nation*

WORD CONNECTIONS		
ADJ + **nation**		

a **wealthy** nation
a **powerful** nation
a **developed** nation
an **industrialized** nation
❑ *America was emerging as the world's most powerful nation.*

a **poor** nation
a **developing** nation
❑ *Many people in developing nations live in extreme poverty.*

WORD FAMILIES	
nation NOUN	The Arab **nations** agreed to meet in Baghdad.
national ADJ	These issues are of **national** and international importance.
international ADJ	They ratified an **international** agreement banning chemical weapons.
nationally ADV	The problem of youth unemployment needs to be addressed both locally and **nationally**.
internationally ADV	He is famous as a designer and inventor both in the UK and **internationally**.
nationalism NOUN	The British government responded to a rise in support for Scottish **nationalism**.
nationalist ADJ	The crisis set off a wave of **nationalist** feeling in Quebec.

❍ **na·tion·al** ◆◆◆ /ˈnæʃənəl/ ADJ, NOUN
[ADJ] **1** **National** means relating to the whole of a country or nation rather than to part of it or to other nations. ≠ local, international ❑ *major national and international issues* ❑ *national and local elections* ❑ *a member of the U.S. national team* **2** [national + N] **National** means typical of the people or customs of a particular country or nation. ❑ *the national characteristics and history of the country*
[NOUN] [C] (**nationals**) You can refer to someone who is legally a citizen of a country as a **national** of that country. = citizen ❑ *a Sri Lankan national*

N

✦ **na·tion·al·ly** /'næʃənəli/ ADV ▫ *a nationally televised speech* ▫ *Duncan Campbell is nationally known for his investigative work.*

na·tion·al·ism /'næʃənəlɪzəm/ NOUN [U] **1** You can refer to a person's great love for their nation as **nationalism**. It is often associated with the belief that a particular nation is better than any other nation, and in this case is often used showing disapproval. ▫ *This kind of fierce nationalism is a powerful and potentially volatile force.* **2** **Nationalism** is the desire for political independence of people who feel they are historically or culturally a separate group within a country. ▫ *The rising tide of Slovak nationalism may also help the party to win representation in parliament.*

na·tion·al·ist ◆◇◇ /'næʃənəlɪst/ ADJ, NOUN
[ADJ] **1** [nationalist + N] **Nationalist** means connected with the desire of a group of people within a country for political independence. ▫ *The crisis has set off a wave of nationalist feelings in Quebec.* **2** [nationalist + N] **Nationalist** means connected with a person's great love for their nation. It is often associated with the belief that their nation is better than any other nation, and in this case is often used showing disapproval. ▫ *Political life has been infected by growing nationalist sentiment.*
[NOUN] [C] (**nationalists**) **1** A **nationalist** is a member of a group of people within a country who desire political independence. ▫ *demands by nationalists for an independent state* **2** A **nationalist** is someone with a great love for their nation. This is often associated with the belief that their nation is better than any other nation, and in this case is often used showing disapproval. ▫ *The parliament is composed mainly of extreme nationalists.*

✦ **na·tion·al·ity** /,næʃə'næliti/ NOUN [C, U] (**nationalities**) **1** [C, U] If you have the **nationality** of a particular country, you were born there or have the legal right to be a citizen. = ethnicity, background, origin ▫ *Asked his nationality, he said American.* ▫ *The crew are of different nationalities and have no common language.* ▫ *a resident who held dual Iranian-Canadian nationality* **2** [C] You can refer to people who have the same racial origins as a **nationality**, especially when they do not have their own independent country. = race ▫ *the many nationalities that comprise Ethiopia*

na·tion·al·ize /'næʃənəlaɪz/ also **nationalise** VERB
[T] (**nationalizes, nationalizing, nationalized**) (*business*) If a government **nationalizes** a private company or industry, that company or industry becomes owned by the state and controlled by the government. ▫ *In 1987, Garcia introduced legislation to nationalize Peru's banking and financial systems.*
na·tion·ali·za·tion /,næʃənəlaɪ'zeɪʃən/ NOUN [U] ▫ *the campaign for the nationalization of the coal mines*

na·tion·al park NOUN [C] (**national parks**) A **national park** is a large area of land which is protected by the government because of its natural beauty, plants, or animals, and which the public can usually visit. ▫ *Roads into Yosemite National Park are closed due to landslides.*

nation·wide /,neɪʃən'waɪd/ ADJ, ADV
[ADJ] **Nationwide** activities or situations happen or exist in all parts of a country. = national ▫ *The rising number of car crimes is a nationwide problem.*
[ADV] If an activity or situation happens or exists **nationwide**, it happens or exists in all parts of a country. = nationally ▫ *The figures show unemployment falling nationwide last month.*

✦ **na·tive** ◆◇◇ /'neɪtɪv/ ADJ, NOUN
[ADJ] **1** [native + N] Your **native** country or area is the country or area where you were born and brought up. ▫ *It was his first visit to his native country since 1948.* **2** [native + N] **Native** is used to describe someone who was born in a particular country or region. ▫ *Joshua Halpern is a native Northern Californian.* **3** [native + N] Some European people use **native** to describe a person living in a non-Western country who belongs to the race or tribe that the majority of people there belong to. This use could cause offence. = indigenous ▫ *Native people were allowed to retain some sense of their traditional culture and religion.* **4** [native + N] Your **native** language or tongue is the first

language that you learned to speak when you were a child. = mother; ≠ non-native ▫ *She spoke not only her native language, Swedish, but also English and French.* ▫ *French is not my native tongue.* **5** [native + N, V-LINK + native 'to' N] Plants or animals that are **native to** a particular region live or grow there naturally and were not brought there. = indigenous; ≠ non-native ▫ *a project to create a 50 acre forest of native Caledonian pines* ▫ *Many of the plants are native to Brazil.*
[NOUN] [C] (**natives**) **1** A **native of** a particular country or region is someone who was born in that country or region. ▫ *Dr Aubin is a native of St Louis.* **2** Some European people use **native** to refer to a person living in a non-Western country who belongs to the race or tribe that the majority of people there belong to. This use could cause offence. ▫ *They used force to banish the natives from the more fertile land.* **3** If a plant or animal is a **native of** a particular region, it lives or grows there naturally and was not brought there. ▫ *The coconut palm is a native of Malaysia.*

✦ **natu·ral** ◆◆◇ /'nætʃərəl/ ADJ, NOUN
[ADJ] **1** If you say that it is **natural** for someone to act in a particular way or for something to happen in that way, you mean that it is reasonable in the circumstances. = normal ▫ *It is only natural for youngsters to crave the excitement of driving a fast car.* ▫ *It is only natural that he should resent you.* **2** **Natural** behaviour is shared by all people or all animals of a particular type and has not been learned. ▫ *the insect's natural instinct to feed* **3** Someone with a **natural** ability or skill was born with that ability and did not have to learn it. = instinctive ▫ *She has a natural ability to understand the motives of others.* **4** If someone's behaviour is **natural**, they appear to be relaxed and are not trying to hide anything. = genuine ▫ *Bethan's sister was as friendly and natural as the rest of the family.* **5** [natural + N] **Natural** things exist or occur in nature and are not made or caused by people. ≠ artificial, man-made, synthetic ▫ *The gigantic natural harbour is a haven for boats.* ▫ *The typhoon was the worst natural disaster in South Korea in many years.*
[PHRASE] **natural causes** If someone dies **of** or **from natural causes**, they die because they are ill or old rather than because of an accident or violence. ▫ *Your brother died of natural causes.*
[NOUN] [C] (**naturals**) If you say that someone is **a natural**, you mean that they do something very well and very easily. ▫ *He's a natural with any kind of engine.*
natu·ral·ness /'nætʃərəlnəs/ NOUN [U] ▫ *The critics praised the reality of the scenery and the naturalness of the acting.*

natu·ral·ly ◆◇◇ /'nætʃərəli/ ADV
[ADV] **1** [naturally after V] If someone behaves **naturally**, they appear to be relaxed and are not trying to hide anything. ▫ *For pictures of people behaving naturally, not posing for the camera, it is essential to shoot unnoticed.* **2** If something exists or occurs **naturally**, it exists or occurs in nature and is not made or caused by people. ▫ *Nitrates are chemicals that occur naturally in water and the soil.* **3** You use **naturally** to indicate that you think something is very obvious and not at all surprising under the circumstances. ▫ *When things go wrong, all of us naturally feel disappointed and frustrated.* ▫ *Naturally these comings and goings excited some curiosity.* **4** [naturally after V] If one thing develops **naturally** from another, it develops as a normal consequence or result of it. = logically ▫ *A study of yoga leads naturally to meditation.* **5** [naturally + ADJ] You can use **naturally** to talk about a characteristic of someone's personality when it is the way that they normally act. ▫ *He has a lively sense of humour and appears naturally confident.* **6** [naturally + ADJ] If someone is **naturally** good at something, they learn it easily and quickly and do it very well. ▫ *Some individuals are naturally good communicators.*
[PHRASE] **come naturally** If something **comes naturally to** you, you find it easy to do and quickly become good at it. ▫ *Humanitarian work comes naturally to them.*

✦ **na·ture** ◆◆◇ /'neɪtʃə/ NOUN
[NOUN] [U, SING] (**natures**) **1** [U] **Nature** is all the animals,

n

plants, and other things in the world that are not made by people, and all the events and processes that are not caused by people. = the environment ❑ *The most amazing thing about nature is its infinite variety.* ❑ *grasses that grow wild in nature* ❑ *the ecological balance of nature* **2** [SING] The **nature** of something is its basic quality or character. ❑ *Mr Sharp would not comment on the nature of the issues being investigated.* ❑ *The rise of a major power is both economic and military in nature.* ❑ *the ambitious nature of the programme* **3** [SING] [with POSS, also 'by' nature] Someone's **nature** is their character, which they show by the way they behave. ❑ *Jeya feels that her ambitious nature made her unsuitable for an arranged marriage.* ❑ *She trusted people. That was her nature.*

PHRASES **by its nature** If you say that something has a particular characteristic **by its nature** or **by its very nature**, you mean that things of that type always have that characteristic. ❑ *Peacekeeping, by its nature, makes pre-planning difficult.*

in the nature of things If you say that something is in **the nature of things**, you mean that you would expect it to happen in the circumstances mentioned. ❑ *Of course, in the nature of things, and with a lot of drinking going on, people failed to notice.*

in the nature of something If you say that one thing is **in the nature of** another, you mean that it is like the other thing. ❑ *There is movement towards, I think, something in the nature of a pluralistic system.*

second nature If a way of behaving is **second nature** to you, you do it almost without thinking because it is easy for you or obvious to you. ❑ *Planning ahead had always come as second nature to her.*

USAGE NOTE

nature

When you use **nature** to talk about all living things, you do not use 'the' in front of it.

*the ecological balance of **nature***

You do not use **nature** to talk about land which is situated away from towns and cities. You refer to this land as **the country** or **the countryside**.

*We live in **the country**.*

*Sometimes he would drive out into **the countryside**.*

---

nau•ti•cal /ˈnɔːtɪkəl/ ADJ **Nautical** means relating to ships and sailing. ❑ *a nautical chart of the region you sail*

na•val ♦◇◇ /ˈneɪvəl/ ADJ [naval + N] **Naval** means belonging to, relating to, or involving a country's navy. ❑ *He was the senior serving naval officer.*

navi•gate /ˈnævɪɡeɪt/ VERB [I, T] (**navigates, navigating, navigated**) **1** [I, T] When someone **navigates** a ship or an aircraft somewhere, they decide which course to follow and steer it there. ❑ *Captain Cook was responsible for safely navigating his ship without accident for 100 voyages.* ❑ *The purpose of the visit was to navigate into an ice-filled fiord.* **2** [I, T] When a ship or boat **navigates** an area of water, it sails on or across it. = sail ❑ *a lock system to allow sea-going craft to navigate the upper reaches of the river* ❑ *Such boats can navigate on the Hudson.* **3** [I] When someone in a car **navigates**, they decide what roads the car should be driven along in order to get somewhere. ❑ *When travelling on fast roads at night it is impossible to drive and navigate at the same time.* ❑ *the relief at successfully navigating across the Golden Gate Bridge to arrive here* **4** [I] When fish, animals, or insects **navigate** somewhere, they find the right direction to go and travel there. ❑ *In tests, the bees navigate back home after being placed in a field a mile away.* **5** [T] If you **navigate** an obstacle, you move carefully in order to avoid hitting the obstacle or hurting yourself. = negotiate ❑ *He's got to learn how to navigate his way around the residence.*

navi•ga•tion /ˌnævɪˈɡeɪʃən/ NOUN [C, U] (**navigations**) **1** [C, U] The **navigation** of a ship or an aircraft is the act of deciding which course to follow and steering it. ❑ *The expedition was wrecked by bad planning and poor navigation.* **2** [U] You can refer to the movement of ships as **navigation**. ❑ *Pack ice around Iceland was becoming a threat to navigation.*

○ **navy** ♦♦◇ /ˈneɪvi/ NOUN, COLOUR

NOUN [C] (**navies**) A country's **navy** consists of the people it employs to fight at sea, and the ships they use. ❑ *The operation was organized by the US Navy.* ❑ *Her own son was also in the navy.* ❑ *The government announced an order for three Type 23 frigates for the Royal Navy yesterday.*

COLOUR Something that is **navy** or **navy-blue** is very dark blue. ❑ *When I was a fashion editor, I mostly wore white shirts and black or navy trousers.*

○ **NB** /ˌen ˈbiː/ You write **NB** to draw someone's attention to what you are about to say or write. ❑ *NB: The opinions stated in this essay do not necessarily represent those of the Church of God Missionary Society.* ❑ *NB: The above course is subject to approval.*

near ♦♦♦ /nɪə/ PREP, ADV, ADJ, VERB, NOUN

PREP **1** If something is **near** a place, thing, or person, it is a short distance from them. ❑ *Don't come near me.* ❑ *He drew his chair nearer the fire.* **2** If someone or something is **near** a particular state, they have almost reached it. ❑ *He was near tears.* ❑ *For almost a month he lay near death.* **3** If something is similar to something else, you can say that it is **near** it. ❑ *Often her feelings were nearer hatred than love.* **4** If something happens **near** a particular time, it happens just before or just after that time. ❑ *Performance is lowest between 3 a.m. and 5 a.m., and reaches a peak near midday.* ❑ *'Since I retired to this place,' he wrote near the end of his life, 'I have never been out of these mountains.'* **5** You use **near** to say that something is a little more or less than an amount or number stated. ❑ *to increase manufacturing from about 2.5 million cars a year to nearer 4.75 million* **6** [with BRD-NEG] You can say that someone will **not go near** a person or thing when you are emphasizing that they refuse to see them or go there. ❑ *He will absolutely not go near a hospital.*

PHRASE **nowhere near** or **not anywhere near** (*emphasis*) You use **nowhere near** and **not anywhere near** to emphasize that something is not the case. ❑ *They are nowhere near good enough.* ❑ *It was nowhere near as painful as David had expected.*

ADV (**nearer, nearest**) **1** If something is **near**, it is a short distance from a place, thing, or person. ❑ *He crouched as near to the door as he could.* ❑ *She took a step nearer to the barrier.* **2** (*written*) If a time or event draws **near**, it will happen soon. ❑ *The time for my departure from Japan was drawing nearer every day.* **3** [near + ADJ] You use **near** to indicate that something is almost the thing mentioned. ❑ *his near fatal accident two years ago*

PHRASE **near to 1** If someone or something is **near to** a particular state, they have almost reached it. = close ❑ *After the war, the firm came near to bankruptcy.* ❑ *The repairs to the Hafner machine were near to completion.* **2** If something is similar to something else, you can say that it is **near to** it. ❑ *It combined with the resinous cedar smell of the logs to produce a sickening sensation that was near to nausea.*

ADJ (**nearer, nearest**) **1** [nearest + N, 'the' nearer 'of' N] You use **near** to refer to something that is a short distance away in comparison with other things of the same type. ❑ *He collapsed into the nearest chair.* ❑ *The nearer of the two barges was perhaps a mile away.* **2** ['the' nearest + N 'to' N, 'the' nearest 'to' N] You describe the thing most similar to something as **the nearest** thing **to** it when there is no example of the thing itself. ❑ *It would appear that the legal profession is the nearest thing to a recession-proof industry.* **3** [DET + near + N] The **near** one of two things is the one that is closer. ❑ *a mighty beech tree on the near side of the little clearing* **4** [near + N] You use **near** to indicate that something is almost the thing mentioned. ❑ *She was believed to have died in near poverty.* **5** [near + N] In a contest, your **nearest** rival or challenger is the person or team that is most likely to defeat you. ❑ *He completed the lengthy course some three seconds faster than his nearest rival, Jonathon Ford.*

PHRASE **in the near future** If you say that something will happen in the **near future**, you mean that it will happen quite soon. ❑ *The controversy regarding vitamin C is unlikely to be resolved in the near future.*

VERB [T, I] (**nears, nearing, neared**) **1** [T] (*literary*) When you **near** a place, you get quite near to it. ❑ *As he neared*

the stable, he slowed the horse and patted it on the neck.
2 [T] When someone or something **nears** a particular
stage or point, they will soon reach that stage or point.
= approach □ His age was hard to guess – he must have been
nearing fifty. □ You are nearing the end of your training and you
haven't attempted any assessments yet. **3** [I] (literary) You say
that an important time or event **nears** when it is going to
occur quite soon. = approach □ As half time neared,
Hardyman almost scored twice.
NOUN
PHRASE **near and far** You use **near and far** to indicate that
you are referring to a very large area or distance. □ People
would gather from near and far.

near·by ◆◇◇ /ˌnɪəˈbaɪ/ ADV, ADJ
ADV If someone, for example, lives or parks their car
nearby, they live or park their car only a short distance
away. □ He might easily have been seen by someone who lived
nearby. □ The helicopter crashed to earth nearby.
ADJ [nearby + N] If something is **nearby**, it is only a short
distance away. □ At a nearby table a man was complaining in
a loud voice.

near·ly ◆◆◇ /ˈnɪəli/ ADV **1** **Nearly** is used to indicate that
something is not quite the case, or not completely the
case. = almost, practically □ Goldsworth stared at me in
silence for nearly twenty seconds. □ Hunter knew nearly all of
this already. □ The beach was nearly empty. **2** **Nearly** is used
to indicate that something will soon be the case. = almost
□ It was already nearly eight o'clock. □ I was nearly asleep.
□ I've nearly finished the words for your song.

neat ◆◇◇ /niːt/ ADJ (**neater, neatest**) **1** A **neat** place,
thing, or person is organized and clean, and has
everything in the correct place. □ So they left her in the neat
little house, alone with her memories. □ Everything was neat
and tidy and gleamingly clean. **2** Someone who is **neat**
keeps their home or possessions organized and clean, with
everything in the correct place. □ 'That's not like Alf,' he
said, 'leaving papers muddled like that. He's always so neat.'
3 A **neat** object, part of the body, or shape is quite small
and has a smooth outline. □ neat handwriting **4** A **neat**
movement or action is done accurately and skilfully, with
no unnecessary movements. □ 'Did you have any trouble?'
Byron asked, driving into a small parking space and changing
the subject in the same neat manoeuvre. **5** A **neat** way of
organizing, achieving, explaining, or expressing
something is clever and convenient. = nice □ It had been
such a neat, clever plan. □ Neat solutions are not easily found
to these issues. **6** (mainly BrE; in AmE, usually use **straight**)
When someone drinks strong alcohol **neat**, they do not
add a weaker liquid such as water to it. **7** (AmE, informal,
approval) If you say that something is **neat**, you mean that
it is very good. = great, cool □ He thought Mick was a
really neat guy.
neat·ly /ˈniːtli/ ADV **1** [neatly with v] □ He folded his paper
neatly and sipped his coffee. **2** [neatly with v] □ I followed
her into that room which her mother had maintained so neatly.
3 [neatly with v] □ He watched her peel and dissect a pear
neatly, no mess, no sticky fingers. **4** [neatly with v] □ Real
people do not fit neatly into these categories.
neat·ness /ˈniːtnəs/ NOUN [U] **1** The grounds were a perfect
balance between neatness and natural wildness. **2** a paragon
of neatness, efficiency, and reliability

nec·es·sar·i·ly ◆◇◇ /ˌnesɪˈserɪli, ˈnesɪsrɪli/ ADV
ADV **1** (vagueness) If you say that something is **not
necessarily** the case, you mean that it may not be the case
or is not always the case. □ Anger is not necessarily the most
useful or acceptable reaction to such events. **2** If you say that
something **necessarily** happens or is the case, you mean
that it has to happen or be the case and cannot be any
different. = inevitably □ Brookman & Langdon were said to
manufacture the most desirable pens and these necessarily
commanded astonishingly high prices.
CONVENTION **not necessarily** If you reply 'Not necessarily',
you mean that what has just been said or suggested may
not be true. □ 'He was lying, of course.'—'Not necessarily.'

⊙**nec·es·sary** ◆◆◇ /ˈnesɪsəri/ ADJ **1** Something that is
necessary is needed in order for something else to happen.
= essential, obligatory, required; ≠ unnecessary □ I kept

the engine running because it might be necessary to leave fast.
□ Make the necessary arrangements. □ We will do whatever is
necessary to stop them. □ the skills necessary for writing
2 [necessary + N] A **necessary** consequence or connection
must happen or exist, because of the nature of the things
or events involved. □ Scientific work is differentiated from art
by its necessary connection with the idea of progress.

WORD FAMILIES		
necessary ADJ	We will do whatever is **necessary** to stop them.	
unnecessary ADJ	Don't take any **unnecessary** risks.	
necessarily ADV	The cheapest solution is not **necessarily** the best.	
unnecessarily ADV	We must never endanger the lives of our troops **unnecessarily**.	
necessity NOUN	There is agreement on the **necessity** of reforms.	
necessitate VERB	A prolonged drought had **necessitated** the introduction of water rationing.	

ne·ces·si·tate /nɪˈsesɪteɪt/ VERB [T] (**necessitates,
necessitating, necessitated**) (formal) If something
necessitates an event, action, or situation, it makes it
necessary. = require □ A prolonged drought had necessitated
the introduction of water rationing.

ne·ces·si·ty /nɪˈsesɪti/ NOUN
NOUN [U, c] (**necessities**) **1** [U] The **necessity** of something
is the fact that it must happen or exist. □ There is agreement
on the necessity of reforms. □ As soon as the necessity for action
is over the troops must be withdrawn. **2** [c] A **necessity** is
something that you must have in order to live properly or
do something. = essential □ Water is a basic necessity of
life. **3** [c] A situation or action that is a **necessity** is
necessary and cannot be avoided. □ The president pleaded
that strong rule from the centre was a necessity.
PHRASE **of necessity** (formal) If you say that something is
of necessity the case, you mean that it is the case because
nothing else is possible or practical under the
circumstances. □ large families where children, of necessity,
shared a bed

neck ◆◇◇ /nek/ NOUN
NOUN [c] (**necks**) **1** Your **neck** is the part of your body
which joins your head to the rest of your body. □ She
threw her arms around his neck and hugged him warmly.
2 The **neck** of an article of clothing such as a shirt, dress,
or sweater is the part which surrounds your neck. □ the
low, ruffled neck of her blouse **3** The **neck** of something such
as a bottle or a guitar is the long narrow part at one end of
it. □ Catherine gripped the broken neck of the bottle.
PHRASES **be breathing down someone's neck** If you say
that someone **is breathing down** your **neck**, you mean
that they are watching you very closely and checking
everything you do. □ Most farmers have bank managers
breathing down their necks.
neck and neck In a competition, especially an election, if
two or more competitors are **neck and neck**, they are level
with each other and have an equal chance of winning.
□ The latest polls indicate that the two main parties are neck
and neck.
stick your neck out (informal) If you **stick** your **neck out**,
you bravely say or do something that might be criticized
or might turn out to be wrong. □ During my political life I've
earned myself a reputation as someone who'll stick his neck out,
a bit of a rebel.

need ◆◆◆ /niːd/ VERB, NOUN

Need sometimes behaves like an ordinary verb, for
example 'She needs to know' and 'She doesn't need to
know' and sometimes like a modal, for example
'No-one need know', 'She needn't know', or, in more
formal English, 'She need not know'.

n

VERB [T, MODAL] (**needs**, **needing**, **needed**) **1** [T] If you **need** something, or **need to** do something, you cannot successfully achieve what you want or live properly without it. ❑ *He desperately needed money.* ❑ *I need to make a phone call.* ❑ *I need you to do something for me.* ❑ *I need you here, Wally.* **2** [T] If an object or place **needs** something done to it, that action should be done to improve the object or place. If a task **needs** doing, it should be done to improve a particular situation. ❑ *The building needs quite a few repairs.* ❑ *a garden that needs tidying* **3** [T] If you say that someone does not **need to** do something, you are telling them not to do it, or advising or suggesting that they should not do it. ❑ *Well, for Heaven's sake, you don't need to apologize.* **4** [MODAL] [NO CONT, with NEG] If you say that someone **needn't** do something, you are telling them not to do it, or advising or suggesting that they should not do it. ❑ *'I'll put the key in the window.'—'You needn't bother,' he said gruffly.* ❑ *Look, you needn't shout.* **5** [T] If you tell someone that they don't **need to** do something, or that something **need** not happen, you are telling them that that thing is not necessary, in order to make them feel better. ❑ *He replied, with a reassuring smile, 'Oh, you don't need to worry about them.'* **6** [MODAL] [with BRD-NEG] If you tell someone that they **needn't** do something, or that something **needn't** happen, you are telling them that that thing is not necessary, in order to make them feel better. ❑ *You needn't worry.* ❑ *We have learned that a market crash need not lead to economic disaster.* **7** [T] You use don't **need to** when you are giving someone permission not to do something. ❑ *You don't need to wait for me.* **8** [MODAL] [with NEG] If you tell someone that they **needn't** do something, you are giving them permission not to do something. ❑ *You needn't come again, if you don't want to.* **9** [MODAL] [with NEG] If someone **needn't have** done something, they didn't need to do it. ❑ *She could have made the sandwich herself; her mother needn't have bothered to do anything.* ❑ *I was a little nervous when I announced my engagement to Grace, but I needn't have worried.* **10** [T] If someone **didn't need to** do something, it wasn't necessary or useful for them to do it, although they did it. ❑ *You didn't need to give me any more money you know, but thank you.* **11** [MODAL] You use **need** in expressions such as **I need hardly say** and **I needn't add** to emphasize that the person you are talking to already knows what you are going to say. ❑ *I needn't add that if you fail to do as I ask, you will suffer the consequences.* **12** [T] You use **need** in the expression **I hardly need to say** to emphasize that the person you are talking to already knows what you are going to say. ❑ *I hardly need to say that I have never lost contact with him.* **NOUN** [C, SING] (**needs**) **1** [C] The **need for** something, or the **need to** do something, is the situation of being unable to successfully achieve what you want or live properly without it. ❑ *Charles has never felt the need to compete with anyone.* ❑ *the child who never had his need for attention and importance satisfied* **2** [SING] If there is a **need for** something, that thing would improve a situation or something cannot happen without it. ❑ *Mr Forrest believes there is a need for other similar schools throughout the country.* ❑ *'I think we should see a specialist.'—'I don't think there's any need for that.'* **PHRASES** **in need** People **in need** do not have enough of essential things such as money, food, or good health. ❑ *The portable clinic will take doctors to children in need.* **in need of** If you are **in need of** something, you need it or ought to have it. ❑ *I was all right but in need of rest.* ❑ *He was badly in need of a shave.* **if need be** If you say that you will do something, especially an extreme action, **if need be**, you mean that you will do it if it is necessary. ❑ *They will act as my legal advisers if need be.*

nee·dle /ˈniːdəl/ NOUN [C] (**needles**) **1** A **needle** is a small, very thin piece of polished metal which is used for sewing. It has a sharp point at one end and a hole in the other for a thread to go through. ❑ *He took a needle and thread and sewed it up.* **2** A **needle** is a thin, hollow, metal rod with a sharp point, which is part of a medical instrument called a syringe. It is used to put a drug into someone's body, or to take blood out. ❑ *the transmission of*

the AIDS virus through dirty needles **3** Knitting **needles** are thin sticks that are used for knitting. They are usually made of plastic or metal and have a point at one end. ❑ *a pair of knitting needles* **4** A **needle** is a thin metal rod with a point which is put into a patient's body during acupuncture. ❑ *I gave Kevin a course of acupuncture using six needles strategically placed on the scalp.* **5** On an instrument which measures something such as speed or weight, the **needle** is the long strip of metal or plastic on the dial that moves backwards and forwards, showing the measurement. ❑ *She kept looking at the dial on the boiler. The needle had reached 250 degrees.* **6** The **needles** of a fir or pine tree are this thin, hard, pointed leaves. ❑ *The carpet of pine needles was soft underfoot.*

✪ **need·less** /ˈniːdləs/ ADJ
ADJ Something that is **needless** is completely unnecessary. = unnecessary, useless; ≠ essential, necessary ❑ *But his death was so needless.* ❑ *It has taken many centuries of needless suffering to close the gap of medical ignorance.* **PHRASE** **needless to say** You use **needless to say** when you want to emphasize that what you are about to say is obvious and to be expected in the circumstances. = of course, obviously ❑ *Soon the story was in all the papers, and the book, needless to say, became a best-seller.* ❑ *Needless to say, the differences in diet between these two populations goes far beyond the amount of fat in it.* ❑ *Our budgie got out of its cage while our cat was in the room. Needless to say, the cat moved quicker than me and caught it.*
✪ **need·less·ly** /ˈniːdləsli/ ADV = unnecessarily ❑ *Half a million women die needlessly each year during childbirth.*

needy /ˈniːdi/ ADJ, NOUN
ADJ (**needier**, **neediest**) **Needy** people do not have enough food, medicine, or clothing, or adequate houses. ❑ *a multinational force aimed at ensuring that food and medicine get to needy Somalis* **NOUN** [PL] The **needy** are people who are needy. ❑ *There will be efforts to get larger amounts of food to the needy.*

✪ **ne·gate** /nɪˈɡeɪt/ VERB [T] (**negates**, **negating**, **negated**) (*academic word, formal*) **1** If one thing **negates** another, it causes that other thing to lose the effect or value that it had. = nullify, invalidate, cancel, neutralize; ≠ confirm, affirm ❑ *These weaknesses negated his otherwise progressive attitude towards the staff.* ❑ *An amendment to the bill effectively negated federal regulations that require organic feed for farm animals.* **2** If someone **negates** something, they say that it does not exist. ❑ *He warned that to negate the results of elections would only make things worse.*

✪ **ne·ga·tion** /nɪˈɡeɪʃən/ NOUN [SING, U] (*formal*) **1** [SING] [negation 'of' N] The **negation of** something is its complete opposite or something which destroys it or makes it lose its effect. = opposite, denial, contradiction; ≠ confirmation, affirmation ❑ *Badly written legislation is the negation of the rule of law and of democracy.* ❑ *The very foundation of this agency is a complete negation of the Quebec identity.* **2** [U] **Negation** is disagreement, refusal, or denial. ❑ *Irena shook her head, but in bewilderment, not negation.*

✪ **nega·tive** ◆◇◇ /ˈneɡətɪv/ ADJ, NOUN (*academic word*)
ADJ **1** A fact, situation, or experience that is **negative** is unpleasant, depressing, or harmful. = adverse; ≠ positive ❑ *The news from overseas is overwhelmingly negative.* ❑ *All this had an extremely negative effect on the criminal justice system.* **2** If someone is **negative** or has a **negative** attitude, they consider only the bad aspects of a situation, rather than the good ones. ❑ *When asked for your views about your current job, on no account must you be negative about it.* **3** A **negative** reply or decision indicates the answer 'no'. ❑ *Dr Velayati gave a vague but negative response.* ❑ *Upon a negative decision, the applicant loses the protection offered by Belgian law.* **4** In grammar, a **negative** clause contains a word such as 'not', 'never', or 'no one'. **5** If a medical test or scientific test is **negative**, it shows no evidence of the medical condition or substance that you are looking for. ❑ *So far 57 have taken the test and all have been negative.* **6** A **negative** charge or current has the same electrical charge as an electron. ❑ *Stimulate the injury or site of greatest pain with a small negative current.* **7** A **negative** number, quantity, or measurement is less than zero. = minus

❑ *Difficult texts record a positive score and simple ones score negative numbers.*

NOUN [C] (**negatives**) **1** A **negative** is a word, expression, or gesture that means 'no' or 'not'. ❑ *In the past we have heard only negatives when it came to following a healthy diet.* **2** In photography, a **negative** is an image that shows dark areas as light and light areas as dark. Negatives are made from camera film, and are used to print photographs. ❑ *negatives of Diana's wedding dress*

PHRASE **in the negative** If an answer is **in the negative**, it is 'no' or means 'no'. ❑ *The Council answered those questions in the negative.*

◆**neg·a·tive·ly** /ˈnegətɪvli/ ADV **1** [negatively with v] = adversely; ≠ positively ❑ *This will negatively affect the result over the first half of the year.* **2** *A few weeks later he said that maybe he viewed all his relationships rather negatively.* **3** [negatively after v] ❑ *Sixty per cent of people answered negatively.* **4** [negatively + -ED] ❑ *As these electrons are negatively charged they will attempt to repel each other.*

neg·a·tiv·ity /ˌnegəˈtɪvɪti/ NOUN [U] ❑ *I loathe negativity. I can't stand people who moan.*

✦ HIV negative → see HIV

◆**ne·glect** /nɪˈglekt/ VERB, NOUN

VERB [T] (**neglects, neglecting, neglected**) **1** If you **neglect** someone or something, you fail to take care of them properly. = disregard; ≠ look after ❑ *The woman denied that she had neglected her child.* ❑ *Feed plants and they grow, neglect them and they suffer.* **2** If you **neglect** someone or something, you fail to give them the amount of attention that they deserve. ❑ *He'd given too much to his career, worked long hours, neglected her.* **3** If you **neglect to** do something that you ought to do or **neglect** your duty, you fail to do it. ❑ *We often neglect to make proper use of our bodies.*

NOUN [U] If something suffers from **neglect** it has not been taken care of properly. = disregard; ≠ care ❑ *The town's old quayside is collapsing after years of neglect.* ❑ *Niwano's business began to suffer from neglect.*

ne·glect·ed /nɪˈglektɪd/ ADJ = forgotten ❑ *The fact that she is not coming today makes her grandmother feel lonely and neglected.* ❑ *a neglected aspect of the city's forgotten history* ❑ *an ancient and neglected church*

◆**neg·li·gence** /ˈneglɪdʒəns/ NOUN [U] (formal) If someone is guilty of **negligence**, they have failed to do something which they ought to do. = carelessness, failure, dereliction, omission, oversight ❑ *The soldiers were ordered to appear before a disciplinary council on charges of negligence.* ❑ *He now stands accused of treating classified secrets with gross negligence.*

◆**neg·li·gent** /ˈneglɪdʒənt/ ADJ If someone in a position of responsibility is **negligent**, they do not do something which they ought to do. = neglectful, careless, remiss; ≠ careful, attentive ❑ *The jury determined that the airline was negligent in training and supervising the crew.* ❑ *The Council had acted in a negligent manner.* ❑ *claims against a negligent third party for personal injury*

neg·li·gent·ly /ˈneglɪdʒəntli/ ADV [negligently with v] ❑ *A manufacturer negligently made and marketed a car with defective brakes.*

◆**neg·li·gible** /ˈneglɪdʒɪbl/ ADJ An amount or effect that is **negligible** is so small that it is not worth considering or worrying about. = minimal ❑ *The pay that the soldiers received was negligible.* ❑ *Senior managers are convinced that the strike will have a negligible impact.* ❑ *cut down to negligible proportions*

ne·go·tiable /nɪˈgəʊʃəbl/ ADJ Something that is **negotiable** can be changed or agreed upon when people discuss it. ❑ *He warned that his economic programme for the country was not negotiable.*

◆**ne·go·ti·ate** ◆◆◇ /nɪˈgəʊʃieɪt/ VERB [RECIP, T] (**negotiates, negotiating, negotiated**) **1** [RECIP] If people **negotiate with** each other or **negotiate** an agreement, they talk about a problem or a situation such as a business arrangement in order to solve the problem or complete the arrangement. = discuss, hold talks, settle ❑ *It is not clear whether the president is willing to negotiate with the Democrats.* ❑ *When you have two adversaries negotiating, you need to be on neutral territory.* ❑ *The local government and the army negotiated a truce.* ❑ *Western governments have this week urged him to negotiate and avoid force.* **2** [T] If you **negotiate** an area of land, a place, or an obstacle, you successfully travel across it or around it. = navigate ❑ *Frank Mariano negotiates the desert terrain in his battered pickup.* ❑ *I negotiated the corner on my motorcycle and pulled to a stop.*

WORD CONNECTIONS

negotiate + NOUN

negotiate a **deal**
negotiate an **agreement**
negotiate a **settlement**
negotiate a **solution**
❑ *It took three weeks to negotiate an agreement acceptable to all sides.*

ADV + **negotiate**

successfully negotiate
directly negotiate
❑ *We are confident that we can successfully negotiate a deal.*

◆**ne·go·tia·tion** ◆◆◇ /nɪˌgəʊʃiˈeɪʃən/ NOUN [C, U] (**negotiations**) **Negotiations** are formal discussions between people who have different aims or intentions, especially in business or politics, during which they try to reach an agreement. = bargaining, discussion, mediation, arbitration ❑ *Warren said, 'We have had meaningful negotiations and I believe we are very close to a deal.'* ❑ *After 10 years of negotiation, the Senate ratified the strategic arms reduction treaty.*

WORD CONNECTIONS

NOUN + **negotiation**

peace negotiations
trade negotiations
❑ *Peace negotiations will resume again next week.*

ADJ + **negotiation**

successful negotiations
❑ *The successful negotiations are a huge boost to the project.*

intense negotiations
protracted negotiations
❑ *After hours of intense negotiations, an agreement was reached.*

VERB + **negotiation**

conclude negotiations
resume negotiations
❑ *They hope to conclude negotiations by May or June.*

◆**ne·go·tia·tor** /nɪˈgəʊʃieɪtə/ NOUN [C] (**negotiators**) **Negotiators** are people who take part in political or financial negotiations. = mediator, intermediary ❑ *On Thursday night the rebels' chief negotiator at the peace talks announced that dialogue had gone as far as it could go.* ❑ *The two American negotiators are calling for substantial cuts in external subsidies.*

neigh·bour /ˈneɪbə/ (BrE; in AmE, use **neighbor**) NOUN [C] (**neighbours**) **1** Your **neighbour** is someone who lives near you. ❑ *My neighbour spies on me through a crack in the fence.* **2** You can refer to the person who is standing or sitting next to you as your **neighbour**. ❑ *The woman prodded her neighbour and whispered urgently in his ear.* **3** You can refer to something which stands next to something else of the same kind as its **neighbour**. ❑ *its big oil-rich neighbour*

◆**neigh·bour·hood** ◆◆◇ /ˈneɪbəhʊd/ (BrE; in AmE, use **neighborhood**) NOUN

NOUN [C] (**neighbourhoods**) **1** A **neighbourhood** is one of the parts of a town where people live. = area, district ❑ *There is no neighbourhood which is really safe.* ❑ *It seemed like a good neighbourhood to raise my children.* **2** The **neighbourhood** of a place or person is the area or the people around them. ❑ *a suburban Boston neighbourhood close to where I live*

PHRASE **in the neighbourhood of** **1** In the **neighbourhood of** a number means approximately that number. = roughly, about ❑ *The album's now sold something in the neighbourhood of 2 million copies.* **2** A place that is **in the neighbourhood of** another place is near it. ❑ *We went to visit two charming young ladies who lived in the neighbourhood of our camp.*

⊕**neigh·bour·ing** /ˈneɪbərɪŋ/ (*BrE; in AmE, use* **neighboring**) ADJ [neighbouring + N] **Neighbouring** places or things are near other things of the same kind. = nearby, adjacent ❑ *He is on his way back to Beijing after a tour of neighbouring Asian capitals.* ❑ *Rwanda is to hold talks with leaders of neighbouring countries next week.* ❑ *Some Liberians sought refuge in the neighbouring Ivory Coast.*

nei·ther ◆◇◇ /ˈnaɪðə, ˈniːðə/ CONJ, DET, QUANT, PRON
CONJ **1** You use **neither** in front of the first of two or more words or expressions when you are linking two or more things which are not true or do not happen. The other thing is introduced by 'nor'. ❑ *Professor Hisamatsu spoke neither English nor German.* **2** If you say that one person or thing does not do something and **neither** does another, what you say is true of all the people or things that you are mentioning. = nor ❑ *I never learned to swim and neither did they.* **3** (*formal*) You use **neither** after a negative statement to emphasize that you are introducing another negative statement. = nor ❑ *I can't ever recall Dad hugging me. Neither did I sit on his knee.*
DET You use **neither** to refer to each of two things or people, when you are making a negative statement that includes both of them. ❑ *At first, neither man could speak.*
QUANT You use **neither of us**, **neither of** you, or **neither of** them to refer to each of two things or people, when you are making a negative statement that includes both of them. ❑ *Neither of us felt like going out.*
PRON You use **neither** to refer to each of two things or people, when you are making a negative statement that includes both of them. ❑ *They both smiled; neither seemed likely to be aware of my absence for long.*

neo·na·tal /ˌniːəʊˈneɪtəl/ ADJ [neonatal + N] **Neonatal** means relating to the first few days of life of a new born baby. ❑ *the neonatal intensive care unit*

neph·ew /ˈnefjuː, ˈnev-/ NOUN [c] (**nephews**) Someone's **nephew** is the son of their sister or brother. ❑ *I am planning a 25th birthday party for my nephew.*

⊕**nerve** ◆◇◇ /nɜːv/ NOUN
NOUN [c, PL, u] (**nerves**) **1** [c] **Nerves** are long thin fibres that transmit messages between your brain and other parts of your body. ❑ *spinal nerves* ❑ *in cases where the nerve fibres are severed* **2** [PL] If you refer to someone's **nerves**, you mean their ability to cope with problems such as stress, worry, and danger. ❑ *Jill's nerves are stretched to breaking point.* **3** [PL] You can refer to someone's feelings of anxiety or tension as **nerves**. = nervousness ❑ *I just played badly. It wasn't nerves.* **4** [u] **Nerve** is the courage that you need in order to do something difficult or dangerous. = courage ❑ *The brandy made him choke, but it restored his nerve.*
PHRASES **get on someone's nerves** (*informal*) If someone or something **gets on** your **nerves**, they annoy or irritate you. ❑ *Lately he hasn't done a thing and it's getting on my nerves.*
have a nerve (*informal, disapproval*) If you say that someone **has a nerve** or **has the nerve** to do something, you are criticizing them for doing something which you feel they had no right to do. ❑ *He told his critics they had a nerve complaining about him.*
lose your nerve If you **lose your nerve**, you suddenly panic and become too afraid to do something that you were about to do. ❑ *The bomber had lost his nerve and fled.*

nerv·ous ◆◇◇ /ˈnɜːvəs/ ADJ **1** If someone is **nervous**, they are frightened or worried about something that is happening or might happen, and show this in their behaviour. = anxious ❑ *The party has become deeply nervous about its prospects of winning the next election.* **2** A **nervous** person is very tense and easily upset. ❑ *She was apparently a very nervous woman, and that affected her career.* **3** [nervous + N] A **nervous** illness or condition is one that

affects your emotions and your mental state. ❑ *The number of nervous disorders was rising in the region.*
nerv·ous·ly /ˈnɜːvəsli/ ADV [nervously with v] ❑ *Brunhilde stood up nervously as the men came into the room.*
nerv·ous·ness /ˈnɜːvəsnəs/ NOUN [u] ❑ *I smiled warmly so he wouldn't see my nervousness.*

⊕**nerv·ous sys·tem** NOUN [c] (**nervous systems**) Your **nervous system** consists of all the nerves in your body together with your brain and spinal cord. ❑ *So it is possible that the symptoms will not finally go until your nervous system is in a better state.* ❑ *It is oxygen that powers the nervous system and feeds the brain.* ❑ *diseases of the brain and nervous system*

⊕**nest** /nest/ NOUN, VERB
NOUN [c] (**nests**) **1** A bird's **nest** is the home that it makes to lay its eggs in. ❑ *I can see an eagle's nest on the rocks.* ❑ *These birds build nests of twigs and leaves in hollows and clefts.* **2** A **nest** is a home that a group of insects or other creatures make in order to live in and give birth to their young in. ❑ *Some solitary bees make their nests in burrows in the soil.* ❑ *a rat's nest*
VERB [I] (**nests, nesting, nested**) When a bird **nests** somewhere, it builds a nest and settles there to lay its eggs. ❑ *Some species may nest in close proximity to each other.* ❑ *nesting sites*

⊕**net** ◆◇◇ /net/ NOUN, VERB, ADJ, ADV
NOUN [u, c, SING] (**nets**) **1** [u] **Net** is a kind of cloth that you can see through. It is made of fine threads woven together so that there are small equal spaces between them. **2** [c] A **net** is a piece of netting which is used as a protective covering for something, for example to protect vegetables from birds. ❑ *I threw aside my mosquito net, jumped out of bed and drew up the blind.* **3** [c] A **net** is a piece of netting which is used for catching fish, insects, or animals. ❑ *Several fishermen sat on wooden barrels, tending their nets.* **4** [SING] **The Net** is the same as the **Internet.**
VERB [T] (**nets, netting, netted**) **1** If you **net** a fish or other animal, you catch it in a net. = land ❑ *I'm quite happy to net a fish and then let it go.* **2** If you **net** something, you manage to get it, especially by using skill. **3** If you **net** a particular amount of money, you gain it as profit after all expenses have been paid. = make ❑ *He netted profit of $1.85 billion from three large sales of stock.*
ADJ (*in BrE, also use* **nett**) **1** [net + N, V-LINK + net 'of' N] A **net** amount is one which remains when everything that should be subtracted from it has been subtracted. ❑ *a rise in sales and net profit* ❑ *What you actually receive is net of deductions.* ❑ *At the year end, net assets were £18 million.* **2** [net + N] The **net** weight of something is its weight without its container or the material that has been used to wrap it. ❑ *350 mg net weight* ❑ *the net weight of snacks packed* **3** [net + N] A **net** result is a final result after all the details have been considered or included. = overall, eventual, final, remaining ❑ *There has been a net gain in jobs in our country.*
ADV (*in BrE, also use* **nett**) A particular amount **net** is what remains when everything that has been subtracted from it has been subtracted. ❑ *Balances of $5,000 and above will earn 11 per cent gross, 8.25 per cent net.* ❑ *a first year profit of around £50,000 net* ❑ *They pay him around $2 million net.* ❑ *All bank and building society interest is paid net.*

nett /net/ (*BrE*) → See **net**

⊕**net·work** ◆◆◇ /ˈnetwɜːk/ NOUN, VERB (*academic word*)
NOUN [c] (**networks**) **1** A radio or television **network** is a company or group of companies that broadcast radio or television programmes throughout an area. ❑ *Los Angeles-based Univision is a Spanish-language broadcast television network.* **2** A **network** of people or institutions is a large number of them that have a connection with each other and work together as a system. = system ❑ *Distribution of the food is going ahead using a network of local church people and other volunteers.* ❑ *He is keen to point out the benefits which the family network can provide.* **3** A particular **network** is a system of things which are connected and which operate together. For example, a **computer network** consists of a number of computers that are part of the same system. = system ❑ *a computer*

N

network with 154 terminals ◻ Huge sections of the rail network are out of action. **4** A **network of** lines, roads, veins, or other long thin things is a large number of them which cross each other or meet at many points. = web, grid ◻ Strasbourg, with its rambling network of medieval streets ◻ a rich network of blood vessels and nerves **VERB** [i] (**networks, networking, networked**) (business) If you **network**, you try to meet new people who might be useful to you in your job. ◻ In business, it is important to network with as many people as possible on a face to face basis.

◒ neu·ral /ˈnjʊərəl, AmE ˈnʊ-/ ADJ **Neural** means relating to a nerve or to the nervous system. ◻ neural pathways in the brain ◻ Brains consist of multiple neural networks. ◻ Folic acid is important for helping to prevent neural tube defects such as spina bifida.

◒ neu·rol·ogy /njʊəˈrɒlədʒi, AmE nʊ-/ NOUN [u] (medical) **Neurology** is the study of the structure, function, and diseases of the nervous system. ◻ He trained in neurology at the National Hospital for Nervous Diseases. ◻ the university's department of clinical neurology

◒ neu·rol·o·gist /njʊəˈrɒlədʒɪst, AmE nʊ-/ NOUN [c] (**neurologists**) ◻ Someone with suspected MS should see a neurologist specializing in the disease. ◻ Neurologists examine the nerves of the head and neck, muscle movement, balance, and other cognitive abilities. ◻ Dr Simon Shorvon, consultant neurologist of the Chalfont Centre for Epilepsy

---

WORD PARTS

The prefix **neuro-** appears in words for things that relate to a nerve or to the nervous system:
neurology (NOUN)
neurolinguistics (NOUN)
neurosurgeon (NOUN)

◒ neu·tral /ˈnjuːtrəl, AmE ˈnuːt-/ ADJ, NOUN, COLOUR (academic word)

ADJ **1** If a person or country adopts a **neutral** position or remains **neutral**, they do not support anyone in a disagreement, war, or contest. = impartial, unbiased; ≠ biased ◻ Let's meet on neutral territory. ◻ Those who decided to remain neutral in the struggle now found themselves required to take sides. **2** If someone speaks in a **neutral** voice or if the expression on their face is **neutral**, they do not show what they are thinking or feeling. ◻ Isabel put her magazine down and said in a neutral voice, 'You're very late, darling.' **3** If you say that something is **neutral**, you mean that it does not have any effect on other things because it lacks any significant qualities of its own, or it is an equal balance of two or more different qualities, amounts, or ideas. ◻ Three in every five interviewed felt that the budget was neutral and they would be no better off. ◻ ICI is making a profit of £190m on the sale, which will have a neutral impact on its earnings. **4** In an electrical device or system, the **neutral** wire is one of the three wires needed to complete the circuit so that the current can flow. The other two wires are called the earth wire and the live or positive wire. ◻ The earth wire in the house is connected to the neutral wire. **5** In chemistry, **neutral** is used to describe things that are neither acid nor alkaline. ◻ Pure water is neutral with a pH of 7. **NOUN** [u, c] (**neutrals**) **1** [u, c] A **neutral** is someone who is neutral. ◻ It was a good game to watch for the neutrals. **2** [u] **Neutral** is the position between the gears of a vehicle such as a car, in which the gears are not connected to the engine. ◻ Graham put the van in neutral and jumped out into the road. **COLOUR** **Neutral** is used to describe things that have a pale colour such as cream or grey, or that have no colour at all. ◻ At the horizon the land mass becomes a continuous pale neutral grey, almost blending with the sky.

neu·tral·ity /njuːˈtræləti, AmE nuː-/ NOUN [u] **1** I noticed, behind the neutrality of his gaze, a deep weariness. **2** a reputation for political neutrality and impartiality

neu·tral·ize /ˈnjuːtrəlaɪz, AmE ˈnuːt-/ also **neutralise** VERB [T] (**neutralizes, neutralizing, neutralized**) **1** To **neutralize** something means to prevent it from having any effect or from working properly. ◻ The US is trying to neutralize the resolution in the UN Security Council.

2 When a chemical substance **neutralizes** an acid, it makes it less acid. ◻ Antacids are alkaline and they relieve pain by neutralizing acid in the contents of the stomach.

◒ neu·tron /ˈnjuːtrɒn, AmE ˈnuːt-/ NOUN [c] (**neutrons**) A **neutron** is an atomic particle that has no electrical charge. ◻ Each atomic cluster is made up of neutrons and protons. ◻ A typical neutron star is a mere 20 km in diameter, but contains as much mass as one or two Suns.

nev·er ◆◆◆ /ˈnevə/ ADV **ADV** **1** **Never** means at no time in the past or at no time in the future. ◻ I have never lost the weight I put on in my teens. ◻ Never had he been so free of worry. ◻ That was a mistake. We'll never do it again. **2** **Never** means 'not in any circumstances at all'. ◻ I would never do anything to hurt him. ◻ Divorce is never easy for children. **3** **Never** is used to refer to the past and means 'not'. ◻ He never achieved anything. ◻ I never knew him. **PHRASE** **never ever** (emphasis) **Never ever** is an emphatic way of saying 'never'. ◻ I never, ever sit around thinking, 'What shall I do next?'
◆ never mind → see mind

◒ never·the·less ◆◇◇ /ˌnevəðəˈles/ ADV [nevertheless with CL] (academic word, formal) You use **nevertheless** when saying something that contrasts with what has just been said. = nonetheless, even so, still, yet ◻ Although the market has been flat, residential property costs remain high. Nevertheless, the fall-off in demand has had an impact on resale values. ◻ Most marriages fail after between five and nine years. Nevertheless, people continue to get married. ◻ There had been no indication of any loss of mental faculties. His whole life had nevertheless been clouded with a series of illnesses.

new ◆◆◆ /njuː, AmE nuː-/ ADJ (**newer, newest**) **1** Something that is **new** has been recently created, built, or invented or is in the process of being created, built, or invented. ◻ They've just opened a new hotel in the area. ◻ These ideas are nothing new. **2** Something that is **new** has not been used or owned by anyone. ◻ That afternoon she went out and bought a new dress. ◻ There are many boats, new and used, for sale. **3** You use **new** to describe something which has replaced another thing, for example because you no longer have the old one, or it no longer exists, or it is no longer useful. ◻ Under the new rules, some factories will cut emissions by as much as 90 per cent. ◻ I had to find somewhere new to live. ◻ Rachel has a new boyfriend. **4** **New** is used to describe something that has only recently been discovered or noticed. ◻ The new planet is about ten times the size of the earth. **5** [new + N] A **new** day or year is the beginning of the next day or year. ◻ The start of a new year is a good time to reflect on the many achievements of the past. **6** [new + N] **New** is used to describe someone or something that has recently acquired a particular status or position. ◻ the usual exhaustion of a new mother **7** [V-LINK + new] If you are **new to** a situation or place, or if the situation or place is **new to** you, you have not previously seen it or had any experience with it. ◻ She wasn't new to the company. ◻ His name was new to me then and it stayed in my mind. **8** [new + N] **New** potatoes, carrots, or peas are produced early in the season for such vegetables and are usually small with a sweet flavour. ◻ Serve with a salad and new potatoes.
→ See also brand-new
◆ as good as new → see good

new·born /ˈnjuːbɔːn, AmE ˈnuː-/ ADJ, NOUN **ADJ** A **newborn** baby or animal is one that has just been born. ◻ The electronic sensor has been adapted to fit on a newborn baby. **NOUN** [PL] (**newborns**) The **newborn** are babies or animals who are newborn. ◻ Mild jaundice in the newborn is common and often clears without treatment.

new·comer /ˈnjuːkʌmə, AmE ˈnuː-/ NOUN [c] (**newcomers**) A **newcomer** is a person who has recently arrived in a place, joined an organization, or started a new activity. ◻ He must be a newcomer to town and he obviously didn't understand our local customs.

new·ly ◆◇◇ /ˈnjuːli, AmE ˈnuːli/ ADV [newly + -ED/ADJ] **Newly** is used before a past participle or an adjective to indicate that a particular action is very recent, or that a particular state of affairs has very recently begun to exist. = **recently** ❑ *She was young at the time, and newly married.*

news ♦♦♦ /njuːz, *AmE* nuːz/ NOUN

NOUN [U, SING] **1** [U] **News** is information about a recently changed situation or a recent event. ❑ *We waited and waited for news of him.* ❑ *They still haven't had any news about when they'll be able to go home.* **2** [U] [also 'the' news] **News** is information that is published in newspapers and broadcast on radio and television about recent events in the country or world or in a particular area of activity. ❑ *Foreign News is on page 16.* ❑ *Those are some of the top stories in the news.* **3** [SING] **The news** is a television or radio broadcast which consists of information about recent events in the country or the world. ❑ *I heard all about the bombs on the news.* **4** [U] (*informal*) If you say that someone or something is **news**, you mean that they are considered to be interesting and important at the moment, and that people want to hear about them on the radio and television and in newspapers. ❑ *A murder was big news.* PHRASES **bad news** or **good news** If you say that something is **bad news**, you mean that it will cause you trouble or problems. If you say that something is **good news**, you mean that it will be useful or helpful to you. ❑ *The drop in travel is bad news for the airline industry.* **be news to someone** If you say that something is **news to** you, you mean that you did not previously know what you have just been told, especially when you are surprised or annoyed about it. ❑ *I'd certainly tell you if I knew anything, but I don't. What you're saying is news to me.*

news agen·cy ♦◇◇ NOUN [C] (**news agencies**) A **news agency** is an organization that gathers news stories from a particular country or from all over the world and supplies them to journalists. ❑ *A correspondent for Reuters news agency says he saw a number of demonstrators being beaten.*

news·caster ♦♦♦ /ˈnjuːzkɑːstə, *AmE* ˈnuːzkæstə/ (in *BrE*, also use **newsreader**) NOUN [C] (**newscasters**) A **newscaster** is a person who reads the news on the radio or on television. ❑ *TV newscaster Barbara Walters*

news con·fer·ence NOUN [C] (**news conferences**) A **news conference** is a meeting held by a famous or important person in which they answer journalists' questions. = **press conference** ❑ *He is due to hold a news conference in about an hour.*

news·paper ♦♦◇ /ˈnjuːspeɪpə, *AmE* ˈnuːz-/ NOUN [C, U] (**newspapers**) **1** [C] A **newspaper** is a publication consisting of a number of large sheets of folded paper, on which news, advertisements, and other information are printed. ❑ *He was carrying a newspaper.* ❑ *They read their daughter's allegations in the newspaper.* **2** [C] A **newspaper** is an organization that produces a newspaper. ❑ *It is the nation's fastest growing national daily newspaper.* **3** [U] **Newspaper** consists of pieces of old newspapers, especially when they are being used for another purpose such as wrapping things up. ❑ *He found two pots, each wrapped in newspaper.*

news·reel /ˈnjuːzriːl, *AmE* ˈnuːz-/ NOUN [C] (**newsreels**) [oft newsreel + N] A **newsreel** is a short film of national or international news events. In the past newsreels were made for showing in cinemas.

New Year NOUN [U, SING] **1** [U] [also 'the' New Year] **New Year** or the **New Year** is the time when people celebrate the start of a year. ❑ *Happy New Year, everyone.* ❑ *The restaurant was closed over the New Year.* **2** [SING] **The New Year** is the first few weeks of a year. ❑ *Isabel was expecting their baby in the New Year.*

next ♦♦♦ /nekst/ ADJ, DET, ADJ, PRON, ADV

ADJ The **next** period of time, event, person, or thing is the one that comes immediately after the present one or after the previous one. ❑ *I got up early the next morning.* ❑ *the next available flight* ❑ *Who will be the next mayor?* PHRASE **as the next** (*emphasis*) If you say that you do something or experience something as much **as the next** person, you mean that you are no different from anyone else in the respect mentioned. ❑ *I enjoy pleasure as much as the next person.* DET You use **next** in expressions such as **next Friday**, **next day** and **next year** to refer, for example, to the first Friday,

day, or year that comes after the present or previous one. ❑ *Let's plan a big night next week.* ❑ *He retires next January.* ADJ **1** [N + next] You use **next** in expressions such as **Friday next** to refer, for example, to the first Friday that comes after the present or previous one. ❑ *I'll be 26 years old on Friday next.* **2** [DET + next] **The next** place or person is the one that is nearest to you or that is the first one that you come to. ❑ *Grace sighed so heavily that Trish could hear it in the next room.* ❑ *The man in the next chair was asleep.* PRON You use **next** after expressions such as **this month** and **this year** to refer, for example, to the first month or year that comes after the present one. ❑ *He predicted that the region's economy would grow by about six per cent both this year and next.* PHRASE **after next** You use **after next** in expressions such as **the week after next** to refer to a period of time after the next one. For example, when it is May, the month after next is July. ❑ *the party's annual conference, to be held the week after next* ADV **1** The thing that happens **next** is the thing that happens immediately after something else. ❑ *Next, close your eyes then screw them up tight.* ❑ *I don't know what to do next.* **2** [next before V] When you **next** do something, you do it for the first time since you last did it. ❑ *I next saw him at his house in Vermont.* **3** [next + ADJ-SUPERL] You use **next** to say that something has more of a particular quality than all other things except one. For example, the thing that is **next** best is the one that is the best except for one other thing. = **second** ❑ *The one thing he didn't have was a son. I think he's felt that a grandson is the next best thing.* PHRASE **next to** **1** If one thing is **next to** another thing, it is at the other side of it. = **beside** ❑ *She sat down next to him on the sofa.* ❑ *at the southern end of the Gaza Strip next to the Egyptian border* **2** You use **next to** in order to give the most important aspect of something when comparing it with another aspect. = **after** ❑ *Her children were the number two priority in her life next to her career.* **3** You use **next to** before a negative, or a word that suggests something negative, to mean almost, but not completely. = **virtually** ❑ *Johnson still knew next to nothing about tobacco.*

next door ADV, ADJ

> The adjective is usually spelled **next-door**.

ADV **1** If a room or building is **next door**, it is the next one to the right or left. ❑ *I went next door to the bathroom.* ❑ *the old lady who lived next door* **2** [N + next door] The people **next door** are the people who live in the house or flat to the right or left of yours. ❑ *The neighbours thought the family next door had moved.* PHRASES **next door to** If a room or building is **next door to** another one, it is the next one to the left or right. ❑ *The kitchen is right next door to the dining room.* **the boy next door** or **the girl next door** If you refer to someone as **the boy next door** or **the girl next door**, you mean that they are pleasant, respectable, and likeable. ❑ *He was dependable, straightforward, the boy next door.* ADJ **1** [next door + N] A **next-door** room or building is the next one to the right or left. ❑ *a thud like a cellar door slamming shut in a next-door house* **2** [next door + N] Your **next-door** neighbour is the person who lives in the house or flat to the right or left of yours. ❑ *Even your next-door neighbour didn't see through your disguise.*

next of kin NOUN [U] (*formal*) **Next of kin** is sometimes used to refer to the person who is your closest relative, especially in official or legal documents. ❑ *We have notified the next of kin.*

nice ♦♦◇ /naɪs/ ADJ (**nicer, nicest**) **1** If you say that something is **nice**, you mean that you find it attractive, pleasant, or enjoyable. ❑ *I think silk ties can be quite nice.* ❑ *It's nice to be here together again.* **2** If you say that it is **nice of** someone to say or do something, you are saying that they are being kind and thoughtful. This is often used as a way of thanking someone. = **kind** ❑ *It's awfully nice of you to come all this way to see me.* ❑ *'How are your boys?'—'How nice of you to ask.'* **3** If you say that someone is **nice**, you mean that you like them because they are

N

friendly and pleasant. ❏ *I've met your father and he's rather nice.* **4** [V-LINK + nice] If you are **nice** to people, you are friendly, pleasant, or polite towards them. ❏ *She met Mr and Mrs Ricciardi, who were very nice to her.* **5** When the weather is **nice**, it is warm and pleasant. ❏ *He nodded to us and said, 'Nice weather we're having.'* **6** You can use **nice** to emphasize a particular quality that you like. ❏ *With a nice dark colour, the wine is medium to full bodied.* ❏ *I'll explain it nice and simply so you can understand.* **7** ['it' V-LINK + nice + to-INF] You can use **nice** when you are greeting people. For example, you can say '**Nice to meet you**', '**Nice to have met you**', or '**Nice to see you**'. ❏ *Good morning. Nice to meet you and thanks for being with us this weekend.*

nice·ly /'naɪsli/ ADV
ADV **1** If you say that something is done **nicely**, you mean that you think it is done in an attractive, pleasant, or enjoyable manner. ❏ *He's just written a book, nicely illustrated and not too technical.* **2** If you treat someone **nicely**, you are friendly, pleasant, or polite towards them. ❏ *He treated you very nicely and acted like a decent guy.* **3** [nicely with v] If something is happening or working **nicely**, it is happening or working in a satisfactory way or in the way that you want it to. ❏ *She has a bit of private money, so they manage quite nicely.*
PHRASE **do nicely** If someone or something **is doing nicely**, they are being successful. ❏ *another hotel owner who is doing very nicely*

⬦ **niche** /niːʃ, AmE nɪtʃ/ NOUN, ADJ
NOUN [c] (**niches**) **1** (*business*) A **niche** in the market is a specific area of marketing which has its own particular requirements, customers, and products. ❏ *I think we have found a niche in the toy market.* ❏ *Small companies can do extremely well if they can fill a specific market niche.* **2** A **niche** is a hollow area in a wall which has been made to hold a statue, or a natural hollow part in a hill or cliff. ❏ *Above him, in a niche on the wall, sat a tiny veiled Ganesh, the elephant god.* **3** Your **niche** is the job or activity which is exactly suitable for you. ❏ *Simon Lane quickly found his niche as a busy freelance model maker.*
ADJ [niche + N] (*business*) **Niche** marketing is the practice of dividing the market into specialized areas for which particular products are made. A **niche** market is one of these specialized areas. ❏ *Many media experts see such all-news channels as part of a general move towards niche marketing.* ❏ *The Japanese are able to supply niche markets because of their flexible production methods.*

nick /nɪk/ VERB, NOUN
VERB [T] (**nicks, nicking, nicked**) **1** (*BrE, informal*) If someone **nicks** something, they steal it. ❏ *He smashed a window to get in and nicked a load of silver cups.* **2** If you **nick** something or **nick** yourself, you accidentally make a small cut in the surface of the object or your skin. ❏ *When I pulled out of the space, I nicked the rear bumper of the car in front of me.* ❏ *A sharp blade is likely to nick the skin and draw blood.*
NOUN [c] (**nicks**) A **nick** is a small cut made in the surface of something, usually in someone's skin. ❏ *The barbed wire had left only the tiniest nick just below my right eye.*

nick·el /'nɪkəl/ NOUN [u, c] (**nickels**) **1** [u] Nickel is a silver-coloured metal that is used in making steel. **2** [c] In the United States and Canada, a **nickel** is a coin worth five cents. ❏ *a large glass jar filled with pennies, nickels, dimes, and quarters*

nick·name /'nɪkneɪm/ NOUN, VERB
NOUN [c] (**nicknames**) A **nickname** is an informal name for someone or something. ❏ *Red got his nickname for his red hair.*
VERB [T] (**nicknames, nicknaming, nicknamed**) If you **nickname** someone or something, you give them an informal name. ❏ *When he got older I nicknamed him Little Alf.*

nico·tine /'nɪkətiːn/ NOUN [u] **Nicotine** is the substance in tobacco that people can become addicted to. ❏ *Nicotine produces a feeling of well-being in the smoker.*

niece /niːs/ NOUN [c] (**nieces**) Someone's **niece** is the daughter of their sister or brother. ❏ *his niece, the daughter of his eldest sister*

night ♦♦♦ /naɪt/ NOUN
NOUN [c, u] (**nights**) **1** [c, u] The **night** is the part of each day when the sun has set and it is dark outside, especially the time when people are sleeping. ❏ *The fighting began in the late afternoon and continued all night.* ❏ *Finally night fell.* **2** [c] The **night** is the period of time between the end of the afternoon and the time that you go to bed, especially the time when you relax before going to bed. ❏ *So whose party was it last night?* **3** [c] A particular **night** is a particular evening when a special event takes place, such as a show or a play. ❏ *The first night crowd packed the building.*
PHRASES **at night** **1** If it is a particular time **at night**, it is during the time when it is dark and is before midnight. ❏ *It's eleven o'clock at night in Moscow.* **2** If something happens **at night**, it happens regularly during the evening or night. ❏ *He was going to college at night, in order to become an accountant.*
day and night or **night and day** If something happens **day and night** or **night and day**, it happens all the time without stopping. ❏ *Dozens of doctors and nurses have been working day and night for weeks.*
an early night or **a late night** If you have **an early night**, you go to bed early. If you have **a late night**, you go to bed late. ❏ *I've had a hell of a day, and all I want is an early night.*
✦ **morning, noon and night** → see **morning**

night·club /'naɪtklʌb/ NOUN [c] (**nightclubs**) A **nightclub** is a place where people go late in the evening to drink and dance.

night·mare ♦◇◇ /'naɪtmeə/ NOUN [c] (**nightmares**) **1** A **nightmare** is a very frightening dream. ❏ *All the victims still suffered nightmares.* **2** If you refer to a situation as a **nightmare**, you mean that it is very frightening and unpleasant. ❏ *The years in prison were a nightmare.* **3** If you refer to a situation as a **nightmare**, you are saying in a very emphatic way that it is irritating because it causes you a lot of trouble. ❏ *Taking my son Peter to a restaurant was a nightmare.*

nil /nɪl/ NOUN [u] If you say that something **is nil**, you mean that it does not exist at all. = nonexistent ❏ *Their legal rights are virtually nil.*

nine ♦♦♦ /naɪn/ NUM (**nines**) Nine is the number 9. ❏ *We still sighted nine yachts.*

nine·teen ♦♦♦ /ˌnaɪn'tiːn/ NUM (**nineteens**) Nineteen is the number 19. ❏ *They have nineteen days to make up their minds.*

nine·teenth ♦♦◇ /ˌnaɪn'tiːnθ/ ADJ The **nineteenth** item in a series is the one that you count as number nineteen. ❏ *my nineteenth birthday*

nine·ti·eth ♦♦◇ /'naɪntiəθ/ ADJ The **ninetieth** item in a series is the one that you count as number ninety. ❏ *He celebrates his ninetieth birthday on Friday.*

nine·ty ♦♦♦ /'naɪnti/ NUM, NOUN
NUM Ninety is the number 90. ❏ *It was decided she had to stay another ninety days.*
NOUN [PL] (**nineties**) **1** When you talk about the **nineties**, you are referring to numbers between 90 and 99. For example, if you are in your **nineties**, you are aged between 90 and 99. If the temperature is **in the nineties**, the temperature is between 90 and 99 degrees. ❏ *By this time she was in her nineties and needed help more and more frequently.* **2** The **nineties** is the decade between 1990 and 1999. ❏ *These trends only got worse as we moved into the nineties.*

ninth ♦♦◇ /naɪnθ/ ADJ, NOUN
ADJ The **ninth** item in a series is the one that you count as number nine. ❏ *January the ninth* ❏ *the ninth century*
NOUN [c] (**ninths**) A **ninth** is one of nine equal parts of something. ❏ *The dollar rose by a ninth of a cent.*

no ♦♦♦ /nəʊ/ CONVENTION, EXCLAM, DET, ADV, NOUN
CONVENTION **1** You use **no** to give a negative response to a question. ❏ *'Any problems?'—'No, I'm OK.'* **2** You use **no** to say that something that someone has just said is not true. ❏ *'We thought you'd emigrated.'—'No, no.'* **3** You use **no** to refuse an offer or a request, or to refuse permission. ❏ *'Here, have mine.'—'No, this is fine.'* ❏ *'Can you just get the*

n

message through to Pete for me?'—'No, no I can't.' **4** You use **no** to acknowledge a negative statement or to show that you accept and understand it. = right ☐ 'We're not on the main campus.'—'No.' ☐ 'It's not one of my favourite forms of music.'—'No.' **5** You use **no** before correcting what you have just said. ☐ I was twenty-two – no, twenty-one.
EXCLAM 1 You use **no** to indicate that you do not want someone to do something. ☐ No. I forbid it. You cannot.
2 You use **no** to express shock or disappointment at something you have just been told. ☐ 'We went with Sarah and the married man that she's currently seeing.'—'Oh no.'
DET 1 You use **no** to mean not any or not one person or thing. ☐ He had no intention of paying the cash. ☐ No job has more influence on the future of the world. **2** You use **no** to emphasize that someone or something is not the type of thing mentioned. ☐ He is no singer. ☐ I make it no secret that our worst consultants earn nothing. **3** You use **no** in front of an adjective and noun to make the noun group mean its opposite. ☐ Sometimes a bit of selfishness, if it leads to greater self-knowledge, is no bad thing. **4** **No** is used in notices or instructions to say that a particular activity or thing is forbidden. ☐ The captain turned out the 'no smoking' signs. ☐ No talking after lights out.
PHRASE **there is no** (emphasis) If you say **there is no** doing a particular thing, you mean that it is very difficult or impossible to do that thing. ☐ There is no going back to the life she had.
ADV [no + COMPAR] You can use **no** to make the negative form of a comparative. ☐ It is to start broadcasting no later than the end of 1994. ☐ Yesterday no fewer than thirty climbers reached the summit.
NOUN [c] (**noes** or **no's**) A **no** is a person who has answered 'no' to a question or who has voted against something. **No** is also used to refer to their answer or vote. ☐ According to the latest opinion polls, the noes have 50 per cent, the yeses 35 per cent.
♦ **not to take no for an answer** → see **answer**; **no longer** → see **long**; **in no way** → see **way**; **there's no way** → see **way**; **no way** → see **way**

no·ble /'nəʊbəl/ ADJ (**nobler, noblest**) **1** (approval) If you say that someone is a **noble** person, you admire and respect them because they are unselfish and morally good. ☐ He was an upright and noble man who was always willing to help in any way he could. **2** (approval) If you say that something is a **noble** idea, goal, or action, you admire it because it is based on high moral principles. ☐ He had implicit faith in their noble intentions. ☐ We'll always justify our actions with noble sounding theories. **3** If you describe something as **noble**, you think that its appearance or quality is very impressive, making it superior to other things of its type. = fine ☐ the great parks with their noble trees **4** **Noble** means belonging to a high social class and having a title. = aristocratic ☐ rich and noble families
no·bly /'nəʊbli/ ADV [nobly with v] ☐ Eric's sister had nobly volunteered to help with the gardening.

no·body ♦♦◇ /'nəʊbʊdi/ PRON, NOUN
PRON **Nobody** means not a single person, or not a single member of a particular group or set. = no one ☐ They were shut away in a little room where nobody could overhear. ☐ Nobody realizes how bad things are.
NOUN [c] (**nobodies**) (disapproval) If someone says that a person is a **nobody**, they are saying in an unkind way that the person is not at all important. ☐ A man in my position has nothing to fear from a nobody like you.

noc·tur·nal /nɒk'tɜːnəl/ ADJ **1** **Nocturnal** means occurring at night. ☐ The dog's main duty will be to accompany me on long nocturnal walks. **2** **Nocturnal** creatures are active mainly at night. ☐ When there is a full moon, this nocturnal rodent is careful to stay in its burrow.

nod ♦◇◇ /nɒd/ VERB, NOUN
VERB [i, t] (**nods, nodding, nodded**) **1** [i, t] If you **nod**, you move your head downwards and upwards to show that you are answering 'yes' to a question, or to show agreement, understanding, or approval. ☐ 'Are you okay?' I asked. She nodded and smiled. ☐ Jacques tasted one and nodded his approval. **2** [i] If you **nod** in a particular direction, you bend your head once in that direction in

order to indicate something or to give someone a signal. ☐ 'Does it work?' he asked, nodding at the piano. ☐ She nodded towards the dining room. 'He's in there.' **3** [i, t] If you **nod**, you bend your head once, as a way of saying hello or goodbye. ☐ All the girls nodded and said 'Hi.' ☐ Both of them smiled and nodded a greeting. ☐ Tom nodded a greeting.
PHRASAL VERB **nod off** (informal) If you **nod off**, you fall asleep, especially when you had not intended to. = doze off ☐ The judge appeared to nod off yesterday while a witness was being cross-examined.
NOUN [c] (**nods**) A **nod** is a movement of your head downwards and upwards to show that you are answering 'yes' to a question, or to show agreement, understanding, or approval. ☐ She gave a nod and said, 'I see.' ☐ 'Probably,' agreed Hunter, with a slow nod of his head.

noise ♦◇◇ /nɔɪz/ NOUN
NOUN [u, c, PL] (**noises**) **1** [u] **Noise** is a loud or unpleasant sound. ☐ There was too much noise in the room and he needed peace. ☐ The noise of bombs and guns was incessant. **2** [c] A **noise** is a sound that someone or something makes. ☐ Gerald made a small noise in his throat. ☐ birdsong and other animal noises **3** [PL] If someone **makes noises** of a particular kind about something, they say things that indicate their attitude to it in a rather indirect or vague way. ☐ The president took care to make encouraging noises about the future.
PHRASE **make the right noises** or **make all the right noises** If you say that someone **makes the right noises** or **makes all the right noises**, you think that they are showing concern or enthusiasm about something because they feel they ought to rather than because they really want to. ☐ But at the annual party conference he always made the right noises.

noisy /'nɔɪzi/ ADJ (**noisier, noisiest**) **1** A **noisy** person or thing makes a lot of loud or unpleasant noise. ☐ my noisy old typewriter **2** A **noisy** place is full of a lot of loud or unpleasant noise. ☐ It's a noisy place with film clips showing constantly on one of the cafe's giant screens. ☐ The baggage hall was crowded and noisy. **3** If you describe someone as **noisy**, you are critical of them for trying to attract attention to their views by frequently and forcefully discussing them. = strident ☐ It might, at last, silence the small but noisy intellectual clique.
nois·i·ly /'nɔɪzɪli/ ADV ☐ The students on the grass bank cheered noisily.

no·mad·ic /nəʊ'mædɪk/ ADJ **1** **Nomadic** people travel from place to place rather than living in one place all the time. ☐ the great nomadic tribes of the Western Sahara **2** If someone has a **nomadic** way of life, they travel from place to place and do not have a settled home. ☐ The daughter of a railway engineer, she at first had a somewhat nomadic childhood.

nomi·nal /'nɒmɪnəl/ ADJ **1** You use **nominal** to indicate that someone or something is supposed to have a particular identity or status, but in reality does not have it. ☐ As he was still not allowed to run a company, his wife became its nominal head. **2** [nominal + N] A **nominal** price or sum of money is very small in comparison with the real cost or value of the thing that is being bought or sold. ☐ I am prepared to sell my shares at a nominal price. **3** [nominal + N] In economics, the **nominal** value, rate, or level of something is the one expressed in terms of current prices or figures, without taking into account general changes in prices that take place over time. ☐ Inflation would be lower and so nominal rates would be more attractive in real terms.
nomi·nal·ly /'nɒmɪnəli/ ADV = technically ☐ The sultan was still nominally the chief of staff. ☐ The road is nominally under the control of UN peacekeeping troops.

nomi·nate /'nɒmɪneɪt/ VERB [T] (**nominates, nominating, nominated**) **1** If someone **is nominated** for a job or position, their name is formally suggested as a candidate for it. = propose ☐ This week one of them will be nominated by the Democratic Party for the presidency of the United States. ☐ The Security Council can nominate anyone for secretary-general. **2** If you **nominate** someone to a job or position, you formally choose them to hold that job or position. = appoint ☐ In 1967 Johnson nominated Thurgood Marshall to the Supreme Court. ❑ *She was nominated by the president as ambassador to Barbados.* **3** *If someone or something such as an actor or a film* **is nominated** *for an award, someone formally suggests that they should be given that award.* = put forward ❑ *Practically every film he made was nominated for an Oscar.*

nomi·na·tion /ˌnɒmɪˈneɪʃən/ NOUN [C, U] (**nominations**) **1** [c] A **nomination** is an official suggestion of someone as a candidate in an election or for a job. ❑ *his candidacy for the Republican presidential nomination* **2** [c] A **nomination** for an award is an official suggestion that someone or something should be given that award. ❑ *They say he's certain to get a nomination for best supporting actor.* **3** [c, U] The **nomination** of someone to a particular job or position is their appointment to that job or position. ❑ *the nomination of Texas Senator Lloyd Bentsen to be treasury secretary*

nomi·nee /ˌnɒmɪˈniː/ NOUN [c] (**nominees**) A **nominee** is someone who is nominated for a job, position, or award. ❑ *His nominee for vice president was elected only after a second ballot.*

none ♦♦◇ /nʌn/ QUANT, PRON
QUANT [none 'of' DEF-N] **None of** something means not even a small amount of it. **None of** a group of people or things means not even one of them. ❑ *None of us knew how to treat her.*
PRON When **none** is used to refer to something, it means not even a small amount of it. When **none** is used to refer to a group of people or things, it means not even one of them. ❑ *I searched bookshops and libraries for information, but found none.* ❑ *No one could imagine a great woman painter. None had existed yet.*
PHRASES **have none of** (*informal*) If you say that someone **will have none of** something, or is **having none of** something, you mean that they refuse to accept it. ❑ *He knew his own mind and was having none of their attempts to keep him at home.*
none too (*formal, emphasis*) You use **none too** in front of an adjective or adverb in order to emphasize that the quality mentioned is not present. ❑ *He was none too thrilled to hear from me at that hour.*
none the You use **none the** to say that someone or something does not have any more of a particular quality than they did before. = no ❑ *You could end up none the wiser about managing your finances.*
✦ **second to none → see second**

⊘none·the·less /ˌnʌnðəˈles/ ADV [nonetheless with CL] (*academic word, formal*) **Nonetheless** means the same as **nevertheless.** = nevertheless, however ❑ *There was still a long way to go. Nonetheless, some progress had been made.* ❑ *Many a country awash in violence has nonetheless managed the transition to democracy.* ❑ *a second-hand gift, but nonetheless pleasurable for its recipient*

non·sense /ˈnɒnsəns/ NOUN
NOUN [u] **1** (*disapproval*) If you say that something spoken or written is **nonsense,** you mean that you consider it to be untrue or silly. ❑ *Most orthodox doctors however dismiss this as complete nonsense.* ❑ *all that poetic nonsense about love* **2** [also 'a' nonsense, usu SUPP + nonsense] (*disapproval*) You can use **nonsense** to refer to something that you think is foolish or that you disapprove of. ❑ *Surely it is an economic nonsense to deplete the world of natural resources.* **3** You can refer to spoken or written words that do not mean anything because they do not make sense as **nonsense.** ❑ *a children's nonsense poem by Charles E Carryl*
PHRASE **make a nonsense of something** To make a **nonsense of** something or to **make nonsense of** it means to make it seem ridiculous or pointless. ❑ *The fighting made a nonsense of peace pledges made last week.*

noon /nuːn/ NOUN, ADJ
NOUN [u] **Noon** is twelve o'clock in the middle of the day. = midday ❑ *The long day of meetings started at noon.*
ADJ [noon + N] **Noon** means happening or appearing in the middle part of the day. = midday ❑ *The noon sun was fierce.*
✦ **morning, noon and night → see morning**

no one ♦♦◇ (in BrE, also use **no-one**) PRON **No one** means not a single person, or not a single member of a particular group or set. = nobody ❑ *Everyone wants to be a hero, but no one wants to die.*

nor ♦♦◇ /nɔː/ CONJ **1** You use **nor** after 'neither' in order to introduce the second alternative or the last of a number of alternatives in a negative statement. ❑ *Neither Mr Rose nor Mr Woodhead was available for comment yesterday.* ❑ *I can give you neither an opinion nor any advice.* **2** You use **nor** after a negative statement in order to introduce another negative statement which adds information to the previous one. = neither ❑ *Cooking up a quick dish doesn't mean you have to sacrifice flavour. Nor does fast food have to be junk food.* **3** You use **nor** after a negative statement in order to indicate that the negative statement also applies to you or to someone or something else. = neither ❑ *'None of us has any idea how long we're going to be here.'—'Nor do I.'* ❑ *'If my husband has no future,' she said, 'then nor do my children.'*

⊘norm /nɔːm/ NOUN [C, SING] (**norms**) (*academic word*) **1** [c] **Norms** are ways of behaving that are considered normal in a particular society. = average, rule, value ❑ *The actions taken depart from what she called the commonly accepted norms of democracy.* ❑ *a social norm that says drunkenness is inappropriate behaviour* **2** [SING] If you say that a situation is **the norm,** you mean that it is usual and expected. ❑ *Families of six or seven are the norm in Borough Park.* **3** [c] A **norm** is an official standard or level that organizations are expected to reach. = standard, rule ❑ *About 32 per cent of students meet national norms in reading.* ❑ *an agency which would establish European norms and co-ordinate national policies to halt pollution.*

⊘nor·mal ♦♦◇ /ˈnɔːməl/ ADJ (*academic word*) **1** Something that is **normal** is usual and ordinary, and is what people expect. = usual, ≠ unusual, abnormal ❑ *The two countries resumed normal diplomatic relations.* ❑ *Her height and weight were normal for her age.* ❑ *In November, Clean's bakery produced 50 per cent more bread than normal.* **2** A **normal** person has no serious physical or mental health problems. = healthy ❑ *Statistics indicate that depressed patients are more likely to become ill than are normal people.*

WORD CONNECTIONS
ADV + **normal**
perfectly normal **completely** normal **quite** normal ❑ *It is perfectly normal for couples to have arguments.*
relatively normal ❑ *Until a few years ago he lived a relatively normal life.*

nor·mal·ity /nɔːˈmælɪti/ NOUN [u] **Normality** is a situation in which everything is normal. ❑ *A semblance of normality has returned with people going to work and shops reopening.*

⊘nor·mal·ly ♦◇◇ /ˈnɔːməli/ ADV **1** If you say that something **normally** happens or that you **normally** do a particular thing, you mean that it is what usually happens or what you usually do. ❑ *All airports in the country are working normally today.* ❑ *Social progress is normally a matter of struggles and conflicts.* ❑ *Normally, the transportation system in Paris carries 950,000 passengers a day.* **2** [normally after V] If you do something **normally,** you do it in the usual or conventional way. = as normal, as usual; ≠ abnormally ❑ *failure of the blood to clot normally*

⊘north ♦♦♦ /nɔːθ/ also **North** NOUN, ADV, ADJ
NOUN [u, SING] **1** [u] [also 'the' north] The **north** is the direction which is on your left when you are looking

towards the direction where the sun rises. ❑ *In the north the ground becomes very cold as the winter snow and ice covers the ground.* ❑ *Birds usually migrate from north to south.* **2** [SING] **The north** of a place, country, or region is the part which is in the north. ❑ *The plan mostly benefits people in the North and Midwest.* ❑ *a tiny house in a village in the north of France* **3** [SING] ['the' north] **The North** is used to refer to the richer, more developed countries of the world. ❑ *Malaysia has emerged as the toughest critic of the North's environmental attitudes.* ADV **1** [north after V] If you go **north**, you travel towards the north. ❑ *Anita drove north up Pacific Highway.* **2** Something that is **north** of a place is positioned to the north of it. ❑ *a little village a few miles north of Portland* ADJ **1** [north + N] The **north** edge, corner, or part of a place or country is the part which is towards the north. ❑ *the north side of the mountain* **2** [north + N] '**North**' is used in the names of some countries, states, and regions in the north of a larger area. ❑ *There were demonstrations this weekend in cities throughout North America, Asia and Europe.* **3** [north + N] A **north** wind is a wind that blows from the north. ❑ *a bitterly cold north wind*

north·east ♦♦◇ /ˌnɔːθˈiːst/ (in BrE, also use **north-east**) NOUN, ADJ, ADJ

NOUN [U, SING] **1** [U] [also 'the' northeast] The **northeast** is the direction which is halfway between north and east. ❑ *the warm waters of Salt Springs Island to the northeast* **2** [SING] The **northeast** of a place, country, or region is the part which is in the northeast. ❑ *The northeast has been particularly hard hit.* ADV **1** [northeast after V] If you go **northeast**, you travel towards the northeast. ❑ *'We're going northeast,' Paula told them, before they started.* **2** [northeast 'of' N] Something that is **northeast of** a place is positioned to the northeast of it. ❑ *This latest attack was at Careysburg, twenty miles northeast of the capital, Monrovia.* ADJ [northeast + N] The **northeast** edge, corner, or part of a place is the part which is towards the northeast. = northeastern ❑ *a climate like that of our northeast coast*

north·eastern /ˌnɔːθˈiːstən/ (in BrE, also use **north-eastern**) ADJ **Northeastern** means in or from the northeast of a region or country. ❑ *on the northeastern coast of Florida*

○**north·ern** ♦♦◇ /ˈnɔːðən/ also **Northern** ADJ [northern + N] **Northern** means in or from the north of a region, state, or country. ❑ *Their two children were immigrants to Northern Ireland from Pennsylvania.* ❑ *Prices at three-star hotels fell furthest in several northern cities.*

north·ward /ˈnɔːθwəd/ ADV, ADJ

The form **northwards** is also used for the adverb.

ADV **Northward** or **northwards** means towards the north. ❑ *Tropical storm Marco is pushing northward up Florida's coast.* ADJ [northward + N] A **northward** direction or course is one that goes towards the north. ❑ *The northward journey from Jalalabad was no more than 120 miles.*

north·west ♦♦◇ /ˌnɔːθˈwest/ (in BrE, also use **north-west**) NOUN, ADV, ADJ

NOUN [U, SING] **1** [U] [also 'the' northwest] The **northwest** is the direction which is halfway between north and west. ❑ *four miles to the northwest* **2** [SING] The **northwest** of a place, country, or region is the part which is towards the northwest. ❑ *in the extreme northwest of the country* ADV **1** [northwest after V] If you go **northwest**, you travel towards the northwest. ❑ *Take the narrow lane going northwest parallel with the railway line.* **2** [northwest 'of' N] Something that is **northwest of** a place is positioned to the northwest of it. ❑ *Just a couple of hours to the northwest of the capital is the wine-growing area of Hunter Valley.* ADJ [northwest + N] The **northwest** part of a place, country, or region is the part which is towards the northwest. = northwestern ❑ *the northwest coast of the United States*

north·western /ˌnɔːθˈwestən/ (in BrE, also use **north-western**) ADJ **Northwestern** means in or from the northwest of a region or country. ❑ *Virtually every river in northwestern Oregon was near flood stage.*

nose ♦◇◇ /nəʊz/ NOUN, VERB

NOUN [C] (**noses**) **1** Your **nose** is the part of your face which sticks out above your mouth. You use it for smelling and breathing. ❑ *She wiped her nose with a tissue.* **2** The **nose** of a vehicle such as an aeroplane or a boat is the front part of it. ❑ *They went over to the aeroplane and stood near its nose.* **3** You can refer to your sense of smell as your **nose**. ❑ *The river that runs through Middlesbrough became ugly on the eye and hard on the nose.*

PHRASES **keep your nose clean** (informal) If you **keep your nose clean**, you behave well and stay out of trouble. ❑ *If you kept your nose clean, you had a job for life.*

follow your nose 1 If you **follow** your **nose** to get to a place, you go straight ahead or follow the most obvious route. ❑ *Just follow your nose and in about five minutes you're at the old railway.* **2** If you **follow** your **nose**, you do something in a particular way because you feel it should be done like that, rather than because you are following any plan or rules. ❑ *You won't have to think, just follow your nose.*

have a nose for something If you say that someone **has a nose for** something, you mean that they have a natural ability to find it or recognize it. ❑ *He had a nose for trouble and a brilliant tactical mind.*

look down your nose at someone (disapproval) If you say that someone **looks down** their **nose** at something or someone, you mean that they believe they are superior to that person or thing and treat them with disrespect. ❑ *I don't look down my nose at comedy.*

pay through the nose (informal, emphasis) If you say that you **paid through the nose** for something, you are emphasizing that you had to pay what you consider too high a price for it. ❑ *We don't like paying through the nose for our wine when eating out.*

poke your nose into something or **stick your nose into something** (informal, disapproval) If someone **pokes** their **nose into** something or **sticks** their **nose into** something, they try to interfere with it even though it does not concern them. = meddle ❑ *We don't like strangers who poke their noses into our affairs.*

rub someone's nose in it (informal) To **rub** someone's **nose in** something that they do not want to think about, such as a failing or a mistake they have made, means to remind them repeatedly about it. ❑ *His enemies will attempt to rub his nose in past policy statements.*

turn up one's nose at something If you **turn up** your **nose** at something, you reject it because you think that it is not good enough for you. ❑ *I'm not in a financial position to turn up my nose at several hundred thousand dollars.*

under someone's nose If you do something under someone's **nose**, you do it right in front of them, without trying to hide it from them. ❑ *We've been married 25 years and this carrying on under my nose was the last straw.*

nose to tail (mainly BrE; in AmE, use **bumper-to-bumper**) If vehicles are **nose to tail**, the front of one vehicle is close behind the back of another.

VERB [I, T] (**noses, nosing, nosed**) If a vehicle **noses** in a certain direction or if you **nose** it there, you move it slowly and carefully in that direction. ❑ *He could not see the driver as the car nosed forward.* ❑ *A motorboat nosed out of the mist and nudged into the branches of a tree.*

PHRASAL VERB **nose around** (informal) If you **nose around** a place that belongs to someone else, you look around it to see if you can find something interesting. ❑ *I wondered what else he'd taken and nosed around his bureau.* ❑ *He had thought to just nose around, see what he could.*

✦ put someone's nose out of joint → see joint

nosy /ˈnəʊzi/ also **nosey** ADJ (**nosier, nosiest**) (informal, disapproval) If you describe someone as **nosy**, you mean that they are interested in things which do not concern them. ❑ *He was having to whisper in order to avoid being overheard by their nosy neighbours.*

not ♦♦♦ /nɒt/ ADV

Not is often shortened to **n't** in spoken English, and added to the auxiliary or modal verb. For example, 'did not' is often shortened to 'didn't'.

ADV 1 You use **not** with verbs to form negative statements. ◻ *The sanctions are not working the way they were intended.* ◻ *I don't trust my father anymore.* **2** You use **not** to form questions to which you expect the answer 'yes'. ◻ *Haven't they got enough problems there already?* ◻ *Didn't I see you at the party last week?* **3** You use **not**, usually in the form **n't**, in questions which imply that someone should have done something, or to express surprise that something is not the case. ◻ *Why didn't you do it months ago?* ◻ *Why couldn't he listen to her?* **4** You use **not**, usually in the form **n't**, in question tags after a positive statement. ◻ *It's crazy, isn't it?* ◻ *I've been a great husband, haven't I?* **5** You use **not**, usually in the form **n't**, in polite suggestions. ◻ *Actually we do have a position in mind. Why don't you fill out our application?* **6** You use **not** to represent the negative of a word, group, or clause that has just been used. ◻ *'Have you found Paula?'—'I'm afraid not, Kate.'* **7** You can use **not** in front of 'all' or 'every' when you want to say something that applies only to some members of the group that you are talking about. ◻ *Not all the money, to put it mildly, has been used wisely.* **8** If something is **not** always the case, you mean that sometimes it is the case and sometimes it is not. ◻ *He didn't always win the arguments, but he often was right.* ◻ *She couldn't always afford a babysitter.* **9** You can use **not** or **not even** in front of 'a' or 'one' to emphasize that there is none at all of what is being mentioned. ◻ *no office, no phone, not even a shelf on which to put my meagre belongings* ◻ *I sent report after report. But not one word was published.* **10** [not + AMOUNT] You can use **not** in front of a word referring to a distance, length of time, or other amount to say that the actual distance, time, or amount is less than the one mentioned. ◻ *The tug crossed our stern not fifty yards away.* ◻ *a large crowd not ten yards away waiting for a bus* **11** You use **not** when you are contrasting something that is true with something that is untrue. You use this especially to indicate that people might think that the untrue statement is true. ◻ *He has his place in the Asian team not because he is white but because he is good.* ◻ *Training is an investment not a cost.* **12** You use **not** in expressions such as 'not only', 'not just', and 'not simply' to emphasize that something is true, but it is not the whole truth. ◻ *These films were not only making money; they were also perceived to be original.* ◻ *What's it going to cost us, not just in terms of money, but in terms of lives?*

PHRASE not that You use **not that** to introduce a negative clause that contradicts something that the previous statement implies. ◻ *His death took me a year to get over; not that you're ever really over it.*

CONVENTION not at all 1 (emphasis) **Not at all** is an emphatic way of saying 'No' or of agreeing that the answer to a question is 'No'. ◻ *'Sorry. I sound like Abby, don't I?'—'No. Not at all.'* **2** (formulae) **Not at all** is a polite way of acknowledging a person's thanks. ◻ *'Thank you very much for speaking with us.'—'Not at all.'*

✦ **if not** → see if; **more often than not** → see often

⊕ **no·table** /ˈnəʊtəbəl/ ADJ Someone or something that is **notable** is important or interesting. = noteworthy, remarkable, marked, striking; ≠ unremarkable ◻ *The proposed new structure is notable not only for its height, but for its shape.* ◻ *Mo did not want to be ruled by anyone and it is notable that she never allowed the men in her life to eclipse her.* ◻ *With a few notable exceptions, doctors are a pretty sensible lot.*

⊕ **no·tably** /ˈnəʊtəbli/ ADV **1** [notably + GROUP/CL] You use **notably** to specify an important or typical example of something that you are talking about. = particularly ◻ *The divorce would be granted when more important problems, notably the fate of the children, had been decided.* ◻ *It was a question of making sure certain needs were addressed, notably in the pensions area.* **2** [notably + ADJ/ADV] You can use **notably** to emphasize a particular quality that someone or something has. = strikingly ◻ *Old established friends are notably absent, so it's a good opportunity to make new contacts.*

⊕ **note** ♦♦◇ /nəʊt/ NOUN, VERB

NOUN [C, SING] (notes) **1** [C] A **note** is a short letter. = message ◻ *Stevens wrote him a note asking him to come to his flat.* **2** [C] A **note** is something that you write down to remind yourself of something. = reminder ◻ *I knew that if I didn't make a note I would lose the thought so I asked to borrow a pen or pencil.* ◻ *She wasn't taking notes on the lecture.* **3** [C] In a book or article, a **note** is a short piece of additional information. = footnote, endnote ◻ *See Note 16 on p. 223.* ◻ *'Exiles' by James Joyce, edited with an Introduction and notes by J C C Mays* **4** [C] A **note** is a short document that has to be signed by someone and that gives official information about something. ◻ *Since Mr Bennett was going to need some time off work, he asked for a sick note.* **5** [C] In music, a **note** is the sound of a particular pitch, or a written symbol representing this sound. ◻ *She has a deep voice and doesn't even try for the high notes.* **6** [SING] You can use **note** to refer to a particular quality in someone's voice that shows how they are feeling. = tone ◻ *There is an unmistakable note of nostalgia in his voice when he looks back on the early years of the family business.* **7** [SING] You can use **note** to refer to a particular feeling, impression, or atmosphere. ◻ *Yesterday's testimony began on a note of passionate but civilized disagreement.* ◻ *Somehow he tells these stories without a note of horror.* **8** [C] (mainly BrE; in AmE, usually use **bill**) You can refer to a banknote as a **note**.

PHRASES of note Someone or something that is **of note** is important, worth mentioning, or well-known. ◻ *politicians of note*

take note If you **take note of** something, you pay attention to it because you think that it is important or significant. ◻ *Take note of the weather conditions.*

VERB [T] (notes, noting, noted) **1** If you **note** a fact, you become aware of it. = notice ◻ *The White House has noted his promise to support any attack that was designed to enforce the UN resolutions.* ◻ *Suddenly, I noted that the rain had stopped.* **2** If you tell someone to **note** something, you are drawing their attention to it. ◻ *Note the statue to Sallustio Bandini, a prominent Sienese.* ◻ *Note how the average level of job performance increases as the SR decreases.* **3** If you **note** something, you mention it in order to draw people's attention to it. = observe ◻ *The report notes that export and import volumes picked up in leading economies.* ◻ *The yearbook also noted a sharp drop in reported cases of sexually transmitted disease.* **4** When you **note** something, you write it down as a record of what has happened. ◻ *'He has had his tonsils out and has been ill, too,' she noted in her diary.* ◻ *They never noted the building's history of problems.*

PHRASAL VERB note down If you **note down** something, you write it down quickly, so that you have a record of it. ◻ *She had noted down the names and she told me the story simply and factually.* ◻ *If you find a name that's on the list I've given you, note it down.*

→ See also **noted**

note·book /ˈnəʊtbʊk/ NOUN [C] (notebooks) **1** A **notebook** is a small book for writing notes in. ◻ *He brought out a notebook and pen from his pocket.* **2** (computing) A **notebook** computer is a small personal computer. ◻ *a range of notebook computers which allows all your important information to travel safely with you*

not·ed ♦◇◇ /ˈnəʊtɪd/ ADJ To be **noted for** something you do or have means to be well known and admired for it. = renowned ◻ *a television programme noted for its attacks on organized crime*

note·worthy /ˈnəʊtwɜːði/ ADJ (formal) A fact or event that is **noteworthy** is interesting, remarkable, or significant in some way. = notable ◻ *It is noteworthy that the programme has been shifted from its original August slot to July.* ◻ *I found nothing particularly noteworthy to report.* ◻ *The most noteworthy feature of the list is that there are no women on it.*

noth·ing ♦♦♦ /ˈnʌθɪŋ/ PRON, NOUN

PRON 1 Nothing means not a single thing, or not a single part of something. ◻ *I've done nothing much since this morning.* ◻ *There is nothing wrong with the car.* **2** You use **nothing** to indicate that something or someone is not important or significant. ◻ *Because he had always had money it meant nothing to him.* ◻ *Do our years together mean nothing?* **3** If you say that something cost **nothing** or is worth **nothing**, you are indicating that it cost or is worth a surprisingly small amount of money. ◻ *The furniture was threadbare; he'd obviously picked it up for nothing.* **4** You use **nothing** before an adjective or 'to'-infinitive to say that

n

something or someone does not have the quality indicated. ❑ *Around the lake the countryside generally is nothing special.* ❑ *There was nothing remarkable about him.* **5** You can use **nothing** before 'so' and an adjective or adverb, or before a comparative, to emphasize how strong or great a particular quality is. ❑ *Youngsters learn nothing so fast as how to beat the system.* ❑ *I consider nothing more important in my life than songwriting.*

PHRASES **all or nothing** You can use **all or nothing** to say that either something must be done fully and completely or else it cannot be done at all. ❑ *Either he went through with this thing or he did not; it was all or nothing.*

be better than nothing If you say that something is **better than nothing**, you mean that it is not what is required, but that it is better to have that thing than to have nothing at all. ❑ *After all, 15 minutes of exercise is better than nothing.*

nothing but You use **nothing but** in front of a noun, an infinitive without 'to', or an '-ing' form to mean 'only'. ❑ *All that money brought nothing but sadness and misery and tragedy.* ❑ *It did nothing but make us ridiculous.* ❑ *He is focused on nothing but winning.*

nothing to it If you say about a story or report that there is **nothing to it**, you mean that it is untrue. ❑ *It's all superstition, and there's nothing to it.*

nothing to it If you say about an activity that there is **nothing to it**, you mean that it is extremely easy. ❑ *If you've shied away from making pancakes in the past, don't be put off – there's really nothing to it!*

nothing of the sort (*emphasis*) **Nothing of the sort** is used when strongly contradicting something that has just been said. ❑ *'We're going to talk this over in my office.' – 'We're going to do nothing of the sort.'*

CONVENTION **it's nothing** (*formulae*) People sometimes say **'It's nothing'** as a polite response after someone has thanked them for something they have done. ❑ *'Thank you for the wonderful dinner.' – 'It's nothing,' Sarah said.*

NOUN [C] (**nothings**) A **nothing** is something or someone that is not important or significant. ❑ *It is the picture itself that is the problem; so small, so dull. It's a nothing, really.*

✦ **nothing to write home about** → see **home**; **stop at nothing** → see **stop**; **think nothing of** → see **think**

no·tice ◆◆◇ /ˈnəʊtɪs/ VERB, NOUN

VERB [I, T] (**notices, noticing, noticed**) If you **notice** something or someone, you become aware of them. ❑ *He stressed that people should not hesitate to contact the police if they've noticed any strangers recently.* ❑ *I noticed that most academics were writing papers during the summer.* ❑ *Luckily, I'd noticed where you left the car.* ❑ *If he thought no one would notice, he's wrong.*

NOUN [C, U] (**notices**) **1** [C] A **notice** is a written announcement in a place where everyone can read it. ❑ *Notices in the waiting room requested that you neither smoke nor spit.* ❑ *A few guest houses had 'No Vacancies' notices in their windows.* **2** [U] If you give **notice** about something that is going to happen, you give a warning in advance that it is going to happen. ❑ *Interest is paid monthly. Three months' notice is required for withdrawals.* ❑ *The insured must be given at least 10 days' notice of cancellation.* **3** [C] A **notice** is a formal announcement in a newspaper or magazine about something that has happened or is going to happen. = announcement ❑ *I spotted a notice in a local newspaper.* **4** [C] A **notice** is one of a number of letters that are similar or exactly the same which an organization sends to people in order to give them information or ask them to do something. ❑ *Bonus notices were issued each year from head office to local agents.* **5** [C] (*BrE*; in *AmE*, use **review**) A **notice** is a written article in a newspaper or magazine in which someone gives their opinion of a play, film, or concert.

PHRASES **on short notice** or **at a moment's notice** or **at twenty-four hours' notice** Notice is used in expressions such as 'on short notice', 'at a moment's notice', or 'at twenty-four hours' notice', to indicate that something can or must be done within a short period of time. ❑ *There's no one available on such short notice to take her class.* ❑ *I live just a mile away, so I can usually be available on short notice.*

until further notice If a situation is said to exist **until**

further notice, it will continue for an uncertain length of time until someone changes it. ❑ *The bad news was that all flights had been cancelled until further notice.*

give someone notice (*business*) If an employer **gives** an employee **notice**, the employer tells the employee that he or she must leave his or her job within a short fixed period of time. ❑ *The next morning I telephoned him and gave him his notice.*

give notice or **hand in notice** (*business*) If you **give notice** or **hand in notice** you tell your employer that you intend to leave your job soon, within a set period of time. You can also **hand in** your **notice**. = quit ❑ *He handed in his notice at the bank and ruined his promising career.*

take notice If you **take notice** of a particular fact or situation, you behave in a way that shows that you are aware of it. ❑ *We want the government to take notice of what we think they should plan for single parents.*

take no notice If you **take no notice** of someone or something, you do not consider them to be important enough to affect what you think or what you do. = ignore ❑ *They took no notice of him, he did not stand out, he was in no way remarkable.*

no·tice·able /ˈnəʊtɪsəbəl/ ADJ Something that is **noticeable** is very obvious, so that it is easy to see, hear, or recognize. ❑ *It is noticeable that women do not have the rivalry that men have.*

no·tice·ably /ˈnəʊtɪsəbli/ ADV ❑ *Standards of living were deteriorating rather noticeably.*

no·ti·fi·ca·tion /ˌnəʊtɪfɪˈkeɪʃən/ NOUN [C, U] (**notifications**) If you are given **notification** of something, you are officially informed of it. ❑ *Names of the dead and injured are being withheld pending notification of relatives.*

no·ti·fy /ˈnəʊtɪfaɪ/ VERB [T] (**notifies, notifying, notified**) (*formal*) If you **notify** someone of something, you officially inform them about it. = inform ❑ *The skipper notified the coastguard of the tragedy.* ❑ *Earlier this year they were notified that their homes were to be cleared away.*

✪ **no·tion** ◆◇◇ /ˈnəʊʃən/ NOUN [C] (**notions**) (*academic word*) A **notion** is an idea or belief about something. = idea, concept ❑ *We each have a notion of just what kind of person we'd like to be.* ❑ *I reject absolutely the notion that privatization of our industry is now inevitable.*

✪ **no·tion·al** /ˈnəʊʃənəl/ ADJ (*formal*) Something that is **notional** exists only in theory or as a suggestion or idea, but not in reality. = theoretical; ≠ actual, real ❑ *the notional value of state assets* ❑ *He made around two hundred thousand pounds notional profit last year.* ❑ *a notional concept of what makes good parents*

✪ **no·tion·al·ly** /ˈnəʊʃənəli/ ADV = theoretically; ≠ actually ❑ *those who notionally supported the republic but did nothing in terms of action* ❑ *That meant that he, notionally at least, outranked them all.*

no·to·ri·ety /ˌnəʊtəˈraɪɪti/ NOUN [U] To achieve **notoriety** means to become well known for something bad. ❑ *He achieved notoriety as chief counsel to President Nixon in the Watergate break-in.*

no·to·ri·ous /nəʊˈtɔːriəs/ ADJ To be **notorious** means to be well known for something bad. = infamous ❑ *an area notorious for drugs, crime, and violence*

no·to·ri·ous·ly /nəʊˈtɔːriəsli/ ADV ❑ *The train company is overstaffed and notoriously inefficient.* ❑ *He worked mainly in New York City where living space is notoriously at a premium.*

✪ **not·with·stand·ing** /ˌnɒtwɪðˈstændɪŋ/ PREP, ADV (*academic word*)

PREP (*formal*) If something is true **notwithstanding** something else, it is true in spite of that other thing. = in spite of, despite ❑ *He despised William Pitt, notwithstanding the similar views they both held.* ❑ *Millen expected they would take action notwithstanding his absence.*

ADV [N + notwithstanding] If something is true **notwithstanding** something, it is true in spite of it. ❑ *His relations with colleagues, differences of opinion notwithstanding, were unfailingly friendly.*

noun /naʊn/ NOUN [C] (**nouns**) A **noun** is a word such as 'car', 'love', or 'Anne' which is used to refer to a person or thing.

nour·ish /ˈnʌrɪʃ, AmE ˈnɜːrɪʃ/ VERB [T] (**nourishes, nourishing, nourished**) To nourish a person, animal, or plant means to provide them with the food that is necessary for life, growth, and good health. ❑ *The food she eats nourishes both her and the baby.*
nour·ish·ing /ˈnʌrɪʃɪŋ, AmE ˈnɜːrɪʃɪŋ/ ADJ ❑ *Most of these nourishing substances are in the yolk of the egg.*

nour·ish·ment /ˈnʌrɪʃmənt, AmE ˈnɜːr-/ NOUN [U] **1** If something provides a person, animal, or plant with nourishment, it provides them with the food that is necessary for life, growth, and good health. ❑ *The mother provides the embryo with nourishment and a place to grow.* **2** The action of nourishing someone or something, or the experience of being nourished, can be referred to as nourishment. ❑ *Sugar gives quick relief to hunger but provides no lasting nourishment.*

✪**nov·el** ♦♦◇ /ˈnɒvəl/ NOUN, ADJ
[NOUN] [C] (**novels**) A novel is a long written story about imaginary people and events. = story, book, narrative ❑ *a novel by Herman Hesse* ❑ *historical novels set in the time of the Pharaohs*
[ADJ] Novel things are new and different from anything that has been done, experienced, or made before. ❑ *Protesters found a novel way of demonstrating against steeply rising oil prices.*

nov·el·ist /ˈnɒvəlɪst/ NOUN [C] (**novelists**) A novelist is a person who writes novels. ❑ *The key to success as a romantic novelist is absolute belief in your story.*

nov·el·ty /ˈnɒvəlti/ NOUN [U, C] (**novelties**) **1** [U] Novelty is the quality of being different, new, and unusual. ❑ *In the contemporary western world, rapidly changing styles cater to a desire for novelty and individualism.* **2** [C] A novelty is something that is new and therefore interesting. ❑ *Stores really like orange cauliflower because it's a novelty, it's something different.* **3** [C] Novelties are cheap toys, ornaments, or other objects that are sold as presents or souvenirs. ❑ *At Easter, we give them plastic eggs filled with small toys, novelties, and coins.*

nov·ice /ˈnɒvɪs/ NOUN [C] (**novices**) **1** A novice is someone who has been doing a job or other activity for only a short time and so is not experienced at it. ❑ *I'm a novice at these things, Lieutenant. You're the professional.* **2** In a monastery or convent, a novice is a person who is preparing to become a monk or nun.

now ♦♦♦ /naʊ/ ADV, PRON, CONJ
[ADV] **1** You use now to refer to the present time, often in contrast to a time in the past or the future. ❑ *She's a widow now.* ❑ *But we are now a much more fragmented society.* **2** [now after V] If you do something now, you do it immediately. ❑ *I'm sorry, but I must go now.* **3** You use now to indicate that a particular situation is the result of something that has recently happened. ❑ *Mrs Chandra has received one sweater for each of her five children and says that the winter will not be so hard now.* ❑ *She told me not to repeat it, but now I don't suppose it matters.* **4** In stories and accounts of past events, now is used to refer to the particular time that is being written or spoken about. ❑ *She felt a little better now.* ❑ *It was too late now for Blake to lock his room door.* **5** You use now in statements which specify the length of time up to the present that something has lasted. ❑ *They've been married now for 30 years.* ❑ *They have been missing for a long time now.* **6** [now + CL] (*spoken*) You say 'Now' or 'Now then' to indicate to the person or people you are with that you want their attention, or that you are about to change the subject. ❑ *'Now then,' Max said, 'to get back to the point.'* ❑ *Now then, what's the trouble?* **7** [now with CL] (*spoken*) You use now to give a slight emphasis to a request or command. ❑ *Come on now. You know you must be hungry.* ❑ *Come and sit down here, now.* **8** [now + CL] (*spoken*) You can say 'Now' to introduce information which is relevant to the part of a story or account that you have reached, and which needs to be known before you can continue. ❑ *My son went to Aspen, in Colorado. Now he and his wife are people who love a quiet vacation.* **9** [now + CL] (*spoken*) You say 'Now' to introduce something which contrasts with what you have just said. ❑ *Now, if it was me, I'd want to do more than just change the locks.*

[PHRASES] **now and then** or **now and again** or **every now and again** If you say that something happens now and then or every now and again, you mean that it happens sometimes but not very often or regularly. ❑ *My father has a collection of magazines to which I return every now and then.*
any day now or **any moment now** or **any time now** If you say that something will happen any day now, any moment now, or any time now, you mean that it will happen very soon. ❑ *Jim expects to be sent to Europe any day now.*
just now (*spoken*) **1** Just now means a very short time ago. ❑ *You looked pretty upset just now.* ❑ *I spoke just now of being in love.* **2** You use just now when you want to say that a particular situation exists at the time when you are speaking, although it may change in the future. ❑ *I'm pretty busy just now.*
now for (*spoken*) People such as television presenters sometimes use now for when they are going to start talking about a different subject or start presenting a new activity. ❑ *And now for something completely different.*
[PRON] **1** You use now to refer to the present time, often in contrast to a time in the past or the future. ❑ *Now is the time when we must all live as economically as possible.* **2** You can use now to refer to the immediate future. ❑ *Now is your chance to talk to him.*
[CONJ] You use now or now that to indicate that an event has occurred and as a result something else may or will happen. ❑ *Now you're settled, why don't you take up some serious study?*

✪**nowa·days** ♦◇◇ /ˈnaʊədeɪz/ ADV [nowadays with CL] Nowadays means at the present time, in contrast with the past. = at the present time, currently, these days ❑ *Nowadays it's acceptable for women to be ambitious. But it wasn't then.* ❑ *This method is seldom used nowadays.*

no·where ♦◇◇ /ˈnəʊweə/ ADV
[ADV] **1** (*emphasis*) You use nowhere to emphasize that a place has more of a particular quality than any other place, or that it is the only place where something happens or exists. ❑ *Nowhere is language a more serious issue than in Hawaii.* ❑ *This kind of forest exists nowhere else in the world.* **2** You use nowhere when making negative statements to say that a suitable place of the specified kind does not exist. ❑ *There was nowhere to hide and nowhere to run.* ❑ *I have nowhere else to go, nowhere in the world.* **3** You use nowhere to indicate that something or someone cannot be seen or found. ❑ *Michael glanced anxiously down the corridor, but Wilfred was nowhere to be seen.* ❑ *The escaped prisoner was nowhere in sight.* **4** You can use nowhere to refer in a general way to small, unimportant, or uninteresting places. ❑ *endless paths that led nowhere in particular* **5** ['from/out of' nowhere] If you say that something or someone appears from nowhere or out of nowhere, you mean that they appear suddenly and unexpectedly. ❑ *A car came from nowhere, and I had to jump back into the hedge just in time.* **6** (*emphasis*) You use nowhere to mean not in any part of a text, speech, or argument. ❑ *He nowhere offers concrete historical background to support his arguments.* ❑ *Point taken, but nowhere did we suggest that this yacht's features were unique.*
[PHRASES] **the middle of nowhere** If you say that a place is in the middle of nowhere, you mean that it is a long way from other places. ❑ *At dusk we pitched camp in the middle of nowhere.*
nowhere near (*emphasis*) If you use nowhere near in front of a word or expression, you are emphasizing that the real situation is very different from, or has not yet reached, the state which that word or expression suggests. ❑ *He's nowhere near recovered yet from his experiences.*

✪**nu·ance** /ˈnjuːɑːns, AmE ˈnuː-/ NOUN [C, U] (**nuances**) A nuance is a small difference in sound, feeling, appearance, or meaning. = subtlety ❑ *We can use our eyes and facial expressions to communicate virtually every subtle nuance of emotion there is.* ❑ *If you read the Koran or the Torah simply in translation, you miss the nuances of the original language.*

✪**nu·clear** ♦♦◇ /ˈnjuːkliə, AmE ˈnuːk-/ ADJ (*academic word*) **1** [nuclear + N] Nuclear means relating to the nuclei of atoms, or to the energy released when these nuclei are

n

split or combined. = atomic ❑ *a nuclear power station* ❑ *nuclear energy* ❑ *nuclear physics* **2** [nuclear + N] **Nuclear** means relating to weapons that explode by using the energy released when the nuclei of atoms are split or combined. = atomic ❑ *They rejected a demand for the removal of all nuclear weapons.* ❑ *nuclear testing*

nui•sance /'nju:səns, AmE 'nu:-/
NOUN [c] (**nuisances**) If you say that someone or something is a **nuisance**, you mean that they annoy you or cause you a lot of problems. = pain ❑ *He could be a bit of a nuisance when he was drunk.* ❑ *Sorry to be a nuisance.*
PHRASE **make a nuisance of oneself** If someone **makes a nuisance of** themselves, they behave in a way that annoys other people.

✪ **num•ber** ◆◆◆ /'nʌmbə/ NOUN, VERB
NOUN [c, SING, u] (**numbers**) **1** [c] A **number** is a word such as 'two', 'nine', or 'twelve', or a symbol such as 1, 3, or 47. You use numbers to say how many things you are referring to or where something comes in a series. = figure ❑ *No, I don't know the room number.* ❑ *Stan Laurel was born at number 3, Argyll Street.* ❑ *The number 47 bus leaves in 10 minutes.* **2** [c] You use **number** with words such as 'large' or 'small' to say approximately how many things or people there are. = amount, quantity ❑ *Quite a considerable number of interviews are going on.* ❑ *I have had an enormous number of letters from single parents.* ❑ *growing numbers of people* **3** [SING] If there are **a number of** things or people, there are several of them. If there are **any number of** things or people, there is a large quantity of them. ❑ *I seem to remember that Sam told a number of lies.* **4** [u] You can refer to someone's or something's position in a list of the most successful or most popular of a particular type of thing as, for example, **number** one or **number** two. ❑ *Martin now faces the world number one, Jansher Khan of Pakistan.* ❑ *Before you knew it, the single was at number 90 in the US singles charts.* **5** [c] A **number** is the series of numbers that you dial when you are making a telephone call. ❑ *a list of names and telephone numbers* ❑ *My number is 414-3925.* **6** [c] You can refer to a short piece of music, a song, or a dance as a **number**. ❑ *'Unforgettable', a number that was written and performed in 1951* VERB [T] (**numbers, numbering, numbered**) **1** If a group of people or things **numbers** a particular total, that is how many there are. ❑ *They told me that their village numbered 100.* **2** (*formal*) If someone or something **is numbered among** a particular group, they are believed to belong in that group. ❑ *Lech Walesa and Nelson Mandela are numbered among my personal heroes.* **3** If you **number** something, you mark it with a number, usually starting at 1. ❑ *He cut his paper up into tiny squares, and he numbered each one.*

WORD CONNECTIONS
ADJ + **number**

a **high** number
a **large** number
a **significant** number
❑ *A high number of their students get into university.*

a **small** number
a **low** number
❑ *Most people are satisfied, but a small number are not.*

a **rising** number
a **growing** number
an **increasing** number
❑ *A growing number of people are working from home.*

a **falling** number
❑ *More and more people were competing for a falling number of jobs.*

USAGE NOTE
number

Do not use 'a number of' before an uncountable noun, as in 'a number of information'.

*The report contains **a lot of information** about the influence of advertising.*

num•ber one ADJ, NOUN
ADJ [number one + N] (*informal*) **Number one** means better, more important, or more popular than anything else or anyone else of its kind. ❑ *The economy is the number one issue by far.*
NOUN [c] (**number ones**) (*informal*) In popular music, the **number one** is the best-selling recording in any one week, or the group or person who has made that recording. ❑ *Paula is the only artist to achieve four number ones from a debut album.*

nu•mera•cy /'nju:mərəsi, AmE 'nu:-/ NOUN [u] [oft numeracy + N] **Numeracy** is the ability to do arithmetic. ❑ *Six months later John had developed literacy and numeracy skills, plus confidence.*

✪ **nu•mer•al** /'nju:mərəl, AmE 'nu:-/ NOUN [c] (**numerals**) **Numerals** are written symbols used to represent numbers. = number, digit ❑ *a flat, square wristwatch with classic Roman numerals* ❑ *the numeral 6*

nu•mer•ate /'nju:mərət, AmE 'nu:-/ ADJ Someone who is **numerate** is able to do arithmetic. ❑ *Your children should be literate and numerate.*

✪ **nu•mer•ous** ◆◇◇ /'nju:mərəs, AmE 'nu:m-/ ADJ If people or things are **numerous**, they exist or are present in large numbers. ❑ *Sex crimes were just as numerous as they are today.* ❑ *Numerous tests had been made, but no physical cause for her symptoms could be found.*

USAGE NOTE
numerous

Numerous is followed directly by a noun. Do not say 'numerous of'.

*The development would bring **numerous benefits** to rural communities.*

nun /nʌn/ NOUN [c] (**nuns**) A **nun** is a member of a female religious community. ❑ *Mr Thomas was taught by the Catholic nuns whose school he attended to work and study hard.*

nurse ◆◇◇ /nɜːs/ NOUN, VERB
NOUN [c] (**nurses**) A **nurse** is a person whose job is to care for people who are ill. ❑ *She had spent 29 years as a nurse.* VERB [T] (**nurses, nursing, nursed**) **1** If you **nurse** someone, you care for them when they are ill. ❑ *All the years he was sick my mother had nursed him.* **2** If you **nurse** an illness or injury, you allow it to get better by resting as much as possible. ❑ *We're going to go home and nurse our colds.* **3** If you **nurse** an emotion or desire, you feel it strongly for a long time. = harbour ❑ *Jane still nurses the pain of rejection.*

nurs•ery /'nɜːsəri/ NOUN [c, u] (**nurseries**) **1** [c] A **nursery** is a room in a family home in which the young children of the family sleep or play. ❑ *He has painted murals in his children's nursery.* **2** [c] [also 'at/from/to' nursery] A **nursery** is a place where children who are not old enough to go to school are cared for. ❑ *She puts her baby in this nursery and then goes back to work.* **3** [c, u] (BrE; in AmE, use **nursery school**) **Nursery** is a school for very young children. **4** [c] A **nursery** is a place where plants are grown in order to be sold. ❑ *The garden, developed over the past 35 years, includes a nursery.*

nurs•ing /'nɜːsɪŋ/ NOUN [u] **Nursing** is the profession of caring for people who are ill. ❑ *She had no aptitude for nursing.*

✪ **nur•ture** /'nɜːtʃə/ VERB, NOUN
VERB [T] (**nurtures, nurturing, nurtured**) (*formal*) **1** If you **nurture** something such as a young child or a young plant, you care for it while it is growing and developing. = care for; ≠ neglect ❑ *Parents want to know the best way to nurture and raise their child to adulthood.* ❑ *The modern conservatory is not an environment for nurturing plants.* **2** If you **nurture** plans, ideas, or people, you encourage them or help them to develop. ❑ *She had always nurtured great ambitions for her son.* ❑ *parents whose political views were nurtured in the sixties* NOUN [u] **Nurture** is care and encouragement that is given to someone while they are growing and developing. = care, rearing ❑ *The human organism learns partly by nature, partly by nurture.* ❑ *Young men were living without*

maternal nurture. ❑ *Visiting the doctor can be a way of getting the nurture and attention you feel unable to ask for any other way.*

nut /nʌt/ NOUN, ADJ

NOUN [c] (nuts) **1** The firm, shelled fruit of some trees and bushes are called **nuts**. Some nuts can be eaten. ❑ *Nuts and seeds are good sources of vitamin E.* **2** A **nut** is a thick, metal ring which you screw onto a metal rod called a bolt. Nuts and bolts are used to hold things such as pieces of machinery together. ❑ *If you want to repair the wheels you just undo the four nuts.* **3** (*informal*) If you describe someone as, for example, a baseball **nut** or a health **nut**, you mean that they re extremely enthusiastic about the thing mentioned. = fanatic ❑ *Annie, the girlfriend who was a true baseball nut*

ADJ **1** [V-LINK + nuts 'about' N] (*informal, feelings*) If you are **nuts about** something or someone, you like them very much. ❑ *They're nuts about the car.* **2** [V-LINK + nuts] If you say that someone goes **nuts** or is **nuts**, you mean that they go crazy or are very foolish. ❑ *You guys are nuts.*

PHRASE **go nuts** or **do one's nut** (*informal*) If someone goes **nuts**, they become extremely angry. ❑ *My father would go nuts if he saw bruises on me.*

✪**nu·tri·ent** /ˈnjuːtriənt, AmE ˌnuː-/ NOUN [c] (**nutrients**) **Nutrients** are substances that help plants and animals to grow. ❑ *In her first book she explained the role of vegetable fibres, vitamins, minerals, and other essential nutrients.* ❑ *Studies show that a depressed person often lacks several key nutrients.* ❑ *daily nutrient intakes*

✪**nu·tri·tion** /njuːˈtrɪʃən, AmE ˌnuː-/ NOUN [u] **Nutrition** is the process of taking food into the body and absorbing the nutrients in those foods. = nourishment ❑ *There are alternative sources of nutrition to animal meat.*

✪**nu·tri·tion·al** /njuːˈtrɪʃənəl, AmE ˌnuː-/ ADJ The **nutritional** content of food is all the substances that are in it which help you to remain healthy. ❑ *It does sometimes help to know the nutritional content of foods.* ❑ *Cooking vegetables reduces their nutritional value.*

nu·tri·tion·al·ly /njuːˈtrɪʃənəli, AmE ˌnuː-/ ADV ❑ *a nutritionally balanced diet*

✪**nu·tri·tious** /njuːˈtrɪʃəs, AmE nuː-/ ADJ **Nutritious** food contains substances which help your body to be healthy. = nourishing ❑ *It is always important to choose enjoyable, nutritious foods.* ❑ *Some ready made meals are nutritious and very easy to prepare.*

ny·lon /ˈnaɪlɒn/ NOUN [u, pl] (**nylons**) **1** [u] **Nylon** is a strong, flexible artificial fibre. ❑ *The chair is made of lightweight nylon.* **2** [pl] (*old-fashioned*) **Nylons** are stockings made of nylon. ❑ *She wore a long skirt with pink pumps and black nylons.*

n

Oo

O also **o** /əʊ/ NOUN [C, U] (**O's, o's**) **O** is the fifteenth letter of the English alphabet.

oak /əʊk/ NOUN [C, U] (**oaks**) **1** [C, U] An **oak** or an **oak tree** is a large tree that often grows in forests and has strong, hard wood. ❑ *Many large oaks were felled during the war.* **2** [U] **Oak** is the wood of this tree. ❑ *The cabinet was made of oak and was hand-carved.*

obedi•ent /əʊ'biːdiənt/ ADJ A person or animal who is **obedient** does what they are told to do. ❑ *He was very respectful at home and obedient to his parents.*
○ **obedi•ence** /əʊ'biːdiəns/ NOUN [U] ❑ *unquestioning obedience to the law*
○ **obedi•ent•ly** /əʊ'biːdiəntli/ ADV [obediently with v] ❑ *He was looking obediently at Keith, waiting for orders.*

❖ **obese** /əʊ'biːs/ ADJ If someone is **obese**, they are extremely fat. ❑ *Obese people tend to have higher blood pressure than lean people.* ❑ *The tendency to become obese is at least in part hereditary.* ❑ *More than 300 million people globally were considered obese in 2000.*
❖ **obesity** /əʊ'biːsɪti/ NOUN [U] ❑ *the excessive consumption of sugar that leads to problems of obesity* ❑ *There is a real obesity epidemic in Eastern Europe, where they have 35% obesity in some regions.*

obey /əʊ'beɪ/ VERB [I, T] (**obeys, obeying, obeyed**) If you **obey** a person, a command, or an instruction, you do what you are told to do. ❑ *Cissie obeyed her mother without question.* ❑ *Most people obey the law.* ❑ *It was his duty to obey.*

obi•tu•ary /əʊ'bɪtʃuəri, AmE -ʃueri/ NOUN [C] (**obituaries**) Someone's **obituary** is an account of their life and character which is presented in a newspaper or broadcast soon after they die. ❑ *His obituary was published in one edition of his own newspaper before it was discovered that he was alive.*

❖ **ob•ject** ♦♦◇ NOUN, VERB
NOUN /'ɒbdʒɪkt/ [C] (**objects**) **1** An **object** is anything that has a fixed shape or form, that you can touch or see, and that is not alive. = thing ❑ *He squinted his eyes as though he were studying an object on the horizon.* ❑ *an object the shape of a coconut* ❑ *In the cosy consulting room the children are surrounded by familiar objects.* ❑ *household objects such as lamps and ornaments* **2** The **object** of what someone is doing is their aim or purpose. = purpose, aim, point ❑ *The object of the exercise is to raise money for the charity.* ❑ *He made it his object in life to find the island.* ❑ *My object was to publish a scholarly work on Peter Mourne.* **3** The **object** of a particular feeling or reaction is the person or thing it is directed towards or that causes it. ❑ *The object of her hatred was 24-year-old model Ros French.* ❑ *The object of great interest at the temple was a large marble tower built in memory of Buddha.* **4** In grammar, the **object** of a verb or a preposition is the word or phrase which completes the structure begun by the verb or preposition.
PHRASE **money is no object** (*emphasis*) If you say that **money is no object** or **distance is no object**, you are emphasizing that you are willing or able to spend as much money as necessary or travel whatever distance is required. ❑ *This was a very impressive programme in which money seems to have been no object.*
VERB /əb'dʒekt/ [I] (**objects, objecting, objected**) If you

object to something, you express your dislike or disapproval of it. = protest, argue ❑ *A lot of people will object to the book.* ❑ *Cullen objected that his small staff would be unable to handle the added work.* ❑ *We objected strongly but were outvoted.*

❖ **ob•jec•tion** /əb'dʒekʃən/ NOUN [C, U] (**objections**) **1** [C, U] If you express or raise an **objection to** something, you say that you do not like it or agree with it. = protest, opposition, complaint ❑ *Despite objections by the White House, the Senate voted today to cut off aid.* ❑ *Some managers have recently raised objections to the PFA handling these negotiations.* **2** [U] If you say that you have **no objection to** something, you mean that you are not annoyed or bothered by it. ❑ *I have no objection to banks making money.*

❖ **ob•jec•tive** ♦◇◇ /əb'dʒektɪv/ NOUN, ADJ (*academic word*)
NOUN [C] (**objectives**) Your **objective** is what you are trying to achieve. = aim, purpose, goal ❑ *Our main objective was the recovery of the child safe and well.* ❑ *Our objective is to become the number-one digital corporation.*
ADJ **1** [objective + N] **Objective** information is based on facts. = factual ❑ *He had no objective evidence that anything extraordinary was happening.* ❑ *It is futile to look for objective causes of drug addiction.* **2** If someone is **objective**, they base their opinions on facts rather than on their personal feelings. = impartial, unbiased, unprejudiced, open-minded; ≠ subjective ❑ *I believe that a journalist should be completely objective.* ❑ *I would really like to have your objective opinion on this.*
❖ **ob•jec•tive•ly** /əb'dʒektɪvli/ ADV **1** = impartially; ≠ subjectively ❑ *We simply want to inform people objectively about events.* **2** *Try to view situations more objectively, especially with regard to work.*
❖ **ob•jec•tiv•ity** /ˌɒbdʒek'tɪvɪti/ NOUN [U] **1** = impartiality; ≠ subjectivity ❑ *The poll, whose objectivity is open to question, gave the party a 39% share of the vote.* **2** *The psychiatrist must learn to maintain an unusual degree of objectivity.*

VOCABULARY BUILDER

objective ADJ
If someone is **objective**, they base their opinions on facts rather than on their personal feelings.
❑ *There has been no way to verify by objective observers any of this information.*

impartial ADJ
Someone who is **impartial** is not directly involved in a particular situation, and is therefore able to give a fair opinion or decision about it.
❑ *Careers advisers offer impartial advice, guidance and information to all pupils.*

unbiased ADJ
If you describe someone or something as **unbiased**, you mean they are fair and not likely to support one particular person or group involved in something.
❑ *There is no clear and unbiased information available for consumers.*

open-minded ADJ

If you describe someone as **open-minded**, you approve of them because they are willing to listen to and consider other people's ideas and suggestions.

❏ He was very open-minded about other people's work.

ob·li·ga·tion /ˌɒblɪˈɡeɪʃən/ NOUN

NOUN [c, u] (**obligations**) **1** If you have an **obligation to** do something, it is your duty to do that thing. ❏ When teachers assign homework, students usually feel an obligation to do it. **2** If you have an **obligation to** a person, it is your duty to take care of them or protect their interests. = responsibility ❏ The United States will do that which is necessary to meet its obligations to its own citizens. PHRASE **without obligation** In advertisements, if a product or a service is available **without obligation**, you do not have to pay for that product or service until you have tried it and are satisfied with it. ❏ If you are selling your property, why not call us for a free valuation without obligation.

✪ **ob·liga·tory** /əˈblɪɡətri, AmE -tɔːri/ ADJ If something is **obligatory**, you must do it because of a rule or a law. = compulsory, necessary; ≠ optional, voluntary ❏ Most women will be offered an ultrasound scan during pregnancy, although it's not obligatory. ❏ These rates do not include the charge for obligatory medical consultations.

oblige /əˈblaɪdʒ/ VERB

VERB [T, I] (**obliges, obliging, obliged**) **1** [T] If you **are obliged to** do something, a situation, rule, or law makes it necessary for you to do that thing. = compel ❏ The storm got worse and worse. Finally, I was obliged to abandon the car and continue on foot. **2** [I, T] To **oblige** someone means to be helpful to them by doing what they have asked you to do. ❏ Mr Oakley has always been ready to oblige journalists with information. ❏ We called up three economists to ask how to eliminate the deficit and they obliged with very straightforward answers. CONVENTION **would be obliged** or **should be obliged** (formal, politeness) If you tell someone that you **would be obliged** or **should be obliged** if they would do something, you are telling them in a polite but firm way that you want them to do it. ❏ I would be obliged if you could read it to us.

ob·scure /ɒbˈskjʊə/ ADJ, VERB

ADJ (**obscurer, obscurest**) **1** If something or someone is **obscure**, they are unknown, or are known by only a few people. ❏ The origin of the custom is obscure. **2** Something that is **obscure** is difficult to understand or deal with, usually because it involves so many parts or details. ❏ The contracts are written in obscure language. VERB [T] (**obscures, obscuring, obscured**) **1** If one thing **obscures** another, it prevents it from being seen or heard properly. ❏ Trees obscured his vision; he couldn't see much of the square's southern half. **2** To **obscure** something means to make it difficult to understand. ❏ the jargon that frequently obscures educational writing

ob·ser·vant /əbˈzɜːvənt/ ADJ Someone who is **observant** pays a lot of attention to things and notices more about them than most people do. ❏ That's a good description, Mrs Drummond. You're very observant.

✪ **ob·ser·va·tion** /ˌɒbzəˈveɪʃən/ NOUN [U, C] (**observations**) **1** [U] **Observation** is the action or process of carefully watching someone or something. = study, surveillance ❏ careful observation of the movement of the planets ❏ In hospital she'll be under observation all the time. **2** [c] An **observation** is something that you have learned by seeing or watching something and thinking about it. ❏ This book contains observations about the causes of addictions. **3** [c] If a person makes an **observation**, they make a comment about something or someone, usually as a result of watching how they behave. ❏ Is that a criticism or just an observation? **4** [u] **Observation** is the ability to pay a lot of attention to things and to notice more about them than most people do. ❏ She has good powers of observation.

✪ **ob·serve** ◆◇◇ /əbˈzɜːv/ VERB [T] (**observes, observing, observed**) **1** If you **observe** a person or thing, you watch them carefully, especially in order to learn something about them. = study, monitor ❏ Olson also studies and observes the behaviour of babies. ❏ Are there any classes I could observe? ❏ I got a chance to observe how a detective actually works. **2** (formal) If you **observe** someone or something, you see or notice them. ❏ In 1664 Hooke observed a reddish spot on the surface of the planet. **3** (formal) If you **observe** that something is the case, you make a remark or comment about it, especially when it is something you have noticed and thought about a lot. ❏ We observe that the first calls for radical transformation did not begin until the period of the industrial revolution. **4** If you **observe** something such as a law or custom, you obey it or follow it. ❏ Imposing speed restrictions is easy, but forcing drivers to observe them is trickier. ❏ The army was observing a ceasefire. **5** If you **observe** an important day such as a holiday or anniversary, you do something special in order to honour or celebrate it. ❏ where he will observe Thanksgiving with family members

✪ **ob·serv·er** ◆◇◇ /əbˈzɜːvə/ NOUN [c] (**observers**) **1** You can refer to someone who sees or notices something as an **observer**. = witness ❏ A casual observer would have taken them to be three men out for an evening stroll. ❏ He argues that truly objective science is impossible: the observer affects the system he or she observes. **2** (journalism) An **observer** is someone who studies current events and situations, especially in order to comment on them and predict what will happen next. ❏ Observers say the events of the weekend seem to have increased support for the opposition. **3** An **observer** is a person who is sent to observe an important event or situation, especially in order to make sure it happens as it should, or to tell other people about it. ❏ The president suggested that a UN observer should attend the conference.

ob·sess /əbˈses/ VERB [I, T] (**obsesses, obsessing, obsessed**) If something **obsesses** you or if you **obsess about** something, you keep thinking about it and find it difficult to think about anything else. ❏ A string of scandals is obsessing America. ❏ She stopped drinking but began obsessing about her weight.

ob·ses·sion /əbˈseʃən/ NOUN [c, u] (**obsessions**) If you say that someone has an **obsession** with a person or thing, you think they are spending too much time thinking about them. ❏ She would try to forget her obsession with Christopher.

ob·ses·sive /əbˈsesɪv/ ADJ, NOUN

ADJ If someone's behaviour is **obsessive**, they cannot stop doing a particular thing or behaving in a particular way. ❏ Williams is obsessive about motor racing. NOUN [c] (**obsessives**) An **obsessive** is someone who is obsessive about something or who behaves in an obsessive way. ❏ Obsessives, in any area, are invariably as boring as their hobbies.

ob·ses·sive·ly /əbˈsesɪvli/ ADV ❏ He couldn't help worrying obsessively about what would happen.

✪ **ob·sta·cle** /ˈɒbstəkəl/ NOUN [c] (**obstacles**) **1** An **obstacle** is an object that makes it difficult for you to go where you want to go, because it is in your way. ❏ Most competition cars will only roll over if they hit an obstacle. ❏ He left her to navigate her own way round the trolleys and other obstacles. **2** You can refer to anything that makes it difficult for you to do something as an **obstacle**. = hindrance ❏ Overcrowding remains a large obstacle to improving conditions. ❏ To succeed, you must learn to overcome obstacles.

✪ **ob·struct** /əbˈstrʌkt/ VERB [T] (**obstructs, obstructing, obstructed**) **1** If something **obstructs** a road or path, it blocks it, stopping people or vehicles getting past. = block ❏ A knot of black and white cars obstructed the junction. **2** To **obstruct** someone or something means to make it difficult for them to move forward by blocking their path. = block ❏ A number of local people have been arrested for trying to obstruct trucks loaded with logs. ❏ Drivers who park their cars illegally, particularly obstructing traffic flow, deserve to be punished. **3** To **obstruct** progress or a process means to prevent it from happening properly. = prevent, hinder ❏ The authorities are obstructing a United Nations

o

investigation. ❑ *He was convicted of obstructing justice for trying to evade a DNA test.* **4** If someone or something **obstructs** your view, they are positioned between you and the thing you are trying to look at, stopping you from seeing it completely. = block ❑ *Claire positioned herself so as not to obstruct David's line of sight.*

⬥**ob·struc·tion** /ɒb'strʌkʃən/ NOUN [C, U] (obstructions) **1** [C] An **obstruction** is something that blocks a road or path. ❑ *John was irritated by drivers parking near his house and causing an obstruction.* **2** [C, U] An **obstruction** is something that blocks a passage in your body. = blockage ❑ *The boy was suffering from a bowel obstruction.* **3** [U] **Obstruction** is the act of deliberately delaying something or preventing something from happening, usually in business, law, or government. = prevention, hindrance ❑ *Mr Anderson refused to let them in and now faces a criminal charge of obstruction.*

⬥**ob·tain** ⬥◇◇ /ɒb'teɪn/ VERB [T] (obtains, obtaining, obtained) (*academic word, formal*) To **obtain** something means to get it or achieve it. = get, acquire, achieve ❑ *Evans was trying to obtain a false passport and other documents.* ❑ *The perfect body has always been difficult to obtain.*

⬥**ob·vi·ous** ⬥⬥◇ /'ɒbviəs/ ADJ, NOUN (*academic word*)
ADJ **1** If something is **obvious**, it is easy to see or understand. = clear, plain; ≠ unclear, obscure ❑ *the need to rectify what is an obvious injustice* ❑ *More and more healthy troops were dying for no obvious reason.* ❑ *The answer is obvious.* **2** If you describe something that someone says as **obvious**, you are being critical of it because you think it is unnecessary or shows lack of imagination. ❑ *Such an explanation seems too simple, and too obvious.*
NOUN
PHRASE **state the obvious** If you say that someone **is stating the obvious**, you mean that they are saying something that everyone already knows and understands.

⬥**ob·vi·ous·ly** ⬥⬥◇ /'ɒbviəsli/ ADV **1** [obviously with CL] (*emphasis*) You use **obviously** when you are stating something that you expect the person who is listening to know already. = clearly, of course ❑ *Obviously, they've had sponsorship from some big companies.* ❑ *As a private hospital it obviously needs to balance its budget each year.* **2** [obviously with CL/GROUP] You use **obviously** to indicate that something is easily noticed, seen, or recognized. ❑ *They obviously appreciate you very much.*

⬥**oc·ca·sion** ⬥⬥◇ /ə'keɪʒən/ NOUN
NOUN [C] (occasions) **1** An **occasion** is a time when something happens, or a case of it happening. ❑ *I often think fondly of an occasion some years ago in New Orleans.* ❑ *The team repeated the experiment on three separate occasions, with the same results.* ❑ *Mr Davis has been asked on a number of occasions.* **2** An **occasion** is an important event, ceremony, or celebration. ❑ *Taking her with me on official occasions has been a challenge.* **3** (*formal*) An **occasion for** doing something is an opportunity for doing it. ❑ *It is an occasion for all the family to celebrate.*
PHRASES **have occasion** If you **have occasion to** do something, you have the opportunity to do it or have a need to do it. ❑ *Over the next few years many people had occasion to reflect on the truth of his warnings.*
rise to the occasion If you say that someone **rose to the occasion**, you mean that they did what was necessary to successfully overcome a difficult situation. ❑ *Colorado rose to the occasion with four players scoring 16 points or more.*

WHICH WORD?
occasion, opportunity, or chance?

An **occasion** is a time when a particular event happens.
❑ *I met her on several occasions.*

You do not use **occasion** to refer to a situation in which it is possible for someone to do something. Instead, you use **opportunity** or **chance**.
❑ *I'm grateful to have had the opportunity to work with Paul.*
❑ *She put the phone down before I had a chance to reply.*

⬥**oc·ca·sion·al** ⬥◇◇ /ə'keɪʒənəl/ ADJ **Occasional** means happening sometimes, but not regularly or often. ❑ *I've had occasional mild headaches all my life.*
oc·ca·sion·al·ly /ə'keɪʒənəli/ ADV ❑ *He still misbehaves occasionally.*

⬥**oc·cu·pant** /'ɒkjʊpənt/ NOUN [C, PL] (occupants) **1** [C] The **occupants** of a building or room are the people who live or work there. = occupier ❑ *Most of the occupants had left before the fire broke out.* ❑ *The filing cabinets had all gone with the previous occupants.* **2** [PL] You can refer to the people who are in a place such as a room, vehicle, or bed at a particular time as the **occupants**. ❑ *He wanted the occupants of the vehicle to get out.*

⬥**oc·cu·pa·tion** ⬥◇◇ /,ɒkjʊ'peɪʃən/ NOUN [C, U] (occupations) (*academic word*) **1** [C] Your **occupation** is your job or profession. = profession, work ❑ *I suppose I was looking for an occupation which was going to be an adventure.* ❑ *Occupation: administrative assistant.* **2** [C] An **occupation** is something that you spend time doing, either for pleasure or because it needs to be done. ❑ *Parachuting is a dangerous occupation.* **3** [U] The **occupation** of a country happens when it is entered and controlled by a foreign army. ❑ *the occupation of Poland*

⬥**oc·cu·pa·tion·al** /,ɒkjʊ'peɪʃənəl/ ADJ **Occupational** means relating to a person's job or profession. = job-related ❑ *Some received substantial occupational assistance in the form of low-interest loans.* ❑ *Catching frequent colds is unfortunately an occupational hazard in this profession.*

oc·cu·pi·er /'ɒkjʊpaɪə/ (*BrE; in AmE, use* occupant; *formal*) NOUN [C] (occupiers) The **occupier** of a house, flat, or piece of land is the person who lives or works there. = occupant

⬥**oc·cu·py** ⬥⬥◇ /'ɒkjʊpaɪ/ VERB [T, PASSIVE] (occupies, occupying, occupied) (*academic word*) **1** [T] The people who **occupy** a building or a place are the people who live or work there. = inhabit ❑ *There were over 40 tenants, all occupying one wing of the building.* ❑ *Land is, in most instances, purchased by those who occupy it.* **2** [PASSIVE] If a room or something such as a seat is **occupied**, someone is using it, so that it is not available for anyone else. ❑ *The hospital bed is occupied by his wife.* **3** [T] If a group of people or an army **occupies** a place or country, they move into it, using force in order to gain control of it. ❑ *US forces now occupy a part of the country.* **4** [T] If someone or something **occupies** a particular place in a system, process, or plan, they have that place. = hold ❑ *Many men still occupy more positions of power than women.* ❑ *We occupy a quality position in the market place.* **5** [T] If something **occupies** you, or if you **occupy** yourself, your time, or your mind with it, you are busy doing that thing or thinking about it. ❑ *Her career occupies all of her time.* ❑ *He occupied himself with packing the car.* **6** [T] If something **occupies** you, it requires your efforts, attention, or time. ❑ *I had other matters to occupy me, during the day at least.* **7** [T] If something **occupies** a particular area or place, it fills or covers it, or exists there. = take up ❑ *Even small aircraft occupy a lot of space.* ❑ *Bookshelves occupied most of the living room walls.*
oc·cu·pied /'ɒkjʊpaɪd/ ADJ ❑ *Keep the brain occupied.*

⬥**oc·cur** ⬥⬥◇ /ə'kɜ:/ VERB [I] (occurs, occurring, occurred) (*academic word*) **1** When something **occurs**, it happens. ❑ *If headaches only occur at night, lack of fresh air and oxygen is often the cause.* ❑ *The crash occurred when the crew shut down the wrong engine.* **2** When something **occurs** in a particular place, it exists or is present there. = exist ❑ *These snails do not occur on low-lying coral islands.* **3** If a thought or idea **occurs to** you, you suddenly think of it or realize it. ❑ *It did not occur to me to check my insurance policy.*

⬥**oc·cur·rence** /ə'kʌrəns, AmE -'kɜ:r-/ NOUN [C] (occurrences) **1** (*formal*) An **occurrence** is something that happens. = incident, happening, event, phenomenon ❑ *Complaints seemed to be an everyday occurrence.* **2** The **occurrence of** something is the fact that it happens or is present. = instance ❑ *The greatest occurrence of coronary heart disease is in those over 65.* ❑ *There is no general agreed explanation for the occurrence of hallucinations.*

O

VOCABULARY BUILDER

occurrence NOUN (*mainly written*)

An **occurrence** is something that happens.

❏ *This was a familiar, even a routine, occurrence to him.*

incident NOUN (*formal*)

An **incident** is something that happens, often something that is unpleasant.

❏ *The attack was the worst in a series of violent incidents.*

event NOUN

An **event** is something that happens, especially when it is unusual or important.

❏ *A new inquiry into the events of the day was opened in 2002.*

phenomenon NOUN (*formal*)

A **phenomenon** is something that is observed to happen or exist.

❏ *scientific explanations of natural phenomena*

❖ **ocean** ◆◇◇ /ˈəʊʃən/ NOUN

NOUN [SING, C] (**oceans**) **1** [SING] The **ocean** is the sea. = the sea ❏ *There were few sights as beautiful as the calm ocean on a warm night.* ❏ *new technology used to explore the deep ocean* ❏ *a fish's habitat on the ocean floor* **2** [C] An **ocean** is one of the five very large areas of sea on the Earth's surface. = a sea ❏ *They spent months cruising the northern Pacific Ocean.* ❏ *a small island in the Indian ocean* **3** [C] (*informal, emphasis*) If you say that there is an **ocean** of something, you are emphasizing that there is a very large amount of it. ❏ *I had cried oceans of tears.*

PHRASE **a drop in the ocean** (*emphasis*) If you say that something is **a drop in the ocean**, you mean that it is a very small amount which is unimportant compared to the cost of other things or is so small that it has very little effect on something. ❏ *His fee is a drop in the ocean compared with the real cost of broadcasting.*

o'clock ◆◇◇ /əˈklɒk/ ADV [NUM + o'clock] You use **o'clock** after numbers from one to twelve to say what time it is. For example, if you say that it is 9 o'clock, you mean that it is nine hours after midnight or nine hours after noon. ❏ *The trouble began just after ten o'clock last night.*

❖ **odd** ◆◆◇ /ɒd/ ADJ, ADV (*academic word*)

ADJ (**odder, oddest**) **1** If you describe someone or something as **odd**, you think that they are strange or unusual. = peculiar ❏ *He'd always been odd, but not to this extent.* ❏ *What an odd coincidence that he should have known your family.* **2** [DET + odd] You use **odd** before a noun to indicate that you are not mentioning the type, size, or quality of something because it is not important. = occasional ❏ *moving from place to place where she could find the odd bit of work* ❏ *He had various odd cleaning jobs around the place.* **3** **Odd** numbers, such as 3 and 17, are those which cannot be divided exactly by the number two. ❏ *The odd numbers are on the left as you walk up the street.* ❏ *Multiplying an odd number by an odd number always gives an odd number.* ❏ *There's an odd number of candidates.* **4** You say that two things are **odd** when they do not belong to the same set or pair. ❏ *I'm wearing odd socks today by the way.*

PHRASE **the odd man out** or **the odd woman out** or **the odd one out** The **odd man out**, the **odd woman out**, or the **odd one out** in a particular situation is a person who is different from the other people in it. ❏ *Azerbaijan has been the odd man out, the one republic not to hold democratic elections.*

ADV [NUM + odd] (*informal*) You use **odd** after a number to indicate that it is only approximate. ❏ *How many pages was it, 500 odd?* ❏ *He has now appeared in sixty odd films.* → See also **odds**

odd·ly /ˈɒdli/ ADV **1** [oddly with V] If someone or something acts or is formed **oddly**, they act or are formed in a strange or unusual way. ❏ *an oddly shaped hill* **2** You use **oddly** to indicate that what you are saying is true, but that it is not what you expected. = strangely ❏ *He said no*

and seemed oddly reluctant to talk about it. ❏ *Oddly, Emma says she never considered her face to be attractive.*

odds /ɒdz/ NOUN

NOUN [PL] **1** You refer to how likely something is to happen as the **odds** that it will happen. ❏ *What are the odds of finding a parking space right outside the door?* **2** In betting, **odds** are expressions with numbers such as '10 to 1' and '7 to 2' that show how likely something is thought to be, for example, how likely a particular horse is to lose or win a race. ❏ *We are offering odds of 6-1 on the fight ending in a knockout.*

PHRASES **against all odds** If something happens **against all odds**, it happens or succeeds although it seemed impossible or very unlikely. ❏ *families in terrible circumstances, who have stayed together against all odds*

at odds If someone is **at odds** with someone else, or if two people are **at odds**, they are disagreeing or arguing with each other. ❏ *He was at odds with the boss.*

the odds are against If you say that **the odds are against** something or someone, you mean that they are unlikely to succeed. ❏ *He reckons the odds are against the plan going ahead.*

the odds are in someone's favour If you say that **the odds are in** someone's **favour**, you mean that they are likely to succeed in what they are doing. ❏ *The troops will only engage in a ground battle when all the odds are in their favour.*

odour /ˈəʊdə/ (in AmE, use **odor**) NOUN [C, U] (**odours**) An **odour** is a particular and distinctive smell. ❏ *the lingering odour of car exhaust*

of ◆◆◆ /əv, STRONG ɒv, AmE ʌv/ PREP

In addition to the uses shown below, **of** is used in phrasal prepositions such as 'because of', 'instead of', and 'in spite of', and in phrasal verbs such as 'make of' and 'dispose of'.

1 [N + of + N] You use **of** to combine two nouns when the first noun identifies the feature of the second noun that you want to talk about. ❏ *The average age of the women interviewed was only 21.5.* ❏ *the population of this town* **2** [N + of + N/-ING] You use **of** to combine two nouns, or a noun and a present participle, when the second noun or present participle defines or gives more information about the first noun. ❏ *She let out a little cry of pain.* ❏ *the problem of having a national shortage of teachers* **3** [N + of + N] You use **of** after nouns referring to actions to specify the person or thing that is affected by the action or that performs the action. For example, 'the kidnapping of the child' refers to an action affecting a child; 'the arrival of the next train' refers to an action performed by a train. ❏ *It sets targets for reduction of greenhouse-gas emissions.* **4** You use **of** after words and phrases referring to quantities or groups of things to indicate the substance or thing that is being measured. ❏ *dozens of people* ❏ *a collection of short stories* **5** [N + of + N] You use **of** after the name of someone or something to introduce the institution or place they belong to or are connected with. ❏ *the governor of Missouri* **6** [N + of + N] You use **of** after a noun referring to a container to form an expression referring to the container and its contents. ❏ *a box of tissues* ❏ *a roomful of people* **7** [N + of + N] You use **of** after a countable noun and before an uncountable noun when you want to talk about an individual piece or item. ❏ *a blade of grass* ❏ *Marina ate only one slice of bread.* **8** [N + of + N] You use **of** to indicate the materials or things that form something. ❏ *local decorations of wood and straw* ❏ *loose-fitting garments of linen* **9** [N + of + N] You use **of** after a noun which specifies a particular part of something, to introduce the thing that is a part of. ❏ *the other side of the square* ❏ *the beginning of the year* **10** You use **of** after some verbs to indicate someone or something else involved in the action. ❏ *He'd been dreaming of her.* ❏ *Listen, I shall be thinking of you always.* **11** [ADJ + of + N/-ING] You use **of** after some adjectives to indicate the thing that a feeling or quality relates to. ❏ *I have grown very fond of Alec.* ❏ *His father was quite naturally very proud of him.* **12** You use **of** before a word referring to the person

o

who performed an action when saying what you think about the action. ❑ *This has been so nice, so terribly kind of you.* **13** ['more/less' of 'a' N] If something is **more** of or **less of** a particular thing, it is that thing to a greater or smaller degree. ❑ *Your extra fat may be more of a health risk than you realize.* **14** You use **of** to indicate a characteristic or quality that someone or something has. ❑ *the worth of their music* ❑ *She is a woman of enviable beauty.* **15** [N + of + AMOUNT] You use **of** to specify an amount, value, or age. ❑ *Last Thursday, Nick announced record revenues of $3.4 billion.* ❑ *young people under the age of 16 years* **16** [N + of + N/-ING] You use **of** after a noun such as 'month' or 'year' to indicate the length of time that some state or activity continues. ❑ *eight bruising years of war*

of course ♦♦♦ ADV, CONVENTION

ADV *(spoken)* **1** [of course with CL] You say **of course** to suggest that something is normal, obvious, or well-known, and should therefore not surprise the person you are talking to. = naturally ❑ *Of course there were lots of other interesting things at the exhibition.* ❑ *'I have read about you in the newspapers of course,' Charlie said.* **2** *(emphasis)* You use **of course** in order to emphasize a statement that you are making, especially when you are agreeing or disagreeing with someone. ❑ *'I suppose you're right.'—'Of course I'm right!'* ❑ *Of course I'm not afraid!*

CONVENTION *(spoken)* **1** *(formulae)* You use **of course** as a polite way of giving permission. ❑ *'Can I just say something about the game on Saturday?'—'Yes, of course you can.'* **2** *(emphasis)* **Of course not** is an emphatic way of saying no. ❑ *'You're not really seriously considering this thing, are you?'—'No, of course not.'*

off ♦♦♦ /ɒf/ PREP, ADV, ADJ

PREP **1** If something is taken **off** something else or moves **off** it, it is no longer touching that thing. = from ❑ *He took his feet off the desk.* ❑ *I took the key for the room off a rack above her head.* **2** When you get **off** a bus, train, or plane, you come out of it or leave it after you have been travelling on it. ❑ *Don't try to get on or off a moving train!* **3** If you keep **off** a street or piece of land, you do not step on it or go there. ❑ *Locking up men does nothing more than keep them off the streets.* **4** If something is situated **off** a place such as a coast, room, or road, it is near to it or next to it, but not exactly in it. ❑ *The boat was anchored off the northern coast of the peninsula.* ❑ *Lily lives in a penthouse just off Park Avenue.* **5** If you have time **off** work or school, you do not go to work or school, for example, because you are sick or it is a day when you do not usually work. ❑ *He could not get time off work to go on vacation.* **6** If you keep **off** a subject, you deliberately avoid talking about it. ❑ *Keep off the subject of politics.* **7** [AMOUNT + off + N] If there is money **off** something, its price is reduced by the amount specified. ❑ *20 per cent off all jackets this Saturday.* **8** *(spoken)* If you get something **off** someone, you obtain it from them. = from ❑ *I don't really get a lot of information, and if I do I get it off Mark.* **9** If someone is **off** something harmful such as a drug, they have stopped taking or using it. ❑ *She felt better and the psychiatrist took her off antidepressants.* **10** If you are **off** something, you have stopped liking it. ❑ *I'm off coffee at the moment.* **11** [V + off + N] If you live **off** a particular kind of food, you eat it in order to live. If you live **off** a particular source of money, you use it to live. = on ❑ *Her husband's memories are of living off roast chicken and drinking whisky.* **12** [V + off + N] If a machine runs **off** a particular kind of fuel or power, it uses that power in order to function. ❑ *The electric armour runs off the tank's power supply.*

ADV **1** [off after v] If something is taken **off** or moves **off**, it is no longer touching something. ❑ *Lee broke off a small piece of orange and held it out to him.* **2** [off after V] If someone gets **off**, they leave a bus, train, or plane after they have been travelling on it. ❑ *At the next stop the man got off too and introduced himself.* **3** If you keep **off**, you do not step on or go into a street or a piece of land. ❑ *a sign saying 'Keep Off'* **4** If you go **off**, you leave a place. ❑ *He was just about to drive off when the secretary came running out.* ❑ *She was off again, to Kenya.* **5** [off after V] When you take **off** clothing or jewellery that you are wearing, you remove it from your body. ❑ *He took off his spectacles and rubbed*

frantically at the lens. **6** If you have time **off** or a particular day **off**, you do not go to work or school, for example, because you are sick or it is a day when you do not usually work. ❑ *The rest of the men had the day off.* ❑ *I'm off tomorrow.* **7** If an amount of money is taken **off**, the price of something is reduced by the amount specified. ❑ *If you pay in cash, I can knock £50 off.* **8** [N/AMOUNT + off] If something is a long way **off**, it is a long distance away from you. = away ❑ *Florida was a long way off.* **9** [N/AMOUNT + off] If something is a long time **off**, it will not happen for a long time. ❑ *An end to the crisis seems a long way off.* **10** If something such as an agreement or a sports event is **off**, it is cancelled. ❑ *Until Pointon is completely happy, however, the deal's off.* **11** When something such as a machine or electric light is **off**, it is not functioning or in use. When you switch it **off**, you stop it from functioning. ❑ *As he pulled into the driveway, he saw her bedroom light was off.* ❑ *We used sail power and turned the engine off to save our fuel.*

PHRASE **on and off** or **off and on** If something happens **on and off**, or **off and on**, it happens occasionally, or only for part of a period of time, not in a regular or continuous way. ❑ *I was still working on and off as a waitress to support myself.*

ADJ *(mainly BrE; in AmE, usually use* **spoiled***)* If food has gone **off**, it tastes and smells bad because it is no longer fresh enough to be eaten. = bad

✪ of·fence ♦◇◇ /əˈfens/ *(BrE; in AmE, use* **offense***)* NOUN

NOUN [C, U] *(offences)* **1** [C] An **offence** is a crime that breaks a particular law and requires a particular punishment. = crime ❑ *A first offence carries a fine of $1,000.* ❑ *In Britain the Consumer Protection Act makes it a criminal offence to sell goods that are unsafe.* **2** [C, U] **Offence** or an **offence** is behaviour that causes people to be upset or embarrassed. ❑ *He said he didn't mean to give offence.*

PHRASE **take offence** If someone **takes offence at** something you say or do, they feel upset, often unnecessarily, because they think you are being rude to them. ❑ *Instead of taking offence, the woman smiled.*

CONVENTION **no offence** *(formulae)* Some people say '**no offence**' to make it clear that they do not want to upset you, although what they are saying may seem rude. ❑ *'No offence,' she said, 'but your sister seems a little gloomy.'*

✪ of·fend /əˈfend/ VERB [I, T] *(offends, offending, offended)*

1 [I, T] If you **offend** someone, you say or do something rude which upsets or embarrasses them. ❑ *He apologizes for his comments and says he had no intention of offending the community.* ❑ *In the great effort not to offend, we end up saying nothing.* **2** [I] *(formal)* If someone **offends**, they commit a crime. = break the law ❑ *In Western countries girls are far less likely to offend than boys.* ❑ *Victims wanted assurances their attackers would never offend again.*

of·fend·ed /əˈfendɪd/ ADJ ❑ *She is terribly offended, angered and hurt by this.*

✪ of·fend·er /əˈfendə/ NOUN [C] *(offenders)*

1 An **offender** is a person who has committed a crime. = criminal ❑ *The authorities often know that sex offenders will attack again when they are released.* ❑ *an experimental scheme for young offenders* **2** You can refer to someone or something which you think is causing a problem as an **offender**. = culprit ❑ *The plant's leaves can often turn brown, and I sometimes cut off the worst offenders.*

of·fen·sive ♦◇◇ /əˈfensɪv/ ADJ, NOUN

ADJ Something that is **offensive** upsets or embarrasses people because it is rude or insulting. ❑ *Some friends of his found the play horribly offensive.*

NOUN [C] *(offensives)* **1** A military **offensive** is a carefully planned attack made by a large group of soldiers. ❑ *Its latest military offensive against rebel forces is aimed at re-opening important trade routes.* **2** If you conduct an **offensive**, you take strong action to show how angry you are about something or how much you disapprove of something. ❑ *Republicans acknowledged that they had little choice but to mount an all-out offensive on the Democratic nominee.*

PHRASE **go on the offensive** If you **go on the offensive** or **take the offensive**, you begin to take strong action against people who have been attacking you. ❑ *The West African* *forces went on the offensive in response to attacks on them.*

of·fer ♦♦♦ /ˈɒfə, AmE ˈɔːfər/ VERB, NOUN

VERB [T] (**offers, offering, offered**) **1** If you **offer** something to someone, you ask them if they would like to have it or use it. ❑ *He has offered seats at the conference table to the Russian leader and the president of Kazakhstan.* ❑ *The number of companies offering them work increased.* **2** If you **offer to** do something, you say that you are willing to do it. ❑ *Peter offered to teach them water-skiing.* **3** If you **offer** someone information, advice, or praise, you give it to them, usually because you feel that they need it or deserve it. ❑ *They manage a company offering advice on mergers and acquisitions.* ❑ *She offered him emotional and practical support in countless ways.* **4** If you **offer** someone something such as love or friendship, you show them that you feel that way towards them. ❑ *The president has offered his sympathy to the Georgian people.* ❑ *It must be better to be able to offer them love and security.* **5** If people **offer** prayers, praise, or a sacrifice to God or a god, they speak to or give something to their god. ❑ *Church leaders offered prayers and condemned the bloodshed.* **6** If an organization **offers** something such as a service or product, it provides it. ❑ *We have been successful because we are offering a quality service.* ❑ *The store is offering customers 1p for each shopping bag re-used.* **7** If you **offer** a particular amount of money for something, you say that you will pay that much to buy it. ❑ *He is in a position to offer $825,000 for the bankrupt airline's assets.* ❑ *They are offering farmers $2.15 a bushel for corn.*

PHRASE **have something to offer** If you **have** something **to offer**, you have a quality or ability that makes you important, attractive, or useful. ❑ *In your free time, explore all that this incredible city has to offer.*

PHRASAL VERB **offer up** Offer up means the same as **offer** VERB 5. ❑ *He should consider offering up a prayer to St Lambert.*

NOUN [c] (**offers**) **1** An **offer** is something that someone says they will give you or do for you. ❑ *The offer of talks with Moscow marks a significant change from the previous Western position.* ❑ *'I ought to reconsider her offer to move in,' he mused.* **2** [oft SUPP + offer, also 'on' offer] An **offer** in a store is a specially low price for a specific product or something extra that you get if you buy a certain product. ❑ *This month's offers include a pork loin and avocados.* ❑ *Today's special offer gives you a choice of three destinations.* **3** An **offer** is the amount of money that someone says they will pay to buy something. ❑ *The estate agent says no one else will make me an offer.*

PHRASES **on offer** If there is something **on offer**, it is available to be used or bought. ❑ *They are making trips to check out the merchandise on offer.*

open to offers If you are **open to offers**, you are willing to do something if someone will pay you an amount of money that you think is reasonable. ❑ *It seems that while the Dodgers are eager to have him, he is still open to offers.*

of·fer·ing ♦♢♢ /ˈɒfərɪŋ, AmE ˈɔːf-/ NOUN [c] (**offerings**) **1** An **offering** is something that is being sold. ❑ *It was very, very good, far better than vegetarian offerings in many an expensive restaurant.* **2** An **offering** is a gift that people offer to their God or gods as a form of worship. ❑ *the holiest of the Shinto rituals, where offerings are made at night to the great Sun*

○**of·fice** ♦♦♦ /ˈɒfɪs, AmE ˈɔːf-/ NOUN [c, u] (**offices**) **1** [c] An **office** is a room or a part of a building where people work sitting at desks. ❑ *By the time Flynn arrived at his office it was 5.30.* ❑ *Telephone their head office for more details.* **2** [c] An **office** is a department of an organization, especially the government, where people deal with a particular kind of administrative work. = department ❑ *Thousands have registered with unemployment offices.* ❑ *the Congressional Budget Office* ❑ *Downing Street's press office* **3** [c] An **office** is a small building or room where people can go for information, tickets, or a service of some kind. ❑ *The tourist office operates a useful room-finding service.* **4** [u] If someone holds **office** in a government, they have an important job or position of authority. ❑ *The events to mark the president's four years in office went ahead as planned.* ❑ *The treasurer shall hold office for five years.*

→ See also **post office**

of·fic·er ♦♦♦ /ˈɒfɪsə, AmE ˈɔːf-/ NOUN [c] (**officers**) **1** In the armed forces, an **officer** is a person in a position of authority. ❑ *a retired army officer* **2** Members of the police force can be referred to as **officers**. ❑ *The officer saw no obvious signs of a break-in.* ❑ *Officer Montoya was first on the scene.* **3** An **officer** is a person who has a responsible position in an organization, especially a government organization. ❑ *a local authority education officer*

→ See also **police officer**

○**of·fi·cial** ♦♦♦ /əˈfɪʃəl/ ADJ, NOUN

ADJ **1** **Official** means approved by the government or by someone in authority. = authorized; ≠ unofficial, informal ❑ *According to the official figures, over one thousand people died during the revolution.* ❑ *An official announcement is expected in the next few days.* **2** [official + N] **Official** activities are carried out by a person in authority as part of their job. ❑ *The president is in Brazil for an official two-day visit.* **3** [official + N] **Official** things are used by a person in authority as part of their job. ❑ *the official residence of the head of state* **4** [official + N] If you describe someone's explanation or reason for something as the **official** explanation, you are suggesting that it is probably not true, but is used because the real explanation is embarrassing. ❑ *They realized that the official explanation left facts unexplained.*

NOUN [c] (**officials**) **1** An **official** is a person who holds a position of authority in an organization. ❑ *A senior UN official hopes to visit Baghdad this month.* ❑ *Local officials say the shortage of water restricts the kind of businesses they can attract.* **2** An **official** at a sports event is a referee, umpire, or other person who checks that the players follow the rules. ❑ *Officials suspended the game because of safety concerns.*

○**of·fi·cial·ly** /əˈfɪʃəli/ ADV **1** = ceremoniously; ≠ unofficially, informally ❑ *The election results have still not been officially announced.* ❑ *The nine-year civil war is officially over.* **2** Officially, the guard was to protect us. In fact, they were there to report on our movements.

○**off·set** /ˌɒfˈset, AmE ˌɔːf-/ VERB [T] (**offsets, offsetting, offset**) (*academic word*) If one thing **is offset** by another, the effect of the first thing is reduced by the second, so that any advantage or disadvantage is cancelled out. = balance, counteract ❑ *The increase in pay costs was more than offset by higher productivity.* ❑ *The move is designed to help offset the shortfall in world oil supplies caused by the UN embargo.*

off·shore /ˌɒfˈʃɔː, AmE ˌɔːf-/ ADJ, ADV

ADJ **1** [offshore + N] **Offshore** means situated or happening in the sea, near to the coast. ❑ *the offshore oil industry* **2** [offshore + N] (*business*) **Offshore** investments or companies are located in a place, usually an island, which has fewer tax regulations than most other countries. ❑ *The island offers a wide range of offshore banking facilities.*

ADV If something is done **offshore**, it is done in the sea, near to the coast. ❑ *One day a larger ship anchored offshore.*

off·spring /ˈɒfsprɪŋ, AmE ˈɔːf-/ NOUN [c] (**offspring**) (*formal*) You can refer to a person's children or to an animal's young as their **offspring**. ❑ *Eleanor was now less anxious about her offspring than she had once been.*

of·ten ♦♦♦ /ˈɒfən, AmE ˈɔːf-/ ADV

> **Often** is usually used before the verb, but it may be used after the verb when it has a word like 'less' or 'more' before it, or when the clause is negative.

ADV **1** If something **often** happens, it happens many times or much of the time. ❑ *They often spent Christmas together.* ❑ *That doesn't happen very often.* **2** You use **how often** to ask questions about frequency. You also use **often** in reported clauses and other statements to give information about the frequency of something. ❑ *How often do you brush your teeth?*

PHRASES **every so often** If something happens **every so often**, it happens regularly, but with fairly long intervals between each occasion. = occasionally ❑ *She's going to come back every so often.*

o

as often as not or **more often than not** If you say that something happens **as often as not**, or **more often than not**, you mean that it happens fairly frequently, and that this can be considered as typical. ◻ *Yet, as often as not, they find themselves the target of persecution rather than praise.*

✪ **oil** ◆◆◆ /ɔɪl/ NOUN, VERB

NOUN [C, U] (**oils**) **1** **Oil** is a smooth, thick liquid that is used as a fuel and for making the parts of machines move smoothly. Oil is found underground. ◻ *The company buys and sells about 600,000 barrels of oil a day.* ◻ *the rapid rise in prices for oil and petrol* ◻ *The Iraqi economy is almost totally dependent on oil production.* **2** **Oil** is a smooth, thick liquid made from plants and is often used for cooking. ◻ *Combine the beans, chopped mint, and oil in a large bowl.* **3** **Oil** is a smooth, thick liquid, often with a pleasant smell, that you rub into your skin or add to your bath. ◻ *Try a hot bath with some relaxing bath oil.*

VERB [T] (**oils, oiling, oiled**) If you **oil** something, you put oil onto or into it, for example, to make it work smoothly or to protect it. ◻ *A crew of assistants oiled and adjusted the release mechanism until it worked perfectly.*

✦ **burn the midnight oil** → see **midnight**

oily /ˈɔɪli/ ADJ (**oilier, oiliest**) **1** Something that is **oily** is covered with oil or contains oil. ◻ *He was wiping his hands on an oily rag.* **2** **Oily** means looking, feeling, tasting, or smelling like oil. ◻ *traces of an oily substance*

okay ◆◆◇ /ˌəʊˈkeɪ/ also **OK, O.K., ok** ADJ, ADV, CONVENTION, VERB, NOUN

ADJ (*informal*) **1** If you say that something is **okay**, you find it satisfactory or acceptable. = all right ◻ *a shooting range where it's OK to use weapons* ◻ *Is it okay if I come by myself?* **2** [V-LINK + okay] If you say that someone is **okay**, you mean that they are safe and well. = all right ◻ *Check that the baby's okay.*

ADV [okay after V] **Okay** means in a satisfactory or acceptable manner. = all right ◻ *We seemed to manage okay for the first year or so after David was born.*

CONVENTION (*informal*) **1** (*formulae*) You can say '**Okay**' to show that you agree to something. = all right ◻ *'Just tell him I would like to talk to him.'—'OK.'* **2** You can say '**Okay?**' to check whether the person you are talking to understands what you have said and accepts it. = all right ◻ *We'll get together next week, OK?* **3** You can use **okay** to indicate that you want to start talking about something else or doing something else. = right ◻ *OK. Now, let's talk some business.* **4** You can use **okay** to stop someone from arguing with you by showing that you accept the point they are making, though you do not necessarily regard it as very important. ◻ *Okay, there is a slight difference.*

VERB [T] (**okays, okaying, okayed**) (*informal*) If someone in authority **okays** something, they officially agree to it or allow it to happen. ◻ *His doctor wouldn't OK the trip.*

NOUN [SING] If someone in authority **gives** something **the okay**, they officially agree to it or allow it to happen. ◻ *He gave the okay to issue a new press release.*

old ◆◆◆ /əʊld/ ADJ, NOUN

ADJ (**older, oldest**) **1** Someone who is **old** has lived for many years and is no longer young. = elderly ◻ *a white-haired old man* **2** You use **old** to talk about how many days, weeks, months, or years someone or something has lived or existed. ◻ *He was abandoned by his father when he was three months old.* ◻ *How old are you now?* ◻ *Bill was six years older than David.* **3** Something that is **old** has existed for a long time. ◻ *She loved the big old house.* ◻ *These books must be very old.* **4** Something that is **old** is no longer in good condition because of its age or because it has been used a lot. ◻ *He took a bunch of keys from the pocket of his old corduroy trousers.* **5** [old + N] You use **old** to refer to something that is no longer used, that no longer exists, or that has been replaced by something else. ◻ *The old road had disappeared under grass and heather.* **6** [POSS + old + N] You use **old** to refer to something that used to belong to you, or to a person or thing that used to have a particular role in your life. ◻ *I'll make up the bed in your old room.* ◻ *I still have affection for my old school.* **7** [old + N] An **old** friend, enemy, or rival is someone who has been your friend, enemy, or rival for a long time. ◻ *I called my old*

friend John Horner.* ◻ *Mr Brownson, I assure you, King's an old enemy of mine.* **8** (BrE, *informal, feelings*) You can use **old** to express affection when talking to or about someone you know. ◻ *Are you all right, old pal?*

NOUN [PL] **The old** are people who are old. ◻ *providing a caring response for the needs of the old and the handicapped*

PHRASES **any old** (*informal, emphasis*) You use **any old** to emphasize that the quality or type of something is not important. If you say that a particular thing is **not any old** thing, you are emphasizing how special or famous it is. ◻ *Any old paper will do.*

in the old days **In the old days** means in the past, before things changed. ◻ *In the old days, doctors made house calls.*

the good old days When people refer to **the good old days**, they are referring to a time in the past when they think that life was better than it is now. ◻ *He remembers the good old days when everyone in his village knew each other and you could leave your door open at night.*

✦ **good old** → see **good**; **settle an old score** → see **score**

USAGE NOTE

old

The use of **old** to describe someone who has lived for many years can sound impolite. 'Elderly' is a more polite word.
*The province has a high proportion of **elderly** residents.*

✪ **old age** NOUN [U] Your **old age** is the period of years towards the end of your life. ◻ *They worry about how they will support themselves in their old age.* ◻ *increased risk of Alzheimer's in old age*

✪ **old-fashioned** ADJ **1** Something such as a style, method, or device that is **old-fashioned** is no longer used, done, or admired by most people, because it has been replaced by something that is more modern. ◻ *The house was dull, old-fashioned and in bad condition.* ◻ *There are some traditional farmers left who still make cheese the old-fashioned way.* **2** **Old-fashioned** ideas, customs, or values are the ideas, customs, and values of the past. = traditional; ≠ modern ◻ *She has some old-fashioned values and can be a strict disciplinarian.* ◻ *good old-fashioned English cooking*

ol·ive /ˈɒlɪv/ NOUN, COLOUR, COMB, ADJ

NOUN [C, U] (**olives**) **1** [C, U] **Olives** are small green or black fruits with a bitter taste. Olives are often pressed to make olive oil. ◻ *a pile of black olives* **2** [C] An **olive tree** or an **olive** is a tree on which olives grow. ◻ *Olives look romantic on a hillside in Provence.*

COLOUR Something that is **olive** is yellowish-green in colour. ◻ *glowing colours such as deep red, olive, saffron and ochre*

COMB **Olive-green** means the same as **olive**. ◻ *She wore an olive-green T-shirt.*

ADJ If someone has **olive** skin, the colour of their skin is yellowish brown. ◻ *They are handsome with dark, shining hair, olive skin and fine brown eyes.*

omen /ˈəʊmen/ NOUN [C] (**omens**) If you say that something is an **omen**, you think it indicates what is likely to happen in the future and whether it will be good or bad. ◻ *Her appearance at this moment is an omen of disaster.*

omi·nous /ˈɒmɪnəs/ ADJ If you describe something as **ominous**, you mean that it worries you because it makes you think that something bad is going to happen. ◻ *There was an ominous silence at the other end of the phone.*
omi·nous·ly /ˈɒmɪnəsli/ ADV ◻ *The bar seemed ominously quiet.*

✪ **omis·sion** /əʊˈmɪʃən/ NOUN [C, U] (**omissions**) **1** [C] An **omission** is something that has not been included or has not been done, either deliberately or accidentally. = exclusion ◻ *He was surprised by his wife's omission from the guest list.* ◻ *Williams is the most notable omission from the 33-strong party announced yesterday.* **2** [U] **Omission** is the act of not including a particular person or thing or of not doing something. = exclusion; ≠ inclusion ◻ *the prosecution's seemingly malicious omission of recorded evidence* ◻ *This scrupulous omission of certain facts is not unusual.*

✪ **omit** /əʊˈmɪt/ VERB [T] (**omits, omitting, omitted**) **1** If you **omit** something, you do not include it in an activity or piece of work, deliberately or accidentally. **= leave out** ❑ *Omit the salt in this recipe.* ❑ *Some details of the initial investment were inadvertently omitted from the financial statements.* ❑ *Our apologies to David Pannick for omitting his name from last week's article.* **2** (*formal*) If you **omit to** do something, you do not do it. **= fail** ❑ *His new girlfriend had omitted to tell him she was married.*

✪ **om·ni·vore** /ˈɒmnɪˌvɔː/ NOUN [C] (**omnivores**)
(*technical*) An **omnivore** is an animal that eats both meat and plants. ❑ *It is a tree-dwelling omnivore with a body resembling a cat's and the face of a weasel.* ❑ *These teeth replace the premolars and molars found in herbivores and omnivores.*

WORD PARTS

The prefix **omni-** often appears in words that have 'all' as part of their meaning:

omnivore (NOUN)

omnipresent (ADJ)

omnipotent (ADJ)

✪ **om·niv·or·ous** /ɒmˈnɪvərəs/ ADJ (*formal*)
1 (*technical*) An **omnivorous** person or animal eats all kinds of food, including both meat and plants. ❑ *Brown bears are omnivorous, eating anything that they can get their paws on.* ❑ *Like other starlings this species is omnivorous.* **2** **Omnivorous** means liking a wide variety of things of a particular type. ❑ *As a child, Coleridge developed omnivorous reading habits.*

on ♦♦♦ /ɒn/ PREP, ADV, ADJ
PREP **1** If someone or something is **on** a surface or object, the surface or object is immediately below them and is supporting their weight. ❑ *He is sitting beside her on the sofa.* ❑ *On top of the cupboards are straw baskets.* **2** If something is **on** a surface or object, it is stuck to it or attached to it. ❑ *I stared at the peeling paint on the ceiling.* ❑ *The clock on the wall showed one minute to twelve.* **3** If you put, throw, or drop something **on** a surface, you move it or drop it so that it is then supported by the surface. **= onto** ❑ *He got his winter jacket from the wardrobe and dropped it on the sofa.* **4** You use **on** to say what part of your body is supporting your weight. ❑ *He continued to lie on his back and look at clouds.* ❑ *He raised himself on his elbows, squinting into the sun.* **5** You use **on** to say that someone or something touches a part of a person's body. ❑ *He leaned down and kissed her lightly on the mouth.* **6** [N + on + N] If someone has a particular expression **on** their face, their face has that expression. ❑ *The maid looked at him, a nervous smile on her face.* **7** [on + PRON] You can say that you have something **on** you if you are carrying it in your pocket or in a purse. ❑ *I didn't have any money on me.* **8** If someone's eyes are **on** you, they are looking or staring at you. ❑ *Everyone's eyes were fixed on him.* **9** If you hurt yourself **on** something, you accidentally hit a part of your body against it and that thing causes damage to you. ❑ *Mr Pendle hit his head on a wall as he fell.* **10** If you are **on** an area of land, you are there. ❑ *He was able to spend only a few days on the island.* ❑ *You lived on the farm until you came back to America?* **11** If something is situated **on** a place such as a road or coast, it forms part of it or is by the side of it. ❑ *Bergdorf Goodman has opened a men's store on Fifth Avenue.* ❑ *The hotel is on the coast.* **12** If you get **on** a bus, train, or plane, you go into it in order to travel somewhere. If you are **on** it, you are travelling in it. ❑ *We waited till twelve and we finally got on the plane.* **13** If there is something **on** a piece of paper, it has been written or printed there. ❑ *The writing on the back of the card was cramped but scrupulously neat.* **14** If something is **on** a list, it is included in it. ❑ *I've seen your name on the list of deportees.* **15** You use **on** to introduce the method, principle, or system which is used to do something. ❑ *a television that we bought on credit two months ago* ❑ *They want all groups to be treated on an equal basis.* **16** If something is done on an instrument or a machine, it is done using that instrument or machine. ❑ *songs that I could just sit down and play on the piano* **17** If information is, for example, **on** tape or **on** computer, that is the way that it is stored. ❑ *We've got her statement on tape.* **18** If something is **on** the radio or television, it is

being broadcast. ❑ *Every sporting event on television and satellite over the next seven days is listed.* **19** You use **on** to introduce an activity that someone is doing, particularly travelling. ❑ *I've always wanted to go on a cruise.* ❑ *We're going on a trip next month.* **20** You can indicate when something happens by saying that it happens **on** a particular day, date, or part of the week. ❑ *This year's event will take place on June 19th, a week earlier than usual.* ❑ *I was born on Christmas Day.* ❑ *The road is often lined with cars on the weekend.* **21** [on + N/-ING] You use **on** when mentioning an event that was followed by another one. ❑ *She waited in her hotel to welcome her children on their arrival from Vancouver.* **22** Books, discussions, or ideas **on** a particular subject are concerned with that subject. ❑ *They offer free counselling on legal matters.* ❑ *He declined to give any information on the presidential election.* **23** If you are **on** a committee or council, you are a member of it. ❑ *Claire and Alita were on the organizing committee.* **24** Someone who is **on** a drug takes it regularly. ❑ *She was on antibiotics for an eye infection that wouldn't go away.* **25** [V + on + N] If you live **on** a particular kind of food, you eat it. If a machine runs on a particular kind of power or fuel, it uses it in order to function. **= off** ❑ *The caterpillars feed on a wide range of trees, shrubs and plants.* ❑ *He lived on a diet of water and canned fish.* **26** (*BrE*) If you are **on** a particular income, that is the income that you have. ❑ *young people who are unemployed or on low wages* ❑ *He's on three hundred a week.* **27** [N + on + N] Taxes or profits that are obtained from something are referred to as taxes or profits **on** it. ❑ *a general strike to protest about a tax on food and medicine* **28** [on + N/-ING] When you buy something or pay for something, you spend money **on** it. ❑ *I resolved not to waste money on a hotel.* ❑ *He spent more on feeding the dog than he spent on feeding himself.* **29** [on + N/-ING] When you spend time or energy **on** a particular activity, you spend time or energy doing it. ❑ *People complain about how children spend so much time on computer games.* ❑ *You all know why I am here, so I won't waste time on preliminaries.*

ADV **1** [on after V] You use **on** to say that something is stuck to or attached to a surface or object. ❑ *I know how to sew a button on.* **2** [on after V] When you put a piece of clothing **on**, you place it over part of your body in order to wear it. If you have it **on**, you are wearing it. ❑ *He put his coat on while she opened the front door.* **3** [on after V] You can say that you get **on**, when you go into a bus, train, or plane in order to travel somewhere. ❑ *He showed his ticket to the conductor and got on.* **4** (*spoken*) You use **on** in expressions such as '**have a lot going on**' and '**not have very much on**' to indicate how busy someone is. ❑ *I have a lot on in the next week.* **5** [on after V] You use **on** to say that someone is continuing to do something. ❑ *They walked on in silence for a while.* ❑ *We worked on into the night.* **6** ['from' N + on] You use **on** in expressions such as **from now on** and **from then on** to indicate that something starts to happen at the time mentioned and continues to happen afterwards. ❑ *Perhaps it would be best not to see much of you from now on.* ❑ *We can expect trouble from this moment on.* **7** [ADV + on] You often use **on** after the adverbs 'early', 'late', 'far', and their comparative forms, especially at the beginning or end of a sentence, or before a preposition. ❑ *The market square is a riot of colour and animation from early on in the morning.* ❑ *Later on I learned how to read music.* **8** When something such as a machine or an electric light is **on**, it is functioning or in use. When you switch it **on**, it starts functioning. ❑ *The light was on and the door was open.* ❑ *The heating's been turned off. I've turned it on again.*

PHRASE **on and on** If you say that something happens **on and on**, you mean that it continues to happen for a very long time. ❑ *designers, builders, fitters – the list goes on and on* ❑ *Lobell drove on and on through the dense and blowing snow.*

ADJ **1** [V-LINK + on] If a radio or television programme is **on** it is being broadcast by radio or television. ❑ *teenagers complaining there's nothing good on* **2** [V-LINK + on] When an activity is taking place, you can say that it is **on**. ❑ *There's an exciting match on at Wimbledon right now.*

PHRASE **not on** or **just not on** (*BrE, informal*) If you say

that something is **not on** or is **just not on**, you mean that it is unacceptable or impossible.
♦ **on behalf of someone** → see **behalf**; **on and off** → see **off**; **and so on** → see **so**; **on top of** → see **top**

once ♦♦♦ /wʌns, wɒns/ ADV, PRON, CONJ
ADV **1** [once with v] If something happens **once**, it happens one time only. □ *I met Miquela once, briefly.* □ *Since that evening I haven't once slept through the night.* **2** [once 'a' N] You use **once** with 'a' and words like 'day', 'week', and 'month' to indicate that something happens regularly, one time in each day, week, or month. □ *Lung cells die and are replaced about once a week.* **3** If something was **once** true, it was true at some time in the past, but is no longer true. □ *Her parents once ran a shop.* □ *I lived there once myself, before I got married.* **4** [once with v] If someone **once** did something, they did it at some time in the past. □ *I once went camping at Lake Michigan with a friend.* □ *We once walked across the frozen pond at two in the morning.*
PHRASES **once again** or **once more** If something happens **once again** or **once more**, it happens again. □ *Amy picked up the hairbrush and brushed her hair once more.*
once and for all (*emphasis*) If something happens **once and for all**, it happens completely or finally. □ *We have to resolve this matter once and for all.*
once in a while If something happens **once in a while**, it happens sometimes, but not very often. □ *Your body, like any other machine, needs a full service once in a while.*
once or twice If you have done something **once or twice**, you have done it a few times, but not very often. □ *I visited once or twice.* □ *Once or twice she had caught a flash of interest in William's eyes.*
PRON ['the/this' once] If something happens **the once** it happens one time only. □ *'Have they been to visit you yet?'—'Just the once, yeah.'*
PHRASES **all at once** If something happens **all at once**, it happens suddenly, often when you are not expecting it to happen. □ *All at once there was someone knocking at the door.*
at once If you do something **at once**, you do it immediately. = immediately □ *I have to go at once.* □ *Remove from the heat, add the parsley, toss and serve at once.*
at once or **all at once** If a number of different things happen **at once** or **all at once**, they all happen at the same time. □ *You can't be doing two things at once.*
for once (*emphasis*) **For once** is used to emphasize that something happens on this particular occasion, that it has never happened before, and may never happen again. □ *For once, Dad is not complaining.*
CONJ If something happens **once** another thing has happened, it happens immediately afterwards. □ *The decision had taken about 10 seconds once he'd read a market research study.*

one ♦♦♦ /wʌn/ NUM, ADJ, DET, PRON, QUANT
NUM (ones) **One** is the number 1. □ *They had three sons and one daughter.* □ *one thousand years ago*
PHRASES **a hundred and one** or **a thousand and one** or **a million and one** (*emphasis*) You can use expressions such as **a hundred and one**, **a thousand and one**, and **a million and one** to emphasize that you are talking about a large number of things or people. □ *There are a hundred and one ways in which you can raise money.*
in one You can use **in one** to indicate that something is a single unit, but is made up of several different parts or has several different functions. □ *a love story and an adventure all in one*
one or two **One or two** means a few. □ *We may make one or two changes.* □ *I've also sold one or two to a publisher.*
be one up on someone If you try to get **one up on** someone, you try to gain an advantage over them. □ *the competitive kind who will see this as the opportunity to be one up on you*
ADJ [DET + one] (*emphasis*) If you say that someone or something is the **one** person or thing of a particular kind, you are emphasizing that they are the only person or thing of that kind. = only □ *They had alienated the one man who knew the business.*
PHRASE **the one and only** **The one and only** can be used in front of the name of an actor, singer, or other famous person when they are being introduced on a show. □ *one of the greatest ever rock performers, the one and only Tina Turner*
DET (*emphasis*) **1** **One** can be used instead of 'a' to emphasize the following noun. □ *There is one thing I would like to know – What is it about Tim that you find so irresistible?* **2** (*informal, emphasis*) You can use **one** instead of 'a' to emphasize the following adjective or expression. □ *If we ever get married we'll have one terrific wedding.* **3** You can use **one** to refer to the first of two or more things that you are comparing. □ *Prices vary from one shop to another.* **4** You can use **one** when you have been talking or writing about a group of people or things and you want to say something about a particular member of the group. □ *'A college degree isn't enough,' said one honours student.* **5** You can use **one** when referring to a time in the past or in the future. For example, if you say that you did something **one day**, you mean that you did it on a day in the past. □ *How would you like to have dinner one night, just you and me?*
PRON **1** You can use **one** to refer to the first of two or more things that you are comparing. □ *The twins were dressed differently and one was thinner than the other.* **2** You can use **one** or **ones** instead of a noun when it is clear what type of thing or person you are referring to and you are describing them or giving more information about them. □ *They are selling their house to move to a smaller one.* **3** You use **ones** to refer to people in general. □ *We are the only ones who know.* **4** [one 'of' N, one 'that'] You can use **one** instead of a noun group when you have just mentioned something and you want to describe it or give more information about it. □ *The issue of land reform was one that dominated Hungary's parliamentary elections.* **5** You can use **one** when you have been talking or writing about a group of people or things and you want to say something about a particular member of the group. □ *Some of them couldn't eat a thing. One couldn't even drink.* **6** (*formal*) You use **one** to make statements about people in general which also apply to themselves. **One** can be used as the subject or object of a sentence. □ *If one looks at the bigger picture, a lot of positive things are happening.* □ *Where does one go from there?*
PHRASES **for one** (*emphasis*) You can use **for one** to emphasize that a particular person is definitely reacting or behaving in a particular way, even if other people are not. □ *I, for one, hope you don't get the job.*
one after the other or **one after another** You use **one after the other** or **one after another** to say that actions or events happen with very little time between them. □ *My three guitars broke one after the other.*
one by one You can use **one by one** to indicate that people do things or that things happen in sequence, not all at the same time. □ *We went into the room one by one.*
QUANT [one 'of' ADJ-SUPERL] You use **one** in expressions such as 'one of the biggest airports' or 'one of the most experienced players' to indicate that something or someone is bigger or more experienced than most other things or people of the same kind. □ *Subaru is one of the smallest Japanese car makers.*
PHRASE **one or other** You use **one or other** to refer to one or more things or people in a group, when it does not matter which particular one or ones are thought of or chosen. □ *One or other of the two women was wrong.*
♦ **one day** → see **day**; **one thing after another** → see **another**; **of one mind** → see **mind**; **in one piece** → see **piece**

one-off NOUN, ADJ
NOUN [c] (one-offs) You can refer to something as a **one-off** when it is made or happens only once. □ *Our survey revealed that these allergies were mainly one-offs.*
ADJ (*mainly BrE; in AmE, usually* use **one-time**) A **one-off** thing is made or happens only once.

on•er•ous /ˈəʊnərəs, AmE ˈɑːn-/ ADJ (*formal*) If you describe a task as **onerous**, you dislike having to do it because you find it difficult or unpleasant. □ *parents who have had the onerous task of bringing up a very difficult child*

one's ♦♦♢ /wʌnz/ DET (*formal*) Speakers and writers use

one's to indicate that something belongs or relates to people in general, or to themselves in particular. = your ❑ *a feeling of responsibility for the welfare of others in one's community*

one·self /wʌnˈself/ PRON (formal)

Oneself is a third person singular reflexive pronoun.

1 **Oneself** is used to mean 'any person in general' as the object of a verb or preposition, when this refers to the same person as the subject of the verb. ❑ *One must apply oneself to the present and keep one's eyes firmly fixed on one's future goals.* **2** **Oneself** is used to mean 'any person in general' as the object of a verb or preposition, when 'one' is not present but is understood to be the subject of the verb. ❑ *The historic feeling of the town makes it a pleasant place to base oneself for summer holidays.*

one-time also **onetime** ADJ [one-time + N] (journalism) **One-time** is used to describe something which happened in the past, or something such as a job, position, or role which someone used to have. = former ❑ *The legislative body had voted to oust the country's onetime rulers.*

✪ **on·go·ing** /ˈɒnɡəʊɪŋ/ ADJ (academic word) An **ongoing** situation has been happening for quite a long time and seems likely to continue for some time in the future. = continuing ❑ *There is an ongoing debate on the issue.* ❑ *That research is ongoing.*

on·ion /ˈʌnjən/ NOUN [C, U] (onions) An **onion** is a round vegetable with a light brown skin. It has many white layers on its inside which have a strong, sharp smell and taste. ❑ *You grind the onion and the raw cranberries together.*

✪ **on·line** ♦♦♦ /ˌɒnˈlaɪn/ also **on-line** ADJ, ADV
ADJ (computing) **1** (business) An **online** company provides services on the Internet. ❑ *the first online bank* ❑ *an online shopping centre* **2** If you are **online**, your computer is connected to the Internet. ❑ *You can chat to other people who are online.* ❑ *Approximately 85 per cent of UK households are now online.*
ADV [online after V] If you can get a service **online**, it is available on the Internet. = on the internet, web-based; ≠ offline ❑ *the cool stuff you find online* ❑ *The study was published online by the British Medical Journal.*

only ♦♦♦ /ˈəʊnli/ ADV, ADJ, CONJ

In written English, **only** is usually placed immediately before the word it qualifies. In spoken English, however, you can use stress to indicate what **only** qualifies, so its position is not so important.

ADV **1** You use **only** to indicate the one thing that is true, appropriate, or necessary in a particular situation, in contrast to all the other things that are not true, appropriate, or necessary. ❑ *Only the president could authorize the use of the atomic bomb.* ❑ *A business can only be built and expanded on a sound financial base.* **2** [only + CL/PREP] You use **only** to introduce the thing which must happen before the thing mentioned in the main part of the sentence can happen. ❑ *The lawyer is paid only if he wins.* ❑ *The Bank of England insists that it will cut interest rates only when it is ready.* **3** You use **only** to indicate that something is no more important, interesting, or difficult, for example, than you say it is, especially when you want to correct a wrong idea that someone has or may get. = just ❑ *At the moment it is only a theory.* ❑ *'I'm only a sergeant,' said Clements.* **4** [only + N/ADV] You use **only** to emphasize how small an amount is or how short a length of time is. ❑ *Child car seats only cost about $10 a week to rent.* ❑ *spacecraft guidance systems weighing only a few grams* **5** [only + N] You use **only** to emphasize that you are talking about a small part of an amount or group, not the whole of it. ❑ *These are only a few of the possibilities.* **6** [MODAL + only + INF] **Only** is used after 'can' or 'could' to emphasize that it is impossible to do anything except the rather inadequate or limited action that is mentioned. ❑ *For a moment I could say nothing. I could only stand and look.* **7** [only before V] You can use **only** in the expressions **I only wish** or **I only hope** in order to emphasize what you are hoping or wishing. = just ❑ *I only wish he were here now that things are getting better for me.* **8** [only + to-INF]

You can use **only** before an infinitive to introduce an event which happens immediately after one you have just mentioned, and which is surprising or unfortunate. ❑ *Ron tried the embassy, only to be told that Hugh was in a meeting.* **9** You can use **only** to emphasize how appropriate a certain course of action or type of behaviour is. ❑ *It's only fair to let her know that you intend to apply.* **10** [only before V] You can use **only** in front of a verb to indicate that the result of something is unfortunate or undesirable and is likely to make the situation worse rather than better. = just ❑ *The embargo would only hurt innocent civilians.*
PHRASES **only have to** (emphasis) If you say you **only have to** do one thing in order to achieve or prove a second thing, you are emphasizing how easily the second thing can be achieved or proved. ❑ *Any time you want a babysitter, dear, you only have to ask.*

only just (emphasis) **1** You can say that something has **only just** happened when you want to emphasize that it happened a very short time ago. ❑ *I've only just arrived.* **2** You use **only just** to emphasize that something is true, but by such a small degree that it is almost not true at all. ❑ *For centuries farmers there have only just managed to survive.* ❑ *I am old enough to remember the War, but only just.*

only too (emphasis) **1** You can use **only too** to emphasize that something is true or exists to a much greater extent than you would expect or like. ❑ *I know only too well that plans can easily go wrong.* **2** You can say that you are **only too** happy to do something to emphasize how willing you are to do it. ❑ *I'll be only too pleased to help them out with any questions.*

ADJ **1** [DET + only] If you talk about the **only** person or thing involved in a particular situation, you mean there are no others involved in it. ❑ *She was the only woman in Shell's legal department.* **2** [only + N] An **only** child is a child who has no brothers or sisters. ❑ *The actor, an only child, grew up in the Bronx.*
CONJ **1** (informal) **Only** can be used to add a comment which slightly changes or limits what you have just said. = but, except ❑ *It's just as dramatic as a movie, only it's real.* ❑ *It's a bit like my house, only nicer.* **2** (spoken) **Only** can be used after a clause with 'would' to indicate why something is not done. = but ❑ *I'd invite you to come with me, only it's such a long way.*
✦ if only → see if; the one and only → see one

on·set /ˈɒnset/ NOUN [SING] The **onset of** something is the beginning of it, used especially to refer to something unpleasant. ❑ *Most of the passes have been closed with the onset of winter.*

on·slaught /ˈɒnslɔːt/ NOUN [C] (onslaughts) **1** An **onslaught** on someone or something is a very violent, forceful attack against them. = assault ❑ *The press launched another vicious onslaught on the president.* **2** If you refer to an **onslaught of** something, you mean that there is a large amount of it, often so that it is very difficult to deal with. = barrage ❑ *the constant onslaught of ads on TV*

onto ♦◇◇ /ˈɒntuː/ PREP

The spelling **on to** is also used.

In addition to the uses shown below, **onto** is used in phrasal verbs such as 'hold onto' and 'latch onto'.

1 If something moves **onto** or is put **onto** an object or surface, it is then on that object or surface. ❑ *I took my bags inside, lowered myself onto the bed and switched on the TV.* **2** You can sometimes use **onto** to mention the place or area that someone moves into. ❑ *The players jogged onto the field.* ❑ *At exactly 6:00 p.m., Marcia drove onto the motorway.* **3** You can use **onto** to introduce the place towards which a light or someone's look is directed. ❑ *the metal part of the door onto which the sun had been shining* ❑ *The colours rotated around on a disc and were reflected onto the wall behind.* **4** [V + onto + N] If a door or room opens **onto** a place, that place is directly in front of it. ❑ *The door opened onto a well-lit hallway.* **5** When you change the position of your body, you use **onto** to introduce the part your body which is now supporting you. ❑ *As he stepped backwards she fell onto her knees, then onto her face.* ❑ *Puffing a little, Mabel shifted her weight onto her feet.* **6** When you get **onto** a bus, train, or plane, you enter it in order to travel somewhere. ❑ *As he got on to the plane, he asked me how I was feeling.* **7** **Onto** is used after verbs such as 'hold', 'hang', and 'cling' to indicate what someone is holding firmly or where something is being held firmly. ❑ *The reflector is held onto the sides of the spacecraft with a frame.* **8** If people who are talking get **onto** a different subject, they begin talking about it. ❑ *Let's get on to more important matters.* **9** You can sometimes use **onto** to indicate that something or someone becomes included as a part of a list or system. ❑ *The Macedonian question had failed to get on to the agenda.* ❑ *The pill itself has changed a lot since it first came onto the market.* **10** ['be' onto + N] (*informal*) If someone **is onto** something, they are about to discover something important. ❑ *He leaned across the table and whispered to me, 'I'm really onto something.'* **11** ['be' onto + N] (*informal*) If someone **is onto** you, they have discovered that you are doing something illegal or wrong. ❑ *I had told people what he had been doing, so now the police were onto him.*

on·ward /ˈɒnwəd/ ADJ, ADV

The form **onwards** can also be used for the adverb.

ADJ **1** **Onward** means moving forward or continuing a journey. ❑ *American Airlines have two flights a day to Bangkok, and there are onward flights to Phnom Penh.* **2** **Onward** means developing, progressing, or becoming more important over a period of time. ❑ *the onward march of progress in the aircraft industry* **ADV** **1** [onward after V] If something or someone moves **onward**, move forward or continue a journey. = on ❑ *The bus continued onward.* **2** [onward after V] If something or someone moves **onward**, they develop, progress, or become more important or successful over a period of time. ❑ *From here, it has been onward and upward all the way.* **3** ['from' N + onward] If something happens from a particular time **onward** or **onwards**, it begins to happen at that time and continues to happen afterwards. ❑ *From the turn of the century onward, she shared the life of the aborigines.*

on·wards ♦♦♦ /ˈɒnwədz/ → See onward

open ♦♦♦ /ˈəʊpən/ VERB, ADJ, NOUN

VERB [I, T] (**opens, opening, opened**) **1** [I, T] If you **open** something such as a door, window, or lid, or if it **opens**, its position is changed so that it no longer covers a hole or gap. ❑ *He opened the window and looked out.* **2** [T] If you **open** something such as a bottle, box, parcel, or envelope, you move, remove, or cut part of it so you can take out what is inside. ❑ *I opened the letter.* **3** [I, T] If you **open** something such as a book, an umbrella, or your hand, or if it **opens**, the different parts of it move away from each other so that the inside of it can be seen. ❑ *He opened the heavy Bible.* ❑ *The flower opens to reveal a bee.* **4** [T] (*computing*) If you **open** a computer file, you give the computer an instruction to display it on the screen. ❑ *Double click on the icon to open the file.* **5** [I, T] When you **open** your eyes or your eyes **open**, you move your eyelids upward, for example, when you wake up, so that you can see. ❑ *When I opened my eyes I saw Melissa standing at the end of my bed.* **6** [T] If you **open** your arms, you stretch them wide apart in front of you, usually in order to put them around someone. ❑ *She opened her arms and gave me a big hug.* **7** [T] If you **open** your shirt or coat, you undo the buttons or pull down the zip. ❑ *I opened my coat and let him see the belt.* **8** [I, T] If people **open** something such as a blocked road or a border, or if it **opens**, people can then pass along it or through it. ❑ *The rebels have opened the road from Monrovia to the Ivory Coast.* **9** [I] If a place **opens into** another, larger place, you can move from one directly into the other. ❑ *The corridor opened into a low smoky room.* **10** [I, T] When a shop, office, or public building **opens** or **is opened**, its doors are unlocked and the public can go in. ❑ *Banks closed on Friday afternoon and did not open again until Monday morning.* ❑ *I'd been waiting for him to open the shop.* **11** [I, T] When a public building, factory, or company **opens** or when someone **opens** it, it starts operating for the first time. ❑ *The original station opened in 1954.* ❑ *The complex opens to the public tomorrow.*

12 [I, T] If something such as a meeting or series of talks **opens**, or if someone **opens** it, it begins. ❑ *an emergency session of the Russian Parliament due to open later this morning* **13** [I, T] If an event such as a meeting or discussion **opens with** a particular activity, that activity is the first thing that happens or is dealt with. You can also say that someone such as a speaker or singer **opens by** doing a particular thing. = begin ❑ *The service opened with a hymn.* ❑ *I opened by saying, 'Honey, you look sensational.'* **14** [I] (*business*) On the stock exchange, the price at which currencies, shares, or commodities **open** is their value at the start of that day's trading. ❑ *Gold declined $2 in Zurich to open at $385.50.* **15** [I] When a film, play, or other public event **opens**, it begins to be shown, be performed, or take place for a limited period of time. ❑ *A photographic exhibition opens at the Smithsonian on Wednesday.* **16** [T] If you **open** an account with a bank or a commercial organization, you begin to use their services. ❑ *He tried to open an account at the branch of his bank nearest to his workplace.*

PHRASAL VERBS **open out** **1** **Open out** means the same as **open** VERB 3. ❑ *Keith took a map from the dashboard and opened it out on his knees.* **2** **Open out** means the same as **open** VERB 9. ❑ *narrow streets opening out into charming squares*

open up **1** **Open up** means the same as **open** VERB 2. ❑ *He opened up a cage and lifted out a 6ft python.* **2** **Open up** means the same as **open** VERB 8. ❑ *As rescue workers opened up roads today, it became apparent that some small towns were totally devastated.* **3** If a place, economy, or area of interest **opens up**, or if someone **opens** it **up**, more people can go there or become involved in it. ❑ *As the market opens up, I think people are going to be able to spend more money on consumer goods.* ❑ *He said he wanted to see how Albania was opening up to the world.* **4** If something **opens up** opportunities, or if they **open up**, they are created. ❑ *It was also felt that the collapse of the system opened up new possibilities.* **5** When you **open up** a building, you unlock and open the door so that people can get in. ❑ *Several customers were waiting when I arrived to open up the shop.* **6** If someone **opens up**, they start to say exactly what they think or feel. ❑ *Lorna found that people were willing to open up to her.*

ADJ **1** If something such as a door, window, or lid is **open**, it does not cover a hole or gap. ❑ *an open window* **2** If something such as a bottle, box, parcel, or envelope is **open**, part of it has been removed or cut away so that you can take out what is inside. ❑ *an open bottle of milk* **3** If something such as a book, an umbrella, or your hand is **open**, the different parts of it have been moved away from each other so that the inside of it can be seen. ❑ *Without warning, Bardo smacked his fist into his open hand.* **4** When your eyes are **open**, you have moved your eyelids upward, for example, when you wake up, so that you can see. ❑ *As soon as he saw that her eyes were open he sat up.* **5** [open + N, V-LINK + open] If your shirt or coat is **open**, you have undone the buttons or pulled down the zip. ❑ *The top can be worn buttoned up or open over a T-shirt.* **6** If a road or a border is **open**, people can pass along it or through it. ❑ *We were part of an entire regiment that had nothing else to do but to keep that highway open.* **7** An **open** area is a large area that does not have many buildings or trees in it. ❑ *Officers will also continue their search of nearby open ground.* **8** [open + N] An **open** structure or object is not covered or enclosed. ❑ *Don't leave a child alone in a room with an open fire.* **9** If a shop, office, or public building is **open**, its doors are unlocked and the public can go in. ❑ *The gallery is open from Monday to Friday, 9 a.m. to 6 p.m.* **10** [V-LINK + open] If a factory or company remains **open**, it continues to operate. ❑ *The government says it's no longer willing to spend $170 million a month to keep the pits open.* ❑ *any operating subsidy required to keep the airline open* **11** If you describe a person or their character as **open**, you mean they are honest and do not want or try to hide anything or to deceive anyone. ❑ *He had always been open with her and she always felt she would know if he lied.* **12** [open + N] If you describe a situation, attitude, or way of behaving as **open**, you mean it is not kept hidden or

secret. ❏ *The action is an open violation of the Vienna Convention.* **13** [V-LINK + open 'to' N] If you are **open to** suggestions or ideas, you are ready and willing to consider or accept them. = receptive ❏ *They are open to suggestions on how working conditions might be improved.* **14** [V-LINK + open 'to' N] If you say that a system, person, or idea is **open to** something such as abuse or criticism, you mean they might receive abuse or criticism because of their qualities, effects, or actions. = susceptible ❏ *The system, though well-meaning, is open to abuse.* **15** If you say that a fact or question is **open to** debate, interpretation, or discussion, you mean that people are uncertain whether it is true, what it means, or what the answer is. ❏ *Her interpretation of the facts may be open to doubt.* **16** You can use **open** to describe something that anyone is allowed to take part in or accept. ❏ *It's an open meeting, everybody's invited.* ❏ *an open invitation* **17** [V-LINK + open] If something such as an offer or job is **open**, it is available for someone to accept or apply for. ❏ *The offer will remain open until further notice.* **18** [V-LINK + open 'to' N] If an opportunity or choice **is open to** you, you are able to do a particular thing if you choose to. ❏ *There are a wide range of career opportunities open to young people.*
PHRASE **wide open** **1** If something is **wide open**, it is open to its full extent. ❏ *The child had left the inner door wide open.* **2** If you say that a competition, race, or election is **wide open**, you mean that anyone could win it, because there is no competitor who seems to be much better than the others. ❏ *The competition has been thrown wide open by the absence of the world champion.*
NOUN
PHRASES **in the open** If you do something **in the open** or **out in the open**, you do it outdoors rather than in a house or other building. ❏ *Many are sleeping in the open because they have no shelter.*
in the open or **out in the open** If an attitude or situation is **in the open** or **out in the open**, people know about it and it is no longer kept secret. ❏ *They had advised us to keep it a secret, but we wanted it out in the open.*
open·ness /'əʊpənnəs/ NOUN [U] **1** *a relationship based on honesty and openness* **2** *the new climate of political openness*
✦ **with open arms** → see **arm**; **keep your eyes open** → see **eye**; **with your eyes open** → see **eye**; **open your eyes** → see **eye**; **open fire** → see **fire**; **open your heart** → see **heart**; **the heavens open** → see **heaven**; **an open mind** → see **mind**; **open your mind** → see **mind**; **keep your options open** → see **option**

open·ing ♦♢♢ /'əʊpənɪŋ/ ADJ, NOUN
ADJ [opening + N] The **opening** event, item, day, or week in a series is the first one. ❏ *They returned to play in the season's opening game.*
NOUN [SING, C] (**openings**) **1** [SING] The **opening** of something such as a meeting or a series of talks is its beginning. ❏ *a statement issued at the opening of the talks* **2** [SING] The **opening** of a film, play, or other public event is the time when it starts to be shown, be performed, or take place. ❏ *He is due to attend the opening of the Asian Games on Saturday.* **3** [C] The **opening** of a public building, factory, or company is the occasion when it starts to operate for the first time. ❏ *He was there, though, for the official opening.* **4** [C] **The opening of** something such as a book, play, or concert is the first part of it. ❏ *The opening of the scene depicts Akhnaten and his family in a moment of intimacy.* **5** [C] An **opening** is a hole or empty space through which things or people can pass. ❏ *He squeezed through a narrow opening in the fence.* **6** [C] An **opening** is a good opportunity to do something, for example, to show people how good you are. = opportunity ❏ *Her capabilities were always there; all she needed was an opening to show them.* **7** [C] An **opening** is a job that is available. ❏ *We don't have any openings now, but we'll call you if something comes up.*

open·ly /'əʊpənli/ ADV If you do something **openly**, you do it without hiding any facts or hiding your feelings. ❏ *She openly criticized other athletes.*

open-minded ADJ (approval) If you describe someone as **open-minded**, you approve of them because they are

willing to listen to and consider other people's ideas and suggestions. ❏ *He was very open-minded about other people's work.*
open-mindedness NOUN [U] ❏ *He was praised for his enthusiasm and his open-mindedness.*

✪ **op·era** ♦♢♢ /'ɒpərə/ NOUN [C, U] (**operas**) An **opera** is a play with music in which all the words are sung. ❏ *a one-act opera about contemporary women in America* ❏ *Donizetti's opera 'Lucia di Lammermoor'* ❏ *He was also learned in classical music with a great love of opera.* ❏ *an opera singer*

✪ **op·er·ate** ♦♦♦ /'ɒpəreɪt/ VERB [I, T] (**operates, operating, operated**) **1** [I, T] If you **operate** a business or organization, you work to keep it running. If a business or organization **operates**, it carries out its work. ❏ *Until his death in 1986 Greenwood owned and operated an enormous pear orchard.* ❏ *allowing commercial banks to operate in the country* ❏ *Operating costs jumped from £85.3m to £95m.* **2** [I] The way that something **operates** is the way that it works or has a particular effect. ❏ *Ceiling and wall lights can operate independently.* ❏ *How do accounting records operate?* ❏ *The world of work doesn't operate that way.* **3** [I, T] When you **operate** a machine or device, or when it **operates**, you make it work. = run, work, function ❏ *A massive rock fall trapped the men as they operated a tunnelling machine.* ❏ *The number of these machines operating around the world has now reached ten million.* **4** [I] When surgeons **operate on** a patient in a hospital, they cut open a patient's body in order to remove, replace, or repair a diseased or damaged part. ❏ *In March 2005, surgeons operated on Max for a brain aneurysm.*

✪ **op·era·tion** ♦♦♦ /,ɒpə'reɪʃən/ NOUN
NOUN [C, U] (**operations**) **1** [C] An **operation** is a highly organized activity that involves many people doing different things. ❏ *The rescue operation began on Friday afternoon.* ❏ *The soldiers were engaged in a military operation close to the Ugandan border.* **2** [C] (business) A business or company can be referred to as an **operation**. ❏ *Thorn's electronics operation employs around 5,000 people.* **3** [C] When a patient has an **operation**, a surgeon cuts open their body in order to remove, replace, or repair a diseased or damaged part. ❏ *Charles was in hospital recovering from an operation on his arm.* **4** [U] The **operation** of a business or organization is the act of making it work. ❏ *Company finance is to provide funds for the everyday operation of the business.* ❏ *Part-time work is made difficult by the operation of the benefit system.* **5** [U] The **operation** of something is the way that it works or has a particular effect. ❏ *No money can be spent on the construction and operation of the tram.* **6** [U] The **operation** of a machine or device is the act of making it work. ❏ *over 1,000 dials monitoring every aspect of the operation of the aeroplane* **7** [U] If a system is **in operation**, it is being used. ❏ *the free banking system that has been in operation since the early eighties* **8** [U] If a machine or device is **in operation**, it is working. ❏ *There are three ski lifts in operation.*
PHRASE **come into operation** or **put something into operation** When a rule, system, or plan **comes into operation** or you **put it into operation**, you begin to use it. ❏ *The Financial Services Act came into operation four years ago.*

op·era·tion·al /,ɒpə'reɪʃənəl/ ADJ **1** A machine or piece of equipment that is **operational** is in use or is ready for use. ❏ *The whole system will be fully operational by December.* **2** **Operational** factors or problems relate to the working of a system, device, or plan. ❏ *The nuclear industry was required to prove that every operational and safety aspect had been fully researched.*
op·era·tion·al·ly /,ɒpə'reɪʃənəli/ ADV ❏ *goods which are economically or operationally impractical to transport*

op·era·tive /'ɒpərətɪv/ ADJ, NOUN
ADJ (formal) A system or service that is **operative** is working or having an effect. ❏ *The commercial telephone service was no longer operative.*
PHRASE **the operative word** If you describe a word as **the operative word**, you want to draw attention to it because you think it is important or exactly true in a particular

o

situation. ❑ As long as the operative word is 'greed', you can't count on people keeping the costs down.

NOUN [c] (**operatives**) **1** (formal) An **operative** is a worker, especially one who does work with their hands. ❑ In an automated car plant there is not a human operative to be seen. **2** (mainly AmE) An **operative** is someone who works for a government agency such as the intelligence service. ❑ Naturally the CIA wants to protect its operatives.

op·era·tor ♦◇◇ /ˈɒpəreɪtə/ NOUN [c] (**operators**) **1** An **operator** is a person who connects telephone calls at a telephone exchange or in a place such as an office or hotel. ❑ He dialled the operator and put in a call to Rome. **2** An **operator** is a person who is employed to operate or control a machine. ❑ computer operators **3** (business) An **operator** is a person or a company that runs a business. ❑ the nation's largest cable TV operator **4** (informal) If you call someone a smooth or shrewd **operator**, you mean that they are skilful at achieving what they want, often in a slightly dishonest way. ❑ He is a smooth operator. Don't underestimate him.

☢ opin·ion ♦♦◇ /əˈpɪnjən/ NOUN

NOUN [c, SING, u] (**opinions**) **1** [c] Your **opinion** about something is what you think or believe about it. = feeling, belief, view, point of view ❑ I wasn't asking for your opinion, Mike. ❑ He held the opinion that a government should think before introducing a tax. ❑ Most who expressed an opinion spoke favourably of Thomas. **2** [SING] Your **opinion of** someone is your judgment of their character or ability. = estimation ❑ That improved Mrs Goole's already favourable opinion of him. **3** [u] You can refer to the beliefs or views that people have as **opinion**. ❑ Some, I suppose, might even be in positions to influence opinion. **4** [c] An **opinion** from an expert is the advice or judgment that they give you in the subject that they know a lot about. ❑ Even if you have had a regular physical check-up recently, you should still seek a medical opinion.

PHRASES **in someone's opinion** You add expressions such as '**in my opinion**' or '**in their opinion**' to a statement in order to indicate that it is what you or someone else thinks, and is not necessarily a fact. ❑ The book is, in Henry's opinion, the best book on the subject.

of the opinion (formal) If someone is **of the opinion that** something is the case, that is what they believe. ❑ Frank is of the opinion that Romero should have won.

→ See also **public opinion**

VOCABULARY BUILDER

opinion NOUN

Your **opinion** about something is what you think or believe about it.

❑ He rang his cameraman and asked him to give his frank opinion of the film.

feeling NOUN

Feeling is used to refer to a general opinion that a group of people has about something.

❑ There is still some feeling in the art world that the market for such works may be declining.

belief NOUN (fairly formal)

If it is your **belief** that something is the case, it is your strong opinion that it is the case.

❑ It is our belief that improvements in health care are needed.

judgment NOUN

A **judgment** is an opinion that you have or express after thinking carefully about something.

❑ In your judgment, what has changed over the past few years?

viewpoint NOUN

Someone's **viewpoint** is the way that they think about things in general, or the way they think about a particular thing.

❑ The novel is shown from the girl's viewpoint.

☢ opin·ion poll NOUN [c] (**opinion polls**) An **opinion poll** involves asking people's opinions on a particular subject, especially one concerning politics. = poll ❑ Nearly three-quarters of people questioned in an opinion poll agreed with the government's decision. ❑ So, though the opinion polls suggested otherwise, Major won, taking power with a majority of twenty-one.

op·po·nent ♦◇◇ /əˈpəʊnənt/ NOUN [c] (**opponents**) **1** A politician's **opponents** are other politicians who belong to a different party or who have different aims or policies. ❑ Mr Kennedy's opponent in the leadership contest **2** In a sports contest, your **opponent** is the person who is playing against you. ❑ Norris twice knocked down his opponent in the early rounds of the fight. **3** The **opponents of** an idea or policy do not agree with it and do not want it to be carried out. ❑ opponents of the spread of nuclear weapons

☢ op·por·tu·nity ♦♦◇ /ˌɒpəˈtjuːnɪti, AmE -ˈtuːn-/ NOUN [c, u] (**opportunities**) An **opportunity** is a situation in which it is possible for you to do something that you want to do. = chance ❑ I had an opportunity to go to New York and study. ❑ equal opportunities in employment ❑ Participants must have the opportunity to take part in the discussion. ❑ I want to see more opportunities for young people.

WORD CONNECTIONS

VERB + opportunity

have an opportunity
❑ Poor children do not have the same opportunities as others.

take an opportunity
seize an opportunity
❑ The government seized the opportunity to act.

miss an opportunity
waste an opportunity
❑ He always felt that he had wasted an opportunity

give an opportunity
offer an opportunity
❑ Working in a group gives people an opportunity to share their skills.

ADJ + opportunity

a **golden** opportunity
an **ideal** opportunity
a **perfect** opportunity
❑ Hooke failed to take advantage of this golden opportunity.

a **rare** opportunity
a **unique** opportunity
❑ The region provides a rare opportunity to see inland waterways still being used.

☢ op·pose ♦◇◇ /əˈpəʊz/ VERB [T] (**opposes, opposing, opposed**) If you **oppose** someone or **oppose** their plans or ideas, you disagree with what they want to do and try to prevent them from doing it. ≠ support ❑ Mr Taylor was not bitter towards those who had opposed him. ❑ Many parents oppose bilingual education.

WORD FAMILIES

oppose VERB	Protesters say they **oppose** the regime but do not believe military action should be taken against it.
opposed ADJ	I am utterly **opposed** to any form of terrorism.
opposing ADJ	The Georgian leader said that he still favoured dialogue between the **opposing** sides.
opposition NOUN	There is bitter **opposition** from local business to the plan.

☢ op·posed ♦◇◇ /əˈpəʊzd/ ADJ

ADJ **1** [V-LINK + opposed 'to' N/-ING] If you **are opposed to** something, you disagree with it or disapprove of it. = against; ≠ in favour of ❑ I am utterly opposed to any form of terrorism. ❑ We are strongly opposed to the presence of

O

America in this region. **2** You say that two ideas or systems are **opposed** when they are opposite to each other or very different from each other. = opposite ❏ *people with policies almost diametrically opposed to his own*

PHRASE **as opposed to** You use **as opposed to** when you want to make it clear that you are talking about one particular thing and not something else. ❏ *We ate in the restaurant, as opposed to the bistro.*

op·pos·ing /əˈpəʊzɪŋ/ ADJ **1** [opposing + N] **Opposing** ideas or tendencies are totally different from each other. = opposite ❏ *I have a friend who has the opposing view and felt that the war was immoral.* **2** [opposing + N] **Opposing** groups of people disagree about something or are in competition with one another. ❏ *The Georgian leader said in a radio broadcast that he still favoured dialogue between the opposing sides.* ❏ *the opposing team*

op·po·site ♦♦◇ /ˈɒpəzɪt/ PREP, ADV, ADJ, NOUN
PREP If one thing is **opposite** another, it is on the other side of a space from it. ❏ *Jennie had sat opposite her at breakfast.*
ADV Someone or something **opposite** is on the other side. ❏ *He looked up at the buildings opposite, but could see no open window.*
ADJ **1** [opposite + N] The **opposite** side or part of something is the side or part that is furthest away from you. = far ❏ *the opposite corner of the room* ❏ *Cassiopeia lies on the opposite side of the Pole Star from Ursa Major.* **2** **Opposite** is used to describe things of the same kind which are completely different in a particular way. For example, north and south are opposite directions, and winning and losing are opposite results in a game. = different, other, contrary; ≠ same, identical ❏ *All the cars driving in the opposite direction had their headlights on.* ❏ *directly opposite points of view*
NOUN [c] (**opposites**) The **opposite of** someone or something is the person or thing that is most different from them. ❏ *Ritter was a very complex man but Marius was the opposite, a simple farmer.* ❏ *Well, whatever he says you can bet he's thinking the opposite.*

op·po·si·tion ♦♦◇ /ˌɒpəˈzɪʃən/ NOUN [U, c, SING] (**oppositions**) **1** [U] **Opposition** is strong, angry, or violent disagreement and disapproval. = hostility, resistance; ≠ support ❏ *There is bitter opposition from local business to the plan.* ❏ *The government is facing a new wave of opposition in the form of a student strike.* ❏ *Much of the opposition to this plan has come from the media.* **2** [c] **The opposition** is the political parties or groups that are opposed to a government. ❏ *The main opposition parties boycotted the election, saying it would not be conducted fairly.* **3** [c] In countries with a parliament, such as Britain, **the opposition** refers to the politicians or political parties that form part of the parliament, but are not the government. ❏ *the Leader of the Opposition* **4** [SING] **The opposition** is the person or team you are competing against in a sports event. ❏ *The coach says his team is not underestimating the opposition.*

WORD CONNECTIONS
VERB + **opposition**
face opposition
❏ *These were unpopular reforms and the government faced a lot of opposition.*
ADJ + **opposition**
strong opposition
stiff opposition
fierce opposition
❏ *The plans were met with stiff opposition from teachers.*
political opposition
❏ *There was growing political opposition to Churchill.*

op·press /əˈpres/ VERB [T] (**oppresses, oppressing, oppressed**) To **oppress** people means to treat them cruelly, or to prevent them from having the same opportunities, freedom, and benefits as others. ❏ *These people are often oppressed by the governments of the countries they find themselves in.*

op·pres·sion /əˈpreʃən/ NOUN [U] **Oppression** is the cruel or unfair treatment of a group of people. ❏ *an attempt to escape political oppression*

op·pres·sive /əˈpresɪv/ ADJ **1** If you describe a society, its laws, or customs as **oppressive**, you think they treat people cruelly and unfairly. = repressive ❏ *The new laws will be just as oppressive as those they replace.* **2** If you describe the weather or the atmosphere in a room as **oppressive**, you mean that it is unpleasantly hot and damp. = stifling ❏ *The oppressive afternoon heat had tired him out.* **3** An **oppressive** situation makes you feel depressed and uncomfortable. ❏ *the oppressive sadness that weighed upon him like a physical pain*

opt ♦◇◇ /ɒpt/ VERB
VERB [I, T] (**opts, opting, opted**) If you **opt for** something, or **opt to** do something, you choose it or decide to do it in preference to anything else. ❏ *Depending on your circumstances you can opt for one method or the other.* ❏ *Our students can also opt to stay in residence.*
PHRASAL VERB **opt out** If you **opt out of** something, you choose to be no longer involved in it. ❏ *The rich can opt out of the public school system.*

op·ti·cal /ˈɒptɪkəl/ ADJ **Optical** devices, processes, and effects involve or relate to vision, light, or images. ❏ *optical telescopes* ❏ *an optical scanner* ❏ *the optical effects of volcanic dust in the stratosphere* ❏ *An optical zoom physically adjusts the lens to magnify a distant object.*

op·ti·mal /ˈɒptɪməl/ → See optimum

op·ti·mism /ˈɒptɪmɪzəm/ NOUN [U] **Optimism** is the feeling of being hopeful about the future or about the success of something in particular. ❏ *The Indian prime minister has expressed optimism about India's future relations with the US.*

op·ti·mist /ˈɒptɪmɪst/ NOUN [c] (**optimists**) An **optimist** is someone who is hopeful about the future. ❏ *He has the upbeat manner of an eternal optimist.*

op·ti·mis·tic ♦◇◇ /ˌɒptɪˈmɪstɪk/ ADJ Someone who is **optimistic** is hopeful about the future or the success of something in particular. ❏ *The president says she is optimistic that an agreement can be worked out soon.*
op·ti·mis·ti·cal·ly /ˌɒptɪˈmɪstɪkli/ ADV [optimistically with V] ❏ *Both sides have spoken optimistically about the talks.*

op·ti·mize /ˈɒptɪmaɪz/ also **optimise** VERB [T] (**optimizes, optimizing, optimized**) (formal) To **optimize** a plan, system, or machine means to arrange or design it so that it operates as smoothly and efficiently as possible. ❏ *The new systems have been optimized for running Microsoft Windows.* ❏ *Doctors are concentrating on understanding the disease better, and on optimizing the treatment.*

op·ti·mum /ˈɒptɪməm/ or **optimal** ADJ (formal) The **optimum** or **optimal** level or state of something is the best level or state that it could achieve. = ideal; ≠ worst ❏ *Try to do some physical activity three times a week for optimum health.* ❏ *regions in which optimal conditions for farming could be created*

op·tion ♦♦◇ /ˈɒpʃən/ NOUN (academic word)
NOUN [c, SING] (**options**) **1** [c] An **option** is something that you can choose to do in preference to one or more alternatives. = alternative, choice ❏ *He's argued from the start that the US and its allies are putting too much emphasis on the military option.* ❏ *What other options do you have?* **2** [SING] If you have the **option** of doing something, you can choose whether to do it or not. = choice ❏ *Criminals are given the option of going to jail or facing public humiliation.* **3** [c] (business) In business, an **option** is an agreement or contract that gives someone the right to buy or sell something such as property or shares at a future date. ❏ *Each bank has granted the other an option on 19.9% of its shares.* **4** [c] (mainly BrE) An **option** is one of a number of subjects which a student can choose to study as a part of his or her course. ❏ *Several options are offered for the student's senior year.* ❏ *You may choose options such as Conversation, Grammar, or Examination Preparation.*
PHRASE **keep your options open** or **leave your options open** If you **keep** your **options open** or **leave** your **options open**, you delay making a decision about something. ❏ *I am*

O

keeping my options open; I can decide in a few months.

✪ **op·tion·al** /ˈɒpʃənəl/ ADJ If something is **optional**, you can choose whether or not you do it or have it. ☐ *Sex education is a sensitive area for some parents, and thus it should remain optional.* ☐ *Finally, it becomes economic to offer the customer optional extras.* ☐ *The violin part is more than an optional accompaniment.*

or ♦♦♦ /ɔː, ə/ CONJ

CONJ **1** You use **or** to link two or more alternatives. ☐ *'Tea or coffee?' John asked.* ☐ *He said he would try to write or call as soon as he reached the Canary Islands.* **2** You use **or** to give another alternative, when the first alternative is introduced by 'either' or 'whether'. ☐ *Items like bread, milk, and meat were either unavailable or could be obtained only on the black market.* ☐ *Either you can talk to him, or I will.* **3** You use **or** between two numbers to indicate that you are giving an approximate amount. ☐ *Everyone benefited from limiting their intake of coffee to just one or two cups a day.* ☐ *When I was nine or ten someone explained to me that when you are grown up you have to work.* **4** You use **or** to introduce a comment which corrects or modifies what you have just said. ☐ *The man was a fool, he thought, or at least incompetent.* **5** If you say that someone should do something **or** something bad will happen, you are warning them that if they do not do it, the bad thing will happen. = otherwise ☐ *She had to have the operation, or she would die.* **6** You use **or** to introduce something which is evidence for the truth of a statement you have just made. = otherwise ☐ *He must have thought Jane was worth it or he wouldn't have wasted time on her, I suppose.*

PHRASES **or not** (*emphasis*) You use **or not** to emphasize that a particular thing makes no difference to what is going to happen. ☐ *Like it or not, you're in charge.*

or no You use **or no** between two occurrences of the same noun in order to say that whether something is true or not makes no difference to a situation. ☐ *The next day, rain or no rain, it was business as usual.*

✦ **or other** → see **other**; **or so** → see **so**

✪ **oral** /ˈɔːrəl/ ADJ, NOUN

ADJ **1 Oral** communication is spoken rather than written. = spoken ☐ *the written and oral traditions of ancient cultures* ☐ *an oral agreement* ☐ *our reliance upon oral records* **2** You use **oral** to indicate that something is done with a person's mouth or relates to a person's mouth. ☐ *good oral hygiene* ☐ *Standard treatment is oral antibiotics.*

NOUN [C] (**orals**) An **oral** is an examination, especially in a foreign language, that is spoken rather than written. ☐ *I spoke privately to the candidate after the oral.*

✪ **oral·ly** /ˈɔːrəli/ ADV **1** [orally after v] ☐ *their ability to present ideas orally and in writing* **2** *antibiotic tablets taken orally*

or·ange ♦♦◇ /ˈɒrɪndʒ, AmE ˈɔːr-/ COLOUR, NOUN

COLOUR Something that is **orange** is of a colour between red and yellow. ☐ *men in bright orange uniforms*

NOUN [C, U] (**oranges**) An **orange** is a round juicy fruit with a thick, orange-coloured skin. ☐ *orange trees*

✪ **or·bit** /ˈɔːbɪt/ NOUN, VERB

NOUN [C] (**orbits**) [also 'in/into' orbit] An **orbit** is the curved path in space that is followed by an object going around and around a planet, moon, or star. ☐ *Mars and Earth have orbits which change with time.* ☐ *The planet is probably in orbit around a small star.* ☐ *the radius of the orbit of the planet Jupiter round the sun*

VERB [T] (**orbits, orbiting, orbited**) If something such as a satellite **orbits** a planet, moon, or sun, it moves around it in a continuous, curving path. = circle ☐ *In 1957 the Soviet Union launched the first satellite to orbit the earth.* ☐ *About 120 planets have been discovered orbiting other stars.*

✪ **or·ches·tra** /ˈɔːkɪstrə/ NOUN [C] (**orchestras**) An **orchestra** is a large group of musicians who play a variety of different instruments together. Orchestras usually play classical music. ☐ *the Los Angeles Philharmonic Orchestra* ☐ *The orchestra played extracts from Beethoven and Brahms.* ☐ *an orchestra conducted by Yakov Kreizberg*

✪ **or·ches·tral** /ɔːˈkestrəl/ ADJ [orchestral + N] **Orchestral** means relating to an orchestra and the music it plays. ☐ *an orchestral concert* ☐ *It was performed in 1901 as*

an orchestral work. ☐ *an orchestral arrangement of Puccini's score*

or·deal /ɔːˈdiːl/ NOUN [C] (**ordeals**) If you describe an experience or situation as an **ordeal**, you think it is difficult and stressful. ☐ *the painful ordeal of the last eight months*

✪ **or·der** ♦♦◇ /ˈɔːdə/ VERB, NOUN

VERB [T, I] (**orders, ordering, ordered**) **1** [T] If a person in authority **orders** someone **to** do something, they tell them to do it. = command ☐ *Williams ordered him to leave.* **2** [T] If someone in authority **orders** something, they give instructions that it should be done. ☐ *The president has ordered a full investigation.* **3** [I, T] When you **order** something that you are going to pay for, you ask for it to be brought to you, sent to you, or obtained for you. ☐ *The couple ordered a new set of sterling silver rings from Tiffany for $200 each.* ☐ *The waitress appeared. 'Are you ready to order?'* **4** [T] The way that something **is ordered** is the way that it is organized and structured. = organize, structure ☐ *a society which is ordered by hierarchy* ☐ *We know the French order things differently.* ☐ *a carefully ordered system in which everyone has his place*

PHRASAL VERB **order around** If you say that someone **is ordering** you **around**, you mean they are telling you what to do as if they have authority over you, and you dislike this. ☐ *When we're out he gets really bossy and starts ordering me around.*

NOUN [C, U, SING] (**orders**) **1** [C] If someone in authority gives you an **order**, they tell you to do something. = command, instruction ☐ *The activists were shot when they refused to obey an order to halt.* ☐ *As darkness fell, Clinton gave orders for his men to rest.* **2** [C] A court **order** is a legal instruction stating that something must be done. ☐ *She has decided not to appeal against a court order banning her from keeping animals.* **3** [C] An **order** is a request for something to be brought, made, or obtained for you in return for money. ☐ *The city is going to place an order for a hundred and eighty-eight buses.* **4** [C] Someone's **order** is what they have asked to be brought, made, or obtained for them in return for money. ☐ *The waiter returned with their order and Graham signed the bill.* **5** [U] [also 'an' order] If a set of things are arranged or done in a particular **order**, they are arranged or done so one thing follows another, often according to a particular factor such as importance. ☐ *Write down (in order of priority) the qualities you'd like to have.* ☐ *Music shops should arrange their recordings in simple alphabetical order, rather than by category.* ☐ *The table shows the factors ranked in order of importance.* **6** [U] **Order** is the situation that exists when everything is in the correct or expected place, or happens at the correct or expected time. ☐ *The wish to impose order upon confusion is a kind of intellectual instinct.* **7** [U] **Order** is the situation that exists when people obey the law and do not fight or riot. ☐ *Troops were sent to the islands to restore order last November.* **8** [SING] When people talk about a particular **order**, they mean the way society is organized at a particular time. ☐ *The end of the Cold War has produced the prospect of a new world order based on international co-operation.* **9** [C] A religious **order** is a group of monks or nuns who live according to a particular set of rules. ☐ *the Benedictine order of monks*

PHRASES **in order to 1** If you do something **in order to** achieve a particular thing or **in order that** something can happen, you do it because you want to achieve that thing. = so that ☐ *Most schools are extremely unwilling to cut down on staff in order to cut costs.* ☐ *There are increased funds available in order that these targets are met.* **2** If someone must be in a particular situation **in order to** achieve something they want, they cannot achieve that if they are not in that situation. ☐ *We need to get rid of the idea that we must be liked all the time in order to be worthwhile.* **3** If something must happen **in order for** something else to happen, the second thing cannot happen if the first thing does not happen. ☐ *In order for their computers to trace a person's records, they need both the name and address of the individual.*

on order Something that is **on order** at a shop or factory has been asked for but has not yet been supplied. ☐ *The* airlines still have 2,500 new planes on order.

to order If you do something **to order**, you do it whenever you are asked to do it. ❏ She now makes wonderful dried flower arrangements to order.

under orders If you are **under orders** to do something, you have been told to do it by someone in authority. ❏ I am under orders not to discuss his mission or his location with anyone.

in order ◼ If you put or keep something **in order**, you make sure that it is neat or well organized. ❏ Now he has a chance to put his life back in order. ◾ If you think something is **in order**, you think it should happen or be provided. ❏ Reforms are clearly in order.

in the order of something or **of the order of something** You use **in the order of** or **of the order of** when mentioning an approximate figure. ❏ They borrowed something in the order of $10 million.

in good order If something is in **good order**, it is in good condition. ❏ The vessel's safety equipment was not in good order.

in working order A machine or device that is in **working order** is functioning properly and is not broken. ❏ Only half of the spacecraft's six science instruments are still in working order.

out of order ◼ A machine or device that is **out of order** is broken and does not work. ❏ Their phone's out of order. ◾ (informal) If you say that someone or their behaviour is **out of order**, you mean that their behaviour is unacceptable. ❏ Kent, you're out of order.
→ See also **law and order**, **mail order**
✦ a tall order → see **tall**; put your house in order → see **house**; order of magnitude → see **magnitude**

or•der•ly /ˈɔːdəli/ ADJ, NOUN
ADJ ◼ If something is done in an **orderly** fashion or manner, it is done in a well-organized and controlled way. ❏ The organizers guided them in an orderly fashion out of the building. ◾ Something that is **orderly** is neat or arranged in a neat way. ❏ It's a beautiful, clean, and orderly city.
NOUN [c] (**orderlies**) An **orderly** is a person who works in a hospital and does jobs that do not require special medical training. ❏ For most of his life, he was a hospital orderly.
or•der•li•ness /ˈɔːdəlinəs/ NOUN [u] ❏ A balance is achieved in the painting between orderliness and unpredictability.

⊙**or•di•nar•i•ly** /ˈɔːdɪnrəli, AmE -ˈnerɪli/ ADV If you say what is **ordinarily** the case, you are saying what is normally the case. = normally, usually ❏ The streets would ordinarily have been full of people, but now they were empty. ❏ Similar arrangements apply to students who are ordinarily resident in Scotland. ❏ places where the patient does not ordinarily go

⊙**or•di•nary** ◆◇◇ /ˈɔːdɪnri, AmE -neri/ ADJ
ADJ **Ordinary** people or things are normal and not special or different in any way. = normal, everyday; ≠ special, extraordinary ❏ I strongly suspect that most ordinary people would agree with me. ❏ It has 25 calories less than ordinary ice cream.
PHRASE **out of the ordinary** Something that is **out of the ordinary** is unusual or different. = unusual ❏ The boy's knowledge was out of the ordinary.

⊙**or•gan** /ˈɔːgən/ NOUN [c] (**organs**) ◼ An **organ** is a part of your body that has a particular purpose or function, for example, your heart or lungs. ❏ damage to the muscles and internal organs ❏ the reproductive organs ❏ Fewer than one in ten of donated organs could be used. ❏ Over 150,000 people in the world need organ transplants. ◾ An **organ** is a large musical instrument with pipes of different lengths through which air is forced. It has keys and pedals like a piano. ❏ the church organ ◼ You refer to a newspaper or organization as **the organ** of the government or another group when it is used by them as a means of giving information or getting things done. = mouthpiece ❏ according to the People's Daily, the official organ of the Chinese communist party

⊙**or•gan•ic** /ɔːˈgænɪk/ ADJ ◼ **Organic** methods of farming and gardening do not use pesticides, chemical fertilizers, growth hormones, or antibiotics, so that the food produced does not contain toxic chemicals. ❏ Organic farming is expanding everywhere. ❏ organic fruit and vegetables ◾ **Organic** substances are produced by or found in living things. = natural; ≠ man-made, synthetic ❏ Incorporating organic material into chalky soils will reduce the alkalinity. ❏ Strong acids tend to destroy organic compounds. ◼ (formal) **Organic** change or development happens gradually and naturally rather than suddenly. ❏ to manage the company and supervise its organic growth
or•gani•cal•ly /ɔːˈgænɪkli/ ADV ❏ organically grown vegetables

⊙**or•gan•ism** /ˈɔːgənɪzəm/ NOUN [c] (**organisms**) An **organism** is an animal or plant, especially one that is so small that you cannot see it without using a microscope. = creature ❏ Not all chemicals normally present in living organisms are harmless. ❏ insect-borne organisms that cause sleeping sickness

⊙**or•gani•za•tion** ◆◆◇ /ˌɔːgənaɪˈzeɪʃən/ also **organisation** NOUN [c, u] (**organizations**) ◼ [c] An **organization** is an official group of people, for example, a political party, a business, a charity, or a club. = group ❏ Most of the food for the homeless is provided by voluntary organizations. ❏ a report by the International Labour Organization ◾ [u] The **organization** of an event or activity involves making all the necessary arrangements for it. ❏ the exceptional attention to detail that goes into the organization of this event ◼ [u] The **organization** of something is the way in which its different parts are arranged or relate to each other. = structure, arrangement ❏ I am aware that the organization of the book leaves something to be desired. ❏ The economic organization of a society is critical to the society's success or failure.

or•gani•za•tion•al /ˌɔːgənaɪˈzeɪʃənəl/ also **organisational** ADJ ◼ [organizational + N] **Organizational** abilities and methods relate to the way that work, activities, or events are planned and arranged. ❏ Evelyn's excellent organizational skills were soon spotted by her employers. ◾ [organizational + N] **Organizational** means relating to the structure of an organization. ❏ The police now recognize that big organizational changes are needed. ◼ [organizational + N] **Organizational** means relating to organizations, rather than individuals. ❏ This problem needs to be dealt with at an organizational level.

⊙**or•gan•ize** ◆◆◇ /ˈɔːgənaɪz/ also **organise** VERB [T] (**organizes, organizing, organized**) ◼ If you **organize** an event or activity, you make sure that the necessary arrangements are made. ❏ In the end, we all decided to organize a concert for Easter. ❏ a two-day meeting organized by the United Nations ❏ The Commission will organize a conference on rural development. ❏ The initial mobilization was well organized. ◾ If you **organize** something that someone wants or needs, you make sure that it is provided. ❏ I will organize transportation. ◼ If you **organize** a set of things, you arrange them in an ordered way or give them a structure. = plan, arrange, order, structure ❏ He began to organize his materials. ❏ She took a hasty cup of coffee and tried to organize her scattered thoughts. ❏ a method of organizing a file ❏ the way in which the Army is organized ◼ If you **organize** yourself, you plan your work and activities in an ordered, efficient way. ❏ changing the way you organize yourself ❏ Go right ahead, I'm sure you don't need me to organize you.

or•ga•nized ◆◇◇ /ˈɔːgənaɪzd/ also **organised** ADJ ◼ [organized + N] An **organized** activity or group involves a number of people doing something together in a structured way, rather than doing it by themselves. ❏ organized groups of art thieves ❏ organized religion ◾ Someone who is **organized** plans their work and activities efficiently. ❏ These people are very efficient, very organized, and excellent time managers.

or•gan•iz•er ◆◇◇ /ˈɔːgənaɪzə/ also **organiser** NOUN [c] (**organizers**) The **organizer** of an event or activity is the person who makes sure that the necessary arrangements are made. ❏ He became an organizer for the Democratic Party.

⊙**ori•ent** /ˈɔːrient/ or **orientate** /ˈɔːriənteɪt/ VERB [T] (**orients, orienting, oriented**) (academic word, formal) When you **orient yourself to** a new situation or course of

o

action, you learn about it and prepare to deal with it.
= accustom, familiarize ❑ *You will need the time to orient yourself to your new way of eating.* ❑ *orienting students to new ways of thinking about their participation in classroom learning* ❑ *Anxiety comes from not being able to orient yourself in your own existence.*
→ See also **oriented**

ori·en·tal /ˌɔːriˈentəl/ ADJ **Oriental** means coming from or associated with eastern Asia, especially China and Japan. = eastern ❑ *There were Oriental carpets on the floors.*

✪**ori·en·tate** /ˈɔːrienteɪt/ IRREG FORM **Orientate** means the same as **orient**

✪**ori·en·tat·ed** /ˈɔːrienteɪtɪd/ IRREG FORM **Orientated** means the same as **oriented**.

✪**ori·en·ta·tion** /ˌɔːrienˈteɪʃən/ NOUN [C, U] (**orientations**) **1** [C, U] If you talk about the **orientation** of an organization or country, you are talking about the kinds of aims and interests it has. = inclination ❑ *a marketing orientation* ❑ *To a society which has lost its orientation he has much to offer.* ❑ *The movement is liberal and social democratic in orientation.* **2** [C, U] Someone's **orientation** is their basic beliefs or preferences. = inclination ❑ *legislation that would have made discrimination on the basis of sexual orientation illegal* **3** [U] **Orientation** is basic information or training that is given to people starting a new job, school, or course. = induction ❑ *They give their new employees a day or two of orientation.* **4** [C] The **orientation** of a structure or object is the direction it faces. ❑ *Farnese had the orientation of the church changed so that the front would face a square.*

✪**ori·ent·ed** /ˈɔːrientɪd/ ADJ

The form **orientated** is also used.

[V-LINK + oriented 'towards/to' N] If someone **is oriented towards** or **oriented to** a particular thing or person, they are mainly concerned with that thing or person. ❑ *It seems almost inevitable that North African economies will still be primarily oriented toward Europe.* ❑ *Most students here are oriented to computers.*

✪**ori·gin** ◆◇◇ /ˈɒrɪdʒɪn, AmE ˈɔːr-/ NOUN [C] (**origins**) **1** You can refer to the beginning, cause, or source of something as its **origin** or **origins**. = beginning, source ❑ *theories about the origin of life* ❑ *Their medical problems are basically physical in origin.* ❑ *The disorder in military policy had its origins in Truman's first term.* ❑ *Most of the thickeners are of plant origin.* **2** [usu POSS + origin, also 'of/in' origin] When you talk about a person's **origin** or **origins**, you are referring to the country, race, or living conditions of their parents or ancestors. ❑ *Thomas has not forgotten his humble origins.* ❑ *people of Asian origin*

✪**origi·nal** ◆◆◇ /əˈrɪdʒɪnəl/ ADJ, NOUN
ADJ **1** [DET + original] You use **original** when referring to something that existed at the beginning of a process or activity, or the characteristics that something had when it began or was made. = first, early; ≠ latest, new ❑ *The original plan was to go by bus.* ❑ *The inhabitants have voted overwhelmingly to restore the city's original name of Chemnitz.* ❑ *the ancient history of Australia's original inhabitants* **2** An **original** document or work of art is not a copy. ❑ *an original movie poster* **3** An **original** piece of writing or music was written recently and has not been published or performed before. ❑ *with catchy original songs by Richard Warner* **4** If you describe someone or their work as **original**, you mean that they are very imaginative and have new ideas. = innovative ❑ *It is one of the most original works of imagination in the language.*
NOUN [C] (**originals**) If something such as a document, a work of art, or a piece of writing is an **original**, it is not a copy or a later version. ❑ *When you have filled in the questionnaire, copy it and send the original to your employer.*
origi·nal·ity /əˌrɪdʒɪˈnælɪti/ NOUN [U] ❑ *He was capable of writing things of startling originality.*

✪**origi·nal·ly** ◆◇◇ /əˈrɪdʒɪnəli/ ADV When you say what happened or was the case **originally**, you are saying what happened or was the case when something began or came into existence, often to contrast it with what happened later. = initially; ≠ subsequently ❑ *The plane has been kept*

in service far longer than originally intended. ❑ *The castle was originally surrounded by a triple wall, only one of which remains.*

✪**origi·nate** /əˈrɪdʒɪneɪt/ VERB [I, T] (**originates, originating, originated**) (formal) When something **originates** or when someone **originates** it, it begins to happen or exist. = begin, start, invent, create ❑ *The disease originated in Africa.* ❑ *All carbohydrates originate from plants.* ❑ *No one has any idea who originated the story.*

or·na·ment /ˈɔːnəmənt/ NOUN [C, U] (**ornaments**) **1** [C] An **ornament** is an attractive object that you display in your home or in your garden. ❑ *a shelf containing a few photographs and ornaments* **2** [U] (formal) Decorations and patterns on a building or a piece of furniture can be referred to as **ornament**. ❑ *walls of glass overlaid with ornament*

or·na·men·tal /ˌɔːnəˈmentəl/ ADJ Something that is **ornamental** is attractive and decorative. ❑ *an ornamental fountain*

or·nate /ɔːˈneɪt/ ADJ An **ornate** building, piece of furniture, or object is decorated with complicated patterns or shapes. = elaborate ❑ *an ornate iron staircase*

or·phan /ˈɔːfən/ NOUN, VERB
NOUN [C] (**orphans**) An **orphan** is a child whose parents are dead. ❑ *a young orphan girl brought up by peasants*
VERB [PASSIVE] (**orphans, orphaned**) If a child **is orphaned**, their parents die, or their remaining parent dies. ❑ *a fifteen-year-old boy left orphaned by the recent disaster*

✪**ortho·dox** /ˈɔːθədɒks/ ADJ

The spelling **Orthodox** is also used for meanings 2 and 3.

1 **Orthodox** beliefs, methods, or systems are ones which are accepted or used by most people. = conventional ❑ *Many of these ideas are now being incorporated into orthodox medical treatment.* ❑ *Payne gained a reputation for sound, if orthodox, views.* ❑ *orthodox police methods* **2** If you describe someone as **orthodox**, you mean that they hold the older and more traditional ideas of their religion or party. = conservative, traditional ❑ *Orthodox Jews* **3** The **Orthodox** churches are Christian churches from Eastern Europe which separated from the western church in the eleventh century. ❑ *the Greek Orthodox Church*

oth·er ◆◆◆ /ˈʌðə/ ADJ, PRON
ADJ **1** [DET + other, other + N] You use **other** to refer to an additional thing or person of the same type as one that has been mentioned or is known about. ❑ *They were just like any other young couple.* **2** [DET + other, other + N] You use **other** to indicate that a thing or person is not the one already mentioned, but a different one. ❑ *The authorities insist that the discussions must not be linked to any other issue.* ❑ *He would have to accept it; there was no other way.* **3** [DET + other] You use **the other** to refer to the second of two things or people when the identity of the first is already known or understood, or has already been mentioned. ❑ *The captain was at the other end of the room.* ❑ *You deliberately went in the other direction.* **4** [DET + other, other + N] You use **other** at the end of a list or a group of examples, to refer generally to people or things like the ones just mentioned. ❑ *The new Station Centre will have shops, restaurants and other amenities.* **5** [DET + other] You use **the other** to refer to the rest of the people or things in a group, when you are talking about one particular person or thing. ❑ *When the other kids were taken to the zoo, he was left behind.* **6** [other + N] **Other** people are people in general, as opposed to yourself or a person you have already mentioned. ❑ *The suffering of other people appals me.* **7** ['the' other + N] You use **other** in informal expressions of time such as **the other day, the other evening,** or **the other week** to refer to a day, evening, or week in the recent past. ❑ *I called her the other day and she said she'd like to come over.*
PHRASES **every other day** or **every other week** or **every other month** If something happens, for example, **every other day** or **every other month**, there is a day or month when it does not happen between each day or month when it happens. ❑ *Their food is adequate. It includes meat at least every other day, vegetables and fruit.*
every other (emphasis) You use **every other** to emphasize that you are referring to all the rest of the people or things

in a group. ❏ *The same will apply in every other country.* **PRON** (**others**) **1** You use **other** to refer to an additional thing or person of the same type as one that has been mentioned or is known about. ❏ *Four crewmen were killed, one other was injured.* **2** You use **other** to indicate that a thing or person is not the one already mentioned, but a different one. ❏ *This issue, more than any other, has divided her cabinet.* **3** ['the' other] You use **the other** to refer to the second of two things or people when the identity of the first is already known or understood, or has already been mentioned. ❏ *Almost everybody had a cigarette in one hand and a martini in the other.* **4** You use **others** at the end of a list or a group of examples, to refer generally to people or things like the ones just mentioned. ❏ *Descartes received his stimulus from the new physics and astronomy of Copernicus, Galileo, and others.* **5** ['the' others] You use **the others** to refer to the rest of the people or things in a group, when you are talking about one particular person or thing. ❏ *Aubrey's on his way here, with the others.* **6** You can use **others** to refer to people in general, as opposed to yourself or a person you have already mentioned. ❏ *His humour depended on contempt for others.*

PHRASES **among other things** or **among others** (*vagueness*) You use expressions like **among other** things or **among others** to indicate that there are several more facts, things, or people like the one or ones mentioned, but that you do not intend to mention them all. ❏ *He moved to Ohio in 2005 where, among other things, he worked as a journalist.* ❏ *His travels took him to Peru, among other places.* **nothing other than** or **no other than** (*emphasis*) You use **nothing other than** and **no other than** when you are going to mention a course of action, decision, or description and emphasize that it is the only one possible in the situation. ❏ *Nothing other than an immediate custodial sentence could be justified.* ❏ *The rebels would not be happy with anything other than the complete removal of the current regime.* **or other** or **somehow or other** or **someone or other** (*vagueness*) You use **or other** in expressions like **somehow or other** and **someone or other** to indicate that you cannot or do not want to be more precise about the information that you are giving. ❏ *I was going to have him called away from the house on some pretext or other.* ❏ *The foundation is holding a dinner in honour of something or other.* **other than** You use **other than** after a negative statement to say that the person, item, or thing that follows is the only exception to the statement. ❏ *She makes no reference to any feminist work other than her own.*

✦ **one after the other** → see **one; one or other** → see **one; in other words** → see **word**

oth·er·wise ◆◆◇ /ˈʌðəwaɪz/ ADV

ADV **1** [otherwise with CL] You use **otherwise** after mentioning a situation or telling someone to do something, in order to say what the result or consequence would be if the situation did not exist or the person did not do as you say. ❏ *Make a note of the questions you want to ask; you will invariably forget some of them otherwise.* ❏ *I'm lucky that I'm interested in school work, otherwise I'd go crazy.* **2** [otherwise + GROUP] You use **otherwise** before stating the general condition or quality of something, when you are also mentioning an exception to this general condition or quality. ❏ *The decorations for the games have lent a splash of colour to an otherwise drab city.* **3** [otherwise with V] (*written*) You use **otherwise** to refer in a general way to actions or situations that are very different from, or the opposite to, your main statement. ❏ *Take approximately 60 mg up to four times a day, unless advised otherwise by a doctor.* ❏ *There is no way anything would ever happen between us, and believe me I've tried to convince myself otherwise.* **4** [otherwise before V] You use **otherwise** to indicate that other ways of doing something are possible in addition to the way already mentioned. ❏ *The studio could punish its players by keeping them out of work, and otherwise controlling their lives.*

PHRASE **or otherwise** or **and otherwise** You use **or otherwise** or **and otherwise** to mention something that is not the thing just referred to or is the opposite of that thing. ❏ *It was for the police to assess the validity or otherwise of the evidence.*

ought ◆◇◇ /ɔːt/ VERB

> **Ought to** is a phrasal modal verb. It is used with the base form of a verb.

PHRASE **ought to** **1** You use **ought to** to mean that it is morally right to do a particular thing or that it is morally right for a particular situation to exist, especially when giving or asking for advice or opinions. = **should** ❏ *Mark, you've got a good wife. You ought to take care of her.* ❏ *The people who already own a bit of money or land ought to have a voice in saying where it goes.* **2** You use **ought to** when saying that you think it is a good idea and important for you or someone else to do a particular thing, especially when giving or asking for advice or opinions. = **should** ❏ *You don't have to be alone with him and I don't think you ought to be.* ❏ *You ought to ask a lawyer's advice.* **3** You use **ought to** to indicate that you expect something to be true or to happen. = **should** ❏ *'This ought to be fun,' he told Alex, eyes gleaming.* **4** You use **ought to** to indicate that you think that something should be the case, but might not be. = **should** ❏ *They ought to win easily today, but nothing in life is certain.* **5** (*vagueness*) You use **ought to** to indicate that you think that something has happened because of what you know about the situation, but are not certain. = **should** ❏ *He ought to have reached the house some time ago.* **6** You use **ought to have** with a past participle to indicate that something was expected to happen or be the case, but it did not happen or was not the case. ❏ *Basically the system ought to have worked.* **7** You use **ought to have** with a past participle to indicate that although it was best or correct for someone to do something in the past, they did not actually do it. ❏ *I realize I ought to have told you about it.* ❏ *I ought not to have asked you a thing like that. I'm sorry.* **8** (*politeness*) You use **ought to** when politely telling someone that you must do something, for example, that you must leave. = **should** ❏ *I really ought to be getting back now.*

ounce /aʊns/ NOUN [C, SING] (**ounces**) **1** [C] An **ounce** is a unit of weight used in the US and Britain. There are sixteen ounces in a pound and one ounce is equal to 28.35 grams. ❏ *four ounces of sugar* **2** [SING] You can refer to a very small amount of something, such as a quality or characteristic, as an **ounce**. ❏ *If only my father had possessed an ounce of business sense.*

our ◆◆◆ /aʊə/ DET

> **Our** is the first person plural possessive determiner.

1 You use **our** to indicate that something belongs or relates both to yourself and to one or more other people. ❏ *We're expecting our first baby.* **2** A speaker or writer sometimes uses **our** to indicate that something belongs or relates to people in general. ❏ *We are all entirely responsible for our actions, and for our reactions.*

ours /aʊəz/ PRON

> **Ours** is the first person plural possessive pronoun.

You use **ours** to refer to something that belongs or relates both to yourself and to one or more other people. ❏ *That car is ours.* ❏ *There are few strangers in a town like ours.*

our·selves ◆◇◇ /aʊəˈselvz/ PRON

> **Ourselves** is the first person plural reflexive pronoun.

1 [V + ourselves, PREP + ourselves] You use **ourselves** to refer to yourself and one or more other people as a group. ❏ *We sat around the fire to keep ourselves warm.* **2** [V + ourselves, PREP + ourselves] A speaker or writer sometimes uses **ourselves** to refer to people in general. **Ourselves** is used as the object of a verb or preposition when the subject refers to the same people. ❏ *We all know that when we exert ourselves our heart rate increases.* **3** You use **ourselves** to emphasize a first person plural subject. In more formal English, **ourselves** is sometimes used instead of 'us' as the object of a verb or preposition, for emphasis. ❏ *Others are feeling just the way we ourselves would feel in the same situation.* **4** If you say something such as 'We did it **ourselves**', you are indicating that the people you are referring to did it, rather than anyone else.

❑ *We villagers built that ourselves, we had no help from anyone.*

oust /aʊst/ VERB [T] (**ousts, ousting, ousted**) (*journalism*) If someone **is ousted** from a position of power, job, or place, they are forced to leave it. ❑ *The leaders have been ousted from power by nationalists.* ❑ *The Republicans may oust him in November.*

oust·ing /'aʊstɪŋ/ NOUN [U] = removal ❑ *The ousting of his predecessor was one of the most dramatic coups the business world had seen in years.*

out ♦♦♦ /aʊt/ ADV, ADJ

> **Out** is often used with verbs of movement, such as 'walk' and 'pull', and also in phrasal verbs such as 'give out' and 'run out'.

> **Out of** is used with verbs of movement, such as 'walk' and 'pull', and also in phrasal verbs such as 'get out of' and 'grow out of'. **Out** is often used instead of **out of**, for example in 'He looked out the window'.

ADV **1** [out after v] When something is in a particular place and you take it **out**, you remove it from that place. ❑ *I like the pop you get when you pull out a cork.* ❑ *He took out his notebook and flipped the pages.* **2** [out after v] You can use **out** to indicate that you are talking about the situation outside, rather than inside buildings. = outside ❑ *It's hot out – very hot, very humid.* **3** If you are **out**, you are not at home or not at your usual place of work. ❑ *I tried to get in touch with you yesterday evening, but I think you were out.* **4** [out + ADV/PREP] If you say that someone is **out** in a particular place, you mean that they are in a different place, usually one far away. ❑ *The police tell me they've finished their investigations out there.* **5** When the sea or tide goes **out**, the sea moves away from the shore. ❑ *The tide was out and they walked among the rock pools.* **6** [out after v] If flowers come **out**, their petals have opened. ❑ *I usually put it in my diary when I see the wild flowers coming out.* **7** [out after v] If something such as a book or CD comes **out**, it becomes available for people to buy. ❑ *The French edition came out in early 2006.*

PHRASE **out of 1** If you go **out of** a place, you leave it. ❑ *She let him out of the house.* **2** If you take something **out of** the container or place where it has been, you remove it so that it is no longer there. ❑ *I always took my key out of my bag and put it in my pocket.* **3** If you look or shout **out of** a window, you look or shout away from the room where you are towards the outside. ❑ *He went on staring out of the window.* **4** If you are **out of** the sun, the rain, or the wind, you are sheltered from it. ❑ *People can keep out of the sun to avoid skin cancer.* **5** If someone or something gets **out of** a situation, especially an unpleasant one, they are then no longer in it. If they keep **out of** it, they do not start being in it. ❑ *In the past army troops have relied heavily on air support to get them out of trouble.* ❑ *The economy is starting to climb out of recession.* **6** You can use **out of** to say that someone leaves an institution. ❑ *That is precisely what I came out of college thinking I was supposed to do.* **7** If you are **out of** range of something, you are beyond the limits of that range. ❑ *Shaun was in the bedroom, out of earshot, watching television.* **8** You use **out of** to say what feeling or reason causes someone to do something. For example, if you do something **out of** pity, you do it because you pity someone. ❑ *He took up office out of a sense of duty.* **9** If you get something such as information or work **out of** someone, you manage to make them give it to you, usually when they are unwilling to give it. ❑ *'Where is she being held prisoner?' I asked. 'Did you get it out of him?'* **10** If you get pleasure or an advantage **out of** something, you get it as a result of being involved with that thing or making use of it. = from ❑ *Jenkins hasn't let the pressure take the fun out of the sport.* **11** If you are **out of** something, you no longer have any of it. ❑ *I can't find the sugar – and we're out of milk.* **12** If something is made **out of** a particular material, it consists of that material because it has been formed or constructed from it. = from ❑ *Would you advise people to make a building out of wood or stone?* **13** You use **out of** to indicate what proportion of a group of things something is true of. For example, if something is true of one **out of** five things, it is true of one fifth of all

things of that kind. = in ❑ *Two out of five thought the business would be sold privately on their retirement or death.*

ADJ **1** [V-LINK + out] If a light or fire is **out** or goes **out**, it is no longer shining or burning. ❑ *All the lights were out in the house.* **2** [V-LINK + out] If flowers are **out**, their petals have opened. ❑ *Well, the daffodils are out in the gardens and they're always a beautiful show.* **3** [V-LINK + out] If something such as a book or CD is **out**, it is available for people to buy. ❑ *Their new album is out now.* **4** [V-LINK + out] In a game or sport, if someone is **out**, they can no longer take part either because they are unable to or because they have been defeated. **5** [V-LINK + out] If you say that a proposal or suggestion is **out**, you mean that it is unacceptable. ❑ *That idea is out, I'm afraid.* **6** [V-LINK + out] If you say that a particular thing is **out**, you mean that it is no longer fashionable at the present time. ❑ *Romance is making a comeback. Reality is out.* **7** [V-LINK + out] If you say that a calculation or measurement is **out**, you mean that it is incorrect. ❑ *When the two ends of the tunnel met in the middle they were only a few inches out.* **8** [V-LINK + out + to-INF] (*informal*) If someone is **out** to do something, they intend to do it. ❑ *Most companies these days are just out to make a quick profit.* **9** [V-LINK + out] If news or information about something is **out**, information about it has been made public. ❑ *The word is out that she has fled the country.*

out·break /'aʊtbreɪk/ NOUN [C] (**outbreaks**) If there is an **outbreak of** something unpleasant, such as violence or a disease, it suddenly starts to happen. ❑ *The four-day festival ended a day early after an outbreak of violence involving hundreds of youths.* ❑ *an outbreak of chickenpox*

out·burst /'aʊtbɜːst/ NOUN [C] (**outbursts**) **1** An **outburst** of an emotion, especially anger, is a sudden strong expression of that emotion. ❑ *a spontaneous outburst of cheers and applause* **2** An **outburst** of violent activity is a sudden period of this activity. = eruption ❑ *Five people were reported killed today in a fresh outburst of violence.*

✪ **out·come** ♦◇◇ /'aʊtkʌm/ NOUN [C] (**outcomes**) (*academic word*) The **outcome** of an activity, process, or situation is the situation that exists at the end of it. = result, conclusion ❑ *Mr Singh said he was pleased with the outcome.* ❑ *It's too early to know the outcome of her illness.* ❑ *a successful outcome*

out·cry /'aʊtkraɪ/ NOUN [C, U] (**outcries**) An **outcry** is a reaction of strong disapproval and anger shown by the public or media about a recent event. ❑ *The killing caused an international outcry.*

out·dat·ed /ˌaʊt'deɪtɪd/ ADJ If you describe something as **outdated**, you mean that you think it is old-fashioned and no longer useful or relevant to modern life. ❑ *outdated and inefficient factories* ❑ *outdated attitudes*

✪ **out·door** /ˌaʊt'dɔː/ ADJ [outdoor + N] **Outdoor** activities or things happen or are used outside and not in a building. ❑ *If you enjoy outdoor activities, this is the trip for you.* ❑ *There were outdoor cafes on almost every block.*

out·doors /ˌaʊt'dɔːz/ ADV, NOUN

ADV If something happens **outdoors**, it happens outside in the fresh air rather than in a building. ❑ *It was warm enough to be outdoors all afternoon.*

NOUN [SING] You refer to the **outdoors** when talking about activities that take place outside, away from buildings. ❑ *I'm a lover of the outdoors.*

✪ **out·er** /'aʊtə/ ADJ [outer + N] The **outer** parts of something are the parts which contain or enclose the other parts, and which are furthest from the centre. ≠ inside ❑ *He heard a voice in the outer room.* ❑ *burns that damage the outer layer of skin* ❑ *the outer suburbs of the city* ❑ *an old building with solid outer walls*

out·fit /'aʊtfɪt/ NOUN [C] (**outfits**) **1** An **outfit** is a set of clothes. ❑ *She was wearing an outfit she'd bought the previous day.* **2** You can refer to an organization as an **outfit**. ❑ *He works for a private security outfit.*

out·going /ˌaʊt'gəʊɪŋ/ ADJ **1** [outgoing + N] **Outgoing** things such as planes, mail, and passengers are leaving or being sent somewhere. ❑ *All outgoing flights were grounded.* **2** Someone who is **outgoing** is very friendly and likes meeting and talking to people. = extrovert ❑ *She's very outgoing.* **3** [outgoing + N] You use **outgoing** to describe a person in charge of something who is soon going to leave that position. ❑ *the outgoing director of the International Folk Festival*

out·go·ings /ˈaʊtɡəʊɪŋz/ (*BrE*; in *AmE*, use **outlay**) NOUN [PL] Your **outgoings** are the regular amounts of money which you have to spend every week or every month, for example, in order to pay your rent or bills.

out·ing /ˈaʊtɪŋ/ NOUN [C] (**outings**) An **outing** is a short trip, usually with a group of people, away from your home, school, or place of work. ❑ *One evening, she made a rare outing to the local night club.*

out·law /ˈaʊtlɔː/ VERB, NOUN

  VERB [T] (**outlaws, outlawing, outlawed**) When something **is outlawed**, it is made illegal. = ban ❑ *In some states gambling was outlawed.* ❑ *The German government has outlawed some fascist groups.*

  NOUN [C] (**outlaws**) (*old-fashioned*) An **outlaw** is a criminal who is hiding from the authorities. ❑ *Jesse was an outlaw, a bandit, a criminal.*

out·let /ˈaʊtlet/ NOUN [C] (**outlets**) **1** An **outlet** is a shop or organization which sells the goods made by a particular manufacturer or at a discount price, often direct from the manufacturer. ❑ *the largest retail outlet in the city* ❑ *At the factory outlet you'll find discounted items at up to 75% off regular prices.* **2** If someone has an **outlet for** their feelings or ideas, they have a means of expressing and releasing them. = channel ❑ *Her father had found an outlet for his ambition in his work.* **3** An **outlet** is a hole or pipe through which liquid or air can flow away. ❑ *a warm air outlet*

out·line ♦◇◇ /ˈaʊtlaɪn/ VERB, NOUN

  VERB [T, PASSIVE] (**outlines, outlining, outlined**) **1** [T] If you **outline** an idea or a plan, you explain it in a general way. ❑ *The mayor outlined his plan to clean up the town's image.* **2** [PASSIVE] You say that an object **is outlined** when you can see its general shape because there is light behind it. ❑ *The Ritz was outlined against the lights up there.*

  NOUN [C] (**outlines**) **1** [also 'in' outline] An **outline** is a general explanation or description of something. ❑ *Following is an outline of the survey findings.* **2** The **outline** of something is its general shape, especially when it cannot be clearly seen. ❑ *He could see only the hazy outline of the goalposts.*

⊕ **out·look** /ˈaʊtlʊk/ NOUN [C, SING] (**outlooks**) **1** [C] [usu sing, with SUPP, also 'in' outlook] Your **outlook** is your general attitude towards life. ❑ *I adopted a positive outlook on life.* **2** [SING] The **outlook** for something is what people think will happen in relation to it. = prospect, forecast ❑ *The economic outlook is one of rising unemployment.* ❑ *the uncertain outlook for the motor industry*

out of date also **out-of-date** ADJ Something that is **out of date** is old-fashioned and no longer useful. ❑ *The regulations were out of date and confusing.*

out of touch ADJ **1** [V-LINK + out of touch] Someone who is **out of touch with** a situation is not aware of recent changes in it. ❑ *Washington politicians are out of touch with the American people.* **2** [V-LINK + out of touch] If you are **out of touch** with someone, you have not been in contact with them recently and are not familiar with their present situation. ❑ *James and I have been out of touch for years.*

⊕ **out·put** ♦◇◇ /ˈaʊtpʊt/ NOUN [C, U] (**outputs**) (*academic word*) **1** Output is used to refer to the amount of something that a person or thing produces. ≠ input ❑ *Government statistics show the largest drop in industrial output for ten years.* ❑ *The gland enlarges in an attempt to increase the output of hormone.* **2** The **output** of a computer or word processor is the information that it displays on a screen or prints on paper as a result of a particular program. ≠ input ❑ *You run the software, you look at the output, you make modifications.* ❑ *Screen copy is the output from a computer as seen on a screen.*

out·rage VERB, NOUN

  VERB /ˌaʊtˈreɪdʒ/ [T] (**outrages, outraging, outraged**) If you **are outraged** by something, it makes you extremely angry and shocked. ❑ *Many people have been outraged by*

some of the things that have been said.

  NOUN /ˈaʊtreɪdʒ/ [U, C] (**outrages**) **1** [U] **Outrage** is an intense feeling of anger and shock. ❑ *The decision provoked outrage from women and human rights groups.* **2** [C] You can refer to an act or event that angers and shocks you as an **outrage**. ❑ *The latest outrage was to have been a coordinated gun and bomb attack on the station.*

out·raged /ˌaʊtˈreɪdʒt/ ADJ ❑ *He is truly outraged about what's happened to him.*

out·ra·geous /aʊtˈreɪdʒəs/ ADJ (*emphasis*) If you describe something as **outrageous**, you are emphasizing that it is unacceptable or very shocking. ❑ *By diplomatic standards, this was outrageous behaviour.*

out·ra·geous·ly /aʊtˈreɪdʒəsli/ ADV ❑ *outrageously expensive skin care items*

out·right ADJ, ADV

  ADJ /ˈaʊtraɪt/ **1** [outright + N] You use **outright** to describe behaviour and actions that are open and direct, rather than indirect. ❑ *Kawaguchi finally resorted to an outright lie.* **2** [outright + N] **Outright** means complete and total. = absolute ❑ *She had failed to win an outright victory.*

  ADV /ˌaʊtˈraɪt/ **1** [outright after v] When referring to behaviour and actions, **outright** means openly and directly, rather than indirectly. ❑ *Why are you so mysterious? Why don't you tell me outright?* **2** [outright after v] **Outright** means completely and totally. ❑ *The peace plan wasn't rejected outright.*

  PHRASE **be killed outright** If someone **is killed outright**, they die immediately, for example, in an accident.

out·set /ˈaʊtset/ NOUN

  PHRASE **at the outset** or **from the outset** If something happens **at the outset** of an event, process, or period of time, it happens at the beginning of it. If something happens **from the outset** it happens from the beginning and continues to happen. ❑ *Decide at the outset what kind of learning programme you want to follow.*

out·side ♦♦♦ /ˌaʊtˈsaɪd/ NOUN, ADJ, ADV, PREP

> The form **outside of** can also be used as a preposition.

  NOUN [C, SING] (**outsides**) **1** [C] The **outside** of something is the part which surrounds or encloses the rest of it. ❑ *the outside of the building* **2** [SING] ['the' outside] **The outside** means the people or things that are not in a country, town, or region. ❑ *Peace cannot be imposed from the outside by the United States or anyone else.*

  ADJ **1** [outside + N] The **outside** part of something is the part which is on the exterior of it. ❑ *high up on the outside wall* **2** [outside + N] The **outside** air or temperature is not inside a building or structure, but quite close. ❑ *the outside temperature* **3** [outside + N] When you talk about the **outside** world, you are referring to things that happen or exist in places other than your own home or community. ❑ *a side of Morris's character she hid carefully from the outside world* **4** [outside + N] **Outside** people or organizations are not part of a particular organization or group. ❑ *The company now makes much greater use of outside consultants.*

  ADV **1** If you are **outside**, you are not inside a building but are quite close to it. ❑ *I stepped outside and pulled up my collar against the cold mist.* ❑ *Outside, the light was fading rapidly.* **2** If you are **outside**, you are not in a room, but in the passage next to it. ❑ *They heard voices coming from outside in the corridor.* **3** [outside after v] **Outside** refers to places other than your own home or community. ❑ *The scheme was good for the prisoners because it brought them outside into the community.*

  PREP **1** If you are **outside** a building, you are not inside it but are quite close to it. ❑ *The victim was outside a shop when he was attacked.* **2** If you are **outside** a room, you are not in it but are in the passage or area next to it. ❑ *She'd sent him outside the classroom.* **3** [N/-ED + outside + N] People or things **outside** a country, town, or region are not in it. ❑ *an old castle outside Budapest* **4** People who are **outside** a particular organization or group are not part of that organization or group. ❑ *He is hoping to recruit a chairman from outside the company.* **5** **Outside** a particular institution or field of activity means in other fields of activity or in general life. ❑ *the largest merger ever to take*

o

place outside the oil industry **6** Something that is **outside** a particular range of things is not included within it. = **beyond** ❑ *She is a beautiful boat, but way, way outside my price range.* **7** Something that happens **outside** a particular period of time happens at a different time from the one mentioned. ❑ *They are open outside normal daily banking hours.*

out·sid·er /ˌaʊtˈsaɪdə/ NOUN [c] (**outsiders**) **1** An **outsider** is someone who does not belong to a particular group or organization. ❑ *The most likely outcome may be to subcontract much of the work to an outsider.* **2** An **outsider** is someone who is not accepted by a particular group, or who feels that they do not belong in it. ❑ *Malone, a cop, felt as much an outsider as any of them.* **3** In a competition, an **outsider** is a competitor who is unlikely to win. ❑ *He was an outsider in the race to be the new UN Secretary-General.*

out·skirts /ˈaʊtskɜːts/ NOUN [PL] **The outskirts of** a city or town are the parts of it that are farthest away from its centre. ❑ *Hours later we reached the outskirts of New York.*

out·spo·ken /ˌaʊtˈspəʊkən/ ADJ Someone who is **outspoken** gives their opinions about things openly and honestly, even if they are likely to shock or offend people. = **forthright** ❑ *Some church leaders have been outspoken in their support for political reform in Kenya.*
out·spo·ken·ness /ˌaʊtˈspəʊkənnəs/ NOUN [u] ❑ *Their outspokenness on behalf of civil rights sometimes cost them their jobs.*

out·stand·ing ♦◇◇ /ˌaʊtˈstændɪŋ/ ADJ **1** If you describe someone or something as **outstanding**, you think that they are very remarkable and impressive. ❑ *Derartu is an outstanding athlete and deserved to win.* **2** Money that is **outstanding** has not yet been paid and is still owed to someone. ❑ *The total debt outstanding is $70 billion.* **3** **Outstanding** issues or problems have not yet been resolved. ❑ *We still have some outstanding issues to resolve before we'll have a treaty that is ready to sign.* **4** **Outstanding** means very important or obvious. ❑ *The company is an outstanding example of a small business that grew into a big one.*

out·ward /ˈaʊtwəd/ ADJ, ADV

> The form **outwards** can also be used for the adverb.

ADJ **1** [outward + N] The **outward** feelings, qualities, or attitudes of someone or something are the ones they appear to have rather than the ones that they actually have. ❑ *In spite of my outward calm I was very shaken.* **2** [outward + N] The **outward** features of something are the ones that you can see from the outside. ❑ *Mark was lying unconscious but with no outward sign of injury.* **3** [outward + N] An **outward** flight or journey is one that you make away from a place that you are intending to return to later.
ADV **1** [outward after V] If something moves or faces **outward**, it moves or faces away from the place you are in or the place you are talking about. ❑ *The top door opened outward.* **2** [outward after V] If you say that a person or a group of people, such as a government, looks **outward**, you mean that they turn their attention to another group that they are interested in or would like greater involvement with. ❑ *Other poor countries looked outward, strengthening their ties to the economic superpowers.*

out·ward·ly /ˈaʊtwədli/ ADV You use **outwardly** to indicate the feelings or qualities that a person or situation may appear to have, rather than the ones that they actually have. ❑ *They may feel tired, and though outwardly calm, can be irritable.*

out·weigh /ˌaʊtˈweɪ/ VERB [T] (**outweighs**, **outweighing**, **outweighed**) **1** (formal) If one thing **outweighs** another, the first thing is of greater importance, benefit, or significance than the second thing. = **override**, **cancel out**, **balance out** ❑ *The advantages of this deal largely outweigh the disadvantages.* ❑ *The medical benefits of x-rays far outweigh the risk of having them.* **2** If you **outweigh** someone, you are heavier than them. ❑ *Young outweighed her opponent by about 60 pounds.*

out·wit /ˌaʊtˈwɪt/ VERB [T] (**outwits**, **outwitting**, **outwitted**) If you **outwit** someone, you use your

intelligence or a trick to defeat them or to gain an advantage over them. ❑ *To win the presidency he first had to outwit his rivals within the Socialist Party.*

oval /ˈəʊvəl/ ADJ, NOUN
ADJ **Oval** things have a shape that is like a circle but is wider in one direction than the other. = **elliptical** ❑ *the small oval framed picture of a little boy* ❑ *For prescription eyewear, the shapes are mainly geometric, often rectangular, as well as oval and round.*
NOUN [c] (**ovals**) An **oval** is a shape that is like a circle but is wider in one direction than the other. ❑ *Using 2 spoons, form the cheese into small balls or ovals.*

oven /ˈʌvən/ NOUN [c] (**ovens**) An **oven** is a device for cooking that is like a box with a door. You heat it and cook food inside it. ❑ *Put the onions and ginger in the oven and let them roast for thirty minutes.*

over ♦♦♦ /ˈəʊvə/ PREP, ADV, ADJ, CONVENTION

> In addition to the uses shown below, **over** is used in phrasal verbs such as 'hand over' and 'glaze over'.

PREP **1** If one thing is **over** another thing or is moving **over** it, the first thing is directly above the second, either resting on it, or with a space between them. ❑ *He looked at himself in the mirror over the table.* **2** If one thing is **over** another thing, it is supported by it and its ends are hanging down on each side of it. ❑ *A grey raincoat was folded over her arm.* **3** If one thing is **over** another thing, it covers part or all of it. ❑ *Mix the ingredients and pour over the mushrooms.* ❑ *He was wearing a light-grey suit over a shirt.* **4** [V + over + N] If you lean **over** an object, you bend your body so that the top part of it is above the object. ❑ *They stopped to lean over a gate.* **5** If you look **over** or talk **over** an object, you look or talk across the top of it. ❑ *I went and stood beside him, looking over his shoulder.* **6** [N + over + N, V + over + N] If a window has a view **over** an area of land or water, you can see the land or water through the window. = **onto** ❑ *a light and airy bar with a wonderful view over the river* **7** [V + over + N] If someone or something goes **over** a barrier, obstacle, or boundary, they get to the other side of it by going across it, or across the top of it. ❑ *I stepped over a broken piece of wood.* ❑ *Nearly one million people crossed over the river into Moldavia.* **8** If someone or something moves **over** an area or surface, they move across it, from one side to the other. = **across** ❑ *She ran swiftly over the lawn to the gate.* **9** If something is on the opposite side of a road or river, you can say that it is **over** the road or river. = **across** ❑ *a fashionable neighbourhood, just over the river from Manhattan* **10** [over + AMOUNT] If something is **over** a particular amount, measurement, or age, it is more than that amount, measurement, or age. ❑ *They say that tobacco will kill over 4 million people worldwide this year.* ❑ *His family have accumulated property worth well over $1 million.* **11** If you are **over** an illness or an experience, it has finished and you have recovered from its effects. ❑ *I'm glad that you're over the flu.* **12** [N + over + N] If you have control or influence **over** someone or something, you are able to control them or influence them. ❑ *He's never had any influence over her.* **13** [N + over + N, V + over + N] You use **over** to indicate what a disagreement or feeling relates to or is caused by. = **about** ❑ *concern over recent events in the Dominican Republic* ❑ *Staff at some air and sea ports are beginning to protest over pay.* **14** If something happens **over** a particular period of time or **over** something such as a meal, it happens during that time or during the meal. ❑ *The number of attacks on the capital had gone down over the past week.* **15** You use **over** to indicate that you give or receive information using a telephone, radio, or other piece of electrical equipment. = **on** ❑ *I'm not prepared to discuss this over the telephone.* ❑ *The head of state addressed the nation over the radio.*

PHRASES **all over** All over a place means in every part of it. ❑ *doctors who work all over the country*

over here Over here means near you, or in the country you are in. ❑ *Why don't you come over here tomorrow evening.*

over there Over there means in a place a short distance away from you, or in another country. ❑ *The cafe is just across the road over there.*

over and above Over and above an amount, especially a normal amount, means more than that amount or in addition to it. ❑ *Expenditure on education has gone up by seven point eight per cent over and above inflation.*

ADV **1** [over after v] If something moves **over**, it moves directly above another thing, either resting on it, or with a space between them. ❑ *planes flying over every 10 or 15 minutes* **2** [over after v] You can use **over** to indicate that something is moved so that it covers part or all of another thing. ❑ *Heat this syrup and pour it over.* **3** [over after v] If you lean **over**, you bend your body so that the top part of it is above another object. ❑ *Sam leaned over to open the door of the car.* **4** [over after v] You can use **over** to indicate that someone gets to the other side of something by going across it, or across the top of it. ❑ *I climbed over into the back seat.* **5** If you go **over** to a place, you go to that place. ❑ *I got out of the car and drove over to Greg's place.* ❑ *I thought you might have invited her over.* **6** You can use **over** to indicate a particular position or place a short distance away from someone or something. ❑ *He noticed Rolfe standing silently over by the window.* ❑ *John reached over and took Joanna's hand.* **7** [over after v] You use **over** to say that someone or something falls towards or onto the ground, often suddenly or violently. ❑ *If he drinks more than two glasses of wine he falls over.* ❑ *She pushed past me, almost knocking me over.* **8** [over after v] If something rolls **over** or is turned **over**, its position changes so that the part that was facing upward is now facing downward. ❑ *His car rolled over after a tyre was punctured.* **9** [AMOUNT 'and' over] You can use **over** to indicate that something is more than a particular amount, measurement, or age. ❑ *people aged 65 and over* **10** If you say that you have some food or money **over** or left **over**, you mean that it remains after you have used all that you need. ❑ *The Larsons pay me well enough, but there's not much left over for luxuries.*

PHRASES **twice over** (mainly BrE, emphasis) If you say that something happened **twice over**, **three times over** and so on, you are stating the number of times that it happened and emphasizing that it happened more than once. ❑ *James had to have everything spelled out twice over for him.*

over again If you do something **over again**, you do it again or start doing it again from the beginning. ❑ *If I could live my life over again, I would do things exactly the same way.*

all over again (emphasis) If you say that something is happening **all over again**, you are emphasizing that it is happening again, and you are suggesting that it is tiring, boring, or unpleasant. ❑ *The whole process started all over again.*

over and over (emphasis) If you say that something happened **over and over** or **over and over again**, you are emphasizing that it happened many times. ❑ *He plays the same songs over and over.*

ADJ [V-LINK + over] If an activity is **over** or **all over**, it is completely finished. ❑ *Warplanes that have landed there will be kept until the war is over.* ❑ *I am glad it's all over.*

CONVENTION **1** (formulae) When people such as the police or the army are using a radio to communicate, they say 'Over' to indicate that they have finished speaking and are waiting for a reply. **2** The presenter of a radio or television programme says 'over to someone' to indicate the person who will speak next. ❑ *With the rest of the sports news, over to Mike Martinez.*

❍ **over‧all** ♦♦◇ ADJ, ADV, NOUN (academic word)

ADJ /ˈəʊvərɔːl/ [overall + N] You use **overall** to indicate that you are talking about a situation in general or about the whole of something. = general; ≠ specific ❑ *the overall rise in unemployment* ❑ *A company must have both an overall strategy and local strategies for each unit.* ❑ *It is usually the woman who assumes overall care of the baby.*

ADV /ˌəʊvərˈɔːl/ [overall with CL] You use **overall** to show that you are talking about a situation in general or about the whole of something. ❑ *Overall I was disappointed.* ❑ *The college has few ways to assess the quality of education overall.* ❑ *The review omitted some studies. Overall, however, the evidence was persuasive.*

NOUN /ˈəʊvərɔːl/ [PL] (overalls) [also 'a pair of' overalls] **Overalls** consist of a single piece of clothing that combines trousers and a jacket. You wear overalls over your clothes in order to protect them while you are working.

over‧came /ˌəʊvəˈkeɪm/ IRREG FORM **Overcame** is the past tense of **overcome**.

❍ **over‧come** ♦◇◇ /ˌəʊvəˈkʌm/ VERB [T] (overcomes, overcoming, overcame, overcome) **1** If you **overcome** a problem or a feeling, you successfully deal with it and control it. = defeat, beat, conquer, survive ❑ *Molly had fought and overcome her fear of flying.* ❑ *One way of helping children to overcome shyness is to boost their self-confidence.* **2** If you **are overcome by** a feeling or event, it is so strong or has such a strong effect that you cannot think clearly. = overwhelm ❑ *The night before the test I was overcome by fear and despair.* **3** If you **are overcome by** smoke or a poisonous gas, you become very ill or die from breathing it in. ❑ *The residents were trying to escape from the fire but were overcome by smoke.*

over‧crowd‧ed /ˌəʊvəˈkraʊdɪd/ ADJ An **overcrowded** place has too many things or people in it. ❑ *a windswept, overcrowded, unattractive beach*

WORD PARTS

The prefix **over-** often appears in words for qualities or actions that are too much or too great:

overcrowded (ADJ)

overeat (VERB)

over-cautious (ADJ)

over‧dose /ˈəʊvədəʊs/ NOUN, VERB

NOUN [C] (overdoses) **1** If someone takes an **overdose** of a drug, they take more of it than is safe. ❑ *Each year, one in 100 girls ages 15-19 takes an overdose.* **2** You can refer to too much of something, especially something harmful, as an **overdose**. ❑ *An overdose of sun, sea, sand, and chlorine can give lighter hair a green tinge.*

VERB [I] (overdoses, overdosing, overdosed) **1** If someone **overdoses on** a drug, they take more of it than is safe. ❑ *He'd overdosed on heroin.* **2** You can say that someone **overdoses on** something if they have or do too much of it. ❑ *The city, he concluded, had overdosed on design.*

over‧draft /ˈəʊvədrɑːft, -dræft/ NOUN [C] (overdrafts) If you have an **overdraft**, you have spent more money than you have in your bank account, and so you are in debt to the bank. ❑ *Her bank warned that unless she repaid the overdraft she could face legal action.*

over‧drawn /ˌəʊvəˈdrɔːn/ ADJ If you are **overdrawn** or if your bank account is **overdrawn**, you have spent more money than you have in your account, and so you are in debt to the bank. ❑ *Nick's bank sent him a letter saying he was $500 overdrawn.*

❍ **over‧due** /ˌəʊvəˈdjuː, -ˈduː/ ADJ **1** If you say that a change or an event is **overdue**, you mean that you think it should have happened before now. = belated ❑ *This debate is long overdue.* ❑ *Total revision of the law in this area is long overdue.* **2** **Overdue** sums of money have not been paid, even though it is later than the date on which they should have been paid. = unpaid ❑ *There is a 2% interest charge on overdue balances.* ❑ *Teachers have joined a strike aimed at forcing the government to pay overdue salaries and allowances.* ❑ *Companies can claim up to £100 compensation for each overdue bill.* **3** An **overdue** library book has not been returned to the library, even though the date on which it should have been returned has passed. ❑ *a library book now weeks overdue*

over‧eat /ˌəʊvərˈiːt/ VERB [I] (overeats, overeating, overate, overeaten) If you say that someone **overeats**, you mean they eat more than they need to or more than is healthy. ❑ *If you tend to overeat because of depression, first*

O

take steps to recognize the source of your sadness.

over·flow VERB, NOUN

VERB /ˌəʊvəˈfləʊ/ [I, T] (**overflows, overflowing, overflowed**) **1** [I, T] If a liquid or a river **overflows**, it flows over the edges of the container or place it is in. ❑ *Pour in some of the broth, but not all of it, because it will probably overflow.* ❑ *The rivers overflowed their banks.* **2** [I] If a place or container **is overflowing with** people or things, it is too full of them. ❑ *Schreiber addressed an auditorium overflowing with journalists.*
PHRASE **to overflowing** If a place or container is filled **to overflowing**, it is so full of people or things that no more can fit in. ❑ *The kitchen garden was full to overflowing with fresh vegetables.*
NOUN /ˈəʊvəfləʊ/ [C] (**overflows**) The **overflow** is the extra people or things that something cannot contain or deal with because it is not large enough. ❑ *Tents have been set up next to hospitals to handle the overflow.*

over·haul VERB, NOUN

VERB /ˌəʊvəˈhɔːl/ [T] (**overhauls, overhauling, overhauled**) **1** If a piece of equipment **is overhauled**, it is cleaned, checked thoroughly, and repaired if necessary. = service ❑ *They had ensured the plumbing was overhauled a year ago.* **2** If you **overhaul** a system or method, you examine it carefully and make many changes in it in order to improve it. ❑ *proposals to overhaul bank regulations*
NOUN /ˈəʊvəhɔːl/ [C] (**overhauls**) **1** The **overhaul** of a piece of equipment is when it is cleaned, checked thoroughly, and repaired if necessary. ❑ *the overhaul of a cruiser* **2** The **overhaul** of a system or method is when you examine it carefully and make many changes in it in order to improve it. ❑ *The study says there must be a complete overhaul of air traffic control systems.*

over·head ADJ, ADV

ADJ /ˈəʊvəhed/ [overhead + N] You use **overhead** to indicate that something is above you or above the place that you are talking about. ❑ *She turned on the overhead light and looked around the little room.*
ADV /ˌəʊvəˈhed/ If something passes **overhead**, it passes above you or above the place that you are talking about. ❑ *planes passing overhead*

over·heads /ˈəʊvəhedz/ (in AmE, use **overhead**) NOUN

[PL] (*business*) The **overheads** of a business are its regular and essential expenses, such as salaries, rent, electricity, and telephone bills. ❑ *Private insurers spend 27 pence in every pound on overheads.*

✪ over·lap VERB, NOUN (academic word)

VERB /ˌəʊvəˈlæp/ [RECIP] (**overlaps, overlapping, overlapped**) **1** If one thing **overlaps** another, or if you **overlap** them, a part of the first thing occupies the same area as a part of the other thing. You can also say that two things **overlap**. ❑ *When the bag is folded, the bottom overlaps one side.* ❑ *Overlap the slices carefully so there are no gaps.* **2** If one idea or activity **overlaps** another, or **overlaps** with another, they involve some of the same subjects, people, or periods of time. = coincide ❑ *Christian Holy Week overlaps with the beginning of the Jewish holiday of Passover.* ❑ *The needs of patients invariably overlap.* ❑ *Their life-spans overlapped by six years.*
NOUN /ˈəʊvəlæp/ [C, U] (**overlaps**) An **overlap** between ideas or activities is when they share some subjects, people, or periods of time. ❑ *the overlap between civil and military technology*

over·look /ˌəʊvəˈlʊk/ VERB [T] (**overlooks, overlooking, overlooked**)

1 If a building or window **overlooks** a place, you can see the place clearly from the building or window. ❑ *Pretty and comfortable rooms overlook a flower-filled garden.* **2** If you **overlook** a fact or problem, you do not notice it, or do not realize how important it is. ❑ *We overlook all sorts of warning signals about our own health.* **3** If you **overlook** someone's faults or bad behaviour, you forgive them and take no action. ❑ *satisfying relationships that enable them to overlook each other's faults*

over·ly /ˈəʊvəli/ ADV [overly + ADJ/ADV/-ED] **Overly**

means more than is normal, necessary, or reasonable. = excessively ❑ *Employers may become overly cautious about taking on new staff.*

over·night ♦◇◇ /ˌəʊvəˈnaɪt/ ADV, ADJ

ADV **1** [overnight after v] If something happens **overnight**, it happens throughout the night or at some point during the night. ❑ *The decision was reached overnight.* **2** [overnight after v] You can say that something happens **overnight** when it happens very quickly and unexpectedly. ❑ *The rules are not going to change overnight.*
ADJ **1** [overnight + N] **Overnight** means happening in or throughout the night, or lasting the night. ❑ *Travel and overnight accommodation are included.* **2** [overnight + N] An **overnight** success or sensation happens very quickly and unexpectedly. ❑ *In 1970 he became an overnight success in America.* **3** [overnight + N] **Overnight** bags or clothes are ones that you take when you go and stay somewhere for one or two nights. ❑ *He realized he'd left his overnight bag at Mary's house.*

✪ over·popu·la·tion /ˌəʊvəpɒpjʊˈleɪʃən/ NOUN [U] If

there is a problem of **overpopulation** in an area, there are more people living there than can be supported properly. = overcrowding ❑ *young people who are concerned about overpopulation in the world* ❑ *Bavaria, like all the German regions, was by 1600 suffering from alarming overpopulation, causing food shortages.*

over·run /ˌəʊvəˈrʌn/ VERB, ADJ

VERB [T, I] (**overruns, overrunning, overran**) **1** [T] If an army or an armed force **overruns** a place, area, or country, it succeeds in occupying it very quickly. ❑ *A group of rebels overran the port area and most of the northern suburbs.* **2** [I] (*BrE*) If an event or meeting **overruns** by, for example, ten minutes, it continues for ten minutes longer than it was intended to. = run over **3** [I, T] (*business*) If costs **overrun**, they are higher than was planned or expected. ❑ *We should stop the nonsense of taxpayers trying to finance joint weapons whose costs always overrun hugely.* ❑ *Costs overran the budget by about 30%.*
ADJ [V-LINK + overrun] If you say that a place **is overrun with** things that you consider undesirable, you mean that there are a large number of them there. ❑ *The hotel has been ordered to close because it is overrun by mice and rats.*

✪ over·seas ♦◇◇ /ˌəʊvəˈsiːz/ ADJ, ADV (academic word)

ADJ **1** [overseas + N] You use **overseas** to describe things that involve or are in foreign countries, usually across a sea or an ocean. = foreign ❑ *He has returned to South Africa from his long overseas trip.* ❑ *overseas trade figures* **2** [overseas + N] An **overseas** student or visitor comes from a foreign country, usually across a sea or an ocean. = foreign ❑ *Every year nine million overseas visitors come to the city.* ❑ *firmly targeted at overseas buyers*
ADV If you go **overseas**, you go to a foreign country, usually across a sea or an ocean. = abroad ❑ *If you're staying for more than three months or working overseas, a full 10-year passport is required.*

over·see /ˌəʊvəˈsiː/ VERB [T] (**oversees, overseeing, oversaw, overseen**)

If someone in authority **oversees** a job or an activity, they make sure that it is done properly. = supervise ❑ *Use a surveyor or architect to oversee and inspect the different stages of the work.*

over·shad·ow /ˌəʊvəˈʃædəʊ/ VERB [T] (**overshadows, overshadowing, overshadowed**)

1 If an unpleasant event or feeling **overshadows** something, it makes it less happy or enjoyable. = cloud ❑ *Fears for the president's safety could overshadow his peace-making mission.* **2** If you **are overshadowed** by a person or thing, you are less successful, important, or impressive than they are. = eclipse ❑ *Hester is overshadowed by her younger and more attractive sister.* **3** If one building, tree, or large structure **overshadows** another, it stands near it, is much taller than it, and casts a shadow over it. ❑ *She said stations should be in the open, near housing, not overshadowed by trees or walls.*

over·spend VERB, NOUN

VERB /ˌəʊvəˈspend/ [I] (**overspends, overspending, overspent**) If you **overspend**, you spend more money than you can afford to. ❑ *Don't overspend on your home and expect to get the money back when you sell.*
NOUN /ˈəʊvəspend/ [C] (**overspends**) (*BrE; in AmE, use* **overrun**; *business*) If an organization or business has an

overspend, it spends more money than was planned or allowed in its budget.

over·take /ˌəʊvəˈteɪk/ VERB [I, T] (**overtakes, overtaking, overtook, overtaken**) **1** [I, T] (*mainly BrE; in AmE, usually use* **pass**) If you **overtake**, or **overtake** a vehicle or a person that is ahead of you and moving in the same direction, you pass them. **2** [T] If someone or something **overtakes** a competitor, they become more successful than them. □ *Lung cancer has now overtaken breast cancer as a cause of death for women in the US.* **3** [T] (*literary*) If a feeling **overtakes** you, it affects you very strongly. = engulf, overwhelm □ *Something like panic overtook me in a flood.*

over·throw VERB, NOUN
VERB /ˌəʊvəˈθrəʊ/ [T] (**overthrows, overthrowing, overthrew, overthrown**) When a government or leader **is overthrown**, they are removed from power by force. □ *That government was overthrown in a military coup three years ago.*
NOUN /ˈəʊvəθrəʊ/ [SING] The **overthrow** of a government or leader is their removal from power by force. □ *They were charged with plotting the overthrow of the state.*

over·time /ˈəʊvətaɪm/ NOUN
NOUN [U] **Overtime** is time that you spend doing your job in addition to your normal working hours. □ *He would work overtime, without pay, to finish a job.*
PHRASE **work overtime** (*informal*) If you say that someone **is working overtime** to do something, you mean that they are using a lot of energy, effort, or enthusiasm trying to do it. □ *We had to battle very hard and our defence worked overtime to keep us in the game.*

over·took /ˌəʊvəˈtʊk/ IRREG FORM **Overtook** is the past tense of **overtake**.

over·turn /ˌəʊvəˈtɜːn/ VERB [I, T] (**overturns, overturning, overturned**) **1** [I, T] If something **overturns** or if you **overturn** it, it turns upside down or on its side. □ *The motorcycle veered out of control, overturned and smashed into a wall.* □ *Alex jumped up so violently that he overturned his glass of wine.* **2** [T] If someone in authority **overturns** a legal decision, they officially decide that that decision is incorrect or not valid. = overrule □ *When the courts overturned his decision, he backed down.*

⊙ over·view /ˈəʊvəvjuː/ NOUN [C] (**overviews**) An **overview** of a situation is a general understanding or description of it as a whole. = survey □ *The central section of the book is a historical overview of drug use.* □ *The purpose of this book is to provide an overview of the mammals of the world.*

⊙ over·weight /ˌəʊvəˈweɪt/ ADJ Someone who is **overweight** weighs more than is considered healthy or attractive. = obese; ≠ slim □ *Being even moderately overweight increases your risk of developing high blood pressure.* □ *Studies show that overweight children are generally teased more on average than their peers.*

over·whelm /ˌəʊvəˈwelm/ VERB [T] (**overwhelms, overwhelming, overwhelmed**) **1** If you **are overwhelmed by** a feeling or event, it affects you very strongly, and you do not know how to deal with it. □ *He was overwhelmed by a longing for times past.* **2** If a group of people **overwhelm** a place or another group, they gain complete control or victory over them. □ *It was clear that one massive Allied offensive would overwhelm the weakened enemy.*
over·whelmed /ˌəʊvəˈwelmd/ ADJ □ *Sightseers may be a little overwhelmed by the crowds and noise.*

over·whelm·ing ◆◇◇ /ˌəʊvəˈwelmɪŋ/ ADJ
1 If something is **overwhelming**, it affects you very strongly, and you do not know how to deal with it. = overpowering □ *The task won't feel so overwhelming if you break it down into small, easy-to-accomplish steps.* **2** You can use **overwhelming** to emphasize that an amount or quantity is much greater than other amounts or quantities. □ *The overwhelming majority of small businesses go broke within the first twenty-four months.*
over·whelm·ing·ly /ˌəʊvəˈwelmɪŋli/ ADV
1 [overwhelmingly + ADJ] □ *The other women all seemed overwhelmingly confident.* **2** *The people voted overwhelmingly for change.*

owe ◆◇◇ /əʊ/ VERB
VERB [T] (**owes, owing, owed**) **1** If you **owe** money **to** someone, they have lent it to you and you have not yet paid it back. □ *The company owes money to more than 60 banks.* □ *Blake already owed him nearly $50.* **2** If someone or something **owes** a particular quality or their success **to** a person or thing, they only have it because of that person or thing. □ *I always suspected she owed her first job to her friendship with Roger.* □ *He owed his survival to his strength as a swimmer.* **3** If you say that you **owe** a great deal **to** someone or something, you mean that they have helped you or influenced you a lot, and you feel very grateful to them. □ *As a musician I owe much to the radio station in my home town.* **4** If you say that something **owes** a great deal to a person or thing, you mean that it exists, is successful, or has its particular form mainly because of them. □ *The island's present economy owes a good deal to tourism.* **5** If you say that you **owe** someone gratitude, respect, or loyalty, you mean that they deserve it from you. □ *Perhaps we owe these people more respect.* □ *I owe you an apology; you must have found my attitude very annoying.* **6** If you say that you **owe it to** someone to do something, you mean that you should do that thing because they deserve it. □ *I can't go; I owe it to him to stay.* □ *You owe it to yourself to get some professional help.*
PHRASE **owing to** You use **owing to** when you are introducing the reason for something. □ *Owing to staff shortages, there was no food on the plane.*

⊙ own ◆◆◆ /əʊn/ ADJ, PRON, VERB
ADJ **1** [POSS + own] You use **own** to indicate that something belongs to a particular person or thing. □ *My wife decided I should have my own shop.* □ *He could no longer trust his own judgement.* **2** [POSS + own] You use **own** to indicate that something is used by, or is characteristic of, only one person, thing, or group. □ *Jennifer insisted on her own room.* □ *Each nation has its own peculiarities when it comes to doing business.* **3** [POSS + own] You use **own** to indicate that someone does something without any help from other people. □ *They enjoy making their own decisions.*
PRON **1** [POSS + own] Something that is your **own** belongs to you. □ *He saw the major's face a few inches from his own.* **2** [POSS + own] Something that is your **own** is only used by you or is characteristic of you alone. □ *This young lady has a sense of style that is very much her own.* **3** [POSS + own] Something that is your **own** is done or made without any help from other people. □ *There's no career structure; you have to create your own.*
PHRASES **call something your own** If you have something you can **call** your **own**, it belongs only to you, rather than being controlled by or shared with someone else. □ *I would like a place I could call my own.*
come into one's own or **come into its own** If someone or something **comes into** their **own**, they become very successful or start to perform very well because the circumstances are right. □ *Many women have come into their own as teachers, healers, and leaders.*
get your own back (*BrE, informal*) If you **get** your **own back** on someone, you have your revenge on them because of something bad that they have done to you.
of one's own If you say that someone has a particular thing of their **own**, you mean that that thing belongs or relates to them, rather than to other people. □ *He set out in search of ideas for starting a company of his own.*
of one's own or **all of one's own** If someone or something has a particular quality or characteristic **of** their **own**, that quality or characteristic is especially theirs, rather than being shared by other things or people of that type. □ *The cries of the seagulls gave this part of the harbour a fascinating character of its own.*
on one's own **1** When you are **on** your **own**, you are alone. = alone □ *He lives on his own.* □ *I felt pretty lonely last year being on my own.* **2** If you do something **on** your **own**, you do it without any help from other people. □ *I work best on my own.*
VERB [T] (**owns, owning, owned**) If you **own** something, it is your property. = possess □ *His father owns a local video shop.* □ *farmers who own land* □ *At least three British golf courses are now owned by the Japanese.*

O

PHRASAL VERB **own up** If you **own up** to something wrong that you have done, you admit that you did it. ▢ *The teacher is waiting for someone to own up to the graffiti.*

✦ **hold your own** → see **hold**

⬡**own·er** ◆◆◇ /ˈəʊnə/ NOUN [c] (**owners**) If you are the **owner** of something, it belongs to you. ▢ *The owner of the shop was sweeping his floor when I walked in.* ▢ *Owners of property will lose financially if their property is damaged.* ▢ *New owners will have to wait until September before moving in.*

own·er·ship ◆◇◇ /ˈəʊnəʃɪp/ NOUN [u] **Ownership** of something is the state of owning it. ▢ *On January 23rd, the US decided to relax its rules on the foreign ownership of its airlines.* ▢ *the growth of home ownership*

⬡**oxy·gen** /ˈɒksɪdʒən/ NOUN [u] **Oxygen** is a colourless gas that exists in large quantities in the air. All plants and animals need oxygen in order to live. ▢ *The human brain needs to be without oxygen for only four minutes before permanent damage occurs.* ▢ *The baby was put in an incubator with an oxygen mask.* ▢ *the ability of the blood to carry oxygen to the heart*

oz ABBREVIATION **Oz** is a written abbreviation for **ounce**. ▢ *Whisk 1 oz of butter into the sauce.*

ozone /ˈəʊzəʊn/ NOUN [u] **Ozone** is a colourless gas which is a form of oxygen. There is a layer of ozone high above the Earth's surface, that protects us from harmful radiation from the sun. ▢ *What they find could provide clues to what might happen worldwide if ozone depletion continues.*

⬡**ozone lay·er** NOUN [SING] **The ozone layer** is the part of the Earth's atmosphere that has the most ozone in it. The ozone layer protects living things from the harmful radiation of the sun. ▢ *the hole in the ozone layer* ▢ *damage to the ozone layer*

O

Pp

P also **p** /piː/ NOUN [C, U] (**P's, p's**) P is the sixteenth letter of the English alphabet.

✪ pace ♦◇◇ /peɪs/ NOUN, VERB

NOUN [SING, C] (**paces**) **1** [SING] [usu with SUPP] The **pace** of something is the speed at which it happens or is done. = speed □ *Many people were not satisfied with the pace of change.* □ *They could not stand the pace or the workload.* □ *Interest rates would come down as the recovery gathered pace.* **2** [SING] [usu with SUPP] Your **pace** is the speed at which you walk. □ *He moved at a brisk pace down the rue St Antoine.* **3** [C] [usu with SUPP] A **pace** is the distance that you move when you take one step. □ *He'd only gone a few paces before he stopped again.*

PHRASES **keep pace 1** If something **keeps pace with** something else that is changing, it changes quickly in response to it. = keep up □ *The earnings of the average American have failed to keep pace with the rate of inflation.* **2** If you **keep pace with** someone who is walking or running, you succeed in going as fast as them, so that you remain close to them. = keep up □ *With four laps to go, he kept pace with the leaders.*

at one's own pace If you do something **at** your **own pace**, you do it at a speed that is comfortable for you. □ *The computer will give students the opportunity to learn at their own pace.*

VERB [I, T] (**paces, pacing, paced**) **1** [I, T] If you **pace** a small area, you keep walking up and down it, because you are anxious or impatient. □ *As they waited, Kravis paced the room nervously.* □ *He found John pacing around the house, unable to sleep.* **2** [T] If you **pace yourself** when doing something, you do it at a steady rate. □ *It was a tough race and I had to pace myself.*

paci·fism /'pæsɪfɪzəm/ NOUN [U] **Pacifism** is the belief that war and violence are always wrong. □ *a leading exponent of pacifism*

pack ♦♦◇ /pæk/ VERB, NOUN

VERB [I, T] (**packs, packing, packed**) **1** [I, T] When you **pack** a bag, you put clothes and other things into it, because you are leaving a place or going on holiday. □ *When I was 17, I packed my bags and left home.* □ *I began to pack a few things for the trip.* **2** [T] When people **pack** things, for example, in a factory, they put them into containers or boxes so that they can be transported and sold. □ *They offered me a job packing boxes in a warehouse.* □ *Machines now exist to pack olives in jars.* **3** [I, T] If people or things **pack into** a place or if they **pack** a place, there are so many of them that the place is full. = cram □ *Hundreds of people packed into the mosque.*

PHRASE **send someone packing** (*informal*) If you **send** someone **packing**, you make them go away. □ *I decided I wanted to live alone and I sent him packing.*

NOUN [C] (**packs**) **1** A **pack of** things is a collection of them that is sold or given together in a box or bag. □ *The club will send a free information pack.* □ *a pack of cigarettes* **2** You can refer to a group of people who go around together as a **pack**, especially when it is a large group that you feel threatened by. □ *He thus avoided a pack of journalists eager to question him.* **3** A **pack of** wolves or dogs is a group of them that hunt together. □ *a pack of stray dogs* **4** (*mainly BrE; in AmE, usually use* **deck**) A **pack of** playing cards is a complete set of playing cards.

PHRASE **a pack of lies** If you say that an account is **a pack of lies**, you mean that it is completely untrue. □ *You told me a pack of lies.*

→ See also **packed, packing**

pack·age ♦♦◇ /'pækɪdʒ/ NOUN, VERB

NOUN [C] (**packages**) **1** A **package** is something wrapped in paper, in a bag or large envelope, or in a box, usually so that it can be sent to someone by post. □ *I tore open the package.* **2** A **package** is a set of proposals that are made by a government or organization and that must be accepted or rejected as a group. □ *a package of measures to help the film industry* **3** A **package** tour is a holiday in which your travel and your accommodation are booked for you. □ *package tours to Egypt*

VERB [T] (**packages, packaging, packaged**) **1** When a product **is packaged**, it is put into containers to be sold. □ *The beans are then ground and packaged for sale as ground coffee.* **2** If something **is packaged** in a particular way, it is presented or advertised in that way in order to make it seem attractive or interesting. □ *A city is like any product, it has to be packaged properly to be attractive to the consumer.*

pack·ag·ing /'pækɪdʒɪŋ/ NOUN [U] **Packaging** is the container or covering that something is sold in. □ *It is selling very well, in part because the packaging is so attractive.*

packed /pækt/ ADJ **1** A place that is **packed** is very crowded. □ *The place is packed at lunchtime.* □ *a packed meeting in Detroit* **2** [V-LINK + packed 'with' N] Something that is **packed with** things contains a very large number of them. □ *The encyclopedia is packed with clear illustrations and over 250 recipes.*

pack·et /'pækɪt/ NOUN [C] (**packets**) (*mainly BrE*)
1 A **packet** is a small container in which a quantity of something is sold. Packets are either small boxes made of thin cardboard, or bags or envelopes made of paper or plastic. = pack □ *sugar packets* **2** (*in AmE, usually use* **pack**) You can use **packet** to refer to a packet and its contents, or to the contents only. = pack

pack·ing /'pækɪŋ/ NOUN [U] **1 Packing** is the act of putting clothes and other things into a bag, because you are leaving a place or going on holiday. □ *She left Frances to finish her packing.* **2 Packing** is the act of putting things into containers or boxes so that they can be transported and sold. □ *The shipping and packing costs are passed along in the item price.* **3 Packing** is the paper, plastic, or other material that is put around things that are being sent somewhere to protect them. □ *My fingers shook as I pulled the packing from the box.*

pact ♦◇◇ /pækt/ NOUN [C] (**pacts**) A **pact** is a formal agreement between two or more people, organizations, or governments to do a particular thing or to help each other. □ *Last month he signed a new non-aggression pact with Germany.*

pad /pæd/ NOUN, VERB

NOUN [C] (**pads**) **1** A **pad** is a fairly thick, flat piece of a material such as cloth or rubber. Pads are used, for example, to clean things, to protect things, or to change their shape. □ *He withdrew the needle and placed a pad of cotton over the spot.* □ *a scouring pad* **2** A **pad** of paper is a number of pieces of paper attached together along the top or the side, so that each piece can be torn off when it has been used. □ *She wrote on a pad of paper.* □ *Have a pad and* pencil ready and jot down some of your thoughts. **3** A **pad** is a platform or an area of flat, hard ground where helicopters take off and land or rockets are launched. □ *a little round helicopter pad* □ *a landing pad on the back of the ship* **4** The **pads of** a person's fingers and toes or of an animal's feet are the soft, fleshy parts of them. □ *Tap your cheeks all over with the pads of your fingers.*

VERB [I, T] (**pads, padding, padded**) **1** [I] When someone **pads** somewhere, they walk there with steps that are fairly quick, light, and quiet. □ *Freddy speaks very quietly and pads around in soft velvet slippers.* □ *a dog padding through the streets* **2** [T] If you **pad** something, you put something soft in it or over it in order to make it less hard, to protect it, or to give it a different shape. □ *Pad the back of a car seat with a pillow.* **3** [T] If you **pad** or **pad out** a piece of writing or a speech **with** unnecessary words or pieces of information, you include them to make it longer and hide the fact that you do not have very much to say. □ *Quotations should be used to make points, not to pad the essay.* □ *The reviewer padded out his review with a lengthy biography of the author.* **4** [T] If an employee with an expense account **pads** their expenses, they claim that their expenses are greater than they really are in order to get more money from their employer. □ *She was fired for padding her expenses.*

PHRASAL VERB **pad out** → See **pad** VERB 3
pad·ded /'pædɪd/ ADJ □ *a padded jacket*

page ♦♦♦ /peɪdʒ/ NOUN, VERB
NOUN [C] (**pages**) **1** A **page** is one side of one of the pieces of paper in a book, magazine, or newspaper. Each page usually has a number printed at the top or bottom. □ *Take out your book and turn to page 4.* □ *the front page of USA Today* **2** The **pages** of a book, magazine, or newspaper are the pieces of paper it consists of. □ *He turned the pages of his notebook.* **3** (*literary*) You can refer to an important event or period of time as a **page** of history. □ *a new page in the country's political history* **4** A **page** is a small boy who accompanies the bride at a wedding.
VERB [T] (**pages, paging, paged**) If someone who is in a public place is **paged**, they receive a message, often over a speaker, telling them that someone is trying to contact them. □ *He was paged repeatedly as the flight was boarding.*

paid /peɪd/ IRREG FORM, ADJ
IRREG FORM **Paid** is the past tense and past participle of **pay**.
ADJ **1** [paid + N] **Paid** workers, or people who do **paid** work, receive money for the work that they do. □ *Apart from a small team of paid staff, the organization consists of unpaid volunteers.* **2** [paid + N] If you are given **paid** holiday, you get your wages or salary even though you are not at work. □ *He agreed to hire her at slightly over the minimum wage with two weeks' paid holiday.* **3** [ADV + paid] If you are well **paid**, you receive a lot of money for the work that you do. If you are badly **paid**, you do not receive much money. □ *a well-paid accountant* □ *Travel and tourism employees are among the worst paid in the developed world.*

○ **pain** ♦♦◇ /peɪn/ NOUN, VERB
NOUN [C, U] (**pains**) **1** [C, U] **Pain** is the feeling of great discomfort you have, for example, when you have been hurt or when you are ill. = suffering, discomfort, agony □ *back pain* □ *To help ease the pain, heat can be applied to the area with a hot water bottle.* □ *I felt a sharp pain in my lower back.* □ *a bone disease that caused excruciating pain* **2** [U] **Pain** is the feeling of unhappiness that you have when something unpleasant or upsetting happens. = anguish □ *grey eyes that seemed filled with pain*
PHRASES **be in pain** If you are **in pain**, you feel pain in a part of your body because you are injured or ill. □ *She was writhing in pain, bathed in perspiration.*
a pain or **a pain in the neck** (*informal, disapproval*) In informal English, if you call someone or something **a pain** or **a pain in the neck**, you mean that they are very annoying or irritating. □ *Getting rid of unwanted applications from your PC can be a real pain.*
take pains to do something or **go to great pains to do something** If you **take pains to** do something or **go to great pains to** do something, you try hard to do it, because you think it is important to do it.

□ *He took great pains to see that he got it right.*
VERB [T] (**pains, pained**) If a fact or idea **pains** you, it makes you feel upset and disappointed. □ *This public acknowledgment of Ted's disability pained my mother.*

○ **pain·ful** ♦◇◇ /'peɪnfʊl/ ADJ **1** If a part of your body is **painful**, it hurts because it is injured or because there is something wrong with it. = sore □ *Her glands were swollen and painful.* **2** If something such as an illness, injury, or operation is **painful**, it causes you a lot of physical pain. □ *a painful back injury* □ *Sunburn is painful and potentially dangerous.* **3** Situations, memories, or experiences that are **painful** are difficult and unpleasant to deal with, and often make you feel sad and upset. □ *Remarks like that brought back painful memories.* □ *the painful transition to democracy*

○ **pain·ful·ly** /'peɪnfʊli/ ADV **1** [painfully with V] If an injured part of the body reacts **painfully**, it hurts. □ *His tooth had started to throb painfully again.* **2** [painfully with V] If something happens **painfully**, it causes you a lot of physical pain. □ *cracking his head painfully against the cupboard* **3** [painfully with V] If you experience something **painfully**, you find it difficult and unpleasant to deal with, and it makes you feel sad and upset. □ *their old relationship, which he had painfully broken off* **4** [painfully + ADV/ADJ] (*emphasis*) You use **painfully** to emphasize a quality or situation that is undesirable. □ *Things are moving painfully slowly.* □ *a painfully shy young man*

pain·kill·er /'peɪnkɪlə/ NOUN [C] (**painkillers**) A painkiller is a drug that reduces or stops physical pain.

pain·less /'peɪnləs/ ADJ **1** If something such as a treatment is **painless** it causes no physical pain. □ *Acupuncture treatment is gentle, painless, and relaxing.* □ *The operation itself is a brief, painless procedure.* **2** If a process or activity is **painless**, there are no difficulties involved, and you do not have to make a great effort or suffer in any way. □ *The journey is relatively painless, even with children.*
pain·less·ly /'peɪnləsli/ ADV **1** [painlessly with V] □ *a technique to eliminate unwanted facial hair quickly and painlessly* **2** [painlessly with V] □ *a game for children that painlessly teaches essential pre-reading skills*

pains·taking /'peɪnsteɪkɪŋ/ ADJ A **painstaking** search, examination, or investigation is done extremely carefully and thoroughly. = thorough □ *Forensic experts carried out a painstaking search of the debris.*
pains·taking·ly /'peɪnsteɪkɪŋli/ ADV □ *Broken bones were painstakingly pieced together and reshaped.*

paint ♦♦◇ /peɪnt/ NOUN, VERB
NOUN [C, U, SING] (**paints**) **1** [C, U] **Paint** is a coloured liquid that you put onto a surface with a brush in order to protect the surface or to make it look nice, or that you use to produce a picture. □ *a can of red paint* □ *They saw some large letters in white paint.* **2** [SING] On a wall or object, the **paint** is the covering of dried paint on it. □ *The paint was peeling on the window frames.*
VERB [I, T] (**paints, painting, painted**) **1** [I, T] If you **paint** a wall or an object, you cover it with paint. □ *They started to mend the woodwork and paint the walls.* □ *I had come here to paint.* **2** [T] If you **paint** something or **paint** a picture of it, you produce a picture of it using paint. □ *He is painting a huge volcano.* □ *Why do people paint pictures?* **3** [T] When you **paint** a design or message on a surface, you put it on the surface using paint. □ *a machine for painting white lines on roads* □ *They went around painting rude slogans on cars.* **4** [T] If you **paint** a grim or vivid picture of something, you give a description of it that is grim or vivid. □ *The report paints a grim picture of life there.*
→ See also **painting**

paint·er /'peɪntə/ NOUN [C] (**painters**) **1** A **painter** is an artist who paints pictures. □ *the French painter Claude Monet* **2** A **painter** is someone who paints walls, doors, and some other parts of buildings as their job. □ *the son of a painter and decorator*

paint·ing ♦♦◇ /'peɪntɪŋ/ NOUN [C, U] (**paintings**) **1** [C] A **painting** is a picture that someone has painted. □ *a large painting of Dwight Eisenhower* **2** [U] **Painting** is the activity of painting pictures. □ *two hobbies she really enjoyed,* painting and gardening **3** [U] **Painting** is the activity of painting doors, walls, and some other parts of buildings. ❑ *painting and decorating*

pair ♦♦◇ /peə/ NOUN, VERB

NOUN [c, SING] (**pairs**) **1** [c] A **pair** of things are two things of the same size and shape that are used together or are both part of something, for example, shoes, earrings, or parts of the body. ❑ *a pair of socks* ❑ *earrings that cost $142.50 a pair* **2** [c] Some objects that have two main parts of the same size and shape are referred to as a **pair**, for example, **a pair of trousers** or **a pair of scissors**. ❑ *a pair of faded jeans* **3** [SING] You can refer to two people as a **pair** when they are standing or walking together or when they have some kind of relationship with each other. ❑ *A pair of teenage boys were smoking cigarettes.* ❑ *The pair admitted that their three-year-old marriage was going through 'a difficult time.'*

VERB [T] (**pairs, pairing, paired**) If one thing **is paired with** another, it is put with it or considered with it. ❑ *The trainees will then be paired with experienced managers.*

pal·ace ♦◇◇ /ˈpælɪs/ NOUN [c] (**palaces**) A **palace** is a very large impressive house, especially one that is the official home of a king, queen, or president. ❑ *Buckingham Palace*

pale ♦◇◇ /peɪl/ ADJ, COMB, VERB

ADJ (**paler, palest**) **1** If something is **pale**, it is very light in colour or almost white. ❑ *Migrating birds filled the pale sky.* ❑ *As we age, our skin becomes paler.* **2** If someone looks **pale**, their face looks a lighter colour than usual, usually because they are ill, frightened, or shocked. ❑ *She looked pale and tired.*

COMB **Pale** can be used with a colour to indicate that there is a lot of white in the colour and it is not at all strong and vibrant. ❑ *a pale blue sailor dress*

VERB [I] (**pales, paling, paled**) If one thing **pales** in comparison with another, it is made to seem much less important, serious, or good by it. ❑ *When someone you love has a life-threatening illness, everything else pales in comparison.*

palm /pɑːm/ NOUN

NOUN [c] (**palms**) **1** A **palm** or a **palm tree** is a tree that grows in hot countries. It has long leaves growing at the top, and no branches. ❑ *golden sands and swaying palms* **2** The **palm** of your hand is the inside part of your hand, between your fingers and your wrist. ❑ *Dornberg slapped the table with the palm of his hand.*

PHRASE **in the palm of one's hand** If you have someone or something **in the palm of** your **hand**, you have control over them. ❑ *Johnson thought he had the board of directors in the palm of his hand.*

pam·phlet /ˈpæmflət/ NOUN [c] (**pamphlets**) A **pamphlet** is a very thin book with a paper cover that gives information about something. = **booklet** ❑ *a pamphlet about smoking*

pan ♦◇◇ /pæn/ NOUN, VERB

NOUN [c] (**pans**) A **pan** is a round metal container with a long handle, that is used for cooking things in, usually on top of a stove. = **saucepan** ❑ *Heat the butter and oil in a large pan.*

VERB [T, I] (**pans, panning, panned**) **1** [T] (*informal*) If something such as a film or a book **is panned** by journalists, they say it is very bad. ❑ *His first high-budget movie, called 'Brain Donors', was panned by the critics.* **2** [I, T] If you **pan** a film or television camera or if it **pans** somewhere, it moves slowly around so that a wide area is filmed. ❑ *The camera panned along the line of players.* ❑ *A television camera panned the stadium.*

pan·dem·ic /pænˈdemɪk/ NOUN [c] (**pandemics**) A **pandemic** is an occurrence of a disease that affects many people over a very wide area. ❑ *They feared a new cholera pandemic.*

WORD PARTS

The prefix *pan-* often appears in words that describe something as being connected with all places or people of a particular kind:

pandemic (NOUN)
pan-African (ADJ)
pan-Hellenic (ADJ)

---

pane /peɪn/ NOUN [c] (**panes**) A **pane** of glass is a flat sheet of glass in a window or door. ❑ *I watch my reflection in a pane of glass.*

⊙ **pan·el** ♦◇◇ /ˈpænəl/ NOUN [c] (**panels**) (*academic word*) **1** A **panel** is a small group of people who are chosen to do something, for example, to discuss something in public or to make a decision. ❑ *He assembled a panel of scholars to advise him.* ❑ *All the writers on the panel agreed that Quinn's book should be singled out for special praise.* ❑ *The advisory panel disagreed with the decision.* **2** A **panel** is a flat rectangular piece of wood or other material that forms part of a larger object such as a door. ❑ *the frosted glass panel set in the centre of the door* ❑ *The craft relies on the solar panels for energy.* **3** [N + panel] A control **panel** or instrument **panel** is a board or surface that contains switches and controls to operate a machine or piece of equipment. ❑ *The equipment was extremely sophisticated and was monitored from a central control panel.*

pan·ic ♦◇◇ /ˈpænɪk/ NOUN, VERB

NOUN [c, U] (**panics**) **1** [c, U] **Panic** is a very strong feeling of anxiety or fear that makes you act without thinking carefully. ❑ *An earthquake has hit the capital, causing damage to buildings and panic among the population.* **2** [U] [also 'a' panic] **Panic** or **a panic** is a situation in which people are affected by a strong feeling of anxiety. ❑ *There was a moment of panic as it became clear just how vulnerable the nation was.* ❑ *I'm in a panic about getting everything done in time.*

VERB [I, T] (**panics, panicking, panicked**) If you **panic** or if someone **panics** you, you suddenly feel anxious or afraid, and act quickly and without thinking carefully. ❑ *Guests panicked and screamed when the bomb exploded.* ❑ *The unexpected and sudden memory briefly panicked her.*

⊙ **pa·per** ♦♦♦ /ˈpeɪpə/ NOUN, ADJ, VERB

NOUN [U, c, PL] (**papers**) **1** [U] **Paper** is a material that you write on or wrap things with. The pages of this book are made of paper. ❑ *He wrote his name down on a piece of paper for me.* ❑ *a paper bag* **2** [c] A **paper** is a newspaper. ❑ *I might get a paper in the town.* **3** [c] You can refer to newspapers in general as **the paper** or **the papers**. ❑ *You can't believe everything you read in the paper.* **4** [PL] Your **papers** are sheets of paper with information on them that you might keep in a safe place at home. ❑ *After her death, her papers – including unpublished articles and correspondence – were deposited at the library.* **5** [PL] Your **papers** are official documents, such as your passport or identity card, that prove who you are or that give you official permission to do something. = **identification** ❑ *A young Moroccan stopped by police refused to show his papers.* **6** [c] A **paper** is a long, formal piece of writing about an academic subject. ❑ *He just published a paper in the journal Nature analyzing the fires.* ❑ *a controversial paper suggesting that many SIDS cases are caused by a rare inherited condition* **7** [c] (*mainly AmE*) A **paper** is an essay written by a student. ❑ *the ten common errors that appear most frequently in student papers* **8** [c] A **paper** prepared by a government or a committee is a report on a question they have been considering or a set of proposals for changes in the law. ❑ *a new government paper on electoral reform*

PHRASE **on paper** **1** If you put your thoughts down **on paper**, you write them down. ❑ *It is important to get something down on paper.* **2** If something seems to be the case **on paper**, it seems to be the case from what you read or hear about it, but it may not really be the case. ❑ *On paper, their country is a multi-party democracy.*

ADJ [paper + N] **Paper** agreements, qualifications, or profits are ones that are stated by official documents to exist, although they may not really be effective or useful. ❑ *They expressed deep mistrust of the paper promises.*

VERB [T] (**papers, papering, papered**) If you **paper** a wall, you put wallpaper on it. ❑ *We papered all four bedrooms.* ❑ *We have papered this bedroom in softest grey.*

paper·back /ˈpeɪpəbæk/ NOUN [c] (**paperbacks**) [also 'in' paperback] A **paperback** is a book with a thin cardboard or paper cover. Compare **hardback**. ❑ *She said she would buy the book when it comes out in paperback.*

paper·work /ˈpeɪpəwɜːk/ NOUN [U] **Paperwork** is the

p

routine part of a job that involves writing or dealing with letters, reports, and records. ❑ *At every stage in the production there will be paperwork – forms to fill in, permissions to obtain, letters to write.*

par /pɑː/ NOUN

NOUN [U] [par with NUM, 'under/over' par] In golf, **par** is the number of strokes that a good player should take to get the ball into a hole or into all the holes on a particular golf course. ❑ *He was five under par after the first round.* PHRASES **on a par with** If you say that two people or things are **on a par with** each other, you mean that they are equally good or bad, or equally important. ❑ *The water park will be on a par with some of the best public swimming facilities around.*

below par or **under par** If you say that someone or something is **below par** or **under par**, you are disappointed in them because they are below the standard you expected. ❑ *Duffy's primitive guitar playing is well below par.* ❑ *A teacher's job is relatively safe, even if they perform under par in the classroom.*

up to par If you say that someone or something is not **up to par**, you are disappointed in them because they are below the standard you expected. ❑ *It's a constant struggle to try to keep them up to par.*

below par or **under par** or **not up to par** If you feel **below par** or **under par** or **not up to par**, you feel tired and unable to perform as well as you normally do. ❑ *After the birth of her baby she felt generally under par.*

pa·rade /pəˈreɪd/ NOUN, VERB

NOUN [C, U] (**parades**) **1** [C] A **parade** is a procession of people or vehicles moving through a public place in order to celebrate an important day or event. ❑ *A military parade marched slowly and solemnly down Pennsylvania Avenue.* **2** [C, U] [oft 'on' parade] **Parade** is a formal occasion when soldiers stand in lines to be seen by an officer or important person, or march in a group. ❑ *He had them on parade at six o'clock in the morning.*

VERB [I, T] (**parades, parading, paraded**) **1** [I] When people **parade** somewhere, they walk together in a formal group or a line, usually with other people watching them. ❑ *More than four thousand soldiers, sailors, and airmen paraded down the Champs Elysées.* **2** [T] If prisoners **are paraded** through the streets of a town or on television, they are shown to the public, usually in order to make the people who are holding them seem more powerful or important. ❑ *Five leading fighter pilots have been captured and paraded before the media.* **3** [T] If you say that someone **parades** a person, you mean that they show that person to others only in order to gain some advantage for themselves. ❑ *Captured prisoners were paraded before television cameras.* **4** [T] If people **parade** something, they show it in public so that it can be admired. = show off ❑ *Valentino is eager to see celebrities parading his clothes at big occasions.* **5** [I, T] If you say that something **parades as** or **is paraded as** a good or important thing, you mean that some people say that it is good or important but you think it probably is not. ❑ *all the fashions that parade as modern movements in art*

❖**par·a·digm** /ˈpærədaɪm/ NOUN [C, U] (**paradigms**) (*academic word, formal*) A **paradigm** is a model for something that explains it or shows how it can be produced. = model, pattern ❑ *a new paradigm of production* ❑ *a course that challenges the traditional paradigm adopted in conventional faculties*

WORD PARTS

The prefix ***para-*** often appears in words for people or things that are similar to other things:

paradigm (NOUN)
paramilitary (ADJ)
paramedic (NOUN)
paralegal (NOUN)

---

par·a·dise /ˈpærədaɪs/ NOUN [U, C] (**paradises**) **1** [U] According to some religions, **paradise** is a wonderful place where people go after they die, if they have led good lives. = heaven ❑ *The Koran describes paradise as a place containing a garden of delight.* **2** [C, U] You can refer to a place or situation that seems beautiful or perfect as **paradise** or **a paradise**. ❑ *Bali is one of the world's great natural paradises.*

para·dox /ˈpærədɒks/ NOUN [C, U] (**paradoxes**) **1** [C] You describe a situation as a **paradox** when it involves two or more facts or qualities that seem to contradict each other. ❑ *The paradox is that the region's most dynamic economies have the most primitive financial systems.* ❑ *The paradox of exercise is that while using a lot of energy it seems to generate more.* **2** [C, U] A **paradox** is a statement in which it seems that if one part of it is true, the other part of it cannot be true. ❑ *The story contains many levels of paradox.*

para·dox·i·cal /ˌpærəˈdɒksɪkəl/ ADJ If something is **paradoxical**, it involves two facts or qualities that seem to contradict each other. ❑ *Some sedatives produce the paradoxical effect of making the person more anxious.* **para·doxi·cal·ly** /ˌpærəˈdɒksɪkli/ ADV ❑ *Paradoxically, the less you have to do the more you may resent the work that does come your way.*

❖**para·graph** /ˈpærəɡrɑːf, -ɡræf/ NOUN [C] (**paragraphs**) (*academic word*) A **paragraph** is a section of a piece of writing. A paragraph always begins on a new line and contains at least one sentence. = section ❑ *The length of a paragraph depends on the information it conveys.* ❑ *Paragraph 81 sets out the rules that should apply if a gift is accepted.*

❖**par·al·lel** /ˈpærəlel/ NOUN, VERB, ADJ (*academic word*)
NOUN [C] (**parallels**) **1** If something has a **parallel**, it is similar to something else, but exists or happens in a different place or at a different time. If it has **no parallel** or is **without parallel**, it is not similar to anything else. ❑ *Readers familiar with military conflict will find a vague parallel to the Vietnam War.* ❑ *It's an ecological disaster with no parallel anywhere else in the world.* **2** If there are **parallels** between two things, they are similar in some ways. ❑ *Detailed study of folk music from a variety of countries reveals many close parallels.* ❑ *There are significant parallels with the 1980s.* **3** [usu 'the' ORD + parallel] A **parallel** is an imaginary line round the earth that is parallel to the equator. Parallels are shown on maps. ❑ *the area south of the 38th parallel* VERB [T] (**parallels, parallelling, parallelled**) If one thing **parallels** another, they happen at the same time or are similar, and often seem to be connected. = echo ❑ *Often there are emotional reasons parallelling the financial ones.* ❑ *His remarks parallelled those of the president.* ADJ **1** **Parallel** events or situations happen at the same time as one another, or are similar to one another. ❑ *parallel talks between the two countries' foreign ministers* ❑ *Their instincts do not always run parallel with ours.* **2** If two lines, two objects, or two lines of movement are **parallel**, they are the same distance apart along their whole length. ❑ *seventy-two ships, drawn up in two parallel lines* ❑ *Remsen Street is parallel with Montague Street.* ❑ *The Andes form a mountain range parallel with the coast.*

para·lyse /ˈpærəlaɪz/ (in AmE, use **paralyze**) VERB [T] (**paralyses, paralysing, paralysed**) **1** If someone **is paralysed** by an accident or an illness, they have no feeling in their body, or in part of their body, and are unable to move. ❑ *She is paralysed from the waist down.* **2** If a person, place, or organization **is paralysed by** something, they become unable to act or function properly. ❑ *The city has been virtually paralysed by sudden snowstorms.* ❑ *She was paralysed by fear and love.* **para·lysed** /ˈpærəlaɪzd/ ADJ **1** *A guy with paralysed legs is not supposed to ride horses.* **2** *He sat in his chair, paralysed with dread.*

pa·ral·y·sis /pəˈræləsɪs/ NOUN [U] **1** **Paralysis** is the loss of the ability to move and feel in all or part of your body. ❑ *paralysis of the leg* **2** **Paralysis** is the state of being unable to act or function properly. ❑ *The paralysis of the leadership leaves the army without its supreme command.*

❖**pa·ram·e·ter** /pəˈræmɪtə/ NOUN [C] (**parameters**) (*academic word, formal*) **Parameters** are factors or limits that affect the way something can be done or made. = limits ❑ *some of the parameters that determine the taste of a wine* ❑ *That would be enough to make sure we fell within the parameters of our loan agreement.*

para·mili·tary /ˌpærəˈmɪlɪtri, *AmE* -teri/ ADJ, NOUN
ADJ **1** [paramilitary + N] A **paramilitary** organization is organized like an army and performs either civil or military functions in a country. □ *Searches by the army and paramilitary forces have continued today.* **2** [paramilitary + N] A **paramilitary** organization is an illegal group that is organized like an army. □ *a law which said that all paramilitary groups must be disarmed*
NOUN [c] (**paramilitaries**) **Paramilitaries** are members of a paramilitary organization. □ *Paramilitaries and army recruits patrolled the village.* □ *Paramilitaries were blamed for the shooting.*

para·mount /ˈpærəmaʊnt/ ADJ Something that is **paramount** or of **paramount** importance is more important than anything else. □ *The children's welfare must be seen as paramount.*

✪para·phrase /ˈpærəfreɪz/ VERB, NOUN
VERB [T] (**paraphrases, paraphrasing, paraphrased**) If you **paraphrase** someone or **paraphrase** something that they have said or written, you express what they have said or written in a different way. = summarize □ *To paraphrase President Bush, we must restore confidence in our economic sector.* □ *Baxter paraphrased the contents of the press release.* □ *Parents, to paraphrase Philip Larkin, can seriously damage your health.*
NOUN [c] (**paraphrases**) A **paraphrase** of something written or spoken is the same thing expressed in a different way. = summary, rewording □ *The last two clauses were an exact quote rather than a paraphrase of Mr Forth's remarks.* □ *In addition, quotations and paraphrases from an interview can give your paper immediacy and authority.* □ *You must remember to cite all your paraphrases and summaries of other writers' ideas.*

✪para·site /ˈpærəsaɪt/ NOUN [c] (**parasites**) **1** A **parasite** is a small animal or plant that lives on or inside a larger animal or plant, and gets its food from it. □ *Kangaroos harbour a vast range of parasites.* □ *Victims have tested positive for intestinal parasites, bacterial infection and viruses which cause fever and diarrhoea.* □ *The infection is caused by a tiny parasite which can affect humans and pets.* **2** If you disapprove of someone because you think that they get money or other things from other people but do not do anything in return, you can call them a **parasite**. □ *a parasite, who produced nothing but lived on the work of others*

✪para·sit·ic /ˌpærəˈsɪtɪk/ also **parasitical** ADJ **1** **Parasitic** diseases are caused by parasites. □ *Will global warming mean the spread of tropical parasitic diseases?* **2** **Parasitic** animals and plants live on or inside larger animals or plants and get their food from them. □ *tiny parasitic insects* **3** If you describe a person or organization as **parasitic**, you mean that they get money or other things from people without doing anything in return. □ *a parasitic new middle class of consultants and experts*

par·cel /ˈpɑːsəl/ NOUN
NOUN [c] (**parcels**) A **parcel** is something wrapped in paper, in a bag or large envelope, or in a box, usually so that it can be sent to someone by post. □ *They also sent parcels of food and clothing.*
PHRASE **part and parcel** (*emphasis*) If you say that something is **part and parcel of** something else, you are emphasizing that it is involved in or included in it. □ *Learning about life in a new culture is part and parcel of what newcomers to America face.*

par·don /ˈpɑːdən/ VERB, NOUN
VERB [T] (**pardons, pardoning, pardoned**) If someone who has been found guilty of a crime **is pardoned**, they are officially allowed to go free and are not punished. □ *Hundreds of political prisoners were pardoned and released.*
CONVENTION **pardon me** (*spoken, formulae*) Some people say '**Pardon me**' instead of 'Excuse me' when they want to politely get someone's attention or interrupt them. □ *Pardon me, are you finished, madam?*
NOUN [c] (**pardons**) A **pardon** is when someone who has been found guilty of a crime is allowed to go free and are not punished. □ *They lobbied the government on his behalf and he was granted a presidential pardon.*

CONVENTION **I beg your pardon** (*spoken*) **1** (*formulae*) You say **Pardon?, I beg your pardon?,** or **Pardon me?** when you want someone to repeat what they have just said because you have not heard or understood it. □ *'Will you let me open it?'—'Pardon?'—'Can I open it?'* **2** (*feelings*) People say '**I beg your pardon?**' when they are surprised or offended by something that someone has just said. □ *'Would you get undressed, please?'—'I beg your pardon?'— 'Will you get undressed?'* **3** (*formulae*) You say '**I beg your pardon**' as a way of apologizing for accidentally doing something wrong, such as disturbing someone or making a mistake. □ *I beg your pardon. I thought you were someone else.*

✪par·ent ◆◆◆ /ˈpeərənt/ NOUN, ADJ
NOUN [c] (**parents**) Your **parents** are your mother and father. □ *Children need their parents.* □ *This is where a lot of parents go wrong.* □ *When you become a parent the things you once cared about seem to have less value.*
ADJ [parent + N] An organization's **parent** organization is the organization that created it and usually still controls it. □ *Each unit including the parent company has its own, local management.*
→ See also **single parent**

✪pa·ren·tal /pəˈrentəl/ ADJ **Parental** is used to describe something that relates to parents in general, or to one or both of the parents of a particular child. □ *Medical treatment was sometimes given to children without parental consent.* □ *Parental attitudes vary widely.* □ *the removal of children from the parental home*

par·ent·hood /ˈpeərənthʊd/ NOUN [u] **Parenthood** is the state of being a parent. □ *She may feel unready for the responsibilities of parenthood.*

par·ent·ing /ˈpeərəntɪŋ/ NOUN [u] **Parenting** is the activity of bringing up and taking care of your child. □ *Parenting is not fully valued by society.*

par·ish /ˈpærɪʃ/ NOUN [c] (**parishes**) A **parish** is part of a city or town that has its own vicar or priest. □ *Good Shepherd, a parish of about 450 members* □ *a parish priest*

park ◆◆◇ /pɑːk/ NOUN, VERB
NOUN [c] (**parks**) **1** A **park** is a public area of land with grass and trees, usually in a town, where people go in order to relax and enjoy themselves. □ *Central Park* □ *a brisk walk with the dog around the park* **2** [SUPP + park] You can refer to a place where a particular activity is carried out as a **park**. □ *a science and technology park*
VERB [I, T] (**parks, parking, parked**) **1** [I, T] When you **park** a vehicle or **park** somewhere, you drive the vehicle into a position where it can stay for a period of time, and leave it there. □ *Greenfield turned into the next side street and parked.* □ *He found a place to park the car.* **2** [T] (*informal*) If you **park yourself** somewhere, you sit there. □ *Every Friday, I would park myself in front of the TV.*
→ See also **national park**

park·ing /ˈpɑːkɪŋ/ NOUN [u] **1** **Parking** is the action of moving a vehicle into a place in a garage or by the side of the road where it can be left. □ *In many towns parking is allowed only on one side of the street.* **2** **Parking** is space for parking a vehicle in. □ *Cars allowed, but parking is limited.*

✪par·lia·ment ◆◆◇ /ˈpɑːləmənt/ also **Parliament**
NOUN [c] (**parliaments**) **1** The **parliament** of some countries is the group of people who make or change its laws, and decide what policies the country should follow. □ *The Bangladesh Parliament today approved the policy, but it has not yet become law.* □ *The new European parliament convenes in three weeks' time.* **2** A particular **parliament** is a particular period of time in which a parliament is doing its work, between two elections or between two periods of holiday. □ *The legislation is expected to be passed in the next parliament.*
→ See also **Member of Parliament**

✪par·lia·men·ta·ry ◆◇◇ /ˌpɑːləˈmentəri/ ADJ [parliamentary + N] **Parliamentary** is used to describe things that are connected with a parliament or with members of parliament. □ *He used his influence to make sure she was not selected as a parliamentary candidate.* □ *last month's parliamentary elections*

p

○part ◆◆◆ /pɑːt/ NOUN, QUANT, ADV, VERB

NOUN [C, SING, U] (**parts**) **1** [C] A **part** of something is one of the pieces, sections, or elements that it consists of. = piece, portion, section, element; ≠ whole, entirety □ *I like that part of Cape Town.* □ *Respect is a very important part of any relationship.* **2** [C] A **part** for a machine or vehicle is one of the smaller pieces that is used to make it. = component □ *spare parts for military equipment* **3** [C] You can use **part** when you are talking about the proportions of substances in a mixture. For example, if you are told to use five **parts** water to one **part** paint, the mixture should contain five times as much water as paint. □ *Use turpentine and linseed oil, three parts to two.* **4** [C] A **part** in a play or film is one of the roles in it which an actor or actress can perform. = role □ *Alf Sjoberg offered her a large part in the play he was directing.* **5** [SING] [POSS + part 'in' N] Your **part** in something that happens is your involvement in it. = involvement □ *If only he could conceal his part in the accident.* **6** [U] [also 'a' part, part 'of' N] If something or someone is **part** of a group or organization, they belong to it or are included in it. □ *Annie had never been part of the in-crowd.*

PHRASES **play a part** If something or someone **plays** a large or important **part in** an event or situation, they are very involved in it and have an important effect on what happens. □ *These days work plays an important part in a single woman's life.*

take part If you **take part in** an activity, you do it together with other people. □ *Thousands of students have taken part in demonstrations.*

do your part If you **do** your **part**, you do something that, to a small or limited extent, helps to achieve something. □ *Each of you is going to have to do your part in keeping the community crime-free.*

for someone's part (*formal*) When you are describing people's thoughts or actions, you can say **for** her **part** or **for** my **part**, for example, to introduce what a particular person thinks or does. □ *For my part, I feel elated and close to tears.*

on someone's part If you talk about a feeling or action **on** someone's **part**, you are referring to something that they feel or do. □ *techniques on their part to keep us from knowing exactly what's going on* □ *There is no need for any further instructions on my part.*

in part (*formal*) You use **in part** to indicate that something exists or happens to some extent but not completely. □ *The levels of blood glucose depend in part on what you eat and when you eat.*

QUANT **Part** of something is some of it. □ *It was a very severe accident and he lost part of his foot.* □ *Perry spent part of his childhood in Canada.*

ADV If you say that something is **part** one thing, **part** another, you mean that it is to some extent the first thing and to some extent the second thing. = half □ *The television producer today has to be part news reporter, part educator.*

VERB [I, T, RECIP] (**parts, parting, parted**) **1** [I, T] If things that are next to each other **part** or if you **part** them, they move in opposite directions, so that there is a space between them. = open □ *Her lips parted as if she were about to take a deep breath.* **2** [T] If you **part** your hair in the middle or at one side, you make it lie in two different directions so that there is a straight line running from the front of your head to the back. □ *Picking up a brush, Joanna parted her hair.* **3** [RECIP] (*formal*) When two people **part**, or if one person **parts** from another, they leave each other. □ *He gave me the envelope and we parted.* **4** [RECIP] If you are **parted from** someone you love, you are prevented from being with them. = separated □ *I don't believe Laverne and I will ever be parted.*

PHRASAL VERB **part with** If you **part with** something that is valuable or that you would prefer to keep, you give it or sell it to someone else. □ *Buyers might require further assurances before parting with their cash.*

→ See also **parting**

✦ **part and parcel** → see **parcel**

WORD PARTS

The prefix **part-** appears in words which refer to something that is partly but not completely a particular thing:

part-baked (ADJ)

part exchange (NOUN)

part-time (ADJ)

P

VOCABULARY BUILDER

part NOUN

A **part** of something is one of the pieces, sections, or elements that it consists of.

□ *I told her part of the story, but not all of it.*

component NOUN (*formal*)

The **components** of something are the parts that it is made of.

□ *Enriched uranium is a key component of a nuclear weapon.*

ingredient NOUN (*mainly written*)

Ingredients are the things that are used to make something, especially all the different foods you use when you are cooking a particular dish.

□ *The meeting had all the ingredients of high political drama.*

piece NOUN

A **piece** of an object is one of the individual parts or sections that it is made of, especially a part that can be removed.

□ *assembling objects out of standard pieces*

portion NOUN (*fairly formal*)

A **portion** of something is a part of it.

□ *I have spent a considerable portion of my life here.*

section NOUN (*often formal*)

A **section** of something is one of the parts into which it is divided or from which it is formed.

□ *a large orchestra, with a vast percussion section*

○par·tial /ˈpɑːʃəl/ ADJ **1** You use **partial** to refer to something that is not complete or whole. = incomplete; ≠ complete, total □ *He managed to reach a partial agreement with both republics.* □ *a partial ban on the use of cars in the city* **2** [V-LINK + partial 'to' N/-ING] If you are **partial to** something, you like it. □ *He's partial to sporty women with blue eyes.* □ *Mollie confesses she is rather partial to pink.* **3** [V-LINK + partial] Someone who is **partial** supports a particular person or thing, for example, in a competition or dispute, instead of being completely fair. = biased □ *I might be accused of being partial.*

○par·tial·ly /ˈpɑːʃəli/ ADV [partially with CL/GROUP] If something happens or exists **partially**, it happens or exists to some extent, but not completely. = partly; ≠ completely □ *Lisa is deaf in one ear and partially blind.* □ *He was born with a rare genetic condition which has left him partially sighted.* □ *partially hydrogenated oils*

○par·tici·pant /pɑːˈtɪsɪpənt/ NOUN [C] (**participants**) The **participants** in an activity are the people who take part in it. ≠ observer □ *40 of the course participants are offered employment with the company.* □ *Conference participants agreed that Canada faces an urgent situation with respect to health-care provision.*

○par·tici·pate ◆◇◇ /pɑːˈtɪsɪpeɪt/ VERB [I] (**participates, participating, participated**) (*academic word*) If you **participate in** an activity, you take part in it. = take part □ *They expected him to participate in the ceremony.* □ *Over half the population of this country participate in sports.* □ *Hundreds of faithful Buddhists participated in the annual ceremony.* □ *lower rates for participating corporations*

○par·tici·pa·tion /pɑːˌtɪsɪˈpeɪʃən/ NOUN [U] = involvement, inclusion; ≠ exclusion □ *participation in religious activities* □ *a higher level of participation of women in the labour force*

○par·ti·cle /ˈpɑːtɪkəl/ NOUN [C] (**particles**) **1** A **particle** of something is a very small piece or amount of it. □ *a particle of hot metal* □ *There is a particle of truth in his statement.* □ *food particles* **2** (*technical*) In physics, a **particle** is a piece of matter smaller than an atom such as an electron or a proton. □ *the sub-atomic particles that make up matter* □ *Fewer cosmic rays reach the Earth when the Sun is very active, because the charged particles from the Sun deflect them.* □ *Molecules, atoms and even elementary particles all fall to bits at high temperatures.*

✪par·ticu·lar ♦♦◇ /pəˈtɪkjʊlə/ ADJ

ADJ **1** [particular + N] (emphasis) You use **particular** to emphasize that you are talking about one thing or one kind of thing rather than other similar ones. = specific; ≠ general ❑ I remembered a particular story about a postman who was a murderer. ❑ I have to know exactly why it is I'm doing a particular job. ❑ People with a particular blood type (HLA B27) are much more at risk. **2** [particular + N] If a person or thing has a **particular** quality or possession, it is distinct and belongs only to them. ❑ I have a particular responsibility to ensure I make the right decision. **3** [particular + N] (emphasis) You can use **particular** to emphasize that something is greater or more intense than usual. ❑ Particular emphasis will be placed on oral language training. **4** If you say that someone is **particular**, you mean that they choose things and do things very carefully, and are not easily satisfied. ❑ Ted was very particular about the colours he used.

PHRASE **in particular** You use **in particular** to indicate that what you are saying applies especially to one thing or person. = particularly ❑ The situation in Ethiopia in particular is worrisome. ❑ Why should he notice her car in particular?

→ See also **particulars**

✪par·ticu·lar·ly ♦♦◇ /pəˈtɪkjʊləli/ ADV **1** [particularly with CL/GROUP] You use **particularly** to indicate that what you are saying applies especially to one thing or situation. = especially ❑ Keep your office space looking good, particularly your desk. ❑ More local employment will be created, particularly in service industries. **2** [particularly with CL/GROUP] **Particularly** means more than usual or more than other things. = especially ❑ Progress has been particularly disappointing. ❑ I particularly liked the wooden chests and chairs.

par·ticu·lars /pəˈtɪkjʊləz/ NOUN [PL] The **particulars** of something or someone are facts or details about them that are written down and kept as a record. ❑ You will find all the particulars in Chapter 9.

part·ing /ˈpɑːtɪŋ/ NOUN, ADJ

NOUN [C, U] (partings) **1** [C, U] **Parting** is the act of leaving a particular person or place. A **parting** is an occasion when this happens. ❑ Parting from any one of you for even a short time is hard. **2** [C] (BrE; in AmE, use **part**) The **parting** in someone's hair is the line running from the front to the back of their head where their hair lies in different directions.

ADJ [parting + N] Your **parting** words or actions are the things that you say or do as you are leaving a place or person. ❑ Her parting words left him feeling empty and alone.

par·ti·san /ˌpɑːtɪˈzæn, AmE ˈpɑːrtɪzən/ ADJ, NOUN

ADJ Someone who is **partisan** strongly supports a particular person or cause, often without thinking carefully about the matter. ❑ He is clearly too partisan to be a referee.

NOUN [C] (partisans) **Partisans** are ordinary people, rather than soldiers, who join together to fight enemy soldiers who are occupying their country. ❑ He was rescued by some Italian partisans.

par·ti·tion /pɑːˈtɪʃən/ NOUN, VERB

NOUN [C, U] (partitions) **1** [C] A **partition** is a wall, screen, or divider that separates one part of a room, vehicle, or other space from another. ❑ new offices divided only by glass partitions **2** [U] The **partition** of a country is when it is divided into two or more independent countries. ❑ fighting which followed the partition of India

VERB [T] (partitions, partitioning, partitioned) **1** If you **partition** a room, you separate one part of it from another by means of a partition. ❑ Bedrooms have again been created by partitioning a single larger room. **2** If a country **is partitioned**, it is divided into two or more independent countries. ❑ Korea was partitioned in 1945. ❑ Churchill's plans to partition the German state

part·ly ♦◇◇ /ˈpɑːtli/ ADV [partly with CL/GROUP] You use **partly** to indicate that something happens or exists to some extent, but not completely. = partially ❑ It's partly my fault. ❑ I have not worried so much this year, partly because I have had other things to think about.

part·ner ♦♦◇ /ˈpɑːtnə/ NOUN, VERB (academic word)

NOUN [C] (partners) **1** Your **partner** is the person you are married to or are having a romantic or sexual relationship with. ❑ Wanting other friends doesn't mean you don't love your partner. **2** Your **partner** is the person you are doing something with, for example, dancing with or playing with in a game against two other people. ❑ to dance with a partner ❑ Her partner for the game was Venus Williams. **3** (business) The **partners** in a firm or business are the people who share the ownership of it. ❑ He's a partner in a Chicago law firm. **4** The **partner** of a country or organization is another country or organization with which they work or do business. ❑ Spain has been one of Cuba's major trading partners.

VERB [T] (partners, partnering, partnered) If you **partner** someone, you are their partner in a game or in a dance. ❑ He had partnered the famous Russian ballerina. ❑ He will be partnered by Ian Baker, the defending champion.

✪part·ner·ship ♦◇◇ /ˈpɑːtnəʃɪp/ NOUN [C, U] (partnerships) (academic word) **Partnership** or a **partnership** is a relationship in which two or more people, organizations, or countries work together as partners. = relationship, association, collaboration ❑ the partnership between Germany's banks and its businesses ❑ a new partnership between universities and the private sector

✪part-time ADJ, ADV

> The adverb is also spelled **part time**.

ADJ If someone is a **part-time** worker or has a **part-time** job, they work for only part of each day or week. ≠ full-time ❑ Many businesses are cutting back by employing lower-paid part-time workers. ❑ Part-time work is generally hard to find. ❑ I'm part-time. I work three days a week.

ADV [part-time after V] If someone works **part-time**, they work for only part of each day or week. ≠ full-time ❑ I want to work part-time.

✪par·ty ♦♦♦ /ˈpɑːti/ NOUN, VERB

NOUN [C] (parties) **1** A **party** is a political organization whose members have similar aims and beliefs. Usually the organization tries to get its members elected to the legislature of a country. ❑ a member of the Republican Party ❑ opposition parties ❑ India's ruling party ❑ her resignation as party leader **2** A **party** is a social event, often in someone's home, at which people enjoy themselves doing things such as eating, drinking, dancing, talking, or playing games. ❑ The couple met at a party. ❑ We threw a huge birthday party. **3** A **party of** people is a group of people who are doing something together, for example, travelling together. ❑ They became separated from their party. ❑ a party of sightseers **4** (legal) One of the people involved in a legal agreement or dispute can be referred to as a particular **party**. ❑ It has to be proved that they are the guilty party. ❑ He was the injured party.

PHRASE **be a party to something** or **be party to something** Someone who **is a party to** or **is party to** an action or agreement is involved in it, and therefore partly responsible for it. ❑ You were the one that brought up the idea of blackmail. I'd never be a party to such a thing.

VERB [I] (parties, partying, partied) If you **party**, you enjoy yourself doing things such as going out to parties, drinking, dancing, and talking to people. ❑ They come to eat and drink, to swim, to party.

pass ♦♦♦ /pɑːs, pæs/ VERB, NOUN

VERB [I, T] (passes, passing, passed) **1** [I, T] To **pass** someone or something means to go past them without stopping. ❑ As she passed the library door, the telephone began to ring. ❑ Jane stood aside to let her pass. **2** [I] When someone or something **passes** in a particular direction, they move in that direction. = go ❑ He passed through the doorway into the kitchen. ❑ He passed down the tunnel. **3** [I] If something such as a road or pipe **passes** along a particular route, it goes along that route. ❑ A dirt road passes through the town. **4** [T] If you **pass** something through, over, or around something else, you move or push it through, over, or around that thing. ❑ She passed the needle through the rough cloth, back and forth. ❑ 'I don't understand,' the detective mumbled, passing a hand through

p

his hair. **5** [T] If you **pass** something **to** someone, you take it in your hand and give it to them. = hand ❑ *Ken passed the books to Sergeant Wong.* **6** [I, T] If something **passes** or **is passed from** one person **to** another, the second person then has it instead of the first. ❑ *His mother's small estate had passed to him after her death.* ❑ *These powers were eventually passed to municipalities.* **7** [T] If you **pass** information **to** someone, you give it to them because it concerns them. ❑ *Officials failed to pass vital information to their superiors.* **8** [I, T] If you **pass**, or **pass** the ball **to** someone on your team in a game such as football or basketball, you kick or throw it to them. ❑ *Your partner should then pass the ball back to you.* **9** [I] When a period of time **passes**, it happens and finishes. = go by ❑ *He couldn't imagine why he had let so much time pass without contacting her.* ❑ *As the years passed he felt trapped by certain realities of marriage.* **10** [T] If you **pass** a period of time in a particular way, you spend it in that way. ❑ *The children passed the time playing in the streets.* **11** [I] If you **pass through** a stage of development or a period of time, you experience it. = go ❑ *The country was passing through a grave crisis.* **12** [T] If an amount **passes** a particular total or level, it becomes greater than that total or level. = exceed ❑ *They became the first company in their field to pass the $2 billion turnover mark.* **13** [T] If someone or something **passes** a test, they are considered to be of an acceptable standard. ❑ *Kevin has just passed his driving test.* ❑ *new drugs which have passed early tests to show that they are safe* **14** [T] If someone in authority **passes** a person or thing, they declare that they are of an acceptable standard or have reached an acceptable standard. ❑ *Several popular beaches were found unfit for swimming although the government passed them last year.* **15** [T] When people in authority **pass** a new law or a proposal, they formally agree to it or approve it. ❑ *The Estonian parliament has passed a resolution declaring the republic fully independent.* **16** [T] When a judge **passes** sentence on someone, he or she says what their punishment will be. ❑ *Passing sentence, the judge said it all had the appearance of a con trick.* **17** [I] If someone or something **passes for** or **passes as** something that they are not, they are accepted as that thing or mistaken for that thing. ❑ *Children's toy guns now look so realistic that they can often pass for the real thing.* ❑ *It is doubtful whether Ted, even with his fluent French, passed for one of the locals.* **18** [I] (*informal*) If someone makes you an offer or asks you a question and you say that you will **pass on** it, you mean that you do not want to accept or answer it now. ❑ *I think I'll pass on the swimming.* ❑ *'You can join us if you like.' Brad shook his head. 'I'll pass, thanks.'* **19** [I] In some card games and other games, if you **pass**, you choose not to play at that stage in the game. **20** [T] (*BrE*) If you **pass** comment or **pass** a comment, you say something.

PHRASAL VERBS **pass away** You can say that someone **passed away** to mean that they died, if you want to avoid using the word 'die' because you think it might upset or offend people. ❑ *He unfortunately passed away last year.*

pass off (*BrE*) If an event **passes off** without any trouble, it happens and ends without any trouble.

pass off as If you **pass** something **off as** another thing, you convince people that it is that other thing. ❑ *He passed himself off as a senior psychologist.* ❑ *I've tried to pass off my accent as a New York one.*

pass on **1** **Pass on** means the same as **pass** VERB **7**. ❑ *I do not know what to do with the information if I cannot pass it on.* ❑ *From time to time he passed on confidential information to him.* **2** If you **pass** something **on to** someone, you give it to them so that they have it instead of you. ❑ *The winner is passing the money on to a selection of her favourite charities.* ❑ *The late governor passed on much of his fortune to his daughter.* **3** You can say that someone **passed on** to mean that they died, if you want to avoid using the word 'die' because you think it might upset or offend people. = pass away ❑ *He passed on at the age of 72.*

pass out If you **pass out**, you faint or collapse. ❑ *He felt sick and dizzy and then passed out.*

pass over **1** If someone **is passed over for** a job or position, they do not get the job or position and someone younger or less experienced is chosen instead. ❑ *She claimed she was repeatedly passed over for promotion while less experienced white male colleagues were made partners.* **2** If you **pass over** a topic in a conversation or speech, you do not talk about it. ❑ *He largely passed over the government's record.*

pass up If you **pass up** a chance or an opportunity, you do not take advantage of it. ❑ *The official urged the government not to pass up the opportunity that has now presented itself.*

NOUN [C] (**passes**) **1** A **pass** in an examination, test, or course is a successful result in it. ❑ *He's been allowed to re-take the exam, and he's going to get a pass.* **2** A **pass** is a document that allows you to do something. ❑ *I got myself a pass into the barracks.* **3** A **pass** in a game such as football or basketball is an act of kicking or throwing the ball to someone on your team. ❑ *Hirst rolled a short pass to Merson.* **4** A **pass** is a narrow path or route between mountains. ❑ *The monastery is in a remote mountain pass.* ✦ **pass the buck** → see **buck**; **pass judgment** → see **judgment**

⊙ **pas·sage** ♦◇◇ /'pæsɪdʒ/ NOUN [C, U, SING] (**passages**) **1** [C] A **passage** is a long narrow space with walls or fences on both sides, that connects one place or room with another. = passageway, corridor ❑ *Harry stepped into the passage and closed the door behind him.* **2** [C] A **passage** in a book, speech, or piece of music is a section of it that you are considering separately from the rest. = excerpt, extract, section ❑ *He read a passage from Emerson.* ❑ *the passage in which the author speaks of the world of imagination* **3** [C] A **passage** is a long narrow hole or tube in your body, that air or liquid can pass along. ❑ *cells that line the air passages* **4** [C] A **passage through** a crowd of people or things is an empty space that allows you to move through them. = way ❑ *He cleared a passage for himself through the crammed streets.* **5** [U] The **passage** of someone or something is their movement from one place to another. ❑ *Germany had not requested Franco's consent for the passage of troops through Spain.* **6** [U] The **passage** of someone or something is their progress from one situation or one stage in their development to another. = transition ❑ *to ease their passage to a market economy* **7** [U] The **passage** of a bill is its progress through parliament so that it can become a law. ❑ *a Medicare bill expected to get final passage in Congress today* **8** [SING] The **passage of** a period of time is its passing. = passing ❑ *an asset that increases in value with the passage of time* **9** [C] A **passage** is a journey by ship. = crossing ❑ *We'd arrived the day before after a 10-hour passage from Anchorage.* **10** [U] If you are granted **passage** through a country or area of land, you are given permission to go through it. ❑ *Mr Thomas would be given safe passage to and from Jaffna.*

⊙ **pas·sen·ger** ♦◇◇ /'pæsɪndʒə/ NOUN, ADJ
NOUN [C] (**passengers**) A **passenger** in a vehicle such as a bus, boat, or plane is a person who is travelling in it, but who is not driving it or working on it. = traveller ❑ *Mr Fullemann was a passenger in the car when it crashed.* ❑ *a flight from Milan with more than forty passengers on board* **ADJ** [passenger + N] **Passenger** is used to describe something that is designed for passengers, rather than for drivers or freight. ❑ *I sat in the passenger seat.*

pass·ing /'pɑːsɪŋ, 'pæs-/ ADJ, NOUN
ADJ **1** [passing + N] A **passing** fashion, activity, or feeling lasts for only a short period of time and is not worth taking very seriously. ❑ *Hamnett does not believe environmental concern is a passing fad.* **2** [passing + N] A **passing** mention or reference is brief and is made while you are talking or writing about something else. = casual ❑ *It was just a passing comment, he didn't expand.* **NOUN** [SING] **1** The **passing** of something such as a time or system is the fact of its coming to an end. ❑ *It was an historic day, yet its passing was not marked by the slightest excitement.* **2** You can refer to someone's death as their **passing**, if you want to avoid using the word 'death' because you think it might upset or offend people. ❑ *His passing will be mourned by many people.* **3** The **passing of** a period of time is the fact or process of its going by. = passage ❑ *The passing of time brought a sense of emptiness.* **PHRASE** **in passing** If you mention something **in passing**,

you mention it briefly while you are talking or writing about something else. = incidentally ❑ *The army is only mentioned in passing.*

pas·sion ◆◇◇ /'pæʃən/ NOUN [U, C] (**passions**) **1** [U] [also passions] **Passion** is strong sexual feelings towards someone. ❑ *my passion for a dark-haired, slender boy named Josh* ❑ *the expression of love and passion* **2** [U] [also passions] **Passion** is a very strong feeling about something or a strong belief in something. ❑ *He spoke with great passion.* **3** [C] If you have a **passion for** something, you have a very strong interest in it and like it very much. ❑ *She had a passion for gardening.*

pas·sion·ate /'pæʃənət/ ADJ **1** A **passionate** person has very strong feelings about something or a strong belief in something. ❑ *his passionate commitment to peace* ❑ *He is very passionate about the project.* **2** A **passionate** person has strong romantic or sexual feelings and expresses them in their behaviour. ❑ *a beautiful, passionate woman of twenty-six*

pas·sion·ate·ly /'pæʃənətli/ ADV **1** *I am passionately opposed to the death penalty.* **2** *He was passionately in love with her.*

✪ pas·sive /'pæsɪv/ ADJ, NOUN (academic word)
ADJ **1** (disapproval) If you describe someone as **passive**, you mean that they do not take action but instead let things happen to them. ❑ *His passive attitude made things easier for me.* ❑ *Even passive acceptance of the regime was a kind of collaboration.* **2** [passive + N] A **passive** activity involves watching, looking at, or listening to things rather than doing things. ❑ *They want less passive ways of filling their time.* **3** [passive + N] **Passive** resistance involves showing opposition to the people in power in your country by not cooperating with them and protesting in nonviolent ways. = peaceful ❑ *They made it clear that they would only exercise passive resistance in the event of a military takeover.* ❑ *a policy of passive resistance or peaceful demonstration for political purposes*
NOUN [SING] In grammar, **the passive** or **the passive voice** is formed using 'be' and the past participle of a verb. The subject of a passive clause does not perform the action expressed by the verb but is affected by it. For example, in 'He's been murdered', the verb is in the passive. Compare **active**.

pas·sive·ly /'pæsɪvli/ ADV ❑ *He sat there passively, content to wait for his father to make the opening move.*

pass·port /'pɑːspɔːt, 'pæs-/ NOUN [C] (**passports**) Your **passport** is an official document containing your name, photograph, and personal details, which you need to show when you enter or leave a country. ❑ *You should take your passport with you when changing money.*

pass·word /'pɑːswɜːd, 'pæs-/ NOUN [C] (**passwords**) A **password** is a secret word or phrase that you must know in order to be allowed to enter a place such as a military base, or to be allowed to use a computer system. ❑ *Advance and give the password.*

✪ past ◆◆◆ /pɑːst, pæst/ NOUN, ADJ, PREP, ADV

> In addition to the uses shown below, **past** is used in the phrasal verb 'run past'.

NOUN [SING, C] (**pasts**) **1** **The past** is the time before the present, and the things that have happened. = history ❑ *In the past, about a third of the babies born to women with diabetes died.* ❑ *He should learn from the mistakes of the past. We have been here before.* **2** [C] Your **past** consists of all the things that you have done or that have happened to you. ❑ *revelations about his past* ❑ *Germany's recent past*
PHRASE **live in the past** (disapproval) If you accuse someone of **living in the past**, you mean that they think too much about the past or believe that things are the same as they were in the past. ❑ *What was the point in living in the past, thinking about what had or had not happened?*
ADJ **1** [past + N] **Past** events and things happened or existed before the present time. = previous, earlier; ≠ current, future ❑ *I knew from past experience that alternative therapies could help.* ❑ *a return to the turbulence of past centuries* **2** [DET + past + N] You use **past** to talk about

a period of time that has just finished. For example, if you talk about the **past five years**, you mean the period of five years that has just finished. = last ❑ *Most shops have remained closed for the past three days.*
PREP **1** [NUM + past + NUM] You use **past** when you are stating a time that is thirty minutes or less after a particular hour. For example, if it is **twenty past** six, it is twenty minutes after six o'clock. ❑ *It's ten past eleven.* **2** If it is **past** a particular time, it is later than that time. = gone, after ❑ *It was past midnight.* **3** If you go **past** someone or something, you go near them and keep moving, so that they are then behind you. = by ❑ *I dashed past him and out of the door.* ❑ *A steady procession of people filed past the coffin.* **4** [V + past + N] If you look or point **past** a person or thing, you look or point at something behind them. ❑ *She stared past Christine at the bed.* **5** [V-LINK + past + N] If something is **past** a place, it is on the other side of it. ❑ *Go north on I-15 to the exit just past Barstow.* **6** If someone or something is **past** a particular point or stage, they are no longer at that point or stage. ❑ *He was well past retirement age.*
ADV **1** [NUM + past] You use **past** when you are stating a time that is thirty minutes or less after the hour nearest to the present time. For example, if it is four o'clock and you say that you are leaving at **twenty past**, it means that you are leaving at twenty past four. ❑ *I have my lunch at half past.* **2** If something goes **past**, it comes near you and then keeps moving, so that you are then behind it. = by ❑ *An ambulance drove past.*

pas·ta /'pæstə, AmE 'pɑːstə/ NOUN [C, U] (**pastas**) **Pasta** is a type of food made from a mixture of flour, eggs, and water that is formed into different shapes and then boiled. Spaghetti, macaroni, and noodles are types of pasta.

paste /peɪst/ NOUN, VERB
NOUN [C, U] (**pastes**) **1** **Paste** is a soft, wet, sticky mixture of a substance and a liquid, that can be spread easily. Some types of paste are used to stick things together. ❑ *Blend a little milk with the custard powder to form a paste.* **2** **Paste** is a soft smooth mixture made of crushed meat, fruit, or vegetables. You can, for example, spread it onto bread or use it in cooking. ❑ *tomato paste*
VERB [T] (**pastes, pasting, pasted**) If you **paste** something on a surface, you put glue or paste on it and stick it on the surface. ❑ *pasting labels on bottles*

pas·try /'peɪstri/ NOUN [U, C] (**pastries**) **1** [U] **Pastry** is a food made from flour, fat, and water that is mixed together, rolled flat, and baked in the oven. It is used, for example, for making pies. **2** [C] A **pastry** is a small cake made with sweet pastry. ❑ *a wide range of cakes and pastries*

pas·ture /'pɑːstʃə, 'pæs-/ NOUN [C, U] (**pastures**) **Pasture** is land with grass growing on it for farm animals to eat. ❑ *The cows are out now, grazing in the pasture.*

pat /pæt/ VERB, NOUN
VERB [T] (**pats, patting, patted**) If you **pat** something or someone, you tap them lightly, usually with your hand held flat. ❑ *'Don't you worry about any of this,' she said patting me on the knee.* ❑ *The landlady patted her hair nervously.*
NOUN [C] (**pats**) **1** A **pat** is when you tap someone or something lightly, usually with your hand held flat. ❑ *He gave her an encouraging pat on the shoulder.* **2** A **pat of** butter or something else that is soft is a small lump of it. ❑ *Terreano put a pat of butter on his plate.*
PHRASE **a pat on the back** or **pat someone on the back** (approval) If you give someone **a pat on the back** or if you **pat** them **on the back**, you show them that you think they have done well and deserve to be praised. ❑ *The players deserve a pat on the back.*

patch /pætʃ/ NOUN, VERB
NOUN [C] (**patches**) **1** A **patch** on a surface is a part of it that is different in appearance from the area around it. ❑ *the bald patch on the top of his head* ❑ *There was a small patch of blue in the grey clouds.* **2** A **patch of** land is a small area of land where a particular plant or crop grows. ❑ *a patch of land covered in forest* ❑ *the little vegetable patch in her backyard* **3** A **patch** is a piece of material that you use to cover a hole in something. ❑ *jackets with patches on the*

elbows **4** A **patch** is a small piece of material that you wear to cover an injured eye. ❑ *She went to the hospital and found him lying down with a patch over his eye.* **5** (*computing*) A **patch** is a piece of computer program code written as a temporary solution for dealing with a computer virus and distributed by the makers of the original program. ❑ *Older machines will need a software patch to correct the date.*

PHRASE **a rough patch** If you have or go through **a rough patch**, you have a lot of problems for a time. ❑ *His marriage was going through a rough patch.*

VERB [T] (**patches, patching, patched**) If you **patch** something that has a hole in it, you repair it by fastening a patch over the hole. ❑ *He and Walker patched the barn roof.* ❑ *One of the mechanics took off the damaged tyre, and took it back to the station to be patched.*

PHRASAL VERB **patch up** **1** If you **patch up** an argument or relationship, you try to be friendly again and not to argue anymore. ❑ *She has gone on holiday with her husband to try to patch up their marriage.* ❑ *France patched things up with New Zealand.* **2** If you **patch up** something that is damaged, you repair it or patch it. ❑ *We can patch up those holes.* **3** If doctors **patch** someone **up** or **patch** their wounds **up**, they treat their injuries. ❑ *the medical staff who patched her up after the accident*

✪**pa·tent** /ˈpeɪtənt, AmE ˈpæt-/ NOUN, VERB, ADJ
NOUN [c] (**patents**) A **patent** is an official right to be the only person or company allowed to make or sell a new product for a certain period of time. ❑ *P&G applied for a patent on its invention.* ❑ *He held a number of patents for his many innovations.* ❑ *It sued Centrocorp for patent infringement.*
VERB [T] (**patents, patenting, patented**) If you **patent** something, you obtain a patent for it. ❑ *He patented the idea that the atom could be split.* ❑ *The invention has been patented by the university.* ❑ *a patented machine called the VCR II*
ADJ (*emphasis*) You use **patent** to describe something, especially something bad, in order to indicate in an emphatic way that you think its nature or existence is clear and obvious. = obvious ❑ *This was patent nonsense.*
pa·tent·ly /ˈpeɪtəntli/ ADV = clearly ❑ *He made his displeasure patently obvious.*

✪**pa·ter·nal** /pəˈtɜːnəl/ ADJ **1** **Paternal** is used to describe feelings or actions that are typical of those of a kind father towards his child. = fatherly ❑ *paternal love for his children* ❑ *Maternal and paternal instincts are those behaviours which a mother or father performs without conscious thought.* **2** [paternal + N] A **paternal** relative is one that is related through a person's father rather than their mother. ❑ *my paternal grandparents* ❑ *His paternal uncle had been diagnosed with cancer.*

path ♦◇◇ /pɑːθ, pæθ/ NOUN [c] (**paths**) **1** A **path** is a long strip of ground that people walk along to get from one place to another. ❑ *We followed the path along the clifftops.* ❑ *Feet had worn a path in the rock.* **2** Your **path** is the space ahead of you as you move along. ❑ *A group of reporters blocked his path.* **3** The **path** of something is the line that it moves along in a particular direction. ❑ *He stepped without looking into the path of a reversing car.* ❑ *people who live near airports or under the flight path of aeroplanes* **4** A **path** that you take is a particular course of action or way of achieving something. = road, route ❑ *They appear to have chosen the path of cooperation rather than confrontation.*

pa·thet·ic /pəˈθetɪk/ ADJ **1** If you describe a person or animal as **pathetic**, you mean that they are sad and weak or helpless, and they make you feel very sorry for them. ❑ *a pathetic little dog with a curly tail* ❑ *The small group of onlookers presented a pathetic sight.* **2** If you describe someone or something as **pathetic**, you mean that they make you feel impatient or angry, often because they are weak or not very good. ❑ *What pathetic excuses.* ❑ *Don't be so pathetic.*
pa·theti·cal·ly /pəˈθetɪkli/ ADV **1** *She was pathetically thin.* **2** [pathetically + ADJ] ❑ *Five women in a group of 18 people is a pathetically small number.*

✪**pa·thol·o·gist** /pəˈθɒlədʒɪst/ NOUN [c] (**pathologists**) A **pathologist** is someone who studies or investigates diseases and illnesses, or who examines dead bodies in order to find out the cause of death. ❑ *But a pathologist found that a 6cm cut on her head was consistent with a blow, possibly from a hammer.* ❑ *Most forensic pathologists have little experience in examining infant deaths.*

✪**pa·thol·o·gy** /pəˈθɒlədʒi/ NOUN [u] **Pathology** is the study of the way diseases and illnesses develop. ❑ *Anatomy, physiology, and pathology are studied to a similar level.* ❑ *One part was sent to a pathology laboratory for viewing under a microscope.*

pa·tience /ˈpeɪʃəns/ NOUN
NOUN [u] If you have **patience**, you are able to stay calm and not get annoyed, for example, when something takes a long time, or when someone is not doing what you want them to do. ❑ *He doesn't have the patience to wait.*
PHRASE **try someone's patience** or **test someone's patience** If someone **tries** your **patience** or **tests** your **patience**, they annoy you so much that it is very difficult for you to stay calm. ❑ *He tended to stutter whenever he spoke to her, which tried her patience.*

✪**pa·tient** ♦♦◇ /ˈpeɪʃənt/ NOUN, ADJ
NOUN [c] (**patients**) A **patient** is a person who is receiving medical treatment from a doctor or hospital. A **patient** is also someone who is taken care of by a particular doctor. = case, invalid ❑ *The earlier the treatment is given, the better the patient's chances.* ❑ *He specialized in the treatment of cancer patients.* ❑ *She was tough but wonderful with her patients.*
ADJ If you are **patient**, you stay calm and do not get annoyed, for example, when something takes a long time, or when someone is not doing what you want them to do. ❑ *Please be patient – your cheque will arrive.*
pa·tient·ly /ˈpeɪʃəntli/ ADV [patiently with v] ❑ *She waited patiently for Frances to finish.*

WORD CONNECTIONS
VERB + **patient**
treat a patient
diagnose a patient
help a patient
❑ *A team of doctors decides what is the best way of treating a cancer patient.*
ADJ + **noun**
a **sick** patient
an **ill** patient
❑ *These hospitals often deal with the sickest patients.*
an **elderly** patient
❑ *The nurses are very experienced at dealing with elderly patients.*

pa·tri·ot /ˈpætriət, ˈpeɪt-/ NOUN [c] (**patriots**) Someone who is a **patriot** loves their country and feels very loyal towards it. ❑ *It has been suggested the founders were not true patriots but men out to protect their own interests.*

pat·ri·ot·ic /ˌpætriˈɒtɪk, ˌpeɪt-/ ADJ Someone who is **patriotic** loves their country and feels very loyal towards it. ❑ *Winona is fiercely patriotic.*

pat·ri·ot·ism /ˈpætriətɪzəm, ˈpeɪt-/ NOUN [u] **Patriotism** is love for your country and loyalty towards it. ❑ *He was a country boy who had joined the army out of a sense of patriotism and adventure.*

pa·trol /pəˈtrəʊl/ VERB, NOUN
VERB [T] (**patrols, patrolling, patrolled**) When soldiers, police, or guards **patrol** an area or building, they move around it in order to make sure that there is no trouble there. ❑ *Prison officers continued to patrol the grounds within the jail.*
NOUN [c] (**patrols**) **1** A **patrol** is when soldiers, police, or guards move around an area or building in order to make sure that there is no trouble in it. ❑ *He failed to return from a patrol.* **2** A **patrol** is a group of soldiers or vehicles that are patrolling an area. ❑ *Guerrillas attacked a patrol with hand grenades.*
PHRASE **on patrol** Soldiers, police, or guards who are **on patrol** are patrolling an area. ❑ *The army is now on patrol in Srinagar and a curfew has been imposed.*

pa·tron /ˈpeɪtrən/ NOUN [C] (**patrons**) **1** A **patron** is a person who supports and gives money to artists, writers, or musicians. = sponsor □ *Catherine the Great was a patron of the arts and sciences.* **2** The **patron** of a charity, group, or campaign is an important person who allows his or her name to be used for publicity. □ *He has now become one of the patrons of the association.* **3** The **patrons** of a place such as a bar or hotel are its customers. □ *Few patrons of a high-priced hotel can be led to expect anything other than luxury service.*

pat·ron·age /ˈpætrənɪdʒ, ˈpeɪt-/ NOUN [U] **Patronage** is the support and money given by someone to a person or to a group such as a charity. = sponsorship □ *government patronage of the arts in Europe*

pat·ron·ize /ˈpætrənaɪz, AmE ˈpeɪt-/ also **patronise** VERB [T] (**patronizes, patronizing, patronized**) **1** (*disapproval*) If someone **patronizes** you, they speak or behave towards you in a way that seems friendly, but that shows that they think they are superior to you in some way. □ *Don't you patronize me!* **2** (*formal*) Someone who **patronizes** artists, writers, or musicians supports them and gives them money. □ *The Japanese imperial family patronizes the Japanese Art Association.* **3** If someone **patronizes** a place such as a bar, shop, or hotel, they are one of its customers. = frequent □ *The ladies of Berne liked to patronize the palace for tea and little cakes.*

pat·ron·iz·ing /ˈpætrənaɪzɪŋ, AmE ˈpeɪt-/ also **patronising** ADJ (*disapproval*) If someone is **patronizing**, they speak or behave towards you in a way that seems friendly, but that shows that they think they are superior to you. □ *The tone of the interview was unnecessarily patronizing.*

✪ **pat·tern** ♦♦◇ /ˈpætən/ NOUN [C] (**patterns**) **1** A **pattern** is the repeated or regular way in which something happens or is done. = arrangement, order □ *All three attacks followed the same pattern.* □ *A change in the pattern of his breathing became apparent.* **2** A **pattern** is an arrangement of lines or shapes, especially a design in which the same shape is repeated at regular intervals over a surface. □ *a golden robe embroidered with red and purple thread stitched into a pattern of flames* **3** A **pattern** is a diagram or shape that you can use as a guide when you are making something such as a model or a piece of clothing. □ *cutting out a pattern for slacks* □ *Send for our free patterns to knit yourself.*

WORD CONNECTIONS
VERB + **pattern**
follow a pattern
fit a pattern
□ *The killings seemed to follow a pattern.*
see a pattern
□ *As he looked at the statistics, he saw a pattern developing.*
change a pattern
□ *It can be difficult to change established patterns of behaviour.*
ADJ + **pattern**
a **familiar** pattern
a **normal** pattern
a **typical** pattern
□ *His life had reverted to an old and familiar pattern.*
the **same** pattern
a **similar** pattern
□ *Not every relationship has to follow the same pattern.*
a **different** pattern
□ *The two countries have have pursued different patterns of development.*

pause ♦◇◇ /pɔːz/ VERB, NOUN
VERB [I] (**pauses, pausing, paused**) If you **pause** while you are doing something, you stop for a short period and then continue. □ *'It's rather embarrassing,' he began, and paused.* □ *He talked for two hours without pausing for breath.*

NOUN [C] (**pauses**) A **pause** is a short period when you stop doing something before continuing. □ *After a pause Al said sharply: 'I'm sorry if I've upset you.'*

pave /peɪv/ VERB [T] (**paves, paving, paved**) If a road or an area of ground **has been paved**, it has been covered with asphalt or concrete, so that it is suitable for walking or driving on. □ *The avenue had never been paved, and deep mud made it impassable in winter.*

pave·ment /ˈpeɪvmənt/ (*BrE*; in *AmE*, use **sidewalk**) NOUN [C] (**pavements**) A **pavement** is a path with a hard surface, usually by the side of a road.

pay ♦♦♦ /peɪ/ VERB, NOUN
VERB [I, T] (**pays, paying, paid**) **1** [I, T] When you **pay** an amount of money **to** someone, you give it to them because you are buying something from them or because you owe it to them. When you **pay** something such as a bill or a debt, you pay the amount that you owe. □ *Owners who have already paid for repairs will be reimbursed.* □ *The wealthier may have to pay a little more in taxes.* **2** [T] When you **are paid**, you get your wages or salary from your employer. □ *The lawyer was paid a huge salary.* □ *I get paid monthly.* **3** [T] If you **are paid to** do something, someone gives you some money so that you will help them or perform some service for them. □ *There are people who are paid to sit around and play games.* **4** [I] If a government or organization makes someone **pay for** something, it makes them responsible for providing the money for it, for example, by increasing prices or taxes. □ *a legally binding international treaty that establishes who must pay for environmental damage* **5** [I, T] If a job, deal, or investment **pays** a particular amount, it brings you that amount of money. □ *We're stuck in jobs that don't pay very well.* □ *The banks don't pay interest on those accounts.* **6** [I] If a job, deal, or investment **pays**, it brings you a profit or earns you some money. □ *There are some agencies now specializing in helping older people to find jobs which pay.* **7** [I, T] If a course of action **pays**, it results in some advantage or benefit for you. □ *It pays to invest in protective clothing.* □ *We must demonstrate that aggression will not pay.* **8** [I, T] If you **pay for** something that you do or have, you suffer as a result of it. □ *He was to pay dearly for his lack of resolve.* □ *Why should I pay the penalty for somebody else's mistake?* **9** [T] You use **pay** with some nouns, such as in the expressions **pay a visit** and **pay attention**, to indicate that something is given or done. □ *Pay us a visit next time you're in Portland.* □ *He felt a heavy bump, but paid no attention to it.*

PHRASE **pay for itself** If something that you buy or invest in **pays for itself** after a period of time, the money you gain from it, or save because you have it, is greater than the amount you originally spent or invested. □ *investments in energy efficiency that would pay for themselves within five years*

PHRASAL VERBS **pay back** **1** If you **pay back** some money that you have borrowed or taken from someone, you give them an equal sum of money at a later time. □ *He burst into tears, begging her to forgive him and swearing to pay back everything he had stolen.* **2** If you **pay** someone **back for** doing something unpleasant to you, you take your revenge on them or make them suffer for what they did. □ *Some day I'll pay you back for this!*
pay off **1** If you **pay off** a debt, you give someone all the money that you owe them. □ *It would take him the rest of his life to pay off that loan.* **2** If an action **pays off**, it is successful or profitable after a period of time. □ *Sandra was determined to become a doctor and her persistence paid off.*
pay out If you **pay out** money, usually a large amount, you spend it on something. □ *The insurance industry will pay out billions of dollars for damage caused by Hurricane Katrina.*
pay up If you **pay up**, you give someone the money that you owe them or that they are entitled to, even though you would prefer not to give it. □ *We claimed a refund from the association, but they would not pay up.*

NOUN [U] Your **pay** is the money that you get from your employer as wages or salary. □ *their complaints about their pay and conditions*
→ See also **paid**
✦ **pay dividends** → see **dividend**; **pay through the nose** → see **nose**

p

pay·able /ˈpeɪəbəl/ ADJ **1** [V-LINK + payable] If an amount of money is **payable**, it has to be paid or it can be paid. ☐ *The money is not payable until January 31.* **2** [V N + payable, N + payable, payable 'to' N] If a cheque or money order is made **payable to** you, it has your name written on it to indicate that you are the person who will receive the money. ☐ *Make your cheque payable to 'Stanford Alumni Association'.*

pay·back /ˈpeɪbæk/ NOUN, ADJ

NOUN [c] (**paybacks**) (*mainly AmE*) You can use **payback** to refer to the profit or benefit that you obtain from something that you have spent money, time, or effort on. ☐ *There is a substantial payback in terms of employee and union relations.* ADJ [payback + N] The **payback** period of a loan is the time in which you are required or allowed to pay it back. ☐ *The payback period can be as short as seven years.* PHRASE **payback time** (*informal*) **Payback time** is when someone has to take the consequences of what they have done in the past. You can use this expression to talk about good or bad consequences. ☐ *This was payback time. I've proved once and for all I can become champion.*

pay·ment ♦♦◇ /ˈpeɪmənt/ NOUN [c, u] (**payments**) **1** A **payment** is an amount of money that is paid to someone, or the act of paying this money. ☐ *Thousands of its customers are behind with loans and mortgage payments.* **2** [u] **Payment** is the act of paying money to someone or of being paid. ☐ *He had sought to obtain payment of a sum which he had claimed was owed to him.*

pea /piː/ NOUN [c] (**peas**) **Peas** are round green seeds that grow in long thin cases and are eaten as a vegetable.

⊕ **peace** ♦♦♦ /piːs/ NOUN

NOUN [u] **1** If countries or groups involved in a war or violent conflict are discussing **peace**, they are talking to each other in order to try to end the conflict. ≠ war ☐ *Peace talks involving other rebel leaders and government representatives broke up without agreement last week, but are due to resume shortly.* ☐ *Leaders of some rival factions signed a peace agreement last week.* ☐ *They hope the treaty will bring peace and stability to Southeast Asia.* **2** If there is **peace** in a country or in the world, there are no wars or violent conflicts going on. ☐ *The president spoke of a shared commitment to world peace and economic development.* **3** If you disapprove of weapons, especially nuclear weapons, you can use **peace** to refer to campaigns and other activities intended to reduce their numbers or stop their use. ☐ *two peace campaigners accused of causing damage to an F1-11 nuclear bomber* **4** If you have **peace**, you are not being disturbed and you are in calm, quiet surroundings. ☐ *All I want is to have some peace and quiet and spend a couple of nice days with my grandchildren.* **5** If you have a feeling of **peace**, you feel contented and calm and not at all worried. You can also say that you are **at peace**. ☐ *I had a wonderful feeling of peace and serenity when I saw my husband.* **6** If there is **peace** among a group of people, they live or work together in a friendly way and do not argue. You can also say that people live or work **in peace with** each other. ☐ *a period of relative peace in the country's industrial relations* PHRASES **keep the peace** If someone in authority, such as the army or the police, **keeps the peace**, they make sure that people behave and do not fight or quarrel with each other. ☐ *the first UN contingent assigned to help keep the peace in Cambodia*

peace of mind If something gives you **peace of mind**, it stops you from worrying about a particular problem or difficulty. ☐ *The main appeal these bonds hold for individual investors is the safety and peace of mind they offer.*

WORD CONNECTIONS

VERB + **peace**

bring peace
keep the peace
☐ *We don't need guns or bombs to bring peace to the world.*

ADJ + **peace**

a lasting peace
a permanent peace
☐ *Their purpose is to ensure a lasting peace.*

an **uneasy** peace
☐ *There had been peace, but it was an uneasy peace.*

peace·ful ♦◇◇ /ˈpiːsful/ ADJ **1** **Peaceful** activities and situations do not involve war. ☐ *He has attempted to find a peaceful solution to the Ossetian conflict.* **2** **Peaceful** occasions happen without violence or serious disorder. ☐ *The farmers staged a noisy but peaceful protest outside the headquarters of the organization.* **3** **Peaceful** people are not violent and try to avoid arguing or fighting with other people. ☐ *warriors who killed or enslaved the peaceful farmers* **4** A **peaceful** place or time is quiet, calm, and free from disturbance. ☐ *a peaceful house in the heart of the Ozarks*

peace·ful·ly /ˈpiːsfuli/ ADV **1** [peacefully after V] If you do something **peacefully**, you do it without fighting. ☐ *The US military expects the matter to be resolved peacefully.* **2** [peacefully after V] If an occasion passes **peacefully**, it happens without violence or serious disorder. ☐ *The governor asked the crowd of protestors to leave peacefully.* **3** [peacefully after V] If you live **peacefully**, you try to avoid arguing or fighting with other people. ☐ *They've been living and working peacefully with members of various ethnic groups.* **4** [peacefully after V] If a time passes **peacefully**, it is quiet, calm, and free from disturbance. ☐ *Except for traffic noise the night passed peacefully.* **5** [peacefully after V] If you say that someone died **peacefully**, you mean that they suffered no pain or violence when they died. ☐ *He died peacefully on December 10 after a short illness.*

peach /piːtʃ/ NOUN, COLOUR

NOUN [c] (**peaches**) A **peach** is a soft, round, slightly furry fruit with sweet yellow flesh and pinky-orange skin. Peaches grow in warm countries. COLOUR Something that is **peach** is pale pinky-orange in colour. ☐ *a peach silk blouse*

⊕ **peak** ♦◇◇ /piːk/ NOUN, VERB, ADJ

NOUN [c] (**peaks**) **1** The **peak** of a process or an activity is the point at which it is at its strongest, most successful, or most fully developed. = prime, high point; ≠ low point, trough ☐ *The firm has slashed its workforce from a peak of 150,000 in 2000.* ☐ *a flourishing career that was at its peak at the time of his death* ☐ *The party's membership has fallen from a peak of fifty thousand.* ☐ *At the peak of the boom in 2000, revenues were $27.9 billion.* **2** A **peak** is a mountain or the top of a mountain. ☐ *the snow-covered peaks* VERB [I] (**peaks, peaking, peaked**) When something **peaks**, it reaches its highest value or its highest level. ☐ *Temperatures have peaked at over 90 degrees.* ☐ *The crisis peaked in July 2008.* ☐ *His career peaked during the 1990's.* ADJ **1** [peak + N] The **peak** level or value of something is its highest level or value. ☐ *Today's price is 59% lower than the peak level of $1.5 million.* **2** [peak + N] **Peak** times are the times when there is most demand for something or most use of something. ☐ *It's always crowded at peak times.*

pearl /pɜːl/ NOUN, ADJ

NOUN [c] (**pearls**) A **pearl** is a hard round object that is shiny and creamy white in colour. Pearls grow inside the shell of an oyster and are used for making expensive jewellery. ☐ *She wore a string of pearls at her throat.* ADJ **Pearl** is used to describe something that looks like a pearl. ☐ *tiny pearl buttons*

peas·ant /ˈpezənt/ NOUN [c] (**peasants**) A **peasant** is a poor person of low social status who works on the land; used to refer to people who live in countries where farming is still a common way of life. ☐ *the peasants in the Peruvian highlands*

pe·cu·liar /prˈkjuːliə/ ADJ **1** If you describe someone or something as **peculiar**, you think that they are strange or unusual, sometimes in an unpleasant way. = odd, strange ☐ *Mr Kennet has a rather peculiar sense of humour.* **2** If something is **peculiar to** a particular thing, person, or situation, it belongs or relates only to that thing, person, or situation. = unique ☐ *Punks, soldiers, hippies, and Sumo wrestlers all have distinct hair styles, peculiar to their group.*

pe·cu·liar·ly /prˈkjuːliəli/ ADV **1** *His face had become peculiarly expressionless.* **2** *a peculiarly American conservatism*

pe·cu·li·ar·ity /prˌkjuːliˈærɪti/ NOUN [c] (**peculiarities**)

P

1 A **peculiarity** that someone or something has is a strange or unusual characteristic or habit. ❑ *Joe's other peculiarity was that he was constantly munching hard candy.* **2** A **peculiarity** is a characteristic or quality that belongs or relates only to one person or thing. ❑ *a strange peculiarity of the US system*

ped·al /ˈpedəl/ NOUN, VERB
NOUN [c] (**pedals**) **1** The **pedals** on a bicycle are the two parts that you push with your feet in order to make the bicycle move. **2** A **pedal** in a car or on a machine is a lever that you press with your foot in order to control the car or machine. ❑ *the brake or accelerator pedals*
VERB [I, T] (**pedals, pedalling, pedalled**; in *AmE*, use **pedaling, pedaled**) When you **pedal** a bicycle, you push the pedals around with your feet to make it move. ❑ *She climbed on her bike with a feeling of pride and pedalled the five miles home.*

ped·es·tal /ˈpedɪstəl/ NOUN [c] (**pedestals**) **1** A **pedestal** is the base on which something such as a statue stands. ❑ *a larger than life-sized bronze statue on a granite pedestal* **2** If you put someone **on a pedestal**, you admire them very much and think that they cannot be criticized. If someone is knocked **off** a **pedestal** they are no longer admired. ❑ *Since childhood, I put my own parents on a pedestal. I felt they could do no wrong.*

pe·des·trian /pɪˈdestriən/ NOUN, ADJ
NOUN [c] (**pedestrians**) A **pedestrian** is a person who is walking, especially in a town or city, rather than travelling in a vehicle. ❑ *Ingrid was a walker, even in Los Angeles, where a pedestrian is a rare sight.*
ADJ (*disapproval*) If you describe something as **pedestrian**, you mean that it is ordinary and not at all interesting. ❑ *His style is so pedestrian that the book becomes a real bore.*

peel /piːl/ NOUN, VERB
NOUN [c, u] The **peel** of a fruit such as a lemon or an apple is its skin. You can also refer to a **peel**. ❑ *grated lemon peel* ❑ *a banana peel*
VERB [T, I] (**peels, peeling, peeled**) **1** [T] When you **peel** fruit or vegetables, you remove their skins. ❑ *She sat down in the kitchen and began peeling potatoes.* **2** [I, T] If you **peel off** something that has been sticking to a surface or if it **peels off**, it comes away from the surface. ❑ *One of the kids was peeling plaster off the wall.* ❑ *It took me two days to peel off the labels.* ❑ *Paint was peeling off the walls.* **3** [I] If a surface **is peeling**, the paint on it is coming away. ❑ *Its once-elegant white pillars are peeling.* **4** [I] If you **are peeling** or if your skin **is peeling**, small pieces of skin are coming off, usually because you have been burned by the sun. ❑ *His face was peeling from sunburn.*

peer ◆◇◇ /pɪə/ VERB, NOUN
VERB [I] (**peers, peering, peered**) If you **peer at** something, you look at it very hard, usually because it is difficult to see clearly. ❑ *I had been peering at a computer print-out that made no sense at all.*
NOUN [c] (**peers**) Your **peers** are the people who are the same age as you or who have the same status as you. = associate, colleague ❑ *His engaging personality made him popular with his peers.* ❑ *children who are much cleverer than their peers*

peer re·view NOUN [u] **Peer review** is the evaluation by fellow specialists of research that someone has done in order to assess its suitability for publication or further development. ❑ *Future funding is influenced by the process of peer review.* ❑ *At the research end most decisions are made by some form of peer review.*

peg ◆◇◇ /peg/ NOUN, VERB
NOUN [c] (**pegs**) **1** A **peg** is a small piece of wood or metal that is used for fastening something to something else. ❑ *He builds furniture using wooden pegs instead of nails.* **2** A **peg** is a small hook or knob that is attached to a wall or door and is used for hanging things on. ❑ *His work jacket hung on the peg in the kitchen.* **3** (*mainly BrE*; in *AmE*, usually use **clothespin**) A **peg** is a small device that you use to fasten clothes to a clothes line.
VERB [T] (**pegs, pegging, pegged**) **1** If you **peg** something somewhere or **peg** it **down**, you fix it there with pegs. ❑ *Peg down netting over the top to keep out leaves.* ❑ *a tent*

pegged to the ground nearby for the kids **2** If a price or amount of something **is pegged at** a particular level, it is fixed at that level. ❑ *Its currency is pegged to the dollar.* ❑ *The Bank wants to peg rates at 9%.*

pen ◆◇◇ /pen/ NOUN, VERB
NOUN [c] (**pens**) **1** A **pen** is a long thin object which you use to write in ink. **2** A **pen** is a small area with a fence around it in which farm animals are kept for a short time. = enclosure ❑ *a holding pen for sheep*
VERB [T] (**pens, penning, penned**) **1** (*formal*) If someone **pens** a letter, article, or book, they write it. ❑ *I really intended to pen this letter to you early this morning.* **2** If people or animals **are penned** somewhere or **are penned up**, they are forced to remain in a very small area. ❑ *The cattle were penned for the night.* ❑ *The animals were penned up in cages.*

pe·nal·ize /ˈpiːnəlaɪz/ also **penalise** VERB [T] (**penalizes, penalizing, penalized**) If a person or group **is penalized** for something, they are made to suffer in some way because of it. = punish ❑ *Some of the players may, on occasion, break the rules and be penalized.*

⭘ **pen·al·ty** ◆◇◇ /ˈpenəlti/ NOUN [c] (**penalties**) **1** A **penalty** is a punishment that someone is given for doing something which is against a law or rule. = punishment; ≠ reward ❑ *One of those arrested could face the death penalty.* ❑ *The maximum penalty is up to 7 years' imprisonment or an unlimited fine.* **2** In sports such as football and hockey, a **penalty** is a disadvantage forced on the team that breaks a rule. ❑ *Referee Michael Reed had no hesitation in awarding a penalty.* **3** The **penalty** that you pay for something you have done is something unpleasant that you experience as a result. ❑ *Why should I pay the penalty for somebody else's mistake?*

pence /pens/ NOUN [PL] **Pence** is the plural form of penny, a British coin worth one hundredth of a pound. ❑ *Matches cost only a few pence.*

pen·cil /ˈpensəl/ NOUN [c] (**pencils**) [also 'in' pencil] A **pencil** is an object that you write or draw with. It consists of a thin piece of wood with a rod of a black or coloured substance through the middle. If you write or draw something **in pencil**, you do it using a pencil. ❑ *I found a pencil and some blank paper in her desk.*

pend·ing /ˈpendɪŋ/ ADJ, PREP
ADJ (*formal*) **1** If something such as a legal procedure is **pending**, it is waiting to be dealt with or settled. ❑ *She had a libel action against the magazine pending.* ❑ *In 2006, the court had 600 pending cases.* **2** Something that is **pending** is going to happen soon. = imminent ❑ *A growing number of customers have been inquiring about the pending price rises.*
PREP (*formal*) If something is done **pending** a future event, it is done until that event happens. ❑ *A judge has suspended the ban pending a full inquiry.*

pen·etrate /ˈpenɪtreɪt/ VERB [T] (**penetrates, penetrating, penetrated**) **1** If something or someone **penetrates** a physical object or an area, they succeed in getting into it or passing through it. ❑ *X-rays can penetrate many objects.* **2** If someone **penetrates** an organization, a group, or a profession, they succeed in entering it although it is difficult to do so. ❑ *the continuing failure of women to penetrate the higher levels of engineering* **3** If someone **penetrates** an enemy group or a rival organization, they succeed in joining it in order to get information or cause trouble. = infiltrate ❑ *The CIA had requested our help to penetrate a drug ring operating out of Munich.* **4** (*business*) If a company or country **penetrates** a market or area, they succeed in selling their products there. ❑ *There have been around 15 attempts from outside Idaho to penetrate the market.* **pen·etra·tion** /ˌpenɪˈtreɪʃən/ NOUN [u] **1** *The thick walls prevented penetration by debris from the hurricane.* **2** *the successful penetration by the KGB of the French intelligence service* **3** *import penetration across a broad range of heavy industries*

pen·in·su·la /pəˈnɪnsjʊlə/ NOUN [c] (**peninsulas**) A **peninsula** is a long narrow piece of land that sticks out from a larger piece of land and is almost completely surrounded by water. ❑ *the political situation in the Korean peninsula*

p

pen·ny ♦◇◇ /'peni/ NOUN [C, SING] (**pennies** or **pence**) **1** [C] A **penny** is one hundredth of a British pound. ❑ *He gave a penny in change.* **2** [SING] If you say, for example, that you do not have a **penny**, or that something does not cost a **penny**, you are emphasizing that you do not have any money at all, or that something did not cost you any money at all. ❑ *From the day you arrive at my house, you need not spend a single penny.*

○pen·sion ♦◇◇ /'penʃən/ NOUN [C] (**pensions**) Someone who has a **pension** receives a regular sum of money from the government or a former employer because they have retired or because they are widowed or disabled. = allowance, support ❑ *struggling by on a pension* ❑ *a company pension scheme*

○pen·sion·er /'penʃənə/ NOUN [C] (**pensioners**) (*mainly BrE*) A **pensioner** is someone who receives a pension, especially a pension paid by the state to retired people. = OAP ❑ *Nearly a third of Britain's pensioners live on less than £10,000 a year.*

Pen·ta·gon NOUN [SING] **The Pentagon** is the main building of the US Defense Department, in Washington DC. The US Defense Department is often referred to as **the Pentagon**. ❑ *a news conference at the Pentagon*

○pen·ta·gon /'pentəgən, AmE -gɑːn/ NOUN [C] (**pentagons**) A **pentagon** is a shape with five sides. ❑ *Workspace for each module of the spacecraft is physically arranged as a pentagon seating five persons.* ❑ *One thinks of the common soccer ball which is actually composed of a pattern of hexagons and pentagons.*

○pe·nul·ti·mate /pe'nʌltɪmət/ ADJ [DET + penultimate] (*formal*) The **penultimate** thing in a series of things is the second to the last. ❑ *on the penultimate day of the Asian Games* ❑ *in the penultimate chapter*

○peo·ple ♦♦♦ /'piːpəl/ NOUN, VERB NOUN [PL, C] (**peoples**) **1** [PL] **People** are men, women, and children. **People** is normally used as the plural of **person**, instead of 'persons'. ❑ *Millions of people have lost their homes.* ❑ *the people of Angola* ❑ *I don't think people should make promises they don't mean to keep.* **2** [PL] **The people** is sometimes used to refer to ordinary men and women, in contrast to the government or the military. ❑ *the will of the people* **3** [C] A **people** is all the men, women, and children of a particular country or race. = community, population, race, ethnic group ❑ *the native peoples of Central and South America* ❑ *It's a triumph for the American people.* VERB [T] (**peoples, peopling, peopled**) If a place or country **is peopled by** a particular group of people, that group of people live there. = populate ❑ *It was peopled by a fiercely independent race of peace-loving Buddhists.*

pep·per ♦◇◇ /'pepə/ NOUN, VERB NOUN [U, C] (**peppers**) **1** [U] **Pepper** or **black pepper** is a hot-tasting spice used to flavour food. ❑ *Season with salt and pepper.* **2** [C] A **pepper** is a hollow green, red, yellow, or orange vegetable with seeds inside it. ❑ *2 red or green peppers, sliced* VERB [T] (**peppers, peppering, peppered**) If something **is peppered with** small objects, a lot of those objects hit it. ❑ *He was wounded in both legs and severely peppered with shrapnel.*

per an·num /pər 'ænəm/ ADV [AMOUNT + per annum] A particular amount **per annum** means that amount each year. ❑ *a fee of $35 per annum*

○per capi·ta /pə 'kæpɪtə/ ADJ, ADV ADJ [per capita + N] The **per capita** amount of something is the total amount of it in a country or area divided by the number of people in that country or area. ❑ *They have the world's largest per capita income.* ❑ *The per capita consumption of alcohol has dropped over the past two years.* ADV [N + per capita] You use **per capita** after a noun when the amount of something in a country or area is being considered in proportion to the number of people in that country or area. = per head ❑ *Ethiopia has almost the lowest oil consumption per capita in the world.*

○per·ceive /pə'siːv/ VERB [T] (**perceives, perceiving, perceived**) (*academic word*) **1** If you **perceive** something, you see, notice, or realize it, especially when it is not

obvious. ❑ *Students must perceive for themselves the relationship between success and effort.* **2** If you **perceive** someone or something **as** doing or being a particular thing, it is your opinion that they do this thing or that they are that thing. = believe, consider ❑ *Stress is widely perceived as contributing to coronary heart disease.* ❑ *Bioterrorism is perceived as a real threat in the United States.*

○per cent ♦♦♦ /pə'sent/ also **percent** NOUN, ADJ, ADV (*academic word*) NOUN [C] (**per cent**) You use **per cent** to talk about amounts. For example, if an amount is 10 per cent (10%) of a larger amount, it is equal to 10 hundredths of the larger amount. ❑ *Sixteen per cent of children live in poverty in this country.* ❑ *Sales of new homes fell by 1.4 per cent in August.* ADJ [per cent + N] A 10 **per cent** (10%) increase or decrease is an increase or decrease by 10 hundredths of the original amount. ❑ *a 15 per cent increase in border patrols* ADV [per cent with V] If something increases or decreases 10 **per cent** (10%), it increases or decreases by 10 hundredths of the original amount. ❑ *He predicted sales will fall 2 per cent to 6 per cent in the second quarter.*

○per·cent·age ♦◇◇ /pə'sentɪdʒ/ NOUN [C] (**percentages**) A **percentage** is a fraction of an amount expressed as a particular number of hundredths of that amount. = proportion, amount ❑ *Only a few vegetable-origin foods have such a high percentage of protein.* ❑ *A large percentage of the population speaks fluent English.*

○per·cep·ti·ble /pə'septɪbəl/ ADJ Something that is **perceptible** can barely be seen or noticed. = discernible, noticeable; ≠ indiscernible, imperceptible ❑ *Pasternak gave him a barely perceptible smile.* ❑ *a perceptible shift in US policy* ❑ *There was no perceptible difference in temperature.*

○per·cep·ti·bly /pə'septɪbli/ ADV [perceptibly with V] = discernibly, noticeably; ≠ imperceptibly ❑ *The tension was mounting perceptibly.* ❑ *After 1865 the growth of national craft unions quickened perceptibly.* ❑ *America's attitude to European issues shifted perceptibly as a result of the end of the Cold War.*

○per·cep·tion /pə'sepʃən/ NOUN [C, U] (**perceptions**) **1** [C] Your **perception** of something is the way that you think about it or the impression you have of it. = impression ❑ *He is interested in how our perceptions of death affect the way we live.* ❑ *There was still a perception among the public that the city was unsafe.* **2** [U] Someone who has **perception** realizes or notices things that are not obvious. = understanding ❑ *It did not require a lot of perception to realize the interview was over.* **3** [U] **Perception** is the recognition of things using your senses, especially the sense of sight.

perch /pɜːtʃ/ VERB, NOUN

> The form **perch** is used for both the singular and plural in meaning 2 of the noun.

VERB [I, T] (**perches, perching, perched**) **1** [I] If you **perch on** something, you sit down lightly on the very edge or tip of it. ❑ *He lit a cigarette and perched on the corner of the desk.* **2** [I] To **perch** somewhere means to be on the top or edge of something. ❑ *the vast slums that perch precariously on top of the hills around which the city was built* **3** [T] If you **perch** something on something else, you put or balance it on the top or edge of that thing. ❑ *The use of steel and concrete has allowed the builders to perch a light concrete dome on eight slender columns.* **4** [I] When a bird **perches on** something such as a branch or a wall, it lands on it and stands there. ❑ *A blackbird flew down and perched on the parapet outside his window.* NOUN [C] (**perches**) **1** A **perch** is a short rod for a bird to stand on. ❑ *A small, yellow bird in a cage sat on its perch outside the house.* **2** A **perch** is an edible fish. There are several kinds of perch.

per·en·nial /pə'reniəl/ ADJ, NOUN ADJ **1** You use **perennial** to describe situations or states that keep occurring or that seem to exist all the time; used especially to describe problems or difficulties. = constant ❑ *the perennial urban problems of drugs and homelessness* **2** A **perennial** plant lives for several years and has flowers

P

each year. ❑ *a perennial herb with greenish-yellow flowers* NOUN [C] (**perennials**) A **perennial** is a plant that lives for several years and has flowers each year. ❑ *a low-growing perennial*

per·fect ◆◆◇ ADJ, VERB

ADJ /'pɜːfɪkt/ **1** Something that is **perfect** is as good as it could possibly be. ❑ *He spoke perfect English.* ❑ *Nobody is perfect.* **2** If you say that something is **perfect for** a particular person, thing, or activity, you are emphasizing that it is very suitable for them or for that activity. = ideal ❑ *The pool area is perfect for entertaining.* **3** If an object or surface is **perfect**, it does not have any marks on it, or does not have any lumps, hollows, or cracks in it. ❑ *Use only clean, Grade A, perfect eggs.* **4** [perfect + N] You can use **perfect** to give emphasis to the noun following it. = complete, total ❑ *She was a perfect fool.* ❑ *Some people are always coming up to perfect strangers and asking them what they do.*

VERB /pə'fekt/ [T] (**perfects, perfecting, perfected**) If you **perfect** something, you improve it so that it becomes as good as it can possibly be. ❑ *We perfected a hand-signal system so that he could keep me informed of hazards.* ❑ *I removed the fibroid tumours, using the techniques that I have perfected.*

per·fec·tion /pə'fekʃən/ NOUN [U] **1** Perfection is the quality of being as good as it is possible for something of a particular kind to be. ❑ *His quest for perfection is relentless.* **2** The **perfection of** something such as a skill, system, or product involves making it as good as it could possibly be. ❑ *Madame Clicquot is credited with the perfection of this technique.*

per·fect·ly ◆◇◇ /'pɜːfɪktli/ ADV **1** [perfectly + ADJ/ADV] (*emphasis*) You can use **perfectly** to emphasize an adjective or adverb, especially when you think the person you are talking to might doubt what you are saying. = quite ❑ *There's no reason why you can't have a perfectly normal child.* ❑ *You know perfectly well what happened.* **2** [perfectly with V] If something is done **perfectly**, it is done so well that it could not possibly be done better. ❑ *This ambitious adaptation perfectly captures the spirit of Kurt Vonnegut's acclaimed novel.*

✪**per·form** ◆◆◇ /pə'fɔːm/ VERB [T, I] (**performs, performing, performed**) **1** [T] When you **perform** a task or action, especially a complicated one, you do it. ❑ *We're looking for people of all ages who have performed outstanding acts of bravery, kindness, or courage.* ❑ *His council had had to perform miracles on a tiny budget.* ❑ *A robot capable of performing the most complex brain surgery was unveiled by scientists yesterday.* **2** [T] If something **performs** a particular function, it has that function. = carry out, undertake ❑ *An engine has many parts, each performing a different function.* ❑ *Software can be run on a computer to enable it to perform various tasks.* **3** [T] If you **perform** a play, a piece of music, or a dance, you do it in front of an audience. = act, present ❑ *Gardiner has pursued relentlessly high standards in performing classical music.* ❑ *This play was first performed in 411 BC.* ❑ *He began performing in the early fifties, singing and playing guitar.* **4** [I] If someone or something **performs well**, they work well or achieve a good result. If they **perform badly**, they work badly or achieve a poor result. ❑ *He had not performed well in his exams.* ❑ *State-owned industries will always perform poorly.*

✪**per·for·mance** ◆◆◇ /pə'fɔːməns/ NOUN [C, U, SING] (**performances**) **1** [C] A **performance** involves entertaining an audience by doing something such as singing, dancing, or acting. = production, show ❑ *Inside the theatre, they were giving a performance of Bizet's Carmen.* ❑ *her performance as the betrayed Medea* **2** [C, U] Someone's or something's **performance** is how successful they are or how well they do something. ❑ *That study looked at the performance of 18 surgeons.* ❑ *The poor performance has been blamed on the recession and cheaper sports car imports.* ❑ *The job of the new director-general was to ensure that performance targets were met.* **3** [SING] **The performance of** a task is the fact or action of doing it. ❑ *He devoted in excess of seventy hours a week to the performance of his duties.* ❑ *The people believe that the performance of this ritual is the will of the Great Spirit.*

✪**per·form·er** /pə'fɔːmə/ NOUN [C] (**performers**) **1** A **performer** is a person who acts, sings, or does other entertainment in front of audiences. = entertainer, actor, artist ❑ *A performer plays classical selections on the violin.* **2** You can use **performer** when describing someone or something in a way that indicates how well they do a particular thing. ❑ *Until 1987, Canada's industry had been the star performer.*

✪**per·form·ing arts** NOUN [PL] [usu 'the' performing arts] Dance, drama, music, and other forms of entertainment that are usually performed live in front of an audience are referred to as **the performing arts**.

per·fume /'pɜːfjuːm, pə'fjuːm/ NOUN, VERB

NOUN [C, U] (**perfumes**) **1** Perfume is a pleasant-smelling liquid that women put on their skin to make themselves smell nice. = scent ❑ *The hall smelled of her mother's perfume.* ❑ *a bottle of perfume* **2** Perfume is the ingredient that is added to some products to make them smell nice. ❑ *a delicate white soap without perfume*

VERB [T] (**perfumes, perfuming, perfumed**) If something is used to **perfume** a product, it is added to the product to make it smell nice. ❑ *The oil is used to flavour and perfume soaps, foam baths, and scents.*

per·haps ◆◆◆ /pə'hæps, præps/ ADV **1** [perhaps with CL/GROUP] (*vagueness*) You use **perhaps** to express uncertainty, for example, when you do not know that something is definitely true, or when you are mentioning something that may possibly happen in the future in the way you describe. = maybe ❑ *In the end they lose millions, perhaps billions.* ❑ *Perhaps, in time, the message will get through.* **2** [perhaps with CL/GROUP] (*vagueness*) You use **perhaps** in opinions and remarks to make them appear less definite or more polite. ❑ *Perhaps the most important lesson to be learned is that you simply cannot please everyone.* ❑ *His very last paintings are perhaps the most puzzling.* **3** [perhaps with CL] (*politeness*) You use **perhaps** when you are making suggestions or giving advice. **Perhaps** is also used in formal English to introduce requests. ❑ *Perhaps I may be permitted a few suggestions.* ❑ *Well, perhaps you'll come and see us at our place?*

✪**pe·rim·eter** /pə'rɪmɪtə/ NOUN [C] (**perimeters**) The **perimeter** of an area of land is the whole of its outer edge or boundary. = boundary, edge ❑ *the perimeter of the*

p

airport ❑ *Officers dressed in riot gear are surrounding the perimeter fence.*

✪ **pe·ri·od** ◆◆◇ /ˈpɪəriəd/ NOUN, ADJ (*academic word*)

NOUN [C] (**periods**) **1** [usu with SUPP] A **period** is a length of time. = duration, time, spell, while ❑ *This crisis might last for a long period of time.* ❑ *a period of a few months* ❑ *for a limited period only* **2** A **period** in the life of a person, organization, or society is a length of time that is remembered for a particular situation or activity. ❑ *a period of economic good health and expansion* ❑ *He went through a period of wanting to be accepted.* ❑ *The South African years were his most creative period.* **3** A particular length of time in history is sometimes called a **period**. For example, you can talk about **the Civil War period** or the **Prohibition period** in the US ❑ *The novel is set in the Roman period.* ❑ *No reference to their existence appears in any literature of the period.* **4** Exercise, training, or study **periods** are lengths of time that are set aside for exercise, training, or study. ❑ *They accompanied him during his exercise periods.* **5** When a woman has a **period**, she bleeds from her uterus. This usually happens once a month, unless she is pregnant. ❑ *Can you get pregnant if you have sex during your period?*

ADJ [period + N] **Period** costumes, furniture, and instruments were made at an earlier time in history, or look as if they were made then. ❑ *The characters were dressed in full period costume.*

✪ **pe·ri·od·ic** /ˌpɪəriˈɒdɪk/ ADJ (*academic word*) **Periodic** events or situations happen occasionally, at fairly regular intervals. = regular, periodical ❑ *Periodic checks are made to ensure that high standards are maintained.*

✪ **pe·ri·odi·cal** /ˌpɪəriˈɒdɪkəl/ NOUN, ADJ

NOUN [C] (**periodicals**) **Periodicals** are magazines, especially serious or academic ones, that are published at regular intervals. ❑ *The walls would be lined with books and periodicals.*

ADJ **Periodical** events or situations happen occasionally, at fairly regular intervals. = periodic, regular ❑ *She made periodical visits to her dentist.*

✪ **pe·ri·odi·cal·ly** /ˌpɪəriˈɒdɪkli/ ADV [periodically with V] If events or situations happen **periodically**, they happen occasionally, at fairly regular intervals. = regularly ❑ *Meetings are held periodically to monitor progress on the case.*

✪ **pe·ri·od·ic ta·ble** NOUN [SING] [ˈthe' periodic table] In chemistry, **the periodic table** is a table showing the chemical elements arranged according to their atomic numbers. ❑ *The periodic table once predicted the existence of elements that had yet to be discovered.*

pe·riph·er·al /pəˈrɪfərəl/ ADJ, NOUN

ADJ **1** A **peripheral** activity or issue is one that is not very important compared with other activities or issues. ❑ *Companies are increasingly eager to contract out peripheral activities like training.* ❑ *peripheral and boring information* **2** **Peripheral** areas of land are ones that are on the edge of a larger area. ❑ *urban development in the outer peripheral areas of large towns*

NOUN [C] (**peripherals**) (*computing*) **Peripherals** are devices that can be attached to computers. ❑ *peripherals to expand the use of our computers*

per·ish /ˈperɪʃ/ VERB [I] (**perishes, perishing, perished**) (*written*) If people or animals **perish**, they die as a result of very harsh conditions or as the result of an accident. ❑ *Most of the butterflies perish in the first frosts of autumn.*

per·jury /ˈpɜːdʒəri/ NOUN [U] (*legal*) If someone who is giving evidence in a court of law commits **perjury**, they lie. ❑ *This witness has committed perjury and no reliance can be placed on her evidence.*

✪ **perk** /pɜːk/ NOUN

NOUN [C] (**perks**) **Perks** are special benefits that are given to people who have a particular job or belong to a particular group. = advantage, benefit ❑ *a company car, health insurance and other perks* ❑ *One of the perks of being a student is cheap travel.*

PHRASAL VERB **perk up** (**perks, perking, perked**) **1** If something **perks** you **up** or if you **perk up**, you become cheerful and lively, after feeling tired, bored, or depressed.

❑ *He perks up and jokes with them.* **2** If you **perk** something **up**, you make it more interesting. ❑ *To make the bland taste more interesting, the locals began perking it up with local produce.* **3** (*journalism*) If sales, prices, or economies **perk up**, or if something **perks** them **up**, they begin to increase or improve. ❑ *House prices could perk up during the autumn.*

✪ **per·ma·nent** ◆◇◇ /ˈpɜːmənənt/ ADJ **1** Something that is **permanent** lasts forever. = ongoing, lasting; ≠ non-permanent, transient ❑ *Heavy drinking can cause permanent damage to the brain.* ❑ *a permanent solution to the problem* ❑ *The ban is intended to be permanent.* **2** You use **permanent** to describe situations or states that keep occurring or that seem to exist all the time; used especially to describe problems or difficulties. = constant ❑ *a permanent state of tension* ❑ *They feel under permanent threat.* **3** [permanent + N] A **permanent** employee is one who is employed for an unlimited length of time. ❑ *At the end of the probationary period you will become a permanent employee.* ❑ *a permanent job* **4** [permanent + N] Your **permanent** home or your **permanent** address is the one at which you spend most of your time or the one that you return to after having stayed in other places. ❑ *They had no permanent address.*

✪ **per·ma·nent·ly** /ˈpɜːmənəntli/ ADV **1** = forever ❑ *His confidence had been permanently affected by the ordeal.* **2** *the heavy, permanently locked gate* **3** *permanently employed lifeguards*

per·ma·nence /ˈpɜːmənəns/ NOUN [U] ❑ *Anything which threatens the permanence of the treaty is a threat to stability and to peace.*

✪ **per·me·able** /ˈpɜːmiəbəl/ ADJ If a substance is **permeable**, something such as water or gas can pass through it or soak into it. ❑ *A number of products have been developed which are permeable to air and water.* ❑ *Selectively permeable membranes are thought to have tiny pores which allow the rapid passage of small water molecules.*

✪ **per·me·ate** /ˈpɜːmieɪt/ VERB [T] (**permeates, permeating, permeated**) **1** If an idea, feeling, or attitude **permeates** a system or **permeates** society, it affects every part of it or is present throughout it. ❑ *Bias against women permeates every level of the judicial system.* ❑ *An obvious change of attitude at the top will permeate through the system.* **2** If something **permeates** a place, it spreads throughout it. ❑ *The smell of roast beef permeated the air.*

✪ **per·mis·sion** ◆◇◇ /pəˈmɪʃən/ NOUN [U] If someone who has authority over you gives you **permission to** do something, they say that they will allow you to do it. = authorization, consent; ≠ refusal, denial ❑ *He asked permission to leave the room.* ❑ *They cannot leave the country without permission.* ❑ *Police said permission for the march had not been granted.*

✪ **per·mit** ◆◇◇ VERB, NOUN

VERB /pəˈmɪt/ [T, I] (**permits, permitting, permitted**) (*formal*) **1** [T] If someone **permits** something, they allow it to happen. If they **permit** you **to** do something, they allow you to do it. = allow, let; ≠ forbid, prohibit ❑ *He can let the court's decision stand and permit the execution.* ❑ *The guards permitted me to bring my camera and tape recorder.* ❑ *Employees are permitted to use the golf course during their free hours.* ❑ *No outside journalists have been permitted into the country.* **2** [I, T] If a situation **permits** something, it makes it possible for that thing to exist, happen, or be done or it provides the opportunity for it. = allow ❑ *Try to go out for a walk at lunchtime, if the weather permits.* ❑ *This method of cooking also permits heat to penetrate evenly from both sides.*

NOUN /ˈpɜːmɪt/ [C] (**permits**) A **permit** is an official document which says that you may do something. For example, you usually need a **permit** to work in a foreign country. = warrant, licence ❑ *He has to apply for a permit, and we have to find him a job.* ❑ *The majority of foreign nationals working here have work permits.*

✪ **per·pe·trate** /ˈpɜːpɪtreɪt/ VERB [T] (**perpetrates, perpetrating, perpetrated**) (*formal*) If someone **perpetrates** a crime or any other immoral or harmful act, they do it. = commit ❑ *A high proportion of crime in any country is perpetrated by young males in their teens and*

P

twenties. ❏ *Tremendous wrongs were being perpetrated on the poorest and least privileged human beings.*

○**per·pe·tra·tor** /'pɜːpɪtreɪtə/ NOUN [c] (**perpetrators**) = **culprit** ❏ *The perpetrator of the crime does not have to be traced before you can claim compensation.*

per·pet·ual /pə'petʃuəl/ ADJ **1** A **perpetual** feeling, state, or quality is one that never ends or changes. = **permanent** ❏ *the creation of a perpetual union* **2** A **perpetual** act, situation, or state is one that happens again and again and so seems never to end. = **continual** ❏ *I thought her perpetual complaints were going to prove too much for me.*
per·pet·ual·ly /pə'petʃuəli/ ADV **1** = **permanently** ❏ *They were all perpetually starving.* **2** *He perpetually interferes in political affairs.*

per·petu·ate /pə'petʃueɪt/ VERB [T] (**perpetuates, perpetuating, perpetuated**) If someone or something **perpetuates** a situation, system, or belief, especially a bad one, they cause it to continue. ❏ *We must not perpetuate the religious divisions of the past.*

per·plex /pə'pleks/ VERB [T] (**perplexes, perplexing, perplexed**) If something **perplexes** you, it confuses and worries you because you do not understand it or because it causes you difficulty. ❏ *It perplexed him because he was tackling it the wrong way.*

per·plexed /pə'plekst/ ADJ If you are **perplexed**, you feel confused and slightly worried by something because you do not understand it. ❏ *She is perplexed about what to do for her daughter.*

per·secute /'pɜːsɪkjuːt/ VERB [T] (**persecutes, persecuting, persecuted**) If someone **is persecuted**, they are treated cruelly and unfairly, often because of their race or beliefs. ❏ *Mr Weaver and his family have been persecuted by the authorities for their beliefs.* ❏ *They began by brutally persecuting the Catholic Church.*

per·secu·tion /ˌpɜːsɪ'kjuːʃən/ NOUN [u] **Persecution** is cruel and unfair treatment of a person or group, especially because of their religious or political beliefs, or their race. ❏ *the persecution of minorities* ❏ *victims of political persecution*

per·sever·ance /ˌpɜːsɪ'vɪərəns/ NOUN [u] **Perseverance** is the quality of continuing with something even though it is difficult. = **persistence** ❏ *He has never stopped trying and showed great perseverance.*

per·severe /ˌpɜːsɪ'vɪə/ VERB [i] (**perseveres, persevering, persevered**) If you **persevere with** something, you keep trying to do it and do not give up, even though it is difficult. = **persist** ❏ *This ability to persevere despite obstacles and setbacks is the quality people most admire in others.* ❏ *a school with a reputation for persevering with difficult and disruptive children*

○**per·sist** /pə'sɪst/ VERB [i] (**persists, persisting, persisted**) (*academic word*) **1** If something undesirable **persists**, it continues to exist. = **continue, exist, endure** ❏ *Contact your doctor if the cough persists.* ❏ *These problems persisted for much of the decade.* ❏ *The ceremony still persists in some parishes.* **2** If you **persist in** doing something, you continue to do it, even though it is difficult or other people are against it. ❏ *Why do people persist in begging for money in the street?* ❏ *He urged the United States to persist with its efforts to bring about peace.*

per·sis·tence /pə'sɪstəns/ NOUN [u] **1** If you have **persistence**, you continue to do something even though it is difficult or other people are against it. = **perseverance** ❏ *Skill comes only with practice, patience, and persistence.* **2** The **persistence of** something, especially something bad, is the fact of it continuing to exist for a long time. ❏ *an expression of concern at the persistence of inflation and high interest rates*

○**per·sis·tent** /pə'sɪstənt/ ADJ **1** Something that is **persistent** continues to exist or happen for a long time; used especially about bad or undesirable states or situations. = **continuous, constant, relentless, perpetual, incessant** ❏ *Her position as national leader has been weakened by persistent fears of another coup attempt.* ❏ *His cough grew more persistent until it never stopped.* ❏ *The public has to be reassured that children are safe from persistent*

predatory offenders. **2** Someone who is **persistent** continues trying to do something, even though it is difficult or other people are against it. ❏ *a persistent critic of the president*

persistent ADJ
Something that is **persistent** continues to exist or happen for a long time; used especially about bad or undesirable states or situations.
❏ *The main economic, social and political problem in Europe is high and persistent unemployment.*

continuous ADJ
A **continuous** process or event continues for a period of time without stopping.
❏ *Residents report that they heard continuous gunfire.*

constant ADJ (*often formal*)
You use **constant** to describe something that happens all the time or is always there.
❏ *Inflation is a constant threat.*

relentless ADJ (*formal*)
Something bad that is **relentless** never stops or never becomes less intense.
❏ *The pressure now was relentless.*

perpetual ADJ (*mainly written*)
A **perpetual** act, situation, or state is one that happens again and again and so seems never to end.
❏ *I thought her perpetual complaints were going to prove too much for me.*

○**per·sis·tent·ly** /pə'sɪstəntli/ ADV **1** If something happens **persistently**, it happens again and again or for a long time. ❏ *The allegations have been persistently denied by ministers.* ❏ *People with rail season tickets will get refunds if trains are persistently late.* **2** [persistently with v] If someone does something **persistently**, they do it with determination even though it is difficult or other people are against it. ❏ *Rachel gently but persistently imposed her will on Doug.*

per·son ◆◆◆ /'pɜːsən/ NOUN

The usual word for 'more than one person' is **people**. The form **persons** is used as the plural in formal or legal language.

NOUN [c, PL] (**people** or **persons**) **1** [c] A **person** is a man, woman, or child. ❏ *At least one person died and several others were injured.* ❏ *They were both lovely, friendly people.* **2** [PL] **Persons** is used as the plural of **person** in formal, legal, and technical writing. ❏ *removal of the right of accused persons to remain silent* **3** [c] If you talk about someone **as a person**, you are considering them from the point of view of their real nature. ❏ *Robin didn't feel good about herself as a person.* **4** [c] (*formal*) Your **person** is your body. ❏ *The suspect had refused to give any details of his identity and had carried no documents on his person.* **5** [c] In grammar, we use the term **first person** when referring to 'I' and 'we', **second person** when referring to 'you', and **third person** when referring to 'he', 'she', 'it', 'they', and all other noun groups. **Person** is also used like this when referring to the verb forms that go with these pronouns and noun groups.

PHRASE **in person 1** If you do something **in person**, you do it yourself rather than letting someone else do it for you. ❏ *You must collect the post in person and take along some form of identification.* **2** If you meet, hear, or see someone **in person**, you are in the same place as them, rather than, for example, speaking to them on the telephone, writing to them, or seeing them on television. ❏ *It was the first time she had seen him in person.*

○**per·son·al** ◆◆◇ /'pɜːsənəl/ ADJ **1** [personal + N] A **personal** opinion, quality, or thing belongs or relates to one particular person rather than to other people. ❏ *He learned this lesson the hard way – from his own personal*

p

experience. ❏ *That's my personal opinion.* ❏ *books, furniture, and other personal belongings* **2** If you give something your **personal** care or attention, you deal with it yourself rather than letting someone else deal with it. ❏ *a business that requires a lot of personal contact* ❏ *a personal letter from the president's secretary* **3 Personal** matters relate to your feelings, relationships, and health. = private, individual; ≠ public ❏ *teaching young people about marriage and personal relationships* ❏ *You never allow personal problems to affect your performance.* ❏ *Mr Knight said that he had resigned for personal reasons.* **4 Personal** comments refer to someone's appearance or character in an offensive way. ❏ *Newspapers resorted to personal abuse.* **5** [personal + N] **Personal** care involves taking care of your body and appearance. ❏ *the new breed of men who take as much time and trouble over personal hygiene as the women in their lives* **6** A **personal** relationship is one that is not connected with your job or public life. ❏ *He was a great and valued personal friend whom I've known for many years.* **7** [personal + N] If someone has a **personal** shopper or a **personal** trainer, they employ another person to shop for them or to help them keep fit. ❏ *Another way of escaping the crowds and the changing rooms is to employ a personal shopper.* ❏ *The best clubs also offer personal trainers to help motivate and ensure that exercises are properly performed.*

per·son·al com·put·er NOUN [c] (**personal computers**) A **personal computer** is a computer that is used by one person at a time in a business, a school, or at home. The abbreviation **PC** is also used.

✪ per·son·al·ity ♦◇◇ /ˌpɜːsəˈnælɪti/ NOUN [c, u] (**personalities**) **1** [c, u] Your **personality** is your whole character and nature. = temperament, character ❏ *She has such a kind, friendly personality.* ❏ *The contest was as much about personalities as it was about politics.* ❏ *These personality traits get passed on from generation to generation.* **2** [c, u] If someone has **personality** or is **a personality**, they have a strong and lively character. = character ❏ *a woman of great personality* **3** [c] You can refer to a famous person, especially in entertainment, broadcasting, or sports, as a **personality**. ❏ *the radio and television personality, Johnny Carson*

per·son·al·ly ♦◇◇ /ˈpɜːsənəli/ ADV **1** [personally with CL] (*emphasis*) You use **personally** to emphasize that you are giving your own opinion. ❏ *Personally I think it's a waste of time.* ❏ *You can disagree about them, and I personally do, but they are great ideas that have made people think.* **2** [personally with V] If you do something **personally**, you do it yourself rather than letting someone else do it. ❏ *He is returning to Paris to answer the allegations personally.* ❏ *When the great man arrived, the club's manager personally escorted him upstairs.* **3** [personally with V] If you meet or know someone **personally**, you meet or know them in real life, rather than knowing about them or knowing their work. ❏ *He did not know them personally, but he was familiar with their reputation.* **4** You can use **personally** to say that something refers to an individual person rather than to other people. ❏ *He was personally responsible for all that people suffered under his rule.* **5** You can use **personally** to show that you are talking about someone's private life rather than their professional or public life. ❏ *This has taken a great toll on me personally and professionally.* PHRASE **take something personally** If you **take** someone's remarks **personally**, you are upset because you think that they are criticizing you in particular. ❏ *I take everything too personally.*

per·son·nel ♦◇◇ /ˌpɜːsəˈnel/ NOUN [PL, u] **1** [PL] The **personnel** of an organization are the people who work for it. = staff ❏ *Since 1954 Japan has never dispatched military personnel abroad.* ❏ *There has been very little renewal of personnel in higher education.* **2** [u] (*old-fashioned, business*) **Personnel** is the department in a large company or organization that deals with employees, keeps their records, and helps with any problems they might have. = human resources ❏ *Her first job was in personnel.*

✪ per·spec·tive ♦◇◇ /pəˈspektɪv/ NOUN (*academic word*)
NOUN [c] (**perspectives**) A particular **perspective** is a

particular way of thinking about something, especially one that is influenced by your beliefs or experiences. = viewpoint, position ❏ *He says the death of his father 18 months ago has given him a new perspective on life.* ❏ *two different perspectives on the nature of adolescent development* ❏ *Most literature on the subject of immigrants in France has been written from the perspective of the French themselves.* ❏ *I would like to offer a historical perspective.*
PHRASE **in perspective** or **into perspective** or **out of perspective** If you get something **in perspective** or **into perspective**, you judge its real importance by considering it in relation to everything else. If you get something **out of perspective**, you fail to judge its real importance in relation to everything else. ❏ *Remember to keep things in perspective.* ❏ *I let things get out of perspective.*

per·spi·ra·tion /ˌpɜːspɪˈreɪʃən/ NOUN [u] (*formal*) **Perspiration** is the liquid that comes out on the surface of your skin when you are hot or frightened. = sweat ❏ *His hands were wet with perspiration.*

✪ per·suade ♦◇◇ /pəˈsweɪd/ VERB [T] (**persuades, persuading, persuaded**) **1** If you **persuade** someone **to** do something, you cause them to do it by giving them good reasons for doing it. = convince, cajole, urge; ≠ dissuade ❏ *My husband persuaded me to come.* ❏ *We're trying to persuade manufacturers to sell them here.* **2** If something **persuades** someone **to** take a particular course of action, it causes them to take that course of action because it is a good reason for doing so. ❏ *It was the lack of privacy that eventually persuaded us to move after Ben was born.* **3** If you **persuade** someone that something is true, you say things that eventually make them believe that it is true. = convince ❏ *I've persuaded Mrs Tennant that it's time she retired.* ❏ *We had managed to persuade them that it was worth working with us.*

✪ per·sua·sion /pəˈsweɪʒən/ NOUN [u, c] (**persuasions**) **1** [u] **Persuasion** is the act of persuading someone to do something or to believe that something is true. = influence ❏ *Only after much persuasion from Ellis had she agreed to hold a show at all.* ❏ *Mr Gorbachev needed more persuasion to abandon Soviet plans.* ❏ *She was using all her powers of persuasion to induce the Griffins to remain in Rollway.* **2** [c] (*formal*) If you are of a particular **persuasion**, you have a particular belief or set of beliefs. ❏ *It is a national movement and has within it people of all political persuasions.*

✪ per·sua·sive /pəˈsweɪsɪv/ ADJ Someone or something that is **persuasive** is likely to persuade a person to believe or do a particular thing. = compelling, convincing, influential; ≠ ineffective, unconvincing ❏ *What do you think were some of the more persuasive arguments on the other side?* ❏ *I can be very persuasive when I want to be.*
per·sua·sive·ly /pəˈsweɪsɪvli/ ADV [persuasively with V] ❏ *a trained lawyer who can present arguments persuasively*

per·ti·nent /ˈpɜːtɪnənt/ ADJ (*formal*) Something that is **pertinent** is relevant to a particular subject. ❏ *She had asked some pertinent questions.* ❏ *name, address, and other pertinent information*

per·vade /pəˈveɪd/ VERB [T] (**pervades, pervading, pervaded**) (*formal*) If something **pervades** a place or thing, it is a noticeable feature throughout it. ❏ *The smell of sawdust and glue pervaded the factory.*

✪ per·va·sive /pəˈveɪsɪv/ ADJ (*formal*) Something, especially something bad, that is **pervasive** is present or felt throughout a place or thing. ❏ *the pervasive influence of the army in national life*

pes·si·mism /ˈpesɪmɪzəm/ NOUN [u] **Pessimism** is the belief that bad things are going to happen. ❏ *universal pessimism about the economy*

pes·si·mist /ˈpesɪmɪst/ NOUN [c] (**pessimists**) A **pessimist** is someone who thinks that bad things are going to happen. ❏ *I'm a natural pessimist; I usually expect the worst.*

pes·si·mis·tic /ˌpesɪˈmɪstɪk/ ADJ Someone who is **pessimistic** thinks that bad things are going to happen. ❏ *Not everyone is so pessimistic about the future.* ❏ *Hardy has often been criticized for an excessively pessimistic view of life.*

pest /pest/ NOUN [c] (**pests**) **1 Pests** are insects or small animals that damage crops or food supplies. ❑ *crops which are resistant to some of the major insect pests and diseases* ❑ *Each year ten per cent of the crop is lost to a pest called corn rootworm.* **2** (*informal, disapproval*) You can describe someone, especially a child, as a **pest** if they keep bothering you. = nuisance ❑ *He climbed on the table, pulled my hair, and was generally a pest.*

pes·ter /ˈpestə/ VERB [T] (**pesters, pestering, pestered**) (*disapproval*) If you say that someone **is pestering** you, you mean that they keep asking you to do something, or keep talking to you, and you find this annoying. ❑ *I thought she'd stop pestering me, but it only seemed to make her worse.* ❑ *I know he gets fed up with people pestering him for money.*

✪ **pes·ti·cide** /ˈpestɪsaɪd/ NOUN [C, U] (**pesticides**) **Pesticides** are chemicals that farmers put on their crops to kill harmful insects. ❑ *Many environmental activists and food experts are keen to ban pesticides from British farming.*

pet ♦◊◊ /pet/ NOUN, ADJ, VERB

NOUN [C] (**pets**) A **pet** is an animal that you keep in your home to give you company and pleasure. ❑ *It is plainly cruel to keep turtles as pets.* ❑ *a bachelor living alone in a house with his pet dog*

ADJ Someone's **pet** theory, project, or subject is one that they particularly support or like. ❑ *He would not stand by and let his pet project be killed off.*

VERB [T] (**pets, petting, petted**) If you **pet** a person or animal, you touch them in an affectionate way. ❑ *The policeman reached down and petted the wolfhound.*

pe·ti·tion /pəˈtɪʃən/ NOUN, VERB

NOUN [C] (**petitions**) **1** A **petition** is a document signed by a lot of people that asks a government or other official group to do a particular thing. ❑ *People feel so strongly that we recently presented the government with a petition signed by 4,500 people.* **2** (*legal*) A **petition** is a formal request made to a court of law for some legal action to be taken. ❑ *His lawyers filed a petition for all charges to be dropped.*

VERB [I, T] (**petitions, petitioning, petitioned**) (*legal*) If you **petition** someone in authority, you make a formal request to them. ❑ *couples petitioning for divorce* ❑ *All the attempts to petition Congress had failed.*

✪ **Petri dish** /ˈpiːtri dɪʃ/ NOUN [C] (**Petri dishes**) (*technical*) A **Petri dish** is a shallow circular dish that is used in laboratories for producing groups of microorganisms. ❑ *The embryos are placed in Petri dishes which have tags attached to the bottom.*

pet·rol /ˈpetrəl/ NOUN [U] **Petrol** is the fuel that is used to power motor vehicles. ❑ *The price of petrol is due to rise again at the end of the month.*

pe·tro·leum /pəˈtrəʊliəm/ NOUN [U] **Petroleum** is oil that is found under the surface of the earth or under the sea bed. Petrol and kerosene are obtained from petroleum.

pet·ty /ˈpeti/ ADJ (**pettier, pettiest**) **1** (*disapproval*) You can use **petty** to describe things such as problems, rules, or arguments that you think are unimportant or relate to unimportant things. ❑ *He was miserable all the time and fights would start over petty things.* ❑ *endless rules and petty regulations* **2** (*disapproval*) If you describe someone's behaviour as **petty**, you mean that they care too much about small, unimportant things and perhaps that they are unnecessarily unkind. ❑ *He was petty-minded and obsessed with detail.* **3** [petty + N] **Petty** is used of people or actions that are less important, serious, or great than others. ❑ *petty crime, such as bag-snatching and minor break-ins*
pet·ti·ness /ˈpetinəs/ NOUN [U] ❑ *Never had she met such spite and pettiness.*

✪ **phar·ma·ceu·ti·cal** /ˌfɑːməˈsuːtɪkəl/ ADJ, NOUN
ADJ [pharmaceutical + N] **Pharmaceutical** means connected with the industrial production of medicines. ❑ *a Swiss pharmaceutical company* ❑ *The pharmaceutical industry is the second-largest industry in the world.*
NOUN [PL] (**pharmaceuticals**) **Pharmaceuticals** are medicines. ❑ *Antibiotics were of no use, neither were other pharmaceuticals.*

phar·ma·cist /ˈfɑːməsɪst/ NOUN [C] (**pharmacists**) A **pharmacist** is a person who is qualified to prepare and sell medicines. ❑ *Ask your pharmacist for advice.*

✪ **phar·ma·col·ogy** /ˌfɑːməˈkɒlədʒi/ NOUN [U] **Pharmacology** is the branch of science relating to drugs and medicines. ❑ *Their eldest daughter studied pharmacology and English at London University before becoming a fashion journalist.* ❑ *He was appointed professor of clinical pharmacology in Aberdeen in 1985.*
✪ **phar·ma·co·logi·cal** /ˌfɑːməkəˈlɒdʒɪkəl/ ADJ [pharmacological + N] ❑ *As little as 50 mg of caffeine can produce pharmacological effects.* ❑ *Pharmacological treatment of schizophrenia and related psychoses is usually for the long-term.*
✪ **phar·ma·colo·gist** /ˌfɑːməˈkɒlədʒɪst/ NOUN [C] (**pharmacologists**) ❑ *a pharmacologist from the University of California* ❑ *This clinical pharmacologist says there's no biological reason why antibiotics should cause cancer.*

✪ **phase** ♦◊◊ /feɪz/ NOUN (*academic word*)
NOUN [C] (**phases**) A **phase** is a particular stage in a process or in the gradual development of something. = stage, period ❑ *This autumn, 6,000 residents will participate in the first phase of the project.* ❑ *The crisis is entering a crucial, critical phase.*
PHRASAL VERBS **phase in** (**phases, phasing, phased**) If a new way of doing something **is phased in**, it is introduced gradually. ❑ *The reforms would be phased in over three years.*
phase out If something **is phased out**, people gradually stop using it. ❑ *They said the present system of military conscription should be phased out.*

✪ **PhD** /ˌpiː eɪtʃ ˈdiː/ also **Ph.D.** NOUN [C] (**PhDs**) **1** A **PhD** is a degree awarded to people who have done advanced research into a particular subject. **PhD** is an abbreviation for **Doctor of Philosophy**. = doctorate ❑ *He is more highly educated, with a PhD in chemistry.* ❑ *an unpublished PhD thesis* **2** **PhD** is written after someone's name to indicate that they have a PhD. ❑ *R.D. Combes, PhD*

phe·nom·enal /fɪˈnɒmɪnəl/ ADJ (*emphasis*) Something that is **phenomenal** is unusually great or good. = incredible ❑ *Exports of Australian wine are growing at a phenomenal rate.*
phe·nom·enal·ly /fɪˈnɒmɪnəli/ ADV ❑ *Annie, 37, has recently re-launched her phenomenally successful singing career.*

✪ **phe·nom·enon** /fɪˈnɒmɪnən, AmE -nɑːn/ NOUN [C] (**phenomena**) (*academic word, formal*) A **phenomenon** is something that is observed to happen or exist. ❑ *scientific explanations of natural phenomena*

✪ **phi·loso·pher** /fɪˈlɒsəfə/ NOUN [C] (**philosophers**) **1** A **philosopher** is a person who studies or writes about philosophy. ❑ *the Greek philosopher Plato* ❑ *However, many philosophers have argued that freedom is an illusion.* **2** If you refer to someone as a **philosopher**, you mean that they think deeply and seriously about life and other basic matters. ❑ *Carlos was something of a philosopher.*

philo·sophi·cal /ˌfɪləˈsɒfɪkəl/ ADJ **1** **Philosophical** means concerned with or relating to philosophy. ❑ *He was more accustomed to cocktail party chatter than to political or philosophical discussions.* **2** Someone who is **philosophical** does not get upset when disappointing or disturbing things happen. ❑ *Lewis has grown philosophical about life.*
philo·sophi·cal·ly /ˌfɪləˈsɒfɪkli/ ADV **1** ❑ *Wilbur says he's not a coward, but that he's philosophically opposed to war.* **2** [philosophically after V] ❑ *She says philosophically, 'It could have been far worse.'*

✪ **phi·loso·phy** ♦◊◊ /fɪˈlɒsəfi/ NOUN [U, C] (**philosophies**) (*academic word*) **1** [U] **Philosophy** is the study or creation of theories about basic things such as the nature of existence, knowledge, and thought, or about how people should live. ❑ *He studied philosophy and psychology at Yale.* ❑ *traditional Chinese philosophy* **2** [C] A **philosophy** is a particular set of ideas that a philosopher has. ❑ *the philosophies of Socrates, Plato, and Aristotle* **3** [C] A **philosophy** is a particular theory that someone has about how to live or how to deal with a particular situation. ❑ *The best philosophy is to change your food habits to a low-sugar diet.*

pho·bia /ˈfəʊbiə/ NOUN [C] (**phobias**) A **phobia** is a very strong irrational fear or hatred of something. ❑ *The man had a phobia about flying.*

phone ♦♦◇ /fəʊn/ NOUN, VERB

NOUN [SING, c] (**phones**) **1** [SING] [usu 'the' phone, also 'by' phone] The **phone** is an electrical system that you use to talk to someone else in another place, by dialling a number on a piece of equipment and speaking into it. = telephone □ *'I didn't tell you over the phone', she said. 'I didn't know who might be listening.'* □ *She looked forward to talking to her daughter by phone.* **2** [c] The **phone** is the piece of equipment that you use when you dial someone's phone number and talk to them. = telephone □ *Two minutes later the phone rang.* **3** [SING] If you say that someone picks up or puts down **the phone**, you mean that they lift or replace the receiver. = receiver □ *She picked up the phone, and began to dial Maurice's number.*

PHRASE **on the phone** If you say that someone is **on the phone**, you mean that they are speaking to someone by phone. □ *She's always on the phone, wanting to know what I've been up to.*

VERB [I, T] (**phones, phoning, phoned**) When you **phone** someone, you dial their phone number and speak to them by phone. = telephone □ *He'd phoned Laura to see if she was better.*

PHRASAL VERBS **phone in** **1** If you **phone in** to a radio or television show, you telephone the show in order to give your opinion on a matter that the show has raised. □ *Listeners have been invited to phone in to pick the winner.* **2** If you **phone in** to a place, you make a telephone call to that place. □ *He has phoned in to say he is thinking over his options.* **3** If you **phone in** an order for something, you place the order by telephone. □ *Just phone in your order three or more days prior to departure.*

phone up When you **phone** someone **up**, you dial their phone number and speak to them by phone. □ *Phone him up and tell him to come and have dinner with you one night.*

phone call NOUN [c] (**phone calls**) If you make a **phone call**, you dial someone's phone number and speak to them by phone. □ *Wait there for a minute. I have to make a phone call.*

pho·to ♦♦♦ /ˈfəʊtəʊ/ NOUN [c] (**photos**) A **photo** is the same as a **photograph**. □ *Let's take a photo!*

photo·copy /ˈfəʊtəʊkɒpi/ NOUN, VERB

NOUN [c] (**photocopies**) A **photocopy** is a copy of a document made using a photocopier. □ *He was shown a photocopy of the certificate.*

VERB [T] (**photocopies, photocopying, photocopied**) If you **photocopy** a document, you make a copy of it using a photocopier. □ *Staff photocopied the cheque before cashing it.*

WORD PARTS

The prefix **photo-** often appears in words for things that involve light:

photocopy (NOUN)

photograph (NOUN)

photosynthesis (NOUN)

---

photo·graph ♦♦◇ /ˈfəʊtəɡrɑːf, -ɡræf/ NOUN, VERB

NOUN [c] (**photographs**) A **photograph** is a picture that is made using a camera. □ *He wants to take some photographs of the house.*

VERB [T] (**photographs, photographing, photographed**) (*formal*) When you **photograph** someone or something, you use a camera to obtain a picture of them. □ *She photographed the children.* □ *I hate being photographed.*

pho·tog·ra·pher ♦◇◇ /fəˈtɒɡrəfə/ NOUN [c] (**photographers**) A **photographer** is someone who takes photographs as a job or hobby. □ *a professional photographer* □ *an amateur photographer*

photo·graph·ic /ˌfəʊtəˈɡræfɪk/ ADJ **1** **Photographic** means connected with photographs or photography. □ *photographic equipment* **2** If you have a **photographic memory**, you are able to remember things in great detail after you have seen them. □ *He had a photographic memory for maps.*

pho·tog·ra·phy /fəˈtɒɡrəfi/ NOUN [u] **Photography** is the skill, job, or process of producing photographs. □ *Photography is one of her hobbies.*

○**photo·syn·the·sis** /ˌfəʊtəʊˈsɪnθəsɪs/ NOUN [u] (*technical*) **Photosynthesis** is the way that green plants make their food using sunlight. □ *Chloroplasts contain the green pigment chlorophyll and photosynthesis occurs in them.*

phrase ♦◇◇ /freɪz/ NOUN, VERB

NOUN [c] (**phrases**) **1** A **phrase** is a short group of words that people often use as a way of saying something. The meaning of a phrase is often not obvious from the meaning of the individual words in it. □ *He used a phrase I hate: 'You have to be cruel to be kind.'* **2** A **phrase** is a small group of words that forms a unit, either on its own or within a sentence. □ *A writer spends many hours going over and over a scene – changing a phrase here, a word there.*

PHRASE **turn of phrase** If someone has a particular **turn of phrase**, they have a particular way of expressing themselves in words. □ *Schwarzkopf's distinctive turn of phrase*

VERB [T] (**phrases, phrasing, phrased**) If you **phrase** something in a particular way, you express it in words in that way. □ *I would have phrased it quite differently.* □ *The speech was carefully phrased.*

✦ coin a phrase → see coin

○**physi·cal** ♦♦◇ /ˈfɪzɪkəl/ ADJ, NOUN (*academic word*)

ADJ **1** **Physical** qualities, actions, or things are connected with a person's body, rather than with their mind. □ *the physical and mental problems caused by the illness* □ *Physical activity promotes good health.* **2** **Physical** things are real things that can be touched and seen, rather than ideas or spoken words. □ *Physical and ideological barriers had come down in Eastern Europe.* □ *physical evidence to support the story* **3** [physical + N] **Physical** means relating to the structure, size, or shape of something that can be touched and seen. □ *the physical characteristics of the terrain* **4** [physical + N] **Physical** means connected with physics or the laws of physics. □ *the physical laws of combustion and thermodynamics* **5** Someone who is **physical** touches people a lot, either in an affectionate way or in a rough way. □ *We decided that in the game we would be physical and aggressive.* **6** [physical + N] **Physical** is used in expressions such as **physical love** and **physical relationships** to refer to sexual relationships between people. □ *It had been years since they had shared any meaningful form of physical relationship.*

NOUN [c] (**physicals**) A **physical** is a medical examination by your doctor to make sure that there is nothing wrong with your health, or a medical examination to make sure you are fit enough to do a particular job. = medical □ *Bob failed his physical.*

○**physi·cal·ly** /ˈfɪzɪkli/ ADV **1** = bodily; ≠ mentally, emotionally, psychologically □ *You may be physically and mentally exhausted after a long flight.* □ *disabled people who cannot physically use a telephone* **2** *physically cut off from every other country*

phy·si·cian /fɪˈzɪʃən/ NOUN [c] (**physicians**) (*formal*) A **physician** is a medical doctor. □ *your family physician*

○**physi·cist** /ˈfɪzɪsɪst/ NOUN [c] (**physicists**) A **physicist** is a person who does research connected with physics or who studies physics. □ *a nuclear physicist* □ *types of sub-atomic particle discovered by physicists*

○**phys·ics** /ˈfɪzɪks/ NOUN [u] **Physics** is the scientific study of forces such as heat, light, sound, pressure, gravity, and electricity, and the way that they affect objects. □ *the laws of physics* □ *experiments in particle physics*

○**physio·thera·py** /ˌfɪziəʊˈθerəpi/ NOUN [u] **Physiotherapy** is medical treatment for problems of the joints, muscles, or nerves, which involves doing exercises or having part of your body massaged or warmed. □ *He'll need intensive physiotherapy.*

○**physio·thera·pist** /ˌfɪziəʊˈθerəpɪst/ NOUN [c] (**physiotherapists**) **1** Chartered physiotherapists are trained to degree level which is followed by two years experience in an NHS hospital. □ *Disabling conditions such as cerebral palsy and Parkinson's disease are treated by physiotherapists.*

phy·sique /fɪˈziːk/ NOUN [c] (**physiques**) Someone's **physique** is the shape and size of their body. = build □ *He has the physique and energy of a man half his age.*

P

pi·ano /pi'ænəʊ/ NOUN [C, U] (**pianos**) A **piano** is a large musical instrument with a row of black and white keys. When you press these keys with your fingers, little hammers hit wire strings inside the piano which vibrate to produce musical notes. ❑ *I taught myself how to play the piano.* ❑ *He started piano lessons at the age of 7.*

pick ◆◆◇ /pɪk/ VERB, NOUN

VERB [T] (**picks, picking, picked**) **1** If you **pick** a particular person or thing, you choose that one. ❑ *Mr Nowell had picked ten people to interview for six sales jobs in Dallas.* **2** When you **pick** flowers, fruit, or leaves, you break them off the plant or tree and collect them. ❑ *She used to pick flowers in the Adirondacks.* **3** If you **pick** something from a place, you remove it from there with your fingers or your hand. ❑ *He picked the napkin from his lap and placed it alongside his plate.* **4** If you **pick** your **nose** or **teeth**, you remove substances from inside your nose or between your teeth. ❑ *Edgar, don't pick your nose, dear.* **5** If you **pick** a fight **with** someone, you deliberately cause one. ❑ *He picked a fight with a waiter and landed in jail.* **6** If someone such as a thief **picks** a lock, they open it without a key, for example, by using a piece of wire. ❑ *He picked each lock deftly, and rifled the papers within each drawer.*
PHRASE **pick up speed** When a vehicle **picks up speed**, it begins to move more quickly. = accelerate ❑ *Brian started the engine and pulled away slowly, but picked up speed once he entered Oakwood Drive.*
PHRASAL VERBS **pick on** (*informal*) If someone **picks on** you, they repeatedly criticize you unfairly or treat you unkindly. ❑ *Bullies pick on younger children.*
pick out **1** If you **pick out** someone or something, you recognize them when it is difficult to see them, for example, because they are among a large group. ❑ *The detective picked out the words with difficulty.* **2** If you **pick out** someone or something, you choose them from a group of people or things. = select ❑ *I have been picked out to represent the whole team.*
pick up **1** When you **pick** something **up**, you lift it up. ❑ *He picked his cap up from the floor and stuck it back on his head.* **2** When you **pick yourself up** after you have fallen or been knocked down, you stand up rather slowly. ❑ *Tony picked himself up and set off along the track.* **3** When you **pick up** someone or something that is waiting to be collected, you go to the place where they are and take them away, often in a car. ❑ *She was going over to her parents' house to pick up some clean clothes for Oskar.* **4** If someone **is picked up** by the police, they are arrested and taken to a police station. ❑ *Rawlings had been picked up by police at his office.* **5** (*informal*) If you **pick up** something such as a skill or an idea, you acquire it without effort over a period of time. ❑ *Where did you pick up your English?* **6** (*informal*) If you **pick up** someone you do not know, you talk to them and try to start a sexual relationship with them. ❑ *He had picked her up at a nightclub, where she worked as a singer.* **7** If you **pick up** an illness, you get it from somewhere or something. = catch ❑ *They've picked up a really nasty infection from something they've eaten.* **8** If a piece of equipment, for example, a radio or a microphone, **picks up** a signal or sound, it receives it or detects it. ❑ *We can pick up Mexican television.* **9** If you **pick up** something, such as a feature or a pattern, you discover or identify it. ❑ *Some groups of consumers are slow to pick up trends in the use of information technology.* **10** If someone **picks up** a point or topic that has already been mentioned, or if they **pick up on** it, they refer to it or develop it. ❑ *Can I just pick up that guy's point?* **11** If trade or the economy of a country **picks up**, it improves. ❑ *Industrial production is beginning to pick up.* **12** → See also **pickup**
NOUN [SING, C] (**picks**) **1** [SING] You can refer to the best things or people in a particular group as **the pick of** that group. ❑ *The boys here are the pick of the high school's soccer players.* **2** [C] A **pick** is a large tool consisting of a curved, pointed piece of metal with a long handle joined to the middle. Picks are used for breaking up rocks or the ground.
PHRASE **take one's pick** If you are told to **take** your **pick**, you can choose any one that you like from a group of things. ❑ *Accountants can take their pick of company cars.*
✦ **pick holes in something** → see **hole**; **pick someone's pocket** → see **pocket**

pick·et /'pɪkɪt/ VERB, NOUN

VERB [I, T] (**pickets, picketing, picketed**) When a group of people, usually trade union members, **picket**, or **picket** a place of work, they stand outside it in order to protest about something, to prevent people from going in, or to persuade the workers to join a strike. ❑ *A few dozen employees picketed the company's headquarters.*
NOUN [C] (**pickets**) **1** A **picket** is when a group of people, usually trade union members, stand outside a place of work to protest about something, to stop people from going in, or to persuade workers to join a strike. ❑ *forty demonstrators who have set up a twenty-four hour picket* **2** **Pickets** are people who are picketing a place of work. ❑ *The strikers agreed to remove their pickets and hold talks with the company.*

pick·et line NOUN [C] (**picket lines**) A **picket line** is a group of pickets outside a place of work. ❑ *No one tried to cross the picket lines.*

pick·up ◆◇◇ /'pɪkʌp/ NOUN [C, SING] (**pickups**) **1** [C] A **pickup** or a **pickup truck** is a small truck with low sides that can be easily loaded and unloaded. **2** [SING] A **pickup in** trade or **in** a country's economy is an improvement in it. ❑ *a pickup in the housing market* **3** [C] A **pickup** takes place when someone picks up a person or thing that is waiting to be collected. ❑ *The company had pickup points in most cities.*

pic·nic /'pɪknɪk/ NOUN, VERB

NOUN [C] (**picnics**) When people have a **picnic**, they eat a meal outdoors, usually in a park or a forest, or at the beach. ❑ *We're going on a picnic tomorrow.*
VERB [I] (**picnics, picnicking, picnicked**) When people **picnic** somewhere, they have a picnic. ❑ *Afterwards, we picnicked on the riverbank.*

pic·ture ◆◆◇ /'pɪktʃə/ NOUN, VERB

NOUN [C, SING] (**pictures**) **1** [C] A **picture** consists of lines and shapes that are drawn, painted, or printed on a surface and show a person, thing, or scene. ❑ *drawing a small picture with coloured chalk* **2** [C] A **picture** is a photograph. ❑ *The tourists have nothing to do but take pictures of each other.* **3** [C] Television **pictures** are the scenes that you see on a television screen. ❑ *heartrending television pictures of human suffering* **4** [C] You can refer to a film as a **picture**. ❑ *a director of epic action pictures* **5** [C] If you have a **picture** of something in your mind, you have a clear idea or memory of it in your mind as if you were actually seeing it. = image ❑ *We are just trying to get our picture of the whole afternoon straight.* **6** [C] A **picture** of something is a description of it or an indication of what it is like. ❑ *I'll try and give you a better picture of what the boys do.* **7** [SING] When you refer to the **picture** in a particular place, you are referring to the situation there. = situation ❑ *It's a similar picture across the border in Ethiopia.*
PHRASES **in the picture** or **out of the picture** [V-LINK + in/out of the picture] If you say that someone is **in the picture**, you mean that they are involved in the situation that you are talking about. If you say that they are **out of the picture**, you mean that they are not involved in the situation you are talking about. ❑ *Meyerson is back in the picture after disappearing in July.* ❑ *His dad had been out of the picture since he was eight.*
put someone in the picture If you **put** someone **in the picture**, you tell them about a situation which they need to know about. ❑ *Has anyone put you in the picture?*
VERB [T] (**pictures, picturing, pictured**) **1** To be **pictured** somewhere, for example, in a newspaper or magazine, means to appear in a photograph or picture. ❑ *The golfer is pictured on many of the front pages, kissing his trophy as he holds it aloft.* ❑ *a woman who claimed she had been pictured dancing with a celebrity in a nightclub* **2** If you **picture** something in your mind, you think of it and have such a clear memory or idea of it that you seem to be able to see it. = imagine ❑ *He pictured her with long black braided hair.* ❑ *He pictured Carrie sitting out in the car, waiting for him.*

pic·tur·esque /ˌpɪktʃə'resk/ ADJ, NOUN

ADJ A **picturesque** place is attractive and interesting, and has no ugly modern buildings. ❑ *a picturesque mountain village*

p

NOUN [SING] You can refer to picturesque things as **the picturesque**. ❏ *lovers of the picturesque*

pie /paɪ/ NOUN [C, U] (**pies**) A **pie** consists of fruit, meat, or vegetables baked in pastry. ❏ *a slice of apple pie*
✦ **eat humble pie** → see **humble**

piece ♦♦◇ /piːs/ NOUN
NOUN [C] (**pieces**) **1** A **piece of** something is an amount of it that has been broken off, torn off, or cut off. ❏ *a piece of cake* ❏ *Cut the ham into pieces.* **2** A **piece** of an object is one of the individual parts or sections that it is made of, especially a part that can be removed. = bit ❏ *assembling objects out of standard pieces* **3** A **piece** of land is an area of land. ❏ *People struggle to get the best piece of land.* **4** You can use **piece of** with many uncount nouns to refer to an individual thing of a particular kind. For example, you can refer to some advice as a **piece of advice**. ❏ *When I produced this piece of work, my lecturers were very critical.* ❏ *an interesting piece of information* **5** You can refer to an article in a newspaper or magazine, some music written by someone, a broadcast, or a play as a **piece**. ❏ *She wrote a piece on Gwyneth Paltrow for the New Yorker.* ❏ *a vaguely familiar orchestral piece* **6** (*formal*) You can refer to a work of art as a **piece**. ❏ *Each piece is unique, an exquisite painting of a real person, done on ivory.* **7** You can refer to specific coins as **pieces**. For example, a 5 cent **piece** is a coin that is worth 5 cents. ❏ *lots of 10 cent, 20 cent, and 50 cent pieces* **8** The **pieces** that you use when you play a board game such as chess are the specially made objects that you move around on the board. ❏ *How many pieces does each player have in backgammon?*
PHRASES **give someone a piece of your mind** (*informal*) If you **give** someone **a piece of** your **mind**, you tell them very clearly that you think they have behaved badly. ❏ *How very thoughtless. I'll give him a piece of my mind.*
in one piece If someone or something is still **in one piece** after a dangerous journey or experience, they are safe and not damaged or hurt. = intact ❏ *providing that my brother gets back alive and in one piece from his mission*
to pieces You use **to pieces** in expressions such as 'smash to pieces', or 'take something to pieces', when you are describing how something is broken or comes apart so that it is in separate parts.
go to pieces (*informal*) If you **go to pieces**, you are so upset or nervous that you lose control of yourself and cannot do what you should do. ❏ *She's a strong woman, but she nearly went to pieces when Arnie died.*
PHRASAL VERB **piece together** (**pieces, piecing, pieced**) **1** If you **piece together** the truth about something, you gradually discover it. ❏ *They've pieced together his movements for the last few days before his death.* ❏ *In the following days, Frankie was able to piece together what had happened.* **2** If you **piece** something **together**, you gradually make it by joining several things or parts together. ❏ *This process is akin to piecing together a jigsaw puzzle.*
✦ **a piece of the action** → see **action**; **bits and pieces** → see **bit**

♥ pie chart NOUN [C] (**pie charts**) A **pie chart** is a circle divided into sections to show the relative proportions of a set of things. ❏ *The pie chart above shows how much more Britain has saved in shares than bonds.*

pierce /pɪəs/ VERB [T] (**pierces, piercing, pierced**) **1** If a sharp object **pierces** something, or if you **pierce** something **with** a sharp object, the object goes into it and makes a hole in it. ❏ *One bullet pierced the left side of his chest.* **2** If you have your ears or some other part of your body **pierced**, you have a small hole made through them so that you can wear a piece of jewellery in them. ❏ *I'm having my ears pierced on Saturday.*
pierc·ing /ˈpɪəsɪŋ/ NOUN [C, U] (**piercings**) ❏ *health risks from needles used in piercing and tattooing* ❏ *barefoot girls with braids and piercings*

pig /pɪg/ NOUN
NOUN [C] (**pigs**) **1** A **pig** is a pink or black animal with short legs and not much hair on its skin. Pigs are often kept on farms for their meat, which is called pork, ham, or bacon. = hog ❏ *the grunting of the pigs* **2** (*informal,*

disapproval) If you call someone a **pig**, you think that they are unpleasant in some way, especially that they are greedy or unkind. ❏ *These guys destroyed the company. They're all a bunch of greedy pigs.*
PHRASES **when pigs fly** (*humorous, informal, emphasis*) If you say '**when pigs fly**' after someone has said that something might happen, you are emphasizing that you think it is very unlikely. ❏ *When would they be hired again? Perhaps, as the saying goes, when pigs fly.*
make a pig of oneself (*informal, disapproval*) If you say that someone **is making a pig of themselves**, you are criticizing them for eating a very large amount at one meal. ❏ *I'm afraid I made a pig of myself at dinner.*
PHRASAL VERB **pig out** (**pigs, pigging, pigged**) (*informal, disapproval*) If you say that people **are pigging out**, you are criticizing them for eating a very large amount at one meal or over a short period of time. ❏ *Some are so accustomed to pigging out, they can't cut back.*

pile ♦◇◇ /paɪl/ NOUN, VERB
NOUN [C, SING] (**piles**) **1** [C] A **pile of** things is a mass of them that is high in the middle and has sloping sides. = heap, mound ❏ *a pile of sand* ❏ *a little pile of crumbs* **2** [C] A **pile of** things is a quantity of things that have been put neatly somewhere so that each thing is on top of the one below. ❏ *a pile of boxes* ❏ *We sat in Sam's study, among the piles of books.* **3** [C] **Piles** are wooden, concrete, or metal posts that are pushed into the ground and on which buildings or bridges are built. Piles are often used in very wet areas so that the buildings do not flood. ❏ *settlements of wooden houses, set on piles along the shore* **4** [SING] The **pile** of a carpet or of a fabric such as velvet is its soft surface. It consists of a lot of little threads standing on end. ❏ *the carpet's thick pile*
PHRASE **be at the bottom of the pile** or **be at the top of the pile** (*informal*) Someone who is **at the bottom of the pile** is low down in society or low down in an organization. Someone who is **at the top of the pile** is high up in society or high up in an organization. ❏ *These workers are fed up with being at the bottom of the pile when it comes to pay.*
VERB [T, I] (**piles, piling, piled**) **1** [T] If you **pile** things somewhere, you put them there so that they form a pile. ❏ *He was piling clothes into the suitcase.* **2** [T] If something **is piled with** things, it is covered or filled with piles of things. ❏ *Tables were piled with local produce.* **3** [I] If a group of people **pile into** or **out of** a vehicle, they all get into it or out of it in a disorganized way. ❏ *They all piled into Jerry's car.*
PHRASAL VERB **pile up** **1** If you **pile up** a quantity of things or if they **pile up**, they gradually form a pile. ❏ *Bulldozers piled up huge mounds of dirt.* **2** If you **pile up** work, problems, or losses or if they **pile up**, you get more and more of them. ❏ *Problems were piling up at work.*

pill ♦◇◇ /pɪl/ NOUN
NOUN [C, SING] (**pills**) **1** [C] **Pills** are small solid round masses of medicine or vitamins that you swallow without chewing. = tablet ❏ *Why do I have to take all these pills?* **2** [SING] If a woman is **on the pill**, she takes a special pill that prevents her from becoming pregnant. ❏ *She had been on the pill for three years.*
PHRASES **a bitter pill** or **a bitter pill to swallow** If a person or group has to accept a failure or an unpleasant piece of news, you can say that it was **a bitter pill** or a **bitter pill to swallow**. ❏ *You're too old to be given a job. That's a bitter pill to swallow.*
sweeten the pill If someone does something to **sweeten the pill**, they do it to make some unpleasant news or an unpleasant measure more acceptable. ❏ *A few words of praise help to sweeten the pill of criticism.*

pil·lar /ˈpɪlə/ NOUN [C] (**pillars**) **1** A **pillar** is a tall solid structure that is usually used to support part of a building. = column ❏ *the pillars supporting the roof* **2** If something is the **pillar of** a system or agreement, it is the most important part of it or what makes it strong and successful. ❏ *The pillar of her economic policy was keeping tight control over money supply.* **3** If you describe someone as a **pillar of** society or as a **pillar of** the community, you approve of them because they play an important and active part in society or in the community. ❑ *My father is a pillar of the community.*

pil·low /ˈpɪləʊ/ NOUN [c] (pillows) A pillow is a rectangular cushion that you rest your head on when you are in bed.

pi·lot ♦♦◇ /ˈpaɪlət/ NOUN, VERB, ADJ
NOUN [c] (pilots) **1** A pilot is a person who is trained to fly an aircraft. ❑ *He spent seventeen years as an airline pilot.* **2** A pilot is a person who steers a ship through a difficult stretch of water, for example, the entrance to a harbour. ❑ *It seemed that the pilot had another ship to take up the river that evening.*
VERB [T] (pilots, piloting, piloted) **1** If someone pilots an aircraft or ship, they act as its pilot. ❑ *He piloted his own plane part of the way to Washington.* **2** If a government or organization pilots a programme or project, they test it, before deciding whether to introduce it on a larger scale. ❑ *Teachers are piloting a literature-based reading programme.*
ADJ A pilot plan or a pilot project is one that is used to test an idea before deciding whether to introduce it on a larger scale. ❑ *The plan is to launch a pilot programme next summer.*

⊕**pi·lot study** NOUN (pilot studies) A pilot study is a small-scale experiment or set of observations undertaken to decide how and whether to launch a full-scale project. ❑ *The trials follow the success of a pilot study, revealed by New Scientist in 1999.* ❑ *This child is one of a number who are taking part in a pilot study of children exposed to drugs in the womb.*

pin ♦◇◇ /pɪn/ NOUN, VERB
NOUN [c] (pins) **1** Pins are very small thin pointed pieces of metal. They are used in sewing to fasten pieces of material together until they have been sewn. ❑ *a box of needles and pins* **2** A pin is any long narrow piece of metal or wood that is not sharp, especially one that is used to fasten two things together. ❑ *the 18-inch steel pin holding his left leg together*
VERB [T] (pins, pinning, pinned) **1** If you pin something on or to something, you attach it with a pin, a safety pin, or a drawing pin. ❑ *They pinned a notice to the door.* ❑ *Everyone was supposed to dance with the bride and pin money on her dress.* **2** If someone pins you to something, they press you against a surface so that you cannot move. ❑ *I pinned him against the wall.* ❑ *I'd try to get away and he'd pin me down, saying he would kill me.* **3** If someone tries to pin something on you or to pin the blame on you, they say, often unfairly, that you were responsible for something bad or illegal. ❑ *They're trying to pin it on us.* **4** If you pin your hopes on something or pin your faith on something, you hope very much that it will produce the result you want. ❑ *The Democrats are pinning their hopes on the next election.*
PHRASAL VERB **pin down 1** If you try to pin something down, you try to discover exactly what, where, or when it is. ❑ *It has taken until now to pin down its exact location.* ❑ *I can only pin it down to between 1936 and 1942.* **2** If you pin someone down, you force them to make a decision or to tell you what their decision is, when they have been trying to avoid doing this. ❑ *She couldn't pin him down to a date.*

pinch /pɪntʃ/ VERB, NOUN
VERB [T] (pinches, pinching, pinched) **1** If you pinch a part of someone's body, you take a piece of their skin between your thumb and first finger and give it a short squeeze. ❑ *She pinched his arm as hard as she could.* **2** (*informal*) To pinch something, especially something of little value, means to steal it. ❑ *Do you remember when I pinched your glasses?*
NOUN [c] (pinches) **1** If you give someone a pinch, you take a piece of their skin between your thumb and first finger and give it a short squeeze. ❑ *She gave him a little pinch.* **2** A pinch of an ingredient such as salt is the amount of it that you can hold between your thumb and your first finger. ❑ *Put all the ingredients, including a pinch of salt, into a food processor.*
PHRASE **feel the pinch** If a person or company is feeling the pinch, they do not have as much money as they used

to, and so they cannot buy the things they would like to buy. ❑ *Consumers are spending less and retailers are feeling the pinch.*

pine /paɪn/ NOUN, VERB
NOUN [c, u] (pines) **1** [c, u] A pine tree or a pine is a tall tree that has very thin, sharp leaves called needles and a fresh smell. Pine trees have leaves all year round. ❑ *high mountains covered in pine trees* **2** [u] Pine is the wood of this tree. ❑ *a big pine table*
VERB [I] (pines, pining, pined) **1** If you pine for someone who has died or gone away, you want them to be with you very much and feel sad because they are not there. ❑ *She'd be sitting at home pining for her lost husband.* **2** If you pine for something, you want it very much, especially when it is unlikely that you will be able to have it. ❑ *I pine for the countryside.*

pink ♦♦◇ /pɪŋk/ COLOUR, ADJ
COLOUR Pink is the colour between red and white. ❑ *pink lipstick* ❑ *white flowers edged in pink*
ADJ (pinker, pinkest) (*BrE*) Pink is used to refer to things relating to or connected with gay people. ❑ *the pink pound*

⊕**pin·point** /ˈpɪnpɔɪnt/ VERB [T] (pinpoints, pinpointing, pinpointed) **1** If you pinpoint the cause of something, you discover or explain the cause exactly. = identify ❑ *It was almost impossible to pinpoint the cause of death.* ❑ *if you can pinpoint exactly what the anger is about* ❑ *The commission pinpoints inadequate housing as a basic problem threatening village life.* **2** If you pinpoint something or its position, you discover or show exactly where it is. ❑ *I could pinpoint his precise location on a map.*

⊕**pint** /paɪnt/ NOUN [c] (pints) A pint is a unit of measurement for liquids. In Britain, it is equal to 568 cubic centimetres or one eighth of an imperial gallon. In America, it is equal to 473 cubic centimetres or one eighth of an American gallon. ❑ *a pint of ice cream*

⊕**pio·neer** /ˌpaɪəˈnɪə/ NOUN, VERB
NOUN [c] (pioneers) **1** Someone who is referred to as a pioneer in a particular area of activity is one of the first people to be involved in it and develop it. ❑ *one of the leading pioneers of photo journalism* ❑ *an aeronautics pioneer* **2** Pioneers are people who leave their own country or the place where they were living, and go and live in a place that has not been lived in before. ❑ *abandoned settlements of early European pioneers*
VERB [T] (pioneers, pioneering, pioneered) Someone who pioneers a new activity, invention, or process is one of the first people to do it. = develop ❑ *Professor Alec Jeffreys, who invented and pioneered DNA tests* ❑ *the folk-tale writing style pioneered by Gabriel Garcia Marquez*

⊕**pio·neer·ing** /ˌpaɪəˈnɪərɪŋ/ ADJ Pioneering work or a pioneering individual does something that has not been done before, for example, by developing or using new methods or techniques. = leading, innovative ❑ *The school has won awards for its pioneering work with the community.* ❑ *a pioneering Scottish surgeon and anatomist named John Hunter*

pipe ♦◇◇ /paɪp/ NOUN, VERB
NOUN [c] (pipes) **1** A pipe is a long, round, hollow object, usually made of metal or plastic, through which a liquid or gas can flow. ❑ *The liquid can't escape into the air, because it's inside a pipe.* **2** A pipe is an object that is used for smoking tobacco. You put the tobacco into the cup-shaped part at the end of the pipe, light it, and breathe in the smoke through a narrow tube. ❑ *Do you smoke a pipe?* **3** A pipe is a simple musical instrument in the shape of a tube with holes in it. You play a pipe by blowing into it while covering and uncovering the holes with your fingers. **4** An organ pipe is one of the long hollow tubes in which air vibrates and produces a musical note.
VERB [T] (pipes, piping, piped) If liquid or gas is piped somewhere, it is transferred from one place to another through a pipe. ❑ *The heated gas is piped through a coil surrounded by water.* ❑ *The Communists brought electricity to his village and piped in drinking water from the reservoir.*

pipe·line /ˈpaɪplaɪn/ NOUN
NOUN [c] (pipelines) A pipeline is a large pipe that is used for carrying oil or gas over a long distance, often

p

underground. ❏ *A consortium plans to build a natural-gas pipeline from Russia to supply eastern Germany.* **PHRASE** **in the pipeline** If something is **in the pipeline**, it has already been planned or begun. ❏ *Already in the pipeline is a 2.9 per cent pay increase for teachers.*

pi·rate /'paɪrət/ NOUN, VERB, ADJ

NOUN [c] (**pirates**) **Pirates** are sailors who attack other ships and steal property from them. ❏ *In the nineteenth century, pirates roamed the seas.* **VERB** [T] (**pirates, pirating, pirated**) Someone who **pirates** CDs, DVDs, books, or computer programs copies and sells them when they have no right to do so. ❏ *Computer crimes include data theft and pirating software.* **ADJ** [pirate + N] A **pirate** version of something is an illegal copy of it. ❏ *Pirate copies of the DVD are already being sold.* **pi·rat·ed** /'paɪrətɪd/ ADJ ❏ *New technology makes it possible to make pirated copies of music and films.*

pis·tol /'pɪstəl/ NOUN [c] (**pistols**) A **pistol** is a small gun.

pit ♦◇◇ /pɪt/ NOUN, VERB

NOUN [c, PL] (**pits**) **1** [c] A **pit** is the underground part of a mine, especially a coal mine. **2** [c] A **gravel pit** or **clay pit** is a very large hole that is left where gravel or clay has been dug from the ground. ❏ *This area of former farmland was worked as a gravel pit until 1964.* **3** [c] A **pit** is a large hole that is dug in the ground. ❏ *Eric lost his footing and began to slide into the pit.* **4** [PL] In motor racing, **the pits** are the areas at the side of the track where drivers stop to get more fuel and to repair their cars during races. ❏ *He moved quickly into the pits and climbed rapidly out of the car.* **PHRASE** **in the pit of one's stomach** If you have a feeling **in the pit of** your **stomach**, you have a tight or sick feeling in your stomach, usually because you are afraid or anxious. ❏ *I had a funny feeling in the pit of my stomach.* **VERB** [T] (**pits, pitting, pitted**) If two opposing things or people **are pitted against** one another, they are in conflict. ❏ *You will be pitted against two, three, or four people who are every bit as good as you are.* **PHRASE** **pit one's wits against someone** If you pit your **wits against** someone, you compete with them in a test of knowledge or intelligence. ❏ *I'd like to manage at the very highest level and pit my wits against the best.*

pitch ♦◇◇ /pɪtʃ/ VERB, NOUN

VERB [T, I] (**pitches, pitching, pitched**) **1** [T] If you **pitch** something somewhere, you throw it with some force, usually aiming it carefully. ❏ *Simon pitched the empty bottle into the lake.* **2** [T] In the game of baseball, when you **pitch** the ball, you throw it to the batter for them to hit it. ❏ *We passed long, hot afternoons pitching a baseball.* **3** [I] To **pitch** somewhere means to fall forwards suddenly and with a lot of force. ❏ *The movement took him by surprise, and he pitched forwards.* ❏ *Alan staggered sideways, pitched head-first over the low wall and fell into the lake.* **4** [T] If someone **is pitched into** a new situation, they are suddenly forced into it. ❏ *They were being pitched into a new adventure in which they would have to fight the whole world.* **5** [T] If a sound **is pitched at** a particular level, it is produced at the level indicated. ❏ *His cry is pitched at a level that makes it impossible to ignore.* ❏ *His voice was pitched high, the words muffled by his crying.* **6** [T] If something **is pitched at** a particular level or degree of difficulty, it is set at that level. ❏ *While this is very important material I think it's probably pitched at too high a level for our students.* **7** [T] If someone **pitches** an idea for something such as a new product, they try to persuade people to accept the idea. ❏ *My agent has pitched the idea to my editor in New York.* **PHRASAL VERBS** **pitch for** If someone is **pitching for** something, they are trying to persuade other people to give it to them. ❏ *It was middle-class votes they were pitching for.* **pitch in** (*informal*) If you **pitch in**, you join in and help with an activity. ❏ *The agency says international relief agencies also have pitched in.* **NOUN** [U, SING, c] (**pitches**) **1** [U] The **pitch** of a sound is how high or low it is. ❏ *He raised his voice to an even higher pitch.* **2** [SING] If something such as a feeling or a situation rises to a high **pitch**, it rises to a high level. ❏ *The public's feelings were at a high pitch of indignation.* **3** [c] (*BrE*; in *AmE*

use **field**) A **pitch** is an area of ground that is marked out and used for playing a game such as football, cricket, or hockey. **PHRASE** **make a pitch** or **make one's pitch** If someone **makes a pitch for** something, they try to persuade people to do or buy it. ❏ *The president speaks in New York today, making another pitch for his economic programme.*

pit·fall /'pɪtfɔːl/ NOUN [c] (**pitfalls**) The **pitfalls** involved in a particular activity or situation are the things that may go wrong or may cause problems. ❏ *The pitfalls of working abroad are numerous.*

piti·ful /'pɪtɪfʊl/ ADJ **1** Someone or something that is **pitiful** is so sad, weak, or small that you feel pity for them. ❏ *He sounded both pitiful and eager to get what he wanted.* **2** If you describe something as **pitiful**, you mean that it is completely inadequate. ❏ *The choice is pitiful and the quality of some of the products is very low.* **piti·ful·ly** /'pɪtɪfəli/ ADV **1** *His legs were pitifully thin compared to the rest of his bulk.* **2** *State help for mentally handicapped people is pitifully inadequate.*

pity /'pɪti/ NOUN, VERB

NOUN [U, SING] **1** [U] If you feel **pity for** someone, you feel very sorry for them. ❏ *He felt a sudden tender pity for her.* **2** [SING] If you say that it is a **pity** that something is the case, you mean that you feel disappointment or regret about it. ❏ *It is a great pity that all students in the city cannot have the same chances.* ❏ *It's a pity you've arrived so late in the year.* **3** [U] If someone shows **pity**, they do not harm or punish someone they have power over. ❏ *Noncommunist forces have some pity towards people here.* **PHRASE** **take pity on someone** If you **take pity on** someone, you feel sorry for them and help them. ❏ *No woman had ever felt the need to take pity on him before.* **VERB** [T] (**pities, pitying, pitied**) If you **pity** someone, you feel very sorry for them. ❏ *I don't know whether to hate or pity him.*

piv·ot /'pɪvət/ NOUN, VERB

NOUN [c] (**pivots**) **1** The **pivot** in a situation is the most important thing that everything else is based on or arranged around. ❏ *Forming the pivot of the exhibition is a large group of watercolours.* **2** A **pivot** is the pin or the central point on which something balances or turns. ❏ *The pedal had sheared off at the pivot.* **VERB** [I] (**pivots, pivoting, pivoted**) If something or someone **pivots**, they balance or turn on a central point. ❏ *The wheels pivot for easy manoeuvring.* ❏ *He pivoted on his heels and walked on down the hall.*

✪ piv·ot·al /'pɪvətəl/ ADJ A **pivotal** role, point, or figure in something is one that is very important and affects the success of that thing. = critical, crucial; ≠ peripheral ❏ *The elections may prove to be pivotal in Colombia's political history.* ❏ *The Court of Appeal has a pivotal role in the English legal system.*

piz·za /'piːtsə/ NOUN [c, U] (**pizzas**) A **pizza** is a flat, round piece of dough covered with tomatoes, cheese, and other toppings, and then baked in an oven. ❏ *the last piece of pizza*

plac·ard /'plækɑːd/ NOUN [c] (**placards**) A **placard** is a large notice that is carried in a march or displayed in a public place. ❏ *The protesters sang songs and waved placards.*

place ♦♦♦ /pleɪs/ NOUN, VERB

NOUN [c, SING] (**places**) **1** [c] A **place** is any point, building, area, town, or country. ❏ *a list of museums and places of interest* ❏ *We're going to a place called Platoro.* ❏ *The pain is always in the same place.* **2** [SING] You can use the **place** to refer to the point, building, area, town, or country that you have already mentioned. ❏ *Except for the remarkably tidy kitchen, the place was a mess.* **3** [c] You can refer to somewhere that provides a service, such as a hotel, restaurant, or institution, as a particular kind of **place**. ❏ *He found a bed-and-breakfast place.* ❏ *My wife and I discovered some superb places to eat.* **4** [c] You can refer to the position where something belongs, or where it is supposed to be, as its **place**. ❏ *He returned the album to its place on the shelf.* **5** [c] A **place** is a seat or position that is available for someone to occupy. ❏ *He walked back to the table and sat at the nearest of two empty places.*

P

6 [c] Someone's or something's **place** in a society, system, or situation is their position in relation to other people or things. □ *They want to see more women take their place higher up the corporate or professional ladder.* **7** [c] Your **place** in a race or competition is your position in relation to the other competitors. If you are in first place, you are ahead of all the other competitors. □ *He has risen to second place in the opinion polls.* **8** [c] If you get a **place** on a team, on a committee, or in an institution, for example, you are accepted as a member of the team or committee or as a resident of the institution. □ *Derek had lost his place on the team.* □ *They should be in residential care but there are no places available.* **9** [SING] A good **place to** do something in a situation or activity is a good time or stage at which to do it. = time □ *It seemed an appropriate place to end somehow.* **10** [c] (*informal*) Your **place** is the house or flat where you live. □ *Let's all go back to my place!* **11** [c] Your **place** in a book or speech is the point you have reached in reading the book or making the speech. □ *her finger marking her place in the book* **12** [c] If you say how many decimal **places** there are in a number, you are saying how many numbers there are to the right of the decimal point. □ *A pocket calculator only works to eight decimal places.*

PHRASES **take place** When something **takes place**, it happens, especially in a controlled or organized way. □ *The discussion took place in a famous villa on the lake's shore.* □ *She wanted Randy's wedding to take place quickly.*

all over the place 1 If something is happening **all over the place**, it is happening in many different places. □ *Businesses are closing down all over the place.* **2** If things are **all over the place**, they are spread over a very large area, usually in a disorganized way. □ *Our fingerprints are probably all over the place.*

change places If you **change places with** another person, you start being in their situation or role, and they start being in yours. = swap □ *With his door key in his hand, knowing Millie and the kids awaited him, he wouldn't change places with anyone.*

fall into place or **click into place** or **fit into place** If you have been trying to understand something puzzling and then everything **falls into place** or **clicks into place**, you suddenly understand how different pieces of information are connected and everything becomes clearer. □ *When the reasons behind the decision were explained, of course, it all fell into place.*

fall into place If things **fall into place**, events happen naturally to produce a situation you want. □ *Once the decision was made, things fell into place rapidly.*

go places If you say that someone **is going places**, you mean that they are showing a lot of talent or ability and are likely to become very successful. □ *You always knew Barbara was going places, she was different.*

in high places People **in high places** are people who have powerful and influential positions in a government, society, or organization. □ *He had friends in high places.*

in place or **into place** or **out of place** If something is **in place**, it is in its correct or usual position. If it is **out of place**, it is not in its correct or usual position. □ *Gary hastily pushed the drawer back into place.*

in place If something such as a law, a policy, or an administrative structure is **in place**, it is working or able to be used. □ *Similar legislation is already in place in Utah.*

in place of If one thing or person is used or does something **in place of** another, they replace the other thing or person. □ *Cooked kidney beans can be used in place of French beans.*

in places If something has particular characteristics or features **in places**, it has them at several points within an area. □ *Even now the snow along the roadside was five or six feet deep in places.*

in someone's place If you say what you would have done **in someone else's place**, you say what you would have done if you had been in their situation and had been experiencing what they were experiencing. □ *In her place I wouldn't have been able to resist it.*

in the first place You say **in the first place** when you are talking about the beginning of a situation or about the situation as it was before a series of events. □ *What brought you to Washington in the first place?*

in the first place or **in the second place** You say **in the first place** and **in the second place** to introduce the first and second in a series of points or reasons. **In the first place** can also be used to emphasize a very important point or reason. □ *In the first place you are not old, Conway. And in the second place, you are a very strong and appealing man.*

not someone's place to do something If you say that it **is not** your **place to** do something, you mean that it is not right or appropriate for you to do it, or that it is not your responsibility to do it. □ *He says that it is not his place to comment on government commitment to further funds.*

out of place If someone or something seems **out of place** in a particular situation, they do not seem to belong there or to be suitable for that situation. □ *I felt out of place in my suit and tie.*

put someone in their place If you **put** someone **in** their **place**, you show them that they are less important or clever than they think they are. □ *In a few words she had put him in his place.*

show someone their place or **keep someone in their place** If you say that someone should **be shown** their **place** or **be kept** in their **place**, you are saying, often in a humorous way, that they should be made aware of their low status. □ *an uppity bartender who needs to be shown his place*

take second place If one thing **takes second place to** another, it is considered to be less important and is given less attention than the other thing. □ *My personal life has had to take second place to my career.*

take the place of or **take someone's place** If one thing or person **takes the place of** another or **takes** another's **place**, they replace the other thing or person. □ *Optimism was gradually taking the place of pessimism.*

VERB [T] (**places**, **placing**, **placed**) **1** If you **place** something somewhere, you put it in a particular position, especially in a careful, firm, or deliberate way. □ *Brand folded it in his handkerchief and placed it in the inside pocket of his jacket.* **2** To **place** a person or thing in a particular state means to cause them to be in it. = put □ *Widespread protests have placed the president under serious pressure.* □ *The crisis could well place the relationship at risk.* **3** You can use **place** instead of 'put' or 'lay' in certain expressions where the meaning is carried by the following noun. For example, if you **place emphasis** on something, you emphasize it, and if you **place the blame on** someone, you blame them. = put □ *He placed great emphasis on the importance of family life and ties.* □ *She seemed to be placing most of the blame on her mother.* **4** If you **place** someone or something in a particular class or group, you label or judge them in that way. = put □ *The authorities have placed the drug in Class A, the same category as heroin and cocaine.* **5** If a competitor in a race or competition **is placed** first, second, or third, they finish first, second or third. □ *I had been placed 2nd and 3rd a few times but had never won.* **6** If you **place an order for** a product or **for** a meal, you ask for it to be sent or brought to you. □ *It is a good idea to place your order well in advance as delivery can often take months rather than weeks.* **7** If you **place an advertisement** in a newspaper, you arrange for the advertisement to appear in the newspaper. = put □ *They placed an advertisement in the local paper for a secretary.* **8** If you **place a bet**, you bet money on something. □ *For this race, though, he had already placed a bet on one of the horses.* **9** If an agency or organization **places** someone, it finds them a job or somewhere to live. □ *They managed to place fourteen women in paid positions.*

PHRASE **place something above something** or **place something before something** or **place something over something** If you **place** one thing **above**, **before**, or **over** another, you think that the first thing is more important than the second and you show this in your behaviour. = put □ *He continued to place security above all other objectives.*

pla·cebo /pləˈsiːbəʊ/ NOUN [c] (**placebos**) A **placebo** is a substance with no chemical effects that a doctor gives to a patient instead of a drug. Placebos are used when testing

p

new drugs or sometimes when a patient has imagined their illness.

place·ment /ˈpleɪsmənt/ NOUN [U, C] (**placements**)
1 [U] The **placement of** something or someone is the act of putting them in a particular place or position. ◻ *The treatment involves the placement of twenty-two electrodes in the inner ear.* **2** [U] The **placement** of someone in a job, home, or school is the act or process of finding them a job, home, or school. ◻ *The children were waiting for placement in a foster care home.* **3** [C] If someone gets a **placement**, they get a job for a short period of time to gain experience. ◻ *He spent a year studying Japanese in Tokyo, followed by a six-month work placement with the Japanese government.*

◆**pla·gia·rism** /ˈpleɪdʒərɪzəm/ NOUN [U] **Plagiarism** is the practice of using or copying someone else's idea or work and pretending that you thought of it or created it. ◻ *Now he's in real trouble. He's accused of plagiarism.* ◻ *'It's almost impossible to control or contain plagiarism now,' he said.*

◆**pla·gia·rize** /ˈpleɪdʒəraɪz/ also **plagiarise** VERB [T] (**plagiarizes, plagiarizing, plagiarized**) If someone **plagiarizes** another person's idea or work, they use it or copy it and pretend that they thought of it or created it. = copy, steal ◻ *The students denied plagiarizing papers.* ◻ *Moderates are plagiarizing his ideas in hopes of wooing voters.* ◻ *The poem employs as its first lines a verse plagiarized from a billboard.*

plague /pleɪg/ NOUN, VERB
NOUN [U, C] (**plagues**) **1** [U] [also 'the' plague] **Plague** or **the plague** is a very infectious disease that usually results in death. The patient has a severe fever and swellings on his or her body. ◻ *a fresh outbreak of plague* **2** [C] A **plague of** unpleasant things is a large number of them that arrive or happen at the same time. = epidemic ◻ *The city is under threat from a plague of rats.*
VERB [T] (**plagues, plaguing, plagued**) If you **are plagued by** unpleasant things, they continually cause you a lot of trouble or suffering. ◻ *She was plagued by weakness, fatigue, and dizziness.*

plain ◆◇◇ /pleɪn/ ADJ, NOUN
ADJ (**plainer, plainest**) **1** A **plain** object, surface, or fabric is entirely in one colour and has no pattern, design, or writing on it. ◻ *In general, a plain carpet makes a room look bigger.* ◻ *He placed the paper in a plain envelope.* **2** Something that is **plain** is very simple in style. ◻ *It was a plain, grey stone house.* **3** If a fact, situation, or statement is **plain**, it is easy to recognize or understand. = clear ◻ *It was plain to him that I was having a nervous breakdown.* **4** If you describe someone as **plain**, you think they look ordinary and not at all beautiful. ◻ *a shy, rather plain girl with a pale complexion*
PHRASE **in plain clothes** If a police officer is **in plain clothes**, he or she is wearing ordinary clothes instead of a police uniform. ◻ *Three officers in plain clothes told me to get out of the car.*
NOUN [C] (**plains**) A **plain** is a large flat area of land with very few trees on it. ◻ *Once there were 70 million buffalo on the plains.*
✦ **plain sailing** → see **sailing**

plain·ly /ˈpleɪnli/ ADV **1** (emphasis) You use **plainly** to indicate that you believe something is obviously true, often when you are trying to convince someone else that it is true. ◻ *The judge's conclusion was plainly wrong.* ◻ *Plainly, a more objective method of description must be adopted.* **2** (emphasis) You use **plainly** to indicate that something is easily seen, noticed, or recognized. = clearly ◻ *He was plainly annoyed.* ◻ *I could plainly see him turning his head to the right and left.* **3** [plainly + -ED] Something that is **plainly** presented is presented in a very simple style. ◻ *He was very tall and plainly dressed.*

◆**plan** ◆◆◆ /plæn/ NOUN, VERB
NOUN [C, PL] (**plans**) **1** [C] A **plan** is a method of achieving something that you have worked out in detail beforehand. = aim, procedure, strategy ◻ *The three leaders had worked out a peace plan.* ◻ *He maintains that everything is going according to plan.* ◻ *a detailed plan of action for restructuring the group* **2** [PL] If you have **plans**, you are intending to do a particular thing. ◻ *'I'm sorry,' she said. 'I have plans for*

tonight.'* **3** [C] A **plan of** something that is going to be built or made is a detailed diagram or drawing of it. ◻ *when you have drawn a plan of the garden*
VERB [I, T] (**plans, planning, planned**) **1** [I, T] If you **plan** what you are going to do, you decide in detail what you are going to do, and you intend to do it. = prepare, arrange, organize ◻ *If you plan what you're going to eat, you reduce your chances of overeating.* ◻ *He planned to leave Baghdad on Monday.* ◻ *Moderate Republicans gathered together to plan for the future.* ◻ *I had been planning a trip to the West Coast.* ◻ *A planned demonstration has been called off by its organisers.* **2** [T] When you **plan** something that you are going to make, build, or create, you decide what the main parts of it will be and do a drawing of how it should be made. ◻ *It is no use trying to plan an 18-hole golf course on a 120-acre site if you have to ruin the environment to do it.*
PHRASAL VERB **plan on** If you **plan on** doing something, you intend to do it. ◻ *They were planning on getting married.*
→ See also **planning**

WORD CONNECTIONS
VERB + **plan**
announce a plan **unveil** a plan **outline** a plan ◻ *The company has announced plans to take on 50 new staff.*
follow a plan **implement** a plan ◻ *The government wasted little time implementing plans for reform.*
ADJ + **plan**
an **ambitious** plan a **detailed** plan ◻ *His ambitious plan failed.*
a **long-term** plan an **immediate** plan ◻ *We have no immediate plans to leave.*
the **original** plan ◻ *The original plan was to sail to Sydney.*
plan + OF + NOUN
a plan of **action** a plan of **attack** ◻ *They needed to decide on the best plan of action.*

plane ◆◆◇ /pleɪn/ NOUN, VERB
NOUN [C, SING] (**planes**) **1** [C] A **plane** is a vehicle with wings and one or more engines that can fly through the air. = aeroplane ◻ *He had plenty of time to catch his plane.* ◻ *Her mother was killed in a plane crash.* **2** [C] A **plane** is a flat, level surface that may be sloping at a particular angle. ◻ *a building with angled planes* **3** [SING] If a number of points are in the same **plane**, one line or one flat surface could pass through them all. ◻ *All the planets orbit the Sun in roughly the same plane, around its equator.* **4** [C] A **plane** is a tool that has a flat bottom with a sharp blade in it. You move the plane over a piece of wood in order to remove thin pieces of its surface. **5** [C] A **plane** or a **plane tree** is the same as a sycamore.
VERB [T] (**planes, planing, planed**) If you **plane** a piece of wood, you make it smaller or smoother by using a plane. ◻ *She watches him plane the surface of a walnut board.*

◆**plan·et** ◆◇◇ /ˈplænɪt/ NOUN [C] (**planets**) A **planet** is a large, round object in space that moves around a star. The Earth is a planet. ◻ *The picture shows six of the eight planets in the solar system.*

plan·ner /ˈplænə/ NOUN [C] (**planners**) **Planners** are people whose job is to make decisions about what is going to be done in the future. For example, town planners decide how land should be used and what new buildings should be built. ◻ *a panel that includes city planners, art experts, and historians*

◆**plan·ning** ◆◇◇ /ˈplænɪŋ/ NOUN [U] **1 Planning** is the

process of deciding in detail how to do something before you actually start to do it. = preparation, arrangement ❑ *The trip needs careful planning.* **2** *The new system is still in the planning stages.* **2 Planning** is control by the local government of the way that land is used in an area and of what new buildings are built there. ❑ *New York City's Planning Commissions rejected the builder's proposals.*

⊕ **plant** ◆◆◆ /plɑːnt, plænt/ NOUN, VERB
NOUN [U, C] (**plants**) **1** [U, C] A **plant** is a living thing that grows in the earth and has a stem, leaves, and roots. ❑ *Water each plant as often as required.* **2** *Exotic plants thrive in humid air.* **2** [C] A **plant** is a factory or a place where power is produced. = factory ❑ *Ford's car assembly plants* ❑ *The plant provides forty per cent of the country's electricity.* **3** [U] **Plant** is large machinery that is used in industrial processes. = machinery ❑ *Companies may start to invest in plant and equipment abroad where costs may be lower.* VERB [T] (**plants, planting, planted**) **1** When you **plant** a seed, plant, or young tree, you put it into the ground so that it will grow there. ❑ *He says he plans to plant fruit trees and vegetables.* **2** When someone **plants** land **with** a particular type of plant or crop, they put plants, seeds, or young trees into the land to grow them there. ❑ *They plan to plant the area with grass and trees.* ❑ *Recently much of their energy has gone into planting a large vegetable garden.* **3** If you **plant** something somewhere, you put it there firmly. ❑ *She planted her feet wide and bent her knees slightly.* **4** To **plant** something such as a bomb means to hide it somewhere so that it explodes or works there. ❑ *So far no one has admitted planting the bomb.* **5** If something such as a weapon or drugs **is planted** on someone, it is put among their possessions or in their house so that they will be wrongly accused of a crime. ❑ *He always protested his innocence and claimed that the drugs had been planted to incriminate him.* **6** If an organization **plants** someone somewhere, they send that person there so that they can get information or watch someone secretly. ❑ *Journalists informed police who planted an undercover detective to trap Smith.*
plant·ing /ˈplɑːntɪŋ, ˈplæntɪŋ/ NOUN [U] ❑ *Extensive flooding in the country has delayed planting and many crops are still under water.*

plan·ta·tion /plɑːnˈteɪʃən, plæn-/ NOUN [C] (**plantations**) **1** A **plantation** is a large piece of land, especially in a tropical country, where crops such as rubber, coffee, tea, or sugar are grown. ❑ *banana plantations in Costa Rica* **2** A **plantation** is a large number of trees that have been planted together. ❑ *a plantation of almond trees*

plas·ter /ˈplɑːstə, ˈplæs-/ NOUN, VERB
NOUN [U, C] (**plasters**) **1** [U] **Plaster** is a smooth paste made of sand, lime, and water that gets hard when it dries. Plaster is used to cover walls and ceilings and is also used to make sculptures. ❑ *There were huge cracks in the plaster, and the green shutters were faded.* **2** [C] (*BrE*; in *AmE*, usually use **Band-aid**) A **plaster** is a strip of sticky material used for covering small cuts or sores on your body.
VERB [T] (**plasters, plastering, plastered**) **1** If you **plaster** a wall or ceiling, you cover it with a layer of plaster. ❑ *The ceiling he had just plastered fell in and knocked him off his ladder.* **2** If you **plaster** a surface or a place **with** posters or pictures, you stick a lot of them all over it. ❑ *He has plastered the city with posters proclaiming his qualifications and experience.* **3** If you **plaster yourself in** some kind of sticky substance, you cover yourself in it. ❑ *She gets sunburned even when she plasters herself from head to toe in factor 7 sun lotion.*

plas·tic ◆◇◇ /ˈplæstɪk/ NOUN, ADJ
NOUN [C, U] (**plastics**) **1** [C, U] **Plastic** is a material that is produced from oil by a chemical process and that is used to make many objects. It is light in weight and does not break easily. ❑ *a wooden crate, sheltered from rain by sheets of plastic* ❑ *A lot of the plastics that carmakers are using cannot be recycled.* **2** [U] (*informal*) If you use **plastic** or **plastic money** to pay for something, you pay for it with a credit card instead of using cash. ❑ *Using plastic to pay for an order is simplicity itself.*

ADJ **1** (*disapproval*) If you describe something as **plastic**, you mean that you think it looks or tastes unnatural or not real. ❑ *You wanted proper home-cooked meals, you said you had enough plastic hotel food and airline food.* **2** Something that is **plastic** is soft and can easily be made into different shapes. ❑ *You can also enjoy mud packs with the natural mud, smooth, grey, soft, and plastic as butter.*

plas·tic sur·gery NOUN [U] **Plastic surgery** is the practice of performing operations to repair or replace skin that has been damaged, or to improve people's appearance. ❑ *She even had plastic surgery to change the shape of her nose.*

plate ◆◇◇ /pleɪt/ NOUN
NOUN [C] (**plates**) **1** A **plate** is a round or oval flat dish that is used to hold food. ❑ *Anita pushed her plate away; she had eaten virtually nothing.* **2** A **plate of** food is the amount of food on a plate. ❑ *a huge plate of bacon and eggs* **3** A **plate** is a flat piece of metal, especially on machinery or a building. ❑ *a recess covered by a brass plate* **4** A **plate** is a small, flat piece of metal with someone's name written on it, which you usually find beside the front door of an office or house. ❑ *a brass plate by the front door bearing his name* **5** A **plate** in a book is a picture or photograph that takes up a whole page and is usually printed on better quality paper than the rest of the book. ❑ *The book has 55 colour plates.*
PHRASE **have enough on one's plate** or **have a lot on one's plate** If you **have enough on** your **plate** or **have a lot on** your **plate**, you have a lot of work to do or a lot of things to deal with. ❑ *We have enough on our plate. There is plenty of work to be done on what we have.*

pla·teau /ˈplætəʊ, AmE plæˈtəʊ/ NOUN [C] (**plateaus** or **plateaux**) **1** A **plateau** is a large area of high and fairly flat land. ❑ *A broad valley opened up leading to a high, flat plateau of cultivated land.* **2** If you say that an activity or process has reached a **plateau**, you mean that it has reached a stage where there is no further change or development. ❑ *The US heroin market now appears to have reached a plateau.*

plat·form ◆◇◇ /ˈplætfɔːm/ NOUN [C] (**platforms**) **1** A **platform** is a flat raised structure, usually made of wood, that people stand on when they make speeches or give a performance. ❑ *Nick finished what he was saying and jumped down from the platform.* **2** A **platform** is a flat raised structure or area, usually one that something can stand on or land on. ❑ *They found a spot on a rocky platform where they could pitch their tents.* **3** A **platform** is a structure built for people to work and live on when drilling for oil or gas at sea, or when extracting it. ❑ *The platform began to produce oil in 1994.* **4** A **platform** in a train or subway station is the area beside the tracks where you wait for or get off a train. ❑ *The train was about to leave and I was not even on the platform.* **5** The **platform** of a political party is what they say they will do if they are elected. = programme ❑ *The party has announced a platform of political and economic reforms.* **6** If someone has a **platform**, they have an opportunity to tell people what they think or want. ❑ *The demonstration provided a platform for a broad cross-section of speakers.*

plau·sible /ˈplɔːzɪbəl/ ADJ **1** An explanation or statement that is **plausible** seems likely to be true or valid. = reasonable ❑ *A more plausible explanation would seem to be that people are fed up with the administration.* **2** If you say that someone is **plausible**, you mean that they seem to be telling the truth and to be sincere and honest. = believable ❑ *All I can say is that he was so plausible it wasn't just me that he conned.*
plau·sibly /ˈplɔːzɪbli/ ADV [plausibly with V] ❑ *Having bluffed his way in without paying, he could not plausibly demand his money back.*
plau·sibil·ity /ˌplɔːzɪˈbɪlɪti/ NOUN [U] = credibility ❑ *the plausibility of the theory*

⊕ **play** ◆◆◆ /pleɪ/ VERB, NOUN
VERB [I, RECIP, T, LINK] (**plays, playing, played**) **1** [I] When children, animals, or adults **play**, they spend time doing enjoyable things, such as using toys and taking part in games. ❑ *invite the children over to play* ❑ *They played in the little garden.* **2** [RECIP] When you **play** a sport, game, or

p

match, you take part in it. ❑ *While the twins played cards, Leona sat reading.* ❑ *I used to play basketball.* **3** [I, T] When one person or team **plays** another or **plays against** them, they compete against them in a sport or game. ❑ *Dallas will play Green Bay.* **4** [T] If you **play** a joke or a trick on someone, you deceive them or give them a surprise in a way that you think is funny, but that often causes problems for them or annoys them. ❑ *Someone had played a trick on her, stretched a piece of string at the top of those steps.* **5** [I] If you **play with** an object or with your hair, you keep moving it or touching it with your fingers, perhaps because you are bored or nervous. ❑ *She stared at the floor, idly playing with the strap of her handbag.* **6** [T] If an actor **plays** a role or character in a play or film, he or she performs the part of that character. = act, perform, portray ❑ *Dr Jekyll and Mr Hyde, in which he played Hyde* ❑ *His ambition is to play the part of Dracula.* **7** [LINK] You can use **play** to describe how someone behaves, when they are deliberately behaving in a certain way or like a certain type of person. For example, to **play the innocent** means to pretend to be innocent, and to **play deaf** means to pretend not to hear something. = act ❑ *Hill tried to play the peacemaker.* ❑ *She was just playing the devoted mother.* **8** [T] You can describe how someone deals with a situation by saying that they **play it** in a certain way. For example, if someone **plays it cool**, they keep calm and do not show much emotion, and if someone **plays it straight**, they behave in an honest and direct way. ❑ *Investors are playing it cautious, and they're playing it smart.* **9** [I, T] If you **play** a musical instrument or **play** a tune on a musical instrument, or if a musical instrument **plays**, music is produced from it. ❑ *Nina had been playing the piano.* ❑ *He played for me.* **10** [I, T] If you **play** a record, a CD, or a DVD, you put it into a machine and sound and sometimes pictures are produced. If a record, CD, or DVD **is playing**, sound and sometimes pictures are being produced from it. ❑ *She played her records too loudly.* ❑ *There is classical music playing in the background.* **11** [I, T] If a musician or group of musicians **plays** or **plays** a concert, they perform music for people to listen or dance to. ❑ *A band was playing.* ▸ PHRASE **play a part** or **play a role** If something or someone **plays a part** or **plays a role in** a situation, they are involved in it and have an effect on it. ❑ *They played a part in the life of their community.* ❑ *The UN would play a major role in monitoring a ceasefire.*

▸ PHRASAL VERBS **play around** (*informal*) **1** If you **play around**, you behave in a silly way to amuse yourself or other people. ❑ *Stop playing around and eat!* ❑ *There was no doubt he was serious, it wasn't just playing around.* **2** If you **play around with** a problem or an arrangement of objects, you try different ways of organizing it in order to find the best solution or arrangement. ❑ *I can play around with the pictures in all sorts of ways to make them more eye-catching.*

play at 1 (*disapproval*) If you say that someone **is playing at** something, you disapprove of the fact that they are doing it casually and not very seriously. ❑ *We were still playing at war – dropping leaflets instead of bombs.* **2** If someone, especially a child, **plays at** being someone or doing something, they pretend to be that person or do that thing as a game. ❑ *Ed played at being a pirate.* **3** (*informal*) If you do not know what someone **is playing at**, you do not understand what they are doing or what they are trying to achieve. ❑ *She began to wonder what he was playing at.*

play back When you **play back** a tape or film, you listen to the sounds or watch the pictures after recording them. ❑ *He bought an answering machine that plays back his messages when he calls.* ❑ *Ted might benefit from hearing his own voice recorded and played back.*

play down If you **play down** something, you try to make people believe that it is not particularly important. ❑ *Western diplomats have played down the significance of the reports.*

play on If you **play on** someone's fears, weaknesses, or faults, you deliberately use them in order to persuade that person to do something, or to achieve what you want. = exploit ❑ *a campaign which plays on the population's fear of change*

play up If you **play up** something, you emphasize it and try to make people believe that it is important. ❑ *The media played up the prospects for a settlement.*

NOUN [U, C] (**plays**) **1** [U] **Play** is the activity of spending time doing enjoyable things, such as using toys and taking part in games. ❑ *a few hours of play until the babysitter puts them to bed* **2** [U] **Play** is the action of taking part in a sport or game. ❑ *They've got more exciting players and a more exciting style of play.* **3** [U] **Play** is the activity of competing against another person or team in a sport or game. ❑ *Fischer won after 5 hours and 41 minutes of play.* **4** [C] A **play** is a piece of writing performed in a theatre, on the radio, or on television. = show, drama, performance ❑ *It's my favourite Shakespeare play.* ❑ *The company put on a play about the homeless.*

PHRASE **come into play** or **be brought into play** When something **comes into play** or **is brought into play**, it begins to be used or to have an effect. ❑ *The real existence of a military option will come into play.*

✦ **play the fool** → see fool; **play to the gallery** → see gallery; **play hard to get** → see hard; **play havoc** → see havoc; **play host** → see host; **play safe** → see safe

play·er ◆◆◆ /ˈpleɪə/ NOUN [C] (**players**) **1** A **player** in a sport or game is a person who takes part, either as a job or for fun. ❑ *his greatness as a player* ❑ *She was a good golfer and tennis player.* **2** You can use **player** to refer to a musician. For example, a **piano player** is someone who plays the piano. ❑ *a professional trumpet player* **3** If a person, country, or organization is a **player** in something, they are involved in it and important in it. ❑ *Big business has become a major player in the art market.*

play·ful /ˈpleɪfʊl/ ADJ **1** A **playful** gesture or person is friendly or humorous. ❑ *a playful kiss on the tip of his nose* ❑ *a playful fight* **2** A **playful** animal is lively and cheerful. ❑ *a playful puppy*
play·ful·ly /ˈpleɪfəli/ ADV ❑ *She pushed him away playfully.*
play·ful·ness /ˈpleɪfəlnəs/ NOUN [U] ❑ *the child's natural playfulness*

play·ground /ˈpleɪgraʊnd/ NOUN [C] (**playgrounds**) A **playground** is a piece of land, at school or in a public area, where children can play. ❑ *a seven-year-old boy playing in a school playground*

play·off ◆◆◇ /ˈpleɪˌɒf/ NOUN [C] (**playoffs**) **1** A **playoff** is an extra game that is played to decide the winner of a sports competition when two or more people have the same score. ❑ *Nick Faldo was beaten by Peter Baker in a playoff.* **2** You use **playoffs** to refer to a series of games that are played to decide the winner of a championship. ❑ *It's been a long time since these two teams faced each other in the playoffs.*

✪ **play·wright** /ˈpleɪraɪt/ NOUN [C] (**playwrights**) A **playwright** is a person who writes plays. = dramatist ❑ *Diniso is an award-winning playwright, director and actor.* ❑ *The film is scripted by the playwright Wendy Wasserstein.*

✪ **plea** /pliː/ NOUN [C] (**pleas**) **1** (*journalism*) A **plea** is an appeal or request for something, made in an intense or emotional way. = appeal ❑ *Mr Nicholas made his emotional plea for help in solving the killing.* **2** In a court of law, a person's **plea** is the answer that they give when they have been charged with a crime, saying whether or not they are guilty of that crime. ❑ *The judge questioned him about his guilty plea.* ❑ *We will enter a plea of not guilty.* ❑ *Her plea of guilty to manslaughter through provocation was rejected.* **3** A **plea** is a reason given, to a court of law or to other people, as an excuse for doing something or for not doing something. ❑ *Phillips murdered his wife, but got off on a plea of insanity.* ❑ *Mr Dunn's pleas of poverty are only partly justified.*

✪ **plead** /pliːd/ VERB [I, T] (**pleads, pleading, pleaded, pled**) **1** [I] If you **plead with** someone to do something, you ask them in an intense, emotional way to do it. = beg ❑ *The lady pleaded with her daughter to come back home.* ❑ *He was kneeling on the floor pleading for mercy.* **2** [I] When someone charged with a crime **pleads guilty** or **not guilty** in a court of law, they officially state that they are guilty or not guilty of the crime. ❑ *Morris had pleaded guilty to robbery.* ❑ *They consistently pleaded innocent and were finally cleared at* a hearing in Cartagena yesterday. **3** [T] If you **plead the case** or **cause** of someone or something, you speak out in their support or defence. ❑ *He appeared before the committee to plead his case.* **4** [T] If you **plead** a particular thing as the reason for doing or not doing something, you give it as your excuse. ❑ *Mr. Giles pleads ignorance as his excuse.*

pleas·ant ◆◇◇ /ˈplezənt/ ADJ (**pleasanter, pleasantest**) **1** Something that is **pleasant** is nice, enjoyable, or attractive. ❑ *I've got a pleasant little apartment.* **2** Someone who is **pleasant** is friendly and likeable. ❑ *The woman had a pleasant face.*

pleas·ant·ly /ˈplezəntli/ ADV ❑ *We talked pleasantly of old times.*

please ◆◆◇ /pliːz/ ADV, CONVENTION, VERB
ADV **1** [please with CL] (*politeness*) You say **please** when you are politely asking or inviting someone to do something. ❑ *Can you help us please?* ❑ *Please come in.* ❑ *Can we have the bill please?* **2** (*formulae*) You say **please** when you are accepting something politely. ❑ *'Tea?'—'Yes, please.'*
CONVENTION **1** (*feelings*) You can say **please** to indicate that you want someone to stop doing something or stop speaking. You would say this if, for example, what they are doing or saying makes you angry or upset. ❑ *Please, Mary, this is all so unnecessary.* **2** (*politeness*) You can say **please** in order to attract someone's attention politely. ❑ *Please, Miss Smith, a moment.*
VERB [I, T] (**pleases, pleasing, pleased**) If someone or something **pleases** you, they make you feel happy and satisfied. ❑ *More than anything, I want to please you.* ❑ *It pleased him to talk to her.* ❑ *He appeared anxious to please.*
PHRASE **as you please** or **whatever you please** or **anything you please** You use **please** in expressions such as **she pleases, whatever you please,** and **anything he pleases** to indicate that someone can do or have whatever they want. ❑ *Women should be free to dress and act as they please.* ❑ *He does whatever he pleases.*

pleased ◆◇◇ /pliːzd/ ADJ
ADJ **1** If you are **pleased**, you are happy about something or satisfied with something. ❑ *Felicity seemed pleased at the suggestion.* ❑ *I think he's going to be pleased that we identified the real problems.* **2** [V-LINK + pleased + to-INF] If you say you will be **pleased to** do something, you are saying in a polite way that you are willing to do it. = happy ❑ *We will be pleased to answer any questions you may have.* **3** [V-LINK + pleased] You can tell someone that you are **pleased with** something they have done in order to express your approval. = happy ❑ *I'm pleased with the way things have been going.* ❑ *I am very pleased about the result.* ❑ *We are pleased that the problems have been resolved.* **4** [V-LINK + pleased + to-INF] When you are about to give someone some news that you know will please them, you can say that you are **pleased to** tell them the news or that they will be **pleased to** hear it. = happy ❑ *I'm pleased to say that he is now doing well.* **5** [V-LINK + pleased + to-INF] In official letters, people often say they will be **pleased to** do something, as a polite way of introducing what they are going to do or inviting people to do something. ❑ *We will be pleased to delete the charge from the original invoice.*
PHRASE **pleased with oneself** If someone seems very satisfied with something they have done, you can say that they are **pleased with themselves,** especially if you think they are more satisfied than they should be. ❑ *'Sophie was glad to see you', he said, pleased with himself again for having remembered her name.*
CONVENTION **pleased to meet you** (*formulae*) You can say 'Pleased to meet you' as a polite way of greeting someone who you are meeting for the first time.

pleas·ure ◆◇◇ /ˈpleʒə/ NOUN
NOUN [U, C] (**pleasures**) **1** [U] If something gives you **pleasure**, you get a feeling of happiness, satisfaction, or enjoyment from it. ❑ *Watching sports gave him great pleasure.* ❑ *Everybody takes pleasure in eating.* **2** [U] **Pleasure** is the activity of enjoying yourself, especially rather than working or doing what you have a duty to do. ❑ *He mixed business and pleasure in a perfect and dynamic way.* **3** [C] A **pleasure** is an activity, experience, or aspect of something

that you find very enjoyable or satisfying. ❑ *Watching TV is our only pleasure.* ❑ *the pleasure of seeing a smiling face*
CONVENTION **a pleasure** or **the pleasure 1** (*politeness*) If you meet someone for the first time, you can say, as a way of being polite, that it is **a pleasure to meet** them. You can also ask for **the pleasure of** someone's **company** as a polite and formal way of inviting them somewhere. ❑ *'A pleasure to meet you, sir,' he said.* **2** (*formulae*) You can say '**It's a pleasure**' or '**My pleasure**' as a polite way of replying to someone who has just thanked you for doing something. ❑ *'Thanks very much anyhow.'—'It's a pleasure.'*

pledge ◆◇◇ /pledʒ/ NOUN, VERB
NOUN [C] (**pledges**) **1** When someone makes a **pledge**, they make a serious promise that they will do something. = promise ❑ *The meeting ended with a pledge to step up cooperation between the six states of the region.* **2** A **pledge** is a promise to pay an amount of money to an organization or activity at a particular time or over a particular period. ❑ *a pledge of forty two million dollars a month*
VERB [T] (**pledges, pledging, pledged**) **1** When someone **pledges to** do something, they promise in a serious way to do it. When they **pledge** something, they promise to give it. ❑ *The Communists have pledged to support the opposition's motion.* ❑ *Philip pledges support and offers to help in any way that he can.* **2** If you **pledge** a sum of money to an organization or activity, you promise to pay that amount of money to it at a particular time or over a particular period. ❑ *The French president is pledging $150 million in French aid next year.* **3** If you **pledge yourself to** something, you commit yourself to following a particular course of action or to supporting a particular person, group, or idea. = commit ❑ *The president pledged himself to increase taxes for the rich but not the middle classes.* **4** If you **pledge** something such as a valuable possession or a sum of money, you leave it with someone as a guarantee that you will repay money that you have borrowed. ❑ *He asked her to pledge the house as security for a loan.*

plen·ti·ful /ˈplentɪfʊl/ ADJ Things that are **plentiful** exist in such large amounts or numbers that there is enough for people's wants or needs. ❑ *Fish are plentiful in the lake.*

plen·ty ◆◇◇ /ˈplenti/ QUANT, PRON
QUANT If there is **plenty of** something, there is a large amount of it. If there are **plenty of** things, there are many of them. **Plenty** is used especially to indicate that there is enough of something, or more than you need. ❑ *There was still plenty of time to take Jill out for pizza.* ❑ *Most businesses face plenty of competition.*
PRON If something is **plenty**, there is enough of it or more than enough of it. ❑ *I don't believe in long interviews. Fifteen minutes is plenty.*

plight /plaɪt/ NOUN [C] (**plights**) If you refer to someone's **plight,** you mean that they are in a difficult or distressing situation that is full of problems. ❑ *The nation saw the plight of the farmers, whose crops had died.*

⊙ **plot** ◆◇◇ /plɒt/ NOUN, VERB
NOUN [C, U] (**plots**) **1** [C] A **plot** is a secret plan by a group of people to do something that is illegal or wrong, usually against a person or a government. ❑ *Security forces have uncovered a plot to overthrow the government.* **2** [C, U] The **plot** of a film, novel, or play is the connected series of events which make up the story. = storyline ❑ *He began to tell me the plot of his new book.* ❑ *The special effects don't compensate for a basic lack of plot development.* ❑ *an unexpected plot twist* **3** [C] A **plot** of land is a small piece of land, especially one that has been measured or marked out for a special purpose, such as building houses or growing vegetables. ❑ *I thought that I'd buy myself a small plot of land and build a house on it.*
VERB [T] (**plots, plotting, plotted**) **1** If people **plot to** do something or **plot** something that is illegal or wrong, they plan secretly to do it. ❑ *Prosecutors in the trial allege the defendants plotted to overthrow the government.* ❑ *The military were plotting a coup.* **2** When people **plot** a strategy or a course of action, they carefully plan each step of it. ❑ *Yesterday's meeting was intended to plot a survival strategy for the party.* **3** When someone **plots** something on a graph, they mark certain points on it and then join the

p

points up. ❑ *We plotted about eight points on the graph.* ❑ *The graph above plots UK stock market returns against economic growth in the developed world.* ◢ When someone **plots** the position or course of a plane or ship, they mark it on a map using instruments to obtain accurate information. ❑ *We were trying to plot the course of the submarine.* ◢ If someone **plots** the progress or development of something, they make a diagram or a plan which shows how it has developed in order to give some indication of how it will develop in the future. ❑ *They used a computer to plot the movements of everyone in the police station on December 24, 1990.*

plough /plaʊ/ (in AmE, use **plow**) NOUN, VERB

[NOUN] [c] (**ploughs**) A **plough** is a large farming tool with sharp blades that is pulled across the soil to turn it over, usually before seeds are planted. ❑ *There are new tractors and new ploughs in the machinery lot.*

[VERB] [T] (**ploughs, ploughing, ploughed**) When someone **ploughs** an area of land, they turn over the soil using a plough. ❑ *They were no longer using mules and horses to plough their fields.*

[PHRASAL VERB] **plough back** (*business*) If profits **are ploughed back into** a business, they are used to increase the size of the business or to improve it. ❑ *cash profits that are quickly ploughed back into the market*

plug /plʌg/ NOUN, VERB

[NOUN] [c] (**plugs**) ◢ A **plug** on a piece of electrical equipment is a small plastic object with three or two metal pins that fit into the holes of an electrical socket and connects the equipment to the electricity supply. ❑ *I used to go around and take every plug out at night.* ◢ A **plug** is a thick, circular piece of rubber or plastic that you use to block the hole in a bath or sink when it is filled with water. ❑ *She put the plug in the sink and filled it with cold water.* ◢ A **plug** is a small, round piece of wood, plastic, or wax that is used to block holes. ❑ *A plug had been inserted in the drill hole.* ◢ A **plug** is when someone praises a commercial product, especially a book or a film, in order to encourage people to buy it or see it because they have an interest in it doing well. ❑ *Let's do this show tonight and it'll be a great plug, a great promotion.*

[PHRASE] **pull the plug** If someone in a position of power **pulls the plug on** a project or **on** someone's activities, they use their power to stop them from continuing. ❑ *The banks have the power to pull the plug on the project.*

[VERB] [T] (**plugs, plugging, plugged**) ◢ If you **plug** a hole, you block it with something. ❑ *Crews are working to plug a major oil leak.* ◢ If someone **plugs** a commercial product, especially a book or a film, they praise it in order to encourage people to buy it or see it because they have an interest in it doing well. = promote ❑ *We did not want people on the show who are purely interested in plugging a book or film.*

[PHRASAL VERB] **plug in** or **plug into** ◢ If you **plug** a piece of electrical equipment **into** an electricity supply or if you **plug** it **in**, you push its plug into an electric socket so that it can work. ❑ *They plugged in their tape-recorders.* ❑ *I had a TV set but there was no place to plug it in.* ◢ If you **plug** one piece of electrical equipment **into** another or if you **plug** it **in**, you make it work by connecting the two. ❑ *They plugged their guitars into amplifiers.* ◢ If one piece of electrical equipment **plugs in** or **plugs into** another piece of electrical equipment, it works by being connected by an electrical cord or lead to an electricity supply or to the other piece of equipment. ❑ *The device looks like a video recorder and plugs into the home television and stereo system.* ❑ *They plug into a laptop, desktop, or handheld computer.* ◢ If you **plug** something **into** a hole, you push it into the hole. ❑ *Her instructor plugged live bullets into the gun's chamber.*

✪ **plum·met** /ˈplʌmɪt/ VERB [I] (**plummets, plummeting, plummeted**) (*journalism*) If an amount, rate, or price **plummets**, it decreases quickly by a large amount. = plunge, drop, fall; ≠ rise, soar ❑ *In Tokyo share prices have plummeted for the sixth successive day.* ❑ *The president's popularity has plummeted to an all-time low in recent weeks.*

plump /plʌmp/ ADJ, VERB

[ADJ] (**plumper, plumpest**) You can describe someone or

something as **plump** to indicate that they are somewhat fat or rounded. ❑ *Maria was a pretty little thing, small and plump with a mass of curly hair.* ❑ *He pushed a plump little hand towards me.*

[VERB] [T] (**plumps, plumping, plumped**) If you **plump** a pillow or cushion, you shake it and hit it gently so that it goes back into a rounded shape. ❑ *She patted all the seats and plumped all the cushions.*

[PHRASAL VERB] **plump up** Plump up means the same as **plump** VERB. ❑ *'You need to rest,' she told him reassuringly as she moved to plump up his pillows.*

plun·der /ˈplʌndə/ VERB, NOUN

[VERB] [T] (**plunders, plundering, plundered**) (*literary*) If someone **plunders** a place or **plunders** things **from** a place, they steal things from it. = loot ❑ *He plundered the palaces and ransacked the treasuries.* ❑ *She faces charges of helping to plunder her country's treasury of billions of dollars.*

[NOUN] [U] **Plunder** is the act of stealing things from a place. ❑ *a guerrilla group infamous for torture and plunder*

plunge ◆◇◇ /plʌndʒ/ VERB, NOUN

[VERB] [I, T] (**plunges, plunging, plunged**) ◢ [I] If something or someone **plunges** in a particular direction, especially into water, they fall, rush, or throw themselves in that direction. ❑ *At least 50 people died when a bus plunged into a river.* ◢ [T] If you **plunge** an object **into** something, you push it quickly or violently into it. ❑ *A soldier plunged a bayonet into his body.* ❑ *She plunged her face into a bowl of cold water.* ◢ [I, T] If a person or thing **is plunged into** a particular state or situation, or if they **plunge into** it, they are suddenly in that state or situation. ❑ *The government's political and economic reforms threaten to plunge the country into chaos.* ❑ *Eddy found himself plunged into a world of brutal violence.* ◢ [I, T] If you **plunge into** an activity or **are plunged into** it, you suddenly get very involved in it. ❑ *The two men plunged into discussion.* ❑ *The prince should be plunged into work.* ◢ [I] If an amount or rate **plunges**, it decreases quickly and suddenly. = plummet ❑ *His weight began to plunge.* ❑ *The Peso plunged to a new low on the foreign exchange markets yesterday.*

[NOUN] [c] (**plunges**) ◢ A **plunge** is when something or someone falls, rushes, or throws themselves in a particular direction. ❑ *a plunge into cold water* ◢ A **plunge** into a particular state or situation is when a person or thing is suddenly in that state or situation. ❑ *That peace often looked like a brief truce before the next plunge into war.* ◢ A **plunge** into an activity is the act of suddenly getting very involved in it. ❑ *His sudden plunge into the field of international diplomacy is a major surprise.* ◢ A **plunge** is a quick and sudden decrease in an amount or rate. ❑ *Japan's banks are in trouble because of bad loans and the stock market plunge.*

[PHRASE] **take the plunge** If you **take the plunge**, you decide to do something that you consider difficult or risky. ❑ *If you have been thinking about buying mutual funds, now could be the time to take the plunge.*

plu·ral /ˈplʊərəl/ ADJ, NOUN

[ADJ] The **plural** form of a word is the form that is used when referring to more than one person or thing. ❑ *'Data' is the Latin plural form of 'datum'.*

[NOUN] [c] (**plurals**) The **plural** of a noun is the form of it that is used to refer to more than one person or thing. ❑ *What is the plural of 'person'?*

✪ **plus** ◆◆◇ /plʌs/ CONJ, ADJ, NOUN (*academic word*)

[CONJ] ◢ You say **plus** to show that one number or quantity is being added to another. ❑ *$5 for a small locker, plus a $3 deposit* ❑ *36 plus 5 squared is 61.* ◢ (*informal*) You can use **plus** when mentioning an additional item or fact. = and ❑ *There's easily enough room for two adults and three children, plus a dog in the trunk.*

[ADJ] ◢ [plus + AMOUNT] **Plus** before a number or quantity means that the number or quantity is greater than zero. ❑ *The aircraft was subjected to temperatures of minus 65 degrees and plus 120 degrees.* ◢ [AMOUNT + plus] You use **plus** after a number or quantity to indicate that the actual number or quantity is greater than the one mentioned. ❑ *There are only 35 staff to serve 30,000-plus customers.* ◢ Teachers use **plus** in marking work in schools and colleges. 'B plus' is a better mark than 'B', but it is not as good as 'A'.

NOUN [C] (**pluses** or **plusses**) (*informal*) A **plus** is an advantage or benefit. ◻ *Well-known figures would be a big plus for the new board.*

p.m. /ˌpiːˈem/ also **pm** ADV [NUM + p.m.] **p.m.** is used after a number to show that you are referring to a particular time between 12 noon and 12 midnight. Compare **a.m.** ◻ *The spa is open from 7.00 a.m. to 9.00 p.m. every day of the year.*

pneu·mo·nia /njuːˈməʊniə/ NOUN [U] **Pneumonia** is a serious disease that affects your lungs and makes it difficult for you to breathe. ◻ *She nearly died of pneumonia.*

pock·et ◆◇◇ /ˈpɒkɪt/ NOUN, ADJ, VERB

NOUN [C] (**pockets**) **1** A **pocket** is a kind of small bag that forms part of a piece of clothing, and that is used for carrying small things such as money or a handkerchief. ◻ *He took his torch from his jacket pocket and switched it on.* **2** You can use **pocket** in a lot of different ways to refer to money that people have, get, or spend. For example, if someone gives or pays a lot of money, you can say that they **dig deep into** their **pocket**. If you approve of something because it is very cheap to buy, you can say that it **suits people's pockets**. ◻ *When you come to choosing a dining table, it really is worth digging deep into your pocket for the best you can afford.* ◻ *ladies' fashions to suit all shapes, sizes, and pockets* **3** A **pocket** of something is a small area where something is happening, or a small area which has a particular quality, and which is different from the other areas around it. ◻ *Trapped in a pocket of air, they had only 40 minutes before the tide flooded the chamber.*

PHRASES **deep pockets** If you say that a person or organization has **deep pockets**, you mean that they have a lot of money with which to pay for something. ◻ *The church will do anything to avoid scandal – and everyone knows it has deep pockets.* ◻ *investors with deep pockets*

out of pocket If you are **out of pocket**, you have less money than you should have or than you intended, for example, because you have spent too much or because of a mistake. ◻ *Make sure you are not out of pocket for your expenses.*

pick someone's pocket If someone **picks** your **pocket**, they steal something from your pocket, usually without you noticing. ◻ *They were more in danger of having their pockets picked than being shot at.*

ADJ [pocket + N] You use **pocket** to describe something that is small enough to fit into a pocket, often something that is a smaller version of a larger item. ◻ *a pocket calculator*

VERB [T] (**pockets, pocketing, pocketed**) **1** If someone who is in possession of something valuable such as a sum of money **pockets** it, they steal it or take it for themselves, even though it does not belong to them. ◻ *Banks have passed some of the savings on to customers and pocketed the rest.* **2** (*journalism*) If you say that someone **pockets** something such as a prize or sum of money, you mean that they win or obtain it, often without needing to make much effort or in a way that seems unfair. ◻ *He pocketed more money from this tournament than in his entire three years as a professional.* **3** If someone **pockets** something, they put it in their pocket, for example, because they want to steal it or hide it. ◻ *Anthony snatched his letters and pocketed them.*

⊘poem ◆◇◇ /ˈpəʊɪm/ NOUN [C] (**poems**) A **poem** is a piece of writing in which the words are chosen for their beauty and sound and are carefully arranged, often in short lines that rhyme. = ode, verse ◻ *a book of love poems*

⊘poet ◆◇◇ /ˈpəʊɪt/ NOUN [C] (**poets**) A **poet** is a person who writes poems. = bard, lyricist ◻ *He was a painter and poet.* ◻ *a survey of women poets writing in English*

po·et·ic /pəʊˈetɪk/ ADJ **1** Something that is **poetic** is very beautiful and expresses emotions in a sensitive or moving way. ◻ *Nikolai Demidenko gave an exciting yet poetic performance.* **2** **Poetic** means relating to poetry. ◻ *Keats' famous poetic lines*

⊘po·et·ry ◆◇◇ /ˈpəʊɪtri/ NOUN [U] **1** Poems, considered

as a form of literature, are referred to as **poetry**. = verse; ≠ prose ◻ *Russian poetry* ◻ *Lawrence Durrell wrote a great deal of poetry.* **2** You can describe something very beautiful as **poetry**. ◻ *His music is purer poetry than a poem in words.*

poign·ant /ˈpɔɪnjənt/ ADJ Something that is **poignant** affects you deeply and makes you feel sadness or regret. ◻ *a poignant combination of beautiful surroundings and tragic history* ◻ *a poignant love story*

⊘point ◆◆◆ /pɔɪnt/ NOUN, VERB, CONVENTION

NOUN [C, SING, PL] (**points**) **1** [C] You use **point** to refer to something that someone has said or written. ◻ *We disagree with every point she makes.* ◻ *The following account will clearly illustrate this point.* ◻ *Dave Hill's article makes the right point about the Taylor Report.* **2** [SING] If you say that someone **has a point**, or if you **take** their **point**, you mean that you accept that what they have said is important and should be considered. ◻ *'If he'd already killed once, surely he'd have killed Sarah?' She had a point there.* **3** [SING] **The point** of what you are saying or discussing is the most important part that provides a reason or explanation for the rest. ◻ *'Did I ask you to talk to me?'—'That's not the point.'* **4** [SING] If you ask what **the point of** something is, or say that there is **no point in** it, you are indicating that a particular action has no purpose or would not be useful. ◻ *What was the point of thinking about him?* **5** [C] A **point** is a detail, aspect, or quality of something or someone. ◻ *Many of the points in the report are correct.* ◻ *The most interesting point about the village was its religion.* ◻ *Several key points emerged from the Oxfordshire experiment.* **6** [C] A **point** is a particular place or position where something happens. ◻ *I'm sure there's another point we could meet at, but not there.* **7** [SING] You use **point** to refer to a particular time, or to a particular stage in the development of something. ◻ *We're all going to die at some point.* ◻ *It got to the point where he had to leave.* **8** [C] The **point** of something such as a pin, needle, or knife is the thin, sharp end of it. ◻ *Put the tomatoes into a bowl and stab each one with the point of a knife.* **9** [C] In some sports, competitions, and games, a **point** is one of the single marks that are added together to give the total score. ◻ *Chamberlain scored 50 or more points four times in the season.* **10** [C] The **points of the compass** are directions such as North, South, East, and West. ◻ *Sightseers arrived from all points of the compass.* **11** [PL] (*BrE*; in *AmE*, use **switches**) On a railway track, the **points** are the levers and rails at a place where two tracks join or separate. The points enable a train to move from one track to another.

PHRASES **beside the point** If you say that something is **beside the point**, you mean that it is not relevant to the subject that you are discussing. = irrelevant ◻ *Brian didn't like it, but that was beside the point.*

come to the point or **get to the point** When someone **comes to the point** or **gets to the point**, they start talking about the thing that is most important to them. ◻ *He came to the point at once. 'You did a splendid job on this case.'*

make one's point or **prove one's point** If you **make** your **point** or **prove** your **point**, you prove that something is true, either by arguing about it or by your actions or behaviour. ◻ *I think you've made your point, dear.* ◻ *Dr David McCleland studied one-hundred people, aged eighteen to sixty, to prove the point.*

make a point of If you **make a point of** doing something, you do it in a very deliberate or obvious way. ◻ *She made a point of spending as much time as possible away from Oklahoma.*

on the point of If you are **on the point of** doing something, you are about to do it. ◻ *He was on the point of saying something when the phone rang.*

to the point Something that is **to the point** is relevant to the subject that you are discussing, or expressed neatly without wasting words or time. ◻ *The description which he had been given was brief and to the point.*

up to a point If you say that something is true **up to a point**, you mean that it is partly but not completely true. ◻ *'Was she good?'—'Mmm. Up to a point.'*

VERB [I, T] (**points, pointing, pointed**) **1** [I] If you **point at** a person or thing, you hold out your finger towards them in order to make someone notice them. ◻ *I pointed at the*

p

boy sitting nearest me. ❏ He pointed at me with the stem of his pipe. **2** [T] If you **point** something **at** someone, you aim the tip or end of it towards them. ❏ David pointed his finger at Mary. **3** [I] If something **points to** a place or **points** in a particular direction, it shows where that place is or it faces in that direction. ❏ An arrow pointed to the toilets. ❏ He controlled the car until it was pointing forward again. **4** [I] If something **points to** a particular situation, it suggests that the situation exists or is likely to occur. ❏ Earlier reports pointed to students working harder, more continuously, and with enthusiasm. **5** [I] If you **point to** something that has happened or that is happening, you are using it as proof that a particular situation exists. ❏ George Fodor points to other weaknesses in the campaign.

PHRASAL VERB **point out** **1** If you **point out** an object or place, you make people look at it or show them where it is. ❏ They kept standing up to take pictures and point things out to each other. **2** If you **point out** a fact or mistake, you tell someone about it or draw their attention to it. ❏ I should point out that these estimates cover just the hospital expenditures. ❏ Dr Newlinds pointed out that in 1960 doctors had not known of any drugs causing major defects in the newborn.

CONVENTION In spoken English, you use **point** to refer to the dot or mark in a decimal number that separates the whole numbers from the fractions. ❏ This is FM stereo one oh three point seven.
→ See also **focal point, pointed, point of view**
✦ **in point of fact** → see **fact; point the finger at someone** → see **finger; a sore point** → see **sore**

point·ed /'pɔɪntɪd/ ADJ **1** Something that is **pointed** has a point at one end. ❏ a pointed roof **2** **Pointed** comments or behaviour express criticism in a clear and direct way. ❏ I couldn't help notice the pointed remarks slung in my direction.
point·ed·ly /'pɔɪntɪdli/ ADV ❏ They were pointedly absent from the news conference.

point·less /'pɔɪntləs/ ADJ (disapproval) If you say that something is **pointless**, you are criticizing it because it has no sense or purpose. ❏ Violence is always pointless. ❏ Without an audience the performance is pointless.
point·less·ly /'pɔɪntləsli/ ADV ❏ Chemicals were pointlessly poisoning the soil.

point of view ◆◇◇ NOUN [C] (points of view) **1** You can refer to the opinions or attitudes that you have about something as your **point of view**. = viewpoint ❏ Thanks for your point of view, John. **2** If you consider something **from** a particular **point of view**, you are using one aspect of a situation in order to judge that situation. ❏ Do you think that, from the point of view of results, this exercise was worth the cost?

poise /pɔɪz/ NOUN [U] If someone has **poise**, they are calm, dignified, and self-controlled. ❏ What amazed him even more than her appearance was her poise.

poised /pɔɪzd/ ADJ **1** If a part of your body is **poised**, it is completely still but ready to move at any moment. ❏ He studied the keyboard carefully, one finger poised. **2** [V-LINK + poised] If someone is **poised to** do something, they are ready to take action at any moment. ❏ US forces are poised for a massive air, land, and sea assault. **3** If you are **poised**, you are calm, dignified, and self-controlled. ❏ She was self-assured, poised, almost self-satisfied.

poi·son /'pɔɪzən/ NOUN, VERB
NOUN [C, U] (poisons) **Poison** is a substance that harms or kills people or animals if they swallow or absorb it. ❏ Poison from the fish causes paralysis, swelling, and nausea.
VERB [T] (poisons, poisoning, poisoned) **1** If someone **poisons** another person, they kill the person or make them ill by giving them poison. ❏ The rumours that she had poisoned him could never be proved. **2** If you **are poisoned by** a substance, it makes you very ill and sometimes kills you. ❏ Employees were taken to the hospital yesterday after being poisoned by fumes. **3** If someone **poisons** a food, drink, or weapon, they add poison to it so that it can be used to kill someone. ❏ If I was your wife I would poison your coffee. **4** To **poison** water, air, or land means to damage it with harmful substances such as chemicals. ❏ the textile

and fibre industries that taint the air, poison the water, and use vast amounts of natural resources ❏ The land has been completely poisoned by chemicals. **5** Something that **poisons** a good situation or relationship spoils it or destroys it. ❏ The whole atmosphere has really been poisoned.
poi·son·ing /'pɔɪzənɪŋ/ NOUN [U] **1** She was sentenced to twenty years' imprisonment for poisoning and attempted murder. **2** acute alcohol poisoning

poi·son·ous /'pɔɪzənəs/ ADJ **1** Something that is **poisonous** will kill you or make you ill if you swallow or absorb it. ❏ All parts of the yew tree are poisonous, including the berries. **2** An animal that is **poisonous** produces a poison that will kill you or make you ill if the animal bites you. ❏ There are hundreds of poisonous spiders and snakes. **3** If you describe something as **poisonous**, you mean that it is extremely unpleasant and likely to spoil or destroy a good relationship or situation. ❏ poisonous comments ❏ lying awake half the night tormented by poisonous suspicions

poke /pəʊk/ VERB, NOUN
VERB [T, I] (pokes, poking, poked) **1** [T] If you **poke** someone or something, you quickly push them with your finger or with a sharp object. = jab ❏ Lindy poked him in the ribs. **2** [T] If you **poke** one thing **into** another, you push the first thing into the second thing. ❏ He poked his finger into the hole. **3** [I] If something **pokes out of** or **through** another thing, you can see part of it appearing from behind or underneath the other thing. ❏ He saw the dog's twitching nose poke out of the basket. **4** [I, T] If you **poke** your head through an opening or if it **pokes** through an opening, you push it through, often so that you can see something more easily. ❏ Julie tapped on my door and poked her head in.
NOUN [C] (pokes) If you give someone or something a **poke**, you quickly push them with your finger or with a sharp object. = prod ❏ John smiled at them and gave Richard a playful poke.
✦ **poke fun at** → see **fun**

⊕**po·lar** /'pəʊlə/ ADJ **1** [polar + N] **Polar** means near the North or South Poles. ❏ the rigours of life in the polar regions ❏ There was a period of excessive warmth which melted some of the polar ice. ❏ the ill-fated polar explorers **2** [polar + N] (formal) **Polar** is used to describe things that are completely opposite in character, quality, or type. ❏ The nomads' lifestyle was the polar opposite of collectivization.

⊕**pole** ◆◇◇ /pəʊl/ NOUN
NOUN [C] (poles) **1** A **pole** is a long thin piece of wood or metal, used especially for supporting things. ❏ The truck crashed into a telegraph pole. **2** The Earth's **poles** are the two opposite ends of its axis, its most northern and southern points. ❏ For six months of the year, there is hardly any light at the poles. **3** The two **poles** of a magnet are the two ends of the magnet where the magnetic force is strongest. ❏ The important fact is that the two poles of the magnet work in opposite ways. **4** The two **poles** of a range of qualities, opinions, or beliefs are the completely opposite qualities, opinions, or beliefs at either end of the range. ❏ The two politicians represent opposite poles of the political spectrum.
PHRASE **poles apart** (emphasis) If you say that two people or things are **poles apart**, you mean that they have completely different beliefs, opinions, or qualities.

⊕**po·lice** ◆◆◆ /pə'liːs/ NOUN, VERB
NOUN [SING, PL] **1** [SING] The **police** are the official organization that is responsible for making sure that people obey the law. = law enforcement, police officers ❏ The police are also looking for a second car. ❏ Police say they have arrested twenty people following the disturbances. **2** [PL] **Police** are men and women who are members of the official organization that is responsible for making sure that people obey the law. ❏ More than one hundred police have ringed the area.
VERB [T] (polices, policing, policed) **1** If the police or military forces **police** an area or event, they make sure that law and order is preserved in that area or at that event. ❏ the tiny UN observer force whose job it is to police the border **2** If a person or group in authority **polices** a law or an area of public life, they make sure that what is done is fair

and legal. ❑ *the self-regulatory body that polices the investment management business*

po·lice force NOUN [C] (**police forces**) A **police force** is the police organization in a particular country or area. ❑ *the Wichita police force*

po·lice·man ◆◇◇ /pə'li:smən/ NOUN [C] (**policemen**) A **policeman** is a man who is a member of the police force.

po·lice of·fic·er ◆◇◇ NOUN [C] (**police officers**) A **police officer** is a member of the police force. ❑ *a meeting of senior police officers*

po·lice sta·tion NOUN [C] (**police stations**) A **police station** is the local office of a police force in a particular area. ❑ *Two police officers arrested him and took him to Gettysburg police station.*

✪ poli·cy ◆◆◆ /'pɒlɪsi/ NOUN [C, U] (**policies**) (*academic word*) **1** [C, U] A **policy** is a set of ideas or plans that is used as a basis for making decisions, especially in politics, economics, or business. ❑ *plans that include changes in foreign policy and economic reforms* ❑ *the UN's policy-making body* **2** [C] An official organization's **policy** on a particular issue or towards a country is their attitude and actions regarding that issue or country. ❑ *the organization's future policy towards South Africa* ❑ *the government's policy on repatriation* **3** [C] (*business*) An insurance **policy** is a document that shows the agreement that you have made with an insurance company. ❑ *You are advised to read the small print of homeowner and car insurance policies.*

WORD CONNECTIONS
ADJ + **policy**
foreign policy
economic policy
monetary policy
social policy
❑ *What effect are the government's economic policies having?*

po·lio /'pəʊliəʊ/ NOUN [U] **Polio** is a serious infectious disease that often makes people unable to use their legs. ❑ *Gladys was crippled by polio at the age of 3.*

pol·ish /'pɒlɪʃ/ NOUN, VERB
NOUN [C, U, SING] (**polishes**) **1** [C, U] **Polish** is a substance that you put on the surface of an object in order to clean it, protect it, and make it shine. ❑ *The still air smelled faintly of furniture polish.* **2** [SING] A **polish** is the act of putting polish on something or rubbing it with a cloth to make it shine. ❑ *He gave his counter a polish with a soft duster.* **3** [U] If you say that a performance or piece of work has **polish**, you mean that it is of a very high standard. ❑ *The opera lacks the polish of his later work.*
VERB [T] (**polishes, polishing, polished**) **1** If you **polish** something, you put polish on it or rub it with a cloth to make it shine. ❑ *Each morning he shaved and polished his shoes.* **2** If you **polish** your technique, performance, or skill at doing something, you work on improving it. ❑ *They just need to polish their technique.*
PHRASAL VERB **polish up** Polish up means the same as polish VERB 2. ❑ *Polish up your writing skills on a one-week professional course.*
pol·ished /'pɒlɪʃt/ ADJ ❑ *a highly polished floor*

po·lite /pə'laɪt/ ADJ (**politer, politest**) Someone who is **polite** has good manners and behaves in a way that is socially correct and not rude to other people. ❑ *Everyone around him was trying to be polite, but you could tell they were all bored.* ❑ *Gonzales, a quiet and very polite young man, made a favourable impression.*
po·lite·ly /pə'laɪtli/ ADV ❑ *'Your home is beautiful', I said politely.*
po·lite·ness /pə'laɪtnəs/ NOUN [U] ❑ *She listened to him, but only out of politeness.*

✪ po·liti·cal ◆◆◆ /pə'lɪtɪkəl/ ADJ **1 Political** means relating to the way power is achieved and used in a country or society. = governmental ❑ *All other political parties there have been completely banned.* ❑ *The government is facing another political crisis.* ❑ *a democratic political system* **2** Someone who is **political** is interested or involved in

politics and holds strong beliefs about it. ❑ *Oh I'm not political, I take no interest in politics.*
po·liti·cal·ly /pə'lɪtɪkli/ ADV = governmentally ❑ *They do not believe the killings were politically motivated.* ❑ *Politically and economically this is an extremely difficult question.*

po·liti·cal asy·lum NOUN [U] **Political asylum** is the right to live in a foreign country and is given by the government of that country to people who have to leave their own country for political reasons. ❑ *a university teacher who is seeking political asylum in California*

✪ poli·ti·cian ◆◆◇ /,pɒlɪ'tɪʃən/ NOUN [C] (**politicians**) A **politician** is a person whose job is in politics, especially a member of the government. = Member of Parliament, MP, statesman ❑ *They have arrested a number of leading opposition politicians.*

✪ poli·tics ◆◆◇ /'pɒlɪtɪks/ NOUN [PL, U] **1** [PL] Politics are the actions or activities concerned with achieving and using power in a country or society. The verb that follows **politics** may be either singular or plural. = domestic affairs, foreign affairs ❑ *Many people think Nixon transformed American politics.* ❑ *He quickly involved himself in local politics.* ❑ *Politics is by no means the only arena in which women are excelling.* **2** [PL] Your **politics** are your beliefs about how a country ought to be governed. ❑ *My politics are well to the left of centre.* **3** [U] Politics is the study of the ways in which countries are governed. ❑ *He began studying politics and medieval history.* **4** [PL] Politics can be used to talk about the ways that power is shared in an organization and the ways it is affected by personal relationships between people who work together. The verb that follows **politics** may be either singular or plural. ❑ *You need to understand how office politics influence the working environment.*

WORD FAMILIES	
politics NOUN	She was involved in **politics** as a local councillor.
politician NOUN	Leading opposition **politicians** called on the minister to resign.
political ADJ	They were making the transition to a democratic **political** system.
politically ADV	They do not believe the killings were **politically** motivated.

WHICH WORD?
politics, policy, or political?
The noun **politics** is usually used to refer to the methods by which people acquire and use power in a country or society.
❑ *They are reluctant to take part in politics.*
Politics can also refer to the study of the ways in which countries are governed.
❑ *Politics is a wide subject.*
There is no noun 'politic'. If you want to refer to a course of action or plan that has been agreed upon by a government or political party, the word you use is **policy**.
❑ *He was criticized for pursuing a policy of reconciliation.*
You also do not use 'politic' to mean 'relating to politics'. The word you use is **political**.
❑ *The Canadian government is facing another political crisis.*

✪ poll ◆◆◇ /pəʊl/ NOUN, VERB
NOUN [C, PL] (**polls**) **1** [C] A **poll** is a survey in which people are asked their opinions about something, usually in order to find out how popular something is or what people want to do in the future. = survey ❑ *Polls show that the European treaty has gained support in Denmark.* ❑ *We are doing a weekly poll on the president, and clearly his popularity has declined.* ❑ *opinion polls on Venezuela's presidential election* **2** [PL] The **polls** means an election for a country's government, or the place where people go to vote in an election. ❑ *Incumbent officeholders are difficult to*

defeat at the polls. ❑ *Voters are due to go to the polls on Sunday to elect a new president.*

VERB [T] (**polls, polling, polled**) **1** If you **are polled on** something, you are asked what you think about it as part of a survey. = survey ❑ *More than 18,000 people were polled.* ❑ *Audiences were going to be polled on which of three pieces of contemporary music they liked best.* **2** If a political party or a candidate **polls** a particular number or percentage of votes, they get that number or percentage of votes in an election. ❑ *The result showed he had polled enough votes to force a second ballot.*

→ See also **opinion poll**

✪**pol·len** /'pɒlən/ NOUN [c, u] (**pollens**) **Pollen** is a fine powder produced by flowers. It fertilizes other flowers of the same species so that they produce seeds. ❑ *Your susceptibility to pollen allergy or other sensitivities can be increased by emotional stresses.* ❑ *The flowers produce no new pollen after they have been cut.*

✪**pol·li·nate** /'pɒlɪneɪt/ VERB [T] (**pollinates, pollinating, pollinated**) To **pollinate** a plant or tree means to fertilize it with pollen. This is often done by insects. ❑ *Many of the indigenous insects are needed to pollinate the local plants.* ❑ *So for the first time bees can be brought into glasshouses to pollinate crops by natural means.*

✪**pol·li·na·tion** /ˌpɒlɪ'neɪʃən/ NOUN [u] ❑ *Without sufficient pollination, the growth of the corn is stunted.* ❑ *The blossom of your chosen varieties must be produced at the same time to ensure successful pollination.*

pol·lu·tant /pə'luːtənt/ NOUN [c, u] (**pollutants**) **Pollutants** are substances that pollute the environment, especially gases from vehicles and poisonous chemicals produced as waste by industrial processes. ❑ *Industrial pollutants are responsible for a sizable proportion of all cancers.*

✪**pol·lute** /pə'luːt/ VERB [T] (**pollutes, polluting, polluted**) To **pollute** water, air, or land means to make it dirty and dangerous to live in or to use, especially with poisonous chemicals or sewage. = contaminate ❑ *Heavy industry pollutes our rivers with noxious chemicals.*

pol·lut·ed /pə'luːtɪd/ ADJ ❑ *The police have warned the city's inhabitants not to bathe in the polluted river.*

✪**pol·lu·tion** /pə'luːʃən/ NOUN [u] **1 Pollution** is the process of polluting water, air, or land, especially with poisonous chemicals. ❑ *The fine was for the company's pollution of the air near its plants.* ❑ *Recycling also helps control environmental pollution by reducing the need for waste dumps.* **2 Pollution** is poisonous or dirty substances that are polluting the water, air, or land somewhere. = emissions, contamination ❑ *The level of pollution in the river was falling.*

WORD CONNECTIONS
VERB + **pollution**
cause pollution
❑ *These chemicals can travel through the atmosphere and cause pollution.*
reduce pollution
cut pollution
combat pollution
❑ *In an effort to combat pollution, cars cannot be driven into the city centre.*
ADJ + **pollution**
atmospheric pollution
environmental pollution
❑ *Environmental pollution contaminates our air, soil, and food.*
industrial pollution
❑ *We need much better control of industrial pollution.*

poly·es·ter /ˌpɒli'estə, AmE 'pɑːlies-/ NOUN [c, u] (**polyesters**) **Polyester** is a type of synthetic cloth used especially to make clothes. ❑ *a green polyester shirt*

po·lyga·my /pə'lɪgəmi/ NOUN [u] **Polygamy** is the custom in some societies in which someone can be legally married to more than one person at the same time. ❑ *In Nicaragua, polygamy is punishable with up to five years in jail.*

WORD PARTS
The prefix **poly-** often appears in words that have 'many' as part of their meaning, including the names of some chemicals that consist of the same structure repeated many times:
polygamy (NOUN)
polyester (NOUN)
polyglot (NOUN)

pond /pɒnd/ NOUN [c, SING] (**ponds**) **1** [c] A **pond** is a small area of water that is smaller than a lake. Ponds are often made artificially. ❑ *She chose a bench beside the duck pond and sat down.* **2** [SING] (mainly journalism) People sometimes refer to the Atlantic Ocean as **the pond**. ❑ *Tourist numbers from across the pond have dropped dramatically.*

pon·der /'pɒndə/ VERB [I, T] (**ponders, pondering, pondered**) If you **ponder** something, you think about it carefully. ❑ *I found myself constantly pondering the question: 'How could anyone do these things?'* ❑ *He pondered over the difficulties involved.*

pony /'pəʊni/ NOUN [c] (**ponies**) A **pony** is a small or young horse.

pool ◆◇◇ /puːl/ NOUN, VERB

NOUN [c] (**pools**) **1** A **pool** is the same as a **swimming pool**. ❑ *a heated indoor pool* **2** A **pool** is a fairly small area of still water. ❑ *The pool had dried up and was full of bracken and reeds.* **3** A **pool of** liquid or light is a small area of it on the ground or on a surface. ❑ *She was found lying in a pool of blood.* ❑ *It was raining quietly and steadily and there were little pools of water on the gravel drive.* **4** A **pool of** people, money, or things is a quantity or number of them that is available for an organization or group to use. ❑ *The available pool of healthy manpower was not as large as military officials had expected.*

VERB [T] (**pools, pooling, pooled**) If a group of people or organizations **pool** their money, knowledge, or equipment, they share it or put it together so that it can be used for a particular purpose. ❑ *We pooled ideas and information.*

✪**poor** ◆◆◇ /pʊə, pɔː/ ADJ, NOUN

ADJ (**poorer, poorest**) **1** Someone who is **poor** has very little money and few possessions. = impoverished, deprived, poverty-stricken; ≠ rich, affluent, wealthy, well-off ❑ *The reason our schools cannot afford better teachers is because people here are poor.* ❑ *He was one of thirteen children from a poor family.* **2** The people in a **poor** country or area have very little money and few possessions. ❑ *Many countries in the Third World are as poor as they have ever been.* ❑ *a settlement house for children in a poor neighbourhood* **3** [poor + N] You use **poor** to express your sympathy for someone. ❑ *I feel sorry for that poor child.* ❑ *It was way too much for the poor guy to overcome.* **4** If you describe something as **poor**, you mean that it is of a low quality or standard or that it is in bad condition. ❑ *the poor state of the economy* ❑ *The gap between the best and poorest childcare provision has widened.* **5** If you describe an amount, rate, or number as **poor**, you mean that it is less than expected or less than is considered reasonable. ❑ *poor wages and working conditions* **6** You use **poor** to describe someone who is not very skilful in a particular activity. ❑ *He was a poor actor.* **7** [V-LINK + poor 'in' N] If something is **poor in** a particular quality or substance, it contains very little of the quality or substance. ❑ *Fats and sugar are very rich in energy but poor in vitamins and minerals.*

NOUN [PL] **The poor** are people who are poor. ❑ *Even the poor have their pride.*

poor·ly /'pʊəli, 'pɔːli/ ADV **1** Some are living in poorly built dormitories, even in tents. **2** During the first week, the evening meetings were poorly attended. **3** [poorly after V] ❑ *Cheetahs breed very poorly in captivity.*

pop ◆◇◇ /pɒp/ NOUN, VERB

NOUN [u, c] (**pops**) **1** [u] **Pop** is modern music that usually has a strong rhythm and uses electronic equipment. ❑ *the perfect combination of Caribbean rhythms, European pop, and American soul* ❑ *a life-size poster of a pop star* **2** [u] (BrE, informal) You can refer to carbonated drinks such as cola as

pop. ❑ *a can of pop* **3** [c] **Pop** is used to represent a short sharp sound such as the sound made by bursting a balloon or by pulling a cork out of a bottle. ❑ *Each corn kernel will make a loud pop when cooked.*

VERB [I, T] (**pops, popping, popped**) **1** [I] If something **pops**, it makes a short sharp sound. ❑ *He untwisted the wire off the champagne bottle, and the cork popped and shot to the ceiling.* **2** [I] (*informal*) If your eyes **pop**, you look very surprised or excited when you see something. ❑ *My eyes popped at the sight of the rich variety of food on show.* **3** [T] (*informal*) If you **pop** something somewhere, you put it there quickly. ❑ *Marianne got a couple of mugs from the cupboard and popped a teabag into each of them.*

PHRASAL VERB **pop up** (*informal*) If someone or something **pops up**, they appear in a place or situation unexpectedly. = appear ❑ *She was startled when Lisa popped up at the door all smiles.*

✦ **pop the question → see question**

pope /pəʊp/ NOUN [c] (**popes**) [usu 'the' pope; POPE] The **pope** is the head of the Roman Catholic Church. ❑ *The highlight of the pope's visit will be his message to the people.*

✪ **popu·lar** ✦✦◇ /ˈpɒpjʊlə/ ADJ **1** Something that is **popular** is enjoyed or liked by a lot of people. = well-liked, sought-after ❑ *Chocolate sauce is always popular with youngsters.* ❑ *This is the most popular ball game ever devised.* **2** Someone who is **popular** is liked by most people, or by most people in a particular group. ❑ *He remained the most popular politician in Arkansas.* **3** [popular + N] **Popular** newspapers, television programmes, or forms of art are aimed at ordinary people and not at experts or intellectuals. ❑ *Once again the popular press in Britain has been rife with stories about their marriage.* ❑ *one of the classics of modern popular music* **4** **Popular** ideas, feelings, or attitudes are approved of or held by most people. ❑ *Contrary to popular belief, the oil companies can't control the price of crude.* ❑ *The military government has been unable to win popular support.* **5** [popular + N] **Popular** is used to describe political activities that involve the ordinary people of a country, and not just members of political parties. ❑ *The late president Ferdinand Marcos was overthrown by a popular uprising in 1986.*

✪ **popu·lar·ity** /ˌpɒpjʊˈlærɪti/ NOUN [u] **1** = acclaim, approval; ≠ unpopularity ❑ *the growing popularity of Australian wines among consumers* ❑ *Walking and golf increased in popularity during the 1980s.* **2** *It is his popularity with ordinary people that sets him apart.* **3** *Over time, though, Watson's views gained in popularity.*

WORD CONNECTIONS
ADV + **popular**
hugely popular
wildly popular
extremely popular
❑ *Computer games are hugely popular among young people.*
increasingly popular
more popular
❑ *Shiatsu is a Japanese therapy which has become increasingly popular over recent years.*

popu·lar·ize /ˈpɒpjʊləraɪz/ also **popularise** VERB [T] (**popularizes, popularizing, popularized**) To **popularize** something means to make a lot of people interested in it and able to enjoy it. ❑ *Irving Brokaw, who had studied figure skating in Europe, returned to the US and popularized the new sport.*
popu·lari·za·tion /ˌpɒpjʊlaraɪˈzeɪʃən/ NOUN [u] ❑ *the popularization of sport through television*

popu·lar·ly /ˈpɒpjʊləli/ ADV **1** [popularly with -ED] If something or someone is **popularly** known as something, most people call them that, although it is not their official name or title. = commonly ❑ *the Mesozoic era, more popularly known as the age of dinosaurs* ❑ *an infection popularly called mad cow disease* **2** [popularly + -ED] If something is **popularly** believed or supposed to be the case, most people believe or suppose it to be the case, although it may not be true. = commonly ❑ *Schizophrenia is not a 'split mind' as is popularly believed.*

3 [popularly + -ED] A **popularly elected** leader or government has been elected by a majority of the people in a country. = democratically ❑ *Walesa was Poland's first popularly elected president.*

✪ **popu·la·tion** ✦✦◇ /ˌpɒpjʊˈleɪʃən/ NOUN [c] (**populations**) **1** The **population** of a country or area is all the people who live in it. ❑ *Bangladesh now has a population of about 110 million.* ❑ *the annual rate of population growth* **2** (*formal*) If you refer to a particular type of **population** in a country or area, you are referring to all the people or animals of that type there. ❑ *75.6 per cent of the male population over sixteen* ❑ *areas with a large black population* ❑ *the elephant populations of Tanzania and Kenya*

porce·lain /ˈpɔːsəlɪn/ NOUN [u] **Porcelain** is a hard, shiny substance made by heating clay. It is used to make delicate cups, plates, and ornaments. ❑ *There were lilies everywhere in tall white porcelain vases.*

pork /pɔːk/ NOUN [u] **Pork** is meat from a pig, usually fresh and not smoked or salted. ❑ *fried pork chops*

✪ **po·rous** /ˈpɔːrəs/ ADJ Something that is **porous** has many small holes in it that water and air can pass through. ❑ *The local limestone is so porous that all the rainwater immediately sinks below ground.* ❑ *Rough porous surfaces will soak up paint more quickly than smooth sealed surfaces.*

port ✦◇◇ /pɔːt/ NOUN, ADJ
NOUN [c, u] (**ports**) **1** [c] A **port** is a town by the sea or on a river that has a harbour. ❑ *the Mediterranean port of Marseilles* **2** [c] A **port** is a harbour area where ships load and unload goods or passengers. ❑ *the bridges that link the port area to the rest of the city* **3** [c] (*computing*) A **port** on a computer is a place where you can attach another piece of equipment such as a printer. ❑ *The devices, attached to a PC through standard ports, print bar codes onto envelopes.* **4** [u] In sailing, the **port** of a ship is the left side when you are on it and facing towards the front. ❑ *USS Ogden turned to port.* **5** [u] **Port** is a type of strong, sweet red wine. ❑ *He asked for a glass of port after dinner.*
ADJ (*technical*) In sailing, the **port** side of a ship is the left side when you are on it and facing towards the front. ❑ *Her official number is carved on the port side of the forecabin.*

port·able /ˈpɔːtəbəl/ ADJ, NOUN
ADJ A **portable** machine or device is designed to be easily carried or moved. ❑ *There was a little portable television switched on behind the bar.*
NOUN [c] (**portables**) A **portable** is something such as a television, radio, or computer that can be easily carried or moved. ❑ *We bought a portable for the bedroom.*

por·ter /ˈpɔːtə/ NOUN [c] (**porters**) **1** A **porter** is a person whose job is to carry things, for example, people's luggage at a train station or in a hotel. ❑ *Our taxi pulled up at Old Delhi station and a porter sprinted to the door.* **2** (*BrE; in AmE, use orderly*) In a hospital, a **porter** is someone whose job is to move patients from place to place. **3** (*BrE; in AmE, use doorman*) A **porter** is a person whose job is to be in charge of the entrance of a building such as a hotel.

port·fo·lio /pɔːtˈfəʊliəʊ/ NOUN [c] (**portfolios**) **1** A **portfolio** is a set of pictures by someone, photographs of their work, or examples of their writing, which they use when entering competitions or applying for work. ❑ *After dinner that evening, Edith showed them a portfolio of her own political cartoons.* **2** (*business*) In finance, a **portfolio** is the combination of investments that a particular person or company owns. ❑ *Roger Early, a portfolio manager at Federated Investors Corp* **3** In politics, a **portfolio** is a high-ranking official's responsibility for a particular area of a government's activities. ❑ *He has held the defence portfolio since the first free elections in 1990.* **4** (*business*) A company's **portfolio** of products or designs is their range of products or designs. ❑ *The company has continued to invest heavily in a strong portfolio of products.*

✪ **por·tion** /ˈpɔːʃən/ NOUN [c] (**portions**) (*academic word*) **1** A **portion** of something is a part of it. = part ❑ *Damage was confined to a small portion of the castle.* ❑ *I have spent a considerable portion of my life here.*

p

2 A **portion** is the amount of food that is given to one person at a meal. ❏ *Desserts can be substituted by a portion of fresh fruit.* ❏ *The portions were generous.*

✪ **por·trait** ◆◇◇ /ˈpɔːtreɪt/ NOUN [c] (**portraits**)
1 A **portrait** is a painting, drawing, or photograph of a particular person. ❏ *badly painted family portraits* ❏ *Lucian Freud was asked to paint a portrait of the Queen.* **2** [usu portrait 'of' N] A **portrait** of a person, place, or thing is a verbal description of them. ❏ *this gripping, funny portrait of Jewish life in 1950s Hoboken*

por·tray /pɔːˈtreɪ/ VERB [T] (**portrays, portraying, portrayed**) **1** When an actor or actress **portrays** someone, he or she plays that person in a play or film. ❏ *In 1975 he portrayed the king in a Los Angeles revival of 'Camelot.'* **2** When a writer or artist **portrays** something, he or she writes a description or produces a painting of it. = depict ❏ *The film portrays a culture of young people who live in lower Manhattan.* **3** If a film, book, or television programme **portrays** someone in a certain way, it represents them in that way. ❏ *complaints about the way women are portrayed in ads*

por·tray·al /pɔːˈtreɪəl/ NOUN [c] (**portrayals**) **1** An actor's **portrayal of** a character in a play or film is the way that he or she plays the character. ❏ *Mr Ying is well-known for his portrayal of a prison guard in the film 'The Last Emperor.'* **2** An artist's **portrayal of** something is a drawing, painting, or photograph of it. ❏ *a moving portrayal of St John the Evangelist by Simone Martini* **3** The **portrayal of** something in a book or film is the act of describing it or showing it. ❏ *an accurate portrayal of family life* **4** The **portrayal of** something in a book, film, or programme is the way that it is made to appear. ❏ *The media persists in its portrayal of us as muggers, dope sellers, and gangsters.*

✪ **pose** ◆◇◇ /pəʊz/ VERB, NOUN (*academic word*)
VERB [T, I] (**poses, posing, posed**) **1** [T] If something **poses** a problem or a danger, it is the cause of that problem or danger. = present ❏ *This could pose a threat to jobs in the coal industry.* ❏ *His ill health poses serious problems for the future.* **2** [T] (*formal*) If you **pose** a question, you ask it. If you **pose** an issue that needs considering, you mention the issue. = put forward ❏ *When I finally posed the question 'Why?', he merely shrugged.* ❏ *the moral issues posed by new technologies* **3** [I] If you **pose as** someone, you pretend to be that person in order to deceive people. ❏ *The team posed as drug dealers to trap the ringleaders.* **4** [I] If you **pose for** a photograph or painting, you stay in a particular position so that someone can photograph you or paint you. ❏ *Before going into their meeting the six foreign ministers posed for photographs.*
NOUN [c] (**poses**) A **pose** is a particular way that you stand, sit, or lie, for example, when you are being photographed or painted. ❏ *We have had several preliminary sittings in various poses.*

✪ **po·si·tion** ◆◆◆ /pəˈzɪʃən/ NOUN, VERB
NOUN [C, SING] (**positions**) **1** [c] The **position** of someone or something is the place where they are in relation to other things. = location, setting, place ❏ *The ship was identified, and its name and position were reported to the Coast Guard.* ❏ *This conservatory enjoys an enviable position overlooking a leafy expanse.* **2** [c] When someone or something is in a particular **position**, they are sitting, lying, or arranged in that way. ❏ *It is crucial that the upper back and neck are held in an erect position to give support for the head.* ❏ *Mr Dambar had raised himself to a sitting position.* **3** [c] Your **position** in society is the role and the importance that you have in it. = standing, role ❏ *Adjustment to their changing role and position in society can be painful for some old people.* ❏ *the profoundly radical changes to the position of women brought about by the Divorce Act of 1857* **4** [c] (*formal*) A **position** in a company or organization is a job. = post ❏ *He left a career in teaching to take up a position with the NEH.* ❏ *Hyundai said this week it is scaling back its US operations by eliminating 50 positions.* **5** [c] Your **position** in a race or competition is how well you did in relation to the other competitors or how well you are doing. ❏ *By the ninth hour the car was running in eighth position.* **6** [c] You can describe your situation at a

particular time by saying that you are in a particular **position**. = situation ❏ *He's going to be in a very difficult position if things go badly for him.* ❏ *Companies should be made to reveal more about their financial position.* **7** [c] (*formal*) Your **position on** a particular matter is your attitude towards it or your opinion of it. = stance ❏ *He could be depended on to take a moderate position on most of the key issues.* ❏ *Mr Howard is afraid to state his true position on the republic, which is that he is opposed to it.* **8** [SING] If you are **in a position to** do something, you are able to do it. If you are **in no position to** do something, you are unable to do it. ❏ *I am not in a position to comment.*
PHRASE **in position** If someone or something is in **position**, they are in their correct or usual place or arrangement. ❏ *28,000 US troops are moving into position.*
VERB [T] (**positions, positioning, positioned**) If you **position** something somewhere, you put it there carefully, so that it is in the right place or position. = place ❏ *Position the cursor where you want the new margins to begin.*

WORD CONNECTIONS
VERB + **position**
advertise a position
❏ *First they advertise the position, and then interviews take place.*
accept a position
❏ *He has accepted a position as a school cleaner.*
take a position **adopt** a position **assume** a position
❏ *The party has not yet taken a position on gay marriage.*
ADJ + **position**
a **difficult** position an **uncomfortable** position
❏ *Some parents find themselves in the uncomfortable position of not liking their children.*
a **financial** position
❏ *The company ended the year in a much improved financial position.*
a **clear** position an **understandable** position
❏ *The government has failed to adopt a clear position on the issue.*
a **moderate** position
❏ *Moscow had taken a more moderate position than France and Germany.*
an **official** position
❏ *Canada's official position has not changed.*

✪ **pos·i·tive** ◆◆◇ /ˈpɒzɪtɪv/ ADJ, NOUN (*academic word*)
ADJ **1** If you are **positive about** things, you are hopeful and confident, and think of the good aspects of a situation rather than the bad ones. ❏ *Be positive about your future and get on with living a normal life.* ❏ *Her husband became much more positive and was soon back in full-time employment.* **2** A **positive** fact, situation, or experience is pleasant and helpful to you in some way. = beneficial, advantageous ❏ *The parting from his sister had a positive effect on John.* ❏ *The project will have a positive impact on the economy.* ❏ *Working abroad should be an exciting and positive experience for all concerned.* **3** If you make a **positive** decision or take **positive** action, you do something definite in order to deal with a task or problem. ❏ *There are positive changes that should be implemented in the rearing of animals.* **4** A **positive** response to something indicates agreement, approval, or encouragement. ❏ *There's been a positive response to the UN Secretary-General's recent peace efforts.* **5** [V-LINK + positive] If you are **positive** about something, you are completely sure about it. ❏ *'Judith's never late. You sure she said eight?'—'Positive.'* **6** [positive + N] **Positive** evidence gives definite proof of the truth or identity of something. = conclusive ❏ *There was no positive evidence that any birth*

defects had arisen as a result of Vitamin A intake. **7** If a medical or scientific test is **positive**, it shows that something has happened or is present. ❑ *If the test is positive, a course of antibiotics may be prescribed.* **8** [positive + N] A **positive** number is greater than zero. ❑ *It's really a simple numbers game with negative and positive numbers.* **9** (technical) If something has a **positive** electrical charge, it has the same charge as a proton and the opposite charge to a neutron.

NOUN [SING] ['the' positive] **The positive** in a situation is the good and pleasant aspects of it. ❑ *He prefers to focus on the positive.*

✦ HIV positive → see HIV

posi·tive·ly /ˈpɒzɪtɪvli/ ADV **1** [positively + ADJ-SUPERL] (emphasis) You use **positively** to emphasize that you really mean what you are saying. = absolutely ❑ *This is positively the last chance for the industry to establish such a system.* **2** (emphasis) You use **positively** to emphasize that something really is the case, although it may sound surprising or extreme. ❑ *Mike's changed since he came back – he seems positively cheerful.* **3** [positively after v] If you act **positively**, you are hopeful and confident, and think of the good aspects of a situation rather than the bad ones. ❑ *You really must try to start thinking positively.* **4** [positively after v] If you respond **positively** to something, you indicate your agreement, approval, or encouragement. ❑ *He responded positively and accepted the fee of $1,000 I had offered.* **5** [positively with v] If you **positively** identify something, you find definite proof of its truth or identity. ❑ *He has positively identified the body as that of his wife.*

❍ **pos·sess** /pəˈzes/ VERB [T] (possesses, possessing, possessed) **1** If you **possess** something, you have it or own it. = own, have ❑ *He was then arrested and charged with possessing an offensive weapon.* ❑ *He is said to possess a fortune of more than two-and-a-half-thousand million dollars.* **2** (formal) If someone or something **possesses** a particular quality, ability, or feature, they have it. ❑ *individuals who are deemed to possess the qualities of sense, loyalty and discretion* ❑ *This figure has long been held to possess miraculous power.*

USAGE NOTE
possess
Possess is mainly used in formal and legal contexts. For general use, it is more natural to use 'have'.
*The area **has** very good schools.*

❍ **pos·ses·sion** /pəˈzeʃən/ NOUN [U, C] (possessions) **1** [U] (formal) If you are **in possession of** something, you have it, because you have obtained it or because it belongs to you. = ownership ❑ *Those documents are now in the possession of the Washington Post.* ❑ *He was also charged with illegal possession of firearms.* ❑ *There is no legal remedy for her to gain possession of the house.* **2** [C] Your **possessions** are the things that you own or have with you at a particular time. = belongings ❑ *People had lost their homes and all their possessions.* ❑ *the acquisition of material possessions*

❍ **pos·si·bil·ity** ♦♦◇ /ˌpɒsɪˈbɪlɪti/ NOUN [C] (possibilities) **1** If you say there is a **possibility that** something is the case or that something will happen, you mean that it might be the case or it might happen. = chance, likelihood; ≠ certainty, impossibility ❑ *We were not in the least worried about the possibility that sweets could rot the teeth.* **2** A **possibility** is one of several different things that could be done. = option ❑ *There were several possibilities open to each manufacturer.*

❍ **pos·si·ble** ♦♦♦ /ˈpɒsɪbəl/ ADJ, NOUN **ADJ 1** If it is **possible** to do something, it can be done. ≠ impossible, unlikely, inconceivable ❑ *If it is possible to find out where your brother is, we will.* ❑ *Everything is possible if we want it enough.* ❑ *anaesthetics which have made modern surgery possible* **2** A **possible** event is one that might happen. ❑ *He referred the matter to the attorney general for possible action against several newspapers.* ❑ *One possible solution, if all else fails, is to take legal action.* **3** [V-LINK + possible] If you say that it is **possible that** something is

true or correct, you mean that although you do not know whether it is true or correct, you accept that it might be. = conceivable ❑ *It is possible that there's an explanation for all this.* **4** ['as' ADV/PRON 'as' possible] If you do something **as** soon **as possible**, you do it as soon as you can. If you get **as** much **as possible** of something, you get as much of it as you can. ❑ *Please make your decision as soon as possible.* ❑ *Mrs Pollard decided to learn as much as possible about the country before going there.* **5** You use **possible** with superlative adjectives to emphasize that something has more or less of a quality than anything else of its kind. ❑ *They have joined the job market at the worst possible time.* ❑ *We expressed in the clearest possible way our disappointment, hurt, and anger.* **6** [possible + N] If you describe someone as, for example, a **possible** governor, you mean that they could be elected as governor. = potential ❑ *Government sources are now openly speculating about a possible successor for Dr Lawrence.*

NOUN [C, SING] (possibles) **1** [C] A **possible** is someone who could be elected or chosen for a particular job or role. ❑ *Kennedy, who divorced wife Joan in 1982, was tipped as a presidential possible.* **2** [SING] **The possible** is everything that can be done in a situation. ❑ *He is a Democrat with the skill, nerve, and ingenuity to push the limits of the possible.*

WORD CONNECTIONS
ADV + **possible**
perfectly possible
entirely possible
❑ *It is perfectly possible to survive a nuclear explosion.*
remotely possible
❑ *It is remotely possible, but unlikely, that they will win.*
humanly possible
❑ *They had done everything humanly possible for their son.*
physically possible
technically possible
❑ *It is technically possible to select an embryo with certain genetic characteristics.*

❍ **pos·sibly** ♦♦◇ /ˈpɒsɪbli/ ADV **1** (vagueness) You use **possibly** to indicate that you are not sure whether something is true or might happen. = perhaps; ≠ definitely ❑ *Exercise will not only lower blood pressure but possibly protect against heart attacks.* ❑ *They were casually dressed; possibly students.* ❑ *a painful and possibly fatal operation* ❑ *Do you think that he could possibly be right?* **2** [possibly before v] (emphasis) You use **possibly** to emphasize that you are surprised, puzzled, or shocked by something that you have seen or heard. ❑ *It was the most unexpected piece of news one could possibly imagine.* **3** [possibly before v] (emphasis) You use **possibly** to emphasize that someone has tried their hardest to do something, or has done it as well as they can. ❑ *They've done everything they can possibly think of.* **4** [with BRD-NEG, possibly before v] (emphasis) You use **possibly** to emphasize that something definitely cannot happen or definitely cannot be done. ❑ *No I really can't possibly answer that!*

post ♦♦◇ /pəʊst/ VERB, NOUN **VERB** [T] (posts, posting, posted) **1** If you **post** notices, signs, or other pieces of information somewhere, you attach them to a wall or board so that everyone can see them. ❑ *Officials began posting warning notices.* **2** (computing) If you **post** information on the Internet, you make the information available to other people on the Internet. ❑ *A consultation paper has been posted on the Internet inviting input from users.* **3** (mainly BrE; in AmE, usually use mail) If you **post** a letter or package, you send it to someone by putting it in a postbox or by taking it to a post office. **4** If you **are posted** somewhere, you are sent there by the organization that you work for and usually work there for several years. ❑ *After training she was posted to Biloxi.* **5** If a soldier, guard, or other person **is posted** somewhere, they are told to stand there, in order to supervise an activity or guard a place. ❑ *Police have now been posted outside all temples.* ❑ *They had to post a signalman at the entrance to the tunnel.*

p

PHRASE **keep someone posted** If you **keep** someone **posted**, you keep giving them the latest information about a situation that they are interested in. □ *Keep me posted on your progress.*

PHRASAL VERB **post up** Post up means the same as post VERB 1. □ *He has posted a sign up that says 'No Fishing.'*

NOUN [U, C, SING] **(posts)** **1** [U] (*mainly BrE; in AmE, usually use* **mail**) You can use **post** to refer to letters and packages that are delivered to you. **2** [C] (*formal*) A **post** in a company or organization is a job or official position in it, usually one that involves responsibility. = position □ *She had earlier resigned her post as President Menem's assistant.* **3** [C] A **post** is a strong upright pole made of wood or metal that is dug into the ground. □ *The device is fixed to a post.* **4** [SING] On a horse-racing track, **the post** is a pole that marks the finishing point.
→ See also **posting**

post·age /ˈpəʊstɪdʒ/ NOUN [U] **Postage** is the money that you pay for sending letters and packages by post. □ *All prices include postage and handling.*

post·al /ˈpəʊstəl/ ADJ **1** [postal + N] **Postal** is used to describe things or people connected with the public service of carrying letters and packages from one place to another. □ *Compensation for lost or damaged mail will be handled by the postal service.* **2** [postal + N] **Postal** is used to describe activities that involve sending things by post. □ *free postal delivery*

post·card /ˈpəʊstkɑːd/ *also* **post card** NOUN [C] **(postcards)** A **postcard** is a thin card, often with a picture on one side, which you can write on and post to people without using an envelope.

post·code /ˈpəʊstkəʊd/ *also* **post code** (*BrE; in AmE, use* **zip code**) NOUN [C] **(postcodes)** A **postcode** is a short sequence of numbers and letters at the end of an address.

post·er /ˈpəʊstə/ NOUN [C] **(posters)** A **poster** is a large notice or picture that you stick on a wall or board, often in order to advertise something. □ *I had seen the poster for the jazz festival in Monterey.*

✪ **post·gradu·ate** /ˌpəʊstˈɡrædʒuət/ *also* **post-graduate** ADJ, NOUN
ADJ [postgraduate + N] **Postgraduate** study or research is done by a student who has a bachelor's degree and is studying or doing research at a more advanced level. □ *postgraduate courses* □ *Dr Hoffman did his postgraduate work at Leicester University.*
NOUN [C] **(postgraduates)** (*BrE; in AmE, use* **graduate student**) A **postgraduate** or a **postgraduate student** is a student with a first degree from a university who is studying or doing research at a more advanced level. □ *In contrast to the undergraduates, the postgraduates who went abroad were chiefly engineers and physicists.* □ *as a postgraduate studying International Relations at Oxford*

WORD PARTS

The prefix ***post-*** often appears in words for something that takes place after a particular date, period, or event:
postgraduate (NOUN)
postwar (ADJ)
postmodern (ADJ)

---

post·ing /ˈpəʊstɪŋ/ NOUN [C] **(postings)** **1** If a member of an armed force gets a **posting** to a particular place, they are sent to live and work there for a period. □ *awaiting his posting to a field ambulance corps in early 1941* **2** (*computing*) A **posting** is a message that is placed on the Internet, for example, on a newsgroup or website, for everyone to read. □ *Postings on the Internet can be accessed from anywhere in the world.* **3** (*mainly BrE; in AmE, usually use* **assignment**) If you get a **posting** to a different town or country, your employers send you to work there, usually for several years.

post of·fice NOUN [C, SING] **(post offices)** **1** [C] A **post office** is a building where you can buy stamps, post letters and packages, and use other services provided by the national postal service. □ *She rushed to get to the post office before it closed.* **2** [SING] **The Post Office** is sometimes used

to refer to the company which operates post offices. □ *The Post Office has confirmed that up to fifteen thousand jobs could be lost.*

✪ **post·pone** /pəʊsˈpəʊn/ VERB [T] **(postpones, postponing, postponed)** If you **postpone** an event, you delay it or arrange for it to take place at a later time than was originally planned. = delay □ *He decided to postpone the expedition until the following day.* □ *The visit has now been postponed indefinitely.*

✪ **post·pone·ment** /pəʊsˈpəʊnmənt/ NOUN [C, U] **(postponements)** The **postponement** of an event is the act of delaying it or arranging for it to take place at a later time than originally planned. = delay □ *The postponement was due to a dispute over where the talks should be held.* □ *Mandela agreed to the postponement of undiluted one man one vote majority rule.*

✪ **pos·tur·al** /ˈpɒstʃərəl/ ADJ [postural + N] (*formal*) **Postural** means relating to the way a person stands or sits. □ *Children can develop bad postural habits from quite an early age.* □ *With her back held in the correct postural alignment she rose from the sofa.*

✪ **pos·ture** /ˈpɒstʃə/ NOUN, VERB
NOUN [C, U] **(postures)** **1** [C, U] Your **posture** is the position in which you stand or sit. □ *You can make your stomach look flatter instantly by improving your posture.* □ *Exercise, fresh air, and good posture are all helpful.* □ *Sit in a relaxed upright posture.* **2** [C] (*formal*) A **posture** is an attitude that you have towards something. = position, stance □ *The military machine is ready to change its defensive posture to one prepared for action.*
VERB [I] **(postures, posturing, postured)** (*formal, disapproval*) You can say that someone **is posturing** when you disapprove of their behaviour because you think they are trying to give a particular impression in order to deceive people. □ *She says the president may just be posturing.*

post·war /ˌpəʊstˈwɔː, ˌpəʊstˈwɔː/ ADJ **Postwar** is used to describe things that happened, existed, or were made in the period immediately after a war, especially World War II, 1939-45. □ *Anaesthetics and bottle feeding were popular in the early postwar years.*

pot ◆◇◇ /pɒt/ NOUN, VERB
NOUN [C, U, SING] **(pots)** **1** [C] A **pot** is a deep round container used for cooking stews, soups, and other food. □ *metal cooking pots* **2** [C] You can use **pot** to refer to the pot and its contents, or to the contents only. □ *He was stirring a pot of soup.* **3** [C] A **pot** of coffee or tea is an amount of it contained in a pot. □ *He spilt a pot of coffee.* **4** [C] You can use **pot** to refer to a coffeepot or teapot. □ *There's tea in the pot.* **5** [U] (*informal*) **Pot** is sometimes used to refer to the drug marijuana or the cannabis plant. □ *I started smoking pot when I was about eleven.* **6** [SING] ['the' pot] In a card game, **the pot** is the money from all the players which the winner of the game will take as a prize.
VERB [T] **(pots, potting, potted)** If you **pot** a young plant, or part of a plant, you put it into a container filled with soil, so it can grow there. □ *Pot the cuttings individually.* **pot·ted** /ˈpɒtɪd/ ADJ □ *potted plants*

po·ta·to ◆◇◇ /pəˈteɪtəʊ/ NOUN
NOUN [C, U] **(potatoes)** **Potatoes** are round vegetables with brown or red skins and white insides. They grow under the ground.
PHRASE **hot potato** You can refer to a difficult subject that people disagree on as a **hot potato**. □ *a political hot potato such as abortion*

po·tent /ˈpəʊtənt/ ADJ Something that is **potent** is very effective and powerful. = powerful □ *Their most potent weapon was the Exocet missile.*

✪ **po·ten·tial** ◆◆◇ /pəˈtenʃəl/ ADJ, NOUN (*academic word*)
ADJ [potential + N] You use **potential** to say that someone or something is capable of developing into the particular kind of person or thing mentioned. = possible □ *The company has identified 60 potential customers.* □ *We are aware of the potential problems and have taken every precaution.*
NOUN [U] **1** If you say that someone or something has

P

potential, you mean that they have the necessary abilities or qualities to become successful or useful in the future. ❑ *The boy has great potential.* ❑ *The school strives to treat students as individuals and to help each one to achieve their full potential.* **2** If you say that someone or something has **potential for** doing a particular thing, you mean that it is possible they may do it. If there is **the potential for** something, it may happen. ❑ *John seemed as horrified as I about his potential for violence.* ❑ *The meeting has the potential to be a watershed event.*
✪ **po·ten·tial·ly** /pə'tenʃəli/ ADV = possibly ❑ *Clearly this is a potentially dangerous situation.* ❑ *Potentially this could damage the reputation of the whole industry.*

pot·tery /'pɒtəri/ NOUN [U, C] (**potteries**) **1** [U] You can use **pottery** to refer to pots, dishes, and other objects made from clay and then baked in an oven until they are hard. ❑ *a fine range of pottery* **2** [U] You can use **pottery** to refer to the hard clay that some pots, dishes, and other objects are made of. ❑ *Some bowls were made of pottery and wood.* **3** [U] **Pottery** is the craft or activity of making objects out of clay. ❑ *He became interested in sculpting and pottery.* **4** [C] A **pottery** is a factory or other place where pottery is made. ❑ *the many galleries and potteries which sell pieces by local artists*

poul·try /'pəultri/ NOUN [PL, U] **1** [PL] You can refer to chickens, ducks, and other birds that are kept for their eggs and meat as **poultry**. ❑ *a poultry farm* **2** [U] Meat from these birds is also referred to as **poultry**. ❑ *The menu features roast meats and poultry.*

pounce /pauns/ VERB [I] (**pounces, pouncing, pounced**) **1** If someone **pounces on** you, they come up towards you suddenly and take hold of you. ❑ *He pounced on the photographer, beat him up, and smashed his camera.* **2** If someone **pounces on** something such as a mistake, they quickly draw attention to it, usually in order to gain an advantage for themselves or to prove that they are right. ❑ *The Democrats were ready to pounce on any Republican failings or mistakes.* **3** When an animal or bird **pounces on** something, it jumps on it and holds it, in order to kill it. ❑ *like a tiger pouncing on its prey*

pound ◆◆◆ /paund/ NOUN, VERB
NOUN [C, SING] (**pounds**) **1** [C] A **pound** is a unit of weight used mainly in Britain, the US, and other countries where English is spoken. One pound is equal to 0.454 kilograms. A **pound of** something is a quantity of it that weighs one pound. ❑ *Her weight was under ninety pounds.* ❑ *a pound of cheese* **2** [C] The **pound** is the unit of money which is used in Britain. It is represented by the symbol £. One British pound is divided into a hundred pence. Some other countries, for example, Egypt, also have a unit of money called a **pound**. ❑ *multi-million pound profits* **3** [SING] The **pound** is used to refer to the British currency system, and sometimes to the currency systems of other countries which use pounds. ❑ *The pound is expected to continue to increase against most other currencies.* **4** [C] A **pound** is a place where dogs and cats found wandering in the street are taken and kept until they are claimed by their owners. ❑ *cages at the local pound* **5** [C] A **pound** is a place where cars that have been parked illegally are taken by the police and kept until they have been claimed by their owners. ❑ *The car remained in the police pound for a month.*
VERB [I, T] (**pounds, pounding, pounded**) **1** [I, T] If you **pound** something or **pound on** it, you hit it with great force, usually loudly and repeatedly. ❑ *He pounded the table with his fist.* ❑ *Somebody began pounding on the front door.* **2** [T] If you **pound** something, you crush it into a paste or a powder or into very small pieces. ❑ *She pounded the corn kernels.* **3** [I] If your heart **is pounding**, it is beating with an unusually strong and fast rhythm, usually because you are afraid. ❑ *I'm sweating, my heart is pounding. I can't breathe.*

pour ◆◆◇ /pɔː/ VERB
VERB [T, I] (**pours, pouring, poured**) **1** [T] If you **pour** a liquid or other substance, you make it flow steadily out of a container by holding the container at an angle. ❑ *Pour a pool of sauce on two plates and arrange the meat neatly.* ❑ *Don poured a generous measure of Scotch into a fresh glass.*

2 [T] If you **pour** someone a drink, you put some of the drink in a cup or glass so that they can drink it. ❑ *He got up and poured himself another drink.* ❑ *She asked Tillie to pour her a cup of coffee.* **3** [I] When a liquid or other substance **pours** somewhere, for example, through a hole, it flows quickly and in large quantities. ❑ *Blood was pouring from his broken nose.* ❑ *Tears poured down both our faces.* **4** [I] When it rains very heavily, you can say that **it is pouring**. ❑ *It was still pouring outside.* ❑ *The rain was pouring down.* **5** [I] If people **pour** into or out of a place, they go there quickly and in large numbers. = stream ❑ *Any day now, the Northern forces may pour across the new border.* ❑ *At six pm large groups poured from the numerous offices.* **6** [I] If something such as information **pours** into a place, a lot of it is obtained or given. = flood ❑ *Martin, 78, died yesterday. Tributes poured in from around the globe.*
PHRASAL VERB **pour out** **1** If you **pour out** a drink, you put some of it in a cup or glass. ❑ *Larry was pouring out four glasses of champagne.* **2** If you **pour out** your thoughts, feelings, or experiences, you tell someone all about them. ❑ *I poured my thoughts out on paper in an attempt to rationalize my feelings.*
✦ **pour cold water on something** → see **water**

✪ **pov·er·ty** ◆◇◇ /'pɒvəti/ NOUN [U, SING] **1** [U] **Poverty** is the state of being extremely poor. = deprivation, destitution, penury; ≠ affluence ❑ *According to World Bank figures, 41 per cent of Brazilians live in absolute poverty.* ❑ *More than 300 million Indians live below the poverty line.* **2** [SING] [also no DET, poverty 'of' N] (*formal*) You can use **poverty** to refer to any situation in which there is not enough of something or its quality is poor. ❑ *a poverty of ideas*

WORD CONNECTIONS
VERB + **poverty**
live in poverty
❑ *Too many people are still living in poverty.*
alleviate poverty **eradicate** poverty **tackle** poverty
❑ *Are people willing to pay more in tax to help alleviate poverty?*
ADJ + **poverty**
abject poverty **extreme** poverty **absolute** poverty
❑ *Stalin was born into abject poverty.*
global poverty **world** poverty
❑ *Eradicating global poverty is in everyone's interest.*

pow·der /'paudə/ NOUN, VERB
NOUN [C, U] (**powders**) **Powder** consists of many tiny particles of a solid substance. ❑ *Put a small amount of the powder into a container and mix with water.* ❑ *cocoa powder*
VERB [T] (**powders, powdering, powdered**) If a woman **powders** her face or some other part of her body, she puts face powder or talcum powder on it. ❑ *She powdered her face and applied her lipstick and rouge.*

✪ **pow·er** ◆◆◆ /'pauə/ NOUN, VERB, ADJ
NOUN [U, C, SING] (**powers**) **1** [U] If someone has **power**, they have a lot of control over people and activities. = influence, control, command ❑ *In a democracy, power must be divided.* ❑ *a political power struggle between the Liberals and National Party* **2** [U] Your **power to** do something is your ability to do it. ❑ *Human societies have the power to solve the problems confronting them.* ❑ *Fathers have the power to dominate children and young people.* **3** [U] If it is **in** or **within** your **power to** do something, you are able to do it or you have the resources to deal with it. ❑ *Your debt situation is only temporary, and it is within your power to resolve it.* **4** [U] [also powers] If someone in authority has the **power** to do something, they have the legal right to do it. ❑ *The police have the power of arrest.* **5** [U] If people take **power** or come to **power**, they take charge of a country's affairs. If a group of people are in

p

power, they are in charge of a country's affairs. ☐ *Idi Amin came into power several years later.* ☐ *He first assumed power in 1970.* **6** [c] You can use **power** to refer to a country that is very rich or important, or has strong military forces. ☐ *the emergence of the new major economic power, Japan* **7** [U] The **power** of something is the ability that it has to move or affect things. ☐ *The vehicle had better power, better tyres, and better brakes.* ☐ *massive computing power* **8** [U] **Power** is energy, especially electricity, that is obtained in large quantities from a fuel source and used to operate lights, heating, and machinery. = energy ☐ *Nuclear power is cleaner than coal.* ☐ *Power has been restored to most parts that were hit last night by high winds.* ☐ *Solar power is an example of a renewable source of energy.* **9** [SING] In mathematics, **power** is used in expressions such as **2 to the power of 4** or **2 to the 4th power** to indicate that 2 must be multiplied by itself 4 times. This is written in numbers as 2^4, or $2 \times 2 \times 2 \times 2$, which equals 16. ☐ *Any number to the power of nought is equal to one.* ☐ *A trillion is 10 raised to the 12th power.*
VERB [T] (**powers**, **powering**, **powered**) The device or fuel that **powers** a machine provides the energy that the machine needs in order to work. = operate ☐ *The 'flywheel' battery, it is said, could power an electric car for 600 miles on a single charge.* ☐ *Vehicles can be powered by hydrogen and batteries.*
PHRASAL VERB **power up** When you **power up** something such as a computer or a machine, you connect it to a power supply and switch it on. = switch on ☐ *Simply power up your laptop and continue work.*
ADJ [power + N] **Power** tools are operated by electricity. ☐ *large power tools, such as chainsaws*

○ **pow·er·ful** ♦♦◇ /'paʊəfʊl/ ADJ **1** A **powerful** person or organization is able to control or influence people and events. = strong, influential; ≠ weak, ineffective ☐ *You're a powerful man – people will listen to you.* ☐ *Russia and India, two large, powerful countries* ☐ *Hong Kong's powerful business community* ☐ *He is a powerful figure in the world of animal conservation.* **2** You say that someone's body is **powerful** when it is physically strong. ☐ *Hans flexed his powerful muscles.* **3** A **powerful** machine or substance is effective because it is very strong. = strong, potent; ≠ weak ☐ *The more powerful the car the more difficult it is to handle.* ☐ *powerful computer systems* ☐ *Alcohol is also a powerful and fast-acting drug.* **4** A **powerful** smell is very strong. = strong ☐ *There was a powerful smell of stale beer.* **5** A **powerful** voice is loud and can be heard from a long way away. = loud ☐ *At that moment Mrs Jones's powerful voice interrupted them, announcing a visitor.* **6** You describe a piece of writing, speech, or work of art as **powerful** when it has a strong effect on people's feelings or beliefs. ☐ *a powerful 11-part drama about a corrupt city leader*
○ **pow·er·ful·ly** /'paʊəfəli/ ADV **1** [powerfully with V] = strongly; ≠ weakly ☐ *He is described as a strong, powerfully-built man of 60.* **2** [powerfully + ADJ] ☐ *Crack is a much cheaper, smokable form of cocaine which is powerfully addictive.* ☐ *This drug is powerfully hallucinogenic.* **3** [powerfully after V] ☐ *The air smelled powerfully of dry dust.* **4** *It's a play – painful, funny, and powerfully acted.*

pow·er·less /'paʊələs/ ADJ **1** Someone who is **powerless** is unable to control or influence events. ☐ *If you don't have money, you're powerless.* **2** [powerless + to-INF] If you are **powerless** to do something, you are completely unable to do it. = unable ☐ *People are being murdered every day and I am powerless to stop it.*
pow·er·less·ness /'paʊələsnəs/ NOUN [U] = impotence, helplessness ☐ *If we can't bring our problems under control, feelings of powerlessness and despair often ensue.*

pow·er sta·tion NOUN [c] (**power stations**) A **power station** is a place where electricity is produced. = power plant

pp. ♦◇◇ (*written*) **pp.** is the plural of 'p.' and means 'pages.' ☐ *See chapter 6, pp. 137-141.*

PR /ˌpiː 'ɑː/ NOUN [U] (*business*) **PR** is an abbreviation for public relations. ☐ *It will be good PR.*

prac·ti·cal ♦◇◇ /'præktɪkəl/ ADJ **1** The **practical** aspects of something involve real situations and events, rather than just ideas and theories. ☐ *practical suggestions on how to increase the fibre in your daily diet* **2** You describe people as **practical** when they make sensible decisions and deal effectively with problems. = down-to-earth ☐ *You were always so practical, Maria.* ☐ *How could she be so practical when he'd just told her something so shattering?* **3** **Practical** ideas and methods are likely to be effective or successful in a real situation. ☐ *Although the causes of cancer are being uncovered, we do not yet have any practical way to prevent it.* **4** You can describe clothes and things in your house as **practical** when they are suitable for a particular purpose rather than just being fashionable or attractive. ☐ *lightweight, practical clothes*

prac·ti·cal·ity /ˌpræktɪ'kælɪti/ NOUN [c, u] (**practicalities**) The **practicalities of** a situation are the practical aspects of it, as opposed to its theoretical aspects. ☐ *Decisions about your children should be based on the practicalities of everyday life.*

prac·ti·cal·ly /'præktɪkəli/ ADV **1** [practically with GROUP/CL] **Practically** means almost, but not completely or exactly. = almost ☐ *He'd known the old man practically all his life.* **2** [practically + ADJ/-ED] You use **practically** to describe something that involves real actions or events rather than ideas or theories. ☐ *The course is more practically based than the master's degree.*

○ **prac·tice** ♦♦◇ /'præktɪs/ NOUN
NOUN [c, u] (**practices**) **1** [c] You can refer to something that people do regularly as a **practice**. = custom, habit, procedure, system ☐ *Some firms have reached agreements to cut workers' pay below the level set in their contract, a practice that is illegal in Germany.* ☐ *The prime minister demanded a public inquiry into bank practices.* **2** [c, u] **Practice** means doing something regularly in order to be able to do it better. A **practice** is one of these periods of doing something. ☐ *She was taking all three of her daughters to basketball practice every day.* ☐ *the hard practice necessary to develop from a learner to an accomplished musician* **3** [u] The work done by doctors and lawyers is referred to as the **practice** of medicine and law. People's religious activities are referred to as the **practice** of a religion. ☐ *maintaining or improving his skills in the practice of internal medicine* ☐ *I eventually realized I had to change my attitude toward medical practice.* **4** [c] A doctor's or lawyer's **practice** is his or her business, often shared with other doctors or lawyers. ☐ *The new doctor's practice was miles away from where I lived.*
PHRASES **in practice** What happens **in practice** is what actually happens, in contrast to what is supposed to happen. ☐ *the difference between foreign policy as presented to the public and foreign policy in actual practice*
put into practice If you **put** a belief or method **into practice**, you behave or act in accordance with it. ☐ *Now that he is back, the mayor has another chance to put his new ideas into practice.*

WHICH WORD?
practice or practise?

Do not confuse **practice** and **practise**.

Practice is a noun and **practise** is a verb.

Practice involves doing something regularly in order to improve your ability at it.

☐ *Skating's just a matter of **practice**.*

A **practice** is something that is done regularly, for example as a custom.

☐ *Benn began the **practice** of holding regular meetings.*

If you **practise** something, you do it or take part in it regularly.

☐ *I played the piece I had been **practising** for months.*

○ **prac·tise** /'præktɪs/ (*BrE*; in *AmE*, use **practice**) VERB [I, T] (**practises**, **practising**, **practised**) **1** [I, T] If you **practise**, or **practise** something, you keep doing it regularly in order to be able to do it better. ☐ *She practised the piano in the basement.* **2** [T] When people **practise** something such as a custom, craft, or religion, they take part in the activities associated with it. ☐ *Her parents had* yearned to be free to practise their religion. ◻ He was brought up in a family that practised traditional Judaism. ◻ countries which practise multi-party politics ◻ Acupuncture was practised in China as long ago as the third millennium BC. **3** [T] If something cruel is regularly done to people, you can say that it **is practised on** them. ◻ Female circumcision is practised on 2 million girls a year. **4** [I, T] Someone who **practises** medicine or law works as a doctor or a lawyer. ◻ He doesn't practise medicine for the money. ◻ the obligations of my licence to practise as a lawyer

✪**prac·ti·tion·er** /præk'tɪʃənə/ NOUN [c] (**practitioners**) (academic word, formal) Doctors are sometimes referred to as **practitioners** or **medical practitioners**. ◻ Some orthodox medical practitioners claim that a balanced diet will provide all the necessary vitamins. ◻ If in doubt consult a qualified practitioner.

✪**prag·mat·ic** /præg'mætɪk/ ADJ A **pragmatic** way of dealing with something is based on practical considerations, rather than theoretical ones. A **pragmatic** person deals with things in a practical way. = realistic, practical ◻ Robin took a pragmatic look at her situation. ◻ a pragmatic approach to the problems faced by Latin America ◻ a thoroughly pragmatic politician with an acute instinct for the popular mood

✪**prag·mat·i·cal·ly** /præg'mætɪkli/ ADV = realistically, practically ◻ 'I can't ever see us doing anything else,' stated Brian pragmatically. ◻ Pragmatically, MTV's survival depends on selling the youth market to advertisers.

✪**prag·ma·tism** /'prægmətɪzəm/ NOUN [u] (formal) **Pragmatism** means thinking of or dealing with problems in a practical way, rather than by using theory or abstract principles. ◻ She had a reputation for clear thinking and pragmatism. ◻ The search for a middle road is not just political pragmatism.

prag·ma·tist /'prægmətɪst/ NOUN [c] (**pragmatists**) ◻ He is a political pragmatist, not an idealist.

praise ◆◇◇ /preɪz/ VERB, NOUN

VERB [T] (**praises, praising, praised**) If you **praise** someone or something, you express approval for their achievements or qualities. ◻ The American president praised Turkey for its courage. ◻ Many others praised Sanford for taking a strong stand.

NOUN [u] **Praise** is what you say or write about someone when you are praising them. = commendation ◻ All the ladies had a lot of praise for the staff and service they received. ◻ I have nothing but praise for the police.

pray /preɪ/ VERB [I, T] (**prays, praying, prayed**) **1** [I] When people **pray**, they speak to God in order to give thanks or to ask for his help. ◻ He spent his time in prison praying and studying. ◻ Now all we have to do is help ourselves and pray to God. **2** [T] When someone is hoping very much that something will happen, you can say that they **are praying** that it will happen. = hope ◻ I'm just praying that somebody in Congress will do something before it's too late.

prayer /preə/ NOUN [u, c, pl] (**prayers**) **1** [u] **Prayer** is the activity of speaking to God. ◻ They had joined a religious order and dedicated their lives to prayer and good works. **2** [c] A **prayer** is the words a person says when they speak to God. ◻ They should take a little time and say a prayer for the people on both sides. **3** [c] You can refer to a strong hope that you have as your **prayer**. ◻ This drug could be the answer to our prayers. **4** [pl] A short religious service at which people gather to pray can be referred to as **prayers**. ◻ He promised that the boy would be back at school in time for evening prayers.

preach /priːtʃ/ VERB [I, T] (**preaches, preaching, preached**) **1** [I, T] When a member of the clergy **preaches** a sermon, he or she gives a talk on a religious or moral subject during a religious service. ◻ At High Mass the priest preached a sermon on the devil. ◻ The bishop preached to a crowd of several hundred local people. **2** [I, T] When people **preach** a belief or a course of action, they try to persuade other people to accept the belief or to take the course of action. ◻ He said he was trying to preach peace and tolerance to his people. ◻ Health experts are now preaching that even a little exercise is far better than none at all. **3** [I] If someone gives you advice in a very serious, boring way, you can say that

they **are preaching at** you. ◻ 'Don't preach at me', he shouted.

✪**pre·cau·tion** /prɪ'kɔːʃən/ NOUN [c] (**precautions**) A **precaution** is an action that is intended to prevent something dangerous or unpleasant from happening. ◻ Could he not, just as a precaution, move to a place of safety? ◻ He took elaborate precautions to conceal his true persona. ◻ Extra safety precautions are essential in homes where older people live.

✪**pre·cau·tion·ary** /prɪ'kɔːʃənri, AmE -neri/ ADJ [usu precautionary + N] (formal) **Precautionary** actions are taken in order to prevent something dangerous or unpleasant from happening. ◻ The local administration says the curfew is a precautionary measure. ◻ the process of taking precautionary steps to ensure that no one will be blamed if something goes wrong

✪**pre·cede** /prɪ'siːd/ VERB [T] (**precedes, preceding, preceded**) (academic word) **1** (formal) If one event or period of time **precedes** another, it happens before it. ◻ Intensive negotiations between the main parties preceded the vote. ◻ The earthquake was preceded by a loud roar and lasted 20 seconds. ◻ Industrial orders had already fallen in the preceding months. **2** (formal) If you **precede** someone somewhere, you go in front of them. ◻ He gestured to Alice to precede them from the room. **3** A sentence, paragraph, or chapter that **precedes** another one comes just before it. ◻ Look at the information that precedes the paragraph in question.

WORD PARTS
The prefix **pre-** often appears in words for something that takes place before a particular date, period, or event: **pre-**Christmas (ADJ) **pre**historic (ADJ) **pre-**tax (ADJ)

✪**prec·edence** /'presɪdəns/ NOUN [u] If one thing takes **precedence over** another, it is regarded as more important than the other thing. = priority ◻ Have as much fun as possible at college, but don't let it take precedence over work. ◻ The shocking, glamorous, or the extreme is always given precedence over the true and the mundane. ◻ As the King's representative he took precedence over everyone else on the island.

✪**prec·edent** /'presɪdənt/ NOUN [c, u] (**precedents**) (formal) If there is a **precedent for** an action or event, it has happened before, and this can be regarded as an argument for doing it again. ◻ The trial could set an important precedent for dealing with similar cases. ◻ There are plenty of precedents in Hollywood for letting people out of contracts.

pre·ced·ing /prɪ'siːdɪŋ/ ADJ You refer to the period of time or the thing immediately before the one that you are talking about as the **preceding** one. ◻ As we saw in the preceding chapter, groups can be powerful agents of socialization. ◻ She informed us that eighteen members of the staff had left during the preceding year.

pre·cious /'preʃəs/ ADJ **1** If you say that something such as a resource is **precious**, you mean that it is valuable and should not be wasted or used badly. ◻ After four months in foreign parts, every hour at home was precious. ◻ A family break allows you to spend precious time together. **2** **Precious** objects and materials are worth a lot of money because they are rare. = valuable ◻ jewellery and precious objects belonging to her mother **3** If something is **precious** to you, you regard it as important and do not want to lose it. ◻ Her family's support is particularly precious to Josie.

✪**pré·cis** /'preɪsiː, AmE preɪ'siː/ NOUN [c] (oft précis 'of' N) (formal) A **précis** is a short written or spoken account of something, that gives the important points but not the details. = summary ◻ A précis of the manuscript was sent to the magazine New Idea. ◻ The power of this book cannot be judged from a précis of its plot.

✪**pre·cise** /prɪ'saɪs/ ADJ (academic word) **1** [precise + N] (emphasis) You use **precise** to emphasize that you are referring to an exact thing, rather than something vague. = exact, accurate; ≠ imprecise, inexact, inaccurate, vague

p

❏ *I can remember the precise moment when my daughter came to see me and her new baby brother in the hospital.* ❏ *The precise location of the wreck was discovered in 1988.* ❏ *He was not clear on the precise nature of his mission.* ❏ *We will never know the precise details of his death.* **2** Something that is **precise** is exact and accurate in all its details. ❏ *They speak very precise English.* ❏ *His comments were precise and to the point.*

✪ **pre·cise·ly** ♦◇◇ /prɪˈsaɪsli/ ADV **1** **Precisely** means accurately and exactly. = exactly, accurately; ≠ imprecisely, inaccurately ❏ *Nobody knows precisely how many people are still living in the camp.* ❏ *The first bell rang at precisely 10:29 am.* **2** [precisely with CL/GROUP] You can use **precisely** to emphasize that a reason or fact is the only important one there is, or that it is obvious. ❏ *Children come to zoos precisely to see captive animals.* ❏ *That is precisely the result the system is designed to produce.* **3** [as reply] You can say '**precisely**' to confirm in an emphatic way that what someone has just said is true. = exactly ❏ *'All I did was write the truth.'—'Precisely! Now everyone knows.'*

✪ **pre·ci·sion** /prɪˈsɪʒən/ NOUN [U] If you do something with **precision**, you do it exactly as it should be done. = exactness, accuracy; ≠ imprecision, inaccuracy ❏ *The choir sang with precision.* ❏ *The interior is planned with military precision.*

✪ **pre·date** /ˌpriːˈdeɪt/ VERB [T] (predates, predating, predated) If you say that one thing **predated** another, you mean that the first thing happened or existed some time before the second thing. ❏ *His troubles predated the recession.* ❏ *The monument predates the arrival of the druids in Britain.*

✪ **preda·tor** /ˈpredətə/ NOUN [C] (predators) **1** A **predator** is an animal that kills and eats other animals. ❏ *With no natural predators on the island, the herd increased rapidly.* ❏ *The mites in turn were eaten by other arachnid predators.* ❏ *Tomato growers are using natural predators to control the pests which could otherwise destroy the crop.* **2** People sometimes refer to predatory people or organizations as **predators**. ❏ *Rumours of a takeover by Hanson are probably far-fetched, but the company is worried about other predators.*

✪ **preda·tory** /ˈpredətri, AmE -tɔːri/ ADJ **1** **Predatory** animals live by killing other animals for food. ❏ *predatory birds like the eagle* ❏ *the predatory instincts of foxes* ❏ *non-lethal solutions for controlling predatory marine mammals* **2** **Predatory** people or organizations are eager to gain something out of someone else's weakness or suffering. ❏ *People will not set up new businesses while they are frightened by the predatory behaviour of the banks.*

pre·de·ces·sor /ˈpriːdɪsesə, AmE ˈpred-/ NOUN [C] (predecessors) **1** Your **predecessor** is the person who had your job before you. ❏ *He maintained that he learned everything he knew from his predecessor.* **2** The **predecessor** of an object or machine is the object or machine that came before it in a sequence or process of development. = forerunner ❏ *Although the car is some 2 inches shorter than its predecessor, its boot is 20 per cent larger.*

pre·dica·ment /prɪˈdɪkəmənt/ NOUN [C] (predicaments) If you are in a **predicament**, you are in an unpleasant situation that is difficult to get out of. ❏ *Hank explained our predicament.*

✪ **pre·dict** ♦◇◇ /prɪˈdɪkt/ VERB [T] (predicts, predicting, predicted) (academic word) If you **predict** an event, you say that it will happen. = forecast, foresee ❏ *The latest opinion polls are predicting a very close contest.* ❏ *He predicted that my hair would grow back 'in no time'.* ❏ *Chinese seismologists have predicted earthquakes this year in Western China.* ❏ *Some analysts were predicting that online sales during the holiday season could top $10 billion.* ❏ *tests that accurately predict when you are most fertile*

WORD CONNECTIONS

predict + NOUN

predict an **event**
predict an **outcome**
❏ *Ever since ancient times, psychics have predicted future events.*

---

predict a **fall**
predict a **drop**
predict a **decline**
❏ *Economists are predicting a fall in economic growth this quarter.*

---

predict a **rise**
predict an **upturn**
predict a **recovery**
❏ *The government predicts a 20% rise in traffic on major roads this weekend.*

ADV + **predict**

accurately predict
correctly predict
rightly predict
❏ *They rightly predicted that Brazil would win the contest.*

---

confidently predict
❏ *The polls had confidently predicted a Labour victory.*

✪ **pre·dict·able** /prɪˈdɪktəbəl/ ADJ If you say that an event is **predictable**, you mean that it is obvious in advance that it will happen. ❏ *This was a predictable reaction, given the bitter hostility between the two countries.* ❏ *The result was entirely predictable.*
pre·dict·ably /prɪˈdɪktəbli/ ADV ❏ *His article is, predictably, a scathing attack on capitalism.*
pre·dict·abil·ity /prɪˌdɪktəˈbɪlɪti/ NOUN [U] ❏ *Your mother values the predictability of your Sunday calls.*

✪ **pre·dic·tion** /prɪˈdɪkʃən/ NOUN [C, U] (predictions) If you make a **prediction** about something, you say what you think will happen. = forecast, prophesy ❏ *He was unwilling to make a prediction for the coming year.* ❏ *Weather prediction has never been a perfect science.*

✪ **pre·domi·nant** /prɪˈdɒmɪnənt/ ADJ (academic word) If something is **predominant**, it is more important or noticeable than anything else in a set of people or things. = main ❏ *Mandy's predominant emotion was confusion.* ❏ *The third survivor is Hope, who manifests the predominant symptoms of multiple personality disorder.* ❏ *The predominant theme of this book is the idea of the sacred or god.*

✪ **pre·domi·nant·ly** /prɪˈdɒmɪnəntli/ ADV You use **predominantly** to indicate which feature or quality is most noticeable in a situation. = mainly, largely ❏ *The landscape has remained predominantly rural in appearance.* ❏ *a predominantly female profession* ❏ *Although it is predominantly a teenage problem, acne can occur in early childhood.*

pre·domi·nate /prɪˈdɒmɪneɪt/ VERB [I] (predominates, predominating, predominated) (formal) **1** If one type of person or thing **predominates** in a group, there is more of that type of person or thing in the group than of any other. ❏ *In older age groups women predominate because men tend to die younger.* **2** When a feature or quality **predominates**, it is the most important or noticeable one in a situation. ❏ *He wants to create a society where Islamic principles predominate.*

pref·ace /ˈprefɪs/ NOUN, VERB
NOUN [C] (prefaces) A **preface** is an introduction at the beginning of a book that explains what the book is about or why it was written. = foreword ❏ *the preface to Kelman's novel*
VERB [T] (prefaces, prefacing, prefaced) If you **preface** an action or speech **with** something else, you do or say this other thing first. ❏ *I will preface what I am going to say with a few lines from Shakespeare.*

✪ **pre·fer** ♦♦◇ /prɪˈfɜː/ VERB [T] (prefers, preferring, preferred) If you **prefer** someone or something, you like that person or thing better than another, and so you are more likely to choose them if there is a choice. = favour, choose; ≠ reject, dislike ❏ *Does he prefer a particular sort of music?* ❏ *Centipedes are nocturnal and generally prefer moist conditions such as forests or woodlands.* ❏ *I prefer to go on self-catering holidays.* ❏ *I became a teacher because I preferred books and people to politics.* ❏ *I prefer to think of peace not war.* ❏ *I would prefer him to be with us next season.*

pref·er·able /ˈprefrəbəl/ ADJ If you say that one thing is

preferable to another, you mean that it is more desirable or suitable. ❏ *Prevention of a problem is always preferable to trying to cure it.*

pref·er·ably /'prefrəbli/ ADV ❏ *Do something creative or take exercise, preferably in the fresh air.*

✪**pref·er·ence** /'prefərəns/ NOUN [c, u] (**preferences**) **1** [c, u] If you have a **preference** for something, you would like to have or do that thing rather than something else. = choice, selection; ≠ rejection ❏ *It upset her when men revealed a preference for her sister.* ❏ *Parents can express a preference for the school their child attends.* **2** [u] If you **give preference to** someone with a particular qualification or feature, you choose them rather than someone else. = priority ❏ *The Pentagon has said it will give preference to companies with which it can do business electronically.*

pref·er·en·tial /,prefə'renʃəl/ ADJ If you get **preferential** treatment, you are treated better than other people and therefore have an advantage over them. = special ❏ *Firstborn sons received preferential treatment.*

preg·nan·cy ◆◇◇ /'pregnənsi/ NOUN [c, u] (**pregnancies**) **Pregnancy** is the condition of being pregnant or the period of time during which a female is pregnant. ❏ *It would be wiser to cut out all alcohol during pregnancy.*

preg·nant ◆◇◇ /'pregnənt/ ADJ **1** If a woman or female animal is **pregnant**, she has a baby or babies developing in her body. ❏ *Lena got pregnant and married.* **2** [pregnant + N, V-LINK + pregnant 'with' N] A **pregnant** silence or moment has a special meaning that is not obvious but that people are aware of. ❏ *There was a long, pregnant silence, which Mrs Madrigal punctuated by reaching for the bill.*

✪**pre·his·tor·ic** /,pri:hɪ'stɒrɪk, AmE -'tɔ:r-/ ADJ **Prehistoric** people and things existed at a time before information was written down. ❏ *the famous prehistoric cave paintings of Lascaux* ❏ *Many of our prehistoric ancestors ate high-protein diets.*

✪**preju·dice** /'predʒʊdɪs/ NOUN, VERB
[NOUN] [c, u] (**prejudices**) **Prejudice** is an unreasonable dislike of a particular group of people or things, or a preference for one group of people or things over another. ❏ *There was a deep-rooted racial prejudice long before the two countries went to war.* ❏ *There is widespread prejudice against workers over 45.*
[VERB] [T] (**prejudices, prejudicing, prejudiced**) **1** If you **prejudice** someone or something, you influence them so that they are unfair in some way. ❏ *I think your upbringing has prejudiced you.* ❏ *The report was held back for fear of prejudicing his trial.* **2** (formal) If someone **prejudices** another person's situation, they do something that makes it worse than it should be. ❏ *Her study was not in any way intended to prejudice the future development of the college.*

✪**preju·diced** /'predʒʊdɪst/ ADJ A person who is **prejudiced** against someone from a different racial group has an unreasonable dislike of them. ❏ *Some landlords and landladies are racially prejudiced.* ❏ *The law is also making prejudiced attitudes less acceptable.*

✪**preju·di·cial** /,predʒʊ'dɪʃəl/ ADJ (formal) If an action or situation is **prejudicial** to someone or something, it is harmful to them. = harmful; ≠ harmless ❏ *You could face up to eight years in jail for spreading rumours considered prejudicial to security.* ❏ *The judge agreed with the prosecution that such information would be too prejudicial for the jury to hear.*

✪**pre·limi·nary** /prɪ'lɪmɪnri, AmE -neri/ ADJ, NOUN (academic word)
[ADJ] **Preliminary** activities or discussions take place at the beginning of an event, often as a form of preparation. = initial; ≠ concluding ❏ *Preliminary results show the Republican Party with 11 per cent of the vote.* ❏ *Preliminary talks on the future of the bases began yesterday.*
[NOUN] [c] (**preliminaries**) A **preliminary** is something that you do at the beginning of an activity, often as a form of preparation. ❏ *You all know why I am here. So I won't waste time on preliminaries.*

prel·ude /'prelju:d, AmE 'preɪlu:d/ NOUN [c] (**preludes**) You can describe an event as a **prelude to** another event or

activity when it happens before it and acts as an introduction to it. ❏ *For him, reading was a necessary prelude to sleep.*

prema·ture /,premə'tʃʊə, AmE ,pri:-/ ADJ **1** Something that is **premature** happens earlier than usual or earlier than people expect. ❏ *Accidents are still the number one cause of premature death for Americans.* ❏ *His career was brought to a premature end by a succession of knee injuries.* **2** You can say that something is **premature** when it happens too early and is therefore inappropriate. ❏ *It now seems their optimism was premature.* **3** A **premature** baby is one that was born before the date when it was expected to be born. ❏ *Even very young premature babies respond to their mother's presence.*

prema·ture·ly /,premə'tʃʊəli, AmE ,pri:-/ ADV **1** *The war and the years in the harsh mountains had prematurely aged him.* **2** *He was careful not to celebrate prematurely.* **3** [prematurely after V] ❏ *Danny was born prematurely, weighing only 3lb 3oz.*

prem·ier ◆◇◇ /'premiə, AmE prɪ'mɪr/ NOUN, ADJ
[NOUN] [c] (**premiers**) The leader of the government of a country is sometimes referred to as the country's **premier**. ❏ *Australian premier Tony Abbott*
[ADJ] [premier + N] **Premier** is used to describe something that is considered to be the best or most important thing of a particular type. = principal, leading ❏ *the country's premier opera company*

premi·ere /'premiə, AmE prɪm'jer/ NOUN, VERB
[NOUN] [c] (**premieres**) The **premiere** of a new play or film is the first public performance of it. ❏ *Four astronauts visited for last week's premiere of the movie Space Station.*
[VERB] [I, T] (**premieres, premiering, premiered**) When a film or show **premieres** or is **premiered**, it is shown to an audience for the first time. ❏ *The documentary premiered at the Jerusalem Film Festival.*

prem·ise /'premɪs/ NOUN [PL, c] (**premises**) **1** [PL] The **premises** of a business or an institution are all the buildings and land that it occupies in one place. ❏ *There is a kitchen on the premises.* **2** [c] (formal) A **premise** is something that you suppose is true and that you use as a basis for developing an idea. = assumption ❏ *The premise is that schools will work harder to improve if they must compete.*

pre·mium ◆◇◇ /'pri:miəm/ NOUN, ADJ
[NOUN] [c] (**premiums**) **1** A **premium** is a sum of money that you pay regularly to an insurance company for an insurance policy. ❏ *It is too early to say whether insurance premiums will be affected.* **2** A **premium** is a sum of money that you have to pay for something in addition to the normal cost. ❏ *Even if customers want 'solutions', most are not willing to pay a premium for them.*
[PHRASE] **at a premium 1** If something is **at a premium**, it is wanted or needed, but is difficult to get or achieve. = scarce ❏ *If space is at a premium, choose adaptable furniture that won't fill the room.* **2** If you buy or sell something **at a premium**, you buy or sell it at a higher price than usual, for example, because it is in short supply. ❏ *He eventually sold the shares back to the bank at a premium.*
[ADJ] [premium + N] **Premium** products are of a higher than usual quality and are often expensive. = luxury ❏ *At the premium end of the market, business is booming.*

pre·oc·cu·pa·tion /pri,ɒkjʊ'peɪʃən/ NOUN [c, u] (**preoccupations**) **1** [c] If you have a **preoccupation with** something or someone, you keep thinking about them because they are important to you. ❏ *Karouzos's poetry shows a profound preoccupation with the Orthodox Church.* **2** [u] **Preoccupation** is a state of mind in which you think about something so much that you do not consider other things to be important. = obsession ❏ *The arrest of Senator Pinochet has created a climate of preoccupation among our citizens.*

pre·oc·cu·pied /pri'ɒkjʊpaɪd/ ADJ If you are **preoccupied**, you are thinking a lot about something or someone, and so you hardly notice other things. ❏ *Tom Banbury was preoccupied with the missing Shepherd child and did not want to devote time to the new murder.*

pre·oc·cu·py /pri'ɒkjʊpaɪ/ VERB [T] (**preoccupies, preoccupying, preoccupied**) If something **is preoccupying**

p

you, you are thinking about it a lot. ❑ *Crime and the fear of crime preoccupy the community.*

⦿**prepa·ra·tion** ◆◇◇ /ˌprepəˈreɪʃən/ NOUN [U, PL, C] (**preparations**) **1** [U] **Preparation** is the process of getting something ready for use or for a particular purpose, or making arrangements for something. = arrangement ❑ *Rub the surface of the wood in preparation for the varnish.* ❑ *Few things distracted the pastor from the preparation of his weekly sermons.* ❑ *Behind any successful event lay months of preparation.* **2** [PL] **Preparations** are all the arrangements that are made for a future event. = arrangements ❑ *The United States is making preparations for a large-scale airlift of 1,200 American citizens.* ❑ *Final preparations are underway for celebrations to mark German unification.* **3** [C] A **preparation** is a mixture that has been prepared for use as food, medicine, or a cosmetic. ❑ *anti-aging creams and sensitive-skin preparations*

⦿**pre·pare** ◆◆◇ /prɪˈpeə/ VERB [T, I] (**prepares, preparing, prepared**) **1** [T] If you **prepare** something, you make it ready for something that is going to happen. ❑ *Two technicians were preparing a videotape recording of last week's programme.* ❑ *On average each report requires 1,000 hours to prepare.* ❑ *The crew of the Iowa has been preparing the ship for storage.* **2** [I, T] If you **prepare for** an event or action that will happen soon, you get yourself ready for it or make the necessary arrangements. = plan, arrange ❑ *The party leadership is using management consultants to help prepare for the next election.* ❑ *He had to go back to his hotel and prepare to catch a train for New York.* ❑ *We are preparing to map the entire genetic structure of the human species.* ❑ *His doctor had told him to prepare himself for surgery.* **3** [T] When you **prepare** food, you get it ready to be eaten, for example, by cooking it. ❑ *She made her way to the kitchen, hoping to find someone preparing dinner.*

WORD CONNECTIONS
prepare + NOUN
prepare a **report**
prepare a **document**
prepare a **statement**
prepare a **plan**
❑ *The committee had prepared a report concluding that there was no hard evidence of her involvement.*
prepare + FOR + NOUN
prepare for a **possibility**
prepare for an **eventuality**
❑ *The department is already preparing for the possibility of another busy year.*
prepare for a **fight**
❑ *His party is prepared for a fight to stay in power.*

pre·pared ◆◆◇ /prɪˈpeəd/ ADJ **1** [V-LINK + prepared + TO-INF] If you are **prepared to** do something, you are willing to do it if necessary. = willing ❑ *Are you prepared to take industrial action?* **2** [V-LINK + prepared 'for' N] If you are **prepared for** something that you think is going to happen, you are ready for it. ❑ *Police are prepared for large numbers of demonstrators.* **3** [prepared + N] You can describe something as **prepared** when it has been done or made beforehand, so that it is ready when it is needed. ❑ *He ended his prepared statement by thanking the police.*

prepo·si·tion /ˌprepəˈzɪʃən/ NOUN [C] (**prepositions**) A **preposition** is a word such as 'by', 'for', 'into', or 'with' that usually has a noun group as its object. ❑ *There is nothing in the rules of grammar to suggest that ending a sentence with a preposition is wrong.*

pre·scribe /prɪˈskraɪb/ VERB [T] (**prescribes, prescribing, prescribed**) **1** If a doctor **prescribes** medicine or treatment for you, he or she tells you what medicine or treatment to have. ❑ *The doctor examines the patient then diagnoses the disease and prescribes medication.* ❑ *She took twice the prescribed dose of sleeping tablets.* **2** (formal) If a person or set of laws or rules **prescribes** an action or duty, they state that it must be carried out. ❑ *article II of the constitution, which prescribes the method of electing a president*

pre·scrip·tion /prɪˈskrɪpʃən/ NOUN
[C] (**prescriptions**) **1** A **prescription** is the piece of paper on which your doctor writes an order for medicine and which you give to a pharmacist to get the medicine. ❑ *The new drug will not require a doctor's prescription.* **2** A **prescription** is a medicine that a doctor has told you to take. ❑ *I'm not sleeping even with the prescription Ackerman gave me.* **3** A **prescription** is a proposal or a plan that gives ideas about how to solve a problem or improve a situation. ❑ *There's not much difference in the economic prescriptions of Ireland's two main political parties.*
PHRASE **on prescription** If a medicine is available **by** or **on prescription**, you can only get it from a pharmacist if a doctor gives you a prescription for it.

⦿**pres·ence** ◆◆◇ /ˈprezəns/ NOUN
[SING, U, C] (**presences**) **1** [SING] Someone's **presence** in a place is the fact that they are there. ❑ *They argued that his presence in the town could only stir up trouble.* ❑ *Her Majesty later honoured the Headmaster with her presence at lunch.* **2** [U] If you say that someone has **presence**, you mean that they impress people by their appearance and manner. ❑ *They do not seem to have the vast, authoritative presence of those great men.* **3** [C] (*literary*) A **presence** is a person or creature that you cannot see, but that you are aware of. ❑ *She started to be affected by the ghostly presence she could feel in the house.* **4** [SING] If a country has a military **presence** in another country, it has some of its armed forces there. ❑ *The Philippine government wants the US to maintain a military presence in Southeast Asia.* **5** [U] If you refer to the **presence** of a substance in another thing, you mean that it is in that thing. ❑ *The somewhat acid flavour is caused by the presence of lactic acid.* ❑ *the presence of a carcinogen in the water* ❑ *Although the fluid presents no symptoms to the patient, its presence can be detected by a test.*
PHRASE **in someone's presence** If you are **in** someone's **presence**, you are in the same place as that person, and are close enough to them to be seen or heard. ❑ *The talks took place in the presence of a diplomatic observer.*

⦿**pres·ent** ◆◆◇ ADJ, NOUN, VERB
ADJ /ˈprezənt/ **1** [present + N] You use **present** to describe things and people that exist now, rather than those that existed in the past or those that may exist in the future. = current ❑ *He has brought much of the present crisis on himself.* ❑ *the government's present economic difficulties* ❑ *It has been skilfully renovated by the present owners.* ❑ *No statement can be made at the present time.* **2** [V-LINK + present] If someone is **present at** an event, they are there. ❑ *The president was not present at the meeting.* ❑ *Nearly 85 per cent of men are present at the birth of their children.* ❑ *The whole family was present.* **3** [V-LINK + present] If something, especially a substance or disease, is **present in** something else, it exists within that thing. ❑ *This special form of vitamin D is naturally present in breast milk.* ❑ *If the gene is present, a human embryo will go on to develop as a male.*
PHRASE **the present day** The **present day** is the period of history that we are in now. = today ❑ *Western European art from the period of Giotto to the present day*
NOUN /ˈprezənt/ [SING, C] (**presents**) **1** [SING] The **present** is the period of time that we are in now and the things that are happening now. ❑ *his struggle to reconcile the past with the present* ❑ *continuing right up to the present* **2** [C] A **present** is something that you give to someone, for example, at Christmas or when they visit them. = gift ❑ *The carpet was a wedding present from Jack's parents.* ❑ *She bought a birthday present for her mother.*
PHRASES **at present** A situation that exists **at present** exists now, although it may change. ❑ *There is no way at present of predicting which individuals will develop the disease.*
for the present Something that exists or will be done **for the present** exists now or will continue for a while, although the situation may change later. ❑ *The cabinet had expressed the view that sanctions should remain in place for the present.*
VERB /prɪˈzent/ [T] (**presents, presenting, presented**) **1** If you **present** someone **with** something such as a prize or document, or if you **present** it **to** them, you formally give

it to them. ❑ *The mayor presented him with a gold medal at an official city reception.* ❑ *Betty will present the prizes to the winners.* **2** If something **presents** a difficulty, challenge, or opportunity, it causes it or provides it. ❑ *This presents a problem for many financial consumers.* ❑ *The future is going to be one that presents many challenges.* **3** If an opportunity or problem **presents** itself, it occurs, often when you do not expect it. ❑ *Their colleagues insulted them whenever the opportunity presented itself.* **4** When you **present** information, you give it to people in a formal way. = offer, provide, submit ❑ *We spend the time collating and presenting the information in a variety of chart forms.* ❑ *We presented three options to the unions for discussion.* ❑ *In effect, Parsons presents us with a beguilingly simple outline of social evolution.* **5** If you **present** someone or something in a particular way, you describe them in that way. ❑ *The government has presented these changes as major reforms.* **6** The way you **present yourself** is the way you speak and act when meeting new people. ❑ *all those tricks which would help him to present himself in a more confident way in public* **7** If someone or something **presents** a particular appearance or image, that is how they appear or try to appear. ❑ *The small group of onlookers presented a pathetic sight.* ❑ *Cohen was making an effort to present a kinder, gentler image.* **8** If you **present yourself** somewhere, you officially arrive there, for example, for an appointment. ❑ *Get word to him right away that he's to present himself at City Hall by tomorrow afternoon.* **9** (*mainly BrE; in AmE, usually use* **host**) If someone **presents** a programme on television or radio, they introduce each item in it. **10** When someone **presents** something such as a production of a play or an exhibition, they organize it. ❑ *They threatened to close any theatre presenting a play with gay characters.* **11** If you **present** someone **to** someone else, often an important person, you formally introduce them. = introduce ❑ *Fox stepped forward, welcomed him in Malay, and presented him to Jack.*

WORD CONNECTIONS

ADV + **present**

naturally present
❑ *Vitamin D is naturally present in breast milk.*

commonly present
rarely present
❑ *This harmful bacteria is commonly present in meat and dairy products.*

USAGE NOTE

present

Note that the verb **present** is not used to introduce indirect speech. Do not say 'The speaker presented that the problem could be solved easily'.
*The speaker **explained that** the problem could be solved easily.*

⭘ **pres·en·ta·tion** /ˌprezənˈteɪʃən, AmE ˌpriːzen-/ NOUN [U, C] (**presentations**) **1** [U] The **presentation** of something such as a prize or document is the formal act of giving it to someone. ❑ *Then came the presentation of the awards by the First Lady.* **2** [C, U] The **presentation** of information is the act of giving it to people in a formal way. ❑ *in his first presentation of the theory to the Berlin Academy* ❑ *a fair presentation of the facts to a jury* **3** [U] **Presentation** is the appearance of something, that someone has worked to create. ❑ *We serve traditional French food cooked in a lighter way, keeping the presentation simple.* **4** [C] A **presentation** is a formal event at which someone is given a prize or award. ❑ *after receiving his award at a presentation in Kansas City yesterday* **5** [C] When someone gives a **presentation**, they give a formal talk, often in order to sell something or get support for a proposal. ❑ *James Watson, Philip Mayo and I gave a slide and video presentation.*

⭘ **present-day** ADJ [present-day + N] **Present-day** things, situations, and people exist at the time in history we are now in. = contemporary, modern; ≠ historical ❑ *Even by present-day standards these were large aircraft.* ❑ *a huge area*

of northern India, stretching from present-day Afghanistan to Bengal

pre·sent·er /prɪˈzentə/ (*mainly BrE; in AmE, usually use* **host**) NOUN [C] (**presenters**) A radio or television **presenter** is a person who introduces the items in a particular programme.

pres·ent·ly /ˈprezntli/ ADV **1** If you say that something is **presently** happening, you mean that it is happening now. = currently ❑ *She is presently developing a number of projects.* ❑ *The island is presently uninhabited.* **2** [presently with CL] (*written*) You use **presently** to indicate that something happened a short time after the time or event that you have just mentioned. ❑ *He was shown to a small office. Presently, a young woman in a white coat came in.*

pre·serva·tive /prɪˈzɜːvətɪv/ NOUN [C, U] (**preservatives**) A **preservative** is a chemical that prevents things from decaying. Some preservatives are added to food, and others are used to treat wood or metal. ❑ *Nitrates are used as preservatives in food processing.*

⭘ **pre·serve** ◆◇◇ /prɪˈzɜːv/ VERB, NOUN
VERB [T] (**preserves, preserving, preserved**) **1** If you **preserve** a situation or condition, you make sure that it remains as it is, and does not change or end. = maintain, protect; ≠ neglect ❑ *We will do everything to preserve peace.* **2** If you **preserve** something, you take action to save it or protect it from damage or decay. = maintain, save, protect; ≠ neglect, waste ❑ *We need to preserve the forest.* ❑ *the Government's aim of preserving biodiversity* ❑ *The current administration has done little to preserve forest ecosystems.* **3** If you **preserve** food, you treat it in order to prevent it from decaying so that you can store it for a long time. ❑ *I like to make puree, using only enough sugar to preserve the plums.*
NOUN [C, PL] (**preserves**) **1** [C, PL] **Preserves** are foods made by cooking fruit with a large amount of sugar so that they can be stored for a long time. ❑ *She decided to make peach preserves for Christmas gifts.* **2** [C] If you say that a job or activity is the **preserve** of a particular person or group of people, you mean that they are the only ones who take part in it. ❑ *The making and conduct of foreign policy is largely the preserve of the president.*

⭘ **pres·er·va·tion** /ˌprezəˈveɪʃən/ NOUN [U] **1** = maintenance ❑ *the preservation of the status quo* **2** = maintenance, protection; ≠ neglect ❑ *the preservation of buildings of architectural or historic interest*

VOCABULARY BUILDER

preserve VERB (*mainly formal*)
If you **preserve** a situation or condition, you make sure that it remains as it is, and does not change or end.
❑ *The Fund seeks to preserve the value of your investment at $1.00 per share.*

maintain VERB (*mainly formal*)
If you **maintain** something, you continue to have it, and do not let it stop or grow weaker.
❑ *emergency powers to try to maintain law and order*

save VERB
If you **save** something, you keep it because it will be needed later.
❑ *Try to get into the habit of saving your work regularly.*

protect VERB
To **protect** someone or something means to prevent them from being harmed or damaged.
❑ *A purple headscarf protected her against the wind.*

---
pre·side /prɪˈzaɪd/ VERB [I] (**presides, presiding, presided**) If you **preside over** a meeting or an event, you are in charge. ❑ *The PM returned to Downing Street to preside over a meeting of his inner cabinet.*

presi·den·cy ◆◇◇ /ˈprezɪdənsi/ NOUN [C] (**presidencies**) The **presidency** of a country or organization is the position of being the president or the period of time during which someone is president. ❑ *He is a candidate for the presidency of the organization.*

p

✪pres·i·dent ✦✦✦ /ˈprezɪdənt/ NOUN [c] (**presidents**)
1 [oft 'the' president; President] The **president** of a country that has no king or queen is the person who is the head of state of that country. = leader, head of state, premier, chief, CEO ❑ *President Mubarak* ❑ *The White House says the president would veto the bill.* **2** The **president** of an organization is the person who has the highest position in it. ❑ *Alexandre de Merode, the president of the medical commission*

pres·i·den·tial ✦✦◇ /ˌprezɪˈdenʃəl/ ADJ [presidential + N] **Presidential** activities or things relate or belong to a president. ❑ *campaigning for Peru's presidential election*

✪press ✦✦✦ /pres/ VERB, NOUN
VERB [T, I] (**presses, pressing, pressed**) **1** [T] If you **press** something somewhere, you push it firmly against something else. ❑ *He pressed his back against the door.* **2** [T] If you **press** a button or switch, you push it with your finger in order to make a machine or device work. ❑ *Drago pressed a button and the door closed.* **3** [I, T] If you **press** something or **press down on** it, you push hard against it with your foot or hand. ❑ *The engine stalled. He pressed the accelerator hard.* **4** [I] If you **press for** something, you try hard to persuade someone to give it to you or to agree to it. = push ❑ *Police might now press for changes in the law.* **5** [T] If you **press** someone, you try hard to persuade them to do something. ❑ *Trade unions are pressing him to stand firm.* ❑ *Mr. Kurtz seems certain to be pressed for further details.* **6** [T] If someone **presses** their claim, demand, or point, they state it in a very forceful way. ❑ *The protest campaign has used mass strikes and demonstrations to press its demands.* **7** [T] If you **press** something **on** someone, you give it to them and insist that they take it. ❑ *All I had was money, which I pressed on her reluctant mother.* **8** [T] If you **press** clothes, you iron them in order to get rid of the creases. = iron ❑ *Vera pressed his shirt.* ❑ *There's a couple of dresses to be pressed.*
PHRASE **press charges against** If you **press charges against** someone, you make an official accusation against them that has to be decided in a court of law. ❑ *I could have pressed charges against him.*
NOUN [C, SING] (**presses**) **1** [c] A **press** is a firm push. ❑ *a TV which rises from a table at the press of a button* **2** [SING] ['the' press] Newspapers are referred to as the **press**. = newspapers, the media ❑ *interviews in the local and foreign press* ❑ *freedom of the press* ❑ *Today the British press is full of articles on India's new prime minister.* ❑ *Press reports revealed that ozone levels in the upper atmosphere fell during the past month.* **3** [SING] Journalists and reporters are referred to as **the press**. ❑ *Christie looked relaxed and calm as she faced the press afterwards.* **4** [c] A **press** or a **printing press** is a machine used for printing things such as books and newspapers.
PHRASES **get bad press** or **get good press** If someone or something **gets bad press**, they are criticized, especially in the newspapers, on television, or on radio. If they **get good press**, they are praised. ❑ *the bad press that career women consistently get in this country*
go to press When a newspaper or magazine **goes to press**, it starts being printed. ❑ *We check prices at the time of going to press.*
→ See also **pressing**

press con·fer·ence NOUN [c] (**press conferences**)
A **press conference** is a meeting held by a famous or important person in which they answer reporters' questions. ❑ *She gave her reaction to his release at a press conference.*

✪press·ing /ˈpresɪŋ/ ADJ A **pressing** problem, need, or issue has to be dealt with immediately. = urgent ❑ *It is one of the most pressing problems facing this country.* ❑ *There is a pressing need for more funds.*
→ See also **press**

✪pres·sure ✦✦✦ /ˈpreʃə/ NOUN, VERB
NOUN [u] (**pressures**) **1** Pressure is force that you produce when you press hard on something. ❑ *She kicked at the door with her foot, and the pressure was enough to open it.* ❑ *The pressure of his fingers had relaxed.* ❑ *The best way to treat such bleeding is to apply firm pressure.* **2** [also pressures]

The **pressure** in a place or container is the force produced by the quantity of gas or liquid in that place or container. ❑ *The window in the cockpit had blown in and the pressure dropped dramatically.* ❑ *Warm air is now being drawn in from another high pressure area over the North Sea.* **3** [also pressures] If there is **pressure on** a person, someone is trying to persuade or force them to do something. ❑ *He may have put pressure on her to agree.* ❑ *A lot of dot-coms were under pressure from their investors.* **4** [also pressures] If you are experiencing **pressure**, you feel that you must do a lot of tasks or make a lot of decisions in very little time, or that people expect a lot from you. ❑ *Can you work under pressure?* ❑ *Even if I had the talent to play tennis I couldn't stand the pressure.*
VERB [T] (**pressures, pressuring, pressured**) If you **pressure** someone **to** do something, you try forcefully to persuade them to do it. ❑ *He will never pressure you to get married.* ❑ *The Senate should not be pressured into making hasty decisions.*
pres·sured /ˈpreʃəd/ ADJ ❑ *You're likely to feel anxious and pressured.*
→ See also **blood pressure**

pres·sure group NOUN [c] (**pressure groups**) A **pressure group** is an organized group of people who are trying to persuade a government or other authority to do something, for example to change a law. ❑ *the environmental pressure group Greenpeace*

pres·tige /preˈstiːʒ/ NOUN, ADJ
NOUN [U] If a person, a country, or an organization has **prestige**, they are admired and respected because of the position they hold or the things they have achieved. ❑ *efforts to build up the prestige of the United Nations* ❑ *It was his responsibility for foreign affairs that gained him international prestige.*
ADJ [prestige + N] **Prestige** is used to describe products, places, or activities that people admire because they are associated with being rich or having a high social position. = luxury ❑ *such prestige cars as Cadillac, Mercedes, Porsche, and Jaguar*

pres·tig·ious /preˈstɪdʒəs/ ADJ A **prestigious** institution, job, or activity is respected and admired by people. ❑ *It's one of the best equipped and most prestigious schools in the country.*

pre·sum·ably ✦◇◇ /prɪˈzjuːməbli, AmE -ˈzuːm-/ ADV (*vagueness*) If you say that something is **presumably** the case, you mean that you think it is very likely to be the case, although you are not certain. ❑ *The spear is presumably the murder weapon.*

✪pre·sume /prɪˈzjuːm, AmE -ˈzuːm/ VERB [T] (**presumes, presuming, presumed**) (*academic word*) **1** If you **presume that** something is the case, you think that it is the case, although you are not certain. = assume ❑ *I presume you're here on business.* ❑ *'Had he been home all week?'— 'I presume so.'* ❑ *In Madagascar, nearly half of 176 indigenous palm species are endangered or presumed extinct.* ❑ *areas that have been presumed to be safe* ❑ *It is presumed that the hormone melatonin is involved.* **2** (*formal*) If you say that someone **presumes to** do something, you mean that they do it even though they have no right to do it. ❑ *They're resentful that outsiders presume to meddle in their affairs.* **3** (*formal*) If an idea, theory, or plan **presumes** certain facts, it regards them as true so that they can be used as a basis for further ideas and theories. ❑ *The legal definition of 'know' often presumes mental control.*

✪pre·sump·tion /prɪˈzʌmpʃən/ NOUN [c] (**presumptions**) A **presumption** is something that is accepted as true but is not certain to be true. = assumption ❑ *the presumption that a defendant is innocent until proved guilty* ❑ *stories that challenge presumptions and preconceptions*

pre·tax /ˈpriːˌtæks/ also **pre-tax** ADJ, ADV
ADJ [pretax + N] (*business*) **Pretax** profits or losses are the total profits or losses made by a company before tax has been taken away. ❑ *They announced a fall in pretax profits.*
ADV [pretax after V] If a company makes a certain profit or loss **pretax**, this is the total profit or loss it made before tax has been taken away. ❑ *Last year it made $2.5 million pretax.*

P

pre·tence /prɪˈtens, *AmE* ˈpriːtens/ (*BrE*; in *AmE*, use **pretense**) NOUN

NOUN [C, U] (**pretences**) A **pretence** is an action or way of behaving that is intended to make people believe something that is not true. ◻ *He goes to the library and makes a pretence of reading some Thoreau.* ◻ *On the eighth day of questioning, she dropped the pretence that she was Japanese.*

PHRASE **false pretences** If you do something **under false pretences**, you do it when people do not know the truth about you and your intentions. ◻ *This interview was conducted under false pretences.*

pre·tend /prɪˈtend/ VERB [T] (**pretends, pretending, pretended**) **1** If you **pretend that** something is the case, you act in a way that is intended to make people believe that it is the case, although in fact it is not. ◻ *I pretend that things are really okay when they're not.* ◻ *Sometimes the boy pretended to be asleep.* **2** If children or adults **pretend that** they are doing something, they imagine that they are doing it, for example as part of a game. ◻ *She can sunbathe and pretend she's in Cancun.* **3** If you do not **pretend that** something is the case, you do not claim that it is the case. ◻ *We do not pretend that the past six years have been without problems for us.*

pre·ten·sion /prɪˈtenʃən/ NOUN [C, U, PL] (**pretensions**) **1** [C, U] (*disapproval*) If you say that someone has **pretensions**, you disapprove of them because they claim or pretend that they are more important than they really are. ◻ *Her wide-eyed innocence soon exposes the pretensions of the art world.* **2** [PL] If someone has **pretensions to** something, they claim to be or do that thing. ◻ *The city has unrealistic pretensions to world-class status.*

pre·ten·tious /prɪˈtenʃəs/ ADJ (*disapproval*) If you say that someone or something is **pretentious**, you mean that they try to seem important or significant, but you do not think that they are. ◻ *His response was full of pretentious nonsense.*

pre·text /ˈpriːtekst/ NOUN [C] (**pretexts**) A **pretext** is a reason that you pretend has caused you to do something. ◻ *They wanted a pretext for subduing the region by force.*

pret·ty ◆◆◇ /ˈprɪti/ ADJ, ADV

ADJ (**prettier, prettiest**) **1** If you describe someone, especially a girl, as **pretty**, you mean that they look nice and are attractive in a delicate way. ◻ *She's a very charming and very pretty girl.* **2** A place or a thing that is **pretty** is attractive and pleasant, in a charming but not particularly unusual way. ◻ *a very pretty little town*

ADV [pretty + ADJ/ADV] (*informal*) You can use **pretty** before an adjective or adverb to slightly lessen its force. ◻ *I had a pretty good idea what she was going to do.*

pret·ti·ly /ˈprɪtɪli/ ADV **1** *She smiled again, prettily.* **2** *The living-room was prettily decorated.*

pre·vail /prɪˈveɪl/ VERB [I] (**prevails, prevailing, prevailed**) **1** If a proposal, principle, or opinion **prevails**, it gains influence or is accepted, often after a struggle or argument. = triumph ◻ *We hoped that common sense would prevail.* ◻ *Rick still believes that justice will prevail.* **2** If a situation, attitude, or custom **prevails** in a particular place at a particular time, it is normal or most common in that place at that time. ◻ *A similar situation prevails in Canada.* ◻ *the confusion which had prevailed at the time of the revolution* **3** If one side in a battle, contest, or dispute **prevails**, it wins. ◻ *He appears to have the votes he needs to prevail.*

preva·lent /ˈprevələnt/ ADJ A condition, practice, or belief that is **prevalent** is common. ◻ *This condition is more prevalent in women than in men.* ◻ *Smoking is becoming increasingly prevalent among younger women.*

preva·lence /ˈprevələns/ NOUN [U] ◻ *the prevalence of cocaine abuse in the 1980s*

pre·vent ◆◆◇ /prɪˈvent/ VERB [T] (**prevents, preventing, prevented**) **1** To **prevent** something means to ensure that it does not happen. = stop, hinder; ≠ cause, encourage, promote ◻ *These methods prevent pregnancy.* ◻ *Further treatment will prevent cancer from developing.* ◻ *We recognized the possibility and took steps to prevent it happening.* **2** To **prevent** someone **from** doing something means to make it

impossible for them to do it. ◻ *He said this would prevent companies from creating new jobs.* ◻ *Its nationals may be prevented from leaving the country.*

pre·ven·tion /prɪˈvenʃən/ NOUN [U] ≠ encouragement, promotion ◻ *the prevention of heart disease* ◻ *crime prevention*

WORD CONNECTIONS
prevent + NOUN
prevent a **disease**   prevent **infection**   prevent **cancer**   prevent **injury**   ◻ *Fibre seems to play a large part in preventing cancer.*
prevent an **attack**   prevent **war**   ◻ *The government had done everything possible to prevent war.*
prevent the **spread** of …   prevent a **repeat** of …   ◻ *The fish are given doses of antibiotics to prevent the spread of disease.*

pre·vent·able /prɪˈventəbəl/ ADJ **Preventable** diseases, illnesses, or deaths could be stopped from occurring. ◻ *Forty thousand children a day die from preventable diseases.*

pre·ven·ta·tive /prɪˈventətɪv/ or **preventive** /prɪˈventɪv/ ADJ **Preventative** actions are intended to help prevent things such as disease or crime. ◻ *Too much is spent on curative medicine and too little on preventative medicine.*

pre·view /ˈpriːvjuː/ NOUN [C] (**previews**) A **preview** is an opportunity to see something such as a film, exhibition, or invention before it is open or available to the public. ◻ *He had gone to see the preview of a play.*

pre·vi·ous ◆◆◇ /ˈpriːviəs/ ADJ (*academic word*) **1** [previous + N] A **previous** event or thing is one that happened or existed before the one that you are talking about. = earlier, former; ≠ current, later, subsequent ◻ *She has a teenage daughter from a previous marriage.* ◻ *Previous studies have shown that organic farming methods can benefit the wildlife around farms.* **2** [DET + previous] You refer to the period of time or the thing immediately before the one that you are talking about as the **previous** one. = preceding; ≠ following ◻ *It was a surprisingly dry day after the rain of the previous week.*

pre·vi·ous·ly ◆◆◇ /ˈpriːviəsli/ ADV **1** **Previously** means at some time before the period that you are talking about. = earlier, formerly; ≠ currently, subsequently ◻ *Guyana's railways were previously owned by private companies.* ◻ *The contract was awarded to a previously unknown company.* ◻ *a collection of previously unpublished poems* **2** [N + previously] You can use **previously** to say how much earlier one event was than another event. = earlier ◻ *He had first entered the House 12 years previously.*

prey /preɪ/ NOUN, VERB

NOUN [U] **1** A creature's **prey** are the creatures that it hunts and eats in order to live. ◻ *Electric rays stun their prey with huge electrical discharges.* ◻ *These animals were the prey of hyenas.* **2** You can refer to the people who someone tries to harm or trick as their **prey**. ◻ *Police officers lie in wait for the gangs who stalk their prey at night.*

VERB [I] (**preys, preying, preyed**) **1** A creature that **preys on** other creatures lives by catching and eating them. = feed, hunt ◻ *The effect was to disrupt the food chain, starving many animals and those that preyed on them.* ◻ *The larvae prey upon small aphids.* **2** If someone **preys on** other people, especially people who are unable to protect themselves, they take advantage of them or harm them in some way. ◻ *Pam had never learned that there were men who preyed on young runaways.* **3** If something **preys on** your mind, you cannot stop thinking and worrying about it. = weigh ◻ *It was a misunderstanding and it preyed on his conscience.*

price ◆◆◇ /praɪs/ NOUN, VERB

NOUN [SING, C] (**prices**) **1** [SING, C] The **price** of something is the amount of money that you have to pay in order to buy it. ❑ *a sharp increase in the price of gas* ❑ *They expected house prices to rise.* ■ [SING] The **price** that you pay for something that you want is an unpleasant thing that you have to do or suffer in order to get it. = **penalty** ❑ *There may be a price to pay for such relentless activity, perhaps ill health or even divorce.*

PHRASES **at any price** If you want something **at any price**, you are determined to get it, even if unpleasant things happen as a result. ❑ *If they wanted a deal at any price, they would have to face the consequences.*

at a price ■ If you get something that you want **at a price**, you get it but something unpleasant happens as a result. ❑ *Fame comes at a price.* ■ If you can buy something that you want **at a price**, it is for sale, but it is extremely expensive. ❑ *Most goods are available, but at a price.*

VERB [T] (**prices, pricing, priced**) If something **is priced at** a particular amount, the price is set at that amount. ❑ *The bond is currently priced at $900.* ❑ *Analysts predict that Digital will price the new line at less than half the cost of comparable IBM mainframes.*

pric·ing /'praɪsɪŋ/ NOUN [U] ❑ *It's hard to maintain competitive pricing.*

✦ **price yourself out of the market** → see **market**

WHICH WORD?

price or cost?

The **price** or **cost** of something is the amount of money you must pay to buy it.

❑ the **price** of sugar

❑ an increase in the **cost** of fertilizer

You can also use **cost** to refer to the amount of money needed to do or make something. You do not use **price** in this way.

❑ The building was recently restored at a **cost** of £500,000.

You use the plural noun **costs** when you are referring to the total amount of money needed to run a business.

❑ She decided she needed to cut her **costs** by half.

---

prick /prɪk/ VERB, NOUN

VERB [T] (**pricks, pricking, pricked**) ■ If you **prick** something or **prick** holes in it, you make small holes in it with a sharp object such as a pin. ❑ *Prick the potatoes and rub the skins with salt.* ■ If something sharp **pricks** you or if you **prick yourself** with something sharp, it sticks into you or presses your skin and causes you pain. ❑ *She had just pricked her finger with the needle.*

NOUN [C] (**pricks**) A **prick** is a small, sharp pain that you get when something pricks you. ❑ *At the same time she felt a prick on her neck.*

pride ✦◇◇ /praɪd/ NOUN, VERB

NOUN [U] ■ **Pride** is a feeling of satisfaction that you have because you or people close to you have done something good or possess something good. ❑ *the sense of pride in a job well done* ❑ *We take pride in offering you the highest standards.* ■ **Pride** is a sense of the respect that other people have for you, and that you have for yourself. = **self-esteem** ❑ *Davis had to salvage his pride.* ■ Someone's **pride** is the feeling that they have that they are better or more important than other people. = **arrogance** ❑ *His pride may still be his downfall.*

VERB [T] (**prides, priding, prided**) If you **pride** yourself **on** a quality or skill that you have, you are very proud of it. ❑ *Suarez prides himself on being able to organize his own life.*

priest ✦◇◇ /priːst/ NOUN [C] (**priests**) ■ A **priest** is a member of the Christian clergy in the Catholic, Anglican, or Orthodox church. ❑ *He had trained to be a Catholic priest.* ■ In many non-Christian religions a **priest** is a man who has particular duties and responsibilities in a place where people worship. ❑ *a New Age priest or priestess*

✪**pri·mari·ly** /'praɪmərɪli, AmE praɪ'merɪli/ ADV You use **primarily** to say what is mainly true in a particular situation. = **mainly, principally, chiefly** ❑ *a book aimed primarily at high-energy physicists* ❑ *Public order is primarily an urban problem.* ❑ *Investment remains tiny primarily because of the exorbitant cost of land.*

✪**pri·ma·ry** ✦◇◇ /'praɪməri, AmE -meri/ ADJ (*academic word*) ■ [primary + N] (*formal*) You use **primary** to describe something that is very important. = **main, principal** ❑ *That's the primary reason the company's share price has held up so well.* ❑ *His misunderstanding of language was the primary cause of his other problems.* ❑ *The family continues to be the primary source of care and comfort for people as they grow older.* ■ [primary + N] **Primary** education is the first few years of formal education for children. ❑ *The content of primary education should be the same for everyone.* ❑ *Ninety-nine per cent of primary pupils now have hands-on experience of computers.* ■ [primary + N] **Primary** is used to describe something that occurs first. ❑ *It is not the primary tumour that kills, but secondary growths elsewhere in the body.*

✪**pri·ma·ry school** (*mainly BrE; in AmE, usually use* **elementary school**) NOUN [C, U] (**primary schools**) A **primary school** is a school for children between the ages of 4 or 5 and 11. ❑ *eight-to nine-year-olds in their third year at primary school* ❑ *Greenside Primary School*

✪**prime** ✦◇◇ /praɪm/ ADJ, NOUN, VERB (*academic word*) **ADJ** ■ [prime + N] You use **prime** to describe something that is most important in a situation. = **main, principal** ❑ *Political stability, meanwhile, will be a prime concern.* ❑ *It could be a prime target for guerrilla attack.* ❑ *The prime objective of the organization is to increase profit.* ■ [prime + N] You use **prime** to describe something that is of the best possible quality. ❑ *The location of these beaches makes them prime sites for development.* ■ [prime + N] You use **prime** to describe an example of a particular kind of thing that is absolutely typical. = **classic** ❑ *The prime example is Macy's, once the undisputed king of California retailers.* **NOUN** [U] If someone or something is in their **prime**, they are at the stage in their existence when they are at their strongest, most active, or most successful. ❑ *Maybe I'm just coming into my prime now.* ❑ *We've had a series of athletes trying to come back well past their prime.* **VERB** [T] (**primes, priming, primed**) ■ If you **prime** someone **to** do something, you prepare them to do it, for example, by giving them information about it beforehand. = **brief** ❑ *Claire wished she'd primed Sarah beforehand.* ❑ *Marianne had not known until Arnold primed her for her duties that she was to be the sole female.* ■ If someone **primes a bomb** or **a gun**, they prepare it so that it is ready to explode or fire. ❑ *He was priming the bomb to go off in an hour's time.* ❑ *He kept a primed shotgun in his office.*

prime min·is·ter ✦✦✦ NOUN [C] (**prime ministers**) The leader of the government in some countries is called the **prime minister**. = **PM, premier** ❑ *the former prime minister of Pakistan, Miss Benazir Bhutto*

✪**prime num·ber** NOUN [C] (**prime numbers**) In mathematics, a **prime number** is a whole number greater than 1 that cannot be divided exactly by any whole number except itself and the number 1, such as 17. ❑ *The progress takes the project tantalisingly close to finding the first 10 million-digit prime number.* ❑ *his work on prime numbers, the building blocks of arithmetic*

✪**primi·tive** /'prɪmɪtɪv/ ADJ ■ **Primitive** means belonging to a society in which people live in a very simple way, usually without industries or a writing system. ❑ *studies of primitive societies* ❑ *Weston A. Price, who studied the health of many primitive tribes in Central and Southern America* ■ **Primitive** means belonging to a very early period in the development of an animal or plant. ❑ *primitive whales* ❑ *Primitive humans needed to be able to react like this to escape from dangerous animals.* ■ If you describe something as **primitive**, you mean that it is very simple in style or very old-fashioned. ❑ *The conditions are primitive by any standards.*

prince ✦✦◇ /prɪns/ NOUN [C] (**princes**) ■ A **prince** is a male member of a royal family, especially the son of the king or queen of a country. ❑ *Prince Edward and other royal guests* ■ A **prince** is the male royal ruler of a small country or state. ❑ *He was speaking without the prince's authority.*

prin·cess ✦✦◇ /ˌprɪn'ses, AmE 'prɪnsəs/ NOUN [C] (**princesses**) A **princess** is a female member of a royal family, usually the daughter of a king or queen or the wife of a prince. ❑ *Princess Anne topped the guest list.*

⊙prin·ci·pal ◆◇◇ /ˈprɪnsɪpəl/ ADJ, NOUN (*academic word*)
 ADJ [principal + N] **Principal** means first in order of importance. = **main, chief** ❑ *The principal reason for my change of mind is this.* ❑ *the country's principal source of foreign exchange earnings* ❑ *Their principal concern is bound to be that of winning the next general election.*
 NOUN [c] (**principals**) **1** The **principal** of a school is the person in charge of the school or college. ❑ *Donald King is the principal of Dartmouth High School.* **2** [usu sing] (*business*) The **principal** of a loan is the original amount of the loan, on which you pay interest.

⊙prin·ci·pal·ly /ˈprɪnsɪpəli/ ADV [principally with CL/GROUP] **Principally** means more than anything else. = **chiefly, mainly** ❑ *This is principally because the major export markets are slowing.* ❑ *Embryonic development seems to be controlled principally by a very small number of master genes.*

⊙prin·ci·ple ◆◆◇ /ˈprɪnsɪpəl/ NOUN (*academic word*)
 NOUN [c, u] (**principles**) **1** [c, u] A **principle** is a general belief about the way you should behave, which influences your behaviour. ❑ *Buck never allowed himself to be bullied into doing anything that went against his principles.* ❑ *It's not just a matter of principle.* **2** [c] The **principles of** a particular theory or philosophy are its basic rules or laws. ❑ *a violation of the basic principles of Marxism* ❑ *The doctrine was based on three fundamental principles.* **3** [c] Scientific **principles** are general scientific laws which explain how something happens or works. = **rule, law** ❑ *These people lack all understanding of scientific principles.* ❑ *the principles of quantum theory*
 PHRASES **in principle** **1** If you agree with something **in principle**, you agree in general terms to the idea of it, although you do not yet know the details or know if it will be possible. = **in theory**; ≠ **in practice** ❑ *I agree with it in principle but I doubt if it will happen in practice.* **2** If something is possible **in principle**, there is no known reason why it should not happen, even though it has not happened before. ❑ *Even assuming this to be in principle possible, it will not be achieved soon.*
 on principle If you refuse to do something **on principle**, you refuse to do it because of a particular belief that you have. ❑ *He would vote against it on principle.*

print ◆◆◇ /prɪnt/ VERB, NOUN, ADJ
 VERB [T] (**prints, printing, printed**) **1** If someone **prints** something such as a book or newspaper, they produce it in large quantities using a machine. ❑ *He started to print his own posters to distribute abroad.* ❑ *Our brochure is printed on environmentally friendly paper.* **2** If a newspaper or magazine **prints** a piece of writing, it includes it or publishes it. = **publish** ❑ *We can only print letters which are accompanied by the writer's name and address.* **3** If numbers, letters, or designs **are printed on** a surface, they are put on it in ink or dye using a machine. You can also say that a surface **is printed with** numbers, letters, or designs. ❑ *the number printed on the receipt* ❑ *The company has for some time printed its phone number on its products.* **4** When you **print** a photograph, you produce it from a negative. ❑ *Printing a black-and-white negative on to colour paper produces a similar monochrome effect.* **5** If you **print** words, you write in letters that are not joined together. ❑ *Print your name and address on a postcard and send it to us.*
 PHRASAL VERB **print out** If a computer or a machine attached to a computer **prints** something **out**, it produces a copy of it on paper. ❑ *You measure yourself, enter measurements and the computer will print out the pattern.*
 NOUN [u, c] (**prints**) **1** [u, c] A **print** is a piece of clothing or material with a pattern printed on it. You can also refer to the pattern itself as a **print**. ❑ *Her mother wore one of her dark summer prints.* ❑ *In this living room we've mixed glorious floral prints.* **2** [c] A **print** is a photograph from a film that has been developed. ❑ *black and white prints of Margaret and Jean as children* **3** [c] A **print** is one of a number of copies of a particular picture. It can be either a photograph, something such as a painting, or a picture made by an artist who puts ink on a prepared surface and presses it against paper. ❑ *12 original copper plates engraved*

by William Hogarth for his famous series of prints **4** [u] **Print** is used to refer to letters and numbers as they appear on the pages of a book, newspaper, or printed document. ❑ *columns of tiny print* **5** [c] You can refer to a mark left by someone's foot as a **print**. = **footprint** ❑ *He crawled from print to print, sniffing at the earth, following the scent left in the tracks.* **6** [c] You can refer to oily marks left by someone's fingers as their **prints**. = **fingerprint** ❑ *Fresh prints of both girls were found in the house.*
 PHRASES **in print** If you appear **in print**, or get **into print**, what you say or write is published in a book, newspaper, or magazine. ❑ *Many of these poets appeared in print only long after their deaths.*
 small print or **fine print** The **small print** or the **fine print** of something such as an advertisement or a contract consists of the technical details and legal conditions, which are often printed in much smaller letters than the rest of the text. ❑ *I'm looking at the small print; I don't want to sign anything that I shouldn't sign.*
 ADJ [print + N] The **print** media consists of newspapers and magazines, but not television or radio. ❑ *I have been convinced that the print media are more accurate and more reliable than television.*

print·ing /ˈprɪntɪŋ/ NOUN [u] ❑ *His brother ran a printing and publishing company.*

print·er /ˈprɪntə/ NOUN [c] (**printers**) **1** A **printer** is a machine that can be connected to a computer in order to make copies on paper of documents or other information held by the computer. **2** A **printer** is a person or company whose job is printing things such as books. ❑ *The manuscript had already been sent off to the printer.*

⊙pri·or ◆◇◇ /ˈpraɪə/ ADJ (*academic word*)
 ADJ **1** [prior + N] You use **prior** to indicate that something has already happened, or must happen, before another event takes place. = **previous** ❑ *He claimed he had no prior knowledge of the protest.* ❑ *The Constitution requires the president to seek the prior approval of Congress for military action.* ❑ *Prior knowledge of the programme is not essential.* ❑ *For the prior year, they reported net income of $1.1 million.* **2** [prior + N] A **prior** claim or duty is more important than other claims or duties and needs to be dealt with first. ❑ *The firm I wanted to use had prior commitments.*
 PHRASE (*formal*) If something happens **prior to** a particular time or event, it happens before that time or event. = **before**; ≠ **after** ❑ *A death prior to 65 is considered to be a premature death.* ❑ *Prior to his Japan trip, he went to New York.* ❑ *This is the preliminary investigation prior to the official inquiry.*

⊙pri·ori·tize /praɪˈɒrɪtaɪz, AmE -ˈɔːr-/ also **prioritise** VERB [T] (**prioritizes, prioritizing, prioritized**) **1** If you **prioritize** something, you treat it as more important than other things. ❑ *Prioritize your own wants rather than constantly thinking about others.* ❑ *The government is prioritizing the service sector, rather than investing in industry and production.* **2** If you **prioritize** the tasks that you have to do, you decide which are the most important and do them first. ❑ *Make lists of what to do and prioritize your tasks.*

⊙pri·ori·ti·za·tion also **prioritisation** /praɪˌɒrɪtaɪˈzeɪʃən/ NOUN [u] ❑ *the government's prioritization of resource allocation* ❑ *The plan does not suggest prioritization based on age.*

⊙pri·ori·ty ◆◆◇ /praɪˈɒriti, AmE -ˈɔːr-/ NOUN (*academic word*)
 NOUN [c] (**priorities**) If something is a **priority**, it is the most important thing you have to do or deal with, or must be done or dealt with before everything else you have to do. ❑ *Being a parent is her first priority.* ❑ *The government's priority is to build more power plants.* ❑ *You may be surprised to find that your priorities change after having a baby.*
 PHRASES **give priority** If you **give priority to** something or someone, you treat them as more important than anything or anyone else. ❑ *Women are more likely to give priority to child care and education policies.*
 take priority or **have priority** If something **takes priority** or **has priority over** other things, it is regarded as being more important than them and is dealt with first. ❑ *The fight against inflation took priority over measures to combat the deepening recession.*

p

✪**pris·on** ♦♦◇ /'prɪzən/ NOUN [C, U] (**prisons**) A **prison** is a building where criminals are kept as punishment. = jail ❑ *The prison's inmates are being kept in their cells.* ❑ *He was sentenced to life in prison.*

✪**pris·on·er** ♦♦◇ /'prɪzənə/ NOUN [C] (**prisoners**) **1** A **prisoner** is a person who is kept in a prison as a punishment for a crime that they have committed. = inmate, convict, criminal ❑ *The committee is concerned about the large number of prisoners sharing cells.* **2** [also 'hold/take' N + prisoner] A **prisoner** is a person who has been captured by an enemy, for example, in war. ❑ *wartime hostages and concentration-camp prisoners*

pri·va·cy /'prɪvəsi, AmE 'praɪ-/ NOUN [U] If you have **privacy**, you are in a place or situation that allows you to do things without other people seeing you or disturbing you. ❑ *He resented the publication of this book, which he saw as an embarrassing invasion of his privacy.* ❑ *Thatched pavilions provide shady retreats for relaxing and reading in privacy.*

✪**pri·vate** ♦♦◇ /'praɪvɪt/ ADJ, NOUN
[ADJ] **1** (*business*) **Private** industries and services are owned or controlled by an individual person or a commercial company, rather than by the state or an official organization. ≠ public ❑ *a joint venture with private industry* ❑ *They sent their children to private schools.* ❑ *Bupa runs private hospitals in Britain.* ❑ *Brazil says its constitution forbids the private ownership of energy assets.* **2** [private + N] **Private** individuals are acting only for themselves, and are not representing any group, company, or organization. ❑ *Private individuals with money to lend are more difficult to find than traditional lenders.* ❑ *The king was on a private visit to enable him to pray at the tombs of his ancestors.* **3** Your **private** things belong only to you, or may only be used by you. ❑ *They want more state control over private property.* **4** **Private** places or gatherings may be attended only by a particular group of people, rather than by the general public. ❑ *673 private golf clubs took part in a recent study.* ❑ *The door is marked 'Private'.* **5** **Private** meetings, discussions, and other activities involve only a small number of people, and very little information about them is given to other people. ❑ *Don't bug private conversations, and don't buy papers that reprint them.* **6** Your **private life** is that part of your life that is concerned with your personal relationships and activities, rather than with your work or business. = personal ❑ *I've always kept my private and professional life separate.* **7** Your **private** thoughts or feelings are ones that you do not talk about to other people. ❑ *We all felt as if we were intruding on his private grief.* **8** If you describe a place as **private**, or as somewhere where you can be **private**, you mean that it is a quiet place and you can be alone there without being disturbed. ❑ *It was the only reasonably private place they could find.* **9** If you describe someone as a **private** person, you mean that they are very quiet by nature and do not reveal their thoughts and feelings to other people. ❑ *Gould was an intensely private individual.*
[NOUN] [C] (**privates**) A **private** is a soldier of the lowest rank in an army or the marines. ❑ *He was a private in the US Army.*
[PHRASE] **in private** If you do something **in private**, you do it without other people being present, often because it is something that you want to keep secret. ❑ *Some of what we're talking about might better be discussed in private.*

WORD FAMILIES	
private ADJ	This action requires co-operation between the government and **private** industry.
privately ADV	No other European country had so much state ownership and so few **privately** owned businesses.
privatize VERB	The new government pledged to **privatize** many state-owned industries.
privatization NOUN	He called for **privatization** of the state water authority.

✪**pri·vate·ly** /'praɪvɪtli/ ADV **1** [privately with v] If an industry or service is **privately** owned, it is controlled by an individual person or a commercial company, rather than by the state or an official organization. ≠ publicly ❑ *No other European country had so much state ownership and so few privately owned businesses.* ❑ *She was privately educated at schools in Ireland and Paris.* **2** If people meet or discuss things **privately**, they do so without involving or giving information to other people. ❑ *Few senior figures have issued any public statements but privately the resignation's been welcomed.* **3** If you think or feel something **privately**, you do not talk about to other people about your thoughts or feelings. ❑ *Privately, she worries about whether she's really good enough.* **4** [privately after v] If you buy or sell something **privately**, you buy it from or sell it to another person directly, rather than in a store or through a business. ❑ *The whole process makes buying a car privately as painless as buying from a garage.*

pri·vate sec·tor NOUN [SING] (*business*) The **private sector** is the part of a country's economy that consists of industries and commercial companies that are not owned or controlled by the government. ❑ *small firms in the private sector*

✪**pri·vat·ize** ♦◇◇ /'praɪvətaɪz/ also **privatise** VERB [T] (**privatizes**, **privatizing**, **privatized**) (*business*) If a company, industry, or service that is owned by the state **is privatized**, the government sells it and makes it a private company. ❑ *Many state-owned companies were privatized.* ❑ *a move to privatize prisons* ❑ *The water boards are about to be privatized.* ❑ *a pledge to privatize the rail and coal industries* ❑ *the newly privatized FM radio stations*
✪**pri·vati·za·tion** /ˌpraɪvətaɪˈzeɪʃən/ also **privatisation** NOUN [C, U] (**privatizations**) ❑ *the privatization of government services* ❑ *the privatization of British Rail* ❑ *fresh rules governing the conduct of future privatizations*

✪**privi·lege** /'prɪvɪlɪdʒ/ NOUN [C, U, SING] (**privileges**) **1** [C] A **privilege** is a special right or advantage that only one person or group has. ❑ *The Russian Federation has issued a decree abolishing special privileges for government officials.* ❑ *the ancient powers and privileges of the House of Commons* **2** [U] If you talk about **privilege**, you are talking about the power and advantage that only a small group of people have, usually because of their wealth or their connections with powerful people. ❑ *Pironi was the son of privilege and wealth, and it showed.* ❑ *Having been born to privilege in old Hollywood, she was carrying on a family tradition by acting.* **3** [SING] You can use **privilege** in expressions such as **be a privilege** or **have the privilege** when you want to show your appreciation of someone or something, or to show your respect. ❑ *It must be a privilege to know such a man.*

✪**privi·leged** /'prɪvɪlɪdʒd/ ADJ, NOUN
[ADJ] **1** Someone who is **privileged** has an advantage or opportunity that most other people do not have, often because of their wealth or connections with powerful people. ❑ *They were, by and large, a very wealthy, privileged elite.* ❑ *She was born in Croydon to Scottish parents and had a fairly privileged upbringing.* **2** **Privileged** information is known by only a small group of people, who are not legally required to give it to anyone else. = confidential ❑ *The data is privileged information, not to be shared with the general public.* ❑ *Mr Nixon argued the tapes were privileged.*
[NOUN] [PL] **The privileged** are people who are privileged. ❑ *They are only interested in preserving the power of the privileged and the well off.* ❑ *Family problems are found in every class, he said, but were more common among the less privileged.*

prize ♦♦◇ /praɪz/ NOUN, ADJ, VERB
[NOUN] [C] (**prizes**) **1** A **prize** is money or something valuable that is given to someone who has the best results in a competition or game, or as a reward for doing good work. ❑ *You must claim your prize by telephoning our claims line.* ❑ *He was awarded the Nobel Prize for Physics in 1985.* **2** You can refer to someone or something as a **prize** when people consider them to be of great value or importance. ❑ *With no lands of his own, he was no great matrimonial prize.*
[ADJ] [prize + N] You use **prize** to describe things that are of such good quality that they win prizes or deserve to win prizes. ❑ *a prize bull*

P

VERB [T] (**prizes, prizing, prized**) **1** Something that **is prized** is wanted and admired because it is considered to be very valuable or very good quality. □ *Military figures made out of lead are prized by collectors.* **2** (*mainly BrE; in AmE, usually use* **pry**) If you **prize** something **open** or **prize** it away from a surface, you force it to open or force it to come away from the surface.

pro /prəʊ/ NOUN, PREP
NOUN [C] (**pros**) (*informal*) A **pro** is a professional. □ *In the professional theatre, there is a tremendous need to prove that you're a pro.*
PHRASE **pros and cons** The **pros and cons** of something are its advantages and disadvantages, which you consider carefully so that you can make a sensible decision. □ *Motherhood has both its pros and cons.*
PREP If you are **pro** a particular course of action or belief, you agree with it or support it. = for □ *Americans have always been very pro business, pro competition, pro free market.*

WORD PARTS
The prefix **pro-** often appears in words to show that someone supports a particular person or thing: **pro-choice** (ADJ)   **pro-European** (ADJ)   **pro-Communism** (ADJ)

pro·ac·tive /prəʊˈæktɪv/ ADJ **Proactive** actions are intended to cause changes, rather than just reacting to change. □ *In order to survive the competition a company should be proactive not reactive.*

⚫**prob·abil·ity** /ˌprɒbəˈbɪlɪti/ NOUN
NOUN [C, U] (**probabilities**) **1** The **probability** of something happening is how likely it is to happen, sometimes expressed as a fraction or a percentage. = chance, likelihood, possibility; ≠ improbability □ *Without a transfusion, the victim's probability of dying was 100%.* □ *The probabilities of crime or victimization are higher with some situations than with others.* **2** You say that there is a **probability that** something will happen when it is likely to happen. □ *If you've owned property for several years, the probability is that values have increased.* □ *Formal talks are still said to be a possibility, not a probability.*
PHRASE **in all probability** (*vagueness*) If you say that something will happen **in all probability**, you mean that you think it is very likely to happen. □ *The Republicans had better get used to the fact that in all probability, they are going to lose.*

⚫**prob·able** /ˈprɒbəbəl/ ADJ **1** (*vagueness*) If you say that something is **probable**, you mean that it is likely to be true or likely to happen. = likely; ≠ improbable, unlikely □ *It is probable that the medication will suppress the symptom without treating the condition.* □ *A bomb was the incident's most probable cause.* **2** [probable + N] You can use **probable** to describe a role or function that someone or something is likely to have. = likely □ *their probable presidential candidate*

⚫**prob·ably** ♦♦♦ /ˈprɒbəbli/ ADV (*vagueness*) **1** [probably with CL/GROUP] If you say that something is **probably** the case, you think that it is likely to be the case, although you are not sure. = perhaps, possibly; ≠ certainly □ *The White House probably won't make this plan public until July.* □ *Van Gogh is probably the best-known painter in the world.* **2** [probably with CL/GROUP] You can use **probably** when you want to make your opinion sound less forceful or definite, so that you do not offend people. □ *What would he think of their story? He'd probably think she and Lenny were both crazy!*

probe /prəʊb/ VERB, NOUN
VERB [I, T] (**probes, probing, probed**) **1** [I] If you **probe into** something, you ask questions or try to discover facts about it. □ *The more they probed into his background, the more inflamed their suspicions would become.* □ *For three years, I have probed for understanding.* **2** [I] If a doctor or dentist **probes**, he or she uses a long instrument to examine part of a patient's body. □ *The surgeon would pick up his instruments, probe, repair, and stitch up again.* □ *Dr Amid probed around the sensitive area.* **3** [T] If you **probe** a place,

you search it in order to find someone or something that you are looking for. □ *A flashlight beam probed the underbrush only yards away from their hiding place.*
NOUN [C] (**probes**) **1** A **probe into** something is the act of asking questions or trying to discover facts about it. □ *a federal grand-jury probe into corruption within the FDA* **2** A **probe** is a long thin instrument that doctors and dentists use to examine parts of the body. □ *a fibre-optic probe*

⚫**prob·lem** ♦♦♦ /ˈprɒbləm/ NOUN [C] (**problems**)
1 A **problem** is a situation that is unsatisfactory and causes difficulties for people. = difficulty, concern □ *the economic problems of the inner city* □ *I do not have a simple solution to the drug problem.* □ *The main problem is unemployment.* □ *He told Americans that solving the energy problem was very important.* **2** A **problem** is a puzzle that requires logical thought or mathematics to solve it. □ *With mathematical problems, you can save time by approximating.*

WORD CONNECTIONS
VERB + **problem**
have a problem   **face** a problem   □ *We will face serious problems if we do not deal with the issue now.*
cause a problem   □ *Too much stretching all at once can cause problems.*
solve a problem   **resolve** a problem   **tackle** a problem   **address** a problem   □ *Resolving the problem may be extremely difficult.*
ADJ + **problem**
a **major** problem   a **serious** problem   a **real** problem   □ *Ticks are a major problem for cattle worldwide.*
the **main** problem   the **biggest** problem   □ *The main problem is that she refuses to listen.*
financial problems   **economic** problems   **medical** problems   □ *Eventually, financial problems caused the the theatre to close.*

WHICH WORD?
problem or question?
Do not confuse **problem** and **question**.   A **problem** is a situation that is unsatisfactory and causes difficulties for people.   □ *the **problem** of refugees*   □ *They have financial **problems**.*   A **question** is something that you say or write in order to ask a person about something.   □ *A panel of experts will answer **questions** on education.*

⚫**prob·lem·at·ic** /ˌprɒbləˈmætɪk/ ADJ Something that is **problematic** involves problems and difficulties. ≠ unproblematic □ *Some places are more problematic than others for women travelling alone.* □ *the problematic business of running an economy*

⚫**pro·cedur·al** /prəˈsiːdʒərəl/ ADJ (*formal*) **Procedural** means involving a formal procedure. □ *A Spanish judge rejected the suit on procedural grounds.* □ *The Paris talks will mainly be about procedural matters.*

⚫**pro·cedure** ♦◇◇ /prəˈsiːdʒə/ NOUN [C, U] (**procedures**) A **procedure** is a way of doing something, especially the usual or correct way. = method, process □ *A biopsy is usually a minor surgical procedure.* □ *Police insist that Michael did not follow the correct procedure in applying for a visa.*

⚫**pro·ceed** ♦◇◇ VERB, NOUN (*academic word*)
VERB /prəˈsiːd/ [T, I] (**proceeds, proceeding, proceeded**)

p

1 [T] If you **proceed to** do something, you do it, often after doing something else first. ❑ *He proceeded to tell me of my birth.* **2** [I] (*formal*) If you **proceed with** a course of action, you continue with it. = continue; ≠ stop, discontinue ❑ *The group proceeded with a march they knew would lead to bloodshed.* ❑ *The trial has been delayed until November because the defence is not ready to proceed.* **3** [I] If an activity, process, or event **proceeds**, it goes on and does not stop. ❑ *The ideas were not new. Their development had proceeded steadily since the war.*

NOUN /'prəʊsiːdz/ [PL] (**proceeds**) The **proceeds** of an event or activity are the money that has been obtained from it. ❑ *The proceeds of the concert went to charity.*

✪ **pro·ceed·ing** /prə'siːdɪŋ/ NOUN [C, PL] (**proceedings**) (*academic word*) **1** [C] (*formal*) Legal **proceedings** are legal action taken against someone. = action ❑ *criminal proceedings against the former prime minister* **2** [C] (*formal*) The **proceedings** are an organized series of events that take place in a particular place. ❑ *The proceedings of the inquiry will take place in private.* **3** [PL] You can refer to a written record of the discussions at a meeting or conference as **the proceedings**. ❑ *The Department of Transport is to publish the conference proceedings.*

✪ **pro·cess** ♦♦♦ /'prəʊses, AmE 'prɑːses/ NOUN, VERB (*academic word*)

NOUN [C] (**processes**) **1** A **process** is a series of actions which are carried out in order to achieve a particular result. ❑ *There was total agreement to start the peace process as soon as possible.* ❑ *They decided to spread the building process over three years.* ❑ *The best way to proceed is by a process of elimination.* **2** A **process** is a series of things that happen naturally and result in a biological or chemical change. = course, procedure ❑ *It occurs in elderly men, apparently as part of the aging process.* **3** [usu with SUPP] A **process** is the preparation of raw materials or foods in factories before they are used or sold. ❑ *the cost of reengineering the production process*

PHRASES **in the process of** If you are **in the process of** doing something, you have started to do it and are still doing it. ❑ *The administration is in the process of drawing up a peace plan.* **in the process** If you are doing something and you do something else **in the process**, you do the second thing as part of doing the first thing. ❑ *You have to let us struggle for ourselves, even if we must die in the process.*

VERB [T] (**processes, processing, processed**) **1** When raw materials or foods **are processed**, they are prepared in factories before they are used or sold. ❑ *fish which are processed by the best methods: from freezing to canning and smoking* ❑ *The material will be processed into plastic pellets.* **2** When people **process** information, they put it through a system or into a computer in order to deal with it. ❑ *facilities to process the data, and the right to publish the results* **3** When people **are processed** by officials, their case is dealt with in stages and they pass from one stage of the process to the next. ❑ *Patients took more than two hours to be processed through the department.*

pro·cess·ing /'prəʊsesɪŋ, AmE 'prɑːsesɪŋ/ NOUN [U] **1** *America sent cotton to England for processing.* **2** *data processing*

WORD CONNECTIONS
VERB + **process**
participate in a process **control** a process ❑ *They refused to participate in the peace process.*
start a process **complete** a process ❑ *We started the process of pumping fuel out of the tanks.*
describe a process ❑ *The author describes the process of designing and creating training programmes.*
ADJ + **process**
a **difficult** process a **complicated** process a **long** process ❑ *Then began the difficult process of identifying the bodies.*

a **slow** process
a **gradual** process
❑ *Losing weight should be a gradual process.*

pro·ces·sion /prə'seʃən/ NOUN [C] (**processions**) A **procession** is a group of people who are walking, riding, or driving in a line as part of a public event. ❑ *a funeral procession*

pro·ces·sor /'prəʊsesə, AmE 'prɑːs-/ NOUN [C] (**processors**) **1** (*computing*) A **processor** is the part of a computer that interprets commands and performs the processes the user has requested. = CPU **2** A **processor** is someone or something which carries out a process. ❑ *The frozen-food industry could be supplied entirely by growers and processors outside the country.*

pro·claim /prəʊ'kleɪm/ VERB [T] (**proclaims, proclaiming, proclaimed**) **1** If people **proclaim** something, they formally make it known to the public. = declare ❑ *The new government in Venezuela set up its own army and proclaimed its independence.* ❑ *Britain proudly proclaims that it is a nation of animal lovers.* **2** If you **proclaim** something, you state it in an emphatic way. ❑ *'I think we have been heard today,' he proclaimed.*

prod /prɒd/ VERB, NOUN

VERB [T] (**prods, prodding, prodded**) **1** If you **prod** someone or something, you give them a quick push with your finger or with a pointed object. = poke ❑ *He prodded Murray with the shotgun.* ❑ *Prod the windowsills to check for signs of rot.* **2** If you **prod** someone **into** doing something, you remind or persuade them to do it. ❑ *The question is intended to prod students into examining the concept of freedom.*

NOUN [C] (**prods**) A **prod** is a quick push of someone or something with your finger or with a pointed object. = poke ❑ *He gave the donkey a mighty prod in the backside.*

✪ **pro·duce** ♦♦♦ VERB, NOUN

VERB /prə'djuːs/ [T] (**produces, producing, produced**) **1** To **produce** something means to cause it to happen. = cause, induce ❑ *The drug is known to produce side-effects in women.* ❑ *Talks aimed at producing a new world trade treaty have been under way for six years.* **2** If you **produce** something, you make or create it. = make, manufacture, create; ≠ consume ❑ *The company produced circuitry for communications systems.* **3** When things or people **produce** something, it comes from them or slowly forms from them, especially as the result of a biological or chemical process. ❑ *These plants are then pollinated and allowed to mature and produce seed.* **4** If you **produce** evidence or an argument, you show it or explain it to people in order to make them agree with you. ❑ *They challenged him to produce evidence to support his allegations.* **5** If you **produce** an object from somewhere, you show it or bring it out so that it can be seen. ❑ *To hire a car you must produce a passport and a current driver's licence.* **6** If someone **produces** something such as a film, a magazine, or a CD, they organize it and decide how it should be done. ❑ *He has produced his own sports magazine.*

NOUN /'prɒdjuːs/ [U] **Produce** is fruit and vegetables that are grown in large quantities to be sold. ❑ *We manage to get most of our produce in farmers' markets.*

WORD FAMILIES	
produce VERB	*The company produced circuitry for communications systems.*
producer NOUN	*Saudi Arabia is the world's leading oil producer.*
product NOUN	*South Korea's imports of consumer products increased by 33% this year.*
production NOUN	*There were tax incentives to encourage domestic production of oil.*
productive ADJ	*More productive farmers have been able to provide cheaper food.*

P

productivity NOUN	The third-quarter results reflect continued improvements in **productivity**.

❂ **pro·duc·er** ◆◆◇ /prə'dju:sə, AmE -'du:s-/ NOUN [c] **(producers)** ❶ A **producer** is a person whose job is to produce plays, films, programmes, or CDs. ❑ *a freelance film producer* ❷ A **producer** of a food or material is a company or country that grows or manufactures a large amount of it. = manufacturer ❑ *Saudi Arabia, the world's leading oil producer*

❂ **prod·uct** ◆◆◆ /'prɒdʌkt/ NOUN [c] **(products)** ❶ A **product** is something that is produced and sold in large quantities, often as a result of a manufacturing process. = goods ❑ *Try to get the best product at the lowest price.* ❑ *South Korea's imports of consumer products increased by 33% this year.* ❷ If you say that someone or something is a **product** of a situation or process, you mean that the situation or process has had a significant effect in making them what they are. ❑ *We are all products of our time.* ❑ *The bank is the product of a 1971 merger of two Japanese banks.*

USAGE NOTE
product
Note that **product** is a noun and not a verb. The related verb is 'produce'.
*The system will help workers to create a better **product**.*
*The system will help workers to **produce** bettter quality goods.*

❂ **pro·duc·tion** ◆◆◇ /prə'dʌkʃən/ NOUN
NOUN [u, c] **(productions)** ❶ [u] **Production** is the process of manufacturing or growing something in large quantities. ❑ *That model won't go into production before late 2017.* ❑ *tax incentives to encourage domestic production of oil* ❷ [u] **Production** is the amount of goods manufactured or grown by a company or country. = manufacturing, output ❑ *We needed to increase the volume of production.* ❸ [u] The **production of** something is its creation as the result of a natural process. ❑ *These proteins stimulate the production of blood cells.* ❹ [u] **Production** is the process of organizing and preparing a play, film, programme, or CD, in order to present it to the public. ❑ *She is head of the production company.* ❺ [c] A **production** is a play, opera, or other show that is performed in a theatre. ❑ *a critically acclaimed production of Othello*
PHRASE **on production of something** or **on the production of something** When you can do something **on production of** or **on the production of** documents, you need to show someone those documents in order to be able to do that thing. ❑ *Entry to the show is free to members on production of their membership cards.*

WORD CONNECTIONS
VERB + **production**
go into production
❑ *The new car will go into production early next year.*
increase production
boost production
stimulate production
❑ *The reduction in the tax rate will stimulate production and investment.*
ADJ + **production**
industrial production
agricultural production
commercial production
❑ *Industrial production declined sharply.*
mass production
❑ *Some drugs are far too expensive for mass production.*

pro·duc·tive /prə'dʌktɪv/ ADJ ❶ Someone or something that is **productive** produces or does a lot for the amount of resources used. ❑ *Training makes workers highly productive.* ❑ *More productive farmers have been able to provide cheaper food.* ❷ If you say that a relationship between people is

productive, you mean that a lot of good or useful things happen as a result of it. = fruitful ❑ *He was hopeful that the next round of talks would also be productive.*

prod·uc·tiv·ity /ˌprɒdʌk'tɪvɪti/ NOUN [u] **Productivity** is the rate at which goods are produced. = output ❑ *The third-quarter results reflect continued improvements in productivity.*

pro·fes·sion ◆◆◇ /prə'feʃən/ NOUN [c] **(professions)** ❶ [also 'by' profession] A **profession** is a type of job that requires advanced education or training. ❑ *Harper was a teacher by profession.* ❷ You can use **profession** to refer to all the people who have the same profession. ❑ *The attitude of the medical profession is very much more liberal now.*

❂ **pro·fes·sion·al** ◆◆◇ /prə'feʃənəl/ ADJ, NOUN **(academic word)**
ADJ ❶ [professional + N] **Professional** means relating to a person's work, especially work that requires special training. ❑ *His professional career started at Colgate University.* ❷ [professional + N] **Professional** people have jobs that require advanced education or training. = qualified; ≠ amateur ❑ *highly qualified professional people like doctors and engineers* ❸ You use **professional** to describe people who do a particular thing to earn money rather than as a hobby. ❑ *This has been my worst time for injuries since I started as a professional player.* ❹ [professional + N] **Professional** sports are played for money rather than as a hobby. ❑ *an art student who had played professional football for a short time* ❺ If you say something that someone does or produces is **professional**, you approve of it because you think that it is of a very high standard. ❑ *They run it with a truly professional but personal touch.*
NOUN [c] **(professionals)** ❶ A **professional** is someone who has a job that requires advanced education or training. ❑ *My father wanted me to become a professional and have more stability.* ❷ [professional after V] A **professional** is someone who does something to earn money rather than as a hobby. ❑ *He had been a professional since March 1985.* ❸ [professional with V] A **professional** is someone who does or produces something that you think is of a very high standard. ❑ *a dedicated professional who worked harmoniously with the cast and crew*
pro·fes·sion·al·ly /prə'feʃnəli/ ADV ❶ *a professionally-qualified architect* ❷ *By age 16 he was playing professionally with bands in Greenwich Village.* ❸ *These tickets have been produced very professionally.*

❂ **pro·fes·sor** ◆◆◇ /prə'fesə/ NOUN [c] **(professors)** ❶ A **professor** in a British university is the most senior teacher in a department. ❑ *Professor Cameron* ❑ *Ross is a university professor who specializes in defence issues.* ❑ *In 1979, only 2% of British professors were female.* ❷ A **professor** in an American or Canadian university or college is a teacher of the highest rank. ❑ *Robert Dunn is a professor of economics at George Washington University.* ❑ *Typically, the young college professor takes a job for a few years.*

pro·fi·cien·cy /prə'fɪʃənsi/ NOUN [u] If you show **proficiency in** something, you show ability or skill at it. = ability ❑ *Evidence of basic proficiency in English is part of the admissions requirement.*

pro·fi·cient /prə'fɪʃənt/ ADJ If you are **proficient in** something, you can do it well. = competent ❑ *A great number of Egyptians are proficient in foreign languages.*

❂ **pro·file** ◆◇◇ /'prəʊfaɪl/ NOUN
NOUN [u, c] **(profiles)** ❶ [u, c] Your **profile** is the outline of your face as it is seen when someone is looking at you from the side. ❑ *His handsome profile was turned away from us.* ❷ [u] If you see someone **in profile**, you see them from the side. ❑ *This picture shows the girl in profile.* ❸ [c] A **profile of** someone is a short article or programme in which their life and character are described. ❑ *A Washington newspaper published comparative profiles of the candidates' wives.* ❹ [c] [oft profile 'of' N] If the police make a **profile** of someone they are looking for, they write a description of the sort of person they are looking for. ❑ *the FBI profile of the anthrax killer* ❺ [c] A **profile** is a description of a person or group detailing their features or characteristics. = description ❑ *Members can browse profiles online.* ❑ *Forensic scientists create a DNA profile of an individual from a sample of saliva or hair.*

p

PHRASE **high profile** or **low profile** If someone has a **high profile**, people notice them and what they do. If you **keep a low profile**, you avoid doing things that will make people notice you. ❑ *a move that would give Egypt a much higher profile in the upcoming peace talks*

pro·fil·ing /ˈprəʊfaɪlɪŋ/ NOUN [U] ❑ *a former FBI agent who pioneered psychological profiling in the 1970s* ❑ *DNA profiling would now be added to the struggle against vandalism.*

✪**prof·it** ♦♦◇ /ˈprɒfɪt/ NOUN, VERB

NOUN [C, U] (**profits**) A **profit** is an amount of money that you gain when you are paid more for something than it cost you to make, get, or do it. = income, takings; ≠ loss ❑ *The bank made pre-tax profits of $6.5 million.* ❑ *You can improve your chances of profit by sensible planning.*

VERB [I, T] (**profits, profiting, profited**) ❶ [I] If you **profit from** something, you earn a profit from it. ❑ *No one was profiting inordinately from the war effort.* ❑ *He has profited by selling his holdings to other investors.* ❑ *Footballers are accustomed to profiting handsomely from bonuses.* ❷ [I, T] (*formal*) If you **profit from** something, or it **profits** you, you gain some advantage or benefit from it. ❑ *Jennifer wasn't yet totally convinced that she'd profit from a more relaxed lifestyle.* ❑ *So far the French alliance had profited the rebels little.*

✪**prof·it·able** /ˈprɒfɪtəbəl/ ADJ ❶ A **profitable** organization or practice makes a profit. = lucrative; ≠ unprofitable ❑ *Drug manufacturing is the most profitable business in the US.* ❑ *It was profitable for them to produce large amounts of food.* ❷ Something that is **profitable** results in some benefit for you. ❑ *close collaboration with industry which leads to a profitable exchange of personnel and ideas* **prof·it·ably** /ˈprɒfɪtəbli/ ADV ❶ [profitably with v] ❑ *The 28 French stores are trading profitably.* ❷ [profitably with v] ❑ *In fact he could scarcely have spent his time more profitably.* **prof·it·abil·ity** /ˌprɒfɪtəˈbɪlɪti/ NOUN [U] ❑ *Changes were made in operating methods in an effort to increase profitability.*

✪**pro·found** /prəˈfaʊnd/ ADJ (**profounder, profoundest**) ❶ (*emphasis*) You use **profound** to emphasize that something is very great or intense. = deep, intense, extreme ❑ *discoveries which had a profound effect on many areas of medicine* ❑ *profound disagreement* ❑ *The overwhelming feeling is just deep, profound shock and anger.* ❑ *Anna's patriotism was profound.* ❷ A **profound** idea, work, or person shows great intellectual depth and understanding. ❑ *This is a book full of profound, original, and challenging insights.* ✪**pro·found·ly** /prəˈfaʊndli/ ADV = deeply, intensely ❑ *This has profoundly affected my life.* ❑ *In politics, as in other areas, he is profoundly conservative.*

✪**pro·gram** ♦♦◇ /ˈprəʊgræm/ NOUN, VERB

NOUN [C] (**programs**) A **program** is a set of instructions that a computer follows in order to perform a particular task. = software, code ❑ *The chances of an error occurring in a computer program increase with the size of the program.* **VERB** [T] (**programs, programming, programmed**) (*computing*) When you **program** a computer, you give it a set of instructions to make it able to perform a particular task. ❑ *He programmed his computer to compare the 1,431 possible combinations of pairs in this population.* ❑ *45 million people, about half of whom can program their own computers* ❑ *a computer programmed to translate a story given to it in Chinese* **pro·gram·ming** /ˈprəʊgræmɪŋ/ NOUN [U] ❑ *programming skills*

✪**pro·gramme** /ˈprəʊgræm/ (*mainly BrE; in AmE, use* **program**) NOUN, VERB

NOUN [C] (**programmes**) ❶ A **programme** of actions or events is a series of actions or events that are planned to be done. = plan, strategy, schedule ❑ *The nation's largest training and education programme for adults.* ❑ *The general argued that the nuclear programme should still continue.* ❑ *The programme of sell-offs has been implemented by the new chief executive.* ❷ A television or radio **programme** is something that is broadcast on television or radio. ❑ *a network television programme* ❸ A theatre or concert **programme** is a small book or sheet of paper that gives information about the play or concert you are attending. ❑ *When you go to concerts, it's helpful to read the programme.* **VERB** [T] (**programmes, programming, programmed**)

When you **programme** a machine or system, you set its controls so that it will work in a particular way. ❑ *Parents can programme the machine not to turn on at certain times.*

WHICH WORD?

programme or program?

A **programme** is a plan which has been developed for a particular purpose. A television or radio **programme** is a single broadcast, for example a play, discussion, or show. ❑ *The company has major **programmes** of research and development.*

❑ *This is the last **programme** in our series on education.*

These uses of the word are spelled **program** in American English.

A computer **program** is a set of instructions that a computer uses to perform a particular operation. This use of the word is spelled **program** in both British and American English.

✪**pro·gress** ♦♦◇ NOUN, VERB

NOUN /ˈprəʊgres/ [U, SING] ❶ [U] **Progress** is the process of gradually improving or getting nearer to achieving or completing something. = advancement, development; ≠ setback ❑ *The medical community continues to make progress in the fight against cancer.* ❑ *The two sides made little if any progress towards agreement.* ❷ [SING] **The progress of** a situation or action is the way in which it develops. ❑ *The president is reported to have been delighted with the progress of the first day's talks.*

PHRASE **in progress** If something is **in progress**, it has started and is still continuing. ❑ *The game was already in progress when we took our seats.*

VERB /prəˈgres/ [I, T] (**progresses, progressing, progressed**) ❶ [I] To **progress** means to move over a period of time to a stronger, more advanced, or more desirable state. ≠ stall ❑ *He will visit once every two weeks to see how his new employees are progressing.* ❑ *He started with sketching and then progressed to painting.* ❑ *A company spokesman said that talks were progressing well.* ❷ [I] If events **progress**, they continue to happen gradually over a period of time. ❑ *As the evening progressed, sadness turned to rage.* ❸ [T] (*BrE, formal*) If you **progress** something, you cause it to develop.

WORD CONNECTIONS

VERB + **progress**

make progress
❑ *They didn't seem to be making any progress at all.*

ADJ + **progress**

good progress
rapid progress
real progress
steady progress
❑ *This is the first real progress that has been made for years.*

slow progress
❑ *Impatient with the slow progress, Yeltsin unfolded a radical economic programme to the Russian people.*

economic progress
academic progress
❑ *Everyone should share the benefits of economic progress.*

WORD FAMILIES

progress NOUN	The medical community continues to make **progress** in the fight against cancer.
progressive ADJ	He was able to point to the **progressive** changes he had already introduced.
progression NOUN	They have developed a skills strategy which is aimed at improving career **progression**.

P

⚙**pro·gres·sion** /prəˈɡreʃən/ NOUN [C] (**progressions**)
A **progression** is a gradual development from one state to another. = development ❑ *Both drugs slow the progression of HIV, but neither cures the disease.* ❑ *a skills strategy which is aimed at improving career progression*

⚙**pro·gres·sive** /prəˈɡresɪv/ ADJ, NOUN
ADJ ◻ Someone who is **progressive** or has **progressive** ideas has modern ideas about how things should be done, rather than traditional ones. ❑ *a progressive businessman who had voted for Roosevelt in 1932 and 1936* ❑ *Willan was able to point to the progressive changes he had already introduced.* ◼ A **progressive** change happens gradually over a period of time. = gradual ❑ *One prominent symptom of the disease is progressive loss of memory.* ❑ *the progressive development of a common foreign and security policy*
NOUN [C] (**progressives**) A **progressive** is someone who is progressive. ❑ *The Republicans were deeply split between progressives and conservatives.*

⚙**pro·gres·sive·ly** /prəˈɡresɪvli/ ADV = gradually, steadily; ≠ suddenly ❑ *Her symptoms became progressively worse.* ❑ *The amount of grant the council received from the Government was progressively reduced.*

⚙**pro·hib·it** /prəˈhɪbɪt, AmE prəʊ-/ VERB [T] (**prohibits, prohibiting, prohibited**) (*academic word, formal*) If a law or someone in authority **prohibits** something, they forbid it or make it illegal. = forbid ❑ *a law that prohibits tobacco advertising in newspapers and magazines* ❑ *Fishing is prohibited.* ❑ *Federal law prohibits foreign airlines from owning more than 25% of any US airline.*

⚙**pro·hi·bi·tion** /ˌprəʊhɪˈbɪʃən/ NOUN [U, C] (**prohibitions**) ◻ [U] (*formal*) The **prohibition** of something is the act of forbidding it or making it illegal. ❑ *The air force and the navy retain their prohibition of women on air combat missions.* ❑ *the prohibition of alcohol* ◼ [C] A **prohibition** is a law or rule forbidding something. ❑ *a prohibition on discrimination*

⚙**proj·ect** ◆◆◇ NOUN, VERB (*academic word*)
NOUN /ˈprɒdʒekt/ [C] (**projects**) ◻ A **project** is a task that requires a lot of time and effort. = scheme ❑ *Money will also go into local development projects in Vietnam.* ❑ *an international science project* ❑ *a research project on alternative health care* ◼ A **project** is a detailed study of a subject by a student. ❑ *Students complete projects for a personal tutor, working at home at their own pace.*
VERB /prəˈdʒekt/ [T, I] (**projects, projecting, projected**) ◻ [T] If something **is projected**, it is planned or expected. = forecast, expect, estimate ❑ *13% of Americans are over 65; this number is projected to reach 22% by the year 2030.* ❑ *The government had been projecting a 5% consumer price increase for the entire year.* ❑ *The population is projected to more than double by 2025.* ❑ *a projected deficit of $1.5 million* ◼ If you **project** someone or something in a particular way, you try to make people see them in that way. If you **project** a particular feeling or quality, you show it in your behaviour. ❑ *Bradley projects a natural warmth and sincerity.* ❑ *He just hasn't been able to project himself as the strong leader.* ◻ [T] If you **project** a film or picture **onto** a screen or wall, you make it appear there. ❑ *The team tried projecting the maps with two different projectors onto the same screen.* ◻ [I] (*formal*) If something **projects**, it sticks out above or beyond a surface or edge. ❑ *a narrow ledge that projected out from the bank of the river*

⚙**pro·jec·tion** /prəˈdʒekʃən/ NOUN [C, U] (**projections**) ◻ [C] A **projection** is an estimate of a future amount. = forecast, estimate ❑ *the company's projection of 11 million visitors for the first year* ❑ *sales projections* ◼ [U] The **projection** of a film or picture is the act of projecting it onto a screen or wall. ❑ *They took me into a projection room to see a picture.*

pro·jec·tor /prəˈdʒektə/ NOUN [C] (**projectors**)
A **projector** is a machine that projects films or slides onto a screen or wall. ❑ *a slide projector*

pro·lif·er·ate /prəˈlɪfəreɪt/ VERB [I] (**proliferates, proliferating, proliferated**) (*formal*) If things **proliferate**, they increase in number very quickly. ❑ *Computerized databases are proliferating fast.*

pro·lif·era·tion /prəˌlɪfəˈreɪʃən/ NOUN [U] (*formal*) The **proliferation** of something is an increase in its quantity. ❑ *the proliferation of nuclear weapons*

pro·lif·ic /prəˈlɪfɪk/ ADJ ◻ A **prolific** writer, artist, or composer produces a large number of works. ❑ *She is a prolific writer of novels and short stories.* ◼ An animal, person, or plant that is **prolific** produces a large number of babies, young plants, or fruit. ❑ *They are prolific breeders, with many hens laying up to six eggs.*

⚙**pro·long** /prəˈlɒŋ, AmE -ˈlɔːŋ/ VERB [T] (**prolongs, prolonging, prolonged**) To **prolong** something means to make it last longer. = lengthen, extend; ≠ shorten ❑ *Mr Chesler said foreign military aid was prolonging the war.* ❑ *The actual action of the drug can be prolonged significantly.*

⚙**pro·longed** /prəˈlɒŋd, AmE -ˈlɔːŋd/ ADJ A **prolonged** event or situation continues for a long time, or for longer than expected. = lasting; ≠ brief ❑ *a prolonged period of low interest rates* ❑ *a prolonged drought*

⚙**promi·nence** /ˈprɒmɪnəns/ NOUN [U] If someone or something is in a position of **prominence**, they are well-known and important. ❑ *He came to prominence during the World Cup.* ❑ *Crime prevention had to be given more prominence.*

⚙**promi·nent** ◆◇◇ /ˈprɒmɪnənt/ ADJ ◻ Someone who is **prominent** is important and well-known. = well-known ❑ *the children of very prominent or successful parents* ❑ *a prominent member of the Law Society* ◼ Something that is **prominent** is very noticeable or is an important part of something else. ❑ *Here the window plays a prominent part in the design.* ❑ *Romania's most prominent independent newspaper*

⚙**promi·nent·ly** /ˈprɒmɪnəntli/ ADV [prominently with V] ❑ *Trade will figure prominently in the second day of talks in Washington.* ❑ *Entries will be prominently displayed in the exhibition hall.*

prom·ise ◆◆◇ /ˈprɒmɪs/ VERB, NOUN
VERB [I, T] (**promises, promising, promised**) ◻ [I, T] If you **promise that** you will do something, you say to someone that you will definitely do it. ❑ *The post office has promised to resume first-class mail delivery to the area on Friday.* ❑ *He had promised that the rich and privileged would no longer get preferential treatment.* ❑ *Promise me you will not waste your time.* ❑ *I'll call you back, I promise.* ◼ [T] If you **promise** someone something, you tell them that you will definitely give it to them or make sure that they have it. ❑ *In 1920 the great powers promised them an independent state.* ◻ [T] If a situation or event **promises to** have a particular quality or **to** be a particular thing, it shows signs that it will have that quality or be that thing. ❑ *While it will be fun, the seminar also promises to be most instructive.*
NOUN [C, U] (**promises**) ◻ [C] A **promise** is a statement that you make to a person in which you say that you will definitely do something or give them something. ❑ *If you make a promise, you should keep it.* ◼ [U] If someone or something shows **promise**, they seem likely to be very good or successful. = potential ❑ *The boy first showed promise as an athlete in primary school.*

prom·is·ing /ˈprɒmɪsɪŋ/ ADJ Someone or something that is **promising** seems likely to be very good or successful. ❑ *A school has honoured one of its brightest and most promising former students.*

⚙**pro·mote** ◆◆◇ /prəˈməʊt/ VERB [T] (**promotes, promoting, promoted**) (*academic word*) ◻ If people **promote** something, they help or encourage it to happen, increase, or spread. = encourage ❑ *You don't have to sacrifice environmental protection to promote economic growth.* ◼ If a firm **promotes** a product, it tries to increase the sales or popularity of that product. ❑ *a tour to promote his second solo album* ❑ *a special St Lucia week where the island*

p

could be promoted as a tourist destination **3** If someone **is promoted**, they are given a more important job or rank in the organization that they work for. ❑ *I was promoted to editor and then editorial director.*

WORD CONNECTIONS

promote + NOUN

promote **development**
promote **growth**
promote **trade**
promote **competition**
❑ *Government policy is one of promoting competition so that both industry and the consumer can benefit.*

promote **awareness**
promote **understanding**
❑ *The event is aimed at promoting awareness of domestic violence.*

promote **peace**
promote **democracy**
❑ *The two countries must work together to promote peace.*

promote **a product**
❑ *Businesses began to use the Internet to promote their products.*

ADV + **promote**

actively promote
strongly promote
vigorously promote
❑ *The president said one of his goals was to actively promote democracy in the Middle East.*

heavily promote
aggressively promote
❑ *The computer company is heavily promoting its latest operating system.*

---

pro·mot·er /prə'məʊtə/ NOUN [c] (**promoters**) **1** A **promoter** is a person who helps organize and finance an event, especially a sports event. ❑ *one of the top boxing promoters in Las Vegas* **2** The **promoter of** a cause or idea tries to make it become popular. ❑ *Aaron Copland was always the most energetic promoter of American music.*

❍ **pro·mo·tion** ◆◇◇ /prə'məʊʃən/ NOUN [u, c] (**promotions**) **1** [u] The **promotion** of something is the act of helping or encouraging it to happen, increase, or spread. ❑ *The government has pledged to give the promotion of democracy higher priority.* ❑ *disease prevention and health promotion* **2** [c, u] If you are given **promotion** or a **promotion** in your job, you are given a more important job or rank in the organization that you work for. ❑ *Consider changing jobs or trying for promotion.* **3** [c, u] (*business*) A **promotion** is an attempt to make a product or event popular or successful, especially by advertising. ❑ *Advertising and promotion are what American business does best.*

pro·mo·tion·al /prə'məʊʃənəl/ ADJ **Promotional** material, events, or ideas are designed to increase the sales of a product or service. ❑ *'Jeans,' according to one company's promotional material, 'are designed and made to be worn hard.'*

❍ **prompt** ◆◇◇ /prɒmpt/ VERB, ADJ
VERB [T] (**prompts, prompting, prompted**) **1** To **prompt** someone **to** do something means to make them decide to do it. = encourage ❑ *Japan's recession has prompted consumers to cut back on buying cars.* ❑ *The need for villagers to control their own destinies has prompted a new plan.* **2** If you **prompt** someone when they stop speaking, you encourage or help them to continue. If you **prompt** an actor, you tell them what their next line is when they have forgotten what comes next. ❑ *'You wouldn't have wanted to bring those people to justice anyway, would you?' Brand prompted him.*
ADJ **1** A **prompt** action is done without any delay. ❑ *It is not too late, but prompt action is needed.* **2** [V-LINK + prompt] If you are **prompt** to do something, you do it without delay or you are not late. ❑ *You have been so prompt in carrying out all these commissions.*

prompt·ly /'prɒmptli/ ADV **1** [promptly with v] If you do something **promptly**, you do it immediately. = immediately ❑ *Sister Francesca entered the chapel, took her seat, and promptly fell asleep.* **2** If you do something **promptly at** a particular time, you do it at exactly that time. ❑ *Promptly at a quarter past seven, we left the hotel.*

❍ **prone** /prəʊn/ ADJ, COMB
ADJ **1** [V-LINK + prone] To be **prone to** something, usually something bad, means to have a tendency to be affected by it or to do it. ❑ *For all her experience as a television reporter, she was still prone to camera nerves.* ❑ *People with fair skin who sunburn easily are very prone to skin cancer.* **2** [prone after V, prone + N] (*formal*) If you are lying **prone**, you are lying on your front. ❑ *Bob slid from his chair and lay prone on the floor.*
COMB **-prone** combines with nouns to make adjectives that describe people who are frequently affected by something bad. ❑ *the most injury-prone rider on the circuit*

pro·noun /'prəʊnaʊn/ NOUN [c] (**pronouns**) A **pronoun** is a word that you use to refer to someone or something when you do not need to use a noun, often because the person or thing has been mentioned earlier. Examples are 'it', 'she', 'something', and 'myself'.

❍ **pro·nounce** /prə'naʊns/ VERB [T] (**pronounces, pronouncing, pronounced**) **1** To **pronounce** a word means to say it using particular sounds. ❑ *Have I pronounced your name correctly?* ❑ *He pronounced it Per-sha, the way the English do.* **2** (*formal*) If you **pronounce** something to be true, you state that it is the case. = declare ❑ *A specialist has now pronounced him fully fit.*

❍ **pro·nounced** /prə'naʊnst/ ADJ Something that is **pronounced** is very noticeable. = noticeable, marked, distinct, conspicuous; ≠ imperceptible ❑ *Most of the art exhibitions have a pronounced Appalachian theme.* ❑ *a pronounced Australian accent* ❑ *Since then, the contrast between his two careers has become even more pronounced.*

❍ **pro·nounce·ment** /prə'naʊnsmənt/ NOUN [c] (**pronouncements**) **Pronouncements** are public or official statements on an important subject. ❑ *the president's latest pronouncements about the protection of minorities*

❍ **pro·nun·ci·a·tion** /prə,nʌnsi'eɪʃən/ NOUN [c, u] (**pronunciations**) The **pronunciation** of a word or language is the way it is pronounced. ❑ *She gave the word its French pronunciation.* ❑ *the correct pronunciation of 'nuclear'*

❍ **proof** ◆◇◇ /pruːf/ NOUN, ADJ
NOUN [c, u] (**proofs**) **Proof** is a fact, argument, or piece of evidence showing that something is definitely true or definitely exists. = evidence ❑ *You have to have proof of residence in the state of Texas, such as a Texas ID card.* ❑ *This is not necessarily proof that he is wrong.* ❑ *There is no conclusive proof of the Milancovitch theory.* ❑ *Economists have been concerned with establishing proofs for their arguments.*
ADJ [AMOUNT + proof] **Proof** is used after a number of degrees or a percentage, when indicating the strength of a strong alcoholic drink such as whisky. ❑ *a glass of Wild Turkey bourbon: 101 proof*

proof·read /'pruːfriːd/ VERB [I, T] (**proofreads, proofreading, proofread**) When someone **proofreads** something such as a book or an article, they read it before it is published in order to find and mark mistakes that need to be corrected. ❑ *I didn't even have the chance to proofread my own report.*

proof·read·er /'pruːfriːdə/ NOUN [c] (**proofreaders**) ❑ *a proofreader on the Montreal Gazette*

prop /prɒp/ VERB, NOUN
VERB [T] (**props, propping, propped**) If you **prop** an object **on** or **against** something, you support it by putting something underneath it or by resting it somewhere. ❑ *He rocked back in the chair and propped his feet on the desk.*
PHRASAL VERB **prop up 1 Prop up** means the same as **prop**. ❑ *Sam slouched back and propped his elbows up on the bench behind him.* **2** To **prop up** something means to support it or help it to survive. ❑ *Investments in the US money market have propped up the American dollar.*
NOUN [c] (**props**) **1** A **prop** is a stick or other object that you use to support something. ❑ *Using the table as a prop,*

P

he dragged himself to his feet. **2** To be a **prop** for a system, institution, or person means to be the main thing that keeps them strong or helps them survive. ❑ *The army is one of the main props of the government.* **3** The **props** in a play or film are all the objects or pieces of furniture that are used in it. ❑ *the backdrop and props for a stage show*

❂ **prop·a·gan·da** /ˌprɒpəˈɡændə/ NOUN [U] (*disapproval*) Propaganda is information, often inaccurate information, that a political organization publishes or broadcasts in order to influence people. ❑ *The party adopted an aggressive propaganda campaign against its rivals.* ❑ *anti-European propaganda movies*

❂ **pro·pel** /prəˈpel/ VERB, COMB
[VERB] [T] (**propels, propelling, propelled**) To **propel** something in a particular direction means to cause it to move in that direction. ❑ *The tiny rocket is attached to the spacecraft and is designed to propel it towards Mars.* ❑ *the club propels the ball forward rather than up*
[COMB] **-propelled** combines with nouns to form adjectives that indicate how something, especially a weapon, is propelled. = **drive, launch, thrust** ❑ *rocket-propelled grenades* ❑ *the first jet-propelled aeroplane*

pro·pel·ler /prəˈpelə/ NOUN [C] (**propellers**) A **propeller** is a device with blades attached to a boat or aircraft. The engine makes the propeller spin around and causes the boat or aircraft to move. ❑ *a fixed three-bladed propeller*

pro·pen·sity /prəˈpensɪti/ NOUN [C] (**propensities**) (*formal*) A **propensity to** do something or a **propensity for** something is a natural tendency to behave in a particular way. ❑ *Mr Bint has a propensity to put off decisions to the last minute.*

prop·er ◆◇◇ /ˈprɒpə/ ADJ **1** [proper + N] You use **proper** to describe things that you consider to be real and satisfactory rather than inadequate in some way. ❑ *Two out of five people lack a proper job.* **2** [proper + N] The **proper** thing is the one that is correct or most suitable. = **right** ❑ *The Supreme Court will ensure that the proper procedures have been followed.* **3** If you say that a way of behaving is **proper**, you mean that it is considered socially acceptable and right. = **fitting** ❑ *In those days it was not thought entirely proper for a woman to be on the stage.* **4** [N + proper] You can add **proper** after a word to indicate that you are referring to the central and most important part of a place, event, or object and want to distinguish it from other things that are not regarded as being important or central to it. ❑ *A distinction must be made between archaeology proper and science-based archaeology.*

prop·er·ly ◆◇◇ /ˈprɒpəli/ ADV **1** If something is done **properly**, it is done in a correct and satisfactory way. ❑ *You're too thin. You're not eating properly.* **2** [properly after v] If someone behaves **properly**, they behave in a way that is considered acceptable and not rude. = **correctly** ❑ *He's a spoiled brat and it's about time he learned to behave properly.*

❂ **prop·er·ty** ◆◆◇ /ˈprɒpəti/ NOUN [U, C] (**properties**) **1** [U] (*formal*) Someone's **property** is all the things that belong to them or something that belongs to them. = **belongings, possessions** ❑ *Richard could easily destroy her personal property to punish her for walking out on him.* ❑ *Security forces searched thousands of homes, confiscating weapons and stolen property.* **2** [C, U] (*formal*) A **property** is a building and the land belonging to it. = **house, building** ❑ *Cecil inherited a family property near Stamford.* ❑ *privately owned properties* **3** [C] The **properties** of a substance or object are the ways in which it behaves in particular conditions. ❑ *A radio signal has both electrical and magnetic properties.* ❑ *the electromagnetic properties of electrons*

proph·et /ˈprɒfɪt/ NOUN [C] (**prophets**) A **prophet** is a person who is believed to be chosen by God to say the things that God wants to tell people. ❑ *the sacred name of the Holy Prophet of Islam*

pro·phet·ic /prəˈfetɪk/ ADJ If something was **prophetic**, it described or suggested something that did actually happen later. ❑ *This ominous warning soon proved prophetic.*

pro·po·nent /prəˈpəʊnənt/ NOUN [C] (**proponents**) (*formal*) If you are a **proponent of** a particular idea or course of action, you actively support it. = **advocate**

❑ *Halsey was identified as a leading proponent of the values of progressive education.*

❂ **pro·por·tion** ◆◇◇ /prəˈpɔːʃən/ NOUN (*academic word*)
[NOUN] [C, PL] (**proportions**) **1** [C] (*formal*) A **proportion of** a group or an amount is a part of it. ❑ *A large proportion of the dolphins in that area will eventually die.* ❑ *A proportion of the rent is met by the city council.* **2** [C] The **proportion of** one kind of person or thing in a group is the number of people or things of that kind compared to the total number of people or things in the group. = **amount, part, percentage** ❑ *The proportion of women in the profession had risen to 17.3%.* ❑ *A growing proportion of the population is living alone.* **3** [C] The **proportion of** one amount **to** another is the relationship between the size of the two amounts. = **ratio** ❑ *Women's bodies tend to have a higher proportion of fat to water.* **4** [PL] (*written*) If you refer to the **proportions** of something, you are referring to its size, usually when this is extremely large. ❑ *In the tropics plants grow to huge proportions.*
[PHRASES] **in proportion to** **1** If one thing increases or decreases **in proportion to** another thing, it increases or decreases to the same degree as that thing. ❑ *The pressure in the cylinders would go up in proportion to the boiler pressure.* **2** If something is small or large **in proportion to** something else, it is small or large when compared with that thing. = **in relation to** ❑ *Children tend to have relatively larger heads than adults in proportion to the rest of their body.* ❑ *Japan's contribution to the UN budget is much larger in proportion to its economy than that of almost any other country.*
out of all proportion to If you say that something is **out of all proportion to** something else, you think that it is far greater or more serious than it should be. ❑ *The punishment was out of all proportion to the crime.*

❂ **pro·por·tion·al** /prəˈpɔːʃənəl/ ADJ (*academic word, formal*) If one amount is **proportional to** another, the two amounts increase and decrease at the same rate so there is always the same relationship between them. ❑ *Loss of weight is directly proportional to the rate at which the disease is progressing.* ❑ *a proportional fee based on the final sale price*
❂ **pro·por·tion·al·ly** /prəˈpɔːʃənəli/ ADV ❑ *You have proportionally more fat on your thighs and hips than anywhere else on your body.* ❑ *Candidates would be elected proportionally.*

❂ **pro·po·sal** ◆◆◇ /prəˈpəʊzəl/ NOUN [C] (**proposals**) **1** A **proposal** is a plan or an idea, often a formal or written one, which is suggested for people to think about and decide upon. = **plan, idea** ❑ *The president is to put forward new proposals for resolving the country's constitutional crisis.* ❑ *the governor's proposal to restrict cigarette sales* ❑ *the government's proposals to abolish free health care* **2** A **proposal** is the act of asking someone to marry you. ❑ *After a three-weekend courtship, Pam accepted Randy's proposal of marriage.*

❂ **pro·pose** ◆◆◇ /prəˈpəʊz/ VERB [T, I] (**proposes, proposing, proposed**) **1** [T] If you **propose** something such as a plan or an idea, you suggest it for people to think about and decide upon. = **suggest** ❑ *Hamilton proposed a change in the traditional debating format.* ❑ *Britain is about to propose changes to some institutions.* ❑ *It was George who first proposed that we dry clothes in that locker.* **2** [T] If you **propose** to do something, you intend to do it. ❑ *It's still far from clear what action the government proposes to take over the affair.* **3** [T] If you **propose** a motion for debate, or a candidate for election, you begin the debate or the election procedure by formally stating your support for that motion or candidate. ❑ *He has proposed a resolution limiting the role of US troops.* **4** [T] (*formal*) If you **propose** a theory or an explanation, you state that it is possibly or probably true, because it fits in with the evidence that you have considered. ❑ *This highlights a problem faced by people proposing theories of ball lightning.* ❑ *Newton proposed that heavenly and terrestrial motion could be unified with the idea of gravity.* **5** [I, T] If you **propose to** someone, or **propose marriage** to them, you ask them to marry you. ❑ *He proposed to his girlfriend over a public-address system.*

❂ **propo·si·tion** /ˌprɒpəˈzɪʃən/ NOUN [C] (**propositions**) **1** If you describe something such as a task or an activity

p

as, for example, a difficult **proposition** or an attractive **proposition**, you mean that it is difficult or pleasant to do. ❑ *Making easy money has always been an attractive proposition.* **2** *(formal)* A **proposition** is a statement or an idea that people can consider or discuss to decide whether it is true. = statement, idea ❑ *The proposition that democracies do not fight each other is based on a tiny historical sample.* **3** A **proposition** is a question or statement about an issue of public policy that appears on a voting paper so that people can vote for or against it. ❑ *Vote Yes on Proposition 136, but No on Propositions 129, 133, and 134.* **4** A **proposition** is an offer or a suggestion that someone makes to you, usually concerning some work or business that you might be able to do together. ❑ *You came to see me at my office the other day with a business proposition.*

✪ **prose** /prəʊz/ NOUN [U] **Prose** is ordinary written language, in contrast to poetry. ❑ *Shute's prose is stark and chillingly unsentimental.* ❑ *What he has to say is expressed in prose of exceptional lucidity and grace.*

✪ **pros•ecute** /'prɒsɪkjuːt/ VERB [I, T] (**prosecutes, prosecuting, prosecuted**) **1** [I, T] If the authorities **prosecute** someone, they charge them with a crime and put them on trial. ❑ *The police have decided not to prosecute because the evidence is not strong enough.* ❑ *Photographs taken by roadside cameras will soon be enough to prosecute drivers for speeding.* ❑ *He is being prosecuted for two criminal offences.* **2** [T] When a lawyer **prosecutes** a case, he or she tries to prove that the person who is on trial is guilty. ❑ *The lawyer who will prosecute the case says he cannot reveal how much money is involved.*

✪ **pros•ecu•tion** ♦◇◇ /ˌprɒsɪ'kjuːʃən/ NOUN [C, U, SING] (**prosecutions**) **1** [C, U] **Prosecution** is the action of charging someone with a crime and putting them on trial. ❑ *Yesterday the head of government called for the prosecution of those responsible for the deaths.* ❑ *He had fled when facing prosecution for libel.* **2** [SING] The lawyers who try to prove that a person on trial is guilty are called **the prosecution**. ≠ the defence ❑ *The star witness for the prosecution took the stand.* ❑ *Colonel Pugh, for the prosecution, said that the offences occurred over a six-year period.* ❑ *During his trial the prosecution claimed he lay in wait for the burglars before firing his shotgun three times.*

WORD CONNECTIONS
VERB + **prosecution**
avoid prosecution
escape prosecution
❑ *These criminals know exactly what to do to avoid prosecution.*
face prosecution
❑ *Anyone caught shoplifting will face prosecution.*
ADJ + **prosecution**
a **criminal** prosecution
❑ *The case resluted in a criminal prosecution.*
a **successful** prosecution
❑ *Investigations are ongoing, and there have been two successful prosecutions.*

✪ **pros•ecu•tor** /'prɒsɪkjuːtə/ NOUN [C] (**prosecutors**) In some countries, a **prosecutor** is a lawyer or official who brings charges against someone or tries to prove in a trial that they are guilty. ❑ *For the last quarter of a century she has been a state prosecutor in the Parquet at Nantes.* ❑ *Prosecutors allege that cars and lorries were stored at privately-owned depots at government expense.*

✪ **pros•pect** ♦♦◇ NOUN, VERB *(academic word)*
NOUN /'prɒspekt/ [C, U, SING, PL] (**prospects**) **1** [C, U] If there is some **prospect of** something happening, there is a possibility that it will happen. ❑ *Unfortunately, there is little prospect of seeing these big questions answered.* ❑ *The prospects for peace in the country's eight-year civil war are becoming brighter.* ❑ *The prospect of finding a job is slim at present.* **2** [SING] A particular **prospect** is something that you expect or know is going to happen. ❑ *There was a*

mixed reaction to the prospect of having new neighbours. ❑ *They now face the prospect of having to wear a cycling helmet by law.* ❑ *Starting up a company may be a daunting prospect.* **3** [PL] Someone's **prospects** are their chances of being successful, especially in their career. ❑ *I chose to work abroad to improve my career prospects.*

VERB /prə'spekt/ [I] (**prospects, prospecting, prospected**) When people **prospect for** oil, gold, or some other valuable substance, they look for it in the ground or under the sea. ❑ *He had prospected for minerals everywhere from the Gobi Desert to the Transvaal.*

WORD CONNECTIONS
VERB + **prospect**
relish the prospect
welcome the prospect
savour the prospect
❑ *He did not relish the prospect of spending days in bed with nothing to do.*
dread the prospect
❑ *They dreaded the prospect of another German war.*
contemplate the prospect
❑ *She is now contemplating the prospect of 20 years in jail.*
ADJ + **prospect**
a **pleasant** prospect
a **promising** prospect
❑ *A job seemed like a much more pleasant prospect than hanging round the house all day.*
a **bleak** prospect
a **daunting** prospect
a **gloomy** prospect
❑ *The thousand mile race is a daunting prospect for most drivers.*
prospects + FOR + NOUN
the prospects for **recovery**
the prospects for **peace**
the prospects for **growth**
the prospects for **success**
❑ *The prospects for success are not good.*

✪ **pro•spec•tive** /prə'spektɪv, AmE prɑː-/ ADJ **1** [prospective + N] You use **prospective** to describe someone who wants to be the thing mentioned or who is likely to be the thing mentioned. = would-be, future ❑ *The story should act as a warning to other prospective buyers.* ❑ *his prospective employers* **2** [prospective + N] You use **prospective** to describe something that is likely to happen soon. = anticipated ❑ *The terms of the prospective deal are most clearly spelled out in Business Week.* ❑ *prospective economic growth*

pro•spec•tus /prə'spektəs, AmE prɑː-/ NOUN [C] (**prospectuses**) A **prospectus** is a detailed document produced by a company, college, or school, which gives details about it. ❑ *a prospectus for a new issue of stock*

pros•per /'prɒspə/ VERB [I] (**prospers, prospering, prospered**) *(formal)* If people or businesses **prosper**, they are successful and do well. ❑ *His business continued to prosper.*

✪ **pros•per•ity** /prɒ'sperɪti/ NOUN [U] **Prosperity** is a condition in which a person or community is doing well financially. = wealth ❑ *a new era of peace and prosperity* ❑ *Japan's economic prosperity*

✪ **pros•per•ous** /'prɒspərəs/ ADJ *(formal)* **Prosperous** people, places, and economies are rich and successful. = wealthy ❑ *the youngest son of a relatively prosperous family* ❑ *The place looks more prosperous than ever.* ❑ *Australia's economy is prosperous and stable.*

pros•ti•tute /'prɒstɪtjuːt, AmE -tuːt/ NOUN [C] (**prostitutes**) A **prostitute** is a person, usually a woman, who has sex with men in exchange for money. ❑ *He admitted last week he paid for sex with a prostitute.*

✪ **pro•tect** ♦♦◇ /prə'tekt/ VERB [T] (**protects, protecting,** protected) **1** To **protect** someone or something means to prevent them from being harmed or damaged. = defend, shield, safeguard; ≠ endanger, risk □ *So, what can women do to protect themselves from heart disease?* □ *A long thin wool coat and a purple headscarf protected her against the wind.* □ *The contraceptive pill may protect women against cancer.* □ *The government is committed to protecting the interests of tenants.* **2** If an insurance policy **protects** you **against** an event such as death, injury, fire, or theft, the insurance company will give you or your family money if that event happens. □ *Many manufacturers have policies to protect themselves against blackmailers.*

pro·tec·tion ♦♦◇ /prəˈtekʃən/ NOUN [C, U] (protections) **1** [C, U] To give or be **protection** against something unpleasant means to prevent people or things from being harmed or damaged by it. = care □ *Such a diet is widely believed to offer protection against a number of cancers.* □ *It is clear that the primary duty of parents is to provide protection for our children.* **2** [U] [oft protection 'against' N] If an insurance policy gives you **protection against** an event such as death, injury, fire, or theft, the insurance company will give you or your family money if that event happens. □ *Insurance can be purchased to provide protection against such risks.* **3** [U] (*business*) If a government has a policy of **protection**, it helps its own industries by putting a tax on imported goods or by restricting imports in some other way. □ *Over the same period trade protection has increased in the rich countries.*

pro·tec·tive /prəˈtektɪv/ ADJ **1** **Protective** means designed or intended to protect something or someone from harm. = defensive □ *Protective gloves reduce the absorption of chemicals through the skin.* □ *Protective measures are necessary if the city's monuments are to be preserved.* **2** If someone is **protective toward** you, they look after you and show a strong desire to keep you safe. □ *He is very protective towards his mother.*

pro·tec·tor /prəˈtektə/ NOUN [C] (protectors) **1** If you refer to someone as your **protector**, you mean that they protect you from being harmed. □ *Many mothers see their son as a potential protector and provider.* **2** A **protector** is a device that protects someone or something from physical harm. □ *He was the only National League umpire to wear an outside chest protector.*

pro·tein ♦◇◇ /ˈprəʊtiːn/ NOUN [C, U] (proteins) **Protein** is a substance found in food and drink such as meat, eggs, and milk. You need protein in order to grow and be healthy. □ *Fish was a major source of protein for the working man.* □ *a high protein diet*

pro·test ♦♦◇ VERB, NOUN
VERB /prəˈtest/ [I, T] (protests, protesting, protested) **1** [I, T] If you **protest against** something or **about** something, you say or show publicly that you object to it. In American English, you usually say that you **protest** it. = challenge, object, revolt □ *Groups of women took to the streets to protest against the arrests.* □ *The students were protesting at overcrowding in the university hostels.* □ *They were protesting soaring prices.* **2** [T] If you **protest** that something is the case, you insist that it is the case, when other people think that it may not be. □ *When we tried to protest that Mo was beaten up they didn't believe us.* □ *'I never said any of that to her,' he protested.*
NOUN /ˈprəʊtest/ [C, U] (protests) A **protest** is the act of saying or showing publicly that you object to something. = demonstration, rally □ *The opposition now seems too weak to stage any serious protests against the government.* □ *The Mexican president cancelled a trip to Texas in protest at the state's execution of a Mexican national.* □ *The unions called a two-hour strike in protest at the railway authority's announcement.* □ *a protest march*

protest + ADV

protest **peacefully**
protest **angrily**
protest **publicly**
□ *Companies protested angrily about the tax increase.*

protest + AGAINST + NOUN

protest against a **war**
protest against a **killing**
□ *As a student he had protested against the war in Vietnam.*

protest against **injustice**
□ *He believed that citizens should protest against injustice.*

ADJ + **protest**

a **peaceful** protest
□ *The police were assured it would be a peaceful protest.*

a **political** protest
an **organized** protest
an **anti-government** protest
an **anti-war** protest
□ *One afternoon we joined an anti-war protest.*

pro·test·er /prəˈtestə/ also **protestor** NOUN [C] (protesters) **Protesters** are people who protest publicly about an issue. = demonstrator, dissident □ *The protesters say the government is corrupt and inefficient.* □ *anti-abortion protesters*

pro·to·col /ˈprəʊtəkɒl, AmE -kɔːl/ NOUN [C, U] (protocols) (*academic word*) **1** [C, U] **Protocol** is a system of rules about the correct way to act in formal situations. □ *He has become a stickler for the finer observances of Washington protocol.* **2** [C] (*computing*) A **protocol** is a set of rules for exchanging information between computers. □ *a computer protocol which could communicate across different languages* □ *an open source email encryption protocol* □ *A serious problem with the most commonly used internet communications protocol has been revealed by computer experts.* **3** [C] (*formal*) A **protocol** is a written record of a treaty or agreement that has been made by two or more countries. = accord □ *the Montreal Protocol to phase out use and production of CFCs* □ *There are also protocols on the testing of nuclear weapons.*

pro·to·type /ˈprəʊtətaɪp/ NOUN [C] (prototypes) A **prototype** is a new type of machine or device that is not yet ready to be made in large numbers and sold. □ *Chris Retzler has built a prototype of a machine called the wave rotor.* □ *the first prototype aircraft*

WORD PARTS

The prefix **proto-** often appears in words which show that something is in the early stages of its development:

prototype (NOUN)
protogalaxy (NOUN)
Proto-Germanic (NOUN)

pro·tract·ed /prəˈtræktɪd, AmE prəʊ-/ ADJ (*formal*) Something, usually something unpleasant, that is **protracted** lasts a long time, especially longer than usual or longer than you hoped. □ *However, after protracted negotiations Ogden got the deal he wanted.* □ *a protracted civil war*

pro·trude /prəˈtruːd, AmE prəʊ-/ VERB [I] (protrudes, protruding, protruded) (*formal*) If something **protrudes** from somewhere, it sticks out. □ *a huge round mass of smooth rock protruding from the water*

proud ♦◇◇ /praʊd/ ADJ (prouder, proudest) **1** If you feel **proud**, you feel pleased about something good that you possess or have done, or about something good that a person close to you has done. □ *I felt proud of his efforts.* □ *They are proud that she is doing well at school.* **2** [proud + N] Your **proudest** moments or achievements are the ones that you are most proud of. □ *This must have been one of the proudest moments of his busy and hard-working life.* **3** Someone who is **proud** has respect for themselves and does not want to lose the respect that other people have for them. □ *He was too proud to ask his family for help and support.* **4** Someone who is **proud** feels that they are better or more important than other people. = arrogant □ *She was said to be proud and arrogant.*
proud·ly /ˈpraʊdli/ ADV [proudly with V] □ *'That's the first part finished,' he said proudly.*

p

✪**prove** ♦♦◇ /pruːv/ VERB [LINK, T] (**proves, proving, proved, proved** or **proven**) **1** [LINK] If something **proves to** be true or **to** have a particular quality, it becomes clear after a period of time that it is true or has that quality. ❏ *We have been accused of exaggerating before, but unfortunately all our reports proved to be true.* ❏ *In the past this process of transition has often proven difficult.* ❏ *an experiment which was to prove a source of inspiration for many years to come* **2** [T] If you **prove that** something is true, you show by means of argument or evidence that it is definitely true. = show, verify; ≠ disprove ❏ *You brought this charge. You prove it!* ❏ *The results prove that regulation of the salmon farming industry is inadequate.* ❏ *That made me hopping mad and determined to prove him wrong.* ❏ *trying to prove how groups of animals have evolved* ❏ *a proven cause of cancer* **3** [T] If you **prove yourself** to have a certain good quality, you show by your actions that you have it. ❏ *Margie proved herself to be a good mother.* ❏ *As a composer he proved himself adept at large dramatic forms.*

WORD CONNECTIONS
prove + NOUN
prove a **success**
prove a **hit**
❏ *The project proved a great success.*
prove a **blessing**
❏ *In the end, the delay proved a blessing, because they managed to come up with something better.*
prove **innocence**
prove **guilt**
❏ *It is up to the prosecution to prove a defendant's guilt.*
prove + ADV
prove **conclusively**
prove **scientifically**
❏ *A lack of vitamin D appears to be linked with dental decay, although this has not yet been proved conclusively.*

pro·ver·bial /prəˈvɜːbiəl/ ADJ [proverbial + N] You use **proverbial** to show that you know the way you are describing something is one that is often used or is part of a popular saying. ❏ *The limousine sped off down the road in the proverbial cloud of dust.*

✪**pro·vide** ♦♦♦ /prəˈvaɪd/ VERB
VERB [T] (**provides, providing, provided**) **1** If you **provide** something that someone needs or wants, or if you **provide** them **with** it, you give it to them or make it available to them. = supply, give ❏ *I'll be glad to provide a copy of this.* ❏ *They would not provide any details.* ❏ *They provided him with a car and driver.* ❏ *The government was not in a position to provide them with food.* **2** (formal) If a law or agreement **provides that** something will happen, it states that it will happen. ❏ *The treaty provides that, by the end of the century, the United States must have removed its bases.*
PHRASAL VERB **provide for** **1** If you **provide for** someone, you support them financially and make sure that they have the things that they need. ❏ *Elaine wouldn't let him provide for her.* **2** If you **provide for** something that might happen or that might need to be done, you make arrangements to deal with it. ❏ *Jim had provided for just such an emergency.*
→ See also **provided, providing**

USAGE NOTE
provide
Note that you **provide** someone **with** something. You do not 'provide someone something'.
*The embassy **provided** him **with** cash to buy new clothes.*
You can also say that you **provide** something **for** someone.
*Most animals **provide** food **for** their young.*

pro·vid·ed /prəˈvaɪdɪd/ CONJ If you say that something will happen **provided** or **provided that** something else happens, you mean that the first thing will happen only if the second thing also happens. ❏ *The other banks are going*

to be very eager to help, provided that they see that he has a specific plan.

pro·vid·ing /prəˈvaɪdɪŋ/ CONJ If you say that something will happen **providing** or **providing that** something else happens, you mean that the first thing will happen only if the second thing also happens. ❏ *I do believe in people being able to do what they want to do, providing they're not hurting someone else.*

prov·ince ♦◇◇ /ˈprɒvɪns/ NOUN [C, PL, SING] (**provinces**) **1** [C] A **province** is a large section of a country that has its own administration. ❏ *the Algarve, Portugal's southernmost province* **2** [PL] The **provinces** are all the parts of a country except the part where the capital is situated. ❏ *The government plans to transfer some 30,000 government jobs from Paris to the provinces.* **3** [SING] If you say that a subject or activity is a particular person's **province**, you mean that this person has a special interest in it, a special knowledge of it, or a special responsibility for it. ❏ *Tattooing is not just the province of sailors.*

pro·vin·cial /prəˈvɪnʃəl/ ADJ **1** [provincial + N] **Provincial** means connected with the parts of a country away from the capital city. ❏ *the Quebec and Ontario provincial police* **2** If you describe someone or something as **provincial**, you disapprove of them because you think that they are old-fashioned and boring. ❏ *He decided to revamp the company's provincial image.*

✪**pro·vi·sion** ♦◇◇ /prəˈvɪʒən/ NOUN [U, C] (**provisions**) **1** [U] [also 'a' provision] The **provision** of something is the act of giving it or making it available to people who need or want it. ❏ *The department is responsible for the provision of residential care services.* ❏ *nursery provision for children with special needs* **2** [C, U] If you make **provision for** something that might happen or that might need to be done, you make arrangements to deal with it. ❏ *Mr Kurtz asked if it had ever occurred to her to make provision for her retirement.* **3** [U] [also provisions, provision 'for' N] If you make **provision for** someone, you support them financially and make sure that they have the things that they need. ❏ *Special provision should be made for children.* **4** [C] A **provision** in a law or an agreement is an arrangement which is included in it. ❏ *He backed a provision that would allow judges to delay granting a divorce decree in some cases.*

✪**pro·vi·sion·al** /prəˈvɪʒənəl/ ADJ You use **provisional** to describe something that has been arranged or appointed for the present, but may be changed in the future. ❏ *the possibility of setting up a provisional coalition government* ❏ *These times are provisional and subject to confirmation.* ❏ *If you have never held a driving licence before, you should apply for a provisional licence.*
✪**pro·vi·sion·al·ly** /prəˈvɪʒnəli/ ADV [provisionally with V] ❏ *The US and Japan provisionally agreed to add new chartered flights to serve their major cities.* ❏ *A meeting is provisionally scheduled for early next week.*

provo·ca·tion /ˌprɒvəˈkeɪʃən/ NOUN [C, U] (**provocations**) If you describe a person's action as **provocation** or **a provocation**, you mean that it is a reason for someone else to react angrily, violently, or emotionally. ❏ *He denies murder on the grounds of provocation.*

pro·voca·tive /prəˈvɒkətɪv/ ADJ **1** If you describe something as **provocative**, you mean that it is intended to make people react angrily or argue against it. ❏ *He has made a string of outspoken and sometimes provocative speeches in recent years.* **2** If you describe someone's clothing or behaviour as **provocative**, you mean that it is intended to make someone feel sexual desire. ❏ *Some adolescents might be more sexually mature and provocative than others.*

✪**pro·voke** ♦◇◇ /prəˈvəʊk/ VERB [T] (**provokes, provoking, provoked**) **1** If you **provoke** someone, you deliberately annoy them and try to make them behave aggressively. ❏ *He started beating me when I was about fifteen but I didn't do anything to provoke him.* **2** If something **provokes** a reaction, it causes it. = cause, excite, generate ❏ *His election success has provoked a shocked reaction.* ❏ *The destruction of the mosque has provoked anger throughout the Muslim world.*

prow·ess /ˈpraʊɪs/ NOUN [U] (formal) Someone's **prowess** is their great skill at doing something. ❏ *He's always* *bragging about his prowess as a hunter.*

prox·im·ity /prɒkˈsɪmɪti/ NOUN [U] (*formal*) **Proximity to** a place or person is nearness to that place or person. □ *Part of the attraction is Darwin's proximity to Asia.* □ *He became aware of the proximity of the Afghans.* □ *Families are no longer in close proximity to each other.*

proxy /ˈprɒksi/ NOUN [U] If you do something **by proxy**, you arrange for someone else to do it for you. □ *Those not attending the meeting may vote by proxy.*

pru·dence /ˈpruːdəns/ NOUN [U] (*formal*) **Prudence** is care and good sense that someone shows when making a decision or taking action. □ *Western businessmen are showing remarkable prudence in investing in the region.*

pru·dent /ˈpruːdənt/ ADJ Someone who is **prudent** is sensible and careful. □ *It is clearly prudent to take all precautions.*
pru·dent·ly /ˈpruːdəntli/ ADV □ *I believe it is essential that we act prudently.*

prune /pruːn/ NOUN, VERB
NOUN [C] (**prunes**) A **prune** is a dried plum.
VERB [I, T] (**prunes, pruning, pruned**) **1** [I, T] When you **prune**, or **prune** a tree or bush, you cut off some of the branches so that it will grow better the next year. □ *You have to prune a bush if you want fruit.* **2** [T] If you **prune** something, you cut out all the parts that you do not need. □ *Companies are cutting investment and pruning their product ranges.*
PHRASAL VERB **prune back** **1** Prune back means the same as **prune** VERB 1. □ *Apples, pears, and cherries can be pruned back when they've lost their leaves.* **2** Prune back means the same as **prune** VERB 2. □ *The company has pruned back its workforce by 20,000 since 2003.*

pry /praɪ/ VERB [I, T] (**pries, prying, pried**) **1** [I] If someone **pries**, they try to find out about someone else's private affairs, or look at their personal possessions. □ *We do not want people prying into our affairs.* □ *Imelda might think she was prying.* **2** [T] If you **pry** something **open** or **pry** it away from a surface, you force it open or away from a surface. □ *They pried open a sticky can of blue paint.* □ *They pried the bars apart to free the dog.*

pseudo·nym /ˈsjuːdənɪm/ NOUN [C] (**pseudonyms**) A **pseudonym** is a name which someone, usually a writer, uses instead of his or her real name. □ *Both plays were published under the pseudonym of Philip Dayre.*

> ### WORD PARTS
> The prefix *pseudo-* often appears in words to show that something is not really what it seems or claims to be:
> **pseudo**nym (NOUN)
> **pseudo**-science (NOUN)
> **pseudo**pregnancy (NOUN)

psy·chi·at·ric /ˌsaɪkiˈætrɪk/ ADJ **1** [psychiatric + N] **Psychiatric** means relating to psychiatry. □ *We finally insisted that he seek psychiatric help.* **2** [psychiatric + N] **Psychiatric** means involving mental illness. □ *About 4% of the prison population have chronic psychiatric illnesses.*

psy·chia·trist /saɪˈkaɪətrɪst, AmE sɪ-/ NOUN [C] (**psychiatrists**) A **psychiatrist** is a doctor who treats people suffering from mental illness. □ *Alex will probably be seeing a psychiatrist for many months or even years.* □ *Having seen most forms of human perversion and violence, the average forensic psychiatrist doesn't shock easily.*

psy·chia·try /saɪˈkaɪətri, AmE sɪ-/ NOUN [U] **Psychiatry** is the branch of medicine concerned with the treatment of mental illness. □ *The new professions of psychology and psychiatry welcomed the opportunity to extend their work.* □ *a consultant and senior lecturer in child and adolescent psychiatry*

psy·chic /ˈsaɪkɪk/ ADJ, NOUN
ADJ **1** If you believe that someone is **psychic** or has **psychic** powers, you believe that they have strange mental powers, such as being able to read the minds of other people or to see into the future. □ *The woman helped police by using her psychic powers.* **2** **Psychic** means relating to ghosts and the spirits of the dead. □ *He declared his total disbelief in psychic phenomena.*

NOUN [C] (**psychics**) A **psychic** is someone who seems to be psychic. □ *her latest role as a psychic who can foretell the future*

psycho·analy·sis /ˌsaɪkəʊəˈnælɪsɪs/ NOUN [U] **Psychoanalysis** is the treatment of someone who has mental problems by asking them about their feelings and their past in order to try to discover what may be causing their condition. = analysis

> ### WORD PARTS
> The prefix *psycho-* often appears in words that relate to the mind or to mental processes:
> **psycho**analysis (NOUN)
> **psycho**therapist (NOUN)
> **psycho**kinesis (NOUN)

psycho·logi·cal ◆◇◇ /ˌsaɪkəˈlɒdʒɪkəl/ ADJ **1** **Psychological** means concerned with a person's mind and thoughts. = mental □ *John received constant physical and psychological abuse from his father.* □ *Robyn's loss of memory is a psychological problem, rather than a physical one.* **2** [psychological + N] **Psychological** means relating to psychology. □ *psychological testing*
psycho·logi·cal·ly /ˌsaɪkəˈlɒdʒɪkli/ ADV □ *It was very important psychologically for us to succeed.*

psy·cholo·gist /saɪˈkɒlədʒɪst/ NOUN [C] (**psychologists**) A **psychologist** is a person who studies the human mind and tries to explain why people behave in the way that they do. □ *Psychologists tested a group of six-year-olds with a video.*

psy·chol·ogy /saɪˈkɒlədʒi/ NOUN [U] (*academic word*) **1** **Psychology** is the scientific study of the human mind and the reasons for people's behaviour. □ *Professor of Psychology at Haverford College* □ *research in educational psychology* **2** The **psychology of** a person is the kind of mind that they have, which makes them think or behave in the way that they do. □ *a fascination with the psychology of murderers*

pub ◆◇◇ /pʌb/ NOUN [C] (**pubs**) (*mainly BrE*) A **pub** is a building where people can have drinks, especially alcoholic drinks, and talk to their friends. Many pubs also serve food. □ *He was in the pub until closing time.*

pub·lic ◆◆◆ /ˈpʌblɪk/ NOUN, ADJ
NOUN [SING] **1** You can refer to people in general, or to all the people in a particular country or community, as **the public**. = population, community, people □ *The park is now open to the public.* □ *Pure alcohol is not for sale to the general public.* □ *Trade unions are regarding the poll as a test of the public's confidence in the government.* **2** You can refer to a set of people in a country who share a common interest, activity, or characteristic as a particular kind of **public**. □ *Market research showed that 93% of the viewing public wanted a hit film channel.*
PHRASE **in public** If you say or do something **in public**, you say or do it when a group of people are present. □ *I probably won't be performing in public much.*
ADJ **1** [public + N] **Public** means relating to all the people in a country or community. □ *The president is attempting to drum up public support for his economic programme.* □ *The dominance of public opinion resulted in tyranny and mediocrity.* **2** [public + N] **Public** means relating to the government or state, or things that are done for the people by the state. = government, state; ≠ private □ *The social services account for a substantial part of public spending.* □ *the role of religion in shaping public policy* **3** [public + N] **Public** buildings and services are provided for everyone to use. □ *the New York Public Library* □ *The new museum must be accessible by public transport.* □ *a public health service* **4** A **public** place is one where people can go about freely and where you can easily be seen and heard. □ *the heavily congested public areas of international airports* **5** [public + N] If someone is a **public figure** or in **public life**, many people know who they are because they are often mentioned in newspapers and on television. □ *He hit out at public figures who commit adultery.* **6** [public + N] **Public** is used to describe statements, actions, and events that are made or done in such a way that any member of the public can see them or be aware

p

of them. ❑ *a public inquiry into the most grievous breakdown in security our nation has ever known* ❑ *The comments were the governor's first detailed public statement on the subject.* **7** [V-LINK + public] If a fact is made **public** or becomes **public**, it becomes known to everyone rather than being kept secret. ❑ *The facts could cause embarrassment if they ever became public.*

PHRASE go public (*business*) If a company **goes public**, it starts selling its shares on the stock exchange. ❑ *The company went public at $21 per share.*

pub·lic·ly /ˈpʌblɪkli/ ADV **1** *publicly funded legal services* **2** *He never spoke publicly about the affair.*

✪ **pub·li·ca·tion** ◆◇◇ /ˌpʌblɪˈkeɪʃən/ NOUN [U, C] (**publications**) (*academic word*) **1** [U] The **publication** of a book or magazine is the act of printing it and sending it to stores to be sold. ❑ *The guide is being translated into several languages for publication near Christmas.* ❑ *the publication of an article in a physics journal* ❑ *the online publication of the census* **2** [C] A **publication** is a book or magazine that has been published. ❑ *They have started legal proceedings against two publications which spoke of an affair.* ❑ *the ease of access to scientific publications on the internet* ❑ *The magazine, which will be a quarterly publication, has received sponsorship from companies in the US.* **3** [U] The **publication of** something such as information is the act of making it known to the public, for example, by informing journalists or by publishing a government document. ❑ *A spokesman said, 'We have no comment regarding the publication of these photographs.'*

pub·lic·ity ◆◇◇ /pʌˈblɪsɪti/ NOUN [U] **1 Publicity** is information or actions that are intended to attract the public's attention to someone or something. ❑ *Much advance publicity was given to the talks.* ❑ *government publicity campaigns* **2** When the news media and the public show a lot of interest in something, you can say that it is receiving **publicity**. ❑ *The case has generated enormous publicity in Brazil.*

pub·li·cize /ˈpʌblɪsaɪz/ also **publicise** VERB [T] (**publicizes, publicizing, publicized**) If you **publicize** a fact or event, you make it widely known to the public. ❑ *The author appeared on television to publicize her latest book.* ❑ *He never publicized his plans.*

pub·lic opin·ion NOUN [U] **Public opinion** is the opinion or attitude of the public regarding a particular matter. ❑ *He mobilized public opinion all over the world against hydrogen-bomb tests.*

pub·lic re·la·tions NOUN [U, PL] **1** [U] (*business*) **Public relations** is the part of an organization's work that is concerned with obtaining the public's approval for what it does. The abbreviation **PR** is often used. ❑ *The move was good public relations.* **2** [PL] You can refer to the opinion that the public has of an organization as **public relations**. ❑ *Limiting casualties is important for public relations.*

pub·lic school NOUN [C, U] (**public schools**) **1** In Britain, a **public school** is a private school that provides secondary education that parents have to pay for. The students often live at the school during the school term. ❑ *He was headmaster of a public school in the West of England.* **2** In the United States, Australia, and many other countries, a **public school** is a school that is supported financially by the government and usually provides free education. ❑ *Milwaukee's public school system*

pub·lic sec·tor NOUN [SING] (*business*) **The public sector** is the part of a country's economy which is controlled or supported financially by the government. ❑ *Carlos Menem's policy of reducing the public sector and opening up the economy to free-market forces*

✪ **pub·lish** ◆◇◇ /ˈpʌblɪʃ/ VERB [T] (**publishes, publishing, published**) (*academic word*) **1** When a company **publishes** a book or magazine, it prints copies of it, which are sent to shops to be sold. ❑ *They publish reference books.* **2** When the people in charge of a newspaper or magazine **publish** a piece of writing or a photograph, they print it in their newspaper or magazine. ❑ *Womens' magazines just don't publish articles on the harmful effects of smoking.* **3** If someone **publishes** a book or an article that they have written, they arrange to have it published. ❑ *Walker has*

published four books of her verse. ❑ *Dr Peters published the findings of his detailed studies last year.* ❑ *The research was published online in the latest British Medical Journal.* **4** If you **publish** information or an opinion, you make it known to the public by having it printed in a newspaper, magazine, or official document. ❑ *The demonstrators called on the government to publish a list of registered voters.*

WORD CONNECTIONS
publish + NOUN
publish a **book**
publish an **article**
publish a **report**
publish a **paper**
❑ *He published a paper describing his results.*
publish **findings**
publish **figures**
publish **research**
❑ *The team will publish their findings in the Journal of the Geological Society.*

pub·lish·er ◆◇◇ /ˈpʌblɪʃə/ NOUN [C] (**publishers**) A **publisher** is a person or a company that publishes books, newspapers, or magazines. ❑ *The publishers planned to produce the journal on a weekly basis.*

pub·lish·ing ◆◇◇ /ˈpʌblɪʃɪŋ/ NOUN [U] **Publishing** is the profession of publishing books. ❑ *I had a very high-powered job in publishing.*

pud·ding /ˈpʊdɪŋ/ NOUN [C, U] (**puddings**) A **pudding** is a cooked sweet food made from ingredients such as milk, sugar, flour, and eggs, and is served either hot or cold. ❑ *a banana vanilla pudding*

pull ◆◆◇ /pʊl/ VERB, NOUN

VERB [I, T] (**pulls, pulling, pulled**) **1** [I, T] When you **pull** something, you hold it firmly and use force in order to move it towards you or away from its previous position. ❑ *They have pulled out patients' teeth unnecessarily.* ❑ *Erica was solemn, pulling at her blonde curls.* ❑ *I helped pull him out of the water.* ❑ *Someone pulled her hair.* **2** [T] When you **pull** an object from a bag, pocket, or cabinet, you put your hand in and bring the object out. ❑ *Jack pulled the slip of paper from his shirt pocket.* **3** [T] When a vehicle, animal, or person **pulls** a cart or piece of machinery, they are attached to it or hold it, so that it moves along behind them when they move forward. ❑ *He pulls a rickshaw, probably the oldest form of human taxi service.* **4** [T] If you **pull yourself** or **pull** a part of your body in a particular direction, you move your body or a part of your body with effort or force. ❑ *Hughes pulled himself slowly to his feet.* ❑ *He pulled his arms out of the sleeves.* **5** [I] When a driver or vehicle **pulls to** a stop or a halt, the vehicle stops. ❑ *He pulled to a stop behind a pickup truck.* **6** [I] In a race or contest, if you **pull ahead of** or **pull away from** an opponent, you gradually increase the amount by which you are ahead of them. ❑ *He pulled away, extending his lead to 15 seconds.* **7** [T] If you **pull** something **apart**, you break or divide it into small pieces, often in order to put them back together again in a different way. ❑ *If I wanted to improve the car significantly I would have to pull it apart and start again.* **8** [T] (*informal*) To **pull** crowds, viewers, or voters means to attract them. ❑ *The organizers have to employ performers to pull a crowd.*

PHRASAL VERBS pull away 1 When a vehicle or driver **pulls away**, the vehicle starts moving forwards. ❑ *I stood in the driveway and watched him back out and pull away.* **2** If you **pull away from** someone that you have had close links with, you deliberately become less close to them. ❑ *Other daughters, faced with their mother's emotional hunger, pull away.*

pull back 1 If someone **pulls back from** an action, they decide not to do it or continue with it, because it could have bad consequences. ❑ *They will plead with him to pull back from confrontation.* **2** If troops **pull back** or if their leader **pulls** them **back**, they go some or all of the way back to their own territory. ❑ *They were asked to pull back from their artillery positions around the city.*

pull down To **pull down** a building or statue means to deliberately destroy it. = demolish ❑ *They'd pulled the* registrar's office down which then left an open space.

pull in ◼ **Pull in** means the same as **pull** VERB 8. ❑ *They provided a far better news service and pulled in many more viewers.* ◼ When a vehicle or driver **pulls in** somewhere, the vehicle stops there. ❑ *He pulled in at the side of the road.*

pull into When a vehicle or driver **pulls into** a place, the vehicle moves into the place and stops there. ❑ *He pulled into the driveway in front of her garage.*

pull off ◼ If you **pull off** something very difficult, you succeed in achieving it. ❑ *The National League for Democracy pulled off a landslide victory.* ◼ If a vehicle or driver **pulls off** the road, the vehicle stops by the side of the road. ❑ *I pulled off the road at a scenic spot.*

pull out ◼ When a vehicle or driver **pulls out**, the vehicle moves out into the road or nearer the centre of the road. ❑ *She pulled out into the street.* ◼ If you **pull out of** an agreement, a contest, or an organization, you withdraw from it. ❑ *The World Bank should pull out of the project.* ❑ *France was going to pull out of NATO.* ◼ If troops **pull out** of a place or if their leader **pulls** them **out**, they leave it. ❑ *The militia in Lebanon has agreed to pull out of Beirut.* ❑ *Economic sanctions will be lifted once two-thirds of their forces have pulled out.* ◼ If you **pull out of** a bad situation or if someone **pulls** you **out**, you begin to recover from it. ❑ *I pulled out of the depression very quickly with treatment.* ❑ *Sterling has been hit by the economy's failure to pull out of recession.*

pull over When a vehicle or driver **pulls over**, or when a police officer **pulls** them **over**, the vehicle moves closer to the side of the road and stops there. ❑ *He noticed a man behind him in a blue Ford gesticulating to pull over.*

pull through If someone with a serious illness or someone in a very difficult situation **pulls through**, they recover. ❑ *Everyone was very concerned whether he would pull through or not.* ❑ *It is only our determination to fight that has pulled us through.*

pull together ◼ If people **pull together**, they help each other or work together in order to deal with a difficult situation. ❑ *The nation was urged to pull together to avoid a slide into complete chaos.* ◼ If you are upset or depressed and someone tells you to **pull yourself together**, they are telling you to control your feelings and behave calmly again. ❑ *Pull yourself together, you stupid woman!*

pull up ◼ When a vehicle or driver **pulls up**, the vehicle slows down and stops. = draw up ❑ *The cab pulled up and the driver jumped out.* ◼ If you **pull up** a chair, you move it closer to something or someone and sit on it. = draw up ❑ *He pulled up a chair behind her and put his chin on her shoulder.*

NOUN [c] (**pulls**) ◼ A **pull** is a forceful movement made to move something you are holding towards you or away from its previous position. ❑ *The feather must be removed with a straight, firm pull.* ◼ A **pull** is a strong physical force that causes things to move in a particular direction. ❑ *the pull of gravity*

✦ **pull a face** → see **face**; **pull someone's leg** → see **leg**; **pull strings** → see **string**; **pull your weight** → see **weight**

pulse /pʌls/ NOUN, VERB

NOUN [c, SING, PL] (**pulses**) ◼ [c] Your **pulse** is the regular beating of blood through your body, which you can feel when you touch particular parts of your body, especially your wrist. ❑ *Mahoney's pulse was racing, and he felt confused.* ◼ [c] In music, a **pulse** is a regular beat, often produced by a drum. ❑ *the repetitive pulse of the music* ◼ [c] A **pulse** of electric current, light, or sound is a temporary increase in its level. ❑ *The switch works by passing a pulse of current between the tip and the surface.* ◼ [SING] If you refer to **the pulse of** a group in society, you mean the ideas, opinions, or feelings they have at a particular time. ❑ *The White House insists that the president is in touch with the pulse of the black community.* ◼ [PL] (mainly BrE; in AmE, usually use **legumes**) Some seeds that can be cooked and eaten are called **pulses**, for example peas, beans, and lentils.

VERB [I] (**pulses, pulsing, pulsed**) If something **pulses**, it moves, appears, or makes a sound with a strong regular rhythm. = throb ❑ *His temples pulsed a little, threatening a headache.*

pump ◆◇◇ /pʌmp/ NOUN, VERB

NOUN [c] (**pumps**) ◼ A **pump** is a machine or device that is used to force a liquid or gas to flow in a particular direction. ❑ *pumps that circulate the fuel around in the engine* ❑ *There was no water in the building, just a pump in the courtyard.* ◼ A fuel or gas **pump** is a machine with a tube attached to it that you use to fill a car with gasoline. ❑ *The average price for all grades of gas at the pump was $3.49 a gallon.*

VERB [T] (**pumps, pumping, pumped**) ◼ To **pump** a liquid or gas in a particular direction means to force it to flow in that direction using a pump. ❑ *It's not enough to get rid of raw sewage by pumping it out to sea.* ❑ *The money raised will be used to dig bore holes to pump water into the dried-up lake.* ◼ If someone **has** their stomach **pumped**, doctors remove the contents of their stomach, for example because they have swallowed poison or drugs. ❑ *One woman was rushed to the emergency room to have her stomach pumped.*

PHRASAL VERBS **pump out** To **pump out** something means to produce or supply it continually and in large amounts. ❑ *Japanese companies have been pumping out plenty of innovative products.*

pump up If you **pump up** something such as a tyre, you fill it with air using a pump. ❑ *Pump all the tyres up.*

punch ◆◇◇ /pʌntʃ/ VERB, NOUN

VERB [T] (**punches, punching, punched**) ◼ If you **punch** someone or something, you hit them hard with your fist. ❑ *After punching him on the chin she wound up hitting him over the head.* ◼ If you **punch** something such as the buttons on a keyboard, you touch them in order to store information on a machine such as a computer or to give the machine a command to do something. = push, press ❑ *Mrs Baylor strode to the lift and punched the button.* ◼ If you **punch** holes **in** something, you make holes in it by pushing or pressing it with something sharp. ❑ *I took a ballpoint pen and punched a hole in the carton.*

PHRASAL VERB **punch in** If you **punch in** a number on a machine or **punch** numbers **into** it, you push the machine's buttons or keys in order to give it a command to do something. ❑ *You can bank by phone in the US, punching in account numbers on the phone.*

NOUN [c, u] (**punches**) ◼ [c] A **punch** is when you hit someone or something hard with your fist. ❑ *He was hurting Johansson with body punches in the fourth round.* ◼ [c] A **punch** is a tool that you use for making holes in something. ❑ *Make two holes with a hole punch.* ◼ [u] If you say that something has **punch**, you mean that it has force or effectiveness. ❑ *My nervousness made me deliver the vital points of my address without sufficient punch.* ◼ [c, u] **Punch** is a drink made from wine, spirits, or fruit juice, mixed with things such as sugar and spices. ❑ *a bowl of punch*

punc•tu•al /ˈpʌŋktʃuəl/ ADJ If you are **punctual**, you do something or arrive somewhere at the right time and are not late. ❑ *He's always very punctual. I'll see if he's here yet.*
punc•tu•al•ly /ˈpʌŋktʃuəli/ ADV *My guest arrived punctually.*

punc•tu•al•ity /ˌpʌŋktʃuˈæliti/ NOUN [u] **Punctuality** is the quality of being punctual. ❑ *The airline hopes to improve punctuality next year.*

punc•tu•ate /ˈpʌŋktʃueɪt/ VERB [T] (**punctuates, punctuating, punctuated**) (written) If an activity or situation **is punctuated by** particular things, it is interrupted by them at intervals. ❑ *The game was punctuated by a series of injuries.*

punc•tua•tion /ˌpʌŋktʃuˈeɪʃən/ NOUN [u] ◼ **Punctuation** is the use of symbols such as full stops, commas, or question marks to divide written words into sentences and clauses. ❑ *He was known for his poor grammar and punctuation.* ◼ **Punctuation** is the symbols that you use to divide written words into sentences and clauses. ❑ *Jessica had rapidly scanned the lines, none of which boasted a capital letter or any punctuation.*

punc•tua•tion mark NOUN [c] (**punctuation marks**) A **punctuation mark** is a symbol such as a full stop, comma, or question mark that you use to divide written words into sentences and clauses.

p

punc·ture /ˈpʌŋktʃə/ NOUN, VERB
[NOUN] [c] (**punctures**) **1** A **puncture** is a small hole in a car tyre or bicycle tyre that has been made by a sharp object. ❑ *Somebody helped me to mend the puncture.* **2** A **puncture** is a small hole in someone's skin that has been made by or with a sharp object. ❑ *An instrument called a trocar makes a puncture in the abdominal wall.*
[VERB] [T, I] (**punctures, puncturing, punctured**) **1** [T] If a sharp object **punctures** something, it makes a hole in it. ❑ *The bullet punctured the skull.* **2** [I, T] If a car tyre or bicycle tyre **punctures** or if something **punctures** it, a hole is made in the tyre. ❑ *His bike's rear tyre punctured.*

✪**pun·ish** /ˈpʌnɪʃ/ VERB [T] (**punishes, punishing, punished**) **1** To **punish** someone means to make them suffer in some way because they have done something wrong. ≠ reward, pardon ❑ *I don't believe that George ever had to punish the children.* ❑ *According to present law, the authorities can only punish smugglers with small fines.* ❑ *No one should be punished twice for the same offence.* **2** To **punish** a crime means to punish anyone who commits that crime. ❑ *federal laws to punish crimes such as murder and assault*

✪**pun·ish·ment** /ˈpʌnɪʃmənt/ NOUN [U, c] (**punishments**) **1** [U] **Punishment** is the act of punishing someone or of being punished. ≠ reward, leniency ❑ *a group that campaigns against the physical punishment of children* **2** [c, U] A **punishment** is a particular way of punishing someone. ❑ *The government is proposing tougher punishments for officials convicted of corruption.* ❑ *The usual punishment is a fine.* **3** [U] You can use **punishment** to refer to severe physical treatment of any kind. ❑ *Don't expect these boots to take the punishment that gardening will give them.*
→ See also **capital punishment**

✪**pu·pil** ◆◇◇ /ˈpjuːpɪl/ NOUN [c] (**pupils**) **1** A **pupil** of a painter, musician, or other expert is someone who studies under that expert and learns his or her skills. ❑ *After his education, Goldschmidt became a pupil of the composer Franz Schreker.* **2** The **pupils** of a school are the children who go to it. = schoolchild, schoolboy, schoolgirl ❑ *schools with over 1,000 pupils* **3** The **pupils** of your eyes are the small, round, black holes in the centre of them. ❑ *The sick man's pupils were dilated.*

✪**pur·chase** ◆◆◇ /ˈpɜːtʃɪs/ VERB, NOUN (*academic word*)
[VERB] [T] (**purchases, purchasing, purchased**) (*formal*) When you **purchase** something, you buy it. ≠ sell ❑ *He purchased a ticket and went up on the top deck.* ❑ *Nearly three out of every 10 new car buyers are purchasing their vehicles online.* ❑ *Most of those shares were purchased from brokers.*
[NOUN] [c, U] (**purchases**) (*formal*) **1** [c, U] The **purchase of** something is the act of buying it. ❑ *This week he is to visit China to discuss the purchase of military supplies.* **2** [c] A **purchase** is something that you buy. ❑ *She opened the tie box and looked at her purchase. It was silk, with maroon stripes.* ❑ *The latest data reveals that nine in every 10 internet users have made a purchase online.* ❑ *Discounts are available for bulk purchases.*
pur·chas·er /ˈpɜːtʃɪsə/ NOUN [c] (**purchasers**) = buyer ❑ *The broker will get 5% if he finds a purchaser.*

pure ◆◇◇ /pjʊə/ ADJ (**purer, purest**) **1** A **pure** substance is not mixed with anything else. ❑ *a carton of pure orange juice* **2** [with POSS] Something that is **pure** is clean and does not contain any harmful substances. ❑ *In remote regions, the air is pure and the crops are free of poisonous insecticides.* **3** If you describe something such as a colour, a sound, or a type of light as **pure**, you mean that it is very clear and represents a perfect example of its type. ❑ *She was dressed in pure white clothes.* **4** [pure + N] **Pure** science or **pure** research is concerned only with theory and not with how this theory can be used in practical ways. ❑ *Physics isn't just about pure science with no immediate applications.* **5** **Pure** means complete and total. = sheer ❑ *The old man turned to give her a look of pure surprise.*
pu·rity /ˈpjʊərɪti/ NOUN [U] **1** *They worried about the purity of tap water.* **2** *The soaring purity of her voice conjured up the frozen bleakness of the Far North.*

pure·ly /ˈpjʊəli/ ADV [purely with CL/GROUP] (*emphasis*) You use **purely** to emphasize that the thing you are mentioning is the most important feature or that it is the only thing which should be considered. ❑ *It is a racing machine, designed purely for speed.*

purge /pɜːdʒ/ VERB, NOUN
[VERB] [T] (**purges, purging, purged**) **1** To **purge** an organization **of** its unacceptable members means to remove them from it. You can also talk about **purging** people **from** an organization. ❑ *The leadership voted to purge the party of 'hostile and antiparty elements'.* ❑ *He recently purged the armed forces, sending hundreds of officers into retirement.* **2** If you **purge** something **of** undesirable things, you get rid of them. = rid ❑ *He closed his eyes and lay still, trying to purge his mind of anxiety.*
[NOUN] [c] (**purges**) A **purge** is the act of removing from an organization those members considered unacceptable. ❑ *The army have called for a more thorough purge of people associated with the late president.*

pu·ri·fy /ˈpjʊərɪfaɪ/ VERB [T] (**purifies, purifying, purified**) If you **purify** a substance, you make it pure by removing any harmful, dirty, or inferior substances from it. ❑ *I take wheat and yeast tablets daily to purify the blood.*
pu·ri·fi·ca·tion /ˌpjʊərɪfɪˈkeɪʃən/ NOUN [U] ❑ *a water purification plant*

pu·rist /ˈpjʊərɪst/ NOUN, ADJ
[NOUN] [c] (**purists**) A **purist** is a person who wants something to be totally correct or unchanged, especially something they know a lot about. ❑ *The new edition of the dictionary carries 7,000 additions to the language, which purists say is under threat.*
[ADJ] **Purist** attitudes are the kind of attitudes that purists have. ❑ *a peculiarly purist argument*

pu·rity /ˈpjʊərɪti/ → See **pure**

pur·ple ◆◇◇ /ˈpɜːpəl/ COLOUR Something that is **purple** is of a reddish-blue colour. ❑ *She wore purple and green silk.*

pur·port /pəˈpɔːt/ VERB [T] (**purports, purporting, purported**) (*formal*) If you say that someone or something **purports to** do or be a particular thing, you mean that they claim to do or be that thing, although you may not always believe that claim. ❑ *a book that purports to tell the whole truth*

✪**pur·pose** ◆◆◇ /ˈpɜːpəs/ NOUN
[NOUN] [c, U] (**purposes**) **1** [c] The **purpose** of something is the reason for which it is made or done. = reason, objective, aim ❑ *The purpose of the occasion was to raise money for medical supplies.* ❑ *the use of nuclear energy for military purposes* ❑ *Various insurance schemes already exist for this purpose.* ❑ *He was asked about casualties, but said it would serve no purpose to count bodies.* **2** [c] Your **purpose** is the thing that you want to achieve. = aim, objective ❑ *They might well be prepared to do you harm in order to achieve their purpose.* **3** [U] **Purpose** is the feeling of having a definite aim and of being determined to achieve it. ❑ *The teachers are enthusiastic and have a sense of purpose.*
[PHRASE] **on purpose** If you do something **on purpose**, you do it intentionally. = intentionally, deliberately ❑ *Was it an accident or did David do it on purpose?*

WORD CONNECTIONS
VERB + **purpose**
serve a purpose
❑ *Some types of pain serve a useful purpose.*
achieve a purpose
accomplish a purpose
❑ *He was willing to participate in the debate if it achieved the purpose of getting more people involved.*
ADJ + **purpose**
the **main** purpose
the **primary** purpose
❑ *The main purpose of the meeting was to set targets.*
the **real** purpose
the **true** purpose
❑ *The real purpose of her visit was not clear.*

P

the **sole** purpose
- ❑ *Salesmen turn on the charm with the sole purpose of convincing the public to buy.*

VOCABULARY BUILDER

purpose NOUN
The **purpose** of something is the reason for which it is made or done.
- ❑ *The unspoken but clear purpose of this conversation hung in the air between us.*

reason NOUN
The **reason** for something is a fact or situation which explains why it happens.
- ❑ *My parents came to Germany for business reasons.*

objective NOUN (*mainly formal*)
Your **objective** is what you are trying to achieve.
- ❑ *Our objective is to become the number-one digital corporation.*

aim NOUN
The **aim** of something that you do is the result that it is intended to achieve.
- ❑ *The main aim of the present study was to test Boklage's findings.*

---

pur·pose·ful /'pɜːpəsfʊl/ ADJ If someone is **purposeful**, they show that they have a definite aim and a strong desire to achieve it. ❑ *She had a purposeful air, and it became evident that this was not a casual visit.*
pur·pose·ful·ly /'pɜːpəsfəli/ ADV *He strode purposefully towards the barn.*

purse /pɜːs/ NOUN, VERB
NOUN [C, SING] (**purses**) **1** [C] (*mainly BrE; in AmE, usually use* **wallet**) A **purse** is a very small bag that people, especially women, keep their money in. **2** [SING] **Purse** is used to refer to the total amount of money that a country, family, or group has. ❑ *The money could simply go into the public purse, helping to lower taxes.*
VERB [T] (**purses, pursing, pursed**) If you **purse** your **lips**, you move them into a small, rounded shape, usually because you disapprove of something or when you are thinking. ❑ *She pursed her lips in disapproval.*

◆ pur·sue ◆◇◇ /pə'sjuː, -'suː/ VERB [T] (**pursues, pursuing, pursued**) (*academic word, formal*) **1** If you **pursue** an activity, interest, or plan, you carry it out or follow it. = follow, follow up; ≠ drop, abandon ❑ *He said Japan would continue to pursue the policies laid down at the London summit.* **2** If you **pursue** a particular aim or result, you make efforts to achieve it, often over a long period of time. ❑ *He will pursue a trade policy that protects American workers.* ❑ *The implication seems to be that it is impossible to pursue economic reform and democracy simultaneously.* ❑ *Europe must pursue aggressively its programme of economic reform.* **3** If you **pursue** a particular topic, you try to find out more about it by asking questions. = follow up ❑ *If your original request is denied, don't be afraid to pursue the matter.* **4** If you **pursue** a person, vehicle, or animal, you follow them, usually in order to catch them. ❑ *She pursued the man who had stolen a woman's bag.*

◆ pur·suit /pə'sjuːt, AmE -'suːt/ NOUN [U, C] (**pursuits**) **1** [U] Your **pursuit of** something is your attempts at achieving it. If you do something **in pursuit of** a particular result, you do it in order to achieve that result. ❑ *a young man whose relentless pursuit of excellence is conducted with single-minded determination* **2** [U] The **pursuit of** an activity, interest, or plan consists of all the things that you do when you are carrying it out. ❑ *The vigorous pursuit of policies is no guarantee of success.* **3** [U] Someone who is **in pursuit of** a person, vehicle, or animal is chasing them. ❑ *a police officer who drove a patrol car at more than 120 mph in pursuit of a motorcycle* **4** [C] Your **pursuits** are your activities, usually activities that you enjoy when you are not working. ❑ *They both love outdoor pursuits.*

push ◆◆◇ /pʊʃ/ VERB, NOUN
VERB [I, T] (**pushes, pushing, pushed**) **1** [I, T] When you **push** something, you use force to make it move away from you or away from its previous position. ❑ *The woman pushed back her chair and stood up.* ❑ *They pushed him into the car.* ❑ *a pregnant woman pushing a pram* **2** [I, T] If you **push through** things that are blocking your way or **push** your **way through** them, you use force in order to move past them. ❑ *I pushed through the crowds and on to the escalator.* ❑ *Dix pushed forward carrying a glass.* **3** [I] If an army **pushes into** a country or area that it is attacking or invading, it moves further into it. = advance ❑ *One detachment pushed into the eastern suburbs towards the airfield.* **4** [T] To **push** a value or amount **up** or **down** means to cause it to increase or decrease. ❑ *Any shortage could push up grain prices.* ❑ *The government had done everything it could to push down inflation.* **5** [T] If someone or something **pushes** an idea or project in a particular direction, they cause it to develop or progress in a particular way. ❑ *China would use its influence to help push forward the peace process.* **6** [T] If you **push** someone **to** do something or **push** them **into** doing it, you encourage or force them to do it. ❑ *She thanks her parents for keeping her in school and pushing her to study.* ❑ *Jason did not push her into stealing the money.* **7** [I] If you **push for** something, you try very hard to achieve it or to persuade someone to do it. ❑ *Doctors are pushing for a ban on all cigarette advertising.* **8** [T] If someone **pushes** an idea, a point, or a product, they try in a forceful way to convince people to accept it or buy it. ❑ *The commissioners will push the case for opening the plant.* **9** [T] (*informal*) When someone **pushes** drugs, they sell them illegally. = deal ❑ *You would be on the dole with your kids pushing drugs to pay the rent.*
PHRASAL VERBS **push ahead** or **push forward** If you **push ahead** or **push forward with** something, you make progress with it. ❑ *The government intends to push ahead with its reform programme.*
push on When you **push on**, you continue with a trip or task. ❑ *Although the journey was a long and lonely one, Tumalo pushed on.*
push over If you **push** someone or something **over**, you push them so that they fall onto the ground. ❑ *We have had trouble with people damaging hedges, uprooting trees and pushing over walls.*
push through If someone **pushes through** a law, they succeed in getting it accepted although some people oppose it. ❑ *The Democratic majority pushed through a law permitting the sale of arms.*
NOUN [C] (**pushes**) **1** A **push** is a forceful movement to make something move away from you or away from its previous position. ❑ *He gave me a sharp push.* **2** A **push** is a movement by an army further into a country or area that it is attacking or invading. ❑ *All that was needed was one final push, and the enemy would be vanquished once and for all.* **3** If you give someone a **push**, you encourage or force them to do something. ❑ *We need a push to take the first step.* **4** A **push** is an effort to achieve something. ❑ *In its push for economic growth it has ignored projects that would improve living standards.*
✦ **if push comes to shove** → see **shove**

put ◆◆◆ /pʊt/ VERB
VERB [T] (**puts, putting, put**) **1** When you **put** something in a particular place or position, you move it into that place or position. ❑ *Leaphorn put the photograph on the desk.* ❑ *She hesitated, then put her hand on Grace's arm.* **2** If you **put** someone somewhere, you cause them to go there and to stay there for a period of time. ❑ *Rather than put him in the hospital, she had been caring for him at home.* **3** To **put** someone or something in a particular state or situation means to cause them to be in that state or situation. ❑ *This is going to put them out of business.* ❑ *He was putting himself at risk.* **4** To **put** something **on** people or things means to cause them to have it, or to cause them to be affected by it. = place ❑ *He didn't put any pressure on her.* ❑ *Be aware of the terrible strain it can put on a child when you expect the best grades.* **5** If you **put** your trust, faith, or confidence **in** someone or something, you trust them or have faith or confidence in them. = place ❑ *He had*

p

decided long ago that he would put his trust in socialism when the time came. **6** If you **put** time, strength, or energy into an activity, you use it in doing that activity. ❑ *We're not saying that activists should put all their effort and time into party politics.* **7** If you **put** money **into** a business or project, you invest money in it. ❑ *Investors should consider putting some money into an annuity.* **8** When you **put** an idea or remark in a particular way, you express it in that way. You can use expressions like **to put it simply** and **to put it bluntly** before saying something when you want to explain how you are going to express it. ❑ *I had already met Pete a couple of times through – how should I put it – friends in low places.* ❑ *He admitted the security forces might have made some mistakes, as he put it.* **9** When you **put a question to** someone, you ask them the question. ❑ *Is this fair? Well, I put that question today to the mayor.* **10** If you **put** a case, opinion, or proposal, you explain it and list the reasons why you support or believe it. = present ❑ *He always put his point of view with clarity and with courage.* ❑ *He put the case to the Saudi foreign minister.* **11** If you **put** something **at** a particular value or **in** a particular category, you consider that it has that value or that it belongs in that category. ❑ *I would put her age at about 50 or so.* ❑ *All the more technically advanced countries put a high value on science.* **12** If you **put** written information somewhere, you write, type, or print it there. ❑ *Mary's family was so pleased that they put an announcement in the local paper to thank them.* ❑ *I think what I put in that book is now pretty much the agenda for this country.*

PHRASES **put it to someone that** If you **put it to** someone **that** something is true, you suggest that it is true, especially when you think that they will be unwilling to admit this. ❑ *But I put it to you that they're useless.*

put together If you say that something is bigger or better than several other things **put together**, you mean that it is bigger or has more good qualities than all of those other things if they are added together. ❑ *Mary ate more than the rest of us put together.*

PHRASAL VERBS **put across** or **put over** When you **put** something **across** or **put** it **over**, you succeed in describing or explaining it to someone. = get across ❑ *He has taken out a half-page advertisement in his local paper to put his point across.*

put aside If you **put** something **aside**, you keep it to be dealt with or used at a later time. ❑ *Encourage children to put aside some of their allowance to buy Christmas presents.*

put away If you **put** something **away**, you put it into the place where it is normally kept when it is not being used, for example, in a drawer. ❑ *She finished putting the milk away and turned around.* ❑ *'Yes, Mom,' replied Cheryl as she slowly put away her doll.*

put back To **put** something **back** means to delay it or arrange for it to happen later than you previously planned. = delay ❑ *There are always new projects which seem to put the reunion back further.*

put down **1** If you **put** something **down** somewhere, you write or type it there. ❑ *Never put anything down on paper which might be used in evidence against you at a later date.* ❑ *The journalists simply put down what they thought they heard.* **2** If you **put down** some money, you pay part of the price of something, and will pay the rest later. ❑ *He bought an investment property for $100,000 and put down $20,000.* **3** When soldiers, police, or the government **put down** a riot or rebellion, they stop it by using force. ❑ *Soldiers went in to put down a rebellion.* **4** If someone **puts** you **down**, they treat you in an unpleasant way by criticizing you in front of other people or making you appear foolish. ❑ *I know that I do put people down occasionally.* ❑ *Racist jokes come from wanting to put down other kinds of people we feel threatened by.* **5** When an animal **is put down**, it is killed because it is dangerous or very ill. ❑ *The judge ordered their dog Samson to be put down immediately.*

put down to If you **put** something **down to** a particular thing, you believe that it is caused by that thing. ❑ *You may be a sceptic and put it down to life's inequalities.*

put forward If you **put forward** a plan, proposal, or name, you suggest that it should be considered for a

particular purpose or job. = submit ❑ *He has put forward new peace proposals.* ❑ *Various theories have been put forward to account for this apparent anomaly.*

put in **1** If you **put in** an amount of time or effort doing something, you spend that time or effort doing it. ❑ *Wade was going to be paid a salary, instead of by the hour, whether he put in forty hours or not.* ❑ *They've put in time and effort to keep the strike going.* **2** If you **put in** a request or **put in for** something, you formally request or apply for that thing. ❑ *I also put in a request for some overtime.* **3** If you **put in** a remark, you interrupt someone or add to what they have said with the remark. ❑ *'He was a lawyer before that,' Mary Ann put in.*

put off **1** If you **put** something **off**, you delay doing it. = postpone ❑ *Women who put off having a baby often make the best mothers.* **2** If you **put** someone **off**, you make them wait for something that they want. ❑ *The old priest tried to put them off, saying that the hour was late.* **3** If something **puts** you **off** something, it makes you dislike it, or decide not to do or have it. ❑ *The high divorce figures don't seem to be putting people off marriage.* ❑ *His personal habits put them off.* **4** If someone or something **puts** you **off**, they take your attention from what you are trying to do and make it more difficult for you to do it. = distract ❑ *She asked me to be serious – said it put her off if I laughed.*

put on **1** When you **put on** clothing or makeup, you place it on your body in order to wear it. ❑ *She put on her coat and went out.* ❑ *Maximo put on a pair of glasses.* **2** When people **put on** a show, exhibition, or service, they perform it or organize it. ❑ *The band is hoping to put on a show before the end of the year.* **3** If someone **puts on** weight, they become heavier. = gain ❑ *I can eat what I want but I never put on weight.* **4** If you **put on** a piece of equipment or a device, you make it start working, for example, by pressing a switch or turning a knob. ❑ *I put the radio on.* **5** If you **put** a record or CD **on**, you place it in a record or CD player and listen to it. ❑ *She poured them drinks, and put a record on loud.*

put out **1** If you **put out** an announcement or story, you make it known to a lot of people. ❑ *No one put out a press release aimed at the public.* **2** If you **put out** a fire, candle, or cigarette, you make it stop burning. = extinguish ❑ *Firemen tried to free the injured and put out the blaze.* **3** If you **put out** an electric light, you make it stop shining by pressing a switch. = turn out ❑ *He crossed to the nightstand and put out the light.* **4** If you **put out** things that will be needed, you place them somewhere ready to be used. ❑ *Paula had put out her luggage for the bus.* **5** If you **put out** your **hand**, you move it forward, away from your body. = stretch out, extend ❑ *He put out his hand to Alfred.* **6** If you **put** someone **out**, you cause them trouble because they have to do something for you. ❑ *It is a very sociable diet to follow because you don't have to put anyone out.*

put through **1** When someone **puts through** someone who is making a telephone call, they make the connection that allows the telephone call to take place. = connect ❑ *The operator will put you through.* **2** If someone **puts** you **through** an unpleasant experience, they make you experience it. ❑ *She wouldn't want to put them through the ordeal of a huge ceremony.*

put together **1** If you **put** something **together**, you join its different parts to each other so that it can be used. = assemble ❑ *He took it apart brick by brick, and put it back together again.* **2** If you **put together** a group of people or things, you form them into a team or collection. ❑ *It will be able to put together a governing coalition.* **3** If you **put together** an agreement, plan, or product, you design and create it. ❑ *We wouldn't have time to put together an agreement.* ❑ *Reports speak of Berlin putting together an aid package for Moscow.*

put up **1** If people **put up** a wall, building, tent, or other structure, they construct it so that it is upright. ❑ *Protesters have been putting up barricades across a number of major road junctions.* **2** If you **put up** a poster or notice, you attach it to a wall or board. ❑ *They're putting new street signs up.* **3** To **put up** resistance to something means to resist it. ❑ *In the end the Kurds surrendered without putting up any resistance.* ❑ *He'd put up a real fight to keep you there.*

P

4 If you **put up** money for something, you provide the money that is needed to pay for it. = provide ❑ *The state agreed to put up $69,000 to start his company.* **5** To **put up** the price of something means to cause it to increase. = raise, increase ❑ *Their friends suggested they should put up their prices.* **6** If a person or hotel **puts** you **up** or if you **put up** somewhere, you stay there for one or more nights. ❑ *I wanted to know if she could put me up for a few days.* ❑ *Hundreds of commuters had to be put up in hotel rooms.* **7** If a political party **puts up** a candidate in an election or if the candidate **puts up**, the candidate takes part in the election. ❑ *Barnes put up a candidate of his own for this post.*

put up with If you **put up with** something, you tolerate or accept it, even though you find it unpleasant or unsatisfactory. ❑ *They had put up with behaviour from their son which they would not have tolerated from anyone else.*

put out ADJ [V-LINK + put out] If you feel **put out**, you feel annoyed or upset. ❑ *I did not blame him for feeling put out.*

puz•zle /ˈpʌzəl/ VERB, NOUN
  VERB [T, I] (**puzzles, puzzling, puzzled**) **1** [T] If something **puzzles** you, you do not understand it and feel confused. ❑ *My sister puzzles me and causes me anxiety.* **2** [I] If you **puzzle over** something, you try hard to think of the answer to it or the explanation for it. ❑ *In rehearsing Shakespeare, I puzzle over the complexities of his verse and prose.*

NOUN [C, SING] (**puzzles**) **1** [C] [oft SUPP + puzzle] A **puzzle** is a question, game, or toy that you have to think about carefully in order to answer it correctly or put it together properly. ❑ *a word puzzle* **2** [SING] ['a' puzzle] You can describe a person or thing that is hard to understand as **a puzzle**. = mystery ❑ *The rise in accidents remains a puzzle.*
puz•zling /ˈpʌzlɪŋ/ ADJ ❑ *His letter poses a number of puzzling questions.*

puz•zled /ˈpʌzəld/ ADJ Someone who is **puzzled** is confused because they do not understand something. ❑ *Critics remain puzzled by the election results.*

✪**pyra•mid** /ˈpɪrəmɪd/ NOUN [C] (**pyramids**) **1** Pyramids are ancient stone buildings with four triangular sloping sides. The most famous pyramids are those built in ancient Egypt to contain the bodies of their kings and queens. ❑ *We set off to see the Pyramids and Sphinx.* **2** A **pyramid** is a shape, object, or pile of things with a flat base and sloping triangular sides that meet at a point. ❑ *On a plate in front of him was piled a pyramid of flat white crackers.* ❑ *Pei's solitary glass pyramid in the courtyard of the Louvre* **3** You can describe something as a **pyramid** when it is organized so that there are fewer people at each level as you go towards the top. ❑ *Traditionally, the Brahmins, or the priestly class, are set at the top of the social pyramid.*

p

Q also **q** /kjuː/ NOUN [C, U] (**Q's, q's**) Q is the seventeenth letter of the English alphabet.

quad·ru·ple /ˌkwɒˈdruːpəl/ VERB, PREDET, ADJ

VERB [I, T] (**quadruples, quadrupling, quadrupled**) If someone **quadruples** an amount or if it **quadruples**, it becomes four times bigger. □ *China seeks to quadruple its income in twenty years.*

PREDET [quadruple + DET N] If one amount is **quadruple** another amount, it is four times bigger. □ *Fifty-nine per cent of its residents have attended graduate school – quadruple the national average.*

ADJ [quadruple + N] You use **quadruple** to indicate that something has four parts or happens four times. □ *The quadruple murder has replaced property prices as the sole topic of interest.*

✪**quali·fi·ca·tion** /ˌkwɒlɪfɪˈkeɪʃən/ NOUN [C, U] (**qualifications**) **1** [C] Your **qualifications** are the official documents or titles you have that show your level of education and training. = certificate, accreditation □ *'Do you have any qualifications?'—'Yes, I'm certified to teach high school.'* □ *All surgeons who operate on children must obtain a recognized professional qualification for the care of children.* **2** [U] **Qualification** is the act of passing the examinations you need to work in a particular profession. □ *She has met the minimum educational requirements for qualification.* □ *Following qualification, he worked as a social worker.* **3** [C] The **qualifications** you need for an activity or task are the qualities and skills that you need to be able to do it. □ *Responsibility and reliability are necessary qualifications, as well as a friendly and outgoing personality.* **4** [C, U] A **qualification** is a detail or explanation that you add to a statement to make it less strong or less general. □ *The empirical evidence considered here is subject to many qualifications.* **5** [C] (*BrE*) Your **qualifications** are the examinations that you have passed. □ *Lucy Thomson, 16, wants to study theatre but needs more qualifications.*

✪**quali·fied** ♦◇◇ /ˈkwɒlɪfaɪd/ ADJ

ADJ **1** Someone who is **qualified** has a certificate, licence, diploma or degree in order to work in a particular profession. = skilled, trained; ≠ unqualified □ *Demand has far outstripped supply of qualified teachers.* □ *Are you qualified for this job?* □ *The reader should seek the services of a qualified professional for advice.* **2** [qualified + N] If you give someone or something **qualified** support or approval, your support or approval is not total because you have some doubts. □ *The government has in the past given qualified support to the idea of tightening the legislation.*

PHRASE **qualified success** If you describe something as a **qualified success**, you mean that it is only partly successful. □ *Even as a humanitarian mission it has been only a qualified success.*

quali·fi·er /ˈkwɒlɪfaɪə/ NOUN [C] (**qualifiers**) **1** A **qualifier** is someone who is successful in one part of in a competition and goes on to the next stage. □ *Kenya's Robert Kibe was the fastest qualifier for the 800 metres final.* **2** A **qualifier** is an early round or match in some competitions. The players or teams who are successful are able to continue to the next round or to the main competition. □ *Crew Stadium hosted the US–Mexico qualifier.*

✪**quali·fy** ♦◇◇ /ˈkwɒlɪfaɪ/ VERB [I, T] (**qualifies, qualifying, qualified**) **1** [I] If you **qualify** in a competition, you are successful in one part of it and go on to the next stage. □ *We qualified for the final by beating Stanford on Tuesday.* **2** [I, T] To **qualify as** something or to **be qualified as** something means to have all the features that are needed to be that thing. □ *13 per cent of American households qualify as poor, says Mr Mishel.* **3** [T] If you **qualify** a statement, you make it less strong or less general by adding a detail or explanation to it. □ *I would qualify that by putting it into context.* □ *Boyd qualified his opinion, noting that the evidence could be interpreted in other ways.* **4** [I, T] If you **qualify** for something or if something **qualifies** you for it, you have the right to do it or have it. □ *To qualify for maternity leave you must have worked for the same employer for two years.* □ *The basic course does not qualify you to practise as a therapist.* **5** [I] When someone **qualifies**, they pass the examinations that they need to be able to work in a particular profession. □ *But when I'd qualified and started teaching it was a different story.* □ *I qualified as a doctor from London University over 30 years ago.*
→ See also **qualified**

✪**quali·ta·tive** /ˈkwɒlɪtətɪv, AmE -teɪt-/ ADJ (*academic word, formal*) **Qualitative** means relating to the nature or standard of something, rather than to its quantity. □ *There are qualitative differences in the way children of different ages and adults think.* □ *That's the whole difference between quantitative and qualitative research.*

✪**quali·ta·tive·ly** /ˈkwɒlɪtətɪvli, AmE -teɪt-/ ADV □ *The new media are unlikely to prove qualitatively different from the old.* □ *a group with minimal demands for housing, both quantitatively and qualitatively*

✪**qual·ity** ♦♦◇ /ˈkwɒlɪti/ NOUN [U, C] (**qualities**) (*academic word*) **1** [U] The **quality** of something is how good or bad it is. □ *Everyone can greatly improve the quality of life.* □ *Other services vary dramatically in quality.* □ *Employees whose work is of a consistently high quality should not fear unemployment.* □ *high-quality paper and plywood* **2** [U] Something of **quality** is of a high standard. □ *a college of quality* **3** [C] Someone's **qualities** are the good characteristics that they have which are part of their nature. = characteristic □ *Sometimes you wonder where your kids get their good qualities.* **4** [C] You can describe a particular characteristic of a person or thing as a **quality**. = characteristic □ *a childlike quality* □ *the pretentious quality of the poetry* □ *Thyme tea can be used by adults for its antiseptic qualities.*

WORD CONNECTIONS
ADJ + **quality**
high quality
top quality
good quality
□ *We have to ensure we have the very best quality information.*
poor quality
low quality
□ *There were complaints about the poor quality of the food.*
VERB + **quality**
improve the quality of
enhance the quality of
□ *All these factors would enhance the quality of the data.*

> **ensure** the quality of
> ❏ *There are mechanisms in place to ensure the quality of services.*

> **assess** the quality of
> ❏ *The quality of their work is continually assessed.*

qualm /kwɑːm/ NOUN [C] (**qualms**) If you have no **qualms** about doing something, you are not worried that it may be wrong in some way. ❏ *I have no qualms about recommending the same approach to other doctors.*

✪**quan·ti·fi·able** /ˈkwɒntɪfaɪəbəl/ ADJ Something that is **quantifiable** can be measured or counted in a scientific way. = calculable, measurable ❏ *A clearly quantifiable measure of quality is not necessary.*

✪**quan·ti·fy** /ˈkwɒntɪfaɪ/ VERB [T] (**quantifies, quantifying, quantified**) If you try to **quantify** something, you try to calculate how much of it there is. = measure, calculate ❏ *It is difficult to quantify an exact figure as firms are reluctant to declare their losses.* ❏ *The study is the first to quantify how widespread the practice is.*

✪**quan·ti·ta·tive** /ˈkwɒntɪtətɪv, AmE -teɪt-/ ADJ (formal) **Quantitative** means relating to different sizes or amounts of things. ❏ *the advantages of quantitative and qualitative research* ❏ *the quantitative analysis of migration* ❏ *An important distinction must be made between quantitative and qualitative similarities.*

✪**quan·ti·ta·tive·ly** /ˈkwɒntɪtətɪvli, AmE -teɪt-/ ADV ❏ *We cannot predict quantitatively the value or the cost of a new technology.* ❏ *The response was tremendous, quantitatively and qualitatively.*

✪**quan·tity** ♦◇◇ /ˈkwɒntɪti/ NOUN (academic word)
NOUN [C, U] (**quantities**) **1** [C, U] A **quantity** is an amount. = amount ❏ *a small quantity of water* ❏ *huge quantities of narcotics* ❏ *Cheap goods are available, but not in sufficient quantities to satisfy demand.* **2** [U] Things that are produced or available in **quantity** are produced or available in large amounts. ❏ *After some initial problems, acetone was successfully produced in quantity.* **3** [U] You can use **quantity** to refer to the amount of something that there is, especially when you want to contrast it with its quality. = amount ❏ *the less discerning drinker who prefers quantity to quality*
PHRASE **unknown quantity** If you say that someone or something is an **unknown quantity**, you mean that not much is known about what they are like or how they will behave. ❏ *She had known Max for some years now, but he was still pretty much an unknown quantity.*

WHICH WORD?
quantity, amount, or number?

A **quantity** or an **amount** of something is how much of it you have, need, or get.
❏ *There was a large **quantity** of water in the cellar.*
❏ *I was horrified by the **amount** of work I had to do.*
You do not talk about an 'amount' of things or people. For example, you do not say ~~'There was an amount of chairs in the room'~~. You say 'There were a **number** of chairs in the room'.
❏ *A small **number** of law firms have picked up some major deals.*

---

quan·tum /ˈkwɒntəm/ ADJ **1** [quantum + N] In physics, **quantum** theory and **quantum** mechanics are concerned with the behaviour of atomic particles. ❏ *Both quantum mechanics and chaos theory suggest a world constantly in flux.* **2** [quantum + N] A **quantum leap** or **quantum jump** in something is a very great and sudden increase in its size, amount, or quality. ❏ *A vaccine which can halt this suffering represents a quantum leap in healthcare in this country.*

quar·an·tine /ˈkwɒrəntiːn, AmE ˈkwɔːr-/ NOUN, VERB
NOUN [U] If a person or animal is **in quarantine**, they are being kept separate from other people or animals for a set period of time, usually because they have or may have a disease that could spread. ❏ *She was sent home and put in quarantine.*
VERB [T] (**quarantines, quarantining, quarantined**) If people or animals **are quarantined**, they are stopped from having contact with other people or animals. If a place **is quarantined**, people and animals are prevented from entering or leaving it. ❏ *Dogs have to be quarantined for six months before they'll let them in.*

quar·rel /ˈkwɒrəl, AmE ˈkwɔːr-/ NOUN, VERB
NOUN [C, SING] (**quarrels**) **1** [C] A **quarrel** is an angry argument between two or more friends or family members. ❏ *I had a terrible quarrel with my other brothers.* **2** [SING] If you say that you have no **quarrel** with someone or something, you mean that you do not disagree with them. ❏ *We have no quarrel with the people of Spain or of any other country.* **3** [C] (journalism) **Quarrels** between countries or groups of people are disagreements, which may be diplomatic or include fighting. ❏ *New Zealand's quarrel with France over the Rainbow Warrior incident was formally ended.*
VERB [RECIP] (**quarrels, quarrelling, quarrelled**; in AmE, use **quarreling, quarreled**) When two or more people **quarrel**, they have an angry argument. ❏ *At one point we quarrelled, over something silly.*

✪**quar·ter** ♦♦◇ /ˈkwɔːtə/ NOUN, PREDET, ADJ, VERB
NOUN [C, U] (**quarters**) **1** [C] A **quarter** is one of four equal parts of something. ❏ *A quarter of the residents are over 55 years old.* ❏ *Prices have fallen by a quarter since January.* ❏ *a quarter of an hour* ❏ *a unique 'four-in-one' channel that splits your screen into quarters* **2** [C] A **quarter** is a fixed period of three months. Companies often divide their financial year into four quarters. ❏ *The group said results for the third quarter are due on October 29.* ❏ *PeopleSoft announced yesterday that it had performed better than expected in its current financial quarter.* **3** [U] [also 'a' quarter] When you are telling the time, you use **quarter** to talk about the fifteen minutes before or after an hour. For example, 8.15 is **quarter past** eight and 8.45 is **quarter to** nine. ❏ *It was quarter to six.* **4** [C] A **quarter** is an American or Canadian coin that is worth 25 cents. ❏ *I dropped a quarter into the slot of the pay phone.* **5** [C] A particular **quarter** of a town is a part of the town where a particular group of people traditionally live or work. ❏ *We wandered through the Chinese quarter.*
PHRASE **at close quarters** If you do something **at close quarters**, you do it very near to a particular person or thing. ❏ *You can watch aircraft take off or land at close quarters.*
PREDET A **quarter** the size, the weight, etc. of something means that something is only 25 per cent as big, heavy, etc. as something else. ❏ *The largest asteroid is Ceres, which is about a quarter the size of the moon.*
ADJ [quarter + N] **Quarter** describes something that is one of four equal parts of something. ❏ *the past quarter century*
VERB [T] (**quarters, quartering, quartered**) **1** If you **quarter** something such as a fruit or a vegetable, you cut it into four roughly equal parts. ❏ *Chop the mushrooms and quarter the tomatoes.* **2** If the number or size of something **is quartered**, it is reduced to about a quarter of its previous number or size. ❏ *The doses I suggested for adults could be halved or quartered.*

quarter-final NOUN [C] (**quarter-finals**) A **quarter-final** is one of the four matches in a competition which decides which four players or teams will compete in the semi-final. ❏ *The very least I'm looking for at the Open is to reach the quarter-finals.*

✪**quar·ter·ly** /ˈkwɔːtəli/ ADJ, ADV, NOUN
ADJ A **quarterly** event happens four times a year, at intervals of three months. ❏ *the latest Bank of Japan quarterly survey of 5,000 companies* ❏ *The software group last night announced record quarterly profits of $1.98 billion.*
ADV [quarterly after V] Something happening **quarterly** happens four times a year, at intervals of three months. ❏ *It makes no difference whether dividends are paid quarterly or annually.* ❏ *The list will be updated quarterly by the nonprofit Direct Marketing Association.*
NOUN [C] (**quarterlies**) A **quarterly** is a magazine that is published four times a year, at intervals of three months. ❏ *The quarterly had been a forum for sound academic debate.*

quar·tet /kwɔːˈtet/ NOUN [C] (**quartets**) **1** A **quartet** is a group of four people who play musical instruments or sing

q

together. □ *a string quartet* **2** A **quartet** is a piece of music for four instruments or four singers. □ *The String Quartet No. 1 is an early work, composed in California in 1941.*

quay /kiː/ NOUN [C] (**quays**) A **quay** is a long platform beside the sea or a river where boats can be tied up and loaded or unloaded. □ *Jack and Stephen were waiting for them on the quay.*

queen ◆◆◇ /kwiːn/ NOUN [C] (**queens**) **1** A **queen** is a woman who rules a country as its monarch. □ *Queen Victoria* **2** A **queen** is a woman who is married to a king. □ *The king and queen had fled.* **3** If you refer to a woman as **the queen of** a particular activity, you mean that she is well-known for being very good at it. □ *the queen of crime writing* **4** (*informal*) A **queen** is a male homosexual who dresses and speaks rather like a woman. **5** In chess, the **queen** is the most powerful piece. It can be moved in any direction. □ *Chris will either have to take his queen's knight and lose his own knight, or he'll lose a rook.* **6** A **queen** is a playing card with a picture of a queen on it. □ *the queen of spades* **7** A **queen** or a **queen bee** is a large female bee which can lay eggs. □ *Glass hives offer a close-up view of the bees at work, with the queen bee in each hive marked by a white dot.*

⊙**que•ry** /ˈkwɪəri/ NOUN, VERB
NOUN [C] (**queries**) A **query** is a question, especially one that you ask an organization, publication, or expert. = question □ *If you have any queries about this insurance, please contact our call centre.* □ *The major queries on this subject were from Dr Guy Jansen.* □ *The Ministry of Defence is considering the appointment of an official spokesman to answer media queries.*
VERB [T] (**queries, querying, queried**) **1** If you **query** something, you check it by asking about it because you are not sure if it is correct. = question, verify, check □ *It's got a number you can call to query your bill.* □ *Dr Grout had not queried the payments when they were debited from his credit-card account.* □ *Some councillors who are in arrears are querying the amounts reflected in their accounts.* **2** To **query** means to ask a question. □ *'Is there something else?' Ray queried as Helen stopped speaking.*

⊙**ques•tion** ◆◆◆ /ˈkwestʃən/ NOUN, VERB
NOUN [SING, C] (**questions**) **1** [SING, C] A **question** is something that you say or write in order to ask a person about something. □ *They asked a lot of questions about China.* **2** [SING] If you say that there is some **question** about something, you mean that there is doubt or uncertainty about it. If something is **in question** or has been **called into question**, doubt or uncertainty has been expressed about it. □ *There's no question about their success.* □ *Her political future is in question.* □ *My integrity has been called into question by people who have never spoken to me.* □ *The relevance of these studies to the current situation is open to question.* **3** [C] A **question** is a problem, matter, or point which needs to be considered. = issue, point □ *But the whole question of aid is a tricky political one.* □ *That decision raised questions about the secretary of state's powers.* **4** [C] The **questions** on an examination are the problems that test your knowledge or ability. □ *That question did come up on the test.*
PHRASES **in question** The person, thing, or time **in question** is one which you have just been talking about or which is relevant. □ *Add up all the income you've received over the period in question.*
out of the question (*emphasis*) If you say that something is **out of the question**, you are emphasizing that it is completely impossible or unacceptable. □ *For the homeless, private medical care is simply out of the question.*
pop the question (*informal*) If you **pop the question**, you ask someone to marry you. = propose □ *Stuart got serious quickly and popped the question six months later.*
there's no question of doing something (*emphasis*) If you say **there is no question** of something happening, you are emphasizing that it is not going to happen. □ *There was no question of my blaming Janet.*
VERB [T] (**questions, questioning, questioned**) **1** If you **question** someone, you ask them a lot of questions about something. □ *This led the therapist to question Jim about his*

parents and their marriage. **2** If you **question** something, you have or express doubts about whether it is true, reasonable, or worthwhile. = challenge, doubt □ *It never occurs to them to question the doctor's decisions.* □ *Scientists began questioning the validity of the research because they could not reproduce the experiments.*
ques•tion•ing /ˈkwestʃənɪŋ/ NOUN [U] □ *The police have detained thirty-two people for questioning.*

WORD CONNECTIONS
VERB + **question**
ask a question
pose a question
raise a question
beg the question
□ *This begs the question, just who is in control?*
answer a question
□ *She refused to answer any of my questions.*
ADJ + **question**
a **difficult** question
a **good** question
an **important** question
□ *He was forced to answer some very difficult questions.*

ques•tion•able /ˈkwestʃənəbəl/ ADJ (*formal*) If you say that something is **questionable**, you mean that it is not completely honest, reasonable, or acceptable. = dubious □ *He has been dogged by allegations of questionable business practices.*

ques•tion mark NOUN [C] (**question marks**) **1** A **question mark** is the punctuation mark ? which is used in writing at the end of a question. □ *Who invented the question mark?* **2** If there is doubt or uncertainty about something, you can say that there is a **question mark over** it. □ *There are bound to be question marks over his future.*

⊙**ques•tion•naire** /ˌkwestʃəˈneə, ˌkes-/ NOUN [C] (**questionnaires**) A **questionnaire** is a written list of questions which are answered by a lot of people in order to provide information for a report or a survey. = survey □ *Teachers will be asked to fill in a questionnaire.* □ *a questionnaire on key issues*

queue /kjuː/ NOUN, VERB
NOUN [C] (**queues**) **1** (*mainly BrE; in AmE, usually use* **line**) A **queue** is a line of people or vehicles that are waiting for something. **2** (*mainly BrE; in AmE, usually use* **line**) If you say there is a **queue of** people who want to do or have something, you mean that a lot of people are waiting for an opportunity to do it or have it. **3** (*computing*) A **queue** is a list of computer tasks which will be done in order. □ *Your print job has already been sent from your PC to the network print queue.*
VERB [I, T] (**queues, queuing** or **queueing, queued**) **1** [I] (*mainly BrE; in AmE, usually use* **stand in line**) When people **queue**, they stand in a line waiting for something. **2** [T] (*computing*) To **queue** a number of computer tasks means to arrange them to be done in order.
PHRASAL VERB **queue up** Queue up means the same as **queue** VERB 1.

quick ◆◆◆ /kwɪk/ ADJ, ADV
ADJ (**quicker, quickest**) **1** Someone or something that is **quick** moves or does things with great speed. □ *You'll have to be quick. The flight leaves in about three hours.* **2** Something that is **quick** takes or lasts only a short time. □ *He took one last quick look around the room.* **3** **Quick** means happening without delay or with very little delay. = speedy □ *Officials played down any hope for a quick end to the bloodshed.* **4** [V-LINK + quick] If you are **quick to** do something, you do not hesitate to do it. □ *Mark says the ideas are Katie's own, and is quick to praise her talent.* **5** [quick + N] If someone has a **quick** temper, they are easily made angry. □ *He readily admitted to the interviewer that he had a quick temper, with a tendency towards violence.*
ADV **1** [quick after v] (*informal*) **Quicker** is sometimes used to mean 'at a greater speed', and **quickest** to mean 'at the greatest speed'. **Quick** is sometimes used to mean 'with

Q

great speed'. Some people consider this to be non-standard. ❑ *Warm the sugar slightly first to make it dissolve quicker.* **2** [quick after v] **Quick** is sometimes used to mean 'with very little delay'. ❑ *I got away as quick as I could.*

quick·ly /'kwɪkli/ ADV **1** [quickly with v] ❑ *Cussane worked quickly and methodically.* **2** [quickly with v] ❑ *You can get in shape quite quickly and easily.* **3** [quickly with v] ❑ *We need to get it back as quickly as possible.*

quick·ness /'kwɪknəs/ NOUN [U] ❑ *the natural quickness of his mind*

✦ **quick as a flash** → see **flash**

quick·en /'kwɪkən/ VERB [I, T] (**quickens, quickening, quickened**) If something **quickens** or if you **quicken** it, it becomes faster or moves at a greater speed. ❑ *Ann's pulse quickened in alarm.*

qui·et ♦♦◇ /'kwaɪət/ ADJ, NOUN

ADJ (**quieter, quietest**) **1** Someone or something that is **quiet** makes only a small amount of noise. ❑ *Tania kept the children reasonably quiet and contented.* **2** If a place is **quiet**, there is very little noise there. ❑ *She was received in a small, quiet office.* **3** If a place, situation, or time is **quiet**, there is no excitement, activity, or trouble. ❑ *a quiet rural backwater* **4** [V-LINK + quiet] If you are **quiet**, you are not saying anything. ❑ *I told them to be quiet and go to sleep.* **5** A **quiet** person behaves in a calm way and is not easily made angry or upset. = placid ❑ *He's a nice quiet man.*

PHRASE **keep quiet about something** or **keep something quiet** If you **keep quiet about** something or **keep** something **quiet**, you do not say anything about it. ❑ *I told her to keep quiet about it.*

NOUN [U] **Quiet** is silence. ❑ *He called for quiet and announced that the next song was in our honour.*

PHRASE **on the quiet** If something is done **on the quiet**, it is done secretly or in such a way that people do not notice it. ❑ *She'd promised to give him driving lessons, on the quiet, when no one could see.*

qui·et·ly /'kwaɪətli/ ADV **1** ❑ *'This is goodbye, isn't it?' she said quietly.* **2** [quietly with v] ❑ *His most prized time, though, will be spent quietly on his farm.* **3** *Amy stood quietly in the doorway watching him.*

qui·et·ness /'kwaɪətnəs/ NOUN [U] **1** *the smoothness and quietness of the flight* **2** *I miss the quietness of the countryside.* **3** *He stretched, taking pleasure in the quietness of the morning hour.*

WHICH WORD?

quiet or quite?

Do not confuse **quiet** and **quite**.

Quiet is an adjective. Someone or something that is **quiet** makes only a small amount of noise.

❑ *Bal spoke in a **quiet** voice.*

A **quiet** place does not have much activity or trouble.

❑ *It's a **quiet** little village.*

You use **quite** in front of an adjective or adverb to indicate that something is the case to a fairly great extent.

❑ *He was **quite** young.*

❑ *The end of the story can be told **quite** quickly.*

---

qui·et·en /'kwaɪətən/ (BrE) VERB [I, T] (**quietens, quietening, quietened**) **1** [I, T] If someone or something **quietens** or if you **quieten** them, they become less noisy, less active, or silent. ❑ *The wind dropped and the sea quietened.* **2** [T] To **quieten** fears or complaints means to persuade people that there is no good reason for them. ❑ *Supporters of the constitution had to quieten fears that aristocrats plotted to steal the fruits of the revolution.*

quilt /kwɪlt/ NOUN [C] (**quilts**) A **quilt** is a bed cover made by sewing layers of cloth together, usually with different colours sewn together to make a design. ❑ *an old patchwork quilt*

quit /kwɪt/ VERB, NOUN

VERB [I, T] (**quits, quitting, quit**) **1** [I, T] (informal) If you **quit**, or **quit** your job, you choose to leave it. ❑ *He quit his job as an office boy.* **2** [T, I] If you **quit**, or **quit** smoking, you stop doing it. ❑ *A nicotine spray can help smokers quit the habit.* **3** [T] If you **quit** a place, you leave it completely

and do not go back to it. ❑ *Science fiction writers have long dreamed that humans might one day quit the earth to colonize other planets.*

NOUN

PHRASE **call it quits** If you say that you are going to **call it quits**, you mean that you have decided to stop doing something or being involved in something. ❑ *They raised $630,000 through listener donations, and then called it quits.*

quite ♦♦♦ /kwaɪt/ ADV, PREDET

ADV **1** (vagueness) You use **quite** to indicate that something is the case to a fairly great extent. **Quite** is less emphatic than 'very' and 'extremely'. = pretty ❑ *I felt quite bitter about it at the time.* ❑ *Well, actually it requires quite a bit of work and research.* **2** (emphasis) You use **quite** to emphasize what you are saying. ❑ *It is quite clear that we were firing in self defence.* ❑ *My position is quite different.* **3** (vagueness) You use **quite** after a negative to make what you are saying weaker or less definite. ❑ *Something here is not quite right.* **4** [quite as reply] (mainly BrE, spoken, formulae) You can say **quite** to express your agreement with someone. ❑ *'It's your choice, isn't it?'—'Quite.'*

PREDET [quite 'a' N] (approval) You use **quite** in front of a noun group to emphasize that a person or thing is very impressive or unusual. ❑ *'Oh, he's quite a character,' Sean replied.*

✪ **quo·ta** /'kwəʊtə/ NOUN [C] (**quotas**) **1** A **quota** is the limited number or quantity of something which is officially allowed. ❑ *The quota of four tickets per person had been reduced to two.* ❑ *The country now imposes quotas on beef imports to protect its weak farm industry.* **2** A **quota** is a fixed maximum or minimum proportion of people from a particular group who are allowed to do something, such as come and live in a country or work for the government. ❑ *The bill would force employers to adopt a quota system when recruiting workers.* ❑ *The court, on a 5-4 vote, outlawed racial quotas in university admissions.* **3** Someone's **quota of** something is their expected or deserved share of it. = share ❑ *They have the usual quota of human weaknesses, no doubt.*

✪ **quo·ta·tion** /kwəʊ'teɪʃən/ NOUN [C] (**quotations**) **1** A **quotation** is a sentence or phrase taken from a book, poem, speech, or play, which is repeated by someone else. = quote, citation ❑ *He illustrated his argument with quotations from Martin Luther King Jr.* **2** When someone gives you a **quotation**, they tell you how much they will charge to do a particular piece of work. = quote ❑ *Get several written quotations and check exactly what's included in the cost.*

✪ **quote** ♦♦◇ /kwəʊt/ VERB, NOUN (academic word)

VERB [I, T, PASSIVE] (**quotes, quoting, quoted**) **1** [I, T] If you **quote** someone as saying something, you repeat what they have written or said. = cite, reference ❑ *He quoted Mr Polay as saying that peace negotiations were already underway.* ❑ *I gave the letter to the local press and they quoted from it.* ❑ *Mawby and Gill (1987) quote this passage from the Home Office White Paper, 1964.* ❑ *O'Regan cites one exception, quoting from a paper on cancer of the cervix.* **2** [T] If you **quote** something such as a law or a fact, you state it because it supports what you are saying. ❑ *The Congresswoman quoted statistics saying that the standard of living of the poorest people had fallen.* **3** [T] If someone **quotes** a price **for** doing something, they say how much money they would charge you for a service they are offering or for a job that you want them to do. ❑ *A travel agent quoted her $260 for a flight from Boston to New Jersey.* **4** [PASSIVE] (business) If a company's shares, a substance, or a currency **is quoted** at a particular price, that is its current market price. ❑ *In early trading in Hong Kong yesterday, gold was quoted at $368.20 an ounce.*

NOUN [C] (**quotes**) **1** A **quote from** a book, poem, play, or speech is a passage or phrase from it. = quotation, citation ❑ *The paper starts its editorial comment with a quote from an unnamed member of the House.* ❑ *The quote is attributed to the Athenean philosopher Socrates.* **2** A **quote for** a piece of work is the price that someone says they will charge you to do the work. = quotation ❑ *Always get a written quote for any repairs needed.*

q

Rr

R also **r** /ɑː/ NOUN [C, U] (**R's, r's**) **R** is the eighteenth letter of the English alphabet.

✪race ♦♦♦ /reɪs/ NOUN, VERB

NOUN [C, PL, U] (**races**) **1** [C] A **race** is a competition to see who is the fastest, for example in running, swimming, or driving. ❑ *The women's race was won by the only American in the field, Patti Sue Plumer.* **2** [PL] **The races** are a series of horse races that are held in a particular place on a particular day. People go to watch and to bet on which horse will win. ❑ *The high point of this trip was a day at the races.* **3** [C] A **race** is a situation in which people or organizations compete with each other for power or control. ❑ *The race for the White House begins in earnest today.* **4** [C, U] A **race** is one of the major groups which human beings can be divided into according to their physical features, such as the colour of their skin. = ethnicity ❑ *The college welcomes students of all races, faiths, and nationalities.* ❑ *Discrimination by employers on the grounds of race and nationality was illegal.*

PHRASE **a race against time** You describe a situation as a **race against time** when you have to work very fast in order to do something before a particular time, or before another thing happens. ❑ *A spokesman said the rescue operation was a race against time.*

VERB [I, T] (**races, racing, raced**) **1** [I, T] If you **race**, you take part in a race. ❑ *In the 10 years I raced in Europe, 30 drivers were killed.* ❑ *We raced them to the summit.* **2** [I] If you **race** somewhere, you go there as quickly as possible. ❑ *He raced across town to the State House building.* **3** [I] If something **races** towards a particular state or position, it moves very fast towards that state or position. ❑ *Do they realize we are racing towards complete economic collapse?* **4** [T] If you **race** a vehicle or animal, you prepare it for races and make it take part in races. ❑ *He still raced sports cars as often as he could.* **5** [I] If your mind **races**, or if thoughts **race** through your mind, you think very fast about something, especially when you are in a difficult or dangerous situation. ❑ *I made sure I sounded calm but my mind was racing.* **6** [I] If your heart **races**, it beats very quickly because you are excited or afraid. ❑ *Her heart raced uncontrollably.*

→ See also **racing**

✪ra·cial ♦◇◇ /reɪʃəl/ ADJ **Racial** describes things relating to people's race. ❑ *the protection of national and racial minorities* ❑ *the elimination of racial discrimination* ❑ *It was his legal insights that led to racial integration in the United States.* = ethnic

ra·cial·ly /reɪʃəli/ ADV ❑ *We are both children of racially mixed marriages.*

rac·ing ♦◇◇ /reɪsɪŋ/ NOUN [U] **Racing** refers to races between animals, especially horses, or between vehicles. ❑ *Four horse racing tracks operate in Pennsylvania.*

rac·ism /reɪsɪzəm/ NOUN [U] **Racism** is the belief that people of some races are inferior to others, and the behaviour which is the result of this belief. ❑ *There is a feeling among some black people that the level of racism is declining.*

✪rac·ist /reɪsɪst/ ADJ, NOUN

ADJ (disapproval) If you describe people, things, or behaviour as **racist**, you mean that they are influenced by the belief that some people are inferior because they belong to a particular race. ❑ *You have to acknowledge that we live in a racist society.* ❑ *This is an affluent area with no previous racist incidents.* ❑ *his political and racist views*

NOUN [C] (**racists**) A **racist** is someone who is racist. ❑ *He has a hard core of support among white racists.* ❑ *the individuals who are most likely to become bullies, criminals or racists*

rack /ræk/ NOUN, VERB

> The spelling **wrack** is also used for the meaning of the verb shown below.

NOUN [C] (**racks**) A **rack** is a frame or shelf, usually with bars or hooks, that is used for holding things or for hanging things on. ❑ *A luggage rack is a sensible option.*

VERB [T] (**racks, racking, racked**) If someone **is racked by** something such as illness or anxiety, it causes them great suffering or pain. ❑ *His already infirm body was racked by high fever.*

PHRASE **rack your brains** If you **rack** your **brains**, you try very hard to think of something. ❑ *She began to rack her brains to remember what had happened at the nursing home.*

PHRASAL VERB **rack up** If a business **racks up** profits, losses, or sales, it makes a lot of them. If a sportsman, sportswoman, or team **racks up** wins, they win a lot of games or races. ❑ *Lower rates mean that firms are more likely to rack up profits in the coming months.*

ra·dar /reɪdɑː/ NOUN [C, U] (**radars**) **Radar** is a way of discovering the position or speed of objects such as aircraft or ships when they cannot be seen, by using radio signals. ❑ *a ship's radar screen*

✪ra·dia·tion /ˌreɪdiˈeɪʃən/ NOUN [U] **1 Radiation** consists of very small particles of a radioactive substance. Large amounts of radiation can cause illness and death. ❑ *They suffer from health problems and fear the long-term effects of radiation.* ❑ *If the cancer returns, radiation therapy is successful in 90 per cent of cases.* **2 Radiation** is energy, especially heat, that comes from a particular source. ❑ *The $617 million satellite will study energy radiation from the most violent stars in the universe.* ❑ *To measure cosmic radiation in the early 1930s he sent up balloons of rubber.*

✪radi·cal ♦♦◇ /rædɪkəl/ ADJ, NOUN (academic word)

ADJ **1 Radical** changes and differences are very important and great in degree. = fundamental ❑ *The country needs a period of calm without more surges of radical change.* ❑ *The Football League has announced its proposals for a radical reform of the way football is run.* **2 Radical** people believe that there should be great changes in society and try to bring about these changes. ❑ *threats by left-wing radical groups to disrupt the proceedings*

NOUN [C] (**radicals**) A **radical** is someone who has radical views. ❑ *Vanessa and I had been student radicals together at Berkeley from 1965 to 1967.*

✪radi·cal·ly /rædɪkli/ ADV = fundamentally ❑ *two large groups of people with radically different beliefs and cultures* ❑ *The power of the presidency may be radically reduced in certain circumstances.* ❑ *proposals for radically new models*

ra·dio ♦♦♦ /reɪdiəʊ/ NOUN, VERB

NOUN [U, SING, C] (**radios**) **1** [U] **Radio** is the broadcasting of programmes for the public to listen to, by sending out signals from a transmitter. ❑ *The last 12 months have been difficult ones for local radio.* **2** [SING] You can refer to the programmes broadcast by radio stations as **the radio.**

❏ *A lot of people listen to the radio in the mornings.* **3** [c] A **radio** is the piece of equipment that you use in order to listen to radio programmes. ❏ *He sat down in the armchair and turned on the radio.* **4** [u] **Radio** is a system of sending sound over a distance by transmitting electrical signals. ❏ *They are in twice daily radio contact with the rebel leader.* **5** [c] A **radio** is a piece of equipment that is used for sending and receiving messages. ❏ *Judge Bruce Laughland praised the courage of the young policeman, who managed to raise the alarm on his radio.* **VERB** [i, t] (**radios, radioing, radioed**) If you **radio** someone, you send a message to them by radio. ❏ *The officer radioed for advice.*

✪**radio·ac·tive** /ˌreɪdiəʊˈæktɪv/ ADJ Something that is **radioactive** contains a substance that produces energy in the form of powerful and harmful rays. ❏ *The government has been storing radioactive waste at Fernald for 50 years.* ❏ *24.7 tonnes of highly radioactive fuel*
radio·ac·tiv·ity /ˌreɪdiəʊækˈtɪvɪti/ NOUN [u] ❏ *the storage and disposal of solid waste that is contaminated with low levels of radioactivity*

✪**ra·dius** /ˈreɪdiəs/ NOUN [SING, c] (**radii**) **1** [SING] The **radius** around a particular point is the distance from it in any direction. ❏ *Nick has searched for work in a ten-mile radius around his home.* ❏ *within a fifty-mile radius of the town* ❏ *Fragments of twisted metal were scattered across a wide radius.* **2** [c] The **radius** of a circle is the distance from its centre to its outside edge. ❏ *He indicated a semicircle with a radius of about thirty miles.* ❏ *the radius of a circle is equal to one-half its diameter*

rag /ræg/ NOUN [c, u, PL] (**rags**) **1** [c, u] A **rag** is a piece of old cloth which you can use to clean or wipe things. ❏ *He was wiping his hands on an oily rag.* **2** [PL] **Rags** are old torn clothes. ❏ *There were men, women, and small children, some dressed in rags.* **3** [c] (*informal, disapproval*) People refer to a newspaper as a **rag** when they have a poor opinion of it. ❏ *'This man Tom works for a local rag,' he said.*

rage /reɪdʒ/ NOUN, VERB
NOUN [c, u] (**rages**) **1** [c, u] **Rage** is strong anger that is difficult to control. = fury ❏ *He was red-cheeked with rage.* **2** [u] You can refer to the strong anger that someone feels in a particular situation as a particular **rage**, especially when this results in violent or aggressive behaviour. ❏ *Cabin crews are reporting up to nine cases of air rage a week.* **VERB** [i] (**rages, raging, raged**) **1** You say that something powerful or unpleasant **rages** when it continues with great force or violence. ❏ *Train service was halted as the fire raged for more than four hours.* **2** If you **rage** about something, you speak or think very angrily about it. ❏ *Monroe was on the phone, raging about her mistreatment by the brothers.* ❏ *Inside, Frannie was raging.*

rag·ged /ˈrægɪd/ ADJ **1** Someone who is **ragged** looks messy and is wearing clothes that are old and torn. ❏ *The five survivors eventually reached safety, ragged, half-starved, and exhausted.* **2** **Ragged** clothes are old and torn. ❏ *an elderly, bearded man in ragged clothes* **3** You can say that something is **ragged** when it is rough or uneven. = uneven ❏ *O'Brien formed the men into a ragged line.*

raid /reɪd/ VERB, NOUN
VERB [T] (**raids, raiding, raided**) **1** When soldiers **raid** a place, they make a sudden armed attack against it, with the aim of causing damage rather than occupying any of the enemy's land. ❏ *The guerrillas raided banks and destroyed a police barracks and an electricity substation.* **2** If the police **raid** a building, they enter it suddenly and by force in order to look for dangerous criminals or for evidence of something illegal, such as drugs or weapons. ❏ *Police raided their headquarters and other offices.* **NOUN** [c] (**raids**) **1** When soldiers make a **raid** on a place, they make a sudden armed attack against it. ❏ *The rebels attempted a surprise raid on a military camp.* **2** If the police make a **raid** on a building, they enter it suddenly and by force in order to look for dangerous criminals or for evidence of something illegal, such as drugs or weapons. ❏ *They were arrested early this morning after a raid on a house by thirty armed police.*
→ See also **air raid**

rail /reɪl/ NOUN
NOUN [c, u] (**rails**) **1** [c] A **rail** is a horizontal bar attached to posts or around the edge of something as a fence or support. ❏ *They had to walk across an emergency footbridge, holding onto a rope that served as a rail.* **2** [c] A **rail** is a horizontal bar that you hang things on. ❏ *This pair of curtains will fit a rail up to 7 ft 6 in wide.* **3** [c] **Rails** are the steel bars which trains run on. = track ❏ *The train left the rails but somehow forced its way back onto the line.* **4** [u] If you travel or send something **by rail**, you travel or send it on a train. ❏ *The president travelled by rail to his home town.*
PHRASES **back on the rails** (*mainly BrE; in AmE, use* **back on track**; *journalism*) If something is **back on the rails**, it is beginning to be successful again after a period when it almost failed.
go off the rails (*mainly BrE*) If someone **goes off the rails**, they start to behave in a way that other people think is unacceptable or very strange, for example they start taking drugs or breaking the law. ❏ *They've got to do something about these children because clearly they've gone off the rails.*

rail·way /ˈreɪlweɪ/ NOUN [c] (**railways**) **1** (*mainly BrE; in AmE, usually use* **railroad**) A **railway** is a route between two places along which trains travel on steel rails. **2** (*BrE; in AmE, use* **railroad**) A **railway** is a company or organization that operates railway routes. **3** (*mainly AmE*) A **railway** is the system and network of tracks that trains travel on.

rain /reɪn/ NOUN, VERB
NOUN [u, PL] (**rains**) **1** [u] [*also 'the' rain*] **Rain** is water that falls from the clouds in small drops. ❏ *I hope you didn't get soaked standing out in the rain.* **2** [PL] In countries where rain only falls in certain seasons, this rain is sometimes referred to as **the rains**. ❏ *the spring, when the rains came* **VERB** [i, T] (**rains, raining, rained**) **1** [i] When rain falls, you can say that **it is raining**. ❏ *It was raining hard, and she didn't have an umbrella.* **2** [i, T] If someone **rains** blows, kicks, or bombs **on** a person or place, the person or place is attacked by many blows, kicks, or bombs. You can also say that blows, kicks, or bombs **rain on** a person or place. ❏ *The police, raining blows on rioters and spectators alike, cleared the park.*
PHRASAL VERB **Rain down** means the same as **rain** VERB 2. ❏ *Fighter aircraft rained down high explosives.*

rain·bow /ˈreɪnbəʊ/ NOUN [c] (**rainbows**) A **rainbow** is an arch of different colours that you can sometimes see in the sky when it is raining. ❏ *silk and satin in every shade of the rainbow*

rain·fall /ˈreɪnfɔːl/ NOUN [u] **Rainfall** is the amount of rain that falls in a place during a particular period. ❏ *There have been four years of below average rainfall.*

rain forest *also* **rainforest** NOUN [c, u] (**rain forests**) A **rain forest** is a thick forest of tall trees which is found mainly in tropical areas where there is a lot of rain. ❏ *the destruction of the Amazon rain forest*

rainy /ˈreɪni/ ADJ (**rainier, rainiest**) During a **rainy** day, season, or period it rains a lot. ❏ *The rainy season in the Andes normally starts in December.*

✪**raise** /reɪz/ VERB [T] (**raises, raising, raised**) **1** If you **raise** something, you move it so that it is in a higher position. ❏ *He raised his hand to wave.* ❏ *Milton raised the glass to his lips.* **2** If you **raise** a flag, you display it by moving it up a pole or into a high place where it can be seen. ❏ *They had raised the white flag in surrender.* **3** If you **raise yourself**, you lift your body so that you are standing up straight, or so that you are no longer lying flat. = lift ❏ *He raised himself into a sitting position.* **4** If you **raise** the rate or level of something, you increase it. = increase; ≠ lower ❏ *The Federal Reserve Board is expected to raise interest rates.* ❏ *Two incidents in recent days have raised the level of concern.* ❏ *a raised body temperature* **5** To **raise** the standard of something means to improve it. = improve ❏ *a new drive to raise standards of literacy in New York's schools* **6** If you **raise** your voice, you speak more loudly, usually because you are angry. ❏ *Don't you raise your voice to me!* **7** If you **raise money for** a charity or an institution, you ask people for money which you collect on its behalf. ❏ *events held to raise money for flood victims* **8** If a person or company **raises** money that they need, they manage to get it, for example by selling their property or by borrowing. ❑ *They raised the money to buy the house and two hundred acres of land.* ◼ If an event **raises** a particular emotion or question, it makes people feel the emotion or consider the question. = highlight ❑ *The agreement has raised hopes that the war may end soon.* ❑ *The accident again raises questions about the safety of the building.* ◼ If you **raise** a subject, an objection, or a question, you mention it or bring it to someone's attention. ❑ *He had been consulted and had raised no objections.* ◼ Someone who **raises** a child takes care of it until it is grown up. = bring up ❑ *My mother was an amazing woman. She raised four of us kids virtually singlehandedly.* ◼ If someone **raises** a particular type of animal or crop, they breed that type of animal or grow that type of crop. ❑ *He raises 2,000 acres of wheat and hay.*

✦ **raise the alarm** → see **alarm**; **raise your eyebrows** → see **eyebrow**; **raise a finger** → see **finger**

WHICH WORD?

raise, bring up, or educate?

If you **bring up** a child, you take care of it until it is grown up. You can say you **were brought up** somewhere to talk about where you spent your childhood.

❑ *He was brought up on a small farm in Ireland.*

In American English, **raise** can be used with the same meaning.

❑ *She was raised in a small town in the Midwest.*

Do not confuse **raise** or **bring up** with **educate**. To **educate** a child means to teach it various subjects, usually at school or university.

❑ *93 per cent of children in Britain are educated in state schools.*

---

ral·ly ◆◇◇ /ˈræli/ NOUN, VERB

NOUN [c] (**rallies**) ◼ A **rally** is a large public meeting that is held in order to show support for something such as a political party. ❑ *About three thousand people held a rally to mark international human rights day.* ◼ A **rally** is when someone or something begins to recover or improve after having been weak. ❑ *After a brief rally the shares returned to $2.15.* ◼ A **rally** in tennis, badminton, or squash is a continuous series of shots that the players exchange without stopping. ❑ *a long rally* ◼ A **rally** is a competition in which vehicles are driven over public roads. ❑ *Carlos Sainz of Spain has won the New Zealand Motor Rally.*

VERB [I, T] (**rallies, rallying, rallied**) ◼ When people **rally to** something or when something **rallies** them, they unite to support it. ❑ *Her cabinet colleagues have continued to rally to her support.* ◼ [I] When someone or something **rallies**, they begin to recover or improve after having been weak. = recover ❑ *He rallied enough to thank his doctors.*

PHRASAL VERB **rally around** When people **rally around**, they work as a group in order to support someone or something at a difficult time. ❑ *So many people have rallied around to help the family.*

ram·page VERB, NOUN

VERB /ræmˈpeɪdʒ/ [I] When people or animals **rampage** through a place, they rush around there in a wild or violent way, causing damage or destruction. ❑ *Hundreds of youths rampaged through the town, smashing shop windows and overturning cars.*

NOUN /ˈræmpeɪdʒ/

PHRASE **go on a rampage** or **go on the rampage** If people go **on a rampage** or go **on the rampage**, they rush around in a wild or violent way, causing damage or destruction. ❑ *The prisoners went on a rampage destroying everything in their way.*

ram·pant /ˈræmpənt/ ADJ If you describe something bad, such as a crime or disease, as **rampant**, you mean that it is very common and is increasing in an uncontrolled way. ❑ *Inflation is rampant and industry is in decline.*

ran /ræn/ IRREG FORM **Ran** is the past tense of **run**.

ran·dom /ˈrændəm/ ADJ, NOUN (academic word)

ADJ ◼ A **random** sample or method is one in which all the people or things involved have an equal chance of

being chosen. ≠ targeted ❑ *The survey used a random sample of two thousand people across the Midwest.* ❑ *The competitors will be subject to random drug testing.* ◼ If you describe events as **random**, you mean that they do not seem to follow a definite plan or pattern. ❑ *random violence against innocent victims*

NOUN

PHRASE **at random** ◼ If you choose people or things **at random**, you do not use any particular method, so they all have an equal chance of being chosen. ❑ *We received several answers, and we picked one at random.* ◼ If something happens **at random**, it happens without a definite plan or pattern. ❑ *Three African-Americans were killed by shots fired at random from a minibus.*

❖ **ran·dom·ly** /ˈrændəmli/ ADV ◼ [randomly with v] ❑ *interviews with a randomly selected sample of 30 girls aged between 13 and 18* ◼ *They were randomly allotted to one or other of two groups.* ◼ [randomly with v] ❑ *drinks and magazines left scattered randomly around*

rang /ræŋ/ IRREG FORM **Rang** is the past tense of **ring**.

❖ **range** ◆◆◇ /reɪndʒ/ NOUN, VERB (academic word)

NOUN [c] (**ranges**) ◼ A **range** of things is a number of different things of the same general kind. = variety, selection, collection ❑ *A wide range of colours and patterns are available.* ❑ *Office workers face a wide range of health and safety problems.* ❑ *The two men discussed a range of issues.* ◼ A **range** is the complete group that is included between two points on a scale of measurement or quality. ❑ *The average age range is between 35 and 55.* ❑ *products available in this price range* ◼ The **range of** something is the maximum area in which it can reach things or detect things. ❑ *The 120mm mortar has a range of 18,000 yards.* ◼ A **range** of mountains or hills is a line of them. ❑ *the massive mountain ranges to the north* ◼ A rifle **range** or a shooting **range** is a place where people can practise shooting at targets. ❑ *It reminds me of my days on the rifle range preparing for duty in Vietnam.* ◼ A **range** is a large area of open land, especially land in the United States, where cattle are kept. ❑ *He grazed his cattle on the open range.*

PHRASES **in range** or **within range** or **out of range** If something is **in range** or **within range**, it is near enough to be reached or detected. If it is **out of range**, it is too far away to be reached or detected. ❑ *Cars are driven through the mess, splashing everyone within range.*

at close range or **from close range** If you see or hit something **at close range** or **from close range**, you are very close to it when you see it or hit it. If you do something **at a range of** half a mile, for example, you are half a mile away from it when you do it. ❑ *He was shot in the head at close range.*

VERB [I] (**ranges, ranging, ranged**) If things **range between** two points or **range from** one point **to** another, they vary within these points on a scale of measurement or quality. = vary ❑ *They range in price from $3 to $15.* ❑ *offering merchandise ranging from the everyday to the esoteric* ❑ *The cars were all new models and ranged from sports cars to Cadillacs.* ❑ *temperatures ranging between 5°C and 20°C*

WORD CONNECTIONS

ADJ + range

a **broad** range
a **wide** range

❑ *It is important to develop a broad range of skills.*

a **limited** range
a **narrow** range

❑ *They may handle only one product, or a narrow range of products.*

the **full** range
the **whole** range

❑ *Doctors are trained in the full range of child and family problems.*

the **normal** range

❑ *The temperature, although high, was within the normal range.*

❑ *a lawyer who boasts he can beat any rap, for a $5,000 fee*

VERB [I, T] (**raps, rapping, rapped**) **1** [I] Someone who **raps** performs rap music. ❑ *They rap about life in the inner city.* **2** [I, T] If you **rap on** something or **rap** it, you hit it with a series of quick blows. ❑ *Mary Ann turned and rapped on Charlie's door.* ❑ *rapping the glass with the knuckles of his right hand* **3** [T] (*journalism*) If you **rap** someone **for** something, you criticize or blame them for it. ❑ *Water industry chiefs were rapped yesterday for failing their customers.*

PHRASE rap someone's knuckles or **rap someone on the knuckles** (*journalism*) If someone in authority **raps** your **knuckles** or **raps** you **on the knuckles**, they criticize you or blame you for doing something they think is wrong. ❑ *I joined the workers on strike and was rapped on the knuckles.*

rape ◆◇◇ /reɪp/ VERB, NOUN

VERB [T] (**rapes, raping, raped**) If someone **is raped**, they are forced to have sex, usually by violence or threats of violence. ❑ *A young woman was brutally raped in her own home.*

NOUN [C, U] (**rapes**) **1** [C, U] **Rape** is the crime of forcing someone to have sex. ❑ *Almost 90 per cent of all rapes and violent assaults went unreported.* **2** [U] **Rape** is a plant with yellow flowers which is grown as a crop. Its seeds are crushed to make cooking oil.

🟠 **rap·id** ◆◆◇ /ˈræpɪd/ ADJ **1** A **rapid** change is one that happens very quickly. ❑ *the country's rapid economic growth in the 1980s* ❑ *the rapid decline in the birth rate in Western Europe* **2** A **rapid** movement is one that is very fast. ❑ *He walked at a rapid pace along Charles Street.* ❑ *The Tunnel will provide more rapid car transport than ferries.*

🟠 **rap·id·ly** /ˈræpɪdli/ ADV **1** = quickly, swiftly; ≠ slowly ❑ *countries with rapidly growing populations* ❑ *Try to rip it apart as rapidly as possible.* ❑ *'Operating profit is rising more rapidly,' he said.* **2** [rapidly with V] ❑ *He was moving rapidly around the room.*

ra·pid·ity /rəˈpɪdɪti/ NOUN [U] **1** = speed ❑ *the rapidity with which the weather can change* **2** The water rushed through the holes with great rapidity.

rap·port /ræˈpɔː/ NOUN [SING] [also no DET, oft rapport 'with/between' N] If two people or groups have a **rapport**, they have a good relationship in which they are able to understand each other's ideas or feelings very well. ❑ *The success depends on good rapport between interviewer and interviewee.*

🟠 **rare** ◆◇◇ /reə/ ADJ (**rarer, rarest**) **1** Something that is **rare** is not common and is therefore interesting or valuable. ❑ *the black-necked crane, one of the rarest species in the world* ❑ *She collects rare plants.* ❑ *Do you want to know about a particular rare stamp or rare stamps in general?* **2** An event or situation that is **rare** does not occur very often. = scarce, exceptional, uncommon; ≠ common, commonplace, ordinary ❑ *on those rare occasions when he did eat alone* ❑ *Heart attacks were extremely rare in babies, he said.* ❑ *I think it's very rare to have big families nowadays.* **3** [rare + N] You use **rare** to emphasize an extremely good or remarkable quality. ❑ *Ferris has a rare ability to record her observations on paper.* **4** Meat that is **rare** is cooked very lightly so that the inside is still red. ❑ *Thick tuna steaks are eaten rare, like beef.*

rank ◆◇◇ /ræŋk/ NOUN, VERB

NOUN [C, U, PL] (**ranks**) **1** [C, U] Someone's **rank** is the position or grade that they have in an organization. ❑ *He eventually rose to the rank of captain.* **2** [C, U] (*formal*) Someone's **rank** is the social class, especially the high social class, that they belong to. ❑ *He must be treated as a hostage of high rank, not as a common prisoner.* **3** [PL] The **ranks** of a group or organization are the people who belong to it. ❑ *There were some misgivings within the ranks of the media too.* **4** [PL] **The ranks** are the ordinary members of an organization, especially of the armed forces. ❑ *Most shop managers have worked their way up through the ranks.* **5** [C] A **rank of** people or things is a row of them. ❑ *Ranks of police in riot gear stood nervously by.* **6** [C] (*mainly BrE; in AmE, use* **stand**) A **taxi rank** is a place on a city street where taxis park when they are available.

PHRASES break ranks If you say that a member of a group or organization **breaks ranks**, you mean that they disobey the instructions of their group or organization. ❑ *Britain appears unlikely to break ranks with other members of the European Union.*

close ranks If you say that the members of a group **close ranks**, you mean that they are supporting each other only because their group is being criticized. ❑ *Institutions tend to close ranks when a member has been accused of misconduct.*

VERB [I, T] (**ranks, ranking, ranked**) **1** If an official organization **ranks** someone or something 1st, 5th, or 50th, for example, they calculate that the person or thing has that position on a scale. You can also say that someone or something **ranks** 1st, 5th, or 50th, for example. ❑ *The report ranks the US 20th out of 22 advanced nations.* ❑ *the only Canadian woman to be ranked in the top 50 of the women's world rankings* **2** If you say that someone or something **ranks** high or low on a scale, you are saying how good or important you think they are. ❑ *His prices rank high among those of other contemporary photographers.* ❑ *Investors ranked South Korea high among Asian nations.* ❑ *St Petersburg's night life ranks as more exciting than the capital's.*

ran·som /ˈrænsəm/ NOUN, VERB

NOUN [C, U] (**ransoms**) A **ransom** is the money that has to be paid to someone so that they will set free a person they have kidnapped. ❑ *Her kidnapper successfully extorted a $250,000 ransom for her release.*

PHRASE hold someone to ransom If a kidnapper **is holding** a person **to ransom**, they keep that person prisoner until they are given what they want. ❑ *He is charged with kidnapping a businessman last year and holding him to ransom.*

VERB [T] (**ransoms, ransoming, ransomed**) If you **ransom** someone who has been kidnapped, you pay the money to set them free. ❑ *The same system was used for ransoming or exchanging captives.*

rap /ræp/ NOUN, VERB

NOUN [U, C] (**raps**) **1** [U] **Rap** is a type of music in which the words are not sung but are spoken in a rapid, rhythmic way. ❑ *Her favourite music was by Run DMC, a rap group.* **2** [C] A **rap** is a piece of music performed in rap style, or the words that are used in it. ❑ *Every member contributes to the rap, singing either solo or as part of a rap chorus.* **3** [C] A **rap on** something is a sharp quick blow or series of blows. ❑ *There was a sharp rap on the door.* **4** [C] (*journalism*) A **rap** is an act of criticizing or blaming someone or something. ❑ *Bad corks get the rap for as much as 15 per cent of tainted wine.*

PHRASES take the rap (*informal*) If you **take the rap**, you are blamed or punished for something, especially something that is not your fault or for which other people are equally guilty. ❑ *When the client was murdered, his wife took the rap, but did she really do it?*

beat the rap (*informal*) If you **beat the rap**, you avoid being blamed for something wrong that you have done.

WORD CONNECTIONS

ADV + rare

extremely rare
increasingly rare
❑ *Cases like this are extremely rare.*

quite rare
relatively rare
❑ *In those days, it was quite rare for girls to go to university.*

🟠 **rare·ly** ◆◇◇ /ˈreəli/ ADV If something **rarely** happens, it does not happen very often. = seldom, hardly ever ❑ *They battled against other Indian tribes, but rarely fought with the whites.* ❑ *Money was plentiful, and rarely did anyone seem very bothered about levels of expenditure.* ❑ *Adolescent suicide is rarely an impulsive reaction to immediate distress.*

r

rar·ity /'reərɪti/ NOUN [C, U] (**rarities**) **1** [C] (*journalism*) If someone or something is a **rarity**, they are interesting or valuable because they are so unusual. ◻ *Sontag has always been that rarity, a glamorous intellectual.* **2** [U] The **rarity** of something is the fact that it is very uncommon. ◻ *It was a real prize due to its rarity and good condition.*

rash /ræʃ/ ADJ, NOUN

ADJ If someone is **rash** or does **rash** things, they act without thinking carefully first, and therefore make mistakes or behave foolishly. ◻ *It would be rash to rely on such evidence.*

NOUN [C, SING] (**rashes**) **1** [C] A **rash** is an area of red spots that appears on your skin when you are ill or have a bad reaction to something that you have eaten or touched. ◻ *He may break out in a rash when he eats these nuts.* **2** [SING] If you talk about a **rash of** events or things, you mean a large number of unpleasant events or undesirable things, which have happened or appeared within a short period of time. = spate ◻ *one of the few major airlines left untouched by the industry's rash of takeovers*

rash·ly /'ræʃli/ ADV ◻ *I made a lot of money, but I rashly gave most of it away.*

rat /ræt/ NOUN, VERB

NOUN [C] (**rats**) **1** A **rat** is an animal which has a long tail and looks like a large mouse. ◻ *This was demonstrated in a laboratory experiment with rats.* **2** (*informal, disapproval*) If you call someone a **rat**, you mean that you are angry with them or dislike them, often because they have cheated you or betrayed you. ◻ *What did you do with the gun you took from that little rat Turner?*

PHRASE **smell a rat** If you **smell a rat**, you begin to suspect or realize that something is wrong in a particular situation, for example that someone is trying to deceive you or harm you. ◻ *If I don't send a picture, he will smell a rat.*

VERB [I] (**rats, ratting, ratted**) (*informal*) **1** If someone **rats on** you, they tell someone in authority about things that you have done, especially bad things. ◻ *They were accused of encouraging children to rat on their parents.* **2** If someone **rats on** an agreement, they do not do what they said they would do. ◻ *She claims he ratted on their divorce settlement.*

⚙ **rate** ◆◆◆ /reɪt/ NOUN, VERB

NOUN [C] (**rates**) **1** The **rate** at which something happens is the speed with which it happens. = speed, pace ◻ *The rate at which hair grows can be agonizingly slow.* ◻ *The world's tropical forests are disappearing at an even faster rate than experts had thought.* **2** The **rate** at which something happens is the number of times it happens over a period of time. ◻ *New diet books appear at a rate of nearly one a week.* ◻ *His heart rate was 30 beats per minute slower.* ◻ *the highest divorce rate in Europe* **3** A **rate** is the amount of money that is charged for goods or services. ◻ *A special weekend rate is available from mid-November.* **4** (*business*) The **rate** of taxation or interest is the amount of tax or interest that needs to be paid. It is expressed as a percentage of the amount that is earned, gained as profit, or borrowed. = percentage ◻ *The government insisted that it would not be panicked into interest rate cuts.* ◻ *The card has a fixed annual rate of 9.9 % and no annual fee.*

PHRASES **at any rate** You use **at any rate** to indicate that what you have just said might be incorrect or unclear in some way, and that you are now being more precise. ◻ *His friends liked her – well, most of them at any rate.*

at this rate If you say that **at this rate** something bad or extreme will happen, you mean that it will happen if things continue to develop as they have been doing. ◻ *At this rate they'd be lucky to get home before eight-thirty or nine.*

VERB [I, T, PASSIVE] (**rates, rating, rated**) **1** [I, T] If you **rate** someone or something as good or bad, you consider them to be good or bad. You can also say that someone or something **rates** as good or bad. ◻ *Of all the men in the survey, they rate themselves the least fun-loving and the most responsible.* ◻ *Most rated it a hit.* ◻ *We rate him as one of the best.* **2** [PASSIVE] If someone or something **is rated** at a particular position or rank, they are calculated or considered to be in that position on a list. ◻ *He is generally rated the country's No. 3 industrialist.* **3** [T] If you say that someone or something **rates** a particular reaction, you

mean that this is the reaction you consider to be appropriate. = merit ◻ *This is so extraordinary, it rates a medal and a phone call from the president.*

→ See also **exchange rate, rating**

WORD CONNECTIONS

ADJ + **rate**

a **slow** rate
a **steady** rate
a **fast** rate
an **alarming** rate
◻ *Infections are continuing to spread at a steady rate.*

an **average** rate
◻ *Prices were rising at an average rate of 6% per year.*

a **high** rate
a **low** rate
◻ *Storecards charge very high rates of interest.*

a **fixed** rate
a **standard** rate
◻ *There may be a reduction in the standard rate of tax.*

VERB + **rate**

charge a rate
cut a rate
fix a rate
◻ *Some banks charge lower rates than others.*

ra·ther ◆◆◆ /'rɑːðə, 'ræð-/ CONJ, ADV

CONJ You use **rather** when you are describing what a particular situation is not like, after saying what it is. ◻ *She made students think for themselves, rather than telling them what to think.*

ADV **1** [rather with CL/GROUP] You use **rather** when you are correcting something that you have just said, especially when you are describing a particular situation after saying what it is not. ◻ *Twenty million years ago, Idaho was not the arid place it is now. Rather, it was warm and damp, populated by dense primordial forest.* **2** You use **rather** to indicate that something is true to a fairly great extent, especially when you are talking about something unpleasant or undesirable. ◻ *I grew up in rather unusual circumstances.* ◻ *I'm afraid it's a rather long story.* **3** [rather before V] (*mainly BrE, politeness*) You use **rather** before verbs that introduce your thoughts and feelings, in order to express your opinion politely, especially when a different opinion has been expressed. ◻ *I rather think he was telling the truth.*

PHRASES **rather than** You use **rather than** when you are contrasting two things or situations. **Rather than** introduces the thing or situation that is not true or that you do not want. ◻ *The problem was psychological rather than physiological.*

would rather If you say that you **would rather** do something or you**'d rather** do it, you mean that you would prefer to do it. If you say that you **would rather not** do something, you mean that you do not want to do it. ◻ *If it's all the same to you, I'd rather work at home.* ◻ *Kids would rather play than study.*

⚙ **rati·fi·ca·tion** /ˌrætɪfɪ'keɪʃən/ NOUN [C, U] (**ratifications**) The **ratification** of a treaty or written agreement is the process of ratifying it. = approval ◻ *We welcome this development and we look forward to early ratification of the treaty by China.* ◻ *The agreement next required ratification by the parliaments of the provinces.*

⚙ **rati·fy** /'rætɪfaɪ/ VERB [T] (**ratifies, ratifying, ratified**) When national leaders or organizations **ratify** a treaty or written agreement, they make it official by giving their formal approval to it, usually by signing it or voting for it. = approve, affirm; ≠ annul ◻ *The parliaments of Australia and Indonesia have yet to ratify the treaty.* ◻ *Russia formally ratified the Kyoto Protocol on Thursday.*

rat·ing ◆◇◇ /'reɪtɪŋ/ NOUN [C, PL] (**ratings**) **1** [C] A **rating** of something is a score or measurement of how good or popular it is. ◻ *New public opinion polls show the president's approval rating at its lowest point since he took office.*

2 [PL] The **ratings** are the statistics published each week which show how popular each television programme is. □ *CBS's ratings again showed huge improvement over the previous year.*

⭘ **ra·tio** /ˈreɪʃiəʊ, AmE -ʃoʊ/ NOUN [C] (**ratios**) (*academic word*) A **ratio** is a relationship between two things when it is expressed in numbers or amounts. For example, if there are ten boys and thirty girls in a room, the ratio of boys to girls is 1:3, or one to three. = proportion □ *The adult to child ratio is one to six.* □ *In 1978 there were 884 students at a lecturer/student ratio of 1:15.* □ *The bottom chart shows the ratio of personal debt to personal income.*

ra·tion /ˈræʃən/ NOUN, VERB

NOUN [C, PL] (**rations**) **1** [C] When there is not enough of something, your **ration** of it is the amount that you are allowed to have. □ *The meat ration was down to one pound per person per week.* **2** [PL] **Rations** are the food that is given to people who do not have enough food or to soldiers. □ *Aid officials said that the first emergency food rations of wheat and oil were handed out here last month.* **3** [C] Your **ration of** something is the amount of it that you normally have. □ *after consuming his ration of junk food and two cigarettes*

VERB [T] (**rations, rationing, rationed**) When something **is rationed** by a person or government, you are only allowed to have a limited amount of it, usually because there is not enough of it. □ *Staples such as bread, rice, and tea are already being rationed.* □ *The City Council of Moscow has decided that it will begin rationing bread, butter, and meat.*

⭘ **ra·tion·al** /ˈræʃənəl/ ADJ (*academic word*) **1 Rational** decisions and thoughts are based on reason rather than on emotion. = sensible, logical; ≠ irrational □ *He's asking you to look at both sides of the case and come to a rational decision.* □ *Mary was able to short-circuit her stress response by keeping her thoughts calm and rational.* **2** A **rational** person is someone who is sensible and is able to make decisions based on intelligent thinking rather than on emotion. □ *Did he come across as a sane, rational person?*

ra·tion·al·ity /ˌræʃəˈnælɪti/ NOUN [U] □ *We live in an era of rationality.*

⭘ **ra·tion·al·ly** /ˈræʃnəli/ ADV ≠ irrationally □ *It can be very hard to think rationally when you're feeling so vulnerable and alone.* □ *Their ability to look rationally at problems will be a great asset.*

⭘ **ra·tion·ale** /ˌræʃəˈnɑːl, -ˈnæl/ NOUN [C] (**rationales**) (*formal*) The **rationale** for a course of action, practice, or belief is the set of reasons on which it is based. = basis, reasons, justification □ *However, the rationale for such initiatives is not, of course, solely economic.* □ *The best managers explain the rationale behind their decisions.* □ *Overall, we find this paper lacking in a coherent scientific rationale.*

ra·tion·al·ize /ˈræʃənəlaɪz/ also **rationalise** VERB [T] (**rationalizes, rationalizing, rationalized**) If you try to **rationalize** attitudes or actions that are difficult to accept, you think of reasons to justify or explain them. □ *He further rationalized his activity by convincing himself that he was actually promoting peace.*

rat·tle /ˈrætəl/ VERB, NOUN

VERB [I, T] (**rattles, rattling, rattled**) **1** [I, T] When something **rattles** or when you **rattle** it, it makes short, sharp, knocking sounds because it is being shaken or it keeps hitting against something hard. □ *She slams the kitchen door so hard I hear dishes rattle.* **2** [T] If something or someone **rattles** you, they make you nervous. = unnerve □ *Officials are not normally rattled by any reporter's question.*

NOUN [C] (**rattles**) **1** A **rattle** is a series of short, sharp, knocking sounds when something is being shaken or keeps hitting against something hard. □ *There was a rattle of rifle fire.* **2** A **rattle** is a baby's toy with small, loose objects inside which make a noise when the baby shakes it. **rat·tled** /ˈrætəld/ ADJ □ *He swore in Spanish, an indication that he was rattled.*

rav·age /ˈrævɪdʒ/ VERB [T] (**ravages, ravaging, ravaged**) A town, country, or economy that **has been ravaged** is one that has been damaged so much that it is almost completely destroyed. □ *The country has been ravaged by civil war.*

rave /reɪv/ VERB, NOUN

VERB [I, T] (**raves, raving, raved**) **1** If someone **raves**, they talk in an excited and uncontrolled way. □ *She cried and raved for weeks, and people did not know what to do.* □ *'What is wrong with you, acting like that?' she raved.* **2** If you **rave about** something, you speak or write about it with great enthusiasm. □ *Rachel raved about the new foods she ate while she was there.* □ *'I'd no idea Milan was so wonderful,' he raved.*

NOUN [C] (**raves**) A **rave** is a big event at which young people dance to electronic music in a large building or in the open air. Raves are often associated with illegal drugs. □ *an all-night rave*

⭘ **raw** ◆◇◇ /rɔː/ ADJ

ADJ (**rawer, rawest**) **1 Raw** materials or substances are in their natural state before being processed or used in manufacturing. = untreated; ≠ processed □ *We import raw materials and energy and export mainly industrial products.* □ *two ships carrying raw sugar from Cuba* **2 Raw** food is food that is eaten uncooked, that has not yet been cooked, or that has not been cooked enough. □ *a popular dish made of raw fish* **3** If a part of your body is **raw**, it is red and painful, perhaps because the skin has come off or has been burned. □ *the drag of the rope against the raw flesh of my shoulders* **4 Raw** emotions are strong basic feelings or responses which are not weakened by other influences. □ *Her grief was still raw and he did not know how to help her.* **5** If you describe something as **raw**, you mean that it is simple, powerful, and real. □ *the raw power of instinct* **6 Raw** data is facts or information that has not yet been sorted, analysed, or prepared for use. ≠ analysed □ *Analyses were conducted on the raw data.* □ *a statistical model that fully adjusts the census's raw figures* **7** If you describe someone in a new job as **raw**, or as a **raw** recruit, you mean that they lack experience in that job. = inexperienced □ *replacing experienced men with raw recruits* **8 Raw** weather feels unpleasantly cold. = bitter □ *a raw December morning* **9** [raw + N] **Raw** sewage is sewage that has not been treated to make it cleaner. = untreated □ *contamination of drinking water by raw sewage*

PHRASE **a raw deal** (*informal*) If you say that you are getting **a raw deal**, you mean that you are being treated unfairly. □ *I think women have a raw deal.*

ray ◆◇◇ /reɪ/ NOUN [C] (**rays**) **1 Rays** of light are narrow beams of light. □ *The sun's rays can penetrate water up to 10 feet.* **2** A **ray of** hope, comfort, or other positive quality is a small amount of it that you have because it makes a bad situation seem less bad. = glimmer □ *They could provide a ray of hope amid the general economic gloom.* → See also **X-ray**

re /riː/ PREP You use **re** in documents such as business letters, e-mails, faxes and memos to introduce a subject or item which you are going to discuss or refer to in detail. = regarding □ *Dear Mrs Cox, Re: Homeowner's Insurance. We note from our files that we have not yet received your renewal instructions.*

⭘ **reach** ◆◆◆ /riːtʃ/ VERB, NOUN

VERB [T, I] (**reaches, reaching, reached**) **1** [T] When someone or something **reaches** a place, they arrive there. □ *He did not stop until he reached the door.* **2** [T] If someone or something has **reached** a certain stage, level, or amount, they are at that stage, level, or amount. = attain, arrive at □ *The process of political change in South Africa has reached the stage where it is irreversible.* □ *We're told the figure could reach 100,000 next year.* **3** [I] If you **reach** somewhere, you move your arm and hand to take or touch something. □ *Judy reached into her handbag and handed me a small, printed leaflet.* **4** [T] If you can **reach** something, you are able to touch it by stretching out your arm or leg. □ *Can you reach your toes with your fingertips?* **5** [T] If you try to **reach** someone, you try to contact them, usually by telephone. = contact □ *Has the doctor told you how to reach him or her in emergencies?* **6** [I, T] If something **reaches** a place, point, or level, it extends as far as that place, point, or level. □ *a nightshirt that reached to his knees* **7** [T] When people **reach** an agreement or a decision, they succeed in achieving it. □ *A meeting of* *agriculture ministers has so far failed to reach agreement over farm subsidies.* **NOUN** [U] **1** Someone's or something's **reach** is the distance or limit to which they can stretch, extend, or travel. □ *Isabelle placed a wine cup on the table within his reach.* **2** If a place or thing is within **reach**, it is possible to have it or get to it. If it is out of **reach**, it is not possible to have it or get to it. □ *It is located within reach of many important Norman towns, including Bayeux.*

WORD CONNECTIONS

reach + NOUN

reach a **stage**
reach a **level**
reach a **point**
□ *The group has reached a stage where it is eager to expand.*

reach an **agreement**
reach a **conclusion**
reach a **decision**
□ *They could reach a decision as early as today.*

✪ **re·act** ♦◇◇ /ri'ækt/ VERB [I, RECIP] (reacts, reacting, reacted) (*academic word*) **1** [I] When you **react to** something that has happened to you, you behave in a particular way because of it. = respond □ *They reacted violently to the news.* □ *It's natural to react with disbelief if your child is accused of bullying.* **2** [I] If you **react against** someone's way of behaving, you deliberately behave in a different way because you do not like the way they behave. = rebel □ *My father never saved money and perhaps I reacted against that.* **3** [I] If you **react to** a substance such as a drug, or **to** something you have touched, you are affected unpleasantly or made ill by it. □ *Someone allergic to milk is likely to react to cheese.* **4** [RECIP] When one chemical substance **reacts with** another, or when two chemical substances **react**, they combine chemically to form another substance. □ *Calcium reacts with water but less violently than sodium and potassium do.* □ *Under normal circumstances, these two gases react readily to produce carbon dioxide and water.*

WORD CONNECTIONS

react + TO + NOUN

react to the **news**
react to **information**
react to an **announcement**
□ *The opposition were quick to react to the announcement.*

react + WITH + NOUN

react with **anger**
react with **horror**
react with **disbelief**
□ *People reacted with horror to news of the attack.*

react + ADV

react **angrily**
react **quickly**
react **positively**
□ *In general audiences have reacted positively to the film.*

✪ **re·ac·tion** ♦♦◇ /ri'ækʃən/ NOUN [C, U, SING, PL] (reactions) **1** [C, U] Your **reaction to** something that has happened or something that you have experienced is what you feel, say, or do because of it. = response □ *Reaction to the visit is mixed.* □ *The initial reaction of most participants is fear.* **2** [C] A **reaction against** something is a way of behaving or doing something that is deliberately different from what has been done before. □ *All new fashion starts out as a reaction against existing convention.* **3** [SING] [also no DET, reaction 'against' N] If there is a **reaction against** something, it becomes unpopular. □ *Premature moves in this respect might well provoke a reaction against the reform.* **4** [PL] Your **reactions** are your ability to move quickly in response to something, for example when you are in danger. □ *The sport requires very fast reactions.* **5** [U] **Reaction** is the belief that the political or social system of your country should not change. □ *Thus, he aided reaction*

and thwarted progress. **6** [C] A chemical **reaction** is a process in which two substances combine together chemically to form another substance. □ *Ozone is produced by the reaction between oxygen and ultraviolet light.* □ *Catalysts are materials which greatly speed up chemical reactions.* **7** [C] If you have a **reaction to** a substance such as a drug, or **to** something you have touched, you are affected unpleasantly or made ill by it. □ *Every year, 5,000 people have life-threatening reactions to anaesthetics.*

WORD CONNECTIONS

ADJ + **reaction**

a **mixed** reaction
a **negative** reaction
a **positive** reaction
an **initial** reaction
□ *The move has met with a largely positive reaction.*

a **chemical** reaction
a **chain** reaction
□ *A minor explosion occurred which set off a chain reaction.*

VERB + **reaction**

provoke a reaction
trigger a reaction
cause a reaction
□ *His statement provoked an immediate reaction from industry leaders.*

speed up a reaction
slow down a reaction
monitor a reaction
□ *The effect of refrigeration is to slow down the reaction.*

re·ac·tor /ri'æktə/ NOUN [C] (reactors) A nuclear **reactor** is a machine which is used to produce nuclear energy or the place where this machine and other related machinery and equipment is kept.

read ♦♦♦ /ri:d/ VERB, NOUN
VERB [I, T] (reads, reading, read /red/) **1** [I, T] When you **read** something such as a book or article, you look at and understand the words that are written there. □ *Have you read this book?* □ *I read about it in the paper.* □ *She spends her days reading and watching television.* **2** [I, T] When you **read** a piece of writing to someone, you say the words aloud. □ *Jay reads poetry so beautifully.* □ *I like it when she reads to us.* **3** [I, T] People who can **read** have the ability to look at and understand written words. □ *He couldn't read or write.* □ *The kid can read words, but did miserably on the test.* **4** [T] If you can **read** music, you have the ability to look at and understand the symbols that are used in written music to represent musical sounds. □ *Later on I learned how to read music.* **5** [T] (*computing*) When a computer **reads** a file or a document, it takes information from a disk or tape. □ *How can I read an Excel file on a computer that only has Word installed?* **6** [T] You can use **read** when saying what is written on something or in something. For example, if a notice **reads** 'Entrance', the word 'Entrance' is written on it. □ *The sign on the bus read 'Private: Not In Service'.* **7** [I] If you refer to how a piece of writing **reads**, you are referring to its style. □ *The book reads like a ballad.* **8** [T] If something **is read** in a particular way, it is understood or interpreted in that way. = interpret □ *The play is being widely read as an allegory of imperialist conquest.* **9** [T] If you **read** someone's mind or thoughts, you know exactly what they are thinking without them telling you. □ *From behind her, as if he could read her thoughts, Benny said, 'You're free to go any time you like, Madame.'* **10** [T] If you can **read** someone or you can **read** their gestures, you can understand what they are thinking or feeling by the way they behave or the things they say. □ *If you have to work as part of a team, you must learn to read people.* **11** [T] When you **read** a measuring device, you look at it to see what the figure or measurement on it is. □ *It is essential that you are able to read a thermometer.* **12** [T] If a measuring device **reads** a particular amount, it shows that amount. □ *The thermometer read 105 degrees Fahrenheit.*
PHRASAL VERBS **read into** If you **read** a meaning **into**

something, you think it is there although it may not actually be there. ❑ *It is dangerous to read too much into one year's figures.*

read out If you **read out** a piece of writing, you say it aloud. ❑ *He's obliged to take his turn at reading out the announcements.*

read up on If you **read up on** a subject, you read a lot about it so that you become informed about it. ❑ *I've read up on the dangers of all these drugs.*

NOUN [SING, C] (**reads**) **1** [SING] A **read** is the act of reading something such as a book or article. ❑ *I settled down to have a good read.* **2** [C] [ADJ + read] If you say that a book or magazine is a good **read**, you mean that it is very enjoyable to read. ❑ *Ben Okri's latest novel is a good read.*
→ See also **reading**

read·er ♦♦◇ /ˈriːdə/ NOUN [C] (**readers**) **1** The **readers** of a newspaper, magazine, or book are the people who read it. ❑ *These texts give the reader an insight into the Chinese mind.* ❑ *The paper's success is simple: we give our readers what they want.* **2** A **reader** is a person who reads, especially one who reads for pleasure. ❑ *Thanks to that job I became an avid reader.*

read·i·ly /ˈredɪli/ ADV **1** [readily with V] If you do something **readily**, you do it in a way which shows that you are very willing to do it. ❑ *I asked her if she would allow me to interview her, and she readily agreed.* **2** You also use **readily** to say that something can be done or obtained quickly and easily. For example, if you say that something can be readily understood, you mean that people can understand it quickly and easily. = easily ❑ *The components are readily available in hardware stores.*

read·ing ♦♦◇ /ˈriːdɪŋ/ NOUN [U, C] (**readings**) **1** [U] **Reading** is the activity of reading books. ❑ *I have always loved reading.* **2** [C] A **reading** is an event at which poetry or extracts from books are read to an audience. ❑ *a poetry reading* **3** [C] Your **reading of** a word, text, or situation is the way in which you understand or interpret it. ❑ *My reading of her character makes me feel that she was too responsible a person to do those things.* **4** [C] The **reading** on a measuring device is the figure or measurement that it shows. ❑ *The gauge must be giving a faulty reading.*

ready ♦♦◇ /ˈredi/ ADJ, VERB
ADJ (**readier**, **readiest**) **1** [V-LINK + ready] If someone is **ready**, they are properly prepared for something. If something is **ready**, it has been properly prepared and is now able to be used. ❑ *It took her a long time to get ready for church.* ❑ *Are you ready to board, Mr Daly?* **2** [V-LINK + ready] If you are **ready for** something or **ready to** do something, you have enough experience to do it or you are old enough and sensible enough to do it. ❑ *She says she's not ready for marriage.* **3** [V-LINK + ready + to-INF] If you are **ready to** do something, you are willing to do it. = willing ❑ *They were ready to die for their beliefs.* **4** [V-LINK + ready 'for' N] If you are **ready for** something, you need it or want it. ❑ *I don't know about you, but I'm ready for bed.* **5** [V-LINK + ready + to-INF] To be **ready to** do something means to be about to do it or likely to do it. ❑ *She looked ready to cry.* **6** [ready + N] You use **ready** to describe things that are able to be used very quickly and easily. ❑ *I didn't have a ready answer for this dilemma.*
VERB [T] (**readies**, **readying**, **readied**) (*formal*) When you **ready** something, you prepare it for a particular purpose. ❑ *John's soldiers were readying themselves for the final assault.*

real ♦♦♦ /riːl/ ADJ
ADJ 1 Something that is **real** actually exists and is not imagined, invented, or theoretical. ❑ *No, it wasn't a dream. It was real.* **2** If something is **real to** someone, they experience it as though it really exists or happens, even though it does not. ❑ *Whitechild's life becomes increasingly real to the reader.* **3** A material or object that is **real** is natural or functioning, and not artificial or an imitation. = genuine ❑ *the smell of real leather* **4** [real + N] You can use **real** to describe someone or something that has all the characteristics or qualities that such a person or thing typically has. = proper ❑ *his first real girlfriend* **5** [real + N] You can use **real** to describe something that is the true or original thing of its kind, in contrast to one that

someone wants you to believe is true. = true ❑ *This was the real reason for her call.* **6** [real + N] You can use **real** to describe something that is the most important or typical part of a thing. ❑ *When he talks, he only gives glimpses of his real self.* **7** You can use **real** when you are talking about a situation or feeling to emphasize that it exists and is important or serious. ❑ *Global warming is a real problem.* ❑ *The prospect of civil war is very real.* **8** [real + N] You can use **real** to emphasize a quality that is genuine and sincere. ❑ *You've been drifting from job to job without any real commitment.* **9** [real + N] (*mainly spoken, emphasis*) You can use **real** before nouns to emphasize your description of something or someone. ❑ *You must think I'm a real idiot.* **10** [real + N] The **real** cost or value of something is its cost or value after other amounts have been added or subtracted and when factors such as the level of inflation have been considered. = actual, net ❑ *the real cost of borrowing*
PHRASES **in real terms** You can also talk about the cost or value of something **in real terms**. ❑ *In real terms the cost of driving is cheaper than a decade ago.*
for real (*informal*) If you say that someone does something **for real**, you mean that they actually do it and do not just pretend to do it. ❑ *I have gone to premieres in my dreams but I never thought I'd do it for real.*

re·al·ism /ˈriːəlɪzəm/ NOUN [U] **1** (*approval*) When people show **realism** in their behaviour, they recognize and accept the true nature of a situation and try to deal with it in a practical way. ❑ *It was time now to show more political realism.* **2** If things and people are presented with **realism** in paintings, stories, or films, they are presented in a way that is like real life. ❑ *Greene's stories had an edge of realism that made it easy to forget they were fiction.*

re·al·ist /ˈriːəlɪst/ NOUN, ADJ
NOUN [C] (**realists**) (*approval*) A **realist** is someone who recognizes and accepts the true nature of a situation and tries to deal with it in a practical way. ❑ *I see myself not as a cynic but as a realist.*
ADJ [realist + N] A **realist** painter or writer is one who represents things and people in a way that is like real life. ❑ *perhaps the foremost realist painter of our time*

✪ **re·al·is·tic** /ˌriːəˈlɪstɪk/ ADJ **1** If you are **realistic** about a situation, you recognize and accept its true nature and try to deal with it in a practical way. ≠ unrealistic, impractical ❑ *Police have to be realistic about violent crime.* ❑ *a realistic view of what we can afford* **2** Something such as a goal or target that is **realistic** is one that you can sensibly expect to achieve. = sensible ❑ *A more realistic figure is 11 million.* **3** You say that a painting, story, or film is **realistic** when the people and things in it are like people and things in real life. ❑ *extraordinarily realistic paintings of Indians*

✪ **re·al·is·ti·cal·ly** /ˌriːəˈlɪstɪkəli/ ADV [realistically with CL] (*emphasis*) You use **realistically** when you want to emphasize that what you are saying is true, even though you would prefer it not to be true. = frankly; ≠ unrealistically ❑ *Realistically, there is never one right answer.* ❑ *As an adult, you can assess the situation realistically.* ❑ *What results can you realistically expect?* ❑ *the definition of what is realistically possible*
→ See also **realistic**

✪ **re·al·ity** ♦♦◇ /riˈæliti/ NOUN
NOUN [U, C, SING] (**realities**) **1** [U] You use **reality** to refer to real things or the real nature of things rather than imagined, invented, or theoretical ideas. = fact, actuality ❑ *Fiction and reality were increasingly blurred.* ❑ *Psychiatrists become too caught up in their theories to deal adequately with reality.* **2** [C] **The reality of** a situation is the truth about it, especially when it is unpleasant or difficult to deal with. ❑ *the harsh reality of top international competition* **3** [SING] You say that something has become a **reality** when it actually exists or is actually happening. ❑ *the whole procedure that made this book become a reality*
PHRASE **in reality** You can use **in reality** to introduce a statement about the real nature of something, when it contrasts with something incorrect that has just been described. = in fact, actually, in truth ❑ *He came across as*

r

streetwise, but in reality he was not. ❏ *For convenience, we can classify these differences into three groups, although in reality they are innumerable.*

re·al·ize ◆◆◇ /'riːəlaɪz/ also **realise** VERB [I, T] (**realizes, realizing, realized**) **1** [I, T] If you **realize** that something is true, you become aware of that fact or understand it. ❏ *As soon as we realized something was wrong, we moved the children away.* ❏ *People don't realize how serious this recession has actually been.* **2** [T] If your hopes, desires, or fears **are realized**, the things that you hope for, desire, or fear actually happen. ❏ *All his worst fears were realized.* **3** [T] (*formal*) When someone **realizes** a design or an idea, they make or organize something based on that design or idea. ❏ *I knew the technique that I would have to create in order to realize that structure.* **4** [T] If someone or something **realizes** their potential, they do everything they are capable of doing, because they have been given the opportunity to do so. = achieve ❏ *The support systems to enable women to realize their potential at work are seriously inadequate.* **5** [T] (*formal*) If something **realizes** a particular amount of money when it is sold, that amount of money is paid for it. ❏ *A selection of correspondence from PG Wodehouse realized 2,000 dollars.*

re·al·i·za·tion /ˌriːəlaɪˈzeɪʃən/ NOUN [C, U] (**realizations**) **1** [C, U] ❏ *There is now a growing realization that things cannot go on like this for much longer.* **2** [U] ❏ *In Kravis's venomous tone he recognized the realization of his worst fears.* **3** [C, U] ❏ *a total cash realization of about $23 million*

real life NOUN, ADJ

NOUN [U] If something happens **in real life**, it actually happens and is not just in a story or in someone's imagination. ❏ *In real life men like Richard Gere don't marry hookers.* ADJ [real life + N] If you describe something as **real-life**, it means it actually happened and is not just in a story or in someone's imagination. ❏ *a real-life horror story*

re·al·ly ◆◆◆ /'rɪəli/ ADV, CONVENTION

ADV **1** (*spoken, emphasis*) You can use **really** to emphasize a statement. ❏ *I'm very sorry. I really am.* **2** [really + ADJ/ADV] (*emphasis*) You can use **really** to emphasize an adjective or adverb. = very ❏ *It was really good.* **3** You use **really** when you are discussing the real facts about something, in contrast to the ones someone wants you to believe. ❏ *My father didn't really love her.* **4** [really before v] People use **really** in questions and negative statements when they want you to answer 'no'. = honestly ❏ *Do you really think he would be that stupid?* **5** [really before v] If you refer to a time when something **really** begins to happen, you are emphasizing that it starts to happen at that time to a much greater extent and much more seriously than before. ❏ *That's when the pressure really started.* **6** (*spoken, vagueness*) People sometimes use **really** to slightly reduce the force of a negative statement. ❏ *I'm not really surprised.*

CONVENTION (*spoken, feelings*) You can say **really** to express surprise or disbelief at what someone has said. ❏ *'We discovered it was totally the wrong decision.'—'Really?'*

realm /relm/ NOUN [C] (**realms**) (*formal*) **1** You can use **realm** to refer to any area of activity, interest, or thought. ❏ *the realm of politics* **2** A **realm** is a country that has a king or queen. ❏ *Defence of the realm is crucial.*

real world NOUN [SING] If you talk about **the real world**, you are referring to the world and life in general, in contrast to a particular person's own life, experience, and ideas, which may seem untypical and unrealistic. ❏ *When they eventually leave the school they will be totally ill-equipped to deal with the real world.*

rear ◆◇◇ /rɪə/ NOUN, ADJ, VERB

NOUN [SING, C] **1** [SING] The **rear** of something such as a building or vehicle is the back part of it. = back ❏ *He settled back in the rear of the taxi.* **2** [SING] (*formal*) If you are at the **rear** of a moving line of people, you are the last person in it. = back ❏ *Musicians played at the front and rear of the procession.* **3** [C] (*informal*) Your **rear** is the part of your body that you sit on. = behind ❏ *I saw him pat a waitress on her rear.*

PHRASE **bring up the rear** If a person or vehicle is

bringing up the rear, they are the last person or vehicle in a moving line of them. ❏ *police motorcyclists bringing up the rear of the procession*

ADJ [rear + N] **Rear** is used to refer to the part of something such as a building or vehicle that is towards the back or nearest to the back. ❏ *Manufacturers have been obliged to fit rear seat belts in all new cars.*

VERB [T, I] (**rears, rearing, reared**) **1** [T] If you **rear** children, you take care of them until they are old enough to take care of themselves. = bring up, raise ❏ *She reared sixteen children, six her own and ten her husband's.* **2** [T] If you **rear** a young animal, you keep and take care of it until it is old enough to be used for work or food, or until it can look after itself. ❏ *She spends a lot of time rearing animals.* **3** [I] When a horse **rears**, it moves the front part of its body upwards, so that its front legs are high in the air and it is standing on its back legs. ❏ *The horse reared and threw off its rider.*

re·arrange /ˌriːəˈreɪndʒ/ VERB [T] (**rearranges, rearranging, rearranged**) **1** If you **rearrange** things, you change the way in which they are organized or ordered. ❏ *When she returned, she found Malcolm had rearranged all her furniture.* **2** If you **rearrange** a meeting or an appointment, you arrange for it to take place at a different time from that originally intended. = reschedule ❏ *You may cancel or rearrange the appointment.*

WORD PARTS

The prefix **re-** appears in words to show that an action or process is repeated:

rearrange (VERB)

reassess (VERB)

re-read (VERB)

❂**rea·son** ◆◆◆ /'riːzən/ NOUN, VERB

NOUN [C, U] (**reasons**) **1** [C] The **reason for** something is a fact or situation which explains why it happens or what causes it to happen. ❏ *There is a reason for every important thing that happens.* ❏ *Who would have a reason to want to kill her?* ❏ *the reason why Italian tomatoes have so much flavour* ❏ *My parents came to Germany for business reasons.* = grounds, cause, excuse, motive, justification **2** [U] If you say that you have **reason to** believe something or **to** have a particular emotion, you mean that you have evidence for your belief or there is a definite cause of your feeling. ❏ *They had reason to believe there could be trouble.* **3** [U] The ability that people have to think and to make sensible judgments can be referred to as **reason**. ❏ *a conflict between emotion and reason* ❏ *Never underestimate their powers of reason and logic.* ❏ *the man of madness and the man of reason*

PHRASES **by reason of** (*formal*) If one thing happens **by reason of** another, it happens because of it. ❏ *The boss retains enormous influence by reason of his position.*

listen to reason If you try to make someone **listen to reason**, you try to persuade them to listen to sensible arguments and be influenced by them. ❏ *The company's top executives had refused to listen to reason.*

for no reason or **for no good reason** or **for no reason at all** If you say that something happened or was done **for no reason, for no good reason**, or **for no reason at all**, you mean that there was no obvious reason why it happened or was done. ❏ *The guards, he said, would punch them for no reason.*

within reason If you say that you will do anything **within reason**, you mean that you will do anything that is fair or reasonable and not too extreme. ❏ *I will take any job that comes along, within reason.*

VERB [T] (**reasons, reasoning, reasoned**) If you **reason that** something is true, you decide that it is true after thinking carefully about all the facts. ❏ *I reasoned that changing my diet would lower my cholesterol level.*

PHRASAL VERB **reason with** If you try to **reason with** someone, you try to persuade them to do or accept something by using sensible arguments. ❏ *He's impossible. I can't reason with him.*

→ See also **reasoning**

✦ **it stands to reason** → see **stand**

| WORD CONNECTIONS |

WORD CONNECTIONS

ADJ + reason

the **main** reason
the **only** reason
the **real** reason
❏ *The deal has been criticized for two main reasons.*

a **compelling** reason
a **good** reason
❏ *There is a good reason why she makes this claim.*

VERB + reason

give a reason
have a reason
find the reason
❏ *A patient is entitled to refuse treatment without giving a reason.*

FOR + ADJ + reasons

for **safety** reasons
for **tax** reasons
for **health** reasons
for **security** reasons
❏ *The main gate has to be kept locked for security reasons.*

VOCABULARY BUILDER

reason NOUN
The **reason for** something is a fact or situation which explains why it happens or what causes it to happen.
❏ *That wasn't the real reason for my anger.*

grounds NOUN *(formal)*
If something is **grounds** for a feeling or action, it is a reason for it.
❏ *In the interview he gave some grounds for optimism.*

cause NOUN
The **cause** of an event, usually a bad event, is the thing that makes it happen.
❏ *Smoking is the biggest preventable cause of death and disease.*

excuse NOUN
An **excuse** is a reason that you give in order to explain why something has been done or has not been done, or in order to avoid doing something.
❏ *It is easy to find excuses for his indecisiveness.*

motive NOUN *(formal)*
Your **motive** for doing something is your reason for doing it.
❏ *Police have ruled out robbery as a motive for the killing.*

justification NOUN
A **justification** for something is an acceptable reason or explanation for it.
❏ *To me the only justification for a zoo is educational.*

WHICH WORD?
reason or cause?

The **reason** for something is the fact or situation which explains why it happens, exists, or is done.
❏ *I asked the **reason** for the decision.*
The **cause** of an event is the thing that makes it happen.
❏ *Nobody knew the **cause** of the explosion.*

USAGE NOTE
reason

When you use **reason** to explain why something happens or is done, make sure you use the preposition 'for'. Do not use 'the reason of'.
*The **reason for** coming here is to make money.*

✿**rea·son·able** ◆◇◇ /ˈriːzənəbəl/ ADJ **1** If you think that someone is fair and sensible you can say that they are **reasonable**. ❏ *He's a reasonable sort of person.* **2** If you say that a decision or action is **reasonable**, you mean that it is fair and sensible. ❏ *a perfectly reasonable decision* ❏ *At the time, what he'd done had seemed reasonable.* ❏ *reasonable grounds for complaint* **3** If you say that an expectation or explanation is **reasonable**, you mean that there are good reasons why it may be correct. = sensible; ≠ unreasonable ❏ *It seems reasonable to expect rapid urban growth.* ❏ *There must be some other reasonable answer.* **4** If you say that the price of something is **reasonable**, you mean that it is fair and not too high. ❏ *You get a good meal for a reasonable price.* **5** You can use **reasonable** to describe something that is fairly good, but not very good. ❏ *The boy answered him in reasonable French.* **6** A **reasonable** amount of something is a fairly large amount of it. ❏ *They will need a reasonable amount of desk area and good light.*
✿**rea·son·ably** /ˈriːznəbli/ ADV **1** = sensibly; ≠ unreasonably ❏ *'I'm sorry, Andrew,' she said reasonably.* **2** [reasonably with V] ❏ *You can reasonably expect your goods to arrive within six to eight weeks.* ❏ *The panel says he acted reasonably based on the information he had access to.* **3** [reasonably with V] ❏ *reasonably priced accommodations* **4** [reasonably + ADJ/ADV] ❏ *I can dance reasonably well.* **5** [reasonably + ADJ/ADV] ❏ *From now on events moved reasonably quickly.*
rea·son·able·ness /ˈriːznəbəlnəs/ NOUN [U] ❏ *'I can understand how you feel,' Dan said with great reasonableness.*

✿**rea·son·ing** /ˈriːzənɪŋ/ NOUN [C, U] (**reasonings**) **Reasoning** is the process by which you reach a conclusion after thinking about all the facts. = thinking, logic ❏ *the reasoning behind the decision* ❏ *She was not really convinced by this line of reasoning.*

✿**re·as·sess** /ˌriːəˈses/ VERB [T] (**reassesses, reassessing, reassessed**) *(academic word)* If you **reassess** something, you think about it and decide whether you need to change your opinion about it. = reappraise, review ❏ *I will reassess the situation when I get home.* ❏ *But yesterday they admitted that it might be time to reassess the situation.* ❏ *Security in the area will have to be reassessed.*

✿**re·as·sess·ment** /ˌriːəˈsesmənt/ NOUN [C, U] (**reassessments**) If you make a **reassessment** of something, you think about it and decide whether you need to change your opinion about it. = reappraisal ❏ *There's a total reassessment of what people want out of life.* ❏ *a major reassessment of the impact of nuclear weapons on military doctrine* ❏ *There are three questions in particular which should concern the Prime Minister and prompt a reassessment of policy.*

re·assur·ance /ˌriːəˈʃʊərəns/ NOUN [U, C] (**reassurances**) **1** [U] If someone needs **reassurance**, they are very worried and need someone to help them stop worrying by saying kind or helpful things. ❏ *She needed reassurance that she belonged somewhere.* **2** [C] **Reassurances** are things that you say to help people stop worrying about something. ❏ *reassurances that pesticides are not harmful*

re·assure /ˌriːəˈʃʊə/ VERB [T] (**reassures, reassuring, reassured**) If you **reassure** someone, you say or do things to make them stop worrying about something. ❏ *I tried to reassure her, 'Don't worry about it. We won't let it happen again.'*

re·assur·ing /ˌriːəˈʃʊərɪŋ/ ADJ If you find someone's words or actions **reassuring**, they make you feel less worried about something. ❏ *It was reassuring to hear John's familiar voice.*
re·assur·ing·ly /ˌriːəˈʃʊərɪŋli/ ADV ❏ *'It's okay now,' he said reassuringly.*

re·bate /ˈriːbeɪt/ NOUN [C] (**rebates**) A **rebate** is an amount of money which is returned to you after you have paid for goods or services or after you have paid tax or rent. = refund ❏ *Citicorp will guarantee its credit card customers a rebate on a number of products.*

✿**re·bel** ◆◆◇ NOUN, VERB
NOUN /ˈrebəl/ [C] (**rebels**) **1** **Rebels** are people who are fighting against their own country's army in order to change the political system there. = revolutionary, insurgent ❏ *fighting between rebels and government forces*

r

❑ *Before any instructions could be given, the rebels attacked again, with a much larger force.* **2** Politicians who oppose some of their own party's policies can be referred to as **rebels**. ❑ *The rebels want another 1% cut in interest rates.* **3** You can say that someone is a **rebel** if you think that they behave differently from other people and have rejected the values of society or of their parents. ❑ *She had been a rebel at school.*
[VERB] /rɪˈbel/ [i] (**rebels, rebelling, rebelled**) **1** If politicians **rebel** against one of their own party's policies, they show that they oppose it. ❑ *Voters rebelled against high property taxes.* **2** When someone **rebels**, they start to behave differently from other people and reject the values of society or of their parents. ❑ *The child who rebels is unlikely to be overlooked.*

✪ **re·bel·lion** /rɪˈbeliən/ NOUN [c, u] (**rebellions**) **1** A **rebellion** is a violent organized action by a large group of people who are trying to change their country's political system. = revolt, uprising, insurrection, insurgency ❑ *The government soon put down the rebellion.* ❑ *the ruthless and brutal suppression of rebellion* **2** A situation in which people show their opposition to the way things have been done in the past can be referred to as a **rebellion**. = revolt ❑ *Women are waging a quiet rebellion against the traditional roles their mothers have played.*

re·bel·lious /rɪˈbeliəs/ ADJ **1** If you think someone behaves in an unacceptable way and does not do what they are told, you can say they are **rebellious**. ❑ *a rebellious teenager* **2** [rebellious + N] A **rebellious** group of people is a group involved in taking violent action against the rulers of their own country, usually in order to change the system of government there. ❑ *The rebellious officers, having seized the radio station, broadcast the news of the overthrow of the monarchy.*
re·bel·lious·ness /rɪˈbeliəsnəs/ NOUN [u] ❑ *the normal rebelliousness of youth*

re·birth /ˌriːˈbɜːθ/ NOUN [u] You can refer to a change that leads to a new period of growth and improvement in something as its **rebirth**. ❑ *the rebirth of democracy in Latin America*

re·bound /rɪˈbaʊnd/ VERB [i] (**rebounds, rebounding, rebounded**) **1** If something **rebounds** from a solid surface, it bounces or springs back from it. ❑ *His shot in the 21st minute of the game rebounded from a post.* **2** If an action or situation **rebounds on** you, it has an unpleasant effect on you, especially when this effect was intended for someone else. ❑ *Mia realized her trick had rebounded on her.*

re·build /ˌriːˈbɪld/ VERB [t] (**rebuilds, rebuilding, rebuilt**) **1** When people **rebuild** something such as a building or a city, they build it again after it has been damaged or destroyed. ❑ *They say they will stay to rebuild their homes rather than retreat to refugee camps.* ❑ *The old south grandstand must be rebuilt.* **2** When people **rebuild** something such as an institution, a system, or an aspect of their lives, they take action to bring it back to its previous condition. ❑ *The president's message was that everyone would have to work hard together to rebuild the economy.*

✪ **re·call** ♦♦◇ VERB, NOUN
[VERB] /rɪˈkɔːl/ [i, t] (**recalls, recalling, recalled**) **1** [i, t] When you **recall** something, you remember it and tell others about it. = remember, relate ❑ *Henderson recalled that he first met Pollard during a business trip to Washington.* ❑ *His mother later recalled: 'He used to stay up until two o'clock in the morning playing these war games.'* ❑ *'What was his name?'—'I don't recall.'* ❑ *Colleagues today recall with humour how meetings would crawl into the early morning hours.* **2** [t] If you **are recalled** to your home, country, or the place where you work, you are ordered to return there. ❑ *The US envoy was recalled to Washington.* **3** [t] If a company **recalls** a product, it asks the shops or the people who have bought that product to return it because there is something wrong with it. ❑ *The company said it was recalling one of its drugs and had stopped selling two others.*
[NOUN] /ˈriːkɔːl/ [u, sing, c] **1** [u] **Recall** is the ability to remember something that has happened in the past or the act of remembering it. ❑ *He had a good memory, and total recall of her spoken words.* ❑ *He was impressed by her effortless*

recall of detail. ❑ *his encyclopaedic recall* **2** [sing] **Recall** is when you are ordered to return to your home, country, or the place where you work. ❑ *The recall of Ambassador Alan Green is a public signal of America's concern.* **3** [c] A **recall** is an occasion when a company asks the shops or people who have bought a particular product to return it because there is something wrong with it. ❑ *a recall of the laptops due to defective supply parts*

re·cap /ˈriːkæp/ VERB, NOUN
[VERB] [i, t] (**recaps, recapping, recapped**) You can say that you are going to **recap** when you want to draw people's attention to the fact that you are going to repeat the main points of an explanation, argument, or description, as a summary of it. = sum up, recapitulate ❑ *To recap briefly, the agreement was rejected 10 days ago.* ❑ *Can you recap the points included in the proposal?*
[NOUN] [sing] A **recap** is the repetition of the main points of an explanation, argument, or description, as a summary of it. ❑ *Each report starts with a recap of how we did versus our projections.*

re·cap·ture /ˌriːˈkæptʃə/ VERB, NOUN
[VERB] [t] (**recaptures, recapturing, recaptured**) **1** When soldiers **recapture** an area of land or a place, they gain control of it again from an opposing army who had taken it from them. ❑ *They said the bodies were found when rebels recaptured the area.* **2** When people **recapture** something that they have lost to a competitor, they get it back again. ❑ *I believe that he would be the best possibility to recapture the centre vote in the upcoming election.* **3** To **recapture** a person or animal which has escaped from somewhere means to catch them again. ❑ *Police have recaptured Alan Lewis, who escaped from a jail cell in Boston.*
[NOUN] [sing] **1** The **recapture** of an area of land or a place is when soldiers gain control of it again from an opposing army who had taken it from them. ❑ *an offensive to be launched for the recapture of the city* **2** The **recapture** of a person or animal happens when they have escaped from somewhere and they are caught again. ❑ *the recapture of a renegade police chief in Panama*

re·cede /rɪˈsiːd/ VERB [i] (**recedes, receding, receded**) **1** When something **recedes** from you, it moves away. ❑ *Luke's footsteps receded into the night.* ❑ *As she receded he waved goodbye.* **2** When something such as a quality, problem, or illness **recedes**, it becomes weaker, smaller, or less intense. ❑ *Just as I started to think that I was never going to get well, the illness began to recede.* **3** If a man's hair starts to **recede**, it no longer grows on the front of his head. ❑ *a youngish man with dark hair just beginning to recede*

re·ceipt /rɪˈsiːt/ NOUN
[NOUN] [c, pl, u] (**receipts**) **1** [c] A **receipt** is a piece of paper that you get from someone as proof that they have received money or goods from you. ❑ *I wrote her a receipt for the money.* **2** [pl] **Receipts** are the amount of money received during a particular period, for example by a shop or theatre. = takings ❑ *He was tallying the day's receipts.* **3** [u] (formal) The **receipt** of something is the act of receiving it. ❑ *Goods should be supplied within 28 days after the receipt of your order.*
[PHRASE] **in receipt of** (formal) If you are **in receipt of** something, you have received it or you receive it regularly. ❑ *We are taking action, having been in receipt of a letter from him.*

✪ **re·ceive** ♦♦♦ /rɪˈsiːv/ VERB
[VERB] [t] (**receives, receiving, received**) **1** When you **receive** something, you get it after someone gives it to you or sends it to you. = get; ≠ give, present ❑ *They will receive their awards at a ceremony in Stockholm.* ❑ *I received your letter of November 7.* ❑ *Users receive text messages with regular updates.* **2** You can use **receive** to say that certain kinds of things happen to someone. For example if they are injured, you can say that they **received** an injury. ❑ *He received more of the blame than anyone when the plan failed to work.* **3** When you **receive** a visitor or a guest, you greet them. ❑ *The following evening the hotel was again receiving guests.* **4** If you say that something **is received** in a particular way, you mean that people react to it in that way. ❑ *The resolution had been received with great disappointment within*

the PLO. **5** When a radio or television **receives** signals that are being transmitted, it picks them up and converts them into sound or pictures. ❏ *The reception was a little faint but clear enough for him to receive the signal.*

PHRASE **be on the receiving end** or **be at the receiving end** If you **are on the receiving end** or **at the receiving end** of something unpleasant, you are the person that it happens to. ❏ *You saw hate in their eyes and you were on the receiving end of that hate.*

re·ceiv·er /rɪˈsiːvə/ NOUN [c] (**receivers**) **1** A telephone's **receiver** is the part that you hold near to your ear and speak into. ❏ *She picked up the receiver and started to dial.* **2** A **receiver** is the part of a radio or television that picks up signals and converts them into sound or pictures. ❏ *Auto-tuning VHF receivers are now common in cars.* **3** [usu 'the' receiver] (*business*) **The receiver** is someone who is appointed by a court of law to manage the affairs of a business, usually when it is facing financial failure. ❏ *the receivers handling his bankruptcy case*

✪**re·cent** ♦♦♦ /ˈriːsənt/ ADJ A **recent** event or period of time happened only a short while ago. ❏ *In the most recent attack, one man was shot dead and two others were wounded.* ❏ *Sales have fallen by more than 75 per cent in recent years.*

✪**re·cent·ly** ♦♦◇ /ˈriːsəntli/ ADV If you have done something **recently** or if something happened **recently**, it happened only a short time ago. ❏ *The bank recently opened a branch in Miami.* ❏ *He was until very recently the most powerful banker in the city.*

re·cep·tion /rɪˈsepʃən/ NOUN [c, SING, u] (**receptions**) **1** [c] A **reception** is a formal party which is given to welcome someone or to celebrate a special event. ❏ *At the reception they served smoked salmon.* **2** [SING] ['the' reception, oft reception + N, also 'at' reception] **Reception** in a hotel is the desk or office that books rooms for people and answers their questions. = front desk ❏ *Have him bring a car around to reception.* **3** [SING] ['the' reception, oft reception + N, also 'at' reception] **Reception** in an office or hospital is the place where people's appointments and questions are dealt with. = reception desk ❏ *Wait at reception for me.* **4** [c] If someone or something has a particular kind of **reception**, that is the way that people react to them. ❏ *Mr Mandela was given a warm reception in Washington.* **5** [u] If you get good **reception** from your radio or television, the sound or picture is clear because the signal is strong. If the **reception** is poor, the sound or picture is unclear because the signal is weak. ❏ *poor radio reception*

re·cep·tion·ist /rɪˈsepʃənɪst/ NOUN [c] (**receptionists**) **1** In an office or hospital, the **receptionist** is the person whose job is to answer the telephone, arrange appointments, and deal with people when they first arrive. **2** In a hotel, the **receptionist** is the person whose job is to reserve rooms for people and answer their questions.

re·cep·tive /rɪˈseptɪv/ ADJ **1** Someone who is **receptive** to new ideas or suggestions is prepared to consider them or accept them. ❏ *The voters had seemed receptive to his ideas.* **2** [V-LINK + receptive 'to' N] If someone who is ill is **receptive** to treatment, they start to get better when they are given treatment. ❏ *For those patients who are not receptive to treatment, the chance for improvement is small.*

✪**re·ces·sion** ♦♦◇ /rɪˈseʃən/ NOUN [c, u] (**recessions**) A **recession** is a period when the economy of a country is doing badly, for example because industry is producing less and more people are becoming unemployed. = depression, slump; ≠ boom ❏ *The oil price increases sent Europe into deep recession.* ❏ *The recession caused sales to drop off.* ❏ *We should concentrate on sharply reducing interest rates to pull the economy out of recession.*

reci·pe /ˈresɪpi/ NOUN [c, SING] (**recipes**) **1** [c] A **recipe** is a list of ingredients and a set of instructions that tell you how to cook something. ❏ *a traditional recipe for buttermilk biscuits* **2** [SING] If you say that something is **a recipe for** a particular situation, you mean that it is likely to result in that situation. ❏ *Large-scale inflation is a recipe for disaster.*

re·cipi·ent /rɪˈsɪpiənt/ NOUN [c] (**recipients**) (*formal*) The **recipient** of something is the person who receives it. ❏ *the largest recipient of US foreign aid*

re·cip·ro·cal /rɪˈsɪprəkəl/ ADJ (*formal*) A **reciprocal** action or agreement involves two people or groups who do the same thing to each other or agree to help each other in a similar way. ❏ *They expected a reciprocal gesture before more hostages could be freed.*

reck·less /ˈrekləs/ ADJ If you say that someone is **reckless**, you mean that they act in a way which shows that they do not care about danger or the effect their behaviour will have on other people. ❏ *He is charged with reckless driving.*
reck·less·ly /ˈrekləsli/ ADV ❏ *He was leaning recklessly out of the open window.*
reck·less·ness /ˈrekləsnəs/ NOUN [u] ❏ *He felt a surge of recklessness.*

reck·on ♦◇◇ /ˈrekən/ VERB
VERB [T] (**reckons, reckoning, reckoned**) **1** (*informal*) If you **reckon** that something is true, you think that it is true. = think ❏ *Toni reckoned that it must be about three o'clock.* **2** If something **is reckoned** to be a particular figure, it is calculated to be roughly that amount. ❏ *The market is reckoned to be worth $1.4 bn in the US alone.*
PHRASAL VERB **reckon with** If you say that you had not **reckoned with** something, you mean that you had not expected it and so were not prepared for it. = bargain for, bargain on ❏ *Gary had not reckoned with the strength of Sally's feelings for him.*
PHRASE **to be reckoned with** If you say that there is someone or something **to be reckoned with**, you mean that they must be dealt with and it will be difficult. ❏ *This act was a signal to his victim's friends that he was someone to be reckoned with.*

reck·on·ing /ˈrekənɪŋ/ NOUN [c, u] (**reckonings**) Someone's **reckoning** is a calculation they make about something, especially a calculation that is not very exact. ❏ *By my reckoning we were seven or eight miles from the campground.*

re·claim /rɪˈkleɪm/ VERB [T] (**reclaims, reclaiming, reclaimed**) **1** If you **reclaim** something that you have lost or that has been taken away from you, you succeed in getting it back. ❏ *In 1986, they got the right to reclaim South African citizenship.* **2** If you **reclaim** an amount of money, for example tax that you have paid, you claim it back. ❏ *The good news for the industry was that investors don't seem to be in any hurry to reclaim their money.* **3** When people **reclaim** land, they make it suitable for a purpose such as farming or building, for example by draining it or by building a barrier against the sea. ❏ *The Netherlands has been reclaiming farmland from water.* **4** If a piece of land that was used for farming or building **is reclaimed by** a desert, forest, or the sea, it turns back into desert, forest, or sea. ❏ *The diamond towns are gradually being reclaimed by the desert.*

✪**rec·og·ni·tion** ♦◇◇ /ˌrekəgˈnɪʃən/ NOUN
NOUN [u] **1** **Recognition** is the act of recognizing someone or identifying something when you see it. ❏ *He searched for a sign of recognition on her face, but there was none.* **2** **Recognition of** something is an understanding and acceptance of it. = acknowledgement ❏ *Recognition of the importance of career development is increasing.* ❏ *The CBI welcomed the Chancellor's recognition of the recession.* ❏ *This agreement was a formal recognition of an existing state of affairs.* **3** When a government gives diplomatic **recognition** to another country, they officially accept that its status is valid. ❏ *His government did not receive full recognition by the United States until July.* **4** When a person receives **recognition** for the things that they have done, people acknowledge the value or skill of their work. ❏ *At last, her father's work has received popular recognition.*
PHRASE **in recognition of** If something is done **in recognition of** someone's achievements, it is done as a way of showing official appreciation of them. ❏ *a small plaque in recognition of her contribution to the university*

rec·og·niz·able /ˌrekəgˈnaɪzəbəl/ also **recognisable** ADJ If something can be easily recognized or identified, you can say that it is easily **recognizable**. ❏ *The vault was opened and the body found to be well preserved, his features easily recognizable.*

r

✪ **rec•og•nize** ♦♦◇ /ˈrekəgnaɪz/ also **recognise** VERB
[T] (**recognizes**, **recognizing**, **recognized**) **1** If you
recognize someone or something, you know who that
person is or what that thing is. ❑ *The receptionist recognized
him at once.* **2** If someone says that they **recognize**
something, they acknowledge that it exists or that it is
true. = acknowledge ❑ *I recognize my own shortcomings.*
❑ *We recognized that the situation was becoming increasingly
dangerous.* ❑ *Well, of course I recognize that evil exists.* **3** If
people or organizations **recognize** something as valid,
they officially accept it or approve of it. = accept ❑ *Many
doctors recognize homeopathy as a legitimate form of medicine.*
❑ *France is on the point of recognizing the independence of the
Baltic States.* ❑ *a nationally recognized expert on psychology*
4 When people **recognize** the work that someone has
done, they show their appreciation of it, often by giving
that person an award of some kind. ❑ *The army recognized
him as an outstandingly able engineer.*

WHICH WORD?
recognize, realize, or understand?

If you **recognize** someone or something, you know who
or what they are because you have seen them before, or
because they have been described to you.
❑ *She didn't **recognize** me at first.*
If you **recognize** something such as a problem, you
accept that it exists.
❑ *Governments are beginning to **recognize** the problem.*
If you can **understand** someone, you know what they mean.
❑ *His lecture was confusing; no one could **understand** it.*
If you say that you **understand** that something is true, you
mean that you have been told that it is true.
❑ *I **understand** he's been married before.*
If you become aware of a fact, you do not say that you
'recognize' it or 'understand' it. You say that you **realize** it.
❑ *As soon as I saw him, I **realized** that I'd seen him before.*

re•coil VERB, NOUN
VERB /rɪˈkɔɪl/ [I] (**recoils**, **recoiling**, **recoiled**) **1** If
something makes you **recoil**, you move your body quickly
away from it because it frightens, offends, or hurts you.
❑ *For a moment I thought he was going to kiss me. I recoiled in
horror.* **2** If you **recoil from** doing something or **recoil at**
the idea of something, you refuse to do it or accept it
because you dislike it so much. ❑ *People used to recoil from
the idea of getting into debt.*
NOUN /ˈriːkɔɪl/ [U] The act of **recoil** is when your body
moves quickly away from something because it frightens,
offends, or hurts you. ❑ *his small body jerking in recoil from
the volume of his shouting*

rec•ol•lect /ˌrekəˈlekt/ VERB [T] (**recollects**, **recollecting**,
recollected) If you **recollect** something, you remember it.
= remember ❑ *Ramona spoke with warmth when she
recollected the doctor who used to be at the community hospital.*

rec•ol•lec•tion /ˌrekəˈlekʃən/ NOUN [C, U] (**recollections**)
If you have a **recollection of** something, you remember it.
= memory ❑ *Pat has vivid recollections of the trip, and
remembers some of the frightening aspects I had forgotten.*

✪ **rec•om•mend** ♦♦◇ /ˌrekəˈmend/ VERB [T]
(**recommends**, **recommending**, **recommended**) **1** If
someone **recommends** a person or thing to you, they
suggest that you would find that person or thing good or
useful. = put forward, suggest, commend, advise, advocate
❑ *I just spent a holiday there and would recommend it to anyone.*
❑ *'You're a good worker,' he told him. 'I'll recommend you for
a promotion.'* ❑ *foods that are recommended for diabetics*
❑ *Ask your doctor to recommend a suitable therapist.* **2** If you
recommend that something is done, you suggest that it
should be done. ❑ *The judge recommended that he serve 20
years in prison.* ❑ *We strongly recommend reporting the incident
to the police.* **3** If something or someone has a particular
quality to **recommend** them, that quality makes them
attractive or gives them an advantage over similar things or
people. ❑ *La Cucina restaurant has much to recommend it.*
rec•om•mend•ed /ˌrekəˈmendɪd/ ADJ ❑ *Though ten years
old, this book is highly recommended.*

WORD CONNECTIONS

ADV + **recommend**

highly recommend
strongly recommend

❑ *We would strongly recommend this book to anyone with an
interest in the subject.*

NOUN + **recommend**

doctors recommend
experts recommend

❑ *Doctors recommend eating at least five portions of fruit and
vegetables per day.*

recommend + NOUN

recommend **changes**

❑ *Management consultants visited the company and
recommended changes.*

VOCABULARY BUILDER

recommend VERB
If you **recommend** that something is done, you suggest
that it should be done.
❑ *On 16 December Dr Spencer recommended the suspension
of the programme.*

put forward VERB
If you **put forward** a plan or a proposal, you describe it
and explain how it could be used for a particular purpose.
❑ *He has put forward new peace proposals.*

suggest VERB
If you **suggest** something, you put forward a plan or idea
for someone to think about.
❑ *I suggest you ask him some specific questions about his
past.*

commend VERB (formal)
If someone **commends** a person or thing to you, they tell
you that you will find them good or useful.
❑ *I can commend it to him as a realistic course of action.*

advise VERB
If you **advise** someone to do something, you tell them
what you think they should do.
❑ *The minister advised him to leave as soon as possible.*

advocate VERB (formal)
If you **advocate** a particular action or plan, you
recommend it publicly.
❑ *Mr Williams advocates fewer government controls on
business.*

✪ **rec•om•men•da•tion** ♦◇◇ /ˌrekəmenˈdeɪʃən/ NOUN
[C, U] (**recommendations**) **1** The **recommendations** of a
person or a committee are their suggestions or advice on
what is the best thing to do. = suggestion, advice ❑ *The
committee's recommendations are unlikely to be made public.*
❑ *The decision was made on the recommendation of the Interior
Minister.* **2** A **recommendation** of something is the
suggestion that someone should have or use it because it is
good. ❑ *The best way of finding a lawyer is through personal
recommendation.*

rec•on•cile /ˈrekənsaɪl/ VERB [T, RECIP-PASSIVE] (**reconciles**,
reconciling, **reconciled**) **1** [T] If you **reconcile** two beliefs,
facts, or demands that seem to be opposed or completely
different, you find a way in which they can both be true
or both be successful. ❑ *It's difficult to reconcile the demands
of my job and the desire to be a good father.* **2** [RECIP-PASSIVE] If
you **are reconciled with** someone, you become friendly
with them again after a quarrel or disagreement. ❑ *He
never believed he and Susan would be reconciled.* **3** [T] If you
reconcile two people, you make them become friends
again after a quarrel or disagreement. ❑ *my attempt to
reconcile him with Toby* **4** [T] If you **reconcile yourself to** an
unpleasant situation, you accept it, although it does not

R

make you happy to do so. ❑ *She had reconciled herself to never seeing him again.*

rec·on·ciled /ˈrekənsaɪld/ ADJ ❑ *She felt, if not grateful for her own situation, at least a little more reconciled to it.*

rec·on·cil·ia·tion /ˌrekənsɪliˈeɪʃən/ NOUN [C, U, SING] (reconciliations) **1** [C, U] Reconciliation between two people or countries who have quarrelled is the process of their becoming friends again. A **reconciliation** is an instance of this. ❑ *an appeal for reconciliation between Catholics and Protestants* **2** [SING] The **reconciliation** of two beliefs, facts, or demands that seem to be opposed is the process of finding a way in which they can both be true or both be successful. ❑ *the ideal of democracy based upon a reconciliation of the values of equality and liberty*

re·con·sid·er /ˌriːkənˈsɪdə/ VERB [I, T] (reconsiders, reconsidering, reconsidered) If you **reconsider** a decision or opinion, you think about it and try to decide whether it should be changed. ❑ *We want you to reconsider your decision to resign from the board.* ❑ *If at the end of two years you still feel the same, we will reconsider.*

re·con·struc·tion /ˌriːkənˈstrʌkʃən/ NOUN [U, C] (reconstructions) **1** [U] Reconstruction is the process of making a country normal again after a war, for example by making the economy stronger and by replacing buildings that have been damaged. ❑ *America's part in the postwar reconstruction of Germany* ❑ *the Reconstruction period immediately following the civil war* **2** [U] The **reconstruction** of a building, structure, or road is the activity of building it again, because it has been damaged. ❑ *Work began on the reconstruction of the road.* **3** [C] The **reconstruction** of a crime or event is when people try to understand or show exactly what happened, often by acting it out. ❑ *Mrs Kerr was too upset to take part in a reconstruction of her ordeal.*

⭐**rec·ord** ♦♦♦ NOUN, VERB, ADJ

NOUN /ˈrekɔːd, [C] (AmE) -kərd/ (records) **1** If you keep a **record of** something, you keep a written account or photographs of it so that it can be referred to later. = document, journal, database, register, file ❑ *Keep a record of all the payments.* ❑ *There's no record of any marriage or children.* ❑ *The result will go on your medical records.* **2** A **record** is a round, flat piece of black plastic on which sound, especially music, is stored, and which can be played on a record player. You can also refer to the music stored on this piece of plastic as a **record**. ❑ *This is one of my favourite records.* **3** A **record** is the best result that has ever been achieved in a particular sport or activity, for example the fastest time, the farthest distance, or the greatest number of victories. ❑ *Roger Kingdom set the world record of 12.92 seconds.* **4** Someone's **record** is the facts that are known about their achievements or character. ❑ *His record reveals a tough streak.* **5** If someone has a criminal **record**, it is officially known that they have committed crimes in the past. ❑ *a heroin addict with a criminal record going back 15 years*

PHRASES **for the record 1** If you say that what you are going to say next is **for the record**, you mean that you are saying it publicly and officially and you want it to be written down and remembered. ❑ *We're willing to state for the record that it has enormous value.* **2** If you give some information **for the record**, you give it in case people might find it useful at a later time, although it is not a very important part of what you are talking about. ❑ *For the record, most Moscow girls leave school at about 18.*

off the record If something that you say is **off the record**, you do not intend it to be considered as official, or published with your name attached to it. ❑ *May I speak off the record?*

on record 1 If you are **on record as** saying something, you have said it publicly and officially and it has been written down. ❑ *The president is on record as saying that the increase in unemployment is 'a price worth paying' to keep inflation down.* **2** If you keep information **on record**, you write it down or store it in a computer so that it can be used later. ❑ *The practice is to keep on record any analysis of samples.*

VERB /rɪˈkɔːd/ [T] (records, recording, recorded) **1** If you **record** a piece of information or an event, you write it

down, photograph it, or put it into a computer so that in the future people can refer to it. = document, report ❑ *Her letters record the domestic and social details of diplomatic life in China.* ❑ *Up to five wives, and sometimes in excess of twenty, are recorded in some tribes.* ❑ *a place which has rarely suffered a famine in its recorded history* **2** If you **record** something such as a speech or performance, you put it on tape or film so that it can be heard or seen again later. ❑ *There is nothing to stop viewers from recording the films on videotape.* **3** If a musician or performer **records** a piece of music or a television or radio show, they perform it so that it can be put onto CD, tape, or film. ❑ *It took the musicians two and a half days to record their soundtrack for the film.* **4** If a dial or other measuring device **records** a certain measurement or value, it shows that measurement or value. ❑ *The test records the electrical activity of the brain.* ADJ /ˈrekɔːd, AmE -kərd/ [record + N] You use **record** to say that something is higher, lower, better, or worse than has ever been achieved before. ❑ *Profits were at record levels.* → See also **recording**

re·cord·er /rɪˈkɔːdə/ NOUN [C, U] (recorders) **1** [C] You can refer to a cassette recorder, a tape recorder, or a video recorder as a **recorder**. ❑ *Rodney put the recorder on the desk top and pushed the play button.* **2** [C, U] A **recorder** is a wooden or plastic musical instrument in the shape of a pipe. You play the recorder by blowing into the top of it and covering and uncovering the holes with your fingers. **3** [C] A **recorder** is a machine or instrument that keeps a record of something, for example in an experiment or on a vehicle. ❑ *Data recorders also pinpoint mechanical faults rapidly, reducing repair times.*

re·cord·ing ♦◇◇ /rɪˈkɔːdɪŋ/ NOUN [C, U] (recordings) **1** [C] A **recording** of something is a record, CD, tape, or video of it. ❑ *a video recording of a police interview* **2** [U] Recording is the process of making records, CDs, tapes, or videos. ❑ *the recording industry*

⭐**re·cov·er** ♦◇◇ /rɪˈkʌvə/ VERB [I, T] (recovers, recovering, recovered) (academic word) **1** [I] When you **recover from** an illness or an injury, you become well again. = recuperate; ≠ relapse ❑ *He is recovering from a knee injury.* ❑ *A policeman was recovering in hospital last night after being stabbed.* ❑ *He is fully recovered from the virus.* **2** [I] If you **recover from** an unhappy or unpleasant experience, you stop being upset by it. ❑ *a tragedy from which he never fully recovered* **3** [I] If something **recovers from** a period of weakness or difficulty, it improves or gets stronger again. = rally ❑ *He recovered from a 4-2 deficit to reach the quarter-finals.* ❑ *The stock market index fell by 80% before it began to recover.* **4** [T] If you **recover** something that has been lost or stolen, you find it or get it back. = retrieve ❑ *Police raided five houses in Brooklyn and recovered stolen goods.* **5** [T] If you **recover** a mental or physical state, it comes back again. For example, if you **recover** consciousness, you become conscious again. = regain ❑ *She had a severe attack of asthma and it took an hour to recover her breath.* **6** [T] If you **recover** money that you have spent, invested, or lent to someone, you get the same amount back. = recoup ❑ *Legal action is being taken to recover the money.*

WORD CONNECTIONS
recover + FROM + NOUN
recover from an **illness** recover from an **injury** recover from an **operation** ❑ *She is at home recovering from an illness.*
recover from **recession** recover from a **setback** ❑ *Property prices are rising again after recovering from a setback last quarter.*
ADV + **recover**
quickly recover **fully** recover **completely** recover ❑ *It could take him months to fully recover from his injuries.*

r

✪ re·cov·ery ◆◇◇ /rɪˈkʌvəri/ NOUN

NOUN [c, u] (**recoveries**) **1** [c, u] If a sick person makes a **recovery**, he or she becomes well again. ❑ *He made a remarkable recovery from a shin injury.* ❑ *He had been given less than a one in 500 chance of recovery by his doctors.* **2** [c, u] When there is a **recovery** in a country's economy, it improves. ❑ *Interest-rate cuts have failed to bring about economic recovery.* ❑ *In many sectors of the economy the recovery has started.* **3** [u] You talk about the **recovery of** something when you get it back after it has been lost or stolen. ❑ *A substantial reward is being offered for the recovery of a painting by Turner.* **4** [u] You talk about the **recovery of** someone's physical or mental state when they return to this state. ❑ *the abrupt loss and recovery of consciousness*

PHRASE **in recovery** If someone is **in recovery**, they are being given a course of treatment to help them recover from something such as a drug habit or mental illness. ❑ *Carole, a compulsive pot smoker and alcoholic in recovery*

WORD CONNECTIONS
ADJ + **recovery**
a **rapid** recovery
a **remarkable** recovery
a **full** recovery
❑ *His doctors expect him to make a full recovery.*
an **economic** recovery
a **sustainable** recovery
❑ *There are encouraging signs of economic recovery.*
VERB + **recovery**
make a recovery
❑ *The surgery is straightforward and most patients make a rapid recovery.*
predict a recovery
expect a recovery
bring about recovery
❑ *Most economists are predicting a recovery in the new year.*

re·cre·ate /ˌriːkriˈeɪt/ VERB [T] (**recreates, recreating, recreated**) If you **recreate** something, you succeed in making it exist or seem to exist in a different time or place from its original time or place. ❑ *I am trying to recreate family life far from home.*

rec·rea·tion NOUN [c, u] (**recreations**) **1** /ˌrekriˈeɪʃən/ [c, u] **Recreation** consists of things that you do in your spare time to relax. ❑ *Saturday afternoon is for recreation and outings.* **2** /ˌriːkriˈeɪʃən/ [c] A **recreation of** something is the process of making it exist or seem to exist again in a different time or place. ❑ *They are planning to build a faithful recreation of the original frontier town.*

rec·rea·tion·al /ˌrekriˈeɪʃənəl/ ADJ **Recreational** means relating to things people do in their spare time to relax. ❑ *parks and other recreational facilities*

re·cruit ◆◇◇ /rɪˈkruːt/ VERB, NOUN

VERB [T] (**recruits, recruiting, recruited**) If you **recruit** people for an organization, you select them and persuade them to join it or work for it. ❑ *The police are trying to recruit more black and Hispanic officers.* ❑ *She set up her stand to recruit students to the Anarchist Association.*

NOUN [c] (**recruits**) A **recruit** is a person who has recently joined an organization or an army. ❑ *a new recruit to the LA Police Department*

re·cruit·ing /rɪˈkruːtɪŋ/ NOUN [u] ❑ *A bomb exploded at an army recruiting office.*

re·cruit·ment /rɪˈkruːtmənt/ NOUN [u] The **recruitment** of workers, soldiers, or members is the act or process of selecting them for an organization or army and persuading them to join. ❑ *the examination system for the recruitment of civil servants*

✪ rec·tan·gle /ˈrektæŋɡəl/ NOUN [c] (**rectangles**) A **rectangle** is a four-sided shape whose corners are all ninety-degree angles. Each side of a rectangle is the same length as the one opposite to it. ❑ *a long rectangle of grass* ❑ *a number of regularly spaced rectangles* = oblong

✪ rec·tan·gu·lar /rekˈtæŋɡjʊlə/ ADJ Something that is **rectangular** is shaped like a rectangle. ❑ *a rectangular table* ❑ *a pattern of lines and rectangular shapes*

rec·ti·fy /ˈrektɪfaɪ/ VERB [T] (**rectifies, rectifying, rectified**) If you **rectify** something that is wrong, you change it so that it becomes correct or satisfactory. ❑ *Only an act of Congress could rectify the situation.*

re·cu·per·ate /rɪˈkuːpəreɪt/ VERB [I] (**recuperates, recuperating, recuperated**) When you **recuperate**, you recover your health or strength after you have been ill or injured. = recover ❑ *I went away to the country to recuperate.*

re·cu·pera·tion /rɪˌkuːpəˈreɪʃən/ NOUN [u] = recovery ❑ *Leonard was very pleased with his powers of recuperation.*

re·cur /rɪˈkɜː/ VERB [I] (**recurs, recurring, recurred**) If something **recurs**, it happens more than once. ❑ *a theme that was to recur frequently in his work*

re·cur·rence /rɪˈkʌrəns, AmE -ˈkɜːr-/ NOUN [c, u] (**recurrences**) If there is a **recurrence** of something, it happens again. ❑ *Police are out in force to prevent a recurrence of the violence.*

re·cur·rent /rɪˈkʌrənt, AmE -ˈkɜːr-/ ADJ A **recurrent** event or feeling happens or is experienced more than once. ❑ *Race is a recurrent theme in the work.*

✪ re·cy·cle /ˌriːˈsaɪkəl/ VERB [T] (**recycles, recycling, recycled**) If you **recycle** things that have already been used, such as bottles or sheets of paper, you process them so that they can be used again. = reuse ❑ *The objective would be to recycle 98 per cent of domestic waste.* ❑ *All glass bottles which can't be refilled can be recycled.* ❑ *printed on recycled paper*

✪ re·cy·cling /ˌriːˈsaɪklɪŋ/ NOUN [u] ❑ *a recycling plan* ❑ *a plan to increase recycling of household waste*

red ◆◆◆ /red/ COLOUR, ADJ, NOUN

COLOUR Something that is **red** is the colour of blood or fire. ❑ *a bunch of red roses*

PHRASES **in the red** If a person or company is **in the red** or if their bank account is **in the red**, they have spent more money than they have in their account and therefore they owe money to the bank. ❑ *The theatre is $500,000 in the red.*

see red If you **see red**, you suddenly become very angry. ❑ *I didn't mean to break his nose. I just saw red.*

ADJ (**redder, reddest**) **1** If you say that someone's face is **red**, you mean that it is redder than its normal colour, because they are embarrassed, angry, or out of breath. ❑ *With a bright red face I was forced to admit that I had no real idea.* **2** You describe someone's hair as **red** when it is between red and brown in colour. ❑ *a girl with red hair*

NOUN [c, u] (**reds**) You can refer to red wine as **red**. ❑ *The spicy flavours in these dishes call for reds rather than whites.*

✪ re·de·fine /ˌriːdɪˈfaɪn/ VERB [T] (**redefines, redefining, redefined**) (*academic word*) If you **redefine** something, you cause people to consider it in a new way. = reinvent ❑ *Feminists have redefined the role of women.* ❑ *We will finally have to redefine our relationship with neighbouring states in north Africa.*

re·devel·op·ment /ˌriːdɪˈveləpmənt/ NOUN [u] When **redevelopment** takes place, the buildings in one area of a town are knocked down and new ones are built in their place. ❑ *The group's intention is to clear the site for redevelopment.*

✪ re·dis·trib·ute /ˌriːdɪˈstrɪbjuːt/ VERB [T] (**redistributes, redistributing, redistributed**) (*academic word*) If something such as money or property **is redistributed**, it is shared among people or organizations in a different way from the way that it was previously shared. ❑ *Wealth was redistributed more equitably among society.* ❑ *Taxes could be used to redistribute income.*

✪ re·dis·tri·bu·tion /ˌriːdɪstrɪˈbjuːʃən/ NOUN [u] ❑ *One of government's primary duties is the redistribution of income, so that the better off can help the worse off out of poverty.* ❑ *Others also believe that Labour has now abandoned support for the redistribution of power and wealth.*

re·dress /rɪˈdres/ VERB, NOUN

VERB [T] (**redresses, redressing, redressed**) (*formal*) **1** If

R

you **redress** something such as a wrong or a complaint, you do something to correct it or to improve things for the person who has been badly treated. ☐ *More and more victims turn to litigation to redress wrongs done to them.* **2** If you **redress** the balance or the imbalance between two things that have become unfair or unequal, you make them fair and equal again. ☐ *So we're trying to redress the balance and to give teachers a sense that both spoken and written language are equally important.* **NOUN** [u] (*formal*) **Redress** is money that someone pays you because they have caused you harm or loss. = compensation ☐ *They are continuing their legal battle to seek some redress from the government.*

red tape NOUN [u] (*disapproval*) You refer to official rules and procedures as **red tape** when they seem unnecessary and cause delay. ☐ *The little money that was available was tied up in bureaucratic red tape.*

⭐**re·duce** ♦♦◇ /rɪ'dju:s, *AmE* -'du:s/ VERB
VERB [T, I] (**reduces, reducing, reduced**) **1** [T] If you **reduce** something, you make it smaller in size or amount, or less in degree. = decrease, lessen, lower ☐ *It reduces the risks of heart disease.* ☐ *Consumption is being reduced by 25 per cent.* ☐ *The reduced consumer demand is also affecting company profits.* **2** [T] If someone **is reduced to** a weaker or inferior state, they become weaker or inferior as a result of something that happens to them. ☐ *They were reduced to extreme poverty.* **3** [T] If you say that someone **is reduced to** doing something, you mean that they have to do it, although it is unpleasant or embarrassing. ☐ *He was reduced to begging for a living.* **4** [T] If something is changed to a different or less complicated form, you can say that it **is reduced to** that form. ☐ *All the buildings in the town have been reduced to rubble.* **5** [I, T] If you **reduce** liquid when you are cooking, or if it **reduces**, it is boiled in order to make it less in quantity and thicker. ☐ *Boil the liquid in a small saucepan to reduce it by half.*
PHRASE **reduce to tears** If someone or something **reduces** you **to tears**, they make you feel so unhappy that you cry. ☐ *The attentions of the media reduced her to tears.*

WORD CONNECTIONS

reduce + NOUN

reduce the **number**
reduce the **rate**
reduce the **level**
☐ *The aim of the campaign is to reduce the number of deaths caused by fire.*

reduce **costs**
reduce **waste**
reduce **emissions**
☐ *The company set an objective of reducing emissions by 10% within 12 months.*

ADV + **reduce**

dramatically reduce
significantly reduce
substantially reduce
☐ *The chemical, which is harmless to livestock, could dramatically reduce mosquito populations.*

⭐**re·duc·tion** ♦♦◇ /rɪ'dʌkʃən/ NOUN [c, u] (**reductions**)
1 [c] When there is a **reduction** in something, it is made smaller. = decrease, lowering ☐ *a future reduction in interest rates* ☐ *This morning's inflation figures show a reduction of 0.2 per cent from 5.8 per cent to 5.6.* ☐ *Many companies have announced dramatic reductions in staff.* **2** [u] **Reduction** is the act of making something smaller in size or amount, or less in degree. ☐ *a new strategic arms reduction agreement*

WORD CONNECTIONS

reduction + IN + NOUN

a reduction in **mortality**
a reduction in **emissions**
a reduction in a **rate**
☐ *We have already achieved a 30% reduction in emissions.*

VERB + **reduction**

achieve a reduction
announce a reduction
mean a reduction
☐ *The cuts will mean a reduction in staff numbers.*

ADJ + **reduction**

a **significant** reduction
a **dramatic** reduction
a **further** reduction
☐ *Campaigners have called for a further reduction in fuel prices.*

⭐**re·dun·dan·cy** /rɪ'dʌndənsi/ NOUN [u, c]
(**redundancies**) (*business*) **1** [u] **Redundancy** means being made redundant. ☐ *Thousands of bank employees are facing redundancy as their employers cut costs.* ☐ *The company has had to make redundancy payments of £472 million.* **2** [c] (*BrE*; in *AmE*, use **dismissals**) When there are **redundancies**, an organization tells some of its employees to leave because their jobs are no longer necessary or because the organization can no longer afford to pay them. ☐ *The ministry has said it hopes to avoid compulsory redundancies.*

⭐**re·dun·dant** /rɪ'dʌndənt/ ADJ **1** Something that is **redundant** is unnecessary, for example, because it is no longer needed or because its job is being done by something else. ☐ *Changes in technology may mean that once-valued skills are now redundant.* ☐ *the conversion of redundant buildings to residential use* **2** (*BrE*; in *AmE*, use **be dismissed**; *business*) If you are made **redundant**, your employer tells you to leave because your job is no longer necessary or because your employer cannot afford to keep paying you. ☐ *My husband was made redundant late last year.* ☐ *a redundant miner*

reel ♦◇◇ /ri:l/ NOUN, VERB
NOUN [c] (**reels**) A **reel** is a cylindrical object around which you wrap something such as film tape, magnetic tape, or fishing line. ☐ *a 30-metre reel of cable*
VERB [I] (**reels, reeling, reeled**) **1** If someone **reels**, they move about in an unsteady way as if they are going to fall. ☐ *He is reeling a little. He must be very drunk.* **2** If you **are reeling** from a shock, you are feeling extremely surprised or upset because of it. ☐ *I'm still reeling from the shock of hearing about it.* **3** If you say that your brain or your mind **is reeling**, you mean that you are very confused because you have too many things to think about. ☐ *His mind reeled at the question.*
PHRASAL VERB **reel off** If you **reel off** information, you repeat it from memory quickly and easily. ☐ *She reeled off the titles of a dozen or so of the novels.*

re·elect VERB [T] (**re-elects, re-electing, re-elected**) When someone such as a politician or an official who has been elected **is re-elected**, they win another election and are therefore able to continue in their position as, for example, president, or an official in an organization. ☐ *He needs 51 per cent to be re-elected.* ☐ *James Rhodes was re-elected governor of Ohio.*

re·election NOUN [u] The **re-election** of someone such as a politician or a public official, is the act of winning another election which allows them to continue in their position. ☐ *He is heavily favoured to win re-election.*

⭐**re·fer** ♦♦◇ /rɪ'fɜ:/ VERB [I, T] (**refers, referring, referred**)
1 [I] If you **refer to** a particular subject or person, you talk about them or mention them. = mention, cite ☐ *In his speech, he referred to a recent trip to Canada.* ☐ *'What precisely is your interest in the patient referred to here?'* **2** [I] If you **refer to** someone or something **as** a particular thing, you use a particular word, expression, or name to mention or describe them. = allude, call, describe ☐ *Marcia had referred to him as a dear friend.* ☐ *Our economy is referred to as a free market.* **3** [I] If a word **refers to** a particular thing, situation, or idea, it describes it in some way. = describe, relate to, apply to ☐ *The term electronics refers to electrically induced action.* ☐ *English prefers nouns to verbs – that is, words which refer to objects rather than words which refer to actions.* **4** [T] If a person who is ill **is referred to** a hospital or a

r

specialist, they are sent there by a doctor in order to be treated. ❑ *She was referred to the hospital by a neighbourhood clinic.* **5** [T] If you **refer** a task or a problem **to** a person or an organization, you formally tell them about it, so that they can deal with it. ❑ *He could refer the matter to the high court.* **6** [T] If you **refer** someone **to** a person or organization, you send them there for the help they need. ❑ *Now and then I referred a client to him.* **7** [I] If you **refer to** a book or other source of information, you look at it in order to find something out, often to mention it in your own work. = allude to, mention, cite ❑ *He referred briefly to his notebook.* ❑ *Concerning its origins we should like to refer to E F Schumacher, to the fieldwork of K Hart and to the theoretical work of M Lipton.* **8** [T] If you **refer** someone **to** a source of information, you tell them the place where they will find the information they need or that you think will interest them. ❑ *Mr Bryan also referred me to a book by the American journalist Anthony Scaduto.*

VOCABULARY BUILDER

refer VERB *(fairly formal)*

If you **refer to** a particular subject or person, you talk or write about them.

❑ *The newspaper headline referred to events of the preceding Thursday.*

mention VERB

If you **mention** something, you say or write something about it, usually briefly.

❑ *Sydney University's Professor of Medicine did not even mention insulin when lecturing on diabetes in 1923.*

cite VERB

If you **cite** a particular subject or person, you talk or write about them.

❑ *The researchers cite various examples of this phenomenon.*

touch on VERB

If you **touch on** a particular subject or problem, you speak or write briefly about it, but it is not your main subject.

❑ *The film touches on these issues, but only superficially.*

quote VERB

If you **quote** someone as saying something, you repeat what they have written or said.

❑ *Mawby and Gill (1987) quote this passage from the Home Office White Paper, 1964.*

ref•er•ee /ˌrefəˈriː/ NOUN, VERB

NOUN [c] **(referees)** **1** The **referee** is the official who controls a sports event such as a football game or a boxing match. **2** *(BrE; in AmE, use reference)* A **referee** is a person who gives you a reference, for example when you are applying for a job.

VERB [I, T] **(referees, refereeing, refereed)** When someone **referees** a sports event or contest, they act as referee. ❑ *Vautrot has refereed in two World Cups.*

✪**ref•er•ence** ◆◇◇ /ˈrefərəns/ NOUN, ADJ

NOUN [c, u] **(references)** **1** [c, u] **Reference to** someone or something is the act of talking about them or mentioning them. A **reference** is a particular example of this. ❑ *He made no reference to any agreement.* **2** [u] **Reference** is the act of consulting someone or something in order to get information or advice. ❑ *Please keep this sheet in a safe place for reference.* **3** [c] A **reference** is a word, phrase, or idea which comes from something such as a book, poem, or play and which you use when making a point about something. = quote, allusion ❑ *a reference from the Koran* ❑ *historical references* ❑ *In Doyle's prison file there's a reference to a military intelligence report.* **4** [c] A **reference** is something such as a number or a name that tells you where you can obtain the information you want. ❑ *Make a note of the reference number shown on the form.* **5** [c] A **reference** is a letter that is written by someone who knows you and which describes your character and abilities. When you apply for a job, an employer might ask for **references**. ❑ *The firm offered to give her a reference.*

PHRASE **with reference to** or **in reference to** You use **with reference to** or **in reference to** in order to indicate what something relates to. ❑ *I am writing with reference to your article on salaries for scientists.*

ADJ [reference + N] **Reference** books are ones that you look at when you need specific information or facts about a subject. ❑ *a useful reference work for teachers*

ref•er•en•dum ◆◇◇ /ˌrefəˈrendəm/ NOUN [c] **(referendums** or **referenda)** If a country holds a **referendum** on a particular policy, they ask the people to vote on the policy and show whether or not they agree with it. ❑ *Estonia said today it too plans to hold a referendum on independence.*

re•fill VERB, NOUN

VERB /riːˈfɪl/ [T] **(refills, refilling, refilled)** If you **refill** something, you fill it again after it has been emptied. ❑ *I refilled our wine glasses.*

NOUN /ˈriːfɪl/ [c] **(refills)** **1** *(informal)* A **refill** is the act of refilling something again after it has been emptied. ❑ *Max held out his cup for a refill.* **2** A **refill** of a particular product is a quantity of that product sold in a cheaper container than the one it is usually sold in. You use a refill to fill the more permanent container when it is empty. ❑ *Refill packs are cheaper and lighter.*

✪**re•fine** /rɪˈfaɪn/ VERB [T] **(refines, refining, refined)** *(academic word)* **1** When a substance **is refined**, it is made pure by having all other substances removed from it. = process ❑ *Oil is refined to remove naturally occurring impurities.* ❑ *All white sugar is refined, however, this refined sugar may then be ground or coloured.* **2** If something such as a process, theory, or machine **is refined**, it is improved by having small changes made to it. = improve ❑ *Surgical techniques are constantly being refined.* ❑ *Twentieth century botanists have continually refined these classifications.* **re•fin•ing** /rɪˈfaɪnɪŋ/ NOUN [u] ❑ *oil refining*

re•fined /rɪˈfaɪnd/ ADJ **1** A **refined** substance has been made pure by having other substances removed from it. ❑ *refined sugar* **2** If you say that someone **is refined**, you mean that they are very polite and have good manners and good taste. = genteel ❑ *refined and well-dressed ladies* **3** If you describe a machine or a process as **refined**, you mean that it has been carefully developed and is therefore very efficient or elegant. ❑ *This technique is becoming more refined and more acceptable all the time.*

✪**re•fine•ment** /rɪˈfaɪnmənt/ NOUN [c, u] **(refinements)** **1** [c, u] **Refinements** are small changes or additions that you make to something in order to improve it. **Refinement** is the process of making refinements. = improvement ❑ *Older cars inevitably lack the latest safety refinements.* ❑ *development and refinement of the game* **2** [u] **Refinement** is politeness and good manners.

✪**re•flect** ◆◆◇ /rɪˈflekt/ VERB [T, I] **(reflects, reflecting, reflected)** **1** [T] If something **reflects** an attitude or situation, it shows that the attitude or situation exists or it shows what it is like. = show ❑ *A newspaper report seems to reflect the view of most members of Congress.* ❑ *The Los Angeles riots reflected the bitterness between the black and Korean communities in the city.* ❑ *Concern at the economic situation was reflected in the government's budget.* **2** [I, T] When light, heat, or other rays **reflect** off a surface or when a surface **reflects** them, they are sent back from the surface and do not pass through it. ❑ *The sun reflected off the snow-covered mountains.* ❑ *The glass appears to reflect light naturally.* **3** [T] When something **is reflected** in a mirror or in water, you can see its image in the mirror or in the water. ❑ *His image was reflected many times in the mirror.* **4** [I] When you **reflect on** something, you think deeply about it. ❑ *We should all give ourselves time to reflect.* **5** [T] You can use **reflect** to indicate that a particular thought occurs to someone. ❑ *Things were very much changed since before the war, he reflected.* **6** [I] If an action or situation **reflects** in a particular way **on** someone or something, it gives people a good or bad impression of them. ❑ *The affair hardly reflected well on the president.*

✪**re•flec•tion** /rɪˈflekʃən/ NOUN

NOUN [c, u, SING] **(reflections)** **1** [c] A **reflection** is an image that you can see in a mirror or in glass or water.

❏ *Meg stared at her reflection in the bedroom mirror.* **2** [U] **Reflection** is the process by which light and heat are sent back from a surface and do not pass through it. ❏ *the reflection of a beam of light off a mirror* **3** [C] If you say that something is a **reflection of** a particular person's attitude or **of** a situation, you mean that it is caused by that attitude or situation and therefore reveals something about it. = indication ❏ *Inhibition in adulthood seems to be a reflection of a person's experiences as a child.* **4** [SING] If something is a **reflection** or a **sad reflection on** a person or thing, it gives a bad impression of them. ❏ *Infection with head lice is no reflection on personal hygiene.* **5** [U] [also reflections] **Reflection** is careful thought about a particular subject. Your **reflections** are your thoughts about a particular subject. ❏ *After days of reflection she decided to write back.*

PHRASE **on reflection** If someone admits or accepts something **on reflection**, they admit or accept it after having thought carefully about it. ❏ *While the news at first shocked me, on reflection it made perfect sense.*

re·flec·tive /rɪˈflektɪv/ ADJ **1** (written) If you are **reflective**, you are thinking deeply about something. ❏ *I walked on in a reflective mood to the car, thinking about the poor honeymooners.* **2** [V-LINK + reflective 'of' N] If something is **reflective of** a particular situation or attitude, it is typical of that situation or attitude, or is a consequence of it. ❏ *The German government's support of the US is not entirely reflective of German public opinion.* **3** (formal) A **reflective** surface or material sends back light or heat. ❏ *Avoid using pans with a shiny, reflective base as the heat will be reflected back.*

❍ **re·form** ◆◆◇ /rɪˈfɔːm/ NOUN, VERB
NOUN [C, U] (reforms) **Reform** consists of changes and improvements to a law, social system, or institution. A **reform** is an instance of such a change or improvement. = improvement, amendment, reorganization ❏ *The party embarked on a programme of economic reform.* ❏ *He has urged reform of the welfare system.* ❏ *The Socialists introduced fairly radical reforms.*
VERB [T, I] (reforms, reforming, reformed) **1** [T] If someone **reforms** something such as a law, social system, or institution, they change or improve it. = improve, amend, reorganize ❏ *his plans to reform the country's economy* ❏ *A reformed party would have to win the approval of the people.* ❏ *proposals to reform the tax system* **2** [I, T] When someone **reforms** or when something **reforms** them, they stop doing things that society does not approve of, such as breaking the law or drinking too much alcohol. ❏ *When his court case was coming up, James promised to reform.*
re·formed /rɪˈfɔːmd/ ADJ ❏ *a reformed alcoholic*

WORD CONNECTIONS
VERB + **reform**
need reform
promise reform
demand reform
❏ *The country's education system is failing and desperately needs reform.*
introduce reform
implement reform
❏ *The new government-introduced reforms aimed at making the judiciary constitutionally independent.*
ADJ + **reform**
economic reform
political reform
electoral reform
❏ *His party have been the main proponents of electoral reform.*
NOUN + **reform**
education reform
welfare reform
tax reform
❏ *Congress introduced sweeping tax reforms, including a plan to eliminate estate tax.*

❍ **re·form·er** /rɪˈfɔːmə/ NOUN [C] (reformers) A **reformer** is someone who tries to change and improve something such as a law or a social system. ❏ *How could he be a reformer and a defender of established interests at the same time?* ❏ *Charles Dickens, novelist and social reformer* ❏ *Political reformers, in attacking the wrong issue, only made the situation worse.*

re·frain /rɪˈfreɪn/ VERB, NOUN
VERB [I] (refrains, refraining, refrained) If you **refrain from** doing something, you deliberately do not do it. ❏ *Mrs Hardie refrained from making any comment.*
NOUN [C] (refrains) **1** A **refrain** is a short, simple part of a song, which is repeated many times. ❏ *a refrain from an old song* **2** A **refrain** is a comment or saying that people often repeat. ❏ *Rosa's constant refrain is that she doesn't have a life.*

re·fresh /rɪˈfreʃ/ VERB [T] (refreshes, refreshing, refreshed) **1** If something **refreshes** you when you are hot, tired, or thirsty, it makes you feel cooler or more energetic. ❏ *The lotion cools and refreshes the skin.* **2** If you **refresh** something old or dull, you make it as good as it was when it was new. ❏ *Many view these meetings as an occasion to share ideas and refresh friendship.* **3** If someone **refreshes** your memory, they tell you something that you had forgotten. ❏ *He walked on the opposite side of the street to refresh his memory of the building.* **4** (computing) If you **refresh** a web page, you click a button in order to get the most recent version of the page. ❏ *I've refreshed the page a few times and still see no comments.*
re·freshed /rɪˈfreʃt/ ADJ ❏ *He awoke feeling completely refreshed.*

re·fresh·ing /rɪˈfreʃɪŋ/ ADJ **1** You say that something is **refreshing** when it is pleasantly different from what you are used to. ❏ *It's refreshing to hear somebody speaking common sense.* **2** A **refreshing** bath or drink makes you feel energetic or cool again after you have been tired or hot. ❏ *Herbs have been used for centuries to make refreshing drinks.*
re·fresh·ing·ly /rɪˈfreʃɪŋli/ ADV ❏ *He was refreshingly honest.*

re·fresh·ment /rɪˈfreʃmənt/ NOUN [PL, U] (refreshments) **1** [PL] **Refreshments** are drinks and small amounts of food that are provided, for example during a meeting or a trip. ❏ *Lunch and refreshments will be provided.* **2** [U] (formal) You can refer to food and drink as **refreshment**. ❏ *May I offer you some refreshment?*

re·frig·era·tor /rɪˈfrɪdʒəreɪtə/ NOUN [C] (refrigerators) A **refrigerator** is a large container which is kept cool inside, usually by electricity, so that the food and drink in it stay fresh. = fridge

re·fu·el /ˌriːˈfjuːəl/ VERB [I, T] (refuels, refuelling, refuelled; in AmE, use refueling, refueled) When an aircraft or other vehicle **refuels** or when someone **refuels** it, it is filled with more fuel so that it can continue its journey. ❏ *His plane stopped in Hawaii to refuel.*
re·fu·el·ling /ˌriːˈfjuːəlɪŋ/ NOUN [U] ❏ *nighttime refuelling of vehicles*

ref·uge /ˈrefjuːdʒ/ NOUN [U, C] (refuges) **1** [U] If you take **refuge** somewhere, you try to protect yourself from physical harm by going there. ❏ *They took refuge in a bomb shelter.* **2** [C] A **refuge** is a place where you go for safety and protection, for example from violence or from bad weather. = shelter ❏ *Eventually Suzanne fled to a refuge for battered women.* **3** [U] If you take **refuge in** a particular way of behaving or thinking, you try to protect yourself from unhappiness or unpleasantness by behaving or thinking in that way. ❏ *All too often, they get bored and seek refuge in drink and drugs.*

❍ **refu·gee** ◆◆◇ /ˌrefjuˈdʒiː/ NOUN [C] (refugees) **Refugees** are people who have been forced to leave their homes or their country, either because there is a war there, because of their political or religious beliefs, or because of natural disaster. ❏ *A political refugee from Cameroon has moved into our neighbourhood.* ❏ *Thousands of Hungarian refugees fled to the West, and armed resistance in Hungary was soon crushed.*

re·fund NOUN, VERB
NOUN /ˈriːfʌnd/ [C] (refunds) A **refund** is a sum of money

r

that is returned to you, for example because you have paid too much or because you have returned goods to a store. ❑ *Face it – you'll just have to take those cowboy boots back and ask for a refund.*
  VERB /rɪˈfʌnd/ [T] (**refunds, refunding, refunded**) If someone **refunds** your money, they return it to you, for example because you have paid too much or because you have returned goods to a store. ❑ *We guarantee to refund your money if you're not delighted with your purchase.*

re·fur·bish /riːˈfɜːbɪʃ/ VERB [T] (**refurbishes, refurbishing, refurbished**) To **refurbish** a building or room means to clean it and decorate it and make it more attractive or better equipped. ❑ *We have spent money on refurbishing the offices.*

re·fus·al /rɪˈfjuːzəl/ NOUN
  NOUN [C, U] (**refusals**) Someone's **refusal to** do something is the fact of them showing or saying that they will not do it, allow it, or accept it. ❑ *Her country suffered through her refusal to accept change.*
  PHRASE **first refusal** If someone has **first refusal** on something that is being sold or offered, they have the right to decide whether or not to buy it or take it before it is offered to anyone else. ❑ *A tenant may have a right of first refusal if a property is offered for sale.*

❂**re·fuse** ◆◆◇ VERB, NOUN
  VERB /rɪˈfjuːz/ [I, T] (**refuses, refusing, refused**) ◼ [I, T] If you **refuse to** do something, you deliberately do not do it, or you say firmly that you will not do it. ❑ *He refused to comment after the trial.* ❑ *I could hardly refuse, could I?* ◼ [T] If someone **refuses** you something, they do not give it to you or do not allow you to have it. ❑ *The United States has refused him a visa.* ◼ [T] If you **refuse** something that is offered to you, you do not accept it. = **turn down** ❑ *The patient has the right to refuse treatment.*
  NOUN /ˈrefjuːs/ [U] **Refuse** consists of the rubbish and all the things that are not wanted in a house, shop, or factory, and that are regularly thrown away; used mainly in official language. = **waste, rubbish** ❑ *The town made a weekly collection of refuse.* ❑ *Vast amounts of unwanted domestic refuse including TVs and washing machines have been dumped on the path.*

re·gain /rɪˈɡeɪn/ VERB [T] (**regains, regaining, regained**) If you **regain** something that you have lost, you get it back again. ❑ *Troops have regained control of the city.*

❂**re·gard** ◆◆◇ /rɪˈɡɑːd/ VERB, NOUN
  VERB [T] (**regards, regarding, regarded**) ◼ If you **regard** someone or something **as** being a particular thing or **as** having a particular quality, you believe that they are that thing or have that quality. ❑ *He was regarded as the most successful president of modern times.* ❑ *I regard creativity both as a gift and as a skill.* ◼ If you **regard** something or someone **with** a feeling such as dislike or respect, you have that feeling about them. ❑ *He regarded drug dealers with loathing.*
  PHRASE **as regards** You can use **as regards** to indicate the subject that is being talked or written about. ❑ *As regards the war, Haig believed in victory at any price.*
  NOUN [U, PL] (**regards**) ◼ [U] If you have **regard for** someone or something, you respect them and care about them. If you hold someone **in high regard**, you have a lot of respect for them. ❑ *I have a very high regard for him and what he has achieved.* ◼ [PL] **Regards** are greetings. You use **regards** in expressions such as **best regards** and **with kind regards** as a way of expressing friendly feelings towards someone, especially in a letter. ❑ *Give my regards to your family.*
  PHRASE **with regard to** or **in regard to** You can use **with regard to** or **in regard to** to indicate the subject that is being talked or written about. = **regarding** ❑ *The department is reviewing its policy with regard to immunization.*

USAGE NOTE

regard

When you explain how you feel about something, you say that you 'regard it as' something or that you 'regard it to be' something. Do not use 'regard that'.

*I **regard this as** a massive improvement.*
The 29-year-old Italian is widely regarded to be the best runner in the race.

❂**re·gard·ing** /rɪˈɡɑːdɪŋ/ PREP You can use **regarding** to indicate the subject that is being talked or written about. = **concerning** ❑ *He refused to divulge any information regarding the man's whereabouts.* ❑ *There are conflicting reports regarding the number of terrorists involved.*

❂**re·gard·less** /rɪˈɡɑːdləs/ ADV
  ADV [regardless after V] If you say that someone did something **regardless**, you mean that they did it even though there were problems or factors that could have stopped them, or perhaps should have stopped them. ❑ *Despite her recent surgery she has been carrying on regardless.*
  PHRASE **regardless of** If something happens **regardless of** something else, it is not affected or influenced at all by that other thing. ❑ *It takes in anybody regardless of religion, colour, or creed.* ❑ *Regardless of whether he is right or wrong, we have to abide by his decisions.*

re·gen·er·ate /rɪˈdʒenəreɪt/ VERB [I, T] (**regenerates, regenerating, regenerated**) ◼ To **regenerate** something means to develop and improve it to make it more active, successful, or important, especially after a period when it has been getting worse. ❑ *The government will continue to try to regenerate inner-city areas.* ◼ If organs or tissues **regenerate** or if something **regenerates** them, they heal and grow again after they have been damaged. ❑ *Nerve cells have limited ability to regenerate if destroyed.*
  re·gen·era·tion /rɪˌdʒenəˈreɪʃən/ NOUN [U] ◼ the physical and economic regeneration of the area ◼ Vitamin B assists in red-blood-cell regeneration.

❂**re·gime** ◆◇◇ /reɪˈʒiːm/ NOUN [C] (**regimes**) (*academic word*) ◼ (*disapproval*) If you refer to a government or system of running a country as a **regime**, you are critical of it because you think it is not democratic and uses unacceptable methods. = **government, system, administration** ❑ *the collapse of the Fascist regime at the end of the war* ❑ *Pujol was imprisoned and tortured under the Franco regime.* ◼ A **regime** is the way that something such as an institution, company, or economy is run, especially when it involves tough or severe action. ❑ *The authorities moved him to the less rigid regime of an open prison.* ◼ A **regime** is a set of rules about food, exercise, or beauty that some people follow in order to stay healthy or attractive. ❑ *He has a new fitness regime to strengthen his back.*

❂**re·gion** ◆◆◇ /ˈriːdʒən/ NOUN (*academic word*)
  NOUN [C] (**regions**) ◼ A **region** is a large area of land that is different from other areas of land, for example because it is one of the different parts of a country with its own customs and characteristics, or because it has a particular geographical feature. = **area, province, country** ❑ *Barcelona, capital of the autonomous region of Catalonia* ❑ *a remote mountain region* ◼ You can refer to a part of your body as a **region**. = **area** ❑ *the pelvic region*
  PHRASE **in the region of** (*vagueness*) You say **in the region of** to indicate that an amount that you are stating is approximate. = **around** ❑ *The plan will cost in the region of six million dollars.*

WORD CONNECTIONS
VERB + **region**
visit a region
explore a region
❑ *The prime minister plans to visit the region.*
affect a region
destabilize a region
devastate a region
❑ *Last month an earthquake devastated the region.*
ADJ + **region**
a **remote** region
a **mountainous** region
a **coastal** region
❑ *Flooding is a problem in coastal regions of the country.*
a **disputed** region
a **troubled** region
❑ *Fighting broke out again in the disputed region near the border with Eritrea.*

R

✪**re·gion·al** ♦♦◇ /'riːdʒənəl/ ADJ| **Regional** is used to describe things which relate to a particular area of a country or of the world. = local, district, provincial ❑ *The Garden's menu is based on Hawaiian regional cuisine.* ❑ *the autonomous regional government of Andalucia* ❑ *Many people in Minnesota and Tennessee have noticeable regional accents.*

✪**reg·is·ter** ♦◇◇ /'redʒɪstə/ NOUN, VERB *(academic word)* **NOUN** [c] **(registers)** A **register** is an official list or record of people or things. ❑ *registers of births, deaths, and marriages* **VERB** [I, T] **(registers, registering, registered)** ❚ [I, T] If you **register** to do something, you put your name on an official list, in order to be able to do that thing or to receive a service. = enrol, enlist, sign up ❑ *Have you come to register at the school?* ❑ *Thousands lined up to register to vote.* ❑ *Many students register for these courses to widen skills for use in their current job.* ❙ [T] If you **register** something, such as the name of a person who has just died or information about something you own, you have these facts recorded on an official list. = license, record ❑ *In order to register a car in Japan, the owner must have somewhere to park it.* ❑ *They registered his birth.* ❑ *a registered charity* ❘ [I, T] When something **registers on** a scale or measuring instrument, it shows on the scale or instrument. = show ❑ *It will only register on sophisticated X-ray equipment.* ❑ *The earthquake registered 5.7 on the Richter scale.* ❑ *The scales registered a gain of 1.3 kilograms.* ❙ [T] If you **register** your feelings or opinions about something, you do something that makes them clear to other people. ❑ *Voters wish to register their dissatisfaction with the ruling party.* ❙ [I] If a feeling **registers on** someone's face, their expression shows clearly that they have that feeling. = show ❑ *Surprise again registered on Rodney's face.* ❙ [I, T] If a piece of information does not **register** or if you do not **register** it, you do not really pay attention to it, and so you do not remember it or react to it. ❑ *It wasn't that she couldn't hear me, it was just that what I said sometimes didn't register in her brain.*

→ See also **cash register**

✪**reg·is·tra·tion** /ˌredʒɪ'streɪʃən/ NOUN [U] The **registration** of something such as a person's name or the details of an event is the recording of it in an official list. = licensing ❑ *They have campaigned strongly for compulsory registration of dogs.* ❑ *With the high voter registration, many will be voting for the first time.* ❑ *fill in the registration forms*

re·gret ♦◇◇ /rɪ'gret/ VERB, NOUN **VERB** [T] **(regrets, regretting, regretted)** ❚ If you **regret** something that you have done, you wish that you had not done it. ❑ *I simply gave in to him, and I've regretted it ever since.* ❑ *Ellis seemed to be regretting that he had asked the question.* ❙ You can say that you **regret** something as a polite way of saying that you are sorry about it. You use expressions such as **I regret to say** or **I regret to inform you** to show that you are sorry about something. ❑ *'I very much regret the injuries he sustained,' he said.* ❑ *I regret that the United States has added its voice to such protests.* **NOUN** [c, u] **(regrets) Regret** is a feeling of sadness or disappointment, which is caused by something that has happened or something that you have done or not done. ❑ *Larry said he had no regrets about retiring.*

✪**regu·lar** ♦♦◇ /'regjʊlə/ ADJ, NOUN **ADJ** ❚ **Regular** events have equal amounts of time between them, so that they happen, for example, at the same time each day or each week. = frequent; ≠ irregular ❑ *Get regular exercise.* ❑ *We're going to be meeting there on a regular basis.* ❑ *The cartridge must be replaced at regular intervals.* ❙ **Regular** events happen often. ❑ *Although it may look unpleasant, this condition is harmless and usually clears up with regular shampooing.* ❘ [regular + N] If you are, for example, a **regular** customer at a shop or a **regular** visitor to a place, you go there often. ❑ *She has become a regular visitor to Houghton Hall.* ❙ [DET + regular + N] You use **regular** when referring to the thing, person, time, or place that is usually used by someone. For example, someone's **regular** place is the place where they usually sit. = usual ❑ *The man shook his hand and then sat at his regular table near the windows.* ❙ A **regular** rhythm consists of a series of sounds or movements with equal periods of time between them.

❑ *a very regular beat* ❘ [regular + N] *(mainly AmE)* **Regular** is used to mean 'normal.' = ordinary ❑ *The product looks and burns like a regular cigarette.* ❙ [regular + N] *(mainly AmE)* In some restaurants, a **regular** drink or quantity of food is of medium size. ❑ *a cheeseburger and regular fries* ❙ A **regular** pattern or arrangement consists of a series of things with equal spaces between them. ❑ *The village was laid out in regular patterns.* ❙ If something has a **regular** shape, both halves are the same and it has straight edges or a smooth outline. ❑ *some regular geometrical shape* ❙ In grammar, a **regular** verb, noun, or adjective inflects in the same way as most verbs, nouns, or adjectives in the language. **NOUN** [c] **(regulars)** The **regulars** at a place or on a team are the people who often go to the place or are often on the team. ❑ *Regulars at his local bar have set up a fund to help out.*

regu·lar·ity /ˌregjʊ'lærɪti/ NOUN [U] ❚ The overdraft arrangements had been generous because of the regularity of the half-yearly payments. ❙ *Closures and job losses are again being announced with monotonous regularity.* ❘ *Experimenters have succeeded in controlling the rate and regularity of the heartbeat.* ❙ *the chessboard regularity of their fields*

✪**regu·lar·ly** /'regjʊləli/ ADV ❚ [regularly with v] = frequently, routinely; ≠ occasionally ❑ *He also writes regularly for 'International Management' magazine.* ❙ *Exercise regularly.* ❘ [regularly with v] ❑ *Fox, badger, and weasel are regularly seen here.* ❙ [regularly with v] ❑ *Remember to breathe regularly.*

WORD FAMILIES	
regular ADJ|	It is important to get **regular** exercise.
irregular ADJ|	She was taken to hospital suffering from an **irregular** heartbeat.
regularly ADV	He also writes **regularly** for 'International Management' magazine.
irregularly ADV	He was eating **irregularly**, steadily losing weight.
regularity NOUN	Experimenters have succeeded in controlling the rate and **regularity** of the heartbeat.
irregularity NOUN	His creditors became impatient with the **irregularity** of his payments.

✪**regu·late** /'regjʊleɪt/ VERB [T] **(regulates, regulating, regulated)** *(academic word)* To **regulate** an activity or process means to control it, especially by means of rules. = control, manage ❑ *Under such a plan, the government would regulate competition among insurance companies so that everyone gets care at a lower cost.* ❑ *As we get older the temperature-regulating mechanisms in the body tend to become a little less efficient.* ❑ *regulating cholesterol levels*

✪**regu·lat·ed** /'regjʊleɪtɪd/ ADJ| = controlled; ≠ non-regulated ❑ *a planned, state-regulated economy* ❑ *It's a treatment that can carry risks, and in Britain it's strictly regulated.*

regu·la·tion ♦◇◇ /ˌregjʊ'leɪʃən/ NOUN [c, u] **(regulations)** *(academic word)* ❚ [c] **Regulations** are rules made by a government or other authority in order to control the way something is done or the way people behave. = rule, law, guideline, requirement ❑ *The European Union has proposed new regulations to control the hours worked by its employees.* ❑ *Under pressure from the government, the manufacturers obeyed the new safety regulations.* ❙ [u] **Regulation** is the controlling of an activity or process, usually by means of rules. ❑ *Some in the market now want government regulation in order to reduce costs.*

WORD CONNECTIONS
VERB + **regulation**
introduce regulations
adopt regulations
impose regulations
❑ *The government introduced regulations on the labelling of genetically modified foods.*

r

ignore regulations
disregard regulations
breach regulations
❑ *The company is said to have breached health and safety regulations.*

ADJ + **regulation**

new regulations
current regulations
strict regulations
❑ *Strict regulations govern the use of explosives in offshore drilling.*

NOUN + **regulation**

banking regulation
government regulation
industry regulation
❑ *Poor banking regulation has allowed banks to run up too much debt.*

✪**regu·la·tor** ◆◇◇ /ˈreɡjʊleɪtə/ NOUN [C] (**regulators**)
A **regulator** is a person or organization appointed by a government to regulate an area of activity such as banking or industry. ❑ *An independent regulator will be appointed to ensure fair competition.* ❑ *Congress is being asked to investigate why it took so long for government regulators to shut the plant down.*

✪**regu·la·tory** /ˌreɡjʊˈleɪtəri, AmE ˈreɡjʊlətɔːri/ ADJ
[regulatory + N] ❑ *the US's financial regulatory system* ❑ *This new regulatory regime was designed to protect the public.*

re·ha·bili·tate /ˌriːhəˈbɪlɪteɪt/ VERB [T] (**rehabilitates, rehabilitating, rehabilitated**) To **rehabilitate** someone who has been ill or in prison means to help them to live a normal life again. To **rehabilitate** someone who has a drug or alcohol problem means to help them stop using drugs or alcohol. ❑ *Considerable efforts have been made to rehabilitate patients who have suffered in this way.*

re·ha·bili·ta·tion /ˌriːhəbɪlɪˈteɪʃən/ NOUN [U] The **rehabilitation** of someone who has been ill or in prison is the process of allowing them to live a normal life again. The **rehabilitation** of someone who has a drug or alcohol problem is the process of helping them stop using drugs or alcohol. ❑ *A number of other techniques are now being used by psychologists in the rehabilitation of young offenders.*

re·hears·al /rɪˈhɜːsəl/ NOUN [C, U] (**rehearsals**) ◼ [C, U] A **rehearsal** of a play, dance, or piece of music is a practice of it in preparation for a performance. ❑ *The band was scheduled to begin rehearsals for a concert tour.* ◼ [C] You can describe an event or object that is a preparation for a more important event or object as a **rehearsal** for it.
❑ *Daydreams may seem to be rehearsals for real-life situations, but we know they are not.*

re·hearse /rɪˈhɜːs/ VERB [I, T] (**rehearses, rehearsing, rehearsed**) ◼ [I, T] When people **rehearse** a play, dance, or piece of music, they practice in it order to prepare for a performance. ❑ *In his version, a group of actors are rehearsing a play about Joan of Arc.* ❑ *Tens of thousands of people have been rehearsing for the opening ceremony in the new stadium.* ◼ [T] If you **rehearse** something that you are going to say or do, you silently practise it by imagining that you are saying or doing it. ❑ *Anticipate any tough questions and rehearse your answers.*

reign /reɪn/ VERB, NOUN
VERB [I] (**reigns, reigning, reigned**) ◼ (*written*) If you say, for example, that silence **reigns** in a place or confusion **reigns** in a situation, you mean that the place is silent or the situation is confused. ❑ *Last night confusion reigned about how the debate, which continues today, would end.* ◼ When a king or queen **reigns**, he or she rules a country. ❑ *Henry II, who reigned from 1154 to 1189*
NOUN [C] (**reigns**) The **reign** of a king or queen is the period he or she rules a particular country. ❑ *Queen Victoria's reign*

✪**re·im·burse** /ˌriːɪmˈbɜːs/ VERB [T] (**reimburses, reimbursing, reimbursed**) (*formal*) If you **reimburse** someone **for** something, you pay them back the money that they have spent or lost because of it. = refund
❑ *I'll be happy to reimburse you for any expenses you've had.*
❑ *Participants will be reimbursed for any out-of-pocket expenses such as travel.* ❑ *The funds are supposed to reimburse policyholders in the event of insurer failure.*

✪**re·im·burse·ment** /ˌriːɪmˈbɜːsmənt/ NOUN [C, U] (**reimbursements**) (*formal*) If you receive **reimbursement** for money that you have spent, you get your money back, for example because the money should have been paid by someone else. = compensation, refund ❑ *She is demanding reimbursement for medical and other expenses.*
❑ *It can take up to six months before reimbursements are paid.*

rein /reɪn/ NOUN
NOUN [PL] (**reins**) ◼ **Reins** are the thin leather straps attached around a horse's neck which are used to control the horse. ❑ *Cord held the reins while the stallion tugged and snorted.* ◼ Journalists sometimes use the expression **the reins** or **the reins of power** to refer to the control of a country or organization. ❑ *He was determined to see the party keep a hold on the reins of power.*
PHRASES **give someone free rein** If you **give free rein to** someone, you give them a lot of freedom to do what they want. ❑ *The government continued to believe it should give free rein to the private sector in transport.*
keep a tight rein on If you **keep a tight rein on** someone, you control them firmly. ❑ *Her parents kept her on a tight rein with their narrow and inflexible views.*
PHRASAL VERBS **rein back** (**reins, reining, reined**) To **rein back** something such as spending means to control it strictly. = check ❑ *He promised that between now and the end of the year the government would try to rein back inflation.*
rein in To **rein in** something means to control it. ❑ *Many people have begun looking for long-term ways to rein in spending.*

✪**re·inforce** /ˌriːɪnˈfɔːs/ VERB [T] (**reinforces, reinforcing, reinforced**) (*academic word*) ◼ If something **reinforces** a feeling, situation, or process, it makes it stronger or more intense. = strengthen; ≠ weaken ❑ *I hope this will reinforce Indonesian determination to deal with this kind of threat.* ❑ *A stronger European Parliament would, they fear, only reinforce the power of the larger countries.* ❑ *This sense of privilege tends to be reinforced by the outside world.* ◼ If something **reinforces** an idea or point of view, it provides more evidence or support for it. = support; ≠ undermine ❑ *The delegation hopes to reinforce the idea that human rights are not purely internal matters.* ◼ To **reinforce** an object means to make it stronger or harder. ❑ *Eventually, they had to reinforce the walls with exterior beams.* ◼ To **reinforce** an army or a police force means to make it stronger by increasing its size or providing it with more weapons. To **reinforce** a position or place means to make it stronger by sending more soldiers or weapons. ❑ *Both sides have been reinforcing their positions after yesterday's fierce fighting.*

✪**re·inforce·ment** /ˌriːɪnˈfɔːsmənt/ NOUN [PL, C, U] (**reinforcements**) ◼ [PL] **Reinforcements** are soldiers or police officers who are sent to join an army or group of police in order to make it stronger. ❑ *Mr Vlok promised new measures to protect residents, including the dispatch of police and troop reinforcements.* ◼ [C, U] The **reinforcement** of something is the process of making it stronger. = support ❑ *I am sure that this meeting will contribute to the reinforcement of peace and security all over the world.* ❑ *What the teacher now has to do is remove the reinforcement for this bad behaviour.*

re·instate /ˌriːɪnˈsteɪt/ VERB [T] (**reinstates, reinstating, reinstated**) ◼ If you **reinstate** someone, you give them back a job or position that had been taken away from them. ❑ *The governor is said to have agreed to reinstate five senior workers who were dismissed.* ◼ To **reinstate** a law, facility, or practice means to start having it again. = restore ❑ *She says the public response was a factor in the decision to reinstate the grant.*

re·it·er·ate /riˈɪtəreɪt/ VERB [T] (**reiterates, reiterating, reiterated**) (*formal, journalism*) If you **reiterate** something, you say it again, usually in order to emphasize it. = repeat ❑ *He reiterated his opposition to the creation of a central bank.*

✪**re·ject** ◆◆◇ VERB, NOUN (*academic word*)
VERB /rɪˈdʒekt/ [T] (**rejects, rejecting, rejected**) ◼ If you **reject** something such as a proposal, a request, or an offer,

you do not accept it or you do not agree to it. = deny, turn down, decline; ≠ accept, approve ❏ *The government is expected to reject the idea of state subsidy for a new high-speed railway.* ❏ *Seventeen publishers rejected the manuscript before Jenks saw its potential.* ❏ *reject the possibility of failure* **2** If you **reject** a belief or a political system, you refuse to believe in it or to live by its rules. ❏ *the children of Eastern European immigrants who had rejected their parents' political and religious beliefs* **3** If someone **is rejected** for a job or course of study, it is not offered to them. ❏ *One of my most able students was rejected by another university.* **4** If someone **rejects** another person who expects affection from them, they are cold and unfriendly towards them. ❏ *people who had been rejected by their lovers* **5** If a person's body **rejects** something such as a new heart that has been transplanted into it, it tries to attack and destroy it. ❏ *It was feared his body was rejecting a kidney he received in a transplant four years ago.*

NOUN /ˈriːdʒekt/ [c] (**rejects**) A **reject** is a product that has not been accepted for use or sale, because there is something wrong with it. ❏ *The checked shirt is a reject – too small.*

❍**re·jec·tion** /rɪˈdʒekʃən/ NOUN [c, u] (**rejections**) **1** [c, u] = denial; ≠ acceptance, approval ❏ *The rejection of such initiatives by no means indicates that voters are unconcerned about the environment.* **2** [c, u] ❏ *His rejection of our values is far more complete than that of D H Lawrence.* **3** [u] ❏ *Be prepared for lots of rejections before you land a job.* **4** [c, u] ❏ *These feelings of rejection and hurt remain.* ❏ *the chances of criticism and rejection* **5** [c, u] ❏ *a special drug which stops rejection of transplanted organs*

WORD CONNECTIONS

reject + NOUN

reject an **offer**
reject a **plan**
reject a **proposal**
reject a **claim**

❏ *The seller is free to either accept or reject the proposal.*

NOUN + **reject**

voters reject
shareholders reject
the **board** rejects
a **judge** rejects

❏ *She sued for a share of the business but the judge rejected her claim.*

ADV + **reject**

flatly reject
firmly reject
unanimously reject

❏ *Many scientists firmly reject these arguments.*

---

re·joice /rɪˈdʒɔɪs/ VERB [i, t] (**rejoices, rejoicing, rejoiced**) If you **rejoice**, you are very pleased about something and you show it in your behaviour. ❏ *Garbo plays the queen, rejoicing in the love she has found with Antonio.* ❏ *Party activists in New Hampshire rejoiced that the presidential campaign had finally started.*

re·joic·ing /rɪˈdʒɔɪsɪŋ/ NOUN [u] ❏ *There was general rejoicing at the news.*

re·lapse VERB, NOUN

VERB /rɪˈlæps/ [i] (**relapses, relapsing, relapsed**) **1** If you say that someone **relapses into** a way of behaving that is undesirable, you mean that they start to behave in that way again. ❏ *'I wish I did,' said Phil Jordan, relapsing into his usual gloom.* **2** If a sick person **relapses**, their health suddenly gets worse after it had been improving. ❏ *In 90 per cent of cases the patient will relapse within six months.*

NOUN /ˈriːlæps, rɪˈlæps/ [c, u] (**relapses**) **1** [c] If you say that someone has had a **relapse** into a way of behaving that is undesirable, you mean that they have started to behave in that way again. ❏ *a relapse into the nationalism of the nineteenth century* **2** [c, u] If a sick person has a **relapse**, their health suddenly gets worse after it had been improving. ❏ *The treatment is usually given to women with a high risk of relapse after surgery.*

❍**re·late** ♦◇◇ /rɪˈleɪt/ VERB [i, RECIP] (**relates, relating, related**) **1** [i] If something **relates to** a particular subject, it concerns that subject. = concern, involve ❏ *Other recommendations relate to the details of how such data is stored.* ❏ *It does not matter whether the problem you have relates to food, drink, smoking or just living.* **2** [RECIP] The way that two things **relate**, or the way that one thing **relates to** another, is the sort of connection that exists between them. = connect ❏ *I don't think he understood the dynamics of how the police and the city administration relate.* ❏ *Trainees should be invited to relate new ideas to their past experiences.* ❏ *More studies will be required before we know what the functions of these genes are and whether they relate to each other.* ❏ *Cornell University offers a course that investigates how language relates to particular cultural codes.* **3** [RECIP] If you can **relate to** someone, you can understand how they feel or behave so that you are able to communicate with them or deal with them easily. ❏ *He is unable to relate to other people.*

❍**re·lat·ed** ♦◇◇ /rɪˈleɪtɪd/ ADJ **1** If two or more things are **related**, there is a connection between them. = connected; ≠ unrelated ❏ *The philosophical problems of chance and of free will are closely related.* ❏ *equipment and accessories for diving and related activities* **2** [V-LINK + related] People who are **related** belong to the same family. ❏ *The children, although not related to us by blood, had become as dear to us as our own.* **3** If you say that different types of things, such as languages, are **related**, you mean that they developed from the same language. ❏ *He recognized that Sanskrit, the language of India, was related very closely to Latin, Greek, and the Germanic and Celtic languages.*

❍**re·la·tion** ♦♦◇ /rɪˈleɪʃən/ NOUN

NOUN [c] (**relations**) **1 Relations** between people, groups, or countries are contacts between them and the way in which they behave towards each other. = contact, link ❏ *Greece has established full diplomatic relations with Israel.* ❏ *Apparently relations between husband and wife had not improved.* ❏ *The company has a track record of good employee relations.* **2** If you talk about the **relation** of one thing to another, you are talking about the ways in which they are connected. = concerning, regarding, with regard to, in respect of ❏ *It is a question of the relation of ethics to economics.* ❏ *a relation between youthful unemployment and drug-related offences.* ❏ *This theory bears no relation to reality.* **3** Your **relations** are the members of your family. = relative ❏ *visits to friends and relations*

PHRASE **in relation to 1** You can talk about something **in relation to** something else when you want to compare the size, condition, or position of the two things. = in comparison to ❏ *The money he'd been ordered to pay was minimal in relation to his salary.* ❏ *women's position in relation to men in the context of the family* **2** If something is said or done **in relation to** a subject, it is said or done in connection with that subject. ❏ *a question that has been asked many times in relation to Irish affairs*

→ See also **industrial relations, public relations**

WHICH WORD?

relation, relative, or relationship?

Your **relations** or **relatives** are the members of your family. ❏ *His wife had to visit some of her relatives.*

The **relations** or **relationship** between people or groups are the contacts between them.

❏ *The unions should have close relations with the management.*

❏ *Pakistan's relationship with India has changed dramatically.*

A **relationship** is also a close friendship between two people.

❏ *The couple's relationship broke down soon after the birth of their son.*

WORD CONNECTIONS

ADJ + **relations**

diplomatic relations
public relations
industrial relations
international relations

❏ *Many organizations exist with the aim of fostering peaceful international relations.*

r

friendly relations
good relations
normal relations
❑ *The council endorsed the resumption of normal relations with Cuba.*

VERB + **relations**

improve relations
restore relations
establish relations
❑ *The majority believe that the initiative has improved relations between the community and police.*

relations + VERB

relations **deteriorate**
relations **worsen**
relations **improve**
❑ *Industrial relations deteriorated during the period and strikes were common.*

✪ **re·la·tion·ship** ◆◆◇ /rɪˈleɪʃənʃɪp/ NOUN [c] (**relationships**) **1** The **relationship** between two people or groups is the way in which they feel and behave towards each other. = bond, partnership ❑ *the friendly relationship between France and Britain* ❑ *family relationships* **2** A **relationship** is a close friendship between two people, especially one involving romantic or sexual feelings. ❑ *We had been together for two years, but both of us felt the relationship wasn't really going anywhere.* **3** The **relationship** between two things is the way in which they are connected. = connection, association, link ❑ *A number of small-scale studies have already indicated that there is a relationship between diet and cancer.* ❑ *an analysis of market mechanisms and their relationship to state capitalism and political freedom*

WORD CONNECTIONS

VERB + **relationship**

develop a relationship
start a relationship
form a relationship
establish a relationship
build a relationship
❑ *The company is trying to develop closer relationships with its customers.*

maintain a relationship
sustain a relationship
❑ *It is important for a manager to maintain good relationships with his or her employees.*

strengthen a relationship
improve a relationship
❑ *A series of official visits has improved the relationship between the two countries.*

ADJ + **relationship**

a **close** relationship
a **strong** relationship
an **important** relationship
a **complex** relationship
❑ *There is a close relationship between poverty and lack of education.*

VOCABULARY BUILDER

relationship NOUN
The **relationship** between two things is the way in which they are connected.
❑ *The report links the relationship between age, income, housing costs and levels of investment in home ownership.*

connection NOUN
A **connection** is the fact that two or more things, people, or groups are connected in some way.
❑ *The police say he had no connection with the security forces.*

association NOUN (*formal*)
Your **association** with a person or a thing such as an organization is the connection that you have with them.
❑ *the company's six-year association with retailer J.C. Penney Co*

link NOUN
If there is a **link** between two things or situations, there is a relationship between them, for example, because one thing causes or affects the other.
❑ *the link between smoking and lung cancer*

✪ **rela·tive** ◆◇◇ /ˈrelətɪv/ NOUN, ADJ
NOUN [c] (**relatives**) **1** Your **relatives** are the members of your family. = relation ❑ *Get a relative to look after the children.* ❑ *We need to inform his relatives.* ❑ *I was taken in by my mother's only relative.* ❑ *a counselling service for relatives and friends as well as the drug abusers themselves* **2** If one animal, plant, language, or invention is a **relative of** another, they have both developed from the same type of animal, plant, language, or invention. ❑ *The pheasant is a close relative of the guinea hen.*
ADJ **1** [relative + N] You use **relative** to say that something is true to a certain degree, especially when compared with other things of the same kind. = comparative ❑ *The fighting resumed after a period of relative calm.* ❑ *It is a cancer that can be cured with relative ease.* **2** [relative + N] You use **relative** when you are comparing the quality or size of two things. = comparative, corresponding ❑ *They chatted about the relative merits of London and Paris as places to live.* ❑ *I reflected on the relative importance of education in 50 countries.* **3** If you say that something is **relative**, you mean that it needs to be considered and judged in relation to other things. ❑ *Fitness is relative; one must always ask 'Fit for what?'*
PHRASE **relative to** Relative to something means with reference to it or in comparison with it. = in relation to ❑ *Japanese interest rates rose relative to America's.* ❑ *House prices now look cheap relative to earnings.* ❑ *The satellite remains in one spot relative to the earth's surface.*

✪ **rela·tive·ly** ◆◇◇ /ˈrelətɪvli/ ADV [relatively + ADJ/ADV] **Relatively** means to a certain degree, especially when compared with other things of the same kind. = comparatively ❑ *The sums needed are relatively small.* ❑ *Such an explanation makes it relatively easy for a child to absorb metaphysical information.*

re·launch /riːˈlɔːntʃ/ VERB, NOUN
VERB [T] (**relaunches, relaunching, relaunched**) To **relaunch** something such as a company, a product, or a programme means to start it again or to produce it in a different way. ❑ *He is hoping to relaunch his film career with a remake of the 1971 British thriller.*
NOUN [c] (**relaunches**) A **relaunch** of something such as a company, a product, or a programme is the act of starting it again or producing it in a different way. ❑ *Relaunches are often simply a way of boosting sales.*

✪ **re·lax** ◆◇◇ /rɪˈlæks/ VERB [I, T] (**relaxes, relaxing, relaxed**) (*academic word*) **1** [I, T] If you **relax** or if something **relaxes** you, you feel more calm and less worried or tense. ❑ *I ought to relax and stop worrying about it.* **2** [I, T] When a part of your body **relaxes**, or when you **relax** it, it becomes less stiff or firm. ❑ *Massage is used to relax muscles, relieve stress and improve the circulation.* **3** [T] If you **relax** your grip or hold on something, you hold it less tightly than before. ❑ *He gradually relaxed his grip on the arms of the chair.* **4** [I, T] If you **relax** a rule or your control over something, or if it **relaxes**, it becomes less firm or strong. = loosen ❑ *Rules governing student conduct have relaxed somewhat in recent years.* ❑ *How much can the President relax his grip over the nation?* ❑ *Some analysts believe that the government soon will begin relaxing economic controls.*
→ See also **relaxed, relaxing**

✪ **re·laxa·tion** /ˌriːlækˈseɪʃən/ NOUN [U] **1** Relaxation is a way of spending time in which you rest and feel comfortable. ❑ *You should be able to find the odd moment for relaxation.* **2** If there is **relaxation** of a rule or control, it is made less firm or strong. = easing; ≠ tightening ❑ *The*

R

relaxation of travel restrictions means they are free to travel and work. ❏ *This year's pork price crash was directly related to the relaxation of laws prohibiting pig meat imports.*

re•laxed /rɪˈlækst/ ADJ **1** If you are **relaxed**, you are calm and not worried or tense. ❏ *As soon as I had made the final decision, I felt a lot more relaxed.* **2** If a place or situation is **relaxed**, it is calm and peaceful. ❏ *The atmosphere at lunch was relaxed.*

re•lax•ing /rɪˈlæksɪŋ/ ADJ Something that is **relaxing** is pleasant and helps you to relax. ❏ *I find cooking very relaxing.*

re•lay NOUN, VERB
NOUN /ˈriːleɪ/ [C] (**relays**) A **relay** or a **relay race** is a race between two or more teams, for example teams of runners or swimmers. Each member of the team runs or swims one section of the race. ❏ *Britain's prospects of beating the United States in the relay looked poor.*
VERB /rɪˈleɪ/ [T] (**relays, relaying, relayed**) **1** To **relay** television or radio signals means to send them or broadcast them. ❏ *The satellite will be used mainly to relay television programmes.* **2** (*formal*) If you **relay** something that has been said to you, you repeat it to another person. ❏ *She relayed the message, then frowned.*

✪**re•lease** ◆◆◆ /rɪˈliːs/ VERB, NOUN (*academic word*)
VERB [T] (**releases, releasing, released**) **1** If a person or animal **is released** from somewhere where they have been locked up or cared for, they are set free or allowed to go. = set free, free, liberate; ≠ imprison ❏ *He was released from custody the next day.* ❏ *He is expected to be released from hospital today.* ❏ *He was released on bail.* **2** (*formal*) If someone or something **releases** you **from** a duty, task, or feeling, they free you from it. ❏ *Divorce releases both the husband and wife from all marital obligations to each other.* **3** To **release** feelings or abilities means to allow them to be expressed. ❏ *Becoming your own person releases your creativity.* **4** If someone in authority **releases** something such as a document or information, they make it available. = issue, publish, announce ❏ *They're not releasing any more details yet.* ❏ *Figures released yesterday show retail sales were down in March.* **5** (*formal*) If you **release** someone or something, you stop holding them. ❏ *He stopped and faced her, releasing her wrist.* **6** If something **releases** gas, heat, or a substance, it causes it to leave its container or the substance that it was part of and enter the surrounding atmosphere or area. = discharge ❏ *a weapon that releases toxic nerve gas* ❏ *The contraction of muscles uses energy and releases heat.* **7** When an entertainer or company **releases** a new CD, DVD, or film, it becomes available so that people can buy it or see it. ❏ *He is releasing an album of love songs.*
NOUN [C, U] (**releases**) **1** [C] [with SUPP] When someone is released, you refer to their **release**. = liberation, discharge; ≠ imprisonment ❏ *He called for the immediate release of all political prisoners.* ❏ *Serious complications have delayed his release from hospital.* **2** [U] [also 'a' release, oft release 'from' N] If someone or something **releases** you from a duty, task, or feeling, you call this a **release**. ❏ *Our therapeutic style offers release from stored tensions, traumas, and grief.* **3** [U] If you **release** feelings or abilities, allowing them to be expressed, this is called a **release**. ❏ *She felt the sudden sweet release of her own tears.* **4** [C] The **release** of a document or information by someone in authority is when they make it available to the public. = issue, publication, announcement ❏ *Action had been taken to speed up the release of cheques.* **5** [C] A **release** of gas, heat, or a substance happens when something causes it to leave its container or the substance that it was part of and enter the surrounding atmosphere or area. = discharge ❏ *Under the agreement, releases of cancer-causing chemicals will be cut by about 80 per cent.* **6** [C] A new **release** is a new CD, DVD, or film that has just become available for people to buy or see. ❏ *Of the new releases that are out there now, which do you think are really good?*

rel•egate /ˈrelɪɡeɪt/ VERB [T] (**relegates, relegating, relegated**) If you **relegate** someone or something to a less important position, you give them this position. ❏ *Might it not be better to relegate the king to a purely ceremonial function?*

re•lent /rɪˈlent/ VERB [I] (**relents, relenting, relented**) If you **relent**, you allow someone to do something that you had previously refused to allow them to do. ❏ *Finally his mother relented and gave permission for her youngest son to marry.*

re•lent•less /rɪˈlentləs/ ADJ **1** Something bad that is **relentless** never stops or never becomes less intense. ❏ *The pressure now was relentless.* **2** Someone who is **relentless** is determined to do something and refuses to give up, even if what they are doing is unpleasant or cruel. ❏ *Relentless in his pursuit of quality, his technical ability was remarkable.*
re•lent•less•ly /rɪˈlentləsli/ ADV **1** *The sun is beating down relentlessly.* **2** *She always questioned me relentlessly.*

✪**rel•evance** /ˈreləvəns/ NOUN [U] Something's **relevance to** a situation or person is its importance or significance in that situation or to that person. = appropriateness; ≠ irrelevance ❏ *Politicians' private lives have no relevance to their public roles.* ❏ *There are additional publications of special relevance to new graduates.*

✪**rel•evant** /ˈreləvənt/ ADJ (*academic word*) Something that is **relevant to** a situation or person is important or significant in that situation or to that person. = pertinent ❏ *We have passed all relevant information on to the police.*
rel•evant•ly /ˈreləvəntli/ ADV ❏ *More relevantly, the past months have reinforced some important truths.*

✪**re•li•able** ◆◇◇ /rɪˈlaɪəbl/ ADJ (*academic word*) **1** People or things that are **reliable** can be trusted to work well or to behave in the way that you want them to. ❏ *She was efficient and reliable.* **2** Information that is **reliable** or that is from a **reliable** source is very likely to be correct. = trustworthy; ≠ unreliable ❏ *There is no reliable information about civilian casualties.* ❏ *It's very difficult to give a reliable estimate.* ❏ *We have reliable sources.*
re•li•ably /rɪˈlaɪəbli/ ADV **1** *It's been working reliably for years.* **2** *Sonia, we are reliably informed, loves her family very much.*
✪**re•li•abil•ity** /rɪˌlaɪəˈbɪlɪti/ NOUN [U] **1** *He's not at all worried about his car's reliability.* **2** = trustworthiness; ≠ unreliability ❏ *Both questioned the reliability of recent opinion polls.* ❏ *the reliability of her testimony* ❏ *Check the figures and set them beside other data to get some idea of their reliability.*

✪**re•li•ance** /rɪˈlaɪəns/ NOUN [U] A person's or thing's **reliance on** something is the fact that they need it and often cannot live or work without it. = dependence ❏ *the country's increasing reliance on foreign aid* ❏ *The attack did signal a growing reliance upon political assassination in the province.*

✪**re•li•ant** /rɪˈlaɪənt/ ADJ [V-LINK + reliant 'on/upon' N] A person or thing that is **reliant on** something needs it and often cannot live or work without it. = dependent; ≠ independent ❏ *These people are not wholly reliant on Western charity.* ❏ *Lithuania is heavily reliant on Moscow for almost all its oil.*

re•lief ◆◆◇ /rɪˈliːf/ NOUN [U, C] (**reliefs**) **1** [U] [also 'a' relief] If you feel a sense of **relief**, you feel happy because something unpleasant has not happened or is no longer happening. ❏ *I breathed a sigh of relief.* **2** [U] If something provides **relief from** pain or distress, it stops the pain or distress. ❏ *a self-help programme which can give lasting relief from the torment of hay fever* **3** [U] **Relief** is money, food, or clothing that is provided for people who are very poor, or who have been affected by war or a natural disaster. ❏ *Relief agencies are stepping up efforts to provide food, shelter, and agricultural equipment.* **4** [C] A **relief** worker is someone who does your work when you go home, or who is employed to do it instead of you when you are sick. ❏ *No relief drivers were available.*

re•lieve /rɪˈliːv/ VERB [T] (**relieves, relieving, relieved**) **1** If something **relieves** an unpleasant feeling or situation, it makes it less unpleasant or causes it to disappear completely. ❏ *Drugs can relieve much of the pain.* **2** If someone or something **relieves** you **of** an unpleasant feeling or difficult task, they take it from you. ❏ *A part-time bookkeeper will relieve you of the burden of chasing unpaid invoices.* **3** If you **relieve** someone, you take their

r

place and continue to do the job or duty that they have been doing. ❑ *At seven o'clock the night nurse came in to relieve her.* **4** *(formal)* If someone **is relieved of** their duties or **is relieved of** their post, they are told that they are no longer required to continue in their job. ❑ *The officer involved was relieved of his duties because he had violated strict guidelines.*

re·lieved /rɪˈliːvd/ ADJ If you are **relieved**, you feel happy because something unpleasant has not happened or is no longer happening. ❑ *We are all relieved to be back home.*

✪**re·li·gion** ◆◇◇ /rɪˈlɪdʒən/ NOUN [U, C] (**religions**) **1** [U] **Religion** is belief in a god or gods and the activities that are connected with this belief, such as praying or worshipping in a building such as a church or temple. ❑ *his understanding of Indian philosophy and religion* ❑ *Avoid subjects such as religion, sex or politics.* **2** [C] A **religion** is a particular system of belief in a god or gods and the activities that are connected with this system. ❑ *the Christian religion* = faith, belief, creed

✪**re·li·gious** ◆◆◇ /rɪˈlɪdʒəs/ ADJ **1** [religious + N] You use **religious** to describe things that are connected with religion or with one particular religion. ❑ *Religious groups are now able to meet quite openly.* ❑ *different religious beliefs* **2** Someone who is **religious** has a strong belief in a god or gods. ❑ *They are both very religious and felt it was a gift from God.*

rel·ish /ˈrelɪʃ/ VERB, NOUN

VERB [T] (**relishes, relishing, relished**) If you **relish** something, you get a lot of enjoyment from it. ❑ *I relish the challenge of doing jobs that others turn down.* NOUN [U] **Relish** means enjoyment. ❑ *The three men ate with relish.*

re·lo·cate /ˌriːləʊˈkeɪt, AmE -ˈləʊkeɪt/ VERB [I, T] (**relocates, relocating, relocated**) If people or businesses **relocate** or if someone **relocates** them, they move to a different place. ❑ *If the company was to relocate, most employees would move.* **re·lo·ca·tion** /ˌriːləʊˈkeɪʃən/ NOUN [U] ❑ *The company says the cost of relocation will be negligible.*

✪**re·luc·tant** ◆◇◇ /rɪˈlʌktənt/ ADJ *(academic word)* If you are **reluctant to** do something, you are unwilling to do it and hesitate before doing it, or do it slowly and without enthusiasm. = unwilling; ≠ willing ❑ *Mr Spero was reluctant to ask for help.* ❑ *The police are very reluctant to get involved in this sort of thing.* ✪**re·luc·tant·ly** /rɪˈlʌktəntli/ ADV [reluctantly with v] = unwillingly, grudgingly; ≠ willingly ❑ *We have reluctantly agreed to let him go.* ❑ *Rescuers reluctantly ended their search Thursday morning.* ✪**re·luc·tance** /rɪˈlʌktəns/ NOUN [U] = unwillingness; ≠ willingness ❑ *Committee members have shown extreme reluctance to explain their position to the media.* ❑ *British officials have indicated reluctance to lift the ban.*

✪**rely** ◆◇◇ /rɪˈlaɪ/ VERB [I] (**relies, relying, relied**) *(academic word)* **1** If you **rely on** someone or something, you need them and depend on them in order to live or work properly. ❑ *They relied heavily on the advice of their professional advisers.* ❑ *The Association relies on member subscriptions for most of its income.* **2** If you can **rely on** someone to work well or to behave as you want them to, you can trust them to do this. ❑ *I know I can rely on you to sort it out.*

✪**re·main** ◆◆◆ /rɪˈmeɪn/ VERB, NOUN VERB [LINK, I] (**remains, remaining, remained**) **1** [LINK] If someone or something **remains** in a particular state or condition, they stay in that state or condition and do not change. = continue ❑ *The three men remained silent.* ❑ *The government remained in control.* ❑ *He remained a formidable opponent.* **2** [I] If you **remain** in a place, you stay there and do not move away. ❑ *They have asked the residents to remain in their homes.* **3** [I] You can say that something **remains** when it still exists. ❑ *The wider problem remains.* **4** [LINK] If something **remains to be** done, it has not yet been done and still needs to be done. ❑ *Major questions remain to be answered about his work.* NOUN [PL] (**remains**) **1** The **remains of** something are the parts of it that are left after most of it has been taken away

or destroyed. ❑ *They were cleaning up the remains of their picnic.* **2** The **remains** of a person or animal are the parts of their body that are left after they have died, sometimes after they have been dead for a long time. ❑ *The unrecognizable remains of a man had been found.*
→ See also **remaining**

WHICH WORD?

remain or stay?

Remain and **stay** both mean to continue in the same state or condition. **Remain** is more formal than **stay**.
❑ *Oliver remained silent.*
❑ *I stayed awake.*
If something continues to exist, you can say it **remains**. You do not say it 'stays'.
❑ *Many of the problems still remain.*
If you **stay** in a town, hotel or house, you live there for a short time. You do not use **remain** with this meaning.
❑ *He was staying in the same hotel as I was.*

---

re·main·der /rɪˈmeɪndə/ QUANT, PRON
QUANT ['the' remainder 'of' DEF-N] **The remainder of** a group are the things or people that still remain after the other things or people have gone or have been dealt with. = rest ❑ *He gulped down the remainder of his coffee.* PRON If you use **the remainder** to refer to part of a group, you are referring to the things or people that still remain after the other things or people have already been mentioned or dealt with. ❑ *Only 5.9 per cent of the area is now covered in trees. Most of the remainder is farmland.*

re·main·ing ◆◇◇ /rɪˈmeɪnɪŋ/ ADJ [remaining + N] The **remaining** things or people out of a group are the things or people that still exist, are still present, or have not yet been dealt with. ❑ *The three parties will meet next month to work out remaining differences.*
→ See also **remain**

re·mark ◆◇◇ /rɪˈmɑːk/ VERB, NOUN
VERB [I, T] (**remarks, remarking, remarked**) If you **remark** that something is the case, you say that it is the case. ❑ *I remarked that I would go shopping that afternoon.* ❑ *On several occasions she had remarked on the boy's improvement.* NOUN [C] (**remarks**) If you make a **remark** about something, you say something about it. = comment ❑ *She has made outspoken remarks about the legalization of marijuana.*

re·mark·able ◆◇◇ /rɪˈmɑːkəbəl/ ADJ Someone or something that is **remarkable** is unusual or special in a way that makes people notice them and be surprised or impressed. ❑ *He was a remarkable man.* **re·mark·ably** /rɪˈmɑːkəbli/ ADV ❑ *Herbal remedies are remarkably successful in treating eczema.*

✪**rem·edy** /ˈremədi/ NOUN, VERB
NOUN [C] (**remedies**) **1** A **remedy** is a successful way of dealing with a problem. = solution ❑ *The remedy lies in the hands of the government.* ❑ *a remedy for economic ills* **2** A **remedy** is something that is intended to cure you when you are ill or in pain. = cure, treatment ❑ *There are many different kinds of natural remedies to help overcome winter infections.* ❑ *St John's wort is a popular herbal remedy for depression.* VERB [T] (**remedies, remedying, remedied**) If you **remedy** something that is wrong or harmful, you correct it or improve it. ❑ *A great deal has been done internally to remedy the situation.*

re·mem·ber ◆◆◆ /rɪˈmembə/ VERB [I, T] (**remembers, remembering, remembered**) **1** [I, T] If you **remember** people or events from the past, you still have an idea of them in your mind and you are able to think about them. ❑ *You wouldn't remember me. I was in another group.* ❑ *I remembered that we had made the last of the coffee the day before.* ❑ *What a day that was, do you remember?* **2** [T] If you **remember** that something is the case, you become aware of it again after a time when you did not think about it. ❑ *She remembered that she was going to the club that evening.* **3** [I, T] If you cannot **remember** something, you are not able to bring it back into your mind when you make an effort to do so. ❑ *If you can't remember your number, write it in code in an appointment book.* ❑ *I can't remember what I said.* ❑ *Don't tell me you can't remember.* **4** [T] If you **remember to** do something, you do it when you intend to. ❑ *Please remember to enclose a stamped self-addressed envelope when writing.* **5** [T] You tell someone to **remember that** something is the case when you want to emphasize its importance. It may be something that they already know about or a new piece of information. ❑ *It is important to remember that each person reacts differently.*

WHICH WORD?
remember or remind?

Do not confuse the verbs **remember** and **remind**. If you **remember** something, you have it in your own mind.
❑ *He couldn't **remember** the name of the restaurant.*

If you do not want someone to forget something, you **remind** them about it.
❑ *She **reminded** me to sign the visitor's book.*

---

re·mind ♦◇◇ /rɪˈmaɪnd/ verb [T] (**reminds, reminding, reminded**) **1** If someone **reminds** you **of** a fact or event that you already know about, they say something which makes you think about it. ❑ *So she simply welcomed Tim and reminded him of the last time they had met.* **2** (*spoken, emphasis*) You use **remind** in expressions such as **Let me remind you that** and **May I remind you that** to introduce a piece of information that you want to emphasize. It may be something that the hearer already knows about or a new piece of information. Sometimes these expressions can sound unfriendly. ❑ *'Let me remind you,' said Marianne, 'that Milwaukee is also my home town.'* **3** If someone **reminds** you **to** do a particular thing, they say something which makes you remember to do it. ❑ *Can you remind me to buy a bottle of wine?* **4** If you say that someone or something **reminds** you **of** another person or thing, you mean that they are similar to the other person or thing and that they make you think about them. ❑ *She reminds me of the wife of the pilot who used to work for you.*

re·mind·er /rɪˈmaɪndə/ noun [c] (**reminders**) **1** (*written*) Something that serves as a **reminder of** another thing makes you think about the other thing. ❑ *The last thing you'd want is a constant reminder of a bad experience.* **2** A **reminder** is a letter or note that is sent to tell you that you have not done something such as pay a bill or return library books. ❑ *the final reminder for the gas bill*

remi·nis·cent /ˌremɪˈnɪsənt/ adj [V-LINK + reminiscent 'of' N] (*formal*) If you say that one thing is **reminiscent of** another, you mean that it reminds you of it. ❑ *We drank from wax-coated paper cups reminiscent of a visit to the dentist.*

re·mit /ˈriːmɪt/ noun [c] (**remits**) (BrE) Someone's **remit** is the area of activity which they are expected to deal with, or which they have authority to deal with. ❑ *That issue is not within my remit.*

rem·nant /ˈremnənt/ noun [c] (**remnants**) The **remnants of** something are small parts of it that are left over when the main part has disappeared or has been used or destroyed. ❑ *Beneath the present church were remnants of Roman flooring.*

✪ **re·mote** ♦◇◇ /rɪˈməʊt/ adj (**remoter, remotest**) **1** **Remote** areas are far away from cities and places where most people live, and are therefore difficult to get to. = isolated, inaccessible ❑ *Landslides have cut off many villages in remote areas.* ❑ *a remote farm in the Yorkshire dales* **2** The **remote** past or **remote** future is a time that is many years distant from the present. = distant ❑ *Slabs of rock had slipped sideways in the remote past and formed this hole.* **3** If something is **remote from** a particular subject or area of experience, it is not relevant to it because it is very different. ❑ *This government depends on the wishes of a few who are remote from the people.* **4** If you say that there is a **remote** possibility or chance that something will happen, you are emphasizing that there is only a very small chance that it will happen. ❑ *I use sunscreen whenever there is even a remote possibility that I will be in the sun.* **5** If you describe someone as **remote**, you mean that they behave as if they do not want to be friendly or closely involved with other

people. ❑ *She looked so beautiful, and at the same time so remote.*

✪ **re·mov·al** /rɪˈmuːvəl/ noun [u, c] (**removals**) **1** [u] The **removal** of something is the act of removing it. = extraction, eradication ❑ *What they expected to be the removal of a small lump turned out to be major surgery.* ❑ *The most common type of oxidation involves the removal of hydrogen atoms from a substance.* **2** [c, u] (BrE; in AmE, use **moving**) **Removal** is the process of transporting furniture or equipment from one building to another.

✪ **re·move** ♦◇◇ /rɪˈmuːv/ verb [T] (**removes, removing, removed**) (*academic word*) **1** (*written*) If you **remove** something from a place, you take it away. = take away, take out, extract ❑ *As soon as the cake is done, remove it from the oven.* ❑ *attempts to remove carbon dioxide from the atmosphere* ❑ *Three bullets were removed from his wounds.* **2** (*written*) If you **remove** clothing, you take it off. ❑ *He removed his jacket.* **3** If you **remove** a stain from something, you make the stain disappear by treating it with a chemical or by washing it. ❑ *This treatment removes the most stubborn stains.* **4** If people **remove** someone **from** power or **from** something such as a committee, they stop them from being in power or being a member of the committee. ❑ *The student senate voted to remove Fuller from office.* **5** If you **remove** an obstacle, a restriction, or a problem, you get rid of it. ❑ *The agreement removes the last serious obstacle to the signing of the arms treaty.*

re·nais·sance /rɪˈneɪsɒns, AmE ˌreniˈsɑːns/ noun [SING] **1** If something experiences a **renaissance**, it becomes popular or successful again after a time when people were not interested in it. = revival ❑ *Popular art is experiencing a renaissance.* **2** The **Renaissance** was the period in Europe, especially Italy, in the 14th, 15th, and 16th centuries, when there was a new interest in art, literature, science, and learning. ❑ *the Renaissance masterpieces in London's galleries*

ren·der /ˈrendə/ verb [T] (**renders, rendering, rendered**) You can use **render** with an adjective that describes a particular state to say that someone or something is changed into that state. For example, if someone or something makes a thing harmless, you can say that they **render** it harmless. = make ❑ *It contained so many errors as to render it worthless.*

re·new ♦◇◇ /rɪˈnjuː, AmE -ˈnuː/ verb [T, RECIP] (**renews, renewing, renewed**) **1** [T] If you **renew** an activity, you begin it again. ❑ *He renewed his attack on government policy towards Europe.* **2** [RECIP] If you **renew** a relationship **with** someone, you start it again after you have not seen them or have not been friendly with them for some time. = resume ❑ *When the two men met again after the war they renewed their friendship.* **3** [T] When you **renew** something such as a licence or a contract, you extend the period of time for which it is valid. ❑ *Larry's landlord threatened not to renew his lease.* **4** [T] You can say that something **is renewed** when it grows again or is replaced after it has been destroyed or lost. ❑ *Nature's repair process is slow and steady, with cells being constantly renewed.*

✪ **re·new·able** /rɪˈnjuːəbəl, AmE -ˈnuː-/ adj **1** **Renewable** resources are natural ones such as wind, water, and sunlight which are always available. ≠ non-renewable ❑ *renewable energy sources* ❑ *each winter's endlessly renewable supply of frozen water* **2** If a contract or agreement is **renewable**, it can be extended when it reaches the end of a fixed period of time. ❑ *A formal contract is signed which is renewable annually.*

re·new·al /rɪˈnjuːəl, -ˈnuː-/ noun [SING, c, u] (**renewals**) **1** [SING] If there is a **renewal of** an activity or a situation, it starts again. ❑ *They will discuss the possible renewal of diplomatic relations.* **2** [c, u] The **renewal** of a document such as a licence or a contract is an official increase in the period of time for which it remains valid. ❑ *His contract came up for renewal.* **3** [u] **Renewal** of something lost, dead, or destroyed is the process of it growing again or being replaced. ❑ *a political lobbyist concentrating on urban renewal and regeneration*

re·nounce /rɪˈnaʊns/ verb [T] (**renounces, renouncing, renounced**) If you **renounce** a belief or a way of behaving,

r

you decide and declare publicly that you no longer have that belief or will no longer behave in that way. ❑ *After a period of imprisonment she renounced terrorism.*

reno·vate /'renəveɪt/ VERB [T] (**renovates, renovating, renovated**) If someone **renovates** an old building, they repair and improve it and get it back into good condition. ❑ *The couple spent thousands renovating the house.*
reno·va·tion /ˌrenə'veɪʃən/ NOUN [C, U] (**renovations**) ❑ *a property which will need extensive renovation*

re·nowned /rɪ'naʊnd/ ADJ A person or place that is **renowned for** something, usually something good, is well known because of it. ❑ *The area is renowned for its Romanesque churches.*

rent ◆◇◇ /rent/ VERB, NOUN
VERB [T] (**rents, renting, rented**) If you **rent** something, you regularly pay its owner a sum of money in order to be able to have it and use it yourself. ❑ *She rents a house with three other girls.* If you **rent** something **to** someone, you let them have it and use it in exchange for a sum of money which they pay you regularly. ❑ *She rented rooms to university students.*
PHRASAL VERB **rent out** Rent out means the same as **rent** VERB 2. ❑ *Last summer Brian Williams rented out his house and went camping.*
NOUN [C, U] (**rents**) **Rent** is the amount of money that you pay regularly to use a house, flat, or piece of land. ❑ *She worked to pay the rent while I went to college.*
PHRASE **for rent** (mainly AmE; in BrE, usually use **for hire**) If something is **for rent**, it is available for you to use in exchange for a sum of money. ❑ *Helmets will be available for rent at all Vail Resort ski areas.*

rent·al /'rentəl/ NOUN, ADJ
NOUN [U, C] (**rentals**) [U] [also rentals] The **rental** of something such as a car or piece of equipment is the activity or process of renting it. ❑ *We can arrange car rental from Chicago's O'Hare Airport.* [C] The **rental** is the amount of money that you pay when you rent something such as a car, property, or piece of equipment. ❑ *It has been let at an annual rental of $393,000.*
ADJ [rental + N] You use **rental** to describe things that are connected with the renting out of goods, properties, and services. ❑ *A friend drove her to Atlanta, where she picked up a rental car.*

re·or·gan·ize /ri'ɔːɡənaɪz/ also **reorganise** VERB [I, T] (**reorganizes, reorganizing, reorganized**) To **reorganize** something means to change the way in which it is organized, arranged, or done. ❑ *It is the mother who is expected to reorganize her busy schedule.* ❑ *Four thousand troops have been reorganized into a fighting force.*
re·or·gani·za·tion /ri,ɔːɡənaɪ'zeɪʃən/ NOUN [C, U] (**reorganizations**) ❑ *the reorganization of the legal system*

re·paid /rɪ'peɪd/ IRREG FORM **Repaid** is the past tense and past participle of **repay**.

re·pair ◆◇◇ /rɪ'peə/ VERB, NOUN
VERB [T] (**repairs, repairing, repaired**) If you **repair** something that has been damaged or is not working properly, you fix it. ❑ *Goldsmith has repaired the roof to ensure the house is windproof.* If you **repair** a relationship or someone's reputation after it has been damaged, you do something to improve it. ❑ *The administration continued to try to repair the damage caused by the secretary's interview.*
NOUN [C, U] (**repairs**) A **repair** is something that you do to mend a machine, building, piece of clothing, or other thing that has been damaged or is not working properly. ❑ *Many women know how to make repairs on their cars.*
re·pair·er /rɪ'peərə/ NOUN [C] (**repairers**) ❑ *services provided by builders, plumbers, and TV repairers*

re·pat·ri·ate /ˌriː'pætrieɪt, AmE -'peɪt-/ VERB [T] (**repatriates, repatriating, repatriated**) If a country **repatriates** someone, it sends them back to their home country. ❑ *It was not the policy of the government to repatriate genuine refugees.* If someone **repatriates** money that is invested in another country, they change their investments so that the money is invested in their own country.
re·pat·ria·tion /ˌriː'pætri'eɪʃən, AmE -'peɪt-/ NOUN [C, U] (**repatriations**) ❑ *Today they begin the forced repatriation of Vietnamese boat people.*

re·pay /rɪ'peɪ/ VERB [T] (**repays, repaying, repaid**) If you **repay** a loan or a debt, you pay back the money that you owe to the person who you borrowed or took it from. ❑ *He advanced funds of his own to his company, which was unable to repay him.* If you **repay** a favour that someone did for you, you do something for them in return. ❑ *It was very kind. I don't know how I can ever repay you.*

re·pay·ment /rɪ'peɪmənt/ NOUN [C, U] (**repayments**) [C] (mainly BrE; in AmE, usually use **payment**) **Repayments** are amounts of money which you pay at regular intervals to a person or organization in order to repay a debt. [U] The **repayment of** money is the act or process of paying it back to the person you owe it to. ❑ *He failed to meet last Friday's deadline for repayment of a $114 million loan.*

✪ **re·peat** ◆◆◇ /rɪ'piːt/ VERB, NOUN, ADJ
VERB [T, I] (**repeats, repeating, repeated**) [T] If you **repeat** something, you say or write it again. You can say **I repeat** to show that you feel strongly about what you are repeating. = reiterate, restate ❑ *He repeated that he had been misquoted.* ❑ *She repeated her call yesterday for an investigation into the incident.* ❑ *The Libyan leader repeated his call for the release of hostages.* [T] If you **repeat** something that someone else has said or written, you say or write the same thing, or tell it to another person. ❑ *She had an irritating habit of repeating everything I said to her.* ❑ *I trust you not to repeat that to anyone else.* [T] If you **repeat yourself**, you say something which you have said before, usually by mistake. ❑ *He spoke well to begin with, but then started rambling and repeating himself.* [I, T] If you **repeat** an action, you do it again. ❑ *The next day I repeated the procedure.* ❑ *Move the leg up and down several times and rotate the foot. Repeat on the right leg.* ❑ *He said Japan would never repeat its mistakes.* [T] If an event or series of events **repeats itself**, it happens again. ❑ *The UN will have to work hard to stop history from repeating itself.*
NOUN [C] (**repeats**) If there is a **repeat of** an event, usually an undesirable event, it happens again. = repetition ❑ *There were fears that there might be a repeat of last year's campaign of strikes.* A **repeat** is a television or radio programme that has been broadcast before. ❑ *There's nothing except sport and repeats on TV.*
ADJ [repeat + N] (business) If a company gets **repeat** business or **repeat** customers, people who have bought their goods or services before buy them again. ❑ *Nearly 60% of our bookings come from repeat business and personal recommendation.*

re·peat·ed /rɪ'piːtɪd/ ADJ [repeat + N] **Repeated** actions or events are ones that happen many times. = frequent ❑ *Mr Lawssi apparently did not return the money, despite repeated reminders.*

re·peat·ed·ly /rɪ'piːtɪdli/ ADV [repeatedly with v] If you do something **repeatedly**, you do it many times. ❑ *Both men have repeatedly denied the allegations.*

re·pel /rɪ'pel/ VERB [T, RECIP] (**repels, repelling, repelled**) [T] (formal) When an army **repels** an attack, they successfully fight and drive back soldiers from another army who have attacked them. ❑ *They have fifty thousand troops along the border ready to repel any attack.* [T] If something **repels** you, you find it horrible and disgusting. = revolt ❑ *a violent excitement that frightened and repelled her* [RECIP] (technical) When a magnetic pole **repels** another magnetic pole, it gives out a force that pushes the other pole away. You can also say that two magnetic poles **repel** each other or that they **repel**.
re·pelled /rɪ'peld/ ADJ ❑ *She was very striking but in some way I felt repelled.*

re·pent /rɪ'pent/ VERB [I] (**repents, repenting, repented**) If you **repent**, you show or say that you are sorry for something wrong you have done. ❑ *Those who refuse to repent, he said, will be punished.*

✪ **re·per·cus·sion** /ˌriːpə'kʌʃən/ NOUN [C] (**repercussions**) [usu pl] (formal) If an action or event has **repercussions**, it causes unpleasant things to happen some time after the original action or event. = consequence ❑ *It was an effort which was to have painful repercussions.*

❏ *Members of congress were warned of possible repercussions if their vote went through.*

rep·er·toire /ˈrepətwɑː/ NOUN [C] (**repertoires**) A performer's **repertoire** is all the plays or pieces of music that he or she has learned and can perform. = repertory ❏ *Meredith D'Ambrosio has thousands of songs in her repertoire.*

✪ **rep·eti·tion** /ˌrepɪˈtɪʃən/ NOUN [C, U] (**repetitions**) **1** If there is a **repetition** of an event, usually an undesirable event, it happens again. ❏ *Today the city government has taken measures to prevent a repetition of last year's confrontation.* ❏ *He wants to avoid repetition of the confusion that followed the discovery of the cystic fibrosis gene.* **2 Repetition** means using the same words again. = duplication, reiteration, recurrence ❏ *He could also have cut out much of the repetition and thus saved many pages.* ❏ *Unnecessary repetition weakens sentences.*

✪ **rep·eti·tive** /rɪˈpetɪtɪv/ ADJ **1** (*disapproval*) Something that is **repetitive** involves actions or elements that are repeated many times and is therefore boring. ❏ *factory workers who do repetitive jobs* ❏ *Suddenly music that seemed dull and repetitive comes alive.* **2 Repetitive** movements or sounds are repeated many times. ❏ *This technique is particularly successful where problems occur as the result of repetitive movements.* ❏ *The repetitive nature of a chant*
rep·eti·tive·ly /rɪˈpetɪtɪvli/ ADV ❏ *I heard him babbling repetitively above the car radio.*

✪ **re·place** ♦♦◇ /rɪˈpleɪs/ VERB [T] (**replaces, replacing, replaced**) **1** If one thing or person **replaces** another, the first is used or acts instead of the second. = substitute ❏ *One species of tree replaces another as a forest ages.* ❏ *the lawyer who replaced Robert as chairman of the company* ❏ *They were planning to pull down the building and replace it with shops and offices.* ❏ *The council tax replaces the poll tax next April.* **2** If you **replace** one thing or person **with** another, you put something or someone else in their place to do their job. ❏ *I clean out all the grease and replace it with oil so it works better in very low temperatures.* **3** If you **replace** something that is broken, damaged, or lost, you get a new one to use instead. ❏ *The shower that we put in a few years back has broken and we cannot afford to replace it.* **4** If you **replace** something, you put it back where it was before. ❏ *Replace the caps on the bottles.*

✪ **re·place·ment** ♦◇◇ /rɪˈpleɪsmənt/ NOUN [U, C] (**replacements**) **1** [U] [with SUPP] If you refer to the **replacement** of one thing by another, you mean that the second thing takes the place of the first. = substitution, exchange ❏ *the replacement of damaged or lost books* **2** [C] Someone who takes someone else's place in an organization, government, or team can be referred to as their **replacement**. ❏ *Taylor has nominated Adams as his replacement.*

re·play VERB, NOUN
▸ VERB /ˌriːˈpleɪ/ [T] (**replays, replaying, replayed**) **1** If a game or match between two sports teams **is replayed**, the two teams play it again, because neither team won the first time, or because the game was stopped because of bad weather. ❏ *The game had to be replayed at the end of the season.* **2** If you **replay** something that you have recorded on film or tape, you play it again in order to watch it or listen to it. ❏ *He stopped the machine and replayed the message.* **3** If you **replay** an event in your mind, you think about it again and again. ❏ *She spends her nights lying in bed, replaying the fire in her mind.*
▸ NOUN /ˈriːpleɪ/ [C] (**replays**) **1** You can refer to a game that is replayed as a **replay**. ❏ *If there has to be a replay we are confident of victory.* **2** If you watch a **replay** of something that you have recorded on film or tape, you play it again in order to watch it or listen to it. ❏ *I watched a slow-motion videotape replay of his fall.*

re·plen·ish /rɪˈplenɪʃ/ VERB [T] (**replenishes, replenishing, replenished**) (*formal*) If you **replenish** something, you make it full or complete again. ❏ *Three hundred thousand tons of cereals are needed to replenish stocks.*

✪ **rep·li·cate** /ˈreplɪkeɪt/ VERB [T] (**replicates, replicating, replicated**) (*formal*) If you **replicate** someone's experiment, work, or research, you do it yourself in exactly the same way. = duplicate, reproduce, repeat ❏ *He invited her to his laboratory to see if she could replicate the experiment.*

❏ *Tests elsewhere have not replicated the findings.*

re·ply ♦♦◇ /rɪˈplaɪ/ VERB, NOUN
▸ VERB [I, T] (**replies, replying, replied**) **1** [I, T] When you **reply to** something that someone has said or written to you, you say or write an answer to them. = answer ❏ *'That's a nice dress,' said Michael. 'Thanks,' she replied solemnly.* ❏ *He replied that this was absolutely impossible.* ❏ *He never replied to the letters.* **2** [I] If you **reply to** something such as an attack **with** violence or **with** another action, you do something in response. ❏ *During a number of violent incidents farmers threw eggs and empty bottles at police, who replied with tear gas.*
▸ NOUN [C] (**replies**) [oft reply 'to/from' N, also 'in' reply] A **reply** is something that you say or write when you answer someone or answer a letter or advertisement. = response ❏ *I called out a challenge, but there was no reply.* ❏ *He said in reply that the question was unfair.*

✪ **re·port** ♦♦♦ /rɪˈpɔːt/ VERB, NOUN
▸ VERB [T, I] (**reports, reporting, reported**) **1** [T] If you **report** something that has happened, you tell people about it. = relate, inform, communicate ❏ *I reported the theft to the police.* ❏ *The officials also reported that two more ships were apparently heading for Malta.* ❏ *'He seems to be all right now', reported a relieved Taylor.* ❏ *She reported him missing the next day.* ❏ *Researchers reported that the incidence of the condition was rising significantly.* ❏ *New cases are being reported more accurately.* ❏ *The foreign secretary is reported as saying that force will have to be used if diplomacy fails.* **2** [I] If you **report on** an event or subject, you tell people about it, because it is your job or duty to do so. ❏ *Many journalists based outside of Sudan have been refused visas to enter the country to report on political affairs.* **3** [T] If someone **reports** you **to** a person in authority, they tell that person about something wrong that you have done. ❏ *His ex-wife reported him to police a few days later.* **4** [I] If you **report to** a person or place, you go to that person or place and say that you are ready to start work or say that you are present. ❏ *Mr Ashwell has to surrender his passport and report to the police every five days.* **5** [I] (*formal*) If you say that one employee **reports to** another, you mean that the first employee is told what to do by the second one and is responsible to them. ❏ *He reported to a section chief, who reported to a division chief, and so on up the line.*
▸ NOUN [C] (**reports**) **1** A **report** is a news article or broadcast which gives information about something that has just happened. ❏ *According to a report in the newspaper, he still has control over the remaining shares.* **2** A **report** is an official document which a group of people issue after investigating a situation or event. = analysis, account ❏ *The education committee will today publish its report on the supply of teachers for the next decade.* ❏ *After an inspection, the inspectors must publish a report.* ❏ *A report by the Association of University Teachers finds that only 22 per cent of lecturers in our universities are women.* **3** If you give someone a **report on** something, you tell them what has been happening. ❏ *She came back to give us a progress report on how the project is going.* **4** If you say that there are **reports** that something has happened, you mean that some people say it has happened but you have no direct evidence of it. ❏ *There are unconfirmed reports that two people have been shot in the neighbouring town of Springfield.*
→ See also **reporting**

WORD CONNECTIONS
VERB + **report**
produce a report
publish a report
release a report
❏ *The group was asked to produce a report on the company's environmental impact.*
report + VERB
a report **suggests**
a report **concludes**
a report **recommends**
❏ *A recent UN report suggests that the number of infections worldwide is rising.*

r

a report **shows**
a report **reveals**
a report **finds**
❏ *The report reveals that even women with full-time jobs still do the great majority of housework.*

ADJ + **report**

a **recent** report
an **annual** report
a **special** report
❏ *The company publishes an annual report.*

✪ **re·port·ed·ly** ♦◇ /rɪˈpɔːtɪdli/ ADV (*formal, vagueness*) If you say that something is **reportedly** true, you mean that someone has said that it is true, but you have no direct evidence of it. ❏ *More than two hundred people have reportedly been killed in the past week's fighting.* ❏ *Now Moscow has reportedly agreed that the sale can go ahead.* ❏ *General Breymann had been shot dead, reportedly by one of his own men.*

re·port·er ♦♦◇ /rɪˈpɔːtə/ NOUN [C] (**reporters**) A **reporter** is someone who writes news articles or who broadcasts news reports. ❏ *a TV reporter*

re·port·ing ♦♦◇ /rɪˈpɔːtɪŋ/ NOUN [U] **Reporting** is the presenting of news in newspapers, on radio, and on television. ❏ *This newspaper has achieved a reputation for honest and impartial political reporting.*

✪ **rep·re·sent** ♦♦◇ /ˌreprɪˈzent/ VERB [T, PASSIVE] (**represents, representing, represented**) **1** [T] If someone such as a lawyer or a politician **represents** a person, a group of people, or a place, they act on behalf of that person, group, or place. ❏ *the politicians we elect to represent us* ❏ *Richard Bolling, a Democrat who represented Missouri in Congress* ❏ *The offer was accepted by the lawyers representing the victims.* **2** [T] If you **represent** a person or group at an official event, you go there on their behalf. ❏ *The general secretary may represent the president at official ceremonies.* **3** [T] If you **represent** your country or city in a competition or sports event, you take part in it on behalf of the country or city where you live. ❏ *My only aim is to represent the United States at the Olympics.* **4** [PASSIVE] If a group of people or things **is** well **represented** in a particular activity or in a particular place, a lot of them can be found there. ❏ *Women are already well represented in the area of TV drama.* **5** [T] If a sign or symbol **represents** something, it is accepted as meaning that thing. = symbolize, signify ❏ *A black dot in the middle of the circle is supposed to represent the source of the radiation.* **6** [T] To **represent** an idea or quality means to be a symbol or an expression of that idea or quality. = embody ❏ *New York represents everything that's great about America.* **7** [T] If you **represent** a person or thing **as** a particular thing, you describe them as being that thing. = portray ❏ *The popular press tends to represent him as an environmental guru.* **8** [T] [oft represent + N] (*formal, written*) If you say that something **represents** a change, achievement, or victory, you mean that it is a change, achievement, or victory. ❏ *These developments represented a major change in the established order.*

rep·re·sen·ta·tion /ˌreprɪzenˈteɪʃən/ NOUN [U, C] (**representations**) **1** [U] If a group or person has **representation** in a legislature or on a committee, someone in the legislature or on the committee supports them and makes decisions on their behalf. ❏ *Puerto Ricans are US citizens but they have no representation in Congress.* **2** [C] (*formal*) You can describe a picture, model, or statue of a person or thing as a **representation** of them. ❏ *a lifelike representation of Christ*

✪ **rep·re·sen·ta·tive** ♦♦◇ /ˌreprɪˈzentətɪv/ NOUN, ADJ
NOUN [C] (**representatives**) **1** A **representative** is a person who has been chosen to act or make decisions on behalf of another person or a group of people. = agent ❏ *trade union representatives* ❏ *Employees from each department elect a representative.* **2** (*formal*) A **representative** is a person whose job is to sell a company's products or services, especially by travelling around and visiting other companies. ❏ *She had a stressful job as a sales representative.*

3 In the United States, a **representative** is a member of the House of Representatives, the less powerful of the two parts of Congress. ❏ *a Republican representative from Wyoming*
ADJ **1** [representative + N] A **representative** group consists of a small number of people who have been chosen to make decisions on behalf of a larger group. ❏ *The new head of state should be chosen by an 87-member representative council.* **2** Someone who is typical of the group to which they belong can be described as **representative**. = typical, characteristic; ≠ unrepresentative, atypical, uncharacteristic ❏ *He was in no way representative of dog trainers in general.* ❏ *fairly representative groups of adults*

WORD CONNECTIONS

VERB + **representative**

elect a representative
appoint a representative
send a representative
❏ *Shareholders have the right to appoint their own representatives to the board.*

ADJ + **representative**

a **legal** representative
an **authorized** representative
❏ *Their legal representatives can give consent on their behalf.*

re·pressed /rɪˈprest/ ADJ A **repressed** person is someone who does not allow themselves to have natural feelings and desires, especially sexual ones. ❏ *Some have charged that the Puritans were sexually repressed.*

re·pres·sion /rɪˈpreʃən/ NOUN [U] **1** (*disapproval*) **Repression** is the use of force to restrict and control a society or other group of people. = oppression ❏ *a society conditioned by violence and repression* **2** **Repression** of feelings, especially sexual ones, is a person's unwillingness to allow themselves to have natural feelings and desires. ❏ *Much of the anger he's felt during his life has stemmed from the repression of his feelings about men.*

re·pres·sive /rɪˈpresɪv/ ADJ (*disapproval*) A **repressive** government is one that restricts people's freedom and controls them by using force. ❏ *The military regime in power was unpopular and repressive.*

re·prieve /rɪˈpriːv/ VERB, NOUN
VERB [T] (**reprieves, reprieving, reprieved**) If someone who has been sentenced in a court **is reprieved**, their punishment is officially delayed or cancelled. ❏ *Fourteen people, waiting to be hanged for the murder of a former prime minister, have been reprieved.*
NOUN [C, U] (**reprieves**) **1** [C, U] If someone who has been sentenced in a court is given a **reprieve**, their punishment is officially delayed or cancelled. ❏ *A man awaiting death by lethal injection has been saved by a last-minute reprieve.* **2** [C] A **reprieve** is a delay before a very unpleasant or difficult situation which may or may not take place. ❏ *It looked as though the college would have to shut, but this week it was given a reprieve.*

rep·ri·mand /ˈreprɪmɑːnd, ˌreprɪˈmænd/ VERB, NOUN
VERB [T] (**reprimands, reprimanding, reprimanded**) (*formal*) If someone **is reprimanded**, they are spoken to angrily or seriously for doing something wrong, usually by a person in authority. ❏ *He was reprimanded by a teacher for talking in the corridor.*
NOUN [C, U] (**reprimands**) If someone is given a **reprimand**, they are spoken to angrily or seriously for doing something wrong, usually by a person in authority. ❏ *He has been fined five thousand dollars and given a severe reprimand.*

✪ **re·pro·duce** /ˌriːprəˈdjuːs, AmE -ˈduːs/ VERB [T, I] (**reproduces, reproducing, reproduced**) **1** [T] If you try to **reproduce** something, you try to copy it. = imitate, copy ❏ *The effect has proved hard to reproduce.* ❏ *I shall not try to reproduce the policemen's English.* **2** [T] If you **reproduce** a picture, speech, or piece of writing, you make a photograph or printed copy of it. ❏ *We are grateful to you for permission to reproduce this article.* **3** [T] If you **reproduce** an action or an achievement, you repeat it. = repeat ❏ *If we can reproduce the form we have shown in the last couple of months*

R

we will be successful. **4** [I, T] When people, animals, or plants **reproduce**, they produce young. = breed ☐ *a society where women are defined by their ability to reproduce* ☐ *We are reproducing ourselves at such a rate that our numbers threaten the ecology of the planet.*

❖**re·pro·duc·tion** /ˌriːprəˈdʌkʃən/ NOUN [U, C] (**reproductions**) **1** [U] **Reproduction** is the process by which people, animals, or plants produce young. ☐ *Treatments using assisted reproduction techniques jumped 30 per cent.* ☐ *Genes are those tiny bits of biological information swapped in sexual reproduction.* ☐ *the acids which are vital for normal cell reproduction* **2** [C] A **reproduction** is a copy of something such as a piece of furniture or a work of art. ☐ *a reproduction of a popular religious painting*

❖**rep·tile** /ˈreptaɪl, AmE -tɪl/ NOUN [C] (**reptiles**) Reptiles are a group of cold-blooded animals which lay eggs and have skins covered with small, hard plates called scales. Snakes, lizards, and crocodiles are reptiles.

❖**re·pub·lic** ♦♦◇ /rɪˈpʌblɪk/ NOUN [C] (**republics**) (*academic word*) A **republic** is a country where power is held by the people or the representatives that they elect. Republics have presidents who are elected, rather than kings or queens. ☐ *In 1918, Austria became a republic.* ☐ *the Baltic republics* ☐ *the Republic of Ireland*

❖**re·pub·li·can** ♦♦◇ /rɪˈpʌblɪkən/ ADJ, NOUN
[ADJ] **Republican** means relating to a republic. In **republican** systems of government, power is held by the people or the representatives that they elect. ☐ *the nations that had adopted the republican form of government*
[NOUN] [C] (**republicans**) In the United States, a **Republican** is someone who supports or belongs to the Republican Party. ☐ *What made you decide to become a Republican, as opposed to a Democrat?*

re·pul·sive /rɪˈpʌlsɪv/ ADJ If you describe something or someone as **repulsive**, you mean that they are horrible and disgusting and you want to avoid them. = revolting, disgusting ☐ *repulsive, fat, white slugs*

repu·table /ˈrepjʊtəbəl/ ADJ A **reputable** company or person is reliable and can be trusted. ☐ *You are well advised to buy your car through a reputable dealer.*

❖**repu·ta·tion** ♦◇◇ /ˌrepjʊˈteɪʃən/ NOUN
[NOUN] [C] (**reputations**) **1** To have a **reputation for** something means to be known or remembered for it. ☐ *Alice Munro has a reputation for being a very depressing writer.* ☐ *Barcelona's reputation as a design-conscious, artistic city* **2** Something's or someone's **reputation** is the opinion that people have about how good they are. If they have a good reputation, people think they are good. = name, image, standing ☐ *This college has a good academic reputation.* ☐ *The stories ruined his reputation.*
[PHRASE] **by reputation** If you know someone **by reputation**, you have never met them but you have heard of their reputation. ☐ *She was by reputation a good organizer.*

re·put·ed /rɪˈpjuːtɪd/ VERB [PASSIVE] (*formal, vagueness*) If you say that something **is reputed** to be true, you mean that people say it is true, but you do not know if it is definitely true. ☐ *He was reputed to be a fine cook.*

re·put·ed·ly /rɪˈpjuːtɪdli/ ADV ☐ *He reputedly earns two million dollars a year.*

❖**re·quest** ♦♦◇ /rɪˈkwest/ VERB, NOUN
[VERB] [T] (**requests, requesting, requested**) (*formal*) **1** If you **request** something, you ask for it politely or formally. = ask for ☐ *Mr Dennis said he had requested access to a telephone.* ☐ *The governor had requested a police presence to ensure external security.* ☐ *The Prime Minister requested that a State of Emergency be declared.* **2** If you **request** someone **to** do something, you politely or formally ask them to do it. ☐ *Students are requested to park at the rear of the building.*
[NOUN] [C] (**requests**) If you make a **request**, you politely or formally ask someone to do something. = appeal ☐ *France had agreed to his request for political asylum.* ☐ *Vietnam made an official request that the meeting be postponed.* ☐ *a request, not a demand*
[PHRASES] **at someone's request** or **at the request of someone** If you do something **at someone's request**, you do it because they have asked you to. ☐ *The evacuation is being*

organized at the request of the United Nations Secretary General.
on request If something is given or done **on request**, it is given or done whenever you ask for it. ☐ *Details are available on request.*

❖**re·quire** ♦♦◇ /rɪˈkwaɪə/ VERB [T] (**requires, requiring, required**) (*academic word, formal*) **1** If you **require** something or if something **is required**, you need it or it is necessary. = need ☐ *If you require further information, you should consult the registrar.* ☐ *This isn't the kind of crisis that requires us to drop everything else.* **2** If a law or rule **requires** you **to** do something, you have to do it. = order, demand, oblige, instruct ☐ *The rules also require employers to provide safety training.* ☐ *At least 35 manufacturers have flouted a law requiring prompt reporting of such malfunctions.* ☐ *The law now requires that parents serve on the committees that plan and evaluate school programmes.* ☐ *Then he'll know exactly what's required of him.*

VOCABULARY BUILDER

require VERB (*formal*)
If a law or rule **requires** you **to** do something, you have to do it.
☐ *No operating instruments were provided, as each surgeon was required to bring along his own.*

order VERB
If a person in authority **orders** someone to do something, they tell them to do it.
☐ *Williams ordered him to leave.*

demand VERB (*formal*)
If you **demand** something such as information or action, you ask for it in a very forceful way.
☐ *Russia demanded that UNITA send a delegation to the peace talks.*

oblige VERB (*formal*)
If you are **obliged** to do something, a situation, rule, or law makes it necessary for you to do that thing.
☐ *The storm got worse and I was obliged to abandon the car.*

instruct VERB (*formal*)
If you **instruct** someone to do something, you formally tell them to do it.
☐ *A doctor will often instruct patients to exercise.*

❖**re·quire·ment** ♦◇◇ /rɪˈkwaɪəmənt/ NOUN [C] (**requirements**) **1** A **requirement** is a quality or qualification that you must have in order to be allowed to do something or to be suitable for something. = condition, qualification, stipulation, specification ☐ *Its products met all legal requirements.* ☐ *Graduate status is the minimum requirement for entry to the teaching profession.* **2** (*formal*) Your **requirements** are the things that you need. = necessity, essential ☐ *Variations of this programme can be arranged to suit your requirements.* ☐ *a packaged food which provides 100 per cent of your daily requirement of one vitamin*

WORD CONNECTIONS

VERB + **requirement**

meet a requirement
satisfy a requirement
fulfil a requirement
☐ *Waste disposal systems must satisfy certain safety requirements.*

impose a requirement
introduce a requirement
☐ *The government does not impose any requirement on companies to train their workers.*

ADJ + **requirement**

a legal requirement
a statutory requirement
a minimum requirement
☐ *In most countries recording of a death is a statutory requirement.*

r

a **daily** requirement
an **essential** requirement
a **basic** requirement
❏ *What are the essential requirements for healthy adolescent development?*

res·cue ◆◇◇ /ˈreskjuː/ VERB, NOUN

VERB [T] (**rescues, rescuing, rescued**) If you **rescue** someone, you get them out of a dangerous or unpleasant situation. ❏ *Helicopters rescued nearly 20 people from the roof of the burning building.*

NOUN [C, U] (**rescues**) **1** [C, U] **Rescue** is help which gets someone out of a dangerous or unpleasant situation. ❏ *A big rescue operation has been launched for a trawler missing in the North Atlantic.* **2** [C] A **rescue** is an attempt to save someone from a dangerous or unpleasant situation. ❏ *A major air-sea rescue is under way.*

PHRASE **go to someone's rescue** or **come to someone's rescue** If you **go to** someone's **rescue** or **come to** their **rescue**, you help them when they are in danger or difficulty. ❏ *The 23-year-old's screams alerted a passer-by who went to her rescue.*

res·cu·er /ˈreskjuːə/ NOUN [C] (**rescuers**) ❏ *It took rescuers 90 minutes to reach the trapped men.*

re·search ◆◆◆ /rɪˈsɜːtʃ/ NOUN, VERB (*academic word*)

NOUN [U] (**researches**) [also researches] **Research** is work that involves studying something and trying to discover facts about it. = analysis, investigation ❏ *Sixty-five per cent of the 1987 budget went on nuclear weapons research and production.* ❏ *money spent on cancer research* ❏ *a centre which conducts animal research into brain diseases*

VERB [I, T] (**researches, researching, researched**) If you **research** something, you try to discover facts about it. = investigate, examine, explore, study, analyse ❏ *She spent two years in South Florida researching and filming her documentary.* ❏ *So far we haven't been able to find anything, but we're still researching.* ❏ *a meticulously researched study*

re·search·er /rɪˈsɜːtʃə/ NOUN [C] (**researchers**) = analyst, scientist ❏ *He chose to join the company as a market researcher.* ❏ *Researchers have found that vitamin A can protect the lungs from cancer.*

WORD CONNECTIONS

VERB + **research**

conduct research
undertake research
carry out research
❏ *She carried out research into the use of ICT in the classroom.*

research + VERB

research **suggests**
research **shows**
research **reveals**
research **indicates**
❏ *Research suggests that both genetic factors and environmental influences play a part.*

ADJ + **research**

new research
recent research
current research
❏ *According to recent research, long-term unemployment can cause serious psychological damage.*

clinical research
medical research
scientific research
❏ *Sustainable energy technologies are currently the focus of much scientific research.*

research + NOUN

a research **scientist**
a research **facility**
a research **laboratory**
❏ *The hospital has its own medical research facility.*

---

research **findings**
research **methods**
❏ *His research findings were widely published in scientific journals.*

VOCABULARY BUILDER

research VERB

If you **research** something, you try to discover facts about it.
❏ *You can check your email in the study while the kids research their homework in the front room.*

investigate VERB (*formal*)

If someone, especially an official, **investigates** an event, situation, or claim, they try to find out what happened or what is the truth.
❏ *They're still investigating the accident.*

examine VERB

If an idea, proposal, or plan is **examined**, it is considered very carefully.
❏ *I have given the matter much thought, examining all the possible alternatives.*

explore VERB (*formal*)

If you **explore** an idea or suggestion, you think about it or comment on it in detail, in order to assess it carefully.
❏ *The film explores the relationship between artist and instrument.*

study VERB

If you **study** something, you consider it or observe it carefully in order to be able to understand it fully.
❏ *I invite every citizen to carefully study the document.*

analyse VERB

If you **analyse** something, you examine it using scientific methods in order to find out what it consists of.
❏ *Over decades Darwin obsessively collected, classified and analysed his findings.*

USAGE NOTE

research

Research is an uncountable noun. Do not use 'a research'.
*They set up an organization to conduct **research** into agriculture.*

re·sem·blance /rɪˈzembləns/ NOUN [C, U] (**resemblances**) If there is a **resemblance** between two people or things, they are similar to each other. = similarity ❏ *There was a remarkable resemblance between him and Pete.* ❏ *Our tour prices bore little resemblance to those in the holiday brochures.*

re·sem·ble /rɪˈzembəl/ VERB [T] (**resembles, resembling, resembled**) If one thing or person **resembles** another, they are similar to each other. ❏ *Some of the commercially produced venison resembles beef in flavour.* ❏ *It is true that both therapies do closely resemble each other.*

re·sent /rɪˈzent/ VERB [T] (**resents, resenting, resented**) If you **resent** someone or something, you feel bitter and angry about them. ❏ *She resents her mother for being so tough on her.*

re·sent·ment /rɪˈzentmənt/ NOUN [U] **Resentment** is bitterness and anger that someone feels about something. ❏ *She expressed resentment at being interviewed by a social worker.*

res·er·va·tion /ˌrezəˈveɪʃən/ NOUN [C, U] (**reservations**) **1** [C, U] If you have **reservations about** something, you are not sure that it is entirely good or right. ❏ *I told him my main reservation about his film was the ending.* **2** [C] If you make a **reservation**, you arrange for something such as a table in a restaurant or a room in a hotel to be kept for you. = booking ❏ *He went to the desk to inquire and make a reservation.* **3** [C] A **reservation** is an area of land that is kept separate for a particular group of people to live in.

R

❏ *Seventeen thousand Indians live in Arizona on a reservation.*

⊙ **re·serve** ♦♦◇ /rɪˈzɜːv/ VERB, NOUN

VERB [T] (**reserves, reserving, reserved**) **1** If something **is reserved for** a particular person or purpose, it is kept specially for that person or purpose. = set aside ❏ *A double room with a balcony overlooking the sea had been reserved for him.* **2** If you **reserve** something such as a table, ticket, or magazine, you arrange for it to be kept specially for you, rather than sold or given to someone else. ❏ *I'll reserve a table for five.*

NOUN [C, U] (**reserves**) **1** [C] A **reserve** is a supply of something that is available for use when it is needed. = store, stock, supply ❏ *The Persian Gulf has 65 per cent of the world's oil reserves.* ❏ *Having a reserve of 24 hours' worth of water is the standard across Canada.* **2** [C] (*mainly BrE*; *in AmE, use* **preserve**) A nature **reserve** is an area of land where the animals, birds, and plants are officially protected. **3** [U] If someone shows **reserve**, they keep their feelings hidden. ❏ *I hope that you'll overcome your reserve and let me know.*

PHRASE in reserve If you have something **in reserve**, you have it available for use when it is needed. ❏ *He poked around the top of his cabinet for the bottle of whisky that he kept in reserve.*

✦ **reserve judgment** → see **judgment**; **reserve the right** → see **right**

re·served /rɪˈzɜːvd/ ADJ **1** Someone who is **reserved** keeps their feelings hidden. ❏ *He was unemotional, quiet, and reserved.* **2** A table in a restaurant or a seat in a theatre that is **reserved** is being kept for someone rather than given or sold to anyone else. ❏ *Seats, or sometimes entire tables, were reserved.*

res·er·voir /ˈrezəvwɑː/ NOUN [C] (**reservoirs**) **1** A **reservoir** is a lake that is used for storing water before it is supplied to people. **2** A **reservoir of** something is a large quantity of it that is available for use when needed. ❏ *the huge oil reservoir beneath the Kuwaiti desert*

resi·dence /ˈrezɪdəns/ NOUN

NOUN [C, U] (**residences**) **1** [C] (*formal*) A **residence** is a house where people live. ❏ *The house is currently run as a country inn, but could easily convert back into a private residence.* **2** [U] (*formal*) Your place of **residence** is the place where you live. ❏ *There were significant differences among women based on age, place of residence, and educational levels.* **3** [U] Someone's **residence** in a particular place is the fact that they live there or that they are officially allowed to live there. ❏ *They had entered the country and had applied for permanent residence.*

PHRASE in residence If someone is **in residence** in a particular place, they are living there. ❏ *The king and queen of Jordan are in residence.*

⊙ **resi·dent** ♦♦◇ /ˈrezɪdənt/ NOUN, ADJ (*academic word*)

NOUN [C] (**residents**) The **residents** of a house or area are the people who live there. = inhabitant, citizen ❏ *The archbishop called on the government to build more low cost homes for local residents.* ❏ *More than 10 per cent of Munich residents live below the poverty line.*

ADJ [V-LINK + resident] Someone who is **resident in** a country or a town lives there. ❏ *He moved to the United States in 1990 to live with his son, who had been resident in Baltimore since 1967.*

resi·den·tial /ˌrezɪˈdenʃəl/ ADJ **1** A **residential** area contains houses rather than offices or factories. ❏ *a posh residential area 20 minutes from the White House* **2** A **residential** institution is one where people live while they are studying there or being cared for there. ❏ *Training involves a two-year residential course.*

re·sid·ual /rɪˈzɪdjuəl/ ADJ **Residual** is used to describe what remains of something when most of it has gone. ❏ *residual radiation from nuclear weapons testing*

resi·due /ˈrezɪdjuː, *AmE* -duː/ NOUN [C] (**residues**) A **residue** of something is a small amount that remains after most of it has gone. ❏ *Always using the same shampoo means that a residue can build up on the hair.*

re·sign ♦◇◇ /rɪˈzaɪn/ VERB [I, T] (**resigns, resigning, resigned**) **1** [I, T] If you **resign** from a job or position, you

formally announce that you are leaving it. = quit ❏ *A hospital administrator has resigned over claims he lied to get the job.* ❏ *Mr Robb resigned his position last month.* **2** [T] If you **resign yourself to** an unpleasant situation or fact, you accept it because you realize that you cannot change it. = reconcile ❏ *Pat and I resigned ourselves to yet another summer without a boat.*

→ See also **resigned**

res·ig·na·tion ♦◇◇ /ˌrezɪɡˈneɪʃən/ NOUN [C, U] (**resignations**) **1** [C, U] Your **resignation** is a formal statement of your intention to leave a job or position. ❏ *Bob Morgan has offered his resignation and it has been accepted.* **2** [U] **Resignation** is the acceptance of an unpleasant situation or fact because you realize that you cannot change it. ❏ *He sighed with profound resignation.*

re·signed /rɪˈzaɪnd/ ADJ If you are **resigned to** an unpleasant situation or fact, you accept it without complaining because you realize that you cannot change it. = reconciled ❏ *He is resigned to the noise, the mess, the constant upheaval.*

re·sili·ent /rɪˈzɪliənt/ ADJ **1** Something that is **resilient** is strong and not easily damaged by being hit, stretched, or squeezed. ❏ *an armchair of some resilient plastic material* **2** People and things that are **resilient** are able to recover easily and quickly from unpleasant or damaging events. ❏ *When the US stock market collapsed in October 1987, the Japanese stock market was the most resilient.*

re·sili·ence /rɪˈzɪliəns/ NOUN [U] **1** [also 'a' resilience] ❏ *Do you feel that your muscles do not have the strength and resilience that they should have?* **2** [also 'a' resilience] ❏ *the resilience of human beings to fight after they've been attacked*

⊙ **re·sist** ♦◇◇ /rɪˈzɪst/ VERB [T, I] (**resists, resisting, resisted**) **1** [T] If you **resist** something such as a change, you refuse to accept it and try to prevent it. = oppose ❏ *They resisted our attempts to modernize the distribution of books.* ❏ *She says she will resist a single European currency being imposed.* **2** [I, T] If you **resist** someone or **resist** an attack by them, you fight back against them. ❏ *The man was shot outside his house as he tried to resist arrest.* ❏ *When she attempted to cut his nails he resisted.* **3** [T] If you **resist** doing something, or **resist** the temptation to do it, you stop yourself from doing it although you would like to do it. ❏ *Congress should resist the temptation to try quick economic fixes.* **4** [T] If someone or something **resists** damage of some kind, they are not damaged. = withstand ❏ *bodies trained and toughened to resist the cold* ❏ *Chemicals form a protective layer that resists both oil and water-based stains.*

⊙ **re·sist·ance** ♦◇◇ /rɪˈzɪstəns/ NOUN [U, C] (**resistances**) **1** [U] **Resistance** to something such as a change or a new idea is a refusal to accept it. = opposition ❏ *The US wants big cuts in European agricultural export subsidies, but this is meeting resistance.* ❏ *stubborn resistance to social reform* **2** [U] **Resistance** to an attack consists of fighting back against the people who have attacked you. ❏ *A CBS correspondent in Colombo says the troops are encountering stiff resistance.* **3** [U] The **resistance** of your body **to** germs or diseases is its power to remain unharmed or unaffected by them. ❏ *This disease is surprisingly difficult to catch, as most people have a natural resistance to it.* **4** [U] Wind or air **resistance** is a force which slows down a moving object or vehicle. ❏ *The design of the bicycle reduces the effects of wind resistance and drag.* **5** [C, U] In electrical engineering or physics, **resistance** is the ability of a substance or an electrical circuit to stop the flow of an electrical current through it. ❏ *The salt reduces the electrical resistance of the water.*

⊙ **re·sist·ant** /rɪˈzɪstənt/ ADJ **1** Someone who is **resistant to** something is opposed to it and wants to prevent it. = opposed ❏ *Some people are very resistant to the idea of exercise.* **2** If something is **resistant to** a particular thing, it is not harmed by it. ❏ *how to improve plants to make them more resistant to disease* ❏ *The body may be less resistant if it is cold.*

reso·lute /ˈrezəluːt/ ADJ (*formal*) If you describe someone as **resolute**, you approve of them because they are very determined not to change their mind or not to give up a

r

course of action. = determined ☐ *Voters perceive him as a decisive and resolute international leader.*

reso·lute·ly /ˈrezəluːtli/ ADV ☐ *He resolutely refused to speak English unless forced to.*

✪ **reso·lu·tion** ◆◆◇ /ˌrezəˈluːʃən/ NOUN [C, U, SING] (resolutions) **1** [C] A **resolution** is a formal decision made at a meeting by means of a vote. = decision ☐ *He replied that the UN had passed two major resolutions calling for a complete withdrawal.* ☐ *a draft resolution on the occupied territories* **2** [C] If you make a **resolution**, you decide to try very hard to do something. ☐ *They made a resolution to lose all the weight gained during the Christmas holidays.* **3** [U] **Resolution** is determination to do something or not do something. ☐ *'I think I'll try a hypnotist,' I said with sudden resolution.* **4** [SING] (formal) The **resolution** of a problem or difficulty is the final solving of it. = solution, settlement ☐ *the successful resolution of a dispute involving UN inspectors in Baghdad* ☐ *in order to find a peaceful resolution to the crisis* ☐ *Most problems don't require instant resolution.*

✪ **re·solve** ◆◇◇ /rɪˈzɒlv/ VERB, NOUN (academic word) VERB [T] (resolves, resolving, resolved) (formal) **1** To **resolve** a problem, argument, or difficulty means to find a solution to it. ☐ *We must find a way to resolve these problems before it's too late.* ☐ *They hoped the crisis could be resolved peacefully.* **2** If you **resolve to** do something, you make a firm decision to do it. = decide ☐ *She resolved to report the matter to the hospital's nursing supervisor.* ☐ *The Prime Minister had finally resolved to retire.*
NOUN [C, U] (resolves) (formal) **Resolve** is determination to do what you have decided to do. = determination ☐ *So you're saying this will strengthen the American public's resolve to go to war if necessary?*

re·sort ◆◇◇ /rɪˈzɔːt/ VERB, NOUN
VERB [I] (resorts, resorting, resorted) If you **resort to** a course of action that you do not really approve of, you adopt it because you cannot see any other way of achieving what you want. ☐ *His punishing work schedule had made him resort to drugs.*
NOUN [U, C] (resorts) **1** [U] If you achieve something without **resort to** a particular course of action, you succeed without carrying out that action. To have **resort to** a particular course of action means to have to do that action in order to achieve something. = recourse ☐ *Congress has a responsibility to ensure that all peaceful options are exhausted before resort to war.* **2** [C] A **resort** is a place where a lot of people spend their holidays. ☐ *The ski resorts are expanding to meet the growing number of skiers that come here.*
PHRASE **as a last resort** If you do something **as a last resort**, you do it because you can find no other way of getting out of a difficult situation or of solving a problem. ☐ *Nuclear weapons should be used only as a last resort.*

✪ **re·source** ◆◆◇ /rɪˈzɔːs, AmE ˈriːsɔːrs/ NOUN [C] (resources) (academic word) **1** The **resources** of an organization or person are the materials, money, and other things that they have and can use in order to function properly. = supplies ☐ *Some families don't have the resources to feed themselves adequately.* **2** A country's **resources** are the things that it has and can use to increase its wealth, such as coal, oil, or land. = assets, materials ☐ *resources like coal, tungsten, oil, and copper* ☐ *Today we are overpopulated, straining the earth's resources.*

WORD CONNECTIONS

ADJ + resource

financial resources
economic resources
limited resources
☐ *The organization has achieved a great deal with very limited financial resources.*

natural resources
mineral resources
energy resources
☐ *Some countries are poor despite abundant natural resources.*

VERB + resources

allocate resources
devote resources
lack resources
☐ *Resources must be allocated in such a way as to produce maximum profit.*

✪ **re·spect** ◆◆◇ /rɪˈspekt/ VERB, NOUN
VERB [T] (respects, respecting, respected) **1** If you **respect** someone, you have a good opinion of their character or ideas. ☐ *I want him to respect me as a career woman.* **2** If you **respect** someone's wishes, rights, or customs, you avoid doing things that they would dislike or regard as wrong. = honour ☐ *Finally, trying to respect her wishes, I said I'd leave.* ☐ *It is our policy to respect the privacy of every customer.* **3** If you **respect** a law or moral principle, you agree not to break it. = recognise, honour, acknowledge; ≠ break, breach ☐ *It is about time tour operators respected the law and their own code of conduct.* ☐ *pledges by both sides to respect the ceasefire*
NOUN [U] (respects) **1** If you have **respect for** someone, you have a good opinion of them. ☐ *I have tremendous respect for Dean.* **2** If you show **respect for** someone's wishes, rights, or customs, you avoid doing anything they would dislike or regard as wrong. = regard; ≠ disrespect ☐ *They will campaign for respect for aboriginal rights and customs.* **3** **Respect** is agreeing not to break a law or moral principle. ☐ *respect for the law and the rejection of the use of violence*
PHRASES **with all due respect** (politeness) You can say with **all due respect** when you are politely disagreeing with someone or criticizing them. ☐ *With all due respect, I hardly think that's the point.*

pay one's respects (formal) If you pay your **respects to** someone, you go to see them or speak to them. You usually do this to be polite, and not necessarily because you want to do it. ☐ *Carl had asked him to visit the hospital and to pay his respects to Francis.*

in this respect or **in many respects** You use expressions like **in this respect** and **in many respects** to indicate that what you are saying applies to the feature you have just mentioned or to many features of something. ☐ *Within the Department of Justice are several drug-fighting agencies. The lead agency in this respect is the DEA.* ☐ *The children are not unintelligent – in fact, they seem quite normal in this respect.* ☐ *In many respects Asian women see themselves as equal to their men.*

with respect to (formal) You use **with respect to** or in **respect of** to say what something relates to. = concerning, regarding, apropos of ☐ *Parents often have little choice with respect to the way their child is medically treated.* ☐ *Where Dr Shapland feels the system is not working most effectively is in respect of professional training.*
→ See also **respected**

re·spect·able /rɪˈspektəbəl/ ADJ **1** Someone or something that is **respectable** is approved of by society and considered to be morally correct. ☐ *He came from a perfectly respectable middle-class family.* **2** You can say that something is **respectable** when you mean that it is good enough or acceptable. = decent ☐ *investments that offer respectable and highly attractive rates of return*
re·spect·abil·ity /rɪˌspektəˈbɪlɪti/ NOUN [U] ☐ *If she divorced Tony, she would lose the respectability she had as Mrs Tony Tatterton.*

re·spect·ed /rɪˈspektɪd/ ADJ Someone or something that is **respected** is admired and considered important by many people. ☐ *He is highly respected for his novels and plays as well as his translations of American novels.*

re·spect·ful /rɪˈspektfʊl/ ADJ If you are **respectful**, you show respect for someone. ☐ *The children in our family are always respectful to their elders.*
re·spect·ful·ly /rɪˈspektfəli/ ADV ☐ *'You are an artist,' she said respectfully.*

✪ **re·spec·tive** /rɪˈspektɪv/ ADJ [respective + N] **Respective** means relating or belonging separately to the individual people you have just mentioned. = own, particular, relevant, corresponding ☐ *Steve and I were at very different stages in our respective careers.*

R

❑ *the respective roles of men and women*

✪ **re·spec·tive·ly** /rɪˈspektɪvli/ ADV [respectively with CL/GROUP] **Respectively** means in the same order as the items that you have just mentioned. = correspondingly ❑ *Their sons, Ben and Jonathan, were three and six respectively.* ❑ *Obesity and high blood pressure occurred in 16 per cent and 14 per cent of Australian adults, respectively.*

✪ **res·pi·ra·tion** /ˌrespɪˈreɪʃən/ NOUN [U] (*medical*) Your **respiration** is your breathing. = breathing ❑ *His respiration grew fainter throughout the day.*

✪ **res·pira·tory** /ˈrespərətri, AmE -tɔri/ ADJ [respiratory + N] (*medical*) **Respiratory** means relating to breathing. = breathing ❑ *people with severe respiratory problems* ❑ *If you smoke then the whole respiratory system is constantly under attack.* ❑ *complete respiratory failure*

res·pite /ˈrespaɪt, -pɪt/ NOUN [SING] (*formal*) **1** [also no DET, oft respite 'from' N] A **respite** is a short period of rest from something unpleasant. ❑ *It was some weeks now since they'd had any respite from shellfire.* **2** [also no DET] A **respite** is a short delay before a very unpleasant or difficult situation which may or may not take place. = reprieve ❑ *Devaluation would only give the economy a brief respite.*

✪ **re·spond** ♦♦◇ /rɪˈspɒnd/ VERB [I, T] (**responds, responding, responded**) (*academic word*) **1** [I, T] When you **respond** to something that is done or said, you react to it by doing or saying something yourself. = react ❑ *They are likely to respond positively to the president's request for aid.* ❑ *The army responded with gunfire and tear gas.* ❑ *'I have no idea,' she responded.* **2** [I] When you **respond to** a need, crisis, or challenge, you take the necessary or appropriate action. = react ❑ *This modest group size allows our teachers to respond to the needs of each student.* **3** [I] If a patient or their injury or illness **is responding to** treatment, the treatment is working and they are getting better. ❑ *I'm pleased to say that he is now doing well and responding to treatment.*

✪ **re·spond·ent** /rɪˈspɒndənt/ NOUN [C] (**respondents**) [usu pl] A **respondent** is a person who replies to something such as a survey or set of questions. ❑ *Sixty per cent of the respondents said they disapproved of the president's performance.* ❑ *Three hundred and fifty questionnaire respondents were asked four questions.* ❑ *the medical background of the respondents*

✪ **re·sponse** ♦♦◇ /rɪˈspɒns/ NOUN [C] (**responses**) [oft response 'to/from' N, also 'in' response] Your **response** to an event or to something that is said is your reply or reaction to it. = reaction ❑ *There has been no response to his remarks from the government.* ❑ *Your positive response will reinforce her actions.* ❑ *The meeting was called in response to a request from Venezuela.*

✪ **re·spon·sibil·ity** ♦♦◇ /rɪˌspɒnsɪˈbɪlɪti/ NOUN [U, PL, SING] (**responsibilities**) **1** [U] If you have **responsibility** for something or someone, or if they are your **responsibility**, it is your job or duty to deal with them and to make decisions relating to them. = duty, obligation ❑ *Each manager had responsibility for just under 600 properties.* ❑ *We need to take responsibility for looking after our own health.* ❑ *'She's not your responsibility', he said gently.* **2** [U] If you accept **responsibility for** something that has happened, you agree that you were to blame for it or you caused it. = accountability, guilt, blame, fault, liability ❑ *No one admitted responsibility for the attacks.* ❑ *Someone had to give orders and take responsibility for mistakes.* **3** [PL] Your **responsibilities** are the duties that you have because of your job or position. = duties, obligations ❑ *I am told that he handled his responsibilities as a counsellor in a highly intelligent and caring fashion.* ❑ *programmes to help employees balance work and family responsibilities* **4** [U] If someone is given **responsibility**, they are given the right or opportunity to make important decisions or to take action without having to get permission from anyone else. ❑ *She would have loved to have a better-paying job with more responsibility.* **5** [SING] If you think that you have a **responsibility to** do something, you feel that you ought to do it because it is morally right to do it. = duty ❑ *The court feels it has a responsibility to ensure that customers are not misled.* **6** [SING] If you think that you have a **responsibility**

to someone, you feel that it is your duty to take action that will protect their interests. ❑ *She had decided that as a doctor she had a responsibility to her fellow creatures.*

have responsibility
take responsibility
assume responsibility
❑ *Parents must assume responsibility for the well-being of their children.*

give responsibility
delegate responsibility
assign responsibility
❑ *The project manager assigns responsibility for different tasks to team members.*

admit responsibility
accept responsibility
claim responsibility
deny responsibility
❑ *The company denied responsibility for the accident.*

VOCABULARY BUILDER

responsibility NOUN
If you accept **responsibility for** something that has happened, you agree that you were to blame for it or you caused it.
❑ *The Ministry of Defence paid an out-of-court settlement, but did not admit responsibility.*

guilt NOUN (*fairly formal*)
Guilt is the fact that you have done something wrong or illegal.
❑ *The trial is concerned only with the determination of guilt.*

blame NOUN
The **blame** for something bad that has happened is the responsibility for causing it or letting it happen.
❑ *I'm not going to take the blame for a mistake he made.*

fault NOUN
If a bad or undesirable situation is your **fault**, you caused it or are responsible for it.
❑ *There was no escaping the fact: it was all his fault.*

liability NOUN (*formal*)
Liability for something such as a debt is a legal duty to settle it.
❑ *He is claiming damages from London Underground, which has admitted liability.*

✪ **re·spon·sible** ♦♦◇ /rɪˈspɒnsɪbəl/ ADJ **1** [V-LINK + responsible] If someone or something is **responsible for** a particular event or situation, they are the cause of it or they can be blamed for it. = to blame, guilty; ≠ innocent ❑ *He still felt responsible for her death.* ❑ *I want you to do everything you can to find out who's responsible.* **2** [V-LINK + responsible] If you are **responsible for** something, it is your job or duty to deal with it and make decisions relating to it. = accountable ❑ *the cabinet member responsible for the environment* ❑ *The man responsible for finding the volunteers is Dr Charles Weber.* **3** [V-LINK + responsible 'to' N] If you are **responsible to** a person or group, they have authority over you and you have to report to them about what you do. ❑ *I'm responsible to my board of directors.* **4** **Responsible** people behave properly and sensibly, without needing to be supervised. ❑ *He feels that the media should be more responsible in what they report.* **5** [responsible + N] **Responsible** jobs involve making important decisions or carrying out important tasks. ❑ *You are too young for such a responsible position.*
re·spon·sibly /rɪˈspɒnsɪbli/ ADV [responsibly with V] ❑ *He urged everyone to act responsibly.*

rest ♦♦◇ /rest/ QUANT, PRON, VERB, NOUN
QUANT ['the' rest 'of' DEF-N] **The rest** is used to refer to all

the parts of something or all the things in a group that remain or that you have not already mentioned. ◻ *It was an experience I will treasure for the rest of my life.* **PRON** **The rest** is used to refer to all the parts of something or all the things in a group that remain or that you have not already mentioned. ◻ *The first payment was made yesterday, and the rest will be paid next month.* **PHRASE** **and the rest** or **all the rest of it** (*spoken, vagueness*) You can add **and the rest** or **all the rest of it** to the end of a statement or list when you want to refer in a vague way to other things that are associated with the ones you have already mentioned. ◻ *a man with nice clothes, an SUV, and the rest* **VERB** [I, T] (**rests, resting, rested**) **1** [I, T] If you **rest** or if you **rest** your body, you do not do anything active for a time. ◻ *He's tired and exhausted, and has been advised to rest for two weeks.* **2** [I] (*formal*) If something such as a theory or someone's success **rests on** a particular thing, it depends on that thing. = **depend** ◻ *Such a view rests on a number of incorrect assumptions.* **3** [I] (*formal*) If authority, a responsibility, or a decision **rests with** you, you have that authority or responsibility, or you are the one who will make that decision. ◻ *The final decision rested with the president.* **4** [T] If you **rest** something somewhere, you put it there so that its weight is supported. = **lean** ◻ *He rested his arms on the back of the chair.* **5** [I, T] If something **is resting** somewhere, or if you **are resting** it there, it is in a position where its weight is supported. ◻ *His head was resting on her shoulder.* **6** [I] If you **rest** on or against someone or something, you lean on them so that they support the weight of your body. = **lean** ◻ *He rested on his pick for a while.* **7** [I] (*written*) If your eyes **rest on** a particular person or object, you look directly at them, rather than somewhere else. ◻ *As she spoke, her eyes rested on her husband's face.* **PHRASE** **let something rest** If someone refuses to **let** a subject **rest**, they refuse to stop talking about it, especially after they have been talking about it for a long time. = **drop** ◻ *I am not prepared to let this matter rest.* **NOUN** [C, U] (**rests**) **1** [C, U] If you get some **rest** or have a **rest**, you do not do anything active for a time. ◻ *'You're worn out, Laura,' he said. 'Go home and get some rest.'* **2** [C] A **rest** is an object that is used to support something, especially your head, arms, or feet. ◻ *When you are sitting, keep your elbow on the arm rest.* **PHRASES** **come to rest** (*formal*) When an object that has been moving **comes to rest**, it finally stops. ◻ *The plane had ploughed a path through a patch of forest before coming to rest in a field.* **put someone's mind at rest** or **set someone's mind at rest** To put someone's **mind at rest** or set their **mind at rest** means to tell them something that stops them from worrying. = **reassure** ◻ *A brain scan last Friday finally set his mind at rest.* ✦ **rest assured** → see **assured**

res·tau·rant ♦♦◇ /ˈrestərɒnt, AmE -rənt/ NOUN [C] (**restaurants**) A **restaurant** is a place where you can eat a meal and pay for it. In restaurants, your food is usually served to you at your table by a waiter or waitress. ◻ *They ate in an Italian restaurant in Forth Street.*

rest·less /ˈrestləs/ ADJ **1** If you are **restless**, you are bored, impatient, or dissatisfied, and you want to do something else. ◻ *By 1982, she was restless and needed a new impetus for her talent.* **2** If someone is **restless**, they keep moving around because they find it difficult to keep still. ◻ *My father seemed very restless and excited.*
rest·less·ness /ˈrestləsnəs/ NOUN [U] **1** *From the audience came increasing sounds of restlessness.* **2** *Karen complained of hyperactivity and restlessness.*
rest·less·ly /ˈrestləsli/ ADV ◻ *He paced up and down restlessly, trying to put his thoughts in order.*

✪ **re·store** ♦◇◇ /rɪˈstɔː/ VERB [T] (**restores, restoring, restored**) (*academic word*) **1** To **restore** a situation or practice means to cause it to exist again. = **bring back, reinstate, re-establish;** ≠ **abolish** ◻ *The army has recently been brought in to restore order.* ◻ *restore the status quo* ◻ *The death penalty was never restored.* **2** To **restore** someone or

something **to** a previous condition or place means to cause them to be in that condition or place once again. = **reinstate, return** ◻ *We will restore her to health but it may take time.* ◻ *He said the ousted president must be restored to power.* ◻ *His country desperately needs Western aid to restore its ailing economy.* **3** When someone **restores** something such as an old building, painting, or piece of furniture, they repair and clean it, so that it looks like it did when it was new. ◻ *experts who specialize in examining and restoring ancient parchments* **4** (*formal*) If something that was lost or stolen **is restored to** its owner, it is returned to them. = **return** ◻ *The following day their horses and goods were restored to them.*
✪ **res·to·ra·tion** /ˌrestəˈreɪʃən/ NOUN [U, C] **1** [U] ◻ *His visit is expected to lead to the restoration of diplomatic relations.* ◻ *They were committed to the eventual restoration of a traditional monarchy.* **2** [U] ◻ *I owe the restoration of my hearing to this remarkable new technique.* **3** [C, U] ◻ *I specialized in the restoration of old houses.*
re·stored /rɪˈstɔːd/ ADJ ◻ *The restored building helps people understand the historic significance of our neighbourhood.*

✪ **re·strain** /rɪˈstreɪn/ VERB [T] (**restrains, restraining, restrained**) (*academic word*) **1** If you **restrain** someone, you stop them from doing what they intended or wanted to do, usually by using your physical strength. ◻ *Wally gripped my arm, partly to restrain me and partly to reassure me.* ◻ *One onlooker had to be restrained by police.* ◻ *One MP was physically restrained during an argument with a minister.* ◻ *the bare minimum of force necessary to restrain the attackers* **2** If you **restrain** an emotion or you **restrain yourself from** doing something, you prevent yourself from showing that emotion or doing what you wanted or intended to do. ◻ *She was unable to restrain her desperate anger.* **3** To **restrain** something that is growing or increasing means to prevent it from getting too large. = **limit, check;** ≠ **encourage** ◻ *The radical 500-day plan was very clear on how it intended to try to restrain inflation.* ◻ *In the 1970s, the government tried to restrain corruption.* ◻ *to restrain the growth in state spending*

✪ **re·straint** /rɪˈstreɪnt/ NOUN [C, U] (**restraints**) **1** [C, U] **Restraints** are rules or conditions that limit or restrict someone or something. = **limitation, check, constraint;** ≠ **freedom** ◻ *The president is calling for spending restraints in some areas.* ◻ *With open frontiers and lax visa controls, criminals could cross into the country without restraint.* ◻ *free of any restraints which social convention might impose* **2** [U] **Restraint** is calm, controlled, and unemotional behaviour. ◻ *They behaved with more restraint than I'd expected.*

✪ **re·strict** /rɪˈstrɪkt/ VERB [T] (**restricts, restricting, restricted**) (*academic word*) **1** If you **restrict** something, you put a limit on it in order to reduce it or prevent it from becoming too great. = **limit** ◻ *There is talk of raising the admission requirements to restrict the number of students on campus.* ◻ *The French, I believe, restrict Japanese imports to a maximum of 3 per cent of their market.* **2** To **restrict** the movement or actions of someone or something means to prevent them from moving or acting freely. = **limit, restrain** ◻ *The government imprisoned dissidents, forbade travel, and restricted the press.* ◻ *Villagers say the fence would restrict public access to the hills.* ◻ *These dams restricted the flow of the river downstream.* **3** If you **restrict** someone or their activities **to** one thing, they can only do, have, or deal with that thing. If you **restrict** them **to** one place, they cannot go anywhere else. = **confine** ◻ *For the first two weeks, patients are restricted to the grounds.* **4** If you **restrict** something **to** a particular group, only that group can do it or have it. If you **restrict** something **to** a particular place, it is allowed only in that place. = **limit** ◻ *Trustees had decided to restrict university entry to about 30 percent of applicants.*

re·strict·ed /rɪˈstrɪktɪd/ ADJ **1** Something that is **restricted** is quite small or limited. ◻ *the monotony of a heavily restricted diet* **2** [V-LINK + restricted 'to' N] If something is **restricted to** a particular group, only members of that group have it. If it is **restricted to** a particular place, it exists only in that place. ◻ *Discipline*

R

problems are by no means restricted to children in families dependent on benefits. **3** A **restricted** area is one that only people with special permission can enter. □ *a highly restricted area close to the old naval airfield*

✪ re·stric·tion ◆◇◇ /rɪˈstrɪkʃən/ NOUN [C, U] (**restrictions**) **1** [C] A **restriction** is an official rule that limits what you can do or that limits the amount or size of something. □ *the lifting of restrictions on political parties and the news media* **2** [C] You can refer to anything that limits what you can do as a **restriction**. = limitation □ *His parents are trying to make up to him for the restrictions of urban living.* **3** [U] The **restriction** of something is the act of putting a limit on it in order to reduce it or prevent it from becoming too great. □ *Since the costs of science were rising faster than inflation, some restriction on funding was necessary.* **4** [U] **Restriction** of someone's or something's movement or actions is the act of preventing them from moving or acting freely. = limitation, control; ≠ freedom □ *the justification for this restriction of individual liberty*

✪ re·struc·ture /ˌriːˈstrʌktʃə/ VERB [I, T] (**restructures, restructuring, restructured**) (*academic word*) To **restructure** an organization or system means to change the way it is organized, usually in order to make it work more effectively. = reorganize □ *The president called on educators and politicians to help him restructure American education.* □ *At the same time as firms were restructuring, popular attitudes towards saving and investing were changing.* □ *an effort to restructure or re-engineer their businesses*

✪ re·struc·tur·ing /ˌriːˈstrʌktʃərɪŋ/ NOUN [C, U] (**restructurings**) The **restructuring** of an organization or system is a change in the way it is organized, usually in order to make it work more effectively. = reorganization □ *The company is to lay off 1,520 workers as part of a restructuring.* □ *In an effort to increase profitability, it announced a broad restructuring aimed at lowering expenses.*

✪ re·sult ◆◆◆ /rɪˈzʌlt/ NOUN, VERB
NOUN [C] (**results**) **1** A **result** is something that happens or exists because of something else that has happened. = by-product, consequence □ *Compensation is available for people who have developed asthma as a direct result of their work.* □ *Cancer is the end result of a long degenerative process.* **2** A **result** is the situation that exists at the end of a contest. □ *The final election results will be announced on Friday.* **3** A **result** is the number that you get when you do a calculation. = answer □ *They found their computers producing different results from exactly the same calculation.* **4** A **result** is the information that you get when you carry out an experiment or some research. = findings □ *There were some experimental errors on my part, invalidating the results.* □ *Here he published the results of his meticulous research.* **5** (*mainly BrE; in AmE, usually use* **scores**) Your **results** are the marks or grades that you get for examinations you have taken.
VERB [I] (**results, resulting, resulted**) **1** If something **results in** a particular situation or event, it causes that situation or event to happen. = cause, lead to □ *Fifty per cent of road accidents result in head injuries.* □ *Continuous rain resulted in the land becoming submerged.* **2** If something **results from** a particular event or action, it is caused by that event or action. = follow, develop, ensue □ *Many hair problems result from what you eat.* □ *Ignore the early warnings and illness could result.*

WORD CONNECTIONS

ADJ + **result**

a **direct** result
the **final** result
the **end** result
□ *The final result is that the overall levels remain unchanged.*

a **disappointing** result
a **surprising** result
an **impressive** result
a **positive** result
□ *The therapy produces impressive results in some patients.*

VERB + **result**

get results
achieve results
produce results
yield results
□ *Researchers using this method have achieved some very good results.*

result + OF + NOUN

the results of a **study**
the results of a **survey**
the results of an **experiment**
□ *They presented the results of a study of flight data.*

result + IN + NOUN

result in an **increase**
result in a **loss**
result in a **reduction**
□ *An increase of pressure results in an increase of the rate of reaction.*

WHICH WORD?

result or effect?

A **result** of something is an event or situation that happens or exists because of it.
□ *The **result** of this was months of anguish and guilt.*
When something produces a change in a thing or person, you do not refer to this change as a 'result' on the thing or person. The word you use is **effect**.
□ *Road transport has a considerable **effect** on our daily lives.*

✪ re·sult·ant /rɪˈzʌltənt/ ADJ [resultant + N] (*formal*) **Resultant** means caused by the event just mentioned. = consequent, ensuing □ *At least a quarter of a million people have died in the fighting and the resultant famines.*

re·sume ◆◇◇ /rɪˈzjuːm, AmE -ˈzuːm/ VERB [I, T] (**resumes, resuming, resumed**) (*formal*) **1** [I, T] If you **resume** an activity or if it **resumes**, it begins again. □ *After the war he resumed his duties at Wellesley College.* **2** [T] If you **resume** your seat or position, you return to the seat or position you were in before you moved. □ *'I changed my mind,'* Blanche said, resuming her seat.

re·sump·tion /rɪˈzʌmpʃən/ NOUN [U] □ *It is premature to speculate about the resumption of negotiations.*

✪ re·tail ◆◇◇ /ˈriːteɪl/ NOUN, ADV, VERB
NOUN [U] (*business*) **Retail** is the activity of selling products direct to the public, usually in small quantities. Compare **wholesale**. □ *Retail stores usually count on the Christmas season to make up to half of their annual profits.* □ *Retail sales grew just 3.8 per cent last year.* □ *The companies had come to sell – retail, wholesale, or export.*
ADV [retail after V] (*business*) If something is sold **retail**, it is sold in ordinary shops direct to the public. □ *We sell wholesale to several chains that sell retail to the public.*
VERB [I] (**retails, retailing, retailed**) (*business*) If an item in a shop **retails at** or **for** a particular price, it is for sale at that price. = sell □ *It originally retailed at $23.50.*

✪ re·tail·er /ˈriːteɪlə/ NOUN [C] (**retailers**) (*business*) A **retailer** is a person or business that sells goods to the public. □ *Furniture and carpet retailers are among those reporting the sharpest annual decline in sales.* □ *These can be purchased at many retailers and specialist medical suppliers.*

✪ re·tain ◆◇◇ /rɪˈteɪn/ VERB [T] (**retains, retaining, retained**) (*academic word, formal*) To **retain** something means to continue to have that thing. = keep, maintain, preserve; ≠ lose □ *The interior of the shop still retains a nineteenth-century atmosphere.* □ *Other countries retained their traditional and habitual ways of doing things.*

re·tali·ate /rɪˈtælieɪt/ VERB [I] (**retaliates, retaliating, retaliated**) If you **retaliate** when someone harms or annoys you, you do something which harms or annoys them in return. □ *I was sorely tempted to retaliate.* □ *The company would retaliate against employees who joined a union.*

re·talia·tion /rɪˌtæliˈeɪʃən/ NOUN [U] □ *Police said they*

r

believed the attack was in retaliation for the death of the drug trafficker.

⊕re·ten·tion /rɪˈtenʃən/ NOUN [U] (*formal*) The **retention** of something is the keeping of it. ▢ *The Citizens' Forum supported special powers for Quebec but also argued for the retention of a strong central government.* ▢ *A deficiency in magnesium increases lead absorption and retention.*

re·think /ˌriːˈθɪŋk/ VERB, NOUN

VERB [T] (**rethinks, rethinking, rethought**) If you **rethink** something such as a problem, a plan, or a policy, you think about it again and change it. ▢ *Both major political parties are having to rethink their policies.*

NOUN [SING] (*journalism*) If you have a **rethink** of a problem, a plan, or a policy, you think about it again and change it. ▢ *There must be a rethink of government policy towards this vulnerable group.*

⊕re·tire ◆◇◇ /rɪˈtaɪə/ VERB [I] (**retires, retiring, retired**)
1 When older people **retire**, they leave their job and usually stop working completely. = finish, leave, stop, quit ▢ *At the age when most people retire, he is ready to face a new career.* ▢ *Many said they plan to retire at 50.* ▢ *In 1974 he retired from the museum.* **2** When an athlete **retires from** their sport, they stop playing in competitions. When they **retire from** a race or a game, they stop competing in it. ▢ *I have decided to retire from Formula One racing at the end of the season.* **3** When a jury in a court of law **retires**, its members leave the court in order to decide whether someone is guilty or innocent. ▢ *The jury will retire to consider its verdict today.*
→ See also **retired**

re·tired /rɪˈtaɪəd/ ADJ A **retired** person is an older person who has left his or her job and has usually stopped working completely. ▢ *a seventy-three-year-old retired teacher from Florida*
→ See also **retire**

⊕re·tire·ment ◆◇◇ /rɪˈtaɪəmənt/ NOUN [C, U] (**retirements**) **1** [C, U] **Retirement** is the time when a worker retires. ▢ *The proportion of the population who are over retirement age has grown tremendously in the past few years.* ▢ *The Governor of the prison is to take early retirement.* **2** [U] A person's **retirement** is the period in their life after they have retired. ▢ *'Growing Older' considered the needs of the elderly for financial support during retirement.*

re·tort /rɪˈtɔːt/ VERB, NOUN

VERB [T] (**retorts, retorting, retorted**) (*written*) To **retort** means to reply angrily to someone. ▢ *'You can't smoke in here,' Shaw said. 'Don't worry, it's not tobacco,' he retorted.*

NOUN [C] (**retorts**) A **retort** is an angry reply to someone. ▢ *His sharp retort clearly made an impact.*

re·tract /rɪˈtrækt/ VERB [I, T] (**retracts, retracting, retracted**) (*formal*) **1** If you **retract** something that you have said or written, you say that you did not mean it. ▢ *Mr Smith hurriedly sought to retract the statement, but it had just been broadcast on national radio.* ▢ *He's hoping that if he makes me feel guilty, I'll retract.* **2** When a part of a machine or a part of a person's body **retracts** or **is retracted**, it moves inwards or becomes shorter. ▢ *Torn muscles retract and lose strength, structure, and tightness.*

re·trac·tion /rɪˈtrækʃən/ NOUN [C] (**retractions**)
= withdrawal ▢ *Miss Pearce said she expected an unqualified retraction of his comments within twenty-four hours.*

re·treat ◆◇◇ /rɪˈtriːt/ VERB, NOUN

VERB [I] (**retreats, retreating, retreated**) **1** If you **retreat**, you move away from something or someone. ▢ *'I've already got a job,' I said quickly, and retreated from the room.* **2** When an army **retreats**, it moves away from enemy forces in order to avoid fighting them. ▢ *The French, suddenly outnumbered, were forced to retreat.* **3** If you **retreat from** something such as a plan or a way of life, you give it up, usually in order to do something safer or less extreme. ▢ *She retreated from public life.*

NOUN [C, U] (**retreats**) **1** [C, U] The **retreat** of an army is the act of moving away from enemy forces in order to avoid fighting them. ▢ *In June 1942, the British 8th Army was in full retreat.* **2** [C, U] A **retreat** from something such as a plan or position is the act of changing your mind and giving it up, usually in order to do or adopt something

safer or less extreme. ▢ *The president's remarks appear to signal that there will be no retreat from his position.* **3** [C] A **retreat** is a quiet, isolated place that you go to in order to rest or to do things in private. ▢ *He spent yesterday hidden away in his country retreat.*

⊕re·triev·al /rɪˈtriːvəl/ NOUN [U] **1** The **retrieval** of information from a computer is the process of getting it back. ▢ *electronic storage and retrieval systems* ▢ *the study of the organization and retrieval of memories* **2** The **retrieval** of something is the process of getting it back from a particular place, especially from a place where it should not be. = recovery ▢ *Its real purpose is the launching and retrieval of small airplanes in flight.*

⊕re·trieve /rɪˈtriːv/ VERB [T] (**retrieves, retrieving, retrieved**) **1** If you **retrieve** something, you get it back from the place where you left it. = recover ▢ *The men were trying to retrieve weapons left when the army abandoned the island.* **2** If you manage to **retrieve** a situation, you succeed in bringing it back into a more acceptable state. ▢ *He, the one man who could retrieve that situation, might receive the call.* **3** To **retrieve** information from a computer or from your memory means to get it back. ▢ *Computers can instantly retrieve millions of information bits.* ▢ *As the child gets older, so his or her strategies for storing and retrieving information improve.*

⊕retro·spect /ˈretrəspekt/ NOUN

PHRASE **in retrospect** When you consider something **in retrospect**, you think about it afterwards, and often have a different opinion about it from the one that you had at the time. = with hindsight; ≠ with foresight ▢ *In retrospect, I wish that I had thought about alternative courses of action.* ▢ *In retrospect, it was a role he should have avoided, but fatigue and a lack of direction played their part in the choice.*

⊕retro·spec·tive /ˌretrəˈspektɪv/ NOUN, ADJ

NOUN [C] (**retrospectives**) A **retrospective** is an exhibition or showing of work done by an artist over many years, rather than his or her most recent work. ▢ *a retrospective of the films of Judy Garland*

ADJ **1 Retrospective** feelings or opinions concern things that happened in the past. ≠ prospective ▢ *Afterwards, retrospective fear of the responsibility would make her feel almost faint.* ▢ *The examples I have cited have been based on retrospective accounts.* **2** (*mainly BrE; in AmE, use* **retroactive**) **Retrospective** laws or legal actions take effect from a date before the date when they are officially approved.

⊕retro·spec·tive·ly /ˌretrəˈspektɪvli/ ADV = in retrospect, with hindsight ▢ *Retrospectively, it seems as if they probably were negligent.* ▢ *To ascribe opinions retrospectively is of course very dangerous.*

⊕re·turn ◆◆◆ /rɪˈtɜːn/ VERB, NOUN, ADJ

VERB [I, T] (**returns, returning, returned**) **1** [I] When you **return to** a place, you go back there after you have been away. ▢ *There are unconfirmed reports that Aziz will return to Moscow within hours.* **2** [T] If you **return** something that you have borrowed or taken, you give it back or put it back. ▢ *I enjoyed the book and said so when I returned it.* **3** [T] If you **return** something somewhere, you put it back where it was. ▢ *He returned the notebook to his jacket.* **4** [T] If you **return** someone's action, you do the same thing to them as they have just done to you. If you **return** someone's feelings, you feel the same way towards them as they feel towards you. ▢ *Back at the station the chief inspector returned the call.* **5** [I] If a feeling or situation **returns**, it comes back or happens again after a period when it was not present. ▢ *Official reports in Algeria suggest that calm is returning to the country.* **6** [I] If you **return to** a state that you were in before, you start being in that state again. ▢ *Life has improved and returned to normal.* **7** [I] If you **return to** a subject that you have mentioned before, you begin talking about it again. ▢ *The power of the church is one theme all these writers return to.* **8** [I] If you **return to** an activity that you were doing before, you start doing it again. ▢ *At that stage he will be 52, young enough to return to politics if he wishes to do so.* **9** [T] When a judge or jury **returns** a verdict, they announce whether they think the person on trial is guilty or not. ▢ *They returned a verdict of not guilty.*

R

NOUN [SING, c] (**returns**) **1** [SING] Your **return** is your arrival back at a place where you had been before. ❑ *Kenny explained the reason for his sudden return to Dallas.* **2** [SING] The **return** of something you have borrowed or taken is when you give it back or put it back. ❑ *The main demand of the Indians is for the return of one-and-a-half-million acres of forest to their communities.* **3** [SING] The **return** of a feeling or situation is when it comes back or happens again after a period when it was not present. ❑ *It was like the return of his youth.* **4** [SING] The **return** of a state you were in before is when you start being in that state again. ❑ *He made an uneventful return to normal health.* **5** [SING] A **return** to an activity you were doing before is when you start doing it again. ❑ *He has not ruled out the shock possibility of a return to football.* **6** [c] (*business*) The **return on** an investment is the profit that you get from it. = profit; ≠ loss ❑ *Profits have picked up this year but the return on capital remains tiny.* ❑ *Higher returns and higher risk usually go hand in hand.*

PHRASE **in return** If you do something **in return for** what someone else has done for you, you do it because they did that thing for you. ❑ *You pay regular premiums and in return the insurance company will pay out a lump sum.*

ADJ **1** (*mainly BrE; in AmE, usually use* **round trip**) A **return** ticket is a ticket for a trip from one place to another and then back again. **2** [return + N] The **return** trip is the part of a trip that takes you back to where you started from. ❑ *Buy an extra ticket for the return trip.*

✦ **return fire** → see **fire**

re·use VERB, NOUN

VERB /riːˈjuːz/ [T] (**reuses, reusing, reused**) When you **reuse** something, you use it again instead of throwing it away. ❑ *Try where possible to reuse paper.*

NOUN /riːˈjuːs/ [U] The **reuse** of something is the act or process of using something again instead of throwing it away. ❑ *Copper, brass, and aluminium are separated and remelted for reuse.*

⊕ **re·veal** ◆◆◇ /rɪˈviːl/ VERB [T] (**reveals, revealing, revealed**) (*academic word*) **1** To **reveal** something means to make people aware of it. = disclose, divulge, uncover; ≠ hide ❑ *She has refused to reveal the whereabouts of her daughter.* ❑ *A survey of the American diet has revealed that a growing number of people are overweight.* ❑ *No test will reveal how much of the drug was taken.* **2** If you **reveal** something that has been out of sight, you uncover it so that people can see it. = show ❑ *In the main room, a grey carpet was removed to reveal the original pine floor.*

re·veal·ing /rɪˈviːlɪŋ/ ADJ A **revealing** statement, account, or action tells you something that you did not know, especially about the person doing it or making it. ❑ *a revealing interview*

rev·e·la·tion /ˌrevəˈleɪʃən/ NOUN [c, U, SING] (**revelations**) **1** [c] A **revelation** is a surprising or interesting fact that is made known to people. ❑ *the seemingly everlasting revelations about his private life* **2** [c, U] The **revelation of** something is the act of making it known. ❑ *following the revelation of his affair with a former secretary* **3** [SING] If you say that something you experienced was **a revelation**, you are saying that it was very surprising or very good. ❑ *Degas's work had been a revelation to her.*

re·venge /rɪˈvendʒ/ NOUN, VERB

NOUN [U] **Revenge** involves hurting or punishing someone who has hurt or harmed you. ❑ *The attackers were said to be taking revenge on the 14-year-old, claiming he was a school bully.*

VERB [T] (**revenges, revenging, revenged**) (*written*) If you **revenge** yourself on someone who has hurt you, you hurt them in return. = avenge ❑ *The paper accused her of trying to revenge herself on her former lover.*

⊕ **rev·e·nue** ◆◇◇ /ˈrevənjuː/ NOUN [U] [also revenues] (*academic word, business*) **Revenue** is money that a company, organization, or government receives from people. = profit, income, proceeds; ≠ expenditure ❑ *a boom year at the cinema, with record advertising revenue and the highest ticket sales since 1980* ❑ *Fishing is the main industry, with seal-hunting in season an additional source of revenue.* ❑ *The government would gain about $12 billion in tax revenues over five years.*

⊕ **re·ver·sal** /rɪˈvɜːsəl/ NOUN [c] (**reversals**) **1** A **reversal of** a process, policy, or trend is a complete change in it. ≠ implementation ❑ *The paper says the move represents a complete reversal of previous US policy.* ❑ *This marked a 7% increase on the previous year and the reversal of a steady five-year downward trend.* **2** When there is a role **reversal** or a **reversal of** roles, two people or groups exchange their positions or functions. ❑ *When children end up taking care of their parents, it is a strange role reversal indeed.*

⊕ **re·verse** ◆◇◇ /rɪˈvɜːs/ VERB, NOUN, ADJ

VERB [T, I] (**reverses, reversing, reversed**) (*academic word*) **1** [T] When someone or something **reverses** a decision, policy, or trend, they change it to the opposite decision, policy, or trend. = change, overrule, overturn ❑ *They have made it clear they will not reverse the decision to increase prices.* ❑ *The rise, the first in 10 months, reversed the downward trend in Belgium's jobless rate.* **2** [T] If you **reverse** the order of a set of things, you arrange them in the opposite order, so that the first thing comes last. ❑ *Because the normal word order is reversed in passive sentences, they are sometimes hard to follow.* **3** [T] If you **reverse** the positions or functions of two things, you change them so that each thing has the position or function that the other one had. ❑ *He reversed the position of the two stamps.* **4** [I, T] (*mainly BrE; in AmE, usually use* **back up**) When a car **reverses** or when you **reverse** it, the car is driven backwards.

PHRASE **reverse the charges** (*mainly BrE; in AmE, usually use* **call collect**) If you **reverse the charges** when you make a telephone call, the person who you are phoning pays the cost of the call and not you.

NOUN [U, SING] **1** [U] If your car is **in reverse**, you have changed gears so that you can drive it backwards. ❑ *He lurched the car in reverse along the ruts to the access road.* **2** [SING] If you say that one thing is **the reverse** of another, you are emphasizing that the first thing is the complete opposite of the second thing. ❑ *He was not at all jolly. Quite the reverse.* **3** [SING] The **reverse** or the **reverse side** of a flat object which has two sides is the less important or the other side. = back ❑ *A chart on the reverse of this letter highlights your savings.*

PHRASE **in reverse** If something happens **in reverse** or goes **into reverse**, things happen in the opposite way from what usually happens or from what has been happening. ❑ *Amis tells the story in reverse, from the moment the man dies.*

ADJ **Reverse** means opposite from what you expect or to what has just been described. = opposite ❑ *The wrong attitude will have exactly the reverse effect.*

re·vert /rɪˈvɜːt/ VERB [I] (**reverts, reverting, reverted**) **1** When people or things **revert to** a previous state, system, or type of behaviour, they go back to it. ❑ *Jackson said her boss became increasingly depressed and reverted to smoking heavily.* **2** (*written*) When someone **reverts to** a previous topic, they start talking or thinking about it again. ❑ *In the car she reverted to the subject uppermost in her mind. 'You know, I really believe what Grandma told you.'* **3** (*legal*) If property, rights, or money **revert to** someone, they become that person's again after someone else has had them for a period of time. ❑ *When the lease ends, the property reverts to the owner.*

⊕ **re·view** ◆◆◇ /rɪˈvjuː/ NOUN, VERB

NOUN [c] (**reviews**) **1** [oft review 'of' N, also PREP + review] A **review of** a situation or system is its formal examination by people in authority. This is usually done in order to see whether it can be improved or corrected. = revision, reassessment, evaluation ❑ *The president ordered a review of US economic aid to Jordan.* ❑ *The White House quickly announced that the policy is under review.* **2** A **review** is a report in the media in which someone gives their opinion of something such as a new book or film. ❑ *We've never had a good review in the music press.* **3** A literature **review** is a summary of what has been written before on a subject. ❑ *Literature reviews form a substantial part of any higher degree dissertation.*

VERB [T] (**reviews, reviewing, reviewed**) **1** If you **review** a situation or system, you consider it carefully to see what is wrong with it or how it could be improved. ❑ *The president* reviewed the situation with his cabinet yesterday. ❑ *The next day we reviewed the previous day's work.* **2** If someone **reviews** something such as a new book or film, they write a report or give a talk on television or radio in which they express their opinion of it. ❑ *Richard Coles reviews all the latest video releases.*

WORD CONNECTIONS

VERB + **review**

conduct a review
launch a review
order a review

❑ *A team was appointed to conduct a review of the planning system.*

ADJ + **review**

a **judicial** review
an **independent** review

❑ *All his decisions are subject to an independent review.*

NOUN + **review**

a **spending** review
a **pay** review

❑ *The government is to carry out a spending review aimed at cutting costs across all departments.*

review + NOUN

a review **panel**
a review **board**
a review **process**

❑ *Approval from the hospital's medical ethics review board will be required.*

✪**re·vise** /rɪ'vaɪz/ VERB [T, I] (revises, revising, revised) (*academic word*) **1** [T] If you **revise** the way you think about something, you adjust your thoughts, usually in order to make them better or more suited to how things are. = change ❑ *With time he came to revise his opinion of the profession.* **2** [T] If you **revise** a price, amount, or estimate, you change it to make it more fair, realistic, or accurate. = change, alter, amend ❑ *They realized that some of their prices were higher than their competitors' and revised prices accordingly.* ❑ *The United Nations has been forced to revise its estimates of population growth upwards.* **3** [T] When you **revise** an article, a book, a law, or a piece of music, you change it in order to improve it, make it more modern, or make it more suitable for a particular purpose. = change ❑ *Three editors handled the work of revising the articles for publication.* ❑ *The staff should work together to revise the school curriculum.* **4** [I] (*BrE; in AmE, use* review) When you **revise for** an examination, you read things again and make notes in order to be prepared for the examination.

VOCABULARY BUILDER

revise VERB

If you **revise** something, such as an opinion, a law, or an article, you change it to make it more useful.

❑ *The glossary was revised in 1990 with the help of the present writer.*

change VERB

When something **changes** or when you **change** it, it becomes different.

❑ *They should change the law.*

alter VERB (*fairly formal*)

If something **alters** or if you **alter** it, it changes.

❑ *attempts to genetically alter the caffeine content of coffee plants*

amend VERB

If you **amend** something that has been written, such as a law, or something that is said, you change it in order to improve it or make it more accurate.

❑ *The president agreed to amend the constitution.*

✪**re·vi·sion** /rɪ'vɪʒən/ NOUN [C, U] (revisions) **1** [C, U] To make a **revision of** something that is written or something that has been decided means to make changes to it in order to improve it, make it more modern, or make it more suitable for a particular purpose. = editing, correction, alteration ❑ *The phase of writing that is actually most important is revision.* ❑ *A major addition to the earlier revisions of the questionnaire is the job requirement exercise.* **2** [U] (*BrE; in AmE, use* review) When people who are studying do **revision**, they read things again and make notes in order to prepare for an examination.

re·vis·it /,riː'vɪzɪt/ VERB [T] (revisits, revisiting, revisited) **1** If you **revisit** a place, you return there for a visit after you have been away for a long time, often after the place has changed a lot. ❑ *In the summer, when we returned to Canada, we revisited this lake at dawn.* **2** If you **revisit** a subject or topic, you discuss it again or consider it again. ❑ *The committee agreed to revisit the issue at their next meeting.*

re·vi·tal·ize /,riː'vaɪtəlaɪz/ *also* **revitalise** VERB [T] (revitalizes, revitalizing, revitalized) To **revitalize** something that has lost its activity or its health means to make it active or healthy again. = revive ❑ *This hair conditioner is excellent for revitalizing dry, lifeless hair.*

re·viv·al /rɪ'vaɪvəl/ NOUN [C, U] (revivals) **1** [C] When there is a **revival** of something, it becomes active or popular again. ❑ *This return to realism has produced a revival of interest in a number of artists.* **2** [C] A **revival** is a new production of a play, an opera, or a ballet. ❑ *John Clement's revival of Chekhov's 'The Seagull'* **3** [U] A **revival** meeting is a public religious event that is intended to make people more interested in Christianity. ❑ *He toured the country organizing revival meetings.*

re·vive /rɪ'vaɪv/ VERB [I, T] (revives, reviving, revived) **1** [I, T] When something such as the economy, a business, a trend, or a feeling **is revived** or when it **revives**, it becomes active, popular, or successful again. ❑ *an attempt to revive the economy* **2** [T] When someone **revives** a play, an opera, or a ballet, they present a new production of it. ❑ *His plays continue to be revived both here and abroad.* **3** [I, T] If you **revive** someone who has fainted or if they **revive**, they become conscious again. ❑ *She and a neighbour tried in vain to revive him.*

re·voke /rɪ'vəʊk/ VERB [T] (revokes, revoking, revoked) (*formal*) When people in authority **revoke** something such as a licence, a law, or an agreement, they cancel it. ❑ *The government revoked her husband's licence to operate migrant labour crews.*

re·volt /rɪ'vəʊlt/ NOUN, VERB
NOUN [C, U] (revolts) **1** A **revolt** is an illegal and often violent attempt by a group of people to change their country's political system. = rebellion ❑ *It was undeniably a revolt by ordinary people against their leaders.* **2** A **revolt** by a person or group against someone or something is a refusal to accept the authority of that person or thing. = rebellion ❑ *Conservative Republicans had led the revolt against the budget package.*
VERB [I] (revolts, revolting, revolted) **1** When people **revolt**, they make an illegal and often violent attempt to change their country's political system. ❑ *In 1375 the townspeople revolted.* **2** When people **revolt against** someone or something, they reject the authority of that person or reject that thing. = rebel ❑ *In 1978 California taxpayers revolted against higher taxes.*

✪**revo·lu·tion** ◆◇◇ /,revə'luːʃən/ NOUN [C] (revolutions) (*academic word*) **1** A **revolution** is a successful attempt by a large group of people to change the political system of their country by force. = revolt, uprising ❑ *The period since the revolution has been one of political turmoil.* ❑ *after the French Revolution* ❑ *before the 1917 Revolution* **2** A **revolution** in a particular area of human activity is an important change in that area. = transformation, reformation ❑ *The nineteenth century witnessed a revolution in ship design and propulsion.* ❑ *the industrial revolution*

R

WORD CONNECTIONS

ADJ + revolution

a **technological** revolution
a **cultural** revolution
an **industrial** revolution
a **digital** revolution
❏ The digital revolution has slashed the cost of long-distance communication.

VERB + revolution

undergo a revolution
❏ With nanotechnology, surgery will undergo a revolution.

✪ revo·lu·tion·ary ◆◇◇ /ˌrevəˈluːʃənri, AmE -neri/ ADJ, NOUN

ADJ **1** **Revolutionary** activities, organizations, or people have the aim of causing a political revolution. = rebel, radical ❏ Do you know anything about the revolutionary movement? ❏ the Cuban revolutionary leader, Jose Marti **2** **Revolutionary** ideas and developments involve great changes in the way that something is done or made. = innovative, radical, ground-breaking ❏ Invented in 1951, the rotary engine is a revolutionary concept in internal combustion.
NOUN [c] (**revolutionaries**) A **revolutionary** is a person who tries to cause a revolution or who takes an active part in one. ❏ The revolutionaries laid down their arms and their leaders went into voluntary exile.

VOCABULARY BUILDER

revolutionary ADJ

Revolutionary ideas and developments involve great changes in the way that something is done, made, or thought about.
❏ Somewhat more revolutionary was Freud's idea that we have a death instinct.

innovative ADJ (formal)

Something that is **innovative** is new and original.
❏ products which are cheaper, more innovative, and more reliable

radical ADJ (fairly formal)

Radical changes and differences are very important and great in degree.
❏ the Football League's proposals for a radical reform of the way football is run

progressive ADJ (fairly formal)

Someone who is **progressive** or has **progressive** ideas has modern ideas about how things should be done, rather than traditional ones.
❏ He was able to point to the progressive changes he had already introduced.

✪ revo·lu·tion·ize /ˌrevəˈluːʃənaɪz/ also **revolutionise** VERB [T] (**revolutionizes, revolutionizing, revolutionized**) When something **revolutionizes** an activity, it causes great changes in the way that it is done. = transform ❏ Over the past forty years plastics have revolutionized the way we live. ❏ Automation revolutionized the olive industry in the early 1970s.

re·volve /rɪˈvɒlv/ VERB [I, T] (**revolves, revolving, revolved**) **1** [I] If you say that one thing **revolves around** another thing, you mean that the second thing is the main feature or focus of the first thing. ❏ Since childhood, her life has revolved around tennis. **2** [I] If a discussion or conversation **revolves around** a particular topic, it is mainly about that topic. ❏ The debate revolves around specific accounting techniques. **3** [I] If one object **revolves around** another object, the first object turns in a circle around the second object. ❏ The satellite revolves around the earth once every hundred minutes. **4** [I, T] When something **revolves** or when you **revolve** it, it moves or turns in a circle around a central point or line. ❏ Overhead, the fan revolved slowly.

re·vul·sion /rɪˈvʌlʃən/ NOUN [U] Someone's **revulsion** at something is the strong feeling of disgust or disapproval they have towards it. = disgust ❏ their revulsion at the act of desecration

✪ re·ward ◆◇◇ /rɪˈwɔːd/ NOUN, VERB

NOUN [c] (**rewards**) **1** A **reward** is something that you are given, for example because you have behaved well, worked hard, or provided a service to the community. = bonus, prize; ≠ punishment ❏ A bonus of up to five per cent can be added to a student's final exam score as a reward for good spelling, punctuation, and grammar. ❏ He was given the job as a reward for running a successful leadership bid. **2** A **reward** is a sum of money offered to anyone who can give information about lost or stolen property, a missing person, or someone who is wanted by the police. ❏ The firm last year offered a $10,000 reward for information leading to the conviction of the killer. **3** The **rewards** of something are the benefits that you receive as a result of doing or having that thing. ❏ The company is just starting to reap the rewards of long-term investments.
VERB [T] (**rewards, rewarding, rewarded**) If you do something and **are rewarded** with a particular benefit, you receive that benefit as a result of doing that thing. ❏ Make the extra effort to impress the buyer and you will be rewarded with a quicker sale at a better price.

re·ward·ing /rɪˈwɔːdɪŋ/ ADJ An experience or action that is **rewarding** gives you satisfaction or brings you benefits. = satisfying ❏ a career that she found stimulating and rewarding

re·work /ˌriːˈwɜːk/ VERB [T] (**reworks, reworking, reworked**) If you **rework** something such as an idea or a piece of writing, you reorganize it and make changes to it in order to improve it or bring it up to date. = revise ❏ See if you can rework your schedule and come up with practical ways to reduce the number of hours you're on call.

re·write /ˌriːˈraɪt/ VERB [T] (**rewrites, rewriting, rewrote, rewritten**) **1** If someone **rewrites** a piece of writing such as a book, an article, or a law, they write it in a different way in order to improve it. = rework ❏ Following this critique, students rewrite their papers and submit them for final evaluation. **2** If you accuse someone such as a government of **rewriting** history, you are criticizing them for selecting and presenting particular historical events in a way that suits their own purposes. ❏ We have always been an independent people, no matter how they rewrite history.

✪ rhet·o·ric /ˈretərɪk/ NOUN [U] **1** (disapproval) If you refer to speech or writing as **rhetoric**, you disapprove of it because it is intended to convince and impress people but may not be sincere or honest. ❏ The change is largely cosmetic, a matter of acceptable political rhetoric rather than social reality. ❏ What is required is immediate action, not rhetoric. ❏ The harsh rhetoric had so soured officials that the two sides were barely speaking. **2** (formal) **Rhetoric** is the skill or art of using language effectively. ❏ the noble institutions of political life, such as political rhetoric, public office, and public service ❏ the absence of rhetoric and symbol, which poets and other writers may redress

✪ rhe·tori·cal /rɪˈtɒrɪkəl, AmE -ˈtɔːr-/ ADJ **1** A **rhetorical** question is one that is asked in order to make a statement rather than to get an answer. ❏ He grimaced slightly, obviously expecting no answer to his rhetorical question. ❏ He made no answer to the Commandante's question, which had been rhetorical in any case. **2** (formal) **Rhetorical** language is intended to be grand and impressive. ❏ These arguments may have been used as a rhetorical device to argue for a perpetuation of a United Nations role. ❏ Some of Larkin's poetry denies itself the traditional rhetorical flourishes of poetry.
rhe·tori·cal·ly /rɪˈtɒrɪkli, AmE -ˈtɔːr-/ ADV **1** [rhetorically with v] ❏ 'Do these kids know how lucky they are?' Jackson asked rhetorically. **2** Suddenly, the narrator speaks in his most rhetorically elevated mode.

rhythm ◆◇◇ /ˈrɪðəm/ NOUN [c, u] (**rhythms**) **1** [c, u] A **rhythm** is a regular series of sounds or movements. ❏ His music of that period fused the rhythms of jazz with classical forms. **2** [c] A **rhythm** is a regular pattern of changes, for example changes in your body, in the seasons, or in the tides. ❏ Begin to listen to your own body rhythms.

r

rhyth·mic /ˈrɪðmɪk/ or **rhythmical** /ˈrɪðmɪkəl/ ADJ
A **rhythmic** movement or sound is repeated at regular intervals, forming a regular pattern or beat. ▢ *Good breathing is slow, rhythmic, and deep.*
rhyth·mi·cal·ly /ˈrɪðmɪkli/ ADV [rhythmically after V] ▢ *She stood, swaying her hips, moving rhythmically.*

rib /rɪb/ NOUN [c] (**ribs**) **1** Your **ribs** are the 12 pairs of curved bones that surround your chest. ▢ *Her heart was thumping against her ribs.* **2** A **rib of** meat such as beef or pork is a piece that has been cut to include one of the animal's ribs. ▢ *a rib of beef* ▢ *pork ribs*

rib·bon /ˈrɪbən/ NOUN [c, u] (**ribbons**) **1** [c, u] A ribbon is a long, narrow piece of cloth that you use for tying things together or as a decoration. ▢ *She had tied back her hair with a peach satin ribbon.* **2** [c] A typewriter or printer **ribbon** is a long, narrow piece of cloth containing ink and is used in a typewriter or printer.

rice ♦◇◇ /raɪs/ NOUN [c, u] **Rice** consists of white or brown grains taken from a cereal plant. You cook rice and usually eat it with meat or vegetables. ▢ *a meal consisting of chicken, rice, and vegetables*

⊕**rich** ♦♦◇ /rɪtʃ/ ADJ, NOUN
ADJ (**richer, richest**) **1** A **rich** person has a lot of money or valuable possessions. = wealthy, well-off, affluent ▢ *You're going to be a very rich man.* ▢ *Their one aim in life is to get rich.* ▢ *the kind of treatment that only rich people could afford* **2** A **rich** country has a strong economy and produces a lot of wealth, so many people who live there have a high standard of living. = developed; ≠ developing ▢ *There is hunger in many parts of the world, even in rich countries.* ▢ *the means by which the rich nations dictate economic policy to the poor* **3** [V-LINK + rich 'in' N, rich + N] If something is **rich in** a useful or valuable substance or is a **rich source** of it, it contains a lot of it. ▢ *Liver and kidneys are particularly rich in vitamin A.* **4** Rich food contains a lot of fat or oil. ▢ *Additional cream would make it too rich.* **5** Rich soil contains large amounts of substances that make it good for growing crops or flowers. ▢ *Farmers grow rice in the rich soil.* **6** A **rich** deposit of a mineral or other substance is a large amount of it. ▢ *the country's rich deposits of the metal lithium* **7** [rich + N] If you say that something is a **rich** vein or source of something such as humour, ideas, or information, you mean that it can provide a lot of that thing. ▢ *The director discovered a rich vein of sentimentality.* **8** Rich smells are strong and very pleasant. **Rich** colours and sounds are deep and very pleasant. ▢ *a rich and luxuriously perfumed bath essence* **9** A **rich** life or history is one that is interesting because it is full of different events and activities. ▢ *A rich and varied cultural life is essential for this couple.* **10** A **rich** collection or mixture contains a wide and interesting variety of different things. ▢ *Visitors can view a rich and colourful array of aquatic plants and animals.*
NOUN [PL] (**riches**) **1** The **rich** are rich people. ▢ *This is a system in which the rich are taken care of and the poor are left to suffer.* **2** Riches are valuable possessions or large amounts of money. ▢ *An Olympic gold medal can lead to untold riches for an athlete.* **3** If you talk about the Earth's **riches**, you are referring to things that exist naturally in large quantities and that are useful and valuable, for example minerals, wood, and oil. ▢ *Russia's vast natural riches*
rich·ness /ˈrɪtʃnəs/ NOUN [u] **1** A squeeze of fresh lime juice cuts the richness of the avocado. **2** the richness of Tibet's mineral deposits **3** His musicals were infused with richness of colour and visual detail. **4** It all adds to the richness of human life. **5** a huge country, containing a richness of culture and diversity of landscape

rich·ly /ˈrɪtʃli/ ADV **1** If something is **richly** coloured, flavoured, or perfumed, it has a pleasantly strong colour, flavour, or perfume. ▢ *Renaissance masterpieces, so richly coloured and lustrous* **2** If something is **richly** decorated, patterned, or furnished, it has a lot of elaborate and beautiful decoration, patterns, or furniture. = lavishly ▢ *Coffee steamed in the richly decorated silver pot.* **3** If you say that someone **richly** deserves an award, success, or victory, you approve of what they have done and feel very

strongly that they deserve it. ▢ *He achieved the success he so richly deserved.* **4** If you are **richly** rewarded for doing something, you get something very valuable or pleasant in return for doing it. ▢ *It is a difficult book to read, but it richly rewards the effort.*

rid ♦◇◇ /rɪd/ VERB, ADJ
VERB [T] (**rids, ridding, rid**) **1** If you **rid** a place or person **of** something undesirable or unwanted, you succeed in removing it completely from that place or person. = free ▢ *The proposals are an attempt to rid the country of political corruption.* **2** If you **rid yourself of** something you do not want, you take action so that you no longer have it or are no longer affected by it. = free ▢ *Why couldn't he ever rid himself of those thoughts, those worries?*
ADJ [V-LINK + rid 'of' N] If you are **rid of** someone or something that you did not want or that caused problems for you, they are no longer with you or causing problems for you. ▢ *The family had sought a way to be rid of her and the problems she had caused them.*
PHRASES **get rid of something** When you **get rid of** something that you do not want or do not like, you take action so that you no longer have it or suffer from it. ▢ *The owner needs to get rid of the car for financial reasons.*
get rid of someone If you **get rid of** someone who is causing problems for you or who you do not like, you do something to prevent them from affecting you anymore, for example by making them leave. ▢ *He believed that his manager wanted to get rid of him for personal reasons.*

rid·den /ˈrɪdən/ IRREG FORM **Ridden** is the past participle of ride.

ride ♦♦◇ /raɪd/ VERB, NOUN
VERB [I, T] (**rides, riding, rode, ridden**) **1** [I, T] When you **ride** a horse, you sit on it and control its movements. ▢ *I saw a girl riding a horse.* **2** Can you ride? **2** [I, T] When you **ride** a bicycle or a motorcycle, you sit on it, control it, and travel along on it. ▢ *Riding a bike is great exercise.* ▢ *Two men riding on motorcycles opened fire on him.* **3** [I] When you **ride in** a vehicle such as a car, you travel in it. ▢ *He prefers travelling on the underground to riding in a limousine.* **4** [I] If you say that one thing **is riding on** another, you mean that the first thing depends on the second thing. = depend ▢ *Billions of dollars are riding on the outcome of the election.*
PHRASAL VERB **ride out** If someone **rides out** a storm or a crisis, they manage to survive a difficult period without suffering serious harm. ▢ *The Republicans think they can ride out the political storm.*
NOUN [c] (**rides**) **1** A **ride** is a trip on a horse or bicycle, or in a vehicle. ▢ *She took some friends for a ride in the family car.* **2** In an amusement park, a **ride** is a large machine that people ride on for fun. ▢ *roller coasters or other thrill rides at amusement parks*
PHRASES **a rough ride** (*informal*) If you say that someone faces **a rough ride**, you mean that things are going to be difficult for them because people will criticize them a lot or treat them badly. ▢ *The president could face a rough ride unless the plan works.*
a free ride (*informal*) If you describe something as **a free ride**, you mean that things are going to be very easy and that people will take advantage of this. ▢ *I've had an opponent every time. I've never had a free ride. I've had to fight.*
be taken for a ride (*informal*) If you say that someone **has been taken for a ride**, you mean that they have been deceived or cheated. ▢ *You got taken for a ride. Why did you give him five thousand dollars?*
→ See also riding

rid·er ♦◇◇ /ˈraɪdə/ NOUN [c] (**riders**) A **rider** is someone who rides a horse, a bicycle, or a motorcycle as a hobby or job. You can also refer to someone who is riding a horse, a bicycle, or a motorcycle as a rider. ▢ *She is a very good and experienced rider.*

ridge /rɪdʒ/ NOUN [c] (**ridges**) **1** A **ridge** is a long, narrow piece of raised land. ▢ *a high road along a mountain ridge* **2** A **ridge** is a raised line on a flat surface. ▢ *the bony ridge of the eye socket*

ridi·cule /ˈrɪdɪkjuːl/ VERB, NOUN
VERB [T] (**ridicules, ridiculing, ridiculed**) If you **ridicule**

R

someone or **ridicule** their ideas or beliefs, you make fun of them in an unkind way. = mock □ *I admired her all the more for allowing them to ridicule her and never striking back.* NOUN [U] If someone or something is an object of **ridicule** or is held up to **ridicule**, someone makes fun of them in an unkind way. □ *As a heavy child, she became the object of ridicule from classmates.*

ri•dic•u•lous /rɪˈdɪkjʊləs/ ADJ If you say that something or someone is **ridiculous**, you mean that they are very foolish. = absurd □ *It is ridiculous to suggest we are having a romance.*

rid•ing /ˈraɪdɪŋ/ NOUN [U] **Riding** is the activity or sport of riding horses. □ *The next morning we went riding again.*

ri•fle /ˈraɪfəl/ NOUN, VERB

NOUN [C] (**rifles**) A **rifle** is a gun with a long barrel. □ *They shot him at point blank range with an automatic rifle.* VERB [I, T] (**rifles, rifling, rifled**) If you **rifle through** things or **rifle** them, you make a quick search among them in order to find something or steal something. □ *I discovered my husband rifling through the filing cabinet.*

rig /rɪg/ VERB, NOUN

VERB [T] (**rigs, rigging, rigged**) If someone **rigs** an election, a job appointment, or a game, they dishonestly arrange it to get the result they want or to give someone an unfair advantage. □ *She accused her opponents of rigging the vote.* NOUN [C] (**rigs**) A **rig** is a large structure that is used for looking for oil or gas and for taking it out of the ground or the sea bed. □ *a supply vessel for oil rigs in the Gulf of Mexico*

⊙**right** ♦♦♦ /raɪt/ ADJ, ADV, NOUN, VERB, CONVENTION

The spelling **Right** is also used for meaning 3 of the noun.

ADJ **1** If something is **right**, it is correct and agrees with the facts. = correct □ *That's absolutely right.* □ *Clocks never told the right time.* **2** If you do something in the **right** way or in the **right** place, you do it as or where it should be done or was planned to be done. = correct □ *Walking, done in the right way, is a form of aerobic exercise.* □ *They have computerized systems to ensure delivery of the right pizza to the right place.* **3** If you say that someone is seen in **all the right** places or knows **all the right** people, you mean that they go to places that are socially acceptable or know people who are socially acceptable. □ *He was always to be seen in the right places.* **4** If someone is **right about** something, they are correct in what they say or think about it. □ *Ron has been right about the result of every general election but one.* **5** If something such as a choice, action, or decision is the **right** one, it is the best or most suitable one. □ *She'd made the right choice in leaving New York.* **6** [V-LINK + right, with BRD-NEG] If something is **not right**, there is something unsatisfactory about the situation or thing that you are talking about. □ *Ratatouille doesn't taste right with any other oil.* **7** [V-LINK + right] If you think that someone was **right** to do something, you think that there were good moral reasons why they did it. □ *You were right to do what you did, under the circumstances.* **8** [V-LINK + right, oft with BRD-NEG] **Right** is used to refer to activities or actions that are considered to be morally good and acceptable. □ *It's not right, leaving her like this.* **9** [right + N] The **right** side of a material is the side that is intended to be seen and that faces outward when it is made into something. □ *Trim off excess fabric and turn the right side out.* **10** [right + N] Your **right** arm, leg, or ear, for example, is the one which is on the right side of your body. Your **right** shoe or glove is the one which is intended to be worn on your right foot or hand. □ *She shattered her right leg in a fall.*

ADV **1** [right after V] If something happens or is done **right**, it is correct and agrees with the facts. □ *He guessed right about some things.* **2** [right after V] If you do something **right**, you do it as or where it should be done or was planned to be done. = correctly □ *To make sure I did everything right, I bought a fat instruction book.* **3** [right after V] **Right** is also an adverb. If something goes or is situated **right**, it goes to the right or is situated to the right side of something. □ *Turn right into the street.* **4** [right + CL] (spoken) You use **right** in order to attract someone's

attention or to indicate that you have dealt with one thing so you can go on to another. □ *Right, I'll be back in a minute.* **5** [right as reply] (spoken) You can say '**right**' to show that you are listening to what someone is saying and that you accept it or understand it. = yes □ *'It was probably much harder for older people. Don't you think?'— 'Right.'* **6** [right + ADV/PREP] You can use **right** to emphasize the precise place, position, or time of something. □ *The back of a car appeared right in front of him.* **7** [right + PREP/ADV] You can use **right** to emphasize how far something moves or extends or how long it continues. □ *the highway that runs through the neutral zone right to the army positions* **8** [right + ADV/PREP] You can use **right** to emphasize that an action or state is complete. □ *The candle had burned right down.* **9** [right + PREP/ADV] If you say that something happened **right after** a particular time or event or **right before** it, you mean that it happened immediately after or before it. = just □ *All of a sudden, right after the summer, Mother gets married.* **10** [right + ADV] If you say **I'll be right there** or **I'll be right back**, you mean that you will get to a place or get back to it in a very short time. □ *I'm going to get some water. I'll be right back.*

PHRASES **go right** If you say that things are **going right**, you mean that your life or a situation is developing as you intended or expected and you are pleased with it. □ *I can't think of anything in my life that's going right.*

put something right If you **put** something **right**, you correct something that was wrong or that was causing problems. □ *We've discovered what went wrong and are going to put it right.*

right away (informal, emphasis) If you do something **right away**, you do it immediately. □ *He wants to see you right away.*

right now (informal, emphasis) You can use **right now** to emphasize that you are referring to the present moment. □ *Right now I'm feeling very excited.*

NOUN [U, SING, PL] (**rights**) **1** [U] **Right** is used to refer to activities or actions that are considered to be morally good and acceptable. □ *At least he knew right from wrong.* **2** [SING] The **right** is one of two opposite directions, sides, or positions. If you are facing north and you turn to the right, you will be facing east. In the word 'to', the 'o' is to the right of the 't'. □ *Ahead of you on the right will be a lovely garden.* **3** [SING] You can refer to people who support the political ideals of capitalism and conservatism as **the right**. They are often contrasted with **the left**, who support the political ideals of socialism. □ *The Republican Right despise him.* **4** [PL] Your **rights** are what you are morally or legally entitled to do or to have. = entitlements; ≠ duties □ *They don't know their rights.* □ *You must stand up for your rights.* □ *voting rights* **5** [SING] If you have a **right to** do or to have something, you are morally or legally entitled to do it or to have it. = entitlement; ≠ duty □ *a woman's right to choose* □ *People have the right to read any kind of material they wish.* **6** [PL] If someone has **the rights to** a story or book, they are legally allowed to publish it or reproduce it in another form, and nobody else can do so without their permission. □ *An agent bought the rights to his life.*

PHRASES **by rights** If something is not the case but you think that it should be, you can say that **by rights** it should be the case. □ *She did work which by rights should be done by someone else.*

in one's own right If someone is a successful or respected person **in** their **own right**, they are successful or respected because of their own efforts and talents rather than those of the people they are closely connected with. □ *Although now a celebrity in her own right, actress Lynn Redgrave knows the difficulties of living in the shadow of her famous older sister.*

reserve the right If you say that you **reserve the right** to do something, you mean that you will do it if you feel that it is necessary. □ *He reserved the right to change his mind.*

within one's rights If you say that someone is **within** their **rights to** do something, you mean that they are morally or legally entitled to do it. = justified □ *You were quite within your rights to refuse to cooperate with him.*

VERB [T] (**rights, righting, righted**) **1** If you **right** something or if it **rights itself**, it returns to its normal or

r

correct state, after being in an undesirable state. ❑ *They recognize the urgency of righting the economy.* **2** If you **right** a wrong, you do something to make up for a mistake or something bad that you did in the past. = rectify ❑ *We've made progress in righting the wrongs of the past.* **3** If you **right** something that has fallen or rolled over, or if it **rights itself**, it returns to its normal upright position. ❑ *He righted the yacht and continued the race.*

CONVENTION (*spoken*) You can use **right** to check whether what you have just said is correct. ❑ *They have a small plane, right?*

right·ness /'raɪtnəs/ NOUN [U] ❑ *Many people have very strong opinions about the rightness or wrongness of abortion.*
→ See also **all right**
✦ **heart in the right place** → see **heart**; **it serves you right** → see **serve**

WORD CONNECTIONS
VERB + **right**
have the right
earn the right
win the right
❑ *Women in many countries won the right to vote early in the 20th century.*
protect a right
respect a right
violate a right
❑ *They argue that the second amendment protects their right to own a gun.*
ADJ + **right**
equal rights
basic rights
❑ *All citizens should possess equal rights under the law.*
human rights
civil rights
gay rights
women's rights
❑ *Torture is a grotesque violation of human rights.*

right·ful /'raɪtfʊl/ ADJ [rightful + N] If you say that someone or something has returned to its **rightful** place or position, they have returned to the place or position that you think they should have. ❑ *We have restored Hamill to his rightful place as editor.*

right·ful·ly /'raɪtfəli/ ADV ❑ *Jealousy is the feeling that someone else has something that rightfully belongs to you.*

right-hand ADJ [right-hand + N] If something is on the **right-hand** side of something, it is positioned on the right of it. ❑ *a church on the right-hand side of the road*

right-handed ADJ, ADV
1 ADJ Someone who is **right-handed** uses their right hand rather than their left hand for activities such as writing and sports, and for picking things up.
2 ADV [right-handed after v] If you do something **right-handed**, such as writing, sports, or picking things up, you use your right hand rather than your left hand. ❑ *I batted left-handed and bowled right-handed.*

⊕ **right-wing** ◆◇◇ ADJ, NOUN

The spelling **right wing** is used for the noun.

1 ADJ A **right-wing** person or group has conservative or capitalist views. = conservative, reactionary ❑ *a right-wing government* ❑ *Liberals say the paper is too right-wing.*
2 NOUN [SING] The **right wing** of a political party consists of the members who have the most conservative or the most capitalist views. ❑ *the right wing of the Republican Party*

⊕ **rig·id** /'rɪdʒɪd/ ADJ (*academic word*) **1** (*disapproval*) Laws, rules, or systems that are **rigid** cannot be changed or varied, and are therefore considered to be rather severe. = strict, inflexible ❑ *Several colleges in our study have rigid rules about student conduct.* ❑ *Hospital routines for nurses are very rigid.* **2** (*disapproval*) If you disapprove of someone because you think they are not willing to change their way of thinking or behaving, you can describe them as **rigid**.

❑ *She was a fairly rigid person who had strong religious views.* **3** A **rigid** substance or object is stiff and does not bend, stretch, or twist easily. ❑ *rigid plastic containers* ❑ *These plates are fairly rigid.*

⊕ **ri·gid·ity** /rɪ'dʒɪdɪti/ NOUN [U] **1** = inflexibility; ≠ flexibility ❑ *the rigidity of government policy* **2** = inflexibility; ≠ flexibility ❑ *the strength and rigidity of glass*

⊕ **rig·id·ly** /'rɪdʒɪdli/ ADV [rigidly with v] = strictly, stiffly ❑ *The caste system was so rigidly enforced that non-Hindus were not even allowed inside a Hindu house.* ❑ *The soldiers stood rigidly, awaiting orders.*

⊕ **rig·or·ous** /'rɪgərəs/ ADJ **1** A test, system, or procedure that is **rigorous** is very thorough and strict. = thorough, strict, tough; ≠ soft, careless ❑ *The selection process is based on rigorous tests of competence and experience.* ❑ *a rigorous system of blood analysis* ❑ *rigorous military training* **2** If someone is **rigorous** in the way that they do something, they are very careful and thorough. ❑ *He is rigorous in his control of expenditure.*

⊕ **rig·or·ous·ly** /'rɪgərəsli/ ADV = thoroughly ❑ *rigorously conducted research* ❑ *A car must be very rigorously tested before the company making it is allowed to sell it to the public.*

⊕ **ri·gour** /'rɪgə/ (*mainly BrE; in AmE, use* **rigor**) NOUN [PL, U] (**rigours**) **1** [PL] If you refer to **the rigours of** an activity or job, you mean the difficult, demanding, or unpleasant things that are associated with it. ❑ *They're accustomed to the rigours of army life.* **2** [U] If something is done with **rigour**, it is done in a strict, thorough way. = strictness, thoroughness ❑ *The prince had performed his social duties with professional rigour.* ❑ *The new current affairs series promises to address challenging issues with freshness and rigour.* ❑ *They must believe you will pursue injustice with rigour and not be nudged off course.*

rim /rɪm/ NOUN [C] (**rims**) **1** The **rim** of a container such as a cup or glass is the edge that goes all the way around the top. ❑ *She looked at him over the rim of her glass.* **2** The **rim** of a circular object is its outside edge. ❑ *a round mirror with white metal rim*

ring ◆◆◇ /rɪŋ/ VERB, NOUN

The form **ringed** is used as the past tense and past participle for meaning 5 of the verb.

VERB [I, T] (**rings, ringing, rang** or **ringed, rung** or **ringed**) **1** [I] When a telephone **rings**, it makes a sound to let you know that someone is phoning you. ❑ *As soon as he got home, the phone rang.* **2** [I, T] (*mainly BrE; in AmE, usually use* **call**) When you **ring** someone, you telephone them. = phone **3** [I, T] When you **ring** a bell or when a bell **rings**, it makes a sound. ❑ *He heard the school bell ring.* **4** [I] (*literary*) If you say that a place **is ringing with** sound, usually pleasant sound, you mean that the place is completely filled with that sound. ❑ *The whole place was ringing with music.* **5** [T] If a building or place **is ringed with** or **by** something, it is surrounded by it. ❑ *The areas are sealed off and ringed by troops.*

PHRASE **ring true** or **ring hollow** If a statement **rings true**, it seems to be true or genuine. If it **rings hollow**, it does not seem to be true or genuine. ❑ *Joanna's denial rang true.*

PHRASAL VERBS **ring back** [no passive] (*BrE; in AmE, use* **call back**) If you **ring** someone **back**, you phone them either because they phoned you earlier and you were not there or because you did not finish an earlier telephone conversation.

ring in (*BrE; in AmE, use* **call in**) If you **ring in**, you phone a place, such as the place where you work.

ring off (*BrE; in AmE, use* **hang up**) When you **ring off**, you put down the receiver at the end of a telephone call.

ring round or **ring around** (*BrE; in AmE, use* **call around**) If you **ring round** or **ring around**, you phone several people, usually when you are trying to organize something or to find some information.

ring up **1** Ring up means the same as **ring** VERB 2. **2** If a shop assistant **rings up** a sale on a cash register, he or she presses the keys in order to record the amount that is being spent. ❑ *She was ringing up her sale on an ancient cash register.* **3** If a company **rings up** an amount of money, usually a large amount of money, it makes that amount of money in sales or profits. ❑ *The advertising agency rang up 1.4 billion dollars in yearly sales.*

NOUN [SING, C] (**rings**) **1** [SING, C] A **ring** is the sound that a telephone makes to let you know that someone is phoning you. ❑ *After at least eight rings, an ancient-sounding maid answered the phone.* **2** [C] The **ring** of a bell is the sound that it makes. ❑ *There was a ring of the bell.* **3** [SING] You can use **ring** to describe a quality that something such as a statement, discussion, or argument seems to have. For example, if an argument **has a familiar ring**, it seems familiar. = feel ❑ *His proud boast of leading 'the party of low taxation' has a hollow ring.* **4** [C] A **ring** is a small circle of metal or other substance that you wear on your finger as jewellery. ❑ *a gold wedding ring* **5** [C] An object or substance that is in the shape of a circle can be described as a **ring**. ❑ *Frank took a large ring of keys from his pocket.* **6** [C] A group of people or things arranged in a circle can be described as a **ring**. = circle ❑ *They then formed a ring around the square.* **7** [C] At a boxing or wrestling match or a circus, the **ring** is the place where the contest or performance takes place. It consists of an enclosed space with seats around it. ❑ *He will never again be allowed inside a boxing ring.* **8** [C] You can refer to an organized group of people who are involved in an illegal activity as a **ring**. ❑ *Police are investigating the suspected drugs ring at the school.* **9** [C] (*BrE*; in *AmE*, usually use **burner**) A gas or electric **ring** is one of the small flat areas on top of a stove which heat up and which you use for cooking. **PHRASE** **give someone a ring** (*mainly BrE*; in *AmE*, usually use **call**; *informal*) If you **give** someone **a ring**, you phone them. ❑ *We'll give him a ring as soon as we get back.*

ring·ing /ˈrɪŋɪŋ/ NOUN [U] **1** *She was jolted out of her sleep by the ringing of the telephone.* **2** *the ringing of church bells*
✦ **ring a bell** → see **bell**

rinse /rɪns/ VERB, NOUN

VERB [T] (**rinses, rinsing, rinsed**) **1** When you **rinse** something, you wash it in clean water in order to remove dirt or soap from it. ❑ *It's important to rinse the rice to remove the starch.* **2** If you **rinse** your mouth, you wash it by filling your mouth with water or with a liquid that kills germs, then spitting it out. ❑ *Use a toothbrush on your tongue as well, and rinse your mouth frequently.*
PHRASAL VERB **rinse out** Rinse out means the same as **rinse** VERB 2. ❑ *After her meal she invariably rinsed out her mouth.*
NOUN [C] (**rinses**) If you give something a **rinse**, you wash it in clean water in order to remove dirt or soap from it. ❑ *Clean skin means plenty of lather followed by a rinse with water.*

riot ◆◇◇ /ˈraɪət/ NOUN, VERB

NOUN [SING, C] (**riots**) **1** [SING, C] When there is a **riot**, a crowd of people behave violently in a public place, for example they fight, throw stones, or damage buildings and vehicles. ❑ *Twelve inmates have been killed during a riot at the prison.* **2** [SING] If you say that there is **a riot of** something pleasant such as colour, you mean that there is a large amount of various types of it. ❑ *It would be a riot of colour, of poppies and irises and flowers of every kind.*
PHRASES **read someone the riot act** If someone in authority **reads** you **the riot act**, they tell you that you will be punished unless you start behaving properly. ❑ *I'm glad you read the riot act to Billy. He's still a kid and still needs to be told what to do.*
run riot **1** If something such as your imagination **runs riot**, it is not limited or controlled, and produces ideas that are new or exciting, rather than sensible. ❑ *She dressed strictly for comfort and economy, but let her imagination run riot with costume jewellery.* **2** If people **run riot**, they behave in a wild and uncontrolled manner. ❑ *Rampaging prisoners ran riot through the jail.*
VERB [I] (**riots, rioting, rioted**) If people **riot**, they behave violently in a public place. ❑ *Last year 600 inmates rioted, starting fires and building barricades.*
ri·ot·er /ˈraɪətə/ NOUN [C] (**rioters**) ❑ *The militia dispersed the rioters.*
ri·ot·ing /ˈraɪətɪŋ/ NOUN [U] ❑ *At least fifteen people are now known to have died in three days of rioting.*

rip /rɪp/ VERB, NOUN

VERB [I, T] (**rips, ripping, ripped**) **1** [I, T] When something **rips** or when you **rip** it, you tear it forcefully with your hands or with a tool such as a knife. = tear ❑ *I felt the banner rip as we were pushed in opposite directions.* **2** [T] If you **rip** something away, you remove it quickly and forcefully. = tear ❑ *He ripped away a wire that led to the alarm button.* **3** [I] If something **rips** into someone or something or **rips** through them, it enters that person or thing so quickly and forcefully that it often goes completely through them. = tear ❑ *A volley of bullets ripped into the facing wall.*
PHRASE **let it rip** (*informal*) If you **let it rip**, you do something forcefully and without trying to control yourself. ❑ *Turn the guitars up full and let it rip.*
PHRASAL VERBS **rip off** (*informal*) If someone **rips** you **off**, they cheat you by charging you too much money for something or by selling you something that is broken or damaged. ❑ *The bigger, more reputable online casinos are not going to rip you off.*
rip up If you **rip** something **up**, you tear it into small pieces. = tear up ❑ *If we wrote, I think he would rip up the letter.*
NOUN [C] (**rips**) A **rip** is a long cut or split in something made of cloth or paper. = tear ❑ *Looking at the rip in her new dress, she flew into a rage.*

ripe /raɪp/ ADJ

ADJ (**riper, ripest**) **1** Ripe fruit or grain is fully grown and ready to eat. ❑ *Always choose firm, but ripe fruit.* **2** [V-LINK + ripe 'for' N/-ING] If a situation is **ripe for** a particular development or event, you mean that development or event is likely to happen soon. ❑ *A hospital consultant said conditions were ripe for an outbreak of cholera and typhoid.*
PHRASE **ripe old age** If someone lives to a **ripe old age**, they live until they are very old. ❑ *He lived to the ripe old age of 95.*

rip·en /ˈraɪpən/ VERB [I, T] (**ripens, ripening, ripened**) When crops **ripen** or when the sun **ripens** them, they become ripe. ❑ *I'm waiting for the apples to ripen.*

✪ rise ◆◆◆ /raɪz/ VERB, NOUN

VERB [I] (**rises, rising, rose, risen**) **1** If something **rises**, it moves upwards. ❑ *Wilson's ice-cold eyes watched the smoke rise from his cigarette.* **2** (*formal*) When you **rise**, you stand up. ❑ *Luther rose slowly from the chair.* **3** (*formal*) When you **rise**, you get out of bed. ❑ *Tony had risen early and gone to the cottage to work.* **4** When the sun or moon **rises**, it appears in the sky. ❑ *He wanted to be over the line of the ridge before the sun had risen.* **5** (*literary*) You can say that something **rises** when it appears as a large, tall shape. ❑ *The building rose before him, tall and stately.* **6** If the level of something such as the water in a river **rises**, it becomes higher. ❑ *The waters continue to rise as more than 1,000 people are evacuated.* **7** If land **rises**, it slopes upward. ❑ *He looked up the slope of land that rose from the house.* **8** If an amount **rises**, it increases. = increase ❑ *Interest rates rise from 4% to 5%.* ❑ *Tourist trips of all kinds rose by 10.5% between 1977 and 1987.* ❑ *Exports rose 23%.* ❑ *Pre-tax profits rose from £842,000 to £1.82m.* ❑ *The number of business failures has risen.* ❑ *rising costs* **9** If the wind **rises**, it becomes stronger. ❑ *The wind was still rising, approaching a force nine gale.* **10** If a sound **rises** or if someone's voice **rises**, it becomes louder or higher. ❑ *'Bernard?' Her voice rose hysterically.* **11** When the people in a country **rise**, they try to defeat the government or army that is controlling them. ❑ *President Bush had encouraged the Panamanian military to rise against General Noriega.* **12** If someone **rises to** a higher position or status, they become more important, successful, or powerful. ❑ *She is a strong woman who has risen to the top of a deeply sexist organization.*
PHRASAL VERBS **rise above** If you **rise above** a difficulty or problem, you manage not to let it affect you. ❑ *It tells the story of an aspiring young man's attempt to rise above the squalor of the street.*
rise up **1** Rise up means the same as **rise** VERB 1. ❑ *Spray rose up from the surface of the water.* **2** Rise up means the same as **rise** VERB 2. ❑ *The only thing I wanted was to rise up from the table and leave this house.* **3** Rise up means the

r

same as **rise** VERB **5**. ❑ *The White Mountains rose up before me.* **4** **Rise up** means the same as **rise** VERB **11**. ❑ *He warned that if the government moved against him the people would rise up.* **5** **Rise up** means the same as **rise** VERB **12**. ❑ *I started with Hoover 26 years ago in sales and rose up through the ranks.* NOUN [C, SING] (**rises**) **1** [C] A **rise** in the amount of something is an increase in it. = increase; ≠ fall ❑ *the prospect of another rise in interest rates* ❑ *a sharp rise in violence* **2** [SING] The **rise of** a movement or activity is an increase in its popularity or influence. = increase ❑ *The rise of racism in America is a serious concern.* **3** [C] (*BrE*; in *AmE*, use **raise**) A **rise** is an increase in your wages or your salary. = increase **4** [SING] The **rise** of someone is the process by which they become more important, successful, or powerful. ❑ *Haig's rise was fuelled by an all-consuming sense of patriotic duty.* PHRASE **give rise to** If something **gives rise to** an event or situation, it causes that event or situation to happen. ❑ *Low levels of choline in the body can give rise to high blood pressure.* ✦ **rise to the challenge** → see **challenge**; **rise to the occasion** → see **occasion**

WORD CONNECTIONS

NOUN + **rise**

costs rise
prices rise
rates rise
❑ *There is bad news for consumers as food prices continue to rise.*

unemployment rises
inflation rises
demand rises
crime rises
❑ *As demand rises, the price falls.*

the temperature rises
tension rises
❑ *The temperature rose to almost 40 degrees at midday.*

rise + ADV

rise sharply
rise dramatically
rise steadily
❑ *Survival rates for cancer have risen steadily with the introduction of new treatments.*

ADJ + **rise**

a sharp rise
a rapid rise
a further rise
❑ *The rapid rise in obesity is leading to an increasing prevalence of diabetes.*

NOUN + **rise**

a pay rise
a price rise
an interest-rate rise
❑ *Interest-rate rises make the cost of borrowing higher.*

rise + IN + NOUN

a rise in profits
a rise in prices
a rise in costs
❑ *People who bought houses in the 1970s profited from a dramatic rise in property prices.*

a rise in unemployment
a rise in crime
❑ *People feel more insecure even though there has been no rise in crime.*

VERB + **rise**

see a rise
report a rise
expect a rise
❑ *Hospitals reported a rise in the number of measles cases.*

WHICH WORD?
rise or raise?

Do not confuse **rise** and **raise**.
Rise is an intransitive verb. If something **rises**, it moves upwards or increases.
❑ *Thick columns of smoke **rise** from the houses.*
❑ *Prices are expected to **rise**.*
Raise is a transitive verb. If you **raise** something, you move it to a higher position or increase it.
❑ *She **raised** her eyebrows in surprise.*
❑ *We need to **raise** standards in schools.*

❂ **risk** ✦✦◇ /rɪsk/ NOUN, VERB
NOUN [C, U] (**risks**) **1** [C, U] If there is a **risk of** something unpleasant, there is a possibility that it will happen. ❑ *There is a small risk of brain damage from the procedure.* ❑ *In all the confusion, there's a serious risk that the main issues will be forgotten.* ❑ *People do it because there is that element of danger and risk.* **2** [C] If something that you do is a **risk**, it might have unpleasant or undesirable results. ❑ *You're taking a big risk showing this to Kravis.* ❑ *This was one risk that paid off.* **3** [C] If you say that something or someone is a **risk**, you mean they are likely to cause harm. = gamble, danger, hazard ❑ *It's being obese that constitutes a health risk.* ❑ *The restaurant has been refurbished because it was found to be a fire risk.* ❑ *a risk to national security* **4** [C] If you are considered a good **risk**, a bank or shop thinks that it is safe to lend you money or let you have goods without paying for them at the time. ❑ *Before providing the cash, they will have to decide whether you are a good or bad risk.* PHRASES **at risk** To be **at risk** means to be in a situation where something unpleasant might happen. ❑ *Up to 25,000 jobs are still at risk.* **at the risk of something** If you do something **at the risk of** something unpleasant happening, you do it even though you know that the unpleasant thing might happen as a result. ❑ *At the risk of being repetitive, I will say again that statistics are only a guide.* **at one's own risk** If you tell someone that they are doing something **at their own risk**, you are warning them that, if they are harmed, it will be their own responsibility. ❑ *Those who wish to come here will do so at their own risk.* **run a risk** If you **run the risk of** doing or experiencing something undesirable, you do something knowing that the undesirable thing might happen as a result. ❑ *The officers had run the risk of being dismissed.* VERB [T] (**risks**, **risking**, **risked**) **1** If you **risk** something unpleasant, you do something which might result in that thing happening or affecting you. ❑ *Those who fail to register risk severe penalties.* **2** If you **risk** doing something, you do it, even though you know that it might have undesirable consequences. ❑ *The skipper was not willing to risk taking his ship through the straits until he could see where he was going.* **3** If you **risk** your life or something else important, you behave in a way that might result in it being lost or harmed. ❑ *She risked her own life to help a disabled woman.*

WORD CONNECTIONS

VERB + **risk**

pose a risk
involve risk
❑ *Investments always involve some degree of risk.*

reduce the risk
increase the risk
❑ *You can reduce the risk of heart disease by cutting the amount of salt in your diet.*

take a risk
run a risk
❑ *If the company changes the brand image they run the risk of alienating loyal customers.*

R

risky /ˈrɪski/ ADJ (**riskier**, **riskiest**) If an activity or action is **risky**, it is dangerous or likely to fail. ❏ *Investing in airlines is a very risky business.*

rite /raɪt/ NOUN [C] (**rites**) A **rite** is a traditional ceremony that is carried out by a particular group or within a particular society. ❏ *Most traditional societies have transition rites at puberty.*

❖**rit·u·al** /ˈrɪtʃuəl/ NOUN, ADJ
NOUN [C, U] (**rituals**) **1** A **ritual** is a religious service or other ceremony which involves a series of actions performed in a fixed order. = ceremony, custom, rite ❏ *This is the most ancient, and holiest of the Shinto rituals.* ❏ *These ceremonies were already part of pre-Christian ritual in Mexico.* **2** A **ritual** is a way of behaving or a series of actions that people regularly carry out in a particular situation, because it is their custom to do so. ❏ *The whole Italian culture revolves around the ritual of eating.*
ADJ **1** [ritual + N] **Ritual** activities happen as part of a ritual or tradition. ❏ *fasting and ritual dancing* **2** [ritual + N] You can describe something as a **ritual** action when it is done in exactly the same way whenever a particular situation occurs. ❏ *I realized that here the conventions required me to make the ritual noises.*

❖**ri·val** ◆◆◇ /ˈraɪvəl/ NOUN, VERB
NOUN [C] (**rivals**) **1** Your **rival** is a person, business, or organization who you are competing or fighting against in the same area or for the same things. = opponent, contender, adversary ❏ *The world champion finished more than two seconds ahead of his nearest rival.* ❏ *He eliminated his rivals in a brutal struggle for power.* ❏ *The two are rivals for the leadership of the party.* **2** If you say that someone or something has **no rivals** or is **without rival**, you mean that it is best of its type. ❏ *The area is famous for its wonderfully fragrant wine which has no rivals in the Rhone.*
VERB [T] (**rivals**, **rivalling**, **rivalled**; in *AmE*, use **rivaling**, **rivaled**) If you say that one thing **rivals** another, you mean that they are both of the same standard or quality. ❏ *Cassette recorders cannot rival the sound quality of CDs.*

❖**ri·val·ry** /ˈraɪvəlri/ NOUN [C, U] (**rivalries**) **Rivalry** is competition or fighting between people, businesses, or organizations who are in the same area or want the same things. = competition, competitiveness ❏ *The rivalry between the Inkatha and the ANC has resulted in violence in the black townships.* ❏ *The rivalry among her peers was intense.* ❏ *a city torn by deep ethnic rivalries*

riv·er ◆◆◇ /ˈrɪvə/ NOUN [C] (**rivers**) A **river** is a large amount of fresh water flowing continuously in a long line across the land. ❏ *a chemical plant on the banks of the river*

river·side /ˈrɪvəsaɪd/ NOUN [SING] The **riverside** is the area of land by the banks of a river. ❏ *They walked back along the riverside.*

road ◆◆◆ /rəʊd/ NOUN
NOUN [C] (**roads**) **1** A **road** is a long piece of hard ground that is built between two places so that people can drive or ride easily from one place to the other. ❏ *There was very little traffic on the roads.* ❏ *We just go straight up the Boston Post Road.* **2** The **road to** a particular result is the means of achieving it or the process of achieving it. ❏ *We are bound to see some ups and downs along the road to recovery.*
PHRASE **on the road** If you say that someone is **on the road to** something, you mean that they are likely to

achieve it. ❏ *The government took another step on the road to political reform.*
✦ **the end of the road** → see **end**

roam /rəʊm/ VERB [I, T] (**roams**, **roaming**, **roamed**) If you **roam** an area or **roam around** it, you wander or travel around it without having a particular purpose. ❏ *Barefoot children roamed the streets.* ❏ *I spent a couple of years roaming around the countryside.*

roar /rɔː/ VERB, NOUN
VERB [I, T] (**roars**, **roaring**, **roared**) **1** [I] (*written*) If something, usually a vehicle, **roars** somewhere, it goes there very fast, making a loud noise. ❏ *A police car roared past.* **2** [I] (*written*) If something **roars**, it makes a very loud noise. ❏ *The engine roared, and the vehicle leapt forward.* **3** [I] If someone **roars with** laughter, they laugh in a very noisy way. ❏ *Max threw back his head and roared with laughter.* **4** [I, T] (*written*) If someone **roars**, they shout something in a very loud voice. ❏ *'I'll kill you for that!' he roared.* ❏ *During the playing of the national anthem the crowd roared and whistled.* **5** [I] When a lion **roars**, it makes the loud sound that lions typically make. ❏ *The lion roared once, and sprang.*
NOUN [C] (**roars**) **1** The **roar** of a vehicle or of traffic is the loud noise it makes when travelling fast. ❏ *the roar of traffic* **2** A **roar** of laughter is a very noisy laugh. ❏ *There were roars of laughter as he stood up.* **3** A **roar** is a very loud shout. ❏ *There was a roar of approval.* **4** A **roar** is the loud sound that lions typically make. ❏ *the roar of lions in the distance*

roast /rəʊst/ VERB, ADJ, NOUN
VERB [T] (**roasts**, **roasting**, **roasted**) When you **roast** meat or other food, you cook it by dry heat in an oven or over a fire. ❏ *I personally would rather roast a chicken whole.*
ADJ [roast + N] **Roast** meat has been cooked by roasting. ❏ *They serve the most delicious roast beef.*
NOUN [C] (**roasts**) A **roast** is a piece of meat that is cooked by roasting. ❏ *Come into the kitchen. I've got to put the roast in.*

rob /rɒb/ VERB [T] (**robs**, **robbing**, **robbed**) **1** If someone **is robbed**, they have money or property stolen from them. ❏ *Mrs Yacoub was robbed of her designer watch at her Westchester home.* **2** If someone **is robbed of** something that they deserve, have, or need, it is taken away from them. ❏ *When Miles Davis died, jazz was robbed of its most distinctive voice.*

rob·bery /ˈrɒbəri/ NOUN [C, U] (**robberies**) **Robbery** is the crime of stealing money or property from a bank, shop, or vehicle, often by using force or threats. ❏ *The gang members committed dozens of armed robberies over the past year.*

ro·bot /ˈrəʊbɒt, *AmE* -bət/ NOUN [C] (**robots**) A **robot** is a machine that is programmed to move and perform certain tasks automatically. ❏ *very lightweight robots that we could send to the moon for planetary exploration*

ro·bust /rəʊˈbʌst, ˈrəʊbʌst/ ADJ **1** Someone or something that is **robust** is very strong or healthy. ❏ *He was always the robust one, physically strong and mentally sharp.* **2** **Robust** views or opinions are strongly held and forcefully expressed. ❏ *The Secretary of State has made a robust defence of the agreement.*

❖**rock** ◆◆◇ /rɒk/ NOUN, VERB
NOUN [U, C] (**rocks**) **1** [U] **Rock** is the hard substance which the earth is made of. = stone ❏ *The hills above the valley are bare rock.* ❏ *A little way below the ridge was an outcrop of rock that made a rough shelter.* **2** [C] A **rock** is a large piece of rock that sticks up out of the ground or the sea, or that has broken away from a mountain or a cliff. ❏ *She sat cross-legged on the rock.* **3** [C] A **rock** is a piece of rock that is small enough for you to pick up. ❏ *She bent down, picked up a rock, and threw it into the trees.* **4** [U] **Rock** is loud music with a strong beat that is usually played and sung by a small group of people using instruments such as electric guitars and drums. ❏ *a rock concert*
VERB [I, T] (**rocks**, **rocking**, **rocked**) **1** [I, T] When something **rocks** or when you **rock** it, it moves slowly and regularly backward and forward or from side to side. ❏ *His body rocked from side to side with the train.* **2** [I, T]

(*journalism*) If an explosion or an earthquake **rocks** a building or an area, it causes the building or area to shake. ❑ *Three people were injured yesterday when an explosion rocked the factory.* ❑ *In Taipei buildings rocked back and forth.* **3** [T] (*journalism*) If an event or a piece of news **rocks** a group or society, it shocks them or makes them feel less secure. ❑ *His death rocked the fashion business.*

rock·et ◆◇◇ /ˈrɒkɪt/ NOUN, VERB

NOUN [c, u] (**rockets**) **1** [c] A **rocket** is a space vehicle that is shaped like a long tube. ❑ *the Apollo 12 rocket that took astronauts to the moon* **2** [c] A **rocket** is a missile containing explosives that is powered by gas. ❑ *There has been a renewed rocket attack on the capital.* **3** [c] A **rocket** is a firework that quickly goes high into the air and then explodes. **4** [u] (*BrE*; in *AmE*, use **arugula**) **Rocket** is an edible Mediterranean plant of the cabbage family, whose leaves are eaten in salads.

VERB [I] (**rockets, rocketing, rocketed**) **1** (*journalism*) If things such as prices or social problems **rocket**, they increase very quickly and suddenly. = soar ❑ *Fresh food is so scarce that prices have rocketed.* **2** If something such as a vehicle **rockets** somewhere, it moves there very quickly. ❑ *A train rocketed by, shaking the walls of the houses.*

rod /rɒd/ NOUN [c] (**rods**) A **rod** is a long, thin, metal or wooden bar. ❑ *a 15-foot thick roof that was reinforced with steel rods*

rode /rəʊd/ IRREG FORM **Rode** is the past tense of **ride**.

rogue /rəʊg/ NOUN, ADJ

NOUN [c] (**rogues**) **1** A **rogue** is a man who behaves in a dishonest or criminal way. ❑ *Mr Ward wasn't a rogue at all.* **2** If a man behaves in a way that you do not approve of but you still like him, you can refer to him as a **rogue**. ❑ *Falstaff, the lovable rogue*

ADJ [rogue + N] A **rogue** element is someone or something that behaves differently from others of its kind, often causing damage. ❑ *Computer systems throughout the country are being affected by a series of mysterious rogue programs, known as viruses.*

✪ **role** ◆◆◆ /rəʊl/ NOUN [c] (**roles**) (*academic word*) **1** If you have a **role** in a situation or in society, you have a particular position and function in it. ❑ *Until now scientists had very little clear evidence about the drug's role in preventing more serious effects of infection.* ❑ *Both sides have roles to play.* **2** A **role** is one of the characters that an actor or singer can play in a film, play, or opera. ❑ *She has just landed the lead role in their latest production.*

WORD CONNECTIONS

VERB + **role**

play a role
have a role
take a role
❑ *Folic acid has a key role in the synthesis of DNA.*

ADJ + **role**

an **important** role
a **key** role
a **vital** role
a **major** role
❑ *The media plays a major role in shaping public attitudes.*

an **active** role
a **positive** role
❑ *We want to encourage students to take an active role in deciding school policy.*

---

roll ◆◆◇ /rəʊl/ VERB, NOUN

VERB [I, T] (**rolls, rolling, rolled**) **1** [I, T] When something **rolls** or when you **roll** it, it moves along a surface, turning over many times. ❑ *The ball rolled into the net.* **2** [I] If you **roll** somewhere, you move on a surface while lying down, turning your body over and over, so that you are sometimes on your back, sometimes on your side, and sometimes on your front. ❑ *When I was a little kid I rolled down a hill and broke my leg.* **3** [I] When vehicles **roll** along, they move along slowly. ❑ *The truck quietly rolled forward and demolished all the old wooden fencing.* **4** [I] If a machine

rolls, it is operating. ❑ *He slipped and fell on the step as the cameras rolled.* **5** [I] If drops of liquid **roll** down a surface, they move quickly down it. ❑ *She looked at Ginny and tears rolled down her cheeks.* **6** [T] If you **roll** something flexible **into** a cylinder or a ball, you form it into a cylinder or a ball by wrapping it several times around itself or by shaping it between your hands. ❑ *He took off his sweater, rolled it into a pillow, and lay down on the grass.* **7** [T] If you **roll up** something such as a car window or a blind, you cause it to move upwards by turning a handle. If you **roll** it **down**, you cause it to move downwards by turning a handle. ❑ *In mid-afternoon, shopkeepers began to roll down their shutters.* **8** [I, T] (*written*) If you **roll** your eyes or if your eyes **roll**, they move around and upwards. People sometimes roll their eyes when they are frightened, bored, or annoyed. ❑ *People may roll their eyes and talk about overprotective, interfering grandmothers.*

PHRASE **rolled into one** If something is several things **rolled into one**, it combines the main features or qualities of those things. ❑ *This is our kitchen, living room, and dining room all rolled into one.*

PHRASAL VERBS **roll back** (*mainly AmE*) To **roll back** prices, taxes, or benefits means to reduce them. ❑ *One provision of the law was to roll back taxes to the 1975 level.*

roll in (*informal*) If something such as money **is rolling in**, it is appearing or being received in large quantities. ❑ *Don't forget, I have always kept the money rolling in.*

roll out If a company **rolls out** a new product or service, or if the product or service **rolls out**, it is made available to the public. ❑ *On Thursday Microsoft rolls out its new operating system.* ❑ *Northern Telecom says its products will roll out over 18 months beginning early next year.*

roll over **1** If you are lying down and you **roll over**, you turn your body so that a different part of you is facing upward. ❑ *I rolled over and went back to sleep.* **2** If a moving vehicle such as a car **rolls over**, it turns over many times, usually because it has crashed. ❑ *Those kinds of vehicles are more likely to roll over than passenger cars.* **3** If you say that someone **rolls over**, you mean that they stop resisting someone and do what the other person wants them to do. ❑ *That's why most people and organizations just roll over and give up when they're challenged or attacked by the I.R.S.* **4** (*business*) If you **roll over** a loan or other financial arrangement, you extend it, for example by adding it to another loan. ❑ *There seems to be no way to spread out the tax or roll over the cash into another pension plan.* **5** In lotteries and similar games, if a jackpot **rolls over**, it is not won by anyone and the money is added to the prize money for the next lottery. ❑ *If the jackpot isn't won this week it will roll over again to next week.*

roll up **1** Roll up means the same as **roll** VERB 6. ❑ *Stein rolled up the paper bag with the money inside.* **2** If you **roll up** your sleeves or trouser legs, you fold the ends back several times, making them shorter. ❑ *The jacket was too big for him so he rolled up the cuffs.* **3** (*informal*) If people **roll up** somewhere, they arrive there, especially in a car and often late. ❑ *They eventually rolled up two hours late.*

NOUN [c] (**rolls**) **1** A **roll** of paper, plastic, cloth, or wire is a long piece of it that has been wrapped many times around itself or around a tube. ❑ *The photographers had already shot a dozen rolls of film.* **2** A **roll** is a small piece of bread that is round or long and is made to be eaten by one person. Rolls can be eaten plain, with butter, or with a filling. ❑ *He sipped at his coffee and spread butter and marmalade on a roll.* **3** A **roll** of drums is a long, low, fairly loud sound made by drums. ❑ *As the town clock struck two, they heard the roll of drums.* **4** A **roll** is an official list of people's names. = register ❑ *Pro-democracy activists say a new electoral roll should be drawn up.*

✦ **heads will roll** → see **head**

roll·er /ˈrəʊlə/ NOUN [c] (**rollers**) **1** A **roller** is a cylinder that turns around in a machine or device. **2** Rollers are hollow tubes that women roll their hair round in order to make it curly. ❑ *She gets up every morning and puts her hair in rollers.*

Ro·man ◆◇◇ /ˈrəʊmən/ ADJ, NOUN

ADJ **1** **Roman** means related to or connected with ancient Rome and its empire. ❑ *the fall of the Roman Empire*

2 **Roman** means related to or connected with modern Rome. ❑ *a Roman hotel room*
NOUN [c] (**Romans**) **1** A **Roman** was a citizen of ancient Rome or its empire. ❑ *When they conquered Britain, the Romans brought this custom with them.* **2** A **Roman** is someone who lives in or comes from Rome. ❑ *football-mad Romans*

ro•mance /rə'mæns, 'rəʊmæns/ NOUN [c, u] (**romances**)
1 [c] A **romance** is a relationship between two people who are in love with each other but who are not married to each other. ❑ *After a whirlwind romance the couple announced their engagement in July.* **2** [u] **Romance** refers to the actions and feelings of people who are in love, especially behaviour that is very caring or affectionate. ❑ *He still finds time for romance by cooking candlelit dinners for his girlfriend.*
3 [u] You can refer to the pleasure and excitement of doing something new or exciting as **romance**. ❑ *We want to recreate the romance and excitement that used to be part of rail journeys.* **4** [c] A **romance** is a novel or film about a love affair. ❑ *Her taste in fiction was for chunky historical romances.*

Ro•man nu•mer•al NOUN [c] (**Roman numerals**) [usu pl] **Roman numerals** are the letters used by the ancient Romans to represent numbers, for example I, IV, VIII, and XL, which represent 1, 4, 8, and 40. Roman numerals are still sometimes used today. ❑ *'VII', the Roman numeral for seven* ❑ *The date was written in Roman numerals as MIIM for 1998.* ❑ *a Roman numeral indicating the order in which the enzyme was discovered*

ro•man•tic ◆◇◇ /rəʊ'mæntɪk/ ADJ, NOUN
ADJ **1** Someone who is **romantic** or does **romantic** things says and does things that make their wife, husband, girlfriend, or boyfriend feel special and loved. ❑ *When we're together, all he talks about is business. I wish he were more romantic.* **2** [romantic + N] **Romantic** means connected with sexual love. ❑ *He was not interested in a romantic relationship with Ingrid.* **3** [romantic + N] A **romantic** play, film, or story describes or represents a love affair. ❑ *It is a lovely romantic comedy, well worth seeing.*
4 (disapproval) If you say that someone has a **romantic** view or idea of something, you are critical of them because their view of it is unrealistic and they think that thing is better or more exciting than it really is. ❑ *He has a romantic view of rural society.* **5** Something that is **romantic** is beautiful in a way that strongly affects your feelings.
❑ *It is considered one of the most romantic restaurants in the city.*
NOUN [c] (**romantics**) A **romantic** is a person who has romantic views. ❑ *You're a hopeless romantic.*
ro•man•ti•cal•ly /rəʊ'mæntɪkli/ ADV **1** *We are not romantically involved.* **2** *the romantically named, but very muddy, Cave of the Wild Horses*

roof ◆◇◇ /ruːf/ NOUN
NOUN [c] (**roofs**) **1** The **roof** of a building is the covering on top of it that protects the people and things inside from the weather. ❑ *a small stone cottage with a red slate roof* **2** The **roof** of a car or other vehicle is the top part of it, which protects passengers or goods from the weather. ❑ *The car rolled onto its roof, trapping him.* **3** The **roof of** your mouth is the highest part of the inside of your mouth. = palate ❑ *She clicked her tongue against the roof of her mouth.*
PHRASES **go through the roof** (informal) If the level of something such as the price of a product or the rate of inflation **goes through the roof**, it suddenly increases very rapidly indeed. ❑ *Prices for Korean art have gone through the roof.*
hit the roof or **go through the roof** (informal) If you **hit the roof** or **go through the roof**, you become very angry, and usually show your anger by shouting at someone. ❑ *Sergeant Long will hit the roof when I tell him you've gone off.*
under one roof or **under the same roof** If a number of things or people are **under one roof** or **under the same roof**, they are in the same building. ❑ *The firms intend to open either together under one roof or alongside each other in shopping centres.*

room ◆◆◆ /ruːm, rʊm/ NOUN [c, u] (**rooms**) **1** [c] A **room** is one of the separate sections or parts of the inside of a building. Rooms have their own walls, ceilings, floors, and doors, and are usually used for particular activities. You can refer to all the people who are in a room as **the room**. ❑ *A minute later he excused himself and left the room.* ❑ *The largest conference room could seat 5,000 people.* **2** [c] If you talk about your **room**, you are referring to the room that you alone use, especially your bedroom at home or your office at work. ❑ *If you're running upstairs, go to my room and bring down my sweater, please.* **3** [c] A **room** is a bedroom in a hotel. ❑ *Toni reserved a room in a hotel not far from Arzfeld.* **4** [u] If there is **room** somewhere, there is enough empty space there for people or things to be fitted in, or for people to move freely or do what they want to. ❑ *There is usually room to accommodate up to 80 visitors.*
5 [u] If there is **room for** a particular kind of behaviour or action, people are able to behave in that way or to take that action. ❑ *The intensity of the work left little room for personal grief or anxiety.*
→ See also **dining room, living room**

root ◆◇◇ /ruːt/ NOUN, VERB, ADJ
NOUN [c, PL] (**roots**) **1** [c] The **roots** of a plant are the parts of it that grow under the ground. = tuber, rhizome ❑ *the twisted roots of an apple tree* ❑ *Mint roots spread rapidly.*
2 [c] The **root** of a hair or tooth is the part of it that is underneath the skin. ❑ *decay around the roots of teeth*
3 [PL] You can refer to the place or culture that a person or their family comes from as their **roots**. ❑ *I am proud of my Brazilian roots.* **4** [c] You can refer to the cause of a problem or of an unpleasant situation as **the root of** it or **the roots of** it. ❑ *We got to the root of the problem.*
PHRASES **put down roots** If someone **puts down roots**, they make a place their home, for example by taking part in activities there or by making a lot of friends there.
= settle down ❑ *When they got to Montana, they put down roots and built a life.*
take root If an idea, belief, or custom **takes root**, it becomes established among a group of people. ❑ *Time would be needed for democracy to take root.*
VERB [I, T] (**roots, rooting, rooted**) **1** [I, T] If you **root** a plant or cutting or if it **roots**, roots form on the bottom of its stem and it starts to grow. ❑ *Most plants will root in about six to eight weeks.* **2** [I] If you **root through** or **in** something, you search for something by moving other things around. = rummage ❑ *She rooted through the bag, found what she wanted, and headed towards the door.*
PHRASAL VERB **root out** **1** If you **root out** a person, you find them and force them from the place they are in, usually in order to punish them. ❑ *The generals have to root out traitors.* **2** If you **root out** a problem or an unpleasant situation, you find out who or what is the cause of it and put an end to it. ❑ *There would be a major drive to root out corruption.*
ADJ [root + N] **Root** vegetables or **root** crops are grown for their roots, which are large and can be eaten. ❑ *root crops such as carrots and potatoes*

rope /rəʊp/ NOUN, VERB
NOUN [c, u] (**ropes**) A **rope** is a thick cord or wire that is made by twisting together several thinner cords or wires. Ropes are used for jobs such as pulling cars, tying up boats, or tying things together. ❑ *He tied the rope around his waist.*
PHRASES **give someone enough rope to hang** If you **give** someone **enough rope to hang** themselves, you give them the freedom to do a job in their own way because you hope that their attempts will fail and that they will look foolish. ❑ *The king has merely given the politicians enough rope to hang themselves.*
learn the ropes (informal) If you **are learning the ropes**, you are learning how a particular task or job is done. ❑ *He tried hiring more salesmen to push his radio products, but they took too much time to learn the ropes.*
know the ropes (informal) If you **know the ropes**, you know how a particular job or task should be done. ❑ *The moment she got to know the ropes, there was no stopping her.*
show someone the ropes (informal) If you **show** someone **the ropes**, you show them how to do a particular job or task.

r

❑ *We had a patrol out on the border, breaking in some young soldiers, showing them the ropes.*

VERB [T] (**ropes, roping, roped**) If you **rope** one thing **to** another, you tie the two things together with a rope. ❑ *I roped myself to the chimney.*

PHRASAL VERB **rope in** (*informal*) If you say that you **were roped in to** do a particular task, you mean that someone persuaded you to help them do that task. ❑ *Visitors were roped in for potato picking and harvesting.*

rose ◆◇◇ /rəʊz/ IRREG FORM, NOUN, COLOUR

IRREG FORM Rose is the past tense of **rise**.

NOUN [c] (**roses**) **1** A **rose** is a flower, often with a pleasant smell, which grows on a bush with stems that have sharp points called thorns on them. ❑ *She bent to pick a red rose.* **2** A **rose** is a bush that roses grow on. ❑ *Prune rambling roses when the flowers have faded.*

PHRASE **bed of roses** If you say that a situation is not **a bed of roses**, you mean that it is not as pleasant as it seems, and that there are some unpleasant aspects to it. ❑ *We all knew that life was unlikely to be a bed of roses back in Nebraska.*

COLOUR (*literary*) Something that is **rose** is reddish pink in colour. ❑ *the rose and violet hues of a twilight sky*

rot /rɒt/ VERB, NOUN

VERB [i, t] (**rots, rotting, rotted**) **1** [i, t] When food, wood, or another substance **rots**, or when something **rots** it, it becomes softer and is gradually destroyed. ❑ *If we don't unload it soon, the grain will start rotting in the silos.* **2** [i] If you say that someone is being left to **rot** in a particular place, especially in a prison, you mean that they are being left there and their physical and mental condition is being allowed to get worse and worse. ❑ *Most governments simply leave the long-term jobless to rot.*

NOUN [u, SING] **1** [u] If there is **rot** in something, especially something that is made of wood, parts of it have decayed and fallen apart. ❑ *Investigations had revealed extensive rot in the beams under the ground floor.* **2** [SING] You can use the **rot** to refer to the way something gradually gets worse. For example, if you are talking about the time when **the rot set in**, you are talking about the time when a situation began to get steadily worse and worse. ❑ *In many schools, the rot is beginning to set in. Standards are falling all the time.*

✪ ro•tate /rəʊˈteɪt, AmE ˈrəʊteɪt/ VERB [i, t] (**rotates, rotating, rotated**) **1** When something **rotates** or when you **rotate** it, it turns with a circular movement. = revolve, turn, spin ❑ *The Earth rotates around the sun.* ❑ *Take each foot in both your hands and rotate it to loosen and relax the ankle.* **2** If people or things **rotate**, or if someone **rotates** them, they take turns to do a particular job or serve a particular purpose. ❑ *The members of the club can rotate and one person can do all the preparation for the evening.*

✪ ro•ta•tion /rəʊˈteɪʃən/ NOUN [c, u] (**rotations**) **1** [c, u] **Rotation** is circular movement. A **rotation** is the movement of something through one complete circle. = revolution, gyration, spinning ❑ *the daily rotation of the earth upon its axis* ❑ *the point of rotation of the lever arms* **2** [u] The **rotation** of a group of things or people is the fact of them taking turns to do a particular job or serve a particular purpose. If people do something **in rotation**, they take turns to do it. ❑ *He grew a different crop on the same field five years in a row, what researchers call crop rotation.*

rot•ten /ˈrɒtən/ ADJ **1** If food, wood, or another substance is **rotten**, it has decayed and can no longer be used. ❑ *The smell outside this building is overwhelming – like rotten eggs.* **2** (*informal*) If you describe something as **rotten**, you think it is very unpleasant or of very poor quality. ❑ *I personally think it's a rotten idea.* **3** (*informal*) If you feel **rotten**, you feel bad, either because you are ill or because you are sorry about something. = awful ❑ *I had rheumatic fever and spent that year feeling rotten.*

✪ rough ◆◇◇ /rʌf/ ADJ, ADV, VERB

ADJ (**rougher, roughest**) **1** If a surface is **rough**, it is uneven and not smooth. ❑ *His hands were rough and callused, from years of karate practice.* **2** You say that people or their actions are **rough** when they use too much force and not enough care or gentleness. ❑ *Football's a rough game at the best of times.* **3** A **rough** area, city, school, or

other place is unpleasant and dangerous because there is a lot of violence or crime there. ❑ *It was quite a rough part of our town.* **4** If you say that someone has had a **rough** time, you mean that they have had some difficult or unpleasant experiences. = tough ❑ *All women have a rough time in our society.* **5** A **rough** calculation or guess is approximately correct, but not exact. = approximate, vague; ≠ exact ❑ *We were only able to make a rough estimate of how much fuel would be required.* ❑ *As a rough guide, a horse needs 2.5 per cent of his body weight in food every day.* **6** If you give someone a **rough** idea, description, or drawing of something, you indicate only the most important features, without much detail. ❑ *I've got a rough idea of what he looks like.* **7** You can say that something is **rough** when it is not neat and well made. ❑ *The bench had a rough wooden table in front of it.* **8** If the sea or the weather at sea is **rough**, the weather is windy or stormy and there are very big waves. ❑ *A fishing vessel and a cargo ship collided in rough seas.*

VERB (**roughs, roughing, roughed**)

PHRASE **rough it** (*informal*) If you have to **rough it**, you have to live without the possessions and comforts that you normally have. ❑ *There is a campsite but, if you prefer not to rough it, the Lake Hotel is nearby.*

PHRASAL VERB **rough up** (*informal*) If someone **roughs** you **up**, they attack you and hit or beat you. ❑ *They threw him in a cell and roughed him up a bit.* ❑ *He was fired from his job after roughing up a colleague.*

✪ rough•ly /ˈrʌfli/ ADV **1** ❑ *They roughly pushed her forward.* **2** [roughly with CL/GROUP] = approximately; ≠ exactly ❑ *Gambling and tourism pay roughly half the entire state budget.* ❑ *Ukraine is roughly equal to France in size and population.* ❑ *a period of very roughly 30 million years* **3** He knew roughly what was about to be said. **4** [roughly with V] ❑ *Roughly chop the tomatoes and add them to the casserole.*

rough•ness /ˈrʌfnəs/ NOUN [u] **1** *She rested her cheek against the roughness of his jacket.* **2** *He regretted his roughness.*

round ◆◆◇ /raʊnd/ NOUN, ADJ, ADV, VERB

NOUN [c] (**rounds**) **1** A **round** of events is a series of related events, especially one which comes after or before a similar series of events. ❑ *It was agreed that another round of preliminary talks would be held in Beijing.* **2** In sports, a **round** is a series of games in a competition. Often, the winners of these games go on to play in the next round, and so on, until only one player or team is left. = heat ❑ *in the third round of the Ryder Cup* **3** In a boxing or wrestling match, a **round** is one of the periods during which the boxers or wrestlers fight. ❑ *He was declared the victor in the 11th round.* **4** A **round** of golf is one game, usually including 18 holes. ❑ *two rounds of golf* **5** If you do your **rounds** or your **round**, you make a series of visits to different places or people, for example as part of your job. ❑ *The doctors still did their morning rounds.* **6** If you buy a **round** of drinks, you buy a drink for each member of the group of people that you are with. ❑ *They sat on the clubhouse terrace, downing a round of drinks.* **7** A **round** of ammunition is the bullet or bullets released when a gun is fired. ❑ *firing 1,650 rounds of ammunition during a period of ten minutes* **8** If there is a **round of applause**, everyone claps their hands to welcome someone or to show that they have enjoyed something. ❑ *Sue got a sympathetic round of applause.*

PHRASE **make the rounds** If you **make the rounds** or **do the rounds**, you visit a series of different places. ❑ *After school, I had picked up Nick and Ted and made the rounds of the dry cleaner and the food shops.*

ADJ (**rounder, roundest**) **1** Something that is **round** is shaped like a circle or ball. ❑ *She had small feet and hands and a flat, round face.* **2** [round + N] A **round** number is a multiple of 10, 100, 1,000, and so on. Round numbers are used instead of precise ones to give the general idea of a quantity or proportion. ❑ *I asked how much silver could be bought for a million dollars, which seemed a suitably round number.*

ADV

PHRASE **all year round** If something happens **all year round**, it happens throughout the year. ❑ *Many of these* *plants are evergreen, so you can enjoy them all year round.* **VERB** [T] (**rounds, rounding, rounded**) **1** If you **round** a place or obstacle, you move in a curve past the edge or corner of it. = go round ❑ *The house disappeared from sight as we rounded a corner.* **2** If you **round** an amount **up** or **down**, or if you **round** it **off**, you change it to the nearest whole number or nearest multiple of 10, 100, 1000, and so on. ❑ *We needed to do decimals to round up and round down numbers.* ❑ *The fraction was then multiplied by 100 and rounded to the nearest half or whole number.* **PHRASAL VERB** **round up** **1** If the police or army **round up** a number of people, they arrest or capture them. ❑ *The police rounded up a number of suspects.* **2** If you **round up** animals or things, you gather them together. ❑ *He had sought work as a cowboy, rounding up cattle.*

round·about /ˈraʊndəbaʊt/ ADJ, NOUN
ADJ **1** If you go somewhere by a **roundabout** route, you do not go there by the shortest and quickest route. ❑ *He left today on a roundabout route for Jordan and is also due soon in Egypt.* **2** If you do or say something in a **roundabout** way, you do not do or say it in a simple, clear, and direct way. ❑ *We made a little fuss in a roundabout way.*
NOUN [C] (**roundabouts**) (*BrE*) **1** (in *AmE*, use **traffic circle, rotary**) A **roundabout** is a circular structure in the road at a place where several roads meet. You drive around it until you come to the road that you want. **2** (in *AmE*, use **merry-go-round**) A **roundabout** at an amusement park is a large, circular mechanical device with seats, often in the shape of animals or cars, on which children sit and go around and around. **3** (in *AmE*, use **merry-go-round**) A **roundabout** in a park or school play area is a circular platform that children sit or stand on. People push the platform to make it spin round.

rout /raʊt/ VERB, NOUN
VERB [T] (**routs, routing, routed**) If an army, sports team, or other group **routs** its opponents, it defeats them completely and easily. ❑ *the Battle of Hastings at which the Norman army routed the English opposition*
NOUN [C] (**routs**) A **rout** is when an army, sports team, or other group defeats its opponents completely and easily. ❑ *One after another the Italian bases in the desert fell as the retreat turned into a rout.*

⊘ **route** ◆◆◇ /ruːt, *AmE* raʊt/ NOUN, VERB (*academic word*)
NOUN [C] (**routes**) **1** A **route** is a way from one place to another. ❑ *the most direct route to the centre of town* ❑ *All escape routes were blocked by armed police.* ❑ *Tens of thousands lined the route from Dublin airport.* **2** A bus, air, or shipping **route** is the way between two places along which buses, planes, or ships travel regularly. ❑ *the main shipping routes to Japan* **3** You can refer to a way of achieving something as a **route**. = road ❑ *Researchers are trying to get at the same information through an indirect route.* **4** In the United States, **Route** is used in front of a number in the names of main roads between major cities. ❑ *From San Francisco take the freeway to the Broadway-Webster exit on Route 580.*
PHRASE **en route** **1** **En route to** a place means on the way to that place. **En route** is sometimes spelled **on route** in nonstandard English. ❑ *They have arrived in London en route to the United States.* **2** Journalists sometimes use **en route** when they are mentioning an event that happened as part of a longer process or before another event. ❑ *The German set three tournament records and equalled two others en route to grabbing golf's richest prize.*
VERB [T] (**routes, routing, routed**) If vehicles, goods, or passengers **are routed** in a particular direction, they are made to travel in that direction. ❑ *Trains are taking a lot of freight that used to be routed via lorries.*

WORD CONNECTIONS
VERB + **route**

take a route
follow a route
choose a route
❑ *The missile takes the shortest possible route to the target.*

ADJ + **route**

the **main** route
a **direct** route
an **alternative** route
❑ *The system informs the commuter of heavy traffic and suggests an alternative route.*

rou·tine ◆◇◇ /ruːˈtiːn/ NOUN, ADJ
NOUN [C, U] (**routines**) **1** [C, U] A **routine** is the usual series of things that you do at a particular time. A **routine** is also the practice of regularly doing things in a fixed order. ❑ *The players had to change their daily routine and lifestyle.* **2** [C, U] You use **routine** to refer to a way of life that is uninteresting and ordinary, or hardly ever changes. ❑ *the mundane routine of her life* **3** [C] (*computing*) A **routine** is a computer program, or part of a program, that performs a specific function. ❑ *an installation routine* **4** [C] A **routine** is a short sequence of jokes, remarks, actions, or movements that forms part of a longer performance. ❑ *an athletic dance routine*
ADJ **1** You use **routine** to describe activities that are done as a normal part of a job or process. ❑ *a series of routine medical tests including X-rays and blood tests* **2** A **routine** situation, action, or event is one which seems completely ordinary, rather than interesting, exciting, or different. = ordinary ❑ *So many days are routine and uninteresting, especially in winter.*

rou·tine·ly /ruːˈtiːnli/ ADV **1** If something is **routinely** done, it is done as a normal part of a job or process. ❑ *Vitamin K is routinely given in the first week of life to prevent bleeding.* **2** [routinely with V] If something happens **routinely**, it happens repeatedly and is not surprising, unnatural, or new. ❑ *Any outside criticism is routinely dismissed as interference.*

⊘ **row** ◆◇◇ /rəʊ/ NOUN, VERB
NOUN [C] (**rows**) **1** A **row** of things or people is a number of them arranged in a line. ❑ *a row of pretty little cottages* ❑ *a row of plants* ❑ *Several men are pushing school desks and chairs into neat rows.* **2** **Row** is sometimes used in the names of streets. ❑ *the house at 236 Larch Row* **3** /raʊ/ (*BrE*) A **row** is a serious argument between people or organizations. ❑ *a row about the bank's role in the affair* **4** If you go for a **row** or take someone for a **row**, you sit in a boat and make it move through the water by using oars. ❑ *I took Daniel for a row.*
PHRASE **in a row** If something happens several times **in a row**, it happens that number of times without a break. If something happens several days **in a row**, it happens on each of those days. ❑ *They have won five championships in a row.*
VERB [I, T] (**rows, rowing, rowed**) When you **row**, you sit in a boat and make it move through the water by using oars. If you **row** someone somewhere, you take them there in a boat, using oars. ❑ *He rowed as quickly as he could to the shore.* ❑ *The boatman refused to row him back.*

roy·al ◆◆◇ /ˈrɔɪəl/ ADJ, NOUN
ADJ **1** **Royal** is used to indicate that something is connected with a king, queen, or emperor, or their family. A **royal** person is a king, queen, or emperor, or a member of their family. ❑ *an invitation to a royal garden party* **2** [royal + N] **Royal** is used in the names of institutions or organizations that are officially appointed or supported by a member of a royal family. ❑ *the Royal Academy of Music*
NOUN [C] (**royals**) (*informal*) Members of the royal family are sometimes referred to as **royals**. ❑ *The royals have always been patrons of charities pulling in large donations.*

roy·al·ty /ˈrɔɪəlti/ NOUN [U, PL, C] (**royalties**) **1** [U] The members of royal families are sometimes referred to as **royalty**. ❑ *Royalty and government leaders from all around the world are gathering in Japan.* **2** [PL] **Royalties** are payments made to authors and musicians when their work is sold or performed. They usually receive a fixed percentage of the profits from these sales or performances. ❑ *I lived on about $5,000 a year from the royalties on my book.* **3** [C] Payments made to someone whose invention, idea, or property is used by a commercial company can be referred to as **royalties**. ❑ *The royalties enabled the inventor to re-establish himself in business.*

r

rub /rʌb/ VERB, NOUN

VERB [I, T] (**rubs, rubbing, rubbed**) **1** [I, T] If you **rub** a part of your body or if you **rub** at it, you move your hand or fingers backwards and forwards over it while pressing firmly. ❑ *He rubbed his arms and stiff legs.* **2** [I, T] If you **rub against** a surface or **rub** a part of your body **against** a surface, you move it backwards and forwards while pressing it against the surface. ❑ *A cat was rubbing against my leg.* **3** [I, T] If you **rub** an object or a surface or you **rub** at it, you move a cloth backwards and forwards over it in order to clean or dry it. ❑ *She took off her glasses and rubbed them hard.* **4** [T] If you **rub** a substance **into** a surface or **rub** something such as dirt **from** a surface, you spread it over the surface or remove it from the surface using your hand or something such as a cloth. ❑ *He rubbed oil into my back.* **5** [I, T] If you **rub** two things **together** or if they **rub together**, they move backwards and forwards, pressing against each other. ❑ *He rubbed his hands together a few times.* **6** [I] If something you are wearing or holding **rubs**, it makes you sore because it keeps moving backwards and forwards against your skin. ❑ *It should be comfortable against the skin without rubbing, chafing, or cutting into anything.*

PHRASES **rub shoulders with** If you **rub shoulders with** famous people, you meet them and talk to them. ❑ *He regularly rubbed shoulders with the likes of Elizabeth Taylor and Kylie Minogue.*

rub someone up the wrong way (*informal*) If you **rub** someone **the wrong way**, you offend or annoy them without intending to. = annoy ❑ *What are you going to get out of him if you rub him the wrong way?*

PHRASAL VERB **rub out** (*BrE*; in *AmE*, use **erase**) If you **rub out** something that you have written on paper or a board, you remove it using an eraser.

NOUN [c] (**rubs**) A massage can be referred to as a **rub**. ❑ *She sometimes asks if I want a back rub.*

✦ **rub someone's nose in it** → see **nose**

rub·ber /'rʌbə/ NOUN [U, c] (**rubbers**) **1** [U] **Rubber** is a strong, waterproof, elastic substance made from the juice of a tropical tree or produced chemically. It is used for making tyres, boots, and other products. ❑ *the smell of burning rubber* **2** [c] (*BrE*; in *AmE*, use **eraser**) A **rubber** is a small piece of rubber or other material that is used to remove mistakes that you have made while drawing, or typing.

rub·bish /'rʌbɪʃ/ NOUN, VERB

NOUN [U] (*mainly BrE*; in *AmE*, usually use **garbage, trash**) **Rubbish** consists of unwanted things or waste material such as used paper, empty cans and bottles, and waste food. = refuse **2** (*BrE*; *informal*) If you think that something is of very poor quality, you can say that it is **rubbish**.

VERB [T] (**rubbishes, rubbishing, rubbished**) (*BrE*; in *AmE*, use **trash**; *informal*) If you **rubbish** a person, their ideas or their work, you say they are of little value.

rub·bish tip (*BrE*; in *AmE*, use **garbage dump**) NOUN [c] (**rubbish tips**) A **rubbish tip** is a place where waste material is left.

rude /ruːd/ ADJ (**ruder, rudest**) **1** When people are **rude**, they act in an impolite way towards other people or say impolite things about them. ❑ *He's rude to her friends and obsessively jealous.* **2** **Rude** is used to describe words and behaviour that are likely to embarrass or offend people, because they relate to sex or to body functions. = obscene, vulgar ❑ *Fred keeps cracking rude jokes with the guests.* **3** [rude + N] If someone receives a **rude** shock, something unpleasant happens unexpectedly. ❑ *It will come as a rude shock when their salary or income-tax refund cannot be cashed.*

rude·ly /'ruːdli/ ADV **1** *I could not understand why she felt compelled to behave so rudely to a friend.* **2** People were rudely awakened by a siren just outside their window.

rude·ness /'ruːdnəs/ NOUN [U] ❑ *Mother is annoyed at Caleb's rudeness, but I can forgive it.*

ru·di·men·ta·ry /ˌruːdɪˈmentri/ ADJ (*formal*) **1** **Rudimentary** things are very basic or simple and are therefore unsatisfactory. ❑ *The earth surface of the courtyard* extended into a kind of rudimentary kitchen. **2** **Rudimentary** knowledge includes only the simplest and most basic facts. = basic ❑ *He had only a rudimentary knowledge of French.*

rug /rʌg/ NOUN

NOUN [c] (**rugs**) **1** A **rug** is a piece of thick material that you put on a floor. It is like a carpet but covers a smaller area. ❑ *A Persian rug covered the hardwood floors.* **2** (*mainly BrE*) A **rug** is a small blanket which you use to cover your shoulders or your knees to keep them warm. ❑ *The old lady was seated in her chair at the window, a rug over her knees.*

PHRASE **pull the rug from under someone** or **pull the rug from under someone's feet** If someone **pulls the rug from under** a person or thing or **pulls the rug from under** someone's **feet**, they stop giving their help or support. ❑ *If the banks opt to pull the rug from under the ill-fated project, it will go into liquidation.*

✦ **sweep something under the rug** → see **sweep**

rug·by ✦◇◇ /'rʌgbi/ NOUN [U] **Rugby** or **rugby football** is a game played by two teams using an oval ball. Players try to score points by carrying the ball to their opponents' end of the field, or by kicking it over a bar fixed between two posts.

ruin ✦◇◇ /'ruːɪn/ VERB, NOUN

VERB [T] (**ruins, ruining, ruined**) **1** To **ruin** something means to severely harm, damage, or spoil it. ❑ *My wife was ruining her health through worry.* **2** To **ruin** someone means to cause them to no longer have any money. ❑ *She accused him of ruining her financially with his taste for the high life.*

NOUN [U, PL, c] (**ruins**) **1** [U] **Ruin** is the state of no longer having any money. ❑ *The farmers say recent inflation has driven them to the brink of ruin.* **2** [U] **Ruin** is the state of being severely damaged or spoiled, or the process of reaching this state. ❑ *The vineyards were falling into ruin.* **3** [PL] The **ruins** of something are the parts of it that remain after it has been severely damaged or weakened. ❑ *The new Turkish republic he helped to build emerged from the ruins of a great empire.* **4** [c] The **ruins** of a building are the parts of it that remain after the rest has fallen down or been destroyed. ❑ *One dead child was found in the ruins almost two hours after the explosion.*

PHRASE **in ruins** **1** If something is **in ruins**, it is completely spoiled. ❑ *Its heavily subsidized economy is in ruins.* **2** If a building or place is **in ruins**, most of it has been destroyed and only parts of it remain. ❑ *The abbey was in ruins.*

★**rule** ✦✦✦ /ruːl/ NOUN, VERB

NOUN [c, SING, U] (**rules**) **1** [c] **Rules** are instructions that tell you what you are allowed to do and what you are not allowed to do. ❑ *a thirty-two-page pamphlet explaining the rules of basketball* **2** [c] A **rule** is a statement telling people what they should do in order to achieve success or a benefit of some kind. ❑ *An important rule is to drink plenty of water during any flight.* **3** [c] The **rules of** something such as a language or a science are statements that describe the way that things usually happen in a particular situation. ❑ *according to the rules of quantum theory* ❑ *Children often apply grammatical rules correctly in order to express what they want.* **4** [SING] If something is **the rule**, it is the normal state of affairs. ❑ *However, for many Americans today, weekend work has unfortunately become the rule rather than the exception.* **5** [U] When a person or group controls the affairs of a country, you call this their **rule**. A person's or a group's **rule** is also the length of time during which they rule a country. ❑ *demands for an end to one-party rule*

PHRASES **as a rule** If you say that something happens **as a rule**, you mean that it usually happens. = generally, usually ❑ *As a rule, however, such attacks have been aimed at causing damage rather than taking life.*

bend the rules or **stretch the rules** If someone in authority **bends the rules** or **stretches the rules**, they do something even though it is against the rules. ❑ *There happens to be a particular urgency in this case, and it would help if you could bend the rules.*

rule of thumb A **rule of thumb** is a rule or principle that

you follow which is not based on exact calculations, but rather on experience. ❑ *A good rule of thumb is that a broker must generate sales of ten times his salary if his employer is to make a profit.* **VERB** [I, T] (**rules, ruling, ruled**) **1** [I, T] The person or group that **rules** a country controls its affairs. ❑ *For four centuries, he says, foreigners have ruled Angola.* ❑ *He ruled for eight months.* **2** [T] If something **rules** your life, it influences or restricts your actions in a way that is not good for you. ❑ *Scientists have always been aware of how fear can rule our lives and make us ill.* **3** [I, T] (formal) When someone in authority **rules** that something is true or should happen, they state that they have officially decided that it is true or should happen. = pronounce, decide, judge ❑ *The court ruled that laws passed by the assembly remained valid.* ❑ *The Israeli court has not yet ruled on the case.* ❑ *A provincial magistrates' court last week ruled it unconstitutional.* ❑ *The committee ruled against all-night opening mainly on safety grounds.* **4** [T] If you **rule** a straight line, you draw it using something that has a straight edge. ❑ *a ruled grid of horizontal and vertical lines*
PHRASAL VERB **rule out** **1** If you **rule out** a course of action, an idea, or a solution, you decide that it is impossible or unsuitable. ❑ *The Treasury Department has ruled out using a weak dollar as the main solution for the country's trade problems.* **2** If something **rules out** a situation, it prevents it from happening or from being possible. ❑ *A serious car accident in 1986 ruled out a permanent future for him in farming.*
→ See also **ruling**

rul·er /ˈruːlə/ NOUN [c] (**rulers**) **1** The **ruler** of a country is the person who rules the country. ❑ *The former military ruler of Lesotho has been placed under house arrest.* **2** A **ruler** is a long, flat piece of wood, metal, or plastic with straight edges marked in inches or centimetres. Rulers are used to measure things and to draw straight lines. ❑ *a twelve-inch ruler*

rul·ing ◆◇◇ /ˈruːlɪŋ/ ADJ, NOUN
ADJ **1** [ruling + N] The **ruling** group of people in a country or organization is the group that controls its affairs. ❑ *the Mexican voters' growing dissatisfaction with the ruling party* **2** [ruling + N] Someone's **ruling** passion or emotion is the feeling they have most strongly, which influences their actions. ❑ *Even my love of literary fame, my ruling passion, never soured my temper.*
NOUN [c] (**rulings**) A **ruling** is an official decision made by a judge or court. ❑ *Goodwin tried to have the court ruling overturned.*

ru·mour /ˈruːmə/ (BrE; in AmE, use **rumor**) NOUN [c, u] (**rumours**) A **rumour** is a story or piece of information that may or may not be true, but that people are talking about. ❑ *US officials are discounting rumours of a coup.*

run ◆◆◆ /rʌn/ VERB, NOUN
VERB [I, T] (**runs, running, ran, run**) **1** [I, T] When you **run**, you move more quickly than when you walk, for example because you are in a hurry to get somewhere, or for exercise. ❑ *I excused myself and ran back to the telephone.* ❑ *He ran the last block to the White House with two cases of gear.* **2** [I, T] When someone **runs** in a race, they run in competition with other people. ❑ *when I was running in the New York Marathon* ❑ *He ran a tremendous race.* **3** [I, T] When a horse **runs** in a race or when its owner **runs** it, it competes in a race. ❑ *He was overruled by the owner, Peter Bolton, who insisted on Cool Ground running in the Gold Cup.* **4** [I] If you say that something long, such as a road, **runs** in a particular direction, you are describing its course or position. You can also say that something **runs** the length or width of something else. ❑ *the sun-dappled trail which ran through the beech woods* **5** [T] If you **run** a wire or tube somewhere, you attach it or pull it from, to, or across a particular place. ❑ *Our host ran a long extension cord out from the house and set up a screen and a projector.* **6** [T] If you **run** your hand or an object **through** something, you move your hand or the object through it. ❑ *He laughed and ran his fingers through his hair.* **7** [T] If you **run** something through a machine, process, or series of tests, you make it go through the machine, process, or tests.

❑ *They have gathered the best statistics they can find and run them through their own computers.* **8** [I] If someone **runs for** office in an election, they take part as a candidate. ❑ *It was only last February that he announced he would run for president.* **9** [T] If you **run** something such as a business or an activity, you are in charge of it or you organize it. ❑ *His stepfather ran a prosperous paint business.* ❑ *a well-run, profitable organization* **10** [I] If you talk about how a system, an organization, or someone's life **is running**, you are saying how well it is operating or progressing. ❑ *Officials in charge of the camps say the system is now running extremely smoothly.* **11** [I, T] If you **run** an experiment, computer program, or other process, you start it and let it continue. ❑ *He ran a lot of tests and it turned out I had an infection called mycoplasma.* **12** [I, T] When a machine **is running** or when you **are running** it, it is switched on and is working. ❑ *We told him to wait outside with the engine running.* **13** [I] A machine or equipment that **runs on** or **off** a particular source of energy functions using that source of energy. ❑ *The buses run on diesel.* **14** [I] When you say that vehicles such as trains and buses **run** from one place to another, you mean they regularly travel along that route. ❑ *A shuttle bus runs frequently between the inn and the country club.* **15** [T] (informal) If you **run** someone somewhere in a car, you drive them there. = drive ❑ *Could you run me up to Baltimore?* **16** [I] (informal) If you **run** over or down to a place that is quite near, you drive there. = drive ❑ *I'll run over to Short Mountain and check on Mrs Adams.* **17** [I] If a liquid **runs** in a particular direction, it flows in that direction. = flow ❑ *Tears were running down her cheeks.* **18** [T] If you **run** water, or if you **run** a tap or a bath, you cause water to flow from a tap. ❑ *She went to the sink and ran water into her empty glass.* **19** [I] If a tap or a bath **is running**, water is coming out of a tap. ❑ *The kitchen sink had been stopped up and the tap left running, so water spilled over onto the floor.* **20** [I] If your nose **is running**, liquid is flowing out of it, usually because you have a cold. ❑ *Timothy was crying, mostly from exhaustion, and his nose was running.* **21** [I] If a surface **is running with** a liquid, that liquid is flowing down it. ❑ *After an hour he realized he was completely running with sweat.* **22** [I, T] When you **run** a cassette or videotape or when it **runs**, it moves through the machine as the machine operates. = play ❑ *Leaphorn pushed the play button again, ran the tape, pushed stop, pushed rewind.* **23** [I] If the dye in some cloth or the ink on some paper **runs**, it comes off or spreads when the cloth or paper gets wet. ❑ *The ink had run on the wet paper.* **24** [I] If a feeling **runs through** your body or a thought **runs through** your mind, you experience it or think it quickly. = go ❑ *She felt a surge of excitement run through her.* **25** [I] If a feeling or noise **runs through** a group of people, it spreads among them. = go ❑ *A buzz of excitement ran through the crowd.* **26** [I] If a theme or feature **runs through** something such as someone's actions or writing, it is present in all of it. ❑ *Another thread running through this series is the role of doctors in the treatment of the mentally ill.* **27** [I, T] When newspapers or magazines **run** a particular item or story or if it **runs**, it is published or printed. ❑ *The New Orleans Times-Picayune ran a series of four scathing editorials entitled 'The Choice of Our Lives'.* **28** [I] If an amount **is running** at a particular level, it is at that level. = stand ❑ *Today's figures show inflation running at 10.9 per cent.* **29** [I] If a play, event, or legal contract **runs** for a particular period of time, it lasts for that period of time. ❑ *It pleased critics but ran for only three months on Broadway.* ❑ *The contract was to run from 1992 to 2020.* **30** [I] If someone or something **is running** late, they have taken more time than had been planned. If they **are running** on time or ahead of time, they have taken the time planned or less than the time planned. ❑ *Tell her I'll call her back later, I'm running late again.* **31** [T] If you **are running** a temperature or a fever, you have a high temperature because you are ill. ❑ *The little girl is running a fever and she needs help.*
PHRASES **run someone a close second** or **run a close second** If you **run** someone **a close second**, or **run a close second**, you almost beat them in a race or competition. ❑ *While 'Nightly' has led in the ratings all season, 'World News Tonight' is running a close second.*

r

run dry ◼ If a river or well **runs dry**, it no longer has any water in it. If an oil well **runs dry**, it no longer produces any oil. = dry up ❑ *Streams had run dry for the first time in memory.* ◼ If a source of information or money **runs dry**, no more information or money can be obtained from it. = dry up ❑ *Three days into production, the kitty had run dry.*

run in someone's family If a characteristic **runs in** someone's **family**, it often occurs in members of that family, in different generations. ❑ *The insanity which ran in his family haunted him.*

run high If people's feelings **are running high**, they are very angry, concerned, or excited. ❑ *Feelings there have been running high in the wake of last week's killing.*

be running short or **be running low** If you **are running short** of something or **running low on** something, you do not have much of it left. If a supply of something is **running short** or **running low**, there is not much of it left. ❑ *Government forces are running short of ammunition and fuel.*

run off at the mouth [v inflects] (*disapproval*) If you say that someone **is running off at the mouth**, you are criticizing them for talking too much. ❑ *That was when she really started running off at the mouth. I'll bet she hasn't shut up yet.*

PHRASAL VERBS **run across** If you **run across** someone or something, you meet them or find them unexpectedly. = come across ❑ *We ran across some old friends in the village.*

run around If you **run around**, you go to a lot of places and do a lot of things, often in a rushed or disorganized way. ❑ *We had been running around cleaning up.* ❑ *Jessica was running around with the camera snapping pictures.* ❑ *I will not have you running around the countryside without my authority.*

run away ◼ If you **run away** from a place, you leave it because you are unhappy there. ❑ *I ran away from home when I was sixteen.* ❑ *After his beating, Colin ran away and hasn't been heard of since.* ◼ If you **run away** with someone, you secretly go away with them in order to live with them or marry them. = run off ❑ *She ran away with a man called McTavish last year.* ◼ If you **run away from** something unpleasant or new, you try to avoid dealing with it or thinking about it. ❑ *They run away from the problem, hoping it will disappear of its own accord.*

run away with If you let your imagination or your emotions **run away with** you, you fail to control them and cannot think sensibly. ❑ *You're letting your imagination run away with you.*

run by If you **run** something **by** someone, you tell them about it or mention it, to see if they think it is a good idea, or can understand it. ❑ *I'm definitely interested, but I'll have to run it by Larry Estes.*

run down ◼ If you **run** people or things **down**, you criticize them strongly. ❑ *I'm always running myself down.* ◼ If a vehicle or its driver **runs** someone **down**, the vehicle hits them and injures them. = knock down, run over ❑ *Lozano claimed that motorcycle driver Clement Lloyd was trying to run him down.* ◼ If a machine or device **runs down**, it gradually loses power or works more slowly. ❑ *The batteries are running down.* ◼ If people **run down** an industry or an organization, they deliberately reduce its size or the amount of work that it does. ❑ *The government is cynically running down Sweden's welfare system.* ◼ If someone **runs down** an amount of something, they reduce it or allow it to decrease. ❑ *But the survey also revealed firms were running down stocks instead of making new products.*

run into ◼ If you **run into** problems or difficulties, you unexpectedly begin to experience them. ❑ *Wang agreed to sell IBM Systems last year after it ran into financial problems.* ◼ If you **run into** someone, you meet them unexpectedly. = meet, bump into ❑ *He ran into Krettner in the corridor a few minutes later.* ◼ If a vehicle **runs into** something, it accidentally hits it. ❑ *The driver failed to negotiate a bend and ran into a tree.* ◼ You use **run into** when indicating that the cost or amount of something is very great. ❑ *He said companies should face punitive civil penalties running into millions of dollars.*

run off ◼ If you **run off** with someone, you secretly go away with them in order to live with them or marry them. = run away ❑ *The last thing I'm going to do is run off with somebody's husband.* ◼ If you **run off** copies of a piece of

writing, you produce them using a machine. ❑ *If you want to run off a copy sometime today, you're welcome to.*

run out ◼ If you **run out of** something, you have no more of it left. ❑ *They have run out of ideas.* ❑ *We're running out of time.* ◼ If something **runs out**, it becomes used up so that there is no more left. ❑ *Conditions are getting worse and supplies are running out.* ◼ When a legal document **runs out**, it stops being valid. = expire ❑ *When the lease ran out the family moved to Cleveland.*

run over If a vehicle or its driver **runs** a person or animal **over**, it knocks them down or drives over them. = knock down, run down ❑ *You can always run him over and make it look like an accident.*

run through ◼ If you **run through** a list of items, you read or mention all the items quickly. = go through ❑ *I ran through the options with him.* ◼ If you **run through** a performance or a series of actions, you practise it. = go through ❑ *Doug stood still while I ran through the handover procedure.*

run up ◼ If someone **runs up** bills or debts, they acquire them by buying a lot of things or borrowing money. ❑ *She managed to run up a credit card debt of $60,000.* ◼ → See also **run-up**

run up against If you **run up against** problems, you suddenly begin to experience them. = encounter ❑ *I ran up against the problem of getting taken seriously long before I became a writer.*

NOUN [c, sing] (**runs**) ◼ [c] A **run** is a time when you move somewhere on foot more quickly than when you walk, usually for exercise. ❑ *After a six-mile run, Jackie returns home for a substantial breakfast.* ◼ [sing] [run 'for' N] (*mainly AmE; in BrE, usually use* **bid**) A **run for** office is an attempt to be elected to office. ❑ *He was already preparing his run for the presidency.* ◼ [c] A **run** is a trip somewhere. ❑ *doing the morning school run* ◼ [c] A **run** of a play or television programme is the period of time during which performances are given or programmes are shown. ❑ *The show will transfer to Broadway on October 9, after a month's run in Philadelphia.* ◼ [sing] A **run of** successes or failures is a series of successes or failures. ❑ *The team is haunted by a run of low scores.* ◼ [c] A **run** of a product is the amount that a company or factory decides to produce at one time. ❑ *Wayne plans to increase the print run to 1,000.* ◼ [c] In cricket or baseball, a **run** is a score of one, which is made by players running between marked places on the field after hitting the ball. ❑ *Pakistan has beaten Sri Lanka by fifty runs.* ◼ [sing] If someone gives you **the run of** a place, they give you permission to go where you like in it and use it as you wish. ❑ *He had the run of the house and the pool.* ◼ [sing] If there is a **run on** something, a lot of people want to buy it or get it at the same time. ❑ *A run on the dollar has killed off hopes of a rate cut.* ◼ [c] A **run** is a hole or torn part in a woman's stocking or tights, where some the vertical threads have broken, leaving only the horizontal threads. ❑ *I had a run in my stocking.* ◼ [c] A ski **run** or bobsled **run** is a course or route that has been designed for skiing or for riding in a bobsled. ❑ *an avalanche on Colorado's highest ski run*

PHRASES **make a run for it** or **run for it** If you **make a run for it** or if you **run for it**, you run away in order to escape from someone or something. ❑ *A helicopter hovered overhead as one of the gang made a run for it.*

in the long run or **in the short run** If you talk about what will happen **in the long run**, you are saying what you think will happen over a long period of time in the future. If you talk about what will happen **in the short run**, you are saying what you think will happen in the near future. ❑ *Sometimes expensive drugs or other treatments can be economical in the long run.*

give someone a run for their money If you say that someone could **give** someone else **a run for** their **money**, you mean you think they are almost as good as the other person. ❑ *a youngster who even now could give Meryl Streep a run for her money*

on the run ◼ If someone is **on the run**, they are trying to escape or hide from someone such as the police or an enemy. ❑ *Fifteen-year-old Danny is on the run from a juvenile detention centre.* ◼ If someone is **on the run**, they are being severely defeated in a contest or competition. ❏ *I knew I had him on the run.*

→ See also **running**

✦ **run deep** → see **deep**; **run a risk** → see **risk**; **run out of steam** → see **steam**

rung /rʌŋ/ IRREG FORM, NOUN

IRREG FORM **Rung** is the past participle of **ring**.

NOUN [c] (**rungs**) **1** The **rungs** on a ladder are the wooden or metal bars that form the steps. ❏ *I swung myself onto the ladder and felt for the next rung.* **2** If you reach a particular **rung** in your career, in an organization, or in a process, you reach that level in it. ❏ *I first worked with him in 1971 when we were both on the lowest rung of our careers.*

run-in NOUN [c] (**run-ins**) (*informal*) A **run-in** is an argument or quarrel with someone. ❏ *I had a monumental run-in with him a couple of years ago.*

run·ner ♦◇◇ /'rʌnə/ NOUN [c] (**runners**) **1** A **runner** is a person who runs, especially for sport or pleasure. ❏ *a marathon runner* **2** The **runners** in a horse race are the horses taking part. ❏ *There are 18 runners in the top race of the day.* **3** A drug **runner** or gun **runner** is someone who illegally takes drugs or guns into a country. ❏ *a gang of evil gun runners* **4** Someone who is a **runner** for a particular person or company is employed to take messages, collect money, or do other small tasks for them. ❏ *a bookie's runner* **5 Runners** are thin strips of wood or metal underneath something which help it to move smoothly. ❏ *the runners of his sled*

runner-up NOUN [c] (**runners-up**) A **runner-up** is someone who has finished in second place in a race or competition. ❏ *The ten runners-up will receive a case of wine.*

run·ning ♦♦◇ /'rʌnɪŋ/ NOUN, ADJ, ADV

NOUN [U, SING] **1** [U] **Running** is the activity of moving fast on foot, especially as a sport. ❏ *We chose to do cross-country running.* **2** [SING] **The running of** something such as a business is the managing or organizing of it. ❏ *the committee in charge of the day-to-day running of the party* PHRASE **in the running** or **out of the running** If someone is **in the running for** something, they have a good chance of winning or obtaining it. If they are **out of the running for** something, they have no chance of winning or obtaining it. ❏ *Until this week he appeared to have ruled himself out of the running because of his age.* ADJ **1** [running + N] You use **running** to describe things that continue or keep occurring over a period of time. = ongoing ❏ *He also began a running feud with Dean Acheson.* **2** [running + N] A **running** total is a total which changes because numbers keep being added to it as something progresses. ❏ *He kept a running tally of who had called him, who had visited, who had sent flowers.* **3** [running + N] **Running** water is water that is flowing rather than standing still. ❏ *The forest was filled with the sound of running water.* **4** [running + N] If a house has **running** water, water is supplied to the house through pipes and taps. ❏ *a house without electricity or running water in a tiny African village* PHRASE **up and running** If something such as a system or place is **up and running**, it is operating normally. ❏ *We're trying to get the medical facilities up and running again.* ADV [N + running] You can use **running** when indicating that something keeps happening. For example, if something has happened every day for three days, you can say that it has happened for the third day **running** or for three days **running**. ❏ *He said drought had led to severe crop failure for the second year running.*

run-up NOUN [SING] (*mainly BrE*) **The run-up to** an event is the period of time just before it. ❏ *The company believes the products will sell well in the run-up to Christmas.*

rup·ture /'rʌptʃə/ NOUN, VERB

NOUN [c] (**ruptures**) **1** A **rupture** is a severe injury in which an internal part of your body tears or bursts open, especially the part between the bowels and the abdomen. ❏ *He died of an abdominal infection caused by a rupture of his stomach.* **2** If there is a **rupture** between people, relations between them get much worse or end completely. ❏ *The incidents have not yet caused a major rupture in the political ties between countries.*

VERB [I, T] (**ruptures, rupturing, ruptured**) **1** [I, T] If a person or animal **ruptures** a part of their body or if it **ruptures**, it tears or bursts open. ❏ *His stomach might rupture from all the acid.* ❏ *While playing badminton, I ruptured my Achilles tendon.* **2** [T] If you **rupture yourself**, you rupture a part of your body, usually because you have lifted something heavy. ❏ *He ruptured himself playing football.* **3** [I, T] If an object **ruptures** or if something **ruptures** it, it bursts open. = burst ❏ *Certain petrol tanks in lorries can rupture and burn in a collision.* **4** [T] If someone or something **ruptures** relations between people, they damage them, causing them to become worse or to end. ❏ *Brutal clashes between squatters and police yesterday ruptured the city's governing coalition.*

✪ **ru·ral** ♦◇◇ /'rʊərəl/ ADJ **1** Rural places are far away from large towns or cities. ❏ *These plants have a tendency to grow in the more rural areas.* ❏ *the closure of rural schools* **2** [rural + N] **Rural** means having features which are typical of areas that are far away from large towns or cities. ❏ *the old rural way of life*

ruse /ruːz, AmE ruːs/ NOUN [c] (**ruses**) (*formal*) A **ruse** is an action or plan which is intended to deceive someone. ❏ *It is now clear that this was a ruse to divide them.*

rush ♦◇◇ /rʌʃ/ VERB, NOUN

VERB [I, T] (**rushes, rushing, rushed**) **1** [I, T] If you **rush** somewhere, you go there quickly. ❏ *A schoolgirl rushed into a burning apartment to save a man's life.* ❏ *I've got to rush. Got a meeting in a few minutes.* ❏ *I rushed to get the 7:00 a.m. train.* **2** [T] If people **rush to** do something, they do it as soon as they can, because they are very eager to do it. ❏ *Russian banks rushed to buy as many dollars as they could.* **3** [I, T] If you **rush** something, you do it in a hurry, often too quickly and without much care. ❏ *You can't rush a search.* ❏ *Instead of rushing at life, I wanted something more meaningful.* **4** [T] If you **rush** someone or something to a place, you take them there quickly. ❏ *They had rushed him to a hospital for a lifesaving operation.* **5** [I, T] If you **rush into** something or **are rushed into** it, you do it without thinking about it for long enough. ❏ *He will not rush into any decisions.* ❏ *They had rushed in without adequate appreciation of the task.* **6** [I, T] If you **rush** something or someone, or **rush at** them, you move quickly and forcefully at them, often in order to attack them. ❏ *They rushed the entrance and forced their way in.* ❏ *Reporters rushed at him and he ran back inside.* **7** [I] If air or liquid **rushes** somewhere, it flows there suddenly and quickly. ❏ *Water rushes out of huge tunnels.*

NOUN [SING, C] (**rushes**) **1** [SING] A **rush** is a situation in which you need to go somewhere or do something very quickly. ❏ *The men left in a rush.* **2** [SING] If there is a **rush for** something, many people suddenly try to get it or do it. ❏ *Record shops are expecting a huge rush for the single.* **3** [SING] **The rush** is a period of time when many people go somewhere or do something. ❏ *The store's opening coincided with the Christmas rush.* **4** [c] If there is a **rush** of air or liquid somewhere, it flows there suddenly and quickly. ❏ *A rush of air on my face woke me.* **5** [c] If you experience a **rush of** a feeling, you suddenly experience it very strongly. ❏ *A rush of pure affection swept over him.*

rushed /rʌʃt/ ADJ **1** *The report had all the hallmarks of a rushed job.* **2** *At no time did I feel rushed or under pressure.*

rust /rʌst/ NOUN, VERB, COLOUR

NOUN [U] **Rust** is a brown substance that forms on iron or steel, for example when it comes into contact with water. ❏ *a decaying tractor, red with rust*

VERB [I] (**rusts, rusting, rusted**) When a metal object **rusts**, it becomes covered in rust and often loses its strength. ❏ *Copper nails are better than iron nails because the iron rusts.*

COLOUR **Rust** is sometimes used to describe things that are reddish brown in colour. ❏ *rust and gold leaves from the maples*

rut /rʌt/ NOUN [c] (**ruts**) **1** (*disapproval*) If you say that someone is **in a rut**, you disapprove of the fact that they have become fixed in their way of thinking and doing things, and find it difficult to change. You can also say that someone's life or career is **in a rut**. ❏ *I don't like being in a rut – I like to keep moving on.* **2** A **rut** is a deep, narrow mark made in the ground by the wheels of a vehicle. ❑ *Our driver slowed up as we approached the ruts in the road.*

ruth·less /ˈruːθləs/ ADJ **1** (disapproval) If you say that someone is **ruthless**, you mean that you disapprove of them because they are very harsh or cruel, and will do anything that is necessary to achieve what they want. ❑ *The president was ruthless in dealing with any hint of internal political dissent.* **2** A **ruthless** action or activity is done forcefully and thoroughly, without much concern for its effects on other people. ❑ *Her lawyers have been ruthless in thrashing out a divorce settlement.*

ruth·less·ly /ˈruːθləsli/ ADV **1** [ruthlessly with v] ❑ *The party has ruthlessly crushed any sign of organized opposition.* **2** *Gloria showed signs of turning into the ruthlessly efficient woman her father wanted her to be.*

ruth·less·ness /ˈruːθləsnəs/ NOUN [U] **1** *a powerful political figure with a reputation for ruthlessness* **2** *a woman with a brain and business acumen and a certain healthy ruthlessness*

R

Ss

S also **s** /es/ NOUN [C, U] (**S's, s's**) **S** is the nineteenth letter of the English alphabet.

sab·o·tage /'sæbətɑːʒ/ VERB, NOUN
VERB [T] (**sabotages, sabotaging, sabotaged**) **1** If a machine, railway line, or bridge **is sabotaged**, it is deliberately damaged or destroyed, for example, in a war or as a protest. ❑ *The main pipeline supplying water was sabotaged by rebels.* **2** If someone **sabotages** a plan or a meeting, they deliberately prevent it from being successful. ❑ *He accused the opposition of doing everything they could to sabotage the election.*
NOUN [U] **Sabotage** is the act of deliberately damaging or destroying a machine, railway line, or bridge, for example, in a war or as a protest. ❑ *The bombing was a spectacular act of sabotage.*

sack ♦♢♢ /sæk/ NOUN, VERB
NOUN [C, SING] (**sacks**) **1** A **sack** is a large bag made of thick paper or rough material. Sacks are used to carry or store things such as food or groceries. ❑ *a sack of potatoes* **2** [SING] (*mainly BrE, informal*) The **sack** is when your employers tell you that you can no longer work for them because you have done something that they did not like or because your work was not good enough.
VERB [T] (**sacks, sacking, sacked**) (*mainly BrE; in AmE, usually use fire; informal*) If your employers **sack** you, they tell you that you can no longer work for them because you have done something that they did not like or because your work was not good enough. = fire

sa·cred /'seɪkrɪd/ ADJ **1** Something that is **sacred** is believed to be holy and to have a special connection with God. ❑ *The owl is sacred for many Californian Indian people.* **2** [sacred + N] Something connected with religion or used in religious ceremonies is described as **sacred**. ❑ *sacred art* **3** You can describe something as **sacred** when it is regarded as too important to be changed or interfered with. ❑ *My memories are sacred.*

sac·ri·fice ♦♢♢ /'sækrɪfaɪs/ VERB, NOUN
VERB [T] (**sacrifices, sacrificing, sacrificed**) **1** To **sacrifice** an animal or person means to kill them in a special religious ceremony as an offering to a god. ❑ *The priest sacrificed a chicken.* **2** If you **sacrifice** something that is valuable or important, you give it up, usually to obtain something else for yourself or for other people. ❑ *She sacrificed family life to her career.* ❑ *Kitty Aldridge has sacrificed all for her first film.*
NOUN [C, U] (**sacrifices**) **1** [C] The **sacrifice** of an animal or person is the act of killing them in a special religious ceremony as an offering to a god. ❑ *animal sacrifices to the gods* **2** [C, U] If you make a **sacrifice**, you give up something that is valuable or important, usually to obtain something else for yourself or for other people. ❑ *She made many sacrifices to get Anita a good education.*

sad ♦♦♢ /sæd/ ADJ (**sadder, saddest**) **1** If you are **sad**, you feel unhappy, usually because something has happened that you do not like. ❑ *The relationship had been important to me and its loss left me feeling sad and empty.* ❑ *I'm sad that Julie's marriage is on the verge of splitting up.* **2 Sad** stories and **sad** news make you feel sad. ❑ *a desperately humorous, impossibly sad novel* **3** A **sad** event or situation is unfortunate or undesirable. ❑ *It's a sad truth that children are the biggest victims of passive smoking.* **4** (*informal,*

disapproval) If you describe someone as **sad**, you do not have any respect for them and think their behaviour or ideas are ridiculous. = pathetic ❑ *sad old bikers and youngsters who think that Jim Morrison is God*
sad·ly /'sædli/ ADV **1** *a gallant man who will be sadly missed by all his comrades* **2** *Sadly, bamboo plants die after flowering.*
sad·ness /'sædnəs/ NOUN [U] ❑ *It is with a mixture of sadness and joy that I say farewell.*

sad·den /'sædən/ VERB [T] (**saddens, saddened**) If something **saddens** you, it makes you feel sad. ❑ *The cruelty in the world saddens me incredibly.*
sad·dened /'sædənd/ ADJ ❑ *He was disappointed and saddened that legal argument had stopped the trial.*

sad·dle /'sædəl/ NOUN, VERB
NOUN [C] (**saddles**) **1** A **saddle** is a leather seat that you put on the back of an animal so that you can ride the animal. **2** A **saddle** is a seat on a bicycle or motorcycle.
VERB [T] (**saddles, saddling, saddled**) If you **saddle** a horse, you put a saddle on it so that you can ride it. ❑ *Why don't we saddle a couple of horses and go for a ride?*
PHRASAL VERB **saddle up** Saddle up means the same as **saddle** VERB. ❑ *I want to be gone from here as soon as we can saddle up.*

sa·fa·ri /sə'fɑːri/ NOUN [C] (**safaris**) [also 'on' safari] A **safari** is a trip to observe or hunt wild animals, especially in East Africa. ❑ *He'd like to go on safari to photograph snakes and tigers.*

safe ♦♦♢ /seɪf/ ADJ, NOUN
ADJ (**safer, safest**) **1** Something that is **safe** does not cause physical harm or danger. ❑ *Officials arrived to assess whether it is safe to bring emergency food supplies into the city.* ❑ *Most foods that we eat are safe for birds.* **2** [V-LINK + safe] If a person or thing is **safe from** something, they cannot be harmed or damaged by it. ❑ *They are safe from the violence that threatened them.* **3** [V-LINK + safe] If you are **safe**, you have not been harmed, or you are not in danger of being harmed. ❑ *Where is Sophy? Is she safe?* **4** A **safe** place is one where it is unlikely that any harm, damage, or unpleasant things will happen to the people or things that are there. ❑ *The continuing tension has prompted more than half the inhabitants of the refugee camp to flee to safer areas.* **5** [safe + N] If people or things have a **safe** trip, they reach their destination without harm, damage, or unpleasant things happening to them. ❑ *I told him good night, come back any time, and have a safe trip home.* **6** [safe + N] If you are at a **safe** distance from something or someone, you are far enough away from them to avoid any danger, harm, or unpleasant effects. ❑ *I shall conceal myself at a safe distance from the battlefield.* **7** If something you have or expect to obtain is **safe**, you cannot lose it or be prevented from having it. = secure ❑ *We as consumers need to feel confident that our jobs are safe before we will spend spare cash.* **8** A **safe** course of action is one in which there is very little risk of loss or failure. ❑ *Electricity shares are still a safe investment.* **9** [safe before V] If it is **safe** to say or assume something, you can say it with very little risk of being wrong. ❑ *I think it is safe to say that very few students expend the effort to do quality work in school.*
PHRASES **in safe hands** or **safe in someone's hands** If you say that a person or thing is **in safe hands**, or is **safe in someone's hands**, you mean that they are being taken care

of by a reliable person and will not be harmed. ❑ *I had a huge responsibility to ensure these packets remained in safe hands.*

play safe or **play it safe** If you **play safe** or **play it safe**, you do not take any risks. ❑ *If you want to play safe, cut down on the amount of salt you eat.*

be on the safe side If you say you are doing something **to be on the safe side**, you mean that you are doing it in case something undesirable happens, even though this may be unnecessary. ❑ *You might still want to go for an X-ray, however, just to be on the safe side.*

it's better to be safe than sorry or **better safe than sorry** If you say '**it's better to be safe than sorry**', you are advising someone to take action in order to avoid possible unpleasant consequences later, even if this seems unnecessary. ❑ *Don't be afraid to have this checked by a doctor – better safe than sorry!*

safe and sound You say that someone is **safe and sound** when they are still alive or unharmed after being in danger. ❑ *All I'm hoping for is that wherever Trevor is he will come home safe and sound.*

NOUN [c] (**safes**) A **safe** is a strong metal cabinet with special locks, in which you keep money, jewellery, or other valuable things. ❑ *The files are now in a safe to which only he has the key.*

⚙ **safe·guard** /ˈseɪfɡɑːd/ VERB, NOUN

VERB [T] (**safeguards, safeguarding, safeguarded**) (*formal*) To **safeguard** something or someone means to protect them from being harmed, lost, or badly treated. = protect, defend ❑ *They will press for international action to safeguard the ozone layer.* ❑ *They are taking precautionary measures to safeguard their forces from the effects of chemical weapons.*

NOUN [c] (**safeguards**) A **safeguard** is a law, rule, or measure intended to prevent someone or something from being harmed. = protection, defence ❑ *As an additional safeguard against weeds you can always use an underlay of heavy duty polyethylene.* ❑ *A system like ours lacks adequate safeguards for civil liberties.*

safe·ly /ˈseɪfli/ ADV **1** If something is done **safely**, it is done in a way that makes it unlikely that anyone will be harmed. ❑ *The waste is safely locked away until it is no longer radioactive.* ❑ *'Drive safely,' he said and waved goodbye.* **2** You also use **safely** to say that there is no risk of a situation being changed. ❑ *Once events are safely in the past, this idea seems to become less alarming.* **3** If you escape **safely** from a situation, you have not been harmed by it, or you are not in danger of being harmed by it. ❑ *All 140 guests were brought out of the building safely by firemen.* **4** [safely after v] You can use **safely** to indicate that something is in a place where it is unlikely that any harm or damage will happen to it. ❑ *The banker keeps the money tucked safely under his bed.* **5** If people or things arrive or return **safely** after a journey, they reach their destination without harm, damage, or unpleasant things happening to them. ❑ *The space shuttle returned safely today from a 10-day mission.* **6** If you do something **safely**, you do it in such a way that there is very little risk of loss or failure. ❑ *We reveal only as much information as we can safely risk at a given time.* **7** [safely before v] If you can **safely** say or assume something, you can say it with very little risk of being wrong. ❑ *I think you can safely say she will not be appearing in another of my films.*

safe·ty ◆◆◇ /ˈseɪfti/ NOUN, ADJ

NOUN [u, SING] **1** [u] **Safety** is the state of being safe from harm or danger. ❑ *The report goes on to make a number of recommendations to improve safety on aircraft.* **2** [u] If you reach **safety**, you reach a place where you are safe from danger. ❑ *He stumbled through smoke and fumes to pull her to safety.* ❑ *People scurried for safety as the firing started.* **3** [SING] If you are concerned about the **safety** of something, you are concerned that it might be harmful or dangerous. ❑ *Consumers are showing growing concern about the safety of the food they buy.* **4** [SING] If you are concerned for someone's **safety**, you are concerned that they might be in danger. ❑ *There is grave concern for the safety of witnesses.*

ADJ [safety + N] **Safety** features or measures are intended to make something less dangerous. ❑ *The built-in safety device compensates for a fall in water pressure.*

said /sed/ IRREG FORM **Said** is the past tense and past participle of **say**.

sail ◆◇◇ /seɪl/ NOUN, VERB

NOUN [c] (**sails**) **Sails** are large pieces of material attached to the mast of a ship. The wind blows against the sails and pushes the ship along. ❑ *The white sails billow with the breezes they catch.*

PHRASE **set sail** When a ship **sets sail**, it leaves a port. ❑ *He loaded his vessel with another cargo and set sail.*

VERB [I, T] (**sails, sailing, sailed**) **1** [I] You say a ship **sails** when it moves over the sea. ❑ *The trawler had sailed from the port of Zeebrugge.* **2** [I, T] If you **sail** a boat or if a boat **sails**, it moves across water using its sails. ❑ *His crew's job is to sail the boat.* ❑ *I'd buy a big boat and sail around the world.*

PHRASAL VERB **sail through** If someone or something **sails through** a difficult situation or experience, they deal with it easily and successfully. ❑ *While she sailed through her exams, he struggled.*

→ See also **sailing**

sail·ing /ˈseɪlɪŋ/ NOUN

NOUN [u, c] (**sailings**) **1** [u] **Sailing** is the activity or sport of sailing boats. ❑ *There was swimming and sailing down on the lake.* **2** [c] **Sailings** are trips made by a ship carrying passengers. ❑ *Ferry companies are providing extra sailings from Calais.*

PHRASE **plain sailing** If you say that a task was not all **plain sailing**, you mean that it was not very easy. ❑ *Pregnancy wasn't all plain sailing and once again there were problems.*

sail·or /ˈseɪlə/ NOUN [c] (**sailors**) A **sailor** is someone who works on a ship or sails a boat. ❑ *sailors, marines and Coast Guard personnel*

saint ◆◇◇ /seɪnt/ NOUN [c] (**saints**) **1** A **saint** is someone who has died and been officially recognized and honoured by the Christian church because his or her life was a perfect example of the way Christians should live. ❑ *Every parish was named after a saint.* **2** If you refer to a living person as a **saint**, you mean that they are extremely kind, patient, and unselfish. ❑ *My girlfriend Geraldine is a saint to put up with me.*

sake ◆◇◇ /seɪk/ NOUN (**sakes**)

PHRASES **for the sake of something** If you do something **for the sake of** something, you do it for that purpose or in order to achieve that result. You can also say that you do it **for something's sake**. ❑ *Let's assume for the sake of argument that we manage to build a satisfactory database.* ❑ *For the sake of historical accuracy, please permit us to state the true facts.*

for its own sake or **for their own sake** If you do something **for its own sake**, you do it because you want to, or because you enjoy it, and not for any other reason. You can also talk about, for example, **art for art's sake** or **sport for sport's sake**. ❑ *Economic change for its own sake did not appeal to him.*

for someone's sake When you do something **for someone's sake**, you do it in order to help them or make them happy. ❑ *I trust you to do a good job for Stan's sake.*

for God's sake or **for heaven's sake** or **for goodness' sake** or **for Pete's sake** (*informal, feelings*) Some people use expressions such as **for God's sake, for heaven's sake, for goodness' sake**, or **for Pete's sake** in order to express annoyance or impatience, or to add force to a question or request. The expressions 'for God's sake' and 'for Christ's sake' could cause offence. ❑ *For goodness' sake, why didn't you call me?*

sal·ad /ˈsæləd/ NOUN [c, u] (**salads**) A **salad** is a mixture of cold foods such as lettuce, tomatoes, or cold cooked potatoes, cut up and mixed with a dressing. It is often served with other food as part of a meal. ❑ *a salad of tomato, onion, and cucumber*

⚙ **sal·a·ry** ◆◇◇ /ˈsæləri/ NOUN [c, u] (**salaries**) (*business*) A **salary** is the money that someone earns each month or year from their employer. = wage, earnings, income ❑ *The lawyer was paid a huge salary.* ❑ *IT directors can expect to earn average salaries of between £55,000 and £80,000.*

⊙**sale** ◆◆◆ /seɪl/ NOUN

NOUN [SING, PL, C] (**sales**) **1** [SING] The **sale** of goods is the act of selling them for money. ≠ purchase □ *Efforts were made to limit the sale of alcohol.* □ *a proposed arms sale to Saudi Arabia* **2** [PL] The **sales** of a product are the quantity of it that is sold. □ *The newspaper has sales of 1.72 million.* □ *the huge Christmas sales of computer games* □ *Retail sales rose by 3 per cent.* □ *This year's sales figures are better than last.* **3** [PL] The part of a company that deals with **sales** deals with selling the company's products. □ *Until 1983 he worked in sales and marketing.* □ *She was their Dusseldorf sales manager.* **4** [C] A **sale** is an occasion when a shop sells things at less than their normal price. □ *a pair of jeans bought half-price in a sale* **5** [C] A **sale** is an event when goods are sold to the person who offers the highest price. = auction □ *The Old Master was bought by dealers at the Christie's sale.*

PHRASES **for sale** If something is **for sale**, it is being offered to people to buy. □ *The yacht is for sale at a price of 1.7 million dollars.*

on sale Products that are **on sale** can be bought. □ *English textbooks and dictionaries are on sale everywhere.* □ *Tickets go on sale this week.*

up for sale If a property or company is **up for sale**, its owner is trying to sell it. □ *The mansion has been put up for sale.*

sales·man /ˈseɪlzmən/ NOUN [C] (**salesmen**) A **salesman** is a man whose job is to sell things, especially directly to stores or other businesses on behalf of a company. □ *an insurance salesman*

sales·person /ˈseɪlzpɜːsən/ NOUN [C] (**salespeople** or **salespersons**) (*business*) A **salesperson** is a person who sells things, either in a store or directly to customers on behalf of a company. □ *They will usually send a salesperson out to measure your bathroom.*

salm·on /ˈsæmən/ NOUN [C, U] (**salmon**) **1** [C] A **salmon** is a large silver-coloured fish. **2** [U] **Salmon** is the orangey-pink flesh of this fish which is eaten as food. It is often smoked and eaten raw. □ *He gave them a splendid lunch of smoked salmon.*

salt ◆◇◇ /sɔːlt/ NOUN, VERB

NOUN [U, C] (**salts**) **1** [U] **Salt** is a strong-tasting substance, in the form of white powder or crystals, which is used to improve the flavour of food or to preserve it. Salt occurs naturally in sea water. □ *Season lightly with salt and pepper.* **2** [C] **Salts** are substances that are formed when an acid reacts with an alkali. □ *The rock is rich in mineral salts.*

PHRASES **take something with a pinch of salt** or **take something with a grain of salt** If you **take something with a pinch of salt** or **with a grain of salt**, you do not believe that it is completely accurate or true. □ *You have to take these findings with a pinch of salt because respondents tend to give the answers they feel they should.*

worth one's salt If you say, for example, that any doctor **worth** his or her **salt** would do something, you mean that any doctor who was good at his or her job or who deserved respect would do it. □ *No golf teacher worth his salt would ever recommend that you grip the club tightly.*

VERB [T] (**salts, salting, salted**) When you **salt** food, you add salt to it. □ *Salt the stock to your taste and leave it simmering very gently.*

salt·ed /ˈsɔːltɪd/ ADJ □ *Put a pan of salted water on to boil.*

sa·lute /səˈluːt/ VERB, NOUN

VERB [I, T] (**salutes, saluting, saluted**) **1** [I, T] If you **salute** someone, you greet them or show your respect with a formal sign. Soldiers usually salute officers by raising their right hand so that their fingers touch their forehead. □ *One of the company stepped out and saluted the General.* **2** [T] To **salute** a person or their achievements means to publicly show or state your admiration for them. □ *I salute the governor for the leadership role that he is taking.*

NOUN [C] (**salutes**) [also 'in' salute] If you give someone a **salute**, you greet them or show your respect with a formal sign. Soldiers usually do this by raising their right hand so that their fingers touch their forehead. □ *He gave his salute and left.*

sal·vage /ˈsælvɪdʒ/ VERB, NOUN

VERB [T] (**salvages, salvaging, salvaged**) **1** If something is

salvaged, someone manages to save it, for example, from a ship that has sunk, or from a building that has been damaged. □ *The team's first task was to decide what equipment could be salvaged.* **2** If you manage to **salvage** a difficult situation, you manage to get something useful from it so that it is not a complete failure. □ *Officials tried to salvage the situation.* **3** If you **salvage** something such as your pride or your reputation, you manage to keep it even though it seems likely you will lose it, or you get it back after losing it. □ *We definitely wanted to salvage some pride for American tennis.*

NOUN [U] **1 Salvage** is the act of salvaging things from somewhere such as a damaged ship or building. □ *The salvage operation went on.* **2** The **salvage** from somewhere such as a damaged ship or building is the things that are saved from it. □ *They climbed up on the rock with their salvage.*

sal·va·tion /sælˈveɪʃən/ NOUN [U, SING] **1** [U] In Christianity, **salvation** is the fact that Christ has saved a person from evil. □ *The church's message of salvation has changed the lives of many.* **2** [U] The **salvation** of someone or something is the act of saving them from harm, destruction, or an unpleasant situation. □ *those whose marriages are beyond salvation* **3** [SING] If someone or something is your **salvation**, they are responsible for saving you from harm, destruction, or an unpleasant situation. □ *The country's salvation lies in forcing through democratic reforms.*

same ◆◆◆ /seɪm/ ADJ, PRON, CONVENTION

ADJ **1** If two or more things, actions, or qualities are the **same**, or if one is the **same as** another, they are very like each other in some way. □ *The houses were all the same – square, close to the street, needing paint.* □ *People with the same experience in the job should be paid the same.* **2** You use **same** to indicate that you are referring to only one place, time, or thing, and not to different ones. □ *Bernard works at the same institution as Arlette.* □ *It's impossible to get everybody together at the same time.* **3** ['the' same] Something that is still **the same** has not changed in any way. □ *Taking ingredients from the same source means the beers stay the same.* **4** ['the' same] You use **the same** to refer to something that has previously been mentioned or suggested. □ *He's so effective. I admire Ginny for pretty much the same reason.*

PRON ['the' same] You use **the same** to refer to something that has previously been mentioned or suggested. □ *We made the decision which was right for us. Other parents must do the same.* □ *In the United States small bookshops survive quite well. The same applies to small publishers.*

PHRASES **the same as** If something is happening **the same as** something else, the two things are happening in a way that is similar or exactly the same. □ *I mean, it's a relationship, the same as a marriage is a relationship.*

same again (*informal, spoken*) You say '**same again**' when you want to order another drink of the same kind as the one you have just had. □ *Give Roger another pint, Imogen, and I'll have the same again.*

all the same or **just the same** You can say **all the same** or **just the same** to introduce a statement which indicates that a situation or your opinion has not changed, in spite of what has happened or what has just been said. □ *I arranged to pay him the dollars when he got there, a purely private arrangement. All the same, it was illegal.*

all the same to me (*mainly spoken*) If you say '**It's all the same to me**', you mean that you do not care which of several things happens or is chosen. □ *Whether I've got a moustache or not it's all the same to me.*

CONVENTION (*spoken, informal, formulae*) **1** You say '**same here**' in order to suggest that you feel the same way about something as the person who has just spoken to you, or that you have done the same thing. = likewise □ *'Nice to meet you,' said Michael. 'Same here,' said Mary Ann.* **2** You say '**same to you**' in response to someone who wishes you well with something. □ *'Have a nice Easter.'—'And the same to you Bridie.'*

⊙**sam·ple** ◆◇◇ /ˈsɑːmpəl, ˈsæm-/ NOUN, VERB

NOUN [C] (**samples**) **1** A **sample** of a substance or product

is a small quantity of it that shows you what it is like. ❑ *You'll receive samples of paint, curtains and upholstery.* ❑ *We're giving away 2,000 free samples.* **2** A **sample** of a substance is a small amount of it that is examined and analyzed scientifically. = specimen ❑ *They took samples of my blood.* ❑ *a robotic mission that would collect rock and soil samples for more detailed analysis* **3** A **sample** of people or things is a number of them chosen out of a larger group and then used in tests or used to provide information about the whole group. ❑ *We based our analysis on a random sample of more than 200 males.* ❑ *The sample size used in the study was too small.*
VERB [T] (**samples, sampling, sampled**) **1** If you **sample** food or drink, you taste a small amount of it in order to find out if you like it. = taste ❑ *We sampled a selection of different bottled waters.* **2** If you **sample** a place or situation, you experience it for a short time in order to find out about it. = try ❑ *the chance to sample a different way of life*

⊘ sanc·tion ◆◆◇ /ˈsæŋkʃən/ VERB, NOUN
VERB [T] (**sanctions, sanctioning, sanctioned**) If someone in authority **sanctions** an action or practice, they officially approve of it and allow it to be done. = approve ❑ *He may now be ready to sanction the use of force.*
NOUN [U, PL] (**sanctions**) **1** [U] **Sanction** is official approval or permission from someone in authority. = approval ❑ *a newspaper run by citizens without the sanction of the government* **2** [PL] **Sanctions** are measures taken by countries to restrict trade and official contact with a country that has broken international law. ❑ *The continued abuse of human rights has now led the United States to impose sanctions against the regime.* ❑ *He expressed his opposition to the lifting of sanctions.*

sanc·tu·ary /ˈsæŋktʃuəri, AmE -tʃueri/ NOUN [C, U] (**sanctuaries**) **1** [C] A **sanctuary** is a place where people who are in danger from other people can go to be safe. = haven ❑ *His church became a sanctuary for thousands of people who fled the civil war.* **2** [U] **Sanctuary** is the safety provided in a sanctuary. ❑ *Some of them have sought sanctuary in the church.* **3** [C] A **sanctuary** is a place where birds or animals are protected and allowed to live freely. ❑ *a bird sanctuary*

sand ◆◇◇ /sænd/ NOUN, VERB
NOUN [U, PL] (**sands**) **1** [U] **Sand** is a substance that looks like powder, and consists of extremely small pieces of stone. ❑ *They all walked barefoot across the damp sand to the water's edge.* **2** [PL] **Sands** are a large area of sand, for example, a beach. ❑ *miles of golden sands*
VERB [T] (**sands, sanding, sanded**) If you **sand** a wood or metal surface, you rub sandpaper over it in order to make it smooth or clean. ❑ *Sand the surface softly and carefully.*
PHRASAL VERB **sand down** Sand down means the same as **sand** VERB. ❑ *I was going to sand down the chairs and repaint them.*

sand·wich /ˈsænwɪdʒ, -wɪtʃ/ NOUN, VERB
NOUN [C] (**sandwiches**) A **sandwich** usually consists of two slices of bread with a layer of food such as cheese or meat between them. ❑ *a ham sandwich*
VERB [T] (**sandwiches, sandwiching, sandwiched**) If you **sandwich** two things **together** with something else, you put that other thing between them. If you **sandwich** one thing between two other things, you put it between them. ❑ *Carefully split the sponge ring, then sandwich the two halves together with whipped cream.*

sandy /ˈsændi/ ADJ (**sandier, sandiest**) A **sandy** area is covered with sand. ❑ *long, sandy beaches*

sane /seɪn/ ADJ (**saner, sanest**) **1** Someone who is **sane** is able to think and behave normally and reasonably, and is not mentally ill. ❑ *He seemed perfectly sane.* **2** If you refer to a **sane** person, action, or system, you mean one that you think is reasonable and sensible. ❑ *No sane person wishes to see conflict or casualties.*

sang /sæŋ/ IRREG FORM **Sang** is the past tense of **sing**.

sani·ta·tion /ˌsænɪˈteɪʃən/ NOUN [U] **Sanitation** is the process of keeping places clean and healthy, especially by providing a sewage system and a clean water supply. ❑ *the*

hazards of contaminated water and poor sanitation

san·ity /ˈsænɪti/ NOUN [U] A person's **sanity** is their ability to think and behave normally and reasonably. ❑ *He and his wife finally had to move from their flat just to preserve their sanity.*

sank /sæŋk/ IRREG FORM **Sank** is the past tense of **sink**.

sap /sæp/ VERB, NOUN
VERB [T] If something **saps** your strength or confidence, it gradually weakens or destroys them. ❑ *I was afraid the sickness had sapped my strength.*
NOUN [U] **Sap** is the watery liquid in plants and trees. ❑ *The leaves, bark, and sap are also common ingredients of local herbal remedies.*

sar·casm /ˈsɑːkæzəm/ NOUN [U] **Sarcasm** is speech or writing which actually means the opposite of what it seems to say. Sarcasm is usually intended to mock or insult someone. ❑ *Sarcasm and demeaning remarks have no place in parenting.*

sar·cas·tic /sɑːˈkæstɪk/ ADJ Someone who is **sarcastic** says or does the opposite of what they really mean in order to mock or insult someone. ❑ *She poked fun at people's shortcomings with sarcastic remarks.*
sar·cas·ti·cal·ly /sɑːˈkæstɪkli/ ADV *'What a surprise!' Caroline murmured sarcastically.*

sash /sæʃ/ NOUN [C] (**sashes**) A **sash** is a long piece of cloth which people wear around their waist or over one shoulder, especially with formal or official clothes. ❑ *She wore a white dress with a thin blue sash.*

sat /sæt/ IRREG FORM **Sat** is the past tense and past participle of **sit**.

⊘ sat·el·lite ◆◇◇ /ˈsætəlaɪt/ NOUN, ADJ
NOUN [C] (**satellites**) **1** [also 'by' satellite] A **satellite** is an object which has been sent into space in order to collect information or to be part of a communications system. Satellites move continually around the earth or around another planet. ❑ *The rocket launched two communications satellites.* ❑ *The signals are sent by satellite link.* **2** A **satellite** is a natural object in space that moves around a planet or star. = moon ❑ *the satellites of Jupiter* **3** You can refer to a country, area, or organization as a **satellite** when it is controlled by or depends on a larger and more powerful one. ❑ *Some companies are outfitting their satellite offices with wireless LANs.*
ADJ [satellite + N] **Satellite** television is broadcast using a satellite. ❑ *They have four satellite channels.*

sat·is·fac·tion /ˌsætɪsˈfækʃən/ NOUN
NOUN [U] **1** **Satisfaction** is the pleasure that you feel when you do something or get something that you wanted or needed to do or get. ❑ *She felt a small glow of satisfaction.* ❑ *Both sides expressed satisfaction with the progress so far.* **2** If you get **satisfaction** from someone, you get money or an apology from them because you have been treated badly. ❑ *If you can't get any satisfaction, complain to the park owner.*
PHRASE **to someone's satisfaction** If you do something **to** someone's **satisfaction**, they are happy with the way that you have done it. ❑ *She could never seem to do anything right or to his satisfaction.*

⊘ sat·is·fac·tory /ˌsætɪsˈfæktəri/ ADJ Something that is **satisfactory** is acceptable to you or fulfils a particular need or purpose. = acceptable, adequate; ≠ unsatisfactory, inadequate ❑ *I never got a satisfactory answer.* ❑ *The concept of instinct is not a satisfactory explanation of human behaviour.* ❑ *It seemed a very satisfactory arrangement.*
sat·is·fac·to·ri·ly /ˌsætɪsˈfæktərɪli/ ADV ❑ *The wedding was proceeding quite satisfactorily except for one thing.*

⊘ sat·is·fied ◆◇◇ /ˈsætɪsfaɪd/ ADJ **1** If you are **satisfied** with something, you are happy because you have got what you wanted or needed. = pleased, contented; ≠ dissatisfied ❑ *We are not satisfied with these results.* **2** [V-LINK + satisfied] If you are **satisfied that** something is true or has been done properly, you are convinced about this after checking it. ❑ *People must be satisfied that the treatment is safe.*

⊘ sat·is·fy /ˈsætɪsfaɪ/ VERB [T] (**satisfies, satisfying, satisfied**) **1** If someone or something **satisfies** you, they give you enough of what you want or need to make you pleased or contented. ❑ *The pace of change has not been quick enough to satisfy everyone.* **2** To **satisfy** someone **that** something is true or has been done properly means to convince them by giving them more information or by showing them what has been done. **= convince** ❑ *He has to satisfy the environmental lobby that real progress will be made to cut emissions.* ❑ *The statisticians were satisfied that the sample and the evidence were sufficient.* **3** If you **satisfy** the requirements for something, you are good enough to have the right qualities to fulfill these requirements. **= fulfil, meet** ❑ *The executive committee recommends that the procedures should satisfy certain basic requirements.*

sat·is·fy·ing /ˈsætɪsfaɪɪŋ/ ADJ Something that is **satisfying** makes you feel happy, especially because you feel you have achieved something. ❑ *I found wood carving satisfying.*

satu·rate /ˈsætʃʊreɪt/ VERB [T] (**saturates, saturating, saturated**) **1** If people or things **saturate** a place or object, they fill it completely so that no more can be added. ❑ *In the last days before the vote, both sides are saturating the airwaves.* **2** If someone or something is **saturated**, they become extremely wet. ❑ *If the filter has been saturated with motor oil, it should be discarded and replaced.*

satu·ra·tion /ˌsætʃʊˈreɪʃən/ NOUN, ADJ
NOUN [U] **Saturation** is the process or state that occurs when a place or thing is filled completely with people or things, so that no more can be added. ❑ *Japanese car makers have been equally blind to the saturation of their markets at home and abroad.*
ADJ [saturation + N] **Saturation** is used to describe a campaign or other activity that is carried out very thoroughly, so that nothing is missed. ❑ *The concept of saturation marketing makes perfect sense.*

sauce ◆◇◇ /ˈsɔːs/ NOUN [C, U] (**sauces**) A **sauce** is a thick liquid which is served with other food. ❑ *pasta cooked in a sauce of garlic, tomatoes, and cheese*

sau·sage /ˈsɒsɪdʒ, AmE ˈsɔːs-/ NOUN [C, U] (**sausages**) A **sausage** consists of minced meat, usually pork, mixed with other ingredients and contained in a tube made of skin or a similar material. ❑ *sausages and chips*

sav·age /ˈsævɪdʒ/ ADJ, NOUN, VERB
ADJ Someone or something that is **savage** is extremely cruel, violent, and uncontrolled. **= vicious** ❑ *This was a savage attack on a defenceless young girl.* ❑ *the savage wave of violence that swept the country in November 1987*
NOUN [C] (**savages**) (*disapproval*) If you refer to people as **savages**, you dislike them because you think that they do not have an advanced society and are violent. ❑ *their conviction that the area was a frozen desert peopled with uncouth savages*
VERB [T] (**savages, savaging, savaged**) If someone is **savaged** by a dog or other animal, the animal attacks them violently. ❑ *The animal then turned on him and he was savaged to death.*
sav·age·ly /ˈsævɪdʒli/ ADV ❑ *He was savagely beaten.*

sav·age·ry /ˈsævɪdʒri/ NOUN [U] **Savagery** is extremely cruel and violent behaviour. ❑ *the sheer savagery of war*

❂**save** ◆◆◇ /ˈseɪv/ VERB, NOUN
VERB [T, I] (**saves, saving, saved**) **1** [T] If you **save** someone or something, you help them to avoid harm or to escape from a dangerous or unpleasant situation. ❑ *an austerity programme designed to save the country's failing economy* ❑ *The meeting is an attempt to mobilize nations to save children from death by disease and malnutrition.* **2** [I, T] If you **save**, you gradually collect money by spending less than you get, usually in order to buy something that you want. ❑ *The majority of people intend to save, but find that by the end of the month there is nothing left.* ❑ *Tim and Barbara are now saving for a house in the suburbs.* ❑ *I was trying to save money to go to college.* **3** [I, T] If you **save** something such as time or money, you prevent the loss or waste of it. ❑ *It saves time in the kitchen to have things you use a lot within reach.* ❑ *More cash will be saved by shutting studios and selling outside-broadcast vehicles.* ❑ *I'll try to save him the expense of a flight from Perth.* ❑ *A new filter can save on energy bills.*

4 [T] If you **save** something, you keep it because it will be needed later. ❑ *Drain the beans thoroughly and save the stock for soup.* **5** [T] If someone or something **saves** you **from** an unpleasant action or experience, they change the situation so that you do not have to do it or experience it. ❑ *The scanner will reduce the need for exploratory operations which will save risk and pain for patients.* ❑ *She was hoping that something might save her from having to make a decision.* **6** [I, T] (*computing*) If you **save** data in a computer, you give the computer an instruction to store the data on a tape or disk. ❑ *Try to get into the habit of saving your work regularly.* ❑ *Save frequently when you are creating graphics.* **7** [I, T] If a goalkeeper **saves**, or **saves** a shot, they succeed in preventing the ball from going into the goal. ❑ *He saved one shot when the ball hit him on the head.*
PHRASAL VERB **save up** Save up means the same as **save** VERB 2. ❑ *Julie wanted to put some of her money aside for holidays or save up for something special.*
NOUN [C] (**saves**) A **save** is an occasion when a goalkeeper succeeds in preventing the ball from going into the goal. ❑ *The goalie made some great saves.*
✦ **save the day** → see **day**

sav·ing ◆◇◇ /ˈseɪvɪŋ/ NOUN [C, PL] (**savings**) **1** [C] A **saving** is a reduction in the amount of time or money that is used or needed. ❑ *You can enjoy a year's membership for just £28 – a saving of £7 off the regular rate.* **2** [PL] Your **savings** are the money that you have saved, especially in a bank or a building society. ❑ *Her savings were in the First National Bank.*

sav·iour /ˈseɪvjə/ (in AmE, use **savior**) NOUN [C] (**saviours**) A **saviour** is a person who saves someone or something from danger, ruin, or defeat. ❑ *the saviour of his country*

sa·vour /ˈseɪvə/ (in AmE, use **savor**) VERB [T] (**savours, savouring, savoured**) **1** If you **savour** an experience, you enjoy it as much as you can. ❑ *She savoured her newfound freedom.* **2** If you **savour** food or drink, you eat or drink it slowly in order to taste its full flavour and to enjoy it properly. ❑ *Just relax, eat slowly and savour the full flavour of your food.*

sa·voury /ˈseɪvəri/ (in AmE, use **savory**) ADJ **Savoury** food has a salty or spicy flavour rather than a sweet one. ❑ *all sorts of sweet and savoury breads*

saw /sɔː/ IRREG FORM, NOUN, VERB
IRREG FORM **Saw** is the past tense of **see**.
NOUN [C] (**saws**) A **saw** is a tool for cutting wood, which has a blade with sharp teeth along one edge. Some saws are pushed backwards and forwards by hand, and others are powered by electricity.
VERB [I, T] (**saws, sawing, sawed, sawed** or **sawn**) If you **saw** something, you cut it with a saw. ❑ *He escaped by sawing through the bars of his cell.*

sawn /sɔːn/ (*mainly BrE*) IRREG FORM **Sawn** is the past participle of **saw**.

say ◆◆◆ /seɪ/ VERB, NOUN
VERB [T] (**says, saying, said**) **1** When you **say** something, you speak words. ❑ *'I'm sorry,' he said.* ❑ *She said they were very impressed.* ❑ *Forty-one people are said to have been seriously hurt.* ❑ *I packed and said goodbye to Charlie.* **2** You use **say** in expressions such as **I would just like to say** to introduce what you are actually saying, or to indicate that you are expressing an opinion or admitting a fact. If you state that you **can't say** something or you **wouldn't say** something, you are indicating in a polite or indirect way that it is not the case. ❑ *I would just like to say that this is the most hypocritical thing I have ever heard in my life.* ❑ *I must say that rather shocked me, too.* **3** You can mention the contents of a piece of writing by mentioning what it **says** or what someone **says** in it. ❑ *The report says there is widespread and routine torture of political prisoners in the country.* ❑ *You can't have one without the other, as the song says.* **4** If you **say** something **to yourself**, you think it. ❑ *Perhaps I'm still dreaming, I said to myself.* **5** You indicate the information given by something such as a clock, dial, or map by mentioning what it **says**. ❑ *The clock said four minutes past eleven when we set off.* **6** If something **says** something **about** a person, situation, or thing, it gives important information about them. ❑ *I think that says a lot*

S

about how well Safin is playing. **7** If something **says** a lot **for** a person or thing, it shows that this person or thing is very good or has a lot of good qualities. ❑ *That the Escort was still the nation's bestselling car in 1992 said a lot for the power of Ford's marketing people.* **8** You use **say** in expressions such as **I'll say that for them** and **you can say this for them** after or before you mention a good quality that someone has, usually when you think they do not have many good qualities. ❑ *He's usually well-dressed, I'll say that for him.* **9** You can use **say** when you want to discuss something that might possibly happen or be true. = suppose ❑ *Say you were buying a new car, would your discussion begin and end with the monthly payment?*

PHRASES **let's say** You can use **say** or **let's say** when you mention something as an example. ❑ *To see the problem here more clearly, let's look at a different biological system, say, an acorn.*

say it all If you say that something **says it all**, you mean that it shows you very clearly the truth about a situation or someone's feelings. ❑ *This is my third visit in a week, which says it all.*

to be said for something If you say there is a lot **to be said for** something, you mean you think it has a lot of good qualities or aspects. ❑ *There's a lot to be said for being based in the country.*

what does someone have to say for themselves If someone asks **what** you **have to say for yourself**, they are asking what excuse you have for what you have done. ❑ *'Well,' she said eventually, 'what have you to say for yourself?'*

goes without saying If something **goes without saying**, it is obvious. ❑ *It goes without saying that if someone has lung problems they should not smoke.*

that is to say (*formal*) You use **that is to say** or **that's to say** to indicate that you are about to express the same idea more clearly or precisely. ❑ *That would mean voting no, that is to say, using the veto.*

CONVENTIONS **you don't say** (*feelings*) You can use '**You don't say**' to express surprise at what someone has told you. People often use this expression to indicate that in fact they are not surprised. ❑ *'I'm a writer.'—'You don't say. What kind of book are you writing?'*

I wouldn't say no (*informal, formulae*) You use '**I wouldn't say no**' to indicate that you would like something, especially something that has just been offered to you. ❑ *I wouldn't say no to a drink.*

You can say that again (*informal, emphasis*) You can use '**You can say that again**' to express strong agreement with what someone has just said. ❑ *'You are in enough trouble already.'—'You can say that again,' sighed Richard.*

NOUN [SING] [usu 'a' say, also 'more/some' say] If you have **a say** in something, you have the right to give your opinion and influence decisions relating to it. ❑ *You can get married at sixteen, and yet you haven't got a say in the running of the country.*

PHRASE **have one's say** When one of the people or groups involved in a discussion **has** their **say**, they give their opinion. ❑ *Voters were finally having their say today.*

say·ing /ˈseɪɪŋ/ NOUN [c] (**sayings**) A **saying** is a sentence that people often say and that gives advice or information about human life and experience. ❑ *We also realize the truth of that old saying: Charity begins at home.*

scab /skæb/ NOUN [c] (**scabs**) A **scab** is a hard, dry covering that forms over the surface of a wound. ❑ *The area can be very painful until scabs form after about ten days.*

❍scale ◆◆◇ /skeɪl/ NOUN, ADJ, VERB **NOUN** [SING, c] (**scales**) **1** [SING] If you refer to the **scale** of something, you are referring to its size or extent, especially when it is very big. ❑ *However, he under-estimates the scale of the problem.* ❑ *The breakdown of law and order could result in killing on a massive scale.* **2** [c] A **scale** is a set of levels or numbers which are used in a particular system of measuring things or are used when comparing things. ❑ *an earthquake measuring 5.5 on the Richter scale* ❑ *The patient rates the therapies on a scale of zero to ten.* **3** [c] A pay **scale** or **scale of** fees is a list that shows how much someone should be paid, depending, for example, on their age or what work they do. ❑ *those on the high end of the pay*

scale **4** [c] The **scale** of a map, plan, or model is the relationship between the size of something in the map, plan, or model and its size in the real world. ❑ *The map, on a scale of 1:10,000, shows over 5,000 individual paths.* **5** [c] In music, a **scale** is a fixed sequence of musical notes, each one higher than the next, which begins at a particular note. ❑ *the scale of C major* **6** [c] The **scales** of a fish or reptile are the small, flat pieces of hard skin that cover its body. ❑ *Remove any excess scales from the fish skin.* **7** [c] [usu pl] A **scale** is a piece of equipment used for weighing things, for example, for weighing amounts of food that you need in order to make a particular meal. ❑ *a pair of kitchen scales* ❑ *a bathroom scale*

PHRASES **out of scale** If something is **out of scale with** the things near it, it is too big or too small in relation to them. ❑ *The tiny church was out of scale with the new banks and offices around it.*

to scale If the different parts of a map, drawing, or model are **to scale**, they are the right size in relation to each other. ❑ *a miniature garden, with little pagodas and bridges all to scale*

ADJ [scale + N] A **scale** model or **scale** replica of a building or object is a model of it which is smaller than the real thing but has all the same parts and features. ❑ *Franklin made his mother an intricately detailed scale model of the house.*

VERB [T] (**scales, scaling, scaled**) (*written*) If you **scale** something such as a mountain or a wall, you climb up it or over it. = climb ❑ *Rebecca Stephens, the first British woman to scale Everest*

PHRASAL VERBS **scale down** If you **scale down** something, you make it smaller in size, amount, or extent than it used to be. = reduce ❑ *One factory has had to scale down its workforce from six hundred to only six.*

scale up If you **scale up** something, you make it greater in size, amount, or extent than it used to be. = increase ❑ *a major push to scale up treatment programmes for people in poor countries*

→ See also **full-scale, large-scale, small-scale**

❍scan /skæn/ VERB, NOUN **VERB** [I, T] (**scans, scanning, scanned**) **1** [I, T] When you **scan** written material, you look through it quickly in order to find important or interesting information. = skim, browse; ≠ pore over, examine ❑ *She scanned the advertisement pages of the newspapers.* ❑ *I haven't read much into it as yet. I've only just scanned through it.* **2** [I, T] When you **scan** a place or group of people, you look at it carefully, usually because you are looking for something or someone. ❑ *The officer scanned the room.* ❑ *She was nervous and kept scanning the crowd for Paul.* **3** [T] If people **scan** something such as luggage, they examine it using a machine that can show or find things inside it that cannot be seen from the outside. ❑ *Their approach is to scan every checked-in bag with a bomb detector.* **4** [T] (*computing*) If a computer document or disk **is scanned**, a program on the computer checks it to make sure that it does not contain a virus. ❑ *Not all ISPs are equipped to scan for viruses.* **5** [T] (*computing*) If a picture or document **is scanned** into a computer, a machine passes a beam of light over it to make a copy of it in the computer. ❑ *The entire paper contents of all libraries will eventually be scanned into computers.* **6** [T] If a radar or sonar machine **scans** an area, it examines or searches it by sending radar or sonar beams over it. ❑ *The ship's radar scanned the sea ahead.*

NOUN [SING, c] (**scans**) **1** [SING] A **scan** through written material is the action of looking quickly through it in order to find important or interesting information. ❑ *I had a quick scan through your book again.* **2** [c] A **scan** is a medical test in which a machine sends a beam of X-rays over a part of your body in order to check that it is healthy. = X-ray, MRI, CAT scan ❑ *A brain scan revealed the blood clot.*

scan·dal ◆◇◇ /ˈskændəl/ NOUN [c, u] (**scandals**) **1** [c] A **scandal** is a situation or event that is thought to be shocking and immoral and that everyone knows about. ❑ *a financial scandal* **2** [u] **Scandal** is talk about the shocking and immoral aspects of someone's behaviour or something that has happened. ❑ *He loved gossip and scandal.*

scan·dal·ous /ˈskændələs/ ADJ **1** Scandalous behaviour or activity is considered immoral and shocking. ❑ *They would be sacked for criminal or scandalous behaviour.* **2** Scandalous stories or remarks are concerned with the immoral and shocking aspects of someone's behaviour or something that has happened. ❑ *Newspaper columns were full of scandalous tales.*

scan·dal·ous·ly /ˈskændələsli/ ADV [scandalously with V] ❑ *He asked only that Ingrid stop behaving so scandalously.*

scan·ner /ˈskænə/ NOUN [C] (**scanners**) **1** A scanner is a machine which is used to examine, identify, or record things, for example by using a beam of light, sound, or X-rays. ❑ *brain scanners* **2** (computing) A scanner is a piece of computer equipment that you use for copying a picture or document into a computer. ❑ *a colour printer and scanner*

scape·goat /ˈskeɪpɡəʊt/ NOUN, VERB

NOUN [C] (**scapegoats**) If you say that someone is made a scapegoat for something bad that has happened, you mean that people blame them and may punish them for it although it may not be their fault. ❑ *I don't think I deserve to be made the scapegoat for a couple of bad results.*

VERB [T] (**scapegoats, scapegoating, scapegoated**) To scapegoat someone means to blame them publicly for something bad that has happened, even though it was not their fault. ❑ *a climate where ethnic minorities are continually scapegoated for the lack of jobs and housing problems*

scar /skɑː/ NOUN, VERB

NOUN [C] (**scars**) **1** A scar is a mark on the skin which is left after a wound has healed. ❑ *He had a scar on his forehead.* **2** If an unpleasant physical or emotional experience leaves a scar on someone, it has a permanent effect on their mind. ❑ *The early years of fear and the hostility left a deep scar on the young boy.*

VERB [T] (**scars, scarring, scarred**) **1** If your skin is scarred, it is badly marked as a result of a wound. ❑ *He was scarred for life during a fight.* **2** If a surface is scarred, it is damaged and there are ugly marks on it. ❑ *The arena was scarred by deep muddy ruts.* **3** If an unpleasant physical or emotional experience scars you, it has a permanent effect on your mind. ❑ *This is something that's going to scar him forever.*

⊗**scarce** /skeəs/ ADJ

ADJ (**scarcer, scarcest**) If something is scarce, there is not enough of it. ≠ plentiful ❑ *Food was scarce and expensive.* ❑ *Jobs are becoming increasingly scarce.* ❑ *the allocation of scarce resources*

PHRASE **make oneself scarce** (informal) If you **make yourself scarce**, you quickly leave the place you are in, usually in order to avoid a difficult or embarrassing situation. ❑ *It probably would be a good idea if you made yourself scarce.*

scarce·ly /ˈskeəsli/ ADV **1** (emphasis) You use scarcely to emphasize that something is only just true or only just the case. ❑ *He could scarcely breathe.* ❑ *I scarcely knew him.* **2** You can use scarcely to say that something is not true or is not the case, in a humorous or critical way. = hardly ❑ *It can scarcely be coincidence.* **3** [scarcely before V] If you say scarcely had one thing happened when something else happened, you mean that the first event was followed immediately by the second. ❑ *Scarcely had the votes been counted, when the telephone rang.*

scar·city /ˈskeəsɪti/ NOUN [C, U] (**scarcities**) (formal) If there is a scarcity of something, there is not enough of it for the people who need it or want it. = shortage ❑ *an ever increasing scarcity of water*

scare /skeə/ VERB, NOUN

VERB [T] (**scares, scaring, scared**) If something scares you, it frightens or worries you. = frighten ❑ *You're scaring me.* ❑ *The prospect of failure scares me rigid.*

PHRASE **scare the hell out of** or **scare the life out of** (informal, emphasis) If you want to emphasize that something scares you a lot, you can say that it **scares the hell out of** you or **scares the life out of** you.

PHRASAL VERB **scare off** or **scare away** **1** If you **scare off** or **scare away** a person or animal, you frighten them so that they go away. ❑ *an alarm to scare off an attacker* **2** If

you **scare** someone **off**, you accidentally make them unwilling to become involved with you. = put off ❑ *I don't think that revealing your past to your boyfriend scared him off.*

NOUN [SING, C] (**scares**) **1** [SING] If a sudden unpleasant experience gives you a scare, it frightens you. ❑ *Don't you realize what a scare you've given us all?* **2** [C] A scare is a situation in which many people are afraid or worried because they think something dangerous is happening which will affect them all. ❑ *The news set off a continent-wide health scare.* **3** [C] A bomb scare or a security scare is a situation in which there is believed to be a bomb in a place. = alert ❑ *Despite many recent bomb scares, no one has yet been hurt.*

→ See also **scared**

scared /skeəd/ ADJ **1** If you are scared of someone or something, you are frightened of them. = frightened ❑ *I'm certainly not scared of him.* ❑ *I was too scared to move.* **2** If you are scared that something unpleasant might happen, you are nervous and worried because you think that it might happen. = worried ❑ *I was scared that I might be sick.*

scarf /skɑːf/ NOUN [C] (**scarfs** or **scarves**) A scarf is a piece of cloth that you wear around your neck or head, usually to keep yourself warm. ❑ *He reached up to loosen the scarf around his neck.*

scarves /skɑːvz/ IRREG FORM Scarves is a plural of scarf.

scat·ter /ˈskætə/ VERB [T, I] (**scatters, scattering, scattered**) **1** [T] If you scatter things over an area, you throw or drop them so that they spread all over the area. ❑ *She tore the rose apart and scattered the petals over the grave.* ❑ *They've been scattering toys everywhere.* **2** [I, T] If a group of people scatter or if you scatter them, they suddenly separate and move in different directions. ❑ *After dinner, everyone scattered.*

→ See also **scattered**

scat·tered /ˈskætəd/ ADJ **1** [scattered + N] Scattered things are spread over an area in an untidy or irregular way. ❑ *He picked up the scattered toys.* ❑ *Tomorrow there will be a few scattered showers.* **2** [V-LINK + scattered 'with' N] If something is scattered with a lot of small things, they are spread all over it. ❑ *Every surface is scattered with photographs.*

⊗**sce·nar·io** /sɪˈnɑːriəʊ, AmE -ˈner-/ NOUN [C] (**scenarios**) (academic word) If you talk about a likely or possible scenario, you are talking about the way in which a situation may develop. = situation ❑ *The conflict degenerating into civil war is everybody's nightmare scenario.* ❑ *Try to imagine all the possible scenarios and what action you would take.*

⊗**scene** ♦♦◇ /siːn/ NOUN

NOUN [C, SING] (**scenes**) **1** [C] A scene in a play, film, or book is part of it in which a series of events happen in the same place. ❑ *the opening scene of 'A Christmas Carol'* ❑ *Act I, scene 1* ❑ *I found the scene in which Percy proposed to Olive tremendously poignant.* **2** [C] You refer to a place as a scene when you are describing its appearance and indicating what impression it makes on you. ❑ *It's a scene of complete devastation.* ❑ *Thick black smoke billowed over the scene.* **3** [C] You can describe an event that you see, or that is broadcast or shown in a picture, as a scene of a particular kind. ❑ *There were emotional scenes as the refugees enjoyed their first breath of freedom.* ❑ *Television broadcasters were warned to exercise caution over depicting scenes of violence.* **4** [C] The scene of an event is the place where it happened. ❑ *The area has been the scene of fierce fighting for three months.* ❑ *traces left at the scene of a crime* **5** [SING] You can refer to an area of activity as a particular type of scene. ❑ *Sandman's experimentation has made him something of a cult figure on the local music scene.* **6** [C] If you make a scene, you embarrass people by publicly showing your anger about something. ❑ *I'm sorry I made such a scene.*

PHRASES **behind the scenes** **1** If something is done behind the scenes, it is done secretly rather than publicly. ❑ *But behind the scenes Mr Cain will be working quietly to try to get a deal done.* **2** If you refer to what happens behind the scenes, you are referring to what happens during the

S

making of a movie, play, or radio or television programme. ❏ *It's an exciting opportunity to learn what goes on behind the scenes.*

a change of scene If you have **a change of scene**, you go somewhere different after being in a particular place for a long time. ❏ *What you need is a change of scene. Why not go on a cruise?*

set the scene for something Something that **sets the scene for** a particular event creates the conditions in which the event is likely to happen. ❏ *An improving economy helped set the scene for his re-election.*

on the scene or **from the scene** When a person or thing appears **on the scene**, they come into being or become involved in something. When they disappear **from the scene**, they are no longer there or are no longer involved. ❏ *He could react jealously when and if another child comes on the scene.*

scen•ery /'siːnəri/ NOUN
[NOUN] [U] **1** The **scenery** in a country area is the land, water, or plants that you can see around you. ❏ *the island's spectacular scenery* **2** In a theatre, the **scenery** consists of the structures and painted backgrounds that show where the action in the play takes place. ❏ *Instead of stagehands, the actors will move the scenery right in front of the audience.* [PHRASE] **a change of scenery** If you have **a change of scenery**, you go somewhere different after being in a particular place for a long time. ❏ *A change of scenery might do you good.*

sce•nic /'siːnɪk/ ADJ **1** A **scenic** place has attractive scenery. ❏ *This is an extremely scenic part of America.* **2** A **scenic** route goes through attractive scenery and has nice views. ❏ *It was even marked on the map as a scenic route.*

scent /sent/ NOUN, VERB
[NOUN] [C, U] (**scents**) **1** [C] The **scent** of something is the pleasant smell that it has. = fragrance ❏ *Flowers are chosen for their scent as well as their look.* **2** [C, U] **Scent** is a liquid which women put on their necks and wrists to make themselves smell nice. = perfume ❏ *She dabbed herself with scent.* **3** [C, U] The **scent** of a person or animal is the smell that they leave and that other people sometimes follow when looking for them. ❏ *A police dog picked up the murderer's scent.*
[VERB] [T] (**scents, scenting, scented**) **1** If something **scents** a place or thing, it makes it smell pleasant. ❏ *Jasmine flowers scent the air.* **2** When an animal **scents** something, it becomes aware of it by smelling it. = smell ❏ *dogs which scent the hidden birds*

❍**scep•tic** /'skeptɪk/ (mainly BrE; in AmE, use **skeptic**)
NOUN [C] (**sceptics**) A **sceptic** is a person who has doubts about things that other people believe. ≠ believer ❏ *He is a sceptic who tries to keep an open mind.* ❏ *But he now has to convince sceptics that he has a serious plan.*

❍**scep•ti•cal** /'skeptɪkəl/ (in AmE, use **skeptical**) ADJ If you are **sceptical about** something, you have doubts about it. = doubtful; ≠ convinced ❏ *Other archaeologists are sceptical about his findings.* ❏ *scientists who are sceptical of global warming and its alleged consequences*

❍**scep•ti•cism** /'skeptɪsɪzəm/ NOUN [U] (in AmE, use **skepticism**) Scepticism is great doubt about whether something is true or useful. = disbelief, doubt; ≠ belief ❏ *A survey reflects business scepticism about the strength of the economic recovery.* ❏ *There was considerable scepticism about the Chancellor's forecast of a booming economy.* ❏ *The report has inevitably been greeted with scepticism.*

❍**sched•ule** ◆◆◇ /'ʃedjuːl, AmE 'skedʒuːl/ NOUN, VERB (academic word)
[NOUN] [C, U] (**schedules**) **1** [C] A **schedule** is a plan that gives a list of events or tasks and the times at which each one should happen or be done. = timetable ❏ *He has been forced to adjust his schedule.* ❏ *We both have such hectic schedules.* **2** [U] You can use **schedule** to refer to the time or way something is planned to be done. For example, if something is completed **on schedule**, it is completed at the time planned. ❏ *The jet arrived in Johannesburg two minutes ahead of schedule.* ❏ *Everything went according to schedule.* **3** [C] A **schedule** is a written list of things, for example, a list of prices, details, or conditions. = list

❏ *Ticket plans and a pricing schedule will not be released until later this year.* **4** [C] (mainly AmE; in BrE, usually use **timetable**) A **schedule** is a list of all the times when trains, boats, buses, or aircraft are supposed to arrive at or leave at a particular place. ❏ *a bus schedule*
[VERB] [T] (**schedules, scheduling, scheduled**) If something **is scheduled** to happen at a particular time, arrangements are made for it to happen at that time. ❏ *The space shuttle had been scheduled to blast off at 04:38.* ❏ *A presidential election was scheduled for last December.*

❍**sche•mat•ic** /skiː'mætɪk/ ADJ [usu schematic + N] (academic word) A **schematic** diagram or picture shows something in a simple way. ❏ *This is represented in the schematic diagram below.* ❏ *a schematic picture of the solar system*

❍**scheme** ◆◆◇ /skiːm/ NOUN, VERB (academic word)
[NOUN] [C] (**schemes**) **1** A **scheme** is someone's plan for achieving something, especially something that will bring them some benefit. ❏ *a quick money-making scheme to get us through the summer* ❏ *They would first have to work out some scheme for getting the treasure out.* **2** (BrE; in AmE, use **plan**) A **scheme** is a plan or arrangement involving many people which is made by a government or other organization. = plan, system, programme ❏ *a private pension scheme* ❏ *schemes to help combat unemployment* [PHRASE] **the scheme of things** or **the grand scheme of things** When people talk about **the scheme of things** or **the grand scheme of things**, they are referring to the way that everything in the world seems to be organized. ❏ *We realize that we are infinitely small within the scheme of things.*
[VERB] [I, T] (**schemes, scheming, schemed**) (disapproval) If you say that people **are scheming**, you mean that they are making secret plans in order to gain something for themselves. ❏ *Everyone's always scheming and plotting.* ❏ *The bride's family were scheming to prevent a wedding.*

❍**schol•ar** /'skɒlə/ NOUN [C] (**scholars**) (formal) A **scholar** is a person who studies an academic subject and knows a lot about it. ❏ *The library attracts thousands of scholars and researchers.* ❏ *an influential Islamic scholar*

schol•ar•ly /'skɒləli/ ADJ **1** A **scholarly** person spends a lot of time studying and knows a lot about academic subjects. ❏ *He was an intellectual, scholarly man.* **2** A **scholarly** book or article contains a lot of academic information and is intended for academic readers. ❏ *the more scholarly academic journals* **3** **Scholarly** matters and activities involve people who do academic research. ❏ *This has been the subject of intense scholarly debate.*

❍**schol•ar•ship** /'skɒləʃɪp/ NOUN [C, U] (**scholarships**) **1** [C] If you get a **scholarship** to a school or university, your studies are paid for by the school or university or by some other organization. = bursary, grant, funding ❏ *He got a scholarship to the Pratt Institute of Art.* ❏ *Scholarships are awarded on the basis of academic achievement.* **2** [U] **Scholarship** is serious academic study and the knowledge that is obtained from it. ❏ *I want to take advantage of your lifetime of scholarship.*

school ◆◆◆ /skuːl/ NOUN, VERB
[NOUN] [C, U] (**schools**) **1** [C, U] A **school** is a place where children are educated. You usually refer to this place as **school** when you are talking about the time that children spend there and the activities that they do there. ❏ *a boy who was in my class at school* ❏ *Even the good students say homework is what they most dislike about school.* ❏ *a school built in the sixties* **2** [C] A **school** is the students or staff at a school. ❏ *Deirdre, the whole school's going to hate you.* **3** [C] A privately-run place where a particular skill or subject is taught can be referred to as a **school**. ❏ *a riding school* **4** [C, U] A university, college, or university department specializing in a particular type of subject can be referred to as a **school**. ❏ *a lecturer in the school of veterinary medicine at the University of Pennsylvania* **5** [C] [usu with SUPP] A particular **school of** writers, artists, or thinkers is a group of them whose work, opinions, or theories are similar. ❏ *the Chicago school of economists*
[VERB] [T] (**schools, schooling, schooled**) (written) If you **school** someone **in** something, you train or educate them to have a certain skill, type of behaviour, or way of

thinking. ❑ *Many mothers schooled their daughters in the myth of female inferiority.*
→ See also **schooling, high school, primary school, public school**

school·ing /'sku:lɪŋ/ NOUN [U] **Schooling** is education that children receive at school. = education ❑ *His formal schooling continued erratically until he reached the age of eleven.*

school·mate /'sku:lmeɪt/ NOUN [C] (**schoolmates**) [oft with POSS] (*mainly BrE*) A **schoolmate** is a child who goes to the same school as you, especially one who is your friend. = schoolfriend ❑ *He started the magazine with a schoolmate.*

school·teach·er /'sku:lti:tʃə/ NOUN [C] (**schoolteachers**) A **schoolteacher** is a teacher in a school.

❂ **sci·ence** ◆◇◇ /'saɪəns/ NOUN [U, C] (**sciences**) **1** [U] **Science** is the study of the nature and behaviour of natural things and the knowledge that we obtain about them. ❑ *The best discoveries in science are very simple.* ❑ *one of the problems with the way we teach science* **2** [C] A **science** is a particular branch of science such as physics, chemistry, or biology. ❑ *Physics is the best example of a science which has developed strong, abstract theories.* ❑ *recent innovations in medical science* **3** [C] A **science** is the study of some aspect of human behaviour, for example, sociology or anthropology. ❑ *the modern science of psychology*

❂ **sci·en·tif·ic** ◆◇◇ /ˌsaɪən'tɪfɪk/ ADJ **1** **Scientific** is used to describe things that relate to science or to a particular science. ❑ *Scientific research is widely claimed to be the source of the high standard of living in the US.* ❑ *the use of animals in scientific experiments* ❑ *There has been a certain amount of scientific research into meditation.* **2** If you do something in a **scientific** way, you do it carefully and thoroughly, using experiments or tests. = systematic ❑ *It's not a scientific way to test their opinions.*
sci·en·tif·i·cal·ly /ˌsaɪən'tɪfɪkli/ ADV **1** *scientifically advanced countries* **2** *Efforts are being made to research it scientifically.*

❂ **sci·en·tist** ◆◆◇ /'saɪəntɪst/ NOUN [C] (**scientists**) A **scientist** is someone who has studied science and whose job is to teach or to do research in science. ❑ *Scientists say they've already collected more data than had been expected.* ❑ *a senior research scientist at the University of Maryland*

scoop /sku:p/ VERB, NOUN
VERB [T] (**scoops, scooping, scooped**) **1** If you **scoop** something from a container, you remove it with something such as a spoon. ❑ *the sound of a spoon scooping dog food out of a can* **2** If you **scoop** a person or thing somewhere, you put your hands or arms under or around them and quickly move them there. ❑ *Michael knelt next to her and scooped her into his arms.*
PHRASAL VERB **scoop up** If you **scoop** something **up**, you put your hands or arms under it and lift it in a quick movement. ❑ *Use both hands to scoop up the leaves.*
NOUN [C] (**scoops**) **1** A **scoop** is an object like a spoon which is used for picking up a quantity of a food such as ice cream or an ingredient such as flour. ❑ *a small ice-cream scoop* **2** You can use **scoop** to refer to an exciting news story which is reported in one newspaper or on one television programme before it appears anywhere else. ❑ *one of the biggest scoops in the history of newspapers*

❂ **scope** /skəʊp/ NOUN [U, SING] (*academic word*) **1** [U] If there is **scope for** a particular kind of behaviour or activity, people have the opportunity to behave in this way or do that activity. ❑ *He believed in giving his staff scope for initiative.* **2** [SING] The **scope of** an activity, topic, or piece of work is the whole area which it deals with or includes. = scale, extent, range ❑ *Mr Dobson promised to widen the organization's scope of activity.* ❑ *the scope of a novel*

score ◆◆◇ /skɔ:/ VERB, NOUN, QUANT, NUM
VERB [I, T] (**scores, scoring, scored**) **1** [I, T] In a sport or game, if a player **scores** a goal or a point, they gain a goal or point. ❑ *Patten scored his second touchdown of the game.* ❑ *He scored late in the third quarter to cut the gap to 10 points.* **2** [I, T] If you **score** a particular number or amount, for example, as a mark in a test, you achieve that number or amount. ❑ *Kelly had scored an average of 147 on three separate IQ tests.* ❑ *Congress scores low in public opinion polls.*

3 [T] (*written*) If you **score** a success, a victory, or a hit, you are successful in what you are doing. ❑ *His abiding passion was ocean racing, at which he scored many successes.* **4** [T] If you **score** a surface with something sharp, you cut a line or number of lines in it. ❑ *Lightly score the surface of the steaks with a sharp cook's knife.*
NOUN [C] (**scores**) **1** Someone's **score** in a game or test is a number, for example, a number of points or runs, which shows what they have achieved or what level they have reached. ❑ *The US Open golf tournament was won by Ben Hogan, with a score of 287.* ❑ *He won this year's title with a score of 9.687.* **2** The **score** in a game is the result of it or the current situation, as indicated by the number of goals, runs, or points obtained by the two teams or players. ❑ *4-1 was the final score.* ❑ *They beat the Giants by a score of 7 to 3.* **3** The **score** of a film, play, or similar production is the music which is written or used for it. ❑ *The dance is accompanied by an original score by Henry Torgue.* **4** The **score** of a piece of music is the written version of it. ❑ *He recognizes enough notation to be able to follow a score.*
PHRASES **keep score** If you **keep score** of the number of things that are happening in a certain situation, you count them and record them. ❑ *You can keep score of your baby's movements before birth by recording them on a kick chart.*
know the score (*spoken*) If you **know the score**, you know what the real facts of a situation are and how they affect you, even though you may not like them. ❑ *I don't feel sorry for Carl. He knew the score, he knew what he had to do and couldn't do it.*
on that score or **on this score** You can use **on that score** or **on this score** to refer to something that has just been mentioned, especially an area of difficulty or concern. ❑ *I became pregnant easily. At least I've had no problems on that score.*
settle a score or **settle an old score** If you **settle a score** or **settle an old score with** someone, you take revenge on them for something they have done in the past. ❑ *The groups had historic scores to settle with each other.*
QUANT [scores 'of' PL-N] (*written, emphasis*) If you refer to **scores of** things or people, you are emphasizing that there are very many of them. ❑ *Campaigners lit scores of bonfires in ceremonies to mark the anniversary.*
NUM (**score**) (*written*) A **score** is twenty or approximately twenty. ❑ *A score of countries may be either producing or planning to obtain chemical weapons.*

scor·er /'skɔ:rə/ NOUN [C] (**scorers**) **1** In football, hockey, and many other sports and games, a **scorer** is a player who scores a goal, runs, or points. ❑ *David Hirst, the scorer of 11 goals this season* **2** A **scorer** is an official who writes down the score of a game or competition as it is being played.

scorn /skɔ:n/ NOUN, VERB
NOUN [U] If you treat someone or something **with scorn**, you show contempt for them. = contempt ❑ *Researchers greeted the proposal with scorn.*
VERB [T] (**scorns, scorning, scorned**) **1** If you **scorn** someone or something, you feel or show contempt for them. ❑ *Several leading officers have quite openly scorned the peace talks.* **2** If you **scorn** something, you refuse to have it or accept it because you think it is not good enough or suitable for you. ❑ *people who scorned traditional methods*

scorn·ful /'skɔ:nfəl/ ADJ If you are **scornful of** someone or something, you show contempt for them. = contemptuous ❑ *He is deeply scornful of politicians.*

scour /skaʊə/ VERB [T] (**scours, scouring, scoured**) **1** If you **scour** something such as a place or a book, you make a thorough search of it to try to find what you are looking for. = search ❑ *Rescue crews had scoured an area of 30 square miles.* **2** If you **scour** something such as a sink, floor, or pan, you clean its surface by rubbing it hard with something rough. = scrub ❑ *He decided to scour the sink.*

scout /skaʊt/ NOUN, VERB
NOUN [C] (**scouts**) A **scout** is someone who is sent to an area of countryside to find out the position of an enemy army. ❑ *They set off, two men out in front as scouts, two behind in case of any attack from the rear.*
VERB [I, T] (**scouts, scouting, scouted**) If you **scout** somewhere **for** something, you go through that area

S

searching for it. = search ❑ *I wouldn't have time to scout the area for junk.* ❑ *A team of four was sent to scout for a nuclear test site.*

scram·ble /ˈskræmbəl/ VERB, NOUN

VERB [I, T] (**scrambles, scrambling, scrambled**) **1** [I] If you **scramble** over rocks or up a hill, you move quickly over them or up it using your hands to help you. = clamber ❑ *Tourists were scrambling over the rocks looking for the perfect camera angle.* **2** [I] If you **scramble** to a different place or position, you move there in a hurried, awkward way. ❑ *Ann threw back the covers and scrambled out of bed.* **3** [T] If a number of people **scramble for** something, they compete energetically with each other for it. ❑ *More than three million fans are expected to scramble for tickets.* **4** [T] If you **scramble** eggs, you break them, mix them together and then cook them in butter. ❑ *Make the toast and scramble the eggs.* **5** [T] If a device **scrambles** a radio or telephone message, it interferes with the sound so that the message can only be understood by someone with special equipment. ❑ *The system lets you encrypt or scramble the data that's sent between machines.*

NOUN [C] (**scrambles**) A **scramble for something** happens when a number of people compete energetically with each other for it. ❑ *the scramble for jobs*

scram·bled /ˈskræmbəld/ ADJ ❑ *scrambled eggs and bacon*

scrap /skræp/ NOUN, VERB, ADJ

NOUN [C, PL, U] (**scraps**) **1** [C] A **scrap of** something is a very small piece or amount of it. ❑ *A crumpled scrap of paper was found in her handbag.* **2** [PL] **Scraps** are pieces of unwanted food which are thrown away or given to animals. ❑ *the scraps from the Sunday dinner table* **3** [U] **Scrap** is metal from old or damaged machinery or cars. ❑ *Thousands of tanks, artillery pieces and armoured vehicles will be cut up for scrap.* **4** [C] (*informal*) You can refer to a fight or a quarrel as a **scrap**, especially if it is not very serious. ❑ *He had suffered a mild concussion in a scrap for a loose ball.*

VERB [T, I] (**scraps, scrapping, scrapped**) **1** [T] (*journalism*) If you **scrap** something, you get rid of it or cancel it. ❑ *President Hussein called on all countries in the Middle East to scrap nuclear or chemical weapons.* **2** [I] People **scrap** when they fight or quarrel, especially when it is not a very serious fight or quarrel. ❑ *Our guys scrapped and competed and went right to the wire.*

ADJ [scrap + N] **Scrap** metal or paper is no longer wanted for its original purpose, but may have some other use. ❑ *There's always tons of scrap paper in Dad's office.*

scrape /skreɪp/ VERB

VERB [T, I] (**scrapes, scraping, scraped**) **1** [T] If you **scrape** something from a surface, you remove it, especially by pulling a sharp object over the surface. ❑ *She went around the car scraping the frost off the windows.* **2** [I, T] If something **scrapes** against something else, it rubs against it, making a noise or causing slight damage. ❑ *The only sound is that of knives and forks scraping against china.* ❑ *The car hurtled past us, scraping the wall and screeching to a halt.* **3** [T] If you **scrape** a part of your body, you accidentally rub it against something hard and rough, and damage it slightly. = graze ❑ *She stumbled and fell, scraping her palms and knees.*

PHRASAL VERBS **scrape through** If you **scrape through** an examination, you just succeed in passing it. If you **scrape through** a competition or a vote, you just succeed in winning it. ❑ *He was a poor student, barely scraping through his final year.*

scrape together If you **scrape together** an amount of money or a number of things, you succeed in obtaining it with difficulty. ❑ *They only just managed to scrape the money together.*

scratch /skrætʃ/ VERB, NOUN

VERB [T] (**scratches, scratching, scratched**) **1** If you **scratch yourself**, you rub your fingernails against your skin because it is itching. ❑ *He scratched himself under his arm.* ❑ *The old man lifted his cardigan to scratch his side.* **2** If a sharp object **scratches** someone or something, it makes small shallow cuts on their skin or surface. ❑ *The branches tore at my jacket and scratched my hands and face.*

PHRASE **scratch one's head** If you say that someone is

scratching their **head**, you mean that they are thinking hard and trying to solve a problem or puzzle. ❑ *The Institute spends a lot of time scratching its head about how to boost American productivity.*

NOUN [C] (**scratches**) **Scratches** on someone or something are small shallow cuts. ❑ *The seven-year-old was found crying with scratches on his face and neck.*

PHRASE **from scratch** If you do something **from scratch**, you do it without making use of anything that has been done before. ❑ *Building a home from scratch can be both exciting and challenging.*

scream ◆◇◇ /skriːm/ VERB, NOUN

VERB [I, T] (**screams, screaming, screamed**) **1** [I] When someone **screams**, they make a very loud, high-pitched cry, for example, because they are in pain or are very frightened. ❑ *Women were screaming; some of the houses nearest the bridge were on fire.* **2** [T] If you **scream** something, you shout it in a loud, high-pitched voice. ❑ *'Brigid!' she screamed. 'Get up!'*

NOUN [C] (**screams**) A **scream** is a very loud, high-pitched cry, for example, because you are in pain or are very frightened. ❑ *Hilda let out a scream.*

⊙ screen ◆◆◇ /skriːn/ NOUN, VERB

NOUN [SING, C] (**screens**) **1** [SING, C] A **screen** is a flat vertical surface on which pictures or words are shown. Television sets and computers have screens, and films are shown on a screen in cinemas. **2** [SING] ['the' screen, also 'on/off' screen] You can refer to films or television as **the screen**. ❑ *Many viewers have strong opinions about violence on the screen.* **3** [C] A **screen** is a vertical panel which can be moved around. It is used to keep cold air away from part of a room, or to create a smaller area within a room. ❑ *They put a screen in front of me so I couldn't see what was going on.*

VERB [I, T] (**screens, screening, screened**) **1** [I, T] When a film or a television programme **is screened**, it is shown in the cinema or broadcast on television. ❑ *The series is likely to be screened in January.* **2** [T] If something **is screened by** another thing, it is behind it and hidden by it. ❑ *Most of the road behind the hotel was screened by an apartment block.* **3** [I] To **screen for** a disease means to examine people to make sure that they do not have it. = check, examine ❑ *a quick saliva test that would screen for people at risk of tooth decay* ❑ *Men over 50 are routinely screened for prostate abnormalities.* **4** [T] When an organization **screens** people who apply to join it, it investigates them to make sure that they are not likely to cause problems. ❑ *They will screen all their candidates.* **5** [T] To **screen** people or luggage means to check them using special equipment to make sure they are not carrying a weapon or a bomb. ❑ *The airline had not been searching unaccompanied baggage by hand, but only screening it on X-ray machines.*

⊙ screen·ing /ˈskriːnɪŋ/ NOUN [C, U] (**screenings**) **1** [C] ❑ *The film-makers will be present at the screenings to introduce their works.* **2** [C, U] ❑ *Our country has an enviable record on breast screening for cancer.*

screw /skruː/ NOUN, VERB, ADJ

NOUN [C] (**screws**) A **screw** is a metal object similar to a nail, with a raised spiral line around it. You turn a screw using a screwdriver so that it goes through two things, for example, two pieces of wood, and fastens them together. ❑ *Each bracket is fixed to the wall with just three screws.*

VERB [I, T, RECIP] (**screws, screwing, screwed**) **1** [I, T] If you **screw** something somewhere or if it **screws** somewhere, you fix it in place by means of a screw or screws. ❑ *I had screwed the shelf on the wall myself.* ❑ *Screw down any loose floorboards.* **2** [I, T] If you **screw** something somewhere or if it **screws** somewhere, you fix it in place by twisting it around and around. ❑ *'Yes, I know that,' Kelly said, screwing the silencer onto the pistol.* ❑ *Screw down the lid fairly tightly.* **3** [T] If you **screw** something such as a piece of paper **into** a ball, you squeeze or twist it tightly so that it is in the shape of a ball. ❑ *He screwed the paper into a ball and tossed it into the fire.* **4** [T] If you **screw** your face or your eyes **into** a particular expression, you tighten the muscles of your face to form that expression, for example, because you are in pain or because the light is too bright. ❑ *He* screwed his face into an expression of mock pain. **5** [RECIP] (informal, vulgar) If someone **screws** someone else or if two people **screw**, they have sex together. ❏ 'Are you screwing her?' she said. **6** [T] (informal, vulgar, feelings) Some people use **screw** in expressions such as **screw you** or **screw that** to show that they are not concerned about someone or something or that they feel contempt for them. ❏ Something inside me snapped. 'Well, screw you then!' **7** [T] (informal) If someone **screws** something, especially money, **out of** you, they get it from you by putting pressure on you. ❏ After decades of rich nations screwing money out of poor nations, it's about time some went the other way. [PHRASAL VERB] **screw up ❶** If you **screw up** your eyes or your face, you tighten your eye or face muscles, for example, because you are in pain or because the light is too bright. ❏ She had screwed up her eyes, as if she found the sunshine too bright. ❏ Close your eyes and screw them up tight. **❷** If you **screw up** a piece of paper, you squeeze it tightly so that it becomes very creased and no longer flat, usually when you are throwing it away. ❏ He would start writing to his family and would screw the letter up in frustration. **❸** (informal) To **screw** something **up**, or to **screw up**, means to cause something to fail or be spoiled. ❏ You can't open the window because it screws up the air conditioning. ❏ Get out. Haven't you screwed things up enough already, you idiot! [ADJ] [screw + N] A **screw** lid or fitting is one that has a raised spiral line on the inside or outside of it, so that it can be fixed in place by twisting. ❏ an ordinary jam jar with a screw lid

screw·driver /'skruːdraɪvə/ NOUN [c] (**screwdrivers**) A **screwdriver** is a tool that is used for turning screws. It consists of a metal rod with a flat or cross-shaped end that fits into the top of the screw.

script ♦◇◇ /skrɪpt/ NOUN, VERB [NOUN] [c, u] (**scripts**) **❶** [c] The **script** of a play, film, or television programme is the written version of it. ❏ Jenny's writing a film script. **❷** [c, u] [usu ADJ + script] You can refer to a particular system of writing as a particular **script**. ❏ a text in the Malay language but written in Arabic script **❸** [c, u] Script is handwriting in which the letters are joined together. ❏ When you're writing in script, there are four letters of the alphabet that you can't complete in one stroke. [VERB] [T] (**scripts, scripting, scripted**) The person who **scripts** a film or a radio or television play writes it. ❏ James Cameron, who scripted and directed both films

scrounge /skraʊndʒ/ VERB [I, T] (**scrounges, scrounging, scrounged**) (informal, disapproval) If you say that someone **scrounges** something such as food or money, you disapprove of them because they get it by asking for it, rather than by buying it or earning it. ❏ We managed to scrounge every piece of gear you requested.

scrub /skrʌb/ VERB, NOUN [VERB] [T] (**scrubs, scrubbing, scrubbed**) **❶** If you **scrub** something, you rub it hard in order to clean it, using a stiff brush and water. ❏ Surgeons began to scrub their hands and arms with soap and water before operating. **❷** If you **scrub** dirt or stains **off** something, you remove them by rubbing hard. ❏ I started to scrub off the dirt. [NOUN] [SING, u] (**scrubs**) **❶** [SING] A **scrub** is the action of rubbing something hard in order to clean it, using a stiff brush and water. ❏ The walls needed a good scrub. **❷** [u] Scrub consists of low trees and bushes, especially in an area that has very little rain. ❏ There is an area of scrub and woodland beside the railway.

scru·ple /'skruːpəl/ NOUN [c, u] (**scruples**) Scruples are moral principles or beliefs that make you unwilling to do something that seems wrong. ❏ a man with no moral scruples

✪scru·ti·nize /'skruːtɪnaɪz/ also **scrutinise** VERB [T] (**scrutinizes, scrutinizing, scrutinized**) If you **scrutinize** something, you examine it very carefully, often to find out some information from it or about it. = examine ❏ Her purpose was to scrutinize his features to see if he was an honest man. ❏ Lloyds' results were carefully scrutinised as a guide to what to expect from the other banks.

✪scru·ti·ny /'skruːtɪni/ NOUN [u] If a person or thing is under **scrutiny**, they are being studied or observed very

carefully. = examination ❏ His private life came under media scrutiny. ❏ The President promised a government open to public scrutiny.

✪sculp·tor /'skʌlptə/ NOUN [c] (**sculptors**) A **sculptor** is someone who creates sculptures. ❏ The critic at the Washington Post called him the most innovative sculptor of the decade. ❏ He is a glass sculptor, so his true skill lies with glass itself.

✪sculp·ture /'skʌlptʃə/ NOUN [c, u] (**sculptures**) **❶** [c, u] A **sculpture** is a work of art that is produced by carving or shaping stone, wood, clay, or other materials. ❏ stone sculptures of figures and animals ❏ a collection of 20th-century art and sculpture **❷** [u] Sculpture is the art of creating sculptures. ❏ Both studied sculpture. ❏ The Arts Academy offers courses in sculpture and painting.

sea ♦♦◇ /siː/ NOUN [NOUN] [SING, PL, c] (**seas**) **❶** [SING] ['the' sea, also 'by' sea] The **sea** is the salty water that covers about three-quarters of the Earth's surface. ❏ Most of the kids have never seen the sea. **❷** [PL] (literary) You use **seas** when you are describing the sea at a particular time or in a particular area. ❏ He drowned after 30 minutes in the rough seas. **❸** [c] A **sea** is a large area of salty water that is part of an ocean or is surrounded by land. ❏ the North Sea [PHRASES] **at sea** At sea means on or under the sea, far away from land. ❏ The boats remain at sea for an average of ten days at a time. **out to sea** or **to sea** If you go or look out **to sea**, you go or look across the sea. ❏ fishermen who go to sea for two weeks at a time

sea·bed /'siːbed/ also **sea bed** NOUN [SING] The seabed is the ground under the sea. ❏ The wreck was raised from the seabed in June 2000.

sea·food /'siːfuːd/ NOUN [u] Seafood is shellfish such as lobsters, mussels, and crabs, and sometimes other sea creatures that you can eat. ❏ a seafood restaurant

seal ♦◇◇ /siːl/ VERB, NOUN [VERB] [T] (**seals, sealing, sealed**) **❶** When you **seal** an envelope, you close it by folding part of it over and sticking it down, so that it cannot be opened without being torn. ❏ He sealed the envelope and put on a stamp. ❏ Write your letter and seal it in a blank envelope. **❷** If you **seal** a container or an opening, you cover it with something in order to prevent air, liquid, or other material from getting in or out. If you **seal** something **in** a container, you put it inside and then close the container tightly. ❏ She filled the containers, sealed them with a cork, and stuck on labels. ❏ A woman picks them up and seals them in plastic bags. **❸** If someone in authority **seals** an area, they stop people entering or passing through it, for example, by placing barriers in the way. ❏ The soldiers were deployed to help paramilitary police seal the border. **❹** (written) To **seal** something means to make it definite or confirm how it is going to be. ❏ McLaren are close to sealing a deal with Renault. ❏ A general election will be held which will seal his destiny one way or the other. [PHRASAL VERB] **seal off ❶** Seal off means the same as **seal** VERB 3. ❏ Police and troops sealed off the area after the attack. **❷** If one object or area **is sealed off** from another, there is a physical barrier between them, so that nothing can pass between them. ❏ Windows are usually sealed off. [NOUN] [c] (**seals**) **❶** The **seal** on a container or opening is the part where it has been sealed. ❏ When assembling the pie, wet the edges where the two crusts join, to form a seal. **❷** [oft seal 'on' N] A **seal** is a device or a piece of material, for example, in a machine, which closes an opening tightly so that air, liquid, or other substances cannot get in or out. ❏ Check seals on fridges and freezers regularly. **❸** [oft seal 'on' N] A **seal** is something such as a piece of sticky paper or wax that is fixed to a container or door and must be broken before the container or door can be opened. ❏ The seal on the box broke when it fell from its hiding-place. **❹** A **seal** is a special mark or design, for example, on a document, representing someone or something. It may be used to show that something is genuine or officially approved. ❏ a supply of note paper bearing the presidential seal **❺** A **seal** is a large animal with a rounded body and flat legs called flippers. Seals eat fish and live in and near the sea, usually in cold parts of the world.

seam /siːm/ NOUN

NOUN [c] (seams) **1** A **seam** is a line of stitches which joins two pieces of cloth together. ❑ *The skirt ripped along a seam.* **2** A **seam** of coal is a long, narrow layer of it underneath the ground. ❑ *The average coal seam here is three feet thick.*

PHRASES **come apart at the seams** or **fall apart at the seams** If something **is coming apart at the seams** or **is falling apart at the seams,** it is no longer working properly and may soon stop working completely. ❑ *Our university system is in danger of falling apart at the seams.*
bursting at the seams If a place is very full, you can say that it is **bursting at the seams.** ❑ *The hotels of Warsaw, Prague, and Budapest were bursting at the seams.*

seam·less /ˈsiːmləs/ ADJ You use **seamless** to describe something that has no breaks or gaps in it or which continues without stopping. ❑ *It was a seamless procession of wonderful electronic music.*
seam·less·ly /ˈsiːmləsli/ ADV [seamlessly with v] ❑ *It's a class move, allowing new and old to blend seamlessly.*

search ♦♦◇ /sɜːtʃ/ VERB, NOUN

VERB [I, T] (searches, searching, searched) **1** [I] If you **search for** something or someone, you look carefully for them. ❑ *The Turkish security forces have started searching for the missing men.* ❑ *They searched for a spot where they could sit on the floor.* **2** [I, T] If you **search** a place, you look carefully for something or someone there. ❑ *Armed troops searched the hospital yesterday.* ❑ *She searched her desk for the necessary information.* ❑ *Relief workers are still searching through collapsed buildings.* **3** [T] If a police officer or someone else in authority **searches** you, they look carefully to see whether you have something hidden on you. ❑ *The man took her suitcase from her and then searched her.* **4** [I] (computing) If you **search for** information on a computer, you give the computer an instruction to find that information. ❑ *You can use a directory service to search for people on the Internet.*

CONVENTION **search me** (informal, emphasis) You say '**search me**' when someone asks you a question and you want to emphasize that you do not know the answer. ❑ *'So why did he get interested all of a sudden?'—'Search me.'*

NOUN [c] (searches) **1** A **search** is an attempt to find something or someone by looking for them carefully. ❑ *There was no chance of him being found alive and the search was abandoned.* **2** (computing) If you do a **search** for information on a computer, you give the computer an instruction to find that information. ❑ *He came across this story while he was doing a computer search of local news articles.*

PHRASE **in search of** If you go **in search of** something or someone, you try to find them. ❑ *Miserable, and unexpectedly lonely, she went in search of Jean-Paul.*

S

USAGE NOTE

search

Note that you do not say that you 'search' the thing you are trying to find. You can say that you 'search for' it, or that you 'look for' it.

He **is looking for** his phone.

---

search en·gine NOUN [c] (search engines) (computing) A **search engine** is a computer program that searches for documents containing a particular word or words on the Internet.

✪sea·son ♦♦♦ /ˈsiːzən/ NOUN, VERB

NOUN [c] (seasons) **1** The **seasons** are the main periods into which a year can be divided and which each have their own typical weather conditions. ❑ *Autumn is my favourite season.* ❑ *the only region of Brazil where all four seasons are clearly defined* ❑ *The climate is characterized by hot summers with a four-month rainy season.* **2** You can use **season** to refer to the period during each year when a particular activity or event takes place. For example, the planting **season** is the period when a particular plant or crop is planted. = period, time ❑ *birds arriving for the*

breeding season ❑ *For law students, autumn brings the recruiting season.* **3** [N + season, also 'in/out of' season] You can use **season** to refer to the period when a particular fruit, vegetable, or other food is ready for eating and is widely available. ❑ *The plum season is about to begin.* **4** You can use **season** to refer to a fixed period during each year when a particular sport is played or when a particular activity is allowed. ❑ *the baseball season* ❑ *Deer hunting season is only a couple of weeks long.* **5** A **season** is a period in which a play or show, or a series of plays or shows, is performed in one place. ❑ *a season of three new plays* **6** A **season of** films is several of them shown as a series because they are connected in some way. ❑ *a brief season of films in which Artaud appeared* **7** [usu sing, usu SUPP + season, also 'in/out of' season] The holiday **season** is the time when most people take their holiday. ❑ *the peak holiday season*

PHRASE **in season** If a female animal is **in season**, she is in a state where she is ready to have sex. ❑ *There are a few ideas around on how to treat fillies and mares in season.*

VERB [T] (seasons, seasoning, seasoned) If you **season** food with salt, pepper, or spices, you add them to it in order to improve its flavour. ❑ *Season the meat with salt and pepper.*
→ See also **seasoned, seasoning**

sea·son·al /ˈsiːzənəl/ ADJ [seasonal + N] A **seasonal** factor, event, or change occurs during one particular time of the year. ❑ *The figures aren't adjusted for seasonal variations.*
sea·son·al·ly /ˈsiːzənəli/ ADV ❑ *The seasonally adjusted unemployment figures show a rise of twelve hundred.*

sea·soned /ˈsiːzənd/ ADJ You can use **seasoned** to describe a person who has a lot of experience of something. For example, a **seasoned** traveller is a person who has travelled a lot. ❑ *The author is a seasoned academic.*

sea·son·ing /ˈsiːzənɪŋ/ NOUN [c, u] (seasonings) **Seasoning** is salt, pepper, or other spices that are added to food to improve its flavour. ❑ *Mix the meat with the onion, carrot, and some seasoning.*

seat ♦♦◇ /siːt/ NOUN, VERB

NOUN [c, SING] (seats) **1** [c] A **seat** is an object that you can sit on, for example, a chair. ❑ *Stephen returned to his seat.* **2** [c] The **seat** of a chair is the part that you sit on. ❑ *The stool had a torn, red plastic seat.* **3** [SING] [usu 'the' seat 'of' N] The **seat** of a piece of clothing is the part that covers your bottom. ❑ *Then he got up, brushed off the seat of his jeans, and headed slowly down the slope.* **4** [c] When someone is elected to a legislature you can say that they, or their party, have won a **seat**. ❑ *Independent candidates won the majority of seats on the local council.* **5** [c] If someone has a **seat** on the board of a company or on a committee, they are a member of it. ❑ *He has been unsuccessful in his attempt to win a seat on the board of the company.* **6** [c] The **seat** of an organization, a wealthy family, or an activity is its base. ❑ *Gunfire broke out early this morning around the seat of government in Lagos.*

PHRASES **take a back seat** If you **take a back seat,** you allow other people to have all the power and to make all the decisions. ❑ *You need to take a back seat and think about both past and future.*
take a seat (formal) If you **take a seat,** you sit down. ❑ *'Take a seat,' he said in a bored tone.*

VERB [T] (seats, seating, seated) **1** (written) If you **seat yourself** somewhere, you sit down. ❑ *He waved towards a chair, and seated himself at the desk.* **2** A building or vehicle that **seats** a particular number of people has enough seats for that number. ❑ *The theatre seats 570.*
→ See also **deep-seated**

seat belt also **seatbelt** NOUN [c] (seat belts) A **seat belt** is a strap attached to a seat in a car or an aircraft. You fasten it across your body in order to prevent yourself being thrown out of the seat if there is a sudden movement or stop. = safety belt ❑ *The fact I was wearing a seat belt saved my life.*

seat·ing /ˈsiːtɪŋ/ NOUN [u] **1** You can refer to the seats in a place as the **seating.** ❑ *The stadium has been fitted with seating for over eighty thousand spectators.* **2** The **seating** at a public place or a formal occasion is the arrangement of where people will sit. ❑ *She made a mental note to check the seating arrangements before the guests filed into the dining room.*

se·clu·sion /sɪˈkluːʒən/ NOUN [U] If you are living in **seclusion**, you are in a quiet place away from other people. ❑ *She lived in seclusion with her husband on their farm in Panama.*

sec·ond ♦♦♦ /ˈsekənd/ NOUN, ADJ, ADV, VERB

NOUN [C, PL] (**seconds**) **1** [C] A **second** is one of the sixty parts that a minute is divided into. People often say '**a second**' or '**seconds**' when they simply mean a very short time. ❑ *For a few seconds nobody said anything.* ❑ *It only takes forty seconds.* **2** [PL] (*informal*) If you have **seconds**, you have a second helping of food. ❑ *There's seconds if you want them.* **3** [C] **Seconds** are goods that are sold cheaply in shops because they have slight faults. ❑ *These are not seconds, or unbranded goods, but first-quality products.*

ADJ **1** The **second** item in a series is the one that you count as number two. ❑ *the second day of his visit to Delhi* ❑ *their second child* ❑ *the Second World War* **2** [second + ADJ-SUPERL] **Second** is used before superlative adjectives to indicate that there is only one thing better or larger than the thing you are referring to. ❑ *The party is still the second strongest in Italy.*

PHRASES **at second hand** If you experience something **at second hand**, you are told about it by other people rather than experiencing it yourself. ❑ *Most of them, after all, had not been at the battle and had only heard of the massacre at second hand.*

second to none (*emphasis*) If you say that something is **second to none**, you are emphasizing that it is very good indeed or the best that there is. ❑ *Our scientific research is second to none.*

second only to something If you say that something is **second only to** something else, you mean that only that thing is better or greater than it. ❑ *As a major health risk hepatitis is second only to tobacco.*

ADV [second + CL] You say **second** when you want to make a second point or give a second reason for something. ❑ *First, the weapons should be intended for use only in retaliation after a nuclear attack. Second, the possession of the weapons must be a temporary expedient.*

VERB [T] (**seconds**, **seconding**, **seconded**) **1** If you **second** a proposal in a meeting or debate, you formally express your agreement with it so that it can then be discussed or voted on. ❑ *Bryan Sutton, who seconded the motion against fox hunting* **2** If you **second** what someone has said, you say that you agree with them or say the same thing yourself. ❑ *The UN secretary-general seconded the appeal for peace.*

✦ **second nature** → see **nature**; **in the second place** → see **place**

🟠 **sec·ond·ary** /ˈsekəndri, *AmE* -deri/ ADJ **1** If you describe something as **secondary**, you mean that it is less important than something else. ❑ *The street erupted in a huge explosion, with secondary explosions in the adjoining buildings.* ❑ *They argue that human rights considerations are now of only secondary importance.* ❑ *The actual damage to the brain cells is secondary to the damage caused to the blood supply.* **2** **Secondary** diseases or infections happen as a result of another disease or infection that has already happened. ❑ *These patients had been operated on for the primary cancer but there was evidence of secondary tumours.* **3** **Secondary** education is given to pupils between the ages of 11 or 12 and 17 or 18. ❑ *Examinations are taken after about five years of secondary education.*

🟠 **sec·ond·ary school** NOUN [C, U] (**secondary schools**) A **secondary school** is a school for pupils between the ages of 11 or 12 and 17 or 18. = **high school** ❑ *She taught history at a secondary school.*

second-class also **second class** ADJ, ADV, NOUN

ADJ **1** [second-class + N] If someone treats you as a **second-class** citizen, they treat you as if you are less valuable and less important than other people. ❑ *Too many airlines treat our children as second-class citizens.* **2** If you describe something as **second-class**, you mean that it

is of poor quality. = **second-rate** ❑ *I am not prepared to see children in some parts of this country having to settle for a second-class education.* **3** [second-class + N] The **second-class** accommodation on a train or ship is the ordinary accommodation, which is cheaper and less comfortable than the first-class accommodation. ❑ *He sat in the corner of a second-class compartment.* ❑ *Seven second-class passengers prepared to disembark.* **4** [second-class + N] (*BrE*) **Second-class** postage is a slower and cheaper type of postage.

ADV [second class after V] If you travel **second class** on a train or ship, you travel in the ordinary accommodation, which is cheaper and less comfortable than the first-class accommodation. ❑ *I recently travelled second class from Pisa to Ventimiglia.*

NOUN [U] **Second class** is second-class accommodation on a train or ship. ❑ *'Is there any chance of a compartment to myself?'—'Not in second class.'*

sec·ond·ly /ˈsekəndli/ ADV You say **secondly** when you want to make a second point or give a second reason for something. ❑ *It makes you look firstly at how you're treated and secondly how you treat everybody else.*

se·cre·cy /ˈsiːkrəsi/ NOUN [U] **Secrecy** is the act of keeping something secret, or the state of being kept secret. ❑ *The government has thrown a blanket of secrecy over the details.*

se·cret ♦♦◇ /ˈsiːkrət/ ADJ, NOUN

ADJ If something is **secret**, it is known about by only a small number of people, and is not told or shown to anyone else. ❑ *Soldiers have been training at a secret location.*

NOUN [C, SING] (**secrets**) **1** [C] A **secret** is a fact that is known by only a small number of people, and is not told to anyone else. ❑ *I think he enjoyed keeping our love a secret.* **2** [SING] If you say that a particular way of doing things is **the secret of** achieving something, you mean that it is the best or only way to achieve it. ❑ *The secret of success is honesty and fair dealing.* **3** [C] Something's **secrets** are the things about it which have never been fully explained. ❑ *We have an opportunity now to really unlock the secrets of the universe.*

PHRASES **in secret** If you do something **in secret**, you do it without anyone else knowing. ❑ *Dan found out that I had been meeting my ex-boyfriend in secret.*

keep a secret If you say that someone can **keep a secret**, you mean that they can be trusted not to tell other people a secret that you have told them. ❑ *Tom was utterly indiscreet, and could never keep a secret.*

make no secret If you **make no secret** of something, you tell others about it openly and clearly. ❑ *His wife made no secret of her hatred for the formal occasions.*

se·cret·ly /ˈsiːkrətli/ ADV ❑ *He wore a hidden microphone to secretly tape-record conversations.*

sec·re·tary ♦♦♦ /ˈsekrətri, *AmE* -teri/ NOUN [C] (**secretaries**) **1** A **secretary** is a person who is employed to do office work, such as typing letters, answering phone calls, and arranging meetings. **2** The **secretary** of a company is the person who has the legal duty of keeping the company's records. **3** **Secretary** is used in the titles of high officials who are in charge of main government departments. ❑ *a former Venezuelan foreign secretary*

secretary-general ♦◇◇ also **Secretary General** NOUN [C] (**secretaries-general**) The **secretary-general** of an international political organization is the person in charge of its administration. ❑ *the United Nations Secretary-General*

se·cre·tive /ˈsiːkrətɪv, sɪˈkriːt-/ ADJ If you are **secretive**, you like to have secrets and to keep your knowledge, feelings, or intentions hidden. ❑ *Billionaires are usually fairly secretive about the exact amount that they're worth.*

sect /sekt/ NOUN [C] (**sects**) A **sect** is a group of people that has separated from a larger group and has a particular set of religious or political beliefs.

🟠 **sec·tion** ♦♦◇ /ˈsekʃən/ NOUN, VERB (*academic word*)

NOUN [C] (**sections**) **1** A **section** of something is one of the parts into which it is divided or from which it is formed. = **part** ❑ *He said it was wrong to single out any section of society for AIDS testing.* ❑ *the Georgetown section of Washington, D.C.* ❑ *a large orchestra, with a vast percussion*

S

section **2** A **section** is a diagram of something such as a building or a part of the body. It shows how the object would appear to you if it were cut from top to bottom and looked at from the side. ❑ *For some buildings a vertical section is more informative than a plan.* ▭**VERB** [T] (**sections, sectioning, sectioned**) If something is **sectioned**, it is divided into sections. ❑ *It holds vegetables in place while they are being peeled or sectioned.*
→ See also **cross-section**

✪**sec·tor** ◆◆◇ /ˈsektə/ NOUN [C] (**sectors**) (*academic word*)
1 A particular **sector** of a country's economy is the part connected with that specified type of industry. ❑ *the nation's manufacturing sector* ❑ *the service sector of the Hong Kong economy* **2** A **sector** of a large group is a smaller group which is part of it. ❑ *Workers who went to the Gulf came from the poorest sectors of Pakistani society.* **3** A **sector** is an area of a city or country which is controlled by a military force. ❑ *Officers were going to retake sectors of the city.*
→ See also **public sector, private sector**

✪**secu·lar** /ˈsekjʊlə/ ADJ You use **secular** to describe things that have no connection with religion. ❑ *He spoke about preserving the country as a secular state.* ❑ *secular and religious education*

✪**secu·lar·ized** /ˈsekjʊləraɪzd/ also **secularised**
ADJ **Secularized** societies are no longer under the control or influence of religion. ≠ **religious** ❑ *The Pope had no great sympathy for the secularized West.* ❑ *the changes brought about by an increasingly secularized society*

✪**se·cure** ◆◆◇ /sɪˈkjʊə/ VERB, ADJ (*academic word*)
▭**VERB** [T] (**secures, securing, secured**) **1** (*formal*) If you **secure** something that you want or need, you obtain it, often after a lot of effort. = **obtain** ❑ *Federal leaders continued their efforts to secure a ceasefire.* ❑ *Graham's achievements helped secure him the job.* **2** (*formal*) If you **secure** a place, you make it safe from harm or attack. ❑ *Staff withdrew from the main part of the prison but secured the perimeter.* **3** If you **secure** an object, you fasten it firmly to another object. ❑ *He helped her close the cases up, and then he secured the canvas straps as tight as they would go.* **4** (*business*) If a loan **is secured**, the person who lends the money may take property such as a house from the person who borrows the money if they fail to repay it. ❑ *The loan is secured against your home.*
▭**ADJ** **1** A **secure** place is tightly locked or well protected, so that people cannot enter it or leave it. = **safe, guarded, protected** ❑ *We'll make sure our home is as secure as possible from now on.* ❑ *The building has secure undercover parking for 27 vehicles.* **2** If an object is **secure**, it is fixed firmly in position. ❑ *Check that joints are secure and the wood is sound.* **3** If you describe something such as a job as **secure**, it is certain not to change or end. ❑ *demands for secure wages and employment* ❑ *Senior citizens long for a more predictable and secure future.* **4** A **secure** base or foundation is strong and reliable. ❑ *He was determined to give his family a secure and solid base.* **5** If you feel **secure**, you feel safe and happy and are not worried about life. ❑ *She felt secure and protected when she was with him.*

✪**secure·ly** /sɪˈkjʊəli/ ADV **1** = **safely** ❑ *He locked the heavy door securely and kept the key in his pocket.* **2** [securely with V] ❑ *Ensure that the frame is securely fixed to the ground with bolts.*

✪**se·cu·rity** ◆◆◆ /sɪˈkjʊərɪti/ NOUN (*academic word*)
▭**NOUN** [U, PL] (**securities**) **1** [U] **Security** refers to all the measures that are taken to protect a place, or to ensure that only people with permission enter it or leave it. ❑ *They are now under a great deal of pressure to tighten their airport security.* ❑ *Strict security measures are in force in the capital.* **2** [U] A feeling of **security** is a feeling of being safe and free from worry. ❑ *He loves the security of a happy home life.* ❑ *If an alarm gives you that feeling of security, then it's worth carrying.* **3** [U] (*business*) If something is **security** for a loan, you promise to give that thing to the person who lends you money, if you fail to pay the money back. = **collateral** ❑ *The central bank will provide special loans, and the banks will pledge the land as security.* **4** [PL] (*business*) **Securities** are stocks, shares, bonds, or other certificates

that you buy in order to earn regular interest from them or to sell them later for a profit. ❑ *National banks can package their own mortgages and underwrite them as securities.*
▭**PHRASE** **a false sense of security** If something gives you **a false sense of security**, it makes you believe that you are safe when you are not.

se·date /sɪˈdeɪt/ ADJ, VERB
▭**ADJ** **1** If you describe someone or something as **sedate**, you mean that they are quiet and rather dignified, though perhaps a bit dull. ❑ *She took them to visit her sedate, elderly cousins.* ❑ *Her life was sedate, almost mundane.* **2** If you move along at a **sedate** pace, you move slowly, in a controlled way. ❑ *We set off again at a more sedate pace.*
▭**VERB** [T] (**sedates, sedating, sedated**) If someone is **sedated**, they are given a drug to calm them or to make them sleep. ❑ *The patient is sedated with intravenous use of sedative drugs.*

sedi·ment /ˈsedɪmənt/ NOUN [C, U] (**sediments**)
Sediment is solid material that settles at the bottom of a liquid, especially earth and pieces of rock that have been carried along and then left somewhere by water, ice, or wind. ❑ *Many organisms that die in the sea are soon buried by sediment.*

se·duce /sɪˈdjuːs, AmE -ˈduːs/ VERB [T] (**seduces, seducing, seduced**) **1** If something **seduces** you, it is so attractive that it makes you do something that you would not otherwise do. ❑ *The view of the lake and plunging cliffs seduces visitors.* **2** If someone **seduces** another person, they use their charm to persuade that person to have sex with them. ❑ *She has set out to seduce Stephen.*
se·duc·tion /sɪˈdʌkʃən/ NOUN [C, U] (**seductions**) **1** *the seduction of words* **2** *Her methods of seduction are subtle.*

see ◆◆◆ /siː/ VERB
▭**VERB** [I, T] (**sees, seeing, saw, seen**) **1** [I, T] When you see something, you notice it using your eyes. ❑ *You can't see colours at night.* ❑ *She can see, hear, touch, smell, and taste.* **2** [T] If you **see** someone, you visit them or meet them. ❑ *I saw him yesterday.* ❑ *Mick wants to see you in his office right away.* **3** [T] If you **see** an entertainment such as a play, film, concert, or sports match, you watch it. = **watch** ❑ *I haven't been to see a movie in 10 years.* **4** [I, T] If you **see** that something is true or exists, you realize that by observing it that it is true or exists. ❑ *I could see she was lonely.* ❑ *A lot of people saw what was happening but did nothing about it.* ❑ *My taste has changed a bit over the years as you can see.* **5** [T] If you **see** what someone means or **see** why something happened, you understand what they mean or understand why it happened. = **understand** ❑ *Oh, I see what you're saying.* ❑ *I really don't see any reason for changing it.* **6** [T] If you **see** someone or something **as** a certain thing, you have the opinion that they are that thing. ❑ *She saw him as a visionary, but her father saw him as a man who couldn't make a living.* ❑ *Others saw it as a betrayal.* **7** [T] If you **see** a particular quality **in** someone, you believe they have that quality. If you ask what someone **sees in** a particular person or thing, you want to know what they find attractive about that person or thing. ❑ *Frankly, I don't know what Paul sees in her.* **8** [T] If you **see** something happening in the future, you imagine it, or predict that it will happen. = **imagine** ❑ *A good idea, but can you see Taylor trying it?* **9** [T] If a period of time or a person **sees** a particular change or event, it takes place during that period of time or while that person is alive. ❑ *Yesterday saw the resignation of the chief financial officer.* ❑ *He had worked with the general for three years and was sorry to see him go.* **10** [T] If you **see that** something is done or if you **see to it that** it is done, you make sure that it is done. ❑ *See that you take care of him.* **11** [T] If you **see** someone to a particular place, you accompany them to make sure that they get there safely, or to show politeness. ❑ *He didn't offer to see her to her car.* **12** [T] If you **see a lot of** someone, you often meet each other or visit each other. ❑ *We used to see quite a lot of his wife, Carolyn.* **13** [T] If you **are seeing** someone, you spend time with them socially, and are having a romantic or sexual relationship. ❑ *My husband was still seeing her and he was having an affair with her.* **14** [T] **See** is used in books to indicate to readers that

they should look at another part of the book, or at another book, because more information is given there. ❑ *Surveys consistently find that men report feeling safe on the street after dark. See, for example, Hindelang and Garofalo (1978, p.127).* **15** [T] You can use **see** in expressions to do with finding out information. For example, if you say '**I'll see what's happening**', you mean that you intend to find out what is happening. ❑ *Let me just see what the next song is.* ❑ *Every time we asked our mother, she said, 'Well, see what your father says.'* **16** [T] You can use **see** in expressions in which you promise to try and help someone. For example, if you say '**I'll see if I can do it**', you mean that you will try to do the thing concerned. ❑ *I'll see if I can call her for you.* **17** [T] Some writers use **see** in expressions such as **we saw** and **as we have seen** to refer to something that has already been explained or described. ❑ *We saw in Chapter 16 how annual cash budgets are produced.* ❑ *Laws are often not clear, as we saw in Chapter 1.*

PHRASES **seeing that** or **seeing as** (*informal, spoken*) You can use **seeing that** or **seeing as** to introduce a reason for what you are saying. = **since** ❑ *Seeing as Mr Moreton is a doctor, I assume he is reasonably intelligent.*

see sense or **see reason** If you try to make someone **see sense** or **see reason**, you try to make them realize that they are wrong or are being stupid. ❑ *He was hopeful that by sitting together they could both see sense and live as good neighbours.*

CONVENTIONS **I see** (*spoken, formulae*) You can say '**I see**' to indicate that you understand what someone is telling you. ❑ *'He came home in my car.'—'I see.'*

I'll see or **we'll see** People say '**I'll see**' or '**We'll see**' to indicate that they do not intend to make a decision immediately, and will decide later. ❑ *We'll see. It's a possibility.*

let me see or **let's see** People say '**let me see**' or '**let's see**' when they are trying to remember something, or are trying to find something. ❑ *Let's see, they're six – no, make that five hours ahead of us.*

you see (*spoken*) You can say '**you see**' when you are explaining something to someone, to encourage them to listen and understand. ❑ *Well, you see, you shouldn't really feel that way about it.*

see you or **be seeing you** (*informal, spoken, formulae*) '**See you**', '**be seeing you**', and '**see you later**' are ways of saying goodbye to someone when you expect to meet them again soon. = **bye** ❑ *'Talk to you later.'—'All right. See you, love.'*

you'll see You can say '**You'll see**' to someone if they do not agree with you about what you think will happen in the future, and you believe that you will be proved right. ❑ *The thrill wears off after a few years of marriage. You'll see.*

PHRASAL VERBS **see about** When you **see about** something, you arrange for it to be done or provided. ❑ *Tony announced it was time to see about lunch.*

see off When you **see** someone **off**, you go with them to the station, airport, or port that they are leaving from, and say goodbye to them there. ❑ *Ben had planned a steak dinner for himself after seeing Jackie off on her plane.*

see out If you **see out** a period of time, you continue to do what you are doing until that period of time is over. ❑ *The lease runs for 21 years, and they are committed to seeing out that time.*

see through If you **see through** someone or their behaviour, you realize what their intentions are, even though they are trying to hide them. ❑ *I saw through your little ruse from the start.*

see to If you **see to** something that needs attention, you deal with it. ❑ *While Franklin saw to the luggage, Sara took Eleanor home.*

♦ **have seen better days** → see **day**; **be seen dead** → see **dead**; **as far as the eye can see** → see **eye**; **see eye to eye** → see **eye**; **as far as I can see** → see **far**; **see fit** → see **fit**; **see red** → see **red**; **wait and see** → see **wait**

⊙ **seed** ♦♦◇ /siːd/ NOUN, VERB

NOUN [C, U, PL] (**seeds**) **1** [C, U] A **seed** is the small, hard part of a plant from which a new plant grows. ❑ *I sow the seed in pots of soil-based compost.* ❑ *a packet of cabbage seed* **2** [PL] (*literary*) You can refer to the **seeds of** something when you want to talk about the beginning of a feeling or

process that gradually develops and becomes stronger or more important. ❑ *He raised questions meant to plant seeds of doubts in the minds of jurors.* **3** [C] In sports such as tennis or badminton, a **seed** is a player who has been ranked according to his or her ability. ❑ *Roger Federer, Wimbledon's top seed and the world No.1*

PHRASE **go to seed** **1** If vegetable plants **go to seed**, they produce flowers and seeds as well as leaves. ❑ *plants that had long since flowered, gone to seed, and died* **2** If you say that someone or something **has gone to seed**, you mean that they have become much less attractive, healthy, or efficient. ❑ *He says the economy has gone to seed.* ❑ *a retired cop who has gone to seed*

VERB [T] (**seeds, seeding, seeded**) **1** If you **seed** a piece of land, you plant seeds in it. ❑ *Men mowed the wide lawns and seeded them.* ❑ *The primroses should begin to seed themselves down the steep hillside.* **2** When a player or a team **is seeded** in a sports competition, they are ranked according to their ability. ❑ *The Longhorns have won a national title and are seeded first overall.* ❑ *He is seeded second, behind Brad Beven.*

⊙ **seek** ♦◇◇ /siːk/ VERB (*academic word*)

VERB [T] (**seeks, seeking, sought**) (*formal*) **1** If you **seek** something such as a job or a place to live, you try to find one. ❑ *They have had to seek work as labourers.* ❑ *Four people who sought refuge in the Italian embassy have left voluntarily.* ❑ *Candidates are urgently sought for the post of Conservative Party chairman.* ❑ *The couple have sought help from marriage guidance counsellors.* **2** When someone **seeks** something, they try to obtain it. ❑ *The prosecutors have warned they will seek the death penalty.* **3** If you **seek** someone's help or advice, you contact them in order to ask for it. ❑ *Always seek professional legal advice before entering into any agreement.* ❑ *On important issues, they seek a second opinion.* **4** If you **seek to** do something, you try to do it. ❑ *He also denied that he would seek to annex the country.*

PHRASAL VERB **seek out** If you **seek out** someone or something or **seek** them **out**, you keep looking for them until you find them. ❑ *Now is the time for local companies to seek out business opportunities in Europe.*

seek·er /ˈsiːkə/ NOUN [C] (**seekers**) A **seeker** is someone who is looking for or trying to get something. ❑ *I am a seeker after truth.*
→ See also **asylum seeker**

⊙ **seem** ♦♦♦ /siːm/ VERB

VERB [LINK] (**seems, seeming, seemed**) **1** You use **seem** to say that someone or something gives the impression of having a particular quality, or of happening in the way you describe. = **appear** ❑ *The explosions seemed quite close by.* ❑ *To everyone who knew them, they seemed an ideal couple.* ❑ *The calming effect seemed to last for about ten minutes.* ❑ *It seems that the attack was carefully planned.* ❑ *It seemed as if she'd been gone forever.* ❑ *It seems likely that a calcium-rich diet may help prevent osteoporosis.* ❑ *This phenomenon is not as outrageous as it seems.* **2** You use **seem** when you are describing your own feelings or thoughts, or describing something that has happened to you, in order to make your statement less forceful. ❑ *I seem to have lost all my self-confidence.* ❑ *I seem to remember giving you very precise instructions.*

PHRASE **cannot seem** If you say that you **cannot seem** or **could not seem to** do something, you mean that you have tried to do it and were unable to. ❑ *No matter how hard I try I cannot seem to catch up on all the bills.*

USAGE NOTE
seem
Note that you do not use 'as' after **seem**. Do not say, for example, 'It seemed as a good idea'. *It **seemed** a good idea.*

seem·ing·ly /ˈsiːmɪŋli/ ADV **1** [seemingly + ADJ/ADV] If something is **seemingly** the case, you mean that it appears to be the case, even though it may not really be so. = **apparently** ❑ *A seemingly endless line of trucks waits in vain to load up.* **2** You use **seemingly** when you want to say that something seems to be true. ❑ *He has moved to Spain, seemingly to enjoy a slower style of life.*

S

seen /siːn/ IRREG FORM **Seen** is the past participle of **see**.

seep /siːp/ VERB, NOUN

VERB [I] (**seeps, seeping, seeped**) **1** If something such as liquid or gas **seeps** somewhere, it flows slowly and in small amounts into a place where it should not go. ❑ *Radioactive water had seeped into underground reservoirs.* ❑ *The gas is seeping out of the rocks.* **2** If something such as information or an emotion **seeps** into or out of a place, it enters or leaves it gradually. ❑ *Many of us thrive on competition, but it can seep into areas of our lives where we do not want it.*

NOUN [C] (**seeps**) A **seep** happens when something such as liquid or gas flows slowly and in small amounts into a place where it should not go. ❑ *an oil seep*

seethe /siːð/ VERB [I] (**seethes, seething, seethed**) When you **are seething**, you are very angry about something but do not express your feelings about it. ❑ *She took it calmly at first but under the surface was seething.* ❑ *She put a hand on her hip, grinning derisively, while I seethed with rage.*

✪ **seg·ment** ◆◇◇ /ˈsegmənt/ NOUN [C] (**segments**) **1** A **segment of** something is one part of it, considered separately from the rest. = section ❑ *the poorer segments of society* **2** A **segment** of fruit such as an orange or grapefruit is one of the sections into which it is easily divided. ❑ *Peel all the fruit except the lime and separate into segments.* **3** A **segment** of a circle is one of the two parts into which it is divided when you draw a straight line through it. ❑ *The other children stood around the circle, one in each segment.* ❑ *The pie chart is divided into equal segments.* **4** A **segment** of a market is one part of it, considered separately from the rest. = niche, sector ❑ *Three-to-five day cruises are the fastest-growing segment of the market.* ❑ *Women's tennis is the market leader in a growing market segment – women's sports.*

seg·re·gate /ˈsegrɪgeɪt/ VERB [T] (**segregates, segregating, segregated**) To **segregate** two groups of people or things means to keep them physically apart from each other. ❑ *A large detachment of police was used to segregate the two rival camps of protesters.*

seg·re·gat·ed /ˈsegrɪgeɪtɪd/ ADJ **Segregated** buildings or areas are kept for the use of one group of people who are the same race, sex, or religion, and no other group is allowed to use them. ❑ *racially segregated schools*

seg·re·ga·tion /ˌsegrɪˈgeɪʃən/ NOUN [U] **Segregation** is the official practice of keeping people apart, usually people of different sexes, races, or religions. ❑ *The Supreme Court unanimously ruled that racial segregation in schools was unconstitutional.*

seize ◆◇◇ /siːz/ VERB

VERB [T] (**seizes, seizing, seized**) **1** If you **seize** something, you take hold of it quickly, firmly, and forcefully. ❑ *'Leigh,' he said, seizing my arm to hold me back.* **2** When a group of people **seize** a place or **seize** control of it, they take control of it quickly and suddenly, using force. = take ❑ *Troops have seized the airport and railway terminals.* **3** If a government or other authority **seize** someone's property, they take it from them, often by force. ❑ *Police were reported to have seized all copies of this morning's edition of the newspaper.* **4** When someone **is seized**, they are arrested or captured. ❑ *UN officials say two military observers were seized by the Khmer Rouge yesterday.* **5** When you **seize** an opportunity, you take advantage of it and do something that you want to do. ❑ *During the riots hundreds of people seized the opportunity to steal property.*

PHRASAL VERBS **seize on** or **seize upon** If you **seize on** something or **seize upon** it, you show great interest in it, often because it is useful to you. ❑ *Newspapers seized on the results as proof that global warming wasn't really happening.* **seize up 1** If a part of your body **seizes up**, it suddenly stops working, because you have strained it or because you are getting old. ❑ *After two days' exertions, it's the arms and hands that seize up, not the legs.* **2** If something such as an engine **seizes up**, it stops working, because it has not been properly cared for. ❑ *She put diesel fuel, instead of petrol, into the tank causing the motor to seize up.*

✪ **sel·dom** /ˈseldəm/ ADV If something **seldom** happens,

it happens only occasionally. = rarely, hardly ever, infrequently ❑ *They seldom speak.* ❑ *I've seldom felt so happy.* ❑ *The fines were seldom sufficient to force any permanent change.*

✪ **se·lect** ◆◇◇ /sɪˈlekt/ VERB, ADJ (*academic word*)

VERB [T] (**selects, selecting, selected**) **1** If you **select** something, you choose it from a number of things of the same kind. = choose ❑ *Voters are selecting candidates for both US Senate seats and for 52 congressional seats.* ❑ *a randomly selected sample of school children* **2** (*computing*) If you **select** a file or a piece of text on a computer screen, you click on it so that it is marked in a different colour, usually in order for you to give the computer an instruction relating to that file or piece of text. ❑ *I selected a file and pressed the delete key.*

ADJ **1** [select + N] A **select** group is a small group of some of the best people or things of their kind. ❑ *a select group of French cheeses* **2** If you describe something as **select**, you mean it has many desirable features, but is available only to people who have a lot of money or who belong to a high social class. = exclusive ❑ *Christian Lacroix is throwing a very lavish and very select party.*

✪ **se·lec·tion** ◆◇◇ /sɪˈlekʃən/ NOUN [U, C] (**selections**) **1** [U] **Selection** is the act of selecting one or more people or things from a group. = choice ❑ *Darwin's principles of natural selection* ❑ *Dr Sullivan's selection to head the Department of Health was greeted with satisfaction.* **2** [C] A **selection of** people or things is a set of them that have been selected from a larger group. = sample ❑ *this selection of popular songs* ❑ *a random selection of 1,300 Canadian exporters* ❑ *selections from Dickens' A Christmas Carol* **3** [C] The **selection of** goods in a shop is the particular range of goods that it has available and from which you can choose what you want. = range ❑ *It offers the widest selection of antiques of every description in a one-day market.* **4** [C] (*computing*) In computing, a **selection** is an area of the screen that you have highlighted, for example because you want to copy it to another file.

se·lec·tive /sɪˈlektɪv/ ADJ **1** [selective + N] A **selective** process applies only to a few things or people. ❑ *Selective breeding may result in a greyhound running faster and seeing better than a wolf.* **2** When someone is **selective**, they choose things carefully, for example, the things that they buy or do. ❑ *Sales still happen, but buyers are more selective.* **3** If you say that someone has a **selective** memory, you disapprove of the fact that they remember certain facts about something and deliberately forget others, often because it is convenient for them to do so. ❑ *We seem to have a selective memory for the best bits of the past.*

se·lec·tive·ly /sɪˈlektɪvli/ ADV **1** *Within the project, trees are selectively cut on a 25-year rotation.* **2** [selectively with V] ❑ *people on small incomes who wanted to shop selectively* **3** [selectively with V] ❑ *a tendency to remember only the pleasurable effects of the drug and selectively forget all the adverse effects*

self ◆◇◇ /self/ NOUN [C] (**selves**) **1** Your **self** is your basic personality or nature, especially considered in terms of what you are really like as a person. ❑ *You're looking more like your usual self.* **2** A person's **self** is the essential part of their nature which makes them different from everyone and everything else. ❑ *I want to explore and get in touch with my inner self.* ❑ *The face is the true self visible to others.*

self-assured ADJ Someone who is **self-assured** shows confidence in what they say and do because they are sure of their own abilities. = self-confident ❑ *He's a self-assured, confident negotiator.*

WORD PARTS
The prefix **self-** often appears in words to show that something involves yourself or that you do something yourself:
self-assured (ADJ)
self-defence (NOUN)
self-confident (ADJ)

self-confident ADJ Someone who is **self-confident** behaves confidently because they feel sure of their abilities or value. = self-assured ❑ *She'd blossomed into a self-confident young woman.*

self-contained ADJ **1** You can describe someone or something as **self-contained** when they are complete and separate and do not need help or resources from outside. ❑ *He seems completely self-contained and he doesn't miss you when you're not there.* **2** **Self-contained** accommodation such as a flat has all its own facilities, so that a person living there does not have to share rooms such as a kitchen or bathroom with other people. ❑ *Her family lives in a self-contained three-bedroom suite in the back of the main house.*

self-control NOUN [U] **Self-control** is the ability to not show your feelings or not do the things that your feelings make you want to do. ❑ *His self-control, reserve and aloofness were almost inhuman.*

self-defence (in *AmE*, use **self-defense**) NOUN [U] **1** **Self-defence** is the use of force to protect yourself against someone who is attacking you. ❑ *The women acted in self-defence after years of abuse.* **2** **Self-defence** is the action of protecting yourself against something bad. ❑ *Tai Chi is an ancient form of self-defence.*

self-esteem NOUN [U] Your **self-esteem** is how you feel about yourself. For example, if you have low **self-esteem**, you do not like yourself, you do not think that you are a valuable person, and therefore you do not behave confidently. ❑ *Poor self-esteem is at the centre of many of the difficulties we experience in our relationships.*

self-explanatory ADJ Something that is **self-explanatory** is clear and easy to understand without needing any extra information or explanation. ❑ *I hope the graphs on the following pages are self-explanatory.*

self-indulgent ADJ If you say that someone is **self-indulgent**, you mean that they allow themselves to have or do the things that they enjoy very much. ❑ *Why give publicity to this self-indulgent, adolescent oaf?*

self-inflicted ADJ A **self-inflicted** wound or injury is one that you do to yourself deliberately. ❑ *He is being treated for a self-inflicted gunshot wound.*

self·ish /'selfɪʃ/ ADJ (disapproval) If you say that someone is **selfish**, you mean that he or she cares only about himself or herself, and not about other people. ❑ *I think I've been very selfish. I've been mainly concerned with myself.* **self·ish·ly** /'selfɪʃli/ ADV ❑ *Someone has selfishly emptied the biscuit tin.* **self·ish·ness** /'selfɪʃnəs/ NOUN [U] ❑ *The arrogance and selfishness of different interest groups never ceases to amaze me.*

self-sufficient ADJ **1** If a country or group is **self-sufficient**, it is able to produce or make everything that it needs. ❑ *This enabled the country to become self-sufficient in sugar.* **2** Someone who is **self-sufficient** is able to live happily without anyone else. ❑ *Although she had various boyfriends, Madeleine was, and remains, fiercely self-sufficient.*

✪ **sell** ♦♦♦ /sel/ VERB

⟦VERB⟧ [I, T] (**sells, selling, sold**) **1** [I, T] If you **sell** something that you own, you let someone have it in return for money. ≠ buy, purchase ❑ *Catlin sold the paintings to Philadelphia industrialist Joseph Harrison.* ❑ *The directors sold the business for $14.8 million.* ❑ *When is the best time to sell?* **2** [T] If a store **sells** a particular thing, it is available for people to buy there. ❑ *It sells everything from hair ribbons to oriental rugs.* ❑ *Bean sprouts are also sold in cans.* **3** [I] If something **sells for** a particular price, that price is paid for it. ❑ *Unmodernized property can sell for up to 40 per cent of its modernized market value.* **4** [I] If something **sells**, it is bought by the public, usually in fairly large quantities. ❑ *Even if this album doesn't sell and the critics don't like it, we wouldn't ever change.* **5** [I, T] Something that **sells** a product makes people want to buy the product. ❑ *It is only the sensational that sells news magazines.* ❑ *the maxim that safety doesn't sell* **6** [T] If you **sell** someone an idea or proposal, or **sell** someone **on** an idea, you convince them that it is a good idea. ❑ *She tried to sell me the idea of buying my own paper shredder.* ❑ *She is hoping she can sell the idea to clients.*

⟦PHRASES⟧ **sell one's body** If someone **sells** their **body**, they have sex for money. ❑ *85 percent said they would rather not sell their bodies for a living.*

sell one's soul (disapproval) If you talk about someone **selling** their **soul** in order to get something, you are criticizing them for abandoning their principles. ❑ *a man who would sell his soul for political viability*

⟦PHRASAL VERBS⟧ **sell off** If you **sell** something **off**, you sell it because you need the money. ❑ *The company is selling off some sites and concentrating on cutting debts.*

sell on If you buy something and then **sell** it **on**, you sell it to someone else soon after buying it, usually in order to make a profit. ❑ *Mr Farrier bought cars at auctions and sold them on.*

sell out **1** If a store **sells out** of something, it sells all its stocks of it, so that there is no longer any left for people to buy. ❑ *Hardware stores have sold out of water pumps and tarpaulins.* **2** If a performance, sports event, or other entertainment **sells out**, all the tickets for it are sold. ❑ *Football games often sell out well in advance.* **3** When things **sell out**, all of them that are available are sold. ❑ *Sleeping bags sold out almost immediately.* **4** (disapproval) If you accuse someone of **selling out**, you disapprove of the fact that they do something which used to be against their principles, or give in to an opposing group. ❑ *You don't have to sell out and work for some corporation.* **5** If you **sell out**, you sell everything you have, such as your house or your business, because you need the money. ❑ *I'll have a going out of business sale. I'll sell out and move out of here.*

sell·er /'selə/ NOUN [C] (**sellers**) **1** A **seller** of a type of thing is a person or company that sells that type of thing. ❑ *a flower seller* **2** In a business deal, the **seller** is the person who is selling something to someone else. = vendor ❑ *In theory, the buyer could ask the seller to have a test carried out.* **3** If you describe a product as, for example, a big **seller**, you mean that large numbers of it are being sold. ❑ *The gift shop's biggest seller is a photo of Nixon meeting Presley.*

selves /selvz/ IRREG FORM **Selves** is the plural of **self**.

se·mes·ter /sɪ'mestə/ NOUN [C] (**semesters**) In colleges and universities in some countries, a **semester** is one of the two main periods into which the year is divided. ❑ *February 22nd, when most of their students begin their spring semester*

semi-detached also **semidetached** (mainly BrE; in AmE, usually use **duplex**) ADJ, NOUN
⟦ADJ⟧ A **semi-detached** house is a house that is joined to another house on one side by a shared wall.
⟦NOUN⟧ [SING] A **semi-detached** is a house that is joined to another house on one side by a shared wall.

WORD PARTS
The prefix **semi-** often appears in words for people and things that are partly, but not completely, in a particular state: semi-detached (ADJ) semi-conscious (ADJ) semiskilled (ADJ)

semi-final NOUN [C, PL] (**semi-finals**) **1** [C] A **semi-final** is one of the two games or races in a competition that are held to decide who will compete in the final. ❑ *We want to go into the semi-final, no matter who the opponent is.* **2** [PL] The **semi-finals** is the round of a competition in which these two games or races are held. ❑ *Team USA reached the semi-finals by defeating New Zealand in the second round.*

✪ **semi·nal** /'semɪnəl/ ADJ (formal) **Seminal** is used to describe things such as books, works, events, and experiences that have a great influence in a particular field. = significant, ground-breaking, influential ❑ *author of the seminal book 'Animal Liberation'* ❑ *The reforms have been a seminal event in the history of the NHS.*

✪ **semi·nar** /'semɪnɑː/ NOUN [C] (**seminars**) **1** A **seminar** is a meeting where a group of people discuss a problem or topic. = meeting, tutorial, workshop ❑ *a series of half-day seminars to help businessmen get the best value from investing in information technology* ❑ *We conduct seminars on*

S

Immigration and Discrimination Law. **2** A **seminar** is a class at a college or university in which the teacher and a small group of students discuss a topic. □ *Students are asked to prepare material in advance of each weekly seminar.* □ *a seminar on a topic closely related to the course*

semi•skilled /'semi,skɪld/ ADJ (*business*) A **semiskilled** worker has some training and skills, but not enough to do specialized work.

sena•tor ◆◇◇ /'senɪtə/ NOUN [C] (**senators**) A **senator** is a member of a political Senate, for example, in the United States or Australia. □ *Texas' first black senator*

send ◆◆◆ /send/ VERB

  VERB [T] (**sends, sending, sent**) **1** When you **send** someone something, you arrange for it to be taken and delivered to them, for example, by post. □ *Myra Cunningham sent me a note thanking me for dinner.* □ *I sent a copy to the head teacher.* **2** If you **send** someone somewhere, you tell them to go there. □ *Inspector Banbury came up to see her, but she sent him away.* □ *the government's decision to send troops to the region* □ *I suggested that he rest, and sent him for an X-ray.* **3** If you **send** someone **to** an institution such as a school or a prison, you arrange for them to stay there for a period of time. □ *It's his parents' choice to send him to a boarding school, rather than a convenient day school.* **4** To **send** a signal means to cause it to go to a place by means of radio waves or electricity. □ *The transmitters will send a signal automatically to a local base station.* **5** If something **sends** things or people in a particular direction, it causes them to move in that direction. □ *The explosion sent shrapnel flying through the sides of cars on the crowded road.* □ *A left hook sent him reeling.* **6** To **send** someone or something **into** a particular state means to cause them to go into or be in that state. □ *My attempt to fix it sent Lawrence into fits of laughter.* □ *before civil war and famine sent the country plunging into anarchy*

  PHRASAL VERBS **send for** **1** If you **send for** someone, you send them a message asking them to come and see you. □ *I've sent for the doctor.* **2** If you **send for** something, or **send away for** it, or **send off for** it, you write and ask for it to be sent to you. □ *Send for your free catalogue today.* **send in** **1** If you **send in** something such as a competition entry or a letter applying for a job, you post it to the organization concerned. □ *Applicants are asked to send in a CV and a covering letter.* **2** When a government **sends in** troops or police officers, it orders them to deal with a crisis or problem somewhere. □ *He has asked the government to send in troops to end the fighting.* **send off** **1** When you **send off** a letter or parcel, you send it somewhere by post. □ *He sent off copies to various people for them to read and make comments.* **2** (*mainly BrE*; in *AmE*, use **eject**) If a football player is **sent off**, the referee makes them leave the field during a game, as a punishment for seriously breaking the rules. **send out** **1** If you **send out** things such as letters or bills, you send them to a large number of people at the same time. □ *She had sent out well over four hundred invitations that afternoon.* **2** To **send out** a signal, sound, light, or heat means to cause them to produce it. □ *The crew did not send out any distress signals.* **send out for** If you **send out for** food, for example, pizza or sandwiches, you phone and ask for it to be delivered to you. □ *Let's send out for a pizza.*

  ✦ **send someone packing** → see **pack**

send•er /'sendə/ NOUN [C] (**senders**) The **sender** of a letter, parcel, or radio message is the person who sent it. □ *The sender of the best letter every week will win a cheque for £25.*

❂ sen•ior ◆◆◇ /'siːnjə/ ADJ, NOUN

  ADJ **1** [senior + N] The **senior** people in an organization or profession have the highest and most important jobs. □ *senior officials in the Israeli government* □ *the company's senior management* □ *Television and radio needed many more women in senior jobs.* **2** If someone is **senior to** you in an organization or profession, they have a higher and more important job than you or they are considered to be superior to you because they have worked there for longer

and have more experience. □ *The position had to be filled by an officer senior to Haig.* **3** [senior + N] If you take part in a sport at **senior** level, you take part in competitions with adults and people who have reached a high degree of achievement in that sport. □ *This will be his fifth international championship and his third at senior level.*

  NOUN [PL, SING] (**seniors**) **1** [PL] Your **seniors** are the people who are senior to you in an organization or profession. □ *He was described by his seniors as a model officer.* **2** [SING] **Senior** is used when indicating how much older one person is than another. For example, if someone is ten years your **senior**, they are ten years older than you. □ *She became involved with a married man many years her senior.*

sen•sa•tion /sen'seɪʃən/ NOUN [C, U, SING] (**sensations**) **1** [C] A **sensation** is a physical feeling. = **feeling** □ *Floating can be a very pleasant sensation.* **2** [U] **Sensation** is your ability to feel things physically, especially through your sense of touch. = **feeling** □ *The pain was so bad that she lost all sensation.* **3** [C] You can use **sensation** to refer to the general feeling or impression caused by a particular experience. = **feeling** □ *It's a funny sensation to know someone's talking about you in a language you don't understand.* **4** [C] If a person, event, or situation is a **sensation**, it causes great excitement or interest. □ *the film that turned her into an overnight sensation* **5** [SING] If a person, event, or situation causes **a sensation**, they cause great excitement or excitement. □ *She was just 14 when she caused a sensation at the Montreal Olympics.*

sen•sa•tion•al /sen'seɪʃənəl/ ADJ **1** A **sensational** result, event, or situation is so remarkable that it causes great excitement and interest. = **dramatic** □ *The world champions suffered a sensational defeat.* **2** You can describe stories or reports as **sensational** if you disapprove of them because they present facts in a way that is intended to cause feelings of shock, anger, or excitement. □ *sensational tabloid newspaper reports* **3** You can describe something as **sensational** when you think that it is extremely good. = **amazing** □ *Her voice is sensational.*

sen•sa•tion•al•ly /sen'seɪʃənəli/ ADV **1** *The rape trial was sensationally halted yesterday.* **2** *sensationally good food*

❂ sense ◆◆◆ /sens/ NOUN, VERB

  NOUN [C, SING, U] (**senses**) **1** [C] Your **senses** are the physical abilities of sight, smell, hearing, touch, and taste. □ *She stared at him again, unable to believe the evidence of her senses.* □ *Sharks have a keen sense of smell.* **2** [SING] If you have a **sense that** something is the case, you think that it is the case, although you may not have firm, clear evidence for this belief. □ *Suddenly you got this sense that people were drawing themselves away from each other.* **3** [SING] If you have a **sense of** guilt or relief, for example, you feel guilty or relieved. = **feeling** □ *When your child is struggling for life, you feel this overwhelming sense of guilt.* **4** [SING] If you have a **sense of** something such as duty or justice, you are aware of it and believe it is important. □ *My sense of justice was offended.* **5** [SING] [sense 'of' N, also N + sense] Someone who has a **sense of** timing or style has a natural ability with regard to timing or style. You can also say that someone has a bad **sense of** timing or style. □ *He has an impeccable sense of timing.* □ *Her dress sense is appalling.* **6** [U] **Sense** is the ability to make good judgments and to behave sensibly. □ *when he was younger and had a bit more sense* □ *When that doesn't work they sometimes have the sense to seek help.* **7** [SING] If you say that there is no **sense** or little **sense** in doing something, you mean that it is not a sensible thing to do because nothing useful would be gained by doing it. = **point** □ *There's no sense in pretending this doesn't happen.* **8** [C] A **sense** of a word or expression is one of its possible meanings. = **meaning** □ *a noun which has two senses*

  PHRASES **come to one's senses** or **bring someone to their senses** If you say that someone **has come to** their **senses** or **has been brought to** their **senses**, you mean that they have stopped being foolish and are being sensible again. □ *Eventually the world will come to its senses and get rid of them.*

  in a sense **Sense** is used in several expressions to indicate how true your statement is. For example, if you say that something is true **in a sense**, you mean that it is partly true, or true in one way. If you say that something is true **in** a general **sense**, you mean that it is true in a general way. ❑ *In a sense, both were right.* ❑ *Though his background was modest, it was in no sense deprived.*

make sense 1 If something **makes sense**, you can understand it. ❑ *He was sitting there saying, 'Yes, the figures make sense.'* **2** If a course of action **makes sense**, it seems sensible. ❑ *It makes sense to look after yourself.* ❑ *The project should be re-appraised to see whether it made sound economic sense.*

make sense of something When you **make sense of** something, you succeed in understanding it. ❑ *Provided you didn't try to make sense of it, it sounded beautiful.*

talk sense If you say that someone **talks sense**, you mean that what they say is sensible. ❑ *When he speaks, he talks sense.*

have a sense that or **get a sense that** (*mainly spoken*) If you **have a sense that** something is true or **get a sense that** something is true, you think that it is true. ❑ *Do you have the sense that you are loved by the public?*

VERB [T] (**senses, sensing, sensed**) If you **sense** something, you become aware of it or you realize it, although it is not very obvious. ❑ *She probably sensed that I wasn't telling her the whole story.* ❑ *He looks about him, sensing danger.*
→ See also **common sense**

sense·less /ˈsensləs/ ADJ **1** If you describe an action as **senseless**, you think it is wrong because it has no purpose and produces no benefit. = pointless ❑ *people whose lives have been destroyed by acts of senseless violence* **2** If someone is **senseless**, they are unconscious. ❑ *They were knocked to the ground, beaten senseless, and robbed of their wallets.*

sen·si·ble ◆◇◇ /ˈsensɪbəl/ ADJ **1** Sensible actions or decisions are good because they are based on reasons rather than emotions. ❑ *It might be sensible to get a lawyer.* ❑ *The sensible thing is to leave them alone.* **2** Sensible people behave in a sensible way. ❑ *She was a sensible girl and did not panic.* ❑ *Oh come on, let's be sensible about this.* **3** Sensible shoes or clothes are practical and strong rather than fashionable and attractive. ❑ *Wear loose clothing and sensible footwear.*

WHICH WORD?
sensible or sensitive?

Do not confuse **sensible** and **sensitive**. A **sensible** person makes good decisions based on reason.
❑ *The website offers some sensible advice.*

A **sensitive** person is easily upset or affected by their emotions.
❑ *They are very sensitive so try not to be too critical.*

---

sen·si·bly /ˈsensɪbli/ ADV **1** *He sensibly decided to lie low for a while.* **2** *They were not sensibly dressed.*

sen·si·tive ◆◇◇ /ˈsensɪtɪv/ ADJ **1** [oft sensitive 'for' N] (*approval*) If you are **sensitive** to other people's needs, problems, or feelings, you show understanding and awareness of them. ❑ *The classroom teacher must be sensitive to a child's needs.* **2** If you are **sensitive about** something, you are easily worried and offended when people talk about it. ❑ *Young people are very sensitive about their appearance.* **3** [oft sensitive 'of' N] A **sensitive** subject or issue needs to be dealt with carefully because it is likely to cause disagreement or make people angry or upset. ❑ *Employment is a very sensitive issue.* **4** Sensitive documents or reports contain information that needs to be kept secret and dealt with carefully. ❑ *He instructed staff to shred sensitive documents.* **5** Something that is **sensitive to** a physical force, substance, or treatment is easily affected by it and often harmed by it. ❑ *a chemical which is sensitive to light* **6** A **sensitive** piece of scientific equipment is capable of measuring or recording very small changes. ❑ *an extremely sensitive microscope*

sen·si·tive·ly /ˈsensɪtɪvli/ ADV ❑ *The abuse of women needs to be treated seriously and sensitively.*

sen·si·tiv·ity /ˌsensɪˈtɪvɪti/ NOUN [U, c] **1** [U] ❑ *A good* relationship involves concern and sensitivity for each other's feelings. **2** [c, U] ❑ *people who suffer extreme sensitivity about what others think* **3** [U] ❑ *Due to the obvious sensitivity of the issue he would not divulge any details.* **4** [U] ❑ *the sensitivity of cells damaged by chemotherapy* **5** [U] ❑ *the sensitivity of the detector*

sent /sent/ IRREG FORM Sent is the past tense and past participle of **send**.

❂**sen·tence** ◆◆◇ /ˈsentəns/ NOUN, VERB
NOUN [c, U] (**sentences**) **1** [c] A **sentence** is a group of words which, when they are written down, begin with a capital letter and end with a full stop, question mark, or exclamation mark. Most sentences contain a subject and a verb. ❑ *Here we have several sentences incorrectly joined by commas.* **2** [c, U] In a law court, a **sentence** is the punishment that a person receives after they have been found guilty of a crime. = punishment ❑ *They are already serving prison sentences for their part in the assassination.* ❑ *He was given a four-year sentence.* ❑ *The court is expected to pass sentence later today.* ❑ *The offences carry a maximum sentence of 10 years.*
VERB [T] (**sentences, sentencing, sentenced**) When a judge **sentences** someone, he or she states in court what their punishment will be. = convict ❑ *A military court sentenced him to death in his absence.* ❑ *She was sentenced to nine years in prison.* ❑ *He has admitted the charge and will be sentenced later.*
→ See also **death sentence**

sen·ti·ment /ˈsentɪmənt/ NOUN [c, U] (**sentiments**) **1** [c, U] A **sentiment** that people have is an attitude which is based on their thoughts and feelings. = feeling ❑ *Public sentiment rapidly turned anti-American.* ❑ *He's found growing sentiment for military action.* **2** [c] A **sentiment** is an idea or feeling that someone expresses in words. ❑ *I must agree with the sentiments expressed by John Prescott.* **3** [U] Sentiment is feelings such as pity or love, especially for things in the past, and may be considered exaggerated and foolish. ❑ *Laura kept that letter out of sentiment.*

sen·ti·men·tal /ˌsentɪˈmentəl/ ADJ **1** Someone or something that is **sentimental** feels or shows pity or love, sometimes to an extent that is considered exaggerated and foolish. ❑ *I'm trying not to be sentimental about the past.* **2** Sentimental means relating to or involving feelings such as pity or love, especially for things in the past. ❑ *Our paintings and photographs are of sentimental value only.*

sen·ti·men·tal·ly /ˌsentɪˈmentəli/ ADV ❑ *Childhood had less freedom and joy than we sentimentally attribute to it.*

sen·ti·men·tal·ity /ˌsentɪmenˈtælɪti/ NOUN [U] ❑ *In this book there is no sentimentality.*

❂**sepa·rate** ◆◆◇ ADJ, VERB, NOUN
ADJ /ˈsepərət/ **1** If one thing is **separate from** another, there is a barrier, space, or division between them, so that they are clearly two things. ❑ *They are now making plans to form their own separate party.* ❑ *Business bank accounts were kept separate from personal ones.* **2** If you refer to **separate** things, you mean several different things, rather than just one thing. = different, distinct, discrete ❑ *Use separate chopping boards for raw meats, cooked meats, vegetables and salads.* ❑ *Men and women have separate exercise rooms.*
PHRASE **go their separate ways** When two or more people who have been together for some time **go their separate ways**, they go to different places or end their relationship. ❑ *Sue was 27 when she and her husband decided to go their separate ways.*
VERB /ˈsepəreɪt/ [RECIP, T, I] (**separates, separating, separated**) **1** [RECIP] If you **separate** people or things that are together, or if they **separate**, they move apart. = disconnect, sever, split; ≠ join, connect ❑ *Police moved in to separate the two groups.* ❑ *The pans were held in both hands and swirled around to separate gold particles from the dirt.* ❑ *The front end of the car separated from the rest of the vehicle.* **2** [RECIP] If you **separate** people or things that have been connected, or if one **separates from** another, the connection between them is ended. ❑ *They want to separate teaching from research.* ❑ *It's very possible that we may see a movement to separate the two parts of the country.* **3** [RECIP] If a couple who are married or living together

S

separate, they decide to live apart. ❑ *Her parents separated when she was very young.* **4** [T] An object, obstacle, distance, or period of time which **separates** two people, groups, or things exists between them. ❑ *the white-railed fence that separated the yard from the paddock* ❑ *They had undoubtedly made progress in the six years that separated the two periods.* **5** [T] If you **separate** one idea or fact **from** another, you clearly see or show the difference between them. = distinguish ❑ *It is difficult to separate legend from truth.* ❑ *learning how to separate real problems from imaginary illnesses* **6** [T] A quality or factor that **separates** one thing **from** another is the reason why the two things are different from each other. = distinguish ❑ *The single most important factor that separates ordinary photographs from good photographs is the lighting.* **7** [T] If a particular number of points **separate** two teams or competitors, one of them is winning or has won by that number of points. ❑ *In the end only three points separated the two teams.* **8** [I, T] If you **separate** a group of people or things **into** smaller elements, or if a group **separates**, it is divided into smaller elements. = split ❑ *The police wanted to separate them into smaller groups.* ❑ *Let's separate into smaller groups.*

PHRASAL VERB **separate out** **1** Separate out means the same as **separate** VERB **5**. ❑ *How can one ever separate out the act from the attitudes that surround it?* **2** Separate out means the same as **separate** VERB **8**. ❑ *If prepared many hours ahead, the mixture may separate out.* **3** If you **separate out** something from the other things it is with, you take it out. ❑ *The ability to separate out reusable elements from other waste is crucial.*

NOUN /ˈsepərəts/ [PL] (**separates**) **Separates** are clothes such as skirts, trousers, and shirts which cover just the top half or the bottom half of your body. ❑ *She wears coordinated separates instead of a suit.*

→ See also **separated**

VOCABULARY BUILDER

separate ADJ

If you refer to **separate** things, you mean several different things, rather than just one thing.

❑ *Since they could not agree, they wrote four separate reports.*

different ADJ

If two people or things are **different**, they are not like each other in one or more ways.

❑ *London was different from most European capitals.*

discrete ADJ

Discrete ideas or things are separate and distinct from each other.

❑ *The instruction manual breaks down the job into scores of discrete steps.*

distinct ADJ (*formal*)

If something is **distinct** from something else of the same type, it is different from it in an important way.

❑ *This book is divided into two distinct parts.*

---

sepa·rat·ed /ˈsepəreɪtɪd/ ADJ **1** [V-LINK + separated] Someone who is **separated** from their wife or husband lives apart from them, but is not divorced. ❑ *Most single parents are either divorced or separated.* **2** If you are **separated** from someone, for example, your family, you are not able to be with them. ❑ *The idea of being separated from him, even for a few hours, was torture.*

❍ **sepa·rate·ly** /ˈsepərətli/ ADV If people or things are dealt with **separately** or do something **separately**, they are dealt with or do something at different times or places, rather than together. = distinctly ❑ *Cook each vegetable separately until just tender.* ❑ *The software is sold separately.* ❑ *Acid fruits are best eaten separately from sweet fruits.*

❍ **sepa·ra·tion** /ˌsepəˈreɪʃən/ NOUN [C, U] (**separations**) **1** [oft separation 'of/from/between' N] The **separation of** two or more things or groups is the fact that they are separate or become separate, and are not linked. = disconnection, split, division; ≠ connection, link

❑ *He believes in the separation of the races.* ❑ *Early spatial separations of groups of humans facilitated the development of physical variations.* ❑ *a 'Christian republic' in which there was a clear separation between church and state* **2** During a **separation**, people who usually live together are not together. ❑ *She wondered if Harry had been unfaithful to her during this long separation.* **3** If a couple who are married or living together have a **separation**, they decide to live apart. ❑ *They agreed to a trial separation.*

sepa·ra·tist /ˈsepərətɪst/ ADJ, NOUN

ADJ [separatist + N] **Separatist** organizations and activities within a country involve members of a group of people who want to establish their own separate government or are trying to do so. ❑ *Spanish police say they have arrested ten people suspected of being members of the Basque separatist movement.*

NOUN [C] (**separatists**) **Separatists** are people who want their own separate government or are involved in separatist activities. ❑ *The army has come under attack by separatists.*

❍ **se·quence** /ˈsiːkwəns/ NOUN [C] (**sequences**) (*academic word*) **1** A **sequence** of events or things is a number of events or things that come one after another in a particular order. = series ❑ *the sequence of events which led to the murder* ❑ *A flow chart displays the chronological sequence of steps in a process.* **2** A particular **sequence** is a particular order in which things happen or are arranged. ❑ *the colour sequence yellow, orange, purple, blue, green and white* ❑ *a simple numerical sequence*

❍ **se·quen·tial** /sɪˈkwenʃəl/ ADJ [usu sequential + N] (*formal*) Something that is **sequential** follows a fixed order. = consecutive, in order ❑ *the sequential story of the universe* ❑ *In this way the children are introduced to sequential learning.* **se·quen·tial·ly** /sɪˈkwenʃəli/ ADV ❑ *The pages are numbered sequentially.*

se·rene /sɪˈriːn/ ADJ Someone or something that is **serene** is calm and quiet. ❑ *She looked as calm and serene as she always did.* ❑ *He didn't speak much, he just smiled with that serene smile of his.* **se·rene·ly** /sɪˈriːnli/ ADV ❑ *We sailed serenely down the river.* ❑ *She carried on serenely sipping her gin and tonic.* **se·ren·ity** /sɪˈrenɪti/ NOUN [U] ❑ *I had a wonderful feeling of peace and serenity when I saw my husband.*

ser·geant /ˈsɑːdʒənt/ NOUN [C] (**sergeants**) **1** A **sergeant** is a non-commissioned officer of middle rank in the army, marines, or air force. ❑ *A sergeant with a detail of four men came into view.* **2** A **sergeant** is an officer with the rank immediately below a captain. ❑ *A police sergeant patrolling the area spotted flames at the store.*

se·rial /ˈsɪəriəl/ NOUN, ADJ

NOUN [C] (**serials**) A **serial** is a story which is broadcast on television or radio or is published in a magazine or newspaper in a number of parts over a period of time. ❑ *one of television's most popular serials*

ADJ [serial + N] **Serial** killings or attacks are a series of killings or attacks committed by the same person. This person is known as a **serial** killer or attacker. ❑ *serial murders*

❍ **se·ries** ♦♦◇ /ˈsɪəriːz/ NOUN [C] (**series**) (*academic word*) **1** A **series** of things or events is a number of them that come one after the other. = succession ❑ *a series of meetings with students and political leaders* ❑ *a series of explosions* **2** A radio or television **series** is a set of programmes of a particular kind which have the same title. ❑ *Captain Kirk's chair from the TV series 'Star Trek'*

❍ **se·ri·ous** ♦♦♦ /ˈsɪəriəs/ ADJ **1** **Serious** problems or situations are very bad and cause people to be worried or afraid. ❑ *Crime is an increasingly serious problem in Russian society.* ❑ *The government still faces very serious difficulties.* ❑ *Doctors said his condition was serious but stable.* **2** **Serious** matters are important and deserve careful and thoughtful consideration. ❑ *I regard this as a serious matter.* ❑ *Don't laugh boy. This is serious.* **3** When important matters are dealt with in a **serious** way, they are given careful and thoughtful consideration. ❑ *My parents never really faced up to my drug use in any serious way.* ❑ *It was a question which deserved serious consideration.* **4** [serious + N] **Serious** music

S

or literature requires concentration to understand or appreciate it. ❑ *serious classical music* **5** If someone is **serious about** something, they are sincere about what they are saying, doing, or intending to do. ❑ *You really are serious about this, aren't you?* **6 Serious** people are thoughtful and quiet, and do not laugh very often. ❑ *He's quite a serious person.*

se‧ri‧ous‧ness /'sɪəriəsnəs/ NOUN [U] **1** [oft seriousness 'of' N] ❑ *the seriousness of the crisis* **2** In all seriousness, there is nothing else I can do.

◆ **se‧ri‧ous‧ly** ◆◇◇ /'sɪəriəsli/ ADV, CONVENTION

  ADV   **1** [seriously with CL] You use **seriously** to indicate that you are not joking and that you really mean what you say. ❑ *Seriously, I only smoke in the evenings.* **2** If something affects you **seriously**, the situation is very bad and causes you to be worried or afraid. ❑ *If this ban was to come in it would seriously damage my business.* ❑ *They are not thought to be seriously hurt.* **3** [seriously with V] If you treat something **seriously**, you think it is important and give it careful consideration. ❑ *The management will have to think seriously about their positions.* **4** You can use **seriously** to indicate that you are sincere about what you are saying, doing, or intending to do. ❑ *Are you seriously jealous of Erica?* **5** [seriously with V] If someone behaves **seriously**, they are thoughtful and quiet, and do not laugh very often. ❑ *They spoke to me very seriously but politely.*

  CONVENTION   (spoken, feelings) You say '**seriously**' when you are surprised by what someone has said, as a way of asking them if they really mean it. ❑ *'I tried to chat him up in the supermarket.' He laughed. 'Seriously?'*

  PHRASE   **take seriously** If you **take** someone or something **seriously**, you believe that they are important and deserve attention. ❑ *It's hard to take them seriously in their pretty grey uniforms.*

serv‧ant ◆◇◇ /'sɜːvənt/ NOUN [C] (**servants**) **1** A servant is someone who is employed to work at another person's home, for example, as a cleaner or a gardener. ❑ *a large Victorian family with several servants* **2** You can use **servant** to refer to someone or something that provides a service for people or can be used by them. ❑ *Like any other public servants, police must respond to public demand.*
→ See also **civil servant**

serve ◆◆◇ /sɜːv/ VERB, NOUN

  VERB   [T, I] (**serves, serving, served**) **1** [T] If you **serve** your country, an organization, or a person, you do useful work for them. ❑ *It is unfair to soldiers who have served their country well for many years.* **2** [I] If you **serve** in a particular place or as a particular official, you perform official duties, especially in the armed forces, as a civil servant, or as a politician. ❑ *During the second world war he served with 92nd Airborne.* ❑ *They have both served on the school board.* **3** [I, T] If something **serves as** a particular thing or **serves** a particular purpose, it performs a particular function, which is often not its intended function. ❑ *She ushered me into the front room, which served as her office.* ❑ *I really do not think that an inquiry would serve any useful purpose.* **4** [T] If something **serves** people or an area, it provides them with something that they need. ❑ *This could mean the closure of thousands of small businesses which serve the community.* ❑ *improvements in the public water-supply system serving the Nairobi area* **5** [T] Something that **serves** someone's interests benefits them. ❑ *The economy should be organized to serve the interests of all the people.* **6** [I, T] When you **serve** food and drinks, you give people food and drinks. ❑ *Serve it with French bread.* ❑ *Serve the cakes warm.* ❑ *Refrigerate until ready to serve.* **7** [T] **Serve** is used to indicate how much food a recipe produces. For example, a recipe that **serves** six provides enough food for six people. ❑ *Garnish with fresh herbs. Serves 4.* **8** [I, T] Someone who **serves** customers in a shop or a bar helps them and provides them with what they want to buy. ❑ *They wouldn't serve me in any bars because I looked too young.* **9** [T] (legal) When the police or other officials **serve** someone **with** a legal order or **serve** an order **on** them, they give or send the legal order to them. ❑ *Immigration officers tried to serve her with a deportation order.* **10** [T] If you **serve** something such as a prison sentence or an

apprenticeship, you spend a period of time doing it. ❑ *Leo, who is currently serving a life sentence for murder* **11** [I, T] When you **serve** in games such as tennis and badminton, you throw up the ball or shuttlecock and hit it to start play. ❑ *He served 17 double faults.*

  PHRASE   **it serves you right** (feelings) If you say **it serves** someone **right** when something unpleasant happens to them, you mean that it is their own fault and you have no sympathy for them. ❑ *Serves her right for being so stubborn.*

  PHRASAL VERB   **Serve up** means the same as **serve** VERB **6.** ❑ *After all, it is no use serving up TV dinners if the kids won't eat them.*

  NOUN   [C] (**serves**) **1** A **serve** in games such as tennis and badminton is the act of throwing up the ball or shuttlecock and hitting it to start play. ❑ *His second serve clipped the net.* **2** When you describe someone's **serve**, you are indicating how well or how fast they serve a ball or shuttlecock. ❑ *His powerful serve was too much for the defending champion.*
→ See also **serving**

◆ **ser‧vice** ◆◆◆ /'sɜːvɪs/ NOUN, ADJ, VERB

  NOUN   [C, PL, U] (**services**) **1** [C] A **service** is something that the public needs, such as transport, communications facilities, hospitals, or energy supplies, which is provided in a planned and organized way by the government or an official body. ❑ *The postal service has been trying to cut costs.* ❑ *We have started a campaign for better nursery and school services.* ❑ *The authorities have said they will attempt to maintain essential services.* **2** [C] You can sometimes refer to an organization or private company as a particular **service** when it provides something for the public or acts on behalf of the government. ❑ *The Agriculture Department has ultimate control over the Forest Service.* **3** [C] If an organization or company provides a particular **service**, they can do a particular job or a type of work for you. ❑ *The kitchen maintains a twenty-four hour service and can be contacted via reception.* ❑ *The larger firm was capable of providing a better range of services.* **4** [PL] **Services** are activities such as tourism, banking, and selling things which are part of a country's economy, but are not concerned with producing or manufacturing goods. ❑ *Mining rose by 9.1%, manufacturing by 9.4% and services by 4.3%.* ❑ *the doctrine that a highly developed service sector was the sign of a modern economy* **5** [U] The level or standard of **service** provided by an organization or company is the amount or quality of the work it can do for you. ❑ *Taking risks is the only way employees can provide effective and efficient customer service.* **6** [C] A bus or train **service** is a route or regular trip that is part of a transport system. ❑ *The local bus service is well run and extensive.* **7** [PL] Your **services** are the things that you do or the skills that you use in your job, which other people find useful and are usually willing to pay you for. ❑ *I have obtained the services of a top photographer to take our pictures.* **8** [U] [also services, oft service 'to' N] If you refer to someone's **service** or **services to** a particular organization or activity, you mean that they have done a lot of work for it or spent a lot of their time on it. ❑ *You've given a lifetime of service to athletics.* ❑ *Most employees had long service with the company and were familiar with our products.* **9** [C] **The Services** are the army, the navy, the air force and the marines. ❑ *Some of the money could be spent on persuading key specialists to stay in the Services.* **10** [U] **Service** is the work done by people or equipment in the army, navy, or air force, for example, during a war. ❑ *Units are being called up today for service in the Gulf.* **11** [U] When you receive **service** in a restaurant, hotel, or store, an employee asks you what you want or gives you what you have ordered. ❑ *Service was attentive and the meal proceeded at a leisurely pace.* **12** [C] [also no DET] A **service** is a religious ceremony that takes place in a church or synagogue. ❑ *After the hour-long service, his body was taken to a cemetery in the south of the city.* **13** [C] [also no DET] If a vehicle or machine has a **service**, it is examined, adjusted, and cleaned so that it will keep working efficiently and safely. ❑ *The car needs a service.* **14** [C] A **dinner service** or a **tea service** is a complete set of plates, cups, saucers, and other pieces of china. ❑ *a 60-piece dinner service* **15** [C] In tennis, badminton, and some other

S

sports, when it is your **service**, it is your turn to serve. ❑ *She conceded just three points on her service during the first set.*

PHRASES **do someone a service** If you **do** someone **a service**, you do something that helps or benefits them. ❑ *You are doing me a great service, and I'm very grateful to you.* **in service** or **out of service** If a piece of equipment or type of vehicle is **in service**, it is being used or is able to be used. If it is **out of service**, it is not being used, usually because it is not working properly. ❑ *Cuts in funding have meant that equipment has been kept in service long after it should have been replaced.* ❑ *In 1882, the city's first electric tram cars went into service.*

ADJ [service + N] **Service** is used to describe the parts of a building or structure that are used by the staff who clean, repair, or take care of it, and are not usually used by the public. ❑ *I went out through the kitchen and down the service lift.*

VERB [T] (**services, servicing, serviced**) **1** If you have a vehicle or machine **serviced**, you arrange for someone to examine, adjust, and clean it so that it will keep working efficiently and safely. ❑ *I had my car serviced at the local garage.* **2** If someone or something **services** an organization, a project, or a group of people, they provide it with the things that it needs in order to function properly or effectively. ❑ *There are now 400 staff at headquarters, servicing our regional and overseas work.*
→ See also **civil service, emergency services**

ser·vice·man /'sɜːvɪsmən/ NOUN [c] (**servicemen**) A **serviceman** is a man who is in the army, navy, air force, or marines. ❑ *He was an American serviceman based in Vietnam during the war.*

serv·ing /'sɜːvɪŋ/ NOUN, ADJ
NOUN [c] (**servings**) A **serving** is an amount of food that is given to one person at a meal. ❑ *Quantities will vary according to how many servings of soup you want to prepare.*
ADJ [serving + N] A **serving** spoon or dish is used for giving out food at a meal. ❑ *Pile the potatoes into a warm serving dish.*

ses·sion ♦♦◇ /'seʃən/ NOUN [c] (**sessions**) **1** [also 'in' session] A **session** is a meeting of a court, legislature, or other official group. ❑ *After two late night sessions, the Security Council has failed to reach agreement.* ❑ *The Arab League is meeting in emergency session today.* **2** [also 'in' session] A **session** is a period during which the meetings of a court, legislature, or other official group are regularly held. ❑ *From September until December, Congress remained in session.* **3** A **session** of a particular activity is a period of that activity. ❑ *The two leaders emerged for a photo session.*

set ♦♦♦ /set/ NOUN, VERB, ADJ
NOUN [c] (**sets**) **1** A **set** of things is a number of things that belong together or that are thought of as a group. ❑ *There must be one set of laws for the whole of the country.* ❑ *The mattress and base are normally bought as a set.* ❑ *a chess set* **2** In tennis, a **set** is one of the groups of six or more games that form part of a match. ❑ *Graf was leading 5–1 in the first set.* **3** In mathematics, a **set** is a group of mathematical quantities that have some characteristic in common. ❑ *the field of set theory* **4** [also 'on/off' set] The **set** for a play, film, or television programme is the furniture and scenery that is on the stage when the play is being performed or in the studio where filming takes place. ❑ *From the first moment he got on the set, he wanted to be a director too.* ❑ *He achieved fame for his stage sets for the Folies Bergeres.* **5** A **set** is an appliance that receives television or radio signals. For example, a television set is a television. ❑ *Children spend so much time in front of the television set.*
VERB [T, I] (**sets, setting, set**) **1** [T] If you **set** something somewhere, you put it there, especially in a careful or deliberate way. = put, place ❑ *She took the case out of her hand and set it on the floor.* **2** [T] You can use **set** to say that a person or thing causes another person or thing to be in a particular condition or situation. For example, to **set** someone free means to cause them to be free, and to **set** something going means to cause it to start working. **3** [T] When you **set** a clock or control, you adjust it to a

particular point or level. ❑ *Set the volume as high as possible.* **4** [T] If you **set** a date, price, goal, or level, you decide what it will be. ❑ *The conference chairman has set a deadline of noon tomorrow.* ❑ *A date will be set for a future meeting.* **5** [T] If you **set** a certain value **on** something, you think it has that value. ❑ *She sets a high value on autonomy.* **6** [T] If you **set** something such as a record, an example, or a precedent, you do something that people will want to copy or try to achieve. ❑ *Legal experts said her case would not set a precedent because it was an out-of-court settlement.* **7** [T] If someone **sets** you a task or aim or if you **set** yourself a task or aim, you need to succeed in doing it. ❑ *I have to plan my academic work very rigidly and set myself clear objectives.* **8** [I] When something such as jelly, melted plastic, or cement **sets**, it becomes firm or hard. ❑ *You can add ingredients to these desserts as they begin to set.* **9** [I] When the sun **sets**, it goes below the horizon. ❑ *They watched the sun set behind the distant dales.* **10** [T] To **set** a trap means to prepare it to catch someone or something. ❑ *He seemed to think I was setting some sort of trap for him.* **11** [T] When someone **sets** the table, they prepare it for a meal by putting plates and cutlery on it. = lay ❑ *One would shop and cook, another would set the table and another would wash up.* **12** [T] If someone **sets** a poem or a piece of writing to music, they write music for the words to be sung to. ❑ *He has attracted much interest by setting ancient religious texts to music.*

PHRASE **set the scene** or **set the stage** If someone **sets the scene** or **sets the stage for** an event to take place, they make preparations so that it can take place. ❑ *The Democratic convention has set the scene for a ferocious election campaign this autumn.*

PHRASAL VERBS **set aside** **1** If you **set** something **aside for** a special use or purpose, you keep it available for that use or purpose. = put aside ❑ *Some doctors advise setting aside a certain hour each day for worry.* **2** If you **set aside** a belief, principle, or feeling, you decide that you will not be influenced by it. = put aside ❑ *He urged the participants to set aside minor differences for the sake of achieving peace.*
set back **1** If something **sets** you **back** or **sets back** a project or plan, it causes a delay. ❑ *It has set us back in so many respects that I'm not sure how long it will take for us to catch up.* **2** (informal) If something **sets** you **back** a certain amount of money, it costs you that much money. ❑ *A bottle of imported beer will set you back $7.* **3** → See also **setback**
set down **1** If a committee or organization **sets down** rules for doing something, it decides what they should be and officially records them. = lay down ❑ *I like to make suggestions rather than setting down laws and forcing people to follow them.* **2** If you **set down** your thoughts or experiences, you write them all down. = write down ❑ *Old Walter is setting down his memories of village life.*
set in If something unpleasant **sets in**, it begins and seems likely to continue or develop. ❑ *Winter is setting in and the population is facing food and fuel shortages.*
set off **1** When you **set off**, you start a journey. = set out ❑ *Nichols set off for his remote farmhouse in Connecticut.* ❑ *The president's envoy set off on another diplomatic trip.* **2** If something **sets off** something such as an alarm or a bomb, it makes it start working so that, for example, the alarm rings or the bomb explodes. ❑ *Any escape, once it's detected, sets off the alarm.* ❑ *Someone set off a fire extinguisher.* **3** If something **sets off** an event or a series of events, it causes it to start happening. ❑ *The arrival of the charity van set off a minor riot as villagers scrambled for a share of the aid.*
set out **1** When you **set out**, you start a journey. = set off ❑ *When setting out on a long walk, always wear suitable boots.* **2** If you **set out to** do something, you start trying to do it. ❑ *He has achieved what he set out to do three years ago.* **3** If you **set things out**, you arrange or display them somewhere. = arrange ❑ *Set out the cakes attractively, using lacy doilies.* **4** If you **set out** a number of facts, beliefs, or arguments, you explain them in writing or speech in a clear, organized way. ❑ *He has written a letter to The Times setting out his views.*
set up **1** If you **set** something **up**, you create or arrange it. ❑ *The two sides agreed to set up a commission to investigate*

S

claims. ❏ *an organization which sets up meetings about issues of interest to women* **2** If you **set up** a temporary structure, you place it or build it somewhere. ❏ *They took to the streets, setting up roadblocks of burning tyres.* **3** If you **set up** a device or piece of machinery, you do the things that are necessary for it to be able to start working. ❏ *Setting up the camera can be tricky.* **4** If you **set up** somewhere or **set yourself up** somewhere, you establish yourself in a new business or new area. ❏ *The mayor's plan offers incentives to firms setting up in lower Manhattan.* ❏ *He worked as a dance instructor in London before setting himself up in Bucharest.* ❏ *Grandfather set them up in a printing business.* **5** If you **set up** house or home or **set up** shop, you buy a house or business of your own and start living or working there. ❏ *They married, and set up home in Atlanta.* **6** (*informal*) If you **are set up** by someone, they make it seem that you have done something wrong when you have not. ❏ *He claimed yesterday that he had been set up after drugs were discovered at his home.* **7** → See also **setup**

[ADJ] **1** [V-LINK + set + PREP/ADV] If something is **set** in a particular place or position, it is in that place or position. = situated ❏ *The castle is set in 25 acres of beautiful grounds.* **2** [V-LINK + set + PREP/ADV] If something is **set into** a surface, it is fixed there and does not stick out. ❏ *The man unlocked a gate set in a high wall and let me through.* **3** You use **set** to describe something which is fixed and cannot be changed. ❏ *A set period of fasting is supposed to bring us closer to godliness.* **4** [set + N] (*BrE*; in *AmE*, use **required**) A **set** book must be studied by students taking a particular course. **5** [V-LINK + set + PREP/ADV] If a play, film, or story is **set** in a particular place or period of time, the events in it take place in that place or period. ❏ *The play is set in a small Midwestern town.* **6** [V-LINK + set + to-INF] If you are **set to** do something, you are ready to do it or are likely to do it. If something is **set to** happen, it is about to happen or likely to happen. ❏ *Roberto Baggio was set to become one of the greatest players of all time.* **7** [V-LINK + set + 'on/against' N/-ING] If you are **set on** something, you are strongly determined to do or have it. If you are **set against** something, you are strongly determined not to do or have it. ❏ *She was set on going to an all-girls school.*
→ See also **setting**
✦ **set fire to something** → see **fire**; **set foot somewhere** → see **foot**; **set your heart on something** → see **heart**; **set sail** → see **sail**; **set to work** → see **work**

✪ **set·back** /ˈsetbæk/ NOUN [C] (**setbacks**) [oft setback 'for/in/to' N] A **setback** is an event that delays your progress or reverses some of the progress that you have made. = upset, difficulty, hindrance ❏ *The move represents a setback for the Middle East peace process.* ❏ *He has suffered a serious setback in his political career.* ❏ *The incident dealt a serious setback to reconciliation efforts.*

set·ting /ˈsetɪŋ/ NOUN [C] (**settings**) **1** A particular **setting** is a particular place or type of surroundings where something is or takes place. ❏ *Rome is the perfect setting for romance.* **2** A **setting** is one of the positions to which the controls of a device such as a cooker or heater can be adjusted. ❏ *You can boil the fish fillets on a high setting.*

set·tle ♦♦◇ /ˈsetəl/ VERB
[VERB] [T, I] (**settles, settling, settled**) **1** [T] If people **settle** an argument or problem, or if something **settles** it, they solve it, for example, by making a decision about who is right or about what to do. ❏ *They agreed to try to settle their dispute by negotiation.* **2** [I, T] If people **settle** a legal dispute or if they **settle**, they agree to end the dispute without going to a court of law, for example, by paying some money or by apologizing. ❏ *In an attempt to settle the case, Molken has agreed to pay restitution.* ❏ *She got much less than she would have done if she had settled out of court.* **3** [I, T] If you **settle** a bill or debt, you pay the amount that you owe. ❏ *I settled the bill for my coffee and his two glasses of wine.* ❏ *She has now settled with her landlord.* **4** [T] If something **is settled**, it has all been decided and arranged. ❏ *As far as we're concerned, the matter is settled.* **5** [I, T] When people **settle** a place or in a place, or when a government **settles** them there, they start living there permanently. ❏ *Refugees settling in a new country suffer from*

a number of problems. ❏ *He visited Paris and eventually settled there.* **6** [I, T] If you **settle yourself** somewhere or **settle** somewhere, you sit down or make yourself comfortable. ❏ *Albert settled himself on the sofa.* **7** [I, T] If something **settles** or if you **settle** it, it sinks slowly down and becomes still. ❏ *A black dust settled on the walls.* ❏ *Once its impurities had settled, the oil could be graded.* **8** [I] If your eyes **settle on** or **upon** something, you stop looking around and look at that thing for some time. = rest ❏ *The man let his eyes settle upon Blume's face.* **9** [I] When birds or insects **settle on** something, they land on it from above. = light ❏ *Moths flew in front of it, eventually settling on the rough painted metal.*

[PHRASAL VERBS] **settle down 1** When someone **settles down**, they start living a quiet life in one place, especially when they get married or buy a house. ❏ *One day I'll want to settle down and have a family.* **2** If a situation or a person that has been going through a lot of problems or changes **settles down**, they become calm. ❏ *It'd be fun, after the situation in Europe settles down, to take a trip to France.* **3** If you **settle down to** do something or **to** something, you prepare to do it and concentrate on it. ❏ *He got his coffee, came back and settled down to listen.* **4** If you **settle down** for the night, you get ready to lie down and sleep. ❏ *They put up their tents and settled down for the night.*
settle for If you **settle for** something, you choose or accept it, especially when it is not what you really want but there is nothing else available. ❏ *Virginia was a perfectionist. She was just not prepared to settle for anything mediocre.*
settle in If you **settle in**, you become used to living in a new place, doing a new job, or going to a new school. ❏ *I enjoyed school enormously once I'd settled in.*
settle on If you **settle on** a particular thing, you choose it after considering other possible choices. = decide on ❏ *I finally settled on a Mercedes. It's the ideal car for me.*
settle up When you **settle up**, you pay a bill or a debt. ❏ *I'll have to settle up what I owe for the phone.*
→ See also **settled**
✦ **when the dust settles** → see **dust**; **settle a score** → see **score**

set·tled /ˈsetəld/ ADJ **1** If you have a **settled** way of life, you stay in one place, in one job, or with one person, rather than moving around or changing. ❏ *He decided to lead a more settled life with his partner.* **2** A **settled** situation or system stays the same all the time. ❏ *There has been a period of settled weather.*

set·tle·ment ♦♦◇ /ˈsetəlmənt/ NOUN [C, U] (**settlements**) **1** [C] A **settlement** is an official agreement between two sides who were involved in a conflict or argument. ❏ *Our objective must be to secure a peace settlement.* **2** [C] A **settlement** is an agreement to end a disagreement or dispute without going to a court of law, for example, by offering someone money. ❏ *She accepted an out-of-court settlement of $40,000.* **3** [U] The **settlement** of a debt is the act of paying back money that you owe. ❏ *ways to delay the settlement of debts* **4** [C] A **settlement** is a place where people have come to live and have built homes. ❏ *The village is a settlement of just fifty houses.*

set·tler /ˈsetlə/ NOUN [C] (**settlers**) Settlers are people who go to live in a new country. ❏ *The first German village in southwestern Siberia was founded a century ago by settlers from the Volga region.*

set·up ♦♦◇ /ˈsetˌʌp/ also **set-up** NOUN [C, SING] (**setups**) **1** [C] (*informal*) A particular **setup** is a particular system or way of organizing something. ❏ *It appears to be an idyllic domestic setup.* **2** [C] (*informal*) If you describe a situation as a **setup**, you mean that people have planned it in order to deceive you or to make it look as if you have done something wrong. ❏ *He was asked to pick somebody up and bring them to a party, not realizing it was a setup.* **3** [SING] (*computing*) The **setup** of computer hardware or software is the process of installing it and making it ready to use. ❏ *The worst part of the setup is the poor instruction manual.*

sev·en ♦♦♦ /ˈsevən/ NUM (**sevens**) Seven is the number 7. ❏ *Sarah and Ella have been friends for seven years.*

sev·en·teen ♦♦♦ /ˌsevənˈtiːn/ NUM (**seventeens**) Seventeen is the number 17. ❏ *Jenny is seventeen years old.*

S

sev·en·teenth ♦♦◇ /ˌsevənˈtiːnθ/ ADJ, NOUN

ADJ The **seventeenth** item in a series is the one that you count as number seventeen. ❑ *She gave birth to Annabel just after her seventeenth birthday.*

NOUN [C] (**seventeenths**) A **seventeenth** is one of seventeen equal parts of something.

sev·enth ♦♦◇ /ˈsevənθ/ ADJ, NOUN

ADJ The **seventh** item in a series is the one that you count as number seven. ❑ *I was the seventh child in the family.*

NOUN [C] (**sevenths**) A **seventh** is one of seven equal parts of something. ❑ *A million people died, a seventh of the population.*

sev·en·ti·eth ♦♦◇ /ˈsevəntiəθ/ ADJ, NOUN

ADJ The **seventieth** item in a series is the one that you count as number seventy. ❑ *the seventieth anniversary of the discovery of Tutankhamun's tomb*

NOUN [C] (**seventieths**) A **seventieth** is one of seventy equal parts of something.

sev·en·ty ♦♦♦ /ˈsevənti/ NUM, NOUN

NUM **Seventy** is the number 70. ❑ *Seventy people were killed.*

NOUN [PL] (**seventies**) **1** When you talk about the **seventies**, you are referring to numbers between 70 and 79. For example, if you are **in** your **seventies**, you are aged between 70 and 79. If the temperature is **in the seventies**, it is between 70 and 79. ❑ *I thought it was a long way to go for two people in their seventies, but Sylvia loved the idea.* **2** The **seventies** is the decade between 1970 and 1979. ❑ *In the late seventies, things had to be new, modern, revolutionary.*

sev·er /ˈsevə/ VERB [T] (**severs, severing, severed**) (*formal*) **1** To **sever** something means to cut completely through it or to cut it completely off. ❑ *Richardson severed his right foot in a motorcycle accident.* **2** If you **sever** a relationship or connection that you have with someone, you end it suddenly and completely. ❑ *She severed her ties with her homeland.*

❂**sev·er·al** ♦♦♦ /ˈsevrəl/ DET, QUANT, PRON

DET **Several** is used to refer to a number of people or things that is not large but is greater than two. = some, a few ❑ *I had lived two doors away from this family for several years.* ❑ *Several blue plastic boxes under the window were filled with CDs.* ❑ *Several hundred students gathered on campus.*

QUANT [several 'of' PL-N] If you talk about **several of** something, you mean not many but more than two of them. ❑ *The building was picketed by demonstrators, several of whom were well-known actors.*

PRON **Several** means not many but more than two. ❑ *No one drug will suit or work for everyone and sometimes several may have to be tried.*

❂**se·vere** ♦♦◇ /sɪˈvɪə/ ADJ (**severer, severest**) **1** [usu with SUPP] You use **severe** to indicate that something bad or undesirable is great or intense. = extreme, intense, acute, tough; ≠ mild, slight ❑ *a business with severe cash flow problems* ❑ *Shortages of professional staff are very severe in some places.* **2** **Severe** punishments or criticisms are very strong or harsh. ❑ *This was a dreadful crime and a severe sentence is necessary.* ❑ *But perhaps the most severe criticisms have focused upon their military dimensions.*

❂**se·vere·ly** /sɪˈvɪəli/ ADV **1** = extremely, intensely, acutely, harshly; ≠ mildly, slightly ❑ *The UN wants to send food aid to 10 countries in Africa severely affected by the drought.* ❑ *An aircraft overshot the runway and was severely damaged.* **2** [severely with V] ❑ *a campaign to try to change the law to punish dangerous drivers more severely*

❂**se·ver·ity** /sɪˈverɪti/ NOUN [U] **1** = extremity, intensity, toughness, harshness; ≠ mildness ❑ *Several drugs are used to lessen the severity of the symptoms.* **2** He was sickened by the severity of the sentence.

sew /səʊ/ VERB [I, T] (**sews, sewing, sewed, sewn**) When you **sew** something such as clothes, you make them or repair them by joining pieces of cloth together by passing thread through them with a needle. ❑ *She sewed the dresses on the sewing machine.* ❑ *Anyone can sew on a button, including you.*

sew·age /ˈsuːɪdʒ/ NOUN [U] **Sewage** is waste matter such as faeces or dirty water from homes and factories, which flows away through sewers. ❑ *treatment of raw sewage*

sew·er /ˈsuːə/ NOUN [C] (**sewers**) A **sewer** is a large underground channel that carries waste matter and rain water away, usually to a place where it is treated and made harmless. ❑ *the city's sewer system*

sewn /səʊn/ IRREG FORM **Sewn** is the past participle of **sew**.

❂**sex** ♦♦◇ /seks/ NOUN (*academic word*)

NOUN [C, U] (**sexes**) **1** [C] The two **sexes** are the two groups, male and female, into which people and animals are divided according to the function they have in producing young. = gender ❑ *a movie star who appeals to all ages and both sexes* ❑ *differences between the sexes* **2** [C] The **sex** of a person or animal is their characteristic of being either male or female. = gender ❑ *She continually failed to gain promotion because of her sex.* ❑ *The new technique has been used to identify the sex of foetuses.* **3** [U] **Sex** is the physical activity by which people can produce young. = sexual intercourse, copulation, lovemaking ❑ *He was very open in his attitudes about sex.* ❑ *The entire film revolves around drugs, sex and violence.* ❑ *Sex education in schools was made universal.* ❑ *Most diabetics have a normal sex life.*

PHRASE **have sex** If two people **have sex**, they perform the act of sex. ❑ *Have you ever thought about having sex with someone other than your husband?*

PHRASAL VERB **sex up** (**sexes, sexing, sexed**) (*informal*) To **sex** something **up** means to make it seem more attractive or interesting than it actually is. ❑ *Nintendo is sexing up its US advertising to launch the new handheld device.*

❂**sex·ism** /ˈseksɪzəm/ NOUN [U] **Sexism** is the belief that the members of one sex, usually women, are less intelligent or less capable than those of the other sex and need not be treated equally. It is also the behaviour which is the result of this belief. ❑ *Groups like ours are committed to eradicating homophobia, racism and sexism.* ❑ *A small number of women have reached senior positions only to find a glass ceiling or even blatant sexism.*

❂**sex·ist** /ˈseksɪst/ ADJ, NOUN

ADJ (*disapproval*) If you describe people or their behaviour as **sexist**, you mean that they are influenced by the belief that the members of one sex, usually women, are less intelligent or less capable than those of the other sex and need not be treated equally. ❑ *Old-fashioned sexist attitudes are still common.* ❑ *There is a continued reluctance to recognize the racist, sexist and ageist biases in our social system as a whole.*

NOUN [C] (**sexists**) A **sexist** is someone with sexist views or behaviour. ❑ *It's got nothing to do with sexism. You know I'm not a sexist.* ❑ *The judges are, however inadvertently, adopting the logic of generalization, of racists and sexists.*

❂**sex·ual** ♦♦◇ /ˈsekʃuəl/ ADJ **1** **Sexual** feelings or activities are connected with the act of sex or with people's desire for sex. ❑ *This was the first sexual relationship I'd had.* ❑ *Many marriage troubles spring from unsatisfactory sexual relationships.* ❑ *incidents of domestic violence and sexual assault* **2** **Sexual** means relating to the differences between male and female people. ❑ *Women's groups denounced sexual discrimination.* **3** **Sexual** means relating to the differences between heterosexuals and homosexuals. ❑ *couples of all sexual persuasions* **4** **Sexual** means relating to the biological process by which people and animals produce young. ❑ *Girls generally reach sexual maturity two years earlier than boys.*

sex·ual·ly /ˈsekʃuəli/ ADV **1** *sexually transmitted diseases* **2** [sexually with V] ❑ *If you're sexually harassed, you ought to do something about it.* **3** *The first organisms that reproduced sexually were free-floating plankton.*

sex·ual har·ass·ment NOUN [U] **Sexual harassment** is repeated and unwelcome sexual comments, looks, or physical contact at work, usually a man's actions that offend a woman. ❑ *Sexual harassment of women workers by their bosses is believed to be widespread.*

sexu·al·ity /ˌsekʃuˈælɪti/ NOUN [U] **1** A person's **sexuality** is their sexual feelings. ❑ *the growing discussion of women's*

sexuality **2** You can refer to a person's **sexuality** when you are talking about whether they are sexually attracted to people of the same sex or a different sex. ❑ *He believes he has been discriminated against because of his sexuality.*

sexy /ˈseksi/ ADJ (**sexier**, **sexiest**) You can describe people and things as **sexy** if you think they are sexually exciting or sexually attractive. ❑ *She was one of the sexiest women I had seen.*

shab·by /ˈʃæbi/ ADJ (**shabbier**, **shabbiest**) **Shabby** things or places look old and in bad condition. ❑ *His clothes were old and shabby.*

shade ◆◇◇ /ʃeɪd/ NOUN, VERB

NOUN [c, u] (**shades**) **1** [c] A **shade of** a particular colour is one of its different forms. For example, emerald green and olive green are shades of green. ❑ *In the mornings the sky appeared a heavy shade of mottled grey.* ❑ *The walls were painted in two shades of green.* **2** [u] **Shade** is an area of darkness under or next to an object such as a tree, where sunlight does not reach. ❑ *Temperatures in the shade can reach forty-eight degrees Celsius at this time of year.* ❑ *Alexis walked up the coast, and resumed his reading in the shade of an overhanging cliff.* **3** [u] **Shade** is darkness or shadows as they are shown in a picture. ❑ *Rembrandt's skilful use of light and shade to create the atmosphere of movement* **4** [c] The **shades of** something abstract are its many, slightly different forms. ❑ *the capacity to convey subtle shades of meaning*

VERB [T] (**shades**, **shading**, **shaded**) **1** If you say that a place or person **is shaded** by objects such as trees, you mean that the place or person cannot be reached, harmed, or bothered by strong sunlight because those objects are in the way. ❑ *a health resort whose beaches are shaded by palm trees* **2** If you **shade** your eyes, you put your hand or an object partly in front of your face in order to prevent a bright light from shining into your eyes. = shield ❑ *You can't look directly into it; you've got to shade your eyes or close them altogether.*

shad·ow ◆◇◇ /ˈʃædəʊ/ NOUN, VERB, ADJ

NOUN [c, u] (**shadows**) **1** [c] A **shadow** is a dark shape on a surface that is made when something stands between a light and the surface. ❑ *An oak tree cast its shadow over a tiny wool pool.* ❑ *Nothing would grow in the shadow of the grey wall.* **2** [u] **Shadow** is darkness in a place caused by something preventing light from reaching it. = shade ❑ *Most of the lake was in shadow.* **3** [c] A British Member of Parliament who belongs to the main opposition party and takes a special interest in matters which are the responsibility of a particular government minister can be referred to as that minister's **shadow**. ❑ *Clarke swung at his shadow the accusation that he was 'a tabloid politician'.*

PHRASES **a shadow of a doubt** or **a shadow of doubt** (*emphasis*) If you say that something is true **without a shadow of a doubt** or **without a shadow of doubt**, you are emphasizing that there is no doubt at all that it is true. ❑ *It was without a shadow of a doubt the best we've played.* **in the shadow of someone** or **in someone's shadow** If you live **in the shadow of** someone or **in** their **shadow**, their achievements and abilities are so great that you are not noticed or valued. ❑ *He has always lived in the shadow of his brother.*

VERB [T] (**shadows**, **shadowing**, **shadowed**) **1** If something **shadows** a thing or place, it covers it with a shadow. ❑ *The hood shadowed her face.* **2** If someone **shadows** you, they follow you very closely wherever you go. = follow ❑ *The president is constantly shadowed by bodyguards.*

ADJ [shadow + N] A British Member of Parliament who is a member of the **shadow** cabinet or who is a **shadow** cabinet minister belongs to the main opposition party and takes a special interest in matters which are the responsibility of a particular government minister. ❑ *the shadow chancellor*

shad·owy /ˈʃædəʊi/ ADJ **1** A **shadowy** place is dark or full of shadows. ❑ *I watched him from a shadowy corner.* **2** [shadowy + N] A **shadowy** figure or shape is someone or something that you can hardly see because they are in a dark place. ❑ *a tall, shadowy figure silhouetted against the*

pale wall **3** You describe activities and people as **shadowy** when very little is known about them. = mysterious ❑ *the shadowy world of spies*

shaft /ʃɑːft, ʃæft/ NOUN [c] (**shafts**) **1** A **shaft** is a long vertical passage, for example, for a lift. ❑ *The fire began in a lift shaft and spread to the roof.* **2** In a machine, a **shaft** is a rod that turns around continually in order to transfer movement in the machine. ❑ *a drive shaft* **3** A **shaft** is a long, thin piece of wood or metal that forms part of a spear, axe, golf club, or other object. ❑ *golf clubs with steel shafts* **4** A **shaft of** light is a beam of light, for example, sunlight shining through an opening. ❑ *A brilliant shaft of sunlight burst through the doorway.*

shake ◆◆◇ /ʃeɪk/ VERB, NOUN

VERB [T, I] (**shakes**, **shaking**, **shook**, **shaken**) **1** [T] If you **shake** something, you hold it and move it quickly backwards and forwards or up and down. You can also **shake** a person, for example, because you are angry with them or because you want them to wake up. ❑ *The nurse took the thermometer, shook it, and put it under my armpit.* **2** [T] If you **shake yourself** or your body, you make a lot of quick, small, repeated movements without moving from the place where you are. ❑ *As soon as he got inside, the dog shook himself.* **3** [T] If you **shake** your head, you turn it from side to side in order to say 'no' or to show disbelief or sadness. ❑ *'Anything else?' Chris asked. Kathryn shook her head wearily.* **4** [I] If you **are shaking**, or a part of your body **is shaking**, you are making quick, small movements that you cannot control, for example, because you are cold or afraid. ❑ *He roared with laughter, shaking in his chair.* ❑ *My hand shook so much that I could hardly hold the microphone.* **5** [T] If you **shake** your fist or an object such as a stick **at** someone, you wave it in the air in front of them because you are angry with them. ❑ *The colonel rushed up to Earle and shook his gun at him.* **6** [I, T] If a force **shakes** something, or if something **shakes**, it moves from side to side or up and down with quick, small, but sometimes violent movements. ❑ *an explosion that shook buildings several kilometres away* **7** [T] To **shake** something into a certain place or state means to bring it into that place or state by moving it quickly up and down or from side to side. ❑ *She shook some pepper onto her sandwich.* **8** [I] If your voice **is shaking**, you cannot control it properly and it sounds very unsteady, for example, because you are nervous or angry. ❑ *His voice shaking with rage, he asked how the committee could keep such a report from the public.* **9** [T] If an event or a piece of news **shakes** you, or **shakes** your confidence, it makes you feel upset and unable to think calmly. ❑ *There was no doubt that the news of Tandy's escape had shaken them all.* **10** [T] If an event **shakes** a group of people or their beliefs, it causes great uncertainty and makes them question their beliefs. ❑ *The five years she spent as a news correspondent in Moscow were five years that shook the world.*

PHRASES **shake someone's hand** or **shake someone by the hand** If you **shake** someone's **hand** or **shake** someone **by the hand**, you shake hands with them. ❑ *I said congratulations and walked over to him and shook his hand.* **shake hands** If you **shake hands with** someone, you take their right hand in your own for a few moments, often moving it up and down slightly, when you are saying hello or goodbye to them, congratulating them, or agreeing on something. You can also say that two people **shake hands**. ❑ *He nodded greetings to Mary Ann and Michael and shook hands with Burke.*

PHRASAL VERBS **shake off** **1** If you **shake off** something that you do not want such as an illness or a bad habit, you manage to recover from it or get rid of it. ❑ *Businessmen are frantically trying to shake off the bad habits learned under six decades of a protected economy.* **2** If you **shake off** someone who is following you, you manage to get away from them, for example, by running faster than them. ❑ *Although I could pass him I could not shake him off.* **shake up** If someone **shakes up** something such as an organization, an institution, or a profession, they make major changes to it. ❑ *The government wanted to accelerate the reform of the institutions, to find new ways of shaking up the country.*

S

NOUN [c] (**shakes**) **1** If you give something or someone a **shake**, you hold them and move them quickly backwards and forwards or up and down. □ *She picked up the bag of salad and gave it a shake.* **2** If you give **yourself** or your body a **shake**, you make a lot of quick, small, repeated movements without moving from the place where you are. □ *Take some slow, deep breaths and give your body a bit of a shake.* **3** A **shake** of the head is when you turn it from side to side in order to say 'no' or to show disbelief or sadness. □ *'The elm trees are all dying,' said Palmer, with a sad shake of his head.*

shall ♦♦◇ /ʃəl, STRONG ʃæl/ VERB [MODAL]

> **Shall** is a modal verb. It is used with the base form of a verb.

1 You use **shall** with 'I' and 'we' in questions in order to make offers or suggestions, or to ask for advice. □ *Shall I get the keys?* □ *Well, shall we go?* □ *Let's have a nice little stroll, shall we?* **2** (formal) You use **shall**, usually with 'I' and 'we', when you are referring to something that you intend to do, or when you are referring to something that you are sure will happen to you in the future. □ *We shall be landing in Paris in sixteen minutes, exactly on time.* □ *I shall know more next month, I hope.* **3** (formal) You use **shall** with 'I' or 'we' during a speech or piece of writing to say what you are going to discuss or explain later. □ *In Chapter 3, I shall describe some of the documentation that I gathered.* **4** You use **shall** to indicate that something must happen, usually because of a rule or law. You use **shall not** to indicate that something must not happen. □ *The president shall hold office for five years.* **5** You use **shall**, usually with 'you', when you are telling someone that they will be able to do or have something they want. □ *Very well, if you want to go, go you shall.*

shal·low /ˈʃæləʊ/ ADJ (**shallower, shallowest**)
1 A **shallow** container, hole, or area of water measures only a short distance from the top to the bottom. □ *Put the milk in a shallow dish.* **2** (disapproval) If you describe a person, piece of work, or idea as **shallow**, you disapprove of them because they do not show or involve any serious or careful thought. □ *I think he is shallow, vain, and untrustworthy.* **3** If your breathing is **shallow**, you take only a very small amount of air into your lungs at each breath. □ *She began to hear her own taut, shallow breathing.*

sham /ʃæm/ NOUN [c] (**shams**) (disapproval) Something that is a **sham** is not real or is not really what it seems to be. □ *The government's promises were exposed as a hollow sham.*

sham·bles /ˈʃæmbəlz/ NOUN [SING] If a place, event, or situation is **a shambles** or is **in a shambles**, everything is in disorder. = mess □ *The ship's interior was an utter shambles.*

shame ♦◇◇ /ʃeɪm/ NOUN, VERB, CONVENTION
NOUN [U, SING] **1** [U] **Shame** is an uncomfortable feeling that you get when you have done something wrong or embarrassing, or when someone close to you has. □ *She felt a deep sense of shame.* □ *Her father and her brothers would die of shame.* **2** [U] If someone brings **shame on** you, they make other people lose their respect for you. = disgrace □ *I don't want to bring shame on the family name.* **3** [SING] If you say that something is **a shame**, you are expressing your regret about it and indicating that you wish it had happened differently. □ *It's a crying shame that police have to put up with these mindless attacks.*
PHRASE **put someone to shame** If someone **puts** you **to shame**, they make you feel ashamed because they do something much better than you do. □ *His playing really put me to shame.*
VERB [T] (**shames, shaming, shamed**) **1** If something **shames** you, it causes you to feel shame. □ *Her son's affair had humiliated and shamed her.* **2** If you **shame** someone **into** doing something, you force them to do it by making them feel ashamed not to. □ *He would not let neighbours shame him into silence.*
CONVENTION (feelings) You can use **shame** in expressions such as **shame on you** and **shame on him** to indicate that someone ought to feel shame for something they have said or done. □ *He tried to deny it. Shame on him!*

shame·ful /ˈʃeɪmfʊl/ ADJ (disapproval) If you describe a person's action or attitude as **shameful**, you think that it is so bad that the person ought to be ashamed. □ *the most shameful episode in US naval history*
shame·ful·ly /ˈʃeɪmfəli/ ADV □ *At times they have been shamefully neglected.*

shame·less /ˈʃeɪmləs/ ADJ (disapproval) If you describe someone as **shameless**, you mean that they should be ashamed of their behaviour, which is unacceptable to other people. □ *a shameless attempt to stifle democratic debate*
shame·less·ly /ˈʃeɪmləsli/ ADV □ *a shamelessly lazy week-long trip*

shape ♦♦◇ /ʃeɪp/ NOUN, VERB
NOUN [c, SING] (**shapes**) **1** [c] [oft shape 'of' N, also 'in' shape] The **shape** of an object, a person, or an area is the appearance of their outside edges or surfaces, for example, whether they are round, square, curved, or fat. □ *Each mirror is made to order and can be designed to almost any shape or size.* □ *little pens in the shape of baseball bats* □ *sofas and chairs of contrasting shapes and colours* **2** [c] You can refer to something that you can see as a **shape** if you cannot see it clearly, or if its outline is the clearest or most striking aspect of it. □ *The great grey shape of a tank rolled out of the village.* **3** [c] A **shape** is a space enclosed by an outline, for example, a circle, a square, or a triangle. □ *Imagine a sort of a kidney shape.* **4** [SING] The **shape** of something that is planned or organized is its structure and character. □ *The last two weeks have seen a lot of talk about the future shape of Europe.*
PHRASES **in any shape or form** (emphasis) If you say, for example, that you will not accept something **in any shape or form**, or **in any way, shape or form**, you are emphasizing that you will not accept it in any circumstances. □ *I don't condone violence in any shape or form.*
in shape or **in good shape** or **in bad shape** If someone or something is **in shape**, or **in good shape**, they are in a good state of health or in a good condition. If they are **in bad shape**, they are in a bad state of health or in a bad condition. □ *the Fatburner Diet Book, a comprehensive guide to getting in shape* □ *He was still in better shape than many young men.*
lick into shape or **knock into shape** or **whip into shape** If you **lick, knock,** or **whip** someone or something **into shape**, you use whatever methods are necessary to change or improve them so that they are in the condition that you want them to be in. □ *You'll have four months in which to lick the recruits into shape.*
out of shape **1** If something is **out of shape**, it is no longer in its proper or original shape, for example, because it has been damaged or wrongly handled. □ *Once most wires are bent out of shape, they don't return to the original position.* **2** If you are **out of shape**, you are unhealthy and unable to do a lot of physical activity without getting tired. = unfit □ *I weighed 245 pounds and was out of shape.*
take shape When something **takes shape**, it develops or starts to appear in such a way that it becomes fairly clear what its final form will be. □ *In 1912 women's events were added, and the modern Olympic programme began to take shape.*
VERB [T] (**shapes, shaping, shaped**) **1** Someone or something that **shapes** a situation or an activity has a very great influence on the way it develops. □ *Like it or not, our families shape our lives and make us what we are.* **2** If you **shape** an object, you give it a particular shape, using your hands or a tool. □ *Cut the dough in half and shape each half into a loaf.*
PHRASAL VERB **shape up** **1** If something is **shaping up**, it is starting to develop or seems likely to happen. □ *There are also indications that a major tank battle may be shaping up for tonight.* □ *The accident is already shaping up as a significant environmental disaster.* **2** If you ask how someone or something is **shaping up**, you want to know how well they are doing in a particular situation or activity. □ *I did have a few worries about how Hugh and I would shape up as parents.* **3** If you tell someone to **shape up**, you are telling them to

start behaving in a sensible and responsible way. ❏ *They were given a year to shape up or risk losing their scholarships.*
→ See also **shaped**

shaped ◆◇◇ /ʃeɪpt/ ADJ [V-LINK + shaped] Something that is **shaped** like a particular object or in a particular way has the shape of that object or a shape of that type. ❏ *A new perfume from Russia comes in a bottle shaped like a tank.*

✪ **share** ◆◆◆ /ʃeə/ NOUN, VERB
NOUN [c] (**shares**) **1** (*business*) A company's **shares** are the many equal parts into which its ownership is divided. Shares can be bought by people as an investment. ❏ *People in China are eager to buy shares in new businesses.* ❏ *For some months the share price remained fairly static.* **2** If something is divided or distributed among a number of different people or things, each of them has, or is responsible for, a **share of** it. ❏ *Sara also pays a share of the gas, electricity and phone bills.* **3** If you have or do your **share of** something, you have or do an amount that seems reasonable to you, or to other people. ❏ *Women must receive their fair share of training for well-paying jobs.* VERB [RECIP, T, I] (**shares, sharing, shared**) **1** [RECIP] If you **share** something **with** another person, you both have it, use it, or occupy it. You can also say that two people **share** something. ❏ *the small income he had shared with his brother from his father's estate* ❏ *Two Americans will share this year's Nobel Prize for Medicine.* **2** [RECIP] If you **share** a task, duty, or responsibility **with** someone, you each carry out or accept part of it. You can also say that two people **share** something. ❏ *You can find out whether they are prepared to share the cost of the flowers with you.* **3** [RECIP] If you **share** an experience **with** someone, you have the same experience, often because you are with them at the time. You can also say that two people **share** something. ❏ *Yes, I want to share my life with you.* **4** [T] If you **share** someone's opinion, you agree with them. ❏ *The forum's members share his view that business can be a positive force for change in developing countries.* **5** [RECIP] If one person or thing **shares** a quality or characteristic **with** another, they have the same quality or characteristic. You can also say that two people or things **share** something. ❏ *La Repubblica and El Pais are politically independent newspapers which share similar characteristics.* **6** [I, T] If you **share** something that you have **with** someone, you give some of it to them or let them use it. ❏ *He shared his food with the family.* ❏ *Scientists now have to compete for funding, and do not share information among themselves.* ❏ *I wanted everybody to share.* **7** [T] If you **share** something personal such as a thought or a piece of news **with** someone, you tell them about it. ❏ *It can be beneficial to share your feelings with someone you trust.*
PHRASAL VERB **share out** If you **share out** an amount of something, you give each person in a group an equal or fair part of it.
→ See also **market share**

share·holder ◆◇◇ /ˈʃeəhəʊldə/ NOUN [c] (**shareholders**) (*business*) A **shareholder** is a person who owns shares in a company. ❏ *a shareholders' meeting*

✪ **sharp** ◆◆◇ /ʃɑːp/ ADJ, ADV, NOUN
ADJ (**sharper, sharpest**) **1** A **sharp** point or edge is very thin and can cut through things very easily. A **sharp** knife, tool, or other object has a point or edge of this kind. ❏ *With a sharp knife, make diagonal slashes in the chicken breast.* **2** You can describe a shape or an object as **sharp** if part of it or one end of it comes to a point or forms an angle. ❏ *His nose was thin and sharp.* **3** A **sharp** bend or turn is one that changes direction suddenly. = **tight** ❏ *I was approaching a fairly sharp bend that swept downhill to the left.* **4** If you describe someone as **sharp**, you are praising them because they are quick to notice, hear, understand, or react to things. ❏ *He is very sharp, a quick thinker and swift with repartee.* **5** If someone says something in a **sharp** way, they say it suddenly and rather firmly or angrily, for example, because they are warning or criticizing you. ❏ *'Don't contradict your mother,' was Charles's sharp reprimand.* **6** A **sharp** change, movement, or feeling occurs suddenly, and is great in amount, force, or degree. = **dramatic, abrupt, intense**; ≠ **gradual** ❏ *There's been a sharp rise in the rate of inflation.* ❏ *a new*

treatment for chronic, sharp pain associated with nerve injuries ❏ *Tennis requires a lot of short sharp movements.* **7** A **sharp** difference, image, or sound is very easy to see, hear, or distinguish. ❏ *Many people make a sharp distinction between humans and other animals.* ❏ *All the footmarks are quite sharp and clear.* **8** A **sharp** taste or smell is rather strong or bitter, but is often also clear and fresh. ❏ *The apple tasted just as I remembered – sharp, sour, yet sweet.*
ADV **1** [sharp + ADV] To turn or bend **sharp left** or **right** means to change direction suddenly to the left or right. ❏ *Do not cross the bridge but turn sharp left to go down on to the towpath.* **2** [N + sharp] **Sharp** is used after stating a particular time to show that something happens at exactly the time stated. = **precisely** ❏ *She planned to unlock the shop at 8.00 sharp this morning.*
NOUN [c] (**sharps**) **Sharp** is used after a letter representing a musical note to show that the note should be played or sung half a tone higher. **Sharp** is often represented by the symbol ♯. ❏ *A solitary viola plucks a lonely, soft F sharp.*
✪ **sharp·ly** /ˈʃɑːpli/ ADV **1** *'You've known,' she said sharply, 'and you didn't tell me?'* **2** = **dramatically, markedly** ❏ *Unemployment has risen sharply in recent years.* ❏ *The latest survey shows buying plans for homes are sharply lower than in June.* **3** *Opinions on this are sharply divided.* **4** *Room number nine was at the far end of the corridor where it turned sharply to the right.*

sharp·en /ˈʃɑːpən/ VERB [I, T] (**sharpens, sharpening, sharpened**) **1** [I, T] If your senses, understanding, or skills **sharpen** or **are sharpened**, you become better at noticing things, thinking, or doing something. ❏ *Her gaze sharpened, as if she had seen something unusual.* ❏ *He will need to sharpen his diplomatic skills in order to work with Congress.* **2** [T] If you **sharpen** an object, you make its edge very thin or you make its end pointed. ❏ *He started to sharpen his knife.*

shat·ter /ˈʃætə/ VERB [I, T] (**shatters, shattering, shattered**) **1** [I, T] If something **shatters** or **is shattered**, it breaks into a lot of small pieces. ❏ *safety glass that won't shatter if it's broken* ❏ *The car shattered into a thousand burning pieces in a 200 mph crash.* **2** [T] If something **shatters** your dreams, hopes, or beliefs, it completely destroys them. ❏ *A failure would shatter the hopes of many people.*
shat·ter·ing /ˈʃætərɪŋ/ NOUN [u] ❏ *the shattering of glass*
→ See also **shattered**

shat·tered /ˈʃætəd/ ADJ If you are **shattered** by something, you are extremely shocked and upset about it. = **devastated** ❏ *It is desperately sad news and I am absolutely shattered to hear it.*

shave /ʃeɪv/ VERB, NOUN
VERB [I, T] (**shaves, shaving, shaved**) **1** [I, T] When a man **shaves**, he removes the hair from his face using a razor or shaver so that his face is smooth. ❏ *He took a bath and shaved before dinner.* ❏ *He had shaved his face until it was smooth.* **2** [T] If you **shave off** part of a piece of wood or other material, you cut very thin pieces from it. ❏ *I set the log on the ground and shaved off the bark.* **3** [T] If you **shave** a small amount **off** something such as a record, cost, or price, you reduce it by that amount. ❏ *She's already shaved four seconds off the national record for the mile.*
NOUN [c] (**shaves**) When a man has a **shave**, he removes the hair from his face using a razor or shaver so that his face is smooth. ❏ *He never seemed to need a shave.*
PHRASE **a close shave** If you describe a situation as **a close shave**, you mean that there was nearly an accident or a disaster but it was avoided. ❏ *I can't quite believe the close shaves I've had just recently.*
shav·ing /ˈʃeɪvɪŋ/ NOUN [u] ❏ *a range of shaving products*

she ◆◆◆ /ʃi, STRONG ʃiː/ PRON

> **She** is a third person singular pronoun. **She** is used as the subject of a verb.

1 You use **she** to refer to a woman, girl, or female animal who has already been mentioned or whose identity is clear. ❏ *When Ann arrived home that night, she found Brian in the house watching TV.* ❏ *She was seventeen and she had no education or employment.* **2** Some writers may use **she** to refer to a person who is not identified as either male or female. They do this because they wish to avoid using the pronoun 'he' all the time. Some people dislike this use and prefer to use 'he or she' or 'they'. ❑ *The student may show signs of feeling the strain of responsibility and she may give up.* **3** **She** is sometimes used to refer to a country or nation. ❑ *The country needs new leadership if she is to play a role in future development.* **4** Some people use **she** to refer to a car or machine. People who sail often use **she** to refer to a ship or boat. ❑ *The Seaflower was being repaired, but soon she was fit to sail again.*

shed ◆◇◇ /ʃed/ NOUN, VERB
[N] [c] (**sheds**) **1** A **shed** is a small building that is used for storing things such as garden tools. ❑ *a garden shed* **2** A **shed** is a large shelter or building, for example, at a railway station, port, or factory. ❑ *a vast factory shed* [VERB] [T] (**sheds, shedding, shed**) **1** When a tree **sheds** its leaves, it leaves fall off in the autumn. When an animal **sheds** hair or skin, some of its hair or skin drops off. ❑ *Some of the trees were already beginning to shed their leaves.* **2** (formal) To **shed** something means to get rid of it. ❑ *The firm is to shed 700 jobs.* **3** If you **shed** tears, you cry. ❑ *They will shed a few tears at their daughter's wedding.* **4** (formal) To **shed** blood means to kill people in a violent way. If someone **sheds** their blood, they are killed in a violent way, usually when they are fighting in a war. ❑ *young warriors, eager to shed blood*
◆ **shed light on something** → see **light**

sheep /ʃiːp/ NOUN [c] (**sheep**) A **sheep** is a farm animal which is covered with thick, curly hair called wool. Sheep are kept for their wool or for their meat. ❑ *grassland on which a flock of sheep were grazing*

sheer /ʃɪə/ ADJ (**sheerer, sheerest**) **1** [sheer + N] (emphasis) You can use **sheer** to emphasize that a state or situation is complete and does not involve or is not mixed with anything else. = **pure** ❑ *His music is sheer delight.* ❑ *Sheer chance quite often plays an important part in sparking off an idea.* **2** A **sheer** cliff or drop is extremely steep or completely vertical. ❑ *There was a sheer drop just outside my window.* **3** **Sheer** material is very thin, light, and delicate. ❑ *sheer black tights*

sheet ◆◇◇ /ʃiːt/ NOUN [c] (**sheets**) **1** A **sheet** is a large rectangular piece of cotton or other cloth that you sleep on or cover yourself with in a bed. ❑ *Once a week, a maid changes the sheets.* **2** A **sheet** of paper is a rectangular piece of paper. ❑ *a sheet of newspaper* **3** You can use **sheet** to refer to a piece of paper which gives information about something. ❑ *information sheets on each country in the world* **4** A **sheet** of glass, metal, or wood is a large, flat, thin piece of it. ❑ *a cracked sheet of glass* ❑ *Overhead cranes were lifting giant sheets of steel.* **5** A **sheet of** something is a thin wide layer of it over the surface of something else. ❑ *a sheet of ice*
→ See also **spreadsheet**

sheikh /ʃeɪk, AmE ʃiːk/ NOUN [c] (**sheikhs**) A **sheikh** is a male Arab chief or ruler. ❑ *Sheikh Khalifa*

shelf /ʃelf/ NOUN
[N] [c] (**shelves**) A **shelf** is a flat piece of wood, metal, or glass which is attached to a wall or to the sides of a cabinet. Shelves are used for keeping things on. ❑ *He took a book from the shelf.*
[PHRASE] **off the shelf** If you buy something off the shelf, you buy something that is not specially made for you. ❑ *Lower-priced jewellery will be sold off the shelf by this autumn.*

shell ◆◇◇ /ʃel/ NOUN, VERB
[N] [u, c] (**shells**) **1** [u, c] The **shell** of a nut or egg is the hard covering which surrounds it. ❑ *They cracked the nuts and removed their shells.* **2** [u] **Shell** is the substance that a shell is made of. ❑ *beads made from ostrich egg shell* **3** [c] The **shell** of an animal such as a tortoise, snail, or crab is the hard protective covering that it has around its body or on its back. ❑ *the spiral form of a snail shell* **4** [c] **Shells** are hard objects found on beaches. They are usually pink, white, or brown and are the coverings which used to surround small sea creatures. ❑ *I collect shells and interesting seaside items.* **5** [c] If someone comes out of their **shell**, they become more friendly and interested in other people and less quiet, shy, and reserved. ❑ *Her normally shy son*

had come out of his shell. **6** [c] The **shell** of a building, boat, car, or other structure is the outside frame of it. ❑ *the shells of burned buildings* **7** [c] A **shell** is a weapon consisting of a metal container filled with explosives that can be fired from a large gun over long distances. ❑ *Tanks fired shells at the house.*
[VERB] [T] (**shells, shelling, shelled**) **1** If you **shell** nuts, peas, shrimp, or other food, you remove their natural outer covering. ❑ *She shelled and ate a few nuts.* **2** To **shell** a place means to fire explosive shells at it. ❑ *The rebels shelled the densely populated suburbs near the port.*
[PHRASAL VERB] **shell out** (informal) If you **shell out for** something, you spend a lot of money on it. = **fork out** ❑ *You won't have to shell out a fortune for it.* ❑ *an insurance policy which saves you from having to shell out for repairs*
shell·ing /ˈʃelɪŋ/ NOUN [c, u] (**shellings**) ❑ *Out on the streets, the shelling continued.*

shell·fish /ˈʃelfɪʃ/ NOUN [c, u] (**shellfish**) Shellfish are small creatures that live in the sea and have a shell. ❑ *Fish and shellfish are the specialities.*

shel·ter ◆◇◇ /ˈʃeltə/ NOUN, VERB
[N] [c, u] (**shelters**) **1** [c] A **shelter** is a small building or covered place which is made to protect people from bad weather or danger. ❑ *The city's bomb shelters were being prepared for possible air raids.* **2** [u] If a place provides **shelter**, it provides you with a place to stay or live, especially when you need protection from bad weather or danger. ❑ *The number of families seeking shelter rose by 17 per cent.* ❑ *Although horses do not generally mind the cold, shelter from rain and wind is important.* **3** [c] A **shelter** is a building where homeless people can sleep and get food. ❑ *a shelter for homeless women*
[VERB] [i, T] (**shelters, sheltering, sheltered**) **1** [i] If you **shelter** in a place, you stay there and are protected from bad weather or danger. ❑ *a man sheltering in a doorway* **2** [T] If a place or thing **is sheltered** by something, it is protected by that thing from wind and rain. ❑ *a wooden house, sheltered by a low pointed roof* **3** [T] If you **shelter** someone, usually someone who is being hunted by police or other people, you provide them with a place to stay or live. ❑ *A neighbour sheltered the boy for seven days.*

shield /ʃiːld/ NOUN, VERB
[N] [c] (**shields**) **1** Something or someone which is a **shield** against a particular danger or risk provides protection from it. ❑ *He used his left hand as a shield against the reflecting sunlight.* **2** A **shield** is a large piece of metal or leather which soldiers used to carry to protect their bodies while they were fighting. ❑ *He clanged his sword three times on his shield.* **3** A **shield** is a sports prize or badge that is shaped like a shield.
[VERB] [T] (**shields, shielding, shielded**) **1** If something or someone **shields** you **from** a danger or risk, they protect you from it. = **protect** ❑ *He shielded his head from the sun with an old sack.* **2** If you **shield** your eyes, you put your hand above your eyes to protect them from direct sunlight. = **shade** ❑ *He squinted and shielded his eyes.*

❂ shift ◆◇◇ /ʃɪft/ VERB, NOUN (academic word)
[VERB] [i, T] (**shifts, shifting, shifted**) **1** [i, T] If you **shift** something or if it **shifts**, it moves slightly. = **move** ❑ *He stopped, shifting his cane to his left hand.* ❑ *He shifted from foot to foot.* ❑ *Firefighters have been hampered by high temperatures and shifting winds.* **2** [i, T] If someone's opinion, a situation, or a policy **shifts** or **is shifted**, it changes slightly. = **alter, change, adjust** ❑ *Attitudes to mental illness have shifted in recent years.* ❑ *The emphasis should be shifted more towards Parliament.* **3** [T] If someone **shifts** the responsibility or blame for something onto you, they unfairly make you responsible or make people blame you for it, instead of them. ❑ *It was a vain attempt to shift the responsibility for the murder to somebody else.*
[NOUN] [c] (**shifts**) **1** [usu shift + PREP] A **shift** is a slight change in someone's opinion, a situation, or a policy. = **change** ❑ *a shift in government policy* ❑ *The migration towards technology as a service is a cultural shift.* **2** If a group of factory workers, nurses, or other people work **shifts**, they work for a set period before being replaced by another group, so that there is always a group working.

Each of these set periods is called a **shift**. You can also use **shift** to refer to a group of workers who work together on a particular shift. ❑ *His father worked shifts in a steel mill.*

shine /ʃaɪn/ VERB, NOUN

VERB [I, T] (shines, shining, shined or shone) **1** [I] When the sun or a light **shines**, it gives out bright light. ❑ *It is a mild morning and the sun is shining.* **2** [T] If you **shine** a torch or other light somewhere, you point it there, so that you can see something when it is dark. ❑ *One of the men shone a torch in his face.* ❑ *The man walked slowly towards her, shining the torch.* **3** [I] Something that **shines** is very bright and clear because it is reflecting light. = **gleam** ❑ *Her blue eyes shone and caught the light.* ❑ *a pair of patent leather shoes that shone like mirrors* **4** [I] Someone who **shines** at a skill or activity does it extremely well. = **excel** ❑ *Did you shine at school?*

NOUN [SING] Something that has a **shine** is bright and clear because it is reflecting light. = **sheen** ❑ *This gel gives a beautiful shine to the hair.*

→ See also **shining**

shin·ing /ˈʃaɪnɪŋ/ ADJ A **shining** achievement or quality is a very good one which should be greatly admired. ❑ *She is a shining example to us all.*

→ See also **shine**

shiny /ˈʃaɪni/ ADJ (shinier, shiniest) Shiny things are bright and reflect light. ❑ *Her blonde hair was shiny and clean.*

ship ♦♦◇ /ʃɪp/ NOUN, VERB

NOUN [C] (ships) [also 'by' ship] A **ship** is a large boat which carries passengers or cargo. ❑ *Within ninety minutes the ship was ready for departure.* ❑ *We went by ship over to America.*

VERB [T] (ships, shipping, shipped) If people, supplies, or goods **are shipped** somewhere, they are sent there on a ship or by some other means of transportation. ❑ *We'll ship your order to the address we print on your cheques.* ❑ *Food is being shipped to drought-stricken Southern Africa.*

→ See also **shipping**

ship·ment /ˈʃɪpmənt/ NOUN [C, U] (shipments) **1** [C] A **shipment** is an amount of a particular kind of cargo that is sent to another country on a ship, train, plane, or other vehicle. ❑ *After that, food shipments to the port could begin in a matter of weeks.* **2** [U] The **shipment** of a cargo or goods somewhere is the sending of it there by ship, train, plane, or some other vehicle. ❑ *Bananas are packed before being transported to the docks for shipment overseas.*

ship·ping /ˈʃɪpɪŋ/ NOUN [U] **1** [usu with SUPP] **Shipping** is the transportation of cargo or goods as a business, especially on ships. ❑ *the international shipping industry* ❑ *a coupon for free shipping of your catalogue order* **2** You can refer to the amount of money that you pay to a company to transport cargo or goods as **shipping**. ❑ *It is £39.95 plus £3 shipping.*

shirt ♦◇◇ /ʃɜːt/ NOUN [C] (shirts) A **shirt** is a piece of clothing that you wear on the upper part of your body. Shirts have a collar, sleeves, and buttons down the front.

→ See also **T-shirt**

shiv·er /ˈʃɪvə/ VERB, NOUN

VERB [I] (shivers, shivering, shivered) When you **shiver**, your body shakes slightly because you are cold or frightened. = **shake** ❑ *He shivered in the cold.*

NOUN [C] (shivers) A **shiver** is a slight shaking of the body because you are cold or frightened. ❑ *The emptiness here sent shivers down my spine.*

shock ♦♦◇ /ʃɒk/ NOUN, VERB

NOUN [C, U] (shocks) **1** [C] If you have a **shock**, something suddenly happens which is unpleasant, upsetting, or very surprising. ❑ *The extent of the violence came as a shock.* ❑ *He has never recovered from the shock of your brother's death.* **2** [U] **Shock** is a person's emotional and physical condition when something very frightening or upsetting has happened to them. ❑ *The little boy was speechless with shock.* **3** [U] If someone is **in shock**, they are suffering from a serious physical condition in which their blood is not flowing around their body properly, for example, because they have had a bad injury. ❑ *He was found beaten and in*

shock. **4** [C, U] A **shock** is the force of something suddenly hitting or pulling something else. ❑ *Steel barriers can bend and absorb the shock.* **5** [C] A **shock** is the same as an **electric shock**.

VERB [T, I] (shocks, shocking, shocked) **1** [T] If something **shocks** you, it makes you feel very upset, because it involves death or suffering and because you had not expected it. ❑ *After forty years in the police force nothing much shocks me.* **2** [I, T] If someone or something **shocks** you, it upsets or offends you because you think it is vulgar or morally wrong. ❑ *You can't shock me.* ❑ *They were easily shocked in those days.* ❑ *the desire to shock*

shocked /ʃɒkt/ ADJ **1** *This was a nasty attack and the woman is still very shocked.* **2** *Don't look so shocked.*

→ See also **electric shock**

shock·ing /ˈʃɒkɪŋ/ ADJ **1** (informal) You can say that something is **shocking** if you think that it is very bad. = **appalling** ❑ *The media coverage was shocking.* **2** You can say that something is **shocking** if you think that it is morally wrong. ❑ *It is shocking that nothing was said.*

shock·ing·ly /ˈʃɒkɪŋli/ ADV **1** [shockingly + ADJ/ADV] ❑ *His memory was becoming shockingly bad.* **2** Shockingly, this useless and dangerous surgery did not end until the 1930s.

→ See also **shock**

shoe ♦◇◇ /ʃuː/ NOUN

NOUN [C] (shoes) **Shoes** are objects which you wear on your feet. They cover most of your foot and you wear them over socks or stockings. ❑ *a pair of shoes* ❑ *Low-heeled comfortable shoes are best.*

PHRASES fill someone's shoes or **step into someone's shoes** If you **fill** someone's **shoes** or **step into** their **shoes**, you take their place by doing the job they were doing. ❑ *No one has been able to fill his shoes.*

be in someone's shoes If you talk about being **in** someone's **shoes**, you talk about what you would do or how you would feel if you were in their situation. ❑ *I wouldn't want to be in his shoes.*

shone /ʃɒn, AmE ʃoʊn/ IRREG FORM **Shone** is the past tense and past participle of **shine**.

shook /ʃʊk/ IRREG FORM **Shook** is the past tense of **shake**.

shoot ♦♦◇ /ʃuːt/ VERB, NOUN

VERB [T, I] (shoots, shooting, shot) **1** [T] If someone **shoots** a person or an animal, they kill them or injure them by firing a bullet or arrow at them. ❑ *The police had orders to shoot anyone who attacked them.* ❑ *The man was shot dead by the police during a raid on his house.* **2** [I] To **shoot** means to fire a bullet from a weapon such as a gun. ❑ *He taunted armed officers by pointing to his head, as if inviting them to shoot.* ❑ *The police came around the corner and they started shooting at us.* **3** [I] If someone or something **shoots** in a particular direction, they move in that direction quickly and suddenly. ❑ *They had almost reached the boat when a figure shot past them.* **4** [I, T] If you **shoot** something somewhere or if it **shoots** somewhere, it moves there quickly and suddenly. ❑ *Masters shot a hand across the table and gripped his wrist.* ❑ *As soon as she got close, the old woman's hand shot out.* **5** [T] If you **shoot** a look at someone, you look at them quickly and briefly, often in a way that expresses your feelings. ❑ *Mary Ann shot him a rueful look.* **6** [I] If someone **shoots** to fame, they become famous or successful very quickly. ❑ *Alina Reyes shot to fame a few years ago with her extraordinary first novel.* **7** [T] When people **shoot** a film or **shoot** photographs, they make a film or take photographs using a camera. ❑ *He'd love to shoot his film in Cuba.* **8** [I] In sports such as football or basketball, when someone **shoots**, they try to score by kicking or throwing the ball towards the goal or hoop. ❑ *Spencer scuttled away from Singh to shoot wide when he should have scored.*

PHRASAL VERBS shoot down 1 If someone **shoots down** a plane, a helicopter, or a missile, they make it fall to the ground by hitting it with a bullet or missile. ❑ *They claimed to have shot down one incoming missile.* **2** If one person **shoots down** another, they shoot them with a gun. ❑ *He was prepared to suppress rebellion by shooting down protesters.*

shoot up If something **shoots up**, it grows or increases

S

very quickly. ❑ *Sales shot up by 9% last month.*
NOUN [c] (**shoots**) **1** A **shoot** is an occasion when a
professional photographer takes photographs or when a
film or video is being made. ❑ *a barn presently being used
for a video shoot* **2** **Shoots** are plants that are beginning to
grow, or new parts growing from a plant or tree. ❑ *Prune
established plants annually as new shoots appear.*
→ See also **shooting, shot**
✦ **shoot from the hip** → see **hip**

shoot·ing /ˈʃuːtɪŋ/ NOUN [C, U] (**shootings**) **1** [c] A
shooting is an occasion when someone is killed or injured
by being shot with a gun. ❑ *Two more bodies were found
nearby after the shooting.* **2** [u] **Shooting** is hunting
animals with a gun as a leisure activity. ❑ *Grouse shooting
begins in August.* **3** [u] The **shooting** of a film is the act of
filming it. ❑ *Ingrid was busy learning her lines for the next
day's shooting.* **4** [u] In sports such as football and
basketball, a player's **shooting** is their ability to score goals
or points. ❑ *When asked whether the injury affected his
shooting, Iverson said: 'Not at all.'*

shop ♦♦◇ /ʃɒp/ NOUN, VERB
NOUN [c] (**shops**) **1** (*mainly BrE; in AmE, usually use* **store**)
A **shop** is a building or part of a building where things are
sold. = store **2** You can refer to a place where a
particular service is offered as a particular type of **shop**.
❑ *the barber's shop where Rodney sometimes had his hair cut*
❑ *betting shops*
PHRASE **talk shop** If you say that people **are talking shop**,
you mean that they are talking about their work, and this
is boring for other people who do not do the same work.
❑ *Although I get on well with my colleagues, if you hang around
together all the time you just end up talking shop.*
VERB [I] (**shops, shopping, shopped**) When you **shop**, you
go to stores or shops and buy things. ❑ *He always shopped
at the co-op.* ❑ *some advice that's worth bearing in mind when
shopping for a new carpet*
PHRASAL VERB **shop around** If you **shop around**, you go to
different stores or companies in order to compare the
prices and quality of goods or services before you decide to
buy them. ❑ *Prices may vary so it's well worth shopping
around before you buy.*
shop·per /ˈʃɒpə/ NOUN [c] (**shoppers**) ❑ *crowds of Christmas
shoppers*
→ See also **shopping**

USAGE NOTE

shop

Note that you say 'go shopping'. Do not use '~~go to
shopping~~'.
*We **went shopping** at the weekend.*

---

shop·keeper /ˈʃɒpkiːpə/ NOUN [c] (**shopkeepers**)
A **shopkeeper** is a person who owns or manages a shop.
= merchant, storekeeper

shop·lifting /ˈʃɒplɪftɪŋ/ NOUN [u] **Shoplifting** is stealing
from a shop or store by hiding things in a bag or in your
clothes. ❑ *The grocer accused her of shoplifting and demanded
to look in her bag.*

shop·ping ♦◇◇ /ˈʃɒpɪŋ/ NOUN [u] **1** When you do the
shopping, you go to the shops and buy things. ❑ *I'll do the
shopping this afternoon.* **2** (*mainly BrE; in AmE, usually use*
groceries) Your **shopping** is the things that you have
bought from shops, especially food.

shore ♦◇◇ /ʃɔː/ NOUN
NOUN [c] (**shores**) [*also* PREP + shore] The **shores** or the
shore of a sea, lake, or wide river is the land along the
edge of it. Someone who is **on shore** is on the land rather
than on a ship. ❑ *They walked down to the shore.*
❑ *elephants living on the shores of Lake Kariba*
PHRASAL VERB **shore up** (**shores, shoring, shored**) If you
shore up something that is weak or about to fail, you do
something in order to strengthen it or support it. ❑ *The
democracies of the West may find it hard to shore up their
defences.*

short ♦♦♦ /ʃɔːt/ ADJ, ADV, NOUN
ADJ (**shorter, shortest**) **1** If something is **short** or lasts
for a **short** time, it does not last very long. ❑ *The*

announcement was made a short time ago.* ❑ *Kemp gave a
short laugh.* **2** A **short** speech, letter, or book does not
have many words or pages in it. ❑ *They were performing a
short extract from Shakespeare's Two Gentlemen of Verona.*
3 Someone who is **short** is not as tall as most people are.
❑ *I'm tall and thin and he's short and fat.* ❑ *a short, elderly
woman with grey hair* **4** Something that is **short** measures
only a small amount from one end to the other. ❑ *The
restaurant is only a short distance away.* ❑ *A short flight of steps
led to a grand doorway.* **5** [V-LINK + short] If you are **short
of** something or if it is **short**, you do not have enough of
it. If you are running **short of** something or if it is running
short, you do not have much of it left. ❑ *Her father's illness
left the family short of money.* ❑ *Government forces are running
short of ammunition and fuel.* **6** [V-LINK + short 'of' N] If
someone or something is or stops **short of** a place, they
have not quite reached it. If they are or fall **short of** an
amount, they have not quite achieved it. ❑ *He stopped a
hundred yards short of the building.* **7** [V-LINK + short 'for' N]
If a name or abbreviation is **short for** another name, it is
the short version of that name. ❑ *Her friend Kes (short for
Kesewa) was in tears.* **8** If you have a **short** temper, you get
angry very easily. ❑ *an awkward, self-conscious woman with a
short temper* **9** [V-LINK + short] If you are **short with**
someone, you speak briefly and rather rudely to them,
because you are impatient or angry. ❑ *She seemed nervous
or tense, and she was definitely short with me.*
PHRASE **be short on something** (*disapproval*) If someone
or something is **short on** a particular good quality, they do
not have as much of it as you think they should have.
❑ *The proposals were short on detail.*
ADV [short after v] If something is **cut short** or stops **short**,
it is stopped before people expect it to or before it has
finished. ❑ *His glittering career was cut short by a heart
attack.*
PHRASES **short of** Of a particular thing means except
for that thing or without actually doing that thing.
❑ *Short of gagging the children, there was not much she could
do about the noise.*
stop short of If someone **stops short of** doing something,
they come close to doing it but do not actually do it. ❑ *He
stopped short of explicitly criticizing the government.*
NOUN [PL, c] (**shorts**) **1** [PL] [also 'a pair of' shorts] **Shorts**
are trousers with very short legs that people wear in hot
weather or for taking part in sports. ❑ *two women in bright
cotton shorts and tee shirts* **2** [c] A **short** is a short film,
especially one that is shown before the main film at the
cinema.
PHRASES **for short** If a person or thing is called something
for short, that is the short version of their name.
❑ *Opposite me was a woman called Jasminder (Jazzy for short).*
in short You use **in short** when you have been giving a lot
of details and you want to give a conclusion or summary.
❑ *Try tennis, badminton or windsurfing. In short, anything
challenging.*
✦ **short of breath** → see **breath; on short notice** → see
notice; draw the short straw → see **straw; in short supply**
→ see **supply; in the short term** → see **term**

⊘ **short·age** ♦◇◇ /ˈʃɔːtɪdʒ/ NOUN [C, U] (**shortages**) If
there is a **shortage** of something, there is not enough of it.
= lack; ≠ excess, abundance ❑ *A shortage of funds is
preventing the UN from monitoring relief.* ❑ *Vietnam is suffering
from food shortage.*

⊘ **short·coming** /ˈʃɔːtkʌmɪŋ/ NOUN [c] (**shortcomings**)
Someone's or something's **shortcomings** are the faults or
weaknesses which they have. = failing, weakness;
≠ strength ❑ *Marriages usually break down as a result of the
shortcomings of both partners.* ❑ *His book has its shortcomings.*

short·cut /ˈʃɔːtkʌt/ NOUN [c] (**shortcuts**) **1** A **shortcut** is
a quicker way of getting somewhere than the usual route.
❑ *I tried to take a shortcut and got lost.* **2** A **shortcut** is a
method of achieving something more quickly or more
easily than if you use the usual methods. ❑ *Fame can be a
shortcut to love and money.* **3** (*computing*) On a computer, a
shortcut is an icon on the desktop that allows you to go
immediately to a program or document. ❑ *There are any
number of ways to move or copy icons or create shortcuts in*

S

Windows. **4** (*computing*) On a computer, a **shortcut** is a keystroke or a combination of keystrokes that allow you to give commands without using the mouse. ❑ *There is a handy keyboard shortcut to save you having to scroll up to the top of the screen.*

short·en /ˈʃɔːtən/ VERB [I, T] (**shortens, shortening, shortened**) **1** [I, T] If you **shorten** an event or the length of time that something lasts, or if it **shortens**, it does not last as long as it would otherwise do or as it used to do. ❑ *Smoking can shorten your life.* ❑ *The trading day is shortened in observance of the May bank holiday.* **2** [I, T] If you **shorten** an object or if it **shortens**, it becomes smaller in length. ❑ *Her father paid $5,000 for an operation to shorten her nose.* **3** [T] If you **shorten** a name or other word, you change it by removing some of the letters. ❑ *Originally called Lili, she eventually shortened her name to Lee.*

short·fall /ˈʃɔːtfɔːl/ NOUN [C] (**shortfalls**) If there is a **shortfall** in something, there is less of it than you need. = **deficit** ❑ *The government has refused to make up a $30,000 shortfall in funding.*

short·list /ˈʃɔːtlɪst/ NOUN, VERB
NOUN (also **short list**) [C] (**shortlists**) If someone is on a **shortlist**, for example, for a job or a prize, they are one of a small group of people who have been chosen from a larger group. The successful person is then chosen from the small group. ❑ *If you've been asked for an interview you are probably on a shortlist of no more than six.*
VERB [T] (**shortlists, shortlisting, shortlisted**) If someone or something **is shortlisted for** a job or a prize, they are put on a shortlist. ❑ *He was shortlisted for the Nobel Prize for literature several times.*

short-lived ADJ Something that is **short-lived** does not last very long. ❑ *Any hope that the speech would end the war was short-lived.*

short·ly ◆◇◇ /ˈʃɔːtli/ ADV If something happens **shortly** after or before something else, it happens not long after or before it. If something is going to happen **shortly**, it is going to happen soon. ❑ *Their trial will shortly begin.* ❑ *Shortly after moving into her flat, she found a job.*

short·sighted /ˌʃɔːtˈsaɪtɪd/ also **short-sighted** ADJ **1** (*mainly BrE; in AmE*, usually use **nearsighted**) If you are **short-sighted**, you cannot see things properly that are far away, because there is something wrong with your eyes. **2** If someone is **shortsighted** about something, or if their ideas are **shortsighted**, they do not make proper or careful judgments about the future. ❑ *Environmentalists fear that this is a shortsighted approach to the problem of global warming.*

short-term ◆◇◇ ADJ **Short-term** is used to describe things that will last for a short time, or things that will have an effect soon rather than in the distant future. ❑ *Investors weren't concerned about short-term profits over the next few years.* ❑ *The company has 90 staff, almost all on short-term contracts.*

shot ◆◆◇ /ʃɒt/ IRREG FORM, NOUN
IRREG FORM **Shot** is the past tense and past participle of **shoot**.
NOUN [C] (**shots**) **1** A **shot** is an act of firing a gun. ❑ *He had murdered Perceval at point blank range with a single shot.* **2** Someone who is a good **shot** can shoot well. Someone who is a bad **shot** cannot shoot well. ❑ *He was not a particularly good shot because of his eyesight.* **3** In sports such as football, golf, or tennis, a **shot** is an act of kicking, hitting, or throwing the ball, especially in an attempt to score a point. ❑ *He had only one shot at goal.* **4** A **shot** is a photograph or a particular sequence of pictures in a film. ❑ *I decided to try for a more natural shot of a fox peering from the bushes.* **5** (*informal*) If you have a **shot** at something, you attempt to do it. ❑ *The heavyweight champion will be given a shot at Holyfield's world title.* **6** A **shot of** a drug is an injection of it. ❑ *He administered a shot of Nembutal.* **7** A **shot of** a strong alcoholic drink is a small glass of it. ❑ *a shot of vodka*
PHRASES **give something your best shot** (*informal*) If you **give** something your **best shot**, you do it as well as you possibly can. ❑ *I don't expect to win. But I am going to give it my best shot.*

call the shots The person who **calls the shots** is in a position to tell others what to do. ❑ *The directors call the shots and nothing happens without their say-so.*

like a shot (*informal*) If you do something **like a shot**, you do it without any delay or hesitation. ❑ *I heard the key turn in the front door and I was out of bed like a shot.*

a long shot If you describe something as **a long shot**, you mean that it is unlikely to succeed, but is worth trying. ❑ *The deal was a long shot, but Bagley had little to lose.*

by a long shot (*emphasis*) People sometimes use the expression **by a long shot** to emphasize the opinion they are giving. ❑ *The missile-reduction treaty makes sweeping cuts, but the arms race isn't over by a long shot.*

should ◆◆◆ /ʃəd, STRONG ʃʊd/ VERB [MODAL]

> **Should** is a modal verb. It is used with the base form of a verb.

1 You use **should** when you are saying what would be the right thing to do or the right state for something to be in. ❑ *I should exercise more.* ❑ *He's never going to be able to forget it. And I don't think he should.* ❑ *Should our children be taught to swim at school?* **2** You use **should** to give someone an order to do something, or to report an official order. ❑ *18-year-olds are sent reminders that they should register to vote.* **3** If you say that something **should have** happened, you mean that it did not happen, but that you wish it had. If you say that something **should not have** happened, you mean that it did happen, but that you wish it had not. ❑ *I should have gone this morning but I was feeling a bit ill.* ❑ *You should have written to the area manager again.* **4** You use **should** when you are saying that something is probably the case or will probably happen in the way you are describing. If you say that something **should have** happened by a particular time, you mean that it will probably have happened by that time. ❑ *You should have no problem with reading this language.* ❑ *The doctor said it will take six weeks and I should be fine by then.* **5** You use **should** in questions when you are asking someone for advice, permission, or information. ❑ *Should I take out a loan?* ❑ *What should I do?* **6** (*mainly BrE, formal*) You say '**I should**', usually with the expression 'if I were you', when you are giving someone advice by telling them what you would do if you were in their position. ❑ *I should look out if I were you!* **7** (*formal*) You use **should** in conditional clauses when you are talking about things that might happen. ❑ *If you should be fired, your health and pension benefits will not be automatically cut off.* **8** You use **should** in 'that' clauses after certain verbs, nouns, and adjectives when you are talking about a future event or situation. ❑ *He raised his glass and indicated that I should do the same.* ❑ *I insisted that we should have a look at every car.* **9** You use **should** in expressions such as **I should think** and **I should imagine** to indicate that you think something is true but you are not sure. ❑ *I should think it's going to rain soon.* **10** (*spoken, emphasis*) You use **should** in expressions such as **You should have seen us** and **You should have heard him** to emphasize how funny, shocking, or impressive something that you experienced was. ❑ *You should have heard him last night!*

shoul·der ◆◆◇ /ˈʃəʊldə/ NOUN, VERB
NOUN [C, PL, U] (**shoulders**) **1** [C] Your **shoulders** are between your neck and the tops of your arms. ❑ *She led him to an armchair, with her arm round his shoulder.* **2** [PL] When you talk about someone's problems or responsibilities, you can say that they carry them **on** their **shoulders**. ❑ *No one suspected the anguish he carried on his shoulders.* **3** [C, U] A **shoulder** is a cut of meat from the upper part of the front leg of an animal. ❑ *shoulder of lamb*
PHRASES **a shoulder to cry on** If someone offers you **a shoulder to cry on** or is **a shoulder to cry on**, they listen sympathetically as you talk about your troubles. ❑ *Mrs Barrantes longs to be at her daughter's side to offer her a shoulder to cry on.*

head and shoulders If you say that someone or something stands **head and shoulders above** other people or things, you mean that they are a lot better than them. ❑ *The two candidates stood head and shoulders above the rest.*

shoulder to shoulder **1** If two or more people stand

S

shoulder to shoulder, they are next to each other, with their shoulders touching. ❑ *They fell into step, walking shoulder to shoulder with their heads bent against the rain.* **2** If people work or stand **shoulder to shoulder**, they work together in order to achieve something, or support each other. ❑ *They could fight shoulder to shoulder against a common enemy.*

VERB [T, I] (**shoulders, shouldering, shouldered**)
1 [T] If you **shoulder** the responsibility or the blame for something, you accept it. = accept ❑ *He has had to shoulder the responsibility of his father's mistakes.* **2** [I, T] If you **shoulder** someone **aside** or if you **shoulder** your **way** somewhere, you push past people roughly using your shoulder. ❑ *The policemen rushed past him, shouldering him aside.* ❑ *She could do nothing to stop him as he shouldered his way into the house.*
♦ **rub shoulders with** → see **rub**

shout ♦◇◇ /ʃaʊt/ VERB, NOUN
VERB [I, T] (**shouts, shouting, shouted**) If you **shout**, you say something very loudly, usually because you want people a long distance away to hear you or because you are angry. ❑ *He had to shout to make himself heard above the wind.* ❑ *'She's alive!' he shouted triumphantly.* ❑ *Andrew rushed out of the house, shouting for help.*
PHRASAL VERB **shout out** If you **shout** something **out**, you say it very loudly so that people can hear you clearly. ❑ *They shouted out the names of those detained.* ❑ *I shouted out 'I'm OK!'*
NOUN [C] (**shouts**) A **shout** is a loud cry that you usually make because you want people a long distance away to hear you or because you are angry. ❑ *The decision was greeted with shouts of protest from the crowd.*

shove /ʃʌv/ VERB, NOUN
VERB [I, T] (**shoves, shoving, shoved**) **1** [I, T] If you **shove** someone or something, you push them with a quick, violent movement. ❑ *He shoved her out of the way.* ❑ *He's the one who shoved me.* **2** [T] If you **shove** something somewhere, you push it there quickly and carelessly. ❑ *We shoved a copy of the newsletter beneath their door.*
NOUN [C] (**shoves**) If you give someone or something a **shove**, you push them with a quick, violent movement. ❑ *She gave Gracie a shove towards the house.*
PHRASE **if push comes to shove** (*informal*) If you talk about what you think will happen **if push comes to shove**, you are talking about what you think will happen if a situation becomes very bad or difficult. ❑ *If push comes to shove, if you should lose your case in the court, what will you do?*

✪ show ♦♦♦ /ʃəʊ/ VERB, NOUN
VERB [T, I] (**shows, showing, showed, shown**) **1** [T] If something **shows that** a state of affairs exists, it gives information that proves it or makes it clear to people. = indicate, demonstrate ❑ *Research shows that young people still look to parents as their main source for health information.* ❑ *These figures show an increase of over one million in unemployment.* ❑ *It was only later that the drug was shown to be addictive.* **2** [T] If a picture, chart, film, or piece of writing **shows** something, it represents it or gives information about it. = present, represent ❑ *Figure 4.1 shows the respiratory system.* ❑ *The cushions, shown left, measure 20 x 12 inches and cost $39.95.* ❑ *Much of the film shows the painter simply going about his task.* **3** [T] If you **show** someone something, you give it to them, take them to it, or point to it, so that they can see it or know what you are referring to. ❑ *Cut out this article and show it to your boss.* ❑ *He showed me the apartment he shares with Esther.* **4** [T] If you **show** someone to a room or seat, you lead them there. ❑ *It was very good of you to come. Let me show you to my study.* ❑ *Milton was shown into the office.* **5** [T] If you **show** someone how to do something, you do it yourself so that they can watch you and learn how to do it. ❑ *Claire showed us how to make a chocolate cake.* ❑ *There are seasoned professionals who can teach you and show you what to do.* **6** [I, T] If something **shows** or if you **show** it, it is visible or noticeable. ❑ *When he smiled he showed a row of strong white teeth.* ❑ *Faint glimmers of daylight were showing through the trees.* **7** [I, T] If you **show** a particular attitude,

quality, or feeling, or if it **shows**, you behave in a way that makes this attitude, quality, or feeling clear to other people. ❑ *She showed no interest in her children.* ❑ *Ferguson was unhappy and it showed.* ❑ *You show me respect.* **8** [T] If something **shows** a quality or characteristic or if that quality or characteristic **shows itself**, it can be noticed or observed. ❑ *The story shows a strong narrative gift and a vivid eye for detail.* ❑ *Her popularity clearly shows no sign of waning.* **9** [T] If a company **shows** a profit or a loss, its accounts indicate that it has made a profit or a loss. ❑ *It is the only one of the three companies expected to show a profit for the quarter.* **10** [I] (*mainly AmE*) If a person you are expecting to meet does not **show**, they do not arrive at the place where you expect to meet them. = turn up ❑ *There was always a chance he wouldn't show.* **11** [I, T] If someone **shows** a film or television programme, it is broadcast or appears on television or in the cinema. ❑ *The TV news showed the same film clip.* ❑ *The film is now showing at cinemas around the country.* **12** [T] To **show** things such as works of art means to put them in an exhibition where they can be seen by the public. ❑ *50 dealers will show oils, watercolours, drawings and prints from 1900 to 1992.*

PHRASES **have something to show for something** If you **have** something **to show for** your efforts, you have achieved something as a result of what you have done. ❑ *I'm nearly 31 and it's about time I had something to show for my time in my job.*

it just goes to show If you say **it just goes to show** or **it just shows that** something is the case, you mean that what you have just said or experienced demonstrates that it is the case. ❑ *I forgot all about the ring. Which just goes to show that getting good grades in school doesn't mean you're clever.*

PHRASAL VERBS **show off** **1** If you say that someone **is showing off**, you are criticizing them for trying to impress people by showing in a very obvious way what they can do or what they own. ❑ *All right, there's no need to show off.* **2** If you **show off** something that you have, you show it to a lot of people or make it obvious that you have it, because you are proud of it. ❑ *Naomi was showing off her engagement ring.*

show up **1** Show up means the same as **show** VERB **10**. ❑ *We waited until five o'clock, but he did not show up.* **2** If something **shows up** or if something **shows** it **up**, it can be clearly seen or noticed. ❑ *You may have some strange disease that may not show up for 10 or 15 years.* ❑ *The orange colour shows up well against most backgrounds.* **3** If someone or something **shows** you **up**, they make you feel embarrassed or ashamed of them. ❑ *He wanted to teach her a lesson for showing him up in front of Leonov.*

NOUN [C, U] (**shows**) **1** [C] [usu 'a' show 'of' N] A **show of** a feeling or quality is an attempt by someone to make it clear that they have that feeling or quality. ❑ *Miners gathered in the centre of Bucharest in a show of support for the government.* **2** [U] If you say that something is **for show**, you mean that it has no real purpose and is done just to give a good impression. ❑ *The change in government is more for show than for real.* **3** [C] A television or radio **show** is a programme on television or radio. = programme ❑ *I had my own TV show.* ❑ *a popular talk show on a Cuban radio station* **4** [C] A **show** in a theatre is an entertainment or concert, especially one that includes different items such as music, dancing, and comedy. ❑ *How about going shopping and seeing a show?* **5** [C] [also 'on' show] A **show** is a public exhibition of things, such as works of art, fashionable clothes, or things that have been entered in a competition. ❑ *Currently, the show is in Boston.* ❑ *It plans about 30 such fashion shows this autumn in department stores.*
♦ **show someone the door** → see **door**; **show your face** → see **face**

WORD CONNECTIONS
NOUN + **show**
a **study** shows
a **survey** shows
research shows
❑ *Studies have shown that girls do better in subjects that require verbal competence.*

S

figures show
data shows
evidence shows
❏ *The evidence shows that people enormously over-estimate some risks.*

a **picture** shows
a **chart** shows
a **graph** shows
a **map** shows
❏ *The picture on the left shows the site before construction started.*

show + ADV

show **clearly**
show **conclusively**
❏ *The results clearly show an increase in average temperature.*

VOCABULARY BUILDER

show VERB
If something **shows that** a state of affairs exists, it gives information that proves it or makes it clear to people.
❏ *The user breakdown shows that 48 per cent of users work in organizations of 100 people or less.*

demonstrate VERB
To **demonstrate** a fact means to make it clear.
❏ *The study demonstrated a direct link between obesity and mortality.*

illustrate VERB *(formal)*
If you say that something **illustrates** a situation that you are drawing attention to, you mean that it shows that the situation exists.
❏ *The situation illustrates how vulnerable the president is.*

display VERB *(fairly formal)*
If you **display** something, you show it to people.
❏ *She displayed her wound to the jury.*

exhibit VERB
If someone or something shows a particular quality, feeling, or type of behaviour, you can say that they **exhibit** it.
❏ *He has exhibited symptoms of anxiety.*

present VERB *(formal)*
When you **present** information, you give it to people in a formal way.
❏ *We presented three options to the unions for discussion.*

show·er /ˈʃaʊə/ NOUN, VERB
NOUN [C] (showers) **1** A **shower** is a device for washing yourself. It consists of a pipe which ends in a flat cover with a lot of holes in it so that water comes out in a spray. ❏ *She heard him turn on the shower.* **2** A **shower** is a small enclosed area containing a shower. ❏ *Do you sing in the shower?* **3** The **showers** or the **shower** in a place such as a gym is the area containing showers. ❏ *The showers are a mess.* **4** If you have a **shower**, you wash yourself by standing under a spray of water from a shower. ❏ *I think I'll have a shower before dinner.* **5** A **shower** is a short period of rain, especially light rain. ❏ *There'll be bright or sunny spells and scattered showers this afternoon.* **6** You can refer to a lot of things that are falling as a **shower** of them. ❏ *Showers of sparks flew in all directions.* **7** (mainly AmE) A **shower** is a party or celebration at which the guests bring gifts. ❏ *a baby shower*
VERB [I, T] (showers, showering, showered) **1** [I] If you **shower**, you wash yourself by standing under a spray of water from a shower. ❏ *There wasn't time to shower or change clothes.* **2** [T] If you **are showered with** a lot of small objects or pieces, they are scattered over you. ❏ *They were showered with rice in the traditional manner.*

shown /ʃəʊn/ IRREG FORM **Shown** is the past participle of **show**.

shrank /ʃræŋk/ IRREG FORM **Shrank** is the past tense of **shrink**.

shred /ʃred/ VERB, NOUN
VERB [T] (shreds, shredding, shredded) If you **shred** something such as food or paper, you cut it or tear it into very small, narrow pieces. ❏ *They may be shredding documents.*
NOUN [C] (shreds) **1** If you cut or tear food or paper **into shreds**, you cut or tear it into small, narrow pieces. ❏ *Cut the cabbage into fine long shreds.* **2** If there is not a **shred** of something, there is not even a small amount of it. = scrap ❏ *He said there was not a shred of evidence to support such remarks.* ❏ *There is not a shred of truth in the story.*

shrewd /ʃruːd/ ADJ (shrewder, shrewdest) A **shrewd** person is able to understand and judge a situation quickly and to use this understanding to their own advantage. ❏ *She's a shrewd businesswoman.*

shriek /ʃriːk/ VERB, NOUN
VERB [I] (shrieks, shrieking, shrieked) When someone **shrieks**, they make a short, very loud cry, for example, because they are suddenly surprised, are in pain, or are laughing. ❏ *She shrieked and leapt from the bed.*
NOUN [C] (shrieks) A **shriek** is a short, very loud cry that someone makes, for example, because they are suddenly surprised, are in pain, or are laughing. ❏ *Sue let out a terrific shriek and leapt out of the way.*

✪ shrink /ʃrɪŋk/ VERB [I, T] (shrinks, shrinking, shrank, shrunk) **1** [I] If cloth or clothing **shrinks**, it becomes smaller in size, usually as a result of being washed. ❏ *People were short in those days – or else those military uniforms all shrank in the wash!* **2** [I, T] If something **shrinks** or something else **shrinks** it, it becomes smaller. = decrease; ≠ grow ❏ *The vast forests of West Africa have shrunk.* ❏ *Hungary may have to lower its hopes of shrinking its state sector.* **3** [I] If you **shrink away from** someone or something, you move away from them because you are frightened, shocked, or disgusted by them. ❏ *One child shrinks away from me when I try to talk to him.* **4** [I] If you do not **shrink from** a task or duty, you do it even though it is unpleasant or dangerous. ❏ *He is decisive and won't shrink from a fight.*

shrub /ʃrʌb/ NOUN [C] (shrubs) **Shrubs** are plants that have several woody stems. ❏ *flowering shrubs*

shrug /ʃrʌɡ/ VERB, NOUN
VERB [I, T] (shrugs, shrugging, shrugged) If you **shrug**, you raise your shoulders to show that you are not interested in something or that you do not know or care about something. ❏ *I shrugged, as if to say, 'Why not?'*
PHRASAL VERB **shrug off** If you **shrug** something **off**, you ignore it or treat it as if it is not really important or serious. ❏ *He shrugged off the criticism.*
NOUN [C] (shrugs) A **shrug** is the act of raising your shoulders to show that you are not interested in something or that you do not know or care about something. ❏ *'I suppose so,' said Anna with a shrug.*

shrunk /ʃrʌŋk/ IRREG FORM **Shrunk** is the past participle of **shrink**.

shud·der /ˈʃʌdə/ VERB, NOUN
VERB [I] (shudders, shuddering, shuddered) **1** If you **shudder**, you shake with fear, horror, or disgust, or because you are cold. ❏ *Lloyd had urged her to eat caviar. She had shuddered at the thought.* **2** If something such as a machine or vehicle **shudders**, it shakes suddenly and violently. ❏ *The train began to pull out of the station – then suddenly shuddered to a halt.*
NOUN [C] (shudders) **1** [usu sing] If you give a **shudder**, you shake with fear, horror, or disgust, or because you are cold. ❏ *She gave a violent shudder.* **2** If something sends a **shudder** or **shudders** through a group of people, it makes them worried or afraid. ❏ *The next crisis sent a shudder of fear through the UN community.*

shuf·fle /ˈʃʌfəl/ VERB, NOUN
VERB [I, T] (shuffles, shuffling, shuffled) **1** [I] If you **shuffle** somewhere, you walk there without lifting your feet properly off the ground. ❏ *Moira shuffled across the kitchen.* **2** [I, T] If you **shuffle around**, you move your feet about

S

while standing or you move your bottom about while sitting, often because you feel uncomfortable or embarrassed. ❑ *He shuffles around in his chair.* **3** [T] If you **shuffle** playing cards, you mix them up before you begin a game. ❑ *There are various ways of shuffling and dealing the cards.* NOUN [SING] A **shuffle** is an act or instance of walking without lifting your feet properly off the ground. ❑ *She noticed her own proud walk had become a shuffle.*

shut ◆◇◇ /ʃʌt/ VERB, ADJ
VERB [I, T] (**shuts, shutting, shut**) **1** [I, T] If you **shut** something such as a door or if it **shuts**, it moves so that it fills a hole or a space. = close ❑ *Just make sure you shut the gate.* **2** [T] If you **shut** your eyes, you lower your eyelids so that you cannot see anything. = close ❑ *Lucy shut her eyes so she wouldn't see it happen.* **3** [I, T] If your mouth **shuts** or if you **shut** your mouth, you place your lips firmly together. ❑ *Daniel's mouth opened, and then shut again.* **4** [I, T] When a shop, bar, or other public building **shuts** or when someone **shuts** it, it is closed and you cannot use it until it is open again. = close ❑ *There is a tendency to shut museums or shops at a moment's notice.* ❑ *Shops usually shut from noon-3pm, and stay open late.*

PHRASAL VERBS **shut down** If a factory or business **shuts down** or if someone **shuts** it **down**, work there stops or it is no longer in business. ❑ *Smaller contractors had been forced to shut down.* ❑ *It is required by law to shut down banks which it regards as chronically short of capital.*

shut in If you **shut** someone or something **in** a room, you close the door so that they cannot leave it. ❑ *The door enables us to shut the birds in the shelter in bad weather.*

shut off **1** If you **shut off** something such as an engine or an electrical item, you turn it off to stop it from working. = switch off ❑ *They pulled over and shut off the engine.* **2** If you **shut yourself off**, you avoid seeing other people, usually because you are feeling depressed. ❑ *Billy tends to keep things to himself more and shut himself off.* **3** If an official organization **shuts off** the supply of something, they no longer send it to the people they supplied in the past. ❑ *The State Water Project has shut off all supplies to farmers.*

shut out **1** If you **shut** something or someone **out**, you prevent them from getting into a place, for example, by closing the doors. ❑ *'I shut him out of the bedroom,' says Maureen.* **2** If you **shut out** a thought or a feeling, you prevent yourself from thinking or feeling it. = block out ❑ *I shut out the memory which was too painful to dwell on.* **3** If you **shut** someone **out** of something, you prevent them from having anything to do with it. ❑ *She is very reclusive, to the point of shutting me out of her life.* **4** (AmE) In sports such as American football and hockey, if one team **shuts out** the team they are playing against, they win and prevent the opposing team from scoring. ❑ *Harvard shut out Yale, 14–0.*

shut up If someone **shuts up** or if someone **shuts** them **up**, they stop talking. You can say '**shut up**' as an impolite way to tell a person to stop talking. ❑ *Just shut up, will you?* ADJ **1** [V-LINK + shut] If a door or window is **shut**, it has been moved so that it fills a hole or a space. ❑ *They have warned residents to stay inside and keep their doors and windows shut.* **2** [V-LINK + shut] If your eyes are **shut**, you have lowered your eyelids so that you cannot see anything. ❑ *His eyes were shut and he seemed to have fallen asleep.* **3** [V-LINK + shut] If your mouth is **shut**, your lips are pressed firmly together. ❑ *She was silent for a moment, lips tight shut, eyes distant.* **4** [V-LINK + shut] When a shop, bar, or other public building is **shut**, it is closed and you cannot use it until it is open again. ❑ *Make sure you have food to tide you over when the local shop may be shut.*

PHRASE **keep your mouth shut** **1** If someone tells you to **keep** your **mouth shut** about something, they are telling you not to let anyone else know about it. ❑ *I don't have to tell you how important it is for you to keep your mouth shut about all this.* **2** If you **keep** your **mouth shut**, you do not express your opinions about something, even though you would like to. ❑ *If she had kept her mouth shut she would still have her job now.*

shut·ter /ˈʃʌtə/ NOUN [C] (**shutters**) **1 Shutters** are wooden or metal covers fitted on the outside of a window.

They can be opened to let in the light, or closed to keep out the sun or the cold. ❑ *She opened the shutters and gazed out over village roofs.* **2** The **shutter** in a camera is the part which opens to allow light through the lens when a photograph is taken. ❑ *There are a few things you should check before pressing the shutter release.*

shut·tle /ˈʃʌtəl/ NOUN, VERB
NOUN [C] (**shuttles**) A **shuttle** is a plane, bus, or train which makes frequent trips between two places. ❑ *There is a free 24-hour shuttle between the airport terminals.* VERB [I, T] (**shuttles, shuttling, shuttled**) If someone or something **shuttles** or is **shuttled** from one place to another place, they frequently go from one place to the other. ❑ *He and colleagues have shuttled back and forth between the three capitals.*

shy /ʃaɪ/ ADJ
ADJ (**shyer, shyest**) **1** A **shy** person is nervous and uncomfortable in the company of other people. ❑ *She was a shy, quiet girl.* ❑ *She was a shy and retiring person off-stage.* **2** If you are **shy about** or **shy of** doing something, you are unwilling to do it because you are afraid of what might happen. ❑ *They feel shy about showing their feelings.* PHRASAL VERB **shy away from** (**shies, shying, shied**) If you **shy away from** doing something, you avoid doing it, often because you are afraid or not confident enough. ❑ *We frequently shy away from making decisions.*

shy·ly /ˈʃaɪli/ ADV ❑ *The children smiled shyly.*

shy·ness /ˈʃaɪnəs/ NOUN [U] ❑ *Eventually he overcame his shyness.*

✪**sib·ling** /ˈsɪblɪŋ/ NOUN [C] (**siblings**) (formal) Your **siblings** are your brothers and sisters. ❑ *His siblings are in their twenties.* ❑ *Some studies have found that children are more friendly to younger siblings of the same sex.* ❑ *Sibling rivalry often causes parents anxieties.*

sick ◆◇◇ /sɪk/ ADJ, NOUN
ADJ (**sicker, sickest**) **1** If you are **sick**, you are ill. **Sick** usually means physically ill, but it can sometimes be used to mean mentally ill. ❑ *He's very sick. He needs medication.* ❑ *She found herself with two small children, a sick husband, and no money.* **2** [V-LINK + sick] If you are **sick**, the food that you have eaten comes up from your stomach and out of your mouth. If you **feel sick**, you feel as if you are going to be sick. ❑ *She got up and was sick in the sink.* ❑ *The very thought of food made him feel sick.* **3** [V-LINK + sick 'of' N/-ING] (informal, emphasis) If you say that you are **sick of** something or **sick and tired of** something, you are emphasizing that you are very annoyed by it and want it to stop. = fed up ❑ *I am sick and tired of hearing all these people moaning.* **4** If you describe something such as a joke or story as **sick**, you mean that it deals with death or suffering in an unpleasantly humorous way. ❑ *a sick joke about a cat*

PHRASES **make someone sick** (informal) If you say that something or someone **makes** you **sick**, you mean that they make you feel angry or disgusted. ❑ *It makes me sick that this wasn't disclosed.*

off sick [usu V-LINK + off sick] (BrE; in AmE, use **out sick**) If you are **off sick**, you are not at work because you are sick. ❑ *That afternoon she was fired from her job as a nurse, because she'd been off sick so much.*

worried sick (informal, emphasis) If you say that you are **worried sick**, you are emphasizing that you are extremely worried. ❑ *He was worried sick about what our mothers would say.*

NOUN [PL] The **sick** are people who are sick. ❑ *There were no doctors to treat the sick.*

sick·en /ˈsɪkən/ VERB [T] (**sickens, sickening, sickened**) If something **sickens** you, it makes you feel disgusted. = disgust ❑ *The notion that art should be controlled by intellectuals sickened him.*

sick·en·ing /ˈsɪkənɪŋ/ ADJ You describe something as **sickening** when it gives you feelings of horror or disgust, or makes you feel sick. ❑ *the sickening rise in the number of suicide bombings*

sick·ness /ˈsɪknəs/ NOUN [U, C] (**sicknesses**) **1** [U] Sickness is the state of being ill or unhealthy. ❑ *In fifty-two years of working he had one week of sickness.* **2** [u] **Sickness** is the uncomfortable feeling that you are going to vomit. = nausea ❑ *After a while, the sickness gradually passed and she struggled to the mirror.* **3** [c, u] A **sickness** is a particular illness. ❑ *More than 930 local people are registered as suffering from radiation sickness.*

side ◆◆◆ /saɪd/ NOUN, ADJ, VERB

NOUN [c] (**sides**) **1** The **side** of something is a position to the left or right of it, rather than in front of it, behind it, or on it. ❑ *On one side of the main entrance there's a red plaque.* ❑ *a photograph with Joe and Ken on each side of me* ❑ *the nations on either side of the Pacific* **2** The **side** of an object, building, or vehicle is any of its flat surfaces which is not considered to be its front, its back, its top, or its bottom. ❑ *We put a notice on the side of the box.* ❑ *A carton of milk lay on its side.* **3** The **sides** of a hollow or a container are its inside vertical surfaces. ❑ *The rough rock walls were like the sides of a deep canal.* ❑ *Line the base of the dish with greaseproof paper and lightly grease the sides.* **4** The **sides** of an area or surface are its edges. = edge ❑ *Park on the side of the road.* ❑ *a small beach on the north side of the peninsula* **5** The two **sides** of an area, surface, or object are its two halves. = half ❑ *She turned over on her stomach to the other side of the bed.* ❑ *The major centre for language is in the left side of the brain.* **6** The two **sides** of a road are its two halves on which traffic travels in opposite directions. ❑ *It had gone on to the wrong side of the road and hit a car coming in the other direction.* **7** If you talk about the other **side** of a town, a country, or the world, you mean a part of the town, the country, or the world that is very far from where you are. ❑ *He lives on the other side of town.* ❑ *He saw the ship that was to transport them to the other side of the world.* **8** Your **sides** are the parts of your body between your front and your back, from under your arms to your hips. ❑ *His arms were limp at his sides.* **9** If someone is **by** your **side** or **at** your **side**, they stay near you and give you comfort or support. ❑ *He was constantly at his wife's side.* ❑ *He calls me 20 times a day and needs me by his side in the evening.* **10** The two **sides** of something flat, for example, a piece of paper, are its two flat surfaces. You can also refer to one side of a piece of paper filled with writing as one **side** of writing. ❑ *The new copiers only copy onto one side of the paper.* ❑ *Fry the chops until brown on both sides.* **11** One **side** of a tape or record is what you can hear or record if you play the tape or record from beginning to end without turning it over. ❑ *We want to hear side A.* **12** The different **sides** in a war, argument, or negotiation are the groups of people who are opposing each other. ❑ *Both sides appealed for a new ceasefire.* ❑ *Any solution must be acceptable to all sides.* **13** The different **sides** of an argument or deal are the different points of view or positions involved in it. ❑ *His words drew sharp reactions from people on both sides of the issue.* **14** (BrE) In sports, a **side** is a team. = team **15** A particular **side** of something such as a situation or someone's character is one aspect of it. ❑ *He is in charge of the civilian side of the UN mission.* **16** The **mother's side** and the **father's side** of your family are your mother's relatives and your father's relatives. ❑ *So was your father's side more well off?*

PHRASES **side by side 1** If two people or things are **side by side**, they are next to each other. ❑ *We sat side by side on two wicker seats.* **2** If people work or live **side by side**, they work or live closely together in a friendly way. ❑ *areas where different nationalities have lived side by side for centuries*

from side to side If something moves **from side to side**, it moves repeatedly to the left and to the right. ❑ *She was shaking her head from side to side.*

on someone's side If you are **on someone's side**, you are supporting them in an argument or a war. ❑ *He has the Democrats on his side.*

on your side If something is **on** your **side** or if you have it **on** your **side**, it helps you when you are trying to achieve something. ❑ *The weather is rather on our side.*

on the big side or **on the young side** or **on the small side** (politeness) If you say that something is, for example, **on the** small **side**, you are saying politely that you think it

is slightly too small. If you say that someone is **on the** young **side**, you are saying politely that you think they are slightly too young. ❑ *He's quiet and a bit on the shy side.*

on the side If someone does something **on the side**, they do it in addition to their main work. ❑ *ways of making a little bit of money on the side*

put something to one side or **put something on one side** If you **put** something **to one side** or put it **on one side**, you temporarily ignore it in order to concentrate on something else. ❑ *He can now concentrate on a project he'd originally put to one side.*

take someone to one side or **draw someone to one side** If you **take** someone **to one side** or **draw** them **to one side**, you speak to them privately, usually in order to give them advice or a warning. ❑ *He took Sabrina to one side and told her about the safe.*

take sides or **take someone's side** If you **take sides** or **take** someone's **side** in an argument or war, you support one of the sides against the other. ❑ *We cannot take sides in a civil war.*

ADJ [side + N] **Side** is used to describe things that are not the main or most important ones of their kind. ❑ *She slipped in and out of the theatre by a side door.*

VERB [i] (**sides, siding, sided**) If one person or country **sides with** another, they support them in an argument or a war. If people or countries **side against** another person or country, they support each other against them. ❑ *There has been much speculation that they might be siding with the rebels.*

✦ **the other side of the coin** → see **coin**; **be on the safe side** → see **safe**; **someone's side of the story** → see **story**

⊕**side-effect** also **side effect** NOUN [c] (**side-effects**) **1** The **side-effects** of a drug are the effects, usually bad ones, that the drug has on you in addition to its function of curing illness or pain. = reaction ❑ *Side-effects include nausea, tiredness, and dizziness.* ❑ *The treatment has a whole host of extremely unpleasant side-effects including weight gain, acne, skin rashes and headaches.* ❑ *Most patients suffer no side-effects.* **2** A **side-effect of** a situation is something unplanned and usually unpleasant that happens in addition to the main effects of that situation. ❑ *One side effect of modern life is stress.*

side·ways /ˈsaɪdweɪz/ ADV, ADJ

ADV **1** [sideways after v] **Sideways** means from or towards the side of something or someone. ❑ *Piercey glanced sideways at her.* ❑ *The ladder blew sideways.* **2** [sideways after v] If you are moved **sideways** at work, you move to another job at the same level as your old job. ❑ *He would be moved sideways, rather than demoted.*

ADJ **1** [sideways + N] A **sideways** look or push is a look or push towards the side of something or someone. ❑ *Alfred shot him a sideways glance.* **2** [sideways + N] A **sideways** move at work is when you move to another job at the same level as your old job. ❑ *her recent sideways move*

siege /siːdʒ/ NOUN

NOUN [c] (**sieges**) [also 'under' siege] A **siege** is a military or police operation in which soldiers or police surround a place in order to force the people there to come out or give up control of the place. ❑ *We must do everything possible to lift the siege.*

PHRASE **lay siege to something** If police, soldiers, or journalists **lay siege to** a place, they surround it in order to force the people there to come out or give up control of the place. ❑ *The rebels laid siege to the governor's residence.*

sigh ◆◇◇ /saɪ/ VERB, NOUN

VERB [i] (**sighs, sighing, sighed**) When you **sigh**, you let out a deep breath, as a way of expressing feelings such as disappointment, tiredness, or pleasure. ❑ *Michael sighed wearily.* ❑ *Roberta sighed with relief.*

NOUN [c] (**sighs**) When you give a **sigh**, you let out a deep breath, as a way of expressing feelings such as disappointment, tiredness, or pleasure. ❑ *She kicked off her shoes with a sigh.*

PHRASE **breathe a sigh of relief** or **heave a sigh of relief** If people breathe or heave a **sigh of relief**, they feel happy that something unpleasant has not happened or is no longer happening. ❑ *With monetary mayhem now*

S

retreating into memory, European countries can breathe a collective sigh of relief.

⊕**sight** ♦♦◇ /saɪt/ NOUN, VERB

NOUN [U, SING, C, PL] (**sights**) **1** [U] Someone's **sight** is their ability to see. = vision ❏ *My sight is failing, and I can't see to read any more.* ❏ *I use the sense of sound much more than the sense of sight.* **2** [SING] The **sight** of something is the act of seeing it or an occasion on which you see it. ❏ *I faint at the sight of blood.* **3** [C] A **sight** is something that you see. ❏ *The practice of hanging clothes across the street is a common sight in many parts of the city.* ❏ *We encountered the pathetic sight of a family packing up its home.* ❏ *Among the most spectacular sights are the great sea-bird colonies.* **4** [PL] The **sights** are the places that are interesting to see and that are often visited by tourists. ❏ *We'd toured the sights of Paris.* ❏ *I am going to show you the sights of our wonderful city.* ❏ *Once at Elgin day-trippers visit a number of local sights.*

PHRASES **catch sight of** If you **catch sight of** someone, you suddenly see them, often briefly. = see ❏ *Then he caught sight of her small black velvet hat in the crowd.*

at first sight If you say that something seems to have certain characteristics **at first sight**, you mean that it appears to have the features you describe when you first see it but later it is found to be different. ❏ *The theory is not as simple as you might think at first sight.*

in sight or **within sight** or **out of sight** If something is **in sight** or **within sight**, you can see it. If it is **out of sight**, you cannot see it. ❏ *The sandy beach was in sight.* ❏ *The Atlantic coast is within sight of the hotel.*

in sight or **within sight** If a result or a decision is **in sight** or **within sight**, it is likely to happen within a short time. ❏ *An agreement on many aspects of trade policy was in sight.*

lose sight of If you **lose sight of** an important aspect of something, you no longer pay attention to it because you are worrying about less important things. = forget ❏ *In some cases, US industry has lost sight of customer needs in designing products.*

on sight If someone is ordered to do something **on sight**, they have to do it without delay, as soon as a person or thing is seen. ❏ *Troops shot anyone suspicious on sight.*

set one's sights on something If you **set** your **sights on** something, you decide that you want it and try hard to get it. ❏ *They have set their sights on the world record.*

have in your sights If you **have** something **in** your **sights**, you are trying hard to achieve it, and you have a good chance of success. If you **have** someone **in** your **sights**, you are determined to catch, defeat, or overcome them. ❏ *He has the world record in his sights.* ❏ *Is this knowledge of yours the reason the murderer now has you in his sights?*

VERB [T] (**sights, sighting, sighted**) If you **sight** someone or something, you suddenly see them, often briefly. ❏ *The security forces sighted a group of young men that had crossed the border.*

sight·see·ing /ˈsaɪtsiːɪŋ/ NOUN [U] If you go **sightseeing** or do some **sightseeing**, you travel around visiting the interesting places that tourists usually visit. ❏ *a day's sightseeing in Venice*

⊕**sign** ♦♦♦ /saɪn/ NOUN, VERB

NOUN [C, U] (**signs**) **1** [C] A **sign** is a mark or shape that always has a particular meaning, for example, in mathematics or music. = symbol ❏ *Equations are generally written with an equals sign.* **2** [C] A **sign** is a movement of your arms, hands, or head which is intended to have a particular meaning. ❏ *They gave Lavalle the thumbs-up sign.* **3** [C] A **sign** is a piece of wood, metal, or plastic with words or pictures on it. Signs give you information about something, or give you a warning or an instruction. ❏ *a sign saying that the road was closed because of snow* **4** [C, U] If there is a **sign of** something, there is something which shows that it exists or is happening. = indication, symptom ❏ *They are prepared to hand back a hundred prisoners of war a day as a sign of good will.* ❏ *His face and movements rarely betrayed a sign of nerves.* ❏ *Your blood would have been checked for any sign of kidney failure.* **5** [C] In astrology, a **sign** or a **sign of the zodiac** is one of the twelve areas into which the heavens are divided. ❏ *The new moon takes place in your opposite sign of Libra on the 15th.*

PHRASE **no sign of someone** If you say that there is **no sign of** someone, you mean that they have not yet arrived, although you are expecting them to come. ❏ *The train was on time, but there was no sign of my Finnish friend.*

VERB [T, I] (**signs, signing, signed**) **1** [T] If you **sign**, you communicate with someone using sign language. If a programme or performance **is signed**, someone uses sign language so that deaf people can understand it. ❏ *All programmes will be either signed or subtitled.* **2** [T] When you **sign** a document, you write your name on it, usually at the end or in a special space. You do this to indicate that you have written the document, that you agree with what is written, or that you were present as a witness. ❏ *World leaders are expected to sign a treaty pledging to increase environmental protection.* **3** [I, T] If an organization **signs** someone or if someone **signs** for an organization, they sign a contract agreeing to work for that organization for a specified period of time. ❏ *The Minnesota Vikings signed Herschel Walker from the Dallas Cowboys.*

PHRASAL VERBS **sign for** If you **sign for** something, you officially state that you have received it, by signing a form or book. ❏ *When the courier delivers your order, check the parcel before signing for it.*

sign in If you **sign in**, you officially indicate that you have arrived at a hotel or club by signing a book or form. ❏ *I signed in and crunched across the gravel to my room.*

sign over If you **sign** something **over**, you sign documents that give someone else property, possessions, or rights that were previously yours. ❏ *Two years ago, he signed over his art collection to the New York Metropolitan Museum of Art.*

sign up If you **sign up** for an organization or if an organization **signs** you **up**, you sign a contract officially agreeing to do a job or course of study. ❏ *He signed up as a flight attendant with Korean Air.*

→ See also **signing**

⊕**sig·nal** ♦◇◇ /ˈsɪɡnəl/ NOUN, VERB

NOUN [C] (**signals**) **1** A **signal** is a gesture, sound, or action which is intended to give a particular message to the person who sees or hears it. ❏ *They fired three distress signals.* ❏ *As soon as it was dark, Mrs Evans gave the signal.* **2** If an event or action is a **signal of** something, it suggests that this thing exists or is going to happen. = sign ❏ *Kurdish leaders saw the visit as an important signal of support.* **3** A **signal** is a piece of equipment beside a railway, which indicates to train drivers whether they should stop the train or not. ❏ *A signal failure contributed to the crash.* **4** A **signal** is a series of radio waves, light waves, or changes in electrical current which may carry information. ❏ *high-frequency radio signals* ❏ *a means of transmitting television signals using microwave frequencies*

VERB [I, T] (**signals, signalling, signalled**) **1** [I, T] If you **signal to** someone, you make a gesture or sound in order to send them a particular message. ❏ *Mandy started after him, signalling to Jesse to follow.* ❏ *She signalled to Ted that she was moving forward.* **2** [T] If someone or something **signals** an event, they suggest that the event is happening or likely to happen. = indicate ❏ *He seemed to be signalling important shifts in US government policy.*

sig·na·ture /ˈsɪɡnətʃə/ NOUN [C] (**signatures**) Your **signature** is your name, written in your own characteristic way, often at the end of a document to indicate that you wrote the document or that you agree with what it says. ❏ *I was writing my signature at the bottom of the page.*

⊕**sig·nifi·cance** /sɪɡˈnɪfɪkəns/ NOUN [U] The **significance** of something is the importance that it has, usually because it will have an effect on a situation or shows something about a situation. = importance; ≠ insignificance ❏ *Ideas about the social significance of religion have changed over time.* ❏ *The difference did not achieve statistical significance.*

⊕**sig·nifi·cant** ♦♦◇ /sɪɡˈnɪfɪkənt/ ADJ (*academic word*) **1** A **significant** amount or effect is large enough to be important or affect a situation to a noticeable degree. ❏ *Most 11-year-olds are not encouraged to develop reading skills; a small but significant number are illiterate.* ❏ *foods that offer a significant amount of protein* ❏ *The study is too small to* show whether this trend is statistically significant. **2** A **significant** fact, event, or thing is one that is important or shows something. = important; ≠ insignificant ❑ I think it was significant that he never knew his own father. ❑ Time would appear to be the significant factor in this whole drama. ❑ a very significant piece of legislation

❍ **sig·nifi·cant·ly** /sɪɡˈnɪfɪkəntli/ ADV **1** ≠ insignificantly ❑ The number of Senators now supporting him had increased significantly. ❑ The groups differed significantly in two areas. ❑ America's airlines have significantly higher productivity than European ones. **2** Significantly, the company recently opened a huge store in Atlanta.

WORD FAMILIES	
significant ADJ	The study is too small to show whether this trend is statistically **significant**.
insignificant ADJ	In 1949 Bonn was a small, **insignificant** city.
significance NOUN	People were slow to realize the **significance** of the discovery.
insignificance NOUN	Events that seem very important at the time can later fade into **insignificance**.
significantly ADV	The groups differed **significantly** in two areas.

❍ **sig·ni·fy** /ˈsɪɡnɪfaɪ/ VERB [T] (signifies, signifying, signified) (academic word) **1** If an event, a sign, or a symbol **signifies** something, it is a sign of that thing or represents that thing. = indicate ❑ These were not the only changes that signified the end of boyhood. ❑ The contrasting approaches to Europe signified a sharp difference between the major parties. ❑ The symbol displayed outside a restaurant signifies there's excellent cuisine inside. **2** If you **signify** something, you make a sign or gesture in order to communicate a particular meaning. = indicate ❑ Two jurors signified their dissent.

sign·ing /ˈsaɪnɪŋ/ NOUN [U, C] (signings) **1** [U] The **signing** of a document is the act of writing your name to indicate that you agree with what it says or to say that you have been present to witness other people writing their signature. ❑ Spain's top priority is the signing of the treaty. **2** [C] (usu with SUPP] A **signing** is someone who has recently signed a contract agreeing to play for a sports team or work for a record company. ❑ the salary paid to the club's latest signing **3** [U] The **signing** of a player by a sports team or a group by a record company is the act of drawing up a legal document setting out the length and terms of the association between them. ❑ The ranks of professional tennis swelled with the signing of Bobby Riggs. **4** [U] **Signing** is the use of sign language to communicate with someone who is deaf. ❑ The two deaf actors converse solely in signing.

❍ **sign lan·guage** NOUN [C, U] (sign languages) **Sign language** is movements of your hands and arms used to communicate. There are several official systems of sign language, used, for example, by deaf people. Movements are also sometimes invented by people when they want to communicate with someone who does not speak the same language. ❑ Her son used sign language to tell her what happened. ❑ He indicated with sign language that he too would like to go there.

sign·post /ˈsaɪnpəʊst/ NOUN [C] (signposts) A **signpost** is a sign where roads meet that tells you which direction to go in to reach a particular place or different places. = sign ❑ Turn off at the signpost for the East 71st Street exit.

si·lence ◆◇◇ /ˈsaɪləns/ NOUN, VERB

■NOUN■ [C, U] (silences) **1** [C, U] If there is **silence**, nobody is speaking. ❑ They stood in silence. ❑ He never lets those long silences develop during dinner. **2** [U] Someone's **silence** about something is their failure or refusal to speak to other people about it. ❑ The district court ruled that Popper's silence in court today should be entered as a plea of not guilty.

■PHRASE■ **break your silence** If someone **breaks** their **silence** about something, they talk about something that they have not talked about before or for a long time.

■VERB■ [T] (silences, silencing, silenced) If someone **silences** you, they stop you from expressing opinions that they do not agree with. ❑ Like other tyrants, he tried to silence anyone who spoke out against him.

si·lent ◆◇◇ /ˈsaɪlənt/ ADJ

■ADJ■ **1** [V-LINK + silent] Someone who is **silent** is not speaking. ❑ Trish was silent because she was reluctant to put her thoughts into words. ❑ He spoke no English and was completely silent during the visit. **2** A place that is **silent** is completely quiet, with no sound at all. Something that is **silent** makes no sound at all. = quiet ❑ The room was silent except for the TV. **3** [silent + N] A **silent** film has pictures usually accompanied by music but does not have the actors' voices or any other sounds. ❑ one of the famous silent films of Charlie Chaplin

■PHRASE■ **give someone the silent treatment** If you **give** someone **the silent treatment**, you do not speak to them for a period of time because you are annoyed at something they have done. ❑ He fully expected his mother to give him the silent treatment.

si·lent·ly /ˈsaɪləntli/ ADV **1** [silently with v] ❑ She and Ned sat silently for a moment, absorbing the peace of the lake. **2** Strange shadows moved silently in the almost permanent darkness.

❍ **sili·con chip** NOUN [C] (silicon chips) A **silicon chip** is a very small piece of silicon inside a computer. It has electronic circuits on it and can hold large quantities of information or perform mathematical or logical operations. = microchip ❑ Today's silicon chip-based computers can't come close. ❑ This silicon chip implant will perform the same processes as the damaged part of the brain it is replacing. ❑ RFID tags are tiny silicon chips that broadcast a unique identification code when prompted by a reader device.

silk /sɪlk/ NOUN [C, U] (silks) **Silk** is a substance which is made into smooth, fine cloth and sewing thread. You can also refer to this cloth or thread as **silk**. ❑ They continued to get their silks from China. ❑ Pauline wore a silk dress with a strand of pearls.

sil·ly /ˈsɪli/ ADJ (sillier, silliest) If you say that someone or something is **silly**, you mean that they are foolish, childish, or ridiculous. ❑ My best friend tells me that I am silly to be upset about this. ❑ I thought it would be silly to be too rude at that stage.

sil·ver ◆◇◇ /ˈsɪlvə/ NOUN, COLOUR

■NOUN■ [U] **1** **Silver** is a valuable, pale grey metal that is used for making jewellery and ornaments. ❑ a hand-crafted brooch made from silver ❑ amber earrings set in silver **2** **Silver** consists of coins that are made from silver or that look like silver. ❑ the basement where $150,000 in silver was buried **3** [also 'the' silver] You can use **silver** to refer to all the things in a house that are made of silver, especially the cutlery and dishes. ❑ He beat the rugs and polished the silver.

■COLOUR■ **Silver** is used to describe things that are shiny and pale grey in colour. ❑ He had thick, silver hair which needed cutting.

❍ **simi·lar** ◆◆◇ /ˈsɪmɪlə/ ADJ (academic word) If one thing is **similar to** another, or if two things are **similar**, they have features that are the same. = alike; ≠ different ❑ a savoury cake with a texture similar to that of carrot cake ❑ The accident was similar to one that happened in 1973. ❑ a group of similar pictures

WORD FAMILIES	
similar ADJ	The accident was **similar** to one that happened in 1973.
similarly ADV	We tend to think and react **similarly** to people our own age.
similarity NOUN	There was a very basic **similarity** in our philosophies.
dissimilar ADJ	It would be difficult to find two men who were more **dissimilar**.

❍ **simi·lar·ity** /ˌsɪmɪˈlærɪti/ NOUN [U, C] (similarities) **1** [U] If there is a **similarity between** two or more things, they are similar to each other. ≠ difference ❑ the astonishing similarity between my brother and my first-born son ❑ *There was a very basic similarity in our philosophies.* **2** [c] **Similarities** are features that things have which make them similar to each other. ❑ *There were significant similarities between mother and son.* ❑ *The film bears some similarities to Spielberg's 'A.I.'* ❑ *The similarities between Mars and Earth were enough to keep alive hopes of some form of Martian life.*

✪ **simi·lar·ly** /'sɪmɪləli/ ADV **1** You use **similarly** to say that something is similar to something else. ❑ *Most of the men who now gathered around him again were similarly dressed.* ❑ *We tend to think and react similarly to people our own age.* **2** [similarly with CL] You use **similarly** when mentioning a fact or situation that is similar to the one you have just mentioned. = likewise ❑ *A mother recognises the feel of her child's skin. Similarly, she can instantly identify her baby's cry.*

sim·mer /'sɪmə/ VERB, NOUN
VERB [I, T] (**simmers, simmering, simmered**) **1** [I, T] When you **simmer** food or when it **simmers**, you cook it by keeping it at boiling point or just below boiling point. ❑ *Make an infusion by boiling and simmering the rhubarb and camomile together.* **2** [I] If a conflict or a quarrel **simmers**, it does not actually happen for a period of time, but eventually builds up to the point where it does. ❑ *bitter divisions that have simmered for more than half a century* NOUN [SING] When food or a liquid is kept at or brought to a **simmer**, it is kept at or brought to boiling point or just below boiling point. ❑ *Combine the stock, whole onion, and peppercorns in a pan and bring to a simmer.*

✪ **sim·ple** ♦♦◇ /'sɪmpəl/ ADJ (**simpler, simplest**) **1** If you describe something as **simple**, you mean that it is not complicated, and is therefore easy to understand. ❑ *simple pictures and diagrams* ❑ *pages of simple advice on filling in your tax form* ❑ *Buddhist ethics are simple but its practices are very complex to a western mind.* **2** If you describe people or things as **simple**, you mean that they have all the basic or necessary things they require, but nothing extra. = basic, plain; ≠ ornate, elaborate ❑ *He ate a simple dinner of rice and beans.* ❑ *the simple pleasures of childhood* ❑ *Nothing is simpler than a cool white shirt.* **3** If a problem is **simple** or if its solution is **simple**, the problem can be solved easily. ❑ *Some puzzles look difficult but are actually quite simple.* **4** A **simple** task is easy to do. = easy ❑ *The job itself had been simple enough.* ❑ *a simple mathematical task* **5** [simple + N] You use **simple** to emphasize that the thing you are referring to is the only important or relevant reason for something. = plain ❑ *His refusal to talk was simple stubbornness.* **6** In grammar, **simple** tenses are ones which are formed without an auxiliary verb 'be', for example, 'I dressed and went for a walk' and 'This tastes nice'. **Simple** verb groups are used especially to refer to completed actions, regular actions, and situations. Compare **continuous**.

✪ **sim·plic·i·ty** /sɪm'plɪsɪti/ NOUN [U] The **simplicity** of something is the fact that it is not complicated and can be understood or done easily. = clarity, straightforwardness; ≠ complexity, difficulty ❑ *The apparent simplicity of his plot is deceptive.* ❑ *Because of its simplicity, this test could be carried out easily by a family doctor.*

✪ **sim·pli·fi·ca·tion** /ˌsɪmplɪfɪ'keɪʃən/ NOUN [C, U] (**simplifications**) **1** [C] You can use **simplification** to refer to the thing that is produced when you make something simpler or when you reduce it to its basic elements. ❑ *Like any such diagram, it is a simplification.* **2** [U] **Simplification** is the act or process of making something simpler. ≠ complication ❑ *Everyone favours the simplification of court procedures.*

✪ **sim·pli·fy** /'sɪmplɪfaɪ/ VERB [T] (**simplifies, simplifying, simplified**) If you **simplify** something, you make it easier to understand or you remove the things which make it complex. ❑ *Our aim is to simplify the complex social security system.* ❑ *technology for simplifying trade procedures* ❑ *a simplified version of the formula*

sim·plis·tic /sɪm'plɪstɪk/ ADJ A **simplistic** view or interpretation of something makes it seem much simpler than it really is. ❑ *He has a simplistic view of the treatment of eczema.*

✪ **sim·ply** ♦♦◇ /'sɪmpli/ ADV **1** [simply with v] If you explain something **simply**, you explain it so that it is easy to understand. = plainly ❑ *When applying for a visa extension state simply and clearly the reasons why you need an extension.* **2** [simply after v] If something is presented **simply**, it has all the basic or necessary things but nothing extra. ❑ *The living room is furnished simply with white wicker furniture and blue-and-white fabrics.* **3** [simply after v] You can use **simply** to indicate that an action is easy to do. ❑ *We can do things that were not possible before, and can be done simply.* **4** (*emphasis*) You use **simply** to emphasize that something consists of only one thing, happens for only one reason, or is done in only one way. = just ❑ *The table is simply a chipboard circle on a base.* ❑ *Most of the damage that's occurred was simply because of fallen trees.* **5** (*emphasis*) You use **simply** to emphasize what you are saying. = just ❑ *This sort of increase simply cannot be justified.*

✪ **simu·late** /'sɪmjʊleɪt/ VERB [T] (**simulates, simulating, simulated**) (*academic word*) **1** If you **simulate** an action or a feeling, you pretend that you are doing it or feeling it. ❑ *They rolled about on the Gilligan Road, simulating a bloodthirsty fight.* **2** If you **simulate** a set of conditions, you create them artificially, for example, in order to conduct an experiment. = replicate, reproduce, model ❑ *The scientist developed one model to simulate a full year of the globe's climate.* ❑ *Cars are tested to see how much damage they suffer in simulated crashes.*

✪ **simu·la·tion** /ˌsɪmjʊ'leɪʃən/ NOUN [C, U] (**simulations**) **Simulation** is the process of simulating something or the result of simulating it. ❑ *Training includes realistic simulation of casualty procedures.* ❑ *a simulation of the greenhouse effect*

✪ **sim·ul·ta·neous** /ˌsɪməl'teɪniəs, AmE ˌsaɪm-/ ADJ Things which are **simultaneous** happen or exist at the same time. = concurrent; ≠ separate ❑ *the simultaneous release of the book and the CD* ❑ *The theatre will provide simultaneous translation in both English and Chinese.*

✪ **sim·ul·ta·neous·ly** /ˌsɪməl'teɪniəsli, AmE ˌsaɪm-/ ADV If two or more things happen or exist **simultaneously**, they happen or exist at the same time. ❑ *The two guns fired almost simultaneously.* ❑ *a spurt in economic growth that occurred simultaneously with extensive industrial investment*

sin /sɪn/ NOUN, VERB
NOUN [C, U] (**sins**) **1** [C, U] **Sin** or a **sin** is an action or type of behaviour which is believed to break the laws of God. ❑ *The Vatican's teaching on abortion is clear: it is a sin.* **2** [C] A **sin** is any action or behaviour that people disapprove of or consider morally wrong. ❑ *the sin of arrogant hard-heartedness*
VERB [I] (**sins, sinning, sinned**) If you **sin**, you do something that is believed to break the laws of God. ❑ *The Spanish Inquisition charged him with sinning against God and man.*

sin·ner /'sɪnə/ NOUN [C] (**sinners**) ❑ *I was shown that I am a sinner, that I needed to repent of my sins.*

since ♦♦♦ /sɪns/ PREP, ADV, CONJ
PREP **1** You use **since** when you are mentioning a time or event in the past and indicating that a situation has continued from then until now. ❑ *He's been in exile in India since 1959.* ❑ *She had a sort of breakdown some years ago, and since then she has been very shy.* **2** You use **since** to mention a time or event in the past when you are describing an event or situation that has happened after that time. ❑ *The percentage increase in reported crime this year is the highest since the war.*
ADV **1** [since with v] You use **since** when you are mentioning a time or event in the past and indicating that a situation has continued from then until now. ❑ *They worked together in the 1990s, and have kept in contact ever since.* **2** [since with v] When you are talking about an event or situation in the past, you use **since** to indicate that another event happened at some point later in time. ❑ *About six thousand people were arrested, several hundred of whom have since been released.*
CONJ **1** You use **since** when you are mentioning a time or event in the past and indicating that a situation has continued from then until now. ❑ *I've earned my own living since I was seven, doing all kinds of jobs.* **2** When you are

S

talking about an event or situation in the past, you use **since** to indicate that another event happened after that event or situation. ❑ *So much has changed in the sport since I was a teenager.* ❑ *Since I have become a mother, the sound of children's voices has lost its charm.* **3** You use **since** to introduce reasons or explanations. = as ❑ *I'm forever on a diet, since I put on weight easily.*

USAGE NOTE

since

Use the present perfect form of the verb with **since** to say that something has been the case from a particular time until now. Do not use the past simple.
*Results **have improved** greatly since 1999.*

---

sin·cere /sɪnˈsɪə/ ADJ (approval) If you say that someone is **sincere**, you approve of them because they really mean the things they say. You can also describe someone's behaviour and beliefs as **sincere**. = genuine ❑ *He's sincere in his views.*
sin·cer·ity /sɪnˈserɪti/ NOUN [u] ❑ *I was impressed with his deep sincerity.*

sin·cere·ly /sɪnˈsɪəli/ ADV, CONVENTION
ADV If you say or feel something **sincerely**, you really mean or feel it, and are not pretending. ❑ *'Congratulations,'* he said sincerely. ❑ *sincerely held religious beliefs*
CONVENTION People write '**Yours sincerely**' or '**Sincerely**' before their signature at the end of a formal letter when they have addressed it to someone by name. People sometimes write '**Sincerely yours**' instead. ❑ *Yours sincerely, Alan Green.*

sing ♦♦◇ /sɪŋ/ VERB
VERB [I, T] (**sings, singing, sang, sung**) When you **sing**, you make musical sounds with your voice, usually producing words that fit a tune. ❑ *I can't sing.* ❑ *I sing about love most of the time.* ❑ *They were all singing the same song.*
PHRASAL VERB **sing along** If you **sing along with** a piece of music, you sing it while you are listening to someone else perform it. ❑ *We listen to children's shows on the radio, and Janey can sing along with all the tunes.* ❑ *Would-be Elvis Presleys can sing along to 'Jailhouse Rock', 'Love me Tender', and 'Blue Suede Shoes'.*
→ See also **singing**

sing·er ♦◇◇ /ˈsɪŋə/ NOUN [c] (**singers**) A **singer** is a person who sings, especially as a job. ❑ *My mother was a singer in a dance band.*

sing·ing /ˈsɪŋɪŋ/ NOUN [u] **Singing** is the activity of making musical sounds with your voice. ❑ *a people's carnival, with singing and dancing in the streets* ❑ *the singing of a traditional hymn*

⊙ sin·gle ♦♦♦ /ˈsɪŋɡəl/ ADJ, NOUN
ADJ **1** [single + N] (emphasis) You use **single** to emphasize that you are referring to one thing, and no more than one thing. ❑ *A single shot rang out.* ❑ *Over six hundred people were wounded in a single day.* ❑ *She hadn't uttered a single word.* **2** [DET + single] (emphasis) You use **single** to indicate that you are considering something on its own and separately from other things like it. ❑ *Every single house in town had been damaged.* **3** Someone who is **single** is not married. You can also use **single** to describe someone who does not have a girlfriend or boyfriend. ≠ married ❑ *Is it difficult being a single mother?* ❑ *Gay men are now eligible to become foster parents whether they are single or have partners.* **4** A **single** room is a room intended for one person to stay or live in. ❑ *Each guest has her own single room, or shares, on request, a double room.* **5** [single + N] A **single** bed is wide enough for one person to sleep in. ❑ *his bedroom with its single bed* **6** (BrE; in AmE, use **one-way**) A **single** ticket is a ticket for a trip from one place to another but not back again.
NOUN [c, u] (**singles**) **1** [c] A **single** is a room intended for one person to stay or live in. ❑ *It's $65 for a single, $98 for a double and $120 for an entire suite.* **2** [c] (in AmE, use **one-way**) A **single** is a ticket for a trip from one place to another but not back again. **3** [c] A **single** is a small record which has one song on each side. A **single** is also a CD which has a few short songs on it. You can also refer to

the main song on a record or CD as a **single**. ❑ *The winners will pocket a cash sum and get a chance to release their debut CD single.* **4** [u] **Singles** is a game of tennis or badminton in which one player plays another. The plural **singles** can be used to refer to one or more of these matches. ❑ *Lleyton Hewitt won the men's singles.*
PHRASAL VERB **single out** (**singles, singling, singled**) If you **single** someone **out** from a group, you choose them and give them special attention or treatment. ❑ *The gunman had singled Debilly out and waited for him.* ❑ *His immediate superior has singled him out for a special mention.*
✦ in single file → see file

single-handed or **single-handedly** ADV
[single-handed after V] If you do something **single-handed**, you do it on your own, without help from anyone else. ❑ *I brought up my seven children single-handed.*

single-minded ADJ Someone who is **single-minded** has only one aim or purpose and is determined to achieve it. ❑ *They were effective politicians, ruthless and single-minded in their pursuit of political power.*

sin·gle par·ent NOUN [c] (**single parents**) A **single parent** is someone who is bringing up a child on their own, because the other parent is not living with them. ❑ *I was bringing up my three children as a single parent.* ❑ *single-parent families*

sin·gu·lar /ˈsɪŋɡjʊlə/ ADJ, NOUN
ADJ The **singular** form of a word is the form that is used when referring to one person or thing. ❑ *the fifteen case endings of the singular form of the Finnish noun*
NOUN [SING] The **singular** of a noun is the form of it that is used to refer to one person or thing. ❑ *The inhabitants of the Arctic are known as the Inuit. The singular is Inuk.*

sin·is·ter /ˈsɪnɪstə/ ADJ Something that is **sinister** seems evil or harmful. ❑ *There was something sinister about him that she found disturbing.*

sink ♦◇◇ /sɪŋk/ NOUN, VERB
NOUN [c] (**sinks**) A **sink** is a large fixed container, especially in a kitchen, with taps to supply water. ❑ *The sink was full of dirty dishes.*
VERB [I, T] (**sinks, sinking, sank, sunk**) **1** [I, T] If a boat **sinks** or if someone or something **sinks**, it disappears below the surface of a mass of water. ❑ *In a naval battle your aim is to sink the enemy's ship.* ❑ *The boat was beginning to sink fast.* **2** [I] If something **sinks**, it disappears below the surface of a mass of water. ❑ *A fresh egg will sink and an old egg will float.* **3** [I] If something **sinks**, it moves slowly downwards. ❑ *Far off to the west the sun was sinking.* **4** [I] If something **sinks to** a lower level or standard, it falls to that level or standard. = fall ❑ *Share prices would have sunk – hurting small and big investors.* ❑ *Pay increases have sunk to around seven per cent.* **5** [I] If your heart or your spirits **sink**, you become depressed or lose hope. ❑ *My heart sank because I thought he was going to dump me for another girl.* **6** [I, T] If something sharp **sinks** or **is sunk into** something solid, it goes deeply into it. ❑ *I sank my teeth into a peppermint cream.* **7** [T] If someone **sinks** a well, mine, or other large hole, they make a deep hole in the ground, usually by digging or drilling. ❑ *the site where Stephenson sank his first mineshaft* **8** [T] If you **sink** money **into** a business or project, you spend money on it in the hope of making more money. = plough ❑ *He has already sunk $25 million into the project.*
PHRASE **sink or swim** If you say that someone will have to **sink or swim**, you mean that they will have to succeed through their own efforts, or fail. ❑ *I think athletes sink or swim depending on how they motivate themselves.*
PHRASAL VERB **sink in** When a statement or fact **sinks in**, you finally understand or realize it fully. ❑ *The implication took a while to sink in.*
→ See also **sunk**

sip /sɪp/ VERB, NOUN
VERB [I, T] (**sips, sipping, sipped**) If you **sip** a drink or **sip at** it, you drink by taking just a small amount at a time. ❑ *Jessica sipped her drink thoughtfully.* ❑ *He sipped at the glass and then put it down.*
NOUN [c] (**sips**) A **sip** is a small amount of drink that you take into your mouth. ❑ *Harry took a sip of bourbon.*

S

sir ♦♦◇ /sɜː/ NOUN, CONVENTION

NOUN [C] (**sirs**) **1** (*politeness*) People sometimes say **sir** as a polite way of addressing a man whose name they do not know, or an older man. For example, a shop assistant might address a male customer as **sir**. ❏ *Excuse me sir, but would you mind telling me what sort of car that is?* **2** **Sir** is the title used in front of the name of a knight or baronet. ❏ *She introduced me to Sir Tobias and Lady Clarke.*

CONVENTION You use the expression **Dear Sir** at the beginning of a formal letter or a business letter when you are writing to a man. ❏ *Dear Sir, Enclosed is a copy of my CV for your consideration.*

sis·ter ♦♦♦ /ˈsɪstə/ NOUN, ADJ

NOUN [C] (**sisters**) **1** [oft POSS + sister] Your **sister** is a girl or woman who has the same parents as you. ❏ *His sister Sarah helped him.* ❏ *Vanessa Bell, the sister of Virginia Woolf* **2** **Sister** is a title given to a woman who belongs to a religious community. ❏ *Sister Francesca entered the chapel.* **3** You can describe a woman as your **sister** if you feel a connection with her, for example, because she belongs to the same race, religion, country, or profession. ❏ *Modern woman has been freed from many of the duties that befell her sisters in times past.* ADJ [sister + N] You can use **sister** to describe something that is of the same type or is connected in some way to another thing you have mentioned. For example, if a company has a **sister** company, they are connected. ❏ *the International Monetary Fund and its sister organization, the World Bank*

sister-in-law NOUN [C] (**sisters-in-law**) Someone's **sister-in-law** is the sister of their husband or wife, or the woman who is married to their brother.

sit ♦♦♦ /sɪt/ VERB

VERB [I, T] (**sits, sitting, sat**) **1** [I] If you **are sitting** somewhere, for example, in a chair, your bottom is resting on the chair and the upper part of your body is upright. ❏ *Mother was sitting in her chair in the kitchen.* ❏ *They had been sitting watching television.* **2** [I] When you **sit** somewhere, you lower your body until you are sitting on something. ❏ *He set the cases against a wall and sat on them.* ❏ *Eva pulled over a chair and sat beside her husband.* **3** [T] If you **sit** someone somewhere, you tell them to sit there or put them in a sitting position. ❏ *He used to sit me on his lap.* **4** [I] If you **sit on** a committee or other official group, you are a member of it. ❏ *He was asked to sit on numerous committees.* **5** [I] (*formal*) When a legislature, court, or other official body **sits**, it officially carries out its work. ❏ *The court sits under tight security in a former museum.*

PHRASE **sit tight** If you **sit tight**, you remain in the same place or situation and do not take any action, usually because you are waiting for something to happen. ❏ *Sit tight. I'll be right back.*

PHRASAL VERBS **sit back** (*informal*) If you **sit back** while something is happening, you relax and do not become involved in it. ❏ *They didn't have to do anything except sit back and enjoy life.*

sit down **1** Sit down means the same as **sit** VERB 2. ❏ *I sat down, stunned.* **2** To **sit** someone **down** somewhere means to sit them there. **sit** VERB 3 ❏ *She helped him out of the water and sat him down on the rock.*

sit in on If you **sit in on** a lesson, meeting, or discussion, you are present while it is taking place but do not take part in it. ❏ *Will they permit you to sit in on a few classes as an observer?*

sit on (*informal*) If you say that someone **is sitting on** something, you mean that they are delaying dealing with it. ❏ *He had been sitting on the document for at least two months.*

sit out If you **sit** something **out**, you wait for it to finish, without taking any action. ❏ *The only thing I can do is keep quiet and sit this one out.*

sit through If you **sit through** something such as a film, lecture, or meeting, you stay until it is finished although you are not enjoying it. ❏ *films so bad you can hardly bear to sit through them*

sit up **1** If you **sit up**, you move into a sitting position when you have been leaning back or lying down. ❏ *Her* head spins dizzily as soon as she sits up. **2** If you **sit** someone **up**, you move them into a sitting position when they have been leaning back or lying down. ❏ *She sat him up and made him comfortable.* **3** If you **sit up**, you do not go to bed although it is very late. = stay up ❏ *We sat up drinking and talking.*

✦ **sit on the fence** → see **fence**

✪ **site** ♦♦◇ /saɪt/ NOUN, VERB (*academic word*)

NOUN [C] (**sites**) **1** A **site** is a piece of ground that is used for a particular purpose or where a particular thing happens. ❏ *I was working as a foreman on a building site.* ❏ *a bat sanctuary with special nesting sites* **2** The **site** of an important event is the place where it happened. = position, spot, location ❏ *Scientists have described the Aral sea as the site of the worst ecological disaster on earth.* ❏ *Plymouth Hoe is renowned as the site where Drake played bowls before tackling the Spanish Armada.* **3** A **site** is a piece of ground where something such as a statue or building stands or used to stand. ❏ *the site of Moses' tomb* **4** A **site** is the same as a **website**.

PHRASES **on site** If someone or something is **on site**, they are in a particular area or group of buildings where people work, study, or stay. ❏ *It is cheaper to have extra building work done when the builder is on site, rather than bringing him back for a small job.*

off site If someone or something is **off site**, they are away from a particular area or group of buildings where people work, study, or stay. ❏ *There is ample car parking off site.*

VERB [T] (**sites, siting, sited**) If something **is sited** in a particular place or position, it is put there or built there. ❏ *He said chemical weapons had never been sited in Germany.*

sit·ing /ˈsaɪtɪŋ/ NOUN [SING] ❏ *controls on the siting of gas storage vessels*

sit·ting /ˈsɪtɪŋ/ NOUN, ADJ

NOUN [C] (**sittings**) **1** A **sitting** is one of the periods when a meal is served when there is not enough space for everyone to eat at the same time. ❏ *Dinner was in two sittings.* **2** [usu sitting 'of' N] A **sitting** of a legislature, court, or other official body is one of the occasions when it meets in order to carry out its work. = session ❏ *the recent emergency sittings of the UN Security Council* ADJ [sitting + N] A **sitting** president, Member of Parliament, or congressman is a present one, not a future or past one. ❏ *the greatest clash in our history between a sitting president and an ex-president*
→ See also **sit**

situ·ate /ˈsɪtʃueɪt/ VERB [T] (**situates, situating, situated**) (*formal*) If you **situate** something such as an idea or fact in a particular context, you relate it to that context, especially in order to understand it better. ❏ *How do we situate Christianity in the context of modern physics and psychology?*

situ·at·ed /ˈsɪtʃueɪtɪd/ ADJ If something is **situated** in a particular place or position, it is in that place or position. = located ❏ *His hotel is situated in one of the loveliest places on the Loire.*

✪ **situa·tion** ♦♦♦ /ˌsɪtʃuˈeɪʃən/ NOUN [C] (**situations**) You use **situation** to refer generally to what is happening in a particular place at a particular time, or to refer to what is happening to you. = circumstances ❏ *Army officers said the situation was under control.* ❏ *And now for a look at the travel situation in the rest of the country.* ❏ *The local authority faced a difficult financial situation.* ❏ *If you want to improve your situation you must adopt a positive mental attitude.*

WORD CONNECTIONS
ADJ + **situation**
the **current** situation the **present** situation ❏ *Krugmann discusses the current financial situation on his blog.*
a **financial** situation an **economic** situation a **political** situation ❏ *The local authority faces a difficult financial situation.*

S

VERB + **situation**
describe a situation **discuss** a situation ❏ *Murdoch rejected an invitation to discuss the situation.*
handle a situation **improve** a situation **understand** a situation ❏ *If you want to improve your siutation, you must adopt a positive mental attitude.*

situation + VERB
a situation **improves** a situation **changes** a situation **deteriorates** ❏ *By 2005, the economic situation was deteroirating rapidly.*

six ♦♦♦ /sɪks/ NUM (**sixes**) **Six** is the number 6. ❏ *a glorious career spanning more than six decades*

six‧teen ♦♦♦ /ˌsɪks'tiːn/ NUM (**sixteens**) **Sixteen** is the number 16. ❏ *exams taken at the age of sixteen* ❏ *He worked sixteen hours a day.*

six‧teenth ♦♦◇ /ˌsɪks'tiːnθ/ ADJ, NOUN
ADJ The **sixteenth** item in a series is the one that you count as number sixteen. ❏ *the sixteenth century AD*
NOUN [c] (**sixteenths**) A **sixteenth** is one of sixteen equal parts of something. ❏ *a sixteenth of a second*

sixth ♦♦◇ /sɪksθ/ ADJ, NOUN
ADJ The **sixth** item in a series is the one that you count as number six. ❏ *the sixth round of the World Cup*
NOUN [c] (**sixths**) A **sixth** is one of six equal parts of something. ❏ *The company yesterday shed a sixth of its workforce.*

six‧ti‧eth ♦♦◇ /'sɪkstiəθ/ ADJ, NOUN
ADJ The **sixtieth** item in a series is the one that you count as number sixty. ❏ *He is to retire on his sixtieth birthday.*
NOUN [c] (**sixtieths**) A **sixtieth** is one of sixty equal parts of something.

six‧ty ♦♦♦ /'sɪksti/ NUM, NOUN
NUM (**sixties**) **Sixty** is the number 60. ❏ *the sunniest April for more than sixty years*
NOUN [PL] (**sixties**) **1** When you talk about the **sixties**, you are referring to numbers between 60 and 69. For example, if you are **in** your **sixties**, you are aged between 60 and 69. If the temperature is **in the sixties**, it is between 60 and 69 degrees. ❏ *a lively widow in her sixties* **2** The **sixties** is the decade between 1960 and 1969. ❏ *In the sixties there were the deaths of the two Kennedy brothers and Martin Luther King.*

siz‧able /'saɪzəbəl/ → See **sizeable**

size ♦♦◇ /saɪz/ NOUN
NOUN [c, u] (**sizes**) **1** [c, u] The **size of** something is how big or small it is. Something's **size** is determined by comparing it to other things, counting it, or measuring it. ❏ *In 1970 the average size of a French farm was 19 hectares.* ❏ *shelves containing books of various sizes* **2** [u] The **size of** something is the fact that it is very large. ❏ *He knows the size of the task.* **3** [c] A **size** is one of a series of graded measurements, especially for things such as clothes or shoes. ❏ *My sister is the same height but only a size 12.*
PHRASAL VERB **size up** (**sizes, sizing, sized**) (*informal*) If you **size up** a person or situation, you carefully look at the person or think about the situation, so that you can decide how to act. ❏ *Some US manufacturers have been sizing up the UK as a possible market for their clothes.*

size‧able /'saɪzəbəl/ also **sizable** ADJ **Sizeable** means fairly large. = **substantial** ❏ *Harry inherited the house and a sizeable piece of land that surrounds it.*

skate /skeɪt/ NOUN, VERB
NOUN [c] (**skates**) **1 Skates** are ice-skates. **2 Skates** are roller-skates.
VERB [i] (**skates, skating, skated**) If you **skate**, you move around wearing ice-skates or roller-skates. ❏ *I actually skated, and despite some teetering I did not fall on the ice.*
skat‧ing /'skeɪtɪŋ/ NOUN [u] ❏ *They all went skating together in the winter.*
skat‧er /'skeɪtə/ NOUN [c] (**skaters**) ❏ *West Lake, an outdoor*

ice-skating rink, attracts skaters during the day and night.

skel‧eton /'skelɪtən/ NOUN, ADJ
NOUN [c] (**skeletons**) **1** Your **skeleton** is the framework of bones in your body. ❏ *a human skeleton* **2** The **skeleton** of something such as a building or a plan is its basic framework. ❏ *The town of Rudbar had ceased to exist, with only skeletons of buildings remaining.*
ADJ [skeleton + N] A **skeleton** staff is the smallest number of staff necessary in order to run an organization or service. ❏ *Only a skeleton staff remains to show anyone interested around the site.*

sketch /sketʃ/ NOUN, VERB
NOUN [c] (**sketches**) **1** A **sketch** is a drawing that is done quickly without a lot of details. Artists often use sketches as a preparation for a more detailed painting or drawing. ❏ *a sketch of a soldier by Orpen* **2** A **sketch of** a situation, person, or incident is a brief description of it without many details. ❏ *thumbnail sketches of heads of state and political figures* **3** A **sketch** is a short humorous piece of acting, usually forming part of a comedy show. ❏ *a five-minute sketch about a folk singer*
VERB [i, t] (**sketches, sketching, sketched**) **1** [i, t] If you **sketch** something, you make a quick, rough drawing of it. ❏ *Clare and David Astor are sketching a view of far Spanish hills.* **2** [t] If you **sketch** a situation or incident, you give a short description of it, including only the most important facts. = **outline** ❏ *Cross sketched the story briefly, telling the facts just as they had happened.*
PHRASAL VERB **sketch out** **Sketch out** means the same as **sketch** VERB 2. ❏ *He sketched out plans to give consumers more affordable choices.*

ski ♦◇◇ /skiː/ NOUN, VERB, ADJ
NOUN [c] (**skis**) **Skis** are long, flat, narrow pieces of wood, metal, or plastic that are fastened to boots so that you can move easily on snow or water. ❏ *a pair of skis*
VERB [i] (**skis, skiing, skied**) When people **ski**, they move over snow or water on skis. ❏ *They surf, ski, and ride.*
ADJ [ski + N] You use **ski** to refer to things that are concerned with skiing. ❏ *the Swiss ski resort of Klosters* ❏ *a private ski instructor*
ski‧er /'skiːə/ NOUN [c] (**skiers**) ❏ *He is an enthusiastic skier.*
ski‧ing /'skiːɪŋ/ NOUN [u] ❏ *My hobbies were skiing and scuba diving.*

skid /skɪd/ VERB, NOUN
VERB [i] (**skids, skidding, skidded**) If a vehicle **skids**, it slides sideways or forwards while moving, for example, when you are trying to stop it suddenly on a wet road. ❏ *The car pulled up too fast and skidded on the dusty edge of the road.*
NOUN [c] (**skids**) If a vehicle goes into a **skid**, it slides sideways or forwards while moving, for example, when you are trying to stop it suddenly on a wet road. ❏ *I slammed the brakes on and went into a skid.*

skil‧ful /'skɪlfʊl/ (in *AmE*, use **skillful**) ADJ Someone who is **skilful** at something does it very well. ❏ *He actually is quite a skilful campaigner.*

❂ **skill** ♦♦◇ /skɪl/ NOUN [c, u] (**skills**) **1** [c] A **skill** is a type of work or activity which requires special training and knowledge. = **ability, technique** ❏ *Most of us will know someone who is always learning new skills, or studying new fields.* ❏ *Trainees will be taught basic practical skills.* **2** [u] **Skill** is the knowledge and ability that enables you to do something well. ❏ *The cut of a diamond depends on the skill of its craftsman.*

❂ **skilled** /skɪld/ ADJ **1** Someone who is **skilled** has the knowledge and ability to do something well. ❏ *Few doctors are actually trained, and not all are skilled, in helping their patients make choices.* **2 Skilled** work can only be done by people who have had some training. ❏ *New industries demanded skilled labour not available locally.* ❏ *skilled workers, such as plumbers and electricians*

❂ **skim** /skɪm/ VERB
VERB [t, i] (**skims, skimming, skimmed**) **1** [t] If you **skim** something **from** the surface of a liquid, you remove it. ❏ *Rough seas today prevented specially equipped ships from skimming oil off the water's surface.* **2** [i, t] If something **skims** a surface, it moves quickly along just above it.

S

□ *seagulls skimming the waves* **3** [I, T] If you **skim** a piece of writing, you read through it quickly. = scan, browse; ≠ pore over, examine □ *He skimmed the pages quickly, then read them again more carefully.* □ *I only had time to skim through the script before I flew over here.*

PHRASAL VERB **skim off** If someone **skims off** the best part of something, or money which belongs to other people, they take it for themselves. □ *The regime was able to skim off about $10 billion in illegal revenue.* □ *She admitted she skimmed cash off the top of the fees she collected.*

skin ♦♦◇ /skɪn/ NOUN, VERB

NOUN [C, U, SING] (**skins**) **1** [C, U] Your **skin** is the natural covering of your body. □ *His skin is clear and smooth.* □ *There are three major types of skin cancer.* **2** [C, U] An animal **skin** is skin which has been removed from a dead animal. Skins are used to make things such as coats and rugs. □ *That was real crocodile skin.* **3** [C, U] The **skin** of a fruit or vegetable is its outer layer or covering. □ *The outer skin of the orange is called the 'zest'.* **4** [SING] If a **skin** forms on the surface of a liquid, a thin, fairly solid layer forms on it. □ *Stir the custard occasionally to prevent a skin forming.*

VERB [T] (**skins, skinning, skinned**) If you **skin** a dead animal, you remove its skin. □ *with the expertise of a chef skinning a rabbit*

skin·ny /'skɪni/ ADJ (**skinnier, skinniest**) (*informal*) A **skinny** person is extremely thin, often in a way that you find unattractive. □ *He was quite a skinny little boy.*

skip /skɪp/ VERB, NOUN

VERB [T, I] (**skips, skipping, skipped**) **1** [T, I] If you **skip** along, you move almost as if you are dancing, with a series of little jumps from one foot to the other. □ *They saw the man with a little girl skipping along behind him.* □ *We went skipping down the street arm in arm.* **2** [I] (*BrE*; in *AmE*, use **skip rope**) When someone **skips**, they jump up and down over a rope which they or two other people are holding at each end and turning around and around. □ *They skip and play catch, waiting for the bell.* **3** [T] If you **skip** something that you usually do or something that most people do, you decide not to do it. = miss □ *It is important not to skip meals.* **4** [I, T] If you **skip** or **skip over** a part of something you are reading or a story you are telling, you miss it out or pass over it quickly and move on to something else. □ *You might want to skip the exercises in this chapter.* **5** [I] If you **skip from** one subject or activity **to** another, you move quickly from one to the other, although there is no obvious connection between them. = jump □ *She kept up a continuous chatter, skipping from one subject to the next.*

NOUN [C] (**skips**) **1** A **skip** is a little jump from one foot to the other. □ *The boxer gave a little skip as he came out of his corner.* **2** [In *AmE*, use **dumpster**] A **skip** is a large, open, metal container which is used to hold and take away large unwanted items and rubbish.

skip·ping /'skɪpɪŋ/ NOUN [U] □ *We did skipping and things like that.*

skip·per /'skɪpə/ NOUN [C] (**skippers**) You can use **skipper** to refer to the captain of a ship or boat. = captain □ *the skipper of an English fishing boat*

skir·mish /'skɜːmɪʃ/ NOUN, VERB

NOUN [C] (**skirmishes**) A **skirmish** is a minor battle. □ *Border skirmishes between India and Pakistan were common.* **VERB** [RECIP] (**skirmishes, skirmishing, skirmished**) If people **skirmish**, they fight. □ *They were skirmishing close to the minefield now.*

skirt /skɜːt/ NOUN, VERB

NOUN [C] (**skirts**) A **skirt** is a piece of clothing worn by women and girls. It fastens at the waist and hangs down around the legs.

VERB [T] (**skirts, skirting, skirted**) **1** Something that **skirts** an area is situated around the edge of it. □ *We raced across a large field that skirted the slope of a hill.* **2** If you **skirt** a problem or question, you avoid dealing with it. □ *He skirted the hardest issues, concentrating on areas of possible agreement.*

☉ skull /skʌl/ NOUN [C] (**skulls**) Your **skull** is the bony part of your head which encloses your brain. □ *Her husband was later treated for a fractured skull.* □ *I discovered two human skulls, obviously very old and half disintegrated.*

sky ♦◇◇ /skaɪ/ NOUN [C, U] (**skies**) **The sky** is the space around the earth which you can see when you stand outside and look upwards. □ *The sun is already high in the sky.* □ *warm sunshine and clear blue skies*

sky·scrap·er /'skaɪskreɪpə/ NOUN [C] (**skyscrapers**) A **skyscraper** is a very tall building in a city.

slab /slæb/ NOUN [C] (**slabs**) [with SUPP] A **slab of** something is a thick, flat piece of it. □ *slabs of stone*

slack /slæk/ ADJ, VERB

ADJ (**slacker, slackest**) **1** Something that is **slack** is loose and not firmly stretched or tightly in position. □ *The boy's jaw went slack.* **2** A **slack** period is one in which there is not much work or activity. = quiet □ *The workload can be evened out, instead of the shop having busy times and slack periods.* **3** Someone who is **slack** in their work does not do it properly. □ *Many publishers have simply become far too slack.*

VERB [I] (**slacks, slacking, slacked**) (*disapproval*) If someone **is slacking**, they are not working as hard as they should. □ *He had never let a foreman see him slacking.*

PHRASAL VERB **slack off** (*disapproval*) **Slack off** means the same as **slack** VERB. □ *If someone slacks off, Bill comes down hard.*

slack·en /'slækən/ VERB [I, T] (**slackens, slackening, slackened**) **1** If something **slackens** or if you **slacken** it, it becomes slower, less active, or less intense. □ *Inflationary pressures continued to slacken last month.* **2** If your grip or a part of your body **slackens** or if you **slacken** your grip, it becomes looser or more relaxed. □ *Her grip slackened on Arnold's arm.*

slam /slæm/ VERB [I, T] (**slams, slamming, slammed**) **1** [I, T] If you **slam** a door or window or if it **slams**, it shuts noisily and with great force. □ *She slammed the door and locked it behind her.* □ *I was relieved to hear the front door slam.* **2** [T] If you **slam** something **down**, you put it there quickly and with great force. □ *She listened in a mixture of shock and anger before slamming the phone down.* **3** [T] (*journalism*) To **slam** someone or something means to criticize them very severely. □ *The famed filmmaker slammed the claims as 'an outrageous lie'.* **4** [I, T] If one thing **slams** into or against another, it crashes into it with great force. □ *The plane slammed into the building after losing an engine shortly after take-off.*

slan·der /'slɑːndə, 'slæn-/ NOUN, VERB

NOUN [C, U] (**slanders**) **Slander** is an untrue spoken statement about someone which is intended to damage their reputation. Compare **libel**. □ *Dr Bach is now suing the company for slander.*

VERB [T] (**slanders, slandering, slandered**) To **slander** someone means to say untrue things about them in order to damage their reputation. □ *He accused me of slandering him and trying to undermine his position.*

slang /slæŋ/ NOUN [U] **Slang** consists of words, expressions, and meanings that are informal and are used by people who know each other very well or who have the same interests. □ *Archie liked to think he kept up with current slang.*

slant /slɑːnt, slænt/ VERB, NOUN

VERB [I, T] (**slants, slanting, slanted**) **1** [I] Something that **slants** is sloping, rather than horizontal or vertical. □ *The morning sun slanted through the glass roof.* **2** [T] If information or a system **is slanted**, it is made to show favour towards a particular group or opinion. □ *The programme was deliberately slanted to make the home team look good.*

NOUN [SING] (**slants**) **1** If something is **on a slant**, it is in a slanting position. □ *long pockets cut on the slant* **2** A particular **slant** on a subject is a particular way of thinking about it, especially one that is unfair. □ *The political slant at Focus can be described as centre-right.*

slap /slæp/ VERB, NOUN

VERB [T] (**slaps, slapping, slapped**) **1** If you **slap** someone, you hit them with the palm of your hand. □ *He would push or slap her once in a while.* □ *I slapped him hard across the face.* **2** If you **slap** something **onto** a surface, you put it there quickly, roughly, or carelessly. □ *He emptied his*

S

drink and slapped the money on the bar. **3** (informal, disapproval) If journalists say that the authorities **slap** something such as a tax or a ban **on** something, they think it is unreasonable or put on without careful thought. = **stick** ❑ The government slapped a ban on the export of unprocessed logs. **NOUN** [c] (**slaps**) If you give someone a **slap**, you hit them with the palm of your hand. ❑ He reached forward and gave her a slap.

slash /slæʃ/ VERB, NOUN
VERB [T, I] (**slashes, slashing, slashed**) **1** [T] If you **slash** something, you make a long, deep cut in it. ❑ He came within two minutes of bleeding to death after slashing his wrists. **2** [I] If you **slash at** a person or thing, you quickly hit at them with something such as a knife. ❑ He slashed at her, aiming carefully. **3** [T] (journalism) To **slash** something such as costs or jobs means to reduce them by a large amount. = **cut** ❑ Car makers could be forced to slash prices. **NOUN** [c] (**slashes**) **1** A **slash** is a long, deep cut in something. ❑ Make deep slashes in the meat and push in the spice paste. **2** (spoken) You say **slash** to refer to a sloping line that separates letters, words, or numbers. For example, if you are giving the number 340/2/K you say 'Three four zero, slash two, slash K'.

slate /sleɪt/ NOUN, VERB
NOUN [u, c] (**slates**) **1** [u] **Slate** is a dark grey rock that can be easily split into thin layers. Slate is often used for covering roofs. ❑ a stone-built cottage, with a traditional slate roof **2** [c] A **slate** is one of the small, flat pieces of slate that are used for covering roofs. ❑ Thieves had stolen the slates from the roof. **PHRASE a clean slate** If you start **with a clean slate**, you do not take account of previous mistakes or failures and make a fresh start. ❑ The proposal is to pay everything you owe, so that you can start with a clean slate. **VERB** [PASSIVE] (**slates, slating, slated**) (mainly AmE) If something is **slated** to happen, it is planned to happen at a particular time or on a particular occasion. ❑ Bromfield was slated to become US Secretary of Agriculture.

slaugh·ter /ˈslɔːtə/ VERB, NOUN
VERB [T] (**slaughters, slaughtering, slaughtered**) **1** If large numbers of people or animals **are slaughtered**, they are killed in a way that is cruel or unnecessary. ❑ Thirty-four people were slaughtered while lining up to cast their votes. **2** To **slaughter** animals such as cows and sheep means to kill them for their meat. ❑ Lack of chicken feed means that chicken farms are having to slaughter their stock. **NOUN** [u] **1** **Slaughter** is the killing of large numbers of people or animals in a way that is cruel or unnecessary. ❑ This was only a small part of a war where the slaughter of civilians was commonplace. **2** **Slaughter** is the killing of animals such as cows and sheep for their meat. ❑ More than 491,000 sheep were exported for slaughter last year.

slave /sleɪv/ NOUN, VERB
NOUN [c] (**slaves**) **1** A **slave** is someone who is the property of another person and has to work for that person. ❑ The state of Liberia was formed a century and a half ago by freed slaves from the United States. **2** You can describe someone as a **slave** when they are completely under the control of another person or of a powerful influence. ❑ She may no longer be a slave to the studio system, but she still has a duty to her fans. **VERB** [I] (**slaves, slaving, slaved**) If you say that a person is **slaving over** something or is **slaving for** someone, you mean that they are working very hard. ❑ When you're busy all day the last thing you want to do is spend hours slaving over a hot stove. **PHRASAL VERB slave away** Slave away means the same as slave VERB. ❑ He stares at the hundreds of workers slaving away in the intense sun.

slav·ery /ˈsleɪvəri/ NOUN [u] **Slavery** is the system by which people are owned by other people as slaves. ❑ My people have survived 400 years of slavery.

sleaze /sliːz/ NOUN [u] (informal, disapproval) You use **sleaze** to describe activities that you consider immoral, dishonest, or not respectable, especially in politics, business, journalism, or entertainment. ❑ She claimed that

an atmosphere of sleaze and corruption now surrounded the government.

sleek /sliːk/ ADJ (**sleeker, sleekest**) **1** **Sleek** hair or fur is smooth and shiny and looks healthy. ❑ sleek black hair **2** If you describe someone as **sleek**, you mean that they look rich and stylish. ❑ Lord White is as sleek and elegant as any other millionaire businessman. **3** **Sleek** vehicles, furniture, or other objects look smooth, shiny, and expensive. ❑ a sleek white BMW

sleep ♦♦◇ /sliːp/ NOUN, VERB
NOUN [u, c] (**sleeps**) **1** [u] **Sleep** is the natural state of rest in which your eyes are closed, your body is inactive, and your mind does not think. ❑ They were exhausted from lack of sleep. ❑ Be quiet and go to sleep. **2** [c] A **sleep** is a period of sleeping. ❑ I think he may be ready for a sleep soon. **PHRASES get to sleep** If you cannot **get to sleep**, you are unable to sleep. ❑ I can't get to sleep with all that singing. **lose sleep** If you say that you didn't **lose** any **sleep over** something, you mean that you did not worry about it at all. ❑ I didn't lose too much sleep over that investigation. **put something to sleep** If a sick or injured animal **is put to sleep**, it is killed by a vet in a way that does not cause it pain. ❑ I'm going take the dog down to the vet's and have her put to sleep. **VERB** [I, T] (**sleeps, sleeping, slept**) **1** [I] When you **sleep**, you rest with your eyes closed and your mind and body inactive. ❑ During the drive, the baby slept. ❑ I've not been able to sleep for the last few nights. **2** [T] If a building or room **sleeps** a particular number of people, it has beds for that number of people. ❑ The villa sleeps 10. **PHRASE sleep on it** If you are trying to make a decision and you say that you will **sleep on it**, you mean that you will delay making a decision on it until the following day, so you have time to think about it. ❑ I need more time to sleep on it. It's a big decision and I want to make the right one. **PHRASAL VERBS sleep around** (informal, disapproval) If you say that someone **sleeps around**, you disapprove of them because they have sex with a lot of different people. ❑ I don't sleep around. **sleep in** If you **sleep in**, you stay asleep in the morning for longer than you usually do. ❑ Yesterday, few players turned up because most slept in. **sleep off** If you **sleep off** the effects of too much travelling, drink, or food, you recover from it by sleeping. ❑ It's a good idea to spend the first night of your holiday sleeping off the jet lag. **sleep over** If someone, especially a child, **sleeps over** in a place such as a friend's home, they stay there for one night. ❑ She said his friends could sleep over. **sleep together** If two people **are sleeping together**, they are having a sexual relationship, but are not usually married to each other. ❑ I'm pretty sure they slept together before they were married. **sleep with** If you **sleep with** someone, you have sex with them. ❑ He was old enough to sleep with a girl and make her pregnant.

sleep·er /ˈsliːpə/ NOUN [c] (**sleepers**) You can use **sleeper** to indicate how well someone sleeps. For example, if someone is a light **sleeper**, they are easily woken up. ❑ I'm a very light sleeper and I can hardly get any sleep at all.

sleep·less /ˈsliːpləs/ ADJ **1** A **sleepless** night is one during which you do not sleep. ❑ I have sleepless nights worrying about her. **2** Someone who is **sleepless** is unable to sleep. ❑ A sleepless baby can seem to bring little reward.

sleepy /ˈsliːpi/ ADJ (**sleepier, sleepiest**) **1** If you are **sleepy**, you are very tired and are almost asleep. ❑ I was beginning to feel amazingly sleepy. **2** A **sleepy** place is quiet and does not have much activity or excitement. ❑ Valence is a sleepy little town just south of Lyon. **sleep·ily** /ˈsliːpɪli/ ADV [sleepily with v] ❑ Joanna sat up, blinking sleepily.

sleeve /sliːv/ NOUN
NOUN [c] (**sleeves**) **1** The **sleeves** of a coat, shirt, or other item of clothing are the parts that cover your arms. ❑ His sleeves were rolled up to his elbows. **2** (mainly BrE) A record **sleeve** is the stiff cover in which a record is kept. ❑ an album sleeve

S

PHRASE have something up one's sleeve If you have something **up** your **sleeve**, you have an idea or plan which you have not told anyone about. You can also say that someone has **an ace, card,** or **trick up** their **sleeve**. ❏ *He wondered what tricks Shearson had up his sleeve.*

slen·der /'slendə/ ADJ (*written*) **1** (*approval*) A **slender** person is attractively thin and graceful. ❏ *She was slender, with delicate wrists and ankles.* ❏ *a tall, slender figure in a straw hat* **2** You can use **slender** to describe a situation which exists but only to a very small degree. = slim ❏ *The United States held a slender lead.*

slept /slept/ IRREG FORM **Slept** is the past tense and past participle of **sleep**.

slice ♦◇◇ /slaɪs/ NOUN, VERB
NOUN [C] (**slices**) **1** A **slice of** bread, meat, fruit, or other food is a thin piece that has been cut from a larger piece. ❏ *Try to eat at least four slices of bread a day.* **2** You can use **slice** to refer to a part of a situation or activity. ❏ *Fiction takes up a large slice of the publishing market.*
VERB [T] (**slices, slicing, sliced**) If you **slice** bread, meat, fruit, or other food, you cut it into thin pieces. ❏ *Helen sliced the cake.*
PHRASAL VERB **slice up** Slice up means the same as **slice** VERB. ❏ *I sliced up an onion.*

slick /slɪk/ ADJ, NOUN
ADJ (**slicker, slickest**) **1** A **slick** performance, production, or advertisement is skilful and impressive. ❏ *There's a big difference between an amateur video and a slick Hollywood production.* **2** A **slick** action is done quickly and smoothly, and without any obvious effort. ❏ *They were outplayed by the Colombians' slick passing and decisive finishing.* **3** A **slick** person speaks easily in a way that is likely to convince people, but is not sincere. ❏ *Don't be fooled by slick politicians.*
NOUN [C] An oil **slick** is a layer of oil that is floating in the sea or on a lake because it has accidentally come out of a ship or a container. ❏ *Experts are trying to devise ways to clean up the huge slick.*

slide ♦◇◇ /slaɪd/ VERB, NOUN
VERB [I, T] (**slides, sliding, slid**) **1** [I, T] When something **slides** somewhere or when you slide it there, it moves there smoothly over or against something. ❏ *She slid the door open.* ❏ *I slid the wallet into his pocket.* **2** [I] If you **slide** somewhere, you move there smoothly and quietly. ❏ *He slid into the driver's seat.* **3** [I] To **slide into** a particular mood, attitude, or situation means to gradually start to have that mood, attitude, or situation, often without intending to. = slip ❏ *She had slid into a depression.* **4** [I] (*journalism*) If currencies or prices **slide**, they gradually become worse or lower in value. ❏ *The dollar continued to slide.*
NOUN [C] (**slides**) **1** A **slide** in prices or currencies is when they gradually become worse or lower in value. ❏ *the dangerous slide in oil prices* **2** A **slide** is a small piece of photographic film which you project onto a screen so that you can see the picture. ❏ *a slide show* **3** A **slide** is a piece of glass on which you put something that you want to examine through a microscope. ❏ *a drop of blood on a slide* **4** A **slide** is a piece of playground equipment that has a steep slope for children to go down for fun. ❏ *two young children playing on a slide*

⭐**slight** ♦◇◇ /slaɪt/ ADJ, VERB, NOUN
ADJ (**slighter, slightest**) **1** Something that is **slight** is very small in degree or quantity. = small; ≠ large ❏ *Doctors say he has made a slight improvement.* ❏ *a slight increase in the cost of a new car* ❏ *He's not the slightest bit worried.* **2** A **slight** person has a fairly thin and delicate looking body. ❏ *She is smaller and slighter than Christie.*
PHRASE **in the slightest** (*emphasis*) You use **in the slightest** to emphasize a negative statement. ❏ *That doesn't interest me in the slightest.*
VERB [T] (**slights, slighting, slighted**) If you **are slighted**, someone does or says something that insults you by treating you as if your views or feelings are not important. ❏ *They felt slighted by not being adequately consulted.*
NOUN [C] (**slights**) A **slight** is when someone insults you by treating you as if your views or feelings are not

important. ❏ *It's difficult to persuade my husband that it isn't a slight on him that I enjoy my evening class.*

⭐**slight·ly** ♦♦◇ /'slaɪtli/ ADV **1** **Slightly** means to some degree but not to a very large degree. ≠ very, a lot ❏ *His family then moved to a slightly larger house.* ❏ *Each person learns in a slightly different way.* ❏ *The temperature is slightly above freezing.* ❏ *Oil prices rose slightly.* **2** [slightly + -ED] Someone who is **slightly** built has a fairly thin and delicate looking body. ❏ *a slightly built man*

slim ♦◇◇ /slɪm/ ADJ, VERB
ADJ (**slimmer, slimmest**) **1** (*approval*) A **slim** person has an attractively thin and well-shaped body. ❏ *The young woman was tall and slim.* **2** A **slim** book, wallet, or other object is thinner than usual. ❏ *The slim booklets describe a range of services and facilities.* **3** A **slim** chance or possibility is a very small one. = faint ❏ *There's still a slim chance that he may become president.*
VERB [T] (**slims, slimming, slimmed**) (*business*) If an organization **slims** its products or workers, it reduces the number of them that it has. ❏ *The company recently slimmed its product line.*
PHRASAL VERB **slim down** **1** If you **slim down**, you lose weight and become thinner. ❏ *People will lose weight when they slim down with a friend.* **2** (*business*) If a company or other organization **slims down** or is **slimmed down**, it employs fewer people, in order to save money or become more efficient. ❏ *Many firms have had little choice but to slim down.*

sling /slɪŋ/ VERB, NOUN
VERB [T] (**slings, slinging, slung**) **1** If you **sling** something somewhere, you throw it there carelessly. = fling ❏ *Marla was recently seen slinging her shoes at Trump.* **2** If you **sling** something over your shoulder or over something such as a chair, you hang it there loosely. ❏ *She slung her coat over her desk chair.* ❏ *He had a small green backpack slung over one shoulder.* **3** If a rope, blanket, or other object **is slung** between two points, someone has hung it loosely between them. ❏ *two long poles with a blanket slung between them*
NOUN [C] (**slings**) **1** A **sling** is an object made of ropes, straps, or cloth that is used for carrying things. ❏ *They used slings of rope to lower us from one set of arms to another.* **2** A **sling** is a piece of cloth which supports someone's broken or injured arm and is tied around their neck. ❏ *She was back at work with her arm in a sling.*

slip ♦♦◇ /slɪp/ VERB, NOUN
VERB [I, T] (**slips, slipping, slipped**) **1** [I] If you **slip**, you accidentally slide and lose your balance. ❏ *He had slipped on an icy pavement.* **2** [I] If something **slips**, it slides out of place or out of your hand. ❏ *His glasses had slipped.* **3** [I] If you **slip** somewhere, you go there quickly and quietly. ❏ *Amy slipped downstairs and out of the house.* **4** [T] If you **slip** something somewhere, you put it there quickly in a way that does not attract attention. ❏ *I slipped a note under Louise's door.* ❏ *He found a coin in his pocket and slipped it into her hand.* **5** [T] If you **slip** something **to** someone, you give it to them secretly. ❏ *Robert had slipped her a note in school.* **6** [I] To **slip into** a particular state or situation means to pass gradually into it, in a way that is hardly noticed. = slide ❏ *It amazed him how easily one could slip into a routine.* **7** [I, T] If something **slips to** a lower level or standard, it falls to that level or standard. ❏ *Shares slipped to $1.17.* ❏ *In June, producer prices slipped 0.1% from May.* **8** [I, T] If you **slip into** or **out of** clothes or shoes, you put them on or take them off quickly and easily. ❏ *She slipped out of the jacket and tossed it on the couch.*
PHRASES **let slip** If you **let slip** information, you accidentally tell it to someone, when you wanted to keep it secret. ❏ *I bet he let slip that I'd gone to America.*
slip your mind If something **slips** your **mind**, you forget about it. ❏ *The reason for my visit had obviously slipped his mind.*
PHRASAL VERB **slip up** If you **slip up**, you make a small or unimportant mistake. ❏ *There were occasions when we slipped up.*
NOUN [SING, C] (**slips**) **1** [SING] A **slip** in something is a fall to a lower level or standard. ❏ *a slip in consumer confidence* **2** [C] A **slip** is a small or unimportant mistake. ❏ *We must*

S

be well prepared, there must be no slips. **3** [c] A **slip** of paper is a small piece of paper. ❑ *little slips of paper he had torn from a notebook* ❑ *I put her name on the slip.* **4** [c] A **slip** is a thin piece of clothing that a woman wears under her dress or skirt.

slip·pery /'slɪpəri/ ADJ
ADJ **1** Something that is **slippery** is smooth, wet, or oily and is therefore difficult to walk on or to hold. ❑ *The tiled floor was wet and slippery.* **2** You can describe someone as **slippery** if you think that they are dishonest in a clever way and cannot be trusted. ❑ *He is a slippery customer, and should be carefully watched.*
PHRASE **slippery slope** If someone is on a **slippery slope**, they are involved in a course of action that is difficult to stop and that will eventually lead to failure or trouble. ❑ *The company started down the slippery slope of believing that they knew better than the customer.*

slit /slɪt/ VERB, NOUN
VERB [T] (**slits, slitting, slit**) If you **slit** something, you make a long narrow cut in it. ❑ *They say somebody slit her throat.* ❑ *He began to slit open each envelope.*
NOUN [c] (**slits**) **1** A **slit** is a long narrow cut. ❑ *Make a slit in the stem about half an inch long.* **2** A **slit** is a long narrow opening in something. ❑ *She watched them through a slit in the curtains.*

slo·gan /'sləʊgən/ NOUN [c] (**slogans**) A **slogan** is a short phrase that is easy to remember. Slogans are used in advertisements and by political parties and other organizations who want people to remember what they are saying or selling. ❑ *They could campaign on the slogan 'We'll take less of your money.'*

slope /sləʊp/ NOUN, VERB
NOUN [c] (**slopes**) **1** A **slope** is the side of a mountain, hill, or valley. ❑ *Saint-Christo is perched on a mountain slope.* **2** A **slope** is a surface that is at an angle, so that one end is higher than the other. = incline ❑ *The street must have been on a slope.* **3** The **slope** of something is the angle at which it slopes. ❑ *The slope increases as you go up the curve.*
VERB [i] (**slopes, sloping, sloped**) **1** If a surface **slopes**, it is at an angle, so that one end is higher than the other. ❑ *The bank sloped down sharply to the river.* **2** If something **slopes**, it leans to the right or to the left rather than being upright. = slant ❑ *The writing sloped backwards.*
slop·ing /'sləʊpɪŋ/ ADJ ❑ *a brick building, with a sloping roof*
✦ **slippery slope** → see **slippery**

slot /slɒt/ NOUN, VERB
NOUN [c] (**slots**) **1** A **slot** is a narrow opening in a machine or container, for example, a hole that you put coins in to make a machine work. ❑ *He dropped a coin into the slot and dialled.* **2** A **slot** in a schedule or programme is a place in it where an activity can take place. ❑ *Visitors can book a time slot a week or more in advance.*
VERB [i, T] (**slots, slotting, slotted**) If you **slot** something into something else, or if it **slots** into it, you put it into a space where it fits. ❑ *He was slotting a CD into a CD player.* ❑ *The car seat belt slotted into place easily.*

slow /sləʊ/ ADJ, ADV, VERB
ADJ (**slower, slowest**) **1** Something that is **slow** moves, happens, or is done without much speed. ❑ *The traffic is heavy and slow.* ❑ *Electric whisks should be used on a slow speed.* **2** Something that is **slow** takes a long time. ❑ *The distribution of passports has been a slow process.* **3** [V-LINK + slow] If someone is **slow** to do something, they do it after a delay. ❑ *The world community has been slow to respond to the crisis.* **4** Someone who is **slow** is not very clever and takes a long time to understand things. ❑ *He got hit on the head and he's been a bit slow since.* **5** If you describe a situation, place, or activity as **slow**, you mean that it is not very exciting. = quiet ❑ *Don't be faint-hearted when things seem a bit slow or boring.* **6** If a clock or watch is **slow**, it shows a time that is earlier than the correct time. ❑ *The clock is about two and a half minutes slow.*
ADV [slow after v] In informal English, **slower** is used to mean 'at a slower speed' and **slowest** is used to mean 'at the slowest speed'. In nonstandard English, **slow** is used to mean 'with little speed'. ❑ *I began to walk slower and slower.*
VERB [i, T] (**slows, slowing, slowed**) If something **slows** or

if you **slow** it, it starts to move or happen more slowly. ❑ *The rate of bombing has slowed considerably.* ❑ *She slowed the car and began driving up a narrow road.*
PHRASAL VERBS **slow down** **1** If something **slows down** or if something **slows** it down, it starts to move or happen more slowly. = slow up ❑ *The bus slowed down for the next stop.* ❑ *There is no cure for the disease, although drugs can slow down its rate of development.* **2** If someone **slows down** or if something **slows** them down, they become less active. ❑ *You will need to slow down for a while.*
slow up **Slow up** means the same as **slow** VERB. ❑ *Sales are slowing up.*
slow·ly /'sləʊli/ ADV **1** [slowly with v] ❑ *He spoke slowly and deliberately.* **2** [slowly with v] ❑ *My resentment of her slowly began to fade.*
slow·ness /'sləʊnəs/ NOUN [u] **1** *She lowered the glass with calculated slowness.* **2** *the slowness of political and economic progress*
✦ **slowly but surely** → see **surely**

slug·gish /'slʌgɪʃ/ ADJ You can describe something as **sluggish** if it moves, works, or reacts much more slowly than you would like or is normal. ❑ *The economy remains sluggish.* ❑ *Circulation is much more sluggish in the feet than in the hands.*

slum /slʌm/ NOUN [c] (**slums**) A **slum** is an area of a city where living conditions are very bad and where the houses are in bad condition. ❑ *a slum area of St Louis*

slump /slʌmp/ VERB, NOUN
VERB [i] (**slumps, slumping, slumped**) **1** If something such as the value of something **slumps**, it falls suddenly and by a large amount. ❑ *Net profits slumped by 41%.* **2** If you **slump** somewhere, you fall or sit down there heavily, for example, because you are very tired or you feel ill. ❑ *She slumped into a chair.*
NOUN [c] (**slumps**) **1** A **slump in** the value of something is a sudden fall by a large amount. ❑ *The council's land is now worth much less than originally hoped because of a slump in property prices.* **2** A **slump** is a time when many people in a country are unemployed and poor. = recession ❑ *the slump of the early 1980s*

slung /slʌŋ/ IRREG FORM **Slung** is the past tense and past participle of **sling**.

sly /slaɪ/ ADJ **1** A **sly** look, expression, or remark shows that you know something that other people do not know or that was meant to be a secret. ❑ *His lips were spread in a sly smile.* **2** (disapproval) If you describe someone as **sly**, you disapprove of them because they keep their feelings or intentions hidden and are clever at deceiving people. = cunning ❑ *She is devious and sly and manipulative.*
sly·ly /'slaɪli/ ADV ❑ *Anna grinned slyly.*

smack /smæk/ VERB, NOUN, ADV
VERB [T, i] (**smacks, smacking, smacked**) **1** [T] If you **smack** someone, you hit them with your hand. ❑ *She smacked me on the side of the head.* **2** [T] If you **smack** something somewhere, you put it or throw it there so that it makes a loud, sharp noise. ❑ *He smacked his hands down on his knees.* **3** [i] If one thing **smacks of** another thing that you consider bad, it reminds you of it or is like it. ❑ *The engineers' union was unhappy with the motion, saying it smacked of racism.*
PHRASE **smack one's lips** If you **smack** your **lips**, you open and close your mouth noisily, especially before or after eating, to show that you are eager to eat or enjoyed eating. ❑ *'I really want some dessert,' Keaton says, smacking his lips.*
NOUN [c, u] (**smacks**) **1** [c] If you give someone a **smack**, you hit them with your hand. ❑ *Sometimes he just doesn't listen and I end up shouting at him or giving him a smack.* **2** [u] (informal) **Smack** is heroin. ❑ *a smack addict*
ADV [smack + PREP] (informal) Something that is **smack** in a particular place is exactly in that place. ❑ *In part that's because industry is smack in the middle of the city.*

small /smɔːl/ ADJ, NOUN
ADJ (**smaller, smallest**) **1** A **small** person, thing, or amount of something is not large in physical size. ❑ *She is small for her age.* ❑ *Stick them on using a small amount of glue.* **2** A **small** group or quantity consists of only a few people or things. ❑ *A small group of students meets regularly to learn*

S

Japanese. **3** A **small** child is a very young child. = young, little ❑ *I have a wife and two small children.* **4** You use **small** to describe something that is not significant or great in degree. = minor ❑ *It's easy to make quite small changes to the way that you work.* ❑ *No detail was too small to escape her attention.* **5** **Small** businesses or companies employ a small number of people and do business with a small number of clients. ❑ *shops, restaurants and other small businesses* **6** [V-LINK + small] If someone makes you look or feel **small**, they make you look or feel stupid or ashamed. ❑ *This may just be another of her schemes to make me look small.*

NOUN [SING] The **small of** your **back** is the bottom part of your back that curves in slightly. ❑ *Place your hands on the small of your back and breathe in.*

✦ **the small hours** → see **hour**; **small wonder** → see **wonder**

small-scale ADJ A **small-scale** activity or organization is small in size and limited in extent. ❑ *the small-scale production of farmhouse cheeses in Vermont*

smart ◆◇◇ /smɑːt/ ADJ, VERB
ADJ [smarter, smartest] **1** You can describe someone who is clever or intelligent as **smart**. ❑ *He thinks he's smarter than Sarah is.* **2** (mainly BrE) **Smart** people and things are pleasantly neat and clean in appearance. ❑ *He was smart and well groomed but not good looking.* ❑ *I was dressed in a smart navy blue suit.* **3** (mainly BrE) A **smart** place or event is connected with wealthy and fashionable people. ❑ *smart dinner parties*
VERB [I] (smarts, smarting, smarted) **1** If a part of your body or a wound **smarts**, you feel a sharp stinging pain in it. = sting ❑ *My eyes smarted from the smoke.* **2** (journalism) If you **are smarting from** something such as criticism or failure, you feel upset about it. ❑ *The Americans were still smarting from their defeat in the Vietnam War.*
smart·ly /ˈsmɑːtli/ ADV [smartly with V] (mainly BrE) ❑ *He dressed very smartly, which was important in those days.*
✦ **the smart money** → see **money**

smart·en /ˈsmɑːtən/ (smartens, smartening, smartened)
PHRASAL VERB **smarten up** If you **smarten yourself** or a place **up**, you make yourself or the place look neater and tidier. ❑ *a 10-year programme to smarten up the city* ❑ *She had wisely smartened herself up.*

smash ◆◇◇ /smæʃ/ VERB
VERB [I, T] (smashes, smashing, smashed) **1** [I, T] If you **smash** something or if it **smashes**, it breaks into many pieces, for example, when it is hit or dropped. = break ❑ *Someone smashed a bottle.* ❑ *A crowd of youths started smashing windows.* **2** [I, T] If you **smash** through a wall, gate, or door, you get through it by hitting and breaking it. ❑ *The demonstrators used trucks to smash through embassy gates.* **3** [I, T] If something **smashes** or **is smashed** against something solid, it moves very fast and with great force against it. ❑ *The bottle smashed against a wall.* **4** [T] (informal) To **smash** a political group or system means to deliberately destroy it. ❑ *Their attempts to clean up politics and smash the power of party machines failed.*
PHRASAL VERB **smash up 1** If you **smash** something **up**, you completely destroy it by hitting and breaking it into many pieces. ❑ *She took revenge on her ex-boyfriend by smashing up his home.* **2** If you **smash up** your car, you damage it by crashing it into something. ❑ *All you told me was that he'd smashed up yet another car.*

smear /smɪə/ VERB, NOUN
VERB [T] (smears, smearing, smeared) **1** If you **smear** a surface **with** an oily or sticky substance or **smear** the substance onto the surface, you spread a layer of the substance over the surface. ❑ *My sister smeared herself with suntan oil and slept by the swimming pool.* **2** (journalism) To **smear** someone means to spread unpleasant and untrue rumours or accusations about them in order to damage their reputation. ❑ *They planned to smear him by publishing information about his private life.*
NOUN [C] (smears) **1** A **smear** is a dirty or oily mark. ❑ *There was a smear of gravy on his chin.* **2** (journalism) A **smear** is an unpleasant and untrue rumour or accusation that is intended to damage someone's reputation. = slur ❑ *He puts all the accusations down to a smear campaign by his*

political opponents. **3** (BrE; in AmE, use **Pap smear**) A **smear** or a **smear test** is a medical test in which a few cells are taken from a woman's cervix and examined to see if any cancer cells are present.

smell ◆◇◇ /smel/ NOUN, VERB
NOUN [C, U] (smells) **1** [C] The **smell** of something is a quality it has which you become aware of when you breathe in through your nose. ❑ *the smell of freshly baked bread* ❑ *horrible smells* **2** [U] Your sense of **smell** is the ability that your nose has to detect things. ❑ *people who lose their sense of smell*
VERB [LINK, I, T] (smells, smelling, smelled) **1** [LINK] If something **smells** a particular way, it has a quality which you become aware of through your nose. ❑ *The room smelled of lemons.* ❑ *It smells delicious.* **2** [I] If you say that something **smells**, you mean that it smells unpleasant. ❑ *Ma threw that out. She said it smelled.* **3** [T] If you **smell** something, you become aware of it when you breathe in through your nose. ❑ *As soon as we opened the front door we could smell the gas.* **4** [T] If you **smell** something, you put your nose near it and breathe in, so that you can discover its smell. = sniff ❑ *I took a fresh rose out of the vase on our table, and smelled it.*
✦ **smell a rat** → see **rat**

smelly /ˈsmeli/ ADJ (smellier, smelliest) Something that is **smelly** has an unpleasant smell. ❑ *He had extremely smelly feet.*

smile ◆◆◇ /smaɪl/ VERB, NOUN
VERB [I] (smiles, smiling, smiled) When you **smile**, the corners of your mouth curve up and you sometimes show your teeth. People smile when they are pleased or amused, or when they are being friendly. ❑ *When he saw me, he smiled and waved.* ❑ *He rubbed the back of his neck and smiled ruefully at me.*
NOUN [C] (smiles) A **smile** is the expression that you have on your face when you smile. ❑ *She gave a wry smile.* ❑ *'There are some sandwiches if you're hungry,' she said with a smile.*

smog /smɒg/ NOUN [C, U] (smogs) **Smog** is a mixture of fog and smoke which occurs in some busy industrial cities. ❑ *Cars cause pollution, both smog and acid rain.*

smoke ◆◆◇ /sməʊk/ NOUN, VERB
NOUN [U, SING] **1** [U] **Smoke** consists of gas and small bits of solid material that are sent into the air when something burns. ❑ *A cloud of black smoke blew over the city.* **2** [SING] A **smoke** is the act of sucking the smoke from a cigarette, cigar, or pipe into your mouth and blowing it out again. ❑ *Someone came out for a smoke.*
PHRASES **where there's smoke there's fire** If someone says **where there's smoke there's fire**, they mean that there are rumours or signs that something is true so it must be at least partly true. ❑ *A lot of the stuff in the story is not true, but I have to say that where there's smoke there's fire.* **go up in smoke 1** If something **goes up in smoke**, it is destroyed by fire. ❑ *The crew were able to put out the fire only after 25 acres had gone up in smoke.* **2** If something that is very important to you **goes up in smoke**, it fails or ends without anything being achieved. ❑ *I was afraid you'd say no, and my dream would go up in smoke.*
VERB [I, T] (smokes, smoking, smoked) **1** [I] If something **is smoking**, smoke is coming from it. ❑ *The chimney was smoking fiercely.* **2** [I, T] When someone **smokes** a cigarette, cigar, or pipe, they suck the smoke from it into their mouth and blow it out again. If you **smoke**, you regularly smoke cigarettes, cigars, or a pipe. ❑ *He was sitting alone, smoking a big cigar.* ❑ *It's not easy to quit smoking.* **3** [T] If fish or meat **is smoked**, it is hung over burning wood so that the smoke preserves it and gives it a special flavour. ❑ *the grid where the fish were being smoked*
→ See also **smoking**

smok·er /ˈsməʊkə/ NOUN [C] (smokers) A **smoker** is a person who smokes cigarettes, cigars, or a pipe. ❑ *a 64-year-old former smoker*

smok·ing ◆◇◇ /ˈsməʊkɪŋ/ NOUN, ADJ
NOUN [U] **Smoking** is the act or habit of smoking cigarettes, cigars, or a pipe. ❑ *Smoking is now banned in many places of work.*

S

ADJ [smoking + N] A **smoking** area is intended for people who want to smoke. ❑ *California no longer allows smoking areas in restaurants.*
→ See also **smoke**

smoky /ˈsməʊki/ also **smokey** ADJ (**smokier, smokiest**)
1 A place that is **smoky** has a lot of smoke in the air. ❑ *His main problem was the extremely smoky atmosphere at work.* **2** [smoky + N] You can use **smoky** to describe something that looks like smoke, for example, because it is slightly blue or grey or because it is not clear. ❑ *At the centre of the dial is a piece of smoky glass.* **3** Something that has a **smoky** flavour tastes as if it has been smoked. ❑ *The fish had just the right amount of smoky flavour for my taste.*

smooth ◆◇◇ /smuːð/ ADJ, VERB
ADJ (**smoother, smoothest**) **1** A **smooth** surface has no roughness, lumps, or holes. ❑ *a rich cream that keeps skin soft and smooth* ❑ *a smooth surface such as glass* **2** A **smooth** liquid or mixture has been mixed well so that it has no lumps. ❑ *Continue whisking until the mixture looks smooth and creamy.* **3** If you describe a drink such as wine, whisky, or coffee as **smooth**, you mean that it is not bitter and is pleasant to drink. ❑ *This makes the whiskies much smoother.* **4** A **smooth** line or movement has no sudden breaks or changes in direction or speed. ❑ *This exercise is done in one smooth motion.* **5** A **smooth** ride, flight, or sea crossing is very comfortable because there are no unpleasant movements. ❑ *The active suspension system gives the car a very smooth ride.* **6** You use **smooth** to describe something that is going well and is free of problems or trouble. ❑ *Political hopes for a swift and smooth transition to democracy have been dashed.* **7** If you describe a man as **smooth**, you mean that he is extremely smart, confident, and polite, often in a way that you find rather unpleasant. ❑ *Twelve extremely good-looking, smooth young men have been picked as finalists.*
VERB [T] (**smooths, smoothing, smoothed**) If you **smooth** something, you move your hands over its surface to make it smooth and flat. ❑ *She stood up and smoothed down her frock.*
PHRASAL VERBS **smooth out** If you **smooth out** a problem or difficulty, you solve it, especially by talking to the people concerned. ❑ *Baker was smoothing out differences with European allies.*
smooth over If you **smooth over** a problem or difficulty, you make it less serious and easier to deal with, especially by talking to the people concerned. ❑ *an attempt to smooth over the violent splits that have occurred* ❑ *The president is trying to smooth things over.*
smooth·ly /ˈsmuːðli/ ADV **1** [smoothly with V] ❑ *Make sure that you execute all movements smoothly and without jerking.* **2** [smoothly with V] ❑ *So far, talks at GM have gone smoothly.*

smoth·er /ˈsmʌðə/ VERB [T] (**smothers, smothering, smothered**) **1** If you **smother** a fire, you cover it with something in order to put it out. ❑ *The girl's parents were also burned as they tried to smother the flames.* **2** To **smother** someone means to cover their face with something so that they cannot breathe. = **suffocate** ❑ *He tried to smother me with a pillow.* **3** Things that **smother** something cover it completely. ❑ *Once the shrubs begin to smother the little plants, they have to move them.* **4** If you **smother** someone, you show your love for them too much and protect them too much. ❑ *She loved her own children, almost smothering them with love.* **5** If you **smother** an emotion or a reaction, you control it so that people do not notice it. = **stifle** ❑ *She tried to smother her anger and help them resolve their conflicts.*

smoul·der /ˈsməʊldə/ (in AmE, use **smolder**) VERB [I] (**smoulders, smouldering, smouldered**) **1** If something **smoulders**, it burns slowly, producing smoke but not flames. ❑ *The wreckage was still smouldering several hours after the crash.* **2** If a feeling such as anger or hatred **smoulders** inside you, you continue to feel it but do not show it. ❑ *the guilt that had so long smouldered in her heart* **3** If you say that someone **smoulders**, you mean that they are sexually attractive, usually in a mysterious or very intense way. ❑ *He was good-looking, with dark eyes which could smoulder with just the right intimation of passion.*

smug·gle /ˈsmʌɡəl/ VERB [T] (**smuggles, smuggling, smuggled**) If someone **smuggles** things or people into a place or out of it, they take them there illegally or secretly. ❑ *My message is 'If you try to smuggle drugs you are stupid.'* ❑ *Police have foiled an attempt to smuggle a bomb into Belfast airport.*
smug·gling /ˈsmʌɡlɪŋ/ NOUN [U] ❑ *An air hostess was arrested and charged with drug smuggling.*
smug·gler /ˈsmʌɡələ/ NOUN [C] (**smugglers**) **Smugglers** are people who take goods into or out of a country illegally. ❑ *drug smugglers*

snack /snæk/ NOUN, VERB
NOUN [C] (**snacks**) **1** A **snack** is a simple meal that is quick to cook and to eat. ❑ *Lunch was a snack in the fields.* **2** A **snack** is something such as a chocolate bar that you eat between meals. ❑ *Do you eat sweets, cakes, or sugary snacks?*
VERB [I] (**snacks, snacking, snacked**) If you **snack**, you eat snacks between meals. ❑ *Instead of snacking on crisps and chocolate, nibble on celery or carrot.*

snag /snæɡ/ NOUN, VERB
NOUN [C] (**snags**) A **snag** is a small problem or disadvantage. ❑ *A police clampdown on car thieves hit a snag when villains stole one of their cars.*
VERB [I, T] (**snags, snagging, snagged**) If you **snag** part of your clothing **on** a sharp or rough object or if it **snags**, it gets caught on the object and tears. ❑ *She snagged a heel on a root and tumbled to the ground.* ❑ *Brambles snagged his suit.*

snake /sneɪk/ NOUN, VERB
NOUN [C] (**snakes**) A **snake** is a long, thin reptile without legs.
VERB [I] (**snakes, snaking, snaked**) (literary) Something that **snakes** in a particular direction goes in that direction in a line with a lot of bends. = **wind** ❑ *The road snaked through forested mountains.*

snap ◆◇◇ /snæp/ VERB, NOUN, ADJ
VERB [I, T] (**snaps, snapping, snapped**) **1** [I, T] If something **snaps** or if you **snap** it, it breaks suddenly, usually with a sharp cracking noise. ❑ *He shifted his weight and a twig snapped.* ❑ *The brake pedal had just snapped off.* **2** [I, T] If you **snap** something into a particular position, or if it **snaps** into that position, it moves quickly into that position, with a sharp sound. ❑ *He snapped the notebook shut.* ❑ *He snapped the cap on his ballpoint.* **3** [T] If you **snap** your **fingers**, you make a sharp sound by moving your middle finger quickly across your thumb, for example, in order to accompany music or to order someone to do something. = **click** ❑ *She had millions of listeners snapping their fingers to her first single.* ❑ *He snapped his fingers, and Wilson produced a sheet of paper.* **4** [I, T] If someone **snaps at** you, they speak to you in a sharp, unfriendly way. ❑ *'Of course I don't know her,' Roger snapped.* **5** [I] If someone **snaps**, or if something **snaps** inside them, they suddenly stop being calm and become very angry because the situation has become too tense or too difficult for them. ❑ *He finally snapped when they prevented their children from visiting him one weekend.* **6** [I] If an animal such as a dog **snaps at** you, it opens and shuts its jaws quickly near you, as if it were going to bite you. ❑ *His teeth clicked as he snapped at my ankle.*
PHRASAL VERB **snap up** If you **snap** something **up**, you buy it quickly because it is cheap or is just what you want. ❑ *a millionaire ready to snap them up at the premium price of $200 a gallon*
NOUN [SING, C] (**snaps**) **1** [SING] A **snap** is the sharp, cracking noise of something suddenly breaking. ❑ *Every minute or so I could hear a snap, a crack, and a crash as another tree went down.* **2** [SING] If something moves or is moved into a particular position with a **snap**, it moves quickly into that position, with a sharp sound. ❑ *He shut the book with a snap and stood up.* **3** [SING] [snap 'of' N] A **snap of** your **fingers** is a sharp sound made by moving your middle finger quickly across your thumb, for example, in order to accompany music or to order someone to do something. ❑ *I could obtain with the snap of my fingers anything I chose.* **4** [C] (informal) A **snap** is a photograph. = **photo** ❑ *a snap my mother took last year*

S

ADJ [snap + N] A **snap** decision or action is one that is taken suddenly, often without careful thought. ❑ *I think this is too important for a snap decision.*

snatch /snætʃ/ VERB, NOUN

VERB [I, T] (**snatches, snatching, snatched**) **1** [I, T] If you **snatch** something or **snatch at** something, you take it or pull it away quickly. ❑ *Mick snatched the cards from Archie's hand.* ❑ *He snatched up the telephone.* **2** [T] If something **is snatched** from you, it is stolen, usually using force. If a person **is snatched**, they are taken away by force. ❑ *If your bag is snatched, let it go.* **3** [T] If you **snatch** an opportunity, you take it quickly. If you **snatch** something to eat or a rest, you have it quickly in between doing other things. ❑ *I snatched a glance at the mirror.* **4** [T] If you **snatch** victory in a competition, you defeat your opponent by a small amount or just before the end of the contest. ❑ *The American came from behind to snatch victory by a mere eight seconds.*

NOUN [c] (**snatches**) A **snatch of** a conversation or a song is a very small piece of it. ❑ *I heard snatches of the conversation.*

sneak /sniːk/ VERB [I, T] (**sneaks, sneaking, sneaked** or **snuck**)

The form **snuck** is informal.

1 [I] If you **sneak** somewhere, you go there very quietly on foot, trying to avoid being seen or heard. ❑ *Sometimes he would sneak out of his house late at night to be with me.* **2** [T] If you **sneak** something somewhere, you take it there secretly. ❑ *He smuggled papers out each day, photocopied them, and sneaked them back.* **3** [T] If you **sneak** a look at someone or something, you secretly have a quick look at them. = steal ❑ *You sneak a look at your watch to see how long you've got to wait.*

sneeze /sniːz/ VERB, NOUN

VERB [I] (**sneezes, sneezing, sneezed**) When you **sneeze**, you suddenly take in your breath and then blow it down your nose noisily without being able to stop yourself, for example, because you have a cold. ❑ *What exactly happens when we sneeze?*

PHRASE **not to be sneezed at** (*informal*) If you say that something is **not to be sneezed at**, you mean that it is worth having. ❑ *The money's not to be sneezed at.*

NOUN [c] (**sneezes**) A **sneeze** is the act or sound of sneezing. ❑ *Coughs and sneezes spread infections.*

sniff /snɪf/ VERB, NOUN

VERB [I, T] (**sniffs, sniffing, sniffed**) **1** [I] When you **sniff**, you breathe in air through your nose hard enough to make a sound, for example, when you are trying not to cry, or in order to show disapproval. ❑ *She wiped her face and sniffed loudly.* ❑ *Then he sniffed. There was a smell of burning.* **2** [I, T] If you **sniff** something or **sniff at** it, you smell it by sniffing. ❑ *Suddenly, he stopped and sniffed the air.* **3** [T] You can use **sniff** to indicate that someone says something in a way that shows their disapproval or contempt. ❑ *'Tourists!' she sniffed.* **4** [I, T] If you say that something is **not to be sniffed at**, you think it is very good or worth having. If someone **sniffs at** something, they do not think it is good enough, or they express their contempt for it. ❑ *The salary was not to be sniffed at either.* **5** [T] If someone **sniffs** a substance such as glue, they deliberately breathe in the substance or the gases from it as a drug. ❑ *He felt light-headed, as if he'd sniffed glue.*

PHRASAL VERB **sniff out** **1** (*informal*) If you **sniff out** something, you discover it after some searching. ❑ *journalists who are trained to sniff out scandal* **2** When a dog used by a group such as the police **sniffs out** hidden explosives or drugs, it finds them using its sense of smell. ❑ *a police dog trained to sniff out explosives*

NOUN [c] (**sniffs**) A **sniff** is the act of breathing in air through your nose hard enough to make a sound, for example, when you are trying not to cry, or in order to show disapproval. ❑ *At last the sobs ceased, to be replaced by sniffs.*

snip /snɪp/ VERB [I, T] (**snips, snipping, snipped**)
If you **snip** something, or if you **snip at** or **through** something, you cut it quickly using sharp scissors.

❑ *He has now begun to snip away at the piece of paper.*

snob /snɒb/ NOUN [c] (**snobs**) (*disapproval*) If you call someone a **snob**, you disapprove of them because they behave as if they are superior to other people because of their intelligence, taste, or social status. ❑ *She was an intellectual snob.*

snob·bery /ˈsnɒbəri/ NOUN [u] **Snobbery** is the attitude of a snob. ❑ *There has often been an element of snobbery in golf.*

snore /snɔː/ VERB, NOUN

VERB [I] (**snores, snoring, snored**) When someone who is asleep **snores**, they make a loud noise each time they breathe. ❑ *His mouth was open, and he was snoring.*

NOUN [c] (**snores**) A **snore** is a loud noise that someone who is asleep makes each time they breathe. ❑ *Uncle Arthur, after a loud snore, woke suddenly.*

snort /snɔːt/ VERB, NOUN

VERB [I, T] (**snorts, snorting, snorted**) **1** [I] When people or animals **snort**, they breathe air noisily out through their noses. People sometimes snort in order to express disapproval or amusement. ❑ *Harrell snorted with laughter.* **2** [T] To **snort** a drug such as cocaine means to breathe it in quickly through your nose. ❑ *He died of cardiac arrest after snorting cocaine at a party.*

NOUN [c] (**snorts**) A **snort** is the act of breathing air noisily out through the nose. ❑ *snorts of laughter*

snow ♦◇◇ /snəʊ/ NOUN, VERB

NOUN [u] (**snows**) **Snow** consists of a lot of soft white pieces of frozen water that fall from the sky in cold weather. ❑ *Six inches of snow blocked roads.*

VERB [I] (**snows, snowing, snowed**) When **it snows**, snow falls from the sky. ❑ *It had been snowing all night.*

snowy /ˈsnəʊi/ ADJ (**snowier, snowiest**) A **snowy** place is covered in snow. A **snowy** day is a day when a lot of snow has fallen. ❑ *the snowy peaks of the Bighorn Mountains*

snub /snʌb/ VERB, NOUN

VERB [T] (**snubs, snubbing, snubbed**) If you **snub** someone, you deliberately insult them by ignoring them or by behaving or speaking rudely towards them. ❑ *He snubbed her in public and made her feel an idiot.*

NOUN [c] (**snubs**) If you snub someone, your behaviour or your remarks can be referred to as a **snub**. ❑ *Ryan took it as a snub.*

so ♦♦♦ /səʊ/ ADV, CONJ, CONVENTION

ADV **1** [so after v] You use **so** to refer back to something that has just been mentioned. ❑ *'Do you think that much of a difference to the family?'—'I think so.'* ❑ *If you can't play straight, then say so.* **2** [so + CL] You use **so** when you are saying that something which has just been said about one person or thing is also true of another one. ❑ *I enjoy Ann's company and so does Martin.* ❑ *They had a wonderful time and so did I.* **3** [V-LINK + so] If you say that a state of affairs **is so**, you mean that it is the way it has been described. ❑ *In those days English dances as well as songs were taught at school, but that seems no longer to be so.* ❑ *It is strange to think that he held strong views on many things, but it must have been so.* **4** [so after v] You can use **so** with actions and gestures to show a person how to do something, or to indicate the size, height, or length of something. ❑ *Clasp the chain like so.* **5** [so + CL] You can use **so** in conversations to introduce a new topic, or to introduce a question or comment about something that has been said. ❑ *So how was your day?* ❑ *So you're a runner, huh?* **6** [so + CL] You can use **so** in conversations to show that you are accepting what someone has just said. ❑ *'It makes me feel, well, important.'—'And so you are.'* ❑ *'You can't possibly use this word.'—'So I won't.'* **7** [so + ADJ/ADV] You can use **so** in front of adjectives and adverbs to emphasize the quality that they are describing. ❑ *He was surprised they had married – they had seemed so different.* **8** You can use **so...that** and **so...as** to emphasize the degree of something by mentioning the result or consequence of it. ❑ *The tears were streaming so fast she could not see.* ❑ *He's not so stupid as to listen to rumours.*

PHRASES **and so on** or **and so forth** You use **and so on** or **and so forth** at the end of a list to indicate that there are

S

other items that you could also mention. □ *the government's policies on such important issues as health, education, tax, and so on*

so much or **so many** You use **so much** and **so many** when you are saying that there is a definite limit to something but you are not saying what this limit is. □ *There is only so much time in the day for answering letters.* □ *There is only so much fuel in the tank and if you burn it up too quickly you are in trouble.*

not so much You use the structures **not…so much** and **not so much…as** to say that something is one kind of thing rather than another kind. □ *I did not really object to Will's behaviour so much as his personality.*

or so (*vagueness*) You use **or so** when you are giving an approximate amount. □ *Though rates are heading down, they still offer real returns of 8% or so.*

CONJ ■ You use the structures **as…so** and **just as…so** when you want to indicate that two events or situations are similar in some way. □ *As computer systems become even more sophisticated, so too do the methods of those who exploit the technology.* □ *Just as John has changed, so has his wife.* ■ You use **so** and **so that** to introduce the result of the situation you have just mentioned. □ *I am not an emotional type and so cannot bring myself to tell him I love him.* □ *People are living longer than ever before, so even people who are 65 or 70 have a surprising amount of time left.* ■ You use **so**, **so that**, and **so as** to introduce the reason for doing the thing that you have just mentioned. □ *Come to my suite so I can tell you all about this wonderful play I saw in Boston.* □ *He took her arm and hurried her upstairs so that they wouldn't be overheard.*

CONVENTION (*informal*) You say '**So?**' and '**So what?**' to indicate that you think that something that someone has said is unimportant. □ *'My name's Bruno.'—'So?'*

✦ **so much the better** → see **better**; **so far so good** → see **far**; **so long** → see **long**; **so much so** → see **much**; **every so often** → see **often**; **so there** → see **there**

soak /soʊk/ VERB, NOUN
VERB [I, T] (**soaks**, **soaking**, **soaked**) ■ [I, T] If you **soak** something or leave it **to soak**, you put it into a liquid and leave it there. □ *Soak the beans for 2 hours.* ■ [T] If a liquid **soaks** something or if you **soak** something **with** a liquid, the liquid makes the thing very wet. □ *The water had soaked his jacket and shirt.* ■ [I] If a liquid **soaks through** something, it passes through it. □ *There was so much blood it had soaked through my boxer shorts.* ■ [I] If someone **soaks**, they spend a long time in a hot bath, because they enjoy it. □ *What I need is to soak in a hot tub.*
PHRASAL VERB **soak up** ■ If a soft or dry material **soaks up** a liquid, the liquid goes into the substance. □ *The cells will promptly start to soak up moisture.* ■ (*informal*) If you **soak up** the atmosphere in a place that you are visiting, you observe or get involved in the way of life there, because you enjoy it or are interested in it. = absorb □ *Keaton comes here once or twice a year to soak up the atmosphere.* ■ If something **soaks up** something such as money or other resources, it uses a great deal of money or other resources. □ *Defence soaks up 40 per cent of the budget.*
NOUN [C] (**soaks**) A **soak** is a long time spent in a hot bath, because you enjoy it. □ *I was having a long soak in the bath.*

soap /soʊp/ NOUN [C, U] (**soaps**) **Soap** is a substance that you use with water for washing yourself or sometimes for washing clothes. □ *a bar of lavender soap* □ *a large box of soap powder*

✪ **soar** /sɔː/ VERB [I] (**soars**, **soaring**, **soared**) (*journalism*) If the amount, value, level, or volume of something **soars**, it quickly increases by a great deal. = rise; ≠ drop, fall, plummet □ *Insurance claims are expected to soar.* □ *Shares soared on the New York stock exchange.* □ *Figures showed customer complaints had soared to record levels and profits were falling.*

sob /sɒb/ VERB, NOUN
VERB [I] (**sobs**, **sobbing**, **sobbed**) When someone **sobs**, they cry in a noisy way, breathing in short breaths. □ *She began to sob again, burying her face in the pillow.*
NOUN [C] (**sobs**) A **sob** is one of the noises that you make when you are crying. □ *Her sobs grew louder.*

sob·bing /ˈsɒbɪŋ/ NOUN [U] □ *The room was silent except for her sobbing.*

so·ber /ˈsoʊbə/ ADJ
ADJ ■ When you are **sober**, you are not drunk. □ *He'd been drunk when I arrived. Now he was sober.* ■ A **sober** person is serious and thoughtful. □ *We are now far more sober and realistic.* □ *It was a room filled with sad, sober faces.* ■ **Sober** colours and clothes are plain and rather dull. = sombre □ *He dresses in sober grey suits.*
PHRASAL VERB **sober up** (**sobers**, **sobering**, **sobered**) If someone **sobers up**, or if something **sobers** them **up**, they become sober after being drunk. □ *He was left to sober up in a police cell.*

so·ber·ly /ˈsoʊbəli/ ADV ■ *'There's a new development,' he said soberly.* ■ [soberly with v] □ *She saw Ellis, soberly dressed in a well-cut dark suit.*

✪ **so-called** ◆◇◇ also **so called** ADJ (*academic word*) ■ [so-called + N] You use **so-called** to indicate that you think a word or expression used to describe someone or something is in fact wrong. □ *These are the facts that explode their so-called economic miracle.* □ *More and more companies have gone 'green' and started producing so-called environmentally-friendly products.* ■ [so-called + N] You use **so-called** to indicate that something is generally referred to by the name that you are about to use. □ *a summit of the world's seven leading market economies, the so-called G-7* □ *She was one of the so-called Gang of Four.*

soc·cer ◆◇◇ /ˈsɒkə/ NOUN [U] **Soccer** is a game played by two teams of eleven players using a round ball. Players kick the ball to each other and try to score goals by kicking the ball into a large net. The term **soccer** is used mainly in the United States. In other countries, the game is usually referred to as **football**. □ *a soccer match*

so·cia·ble /ˈsoʊʃəbəl/ ADJ **Sociable** people are friendly and enjoy talking to other people. □ *She was, and remained, extremely sociable, enjoying dancing, golf, tennis, skating, and cycling.*

✪ **so·cial** ◆◆◆ /ˈsoʊʃəl/ ADJ ■ [social + N] **Social** means relating to society or to the way society is organized. □ *the worst effects of unemployment, low pay, and other social problems* □ *long-term social change* □ *changing social attitudes* □ *the tightly woven social fabric of small towns* ■ [social + N] **Social** means relating to the status or rank that someone has in society. □ *Higher education is unequally distributed across social classes.* □ *The guests came from all social backgrounds.* ■ [social + N] **Social** means relating to leisure activities that involve meeting other people. □ *We ought to organize more social events.*

✪ **so·cial·ly** /ˈsoʊʃəli/ ADV ■ *Let's face it – drinking is a socially acceptable habit.* □ *one of the most socially deprived areas in Britain* □ *socially disadvantaged children* ■ *For socially ambitious couples this is a problem.* ■ *We have known each other socially for a long time.*

✪ **so·cial·ism** /ˈsoʊʃəlɪzəm/ NOUN [U] **Socialism** is a set of political principles whose general aim is to create a system in which everyone has an equal opportunity to benefit from a country's wealth. Under socialism, the country's main industries are usually owned by the state. = communism, Marxism; ≠ capitalism □ *In the classical exemplar of state socialism, the Soviet Union, private property was almost completely eliminated.*

✪ **so·cial·ist** ◆◇◇ /ˈsoʊʃəlɪst/ ADJ, NOUN
ADJ **Socialist** means based on socialism or relating to socialism. = communist, Marxist, left-wing; ≠ capitalist □ *members of the ruling Socialist Party* □ *low-inflation policies practised by the socialist government*
NOUN [C] (**socialists**) A **socialist** is a person who believes in socialism or who is a member of a socialist party. = communist; ≠ capitalist □ *Esperanto has always been popular among socialists.* □ *The French electorate voted out the socialists.*

so·cial·ize /ˈsoʊʃəlaɪz/ also **socialise** VERB [I] (**socializes**, **socializing**, **socialized**) If you **socialize**, you meet other people socially, for example at parties. □ *an open meeting, where members socialized and welcomed any new members*

so·cial ser·vices NOUN [PL] **Social services** in a district are the services provided by the local authority or government to help people who have serious family problems or financial problems. ☐ *Schools and social services are also struggling to absorb the influx.*

so·cial work NOUN **Social work** is work which involves giving help and advice to people with serious family problems or financial problems.

so·cial work·er NOUN [C] (**social workers**) A **social worker** is a person whose job is to do social work.

✪ **so·ci·e·ty** ♦♦♦ /sə'saɪɪti/ NOUN [U, C] (**societies**) **1** [U] **Society** is people in general, thought of as a large organized group. ☐ *This reflects attitudes and values prevailing in society.* **2** [C, U] A **society** is the people who live in a country or region, their organizations, and their way of life. = community ☐ *We live in a capitalist society.* ☐ *Debate is fundamental to a democratic society.* ☐ *those responsible for destroying our African heritage and the fabric of our society* ☐ *the complexities of South African society* **3** [C] A **society** is an organization for people who have the same interest or aim. = association ☐ *the Atlanta Horticultural Society* **4** [U] **Society** is the rich, fashionable people in a particular place who meet on social occasions. ☐ *The couple quickly became a fixture in society.*

USAGE NOTE
society

Do not use 'a' or 'the' in front of **society** when you are using it to refer to people in general.
Society is only now learning about how the world really works.

---

so·cio·eco·nom·ic /ˌsəʊsiəʊekə'nɒmɪk, -iːkə-/ ADJ [socioeconomic + N] **Socioeconomic** circumstances or developments involve a combination of social and economic factors. ☐ *The age, education, and socioeconomic status of these young mothers led to less satisfactory child care.*

✪ **so·ci·ol·ogy** /ˌsəʊsi'ɒlədʒi/ NOUN [U] **Sociology** is the study of society or of the way society is organized. ☐ *a sociology professor at the University of North Carolina* ☐ *a treatise on the sociology of religion*

✪ **so·cio·logi·cal** /ˌsəʊsiə'lɒdʒɪkəl/ ADJ ☐ *Psychological and sociological studies were emphasizing the importance of the family.* ☐ *Viewed from a sociological perspective, the president's popularity might be a result of the changing nature of our attitude towards authority.*

✪ **so·ci·olo·gist** /ˌsəʊsi'ɒlədʒɪst/ NOUN [C] (**sociologists**) ☐ *By the 1950s some sociologists were confident that they had identified the key characteristics of capitalist society.*

sock /sɒk/ NOUN, VERB
NOUN [C] (**socks**) **Socks** are pieces of clothing which cover your foot and ankle and are worn inside shoes. ☐ *a pair of knee-high socks*
VERB [T] (**socks, socking, socked**) (*informal*) If you **sock** someone or something, you hit them hard. ☐ *Once, after a boy made a comment, she socked him.*

so·dium /'səʊdiəm/ NOUN [U] **Sodium** is a silvery white chemical element which combines with other chemicals. Salt is a sodium compound. ☐ *The fish or seafood is heavily salted with pure sodium chloride.*

sofa /'səʊfə/ NOUN [C] (**sofas**) A **sofa** is a long, comfortable seat with a back and usually with arms, which two or three people can sit on. = settee, couch

soft ♦♦◇ /sɒft, AmE sɔːft/ ADJ (**softer, softest**)
1 Something that is **soft** is pleasant to touch, and not rough or hard. ☐ *Regular use of a body lotion will keep the skin soft and supple.* ☐ *When it's dry, brush the hair using a soft, nylon baby brush.* **2** Something that is **soft** changes shape or bends easily when you press it. ☐ *She lay down on the soft, comfortable bed.* ☐ *Add enough milk to form a soft dough.* **3** Something that has a **soft** appearance has smooth curves rather than sharp or distinct edges. = gentle ☐ *This is a smart, yet soft and feminine look.* **4** Something that is **soft** is very gentle and has no force. For example, a **soft** sound or voice is quiet and not harsh. A **soft** light or colour is pleasant to look at because it is not

bright. = gentle ☐ *There was a soft tapping on my door.* **5** If you are **soft on** someone, you do not treat them as strictly or severely as you should. ☐ *The president says the measure is soft and weak on criminals.* **6** If you say that someone has a **soft heart**, you mean that they are sensitive and sympathetic towards other people. ☐ *Her rather tough and worldly exterior hides a very soft and sensitive heart.* **7** You use **soft** to describe a way of life that is easy and involves very little work. = easy ☐ *a soft life and easy living* **8** **Soft** water does not contain much of the mineral calcium and so makes bubbles easily when you use soap. ☐ *an area where the water is very soft* **9** [soft + N] (*mainly BrE*; in AmE, use **recreational**) **Soft** drugs are drugs, such as cannabis, which are illegal but which many people do not consider to be strong or harmful.

soft·ness /'sɒftnəs, AmE 'sɔːftnəs/ NOUN [U] ☐ *The sea air robbed her hair of its softness.*

soft·ly /'sɒftli, AmE 'sɔːftli/ ADV **1** [softly with V] ☐ *She wore a softly tailored suit.* **2** [softly with V] ☐ *She crossed the softly lit room.*

soft·en /'sɒfən, AmE 'sɔːf-/ VERB [I, T] (**softens, softening, softened**) **1** [I, T] If you **soften** something or if it **softens**, it becomes less hard, stiff, or firm. ☐ *Soften the butter mixture in a small saucepan.* **2** [T] If one thing **softens** the damaging effect of another thing, it makes the effect less severe. ☐ *There were also pledges to soften the impact of the subsidy cuts on the poorer regions.* **3** [I, T] If you **soften** your position, if your position **softens**, or if you **soften**, you become more sympathetic and less hostile or critical. ☐ *The letter shows no sign that the Germans have softened their position.* ☐ *His party's policy has softened a lot in recent years.* **4** [I, T] If your voice or expression **softens** or if you **soften** it, it becomes much more gentle and friendly. ☐ *All at once, Mick's serious expression softened into a grin.* **5** [T] If you **soften** something such as light, a colour, or a sound, you make it less bright or harsh. ☐ *We wanted to soften the light without destroying the overall effect of space.* **6** [T] Something that **softens** your skin makes it very smooth and pleasant to touch. ☐ *products designed to moisturize and soften the skin*

✪ **soft·ware** ♦◇◇ /'sɒftweə, AmE 'sɔːf-/ NOUN [U] (*computing*) Computer programs are referred to as **software**. Compare **hardware**. ☐ *the people who write the software for big computer projects* ☐ *the latest software development technologies*

✪ **soil** ♦◇◇ /sɔɪl/ NOUN [C, U] (**soils**) **Soil** is the substance on the surface of the earth in which plants grow. ☐ *We have the most fertile soil in the county.* ☐ *regions with sandy soils*

✪ **so·lar** /'səʊlə/ ADJ **1** **Solar** is used to describe things relating to the sun. ☐ *A total solar eclipse is due to take place some time tomorrow.* ☐ *Snow and ice reflect 80% to 90% of solar radiation back into space.* **2** **Solar** power is obtained from the sun's light and heat. ☐ *the financial savings from solar energy* ☐ *a government effort to promote solar power* ☐ *A solar water heater reduces electricity consumption.*

✪ **so·lar sys·tem** NOUN [C] (**solar systems**) The **solar system** is the sun and all the planets that go around it. ☐ *Saturn is the second biggest planet in the solar system.* ☐ *All the objects in the solar system shine by reflecting the light coming from the Sun.*

sold /səʊld/ IRREG FORM **Sold** is the past tense and past participle of **sell**.

sol·dier ♦♦◇ /'səʊldʒə/ NOUN [C] (**soldiers**) A **soldier** is a member of an army, especially a person who is not an officer.

✪ **sole** /səʊl/ ADJ, NOUN (*academic word*)
ADJ **1** [sole + N] The **sole** thing or person of a particular type is the only one of that type. = only ☐ *Their sole aim is to destabilize the Indian government.* ☐ *It's the sole survivor of an ancient family of plants.* **2** [sole + N] If you have **sole** charge or ownership of something, you are the only person in charge of it or who owns it. ☐ *Many women are left as the sole providers in families after their husband has died.* ☐ *Chief Hart had sole control over that fund.*
NOUN [C] (**soles**) The **sole** of your foot or of a shoe or sock is the underneath surface of it. ☐ *shoes with rubber soles*

✪ **sole·ly** /ˈsəʊlli/ ADV If something involves **solely** one thing, it involves only this thing and no others. = only ❑ Too often we make decisions based solely upon what we see in the magazines. ❑ This programme is a production of NPR, which is solely responsible for its content.

sol·emn /ˈsɒləm/ ADJ **1** Someone or something that is **solemn** is very serious rather than cheerful or humorous. = serious ❑ His solemn little face broke into smiles. **2** A **solemn** promise or agreement is one that you make in a very formal, sincere way. ❑ She made a solemn promise to him when they became engaged that she would give up cigarettes for good.
so·lem·nity /səˈlemnɪti/ NOUN [U] ❑ The setting for this morning's signing ceremony matched the solemnity of the occasion.

so·lic·i·tor ♦◇◇ /səˈlɪsɪtə/ NOUN [C] (**solicitors**) In Britain, a **solicitor** is a lawyer who advises clients on matters of law, draws up legal documents, prepares cases for barristers, and who may represent clients in certain courts. Compare **barrister**

✪ **sol·id** ♦◇◇ /ˈsɒlɪd/ ADJ, NOUN
ADJ **1** A **solid** substance or object stays the same shape whether it is in a container or not. ❑ the potential of greatly reducing our solid waste problem ❑ weaning infants onto solid food **2** A substance that is **solid** is very hard or firm. ❑ The snow had melted, but the lake was still frozen solid. **3** A **solid** object or mass does not have a space inside it, or holes or gaps in it. = hard, dense; ≠ liquid ❑ a tunnel carved through 50 ft of solid rock ❑ a solid wall of multicoloured trees ❑ a solid mass of colour ❑ The train station was packed solid with people. **4** [solid + N] If an object is made of **solid** gold or **solid** wood, for example, it is made of gold or wood all the way through, rather than just on the outside. ❑ The taps appeared to be made of solid gold. ❑ solid wood doors **5** A structure that is **solid** is strong and is not likely to collapse or fall over. ❑ Banks are built to look solid to reassure their customers. **6** If you describe someone as **solid**, you mean that they are very reliable and respectable. ❑ You want a husband who is solid and stable, someone who will devote himself to you. **7 Solid** evidence or information is reliable because it is based on facts. ❑ We don't have good solid information on where the people are. **8** You use **solid** to describe something such as advice or a piece of work which is useful and reliable. ❑ The organization provides churches with solid advice on a wide range of subjects. **9** You use **solid** to describe something such as the basis for a policy or support for an organization when it is strong, because it has been developed carefully and slowly. = strong ❑ a Democratic nominee with solid support within the party and broad appeal beyond **10** [solid + N, -ED + solid] If you do something for a **solid** period of time, you do it without any pause or interruption throughout that time. ❑ We had worked together for two solid years.
NOUN [C] (**solids**) A **solid** is a substance that stays the same shape whether it is in a container or not. ❑ Solids turn to liquids at certain temperatures.
sol·id·ly /ˈsɒlɪdli/ ADV **1** [solidly with v] ❑ Their house, which was solidly built, resisted the main shock. **2** [solidly with v] Graham is so solidly consistent. **3** [solidly with v] ❑ She's played solidly throughout the spring. **4** [solidly with v] ❑ The Los Alamos district is solidly Republican. **5** [solidly with v] ❑ People who had worked solidly since Christmas enjoyed the chance of a Friday off.
so·lid·ity /səˈlɪdɪti/ NOUN [U] **1** the solidity of walls and floors **2** He had the proverbial solidity of the English. **3** doubts over the solidity of European backing for the American approach

soli·dar·ity /ˌsɒlɪˈdærɪti/ NOUN [U] If a group of people show **solidarity**, they show support for each other or for another group, especially in political or international affairs. ❑ Supporters want to march tomorrow to show solidarity with their leaders.

so·lidi·fy /səˈlɪdɪfaɪ/ VERB [I, T] (**solidifies, solidifying, solidified**) **1** When a liquid **solidifies** or **is solidified**, it changes into a solid. ❑ The thicker lava would have taken two weeks to solidify. ❑ The Energy Department plans to solidify the deadly waste in a high-tech billion-dollar factory. **2** If something such as a position or opinion **solidifies**, or if

something **solidifies** it, it becomes firmer and more definite and unlikely to change. ❑ Her attitudes solidified through privilege and habit. ❑ his attempt to solidify his position as chairman

soli·tary /ˈsɒlɪtri, AmE -teri/ ADJ **1** A person or animal that is **solitary** spends a lot of time alone. ❑ Paul was a shy, pleasant, solitary man. **2** [solitary + N] A **solitary** activity is one that you do alone. ❑ His evenings were spent in solitary drinking. **3** [solitary + N] A **solitary** person or object is alone, with no others near them. = lone ❑ You could see the occasional solitary figure making a study of wildflowers or grasses.

soli·tude /ˈsɒlɪtjuːd, AmE -tuːd/ NOUN [U] **Solitude** is the state of being alone, especially when this is peaceful and pleasant. ❑ He enjoyed his moments of solitude before the pressures of the day began in earnest.

solo /ˈsəʊləʊ/ ADJ, ADV, NOUN
ADJ You use **solo** to indicate that someone does something alone rather than with other people. ❑ He had just completed his final solo album. ❑ Daniel Amokachi's spectacular solo goal
ADV [solo after v] If you do something **solo**, you do it alone rather than with other people. ❑ Charles Lindbergh became the very first person to fly solo across the Atlantic.
NOUN [C] (**solos**) A **solo** is a piece of music or a dance performed by one person. ❑ The original version featured a guitar solo.

sol·uble /ˈsɒljʊbəl/ ADJ, COMB
ADJ A substance that is **soluble** will dissolve in a liquid. ❑ Uranium is soluble in sea water.
COMB If something is **water-soluble** or **fat-soluble**, it will dissolve in water or in fat. ❑ The red dye on the leather is water-soluble.

✪ **so·lu·tion** ♦♦◇ /səˈluːʃən/ NOUN [C] (**solutions**) **1** A **solution** to a problem or difficult situation is a way of dealing with it so that the difficulty is removed. ❑ Although he has sought to find a peaceful solution, he is facing pressure to use greater military force. ❑ the ability to sort out simple, effective solutions to practical problems ❑ The real solution lay in providing affordable accommodation. **2** The **solution to** a puzzle is the answer to it. ❑ We invited readers who completed the puzzle to send in their solutions. **3** [also 'in' solution] A **solution** is a liquid in which a solid substance has been dissolved. ❑ a warm solution of liquid detergent ❑ Vitamins in solution are more affected than those in solid foods.

✪ **solve** ♦◇◇ /sɒlv/ VERB [T] (**solves, solving, solved**) If you **solve** a problem or a question, you find a solution or an answer to it. = work out ❑ Their domestic reforms did nothing to solve the problem of unemployment. ❑ We may now be able to get a much better idea of the true age of the universe, and solve one of the deepest questions of our origins.

som·bre /ˈsɒmbə/ (in AmE, use **somber**) ADJ **1** If someone is **sombre**, they are serious or sad. ❑ Spencer cried as she described the sombre mood of her co-workers. **2 Sombre** colours and places are dark and dull. ❑ His room is sombre and dark.

some ♦♦♦ /səm, STRONG sʌm/ DET, PRON, QUANT, ADV
DET **1** You use **some** to refer to a quantity of something or to a number of people or things, when you are not stating the quantity or number precisely. ❑ Robin opened some champagne. ❑ He went to fetch some books. **2** You use **some** to emphasize that a quantity or number is fairly large. For example, if an activity takes **some** time, it takes quite a lot of time. ❑ I have discussed this topic in some detail. ❑ He remained silent for some time. **3** You use **some** to emphasize that a quantity or number is fairly small. For example, if something happens to **some** extent, it happens a little. ❑ 'Isn't there some chance that William might lead a normal life?' asked Jill. ❑ All mothers share to some extent in the tension of a wedding. **4** If you refer to **some** person or thing, you are referring to that person or thing but in a vague way, without stating precisely which person or thing you mean. ❑ If you are worried about some aspect of your child's health, call us. **5** (informal, feelings) You can use **some** in front of a noun in order to express your approval or disapproval of the person or thing you are mentioning. ❑ 'Some party!'—'Yep. One hell of a party.'

S

PRON **1** You use **some** to refer to a few but not all of the people or things in a group. ❑ *This year all the apples are all red. My niece and nephew are going out this morning with step-ladders to pick some.* **2** You use **some** to refer to a part of a particular thing but not all of it. ❑ *When the chicken is cooked I'll freeze some.*

QUANT If you refer to **some of** the people or things in a group, you mean a few of them but not all of them. If you refer to **some of** a particular thing, you mean a part of it but not all of it. ❑ *Some of the people already in work will lose their jobs.* ❑ *Remove the cover and spoon some of the sauce into a bowl.*

ADV [some + NUM] (*vagueness*) You can use **some** in front of a number to indicate that it is approximate. = about ❑ *I have kept birds for some 30 years.*

some·body ◆◆◇ /'sʌmbədi, AmE -ba:di/ PRON
Somebody means the same as **someone**.

some·how ◆◇◇ /'sʌmhaʊ/ ADV You use **somehow** to say that you do not know or cannot say how something was done or will be done. ❑ *We'll manage somehow, you and me. I know we will.* ❑ *Somehow Karin managed to cope with the demands of her career.*

✦ **somehow or other** → see **other**

some·one ◆◆◇ /'sʌmwʌn/ PRON

The form **somebody** is also used.

1 You use **someone** or **somebody** to refer to a person without saying exactly who you mean. ❑ *Her father was shot by someone trying to rob his shop.* ❑ *I need someone to help me.* **2** If you say that a person is **someone** or **somebody in** a particular kind of work or **in** a particular place, you mean that they are considered to be important in that kind of work or in that place. ❑ *'Before she came on the scene,' she says, 'I was somebody in this town.'*

> **USAGE NOTE**
> **someone**
> **Someone** and **somebody** do not have plural forms. If you want to refer to a general group of people, you say **some people**.
> *Some people can hide their feelings; others can't.*

some·thing ◆◆◆ /'sʌmθɪŋ/ PRON **1** You use **something** to refer to a thing, situation, event, or idea, without saying exactly what it is. ❑ *He realized right away that there was something wrong.* ❑ *There was something vaguely familiar about him.* ❑ *'You said there was something you wanted to ask me,' he said politely.* **2** [something + PREP] You can use **something** to say that the description or amount that you are giving is not exact. ❑ *Clive made a noise, something like a grunt.* ❑ *Their membership seems to have risen to something over 10,000.* **3** (*informal*) If you say that a person or thing is **something** or is really **something**, you mean that you are very impressed by them. ❑ *You're really something.* **4** You can use **something** in expressions like '**that's something**' when you think that a situation is not very good but is better than it might have been. ❑ *Well, at least he was in town. That was something.* **5** [something 'of' N] If you say that a thing is **something of** a disappointment, you mean that it is quite disappointing. If you say that a person is **something of** an artist, you mean that they are quite good at art. ❑ *The city proved to be something of a disappointment.* **6** [something 'in' N] If you say that there is **something in** an idea or suggestion, you mean that it is quite good and should be considered seriously. ❑ *Could there be something in what he said?* **7** You use **something** in expressions such as '**or something**' and '**or something like that**' to indicate that you are referring to something similar to what you have just mentioned but you are not being exact. ❑ *This guy, his name was Briarly or Beardly or something.*

✦ **something like** → see **like**

some·time /'sʌmtaɪm/ ADV You use **sometime** to refer to a time in the future or the past that is unknown or that has not yet been decided. ❑ *The sales figures won't be released until sometime next month.* ❑ *Why don't you come and see me sometime?*

some·times ◆◆◇ /'sʌmtaɪmz/ ADV You use **sometimes** to say that something happens on some occasions rather than all the time. ❑ *During the summer, my skin sometimes gets greasy.* ❑ *Sometimes I think he dislikes me.*

✪ **some·what** ◆◇◇ /'sʌmwɒt/ ADV [somewhat with CL/ GROUP] (*academic word, formal*) You use **somewhat** to indicate that something is the case to a limited extent or degree. = slightly; ≠ extremely ❑ *He concluded that Oswald was somewhat abnormal.* ❑ *He explained somewhat unconvincingly that the company was paying for everything.* ❑ *The results are somewhat surprising.* ❑ *The outcome variables differed somewhat in the three groups.*

some·where ◆◇◇ /'sʌmweə/ ADV
ADV **1** You use **somewhere** to refer to a place without saying exactly where you mean. ❑ *I've got a feeling I've seen him before somewhere.* ❑ *I'm not going home yet. I have to go somewhere else first.* ❑ *I needed somewhere to live.* **2** [somewhere + PREP] You use **somewhere** when giving an approximate amount, number, or time. ❑ *He is believed to be worth somewhere between seven million and ten million dollars.* ❑ *Caray is somewhere between 73 and 80 years of age.*
PHRASE **be getting somewhere** If you say that you **are getting somewhere**, you mean that you are making progress towards achieving something. ❑ *At last they were agreeing, at last they were getting somewhere.*

son ◆◆◆ /sʌn/ NOUN [C] (**sons**) **1** Someone's **son** is their male child. ❑ *He shared a pizza with his son Laurence.* ❑ *Sam is the seven-year-old son of Eric Davies.* **2** (*journalism*) A man, especially a famous man, can be described as a **son** of the place he comes from. ❑ *New Orleans's most famous son, Louis Armstrong* **3** (*informal, feelings*) Some people use **son** as a form of address when they are showing kindness or affection to a boy or a man who is younger than them. ❑ *Don't be frightened by failure, son.*

so·nar /'səʊnɑː/ NOUN [C, U] (**sonars**) **Sonar** is equipment on a ship which can calculate the depth of the sea or the position of an underwater object using sound waves.

song ◆◆◇ /sɒŋ, AmE sɔːŋ/ NOUN
NOUN [C, U] (**songs**) **1** [C] A **song** is words and music sung together. ❑ *a voice singing a Spanish song* **2** [U] **Song** is the art of singing. ❑ *dance, music, mime, and song* **3** [C] A bird's **song** is the pleasant, musical sounds that it makes. ❑ *It's been a long time since I heard a blackbird's song in the evening.*
PHRASE **burst into song** or **break into song** If someone **bursts into song** or **breaks into song**, they start singing. ❑ *I feel as if I should break into song.*

✪ **son·ic** /'sɒnɪk/ ADJ [sonic + N] (*technical*) **Sonic** is used to describe things related to sound. ❑ *the sonic boom of enemy fighter-bombers* ❑ *He activated the door with the miniature sonic transmitter.*

son-in-law NOUN [C] (**sons-in-law**) Someone's **son-in-law** is the husband of their daughter.

soon ◆◆◆ /suːn/ ADV
ADV (**sooner, soonest**) If something is going to happen **soon**, it will happen after a short time. If something happened **soon** after a particular time or event, it happened a short time after it. ❑ *You'll be hearing from us very soon.* ❑ *This chance has come sooner than I expected.*
PHRASES **as soon as** If you say that something happens **as soon as** something else happens, you mean that it happens immediately after the other thing. ❑ *As soon as relations improve they will be allowed to go.*
would just as soon If you say that you **would just as soon** do something or you**'d just as soon** do it, you mean that you would prefer to do it. ❑ *These people could afford to retire to Florida but they'd just as soon stay put.* ❑ *I'd just as soon not have to make this public.*

soothe /suːð/ VERB [T] (**soothes, soothing, soothed**) **1** If you **soothe** someone who is angry or upset, you make them feel calmer. ❑ *He would take her in his arms and soothe her.* **2** Something that **soothes** a part of your body where there is pain or discomfort makes the pain or discomfort less severe. ❑ *body lotion to soothe the dry skin*

sooth·ing /'suːðɪŋ/ ADJ **1** Put on some nice, soothing music. **2** Cold tea is very soothing for burns.

so·phis·ti·cat·ed ♦◇◇ /səˈfɪstɪkeɪtɪd/ ADJ **1** A **sophisticated** machine, device, or method is more advanced or complex than others. ❑ *Honeybees use one of the most sophisticated communication systems of any insect.* **2** Someone who is **sophisticated** is comfortable in social situations and knows about culture, fashion, and other matters that are considered socially important. = refined ❑ *Claude was a charming, sophisticated companion.* **3** A **sophisticated** person is intelligent and knows a lot, so that they are able to understand complicated situations. ❑ *These people are very sophisticated observers of the foreign policy scene.*

so·phis·ti·ca·tion /səˌfɪstɪˈkeɪʃən/ NOUN [u] The **sophistication** of people, places, machines, or methods is their quality of being sophisticated. ❑ *It would take many decades to build up the level of education and sophistication required.*

sore /sɔː/ ADJ, NOUN

ADJ (**sorer, sorest**) **1** If part of your body is **sore**, it causes you pain and discomfort. ❑ *It's years since I've had a sore throat like I did last night.* **2** [V-LINK + sore] (*mainly AmE, informal*) If you are **sore** about something, you are angry and upset about it. = annoyed ❑ *The result is that they are now all feeling very sore at you.*

PHRASE **a sore point** If something is **a sore point with** someone, it is likely to make them angry or embarrassed if you try to discuss it. ❑ *The continuing presence of American troops on Korean soil remains a very sore point with these students.*

NOUN [c] (**sores**) A **sore** is a painful place on the body where the skin is infected. ❑ *Our backs and hands were covered with sores and burns from the ropes.*

sore·ly /ˈsɔːli/ ADV (*emphasis*) **Sorely** is used to emphasize that a feeling such as disappointment or need is very strong. ❑ *I for one was sorely disappointed.* ❑ *He will be sorely missed.*

sor·row /ˈsɒrəʊ/ NOUN [u] **Sorrow** is a feeling of deep sadness or regret. ❑ *Words cannot express my sorrow.*

sor·ry ♦♦◇ /ˈsɒri/ CONVENTION, ADJ

CONVENTION ♦◇◇ **1** (*formulae*) You say '**Sorry**' or '**I'm sorry**' as a way of apologizing to someone for something that you have done which has upset them or caused them difficulties, or when you bump into them accidentally. ❑ *'We're all talking at the same time.'—'Yeah. Sorry.'* ❑ *Sorry I took so long.* ❑ *I'm really sorry if I said anything wrong.* **2** You use **I'm sorry** or **sorry** as an introduction when you are telling a person something that you do not think they will want to hear, for example when you are disagreeing with them or giving them bad news. ❑ *No, I'm sorry, I can't agree with you.* ❑ *'I'm sorry,' he told the estate agent, 'but we really must go now.'* **3** (*feelings*) You say '**I'm sorry**' to express your regret and sadness when you hear sad or unpleasant news. ❑ *I'm afraid he's ill.'—'I'm sorry to hear that.'* **4** (*formulae*) You say '**Sorry?**' when you have not heard something that someone has said and you want them to repeat it. ❑ *Once or twice I heard her muttering, but when I said, 'Sorry? What did you say?' she didn't respond.* **5** You use **sorry** when you correct yourself and use different words to say what you have just said, especially when what you say the second time does not use the words you would normally choose to use. ❑ *Barcelona will be hoping to bring the trophy back to Spain (sorry, Catalonia) for the first time.*

ADJ (**sorrier, sorriest**) **1** [V-LINK + sorry] If you are **sorry** about a situation, you feel regret, sadness, or disappointment about it. ❑ *She was very sorry about all the trouble she'd caused.* ❑ *I'm sorry he's gone.* **2** [V-LINK + sorry 'for' N] If you feel **sorry for** someone who is unhappy or in an unpleasant situation, you feel sympathy and sadness for them. ❑ *I felt sorry for him and his colleagues – it must have been so frustrating for them.* **3** [V-LINK + sorry] You say that someone is feeling **sorry for themselves** when you disapprove of the fact that they keep thinking unhappily about their problems, rather than trying to be cheerful and positive. ❑ *What he must not do is to sit around at home feeling sorry for himself.* **4** [sorry + N] If someone or something is in a **sorry** state, they are in a bad state, mentally or physically. ❑ *The fire left Kuwait's oil industry in a sorry state.*

PHRASE **1 I'm sorry to say** (*feelings*) You use the expression **I'm sorry to say** to express regret together with disappointment or disapproval. ❑ *I've only done half of it, I'm sorry to say.*

✦ **better safe than sorry** → see **safe**

sort ♦♦♦ /sɔːt/ NOUN, VERB

NOUN [c, SING] (**sorts**) **1** [c] If you talk about a particular **sort** of something, you are talking about a class of things that have particular features in common and that belong to a larger group of related things. = type, kind ❑ *What sort of school did you go to?* ❑ *There are so many different sorts of mushrooms available these days.* ❑ *A dozen trees of various sorts were planted.* **2** [SING] [with SUPP] You describe someone as a particular **sort** when you are describing their character. = type, kind ❑ *He seemed to be just the right sort for the job.* ❑ *She was a very vigorous sort of person.*

PHRASES **all sorts All sorts of** things or people means a large number of different things or people. ❑ *There are all sorts of animals, including bears, pigs, kangaroos, and penguins.* ❑ *It was used by all sorts of people.*

of sorts or **of a sort** If you describe something as a thing **of sorts** or as a thing **of a sort**, you are suggesting that the thing is of a rather poor quality or standard. ❑ *He made a living of sorts selling encyclopaedias door-to-door.*

sort of (*informal, vagueness*) You use **sort of** when you want to say that your description of something is not very accurate. ❑ *You could even order windows from a catalogue – a sort of mail order stained glass service.*

VERB [I, T] (**sorts, sorting, sorted**) If you **sort** things, you separate them into different classes, groups, or places, for example so that you can do different things with them. ❑ *He sorted the materials into their folders.* ❑ *He unlatched the box and sorted through the papers.*

PHRASAL VERB **sort out 1** If you **sort out** a group of things, you separate them into different classes, groups, or places, for example so that you can do different things with them. ❑ *Sort out all your bills, receipts, invoices, and expenses as quickly as possible and keep detailed accounts.* ❑ *Davina was sorting out scraps of material.* **2** If you **sort out** a problem or the details of something, you do what is necessary to solve the problem or organize the details. ❑ *India and Nepal have sorted out their trade and security dispute.* **3** If you **sort yourself out**, you organize yourself or calm yourself so that you can act effectively and reasonably. ❑ *We're in a state of complete chaos here and I need a little time to sort myself out.*

✦ **nothing of the sort** → see **nothing**

sought /sɔːt/ IRREG FORM **Sought** is the past tense and past participle of **seek**.

soul ♦◇◇ /səʊl/ NOUN [c, SING, u] (**souls**) **1** [c] Your **soul** is the part of you that consists of your mind, character, thoughts, and feelings. Many people believe that your soul continues existing after your body is dead. ❑ *She went to pray for the soul of her late husband.* **2** [c] You can refer to someone as a particular kind of **soul** when you are describing their character or condition. ❑ *He's a jolly soul.* **3** [SING] You use **soul** in negative statements like **not a soul** to mean nobody at all. ❑ *I've never harmed a soul in my life.* **4** [u] **Soul** is a type of pop music performed originally by black American musicians. It often expresses deep emotions. ❑ *American soul singer Anita Baker*

sound ♦♦♦ /saʊnd/ NOUN, VERB, ADJ, ADV

NOUN [c, u, SING] (**sounds**) **1** [c] A **sound** is something that you hear. ❑ *Peter heard the sound of gunfire.* ❑ *Liza was so frightened she couldn't make a sound.* **2** [u] **Sound** is energy that travels in waves through air, water, or other substances, and can be heard. ❑ *The aeroplane will travel at twice the speed of sound.* **3** [SING] **The sound** on a television, radio, or CD player is what you hear coming from the machine. Its loudness can be controlled. ❑ *She went and turned the sound down.* **4** [c] A singer's or band's **sound** is the distinctive quality of their music. ❑ *They have started showing a strong soul element in their sound.* **5** [SING] You can describe your impression of something you have heard about or read about by talking about **the sound of** it. ❑ *Here's a new idea*

S

we liked the sound of. ❑ *I don't like the sound of Toby Osborne.* **VERB** [I, T, LINK] (**sounds, sounding, sounded**) **1** [I, T] If something such as a horn or a bell **sounds** or if you **sound** it, it makes a noise. ❑ *The buzzer sounded in Daniel's office.* **2** [T] If you **sound** a warning, you publicly give it. If you **sound** a note of caution or optimism, you say publicly that you are cautious or optimistic. ❑ *The archbishop has sounded a warning to world leaders on third world debt.* **3** [LINK] When you are describing a noise, you can talk about the way it **sounds**. ❑ *They heard what sounded like a huge explosion.* ❑ *The creaking of the hinges sounded very loud in that silence.* **4** [LINK] When you talk about the way someone **sounds**, you are describing the impression you have of them when they speak. ❑ *She sounded a bit worried.* ❑ *Murphy sounds like a child.* **5** [LINK] When you are describing your impression or opinion of something you have heard about or read about, you can talk about the way it **sounds**. ❑ *It sounds like a wonderful idea to me, does it really work?* ❑ *It sounds as if they might have made a dreadful mistake.*

PHRASAL VERB **sound out** If you **sound** someone **out**, you question them in order to find out what their opinion is about something. ❑ *He is sounding out Middle Eastern governments on ways to resolve the conflict.*

ADJ (**sounder, soundest**) **1** If a structure, part of someone's body, or someone's mind is **sound**, it is in good condition or healthy. ❑ *When we bought the house, it was structurally sound.* ❑ *Although the car is basically sound, I was worried about certain areas.* **2** **Sound** advice, reasoning, or evidence is reliable and sensible. ❑ *They are trained nutritionists who can give sound advice on diets.* ❑ *Buy a policy only from an insurance company that is financially sound.* **3** If you describe someone's ideas as **sound**, you mean that you approve of them and think they are correct. ❑ *I am not sure that this is sound democratic practice.* **4** [sound + N] If someone is in a **sound** sleep, they are sleeping very deeply. ❑ *She had woken me out of a sound sleep.*

ADV [sound + ADJ] If someone is **sound** asleep, they are sleeping very deeply. ❑ *He was lying in bed, sound asleep.* → See also **soundly**

✦ **sound the alarm** → see **alarm**; **safe and sound** → see **safe**

sound·ly /ˈsaʊndli/ **ADV 1** [soundly + -ED] If someone is **soundly** defeated or beaten, they are defeated or beaten thoroughly. ❑ *Needing just a point from their match at St Helens, they were soundly beaten, going down by 35 points to 10.* **2** [soundly + -ED] If a decision, opinion, or statement is **soundly** based, there are sensible or reliable reasons behind it. ❑ *Changes must be soundly based in economic reality.* **3** If you sleep **soundly**, you sleep deeply and do not wake during your sleep. = deeply ❑ *How can he sleep soundly at night? He's the one responsible for all those crimes.*

soup /suːp/ **NOUN** [C, U] (**soups**) **Soup** is liquid food made by boiling meat, fish, or vegetables in water. ❑ *home-made chicken soup*

sour /saʊə/ **ADJ, VERB**
ADJ 1 Something that is **sour** has a sharp, unpleasant taste like the taste of a lemon. ❑ *The stewed apple was sour even with honey.* **2** **Sour** milk is milk that has an unpleasant taste because it is no longer fresh. ❑ *The milk had gone sour.* **3** Someone who is **sour** is bad-tempered and unfriendly. ❑ *She made a sour face in his direction.* **4** If a situation or relationship **turns sour** or **goes sour**, it stops being enjoyable or satisfactory. ❑ *Everything turned sour for me there.* ❑ *The American dream is beginning to turn sour.* **VERB** [I, T] (**sours, souring, soured**) If a friendship, situation, or attitude **sours** or if something **sours** it, it becomes less friendly, enjoyable, or hopeful. ❑ *If anything sours the relationship, it is likely to be real differences in their world-views.*

sour·ly /ˈsaʊəli/ **ADV** [sourly with V] ❑ *'Leave my mother out of it,' he said sourly.*

✪ source ♦♦◇ /sɔːs/ **NOUN, VERB** (academic word)
NOUN [C] (**sources**) **1** The **source of** something is the person, place, or thing which you get it from. ❑ *Over 40 per cent of adults use television as their major source of information about the arts.* ❑ *Renewable sources of energy must be used.* ❑ *Tourism, which is a major source of income for the*

city, may be seriously affected. **2** A **source** is a person or book that provides information for a news story or for a piece of research. ❑ *Military sources say the boat was heading south at high speed.* ❑ *Carson (2000) made extensive use of secondary data sources.* **3** The **source of** a difficulty is its cause. = root, cause, origin; ≠ result, effect ❑ *This gave me a clue as to the source of the problem.* ❑ *Reactions to ointments are a common source of skin problems.* **4** The **source of** a river or stream is the place where it begins. ❑ *the source of the Tiber*

VERB [T] (**sources, sourcing, sourced**) (business) In business, if a person or firm **sources** a product or a raw material, they find someone who will supply it. ❑ *Together they travel the world, sourcing clothes for the small, privately owned company.*

WORD CONNECTIONS

source + OF + NOUN

a source of **information**
a source of **inspiration**
❑ *This handbook is an invaluable source of information.*

a source of **income**
a source of **revenue**
a source of **funding**
❑ *The web-design business is our main source of income.*

NOUN + **source**

a **heat** source
a **food** source
an **energy** source
❑ *Thermal imagers record heat sources as white 'hot spots'.*

ADJ + **source**

a **renewable** source
an **alternative** source
a **major** source
a **main** source
❑ *Renewable energy sources such as wind, water and the sun are currently in use, but their contribution is small.*

a **primary** source
a **secondary** source
❑ *The primary source for all students of geography is the earth around us.*

VERB + **source**

identify a source
locate a source
quote a source
cite a source
❑ *One source cited by the research paper was the Institute of Fiscal Studies in the UK.*

✪ south ♦♦♦ /saʊθ/ also **South NOUN, ADV, ADJ**
NOUN [U, SING] **1** [U] [also 'the' south] The **south** is the direction which is on your right when you are looking towards the direction where the sun rises. ❑ *The town lies ten miles to the south of here.* ❑ *All around him, from east to west, north to south, the stars glittered in the heavens.* **2** [SING] [usu 'the' south, oft south 'of' N] The **south of** a place, country, or region is the part which is in the south. ❑ *holidays in the south of Mexico* ❑ *oil production in the south of Iraq* **3** [SING] ['the' south] The **South** is used to refer to the poorer, less developed countries of the world. ❑ *The debate will pit the industrial North against developing countries in the South.*

ADV 1 [south after V] If you go **south**, you travel towards the south. ❑ *I drove south on Highway 9.* **2** [south 'of' N] Something that is **south of** a place is positioned to the south of it. ❑ *They now own and operate a farm 50 miles south of Rochester.*

ADJ 1 [south + N] The **south** edge, corner, or part of a place or country is the part which is towards the south. ❑ *the south coast of Long Island* **2** '**South**' is used in the names of some countries, states, and regions in the south of a larger area. ❑ *Next week the president will visit five South American countries in six days.* **3** A **south** wind is a wind that blows from the south. ❑ *a mild south wind*

south·east ♦♦◇ /ˌsaʊθˈiːst/ (in *BrE*, also use **south-east**)
NOUN, ADV, ADJ

NOUN [U, SING] **1** [U] [also 'the' southeast] **The southeast** is the direction which is halfway between south and east. ❑ *It shook buildings as far away as Galveston, 90 miles to the southeast.* **2** [SING] **The southeast** of a place, country, or region is the part which is in the southeast. ❑ *Record levels of rainfall fell over the southeast of the country.*

ADV **1** [southeast after V] If you go **southeast**, you travel towards the southeast. ❑ *I know we have to go southeast, more or less.* **2** [southeast 'of' N] Something that is **southeast of** a place is positioned to the southeast of it. ❑ *a vessel that is believed to have sunk 500 miles southeast of Nova Scotia*

ADJ **1** [southeast + N] The **southeast** part of a place, country, or region is the part which is towards the southeast. ❑ *rural southeast Kansas* ❑ *Southeast Asia* **2** [southeast + N] A **southeast** wind is a wind that blows from the southeast. ❑ *Thick clothes kept the chill southeast wind from freezing his bones.*

south·eastern ♦♦◇ /ˌsaʊθˈiːstən/ (in *BrE*, also use **south-eastern**) ADJ **Southeastern** means in or from the southeast of a region or country. ❑ *this city on the southeastern edge of the United States*

⊙**south·ern** ♦♦◇ /ˈsʌðən/ also **Southern** ADJ [southern + N] **Southern** means in or from the south of a region, state, or country. ❑ *The Everglades National Park stretches across the southern tip of Florida.* ❑ *a place where you can sample southern cuisine*

south·ward /ˈsaʊθwəd/ ADV, ADJ

The form **southwards** is also used for the adverb.

ADV [southward after V] **Southward** or **southwards** means towards the south. ❑ *They drove southward.*
ADJ A **southward** direction or course is one that goes towards the south. ❑ *Instead of her normal southward course towards Alexandria and home, she headed west.*

south·west ♦♦◇ /ˌsaʊθˈwest/ (in *BrE*, also use **south-west**) NOUN, ADV, ADJ

NOUN [U, SING] **1** [U] [also 'the' southwest] **The southwest** is the direction which is halfway between south and west. ❑ *some 500 kilometres to the southwest of Johannesburg* **2** [SING] **The southwest** of a place, country, or region is the part which is towards the southwest. ❑ *the southwest of France*

ADV **1** [southwest after V] If you go **southwest**, you travel towards the southwest. ❑ *We took a plane southwest across the Anatolian plateau to Cappadocia.* **2** [southwest 'of' N] Something that is **southwest of** a place is positioned to the southwest of it. ❑ *It's some 65 miles southwest of Houston.*

ADJ **1** [southwest + N] The **southwest** part of a place, country, or region is the part which is towards the southwest. ❑ *a Labour Day festival in southwest Louisiana* **2** [southwest + N] A **southwest** wind is a wind that blows from the southwest. ❑ *Then the southwest wind began to blow.*

south·western /ˌsaʊθˈwestən/ (in *BrE*, also use **south-western**) ADJ **Southwestern** means in or from the southwest of a region or country. ❑ *remote areas in the southwestern part of the country*

sou·venir /ˌsuːvəˈnɪə, *AmE* ˌsuːvəˈnɪr/ NOUN [C] (**souvenirs**) A **souvenir** is something which you buy or keep to remind you of a holiday, place, or event. ❑ *a souvenir of the summer of 1992*

⊙**sov·er·eign** /ˈsɒvrɪn/ ADJ, NOUN

ADJ **1** A **sovereign** state or country is independent and not under the authority of any other country. = autonomous ❑ *Lithuania and Armenia signed a treaty in Vilnius recognizing each other as independent sovereign states.* ❑ *The Russian Federation declared itself to be a sovereign republic.* **2** **Sovereign** is used to describe the person or institution that has the highest power in a country. ❑ *Sovereign power will continue to lie with the Supreme People's Assembly.*

NOUN [C] (**sovereigns**) A **sovereign** is a king, queen, or other royal ruler of a country. = monarch ❑ *In March*

1889, she became the first British sovereign to set foot on Spanish soil.

sov·er·eign·ty /ˈsɒvrɪnti/ NOUN [U] **Sovereignty** is the power that a country has to govern itself or another country or state. = autonomy ❑ *Concern to protect national sovereignty is far from new.*

sow VERB, NOUN

VERB /səʊ/ [T] (**sows**, **sowing**, **sowed**, **sown**) **1** If you **sow** seeds or **sow** an area of land **with** seeds, you plant the seeds in the ground. ❑ *Sow the seed in a warm place in February/March.* **2** If someone **sows** an undesirable feeling or situation, they cause it to begin and develop. ❑ *He cleverly sowed doubts into the minds of his rivals.*

PHRASE **sow the seeds of something** or **sow the seeds for something** If one thing **sows the seeds of** another, it starts the process which leads eventually to the other thing. ❑ *Rich industrialized countries have sown the seeds of global warming.*

NOUN /saʊ/ [C] (**sows**) A **sow** is an adult female pig.

⊙**space** ♦♦◇ /speɪs/ NOUN, VERB

NOUN [C, U, SING] (**spaces**) **1** [C, U] You use **space** to refer to an area that is empty or available. The area can be any size. For example, you can refer to a large area outside as a large open **space** or to a small area between two objects as a small **space**. ❑ *cutting down yet more trees to make space for houses* ❑ *I had plenty of space to write and sew.* **2** The **space** underneath could be used as a storage area. **2** [C, U] A particular kind of **space** is the area that is available for a particular activity or for putting a particular kind of thing in. ❑ *the high cost of office space* ❑ *You don't want your living space to look like a bedroom.* **3** [U] If a place gives a feeling of **space**, it gives an impression of being large and open. ❑ *Large paintings can enhance the feeling of space in small rooms.* **4** [U] If you give someone **space** to think about something or to develop as a person, you allow them the time and freedom to do this. = room ❑ *You need space to think everything over.* **5** [U] The amount of **space** for a topic to be discussed in a document is the number of pages available to discuss the topic. ❑ *We can't promise to publish a reply as space is limited.* **6** [SING] A **space of** time is a period of time. ❑ *They've come a long way in a short space of time.* **7** [U] **Space** is the area beyond the Earth's atmosphere, where the stars and planets are. ❑ *The six astronauts on board will spend ten days in space.* ❑ *launching satellites into space* ❑ *pictures of the Earth from outer space* **8** [U] **Space** is the whole area within which everything exists. ❑ *She felt herself transcending time and space.*

PHRASE **(staring) into space** If you are staring **into space**, you are looking straight in front of you, without actually looking at anything in particular, for example because you are thinking or because you are feeling shocked. ❑ *He just sat in the dressing room staring into space.*

VERB [T] (**spaces**, **spacing**, **spaced**) If you **space** a series of things, you arrange them so that they are not all together but have gaps or intervals of time between them. ❑ *Women once again are having fewer children and spacing them further apart.*

PHRASAL VERB **space out** Space out means the same as **space** VERB. ❑ *He talks quite slowly and spaces his words out.*
spac·ing /ˈspeɪsɪŋ/ NOUN [U] ❑ *Generous spacing gives healthier trees and better crops.*
→ See also **airspace**, **breathing space**

space·craft /ˈspeɪskrɑːft, -kræft/ NOUN [C] (**spacecraft**) A **spacecraft** is a rocket or other vehicle that can travel in space. ❑ *the world's largest and most expensive unmanned spacecraft*

spa·cious /ˈspeɪʃəs/ ADJ A **spacious** room or other place is large in size or area, so that you can move around freely in it. = roomy ❑ *The house has a spacious kitchen and dining area.*

⊙**span** /spæn/ NOUN, VERB

NOUN [C] (**spans**) **1** A **span** is the period of time between two dates or events during which something exists, functions, or happens. ❑ *The batteries had a life span of six hours.* ❑ *Gradually the time span between sessions will increase.* **2** Your concentration **span** or your attention **span** is the length of time you are able to concentrate on something

S

or be interested in it. ❑ *His ability to absorb information was astonishing, but his concentration span was short.* ❑ *Young children have a limited attention span and can't concentrate on one activity for very long.* **3** [usu with SUPP] The **span** of something that extends or is spread out sideways is the total width of it from one end to the other. ❑ *It is a very pretty butterfly, with a 2 inch wing span.*

VERB [T] (**spans, spanning, spanned**) **1** If something **spans** a long period of time, it lasts throughout that period of time or relates to that whole period of time. ❑ *His professional career spanned 16 years.* **2** If something **spans** a range of things, all those things are included in it. ❑ *Bernstein's compositions spanned all aspects of music, from symphonies to musicals.* **3** A bridge or other structure that **spans** something such as a river or a valley stretches right across it. ❑ *Travellers get from one side to the other by walking across a footbridge that spans a little stream.*

spare ◆◇◇ /speə/ ADJ, NOUN, VERB
ADJ **1** You use **spare** to describe something that is the same as things that you are already using, but that you do not need yet and are keeping ready in case another one is needed. ❑ *If possible keep a spare pair of glasses accessible in case your main pair is broken or lost.* ❑ *He could have taken a spare key.* **2** You use **spare** to describe something that is not being used by anyone, and is therefore available for someone to use. ❑ *They don't have a lot of spare cash.* ❑ *The spare bedroom is on the second floor.*
NOUN [C] (**spares**) A **spare** is something that is the same as things that you are already using, but that you do not need yet and are keeping ready in case another one is needed. ❑ *Give me the boot key and I'll get the spare.*
VERB [I, T] (**spares, sparing, spared**) **1** [I] If you have something such as time, money, or space **to spare**, you have some extra time, money, or space that you have not used or which you do not need. ❑ *You got here with ninety seconds to spare.* **2** [T] If you **spare** time or another resource **for** a particular purpose, you make it available for that purpose. ❑ *She said that she could only spare 35 minutes for our meeting.* **3** [T] (*literary*) If a person or a place **is spared**, they are not harmed, even though other people or places have been. ❑ *We have lost everything, but thank God, our lives have been spared.* **4** [T] If you **spare** someone an unpleasant experience, you prevent them from suffering it. ❑ *I wanted to spare Frances the embarrassment of discussing this subject.* ❑ *Prisoners are spared the indignity of wearing uniforms.*
PHRASE **spare a thought for** If you **spare a thought for** an unfortunate person, you make an effort to think sympathetically about them and their bad luck. ❑ *Spare a thought for the nation's shopkeepers – consumer sales slid again in May.*
→ See also **sparing**

spar·ing /ˈspeərɪŋ/ ADJ Someone who is **sparing with** something uses it or gives it only in very small quantities. ❑ *I'm never sparing with the garlic.*
spar·ing·ly /ˈspeərɪŋli/ ADV [sparingly after V] ❑ *Medication is used sparingly.*

spark ◆◇◇ /spɑːk/ NOUN, VERB
NOUN [C] (**sparks**) **1** A **spark** is a tiny bright piece of burning material that flies up from something that is burning. ❑ *The fire gradually got bigger and bigger. Sparks flew off in all directions.* **2** A **spark** is a flash of light caused by electricity. It often makes a loud sound. ❑ *He passed an electric spark through a mixture of gases.* **3** A **spark** of a quality or feeling, especially a desirable one, is a small but noticeable amount of it. ❑ *His music lacked that vital spark of imagination.*
PHRASE **sparks fly** If **sparks fly** between people, they discuss something in an excited or angry way. ❑ *They are not afraid to tackle the issues or let the sparks fly when necessary.*
VERB [I, T] (**sparks, sparking, sparked**) **1** [I] If something **sparks**, sparks of fire or light come from it. ❑ *The wires were sparking above me.* **2** [T] If a burning object or electricity **sparks** a fire, it causes a fire. = start ❑ *A dropped cigarette may have sparked the fire.* **3** [T] If one thing **sparks** another, the first thing causes the second

thing to start happening. = cause ❑ *My teacher organized a unit on space exploration that really sparked my interest.*
PHRASAL VERB **spark off** Spark off means the same as **spark** VERB **3**. ❑ *That incident sparked it off.*

spar·kle /ˈspɑːkəl/ VERB, NOUN
VERB [I] (**sparkles, sparkling, sparkled**) **1** If something **sparkles**, it is clear and bright and shines with a lot of very small points of light. = glitter ❑ *The jewels on her fingers sparkled.* ❑ *His bright eyes sparkled.* **2** Someone who **sparkles** is lively, intelligent, and witty. ❑ *She sparkles, and has as much zest as a person half her age.*
NOUN [U, C] (**sparkles**) **1** [U] If something has **sparkle**, it is clear and bright and shines with a lot of very small points of light. ❑ *the sparkle of coloured glass* **2** [C] **Sparkles** are small points of light caused by light reflecting off a clear bright surface. ❑ *sparkles of light* **3** [U] **Sparkle** is the quality of being lively, intelligent, and witty. ❑ *There was little sparkle in their performance.*
spar·kling /ˈspɑːklɪŋ/ ADJ ❑ *He is sparkling and versatile in front of the camera.*

sparse /spɑːs/ ADJ (**sparser, sparsest**) Something that is **sparse** is small in number or amount and spread out over an area. ❑ *Many slopes are rock fields with sparse vegetation.* ❑ *He was a tubby little man in his fifties, with sparse hair.*
sparse·ly /ˈspɑːsli/ ADV ❑ *the sparsely populated interior region, where there are few roads*

spat /spæt/ IRREG FORM **Spat** is a past tense and past participle of **spit**.

speak ◆◆◆ /spiːk/ VERB
VERB [I, T, RECIP] (**speaks, speaking, spoke, spoken**)
1 [I] When you **speak**, you use your voice in order to say something. ❑ *He tried to speak, but for once, his voice had left him.* ❑ *I rang the hotel and spoke to Louie.* ❑ *She cried when she spoke of Oliver.* **2** [I] When someone **speaks to** a group of people, they make a speech. ❑ *When speaking to the seminar Mr Franklin spoke of his experience, gained on a recent visit to Trinidad.* ❑ *He's determined to speak at the Democratic Convention.* **3** [I] If you **speak for** a group of people, you make their views and demands known, or represent them. ❑ *He said it was the job of the Church to speak for the underprivileged.* ❑ *I speak for all 7,000 members of our organization.* **4** [T] If you **speak** a foreign language, you know the language and are able to have a conversation in it. ❑ *He doesn't speak English.* **5** [I] People sometimes mention something that has been written by saying what the author **speaks of**. ❑ *Throughout the book Liu speaks of the abuse of Party power.* **6** [RECIP] If two people **are not speaking**, they no longer speak to each other because they have argued. ❑ *He is not speaking to his mother because of her friendship with his ex-wife.* **7** [I] If you say that something **speaks for itself**, you mean that its meaning or quality is so obvious that it does not need explaining or pointing out. ❑ *the figures speak for themselves – bleak prospects at home and a worsening outlook for exports*
PHRASES **be spoken for** If a person or thing **is spoken for** or **has been spoken for**, someone has claimed them or asked for them, so no one else can have them. ❑ *She'd probably drop some comment about her 'fiancé' into the conversation so that he'd think she was already spoken for.*
speak well of someone or **speak highly of someone** or **speak ill of someone** If you **speak well of** someone or **speak highly of**, someone, you say good things about them. If you **speak ill of** someone, you criticize them. ❑ *Both spoke highly of the Russian president.*
so to speak You use **so to speak** to draw attention to the fact that you are describing or referring to something in a way that may be amusing or unusual rather than completely accurate. ❑ *I ought not to tell you but I will, since you're in the family, so to speak.*
speaking as something You can say 'speaking as a parent' or 'speaking as a teacher', for example, to indicate that the opinion you are giving is based on your experience as a parent or as a teacher. ❑ *Well, speaking as a journalist, I'm dismayed by the amount of pressure there is for pictures of combat.*
generally speaking or **technically speaking** You use **speaking** in expressions such as **generally speaking** and

S

technically speaking to indicate which things or which particular aspect of something you are talking about. ❑ *Generally speaking there was no resistance to the idea.*
PHRASAL VERBS **speak out** If you **speak out** against something or in favour of something, you say publicly that you think it is bad or good. ❑ *As tempers rose, he spoke out strongly against some of the radical ideas for selling off state-owned property.*
speak up ◨ If you **speak up**, you say something, especially to defend a person or protest about something, rather than just saying nothing. ❑ *Uncle Herbert never argued, never spoke up for himself.* ◧ If you ask someone to **speak up**, you are asking them to speak more loudly. ❑ *I'm quite deaf – you'll have to speak up.*
✦ **speak your mind** → see **mind**; **speak volumes** → see **volume**

speak·er ◆◇◇ /ˈspiːkə/ NOUN [C] (**speakers**) ◨ A **speaker** at a meeting, conference, or other gathering is a person who is making a speech or giving a talk. ❑ *Among the speakers at the gathering was Treasury Secretary Nicholas Brady.* ❑ *Bruce Wyatt will be the guest speaker at next month's meeting.* ◧ A **speaker of** a particular language is a person who speaks it, especially one who speaks it as their first language. ❑ *in the Ukraine, where a fifth of the population are Russian speakers* ◨ In the legislature or parliament of many countries, the **Speaker** is the person who is in charge of meetings. ❑ *the Speaker of the House* ◪ A **speaker** is a person who is speaking. ❑ *From a simple gesture or the speaker's tone of voice, the Japanese listener gleans the whole meaning.* ◫ A **speaker** is a piece of electrical equipment, for example part of a radio or set of equipment for playing CDs or tapes, through which sound comes out. ❑ *For a good stereo effect, the speakers should not be too wide apart.*

speak·ing ◆◆◇ /ˈspiːkɪŋ/ NOUN [U] **Speaking** is the activity of giving speeches and talks. ❑ *It would also train women union members in public speaking and decision-making.*

spear /spɪə/ NOUN, VERB
NOUN [C] (**spears**) A **spear** is a weapon consisting of a long pole with a sharp metal point attached to the end.
VERB [T] (**spears**, **spearing**, **speared**) If you **spear** something, you push or throw a pointed object into it. ❑ *Spear a piece of fish with a carving fork and dip it in the batter.*

spear·head /ˈspɪəhed/ VERB [T] (**spearheads**, **spearheading**, **spearheaded**) (*journalism*) If someone **spearheads** a campaign or an attack, they lead it. ❑ *She is spearheading a nationwide campaign against domestic violence.*

spe·cial ◆◆◆ /ˈspeʃəl/ ADJ, NOUN
ADJ ◨ Someone or something that is **special** is better or more important than other people or things. ❑ *You're very special to me, darling.* ❑ *My special guest will be Jerry Seinfeld.* ◧ [special + N] **Special** means different from normal. ❑ *In special cases, a husband can deduct the travel expenses of his wife who accompanies him on a business trip.* ❑ *So you didn't notice anything special about him?* ◨ [special + N] You use **special** to describe someone who is officially appointed or who has a particular position specially created for them. ❑ *Due to his wife's illness, he returned to the State Department as special adviser to the president.* ◪ [special + N] You use **special** to describe something that relates to one particular person, group, or place. = unique ❑ *Every anxious person will have his or her own special problems or fears.*
NOUN [C] (**specials**) A **special** is a product, programme, or meal which is not normally available, or which is made for a particular purpose. ❑ *complaints about the Halloween special, 'Ghostwatch'* ❑ *Grocers have to offer enough specials to bring people into the store.*

spe·cial·ist ◆◇◇ /ˈspeʃəlɪst/ NOUN [C] (**specialists**) A **specialist** is a person who has a particular skill or knows a lot about a particular subject. = expert ❑ *Peckham, himself a cancer specialist, is well aware of the wide variations in medical practice.*

spe·ci·al·ity /ˌspeʃiˈælɪti/ (in AmE, use **specialty**) NOUN [C] (**specialities**) ◨ Someone's **speciality** is a particular type of work that they do most or do best, or a subject that they know a lot about. ❑ *His speciality is international law.*

◧ A **speciality** of a particular place is a special food or product that is always very good there. ❑ *seafood, paella, and other specialities*

spe·cial·ize ◆◇◇ /ˈspeʃəlaɪz/ also **specialise** VERB [I] (**specializes**, **specializing**, **specialized**) If you **specialize in** a thing, you know a lot about it and concentrate a great deal of your time and energy on it, especially in your work or when you are studying or training. You also use **specialize** to talk about a restaurant which concentrates on a particular type of food. ❑ *a University professor who specializes in the history of the Russian empire*
spe·ciali·za·tion /ˌspeʃəlaɪˈzeɪʃən/ NOUN [C, U] (**specializations**) ❑ *This degree offers a major specialization in social policy alongside a course in sociology.*

spe·cial·ized /ˈspeʃəlaɪzd/ also **specialised** ADJ Someone or something that is **specialized** is trained or developed for a particular purpose or area of knowledge. ❑ *Cocaine addicts get specialized support from knowledgeable staff.*

spe·cial·ly /ˈspeʃəli/ ADV ◨ If something has been done **specially for** a particular person or purpose, it has been done only for that person or purpose. ❑ *a soap specially designed for those with sensitive skin* ❑ *Patrick needs to use specially adapted computer equipment.* ◧ (*informal*) **Specially** is used to mean more than usually or more than other things. = particularly ❑ *Stay in bed extra late or get up specially early.*

✪ **spe·cies** ◆◇◇ /ˈspiːʃiːz/ NOUN [C] (**species**) A **species** is a class of plants or animals whose members have the same main characteristics and are able to breed with each other. = breed ❑ *Pandas are an endangered species.* ❑ *There are several thousand species of trees here.*

✪ **spe·cif·ic** ◆◆◇ /spɪˈsɪfɪk/ ADJ, COMB (*academic word*)
ADJ ◨ [specific + N] You use **specific** to refer to a particular exact area, problem, or subject. = particular; ≠ general ❑ *Massage may help to increase blood flow to specific areas of the body.* ❑ *the specific needs of the individual* ❑ *There are several specific problems to be dealt with.* ◧ If someone is **specific**, they give a description that is precise and exact. You can also use **specific** to describe their description. = precise ❑ *She declined to be more specific about the reasons for the separation.* ◨ Something that is **specific to** a particular thing is connected with that thing only. = peculiar ❑ *Send your CV with a covering letter that is specific to that particular job.*
COMB **Specific** is also used after nouns to describe something that is connected with that particular thing only. ❑ *Most studies of trade have been country-specific.*

✪ **spe·cifi·cal·ly** ◆◇◇ /spɪˈsɪfɪkli/ ADV ◨ [specifically with V] (*emphasis*) You use **specifically** to emphasize that something is given special attention and considered separately from other things of the same kind. = particularly; ≠ generally ❑ *the first nursing home designed specifically for people with AIDS* ❑ *We haven't specifically targeted school children.* ◧ [specifically with GROUP] You use **specifically** to add something more precise or exact to what you have already said. ❑ *Death frightens me, specifically my own death.* ❑ *the Christian, and specifically Protestant, religion* ❑ *brain cells, or more specifically, neurons* ◨ [specifically + ADJ] You use **specifically** to indicate that something has a restricted nature, as opposed to being more general in nature. ❑ *a specifically female audience* ◪ [specifically with V] If you state or describe something **specifically**, you state or describe it precisely and clearly. ❑ *I specifically asked for this steak rare.*

✪ **speci·fi·ca·tion** /ˌspesɪfɪˈkeɪʃən/ NOUN [C] (**specifications**) A **specification** is a requirement which is clearly stated, for example about the necessary features in the design of something. = requirement ❑ *I'd like to buy some land and have a house built to my specification.* ❑ *Legislation will require UK petrol companies to meet an EU specification for petrol.* ❑ *officials constrained by rigid job specifications*

✪ **speci·fy** /ˈspesɪfaɪ/ VERB [T] (**specifies**, **specifying**, **specified**) (*academic word*) ◨ If you **specify** something, you give information about what is required or should happen in a certain situation. ❑ *They specified a spacious entrance*

S

hall. ❑ *He has not specified what action he would like them to take.* **2** If you **specify** what should happen or be done, you explain it in an exact and detailed way. ❑ *Each recipe specifies the size of egg to be used.* ❑ *A new law specified that houses must be a certain distance back from the water.* ❑ *One rule specifies that learner drivers must be supervised by adults.* ❑ *Patients eat together at a specified time.*

✪**speci•men** /ˈspesɪmɪn/ NOUN [C] (**specimens**)
1 [usu with SUPP] A **specimen** is a single plant or animal which is an example of a particular species or type and is examined by scientists. = sample, example ❑ *200,000 specimens of fungus are kept at the Komarov Botanical Institute.* ❑ *North American fossil specimens* **2** [usu with SUPP] A **specimen** of something is an example of it which gives an idea of what the whole of it is like. ❑ *Job applicants have to submit a specimen of handwriting.* **3** A **specimen** is a small quantity of someone's urine, blood, or other body fluid which is examined in a medical laboratory, in order to find out if they are ill or if they have been drinking alcohol or taking drugs. = sample ❑ *He refused to provide a specimen.*

spec•ta•cle /ˈspektəkəl/ NOUN [C, U, PL] (**spectacles**)
1 [C] A **spectacle** is a strange or interesting sight.
= sight ❑ *It was a spectacle not to be missed.* **2** [C, U] A **spectacle** is a grand and impressive event or performance. = extravaganza ❑ *Ninety-four thousand people turned up for the spectacle.* **3** [PL] [also 'a pair of' spectacles] (*old-fashioned*) Glasses are sometimes referred to as **spectacles**. ❑ *He looked at me over the tops of his spectacles.*

spec•tacu•lar ◆◇◇ /spekˈtækjʊlə/ ADJ, NOUN
ADJ Something that is **spectacular** is very impressive or dramatic. ❑ *spectacular views of the Sugar Loaf Mountain* NOUN [C] (**spectaculars**) [usu N + spectacular] A **spectacular** is a show or performance which is very grand and impressive. = extravaganza ❑ *a television spectacular*
spec•tacu•lar•ly /spekˈtækjʊləli/ ADV ❑ *My turnover increased spectacularly.*

spec•ta•tor /spekˈteɪtə, AmE ˈspekteɪtər/ NOUN [C]
(**spectators**) A **spectator** is someone who watches something, especially a sports event. ❑ *Thirty thousand spectators watched the final game.*

✪**spec•trum** /ˈspektrəm/ NOUN [SING, C] (**spectra** or **spectrums**) **1** [SING] The **spectrum** is the range of different colours which is produced when light passes through a glass prism or through a drop of water. A rainbow shows the colours in the spectrum. ❑ *lights known as ultraviolet because on the colour spectrum they lie above violet* ❑ *Yellow is the most luminous of the colour spectrum.* **2** [C] A **spectrum** is a range of a particular type of thing. = range ❑ *She'd seen his moods range across the emotional spectrum.* ❑ *Politicians across the political spectrum have denounced the act.* ❑ *The term 'special needs' covers a wide spectrum of problems.* **3** [C] A **spectrum** is a range of light waves or radio waves within particular frequencies. ❑ *Vast amounts of energy, from X-rays right through the spectrum down to radio waves, are escaping into space.* ❑ *The individual colours within the light spectrum are believed to have an effect on health.* ❑ *the ultraviolet spectra of hot stars*

✪**specu•late** ◆◇◇ /ˈspekjʊleɪt/ VERB [I, T] (**speculates**, **speculating**, **speculated**) **1** [I, T] If you **speculate** about something, you make guesses about its nature or identity, or about what might happen. ❑ *Critics of the project speculate about how many hospitals could be built instead.* ❑ *The doctors speculate that he died of a cerebral haemorrhage caused by a blow on the head.* ❑ *The researchers speculate that this weather spreads the disease.* **2** [I] If someone **speculates** financially, they buy property, stocks, or shares, in the hope of being able to sell them again at a higher price and make a profit. ❑ *The banks made too many risky loans which now can't be repaid, and they speculated in property whose value has now dropped.*

✪**specu•la•tion** /ˌspekjʊˈleɪʃən/ NOUN [C, U]
(**speculations**) If there is **speculation**, people guess about the nature or identity of something, or about what might happen. ❑ *The president has gone out of his way to dismiss*

speculation over the future of the economy. ❑ *I had published my speculations about the future of the universe in the Review of Modern Physics.*

specu•la•tive /ˈspekjʊlətɪv, AmE -leɪt-/ ADJ **1** A piece of information that is **speculative** is based on guesses rather than knowledge. ❑ *The papers ran speculative stories about the mysterious disappearance of Eddie Donagan.*
2 **Speculative** is used to describe activities which involve buying goods or shares, or buildings and properties, in the hope of being able to sell them again at a higher price and make a profit. ❑ *Thousands of retirees were persuaded to mortgage their homes to invest in speculative bonds.*

specu•la•tor /ˈspekjʊleɪtə/ NOUN [C] (**speculators**)
A **speculator** is a person who speculates financially. ❑ *He sold the contracts to another speculator for a profit.*

sped /sped/ IRREG FORM **Sped** is a past tense and past participle of **speed**.

speech ◆◆◇ /spiːtʃ/ NOUN [U, SING, C] (**speeches**) **1** [U] **Speech** is the ability to speak or the act of speaking. ❑ *the development of speech in children* ❑ *Intoxication interferes with speech and coordination.* **2** [SING] Your **speech** is the way in which you speak. ❑ *His speech became increasingly thick and nasal.* **3** [U] **Speech** is spoken language. ❑ *He could imitate in speech or writing most of those he admired.* **4** [C] A **speech** is a formal talk which someone gives to an audience. ❑ *She is due to make a speech on the economy next week.* ❑ *He delivered his speech in French.*

speech•less /ˈspiːtʃləs/ ADJ If you are **speechless**, you are temporarily unable to speak, usually because something has shocked you. ❑ *Alex was almost speechless with rage and despair.*

✪**speed** ◆◆◇ /spiːd/ NOUN, VERB

> The form of the past tense and past participle is **sped** for the main verb but **speeded** for the phrasal verb.

NOUN [C, U] (**speeds**) **1** [C, U] The **speed** of something is the rate at which it moves or travels. ❑ *He drove off at high speed.* ❑ *Wind speeds reached force five.* ❑ *An electrical pulse in a wire travels close to the speed of light.* **2** [C] The **speed** of something is the rate at which it happens or is done. = rate, pace ❑ *In the late 1850s the speed of technological change quickened.* ❑ *Each learner can proceed at his own speed.* **3** [U] **Speed** is very fast movement or travel. ❑ *Speed is the essential ingredient of all athletics.* ❑ *He put on a burst of speed.* **4** [U] **Speed** is a very fast rate at which something happens or is done. ❑ *I was amazed at his speed of working.*
VERB [I] (**speeds**, **speeding**, **sped** or **speeded**) **1** If you **speed** somewhere, you move or travel there quickly, usually in a vehicle. = race ❑ *Trains will speed through the tunnel at 186 mph.* **2** Someone who **is speeding** is driving a vehicle faster than the legal speed limit. ❑ *This man was not qualified to drive and was speeding.*
PHRASAL VERB **speed up** **1** When something **speeds up** or when you **speed** it **up**, it moves or travels faster. ❑ *You notice that your breathing has speeded up a bit.* **2** When a process or activity **speeds up** or when something **speeds** it **up**, it happens at a faster rate. ❑ *Job losses are speeding up.* ❑ *I had already taken steps to speed up a solution to the problem.*

speed•ing /ˈspiːdɪŋ/ NOUN [U] ❑ *He was fined for speeding last year.*
✦ **pick up speed** → see **pick**

WORD CONNECTIONS
speed + OF + NOUN
the speed of **light**
the speed of **sound**
❑ *An electrical pulse in a wire travels close to the speed of light.*
ADJ + **speed**
top speed
high speed
❑ *Road accidents are common here because of bad roads and high speeds.*

S

NOUN + **speed**

wind speed
□ Trees fell onto roads as wind speeds reached 110 miles an hour.

VERB + **speed**

gather speed
□ The country's economic recovery is likely to gather speed going into the new year.

---

speedy /'spiːdi/ ADJ (speedier, speediest) A speedy process, event, or action happens or is done very quickly. = quick □ We wish Bill a speedy recovery.

spell ◆◇◇ /spel/ VERB, NOUN
VERB [T, I] (spells, spelling, spelled or spelt) **1** [T] When you spell a word, you write or speak each letter in the word in the correct order. □ He gave his name and then helpfully spelled it. □ How do you spell 'potato'? **2** [I, T] Someone who can spell knows the correct order of letters in words. □ It's shocking how students can't spell these days. □ He can't even spell his own name. **3** [T] If something spells a particular outcome, often an unpleasant one, it suggests that this will be the result. □ If the irrigation plan goes ahead, it could spell disaster for the birds.
PHRASAL VERB spell out **1** Spell out means the same as spell VERB 1. □ If I don't know a word, I ask them to spell it out for me. **2** If you spell something out, you explain it in detail or in a very clear way. □ Be assertive and spell out exactly how you feel.
NOUN [C] (spells) **1** A spell of a particular type of weather or a particular activity is a short period of time during which this type of weather or activity occurs. = period □ There has been a long spell of dry weather. **2** A spell is a situation in which events are controlled by a magical power. □ They say she died after a witch cast a spell on her.
→ See also spelling

spell·ing /'spelɪŋ/ NOUN [C, U] (spellings) **1** [C] A spelling is the correct order of the letters in a word. □ In most languages adjectives have slightly different spellings for masculine and feminine. **2** [U] Spelling is the ability to spell words in the correct way. It is also an attempt to spell a word in the correct way. □ His spelling is very bad.
→ See also spell

spelt /spelt/ (mainly BrE) IRREG FORM Spelt is a past tense and past participle form of spell.

spend ◆◆◆ /spend/ VERB [T] (spends, spending, spent) **1** When you spend money, you pay money for things that you want or need. □ By the end of the holiday I had spent all my money. □ Businessmen spend enormous amounts advertising their products. **2** If you spend time or energy doing something, you use your time or effort doing it. □ Engineers spend much time and energy developing brilliant solutions. **3** If you spend a period of time in a place, you stay there for a period of time. □ We spent the night in a hotel.

USAGE NOTE

spend

Note that you say that someone **spends** money **on** something.
He was happy to **spend** money **on** good clothes.

---

spent /spent/ IRREG FORM Spent is the past tense and past participle form of spend.

❖**sphere** /sfɪə/ NOUN [C] (spheres) (academic word) **1** A sphere is an object that is completely round in shape like a ball. = globe □ Because the earth spins, it is not a perfect sphere. □ the volume of a hollow sphere **2** A sphere of activity or interest is a particular area of activity or interest. = field □ the sphere of international politics □ nurses, working in all spheres of the health service

❖**spheri·cal** /'sferɪkəl, AmE 'sfɪr-/ ADJ (formal) Something that is spherical is round like a ball. = globular, round □ purple and gold spherical earrings □ a spherical particle □ Latitude was measured on the assumption that the earth was perfectly spherical.

spice /spaɪs/ NOUN, VERB
NOUN [C, U] (spices) A spice is a part of a plant, or a powder made from that part, which you put in food to give it flavour. Cinnamon, ginger, and paprika are spices. □ herbs and spices
VERB [T] (spices, spicing, spiced) If you spice something that you say or do, you add excitement or interest to it. □ They spiced their conversations and discussions with intrigue.
PHRASAL VERB spice up Spice up means the same as spice VERB. □ Her publisher wants her to spice up her stories with sex.

spicy /'spaɪsi/ ADJ (spicier, spiciest) Spicy food is strongly flavoured with spices. □ Thai food is hot and spicy.

spi·der /'spaɪdə/ NOUN [C] (spiders) A spider is a small creature with eight legs. Most types of spiders make structures called webs in which they catch insects for food.

spike /spaɪk/ NOUN [C] (spikes) A spike is a long piece of metal with a sharp point. □ a 15-foot wall topped with iron spikes

spill /spɪl/ VERB, NOUN
VERB [I, T] (spills, spilling, spilled or spilt) **1** [I, T] If a liquid spills or if you spill it, it accidentally flows over the edge of a container. □ Seventy thousand tons of oil spilled from the tanker. □ He always spilled the drinks. **2** [T] If the contents of a bag, box, or other container spill or are spilled, they come out of the container onto a surface. □ A number of bags had split and were spilling their contents. **3** [I] If people or things spill out of a place, they come out of it in large numbers. □ Tears began to spill out of the boy's eyes.
NOUN [C] (spills) A spill is an amount of liquid that has spilled from a container. □ She wiped a spill of milkshake off the counter.

spill·age /'spɪlɪdʒ/ NOUN [C, U] (spillages) If there is a spillage, a substance such as oil escapes from its container. Spillage is also used to refer to the substance that escapes. □ an oil spillage off the coast of Texas

spin ◆◇◇ /spɪn/ VERB, NOUN
VERB [I, T] (spins, spinning, spun) **1** [I, T] If something spins or if you spin it, it turns quickly around a central point. □ The latest disks, used for small portable computers, spin 3,600 times a minute. □ He spun the wheel sharply and made a U-turn in the middle of the road. **2** [I] If your head is spinning, you feel unsteady or confused, for example because you are drunk, ill, or excited. □ My head was spinning from the wine. **3** [I, T] When people spin, they make thread by twisting together pieces of a fibre such as wool or cotton using a device or machine. □ Michelle will also spin a customer's wool fleece to specification at a cost of $2.25 an ounce.
PHRASAL VERBS spin off (business) To spin off something such as a company means to create a new company that is separate from the original organization. □ He rescued the company and later spun off its textile division into a separate entity.
spin out If you spin something out, you make it last longer than it normally would. = prolong □ My wife's lawyer was anxious to spin things out for as long as possible.
NOUN [C, U, SING] (spins) **1** [C, U] A spin is a swift rotating motion around a central point. □ This driving mode allows you to move off in third gear to reduce wheel-spin in icy conditions. **2** [SING] (informal) If someone puts a certain spin on an event or situation, they interpret it and try to present it in a particular way. □ He interpreted the vote as support for the constitution and that is the spin his supporters are putting on the results today. **3** [U] In politics, spin is the way in which political parties try to present everything they do in a positive way to the public and the media. □ The public is sick of spin and tired of promises. **4** [SING] If you go for a spin or take a car for a spin, you make a short trip in a car just to enjoy yourself. □ Tom Wright celebrated his 99th birthday by going for a spin in his sporty Mazda. **5** [U] In a game such as tennis or baseball, if you put spin on a ball, you deliberately make it spin rapidly when you hit it or throw it. □ He threw it back again, putting a slight spin on the ball.

❖**spi·nal** /'spaɪnəl/ ADJ (spinal + N) Spinal means relating to your spine. □ spinal fluid □ The spinal cord is a cylindrical

S

mass of nerve cells which connect with the brain and also with other parts of the body. ❑ *The boy had been taken into a hospital in Sheffield well known for its work in spinal injuries.*

✪spine /spaɪn/ NOUN [C] (**spines**) **1** Your **spine** is the row of bones down your back. ❑ *injuries to his spine* ❑ *Her spine was severed, but within eight months, she already was back in the saddle, riding again.* ❑ *a degenerative bone disease of the upper spine and neck* **2** The **spine** of a book is the narrow stiff part which the pages and covers are attached to. ❑ *a book with 'Lifestyle' on the spine* **3** **Spines** are also long, sharp points on an animal's body or on a plant. ❑ *An adult hedgehog can boast 7,500 spines.*

✪spi·ral /'spaɪərəl/ NOUN, ADJ, VERB
NOUN [C, SING] (**spirals**) **1** [C] A **spiral** is a shape which winds around and around, with each curve above or outside the previous one. ❑ *The maze is actually two interlocking spirals.* **2** [C] A **spiral** is a movement around and around, with each curve above or outside the previous one. ❑ *Larks were rising in spirals from the ridge.* **3** [SING] A **spiral** is a quick rise in an amount or level, at an increasing rate. ❑ *an inflationary spiral* **4** [SING] A **spiral** is a quick fall in an amount or level, at an increasing rate. ❑ *a spiral of debt*
ADJ [spiral + N] **Spiral** means in a shape which winds around and around, with each curve above or outside the previous one. ❑ *a spiral staircase* ❑ *the Milky Way, a spiral galaxy with 100 billion stars*
VERB [I, T] (**spirals, spiralling, spiralled**) **1** [I, T] If something **spirals** or **is spiralled** somewhere, it grows or moves in a spiral curve. ❑ *Vines spiralled upward towards the roof.* ❑ *The aircraft began spiralling out of control.* ❑ *A joss stick spiralled smoke.* **2** [I] If an amount or level **spirals**, it rises quickly and at an increasing rate. ❑ *Production costs began to spiral.* ❑ *spiralling health care costs* **3** [I] If an amount or level **spirals** downwards, it falls quickly and at an increasing rate. ❑ *House prices will continue to spiral downwards.*

spir·it ◆◆◇ /'spɪrɪt/ NOUN [SING, C, U, PL] (**spirits**) **1** [SING] Your **spirit** is the part of you that is not physical and that consists of your character and feelings. ❑ *The human spirit is virtually indestructible.* **2** [C] A person's **spirit** is the nonphysical part of them that is believed to remain alive after their death. = soul ❑ *His spirit has left him and all that remains is the shell of his body.* **3** [C] A **spirit** is a ghost or supernatural being. = ghost ❑ *In the Middle Ages branches were hung outside country houses as a protection against evil spirits.* **4** [U] **Spirit** is the courage and determination that helps people to survive in difficult times and to keep their way of life and their beliefs. ❑ *She was a very brave girl and everyone who knew her admired her spirit.* **5** [U] **Spirit** is the liveliness and energy that someone shows in what they do. ❑ *They played with spirit.* **6** [SING] The **spirit** in which you do something is the attitude you have when you are doing it. ❑ *Their problem can only be solved in a spirit of compromise.* **7** [U] A particular kind of **spirit** is the feeling of loyalty to a group that is shared by the people who belong to the group. ❑ *There is a great sense of team spirit in the squad.* **8** [SING] A particular kind of **spirit** is the set of ideas, beliefs, and aims that are held by a group of people. ❑ *the real spirit of the anti-war movement* **9** [SING] The **spirit** of something such as a law or an agreement is the way that it was intended to be interpreted or applied. ❑ *The requirement for work permits violates the spirit of the 1950 treaty.* **10** [C] You can refer to a person as a particular kind of **spirit** if they show a certain characteristic or if they show a lot of enthusiasm for what they are doing. ❑ *I like to think of myself as a free spirit.* **11** [PL] Your **spirits** are your feelings at a particular time, especially feelings of happiness or unhappiness. ❑ *At supper, everyone was in high spirits.* **12** [PL] **Spirits** are strong alcoholic drinks such as whisky and gin. ❑ *The only problem here is that they don't serve beer – only wine and spirits.*

spir·i·tu·al ◆◇◇ /'spɪrɪtʃuəl/ ADJ **1** **Spiritual** means relating to people's thoughts and beliefs, rather than to their bodies and physical surroundings. ❑ *She lived entirely by spiritual values, in a world of poetry and imagination.* **2** **Spiritual** means relating to people's religious beliefs.

= religious ❑ *He is the spiritual leader of the world's Catholics.*
spir·i·tu·al·ly /'spɪrɪtʃəli/ ADV ❑ *Our whole programme is spiritually oriented but not religious.*
spir·i·tu·al·i·ty /ˌspɪrɪtʃu'æliti/ NOUN [U] ❑ *the peaceful spirituality of Japanese culture*

spit /spɪt/ NOUN, VERB
NOUN [U, C] (**spits**) **1** [U] **Spit** is the watery liquid produced in your mouth. You usually use **spit** to refer to an amount of it that has been forced out of someone's mouth. = saliva ❑ *A trickle of spit collected at the corner of her mouth.* **2** [C] A **spit** is a long rod which is pushed through a piece of meat and hung over an open fire to cook the meat. ❑ *She roasted the meat on a spit.*
VERB [I, T] (**spits, spitting, spit** or **spat**) **1** [I] If someone **spits**, they force an amount of liquid out of their mouth, often to show hatred or contempt. ❑ *The gang thought of hitting him too, but decided just to spit.* ❑ *They spat at me and taunted me.* **2** [T] If you **spit** liquid or food somewhere, you force a small amount of it out of your mouth. ❑ *Spit out that gum and pay attention.*
PHRASE **spitting image** (*informal*) If you say that one person is the **spitting image** of another, you mean that they look very similar. ❑ *Nina looks the spitting image of Sissy Spacek.*

spite ◆◇◇ /spaɪt/ NOUN, VERB
NOUN [U] If you do something cruel out of **spite**, you do it because you want to hurt or upset someone. ❑ *I refused her a divorce, out of spite I suppose.*
PHRASE **in spite of** **1** You use **in spite of** to introduce a fact which makes the rest of the statement you are making seem surprising. = despite ❑ *Josef Krips at the State Opera hired her in spite of the fact that she had never sung on stage.* **2** If you do something **in spite of yourself**, you do it although you did not really intend to or expect to. ❑ *The blunt comment made Richard laugh in spite of himself.*
VERB [T] If you do something cruel **to spite** someone, you do it in order to hurt or upset them. ❑ *Pantelaras was giving his art collection away for nothing, to spite Marie and her husband.*

WHICH WORD?

in spite of or despite?

In spite of and **despite** are both used to introduce an idea that makes what follows seems surprising. You do not use 'of' after **despite**.

❑ *In spite of poor health, my father was always cheerful.*

❑ *Despite the differences in their ages, they were close friends.*

splash /splæʃ/ VERB, NOUN
VERB [I, T] (**splashes, splashing, splashed**) **1** [I] If you **splash** around or **splash** about in water, you hit or disturb the water in a noisy way, causing some of it to fly up into the air. ❑ *A lot of people were in the water, swimming or simply splashing about.* ❑ *She could hear the voices of her friends as they splashed in a nearby rock pool.* **2** [I, T] If you **splash** a liquid somewhere or if it **splashes**, it hits someone or something and scatters in a lot of small drops. ❑ *He closed his eyes tight, and splashed the water on his face.* ❑ *A little wave, the first of many, splashed in my face.* **3** [T] If a magazine or newspaper **splashes** a story, it prints it in such a way that it is very noticeable. ❑ *The newspapers splashed the story all over their front pages.*
NOUN [SING, C] (**splashes**) **1** [SING] A **splash** is the sound made when something hits water or falls into it. ❑ *There was a splash and something fell clumsily into the water.* **2** [C] A **splash** of a liquid is a small quantity of it that falls on something or is added to something. ❑ *Wallcoverings and floors should be able to withstand steam and splashes.* **3** [C] A **splash** of colour is an area of a bright colour which contrasts strongly with the colours around it. ❑ *shady walks punctuated by splashes of colour*
PHRASE **make a splash** If you **make a splash**, you become noticed or become popular because of something that you have done. ❑ *Now she's made a splash in the television show 'Civil Wars'.*

splen·did /'splendɪd/ ADJ If you say that something is

splendid, you mean that it is very good. = marvellous ❏ *The book includes a wealth of splendid photographs.*

splen·did·ly /'splendɪdli/ ADV [splendidly with V] ❏ *I have heard him tell people that we get along splendidly.*

splen·dour /'splendə/ (in AmE, use **splendor**) NOUN [U, PL] (**splendours**) **1** [U] The **splendour** of something is its beautiful and impressive appearance. ❏ *She gazed down upon the nighttime splendour of the city.* **2** [PL] The **splendours of** a place or way of life are its beautiful and impressive features. ❏ *such splendours as the Acropolis and the Parthenon*

split ◆◆◇ /splɪt/ VERB, ADJ, NOUN

VERB [I, T] (**splits**, **splitting**, **split**) **1** [I, T] If something **splits** or if you **split** it, it is divided into two or more parts. ❏ *In a severe gale the ship split in two.* ❏ *If the chicken is fairly small, you may simply split it in half.* **2** [I, T] If an organization **splits** or **is split**, one group of members disagree strongly with the other members, and may form a group of their own. ❏ *Yet it is feared the Republican leadership could split over the agreement.* **3** [I, T] If something such as wood or a piece of clothing **splits** or **is split**, a long crack or tear appears in it. ❏ *The seat of his grey trousers split.* **4** [T] If two or more people **split** something, they share it between them. ❏ *I would rather pay for a meal than watch nine friends pick over and split a bill.*

PHRASAL VERB **split up** **1** If two people **split up**, or if someone or something **splits** them **up**, they end their relationship or marriage. ❏ *Research suggests that children whose parents split up are more likely to drop out of secondary school.* ❏ *I was beginning to think that nothing could ever split us up.* **2** If a group of people **split up** or **are split up**, they go away in different directions. ❏ *Did the two of you split up in the woods?* ❏ *This situation has split up the family.* **3** If you **split** something **up**, or if it **splits up**, you divide it so that it is in a number of smaller separate sections. ❏ *Any thought of splitting up the company was unthinkable, they said.* ❏ *Even though museums have begged to borrow her collection, she could never split it up.*

ADJ If an organization is **split**, one group of members disagree strongly with the other members. ❏ *The Kremlin is deeply split in its approach to foreign policy.*

NOUN [C, SING] (**splits**) **1** [C] A **split in** an organization is a disagreement between its members. ❏ *They accused both radicals and conservatives of trying to provoke a split in the party.* **2** [SING] A **split between** two things is a division or difference between them. ❏ *a split between what is thought and what is felt* **3** [C] A **split** is a long crack or tear. ❏ *The plastic-covered seat has a few small splits around the corners.*

spoil /spɔɪl/ VERB

VERB [T, I] (**spoils**, **spoiling**, **spoiled** or **spoilt**) **1** [T] If you **spoil** something, you prevent it from being successful or satisfactory. ❏ *It's important not to let mistakes spoil your life.* **2** [T] If you **spoil** children, you give them everything they want or ask for. This is considered to have a bad effect on a child's character. ❏ *Grandparents are often tempted to spoil their grandchildren whenever they come to visit.* **3** [T] If you **spoil yourself** or **spoil** another person, you give yourself or them something nice as a treat or do something special for them. = pamper ❏ *Spoil yourself with a new perfume this summer.* **4** [I, T] If food **spoils** or if it **is spoiled**, it is no longer fit to be eaten. ❏ *We all know that fats spoil by becoming rancid.*

PHRASE **spoiled for choice** or **spoilt for choice** (mainly BrE) If you say that someone is **spoiled for choice** or **spoilt for choice**, you mean that they have a great many things of the same type to choose from.

spoilt /spɔɪlt/ IRREG FORM (BrE) **Spoilt** is a past participle and past tense of **spoil**.

spoke /spəʊk/ IRREG FORM, NOUN

IRREG FORM **Spoke** is the past tense of **speak**.

NOUN [C] [usu pl] The **spokes** of a wheel are the bars that connect the outer ring to the centre.

spo·ken /'spəʊkən/ IRREG FORM, ADJ

IRREG FORM **Spoken** is the past participle of **speak**.

ADJ The **spoken** form of a language is the one that people use when they communicate using their voices. ❏ *a marked decline in the standards of written and spoken English*

spokes·man ◆◆◇ /'spəʊksmən/ NOUN [C] (**spokesmen**) A **spokesman** is a male spokesperson. ❏ *A UN spokesman said that the mission will carry 20 tons of relief supplies.*

❋**spokes·person** /'spəʊkspɜːsən/ NOUN [C] (**spokespersons** or **spokespeople**) A **spokesperson** is a person who speaks as the representative of a group or organization. = speaker, representative ❏ *A spokesperson for Amnesty, Norma Johnston, describes some cases.* ❏ *A company spokesperson confirmed the dismissal.*

spokes·woman ◆◆◇ /'spəʊkswʊmən/ NOUN [C] (**spokeswomen**) A **spokeswoman** is a female spokesperson. ❏ *A United Nations spokeswoman in New York said the request would be considered.*

spon·sor ◆◇◇ /'spɒnsə/ VERB, NOUN

VERB [T] (**sponsors**, **sponsoring**, **sponsored**) **1** If an organization or an individual **sponsors** something such as an event or someone's training, they pay some or all of the expenses connected with it, often in order to get publicity for themselves. = finance ❏ *Dozens of companies, including Hewlett-Packard, are sponsoring the event.* **2** If you **sponsor** someone who is doing something to raise money for charity, for example trying to walk a certain distance, you agree to give them a sum of money for the charity if they succeed in doing it. ❏ *Please could you sponsor me for my school's campaign to help sick children?* **3** If you **sponsor** a proposal or suggestion, you officially put it forward and support it. ❏ *Eight senators sponsored legislation to stop the military funding.* **4** When a country or an organization such as the United Nations **sponsors** negotiations between countries, it suggests holding the negotiations and organizes them. ❏ *Given the strength of pressure on both sides, the superpowers may well have difficulties sponsoring negotiations.* **5** If one country accuses another of **sponsoring** attacks on it, they mean that the other country does not do anything to prevent the attacks, and may even encourage them. = support ❏ *We have to make the states that sponsor terrorism pay a price.* **6** If a company or organization **sponsors** a television programme, they pay to have a special advertisement shown at the beginning and end of the programme, and at each commercial break. ❏ *The company plans to sponsor television programmes as part of its marketing strategy.*

NOUN [C] (**sponsors**) A **sponsor** is a person or organization that sponsors something or someone. ❏ *Race officials announced a handful of new sponsors on Tuesday.*

spon·sor·ship /'spɒnsəʃɪp/ NOUN [U] [also sponsorships] **Sponsorship** is financial support given by a sponsor. ❏ *Campbell is one of an ever-growing number of skiers in need of sponsorship.*

spon·ta·neous /spɒn'teɪniəs/ ADJ **1** **Spontaneous** acts are not planned or arranged, but are done because someone suddenly wants to do them. ❏ *Diana's house was crowded with happy people whose spontaneous outbursts of song were accompanied by lively music.* **2** A **spontaneous** event happens because of processes within something rather than being caused by things outside it. ❏ *I had another spontaneous miscarriage at around the 16th to 18th week.*

spon·ta·neous·ly /spɒn'teɪniəsli/ ADV **1** Many people spontaneously stood up and cheered. **2** [spontaneously after V] ❏ *Usually a woman's breasts produce milk spontaneously after the birth.*

spoon /spuːn/ NOUN, VERB

NOUN [C] (**spoons**) A **spoon** is an object used for eating, stirring, and serving food. One end of it is shaped like a shallow bowl and it has a long handle. ❏ *He stirred his coffee with a spoon.*

VERB [T] (**spoons**, **spooning**, **spooned**) If you **spoon** food into something, you put it there with a spoon. ❏ *He spooned instant coffee into two of the mugs.*

sport ◆◆◇ /spɔːt/ NOUN [C, U] (**sports**) **Sports** are games such as football and basketball and other competitive leisure activities which need physical effort and skill. ❏ *I chose boxing because it is my favourite sport.* ❏ *She excels at sports.*

sport·ing /'spɔːtɪŋ/ ADJ [sporting + N] **Sporting** means

S

relating to sports or used for sports. ❑ *major sporting events, such as the US Open and the World Series*

sports·man /ˈspɔːtsmən/ NOUN [c] (**sportsmen**) A sportsman is a man who takes part in sports.

sports·person /ˈspɔːtspɜːsən/ NOUN [c] (**sportspeople**) A sportsperson is a person who takes part in sports.

spot ♦♦◇ /spɒt/ NOUN, VERB

NOUN [c] (**spots**) **1** Spots are small, round, coloured areas on a surface. ❑ *The leaves have yellow areas on the top and underneath are powdery orange spots.* **2** (in AmE, usually use **pimples**) Spots on a person's skin are small lumps or marks. **3** You can refer to a particular place as a **spot**. ❑ *They stayed at several of the island's top tourist spots.* **4** A spot in a television or radio show is a part of it that is regularly reserved for a particular performer or type of entertainment. = slot ❑ *Unsuccessful at screen writing, he got a spot on a CNN show.* **5** (mainly BrE) A **spot of** a liquid is a small amount of it. ❑ *Spots of rain had begun to fall.*

PHRASE **on the spot** If you do something **on the spot**, you do it immediately. ❑ *James was called to see the producer and got the job on the spot.*

VERB [T] (**spots, spotting, spotted**) If you spot something or someone, you notice them. ❑ *Vicenzo failed to spot the error.*

spot·light /ˈspɒtlaɪt/ NOUN, VERB

NOUN [c] (**spotlights**) A spotlight is a powerful light, for example in a theatre, which can be directed so that it lights up a small area.

PHRASE **in the spotlight** Someone or something that is in the spotlight is getting a great deal of public attention. ❑ *Webb is back in the spotlight.*

VERB [T] (**spotlights, spotlighting, spotlighted**) If something spotlights a particular problem or situation, it makes people notice it and think about it. = highlight ❑ *The budget crisis also spotlighted a weakening economy.*

✪**spouse** /spaʊs/ NOUN [c] (**spouses**) Someone's spouse is the person they are married to. = husband, wife, partner ❑ *You, or your spouse, must be at least 60 to participate.* ❑ *Husbands and wives do not have to pay any inheritance tax when their spouse dies.*

sprang /spræŋ/ IRREG FORM Sprang is the past tense of spring.

sprawl /sprɔːl/ VERB, NOUN

VERB [I] (**sprawls, sprawling, sprawled**) **1** If you sprawl somewhere, you sit or lie down with your legs and arms spread out in a careless way. ❑ *She sprawled on the bed as he had left her, not even moving to cover herself up.* **2** If you say that a place sprawls, you mean that it covers a large area of land. ❑ *The State Recreation Area sprawls over 900 acres on the southern tip of Key Biscayne.*

PHRASAL VERB **sprawl out** Sprawl out means the same as sprawl VERB 1. ❑ *He would take two aspirin and sprawl out on his bed.*

NOUN [u] You can use **sprawl** to refer to an area where a city has grown outwards in an uncontrolled way. ❑ *The whole urban sprawl of Ankara contains over 2.6 million people.*

spray ♦◇◇ /spreɪ/ NOUN, VERB

NOUN [c, u] (**sprays**) **1** [c, u] Spray is a lot of small drops of water which are being thrown into the air. ❑ *The moon was casting a rainbow through the spray from the waterfall.* **2** [c, u] A spray is a liquid kept under pressure in a can or other container, which you can force out in very small drops. ❑ *hair spray* **3** [c] A spray is a piece of equipment for spraying water or another liquid, especially over growing plants. ❑ *Farmers can use the spray to kill weeds without harming the soy crop.*

VERB [I, T] (**sprays, spraying, sprayed**) **1** [I, T] If you spray a liquid somewhere or if it sprays somewhere, drops of the liquid cover a place or shower someone. ❑ *A sprayer hooked to a tractor can spray five gallons onto ten acres.* ❑ *Inmates threw bricks at prison officers who were spraying them with a hose.* **2** [I, T] If a lot of small things spray somewhere or if something sprays them, they are scattered somewhere with a lot of force. ❑ *A shower of mustard seeds sprayed into the air and fell into the grass.* ❑ *The intensity of the blaze shattered windows, spraying glass on the streets below.* **3** [T] If someone sprays bullets somewhere, they fire a lot of

bullets at a group of people or things. ❑ *He ran to the top of the building, spraying bullets into shoppers below.* **4** [T] If something **is sprayed**, it is painted using paint kept under pressure in a container. ❑ *The bare metal was sprayed with several coats of primer.* **5** [I, T] When someone sprays against insects, they cover plants or crops with a chemical which prevents insects from feeding on them. ❑ *He doesn't spray against pests or diseases.* ❑ *Confine the use of insecticides to the evening and do not spray plants that are in flower.*

✪**spread** ♦♦◇ /spred/ VERB, NOUN

VERB [T, I] (**spreads, spreading, spread**) **1** [T] If you spread something somewhere, you open it out or arrange it over a place or surface, so that all of it can be seen or used easily. ❑ *She spread a towel on the sand and lay on it.* **2** [T] If you spread your arms, hands, fingers, or legs, you stretch them out until they are far apart. ❑ *Sitting on the floor, spread your legs as far as they will go without overstretching.* **3** [T] If you spread a substance on a surface or **spread** the surface **with** the substance, you put a thin layer of the substance over the surface. ❑ *Spread the mixture in the cake tin and bake for 30 minutes.* **4** [I, T] If something **spreads** or **is spread** by people, it gradually reaches or affects a larger and larger area or more and more people. = circulate; ≠ contain ❑ *The industrial revolution, which started a couple of hundred years ago in Europe, is now spreading across the world.* ❑ *the sense of fear spreading in residential neighbourhoods* ❑ *He was fed-up with the lies being spread about him.* **5** [I, T] If something such as a liquid, gas, or smoke **spreads** or **is spread**, it moves outwards in all directions so that it covers a larger area. ❑ *Fire spread rapidly after a chemical lorry exploded.* ❑ *A dark red stain was spreading across his shirt.* ❑ *In Northern California, a wildfire has spread a haze of smoke over 200 miles.* **6** [T] If you spread something **over** a period of time, it takes place regularly or continuously over that period, rather than happening at one time. ❑ *There seems to be little difference whether you eat all your calorie allowance at once, or spread it over the day.* **7** [T] If you spread something such as wealth or work, you distribute it evenly or equally. ❑ *policies that spread the state's wealth more evenly*

PHRASAL VERB **spread out** **1** Spread out means the same as spread VERB 1. ❑ *He extracted several glossy prints and spread them out on a low coffee table.* **2** Spread out means the same as spread VERB 2. ❑ *David made a gesture, spreading out his hands as if he were showing that he had no explanation to make.* **3** If people, animals, or vehicles spread out, they move apart from each other. ❑ *Felix watched his men move like soldiers, spreading out into two teams.* **4** If something such as a city or forest spreads out, it gets larger and gradually begins to covers a larger area. ❑ *Cities such as Tokyo are spreading out.*

NOUN [SING, c] (**spreads**) **1** [SING] The **spread** of something is when something gradually affects or reaches a larger and larger area or more and more people. ❑ *The greatest hope for reform is the gradual spread of information.* ❑ *Thanks to the spread of modern technology, trained workers are now more vital than ever.* **2** [SING] The **spread** of something is when it moves outwards in all directions so that it covers a larger area. ❑ *The situation was complicated by the spread of a serious forest fire.* **3** [SING] The **spread** of something such as wealth or work is its even or equal distribution. ❑ *There are easier ways to encourage the even spread of wealth.* **4** [SING] A **spread of** ideas, interests, or other things is a wide variety of them. = range ❑ *A topic-based approach can be hard to assess in schools with a typical spread of ability.* **5** [c] A **spread** is two pages of a book, magazine, or newspaper that are opposite each other when you open it at a particular place. ❑ *There was a double-page spread of a dinner for 46 people.* **6** [SING] (business) Spread is used to refer to the difference between the price that a seller wants someone to pay for a particular stock or share and the price that the buyer is willing to pay. ❑ *Market makers earn their livings from the spread between buying and selling prices.*

✦ spread your wings → see wing

spread·sheet /ˈspredʃiːt/ NOUN [c] (**spreadsheets**) (computing) A **spreadsheet** is a computer program that is used for displaying and dealing with numbers, used, for example, for financial planning.

spring ♦♦◇ /sprɪŋ/ NOUN, VERB

NOUN [c, u] (**springs**) **1** [c, u] **Spring** is the season between winter and summer when the weather becomes warmer and plants start to grow again. ❑ *They are planning to move house next spring.* **2** [c] A **spring** is a spiral of wire which returns to its original shape after it is pressed or pulled. ❑ *Unfortunately, as a standard mattress wears, the springs soften and so do not support your spine.* **3** [c] A **spring** is a place where water comes up through the ground. It is also the water that comes from that place. ❑ *To the north are the hot springs.*

VERB [i, t] (**springs, springing, sprang, sprung**) **1** [i] When a person or animal **springs**, they jump upwards or forwards suddenly or quickly. ❑ *He sprang to his feet, grabbing his keys off the coffee table.* ❑ *The lion roared once and sprang.* **2** [i] If something **springs** in a particular direction, it moves suddenly and quickly. ❑ *Sadly when the lid of the boot sprang open, it was empty.* **3** [i] If one thing **springs from** another thing, it is the result of it. = stem ❑ *Ethiopia's art springs from its early Christian as well as its Muslim heritage.* **4** [t] If you **spring** some news or a surprise **on** someone, you tell them something that they did not expect to hear, without warning them. ❑ *McLaren sprang a new idea on him.*

PHRASAL VERB **spring up** If something **springs up**, it suddenly appears or begins to exist. ❑ *New theatres and arts centres sprang up all over the country.*

✦ **spring to mind** → see **mind**

sprin·kle /ˈsprɪŋkəl/ VERB [t] (**sprinkles, sprinkling, sprinkled**) **1** If you **sprinkle** a thing **with** something such as a liquid or powder, you scatter the liquid or powder over it. ❑ *Sprinkle the meat with salt and place in the pan.* ❑ *At the festival, candles are blessed and sprinkled with holy water.* **2** If something **is sprinkled with** particular things, it has a few of them throughout it and they are far apart from each other. ❑ *Unfortunately, the text is sprinkled with errors.*

sprint /sprɪnt/ NOUN, VERB

NOUN [SING, c] (**sprints**) **1** [SING] **The sprint** is a short, fast running race. ❑ *Rob Harmeling won the sprint in Bordeaux.* **2** [c] A **sprint** is a short race in which the competitors run, drive, ride, or swim very fast. ❑ *Lewis will compete in both sprints in Stuttgart.* **3** [SING] A **sprint** is a fast run that someone does, either at the end of a race or because they are in a hurry. ❑ *Gilles Delion, of France, won the Tour of Lombardy in a sprint finish at Monza yesterday.*

VERB [i] (**sprints, sprinting, sprinted**) If you **sprint**, you run or ride as fast as you can over a short distance. ❑ *Sergeant Horne sprinted to the car.*

sprung /sprʌŋ/ IRREG FORM **Sprung** is the past participle of **spring**.

spun /spʌn/ IRREG FORM **Spun** is the past tense and past participle of **spin**.

spur ♦◇◇ /spɜː/ VERB, NOUN

VERB [t] (**spurs, spurring, spurred**) **1** If one thing **spurs** you **to** do another, it encourages you to do it. = urge ❑ *It's the money that spurs these fishermen to risk a long ocean journey in their flimsy boats.* **2** (journalism) If something **spurs** a change or event, it makes it happen faster or sooner. ❑ *The administration may put more emphasis on spurring economic growth.*

PHRASAL VERB **spur on** Spur on means the same as **spur** VERB **1**. ❑ *Their attitude, rather than reining him back, only seemed to spur Philip on.*

NOUN [c] (**spurs**) Something that acts as a **spur to** something else encourages a person or organization to do that thing or makes it happen more quickly. ❑ *a belief in competition as a spur to efficiency*

PHRASE **spur of the moment** If you do something on the **spur of the moment**, you do it suddenly, without planning it beforehand. ❑ *They admitted they had taken a vehicle on the spur of the moment.*

spy /spaɪ/ NOUN, ADJ, VERB

NOUN [c] (**spies**) A **spy** is a person whose job is to find out secret information about another country or organization. ❑ *He was jailed for five years as an alleged spy.*

ADJ [spy + N] A **spy** satellite or **spy** plane obtains secret information about another country by taking photographs from the sky. ❑ *pictures from unmanned spy planes operated by the US military*

VERB [i] (**spies, spying, spied**) **1** Someone who **spies for** a country or organization tries to find out secret information about another country or organization. ❑ *The agent spied for East Germany for more than twenty years.* ❑ *East and West are still spying on one another.* **2** If you **spy on** someone, you watch them secretly. ❑ *That day he spied on her while pretending to work on the shrubs.*

spy·ing /ˈspaɪɪŋ/ NOUN [u] ❑ *a ten-year sentence for spying*

squad ♦◇◇ /skwɒd/ NOUN [c] (**squads**) **1** A **squad** is a section of a police force that is responsible for dealing with a particular type of crime. ❑ *The building was evacuated and the bomb squad called.* **2** A **squad** is a group of players from which a sports team will be chosen. ❑ *The American squad has pulled out of the four-day basketball tournament.*

✪ **square** ♦♦◇ /skweə/ NOUN, ADJ, VERB

NOUN [c] (**squares**) **1** A **square** is a shape with four sides that are all the same length and four corners that are all right angles. ❑ *Serve the cake warm or at room temperature, cut in squares.* ❑ *There was a calendar on the wall, with large squares around the dates.* ❑ *Most of the rugs are simple cotton squares.* **2** In a town or city, a **square** is a flat open place, often in the shape of a square. ❑ *The house is located in one of the city's prettiest squares.* **3** The **square of** a number is the number produced when you multiply that number by itself. For example, the square of 3 is 9. ❑ *the square of the speed of light, an exceedingly large number*

PHRASE **back to square one** If you are **back to square one**, you have to start dealing with something from the beginning again because the way you were dealing with it has failed. ❑ *If your complaint is not upheld, you may feel you are back to square one.*

ADJ **1** Something that is **square** has a shape the same as a square or similar to a square. ❑ *Round tables seat more people in the same space as a square table.* ❑ *His finger nails were square and cut neatly across.* **2** [square + N] **Square** is used before units of length when referring to the area of something. For example, if something is three feet long and two feet wide, its area is six square feet. ❑ *The new complex will provide 10 million square feet of office space.* **3** [AMOUNT + square] **Square** is used after units of length when you are giving the length of each side of something that is square in shape. ❑ *a linen cushion cover, 45 cm square*

VERB [t, i] (**squares, squaring, squared**) **1** [t] To **square** a number means to multiply it by itself. For example, **3 squared** is 3 x 3, or 9. **3 squared** is usually written as 3^2. ❑ *Take the time in seconds, square it, and multiply by 5.12.* ❑ *A squared plus B squared equals C squared.* **2** [i, t] If you **square** two different ideas or actions **with** each other or if they **square with** each other, they fit or match each other. ❑ *That explanation squares with the facts, doesn't it.* **3** [t] If you **square** something **with** someone, you ask their permission or check with them that what you are doing is acceptable to them. ❑ *I squared it with Dan, who said it was all right so long as I was back next Monday morning.*

✦ **fair and square** → see **fair**

squash /skwɒʃ/ VERB, ADJ, NOUN

VERB [t] (**squashes, squashing, squashed**) **1** If someone or something **is squashed**, they are pressed or crushed with such force that they become injured or lose their shape. ❑ *Robert was lucky to escape with just a broken foot after being squashed against a fence by a car.* ❑ *Whole neighbourhoods have been squashed flat by shelling.* **2** If you **squash** something that is causing you trouble, you put a stop to it, often by force. ❑ *The troops would stay in position to squash the first murmur of trouble.*

ADJ [V-LINK + squashed 'into' N] If people or things are **squashed into** a place, they are put or pushed into a place where there is not enough room for them to be. = cram ❑ *There were 2,000 people squashed into her recent show.*

NOUN [c, u, SING] (**squashes**) **1** [c, u] A **squash** is one of a family of vegetables that have thick skin and soft or firm flesh inside. **2** [u] **Squash** is a game in which two players hit a small rubber ball against the walls of a court using rackets. ❑ *I also play squash.* **3** [SING] (BrE; in AmE, use

S

squeeze; *informal*) If you say that getting a number of people into a small space is **a squash**, you mean that it is only just possible for them all to get into it. = squeeze

squeak /skwiːk/ VERB, NOUN
VERB [I] (**squeaks, squeaking, squeaked**) If something or someone **squeaks**, they make a short, high-pitched sound. ❑ *My boots squeaked a little as I walked.* ❑ *The door squeaked open.*
NOUN [C] (**squeaks**) A **squeak** is a short, high-pitched sound. ❑ *He gave an outraged squeak.*

squeal /skwiːl/ VERB, NOUN
VERB [I] (**squeals, squealing, squealed**) If someone or something **squeals**, they make a long, high-pitched sound. ❑ *Jennifer squealed with delight and hugged me.*
NOUN [C] (**squeals**) A **squeal** is a long, high-pitched sound. ❑ *At that moment there was a squeal of brakes and the angry blowing of a car horn.*

squeeze ♦◇◇ /skwiːz/ VERB, NOUN
VERB [T, I] (**squeezes, squeezing, squeezed**) **1** [T] If you **squeeze** something, you press it firmly, usually with your hands. ❑ *He squeezed her arm reassuringly.* **2** [T] If you **squeeze** a liquid or a soft substance out of an object, you get the liquid or substance out by pressing the object. ❑ *Joe put the plug in the sink and squeezed some washing-up liquid over the dishes.* **3** [I, T] If you **squeeze** a person or thing somewhere or if they **squeeze** there, they manage to get through or into a small space. ❑ *They lowered him gradually into the cockpit. Somehow they squeezed him in the tight space, and strapped him in.*
NOUN [C, SING] (**squeezes**) **1** [C] A **squeeze** is the act of pressing something firmly, usually with your hands. ❑ *I liked her way of reassuring you with a squeeze of the hand.* **2** [SING] (*informal*) If you say that getting a number of people into a small space is **a squeeze**, you mean that it is only just possible for them all to get into it. = squash ❑ *It was a squeeze in the car with five of them.*

stab /stæb/ VERB, NOUN
VERB [T, I] (**stabs, stabbing, stabbed**) **1** [T] If someone **stabs** you, they push a knife or sharp object into your body. ❑ *Somebody stabbed him in the stomach.* ❑ *Dean tried to stab him with a screwdriver.* **2** [I, T] If you **stab** something or **stab at** it, you push at it with your finger or with something pointed that you are holding. ❑ *Bess stabbed a slice of cucumber.* ❑ *Goldstone flipped the pages and stabbed his thumb at the paragraph he was looking for.*
PHRASE **stab someone in the back** If you say that someone **has stabbed** you **in the back**, you mean that they have done something very harmful to you when you thought that you could trust them. You can refer to an action of this kind as **a stab in the back**. ❑ *She felt betrayed, as though her daughter had stabbed her in the back.*
NOUN [SING] **1** (*informal*) If you have a **stab** at something, you try to do it. ❑ *Several tennis stars have had a stab at acting.* **2** (*literary*) You can refer to a sudden, usually unpleasant feeling as a **stab of** that feeling. ❑ *a stab of pain just above his eye*

○sta·bil·ity /stəˈbɪlɪti/ → See stable

○sta·bi·lize /ˈsteɪbɪlaɪz/ also **stabilise** VERB [I, T] (**stabilizes, stabilizing, stabilized**) If something **stabilizes**, or **is stabilized**, it becomes stable. = steady; ≠ destabilize ❑ *Although her illness is serious, her condition is beginning to stabilize.* ❑ *Officials hope the move will stabilize exchange rates.*
sta·bi·li·za·tion /ˌsteɪbɪlaɪˈzeɪʃən/ NOUN [U] ❑ *the stabilization of property prices*

○sta·ble ♦◇◇ /ˈsteɪbəl/ ADJ, NOUN (*academic word*)
ADJ (**stabler, stablest**) **1** If something is **stable**, it is not likely to change or come to an end suddenly. = steady; ≠ unstable ❑ *The price of oil should remain stable for the rest of 1992.* ❑ *a stable marriage* **2** If someone has a **stable** personality, they are calm and reasonable and their mood does not change suddenly. ❑ *Their characters are fully formed and they are both very stable children.* **3** You can describe someone who is seriously ill as **stable** when their condition has stopped getting worse. ❑ *The injured man was in a stable condition.* **4** (*technical*) Chemical substances are described as **stable** when they tend to remain in the same chemical or atomic state. ❑ *The less stable compounds*

were converted into a compound called Delta-A THC. **5** If an object is **stable**, it is firmly fixed in position and is not likely to move or fall. ❑ *This structure must be stable.*
NOUN [C] (**stables**) **1** A **stable** or **stables** is a building in which horses are kept. **2** A **stable** or **stables** is an organization that breeds and trains horses for racing. ❑ *Miss Curling won on two horses from Mick Trickey's stable.*
○sta·bil·ity /stəˈbɪlɪti/ NOUN [U] ≠ instability ❑ *It was a time of political stability and progress.* ❑ *UN peacekeepers were dispatched to ensure stability in the border region.*

stack /stæk/ NOUN, VERB
NOUN [C, PL] (**stacks**) **1** [C] A **stack of** things is a pile of them. ❑ *There were stacks of books on the bedside table and floor.* **2** [PL] (*informal*) If you say that someone has **stacks of** something, you mean that they have a lot of it. ❑ *If the job's that good, you'll have stacks of money.*
VERB [T] (**stacks, stacking, stacked**) If you **stack** a number of things, you arrange them in neat piles. ❑ *Mrs Cathiard was stacking the clean bottles in crates.*
PHRASE **the odds are stacked against someone** or **things are stacked against someone** If you say that **the odds are stacked against** someone, or that particular factors **are stacked against** them, you mean that they are unlikely to succeed in what they want to do because the conditions are not favourable. ❑ *The odds are stacked against civilians getting a fair trial.*
PHRASAL VERB **stack up** Stack up means the same as stack VERB. ❑ *He ordered them to stack up pillows behind his back.*

sta·dium ♦◇◇ /ˈsteɪdiəm/ NOUN [C] (**stadiums** or **stadia**) A **stadium** is a large sports field with rows of seats all around it. ❑ *a baseball stadium*

○staff ♦♦♦ /stɑːf, stæf/ NOUN, VERB
NOUN [C, PL] (**staffs**) **1** [C] The **staff** of an organization are the people who work for it. = employees, workforce, workers ❑ *The staff were very good.* ❑ *The outpatient programme has a staff of six people.* ❑ *staff members* ❑ *the nursing staff of the hospital* ❑ *It has 75 members of staff based at its London office.* **2** [PL] People who are part of a particular staff are often referred to as **staff**. ❑ *10 staff were allocated to the task.* ❑ *A hundred extra staff were taken on.* ❑ *Several senior staff have left.*
VERB [T] (**staffs, staffing, staffed**) If an organization **is staffed by** particular people, they are the people who work for it. ❑ *They are staffed by volunteers.*

> ### USAGE NOTE
> **staff**
>
> You use **staff** to talk about all the people who work for an organization. **Staff** is usually followed by a plural verb. You do not refer to an individual person as 'a staff'. You refer to an individual person as a **member of staff**.
> The hotel **staff** were extremely friendly.
> A **member of staff** will be happy to help you.

staffed /stɑːft, stæft/ ADJ ❑ *The house allocated to them was pleasant and spacious, and well staffed.*
→ See also **chief of staff**

○stage ♦♦♦ /steɪdʒ/ NOUN, VERB
NOUN [C, SING] (**stages**) **1** [C] A **stage of** an activity, process, or period is one part of it. = period, phase ❑ *The way children talk about or express their feelings depends on their age and stage of development.* ❑ *Mr Cook has arrived in Greece on the final stage of a tour which also included Egypt and Israel.* **2** [C] [also 'on' stage] In a theatre, the **stage** is an area where actors or other entertainers perform. ❑ *The road crew needed more than 24 hours to move and rebuild the stage after a concert.* **3** [SING] You can refer to a particular area of activity as a particular **stage**, especially when you are talking about politics. = arena ❑ *He was finally forced off the political stage last year by the deterioration of his physical condition.*
VERB [T] (**stages, staging, staged**) **1** If someone **stages** a play or other show, they organize and present a performance of it. = put on ❑ *Maya Angelou first staged the play 'And I Still Rise' in the late 1970s.* **2** If you **stage** an event or ceremony, you organize and usually take part in it. = hold ❑ *Russian workers have staged a number of*

strikes in protest at the republic's declaration of independence.
✦ **set the stage** → see **set**

stag·ger /ˈstægə/ VERB [I, T] (**staggers, staggering, staggered**) **1** [I] If you **stagger**, you walk very unsteadily, for example because you are ill or drunk. ❑ He lost his balance, staggered back against the rail and toppled over. **2** [T] If something **staggers** you, it surprises you very much. ❑ The whole thing staggers me. **3** [T] To **stagger** things such as people's holidays or hours of work means to arrange them so that they do not all happen at the same time. ❑ During the past few years the university has staggered the summer holiday periods for students.
stag·gered /ˈstægəd/ ADJ ❑ I was simply staggered by the heat of the Argentinian high-summer.

stag·ger·ing /ˈstægərɪŋ/ ADJ Something that is **staggering** is very surprising. = astounding ❑ a staggering $900 million in short- and long-term debt

stag·nate /stægˈneɪt, AmE ˈstægneɪt/ VERB [I] (**stagnates, stagnating, stagnated**) (disapproval) If something such as a business or society **stagnates**, it stops changing or progressing. ❑ Industrial production is stagnating.
stag·na·tion /stægˈneɪʃən/ NOUN [U] ❑ the stagnation of the steel industry

staid /steɪd/ ADJ If you say that someone or something is **staid**, you mean that they are serious, dull, and rather old-fashioned. ❑ a staid seaside resort

stain /steɪn/ NOUN, VERB
NOUN [C] (**stains**) A **stain** is a mark on something that is difficult to remove. ❑ Remove stains by soaking in a mild solution of bleach.
VERB (**stains, staining, stained**) If a liquid **stains** something, the thing becomes coloured or marked by the liquid. ❑ Some foods can stain the teeth, as of course can smoking.
stained /steɪnd/ ADJ ❑ His clothing was stained with mud.

stair /steə/ NOUN [PL] (**stairs**) **Stairs** are a set of steps inside a building which go from one floor to another. ❑ Nancy began to climb the stairs. ❑ We walked up a flight of stairs.

stair·case /ˈsteəkeɪs/ NOUN [C] (**staircases**) A **staircase** is a set of stairs inside a building. ❑ They walked down the staircase together.

⊘ **stake** ♦♦◇ /steɪk/ NOUN, VERB
NOUN [PL, C] (**stakes**) **1** [PL] The **stakes** involved in a contest or a risky action are the things that can be gained or lost. ❑ The game was usually played for high stakes between two large groups. ❑ Detectives now believe the Mafia also had a stake in the plot and killed him when it went wrong. **2** [C] If you have a **stake in** something such as a business, it matters to you, for example because you own part of it or because its success or failure will affect you. ❑ He was eager to return to a more entrepreneurial role in which he had a big financial stake in his own efforts. **3** [PL] You can use **stakes** to refer to something that is like a contest. For example, you can refer to the choosing of a leader as **the** leadership **stakes**. ❑ We are lagging behind in the childcare stakes. **4** [C] A **stake** is a pointed wooden post which is pushed into the ground, for example in order to support a young tree. = post ❑ His arms were tied to wooden stakes to hold him flat.
PHRASE **at stake** If something is **at stake**, it is being risked and might be lost or damaged if you are not successful. ❑ The tension was naturally high for a game with so much at stake.
VERB [T] (**stakes, staking, staked**) If you **stake** something such as your money or your reputation **on** the result of something, you risk your money or reputation on it. ❑ He has staked his political future on an election victory.
PHRASE **stake a claim** If you **stake a claim**, you say that something is yours or that you have a right to it. ❑ Jane is determined to stake her claim as an actress.

⊘ **stake·hold·er** /ˈsteɪkhəʊldə/ NOUN [C] (**stakeholders**) (business) **Stakeholders** are people who have an interest in a company's or organization's affairs. ❑ the Delaware River Port Authority, a major stakeholder in Penn's Landing ❑ The assessment resulted in major stakeholders receiving different percentages of the available equity. ❑ In future, key stakeholders should be part of any plan for fighting the disease, should it ever return.

stale /steɪl/ ADJ (**staler, stalest**) **1 Stale** food is no longer fresh or good to eat. ❑ Their daily diet consisted of a lump of stale bread, a bowl of rice, and stale water. **2 Stale** air or smells are unpleasant because they are no longer fresh. ❑ the smell of stale sweat **3** If you say that a place, an activity, or an idea is **stale**, you mean that it has become boring because it is always the same. ❑ Her relationship with Mark has become stale.

stalk /stɔːk/ NOUN, VERB
NOUN [C] (**stalks**) The **stalk** of a flower, leaf, or fruit is the thin part that joins it to the plant or tree. = stem ❑ A single, pale blue flower grows up from each joint on a long stalk.
VERB [T] (**stalks, stalking, stalked**) **1** If you **stalk** a person or a wild animal, you follow them quietly in order to kill them, catch them, or observe them carefully. = track ❑ He stalks his victims like a hunter after a deer. **2** If someone **stalks** someone else, especially a famous person or a person they used to have a relationship with, they keep following them or contacting them in an annoying and frightening way. ❑ Even after their divorce he continued to stalk and threaten her.

stall /stɔːl/ VERB, NOUN
VERB [I, T] (**stalls, stalling, stalled**) **1** [I, T] If a process **stalls**, or if someone or something **stalls** it, the process stops but may continue at a later time. ❑ The Social Democratic Party has vowed to try to stall the bill until the current session ends. ❑ The peace process stalled. **2** [I] If you **stall**, you try to avoid doing something until later. ❑ Thomas had spent all week stalling over his decision. **3** [T] If you **stall** someone, you prevent them from doing something until a later time. ❑ The store manager stalled the man until the police arrived. **4** [I, T] If a vehicle **stalls** or if you accidentally **stall** it, the engine stops suddenly. ❑ The engine stalled.
NOUN [C, PL] (**stalls**) **1** [C] A **stall** is a large table on which you put goods that you want to sell, or information that you want to give people. ❑ market stalls selling local fruits **2** [PL] (mainly BrE; in AmE, use **orchestra**) **The stalls** in a theatre or concert hall are the seats on the ground floor directly in front of the stage.

stal·wart /ˈstɔːlwət/ NOUN [C] (**stalwarts**) A **stalwart** is a loyal worker or supporter of an organization, especially a political party. ❑ His free-trade policies aroused suspicion among party stalwarts.

stami·na /ˈstæmɪnə/ NOUN [U] **Stamina** is the physical or mental energy needed to do a tiring activity for a long time. ❑ You have to have a lot of stamina to be a top-class dancer.

stamp ♦◇◇ /stæmp/ NOUN, VERB
NOUN [C, SING] (**stamps**) **1** [C] A **stamp** or a **postage stamp** is a small piece of paper which you lick and stick on an envelope or parcel before you mail it to pay for the cost of the postage. ❑ a book of stamps ❑ As of February 3rd, the price of a first class stamp will go up to 60 pence. **2** [C] A **stamp** is a small block of wood or metal which has a pattern or a group of letters on one side. You press it onto a pad of ink and then onto a piece of paper in order to produce a mark on the paper. The mark that you produce is also called a **stamp**. ❑ a date stamp and an ink pad **3** [C] A **stamp** is the act or sound of lifting your foot and putting it down very hard on the ground, for example because you are angry or because your feet are cold ❑ hearing the creak of a door and the stamp of cold feet **4** [SING] If something bears **the stamp of** a particular quality or person, it clearly has that quality or was done by that person. = mark ❑ Most of us want to make our home a familiar place and put the stamp of our personality on its walls.
VERB [T, I] (**stamps, stamping, stamped**) **1** [T] If you **stamp** a mark or word on an object, you press the mark or word onto the object using a stamp or other device. ❑ Car manufacturers stamp a vehicle identification number at several places on new cars to help track down stolen vehicles. **2** [I, T] If you **stamp** or **stamp your foot**, you lift your foot and put it down very hard on the ground, for example because you are angry or because your feet are cold. ❑ Often he teased me till my temper went and I stamped and screamed, feeling furiously helpless. ❑ His foot stamped down on the accelerator.

S

3 [I] If you **stamp** somewhere, you walk there putting your feet down very hard on the ground because you are angry. = stomp □ *'I'm going before things get any worse!' he shouted as he stamped out of the bedroom.* **4** [I] If you **stamp on** something, you put your foot down on it very hard. □ *He received the original ban last week after stamping on the referee's foot during the final.*

PHRASAL VERB **stamp out** If you **stamp** something **out**, you put an end to it. □ *Dr Muffett stressed that he was opposed to bullying in schools and that action would be taken to stamp it out.*

stam·pede /stæmˈpiːd/ NOUN, VERB

NOUN [C] (stampedes) **1** If there is a **stampede**, a group of people or animals run in a wild, uncontrolled way. □ *There was a stampede for the exit.* **2** If a lot of people all do the same thing at the same time, you can describe it as a **stampede**. □ *a stampede of consumers rushing to buy merchandise at bargain prices*

VERB [I, T] (stampedes, stampeding, stampeded) If a group of animals or people **stampede** or if something **stampedes** them, they run in a wild, uncontrolled way. □ *The crowd stampeded and many were crushed or trampled underfoot.* □ *a herd of stampeding cattle*

✪ stance /stæns/ NOUN [C] (stances) **1** Your **stance** on a particular matter is your attitude to it. = position □ *Congress had agreed to reconsider its stance on the armed struggle.* □ *They have maintained a consistently neutral stance.* □ *His stance towards the story is quite similar to ours.* **2** (formal) Your **stance** is the way that you are standing. = position □ *Take a comfortably wide stance and flex your knees a little.*

stand ♦♦♦ /stænd/ VERB, NOUN

VERB [I, T, LINK] (stands, standing, stood) **1** [I] When you **are standing**, your body is upright, your legs are straight, and your weight is supported by your feet. □ *She was standing beside my bed staring down at me.* □ *They told me to stand still and not to turn round.* **2** [I] When someone who is sitting **stands**, they change their position so that they are upright and on their feet. □ *Becker stood and shook hands with Ben.* **3** [I] If you **stand aside** or **stand back**, you move a short distance sideways or backwards, so that you are standing in a different place. □ *I stood aside to let her pass me.* **4** [I] (written) If something such as a building or a piece of furniture **stands** somewhere, it is in that position, and is upright. □ *The house stands alone on top of a small hill.* **5** [I] You can say that a building **is standing** when it remains after other buildings around it have fallen down or been destroyed. □ *The palace, which was damaged by bombs in World War II, still stood.* **6** [T] If you **stand** something somewhere, you put it there in an upright position. = place □ *Stand the plant in the open in a sunny, sheltered place.* **7** [I] If you leave food or a mixture of something **to stand**, you leave it without disturbing it for some time. □ *The salad improves if made in advance and left to stand.* **8** [I] If you ask someone **where** or **how** they **stand on** a particular issue, you are asking them what their attitude or view is. □ *The amendment will force senators to show where they stand on the issue of sexual harassment.* **9** [I] If you do not know **where** you **stand with** someone, you do not know exactly what their attitude to you is. □ *No one knows where they stand with him; he is utterly unpredictable.* **10** [LINK] You can use **stand** instead of 'be' when you are describing the present state or condition of something or someone. □ *The alliance stands ready to do what is necessary.* **11** [I] If a decision, law, or offer **stands**, it still exists and has not been changed or cancelled. □ *Although exceptions could be made, the rule still stands.* **12** [I] If something that can be measured **stands** at a particular level, it is at that level. □ *The inflation rate now stands at 3.6 per cent.* **13** [T] If something can **stand** a situation or a test, it is good enough or strong enough to experience it without being damaged, harmed, or shown to be inadequate. □ *These are the first machines that can stand the wear and tear of continuously crushing glass.* **14** [T] If you cannot **stand** something, you cannot bear it or tolerate it. □ *I can't stand any more. I'm going to run away.* □ *Stoddart can stand any amount of personal criticism.* **15** [T] (informal) If you cannot **stand** someone or something, you dislike

them very strongly. = bear □ *I can't stand that man and his arrogance.* **16** [T] If you **stand to gain** something, you are likely to gain it. If you **stand to lose** something, you are likely to lose it. □ *The management group would stand to gain millions of dollars if the company were sold.* **17** [I] (BrE; in AmE, use run) If you **stand in** an election, you are a candidate in it.

PHRASES **it stands to reason** If you say **it stands to reason** that something is true or likely to happen, you mean that it is obvious. □ *It stands to reason that if you are considerate and friendly to people you will get a lot more back.*

stand in the way of something or **stand in someone's way** If you **stand in the way of** something or **stand in** a person's **way**, you prevent that thing from happening or prevent that person from doing something. □ *The administration would not stand in the way of such a proposal.*

PHRASAL VERBS **stand back** If you **stand back** and think about a situation, you think about it as if you were not involved in it. = step back □ *Stand back and look objectively at the problem.*

stand by **1** If you **are standing by**, you are ready and waiting to provide help or to take action. □ *British and American warships are standing by to evacuate their citizens if necessary.* **2** If you **stand by** and let something bad happen, you do not do anything to stop it. □ *The Secretary of Defence has said that he would not stand by and let democracy be undermined.* **3** If you **stand by** someone, you continue to give them support, especially when they are in trouble. = stick by □ *I wouldn't break the law for a friend, but I would stand by her if she did.* **4** If you **stand by** an earlier decision, promise, or statement, you continue to support it or keep it. = stick by □ *The decision has been made and I have got to stand by it.*

stand down If someone **stands down**, they resign from an important job or position, often in order to let someone else take their place. = step down, resign □ *Four days later, the despised leader finally stood down, just 17 days after taking office.*

stand for **1** If you say that a letter **stands for** a particular word, you mean that it is an abbreviation for that word. □ *AIDS stands for Acquired Immune Deficiency Syndrome.* **2** The ideas or attitudes that someone or something **stands for** are the ones that they support or represent. = represent □ *The party is trying to give the impression that it alone stands for democracy.* **3** If you will **not stand for** something, you will not allow it to happen or continue. □ *It's outrageous, and we won't stand for it any more.*

stand in **1** If you **stand in for** someone, you take their place or do their job, because they are sick or away. □ *I had to stand in for her on Tuesday when she didn't show up.* **2** → See also **stand-in**

stand out **1** If something **stands out**, it is very noticeable. □ *Every tree, wall and fence stood out against dazzling white fields.* **2** If something **stands out** from a surface, it rises up from it. = stick out □ *His tendons stood out like rope beneath his skin.*

stand up **1** **Stand up** means the same as **stand** VERB 1. □ *We waited, standing up, for an hour.* **2** **Stand up** means the same as **stand** VERB 2. □ *When I walked in, they all stood up and started clapping.* **3** If something such as a claim or a piece of evidence **stands up**, it is accepted as true or satisfactory after being carefully examined. □ *He made wild accusations that did not stand up.* **4** (informal) If a boyfriend or girlfriend **stands** you **up**, they fail to keep an arrangement to meet you. □ *We were to have had dinner together yesterday evening, but he stood me up.* **5** → See also **stand-up**

stand up for (approval) If you **stand up for** someone or something, you defend them and make your feelings or opinions very clear. = stick up for □ *They stood up for what they believed to be right.*

stand up to **1** If something **stands up to** bad conditions, it is not damaged or harmed by them. □ *Is this building going to stand up to the strongest gales?* **2** If you **stand up to** someone, especially someone more powerful than you are, you defend yourself against their attacks or demands. □ *He hit me, so I hit him back – the first time in my life I'd stood up to him.*

NOUN [C, SING] (**stands**) **1** [C] If you take or make a **stand**, you do something or say something in order to make it clear what your attitude to a particular thing is. □ *He felt the need to make a stand against racism in South Africa.* **2** [C] A **stand** is a small shop or stall, outdoors or in a large public building. = **stall** □ *He ran a newspaper stand outside the American Express office.* **3** [C] A **stand** at a sports stadium or arena is a large structure where people sit or stand to watch what is happening. = **grandstand** □ *I was sitting in the stand for the first game.* **4** [C] A **stand** is an object or piece of furniture that is designed for supporting or holding a particular kind of thing. □ *The teapot came with a stand to catch the drips.* **5** [C] A **stand** is an area where taxis or buses can wait to pick up passengers. □ *Luckily there was a taxi stand nearby.* **6** [SING] In a law court, **the stand** is the place where a witness sits to answer questions. □ *When the father took the stand today, he contradicted his son's testimony.*

♦ **stand a chance** → see **chance**; **stand firm** → see **firm**; **stand on your own two feet** → see **foot**; **stand your ground** → see **ground**; **stand trial** → see **trial**

✪ stand·ard ♦♦◇ /ˈstændəd/ NOUN, ADJ
NOUN [C, PL] (**standards**) **1** [C] A **standard** is a level of quality or achievement, especially a level that is thought to be acceptable. □ *The standard of professional cricket has never been lower.* □ *improvements in the general standard of living* □ *There will be new national standards for hospital cleanliness.* **2** [C] A **standard** is something that you use in order to judge the quality of something else. = **guideline, level** □ *systems that were by later standards absurdly primitive* **3** [PL] **Standards** are moral principles which affect people's attitudes and behaviour. □ *My father has always had high moral standards.*
ADJ **1** You use **standard** to describe things which are usual and normal. = **normal, regular, usual**; ≠ **non-standard, abnormal, unusual, irregular** □ *It was standard practice for untrained clerks to advise in serious cases such as murder.* □ *the standard format for a scientific paper* **2** [standard + N] A **standard** work or text on a particular subject is one that is widely read and often recommended. □ *At twenty he translated Euler's standard work on algebra into English.*

WORD CONNECTIONS
VERB + **standard**
set a standard
raise a standard
maintain a standard
meet a standard
□ *The pitch area will meet international standards for both rugby and soccer.*
ADJ + **standard**
a high standard
a minimum standard
a strict standard
a national standard
a professional standard
□ *All recruits have to pass a common exam to meet a minimum standard.*
NOUN + **standard**
industry standards
safety standards
living standards
□ *All components comply with stringent safety standards.*

stand·ard·ize /ˈstændədaɪz/ also **standardise** VERB
[T] (**standardizes, standardizing, standardized**) To **standardize** things means to change them so that they all have the same features. □ *There is a drive both to standardize components and to reduce the number of models.*
stand·ardi·za·tion /ˌstændədaɪˈzeɪʃən, AmE -dɪˈz-/ NOUN [U] □ *the standardization of working hours*

stand·ard of liv·ing NOUN [C] (**standards of living**) Your **standard of living** is the level of comfort and wealth which you have. □ *We'll continue to fight for a decent standard of living for our members.*

stand-in NOUN [C] (**stand-ins**) A **stand-in** is a person who takes someone else's place or does someone else's job for a while, for example because the other person is sick or away. □ *He was a stand-in for my regular doctor.*

✪ stand·point /ˈstændpɔɪnt/ NOUN [C] (**standpoints**) From a particular **standpoint** means looking at an event, situation, or idea in a particular way. = **point of view, perspective** □ *He believes that from a military standpoint, the situation is under control.* □ *From a marketing standpoint, store cards have a definite appeal.*

stand·still /ˈstændstɪl/ NOUN [SING] If movement or activity comes **to** or is brought to **a standstill**, it stops completely. = **halt** □ *Abruptly the group ahead of us came to a standstill.*

stand-up also **standup** ADJ, NOUN
ADJ [stand-up + N] A **stand-up** comic or comedian stands alone in front of an audience and tells jokes. □ *He does all kinds of accents, he can do jokes – he could be a stand-up comic.*
NOUN [U, C] (**stand-ups**) **1** [U] **Stand-up** is stand-up comedy. □ *likeability, professionalism and the kind of nerve you need to do stand-up* **2** [C] A **stand-up** is a stand-up comedian. □ *one of the worst stand-ups alive*

✪ sta·ple /ˈsteɪpəl/ ADJ, NOUN, VERB
ADJ [staple + N] A **staple** food, product, or activity is one that is basic and important in people's everyday lives. = **basic** □ *Rice is the staple food of more than half the world's population.* □ *The Chinese also eat a type of pasta as part of their staple diet.* □ *Staple goods are disappearing from the shops.*
NOUN [C] (**staples**) **1** A **staple** is a food, product, or activity that is basic and important in people's everyday lives. = **basic** □ *Fish is a staple in the diet of many Africans.* □ *boutiques selling staples such as jeans and T-shirts* **2** A **staple** is something that forms an important part of something else. □ *Political reporting has become a staple of American journalism.* **3** **Staples** are small pieces of bent wire that are used mainly for holding sheets of paper together firmly. You put the staples into the paper using a device called a stapler.
VERB [T] (**staples, stapling, stapled**) If you **staple** something, you fasten it to something else or fix it in place using staples. □ *Staple some sheets of paper together into a book.*

star ♦♦♦ /stɑː/ NOUN, VERB
NOUN [C, PL] (**stars**) **1** [C] A **star** is a large ball of burning gas in space. Stars appear to us as small points of light in the sky on clear nights. □ *The nights were pure with cold air and lit with stars.* **2** [C] You can refer to a shape or an object as a **star** when it has four, five, or more points sticking out of it in a regular pattern. □ *Children at school receive coloured stars for work well done.* **3** [C] You can say how many **stars** something such as a hotel or restaurant has as a way of talking about its quality, which is often indicated by a number of star-shaped symbols. The more stars something has, the better it is. □ *five-star hotels* **4** [C] Famous actors, musicians, and sports players are often referred to as **stars**. □ *star of the TV series Scrubs* □ *By now Murphy is Hollywood's top male comedy star.* **5** [PL] Predictions about people's lives which are based on astrology and appear regularly in a newspaper or magazine are sometimes referred to as **the stars**. = **horoscope** □ *There was nothing in my stars to say I'd have travel problems!*
VERB [I, T] (**stars, starring, starred**) **1** [I] If an actor or actress **stars in** a play or film, he or she has one of the most important parts in it. □ *The previous year Adolphson had starred in a play in which Ingrid had been an extra.* **2** [T] If a play or film **stars** a famous actor or actress, he or she has one of the most important parts in it. □ *a Hollywood movie, 'The Secret of Santa Vittoria', directed by Stanley Kramer and starring Anthony Quinn*

stare ♦◇◇ /steə/ VERB, NOUN
VERB [I] (**stares, staring, stared**) If you **stare at** someone or something, you look at them for a long time. □ *Tamara stared at him in disbelief, shaking her head.* □ *Ben continued to stare out of the window.*
PHRASE **stare someone in the face** (*informal*) If a situation or the answer to a problem **is staring** you **in the**

S

face, it is very obvious, although you may not be immediately aware of it. ❑ *Then the answer hit me. It had been staring me in the face ever since Lullington.*
NOUN [c] (**stares**) A **stare** is the act of looking at someone or something for a long time. ❑ *Hlasek gave him a long, cold stare.*

stark /stɑːk/ ADJ (**starker**, **starkest**) **1** Stark choices or statements are harsh and unpleasant. = harsh ❑ *Companies face a stark choice if they want to stay competitive.* **2** If two things are in **stark** contrast to one another, they are very different from each other in a way that is very obvious. ❑ *secret cooperation between London and Washington that was in stark contrast to official policy* **3** Something that is **stark** is very plain in appearance. ❑ *the stark white, characterless fireplace in the drawing room*
stark·ly /ˈstɑːkli/ ADV **1** *That issue is presented starkly and brutally by Bob Graham and David Cairns.* **2** *Angus's child-like paintings contrast starkly with his adult subject matter in these portraits.* **3** *The room was starkly furnished.*

start ◆◆◆ /stɑːt/ VERB, NOUN
VERB [T, I] (**starts**, **starting**, **started**) **1** [T] If you **start to** do something, you do something that you were not doing before and you continue doing it. = begin ❑ *John then unlocked the front door and I started to follow him up the stairs.* ❑ *It was 1956 when Susanna started the work on the garden.* **2** [I, T] When something **starts**, or if someone **starts** it, it takes place from a particular time. = begin ❑ *The fire is thought to have started in an upstairs room.* ❑ *All of the passengers started the day with a swim.* **3** [I] If you **start by** doing something, or if you **start with** something, you do that thing first in a series of actions. = begin ❑ *I started by asking how many day-care centres were located in the United States.* **4** [I] You use **start** to say what someone's first job was. For example, if their first job was that of a factory worker, you can say that they **started as** a factory worker. ❑ *Betty started as a shipping clerk at the clothes factory.* **5** [T] When someone **starts** something such as a new business, they create it or cause it to happen. ❑ *George Granger has started a health centre and I know he's looking for qualified staff.* **6** [I, T] If you **start** an engine, car, or machine, or if it **starts**, it begins to work. ❑ *He started the car, which hummed smoothly.* **7** [I] If you **start**, your body suddenly moves slightly as a result of surprise or fear. ❑ *She put the bottle on the coffee table beside him, banging it down hard. He started at the sound, his concentration broken.*
PHRASE **to start with** To start with means at the very first stage of an event or process. ❑ *To start with, the pressure on her was very heavy, but it's eased off a bit now.*
PHRASAL VERBS **start off 1** Start off means the same as start VERB 4. ❑ *Mr Dambar had started off as an assistant to Mrs Spear's husband.* **2** If you **start off by** doing something, you do it as the first part of an activity. ❑ *She started off by accusing him of blackmail but he more or less ignored her.* **3** To **start** someone **off** means to cause them to begin doing something. ❑ *Her mother started her off acting in children's theatre.* **4** To **start** something **off** means to cause it to begin. ❑ *He became more aware of the things that started that tension off.*
start on If you **start on** something that needs to be done, you start dealing with it. ❑ *Before you start on these chapters, clear your head.*
start out 1 If someone or something **starts out as** a particular thing, they are that thing at the beginning although they change later. ❑ *Daly was a fast-talking Irish-American who had started out as a salesman.* **2** If you **start out by** doing something, you do it at the beginning of an activity. ❑ *I'm careful to start out by saying clearly what I want.*
start up 1 Start up means the same as start VERB 5. ❑ *The cost of starting up a day-care centre for children ranges from $150,000 to $300,000.* **2** Start up means the same as start VERB 6. ❑ *He waited until they went inside the building before starting up the car and driving off.* ❑ *Put the key in the ignition and turn it to start the car up.*
NOUN [c, SING] (**starts**) **1** [c] A **start** is when you do something that you were not doing before and you continue doing it. ❑ *After several starts, she read the report properly.* **2** [SING] The **start** of something is the time it

starts. = beginning ❑ *1918, four years after the start of the Great War* **3** [c] A **start** is a sudden slight movement of the body, caused by surprise or fear. ❑ *Sylvia woke with a start.*
PHRASE **for a start** or **to start with** You use **for a start** or **to start with** to introduce the first of a number of things or reasons that you want to mention or could mention. ❑ *You must get her name and address, and that can be a problem for a start.*

start·er /ˈstɑːtə/ NOUN [c] (**starters**) (*mainly BrE*; *in AmE*, usually use **appetizer**) A **starter** is a small quantity of food that is served as the first course of a meal.

start·ing point also **starting-point** NOUN [c] (**starting points**) **1** Something that is a **starting point for** a discussion or process can be used to begin it or act as a basis for it. = basis ❑ *These proposals represent a realistic starting point for negotiation.* **2** When you make a journey, your **starting point** is the place from which you start. ❑ *They had already walked a couple of miles or more from their starting point.*

star·tle /ˈstɑːtəl/ VERB [T] (**startles**, **startling**, **startled**) If something sudden and unexpected **startles** you, it surprises and frightens you slightly. ❑ *The telephone startled him.*
star·tled /ˈstɑːtəld/ ADJ ❑ *Martha gave her a startled look.*

star·tling /ˈstɑːtəlɪŋ/ ADJ Something that is **startling** is so different, unexpected, or remarkable that people react to it with surprise. ❑ *Sometimes the results may be rather startling.*

star·va·tion /stɑːˈveɪʃən/ NOUN [U] **Starvation** is extreme suffering or death, caused by lack of food. ❑ *Over three hundred people have died of starvation since the beginning of the year.*

starve /stɑːv/ VERB [I, T] (**starves**, **starving**, **starved**) **1** [I] If people **starve**, they suffer greatly from lack of food which sometimes leads to their death. ❑ *A number of the prisoners we saw are starving.* ❑ *In the 1930s, millions of Ukrainians starved to death or were deported.* **2** [T] To **starve** someone means not to give them any food. ❑ *He said the only alternative was to starve the people, and he said this could not be allowed to happen.* **3** [T] If a person or thing is **starved of** something that they need, they are suffering because they are not getting enough of it. ❑ *The electricity industry is not the only one to have been starved of investment.*

✪ **state** ◆◆◆ /steɪt/ NOUN, ADJ, VERB
NOUN [c, SING] (**states**) **1** [c] You can refer to countries as **states**, particularly when you are discussing politics. = country ❑ *Mexico is a secular state and does not have diplomatic relations with the Vatican.* ❑ *Some weeks ago I recommended to EU member states that we should have discussions with the Americans.* **2** [c] Some large countries such as the US are divided into smaller areas called **states**. ❑ *Leaders of the Southern states are meeting in Louisville.* ❑ *New York State* **3** [SING] You can refer to the government of a country as **the state**. ❑ *The state does not collect enough revenue to cover its expenditure.* **4** [c] When you talk about the **state of** someone or something, you are referring to the condition they are in or what they are like at a particular time. = condition ❑ *For the first few months after Daniel died, I was in a state of clinical depression.* ❑ *He will be in a state of great emotional shock due to his wife's death.* ❑ *The president declared a state of emergency.*
PHRASES **not in a fit state** If you say that someone is **not in a fit state to** do something, you mean that they are too upset or ill to do it. ❑ *When you left our place, you weren't in a fit state to drive.*
in a state or **into a state** If you are **in a state** or if you get **into a state**, you are very upset or nervous about something. ❑ *I was in a terrible state because nobody could understand why I had this illness.*
lie in state If the dead body of an important person **lies in state**, it is publicly displayed for a few days before it is buried. ❑ *the 30,000 people who filed past the cardinal's body while it lay in state last week*
ADJ **1** [state + N] State industries or organizations are financed and organized by the government rather than private companies. ❑ *reform of the state social-security system*

2 [state + N] A **state** occasion is a formal one involving the head of a country. ❑ *The president of the Czech Republic is in Washington on a state visit.*

VERB [T] (**states, stating, stated**) If you **state** something, you say or write it in a formal or definite way. = declare, relate ❑ *Clearly state your address and telephone number.* ❑ *The police report stated that he was arrested for allegedly assaulting his wife.* ❑ *The table clearly states the amount of fat found in commonly used foods.* ❑ *Buyers who do not apply within the stated period can lose their deposits.*

→ See also **head of state**

✪ state·ment ◆◆◇ /ˈsteɪtmənt/ NOUN [c] (**statements**) **1** A **statement** is something that you say or write which gives information in a formal or definite way. ❑ *Andrew now disowns that statement, saying he was depressed when he made it.* ❑ *'Things are moving ahead.' – I found that statement vague and unclear.* **2** A **statement** is an official or formal announcement that is issued on a particular occasion. ❑ *The statement by the military denied any involvement in last night's attack.* **3** You can refer to the official account of events which a suspect or a witness gives to the police as a **statement**. ❑ *The 350-page report was based on statements from witnesses to the events.* **4** If you describe an action or thing as a **statement**, you mean that it clearly expresses a particular opinion or idea that you have. ❑ *The following recipe is a statement of another kind – food is fun!* **5** A printed document showing how much money has been paid into and taken out of a bank or investment account is called a **statement**. ❑ *the address at the top of your monthly statement*

✪ state-of-the-art ADJ If you describe something as **state-of-the-art**, you mean that it is the best available because it has been made using the most modern techniques and technology. ❑ *the production of state-of-the-art military equipment* ❑ *state-of-the-art technology*

states·man /ˈsteɪtsmən/ NOUN [c] (**statesmen**) A **statesman** is an important and experienced politician, especially one who is widely known and respected. ❑ *Hamilton is a great statesman and political thinker.*

stat·ic /ˈstætɪk/ ADJ, NOUN

ADJ Something that is **static** does not move or change. ❑ *The number of young people obtaining qualifications has remained static or decreased.*

NOUN [U] **1** Static or **static electricity** is electricity which can be caused by things rubbing against each other and which collects on things such as your body or metal objects. ❑ *When the weather turns cold and dry, my clothes develop a static problem.* **2** If there is **static** on the radio or television, you hear a series of loud noises which spoils the sound. ❑ *After only a minute an authoritative voice came through the static on the radio.*

sta·tion ◆◆◇ /ˈsteɪʃən/ NOUN, VERB

NOUN [c] (**stations**) **1** A **station** or a railway **station** is a building by a railway track where trains stop so that people can get on or off. ❑ *Ingrid went with him to the railway station to see him off.* **2** A bus **station** is a building, usually in a town or city, where buses stop, usually for a while, so that people can get on or off. ❑ *I walked the two miles back to the bus station and bought a ticket home.* **3** If you talk about a particular radio or television **station**, you are referring to the company that broadcasts programmes. ❑ *an independent local radio station*

VERB [PASSIVE] (**stations, stationing, stationed**) If soldiers or officials **are stationed** in a place, they are sent there to do a job or to work for a period of time. ❑ *Reports from the capital, Lomé, say troops are stationed on the streets.*

→ See also **police station, power station**

sta·tion·ary /ˈsteɪʃənri, AmE -neri/ ADJ Something that is **stationary** is not moving. ❑ *Stationary cars in traffic jams cause a great deal of pollution.*

sta·tion·ery /ˈsteɪʃənri, AmE -neri/ NOUN [U] **Stationery** is paper, envelopes, and other materials or equipment used for writing. ❑ *envelopes and other office stationery*

✪ sta·tis·tic ◆◇◇ /stəˈtɪstɪk/ NOUN [c, U] (**statistics**) (*academic word*) **1** [c] **Statistics** are facts which are obtained from analysing information expressed in numbers, for example information about the number of times that something happens. = figures, numbers

❑ *Official statistics show real wages declining by 24%.* ❑ *There are no reliable statistics for the number of deaths in the battle.* **2** [U] **Statistics** is a branch of mathematics concerned with the study of information that is expressed in numbers. ❑ *a professor of mathematical statistics*

✪ sta·tis·ti·cal /stəˈtɪstɪkəl/ ADJ **Statistical** means relating to the use of statistics. = numerical ❑ *The report contains a great deal of statistical information.* ❑ *Other controls confirmed the statistical significance of the relationship.* **sta·tis·ti·cal·ly** /stəˈtɪstɪkli/ ADV ❑ *The results are not statistically significant.* ❑ *Statistically, ninety-eight per cent of all acute sunstroke cases are fatal.*

✪ stat·is·ti·cian /ˌstætɪˈstɪʃən/ NOUN [c] (**statisticians**) A **statistician** is a person who studies statistics or who works using statistics. = analyst, economist ❑ *Government statisticians published figures that showed a 0.9 per cent fall in the volume of goods sold in December.*

stat·ue /ˈstætʃuː/ NOUN [c] (**statues**) A **statue** is a large sculpture of a person or an animal, made of stone or metal. ❑ *a bronze statue of an Arabian horse*

stat·ure /ˈstætʃə/ NOUN [U] **1** Someone's **stature** is their height. ❑ *It's more than his physical stature that makes him remarkable.* ❑ *Mother was of very small stature, barely five feet tall.* **2** The **stature** of a person is the importance and reputation that they have. ❑ *Who can deny his stature as the world's greatest cellist?*

✪ sta·tus ◆◆◇ /ˈsteɪtəs/ NOUN [U] (*academic word*) **1** Your **status** is your social or professional position. ❑ *People of higher status tend more to use certain drugs.* ❑ *women and men of wealth and status* ❑ *Metal daggers and horses may have been status symbols of an invading elite.* **2** **Status** is the importance and respect that someone has among the public or a particular group. ❑ *Nurses are undervalued, and they never enjoy the same status as doctors.* **3** The **status** of something is the importance that people give it. = importance, prestige, standing, rank, station ❑ *Those things that can be assessed by external tests are being given unduly high status.* **4** A particular **status** is an official description that says what category a person, organization, or place belongs to, and gives them particular rights or advantages. ❑ *The Snoqualmie tribe regained its status as a federally recognized tribe.* **5** The **status** of something is its state of affairs at a particular time. ❑ *The council unanimously directed city staff to prepare a status report on the project.*

VOCABULARY BUILDER

status NOUN (*formal*)
Status is the importance and respect that someone has among the public or a particular group.
❑ *He felt he had been reduced to the status of an animal.*

importance NOUN
The **importance** of something is its quality of being significant, valued, or necessary in a particular situation.
❑ *Safety is of paramount importance.*

prestige NOUN (*formal*)
If a person, a country, or an organization has **prestige**, they are admired and respected because of the position they hold or the things they have achieved.
❑ *It was his responsibility for foreign affairs that gained him international prestige.*

rank NOUN
Someone's **rank** is the position or grade that they have in an organization.
❑ *He eventually rose to the rank of captain.*

✪ sta·tus quo /ˌsteɪtəs ˈkwəʊ/ NOUN [SING] The **status quo** is the state of affairs that exists at a particular time, especially in contrast to a different possible state of affairs. ❑ *By 492 votes to 391, the federation voted to maintain the status quo.* ❑ *They have no wish for any change in the status quo.* ❑ *We must not return to the status quo.*

stat·ute /ˈstætʃuːt/ NOUN [c, U] (**statutes**) A **statute** is a rule or law which has been made by a government or other organization and formally written down. ❑ *The new*

S

statute covers the care for, raising, and protection of children.

✪ **statu·tory** /ˈstætʃʊtəri, AmE -tɔːri/ ADJ (formal)
Statutory means relating to rules or laws which have been formally written down. ❑ *The FCC has no statutory authority to regulate the Internet.* ❑ *We had a statutory duty to report to Parliament.* ❑ *Compliance with the statutory requirements is necessary to secure the monies.*

staunch /stɔːntʃ/ ADJ (**stauncher, staunchest**)
A **staunch** supporter or believer is very loyal to a person, organization, or set of beliefs, and supports them strongly. = **steadfast** ❑ *He's a staunch supporter of controls on government spending.*
staunch·ly /ˈstɔːntʃli/ ADV ❑ *He was staunchly opposed to a public confession.*

stay ♦♦♦ /steɪ/ VERB, NOUN
VERB [I, LINK] (**stays, staying, stayed**) **1** [I] If you **stay** where you are, you continue to be there and do not leave. ❑ *'Stay here,' Trish said. 'I'll bring the car down the drive to take you back.'* **2** [I] If you **stay** in a town, or hotel, or at someone's house, you live there for a short time. ❑ *Gordon stayed at The Park Hotel, Milan.* ❑ *Can't you stay a few more days?* **3** [LINK] If someone or something **stays** in a particular state or situation, they continue to be in it. = **remain** ❑ *The Republican candidate said he would 'work like crazy to stay ahead'.* ❑ *community care networks that offer classes on how to stay healthy* **4** [I] If you **stay away from** a place, you do not go there. = **keep** ❑ *Management also stayed away from work during the strike.* **5** [I] If you **stay out of** something, you do not get involved in it. ❑ *In the past, the UN has stayed out of the internal affairs of countries unless invited in.*
PHRASES **stay put** If you **stay put**, you remain somewhere. ❑ *He was forced by his condition to stay put and remain out of politics.*
stay the night If you **stay the night** in a place, you sleep there for one night. ❑ *They had invited me to come to supper and stay the night.*
PHRASAL VERBS **stay in** If you **stay in** during the evening, you remain at home and do not go out. ❑ *If I stay in, my boyfriend cooks a wonderful lasagne or chicken or steak.*
stay on If you **stay on** somewhere, you remain there after other people have left or after the time when you were going to leave. ❑ *He had managed to arrange to stay on in Adelaide.*
stay out If you **stay out** at night, you remain away from home, especially when you are expected to be there. ❑ *That was the first time Elliot stayed out all night.*
stay up If you **stay up**, you remain out of bed at a time when most people have gone to bed or at a time when you are normally in bed yourself. ❑ *I used to stay up late with my mum and watch films.*
NOUN [c] A **stay** in a town, or hotel, or at someone's house is a short time you spend living there. ❑ *An experienced Indian guide is provided during your stay.*

stead·fast /ˈstedfɑːst, -fæst/ ADJ If someone is **steadfast** in something that they are doing, they are convinced that what they are doing is right and they refuse to change it or to give up. ❑ *He remained steadfast in his belief that he had done the right thing.*

✪ **steady** ♦♦◇ /ˈstedi/ ADJ, VERB
ADJ (**steadier, steadiest**) **1** A **steady** situation continues or develops gradually without any interruptions and is not likely to change quickly. = **regular, even** ❑ *Despite the steady progress of building work, the campaign against it is still going strong.* ❑ *The improvement in standards has been steady and persistent, but has attracted little comment from educationalists.* ❑ *a steady stream of traffic* **2** If an object is **steady**, it is firm and does not shake or move around. ❑ *Get as close to the subject as you can and hold the camera steady.* **3** If you look at someone or speak to them in a **steady** way, you look or speak in a calm, controlled way. ❑ *'Well, go on,' said Camilla, her voice fairly steady.* **4** If you describe a person as **steady**, you mean that they are sensible and reliable. ❑ *He was firm and steady unlike other men she knew.*
VERB [I, T] (**steadies, steadying, steadied**) **1** [I, T] If you **steady** something or if it **steadies**, it stops shaking or moving around. ❑ *Two men were on the bridge-deck,*

steadying a ladder. **2** [T] If you **steady yourself**, you control your voice or expression, so that people will think that you are calm and not nervous. = **compose** ❑ *Somehow she steadied herself and murmured, 'Have you got a cigarette?'*
✪ **steadi·ly** /ˈstedɪli/ ADV **1** [steadily after v] = **evenly**; ≠ **unevenly** ❑ *Relax as much as possible and keep breathing steadily.* ❑ *Overseas student numbers in Britain have been rising steadily for a decade.* ❑ *The company has steadily been losing market share to Boeing and Airbus.* **2** [steadily after v] ❑ *He moved back a little and stared steadily at Elaine.*

steal ♦♦◇ /stiːl/ VERB [I, T] (**steals, stealing, stole, stolen**) **1** [I, T] If you **steal** something **from** someone, you take it away from them without their permission and without intending to return it. ❑ *He was accused of stealing a small boy's bicycle.* ❑ *People who are drug addicts come in and steal.* **2** [T] If you **steal** someone else's ideas, you pretend that they are your own. ❑ *A writer is suing director Steven Spielberg for allegedly stealing his film idea.*

steam ♦◇◇ /stiːm/ NOUN, VERB
NOUN [U] **Steam** is the hot mist that forms when water boils. **Steam** vehicles and machines are operated using steam as a means of power. ❑ *In an electric power plant the heat converts water into high-pressure steam.*
PHRASES **full steam ahead** If something such as a plan or a project goes **full steam ahead**, it progresses quickly. ❑ *The administration was determined to go full steam ahead with its reform programme.*
run out of steam (*informal*) If you **run out of steam**, you stop doing something because you have no more energy or enthusiasm left. ❑ *I decided to paint the bathroom ceiling but ran out of steam halfway through.*
VERB [I, T] (**steams, steaming, steamed**) **1** [I] If something **steams**, it gives off steam. ❑ *restaurants where coffee pots steamed on their burners* **2** [I, T] If you **steam** food or if it **steams**, you cook it in steam rather than in water. ❑ *Steam the carrots until they are just beginning to be tender.* ❑ *Leave the vegetables to steam over the rice for the 20 minutes cooking time.*
PHRASAL VERB **steam up** When a window, mirror, or pair of glasses **steams up**, it becomes covered with steam or mist. ❑ *the irritation of living with lenses that steam up when you come in from the cold*

steel ♦◇◇ /stiːl/ NOUN, VERB
NOUN [C, U] (**steels**) **Steel** is a very strong metal which is made mainly from iron. Steel is used for making many things, for example bridges, buildings, vehicles, and cutlery. ❑ *steel pipes* ❑ *the iron and steel industry*
VERB [T] (**steels, steeling, steeled**) If you **steel yourself**, you prepare to deal with something unpleasant. ❑ *Those involved are steeling themselves for the coming battle.*

✪ **steep** /stiːp/ ADJ (**steeper, steepest**) **1** A **steep** slope rises at a very sharp angle and is difficult to go up. = **sheer**; ≠ **gradual, gentle** ❑ *San Francisco is built on 40 hills and some are very steep.* ❑ *a narrow, steep-sided valley* **2** A **steep** increase or decrease is something that is a very big increase or decrease. = **sharp**; ≠ **gradual, gentle** ❑ *Consumers are rebelling at steep price increases.* ❑ *Many smaller emerging Asian economies are suffering their steepest economic declines for half a century.* **3** (*informal*) If you say that the price of something is **steep**, you mean that it is expensive. ❑ *The annual premium can be a little steep, but will be well worth it if your dog is injured.*
✪ **steep·ly** /ˈstiːpli/ ADV **1** [steeply with v] ❑ *The road climbs steeply, with good views of Orvieto through the trees.* ❑ *steeply terraced valleys* **2** [steeply with v] ❑ *Unemployment is rising steeply.*

steer /stɪə/ VERB
VERB [T] (**steers, steering, steered**) **1** When you **steer** a car, boat, or plane, you control it so that it goes in the direction that you want. ❑ *What is it like to steer a ship this size?* **2** If you **steer** people towards a particular course of action or attitude, you try to lead them gently in that direction. ❑ *The new government is seen as one that will steer the country in the right direction.* **3** If you **steer** someone in a particular direction, you guide them there. = **guide** ❑ *Nick steered them into the nearest seats.*
PHRASE **steer clear of** If you **steer clear of** someone or

something, you deliberately avoid them. ❑ *I think a lot of people, women in particular, steer clear of these sensitive issues.*

steer·ing wheel NOUN [C] (**steering wheels**) In a car or other vehicle, the **steering wheel** is the wheel which the driver holds when he or she is driving.

❂**stem** ♦◇◇ /stem/ VERB, NOUN

◼VERB◼ [I, T] (**stems, stemming, stemmed**) ◼1◼ [I] If a condition or problem **stems from** something, it was caused originally by that thing. = originate ❑ *All my problems stem from drink.* ❑ *Much of the instability stems from the economic effects of the war.* ❑ *Much of London's energy and resilience stems from the fact that London has always been a city that relied on migrants.* ◼2◼ [T] (formal) If you **stem** something, you stop it spreading, increasing, or continuing. = stop ❑ *Austria has sent three army battalions to its border with Hungary to stem the flow of illegal immigrants.* ❑ *The authorities seem powerless to stem the rising tide of violence.* ❑ *He was still conscious, trying to stem the bleeding with his right hand.*

◼NOUN◼ [C] (**stems**) The **stem** of a plant is the thin, upright part on which the flowers and leaves grow. = stalk ❑ *He stooped down, cut the stem for her with his knife and handed her the flower.* ❑ *Tansy has a tall leafy stem and ferny foliage.*

❂**step** ♦♦♦ /step/ NOUN, VERB

◼NOUN◼ [C, SING] (**steps**) ◼1◼ [C] If you take a **step**, you lift your foot and put it down in a different place, for example when you are walking. ❑ *I took a step towards him.* ❑ *She walked on a few steps.* ◼2◼ [C] **Steps** are a series of surfaces at increasing or decreasing heights, on which you put your feet in order to walk up or down to a different level. ❑ *This little room was along a passage and down some steps.* ◼3◼ [C] A **step** is a raised flat surface in front of a door. ❑ *A little girl was sitting on the step of the end house.* ◼4◼ [C] A **step** is one of a series of actions that you take in order to achieve something. ❑ *He greeted the agreement as the first step towards peace.* ❑ *She is not content with her present lot and wishes to take steps to improve it.* ❑ *The elections were a step in the right direction, but there is a lot more to be done.* ◼5◼ [C] A **step** in a process is one of a series of stages. = stage ❑ *The next step is to put the theory into practice.* ❑ *Aristotle took the scientific approach a step further.* ◼6◼ [C] The **steps** of a dance are the sequences of foot movements which make it up. = movement ❑ *She was a better dancer than Gordon. At least she knew the steps.* ◼7◼ [SING] Someone's **step** is the way they walk. ❑ *He quickened his step.*

◼PHRASES◼ **one step ahead of** If you stay **one step ahead of** someone or something, you manage to achieve more than they do or avoid competition or danger from them. ❑ *Successful travel is partly a matter of keeping one step ahead of the crowd.*

in step or **out of step** ◼1◼ If people who are walking or dancing are **in step**, they are moving their feet forward at exactly the same time as each other. If they are **out of step**, their feet are moving forward at different times. ❑ *They were almost the same height and they moved perfectly in step.* ◼2◼ If people are **in step** with each other, their ideas or opinions are the same. If they are **out of step** with each other, their ideas or opinions are different. ❑ *Moscow is anxious to stay in step with Washington.*

step by step If you do something **step by step**, you do it by progressing gradually from one stage to the next. ❑ *I am not rushing things and I'm taking it step by step.*

watch your step If someone tells you to **watch** your **step**, they are warning you to be careful about how you behave or what you say so that you do not get into trouble. ❑ *He said I'd come to a bad end, if I didn't watch my step.*

◼VERB◼ [I] (**steps, stepping, stepped**) If you **step on** something or **step** in a particular direction, you put your foot on the thing or move your foot in that direction. ❑ *This was the moment when Neil Armstrong became the first man to step on the Moon.* ❑ *She accidentally stepped on his foot on a crowded commuter train.*

◼PHRASAL VERBS◼ **step back** If you **step back** and think about a situation, you think about it as if you were not involved in it. = stand back ❑ *I stepped back and analysed the situation.*

step down or **step aside** If someone **steps down** or **steps**

aside, they resign from an important job or position, often in order to let someone else take their place. = stand down ❑ *Judge Ito said that if his wife was called as a witness, he would step down as trial judge.*

step in If you **step in**, you get involved in a difficult situation because you think you can or should help with it. = intervene ❑ *If no agreement was reached, the army would step in.*

step up If you **step up** something, you increase it or increase its intensity. = increase ❑ *He urged donors to step up their efforts to send aid to Somalia.*

ste·reo /ˈsteriəʊ/ ADJ, NOUN

◼ADJ◼ **Stereo** is used to describe a sound system in which the sound is played through two speakers. ❑ *loudspeakers that give all-round stereo sound*

◼NOUN◼ [C] (**stereos**) A **stereo** is a sound system with two speakers.

❂**ste·reo·type** /ˈsteriətaɪp/ NOUN, VERB

◼NOUN◼ [C] (**stereotypes**) A **stereotype** is a fixed general image or set of characteristics that a lot of people believe represent a particular type of person or thing. ❑ *There's always been a stereotype about successful businessmen.* ❑ *Such a crass observation does nothing but reinforce negative racial stereotypes.* ❑ *the cultural stereotypes of women in contemporary society*

◼VERB◼ [T] (**stereotypes, stereotyping, stereotyped**) If someone **is stereotyped** as something, people form a fixed general idea or image of them, so that it is assumed that they will behave in a particular way. = label, typecast ❑ *He was stereotyped by some as a renegade.* ❑ *Psychiatric patients are often stereotyped as dangerous.* ❑ *Their image in the media is stereotyped and distorted.*

❂**ste·reo·typi·cal** /ˌsteriəʊˈtɪpɪkəl/ ADJ A **stereotypical** idea of a type of person or thing is a fixed general idea that a lot of people have about it, that may be false in many cases. ❑ *These are men whose masculinity does not conform to stereotypical images of the unfeeling male.* ❑ *Dara challenges our stereotypical ideas about gender and femininity.* ❑ *People have a very stereotypical image of scientists as guys in white coats.*

ster·ile /ˈsteraɪl, AmE -rəl/ ADJ ◼1◼ Something that is **sterile** is completely clean and free from germs. ❑ *He always made sure that any cuts were protected by sterile dressings.* ◼2◼ A person or animal that is **sterile** is unable to have or produce babies. ❑ *George was sterile.*

ster·il·ity /stəˈrɪliti/ NOUN [U] ◼1◼ *the antiseptic sterility of the hospital* ◼2◼ *This disease causes sterility in both males and females.*

steri·lize /ˈsterɪlaɪz/ also **sterilise** VERB [T] (**sterilizes, sterilizing, sterilized**) ◼1◼ If you **sterilize** a thing or a place, you make it completely clean and free from germs. ❑ *Sulphur is also used to sterilize equipment.* ◼2◼ If a person or an animal **is sterilized**, they have a medical operation that makes it impossible for them to have or produce babies. ❑ *My wife was sterilized after the birth of her fourth child.*

steri·li·za·tion /ˌsterɪlaɪˈzeɪʃən, AmE -lɪˈz-/ NOUN [U, C] ◼1◼ [U] ❑ *the pasteurization and sterilization of milk* ◼2◼ [C, U] ❑ *In some cases, a sterilization is performed through the vaginal wall.*

ster·ling ♦♦◇ /ˈstɜːlɪŋ/ ADJ, NOUN

◼ADJ◼ (formal, approval) **Sterling** means very good in quality; used to describe someone's work or character. = excellent, outstanding ❑ *Those are sterling qualities to be admired in anyone.*

◼NOUN◼ [U] **Sterling** is the money system of Great Britain. ❑ *The stamps had to be paid for in sterling.*

stern /stɜːn/ ADJ (**sterner, sternest**) ◼1◼ **Stern** words or actions are very severe. ❑ *Mr Monroe issued a stern warning to those who persist in violence.* ◼2◼ Someone who is **stern** is very serious and strict. ❑ *Her father was stern and hard to please.*

stern·ly /ˈstɜːnli/ ADV ❑ *'We will take the necessary steps,' she said sternly.*

ster·oid /ˈsteroɪd, AmE ˈstɪr-/ NOUN [C] (**steroids**) A **steroid** is a type of chemical substance found in your body. Steroids can be artificially introduced into the bodies of athletes to improve their strength.

S

stew /stjuː, AmE stuː/ NOUN, VERB

NOUN [C, U] (**stews**) A **stew** is a meal which you make by cooking meat and vegetables in liquid at a low temperature. ❑ *She served him a bowl of beef stew.*

VERB [T] (**stews, stewing, stewed**) When you **stew** meat, vegetables, or fruit, you cook them slowly in liquid in a covered pot. ❑ *Stew the apple and blackberries to make a thick pulp.*

stew·ard /ˈstjuːəd, AmE ˈstuː-/ NOUN [C] (**stewards**)

1 A **steward** is a man who works on a ship, plane, or train, taking care of passengers and serving meals to them. **2** A **steward** is a man or woman who helps to organize a race, march, or other public event. ❑ *The steward at the march stood his ground while the rest of the marchers decided to run.*

stick ◆◇◇ /stɪk/ NOUN, VERB

NOUN [C] (**sticks**) **1** A **stick** is a thin branch which has fallen off a tree. ❑ *people carrying bundles of dried sticks to sell for firewood* **2** A **stick** is a long thin piece of wood which is used for a particular purpose. ❑ *lollipop sticks* ❑ *drum sticks* **3** Some long thin objects that are used in sports are called **sticks**. ❑ *lacrosse sticks* ❑ *hockey sticks* **4** A **stick of** something is a long thin piece of it. ❑ *a stick of celery* **5** (BrE; in AmE, use **cane**) A **stick** is a long thin piece of wood which is used for supporting someone's weight or for hitting people or animals.

PHRASE **get the wrong end of the stick** or **get hold of the wrong end of the stick** (*informal*) If someone **gets the wrong end of the stick** or **gets hold of the wrong end of the stick**, they do not understand something correctly and get the wrong idea about it. ❑ *I think someone has got the wrong end of the stick. They should have established the facts before speaking out.*

VERB [T, I] (**sticks, sticking, stuck**) **1** [T] (*informal*) If you **stick** something somewhere, you put it there in a rather casual way. ❑ *He folded the papers and stuck them in his desk drawer.* **2** [I, T] If you **stick** a pointed object **in** something, or if it **sticks in** something, it goes into it or through it by making a cut or hole. ❑ *They sent in loads of male nurses and stuck a needle in my back.* **3** [I] If something **is sticking out** from a surface or object, it extends up or away from it. If something **is sticking into** a surface or object, it is partly in it. ❑ *They lay where they had fallen from the crane, sticking out of the water.* **4** [T] If you **stick** one thing to another, you attach it using glue, Sellotape, or another sticky substance. ❑ *Don't forget to clip the token and stick it on your card.* **5** [I] If one thing **sticks to** another, it becomes attached to it and is difficult to remove. = **adhere** ❑ *The soil sticks to the blade and blocks the plough.* ❑ *Peel away the waxed paper if it has stuck to the bottom of the cake.* **6** [I] If something **sticks in** your mind, you remember it for a long time. ❑ *The incident stuck in my mind because it was the first example I had seen of racism in that country.* **7** [I] If something which can usually be moved **sticks**, it becomes fixed in one position. ❑ *The needle on the dial went right around to fifty feet, which was as far as it could go, and there it stuck.*

PHRASE **stick it out** If someone in an unpleasant or difficult situation **sticks it out**, they do not leave or give up. ❑ *I really didn't like New York, but I wanted to stick it out a little bit longer.*

PHRASAL VERBS **stick around** (*informal*) If you **stick around**, you stay where you are, often because you are waiting for something. ❑ *Stick around a while and see what develops.*
stick by 1 If you **stick by** someone, you continue to give them help or support. ❑ *friends who stuck by me during the difficult times* **2** If you **stick by** a promise, agreement, decision, or principle, you do what you said you would do, or do not change your mind. = **stick to** ❑ *But I made my decision then and stuck by it.*
stick out 1 If you **stick out** part of your body, you extend it away from your body. ❑ *She made a face and stuck out her tongue at him.* **2** If something **sticks out**, it is very noticeable because it is unusual. = **stand out** ❑ *What had Cutter done to make him stick out from the crowd?*
stick to 1 If you **stick to** something or someone when you are travelling, you stay close to them. ❑ *Let's stick to the road we know.* **2** If you **stick to** something, you

continue doing, using, saying, or talking about it, rather than changing to something else. ❑ *Perhaps he should have stuck to writing.* **3** If you **stick to** a promise, agreement, decision, or principle, you do what you said you would do, or do not change your mind. = **stick by** ❑ *Immigrant support groups are waiting to see if he sticks to his word.*
stick together If people **stick together**, they stay with each other and support each other. ❑ *If we all stick together, we ought to be okay.*
stick up for If you **stick up for** a person or a principle, you support or defend them forcefully. = **stand up for** ❑ *You would think my own father would stick up for me once in a while.*
stick with 1 If you **stick with** something, you do not change to something else. ❑ *If you're in a job that keeps you busy, stick with it.* **2** If you **stick with** someone, you stay close to them. ❑ *Tugging the woman's arm, she pulled her to her side saying, 'You just stick with me, dear.'*
→ See also **stuck**
◆ **stick your neck out** → see **neck**; **stick to your guns** → see **gun**

stick·er /ˈstɪkə/ NOUN [C] (**stickers**) A **sticker** is a small piece of paper or plastic, with writing or a picture on one side, that you can stick onto a surface. ❑ *a bumper sticker that said, Flowers Make Life Lovelier*

sticky /ˈstɪki/ ADJ (**stickier, stickiest**) **1** A **sticky** substance is soft, or thick and liquid, and can stick to other things. Sticky things are covered with a sticky substance. ❑ *sticky toffee* ❑ *If the dough is sticky, add more flour.* **2** **Sticky** weather is unpleasantly hot and damp. = **muggy** ❑ *four desperately hot, sticky days in the middle of August* **3** (*informal*) A **sticky** situation involves problems or is embarrassing. ❑ *Inevitably the transition will yield some sticky moments.*

stiff /stɪf/ ADJ, ADV

ADJ (**stiffer, stiffest**) **1** Something that is **stiff** is firm or does not bend easily. = **rigid** ❑ *The furniture was stiff, uncomfortable, too delicate, and too neat.* ❑ *His gaberdine trousers were brand new and stiff.* **2** Something such as a door or drawer that is **stiff** does not move as easily as it should. ❑ *Train doors have handles on the inside. They are stiff so that they cannot be opened accidentally.* **3** If you are **stiff**, your muscles or joints hurt when you move, because of illness or because of too much exercise. ❑ *The mud bath is particularly recommended for relieving tension and stiff muscles.* **4** **Stiff** behaviour is rather formal and not very friendly or relaxed. ❑ *They always seemed a little awkward with each other, a bit stiff and formal.* **5** **Stiff** can be used to mean difficult or severe. ❑ *She faces stiff competition in the Best Actress category.* **6** [V N + stiff] If someone bores you **stiff**, worries you **stiff**, or scares you **stiff**, they bore, worry, or scare you very much. ❑ *Even if he bores you stiff, it is good manners not to let him know it.*

ADV [ADJ + stiff] (*informal, emphasis*) If you are bored **stiff**, worried **stiff**, or scared **stiff**, you are extremely bored, worried, or scared. ❑ *Anna tried to look interested. Actually, she was bored stiff.*

stiff·ly /ˈstɪfli/ ADV **1** *Moira sat stiffly upright in her straight-backed chair.* **2** *He climbed stiffly from the Volkswagen.* **3** *'Why don't you borrow your sister's car?' said Cassandra stiffly.*

stiff·en /ˈstɪfən/ VERB

VERB [I, T] (**stiffens, stiffening, stiffened**) **1** [I] If you **stiffen**, you stop moving and stand or sit with muscles that are suddenly tense, for example because you feel afraid or angry. ❑ *Ada stiffened at the sound of his voice.* **2** [I, T] If your muscles or joints **stiffen**, or if something **stiffens** them, they become difficult to bend or move. ❑ *The blood supply to the skin is reduced when muscles stiffen.* **3** [T] If something such as cloth **is stiffened**, it is made firm so that it does not bend easily. ❑ *This special paper was actually thin, soft Sugiwara paper that had been stiffened with a kind of paste.*

PHRASAL VERB **stiffen up** **Stiffen up** means the same as **stiffen** VERB 2. ❑ *These clothes restrict your freedom of movement and stiffen up the whole body.*

sti·fle /ˈstaɪfəl/ VERB [T] (**stifles, stifling, stifled**) **1** (*disapproval*) If someone **stifles** something you consider to be a good thing, they prevent it from continuing. = repress ❑ *Regulations on children stifled creativity.* **2** If you **stifle** a yawn or laugh, you prevent yourself from yawning or laughing. = suppress ❑ *She makes no attempt to stifle a yawn.* **3** If you **stifle** your natural feelings or behaviour, you prevent yourself from having those feelings or behaving in that way. = suppress ❑ *It is best to stifle curiosity and leave birds' nests alone.*

stig·ma /'stɪɡmə/ NOUN [C, U] (**stigmas**) If something has a **stigma** attached to it, people think it is something to be ashamed of. ❑ *There is still a stigma attached to cancer.*

still ♦♦♦ /stɪl/ ADV, ADJ, NOUN

ADV **1** If a situation that used to exist **still** exists, it has continued and exists now. ❑ *I still dream of home.* ❑ *Brian's toe is still badly swollen and he cannot put on his shoe.* **2** [still before v] If something that has not yet happened could **still** happen, it is possible that it will happen. If something that has not yet happened is **still to** happen, it will happen at a later time. ❑ *Big money could still be made if the crisis keeps oil prices high.* ❑ *We could still make it, but we won't get there till three.* **3** ['be' still + N] If you say that there **is still** an amount of something left, you are emphasizing that there is that amount left. ❑ *There are still some outstanding problems.* **4** [still before v] You use **still** to emphasize that something remains the case or is true in spite of what you have just said. = nonetheless ❑ *I'm average for my height. But I still feel I'm fatter than I should be.* **5** [still with CL] You use **still** to indicate that a problem or difficulty is not really worth worrying about. ❑ *Their luck had simply run out. Still, never fear.* **6** [still + N/ADV] You use **still** in expressions such as **still further**, **still another**, and **still more** to show that you find the number or quantity of things you are referring to surprising or excessive. = even ❑ *We look forward to strengthening still further our already close co-operation with the police.* **7** [still with COMPAR] You use **still** with comparatives to indicate that something has even more of a quality than something else. ❑ *Formula One motor racing is supposed to be dangerous. 'Indycar' racing is supposed to be more dangerous still.*

ADJ (**stiller, stillest**) **1** [still after v] If you stay **still**, you stay in the same position and do not move. ❑ *David had been dancing about like a child, but suddenly he stood still and looked at Brad.* **2** If air or water is **still**, it is not moving. ❑ *The night air was very still.* **3** If a place is **still**, it is quiet and shows no sign of activity. = quiet ❑ *In the room it was very still.* **4** Drinks that are **still** do not contain any bubbles of carbon dioxide. ❑ *a glass of still water*

NOUN [C] (**stills**) **1** A **still** is a photograph taken from a film which is used for publicity purposes. ❑ *stills from the James Bond movie series* **2** A **still** is a piece of equipment used to make strong alcoholic drinks by a process called distilling.

still·ness /'stɪlnəs/ NOUN [U] ❑ *Four deafening explosions shattered the stillness of the night air.*

USAGE NOTE

still

You usually put **still** after the first auxiliary in a verb group. Do not say, for example, '~~He still was waiting~~'. He **was still** waiting.

---

stimu·lant /'stɪmjʊlənt/ NOUN [C] (**stimulants**) A **stimulant** is a drug that makes your body work faster, often increasing your heart rate and making you less likely to sleep. ❑ *It is not a good idea to fight fatigue by taking stimulants.*

✪ **stimu·late ♦♢♢** /'stɪmjʊleɪt/ VERB [T] (**stimulates, stimulating, stimulated**) **1** To **stimulate** something means to encourage it to begin or develop further. = encourage ❑ *America's priority is rightly to stimulate its economy.* ❑ *The Russian health service has stimulated public interest in home cures.* **2** If you **are stimulated** by something, it makes you feel full of ideas and enthusiasm. ❑ *Bill was stimulated by the challenge.* **3** If something **stimulates** a part of a person's body, it causes it to move or start working. ❑ *Exercise stimulates the digestive and excretory systems.* ❑ *The body is stimulated to build up resistance.*

✪ **stimu·la·tion** /ˌstɪmjʊ'leɪʃən/ NOUN [U] **1** an economy in need of stimulation **2** Many enjoy the mental stimulation of a challenging job. **3** physical stimulation ❑ *the chemical stimulation of drugs*

stimu·lat·ing /'stɪmjʊleɪtɪŋ/ ADJ **1** *It is a complex yet stimulating book.* **2** *the stimulating effect of adrenaline*

✪ **stimu·lus** /'stɪmjʊləs/ NOUN [C, U] (**stimuli**) A **stimulus** is something that encourages activity in people or things. ❑ *Interest rates could fall soon and be a stimulus to the US economy.* ❑ *It is through our nervous system that we adapt ourselves to our environment and to all external stimuli.*

sting /stɪŋ/ VERB, NOUN

VERB [I, T] (**stings, stinging, stung**) **1** [I, T] If a plant, animal, or insect **stings** you, a sharp part of it, usually covered with poison, is pushed into your skin so that you feel a sharp pain. ❑ *The nettles stung their legs.* **2** [I, T] If a part of your body **stings**, or if a substance **stings** it, you feel a sharp pain there. ❑ *His cheeks were stinging from the icy wind.* **3** [T] If someone's remarks **sting** you, they make you feel hurt and annoyed. = hurt ❑ *Some of the criticism has stung him.*

NOUN [C] (**stings**) **1** The **sting** of an insect or animal is the part that stings you. ❑ *Remove the bee sting with tweezers.* **2** If you feel a **sting**, you feel a sharp pain in your skin or other part of your body. ❑ *This won't hurt – you will just feel a little sting.*

stint /stɪnt/ NOUN [C] (**stints**) A **stint** is a period of time which you spend doing a particular job or activity or working in a particular place. ❑ *He is returning to this country after a five-year stint in Hong Kong.*

stipu·late /'stɪpjʊleɪt/ VERB [T] (**stipulates, stipulating, stipulated**) If you **stipulate** a condition or **stipulate that** something must be done, you say clearly that it must be done. = specify ❑ *She could have stipulated that she would pay when she collected the computer.*

stipu·la·tion /ˌstɪpjʊ'leɪʃən/ NOUN [C] (**stipulations**) = condition ❑ *Clifford's only stipulation is that his clients obey his advice.*

stir ♦♢♢ /stɜː/ VERB, NOUN

VERB [T, I] (**stirs, stirring, stirred**) **1** [T] If you **stir** a liquid or other substance, you move it around or mix it in a container using something such as a spoon. ❑ *Stir the soup for a few seconds.* ❑ *There was Mrs Bellingham, stirring sugar into her tea.* **2** [I] (*written*) If you **stir**, you move slightly, for example because you are uncomfortable or beginning to wake up. = move ❑ *Eileen shook him, and he started to stir.* **3** [I] (*written*) If you do not **stir from** a place, you do not move from it. = move ❑ *She had not stirred from the house that evening.* **4** [I, T] (*written*) If something **stirs** or if the wind **stirs** it, it moves gently in the wind. = move ❑ *Palm trees stir in the soft Pacific breeze.* **5** [I, T] (*written*) If a particular memory, feeling, or mood **stirs** or **is stirred in** you, you begin to think about it or feel it. ❑ *Then a memory stirs in you and you start feeling anxious.* ❑ *Amy remembered the anger he had stirred in her.*

PHRASAL VERB **stir up** **1** If something **stirs up** dust or **stirs up** mud in water, it causes it to rise up and move around. ❑ *They saw first a cloud of dust and then the car that was stirring it up.* **2** If you **stir up** a particular mood or situation, usually a bad one, you cause it. ❑ *As usual, Harriet is trying to stir up trouble.*

NOUN [SING] If an event causes a **stir**, it causes great excitement, shock, or anger among people. = commotion ❑ *His film has caused a stir.*

→ See also **stirring**

stir·ring /'stɜːrɪŋ/ ADJ, NOUN

ADJ A **stirring** event, performance, or account of something makes people very excited or enthusiastic. = rousing ❑ *The president made a stirring speech.*

NOUN [C] (**stirrings**) [usu stirring 'of' N] A **stirring of** a feeling or thought is the beginning of one. ❑ *I feel a stirring of curiosity.*

stitch /stɪtʃ/ VERB, NOUN

VERB [I, T] (**stitches, stitching, stitched**) **1** [I, T] If you **stitch** cloth, you use a needle and thread to join two pieces together or to make a decoration. = sew ❑ *Fold the fabric and stitch the two layers together.* ❑ *We stitched incessantly.*

S

2 [T] When doctors **stitch** a wound, they use a special needle and thread to sew the skin together. ❑ *Jill washed and stitched the wound.*
NOUN [C, U, SING] (**stitches**) **1** [C] **Stitches** are the short pieces of thread that have been sewn in a piece of cloth. ❑ *a row of straight stitches* **2** [C] In knitting and crochet, a **stitch** is a loop made by one turn of wool around a knitting needle or crochet hook. ❑ *Her mother counted the stitches on her knitting needles.* **3** [U] If you sew or knit something in a particular **stitch**, you sew or knit in a way that produces a particular pattern. ❑ *The design can be worked in cross stitch.* **4** [C] A **stitch** is a piece of thread that has been used to sew the skin of a wound together. ❑ *He had six stitches in a head wound.* **5** [SING] A **stitch** is a sharp pain in your side, usually caused by running or laughing a lot. ❑ *One of them was laughing so much he got a stitch.*

stock ♦♦◇ /stɒk/ NOUN, VERB, ADJ
NOUN [C, U] (**stocks**) **1** [C] (*business*) **Stocks** are shares in the ownership of a company, or investments on which a fixed amount of interest will be paid. ❑ *the buying and selling of stocks and shares* **2** [U] (*business*) A company's **stock** is the amount of money which the company has through selling shares. ❑ *Two years later, when Compaq went public, their stock was valued at $38 million.* **3** [U] A shop's **stock** is the total amount of goods which it has available to sell. ❑ *When a nearby shop burned down, our stock was ruined by smoke.* **4** [C] If you have a **stock of** things, you have a supply of them stored in a place ready to be used. ❑ *I keep a stock of cassette tapes describing various relaxation techniques.* **5** [C, U] **Stock** is a liquid, usually made by boiling meat, bones, or vegetables in water, that is used to give flavour to soups and sauces. ❑ *Finally, add the beef stock.*
PHRASES **in stock** or **out of stock** If goods are **in stock**, a shop has them available to sell. If they are **out of stock**, it does not. ❑ *Check that your size is in stock.*
take stock If you **take stock**, you pause to think about all the aspects of a situation or event before deciding what to do next. ❑ *It was time to take stock of the situation.*
VERB [T] (**stocks, stocking, stocked**) **1** If a shop **stocks** particular products, it keeps a supply of them to sell. ❑ *The shop stocks everything from cigarettes to recycled paper.* **2** If you **stock** something such as a cupboard, shelf, or room, you fill it with food or other things. ❑ *I worked stocking shelves in a grocery store.* ❑ *Some families stocked their cellars with food and water.*
PHRASAL VERB **stock up 1** **Stock up** means the same as **stock** VERB 2. ❑ *I had to stock the boat up with food.* **2** If you **stock up on** something, you buy a lot of it, in case you cannot get it later. ❑ *The authorities have urged people to stock up on fuel.*
ADJ [stock + N] A **stock** answer, expression, or way of doing something is one that is very commonly used, especially when someone cannot be bothered to think of something new. = standard ❑ *My boss had a stock response – 'If it ain't broke, don't fix it!'*
✦ **lock, stock, and barrel** → see **barrel**

stock ex·change ♦◇◇ NOUN [C] (**stock exchanges**) (*business*) A **stock exchange** is a place where people buy and sell stocks and shares. **The stock exchange** is also the trading activity that goes on there and the trading organization itself. = stock market ❑ *The shortage of good stock has kept some investors away from the stock exchange.*

stock mar·ket ♦◇◇ NOUN [C] (**stock markets**) (*business*) The **stock market** consists of the general activity of buying stocks and shares, and the people and institutions that organize it. ❑ *He's been studying and playing the stock market since he was 14.*

stole /stəʊl/ IRREG FORM **Stole** is the past tense of **steal**.

sto·len /'stəʊlən/ IRREG FORM, ADJ
IRREG FORM **Stolen** is the past participle of **steal**.
ADJ If you refer to an object as **stolen**, you mean that someone has taken it without the owner's permission and without intending to return it. ❑ *We have now found the stolen car.*

stom·ach ♦◇◇ /'stʌmək/ NOUN, VERB
NOUN [C] (**stomachs**) **1** Your **stomach** is the organ inside your body where food is digested before it moves into the intestines. ❑ *He had an upset stomach.* **2** You can refer to the front part of your body below your waist as your **stomach**. = abdomen ❑ *The children lay down on their stomachs.* **3** If the front part of your body below your waist feels uncomfortable because you are feeling worried or frightened, you can refer to it as your **stomach**. ❑ *His stomach was in knots.* **4** If you say that someone has a strong **stomach**, you mean that they are not disgusted by things that disgust most other people. ❑ *Surgery often demands actual physical strength, as well as the possession of a strong stomach.*
PHRASE **on an empty stomach** If you do something **on an empty stomach**, you do it without having eaten. ❑ *Avoid drinking on an empty stomach.*
VERB [T] (**stomachs, stomaching, stomached**) If you cannot **stomach** something, you cannot accept it because you dislike it or disapprove of it. ❑ *I could never stomach the cruelty involved in the wounding of animals.*

stone ♦♦◇ /stəʊn/ NOUN, VERB
NOUN [C, U] (**stones**) **1** [C, U] **Stone** is a hard, solid substance found in the ground and often used for building houses. ❑ *He could not tell whether the floor was wood or stone.* ❑ *People often don't appreciate that marble is a natural stone.* **2** [C] A **stone** is a small piece of rock that is found on the ground. ❑ *He removed a stone from his shoe.* **3** [C] A **stone** is a large piece of stone put somewhere in memory of a person or event, or as a religious symbol. ❑ *The monument consists of a circle of gigantic stones.* **4** [U] **Stone** is used in expressions such as **set in stone** and **tablets of stone** to suggest that an idea or rule is firm and fixed, and cannot be changed. ❑ *He is merely throwing the idea forward for discussion, it is not cast in stone.* **5** [C] You can refer to a jewel as a **stone**. ❑ *a diamond ring with three stones* **6** [C] A **stone** is a small hard ball of minerals and other substances which sometimes forms in a person's kidneys or gallbladder. ❑ *He had kidney stones.* **7** [C] (*mainly BrE*; in AmE, usually use **pit**) The **stone** in a plum, cherry, or other fruit is the large hard seed in the middle of it.
VERB [T] (**stones, stoning, stoned**) If people **stone** someone or something, they throw stones at them. ❑ *Youths burned cars and stoned police.*

stood /stʊd/ IRREG FORM **Stood** is the past tense and past participle of **stand**.

stop ♦♦♦ /stɒp/ VERB, NOUN
VERB [I, T] (**stops, stopping, stopped**) **1** [I, T] If you have been doing something and then you **stop** doing it, you no longer do it. ❑ *Stop throwing those stones!* ❑ *Does either of the parties want to stop the fighting?* ❑ *She stopped in mid-sentence.* **2** [T] If you **stop** something from happening, or you **stop** something happening, you prevent it from happening or prevent it from continuing. ❑ *He proposed a new diplomatic initiative to try to stop the war.* ❑ *He would do what he must to stop her from destroying him.* **3** [I] If an activity or process **stops**, it is no longer happening. ❑ *The rain had stopped and a star or two was visible over the mountains.* ❑ *The system overheated and filming had to stop.* **4** [I, T] If something such as a machine **stops** or **is stopped**, it is no longer moving or working. ❑ *The clock stopped at 11:59 Saturday night.* ❑ *Arnold stopped the engine and got out of the car.* **5** [I, T] When a moving person or vehicle **stops** or **is stopped**, they no longer move and they remain in the same place. = halt ❑ *The car failed to stop at an army checkpoint.* ❑ *He stopped and let her catch up with him.* **6** [I, T] If someone does not **stop to** think or **to** explain, they continue with what they are doing without taking any time to think about or explain it. = pause ❑ *She doesn't stop to think about what she's saying.* ❑ *There is something rather strange about all this if one stops to consider it.* **7** [I] If you say that a quality or state **stops** somewhere, you mean that it exists or is true up to that point, but no further. = end ❑ *The cafe owner has put up the required 'no smoking' signs, but thinks his responsibility stops there.* **8** [I] If you **stop** somewhere on a journey, you stay there for a short while. ❑ *He insisted we stop at a small restaurant just outside of Atlanta.*
PHRASES **stop at nothing** (*emphasis*) If you say that

someone will **stop at nothing to** get something, you are emphasizing that they are willing to do things that are extreme, wrong, or dangerous in order to get it. ❑ *Their motive is money, and they will stop at nothing to get it.*

know when to stop If you say that someone does not **know when to stop**, you mean that they do not control their own behaviour very well and so they often annoy or upset other people. ❑ *Like many politicians before him, Mr Bentley did not know when to stop.*

PHRASAL VERBS **stop by** or **stop in** (*informal*) If you **stop by** somewhere, you make a short visit to a person or place. ❑ *Perhaps I'll stop by the hospital.*

stop off If you **stop off** somewhere, you stop for a short time in the middle of a trip. ❑ *The president stopped off in Poland on his way to Munich for the economic summit.*

NOUN [SING, C] (**stops**) **1** [SING] If something that is moving comes **to a stop** or is brought **to a stop**, it slows down and no longer moves. = halt ❑ *People often wrongly open doors before the train has come to a stop.* **2** [C] A **stop** is a place where buses or trains regularly stop so that people can get on and off. ❑ *The closest subway stop is Houston Street.* **3** [C] A **stop** is a time or place at which you stop during a journey. ❑ *The last stop in Mr Robinson's lengthy tour was Paris.*

PHRASE **put a stop to something** If you **put a stop to** something that you do not like or approve of, you prevent it from happening or continuing. ❑ *His daughter should have stood up and put a stop to all these rumours.*

✦ **stop dead** → see **dead**; **stop short of** → see **short**; **stop in its tracks** → see **track**

stop·page /ˈstɒpɪdʒ/ NOUN [C] (**stoppages**) **1** (*business*) When there is a **stoppage**, people stop working because of a disagreement with their employers. = strike ❑ *Mineworkers in the Ukraine have voted for a one-day stoppage next month.* **2** (*mainly BrE; in AmE, use* **time out**) In football and some other sports, when there is a **stoppage**, the game stops for a short time, for example because a player is injured. The referee may add some extra time at the end of the game because of this.

✪ **stor·age** /ˈstɔːrɪdʒ/ NOUN [U] **1** If you refer to the **storage** of something, you mean that it is kept in a special place until it is needed. ❑ *the storage of toxic waste* ❑ *Some of the space will at first be used for storage.* **2 Storage** is the process of storing data in a computer. ❑ *His task is to ensure the fair use and storage of personal information held on computer.* ❑ *data-storage devices*

✪ **store** ◆◆◇ /stɔː/ NOUN, VERB
NOUN [C] (**stores**) **1** A **store** is a building or part of a building where things are sold. In British English, **store** is used mainly to refer to a large shop selling a variety of goods, but in American English a **store** can be any size of shop. ❑ *They are selling them for $10 apiece at a few stores in Texas and Oklahoma.* ❑ *grocery stores* **2** A **store of** things is a supply of them that you keep somewhere until you need them. ❑ *I handed over my secret store of chocolate.* **3** A **store** is a place where things are kept while they are not being used. ❑ *a store for spent fuel from submarines*

PHRASE **in store** If something is **in store for** you, it is going to happen at some time in the future. ❑ *Surprises were also in store for me.*

VERB [T] (**stores, storing, stored**) **1** When you **store** things, you put them in a container or other place and leave them there until they are needed. = keep ❑ *Store the biscuits in an airtight tin.* **2** When you **store** information, you keep it in your memory, in a file, or in a computer. = save, keep; ≠ delete ❑ *Where in the brain do we store information about colours?* ❑ *chips for storing data in electronic equipment*

PHRASAL VERBS **store away Store away** means the same as **store** VERB 1. ❑ *He simply stored the tapes away.*
store up If you **store** something **up**, you keep it until you think that the time is right to use it. ❑ *Investors were storing up a lot of cash in anticipation of disaster.*
→ See also **department store**

sto·rey /ˈstɔːri/ (*in AmE, use* **story**) NOUN [C] (**storeys**) A **storey** of a building is one of its different levels, which is situated above or below other levels. ❑ *long brick buildings, two storeys high*

storm ◆◇◇ /stɔːm/ NOUN, VERB
NOUN [C] (**storms**) **1** A **storm** is very bad weather, with heavy rain, strong winds, and often thunder and lightning. ❑ *the violent storms which whipped the East Coast* **2** If something causes a **storm**, it causes an angry or excited reaction from a large number of people. ❑ *The photos caused a storm when they were first published.* **3** A **storm of** applause or other noise is a sudden loud amount of it made by an audience or other group of people in reaction to something. ❑ *His speech was greeted with a storm of applause.*

PHRASE **take something by storm** If someone or something **takes** a place **by storm**, they are extremely successful. ❑ *Kenya's long distance runners have taken the athletics world by storm.*

VERB [T, I] (**storms, storming, stormed**) **1** [T, I] If you **storm into** or **out of** a place, you enter or leave it quickly and noisily, because you are angry. ❑ *After a bit of an argument, he stormed out.* **2** [T] If a place that is being defended **is stormed**, a group of people attack it, usually in order to get inside it. ❑ *Government buildings have been stormed and looted.*

storm·ing /ˈstɔːmɪŋ/ NOUN [U] ❑ *the storming of the Bastille*

sto·ry ◆◆◆ /ˈstɔːri/ NOUN
NOUN [C] (**stories**) **1** A **story** is a description of imaginary people and events, which is written or told in order to entertain. ❑ *The second story in the book is titled 'The Scholar'.* ❑ *I shall tell you a story about four little rabbits.* **2** A **story** is a description of an event or something that happened to someone, especially a spoken description of it. ❑ *The parents all shared interesting stories about their children.* **3** The **story of** something is a description of all the important things that have happened to it since it began. ❑ *the story of the women's movement* **4** If someone invents a **story**, they give a false explanation or account of something. = tale, yarn ❑ *He invented one story about a cousin.* **5** A news **story** is a piece of news in a newspaper or in a news broadcast. ❑ *Those are some of the top stories in the news.* ❑ *They'll do anything for a story.*

PHRASES **a different story** You use a **different story** to refer to a situation, usually a bad one, which exists in one set of circumstances when you have mentioned that it does not exist in another set of circumstances. ❑ *Where Marcella lives, the rents are fairly cheap, but a little further north it's a different story.*
the same old story or **the old story** If you say **it's the same old story** or **it's the old story**, you mean that something unpleasant or undesirable seems to happen again and again. ❑ *It's the same old story. They want one person to do three people's jobs.*
only part of the story or **not the whole story** If you say that something is **only part of the story** or is **not the whole story**, you mean that the explanation or information given is not enough for a situation to be fully understood. ❑ *This may be true but it is only part of the story.*
someone's side of the story If someone tells you their **side of the story**, they tell you why they behaved in a particular way and why they think they were right, when other people think that person behaved wrongly. ❑ *He had already made up his mind before even hearing her side of the story.*

stout /staʊt/ ADJ (**stouter, stoutest**) **1** A **stout** person is rather fat. ❑ *He was a tall, stout man with grey hair.* **2 Stout** shoes, branches, or other objects are thick and strong. = sturdy ❑ *I hope you've both got stout shoes.*

✪ **straight** ◆◆◇ /streɪt/ ADJ, ADV
ADJ (**straighter, straightest**) **1** A **straight** line or edge continues in the same direction and does not bend or curve. ≠ curvy, curved, bent, wavy, twisted ❑ *Keep the boat in a straight line.* ❑ *Using the straight edge as a guide, trim the cloth to size.* ❑ *There wasn't a single straight wall in the building.* ❑ *His teeth were perfectly straight.* **2 Straight** hair has no curls or waves in it. ❑ *Grace had long straight dark hair which she wore in a bun.* **3** [straight + N] If you give someone a **straight** answer, you answer them clearly and honestly. ❑ *What a shifty arguer he is, refusing ever to give a straight answer to a straight question.* **4** [straight + N]

S

Straight means following one after the other, with no gaps or intervals. ❑ *They'd won 12 straight games before they lost.* **5** [straight + N] A **straight** choice or a **straight** fight involves only two people or things. ❑ *It's a straight choice between low-paid jobs and no jobs.* **6** If you describe someone as **straight**, you mean that they are normal and conventional, for example in their opinions and in the way they live. ❑ *Dorothy was described as a very straight woman, a very strict Christian who was married to her job.* ❑ PHRASE **get something straight** (*spoken*) If you **get** something **straight**, you make sure that you understand it properly or that someone else does. ❑ *You need to get your facts straight.* ❑ ADV **1** [straight after v] **Straight** means in a way that does not bend or curve. ❑ *Stand straight and stretch the left hand to the right foot.* **2** [straight + PREP/ADV] You use **straight** to indicate that the way from one place to another is very direct, with no changes of direction. ❑ *squirting the medicine straight to the back of the child's throat* ❑ *He finished his conversation and stood up, looking straight at me.* **3** [straight + PREP/ADV] If you go **straight** to a place, you go there immediately. ❑ *As always, we went straight to the experts for advice.* **4** [straight after v] **Straight** means in a clear and honest way. ❑ *I lost my temper and told him straight that I hadn't been looking for any job.* **5** [N + straight] **Straight** means without any gaps or intervals. ❑ *He called from Washington, having been there for 31 hours straight.*

straight away also **straightaway** ADV [straight away with v] If you do something **straight away**, you do it immediately and without delay. = immediately ❑ *I should go and see a doctor straight away.*

❂ **straight•en** /ˈstreɪtən/ VERB
VERB [T, I] (**straightens, straightening, straightened**) **1** [T] If you **straighten** something, you make it neat or put it in its proper position. ❑ *She sipped her coffee and straightened a picture on the wall.* **2** [I] If you are standing in a relaxed or slightly bent position and then you **straighten**, you make your back or body straight and upright. ❑ *The three men straightened and stood waiting.* **3** [I, T] If you **straighten** something, or it **straightens**, it becomes straight. ≠ curve, bend, twist ❑ *Straighten both legs until they are fully extended.* ❑ *The road straightened and we were on a plateau.* ❑ PHRASAL VERBS **straighten out 1** Straighten out means the same as **straighten** VERB 3. ❑ *No one would dream of straightening out the church's knobbly spire.* **2** If you **straighten out** a confused situation, you succeed in getting it organized and cleaned up. = sort out ❑ *He would make an appointment with him to straighten out a couple of things.* **straighten up 1** Straighten up means the same as **straighten** VERB 1. ❑ *This is my job, to straighten up, to file things.* **2** Straighten up means the same as **straighten** VERB 2. ❑ *He straightened up and slipped his hands in his pockets.*

❂ **straight•forward** /ˌstreɪtˈfɔːwəd/ ADJ (*academic word, approval*) **1** If you describe something as **straightforward**, you approve of it because it is easy to do or understand. = uncomplicated, clear; ≠ complicated ❑ *Disposable nappies are fairly straightforward to put on.* ❑ *The question seemed straightforward enough.* ❑ *Cost accounting is a relatively straightforward process.* ❑ *simple straightforward language* **2** If you describe a person or their behaviour as **straightforward**, you approve of them because they are honest and direct, and do not try to hide their feelings. ❑ *She is very blunt, very straightforward, and very honest.*

❂ **strain** ◆◇◇ /streɪn/ NOUN, VERB
NOUN [C, U, SING] (**strains**) **1** [C, U] If **strain** is put on an organization or system, it has to do more than it is able to do. = pressure ❑ *The prison service is already under considerable strain.* ❑ *The vast expansion in secondary education is putting an enormous strain on the system.* **2** [U] [also strains] **Strain** is a state of worry and tension caused by a difficult situation. = stress ❑ *She was tired and under great strain.* **3** [SING] If you say that a situation is **a strain**, you mean that it makes you worried and tense. ❑ *I sometimes find it a strain to be responsible for the mortgage.* **4** [U] **Strain** is a force that pushes, pulls, or stretches something in a way that may damage it. ❑ *Place your hands under your buttocks to take some of the strain off your*

back. **5** [C, U] **Strain** is an injury to a muscle in your body, caused by using the muscle too much or twisting it. ❑ *Avoid muscle strain by warming up with slow jogging.* **6** [C] A **strain of** a germ, plant, or other organism is a particular type of it. ❑ *Every year new strains of influenza develop.* VERB [T] (**strains, straining, strained**) **1** To **strain** something means to make it do more than it is able to do. = stretch ❑ *The volume of scheduled flights is straining the air traffic control system.* ❑ *Resources will be further strained by new demands for housing.* **2** If you **strain** a muscle, you injure it by using it too much or twisting it. ❑ *He strained his back during a practice session.* **3** If you **strain to** do something, you make a great effort to do it when it is difficult to do. ❑ *I had to strain to hear.* **4** When you **strain** food, you separate the liquid part of it from the solid parts. ❑ *Strain the stock and put it back into the pan.*

strand /strænd/ NOUN, VERB
NOUN [C] (**strands**) A **strand of** something such as hair, wire, or thread is a single thin piece of it. ❑ *She tried to blow a grey strand of hair from her eyes.* VERB [T] (**strands, stranding, stranded**) If you **are stranded**, you are prevented from leaving a place, for example because of bad weather. ❑ *The climbers had been stranded by a storm.*

strange ◆◆◇ /streɪndʒ/ ADJ (**stranger, strangest**) **1** Something that is **strange** is unusual or unexpected, and makes you feel slightly nervous or afraid. = odd ❑ *Then a strange thing happened.* ❑ *There was something strange about the flickering blue light.* **2** [strange + N] A **strange** place is one that you have never been to before. A **strange** person is someone that you have never met before. = unfamiliar ❑ *I ended up alone in a strange city.* **strange•ness** /ˈstreɪndʒnəs/ NOUN [U] ❑ *the breathy strangeness of the music*
→ See also **stranger**

strange•ly /ˈstreɪndʒli/ ADV **1** If someone behaves **strangely**, they do something unusual or unexpected and make you feel slightly nervous or afraid. ❑ *She noticed he was acting strangely.* **2** [strangely with CL] (*emphasis*) You use **strangely** to emphasize that what you are saying is surprising. = surprisingly ❑ *Strangely, they hadn't invited her to join them.*

stran•ger /ˈstreɪndʒə/ NOUN [C, PL] (**strangers**) **1** [C] A **stranger** is someone you have never met before. ❑ *Telling a complete stranger about your life is difficult.* **2** [PL] If two people are **strangers**, they do not know each other. ❑ *The women knew nothing of the dead girl. They were strangers.* **3** [C] If you are a **stranger to** something, you have had no experience of it or do not understand it. ❑ *He is no stranger to controversy.*
→ See also **strange**

stran•gle /ˈstræŋɡəl/ VERB [T] (**strangles, strangling, strangled**) **1** To **strangle** someone means to kill them by squeezing their throat tightly so that they cannot breathe. = throttle ❑ *He tried to strangle a border policeman and steal his gun.* **2** To **strangle** something means to prevent it from succeeding or developing. ❑ *The country's economic plight is strangling its scientific institutions.*

strangle•hold /ˈstræŋɡəlhəʊld/ NOUN [SING] To have a **stranglehold on** something means to have control over it and prevent it from being free or from developing. ❑ *These companies are determined to keep a stranglehold on the banana industry.*

strap /stræp/ NOUN, VERB
NOUN [C] (**straps**) A **strap** is a narrow piece of leather, cloth, or other material. Straps are used to carry things, fasten things together, or to hold a piece of clothing in place. ❑ *Nancy gripped the strap of her beach bag.* ❑ *She pulled the strap of her nightgown onto her shoulder.* VERB [T] (**straps, strapping, strapped**) If you **strap** something somewhere, you fasten it there with a strap. ❑ *She strapped the baby seat into the car.*

❂ **stra•tegic** ◆◇◇ /strəˈtiːdʒɪk/ ADJ **1** **Strategic** means relating to the most important, general aspects of something such as a military operation or political policy, especially when these are decided in advance. = important, critical, key ❑ *the new strategic thinking which NATO leaders* produced at the recent London summit ❑ *The island is of strategic importance to France.* **2 Strategic** weapons are very powerful missiles that can be fired only after a decision to use them has been made by a political leader. ❑ *strategic nuclear weapons* **3** If you put something in a **strategic** position, you place it cleverly in a position where it will be most useful or have the most effect. ❑ *the marble benches Eve had placed at strategic points throughout the gardens, where the views were spectacular*

stra·tegi·cal·ly /strəˈtiːdʒɪkli/ ADV **1** *strategically important roads, bridges and buildings* **2** *We had kept its presence hidden with a strategically placed chair.*

✪**strat·egy** ♦♦◇ /ˈstrætədʒi/ NOUN [C, U] (**strategies**) (*academic word*) **1** [C, U] A **strategy** is a general plan or set of plans intended to achieve something, especially over a long period. = policy, plan ❑ *The energy secretary will present the strategy tomorrow afternoon.* ❑ *Next week, health ministers gather in Amsterdam to agree a strategy for controlling malaria.* ❑ *a customer-led marketing strategy* **2** [U] **Strategy** is the art of planning the best way to gain an advantage or achieve success, especially in war. ❑ *I've just been explaining the basic principles of strategy to my generals.*

straw /strɔː/ NOUN
NOUN [U, C] (**straws**) **1** [U] **Straw** consists of the dried, yellowish stalks from crops such as wheat or barley. ❑ *The barn was full of bales of straw.* ❑ *I stumbled through mud to a yard strewn with straw.* **2** [C] A **straw** is a thin tube of paper or plastic, which you use to suck a drink into your mouth. ❑ *a bottle of lemonade with a straw in it*
PHRASES **clutch at straws** If you **are clutching at straws** or **grasping at straws**, you are trying unusual or extreme ideas or methods because other ideas or methods have failed. ❑ *a badly thought-out plan from an administration clutching at straws*
the last straw or **the straw that broke the camel's back** If an event is **the last straw** or **the straw that broke the camel's back**, it is the latest in a series of unpleasant or undesirable events, and makes you feel that you cannot tolerate a situation any longer. ❑ *For him the Church's decision to allow the ordination of women had been the last straw.*
draw the short straw If you **draw the short straw**, you are chosen from a number of people to perform a job or duty that you will not enjoy. ❑ *if a few of your guests have drawn the short straw and agreed to drive others home after your summer barbecue*

straw·berry /ˈstrɔːbri, AmE -beri/ NOUN [C] (**strawberries**) A **strawberry** is a small, red fruit which is soft and juicy and has tiny yellow seeds on its skin. ❑ *strawberries and cream*

stray /streɪ/ VERB, ADJ, NOUN
VERB [I] (**strays, straying, strayed**) **1** If someone **strays** somewhere, they wander away from where they are supposed to be. ❑ *Tourists often get lost and stray into dangerous areas.* **2** If your mind or your eyes **stray**, you do not concentrate on or look at one particular subject, but start thinking about or looking at other things. = wander ❑ *Even with the simplest cases I find my mind straying.*
ADJ **1** [stray + N] A **stray** dog or cat has wandered away from its owner's home. ❑ *A stray dog came up to him.* **2** [stray + N] You use **stray** to describe something that exists separated from other similar things. ❑ *An 8-year-old boy was killed by a stray bullet.*
NOUN [C] (**strays**) A **stray** is a dog or cat that has wandered away from its owner's home. ❑ *The dog was a stray which had been adopted.*

streak /striːk/ NOUN, VERB
NOUN [C] (**streaks**) **1** A **streak** is a long stripe or mark on a surface which contrasts with the surface because it is a different colour. ❑ *There are these dark streaks on the surface of the moon.* **2** [usu sing, with SUPP] If someone has a **streak** of a particular type of behaviour, they sometimes behave in that way. ❑ *We're both alike – there is a streak of madness in us both.* **3** A winning **streak** or a lucky **streak** is a continuous series of successes, for example in gambling or sport. A losing **streak** or an unlucky **streak** is a series of failures or losses. ❑ *The casinos had better watch out since I'm obviously on a lucky streak!*

VERB [T, I] (**streaks, streaking, streaked**) **1** [T] If something **streaks** a surface, it makes long stripes or marks on the surface. ❑ *Rain had begun to streak the windowpanes.* **2** [I] If something or someone **streaks** somewhere, they move there very quickly. = dart ❑ *A meteorite streaked across the sky.*

stream ♦◇◇ /striːm/ NOUN, VERB
NOUN [C] (**streams**) **1** A **stream** is a small, narrow river. ❑ *There was a small stream at the end of the garden.* **2** A **stream** of smoke, air, or liquid is a narrow moving mass of it. ❑ *He breathed out a stream of cigarette smoke.* **3** A **stream** of vehicles or people is a long moving line of them. ❑ *There was a stream of traffic behind him.* **4** A **stream** of things is a large number of them occurring one after another. ❑ *The discovery triggered a stream of readers' letters.* ❑ *a never-ending stream of jokes*
PHRASE **on stream** If something such as a new factory or a new system comes **on stream** or is brought **on stream**, it begins to operate or becomes available. ❑ *As new mines come on stream, Chile's share of world copper output will increase sharply.*
VERB [I] (**streams, streaming, streamed**) **1** If a liquid **streams** somewhere, it flows or comes out in large amounts. ❑ *Tears streamed down their faces.* **2** If your eyes **are streaming**, liquid is coming from them, for example because you have a cold. You can also say that your nose is **streaming**. ❑ *Her eyes were streaming now from the wind.* **3** If people or vehicles **stream** somewhere, they move there quickly and in large numbers. ❑ *Refugees have been streaming into Travnik for months.* **4** When light **streams** into or out of a place, it shines strongly into or out of it. ❑ *Sunlight was streaming into the courtyard.*

stream·lined /ˈstriːmlaɪnd/ ADJ A **streamlined** vehicle, animal, or object has a shape that allows it to move quickly or efficiently through air or water. ❑ *these beautifully streamlined and efficient cars*

street ♦♦♦ /striːt/ NOUN [C] (**streets**) **1** A **street** is a road in a city, town, or village, usually with houses along it. ❑ *He lived at 66 Bingfield Street.* **2** You can use **street** or **streets** when talking about activities that happen out of doors in a city or town rather than inside a building. ❑ *Changing money on the street is illegal – always use a bank.* ❑ *Their aim is to raise a million dollars to get the homeless off the streets.*

✪**strength** ♦♦◇ /streŋθ/ NOUN
NOUN [U, C] (**strengths**) **1** [U] Your **strength** is the physical energy that you have, which gives you the ability to perform various actions, such as lifting or moving things. ❑ *She has always been encouraged to swim to build up the strength of her muscles.* ❑ *He threw it forward with all his strength.* **2** [U] [also 'a' strength] Someone's **strength** in a difficult situation is their confidence or courage. ❑ *Something gave me the strength to overcome the difficulty.* ❑ *He copes incredibly well. His strength is an inspiration to me in my life.* **3** [U] [also strengths] The **strength** of an object or material is its ability to be treated roughly, or to carry heavy weights, without being damaged or destroyed. ❑ *He checked the strength of the cables.* ❑ *the properties of a material, such as strength or electrical conductivity* **4** [U] [also strengths] The **strength** of a person, organization, or country is the power or influence that they have. = power ❑ *America values its economic leadership, and the political and military strength that goes with it.* ❑ *The alliance, in its first show of strength, drew a hundred thousand-strong crowd to a rally.* ❑ *They have their own independence movement which is gathering strength.* **5** [U] If you refer to the **strength of** a feeling, opinion, or belief, you are talking about how deeply it is felt or believed by people, or how much they are influenced by it. = intensity, depth ❑ *He was surprised at the strength of his own feeling.* ❑ *What makes a mayor successful in Los Angeles is the strength of his public support.* **6** [C, U] Someone's **strengths** are the qualities and abilities that they have which are an advantage to them, or which make them successful. ❑ *Take into account your own strengths and weaknesses.* ❑ *Tact was never Mr. Moore's strength.* **7** [U] If you refer to the **strength** of a currency, economy, or industry, you mean that its value or success is steady or increasing. ❑ *the*

S

long-term competitive strength of the economy **8** [U] [also strength in pl] The **strength** of a group of people is the total number of people in it. ▫ *elite forces, comprising about one-tenth of the strength of the army* **9** [U] [also strengths] The **strength** of a wind, current, or other force is its power or speed. ▫ *Its oscillation depends on the strength of the gravitational field.* **10** [U] [also strengths] The **strength** of a drink, chemical, or drug is the amount of the particular substance in it that gives it its particular effect. ▫ *It is very alcoholic, sometimes near the strength of port.*

PHRASES **go from strength to strength** If a person or organization **goes from strength to strength**, they become more and more successful or confident. ▫ *A decade later, the company has gone from strength to strength.*

full strength If a team or army is at **full strength**, all the members that it needs or usually has are present. ▫ *He needed more time to bring US forces there up to full strength.*

on the strength of If one thing is done **on the strength of** another, it is done because of the influence of that other thing. ▫ *He was elected to power on the strength of his charisma.*

✪strength•en ◆◇◇ /ˈstreŋθən/ VERB [I, T] (**strengthens, strengthening, strengthened**) **1** [I, T] To strengthen something means to make it stronger. If something **strengthens**, it becomes stronger. = reinforce, enhance, fortify; ≠ weaken ▫ *Community leaders want to strengthen controls at external frontiers.* ▫ *The general ordered the troops to strengthen the city's outer defences.* **2** [T] If something **strengthens** a person or group or if they **strengthen** their position, they become more powerful and secure, or more likely to succeed. ▫ *Giving the president the authority to go to war would strengthen his hand for peace.* **3** [T] If something **strengthens** a case or argument, it supports it by providing more reasons or evidence for it. = reinforce ▫ *He does not seem to be familiar with research which might have strengthened his own arguments.* **4** [I, T] If a currency, economy, or industry **strengthens**, or if something **strengthens** it, it increases in value or becomes more successful. ▫ *The dollar strengthened against most other currencies.* **5** [T] If something **strengthens** you or **strengthens** your resolve or character, it makes you more confident and determined. ▫ *Any experience can teach and strengthen you, but particularly the more difficult ones.* ▫ *This merely strengthens our resolve to win the pennant.* **6** [I, T] If something **strengthens** a relationship or link, or if it **strengthens**, it makes it closer and more likely to last for a long time. ▫ *It will draw you closer together, and it will strengthen the bond of your relationship.* **7** [I, T] If something **strengthens** an impression, feeling, or belief, or if it **strengthens**, it becomes greater or affects more people. = deepen ▫ *His speech strengthens the impression he is the main power in the organization.* ▫ *Every day of sunshine strengthens the feelings of optimism.* **8** [T] If something **strengthens** your body or a part of your body, it makes it healthier, often in such a way that you can move or carry heavier things. ▫ *Cycling is good exercise. It strengthens all the muscles of the body.* ▫ *Yoga can be used to strengthen the immune system.* **9** [T] If something **strengthens** an object or structure, it makes it able to be treated roughly or able to support heavy weights, without being damaged or destroyed. = reinforce ▫ *The builders will have to strengthen the existing joists with additional timber.*

WORD CONNECTIONS

strengthen + NOUN

strengthen **ties**
strengthen **co-operation**
strengthen **democracy**
strengthen a **relationship**
strengthen a **bond**
▫ *The programme aims to strengthen the relationship between schools and the wider community.*

strengthen the **economy**
strengthen the **dollar**
strengthen the **pound**
strengthen the **yen**
▫ *Mr Howard said the tax would strengthen an already booming Australian economy.*

ADV + **strengthen**

further strengthen
greatly strengthen
significantly strengthen
immeasurably strengthen
▫ *The leadership's position will be further strengthened by a series of party reforms.*

VOCABULARY BUILDER

strengthen VERB
To **strengthen** something means to make it stronger. If something **strengthens**, it becomes stronger.
▫ *The friendship between Rob and Peter strengthened.*

reinforce VERB (*fairly formal*)
If something **reinforces** a feeling, situation, or process, it makes it stronger.
▫ *This will reinforce Indonesian determination to deal with this kind of threat.*

enhance VERB (*mainly written*)
To **enhance** something means to improve its value, quality, or attractiveness.
▫ *The White House is eager to protect and enhance that reputation.*

fortify VERB (*formal*)
To **fortify** a place means to make it stronger and more difficult to attack, often by building a wall or ditch round it.
▫ *Soldiers are working to fortify an airbase in Bahrain.*

deepen VERB
If a situation or emotion **deepens** or if something **deepens** it, it becomes stronger and more intense.
▫ *If this is not stopped, the financial crisis will deepen.*

strenu•ous /ˈstrenjuəs/ ADJ A **strenuous** activity or action involves a lot of energy or effort. ▫ *Avoid strenuous exercise in the evening.* ▫ *Strenuous efforts had been made to improve conditions in the jail.*

✪stress ◆◆◇ /stres/ VERB, NOUN (*academic word*)
VERB [T] (**stresses, stressing, stressed**) **1** If you **stress** a point in a discussion, you put extra emphasis on it because you think it is important. = emphasize ▫ *The spokesman stressed that the measures did not amount to an overall ban.* ▫ *China's leaders have stressed the need for increased co-operation between Third World countries.* **2** If you **stress** a word or part of a word when you say it, you put emphasis on it so that it sounds slightly louder. ▫ *She stresses the syllables as though teaching a child.*
NOUN [C, U] (**stresses**) **1** [C, U] **Stress** means emphasis on something because you think it is important. = emphasis ▫ *Japanese car makers are laying ever more stress on overseas sales.* **2** [C, U] If you feel under **stress**, you feel worried and tense because of difficulties in your life. = anxiety, worry, strain ▫ *Katy could think clearly when not under stress.* ▫ *a wide range of stress-related problems* ▫ *Relaxation exercises can relieve stress.* **3** [C, U] **Stress** is emphasis that you put on a word or part of a word so that it sounds slightly louder. ▫ *the misplaced stress on the first syllable of this last word* **4** [C] **Stresses** are strong physical pressures applied to an object. ▫ *Earthquakes happen when stresses in rock are suddenly released as the rocks fracture.*

WORD CONNECTIONS

VERB + **stress**

cope with stress
deal with stress
handle stress
▫ *According to the study, men and women handle stress differently.*

cause stress
create stress
▫ *The staff complained of stress caused by overcrowding.*

relieve stress
reduce stress
▫ *Relaxation exercises can relieve stress.*

S

ADJ + **stress**
emotional stress **mental** stress **psychological** stress **work-related** stress ❏ *Emotional stress can have an impact on your blood-sugar levels.*
chronic stress **severe** stress **extreme** stress ❏ *Severe, prolonged stress can affect every system of the body.*

stress•ful /'stresfʊl/ ADJ If a situation or experience is **stressful**, it causes the person involved to feel stress. ❏ *I think I've got one of the most stressful jobs there is.*

stretch ◆◇◇ /stretʃ/ VERB, NOUN
VERB [I, T] (**stretches, stretching, stretched**) **1** [I] Something that **stretches** over an area or distance covers or exists in the whole of that area or distance. = extend ❏ *The procession stretched for several miles.* **2** [I, T] When you **stretch**, you put your arms or legs out straight and tighten your muscles. ❏ *He yawned and stretched.* ❏ *Try stretching your legs and pulling your toes upwards.* **3** [I] If something **stretches** from one time to another, it begins at the first time and ends at the second, which is longer than expected. ❏ *a working day that stretches from seven in the morning to eight at night* **4** [I] If a group of things **stretch from** one type of thing to another, the group includes a wide range of things. = range ❏ *a trading empire, with interests that stretched from chemicals to sugar* **5** [I, T] When something soft or elastic **stretches** or **is stretched**, it becomes longer or bigger as well as thinner, usually because it is pulled. ❏ *The cables are designed not to stretch.* **6** [I, T] If you **stretch** an amount of something or if it **stretches**, you make it last longer than it usually would by being careful and not wasting any of it. ❏ *They're used to stretching their budgets.* **7** [T] If something **stretches** your money or resources, it uses them up so you have hardly enough for your needs. ❏ *The drought there is stretching resources.* **8** [T] If you say that a job or task **stretches** you, you mean that you like it because it makes you work hard and use all your energy and skills so that you do not become bored or achieve less than you should. = push ❏ *I'm trying to move on and stretch myself with something different.*
PHRASAL VERB **stretch out** **1** If you **stretch out** or **stretch yourself out**, you lie with your legs and body in a straight line. ❏ *The bath was too small to stretch out in.* **2** If you **stretch out** a part of your body, you hold it out straight. ❏ *He was about to stretch out his hand to grab me.*
NOUN [C] (**stretches**) **1** A **stretch** of road, water, or land is a length or area of it. ❏ *It's a very dangerous stretch of road.* **2** A **stretch** is the act of extending a limb or other part of the body and tightening the muscles. ❏ *At the end of a workout spend time cooling down with some slow stretches.* **3** A **stretch** of time is a period of time. ❏ *after an 18-month stretch in the army*
PHRASE **by any stretch of the imagination** or **not by any stretch of the imagination** (*emphasis*) If you say that something is not true or possible **by any stretch of the imagination**, you are emphasizing that it is completely untrue or absolutely impossible. ❏ *Her husband was not a womanizer by any stretch of the imagination.*

strick•en /'strɪkən/ IRREG FORM, ADJ, COMB
IRREG FORM **Stricken** is the past participle of some meanings of **strike**.
ADJ If a person or place is **stricken by** something such as an unpleasant feeling, an illness, or a natural disaster, they are severely affected by it. ❏ *a family stricken by genetically inherited cancer*
COMB **Stricken** is used in combination with nouns such as poverty, panic, and grief, and to indicate that someone or something is severely affected by poverty, panic, or grief. ❏ *a leukaemia-stricken child*

✪**strict** ◆◇◇ /strɪkt/ ADJ (**stricter, strictest**) **1** A **strict** rule or order is very clear and precise or severe and must always be obeyed completely. = austere, severe; ≠ lax, lenient ❏ *The officials had issued strict instructions that we were not to get out of the jeep.* ❏ *French privacy laws are very strict.* ❏ *All your replies will be treated in the strictest confidence.* **2** If a parent or other person in authority is **strict**, they regard many actions as unacceptable and do not allow them. ❏ *My parents were very strict.* **3** [strict + N] If you talk about the **strict** meaning of something, you mean the precise meaning of it. ❏ *It's not quite peace in the strictest sense of the word, rather the absence of war.* **4** [strict + N] You use **strict** to describe someone who never does things that are against their beliefs. ❏ *Millions of Americans are now strict vegetarians.*

strict•ly /'strɪktli/ ADV **1** [strictly with V] If a rule or order is enforced **strictly**, it must always be obeyed completely. ❏ *The acceptance of new members is strictly controlled.* **2** [strictly + GROUP] (*emphasis*) You use **strictly** to emphasize that something is of one particular type, or intended for one particular thing or person, rather than any other. = purely ❏ *He seemed fond of her in a strictly professional way.* **3** If a parent or other person in authority acts **strictly**, they regard many actions as unacceptable and do not allow them. ❏ *My own mother was brought up very strictly and correctly.* **4** If you talk about what something **strictly** means, you are referring to its precise meaning. ❏ *Actually, that is not strictly true.*

stride /straɪd/ VERB, NOUN
VERB [I] (**strides, striding, strode**) If you **stride** somewhere, you walk there with quick, long steps. ❏ *They were joined by a newcomer who came striding across a field.*
NOUN [C] (**strides**) **1** A **stride** is a long step which you take when you are walking or running. ❏ *With every stride, runners hit the ground with up to five times their body-weight.* **2** If you **make strides** in something that you are doing, you make rapid progress in it. ❏ *The country has made enormous strides politically but not economically.*
PHRASES **get into one's stride** or **hit one's stride** If you **get into** your **stride** or **hit** your **stride**, you start to do something easily and confidently, after being slow and uncertain. ❏ *The campaign is just getting into its stride.*
take something in your stride If you **take** a problem or difficulty **in** your **stride**, you deal with it calmly and easily. ❏ *He took the ridiculous accusation in his stride.*

stri•dent /'straɪdənt/ ADJ (*disapproval*) If you use **strident** to describe someone or the way they express themselves, you mean that they make their feelings or opinions known in a very strong way that perhaps makes people uncomfortable. ❏ *She was increasingly seen as a strident feminist.*

strife /straɪf/ NOUN [U] (*formal*) **Strife** is strong disagreement or fighting. = conflict ❏ *Money is a major cause of strife in many marriages.*

✪**strike** ◆◆◇ /straɪk/ NOUN, VERB

The form **struck** is the past tense and past participle of the verb. The form **stricken** can also be used as the past participle for meaning 5.

NOUN [C] (**strikes**) **1** (*business*) [also 'on' strike] When there is a **strike**, workers stop doing their work for a period of time, usually in order to try to get better pay or conditions for themselves. = industrial action ❏ *Air traffic controllers have begun a three-day strike in a dispute over pay.* ❏ *Staff at the hospital went on strike in protest at the incidents.* ❏ *a call for strike action* **2** A military **strike** is a military attack, especially an air attack. ❏ *a punitive air strike*
VERB [I, T, RECIP] (**strikes, striking, struck, stricken**) **1** [I] (*business*) When workers **strike**, they go on strike. = go on strike, picket, protest ❏ *their recognition of the workers' right to strike* ❏ *They shouldn't be striking for more money.* ❏ *The government agreed not to sack any of the striking workers.* **2** [T] (*formal*) If you **strike** someone or something, you deliberately hit them. ❏ *She took two quick steps forward and struck him across the mouth.* ❏ *It is impossible to say who struck the fatal blow.* **3** [T] (*formal*) If something that is

S

falling or moving **strikes** something, it hits it. **= hit** ❑ *His head struck the bottom when he dived into the 6 ft end of the pool.* ❑ *One 16-inch shell struck the control tower.* **4** [I, T] (*formal*) If you **strike** one thing against another, or if one thing **strikes** against another, the first thing hits the second thing. **= bang** ❑ *Wilde fell and struck his head on the stone floor.* **5** [I, T] If something such as an illness or disaster **strikes**, it suddenly happens. ❑ *Officials continued to insist that the dollar would soon return to stability but disaster struck.* ❑ *A moderate earthquake struck the northeastern United States early on Saturday.* **6** [I] To **strike** means to attack someone or something quickly and violently. ❑ *He was the only cabinet member out of the country when the terrorists struck.* **7** [T] If an idea or thought **strikes** you, it suddenly comes into your mind. ❑ *A thought struck her. Was she jealous of her mother, then?* **8** [T] If something **strikes** you as being a particular thing, it gives you the impression of being that thing. ❑ *He struck me as a very serious but friendly person.* **9** [T] If you **are struck** by something, you think it is very impressive, noticeable, or interesting. ❑ *She was struck by his simple, spellbinding eloquence.* **10** [RECIP] If you **strike** a deal or a bargain with someone, you come to an agreement with them. ❑ *They struck a deal with their paper supplier, getting two years of newsprint on credit.* ❑ *The two struck a deal in which Rendell took half of what a manager would.* **11** [T] If you **strike** a balance, you do something that is halfway between two extremes. ❑ *At times like that you have to strike a balance between sleep and homework.* **12** [T] If you **strike** a pose or attitude, you put yourself in a particular position, for example when someone is taking your photograph. **= adopt** ❑ *She struck a pose, one hand on her hip and the other waving an imaginary cigarette.* **13** [T] (*literary*) If something **strikes** fear **into** people, it makes them very frightened or anxious. ❑ *If there is a single subject guaranteed to strike fear in the hearts of parents, it is drugs.* **14** [I, T] When a clock **strikes**, its bells make a sound to indicate what the time is. ❑ *The clock struck nine.* **15** [T] (*formal*) If you **strike** words **from** a document or an official record, you remove them. ❑ *Strike that from the minutes.* **16** [T] When you **strike** a match, you make it produce a flame by moving it quickly against something rough. ❑ *Robina struck a match and held it to the crumpled newspaper in the grate.* **17** [T] If someone **strikes** oil or gold, they discover it in the ground as a result of mining or drilling. ❑ *Oil industry sources say that Marathon Oil Company has struck oil in Syria.*

PHRASAL VERBS   **strike down** (*written*) If someone **is struck down**, especially by an illness, they are killed or severely harmed. ❑ *Frank had been struck down by a massive heart attack.*
strike out **1** If you **strike out**, you begin to do something different, often because you want to become more independent. ❑ *She wanted me to strike out on my own, buy a business.* **2** If you **strike out** at someone, you hit, attack, or speak angrily to them. ❑ *He seemed always ready to strike out at anyone and for any cause.* **3** **Strike out** means the same as **strike 15.** ❑ *The censor struck out the next two lines.*
strike up (*written*) When you **strike up** a conversation or friendship with someone, you begin one. ❑ *I trailed her into Penney's and struck up a conversation.*

→ See also **stricken, striker, striking**
✦ **strike a chord** → see **chord; strike home** → see **home**

❍ strik•er /ˈstraɪkə/ NOUN [C] (**strikers**) **1** In football and some other team sports, a **striker** is a player who mainly attacks and scores goals, rather than defends. ❑ *and the striker scored his sixth goal of the season* **2** A **striker** is a worker who has stopped doing their work for a period of time, usually in order to try to get better pay or conditions for themselves. **= protester** ❑ *The strikers want higher wages, which state governments say they can't afford.*

❍ strik•ing ✦◇◇ /ˈstraɪkɪŋ/ ADJ **1** Something that is **striking** is very noticeable or unusual. ❑ *The most striking feature of those statistics is the high proportion of suicides.* ❑ *He bears a striking resemblance to Lenin.* **2** Someone who is **striking** is very attractive, in a noticeable way. ❑ *She was a striking woman with long blonde hair.*

❍ strik•ing•ly /ˈstraɪkɪŋli/ ADV ❑ *In one respect, however, the* men really were strikingly similar. ❑ *Most strikingly, the amount consumers spent in the shops grew much more quickly than anyone expected.* ❑ *a strikingly handsome man*

string ✦◇◇ /strɪŋ/ NOUN
NOUN [C, U, PL] (**strings**) **1** [C, U] **String** is thin rope made of twisted threads, used for tying things together or tying up packages. ❑ *He held out a small bag tied with string.* **2** [C] A **string of** things is a number of them on a piece of string, thread, or wire. ❑ *She wore a string of pearls around her neck.* **3** [C] A **string of** places or objects is a number of them that form a line. ❑ *The landscape is broken only by a string of villages.* **4** [C] A **string of** similar events is a series of them that happen one after the other. ❑ *The incident was the latest in a string of attacks.* **5** [C] The **strings** on a musical instrument such as a violin or guitar are the thin pieces of wire or nylon stretched across it that make sounds when the instrument is played. ❑ *He went off to change a guitar string.* **6** [PL] The **strings** are the section of an orchestra which consists of stringed instruments played with a bow. ❑ *The strings provided a melodic background to the passages played by the soloist.*
PHRASES   **no strings attached** or **no strings** If something is offered to you with **no strings attached** or with **no strings**, it is offered without any special conditions. ❑ *Aid should be given to developing countries with no strings attached.*
pull strings If you **pull strings**, you use your influence with other people in order to get something done, often unfairly. ❑ *Tony is sure he can pull a few strings and get you in.*
PHRASAL VERB   **string together** (**strings, stringing, strung**) If you **string** things **together**, you form something from them by adding them to each other, one at a time. ❑ *As speech develops, the child starts to string more words together.*

strip ✦◇◇ /strɪp/ NOUN, VERB
NOUN [C] (**strips**) **1** A **strip of** something such as paper, cloth, or food is a long, narrow piece of it. ❑ *a new kind of manufactured wood made by pressing strips of wood together and baking them* ❑ *The simplest rag-rugs are made with strips of fabric braided together.* **2** A **strip of** land or water is a long narrow area of it. **= stretch** ❑ *The coastal cities of Liguria sit on narrow strips of land lying under steep mountains.* **3** In a newspaper or magazine, a **strip** is a series of drawings which tell a story. The words spoken by the characters are often written on the drawings. ❑ *the Doonesbury strip*
VERB [I, T] (**strips, stripping, stripped**) **1** [I] If you **strip**, you take off your clothes. ❑ *They stripped completely, and lay and turned in the damp grass.* **2** [T] If someone **is stripped**, their clothes are taken off by another person, for example in order to search for hidden or illegal things. ❑ *One prisoner claimed he'd been dragged to a cell, stripped, and beaten.* **3** [T] To **strip** something means to remove everything that covers it. ❑ *After Mike left for work I stripped the beds and vacuumed the carpets.* **4** [T] If you **strip** an engine or a piece of equipment, you take it to pieces so that it can be cleaned or repaired. ❑ *Volvo's three-man team stripped the car and treated it to a restoration.* **5** [T] To **strip** someone **of** their property, rights, or titles means to take those things away from them. ❑ *The soldiers have stripped the civilians of their passports, and every other type of document.*
PHRASAL VERBS   **strip away** To **strip away** something, especially something that hides the true nature of a thing, means to remove it completely. ❑ *Altman strips away the pretence and mythology to expose the film industry as a business like any other.*
strip down **Strip down** means the same as **strip** VERB **4.** ❑ *In five years I had to strip the water pump down four times.*
strip off **1** **Strip off** means the same as **strip** VERB **1.** ❑ *The children were brazenly stripping off and leaping into the sea.* **2** If you **strip off** your clothes, you take them off. ❑ *He stripped off his wet clothes and stepped into the shower.*

stripe /straɪp/ NOUN [C] (**stripes**) A **stripe** is a long line which is a different colour from the areas next to it. ❑ *She wore a bright green jogging suit with a white stripe down the sides.*

❍ strive /straɪv/ VERB [I, T] (**strives, striving, strove** or **strived, striven** or **strived**) If you **strive to** do something or **strive for** something, you make a great effort to do it or get

S

it. □ *He strives hard to keep himself very fit.* □ *Mr Annan said the region must now strive for economic development as well as peace.*

strode /strəʊd/ IRREG FORM **Strode** is the past tense and past participle of **stride.**

✪ **stroke** ♦◇◇ /strəʊk/ VERB, NOUN

VERB [T] (**strokes, stroking, stroked**) If you **stroke** someone or something, you move your hand slowly and gently over them. □ *Carla, curled up on the sofa, was smoking a cigarette and stroking her cat.*

NOUN [C, SING] (**strokes**) **1** [C] If someone has a **stroke**, a blood vessel in their brain bursts or becomes blocked, which may kill them or make them unable to move one side of their body. □ *He had a minor stroke in 1987, which left him partly paralysed.* □ *He suffered a stroke in 1919 which made it very difficult for him to cope in the last years of his presidency.* **2** [C] The **strokes** of a pen or brush are the movements or marks that you make with it when you are writing or painting. □ *Fill in gaps by using short, upward strokes of the pencil.* **3** [C] When you are swimming or rowing, your **strokes** are the repeated movements that you make with your arms or the oars. □ *I turned and swam a few strokes further out to sea.* **4** [C] A swimming **stroke** is a particular style or method of swimming. □ *She spent hours practising the breast stroke.* **5** [C] The **strokes** of a clock are the sounds that indicate each hour. □ *On the stroke of 12, fireworks suddenly exploded into the night.* **6** [C] In sports such as tennis, baseball, golf, and cricket, a **stroke** is the action of hitting the ball. □ *Compton was sending the ball here, there, and everywhere with each stroke.* **7** [SING] **A stroke of** luck or good fortune is something lucky that happens. □ *It didn't rain, which turned out to be a stroke of luck.* **8** [SING] **A stroke** of genius or inspiration is a very good idea that someone suddenly has. □ *At the time, his appointment seemed a stroke of genius.*

PHRASE **do a stroke** (*informal, emphasis*) If someone does not **do a stroke** of work, they are very lazy and do no work at all. □ *I never did a stroke of work in college.*

stroll /strəʊl/ VERB, NOUN

VERB [I] (**strolls, strolling, strolled**) If you **stroll** somewhere, you walk there in a slow, relaxed way. □ *He collected some orange juice from the refrigerator and, glass in hand, strolled to the kitchen window.*

NOUN [C] (**strolls**) A **stroll** is a slow, relaxed walk somewhere. □ *After dinner, I took a stroll round the city.*

✪ **strong** ♦♦♦ /strɒŋ, AmE strɔːŋ/ ADJ

ADJ (**stronger, strongest** /'strɒŋgɪst, AmE 'strɔːŋgɪst/) **1** Someone who is **strong** is healthy with good muscles and can move or carry heavy things, or do hard physical work. □ *I'm not strong enough to carry him.* **2** Someone who is **strong** is confident and determined, and is not easily influenced or worried by other people. □ *He is sharp and manipulative with a strong personality.* □ *It's up to managers to be strong and do what they believe is right.* **3** **Strong** objects or materials are not easily broken and can support a lot of weight or resist a lot of strain. = sturdy; ≠ weak, fragile □ *The vacuum flask has a strong casing, which won't crack or chip.* □ *Glue the mirror in with a strong adhesive.* **4** A **strong** wind, current, or other force has a lot of power or speed, and can cause heavy things to move. = powerful □ *Strong winds and torrential rain combined to make conditions terrible for golfers in the Scottish Open.* □ *A fairly strong current seemed to be moving the whole boat.* **5** A **strong** impression or influence has a great effect on someone. □ *We're glad if our music makes a strong impression, even if it's a negative one.* □ *There will be a strong incentive to enter into a process of negotiation.* **6** If you have **strong** opinions on something or express them using **strong** words, you have extreme or very definite opinions which you are willing to express or defend. ≠ mild □ *She is known to hold strong views on Cuba.* □ *I am a strong supporter of the president.* □ *There has been strong criticism of the military regime.* □ *It condemned in extremely strong language what it called Britain's iniquitous campaign.* **7** If someone in authority takes **strong** action, they act firmly and severely. □ *The American public deserves strong action from Congress.* **8** If there is a **strong** case or argument for

something, it is supported by a lot of evidence. □ *The testimony presented offered a strong case for acquitting her on grounds of self-defence.* **9** If there is a **strong** possibility or chance that something is true or will happen, it is very likely to be true or to happen. □ *There is a strong possibility that the cat contracted the condition by eating contaminated pet food.* **10** [strong + N] Your **strong** points are your best qualities or talents, or the things you are good at. □ *Discretion is not Jeremy's strong point.* □ *Exports may be the only strong point in the economy over the next six to 12 months.* **11** A **strong** competitor, candidate, or team is good or likely to succeed. □ *She was a strong contender for the Olympic team.* **12** If a relationship or link is **strong**, it is close and likely to last for a long time. □ *He felt he had a relationship strong enough to talk frankly to Sarah.* □ *This has tested our marriage, and we have come through it stronger than ever.* **13** A **strong** currency, economy, or industry has a high value or is very successful. = robust □ *The US dollar continued its strong performance in Tokyo today.* **14** If something is a **strong** element or part of something else, it is an important or large part of it. □ *We are especially encouraged by the strong representation, this year, of women in information technology disciplines.* **15** [NUM + strong] You can use **strong** when you are saying how many people there are in a group. For example, if a group is twenty strong, there are twenty people in it. □ *Ukraine indicated that it would establish its own army, 400,000 strong.* **16** A **strong** drink, chemical, or drug contains a lot of the particular substance which makes it effective. □ *Strong coffee or tea late at night may cause sleeplessness.* **17** A **strong** colour, flavour, smell, sound, or light is intense and easily noticed. □ *As she went past there was a gust of strong perfume.* **18** If someone has a **strong** accent, they speak in a distinctive way that shows very clearly what country or region they come from. = pronounced □ *'Good, Mr. Ryle,' he said in English with a strong French accent.*

PHRASE **going strong** (*informal*) If someone or something is still **going strong**, they are still alive, in good condition, or popular after a long time. □ *The old machinery was still going strong.*

strong·ly /'strɒŋli, AmE 'strɔːŋli/ ADV **1** [strongly + -ED] □ *The fence was very strongly built, with very large posts.* **2** [strongly with V] □ *The metal is strongly attracted to the surface.* **3** [strongly with V] □ *He is strongly influenced by Spanish painters such as Goya and El Greco.* **4** Obviously you feel very strongly about this. □ *Republicans in the House were strongly opposed to lifting the ban.* **5** *He argues strongly for retention of NATO as a guarantee of peace.* **6** [strongly with V] □ *He leaned over her, smelling strongly of sweat.*

strong·hold /'strɒŋhəʊld, AmE 'strɔːŋ-/ NOUN [C] (**strongholds**) If you say that a place or region is a **stronghold of** a particular attitude or belief, you mean that most people there share this attitude or belief. = bastion □ *Florida is a stronghold for pro-choice activists.*

strove /strəʊv/ IRREG FORM **Strove** is a past tense of **strive.**

struck /strʌk/ IRREG FORM **Struck** is the past tense and past participle of **strike.**

✪ **struc·tur·al** /'strʌktʃərəl/ ADJ **Structural** means relating to or affecting the structure of something. □ *The explosion caused little structural damage to the office towers themselves.* □ *structural reform such as privatization*

struc·tur·al·ly /'strʌktʃərəli/ ADV □ *When we bought the house, it was structurally sound, but I decided to redecorate throughout.*

✪ **struc·ture** ♦♦◇ /'strʌktʃə/ NOUN, VERB (*academic word*)

NOUN [C, U] (**structures**) **1** [C, U] The **structure** of something is the way in which it is made, built, or organized. = organization, arrangement □ *The typical family structure of Freud's patients involved two parents and two children.* □ *The chemical structure of this particular molecule is very unusual.* **2** [C] A **structure** is something that consists of parts connected together in an ordered way. □ *The feet are highly specialized structures made up of 26 small delicate bones.* **3** [C] A **structure** is something that has been built. = building □ *About half of those funds has gone to repair public roads, structures, and bridges.*

VERB [T] (**structures, structuring, structured**) If you

S

structure something, you arrange it in a careful, organized pattern or system. = organize □ *By structuring the course this way, we're forced to produce something the companies think is valuable.*

❂ **strug·gle** ♦♦◇ /ˈstrʌɡəl/ VERB, NOUN

VERB [I, T, RECIP] (**struggles, struggling, struggled**) **1** [I, T] If you **struggle to** do something, you try hard to do it, even though other people or things may be making it difficult for you to succeed. = battle, fight □ *They had to struggle against all kinds of adversity.* □ *Those who have lost their jobs struggle to pay their supermarket bills.* **2** [I] If you **struggle** when you are being held, you twist, kick, and move violently in order to get free. □ *I struggled, but he was a tall man, well built.* **3** [RECIP] If two people **struggle with** each other, they fight. □ *She screamed at him to 'stop it' as they struggled on the ground.* **4** [I, T] If you **struggle to** move yourself or to move a heavy object, you try to do it, but it is difficult. □ *I could see the young boy struggling to free himself.* **5** [I, T] If a person or organization **is struggling**, they are likely to fail in what they are doing, even though they might be trying very hard. □ *The company is struggling to find buyers for its new product.* □ *One in five young adults was struggling with everyday mathematics.*

NOUN [C, U, SING] (**struggles**) **1** [C, U] A **struggle** is a long and difficult attempt to achieve something such as freedom or political rights. = battle □ *Life became a struggle for survival.* □ *India's struggle for independence* □ *IT directors now face an uphill struggle to win back respect from their business peers.* □ *a young boy's struggle to support his poverty-stricken family* **2** [C] A **struggle** is a fight between people. □ *He died in a struggle with prison officers less than two months after coming to Britain.* **3** [SING] An action or activity that is **a struggle** is very difficult to do. □ *Losing weight was a terrible struggle.*

strung /strʌŋ/ IRREG FORM **Strung** is the past tense and past participle of **string**.

stub·born /ˈstʌbən/ ADJ **1** Someone who is **stubborn** or who behaves in a **stubborn** way is determined to do what they want and is very unwilling to change their mind. = obstinate □ *He is a stubborn character used to getting his own way.* **2** A **stubborn** stain or problem is difficult to remove or to deal with. = persistent □ *This treatment removes the most stubborn stains.*

stub·born·ly /ˈstʌbənli/ ADV **1** *He stubbornly refused to tell her how he had come to be in such a state.* **2** *Some interest rates have remained stubbornly high.*

stub·born·ness /ˈstʌbənnəs/ NOUN [U] □ *I couldn't tell if his refusal to talk was simple stubbornness.*

stuck /stʌk/ IRREG FORM, ADJ

IRREG FORM **Stuck** is the past tense and past participle of **stick**.

ADJ **1** [V-LINK + stuck] If something is **stuck** in a particular position, it is fixed tightly in this position and is unable to move. □ *He said his car had got stuck in the snow.* **2** [V-LINK + stuck + PREP/ADV] If you are **stuck** in a place, you want to get away from it, but are unable to. □ *I was stuck at home with flu.* **3** [V-LINK + stuck + PREP/ADV] If you are **stuck** in a boring or unpleasant situation, you are unable to change it or get away from it. = trapped □ *I don't want to get stuck in another job like that.* **4** [V-LINK + stuck + PREP/ADV] If something is **stuck** at a particular level or stage, it is not progressing or changing. □ *I think the economy is stuck on a plateau of slow growth.* □ *US unemployment figures for March showed the jobless rate stuck at 7 per cent.* **5** [V-LINK + stuck 'with' N] If you are **stuck with** something that you do not want, you cannot get rid of it. □ *Many people are now stuck with expensive fixed-rate mortgages.* **6** [V-LINK + stuck] If you get **stuck** when you are trying to do something, you are unable to continue doing it because it is too difficult. □ *They will be there to help if you get stuck.*

❂ **stu·dent** ♦♦♦ /ˈstjuːdənt/ AmE ˈstuː-/ NOUN [C] (**students**) **1** A **student** is a person who is studying at a college or university. □ *Warren's eldest son is an art student.* □ *a 23-year-old medical student* **2** Someone who is a **student** of a particular subject is interested in the subject and spends time learning about it. □ *a passionate student of history and an expert on nineteenth-century prime ministers*

stu·dio ♦♦◇ /ˈstjuːdiəʊ, AmE ˈstuː-/ NOUN [C] (**studios**) **1** A **studio** is a room where a painter, photographer, or designer works. □ *She was in her studio again, painting onto a large canvas.* **2** A **studio** is a room where radio or television programmes are recorded, CDs are produced, or films are made. □ *She's much happier performing live than in a recording studio.* **3** You can also refer to film-making or recording companies as **studios**. □ *She wrote to Paramount Studios and asked if they would audition her.* **4** A **studio** or a **studio flat** or a **studio** apartment is a small apartment with one room for living and sleeping in, a kitchen, and a bathroom. □ *Home for a couple of years was a studio apartment.*

❂ **study** ♦♦♦ /ˈstʌdi/ VERB, NOUN

VERB [I, T] (**studies, studying, studied**) **1** [I, T] If you **study**, you spend time learning about a particular subject or subjects. = learn, read □ *a relaxed and happy atmosphere that will allow you to study to your full potential* □ *He studied History and Economics.* □ *The rehearsals make it difficult for her to study for law school exams.* **2** [T] If you **study** something, you look at it or watch it very carefully, in order to find something out. □ *Debbie studied her friend's face for a moment.* **3** [T] If you **study** something, you consider it or observe it carefully in order to be able to understand it fully. = analyse, examine □ *I know that you've been studying chimpanzees for thirty years now.* □ *I invite every citizen to carefully study the document.*

NOUN [U, C, PL] (**studies**) **1** [U] [also studies] **Study** is the activity of studying. □ *the use of maps and visual evidence in the study of local history* **2** [C] A **study** of a subject is a piece of research on it. = analysis □ *Recent studies suggest that as many as 5 in 1,000 new mothers are likely to have this problem.* □ *the first study of English children's attitudes* **3** [PL] You can refer to educational subjects or courses that contain several elements as **studies** of a particular kind. □ *a centre for Islamic studies* **4** [C] A **study** is a room in a house which is used for reading, writing, and studying. □ *That evening we sat together in his study.*

→ See also **case study**

stuff ♦♦◇ /stʌf/ NOUN, VERB

NOUN [U] [usu with SUPP] (*informal*) You can use **stuff** to refer to things such as a substance, a collection of things, events, or ideas, or the contents of something in a general way without mentioning the thing itself by name. □ *I'd like some coffee, and I don't object to the powdered stuff if it's all you've got.* □ *He pointed to a duffle bag. 'That's my stuff.'*

PHRASE **know one's stuff** (*informal, approval*) If you say that someone **knows** their **stuff**, you mean that they are good at doing something because they know a lot about it. □ *These guys know their stuff after seven years of war.*

VERB [T] (**stuffs, stuffing, stuffed**) **1** If you **stuff** something somewhere, you push it there quickly and roughly. = shove □ *I stuffed my hands in my pockets.* **2** If you **stuff** a container or space **with** something, you fill it with something or with a quantity of things until it is full. = cram □ *He grabbed my purse, opened it and stuffed it full, then gave it back to me.* **3** (*informal*) If you **stuff yourself**, you eat a lot of food. □ *I could stuff myself with ten chocolate bars and half an hour later eat a big meal.* **4** If you **stuff** a bird such as a chicken or a vegetable such as a pepper, you put a mixture of food inside it before cooking it. □ *Will you stuff the turkey and shove it in the oven for me?* **5** If a dead animal is

stuffed, it is filled with a substance so that it can be preserved and displayed. □ *his collections of stamps and books and stuffed birds*

stum·ble /ˈstʌmbəl/ VERB, NOUN

VERB [I] (**stumbles, stumbling, stumbled**) If you **stumble**, you put your foot down awkwardly while you are walking or running and nearly fall over. □ *He stumbled and almost fell.*

PHRASAL VERB **stumble across** or **stumble on** If you **stumble across** something or **stumble on**, you find it or discover it unexpectedly. = come across □ *I stumbled across an extremely simple but very exact method for understanding where my money went.*

NOUN [C] (**stumbles**) A **stumble** is when you nearly fall because you put your foot down awkwardly while you are walking or running. □ *I make it into the darkness with only one stumble.*

stum·bling block NOUN [C] (**stumbling blocks**) A **stumbling block** is a problem which stops you from achieving something. □ *The major stumbling block in the talks has been money.*

stump /stʌmp/ NOUN, VERB

NOUN [C] (**stumps**) A **stump** is a small part of something that remains when the rest of it has been removed or broken off. □ *If you have a tree stump, check it for fungus.*

VERB [T] (**stumps, stumping, stumped**) If you **are stumped** by a question or problem, you cannot think of any solution or answer to it. □ *John Diamond is stumped by an unexpected question.*

stun /stʌn/ VERB [T] (**stuns, stunning, stunned**) **1** If you **are stunned** by something, you are extremely shocked or surprised by it and are therefore unable to speak or do anything. □ *He's stunned by today's resignation of his longtime ally.* **2** If something such as a blow on the head **stuns** you, it makes you unconscious or confused and unsteady. □ *Sam stood his ground and got a blow that stunned him.*

stunned /stʌnd/ ADJ □ *When they told me she was missing I was totally stunned.*

→ See also **stunning**

stung /stʌŋ/ IRREG FORM **Stung** is the past tense and past participle of **sting**.

stun·ning /ˈstʌnɪŋ/ ADJ **1** A **stunning** person or thing is extremely beautiful or impressive. □ *She was 55 and still a stunning woman.* **2** A **stunning** event is extremely unusual or unexpected. □ *He resigned last night after a stunning defeat in Sunday's vote.*

stu·pid ♦◇◇ /ˈstjuːpɪd, AmE ˈstuː-/ ADJ (**stupider, stupidest**) **1** If you say that someone or something is **stupid**, you mean that they show a lack of good judgment or intelligence or are not at all sensible. = foolish □ *I'll never do anything so stupid again.* □ *I made a stupid mistake.* **2** You say that something is **stupid** to indicate that you do not like it or that it annoys you. = silly □ *I wouldn't call it art. It's just stupid and tasteless.*

stu·pid·ly /ˈstjuːpɪdli, AmE ˈstuː-/ ADV □ *We had stupidly been looking at the wrong column of figures.*

stu·pid·ity /stjuːˈpɪdɪti, AmE stuː-/ NOUN [C, U] (**stupidities**) □ *I stared at him, astonished by his stupidity.*

stur·dy /ˈstɜːdi/ ADJ (**sturdier, sturdiest**) Someone or something that is **sturdy** looks strong and is unlikely to be easily injured or damaged. = robust □ *She was a short, sturdy woman in her early sixties.*

stur·di·ly /ˈstɜːdɪli/ ADV □ *It was a good table too, sturdily constructed of elm.*

Ⓢ style ♦♦◇ /staɪl/ NOUN, VERB (*academic word*)

NOUN [C, U] (**styles**) **1** The **style** of something is the general way in which it is done or presented, which often shows the attitudes of the people involved. □ *Our children's different needs and learning styles created many problems.* □ *Belmont Park is a broad sweeping track which will suit the European style of running.* **2** [U] If people or places have **style**, they are fashionable and elegant. □ *Boston, you have to admit, has style.* □ *Both love doing things in style.* **3** [C, U] The **style** of a product is its design. □ *His 50 years of experience have given him strong convictions about style.* **4** [C] In the arts, a particular **style** is characteristic of a particular

period or group of people. = method, technique □ *six scenes in the style of a classical Greek tragedy* □ *a mixture of musical styles*

VERB [T] (**styles, styling, styled**) If something such as a piece of clothing, a vehicle, or someone's hair **is styled** in a particular way, it is designed or shaped in that way. □ *His thick blond hair had just been styled before his trip.*

styl·ish /ˈstaɪlɪʃ/ ADJ Someone or something that is **stylish** is elegant and fashionable. □ *a very attractive and very stylish woman of 27*

styl·ish·ly /ˈstaɪlɪʃli/ ADV □ *stylishly dressed middle-aged women*

sub·con·scious /ˌsʌbˈkɒnʃəs/ NOUN, ADJ

NOUN [SING] Your **subconscious** is the part of your mind that can influence you or affect your behaviour even though you are not aware of it. □ *the hidden power of the subconscious*

ADJ A **subconscious** feeling or action exists in or is influenced by your subconscious. □ *He caught her arm in a subconscious attempt to detain her.*

sub·con·scious·ly /ˌsʌbˈkɒnʃəsli/ ADV □ *Subconsciously I had known that I would not be in personal danger.*

WORD PARTS
The prefix **sub-** appears in words for things that are part of a larger thing: **subsidiary** (NOUN) **subcommittee** (NOUN)
The prefix **sub-** also appears in words that have 'under' as part of their meaning: **submarine** (NOUN) **subterranean** (ADJ)
The prefix **sub-** also appears in words that describe people or things that are inferior: **substandard** (ADJ) **suboptimal** (ADJ) **suboptimum** (NOUN)

sub·due /səbˈdjuː, AmE -ˈduː/ VERB [T] (**subdues, subduing, subdued**) **1** If soldiers or the police **subdue** a group of people, they defeat them or bring them under control by using force. □ *Senior government officials admit they have not been able to subdue the rebels.* **2** To **subdue** feelings means to make them less strong. □ *He forced himself to subdue and overcome his fears.*

sub·dued /səbˈdjuːd, AmE -ˈduːd/ ADJ **1** Someone who is **subdued** is very quiet, often because they are sad or worried about something. □ *He faced the press, initially, in a somewhat subdued mood.* **2** **Subdued** lights or colours are not very bright. □ *The lighting was subdued.*

Ⓢ sub·ject ♦♦◇ NOUN, ADJ, VERB

NOUN /ˈsʌbdʒɪkt/ [C] (**subjects**) **1** The **subject** of something such as a conversation, letter, or book is the thing that is being discussed or written about. = topic □ *It was I who first raised the subject of plastic surgery.* □ *the president's own views on the subject* □ *non-fiction books which covered subjects like handicrafts and leisure pursuits* **2** Someone or something that is the **subject of** criticism, study, or an investigation is being criticized, studied, or investigated. □ *Over the past few years, some of the positions Mr. Meredith has adopted have made him the subject of criticism.* □ *the argument that only observable behaviour is a proper subject of psychological investigation* **3** A **subject** is an area of knowledge or study, especially one that you study at school, college, or university. □ *Surprisingly, maths was voted their favourite subject.* □ *a tutor in maths and science subjects* □ *Students must study six academic subjects over two years.* **4** (*formal*) In an experiment or piece of research, the **subject** is the person or animal that is being tested or studied. = participant □ *'White noise' was played into the subject's ears through headphones.* □ *Subjects in the study were asked to follow a modified diet.* **5** An artist's **subjects** are the people, animals, or objects that he or she paints, models, or photographs. □ *Sailboats and fish are popular subjects for local artists.* **6** In grammar, the **subject** of a clause is the noun group that refers to the person or thing that is doing

S

the action expressed by the verb. For example, in 'My cat keeps catching birds', 'my cat' is the subject. **7** The people who live in or belong to a particular country, usually one ruled by a monarch, are the **subjects** of that monarch or country. ❑ *His subjects regarded him as a great and wise monarch.*

PHRASE change the subject When someone involved in a conversation **changes the subject**, they start talking about something else, often because the previous subject was embarrassing. ❑ *He tried to change the subject, but she wasn't to be put off.*

ADJ /ˈsʌbdʒɪkt/ **1** [V-LINK + subject 'to' N] To be **subject to** something means to be affected by it or to be likely to be affected by it. ❑ *Prices may be subject to alteration.* **2** [V-LINK + subject 'to' N] If someone is **subject to** a particular set of rules or laws, they have to obey those rules or laws. ❑ *The tribunal is unique because Mr Jones is not subject to the normal police discipline code.*

PHRASE subject to something If an event will take place **subject to** a condition, it will take place only if that thing happens. ❑ *They denied a report that Egypt had agreed to a summit, subject to certain conditions.*

VERB /səbˈdʒekt/ [T] (**subjects, subjecting, subjected**) If you **subject** someone **to** something unpleasant, you make them experience it. ❑ *the man who had subjected her to four years of beatings and abuse*

✪**sub·jec·tive** /səbˈdʒektɪv/ ADJ Something that is **subjective** is based on personal opinions and feelings rather than on facts. ❑ *We know that taste in art is a subjective matter.* ❑ *The way they interpreted their past was highly subjective.*

✪**sub·jec·tive·ly** /səbˈdʒektɪvli/ ADV ≠ objectively ❑ *Our preliminary results suggest that people do subjectively find the speech clearer.*

✪**sub·jec·tiv·ity** /ˌsʌbdʒəkˈtɪvɪti/ NOUN [U] ≠ objectivity ❑ *They accused her of flippancy and subjectivity in her reporting of events in their country.*

sub·ma·rine /ˌsʌbməˈriːn/ NOUN [C] (**submarines**) A **submarine** is a type of ship that can travel both above and below the surface of the sea. The abbreviation **sub** is also used. ❑ *a nuclear submarine*

sub·merge /səbˈmɜːdʒ/ VERB [I, T] (**submerges, submerging, submerged**) If something **submerges** or if you **submerge** it, it goes below the surface of some water or another liquid. ❑ *Hippos are unable to submerge in the few remaining water holes.*

✪**sub·mis·sion** /səbˈmɪʃən/ NOUN [U, C] (**submissions**) **1** [U] **Submission** is a state in which people can no longer do what they want to do because they have been brought under the control of someone else. ❑ *The army intends to take the city or simply starve it into submission.* **2** [C] The **submission** of a proposal, report, or request to someone is when you send it to them formally so that they can consider it or decide about it. A **submission** is also the proposal, report, or request sent in this way. ❑ *Diploma and certificate courses do not normally require the submission of a dissertation.* ❑ *A written submission has to be prepared.*

sub·mis·sive /səbˈmɪsɪv/ ADJ If you are **submissive**, you obey someone without arguing. ❑ *Most doctors want their patients to be submissive.*

sub·mis·sive·ly /səbˈmɪsɪvli/ ADV ❑ *The troops submissively laid down their weapons.*

✪**sub·mit** /səbˈmɪt/ VERB [I, T] (**submits, submitting, submitted**) (*academic word*) **1** [I] If you **submit to** something, you unwillingly allow something to be done to you, or you do what someone wants, for example because you are not powerful enough to resist. ❑ *In desperation, Mrs Jones submitted to an operation on her right knee to relieve the pain.* **2** [T] If you **submit** a proposal, report, or request to someone, you formally send it to them so that they can consider it or decide about it. = present, hand in ❑ *They submitted their reports to the chancellor yesterday.* ❑ *Head teachers yesterday submitted a claim for a 9 per cent pay rise.*

✪**sub·or·di·nate** NOUN, ADJ, VERB (*academic word*) **NOUN** /səˈbɔːdɪnət/ [C] (**subordinates**) If someone is your **subordinate**, they have a less important position than you

in the organization that you both work for. ❑ *Haig tended not to seek guidance from subordinates.*

ADJ /səˈbɔːdɪnət/ **1** Someone who is **subordinate to** you has a less important position than you and has to obey you. ❑ *Sixty of his subordinate officers followed his example.* **2** Something that is **subordinate to** something else is less important than the other thing. = inferior; ≠ superior ❑ *It was an art in which words were subordinate to images.* ❑ *However, this critique of conspiracy or integrationist theory is subordinate to Connell's main contention.*

VERB /səˈbɔːdɪneɪt/ [T] (**subordinates, subordinating, subordinated**) If you **subordinate** something **to** another thing, you regard it or treat it as less important than the other thing. ❑ *He was both willing and able to subordinate all else to this aim.*

sub·or·di·na·tion /sə,bɔːdɪˈneɪʃən/ NOUN [U] ❑ *the social subordination of women*

sub·scribe /səbˈskraɪb/ VERB [I] (**subscribes, subscribing, subscribed**) **1** If you **subscribe to** an opinion or belief, you are one of a number of people who have this opinion or belief. ❑ *I've personally never subscribed to the view that either sex is superior to the other.* **2** If you **subscribe to** a magazine or a newspaper, you pay to receive copies of it regularly. ❑ *My main reason for subscribing to New Scientist is to keep abreast of advances in science.* **3** (*computing*) If you **subscribe to** an online newsgroup or service, you send a message saying that you wish to receive it or belong to it. ❑ *Usenet is a collection of discussion groups, known as newsgroups, to which anybody can subscribe.* **4** (*business*) If you **subscribe for** shares in a company, you apply to buy shares in that company. ❑ *Employees subscribed for far more shares than were available.*

sub·scrib·er /səbˈskraɪbə/ NOUN [C] (**subscribers**) **1** A magazine's or a newspaper's **subscribers** are the people who pay to receive copies of it regularly. ❑ *I have been a subscriber to Newsweek for many years.* **2** **Subscribers to** a service are the people who pay to receive the service. ❑ *China has almost 15 million subscribers to satellite and cable television.*

sub·scrip·tion /səbˈskrɪpʃən/ NOUN, ADJ **NOUN** [C] (**subscriptions**) A **subscription** is an amount of money that you pay regularly in order to belong to an organization, to help a charity or campaign, or to receive copies of a magazine or newspaper. ❑ *You can become a member by paying the yearly subscription.* **ADJ** [subscription + N] **Subscription** television is television that you can watch only if you pay a subscription. A **subscription** channel is a channel that you can watch only if you pay a subscription. ❑ *Premiere, a subscription channel which began in 1991, shows live football covering the top two divisions.*

✪**sub·se·quent** ♦◇◇ /ˈsʌbsɪkwənt/ ADJ [subsequent + N] (*academic word, formal*) You use **subsequent** to describe something that happened or existed after the time or event that has just been referred to. = following, next; ≠ previous ❑ *the increase of population in subsequent years* ❑ *Those concerns were overshadowed by subsequent events.*

✪**sub·se·quent·ly** /ˈsʌbsɪkwəntli/ ADV ❑ *He subsequently worked on Boeing's 747, 767 and 737 jetliner programmes.* ❑ *She subsequently became the Faculty's President.* ❑ *Kermes were then believed to be berries, but were subsequently discovered to be scale insects.*

✪**sub·sidi·ary** /səbˈsɪdiəri, AmE -dieri/ NOUN, ADJ (*academic word*) **NOUN** [C] (**subsidiaries**) (*business*) A **subsidiary** or a **subsidiary** company is a company which is part of a larger and more important company. ❑ *WM Financial Services is a subsidiary of Washington Mutual.* ❑ *It's one of ten companies that are subsidiaries of Cossack Holdings.* **ADJ** If something is **subsidiary**, it is less important than something else with which it is connected. = secondary ❑ *The marketing department has always played a subsidiary role to the sales department.* ❑ *This character may be pushed into a subsidiary position or even abandoned altogether.*

✪**sub·si·dize** /ˈsʌbsɪdaɪz/ also **subsidise** VERB [T] (**subsidizes, subsidizing, subsidized**) If a government or other authority **subsidizes** something, they pay part of the

S

cost of it. = support ❏ *Around the world, governments have subsidized the housing of middle- and upper-income groups.* ❏ *pensions that are subsidized by the government*

sub·si·dized /'sʌbsɪdaɪzd/ ADJ ❏ *heavily subsidized prices for housing, bread, and meat*

⭕ **sub·si·dy** ◆◇◇ /'sʌbsɪdi/ NOUN [c] (**subsidies**) (*academic word*) A **subsidy** is money that is paid by a government or other authority in order to help an industry or business, or to pay for a public service. = grant, aid ❏ *European farmers are planning a massive demonstration against farm subsidy cuts.* ❏ *They've also slashed state subsidies to utilities and transportation.*

sub·sist·ence /səb'sɪstəns/ NOUN, ADJ

NOUN [U] **Subsistence** is the condition of just having enough food or money to stay alive. ❏ *below the subsistence level*

ADJ [subsistence + N] In **subsistence** farming or **subsistence** agriculture, farmers produce food to eat themselves rather than to sell. ❏ *Many Namibians are subsistence farmers who live in the arid borderlands.*

⭕ **sub·stance** ◆◇◇ /'sʌbstəns/ NOUN [c, u, SING] (**substances**) **1** [c] A **substance** is a solid, powder, liquid, or gas with particular properties. ❏ *There's absolutely no regulation of cigarettes to make sure that they don't include poisonous substances.* ❏ *The substance that's causing the problem comes from the barley.* **2** [U] (*formal*) **Substance** is the quality of being important or significant. ❏ *It's questionable whether anything of substance has been achieved.* **3** [SING] The **substance** of what someone says or writes is the main thing that they are trying to say. ❏ *The substance of his discussions doesn't really matter.* **4** [U] (*formal*) If you say that something has no **substance**, you mean that it is not true. = truth ❏ *There is no substance in any of these allegations.*

⭕ **sub·stan·tial** ◆◇◇ /səb'stænʃəl/ ADJ (*formal*) **Substantial** means large in amount or degree. = significant, considerable; ≠ insubstantial, small ❏ *A substantial number of mothers with young children are deterred from undertaking paid work because they lack access to childcare.* ❏ *a very substantial improvement*

⭕ **sub·stan·tial·ly** /səb'stænʃəli/ ADV (*formal*) If something changes **substantially** or is **substantially** different, it changes a lot or is very different. = significantly, considerably; ≠ slightly ❏ *The percentage of girls in engineering has increased substantially.* ❏ *The price was substantially higher than had been expected.*

sub·stan·ti·ate /səb'stænʃieɪt/ VERB [T] (**substantiates, substantiating, substantiated**) (*formal*) To **substantiate** a statement or a story means to supply evidence which proves that it is true. = validate ❏ *There is little scientific evidence to substantiate the claims.*

⭕ **sub·sti·tute** ◆◇◇ /'sʌbstɪtjuːt, AmE -tuːt/ VERB, NOUN (*academic word*)

VERB [I, T] (**substitutes, substituting, substituted**) If you **substitute** one thing **for** another, or if one thing **substitutes for** another, it takes the place or performs the function of the other thing. ❏ *They were substituting violence for dialogue.* ❏ *He was substituting for the injured William Wales.* ❏ *He substituted different isotopes into the model and charted the changes.*

NOUN [c] (**substitutes**) **1** A **substitute** is something that you have or use instead of something else. = replacement, equivalent ❏ *She is seeking a substitute for the very man whose departure made her cry.* ❏ *The increased use of nuclear energy as a substitute for fossil fuels* ❏ *tests on humans to find a blood substitute made from animal blood* **2** If you say that one thing is no **substitute for** another, you mean that it does not have certain desirable features that the other thing has, and is therefore unsatisfactory. If you say that there is no **substitute for** something, you mean that it is the only thing which is really satisfactory. ❏ *The printed word is no substitute for personal discussion with a great thinker.* **3** In team games such as football, a **substitute** is a player who is brought into a match to replace another player. ❏ *Jefferson came on as a substitute in the 60th minute.*

⭕ **sub·sti·tu·tion** /ˌsʌbstɪ'tjuːʃən, AmE -'tuː-/ NOUN [c, u] (**substitutions**) ❏ *In my experience a straight substitution of*

carob for chocolate doesn't work. ❏ *safety concerns over the substitution of ingredients* ❏ *the nature and pace of technology substitution*

⭕ **sub·tle** /'sʌtəl/ ADJ (**subtler, subtlest**) **1** Something that is **subtle** is not immediately obvious or noticeable. ❏ *the slow and subtle changes that take place in all living things* ❏ *Intolerance can take subtler forms too.* ❏ *There is a subtle distinction between a withdrawal and a retreat.* **2** A **subtle** person cleverly uses indirect methods to achieve something. ❏ *I even began to exploit him in subtle ways.* **3** **Subtle** smells, tastes, sounds, or colours are pleasantly complex and delicate. = delicate; ≠ obvious ❏ *subtle shades of brown* ❏ *delightfully subtle scents*

⭕ **sub·tly** /'sʌtli/ ADV **1** *The truth is subtly different.* ❏ *These substances could subtly alter neural connections* **2** [subtly with V] ❏ *Nathan is subtly trying to turn her against Barry.* **3** *a white sofa teamed with subtly coloured rugs*

⭕ **sub·tle·ty** /'sʌtəlti/ NOUN [c, u] (**subtleties**) **1** [c] **Subtleties** are very small details or differences which are not obvious. = detail ❏ *His fascination with the subtleties of human behaviour makes him a good storyteller.* **2** [u] **Subtlety** is the quality of being not immediately obvious or noticeable, and therefore difficult to describe. = nuance ❏ *African dance is vigorous, but full of subtlety, requiring great strength and control.* ❏ *Many of the resulting wines lack the subtlety of the original model.* **3** [u] **Subtlety** is the ability to notice and recognize things which are not obvious, especially small differences between things. ❏ *She analyses herself with great subtlety.* **4** [u] **Subtlety** is the ability to use indirect methods to achieve something, rather than doing something that is obvious. ❏ *They had obviously been hoping to approach the topic with more subtlety.*

⭕ **sub·tract** /səb'trækt/ VERB [T] (**subtracts, subtracting, subtracted**) If you **subtract** one number **from** another, you do a calculation in which you take it away from the other number. For example, if you subtract 3 from 5, you get 2. = take away; ≠ add ❏ *Mandy subtracted the date of birth from the date of death.* ❏ *We have subtracted £25 per adult to arrive at a basic room rate.*

⭕ **sub·trac·tion** /səb'trækʃən/ NOUN [c, u] (**subtractions**) ≠ addition ❏ *She's ready to learn simple addition and subtraction.* ❏ *I looked at what he'd given me and did a quick subtraction.*

sub·urb /'sʌbɜːb/ NOUN [c, PL] (**suburbs**) **1** [c] A **suburb** of a city or large town is a smaller area which is part of the city or large town but is outside its centre. ❏ *Anna was born in 1923 in a suburb of Philadelphia.* **2** [PL] If you live in the **suburbs**, you live in an area of houses outside the centre of a city or large town. ❏ *His family lived in the suburbs.*

sub·ur·ban /sə'bɜːbən/ ADJ [suburban + N] **Suburban** means relating to a suburb. ❏ *a comfortable suburban home*

sub·ver·sive /səb'vɜːsɪv/ ADJ, NOUN

ADJ Something that is **subversive** is intended to weaken or destroy a political system or government. ❏ *The play was promptly banned as subversive and possibly treasonous.*

NOUN [c] (**subversives**) **Subversives** are people who attempt to weaken or destroy a political system or government. ❏ *Agents regularly rounded up suspected subversives.*

sub·vert /səb'vɜːt/ VERB [T] (**subverts, subverting, subverted**) (*formal*) To **subvert** something means to destroy its power and influence. = undermine ❏ *an alleged plot to subvert the state*

⭕ **suc·ceed** ◆◆◇ /sək'siːd/ VERB [I, T] (**succeeds, succeeding, succeeded**) **1** [I] If you **succeed in** doing something, you manage to do it. = accomplish, manage; ≠ fail ❏ *We have already succeeded in working out ground rules with the Department of Defence.* ❏ *Some people will succeed in their efforts to stop smoking.* **2** [I] If something **succeeds**, it works in a satisfactory way or has the result that is intended. ❏ *The talks can succeed if both sides are flexible and serious.* ❏ *If marriage is to succeed, then people have to recognise the new pressures it is facing.* ❏ *a move which would make any future talks even more unlikely to succeed* **3** [I] Someone who **succeeds** gains a high position in what they do, for example in business or politics. ❏ *the skills and*

S

qualities needed to succeed in small and medium-sized businesses **4** [T] If you **succeed** another person, you are the next person to have their job or position. ❏ *David Rowland is almost certain to succeed him as chairman on January 1.* **5** [T] If one thing **is succeeded by** another thing, the other thing happens or comes after it. ❏ *The presentation was succeeded by a roundtable discussion.*

◆ **suc·cess** ♦♦◇ /sək'ses/ NOUN [U, C] (**successes**) **1** [U] **Success** is the achievement of something that you have been trying to do. ❏ *It's important for the success of any diet that you vary your meals.* ❏ *the success of European business in building a stronger partnership between management and workers* **2** [U] **Success** is the achievement of a high position in a particular field, for example in business or politics. ❏ *We all believed that work was the key to success.* **3** [U] The **success** of something is the fact that it works in a satisfactory way or has the result that is intended. ❏ *We were amazed by the play's success.* **4** [C] Someone or something that is a **success** achieves a high position, makes a lot of money, or is admired a great deal. ❏ *We hope it will be a commercial success.*

WORD CONNECTIONS

VERB + **success**

enjoy success
achieve success
taste success

❏ *The team is on a solid financial footing and should enjoy continued success.*

success + VERB

success **depends on** something
success **lies in** something

❏ *The firm's continuing success depends on long-term productivity.*

ADJ + **success**

huge success
great success

❏ *Her first novel was a huge success.*

success + NOUN

success **rate**

❏ *The treatment has a 75% success rate.*

◆ **suc·cess·ful** ♦♦◇ /sək'sesfʊl/ ADJ **1** Something that is **successful** achieves what it was intended to achieve. Someone who is **successful** achieves what they intended to achieve. ❏ *How successful will this new treatment be?* ❏ *I am looking forward to a long and successful partnership with him.* **2** Something that is **successful** is popular or makes a lot of money. ❏ *the hugely successful movie that brought Robert Redford an Oscar for his directing* **3** Someone who is **successful** achieves a high position in what they do, for example in business or politics. ❏ *Women do not necessarily have to imitate men to be successful in business.* ❏ *She is a successful lawyer.*
suc·cess·ful·ly /sək'sesfəli/ ADV [successfully with V] ❏ *The doctors have successfully concluded preliminary tests.*

WORD CONNECTIONS

ADV + **successful**

hugely successful
highly successful
enormously successful

❏ *Jakob was a highly successful businessman.*

commerically successful
financially successful

❏ *The Apple I was the first commercially successful microcomputer.*

successful + NOUN

a successful **career**
a successful **launch**
a successful **campaign**

❏ *She had a long and successful career in cinema.*

a successful **outcome**
a successful **conclusion**

❏ *A successful outcome would restore the country's confidence in the government.*

a successful **businessman**
a successful **businesswoman**
a successful **applicant**

❏ *The successful applicant will be expected to work closely with both laboratory scientists and IT staff.*

VERB + **successful**

prove successful
become successful

❏ *The treatment proved successful in improving patients' mobility.*

suc·ces·sion /sək'seʃən/ NOUN [SING, U] **1** [SING] [oft succession 'of' N, also 'in' succession] A **succession of** things of the same kind is a number of them that exist or happen one after the other. ❏ *Adams took a succession of jobs which have stood him in good stead.* **2** [U] **Succession** is the act or right of being the next person to have an important job or position. ❏ *She is now seventh in line of succession to the throne.*

◆ **suc·ces·sive** /sək'sesiv/ ADJ (academic word) **Successive** means happening or existing one after another without a break. ❏ *Jackson was the winner for a second successive year.* ❏ *Britain was suffering from the failure of successive governments to co-ordinate a national transport policy.*

suc·ces·sor /sək'sesə/ NOUN [C] (**successors**) (academic word) Someone's **successor** is the person who takes their job after they have left. ❏ *He set out several principles that he hopes will guide his successors.*

◆ **suc·cinct** /sək'sɪŋkt/ ADJ (approval) Something that is **succinct** expresses facts or ideas clearly and in few words. = concise ❏ *The book gives an admirably succinct account of the technology and its history.* ❏ *Weston's essay provides a succinct overview of the historical development of human rights ideas.* ❏ *If you have something to say make sure that it is accurate, succinct and to the point.*
◆ **suc·cinct·ly** /sək'sɪŋktli/ ADV ❏ *He succinctly summed up his manifesto as 'Work hard, train hard and play hard'.* ❏ *Succinctly, the Commission explored real social and legal problems, while developing a theoretical approach.*

suc·cumb /sə'kʌm/ VERB [I] (**succumbs, succumbing, succumbed**) (formal) If you **succumb to** temptation or pressure, you do something that you want to do, or that other people want you to do, although you feel it might be wrong. = give in ❏ *Don't succumb to the temptation to have just one cigarette.*

such ♦♦♦ /sʌtʃ/ DET, PREDET, PRON

When **such** is used as a predeterminer, it is followed by 'a' and a count noun in the singular. When it is used as a determiner, it is followed by a count noun in the plural or by an uncountable noun.

DET **1** You use **such** to refer back to the thing or person that you have just mentioned, or a thing or person like the one that you have just mentioned. You use **such as** and **such...as** to introduce a reference to the person or thing that has just been mentioned. ❏ *There have been previous attempts at coups. We regard such methods as entirely unacceptable.* **2** You use **such...as** or **such as** to link something or someone with a clause in which you give a description of the kind of thing or person that you mean. ❏ *incentive payments for such activities as planting hardwood trees* ❏ *Children do not use inflections such as are used in mature adult speech.* **3** You use **such...as** or **such as** to introduce one or more examples of the kind of thing or person that you have just mentioned. ❏ *such careers as teaching, nursing, hairdressing and catering* ❏ *serious offences, such as assault on a police officer* **4** You use **such** before noun groups to emphasize the extent of something or to emphasize that something is remarkable. ❏ *I think most of us don't want to read what's in the newspaper anyway in such*

S

detail. ☐ One will never be able to understand why these political issues can acquire such force. **5** **Such** is also used before a noun to emphasize the extent of something. ☐ She looked at him in such distress that he had to look away. **6** You use **such...that** or **such that** in order to say what the result or consequence of something that you have just mentioned is. ☐ The operation has uncovered such backstreet dealing in stolen property that police might now press for changes in the law. ☐ Their cost structure is such that they just can't compete with the low-cost carriers.

PREDET **1** [such 'a' N] **Such** is used before **a** or **an** to refer back to something you have just mentioned. ☐ If your request is for information about a child, please contact the registrar to find out how to make such a request. ☐ She has told us that when she goes back to stay with her family, they make her pay rent. We could not believe such a thing. **2** [such 'a' N] **Such** is used with **a** or **an** to emphasize the extent of something. ☐ It was such a pleasant surprise. **3** [such 'a' N 'that'] You use **such...that** or **such that** in order to emphasize the degree of something by mentioning the result or consequence of it. ☐ This is something where you can earn such a lot of money that there is not any risk that you will lose it. ☐ Though Vivaldi had earned a great deal in his lifetime, his extravagance was such that he died in poverty. **4** [such 'a' N 'that'/'as to'] **Such** is used before **a** or **an** to say what the result or consequence of something you have just mentioned is. ☐ He could put an idea in such a way that Alan would believe it was his own.

PRON **Such** is also used before **be** to refer back to something you have just mentioned. ☐ We are scared because we are being watched – such is the atmosphere in Pristina and other cities in Kosovo.

PHRASES **such and such** (spoken, vagueness) You use **such and such** to refer to a thing or person when you do not want to be exact or precise. ☐ I said, 'Well, what time'll I get to Baltimore?' and he said such and such a time but I missed my connection.

as such **1** You use **as such** with a negative to indicate that a word or expression is not a very accurate description of the actual situation. ☐ I am not a learner as such – I used to ride a bike years ago. **2** You use **as such** after a noun to indicate that you are considering that thing on its own, separately from other things or factors. ☐ Mr Simon said he was not against taxes as such, 'but I do object when taxation is justified on spurious or dishonest grounds,' he says.

✦ no such thing → see thing

USAGE NOTE

such

Do not use 'such as' at the beginning of a sentence.
Most Internet users visit government websites to obtain information on subjects **such as** tourism or health.

suck /sʌk/ VERB [I, T, PASSIVE] (**sucks, sucking, sucked**) **1** [I, T] If you **suck** something, you hold it in your mouth and pull at it with the muscles in your cheeks and tongue, for example in order to get liquid out of it. ☐ They waited in silence and sucked their sweets. ☐ He sucked on his cigarette. **2** [T] If something **sucks** a liquid, gas, or object in a particular direction, it draws it there with a powerful force. ☐ The pollution-control team is at the scene and is due to start sucking up oil any time now. **3** [PASSIVE] If you **are sucked into** a bad situation, you are unable to prevent yourself from becoming involved in it. ☐ the extent to which they have been sucked into the cycle of violence

sud·den ✦◇◇ /'sʌdən/ ADJ
ADJ **Sudden** means happening quickly and unexpectedly. ☐ He had been deeply affected by the sudden death of his father-in-law. ☐ It was all very sudden.
PHRASE **all of a sudden** If something happens **all of a sudden**, it happens quickly and unexpectedly. ☐ All of a sudden she didn't look sleepy any more.
sud·den·ness /'sʌdənnəs/ NOUN [U] ☐ The enemy seemed stunned by the suddenness of the attack.

sud·den·ly ✦◇◇ /'sʌdənli/ ADV If something happens **suddenly**, it happens quickly and unexpectedly. ☐ Suddenly, she looked ten years older. ☐ Her expression suddenly altered.

sue /suː/ VERB [I, T] (**sues, suing, sued**) If you **sue** someone, you start a legal case against them, usually in order to claim money from them because they have harmed you in some way. ☐ Mr Warren sued for libel over the remarks. ☐ The company could be sued for damages.

◑ suf·fer ✦✦◇ /'sʌfə/ VERB [I, T] (**suffers, suffering, suffered**) **1** [I, T] If you **suffer** pain, you feel it in your body or in your mind. = be in pain, be affected ☐ Within a few days she had become seriously ill, suffering great pain and discomfort. ☐ He suffered terribly the last few days. ☐ Can you assure me that my father is not suffering? **2** [I] If you **suffer from** an illness or from some other bad condition, you are badly affected by it. ☐ He was eventually diagnosed as suffering from terminal cancer. **3** [T] If you **suffer** something bad, you are in a situation in which something painful, harmful, or very unpleasant happens to you. = endure, experience ☐ The peace process has suffered a serious blow now. **4** [I] If you **suffer**, you are badly affected by an event or situation. ☐ There are few who have not suffered. ☐ It is obvious that Syria will suffer most from this change of heart. **5** [I] If something **suffers**, it becomes worse because it has not been given enough attention or is in a bad situation. ☐ I'm not surprised that your studies are suffering.

WHICH WORD?

suffer, put up with, stand, or bear?

You can say that someone **suffers** pain or an unpleasant experience.
☐ He **suffered** a lot of discomfort.
You do not use **suffer** to say that someone tolerates an unpleasant person. You say that they **put up with** the person.
☐ The local people have to **put up with** gaping tourists.
If you do not like someone at all, you do not say that you 'can't suffer' them. You say that you **can't stand** them or **can't bear** them.
☐ She said she **couldn't stand** him.
☐ I **can't bear** kids.

USAGE NOTE

suffer

Note that **suffer** is only usually followed by 'from' when you are referring to an illness. Do not say that someone 'suffers from poverty' or that they 'are suffering from a disaster'.
In 1934, one third of the human race **suffered from** malaria.
The river is being restocked with fish after **suffering** the worst pollution disaster in its history.

◑ suf·fer·er /'sʌfərə/ NOUN [C] (**sufferers**) [oft sufferer 'from/of' N, N + sufferer] A **sufferer from** an illness or some other bad condition is a person who is affected by the illness or condition. = patient, victim ☐ Frequently sufferers of this kind of allergy are also sufferers of asthma. ☐ hay-fever sufferers

◑ suf·fer·ing /'sʌfərɪŋ/ NOUN [U] (**sufferings**) [also sufferings] **Suffering** is serious pain which someone feels in their body or their mind. = pain, torment, agony ☐ They began to recover slowly from their nightmare of pain and suffering. ☐ It has caused terrible suffering to animals. ☐ His many novels have portrayed the sufferings of his race.

suf·fice /sə'faɪs/ VERB
VERB [I] (**suffices, sufficing, sufficed**) (formal) If you say that something will **suffice**, you mean it will be enough to achieve a purpose or to fulfil a need. = do ☐ A covering letter should never exceed one page; often a far shorter letter will suffice.
PHRASE **suffice it to say** **Suffice it to say** or **suffice to say** is used at the beginning of a statement to indicate that what you are saying is obvious, or that you will only give a short explanation. ☐ Suffice it to say that afterwards we never met again.

S

✪suf·fi·cient ◆◇◇ /səˈfɪʃənt/ ADJ (academic word) If something is **sufficient for** a particular purpose, there is enough of it for the purpose. = enough; ≠ insufficient □ *One yard of fabric is sufficient to cover the exterior of an 18-in-diameter hatbox.* □ *Lighting levels should be sufficient for photography without flash.* □ *There was not sufficient evidence to secure a conviction.*
  ✪suf·fi·cient·ly /səˈfɪʃəntli/ ADV ≠ insufficiently □ *She recovered sufficiently to accompany Chou on his tour of Africa in 1964.* □ *300,000 years after the Big Bang, the Universe had cooled sufficiently for protons and electrons to combine into neutral hydrogen atoms.* □ *The holes were sufficiently large to serve as nests.*

sug·ar ◆◇◇ /ˈʃʊɡə/ NOUN [U, c] (**sugars**) **1** [U] **Sugar** is a sweet substance that is used to make food and drinks sweet. It is usually in the form of small white or brown crystals. □ *bags of sugar* **2** [c] If someone has one **sugar** in their tea or coffee, they have one small spoon of sugar or one sugar lump in it. □ *How many sugars do you take?* **3** [c] **Sugars** are substances that occur naturally in food. When you eat them, the body converts them into energy. □ *Plants produce sugars and starch to provide themselves with energy.*

✪sug·gest ◆◆◆ /səˈdʒest, AmE səˈɡdʒest/ VERB [T] (**suggests, suggesting, suggested**) **1** If you **suggest** something, you put forward a plan or idea for someone to think about. = propose □ *He suggested a link between class size and test results of seven-year-olds.* □ *I suggest you ask him some specific questions about his past.* □ *No one has suggested how this might occur.* □ *I suggested to Mike that we go out for a meal with his colleagues.* **2** If you **suggest** the name of a person or place, you recommend them to someone. □ *Could you suggest someone to advise me how to do this?* **3** If you **suggest that** something is the case, you say something which you believe to be the case. □ *I'm not suggesting that is what is happening.* □ *It is wrong to suggest that there are easy alternatives.* **4** If one thing **suggests** another, it implies it or makes you think that it might be the case. = indicate, imply □ *Earlier reports suggested that a meeting would take place on Sunday.* □ *Its hairy body suggests a mammal.* □ *The scientific evidence suggests otherwise.*

WORD CONNECTIONS
suggest + NOUN
suggest a **possibility**   suggest a **solution**   suggest an **idea**   □ *The report identifies problems and suggests some solutions.*
suggest a **compromise**   suggest an **alternative**   □ *The Commission suggested two possible alternatives to achieve their objective.*
NOUN + **suggest**
evidence suggests   **research** suggests   **data** suggests   **findings** suggest   □ *The findings suggest that the condition is more prevalent than was generally thought.*
a **poll** suggests   a **report** suggests   a **study** suggests   □ *Earlier reports suggested that a meeting would take place on Sunday.*
ADV + **suggest**
strongly suggest   **tentatively** suggest   □ *The evidence strongly suggests that primitive life may have existed on Mars more than 3.6 billion years ago.*

USAGE NOTE
suggest
Note that **suggest** cannot usually be followed by a noun or a pronoun referring to a person. Do not say '~~She suggested me to lie down~~'.   *She **suggested that** I lie down.*

✪sug·ges·tion ◆◇◇ /səˈdʒestʃən, AmE səɡdʒ-/ NOUN [c, SING] (**suggestions**) **1** [c] If you make a **suggestion**, you put forward an idea or plan for someone to think about. = proposal, recommendation, idea, plan □ *The dietitian was helpful, making suggestions as to how I could improve my diet.* □ *Perhaps he'd followed her suggestion of a stroll to the river.* **2** [c] A **suggestion** is something that a person says which implies that something is the case. □ *We reject any suggestion that the law needs amending.* **3** [SING] If there is no **suggestion that** something is the case, there is no reason to think that it is the case. □ *There is no suggestion whatsoever that the two sides are any closer to agreeing.*

sug·ges·tive /səˈdʒestɪv, AmE səɡdʒ-/ ADJ **1** [V-LINK + suggestive 'of' N] Something that is **suggestive of** something else is quite like it or may be a sign of it. □ *The fingers were gnarled, lumpy, with long, curving nails suggestive of animal claws.* **2** **Suggestive** remarks or looks cause people to think about sex, often in a way that makes them feel uncomfortable. □ *another former employee who claims Thomas made suggestive remarks to her*

sui·cid·al /ˌsuːɪˈsaɪdəl/ ADJ People who are **suicidal** want to kill themselves. □ *I was suicidal and just couldn't stop crying.*

sui·cide ◆◇◇ /ˈsuːɪsaɪd/ NOUN [c, U] (**suicides**) People who commit **suicide** deliberately kill themselves because they do not want to continue living. □ *She tried to commit suicide on several occasions.* □ *a case of attempted suicide*

suit ◆◆◇ /suːt/ NOUN, VERB
  NOUN [c] (**suits**) **1** A man's **suit** consists of a jacket, trousers, and sometimes a waistcoat, all made from the same fabric. □ *a dark pin-striped business suit* **2** A woman's **suit** consists of a jacket and skirt, or sometimes trousers, made from the same fabric. □ *I was wearing my tweed suit.* **3** A particular type of **suit** is a piece of clothing that you wear for a particular activity. □ *The six survivors only lived through their ordeal because of the special rubber suits they were wearing.* **4** In a court of law, a **suit** is a case in which someone tries to get a legal decision against a person or company, often so that the person or company will have to pay them money for having done something wrong to them. = lawsuit □ *Up to 2,000 former employees have filed personal injury suits against the company.*
  PHRASE **follow suit** If people **follow suit**, they do the same thing that someone else has just done. □ *Efforts to persuade the remainder to follow suit have continued.*
  VERB [T] (**suits, suiting, suited**) **1** If something **suits** you, it is convenient for you or is the best thing for you in the circumstances. □ *They will only release information if it suits them.* **2** If something **suits** you, you like it. □ *I don't think a sedentary life would altogether suit me.* **3** If a piece of clothing or a particular style or colour **suits** you, it makes you look attractive. □ *Green suits you.* **4** If you **suit yourself**, you do something just because you want to do it, without bothering to consider other people. = please □ *People have tended to suit themselves, not paying much heed to the reformers.*

✪suit·able ◆◇◇ /ˈsuːtəbəl/ ADJ Someone or something that is **suitable for** a particular purpose or occasion is right or acceptable for it. = appropriate, right; ≠ unsuitable, inappropriate □ *Employers usually decide within five minutes whether someone is suitable for the job.* □ *The authority must make suitable accommodation available to the family.*
  ✪suit·abil·ity /ˌsuːtəˈbɪlɪti/ NOUN [U] = fitness; ≠ unsuitability □ *information on the suitability of a product for use in the home* □ *There are some who doubt his suitability for the job.*
  ✪suit·ably /ˈsuːtəbli/ ADV [suitably + ADJ/-ED] You use **suitably** to indicate that someone or something has the right qualities or things for a particular activity, purpose,

S

or situation. = appropriately; ≠ unsuitably, inappropriately □ There are problems in recruiting suitably qualified scientific officers for our laboratories. □ Unfortunately I'm not suitably dressed for gardening.

suit·case /ˈsuːtkeɪs/ NOUN [C] (**suitcases**) A **suitcase** is a box or bag with a handle and a hard frame in which you carry your clothes when you are travelling. □ It did not take Andrew long to pack a suitcase.

suite /swiːt/ NOUN [C] (**suites**) **1** A **suite** is a set of rooms in a hotel or other building. □ They had a fabulous time during their week in a suite at the Paris Hilton. **2** A **suite** is a set of matching furniture. □ a three-piece suite **3** A bathroom **suite** is a matching bath, sink, and toilet. □ the horrible pink suite in the bathroom

suit·ed /ˈsuːtɪd/ ADJ [V-LINK + suited] If something is well **suited** to a particular purpose, it is right or appropriate for that purpose. If someone is well **suited to** a particular job, they are right or appropriate for that job. □ The area is well suited to road cycling as well as off-road riding.

sul·len /ˈsʌlən/ ADJ Someone who is **sullen** is bad-tempered and does not speak much. □ The offenders lapsed into a sullen silence.

sul·phur /ˈsʌlfə/ (mainly BrE; in AmE, use **sulfur**) NOUN [U] **Sulphur** is a yellow chemical which has a strong smell. □ Burning sulphur creates poisonous fumes.

❖sum ◆◇◇ /sʌm/ NOUN (academic word) NOUN [C, SING] (**sums**) **1** [C] A **sum** of money is an amount of money. = amount □ Large sums of money were lost. □ Even the relatively modest sum of £50,000 now seems beyond his reach. **2** [SING] In mathematics, **the sum of** two or more numbers is the number that is obtained when they are added together. □ The sum of all the angles of a triangle is 180 degrees. **3** [SING] **The sum of** something is all of it. You often use **sum** in this way to indicate that you are disappointed because the extent of something is rather small, or because it is not very good. □ To date, the sum of my gardening experience had been futile efforts to rid the flower beds of grass. **4** [C] (BrE) A **sum** is a simple calculation in arithmetic.

PHRASAL VERB **sum up** (**sums, summing, summed**) **1** If you **sum** something **up**, you describe it as briefly as possible. □ One voter in Brasilia summed up the mood – 'Politicians have lost credibility,' he complained. **2** If something **sums** a person or situation **up**, it represents their most typical characteristics. = epitomize □ 'I love my wife, my horse and my dog,' he said, and that summed him up. **3** If you **sum up** after a speech or at the end of a piece of writing, you briefly state the main points again. When a judge **sums up** after a trial, he or she reminds the jury of the evidence and the main arguments of the case they have heard. □ When the judge summed up, it was clear he wanted a guilty verdict.

❖sum·ma·rize /ˈsʌməraɪz/ also **summarise** VERB [I, T] (**summarizes, summarizing, summarized**) If you **summarize** something, you give a summary of it. = sum up, outline □ Table 3.1 summarizes the information given above. □ Basically, the article can be summarized in three sentences.

❖sum·mary /ˈsʌməri/ NOUN, ADJ (academic word) NOUN [C] (**summaries**) A **summary** of something is a short account of it, which gives the main points but not the details. = résumé, abstract, précis □ What follows is a brief summary of the process.

PHRASE **in summary** You use **in summary** to indicate that what you are about to say is a summary of what has just been said. □ In summary, it is my opinion that this complete treatment process was very successful.

ADJ [summary + N] (formal) **Summary** actions are done without delay, often when something else should have been done first or done instead. □ It says torture and summary execution are common.

sum·mer ◆◆◇ /ˈsʌmə/ NOUN [C, U] (**summers**) **Summer** is the season between spring and autumn. In the summer the weather is usually warm or hot. □ I escaped the heatwave in Washington earlier this summer and flew to Maine. □ It was a perfect summer's day.

❖sum·mit ◆◆◇ /ˈsʌmɪt/ NOUN [C] (**summits**) **1** A

summit is a meeting at which the leaders of two or more countries discuss important matters. □ next week's Washington summit □ the NATO summit meeting in Rome □ The Palestinian leader would then be able to attend the Arab summit on March 27th in Beirut. **2** The **summit** of a mountain is the top of it. □ He reached the summit of the mountain at about noon.

sum·mon /ˈsʌmən/ VERB VERB [T] (**summons, summoning, summoned**) **1** (formal) If you **summon** someone, you order them to come to you. □ Howe summoned a doctor and hurried over. □ Suddenly we were summoned to the interview room. **2** If you **summon** a quality, you make a great effort to have it. For example, if you **summon** the courage or strength to do something, you make a great effort to be brave or strong, so that you will be able to do it. □ It took her a full month to summon the courage to tell her mother.

PHRASAL VERB **summon up Summon up** means the same as **summon** VERB 2. □ Painfully shy, he finally summoned up courage to ask her to a game.

sun ◆◆◇ /sʌn/ NOUN [SING, U] **1** [SING] **The sun** is the ball of fire in the sky that the Earth goes around, and that gives us heat and light. □ The sun was now high in the southern sky. □ The sun came out, briefly. **2** [U] You refer to the light and heat that reach us from the sun as **the sun**. □ Dena took them into the courtyard to sit in the sun.

sung /sʌŋ/ IRREG FORM **Sung** is the past participle of **sing**.

sunk /sʌŋk/ IRREG FORM **Sunk** is the past participle of **sink**.

sun·light /ˈsʌnlaɪt/ NOUN [U] **Sunlight** is the light that comes from the sun during the day. □ I saw her sitting at a window table, bathed in sunlight.

sun·ny /ˈsʌni/ ADJ (**sunnier, sunniest**) **1** When it is **sunny**, the sun is shining brightly. = bright □ The weather was surprisingly warm and sunny. **2** **Sunny** places are brightly lit by the sun. □ Most roses like a sunny position in a fairly fertile soil.

sun·rise /ˈsʌnraɪz/ NOUN [U, C] (**sunrises**) **1** [U] **Sunrise** is the time in the morning when the sun first appears in the sky. □ The rain began before sunrise. **2** [C] A **sunrise** is the colours and light that you see in the eastern part of the sky when the sun first appears. □ There was a spectacular sunrise yesterday.

sun·set /ˈsʌnset/ NOUN [U, C] (**sunsets**) **1** [U] **Sunset** is the time in the evening when the sun disappears out of sight from the sky. □ The dance ends at sunset. **2** [C] A **sunset** is the colours and light that you see in the western part of the sky when the sun disappears in the evening. □ There was a red sunset over Paris.

sun·shine /ˈsʌnʃaɪn/ NOUN [U] **Sunshine** is the light and heat that comes from the sun. □ In the marina yachts sparkle in the sunshine. □ She was sitting outside a cafe in bright sunshine.

su·per ◆◇◇ /ˈsuːpə/ ADV, ADJ ADV [super + ADJ] **Super** is used before adjectives to indicate that something has a lot of a quality. □ I'm going to Greece in the summer so I've got to be super slim. ADJ **1** [super + N] **Super** is used before nouns to indicate that something is larger, better, or more advanced than similar things. □ Winners of each regional will advance to the super regionals. **2** (informal, old-fashioned) Some people use **super** to mean very nice or very good. = great □ We had a super time. □ That's a super idea.

su·perb ◆◇◇ /suːˈpɜːb/ ADJ **1** If something is **superb**, its quality is very good indeed. = excellent, outstanding □ There is a superb 18-hole golf course 6 miles away. **2** If you say that someone has **superb** confidence, control, or skill, you mean that they have very great confidence, control, or skill. □ With superb skill he managed to make a perfect landing.

su·perb·ly /suːˈpɜːbli/ ADV **1** The orchestra played superbly. **2** his superbly disciplined opponent

super·fi·cial /ˌsuːpəˈfɪʃəl/ ADJ **1** (disapproval) If you describe someone as **superficial**, you disapprove of them because they do not think deeply, and have little understanding of anything serious or important. □ This guy is a superficial yuppie with no intellect whatsoever.

S

2 If you describe something such as an action, feeling, or relationship as **superficial**, you mean that it includes only the simplest and most obvious aspects of that thing, and not those aspects which require more effort to deal with or understand. □ *Their arguments do not withstand the most superficial scrutiny.* **3 Superficial** is used to describe the appearance of something or the impression that it gives, especially if its real nature is very different. □ *Despite these superficial resemblances, this is a darker work than her earlier novels.* **4 Superficial** injuries are not very serious, and affect only the surface of the body. You can also describe damage to an object as **superficial**. = slight □ *The 69-year-old clergyman escaped with superficial wounds.*

super·fi·cial·ly /ˌsuːpəˈfɪʃəli/ ADV **1** *Her husband Bob was only superficially supportive.* **2** *They superficially resembled ordinary pond frogs – except for one extraordinary feature.*

super·in·ten·dent /ˌsuːpərɪnˈtendənt/ NOUN [c] (**superintendents**) **1** A **superintendent** is a person who is responsible for a particular thing or the work done in a particular department. □ *He became superintendent of the bank's East African branches.* **2** In Britain, a **superintendent** is a senior police officer of the rank above an inspector.

su·peri·or ◆◇◇ /suːˈpɪəriə/ ADJ, NOUN

ADJ **1** If one thing or person is **superior to** another, the first is better than the second. □ *We have a relationship infinitely superior to those of many of our friends.* **2** If you describe something as **superior**, you mean that it is good, and better than other things of the same kind. □ *A few years ago it was virtually impossible to find superior quality coffee in local shops.* **3** A **superior** person or thing is more important than another person or thing in the same organization or system. □ *negotiations between the mutineers and their superior officers* **4** If you describe someone as **superior**, you disapprove of them because they behave as if they are better, more important, or more intelligent than other people. □ *Finch gave a superior smile.* **5** (*formal*) If one group of people has **superior** numbers to another group, the first has more people than the second, and therefore has an advantage over it. □ *The demonstrators fled when they saw the authorities' superior numbers.*

NOUN [c] (**superiors**) Your **superior** in an organization that you work for is a person who has a higher rank than you. □ *Other army units are completely surrounded and cut off from communication with their superiors.*

su·peri·or·ity /suːˌpɪəriˈɒrɪti, AmE -ˈɔːrɪti/ NOUN [u] **1 Superiority** refers to one thing being better than another. □ *The technical superiority of laser discs over tape is well established.* **2 Superiority** is a kind of behaviour when someone acts as if they are better, more important, or more intelligent than other people. □ *a false sense of his superiority over mere journalists* **3** (*formal*) If one side in a war or conflict has **superiority**, it has an advantage over its enemy, for example because it has more soldiers or better equipment. □ *We have air superiority.*

super·man /ˈsuːpəmæn/ NOUN [c] (**supermen**) A **superman** is a man who has very great physical or mental abilities. □ *Collor nurtured the idea that he was a superman, who single-handedly could resolve Brazil's crisis.*

super·mar·ket /ˈsuːpəˌmɑːkɪt/ NOUN [c] (**supermarkets**) A **supermarket** is a large shop which sells all kinds of food and some household goods. □ *Most of us do our food shopping in the supermarket.*

super·natu·ral /ˌsuːpəˈnætʃrəl/ ADJ, NOUN

ADJ **Supernatural** creatures, forces, and events are believed by some people to exist or happen, although they are impossible according to scientific laws. □ *The Nakani were evil spirits who looked like humans and possessed supernatural powers.*

NOUN [SING] The **supernatural** is things that are supernatural. □ *He writes short stories with a touch of the supernatural.*

super·pow·er /ˈsuːpəpaʊə/ NOUN [c] (**superpowers**) A **superpower** is a very powerful and influential country, usually one that is rich and has nuclear weapons. □ *The United States could claim to be both a military and an economic superpower.*

super·sede /ˌsuːpəˈsiːd/ VERB [T] (**supersedes, superseding, superseded**) If something **is superseded by** something newer, it is replaced because it has become old-fashioned or unacceptable. □ *Hand tools are relics of the past that have now been superseded by the machine.*

super·star /ˈsuːpəstɑː/ NOUN [c] (**superstars**) (*informal*) A **superstar** is a very famous entertainer or athlete. □ *He was more than a basketball superstar, he was a celebrity.*

super·sti·tion /ˌsuːpəˈstɪʃən/ NOUN [c, u] (**superstitions**) **Superstition** is belief in things that are not real or possible, for example magic. □ *Fortune-telling is a very much debased art surrounded by superstition.*

super·sti·tious /ˌsuːpəˈstɪʃəs/ ADJ **1** People who are **superstitious** believe in things that are not real or possible, for example magic. □ *Jean was extremely superstitious and believed the colour green brought bad luck.* **2** [superstitious + N] **Superstitious** fears or beliefs are irrational and not based on fact. □ *A wave of superstitious fear spread among the townspeople.*

super·store /ˈsuːpəstɔː/ NOUN [c] (**superstores**) **Superstores** are very large supermarkets or shops selling household goods and equipment. Superstores are usually built outside cities and away from other shops. □ *a Do-It-Yourself superstore*

✪**super·vise** /ˈsuːpəvaɪz/ VERB [T] (**supervises, supervising, supervised**) **1** If you **supervise** an activity or a person, you make sure that the activity is done correctly or that the person is doing a task or behaving correctly. = oversee, direct □ *A team was sent to supervise the elections in Nicaragua.* □ *University teachers have refused to supervise students' examinations.* □ *He supervised and trained more than 400 volunteers.* **2** If you **supervise** a place where work is done, you ensure that the work there is done properly. □ *He makes the wines and supervises the vineyards.*

✪**super·vi·sion** /ˌsuːpəˈvɪʒən/ NOUN [u] **Supervision** is the supervising of people, activities, or places. = control, management □ *A toddler requires close supervision and firm control at all times.* □ *The plan calls for a cease-fire and UN supervision of the country.* □ *First-time licence holders have to work under supervision.*

✪**super·vi·sor** /ˈsuːpəvaɪzə/ NOUN [c] (**supervisors**) A **supervisor** is a person who supervises activities or people, especially workers or students. □ *a full-time job as a supervisor at a factory* □ *Each student has a supervisor to advise on the writing of the dissertation.*

sup·per /ˈsʌpə/ NOUN [c, u] (**suppers**) **1** Some people refer to the main meal eaten in the early part of the evening as **supper**. □ *Some guests like to dress for supper.* **2 Supper** is a simple meal eaten just before you go to bed at night. □ *She gives the children their supper, then puts them to bed.*

sup·ple /ˈsʌpəl/ ADJ (**suppler, supplest**) **1** A **supple** object or material bends or changes shape easily without cracking or breaking. □ *The leather is supple and sturdy enough to last for years.* **2** A **supple** person can move and bend their body very easily. □ *Paul was incredibly supple and strong.*

✪**sup·ple·ment** /ˈsʌplɪmənt/ VERB, NOUN (*academic word*)

VERB [T] (**supplements, supplementing, supplemented**) If you **supplement** something, you add something to it in order to improve it. = augment, enhance, enrich □ *people doing extra jobs outside their regular jobs to supplement their incomes* □ *I suggest supplementing your diet with vitamins E and A.*

NOUN [c] (**supplements**) **1** A **supplement** is an addition to something to improve it. = addition □ *Business sponsorship must be a supplement to, not a substitute for, public funding.* **2** A **supplement** is a pill that you take or a special kind of food that you eat in order to improve your health. ❑ *a multiple vitamin and mineral supplement* **3** A **supplement** is a separate part of a magazine or newspaper, often dealing with a particular topic. ❑ *a special supplement to a monthly financial magazine* **4** A **supplement to** a book is an additional section, written some time after the main text and published either at the end of the book or separately. ❑ *the supplement to the Encyclopedia Britannica* **5** A **supplement** is an extra amount of money that you pay in order to obtain special facilities or services, for example when you are travelling or staying at a hotel. ❑ *If you are travelling alone, the single room supplement is $25 a night.*

⭘ **sup·ple·men·ta·ry** /ˌsʌplɪˈmentri, AmE -teri/ ADJ Supplementary things are added to something in order to improve it. = extra, additional ❑ *the question of whether or not we need to take supplementary vitamins* ❑ *Provide them with additional background or with supplementary information.*

sup·pli·er /səˈplaɪə/ NOUN [c] (suppliers) (business) A **supplier** is a person, company, or organization that sells or supplies something such as goods or equipment to customers. ❑ *one of the country's biggest food suppliers*

⭘ **sup·ply** /səˈplaɪ/ VERB, NOUN
[VERB] [T] (supplies, supplying, supplied) If you **supply** someone with something that they want or need, you give them a quantity of it. ❑ *an agreement not to produce or supply chemical weapons* ❑ *a pipeline which will supply the major Greek cities with Russian natural gas* ❑ *the blood vessels supplying oxygen to the brain*
[NOUN] [PL, c, U] (supplies) **1** [PL] You can use **supplies** to refer to food, equipment, and other essential things that people need, especially when these are provided in large quantities. ❑ *What happens when food and petrol supplies run low?* **2** [c, U] A **supply** of something is an amount of it which someone has or which is available for them to use. ❑ *The brain requires a constant supply of oxygen.* ❑ *Most urban water supplies in the United States now contain fluoride in varying amounts.* **3** [U] (business) **Supply** is the quantity of goods and services that can be made available for people to buy. ❑ *Prices change according to supply and demand.*
[PHRASE] **in short supply** If something is in **short supply**, there is very little of it available and it is difficult to find or obtain. ❑ *Food is in short supply all over the country.*

⭘ **sup·port** ♦♦♦ /səˈpɔːt/ VERB, NOUN
[VERB] [T] (supports, supporting, supported) **1** If you **support** someone or their ideas or aims, you agree with them, and perhaps help them because you want them to succeed. = back, endorse; ≠ oppose ❑ *The vice president insisted that he supported the hard-working people of New York.* ❑ *The National Union of Mineworkers pressed the party to support a total ban on imported coal.* **2** If you **support** someone, you provide them with money or the things that they need. = finance, fund ❑ *I have children to support, money to be earned, and a home to be maintained.* ❑ *She sold everything she'd ever bought in order to support herself through art school.* **3** If a fact **supports** a statement or a theory, it helps to show that it is true or correct. = substantiate, back up ❑ *The Freudian theory about daughters falling in love with their father has little evidence to support it.* ❑ *This observation is supported by the archaeological evidence.* **4** If something **supports** an object, it is underneath the object and holding it up. = hold up ❑ *the thick wooden posts that supported the ceiling* **5** If you **support yourself**, you prevent yourself from falling by holding onto something or by leaning on something. ❑ *He supported himself by means of a nearby post.* **6** If you **support** a sports team, you always want them to win and perhaps go regularly to their games. ❑ *Tim, 17, supports Manchester United.*
[NOUN] [U, c] (supports) **1** [U] If you give your **support** to someone or their ideas or aims, you agree with them, and perhaps help them because you want them to succeed. = backing, endorsement; ≠ opposition ❑ *The president gave his full support to the reforms.* **2** [U] If you give **support** to someone during a difficult or unhappy time, you are kind to them and help them. ❑ *It was hard to come to terms with her death after all the support she gave to me and the family.* **3** [U] Financial **support** is money provided to

enable an organization to continue. = funding ❑ *State agencies continue to cut budgets and support to a number of organizations.* ❑ *the government's proposal to cut agricultural support by only about 15%* **4** [U] **Support** is evidence that helps to show that a statement or theory is true or correct. = evidence ❑ *The two largest powers in any system must always be major rivals. History offers some support for this view.* ❑ *The study did not lend support to the hypothesis.* **5** [c] A **support** is a bar or other object that supports something. ❑ *Each slab was nailed to two straight wooden supports.* **6** [U] If you hold onto or lean on someone or something for **support**, you hold onto or lean on them in order to prevent yourself from falling. ❑ *Alice, very pale, was leaning against him as if for support.*

⭘ **sup·port·er** ♦♦◇ /səˈpɔːtə/ NOUN [c] (supporters) Supporters are people who support someone or something, for example a political leader or a sports team. = proponent, fan; ≠ opponent ❑ *Attacks against opposition supporters are continuing at levels higher than before the election.* ❑ *The fourth night of violence in the German city of Rostock was triggered by football supporters.* ❑ *Bradley was a major supporter of the 1986 tax reform plan.*

sup·port·ive /səˈpɔːtɪv/ ADJ If you are **supportive**, you are kind and helpful to someone at a difficult or unhappy time in their life. ❑ *They were always supportive of each other.*

sup·pose ♦♦◇ /səˈpəʊz/ VERB
[VERB] [T] (supposes, supposing, supposed) **1** You can use **suppose** or **supposing** before mentioning a possible situation or action. You usually then go on to consider the effects that this situation or action might have. = say ❑ *Suppose someone gave you an egg and asked you to describe exactly what was inside.* **2** If you **suppose that** something is true, you believe that it is probably true, because of other things that you know. ❑ *The policy is perfectly clear and I see no reason to suppose that it isn't working.* ❑ *I knew very well that the problem was more complex than I supposed.*
[PHRASES] **I suppose** (spoken) **1** (vagueness) You can say 'I suppose' when you want to express slight uncertainty. ❑ *I suppose I'd better do some homework.* ❑ *'Is that the right way up?'—'Yeah. I suppose so.'* **2** (feelings) You can say 'I suppose' or 'I don't suppose' before describing someone's probable thoughts or attitude, when you are impatient or slightly angry with them. ❑ *I suppose you think you're funny.*
I don't suppose (spoken, politeness) You can say 'I don't suppose' as a way of introducing a polite request. ❑ *I don't suppose you could tell me where James Street is, could you?*
do you suppose (spoken) You can use 'do you suppose' to introduce a question when you want someone to give their opinion about something, although you know that they are unlikely to have any more knowledge or information about it than you. ❑ *Do you suppose he was telling the truth?*

WHICH WORD?
suppose or assume?
If you **suppose** that something is true, you think it is probably true.
❑ *I suppose he'll be going back to New York.*
If you **assume** that something is true, you are fairly sure about it and act as if it were true.
❑ *We assumed the other woman was his wife.*

sup·posed ♦♦◇ ADJ
[ADJ] /səˈpəʊzɪd/ [supposed + N] You can use **supposed** to suggest that something that people talk about or believe in may not in fact exist, happen, or be as it is described. = alleged ❑ *Not all developing countries are willing to accept the supposed benefits of free trade.*
[PHRASE] **be supposed to** /səˈpəʊzd, səˈpəʊst/ **1** If you say that something **is supposed to** happen, you mean that it is planned or expected. Sometimes this use suggests that the thing does not really happen in this way. ❑ *He produced a hand-written list of nine men he was supposed to kill.* **2** If something **was supposed to** happen, it was planned or intended to happen, but did not in fact happen.

S

❑ He was supposed to go back to Bergen on the last bus, but of course the accident prevented him. **3** If you say that something **is supposed to** be true, you mean that people say it is true but you do not know for certain that it is true. ❑ 'The Whipping Block' has never been published, but it's supposed to be a really good poem. **4** (feelings) You can use 'be supposed to' to express annoyance at someone's ideas, or because something is not happening in the right way. ❑ You're supposed to be my friend!

sup·pos·ed·ly /sə'pəʊzɪdli/ ADV ❑ He was more of a victim than any of the women he supposedly offended.

✪sup·press /sə'pres/ VERB [T] (suppresses, suppressing, suppressed) **1** If someone in authority **suppresses** an activity, they prevent it from continuing, by using force or making it illegal. ❑ drug traffickers, who continue to flourish despite international attempts to suppress them ❑ nationwide demonstrations for democracy, suppressed after 7 weeks by the army **2** If a natural function or reaction of your body **is suppressed**, it is stopped, for example by drugs or illness. = inhibit ❑ The reproduction and growth of the cancerous cells can be suppressed by bombarding them with radiation. ❑ the strongest evidence so far that ultraviolet light can suppress human immune responses **3** If you **suppress** your feelings or reactions, you do not express them, even though you might want to. ❑ Liz thought of Barry and suppressed a smile. **4** If someone **suppresses** a piece of information, they prevent other people from learning it. ❑ At no time did they try to persuade me to suppress the information. **5** If someone or something **suppresses** a process or activity, they stop it continuing or developing. ❑ The government is suppressing inflation by increasing interest rates.

✪sup·pres·sion /sə'preʃən/ NOUN [U] **1** people who were imprisoned after the violent suppression of the pro-democracy movement protests **2** Eye problems can indicate an unhealthy lifestyle with subsequent suppression of the immune system. **3** A mother's suppression of her own feelings can cause problems. **4** The inspectors found no evidence which supported any allegation of suppression of official documents.

su·prema·cy /suː'preməsi/ NOUN [U] **1** If one group of people has **supremacy** over another group, they have more political or military power than the other group. ❑ The conservative old guard had re-established its political supremacy. **2** If someone or something has **supremacy** over another person or thing, they are better. = superiority ❑ In the United States Open final, Graf retained overall supremacy.

su·preme ♦♦◊ /suː'priːm/ ADJ **1** [supreme + N] **Supreme** is used in the title of a person or an official group to indicate that they are at the highest level in a particular organization or system. ❑ MacArthur was Supreme Commander for the allied powers in the Pacific. ❑ the Supreme Court **2** You use **supreme** to emphasize that a quality or thing is very great. ❑ Her approval was of supreme importance.

su·preme·ly /suː'priːmli/ ADV [supremely + ADJ/ADV] ❑ She does her job supremely well.

sure ♦♦♦ /ʃʊə/ ADJ, CONVENTION, ADV

ADJ (surer, surest) **1** [V-LINK + sure] If you are **sure** that something is true, you are certain that it is true. If you are not **sure** about something, you do not know for certain what the true situation is. = certain ❑ He'd never been in a class before and he was not even sure that he should have been teaching. ❑ The president has never been sure which direction he wanted to go in on this issue. **2** [V-LINK + sure 'of' -ING/N] If someone is **sure of** getting something, they will definitely get it or they think they will definitely get it. ❑ A lot of people think that it's better to pay for their education so that they can be sure of getting quality. **3** [sure + N] **Sure** is used to emphasize that something such as a sign or ability is reliable or accurate. ❑ Sharpe's leg and shoulder began to ache, a sure sign of rain. **4** [V-LINK + sure] If you tell someone to **be sure to** do something, you mean that they must not forget to do it. ❑ Be sure to read about how mozzarella is made, on page 65.

PHRASES **sure enough** You say **sure enough**, especially when telling a story, to confirm that something was really true or was actually happening. ❑ We found the apple pie pudding too good to resist. Sure enough, it was delicious.

for sure If you say that something is **for sure** or that you know it **for sure**, you mean that it is definitely true. ❑ One thing's for sure, Manilow's vocal style hasn't changed much over the years.

make sure **1** If you **make sure that** something is done, you take action so that it is done. ❑ Make sure that you follow the instructions carefully. **2** If you **make sure that** something is the way that you want or expect it to be, you check that it is that way. ❑ He looked in the bathroom to make sure that he was alone.

be sure of oneself If you are **sure of yourself**, you are very confident about your own abilities or opinions. ❑ I'd never seen him like this, so sure of himself, so in command.

be sure to (emphasis) If you say that something **is sure to** happen, you are emphasizing your belief that it will happen. ❑ With over 80 beaches to choose from, you are sure to find a place to lay your towel.

CONVENTION (formulae) **Sure** is an informal way of saying 'yes' or 'all right.' ❑ 'Do you know where she lives?'—'Sure.'

ADV [sure before V] (informal, emphasis) You can use **sure** in order to emphasize what you are saying. = certainly ❑ 'Has the whole world just gone crazy?'—'Sure looks that way, doesn't it.'

sure·ly ♦◊◊ /'ʃʊəli/ ADV

ADV 1 [surely with CL/GROUP] (emphasis) You use **surely** to emphasize that you think something should be true, and you would be surprised if it was not true. ❑ You're an intelligent woman, surely you realize by now that I'm helping you. ❑ You surely haven't forgotten Dr Walters? **2** (formal) If something will **surely** happen or is **surely** the case, it will definitely happen or is definitely the case. = certainly ❑ He knew that under the surgeon's knife he would surely die.

PHRASE **slowly but surely** If you say that something is happening **slowly but surely**, you mean that it is happening gradually but it is definitely happening. ❑ Slowly but surely she started to fall in love with him.

WHICH WORD?

surely, definitely, or certainly?

You use **surely** for emphasis when you think that something should be true.

❑ **Surely** they could have done something to help her.

When you use **surely**, there may be some doubt. If there is no doubt at all about something, you use **definitely** or **certainly**.

❑ They were **definitely** not for sale.

❑ If nothing is done, there will **certainly** be an economic crisis.

You do not use **surely** as a way of agreeing with someone or saying 'yes'. The word you use is **certainly**.

❑ 'Isn't it ugly?'—'It **certainly** is!'

❑ 'Can you arrange an early morning call, please?'—'Yes, **certainly**.'

✪sur·face ♦♦◊ /'sɜːfɪs/ NOUN, VERB

NOUN [C, SING] (surfaces) **1** [C] The **surface** of something is the flat top part of it or the outside of it. ❑ Ozone forms a protective layer between 12 and 30 miles above the Earth's surface. ❑ tiny little waves on the surface of the water ❑ Its total surface area was seven thousand square feet. **2** [C] A work **surface** is a flat area, for example the top of a table, desk, or kitchen counter, on which you can work. ❑ It can simply be left on the work surface. **3** [SING] When you refer to the **surface** of a situation, you are talking about what can be seen easily rather than what is hidden or not immediately obvious. ❑ Back home, things appear, on the surface, simpler.

VERB [I] (surfaces, surfacing, surfaced) **1** If someone or something under water **surfaces**, they come up to the surface of the water. ❑ He surfaced, gasping for air. **2** When something such as a piece of news, a feeling, or a problem **surfaces**, it becomes known or becomes obvious. = emerge ❑ The paper says the evidence, when it surfaces, is certain to cause uproar.

surge /sɜːdʒ/ NOUN, VERB

NOUN [C] (surges) **1** A **surge** is a sudden large increase in something that has previously been steady, or has only increased or developed slowly. ❑ Specialists see various

reasons for the recent surge in inflation. **2** A **surge** is a sudden powerful movement of a physical force such as wind or water. ❑ *The whole car shuddered with an almost frightening surge of power.*
VERB [I] (**surges, surging, surged**) **1** If something **surges**, it increases suddenly and greatly, after being steady or developing only slowly. ❑ *The Freedom Party's electoral support surged from just under 10 per cent to nearly 17 per cent.* **2** If a crowd of people **surge** forward, they suddenly move forward together. ❑ *The photographers and cameramen surged forward.* **3** If a physical force such as water or electricity **surges** through something, it moves through it suddenly and powerfully. ❑ *Thousands of volts surged through his car after he careered into a lamp post, ripping out live wires.*

❑ **sur·geon** /'sɜːdʒən/ NOUN [C] (**surgeons**) A **surgeon** is a doctor who is specially trained to perform surgery. ❑ *a heart surgeon* ❑ *Two surgeons performed the keyhole surgery.* ❑ *the plastic surgeon who specialized in this type of injury*

❑ **sur·gery** ◆◇◇ /'sɜːdʒəri/ NOUN [U, C] (**surgeries**)
1 [U] **Surgery** is medical treatment in which someone's body is cut open so that a doctor can repair, remove, or replace a diseased or damaged part. ❑ *His father has just recovered from heart surgery.* ❑ *Mr Clark underwent five hours of emergency surgery.* ❑ *the decision to perform this surgery* **2** [C] (*BrE*; in *AmE*, use **doctor's office, dentist's office**) A **surgery** is the room or house where a doctor or dentist works. **3** [C] (*BrE*; in *AmE*, use **office hours**) A doctor's **surgery** is the period of time each day when a doctor sees patients at his or her surgery.
→ See also **cosmetic surgery, plastic surgery**

❑ **sur·gi·cal** /'sɜːdʒɪkəl/ ADJ **1** [surgical + N] **Surgical** equipment and clothing is used in surgery. ❑ *an array of surgical instruments* ❑ *a pair of surgical gloves* **2** [surgical + N] **Surgical** treatment involves surgery. = medical ❑ *A biopsy is usually a minor surgical procedure.* ❑ *surgical removal of a tumour*
❑ **sur·gi·cal·ly** /'sɜːdʒɪkli/ ADV = medically ❑ *In very severe cases, bunions may be surgically removed.*

sur·name /'sɜːneɪm/ NOUN [C] (**surnames**) Your **surname** is the name that you share with other members of your family. In English speaking countries and many other countries it is your last name. ❑ *She'd never known his surname, only his first name.*

❑ **sur·pass** /sə'pɑːs, -'pæs/ VERB [T] (**surpasses, surpassing, surpassed**) **1** If one person or thing **surpasses** another, the first is better than, or has more of a particular quality than, the second. ❑ *He was determined to surpass the achievements of his older brothers.* ❑ *Warwick Arts Centre is the second largest Arts Centre in Britain, surpassed in size only by London's Barbican.* **2** If something **surpasses** expectations, it is much better than it was expected to be. ❑ *Mr Black gave an excellent party that surpassed expectations.*

sur·plus ◆◇◇ /'sɜːpləs/ NOUN, ADJ
NOUN [C, U] (**surpluses**) **1** [C, U] If there is a **surplus of** something, there is more than is needed. ❑ *countries where there is a surplus of labour* **2** [C] If a country has a trade **surplus**, it exports more than it imports. ❑ *Japan's annual trade surplus is in the region of 100 billion dollars.* **3** [C] If a government has a budget **surplus**, it has spent less than it received in taxes. ❑ *Norway's budget surplus has fallen from 5.9% in 1986 to an expected 0.1% this year.*
ADJ **Surplus** is used to describe something that is extra or that is more than is needed. ❑ *Few people have large sums of surplus cash.* ❑ *I sell my surplus birds to a local pet shop.*

sur·prise ◆◆◇ /sə'praɪz/ NOUN, ADJ, VERB
NOUN [C, U] (**surprises**) **1** [C] A **surprise** is an unexpected event, fact, or piece of news. ❑ *I have a surprise for you: We are moving to Switzerland!* ❑ *It may come as a surprise to some that a normal, healthy child is born with many skills.* **2** [U] **Surprise** is the feeling that you have when something unexpected happens. ❑ *The Pentagon has expressed surprise at these allegations.* ❑ *'You mean he's going to vote against her?' Scobie asked in surprise.* **3** [C] If you describe someone or something as a **surprise**, you mean that they are very good or pleasant although you were not expecting it. ❑ *Senga MacFie, one of the surprises of the World Championships three months ago*

PHRASE **take someone by surprise** If something **takes** you **by surprise**, it happens when you are not expecting it or when you are not prepared for it. ❑ *His question took his two companions by surprise.*
ADJ [surprise + N] **Surprise** means unexpected. ❑ *Baxter arrived here this afternoon, on a surprise visit.*
VERB [T] (**surprises, surprising, surprised**) **1** If something **surprises** you, it gives you a feeling of surprise. ❑ *We'll solve the case ourselves and surprise everyone.* ❑ *It surprised me that a driver of Alain's experience should make those mistakes.* **2** If you **surprise** someone, you give them, tell them, or do something pleasant that they are not expecting. ❑ *Surprise a new neighbour with one of your favourite home-made dishes.* **3** If you **surprise** someone, you attack, capture, or find them when they are not expecting it. ❑ *US troops surprised eight enemy fighters in a cave complex.*
→ See also **surprised, surprising**

sur·prised ◆◇◇ /sə'praɪzd/ ADJ If you are **surprised** at something, you have a feeling of surprise, because it is unexpected or unusual. ❑ *This lady was genuinely surprised at what happened to her pet.*
→ See also **surprise**

sur·pris·ing ◆◇◇ /sə'praɪzɪŋ/ ADJ Something that is **surprising** is unexpected or unusual and makes you feel surprised. ❑ *It is not surprising that children learn to read at different rates.*
sur·pris·ing·ly /sə'praɪzɪŋli/ ADV ❑ *The party did surprisingly well in the South.*
→ See also **surprise**

sur·ren·der ◆◇◇ /sə'rendə/ VERB, NOUN
VERB [I, T] (**surrenders, surrendering, surrendered**) **1** [I] If you **surrender**, you stop fighting or resisting someone and agree that you have been beaten. ❑ *General Martin Bonnet called on the rebels to surrender.* **2** [T] If you **surrender** something you would rather keep, you give it up or let someone else have it, for example after a struggle. ❑ *Nadja had to fill out forms surrendering all rights to her property.* **3** [T] (*formal*) If you **surrender** something such as a ticket or your passport, you give it to someone in authority when they ask you to. ❑ *They have been ordered to surrender their passports.*
NOUN [C, U] (**surrenders**) **1** [C, U] **Surrender** is when you stop fighting or resisting someone and agree that you have been beaten. ❑ *the government's apparent surrender to demands made by the religious militants* **2** [U] **Surrender** is when you give up something or let someone have something that you would rather keep. ❑ *the sixteen-day deadline for the surrender of weapons and ammunition*

❑ **sur·round** ◆◆◇ /sə'raʊnd/ VERB [I, T] (**surrounds, surrounding, surrounded**) **1** [I, T] If a person or thing **is surrounded** by something, that thing is situated all around them. = enclose, encompass ❑ *The small churchyard was surrounded by a rusted wrought-iron fence.* ❑ *The shell surrounding the egg has many important functions.* ❑ *Chicago and the surrounding area* ❑ *the snipers and artillerymen in the surrounding hills* **2** [T] If you **are surrounded** by soldiers or police, they spread out so that they are in positions all the way around you. = encircle ❑ *When the car stopped in the town square it was surrounded by soldiers and militiamen.* **3** [T] The circumstances, feelings, or ideas which **surround** something are those that are closely associated with it. ❑ *The decision had been agreed in principle before today's meeting, but some controversy surrounded it.* **4** [T] If you **surround yourself with** certain people or things, you make sure that you have a lot of them near you all the time. ❑ *He had made it his business to surround himself with a hand-picked group of bright young officers.*

❑ **sur·round·ings** /sə'raʊndɪŋz/ NOUN [PL] When you are describing the place where you are at the moment, or the place where you live, you can refer to it as your **surroundings**. = environment, location, setting ❑ *Schumacher adapted effortlessly to his new surroundings.* ❑ *The child's need to interact with immediate surroundings is critical to language development.*

sur·veil·lance /sə'veɪləns/ NOUN [U] **Surveillance** is the careful watching of someone, especially by an organization such as the police or the army. ❑ *He was*

S

arrested after being kept under constant surveillance. ❑ *Police swooped on the home after a two-week surveillance operation.*

✪**sur·vey** ♦♦◇ NOUN, VERB (*academic word*)
    NOUN /'sɜːveɪ/ [c] (**surveys**) **1** If you carry out a **survey**, you try to find out detailed information about a lot of different people or things, usually by asking people a series of questions. = analysis, study ❑ *The council conducted a survey of the uses to which farm buildings are put.* ❑ *According to the survey, overall world trade has also slackened.* **2** If someone carries out a **survey** of an area of land, they examine it and measure it, usually in order to make a map of it. ❑ *the organizer of the geological survey of India* **3** (*mainly BrE*) A **survey** is a careful examination of the condition and structure of a house, usually carried out in order to give information to a person who wants to buy it.
    VERB /sə'veɪ/ [T] (**surveys, surveying, surveyed**) **1** If you **survey** a number of people, companies, or organizations, you try to find out information about their opinions or behaviour, usually by asking them a series of questions. ❑ *Business Development Advisers surveyed 211 companies for the report.* ❑ *Only 18 per cent of those surveyed opposed the idea.* **2** If you **survey** something, you look at or consider the whole of it carefully. ❑ *He pushed himself to his feet and surveyed the room.* **3** If someone **surveys** an area of land, they examine it and measure it, usually in order to make a map of it. ❑ *The city council commissioned geological experts earlier this year to survey the cliffs.* **4** (*mainly BrE*) If someone **surveys** a house, they examine it carefully and report on its structure, usually in order to give advice to a person who is thinking of buying it.

✪**sur·viv·al** ♦◇◇ /sə'vaɪvəl/ NOUN [u] **1** If you refer to the **survival** of something or someone, you mean that they manage to continue or exist in spite of difficult circumstances. ❑ *companies which have been struggling for survival in the advancing recession* **2** If you refer to the **survival** of a person or living thing, you mean that they live through a dangerous situation in which it was possible that they might die. ❑ *If cancers are spotted early there's a high chance of survival.*

✪**sur·vive** ♦♦◇ /sə'vaɪv/ VERB [i, T] (**survives, surviving, survived**) (*academic word*) **1** [i, T] If a person or living thing **survives** in a dangerous situation such as an accident or an illness, they do not die. = live; ≠ die ❑ *the sequence of events that left the eight pupils battling to survive in icy seas for over four hours* ❑ *Those organisms that are most suited to the environment will be those that will survive.* ❑ *Drugs that dissolve blood clots can help people survive heart attacks.* ❑ *He had survived heart bypass surgery.* ❑ *No one survived the crash.* **2** [i, T] If you **survive** in difficult circumstances, you manage to live or continue in spite of them and do not let them affect you very much. ❑ *On my first day here I thought, 'Ooh, how will I survive?'* ❑ *people who are struggling to survive without jobs* **3** [i, T] If something **survives**, it continues to exist even after being in a dangerous situation or existing for a long time. ❑ *When the market economy is introduced, many factories will not survive.* ❑ *The chances of a planet surviving a supernova always looked terribly slim.* **4** [T] If you **survive** someone, you continue to live after they have died. ❑ *Most women will survive their spouses.*

✪**sur·vi·vor** /sə'vaɪvə/ NOUN [c] (**survivors**) **1** A **survivor of** a disaster, accident, or illness is someone who continues to live afterwards in spite of coming close to death. ❑ *Officials said there were no survivors of the plane crash.* **2** A **survivor of** a very unpleasant experience is a person who has had such an experience, and who is still affected by it. ❑ *This book is written with survivors of child sexual abuse in mind.*

sus·cep·tible /sə'septibəl/ ADJ **1** [V-LINK + susceptible 'to' N] If you are **susceptible to** something or someone, you are very likely to be influenced by them. ❑ *Young people are the most susceptible to advertisements.* ❑ *James was extremely susceptible to flattery.* **2** If you are **susceptible to** a disease or injury, you are very likely to be affected by it. = vulnerable ❑ *Walking with weights makes the shoulders very susceptible to injury.*

✪**sus·pect** ♦♦◇ VERB, NOUN, ADJ
    VERB /sə'spekt/ [T] (**suspects, suspecting, suspected**) **1** (*vagueness*) You use **suspect** when you are stating something that you believe is probably true, in order to make it sound less strong or direct. ❑ *I suspect they were right.* ❑ *The above complaints are, I suspect, just the tip of the iceberg.* **2** If you **suspect** that something dishonest or unpleasant has been done, you believe that it has probably been done. If you **suspect** someone **of** doing an action of this kind, you believe that they probably did it. ❑ *He suspected that the woman staying in the flat above was using heroin.* ❑ *It was perfectly all right, he said, because the police had not suspected him of anything.*
    NOUN /'sʌspekt/ [c] (**suspects**) A **suspect** is a person who the police or authorities think may be guilty of a crime. ❑ *Police have arrested a suspect in a series of killings and sexual assaults in the city.*
    ADJ /'sʌspekt/ **Suspect** things or people are ones that you think may be dangerous or may be less good or genuine than they appear. ❑ *Delegates evacuated the building when a suspect package was found.*

✪**sus·pend** ♦◇◇ /sə'spend/ VERB [T] (**suspends, suspending, suspended**) (*academic word*) **1** If you **suspend** something, you delay it or stop it from happening for a while or until a decision is made about it. ❑ *The union suspended strike action this week.* ❑ *A UN official said aid programmes will be suspended until there's adequate protection for relief convoys.* **2** If someone **is suspended**, they are prevented from holding a particular job or position for a fixed length of time or until a decision is made about them. ❑ *Julie was suspended from her job shortly after the incident.* **3** If something **is suspended** from a high place, it is hanging from that place. = hang ❑ *instruments that are suspended on cables* ❑ *a mobile of birds or nursery rhyme characters which could be suspended over the cot* ❑ *chandeliers suspended on heavy chains from the ceiling*

sus·pense /sə'spens/ NOUN
    NOUN [u] **Suspense** is a state of excitement or anxiety about something that is going to happen very soon, for example about some news that you are waiting to hear. ❑ *The suspense over the two remaining hostages ended last night when the police discovered the bullet-ridden bodies.*
    PHRASE **keep someone in suspense** If you **keep** or **leave** someone **in suspense**, you deliberately delay telling them something that they are very eager to know about. ❑ *Keppler kept all his men in suspense until that morning before announcing which two would be going.*

✪**sus·pen·sion** /sə'spenʃən/ NOUN [u, c] (**suspensions**) **1** [u] The **suspension** of something is the act of delaying or stopping it for a while or until a decision is made about it. ❑ *There's been a temporary suspension of flights out of LA.* ❑ *Art experts have appealed for the suspension of plans to restore one of Leonardo da Vinci's most celebrated paintings.* **2** [c, u] Someone's **suspension** is their removal from a job or position for a period of time or until a decision is made about them. ❑ *The minister warned that any civil servant not at his desk faced immediate suspension.* **3** [c, u] A vehicle's **suspension** consists of the springs and other devices attached to the wheels, which give a smooth ride over uneven ground. ❑ *the only small car with independent front suspension*

sus·pi·cion ♦◇◇ /sə'spɪʃən/ NOUN [c, u] (**suspicions**) **1** [c, u] **Suspicion** or a **suspicion** is a belief or feeling that someone has committed a crime or done something wrong. ❑ *There was a suspicion that this runner attempted to avoid the procedures for drug testing.* ❑ *The police said their suspicions were aroused because Mr Owens had other marks on his body.* **2** [c, u] If there is **suspicion** of someone or something, people do not trust them or consider them to be reliable. ❑ *This tendency in his thought is deepened by his suspicion of all Utopian political programmes.* **3** [c] A **suspicion** is a feeling that something is probably true or is likely to happen. ❑ *I have a sneaking suspicion that they are going to succeed.*

sus·pi·cious /sə'spɪʃəs/ ADJ **1** If you are **suspicious of**

someone or something, you do not trust them, and are careful when dealing with them. ❑ *He was rightly suspicious of meeting me until I reassured him I was not writing about him.* **2** If you are **suspicious of** someone or something, you believe that they are probably involved in a crime or some dishonest activity. ❑ *Two officers on patrol became suspicious of two men in a car.* **3** If you describe someone or something as **suspicious**, you mean that there is some aspect of them which makes you think that they are involved in a crime or a dishonest activity. ❑ *He reported that two suspicious-looking characters had approached Callendar.*

sus·pi·cious·ly /sə'spɪʃəsli/ ADV **1** [suspiciously + PREP] If you say that one thing looks or sounds **suspiciously** like another thing, you mean that it probably is that thing, or something very similar to it, although it may be intended to seem different. ❑ *The tan-coloured dog looks suspiciously like a pit bull terrier.* **2** [suspiciously after V] If you treat someone or something **suspiciously**, you deal carefully with them and do not trust them. ❑ *'What is it you want me to do?' Adams asked suspiciously.* **3** [suspiciously + ADJ/ADV] You can use **suspiciously** when you are describing something that you think is slightly strange or not as it should be. ❑ *He lives alone in a suspiciously tidy apartment.*

✪**sus·tain** ✦◇◇ /sə'steɪn/ VERB [T] (**sustains, sustaining, sustained**) (*academic word*) **1** If you **sustain** something, you continue it or maintain it for a period of time. = maintain, continue ❑ *He has sustained his fierce social conscience from young adulthood through old age.* ❑ *Recovery can't be sustained unless more jobs are created.* ❑ *Euphoria cannot be sustained indefinitely.* ❑ *a period of sustained economic growth throughout the year* **2** (*formal*) If you **sustain** something such as a defeat, loss, or injury, it happens to you. ❑ *Every aircraft in there has sustained some damage.* **3** (*formal*) If something **sustains** you, it supports you by giving you help, strength, or encouragement. ❑ *The cash dividends they get from the cash crop would sustain them during the lean season.*

WORD FAMILIES	
sustain VERB	*Recovery can't be **sustained** unless more jobs are created.*
sustainable ADJ	*Try to buy wood that you know has come from a **sustainable** source.*
unsustainable ADJ	*Population growth at this high level is surely **unsustainable**.*
sustainability NOUN	*Planners must take into account the issue of long-term environmental **sustainability**.*

✪**sus·tain·able** /sə'steɪnəbəl/ ADJ **1** You use **sustainable** to describe the use of natural resources when this use is kept at a steady level that is not likely to damage the environment. = environmentally friendly, eco-friendly, ecological; ≠ unsustainable ❑ *the management, conservation and sustainable development of forests* ❑ *Try to buy wood that you know has come from a sustainable source.* **2** A **sustainable** plan, method, or system is designed to continue at the same rate or level of activity without any problems. ≠ unsustainable ❑ *The creation of an efficient and sustainable transport system is critical.* ❑ *a sustainable recovery in consumer spending* ✪**sus·tain·abil·ity** /sə,steɪnə'bɪlɪti/ NOUN [U] **1** *the issue of long-term environmental sustainability* **2** *unease about the sustainability of the American economic recovery*

swal·low /'swɒləʊ/ VERB, NOUN

    VERB [I, T] (**swallows, swallowing, swallowed**) **1** [I, T] If you **swallow** something, you cause it to go from your mouth down into your stomach. ❑ *You are asked to swallow a capsule containing vitamin B.* ❑ *Polly took a bite of the apple, chewed, and swallowed.* **2** [I] If you **swallow**, you make a movement in your throat as if you are swallowing something, often because you are nervous or frightened. ❑ *Nancy swallowed hard and shook her head.* **3** [T] If someone **swallows** a story or a statement, they believe it completely. ❑ *They cast doubt on his words when it suited*

their case, but swallowed them whole when it did not.   PHRASAL VERB **swallow up** **1** If one thing **is swallowed up** by another, it becomes part of the first thing and no longer has a separate identity of its own. ❑ *During the 1980s monster publishing houses started to swallow up smaller companies.* **2** If something **swallows up** money or resources, it uses them entirely while giving very little in return. ❑ *A seven-day TV ad campaign could swallow up the best part of $100,000.*

    NOUN [C] (**swallows**) **1** A **swallow** is a movement that causes something to go from your mouth down into your stomach. ❑ *Jan lifted her glass and took a quick swallow.* **2** A **swallow** is a kind of small bird with pointed wings and a forked tail.

✦ **a bitter pill to swallow** → see **pill**

swam /swæm/ IRREG FORM **Swam** is the past tense of **swim**.

swamp /swɒmp/ NOUN, VERB

    NOUN [C, U] (**swamps**) A **swamp** is an area of very wet land with wild plants growing in it. ❑ *I spent one whole night by a swamp behind the road listening to frogs.*

    VERB [T] (**swamps, swamping, swamped**) **1** If something **swamps** a place or object, it fills it with water. ❑ *Their electronic navigation failed and a rogue wave swamped the boat.* **2** If you **are swamped** by things or people, you have more of them than you can deal with. ❑ *He is swamped with work.*

swap /swɒp/ (in BrE, also use **swop**) VERB, NOUN

    VERB [RECIP, T] (**swaps, swapping, swapped**) **1** [RECIP] If you **swap** something with someone, you give it to them and receive a different thing in exchange. = exchange ❑ *Next week they will swap places and will repeat the switch weekly.* ❑ *I know a sculptor who swaps her pieces for drawings by a well-known artist.* **2** [T] If you **swap** one thing **for** another, you remove the first thing and replace it with the second, or you stop doing the first thing and start doing the second. ❑ *Despite the heat, he'd swapped his overalls for a suit and tie.* ❑ *He has swapped his hectic rock star's lifestyle for that of a country gentleman.*

    NOUN [C] (**swaps**) A **swap** is an exchange. ❑ *Over the long term, a swap of some kind is clearly in the public interest.*

swarm /swɔːm/ NOUN, VERB

    NOUN [C] (**swarms**) **1** A **swarm of** bees or other insects is a large group of them flying together. ❑ *a swarm of locusts* **2** A **swarm of** people is a large group of them moving about quickly. = horde ❑ *A swarm of people encircled the hotel.*

    VERB [I] (**swarms, swarming, swarmed**) **1** When bees or other insects **swarm**, they move or fly in a large group. ❑ *A dark cloud of bees comes swarming out of the hive.* **2** When people **swarm** somewhere, they move there quickly in a large group. ❑ *People swarmed to the shops, buying up everything in sight.* **3** If a place **is swarming with** people, it is full of people moving about in a busy way. ❑ *Within minutes the area was swarming with officers who began searching a nearby wood.*

sway /sweɪ/ VERB, NOUN

    VERB [I, T] (**sways, swaying, swayed**) **1** [I] When people or things **sway**, they lean or swing slowly from one side to the other. ❑ *The people swayed back and forth with arms linked.* ❑ *The whole boat swayed and tipped.* **2** [T] If you **are swayed by** someone or something, you are influenced by them. ❑ *Don't ever be swayed by fashion.*

    NOUN

    PHRASE **hold sway** If someone or something **holds sway**, they have great power or influence over a particular place or activity. ❑ *Powerful traditional chiefs hold sway over more than 15 million people in rural areas.*

swear /sweə/ VERB

    VERB [I, T] (**swears, swearing, swore, sworn**) **1** [I] If someone **swears**, they use language that is considered to be vulgar or offensive, usually because they are angry. ❑ *It's wrong to swear and shout.* **2** [T] If you **swear to** do something, you promise in a serious way that you will do it. ❑ *Alan swore that he would do everything in his power to help us.* ❑ *We have sworn to fight cruelty wherever we find it.* **3** [I, T] If you say that you **swear** that something is true or that you can **swear** to it, you are saying very firmly that it is true. ❑ *I swear I've told you all I know.* ❑ *I swear on all*

I hold dear that I had nothing to do with this. **4** [T] If someone **is sworn to** secrecy or **is sworn to** silence, they promise another person that they will not reveal a secret. ❑ *She was bursting to announce the news but was sworn to secrecy.*

PHRASAL VERBS swear by (*informal*) If you **swear by** something, you believe that it can be relied on to have a particular effect. ❑ *Many people swear by vitamin C's ability to ward off colds.*

swear in When someone **is sworn in**, they formally promise to fulfill the duties of a new job or appointment. ❑ *Mary Robinson was formally sworn in as Ireland's first woman president.*
→ See also **sworn**

sweat /swet/ NOUN, VERB

NOUN [C, U] (**sweats**) **1** [C, U] **Sweat** is the salty colourless liquid which comes through your skin when you are hot, sick, or afraid. ❑ *Both horse and rider were dripping with sweat within five minutes.* **2** [C] If someone is **in a sweat**, they are sweating a lot. ❑ *Every morning I would break out in a sweat.* ❑ *Cool down very gradually after working up a sweat.*

PHRASE in a cold sweat or **in a sweat** If someone is **in a cold sweat** or **in a sweat**, they feel frightened or embarrassed. ❑ *The very thought brought me out in a cold sweat.*

VERB [I] (**sweats, sweating, sweated**) When you **sweat**, sweat comes through your skin. ❑ *Already they were sweating as the sun beat down upon them.*

sweat·ing /ˈswetɪŋ/ NOUN [U] ❑ *symptoms such as sweating, irritability, anxiety, and depression*

sweat·er /ˈswetə/ NOUN [C] (**sweaters**) A **sweater** is a warm knitted piece of clothing which covers the upper part of your body and your arms. = **pullover**

sweep ♦◇◇ /swiːp/ VERB, NOUN

VERB [I, T] (**sweeps, sweeping, swept**) **1** [I, T] If you **sweep** an area of floor or ground, you push dirt or rubbish off it using a brush with a long handle. ❑ *The owner of the shop was sweeping his floor when I walked in.* ❑ *She was in the kitchen sweeping crumbs into a dust pan.* **2** [T] If you **sweep** things off something, you push them off with a quick smooth movement of your arm. ❑ *I swept rainwater off the flat top of a gravestone.* ❑ *With a gesture of frustration, she swept the cards from the table.* **3** [T] If someone with long hair **sweeps** their hair into a particular style, they put it into that style. ❑ *stylish ways of sweeping your hair off your face* **4** [I, T] If your arm or hand **sweeps** in a particular direction, or if you **sweep** it there, it moves quickly and smoothly in that direction. ❑ *His arm swept around the room.* ❑ *Daniels swept his arm over his friend's shoulder.* **5** [T] If wind, a stormy sea, or another strong force **sweeps** someone or something along, it moves them quickly along. ❑ *landslides that buried homes and swept cars into the sea* **6** [T] If you **are swept** somewhere, you are taken there very quickly. ❑ *The visitors were swept past various monuments.* **7** [I] (*written*) If something **sweeps** from one place to another, it moves there extremely quickly. ❑ *An icy wind swept through the streets.* **8** [I, T] If events, ideas, or beliefs **sweep** through a place or **sweep** a place, they spread quickly through it. ❑ *A flu epidemic is sweeping through Moscow.* **9** [I, T] If a person or group **sweeps** an election or **sweeps to** victory, they win the election easily. ❑ *a man who's promised to make radical changes to benefit the poor has swept the election*

PHRASE sweep something under the carpet or **sweep something under the rug** If someone **sweeps** something bad or wrong **under the carpet**, or if they **sweep** it **under the rug**, they try to prevent people from hearing about it. ❑ *For a long time this problem has been swept under the carpet.*

PHRASAL VERB sweep up If you **sweep up** rubbish or dirt, you push it together with a brush and then remove it. ❑ *Get a broom and sweep up that glass will you?*

NOUN [C] (**sweeps**) **1** A **sweep** is a quick and smooth movement of your hand or arm. ❑ *With one sweep of her hand she threw back the sheets.* **2** If someone makes a **sweep of** a place, they search it, usually because they are looking for people who are hiding or for an illegal activity. ❑ *Two of the soldiers swiftly began making a sweep of the premises.*

PHRASE a clean sweep If you **make a clean sweep of** something such as a series of games or tournaments, you win them all. ❑ *the first club to make a clean sweep of all three trophies*
✦ **sweep the board** → see **board**

sweet ♦◇◇ /swiːt/ ADJ, NOUN

ADJ (**sweeter, sweetest**) **1** **Sweet** food and drink contains a lot of sugar. ❑ *a mug of sweet tea* ❑ *If the sauce seems too sweet, add a dash of red wine vinegar.* **2** A **sweet** smell is a pleasant one, for example the smell of a flower. ❑ *the sweet smell of her shampoo* **3** A **sweet** sound is pleasant, smooth, and gentle. ❑ *Her voice was as soft and sweet as a young girl's.* **4** (*written*) If you describe something as **sweet**, you mean that it gives you great pleasure and satisfaction. ❑ *There are few things quite as sweet as revenge.* **5** If you describe someone as **sweet**, you mean that they are pleasant, kind, and gentle towards other people. ❑ *He was a sweet man but when he drank he tended to quarrel.* **6** (*informal*) If you describe a small person or thing as **sweet**, you mean that they are attractive in a simple and unsophisticated way. = **cute** ❑ *a sweet little baby girl*

NOUN [C, U] (**sweets**) **1** [C] (*BrE*; in *AmE*, use **candy**) **Sweets** are small sweet things such as chocolates and mints. **2** [C, U] A **sweet** is the same as a **dessert**.

sweet·ly /ˈswiːtli/ ADV **1** *He sang much more sweetly than he has before.* **2** *I just smiled sweetly and said no.*
✦ **a sweet tooth** → see **tooth**

sweet·en /ˈswiːtən/ VERB [T] (**sweetens, sweetening, sweetened**) **1** If you **sweeten** food or drink, you add sugar, honey, or another sweet substance to it. ❑ *He liberally sweetened his coffee.* **2** If you **sweeten** something such as an offer or a business deal, you try to make someone want it more by improving it or by increasing the amount you are willing to pay. ❑ *Kalon Group has sweetened its takeover offer for Manders.*

sweet·ness /ˈswiːtnəs/ NOUN

NOUN [U] **Sweetness** is the pleasant taste that foods have when they contain a lot of sugar. ❑ *Florida oranges have a natural sweetness.*

PHRASE all sweetness and light If you say that a relationship or situation is not **all sweetness and light**, you mean that it is not as pleasant as it appears to be. ❑ *It has not all been sweetness and light between him and the mayor.*

swell /swel/ VERB

VERB [I, T] (**swells, swelling, swelled, swelled** or **swollen**) **1** [I, T] If the amount or size of something **swells** or if something **swells** it, it becomes larger than it was before. = **increase** ❑ *The human population swelled, at least temporarily, as migrants moved south.* ❑ *His bank balance has swelled by $222,000 in the last three weeks.* **2** [I] If something such as a part of your body **swells**, it becomes larger and rounder than normal. ❑ *Do your ankles swell at night?*

PHRASAL VERB swell up Swell up means the same as **swell** VERB **2**. ❑ *When you develop a throat infection or catch a cold the glands in the neck swell up.*
→ See also **swollen**

swell·ing /ˈswelɪŋ/ NOUN [C, U] (**swellings**) A **swelling** is a raised, curved shape on the surface of your body which appears as a result of an injury or an illness. ❑ *His eye was partly closed, and there was a swelling over his lid.*

swept /swept/ IRREG FORM **Swept** is the past tense and past participle of **sweep**.

swerve /swɜːv/ VERB, NOUN

VERB [I, T] (**swerves, swerving, swerved**) If a vehicle or other moving thing **swerves** or if you **swerve** it, it suddenly changes direction, often in order to avoid hitting something. ❑ *Drivers coming in the opposite direction swerved to avoid the bodies.* ❑ *Her car swerved off the road into a 6 ft high brick wall.*

NOUN [C] (**swerves**) A **swerve** is a sudden change in the direction of a vehicle, often in order to avoid hitting something. ❑ *He swung the car to the left and that swerve saved Malone's life.*

swift /swɪft/ ADJ, NOUN

ADJ (**swifter, swiftest**) **1** A **swift** event or process happens very quickly or without delay. = **quick** ❑ *Our task is to* *challenge the UN to make a swift decision.* **2** Something that is **swift** moves very quickly. = quick □ *With a swift movement, Matthew Jerrold sat upright.*

NOUN [c] (**swifts**) A **swift** is a small bird with long curved wings.

swift·ly /'swɪftli/ ADV **1** *Wall Street reacted swiftly to yesterday's verdict.* **2** [swiftly with V] □ *Lenny moved swiftly and silently across the front lawn.*

swim ◆◇◇ /swɪm/ VERB, NOUN

VERB [I, T] (**swims, swimming, swam, swum**) **1** [I, T] When you **swim**, you move through water by making movements with your arms and legs. □ *She learned to swim when she was really tiny.* □ *He was rescued only when an exhausted friend swam ashore.* □ *I swim a mile a day.* **2** [T] If you **swim** a race, you take part in a swimming race. □ *She swam the 400 metres medley.* **3** [T] If you **swim** a stretch of water, you keep swimming until you have crossed it. □ *By the time we reached the other side, Maram vowed that he would never swim a river again.* **4** [I] When a fish **swims**, it moves through water by moving its body. □ *The barriers are lethal to fish trying to swim upstream.* **5** [I] If your head **is swimming**, you feel unsteady and slightly ill. = spin □ *The musty aroma of incense made her head swim.*

NOUN [SING] A **swim** is a time when you move through water by making movements with your arms and legs. □ *When can we go for a swim?*

✦ **sink or swim** → see **sink**

swim·mer /'swɪmə/ NOUN [c] (**swimmers**) A **swimmer** is a person who swims, especially for sport or pleasure, or a person who is swimming. □ *You don't have to worry about me. I'm a good swimmer.*

swim·ming /'swɪmɪŋ/ NOUN [u] **Swimming** is the activity of swimming, especially as a sport or for pleasure. □ *Swimming is probably the best form of exercise you can get.*

swim·ming pool NOUN [c] (**swimming pools**) A **swimming pool** is a large hole in the ground that has been made and filled with water so that people can swim in it.

swing ◆◇◇ /swɪŋ/ VERB, NOUN

VERB [I, T] (**swings, swinging, swung**) **1** [I, T] If something **swings** or if you **swing** it, it moves repeatedly backwards and forwards or from side to side from a fixed point. □ *The sail of the little boat swung crazily from one side to the other.* □ *She was swinging a bottle of wine by its neck.* **2** [I, T] If something **swings** in a particular direction or if you **swing** it in that direction, it moves in that direction with a smooth, curving movement. □ *The torchlight swung across the little beach and out over the water, searching.* □ *The canoe found the current and swung around.* **3** [I, T] If a vehicle **swings** in a particular direction, or if the driver **swings** it in a particular direction, they turn suddenly in that direction. □ *Joanna swung back on to the main approach and headed for the airport.* **4** [I] If someone **swings around**, they turn around quickly, usually because they are surprised. □ *She swung around to him, spilling her tea without noticing it.* **5** [I] If you **swing at** a person or thing, you try to hit them with your arm or with something that you are holding. □ *Blanche swung at her but she moved her head back and Blanche missed.* **6** [I] If people's opinions, attitudes, or feelings **swing**, they change, especially in a sudden or extreme way. □ *In two years' time there is a presidential election, and the voters could swing again.*

NOUN [c] (**swings**) **1** A **swing** is a repeated movement backwards and forwards or from side to side from a fixed point. □ *a woman in a tight red dress, walking with a slight swing to her hips* **2** A **swing** is a smooth, curving movement. □ *When he's not on the tennis court, you'll find him practising his golf swing.* **3** If you take a **swing** at someone, you try to hit them with your arm or with something that you are holding. = swipe □ *I often want to take a swing at someone to relieve my feelings.* **4** A **swing** is a seat hanging by two ropes or chains from a metal frame or from the branch of a tree. You can sit on the seat and move forwards and backwards through the air. □ *Go to the neighbourhood park. Run around, push the kids on the swings.* **5** A **swing** in people's opinions, attitudes, or feelings is a change in them, especially a sudden or big change. □ *Educational practice is liable to sudden swings and*

changes. □ *Dieters suffer from violent mood swings.*

PHRASES **in full swing** If something is **in full swing**, it is operating fully and is no longer in its early stages. □ *When we returned, the party was in full swing and the dance floor was crowded.*

get into the swing of If you **get into the swing of** something, you become very involved in it and enjoy what you are doing. □ *Everyone understood how hard it was to get back into the swing of things after such a long absence.*

switch ◆◇◇ /swɪtʃ/ NOUN, VERB

NOUN [c] (**switches**) **1** A **switch** is a small control for an electrical device which you use to turn the device on or off. □ *Leona put some detergent into the dishwasher, shut the door, and pressed the switch.* **2** [usu with SUPP] A **switch** is a change to something different. □ *The spokesman implicitly condemned the United States policy switch.*

VERB [I, T] (**switches, switching, switched**) **1** [I, T] If you **switch to** something different, for example to a different system, task, or subject of conversation, you change to it from what you were doing or saying before. = change □ *Estonia is switching to a market economy.* □ *The law would encourage companies to switch from coal to cleaner fuels.* **2** [I, T] If you **switch** your attention from one thing **to** another or if your attention **switches**, you stop paying attention to the first thing and start paying attention to the second. □ *My mother's interest had switched to my health.* **3** [T] If you **switch** two things, you replace one with the other. = swap □ *In half an hour, they'd switched the tags on every cable.*

PHRASAL VERBS **switch off** **1** If you **switch off** a light or other electrical device, you stop it working by operating a switch. = turn off □ *She switched off the coffee machine.* **2** (*informal*) If you **switch off**, you stop paying attention or stop thinking or worrying about something. □ *Thankfully, I've learned to switch off and let it go over my head.*

switch on If you **switch on** a light or other electrical device, you make it start working by operating a switch. = turn on □ *She emptied both their mugs and switched on the electric kettle.*

switch over **Switch over** means the same as **switch** VERB 1. □ *The country will switch over to the new currency next year.*

swol·len /'swəʊlən/ ADJ, IRREG FORM

ADJ **1** If a part of your body is **swollen**, it is larger and rounder than normal, usually as a result of injury or illness. □ *My eyes were so swollen I could hardly see.* **2** A **swollen** river has more water in it and flows faster than normal, usually because of heavy rain. □ *The river, brown and swollen with rain, was running fast.*

IRREG FORM **Swollen** is the past participle of **swell**.

swoop /swuːp/ VERB, NOUN

VERB [I] (**swoops, swooping, swooped**) **1** (*journalism*) If police or soldiers **swoop on** a place, they go there suddenly and quickly, usually in order to arrest someone or to attack the place. □ *The terror ended when armed police swooped on the car.* **2** When a bird or aeroplane **swoops**, it suddenly moves downwards through the air in a smooth curving movement. □ *More than 20 helicopters began swooping in low over the ocean.*

NOUN [c] (**swoops**) A **swoop** is when police or soldiers suddenly and quickly go to a place, usually in order to arrest someone or to attack the place. □ *Police held 10 suspected illegal immigrants after a swoop on a Mexican truck.*

PHRASE **in one fell swoop** If something is done **in one fell swoop**, it is done on a single occasion or by a single action. □ *In one fell swoop the bank wiped away the tentative benefits of this policy.*

sword /sɔːd/ NOUN

NOUN [c] (**swords**) A **sword** is a weapon with a handle and a long sharp blade.

PHRASES **cross swords** If you **cross swords with** someone, you disagree with them and argue with them about something. □ *a candidate who's crossed swords with Labour by supporting the free-trade pact*

a double-edged sword If you say that something is a **double-edged sword**, you mean that it has negative effects as well as positive effects. □ *A person's looks are a* *double-edged sword. Sometimes it works in your favour, sometimes it works against you.*

swore /swɔː/ IRREG FORM Swore is the past tense of **swear**.

sworn /swɔːn/ IRREG FORM, ADJ

IRREG FORM Sworn is the past participle of **swear**. **ADJ 1** [sworn + N] If you make a **sworn** statement or declaration, you swear that everything that you have said in it is true. ❏ *The allegations against them were made in sworn evidence to the inquiry.* **2** [sworn + N] If two people or two groups of people are **sworn** enemies, they dislike each other very much. ❏ *It somehow seems hardly surprising that Ms Player is now his sworn enemy.*

swum /swʌm/ IRREG FORM Swum is the past participle of **swim**.

swung /swʌŋ/ IRREG FORM Swung is the past tense and past participle of **swing**.

❖**syl·la·bus** /'sɪləbəs/ (mainly BrE; in AmE, usually use **curriculum**) NOUN [c] (**syllabuses**) You can refer to the subjects that are studied in a particular course as the **syllabus**. ❏ *the GCSE history syllabus* ❏ *The instructor will follow the syllabus outlined in the students' workbooks.* = curriculum

❖**sym·bol** ♦◇◇ /'sɪmbəl/ NOUN [c] (**symbols**) (*academic word*) **1** Something that is a **symbol of** a society or an aspect of life seems to represent it because it is very typical of it. ❏ *To them, the monarchy is the special symbol of nationhood.* **2** A **symbol** of something such as an idea is a shape or design that is used to represent it. ❏ *Later in this same passage Yeats resumes his argument for the Rose as an Irish symbol.* **3** A **symbol** for an item in a calculation or scientific formula is a number, letter, or shape that represents that item. = sign, representation ❏ *What's the chemical symbol for mercury?* ❏ *mathematical symbols and operations*

❖**sym·bol·ic** /sɪm'bɒlɪk/ ADJ **1** If you describe an event, action, or procedure as **symbolic**, you mean that it represents an important change, although it has little practical effect. ❏ *A lot of Latin-American officials are stressing the symbolic importance of the trip.* ❏ *The move today was largely symbolic.* **2** Something that is **symbolic of** a person or thing is regarded or used as a symbol of them. = representative, iconic, metaphorical; ≠ literal ❏ *Yellow clothes are worn as symbolic of spring.* **3** [symbolic + N] **Symbolic** is used to describe things involving or relating to symbols. ❏ *symbolic representations of landscape* **sym·boli·cal·ly** /sɪm'bɒlɪkli/ ADV **1** *It was a simple enough gesture, but symbolically important.* **2** [symbolically with V] ❏ *Each circle symbolically represents the whole of humanity.*

❖**sym·bol·ize** /'sɪmbəlaɪz/ also **symbolise** VERB [T] (**symbolizes, symbolizing, symbolized**) If one thing **symbolizes** another, it is used or regarded as a symbol of it. = represent, signify ❏ *The fall of the Berlin Wall symbolized the end of the Cold War between East and West.*

sym·pa·thet·ic /ˌsɪmpə'θetɪk/ ADJ **1** If you are **sympathetic** to someone who is in a bad situation, you are kind to them and show that you understand their feelings. ❏ *She was very sympathetic to the problems of adult students.* **2** If you are **sympathetic to** a proposal or action, you approve of it and are willing to support it. ❏ *Many of these early visitors were sympathetic to the Chinese socialist experiment.* **sym·pa·theti·cal·ly** /ˌsɪmpə'θetɪkli/ ADV **1** [sympathetically with V] ❏ *She nodded sympathetically.* **2** [sympathetically with V] ❏ *After a year we will sympathetically consider an application for reinstatement.*

sym·pa·thize /'sɪmpəθaɪz/ also **sympathise** VERB [I] (**sympathizes, sympathizing, sympathized**) **1** If you **sympathize** with someone who is in a bad situation, you show that you are sorry for them. ❏ *I must tell you how much I sympathize with you for your loss, Professor.* **2** If you **sympathize with** someone's feelings, you understand them and are not critical of them. ❏ *Some Europeans sympathize with the Americans over the issue.* **3** If you **sympathize with** a proposal or action, you approve of it and are willing to support it. ❏ *Most of the people living there sympathized with the guerrillas.*

sym·pa·thiz·er /'sɪmpəθaɪzə/ also **sympathiser** NOUN [c] (**sympathizers**) The **sympathizers** of an organization or cause are the people who approve of it and support it. ❏ *Safta Hashmi was a well-known playwright and Communist sympathizer.*

sym·pa·thy ♦◇◇ /'sɪmpəθi/ NOUN [u] (**sympathies**) **1** [also sympathies] If you have **sympathy** for someone who is in a bad situation, you are sorry for them, and show this in the way you behave towards them. ❏ *We expressed our sympathy for her loss.* ❏ *I have had very little help from doctors and no sympathy whatsoever.* **2** [also sympathies, oft sympathy 'with/for' N] If you have **sympathy** with someone's ideas or opinions, you agree with them. ❏ *I have some sympathy with this point of view.* ❏ *Lithuania still commands considerable international sympathy for its cause.* **3** If you take some action **in sympathy with** someone else, you do it in order to show that you support them. ❏ *Several hundred workers struck in sympathy with their colleagues.*

sym·pho·ny /'sɪmfəni/ NOUN [c] (**symphonies**) A **symphony** is a piece of music written to be played by an orchestra. Symphonies are usually made up of four separate sections called movements. ❏ *Beethoven's Ninth Symphony*

sym·po·sium /sɪm'pəʊziəm/ NOUN [c] (**symposia** or **symposiums**) A **symposium** is a conference in which experts or academics discuss a particular subject. ❏ *He had been taking part in an international symposium on population.*

❖**symp·tom** ♦◇◇ /'sɪmptəm/ NOUN [c] (**symptoms**) **1** A **symptom** of an illness is something wrong with your body or mind that is a sign of the illness. = indication ❏ *One of the most common symptoms of schizophrenia is hearing imaginary voices.* ❏ *patients with flu symptoms* **2** A **symptom of** a bad situation is something that happens which is considered to be a sign of this situation. ❏ *Your problem with keeping boyfriends is just a symptom of a larger problem: making and keeping friends.*

symp·to·mat·ic /ˌsɪmptə'mætɪk/ ADJ [V-LINK + symptomatic] (*formal*) If something is **symptomatic of** something else, especially something bad, it is a sign of it. ❏ *The city's problems are symptomatic of the crisis that is spreading throughout the country.*

syn·chro·nize /'sɪŋkrənaɪz/ also **synchronise** VERB [RECIP] (**synchronizes, synchronizing, synchronized**) If you **synchronize** two activities, processes, or movements, or if you **synchronize** one activity, process, or movement **with** another, you cause them to happen at the same time and speed as each other. ❏ *It was virtually impossible to synchronize our lives so as to take holidays and weekends together.* ❏ *Synchronize the score with the film action.*

syn·di·cate NOUN, VERB

NOUN /'sɪndɪkət/ [c] (**syndicates**) **1** A **syndicate** is an association of people or organizations that is formed for business purposes or in order to carry out a project. ❏ *They formed a syndicate to buy the car in which they competed in the race.* ❏ *a syndicate of 152 banks* **2** A press **syndicate** is a group of newspapers or magazines that are all owned by the same person or company.

VERB /'sɪndɪkeɪt/ [T] (**syndicates, syndicating, syndicated**) When newspaper articles or television programmes are **syndicated**, they are sold to several different newspapers or television stations, who then publish the articles or broadcast the programmes. ❏ *Today his programme is syndicated to 500 stations.*

❖**syn·drome** /'sɪndrəʊm/ NOUN [c] (**syndromes**) A **syndrome** is a medical condition that is characterized by a particular group of signs and symptoms. ❏ *Irritable bowel syndrome seems to affect more women than men.* ❏ *The syndrome is more likely to strike those whose immune systems are already below par.*

❖**syn·ony·mous** /sɪ'nɒnɪməs/ ADJ If you say that one thing is **synonymous with** another, you mean that the two things are very closely associated with each other so that one suggests the other or one cannot exist without the other. ❏ *Paris has always been synonymous with elegance, luxury and style.* ❏ *In politics, power and popularity are not synonymous.*

syn·the·sis /'sɪnθɪsɪs/ NOUN [C, U] (**syntheses**) **1** [C] (*formal*) A **synthesis of** different ideas or styles is a mixture or combination of these ideas or styles. ❑ *His novels are a rich synthesis of Balkan history and mythology.* **2** [C, U] (*technical*) The **synthesis** of a substance is the production of it by means of chemical or biological reactions. ❑ *the genes that regulate the synthesis of these compounds*

⊙syn·the·size /'sɪnθɪsaɪz/ also **synthesise** VERB [T] (**synthesizes, synthesizing, synthesized**) **1** (*technical*) To **synthesize** a substance means to produce it by means of chemical or biological reactions. ❑ *After extensive research, Albert Hoffman first succeeded in synthesizing the acid in 1938.* **2** (*formal*) If you **synthesize** different ideas, facts, or experiences, you combine them to form a single idea or impression. = fuse ❑ *The movement synthesized elements of modern art that hadn't been brought together before, such as Cubism and Surrealism.*

⊙syn·thet·ic /sɪn'θetɪk/ ADJ **Synthetic** products are made from chemicals or artificial substances rather than from natural ones. = man-made, artificial; ≠ natural ❑ *Boots made from synthetic materials can usually be washed in a machine.* ❑ *progestogen, the synthetic hormone contained in the pill*

⊙syn·theti·cal·ly /sɪn'θetɪkli/ ADV = artificially; ≠ naturally ❑ *the therapeutic use of natural and synthetically produced hormones* ❑ *Although some vitamins are made from foods, the majority are manufactured synthetically.*

⊙sys·tem ♦♦♦ /'sɪstəm/ NOUN [C, SING] (**systems**) **1** [C] A **system** is a way of working, organizing, or doing something which follows a fixed plan or set of rules. You can use **system** to refer to an organization or institution that is organized in this way. = arrangement, organization ❑ *The present system of funding for higher education is unsatisfactory.* ❑ *a flexible and relatively efficient filing system* ❑ *a multi-party system of government* **2** [C] A **system** is a set of devices powered by electricity, for example a computer or an alarm. ❑ *Viruses tend to be good at surviving when a computer system crashes.* **3** [C] A **system** is a set of equipment or parts such as water pipes or electrical wiring, which is used to supply water, heat, or electricity. ❑ *a central heating system* **4** [C] A **system** is a network of things that are linked together so that people or things can travel from one place to another or communicate. = network ❑ *Australia's road and rail system* **5** [C] Your **system** is your body's organs and other parts that together perform particular functions. ❑ *He had slept for over fourteen hours, and his system seemed to have*

recuperated admirably. **6** [C] A **system** is a particular set of rules, especially in mathematics or science, which is used to count or measure things. ❑ *the decimal system of metric weights and measures* **7** [SING] People sometimes refer to the government or administration of a country as **the system**. ❑ *These feelings are likely to make people attempt to overthrow the system.*

→ See also **ecosystem, immune system, nervous system, solar system**

WORD CONNECTIONS
NOUN + **system**
a **health** system   an **education** system   a **management** system   a **justice** system   a **banking** system   ❑ *With the globalization of the banking system, it becomes more difficult for an individual national authority to control the process.*
a **computer** system   an **alarm** system   a **security** system   ❑ *The virus caused the whole computer system to crash.*
VERB + **system**
design a system   **develop** a system   **implement** a system   **use** a system   ❑ *They developed a system for converting sewage into clean water.*
install a system   ❑ *The system should be installed by a company approved by the National Council for Security Systems.*

⊙sys·tem·at·ic /ˌsɪstə'mætɪk/ ADJ Something that is done in a **systematic** way is done according to a fixed plan, in a thorough and efficient way. = orderly, methodical; ≠ unsystematic ❑ *They went about their business in a systematic way.* ❑ *They had not found any evidence of a systematic attempt to rig the ballot.*

⊙sys·tem·ati·cal·ly /ˌsɪstə'mætɪkli/ ADV = methodically; ≠ unsystematically ❑ *The army has systematically violated human rights.* ❑ *Both Canadian linguistic cultures continue to differ systematically from the American.*

S

Tt

T also **t** /tiː/ NOUN

NOUN [C, U] (**T's, t's**) **T** is the twentieth letter of the English alphabet.

PHRASE **to a T** or **to a tee** (*informal*) You can use **to a T** or **to a tee** to mean perfectly or exactly right. For example, if something suits you **to a T**, it suits you perfectly. If you have an activity or skill **down to a T**, you have succeeded in doing it exactly right. □ *Everything had to be rehearsed down to a T.* □ *The description fits us to a tee.*

tab /tæb/ NOUN

NOUN [C] (**tabs**) **1** A **tab** is a small piece of cloth or paper that is attached to something, usually with information about that thing written on it. = label □ *A clerk had slipped the wrong tab on Tony's X-ray.* **2** A **tab** is the total cost of goods or services that you have to pay, or the bill for those goods or services. = bill □ *At least one estimate puts the total tab at $7 million.*

PHRASES **keep tabs on someone** (*informal*) If someone **keeps tabs on** you, they make sure that they always know where you are and what you are doing, often in order to control you. □ *It was obvious Hill had come over to keep tabs on Johnson and make sure he didn't do anything drastic.*

pick up the tab (*informal*) If you **pick up the tab**, you pay a bill on behalf of a group of people or provide the money that is needed for something. □ *Pollard picked up the tab for dinner that night.*

✪ ta·ble ♦♦◇ /ˈteɪbəl/ NOUN, VERB

NOUN [C] (**tables**) **1** A **table** is a piece of furniture with a flat top that you put things on or sit at. □ *She was sitting at the kitchen table eating a peach.* **2** [also table + NUM] A **table** is a written set of facts and figures arranged in columns and rows. = chart, figure □ *Consult the table on page 104.* □ *Other research supports the figures in Table 3.3.*

VERB [T] (**tables, tabling, tabled**) (*BrE*) If someone **tables** a proposal, they say formally that they want it to be discussed at a meeting. = propose □ *They've tabled a motion criticizing the government for doing nothing about the problem.*

table·spoon /ˈteɪbəlspuːn/ NOUN [C] (**tablespoons**) A **tablespoon** is a fairly large spoon used for serving food and in cooking.

tab·let /ˈtæblət/ NOUN [C] (**tablets**) **1** A **tablet** is a small solid mass of medicine which you swallow. = pill □ *half a tablet of aspirin* **2** Clay **tablets** or stone **tablets** are the flat pieces of clay or stone which people used to write on before paper was invented.

tab·loid /ˈtæblɔɪd/ NOUN [C] (**tabloids**) A **tabloid** is a newspaper that has small pages, short articles, and a lot of photographs. Tabloids are usually considered to be less serious than other newspapers. □ *The tabloids speculated as to whether she was having an affair, and with whom.*

ta·boo /tæˈbuː/ NOUN, ADJ

NOUN [C] (**taboos**) A **taboo** against a subject or activity is a social custom to avoid doing that activity or talking about that subject, because people find them embarrassing or offensive. □ *The topic of addiction remains something of a taboo in our family.*

ADJ A **taboo** subject or activity is one that people avoid because many people find it embarrassing or offensive. □ *Cancer is a taboo subject and people are frightened or embarrassed to talk openly about it.*

tac·it /ˈtæsɪt/ ADJ If you refer to someone's **tacit** agreement or approval, you mean they are agreeing to something or approving it without actually saying so, often because they are unwilling to admit to doing so. □ *The question was a tacit admission that a mistake had indeed been made.*

tac·it·ly /ˈtæsɪtli/ ADV [tacitly with v] □ *He tacitly admitted that the government had breached regulations.*

tack /tæk/ NOUN, VERB

NOUN [C, SING] (**tacks**) **1** [C] A **tack** is a short nail with a broad, flat head, especially one that is used for fastening carpets to the floor. □ *a box of carpet tacks* **2** [SING] [also no DET] If you change **tack** or try a different **tack**, you try a different method for dealing with a situation. = approach □ *Seeing the puzzled look on his face, she tried a different tack.*

VERB [T] (**tacks, tacking, tacked**) **1** If you **tack** something to a surface, you pin it there with tacks or drawing pins. □ *He had tacked this note to her door.* **2** If you **tack** pieces of material together, you sew them together with big, loose stitches in order to hold them firmly or check that they fit, before sewing them permanently. □ *Tack them together with a 1 cm seam.*

PHRASAL VERB **tack on** If you say that something **is tacked on** to something else, you think that it is added in a hurry and in an unsatisfactory way. □ *The child-care bill is to be tacked on to the budget plan now being worked out in the Senate.*

✪ tack·le ♦◇◇ /ˈtækəl/ VERB, NOUN

VERB [T] (**tackles, tackling, tackled**) **1** If you **tackle** a difficult problem or task, you deal with it in a very determined or efficient way. = deal with, confront; ≠ ignore □ *The first reason to tackle these problems is to save children's lives.* □ *the government's latest scheme to tackle crime* **2** If you **tackle** someone in football or hockey, you try to take the ball away from them. If you **tackle** someone in a game such as American football or rugby, you knock them to the ground. □ *Foley tackled the quarterback.* **3** If you **tackle** someone about a particular matter, you speak to them honestly about it, usually in order to get it changed or done. = confront □ *I tackled him about how anyone could live amidst so much poverty.* **4** If you **tackle** someone, you attack them and fight them. □ *Two security guards tackled and apprehended a man suspected of robbing 17 banks.*

NOUN [C, U] (**tackles**) **1** [C] A **tackle** is an attempt to take the ball away from someone in a game such as football or hockey. In games such as American football or rugby a **tackle** is when you knock another player to the ground. □ *a tackle by fullback Brian Burrows* **2** [U] **Tackle** is the equipment that you need for a sport or activity, especially fishing. □ *fishing tackle*

tact /tækt/ NOUN [U] **Tact** is the ability to avoid upsetting or offending people by being careful not to say or do things that would hurt their feelings. = diplomacy □ *Her tact and intuition never failed.*

tact·ful /ˈtæktfʊl/ ADJ (*approval*) If you describe a person or what they say as **tactful** you approve of them because they are careful not to offend or upset another person. = diplomatic □ *He had been extremely tactful in dealing with the financial question.*

tact·ful·ly /ˈtæktfəli/ ADV □ *Alex tactfully refrained from further comment.*

tac·tic ◆◇◇ /ˈtæktɪk/ NOUN [C] (**tactics**) Tactics are the methods that you choose to use in order to achieve what you want in a particular situation. ❑ *The rebels would still be able to use guerrilla tactics to make the country ungovernable.*

tac·ti·cal /ˈtæktɪkəl/ ADJ **1** You use **tactical** to describe an action or plan which is intended to help someone achieve what they want in a particular situation. ❑ *It's not yet clear whether his resignation offer is a serious one, or whether it's simply a tactical move.* **2** [tactical + N] **Tactical** weapons or forces are those which a military leader can decide for themselves to use in a battle, rather than waiting for a decision by a political leader. ❑ *They have removed all tactical nuclear missiles that could strike Europe.* **tac·ti·cal·ly** /ˈtæktɪkli/ ADV ❑ *The electorate is astute enough to vote tactically against the government.*

tag /tæg/ NOUN, VERB
NOUN [C, U] (**tags**) **1** [C] A **tag** is a small piece of card or cloth which is attached to an object or person and has information about that object or person on it. ❑ *Staff wore name tags and called inmates by their first names.* **2** [C] An electronic **tag** is a device that is firmly attached to someone or something and sets off an alarm if that person or thing moves away or is removed. ❑ *Ranchers are testing electronic tags on animals' ears to create a national cattle-tracking system.* **3** [U] **Tag** is a children's game where one child runs to touch or tag the others.
VERB [T] (**tags, tagging, tagged**) If you **tag** something, you attach something to it or mark it so that it can be identified later. ❑ *Professor Orr has developed interesting ways of tagging chemical molecules using existing laboratory lasers.*
PHRASAL VERB **tag along** If someone goes somewhere and you **tag along**, you go with them, especially when they have not asked you to. ❑ *I let him tag along because he had not been too well recently.*

⊘ **tail** ◆◇◇ /teɪl/ NOUN, VERB, ADV
NOUN [C, PL] (**tails**) **1** [C] The **tail** of an animal, bird, or fish is the part extending beyond the end of its body. ❑ *a black dog with a long tail* ❑ *The cattle were swinging their tails to disperse the flies.* **2** [C] You can use **tail** to refer to the end or back of something, especially something long and thin. ❑ *the horizontal stabilizer bar on the plane's tail* **3** [PL] If a man is wearing **tails**, he is wearing a formal jacket which has two long pieces hanging down at the back. ❑ *men in tails and women in party dresses*
VERB [T] (**tails, tailing, tailed**) (*informal*) To **tail** someone means to follow close behind them and watch where they go and what they do. = shadow ❑ *Officers had tailed the gang during a major undercover operation.*
PHRASAL VERB **tail off** When something **tails off**, it gradually becomes less in amount or value, often before coming to an end completely. = wear off, abate; ≠ increase ❑ *Last year, economic growth tailed off to below four per cent.* ❑ *The drug's effect does not tail off after it has been used repeatedly.*
ADV [tail after V] If you toss a coin and it comes down **tails**, you can see the side of it that does not have a picture of a head on it. ❑ *'Heads or tails?'* ❑ *The captain called heads as usual – and the coin came down tails.*
✦ **cannot make head nor tail of something** → see **head**

tai·lor /ˈteɪlə/ NOUN, VERB
NOUN [C] (**tailors**) A **tailor** is a person whose job is to make men's clothes.
VERB [T] (**tailors, tailoring, tailored**) If you **tailor** something such as a plan or system to someone's needs, you make it suitable for a particular person or purpose by changing the details of it. ❑ *We can tailor the programme to the patient's needs.*

tailor-made ADJ **1** If something is **tailor-made**, it has been specially designed for a particular person or purpose. ❑ *Each client's portfolio is tailor-made.* **2** If you say that someone or something is **tailor-made for** a particular task, purpose, or need, you are emphasizing that they are perfectly suitable for it. ❑ *He was tailor-made, it was said, for the task ahead.* **3** **Tailor-made** clothes have been specially made to fit a particular person. ❑ *He was wearing a suit that looked tailor-made.*

taint /teɪnt/ VERB, NOUN
VERB [T] (**taints, tainting, tainted**) **1** If a person or thing is **tainted by** something bad or undesirable, their status or reputation is harmed because they are associated with it. ❑ *Opposition leaders said that the elections had been tainted by corruption.* **2** If an unpleasant substance **taints** food or medicine, the food or medicine is spoiled or damaged by it. ❑ *Rancid oil will taint the flavour.*
NOUN [C] (**taints**) A **taint** is an undesirable quality which ruins the status or reputation of someone or something. ❑ *Her government never really shook off the taint of corruption.*
taint·ed /ˈteɪntɪd/ ADJ ❑ *He came out only slightly tainted by telling millions of viewers he and his wife had had marital problems.*

take ◆◆◆ /teɪk/ VERB, NOUN
VERB [T] (**takes, taking, took, taken**) **1** You can use **take** followed by a noun to talk about an action or event, when it would also be possible to use the verb that is related to that noun. For example, you can say 'she took a shower' instead of 'she showered.' ❑ *She was too tired to take a shower.* ❑ *Betty took a photograph of us.* **2** In ordinary spoken or written English, people use **take** with a range of nouns instead of using a more specific verb. For example, people often say '**he took control**' or '**she took a positive attitude**' instead of 'he assumed control' or 'she adopted a positive attitude.' ❑ *The Patriotic Front took power after a three-month civil war.* ❑ *I felt it was important for women to join and take a leading role.* **3** If you **take** something, you reach out for it and hold it. ❑ *Here, let me take your coat.* ❑ *Colette took her by the shoulders and shook her.* **4** If you **take** something with you when you go somewhere, you carry it or have it with you. ❑ *Mark often took his books to Bess's house to study.* ❑ *You should take your passport with you when changing money.* **5** If a person, vehicle, or path **takes** someone somewhere, they transport or lead them there. ❑ *She took me to a Mexican restaurant.* **6** If something such as a job or interest **takes** you to a place, it is the reason for you going there. ❑ *He was a poor student from Madras whose genius took him to Stanford.* **7** If you **take** something such as your problems or your business to someone, you go to that person when you have problems you want to discuss or things you want to buy. ❑ *You need to take your problems to a trained counsellor.* **8** If one thing **takes** another **to** a particular level, condition, or state, it causes it to reach that level or condition. ❑ *A combination of talent, hard work and good looks have taken her to the top.* **9** If you **take** something from a place, you remove it from there. ❑ *He took a handkerchief from his pocket and lightly wiped his mouth.* **10** If you **take** something from someone who owns it, you steal it or go away with it without their permission. ❑ *He has taken my money, and I have no chance of getting it back.* **11** If an army or political party **takes** something or someone, they win them from their enemy or opponent. ❑ *A Serb army unit took the town.* **12** If you **take** one number or amount from another, you subtract it or deduct it. ❑ *Take off the price of the house, that's another hundred thousand.* **13** If you cannot **take** something difficult, painful, or annoying, you cannot tolerate it without becoming upset, ill, or angry. = stand, bear ❑ *Don't ever ask me to look after those kids again. I just can't take it!* **14** If you **take** something such as damage or loss, you suffer it, especially in war or in a battle. ❑ *They have taken heavy casualties.* **15** If something **takes** a certain amount of time, that amount of time is needed in order to do it. ❑ *Since the roads are very bad, the trip took us a long time.* ❑ *I had heard an appeal could take years.* ❑ *The sauce takes 25 minutes to prepare and cook.* ❑ *It takes 15 minutes to convert the plane into a car by removing the wings and the tail.* **16** If something **takes** a particular quality or thing, that quality or thing is needed in order to do it. = need ❑ *At one time, walking across the room took all her strength.* ❑ *It takes courage to say what you think.* **17** If you **take** something that is given or offered to you, you agree to accept it. = accept ❑ *When I took the job I thought I could change the system, but it's hard.* **18** If you **take** a feeling such as pleasure, pride, or delight in a particular thing or activity, it gives you that feeling. = derive ❑ *They take great pride in their heritage.* **19** If you **take** a prize or medal, you win it. ❑ *'Poison' took*

t

first prize at the 1991 Sundance Film Festival. **20** If you **take** the blame, responsibility, or credit for something, you agree to accept it. = accept ❑ His brother Raoul did it, but Leonel took the blame and kept his mouth shut. **21** If you **take** patients or clients, you accept them as your patients or clients. ❑ Some universities would be forced to take more students than they wanted. **22** If you **take** a telephone call, you speak to someone who is telephoning you. ❑ Douglas telephoned Catherine at her office. She refused to take his calls. **23** If you **take** something in a particular way, you react in the way mentioned to a situation or to someone's beliefs or behaviour. ❑ Unfortunately, no one took my opinion seriously. **24** You use **take** when you are discussing or explaining a particular question, in order to introduce an example or to say how the question is being considered. = consider ❑ There's confusion and resentment, and it's almost never expressed out in the open. Take this office, for example. **25** If you **take** someone's meaning or point, you understand and accept what they are saying. ❑ I had made it as plain as I could so that he could not fail to take my meaning. **26** If you **take** someone **for** something, you believe wrongly that they are that thing. ❑ She had taken him for a journalist. **27** If you **take** a road or route, you choose to travel along it. ❑ From the community college take Old Mill Road to the outskirts of town. **28** If you **take** a car, train, bus, or plane, you use it to go from one place to another. ❑ It's the other end of town so we should take the car. **29** If you **take** a subject or course at school or college, you choose to study it. ❑ Students are allowed to take European history and American history. **30** If you **take** a test or examination, you do it in order to show your knowledge or ability. ❑ She took her driving test yesterday. **31** If someone **takes** drugs, pills, or other medicines, they take them into their body, for example, by swallowing them. ❑ She's been taking sleeping pills. **32** If you **take** a note or a letter, you write down something you want to remember or the words that someone says. ❑ She sat expressionless, carefully taking notes. **33** If you **take** a measurement, you find out what it is by measuring. ❑ By drilling, geologists can take measurements at various depths. **34** If a place or container **takes** a particular amount or number, there is enough space for that amount or number. ❑ The place could just about take 2,000 people. **35** If you **take** a particular size in shoes or clothes, that size fits you. ❑ 'What size do you take?'—'I take a size 7.' **36** (in AmE, usually use **take in**; business) If a shop, restaurant, theatre, or other business **takes** a certain amount of money, they get that amount from people buying goods or services. **37** (informal) If you **are taken by** someone, you are cheated or deceived by them. ❑ They got taken by a scam artist.

PHRASES **take something lying down** If someone **takes** an insult or attack **lying down**, they accept it without protesting. ❑ The government is not taking such criticism lying down.

take a lot out of someone or **take it out of someone** If something **takes a lot out of** you or **takes it out of** you, it requires a lot of energy or effort and makes you feel very tired and weak afterwards. ❑ He looked tired, as if the argument had taken a lot out of him.

take five or **take ten** (mainly AmE, informal) If someone tells you to **take five** or to **take ten**, they are telling you to have a five or ten minute break from what you are doing.

CONVENTION **take it or leave it** If you say to someone 'take it or leave it', you are telling them that they can accept something or not accept it, but that you are not prepared to discuss any other alternatives. ❑ A 72-hour week, 12 hours a day, six days a week, take it or leave it.

PHRASAL VERBS **take after** If you **take after** a member of your family, you resemble them in your appearance, your behaviour, or your character. ❑ She was a smart, brave woman. You take after her.

take apart If you **take** something **apart**, you separate it into the different parts that it is made of. = dismantle ❑ When the clock stopped, he took it apart, found what was wrong, and put the whole thing together again.

take away **1** If you **take** something **away from** someone, you remove it from them, so that they no longer possess it or have it with them. ❑ They're going to take my citizenship away. ❑ 'Give me the toy,' he said softly, 'or I'll take it away from you.' **2** If you **take** one number or amount **away from** another, you subtract one number from the other. = subtract ❑ Add up the bills for each month. Take this away from the income. **3** To **take** someone **away** means to bring them from their home to an institution such as a prison or hospital. = take off ❑ Two men claiming to be police officers went to the pastor's house and took him away.

take back **1** If you **take** something **back**, you return it to the place where you bought it or where you borrowed it from, because it is unsuitable or broken, or because you have finished with it. ❑ If I buy something and he doesn't like it I'll take it back. **2** If you **take** something **back**, you admit that something that you said or thought is wrong. ❑ Take back what you said about Jeremy! **3** If you **take** someone **back**, you allow them to come home again, after they have gone away because of an argument or other problem. ❑ Why did she take him back? **4** If you say that something **takes** you **back**, you mean that it reminds you of a period of your past life and makes you think about it again. ❑ I enjoyed experimenting with colours – it took me back to being five years old.

take down **1** If you **take** something **down**, you reach up and get it from a high place such as a shelf. ❑ Alberto took the portrait down from the wall. **2** If you **take down** a structure, you remove each piece of it. ❑ The Canadian army took down the barricades erected by the Indians. **3** If you **take down** a piece of information or a statement, you write it down. = write down ❑ We've been trying to get back to you, Tom, but we think we took your number down incorrectly.

take in **1** If you **take** someone **in**, you allow them to stay in your house or your country, especially when they do not have anywhere to stay or are in trouble. ❑ He persuaded Jo to take him in. **2** If the police **take** someone **in**, they remove them from their home in order to question them. ❑ The police have taken him in for questioning in connection with the murder of a girl. **3** If you **are taken in by** someone or something, you are deceived by them, so that you get a false impression of them. ❑ I married in my late teens and was taken in by his charm – which soon vanished. **4** If you **take** something **in**, you pay attention to and understand it when you hear it or read it. ❑ Lesley explains possible treatments but you can tell she's not taking it in. **5** If you **take** something **in**, you see all of it. ❑ The eyes behind the lenses were dark and quick-moving, taking in everything at a glance. **6** If people, animals, or plants **take in** air, drink, or food, they allow it to enter their body, usually by breathing or swallowing. ❑ They will certainly need to take in plenty of liquid.

take off **1** When an aeroplane **takes off**, it leaves the ground and starts flying. ❑ We eventually took off at 11 o'clock and arrived in Juneau at 1:30. **2** If something such as a product, an activity, or someone's career **takes off**, it suddenly becomes very successful. ❑ In 1944, he met Edith Piaf, and his career took off. **3** If you **take off** or **take yourself off**, you go away, often suddenly and unexpectedly. ❑ He took off at once and headed back to the motel. **4** If you **take** a garment **off**, you remove it. ❑ He wouldn't take his hat off. **5** If you **take** time **off**, you obtain permission not to go to work for a short period of time. ❑ Mitchel's schedule had not permitted him to take time off.

take on **1** If you **take on** a job or responsibility, especially a difficult one, you accept it. ❑ No other organization was able or willing to take on the job. **2** If something **takes on** a new appearance or quality, it develops that appearance or quality. = assume ❑ Believing he had only a year to live, his writing took on a feverish intensity. **3** If a vehicle such as a bus or ship **takes on** passengers, goods, or fuel, it stops in order to allow them to get on or to be loaded on. ❑ This is a brief stop to take on passengers and water. **4** If you **take** someone **on**, you employ them to do a job. ❑ He's spoken to a publishing company. They're going to take him on. **5** If you **take** someone **on**, you fight them or compete against them, especially when they are bigger or more powerful than you are. ❑ Democrats are reluctant to take on a president whose popularity ratings were historically high. **6** If you **take** something **on** or **upon**

yourself, you decide to do it without asking anyone for permission or approval. ❑ *Knox had taken it on himself to choose the wine.* ❑ *He took upon himself the responsibility for protecting her.*

take out ■ If you **take** something **out**, you remove it permanently from its place. ❑ *I got an abscess so he took the tooth out.* ❷ If you **take out** something such as a loan, a licence, or an insurance policy, you obtain it by fulfilling the conditions and paying the money that is necessary. ❑ *I'll have to stop by the bank and take out a loan.* ❸ If you **take** someone **out**, they go somewhere such as a restaurant or theatre with you after you have invited them, and usually you pay for them. ❑ *Jessica's grandparents took her out for the day.* ❑ *Sophia took me out to lunch.*

take over ■ (*business*) If you **take over** a company, you get control of it, for example, by buying its shares. ❑ *I'm going to take over the company one day.* ❷ If someone **takes over** a country or building, they get control of it by force, for example, with the help of the army. ❑ *The Belgians took over Rwanda under a League of Nations mandate.* ❸ If you **take over** a job or role or if you **take over**, you become responsible for the job after someone else has stopped doing it. ❑ *His widow has taken over the running of his empire, including six theatres.* ❑ *In 2001, I took over from him as governing mayor.* ❹ If one thing **takes over** from something else, it becomes more important, successful, or powerful than the other thing, and eventually replaces it. ❑ *Cars gradually took over from horses.* ❺ → See also **takeover**

take to ■ If you **take to** someone or something, you like them, especially after knowing them or thinking about them for only a short time. ❑ *Did the children take to him?* ❷ If you **take to** doing something, you begin to do it as a regular habit. ❑ *They had taken to wandering through the streets arm-in-arm.*

take up ■ If you **take up** an activity or a subject, you become interested in it and spend time doing it, either as a hobby or as a career. ❑ *He did not particularly want to take up a competitive sport.* ❷ If you **take up** a question, problem, or cause, you act on it or discuss how you are going to act on it. ❑ *If you have a problem with the law, take it up with your legislators.* ❑ *She had taken up the cause of a generation of American youth.* ❸ If you **take up** a job, you begin to work at it. ❑ *He will take up his post as the head of the civil courts at the end of next month.* ❹ If you **take up** an offer or a challenge, you accept it. ❑ *Increasingly, more winemakers are taking up the challenge of growing Pinot Noir.* ❺ If something **takes up** a particular amount of time, space, or effort, it uses that amount. ❑ *I know how busy you must be and naturally I wouldn't want to take up too much of your time.* ❑ *A good deal of my time is taken up with driving the children to soccer games.*

NOUN [C, SING] ■ [C] A **take** is a short piece of action which is filmed in one continuous process for a film. ❑ *She couldn't get it right – she never knew the lines and we had to do several takes.* ❷ [SING] Someone's **take on** a particular situation or fact is their attitude to it or their interpretation of it. = perspective ❑ *What's your take on the new government? Do you think it can work?*

PHRASE **on the take** (*informal*) Someone who is **on the take** is receiving illegal income such as bribes. ❑ *I can also name cops who are on the take.*

✦ **be taken aback** → see **aback**; **take up arms** → see **arm**; **take your hat off to someone** → see **hat**; **be taken for a ride** → see **ride**; **take someone by surprise** → see **surprise**; **take my word for it** → see **word**

tak·en /ˈteɪkən/ IRREG FORM, ADJ
IRREG FORM **Taken** is the past participle of **take**.
ADJ [V-LINK + taken] (*informal*) If you are **taken with** something or someone, you are very interested in them or attracted to them. ❑ *She seems very taken with the idea.*

✪ **take·over** ◆◇◇ /ˈteɪkəʊvə/ NOUN [C] (**takeovers**)
■ (*business*) A **takeover** is the act of gaining control of a company by buying more of its shares than anyone else. = buyout ❑ *He lost his job in a corporate takeover.* ❑ *the government's takeover of the Bank of New England Corporation* ❑ *a hostile takeover bid for NCR, America's fifth-biggest computer-maker* ❷ A **takeover** is the act of taking control of a country, political party, or movement by force. = coup ❑ *There's been a military takeover of some kind.*

tale ◆◇◇ /teɪl/ NOUN [C] (**tales**) ■ A **tale** is a story, often involving magic or exciting events. ❑ *a collection of stories, poems and folk tales* ❷ You can refer to an interesting, exciting, or dramatic account of a real event as a **tale**. = story ❑ *The media have been filled with tales of horror and loss resulting from Monday's earthquake.*

tal·ent ◆◇◇ /ˈtælənt/ NOUN [C, U] (**talents**) Talent is the natural ability to do something well. ❑ *She is proud that both her children have a talent for music.* ❑ *He's got lots of talent.*

tal·ent·ed /ˈtæləntɪd/ ADJ Someone who is **talented** has a natural ability to do something well. = gifted ❑ *Howard is a talented pianist.*

talk ◆◆◆ /tɔːk/ VERB, NOUN
VERB [I, RECIP, T] (**talks, talking, talked**) ■ [I] When you **talk**, you use spoken language to express your thoughts, ideas, or feelings. = speak ❑ *He was too distressed to talk.* ❑ *The boys all began to talk at once.* ❷ [RECIP] If you **talk to** someone, you have a conversation with them. You can also say that two people **talk**. = speak ❑ *We talked and laughed a lot.* ❑ *I talked to him yesterday.* ❑ *When she came back, they were talking about American food.* ❸ [RECIP] If you **talk to** someone, you tell them about the things that are worrying you. You can also say that two people **talk**. ❑ *Your first step should be to talk to a teacher or school counsellor.* ❑ *Do call if you want to talk about it.* ❹ [I] If you **talk on** or **about** something, you make an informal speech telling people what you know or think about it. = speak ❑ *She will talk on the issues she cares passionately about including education and nursery care.* ❺ [RECIP] If one group of people **talks to** another, or if two groups **talk**, they have formal discussions in order to do a deal or produce an agreement. ❑ *We're talking to some people about opening an office in Boston.* ❑ *It triggered speculation that GM and Jaguar might be talking.* ❻ [RECIP] When different countries or different sides in a dispute **talk**, or **talk to** each other, they discuss their differences in order to try and settle the dispute. ❑ *They are collecting information in preparation for the day when the two sides sit down and talk.* ❼ [I] If people **are talking about** another person or **are talking**, they are discussing that person. ❑ *Everyone is talking about him.* ❑ *We'd better not be seen together. People will talk.* ❽ [I] If someone **talks** when they are being held by police or soldiers, they reveal important or secret information, usually unwillingly. ❑ *They'll talk, they'll implicate me.* ❾ [I, T] If you **talk** a particular language or **talk** with a particular accent, you use that language or have that accent when you speak. ❑ *You don't sound like a foreigner talking English.* ❿ [T] If you **talk** something such as politics or sports, you discuss it. ❑ *The guests were mostly middle-aged men talking business.* ⓫ [T] You can use **talk** to say what you think of the ideas that someone is expressing. For example, if you say that someone **is talking sense**, you mean that you think the opinions they are expressing are sensible. ❑ *You must admit George, you're talking absolute nonsense.* ⓬ [T] (*spoken*) You can say that you **are talking** a particular thing to draw attention to your topic or to point out a characteristic of what you are discussing. ❑ *We're talking megabucks this time.*

PHRASES **talk about something** (*informal, emphasis*) You can say **talk about** before mentioning a particular expression or situation, when you mean that something is a very striking or clear example of that expression or situation. ❑ *Took us quite a while to get here, didn't it? Talk about fate moving in a mysterious way!*
talking of You can use the expression **talking of** to introduce a new topic that you want to discuss, and to link it to something that has already been mentioned. = speaking of ❑ *I'll give a prize to the best idea. Talking of good ideas, here's one to break the ice at a wedding reception.*
PHRASAL VERBS **talk back** If you **talk back** to someone in authority such as a parent or teacher, you answer them in a rude way. ❑ *How dare you talk back to me!*
talk down ■ To **talk down** someone who is flying an aircraft in an emergency means to give them instructions

so that they can land safely. ❑ *The pilot began to talk him down by giving instructions over the radio.* **2** If someone **talks down** a particular thing, they make it less interesting, valuable, or likely than it originally seemed. ❑ *They even blame the government for talking down the nation's fourth biggest industry.* ❑ *Businessmen are tired of politicians talking the economy down.*

talk into If you **talk** a person **into** doing something they do not want to do, especially something wrong or stupid, you persuade them to do it. ❑ *He talked me into marrying him. He also talked me into having a baby.*

talk out of If you **talk** someone **out of** doing something they want or intend to do, you persuade them not to do it. ❑ *My mother tried to talk me out of getting a divorce.*

talk over If you **talk** something **over**, you discuss it thoroughly and honestly. ❑ *He always talked things over with his friends.* ❑ *We should go somewhere quiet, and talk it over.*

talk through **1** If you **talk** something **through** with someone, you discuss it with them thoroughly. ❑ *He and I have talked through this whole tricky problem.* ❑ *Now her children are grown-up and she has talked through with them what happened.* **2** If someone **talks** you **through** something that you do not know, they explain it to you carefully. ❑ *Now she must talk her sister through the process a step at a time.*

talk up If someone **talks up** a particular thing, they make it sound more interesting, valuable, or likely than it originally seemed. ❑ *Politicians accuse the media of talking up the possibility of a riot.* ❑ *He'll be talking up his plans for the economy.*

NOUN [U, C, PL] (**talks**) **1** [U] **Talk** is using spoken language to express your thoughts, ideas, or feelings. ❑ *That's not the kind of talk one usually hears from accountants.* **2** [C] A **talk** is a conversation you have with someone. = conversation ❑ *We had a talk with her father, Tony, who was a friend of mine.* **3** [C] If you have a **talk to** or **with** someone, you tell them about the things that are worrying you. ❑ *I think it's time we had a talk.* **4** [C] A **talk on** or **about** something is an informal speech telling people what you know or think about it. ❑ *A guide gives a brief talk on the history of the site.* **5** [PL] **Talks** are formal discussions intended to produce an agreement, usually between different countries or between employers and employees. ❑ *the next round of Middle East peace talks* **6** [U] If there is **talk about** a person, people are discussing that person. ❑ *There has been a lot of talk about me getting married.* **7** [U] If you say that something such as an idea or threat is just **talk**, or **all talk**, you mean that it does not mean or matter much, because people are exaggerating about it or do not really intend to do anything about it. ❑ *Has much of this actually been tried here? Or is it just talk?*

✦ **talk shop** → see **shop**

talka·tive /ˈtɔːkətɪv/ ADJ Someone who is **talkative** talks a lot. ❑ *He suddenly became very talkative, his face slightly flushed, his eyes much brighter.*

tall ♦◇◇ /tɔːl/ ADJ, ADV

ADJ (**taller, tallest**) **1** Someone or something that is **tall** has a greater height than is normal or average. ❑ *Being tall can make you feel incredibly self-confident.* **2** You use **tall** to ask or talk about the height of someone or something. ❑ *How tall are you?*

PHRASE **a tall order** If something is a **tall order**, it is very difficult. ❑ *Financing your studies may seem like a tall order, but there is plenty of help available.*

ADV

PHRASE **walk tall** If you say that someone **walks tall**, you mean that they behave in a way that shows that they have pride in themselves and in what they are doing. ❑ *They shouldn't be disappointed or let their heads fall, but walk tall.*

✪**tal·ly** /ˈtæli/ NOUN, VERB

NOUN [C] (**tallies**) A **tally** is a record of amounts or numbers which you keep changing and adding to as the activity which affects it progresses. ❑ *They do not keep a tally of visitors to the palace, but it is very popular.*

VERB [RECIP] (**tallies, tallying, tallied**) If one number or statement **tallies with** another, they agree with each other or are exactly the same. You can also say that two numbers

or statements **tally**. = correspond, agree, match; ≠ differ, contradict ❑ *Its own estimate of three hundred tallies with that of another survey.* ❑ *The figures didn't seem to tally.*

tame /teɪm/ ADJ, VERB

ADJ (**tamer, tamest**) **1** A **tame** animal or bird is one that is not afraid of humans. ❑ *They never became tame; they would run away if you approached them.* **2** If you say that something or someone is **tame**, you are criticizing them for being weak and uninteresting, rather than forceful or shocking. ❑ *These ideas may seem tame today, but they were inflammatory in his time.*

VERB [T] (**tames, taming, tamed**) If someone **tames** a wild animal or bird, they train it not to be afraid of humans and to do what they say. ❑ *The Amazons were believed to have been the first to tame horses.*

tam·per /ˈtæmpə/ VERB [I] (**tampers, tampering, tampered**) If someone **tampers with** something, they interfere with it or try to change it when they have no right to do so. ❑ *I don't want to be accused of tampering with the evidence.*

tan /tæn/ NOUN, VERB

NOUN [SING] If you have a **tan**, your skin has become darker than usual because you have been in the sun. = suntan ❑ *She is tall and blonde, with a permanent tan.*

VERB [I, T] (**tans, tanning, tanned**) If a part of your body **tans** or if you **tan** it, your skin becomes darker than usual because you spend a lot of time in the sun. ❑ *I have very pale skin that never tans.*

tanned /tænd/ ADJ ❑ *Their skin was tanned and glowing from their weeks at the sea.*

tan·gible /ˈtændʒɪbəl/ ADJ If something is **tangible**, it is clear enough or definite enough to be easily seen, felt, or noticed. ❑ *There should be some tangible evidence that the economy is starting to recover.*

tan·gle /ˈtæŋgəl/ NOUN, VERB

NOUN [C] (**tangles**) A **tangle of** something is a mass of it twisted together in a messy way. ❑ *A tangle of wires is all that remains of the computer and phone systems.*

VERB [I, T] (**tangles, tangling, tangled**) If something is **tangled** or **tangles**, it becomes twisted together in a messy way. ❑ *Animals get tangled in fishing nets and drown.* ❑ *Her hair tends to tangle.*

tank ♦◇◇ /tæŋk/ NOUN [C] (**tanks**) **1** A **tank** is a large container for holding liquid or gas. ❑ *an empty fuel tank* ❑ *Two water tanks provide a total capacity of 400 litres.* **2** A **tank** is a large military vehicle that is equipped with weapons and moves along on metal tracks that are fitted over the wheels.

tank·er /ˈtæŋkə/ NOUN [C] (**tankers**) **1** [oft SUPP + tanker, also 'by' tanker] A **tanker** is a very large ship used for transporting large quantities of gas or liquid, especially oil. ❑ *A Greek oil tanker has run aground.* **2** [usu SUPP + tanker, also 'by' tanker] A **tanker** is a large truck, railway vehicle, or aircraft used for transporting large quantities of a substance. ❑ *aerial refuelling tankers*

tan·ta·lize /ˈtæntəlaɪz/ also **tantalise** VERB [T] (**tantalizes, tantalizing, tantalized**) If someone or something **tantalizes** you, they make you feel hopeful and excited about getting what you want, usually before disappointing you by not letting you have what they appeared to offer. ❑ *the dreams of democracy that have so tantalized them*

tan·ta·liz·ing /ˈtæntəlaɪzɪŋ/ ADJ ❑ *A tantalizing aroma of roast beef fills the air.*

tan·ta·mount /ˈtæntəmaʊnt/ ADJ [V-LINK + tantamount 'to' N/-ING] (*formal, emphasis*) If you say that one thing is **tantamount to** another, more serious, thing you are emphasizing how bad, unacceptable, or unfortunate the first thing is by comparing it to the second thing. ❑ *What Bracey is saying is tantamount to heresy.*

tap ♦◇◇ /tæp/ NOUN, VERB

NOUN [C] (**taps**) **1** (*mainly BrE*; in *AmE*, usually use **faucet**) A **tap** is a device that controls the flow of a liquid or gas from a pipe or container, for example, on a sink or on a cask or barrel. **2** A **tap** is a quick light hit. ❑ *A tap on the* *door interrupted him and Sally Pierce came in.* **3** A **tap** is an act of attaching a special device to a telephone line so that you can secretly listen to someone's conversations. ❑ *He assured us that we were not subjected to phone taps.*

PHRASE **on tap** [usu V-LINK + on tap] If drinks are **on tap**, they come from a tap rather than from a bottle. ❑ *Filtered water is always on tap here.*

VERB [I, T] (**taps, tapping, tapped**) **1** [I, T] If you **tap** something, you hit it with a quick light blow or a series of quick light blows. ❑ *He tapped the table nervously with his fingers.* ❑ *Grace tapped on the bedroom door and went in.* **2** [T] If you **tap** your fingers or feet, you make a regular pattern of sound by hitting a surface lightly and repeatedly with them, especially while you are listening to music. ❑ *The song's so catchy it makes you bounce around the living room or tap your feet.* **3** [T] If someone **taps** your telephone, they attach a special device to the line so that they can secretly listen to your conversations. = bug ❑ *The government passed laws allowing the police to tap telephones.*

tape ♦♦◇ /teɪp/ NOUN, VERB (*academic word*)
NOUN [U, C] (**tapes**) **1** [U] **Tape** is a sticky strip of plastic used for sticking things together. ❑ *strong adhesive tape* **2** [U] **Tape** is a narrow plastic strip covered with a magnetic substance. It is used to record sounds, pictures, and computer information. ❑ *Tape is expensive and loses sound quality every time it is copied.* **3** [C] A **tape** is a cassette or spool with magnetic tape wound around it. ❑ *a new cassette tape* **4** [C] A **tape** is a ribbon that is stretched across the finishing line of a race. ❑ *the finishing tape*
VERB [I, T] (**tapes, taping, taped**) **1** [I, T] If you **tape** music, sounds, or television pictures, you record them using a tape recorder or a video recorder. ❑ *She has just taped an interview.* ❑ *He shouldn't be taping without the singer's permission.* **2** [T] If you **tape** one thing to another, you attach it using adhesive tape. ❑ *I taped the base of the feather onto the velvet.*
→ See also **red tape**

ta·per /ˈteɪpə/ VERB, NOUN
VERB [I, T] (**tapers, tapering, tapered**) If something **tapers**, or if you **taper** it, it becomes gradually thinner at one end. ❑ *Unlike other trees, it doesn't taper very much. It stays fat all the way up.*
NOUN [C] A **taper** is a long, thin candle or a thin wooden strip that is used for lighting fires. ❑ *Taking up a candlestick, he touched the wick to a lighted taper.*
ta·pered /ˈteɪpəd/ ADJ ❑ *the elegantly tapered legs of the dressing-table*

✪ **tar·get** ♦♦◇ /ˈtɑːgɪt/ NOUN, VERB (*academic word*)
NOUN [C] (**targets**) **1** A **target** is something at which someone is aiming a weapon or other object. ❑ *The village lies beside a main road, making it an easy target for bandits.* **2** A **target** is a result that you are trying to achieve. = objective, goal ❑ *She's won back her place too late to achieve her target of 20 goals this season.* ❑ *The budgets should be based on company objectives, and set realistic targets.* ❑ *an export target of $5 billion a year* **3** [oft target 'of/for' N] If someone or something is a **target**, they are being criticized or abused. ❑ *In the past they have been the target of racist abuse.* **4** A **target** group, audience, etc. is the people who you are trying to appeal to or affect. ❑ *Yuppies are a prime target group for marketing strategies.*
PHRASE **on target** If someone or something is **on target**, they are making good progress and are likely to achieve the result that is wanted. ❑ *We were still right on target for our deadline.*
VERB [T] (**targets, targeting** or **targetting, targeted** or **targetted**) **1** To **target** a particular person or thing means to decide to attack or criticize them. = attack, blame, criticize ❑ *Republicans targeted her as vulnerable in her bid for reelection this year.* ❑ *He targets the economy as the root cause of the deteriorating law and order situation.* ❑ *Supermarkets have attached security tags to small, valuable items targeted by thieves.* **2** If you **target** a particular group of people, you try to appeal to those people or affect them. = aim at, focus on ❑ *The campaign will target American insurance companies.* ❑ *The company has targeted adults as its primary customers.*

✪ **tar·iff** /ˈtærɪf/ NOUN [C] (**tariffs**) (*business*) A **tariff** is a tax that a government collects on goods coming into a country. = tax, duty ❑ *America wants to eliminate tariffs on items such as electronics.* ❑ *a rise in import tariffs*

tar·nish /ˈtɑːnɪʃ/ VERB [T, I] (**tarnishes, tarnishing, tarnished**) **1** [T] If you say that something **tarnishes** someone's reputation or image, you mean that it causes people to have a worse opinion of them than they would otherwise have had. ❑ *The affair could tarnish the reputation of the senator.* **2** [I, T] If a metal **tarnishes** or if something **tarnishes** it, it becomes stained and loses its brightness. ❑ *It never rusts or tarnishes.*
tar·nished /ˈtɑːnɪʃt/ ADJ ❑ *He says he wants to improve the tarnished image of his country.*

✪ **task** ♦♦◇ /tɑːsk, tæsk/ NOUN, VERB (*academic word*)
NOUN [C] (**tasks**) A **task** is an activity or piece of work which you have to do, usually as part of a larger project. = chore, job, assignment, duty, responsibility ❑ *Walker had the unenviable task of breaking the bad news to Mark.* ❑ *the massive task of reconstruction after the war* ❑ *She used the day to catch up with administrative tasks.*
VERB [T] (**tasks, tasking, tasked**) If you **are tasked with** doing a particular activity or piece of work, someone in authority asks you to do it. ❑ *Jen was tasked with running a charity basketball tournament.*

t

assignment NOUN (formal)
An **assignment** is a task or piece of work that you are given to do, especially as part of your job or studies. ❑ *The course involves written assignments and practical tests.*

job NOUN
A **job** is the work that someone does to earn money. ❑ *Thousands have lost their jobs.*

duty NOUN
Your **duties** are the activities which you must do as part of your job. ❑ *I carried out my duties conscientiously.*

responsibility NOUN
Your **responsibilities** are the duties that you have of your job or position. ❑ *They are introducing a programme to help employees balance work and family responsibilities.*

taste ♦♦◇ /teɪst/ NOUN, VERB
▪ NOUN [U, C, SING] (**tastes**) **1** [U] **Taste** is one of the five senses that people have. When you have food or drink in your mouth, your sense of **taste** makes it possible for you to recognize what it is. ❑ *a keen sense of taste* **2** [C] The **taste** of something is the individual quality that it has when you put it in your mouth and that distinguishes it from other things. For example, something may have a sweet, bitter, sour, or salty taste. ❑ *I like the taste of wine and enjoy trying different kinds.* **3** [SING] If you have a **taste** of some food or drink, you try a small amount of it in order to see what the flavour is like. ❑ *Yves sometimes gives customers a taste of a wine before they order.* **4** [SING] If you have a **taste of** a particular way of life or activity, you have a brief experience of it. ❑ *This voyage was his first taste of freedom.* **5** [SING] If you have a **taste for** something, you have a liking or preference for it. ❑ *That gave me a taste for reading.* **6** [U] [also tastes] A person's **taste** is their choice in the things that they like or buy, for example, their clothes, possessions, or music. If you say that someone has good **taste**, you mean that you approve of their choices. If you say that they have bad **taste**, you disapprove of their choices. ❑ *His taste in clothes is extremely good.*
▪ PHRASE **in bad taste** or **in poor taste** or **in good taste** If you say that something that is said or done is **in bad taste** or **in poor taste**, you mean that it is offensive, often because it concerns death or sex and is inappropriate for the situation. If you say that something is **in good taste**, you mean that it is not offensive and that it is appropriate for the situation. ❑ *He rejects the idea that his film is in bad taste.*
▪ VERB [I, T] (**tastes, tasting, tasted**) **1** [I] If food or drink **tastes of** something, it has that particular flavour, which you notice when you eat or drink it. ❑ *I drank a cup of tea that tasted of diesel.* **2** [T] If you **taste** some food or drink, you eat or drink a small amount of it in order to try its flavour, for example, to see if you like it or not. ❑ *I tasted the wine the waiter had produced.* **3** [T] If you can **taste** something that you are eating or drinking, you are aware of its flavour. ❑ *You can taste the green chili in the dish but it is a little sweet.* **4** [T] If you **taste** something such as a way of life or a pleasure, you experience it for a short period of time. ❑ *Once you have tasted the outdoor life in southern California, it's hard to return to Montana in winter.*

taste·ful /ˈteɪstfʊl/ ADJ If you say that something is **tasteful**, you consider it to be attractive, elegant, and in good taste. ❑ *The decor is tasteful and restrained.*
taste·ful·ly /ˈteɪstfəli/ ADV ❑ *a large and tastefully decorated home*

taste·less /ˈteɪstləs/ ADJ **1** If you describe something such as furniture, clothing, or the way that a house is decorated as **tasteless**, you consider it to be vulgar and unattractive. ❑ *a house crammed with tasteless furniture* **2** If you describe something such as a remark or joke as **tasteless**, you mean that it is offensive. ❑ *I think that is the most vulgar and tasteless remark I have ever heard in my life.*

3 If you describe food or drink as **tasteless**, you mean that it has very little or no flavour. ❑ *The fish was mushy and tasteless.*

tasty /ˈteɪsti/ ADJ (**tastier, tastiest**) If you say that food is **tasty**, you mean that it has a fairly strong and pleasant flavour which makes it good to eat. ❑ *Try this tasty dish for supper with a crispy salad.*

tat·tered /ˈtætəd/ ADJ If something such as clothing or a book is **tattered**, it is damaged or torn, especially because it has been used a lot over a long period of time. ❑ *He fled wearing only a sarong and a tattered shirt.*

taught /tɔːt/ IRREG FORM **Taught** is the past tense and past participle of **teach**.

taunt /tɔːnt/ VERB, NOUN
▪ VERB [T] (**taunts, taunting, taunted**) If someone **taunts** you, they say unkind or insulting things to you, especially about your weaknesses or failures. ❑ *A gang taunted a disabled man.*
▪ NOUN [C] (**taunts**) A **taunt** is an unkind or insulting remark that someone makes to you, especially about your weaknesses or failures. ❑ *For years they suffered racist taunts.*

✪**tax** ♦♦♦ /tæks/ NOUN, VERB
▪ NOUN [C, U] (**taxes**) (business) **Tax** is an amount of money that you have to pay to the government so that it can pay for public services. = duty, custom ❑ *No-one enjoys paying tax.* ❑ *a pledge not to raise taxes on people below a certain income* ❑ *They are calling for large spending cuts and tax increases.* ❑ *a cut in tax on new cars* ❑ *His decision to return to a form of property tax is the right one.*
▪ VERB [T] (**taxes, taxing, taxed**) (business) When a person or company **is taxed**, they have to pay a part of their income or profits to the government. When goods **are taxed**, a percentage of their price has to be paid to the government. ❑ *Husband and wife may be taxed separately on their incomes.* ❑ *The Bonn government taxes profits of corporations at a rate that is among the highest in Europe.*
→ See also **income tax**

✪**taxa·tion** /tækˈseɪʃən/ NOUN [U] (business) **1 Taxation** is the system by which a government takes money from people and spends it on things such as education, health, and defence. ❑ *the proposed reforms to taxation* **2 Taxation** is the amount of money that people have to pay in taxes. ❑ *The result will be higher taxation.* ❑ *a proposal to increase taxation on fuel*

taxi /ˈtæksi/ NOUN, VERB
▪ NOUN [C] (**taxis**) A **taxi** is a car driven by a person whose job is to take people where they want to go in return for money. = cab ❑ *The taxi drew up in front of the Riviera Club.*
▪ VERB [I, T] (**taxis, taxiing, taxied**) When an aircraft **taxis** along the ground or when a pilot **taxis** a plane somewhere, it moves slowly along the ground. ❑ *She gave permission to the plane to taxi into position and hold for takeoff.*

tax·payer /ˈtækspeɪə/ NOUN [C] (**taxpayers**) (business) **Taxpayers** are people who pay a percentage of their income to the government as tax. ❑ *This is not going to cost the taxpayer anything. The company will bear the costs for the delay.*

tea ♦♦◇ /tiː/ NOUN [C, U] (**teas**) **1 Tea** is a drink made by adding boiling water to tea leaves or tea bags. Tea usually refers to black tea from India or China. Herbal tea is made from various plants. ❑ *a cup of tea* ❑ *Would you like some tea?* ❑ *chamomile tea* **2** The chopped dried leaves of the plant that tea is made from is referred to as **tea**. ❑ *a box of tea*

✪**teach** ♦♦◇ /tiːtʃ/ VERB [T, I] (**teaches, teaching, taught**) **1** [T] If you **teach** someone something, you give them instructions so that they know about it or how to do it. ❑ *She taught me fractions and counting.* ❑ *George had taught him how to ride a horse.* ❑ *The trainers have a programme to teach them vocational skills.* ❑ *the way that children are taught to read* ❑ *The computer has simplified the difficult task of teaching reading to the deaf.* **2** [T] To **teach** someone something means to make them think, feel, or act in a new or different way. ❑ *Their daughter's death had taught him humility.* ❑ *He taught his followers that they could all be*

members of the kingdom of God. **3** [I, T] If you **teach** a subject or **teach**, you help students to learn about it by explaining it or showing them how to do it, usually as a job at a school or college. = educate, instruct; ≠ learn ❏ Ingrid is currently teaching mathematics at the high school. ❏ She taught English to Japanese business people. ❏ She has taught for 34 years. ❏ a twelve-month taught course
→ See also **teaching**
✦ **teach someone a lesson** → see **lesson**

⊘ **teach·er** ♦♦◇ /ˈtiːtʃə/ NOUN [C] (**teachers**) A **teacher** is a person who teaches, usually as a job at a school or similar institution. = tutor, trainer; ≠ pupil, student ❏ I'm a teacher with 21 years' experience. ❏ The shortage of maths teachers is a problem.

⊘ **teach·ing** ♦◇◇ /ˈtiːtʃɪŋ/ NOUN [U, C] (**teachings**) **1** [U] **Teaching** is the work that a teacher does in helping students to learn. = education; ≠ learning ❏ The quality of teaching in the school is excellent. ❏ The Government funds university teaching. ❏ the teaching of English in schools **2** [C] The **teachings** of a particular person, school of thought, or religion are all the ideas and principles that they teach. ❏ the teachings of Jesus

⊘ **team** ♦♦♦ /tiːm/ NOUN (academic word)
NOUN [C] (**teams**) **1** A **team** is a group of people who play a particular sport or game together against other similar groups of people. = group, squad; ≠ individual ❏ a football team ❏ the swimming team **2** You can refer to any group of people who work together as a **team**. ❏ Each specialist has a team of doctors under him or her. ❏ The governors were joined by Mr Hunter and his management team.
PHRASAL VERB **team up** (**teams, teaming, teamed**) If you **team up with** someone, you join them in order to work together for a particular purpose. You can also say that two people or groups **team up**. ❏ Elton teamed up with Eric Clapton to wow thousands at the rock concert.

team·mate /ˈtiːmmeɪt/ also **team-mate** NOUN [C] (**teammates**) In a game or sport, your **teammates** are the other members of your team. ❏ He was always a solid player, a hard worker, a great example to his teammates.

team·work /ˈtiːmwɜːk/ NOUN [U] **Teamwork** is the ability a group of people have to work well together. ❏ Today's complex buildings require close teamwork between the architect and the builders.

tear ♦◇◇ NOUN, VERB
NOUN /tɪə/ [C, PL] (**tears**) **1** [C] **Tears** are the drops of salty liquid that come out of your eyes when you are crying. ❏ Her eyes filled with tears. ❏ I just broke down and wept with tears of joy. **2** [PL] You can use **tears** in expressions such as **in tears**, **burst into tears**, and **close to tears** to indicate that someone is crying or is almost crying. ❏ He was in floods of tears on the phone. ❏ She burst into tears and ran from the kitchen. **3** /teə/ [C] A **tear** in paper, cloth, or another material is a hole that has been made in it. ❏ I peered through a tear in the van's curtains.
VERB /teə/ [I, T, PASSIVE] (**tears, tearing, tore, torn**) **1** [I, T] If you **tear** paper, cloth, or another material, or if it **tears**, you pull it into two pieces or you pull it so that a hole appears in it. ❏ I tore my coat on a nail. **2** [I, T] If you **tear** one of your muscles or ligaments, or if it **tears**, you injure it by accidentally moving it in the wrong way. ❏ He tore a muscle in his right thigh. ❏ If the muscle is stretched again it could even tear. **3** [T] To **tear** something from somewhere means to remove it roughly and violently. ❏ She tore the windscreen wipers from his car. **4** [I] If a person or animal **tears at** something, they pull it violently and try to break it into pieces. = rip ❏ Female fans fought their way past bodyguards and tore at his clothes. **5** [I] If you **tear** somewhere, you run, drive, or move there very quickly. = rush ❏ The door flew open and Miranda tore into the room. **6** [PASSIVE] If you say that a place **is torn by** particular events, you mean that unpleasant events which cause suffering and division among people are happening there. ❏ a country that has been torn by civil war and foreign invasion since its independence
PHRASAL VERBS **tear apart** **1** If something **tears** people **apart**, it causes them to argue or to leave each other. ❏ Her pregnancy was tearing the family apart. **2** If something **tears**

you **apart**, it makes you feel very upset, worried, and unhappy. ❏ Don't think it hasn't torn me apart to be away from you.
tear away If you **tear** someone **away from** a place or activity, you force them to leave the place or stop doing the activity, even though they want to remain there or carry on. ❏ He finally tore himself away from the table long enough to pour me a drink.
tear down If you **tear** something **down**, you destroy it or remove it completely. = pull down ❏ Angry Russians may have torn down the statue of Felix Dzerzhinsky.
tear off If you **tear off** your clothes, you take them off in a rough and violent way. ❏ Totally exhausted, he tore his clothes off and fell into bed.
tear up Tear up means the same as tear VERB **1**. ❏ She tore the letter up. ❏ Don't you dare tear up her ticket!
→ See also **torn**

tease /tiːz/ VERB, NOUN
VERB [T] (**teases, teasing, teased**) **1** To **tease** someone means to laugh at them or make jokes about them in order to embarrass, annoy, or upset them. ❏ He told her how the boys had set on him, teasing him. ❏ He teased me mercilessly about going Hollywood. **2** If someone **teases** their hair, they separate the individual strands from each other, for example by combing it. ❏ Her hair was teased until it stood out and around her face. ❏ two women in party dresses and teased hair
NOUN [C] (**teases**) **1** A **tease** is a joke about someone, made in order to embarrass, annoy, or upset them. ❏ Calling her by her real name had always been one of his teases. **2** If you refer to someone as a **tease**, you mean that they like laughing at people or making jokes about them. = teaser ❏ My brother's such a tease.

tea·spoon /ˈtiːspuːn/ NOUN [C] (**teaspoons**) A **teaspoon** is a small spoon used for putting sugar into tea or coffee, and in cooking. ❏ Drop the dough onto a baking sheet with a teaspoon.

⊘ **tech·ni·cal** ♦◇◇ /ˈteknɪkəl/ ADJ (academic word) **1** Technical means involving the sorts of machines, processes, and materials that are used in industry, transport, and communications. = high-tech, technological, mechanical ❏ In order to reach this limit a number of technical problems will have to be solved. ❏ jobs that require technical knowledge **2** You use **technical** to describe the practical skills and methods used to do an activity such as an art, a craft, or a sport. ❏ Their technical ability is exceptional. **3** Technical language involves using special words to describe the details of a specialized activity. ❏ The technical term for sunburn is erythema. ❏ He's just written a book: large format, nicely illustrated and not too technical.

tech·ni·cal·ity /ˌteknɪˈkælɪti/ NOUN [PL, C] (**technicalities**) **1** [PL] The **technicalities** of a process or activity are the detailed methods used to do it or to carry it out. ❏ the technicalities of classroom teaching **2** [C] A **technicality** is a point, especially a legal one, that is based on a strict interpretation of the law or of a set of rules but that may seem unimportant compared to a larger issue. ❏ The earlier verdict was overturned on a legal technicality.

⊘ **tech·ni·cal·ly** ♦◇◇ /ˈteknɪkəli/ ADV **1** [technically + ADJ] You can use **technically** to indicate activity that involves the sorts of machines, processes, and materials that are used in industry, transport, and communications. = technologically ❏ the largest and most technically advanced furnace company in the world **2** [technically + ADJ] You can use **technically** to indicate the practical skills and methods used to do an activity such as an art, a craft, or a sport. ❏ While Sade's voice isn't technically brilliant it has a quality which is unmistakable. **3** If something is **technically** the case, it is the case according to a strict interpretation of facts, laws, or rules, but may not be important or relevant in a particular situation. = theoretically ❏ More than a third of workers said they called into the office while technically on holiday. ❏ Nude bathing is technically illegal but there are plenty of unspoilt beaches where no one would ever know. ❏ Technically, the two sides have been in a state of war ever since 1949.

t

WORDS IN CONTEXT: TECHNOLOGY

Sales in e-books are growing rapidly as people embrace digital technology. Inevitably, this is likely to result in digital materials replacing the printed book.

To what extent do you agree or disagree?

The growth in e-book sales highlights the advantages of reading a book in **electronic format**. Obtaining an e-book is incredibly simple. Thanks to the **Internet** and **e-commerce**, we can **go online** at any time, **browse** available titles, buy one and start reading it immediately.

The e-book is also just as portable as a printed book. There is no need for an **Internet connection** once the **file** has been **downloaded**, so it can be read **offline** on a **PC**, a **laptop**, a **tablet** or even a **smartphone**. The reading experience on a **screen** can be improved by increasing the font size, and the e-book might be **interactive** with **hyperlinks** to audio, video or extra content on the **Web**. Finally, we can store an almost unlimited number of e-books on our **device**s, so space is not an issue.

However, I still think printed books can survive the **digital revolution**. Many people like the feel of holding a traditional book. The cover design, the printed words, even the smell and feel of the paper make the experience warmer and more intimate than reading on an electronic device. For this reason I think the printed book will be around for some time, although maybe in smaller numbers.

tech·ni·cian /tek'nɪʃən/ NOUN [c] (**technicians**) **1** A technician is someone whose job involves skilled practical work with scientific equipment, for example, in a laboratory. ❑ *a laboratory technician* **2** A technician is someone who is very good at the detailed technical aspects of an activity. ❑ *a versatile, veteran player, a superb technician*

✪tech·nique ♦♦◇ /tek'niːk/ NOUN [c, u] (**techniques**) (*academic word*) **1** [c] A technique is a particular method of doing an activity, usually a method that involves practical skills. = method, style, system, way ❑ *tests performed using a new technique* ❑ *developments in the surgical techniques employed* **2** [u] Technique is skill and ability in an artistic, sporting, or other practical activity that you develop through training and practice. ❑ *He went off to the Amsterdam Academy to improve his technique.*

WORD CONNECTIONS

VERB + **technique**

use a technique
employ a technique
apply a technique
❑ *The Kashmiri weavers used a technique similar to Western tapestry.*

learn a technique
master a technique
perfect a technique
develop a technique
❑ *Once you have mastered the basic technique, you can use it each time you feel anxious.*

ADJ + **technique**

a **modern** technique
a **sophisticated** technique
an **innovative** technique
❑ *Modern techniques can make dental care painless.*

a **traditional** technique
❑ *He liked to do things simply and well, using the traditional techniques his father had taught him.*

a **surgical** technique
a **mathematical** technique
an **investigative** technique
❑ *A new type of investigative technique is being used to detect cancer cells.*

✪tech·no·log·i·cal /ˌteknə'lɒdʒɪkəl/ ADJ [technological + N] Technological means relating to or

associated with technology. = technical ❑ *an era of very rapid technological change* ❑ *workers with technological expertise*
✪tech·no·logi·cal·ly /ˌteknə'lɒdʒɪkli/ ADV = technically ❑ *technologically advanced aircraft*

WORD PARTS

The prefix **techno-** appears in words for things related to technology:

technological (ADJ)
techno-speak (NOUN)
technophobe (NOUN)

✪tech·nol·ogy ♦♦◇ /tek'nɒlədʒi/ NOUN [c, u] (**technologies**) (*academic word*) Technology refers to methods, systems, and devices which are the result of scientific knowledge being used for practical purposes. = electronics, mechanization ❑ *Technology is changing fast.* ❑ *They should be allowed to wait for cheaper technologies to be developed.* ❑ *nuclear weapons technology*

WORD CONNECTIONS

ADJ + **technology**

modern technology
new technology
advanced technology
the **latest** technology
sophisticated technology
❑ *Modern technology has made food production much more efficient.*

digital technology
wireless technology
mobile technology
❑ *Analogue machines are being replaced by digital technology.*

nuclear technology
❑ *Although about half of Sweden's power comes from its reactors, it has never been at ease with nuclear technology.*

VERB + **technology**

use technology
embrace technology
❑ *Banks can use technology to get information about their customers quickly and easily.*

develop a technology
❑ *His team is developing a technology that could help prevent the disease's spread.*

T

te·di·ous /'ti:diəs/ ADJ If you describe something such as a job, task, or situation as **tedious**, you mean it is boring and frustrating. = boring ❏ *Such lists are long and tedious to read.*
te·di·ous·ly /'ti:diəsli/ ADV ❏ *the most tediously boring aspects of international relations*

teem /ti:m/ VERB [I] (**teems, teeming, teemed**) If you say that a place is **teeming with** people or animals, you mean that it is crowded and the people and animals are moving around a lot. = swarm ❏ *For most of the year, the area is teeming with tourists.*

teen /ti:n/ NOUN, ADJ
NOUN [PL] (**teens**) If you are in your **teens**, you are between thirteen and nineteen years old. ❏ *Most people who smoke began smoking in their teens.*
ADJ [teen + N] **Teen** is used to describe things such as films, magazines, bands, or activities that are aimed at or are done by people who are in their teens. = teenage ❏ *There has been an increase in teen pregnancies.*

teen·age /'ti:neɪdʒ/ ADJ **1** [teenage + N] **Teenage** children are aged between thirteen and nineteen years old. ❏ *She looked like any other teenage girl.* **2** [teenage + N] **Teenage** is used to describe things such as movies, magazines, bands, or activities that are aimed at or are done by teenage children. ❏ *'Smash Hits', a teenage magazine*

teen·ager ◆◇◇ /'ti:neɪdʒə/ NOUN [c] (**teenagers**) A **teenager** is someone who is between thirteen and nineteen years old. ❏ *As a teenager he attended Tulse Hill Senior High School.*

tee·ter /'ti:tə/ VERB [I] (**teeters, teetering, teetered**)
1 (*emphasis*) **Teeter** is used in expressions such as **teeter on the brink** and **teeter on the edge** to emphasize that something seems to be in a very unstable situation or position. ❏ *The hotel is teetering on the brink of bankruptcy.*
2 If someone or something **teeters**, they shake in an unsteady way, and seem to be about to lose their balance and fall over. ❏ *Hyde shifted his weight and felt himself teeter forward, beginning to overbalance.*

teeth /ti:θ/ IRREG FORM **Teeth** is the plural of **tooth.**

⊕**tele·com·mu·ni·ca·tions** /ˌtelɪkəmju:nɪ-'keɪʃənz/ NOUN [U]

The form **telecommunication** is used as a modifier.

Telecommunications is the technology of sending signals and messages over long distances using electronic equipment, for example, by radio and telephone. ❏ *the telecommunications industry*

te·lepa·thy /tɪ'lepəθi/ NOUN [U] If you refer to **telepathy**, you mean the direct communication of thoughts and feelings between people's minds, without the need to use speech, writing, or any other normal signals. ❏ *You never tell me what you're thinking. Am I supposed to use telepathy?*

tele·phone ◆◆◇ /'telɪfəʊn/ NOUN, VERB
NOUN [U, c] (**telephones**) **1** [U] The **telephone** is the electrical system of communication that you use to talk directly to someone else in a different place. You use the telephone by dialling a number on a piece of equipment and speaking into it. = phone ❏ *It's easier to reach her by telephone than by email.* ❏ *I hate to think what our telephone bill is going to be.* **2** [c] A **telephone** is the piece of equipment that you use when you talk to someone by telephone. = phone ❏ *He got up and answered the telephone.*
PHRASE **on the telephone** If you are **on the telephone**, you are speaking to someone by telephone. ❏ *Linda remained on the telephone to the police for three hours.*
VERB [I, T] (**telephones, telephoning, telephoned**) If you **telephone** someone, you dial their telephone number and speak to them by telephone. = call, phone ❏ *I felt so badly I had to telephone Owen to say I was sorry.* ❏ *They usually telephone first to see if she's home.*

⊕**tele·scope** /'telɪskəʊp/ NOUN [c] (**telescopes**) A **telescope** is a long instrument shaped like a tube. It has lenses inside it that make distant things seem larger and nearer when you look through it. ❏ *It's hoped that the telescope will enable scientists to see deeper into the universe than ever before.*

tele·vise /'telɪvaɪz/ VERB [T] (**televises, televising, televised**) If an event or programme **is televised**, it is broadcast so that it can be seen on television. ❏ *His comeback fight will be televised on network TV.*

tele·vi·sion ◆◆◇ /'telɪvɪʒən, ˌtelɪ'vɪʒ-/ NOUN [c, U] (**televisions**) **1** [c] A **television** or **television set** is a piece of electrical equipment consisting of a box with a glass screen on it on which you can watch programmes with pictures and sounds. = TV ❏ *She turned the television on and flicked around between news programmes.* **2** [u] **Television** is the system of sending pictures and sounds by electrical signals over a distance so that people can receive them on a television in their home. = TV ❏ *Toy manufacturers began promoting some of their products on television.* **3** [u] **Television** refers to all the programmes that you can watch. = TV ❏ *I don't have much time to watch very much television.* **4** [u] **Television** is the business or industry concerned with making programmes and broadcasting them on television. ❏ *I'd like a job in television.*

tell ◆◆◆ /tel/ VERB
VERB [T, I] (**tells, telling, told**) **1** [T] If you **tell** someone something, you give them information. ❏ *In the evening I returned to tell Phyllis I got the job.* ❏ *I called Andie to tell her how spectacular the stuff looked.* ❏ *Claire had made me promise to tell her the truth.* **2** [T] If you **tell** something such as a joke, a story, or your personal experiences, you communicate it to other people using speech. ❏ *His friends say he was always quick to tell a joke.* ❏ *He told his story to The LA Times and produced photographs.* **3** [T] If you **tell** someone **to** do something, you order or advise them to do it. ❏ *He said officers told him to get out of his car and lean against it.* **4** [T] If you **tell yourself** something, you put it into words in your own mind because you need to encourage or persuade yourself about something. ❏ *'Come on,' she told herself.* **5** [T] If you can **tell** what is happening or what is true, you are able to judge correctly what is happening or what is true. ❏ *It was already impossible to tell where the bullet had entered.* **6** [T] If you can **tell** one thing **from** another, you are able to recognize the difference between it and other similar things. ❏ *I can't really tell the difference between their policies and ours.* ❏ *How do you tell one from another?* **7** [I] (*informal*) If you **tell**, you reveal or give away a secret. ❏ *Many of the children know who they are but are not telling.* **8** [T] If facts or events **tell** you something, they reveal certain information to you through ways other than speech. ❏ *The facts tell us that this is not true.* ❏ *I don't think the unemployment rate ever tells us much about the future.* **9** [I] If an unpleasant or tiring experience begins to **tell**, it begins to have a serious effect. ❏ *It wasn't long before the strain began to tell on our relationship.*
PHRASES **I told you so** (*informal*) If someone disagrees with you or refuses to do what you suggest and you are eventually proved to be right, you can say **'I told you so.'** ❏ *Her parents did not approve of her decision and, if she failed, her mother would say, 'I told you so.'*
I'll tell you what or **I tell you what** (*spoken*) You use **I'll tell you what** or **I tell you what** to introduce a suggestion or a new topic of conversation. ❏ *I tell you what, I'll bring the beer over to your house.*
as far as one can tell or **so far as one can tell** (*vagueness*) You use **as far as I can tell** or **so far as I can tell** to indicate that what you are saying is based on the information you have, but that there may be things you do not know. ❏ *As far as I can tell, Jason is basically a nice guy.*
CONVENTION **I tell you** or **I can tell you** or **I can't tell you** (*informal, emphasis*) You can say **'I tell you', 'I can tell you'**, or **'I can't tell you'** to add emphasis to what you are saying. ❏ *I tell you this, I will not rest until that day has come.*
PHRASAL VERBS **tell apart** If you can **tell** people or things **apart**, you are able to recognize the differences between them and can therefore identify each of them. ❏ *It's easy to tell my pills apart because they're all different colours.*
tell off If you **tell** someone **off**, you speak to them angrily or seriously because they have done something wrong.

t

❑ *He never listened to us when we told him off.* ❑ *I'm always being told off for being so awkward.*

✦ **tell the time** → see **time**; **time will tell** → see **time**

tem·per /ˈtempə/ NOUN

  NOUN [C, U] (**tempers**) **1** If you refer to someone's **temper** or say that they have a **temper**, you mean that they become angry very easily. ❑ *He had a temper and could be nasty.* ❑ *His short temper had become notorious.* **2** Your **temper** is the way you are feeling at a particular time. If you are **in** a good **temper**, you feel cheerful. If you are **in** a bad **temper**, you feel angry and impatient. ❑ *I was in a bad temper last night.*

  PHRASES **in a temper** or **into a temper** If someone is **in a temper** or gets **into a temper**, the way that they are behaving shows that they are feeling angry and impatient. ❑ *She was still in a temper when Colin arrived.*

  lose your temper If you **lose your temper**, you become so angry that you shout at someone or show in some other way that you are no longer in control of yourself. ❑ *I've never seen him get angry or lose his temper.*

tem·pera·ment /ˈtemprəmənt/ NOUN [C, U] (**temperaments**) **1** [C, U] Your **temperament** is your basic nature, especially as it is shown in the way that you react to situations or to other people. ❑ *His impulsive temperament regularly got him into difficulties.* **2** [U] **Temperament** is the tendency to behave in an uncontrolled, bad-tempered, or unreasonable way. ❑ *Some of the models were given to fits of temperament.*

tem·pera·men·tal /ˌtemprəˈmentl/ ADJ

1 (*disapproval*) If you say that someone is **temperamental**, you are criticizing them for not being calm or quiet by nature, but having moods that change often and suddenly. ❑ *He is very temperamental and critical.* **2** If you describe something such as a machine or car as **temperamental**, you mean that it often does not work well. ❑ *The boys couldn't start the temperamental motor.*

❖**tem·per·ate** /ˈtempərit/ ADJ **Temperate** is used to describe a climate or a place which is never extremely hot or extremely cold. ❑ *The Nile Valley keeps a temperate climate throughout the year.* ❑ *crops grown mainly in temperate zones*

❖**tem·pera·ture** ◆◇◇ /ˈtemprətʃə/ NOUN

  NOUN [C, U] (**temperatures**) **1** [C, U] The **temperature** of something is a measure of how hot or cold it is. ❑ *Winter closes in and the temperature drops below freezing.* ❑ *The temperature soared to above 100 degrees in the shade.* ❑ *Coping with severe drops in temperature can be very difficult.* **2** [U] Your **temperature** is the temperature of your body. A normal temperature is about 37°C. ❑ *His temperature continued to rise and the cough worsened until Tania finally persuaded him to see a doctor.* **3** [C] You can use **temperature** to talk about the feelings and emotions that people have in particular situations. ❑ *There's also been a noticeable rise in the political temperature.*

  PHRASES **run a temperature** If you **are running a temperature** or if you **have a temperature**, your temperature is higher than it should be. ❑ *He began to run an extremely high temperature.*

  take someone's temperature If you **take someone's temperature** you use an instrument called a thermometer to measure the temperature of their body in order to see if they are ill. ❑ *He will probably take your child's temperature too.*

→ See also **fever**

tem·ple ◆◇◇ /ˈtempəl/ NOUN [C] (**temples**) **1** A **temple** is a building used for the worship of a god or gods, especially in the Buddhist, Jewish, Mormon, and Hindu religions, and in ancient Greek and Roman times. ❑ *a small Hindu temple* ❑ *We go to temple on Saturdays.* **2** Your **temples** are the flat parts on each side of the front part of your head, near your forehead. ❑ *Threads of silver ran through his beard and the hair at his temples.*

❖**tem·po·rary** ◆◇◇ /ˈtempərəri, AmE -reri/ ADJ

(*academic word*) Something that is **temporary** lasts for only a limited time. = short-term; ≠ permanent, long-term ❑ *His job here is only temporary.* ❑ *Most adolescent problems are temporary.* ❑ *a temporary loss of memory*

❖**tem·po·rari·ly** /ˌtempəˈreərili/ ADV ≠ permanently

❑ *The peace agreement has at least temporarily halted the civil war.* ❑ *Checkpoints between the two zones were temporarily closed.*

tempt /tempt/ VERB [T] (**tempts, tempting, tempted**)

1 Something that **tempts** you attracts you and makes you want it, even though it may be wrong or harmful. ❑ *Cars like that may tempt drivers to speed.* ❑ *It is the fresh fruit that tempts me at this time of year.* **2** If you **tempt** someone, you offer them something they want in order to encourage them to do what you want them to do. ❑ *a million dollar marketing campaign to tempt American tourists back to Britain* ❑ *Don't let credit tempt you to buy something you can't afford.* → See also **tempted**

temp·ta·tion /tempˈteɪʃən/ NOUN [C, U] (**temptations**) If you feel you want to do something or have something, even though you know you really should avoid it, you can refer to this feeling as **temptation**. You can also refer to the thing you want to do or have as a **temptation**. ❑ *Will they be able to resist the temptation to buy?*

tempt·ed /ˈtemptɪd/ ADJ [V-LINK + tempted] If you say that you are **tempted to** do something, you mean that you would like to do it. ❑ *I'm very tempted to sell my house.*

tempt·ing /ˈtemptɪŋ/ ADJ If something is **tempting**, it makes you want to do it or have it. ❑ *In the end, I turned down Raoul's tempting offer of the Palm Beach trip.*

tempt·ing·ly /ˈtemptɪŋli/ ADV ❑ *The good news is that prices are still temptingly low.*

ten ◆◆◆ /ten/ NUM (**tens**) **Ten** is the number 10. ❑ *Over the past ten years things have changed.*

ten·ant /ˈtenənt/ NOUN [C] (**tenants**) A **tenant** is someone who pays rent for the place they live in, or for land or buildings that they use. ❑ *Regulations placed clear obligations on the landlord for the benefit of the tenant.*

❖**tend** ◆◆◇ /tend/ VERB [T, I] (**tends, tending, tended**)

1 [T] If something **tends** to happen, it usually happens or it often happens. = be likely to ❑ *A problem for manufacturers is that lighter cars tend to be noisy.* ❑ *In older age groups women predominate because men tend to die younger.* **2** [I] If you **tend towards** a particular characteristic, you often display that characteristic. ❑ *Artistic and intellectual people tend towards left-wing views.* **3** [T] You can say that you **tend to** think something when you want to give your opinion, but do not want it to seem too forceful or definite. ❑ *I tend to think that our Representatives by and large do a good job.*

❖**ten·den·cy** ◆◆◇ /ˈtendənsi/ NOUN [C] (**tendencies**)

1 A **tendency** is a worrying or unpleasant habit or action that keeps occurring. = trend, habit, disposition ❑ *the government's tendency to secrecy in recent years* **2** A **tendency** is a part of your character that makes you often behave in an unpleasant or worrying way. ❑ *He is spoiled, arrogant and has a tendency towards snobbery.*

ten·der /ˈtendə/ ADJ, NOUN, VERB

  ADJ (**tenderer, tenderest**) **1** Someone or something that is **tender** expresses gentle and caring feelings. ❑ *Her voice was tender, full of pity.* **2** [tender + N] If you say that someone does something at a **tender** age, you mean that they do it when they are still young and have not had much experience. ❑ *He took up the game at the tender age of seven.* **3** Meat or other food that is **tender** is easy to cut or chew. ❑ *Cook for a minimum of 2 hours, or until the meat is tender.* **4** If part of your body is **tender**, it is sensitive and painful when it is touched. = sore ❑ *My tummy felt very tender.*

  NOUN [C, U] (**tenders**) (*business*) A **tender** is a formal offer to supply goods or to do a particular job, and a statement of the price that you or your company will charge. If a contract is **put out to tender**, formal offers are invited. If a company **wins a tender**, their offer is accepted. ❑ *Builders will then be sent the specifications and asked to submit a tender for the work.*

  VERB [I] (**tenders, tendering, tendered**) (*business*) If a company **tenders for** something, it makes a formal offer to supply goods or do a job for a particular price. ❑ *The staff are forbidden to tender for private-sector work.*

T

ten·der·ly /ˈtendəli/ ADV [tenderly with V] ❑ *Mr. White tenderly embraced his wife.*

ten·der·ness /ˈtendənəs/ NOUN [U] **1** *She smiled, politely rather than with tenderness.* **2** *There is still some tenderness in her ankle.*

ten·nis ◆◇◇ /ˈtenɪs/ NOUN [U] Tennis is a game played by two or four players on a rectangular court. The players use an oval racket with strings across it to hit a ball over a net across the middle of the court.

✪tense /tens/ ADJ, VERB, NOUN (*academic word*)
ADJ (tenser, tensest) **1** A tense situation or period of time is one that makes people anxious, because they do not know what is going to happen next. = strained, anxious ❑ *This gesture of goodwill did little to improve the tense atmosphere at the talks.* ❑ *There were a few tense moments before the presentation.* **2** If you are tense, you are anxious and nervous and cannot relax. ❑ *Mark, who had at first been very tense, at last relaxed.* **3** If your body is tense, your muscles are tight and not relaxed. = taut, tight; ≠ loose, relaxed ❑ *A bath can relax tense muscles.*
VERB [I, T] (tenses, tensing, tensed) If your muscles tense, if you tense, or if you tense your muscles, your muscles become tight and stiff, often because you are anxious or frightened. = tauten, tighten; ≠ loosen, relax ❑ *Newman's stomach muscles tensed.* ❑ *Stand with your feet apart and tense your muscles.* ❑ *It involves tensing and relaxing muscle groups, starting with your feet.*
PHRASAL VERB **tense up** Tense up means the same as tense VERB. ❑ *When we are under stress our bodies tend to tense up.*
NOUN [c] (tenses) The tense of a verb group is its form, which usually shows whether you are referring to past, present, or future time. ❑ *It was as though Corinne was already dead: they were speaking of her in the past tense.*

✪ten·sion ◆◇◇ /ˈtenʃən/ NOUN [U, c] (tensions) **1** [U] [also tensions] Tension is a feeling of worry and anxiety which makes it difficult for you to relax. = anxiety ❑ *Smiling and laughing has actually been shown to relieve tension and stress.* **2** [U] [also tensions] Tension is the feeling that is produced in a situation when people are anxious and do not trust each other, and when there is a possibility of sudden violence or conflict. ❑ *The tension between the two countries is likely to remain.* ❑ *years of political tension and conflict* **3** [c, U] If there is a tension between forces, arguments, or influences, there are differences between them that cause difficulties. ❑ *The film explored the tension between public duty and personal affections.* **4** [U] The tension in something such as a rope or wire is the extent to which it is stretched tight. = tightness; ≠ slack ❑ *As the cable wraps itself around the wheel, there is provision for adjusting the tension of the cable.* ❑ *The reassuring tension of the rope moved with him, neither too tight nor too loose.* ❑ *the tension created when tightening the wire*

tent /tent/ NOUN [c] (tents) A tent is a shelter made of canvas or nylon which is held up by poles and ropes, and is used mainly by people who are camping.

✪ten·ta·tive /ˈtentətɪv/ ADJ **1** Tentative agreements, plans, or arrangements are not definite or certain, but have been made as a first step. = provisional, conditional, indefinite; ≠ firm, definite ❑ *Political leaders have reached a tentative agreement to hold a preparatory conference next month.* ❑ *Such theories are still very tentative.* ❑ *The study was adequate to permit at least tentative conclusions.* **2** If someone is tentative, they are cautious and not very confident because they are uncertain or afraid. ❑ *My first attempts at complaining were kind of tentative.*
✪ten·ta·tive·ly /ˈtentətɪvli/ ADV **1** [tentatively with V] = provisionally, conditionally, indefinitely; ≠ firmly, definitely ❑ *The next round of talks is tentatively scheduled to begin on October 21st in Washington.* **2** [tentatively with V] ❑ *Perhaps, he suggested tentatively, they should send for Dr Esteves.*

tenth ◆◇◇ /tenθ/ ADJ, NOUN
ADJ The tenth item in a series is the one that you count as number ten. ❑ *her tenth birthday*
NOUN [c] (tenths) A tenth is one of ten equal parts of something. ❑ *He finished three-tenths of a second behind Prost.*

✪term ◆◆◆ /tɜːm/ NOUN, VERB
NOUN [c, U, PL] (terms) **1** [c] A term is a word or expression with a specific meaning, especially one which is used in relation to a particular subject. = name, word, terminology ❑ *Myocardial infarction is the medical term for a heart attack.* **2** [c, U] A term is one of the periods of time that a school, college, or university divides the year into. ❑ *the summer term* **3** [c] A term is a period of time between two elections during which a particular party or government is in power. = period, duration, session ❑ *Nixon never completed his term of office.* ❑ *Felipe Gonzalez won a fourth term of office in Spain's election.* **4** [c] A term is a period of time that someone spends doing a particular job or in a particular place. = period, duration, session ❑ *a 12 month term of service* ❑ *Offenders will be liable to a seven-year prison term.* **5** [c] A term is the period for which a legal contract or insurance policy is valid. ❑ *Premiums are guaranteed throughout the term of the policy.* **6** [U] The term of a woman's pregnancy is the nine month period that it lasts. Term is also used to refer to the end of the nine month period. ❑ *That makes her the first TV presenter to work the full term of her pregnancy.* **7** [PL] The terms of an agreement, treaty, or other arrangement are the conditions that must be accepted by the people involved in it. ❑ *the terms of the Helsinki agreement*
PHRASES **in terms of** If you talk about something in terms of something or in particular terms, you are specifying which aspect of it you are discussing or from what point of view you are considering it. ❑ *Our goods compete in terms of product quality, reliability and above all variety.* ❑ *Paris has played a dominant role in France, not just in political terms but also in economic power.*
in particular terms If you say something in particular terms, you say it using a particular type or level of language or using language which clearly shows your attitude. ❑ *The video explains in simple terms how the new tax works.*
come to terms with If you come to terms with something difficult or unpleasant, you learn to accept and deal with it. ❑ *She had come to terms with the fact that her husband would always be crippled.*
on equal terms or **on the same terms** If two people or groups compete on equal terms or on the same terms, neither of them has an advantage over the other. ❑ *I had at last found a sport where I could compete on equal terms with able-bodied people.*
on good terms If two people are on good terms or on friendly terms, they are friendly with each other. ❑ *Madeleine is on good terms with Sarah.*
in the long term or **in the short term** or **in the medium term** You use the expressions in the long term, in the short term, and in the medium term to talk about what will happen over a long period of time, over a short period of time, and over a medium period of time. ❑ *Organic fertilizers will have very positive results in the long term.*
on your terms If you do something on your terms, you do it under conditions that you decide because you are in a position of power. ❑ *They will sign the union treaty only on their terms.*
think in terms of If you say that you are thinking in terms of doing a particular thing, you mean that you are considering it. ❑ *You should be thinking in terms of graduating next year.*
VERB [T] (terms, terming, termed) If you say that something is termed a particular thing, you mean that that is what people call it or that is their opinion of it. ❑ *He had been termed a temporary employee.*
✦ in no uncertain terms → see **uncertain**

VOCABULARY BUILDER

term NOUN

A term is a length of time that someone spends doing a particular job or in a particular place.

❑ *The college elected Stephanie Foote to a one-year term as chair of the board of trustees.*

t

period NOUN

A **period** in the life of a person, organization, or society is a length of time that is remembered for a particular situation or activity.

❑ *a period of economic good health and expansion*

duration NOUN *(formal)*

The **duration** of an event or state is the time during which it happens or exists.

❑ *He was given the task of protecting her for the duration of the trial.*

session NOUN

A **session** is a period of time that you spend doing a particular activity.

❑ *He held long question-and-answer sessions with his aides.*

✪**ter·mi·nal** /ˈtɜːmɪnəl/ ADJ, NOUN *(academic word)*

ADJ A **terminal** illness or disease causes death, often slowly, and cannot be cured. ❑ *terminal cancer* ❑ *His illness was terminal.*

NOUN [C] (**terminals**) **1** [usu SUPP + terminal] A **terminal** is a place where vehicles, passengers, or goods begin or end a journey. = station, terminus, depot ❑ *Plans are underway for a new terminal at Dulles airport.* ❑ *a continental ferry terminal* **2** *(computing)* A computer **terminal** is a piece of equipment consisting of a keyboard and a screen that is used for putting information into a computer or getting information from it. ❑ *Carl sits at a computer terminal 40 hours a week.* **3** On a piece of electrical equipment, a **terminal** is one of the points where electricity enters or leaves it. ❑ *the positive terminal of the battery*

ter·mi·nal·ly /ˈtɜːmɪnəli/ ADV [terminally + ADJ] ❑ *The patient is terminally ill.*

✪**ter·mi·nate** /ˈtɜːmɪneɪt/ VERB [I, T] (**terminates, terminating, terminated**) *(academic word)* **1** [I, T] *(formal)* When you **terminate** something or when it **terminates**, it ends completely. = end, discontinue; ≠ begin ❑ *Her next remark abruptly terminated the conversation.* ❑ *the right to terminate an agreement* ❑ *His contract terminates at the end of the season.* **2** [T] *(medical)* To **terminate** a pregnancy means to end it. ❑ *After a lot of agonizing she decided to terminate the pregnancy.* **3** [I] *(formal)* When a train or bus **terminates** somewhere, it ends its journey there. ❑ *This train will terminate at Lamy.*

✪**ter·mi·na·tion** /ˌtɜːmɪˈneɪʃən/ NOUN [U, C] **1** [U] = end, cessation, discontinuation; ≠ beginning ❑ *a dispute which led to the abrupt termination of trade* ❑ *failure to provide reasonable notice of termination of employment* **2** [C, U] ❑ *You should also have a medical check-up after the termination of a pregnancy.*

✪**ter·mi·nol·ogy** /ˌtɜːmɪˈnɒlədʒi/ NOUN [C, U] (**terminologies**) The **terminology** of a subject is the set of special words and expressions used in connection with it. = jargon, vocabulary ❑ *gastritis, which in medical terminology means an inflammation of the stomach* ❑ *In medical terminology a gallop rhythm means that the heart is failing because the cardiac muscle is badly damaged and dilated.*

ter·race /ˈterɪs/ NOUN [C] (**terraces**) **1** A **terrace** is a flat area of stone or grass next to a building where people can sit. ❑ *Some guests recline in deck chairs on the sea-facing terrace.* **2** **Terraces** are a series of flat areas built like steps on the side of a hill so that crops can be grown there. ❑ *massive terraces of corn and millet carved into the mountainside like giant steps*

ter·rain /təˈreɪn/ NOUN [C, U] (**terrains**) **Terrain** is used to refer to an area of land or a type of land when you are considering its physical features. ❑ *The terrain changed quickly from arable land to desert.*

✪**ter·res·trial** /tɪˈrestriəl/ ADJ [terrestrial + N] **Terrestrial** means relating to the planet Earth rather than to some other part of the universe. ≠ extra-terrestrial ❑ *terrestrial life forms* ❑ *Although this is intensely hot by terrestrial standards, it is cool by comparison with the Sun's core.* ❑ *our terrestrial environment*

ter·ri·ble ♦♦◇ /ˈterɪbəl/ ADJ **1** A **terrible** experience or situation is very bad or very unpleasant. = dreadful ❑ *Tens of thousands more suffered terrible injuries in the world's worst industrial disaster.* ❑ *I often have terrible nightmares.* **2** If something is **terrible**, it is very bad or of very poor quality. = dreadful ❑ *She admits her French is terrible.* **3** [terrible + N] You use **terrible** to emphasize the great extent or degree of something. ❑ *I was a terrible fool, you know.*

ter·ri·bly /ˈterɪbli/ ADV **1** [terribly after V] ❑ *My son has suffered terribly. He has lost his best friend.* **2** *I'm terribly sorry to bother you at this hour.*

ter·rif·ic /təˈrɪfɪk/ ADJ **1** *(informal)* If you describe something or someone as **terrific**, you are very pleased with them or very impressed by them. = great ❑ *What a terrific idea!* **2** [terrific + N] **Terrific** means very great in amount, degree, or intensity. = tremendous ❑ *All of a sudden there was a terrific bang and a flash of smoke.*

ter·ri·fy /ˈterɪfaɪ/ VERB [T] (**terrifies, terrifying, terrified**) If something **terrifies** you, it makes you feel extremely frightened. ❑ *Flying terrifies him.*

ter·ri·fied /ˈterɪfaɪd/ ADJ ❑ *He was terrified of heights.* → See also **terror**

ter·ri·fy·ing /ˈterɪfaɪɪŋ/ ADJ If something is **terrifying**, it makes you very frightened. = frightening ❑ *I still find it terrifying to find myself surrounded by large numbers of horses.*

✪**ter·ri·to·rial** /ˌterɪˈtɔːriəl/ ADJ **1** **Territorial** means concerned with the ownership of a particular area of land or water. ❑ *It is the only republic which has no territorial disputes with the others.* ❑ *Both Chile and Argentina feel very strongly about their territorial claims to Antarctica.* **2** If you describe an animal or its behaviour as **territorial**, you mean that it has an area which it regards as its own, and which it defends when other animals try to enter it. ❑ *Two cats or more in one house will also exhibit territorial behaviour.*

✪**ter·ri·tory** ♦♦◇ /ˈterɪtri, AmE -tɔːri/ NOUN [C, U] (**territories**) **1** [C, U] **Territory** is land which is controlled by a particular country or ruler. = land ❑ *The government denies that any of its territory is under rebel control.* ❑ *the view that the US should use military force only when our borders or US territories are attacked* ❑ *Russian territory* **2** [C] A **territory** is a country or region that is controlled by another country. ❑ *He toured some of the disputed territories now under UN control.* **3** [U] [with SUPP] You can use **territory** to refer to an area of knowledge or experience. = terrain ❑ *Following the futuristic 'The Handmaid's Tale', Margaret Atwood's seventh novel, 'Cat's Eye', returns to more familiar territory.* **4** [C, U] An animal's **territory** is an area which it regards as its own and which it defends when other animals try to enter it. ❑ *The territory of a cat only remains fixed for as long as the cat dominates the area.* **5** [U] **Territory** is land with a particular character. ❑ *mountainous territory* ✦ **virgin territory** → see **virgin**

ter·ror ♦♦◇ /ˈterə/ NOUN [U, C] (**terrors**) **1** [U] **Terror** is very great fear. ❑ *I shook with terror whenever I was about to fly in a plane.* **2** [U] **Terror** is violence or the threat of violence, especially when it is used for political reasons. = terrorism ❑ *the war on terror* ❑ *The bomb attack on the capital could signal the start of a pre-election terror campaign.* **3** [C] A **terror** is something that makes you very frightened. ❑ *As a boy, he had a real terror of facing people.*

✪**ter·ror·ism** ♦♦◇ /ˈterərɪzəm/ NOUN [U] *(disapproval)* **Terrorism** is the use of violence, especially murder and bombing, in order to achieve political goals or to force a government to do something. ❑ *the threat of global terrorism* ❑ *the need to combat international terrorism* ❑ *We will fight terrorism and the terrorists who carried out this explosion.* ❑ *He is currently facing terrorism charges in Virginia.*

✪**ter·ror·ist** ♦◇◇ /ˈterərɪst/ NOUN [C] (**terrorists**) *(disapproval)* A **terrorist** is a person who uses violence, especially murder and bombing, in order to achieve political aims. = guerrilla ❑ *One American was killed and three were wounded in terrorist attacks.* ❑ *military action against countries that harbour terrorists* ❑ *the September 11 terrorist atrocities in the US*

ter·ror·ize /ˈterəraɪz/ also **terrorise** VERB [T] (**terrorizes, terrorizing, terrorized**) If someone **terrorizes**

you, they keep you in a state of fear by making it seem likely that they will attack you. ❑ *Bands of gunmen have hijacked food shipments and terrorized relief workers.*

✪ test ◆◆◆ /test/ VERB, NOUN

VERB [T] (**tests, testing, tested**) **1** When you **test** something, you try it, for example, by touching it or using it for a short time, in order to find out what it is, what condition it is in, or how well it works. = check, inspect ❑ *Either measure the temperature with a thermometer or test the water with your wrist.* ❑ *Here the army has its ranges where Rapier missiles and other weaponry are tested.* ❑ *The drug must first be tested in clinical trials to see if it works on other cancers.* **2** If you **test** someone, you ask them questions or tell them to perform certain actions in order to find out how much they know about a subject or how well they are able to do something. ❑ *There was a time when each teacher spent an hour, one day a week, testing students in every subject.* **3** If you **test** someone, you deliberately make things difficult for them in order to see how they react. ❑ *From the first day, Rudolf was testing me, seeing if I would make him tea, bring him a Coke.* **4** If you **are tested for** a particular disease or medical condition, you are examined or go through various procedures in order to find out whether you have that disease or condition. ❑ *My doctor wants me to be tested for diabetes.*

NOUN [C] (**tests**) **1** A **test** is a deliberate action or experiment to find out how well something works. = experiment, inspection ❑ *the banning of nuclear tests* **2** A **test** is a series of questions that you must answer or actions that you must perform in order to show how much you know about a subject or how well you are able to do something. = exam ❑ *Out of a total of 25 students only 15 passed the test.* **3** If an event or situation is a **test of** a person or thing, it reveals their qualities or effectiveness. ❑ *It is a fact that holidays are a major test of any relationship.* **4** A medical **test** is an examination of a part of your body in order to check that you are healthy or to find out what is wrong with you. ❑ *If necessary, X-rays and blood tests will also be used to aid diagnosis.* ❑ *a pregnancy test*

PHRASES **put something to the test** **1** If you **put** something **to the test**, you find out how useful or effective it is by using it. ❑ *The team are now putting their theory to the test.* **2** If new circumstances or events **put** something or someone **to the test**, they put a strain on it and indicate how strong or stable it really is. ❑ *Multiple hijackings are putting air traffic controllers to the test.*

stand the test of time If you say that something **will stand the test of time**, you mean that it is strong or effective enough to last for a very long time. ❑ *It says a lot for her cooking skills that so many of her recipes have stood the test of time.*

✦ **test the waters** → see **water**

tes·ta·ment /ˈtestəmənt/ NOUN

NOUN [C, U] (**testaments**) (*formal*) If one thing is a **testament to** another, it shows that the other thing exists or is true. = testimony ❑ *For him to win the game like that is a testament to his perseverance.*

PHRASE **last will and testament** (*legal*) Someone's **last will and testament** is the most recent will that they have made, especially the last will that they make before they die.

test case NOUN [C] (**test cases**) A **test case** is a legal case which becomes an example for deciding other similar cases. ❑ *It is considered an important test case by both advocates and opponents of gun control.*

test·er /ˈtestə/ NOUN [C] (**testers**) **1** A **tester** is a person who has been asked to test a particular thing. **2** [usu N + tester] A **tester** is a machine or device that you use to test whether another machine or device is working correctly. ❑ *I have a battery tester in my garage.*

✪ tes·ti·fy /ˈtestɪfaɪ/ VERB [I, T] (**testifies, testifying, testified**) When someone **testifies** in a court of law, they give a statement of what they saw someone do or what they know of a situation, after having promised to tell the truth. = witness, declare, certify, state ❑ *Several eyewitnesses testified that they saw the officers hit Miller in*

the face. ❑ *Eva testified to having seen Herndon with his gun on the stairs.* ❑ *He hopes to have his 12-year prison term reduced by testifying against his former colleagues.*

✪ tes·ti·mo·ny /ˈtestɪməni, AmE -məuni/ NOUN [C, U] (**testimonies**) **1** [C, U] In a court of law, someone's **testimony** is a formal statement that they make about what they saw someone do or what they know of a situation, after having promised to tell the truth. = statement ❑ *His testimony was an important element of the prosecution's case.* ❑ *Prosecutors may try to determine if Robb gave false testimony when he appeared before the grand jury.* **2** [U] [also 'a' testimony, usu testimony 'to' N] If you say that one thing is **testimony to** another, you mean that it shows clearly that the second thing has a particular quality. ❑ *The environmental movement is testimony to the widespread feelings of support for nature's importance.*

test·ing ◆◇◇ /ˈtestɪŋ/ ADJ, NOUN

ADJ A **testing** problem or situation is very difficult to deal with and shows a lot about the character of the person who is dealing with it. ❑ *The most testing time is undoubtedly in the early months of your return to work.* **NOUN** [U] **Testing** is the activity of testing something or someone in order to find out information. ❑ *product testing and labelling*

✪ text ◆◇◇ /tekst/ NOUN, VERB (*academic word*)

NOUN [SING, U, C] (**texts**) **1** [SING] The **text** of a book is the main part of it, rather than the introduction, pictures, or notes. ❑ *The text was informative and well written.* **2** [U] **Text** is any written material. = writing ❑ *The machine can recognize handwritten characters and turn them into printed text.* ❑ *A CD-ROM can store more than 250,000 pages of typed text.* **3** [C] The **text** of a speech, broadcast, or recording is the written version of it. ❑ *The text of his recent speech was circulated among leading republicans.* **4** [C] A **text** is a book or other piece of writing, especially one connected with science or learning. = book ❑ *Her text is believed to be the oldest surviving manuscript by a female physician.* ❑ *a tool that can translate English text into spoken Mandarin* **5** [C] A **text** is the same as a **text message**. ❑ *The new system can send a text to a mobile phone, or to another landline phone.* **VERB** [T] (**texts, texting, texted**) If you **text** someone, you send them a text message on a mobile phone. ❑ *Mary texted me when she got home.*

✪ text·book /ˈtekstbʊk/ also **text book** NOUN, ADJ

NOUN [C] (**textbooks**) A **textbook** is a book containing facts about a particular subject that is used by people studying that subject. = course book ❑ *She wrote a textbook on international law.* ❑ *a chemistry textbook* **ADJ** [textbook + N] (*emphasis*) If you say that something is a **textbook** case or example, you are emphasizing that it provides a clear example of a type of situation or event. ❑ *The house is a textbook example of medieval domestic architecture.*

tex·tile /ˈtekstaɪl/ NOUN [C, PL] (**textiles**) **1** [C] **Textiles** are types of cloth or fabric, especially ones that have been woven. ❑ *decorative textiles for the home* **2** [PL] [no DET] **Textiles** are the industries concerned with the manufacture of cloth. ❑ *Another 75,000 jobs will be lost in textiles and clothing.*

text·ing /ˈtekstɪŋ/ NOUN [U] **Texting** is the same as **text messaging.**

text mes·sage NOUN [C] (**text messages**) A **text message** is a message that you send using a mobile phone. ❑ *She has sent text messages to her family telling them not to worry.*

text mes·sag·ing NOUN [U] **Text messaging** is the sending of written messages using a mobile phone. ❑ *the popularity of text messaging*

✪ tex·tu·al /ˈtekstʃuəl/ ADJ [textual + N] **Textual** means relating to written texts, especially literary texts. = literary ❑ *close textual analysis of Shakespeare*

✪ tex·ture /ˈtekstʃə/ NOUN [C, U] (**textures**) **1** The **texture** of something is the way that it feels when you touch it, for example, how smooth or rough it is. ❑ *It is used in moisturizers to give them a wonderfully silky texture.* ❑ *the grainy texture of the paper* **2** The **texture** of something, especially food or soil, is its structure, for example, whether it is light with lots of holes, or very heavy and solid. ❑ *Matured over 18 months, this cheese has an open, crumbly texture with a strong flavour.*

than ◆◆◆ /ðən, STRONG ðæn/ PREP, CONJ

PREP **1** [COMPAR + than + GROUP] You use **than** after a comparative adjective or adverb in order to link two parts of a comparison. ❑ *Children learn faster than adults.* ❑ *The radio only weighs a few ounces and is smaller than a pack of cigarettes.* **2** ['more/less' than + N] You use **than** when you are stating a number, quantity, or value approximately by saying that it is above or below another number, quantity, or value. ❑ *They talked on the phone for more than an hour.* **CONJ** **1** **Than** is used to link two parts of a comparison. ❑ *He wished he could have helped her more than he did.* **2** You use **than** in order to link two parts of a contrast, for example, in order to state a preference. ❑ *The arrangement was more a formality than a genuine partnership of two nations.* ✦ **less than** → see **less**; **more often than not** → see **often**; **other than** → see **other**; **rather than** → see **rather**

thank ◆◆◆ /θæŋk/ CONVENTION, VERB, NOUN

CONVENTION **1** (formulae) You use **thank you** or, in more informal English, **thanks** to express your gratitude when someone does something for you or gives you what you want. ❑ *Thank you very much for your call.* ❑ *Thanks for the information.* **2** (formulae) You use **thank you** or, in more informal English, **thanks** to politely accept something that has just been offered to you. ❑ *'Would you like a cup of coffee?'—'Thank you, I'd love one.'* **3** (formulae) You use **no thank you** or, in more informal English, **no thanks** to politely refuse something that has just been offered to you. ❑ *'Would you like a cigarette?'—'No thank you.'* **4** (emphasis) You use **thank you** or, in more informal English, **thanks** to politely acknowledge what someone has said to you, especially when they have answered your question or said something nice to you. ❑ *'You look very nice indeed.'—'Thank you.'* **5** You use **thank you** or **thank you very much** in order to say firmly that you do not want someone's help or to tell them that you do not like the way that they are behaving towards you. ❑ *I can find my own way home, thank you.* **PHRASE** **thanks to** If you say that something happens **thanks to** a particular person or thing, you mean that they are responsible for it happening or caused it to happen. ❑ *It is thanks to this committee that many new sponsors have come forward.* **VERB** [T] (thanks, thanking, thanked) When you **thank** someone **for** something, you express your gratitude to them for it. ❑ *I thanked them for their long and loyal service.* **PHRASES** **thank God** or **thank goodness** or **thank heavens** (feelings) You say '**thank God**', '**thank goodness**', or '**thank heavens**' when you are very relieved about something. ❑ *I was wrong, thank God.* **have someone to thank** If you say that you **have** someone **to thank for** something, you mean that they caused it to happen. ❑ *I have her to thank for my life.* ❑ *You have only yourself to thank for this mess.* **NOUN** [PL] (thanks) When you express your **thanks** to someone, you express your gratitude to them for something. ❑ *They accepted their certificates with words of thanks.*

thank·ful /'θæŋkfʊl/ ADJ When you are **thankful**, you are very happy and relieved to have something, or that something has happened. **= grateful** ❑ *Most of the time I'm just thankful that I've got a job.*

thank·ful·ly /'θæŋkfʊli/ ADV [thankfully with CL/GROUP] You use **thankfully** in order to express approval or happiness about a statement that you are making. ❑ *Thankfully, she was not injured.*

that ◆◆◆ /ðət, STRONG ðæt/ PRON, DET, ADV, CONJ

PRON **1** You use **that** to refer back to an idea or situation expressed in a previous sentence or sentences. ❑ *They said you particularly wanted to talk to me. Why was that?* ❑ *'There's a party tonight.'—'Is that why you're phoning?'* **2** (formal) You use **that** in expressions such as **that of** and **that which** to introduce more information about something already mentioned, instead of repeating the noun which refers to it.

❑ *A recession like that of 1973–74 could put one in ten American companies into bankruptcy.* **3** You use **that** in front of words or expressions which express agreement, responses, or reactions to what has just been said. ❑ *'She said she'd met you in England.'—'That's true.'* **4** You use **that** when you are referring to someone or something which is a distance away from you in position or time, especially when you indicate or point to them. When there are two or more things near you, **that** refers to the more distant one. ❑ *Leo, what's that you're writing?* **5** You use **that** when you are identifying someone or asking about their identity. ❑ *That's my wife you were talking to.* ❑ *'Who's that with you?'—'A friend of mine.'* **6** (spoken) You can use **that** when you expect the person you are talking to to know what or who you are referring to, without needing to identify the particular person or thing fully. ❑ *That was a terrible case of blackmail in the paper today.* **7** You use **that** to introduce a clause which gives more information to help identify the person or thing you are talking about. ❑ *pills that will make the problem disappear*

PHRASES **and all that** (informal, vagueness) You use **and all that** or **and that** to refer generally to everything else which is associated with what you have just mentioned. ❑ *I'm not a cook myself but I am interested in nutrition and all that.* **at that** (emphasis) You use **at that** after a statement which modifies or emphasizes what you have just said. ❑ *Success never seems to come but through hard work, often physically demanding work at that.* **that is** or **that is to say** You use **that is** or **that is to say** to indicate that you are about to express the same idea more clearly or precisely. ❑ *I am a disappointing, though generally dutiful, student. That is, I do as I'm told.* **that's it** or **that is it** You use **that's it** to indicate that nothing more needs to be done or that the end has been reached. ❑ *When he left the office, that was it, the workday was over.* **just like that** (informal, emphasis) You use **just like that** to emphasize that something happens or is done immediately or in a very simple way, often without much thought or discussion. ❑ *Just like that, I was in love.* **that's that** or **that is that** (spoken) You use **that's that** to say there is nothing more you can do or say about a particular matter. ❑ *'Well, if that's the way you want it,' he replied, tears in his eyes, 'I guess that's that.'* **CONVENTION** **that's it** (formulae) You use **that's it** to express agreement with or approval of what has just been said or done. **= exactly** ❑ *'You got married, right?'—'Yeah, that's it.'* **DET** **1** You use **that** to refer back to an idea or situation expressed in a previous sentence or sentences. ❑ *She's away; for that reason I'm cooking tonight.* **2** You use **that** to refer to someone or something already mentioned. ❑ *The salespeople get between $50,000 and $60,000 a year but that amount can double with commission.* **3** When you have been talking about a particular period of time, you use **that** to indicate that you are still referring to the same period. You use expressions such as **that morning** or **that afternoon** to indicate that you are referring to an earlier period of the same day. ❑ *The story was published in a Sunday newspaper later that week.* **4** You use **that** when you are referring to someone or something which is a distance away from you in position or time, especially when you indicate or point to them. When there are two or more things near you, **that** refers to the more distant one. ❑ *Look at that guy. He's got red socks.* **5** (spoken) You can use **that** when you expect the person you are talking to to know what or who you are referring to, without needing to identify the particular person or thing fully. ❑ *I really thought I was something when I wore that hat and my patent leather shoes.* **ADV** **1** [with BRD-NEG, that + ADJ/ADV] If something is **not that** bad, funny, or expensive for example, it is not as bad, funny, or expensive as it might be or as has been suggested. ❑ *Not even Gary, he said, was that stupid.* **2** [that + ADJ/ADV] (informal, emphasis) You can use **that** to emphasize the degree of a feeling or quality. **= so** ❑ *I would have walked out, I was that angry.* **CONJ** **1** You can use **that** after many verbs, adjectives, nouns, and expressions to introduce a clause in which you report what someone has said, or what they think or feel. ❑ *He called her up one day and said that he and his wife were coming to New York.* **2** You use **that** after 'it' and a linking verb and an adjective to comment on a situation or fact. ❑ *It's interesting that you like him.* **3** You use **that** after expressions with 'so' and 'such' in order to introduce the result or effect of something. ❑ *She became so nervous that she shook violently.*

→ See also **those**

✦ **like that** → see **like**; **this and that** → see **this**

thaw /θɔː/ VERB, NOUN

VERB [I, T] (**thaws, thawing, thawed**) **1** [I] When ice, snow, or something else that is frozen **thaws**, it melts. ❑ *It's so cold the snow doesn't get a chance to thaw.* **2** [I, T] When you **thaw** frozen food or when it **thaws**, you leave it in a place where it can reach room temperature so that it is ready for use. ❑ *Always thaw pastry thoroughly.*

PHRASAL VERB **thaw out Thaw out** means the same as **thaw** VERB 2. ❑ *Thaw it out completely before reheating in a saucepan.*

NOUN [C] (**thaws**) A **thaw** is a period of warmer weather when snow and ice melt, usually at the end of winter. ❑ *We slogged through the mud of an early spring thaw.*

the ◆◆◆ /ðə, ði, STRONG ðiː/ DET

The is the definite article. It is used at the beginning of noun groups. **The** is usually pronounced /ðə/ before a consonant and /ði/ before a vowel, but pronounced /ðiː/ when you are emphasizing it.

1 You use **the** at the beginning of noun groups to refer to someone or something that you have already mentioned or identified. ❑ *Six of the 38 people were US citizens.* **2** You use **the** at the beginning of a noun group when the first noun is followed by an 'of' phrase or a clause which identifies the person or thing. ❑ *There has been a slight increase in the consumption of meat.* **3** You use **the** in front of some nouns that refer to something in our general experience of the world. ❑ *It's always hard to speculate about the future.* **4** You use **the** in front of nouns that refer to people, things, services, or institutions that are associated with everyday life. ❑ *The doctor's on his way.* **5** You use **the** instead of a possessive determiner, especially when you are talking about a part of someone's body or a member of their family. ❑ *'How's the family?'— 'Just fine, thank you.'* **6** You use **the** in front of a singular noun when you want to make a general statement about things or people of that type. ❑ *An area in which the computer has made considerable strides in recent years is in playing chess.* **7** You use **the** with the name of a musical instrument when you are talking about someone's ability to play the instrument. ❑ *Did you play the piano as a child?* **8** You use **the** with nationality adjectives and nouns to talk about the people who live in a country. ❑ *The Japanese, Americans, and even the French and Germans, judge economic policies by results.* **9** You use **the** with words such as 'rich', 'poor', 'old', or 'unemployed' to refer to all people of a particular type. ❑ *Conditions for the poor in Los Angeles have not improved.* **10** If you want to refer to a whole family or to a married couple, you can make their surname into a plural and use **the** in front of it. ❑ *The Taylors decided that they would employ an architect to do the work.* **11** You use **the** in front of an adjective when you are referring to a particular thing that is described by that adjective. ❑ *He knows he's wishing for the impossible.* **12** You use **the** to indicate whether or not you have enough of the thing mentioned for a particular purpose. = sufficient ❑ *She may not have the money to maintain or restore her property.* **13** You use **the** with some titles, place names, and other names. ❑ *the Seattle Times* ❑ *the White House* ❑ *The Great Gatsby* **14** You use **the** in front of numbers such as first, second, and third. ❑ *The meeting should take place on the fifth of May.* **15** You use **the** in front of numbers when they refer to decades. ❑ *It's sometimes hard to imagine how bad things were in the thirties.* **16** You use **the** in front of superlative adjectives and adverbs. ❑ *Brisk daily walks are still the best exercise for young and old alike.* **17** You use **the** in front of each of two comparative adjectives or adverbs when you are describing when one amount or quality changes in relation to another. ❑ *The longer the therapy*

goes on, the more successful it will be. **18** When you express rates, prices, and measurements, you can use **the** to say how many units apply to each of the items being measured. ❑ *cars that get more miles to the gallon* **19** You use **the** to indicate that something or someone is the most famous, important, or best thing of its kind. In spoken English, you put more stress on it, and in written English, you often underline it or write it in capitals or italics. ❑ *The circus is the place to be this Saturday or Sunday.*

✪ **thea·tre** /ˈθiːətə/ (*BrE*; in *AmE*, use **theater**) NOUN [C, SING] (**theatres**) **1** [C] A **theatre** is a building with a stage in it, on which plays, shows, and other performances take place. ❑ *If we went to the theatre it was a very big event.* ❑ *I worked at the Grand Theatre.* **2** [SING] You can refer to work in the theatre such as acting or writing plays as **the theatre**. = drama ❑ *You can move up to work in films and the theatre.*

the·at·ri·cal /θiˈætrɪkəl/ ADJ **1** [theatrical + N] **Theatrical** means relating to the theatre. ❑ *the most outstanding theatrical performances of the year* **2** **Theatrical** behaviour is exaggerated and unnatural, and intended to create an effect. ❑ *In a theatrical gesture Jim clamped his hand over his eyes.*

the·at·ri·cal·ly /θiˈætrɪkli/ ADV **1** *Shaffer's great gift lies in his ability to animate ideas theatrically.* **2** *He looked theatrically at his watch.*

theft /θeft/ NOUN [C, U] (**thefts**) **Theft** is the crime of stealing. ❑ *Over the last decade, car theft has increased by over 56 per cent.*

their ◆◆◆ /ðeə/ DET

Their is the third person plural possessive determiner.

1 You use **their** to indicate that something belongs or relates to the group of people, animals, or things that you are talking about. ❑ *Janis and Kurt have announced their engagement.* **2** You use **their** instead of 'his or her' to indicate that something belongs or relates to a person without saying whether that person is a man or a woman. Some people think this use is incorrect. ❑ *Each student determines their own pace in the yoga class.*

theirs /ðeəz/ PRON

Theirs is the third person plural possessive pronoun.

1 You use **theirs** to indicate that something belongs or relates to the group of people, animals, or things that you are talking about. ❑ *There was a big group of a dozen people at the table next to theirs.* **2** You use **theirs** instead of 'his or hers' to indicate that something belongs or relates to a person without saying whether that person is a man or a woman. Some people think this use is incorrect. ❑ *He would leave the trailer unlocked. If there was something inside that someone wanted, it would be theirs for the taking.*

them ◆◆◆ /ðəm, STRONG ðem/ PRON

Them is a third person plural pronoun. **Them** is used as the object of a verb or preposition.

1 [V + them, PREP + them] You use **them** to refer to a group of people, animals, or things. ❑ *The Beatles – I never get tired of listening to them.* ❑ *Kids these days have no one to tell them what's right and wrong.* **2** [V + them, PREP + them] You use **them** instead of 'him or her' to refer to a person without saying whether that person is a man or a woman. Some people think this use is incorrect. ❑ *It takes great courage to face your child and tell them the truth.*

✪ **the·mat·ic** /θiˈmætɪk/ ADJ [usu thematic + N] (*formal*) **Thematic** means concerned with the subject or theme of something, or with themes and topics in general. ❑ *assembling this material into thematic groups* ❑ *the whole thematic approach to learning*

✪ **the·mati·cal·ly** /θiˈmætɪkli/ ADV ❑ *a thematically-linked threesome of songs* ❑ *Thematically, Miller's work falls into broad categories.*

✪ **theme** ◆◇◇ /θiːm/ NOUN [C] (**themes**) (*academic word*) **1** A **theme** in a piece of writing, a talk, or a discussion is an important idea or subject that runs through it. = topic, subject, motif ❑ *The theme of the conference is renaissance Europe.* **2** A **theme** in an artist's work or in a work of

t

literature is an idea in it that the artist or writer develops or repeats. = topic, subject, motif ❑ *The novel's central theme is the ongoing conflict between men and women.* ◼3 A **theme** is a short simple tune on which a piece of music is based. ❑ *variations on themes from Mozart's The Magic Flute* ◼4 **Theme** music or a **theme** song is a piece of music that is played at the beginning and end of a film or of a television or radio programme. ❑ *the theme from Dr Zhivago*

WORD CONNECTIONS

ADJ + theme

a **central** theme
a **dominant** theme
the **main** theme
a **major** theme
❑ *Love is the central theme of his book.*

a **common** theme
a **recurring** theme
a **universal** theme
❑ *A recurring theme throughout the myths is that of two figures fighting for the hand of one woman.*

an **underlying** theme
❑ *Catholicism is an underlying theme in many of her books.*

VERB + theme

explore a theme
❑ *The novel explores the theme of unrequited love.*

continue a theme
echo a theme
❑ *Douglas echoed the theme of unity at a meeting in Washington.*

VOCABULARY BUILDER

theme NOUN
A **theme** in a piece of writing, a talk, or a discussion is an important idea that runs through it.
❑ *Which line or lines convey to you the theme of the poem?*

topic NOUN
A **topic** is a particular subject that you discuss, study, or write about.
❑ *The weather is a constant topic of conversation in Alaska.*

subject NOUN
The **subject** of something such as a conversation, letter, or book is the thing that is being discussed or written about.
❑ *It was I who first raised the subject of plastic surgery.*

area NOUN
You can use **area** to refer to a particular subject or topic, or to a particular part of a larger, more general situation or activity.
❑ *Awards were presented to writers in every area of the arts.*

field often NOUN
A particular **field** is a particular subject of study or type of activity.
❑ *Each of the authors is an expert in his field.*

them·selves ♦♦♦ /ðəmˈselvz/ PRON

Themselves is the third person plural reflexive pronoun.

◼1 [V + themselves, PREP + themselves] You use **themselves** to refer to people, animals, or things when the object of a verb or preposition refers to the same people or things as the subject of the verb. ❑ *They all seemed to be enjoying themselves.* ◼2 You use **themselves** to emphasize the people or things that you are referring to. **Themselves** is also sometimes used instead of 'them' as the object of a verb or preposition. ❑ *Many mentally ill people are themselves unhappy about the idea of community care.* ◼3 [V + themselves, PREP + themselves] You use **themselves** instead of 'himself or herself' to refer back to the person

who is the subject of the sentence without saying whether it is a man or a woman. Some people think this use is incorrect. ❑ *What can a patient with emphysema do to help themselves?* ◼4 You use **themselves** instead of 'himself or herself' to emphasize the person you are referring to without saying whether it is a man or a woman. **Themselves** is also sometimes used as the object of a verb or preposition. Some people think this use is incorrect. ❑ *Each student makes only one item themselves.*
→ See also ourselves

then ♦♦♦ /ðen/ ADV, ADJ

ADV ◼1 **Then** means at a particular time in the past or in the future. ❑ *He wanted to have a source of income after his retirement; until then, he wouldn't require additional money.* ❑ *Executives pledged to get the company back on track. Since then, though, shares have fallen 30 per cent.* ◼2 [then + GROUP] **Then** is used to refer to something that was true at a particular time in the past but is not true now. ❑ *Richard Strauss, then 76 years old, suffered through the war years in silence.* ◼3 You use **then** to say that one thing happens after another, or is after another on a list. ❑ *Add the oil and then the scallops to the pan, leaving a little space for the garlic.* ◼4 [CL/GROUP + then] You use **then** in conversation to indicate that what you are about to say follows logically in some way from what has just been said or implied. ❑ *'I wasn't a very good scholar in school.'—'Then why did you become a teacher?'* ◼5 [CL/GROUP + then] You use **then** to signal the end of a topic or the end of a conversation. ❑ *'I'll talk to you on Friday anyway.'—'Yep. Okay then.'* ◼6 [ADV + then] You use **then** with words like 'now', 'well', and 'okay', to introduce a new topic or a new point of view. ❑ *Now then, I'm going to explain everything to you before we do it.* ◼7 [then + CL] You use **then** to introduce the second part of a sentence which begins with 'if'. The first part of the sentence describes a possible situation, and **then** introduces the result of the situation. ❑ *If the answer is 'yes', then we need to leave now.* ◼8 [then + CL] You use **then** at the beginning of a sentence or after 'and' or 'but' to introduce a comment or an extra piece of information to what you have already said. ❑ *He sounded sincere, but then, he always did.*

ADJ [then + N] **Then** is used when you refer to something which was true at a particular time in the past but is not true now. ❑ *a tour of the then new airport*
✦ now and then → see now; there and then → see there

⊙**theo·lo·gian** /ˌθiːəˈləʊdʒən/ NOUN [C] (theologians)
A **theologian** is someone who studies the nature of God, religion, and religious beliefs. ❑ *the philosopher and theologian John Henry Newman*

⊙**the·ol·ogy** /θiˈɒlədʒi/ NOUN [U] **Theology** is the study of the nature of God and of religion and religious beliefs. ❑ *questions of theology* ❑ *He began studying theology with a view to becoming a priest.* ❑ *a Christian theology course*
⊙**theo·logi·cal** /ˌθiːəˈlɒdʒɪkəl/ ADJ ❑ *theological books* ❑ *Critics of the Pope said he focused too much power in the hands of the Vatican and smothered theological debate.*

⊙**theo·rem** /ˈθiːərəm/ NOUN [C] (theorems) A **theorem** is a statement in mathematics or logic that can be proved to be true by reasoning. ❑ *the central mathematical theorem underpinning the entire theory* ❑ *The theorem is very easily proved.*

⊙**theo·reti·cal** /ˌθiːəˈretɪkəl/ ADJ ◼1 A **theoretical** study or explanation is based on or uses the ideas and abstract principles that relate to a particular subject, rather than the practical aspects or uses of it. ≠ practical ❑ *theoretical physics* ❑ *There is no theoretical model to explain the impact of inflation on growth.* ◼2 If you describe a situation as a **theoretical** one, you mean that although it is supposed to be true or to exist in the way stated, it may not in fact be true or exist in that way. ❑ *This is certainly a theoretical risk but in practice there is seldom a problem.* ❑ *These fears are purely theoretical.*

theo·reti·cal·ly /ˌθiːəˈretɪkəli/ ADV [theoretically with CL/GROUP] You use **theoretically** to say that although something is supposed to be true or to happen in the way stated, it may not in fact be true or happen in that way. ❑ *Theoretically, the price is supposed to be marked on the shelf.*

❖theo·ry ◆◆◇ /'θɪəri/ NOUN (*academic word*)

NOUN [C, U] (**theories**) **1** [C, U] A **theory** is a formal idea or set of ideas that is intended to explain something. = principle, law, rule ☐ *Marx produced a new theory about historical change based upon conflict between competing groups.* ☐ *Einstein formulated the Theory of Relativity in 1905.* **2** [C] If you have a **theory** about something, you have your own opinion about it which you cannot prove but which you think is true. ☐ *There was a theory that he wanted to marry her.* **3** [U] The **theory** of a practical subject or skill is the set of rules and principles that form the basis of it. ☐ *He taught us music theory.*

PHRASE **in theory** You use **in theory** to say that although something is supposed to be true or to happen in the way stated, it may not in fact be true or happen in that way. = theoretically ☐ *Achieving these goals is relatively easy in theory, yet quite difficult in practice.* ☐ *A school dental service exists in theory, but in practice, there are few dentists to work in it.* ☐ *In theory, the technology is straightforward.*

❖thera·peu·tic /ˌθerə'pjuːtɪk/ ADJ **1** If something is **therapeutic**, it helps you to relax or to feel better about things, especially about a situation that made you unhappy. ☐ *Having a garden is therapeutic.* **2 Therapeutic** treatment is designed to treat an illness or to improve a person's health, rather than to prevent an illness. = healing; ≠ preventative ☐ *therapeutic drugs* ☐ *therapeutic doses of herbs*

❖thera·pist /'θerəpɪst/ NOUN [C] (**therapists**) A **therapist** is a person who is skilled in a particular type of therapy, especially psychotherapy. = counsellor ☐ *My therapist helped me to deal with my anger.* ☐ *the increasing number of people consulting alternative therapists* ☐ *In the view of family therapists, most problems originate in a person's social setting and relationships.*

❖thera·py ◆◇◇ /'θerəpi/ NOUN [U, C] (**therapies**) **1** [U] **Therapy** is the process of talking to a trained counsellor about your emotional and mental problems and your relationships in order to understand and improve the way you feel and behave. = counselling ☐ *Children may need therapy to help them deal with grief and death.* ☐ *Since I've been in therapy, I've grown to be a better husband and father.* **2** [U] **Therapy** is the treatment of someone with mental or physical illness without the use of drugs or operations. = treatment ☐ *a child receiving speech therapy* **3** [C, U] (*medical*) **Therapy** or a **therapy** is a treatment for a particular illness or condition. = treatment ☐ *hormonal therapies* ☐ *conventional drug therapy*

there ◆◆◆ /ðə, STRONG ðeə/ PRON, CONVENTION, ADV

PRON **1** [there 'be' N] **There** is used as the subject of the verb 'be' to say that something exists or does not exist, or to draw attention to it. be ☐ *There are temporary traffic lights now at the school.* ☐ *Are there any biscuits left?* **2** [there + V N] You use **there** in front of certain verbs when you are saying that something exists, develops, or can be seen. Whether the verb is singular or plural depends on the noun which follows the verb. ☐ *There remains considerable doubt over when the road will be completed.*

CONVENTION **1** (*informal*) **There** is used after 'hello' or 'hi' when you are greeting someone. ☐ *'Hello there,' said the woman, smiling at them.—'Hi!' they chorused.* **2** (*spoken*) You say 'there there' to someone who is very upset, especially a small child, in order to comfort them. ☐ *'There, there,' said Mummy. 'You've been having a bad dream.'* **3** (*spoken, formulae*) You say 'there you are' or 'there you go' when you are offering something to someone. ☐ *'There you go, Mr Walters,' she said, giving him his documents.*

ADV **1** If something is **there**, it exists or is available. ☐ *The group of old buildings is still there today.* **2** You use **there** to refer to a place which has already been mentioned. ☐ *The next day we drove 33 miles to Siena (the Villa Arceno is a great place to stay while you are there).* ☐ *'Come on over, if you want.'—'How do I get there?'* **3** You use **there** to indicate a place that you are pointing to or looking at, in order to draw someone's attention to it. ☐ *There it is, on the corner over there.* ☐ *There she is on the left up there.* **4** [there + CL] (*spoken*) You use **there** in expressions such as 'there he was' or 'there we were' to

sum up part of a story or to slow a story down for dramatic effect. ☐ *So there he was all covered in mud, and still in a good mood.* **5** [there with 'be'] You use **there** when speaking on the telephone to ask if someone is available to speak to you. ☐ *Hello, is Gordon there please?* **6** [there after V] You use **there** to refer to a point that someone has made in a conversation. ☐ *I think you're right there John.* **7** You use **there** to refer to a stage that has been reached in an activity or process. ☐ *We are making further investigations and will take the matter from there.* **8** You use **there** to indicate that something has reached a point or level which is completely successful. ☐ *We had hoped to fill the back page with extra news; we're not quite there yet.* **9** [there + CL] (*spoken*) You can use **there** in expressions such as **there you go** or **there we are** when accepting that an unsatisfactory situation cannot be changed. ☐ *This is a little cruel, but there you go.* **10** [there + CL] (*spoken, emphasis*) You can use **there** in expressions such as **there you go** and **there we are** when emphasizing that something proves that you were right. ☐ *You see? There you go. That's why I didn't mention it earlier. I knew you'd take it the wrong way.*

PHRASES **there you go again** (*spoken*) Phrases such as **there you go again** are used to show anger at someone who is repeating something that has annoyed you in the past. ☐ *'There you go again, upsetting the child!' said Shirley.* **so there** (*informal*) You can add 'so there' to what you are saying to show that you have won an argument, or that you will not change your mind about a decision you have made, even though the person you are talking to disagrees with you. This is usually said by children or to be funny. ☐ *I think that's sweet, so there.* ☐ *You see? Mom said I could – so there!* **there and then** or **then and there** If something happens **there and then** or **then and there**, it happens immediately. ☐ *Many felt that he should have resigned there and then.* **be there for someone** (*informal*) If someone **is there for** you, they help and support you, especially when you have problems. ☐ *Despite what happened in the past I want her to know I am there for her.*

USAGE NOTE

there

When **there** is used to show that something exists, it is followed by a form of the verb 'be', such as 'is' or 'are'. Do not say 'there have' or 'there has'.

***There are** more than two hundred and fifty species of shark.*

❖there·after /ˌðeər'ɑːftə, -'æftə/ ADV [thereafter with CL] (*formal*) **Thereafter** means after the event or date mentioned. = afterwards, subsequently ☐ *The plan will help you lose 3–4 pounds the first week, and 1–2 pounds the weeks thereafter.* ☐ *Inflation will fall and thereafter so will interest rates.* ☐ *The woman had surgery and died shortly thereafter.*

❖there·by /ˌðeə'baɪ/ ADV [thereby with CL] (*academic word, formal*) You use **thereby** to introduce an important result or consequence of the event or action you have just mentioned. = thus ☐ *Our bodies can sweat, thereby losing heat by evaporation.* ☐ *A firm might sometimes sell at a loss to drive a competitor out of business, and thereby increase its market power.*

❖there·fore ◆◆◇ /'ðeəfɔː/ ADV [therefore with CL/ GROUP] You use **therefore** to introduce a logical result or conclusion. = thus ☐ *Muscle cells need lots of fuel and therefore burn lots of calories.* ☐ *We expect to continue to gain new customers and therefore also market share.*

ther·mal /'θɜːməl/ ADJ, NOUN

ADJ **1** [thermal + N] **Thermal** means relating to or caused by heat or by changes in temperature. ☐ *thermal power stations* **2** [thermal + N] **Thermal** streams or baths contain water which is naturally hot or warm. ☐ *Volcanic activity has created thermal springs and boiling mud pools.* **3** [thermal + N] **Thermal** clothes are specially designed to keep you warm in cold weather. ☐ *thermal underwear* ☐ *My feet were like blocks of ice despite the thermal socks.*

NOUN [PL, C] (**thermals**) **1** [PL] **Thermals** are thermal clothes. ☐ *Have you got your thermals on?* **2** [C] A **thermal**

t

is a movement of rising warm air. ❏ *Birds use thermals to lift them through the air.*

these ♦♦♦ /ðiːz/ DET, PRON

DET **1** You use **these** at the beginning of noun groups to refer to someone or something that you have already mentioned or identified. ❏ *A committee has been formed. These people can make decisions in ten minutes which would take us months.* **2** You use **these** to introduce people or things that you are going to talk about. ❏ *Your camcorder should have these basic features: autofocus, playback facility, zoom lens.* **3** In spoken English, people use **these** to introduce people or things into a story. ❏ *I was by myself and these guys suddenly came towards me.* **4** You use **these** to refer to people or things that are near you, especially when you touch them or point to them. ❏ *These scissors are awfully heavy.* **5** You use **these** when you refer to something which you expect the person you are talking to to know about, or when you are checking that you are both thinking of the same person or thing. ❏ *You know these last few months when we've been expecting it to warm up a little bit?* **6** You use **these** in the expression **these days** to mean 'at the present time'. ❏ *These days, people appreciate a chance to relax.*

PRON **1** You use **these** to refer to people or things you have already mentioned or identified. ❏ *'I have faith in these guys,' the coach said. 'These are good players.'* **2** You use **these** to introduce people or things you are going to talk about. ❏ *Take care of yourself while you are pregnant. These are some of the things you can do for yourself.* **3** You use **these** when you are identifying a group or asking about their identity. ❏ *These are my children.* **4** You use **these** to refer to people or things that are near you, especially when you touch them or point to them. ❏ *These are the people who are helping us.*

✪ **the·sis** /ˈθiːsɪs/ NOUN [C] (**theses**) (*academic word*) **1** A **thesis** is an idea or theory that is expressed as a statement and is discussed in a logical way. = argument, theory ❏ *This thesis does not stand up to close inspection.* ❏ *One of the arguments used to support the thesis is that students who rely on their parents for money feel great pressure to get good grades.* **2** A **thesis** is a long piece of writing based on your own ideas and research that you do as part of a college degree, especially a higher degree such as a PhD. = dissertation ❏ *He was awarded his PhD for a thesis on industrial robots.*

they ♦♦♦ /ðeɪ/ PRON

They is a third person plural pronoun. **They** is used as the subject of a verb.

1 You use **they** to refer to a group of people, animals, or things. ❏ *Feed the dogs because they haven't eaten.* ❏ *The two men were far more alike than they would ever admit.* ❏ *People matter because of what they are, not what they have.* **2** You use **they** instead of 'he or she' to refer to a person without saying whether that person is a man or a woman. Some people think this use is incorrect. ❏ *The teacher is not responsible for the student's success or failure. They are only there to help the student learn.* **3** You use **they** in expressions such as 'they say' or 'they call it' to refer to people in general when you are making general statements about what people say, think, or do. ❏ *They say there's plenty of opportunities out there, you just have to look carefully and you'll find them.*

thick ♦♦◇ /θɪk/ ADJ, COMB

ADJ (**thicker, thickest**) **1** Something that is **thick** has a large distance between its two opposite sides. ❏ *For breakfast I had a thick slice of bread and butter.* ❏ *He wore thick glasses.* **2** You can use **thick** to talk or ask about how wide or deep something is. ❏ *The folder was two inches thick.* **3** If something that consists of several things is **thick**, it has a large number of them very close together. = dense ❏ *She inherited our father's thick, wavy hair.* **4** [V-LINK + thick 'with' N] If something is **thick with** another thing, the first thing is full of or covered with the second. ❏ *The air is thick with acrid smoke from the fires.* **5** **Thick** clothes are made from heavy cloth, so that they will keep you warm in cold weather. ❏ *In the winter she wears thick socks, boots*

and gloves. **6** **Thick** smoke, fog, or cloud is difficult to see through. ❏ *The smoke was bluish-black and thick.* **7** **Thick** liquids are fairly stiff and solid and do not flow easily. ❏ *It had rained last night, so the garden was thick mud.*

COMB [thick + N] **Thick** is used with an adjective and a noun to describe how wide or deep something is. ❏ *His life was saved by a quarter-inch-thick bullet-proof vest.*

thick·ly /ˈθɪkli/ ADV **1** [thickly with V] ❏ *Slice the meat thickly.* **2** I rounded a bend where the trees and brush grew thickly.

thick·ness /ˈθɪknəs/ NOUN [C, U] (**thicknesses**) ❏ *The size of the fish will determine the thickness of the steaks.*

thick·en /ˈθɪkən/ VERB [I, T] (**thickens, thickening, thickened**) **1** [I, T] When you **thicken** a liquid or when it **thickens**, it becomes stiffer and more solid. ❏ *Thicken the broth with the mashed potato.* **2** [I] If something **thickens**, it becomes more closely grouped together or more solid than it was before. ❏ *The dust behind us grew closer and thickened into a cloud.*

thief /θiːf/ NOUN [C] (**thieves**) A **thief** is a person who steals something from another person. ❏ *The thieves snatched the camera.*

thigh /θaɪ/ NOUN [C] (**thighs**) Your **thighs** are the top parts of your legs, between your knees and your hips. ❏ *The shorts are so small I can't fit my thighs into any of them.*

thin ♦◇◇ /θɪn/ ADJ, VERB

ADJ (**thinner, thinnest**) **1** Something that is **thin** is much narrower than it is long. ❏ *A thin cable carries the signal to a computer.* **2** A person or animal that is **thin** has no extra fat on their body. ❏ *He was a tall, thin man with grey hair that fell in a wild tangle to his shoulders.* **3** Something such as paper or cloth that is **thin** is flat and has only a very small distance between its two opposite surfaces. ❏ *a small, blue-bound book printed in fine type on thin paper* **4** Liquids that are **thin** are weak and watery. ❏ *The soup was thin and clear, yet mysteriously rich.* **5** A crowd or audience that is **thin** does not have many people in it. ❏ *The crowd, which had been thin for the first half of the race, had now grown considerably.* **6** **Thin** clothes are made from light cloth and are not warm to wear. ❏ *Her gown was thin, and she shivered, partly from cold.* **7** If you describe an argument, an explanation, or evidence as **thin**, you mean that it is weak and difficult to believe. = weak ❏ *The police were certain they had the right man, but the evidence was thin.* **8** If someone's hair is described as **thin**, they do not have a lot of hair. ❏ *She had pale thin yellow hair she pulled back into a bun.*

PHRASE **wearing thin** If someone's patience, for example, is **wearing thin**, they are beginning to become impatient or angry with someone. ❏ *War has achieved little, and public patience is wearing thin.*

VERB [I, T] (**thins, thinning, thinned**) When you **thin** something or when it **thins**, it becomes less crowded because people or things have been removed from it. ❏ *It would have been better to have thinned the trees over several winters rather than all at one time.*

PHRASAL VERB **thin out** Thin out means the same as **thin** VERB. ❏ *NATO will continue to thin out its forces.*

thin·ly /ˈθɪnli/ ADV **1** [thinly with V] ❏ *Peel and thinly slice the onion.* **2** [thinly + -ED] ❏ *The island is thinly populated.* **3** *Much of the speech was a thinly disguised attack on environmentalists.*

✦ **on thin ice** → see **ice**; **thin air** → see **air**

thing ♦♦♦ /θɪŋ/ NOUN

NOUN [C, SING, PL] (**things**) **1** [C] You can use **thing** to refer to any object, feature, or event when you cannot, need not, or do not want to refer to it more precisely. ❏ *'What's that thing in the middle of the fountain?'—'Some kind of statue, I guess.'* ❏ *She was in the middle of clearing the breakfast things.* **2** [C] **Thing** is used in lists and descriptions to give examples or to increase the range of what you are referring to. ❏ *They spend their money on things like rent and groceries.* **3** [C] **Thing** is often used after an adjective, where it would also be possible just to use the adjective. For example, you can say 'it's a different thing' instead of 'it's different.' ❏ *Of course, literacy isn't the same thing as intelligence.* **4** [SING] **Thing** is often used instead of the pronouns 'anything' or 'everything' in order to emphasize what you are saying. ❑ *I haven't done a thing all day.* ❑ *It isn't going to solve a single thing.* **5** [C] **Thing** is used in expressions such as **such a thing** or **a thing like that**, especially in negative statements, in order to emphasize the bad or difficult situation you are referring back to. ❑ *I don't believe he would tell Leo such a thing.* **6** [C] (*informal, vagueness*) You can use **thing** to refer in a vague way to a situation, activity, or idea, especially when you want to suggest that it is not very important. ❑ *I'm a bit unsettled tonight. This war thing's upsetting me.* **7** [C] You often use **thing** to indicate to the person you are addressing that you are about to mention something important, or something that you particularly want them to know. ❑ *One thing I am sure of was that she was scared.* **8** [C] A **thing** is often used to refer back to something that has just been mentioned, either to emphasize it or to give more information about it. ❑ *Getting drunk is a thing all young men do.* **9** [C] A **thing** is a physical object that is considered as having no life of its own. ❑ *It's not a thing. It's a human being!* **10** [C] (*spoken, disapproval*) **Thing** is used to refer to something, especially a physical object, when you want to express contempt or anger towards it. ❑ *Turn that thing off!* **11** [C] (*informal*) You can call a person or an animal a particular **thing** when you want to mention a particular quality that they have and express your feelings towards them, usually affectionate feelings. ❑ *She is such a cute little thing.* **12** [PL] Your **things** are your clothes or possessions. ❑ *Sara told him to take all his things and not to return.* **13** [PL] **Things** can refer to the situation or life in general and the way it is changing or affecting you. ❑ *Everyone agrees things are getting better.*

PHRASES **do the right thing** or **do the decent thing** If you **do the right thing** or **do the decent thing** in a situation, you do something which is considered correct or socially acceptable in that situation. ❑ *People want to do the right thing and buy 'green'.*

first thing or **last thing** If you do something **first thing**, you do it at the beginning of the day, before you do anything else. If you do it **last thing**, you do it at the end of the day, before you go to bed or go to sleep. ❑ *I'll go see her, first thing.*

it is a good thing to or **it is a bad thing to** You say **it is a good thing to** do something to introduce a piece of advice or a comment on a situation or activity. ❑ *Can you tell me whether it is a good thing to prune an apple tree?*

be one thing (*emphasis*) You can say that the first of two ideas, actions, or situations **is one thing** when you want to contrast it with a second idea, action, or situation and emphasize that the second one is much more difficult, important, or extreme. ❑ *It was one thing to talk about leaving; it was another to physically walk out the door.*

for one thing You can say **for one thing** when you are explaining a statement or answering a question, to suggest that you are not giving the whole explanation or answer, and that there are other points that you could add to it. ❑ *She was a monster. For one thing, she really enjoyed cruelty.*

one thing and another (*spoken*) You can use the expression 'one thing and another' to suggest that there are several reasons for something or several items on a list, but you are not going to explain or mention them all. ❑ *What with one thing and another, it was fairly late in the day when we got home.*

it is just one of those things or **it is simply one of those things** If you say **it is just one of those things** you mean that you cannot explain something because it seems to happen by chance. ❑ *'I wonder why.' Mr Dambar shrugged. 'It must be just one of those things, I guess.'*

seeing things or **hearing things** If you say that someone **is seeing** or **hearing things**, you mean that they believe they are seeing or hearing something, but it is not really there. ❑ *Dr Payne led Lana back into the examination room and told her she was seeing things.*

no such thing (*emphasis*) You can say there is **no such thing** as something to emphasize that it does not exist or is not possible. ❑ *There really is no such thing as a totally risk-free industry.*

the thing is (*spoken*) You say **the thing is** to introduce an explanation, comment, or opinion, that relates to something that has just been said. **The thing is** is often used to identify a problem relating to what has just been said. ❑ *'What does your market research consist of?'—'Well, the thing is, it depends on our target age group.'*

✦ **other things being equal** → see **equal**

think ◆◆◆ /θɪŋk/ VERB, NOUN

VERB [I, T] (**thinks, thinking, thought**) **1** [I, T] If you **think** that something is the case, you believe that it is the case. = believe ❑ *I certainly think there should be a ban on tobacco advertising.* ❑ *A generation ago, it was thought that babies born this small could not survive.* ❑ *Tell me, what do you think of my theory?* **2** [T] If you say that you **think** that something is true or will happen, you mean that you have the impression that it is true or will happen, although you are not certain of the facts. = believe ❑ *Nora thought he was seventeen years old.* ❑ *The storm is thought to be responsible for as many as four deaths.* **3** [I, T] If you **think** in a particular way, you have those general opinions or attitudes. ❑ *You were probably brought up to think like that.* ❑ *If you think as I do, vote as I do.* ❑ *I don't blame you for thinking that way.* **4** [I] When you **think** about ideas or problems, you make a mental effort to consider them. ❑ *She closed her eyes for a moment, trying to think.* ❑ *I have often thought about this problem.* **5** [I, T] If you **think** in a particular way, you consider things, solve problems, or make decisions in this way, for example, because of your job or your background. ❑ *To make the computer work at full capacity, the programmer has to think like the machine.* ❑ *Why do they think the way they do?* **6** [I, T] If you **think of** something, it comes into your mind or you remember it. ❑ *Nobody could think of anything to say.* ❑ *I was trying to think what else we had to do.* **7** [I] If you **think of** an idea, you make a mental effort and use your imagination and intelligence to create it or develop it. ❑ *He thought of another way of making electricity.* **8** [T] If you **are thinking** something at a particular moment, you have words or ideas in your mind without saying them out loud. ❑ *She must be sick, Tatiana thought.* ❑ *I remember thinking how lovely he looked.* **9** [I, T] If you **think of** someone or something **as** having a particular quality or purpose, you regard them as having this quality or purpose. ❑ *We all thought of him as a father.* ❑ *He thinks of it as his home.* ❑ *I wouldn't have thought him capable of it.* **10** [I, T] If you **think a lot of** someone or something, you admire them very much or think they are very good. ❑ *To tell the truth, I don't think much of psychiatrists.* ❑ *Everyone in my family thought very highly of him.* **11** [I] If you **think of** someone or **about** someone, you show consideration for them and pay attention to their needs. ❑ *I'm only thinking of you.* **12** [I] If you **are thinking of** or **are thinking about** taking a particular course of action, you are considering it as a possible course of action. ❑ *Martin was thinking of taking legal action against Zuckerman.* **13** [I] You can say that you **are thinking of** a particular aspect or subject, in order to introduce an example or explain more exactly what you are talking about. ❑ *The parts of the enterprise which are scientifically the most exciting are unlikely to be militarily useful. I am thinking here of the development of new kinds of lasers.* **14** [I] You use **think** in questions where you are expressing your anger or shock at someone's behaviour. ❑ *What were you thinking of? You shouldn't steal.* **15** [I, T] You use **think** when you are commenting on something which you did or experienced in the past and which now seems surprising, foolish, or shocking to you. ❑ *To think I left you alone in a strange place.* ❑ *When I think of how you've behaved and the trouble you've caused!*

PHRASES **come to think of it** or **when you think about it** or **thinking about it** You use expressions such as **come to think of it**, **when you think about it**, or **thinking about it**, when you mention something that you have suddenly remembered or realized. ❑ *He was her distant relative, as was everyone else on the island, come to think of it.*

I think **1** (*politeness*) You use '**I think**' as a way of being polite when you are explaining or suggesting to someone what you want to do, or when you are accepting or refusing an offer. ❑ *I think I'll go home and have a shower.* **2** (*vagueness*) You use '**I think**' in conversations or speeches to make your statements and opinions sound less

forceful, rude, or direct. ❑ *Thanks, but I think I can handle it.*
just think You say **just think** when you feel excited, fascinated, or shocked by something, and you want the listener to feel the same. = imagine ❑ *Just think; tomorrow we shall walk out of this place and leave it all behind us forever.*
think again If you **think again about** an action or decision, you consider it very carefully, often with the result that you change your mind and decide to do things differently. ❑ *It has forced politicians to think again about the wisdom of trying to evacuate refugees.*
think nothing of If you **think nothing of** doing something that other people might consider difficult, strange, or wrong, you consider it to be easy or normal. ❑ *I thought nothing of betting $1,000 on a horse.*
think nothing of it If something happens and you **think nothing of it**, you do not pay much attention to it or think of it as strange or important, although later you realise that it is. ❑ *When she went off to see her parents for the weekend I thought nothing of it.*
PHRASAL VERBS **think back** If you **think back**, you make an effort to remember things that happened to you in the past. = look back ❑ *I thought back to the time in 1995 when my son was desperately ill.*
think over If you **think** something **over**, you consider it carefully before making a decision. ❑ *She said she needs time to think it over.*
think through If you **think** a situation **through**, you consider it thoroughly, together with all its possible effects or consequences. ❑ *I didn't think through the consequences of promotion.* ❑ *The administration has not really thought through what it plans to do once the fighting stops.*
think up If you **think** something **up**, for example, an idea or plan, you invent it using mental effort. ❑ *Julian has been thinking up new ways of raising money.*
NOUN [SING] ['a' think] When you have a **think** about ideas or problems, you make a mental effort to consider them. ❑ *I'll have a think about that.*
→ See also **thinking**, **thought**
✦ **you can't hear yourself think** → see **hear**; **think better of it** → see **better**; **think big** → see **big**; **think twice** → see **twice**

think·er /ˈθɪŋkə/ NOUN [C] (thinkers) A **thinker** is a person who spends a lot of time thinking deeply about important things, especially someone who is famous for thinking of new or interesting ideas. ❑ *some of the world's greatest thinkers*

think·ing ♦♦◇ /ˈθɪŋkɪŋ/ NOUN [U] **1** **Thinking** is the activity of using your brain by considering a problem or possibility or creating an idea. ❑ *This is a time of decisive action and quick thinking.* **2** The general ideas or opinions of a person or group can be referred to as their **thinking**. ❑ *There was undeniably a strong theoretical dimension to his thinking.*

⊙ **third** ♦♦◇ /θɜːd/ ADJ, NOUN, ADV
ADJ The **third** item in a series is the one that you count as number three. ❑ *I sleep on the third floor.*
NOUN [C] (thirds) **1** A **third** is one of three equal parts of something. ❑ *A third of the cost went into technology and services.* ❑ *Only one third get financial help from their fathers.* **2** A **third** is the lowest honours degree that can be obtained from a British university. ❑ *Ms Hodge, who graduated in 2002 with a third in economics*
ADV You say **third** when you want to make a third point or give a third reason for something. = thirdly ❑ *First, interest rates may take longer to fall than is hoped. Second, lending may fall. Third, bad loans could wipe out much of any improvement.*

third·ly /ˈθɜːdli/ ADV You use **thirdly** when you want to make a third point or give a third reason for something. = third ❑ *First of all, there are not many of them, and secondly, they have little money and, thirdly, they're hungry.*

⊙ **Third World** ♦◇◇ NOUN [SING] The countries of Africa, Asia, and Central and South America are sometimes referred to all together as **the Third World**, especially those parts that are poor, do not have much power, and are not considered to be highly developed. = developing countries ❑ *development in the Third World* ❑ *studies of malnourished mothers in the Third World* ❑ *He urged Britons to*

campaign on the streets to help end Third World poverty.

thirst /θɜːst/ NOUN [C, U] (thirsts) **1** [C, U] **Thirst** is the feeling of wanting to drink something. ❑ *Instead of tea or coffee, drink water to quench your thirst.* **2** [U] **Thirst** is the condition of not having enough to drink. ❑ *They died of thirst on the voyage.*

thirsty /ˈθɜːsti/ ADJ (thirstier, thirstiest) If you are **thirsty**, you feel a need to drink something. ❑ *Drink whenever you feel thirsty during exercise.*

thir·teen ♦♦♦ /ˌθɜːˈtiːn/ NUM (thirteens) **Thirteen** is the number 13.

thir·teenth ♦♦◇ /ˌθɜːˈtiːnθ/ ADJ The **thirteenth** item in a series is the one that you count as number thirteen. ❑ *his thirteenth birthday*

thir·ti·eth ♦♦◇ /ˈθɜːtiəθ/ ADJ The **thirtieth** item in a series is the one that you count as number thirty. ❑ *the thirtieth anniversary of my parents' wedding*

thir·ty ♦♦♦ /ˈθɜːti/ NUM, NOUN
NUM (thirties) **Thirty** is the number 30.
NOUN [PL] (thirties) **1** When you talk about the **thirties**, you are referring to numbers between 30 and 39. For example, if you are **in** your **thirties**, you are aged between 30 and 39. If the temperature is **in the thirties**, the temperature is between 30 and 39 degrees. ❑ *Mozart clearly enjoyed good health throughout his twenties and early thirties.* **2** The **thirties** is the decade between 1930 and 1939. ❑ *She became quite a notable director in the thirties and forties.*

this ♦♦♦ /ðɪs/ DET, PRON, ADV, CONVENTION
DET **1** You use **this** to refer back to a particular person or thing that has been mentioned or implied. ❑ *The entire portfolio is worth $160,312. Of this amount, my investment is worth only $7,748.* **2** You use **this** to introduce someone or something that you are going to talk about. ❑ *This report is from our Science Unit.* **3** You use **this** to refer back to an idea or situation expressed in a previous sentence. ❑ *There have been continual demands to put an end to this situation.* **4** In spoken English, people use **this** to introduce a person or thing into a story. ❑ *I came here by chance and was just watching what was going on, when this girl came up to me.* **5** You use **this** to refer to a person or thing that is near you, especially when you touch them or point to them. When there are two or more people or things near you, **this** refers to the nearest one. ❑ *This church was built by the Emperor Constantine Monomarchus in the eleventh century.* ❑ *I like this coat better than that one.* **6** You use **this** when you refer to the place you are in now or to the present time. ❑ *This country is weird.* ❑ *This place is run like a hotel ought to be run.* **7** You use **this** to refer to the next occurrence in the future of a particular day, month, season, or festival. ❑ *this Sunday's 7:45 performance* **8** You use **this** to refer to the medium of communication that you are using at the time of speaking or writing. ❑ *What I'm going to do in this lecture is focus on something very specific.*
PRON **1** You use **this** to refer back to a particular person or thing that has been mentioned or implied. ❑ *I don't know how bad the injury is, because I have never had one like this before.* **2** You use **this** to introduce someone or something that you are going to talk about. ❑ *This is what I will do. I will telephone Anna and explain.* **3** You use **this** to refer back to an idea or situation expressed in a previous sentence or sentences. ❑ *You feel that it's uneconomical. Why is this?* **4** You use **this** to refer to a person or thing that is near you, especially when you touch them or point to them. When there are two or more people or things near you, **this** refers to the nearest one. ❑ *'If you'd prefer something else I'll gladly have it changed for you.'—'No, this is great.'* **5** [this with 'be'] You use **this** when you refer to a general situation, activity, or event which is happening or has just happened and which you feel involved in. ❑ *I thought, this is why I've travelled thousands of miles.* **6** You use **this** when you refer to the place you are in now or to the present time. ❑ *This is the worst place I've come across.* **7** You use **this is** in order to say who you are or what organization you are representing, when you are speaking on the telephone, radio, or television. ❑ *Hello, this is John Thompson.*
PHRASE **this and that** or **this, that, and the other** If you

say that you are doing or talking about **this and that**, or **this, that, and the other** you mean that you are doing or talking about a variety of things that you do not want to specify. □ *'And what are you doing now?'—'Oh this and that.'* [ADV] **3** [this + ADJ] You use **this** when you are indicating the size or shape of something with your hands. □ *'They'd said the wound was only about this big,' and he showed me with his fingers.* **4** [this + ADV] You use **this** when you are going to specify how much you know or how much you can tell someone. □ *I don't know if it's the best team I've ever had, but I can tell you this much, they're incredible people to be around.* [CONVENTION] (*BrE, formulae*) If you say **this is it**, you are agreeing with what someone else has just said. □ *'You know, people conveniently forget the things they say.'—'Well this is it.'*
→ See also **these**

❂ **thor·ough** ◆◇◇ /ˈθʌrə, AmE ˈθɜːrəʊ/ ADJ **1** A **thorough** action or activity is one that is done very carefully and in a detailed way so that nothing is forgotten. = careful, detailed, exhaustive; ≠ partial, superficial □ *We are making a thorough investigation.* □ *This very thorough survey goes back to 1784.* □ *How thorough is the assessment?* **2** Someone who is **thorough** is always very careful in their work, so that nothing is forgotten. □ *Martin would be a good judge, I thought. He was calm and thorough.* **3** [DET + thorough] **Thorough** is used to emphasize the large degree or extent of something. = complete □ *To me, this seemed like a thorough waste of time.*

❂ **thor·ough·ly** /ˈθʌrəli, AmE ˈθɜːrəʊli/ ADV **1** [thoroughly with V] = carefully; ≠ partially, superficially □ *Food that is being offered hot must be reheated thoroughly.* □ *a thoroughly researched and illuminating biography* **2** I thoroughly enjoy your programme.

thor·ough·ness /ˈθʌrənəs, AmE ˈθɜːrəʊnəs/ NOUN [U] **1** *The thoroughness of the evaluation process we went through was impressive.* **2** *His thoroughness and attention to detail is legendary.*

those ◆◆◆ /ðəʊz/ DET, PRON
[DET] **1** You use **those** to refer to people or things which have already been mentioned. □ *Witnesses said that two people were killed, but those accounts could not be confirmed.* **2** You use **those** when you are referring to people or things that are a distance away from you in position or time, especially when you indicate or point to them. □ *What are those buildings?* **3** (*formal*) You use **those** to refer to someone or something when you are going to give details or information about them. □ *Those people who took up weapons to defend themselves are political prisoners.* **4** You use **those** when you refer to things that you expect the person you are talking to to know about or when you are checking that you are both thinking of the same people or things. □ *He did buy me those daffodils a week or so ago.*
[PRON] **1** You use **those** to refer to people or things which have already been mentioned. □ *I understand that there are a number of projects going on. Could you tell us a little bit about those?* **2** You use **those** when you are referring to people or things that are a distance away from you in position or time, especially when you indicate or point to them. □ *I like these but not those. Where'd you get them?* **3** (*formal*) You use **those** to introduce more information about something already mentioned, instead of repeating the noun which refers to it. □ *The interests he is most likely to enjoy will be those which enable him to show off himself or his talents.* **4** You use **those** to mean 'people'. □ *A little selfish behaviour is unlikely to cause real damage to those around us.*

though ◆◆◆ /ðəʊ/ CONJ **1** You use **though** to introduce a statement in a subordinate clause which contrasts with the statement in the main clause. You often use **though** to introduce a fact which you regard as less important than the fact in the main clause. = although □ *Everything I told them was correct, though I forgot a few things.* □ *I like him. Though he makes me angry sometimes.* **2** You use **though** to introduce a subordinate clause which gives some information that is relevant to the main clause and weakens the force of what it is saying. = although □ *He did reply, though not immediately.*

✦ **as though** → see **as**; **even though** → see **even**

thought ◆◆◆ /θɔːt/ IRREG FORM, NOUN
[IRREG FORM] **Thought** is the past tense and past participle of **think**.
[NOUN] [C, PL, U] (**thoughts**) **1** [C] A **thought** is an idea that you have in your mind. □ *The thought of Nick made her throat tighten.* □ *I've just had a thought.* **2** [PL] A person's **thoughts** are their mind, or all the ideas in their mind when they are concentrating on one particular thing. □ *I jumped to my feet so my thoughts wouldn't start to wander.* □ *Usually at this time our thoughts are on Christmas.* **3** [PL] A person's **thoughts** are their opinions on a particular subject. □ *Many of you have written to us to express your thoughts on the conflict.* **4** [U] **Thought** is the activity of thinking, especially deeply, carefully, or logically. □ *Alice had been so deep in thought that she had walked past her car without even seeing it.* □ *He had given some thought to what she had told him.* **5** [C] A **thought** is an intention, hope, or reason for doing something. □ *Sarah's first thought was to run back and get Max.* **6** [U] **Thought** is the group of ideas and beliefs which belongs, for example, to a particular religion, philosophy, science, or political party. □ *Aristotle's scientific theories dominated Western thought for fifteen hundred years.*

thought·ful /ˈθɔːtfʊl/ ADJ **1** If you are **thoughtful**, you are quiet and serious because you are thinking about something. □ *Nancy, who had been thoughtful for some time, suddenly spoke.* **2** If you describe someone as **thoughtful**, you approve of them because they remember what other people want, need, or feel, and try not to upset them. = considerate □ *a thoughtful and caring man* **3** If you describe something such as a book, film, or speech as **thoughtful**, you mean that it is serious and well thought out. □ *a thoughtful and scholarly book*

thought·ful·ly /ˈθɔːtfəli/ ADV **1** [thoughtfully with V] □ *Daniel nodded thoughtfully.* **2** [thoughtfully with V] □ *the bottle of wine he had thoughtfully purchased for the celebrations* **3** [thoughtfully with V] □ *these thoughtfully designed machines*

thought·less /ˈθɔːtləs/ ADJ (*disapproval*) If you describe someone as **thoughtless**, you are critical of them because they forget or ignore other people's wants, needs, or feelings. □ *a small minority of thoughtless and inconsiderate people* □ *It was a thoughtless remark and I regretted it immediately.*

thought·less·ly /ˈθɔːtləsli/ ADV [thoughtlessly with V] □ *They thoughtlessly planned a picnic without him.*

❂ **thou·sand** ◆◆◆ /ˈθaʊzənd/ NUM, QUANT, PRON

> The plural form is **thousand** after a number, or after a word or expression referring to a number, such as 'several' or 'a few'.

[NUM] (**thousands**) A **thousand** or **one thousand** is the number 1,000. □ *five thousand acres* □ *Visitors can expect to pay about a thousand pounds a year.*
[QUANT] [thousands 'of' PL-N] (*emphasis*) If you refer to **thousands of** things or people, you are emphasizing that there are very many of them. □ *Thousands of refugees are packed into overcrowded towns and villages.*
[PRON] **Thousands** means very many people or things, and is used for emphasis. □ *Hundreds have been killed in the fighting and thousands made homeless.*
✦ **a thousand and one** → see **one**

thou·sandth /ˈθaʊzənθ/ ADJ, NOUN
[ADJ] **1** The **thousandth** item in a series is the one that you count as number one thousand. □ *The magazine has just published its six thousandth edition.* **2** If you say that something has happened for the **thousandth** time, you are emphasizing that it has happened again and that it has already happened a large number of times. □ *The phone rings for the thousandth time.*
[NOUN] [C] (**thousandths**) A **thousandth** is one of a thousand equal parts of something. □ *a dust particle weighing only a thousandth of a gram*

thrash /θræʃ/ VERB
[VERB] [T, I] (**thrashes, thrashing, thrashed**) **1** [T] (*informal*) If one player or team **thrashes** another in a game or

t

contest, they defeat them easily or by a large score. = hammer ❑ *The Kings were thrashed by the Knicks last night.* **2** [T] If you **thrash** someone, you hit them several times as a punishment. ❑ *'Liar!' Sarah screamed, as she thrashed the child. 'You stole it.'* **3** [I, T] If someone **thrashes around** or **thrashes** their arms or legs **around**, they move in a wild or violent way, often hitting against something. You can also say that someone's arms or legs **thrash around.** ❑ *She would thrash around in her hospital bed and remove her intravenous line.* ❑ *Many of the crew died a terrible death as they thrashed about in shark-infested waters.* **4** [I, T] If a person or thing **thrashes** something, or **thrashes at** something, they hit it continually in a violent or noisy way. ❑ *a magnificent paddle-steamer on the mighty Mississippi, her huge wheel thrashing the muddy water*

PHRASAL VERB **thrash out** **1** If people **thrash out** something such as a plan or an agreement, they decide on it after a lot of discussion. = hammer out ❑ *John and Monica have thrashed out a divorce agreement.* **2** If people **thrash out** a problem or a dispute, they discuss it thoroughly until they reach an agreement. = hammer out ❑ *a sincere effort by two people to thrash out differences about which they have strong feelings*

thread /θrɛd/ NOUN, VERB
NOUN [C, U] **(threads)** **1** [C, U] **Thread** or a **thread** is a long very thin piece of a material such as cotton, nylon, or silk, especially one that is used in sewing. ❑ *This time I'll do it right with a spool of thread.* **2** [C] The **thread** of an argument, a story, or a situation is an aspect of it that connects all the different parts together. ❑ *The thread running through many of these proposals was the theme of individual power and opportunity.* **3** [C] A **thread** of something such as liquid, light, or colour is a long thin line or piece of it. ❑ *A thin, glistening thread of moisture ran along the rough concrete sill.* **4** [C] The **thread** on a screw, or on something such as a lid or a pipe, is the raised spiral line of metal or plastic around it which allows it to be fixed in place by twisting. ❑ *The screw threads will be able to get a good grip.* **5** [C] *(computing)* On websites such as newsgroups, a **thread** is one of the subjects that is being written about. ❑ *The dialogues are organized by month so you can go back to previous threads and read them.*
VERB [T, I] **(threads, threading, threaded)** **1** [T] When you **thread** a needle, you put a piece of thread through the hole in the top of the needle in order to sew with it. ❑ *I sit down, thread a needle, snip off an old button.* **2** [I, T] If you **thread** your **way** through a group of people or things, or **thread through** it, you move through it carefully or slowly, changing direction frequently as you move. ❑ *Slowly she threaded her way back through the moving mass of bodies.* **3** [T] If you **thread** a long thin object **through** something, you pass it through one or more holes or narrow spaces. ❑ *threading the laces through the eyelets of his shoes* **4** [T] If you **thread** small objects such as beads onto a string or thread, you join them together by pushing the string through them. ❑ *Wipe the mushrooms clean and thread them on a string.*

✪**threat** ♦♦◇ /θrɛt/ NOUN
NOUN [C, U] **(threats)** **1** [C, U] A **threat to** a person or thing is a danger that something bad might happen to them. A **threat** is also the cause of this danger. ❑ *Some couples see single women as a threat to their relationships.* **2** [C] A **threat** is a statement by someone that they will hurt you in some way, especially if you do not do what they want. ❑ *He may be forced to carry out his threat to resign.* ❑ *The priest remains in hiding after threats by former officials of the ousted dictatorship.*
PHRASE **under threat** If a person or thing is **under threat,** there is a danger that something bad might be done to them, or that they might cease to exist. ❑ *His position as leader is under threat.*

✪**threat·en** ♦♦◇ /θrɛtən/ VERB [T] **(threatens, threatening, threatened)** **1** If a person **threatens to** do something bad to you, or if they **threaten** you, they say or imply that they will hurt you in some way, especially if you do not do what they want. ❑ *He said army officers had threatened to destroy the town.* ❑ *He tied her up and*

threatened her with a six-inch knife. **2** If something or someone **threatens** a person or thing, they are likely to harm that person or thing. = endanger ❑ *The newcomers directly threaten the livelihood of the established workers.* ❑ *30 per cent of reptiles, birds, and fish are currently threatened with extinction.* **3** If something bad **threatens to** happen, it seems likely to happen. ❑ *It's threatening to rain.* ❑ *The fighting is threatening to turn into full-scale war.*
→ See also **threatening**

threat·en·ing ♦◇◇ /θrɛtənɪŋ/ ADJ You can describe someone's behaviour as **threatening** when you think that they are trying to harm you. ❑ *People who engage in threatening behaviour should expect to be arrested.*
→ See also **threaten**

three ♦♦♦ /θriː/ NUM **(threes)** **Three** is the number 3. ❑ *We waited three months before going back to see the specialist.*

✪**three-dimensional** ADJ **1** A **three-dimensional** object is solid rather than flat, because it can be measured in three different directions, usually the height, length, and width. The abbreviation **3-D** can also be used. ❑ *a three-dimensional model* ❑ *the three-dimensional structure of DNA* **2** A **three-dimensional** picture, image, or movie looks as though it is deep or solid rather than flat. The abbreviation **3-D** can also be used. ❑ *The software generates both two-dimensional drawings and three-dimensional images.*

three-quarters QUANT, PRON, ADV
QUANT [three-quarters 'of' N] **Three-quarters** is an amount that is three out of four equal parts of something. ❑ *Three-quarters of the students are African American.*
PRON **Three-quarters** is an amount that is three out of four equal parts of something. ❑ *Applications have increased by three-quarters.*
ADV [three-quarters + ADJ/-ED] If something is **three-quarters** full, it contains three out of the four quarters of the amount or number it can contain. If something is **three-quarters** empty, it contains a quarter of the amount or number it can contain. ❑ *We were left with an open bottle of champagne three-quarters full.* ❑ *The stadium was three-quarters empty when the match began.*

✪**thresh·old** /θrɛʃhəʊld/ NOUN
NOUN [C] **(thresholds)** **1** The **threshold** of a building or room is the floor in the doorway, or the doorway itself. ❑ *He stopped at the threshold of the bedroom.* **2** A **threshold** is an amount, level, or limit on a scale. When the **threshold** is reached, something else happens or changes. = limit, level ❑ *Moss has a high threshold for pain and a history of fast healing.* ❑ *There are many patients whose threshold of pain is very low.* ❑ *The consensus has clearly shifted in favour of raising the nuclear threshold.* ❑ *Fewer than forty per cent voted — the threshold for results to be valid.*
PHRASE **on the threshold of** If you are **on the threshold of** something exciting or new, you are about to experience it. ❑ *We are on the threshold of a new era in astronomy.*

threw /θruː/ IRREG FORM **Threw** is the past tense of **throw.**

thrift /θrɪft/ NOUN [U] **(thrifts)** *(approval)* **Thrift** is the quality and practice of being careful with money and not wasting things. ❑ *They were rightly praised for their thrift and enterprise.*

thrill /θrɪl/ NOUN, VERB
NOUN [C] **(thrills)** If something gives you a **thrill,** it gives you a sudden feeling of great excitement, pleasure, or fear. ❑ *I can remember the thrill of not knowing what I would get on Christmas morning.*
VERB [I, T] **(thrills, thrilling, thrilled)** If something **thrills** you, or if you **thrill at** it, it gives you a feeling of great pleasure and excitement. ❑ *The electric atmosphere both terrified and thrilled him.*
→ See also **thrilled, thrilling**

thrilled /θrɪld/ ADJ [V-LINK + thrilled] If someone is **thrilled,** they are extremely happy and excited about something. ❑ *I was so thrilled to get a good grade from him.*
→ See also **thrill**

thrill·er /θrɪlə/ NOUN [C] **(thrillers)** A **thriller** is a book, film, or play that tells an exciting fictional story about something such as criminal activities or spying. ❑ *a tense psychological thriller*

thrill·ing /ˈθrɪlɪŋ/ ADJ Something that is **thrilling** is very exciting and enjoyable. = exciting ▫ *Our wildlife trips offer a thrilling encounter with wildlife in its natural state.*
→ See also **thrill**

⊕**thrive** /θraɪv/ VERB [i] (**thrives, thriving, thrived**) **1** If someone or something **thrives**, they do well and are successful, healthy, or strong. = succeed, blossom, prosper; ≠ fail ▫ *He appears to be thriving.* ▫ *Today her company continues to thrive.* ▫ *Lavender thrives in poor soil.* ▫ *the river's thriving population of kingfishers* **2** If you say that someone **thrives on** a particular situation, you mean that they enjoy it or that they can deal with it very well, especially when other people find it unpleasant or difficult. ▫ *Many people thrive on a stressful lifestyle.*

throat ◆◇◇ /θrəʊt/ NOUN
NOUN [c] (**throats**) **1** Your **throat** is the back of your mouth and the top part of the tubes that go down into your stomach and your lungs. ▫ *She had a sore throat.* **2** Your **throat** is the front part of your neck. ▫ *His striped tie was loosened at his throat.*
PHRASES **clear your throat** If you **clear** your **throat**, you cough once either to make it easier to speak or to attract people's attention. ▫ *Cross cleared his throat and spoke in low, polite tones.*
ram something down someone's throat or **force something down someone's throat** If you **ram** something **down** someone's **throat** or **force** it **down** their **throat**, you keep mentioning a situation or idea in order to make them accept it or believe it. ▫ *I've always been close to my dad but he's never rammed his career down my throat.*
at each other's throats If two people or groups are **at each other's throats**, they are arguing or fighting violently with each other. ▫ *The idea that we are at each other's throats couldn't be further from the truth.*
✦ **a lump in your throat** → see **lump**

throb /θrɒb/ VERB [i] (**throbs, throbbing, throbbed**) **1** If part of your body **throbs**, you feel a series of strong and usually painful beats there. ▫ *His head throbbed.* **2** (*literary*) If something **throbs**, it vibrates and makes a steady noise. ▫ *The engines throbbed.*

throne /θrəʊn/ NOUN [c, SING] (**thrones**) **1** [c] A **throne** is a decorative chair used by a king, queen, or emperor on important official occasions. **2** [SING] You can talk about **the throne** as a way of referring to the position of king, queen, or emperor. ▫ *the queen's 40th anniversary on the throne*

throt·tle /ˈθrɒtəl/ VERB, NOUN
VERB [T] (**throttles, throttling, throttled**) To **throttle** someone means to kill or injure them by squeezing their throat or tightening something around it and preventing them from breathing. = strangle ▫ *The attacker then tried to throttle her with wire.*
NOUN [c] (**throttles**) The **throttle** of a motor vehicle or aircraft is the device, lever, or pedal that controls the quantity of fuel entering the engine and is used to control the vehicle's speed. ▫ *He gently opened the throttle, and the ship began to ease forward.*

through ◆◆◆ /θruː/ PREP, ADV, ADJ
PREP **1** To move **through** something such as a hole, opening, or pipe means to move directly from one side or end of it to the other. ▫ *The theatre was evacuated when rain poured through the roof.* ▫ *Go straight through that door under the EXIT sign.* **2** To cut **through** something means to cut it in two pieces or to make a hole in it. ▫ *Use a genuine fish knife and fork if possible as they are designed to cut through the flesh but not the bones.* **3** To go **through** a town, area, or country means to travel across it or in it. ▫ *Go through North Carolina and into Virginia.* **4** If you move **through** a group of things or a mass of something, it is on either side of you or all around you. ▫ *We made our way through the crowd to the river.* **5** To get **through** a barrier or obstacle means to get from one side of it to the other. ▫ *Allow twenty-five minutes to get through passport control and customs.* **6** If a driver goes **through** a red light, they keep driving even though they should stop. ▫ *He was killed at a junction by a driver who went through a red light.* **7** If

something goes into an object and comes out of the other side, you can say that it passes **through** the object. ▫ *The ends of the net pass through a wooden bar at each end.* **8** To go **through** a system means to move around it or to pass from one end of it to the other. ▫ *electric currents travelling through copper wires* **9** If you see, hear, or feel something **through** a particular thing, that thing is between you and the thing you can see, hear, or feel. ▫ *Alice gazed pensively through the wet glass.* **10** If something such as a feeling, attitude, or quality happens **through** an area, organization, or a person's body, it happens everywhere in it or affects all of it. ▫ *An atmosphere of anticipation vibrated through the crowd.* **11** If something happens or exists **through** a period of time, it happens or exists from the beginning until the end. ▫ *She kept quiet all through breakfast.* **12** If you go **through** a particular experience or event, you experience it, and if you behave in a particular way **through** it, you behave in that way while it is happening. ▫ *Men go through a change of life emotionally just like women.* **13** [N + through + N] You use **through** in expressions such as **half-way through** and **all the way through** to indicate to what extent an action or task is completed. ▫ *A thirty-nine-year-old competitor collapsed half-way through the marathon.* **14** If something happens because of something else, you can say that it happens **through** it. ▫ *I only succeeded through hard work.* **15** You use **through** when stating the means by which a particular thing is achieved. ▫ *Those who seek to grab power through violence deserve punishment.* **16** If you do something **through** someone else, they take the necessary action for you. = via ▫ *Do I need to go through my doctor to get an appointment?* **17** If something such as a proposal or idea goes **through** a parliament or an official review, it is accepted by people in authority and is made legal or official. ▫ *They want to get the plan through Congress as quickly as possible.* **18** If someone gets **through** an examination or a round of a competition, they succeed or win. ▫ *She was bright, learned languages quickly, and sailed through her exams.* **19** If you look or go **through** a lot of things, you look at them or deal with them one after the other. ▫ *Let's go through the numbers together and see if a workable deal is possible.* **20** If you read **through** something, you read it from beginning to end. ▫ *She read through pages and pages of the music I had brought her.*
ADV **1** [through after v] You can use **through** to indicate that something is moving directly from one side or end of a hole, opening, or pipe to the other. ▫ *There was a hole in the wall and water was seeping through.* **2** [through after v] You can use **through** when you are referring to cutting something in two pieces or making a hole in it. ▫ *Score lightly at first and then repeat, scoring deeper each time until the board is cut through.* **3** [through after v] You can use **through** to indicate travelling across or in a town, area, or country. ▫ *Few know that the tribe was just passing through.* **4** [through after v] You can use **through** to indicate that a group of things or a mass of something is on either side of you or all around you. ▫ *He pushed his way through to the edge of the crowd where he waited.* **5** [through after v] You can use **through** to indicate getting from one side of a barrier or obstacle to the other. ▫ *a maze of concrete and steel barriers, designed to prevent vehicles driving straight through* **6** [through after v] You can use **through** to indicate that something goes into an object and comes out of the other side. ▫ *I bored a hole so that the bolt would pass through.* **7** [through after v] You can use **through** to indicate that something is moving around a system or passing from one end of it to the other. ▫ *Food should be allowed to go through immediately with fewer restrictions.* **8** [through after v] You can use **through** to indicate that something happens or exists from the beginning to the end of a period of time until the end. ▫ *We'll be working right through to the summer.* **9** [N + through] You use **through** in expressions such as **half-way through** and **all the way through** to indicate to what extent an action or task is completed. ▫ *Stir the pork until it turns white all the way through.* **10** [through after v] If something such as a proposal or idea goes **through**, it is accepted by people in authority and is made legal or official. ▫ *We're waiting for*

t

the building permit to go through. **11** [through after v] You can use **through** to indicate that someone has succeeded or won in an examination or a round of a competition. ❏ *Only the top four teams go through.* **12** [through after v] When you get **through** while making a telephone call, the call is connected and you can speak to the person you are phoning. ❏ *Telephones are down so he can't get through.* **13** [through after v] You can use **through** to indicate that you have read something from beginning to end. ❏ *The article had been authored by Raymond Kennedy. He read it right through, looking for any scrap of information that might have passed him by.* **14** [ADJ + through] If you say that someone or something is wet **through**, you are emphasizing how wet they are. ❏ *I returned to the inn cold and wet, soaked through by the drizzling rain.*

ADJ **1** [V-LINK + through] If you are **through with** something or if it is **through**, you have finished doing it. ❏ *We're through with dinner.* ❏ *Are you through with this?* **2** [V-LINK + through] If you are **through with** someone, you do not want to have anything to do with them again. ❏ *I'm through with her; she's bad news!*

○**through·out** ◆◆◇ /θruːˈaʊt/ PREP, ADV
PREP **1** If you say that something happens **throughout** a particular period of time, you mean that it happens during the whole of that period. = during ❏ *The national tragedy of rival groups killing each other throughout 1990.* ❏ *Film music can be made memorable because its themes are repeated throughout the film.* **2** If you say that something happens or exists **throughout** a place, you mean that it happens or exists in all parts of that place. ❏ *'Sight Savers', founded in 1950, now runs projects throughout Africa, the Caribbean and Southeast Asia.* ❏ *As we have tried to show throughout this book, companies that provide outstanding service don't do it by luck.*

ADV **1** [throughout with CL] **Throughout** means during the whole of a particular period of time. ❏ *The first song, 'Blue Moon', didn't go too badly except that everyone talked throughout.* **2** [throughout with CL] **Throughout** means in all parts of a place. ❏ *The route is well sign-posted throughout.*

throw ◆◆◇ /θrəʊ/ VERB, NOUN
VERB [T] (**throws, throwing, threw, thrown**) **1** When you **throw** an object that you are holding, you move your hand or arm quickly and let go of the object, so that it moves through the air. ❏ *He spent hours throwing a tennis ball against a wall.* ❏ *The crowd began throwing stones.* **2** If you **throw** your body or part of your body into a particular position or place, you move it there suddenly and with a lot of force. ❏ *She threw her arms around his shoulders.* ❏ *She threatened to throw herself in front of a train.* **3** If you **throw** something into a particular place or position, you put it there in a quick and careless way. ❏ *He struggled out of his bulky jacket and threw it onto the back seat.* **4** To **throw** someone into a particular place or position means to force them roughly into that place or position. ❏ *He threw me to the ground.* **5** If you say that someone **is thrown into** prison, you mean that they are put there by the authorities. ❏ *Those two should have been thrown in jail.* **6** If a horse **throws** its rider, it makes him or her fall off, by suddenly jumping or moving violently. ❏ *The horse reared, throwing its rider and knocking down a youth standing beside it.* **7** If a person or thing **is thrown into** a bad situation or state, something causes them to be in that situation or state. ❏ *Abidjan was thrown into turmoil because of a protest by taxi drivers.* **8** If something **throws** light or a shadow **on** a surface, it causes that surface to have light or a shadow on it. = cast ❏ *The sunlight is white and blinding, throwing hard-edged shadows on the ground.* **9** If something **throws** doubt **on** a situation, it causes people to doubt or suspect them. = cast ❏ *This new information does throw doubt on their choice.* **10** If you **throw** a look or smile at someone or something, you look or smile at them quickly and suddenly. ❏ *Emily turned and threw her a suggestive grin.* **11** If you **throw** yourself, your energy, or your money **into** a particular job or activity, you become involved in it very actively and enthusiastically. ❏ *She threw herself into a modelling career.* **12** If you **throw** a fit or a tantrum, you suddenly start to behave in an uncontrolled way. ❏ *I used to get very upset and scream and swear, throwing*

tantrums all over the place. **13** If something such as a remark or an experience **throws** you, it surprises you or confuses you because it is unexpected. ❏ *Her sudden change in attitude threw me.* ❏ *This new confession threw me for a loop.* **14** If you **throw** a punch, you punch someone. ❏ *Everything was fine until someone threw a punch.* **15** (*informal*) When someone **throws** a party, they organize one, usually in their own home. ❏ *Why not throw a party for your friends?*

PHRASAL VERBS **throw away** or **throw out** **1** When you **throw away** or **throw out** something that you do not want, you get rid of it, for example, by putting it in the bin. ❏ *I never throw anything away.* **2** If you **throw away** an opportunity, advantage, or benefit, you waste it, rather than using it sensibly. ❏ *Failing to tackle the deficit would be throwing away an opportunity we haven't had for a generation.*
throw out **1** → See **throw away** **2** If a judge **throws out** a case, he or she rejects it and the accused person does not have to stand trial. = dismiss ❏ *The defence wants the district Judge to throw out the case.* **3** If you **throw** someone **out**, you force them to leave a place or group. ❏ *He was thrown out of the Olympic team after testing positive for drugs.* ❏ *I wanted to kill him, but instead I just threw him out of the house.*
throw up **1** When someone **throws up**, they vomit. ❏ *She said she had thrown up after reading reports of the trial.* **2** If something **throws up** dust, stones, or water, when it moves or hits the ground, it causes them to rise up into the air. ❏ *If it had hit the Earth, it would have made a crater 100 miles across and thrown up an immense cloud of dust.*
NOUN [c] (**throws**) A **throw** is when you move your hand or arm quickly and let go of an object you are holding, so that it moves through the air. ❏ *That was a good throw.* ❏ *A throw of the dice allows a player to move himself forward.*
✦ **throw light on something** → see **light**; **throw money at something** → see **money**; **throw in the towel** → see **towel**

thrown /θrəʊn/ IRREG FORM **Thrown** is the past participle of **throw**.

thrust /θrʌst/ VERB, NOUN
VERB [T, I] (**thrusts, thrusting, thrust**) **1** [T] If you **thrust** something or someone somewhere, you push or move them there quickly with a lot of force. = shove ❏ *They thrust him into the back of a jeep.* **2** [T] If you **thrust** your way somewhere, you move there, pushing between people or things which are in your way. = push ❏ *She thrust her way into the crowd.* **3** [I] (*literary*) If something **thrusts** up or out of something else, it sticks up or sticks out in a noticeable way. ❏ *a seedling ready to thrust up into any available light*
NOUN [c, u] (**thrusts**) **1** [c] A **thrust** is a hard strong push of something or someone. ❏ *Two of the knife thrusts were fatal.* **2** [u] **Thrust** is the power or force that is required to make a vehicle move in a particular direction. ❏ *It provides the thrust that makes the craft move forward.*

thud /θʌd/ NOUN, VERB
NOUN [c] (**thuds**) A **thud** is a dull sound, such as that which a heavy object makes when it hits something soft. = thump ❏ *She tripped and fell with a sickening thud.* **VERB** [I] (**thuds, thudding, thudded**) **1** If something **thuds** somewhere, it makes a dull sound, usually when it falls onto or hits something else. ❏ *She ran up the stairs, her bare feet thudding on the wood.* **2** When your heart **thuds**, it beats strongly and somewhat quickly, for example, because you are very frightened or very happy. = pound ❏ *My heart had started to thud, and my mouth was dry.*

thug /θʌg/ NOUN [c] (**thugs**) (*disapproval*) You can refer to a violent person or criminal as a **thug**. ❏ *the cowardly thugs who mug old people*

thumb /θʌm/ NOUN, VERB
NOUN [c] (**thumbs**) Your hand has four fingers and one **thumb**. ❏ *She bit the tip of her left thumb, not looking at me.* **PHRASE** **under someone's thumb** If you are under someone's **thumb**, you are under their control, or very heavily influenced by them. ❏ *I cannot tell you what pain I feel when I see how much my mother is under my father's thumb.*
VERB [T] (**thumbs, thumbing, thumbed**) If you **thumb** a lift

or **thumb** a ride, you stand by the side of the road holding out your thumb until a driver stops and gives you a lift. = hitch ◻ *It may interest you to know that a boy answering Rory's description thumbed a ride to San Antonio.*

✦ **rule of thumb** → see **rule**

thump /θʌmp/ VERB, NOUN

VERB [I, T] (**thumps, thumping, thumped**) **1** [I, T] If you **thump** something, you hit it hard, usually with your fist. = bang ◻ *He thumped my shoulder affectionately, nearly knocking me over.* ◻ *I heard you thumping on the door.* **2** [T] (*informal*) If you **thump** someone, you attack them and hit them with your fist. ◻ *Don't say it serves me right or I'll thump you.* **3** [I, T] If you **thump** something somewhere or if it **thumps** there, it makes a loud, dull sound by hitting something else. ◻ *Their teacher thumped her pen on her book.* **4** [I] When your heart **thumps**, it beats strongly and quickly, usually because you are afraid or excited. = pound, thud ◻ *My heart was thumping wildly but I didn't let my face show any emotion.*

NOUN [C] (**thumps**) **1** A **thump** is a hard hit, usually made with the fist. ◻ *He felt a thump on his shoulder.* **2** A **thump** is a loud, dull sound made by something hitting something else. = thud ◻ *There was a loud thump as the horse crashed into the van.*

thun·der /ˈθʌndə/ NOUN, VERB

NOUN [U] **1 Thunder** is the loud noise that you hear from the sky after a flash of lightning, especially during a storm. ◻ *There was thunder and lightning, and torrential rain.* **2** The **thunder** of something that is moving or making a sound is the loud deep noise it makes. = roar ◻ *The thunder of the sea on the rocks seemed to blank out other thoughts.*

VERB [I] (**thunders, thundering, thundered**) **1** When it **thunders**, a loud noise comes from the sky after a flash of lightning. ◻ *The day was heavy and still. It would probably thunder later.* **2** If something or someone **thunders** somewhere, they move there quickly and with a lot of noise. ◻ *The horses thundered across the valley floor.*

thunder·storm /ˈθʌndəstɔːm/ NOUN [C] (**thunderstorms**) A **thunderstorm** is a storm with thunder and lightning and a lot of heavy rain.

❂ **thus** ♦♦◇ /ðʌs/ ADV (*formal*) **1** [thus with CL/GROUP] You use **thus** to show that what you are about to mention is the result of something else that you have just mentioned. = therefore, hence ◻ *Neither of them thought of turning on the news. Thus Caroline didn't hear of John's death until Peter telephoned.* ◻ *Even in a highly skilled workforce some people will be more capable and thus better paid than others.* ◻ *women's access to the basic means of production and thus to political power* **2** If you say that something is **thus** or happens **thus** you mean that it is, or happens, as you have just described or as you are just about to describe. ◻ *Joanna was pouring the wine. While she was thus engaged, Charles sat on one of the bar-stools.*

thwart /θwɔːt/ VERB [T] (**thwarts, thwarting, thwarted**) If you **thwart** someone or **thwart** their plans, you prevent them from doing or getting what they want. ◻ *The security forces were doing all they could to thwart terrorists.*

tick /tɪk/ VERB, NOUN

VERB [T, I] (**ticks, ticking, ticked**) **1** [T, I] When a clock or watch **ticks**, it makes a regular series of short sounds as it works. ◻ *A wind-up clock ticked busily from the kitchen counter.* **2** [T] (*BrE*; in *AmE*, use **check**) If you **tick** something that is written on a piece of paper, you put a tick next to it.

PHRASAL VERBS **tick away** Tick away means the same as tick VERB 1. ◻ *A grandfather clock ticked away in a corner.*

tick off (*BrE*; in *AmE*, usually use **check off**) If you **tick off** items on a list, you write a tick or other mark next to them, in order to show that they have been dealt with.

NOUN [C] (**ticks**) **1** The **tick** of a clock or watch is the series of short sounds it makes when it is working, or one of those sounds. ◻ *He sat listening to the tick of the grandfather clock.* **2** (*BrE*; in *AmE*, use **check**) A **tick** is a written mark like a V: ✔. It is used to show that something is correct or has been selected or dealt with. **3** A **tick** is a small creature which lives on the bodies of people or animals and uses their blood as food. ◻ *The company produces chemicals that destroy ticks and mites.*

tick·ing /ˈtɪkɪŋ/ NOUN [U] ◻ *the endless ticking of clocks*

tick·et ♦♦◇ /ˈtɪkɪt/ NOUN [C] (**tickets**) **1** [also 'by' ticket] A **ticket** is a small, official piece of paper or card which shows that you have paid to enter a place such as a theatre or a sports stadium, or shows that you have paid for a trip. ◻ *He had a ticket for a flight on Friday.* ◻ *two tickets for the game* **2** A **ticket** is an official piece of paper which orders you to pay a fine or to appear in court because you have committed a driving or parking offence. ◻ *Slow down or you'll get a ticket.* **3** A **ticket** for a game of chance such as a raffle or a lottery is a piece of paper with a number on it. If the number on your ticket matches the number chosen, you win a prize. ◻ *She bought a lottery ticket and won more than $33 million.*

❂ **tid·al** /ˈtaɪdəl/ ADJ **Tidal** means relating to or produced by tides. ◻ *The tidal stream or current gradually decreases in the shallows.* ◻ *the tidal waters of the estuary*

❂ **tide** ♦◇◇ /taɪd/ NOUN [C, SING] (**tides**) **1** [C] The **tide** is the regular change in the level of the sea on the shore. You say the tide is in when water reaches a high point on the land or out when the water leaves the land. ◻ *The tide was at its highest.* ◻ *The tide was going out, and the sand was smooth and glittering.* ◻ *The reserve is inaccessible at high tide.* ◻ *Scientists have found proof that strong tides can trigger earthquakes.* ◻ *State police say that high tides and severe flooding have damaged beaches.* **2** [C] A **tide** is a current in the sea that is caused by the regular and continuous movement of large areas of water towards and away from the shore. = current ◻ *Roman vessels used to sail with the tide from Boulogne to Richborough.* **3** [SING] The **tide of** opinion, for example, is what the majority of people think at a particular time. ◻ *The tide of opinion seems overwhelmingly in his favour.*

tidy /ˈtaɪdi/ (*mainly BrE*) ADJ, VERB

ADJ (**tidier, tidiest**) (in *AmE*, use **neat**) **1** Someone who is **tidy** likes everything to be neat and arranged in an organized way. **2** Something that is **tidy** is neat and is arranged in an organized way.

VERB [T] (**tidies, tidying, tidied**) (in *AmE*, use **clean**) When you **tidy** a place such as a room or cupboard, you make it neat by putting things in their proper places.

PHRASAL VERBS **tidy away** (in *AmE*, use **put away**) When you **tidy** something **away**, you put it in something else so that it is not in the way.

tidy up (in *AmE*, use **clean up**) When you **tidy up** or **tidy** a place **up**, you put things back in their proper places so that everything is neat.

tidi·ness /ˈtaɪdinəs/ NOUN [U] **1** *I'm very impressed by your tidiness and order.* **2** *Employees are expected to maintain a high standard of tidiness in their dress and appearance.*

tidi·ly /ˈtaɪdɪli/ ADV ◻ *books and magazines stacked tidily on shelves*

tie ♦♦◇ /taɪ/ VERB, NOUN

VERB [T, I, RECIP] (**ties, tying, tied**) **1** [T] If you **tie** two things **together** or **tie** them, you fasten them using a knot. ◻ *He tied the ends of the plastic bag together.* **2** [T] If you **tie** something or someone in a particular place or position, you put them there and fasten them using rope or string. ◻ *He had tied the dog to one of the trees near the canal.* **3** [T] If you **tie** a piece of string or cloth around something or **tie** something **with** a piece of string or cloth, you put the piece of string or cloth around it and fasten the ends together. ◻ *She tied her scarf over her head.* ◻ *Roll the meat and tie it with string.* **4** [T] If you **tie** a knot or bow **in** something or **tie** something **in** a knot or bow, you fasten the ends together. ◻ *He took a short length of rope and swiftly tied a slip knot.* ◻ *She tied a knot in a cherry stem.* **5** [I, T] When you **tie** something or when something **ties**, you close or fasten it using a bow or knot. ◻ *He pulled on his heavy suede shoes and tied the laces.* ◻ *a long white thing around his neck that tied in front in a floppy bow* **6** [T] If one thing **is tied to** another or two things **are tied**, the two things have a close connection or link. = link, connect ◻ *Their cancers are not so clearly tied to radiation exposure.* **7** [T] If you **are tied to** a particular place or situation, you are forced to accept it and cannot change it. ◻ *They had children and were consequently tied to the school holidays.*

t

8 [RECIP] If two people **tie** in a competition or game or if they **tie with** each other, they have the same number of points or the same degree of success. = draw ❑ *Ronan Rafferty had tied with Frank Nobilo.*

PHRASAL VERBS **tie down** A person or thing that **ties down** restricts your freedom in some way. ❑ *We'd agreed from the beginning not to tie each other down.* ❑ *He didn't want a family because he didn't want to be tied down.*

tie up **1** When you **tie** something **up**, you fasten string or rope around it so that it is firm or secure. ❑ *He tied up the bag and took it outside.* **2** If someone **ties** another person **up**, they fasten ropes around them so that they cannot move or escape. ❑ *Masked robbers broke in, tied him up, and made off with $8,000.* **3** If you **tie** an animal **up**, you fasten it to a fixed object with a piece of rope so that it cannot run away. = tether ❑ *Would you go and tie your horse up please?*

NOUN [c] (**ties**) **1** A **tie** is a long narrow piece of cloth that is worn around the neck under a shirt collar and tied in a knot at the front. Ties are worn mainly by men. ❑ *Jason had taken off his jacket and loosened his tie.* **2** [usu pl, oft ties + PREP] **Ties** are the connections you have with people or a place. = connection ❑ *Quebec has always had particularly close ties to France.* **3** In a competition or game, it is a **tie** when two people have the same number of points or the same degree of success as each other. ❑ *The first game ended in a tie.* **4** (BrE) In sport, a **tie** is a match that is part of a competition. The losers leave the competition and the winners go on to the next round. ❑ *They'll meet the winners of the first round tie.*

✦ **your hands are tied** → see **hand**

tier /tɪə/ NOUN, COMB

NOUN [c] (**tiers**) **1** A **tier** is a row or layer of something that has other layers above or below it. ❑ *The auditorium with the tiers of seats around and above it* **2** A **tier** is a level in an organization or system. ❑ *Islanders have campaigned for the abolition of one of the three tiers of municipal power on the island.*

COMB **1** You can use **tier** with a number to show how many rows or layers something has. ❑ *a three-tier wedding cake* **2** You can use **tier** with a number to show how many levels there are in an organization or system. ❑ *the possibility of a two-tier system of universities*

tight ✦◇◇ /taɪt/ ADJ, ADV

ADJ (**tighter, tightest**) **1** **Tight** clothes or shoes are small and fit closely to your body. ❑ *She walked off the plane in a miniskirt and tight top.* **2** If you have a **tight** grip or hold of someone or something, you are holding them firmly and securely. ❑ *As he and Hannah passed through the gate he kept a tight hold of her arm.* **3** **Tight** controls or rules are very strict. ❑ *The measures include tight control of media coverage.* ❑ *The government was prepared to keep a tight hold on public sector pay rises.* **4** Skin, cloth, or string that is **tight** is stretched or pulled so that it is smooth or straight. ❑ *My skin feels tight and lacking in moisture.* **5** **Tight** is used to describe a group of things or an amount of something that is closely packed together. ❑ *She curled up in a tight ball, with her knees tucked up at her chin.* **6** If a part of your body is **tight**, it feels uncomfortable and painful, for example, because you are sick, anxious, or angry. = taut ❑ *It is better to stretch the tight muscles first.* **7** A **tight** group of people is one whose members are closely linked by beliefs, feelings, or interests. = close ❑ *We're a tight group, so we do keep in touch.* **8** A **tight** bend or corner is one that changes direction very quickly so that you cannot see very far around it. = sharp ❑ *They collided on a tight bend and both cars were extensively damaged.* **9** A **tight** schedule or budget allows very little time or money for unexpected events or expenses. ❑ *It's difficult to cram everything into a tight schedule.* ❑ *Emma is on a tight budget for clothes.*

ADV **1** If you hold someone or something **tight**, you hold them firmly and securely. ❑ *She just fell into my arms, clutching me tight for a moment.* ❑ *Just hold tight to my hand and follow along.* **2** Something that is shut **tight** is shut very firmly. ❑ *The baby lay on the bed with his eyes closed tight.* ❑ *I keep the flour and sugar in individual jars, sealed tight with their glass lids.* **3** **Tight** is used to describe a group of things or an amount of something that is closely packed

together. ❑ *The people sleep on army cots packed tight, end to end.*

tight·ly /ˈtaɪtli/ ADV **1** [tightly with v] ❑ *He buttoned his collar tightly round his thick neck.* **2** [tightly after v] ❑ *She climbed back into bed and wrapped her arms tightly around her body.* **3** The internal media was tightly controlled by the government during the war. **4** [tightly with v] ❑ *Her sallow skin was drawn tightly across the bones of her face.* **5** [tightly with v] ❑ *Pemberton frowned and closed his eyes tightly.* **6** *Many animals travel in tightly packed trucks and are deprived of food, water and rest.*

→ See also **airtight**

✦ **keep a tight rein on** → see **rein**; **sit tight** → see **sit**

tight·en /ˈtaɪtən/ VERB

VERB [I, T] (**tightens, tightening, tightened**) **1** [I, T] If you **tighten** your grip on something, or if your grip **tightens**, you hold the thing more firmly or securely. ❑ *Luke answered by tightening his grip on her shoulder.* ❑ *Her arms tightened about his neck in gratitude.* **2** [I, T] If you **tighten** a rope or chain, or if it **tightens**, it is stretched or pulled hard until it is straight. ❑ *The anchorman flung his whole weight back, tightening the rope.* **3** [I, T] If a government or organization **tightens** its grip on a group of people or an activity, or if its grip **tightens**, it begins to have more control over it. ❑ *He knows he has considerable support for his plans to tighten his grip on the machinery of central government.* **4** [T] When you **tighten** a screw, nut, or other device, you turn it or move it so that it is more firmly in place or holds something more firmly. ❑ *I used my thumbnail to tighten the screw on my lamp.* **5** [I] If a part of your body **tightens**, the muscles in it become tense and stiff, for example, because you are angry or afraid. ❑ *Sofia's throat had tightened and she couldn't speak.* **6** [T] If someone in authority **tightens** a rule, a policy, or a system, they make it stricter or more efficient. ❑ *The United States plans to tighten the economic sanctions currently in place.*

PHRASAL VERB **tighten up** **1** **Tighten up** means the same as **tighten** VERB 4. ❑ *It's important to tighten up the wheels properly, otherwise they vibrate loose and fall off.* **2** **Tighten up** means the same as **tighten** VERB 6. ❑ *Until this week, every attempt to tighten up the law had failed.*

✦ **tighten your belt** → see **belt**

tile /taɪl/ NOUN [C, U] (**tiles**) **1** **Tiles** are flat, square pieces of baked clay, carpet, cork, or other substance, which are fixed as a covering onto a floor or wall. ❑ *Amy's shoes squeaked on the tiles as she walked down the corridor.* **2** **Tiles** are flat pieces of baked clay which are used for covering roofs. ❑ *a fine building, with a neat little porch and ornamental tiles on the roof*

till ✦◇◇ /tɪl/ PREP, CONJ, NOUN

PREP In spoken English and informal written English, **till** is often used instead of **until**. ❑ *They had to wait till Monday to phone the bank.*

CONJ In spoken English and informal written English, **till** is often used instead of **until**. ❑ *I hadn't left home till I was nineteen.*

NOUN [c] (**tills**) (BrE; in AmE, use **cash register**) In a shop or other place of business, a **till** is a counter or cash register where money is kept, and where customers pay for what they have bought.

tilt /tɪlt/ VERB, NOUN

VERB [I, T] (**tilts, tilting, tilted**) **1** [I, T] If you **tilt** an object or if it **tilts**, it moves into a sloping position with one end or side higher than the other. = lean ❑ *She tilted the mirror and began to comb her hair.* ❑ *Leonard tilted his chair back on two legs and stretched his long body.* **2** [T] If you **tilt** part of your body, usually your head, you move it slightly upwards or to one side. ❑ *Mari tilted her head back so that she could look at him.* ❑ *His wife tilted his head to the side and inspected the wound.* **3** [I, T] If a person or thing **tilts** towards a particular opinion or if something **tilts** them towards it, they change slightly so that they become more in agreement with that opinion or position. ❑ *Political will might finally tilt towards some sort of national health plan.*

NOUN [c] (**tilts**) **1** A **tilt** of the head or part of your body is when you move it slightly upwards or to one side. ❑ *He opened the rear door for me with an apologetic tilt of his head.*

2 The **tilt** of something is the fact that it tilts or slopes, or the angle at which it tilts or slopes. □ *calculations based on our understanding of the tilt of the Earth's axis*

tim·ber /ˈtɪmbə/ NOUN [U] **Timber** is wood that is used for building houses and making furniture. You can also refer to trees that are grown for this purpose as **timber**. □ *These Michigan woods have been exploited for timber since the Great Fire of Chicago.*

time ♦♦♦ /taɪm/ NOUN, CONJ, VERB

NOUN [U, SING, C, PL] (**times**) **1** [U] **Time** is what we measure in minutes, hours, days, and years. □ *a two-week period of time* □ *Time passed, and still Ma did not appear.* **2** [SING] You use **time** to ask or talk about a specific point in the day, which can be stated in hours and minutes and is shown on clocks. □ *'What time is it?'—'Eight o'clock.'* □ *He asked me the time.* **3** [C] The **time** when something happens is the point in the day when it happens or is supposed to happen. □ *Departure times are 08:15 from Baltimore, and 10:15 from Newark.* **4** [U] You use **time** to refer to the system of expressing time and counting hours that is used in a particular part of the world. □ *The incident happened just after ten o'clock local time.* **5** [U] [also 'a' time] You use **time** to refer to the period that you spend doing something or when something has been happening. □ *Adam spent a lot of time in his grandfather's office.* □ *He wouldn't have the time or money to take care of me.* □ *Listen to me, I haven't got much time.* □ *It's obvious that you need more time to think.* **6** [SING] If you say that something has been happening for **a time**, you mean that it has been happening for a fairly long period of time. □ *He was also for a time an art critic.* □ *He stayed for quite a time.* **7** [C] You use **time** to refer to a period of time or a point in time, when you are describing what is happening then. For example, if something happened **at** a particular **time**, that is when it happened. If it happens **at all times**, it always happens. □ *We were in the same college, which was male-only at that time.* □ *By this time he was thirty.* □ *It was a time of terrible uncertainty.* **8** [C] You use **time** or **times** to talk about a particular part in history or in your life. □ *They were hard times and his parents had been struggling to raise their family.* □ *We'll be alone together, just like old times.* **9** [PL] You can use **the times** to refer to the present time and to modern fashions, tastes, and developments. For example, if you say that someone **keeps up with the times**, you mean they are fashionable or aware of modern developments. If you say they are **behind the times**, you mean they are unfashionable or not aware of them. □ *This approach is now seriously out of step with the times.* **10** [C] When you describe the **time** that you had on a particular occasion or during a particular part of your life, you are describing the sort of experience that you had then. □ *Sarah and I had a great time while the kids were away.* **11** [SING] Your **time** is the amount of time that you have to live, or to do a particular thing. □ *Now that Martin has begun to suffer the effects of AIDS, he says his time is running out.* **12** [U] If you say it is **time for** something, **time to** do something, or **time** you did something, you mean that this thing ought to happen or be done now. □ *Opinion polls indicated a feeling among the public that it was time for a change.* □ *It was time for him to go to work.* **13** [C] When you talk about a **time** when something happens, you are referring to a specific occasion when it happens. □ *Every time she travels on the bus it's delayed by at least three hours.* **14** [C] You use **time** after numbers to say how often something happens. □ *It was her job to make tea three times a day.* **15** [PL] You use **times** after numbers when comparing one thing to another and saying, for example, how much bigger, smaller, better, or worse it is. □ *Its profits are rising four times faster than the average company.* **16** [C] Someone's **time** in a race is the amount of time it takes them to finish the race. □ *He was over a second faster than his previous best time.*

PHRASES **about time** (*emphasis*) If you say it is **about time** that something was done, you are saying in an emphatic way that it should happen or be done now, and really should have happened or been done sooner. □ *It's about time a few film makers with original ideas were given a chance.*

ahead of time If you do something **ahead of time**, you do it before a particular event or before you need to, in order to be well prepared. □ *Find out ahead of time what regulations apply to your situation.*

ahead of your time or **before your time** If someone is **ahead of** their **time** or **before** their **time**, they have new ideas a long time before other people start to think in the same way. □ *He was indeed ahead of his time in employing women, ex-convicts, and handicapped people.*

all the time If something happens or is done **all the time**, it happens or is done continually. = continually □ *We can't be together all the time.*

at a time You say **at a time** after an amount to say how many things or how much of something is involved in one action, place, or group. □ *Beat in the eggs, one at a time.*

at any time If something could happen **at any time**, it is possible that it will happen very soon, though nobody can predict exactly when. □ *Conditions are still very tense and the fighting could escalate at any time.*

at one time If you say that something was the case **at one time**, you mean that it was the case during a particular period in the past. □ *At one time 400 men, women and children lived in the village.*

at the same time **1** If two or more things exist, happen, or are true **at the same time**, they exist, happen, or are true together although they seem to contradict each other. □ *I was afraid of her, but at the same time I really liked her.* **2** **At the same time** is used to introduce a statement that slightly changes or contradicts the previous statement. □ *I don't think I set out to come up with a different sound for each CD. At the same time, I do have a sense of what is right for the moment.*

at times You use **at times** to say that something happens or is true on some occasions or at some moments. □ *The debate was highly emotional at times.*

for all time If you say that something will be the case **for all time**, you mean that it will always be the case. □ *He promised to love her for all time.*

for the time being If something is the case or will happen **for the time being**, it is the case or will happen now, but only until something else becomes possible or happens. □ *For the time being, however, immunotherapy is still in its experimental stages.*

from time to time If you do something **from time to time**, you do it occasionally but not regularly. □ *Her daughters visited him from time to time when he was bedridden.*

half the time (*informal*) If you say that something is the case **half the time** you mean that it often is the case. □ *Half the time, I don't have the slightest idea what he's talking about.*

in time If you are **in time for** a particular event, you are not too late for it. □ *I arrived just in time for my flight to Hawaii.*

in time or **given time** If you say that something will happen **in time** or **given time**, you mean that it will happen eventually, when a lot of time has passed. □ *He would sort out his own problems, in time.*

in time or **out of time** If you are playing, singing, or dancing **in time** with a piece of music, you are following the rhythm and speed of the music correctly. If you are **out of time** with it, you are not following the rhythm and speed of the music correctly. □ *Her body swayed in time with the music.*

in a week's time or **in a year's time** or **in a few minutes' time** If you say that something will happen, for example, **in a week's time** or **in two years' time**, you mean that it will happen a week from now or two years from now. □ *Presidential elections are due to be held in ten days' time.*

in good time If you arrive somewhere **in good time**, you arrive early so that there is time to spare before a particular event. □ *We got there in good time for the opening ceremony.*

in no time or **in next to no time** If something happens **in no time** or **in next to no time**, it happens almost immediately or very quickly. □ *He's going to be just fine. At his age he'll heal in no time.*

keep time **1** If you **keep time** when playing or singing music, you follow or play the beat, without going too fast

t

or too slowly. ❑ *As he sang he kept time on a small drum.*
2 When you talk about how well a watch or clock **keeps time**, you are talking about how accurately it measures time. ❑ *Some pulsars keep time better than the Earth's most accurate clocks.*

make time If you **make time for** a particular activity or person, you arrange to have some free time so that you can do the activity or spend time with the person. ❑ *Before leaving the city, be sure to make time for a shopping trip.*

make good time If you say that you **made good time** on a trip, you mean it did not take you very long compared to the length of time you expected it to take. ❑ *They had left early in the morning, on quiet roads, and made good time.*

make up for lost time If someone **is making up for lost time**, they are doing something actively and with enthusiasm because they have not had the opportunity to do it before or when they were younger. ❑ *Five years older than the majority of officers of his same rank, he was determined to make up for lost time.*

nine times out of ten If you say that something happens or is the case **nine times out of ten** or **ninety-nine times out of a hundred**, you mean that it happens on nearly every occasion or is almost always the case. ❑ *When they want something, nine times out of ten they get it.*

of all time If you say that someone or something is, for example, the best writer **of all time**, or the most successful film **of all time**, you mean that they are the best or most successful that there has ever been. ❑ *'Monopoly' is one of the best-selling games of all time.*

on time If you are **on time**, you are not late. ❑ *Don't worry, she'll be on time.*

only a matter of time or **only a question of time** or **just a matter of time** If you say that it is **only a matter of time** or **only a question of time** before something happens, you mean that it cannot be avoided and will definitely happen at some future date. ❑ *It now seems only a matter of time before they resign.*

pass the time If you do something to **pass the time** you do it because you have some time available and not because you really want to do it. ❑ *Without particular interest and just to pass the time, I read a story.*

take time If you say that something will **take time**, you mean that it will take a long time. ❑ *Change will come, but it will take time.*

take your time If you **take** your **time** doing something, you do it slowly and do not hurry. ❑ *'Take your time,' Ted told him. 'I'm in no hurry.'*

tell the time If a child can **tell the time**, they are able to find out what the time is by looking at a clock or watch. ❑ *My four-year-old daughter cannot quite tell the time.*

time after time If something happens **time after time**, it happens in a similar way on many occasions. = repeatedly ❑ *Burns had escaped from jail time after time.*

time flies If you say that **time flies**, you mean that it seems to pass very quickly. ❑ *Time flies when you're having fun.*

no time to lose If you say there is **no time to lose** or **no time to be lost**, you mean you must hurry as fast as you can to do something. ❑ *He rushed home, realizing there was no time to lose.*

time will tell If you say that **time will tell** whether something is true or correct, you mean that it will not be known until some time in the future whether it is true or correct. ❑ *Only time will tell whether Broughton's optimism is justified.*

waste no time If you **waste no time** in doing something, you take the opportunity to do it immediately or quickly. ❑ *Tom wasted no time in telling me why he had come.*

CONJ You use **times** to show multiplication. Three times five is 3x5. ❑ *Four times six is 24.*

VERB [T] (**times, timing, timed**) **1** If you **time** something **for** a particular hour, day, or period, you plan or decide to do it or cause it to happen at this time. ❑ *He timed the election to coincide with new measures to boost the economy.* ❑ *I timed our visit for March 7.* **2** If you **time** an action or activity, you measure how long someone takes to do it or how long it lasts. ❑ *A radar gun timed the speed of the baseball.*

→ See also **timing**
✦ **time and again** → see **again**

◎ **time-consuming** also **time consuming** ADJ If something is **time-consuming**, it takes a lot of time. = arduous, demanding ❑ *It's just very time consuming to get such a large quantity of data.* ❑ *Starting a new business, however small, is a time-consuming exercise.*

time·ly /ˈtaɪmli/ ADJ (approval) If you describe an event as **timely**, it happens exactly at the moment when it is most useful, effective, or relevant. ❑ *The recent outbreaks of cholera are a timely reminder that this disease is still a serious health hazard.*

◎ **time·table** /ˈtaɪmteɪbəl/ NOUN [C] (**timetables**) **1** A **timetable** is a plan of the times when particular events will take place. = schedule, agenda, plan ❑ *The timetable was hopelessly optimistic.* ❑ *Don't you realize we're working to a timetable? We have to have results.* ❑ *The two countries are to try to agree a timetable for formal talks.* **2** (mainly BrE; in AmE, usually use **schedule**) A **timetable** is a list of the times when trains, boats, buses, or aeroplanes are supposed to arrive at or leave from a particular place. **3** (BrE; in AmE, usually use **class schedule**) In a school or college, a **timetable** is a list that shows the times in the week at which particular subjects are taught. You can also refer to the range of subjects that a student learns or the classes that a teacher teaches as their **timetable**. ❑ *Options are offered subject to staff availability and the constraints of the timetable.* ❑ *Members of the union will continue to teach their full timetables.*

tim·id /ˈtɪmɪd/ ADJ **Timid** people are shy, nervous, and lack courage or confidence in themselves. ❑ *A timid child, Isabella had learned obedience at an early age.*

ti·mid·i·ty /tɪˈmɪdɪti/ NOUN [U] ❑ *She doesn't ridicule my timidity.*

tim·id·ly /ˈtɪmɪdli/ ADV ❑ *The little boy stepped forward timidly and shook Leo's hand.*

tim·ing /ˈtaɪmɪŋ/ NOUN [U] **1** **Timing** is the skill or action of judging the right moment in a situation or activity at which to do something. ❑ *His photo is a wonderful happy moment caught with perfect timing.* **2** **Timing** is used to refer to the time at which something happens or is planned to happen, or to the length of time that something takes. ❑ *They had concerns about the timing of the report.*
→ See also **time**

tin /tɪn/ NOUN [U, C] (**tins**) **1** [U] **Tin** is a soft silvery-white metal. ❑ *a factory that turns scrap metal into tin cans* **2** [C] A **tin** is a metal container with a lid in which things such as biscuits, cakes, or tobacco can be kept. ❑ *Store the cakes in an airtight tin.* **3** [C] (mainly BrE; in AmE, usually use **can**) A **tin** is a metal container which is filled with food and sealed in order to preserve the food for long periods of time. **4** [C] (mainly BrE; in AmE, usually use **can**) You can use **tin** to refer to a tin and its contents, or to the contents only. ❑ *a tin of paint* **5** [C] (BrE; in AmE, use **pan**) A baking **tin** is a metal container used for baking things such as cakes and bread in an oven.
✦ **have a tin ear** → see **ear**

tinge /tɪndʒ/ NOUN [C] (**tinges**) A **tinge** of a colour, feeling, or quality is a small amount of it. ❑ *His skin had an unhealthy greyish tinge.*

tint /tɪnt/ NOUN, VERB
NOUN [C] (**tints**) A **tint** is a small amount of colour. ❑ *Its large leaves often show a delicate purple tint.*
VERB [T] (**tints, tinting, tinted**) If something **is tinted**, it

has a small amount of a particular colour or dye in it. ❏ *Eyebrows can be tinted with the same dye.*

tiny ◆◇◇ /'taɪni/ ADJ (**tinier, tiniest**) Something or someone that is **tiny** is extremely small. ❏ *The living room is tiny.* ❏ *Though she was tiny, she had a very loud voice.*

tip ◆◇◇ /tɪp/ NOUN, VERB

NOUN [c] (**tips**) **1** The **tip** of something long and narrow is the end of it. ❏ *The sleeves covered his hands to the tips of his fingers.* **2** If you give a **tip** to someone such as a waiter in a restaurant, you give them some money to thank them for their services. ❏ *I gave the barber a tip.* **3** A **tip** is a useful piece of advice. ❏ *It shows how to prepare a CV, and gives tips on applying for jobs.* **4** (*BrE*; in *AmE*, use **dump**) A **tip** is a place where rubbish is left.

PHRASE **the tip of the iceberg** If you say that a problem is **the tip of the iceberg**, you mean that it is one small part of a much larger problem. ❏ *Unless we're all a lot more careful, the people who have died so far will be just the tip of the iceberg.*

VERB [I, T] (**tips, tipping, tipped**) **1** [I, T] If you **tip** an object or part of your body or if it **tips**, it moves into a sloping position with one end or side higher than the other. ❏ *He leaned away from her, and she had to tip her head back to see him.* **2** [T] If you **tip** something somewhere, you pour it there. ❏ *Tip the vegetables into a bowl.* **3** [T] If you **tip** someone such as a waiter in a restaurant, you give them some money in order to thank them for their services. ❏ *We usually tip 18–20%.*

PHRASE **tip the scales** or **tip the balance** If something **tips the scales** or **tips the balance**, it gives someone a slight advantage. ❏ *Today's slightly shorter race could well help to tip the scales in her favour.*

PHRASAL VERBS **tip off** If someone **tips** you **off**, they give you information about something that has happened or is going to happen. ❏ *Greg tipped police off about a drunk driver.*

tip over If you **tip** something **over** or if it **tips over**, it falls over or turns over. ❏ *He tipped the table over in front of him.* ❏ *Don't tip over that glass.*

tip-off NOUN [c] (**tip-offs**) A **tip-off** is a piece of information or a warning that you give to someone, often privately or secretly. ❏ *The man was arrested at his home after a tip-off to police from a member of the public.*

tire /taɪə/ VERB [I, T] (**tires, tiring, tired**) **1** [I, T] If something **tires** you or you **tire**, you feel that you have used a lot of energy and you want to rest or sleep. ❏ *If driving tires you, take the train.* **2** [I] If you **tire of** something, you no longer wish to do it, because you have become bored with it or unhappy with it. **= weary** ❏ *He felt he would never tire of listening to her stories.*

tired ◆◇◇ /taɪəd/ ADJ **1** If you are **tired**, you feel that you want to rest or sleep. ❏ *Michael is tired and he has to rest after his long trip.* **2** You can describe a part of your body as **tired** if it looks or feels as if you need to rest it or to sleep. ❏ *Cucumber is good for soothing tired eyes.* **3** [V-LINK + tired 'of' N/-ING] If you are **tired of** something, you do not want it to continue because you are bored with it or unhappy with it. **= sick** ❏ *I am tired of all the speculation.* **tired·ness** /taɪədnəs/ NOUN [u] ❏ *He had to cancel some engagements because of tiredness.*

tire·less /taɪələs/ ADJ (*approval*) If you describe someone or their efforts as **tireless**, you approve of the fact that they put a lot of hard work into something, and refuse to give up or take a rest. ❏ *Mother Teresa's tireless efforts to help the poor* **tire·less·ly** /taɪələsli/ ADV [tirelessly with V] ❏ *He worked tirelessly for the cause of health and safety.*

tire·some /taɪəsəm/ ADJ If you describe someone or something as **tiresome**, you mean that you find them irritating or boring. ❏ *the tiresome old lady next door*

tir·ing /taɪərɪŋ/ ADJ If you describe something as **tiring**, you mean that it makes you tired so that you want to rest or sleep. ❏ *It had been a long and tiring day.*

tis·sue ◆◇◇ /tɪʃuː, tɪsjuː/ NOUN [u, c] (**tissues**) **1** [u] [also tissues] In animals and plants, **tissue** consists of cells that are similar to each other in appearance and that have the

same function. ❏ *As we age we lose muscle tissue.* **2** [u] **Tissue paper** is thin paper that is used for wrapping things that are easily damaged, such as objects made of glass or china. ❏ *a small package wrapped in tissue paper* **3** [c] A **tissue** is a piece of thin soft paper that you use to blow your nose. ❏ *a box of tissues*

⊙ ti·tle ◆◆◇ /taɪtəl/ NOUN, VERB

NOUN [c] (**titles**) **1** The **title** of a book, play, film, or piece of music is its name. ❏ *'Patience and Sarah' was first published in 1969 under the title 'A Place for Us'.* **2** Publishers and booksellers often refer to books or magazines as **titles**. ❏ *The magazine has become the biggest publisher of new poetry, with 50 new titles a year.* **3** Someone's **title** is a word such as 'Mr', 'Mrs', or 'Doctor', that is used before their own name in order to show their status or profession. ❏ *Please fill in your name and title.* **4** Someone's **title** is a name that describes their job or status in an organization. ❏ *He was given the title of assistant manager.* **5** If a person or team wins a particular **title**, they win a sports competition that is held regularly. Usually a person keeps a title until someone else defeats them. ❏ *He became Jamaica's first Olympic gold medallist when he won the 400 metre title in 1948.* **6** In Britain, and some other countries, a person's **title** is a word such as 'Sir', 'Lord', or 'Lady', that is used in front of their name, or a phrase that is used instead of their name, and indicates that they have a high rank in society. ❏ *Her husband was also honoured with his title 'Sir Denis'.*

VERB [T] (**titles, titling, titled**) When a writer, composer, or artist **titles** a work, they give it a name. ❏ *Pirandello titled his play 'Six Characters in Search of an Author'.* ❏ *The single is titled 'White Love'.*

to ◆◆◆ /tə, tʊ, STRONG tuː/ PREP, ADV

> In addition to the uses shown below, **to** is used in phrasal verbs such as 'see to' and 'come to'. It is also used with some verbs that have two objects in order to introduce the second object.

PREP **1** You use **to** when indicating the place that someone or something visits, moves towards, or points at. ❏ *Two friends and I drove to Florida during spring break.* ❏ *She went to the window and looked out.* **2** If you go **to** an event, you go where it is taking place. ❏ *We went to a party at the Kurts' house.* ❏ *He came to dinner.* **3** If something is attached **to** something larger or fixed **to** it, the two things are joined together. ❏ *There was a piece of cloth tied to the dog's collar.* **4** You use **to** when indicating the position of something. For example, if something is **to** your left side, it is nearer your left side than your right side. ❏ *Hemingway's studio is to the right.* **5** [V N + to + N] When you give something **to** someone, they receive it. ❏ *He picked up the knife and gave it to me.* **6** [ADJ/N + to + N] You use **to** to indicate who or what an action or a feeling is directed towards. ❏ *Marcus has been really mean to me today.* ❏ *troops loyal to the government* **7** [ADJ/N + to + N] **To** can show who is affected by something. ❏ *He is a witty man, and an inspiration to all of us.* **8** If you say something **to** someone, you want that person to listen and understand what you are saying. ❏ *I will explain to them that I can't pay them.* **9** You use **to** when showing someone's reaction to something or their feelings about a situation or event. For example, if you say that something happens **to** someone's surprise you mean that they are surprised when it happens. ❏ *To his surprise, the bedroom door was locked.* **10** **To** can show whose opinion is being stated. ❏ *It was clear to me that he respected his boss.* **11** You use **to** when indicating what something or someone is becoming, or the state or situation that they are progressing towards. ❏ *The shouts changed to laughter.* ❏ *an old ranch house that has been converted to a nature centre* **12** [N + to + N] **To** can be used as a way of introducing the person or organization you are employed by. ❏ *Rickman worked as a dresser to Nigel Hawthorne.* **13** **To** can show a span of time. ❏ *From 1977 to 1985 the United States gross national product grew 21 per cent.* **14** ['from' N + to + N] You use **to** to show two extreme examples of something. ❏ *I read everything from fiction to history.* **15** ['from' N + to + N] If someone goes from place **to** place or from job **to** job, they go to several places, or

t

work in several jobs, and spend only a short time in each one. ❑ *Larry and Andy had drifted from place to place, working at this and that.* **16** [NUM/N + to + NUM] You use **to** when you are stating a time less than thirty minutes before an hour. For example, if it is 'five to eight', it is five minutes before eight o'clock. ❑ *At twenty to six I was waiting by the entrance to the station.* **17** You use **to** when giving ratios and rates. ❑ *engines that can run at 60 miles to the gallon* **18** You use **to** when indicating that two things happen at the same time. For example, if something is done **to** music, it is done at the same time as music is being played. ❑ *Romeo left the stage, to enthusiastic applause.* **19** You use **to** before the base form of a verb to form the to-infinitive. You use the to-infinitive after certain verbs, nouns, and adjectives, and after words such as 'how', 'which', and 'where'. ❑ *The management wanted to know what I was doing there.* ❑ *She told the family of her decision to resign.* **20** You use **to** before the base form of a verb to indicate the purpose or intention of an action. = in order to ❑ *using the experience of big companies to help small businesses* **21** You use **to** before the base form of a verb when you are commenting on a statement that you are making, for example, when saying that you are being honest or brief, or that you are summing up or giving an example. ❑ *I'm disappointed, to be honest.* **22** You use **to** before the base form of a verb when indicating what situation follows a particular action. ❑ *From the garden you walk down to discover a large and beautiful lake.* **23** You use **to** with 'too' and 'enough' in expressions like **too much to** and **old enough to**; see **too** and **enough**.

CONVENTION **there's nothing to it** (*emphasis*) If you say 'There's nothing to it', 'There's not much to it', or 'That's all there is to it', you are emphasizing how simple you think something is. ❑ *'There is nothing to it,' those I asked about it told me.*

ADV
PHRASE **to and fro** If someone moves **to and fro**, they move repeatedly from one place to another and back again, or from side to side. ❑ *She stood up and began to pace to and fro.*
→ See also **too**

toast /təʊst/ NOUN, VERB
NOUN [U, C] (**toasts**) **1** [U] **Toast** is bread which has been cut into slices and made brown and crisp by cooking at a high temperature. ❑ *a piece of toast* **2** [C] When you drink a **toast** to someone or something, you drink some wine or another alcoholic drink as a symbolic gesture, in order to show your appreciation of them or to wish them success. ❑ *Eleanor and I drank a toast to the bride and groom.*
VERB [T] (**toasts, toasting, toasted**) **1** When you **toast** something such as bread, you cook it at a high temperature so that it becomes brown and crisp. ❑ *Toast the bread lightly on both sides.* **2** When you **toast** someone or something, you drink a toast to them. ❑ *We all toasted his health.*

to·bac·co /təˈbækəʊ/ NOUN [C, U] (**tobaccos**) **1** [C, U] **Tobacco** is dried leaves which people smoke in pipes, cigars, and cigarettes. You can also refer to pipes, cigars, and cigarettes as a whole as **tobacco**. ❑ *Try to do without tobacco and alcohol.* **2** [U] **Tobacco** is the plant from which tobacco is obtained. ❑ *Cuba's tobacco crop*

to·day ♦♦♦ /təˈdeɪ/ ADV, NOUN
ADV **1** [today with CL] You use **today** to refer to this day on which you are speaking or writing. ❑ *How are you feeling today?* **2** You can refer to the present period of history as **today**. ❑ *The United States is in a serious recession today.*
NOUN [U] **1** You use **today** to refer to this day on which you are speaking or writing. ❑ *Today is Friday, September 14th.* **2** You can refer to the present period of history as **today**. ❑ *In today's America, health care is one of the very biggest businesses.*
→ See also **yesterday, tomorrow**

tod·dler /ˈtɒdlə/ NOUN [C] (**toddlers**) A **toddler** is a young child who has only just learned to walk or who still walks unsteadily with small, quick steps. ❑ *I had a toddler at home and two other children at school.*

toe /təʊ/ NOUN
NOUN [C] (**toes**) Your **toes** are the five movable parts at the end of each foot. ❑ *She wiggled her toes against the packed sand.*
PHRASE **keep someone on their toes** If you say that someone or something **keeps** you **on** your **toes**, you mean that they cause you to remain alert and ready for anything that might happen. ❑ *His fiery campaign rhetoric has kept opposition parties on their toes for months.*

to·geth·er ♦♦♦ /təˈgeðə/ ADV, ADJ

In addition to the uses shown below, **together** is used in phrasal verbs such as 'piece together', 'pull together', and 'sleep together'.

ADV **1** If people do something **together**, they do it with each other. ❑ *We went on long bicycle rides together.* ❑ *He and I worked together on a book.* **2** [together after V] If things are joined **together**, they are joined with each other so that they touch or form one whole. ❑ *Mix the ingredients together thoroughly.* **3** [together after V] If things or people are situated **together**, they are in the same place and very near to each other. ❑ *The trees grew close together.* ❑ *Ginette and I gathered our things together.* **4** [together after V] If a group of people are held or kept **together**, they are united with each other in some way. ❑ *He has done a lot to keep the family together.* **5** [together after V] If two things happen or are done **together**, they happen or are done at the same time. ❑ *Three horses crossed the finish line together.* **6** You use **together** when you are adding two or more amounts or things to each other in order to consider a total amount or effect. ❑ *Together we earn $60,000 per year.*
PHRASE **go together** If you say that two things **go together**, or that one thing **goes together with** another, you mean they go well with each other or cannot be separated from each other. ❑ *I can see that some colours go together and some don't.*
ADJ **1** [V-LINK + together] If a group of people are **together**, they are united with each other in some way. = united ❑ *We are together in the way we're looking at this situation.* **2** If two people are **together**, they are married or having a sexual relationship with each other. ❑ *We were together for five years.*
PHRASE **together with** You use **together with** to mention someone or something else that is also involved in an action or situation. ❑ *Every month we'll deliver the very best articles, together with the latest fashion and beauty news.*
✦ **get your act together** → see **act**; **put your heads together** → see **head**

toil /tɔɪl/ VERB
VERB [I, T] (**toils, toiling, toiled**) (*literary*) When people **toil**, they work very hard doing unpleasant or tiring tasks. ❑ *People who toiled in dim, dank factories were too exhausted to enjoy their family life.* ❑ *Workers toiled long hours.*
PHRASAL VERB **toil away** **Toil away** means the same as **toil**. VERB. ❑ *He doesn't spend every minute toiling away at his desk.*

toi·let /ˈtɔɪlət/ NOUN
NOUN [C] (**toilets**) **1** A **toilet** is a large bowl with a seat, or a platform with a hole, which is connected to a water system and which you use when you want to get rid of urine or faeces from your body. ❑ *She made Tina flush the pills down the toilet.* **2** (*mainly BrE; in AmE, usually use* **bathroom**) A **toilet** is a room in a house or public building that contains a toilet.
PHRASE **go to the toilet** (*mainly BrE; in AmE, usually use* **go to the bathroom**) You can say that someone **goes to the toilet** to mean that they get rid of waste substances from their body, especially when you want to avoid using words that you think may offend people.

to·ken /ˈtəʊkən/ ADJ, NOUN
ADJ [token + N] You use **token** to describe things or actions which are small or unimportant but are meant to show particular intentions or feelings which may not be sincere. ❑ *The announcement was welcomed as a step in the right direction, but was widely seen as a token gesture.*
NOUN [C] (**tokens**) **1** A **token** is a round flat piece of metal or plastic that is sometimes used instead of money.

□ *slot-machine tokens* **2** (BrE; in AmE, use **coupon**) A **token** is a piece of paper or card that can be exchanged for goods, either in a particular store or as part of a special offer.

PHRASE **by the same token** You use **by the same token** to introduce a statement that you think is true for the same reasons that were given for a previous statement. □ *If you give up exercise, your muscles shrink and fat increases. By the same token, if you expend more energy you will lose fat.*

told /təʊld/ IRREG FORM

IRREG FORM Told is the past tense and past participle of **tell**. **PHRASE** **all told** You can use **all told** to introduce or follow a summary, general statement, or total. □ *All told there were 104 people on the payroll.*

tol·er·able /ˈtɒlərəbəl/ ADJ If you describe something as **tolerable**, you mean that you can bear it, even though it is unpleasant or painful. □ *Our living conditions are tolerable, but I can't wait to leave.*

tol·er·ably /ˈtɒlərəbli/ ADV □ *Their captors treated them tolerably well.*

✪ tol·er·ance /ˈtɒlərəns/ NOUN [U] **1** (approval) **Tolerance** is the quality of allowing other people to say and do what they like, even if you do not agree with or approve of it. = acceptance □ *his tolerance and understanding of diverse human nature* □ *a unique culture, of which religious tolerance was an important part* **2** **Tolerance** is the ability to bear something painful or unpleasant. □ *There is lowered pain tolerance, lowered resistance to infection.*

✪ tol·er·ant /ˈtɒlərənt/ ADJ **1** (approval) If you describe someone as **tolerant**, you approve of the fact that they allow other people to say and do as they like and that they are willing to accept different races, religions, and lifestyles. = accepting □ *They need to be tolerant of different points of view.* □ *Other changes include more tolerant attitudes to unmarried couples having children.* **2** [V-LINK + tolerant 'of' N] If a plant, animal, or machine is **tolerant** of particular conditions or types of treatment, it is able to bear them without being damaged or hurt. □ *plants which are more tolerant of dry conditions*

✪ tol·er·ate /ˈtɒləreɪt/ VERB [T] (**tolerates, tolerating, tolerated**) **1** If you **tolerate** a situation or person, you accept them although you do not particularly like them. = accept, condone, put up with □ *She can no longer tolerate the position that she's in.* □ *It is vital that councils do not tolerate substandard care.* □ *The Army does not tolerate inappropriate behaviour.* **2** If you can **tolerate** something bad or painful, you are able to bear it. = bear □ *The ability to tolerate pain varies from person to person.*

toll /təʊl/ VERB, NOUN

VERB [I, T] (**tolls, tolling, tolled**) When a bell **tolls** or when someone **tolls** it, it rings slowly and repeatedly, often as a sign that someone has died. □ *Church bells tolled and black flags fluttered.*

NOUN [C] (**tolls**) **1** A **toll** is a sum of money that you have to pay in order to use a particular bridge or road. □ *You can pay a toll to drive on Pike's Peak Highway or relax and take the Pike's Peak Cog Railway.* **2** [toll + N] A **toll** road or **toll** bridge is a road or bridge that you have to pay to use. □ *Most people who drive the toll roads don't use them every day.* **3** (journalism) A **toll** is a total number of deaths, accidents, or disasters that occur in a particular period of time. □ *There are fears that the casualty toll may be higher.* **PHRASE** **take its toll** If you say that something **takes** its **toll** or **takes a heavy toll**, you mean that it has a bad effect or causes a lot of suffering. □ *Winter takes its toll on your health.*

to·ma·to /təˈmɑːtəʊ, AmE -ˈmeɪ-/ NOUN [C, U] (**tomatoes**) **Tomatoes** are soft, red fruit that you can eat raw in salads or cooked as a vegetable.

to·mor·row ♦♦◇ /təˈmɒrəʊ, AmE -ˈmɔːr-/ ADV, NOUN **ADV** **1** [tomorrow with CL] You use **tomorrow** to refer to the day after today. □ *Bye, see you tomorrow.* **2** [tomorrow with CL] You can refer to the future, especially the near future, as **tomorrow**. □ *What is education going to look like tomorrow?*

NOUN [U] (**tomorrows**) **1** You use **tomorrow** to refer to the

day after today. □ *What's on your agenda for tomorrow?* **2** [also tomorrows] You can refer to the future, especially the near future, as **tomorrow**. □ *tomorrow's computer industry*

ton ♦◇◇ /tʌn/ NOUN [C] (**tons**) **1** A **ton** is a unit of weight that is equal to 2,000 pounds. □ *Hundreds of tons of oil spilled into the ocean.* **2** (BrE) A **ton** is the same as a **tonne**, which is 1,000 kilograms.

tone ♦◇◇ /təʊn/ NOUN, VERB

NOUN [C, SING, U] (**tones**) **1** [C] The **tone** of a sound is its particular quality. □ *Cross could hear him speaking in low tones to Sarah.* **2** [C] Someone's **tone** is a quality in their voice which shows what they are feeling or thinking. □ *I still didn't like his tone of voice; he sounded angry and accusing.* **3** [SING] [also 'in' tone] The **tone** of a speech or piece of writing is its style and the opinions or ideas expressed in it. □ *The tone of the letter was very friendly.* **4** [SING] The **tone** of a place or an event is its general atmosphere. □ *There were no shops that would lower the tone of the area.* **5** [U] The **tone** of someone's body, especially their muscles, is its degree of firmness and strength. □ *stretch exercises that improve muscle tone* **6** [C, U] A **tone** is one of the lighter, darker, or brighter shades of the same colour. □ *Each brick also varies slightly in tone, texture and size.* **7** [SING] A **tone** is one of the sounds that you hear when you are using a telephone, for example, the sound that tells you that a number is engaged, or no longer exists. □ *I can't get a dialling tone on this phone.*

VERB [I, T] (**tones, toning, toned**) Something that **tones** your body makes it firm and strong. □ *This movement lengthens your spine and tones the spinal nerves.* □ *Try these toning exercises before you start the day.*

PHRASAL VERBS **tone down** **1** If you **tone down** something that you have written or said, you make it less forceful, severe, or offensive. □ *The fiery right-wing leader toned down his militant statements after the meeting.* **2** If you **tone down** a colour or a flavour, you make it less bright or strong. □ *He was asked to tone down the spices and garlic in his recipes.* **tone up** Tone up means the same as **tone** VERB. □ *Exercise tones up your body.*

tongue /tʌŋ/ NOUN

NOUN [C] (**tongues**) **1** Your **tongue** is the soft movable part inside your mouth which you use for tasting, eating, and speaking. □ *I walked over to the mirror and stuck my tongue out.* **2** You can use **tongue** to refer to the kind of things that a person says. □ *She had a nasty tongue.* **3** (literary) A **tongue** is a language. = language □ *The French feel passionately about their native tongue.* **PHRASE** **tongue in cheek** A tongue-in-cheek remark or attitude is not serious, although it may seem to be. □ *a lighthearted, tongue-in-cheek approach* **♦ bite your tongue** → see **bite**

to·night ♦♦◇ /təˈnaɪt/ ADV, NOUN

ADV **Tonight** is used to refer to the evening of today or the night that follows today. □ *I'm at home tonight.* □ *Tonight he proved what a great player he was.*

NOUN [U] **Tonight** is used to refer to the evening of today or the night that follows today. □ *Tonight is the opening night of the opera.*

✪ tonne /tʌn/ (BrE; in AmE, use **metric ton**) NOUN [C] (**tonnes**) A **tonne** is a metric unit of weight that is equal to 1,000 kilograms. □ *65.5 million tonnes of coal* □ *Top quality Thai rice fetched $340 a tonne.*

→ See also **ton**

too ♦♦♦ /tuː/ ADV

ADV **1** [CL/GROUP + too] You use **too** after mentioning another person, thing, or aspect that a previous statement applies to or includes. = also □ *'Nice to talk to you.'—'Nice to talk to you too.'* □ *'I've got a great feeling about it. Me too.'* **2** [CL/GROUP + too] You use **too** after adding a piece of information or a comment to a statement, in order to emphasize that it is surprising or important. □ *We did learn to read, and quickly too.* **3** You use **too** in order to indicate that there is a greater amount or degree of something than is desirable, necessary, or acceptable. □ *Leather jeans that are too big will make you look larger.* □ *I'm turning up the heat, it's too cold.* **4** [with BRD-NEG, too + ADJ] You use **too** with a

t

negative to make what you are saying sound less forceful or more polite or cautious. = very ❑ *I wasn't too happy with what I'd written so far.*

PHRASE **all too** or **only too** *(emphasis)* You use **all too** or **only too** to emphasize that something happens to a greater extent or degree than is good or desirable. ❑ *She remembered it all too well.*

✦ **none too** → see **none**

took /tʊk/ IRREG FORM **Took** is the past tense of **take**.

tool ◆◇◇ /tuːl/ NOUN [C] (**tools**) **1** A **tool** is any instrument or simple piece of equipment that you hold in your hands and use to do a particular kind of work. For example, spades, hammers, and knives are all tools. ❑ *I find the best tool for the purpose is a pair of shears.* **2** You can refer to anything that you use for a particular purpose as a particular type of **tool**. ❑ *Writing is a good tool for expressing feelings.*

tooth ◆◇◇ /tuːθ/ NOUN
NOUN [C, PL] (**teeth**) **1** [C] Your **teeth** are the hard white objects in your mouth, which you use for biting and chewing. ❑ *She had very pretty straight teeth.* **2** [PL] The **teeth** of something such as a comb, saw, cog, or zip are the parts that stick out in a row on its edge. ❑ *The front cog has 44 teeth.*
PHRASE **a sweet tooth** If you have **a sweet tooth**, you like sweet food very much. ❑ *Add more honey if you have a sweet tooth.*

top ◆◆◆ /tɒp/ NOUN, ADJ, VERB
NOUN [C, SING] (**tops**) **1** [C] The **top** of something is its highest point or part. ❑ *I waited at the top of the stairs.* ❑ *the picture at the top of the page* **2** [C] The **top** of something such as a bottle, jar, or tube is a cap, lid, or other device that fits or screws onto one end of it. ❑ *the plastic tops from soda bottles* **3** [SING] (BrE; in AmE, use **end**) The **top** of a street, garden, bed, or table is the end of it that is farthest away from where you usually enter it or from where you are. = end, head **4** [C] (*informal*) A **top** is a piece of clothing that you wear on the upper half of your body, for example, a blouse or shirt. ❑ *Look at my new top.* **5** [SING] The **top** of an organization or career structure is the highest level in it. ❑ *We started from the bottom and we had to work our way up to the top.* ❑ *his dramatic rise to the top of the military hierarchy* **6** [SING] If someone is **at the top of**, for example, a table or league or is **the top of** the table or league, their performance is better than that of all the other people involved. ❑ *the golfer at the top of the leaderboard*
PHRASES **from top to bottom** *(emphasis)* If you say that you clean or examine something **from top to bottom**, you are emphasizing that you do it completely and thoroughly. ❑ *She would clean the house from top to bottom.*
from top to toe *(emphasis)* You can use **from top to toe** to emphasize that the whole of someone's body is covered or dressed in a particular thing or type of clothing. ❑ *They were sensibly dressed from top to toe in rain gear.*
get on top of When something **gets on top of** you, it makes you feel unhappy or depressed because it is very difficult or worrying, or because it involves more work than you can manage. ❑ *Things have been getting on top of me lately.*
off the top of one's head If you say something **off the top of** your **head**, you say it without thinking about it much before you speak, especially because you do not have enough time. ❑ *It was the best I could think of off the top of my head.*

on top **1** You say that someone is **on top** when they have reached the most important position in an organization or business. ❑ *In such a fast-changing business, it's hard to stay on top.* **2** You can use **on top** or **on top of** to indicate that a particular problem exists in addition to a number of other problems. ❑ *A stepfamily faces all the problems that a normal family has, with a set of additional problems on top.*

on top of **1** If one thing is **on top** of another, it is placed over it or on its highest part. ❑ *He was sound asleep on top of the covers.* **2** If you **are on top of** or **get on top of** something that you are doing, you are dealing with it successfully. ❑ *the government's inability to get on top of the situation*

on top of the world *(emphasis)* If you say that you feel **on top of the world**, you are emphasizing that you feel extremely happy and healthy. ❑ *Two months before she gave birth to Jason she left work feeling on top of the world.*

over the top **1** If one thing is **over the top** of another, it is placed over it so that it is completely covering it. ❑ *I placed a sheet of plastic over the top of the container.* **2** *(informal)* You describe something as **over the top** when you think that it is exaggerated, and therefore unacceptable. = OTT ❑ *The special effects are a bit over the top but I enjoyed it.*

at the top of one's voice If you say something **at the top of** your **voice**, you say it very loudly. ❑ *'Stephen, come back!' shouted Marcia at the top of her voice.*

ADJ **1** [top + N] The **top** part or point of something is the highest part or point of it. ❑ *the top corner of the newspaper* **2** [top + N] The **top** thing or layer in a series of things or layers is the highest one. ❑ *I can't reach the top shelf.* **3** [top + N] You can use **top** to indicate that something or someone is at the highest level of a scale or measurement. ❑ *The vehicles have a top speed of 80 miles per hour.* **4** [top + N] A **top** person or job in an organization is at the highest level in the organization. ❑ *I need to have the top people in this company pull together.* **5** [top + N] You can use **top** to describe the most important or famous people or things in a particular area of work or activity. ❑ *So you want to be a top model.* **6** The **top** person or team is the one which has performed better than all the other people or teams. ❑ *He was the top student in physics.* **7** You can use **top** to indicate that something is the first thing you are going to do, because you consider it to be the most important. ❑ *Cleaning up the water supply is their top priority.* **8** [top + N] You can use **top** to indicate that someone does a particular thing more times than anyone else or that something is chosen more times than anything else. ❑ *Jamillah Lang was Colorado's top scorer.*
PHRASE **top dollar** [V + top dollar, top dollar + N] *(informal)* If someone pays **top dollar** for something, they pay the highest possible price for it. ❑ *People will always pay top dollar for something exclusive.*
VERB [T] (**tops, topping, topped**) *(journalism)* To **top** a list means to be mentioned or chosen more times than anyone or anything else. ❑ *It was the first time in years that a Japanese manufacturer had not topped the list for imported vehicles.*
PHRASAL VERB **top up** *(mainly BrE)* If you **top** something **up**, you make it full again when part of it has been used. ❑ *We topped up the water tanks.*

✪ **top·ic** /ˈtɒpɪk/ NOUN [C] (**topics**) *(academic word)* A **topic** is a particular subject that you discuss, study, or write about. = subject, matter, theme ❑ *The weather is a constant topic of conversation in Alaska.* ❑ *The main topic for discussion is political union.* ❑ *This topic is explored more fully in chapter 5.*

top·i·cal /ˈtɒpɪkəl/ ADJ **Topical** is used to describe something that concerns or relates to events that are happening at the present time. = current ❑ *The newscast covers topical events and entertainment.*

top·ple /ˈtɒpəl/ VERB
VERB [I, T] (**topples, toppling, toppled**) **1** [I, T] If someone or something **topples** somewhere or if you **topple** them, they become unsteady or unstable and fall over. ❑ *He just released his hold and toppled slowly backwards.* **2** [T]

(*journalism*) To **topple** a government or leader, especially one that is not elected by the people, means to cause them to lose power. = overthrow ❑ *the revolution which toppled the regime*

PHRASAL VERB **topple over** means the same as **topple** VERB **1**. ❑ *The tree is so badly damaged they are worried it might topple over.*

torch /tɔːtʃ/ NOUN [c] (**torches**) **1** (*BrE*; in *AmE*, use **flashlight**) A **torch** is a small electric light which is powered by batteries and which you can carry in your hand. **2** A **torch** is a long stick with burning material at one end, used to provide light or to set things on fire. ❑ *The shepherd followed, carrying a torch to light his way.* **3** A **torch** is a device that produces a hot flame and is used for tasks such as cutting or joining pieces of metal. ❑ *The gang worked for up to ten hours with acetylene torches to open the vault.*

tore /tɔː/ IRREG FORM **Tore** is the past tense of **tear**.

tor·ment NOUN, VERB
NOUN /'tɔːment/ [u, c] (**torments**) **1** [u] **Torment** is extreme suffering, usually mental suffering. = anguish ❑ *After years of turmoil and torment, she is finally at peace.* **2** [c] A **torment** is something that causes extreme suffering, usually mental suffering. ❑ *Sooner or later most writers end up making books about the torments of being a writer.*
VERB /tɔː'ment/ [T] (**torments, tormenting, tormented**) If something **torments** you, it causes you extreme mental suffering. = torture ❑ *At times the memories returned to torment her.*

torn /tɔːn/ IRREG FORM, ADJ
IRREG FORM **Torn** is the past participle of **tear**.
ADJ If you are **torn between** two or more things, you cannot decide which to choose, and so you feel anxious or troubled. ❑ *Robb is torn between becoming a doctor and a career in athletics.*

tor·na·do /tɔː'neɪdəʊ/ NOUN [c] (**tornadoes** or **tornados**) A **tornado** is a violent wind storm consisting of a tall column of air which spins around very fast and causes a lot of damage.

tor·ture ♦♢♢ /'tɔːtʃə/ VERB, NOUN
VERB [T] (**tortures, torturing, tortured**) **1** If someone **is tortured**, another person deliberately causes them terrible pain over a period of time, in order to punish them or to make them reveal information. ❑ *Despite being tortured she proclaimed her innocence.* **2** To **torture** someone means to cause them to suffer mental pain or anxiety. = torment ❑ *He would not torture her further by trying to argue with her.*
NOUN [c, u] (**tortures**) **Torture** is deliberately causing someone pain over a period of time, in order to punish them or to make them reveal information. ❑ *alleged cases of torture and murder by the security forces*

toss /tɒs, *AmE* tɔːs/ VERB, NOUN
VERB [T] (**tosses, tossing, tossed**) **1** If you **toss** something somewhere, you throw it there lightly, often in a careless way. ❑ *Just toss it in the rubbish.* **2** If you **toss** your head or **toss** your hair, you move your head backwards, quickly and suddenly, often as a way of expressing an emotion such as anger or contempt. ❑ *'I'm sure I don't know.' Deb tossed her head.* **3** In sports and informal situations, if you decide something by **tossing** a coin, you spin a coin into the air and guess which side of the coin will face upwards when it lands. ❑ *We tossed a coin to decide who would go out and buy the bagels.*
PHRASE **toss and turn** If you **toss and turn**, you keep moving around in bed and cannot sleep, for example, because you are sick or worried. ❑ *I try to go back to sleep and toss and turn for a while.*
NOUN [c] (**tosses**) **1** A **toss** of the head is when you move your head backwards quickly and suddenly. ❑ *With a toss of his head and a few hard gulps, Bob finished the last of his beer.* **2** A **toss** of a coin is the act of spinning it into the air and guessing which side will face upwards when it lands. ❑ *It would be better to decide it on the toss of a coin.*

✪to·tal ♦♦♦ /'təʊtəl/ NOUN, ADJ, VERB
NOUN [c] (**totals**) A **total** is the number that you get when you add several numbers together or when you count how many things there are in a group. = sum ❑ *The companies have a total of 1,776 employees.*
PHRASE **in total** If there are a number of things **in total**, there are that number when you count or add them all together. ❑ *I was with my husband for eight years in total.*
ADJ **1** [total + N] The **total** number or cost of something is the number or cost that you get when you add together or count all the parts in it. = whole, aggregate; ≠ partial ❑ *They said that the total number of cows dying from BSE would be twenty thousand.* ❑ *The total cost of the project would be more than $240 million.* **2** You can use **total** to emphasize that something is as great in extent, degree, or amount as it possibly can be. = complete ❑ *You were a total failure if you hadn't married by the time you were about twenty-three.*
VERB [T] (**totals, totalling, totalled**; in *AmE*, use **totaling, totaled**) If several numbers or things **total** a certain figure, that figure is the total of all the numbers or all the things. ❑ *The unit's exports will total $85 million this year.*

to·tal·ly /'təʊtəli/ ADV = completely ❑ *Young people want something totally different from the old ways.*

to·tali·tar·ian /ˌtəʊtælɪ'teəriən/ ADJ (*disapproval*) A **totalitarian** political system is one in which there is only one political party which controls everything and does not allow any opposition parties. ❑ *a brutal totalitarian regime*

touch ♦♦♢ /tʌtʃ/ VERB, NOUN, QUANT
VERB [I, T, RECIP] (**touches, touching, touched**) **1** [I, T] If you **touch** something, you put your hand onto it in order to feel it or to make contact with it. ❑ *Her tiny hands gently touched my face.* ❑ *Don't touch!* **2** [RECIP] If two things **are touching**, or if one thing **touches** another, or if you **touch** two things, their surfaces come into contact with each other. ❑ *Their knees were touching.* ❑ *A cyclist crashed when he touched wheels with another rider.* **3** [T] To **touch** something means to strike it, usually quite gently. ❑ *He scored the first time he touched the ball.* **4** [T] If something **has** not **been touched**, nobody has dealt with it or taken care of it. ❑ *When John began to restore the house in the 1960s, nothing had been touched for 40 years.* **5** [T] If you say that you did not **touch** someone or something, you are emphasizing that you did not attack, harm, or destroy them, especially when you have been accused of doing so. ❑ *Pearce remained adamant, saying 'I didn't touch him.'* **6** [T] You say that you never **touch** something or that you have not **touched** something for a long time to emphasize that you never use it, or you have not used it for a long time. ❑ *He doesn't drink much and doesn't touch drugs.* **7** [I] If you **touch on** a particular subject or problem, you mention it or write briefly about it. ❑ *The film touches on these issues, but only superficially.* **8** [T] If something **touches** you, it affects you in some way for a short time. ❑ *a guilt that in some sense touches everyone* **9** [T] If something that someone says or does **touches** you, it affects you emotionally, often because you see that they are suffering a lot or that they are being very kind. = move ❑ *It has touched me deeply to see how these people live.*
PHRASAL VERBS **touch down** When an aircraft **touches down**, it lands. = land ❑ *The space shuttle touched down yesterday.*
touch off If something **touches off** a situation or series of events, it causes it to start happening. = spark off ❑ *The lightning could touch off wildfires in Eastern Washington.*
touch up If you **touch** something **up**, you improve its appearance by covering up small marks with paint or another substance. ❑ *editing tools to help people touch up photos* ❑ *The painting has yellowed but the gallery has resisted pressure to touch it up.*
NOUN [c, u, SING] (**touches**) **1** [c] A **touch** is the act of putting your hand onto something in order to feel it or make contact with it. ❑ *Sometimes even a light touch on the face is enough to trigger off this pain.* **2** [u] Your sense of **touch** is your ability to tell what something is like when you feel it with your hands. ❑ *The evidence suggests that our sense of touch is programmed to diminish with age.* **3** [c] [SUPP + touch] A **touch** is a detail which is added to something to improve it. ❑ *They called the event 'a tribute to heroes', which was a nice touch.* **4** [SING] If someone has a particular kind of **touch**, they have a particular way of doing

something. □ *The dishes he produces all have a personal touch.* PHRASES **at the touch of** You use **at the touch of** in expressions such as **at the touch of a button** and **at the touch of a key** to indicate that something is possible by simply touching a switch or one of the keys of a keyboard. □ *Staff will be able to trace calls at the touch of a button.*

in touch If you get **in touch with** someone, you contact them by writing to them or telephoning them. If you are, keep, or stay **in touch with** them, you write, phone, or visit each other regularly. □ *I will get in touch with my lawyer about this.*

in touch or **out of touch** If you are **in touch with** a subject or situation, or if someone keeps you **in touch with** it, you know the latest news or information about it. If you are **out of touch** with it, you do not know the latest news or information about it. □ *keeping the unemployed in touch with the job market*

lose touch **1** If you **lose touch with** someone, you gradually stop writing, telephoning, or visiting them. □ *In my job one tends to lose touch with friends.* **2** If you **lose touch with** something, you no longer have the latest news or information about it. □ *Their leaders have lost touch with what is happening in the country.*

QUANT ['ə' touch 'of' N-UNCOUNT] **A touch of** something is a very small amount of it. □ *She thought she just had a touch of the flu.*

touched /tʌtʃt/ ADJ □ *I was touched to find that he regards me as engaging.*

→ See also **touching**

♦ **the finishing touch** → see finish; **touch wood** → see wood

touch·ing /'tʌtʃɪŋ/ ADJ If something is **touching**, it causes feelings of sadness or sympathy. = moving □ *Her story is the touching tale of a wife who stood by the husband she loved.*

touchy /'tʌtʃi/ ADJ (**touchier, touchiest**) (*disapproval*) If you describe someone as **touchy**, you mean that they are easily upset, offended, or irritated. = sensitive □ *She is very touchy about her past.*

tough ♦♦◇ /tʌf/ ADJ (**tougher, toughest**) **1** A **tough** person is strong and determined, and can tolerate difficulty or suffering. □ *He built up a reputation as a tough businessman.* **2** If you describe someone as **tough**, you mean that they are rough and violent. □ *He had shot three people dead earning himself a reputation as a tough guy.* **3** A **tough** place or area is considered to have a lot of crime and violence. = rough □ *She doesn't seem cut out for this tough neighborhood.* **4** A **tough** way of life or period of time is difficult or full of suffering. = rough □ *She had a pretty tough childhood.* **5** A **tough** task or problem is difficult to do or solve. = hard □ *It was a very tough decision but we feel we made the right one.* **6** **Tough** policies or actions are strict and firm. = strong □ *He is known for taking a tough line on security.* **7** A **tough** substance is strong, and difficult to break, cut, or tear. □ *In industry, diamond can form a tough, non-corrosive coating for tools.* **8** **Tough** meat is difficult to cut and chew. □ *The steak was tough and the peas were like bullets.*

tough·ness /'tʌfnəs/ NOUN [u] □ *Ms Potter has won a reputation for toughness and determination on her way to the top.*

tough·en /'tʌfən/ VERB

VERB [T] (**toughens, toughening, toughened**) **1** If you **toughen** something or if it **toughens**, you make it stronger so that it will not break easily. □ *Months of walking barefoot had toughened his feet.* **2** If a person, institution, or law **toughens** its policies, regulations, or punishments, it makes them firmer or stricter. □ *Talks are under way to toughen trade restrictions.* **3** If an experience **toughens** you, it makes you stronger and more independent in character. □ *They believe that participating in fights toughens boys and shows them how to be men.*

PHRASAL VERB **toughen up** **1** **Toughen up** means the same as **toughen** VERB 2. □ *The new law toughens up penalties for those that misuse guns.* **2** **Toughen up** means the same as **toughen** VERB 3. □ *He thinks boxing is good for kids, that it toughens them up.*

tour ♦♦◇ /tʊə/ NOUN, VERB

NOUN [c] (**tours**) **1** A **tour** is an organized trip that people such as musicians, politicians, or theatre companies go on to several different places, stopping to meet people or perform. □ *The band is currently on a two-month tour of Europe.* **2** A **tour** is a trip during which you visit several places that interest you. □ *It was week five of my tour of the major cities of Europe.* **3** A **tour** is a short trip that you make around a place, for example, around a historical building, so that you can look at it. □ *a guided tour*

PHRASE **on tour** When people are travelling on a tour, you can say that they are **on tour**. □ *The band will be going on tour.*

VERB [i, T] (**tours, touring, toured**) **1** [i, T] When people such as musicians, politicians, or theatre companies **tour**, they go on a tour, for example, in order to perform or to meet people. □ *A few years ago they toured the country with a roadshow.* **2** [T] If you **tour** a place, you go on a trip or journey around it. □ *You can also tour the site on bicycle.*

♦**tour·ism** /'tʊərɪzəm/ NOUN [u] **Tourism** is the business of providing services for people on holiday, for example, hotels, restaurants, and excursions. □ *Tourism is vital for the economy.*

♦**tour·ist** ♦◇◇ /'tʊərɪst/ NOUN [c] (**tourists**) A **tourist** is a person who is visiting a place for pleasure and interest, especially when they are on holiday. = traveller; ≠ local, native □ *a tourist attraction* □ *places frequented by foreign tourists* □ *a heritage site which attracts 300,000 tourists each year*

tour·na·ment ♦◇◇ /'tʊənəmənt/ NOUN [c] (**tournaments**) A **tournament** is a sports competition in which players who win a match continue to play further matches in the competition until just one person or team is left. □ *the biggest golf tournament to be held in Australia*

tow /təʊ/ VERB [T] (**tows, towing, towed**) If one vehicle **tows** another, it pulls it along behind it. □ *He had been using the vehicle to tow his work trailer.* □ *They threatened to tow away my car.*

to·wards ♦♦♦ /tə'wɔːdz, AmE tɔːrdz/ also **toward** PREP

> In addition to the uses shown below, **towards** is used in phrasal verbs such as 'count towards' and 'lean towards'.

1 If you move, look, or point **towards** something or someone, you move, look, or point in their direction. □ *They were all moving towards him down the stairs.* □ *When he looked towards me, I smiled and waved.* **2** [towards + N/-ING] If things develop **towards** a particular situation, that situation becomes nearer in time or more likely to happen. □ *The agreement is a major step towards peace.* **3** If you have a particular attitude **towards** something or someone, you have that attitude when you think about them or deal with them. □ *My attitude towards religion has been shaped by this man.* **4** If something happens **towards** a particular time, it happens just before that time. □ *There was a forecast of cooler weather towards the end of the week.* **5** If something is **towards** part of a place or thing, it is near that part. □ *Gulls are nesting on a small island towards the eastern shore.* **6** If you give money **towards** something, you give it to help pay for that thing. □ *Taxes only get part of the way towards a $50 billion deficit.*

tow·el /taʊəl/ NOUN, VERB

NOUN [c] (**towels**) A **towel** is a piece of thick soft cloth that you use to dry yourself. □ *a bath towel* □ *a hand towel* □ *a beach towel*

PHRASE **throw in the towel** (*informal*) If you **throw in the towel**, you stop trying to do something because you realize that you cannot succeed. □ *It seemed as if the police had thrown in the towel and were abandoning the investigation.*

VERB [T] (**towels, towelling, towelled**; in AmE, use **toweling, toweled**) If you **towel** something or **towel** it dry, you dry it with a towel. □ *James came out of his bedroom, towelling his wet hair.* □ *I towelled myself dry.*

tow·er ♦◇◇ /taʊə/ NOUN, VERB

NOUN [c] (**towers**) **1** A **tower** is a tall, narrow building, that either stands alone or forms part of another building such as a church or castle. □ *an eleventh-century castle with*

120-foot high towers **2** A **tower** is a tall structure that is used for sending radio or television signals. ❑ *Troops are still in control of the television and radio tower.* **3** *(computing)* A **tower** is a tall box that contains the main parts of a computer, such as the hard disk and the drives.

VERB [I] (**towers**, **towering**, **towered**) Someone or something that **towers over** surrounding people or things is a lot taller than they are. ❑ *He stood up and towered over her.*

town ◆◆◆ /taʊn/ NOUN [C, U] (**towns**) **1** [C] A **town** is a place with streets and buildings, where people live and work. Towns are larger than neighbourhoods and smaller than cities. In informal English, cities are sometimes called towns. ❑ *the northern California town of Albany* **2** [C] You can use **the town** to refer to the people of a town. ❑ *The town takes immense pride in recent achievements.* **3** [U] You use **town** in order to refer to the central area of a town where most of the shops and offices are. ❑ *I walked into town.*

→ See also **downtown**

✪ **tox·ic** /ˈtɒksɪk/ ADJ A **toxic** substance is poisonous. = poisonous, dangerous; ≠ non-toxic, safe ❑ *the cost of cleaning up toxic waste* ❑ *These products are not toxic to humans.*

toy ◆◇◇ /tɔɪ/ NOUN

NOUN [C] (**toys**) A **toy** is an object that children play with, for example, a doll or a model car. ❑ *He was really too old for children's toys.*

PHRASAL VERB **toy with** (**toys**, **toying**, **toyed**) **1** If you **toy with** an idea, you consider it casually without making any decisions about it. ❑ *He toyed with the idea of going to China.* **2** If you **toy with** food or drink, you do not eat or drink it with any enthusiasm, but only take a bite or a little drink from time to time. ❑ *She had no appetite, and merely toyed with the bread and cheese.*

✪ **trace** ◆◇◇ /treɪs/ VERB, NOUN *(academic word)*

VERB [T] (**traces**, **tracing**, **traced**) **1** If you **trace** the origin or development of something, you find out or describe how it started or developed. ❑ *The exhibition traces the history of graphic design in America from the 19th century to the present.* ❑ *The psychiatrist successfully traced some of her problems to severe childhood traumas.* **2** If you **trace** someone or something, you find them after looking for them. ❑ *Police are anxious to trace two men seen leaving the house just before 8am.* **3** If you **trace** something such as a pattern or a shape, for example, with your finger or toe, you mark its outline on a surface. ❑ *I traced the course of the river on the map spread out on my briefcase.* **4** If you **trace** a picture, you copy it by covering it with a piece of transparent paper and drawing over the lines underneath. ❑ *She learned to draw by tracing pictures out of old storybooks.*

PHRASAL VERB **trace back** Trace back means the same as **trace** VERB **1**. ❑ *Bronx residents who trace their families back to Dutch settlers* ❑ *Britain's Parliament can trace its history back to the English Parliament of the 13th century.* ❑ *The traditional format of the almanac can be traced back for at least a thousand years.*

NOUN [C] (**traces**) A **trace of** something is a very small amount of it. = vestige, fragment ❑ *Wash them in cold water to remove all traces of sand.* ❑ *The technique could scan luggage at airports for traces of explosives.* ❑ *said without a trace of irony*

PHRASE **disappear without a trace** If you say that someone or something **disappears without a trace**, you mean that they stop existing or stop being successful very suddenly and completely. ❑ *One day he left, disappeared without a trace.*

track ◆◆◇ /træk/ NOUN, VERB

NOUN [C, PL] (**tracks**) **1** [C] A **track** is a rough, unpaved road or path. = path ❑ *We set off once more, over a rough mountain track.* **2** [C] A **track** is a piece of ground, often oval-shaped, that is used for races involving running, cars, bicycles, horses, or dogs called greyhounds. ❑ *the athletics track* **3** [C] Railway **tracks** are the rails that a train travels along. ❑ *A cow stood on the tracks.* **4** [C] A **track** is one of the songs or pieces of music on a CD, record, or tape. ❑ *I only like two of the ten tracks on this CD.* **5** [PL] **Tracks** are

marks left in the ground by the feet of animals or people. ❑ *The only evidence of pandas was their tracks in the snow.*

PHRASES **keep track** If you **keep track of** a situation or a person, you make sure that you have the newest and most accurate information about them all the time. ❑ *With eleven thousand employees, it's very difficult to keep track of them all.*

lose track of If you **lose track of** someone or something, you no longer know where they are or what is happening. ❑ *You become so deeply absorbed in an activity that you lose track of time.*

on track If someone or something is **on track**, they are acting or progressing in a way that is likely to result in success. ❑ *It may take some time to get the economy back on track.*

on the right track or **on the wrong track** If you are **on the right track**, you are acting or progressing in a way that is likely to result in success. If you are **on the wrong track**, you are acting or progressing in a way that is likely to result in failure. ❑ *Guests are returning in increasing numbers – a sure sign that we are on the right track.*

stop dead in your tracks If someone or something **stops** you **in** your **tracks**, or if you **stop dead in your tracks**, you suddenly stop moving because you are very surprised, impressed, or frightened. ❑ *This magnificent church cannot fail to stop you in your tracks.*

stop in its tracks or **stop dead in its tracks** If someone or something **stops** a process or activity **in its tracks**, or if it **stops dead in its tracks**, they prevent the process or activity from continuing. ❑ *Francis felt he would like to stop this conversation in its tracks.*

VERB [T] (**tracks**, **tracking**, **tracked**) **1** If you **track** animals or people, you try to follow them by looking for the signs that they have left behind, for example, the marks left by their feet. ❑ *He thought he had better track this wolf and see where it lived.* **2** To **track** someone or something means to follow their movements by means of a special device, such as a satellite or radar. ❑ *Our radar began tracking the jets.*

PHRASAL VERB **track down** If you **track down** someone or something, you find them, or find information about them, after a difficult or long search. ❑ *She had spent years trying to track down her parents.*

♦ **off the beaten track** → see **beaten**

✪ **trade** ◆◆◆ /treɪd/ VERB, NOUN

VERB [I, RECIP] (**trades**, **trading**, **traded**) **1** [I, RECIP] If someone **trades** one thing for another or if two people **trade** things, they agree to exchange one thing for the other thing. ❑ *They traded land for goods and money.* ❑ *Kids used to trade football cards.* **2** [RECIP] If you **trade places with** someone or if the two of you **trade places**, you move into the other person's position or situation, and they move into yours. = exchange ❑ *Mike asked George to trade places with him so he could ride with Tomas.* **3** [RECIP] If two people or groups **trade** something such as blows, insults, or jokes, they hit each other, insult each other, or tell each other jokes. = exchange ❑ *Children would settle disputes by trading punches or insults in the playground.* **4** [I] *(business)* When people, companies, or countries **trade**, they buy, sell, or exchange goods or services between themselves. = do business ❑ *They may refuse to trade, even when offered attractive prices.* ❑ *They had years of experience of trading with the West.* ❑ *He has been trading in antique furniture for 25 years.*

PHRASAL VERBS **trade down** If someone **trades down**, they sell something such as their car or house and buy a less expensive one. ❑ *They are selling their five-bedroom house and trading down to a two-bedroom apartment.*

trade up If someone **trades up**, they sell something such as their car or their house and buy a more expensive one. ❑ *Petrol prices are discouraging small car owners from trading up to larger cars.*

NOUN [U, C] (**trades**) **1** [U, C] *(business)* **Trade** is the activity of buying, selling, or exchanging goods or services between people, companies, or countries. = commerce, business ❑ *Texas has a long history of trade with Mexico.* ❑ *negotiations on a new international trade agreement* ❑ *The ministry had direct control over every aspect of foreign trade.* **2** [C] *(business)* A **trade** is a particular area of business or industry. ❑ *They've ruined the tourist trade for the next few*

t

years. **3** [C] [oft POSS + trade, also 'by' trade] (*business*) Someone's **trade** is the kind of work that they do, especially when they have been trained to do it over a period of time. □ *He learned his trade as a diver in the North Sea.* **4** [C] (*mainly AmE; in BrE, usually use* **exchange**) A **trade** is an agreement to exchange one thing for another thing. □ *I am willing to make a trade with you.*

trad·ing /ˈtreɪdɪŋ/ NOUN [U] □ *Trading on the stock exchange may be suspended.*

WORD CONNECTIONS

ADJ + trade

international trade
foreign trade
global trade
□ *In 1958 Japan began to expland its foreign trade.*

free trade
fair trade
□ *The Ethical Trading Initiative is an alliance of organizations that promotes free trade.*

illegal trade
illicit trade
□ *Customs officials estimate they detect only about 5% of the illicit trade in tobacco and alcohol.*

---

trade-in NOUN [C] (**trade-ins**) (*business*) A **trade-in** is an arrangement in which someone buys a new car at a reduced price by giving their old one, as well as money, in payment. □ *the trade-in value of the car*

trad·er ◆◇◇ /ˈtreɪdə/ NOUN [C] (**traders**) (*business*) A **trader** is a person whose job is to trade in goods or shares. □ *Market traders display an exotic selection of the island's produce.*

trade un·ion NOUN [C] (**trade unions**) A **trade union** is an organization that represents the rights and interests of workers to their employers, for example in order to improve working conditions or wages. □ *UNISON, the UK's largest trade union*

❂tra·di·tion ◆◇◇ /trəˈdɪʃən/ NOUN [C, U] (**traditions**) (*academic word*) A **tradition** is a custom or belief that has existed for a long time. = custom, heritage, culture, practice, ritual □ *the rich traditions of Afro-Cuban music and dance* □ *Mary has carried on the family tradition of giving away plants.* □ *The story of King Arthur became part of oral tradition.*

WORD CONNECTIONS

VERB + tradition

uphold a tradition
maintain a tradition
preserve a tradition
continue a tradition
□ *He is committed to upholding the traditions of the team.*

ADJ + tradition

a **long** tradition
an **ancient** tradition
a **proud** tradition
□ *Costa Rica has a proud tradition of coffee production.*

an **oral** tradition
□ *These ideas have been kept alive by oral traditions for centuries.*

VOCABULARY BUILDER

tradition NOUN
A **tradition** is a custom or belief that has existed for a long time.
□ *We had strong family traditions; we couldn't escape them.*

custom NOUN
A **custom** is an activity, a way of behaving, or an event which is usual or traditional in a particular society or in particular circumstances.
□ *The custom of lighting the Olympic flame goes back centuries.*

---

heritage NOUN (*formal*)
A country's **heritage** is all the qualities, traditions, or features of life there that have continued over many years and have been passed on from one generation to another.
□ *the rich heritage of Russian folk music*

culture NOUN (*fairly formal*)
The **culture** of a particular organization or group consists of the habits of the people in it and the way they generally behave.
□ *people from different cultures*

practice NOUN
You can refer to something that people do regularly as a **practice**.
□ *parents whose child-rearing practices may be different from those of their grandparents*

ritual NOUN (*formal*)
A **ritual** is a way of behaving or a series of actions that people regularly carry out in a particular situation, because it is their custom to do so.
□ *Often our rules become rituals, regular patterns of behaviour which have a magical quality.*

❂tra·di·tion·al ◆◆◇ /trəˈdɪʃənəl/ ADJ **1** Traditional customs, beliefs, or methods are ones that have existed for a long time without changing. = old-fashioned, conventional; ≠ modern, contemporary □ *Traditional teaching methods sometimes only succeeded in putting students off learning.* □ *traditional Indian music* □ *pipers in traditional highland dress* **2** A **traditional** organization or person prefers older methods and ideas to modern ones. □ *We're still a traditional school in a lot of ways.*

❂tra·di·tion·al·ly /trəˈdɪʃnəli/ ADV **1** [traditionally with CL/GROUP] = conventionally, usually, generally □ *Married women have traditionally been treated as dependent on their husbands.* □ *Some jobs, such as nursing, are traditionally associated with women.* **2** *He is loathed by some of the more traditionally minded officers.*

❂traf·fic ◆◇◇ /ˈtræfɪk/ NOUN, VERB
NOUN [U] **1** [also 'the' traffic] **Traffic** refers to all the vehicles that are moving along the roads in a particular area. = vehicles □ *There was heavy traffic on the roads.* □ *Traffic was unusually light for that time of day.* □ *the problems of city life, such as traffic congestion* **2** **Traffic** refers to the movement of ships, trains, or aircraft between one place and another. **Traffic** also refers to the people and goods that are being transported. □ *Air traffic had returned to normal.* **3** **Traffic in** something such as drugs or stolen goods is an illegal trade in them. □ *the widespread traffic in stolen cultural artifacts*
VERB [I] (**traffics, trafficking, trafficked**) Someone who **traffics in** something such as drugs or stolen goods buys and sells them even though it is illegal to do so. □ *The president said illegal drugs are hurting the entire world and anyone who traffics in them should be brought to justice.*

traf·fick·ing /ˈtræfɪkɪŋ/ NOUN [U] □ *He was sentenced to ten years in prison on charges of drug trafficking.*

trag·e·dy ◆◇◇ /ˈtrædʒɪdi/ NOUN [C, U] (**tragedies**) **1** A **tragedy** is an extremely sad event or situation. □ *They have suffered an enormous personal tragedy.* **2** **Tragedy** is a type of literature, especially drama, that is serious and sad, and often ends with the death of the main character. □ *The story has elements of tragedy and farce.*

trag·ic /ˈtrædʒɪk/ ADJ **1** A **tragic** event or situation is extremely sad, usually because it involves death or suffering. □ *It was just a tragic accident.* □ *the tragic loss of so many lives* **2** [tragic + N] **Tragic** is used to refer to tragedy as a type of literature. □ *Shakespeare's tragic hero, Hamlet*

tragi·cal·ly /ˈtrædʒɪkli/ ADV □ *Tragically, she never saw the completed building because she died before it was finished.*

trail ◆◇◇ /treɪl/ NOUN, VERB
NOUN [C] (**trails**) **1** A **trail** is a rough path across open country or through forests. = track □ *He was following a trail through the trees.* **2** A **trail** is a route along a series of

paths or roads, often one that has been planned and marked out for a particular purpose. □ *a large area of woodland with hiking and walking trails* ◼3 A **trail** is a series of marks or other signs of movement or other activities left by someone or something. □ *Everywhere in the house was a sticky trail of orange juice.* ◼4 You can refer to all the places that a politician visits in the period before an election as their campaign **trail**. □ *During a recent speech on the campaign trail, he was interrupted by hecklers.*

PHRASE on the trail of If you are **on the trail of** a person or thing, you are trying hard to find them or find out about them. □ *The police were hot on his trail.*

VERB [T, I] (**trails, trailing, trailed**) ◼1 [T] If you **trail** someone or something, you follow them secretly, often by finding the marks or signs that they have left. = follow □ *Two detectives were trailing him.* ◼2 [I, T] If you **trail** something or it **trails**, it hangs down loosely behind you as you move along. = drag □ *She came down the stairs slowly, trailing the coat behind her.*

trail·er /ˈtreɪlə/ NOUN [C] (**trailers**) ◼1 A **trailer** is a container on wheels which is pulled by a car or other vehicle and which is used for transporting large or heavy items. ◼2 A **trailer** for a film or television programme is a set of short extracts which are shown to advertise it. = preview □ *a misleadingly violent trailer for the movie*

⭐ **train** ♦♦◇ /treɪn/ NOUN, VERB

NOUN [C] (**trains**) ◼1 [also 'by' train] A **train** is a number of containers on wheels which are all connected together and which are pulled by an engine along a railway. Trains carry people and goods from one place to another. □ *The train pulled into a station.* □ *We can catch the early morning train.* ◼2 A **train** of vehicles, people, or animals is a long line of them travelling slowly in the same direction. □ *In the old days this used to be done with a baggage train of camels.* ◼3 A **train** of thought or a **train** of events is a connected sequence, in which each thought or event seems to occur naturally or logically as a result of the previous one. □ *He lost his train of thought for a moment, then recovered it.*

VERB [I, T] (**trains, training, trained**) ◼1 [I, T] If someone **trains** you to do something, they teach you the skills that you need in order to do it. If you **train to** do something, you learn the skills that you need in order to do it. = educate, teach, prepare □ *He was training us to be soldiers.* □ *The US was ready to train its troops to participate.* □ *Psychiatrists initially train as doctors.* □ *We don't train them only in bricklaying, but also in other building techniques.* □ *I'm a trained nurse.* ◼2 [T] To **train** a natural quality or talent that someone has, for example, their voice or musical ability, means to help them to develop it. □ *I see my degree as something which will train my mind and improve my chances of getting a job.* ◼3 [I, T] If you **train for** a physical activity such as a race or if someone **trains** you **for** it, you prepare for it by doing particular physical exercises. □ *Strachan is training for the new season.* ◼4 [T] If an animal or bird is **trained to** do particular things, it is taught to do them, for example, in order to be able to work for someone or to be a good pet. □ *Sniffer dogs could be trained to track them down.*

-trained /treɪnd/ COMB □ *Michael is a professionally-trained chef.*

→ See also **training**

⭐ **trainee** /treɪˈniː/ NOUN [C] (**trainees**) [oft trainee + N] (*business*) A **trainee** is someone who is employed at a low level in a particular job in order to learn the skills needed for that job. = apprentice, learner □ *He is a 24-year-old trainee reporter.*

train·er /ˈtreɪnə/ NOUN [C] (**trainers**) ◼1 A **trainer** is someone who teaches people the skills that they need in order to do something. □ *a book for both teachers and teacher trainers* ◼2 A **trainer** is someone who helps people to prepare for a physical activity such as a race by doing particular physical exercises. □ *She went to the gym with her personal trainer.* ◼3 A **trainer** is someone who teaches animals or birds to do particular things, for example, in order to be able to work for someone or to be a good pet. □ *The horse made a winning start for his new trainer.* ◼4 (*BrE;*

in *AmE*, use **sneakers**) **Trainers** are shoes that people wear, especially for running and other sports.

⭐ **train·ing** /ˈtreɪnɪŋ/ NOUN [U] ◼1 (*business*) **Training** is the process of learning the skills that you need for a particular job or activity. = education, instruction, teaching, preparation □ *He called for much higher spending on education and training.* □ *Kennedy had no formal training as a decorator.* ◼2 **Training** is physical exercise that you do regularly in order to keep fit or to prepare for an activity such as a race. □ *The emphasis is on developing fitness through exercises and training.*

USAGE NOTE
training
Training is an uncountable noun. Do not use 'trainings' or 'a training'. You can talk about 'a training course', 'a training session' or 'a training programme'.
*Last year, 2000 teachers received basic computer **training**. They meet once a month for workshops and **training sessions**.*

⭐ **trait** /treɪt, treɪ/ NOUN [C] (**traits**) A **trait** is a particular characteristic, quality, or tendency that someone or something has. = characteristic, attribute, quality □ *The study found that some alcoholics had clear personality traits showing up early in childhood.* □ *Do we inherit traits such as agility and sporting excellence, and musical or artistic ability?*

trai·tor /ˈtreɪtə/ NOUN [C] (**traitors**) ◼1 (*disapproval*) If you call someone a **traitor**, you mean that they have betrayed beliefs that they used to hold, or that their friends hold, by their words or actions. □ *Some say he's a traitor to the peace movement.* ◼2 If someone is a **traitor**, they betray their country, friends, or a group of which they are a member by helping its enemies, especially during time of war. □ *rumours that there were traitors among us who were sending messages to the enemy*

trans·ac·tion ♦◇◇ /trænˈzækʃən/ NOUN [C] (**transactions**) (*formal, business*) A **transaction** is a piece of business, for example, an act of buying or selling something. □ *The transaction is completed by payment of the fee.*

WORD PARTS
The prefix **trans-** often appears in words that have movement or change as part of their meaning:
transaction (NOUN)
transform (VERB)

trans·cend /trænˈsend/ VERB [T] (**transcends, transcending, transcended**) Something that **transcends** normal limits or boundaries goes beyond them, because it is more significant than them. □ *issues like disaster relief that transcend party loyalty*

trans·con·ti·nen·tal /ˌtrænskɒntɪˈnentəl/ ADJ [usu transcontinental + N] A **transcontinental** journey or route goes from one side of a continent to the other. □ *in mid-nineteenth-century America, before the transcontinental railway was built*

⭐ **tran·scribe** /trænˈskraɪb/ VERB [T] (**transcribes, transcribing, transcribed**) If you **transcribe** a speech or text, you write it out in a different form from the one in which it exists, for example by writing it out in full from notes or from a tape recording. □ *She is transcribing, from his dictation, the diaries of Simon Forman.* □ *Every telephone conversation will be recorded and transcribed.*

⭐ **tran·script** /ˈtrænskrɪpt/ NOUN [C] (**transcripts**) A **transcript** of a conversation or speech is a written text of it, based on a recording or notes. □ *A transcript of this programme is available through our website.* □ *The data collected for each patient included a transcript of the interview and the interviewer's notes.* □ *reconstructing the case from an array of court transcripts*

⭐ **trans·fer** ♦♦◇ /trænsˈfɜː/ VERB, NOUN (*academic word*)

VERB /trænsˈfɜː/ [I, T] (**transfers, transferring, transferred**) ◼1 [I, T] If you **transfer** something or someone **from** one place **to** another, or they **transfer from** one place **to** another, they go from the first place to the second.

t

= move ❑ *Transfer the meat to a platter and leave in a warm place.* ❑ *He wants to transfer some money to the account of his daughter.* ❑ *The person can transfer from wheelchair to seat with relative ease.* **2** [I, T] If something **is transferred**, or **transfers, from** one person or group of people **to** another, the second person or group gets it instead of the first. = pass ❑ *The decision to transfer the investigation from the police to the district attorney's office is a mutual one.* ❑ *The chances of the disease being transferred to humans is extremely remote.* ❑ *On 1 December the presidency of the Security Council automatically transfers from the US to Yemen.* **3** [I, T] If you **are transferred**, or if you **transfer, to** a different job or place, the company moves you to a different job or you start working in a different part of the same company or organization. ❑ *I was transferred to the book department.* ❑ *I suspect that she is going to be transferred to Fort Meyer.* **4** [T] When information **is transferred onto** a different medium, it is copied from one medium to another. ❑ *Such information is easily transferred onto microfilm.* **NOUN** /'trænsfɜ:/ [C, U] **(transfers) 1** [C, U] [oft transfer 'of' N] **Transfer** is the movement of something or someone from one place to another. ❑ *Arrange for the transfer of medical records to your new doctor.* ❑ *The bank reserves the right to reverse any transfers or payments.* **2** [C, U] **Transfer** is when one person or group gets something after another person or group has had it. ❑ *the transfer of power from the old to the new regimes* **3** [C, U] [oft transfer 'to' N] A **transfer** is when your company moves you to a different job or when you start working in a different part of the same company or organization. ❑ *They will be offered transfers to other locations.* **4** [U] **Transfer** is the copying of information from one medium to another. ❑ *It can be connected to a PC for the transfer of information.*

○**trans·form** ♦◇◇ /træns'fɔːm/ **VERB** [T] **(transforms, transforming, transformed)** (*academic word*) **1** To **transform into** something else means to change or convert it into that thing. = change, convert ❑ *Your metabolic rate is the speed at which your body transforms food into energy.* ❑ *Delegates also discussed transforming them from a guerrilla force into a regular army.* **2** To **transform** something or someone means to change them completely and suddenly so that they are much better or more attractive. = change, convert ❑ *Industrialization transformed the world.* ❑ *The spread of the internet and mobile telephony have transformed society.* ❑ *Yeltsin was committed to completely transforming Russia into a market economy.*
○**trans·for·ma·tion** /ˌtrænsfə'meɪʃən/ **NOUN** [C, U] **(transformations) 1** *Norah made plans for the transformation of an attic room into a study.* **2** = change ❑ *In the last five years he's undergone a personal transformation.* ❑ *one of the most astonishing economic transformations seen since the second world war* ❑ *After 1959, the Spanish economy underwent a profound transformation.*

tran·si·ent /'trænziənt, *AmE* -ʃənt/ **ADJ, NOUN**
ADJ (*formal*) **Transient** is used to describe a situation that lasts only a short time or is constantly changing. ❑ *the transient nature of high fashion*
NOUN [C] **(transients)** [usu pl] (*formal*) **Transients** are people who stay in a place for only a short time and then move somewhere else. ❑ *a dormitory for transients*

trans·it /'trænzɪt/ **NOUN, ADJ** (*academic word*)
NOUN [U] **Transit** is the carrying of goods or people by vehicle from one place to another. ❑ *During their talks, the two presidents discussed the transit of goods between the two countries.* ❑ *a transit time of about 42 minutes*
PHRASE **in transit** If people or things are **in transit**, they are travelling or being taken from one place to another.
ADJ [transit + N] A **transit** area is an area where people wait or where goods are kept between different stages of a journey. ❑ *refugees arriving at the two transit camps*

○**tran·si·tion** ♦◇◇ /træn'zɪʃən/ **NOUN, VERB** (*academic word*)
NOUN [C, U] **(transitions) Transition** is the process in which something changes from one state to another. = shift, change, passage ❑ *The transition from a dictatorship to a multi-party democracy is proving to be difficult.* ❑ *in order to*

ensure a smooth transition from one reign to the next ❑ *a period of transition*
VERB [I] **(transitions, transitioning, transitioned)** (*business*) If someone **transitions from** one state or activity to another, they move gradually from one to the other. ❑ *Most of the discussion was on what needed to be done now as we transitioned from the security issues to the challenging economic issues.*

○**tran·si·tion·al** /træn'zɪʃənəl/ **ADJ** **1** [transitional + N] A **transitional** period is one in which things are changing from one state to another. ❑ *a transitional period following more than a decade of civil war* ❑ *We are still in the transitional stage between the old and new methods.* **2** [transitional + N] **Transitional** is used to describe something that happens or exists during a transitional period. ❑ *The main rebel groups have agreed to join in a meeting to set up a transitional government.*

○**trans·late** /trænz'leɪt/ **VERB** [I, T] **(translates, translating, translated) 1** [I, T] If something said or written **is translated from** one language **into** another, it is said or written again in the second language. = interpret, gloss, render ❑ *Only a small number of Kadare's books have been translated into English.* ❑ *The Spanish word 'acequia' is translated as 'irrigation ditch'.* ❑ *Martin Luther translated the Bible into German.* ❑ *The girls waited for Mr Esch to translate.* **2** [I] If a name, a word, or an expression **translates as** something in a different language, that is what it means in that language. ❑ *His family's Cantonese nickname for him translates as Never Sits Still.* **3** [I, T] If one thing **translates** or **is translated into** another, the second happens or is done as a result of the first. ❑ *Reforming the stagnant economy requires harsh measures that would translate into job losses.*

○**trans·la·tion** /trænz'leɪʃən/ **NOUN** [C, U] **(translations) 1** [C] A **translation** is a piece of writing or speech that has been put into a different language. ❑ *a translation of the Iliad* **2** [U] [also 'in' translation] **Translation** is the act of saying or writing something again in a different second language. ❑ *The papers have been sent to Saudi Arabia for translation.* ❑ *I've only read Solzhenitsyn in translation.*

○**trans·la·tor** /trænz'leɪtə/ **NOUN** [C] **(translators)** A **translator** is a person whose job is translating writing or speech from one language to another. = interpreter ❑ *He works as a Russian translator.*

○**trans·mis·sion** /trænz'mɪʃən/ **NOUN** [U, C] **(transmissions) 1** [U] The **transmission** of something is the passing or sending of it to a different person or place. ❑ *Heterosexual contact is responsible for the bulk of HIV transmission.* ❑ *the fax machine and other forms of electronic data transmission* ❑ *the transmission of knowledge and skills* **2** [U] The **transmission** of television or radio programmes is the broadcasting of them. ❑ *The transmission of the programme was brought forward due to its unexpected topicality.* **3** [C] A **transmission** is a broadcast. ❑ *foreign television transmissions*

○**trans·mit** /trænz'mɪt/ **VERB** [I, T] **(transmits, transmitting, transmitted)** (*academic word*) **1** [I, T] When radio and television programmes, computer data, or other electronic messages **are transmitted**, they are sent from one place to another, using wires, radio waves, or satellites. ❑ *The game was transmitted live.* ❑ *This is currently the most efficient way to transmit certain types of data like electronic mail.* **2** [T] (*formal*) If one person or animal **transmits** a disease to another, they have the disease and cause the other person or animal to have it. = pass, spread ❑ *mosquitoes that transmit disease to humans* ❑ *There was no danger of transmitting the infection through operations.* ❑ *the spread of sexually transmitted diseases* **3** [T] If an object or substance **transmits** something such as sound or electrical signals, the sound or signals are able to pass through it. ❑ *These thin crystals transmit much of the power.*

trans·mit·ter /trænz'mɪtə/ **NOUN** [C] **(transmitters)** A **transmitter** is a piece of equipment that is used for broadcasting television or radio programmes. ❑ *a homemade radio transmitter*

○**trans·par·en·cy** /træns'pærənsi, *AmE* -'per-/ **NOUN** [C, U] **(transparencies) 1** [C] A **transparency** is a small piece of photographic film with a frame around it which can be projected onto a screen so that you can see the picture.

T

= slide ❏ *transparencies of masterpieces from Lizzie's art collection* **2** [U] **Transparency** is the quality that an object or substance has when you can see through it. = clarity ❏ *Cataracts affect the transparency of the eye's lenses.* **3** [U] The **transparency** of a process, situation, or statement is its quality of being easily understood or recognized, for example because there are no secrets connected with it, or because it is expressed in a clear way. ❏ *openness and transparency in the Government's economic decision-making*

⚫**trans·par·ent** /træns'pærənt, AmE -'per-/ ADJ **1** If an object or substance is **transparent**, you can see through it. ❏ *a sheet of transparent coloured plastic* ❏ *a transparent plastic tube* **2** If a situation, system, or activity is **transparent**, it is easily understood or recognized. = open, clear ❏ *The company has to make its accounts and operations as transparent as possible.* ❏ *We are now striving hard to establish a transparent parliamentary democracy.* **3** You use **transparent** to describe a statement or action that is obviously dishonest or wrong, and that you think will not deceive people. If a person is transparent, you can see their true bad motives. ❏ *He thought he could fool people with transparent deceptions.* ❏ *He's so transparent.*

⚫**trans·par·ent·ly** /træns'pærəntli, AmE -'per-/ ADV = openly ❏ *The system was clearly not functioning smoothly or transparently.* ❏ *Government activities must be conducted openly, transparently and effectively.*

tran·spire /træn'spaɪə/ VERB [T, I] (**transpires, transpiring, transpired**) **1** [T] (formal) When it **transpires that** something is the case, people discover that it is the case. = turn out ❏ *It transpired that Kareem had left his driving licence at home.* **2** [I] When something **transpires**, it happens. ❏ *Nothing is known as yet about what transpired at the meeting.*

⚫**trans·plant** NOUN, VERB
  NOUN /'trænsplɑːnt, -plænt/ [C, U] (**transplants**) A **transplant** is a medical operation in which a part of a person's body is replaced because it is diseased. ❏ *He was recovering from a heart transplant operation.* ❏ *several hundred patients awaiting bone marrow transplant operations* ❏ *the controversy over the sale of human organs for transplant*
  VERB /træns'plɑːnt, -'plænt/ [T] (**transplants, transplanting, transplanted**) **1** If doctors **transplant** an organ such as a heart or a kidney, they use it to replace a patient's diseased organ. ❏ *The operation to transplant a kidney is now fairly routine.* ❏ *transplanted organs such as hearts and kidneys* **2** To **transplant** a plant, person, or thing means to move them to a different place. ❏ *I have to transplant the begonias.*

⚫**trans·plan·ta·tion** /ˌtrænzplæn'teɪʃən/ NOUN [U] ❏ *a shortage of kidneys for transplantation* ❏ *Bone marrow transplantation began 20 years ago.*

⚫**trans·port** ◆◆◇ NOUN, VERB (*academic word*)
  NOUN /'trænspɔːt/ [U] (*mainly BrE; in AmE, usually use* **transportation**) **1** **Transport** refers to any vehicle that you can travel in or carry goods in. **2** **Transport** is a system for taking people or goods from one place to another, for example, using buses or trains. ❏ *Campuses are usually accessible by public transport.* **3** **Transport** is the activity of taking goods or people from one place to another in a vehicle. = transportation, carriage ❏ *The extra money could be spent on improving public transport.* ❏ *An efficient transport system is critical to the long-term future of London.* ❏ *Local production virtually eliminates transport costs.*
  VERB /træns'pɔːt/ [T] (**transports, transporting, transported**) To **transport** people or goods somewhere is to take them from one place to another in a vehicle. = move, ship ❏ *They are banned from launching any flights except to transport people.* ❏ *There's no petrol, so it's very difficult to transport goods.* ❏ *They use tankers to transport the oil to Los Angeles.*

WORD PARTS

The prefix **trans-** appears in words which show that something moves or enables travel from one side of an area to another:
transport (VERB)
transmit (VERB)
transcontinental (ADJ)

---

trans·por·ta·tion ◆◆◇ /ˌtrænspɔː'teɪʃən/ (*mainly AmE; in BrE, usually use* **transport**) NOUN [U] **Transportation** is the activity of taking goods or people from one place to another in a vehicle. ❏ *The baggage was being rapidly stowed away for transportation.*

trap ◆◇◇ /træp/ NOUN, VERB
  NOUN [C] (**traps**) **1** A **trap** is a device which is placed somewhere or a hole which is dug somewhere in order to catch animals or birds. ❏ *Nathan's dog got caught in a trap.* **2** A **trap** is a trick that is intended to catch or deceive someone. ❏ *He failed to keep a rendezvous after sensing a police trap.* **3** A **trap** is an unpleasant situation that you cannot easily escape from. ❏ *The government has found that it's caught in a trap of its own making.*
  VERB [T] (**traps, trapping, trapped**) **1** If a person **traps** animals or birds, he or she catches them using traps. ❏ *The locals were encouraged to trap and kill mice to stop the spread of the virus.* **2** If you **trap** someone **into** doing or saying something, you trick them so that they do or say it, although they did not want to. ❏ *Were you just trying to trap her into making some admission?* **3** To **trap** someone, especially a criminal, means to capture them. ❏ *The police knew they had to trap the killer.* **4** If you **are trapped** somewhere, something falls onto you or blocks your way and prevents you from moving or escaping. ❏ *The train was trapped underground by a fire.* ❏ *The light aircraft then cartwheeled, trapping both men.* **5** When something **traps** gas, water, or energy, it prevents it from escaping. ❏ *Wool traps your body heat, keeping the chill at bay.*
  → See also **trapped**

trapped /træpt/ ADJ If you feel **trapped**, you are in an unpleasant situation in which you lack freedom, and you feel you cannot escape from it. ❏ *people who think of themselves as trapped in mundane jobs*
  → See also **trap**

trash /træʃ/ NOUN [U] (*informal*) If you say that something such as a book, painting, or film is **trash**, you mean that it is of very bad quality. ❏ *Pop music doesn't have to be trash; it can be art.*

⚫**trau·ma** /'trɔːmə, AmE 'traʊmə/ NOUN [C, U] (**traumas**) **1** [C, U] **Trauma** is a very severe shock or very upsetting experience, which may cause psychological damage. ❏ *I'd been through the trauma of losing a house.* **2** [U] **Trauma** is a serious injury caused by an accident rather than an illness. = injury ❏ *riding accidents involving head trauma* ❏ *an ambulance for coronary and trauma patients*

trau·mat·ic /trɔː'mætɪk, AmE traʊ-/ ADJ A **traumatic** experience is very shocking and upsetting, and may cause psychological damage. ❏ *I suffered a nervous breakdown. It was a traumatic experience.*

trau·ma·tize /'trɔːmətaɪz, AmE 'traʊ-/ also **traumatise** VERB [T] (**traumatizes, traumatizing, traumatized**) If someone **is traumatized** by an event or situation, it shocks or upsets them very much, and may cause them psychological damage. ❏ *My wife was traumatized by the experience.*

trau·ma·tized /'trɔːmətaɪzd, AmE 'traʊ-/ ADJ ❏ *He left her in the middle of the road, shaking and deeply traumatized.*

trav·el ◆◆◇ /'trævəl/ VERB, NOUN
  VERB [I, T] (**travels, travelling, travelled;** *in AmE, use* **traveling, traveled**) **1** [I, T] If you **travel**, you go from one place to another, often to a place that is far away. ❏ *You had better travel to Nova Scotia tomorrow.* ❏ *I've been travelling all day.* ❏ *Students often travel hundreds of miles to get here.* **2** [T] If you **travel** the world, the country, or the area, you go to many different places in the world or in a particular country or area. ❏ *He was a very wealthy man who had travelled the world.* **3** [I] When light or sound from one place reaches another, you say that it **travels** to the other place. ❏ *When sound travels through water, strange things can happen.* **4** [I] When news becomes known by people in different places, you can say that it **travels** to them. ❏ *News of his work travelled all the way to Asia.*
  PHRASE **travel light** If you **travel light**, you travel without taking much luggage. ❏ *It would be good to be able to travel light, but I end up taking too many clothes.*

NOUN [U, PL] (**travels**) **1** [U] **Travel** is the activity of travelling. ❑ *Information on travel in New Zealand is available at the hotel.* ❑ *He detested air travel.* **2** [PL] Someone's **travels** are the trips that they make to places a long way from their home. ❑ *He also collects things for the house on his travels abroad.*

trav·el·ler ♦◇◇ /ˈtrævələ/ NOUN [C] (**travellers**) A **traveller** is a person who is on a trip or a person who travels a lot. ❑ *Airline travellers need to be confident that their bookings will be honoured.*

tray /treɪ/ NOUN [C] (**trays**) A **tray** is a flat piece of wood, plastic, or metal, which usually has raised edges and which is used for carrying things, especially food and drinks.

treach·er·ous /ˈtretʃərəs/ ADJ **1** (*disapproval*) If you describe someone as **treacherous**, you mean that they are likely to betray you and cannot be trusted. ❑ *He publicly left the party and denounced its treacherous leaders.* **2** If you say that something is **treacherous**, you mean that it is very dangerous and unpredictable. ❑ *The current of the river is fast flowing and treacherous.*

treach·ery /ˈtretʃəri/ NOUN [U] **Treachery** is behaviour or an action in which someone betrays their country or betrays a person who trusts them. ❑ *He was deeply wounded by the treachery of close aides and old friends.*

tread /tred/ NOUN, VERB
NOUN [C, U] (**treads**) The **tread** of a tyre or shoe is the pattern of thin lines cut into its surface that stops it from slipping. ❑ *The fat, broad tyres had a good depth of tread.* **VERB** [I] (**treads, treading, trod, trodden**) **1** (*literary*) If you **tread** in a particular way, you walk that way. ❑ *She trod casually, enjoying the touch of the damp grass on her feet.* **2** If you **tread** carefully, you behave in a careful or cautious way. ❑ *If you are hoping to form a new relationship tread carefully and slowly to begin with.* **3** (*mainly BrE; in AmE, usually use* **step**) If you **tread on** something, you put your foot on it when you are walking or standing. ❑ *He continues to tread an unconventional* **PHRASE** **tread a path** If you **tread** a particular **path**, you take a particular course of action or do something in a particular way. ❑ *He continues to tread an unconventional path.*

trea·son /ˈtriːzən/ NOUN [U] **Treason** is the crime of betraying your country, for example, by helping its enemies or by trying to remove its government using violence. ❑ *They were tried and found guilty of treason.*

treas·ure /ˈtreʒə/ NOUN, VERB
NOUN [U, C] (**treasures**) **1** [U] (*literary*) **Treasure** is a collection of valuable old objects such as gold coins and jewels that has been hidden or lost. ❑ *It was here, the buried treasure, she knew it was.* **2** [C] **Treasures** are valuable objects, especially works of art and items of historical value. ❑ *The house was large and full of art treasures.* **3** [C] [treasure + N] A **treasure** is something that you keep or care for carefully because it gives you great pleasure and you think it is very special. ❑ *His greatest treasure is his collection of rock records.* **VERB** [T] (**treasures, treasuring, treasured**) If you **treasure** something that you have, you keep it or care for it carefully because it gives you great pleasure and you think it is very special. = **cherish** ❑ *She treasures her memories of those joyous days.*

treas·ured /ˈtreʒəd/ ADJ ❑ *These books are still among my most treasured possessions.*

treas·ur·er /ˈtreʒərə/ NOUN [C] (**treasurers**) The **treasurer** of a society or organization is the person who is in charge of its finances and keeps its accounts.

Treas·ury ♦◇◇ /ˈtreʒəri/ NOUN [C] In the United Kingdom, the United States, and some other countries, **the Treasury** is the government department that deals with the country's finances. ❑ *a senior official at the Treasury*

❂treat ♦♦◇ /triːt/ VERB, NOUN
VERB [T] (**treats, treating, treated**) **1** If you **treat** someone or something in a particular way, you behave towards them or deal with them in that way. = **handle, deal with, behave towards** ❑ *Artie treated most women with indifference.* ❑ *The information should be treated with caution.* ❑ *The issues*

should be treated separately. ❑ *Police say they're treating it as a case of attempted murder.* **2** When a doctor or nurse **treats** a patient or an illness, he or she tries to make the patient well again. ❑ *Doctors treated her with aspirin.* ❑ *The boy was treated for a minor head wound.* ❑ *An experienced nurse treats all minor injuries.* **3** If something **is treated with** a particular substance, the substance is put onto or into it in order to clean it, to protect it, or to give it special properties. ❑ *About 70% of the cocoa acreage is treated with insecticide.* **4** If you **treat** someone **to** something special which they will enjoy, you buy it or arrange it for them. ❑ *She was always treating him to ice cream.* ❑ *Tomorrow I'll treat myself to a day's gardening.*
NOUN [C] (**treats**) If you give someone a **treat**, you buy or arrange something special for them which they will enjoy. ❑ *Lettie had never yet failed to return from town without some special treat for him.*

❂treat·ment ♦♦◇ /ˈtriːtmənt/ NOUN [C, U] (**treatments**) **1** [C, U] **Treatment** is medical attention given to a sick or injured person or animal. = **cure, medicine, therapy** ❑ *Many patients are not getting the medical treatment they need.* ❑ *a veterinary surgeon who specializes in the treatment of caged birds* ❑ *an effective treatment for eczema* **2** [U] Your **treatment** of someone is the way you behave towards them or deal with them. = **behaviour** ❑ *We don't want any special treatment.* ❑ *the government's responsibility for the humane treatment of prisoners* **3** [C, U] **Treatment** of something involves putting a particular substance onto or into it, in order to clean it, to protect it, or to give it special properties. ❑ *There should be greater treatment of sewage before it is discharged.*

WORD CONNECTIONS
VERB + **treatment**
get treatment **receive** treatment **undergo** treatment ❑ *She has been receiving treatment for cancer.*
give treatment ❑ *Only a qualified doctor should give treatment.*
ADJ + **treatment**
an **effective** treatment **successful** treatment ❑ *Counselling is the most effective treatment for depression.*
unsuccessful treatment ❑ *Following unsuccessful treatment for infertility, they signed up with an adoption agency.*
medical treatment **dental** treatment ❑ *He received emergency medical treatment as he lay on the pavement.*
equal treatment **fair** treatment **humane** treatment ❑ *She learned how tough it was for women to get fair treatment.*
special treatment **preferential** treatment ❑ *You should expect no special treatment.*
unequal treatment **unfair** treatment **harsh** treatment ❑ *It was difficult for her to talk about the harsh treatment she had received from her strict father.*

❂trea·ty ♦♦◇ /ˈtriːti/ NOUN [C] (**treaties**) A **treaty** is a written agreement between countries in which they agree to do a particular thing or to help each other. = **pact, agreement** ❑ *negotiations over a treaty on global warming* ❑ *the Treaty of Rome, which established the European Community* ❑ *negotiations over a 1992 treaty on global*

T

warming □ *A peace treaty was signed between France and Russia.*

tre•ble /ˈtrebəl/ NOUN, VERB, PREDET

NOUN [C] On a stereo system or radio, the **treble** is the ability to reproduce the higher musical notes. The **treble** is also the knob which controls this.

VERB [I, T] (**trebles, trebling, trebled**) (*mainly BrE; in AmE, use* **triple**) If something **trebles** or if you **treble** it, it becomes three times greater in number or amount than it was. = triple □ *They will have to pay much more when rents treble in January.*

PREDET (*mainly BrE; in AmE, use* **triple**; *formal*) If one thing is **treble** the size or amount of another thing, it is three times greater in size or amount. = triple

tree ♦♦◇ /triː/ NOUN [C] (**trees**) A **tree** is a tall plant that has a hard trunk, branches, and leaves. □ *I planted those apple trees.*

trek /trek/ VERB, NOUN

VERB [I] (**treks, trekking, trekked**) **1** If you **trek** somewhere, you go on a journey across difficult country, usually on foot. □ *trekking through the jungles* **2** If you **trek** somewhere, you go there heavily and unwillingly, usually because you are tired. □ *They trekked from shop to shop in search of white knee-high socks.*

NOUN [C] (**treks**) A **trek** is a journey across difficult country, usually on foot. □ *He is on a trek through the South Gobi desert.*

trem•ble /ˈtrembəl/ VERB, NOUN

VERB [I] (**trembles, trembling, trembled**) **1** If you **tremble**, you shake slightly because you are frightened or cold. = shake □ *His mouth became dry, his eyes widened, and he began to tremble all over.* □ *Lisa was white and trembling with anger.* **2** (*literary*) If something **trembles**, it shakes slightly. = quiver □ *He felt the earth tremble under him.* **3** (*literary*) If your voice **trembles**, it sounds unsteady and uncertain, usually because you are upset or nervous. = shake □ *His voice trembled, on the verge of tears.*

NOUN [SING] **1** A **tremble** in the body or a part of the body is a slight shake caused by fear or cold. □ *I will never forget the look on the patient's face, the tremble in his hand.* **2** (*literary*) If there is a **tremble** in your voice, it sounds unsteady and uncertain, usually because you are upset or nervous. □ *'Please understand this,' she began, a tremble in her voice.*

tre•men•dous ♦◇◇ /trɪˈmendəs/ ADJ **1** (*emphasis*) You use **tremendous** to emphasize how strong a feeling or quality is, or how large an amount is. = terrific □ *I felt a tremendous pressure on my chest.* **2** You can describe someone or something as **tremendous** when you think they are very good or very impressive. = terrific □ *I thought it was absolutely tremendous.*

tre•men•dous•ly /trɪˈmendəsli/ ADV □ *I thought they played tremendously well, didn't you?*

trem•or /ˈtremə/ NOUN [C] (**tremors**) **1** A **tremor** is a small earthquake. □ *The earthquake sent tremors through the region.* **2** If an event causes a **tremor** in a group or organization, it threatens to make the group or organization less strong or stable. □ *News of 160 lay-offs had sent tremors through the community.* **3** A **tremor** is a shaking of your body or voice that you cannot control. □ *The old man has a tremor in his hands.*

❂**trend** ♦◇◇ /trend/ NOUN [C] (**trends**) (*academic word*) **1** A **trend** is a change or development towards something new or different. = tendency, movement □ *This is a growing trend.* □ *a trend towards part-time employment* □ *the upward trend in petrol prices* **2** To set a **trend** means to do something that becomes accepted or fashionable, and that a lot of other people copy. □ *The latest trend is gardening.*

WORD CONNECTIONS
VERB + **trend**
set a trend
start a trend
continue a trend
□ *Sales fell by 5%, continuing a trend that began last year.*

reverse a trend
□ *How can we reverse the trend of rising unemployment?*

ADJ + **trend**
an **overall** trend
□ *With few exceptions, the overall trend is strongly upwards.*

an **upward** trend
a **growing** trend
□ *The findings show a growing trend towards earlier heart disease.*

the **current** trend
a **new** trend
the **latest** trend
a **recent** trend
□ *Despite the current trend for paint, certain kinds of wallpaper are still popular.*

a **disturbing** trend
□ *He warned against a disturbing trend of football-related violence.*

❂**tri•al** ♦♦◇ /ˈtraɪəl/ NOUN

NOUN [C, U] (**trials**) **1** [C, U] A **trial** is a formal meeting in a law court, at which a judge and jury listen to evidence and decide whether a person is guilty of a crime. = case, prosecution, hearing, lawsuit □ *New evidence showed the police lied at the trial.* □ *I have the right to a trial with a jury of my peers.* □ *He's awaiting trial in a military court on charges of plotting against the state.* □ *They believed that his case would never come to trial.* **2** [C, U] A **trial** is an experiment in which you test something by using it or doing it for a period of time to see how well it works. If something is **on trial**, it is being tested in this way. = test □ *They have been treated with this drug in clinical trials.* □ *I took the car out for a trial on the roads.* **3** [C] If you refer to the **trials** of a situation, you mean the unpleasant things that you experience in it. □ *the trials of adolescence*

PHRASES **trial and error** If you do something **by trial and error**, you try several different methods of doing it until you find the method that works best. □ *Many drugs were found by trial and error.*

on trial If someone is **on trial**, they are being tried in a court of law. □ *He is currently on trial for drink driving.*

on trial If you say that someone or something is **on trial**, you mean that they are in a situation where people are observing them to see whether they succeed or fail. □ *The president will be drawn into a damaging battle in which his credentials will be on trial.*

stand trial If someone **stands trial**, they are tried in court for a crime they are accused of. □ *He was found to be mentally unfit to stand trial.*

❂**tri•an•gle** /ˈtraɪæŋgəl/ NOUN [C] (**triangles**) **1** A **triangle** is an object, arrangement, or flat shape with three straight sides and three angles. □ *This design is in pastel colours with three rectangles and three triangles.* □ *Its outline roughly forms an equilateral triangle.* □ *triangles of fried bread* **2** The **triangle** is a musical instrument that consists of a piece of metal shaped like a triangle. You play it by hitting it with a short metal bar. □ *My musical career consisted of playing the triangle at nursery school.*

WORD PARTS
The prefix *tri-* often appears in words for things that have three parts:
triangle (NOUN)
tricycle (NOUN)
triathlon (NOUN)

❂**tri•an•gu•lar** /traɪˈæŋgjʊlə/ ADJ Something that is **triangular** is in the shape of a triangle. □ *a triangular roof* □ *cottages around a triangular green* □ *triangular bandages to make slings*

trib•al /ˈtraɪbəl/ ADJ **Tribal** is used to describe things relating to or belonging to tribes and the way that they are organized. □ *tribal warfare* □ *the Navajo Tribal Council*

tribe /traɪb/ NOUN [C] (**tribes**) **Tribe** is sometimes used to

t

refer to a group of people of the same race, language, and customs, especially in a developing country. Some people disapprove of this use. ❑ *three-hundred members of the Xhosa tribe*

tri·bu·nal /traɪˈbjuːnəl/ NOUN [c] (tribunals) A **tribunal** is a special court or committee that is appointed to deal with particular problems. ❑ *His case comes before an industrial tribunal in March.*

trib·ute /ˈtrɪbjuːt/ NOUN [c, u, SING] (tributes) **1** [c, u] A **tribute** is something that you say, do, or make to show your admiration and respect for someone. ❑ *The song is a tribute to Roy Orbison.* **2** [SING] If one thing is **a tribute to** another, the first thing is the result of the second and shows how good it is. ❑ *His success has been a tribute to hard work, to professionalism.*

trick ♦◇◇ /trɪk/ NOUN, VERB
  NOUN [c] (tricks) **1** A **trick** is an action that is intended to fool or deceive someone. ❑ *We are playing a trick on a man who keeps bothering me.* **2** A **trick** is a clever or skilful action that someone does in order to entertain people. ❑ *magic tricks* ❑ *He shows me card tricks.* **3** A **trick** is a clever way of doing something. ❑ *Everything I cooked was a trick of my mother's.*
  PHRASES **do the trick** (*informal*) If something **does the trick**, it achieves what you wanted. ❑ *Sometimes a few choice words will do the trick.*
  every trick in the book (*informal*) If someone tries **every trick in the book**, they try every possible thing that they can think of in order to achieve something. ❑ *Companies are using every trick in the book to stay one step in front of their competitors.*
  tricks of the trade The **tricks of the trade** are the quick and clever ways of doing something that are known by people who regularly do a particular activity. ❑ *To get you started, we have asked five successful writers to reveal some of the tricks of the trade.*
  VERB [T] (tricks, tricking, tricked) If someone **tricks** you, they deceive you, often in order to make you do something. ❑ *Stephen is going to be pretty upset when he finds out how you tricked him.* ❑ *His family tricked him into going to Pakistan, and once he was there, they took away his passport.*

trick·le /ˈtrɪkəl/ VERB, NOUN
  VERB [I, T] (trickles, trickling, trickled) **1** [I, T] When a liquid **trickles**, or when you **trickle** it, it flows slowly in a thin stream. ❑ *A tear trickled down the old man's cheek.* **2** [I] When people or things **trickle** in a particular direction, they move there slowly in small groups or amounts, rather than all together. ❑ *Some donations are already trickling in.*
  PHRASAL VERB **trickle down** If benefits given to people at the top of a society or system **trickle down**, they are eventually passed on to people lower down the society or system. ❑ *the failure of the prosperity of Las Vegas' casinos to trickle down to poor neighbourhoods*
  NOUN [c] (trickles) **1** A **trickle** of a liquid is a slow, thin stream of it. ❑ *There was not so much as a trickle of water.* **2** If there is a **trickle** of people or things in a particular direction, they move there in small groups or amounts, rather than all together. ❑ *The flood of cars has now slowed to a trickle.*

tricky /ˈtrɪki/ ADJ (trickier, trickiest) If you describe a task or problem as **tricky**, you mean that it is difficult to do or deal with. ❑ *Parking can be tricky in town.*

tried /traɪd/ ADJ [tried 'and' ADJ] **Tried** is used in the expressions **tried and tested**, **tried and trusted**, and **tried and true**, which describe a product or method that has already been used and has been found to be successful. ❑ *over 1,000 tried-and-tested recipes*
→ See also **try**

○**trig·ger** ♦◇◇ /ˈtrɪɡə/ NOUN, VERB (*academic word*)
  NOUN [c] (triggers) **1** The **trigger** of a gun is a small lever which you pull to fire it. ❑ *A man pointed a gun at them and pulled the trigger.* **2** The **trigger** of a bomb is the device which causes it to explode. ❑ *trigger devices for nuclear weapons* **3** If something acts as a **trigger for** another thing such as an illness, event, or situation, the first thing causes the second thing to begin to happen or exist.

❑ *Stress may act as a trigger for these illnesses.*
  VERB [T] (triggers, triggering, triggered) **1** To **trigger** a bomb or system means to cause it to work. = activate ❑ *The thieves must have deliberately triggered the alarm and hidden inside the house.* **2** If something **triggers** an event or situation, it causes it to begin to happen or exist. = spark ❑ *the incident which triggered the outbreak of the First World War* ❑ *The current recession was triggered by a slump in consumer spending.*
  PHRASAL VERB **trigger off** **Trigger off** means the same as **trigger** VERB 2. ❑ *It is still not clear what events triggered off the demonstrations.*

tril·lion /ˈtrɪljən/ NUM (trillions)

> The plural form is **trillion** after a number, or after a word or expression referring to a number, such as 'several' or 'a few'.

A **trillion** is 1,000,000,000,000. ❑ *a 4 trillion dollar debt*

trim /trɪm/ ADJ, VERB, NOUN
  ADJ (trimmer, trimmest) **1** Something that is **trim** is neat and attractive. ❑ *The neighbours' gardens were trim and neat.* **2** If you describe someone's figure as **trim**, you mean that it is attractive because there is no extra fat on their body. ❑ *The driver was a trim young woman of perhaps thirty.*
  VERB [T] (trims, trimming, trimmed) **1** If you **trim** something, for example, someone's hair, you cut off small amounts of it in order to make it look neater. ❑ *My friend trims my hair every eight weeks.* **2** If a government or other organization **trims** something such as a plan, policy, or amount, they reduce it slightly in extent or size. ❑ *American companies looked at ways they could trim these costs.* **3** If something such as a piece of clothing **is trimmed with** a type of material or design, it is decorated with it, usually along its edges. ❑ *jackets, which are then trimmed with crocheted flowers*
  NOUN [SING, c, u] (trims) **1** [SING] If someone gives you a **trim** or gives your hair a **trim**, they cut off small amounts of it in order to make it look neater. ❑ *His hair needed a trim.* **2** [c, u] The **trim** on something such as a piece of clothing is a decoration, for example, along its edges, that is in a different colour or material. = trimming ❑ *a white satin scarf with black trim*

trio /ˈtriːəʊ/ NOUN [c] (trios) A **trio** is a group of three people together, especially musicians or singers, or a group of three things that have something in common. ❑ *classy American songs from a Texas trio*

trip ♦♦◇ /trɪp/ NOUN, VERB
  NOUN [c] (trips) A **trip** is a journey that you make to a particular place. ❑ *We're taking a trip to Montana.* ❑ *On Thursday we went out on a day trip.*
  VERB [I, T] (trips, tripping, tripped) **1** [I] If you **trip** when you are walking, you knock your foot against something and fall or nearly fall. ❑ *She tripped and fell last night and broke her hip.* **2** [T] If you **trip** someone who is walking or running, you put your foot or something else in front of them, so that they knock their own foot against it and fall or nearly fall. ❑ *One guy stuck his foot out and tried to trip me.*
  PHRASAL VERB **trip up** **Trip up** means the same as **trip** VERB 1. ❑ *I tripped up and hurt my foot.* **2** **Trip up** means the same as **trip** VERB 2. ❑ *He made a sudden dive for Uncle Jim's legs to try to trip him up.*

tri·ple /ˈtrɪpl/ ADJ, VERB, PREDET
  ADJ [triple + N] **Triple** means consisting of three things or parts. ❑ *a triple somersault*
  VERB [I, T] (triples, tripling, tripled) If something **triples** or if you **triple** it, it becomes three times as large in size or number. = treble ❑ *I got a fantastic new job and my salary tripled.* ❑ *The exhibition has tripled in size from last year.*
  PREDET [triple 'the' N] If something is **triple the** amount or size of another thing, it is three times as large. = treble ❑ *The mine reportedly had an accident rate triple the national average.*

tri·umph ♦◇◇ /ˈtraɪʌmf/ NOUN, VERB
  NOUN [c, u] (triumphs) **1** [c, u] A **triumph** is a great success or achievement, often one that has been gained with a lot of skill or effort. ❑ *The championships proved to*

be a personal triumph for the coach, Dave Donovan. **2** [U] **Triumph** is a feeling of great satisfaction and pride resulting from a success or victory. ❑ Her sense of triumph was short-lived.
VERB [I] (**triumphs, triumphing, triumphed**) If someone or something **triumphs**, they gain complete success, control, or victory, often after a long or difficult struggle. ❑ All her life, Kelly had stuck with difficult tasks and challenges, and triumphed.

tri·um·phant /traɪˈʌmfənt/ ADJ Someone who is **triumphant** has gained a victory or succeeded in something and feels very happy about it. ❑ The captain's voice was triumphant.
tri·um·phant·ly /traɪˈʌmfəntli/ ADV ❑ They marched triumphantly into the capital.

triv·ial /ˈtrɪviəl/ ADJ If you describe something as **trivial**, you think that it is unimportant and not serious. ❑ The director tried to wave aside these issues as trivial details that could be settled later.

trod /trɒd/ IRREG FORM **Trod** is the past tense of **tread**.

trod·den /ˈtrɒdən/ IRREG FORM **Trodden** is the past participle of **tread**.

trol·ley /ˈtrɒli/ NOUN [C] (**trolleys**) (BrE) **1** (in AmE, use **cart**) A **trolley** is an object with wheels that you use to transport heavy things such as shopping or luggage. **2** (in AmE, use **cart**) A **trolley** is a small table on wheels which is used for serving drinks or food. **3** (in AmE, use **gurney**) A **trolley** is a bed on wheels for moving patients in a hospital.

troop ♦♦◇ /truːp/ NOUN, VERB
NOUN [PL, C] (**troops**) **1** [PL] **Troops** are soldiers, especially when they are in a large organized group doing a particular task. ❑ The next phase of the operation will involve the deployment of more than 35,000 troops from a dozen countries. **2** [C] A **troop** is a group of soldiers. ❑ a troop of American Marines **3** [C] A **troop** of people or animals is a group of them. ❑ The whole troop of men and women wore their hair fairly short.
VERB [I] (**troops, trooping, trooped**) (informal) If people **troop** somewhere, they walk there in a group, often in a sad or tired way. ❑ They all trooped back to the house for a rest.

tro·phy /ˈtrəʊfi/ NOUN [C] (**trophies**) **1** A **trophy** is a prize, for example, a silver cup, that is given to the winner of a competition or race. ❑ The special trophy for the best rider went to Chris Read. **2** A **trophy** is something that you keep in order to show that you have done something very difficult. ❑ His office was lined with animal heads, trophies of his hunting hobby.

✪tropi·cal /ˈtrɒpɪkəl/ ADJ **1** [tropical + N] **Tropical** means belonging to or typical of the tropics. ❑ tropical diseases ❑ a plan to preserve the world's tropical forests **2** **Tropical** weather is hot and damp weather typical of the tropics. ❑ The cool, sweet milk is just what you need in the tropical heat.

✪trop·ics /ˈtrɒpɪks/ NOUN [PL] The **tropics** are the parts of the world that lie between two lines of latitude, the tropic of Cancer, 23½° north of the equator, and the tropic of Capricorn, 23½° south of the equator. ❑ Being in the tropics meant that insects formed a large part of our life.

trou·ble ♦♦◇ /ˈtrʌbəl/ NOUN, VERB
NOUN [U, SING, PL] (**troubles**) **1** [U] [oft 'in' trouble, also troubles] You can refer to problems or difficulties as **trouble**. ❑ I had trouble parking. ❑ You've caused us a lot of trouble. **2** [SING] If you say that one aspect of a situation is **the trouble**, you mean that it is the aspect which is causing problems or making the situation unsatisfactory. = problem ❑ The trouble is that these restrictions have remained while other things have changed. **3** [PL] Your **troubles** are the things that you are worried about. ❑ She tells me her troubles. I tell her mine. **4** [U] If you have kidney **trouble** or back **trouble**, for example, there is something wrong with your kidneys or your back. ❑ An old bed is the most likely cause of back trouble. ❑ Her husband had never before had any heart trouble. **5** [U] [also troubles] If there is **trouble** somewhere, especially in a public place, there is

fighting or rioting there. ❑ Riot police are being deployed throughout the city to prevent any trouble. ❑ Fans who make trouble during the World Cup will be arrested. **6** [U] If you tell someone that it is **no trouble** to do something for them, you are saying politely that you can or will do it, because it is easy or convenient for you. = bother ❑ It's no trouble at all; on the contrary, it will be a great pleasure to help you. **7** [U] If you say that a person or animal is **no trouble**, you mean that they are very easy to look after. ❑ My little grandson is no trouble at all, but his 6-year-old sister is a handful.
PHRASES **in trouble** or **into trouble** If someone is **in trouble**, they are in a situation in which a person in authority is angry with them or is likely to punish them because they have done something wrong. ❑ He was in trouble with his teachers.
take the trouble If you **take the trouble to** do something, you do something which requires a small amount of additional effort. ❑ He did not take the trouble to see the film before he attacked it.
VERB [T] (**troubles, troubling, troubled**) **1** If something **troubles** you, it makes you feel worried. ❑ Is anything troubling you? **2** If a part of your body **troubles** you, it causes you physical pain or discomfort. ❑ The ulcer had been troubling her for several years. **3** If you say that someone does **not trouble to** do something, you are critical of them because they do not do something that they should, and you think that this would require very little effort. ❑ He burps, not troubling to cover his mouth. **4** You use **trouble** in expressions such as **I'm sorry to trouble you** when you are apologizing to someone for disturbing them in order to ask them something. = bother ❑ I'm sorry to trouble you, but I wondered if by any chance you know where he is.
trou·bling /ˈtrʌblɪŋ/ ADJ ❑ But most troubling of all was the simple fact that nobody knew what was going on.

trou·bled /ˈtrʌbəld/ ADJ **1** Someone who is **troubled** is worried because they have problems. ❑ Rose sounded deeply troubled. **2** A **troubled** place, situation, organization, or time has many problems or conflicts. ❑ There is so much we can do to help this troubled country.

trou·ble·some /ˈtrʌbəlsəm/ ADJ You use **troublesome** to describe something or someone that causes annoying problems or difficulties. ❑ He needed surgery to cure a troublesome back injury.

trou·sers /ˈtraʊzəz/ NOUN [PL]

The form **trouser** is used as a modifier.

[also 'a pair of' trousers] (mainly BrE; in AmE, use **pants**) **Trousers** are a piece of clothing that cover the body from the waist downward, and that cover each leg separately. ❑ He was dressed in a shirt, dark trousers and boots.

tru·ant /ˈtruːənt/ NOUN
NOUN [C] (**truants**) A **truant** is a student who stays away from school without permission. ❑ The parents of persistent truants can be put in jail.
PHRASE **play truant** (BrE) If a student **plays truant**, he or she stays away from school without permission. ❑ She was getting into trouble over playing truant from school.

truce /truːs/ NOUN [C] (**truces**) A **truce** is an agreement between two people or groups of people to stop fighting or arguing for a short time. ❑ The fighting of recent days has given way to an uneasy truce between the two sides.

truck ♦◇◇ /trʌk/ NOUN [C] (**trucks**) **1** (BrE; in AmE, use **freight car**) A **truck** is an open vehicle used for carrying goods on a railway. **2** (mainly AmE) A **truck** is a vehicle with a large area in the back for carrying things with low sides to make it easy to load and unload. A **truck** is the same as a **pickup 1**. = pick-up truck ❑ We can only seat two in the truck. ❑ Throw the dogs in the back of the truck.

✪true ♦♦◇ /truː/ ADJ
ADJ (**truer, truest**) **1** If something is **true**, it is based on facts rather than being invented or imagined, and is accurate and reliable. = correct, accurate; ≠ false, invented, untrue ❑ Everything I had heard about him was true. ❑ He said it was true that a collision had happened. ❑ The film tells the true story of a group who survived in the

Andes in sub-zero temperatures. **2** [true + N] You use **true** to emphasize that a person or thing is sincere or genuine, often in contrast to something that is pretended or hidden. = real ❑ I allowed myself to acknowledge my true feelings. **3** [true + N] If you use **true** to describe something or someone, you approve of them because they have all the characteristics or qualities that such a person or thing typically has. = real ❑ This country professes to be a true democracy. ❑ Maybe one day you'll find true love. **4** [V-LINK + true 'of/for' N] If you say that a fact is **true of** a particular person or situation, you mean that it is valid or relevant for them. ❑ I accept that the romance may have gone out of the marriage, but surely this is true of many couples. **5** [V-LINK + true 'to' N] If you are **true to** someone, you remain committed and loyal to them. If you are **true to** an idea or promise, you remain committed to it and continue to act according to it. = faithful ❑ David was true to his wife. ❑ India has remained true to democracy.

PHRASES **come true** If a dream, wish, or prediction **comes true**, it actually happens. ❑ Many of his predictions are coming true.

hold true (formal) If a general statement **holds true** in particular circumstances, or if your previous statement **holds true** in different circumstances, it is true or valid in those circumstances. ❑ This law is known to hold true for galaxies at a distance of at least several billion light years.

too good to be true If you say that something seems **too good to be true**, you are suspicious of it because it seems better than you had expected, and you think there may be something wrong with it that you have not noticed. ❑ On the whole the celebrations were remarkably good-humoured and peaceful. It seemed almost too good to be true.

✦ ring true → see ring

tru·ly ◆◇◇ /'truːli/ ADV
ADV (emphasis) **1** You use **truly** to emphasize that something has all the features or qualities of a particular thing, or is the case to the fullest possible extent. ❑ a truly democratic system ❑ Not all doctors truly understand the reproductive cycle. **2** [truly + ADJ] You can use **truly** in order to emphasize your description of something. ❑ a truly splendid man **3** You use **truly** to emphasize that feelings are genuine and sincere. ❑ Believe me, Susan, I am truly sorry.
CONVENTION **Yours truly** (old-fashioned) You write **Yours truly** at the end of a formal letter, and before signing your name, to someone you do not know very well. ❑ Yours truly, Phil Turner.

✦ well and truly → see well

trum·pet /'trʌmpɪt/ NOUN [C, U] (trumpets) [oft 'the' trumpet] A **trumpet** is a musical instrument of the brass family which plays comparatively high notes. ❑ I played the trumpet in the school orchestra.

trunk /trʌŋk/ NOUN [C, PL] (trunks) **1** [C] The **trunk** of a tree is the large main stem from which the branches grow. ❑ the gnarled trunk of a birch tree **2** [C] A **trunk** is a large, strong case or box used for storing things or for taking on a trip. ❑ Maloney unlocked his trunk and took out some overalls. **3** [C] An elephant's **trunk** is its very long nose that it uses to lift food and water to its mouth. ❑ Manfred the elephant reached out with his trunk and gently scooped up the baby. **4** [PL] **Trunks** are shorts that a man wears when he goes swimming. = swimming trunks **5** [C] [usu sing] (formal) Your **trunk** is the central part of your body, from your neck to your waist. ❑ The leg to be stretched should be positioned behind your trunk with your knee bent.

trust ◆◆◇ /trʌst/ VERB, NOUN
VERB [T, I] (trusts, trusting, trusted) **1** [T] If you **trust** someone, you believe that they are honest and sincere and will not deliberately do anything to harm you. ❑ 'I trust you completely,' he said. **2** [T] If you **trust** someone **to** do something, you believe that they will do it. ❑ That's why I must trust you to keep this secret. **3** [T] If you **trust** someone **with** something important or valuable, you allow them to look after it or deal with it. ❑ This could make your superiors hesitate to trust you with major responsibilities. **4** [T] If you do not **trust** something, you feel that it is not safe or reliable. ❑ She nodded, not trusting her own voice. ❑ For one thing, he didn't trust his legs to hold him up. **5** [T] If you **trust** someone's judgment or advice, you believe that it is

good or right. ❑ Jake has raised two incredible kids and I trust his judgement. **6** [T] (formal) If you say you **trust that** something is true, you mean you hope and expect that it is true. ❑ I trust you will take the earliest opportunity to make a full apology. **7** [I] (formal) If you **trust in** someone or something, you believe strongly in them, and do not doubt their powers or their good intentions. ❑ For a believer, replies to all the questions about life and work are far different because he trusts in God.
NOUN [U, C] (trusts) **1** [U] Your **trust in** someone is your belief that they are honest and sincere and will not deliberately do anything to harm you. ❑ He destroyed me and my trust in men. ❑ You've betrayed their trust. **2** [U] [also 'a' trust] **Trust** is the act of allowing someone to look after or deal with something that is important or valuable to you. ❑ She was organizing and running a large household, a position of trust which was generously paid. **3** [C] [also 'in' trust] (business) A **trust** is a financial arrangement in which a group of people or an organization keeps and invests money for someone. ❑ You could also set up a trust so the children can't spend any inheritance until they are a certain age. **4** [C] (business) A **trust** is a group of people or an organization that has control of an amount of money or property and invests it on behalf of other people or as a charity. ❑ He had set up two charitable trusts.

trus·tee /trʌˈstiː/ NOUN [C] (trustees) (business) A **trustee** is someone with legal control of money or property that is kept or invested for another person, company, or organization. ❑ The trustees of your pension fund decide which fund manager will invest some or all of your future income.

trust·worthy /'trʌstwɜːði/ ADJ A **trustworthy** person is reliable, responsible, and can be trusted completely. ❑ He is a trustworthy and level-headed leader.

✪ **truth** ◆◆◇ /truːθ/ NOUN
NOUN [U, C] (truths) **1** [U] The **truth** about something is all the facts about it, rather than things that are imagined or invented. = facts, accuracy; ≠ falsity, falsehood, lies, fiction ❑ Is it possible to separate truth from fiction? ❑ I must tell you the truth about this business. ❑ The truth of the matter is that we had no other choice. ❑ In the town very few know the whole truth. **2** [U] If you say that there is some **truth in** a statement or story, you mean that it is true, or at least partly true. ❑ There is no truth in this story. ❑ Is there any truth to the rumours? **3** [C] A **truth** is something that is believed to be true. ❑ It is an almost universal truth that the more we are promoted in a job, the less we actually exercise the skills we initially used to perform it.
PHRASE **tell you the truth** You say **to tell you the truth** or **truth to tell** in order to indicate that you are telling someone something in an open and honest way, without trying to hide anything. ❑ To tell you the truth, I was afraid to see him.

WORD CONNECTIONS
VERB + **truth**
accept the truth know the truth ❑ Only Karen knew the truth.
find the truth learn the truth search for the truth ❑ He's bound to learn the truth eventually.
tell the truth ❑ She was clearly telling the truth.
ADJ + **truth**
the plain truth the simple truth the the awful truth the sad truth ❑ The plain truth is that fad dieting is just as bad as overeating.
the whole truth the absolute truth ❑ What she had said was the absolute truth.

T

truth·ful /ˈtruːθfʊl/ ADJ If a person or their comments are **truthful**, they are honest and do not tell any lies. ❑ *Most religions teach you to be truthful.* ❑ *We've all learned to be fairly truthful about our personal lives.*
  truth·ful·ly /ˈtruːθfəli/ ADV [truthfully with V] ❑ *I answered all their questions truthfully.*
  truth·ful·ness /ˈtruːθfəlnəs/ NOUN [U] ❑ *I can say, with absolute truthfulness, that I did my best.*

try ♦♦♦ /traɪ/ VERB, NOUN
  VERB [I, T] (**tries, trying, tried**) **1** [I, T] If you **try** to do something, you want to do it, and you take action which you hope will help you to do it. ❑ *He secretly tried to help her at work.* ❑ *Does it annoy you if others don't seem to try hard enough?* **2** [T] (*informal*) To **try and** do something means to try to do it. ❑ *I must try and see him.* **3** [I] If you **try for** something, you make an effort to get it or achieve it. ❑ *My partner and I have been trying for a baby for two years.* **4** [T] If you **try** something new or different, you use it, do it, or experience it in order to discover its qualities or effects. ❑ *It's best not to try a new recipe for the first time on such an important occasion.* **5** [T] If you **try** a particular place or person, you go to that place or person because you think that they may be able to provide you with what you want. ❑ *Have you tried the local music shops?* **6** [T] If you **try** a door or window, you try to open it. ❑ *Bob tried the door. To his surprise it opened.* **7** [T] When a person **is tried**, he or she has to appear in a law court and is found innocent or guilty after the judge and jury have heard the evidence. When a legal case **is tried**, it is considered in a court of law. ❑ *He suggested that those responsible should be tried for crimes against humanity.* ❑ *Whether he is innocent or guilty is a decision that will be made when the case is tried in court.*
  PHRASAL VERBS **try on** If you **try on** a piece of clothing, you put it on to see if it fits you or if it looks nice. ❑ *Try on clothing and shoes to make sure they fit.*
  try out If you **try** something **out**, you test it in order to find out how useful or effective it is or what it is like. ❑ *I wanted to try the boat out next weekend.* ❑ *Some owners wish they could try out the car on a race track.*
  NOUN [C] (**tries**) **1** A **try** is an action you take in order to help you do something that you want to do. ❑ *It wasn't that she'd really expected to get any money out of him; it had just seemed worth a try.* **2** If you give something new or different a **try**, you use it, do it, or experience it in order to discover its qualities or effects. ❑ *If you're still sceptical about exercising, we can only ask you to trust us and give it a try.* **3** In the game of rugby, a **try** is the action of scoring by putting the ball down behind the goal line of the opposing team. ❑ *The French, who led 21–3 at half time, scored eight tries.*
  → See also **tried**
  ✦ **try your best** → see **best; try your hand** → see **hand; try someone's patience** → see **patience**

T-shirt also **tee-shirt** NOUN [C] (**T-shirts**) A **T-shirt** is a cotton shirt with no collar or buttons. T-shirts usually have short sleeves.

tube ♦♦♦ /tjuːb, AmE tuːb/ NOUN [C, SING] (**tubes**) **1** [C] A **tube** is a long hollow object that is usually round, like a pipe. ❑ *He is fed by a tube that enters his nose.* **2** [C] A **tube** of something such as paste is a long, thin container which you squeeze in order to force the paste out. ❑ *I went out today and bought a tube of toothpaste.* **3** [C] Some long, thin, hollow parts in your body are referred to as **tubes**. ❑ *The lungs are in fact constructed of thousands of tiny tubes.* **4** [SING] (*BrE*) **The tube** is the underground railway system in London.

tuck /tʌk/ VERB, NOUN
  VERB [T] (**tucks, tucking, tucked**) If you **tuck** something somewhere, you put it there so that it is safe, comfortable, or neat. ❑ *He tried to tuck his flapping shirt inside his trousers.*
  PHRASAL VERBS **tuck away** **1** If you **tuck away** something such as money, you store it in a safe place. ❑ *The extra income has meant Phillippa can tuck away the rent.* **2** If someone or something **is tucked away**, they are well hidden in a quiet place where very few people go. ❑ *We were tucked away in a secluded corner of the room.*

tuck in **1** If you **tuck in** a piece of material, you keep it in position by placing one edge or end of it behind or under something else. For example, if you **tuck in** your shirt, you place the bottom part of it inside your trousers or skirt. **2** If you **tuck** a child **in** bed or **tuck** them **in**, you make them comfortable by straightening the sheets and blankets and pushing the loose ends under the mattress. ❑ *I read Lili a story and tucked her in.*
  NOUN [C] (**tucks**) You can use **tuck** to refer to a form of plastic surgery which involves reducing the size of a part of someone's body. ❑ *She'd undergone 13 operations, including a tummy tuck.*

tug /tʌg/
  VERB [I, T] (**tugs, tugging, tugged**) If you **tug** something or **tug at** it, you give it a quick and usually strong pull. ❑ *A little boy came running up and tugged at his sleeve excitedly.*
  NOUN [C] (**tugs**) **1** A **tug** is a strong quick pull on something. ❑ *I felt a tug at my sleeve.* **2** A **tug** or a **tug boat** is a small powerful boat which pulls large ships, usually when they come into a port. ❑ *a 76,000-ton barge pulled by five tug boats*

❂tui·tion /tjuːˈɪʃən, AmE tuː-/ NOUN [U] If you are given **tuition** in a particular subject, you are taught about that subject. = teaching, instruction ❑ *The courses will give you tuition in all types of outdoor photography.* ❑ *You need to pay your tuition fees and to support yourself financially.*

tum·ble /ˈtʌmbəl/ VERB, NOUN
  VERB [I] (**tumbles, tumbling, tumbled**) **1** If someone or something **tumbles** somewhere, they fall there with a rolling or bouncing movement. ❑ *A small boy tumbled off the porch.* **2** (*journalism*) If prices or levels of something **are tumbling**, they are decreasing rapidly. ❑ *Profit after taxes tumbled by half to $15.8 million.* ❑ *Share prices continued to tumble today on the Tokyo stock market.* **3** If water **tumbles**, it flows quickly over an uneven surface. ❑ *Waterfalls crash and tumble over rocks.*
  NOUN [C] (**tumbles**) **1** [usu sing] A **tumble** is a fall with a rolling or bouncing movement. ❑ *He injured his ribs in a tumble from his horse.* **2** (*journalism*) A **tumble** is a rapid decrease in the level or price of something. ❑ *Oil prices took a tumble yesterday.*

tu·mour /ˈtjuːmə, AmE ˈtuː-/ (*BrE; in AmE, use* **tumor**) NOUN [C] (**tumours**) A **tumour** is a mass of diseased or abnormal cells which has grown in a person's or animal's body. ❑ *a malignant brain tumour*

tune ♦♦♦ /tjuːn, AmE tuːn/ NOUN, VERB
  NOUN [C] (**tunes**) **1** A **tune** is a series of musical notes that is pleasant and easy to remember. = melody ❑ *She was humming a merry little tune.* **2** You can refer to a song or a short piece of music as a **tune**. ❑ *She'll also be playing your favourite pop tunes.*
  PHRASES **call the tune** If you say that a person or organization **is calling the tune**, you mean that they are in a position of power or control in a particular situation. ❑ *It is Coulthard who is calling the tune so far this season.*
  change your tune (*disapproval*) If you say that someone **has changed** their **tune**, you are criticizing them because they have changed their opinion or way of doing things. ❑ *You've changed your tune since this morning, haven't you?*
  in tune or **out of tune** A person or musical instrument that is **in tune** produces exactly the right notes. A person or musical instrument that is **out of tune** does not produce exactly the right notes. ❑ *It was just an ordinary voice, but he sang in tune.*
  VERB [T] (**tunes, tuning, tuned**) **1** When someone **tunes** a musical instrument, they adjust it so that it produces the right notes. ❑ *'We do tune our guitars before we go on', he insisted.* **2** When an engine or machine **is tuned**, it is adjusted so that it works well. ❑ *Drivers are urged to make sure that car engines are properly tuned.* **3** If your radio or television **is tuned to** a particular channel or broadcasting station, you are listening to or watching the programmes being broadcast by that station. ❑ *A small colour television was tuned to an afternoon soap opera.*
  PHRASAL VERBS **tune in** **1** If you **tune in** to a particular television or radio station or programme, you watch or listen to it. ❑ *All over the country, youngsters tune in to*

t

Sesame Street every day. **2** If you **tune in to** something such as your own or other people's feelings, you become aware of them. ❑ *You can start now to tune in to your own physical, social and spiritual needs.*

tune out If you **tune out**, you stop listening or paying attention to what is being said. ❑ *Children rapidly tune out if you go beyond them.* ❑ *Rose heard the familiar voice, but tuned out the words.*

tune up 1 Tune up means the same as **tune** VERB **2**. ❑ *The shop charges up to $500 to tune up a Porsche.* **2 Tune up** means the same as **tune** VERB **1**. ❑ *Others were quietly tuning up their instruments.*

tun·nel ♦◇◇ /'tʌnəl/ NOUN, VERB

NOUN [c] **(tunnels)** A **tunnel** is a long passage which has been made under the ground, usually through a hill or under the sea. ❑ *Boston drivers love the tunnel.*

VERB [i] **(tunnels, tunnelling, tunnelled;** in *AmE*, use **tunneling, tunneled)** To **tunnel** somewhere means to make a tunnel there. ❑ *The thieves tunnelled under all the security devices.*

tur·bu·lent /'tɜːbjʊlənt/ ADJ **1** A **turbulent** time, place, or relationship is one in which there is a lot of change, confusion, and disorder. ❑ *They had been together for five or six turbulent years of break-ups and reconciliations.* **2 Turbulent** water or air contains strong currents which change direction suddenly. ❑ *I had to have a boat that could handle turbulent seas.*

tur·moil /'tɜːmɔɪl/ NOUN [c, u] **(turmoils)** **Turmoil** is a state of confusion, disorder, uncertainty, or great anxiety. ❑ *political uncertainty and economic turmoil in Argentina*

turn ♦♦♦ /tɜːn/ VERB, NOUN

VERB [i, t, LINK] **(turns, turning, turned)** **1** [i, t] When you **turn** or when you **turn** part of your body, you move your body or part of your body so that it is facing in a different or opposite direction. ❑ *He turned abruptly and walked away.* ❑ *He sighed, turning away and surveying the sea.* **2** [t] When you **turn** something, you move it so that it is facing in a different or opposite direction, or is in a very different position. ❑ *They turned their telescopes towards other nearby galaxies.* ❑ *She had turned the bedside chair to face the door.* **3** [i, t] When something such as a wheel **turns**, or when you **turn** it, it continually moves around in a particular direction. ❑ *As the wheel turned, the potter shaped the clay.* **4** [i, t] When you **turn** something such as a key, knob, or switch, or when it **turns**, you hold it and twist your hand, in order to open something or make it start working. ❑ *Turn the key three times to the right.* ❑ *Turn the heat to very low and cook for 20 minutes.* **5** [i, t] When you **turn** in a particular direction or **turn** a corner, you change the direction in which you are moving or travelling. ❑ *He turned into the narrow street where he lived.* ❑ *Now turn right to follow West Ferry Road.* **6** [i] The point where a road, path, or river **turns** is the point where it has a bend or curve in it. ❑ *the corner where Tenterfield Road turned into the main road* **7** [i] When the tide **turns**, it starts coming in or going out. ❑ *There was not much time before the tide turned.* **8** [t] When you **turn** a page of a book or magazine, you move it so that it is flat against the previous page, and you can read the next page. ❑ *He turned the pages of a file in front of him.* **9** [t] If you **turn** a weapon or an aggressive feeling **on** someone, you point it at them or direct it at them. ❑ *He tried to turn the gun on me.* **10** [i] If you **turn to** a particular page in a book or magazine, you open it at that page. ❑ *To order, turn to page 236.* **11** [i, t] If you **turn** your attention or thoughts **to** a particular subject or if you **turn to** it, you start thinking about it or discussing it. ❑ *We turned our attention to the practical matters relating to forming a company.* ❑ *We turn now to our primary question.* **12** [i] If you **turn to** someone, you ask for their help or advice. ❑ *For assistance, they turned to one of the city's most innovative museums.* **13** [i] If you **turn to** a particular activity, job, or way of doing something, you start doing or using it. ❑ *These communities are now turning to recycling as a cheaper alternative to landfills.* **14** [i, t] To **turn** or **be turned into** something means to become that thing. ❑ *A prince turns into a frog in this cartoon fairytale.* **15** [LINK] You can use **turn** before an adjective to indicate that something or someone

changes by acquiring the quality described by the adjective. = become ❑ *If the bailiff thinks that things could turn nasty he will enlist the help of the police.* **16** [LINK] If something **turns** a particular colour or if something **turns** it a particular colour, it becomes that colour. ❑ *The sea would turn pale pink and the sky blood red.* **17** [LINK] You can use **turn** to indicate that there is a change to a particular kind of weather. For example, if it **turns** cold, the weather starts being cold. ❑ *If it turns cold, cover the plants.* **18** [t] *(business)* If a business **turns** a profit, it earns more money than it spends. ❑ *The firm will be able to pay off its debts and still turn a modest profit.* **19** [t] When someone **turns** a particular age, they pass that age. When it **turns** a particular time, it passes that time. ❑ *It was his ambition to accumulate a million dollars before he turned thirty.*

PHRASAL VERBS **turn against** If you **turn against** someone or something, or if you **are turned against** them, you stop supporting them, trusting them, or liking them, and sometimes you work against them. ❑ *A kid I used to be friends with turned against me after being told that I'd been insulting him.*

turn around 1 Turn around means the same as **turn** VERB **1**. ❑ *I felt a tapping on my shoulder and I turned around.* **2** If you **turn** something **around**, or if it **turns around**, it is moved so that it faces the opposite direction. ❑ *Bud turned the truck around, and started back for Dalton Pond.* ❑ *He had reached over to turn around a bottle of champagne so that the label didn't show.* **3** *(business)* If something such as a business or economy **turns around**, or if someone **turns** it **around**, it becomes successful, after being unsuccessful for a period of time. ❑ *Turning the company around won't be easy.* ❑ *In his long career, Horton turned around two entire divisions.*

turn away 1 If you **turn** someone **away**, you do not allow them to enter your country, home, or other place. ❑ *Turning Cuban boat people away would be an inhumane action.* **2** To **turn away from** something such as a method or an idea means to stop using it or to become different from it. ❑ *Japanese companies have been turning away from production and have moved into real estate.*

turn back 1 If you **turn back** or if someone **turns** you **back** when you are going somewhere, you change direction and go towards where you started from. ❑ *She turned back towards home.* ❑ *Police attempted to turn back.* **2** If you **cannot turn back**, you cannot change your plans and decide not to do something, because the action you have already taken makes it impossible. ❑ *The Senate has now endorsed the bill and can't turn back.*

turn down 1 If you **turn down** a person or their request or offer, you refuse their request or offer. = reject ❑ *I thanked him for the offer but turned it down.* **2** When you **turn down** a radio, heater, or other piece of equipment, you reduce the amount of sound or heat being produced, by adjusting the controls. ❑ *He kept turning the central heating down.*

turn off 1 If you **turn off** the road or path you are going along, you start going along a different road or path which leads away from it. ❑ *The truck turned off the main road, and went along the gravelly track which led to the farm.* **2** When you **turn off** a piece of equipment or a supply of something, you stop heat, sound, or water from being produced by adjusting the controls. = switch off ❑ *The light's a bit too harsh. You can turn it off.* **3** If something **turns** you **off** a particular subject or activity, it makes you have no interest in it. ❑ *What turns teenagers off science?* ❑ *Greed on the part of owners and athletes turns fans off completely.*

turn on 1 When you **turn on** a piece of equipment or a supply of something, you cause heat, sound, or water to be produced by adjusting the controls. = switch on ❑ *I want to turn on the television.* **2** *(informal)* If someone or something **turns** you **on**, they attract you and make you feel sexually excited. ❑ *The body that turns men on doesn't have to be perfect.* **3** If someone **turns on** you, they suddenly attack you or speak angrily to you. ❑ *Demonstrators turned on police, overturning vehicles and setting fire to them.*

turn out 1 If something **turns out** a particular way, it happens in that way or has the result or degree of success indicated. = **work out** ❑ *If I had known my life was going to turn out like this, I would have let them kill me.* ❑ *I was positive things were going to turn out fine.* **2** If something **turns out** to be a particular thing, it is discovered to be that thing. ❑ *Cosgrave's forecast turned out to be completely wrong.* **3** When you **turn out** something such as a light, you move the switch or knob that controls it so that it stops giving out light or heat. = **turn off** ❑ *The janitor comes around to turn the lights out.*

turn over **1** If you **turn** something **over**, or if it **turns over**, it is moved so that the top part is now facing downwards. ❑ *Liz picked up the blue envelope and turned it over curiously.* ❑ *The buggy turned over and Nancy was thrown out.* **2** If you **turn over**, for example, when you are lying in bed, you move your body so that you are lying in a different position. ❑ *Ann turned over in her bed once more.* **3** If you **turn** something **over** in your mind, you think carefully about it. ❑ *Even when she didn't say anything you could see her turning things over in her mind.* **4** If you **turn** something **over to** someone, you give it to them when they ask for it, because they have a right to it. = **hand over** ❑ *I would have to turn the evidence over to the police.* **5** → See also **turnover**

turn up **1** If you say that someone or something **turns up**, you mean that they arrive unexpectedly or after you have been waiting a long time. = **show up** ❑ *They finally turned up at nearly midnight.* ❑ *Richard had turned up on Christmas Eve with Tony.* **2** If you **turn** something **up** or if it **turns up**, you find, discover, or notice it. ❑ *Investigations have never turned up any evidence.* **3** When you **turn up** a radio, heater, or other piece of equipment, you increase the amount of sound, heat, or power being produced, by adjusting the controls. ❑ *Can you turn up the TV?* ❑ *I turned the volume up.*

NOUN [C, SING] (**turns**) **1** [C] A **turn** is a change of direction when you are travelling or moving. ❑ *You can't do a right-hand turn here.* **2** [C] A **turn** in a road, path, or river is a place where it has a bend or curve in it. ❑ *a sharp turn in the road* **3** [C] If a situation or trend takes a particular kind of **turn**, it changes so that it starts developing in a different or opposite way. ❑ *The scandal took a new turn over the weekend.* **4** [SING] **Turn** is used in expressions such as **the turn of the century** and **the turn of the year** to refer to a period of time when one century or year is ending and the next one is beginning. ❑ *They fled to South America around the turn of the century.* **5** [C] If it is your **turn to** do something, you now have the duty, chance, or right to do it, when other people have done it before you or will do it after you. ❑ *Tonight it's my turn to cook.*

PHRASES **turn of events** If there is a particular **turn of events**, a particular series of things happen. ❑ *They were horrified at this unexpected turn of events.*

at every turn (*emphasis*) If you say that something happens **at every turn**, you are emphasizing that it happens frequently or all the time, usually so that it prevents you from achieving what you want. ❑ *Its operations were hampered at every turn by inadequate numbers of trained staff.*

a good turn If you do someone **a good turn**, you do something that helps or benefits them. ❑ *He did you a good turn by resigning.*

in turn **1** You use **in turn** to refer to actions or events that are in a sequence one after the other, for example, because one causes the other. ❑ *One of the members of the surgical team leaked the story to a fellow physician who, in turn, confided in a reporter.* **2** If each person in a group does something **in turn**, they do it one after the other in a fixed or agreed order. ❑ *There were cheers for each of the women as they spoke in turn.*

take turns If two or more people **take turns to** do something, they do it one after the other at different times, rather than doing it together. ❑ *We took turns driving.*

take a turn for the worse or **take a turn for the better** If a situation **takes a turn for the worse**, it suddenly becomes worse. If a situation **takes a turn for the better**, it suddenly becomes better. ❑ *Her condition took a sharp turn for the worse.*

→ See also **turning**

turn·ing /ˈtɜːnɪŋ/ (*mainly BrE; in AmE, usually use* **turn**) NOUN [C] (**turnings**) If you take a particular **turning**, you go along a road which leads away from the side of another road. = **turn**

turn·ing point NOUN [C] (**turning points**) A **turning point** is a time at which an important change takes place which affects the future of a person or thing. ❑ *The vote yesterday appears to mark a turning point in the war.*

✪turn·over /ˈtɜːnəʊvə/ NOUN [C, U] (**turnovers**) (*business*) **1** The **turnover** of a company is the value of the goods or services sold during a particular period of time. = **revenue** ❑ *The company had a turnover of $3.8 million.* ❑ *Group turnover rose by 13 per cent to £3.7bn.* **2** The **turnover** of people in an organization or place is the rate at which people leave and are replaced. ❑ *Short-term contracts increase staff turnover.*

✪tu·tor /ˈtjuːtə, AmE ˈtuːt-/ NOUN [C] (**tutors**) **1** A **tutor** is someone who gives private lessons to one student or a very small group of students. ❑ *a Spanish tutor* **2** A **tutor** is a teacher at a British university or college. In some American universities or colleges, a **tutor** is a teacher of the lowest rank. = **teacher, lecturer** ❑ *He is course tutor in archaeology at the University of Southampton.* ❑ *Liam surprised his tutors by twice failing a second year exam.*

✪tu·to·rial /tjuːˈtɔːriəl, AmE tuːt-/ NOUN, ADJ NOUN [C] (**tutorials**) **1** In a university or college, a **tutorial** is a regular meeting between a tutor or professor and one or several students, for discussion of a subject that is being studied. ❑ *The methods of study include lectures, tutorials, case studies and practical sessions.* ❑ *Students attend weekly tutorials.* **2** A **tutorial** is part of a book or a computer program which helps you learn something step-by-step without a teacher. ❑ *There is an excellent tutorial section, which carefully walks you through how to play.* ADJ [tutorial + N] **Tutorial** means relating to a tutor or tutors, especially one at a university or college. ❑ *Students may decide to seek tutorial guidance.*

TV ◆◆◇ /ˌtiː ˈviː/ also **T.V.** NOUN [C, U] (**TVs**) **TV** means the same as **television**. ❑ *The TV was on.* ❑ *What's on TV?* ❑ *They watch too much TV.*

twelfth ◆◆◇ /twelfθ/ ADJ, NOUN ADJ The **twelfth** item in a series is the one that you count as number twelve. ❑ *the twelfth anniversary of the April revolution* NOUN [C] (**twelfths**) A **twelfth** is one of twelve equal parts of something. ❑ *She is entitled to a twelfth of the cash.*

twelve ◆◆◆ /twelv/ NUM (**twelves**) **Twelve** is the number 12.

twen·ti·eth ◆◆◇ /ˈtwentiəθ/ ADJ, NOUN ADJ The **twentieth** item in a series is the one that you count as number twenty. ❑ *the twentieth century* NOUN [C] (**twentieths**) A **twentieth** is one of twenty equal parts of something. ❑ *A few twentieths of a gram can be critical.*

twen·ty ◆◆◆ /ˈtwenti/ NUM, NOUN NUM (**twenties**) **Twenty** is the number 20. NOUN [PL] **1** When you talk about the **twenties**, you are referring to numbers between 20 and 29. For example, if you are **in** your **twenties**, you are aged between 20 and 29. If the temperature is **in the twenties**, the temperature is between 20 and 29 degrees. ❑ *They're both in their twenties and both married with children of their own.* **2** The **twenties** is the decade between 1920 and 1929. ❑ *It was written in the Twenties, but it still really stands out.*

✪twice ◆◆◆ /twaɪs/ ADV, PREDET ADV **1** If something happens **twice**, it happens two times, or there are two actions or events of the same kind. = **two times** ❑ *He visited me twice that autumn and called me on the telephone often.* ❑ *The government has twice declined to back the scheme.* ❑ *Thoroughly brush teeth and gums twice daily.* **2** [twice 'a' N] You use **twice** in expressions such as **twice a day** and **twice a week** to indicate that something happens two times in each day or week. ❑ *I phoned twice a day, leaving messages with his wife.* **3** [twice 'as' ADJ/ADV] If one thing is, for example, **twice as** big or old **as** another, the first thing is double the size or age of the second. People sometimes say that one thing is **twice as** good or hard **as**

t

another when they want to emphasize that the first thing is much better or harder than the second. = double; ≠ half ❑ *The figure of seventy-million dollars was twice as big as expected.* ❑ *a report claiming that teachers could be twice as effective if they returned to traditional classroom methods* PHRASE **think twice** If you **think twice** about doing something, you consider it again and decide not to do it, or decide to do it differently. ❑ *From now on, think twice before saying stupid things.* PREDET [twice 'the' N] **Twice** the price, the average, the amount, etc. means double the price, double the average, double the amount, etc. ❑ *Unemployment here is twice the national average.*

✦ once or twice → see once; twice over → see over

twin ◆◇◇ /twɪn/ NOUN, ADJ
 NOUN [c] (**twins**) **Twins** are two people who were born at the same time from the same mother. ❑ *Sarah was looking after the twins.* ❑ *I think there are many positive aspects to being a twin.*
 ADJ **1** [twin + N] **Twin** is used to describe a pair of things that look the same and are close together. ❑ *the twin spires of the cathedral* **2** [twin + N] **Twin** is used to describe two things or ideas that are similar or connected in some way. ❑ *the twin concepts of liberty and equality*

twist ◆◇◇ /twɪst/ VERB, NOUN
 VERB [T, I] (**twists**, **twisting**, **twisted**) **1** [T] If you **twist** something, you turn it to make it a spiral shape, for example, by turning the two ends of it in opposite directions. ❑ *Her hands began to twist the handles of the bag she carried.* **2** [I, T] If you **twist** something, especially a part of your body, or if it **twists**, it moves into an unusual, uncomfortable, or bent position, for example, because of being hit or pushed, or because you are upset. ❑ *He twisted her arms behind her back and clipped a pair of handcuffs on her wrists.* ❑ *Sophia's face twisted in perplexity.* **3** [I, T] If you **twist** part of your body such as your head or your shoulders, you turn that part while keeping the rest of your body still. ❑ *She twisted her head sideways and looked towards the door.* ❑ *Susan twisted round in her seat until she could see Graham behind her.* **4** [T] If you **twist** a part of your body such as your ankle or wrist, you injure it by turning it too sharply, or in an unusual direction. ❑ *He fell and twisted his ankle.* **5** [T] If you **twist** something, you turn it so that it moves around in a circular direction. ❑ *She was staring down at her hands, twisting the ring on her finger.* **6** [I] If a road or river **twists**, it has a lot of sudden changes of direction in it. ❑ *The roads twist around hairpin bends.* **7** [T] If you say that someone **has twisted** something that you have said, you disapprove of them because they have repeated it in a way that changes its meaning, in order to harm you or benefit themselves. = distort ❑ *It's a shame the way the media can twist your words and misrepresent you.*
 NOUN [c] (**twists**) **1** A **twist** of something is a movement in a circular direction. ❑ *Just a twist of the handle is all it takes to wring out the mop.* **2** [usu pl] A **twist** in a road or river is a place where it suddenly changes direction. ❑ *It allows the train to maintain a constant speed through the twists and turns of existing track.* **3** A **twist** in something is an unexpected and significant development. ❑ *The battle of the sexes also took a new twist.*
 ✦ twist someone's arm → see arm

two ◆◆◆ /tuː/ NUM
 NUM (**twos**) **Two** is the number 2.
 PHRASES **it takes two** or **it takes two to tango** If you say **it takes two** or **it takes two to tango**, you mean that a situation or argument involves two people and they are both therefore responsible for it. ❑ *Divorce is never the fault of one partner; it takes two.*
 put two and two together If you **put two and two together**, you work out the truth about something for yourself, by using the information that is available to you. ❑ *Putting two and two together, I assume that this was the car he used.*
 ✦ kill two birds with one stone → see bird

❂**two-dimensional** also **two dimensional** ADJ
 1 [usu two-dimensional + N] A **two-dimensional** object or

figure is flat rather than solid so that only its length and width can be measured. ❑ *new software, which generates both two-dimensional drawings and three-dimensional images* ❑ *The conifers looked like two-dimensional cutouts against the white sky.* **2** If you describe fictional characters as **two-dimensional**, you are critical of them because they are very simple and not realistic enough to be taken seriously. ❑ *I found the characters very two-dimensional and dull.*

❂**type** ◆◆◇ /taɪp/ NOUN, VERB
 NOUN [c, U] (**types**) **1** [c] A **type of** something is a group of those things that have particular features in common. = sort, kind, class ❑ *several types of lettuce* ❑ *There are various types of the disease.* ❑ *In 1990, 25% of households were of this type.* **2** [c] If you refer to a particular thing or person as a **type of** something more general, you are considering that thing or person as an example of that more general group. = sort, kind ❑ *Have you done this type of work before?* ❑ *Rates of interest for this type of borrowing can be high.* **3** [c] If you refer to a person as a particular **type**, you mean that they have that particular appearance, character, or type of behaviour. = sort ❑ *It's the first time I, a fair-skinned, freckly type, have sailed in the sun without burning.* **4** [U] **Type** is printed text as it appears in a book or newspaper, or the small pieces of metal that are used to create this. ❑ *The correction had already been set in type.* ❑ *I can't read this small type.*
 VERB [I, T] (**types**, **typing**, **typed**) If you **type** something, you use a typewriter or computer keyboard to write it. ❑ *I can type your essays for you.* ❑ *I had never really learned to type properly.*
 PHRASAL VERBS **type in** or **type into** If you **type** information **into** a computer or **type** it **in**, you press keys on the keyboard so that the computer stores or processes the information. = key in ❑ *Officials type each passport number into a computer.* ❑ *You have to type in commands, such as 'help' and 'print'.*
 type up If you **type up** a text that has been written by hand, you produce a typed copy of it. ❑ *When the first draft was completed, Nichols typed it up.*

VOCABULARY BUILDER

type NOUN
If you refer to a particular thing or person as a **type of** something more general, you are considering that thing or person as an example of that more general group.
❑ *How familiar are you with this type of software?*

sort NOUN
If you talk about a particular **sort** of something, you are talking about a group of things that have particular features in common and that belong to a larger group of related things.
❑ *There are many different sorts of mushrooms available.*

kind NOUN
If you talk about a particular **kind** of thing, you are talking about one of the types or sorts of that thing.
❑ *The party needs a different kind of leadership.*

class NOUN
A **class** of things is a group of them with similar characteristics.
❑ *the division of the stars into six classes of brightness*

form NOUN (*formal*)
A **form** of something is a type or kind of it.
❑ *He contracted a rare form of cancer.*

❂**ty·phoon** /taɪˈfuːn/ NOUN [c] (**typhoons**) A **typhoon** is a very violent tropical storm. = hurricane, cyclone ❑ *large atmospheric disturbances such as typhoons* ❑ *a powerful typhoon that killed at least 32 people*

❂**typ·i·cal** ◆◇◇ /ˈtɪpɪkəl/ ADJ **1** You use **typical** to describe someone or something that shows the most usual characteristics of a particular type of person or thing, and is therefore a good example of that type. ❑ *Cheney is everyone's image of a typical cop: a big white guy, six feet, 220* pounds. ❑ *A typical soil sample contains the following components.* **2** If a particular action or feature is **typical of** someone or something, it shows their usual qualities or characteristics. = characteristic; ≠ atypical ❑ *This reluctance to move towards a democratic state is typical of totalitarian regimes.* ❑ *With typical energy he found new journalistic outlets.* **3** If you say that something is **typical of** a person, situation, or thing, you are criticizing them or complaining about them and saying that they are just as bad or disappointing as you expected them to be. ❑ *She threw her hands into the air. 'That is just typical of you, isn't it?'*

✪ **typi·cal·ly** /'tɪpɪkəli/ ADV **1** [typically with CL/GROUP] You use **typically** to say that something usually happens in the way that you are describing. = normally, usually; ≠ rarely ❑ *It typically takes a day or two, depending on size.* ❑ *Typically, parents apply to several schools and settle, if need be, for their fourth or fifth choice.* ❑ *Female migrants are typically very young.* **2** [typically + ADJ] You use **typically** to say that something shows all the most usual characteristics of a particular type of person or thing. = normally, usually, characteristically; ≠ rarely ❑ *Philip paced the floor, a typically nervous expectant father.* ❑ *The main course was typically Swiss.* **3** You use **typically** to indicate that someone has behaved in the way that they normally do.

= characteristically ❑ *Typically, the Norwegians were on the mountain two hours before anyone else.*

typi·fy /'tɪpɪfaɪ/ VERB [T] (**typifies, typifying, typified**) If something or someone **typifies** a situation or type of thing or person, they have all the usual characteristics of it and are a typical example of it. = epitomize ❑ *These two buildings typify the rich extremes of local architecture.*

tyr·an·ny /'tɪrəni/ NOUN [C, U] (**tyrannies**) **1** [C, U] A **tyranny** is a cruel, harsh, and unfair government in which a person or small group of people have power over everyone else. ❑ *Self-expression and individuality are the greatest weapons against tyranny.* **2** [U] If you describe someone's behaviour and treatment of others that they have authority over as **tyranny**, you mean that they are severe with them or unfair to them. ❑ *I'm the sole victim of Mother's tyranny.*

ty·rant /'taɪərənt/ NOUN [C] (**tyrants**) You can use **tyrant** to refer to someone who treats the people they have authority over in a cruel and unfair way. ❑ *households where the father was a tyrant*

tyre /taɪə/ (*BrE*; in *AmE*, use **tire**) NOUN [C] (**tyres**) A **tyre** is a thick piece of rubber which is fitted onto the wheels of vehicles such as cars, buses, and bicycles.

Uu

U also **u** NOUN [C, U] (**U's, u's**) **U** is the twenty-first letter of the English alphabet.

ug·ly /'ʌgli/ ADJ (**uglier, ugliest**) **1** If you say that someone or something is **ugly**, you mean that they are very unattractive and unpleasant to look at. ❑ *an ugly little hat* **2** If you refer to an event or situation as **ugly**, you mean that it is very unpleasant, usually because it involves violent or aggressive behaviour. ❑ *There have been some ugly scenes.* ❑ *The confrontation turned ugly.*
ug·li·ness /'ʌglinəs/ NOUN [U] **1** *Dekkeret found the landscape startling in its ugliness.* **2** *the ugliness of sexual harassment*
✦ **rear its ugly head** → see **head**

ul·te·ri·or /ʌl'tɪəriə/ ADJ [ulterior + N] If you say that someone has an **ulterior** motive for doing something, you believe that they have a hidden reason for doing it. ❑ *Sheila had an ulterior motive for trying to help Stan.*

✪ **ul·ti·mate** ✦◇◇ /'ʌltɪmət/ ADJ, NOUN (*academic word*)
ADJ 1 [ultimate + N] You use **ultimate** to describe the final result or aim of a long series of events. **= eventual, final** ❑ *He said it is still not possible to predict the ultimate outcome.* ❑ *The ultimate aim is to expand the network further.* **2** [ultimate + N] You use **ultimate** to describe the original source or cause of something. **= fundamental** ❑ *Plants are the ultimate source of all foodstuffs.* **3** [ultimate + N] You use **ultimate** to describe the most important or powerful thing of a particular kind. **= most important, highest** ❑ *My experience as player, coach and manager has prepared me for this ultimate challenge.* ❑ *the ultimate power of the central government* ❑ *Of course, the ultimate authority remained the presidency.* **4** [ultimate + N] You use **ultimate** to describe the most extreme and unpleasant example of a particular thing. ❑ *Bringing back the death penalty would be the ultimate abuse of human rights.* ❑ *Treachery was the ultimate sin.* **5** [ultimate + N] You use **ultimate** to describe the best possible example of a particular thing. **= definitive** ❑ *Experience the ultimate adventure!*
NOUN
PHRASE **the ultimate in** The ultimate in something is the best or most advanced example of it. ❑ *Ballet is the ultimate in human movement.* ❑ *This hotel is the ultimate in luxury.*

✪ **ul·ti·mate·ly** ✦◇◇ /'ʌltɪmətli/ ADV **1** Ultimately means finally, after a long and often complicated series of events. **= eventually, in the end** ❑ *Whatever the scientists ultimately conclude, all of their data will immediately be disputed.* ❑ *It was a tough but ultimately worthwhile struggle.* **2** [ultimately with CL] You use **ultimately** to indicate that what you are saying is the most important point in a discussion. ❑ *Ultimately, Judge Lewin has the final say.* ❑ *Ultimately, Bismarck's revisionism scarcely affected or damaged British interests at all.*

ul·ti·ma·tum /ˌʌltɪ'meɪtəm/ NOUN [C] (**ultimatums**) An **ultimatum** is a warning to someone that unless they act in a particular way, action will be taken against them. ❑ *They issued an ultimatum to the police to rid the area of racist attackers, or they will take the law into their own hands.*

ul·tra·vio·let /ˌʌltrə'vaɪələt/ ADJ Ultraviolet light or radiation is what causes your skin to become darker in colour after you have been in sunlight. In large amounts ultraviolet light is harmful. ❑ *The sun's ultraviolet rays are responsible for both tanning and burning.*

WORD PARTS
The prefix **ultra-** often appears in words to show that people or things have a very large amount of a quality: **ultraviolet** (ADJ) **ultra-light** (ADJ) **ultrasound** (NOUN)

um·brel·la /ʌm'brelə/ NOUN [C, SING] (**umbrellas**) **1** [C] An **umbrella** is an object which you use to protect yourself from the rain or hot sun. It consists of a long stick with a folding frame covered in cloth. ❑ *Harry held an umbrella over Denise.* **2** [SING] **Umbrella** is used to refer to a single group or description that includes a lot of different organizations or ideas. ❑ *The country's blood banks are under the umbrella of the American Red Cross.*

um·pire /'ʌmpaɪə/ NOUN, VERB
NOUN [C] (**umpires**) An **umpire** is a person whose job is to make sure that a sports contest or game is played fairly and that the rules are not broken. ❑ *The umpire's decision is final.*
VERB [I, T] (**umpires, umpiring, umpired**) To **umpire** means to be the umpire in a sports contest or game. ❑ *He umpired baseball games.*

un·able ✦◇◇ /ʌn'eɪbəl/ ADJ [V-LINK + unable + to-INF] If you are **unable to** do something, it is impossible for you to do it, for example because you do not have the necessary skill or knowledge, or because you do not have enough time or money. ❑ *The military may feel unable to hand over power to a civilian president next year.*

WORD PARTS
The prefix **un-** often gives words the opposite meaning: **unable** (ADJ) **unacceptable** (ADJ) **uncover** (VERB)

un·ac·cep·table /ˌʌnək'septəbəl/ ADJ If you describe something as **unacceptable**, you strongly disapprove of it or object to it and feel that it should not be allowed to continue. ❑ *It is totally unacceptable for children to swear.*

✪ **un·am·big·uous** /ˌʌnæm'bɪgjuəs/ ADJ If you describe a message or comment as **unambiguous**, you mean that it is clear and cannot be understood wrongly. ≠ **ambiguous** ❑ *an election result that sent the party an unambiguous message* ❑ *The instructions were clear and unambiguous.*
✪ **un·am·big·uous·ly** /ˌʌnæm'bɪgjuəsli/ ADV
≠ **ambiguously** ❑ *He has failed to dissociate himself clearly and unambiguously from the attack.* ❑ *The president said that she had stated the US position very clearly and unambiguously.*

✪ **unani·mous** /ju:'nænɪməs/ ADJ **1** When a group of people are **unanimous**, they all agree about something or all vote for the same thing. ❑ *Editors were unanimous in their condemnation of the proposals.* ❑ *Experts are unanimous that money raised through debt should not be allowed to be used for buyback.* **2** A **unanimous** vote, decision, or agreement is one in which all the people involved agree. **= common, agreed, shared, universal; ≠ divided** ❑ *Their decision was unanimous.* ❑ *the unanimous vote for Hungarian membership*
✪ **unani·mous·ly** /ju:'nænɪməsli/ ADV [unanimously with V]

= universally ☐ *The board unanimously approved the project last week.* ☐ *Today its executive committee voted unanimously to reject the proposals.*

un·author·ized /ʌnˈɔːθəraɪzd/ also **unauthorised** ADJ If something is **unauthorized**, it has been produced or is happening without official permission. = unofficial ☐ *a new unauthorized biography of the Russian president* ☐ *It has also been made quite clear that the trip was unauthorized.*

un·avail·able /ˌʌnəˈveɪləbəl/ ADJ When things or people are **unavailable**, you cannot obtain them, meet them, or talk to them. ☐ *Mr Hicks is out of the country and so unavailable for comment.*

un·avoid·able /ˌʌnəˈvɔɪdəbəl/ ADJ If something is **unavoidable**, it cannot be avoided or prevented. ☐ *Managers said the job losses were unavoidable.*

un·aware /ˌʌnəˈweə/ ADJ [V-LINK + unaware] If you are **unaware of** something, you do not know about it. ☐ *Many people are unaware of just how much food and drink they consume.*

un·bear·able /ʌnˈbeərəbəl/ ADJ If you describe something as **unbearable**, you mean that it is so unpleasant, painful, or upsetting that you feel unable to accept it or deal with it. = intolerable ☐ *War has made life almost unbearable for the civilians remaining in the capital.*
un·bear·ably /ʌnˈbeərəbli/ ADV ☐ *By the evening it had become unbearably hot.*

un·beat·en /ʌnˈbiːtən/ ADJ In sports, if a person or their performance is **unbeaten**, nobody else has performed well enough to beat them. ☐ *He's unbeaten in 20 fights.*

un·be·liev·able /ˌʌnbɪˈliːvəbəl/ ADJ **1** (emphasis) If you say that something is **unbelievable**, you are emphasizing that it is very good, impressive, intense, or extreme. = incredible ☐ *His guitar solos are just unbelievable.* ☐ *The pressure they put us under was unbelievable.* **2** (emphasis) You can use **unbelievable** to emphasize that you think something is very bad or shocking. = incredible ☐ *I find it unbelievable that people can accept this sort of behaviour.* **3** [unbelievable with CL/GROUP] If an idea or statement is **unbelievable**, it seems so unlikely to be true that you cannot believe it. = incredible ☐ *I still find this story both fascinating and unbelievable.*
un·be·liev·ably /ˌʌnbɪˈliːvəbli/ ADV **1** [unbelievably with CL/GROUP] = incredibly ☐ *It was unbelievably dramatic as lightning crackled all around the van.* ☐ *Our car was still going unbelievably well.* **2** [unbelievably with CL/GROUP] ☐ *What you did was unbelievably stupid.* **3** [unbelievably with CL/GROUP] ☐ *Lainey was, unbelievably, pregnant again.*

un·bi·ased /ʌnˈbaɪəst/ also **unbiassed** ADJ If you describe someone or something as **unbiased**, you mean they are fair and not likely to support one particular person or group involved in something. = impartial ☐ *There is no clear and unbiased information available for consumers.*

un·bro·ken /ʌnˈbrəʊkən/ ADJ If something is **unbroken**, it is continuous or complete and has not been interrupted or broken. = uninterrupted ☐ *an unbroken string of victories* ☐ *We've had ten days of almost unbroken sunshine.*

un·can·ny /ʌnˈkæni/ ADJ If you describe something as **uncanny**, you mean that it is strange and difficult to explain. ☐ *The hero, Danny, bears an uncanny resemblance to Kirk Douglas.*
un·can·ni·ly /ʌnˈkænɪli/ ADV ☐ *They have uncannily similar voices.*

un·cer·tain /ʌnˈsɜːtən/ ADJ
ADJ **1** If you are **uncertain about** something, you do not know what you should do, what is going to happen, or what the truth is about something. = unsure ☐ *He was uncertain about his brother's intentions.* ☐ *They were uncertain of the total value of the transaction.* **2** If something is **uncertain**, it is not known or definite. ☐ *How much practical help they can give us is uncertain.* ☐ *It's uncertain whether they will accept the plan.*
PHRASE **in no uncertain terms** (emphasis) If you say that someone tells a person something **in no uncertain terms**, you are emphasizing that they say it strongly and clearly so that there is no doubt about what they mean. ☐ *She*

told him in no uncertain terms to go away.
un·cer·tain·ly /ʌnˈsɜːtənli/ ADV ☐ *He entered the hallway and stood uncertainly.*

un·cer·tain·ty /ʌnˈsɜːtənti/ NOUN [C, U] (**uncertainties**) **Uncertainty** is a state of doubt about the future or about what is the right thing to do. ☐ *a period of political uncertainty*

un·changed /ʌnˈtʃeɪndʒd/ ADJ If something is **unchanged**, it has stayed the same for a particular period of time. ☐ *For many years prices have remained virtually unchanged.*

un·char·ac·ter·is·tic /ˌʌnkærɪktəˈrɪstɪk/ ADJ If you describe something as **uncharacteristic of** someone, you mean that it is not typical of them. ☐ *It was uncharacteristic of her father to disappear like this.*
un·char·ac·ter·is·ti·cal·ly /ˌʌnkærɪktəˈrɪstɪkli/ ADV ☐ *Owen has been uncharacteristically silent.*

un·checked /ʌnˈtʃekt/ ADJ If something harmful or undesirable is left **unchecked**, nobody controls it or prevents it from growing or developing. ☐ *If left unchecked, weeds will flourish.* ☐ *a world in which brutality and lawlessness are allowed to go unchecked*

un·cle ♦♦◇ /ˈʌŋkəl/ NOUN [C] (**uncles**) Someone's **uncle** is the brother of their mother or father, or the husband of their aunt. ☐ *My uncle was the mayor of Memphis.* ☐ *An e-mail from Uncle Fred arrived.*

un·clear /ʌnˈklɪə/ ADJ **1** If something is **unclear**, it is not known or not certain. = uncertain ☐ *It is unclear how much popular support they have among the island's population.* ☐ *Just what the soldier was doing there is unclear.* **2** [V-LINK + unclear] If you are **unclear about** something, you do not understand it well or are not sure about it. ☐ *He is still unclear about his own future.*

un·com·fort·able /ʌnˈkʌmftəbəl/ ADJ **1** If you are **uncomfortable**, you are slightly worried or embarrassed, and not relaxed and confident. = awkward ☐ *The request for money made them feel uncomfortable.* ☐ *If you are uncomfortable with your therapist, you must discuss it.* **2** Something that is **uncomfortable** makes you feel slight pain or physical discomfort when you experience it or use it. ☐ *Wigs are hot and uncomfortable to wear constantly.* ☐ *The ride back to the centre of the town was hot and uncomfortable.* **3** If you are **uncomfortable**, you are not physically content and relaxed, and feel slight pain or discomfort. ☐ *I sometimes feel uncomfortable after eating in the evening.*
un·com·fort·ably /ʌnˈkʌmftəbli/ ADV **1** *Sandy leaned across the table, his face uncomfortably close to Brad's.* ☐ *I became uncomfortably aware that the people at the next table were watching me.* **2** [uncomfortably + ADJ] ☐ *The water was uncomfortably cold.* **3** *He felt uncomfortably hot.*

un·com·mon /ʌnˈkɒmən/ ADJ If you describe something as **uncommon**, you mean that it does not happen often or is not often seen. = unusual ☐ *Fortunately, cancer of the breast in young women is uncommon.*

un·com·pro·mis·ing /ʌnˈkɒmprəmaɪzɪŋ/ ADJ **1** If you describe someone as **uncompromising**, you mean that they are determined not to change their opinions or aims in any way. ☐ *Voters have elected an uncompromising nationalist as their new president.* **2** If you describe something as **uncompromising**, you mean that it does not attempt to make something that is shocking or unpleasant any more acceptable to people. ☐ *a film of uncompromising brutality*

un·con·cerned /ˌʌnkənˈsɜːnd/ ADJ If a person is **unconcerned about** something, usually something that most people would care about, they are not interested in it or worried about it. ☐ *Paul was unconcerned about what he had done.*

un·con·di·tion·al /ˌʌnkənˈdɪʃənəl/ ADJ If you describe something as **unconditional**, you mean that the person doing or giving it does not require anything to be done by other people in exchange. ☐ *Children need unconditional love from their parents.*
un·con·di·tion·al·ly /ˌʌnkənˈdɪʃənəli/ ADV [unconditionally with V] ☐ *The hostages were released unconditionally.*

u

un·con·firmed /ˌʌnkənˈfɜːmd/ ADJ If a report or a rumour is **unconfirmed**, there is no definite proof as to whether it is true or not. ◻ There are unconfirmed reports of several small villages buried by mudslides.

un·con·nect·ed /ˌʌnkəˈnektɪd/ ADJ If one thing is **unconnected with** another or the two things are **unconnected**, the things are not related to each other in any way. = unrelated ◻ She had personal problems unconnected with her marriage.

un·con·scious /ʌnˈkɒnʃəs/ ADJ **1** Someone who is **unconscious** is in a state similar to sleep, usually as the result of a serious injury or a lack of oxygen. ◻ By the time the ambulance arrived he was unconscious. **2** [V-LINK + unconscious 'of' N] If you are **unconscious of** something, you are unaware of it. = oblivious ◻ He himself seemed totally unconscious of his failure. **3** If feelings or attitudes are **unconscious**, you are not aware that you have them, but they show in the way that you behave. ◻ my unconscious ambivalence about becoming a mother
un·con·scious·ness /ʌnˈkɒnʃəsnəs/ NOUN [u] ◻ He knew that he might soon lapse into unconsciousness.
un·con·scious·ly /ʌnˈkɒnʃəsli/ ADV **1** 'I was very unsure of myself after the divorce,' she says, unconsciously sweeping back the curls from her forehead. **2** Many women whose fathers left home unconsciously expect to be betrayed by their own mates.

un·con·trol·lable /ˌʌnkənˈtrəʊləbəl/ ADJ **1** If you describe a feeling or physical action as **uncontrollable**, you mean that you cannot control it or prevent yourself from feeling or doing it. ◻ It had been a time of almost uncontrollable excitement. ◻ William was seized with uncontrollable rage. **2** If you describe a person as **uncontrollable**, you mean that their behaviour is bad and that nobody can make them behave more sensibly. ◻ Mark was withdrawn and uncontrollable. **3** If you describe a situation or series of events as **uncontrollable**, you believe that nothing can be done to control them or to prevent things from getting worse. ◻ If political problems are not resolved, the situation may become uncontrollable.
un·con·trol·lably /ˌʌnkənˈtrəʊləbli/ ADV ◻ I started shaking uncontrollably and began to cry.

un·con·trolled /ˌʌnkənˈtrəʊld/ ADJ **1** If you describe someone's behaviour as **uncontrolled**, you mean they appear unable to stop it or to make it less extreme. ◻ His uncontrolled behaviour disturbed the entire class. **2** If a situation or activity is **uncontrolled**, no one is controlling it or preventing it from continuing or growing. = unchecked ◻ The capital, Nairobi, is choking on uncontrolled immigration.

un·con·ven·tion·al /ˌʌnkənˈvenʃənəl/ ADJ **1** If you describe a person or their attitude or behaviour as **unconventional**, you mean that they do not behave in the same way as most other people in their society. ◻ Linus Pauling is an unconventional genius. ◻ He was known for his unconventional behaviour. **2** An **unconventional** way of doing something is not the usual way of doing it, and may be surprising. ◻ The vaccine had been produced by an unconventional technique. ◻ Despite his unconventional methods, he has inspired students more than anyone else.

un·con·vinc·ing /ˌʌnkənˈvɪnsɪŋ/ ADJ **1** If you describe something such as an argument or explanation as **unconvincing**, you find it difficult to believe because it does not seem real. ◻ Mr Patel phoned the university for an explanation, and he was given the usual unconvincing excuses. **2** If you describe a story or a character in a story as **unconvincing**, you think they do not seem likely or real. ◻ an unconvincing love story
un·con·vinc·ing·ly /ˌʌnkənˈvɪnsɪŋli/ ADV [unconvincingly with v] ◻ 'It's not that I don't believe you, Meg,' Jack said, unconvincingly.

un·cov·er /ʌnˈkʌvə/ VERB [T] (**uncovers, uncovering, uncovered**) **1** If you **uncover** something, especially something that has been kept secret, you discover or find out about it. = discover ◻ Auditors said they had uncovered evidence of fraud. **2** To **uncover** something means to remove something that is covering it. ◻ When the seedlings sprout, uncover the tray.

un·daunt·ed /ˌʌnˈdɔːntɪd/ ADJ If you are **undaunted**, you are not at all afraid or worried about dealing with something, especially something that would frighten or worry most people. ◻ Undaunted by the scale of the job, Lesley set about planning how each room should look.

un·de·cid·ed /ˌʌndɪˈsaɪdɪd/ ADJ If someone is **undecided**, they cannot decide about something or have not yet decided about it. ◻ After college she was still undecided as to what career she wanted to pursue.

un·de·ni·able /ˌʌndɪˈnaɪəbəl/ ADJ If you say that something is **undeniable**, you mean that it is definitely true. ◻ Her charm is undeniable.
un·de·ni·ably /ˌʌndɪˈnaɪəbli/ ADV ◻ Bringing up a baby is undeniably hard work.

un·der ♦♦♦ /ˈʌndə/ PREP, ADV

> In addition to the uses shown below, **under** is also used in phrasal verbs such as 'go under' and 'knuckle under'.

PREP **1** If a person or thing is **under** something, they are at a lower level than that thing, and may be covered or hidden by it. ◻ They found a labyrinth of tunnels under the ground. ◻ swimming in the pool or lying under an umbrella ◻ A path runs under the trees. **2** In a place such as an ocean, river, or swimming pool, if someone or something is **under** the water, they are fully in the water and covered by it. ◻ She held her breath for three minutes under the water. **3** If you go **under** something, you move from one side to the other of something that is at a higher level than you. ◻ He went under a brick arch. **4** Something that is **under** a layer of something, especially clothing, is covered by that layer. ◻ I was wearing two sweaters under the green army jacket. ◻ a faded striped shirt under a knitted sweater **5** You can use **under** before a noun to indicate that a person or thing is being affected by something or is going through a particular process. ◻ fishermen whose livelihoods are under threat ◻ Firemen said they had the blaze under control. **6** If something happens **under** particular circumstances or conditions, it happens when those circumstances or conditions exist. ◻ His best friend died under questionable circumstances. ◻ Under normal conditions, only about 20 to 40 per cent of vitamin E is absorbed. **7** If something happens **under** a law, agreement, or system, it happens because that law, agreement, or system says that it should happen. ◻ Under law, your employer has the right to hire a temporary worker to replace you. ◻ Under the new regulations, one in five cars may need repairs costing as much as $120. **8** If something happens **under** a particular person or government, it happens when that person or government is in power. ◻ There would be no new taxes under his leadership. ◻ the realities of life under a brutal dictatorship **9** If you study or work **under** a particular person, that person teaches you or tells you what to do. ◻ Kiefer was just one of the artists who had studied under Beuys in the early Sixties. ◻ General Lewis Hyde had served under General Mitchell. **10** If you do something **under** a particular name, you use that name instead of your real name. ◻ Were any of your books published under the name Amanda Fairchild? **11** You use **under** to say which section of a list, book, or system something is in. ◻ The 'General Diseases of the Eye' study is filed under E. **12** [under + AMOUNT] If something or someone is **under** a particular age or amount, they are less than that age or amount. ◻ jobs for those under 65 ◻ Nearly half of mothers with children under five have a job.
ADV **1** [under after v] In a place such as an ocean, river, or swimming pool, if someone or something goes **under**, they are fully in the water and covered by it. ◻ He took a deep breath before he went under. **2** [AMOUNT 'and' under] If something or someone is a particular age or amount or **under**, they are less than that age or amount. ◻ free or subsidized health insurance for children 13 and under
♦ under wraps → see wrap

under·cur·rent /ˈʌndəkʌrənt, -kɜːr-/ NOUN [C] (**undercurrents**) **1** If there is an **undercurrent of** a feeling, you are hardly aware of the feeling, but it influences the way you think or behave. ◻ the strong undercurrent of pro-business sentiment in Congress **2** An **undercurrent** is a strong current of water that is moving below the surface

U

current and in a different direction to it. ❑ *Karen tried to swim after him but the strong undercurrent swept them apart.*

⊕under·es·ti·mate /ˌʌndərˈestɪmeɪt/ VERB [T] (underestimates, underestimating, underestimated) (*academic word*) **1** If you **underestimate** something, you do not realize how large or great it is or will be. = undervalue; ≠ overestimate, exaggerate ❑ *None of us should ever underestimate the degree of difficulty women face in career advancement.* ❑ *Marx clearly underestimated the importance of population growth.* ❑ *The most common mistake students make in library research is underestimating how long it will take to find the sources they need.* **2** If you **underestimate** someone, you do not realize what they are capable of doing. ❑ *I think a lot of people still underestimate him.*

WORD PARTS

The prefix *under-* often appears in words to show that an amount or value is not enough:

underestimate (VERB)
underpaid (ADJ)
underprivileged (ADJ)

⊕under·go /ˌʌndəˈɡəʊ/ VERB [T] (undergoes, undergoing, underwent, undergone) (*academic word*) If you **undergo** something necessary or unpleasant, it happens to you. ❑ *New recruits have been undergoing training in recent weeks.* ❑ *When cement powder is mixed with water it undergoes a chemical change and sets hard.*

⊕under·gradu·ate /ˌʌndəˈɡrædʒuət/ NOUN [C] (undergraduates) An **undergraduate** is a student at a university or college who is studying for his or her first degree. ❑ *Economics undergraduates are probably the brightest in the university.* ❑ *undergraduate degree programmes*

under·ground ◆◇◇ ADV, ADJ, NOUN
ADV /ˌʌndəˈɡraʊnd/ **1** [underground after V] Something that is **underground** is below the surface of the ground. ❑ *Solid low-level waste will be disposed of deep underground.* **2** [underground after V] If you go **underground**, you hide from the authorities or the police because your political ideas or activities are illegal. ❑ *After the violent clashes of 1981 they either went underground or left the country.*
ADJ /ˈʌndəɡraʊnd/ **1** [underground + N] Something that is **underground** is below the surface of the ground. ❑ *an underground parking garage for 2,100 vehicles* **2** [underground + N] **Underground** groups and activities are secret because their purpose is to oppose the government and they are illegal. ❑ *the underground Kashmir Liberation Front*
NOUN /ˈʌndəɡraʊnd/ [SING] ['the' underground, also 'by' underground] (*BrE*; in *AmE*, use **subway**) **The underground** in a city is the railway system in which electric trains travel below the ground in tunnels.

under·hand /ˌʌndəˈhænd/ or **underhanded** ADJ [usu underhand + N] (*disapproval*) If an action is **underhand** or if it is done in an **underhand** way, it is done secretly and dishonestly. ❑ *underhand financial deals* ❑ *a list of the underhanded ways in which their influence operates in the United States*

under·lie /ˌʌndəˈlaɪ/ VERB [T] (underlies, underlying, underlay, underlain) (*academic word*) If something **underlies** a feeling or situation, it is the cause or basis of it. ❑ *Try to figure out what feeling underlies your anger.*
→ See also **underlying**

⊕under·line /ˌʌndəˈlaɪn/ VERB [T] (underlines, underlining, underlined) **1** If one thing, for example an action or an event, **underlines** another, it draws attention to it and emphasizes its importance. = underscore, emphasize, highlight ❑ *The report underlined his concern that standards were at risk.* ❑ *This incident underlines the danger of travelling in the border area.* ❑ *The incident underlines how easily things can go wrong.* **2** If you **underline** something such as a word or a sentence, you draw a line underneath it in order to make people notice it or to give it extra importance. ❑ *Underline the following that apply to you.*

⊕un·der·ly·ing /ˌʌndəˈlaɪɪŋ/ ADJ (*academic word*) **1** [underlying + N] The **underlying** features of an object, event, or situation are not obvious, and it may be difficult

to discover or reveal them. = basic, fundamental ❑ *To stop a problem you have to understand its underlying causes.* ❑ *I think that the underlying problems are education, unemployment, and bad housing.* **2** [underlying + N] You describe something as **underlying** when it is below the surface of something else. ❑ *hills with the hard underlying rock poking through the turf*
→ See also **underlie**

⊕under·mine ◆◇◇ /ˌʌndəˈmaɪn/ VERB [T] (undermines, undermining, undermined) **1** If you **undermine** something such as a feeling or a system, you make it less strong or less secure than it was before, often by a gradual process or by repeated efforts. = weaken; ≠ strengthen ❑ *Offering advice on each and every problem will undermine her feeling of being adult.* ❑ *Popular culture has helped undermine elitist notions of high culture.* ❑ *The technological sophistication of the Bronzes undermined 19th-century Western European assumptions about primitive Africa.* **2** If you **undermine** someone or **undermine** their position or authority, you make their authority or position less secure, often by indirect methods. ❑ *She undermined him and destroyed his confidence in his own talent.* ❑ *Western intelligence agencies are accused of trying to undermine the government.* **3** If you **undermine** someone's efforts or **undermine** their chances of achieving something, you behave in a way that makes them less likely to succeed. ❑ *The continued fighting threatens to undermine efforts to negotiate an agreement.*

under·neath /ˌʌndəˈniːθ/ PREP, ADV, NOUN
PREP **1** If one thing is **underneath** another, it is directly under it, and may be covered or hidden by it. = beneath ❑ *The device exploded underneath a van.* ❑ *using dogs to locate people trapped underneath collapsed buildings* **2** You use **underneath** when talking about feelings and emotions that people do not show in their behaviour. ❑ *Underneath his outgoing behaviour Luke was shy.*
ADV **1** If one thing has another thing **underneath**, the second thing is directly under the first, and may be covered or hidden by it. ❑ *He has on his jeans and a long-sleeved blue denim shirt with a white T-shirt underneath.* ❑ *The shooting-range is lit from underneath by rows of ruby-red light fixtures.* **2** The part of something which is **underneath** is the part which normally touches the ground or faces towards the ground. ❑ *Check the actual construction of the chair by looking underneath.* ❑ *The sand martin is a brown bird with white underneath.* **3** [underneath with CL] You use **underneath** when talking about feelings and emotions that people do not show in their behaviour. ❑ *He was as violent as Nick underneath.*
NOUN [SING] The **underneath** of something is the part which normally touches the ground or faces towards the ground. ❑ *Now I know what the underneath of a car looks like.*

under·paid /ˌʌndəˈpeɪd/ ADJ People who are **underpaid** are not paid enough money for the job that they do. ❑ *Women are frequently underpaid for the work that they do.*

⊕under·privi·leged /ˌʌndəˈprɪvɪlɪdʒd/ ADJ, NOUN
ADJ [usu underprivileged + N] **Underprivileged** people have less money and fewer possessions and opportunities than other people in their society. = deprived, disadvantaged; ≠ privileged, wealthy ❑ *helping underprivileged children to learn to read* ❑ *the hideous effects of government cuts on underprivileged families*
NOUN [PL] ['the' underprivileged] **The underprivileged** are people who are underprivileged. ❑ *government plans to make more jobs available to the underprivileged*

under·score /ˌʌndəˈskɔː/ (*mainly AmE*; in *BrE*, usually use **underline**) VERB [T] (underscores, underscoring, underscored) If something such as an action or an event **underscores** another, it draws attention to the other thing and emphasizes its importance. = underline ❑ *These figures underscore the shaky state of the economic recovery.*

under·side /ˈʌndəsaɪd/ NOUN [C] (undersides) The **underside** of something is the part of it which normally faces towards the ground. = underneath ❑ *the underside of the car*

⊕under·stand ◆◆◆ /ˌʌndəˈstænd/ VERB [T] (understands, understanding, understood) **1** If you **understand** someone or **understand** what they are saying,

u

you know what they mean. ❏ *I think you heard and also understand me.* ❏ *I don't understand what you are talking about.* **2** If you **understand** a language, you know what someone is saying when they are speaking that language. ❏ *I couldn't read or understand a word of Yiddish, so I asked him to translate.* **3** To **understand** someone means to know how they feel and why they behave in the way that they do. ❏ *It would be nice to have someone who really understood me, a friend.* ❏ *Trish had not exactly understood his feelings.* **4** You say that you **understand** something when you know why or how it happens. = appreciate, comprehend, grasp; ≠ misunderstand ❏ *They are too young to understand what is going on.* ❏ *She didn't understand why the TV was kept out of reach of the patients.* ❏ *In the effort to understand AIDS, attention is moving from the virus to the immune system.* **5** If you **understand** that something is the case, you think it is true because you have heard or read that it is. You can say that something **is understood** to be the case to mean that people generally think it is true. ❏ *We understand that she's in the studio recording her second album.* ❏ *As I understand it, she has a house in the city.* ❏ *The management is understood to be very unwilling to agree to this request.*

under·stand·able /ˌʌndəˈstændəbəl/ ADJ **1** If you describe someone's behaviour or feelings as **understandable**, you think that they have reacted to a situation in a natural way or in the way you would expect. ❏ *His unhappiness was understandable.* **2** If you say that something such as a statement or theory is **understandable**, you mean that people can easily understand it. ❏ *Roger Neuberg writes in a simple and understandable way.*

under·stand·ably /ˌʌndəˈstændəbli/ ADV ❏ *Officials are understandably nervous about the tense situation in the neighbourhood.*

✪**under·stand·ing** ♦◇◇ /ˌʌndəˈstændɪŋ/ NOUN, ADJ
NOUN [C, U, SING] (**understandings**) **1** [C, U] If you have an **understanding** of something, you know how it works or know what it means. = grasp, appreciation, awareness; ≠ ignorance ❏ *They have to have a basic understanding of computers in order to use the advanced technology.* ❏ *testing students' understanding of difficult concepts* **2** [U] If you show **understanding**, you show that you realize how someone feels or why they did something, and are not hostile towards them. ❏ *We would like to thank them for their patience and understanding.* **3** [U] If there is **understanding** between people, they are friendly towards each other and trust each other. ❏ *There was complete understanding between Wilson and myself.* **4** [C] An **understanding** is an informal agreement about something. ❏ *We had not set a date for marriage but there was an understanding between us.* **5** [SING] If you say that it is your **understanding that** something is the case, you mean that you believe it to be the case because you have heard or read that it is. ❏ *It is my understanding that the meeting is Thursday.*
PHRASE **on the understanding (that)** If you agree to do something **on the understanding that** something else will be done, you do it because you have been told that the other thing will definitely be done. ❏ *Poverty forced her to surrender him to foster families, but only on the understanding that she could eventually regain custody.*
ADJ If you are **understanding** towards someone, you are kind and forgiving. = sympathetic ❏ *Her boss, who was very understanding, gave her time off.*

WORD CONNECTIONS

VERB + **understanding**

have an understanding
gain an understanding
develop an understanding
❏ *Scientists are trying to develop a better understanding of the physical forces involved in earthquakes.*

promote understanding
improve understanding
increase understanding
❏ *Measuring the health of children improves our understanding of the health impacts of social changes.*

lack understanding
❏ *Some managers lack a basic understanding of how the system is supposed to work.*

ADJ + **understanding**

a **good** understanding
a **clear** understanding
a **deep** understanding
a **basic** understanding
❏ *Perpetrators need to have a clear understanding of the punishments for their actions.*

under·state /ˌʌndəˈsteɪt/ VERB [T] (**understates, understating, understated**) If you **understate** something, you describe it in a way that suggests that it is less important or serious than it really is. ❏ *The government chooses deliberately to understate the increase in prices.*

under·stat·ed /ˌʌndəˈsteɪtɪd/ ADJ [understated + N] If you describe a style, colour, or effect as **understated**, you mean that it is simple and plain, and does not attract attention to itself. = subtle ❏ *I have always liked understated clothes.*

under·state·ment /ˈʌndəsteɪtmənt/ NOUN [C, U] (**understatements**) **1** [C] If you say that a statement is an **understatement**, you mean that it does not fully express the extent to which something is true. ❏ *To say I'm disappointed is an understatement.* **2** [U] **Understatement** is the practice of suggesting that things have much less of a particular quality than they really have. ❏ *typical British understatement*

un·der·stood /ˌʌndəˈstʊd/ IRREG FORM **Understood** is the past tense and past participle of **understand**.

✪**under·take** /ˌʌndəˈteɪk/ VERB [T] (**undertakes, undertaking, undertook, undertaken**) (*academic word*) **1** When you **undertake** a task or job, you start doing it and accept responsibility for it. = do, carry out ❏ *She undertook the task of monitoring the elections.* ❏ *Students are encouraged to undertake research in areas in which the department has particular expertise.* **2** If you **undertake to** do something, you promise that you will do it. ❏ *He undertook to edit the text himself.*

✪**under·tak·ing** /ˈʌndəteɪkɪŋ/ NOUN [C] (**undertakings**) An **undertaking** is a task or job, especially a large or difficult one. = job, task ❏ *Organizing the show has been a massive undertaking.* ❏ *the nineteenth century's most ambitious scientific undertaking*

un·der·took /ˌʌndəˈtʊk/ IRREG FORM **Undertook** is the past tense of **undertake**.

under·wa·ter /ˌʌndəˈwɔːtə/ ADV, ADJ
ADV Something that exists or happens **underwater** exists or happens below the surface of the sea, a river, or a lake. ❏ *giant submarines able to travel at high speeds underwater* ❏ *Some stretches of beach are completely underwater at high tide.*
ADJ **1** [underwater + N] **Underwater** is used to describe things that exist or happen below the surface of the sea, a river, or a lake. ❏ *underwater exploration* ❏ *underwater fishing with harpoons* **2** [underwater + N] **Underwater** devices are specially made so that they can work in water. ❏ *underwater camera equipment*

under·way /ˌʌndəˈweɪ/ ADJ [V-LINK + underway] If an activity is **underway**, it has already started. If an activity gets **underway**, it starts. ❏ *An investigation is underway to find out how the disaster happened.* ❏ *It was a cold evening, winter well underway.*

un·der·went /ˌʌndəˈwent/ IRREG FORM **Underwent** is the past tense of **undergo**.

under·world /ˈʌndəwɜːld/ NOUN [SING] The **underworld** in a city is the organized crime there and the people who are involved in it. ❏ *a Spanish Harlem underworld of gangs, drugs, and violence* ❏ *Some claim that she still has connections to the criminal underworld.*

under·write /ˌʌndəˈraɪt/ VERB [T] (**underwrites, underwriting, underwrote, underwritten**) (*business*) If an institution or company **underwrites** an activity or **underwrites** the cost of it, they agree to provide any

U

money that is needed to cover losses or buy special equipment, often for an agreed-upon fee. ❑ *The government will have to create a special agency to underwrite small business loans.*

un·de·sir·able /ˌʌndɪˈzaɪərəbəl/ ADJ If you describe something or someone as **undesirable**, you think they will have harmful effects. ❑ *Inflation is considered to be undesirable because of its adverse effects on income distribution.*

un·did /ʌnˈdɪd/ IRREG FORM **Undid** is the past tense of **undo**.

un·dis·closed /ˌʌndɪsˈkləʊzd/ ADJ **Undisclosed** information is not revealed to the public. ❑ *The company has been sold for an undisclosed amount.*

un·dis·put·ed /ˌʌndɪˈspjuːtɪd/ ADJ **1** If you describe a fact or opinion as **undisputed**, you are trying to persuade someone that it is generally accepted as true or correct. ❑ *an undisputed fact* ❑ *his undisputed genius* **2** If you describe someone as the **undisputed** leader or champion, you mean that everyone accepts their position as leader or champion. ❑ *Seles won 10 tournaments, and was the undisputed world champion.* ❑ *At 78 years of age, he's still undisputed leader of his country.*

undo /ʌnˈduː/ VERB [T] (**undoes**, **undoing**, **undid**, **undone**) **1** If you **undo** something that is closed, tied, or held together, or if you **undo** the thing holding it, you loosen or remove the thing holding it. ❑ *I managed secretly to undo a corner of the parcel.* ❑ *I undid the bottom two buttons of my yellow and grey shirt.* **2** To **undo** something that has been done means to reverse its effect. ❑ *A heavy-handed approach from the police could undo that good impression.* ❑ *She knew it would be difficult to undo the damage that had been done.*
→ See also **undoing**

un·do·ing /ʌnˈduːɪŋ/ NOUN [SING] If something is someone's **undoing**, it is the cause of their failure. = downfall ❑ *His lack of experience may prove to be his undoing.*

✪ **un·doubt·ed** /ʌnˈdaʊtɪd/ ADJ (*emphasis*) You can use **undoubted** to emphasize that something exists or is true. = definite, undisputed; ≠ doubtful ❑ *The event was an undoubted success.* ❑ *a man of your undoubted ability*

✪ **un·doubt·ed·ly** /ʌnˈdaʊtɪdli/ ADV (*emphasis*) If something **undoubtedly** exists or is true, it is certain that it exists or is true. = without doubt, certainly ❑ *Undoubtedly, political and economic factors have played their part.* ❑ *These sort of statistics are undoubtedly alarming.* ❑ *It is undoubtedly true that harder times are on the way.*

un·dressed /ʌnˈdrest/ ADJ If you are **undressed**, you are wearing no clothes, or your underwear or pyjamas. If you get **undressed**, you take off your clothes. ❑ *Fifteen minutes later he was undressed and in bed.*

un·due /ʌnˈdjuː, AmE -ˈduː/ ADJ [undue + N] If you describe something bad as **undue**, you mean that it is greater or more extreme than you think is reasonable or appropriate. = excessive ❑ *This would help the families to survive the drought without undue suffering.* ❑ *It is unrealistic to put undue pressure on ourselves by saying we are the best.*

un·du·ly /ʌnˈdjuːli, AmE -ˈduːli/ ADV If you say that something does not happen or is not done **unduly**, you mean that it does not happen or is not done to an excessive or unnecessary extent. ❑ *'But you're not unduly worried about doing this report?'—'No.'* ❑ *This will achieve greater security without unduly burdening consumers or the economy.*

un·ease /ʌnˈiːz/ NOUN [U] **1** If you have a feeling of **unease**, you feel anxious or afraid, because you think that something is wrong. = anxiety ❑ *Sensing my unease about the afternoon ahead, he told me, 'These men are pretty easy to talk to.'* ❑ *We left with a deep sense of unease, because we knew something was being hidden from us.* **2** If you say that there is **unease** in a situation, you mean that people are dissatisfied or angry, but have not yet started to take any action. ❑ *He faces growing unease among the Democrats about the likelihood of war.* ❑ *the depth of public unease about the economy*

un·easy /ʌnˈiːzi/ ADJ **1** If you are **uneasy**, you feel anxious, afraid, or embarrassed, because you think that something is wrong or that there is danger. = uncomfortable ❑ *He said nothing but gave me a sly grin that made me feel terribly uneasy.* ❑ *He looked uneasy and refused to answer questions.* **2** If you are **uneasy about** doing something, you are not sure that it is correct or wise. ❑ *Richard was uneasy about how best to approach his elderly mother.* **3** (*journalism*) If you describe a situation or relationship as **uneasy**, you mean that the situation is not settled and may not last. ❑ *An uneasy calm has settled over Los Angeles.* ❑ *There is an uneasy relationship between us and the politicians.*

un·eas·i·ly /ʌnˈiːzɪli/ ADV **1** Meg shifted uneasily on her chair. **2** *a country whose component parts fit uneasily together*

un·eas·i·ness /ʌnˈiːzinəs/ NOUN [U] **1** With a small degree of uneasiness, he pushed it open and stuck his head inside. **2** *I felt a certain uneasiness about meeting her again.*

un·eco·nomi·cal /ʌnˌiːkəˈnɒmɪkəl, -ˌek-/ ADJ (*business*) If you say that an action, a method, or a product is **uneconomical**, you mean that it does not make a profit. = unprofitable ❑ *It would be uneconomical to send a brand new tape.*

✪ **un·em·ployed** /ˌʌnɪmˈplɔɪd/ ADJ, NOUN
ADJ Someone who is **unemployed** does not have a job. = out of work; ≠ employed ❑ *The problem is millions of people are unemployed.* ❑ *This workshop helps young unemployed people.* ❑ *Have you been unemployed for over six months?*
NOUN [PL] The **unemployed** are people who are unemployed. ❑ *We want to create jobs for the unemployed.*

✪ **un·em·ploy·ment** ♦◇◇ /ˌʌnɪmˈplɔɪmənt/ NOUN [U] **Unemployment** is the fact that people who want jobs cannot get them. ≠ employment ❑ *The state's unemployment rate rose slightly to 7.1 per cent last month.* ❑ *an area that had the highest unemployment rate in Western Europe* ❑ *Unemployment is damaging both to individuals and to communities.*

✪ **un·ethi·cal** /ʌnˈeθɪkəl/ ADJ (*academic word*) If you describe someone's behaviour as **unethical**, you think it is wrong and unacceptable according to a society's rules or people's beliefs. = immoral, corrupt ❑ *It's simply unethical to promote and advertise such a dangerous product.* ❑ *I thought it was unethical for doctors to operate upon their families.* ❑ *It would be unethical to expose humans to radiation in a clinical trial.* ❑ *to investigate widespread unethical and illegal practices in banking* ❑ *accusations of unethical conduct*

un·even /ʌnˈiːvən/ ADJ **1** An **uneven** surface or edge is not smooth, flat, or straight. ❑ *He staggered on the uneven surface.* ❑ *The pathways were uneven, broken, and dangerous.* **2** Something that is **uneven** is not regular or consistent. ❑ *He could hear that her breathing was uneven.* **3** An **uneven** system or situation is unfairly arranged or organized. ❑ *Some of the victims are complaining loudly about the uneven distribution of emergency aid.*

un·event·ful /ˌʌnɪˈventfʊl/ ADJ If you describe a period of time as **uneventful**, you mean that nothing interesting, exciting, or important happened during it. ❑ *The return trip was uneventful, the car running perfectly.*

un·ex·pec·ted ♦◇◇ /ˌʌnɪkˈspektɪd/ ADJ If an event or someone's behaviour is **unexpected**, it surprises you because you did not think that it was likely to happen. ❑ *His death was totally unexpected.* ❑ *He made a brief, unexpected appearance at the office.*

un·ex·pect·ed·ly /ˌʌnɪkˈspektɪdli/ ADV ❑ *Moss had clamped an unexpectedly strong grip on his arm.*

un·ex·plained /ˌʌnɪkˈspleɪnd/ ADJ If you describe something as **unexplained**, you mean that the reason for it or cause of it is unclear or is not known. ❑ *An unexplained death is difficult to come to terms with.* ❑ *The city's water supply has been cut for unexplained reasons.*

un·fair ♦◇◇ /ʌnˈfeə/ ADJ An **unfair** action or situation is not right or fair. ❑ *She was awarded $5,000 in compensation for unfair dismissal.* ❑ *It was unfair that he should suffer so much.*

un·fair·ly /ʌnˈfeəli/ ADV ❑ *He unfairly blamed Frances for the failure.*

u

un·faith·ful /ʌnˈfeɪθfʊl/ ADJ If someone is **unfaithful to** their lover or to the person they are married to, they have a sexual relationship with someone else. ◻ *James had been unfaithful to Christine for the entire four years they'd been together.*

un·fa·mil·iar /ʌnfəˈmɪliə/ ADJ **1** If something is **unfamiliar to** you, you know nothing or very little about it, because you have not seen or experienced it before. ◻ *She grew many wonderful plants that were unfamiliar to me.* **2** [V-LINK + unfamiliar 'with' N] If you are **unfamiliar with** something, you know nothing or very little about it. ◻ *She speaks no Japanese and is unfamiliar with Japanese culture.*

un·fash·ion·able /ʌnˈfæʃənəbəl/ ADJ If something is **unfashionable**, it is not approved of or done by most people because it is out of style. ◻ *Wearing fur has become unfashionable.*

un·fa·vour·able /ʌnˈfeɪvərəbəl/ (in *AmE*, use **unfavorable**) ADJ **1** **Unfavourable** conditions or circumstances cause problems for you and reduce your chances of success. ◻ *The decision to delay the launch stems from unfavourable weather conditions.* ◻ *The whole international economic situation is very unfavourable for the countries in the south.* **2** If you have an **unfavourable** reaction to something, you do not like it. ◻ *The president is drawing unfavourable comments on his new forest policy.* ◻ *views unfavourable to the capitalist system* **3** [unfavourable + N] If you make an **unfavourable** comparison between two things, you say that one thing seems worse than the other. ◻ *I didn't expect unfavourable comparisons between my sons and their friends.*
un·fa·vour·ably /ʌnˈfeɪvərəbli/ ADV **1** [unfavourably after V] ◻ *Other medications or foods may react unfavourably with it.* **2** *Tax rates compare unfavourably with the less heavy-handed North American agreement.*

un·fin·ished /ʌnˈfɪnɪʃt/ ADJ If you describe something such as a work of art or a piece of work as **unfinished**, you mean that it is not complete, for example because it was abandoned or there was no time to complete it. = incomplete ◻ *Jane Austen's unfinished novel* ◻ *The cathedral was eventually completed in 1490, though the Gothic façade remains unfinished.*

un·fit /ʌnˈfɪt/ ADJ **1** If you are **unfit**, your body is not in good condition because you have not been getting regular exercise. ◻ *Many children are so unfit they are unable to do even basic exercises.* **2** If someone is **unfit** for something, he or she is unable to do it because of injury or illness. ◻ *He had a third examination and was declared unfit for duty.* **3** If you say that someone or something is **unfit** for a particular purpose or job, you are criticizing them because they are not good enough for that purpose or job. ◻ *Existing houses are becoming totally unfit for human habitation.* ◻ *They were utterly unfit to govern.*

un·fold /ʌnˈfəʊld/ VERB [I, T] (**unfolds**, **unfolding**, **unfolded**) **1** [I] If a situation **unfolds**, it develops and becomes known or understood. ◻ *The outcome depends on conditions as well as how events unfold.* **2** [I, T] If a story **unfolds** or if someone **unfolds** it, it is told to someone else. ◻ *Don's story unfolded as the cruise got under way.* **3** [I, T] If someone **unfolds** something which has been folded or if it **unfolds**, it is opened out and becomes flat. ◻ *He quickly unfolded the blankets and spread them on the mattress.*

un·fore·see·able /ʌnfɔːˈsiːəbəl/ ADJ An **unforeseeable** problem or unpleasant event is one which you did not expect and could not have predicted. ◻ *This is such an unforeseeable situation that anything could happen.*

un·fore·seen /ʌnfəˈsiːn/ ADJ If something that has happened was **unforeseen**, it was not expected to happen or known about beforehand. = surprising, unpredicted, unexpected; ≠ foreseen, predicted, expected ◻ *Radiation may damage cells in a way that was previously unforeseen.* ◻ *Unfortunately, due to unforeseen circumstances, this year's show has been cancelled.* ◻ *Barring any unforeseen circumstances, interest rates should remain relatively stable in the medium term.*

un·for·get·table /ʌnfəˈgetəbəl/ ADJ If you describe something as **unforgettable**, you mean that it is, for example, extremely beautiful, enjoyable, or unusual, so that you remember it for a long time. You can also refer to extremely unpleasant things as **unforgettable**. ◻ *A visit to the museum is an unforgettable experience.* ◻ *the outdoor activities that will make your holiday unforgettable*

⚪un·for·tu·nate /ʌnˈfɔːtʃʊnət/ ADJ, NOUN
ADJ **1** If you describe someone as **unfortunate**, you mean that something unpleasant or unlucky has happened to them. You can also describe the unpleasant things that happen to them as **unfortunate**. = unlucky, regrettable; ≠ fortunate, lucky ◻ *Some unfortunate person passing below could all too easily be seriously injured.* ◻ *Apparently he had been unfortunate enough to fall victim to a gang of thugs.* ◻ *A few unfortunate individuals will develop the disease.* ◻ *Through some unfortunate accident, the information reached me a day late.* **2** If you describe something that has happened as **unfortunate**, you think that it is inappropriate, embarrassing, awkward, or undesirable. ◻ *It is unfortunate that your flight was cancelled.* ◻ *the unfortunate incident of the upside-down Canadian flag* ◻ *The situation was unfortunate for all concerned.* **3** You can describe someone as **unfortunate** when they are poor or have a difficult life. ◻ *Every year we have fundraisers to raise money for unfortunate people.*
NOUN [c] (**unfortunates**) An **unfortunate** is someone who is unfortunate. ◻ *Dorothy was another of life's unfortunates.*

⚪un·for·tu·nate·ly ♦◇◇ /ʌnˈfɔːtʃʊnətli/ ADV (feelings) You can use **unfortunately** to introduce or refer to a statement when you consider that it is sad or disappointing, or when you want to express regret. = regrettably; ≠ fortunately ◻ *Unfortunately, my time is limited.* ◻ *Unfortunately for him, his title brought obligations as well as privileges.* ◻ *The enclosed photograph is unfortunately not good enough to reproduce.*

un·friend·ly /ʌnˈfrendli/ ADJ If you describe a person, organization, or their behaviour as **unfriendly**, you mean that they behave towards you in an unkind or slightly hostile way. ◻ *Some people were unfriendly to the new recruit.* ◻ *People always complain that the big banks and big companies are unfriendly and unhelpful.*

un·grate·ful /ʌnˈgreɪtfʊl/ ADJ (disapproval) If you describe someone as **ungrateful**, you are criticizing them for not showing thanks or for being unkind to someone who has helped them or done them a favour. ◻ *I thought it was ungrateful of her.*

un·hap·pi·ly /ʌnˈhæpɪli/ ADV **1** If you do something **unhappily**, you feel sad and depressed when you do it. ◻ *'I don't have your imagination,' Kevin said unhappily.* **2** [unhappily with CL] You use **unhappily** to introduce or refer to a statement when you consider it to be sad and wish that it were different. = unfortunately ◻ *On May 23rd, unhappily, the little boy died.* ◻ *Unhappily the facts do not wholly bear out the theory.*

un·hap·py ♦◇◇ /ʌnˈhæpi/ ADJ (**unhappier**, **unhappiest**) **1** If you are **unhappy**, you are sad and depressed. = miserable ◻ *Her marriage is in trouble and she is desperately unhappy.* ◻ *He was a shy, sometimes unhappy man.* **2** [V-LINK + unhappy] If you are **unhappy about** something, you are not pleased about it or not satisfied with it. ◻ *He has been unhappy with his son's political leanings.* ◻ *College students are unhappy with their school bookshops.* **3** [unhappy + N] An **unhappy** situation or choice is not satisfactory or desirable. ◻ *It is our hope that this unhappy chapter in the history of relations between our two countries will soon be closed.* ◻ *The legislation represents in itself an unhappy compromise.*
un·hap·pi·ness /ʌnˈhæpinəs/ NOUN [U] **1** There was a lot of unhappiness in my adolescence. **2** He has, by submitting his resignation, signalled his unhappiness with the government's decision.

un·harmed /ʌnˈhɑːmd/ ADJ [unharmed after V, V-LINK + unharmed] If someone or something is **unharmed** after an accident or violent incident, they are not hurt or damaged in any way. ◻ *They both escaped unharmed.*

un·healthy /ʌnˈhelθi/ ADJ (**unhealthier**, **unhealthiest**) **1** Something that is **unhealthy** is likely to cause illness or bad health. ◻ *Avoid unhealthy foods such as hamburgers and* chips. **2** If you are **unhealthy**, you are sick or not in good physical condition. ☐ *a pale, unhealthy looking man* **3** An **unhealthy** economy or company is financially weak and unsuccessful. **= weak** ☐ *If you have an unhealthy economy, the poor will get hurt worst because they are the weakest.* **4** If you describe someone's behaviour or interests as **unhealthy**, you do not consider them to be normal and think they may involve mental problems. ☐ *Frank has developed an unhealthy relationship with these people.*

un·heard of /ən'hɜːd ɒv/ ADJ [V-LINK + unheard of] An event or situation that is **unheard of** never happens. ☐ *Riots are almost unheard of in Japan.*

un·help·ful /ˌʌn'helpfʊl/ ADJ If you say that someone or something is **unhelpful**, you mean that they do not help you or improve a situation, and may even make things worse. ☐ *The criticism is both unfair and unhelpful.*

un·iden·ti·fied ♦◇◇ /ˌʌnaɪ'dentɪfaɪd/ ADJ **1** If you describe someone or something as **unidentified**, you mean that nobody knows who or what they are. **= unknown** ☐ *He was shot this morning by unidentified intruders at his house.* **2** (*journalism*) If you use **unidentified** to describe people, groups, and organizations, you do not want to give their names. **= unnamed** ☐ *His claims were based on the comments of anonymous and unidentified sources.*

✪ **uni·fi·ca·tion** /ˌjuːnɪfɪ'keɪʃən/ NOUN [U] **Unification** is the process by which two or more countries join together and become one country. **= alliance; ≠ division** ☐ *the process of European unification* ☐ *one of the most difficult obstacles in the unification process*

> **WORD PARTS**
>
> The prefix *uni-* often appears in words that have 'one' as part of their meaning:
>
> unification (NOUN)
>
> unify (VERB)
>
> uniform (ADJ)

✪ **uni·form** ♦◇◇ /'juːnɪfɔːm/ NOUN, ADJ (*academic word*)
NOUN [C, U] (**uniforms**) A **uniform** is a special set of clothes which some people, for example soldiers or the police, wear to work in and which some children wear in school. ☐ *The police wear dark blue uniforms.* ☐ *Felipe was in uniform for the parade.*
ADJ **1** If something is **uniform**, it does not vary, but is even and regular throughout. ☐ *Cut down between the bones so that all the chops are of uniform size.* ☐ *All flowing water, though it appears to be uniform, is actually divided into extensive inner surfaces, or layers, moving against one another.* ☐ *The carbon fibre fabric gives a uniform distribution of heat.* ☐ *The price rises will not be uniform across the country.* **2** If you describe a number of things as **uniform**, you mean that they are all the same. **= identical, even; ≠ uneven, different** ☐ *Along each wall stretched uniform green metal filing cabinets.*
✪ **uni·form·ly** /'juːnɪfɔːmli/ ADV **1** **= evenly** ☐ *Beyond the windows, a November midday was uniformly grey.* ☐ *Microwaves heat water uniformly.* ☐ *the assumption that stars are uniformly distributed in space* **2** They are all about twenty years old, serious, smart, a bit conventional perhaps, but uniformly pleasant. ☐ *a uniformly negative reaction worldwide*

✪ **uni·form·ity** /ˌjuːnɪ'fɔːmɪti/ NOUN [U] **1** If something has **uniformity**, it does not vary, but is even and regular throughout. ☐ *The caramel that was used to maintain uniformity of colour in the brandy* **2** If there is **uniformity** in something such as a system, organization, or group of countries, the same rules, ideas, or methods are applied in all parts of it. ☐ *Spanish liberals sought to create linguistic as well as administrative uniformity.* **3** If there is **uniformity** among a number of things, they are all the same. ☐ *the dull uniformity of the houses*

✪ **uni·fy** /'juːnɪfaɪ/ VERB [I, T] (**unifies, unifying, unified**) (*academic word*) If someone **unifies** different things or parts, or if the things or parts **unify**, they are brought together to form one thing. **= join, unite; ≠ separate** ☐ *He pledged to unify the city's political factions.* ☐ *constitutional reforms designed to unify the country* ☐ *A flexible retirement age is being considered by Ministers to unify*

men's and women's pension rights. ☐ *The plan has been for the rival armies to demobilize, to unify, and then to hold elections to decide who rules.* ☐ *the benefits of unifying with the West*
uni·fied /'juːnɪfaɪd/ ADJ ☐ *a unified system of taxation*

un·im·por·tant /ˌʌnɪm'pɔːtənt/ ADJ If you describe something or someone as **unimportant**, you mean that they do not have much influence, effect, or value, and are therefore not worth serious consideration. ☐ *When they had married, six years before, the difference in their ages had seemed unimportant.*

un·im·pressed /ˌʌnɪm'prest/ ADJ [V-LINK + unimpressed] If you are **unimpressed by** something or someone, you do not think that they are very good, intelligent, or useful. ☐ *He was also very unimpressed by his teachers.*

un·in·hab·it·ed /ˌʌnɪn'hæbɪtɪd/ ADJ An **uninhabited** place is one where nobody lives. **= deserted** ☐ *an uninhabited island in the North Pacific* ☐ *The area is largely uninhabited.*

un·in·hib·it·ed /ˌʌnɪn'hɪbɪtɪd/ ADJ If you describe a person or their behaviour as **uninhibited**, you mean that they express their opinions and feelings openly, and behave as they want to, without worrying what other people think. ☐ *a bold and uninhibited entertainer* ☐ *The dancing is uninhibited and as frenzied as an aerobics class.*

un·in·ten·tion·al /ˌʌnɪn'tenʃənəl/ ADJ Something that is **unintentional** is not done deliberately, but happens by accident. **= inadvertent** ☐ *Perhaps he had slightly misled them, but it was quite unintentional.*
un·in·ten·tion·al·ly /ˌʌnɪn'tenʃənəli/ ADV ☐ *an overblown and unintentionally funny adaptation of 'Dracula'*

✪ **un·ion** ♦♦♦ /'juːnjən/ NOUN [C, U, SING] (**unions**) **1** [C] A **union** is a workers' organization which represents its members and which tries to improve their working conditions and pay. **= trade union** ☐ *Do all teachers have a right to join a union?* ☐ *Women in all types of employment can benefit from joining a union.* ☐ *Union officials criticized management tactics.* **2** [U] When the **union** of two or more things occurs, they are joined together and become one thing. ☐ *In 1918 the Romanian majority in this former czarist province voted for union with Romania.* **3** [SING] When two or more things, for example countries or organizations, have been joined together to form one thing, you can refer to them as a **union**. ☐ *Tanzania is a union of the states of Tanganyika and Zanzibar.*

✪ **unique** ♦◇◇ /juː'niːk/ ADJ (*academic word*) **1** Something that is **unique** is the only one of its kind. ☐ *Each person's signature is unique.* ☐ *The area has its own unique language, Catalan.* **2** You can use **unique** to describe things that you admire because they are very unusual and special. ☐ *She was a woman of unique talent and determination.* **3** [V-LINK + unique 'to' N] If something is **unique** to one thing, person, group, or place, it concerns or belongs only to that thing, person, group, or place. ☐ *No one knows for sure why adolescence is unique to humans.* ☐ *This interesting and charming creature is unique to Borneo.*
✪ **unique·ly** /juː'niːkli/ ADV **1** Because of the extreme cold, the Antarctic is a uniquely fragile environment. **2** There'll never be a shortage of people who consider themselves uniquely qualified to be president of the United States. **3** The problem isn't uniquely American.
unique·ness /juː'niːknəs/ NOUN [U] ☐ *the uniqueness of China's own experience*

✪ **unit** ♦♦◇ /'juːnɪt/ NOUN [C] (**units**) **1** If you consider something as a **unit**, you consider it as a single, complete thing. ☐ *Agriculture was based in the past on the family as a unit.* **2** A **unit** is a group of people who work together at a specific job, often in a particular place. ☐ *the environmental research unit* **3** A **unit** is a group within an armed force or police force, whose members fight or work together or carry out a particular task. ☐ *a firefighting unit* **4** A **unit** is a small machine which has a particular function, often part of a larger machine. ☐ *The unit plugs into any TV set.* **5** A **unit** of measurement is a fixed standard quantity, length, or weight that is used for measuring things. The litre, the metre, and the kilogram are all units. ☐ *The curie became a unit of measurement of radioactivity.* ☐ *the imperial units of measurement* ☐ *a unit of radiation measurement*

u

6 A **unit** is one of the parts that a textbook is divided into. = **module** ❑ *Unit V of this book explains those errors in detail and shows you ways to correct them.*

unite /juːˈnaɪt/ VERB [I, T] (**unites, uniting, united**) If a group of people or things **unite** or if something **unites** them, they join together and act as a group. ❑ *We need to unite against terrorism.*

unit·ed ◆◇◇ /juːˈnaɪtɪd/ ADJ **1** When people are **united** about something, they agree about it and act together. ❑ *The entire Brazilian people are united by their love of football.* **2 United** is used to describe a country which has been formed from two or more states or countries. ❑ *the first elections to be held in a united Germany for fifty eight years*

unity ◆◇◇ /ˈjuːnɪti/ NOUN [U] **1 Unity** is the state of different areas or groups being joined together to form a single country or organization. = **union** ❑ *We have to act to preserve the unity of this nation.* **2** When there is **unity**, people are in agreement and act together for a particular purpose. ❑ *a renewed unity of purpose* ❑ *Speakers at the rally expressed sentiments of unity.*

○uni·ver·sal /juːnɪˈvɜːsəl/ ADJ **1** Something that is **universal** relates to everyone in the world or everyone in a particular group or society. ❑ *The insurance industry has produced its own proposals for universal health care.* ❑ *The desire to look attractive is universal.* **2** Something that is **universal** affects or relates to every part of the world or the universe. = **worldwide** ❑ *universal diseases* ❑ *the law of universal gravitation*

○uni·ver·sal·ly /juːnɪˈvɜːsəli/ ADV **1** If something is **universally** believed or accepted, it is believed or accepted by everyone with no disagreement. ❑ *a universally accepted point of view* ❑ *The scale of the problem is now universally recognised.* **2** If something is **universally** true, it is everywhere in the world or in all situations. ❑ *The disadvantage is that it is not universally available.*

○uni·verse ◆◇◇ /ˈjuːnɪvɜːs/ NOUN [C] (**universes**) **1** The **universe** is the whole of space and all the stars, planets, and other forms of matter and energy in it. ❑ *Einstein's equations showed the universe to be expanding.* **2** If you talk about someone's **universe**, you are referring to the whole of their experience or an important part of it. = **world** ❑ *Good writers suck in what they see of the world, re-creating their own universe on the page.*

○uni·ver·sity ◆◆◆ /juːnɪˈvɜːsiti/ NOUN [C, U] (**universities**) A **university** is an institution where students study for degrees and where academic research is done. = **college** ❑ *Offenbacker earned an education degree at the University of Washington and taught elementary school.* ❑ *She goes to Duke University.* ❑ *exams required to attend university* ❑ *a national conference convened by a major research university*

un·just /ʌnˈdʒʌst/ ADJ If you describe an action, system, or law as **unjust**, you think that it treats a person or group badly in a way that they do not deserve. = **unfair** ❑ *The attack on Charles was unjust.*

un·just·ly /ʌnˈdʒʌstli/ ADV ❑ *She was unjustly accused of stealing money, and then fired.*

un·jus·ti·fied /ʌnˈdʒʌstɪfaɪd/ ADJ If you describe a belief or action as **unjustified**, you think that there is no good reason for having it or doing it. ❑ *Your report last week was unfair. It was based upon wholly unfounded and totally unjustified allegations.*

un·kind /ʌnˈkaɪnd/ ADJ (**unkinder, unkindest**) **1** If someone is **unkind**, they behave in an unpleasant, unfriendly, or slightly cruel way. You can also describe someone's words or actions as **unkind**. ❑ *All last summer he'd been unkind to her.* ❑ *No one has an unkind word to say about him.* **2** (written) If you describe something bad that happens to someone as **unkind**, you mean that they do not deserve it. ❑ *The weather was unkind to those pipers who played in the morning.*

un·kind·ly /ʌnˈkaɪndli/ ADV ❑ *Several viewers commented unkindly on her costumes.*

un·kind·ness /ʌnˈkaɪndnəs/ NOUN [U] ❑ *He realized the unkindness of the remark and immediately regretted having hurt her with it.*

un·known ◆◇◇ /ʌnˈnəʊn/ ADJ, NOUN
ADJ **1** If something is **unknown** to you, you have no knowledge of it. ❑ *An unknown number of demonstrators were arrested.* ❑ *The motive for the killing is unknown.* **2** An **unknown** person is someone whose name you do not know or whose character you do not know anything about. ❑ *the tomb of the unknown soldier* **3** An **unknown** person is not famous or publicly recognized. ❑ *He was an unknown writer.* **4** If you say that a particular problem or situation is **unknown**, you mean that it never occurs. = **unheard of** ❑ *A hundred years ago coronary heart disease was virtually unknown in America.*
NOUN [C, SING] (**unknowns**) **1** [C] An **unknown** is something that is unknown. ❑ *The length of the war is one of the biggest unknowns.* **2** [C] An **unknown** is a person who is unknown. ❑ *Within a short space of time a group of complete unknowns had established a wholly original form of humour.* **3** [SING] **The unknown** refers generally to things or places that people do not know about or understand. ❑ *Ignorance of people brings fear, fear of the unknown.*

un·law·ful /ʌnˈlɔːfʊl/ ADJ (formal) If something is **unlawful**, the law does not allow you to do it. = **illegal** ❑ *employees who believe their dismissal was unlawful*

un·law·ful·ly /ʌnˈlɔːfəli/ ADV [unlawfully with v] ❑ *The government acted unlawfully in imposing the restrictions.*

un·lead·ed /ʌnˈledɪd/ ADJ, NOUN
ADJ **Unleaded** fuel contains a smaller amount of lead than most fuels so that it produces less harmful substances when it is burned. ❑ *He filled up his Toyota with regular unleaded petrol.*
NOUN [U] **Unleaded** is fuel that contains a smaller amount of lead than most fuels so that it produces less harmful substances when it is burned. ❑ *All its V8 engines will run happily on unleaded.*

un·leash /ʌnˈliːʃ/ VERB [T] (**unleashes, unleashing, unleashed**) If you say that someone or something **unleashes** a powerful force, feeling, activity, or group, you mean that they suddenly start it or send it somewhere. ❑ *The announcement unleashed a storm of protest from the public.* ❑ *The officers were still reluctant to unleash their troops in pursuit of a defeated enemy.*

un·less ◆◆◇ /ʌnˈles/ CONJ You use **unless** to introduce the only circumstances in which an event you are mentioning will not take place or in which a statement you are making is not true. ❑ *Unless you are trying to lose weight to please yourself, it's going to be tough to keep your motivation level high.* ❑ *We cannot understand disease unless we understand the person who has the disease.*

un·like ◆◇◇ /ʌnˈlaɪk/ PREP **1** If one thing is **unlike** another thing, the two things have different qualities or characteristics from each other. ❑ *This was a foreign country, so unlike San José.* **2** You can use **unlike** to contrast two people, things, or situations, and show how they are different. ❑ *Unlike aerobics, walking entails no expensive fees for classes or clubs.* **3** If you describe something that a particular person has done as being **unlike** them, you mean that you are surprised by it because it is not typical of their character or normal behaviour. ❑ *It was so unlike him to say something like that, with such intensity, that I was astonished.*

○un·like·ly ◆◆◇ /ʌnˈlaɪkli/ ADJ (**unlikelier, unlikeliest**) If you say that something is **unlikely** to happen or **unlikely** to be true, you believe that it will not happen or that it is not true, although you are not completely sure. ❑ *A military coup seems unlikely.* ❑ *As with many technological revolutions, you are unlikely to be aware of it.* ❑ *It's now unlikely that future parliaments will bring back the death penalty.*

un·lim·it·ed /ʌnˈlɪmɪtɪd/ ADJ If there is an **unlimited** quantity of something, you can have as much or as many of that thing as you want. ❑ *An unlimited number of copies can still be made from the original.* ❑ *You'll also have unlimited access to the swimming pool.*

un·load /ʌnˈləʊd/ VERB [T] (**unloads, unloading, unloaded**) If you **unload** goods from a vehicle, or you **unload** a vehicle, you remove the goods from the vehicle, usually after they have been transported from one place to another. □ *Unload everything from the boat and clean it thoroughly.*

un·lock /ˌʌnˈlɒk/ VERB [T] (**unlocks, unlocking, unlocked**) **1** If you **unlock** something such as a door, a room, or a container that has a lock, you open it using a key. □ *He unlocked the car and threw the coat on to the back seat.* **2** If you **unlock** the potential or the secrets of something or someone, you release them. □ *The point of the competition is to encourage all people to unlock their hidden potential.*

un·lucky /ˌʌnˈlʌki/ ADJ (**unluckier, unluckiest**) **1** If someone is **unlucky**, they have bad luck. = unfortunate □ *You certainly were unlucky to get that horrible illness.* **2** You can use **unlucky** to describe unpleasant things which happen to someone, especially when you feel that the person does not deserve them. □ *Argentina's unlucky defeat by Ireland* **3** **Unlucky** is used to describe something that is thought to cause bad luck. □ *Some people think it is unlucky to walk under a ladder.*

un·mis·tak·able /ˌʌnmɪsˈteɪkəbəl/ also **unmistakeable** ADJ If you describe something as **unmistakable**, you mean that it is so obvious that it cannot be mistaken for anything else. □ *He didn't give his name, but the voice was unmistakable.* **un·mis·tak·ably** /ˌʌnmɪsˈteɪkəbli/ ADV □ *It's still unmistakably a Minnelli film.* □ *an unmistakably American accent*

un·moved /ˌʌnˈmuːvd/ ADJ [V-LINK + unmoved] If you are **unmoved by** something, you are not emotionally affected by it. □ *Mr Bird remained unmoved by the corruption allegations.*

un·named /ˌʌnˈneɪmd/ ADJ **1** **Unnamed** people or things are talked about but their names are not mentioned. □ *Perot accused unnamed US officials of covering up the facts.* **2** **Unnamed** things have not been given a name. □ *unnamed comets and asteroids*

un·natu·ral /ˌʌnˈnætʃərəl/ ADJ **1** If you describe something as **unnatural**, you mean that it is strange and often frightening, because it is different from what you normally expect. □ *The aircraft rose with unnatural speed on takeoff.* **2** Behaviour that is **unnatural** seems artificial and not normal or genuine. = false □ *She gave him a bright, determined smile which seemed unnatural.* **un·natu·ral·ly** /ˌʌnˈnætʃərəli/ ADV **1** [unnaturally + ADJ] □ *The house was unnaturally silent.* **2** [unnaturally with V] □ *Try to avoid shouting or speaking unnaturally.*

❂un·nec·es·sary /ˌʌnˈnesəsri, AmE -seri/ ADJ If you describe something as **unnecessary**, you mean that it is not needed or does not have to be done. = needless □ *The slaughter of whales is unnecessary and inhuman.* □ *She explained that it is quite unnecessary to hurt a patient.* □ *Don't take any unnecessary risks.* **❂un·nec·es·sari·ly** /ˌʌnnesəˈserɪli/ ADV = needlessly □ *I didn't want to upset my husband or my daughter unnecessarily.*

un·no·ticed /ˌʌnˈnəʊtɪst/ ADJ If something happens or passes **unnoticed**, it is not seen or noticed by anyone. □ *I tried to slip up the stairs unnoticed.*

un·ob·tru·sive /ˌʌnəbˈtruːsɪv/ ADJ (formal) If you describe something or someone as **unobtrusive**, you mean that they are not easily noticed or do not draw attention to themselves. □ *The coffee table is glass, to be as unobtrusive as possible.* **un·ob·tru·sive·ly** /ˌʌnəbˈtruːsɪvli/ ADV □ *They slipped away unobtrusively.*

un·of·fi·cial /ˌʌnəˈfɪʃəl/ ADJ An **unofficial** action or statement is not organized or approved by a person or group in authority. □ *Staff voted to continue an unofficial strike in support of seven colleagues who were dismissed last week.* **un·of·fi·cial·ly** /ˌʌnəˈfɪʃəli/ ADV □ *Some workers are legally employed, but the majority work unofficially with neither health insurance nor wage security.*

un·ortho·dox /ˌʌnˈɔːθədɒks/ ADJ If you describe someone's behaviour, beliefs, or customs as **unorthodox**, you mean that they are different from what is generally accepted. = unusual □ *The reality-based show followed the*

unorthodox lives of Ozzy, his wife Sharon, daughter Kelly, and son, Jack.

un·pack /ˌʌnˈpæk/ VERB [I, T] (**unpacks, unpacking, unpacked**) When you **unpack** a suitcase, box, or similar container, or you **unpack** the things inside it, you take the things out of the container. □ *He unpacked his bag.*

un·paid /ˌʌnˈpeɪd/ ADJ **1** [unpaid + N] If you do **unpaid** work or are an **unpaid** worker, you do a job without receiving any money for it. □ *Even unpaid work for charity is better than nothing.* **2** **Unpaid** taxes or bills, for example, are taxes or bills which have not been paid yet. = outstanding □ *millions of dollars in unpaid taxes*

un·par·al·leled /ˌʌnˈpærəleld/ ADJ (emphasis) If you describe something as **unparalleled**, you are emphasizing that it is, for example, bigger, better, or worse than anything else of its kind, or anything that has happened before. = unequalled □ *a period of unparalleled economic growth*

un·pleas·ant /ˌʌnˈplezənt/ ADJ **1** If something is **unpleasant**, it gives you bad feelings, for example by making you feel upset or uncomfortable. □ *The symptoms can be uncomfortable, unpleasant, and serious.* □ *The vacuum has an unpleasant smell.* **2** An **unpleasant** person is very unfriendly and rude. □ *She thought he was an unpleasant man.* **un·pleas·ant·ly** /ˌʌnˈplezəntli/ ADV **1** *The water moved around the body, unpleasantly thick and brown.* □ *The smell was unpleasantly strong.* **2** *Melissa laughed unpleasantly.*

un·popu·lar /ˌʌnˈpɒpjʊlə/ ADJ If something or someone is **unpopular**, most people do not like them. □ *It was a painful and unpopular decision.* □ *In school, I was very unpopular, and I did encounter a little prejudice.* **un·popu·lar·ity** /ˌʌnpɒpjʊˈlærɪti/ NOUN [U] □ *his unpopularity among his colleagues*

❂un·prec·edent·ed /ˌʌnˈpresɪdentɪd/ ADJ **1** If something is **unprecedented**, it has never happened before. = unique, unparalleled □ *Such a move is rare, but not unprecedented.* □ *In 1987 the Socialists took the unprecedented step of appointing a civilian to command the force.* **2** If you describe something as **unprecedented**, you are emphasizing that it is very great in quality, amount, or scale. □ *The mission has been hailed as an unprecedented success.* □ *an instant slaughter unprecedented in the history of mankind*

❂un·pre·dict·able /ˌʌnprɪˈdɪktəbəl/ ADJ [oft with POSS] (academic word) If you describe someone or something as **unpredictable**, you mean that you cannot tell what they are going to do or how they are going to behave. = changeable □ *He is utterly unpredictable.* □ *In macular surgery, outcomes are unpredictable.* □ *Adding more elements into the equation might have unpredictable consequences.* □ *an unpredictable work environment* **un·pre·dict·abil·ity** /ˌʌnprɪˌdɪktəˈbɪlɪti/ NOUN [U] □ *the unpredictability of the weather*

un·pre·pared /ˌʌnprɪˈpeəd/ ADJ **1** If you are **unprepared for** something, you are not ready for it, and you are therefore surprised or at a disadvantage when it happens. □ *I was totally unprepared for the announcement on the next day.* □ *Faculty members complain that their students are unprepared to do university-level work.* **2** [V-LINK + unprepared + to-INF] If you are **unprepared** to do something, you are not willing to do it. □ *They are unprepared to accept the real reasons for their domestic and foreign situation.*

un·quali·fied /ˌʌnˈkwɒlɪfaɪd/ ADJ **1** If you are **unqualified**, you do not have any qualifications, or you do not have the right qualifications for a particular job. □ *She was unqualified for the job.* **2** **Unqualified** means total or unlimited. □ *The event was an unqualified success.*

un·ques·tion·able /ˌʌnˈkwestʃənəbəl/ ADJ (emphasis) If you describe something as **unquestionable**, you are emphasizing that it is so obviously true or real that nobody can doubt it. = undoubted □ *He inspires affection and respect as a man of unquestionable integrity.*

un·ques·tion·ably /ˌʌnˈkwestʃənəbli/ ADV If something is **unquestionably** true or real, it is so obviously

u

true or real that nobody can doubt it. ❑ *They have seen the change as unquestionably beneficial to the country.*

un·re·al·is·tic /ˌʌnrɪəˈlɪstɪk/ ADJ If you say that someone is being **unrealistic**, you mean that they do not recognize the truth about a situation, especially about the difficulties involved in something they want to achieve. ❑ *There are many who feel that the players are being completely unrealistic in their demands.* ❑ *It would be unrealistic to expect such a process ever to be completed.*

un·rea·son·able /ʌnˈriːzənəbəl/ ADJ **1** If you say that someone is being **unreasonable**, you mean that they are behaving in a way that is not fair or sensible. ❑ *The strikers were being unreasonable in their demands, having rejected the deal two weeks ago.* ❑ *It was her unreasonable behaviour with a Texan playboy which broke up her marriage.* **2** An **unreasonable** decision, action, price, or amount seems unfair and difficult to justify. ❑ *unreasonable increases in the price of gas*
un·rea·son·ably /ʌnˈriːzənəbli/ ADV **1** *We unreasonably expect near perfect behaviour from our children.* **2** *The banks' charges are unreasonably high.*

un·re·lat·ed /ˌʌnrɪˈleɪtɪd/ ADJ **1** If one thing is **unrelated to** another, there is no connection between them. You can also say that two things are **unrelated**. = unconnected ❑ *My line of work is entirely unrelated to politics.* **2** (*written*) If one person is **unrelated to** another, they are not members of the same family. You can also say that two people are **unrelated**. ❑ *Jimmy is adopted and thus unrelated to Beth by blood.*

un·re·lent·ing /ˌʌnrɪˈlentɪŋ/ ADJ **1** If you describe someone's behaviour as **unrelenting**, you mean that they are continuing to do something in a very determined way, often without caring whether they hurt or embarrass other people. = relentless ❑ *She established her authority with unrelenting thoroughness.* **2** If you describe something unpleasant as **unrelenting**, you mean that it continues without stopping. ❑ *an unrelenting downpour of rain*

un·re·li·able /ˌʌnrɪˈlaɪəbəl/ ADJ If you describe a person, machine, or method as **unreliable**, you mean that you cannot trust them. ❑ *Diplomats can be a notoriously unreliable and misleading source of information.* ❑ *His judgment was unreliable.*

un·re·solved /ˌʌnrɪˈzɒlvd/ ADJ If a problem or difficulty is **unresolved**, no satisfactory solution has been found to it. ❑ *The murder remains unresolved.*

✪ un·rest /ʌnˈrest/ NOUN [U] (*journalism*) If there is **unrest** in a particular place or society, people are expressing anger and dissatisfaction about something, often by demonstrating or rioting. = instability, discontent ❑ *The real danger is civil unrest in the east of the country.* ❑ *There is growing unrest among students in several major cities.*

un·re·strict·ed /ˌʌnrɪˈstrɪktɪd/ ADJ **1** If an activity is **unrestricted**, you are free to do it in the way that you want, without being limited by any rules. ❑ *Freedom to pursue extracurricular activities is totally unrestricted.* **2** If you have an **unrestricted** view of something, you can see it fully and clearly, because there is nothing in the way. ❑ *Nearly all seats have an unrestricted view.*

un·ru·ly /ʌnˈruːli/ ADJ **1** If you describe people, especially children, as **unruly**, you mean that they behave badly and are difficult to control. ❑ *unruly behaviour* **2** **Unruly** hair is difficult to keep tidy. ❑ *The man had remarkably black, unruly hair.*

un·safe /ʌnˈseɪf/ ADJ **1** If a building, machine, activity, or area is **unsafe**, it is dangerous. = dangerous ❑ *Critics claim the trucks are unsafe.* **2** [V-LINK + unsafe] If you are **unsafe**, you are in danger of being harmed. ❑ *In the larger neighbourhood, I felt very unsafe.*

un·sat·is·fac·tory /ˌʌnsætɪsˈfæktəri/ ADJ If you describe something as **unsatisfactory**, you mean that it is not as good as it should be, and cannot be considered acceptable. = inadequate ❑ *He asked a few more questions, to which he received unsatisfactory answers.*

un·sa·voury /ʌnˈseɪvəri/ (in AmE, use **unsavory**) ADJ (*disapproval*) If you describe a person, place, or thing as **unsavoury**, you mean that you find them unpleasant or

morally unacceptable. ❑ *Police officers meet more unsavoury characters in a week than most of us do in a lifetime.*

un·scathed /ʌnˈskeɪðd/ ADJ [unscathed after V, V-LINK + unscathed] If you are **unscathed** after a dangerous experience, you have not been injured or harmed by it. = unharmed ❑ *Tony emerged unscathed apart from a severely bruised finger.* ❑ *East Los Angeles was left relatively unscathed by the riots.*

un·scru·pu·lous /ʌnˈskruːpjʊləs/ ADJ (*disapproval*) If you describe a person as **unscrupulous**, you are critical of the fact that they are prepared to act in a dishonest or immoral way in order to get what they want. ❑ *These kids are being exploited by very unscrupulous people.*

un·seen /ˌʌnˈsiːn/ ADJ **1** If you describe something as **unseen**, you mean that it has not been seen for a long time. ❑ *a spectacular ballroom, unseen by the public for over 30 years* **2** [unseen + N, unseen after V] You can use **unseen** to describe things which people cannot see. ❑ *For me, a performance is in front of a microphone, over the radio, to an unseen audience.*

un·set·tled /ʌnˈsetəld/ ADJ **1** In an **unsettled** situation, there is a lot of uncertainty about what will happen. = unstable ❑ *The developments leave the airline with several problems, including an unsettled labour situation.* **2** [V-LINK + unsettled] If you are **unsettled**, you cannot concentrate on anything because you are worried. ❑ *To tell the truth, I'm a bit unsettled tonight.* **3** An **unsettled** argument or dispute has not yet been resolved. = unresolved ❑ *They were in the process of resolving all the unsettled issues.* **4** **Unsettled** weather is unpredictable and changes a lot. ❑ *Despite the unsettled weather, we had a marvellous weekend.*

un·skilled /ˌʌnˈskɪld/ ADJ **1** People who are **unskilled** do not have any special training for a job. ❑ *He worked as an unskilled labourer.* **2** **Unskilled** work does not require any special training. ❑ *In the US, minorities and immigrants have generally gone into low-paid, unskilled jobs.*

✪ un·speci·fied /ʌnˈspesɪfaɪd/ ADJ (*academic word*) You say that something is **unspecified** when you are not told exactly what it is. ≠ specified ❑ *The company said that an unspecified number of people were offered jobs.* ❑ *He was arrested on unspecified charges.*

✪ un·spoiled /ˌʌnˈspɔɪld/ or **unspoilt** ADJ If you describe a place as **unspoiled**, you think it is beautiful because it has not been changed or built on for a long time. = untouched; ≠ spoiled ❑ *The port is quiet and unspoiled.* ❑ *a plea for the conservation of unspoiled shorelines.*

un·spoilt /ˌʌnˈspɔɪlt/ (BrE) → See **unspoiled**

un·spo·ken /ˌʌnˈspəʊkən/ ADJ **1** If your thoughts, wishes, or feelings are **unspoken**, you do not speak about them. ❑ *His face was expressionless, but Alex felt the unspoken criticism.* **2** [unspoken + N] When there is an **unspoken** agreement or understanding between people, their behaviour shows that they agree about something or understand it, even though they have never spoken about it. = tacit ❑ *There was an unspoken agreement that he and Viv would look after the frail old couple.*

✪ un·sta·ble /ʌnˈsteɪbəl/ ADJ **1** You can describe something as **unstable** if it is likely to change suddenly, especially if this creates difficulty or danger. = fragile, volatile, unsettled ❑ *The situation is unstable and potentially dangerous.* ❑ *After the fall of the Prime Minister in 1801 there was a decade of unstable government.* **2** **Unstable** objects are likely to move or fall. ❑ *Both clay and sandstone are unstable rock formations.* **3** If people are **unstable**, their emotions and behaviour keep changing because their minds are disturbed or upset. ❑ *He was emotionally unstable.*

un·steady /ʌnˈstedi/ ADJ **1** If you are **unsteady**, you have difficulty doing something, for example walking, because you cannot completely control your legs or your body. ❑ *The boy was very unsteady and had staggered around when he got up.* **2** If you describe something as **unsteady**, you mean that it is not regular or stable, but unreliable or unpredictable. ❑ *His voice was unsteady and only just audible.* **3** **Unsteady** objects are not held, attached, or balanced securely. ❑ *a slightly unsteady table*
un·stead·i·ly /ʌnˈstedɪli/ ADV [unsteadily with V] ❑ *She*

U

pulled herself unsteadily from the bed to the dressing table.

un·suc·cess·ful /ˌʌnsək'sesfəl/ ADJ ◼ Something that is **unsuccessful** does not achieve what it was intended to achieve. ❑ *His efforts were unsuccessful.* ❑ *a second unsuccessful operation on his knee* ◼ Someone who is **unsuccessful** does not achieve what they intended to achieve, especially in their career. ❑ *The difference between successful and unsuccessful people is that successful people put into practice the things they learn.*

un·suc·cess·ful·ly /ˌʌnsək'sesfəli/ ADV [unsuccessfully with v] ❑ *He has been trying unsuccessfully to sell the business in one piece since early last year.*

un·suit·able /ˌʌn'suːtəbəl/ ADJ Someone or something that is **unsuitable** for a particular purpose or situation does not have the right qualities for it. ❑ *Amy's shoes were unsuitable for walking any distance.*

un·sure /ˌʌn'ʃʊə/ ADJ ◼ If you are **unsure of yourself**, you lack confidence. ❑ *The evening show was terrible, with hesitant, unsure performances from all.* ◼ [V-LINK + unsure] If you are **unsure about** something, you feel uncertain about it. ❑ *Fifty-two per cent were unsure about the idea.*

un·sus·pect·ing /ˌʌnsə'spektɪŋ/ ADJ You can use **unsuspecting** to describe someone who is not at all aware of something that is happening or going to happen. ❑ *She threw a surprise party for her unsuspecting husband.*

un·ten·able /ˌʌn'tenəbəl/ ADJ An argument, theory, or position that is **untenable** cannot be defended successfully against criticism or attack. ❑ *This argument is untenable from an intellectual, moral, and practical standpoint.*

un·think·able /ʌn'θɪŋkəbəl/ ADJ, NOUN
  ADJ *(emphasis)* If you say that something is **unthinkable**, you are emphasizing that it cannot possibly be accepted or imagined as a possibility. ❑ *Her strong Catholic beliefs made abortion unthinkable.*
  NOUN [SING] ['the' unthinkable] **The unthinkable** is something that is unthinkable. ❑ *Teresa Zapata told her family the unthinkable; she was going to work in the United States.*

un·ti·dy /ʌn'taɪdi/ *(mainly BrE)* ADJ **(untidier, untidiest)** ◼ If you describe something as **untidy**, you mean that it is not neat or well arranged. ❑ *The place quickly became untidy.* ◼ If you describe a person as **untidy**, you mean that they do not care about whether things are neat and well arranged, for example in their house. ❑ *I'm untidy in most ways.*

un·tie /ʌn'taɪ/ VERB [T] **(unties, untying, untied)** ◼ If you **untie** something that is tied to another thing or if you **untie** two things that are tied together, you remove the string or rope that holds them or that has been tied around them. ❑ *Nicholas untied the boat from her mooring.* ❑ *Just untie my hands.* ◼ If you **untie** something such as string or rope, you undo it so that there is no knot or so that it is no longer tying something. ❑ *She hurriedly untied the ropes binding her ankles.* ◼ When you **untie** your shoelaces or your shoes, you loosen or undo the laces of your shoes. = undo, unfasten ❑ *She untied the laces on one of her trainers.*

un·til ◆◆◆ /ʌn'tɪl/ PREP, CONJ
  PREP ◼ [until + N/PREP] If something happens **until** a particular time, it happens during the period before that time and stops at that time. = till ❑ *Until 2004, she lived in Canada.* ◼ [until after NEG] You use **until** with a negative to emphasize the moment in time after which the rest of your statement becomes true, or the condition which would make it true. = till ❑ *The traffic laws don't take effect until the end of the year.*
  CONJ ◼ If something happens **until** something else happens, it happens during the period before that time and stops at that time. = till ❑ *I waited until it got dark.* ◼ If something is the case **until** something else is done or happens, this emphasizes the moment in time after which the rest of a statement becomes true, or the condition which would make it true. = till ❑ *The government said that it has suspended all aid to Haiti until that country's legitimate government is restored.*
  ✦ up until → see up

un·told /ˌʌn'təʊld/ ADJ *(emphasis)* ◼ [untold + N] You can use **untold** to emphasize how bad or unpleasant something is. ❑ *Landmines have caused untold misery to thousands of innocent people.* ◼ [untold + N] You can use **untold** to emphasize that an amount or quantity is very large, especially when you are not sure how large it is. ❑ *the nation's untold millions of anglers*

un·touched /ˌʌn'tʌtʃt/ ADJ ◼ [V-LINK + untouched, untouched after v] Something that is **untouched by** something else is not affected by it. ❑ *Asian airlines remain untouched by the deregulation that has swept the US.* ◼ [V-LINK + untouched, untouched after v] If something is **untouched**, it is not damaged in any way, although it has been in a situation where it could easily have been damaged. ❑ *Michael pointed out to me that in all the rubble, there was one building that remained untouched.* ◼ An **untouched** area or place is thought to be beautiful because it is still in its original state and has not been changed or damaged in any way. ❑ *Ducie is one of the world's last untouched islands.* ◼ If food or drink is **untouched**, none of it has been eaten or drunk. ❑ *The coffee was untouched, the toast was cold.*

un·true /ˌʌn'truː/ ADJ If a statement or idea is **untrue**, it is false and not based on facts. ❑ *The allegations were completely untrue.* ❑ *It was untrue to say that all political prisoners have been released.*

un·used ADJ ◼ /ˌʌn'juːzd/ Something that is **unused** has not been used or is not being used at the moment. ❑ *unused containers of food* ◼ /ˌʌn'juːst/ [V-LINK + unused 'to' N] If you are **unused** to something, you have not often done it or experienced it before, so it feels unusual and unfamiliar to you. ❑ *My mother was entirely unused to such hard work.*

un·usu·al ◆◇◇ /ʌn'juːʒuəl/ ADJ ◼ If something is **unusual**, it does not happen very often or you do not see it or hear it very often. ❑ *They have replanted many areas with rare and unusual plants.* ◼ If you describe someone as **unusual**, you think that they are interesting and different from other people. ❑ *He was an unusual man with great business talents.*

un·usu·al·ly /ʌn'juːʒuəli/ ADV ◼ [unusually + ADJ] *(emphasis)* You use **unusually** to emphasize that someone or something has more of a particular quality than is usual. ❑ *He was an unusually complex man.* ◼ You can use **unusually** to suggest that something is not what normally happens. ❑ *Unusually for a Japanese politician, he's a fluent English speaker.*

un·veil /ʌn'veɪl/ VERB [T] **(unveils, unveiling, unveiled)** ◼ If someone formally **unveils** something such as a new statue or painting, they draw back the curtain which is covering it. ❑ *a ceremony to unveil a monument to the victims* ◼ If you **unveil** a plan, new product, or some other thing that has been kept secret, you introduce it to the public. ❑ *Mr Werner unveiled his new strategy this week.*

un·want·ed /ˌʌn'wɒntɪd/ ADJ If you say that something or someone is **unwanted**, you mean that you do not want them, or that nobody wants them. ❑ *the misery of unwanted pregnancies* ❑ *She felt unwanted.*

un·wel·come /ʌn'welkəm/ ADJ ◼ An **unwelcome** experience is one that you do not like and did not want. = unwanted ❑ *The mayor delivered the unwelcome news that city employees may have to take unpaid time off.* ◼ If you say that a visitor is **unwelcome**, you mean that you did not want them to come. ❑ *an unwelcome guest*

un·well /ʌn'wel/ ADJ [V-LINK + unwell] If you are **unwell**, you are ill. ❑ *Their grandmother was feeling unwell and had to stay at home.*

un·will·ing /ʌn'wɪlɪŋ/ ADJ ◼ If you are **unwilling** to do something, you do not want to do it and will not agree to do it. ❑ *Initially the government was unwilling to accept the defeat.* ◼ You can use **unwilling** to describe someone who does not really want to do the thing they are doing. = reluctant ❑ *A youthful teacher, he finds himself an unwilling participant in school politics.*

un·will·ing·ness /ʌn'wɪlɪŋnəs/ NOUN [U] ❑ *their unwillingness to accept responsibility for mistakes*

u

un·will·ing·ly /ʌnˈwɪlɪŋli/ ADV = reluctantly ❑ *He accepted his orders very unwillingly.*

un·wind /ʌnˈwaɪnd/ VERB [I, T] (**unwinds, unwinding, unwound**) **1** [I] When you **unwind**, you relax after you have done something that makes you tense or tired. ❑ *It helps them to unwind after a busy day at work.* **2** [I, T] If you unwind a length of something that is wrapped around something else or around itself, you loosen it and make it straight. You can also say that it **unwinds**. ❑ *One of them unwound a length of rope from around his waist.*

un·wise /ʌnˈwaɪz/ ADJ If you describe something as **unwise**, you think that it is foolish and likely to lead to a bad result. ❑ *It would be unwise to expect too much.* ❑ *I think this is extremely unwise.*

un·wise·ly /ʌnˈwaɪzli/ ADV = foolishly ❑ *She accepted that she had acted unwisely.*

un·wit·ting /ʌnˈwɪtɪŋ/ ADJ If you describe a person or their actions as **unwitting**, you mean that the person does something or is involved in something without realizing it. ❑ *We were unwitting collaborators in his plan.*

un·wit·ting·ly /ʌnˈwɪtɪŋli/ ADV If you do something **unwittingly**, you do it without realizing it. ❑ *He was unwittingly caught up in the confrontation.*

un·wor·thy /ʌnˈwɜːði/ ADJ If a person or thing is **unworthy** of something good, they do not deserve it. ❑ *You may feel unworthy of the attention and help people offer you.*

un·writ·ten /ʌnˈrɪtən/ ADJ **1** Something such as a book that is **unwritten** has not been printed or written down. ❑ *Universal has agreed to pay $5 million for Grisham's next, as yet unwritten, novel.* **2** An **unwritten** rule, law, or agreement is one that is understood and accepted by everyone, although it may not have been formally or officially established. ❑ *They obey the one unwritten rule that binds them all – no talking.*

up ♦♦♦ /ʌp/ PREP, ADV, ADJ, VERB

> **Up** is often used with verbs of movement such as 'jump' and 'pull', and also in phrasal verbs such as 'give up' and 'wash up'.

PREP **1** If a person or thing goes **up** something such as a slope, ladder, or chimney, they move away from the ground or to a higher position. ❑ *They were climbing up a narrow mountain road.* ❑ *I ran up the stairs and saw Alison lying at the top.* **2** If a person or thing is **up** something such as a ladder or a mountain, they are near the top of it. ❑ *He was up a ladder sawing off the tops of his apple trees.* **3** [V + up + N] If you go or look **up** something such as a road or river, you go or look along it. If you are **up** a road or river, you are somewhere along it. ❑ *A line of tanks came up the road from the city.* ❑ *We leaned on the wooden rail of the bridge and looked up the river.*

ADV **1** If a person or thing goes **up**, they move away from the ground or to a higher position. ❑ *Finally, after an hour, I went up to Jeremy's room.* ❑ *Intense balls of flame rose up into the sky.* **2** [up after V] If a person or thing is **up**, they are near the top of something. ❑ *a research station perched 4,000 metres up on the lip of the crater* **3** [up after V] You use **up** to indicate that you are looking or facing in a direction that is away from the ground or towards a higher level. ❑ *Keep your head up, and look around you from time to time.* **4** [up after V] If someone stands **up**, they move so that they are standing. ❑ *He stood up and went to the window.* **5** (mainly spoken) If you are travelling to a particular place, you can say that you are going **up** to that place, especially if you are going towards the north or to a higher level of land. If you are already in such a place, you can say that you are **up** there. ❑ *I'll be up to see you tomorrow.* ❑ *He was living up North.* **6** If you go **up** to something or someone, you move to the place where they are and stop there. ❑ *The girl ran the rest of the way across the street and up to the car.* ❑ *On the way out a boy of about ten came up on roller skates.* **7** If an amount of something goes **up**, it increases. If an amount of something is **up**, it has increased and is at a higher level than it was. ❑ *The total budget went up almost $300 million.* ❑ *Tourism is up, jobs are up, individual income is up.*

PHRASES **up and down** If you move **up and down** somewhere, you move there repeatedly in one direction and then in the opposite direction. ❑ *I used to jump up and down to keep warm.* ❑ *I strolled up and down thoughtfully before calling a taxi.*

up to 1 If you feel **up to** doing something, you are well enough to do it. ❑ *Those patients who were up to it could move to the adjacent pool.* ❑ *His fellow directors were not up to running the business without him.* **2** (*informal*) To be **up to** something means to be secretly doing something that you should not be doing. ❑ *Why did you need a room unless you were up to something?* ❑ *They must have known what their father was up to.* **3** If you say that it is **up to** someone to do something, you mean that it is their responsibility to do it. ❑ *It was up to him to make it right, no matter how long it took.* ❑ *I'm sure I'd have spotted him if it had been up to me.* **4** You use **up to** to say how large something can be or what level it has reached. ❑ *Up to twenty thousand students paid between five and six thousand dollars.*

up until Up until or **up to** are used to indicate the latest time at which something can happen, or the end of the period of time that you are referring to. ❑ *Please feel free to call me any time up until 9:30 at night.*

up for 1 If someone or something is **up for** election, review, or discussion, they are about to be considered. ❑ *A third of the Senate and the entire House are up for re-election.* **2** (*informal*) If you are **up for** something, you are willing or eager to do it. ❑ *I'm starved. Who's up for pizza?*

up against If you are **up against** something, you have a very difficult situation or problem to deal with. ❑ *The chairwoman is up against the greatest challenge to her position.*

up and about If someone who has been in bed for some time, for example because they have been sick, is **up and about**, they are now out of bed and living their normal life. ❑ *How are you Lennox? Good to see you up and about.* ADJ **1** [V-LINK + up] If you are **up**, you are not in bed. ❑ *Are you sure you should be up?* ❑ *These days they were up at the crack of dawn.* **2** [V-LINK + up] If a period of time is **up**, it has come to an end. = over ❑ *The moment the half-hour was up, Brooks rose.* **3** [V-LINK + up] If a computer or computer system is **up**, it is working. Compare **down** ADJECTIVE 3 ❑ *The new system is up and ready to run.*

PHRASES **something is up** (*informal*) If you say that **something is up**, you mean that something is wrong or that something worrying is happening. ❑ *What is it then? Something's up, isn't it?*

What's up? (*informal*) If you say to someone 'What's up?' or if you tell someone **what's up**, you are asking them or telling them what is wrong or what is worrying them. ❑ *'What's up?' I said to him. 'Just tired,' he answered.*

VERB [T, I] (**ups, upping, upped**) **1** [T] If you **up** something such as the amount of money you are offering for something, you increase it. = increase ❑ *He upped his offer for the company.* ❑ *Drug stores upped sales by 63 per cent.* **2** [I] If you **up** and leave a place, you go away from it, often suddenly or unexpectedly. ❑ *One day he just upped and left.*

✦ **up in arms** → see **arm**; **up to par** → see **par**

☉**up·bring·ing** /ˈʌpbrɪŋɪŋ/ NOUN [U] Your **upbringing** is the way that your parents treat you and the things that they teach you when you are growing up. = background, childhood ❑ *Martin's upbringing shaped his whole life.* ❑ *John F Kennedy, a naval war hero with a privileged upbringing* ❑ *Proudhon's political ideas were coloured by his upbringing as the son of a poor and irresponsible peasant.* ❑ *his middle-class upbringing in the American Midwest*

☉**up·date** VERB, NOUN

VERB /ʌpˈdeɪt/ [I, T] (**updates, updating, updated**) **1** [I, T] If you **update** something, you make it more modern, usually by adding new parts to it or giving new information. = modernize ❑ *He was back in the office, updating the work schedule on the computer.* ❑ *Airlines would prefer to update rather than retrain crews.* ❑ *an updated edition of the book* ❑ *The guide was updated last year.* **2** [T] If you **update** someone **on** a situation, you tell them the latest developments in that situation. ❑ *We'll update you on the day's top news stories.*

NOUN /ˈʌpdeɪt/ [C] (**updates**) An **update** is a news item

U

containing the latest information about a particular situation. ❑ *She had heard the newsflash on a TV channel's news update.* ❑ *a weather update*

up·grade VERB, NOUN
VERB /ʌpˈgreɪd/ [T, I] (**upgrades, upgrading, upgraded**) **1** [T] If equipment or services **are upgraded**, they are improved or made more efficient. ❑ *Helicopters have been upgraded and modernized.* ❑ *Medical facilities are being reorganized and upgraded.* **2** [T] If someone **is upgraded**, their job or status is changed so that they become more important or receive more money. = promote ❑ *He was upgraded to security guard.* **3** [I, T] If you **upgrade** or **are upgraded**, you change something such as your plane ticket or your hotel room to one that is more expensive. ❑ *His family was upgraded from economy to business class.* NOUN /ˈʌpgreɪd/ [C] (**upgrades**) If equipment or services receive an **upgrade**, they are improved or made more efficient. ❑ *equipment which needs expensive upgrades*

up·heav·al /ʌpˈhiːvəl/ NOUN [C] (**upheavals**) An **upheaval** is a big change which causes a lot of trouble, confusion, and worry. ❑ *Algeria has been going through political upheaval for the past two months.*

up·held /ʌpˈheld/ IRREG FORM **Upheld** is the past tense and past participle of **uphold**.

up·hill /ˌʌpˈhɪl/ ADV, ADJ
ADV If something or someone is **uphill** or is moving **uphill**, they are near the top of a hill or are going up a slope. ❑ *He had been running uphill a long way.* ❑ *The man was no more than ten yards away and slightly uphill.*
ADJ **1** An **uphill** slope or gradient inclines upwards. An **uphill** climb involves going up a slope. ❑ *a long, uphill journey* **2** [uphill + N] If you refer to something as an **uphill** battle or an **uphill** struggle, you mean that it requires a lot of effort and determination, but it should be possible to achieve it. ❑ *It had been an uphill battle to achieve what she had wanted.*

✿ up·hold /ʌpˈhəʊld/ VERB [T] (**upholds, upholding, upheld**) **1** If you **uphold** something such as a law, a principle, or a decision, you support and maintain it. ❑ *Our policy has been to uphold the law.* ❑ *It is the responsibility of every government to uphold certain basic principles.* ❑ *upholding the artist's right to creative freedom* **2** If a court of law **upholds** a legal decision that has already been made, it decides that it was the correct decision. = back, maintain, support; ≠ reject ❑ *The State Supreme Court upheld the Superior Court judge's decision.* ❑ *The judges unanimously upheld the appeal.*

up·load /ʌpˈləʊd/ VERB [T] (**uploads, uploading, uploaded**) (*computing*) If you **upload** data, you transfer it from a disk to your computer or from your computer to another computer. ❑ *All you need to do is upload the files on to your web space.*

upon ◆◆◇ /əˈpɒn/ PREP

In addition to the uses shown below, **upon** is used in phrasal verbs such as 'come upon' and 'look upon', and after some other verbs such as 'decide' and 'depend'.

1 (*literary*) If one thing is **upon** another, it is on it. = on ❑ *He set the tray upon the table.* ❑ *He bent forward and laid a kiss softly upon her forehead.* **2** [upon + -ING/N] (*formal*) You use **upon** when mentioning an event that is followed immediately by another event. = on ❑ *The door on the left, upon entering the church, leads to the Crypt of St Issac.* **3** [N + upon + N] You use **upon** between two occurrences of the same noun in order to say that there are large numbers of the thing mentioned. ❑ *Row upon row of women surged forwards.* **4** [upon + PRON] (*literary*) If an event is **upon** you, it is just about to happen. ❑ *The long-threatened storm was upon us.* ❑ *The wedding season is upon us.*

✿ up·per ◆◇◇ /ˈʌpə/ ADJ
ADJ **1** [upper + N, 'the' upper] You use **upper** to describe something that is above something else. ❑ *There is a good restaurant on the upper floor.* ❑ *his upper lip* ❑ *Students travel on the cheap lower deck and tourists on the upper.* **2** [upper + N] You use **upper** to describe the higher part of something. ❑ *the upper part of the foot* ❑ *the muscles of the upper back and chest*

PHRASE **the upper hand** If you have **the upper hand** in a situation, you have an advantage over other people involved, for example because you have more power or success. ❑ *The home team was beginning to gain the upper hand.*

up·right /ˈʌpraɪt/ ADJ, NOUN
ADJ **1** If you are sitting or standing **upright**, you are sitting or standing with your back straight, rather than bending or lying down. ❑ *Helen sat upright in her chair.* ❑ *He moved into an upright position.* **2** [upright + N] An **upright** vacuum cleaner or freezer is tall rather than wide. **3** An **upright** chair has a straight back and no arms. ❑ *He was sitting on an upright chair beside his bed, reading.* **4** You can describe people as **upright** when they are careful to follow acceptable rules of behaviour and behave in a moral way. ❑ *a very upright, trustworthy man*
NOUN [C] (**uprights**) You can refer to vertical posts or the vertical parts of an object as **uprights**. ❑ *the uprights of a four-poster bed*

up·ris·ing /ˈʌpraɪzɪŋ/ NOUN [C] (**uprisings**) When there is an **uprising**, a group of people start fighting against the people who are in power in their country, because they want to bring about a political change. = rebellion, revolt ❑ *an uprising against the government*

up·roar /ˈʌprɔː/ NOUN [U] **1** [also 'an' uproar, oft 'in' uproar] If there is **uproar**, there is a lot of shouting and noise because people are very angry or upset about something. ❑ *The announcement caused an uproar in the crowd.* **2** [also 'an' uproar] You can also use **uproar** to refer to a lot of public criticism and debate about something that has made people angry. ❑ *The town is in an uproar over the dispute.*

up·root /ʌpˈruːt/ VERB [T] (**uproots, uprooting, uprooted**) **1** If you **uproot yourself** or if you **are uprooted**, you leave, or are made to leave, a place where you have lived for a long time. ❑ *the trauma of uprooting themselves from their homes* ❑ *He had no wish to uproot Dena from her present home.* **2** If someone **uproots** a tree or plant, or if the wind **uproots** it, it is pulled out of the ground. ❑ *They had been forced to uproot their vines and plant wheat.* ❑ *fallen trees which have been uprooted by the storm*

up·set ◆◆◇ ADJ, NOUN, VERB
ADJ /ʌpˈset/ **1** If you are **upset**, you are unhappy or disappointed because something bad has happened to you. ❑ *After she died I felt very, very upset.* ❑ *Marta looked upset.* **2** [upset + N] If you have an **upset** stomach, you experience a slight sickness in your stomach caused by an infection or by something that you have eaten. ❑ *Larry has an upset stomach.*
NOUN /ˈʌpset/ [C] (**upsets**) **1** An **upset** is something that makes you feel worried, unhappy, or disappointed. ❑ *stress and other emotional upsets* **2** An **upset** is an event that causes something such as a procedure or a state of affairs to go wrong. ❑ *Markets are very sensitive to any upsets in the Japanese economic machine.* **3** A stomach **upset** is a slight sickness in your stomach caused by an infection or by something that you have eaten. ❑ *Paul was unwell last night with a stomach upset.*
VERB /ʌpˈset/ [T] (**upsets, upsetting, upset**) **1** If something **upsets** you, it makes you feel worried or unhappy. ❑ *The whole incident had upset me and my fiancée terribly.* ❑ *She warned me not to say anything to upset him.* **2** If events **upset** something such as a procedure or a state of affairs, they cause it to go wrong. ❑ *Political problems could upset agreements between Moscow and Kabul.* **3** If you **upset** an object, you accidentally knock or push it over so that it scatters over a large area. ❑ *Don't upset the piles of sheets under the box.*
up·set·ting /ʌpˈsetɪŋ/ ADJ = distressing ❑ *Childhood sickness can be upsetting for children and parents alike.*

up·shot /ˈʌpʃɒt/ NOUN [SING] The **upshot** of a series of events or discussions is the final result of them, usually a surprising result. = outcome ❑ *The upshot is that we have lots of good but not very happy employees.*

up·side /ˈʌpsaɪd/ NOUN [C] (**upsides**) The **upside** of an unpleasant situation is the aspect of it that is more

u

pleasant or positive. ❑ *Residents said the only upside would be a boost to the island's economy.*

up·side down /ˌʌpsaɪd 'daʊn/ also **upside-down** ADV, ADJ

ADV If something is or has been turned **upside down**, it has been turned round so that the part that is usually lowest is above the part that is usually highest. ❑ *The painting was hung upside down.*

ADJ **Upside down** means in an inverted position, with the part that is usually lowest above the part that is usually highest. ❑ *chandeliers that resemble upside-down wedding cakes*

up·stage /ˌʌp'steɪdʒ/ VERB [T] (**upstages, upstaging, upstaged**) If someone **upstages** you, they draw attention away from you by being more attractive or interesting. ❑ *He had a younger brother who always publicly upstaged him.*

up·stairs /ˌʌp'steəz/ ADV, ADJ, NOUN

ADV [upstairs after v] If you go **upstairs** in a building, you go up a staircase towards a higher floor. ❑ *He went upstairs and changed into clean clothes.* ❷ If something or someone is **upstairs** in a building, they are on a floor that is higher than the ground floor. ❑ *The restaurant is upstairs and consists of a large, open room.*

ADJ [upstairs + N] An **upstairs** room or object is situated on a floor of a building that is higher than the ground floor. ❑ *Marsani moved into the upstairs flat.*

NOUN [SING] The **upstairs** of a building is the floor or floors that are higher than the ground floor. ❑ *Together we went through the upstairs.*

up·stream /ˌʌp'striːm/ ADV, ADJ

ADV Something that is moving **upstream** is moving towards the source of a river against the current, from a point further down the river. Something that is **upstream** is towards the source of a river. ❑ *Salmon manage to swim upstream to lay their eggs.* ❑ *the river police, whose headquarters are just upstream of the Ile St Louis*

ADJ [upstream + N] **Upstream** is used to refer to something that is towards the source of a river. ❑ *We'll go to the upstream side of that big rock.*

up·tight /ˌʌp'taɪt/ ADJ (*informal*) Someone who is **uptight** is tense, nervous, or annoyed about something and so is difficult to be with. ❑ *Penny never got uptight about exams.*

up-to-date also **up to date** ADJ ❶ If something is **up-to-date**, it is the newest thing of its kind. ❑ *the most up-to-date information available on foods today* ❑ *Web services are always up-to-date and available.* ❷ If you are **up-to-date** about something, you have the latest information about it. ❑ *We'll keep you up to date with any news.*

up·ward /'ʌpwəd/ ADJ, ADV

The form **upwards** is also used for the adverb.

ADJ ❶ [upward + N] An **upward** movement or look is directed towards a higher place or a higher level. ❑ *She started once again on the steep, upward climb.* ❑ *She gave him a quick, upward look, then lowered her eyes.* ❷ [upward + N] If you refer to an **upward** trend or an **upward** spiral, you mean that something is increasing in quantity or price. ❑ *the Army's concern that the upward trend in the numbers avoiding military service may continue*

ADV ❶ If someone moves or looks **upward**, they move or look up towards a higher place. ❑ *They climbed upward along the steep cliffs surrounding the village.* ❑ *'There,' said Jack, pointing upwards.* ❷ [upward after v] If an amount or rate moves **upward**, it increases. ❑ *with prices soon heading upward in the shops* ❑ *Unemployment will continue upward for much of this year.*

PHRASE **upwards of** A quantity that is **upwards of** a particular number is more than that number. ❑ *It costs upwards of $40,000 a year to keep some prisoners in prison.*

up·wards /'ʌpwədz/ → See **upward**

ura·nium /jʊ'reɪniəm/ NOUN [U] **Uranium** is a naturally occurring radioactive metal that is used to produce nuclear energy and weapons.

✿**ur·ban** ◆◇◇ /'ɜːbən/ ADJ **Urban** means belonging to, or relating to, a city or town. = city ❑ *For a small state it has a large urban population.* ❑ *Most urban areas are close to a*

park. ❑ *She lived well away from the urban sprawl of London.* ❑ *urban planning*

✿**ur·bani·za·tion** /ˌɜːbənaɪ'zeɪʃən/ also **urbanisation** NOUN [U] **Urbanization** is the process of creating cities or towns in country areas. ❑ *Rapid urbanization is one of the gravest challenges facing governments and communities alike.*

✿**ur·ban·ized** /'ɜːbənaɪzd/ also **urbanised** ADJ ❶ [usu urbanized + N] An **urbanized** country or area has many buildings and a lot of industry and business. ❑ *Zambia is black Africa's most urbanized country.* ❑ *All the nice areas in Florida are becoming more and more urbanized.* ❷ An **urbanized** population consists of people who live and work in a city or town.

urge ◆◆◇ /ɜːdʒ/ VERB, NOUN

VERB [T] (**urges, urging, urged**) ❶ If you **urge** someone **to** do something, you try hard to persuade them to do it. ❑ *They urged Parliament to approve plans for their reform programme.* ❷ If you **urge** someone somewhere, you make them go there by touching them or talking to them. ❑ *He slipped his arm round her waist and urged her away from the window.* ❸ If you **urge** a course of action, you strongly advise that it should be taken. ❑ *He urged restraint on the security forces.*

NOUN [C] (**urges**) If you have an **urge** to do or have something, you have a strong wish to do or have it. ❑ *He had an urge to open a shop of his own.*

ur·gent ◆◇◇ /'ɜːdʒənt/ ADJ ❶ If something is **urgent**, it needs to be dealt with as soon as possible. = pressing ❑ *There is an urgent need for food and water.* ❷ If you speak in an **urgent** way, you show that you are anxious for people to notice something or to do something. ❑ *His voice was low and urgent.*

ur·gen·cy /'ɜːdʒənsi/ NOUN [U] ❶ The **urgency** of finding a cure attracted some of the best minds in medical science. ❷ She was surprised at the **urgency** in his voice.

ur·gent·ly /'ɜːdʒəntli/ ADV ❶ [urgently with v] ❑ *Red Cross officials said they urgently needed bread and water.* ❷ [urgently with v] ❑ *They hastened to greet him and asked urgently, 'Did you find it?'*

urine /'jʊərɪn/ NOUN [U] **Urine** is the liquid that you get rid of from your body when you go to the toilet. ❑ *The doctor took a urine sample and a blood sample.*

us ◆◆◆ /əs, STRONG ʌs/ PRON

Us is the first person plural pronoun. **Us** is used as the object of a verb or a preposition.

❶ [V + us, PREP + us] A speaker or writer uses **us** to refer both to himself or herself and to one or more other people. You can use **us** before a noun to make it clear which group of people you are referring to. ❑ *Neither of us forgot about it.* ❑ *Heather went to the kitchen to get drinks for us.* ❑ *They don't like us much.* ❷ [V + us, PREP + us] **Us** is sometimes used to refer to people in general. ❑ *All of us will struggle fairly hard to survive if we are in danger.* ❸ [V + us, PREP + us] (*mainly formal*) A speaker or writer may use **us** instead of 'me' in order to include the audience or reader in what they are saying. ❑ *This brings us to the second question I asked.*

✿**us·age** /'juːsɪdʒ/ NOUN [U, C] (**usages**) ❶ [U] **Usage** is the way in which words are actually used in particular contexts, especially with regard to their meanings. ❑ *He was a stickler for the correct usage of English.* ❑ *The word 'undertaker' had long been in common usage.* ❷ [C] A **usage** is a meaning that a word has or a way in which it can be used. ❑ *It's very definitely a usage which has come over to Britain from America.* ❸ [U] **Usage** is the degree to which something is used or the way in which it is used. = use ❑ *Parts of the motor wore out because of constant usage.* ❑ *Your water usage may be very small.*

✿**use** ◆◆◆ VERB, NOUN

VERB /juːz/ [T] (**uses, using, used**) ❶ If you **use** something, you do something with it in order to do a job or to achieve a particular result or effect. ❑ *Trim off the excess pastry using a sharp knife.* ❑ *The US has used ships to bring most of its heavy material, like tanks, to the region.* ❑ *He had simply used a little imagination.* ❑ *using personal*

U

computers as teaching tools ❑ *Officials used microphones to call for calm.* **2** If you **use** a supply of something, you finish it so that none of it is left. ❑ *You used all the ice cubes and didn't put the ice trays back.* **3** If someone **uses** drugs, they take drugs regularly, especially illegal ones. = take, do ❑ *He denied he had used drugs.* **4** You can say that someone **uses** the toilet or bathroom as a polite way of saying that they go to the toilet. ❑ *Wash your hands after using the bathroom.* **5** If you **use** a particular word or expression, you say or write it, because it has the meaning that you want to express. ❑ *The judge liked using the word 'wicked' of people he had sent to jail.* **6** If you **use** a particular name, you call yourself by that name, especially when it is not the name that you usually call yourself. ❑ *Now I use a false name if I'm meeting people for the first time.* **7** If you say that someone **uses** people, you disapprove of them because they make others do things for them in order to benefit or gain some advantage from it, and not because they care about the other people. = exploit ❑ *Why do I have the feeling I'm being used again?*

PHRASAL VERB **use up** Use up means the same as use VERB 2. ❑ *It isn't animals who use up the world's resources.*

NOUN /juːs/ [U, SING, C] **(uses)** **1** [U] [also 'a' use, usu use 'of' N] Your **use** of something is the action or fact of your using it. ❑ *The treatment does not involve the use of any artificial drugs.* ❑ *research related to microcomputers and their use in classrooms* ❑ *He said he supported the use of force.* **2** [SING] If you have a **use for** something, you need it or can find something to do with it. ❑ *You will no longer have a use for the magazines.* **3** [C, U] If something has a particular **use**, it is intended for a particular purpose. ❑ *Infrared detectors have many uses.* ❑ *It's an interesting scientific phenomenon, but of no practical use whatever.* ❑ *The report outlined possible uses for the new weapon.* ❑ *We need to recognize that certain uses of the land are simply wrong.* **4** [U] [also 'the' use, usu use 'of' N] If you have the **use of** something, you have the permission or ability to use it. ❑ *She will have the use of the car one night a week.* ❑ *young people who at some point in the past have lost the use of their limbs* **5** [C] A **use** of a word is a particular meaning that it has or a particular way in which it can be used. ❑ *There are new uses of words coming in and old uses dying out.* **6** [U] Your **use** of a particular name is the fact of your calling yourself by it. ❑ *Police have been hampered by Mr Urquhart's use of bogus names.*

PHRASES **for the use of** If something is **for the use of** a particular person or group of people, it is for that person or group to use. ❑ *The facilities are there for the use of guests.*

have its uses (informal) If you say that being something or knowing someone **has its uses**, you mean that it makes it possible for you to do what you otherwise would not be able to do. ❑ *It wasn't a life she particularly enjoyed, but it had its uses.*

in use If something such as a technique, building, or machine is **in use**, it is used regularly by people. If it has gone **out of use**, it is no longer used regularly by people. ❑ *the methods of making champagne which are still in use today*

make use of (written) If you **make use of** something, you do something with it in order to do a job or achieve a particular result or effect. ❑ *Few found jobs in which they could make use of their new skills.*

it's no use If you say **it's no use**, you mean that you have failed to do something and realize that it is useless to continue trying because it is impossible. ❑ *It's no use. Let's hang up and try for another line.*

be of use or **be no use** If something or someone is **of use**, they are useful. If they are **no use**, they are not at all useful. ❑ *The contents of this booklet should be of use to all students.*
→ See also **used**

ADJ + **use**

regular use
frequent use
increased use
❑ *Regular use of painkillers can actually cause headaches.*

recreational use
personal use
unauthorized use
❑ *He had taken company funds for his own personal use.*

practical use
commercial use
❑ *The major commercial uses of carbon dioxide today are in beverages, fire extinguishers, and refrigerants.*

used ◆◆◇ ADJ, VERB

ADJ /juːzd/ **1** A **used** object is dirty or spoiled because it has been used, and usually needs to be thrown away or washed. ❑ *a used cotton wool ball stained with makeup* **2** A **used** car has already had one or more owners. = secondhand ❑ *Would you buy a used car from this man?*

PHRASES **be used to** /juːst/ If you **are used to** something, you are familiar with it because you have done it or experienced it many times before. ❑ *I'm used to having my sleep interrupted.*

get used to /juːst/ If you **get used to** something or someone, you become familiar with it or get to know them, so that you no longer feel that the thing or person is unusual or surprising. ❑ *This is how we do things here. You'll soon get used to it.* ❑ *You quickly get used to using the brakes.*

VERB /juːst/

PHRASES **used to** If something **used to** be done or **used to** be the case, it was done regularly in the past or was the case in the past. ❑ *People used to come and visit him every day.* ❑ *He used to be one of my professors.*

did not use to or **used not to** If something **did not use** to be done, **used to not** be done or **used not to** be done, it was not done in the past. ❑ *Borrowing used to not be recommended.* ❑ *At some point kids start doing things they didn't use to do. They get more independent.*

WHICH WORD?

used to or be used to?

If something **used to** happen, it happened regularly in the past.
❑ *She **used to** tell me stories about people in India and Egypt.*
If you **are used to** something, you are familiar with it and you accept it. With this meaning, **used to** comes after the verb **be**, and is followed by a noun phrase or an '-ing' form.
❑ *The noise doesn't frighten them. They **are used to** it.*
❑ *I **am used to** getting up early.*

✪ use·ful ◆◆◇ /ˈjuːsfʊl/ ADJ

ADJ If something is **useful**, you can use it to do something or to help you in some way. = helpful ❑ *The pressure cooker is very useful for people who go out all day.* ❑ *Hypnotherapy can be useful in helping you give up smoking.* ❑ *The data is useful for planning and scheduling.* ❑ *The police gained a great deal of useful information about the organization.*

PHRASE **come in useful** If an object or skill **comes in useful**, it can help you achieve something in a particular situation. ❑ *Extra blank paper will probably come in useful.*

use·ful·ly /ˈjuːsfəli/ ADV [usefully with V] ❑ *the problems to which computers could be usefully applied*

use·ful·ness /ˈjuːsfəlnəs/ NOUN [U] ❑ *His interest lay in the usefulness of his work, rather than in any personal credit.*

ADJ + **noun**

useful information
useful advice
❑ *The website is full of useful advice on choosing a university course.*

a useful tool
a useful tip
a useful exercise
❑ *The book should prove to be a useful tool for language teachers.*

u

VERB + **useful**
prove useful
find useful
❏ Many people find it useful to draw up a list in order of priority.

use·less /ˈjuːsləs/ ADJ **1** If something is **useless**, you cannot use it. ❏ He realized that their money was useless in this country. **2** If something is **useless**, it does not achieve anything helpful or good. = pointless ❏ She knew it was useless to protest. **3** If you say that someone or something is **useless**, you mean that they are no good at all. ❏ Their education system is useless. **4** If someone feels **useless**, they feel bad because they are unable to help someone or achieve anything. ❏ She sits at home all day, watching TV and feeling useless.

✪**user** ◆◇◇ /ˈjuːzə/ NOUN [C] (**users**) A **user** is a person or thing that uses something such as a place, facility, product, or machine. ❏ Beach users have complained that the bikes are noisy. ❏ a regular user of the subway ❏ a user of electric current, such as an electric motor, a lamp, or a toaster

✪**user-friendly** ADJ If you describe something such as a machine or system as **user-friendly**, you mean that it is well designed and easy to use. = accessible ❏ This is an entirely computer-operated system which is very user-friendly. ❏ user-friendly libraries

ush·er /ˈʌʃə/ VERB, NOUN
▪ VERB [T] (**ushers, ushering, ushered**) (formal) If you **usher** someone somewhere, you show them where they should go by going with them. ❏ I ushered him into the office.
▪ NOUN [C] (**ushers**) An **usher** is a person who shows people where to sit, for example at a wedding or at a concert. ❏ He did part-time work as an usher in a theatre.

✪**usu·al** ◆◆◇ /ˈjuːʒuəl/ ADJ, NOUN
▪ ADJ **Usual** is used to describe what happens or what is done most often in a particular situation. = normal, customary, typical ❏ It is a neighbourhood beset by all the usual inner-city problems. ❏ After lunch there was a little more clearing up to do than usual. ❏ We've had more press coverage than usual in the last three weeks. ❏ It is usual to tip waiters, porters, guides and drivers.
▪ PHRASE **as usual 1** You use **as usual** to indicate that you are describing something that normally happens or that is normally the case. ❏ As usual there will be the local and regional elections on June the twelfth. **2** If something happens **as usual**, it happens in the way that it normally does, especially when other things have changed. ❏ Surgery was scheduled, but life went on as usual.
▪ NOUN [SING] The **usual** is what happens or what is done most often in a particular situation. ❏ The stout barman in a bow tie presented himself to take their order. 'Good morning, sir. The usual?'
✦ business as usual → see business

✪**usu·al·ly** ◆◆◇ /ˈjuːʒuəli/ ADV
▪ ADV If something **usually** happens, it is the thing that most often happens in a particular situation. = generally, normally, typically ❏ The best information about hotels usually comes from friends and acquaintances who have been there. ❏ Usually, the work is boring. ❏ Offering only one loan, usually an instalment loan, is part of the plan.
▪ PHRASE **more than usually** You use **more than usually** to show that something shows even more of a particular quality than it normally does. = unusually ❏ She felt more than usually hungry after her excursion.

✪**util·ity** /juːˈtɪlɪti/ NOUN [C, U] (**utilities**) (academic word) **1** [C] A **utility** is an important service such as water, electricity, or gas that is provided for everyone, and that everyone pays for. ❏ public utilities such as gas, electricity and phones **2** [U] (formal) The **utility** of something is its usefulness. = usefulness; ≠ uselessness ❏ Belief in the utility of higher education is shared by students nationwide. ❏ an emphasis on the practical utility of scientific knowledge ❏ Consumers seek to maximize the utility or satisfaction to be derived from spending a fixed amount of income.

✪**uti·lize** /ˈjuːtɪlaɪz/ also **utilise** VERB [T] (**utilizes, utilizing, utilized**) (academic word, formal) If you **utilize** something, you use it. = use, employ ❏ Sound engineers utilize a range of techniques to enhance the quality of the recordings. ❏ Minerals can be absorbed and utilized by the body in a variety of different forms.
✪**uti·li·za·tion** /ˌjuːtɪlaɪˈzeɪʃən/ also **utilisation** NOUN [U] = use, employment ❏ the utilization of human resources ❏ the economic utilization of atomic energy

ut·most /ˈʌtməʊst/ ADJ, NOUN
▪ ADJ [utmost + N] (emphasis) You can use **utmost** to emphasize the importance or seriousness of something or to emphasize the way that it is done. ❏ It is a matter of the utmost urgency to find out what has happened to these people. ❏ Security matters are treated with the utmost seriousness.
▪ NOUN [SING] (emphasis) If you say that you are doing your **utmost** to do something, you are emphasizing that you are trying as hard as you can to do it. ❏ He would have done his utmost to help her.

ut·ter /ˈʌtə/ VERB, ADJ
▪ VERB [T] (**utters, uttering, uttered**) (literary) If someone **utters** sounds or words, they say them. ❏ He uttered a snorting laugh.
▪ ADJ [utter + N] (emphasis) You use **utter** to emphasize that something is great in extent, degree, or amount. = absolute, total ❏ This, of course, is utter nonsense. ❏ this utter lack of responsibility

ut·ter·ance /ˈʌtərəns/ NOUN [C] (**utterances**) (formal) Someone's **utterances** are the things that they say. ❏ These two utterances communicate the same message.

ut·ter·ly /ˈʌtəli/ ADV (emphasis) You use **utterly** to emphasize that something is very great in extent, degree, or amount. = totally ❏ China is utterly different. ❏ The new laws coming in are utterly ridiculous.

U

V also **v** /viː/ NOUN [C, U] (**V's, v's**) V is the twenty-second letter of the English alphabet.

va·can·cy /ˈveɪkənsi/ NOUN [C] (**vacancies**) **1** A vacancy is a job or position that has not been filled. ☐ *Most vacancies are at the senior level, requiring appropriate qualifications.* **2** If there are **vacancies** at a building such as a hotel, some of the rooms are available to rent. ☐ *This year hotels that usually are jammed had vacancies all summer.*

va·cant /ˈveɪkənt/ ADJ **1** If something is **vacant**, it is not being used by anyone. = empty ☐ *Halfway down the bus was a vacant seat.* **2** If a job or position is **vacant**, no one is doing it or in it at present, and people can apply for it. ☐ *The position of chairman has been vacant for some time.* **3** A **vacant** look or expression is one that suggests that someone does not understand something or that they are not thinking about anything in particular. = blank ☐ *She had a kind of vacant look on her face.*
va·cant·ly /ˈveɪkəntli/ ADV [vacantly after v] ☐ *He looked vacantly out of the window.*

va·cate /veɪˈkeɪt, AmE ˈveɪkeɪt/ VERB [T] (**vacates, vacating, vacated**) (formal) If you **vacate** a place or a job, you leave it or give it up, making it available for other people. = leave ☐ *He quickly vacated the gym after the workout.*

va·ca·tion /vəˈkeɪʃən, AmE veɪ-/ NOUN [C] (**vacations**) **1** A **vacation** is a period of the year when schools, universities, and colleges are officially closed. = holiday ☐ *During the summer vacation he visited Russia.* **2** (AmE) A **vacation** is a period of time during which you relax and enjoy yourself away from home. = holiday ☐ *We went on vacation to Europe.*

⊙**vac·ci·nate** /ˈvæksɪneɪt/ VERB [T] (**vaccinates, vaccinating, vaccinated**) If a person or animal **is vaccinated**, they are given a vaccine, usually by injection, to prevent them from getting a disease. = inoculate ☐ *Dogs must be vaccinated against distemper.* ☐ *Have you had your child vaccinated against whooping cough?* ☐ *Measles and mumps are spreading again because children are not being vaccinated.*
⊙**vac·ci·na·tion** /ˌvæksɪˈneɪʃən/ NOUN [C, U] (**vaccinations**) = inoculation, injection ☐ *Anyone who wants to avoid the flu should consider getting a vaccination.* ☐ *The abandonment of routine vaccination has led to a low immunity among the population.* ☐ *Smallpox was the first disease against which vaccination was shown to be effective.* ☐ *medics who administer vaccinations*

⊙**vac·cine** /ˈvæksiːn, AmE vækˈsiːn/ NOUN [C, U] (**vaccines**) A **vaccine** is a substance containing a harmless form of the germs that cause a particular disease. It is given to people, usually by injection, to prevent them from getting that disease. ☐ *Anti-malarial vaccines are now undergoing trials.* ☐ *Seven million doses of vaccine are annually given to British children.* ☐ *people who normally receive the flu vaccine*

⊙**vacuum** /ˈvækjuːm, -juːəm/ NOUN, VERB
NOUN [C] (**vacuums**) **1** If someone or something creates a **vacuum**, they leave a place or position that then needs to be filled by another person or thing. ☐ *His presence should fill the power vacuum that has been developing over the past few days.* **2** A **vacuum** is a space that contains no air or other gas. = gap, space, void ☐ *Wind is a current of air caused by a vacuum caused by hot air rising.* ☐ *The spinning turbine creates a vacuum.* ☐ *The lenses are processed in a vacuum chamber.*
PHRASE **in a vacuum** If something is done **in a vacuum**, it is not affected by any outside influences or information. ☐ *Moral values cannot be taught in a vacuum.*
VERB [I, T] (**vacuums, vacuuming, vacuumed**) If you **vacuum** something, you clean it using a vacuum cleaner. ☐ *I vacuumed the carpets today.* ☐ *It's important to vacuum regularly.*

⊙**vague** /veɪg/ ADJ (**vaguer, vaguest**) **1** If something written or spoken is **vague**, it does not explain or express things clearly. = imprecise, unclear, ambiguous; ≠ clear ☐ *A lot of the talk was apparently vague and general.* ☐ *The description was pretty vague.* **2** If you have a **vague** memory or idea of something, the memory or idea is not clear. = faint ☐ *They have only a vague idea of the amount of water available.* **3** If you are **vague** about something, you deliberately do not tell people much about it. ☐ *He was vague, however, about just what US forces might actually do.* ☐ *Marx was intentionally vague about the structure and functioning of the socialist economy.* **4** If something such as a feeling is **vague**, you experience it only slightly. ☐ *He was conscious of that vague feeling of irritation again.* **5** A **vague** shape or outline is not clear and is therefore not easy to see. ☐ *The bus was a vague shape in the distance.*

vague·ly /ˈveɪgli/ ADV **1** If you write or speak **vaguely**, you do not explain or express things clearly. ☐ *'I'm not sure,' Liz said vaguely.* **2** [vaguely with v] If you **vaguely** remember something, you cannot remember it clearly. ☐ *Judith could vaguely remember her mother lying on the sofa.* **3** [vaguely + ADJ] **Vaguely** means to some degree but not to a very large degree. ☐ *The voice on the line was vaguely familiar, but Crook couldn't place it at first.*

vain /veɪn/ ADJ
ADJ (**vainer, vainest**) **1** [vain + N] A **vain** attempt or action is one that fails to achieve what was intended. = fruitless ☐ *The drafting committee worked through the night in a vain attempt to finish on schedule.* **2** [vain + N] If you describe a hope that something will happen as a **vain** hope, you mean that there is no chance of it happening. ☐ *He married his fourth wife, Susan, in the vain hope that she would improve his health.* **3** (disapproval) If you describe someone as **vain**, you are critical of their extreme pride in their own beauty, intelligence, or other good qualities. ☐ *He wasn't so vain as to think he was smarter than his boss.*
PHRASE **in vain** **1** If you do something **in vain**, you do not succeed in achieving what you intend. ☐ *He stopped at the door, waiting in vain for her to acknowledge his presence.* **2** If you say that something such as someone's death, suffering, or effort was **in vain**, you mean that it was useless because it did not achieve anything. ☐ *He wants the world to know his son did not die in vain.*
vain·ly /ˈveɪnli/ ADV **1** ☐ *He hunted vainly through his pockets for a piece of paper.* **2** ☐ *He then set out for Virginia for what he vainly hoped would be a peaceful retirement.*

val·iant /ˈvæliənt/ ADJ A **valiant** action is very brave and determined, though it may lead to failure or defeat. ☐ *Despite valiant efforts by the finance minister, inflation rose to 36%.*
val·iant·ly /ˈvæliəntli/ ADV [valiantly with v] = bravely

❏ He suffered further heart attacks and strokes, all of which he fought valiantly.

⊙ **val·id** /'vælɪd/ ADJ (academic word) **1** A **valid** argument, comment, or idea is based on sensible reasoning. = legitimate, sound, solid, reasonable ❏ They put forward many valid reasons for not exporting. ❏ Some of these arguments are valid. ❏ This is a perfectly valid approach, but it has its drawbacks. **2** Something that is **valid** is important or serious enough to make it worth saying or doing. ❏ Most designers share the unspoken belief that fashion is a valid form of visual art. **3** If a ticket or other document is **valid**, it can be used and will be accepted by people in authority. = good ❏ All tickets are valid for two months. **4** If something such as a number is **valid**, it is within an acceptable range of values or restrictions. ≠ invalid ❏ software that generates valid numbers ❏ a valid password ❏ a statistically valid sample

VOCABULARY BUILDER

valid ADJ (formal)

A **valid** argument, comment, or idea is based on sensible reasoning.

❏ She could think of no valid reason for refusing to answer.

legitimate ADJ (formal)

If you say that something such as a feeling or claim is **legitimate**, you think that it is reasonable and justified.

❏ That's a perfectly legitimate fear.

sound ADJ

Sound advice, reasoning, or evidence is reliable and sensible.

❏ nutritionists who can give sound advice on diets

solid ADJ

Solid evidence or information is reliable because it is based on facts.

❏ We don't have solid information on where the people are.

authentic ADJ (formal)

An **authentic** piece of information or account of something comes from a reliable or important person.

❏ I obtained authentic details about the organization.

reasonable ADJ

If you say that an expectation or explanation is **reasonable**, you mean that there are good reasons why it may be correct.

❏ It seems reasonable to expect rapid urban growth.

vali·date /'vælɪdeɪt/ VERB [T] (validates, validating, validated) **1** (formal) To **validate** something such as a claim or statement means to prove or confirm that it is true or correct. = substantiate ❏ This discovery seems to validate the claims of popular astrology. **2** To **validate** a person, state, or system means to prove or confirm that they are valuable or worthwhile. ❏ The Academy Awards appear to validate his career.

vali·da·tion /,vælɪ'deɪʃən/ NOUN [C, U] (validations) **1** When we want validation for our decisions we often turn to friends for advice and approval. **2** I think the film is a validation of our lifestyle.

⊙ **va·lid·ity** /və'lɪdɪti/ NOUN [U] **1** If an argument, comment, or idea has **validity**, it is based on sensible reasoning. = worth, legitimacy, strength ❏ The editorial says this argument has lost much of its validity. ❏ Many scientists are questioning the validity of the claims of the study. **2** The **validity** of something such as a result or a piece of information is whether it can be trusted or believed. ❏ Shocked by the results of the elections, they now want to challenge the validity of the vote. ❏ Some people, of course, denied the validity of any such claim. **3** If an issue has **validity**, it is important or serious enough to make it worth saying or doing. ❏ the validity of making children wear bicycle helmets

val·ley ♦◇◇ /'væli/ NOUN [C] (valleys) A **valley** is a low stretch of land between hills, especially one that has a

river flowing through it. ❏ a wooded valley set against the backdrop of Monte Rosa

⊙ **valu·able** ♦◇◇ /'væljuəbəl/ ADJ **1** If you describe something or someone as **valuable**, you mean that they are very useful and helpful. = useful, helpful ❏ Many of our teachers also have valuable academic links with Heidelberg University. ❏ The experience was very valuable. **2** **Valuable** objects are objects that are worth a lot of money. ❏ Just because a camera is old does not mean it is valuable.

valu·ables /'væljuəbəlz/ NOUN [PL] **Valuables** are things that you own that are worth a lot of money, especially small objects such as jewellery. ❏ Leave your valuables in the hotel safe behind the reception desk.

valua·tion /,vælju'eɪʃən/ NOUN [C, U] (valuations) A **valuation** is a judgment that someone makes about how much money something is worth. ❏ Valuation lies at the heart of all takeovers.

⊙ **value** ♦♦♦ /'vælju:/ NOUN, VERB
NOUN [U, C, PL] (values) **1** [U] [also 'a' value] The **value** of something such as a quality, attitude, or method is its importance or usefulness. If you place a particular **value** on something, that is the importance or usefulness you think it has. = worth ❏ The value of this work experience should not be underestimated. ❏ Further studies will be needed to see if these therapies have any value. ❏ Current sales figures tell us something of value about what is really going on. **2** [C, U] The **value** of something is how much money it is worth. = cost, price, worth ❏ The value of his investment has risen by more than $50,000. ❏ The country's currency went down in value by 3.5 per cent. **3** [U] You use **value** in certain expressions to say whether something is worth the money that it costs. For example, if something is **good value**, or if you get **good value** for your money when you buy something, then it is worth the money that it costs. ❏ We believe that is good value for money for our customers. **4** [C] A **value** is a particular number or amount. = number, amount, figure ❏ Normal values lie between 1.0 and 3.0mg per 100ml blood serum. ❏ These calculations were based on average values for velocity and acceleration. **5** [PL] The **values** of a person or group are the moral principles and beliefs that they think are important. = beliefs, morals ❏ The countries of South Asia also share many common values. ❏ The Health Secretary called for a return to traditional family values. **6** [U] **Value** is used after another noun when mentioning an important or noticeable feature about something. ❏ The script has lost all of its shock value over the intervening 24 years. **PHRASE** **of value** or **of no value** **1** If something is **of value**, it is useful or important. If it is **of no value**, it has no usefulness or importance. ❏ This weekend course will be of value to everyone interested in the Pilgrim Route. **2** If something is **of value**, it is worth a lot of money. If it is **of no value**, it is worth very little money. ❏ a brooch that is really of no value ❏ It might contain something of value.
VERB [T] (values, valuing, valued) **1** If you **value** something or someone, you think that they are important and you appreciate them. = admire, approve of ❏ I value the opinion of my husband and we agree on most things. ❏ a culture in the workplace which values learning and development ❏ Authority is rooted in a patriarchal system; males are highly valued. **2** When experts **value** something, they decide how much money it is worth. ❏ The school board valued the property at $130,000. ❏ I asked him to have my jewellery valued.

VOCABULARY BUILDER

value NOUN (fairly formal)

The **value** of something such as a quality, attitude, or method is its importance or usefulness. If you place a particular **value** on something, that is the importance or usefulness you think it has.

❏ In 1847 Sir James Young Simpson first discovered the value of chloroform as an anaesthetic in childbirth.

importance NOUN

The **importance** of something is how significant, valued, or necessary it is in a particular situation.

❏ Institutions place great importance on symbols of corporate identity.

V

merit NOUN

If something has **merit**, it has good or worthwhile qualities.
❏ *The argument has considerable merit.*

usefulness NOUN

The **usefulness** of something is the degree to which it is helpful.
❏ *His interest lay in the usefulness of his work, rather than in any personal credit.*

valve /vælv/ NOUN [c] (**valves**) A **valve** is a device attached to a pipe or a tube that controls the flow of air or liquid through the pipe or tube.

van ◆◇◇ /væn/ NOUN [c] (**vans**) A **van** is a small or medium-sized road vehicle with one row of seats at the front and a space for carrying goods behind.

van·dal /ˈvændəl/ NOUN [c] (**vandals**) A **vandal** is someone who deliberately damages things, especially public property. ❏ *The street lights were out, smashed by vandals.*

van·dal·ism /ˈvændəlɪzəm/ NOUN [u] **Vandalism** is the deliberate damaging of things, especially public property. ❏ *a 13-year-old boy whose crime file includes violence, theft, vandalism, and bullying*

van·dal·ize /ˈvændəlaɪz/ also **vandalise** VERB [T] (**vandalizes, vandalizing, vandalized**) If something such as a building or part of a building **is vandalized** by someone, it is damaged on purpose. ❏ *The walls had been horribly vandalized with spray paint.*

van·guard /ˈvænɡɑːd/ NOUN [SING] If someone is **in the vanguard of** something such as a revolution or an area of research, they are involved in the most advanced part of it. You can also refer to the people themselves as **the vanguard**. ❏ *Students and intellectuals have been in the vanguard of revolutionary change in China.*

van·ish /ˈvænɪʃ/ VERB [I] (**vanishes, vanishing, vanished**)
1 If someone or something **vanishes**, they disappear suddenly or in a way that cannot be explained. = disappear ❏ *He just vanished and was never seen again.* ❏ *Anne vanished from outside her home last Wednesday.*
2 If something such as a species of animal or a tradition **vanishes**, it stops existing. = disappear ❏ *Many of these species have vanished or are facing extinction.*

van·ity /ˈvænɪti/ NOUN [u] (*disapproval*) If you refer to someone's **vanity**, you are critical of them because they take great pride in their appearance or abilities. ❏ *Men who use steroids are motivated by sheer vanity.*

✪ **va·por·ize** /ˈveɪpəraɪz/ also **vaporise** VERB [I, T] (**vaporizes, vaporizing, vaporized**) If a liquid or solid **vaporizes** or if you **vaporize** it, it changes into vapour or gas. = evaporate ❏ *The benzene vaporized and formed a huge cloud of gas.* ❏ *The blast may have vaporized the meteorite.*

✪ **va·pour** /ˈveɪpə/ (in *AmE*, use **vapor**) NOUN [c, u] (**vapours**) **Vapour** consists of tiny drops of water or other liquids in the air, which appear as mist. = mist, fog ❏ *Cold air can hold very little water vapour compared with warm air.* ❏ *the vapour trail of a jet across the sky*

✪ **vari·able** /ˈveəriəbəl/ ADJ, NOUN
ADJ Something that is **variable** changes quite often, and there usually seems to be no fixed pattern to these changes. ❏ *The potassium content of foodstuffs is very variable.*
NOUN [c] (**variables**) A **variable** is a factor that can change in quality, quantity, or size, that you have to take into account in a situation. = factor ❏ *Decisions could be made on the basis of price, delivery dates, after-sales service or any other variable.* ❏ *Other variables in making forecasts for the industry include the weather and the general economic climate.*
vari·abil·ity /ˌveəriəˈbɪlɪti/ NOUN [u] ❏ *There's a great deal of variability between individuals.*

✪ **vari·ation** /ˌveəriˈeɪʃən/ NOUN [c, u] (**variations**) **1** [c] A **variation on** something is the same thing presented in a slightly different form. ❏ *This delicious variation on an omelette is quick and easy to prepare.* **2** [c, u] A **variation** is a

change or slight difference in a level, amount, or quantity. = difference, diversity; ≠ similarity ❏ *The survey found a wide variation in the prices charged for canteen food.* ❏ *Scotland's employment rate shows significant regional variations.*

✪ **var·ied** /ˈveərɪd/ ADJ Something that is **varied** consists of things of different types, sizes, or qualities. = diverse ❏ *It is essential that your diet is varied and balanced.* ❏ *Before his election to the presidency, Mitterrand had enjoyed a long and varied career.*
→ See also **vary**

✪ **va·ri·ety** ◆◆◇ /vəˈraɪɪti/ NOUN [u, SING, c] (**varieties**)
1 [u] If something has **variety**, it consists of things that are different from each other. = diversity ❏ *Susan's idea of freedom was to have variety in her lifestyle.* **2** [SING] A **variety of** things is a number of different kinds or examples of the same thing. = range ❏ *West Hampstead has a variety of good shops and supermarkets.* ❏ *The island offers such a wide variety of scenery and wildlife.* ❏ *People change their mind for a variety of reasons.* **3** [c] A **variety of** something is a type of it. = kind ❏ *I'm always pleased to try out a new variety.*

WORD CONNECTIONS

ADJ + **variety**

a **wide** variety
a **great** variety
❏ *These slopes are planted with a great variety of crops.*

VERB + **variety**

offer a variety
provide a variety
❏ *The organization provides a variety of services to the community.*

✪ **vari·ous** ◆◆◇ /ˈveəriəs/ ADJ **1** If you say that **various** things, you mean there are several different things of the type mentioned. = different ❏ *His plan is to spread the capital between various building society accounts.* ❏ *He found various species of animals and plants, each slightly different.* ❏ *The school has received various grants from the education department.* **2** If a number of things are described as **various**, they are very different from one another. = varied ❏ *The methods are many and various.*

vari·ous·ly /ˈveəriəsli/ ADV You can use **variously** to introduce a number of different ways that something can be described. ❏ *the crowds, which were variously estimated at two to several thousand*

✪ **vary** ◆◇◇ /ˈveəri/ VERB [I, T] (**varies, varying, varied**) (*academic word*) **1** [I] If things **vary**, they are different from each other in size, amount, or degree. = differ, change ❏ *As they're handmade, each one varies slightly.* ❏ *The text varies from the earlier versions.* ❏ *Assessment practices vary in different schools or colleges.* ❏ *Different writers will prepare to varying degrees.* **2** [I, T] If something **varies** or if you **vary** it, it becomes different or changed. = change ❏ *The cost of the alcohol duty varies according to the amount of wine in the bottle.* ❏ *Company officials should make sure that security routines are varied.*
→ See also **varied**

WORD CONNECTIONS
---

vary + ADV

vary **considerably**
vary **enormously**
vary **greatly**
vary **widely**
❏ *Individuals vary considerably in their response to the disease.*

NOUN + **vary**

prices vary
rates vary
❏ *Unemployment rates vary greatly among advanced capitalist nations.*

V

opinions vary
estimates vary

❏ *Estimates of how much time children spend using the Internet vary widely.*

vast ◆◇◇ /vɑːst, væst/ ADJ (**vaster, vastest**) Something that is **vast** is extremely large. = **huge** ❏ *Afrikaner farmers who own vast stretches of land*

vast·ly /'vɑːstli, 'væst-/ ADV **Vastly** means to an extremely great degree or extent. ❏ *The jury has heard two vastly different accounts.*

veer /vɪə/ VERB [I] (**veers, veering, veered**) **1** If something **veers** in a certain direction, it suddenly moves in that direction. = **swerve** ❏ *The plane veered off the runway and crashed through the perimeter fence.* **2** If someone or something **veers** in a certain direction, they change their position or direction in a particular situation. ❏ *He is unlikely to veer from his boss's strongly held views.*

veg·eta·ble ◆◇◇ /'vedʒtəbəl/ NOUN, ADJ
NOUN [C] (**vegetables**) **1** **Vegetables** are plants such as cabbages, potatoes, and onions that you can cook and eat. ❏ *A good general diet should include plenty of fresh vegetables.* **2** [usu sing] (*informal, offensive*) If someone refers to a brain-damaged person as a **vegetable**, they mean that the person cannot move, think, or speak. = **cabbage**
ADJ (*formal*) **Vegetable** matter comes from plants. ❏ *compounds of animal, vegetable, or mineral origin*

veg·etar·ian /ˌvedʒɪ'teəriən/ ADJ, NOUN
ADJ **1** Someone who is **vegetarian** never eats meat or fish. ❏ *Yasmin sticks to a strict vegetarian diet.* **2** **Vegetarian** food does not contain any meat or fish. ❏ *vegetarian lasagnes*
NOUN [C] (**vegetarians**) A **vegetarian** is someone who is vegetarian. ❏ *a special menu for vegetarians*

⊙veg·eta·tion /ˌvedʒɪ'teɪʃən/ NOUN [U] (*formal*) Plants, trees, and flowers can be referred to as **vegetation**. = **plant life, flora** ❏ *The inn has a garden of semi-tropical vegetation.* ❏ *protection of native vegetation* ❏ *About 6860 hectares of remnant vegetation were cleared.* ❏ *The vegetation cover is much denser in the Subarctic than in the Arctic.*

⊙ve·hi·cle ◆◆◇ /'viːɪkəl/ NOUN [C] (**vehicles**) (*academic word*) **1** A **vehicle** is a machine with an engine, such as a bus, car, or lorry, that carries people or things from place to place. ❏ *a vehicle that was somewhere between a tractor and a truck* ❏ *The vehicle would not be able to make the journey on one tank of fuel.* **2** You can use **vehicle** to refer to something that you use in order to achieve a particular purpose. = **medium** ❏ *Her art became a vehicle for her political beliefs.*

⊙vein /veɪn/ NOUN [C] (**veins**) **1** Your **veins** are the thin tubes in your body through which your blood flows towards your heart. Compare **artery**. ❏ *Many veins are found just under the skin.* ❏ *enlargement of the external jugular veins on either side of the neck* **2** Something that is written or spoken in a particular **vein** is written or spoken in that style or mood. ❏ *It is one of his finest works in a lighter vein.* **3** A **vein of** a particular quality is evidence of that quality that someone often shows in their behaviour or work. ❏ *A rich vein of humour runs through the book.* **4** The **veins** on a leaf are the thin lines on it. ❏ *the serrated edges and veins of the feathery leaves*

vel·vet /'velvɪt/ NOUN [C, U] (**velvets**) **Velvet** is soft material made from cotton, silk, or nylon, that has a thick layer of short cut threads on one side. ❏ *a charcoal-grey overcoat with a velvet collar*

venge·ance /'vendʒəns/ NOUN
NOUN [U] **Vengeance** is the act of killing, injuring, or harming someone because they have harmed you. = **revenge** ❏ *He swore vengeance on everyone involved in the murder.*
PHRASE **with a vengeance** (*emphasis*) If you say that something happens **with a vengeance**, you are emphasizing that it happens to a much greater extent than was expected. ❏ *It began to rain again with a vengeance.*

ven·om /'venəm/ NOUN [U, C] (**venoms**) **1** [U] You can use **venom** to refer to someone's feelings of great bitterness

and anger towards someone. ❏ *He reserved particular venom for critics of his foreign policy.* **2** [C, U] The **venom** of a creature such as a snake or spider is the poison that it puts into your body when it bites or stings you. = **poison** ❏ *snake handlers who grow immune to snake venom*

vent /vent/ NOUN, VERB
NOUN [C] (**vents**) A **vent** is a hole in something through which air can come in and smoke, gas, or smells can go out. = **duct** ❏ *A lot of steam escaped from the vent at the front of the machine.*
PHRASE **give vent to** (*formal*) If you **give vent to** your feelings, you express them forcefully. ❏ *She gave vent to her anger and jealousy.*
VERB [T] (**vents, venting, vented**) If you **vent** your feelings, you express them forcefully. ❏ *She telephoned her best friend to vent her frustration.*

ven·ti·late /'ventɪleɪt/ VERB [T] (**ventilates, ventilating, ventilated**) If you **ventilate** a room or building, you allow fresh air to get into it. ❏ *Ventilate the room properly when stripping paint.*

ven·ti·la·tion /ˌventɪ'leɪʃən/ NOUN [U] **Ventilation** is the movement of fresh air around a room or building. ❏ *The only ventilation comes from tiny sliding windows.*

ven·ture ◆◇◇ /'ventʃə/ NOUN, VERB
NOUN [C] (**ventures**) A **venture** is a project or activity that is new, exciting, and difficult because it involves the risk of failure. ❏ *a Russian-American joint venture*
VERB [I, T] (**ventures, venturing, ventured**) **1** [I] (*literary*) If you **venture** somewhere, you go somewhere that might be dangerous. ❏ *People are afraid to venture out for fear of sniper attacks.* **2** [T] (*written*) If you **venture** a question or statement, you say it in an uncertain way because you are afraid it might be stupid or wrong. ❏ *'So you're Leo's girlfriend?' he ventured.* ❏ *He ventured that plants draw part of their nourishment from the air.* **3** [T] If you **venture** to do something that requires courage or is risky, you do it. = **dare** ❏ *'Don't ask,' he said, whenever Ginny ventured to raise the subject.* **4** [I] If you **venture into** an activity, you do something that involves the risk of failure because it is new and different. ❏ *He enjoyed little success when he ventured into business.*

venue ◆◇◇ /'venjuː/ NOUN [C] (**venues**) The **venue** for an event or activity is the place where it will happen. ❏ *The International Convention Centre is the venue for a three-day arts festival.*

verb /vɜːb/ NOUN [C] (**verbs**) A **verb** is a word such as 'sing', 'feel', or 'die' that is used with a subject to say what someone or something does or what happens to them, or to give information about them.

⊙ver·bal /'vɜːbəl/ ADJ **1** You use **verbal** to indicate that something is expressed in speech rather than in writing or action. = **oral, spoken**; ≠ **written, physical, nonverbal** ❏ *They were jostled and subjected to a torrent of verbal abuse.* ❏ *The West must back up its verbal support with substantial economic aid.* **2** [verbal + n] You use **verbal** to indicate that something is connected with words and the use of words. = **linguistic** ❏ *The test has scores for verbal skills, mathematical skills, and abstract reasoning skills.* ❏ *the verbal dexterity of writers such as O'Brien and Joyce* **3** In grammar, **verbal** means relating to a verb. ❏ *a verbal noun*
ver·bal·ly /'vɜːbəli/ ADV ❏ *Dave drank heavily and became verbally abusive.*

⊙ver·dict ◆◇◇ /'vɜːdɪkt/ NOUN [C] (**verdicts**) **1** In a court of law, the **verdict** is the decision that is given by the jury or judge at the end of a trial. = **decision, decree, ruling** ❏ *The jury returned a unanimous guilty verdict.* ❏ *Three judges will deliver their verdict in October.* **2** Someone's **verdict** on something is their opinion of it, after thinking about it or investigating it. ❏ *The doctor's verdict was that he was entirely healthy.*

verge /vɜːdʒ/ NOUN
NOUN [C] (**verges**) (*BrE*; in *AmE*, use **shoulder**) The **verge** of a road is a narrow piece of ground by the side of a road, which is usually covered with grass or flowers.
PHRASE **on the verge of** If you are **on the verge of** something, you are going to do it very soon or it is likely

V

to happen or begin very soon. = **brink** ❑ *The country was on the verge of becoming prosperous and successful.*
PHRASAL VERB **verge on** (**verges, verging, verged**) If someone or something **verges on** a particular state or quality, they are almost the same as that state or quality. ❑ *a fury that verged on madness*

⭘ **veri·fy** /ˈverɪfaɪ/ VERB [T] (**verifies, verifying, verified**)
1 If you **verify** something, you check that it is true by careful examination or investigation. = **check, confirm** ❑ *I verified the source from which I had that information.* ❑ *continued testing to verify the accuracy of the method* ❑ *A clerk simply verifies that the payment and invoice amount match.* **2** If you **verify** something, you state or confirm that it is true. = **confirm** ❑ *The government has not verified any of those reports.*
⭘ **veri·fi·ca·tion** /ˌverɪfɪˈkeɪʃən/ NOUN [U] = **confirmation** ❑ *All charges against her are dropped pending the verification of her story.* ❑ *the agency's verification procedures*

⭘ **ver·sa·tile** /ˈvɜːsətaɪl, AmE -təl/ ADJ **1** (approval) If you say that a person is **versatile**, you approve of them because they have many different skills. ❑ *He had been one of the game's most versatile athletes.* **2** A tool, machine, or material that is **versatile** can be used for many different purposes. = **adaptable, flexible** ❑ *Never before has computing been so versatile.* ❑ *The most versatile domesticated plant is the coconut palm.*
⭘ **ver·sa·til·ity** /ˌvɜːsəˈtɪlɪti/ NOUN [U] **1** = **adaptability, flexibility** ❑ *Aileen stands out for her incredible versatility as an actress.* **2** *Velvet as a fabric is known for its versatility.* ❑ *the versatility of the software*

⭘ **verse** /vɜːs/ NOUN [U, C] (**verses**) **1** [U] **Verse** is writing arranged in lines that have rhythm and that often rhyme at the end. = **poetry** ❑ *I have been moved to write a few lines of verse.* ❑ *a slim volume of verse* ❑ *Shakespearian blank verse* **2** [C] A **verse** is one of the parts into which a poem, a song, or a chapter of the Bible or the Koran is divided. ❑ *This verse describes three signs of spring.*

⭘ **ver·sion** ♦♦◇ /ˈvɜːʃən, -ʒən/ NOUN [C] (**versions**) (academic word) **1** A **version of** something is a particular form of it in which some details are different from earlier or later forms. ❑ *an updated version of his bestselling book* ❑ *Ludo is a version of an ancient Indian racing game.* ❑ *the film version of Tess of the d'Urbervilles* **2** Someone's **version of** an event is their own description of it, especially when it is different from other people's. ❑ *Some former hostages contradicted the official version of events.*

⭘ **ver·sus** /ˈvɜːsəs/ PREP **1** You use **versus** to indicate that two figures, ideas, or choices are opposed. = **as opposed to, compared with** ❑ *Only 18.8% of the class of 1982 had some kind of diploma four years after high school, versus 45% of the class of 1972.* ❑ *bottle-feeding versus breastfeeding* **2** **Versus** is used to indicate that two teams or people are competing against each other in a sports event. = **against** ❑ *Italy versus Japan is turning out to be a surprisingly well matched competition.* **3** **Versus** is used in a court of law to indicate that two people or organizations are involved in a law suit. The abbreviation **v** is also used. ❑ *That case became known as Healey versus Jones.*

⭘ **ver·ti·cal** /ˈvɜːtɪkəl/ ADJ Something that is **vertical** stands or points straight up. ❑ *The climber inched up a vertical wall of rock.* ❑ *The price variable is shown on the vertical axis.* ❑ *The gadget can be attached to any vertical or near vertical surface.*
⭘ **ver·ti·cal·ly** /ˈvɜːtɪkli/ ADV [vertically after v] = **upwards** ❑ *Cut each bulb in half vertically.* ❑ *Discs should be stored vertically.*

very ♦♦♦ /ˈveri/ ADV, ADJ
ADV (emphasis) **1** [very + ADJ/ADV] **Very** is used to give emphasis to an adjective or adverb. ❑ *The problem and the answer are very simple.* ❑ *I'm very sorry.* ❑ *They are getting the hang of it very quickly.* **2** [very + SUPERL] You use **very** to give emphasis to a superlative adjective or adverb. For example, if you say that something is **the very best**, you are emphasizing that it is the best. ❑ *They will be helped by the very latest in navigation aids.* ❑ *I am feeling in the very best of spirits.*
PHRASES **not very** **Not very** is used with an adjective or

adverb to say that something is not at all true, or that it is true only to a small degree. ❑ *She's not very impressed with them.* ❑ *'How well do you know her?'—'Not very.'*
very much so (emphasis) The expression **very much so** is an emphatic way of answering 'yes' to something or saying that it is true or correct. ❑ *'Are you enjoying your holiday?'—'Very much so.'*
cannot very well do If you say that you **cannot very well** do something, you mean that it would not be right or possible to do it. ❑ *I said yes. I can't very well say no under the circumstances.*
CONVENTION **very well** (formulae) **Very well** is used to say that you agree to do something or you accept someone's answer, even though you might not be completely satisfied with it. = **all right** ❑ *'We need proof, sir.' Another pause. Then, 'Very well.'*
ADJ (emphasis) **1** [very + N] You use **very** with certain nouns in order to specify an extreme position or extreme point in time. ❑ *At the very back of the yard was a wooden shack.* ❑ *I turned to the very end of the book, to read the final words.* **2** [very + N] You use **very** with nouns to emphasize that something is exactly the right one or exactly the same one. ❑ *Everybody says he is the very man for the case.* **3** [very + N] You use **very** with nouns to emphasize the importance or seriousness of what you are saying. ❑ *At one stage his very life was in danger.* ❑ *History is taking place before your very eyes.*

ves·sel ♦◇◇ /ˈvesəl/ NOUN [C] (**vessels**) (formal) A **vessel** is a ship or large boat. ❑ *a New Zealand navy vessel*
→ See also **blood vessel**

vest /vest/ NOUN [C] (**vests**) (BrE; in AmE, use **undershirt**) A **vest** is a piece of underwear that you can wear on the top half of your body in order to keep warm.

ves·tige /ˈvestɪdʒ/ NOUN [C] (**vestiges**) (formal) A **vestige of** something is a very small part that still remains of something that was once much larger or more important. ❑ *We represent the last vestige of what made this nation great – hard work.*

vet /vet/ NOUN, VERB
NOUN [C] (**vets**) (informal) A **vet** is someone who is qualified to treat sick or injured animals. **Vet** is an abbreviation for **veterinary surgeon.** = **veterinarian** ❑ *She's at the vet, with her dog, right now.*
VERB [T] (**vets, vetting, vetted**) (mainly BrE) If someone **is vetted**, they are investigated fully before being given a particular job, role, or position, especially one that involves military or political secrets. = **screen** ❑ *She was secretly vetted before she ever undertook any work for me.*
vet·ting /ˈvetɪŋ/ NOUN [U] ❑ *The government is to make major changes to the procedure for carrying out security vetting.*

vet·er·an ♦◇◇ /ˈvetərən/ NOUN [C] (**veterans**) **1** A **veteran** is someone who has served in the armed forces of their country, especially during a war. ❑ *They approved a $1.1 billion package of pay increases for the veterans of the Persian Gulf War.* **2** You use **veteran** to refer to someone who has been involved in a particular activity for a long time. ❑ *Annette Michelson, the veteran critic and professor of cinema studies at New York University*

vet·eri·nary /ˈvetərənəri, AmE -neri/ ADJ [veterinary + N] **Veterinary** is used to describe the work of a person whose job is to treat sick or injured animals, or to describe the medical treatment of animals. ❑ *It was decided that our veterinary screening of horses at events should be continued.*

⭘ **veto** /ˈviːtəʊ/ VERB, NOUN
VERB [T] (**vetoes, vetoing, vetoed**) If someone in authority **vetoes** something, they forbid it, or stop it from being put into action. = **block, reject**; ≠ **sanction, approve** ❑ *The president vetoed the economic package passed by Congress.* ❑ *the power to veto a bill absolutely*
NOUN [C, U] (**vetoes**) **1** [C] A **veto** is an act of forbidding something or stopping something from being put into action. ≠ **sanction, approval** ❑ *They need 12 votes to override his veto.* ❑ *The veto was a calculated political risk.* ❑ *a presidential veto of legislation* **2** [U] **Veto** is the right that someone in authority has to forbid something. ❑ *the president's power of veto*

⭘ **via** ♦◇◇ /ˈvaɪə, ˈviːə/ PREP (academic word) **1** If someone or something goes somewhere **via** a particular place, they go through that place on the way to their destination. ❑ *We drove via Lovech to the old Danube town of Ruse.* ❑ *Mr Baker will return home via Britain and France.* ❑ *In vertebrates food passes into the stomach from the mouth via the oesophagus.* **2** If you do something **via** a particular means or person, you do it by making use of that means or person. = by way of, through ❑ *The technology to allow relief workers to contact the outside world via satellite already exists.* ❑ *Translators can now work from home, via email systems.*

✪ **vi·able** /ˈvaɪəbəl/ ADJ Something that is **viable** is capable of doing what it is intended to do. = feasible, possible, reasonable ❑ *Cash alone will not make Eastern Europe's banks viable.* ❑ *commercially viable products* ❑ *the argument that plastic is a viable alternative to traditional building materials*
✪ **vi·abil·ity** /ˌvaɪəˈbɪlɪti/ NOUN [u] = feasibility ❑ *the shaky financial viability of the nuclear industry* ❑ *The philosophy behind the development managers is to ensure long-term viability, profitability and sustainability.*

vi·brant /ˈvaɪbrənt/ ADJ **1** Someone or something that is **vibrant** is full of life, energy, and enthusiasm. ❑ *Tom felt himself being drawn towards her vibrant personality.* ❑ *Shakespeare's vibrant language* **2** **Vibrant** colours are very bright and clear. = brilliant ❑ *Horizon blue, corn yellow and pistachio green are just three of the vibrant colours in this range.*
vi·bran·cy /ˈvaɪbrənsi/ NOUN [u] = vitality ❑ *She was a woman with extraordinary vibrancy and extraordinary knowledge.*
vi·brant·ly /ˈvaɪbrəntli/ ADV [vibrantly + ADJ] ❑ *a selection of vibrantly coloured French cast-iron saucepans*

vi·brate /vaɪˈbreɪt, AmE ˈvaɪbreɪt/ VERB [I, T] (**vibrates, vibrating, vibrated**) If something **vibrates** or if you **vibrate** it, it shakes with repeated small, quick movements. ❑ *The ground shook and the cliffs seemed to vibrate.*
vi·bra·tion /vaɪˈbreɪʃən/ NOUN [C, U] (**vibrations**) ❑ *The vibrations of the vehicles rattled the shop windows.*

vic·ar /ˈvɪkə/ NOUN [c] (**vicars**) (*BrE*) In the Church of England, a **vicar** is a clergyman appointed to act as priest of a parish from which, formerly, he did not receive tithes but a stipend.

vice ♦♢♢ /vaɪs/ NOUN [C, u] (**vices**) **1** [c] A **vice** is a habit that is regarded as a weakness in someone's character, but not usually as a serious fault. ❑ *His only vice is to get drunk on champagne after concluding a successful piece of business.* **2** [u] **Vice** refers to criminal activities, especially those connected with pornography or prostitution. ❑ *He said those responsible for offences connected with vice, gaming, and drugs should be deported on conviction.* **3** [c] (*BrE; in AmE*, use **vise**) A **vice** is a tool with a pair of parts that hold an object tightly while you do work on it.

WORD PARTS

The prefix **vice-** often appears in titles or ranks to show that someone is next in importance to the title or rank mentioned:

vice-president (NOUN)
vice-captain (NOUN)
vice-chancellor (NOUN)
---

vice ver·sa /ˌvaɪs ˈvɜːsə/
PHRASE **Vice versa** is used to indicate that the reverse of what you have said is true. For example, 'women may bring their husbands with them, and vice versa' means that men may also bring their wives with them. ❑ *They want to send students from low-income homes into more affluent neighbourhoods, and vice versa.*

vi·cin·ity /vɪˈsɪnɪti/ NOUN [SING] (*formal*) If something is **in the vicinity** of a particular place, it is near it. ❑ *There were a hundred or so hotels in the vicinity of the station.*

vi·cious /ˈvɪʃəs/ ADJ **1** A **vicious** person or a **vicious** blow is violent and cruel. = brutal ❑ *He was a cruel and vicious man.* ❑ *He suffered a vicious attack by a gang of white youths.* **2** A **vicious** remark is cruel and intended to upset someone. = savage ❑ *It is a deliberate, nasty, and vicious attack on a young man's character.*

vi·cious·ly /ˈvɪʃəsli/ ADV **1** *She had been viciously attacked with a hammer.* **2** [viciously with v] ❑ *'He deserved to die,' said Penelope viciously.*
vi·cious·ness /ˈvɪʃəsnəs/ NOUN [u] ❑ *the intensity and viciousness of these attacks*

✪ **vic·tim** ♦♦♢ /ˈvɪktɪm/ NOUN [c] (**victims**) **1** A **victim** is someone who has been hurt or killed. ≠ criminal ❑ *Statistically our chances of being the victims of violent crime are remote.* ❑ *Not all the victims survived.* ❑ *Infectious diseases are spreading among many of the flood victims.* **2** A **victim** is someone who has suffered as a result of someone else's actions or beliefs, or as a result of unpleasant circumstances. ❑ *He was a victim of racial prejudice.* ❑ *He described himself and Altman as victims rather than participants in the scandal.*

WHICH WORD?
victim or casualty?

Do not confuse **victim** and **casualty**.

You refer to someone as a **victim** when they have suffered as the result of a crime, natural disaster, or serious illness.

❑ *About 80% of murder **victims** are men.*

❑ *Please donate money to help the **victims** of famine.*

You do not usually use **victim** to refer to someone who has been injured or killed in a war or accident. The word you use is **casualty**.

❑ *The **casualties** were taken to the nearest hospital.*
---

vic·tim·ize ♦♢♢ /ˈvɪktɪmaɪz/ also **victimise** VERB [T] (**victimizes, victimizing, victimized**) If someone **is victimized**, they are deliberately treated unfairly. ❑ *He felt the students had been victimized because they'd voiced opposition to the government.*
vic·tim·i·za·tion /ˌvɪktɪmaɪˈzeɪʃən/ NOUN [u] ❑ *society's cruel victimization of women*

vic·tor /ˈvɪktə/ NOUN [c] (**victors**) (*literary*) The **victor** in a battle or contest is the person who wins. ❑ *Oliver Townsend and co-driver Kirk Lee eventually emerged as victors after five different cars had led the event.*

vic·to·ri·ous /vɪkˈtɔːriəs/ ADJ You use **victorious** to describe someone who has won a victory in a struggle, war, or competition. = winning ❑ *In 1978 he played for the victorious Argentinian side in the World Cup.*

vic·to·ry ♦♦♢ /ˈvɪktəri/ NOUN
NOUN [C, u] (**victories**) A **victory** is a success in a struggle, war, or competition. ❑ *Union leaders are heading for victory in their battle over workplace rights.*
PHRASE **moral victory** If you say that someone has won a **moral victory**, you mean that although they have officially lost a contest or dispute, they have succeeded in showing they are right about something. ❑ *She said her party had won a moral victory.*

video ♦♦♢ /ˈvɪdiəʊ/ NOUN, VERB
NOUN [C, u] (**videos**) **1** [c] A **video** is a film or television programme recorded on tape for people to watch on a television set. ❑ *sports and exercise videos* **2** [u] **Video** is the system of recording films and events on tape so that people can watch them on a television set. ❑ *She has watched the race on video.* ❑ *manufacturers of audio and video equipment* **3** [c] (*mainly BrE; in AmE*, usually use **VCR**) A **video** is a machine that you can use to record television programmes and play videotapes on a television set. = video recorder, VCR
VERB [T] (**videos, videoing, videoed**) (*mainly BrE; in AmE*, usually use **tape**) If you **video** a television programme or event, you record it on tape using a video recorder or video camera, so that you can watch it later. = videotape, tape

✪ **view** ♦♦♦ /vjuː/ NOUN, VERB
NOUN [C, SING, u] (**views**) **1** [c] Your **views** on something are the beliefs or opinions that you have about it, for example, whether you think it is good, bad, right, or wrong. = opinion, point of view, belief ❑ *Washington and Moscow are believed to have similar views on Kashmir.* ❑ *You should also make your views known to your congressperson.* ❑ *My own view is absolutely clear. What I did was right.*

V

2 [SING] Your **view of** a particular subject is the way that you understand and think about it. □ *The whole point was to get away from a Christian-centred view of religion.* **3** [C] The **view** from a window or high place is everything that can be seen from that place, especially when it is considered to be beautiful. □ *The view from our window was one of beautiful green countryside.* **4** [SING] If you have a **view of** something, you can see it. □ *He stood up to get a better view of the blackboard.* **5** [U] You use **view** in expressions to do with being able to see something. For example, if something is **in view**, you can see it. If something is **in full view of everyone**, everyone can see it. □ *She was lying there in full view of anyone who walked by.* **6** [SING] (*computing*) **View** refers to the way in which a piece of text or graphics is displayed on a computer screen. □ *To see the current document in full-page view, click the Page Zoom Full button.* **PHRASES in my view** You use **in my view** when you want to indicate that you are stating a personal opinion, that other people might not agree with. □ *In my view things won't change.*
in view of You use **in view of** when you are taking into consideration facts that have just been mentioned or are just about to be mentioned. □ *In view of the fact that Hobson was not a trained economist his achievements were remarkable.*
on view If something such as a work of art is **on view**, it is shown in public for people to look at. □ *A significant exhibition of contemporary sculpture will be on view at the Portland Gallery.*
with a view to If you do something **with a view to** doing something else, you do it because you hope it will result in that other thing being done. □ *He has called a meeting of all parties tomorrow, with a view to forming a national reconciliation government.*
VERB [T] (**views, viewing, viewed**) **1** If you **view** something in a particular way, you think of it in that way. = regard □ *First-generation Americans view the United States as a land of golden opportunity.* □ *Abigail's mother Linda views her daughter's talent with a mixture of pride and worry.* □ *Sectors in the economy can be viewed in a variety of ways.* □ *We would view favourably any sensible suggestion for maintaining the business.* **2** (*formal*) If you **view** something, you look at it for a particular purpose. □ *They came back to view the house again.* **3** (*formal*) If you **view** a television programme, DVD, or film, you watch it. □ *We have viewed the video recording of the incident.*

view·er /'vjuːə/ NOUN [C] (**viewers**) **1 Viewers** are people who watch television, or who are watching a particular programme on television. □ *These programmes are each watched by around 19 million viewers every week.* **2** A **viewer** is someone who is looking carefully at a picture or other interesting object. □ *the relationship between the art object and the viewer*

✪view·point /'vjuːpɔɪnt/ NOUN [C] (**viewpoints**) **1** Someone's **viewpoint** is the way that they think about things in general, or the way they think about a particular thing. = point of view, stance □ *The novel is shown from the girl's viewpoint.* **2** to reconcile diverse viewpoints about an issue **2** A **viewpoint** is a place from which you can get a good view of something. = vantage point □ *You have to know where to stand for a good viewpoint.*

vigi·lant /'vɪdʒɪlənt/ ADJ Someone who is **vigilant** gives careful attention to a particular problem or situation and concentrates on noticing any danger or trouble that there might be. = alert □ *He warned the public to be vigilant and report anything suspicious.*
vigi·lance /'vɪdʒɪləns/ NOUN [U] □ *Constant vigilance is needed to combat this evil.*

vig·or·ous /'vɪgərəs/ ADJ **1 Vigorous** physical activities involve using a lot of energy, usually to do short and repeated actions. □ *Very vigorous exercise can increase the risk of heart attacks.* **2** A **vigorous** person does things with great energy and enthusiasm. A **vigorous** campaign or activity is done with great energy and enthusiasm. □ *Theodore Roosevelt was a strong and vigorous politician.*
vig·or·ous·ly /'vɪgərəsli/ ADV **1** [vigorously after v] □ *He shook his head vigorously.* **2** [vigorously with v] □ *The police*

vigorously denied that excessive force had been used.

vig·our /'vɪgə/ (mainly BrE; in AmE, use **vigor**) NOUN [U] **Vigour** is physical or mental energy and enthusiasm. □ *He has approached his job with renewed vigour.*

vil·la /'vɪlə/ NOUN [C] (**villas**) A **villa** is a fairly large house, especially one in a hot country or a resort. □ *He lives in a secluded, five-bedroom, luxury villa.*

vil·lage ♦♦◇ /'vɪlɪdʒ/ NOUN [C] (**villages**) A **village** consists of a group of houses, together with other buildings such as a church and a school, in a country area. □ *He lives quietly in the country in a village near Lahti.*

vil·lain /'vɪlən/ NOUN [C] (**villains**) **1** A **villain** is someone who deliberately harms other people or breaks the law in order to get what he or she wants. □ *I left the room, feeling like a villain and a murderer.* **2** The **villain** in a novel, film, or play is the main bad character. □ *He also played a villain opposite Sylvester Stallone in Demolition Man (1992).*

vin·di·cate /'vɪndɪkeɪt/ VERB [T] (**vindicates, vindicating, vindicated**) (*formal*) If a person or their decisions, actions, or ideas **are vindicated**, they are proved to be correct, after people have said that they were wrong. □ *The director said he had been vindicated by the experts' report.*
vin·di·ca·tion /ˌvɪndɪ'keɪʃən/ NOUN [U] □ *He called the success a vindication of his party's free-market economic policy.*

vin·dic·tive /vɪn'dɪktɪv/ ADJ (*disapproval*) If you say that someone is **vindictive**, you are critical of them because they deliberately try to upset or cause trouble for someone who they think has done them harm. □ *a vindictive woman desperate for revenge against the man who loved and left her*
vin·dic·tive·ness /vɪn'dɪktɪvnəs/ NOUN [U] □ *a dishonest person who is operating completely out of vindictiveness*

vine /vaɪn/ NOUN [C, U] (**vines**) A **vine** is a plant that grows up or over things, especially one that produces grapes. = grapevine □ *Every square metre of soil was used, mainly for olives, vines, and almonds.*

vine·yard /'vɪnjəd/ NOUN [C] (**vineyards**) A **vineyard** is an area of land where grape vines are grown in order to produce wine. You can also use **vineyard** to refer to the set of buildings in which the wine is produced.

vin·tage /'vɪntɪdʒ/ NOUN, ADJ
NOUN [C] (**vintages**) The **vintage** of a good quality wine is the year and place that it was made before being stored to improve it. You can also use **vintage** to refer to the wine that was made in a certain year. □ *This wine is from one of the two best vintages of the decade in this region.*
ADJ **1** [vintage + N] **Vintage** wine is good quality wine that has been stored for several years in order to improve its quality. □ *If you can buy only one case at auction, it should be vintage port.* **2** [vintage + N] **Vintage** cars or planes are old but are admired because they are considered to be the best of their kind. □ *The museum will have a permanent exhibition of 60 vintage and racing cars.* **3** **Vintage** clothing and furniture is old or secondhand, but usually of good quality. □ *collectors of vintage clothing*

✪vio·late ♦◇◇ /'vaɪəleɪt/ VERB [T] (**violates, violating, violated**) (*academic word*) **1** (*formal*) If someone **violates** an agreement, law, or promise, they break it. = breach, break, disobey; ≠ obey □ *They went to prison because they violated the law.* □ *They violated the ceasefire agreement.* **2** (*formal*) If you **violate** someone's privacy or peace, you disturb it. □ *These men were violating her family's privacy.* **3** If someone **violates** a special place such as a grave, they damage it or treat it with disrespect. = desecrate □ *Detectives are still searching for those who violated the graveyard.*
✪vio·la·tion /ˌvaɪə'leɪʃən/ NOUN [C, U] (**violations**) **1** [C, U] □ *To deprive the boy of his education is a violation of state law.* □ *He was in violation of his contract.* □ *allegations of human rights violations* **2** [U] □ *The violation of the graves is not the first such incident.*

✪vio·lence ♦♦◇ /'vaɪələns/ NOUN [U] **1 Violence** is behaviour that is intended to hurt, injure, or kill people. = aggression □ *Twenty people were killed in the violence.* □ *domestic violence between husband and wife* □ *They threaten them with violence.* **2** (*literary*) If you do or say something with **violence**, you use a lot of force and energy in doing

[V in margin]

or saying it, often because you are angry. ❑ *The violence in her tone gave Tyler a shock.*

✪ vio‑lent ◆◇◇ /'vaɪələnt/ ADJ **1** If someone is **violent**, or if they do something that is **violent**, they use physical force or weapons to hurt, injure, or kill other people. = aggressive; ≠ passive, peaceful ❑ *A quarter of current inmates have committed violent crimes.* ❑ *violent anti-government demonstrations* ❑ *Sometimes the men get violent.* **2** A **violent** event happens suddenly and with great force. ❑ *A violent impact hurtled her forward.* **3** If you describe something as **violent**, you mean that it is said, done, or felt very strongly. = intense ❑ *Violent opposition to the plan continues.* ❑ *He had violent stomach pains.* **4** A **violent** death is painful and unexpected, usually because the person who dies has been murdered. ❑ *an innocent man who had met a violent death* **5** A **violent** film or television programme contains a lot of scenes that show violence. ❑ *It was the most violent movie that I have ever seen.*
✪ vio‑lent‑ly /'vaɪələntli/ ADV **1** [violently with v] = aggressively; ≠ peacefully ❑ *Some opposition activists have been violently attacked.* ❑ *Even meek and mild people will sometimes react violently.* **2** [violently with v] ❑ *A nearby volcano erupted violently, sending out a hail of molten rock and boiling mud.* **3** He was violently scolded. **4** [violently with v] ❑ *a girl who had died violently nine years earlier*

VIP /ˌviː aɪ 'piː/ NOUN [c] (**VIPs**) A **VIP** is someone who is given better treatment than ordinary people because they are famous, influential, or important. **VIP** is an abbreviation for 'very important person'. ❑ *such VIPs as Prince Charles and Richard Nixon*

✪ vi‑ral /'vaɪərəl/ ADJ A **viral** disease or infection is caused by a virus. ❑ *a 65-year-old patient suffering from severe viral pneumonia*

vir‑gin /'vɜːdʒɪn/ NOUN, ADJ
NOUN [c] (**virgins**) **1** A **virgin** is someone, especially a woman or girl, who has never had sex. ❑ *I was a virgin until I was thirty years old.* **2** You can use **virgin** to describe someone who has never done or used a particular thing before. ❑ *Until he appeared in 'In the Line of Fire' Malkovich had been an action-movie virgin.*
ADJ You use **virgin** to describe something such as land that has never been used or spoiled. ❑ *Within 40 years there will be no virgin forest left.*
PHRASE **virgin territory** If you say that a situation is **virgin territory**, you mean that you have no experience of it and it is completely new for you. ❑ *The World Cup is virgin territory for Ecuador.*

✪ vir‑tual /'vɜːtʃuəl/ ADJ (academic word) **1** [virtual + N] You can use **virtual** to indicate that something is so nearly true that for most purposes it can be regarded as true. = near ❑ *Argentina came to a virtual standstill while the game was being played.* ❑ *the virtual disappearance of marriage as an institution among poor black people* ❑ *conditions of virtual slavery* **2** [virtual + N] (computing) **Virtual** objects and activities are generated by a computer to simulate real objects and activities. = computerized, online ❑ *Up to four players can compete in a virtual world of role playing.* ❑ *software that generates virtual environments of war zones* ❑ *a virtual shopping centre*
vir‑tu‑al‑ity /ˌvɜːtʃu'æliti/ NOUN [u] ❑ *People speculate about virtuality systems, but we're already working on it.*
✪ vir‑tu‑al‑ly ◆◆◇ /'vɜːtʃuəli/ ADV [virtually with GROUP] You can use **virtually** to indicate that something is so nearly true that for most purposes it can be regarded as true. = almost, nearly, essentially ❑ *Virtually all cooking was done over coal-fired ranges.* ❑ *It would have been virtually impossible to research all the information.*

vir‑tue /'vɜːtʃuː/ NOUN
NOUN [u, c] (**virtues**) **1** [u] **Virtue** is thinking and doing what is right and avoiding what is wrong. = goodness ❑ *Virtue is not confined to the Christian world.* **2** [c] A **virtue** is a good quality or way of behaving. ❑ *His virtue is patience.* **3** [c] The **virtue** of something is an advantage or benefit that it has, especially in comparison with something else. ❑ *There was no virtue in returning to Calvi the way I had come.*
PHRASE **by virtue of** (formal) You use **by virtue of** to

explain why something happens or is true. ❑ *The article stuck in my mind by virtue of one detail.*

vir‑tu‑ous /'vɜːtʃuəs/ ADJ **1** A **virtuous** person behaves in a moral and correct way. = good ❑ *Louis was shown as an intelligent, courageous, and virtuous family man.* **2** If you describe someone as **virtuous**, you mean that they have done what they ought to do and feel very pleased with themselves, perhaps too pleased. ❑ *I cleaned the flat, which left me feeling virtuous.*
vir‑tu‑ous‑ly /'vɜːtʃuəsli/ ADV ❑ *'I've already done that,' said Ronnie virtuously.*

✪ vi‑rus ◆◇◇ /'vaɪərəs/ NOUN [c] (**viruses**) **1** A **virus** is a kind of germ that can cause disease. = illness, disease, infection ❑ *There are many different strains of flu virus.* ❑ *HIV, the virus believed to cause AIDS* **2** (computing) In computer technology, a **virus** is a program that introduces itself into a system, altering or destroying the information stored in it. ❑ *Hackers are said to have started a computer virus.* ❑ *By the time a virus is detected it will almost certainly have infected other disks.*

visa /'viːzə/ NOUN [c] (**visas**) A **visa** is an official document, or a stamp put in your passport, that allows you to enter or leave a particular country. ❑ *His visitor's visa expired.* ❑ *an exit visa*

vis‑ibil‑ity /ˌvɪzɪ'bɪlɪti/ NOUN [u] **1** **Visibility** means how far or how clearly you can see in particular weather conditions. ❑ *Visibility was poor.* **2** If you refer to the **visibility** of something such as a situation or problem, you mean how much it is seen or noticed by other people. ❑ *The plight of the Kurds gained global visibility.*

✪ vis‑ible ◆◇◇ /'vɪzɪbəl/ ADJ (academic word) **1** If something is **visible**, it can be seen. ❑ *The warning lights were clearly visible.* ❑ *They found a bacterium visible to the human eye.* **2** You use **visible** to describe something or someone that people notice or recognize. = clear, evident, noticeable; ≠ invisible, hidden ❑ *The most visible sign of the intensity of the crisis is unemployment.* ❑ *The cabinet is a highly visible symbol of the executive branch of the United States government.*
✪ vis‑ibly /'vɪzɪbli/ ADV = evidently, noticeably ❑ *The Russians were visibly wavering.* ❑ *People dying from cancer or other degenerative disorders grow thin and visibly waste away.* ❑ *They emerged visibly distressed and weeping.*

✪ vi‑sion ◆◇◇ /'vɪʒən/ NOUN [c, u] (**visions**) (academic word) **1** [c] Your **vision** of a future situation or society is what you imagine or hope it would be like, if things were very different from the way they are now. ❑ *I have a vision of a society that is free of exploitation and injustice.* ❑ *That's my vision of how the world could be.* **2** [c] If you have a **vision** of someone in a particular situation, you imagine them in that situation, for example because you are worried that it might happen, or hope that it will happen. = image ❑ *He had a vision of Cheryl, slumped on a plastic chair in the waiting room.* **3** [c] A **vision** is the experience of seeing something that other people cannot see, for example in a religious experience or as a result of madness or taking drugs. ❑ *It was on June 24, 1981 that young villagers first reported seeing the Virgin Mary in a vision.* **4** [u] Your **vision** is your ability to see clearly with your eyes. = sight, eyesight, view; ≠ blindness ❑ *It causes blindness or serious loss of vision.* **5** [u] Your **vision** is everything that you can see from a particular place or position. = view ❑ *Jane blocked Craig's vision and he could see nothing.* ❑ *Your total field of vision is more than 220°.* ❑ *I saw other indistinct shapes that stayed out of vision.*

vis‑it ◆◆◆ /'vɪzɪt/ VERB, NOUN
VERB [i, t] (**visits, visiting, visited**) **1** [i, t] If you **visit** someone, you go to see them and spend time with them. ❑ *He wanted to visit his brother in Worcester.* ❑ *In the evenings, friends would visit.* **2** [i, t] If you **visit** a place, you go there for a short time. ❑ *He'll be visiting four cities including Cagliari in Sardinia.* ❑ *a visiting family from Texas* **3** [t] (computing) If you **visit** a website, you look at it. ❑ *For details visit our website at www.harpercollins.com.* **4** [t] If you **visit** a professional person such as a doctor or lawyer, you go and see them in order to get professional advice. If they **visit** you, they come to see you in order to give you

V

professional advice. = see ❑ *If necessary the patient can then visit his doctor for further advice.*

NOUN [C] (**visits**) **1** If you pay someone a **visit**, you go to see them and spend time with them. ❑ *Helen had recently paid him a visit.* **2** A **visit** is the act of going to a place for a short time. ❑ *the pope's visit to Canada* **3** A **visit** to a professional person such as a doctor or lawyer is when you go and see them in order to get professional advice. A **visit** from them is when they come to see you in order to give you professional advice. ❑ *You may have regular home visits from a neonatal nurse.*

vis·i·tor ♦◇◇ /'vɪzɪtə/ NOUN [C] (**visitors**) A **visitor** is someone who is visiting a person or place. ❑ *The other day we had some visitors from Switzerland.*

✪ vis·u·al /'vɪʒʊəl/ ADJ, NOUN (*academic word*)
ADJ **Visual** means relating to sight, or to things that you can see. ❑ *the graphic visual depiction of violence* ❑ *music, film, dance, and the visual arts* ❑ *people with visual impairment*
NOUN [C] (**visuals**) A **visual** is something such as a picture, diagram, or piece of film that is used to show or explain something. ❑ *Remember you want your visuals to reinforce your message, not detract from what you are saying.*
✪ vis·u·al·ly /'vɪʒʊəli/ ADV ❑ *visually handicapped boys and girls* ❑ *These creatures are visually spectacular.*

vis·u·al·ize /'vɪʒʊəlaɪz/ also **visualise** VERB [T] (**visualizes, visualizing, visualized**) If you **visualize** something, you imagine what it is like by forming a mental picture of it. = imagine ❑ *Susan visualized her wedding day and saw herself walking down the aisle on her father's arm.* ❑ *He could not visualize her as old.*

✪ vi·tal ♦◇◇ /'vaɪtəl/ ADJ If you say that something is **vital**, you mean that it is necessary or very important. = crucial, essential; ≠ unimportant, inessential ❑ *The port is vital to supply relief to millions of drought victims.* ❑ *It is vital that parents give children clear and consistent messages about drugs.* ❑ *It is vital that records are kept.*
✪ vi·tal·ly /'vaɪtəli/ ADV = extremely, utterly ❑ *Lesley's career in the church is vitally important to her.*

vi·tal·ity /vaɪ'tælɪti/ NOUN [U] If you say that someone or something has **vitality**, you mean that they have great energy and liveliness. = vigour ❑ *Without continued learning, graduates will lose their intellectual vitality.*

vita·min ♦◇◇ /'vɪtəmɪn, AmE 'vaɪt-/ NOUN [C] (**vitamins**) **Vitamins** are substances that you need in order to remain healthy, which are found in food or can be eaten in the form of pills. ❑ *Lack of vitamin D is another factor to consider.*

✪ viv·id /'vɪvɪd/ ADJ **1** If you describe memories and descriptions as **vivid**, you mean that they are very clear and detailed. = clear, intense; ≠ vague ❑ *People of my generation who lived through World War II have vivid memories of confusion and incompetence.* ❑ *The play is a vivid portrait of black America in 1969.* ❑ *The poems are full of vivid imagery.* **2** Something that is **vivid** is very bright in colour. ❑ *a vivid blue sky*
✪ viv·id·ly /'vɪvɪdli/ ADV **1** = clearly, strongly, sharply ❑ *I can vividly remember the feeling of panic.* ❑ *The two government studies vividly illustrate that racial discrimination remains widespread in urban areas.* **2** [vividly + -ED/ADJ] ❑ *vividly coloured birds*

✪ vo·cab·u·lary /vəʊ'kæbjʊləri, AmE -leri/ NOUN [C, U, SING] (**vocabularies**) **1** [C, U] Your **vocabulary** is the total number of words you know in a particular language. ❑ *His speech is immature, his vocabulary limited.* ❑ *Listen to the patient's vocabulary, which discloses what they think about their symptoms.* **2** [SING] The **vocabulary** of a language is all the words in it. = lexicon, words, terminology ❑ *a new word in the German vocabulary* ❑ *the grammar and vocabulary of the English language* **3** [C, U] The **vocabulary** of a subject is the group of words that are typically used when discussing it. ❑ *the vocabulary of natural science*

vo·cal /'vəʊkəl/ ADJ **1** You say that people are **vocal** when they speak forcefully about something that they feel strongly about. ❑ *He has been very vocal in his displeasure over the results.* **2** [vocal + N] **Vocal** means involving the use of the human voice, especially in singing. ❑ *a wider range of vocal styles*

vo·ca·tion /vəʊ'keɪʃən/ NOUN [C, U] (**vocations**) **1** If you have a **vocation**, you have a strong feeling that you are especially suited to do a particular job or to fulfil a particular role in life, especially one that involves helping other people. ❑ *It could well be that he has a real vocation.* **2** If you refer to your job or profession as your **vocation**, you feel that you are particularly suited to it. ❑ *Her vocation is her work as an actress.*

✪ vo·ca·tion·al /vəʊ'keɪʃənəl/ ADJ **Vocational** training and skills are the training and skills needed for a particular job or profession. ≠ academic ❑ *a course designed to provide vocational training in engineering* ❑ *Vocational courses are often given more respect and funding than arts or philosophy.*

vogue /vəʊɡ/ NOUN
NOUN [SING] If there is a **vogue for** something, it is very popular and fashionable. = trend, fad ❑ *Despite the vogue for so-called health teas, there is no evidence that they are any healthier.*
PHRASE **in vogue** If something is **in vogue**, it is very popular and fashionable. If it comes **into vogue**, it becomes very popular and fashionable. ❑ *Pale colours are much more in vogue than autumnal bronzes and coppers.*

voice ♦♦◇ /vɔɪs/ NOUN, VERB
NOUN [C] (**voices**) **1** When someone speaks or sings, you hear their **voice**. ❑ *Miriam's voice was strangely calm.* ❑ *'The police are here,' she said in a low voice.* **2** Someone's **voice** is their opinion on a particular topic and what they say about it. ❑ *What does one do when a government simply refuses to listen to the voice of the opposition?*
PHRASES **give voice to** If you **give voice to** an opinion, a need, or a desire, you express it aloud. = express ❑ *a community radio run by the Catholic Church that gave voice to the protests of the slum-dwellers.*
keep one's voice down If someone tells you to **keep** your **voice down**, they are asking you to speak more quietly. ❑ *Keep your voice down, for goodness sake.*
lose one's voice If you **lose** your **voice**, you cannot speak for a while because of an illness. ❑ *I had to be careful not to get a sore throat and lose my voice.*
raise one's voice or **lower one's voice** If you **raise** your **voice**, you speak more loudly. If you **lower** your **voice**, you speak more quietly. ❑ *He raised his voice for the benefit of the other two women.*
at the top of one's voice (*emphasis*) If you say something **at the top of** your **voice**, you say it as loudly as possible. ❑ *'Damn!' he yelled at the top of his voice.*
VERB [T] (**voices, voicing, voiced**) If you **voice** something such as an opinion or an emotion, you say what you think or feel. = express ❑ *Some scientists have voiced concern that the disease could be passed on to humans.*

void /vɔɪd/ NOUN, ADJ, VERB
NOUN [C] (**voids**) **1** If you describe a situation or a feeling as a **void**, you mean that it seems empty because there is nothing interesting or worthwhile about it. ❑ *His death has left a void in the entertainment world that can never be filled.* **2** You can describe a large or frightening space as a **void**. ❑ *He stared into the dark void where the battle had been fought.*
ADJ **1** [V-LINK + void] Something that is **void** or **null and void** is officially considered to have no value or authority. = invalid ❑ *The original elections were declared void by the former military ruler.* **2** [V-LINK + void 'of' N] (*formal*) If you are **void of** something, you do not have any of it. ❑ *He rose, his face void of emotion as he walked towards the door.*
VERB [T] (**voids, voiding, voided**) (*formal*) To **void** something means to officially say that it is not valid. ❑ *The Supreme Court threw out the confession and voided his conviction for murder.*

vol. ♦◇◇ (**vols.**) ABBREVIATION **Vol.** is used as a written abbreviation for **volume** when you are referring to one or more books in a series of books.

✪ vola·tile /'vɒlətaɪl, AmE -təl/ ADJ **1** A situation that is **volatile** is likely to change suddenly and unexpectedly. = unstable, unpredictable; ≠ stable, predictable ❑ *There have been riots before and the situation is volatile.* ❑ *The international oil markets have been highly volatile since the early*

1970s. ❑ *Armed soldiers guard the streets in this volatile atmosphere.* **2** If someone is **volatile**, their mood often changes quickly. ❑ *He accompanied the volatile actress to Hollywood the following year.* **3** (*technical*) A **volatile** liquid or substance is one that will quickly change into a gas. ❑ *The blast occurred when volatile chemicals exploded.* ❑ *volatile organic compounds*

✪**vol·a·til·i·ty** /ˌvɒləˈtɪlɪti/ NOUN [u] = instability, unpredictability; ≠ stability, predictability ❑ *He is keen to see a general reduction in arms sales given the volatility of the region.* ❑ *current stock market volatility* ❑ *Figure 1.5 reveals increased volatility in exchange rates.*

✪**vol·can·ic** /vɒlˈkænɪk/ ADJ **Volcanic** means coming from or created by volcanoes. ❑ *Over 200 people have been killed by volcanic eruptions.* ❑ *Earthquakes and volcanic activity occur at the boundaries between plates.* ❑ *fragments of volcanic rock*

✪**vol·ca·no** /vɒlˈkeɪnəʊ/ NOUN [c] (**volcanoes**) A **volcano** is a mountain from which hot melted rock, gas, steam, and ash from inside the earth sometimes burst. ❑ *The volcano erupted last year killing about 600 people.* ❑ *Etna is Europe's most active volcano.*

✪**volt** /vəʊlt/ NOUN [c] (**volts**) A **volt** is a unit used to measure the force of an electric current. The abbreviation **V** is often used in written notes. ❑ *The power lines were carrying about 15,000 volts of electricity.* ❑ *a 24-volt battery*

✪**volt·age** /ˈvəʊltɪdʒ/ NOUN [c, u] (**voltages**) The **voltage** of an electrical current is its force measured in volts. = electricity, current ❑ *The systems are getting smaller and using lower voltages.* ❑ *high-voltage power lines*

✪**vol·ume** ◆◆◇ /ˈvɒljuːm/ NOUN (*academic word*) **NOUN** [c, u] (**volumes**) **1** [c] The **volume of** something is the amount of it that there is. = amount ❑ *Senior officials will be discussing how the volume of sales might be reduced.* ❑ *the sheer volume of traffic and accidents* **2** [c] The **volume** of an object is the amount of space that it contains or occupies. = capacity ❑ *When egg whites are beaten they can rise to seven or eight times their original volume.* **3** [c] A **volume** is one book in a series of books. The abbreviation **vol.** is used in written notes and bibliographies. ❑ *the first volume of his autobiography* ❑ *The article appeared in volume 41 of the journal Communication Education.* **4** [c] A **volume** is a collection of several issues of a magazine, for example, all the issues for one year. ❑ *bound volumes of the magazine* **5** [u] The **volume** of a radio, television, or sound system is the loudness of the sound it produces. ❑ *He turned down the volume.*

PHRASE **speak volumes** If something such as an action **speaks volumes about** a person or thing, it gives you a lot of information about them. ❑ *What you wear speaks volumes about you.*

✪**vol·un·tary** ◆◇◇ /ˈvɒləntri, AmE -teri/ ADJ (*academic word*) **1** **Voluntary** actions or activities are done because someone chooses to do them and not because they have been forced to do them. = optional; ≠ mandatory ❑ *Attention is drawn to a special voluntary course in Commercial French.* ❑ *The scheme, due to begin next month, will be voluntary.* **2** **Voluntary** work is done by people who are not paid for it, but who do it because they want to do it. = charitable; ≠ paid ❑ *In her spare time she does voluntary work.* ❑ *He'd been working at the local hostel for homeless people on a voluntary basis.* **3** [voluntary + N] A **voluntary** organization is controlled and organized by the people who have chosen to work for it, often without being paid, rather than receiving help or money from the government. ❑ *Some voluntary organizations run workshops for disabled people.*

✪**vol·un·tar·ily** /ˈvɒləntrəli, AmE -ˈterɪli/ ADV [voluntarily with V] ❑ *I would never leave here voluntarily.* ❑ *The company wanted staff to leave voluntarily.*

✪**vol·un·teer** ◆◇◇ /ˌvɒlənˈtɪə/ NOUN, VERB **NOUN** [c] (**volunteers**) **1** A **volunteer** is someone who does work without being paid for it, because they want to do it. ❑ *She now helps in a local school as a volunteer three days a week.* ❑ *Volunteers are needed to help visit elderly people's homes.* **2** A **volunteer** is someone who offers to do a particular task or job without being forced to do it.

❑ *Right. What I want now is two volunteers to come down to the front.* **3** A **volunteer** is someone who chooses to join the armed forces, especially during a war, as opposed to someone who is forced to join by law. ❑ *They fought as volunteers with the Afghan guerrillas.*

VERB [i, t] (**volunteers, volunteering, volunteered**) **1** [i] If you **volunteer** to do something, you offer to do it without being forced to do it. ❑ *Aunt Mary volunteered to clean up the kitchen.* ❑ *He volunteered for the army in 1939.* ❑ *The majority of people will volunteer for early retirement if the financial terms are acceptable.* ❑ *She volunteered as a nurse in a soldiers' rest-home.* **2** [t] (*formal*) If you **volunteer** information, you tell someone something without being asked. ❑ *The room was quiet; no one volunteered any further information.* ❑ *'They were both great supporters of Franco,' Ryle volunteered.*

✪**vote** ◆◆◆ /vəʊt/ NOUN, VERB **NOUN** [sing, c] (**votes**) **1** [sing, c] A **vote** is a choice made by a particular person or group in a meeting or an election. ❑ *He walked to the local polling place to cast his vote.* ❑ *Mr Reynolds was re-elected by 102 votes to 60.* ❑ *The government got a massive majority – well over 400 votes.* **2** [c] A **vote** is an occasion when a group of people make a decision by each person indicating his or her choice. The choice that most people support is accepted by the group. ❑ *Why do you think we should have a vote on that?* **3** [sing] The **vote** is the total number of votes or voters in an election, or the number of votes received or cast by a particular group. ❑ *Opposition parties won fifty-five per cent of the vote.* ❑ *The vote was strongly in favour of the Democratic Party.* ❑ *a huge majority of the white male vote* **4** [sing] If you have **the vote** in an election, or have **a vote** in a meeting, you have the legal right to indicate your choice. = ballot ❑ *Before that, women did not have a vote at all.*

PHRASE **one man one vote** One man one vote or **one person one vote** is a system of voting in which every person in a group or country has the right to cast their vote, and in which each individual's vote is counted and has equal value. ❑ *Mr Gould called for a move towards 'one man one vote'.*

VERB [i, t] (**votes, voting, voted**) **1** [i, t] When you **vote**, you indicate your choice officially at a meeting or in an election, for example, by raising your hand or writing on a piece of paper. ❑ *Two-thirds of the national electorate had the chance to vote in these elections.* ❑ *Nearly two-thirds of this group voted for Buchanan.* ❑ *The residents of Leningrad voted to restore the city's original name of St Petersburg.* **2** [t] If you **vote** a particular political party or leader, or **vote yes** or **no**, you make that choice with the vote that you have. ❑ *52.5% of those questioned said they'd vote Republican.* **3** [t] If people **vote** someone a particular title, they choose that person to have that title. = elect ❑ *His class voted him the man 'who had done the most for Yale'.*

PHRASES **vote with your feet** If you **vote with** your **feet**, you show that you do not support something by leaving the place where it is happening or leaving the organization that is supporting it. ❑ *Thousands of citizens are already voting with their feet, and leaving the country.* **I vote** (*informal*) If you say, for example, '**I vote that** we go' or '**I vote** we stay', you are suggesting that you should go or stay. ❑ *I vote that we all go to Houston immediately.* **vot·ing** /ˈvəʊtɪŋ/ NOUN [u] ❑ *Voting began about two hours ago.*

✪**vot·er** ◆◆◇ /ˈvəʊtə/ NOUN [c] (**voters**) **Voters** are people who have the legal right to vote in elections, or people who are voting in a particular election. = elector ❑ *The turnout was at least 62 per cent of registered voters.* ❑ *Austrian voters went to the polls this weekend to elect a successor to the President.*

vouch /vaʊtʃ/ **PHRASAL VERB** **vouch for** (**vouches, vouching, vouched**) **1** If you say that you can or will **vouch for** someone, you mean that you can guarantee their good behaviour. ❑ *Kim's mother agreed to vouch for Maria and get her a job.* **2** If you say that you can **vouch for** something, you mean that you have evidence from your own personal experience that it is true or correct. ❑ *He cannot vouch for the accuracy of the story.*

vouch·er /ˈvaʊtʃə/ NOUN [C] (**vouchers**) A **voucher** is a ticket or piece of paper that can be used instead of money to pay for something. ❑ *The winners will each receive a voucher for a pair of cinema tickets.*

vow /vaʊ/ VERB, NOUN
VERB [T] (**vows, vowing, vowed**) If you **vow** to do something, you make a serious promise or decision that you will do it. ❑ *While many models vow to go back to college, few do.* ❑ *I solemnly vowed that someday I would return to live in Europe.*
NOUN [C] (**vows**) **1** A **vow** is a serious promise or decision to do a particular thing. ❑ *I made a silent vow to be more careful in the future.* **2** **Vows** are a particular set of serious promises, such as the promises two people make when they are getting married. ❑ *I took my marriage vows and kept them.*

vow·el /ˈvaʊəl/ NOUN [C] (**vowels**) A **vowel** is a sound such as the ones represented in writing by the letters **A**, **E**, **I**, **O**, and **U**, that you pronounce with your mouth open, allowing the air to flow through it. Compare **consonant**. ❑ *The vowel in words like 'my' and 'thigh' is not very difficult.*

voy·age /ˈvɔɪɪdʒ/ NOUN [C] (**voyages**) A **voyage** is a long journey on a ship or in a spacecraft. ❑ *He aims to follow Columbus's voyage to the West Indies.*

vul·gar /ˈvʌlɡə/ ADJ (*disapproval*) **1** If you describe something as **vulgar**, you think it is in bad taste or of poor artistic quality. = tasteless ❑ *I think it's a very vulgar house.*

2 If you describe pictures, gestures, or remarks as **vulgar**, you dislike them because they refer to sex or parts of the body in an offensive way that you find unpleasant. ❑ *The women laughed coarsely at the comedian's vulgar jokes.* **3** If you describe a person or their behaviour as **vulgar**, you mean that they lack taste or behave offensively. = crude ❑ *He was a vulgar old man, but he never swore in front of a woman.*

vul·gar·ity /vʌlˈɡærɪti/ NOUN [U] **1** *I hate the vulgarity of the bright colours in this room.* **2** *Charles was a complete gentleman, incapable of rudeness or vulgarity.* **3** *It's his vulgarity that I can't take.*

✪ **vul·ner·able** ◆◇◇ /ˈvʌlnərəbəl/ ADJ **1** Someone who is **vulnerable** is weak and without protection, with the result that they are easily hurt physically or emotionally. ❑ *Old people are particularly vulnerable members of our society.* **2** If a person, animal, or plant is **vulnerable to** a disease, they are more likely to get it than other people, animals, or plants. = weak, prone, susceptible, exposed; ≠ protected, strong ❑ *People with high blood pressure are especially vulnerable to diabetes.* **3** Something that is **vulnerable** can be easily harmed or affected by something bad. ❑ *Their tanks would be vulnerable to attack from the air.*

✪ **vul·ner·abil·ity** /ˌvʌlnərəˈbɪliti/ NOUN [C, U] (**vulnerabilities**) **1** [C, U] = weakness, susceptibility, exposure; ≠ strength ❑ *David accepts his own vulnerability.* **2** [U] ❑ *Taking long-term courses of certain medicines may increase vulnerability to infection.* **3** [U] ❑ *anxieties about the country's vulnerability to invasion* ❑ *hackers attempting to exploit vulnerabilities in Microsoft products*

v

Ww

W also **w** /ˈdʌbəljuː/ NOUN [c, u] (**W's, w's**) W is the twenty-third letter of the English alphabet.

✪ **wage** ♦◇◇ /weɪdʒ/ NOUN, VERB
- **NOUN** [c] (**wages**) Someone's **wages** are the amount of money that is regularly paid to them for the work that they do. = salary, pay, earnings, income ❑ *His wages have gone up.* ❑ *This may end efforts to set a minimum wage well above the poverty line.*
- **VERB** [T] (**wages, waging, waged**) If a person, group, or country **wages** a campaign or a war, they start it and continue it over a period of time. ❑ *The government, along with the three factions that had been waging a civil war, signed a peace agreement.*

wag·on /ˈwægən/ NOUN [c] (**wagons**) **1** A wagon is a strong vehicle with four wheels, usually pulled by horses or oxen and used for carrying heavy loads. = cart **2** (*BrE*; in *AmE*, use **freight car**) A wagon is a large container on wheels which is pulled by a train.

wail /weɪl/ VERB, NOUN
- **VERB** [i, T] (**wails, wailing, wailed**) **1** [i] If someone **wails**, they make long, loud, high-pitched cries which express sorrow or pain. ❑ *The women began to wail in mourning.* **2** [T] If you **wail** something, you say it in a loud, high-pitched voice that shows that you are unhappy or in pain. ❑ *'Now look what you've done!' Shirley wailed.* **3** [i] If something such as a siren or an alarm **wails**, it makes a long, loud, high-pitched sound. ❑ *Police cars, their sirens wailing, accompanied the trucks.*
- **NOUN** [c, u] (**wails**) **1** [c] A **wail** is a long, loud, high-pitched cry which expresses sorrow or pain. ❑ *Wails of grief were heard as visitors filed past the site of the disaster.* **2** [u] The **wail** of something such as a siren or an alarm is a long, loud, high-pitched sound. ❑ *The wail of the bagpipe could be heard in the distance.*

waist /weɪst/ NOUN [c] (**waists**) **1** Your **waist** is the middle part of your body where it narrows slightly above your hips. ❑ *Ricky kept his arm around her waist.* **2** The **waist** of a garment such as a dress, coat, or pair of trousers is the part of it which covers the middle part of your body. ❑ *She tucked her thumbs into the waist of her trousers.*

wait ♦♦♦ /weɪt/ VERB, NOUN
- **VERB** [i, T] (**waits, waiting, waited**) **1** [i, T] When you **wait** for something or someone, you spend some time doing very little, because you cannot act until that thing happens or that person arrives. ❑ *I walk to a street corner and wait for the school bus.* ❑ *I waited to see how she responded.* ❑ *We had to wait a week before we got the results.* **2** [i, T] If something **is waiting for** you, it is ready for you to use, have, or do. ❑ *There'll be a car waiting for you.* ❑ *When we came home we had a meal waiting for us.* ❑ *He had a car waiting to take him back to the office.* **3** [i] If you say that something can **wait**, you mean that it is not important or urgent and so you will deal with it later. ❑ *I want to talk to you, but it can wait.* **4** [i] You can use **wait** when you are trying to make someone feel excited, or to encourage or threaten them. ❑ *If you think this all sounds very exciting, just wait until you read the book.* **5** [T] (*spoken*) **Wait** is used in expressions such as **wait a minute**, **wait a second**, and **wait a moment** to interrupt someone when they are speaking, for example, because you object to what they are saying or because you want

them to repeat something. = hold on, hang on ❑ *'Wait a minute!' he broke in. 'This is not giving her a fair hearing!'* **6** [i] If an employee **waits on** you, for example, in a restaurant or hotel, they take orders from you and bring you what you want. ❑ *There were plenty of servants to wait on her.*
- **PHRASES** **can't wait** or **can hardly wait** (*spoken, emphasis*) If you say that you **can't wait** to do something or **can hardly wait** to do it, you are emphasizing that you are very excited about it and eager to do it. ❑ *We can't wait to get started.*
  wait and see If you tell someone to **wait and see**, you tell them that they must be patient or that they must not worry about what is going to happen in the future because they have no control over it. ❑ *We'll have to wait and see what happens.*
- **PHRASAL VERBS** **wait around** If you **wait around**, you stay in the same place, usually doing very little, because you cannot act before something happens or before someone arrives. ❑ *The attacker may have been waiting around for an opportunity to strike.* ❑ *I waited around to speak to the doctor.*
  wait up If you **wait up**, you deliberately do not go to bed, especially because you are expecting someone to return home late at night. = stay up ❑ *I hope he doesn't expect you to wait up for him.*
- **NOUN** [c] (**waits**) A **wait** is a period of time in which you do very little, before something happens or before you can do something. ❑ *the four-hour wait for the organizers to declare the result*

USAGE NOTE
wait for
You say that someone **waits for** someone or something. You do not say that someone '~~waits someone or something~~'. *He sat by the telephone **waiting for** the call.*

wait·ing /ˈweɪtɪŋ/ NOUN [u] ❑ *The waiting became almost unbearable.*

wait·er /ˈweɪtə/ NOUN [c] (**waiters**) A **waiter** is a man who works in a restaurant, serving people food and drink.

wait·ing list NOUN [c] (**waiting lists**) A **waiting list** is a list of people who have asked for something that cannot be given to them immediately, such as medical treatment, housing, or training, and who must therefore wait until it is available. ❑ *There were 20,000 people on the waiting list for a home.*

wait·ress /ˈweɪtrəs/ NOUN [c] (**waitresses**) A **waitress** is a woman who works in a restaurant, serving people food and drink.

wake ♦◇◇ /weɪk/ VERB, NOUN
- **VERB** [i, T] (**wakes, waking, woke, woken** or **waked**) When you **wake** or when someone or something **wakes** you, you become conscious again after being asleep. ❑ *It was cold and dark when I woke at 6:30.* ❑ *She went upstairs to wake Milton.*
- **PHRASAL VERB** **wake up** **1** Wake up means the same as **wake** VERB. ❑ *One morning I woke up and felt something was wrong.* **2** If something such as an activity **wakes** you **up**, it makes you more alert and ready to do things after you have been lazy or inactive. ❑ *A cool shower wakes up the body and boosts circulation.*

NOUN [c] (**wakes**) **1** [usu sing, with POSS] The **wake** of a boat or other object moving in the water is the track of waves it makes behind it as it moves through the water. ❏ *Dolphins sometimes play in the wake of the boats.* **2** A **wake** is a gathering or social event that is held before or after someone's funeral. ❏ *A funeral wake was in progress.* **PHRASE** **in the wake of** If one thing follows **in the wake of** another, it happens after the other thing is over, often as a result of it. = following ❏ *The governor has enjoyed a huge surge in the polls in the wake of last week's convention.*

walk ♦♦♦ /wɔːk/ VERB, NOUN
VERB [I, T] (**walks, walking, walked**) **1** [I, T] When you **walk**, you move forward by putting one foot in front of the other in a regular way. ❏ *Rosanna and Forbes walked in silence.* ❏ *We walked into the foyer.* ❏ *I walked a few steps towards the fence.* **2** [T] If you **walk** someone somewhere, you walk there with them in order to show politeness or to make sure that they get there safely. = escort ❏ *She walked me to my car.*
PHRASAL VERBS **walk away** If you **walk away** from a problem or a difficult situation, you do nothing about it or do not face any bad consequences from it. ❏ *The most appropriate strategy may simply be to walk away from the problem.*
walk away with (*journalism*) If you **walk away with** something such as a prize, you win it or get it very easily. = walk off with ❏ *Enter our competition and you could walk away with $10,000.*
walk into If you **walk into** an unpleasant situation, you become involved in it without expecting to, especially because you have been careless. ❏ *He's walking into a situation that he absolutely can't control.*
walk off with (*journalism*) If you **walk off with** something such as a prize, you win it or get it very easily. = walk away with ❏ *We'd like nothing better than to see him walk off with the big prize.*
walk out **1** If you **walk out of** a meeting, a performance, or an unpleasant situation, you leave it suddenly, usually in order to show that you are angry or bored. ❏ *Several dozen councillors walked out of the meeting in protest.* **2** If someone **walks out on** their family or their partner, they leave them suddenly and go to live somewhere else. ❏ *Her husband walked out on her.* **3** If workers **walk out**, they stop doing their work for a period of time, usually in order to try to get better pay or conditions for themselves. = strike ❏ *The miners were furious and threatened to walk out.*
NOUN [c, SING] (**walks**) **1** [c] A **walk** is a trip that you make by walking, usually for pleasure. ❏ *I went for a walk.* **2** [SING] A **walk** of a particular distance is the distance that a person has to walk to get somewhere. ❏ *It was only a three-mile walk to Kabul from there.* **3** [c] A **walk** is a route suitable for walking along for pleasure. ❏ *a 2-mile coastal walk* **4** [SING] A **walk** is the action of walking rather than running. ❏ *She slowed to a steady walk.* **5** [SING] Someone's **walk** is the way that they walk. ❏ *George, despite his great height and gangling walk, was a great dancer.*
✦ **walk tall** → see **tall**

wall ♦♦♦ /wɔːl/ NOUN
NOUN [c] (**walls**) **1** A **wall** is one of the vertical sides of a building or room. ❏ *Kathryn leaned against the wall of the church.* ❏ *The bedroom walls would be papered with chintz.* **2** A **wall** is a long narrow vertical structure made of stone or brick that surrounds or divides an area of land. ❏ *He sat on the wall in the sun.* **3** The **wall** of something that is hollow is its side. ❏ *He ran his fingers along the inside walls of the box.*
PHRASE **drive someone up the wall** (*informal, emphasis*) If you say that something or someone **is driving** you **up the wall**, you are emphasizing that they annoy and irritate you. ❏ *The heat is driving me up the wall.*

wal·let /ˈwɒlɪt/ NOUN [c] (**wallets**) A **wallet** is a small, flat, folded case, usually made of leather or plastic, in which you can keep money and credit cards.

wall·paper /ˈwɔːlpeɪpə/ NOUN, NOUN, VERB
NOUN [c, u] (**wallpapers**) **1** [c, u] **Wallpaper** is thick, coloured or patterned paper that is used for covering and decorating the walls of rooms. ❏ *the wallpaper in the*

bedroom **2** [u] (*computing*) **Wallpaper** is the background on a computer screen. ❏ *preinstalled wallpaper images*
VERB [T] (**wallpapers, wallpapering, wallpapered**) If someone **wallpapers** a room, they cover the walls with wallpaper. ❏ *We were going to wallpaper that room anyway.*

wan·der /ˈwɒndə/ VERB, NOUN
VERB [I, T] (**wanders, wandering, wandered**) **1** [I, T] If you **wander** in a place, you walk around there in a casual way, often without intending to go in any particular direction. ❏ *When he got bored he wandered around the fair.* ❏ *They wandered off in the direction of the nearest shop.* ❏ *People wandered the streets aimlessly.* **2** [I] If a person or animal **wanders** from a place where they are supposed to stay, they move away from the place without going in a particular direction. = stray ❏ *Because Mother is afraid we'll get lost, we aren't allowed to wander far.* **3** [I] If your mind **wanders** or your thoughts **wander**, you stop concentrating on something and start thinking about other things. = stray ❏ *His mind would wander, and he would lose track of what he was doing.* **4** [I] If your eyes **wander**, you stop looking at one thing and start looking around at other things. ❏ *His eyes wandered restlessly around the room.*
NOUN [SING] A **wander** is the act of walking around a place in a casual way, often without intending to go in any particular direction. = stroll ❏ *A wander around any market will reveal stalls piled high with vegetables.*

wane /weɪn/ VERB [I] (**wanes, waning, waned**) If something **wanes**, it becomes gradually weaker or less, often so that it eventually disappears. = fade ❏ *While his interest in these sports began to wane, a passion for lacrosse developed.*

want ♦♦♦ /wɒnt/ VERB, NOUN
VERB [T] (**wants, wanting, wanted**) **1** If you **want** something, you feel a desire or a need for it. ❏ *I want a drink.* ❏ *People wanted to know who this talented designer was.* ❏ *They began to want their father to be the same as other daddies.* ❏ *They didn't want people staring at them as they sat on the lawn, so they put up high walls.* **2** You can say that you **want** to say something to indicate that you are about to say it. ❏ *I want to say how delighted I am that you're having a baby.* **3** If you say to someone that you **want** something, or ask them if they **want to** do it, you are firmly telling them what you want or what you want them to do. ❏ *I want an explanation from you, Jeremy.* ❏ *Do you want to tell me what all this is about?* **4** (*informal*) If you tell someone that they **want to** do a particular thing, you are advising them to do it. = ought ❏ *You want to be very careful not to have a man like Crevecoeur for an enemy.* **5** If someone **is wanted** by the police, the police are searching for them because they are thought to have committed a crime. ❏ *He was wanted for the murder of a judge.*
NOUN [PL] (**wants**) Your **wants** are the things that you want. ❏ *She couldn't lift a spoon without a servant anticipating her wants and getting it for her.*
PHRASE **for want of** If you do something **for want of** something else, you do it because the other thing is not available or not possible. ❏ *The factories shut down for want of fuel and materials.*
want·ed /ˈwɒntɪd/ ADJ ❏ *He is one of the most wanted criminals in Europe.*

✪ war ♦♦♦ /wɔː/ NOUN
NOUN [c, u] (**wars**) **1** A **war** is a period of fighting or conflict between countries or states. = conflict ❏ *He spent part of the war in the National Guard.* ❏ *matters of war and peace* ❏ *They've been at war for the last fifteen years.* **2** **War** is intense economic competition between countries or organizations. ❏ *The most important thing is to reach an agreement and to avoid a trade war.* **3** If you make **war on** someone or something that you are opposed to, you do things to stop them from succeeding. ❏ *She has been involved in the war against organized crime.*
PHRASE **go to war** If a country **goes to war**, it starts fighting a war. ❏ *Do you think this crisis can be settled without going to war?*
→ See also **civil war**, **warring**

ward /wɔːd/ NOUN
NOUN [c] (**wards**) A **ward** is a room in a hospital which

has beds for many people, often people who need similar treatment. ❑ *They transferred her to the psychiatric ward.*

PHRASAL VERB **ward off** (wards, warding, warded) To **ward off** a danger or illness means to prevent it from affecting you or harming you. ❑ *She may have put up a fight to try to ward off her assailant.*

ward·robe /'wɔːdrəʊb/ NOUN [C] (wardrobes) **1** A **wardrobe** is a tall cupboard or cabinet in which you can hang your clothes. **2** Someone's **wardrobe** is the total collection of clothes that they have. ❑ *Her wardrobe consists primarily of huge cashmere sweaters and tiny Italian sandals.*

ware·house /'weəhaʊs/ NOUN [C] (warehouses) A **warehouse** is a large building where raw materials or manufactured goods are stored until they are exported to other countries or distributed to shops to be sold.

war·fare /'wɔːfeə/ NOUN [U] **1** **Warfare** is the activity of fighting a war. ❑ *the threat of chemical warfare* **2** **Warfare** is sometimes used to refer to any violent struggle or conflict. ❑ *Much of the violence is related to drugs and gang warfare.*

warm ♦♦◇ /wɔːm/ ADJ, VERB

ADJ (warmer, warmest) **1** Something that is **warm** has some heat but not enough to be hot. = cool ❑ *Wheat is grown in places which have cold winters and warm, dry summers.* ❑ *Because it was warm, David wore only a white cotton shirt.* **2** **Warm** clothes and blankets are made of a material such as wool that protects you from the cold. ❑ *They have been forced to sleep in the open without food or warm clothing.* **3** **Warm** colours have red or yellow in them rather than blue or green, and make you feel comfortable and relaxed. ❑ *The basement hallway is painted a warm yellow.* **4** A **warm** person is friendly and shows a lot of affection or enthusiasm in their behaviour. ❑ *She was a warm and loving mother.*

VERB [T, I] (warms, warming, warmed) **1** [T] If you **warm** a part of your body or if something hot **warms** it, it stops feeling cold and starts to feel hotter. ❑ *The sun had come out to warm his back.* **2** [I] If you **warm to** a person or an idea, you become fonder of the person or more interested in the idea. ❑ *Those who got to know him better warmed to his openness and honesty.*

PHRASAL VERB **warm up** **1** If you **warm** something **up** or if it **warms up**, it gets hotter. ❑ *He blew on his hands to warm them up.* ❑ *All that she would have to do was warm up the pudding.* **2** If you **warm up** for an event such as a race, you prepare yourself for it by doing exercises or by practising just before it starts. ❑ *In an hour the drivers will be warming up for the main event.* **3** When a machine or engine **warms up** or someone **warms** it **up**, it becomes ready for use a little while after being switched on or started. ❑ *He waited for his car to warm up.*

warm·ly /'wɔːmli/ ADV **1** *Remember to wrap up warmly on cold days.* **2** [warmly with v] ❑ *New members are warmly welcomed.*

warmth /wɔːmθ/ NOUN [U] **1** The **warmth** of something is the heat that it has or produces. ❑ *She went further into the room, drawn by the warmth of the fire.* **2** The **warmth** of something such as a garment or blanket is the protection that it gives you against the cold. ❑ *The blanket will provide additional warmth and comfort in bed.*

♦ warn ♦♦◇ /wɔːn/ VERB [I, T] (warns, warning, warned) **1** If you **warn** someone about something such as a possible danger or problem, you tell them about it so that they are aware of it. = alert, caution ❑ *When I had my first baby friends warned me that children were expensive.* ❑ *They warned him of the dangers of sailing alone.* ❑ *He warned of a possibility of a new terrorist attack.* ❑ *Analysts warned that Europe's most powerful economy may be facing trouble.* ❑ *He also warned of a possible anti-Western backlash.* **2** If you **warn** someone not to do something, you advise them not to do it so that they can avoid possible danger or punishment. ❑ *Mrs Blount warned me not to interfere.* ❑ *'Don't do anything yet,' he warned. 'Too risky.'*

♦ warn·ing ♦◇◇ /'wɔːnɪŋ/ NOUN, ADJ
NOUN [C, U] (warnings) **1** [C] A **warning** is something said

or written to tell people of a possible danger, problem, or other unpleasant thing that might happen. = alert ❑ *The minister gave a warning that if war broke out, it would be catastrophic.* ❑ *He was killed because he ignored a warning to put stronger cords on his parachute.* ❑ *The government has unveiled new health warnings for cigarette packets.* **2** [C, U] A **warning** is an advance notice of something that will happen, often something unpleasant or dangerous. ❑ *The soldiers opened fire without warning.*

ADJ [warning + N] **Warning** actions or signs give a warning. ❑ *She ignored the warning signals and did not check the patient's medical notes.*

WORD CONNECTIONS
VERB + **warning**
issue a warning
give a warning
send a warning
❑ *He issued a stern warning that anyone caught cheating would be disqualified.*
ADJ + **warning**
a **severe** warning
a **stern** warning
a **dire** warning
❑ *There were dire warnings of the threat posed by climate change.*
advance warning
early warning
❑ *It operates an early warning system to alert public health authorities to disease outbreaks.*
NOUN + **warning**
a **weather** warning
a **flood** warning
a **hurricane** warning
a **tsunami** warning
❑ *The meteorological office issued flood warnings for many areas of the country.*
warning + NOUN
a warning **sign**
a warning **signal**
a warning **label**
❑ *It is important that parents and teachers do not ignore warning signs of drug abuse.*

war·rant /'wɒrənt, AmE 'wɔːr-/ VERB, NOUN
VERB [T] (warrants, warranting, warranted) If something **warrants** a particular action, it makes the action seem necessary or appropriate for the circumstances. = merit ❑ *The allegations are serious enough to warrant an investigation.*
NOUN [C] (warrants) [oft warrant 'for' N, also 'by' warrant] A **warrant** is a legal document that allows someone to do something, especially one that is signed by a judge or magistrate and gives the police permission to arrest someone or search their house. ❑ *Police confirmed that they had issued a warrant for his arrest.*

war·ran·ty /'wɒrənti, AmE 'wɔːr-/ NOUN [C] (warranties) [also 'under' warranty] A **warranty** is a written promise by a company that, if you find a fault in something they have sold you within a certain time, they will repair it or replace it free of charge. ❑ *a twelve-month warranty*

war·ring /'wɔːrɪŋ/ ADJ [warring + N] **Warring** is used to describe groups of people who are involved in a conflict or quarrel with each other. ❑ *An official said the warring factions have not yet turned in all their heavy weapons.*

war·ri·or /'wɒriə, AmE 'wɔːr-/ NOUN [C] (warriors) A **warrior** is a fighter or soldier, especially one in former times who was very brave and experienced in fighting. ❑ *the tale of Bima, the great warrior of Indonesian folklore*

war·ship /'wɔːʃɪp/ NOUN [C] (warships) A **warship** is a ship with guns that is used for fighting in wars.

war·time /'wɔːtaɪm/ NOUN [U] **Wartime** is a period of time when a war is being fought. ❑ *The government will commandeer ships only in wartime.*

W

wary /'weəri/ ADJ (**warier, wariest**) If you are **wary of** something or someone, you are cautious because you do not know much about them and you believe they may be dangerous or cause problems. = leery ❑ *People did not teach their children to be wary of strangers.*
wari·ly /'weərɪli/ ADV ❑ *She studied me warily, as if I might turn violent.*

was /wəz, STRONG wɒz, AmE wʌz/ IRREG FORM **Was** is the first and third person singular of the past tense of **be. be**

wash ◆◇◇ /wɒʃ/ VERB, NOUN
[VERB] [T, I] (**washes, washing, washed**) **1** [T] If you **wash** something, you clean it using water and usually a substance such as soap or detergent. ❑ *We did odd jobs like farm work and washing dishes.* ❑ *It took a long time to wash the mud out of his hair.* **2** [I, T] If you **wash** or if you **wash** part of your body, especially your hands and face, you clean part of your body using soap and water. ❑ *They looked as if they hadn't washed in days.* ❑ *She washed her face with cold water.* **3** [I, T] If a sea or river **washes** somewhere, it flows there gently. You can also say that something carried by a sea or river **washes** or **is washed** somewhere. ❑ *The sea washed against the shore.* **4** [I] (*written*) If a feeling **washes over** you, you suddenly feel it very strongly and cannot control it. ❑ *A wave of self-consciousness can wash over her when someone new enters the room.*
[PHRASAL VERBS] **wash away** If rain or floods **wash away** something, they destroy it and carry it away. ❑ *Flood waters washed away one of the main bridges in Pusan.*
wash down **1** If you **wash** something, especially food, **down** with a drink, you drink the drink after eating the food, especially to make the food easier to swallow or digest. ❑ *He took two aspirin immediately and washed them down with three cups of water.* **2** If you **wash down** an object, you wash it all, from top to bottom. ❑ *The prisoner started to wash down the walls of his cell.*
wash up **1** If something **is washed up on** a piece of land, it is carried by a river or sea and left there. ❑ *Thousands of herring and crab are washed up on the beaches during every storm.* **2** (*BrE*; in *AmE*, use **wash the dishes**) If you **wash up**, you wash the plates, cups, cutlery, and pans that have been used for cooking and eating a meal.
[NOUN] [C] (**washes**) **1** If you give something a **wash**, you clean it using water and usually a substance such as soap or detergent. ❑ *The coat could do with a wash.* **2** If you have a **wash**, or if you give part of your body a **wash**, you clean part of your body using soap and water. ❑ *She had a wash and changed her clothes.*
[PHRASE] **be in the wash** (*informal*) If you say that something such as an item of clothing **is in the wash**, you mean that it is being washed, is waiting to be washed, or has just been washed and should therefore not be worn or used. ❑ *Your jeans are in the wash.*
✦ **wash your hands of** → see **hand**

wast·age /'weɪstɪdʒ/ NOUN [U] **Wastage** of something is the act of wasting it or the amount of it that is wasted. ❑ *There was a lot of wastage and many wrong decisions were hastily taken.*

✪ **waste** ◆◆◇ /weɪst/ VERB, NOUN, ADJ
[VERB] [T] (**wastes, wasting, wasted**) **1** If you **waste** something such as time, money, or energy, you use too much of it doing something that is not important or necessary, or is unlikely to succeed. = misuse, squander; ≠ save ❑ *There could be many reasons and he was not going to waste time speculating on them.* ❑ *I resolved not to waste money on a hotel.* ❑ *The system wastes a large amount of water.* **2** If you **waste** an opportunity for something, you do not take advantage of it when it is available. ❑ *Let's not waste an opportunity to see the children.*
[PHRASAL VERB] **waste away** If someone **wastes away**, they become extremely thin or weak because they are ill or worried and are not eating properly. ❑ *Persons dying from cancer grow thin and visibly waste away.*
[NOUN] [SING, U] (**wastes**) **1** [SING] A **waste** of something such as time, money, or energy is when you use too much of it doing something that is not important or necessary, or is unlikely to succeed. ❑ *It is a waste of time going to the doctor with most mild complaints.* **2** [U] **Waste** is the use of

money or other resources on things that do not need it. ❑ *The packets are measured to reduce waste.* ❑ *The department was criticized for inefficiency and waste.* **3** [U] [also **wastes**] **Waste** is material that has been used and is no longer wanted, for example, because the valuable or useful part of it has been taken out. ❑ *Congress passed a law that regulates the disposal of waste.* ❑ *the dangers posed by toxic waste*
[PHRASE] **go to waste** If something **goes to waste**, it remains unused or has to be thrown away. ❑ *So much of his enormous effort and talent will go to waste if we are forced to drop one hour of the film.*
[ADJ] (*BrE*; in *AmE*, use **vacant land**) **Waste** land is land, especially in or near a city, that is not used or taken care of by anyone, and so is covered by wild plants and rubbish.
✦ **waste no time** → see **time**

waste·ful /'weɪstfʊl/ ADJ Action that is **wasteful** uses too much of something valuable such as time, money, or energy. ❑ *This kind of training is ineffective, and wasteful of scarce resources.*

waste·land /'weɪstlænd/ NOUN [C, U] (**wastelands**) **1** [C, U] A **wasteland** is an area of land on which not much can grow or which has been spoiled in some way. ❑ *The pollution has already turned vast areas into a wasteland.* **2** [C] If you refer to a place, situation, or period in time as a **wasteland**, you are criticizing it because you think there is nothing interesting or exciting in it. = desert ❑ *the cultural wasteland of Franco's repressive rule*

watch ◆◆◆ /wɒtʃ/ VERB, NOUN
[VERB] [I, T] (**watches, watching, watched**) **1** [I, T] If you **watch** someone or something, you look at them, usually for a period of time, and pay attention to what is happening. ❑ *The man was standing in his doorway watching him.* ❑ *He seems to enjoy watching me work.* ❑ *Here, now watch how I cut this, OK?* ❑ *He watched as the Yankees rallied for a second comeback victory.* **2** [T] If you **watch** something on television or an event such as a sports contest, you spend time looking at it, especially when you see it from the beginning to the end. ❑ *I'd stayed up late to watch the film.* **3** [I, T] If you **watch** a situation or event, you pay attention to it or you are aware of it, but you do not influence it. ❑ *Human rights groups have been closely watching the case.* ❑ *He watched as nine people were swept into the crevasse.* **4** [T] If you **watch** people, especially children or animals, you are responsible for them, and make sure that they are not in danger. ❑ *Parents can't be expected to watch their children 24 hours a day.* **5** [T] If you tell someone to **watch** a particular person or thing, you are warning them to be careful that the person or thing does not get out of control or do something unpleasant. ❑ *You really ought to watch these quiet types.*
[PHRASES] **watch it** You say '**watch it**' in order to warn someone to be careful, especially when you want to threaten them about what will happen if they are not careful. ❑ *'Now watch it, Patsy,' the sergeant told her.*
you watch or **just watch** You say to someone '**you watch**' or '**just watch**' when you are predicting that something will happen, and you are very confident that it will happen as you say. ❑ *You watch. Things will get worse before they get better.*
[PHRASAL VERBS] **watch for** or **watch out for** If you **watch for** something or **watch out for** it, you pay attention so that you notice it, either because you do not want to miss it or because you want to avoid it. = look out for ❑ *We'll be watching for any developments.*
watch out If you tell someone to **watch out**, you are warning them to be careful, because something unpleasant might happen to them or they might get into difficulties. = look out ❑ *You have to watch out because there are land mines all over the place.*
[NOUN] [C] (**watches**) A **watch** is a small clock that you wear on a strap on your wrist, or on a chain.
[PHRASES] **keep watch** **1** If someone **keeps watch**, they look and listen all the time, while other people are asleep or doing something else, so that they can warn them of danger or an attack. ❑ *Jose, as usual, had climbed a tree to keep watch.* **2** If you **keep watch** on events or a situation, you pay attention to what is happening, so that you can

w

take action at the right moment. ❑ *US officials have been keeping close watch on the situation.*

under watch If someone is being kept **under watch**, they are being guarded or observed all the time. ❑ *Doctors confirmed how serious Josephine's condition was, and she is still being kept under watch.*

✦ **watch your step** → see **step**

watch‧dog /'wɒtʃdɒg, AmE -dɔːg/ NOUN [C] (**watchdogs**) A **watchdog** is a person or committee whose job is to make sure that companies do not act illegally or irresponsibly. ❑ *an anticrime watchdog group funded by New York businesses*

watch‧ful /'wɒtʃfʊl/ ADJ Someone who is **watchful** notices everything that is happening. ❑ *The best thing is to be watchful and see the family doctor for any change in your normal health.*

wa‧ter ♦♦♦ /'wɔːtə/ NOUN, VERB

NOUN [U, PL] (**waters**) **1** [U] **Water** is a clear thin liquid that has no colour or taste when it is pure. It falls from clouds as rain and enters rivers and seas. All animals and people need water in order to live. ❑ *Get me a glass of water.* ❑ *the sound of water hammering on the metal roof* **2** [PL] You use **waters** to refer to a large area of sea, especially the area of sea that is near to a country and that is regarded as belonging to it. ❑ *The ship will remain outside Chinese territorial waters.*

PHRASES **water under the bridge** If you say that an event or incident is **water under the bridge**, you mean that it has happened and cannot now be changed, so there is no point in worrying about it anymore. ❑ *He was relieved his time in jail was over and regarded it as water under the bridge.*

in deep water If you are **in deep water**, you are in a difficult or awkward situation. ❑ *You certainly seem to be in deep water.*

hold water If an argument or theory does not **hold water**, it does not seem to be reasonable or be in accordance with the facts. ❑ *This argument simply cannot hold water in Europe.*

in hot water (*informal*) If you are **in hot water**, you are in trouble. ❑ *The company has already been in hot water over high prices this year.*

pour cold water on something If you **pour cold water on** an idea or suggestion, you show that you have a low opinion of it. ❑ *University economists pour cold water on the idea that the economic recovery has begun.*

test the water or **test the waters** If you **test the water** or **test the waters**, you try to find out what reaction an action or idea will get before you do it or tell it to people. ❑ *You should be cautious when getting involved and test the water before committing yourself.*

VERB [T, I] (**waters, watering, watered**) **1** [T] If you **water** plants, you pour water over them in order to help them to grow. ❑ *He went out to water the plants.* **2** [I] If your eyes **water**, tears build up in them because they are hurting or because you are upset. ❑ *His eyes watered from cigarette smoke.* **3** [I] If you say that your mouth **is watering**, you mean that you can smell or see some nice food that makes you want to eat it. ❑ *cookies to make your mouth water*

PHRASAL VERB **water down** **1** If you **water down** a substance, such as food or drink, you add water to it to make it weaker. = dilute ❑ *You can water down a glass of wine and make it last twice as long.* **2** If something such as a proposal, speech, or statement **is watered down**, it is made much weaker and less forceful, or less likely to make people angry. = tone down ❑ *Proposed legislation affecting bird-keepers has been watered down.*

✦ **like water off a duck's back** → see **duck**; **take to something like a duck to water** → see **duck**

water‧fall /'wɔːtəfɔːl/ NOUN [C] (**waterfalls**) A **waterfall** is a place where water flows over the edge of a steep, high cliff in hills or mountains, and falls into a pool below. ❑ *Angel Falls, the world's highest waterfall*

water‧front /'wɔːtəfrʌnt/ NOUN [C] (**waterfronts**) A **waterfront** is a street or piece of land next to an area of water, such as a harbour or the sea. ❑ *They went for a stroll along the waterfront.*

water‧proof /'wɔːtəpruːf/ ADJ Something that is **waterproof** does not let water pass through it. ❑ *Take*

waterproof clothing – Oregon weather is unpredictable.

watt /wɒt/ NOUN [C] (**watts**) A **watt** is a unit of measurement of electrical power. ❑ *Use a 3 amp fuse for equipment up to 720 watts.*

✪ **wave** ♦♦◇ /weɪv/ VERB, NOUN

VERB [I, T] (**waves, waving, waved**) **1** [I, T] If you **wave** or **wave** your hand, you move your hand from side to side in the air, usually in order to say hello or goodbye to someone. ❑ *Jessica caught sight of Lois and waved to her.* ❑ *He grinned, waved, and said, 'Hi!'* **2** [T] If you **wave** someone away or **wave** them on, you make a movement with your hand to indicate that they should move in a particular direction. ❑ *Leshka waved him away with a show of irritation.* ❑ *He waited for a policeman to stop the traffic and wave the people on.* **3** [T] If you **wave** something, you hold it up and move it rapidly from side to side. ❑ *Hospital staff were outside to welcome him, waving flags and applauding.* **4** [I] If something **waves**, it moves gently from side to side or up and down. = sway ❑ *grass and flowers waving in the wind*

NOUN [C] (**waves**) **1** A **wave** is a movement of the hand from side to side in the air, usually in order to say hello or goodbye to someone. ❑ *Steve stopped him with a wave of the hand.* **2** A **wave** is a raised mass of water on the surface of water, especially the sea, which is caused by the wind or by tides making the surface of the water rise and fall. ❑ *the sound of the waves breaking on the shore* **3** If someone's hair has **waves**, it curves slightly instead of being straight. ❑ *Her blue eyes shone and caught the light, and so did the platinum waves in her hair.* **4** A **wave** is a sudden increase in heat or energy that spreads out from an earthquake or explosion. ❑ *The shock waves of the earthquake were felt in Teheran.* ❑ *the seismic waves generated by natural earthquakes* **5** **Waves** are the form in which things such as sound, light, and radio signals travel. ❑ *Regular repeating actions such as sound waves, light waves, or radio waves have a certain frequency, or number of waves per second.* ❑ *the wave amplitude of light* **6** If you refer to a **wave of** a particular feeling, you mean that it increases quickly and becomes very intense, and then often decreases again. ❑ *She felt a wave of panic, but forced herself to leave the room calmly.* **7** A **wave** is a sudden increase in a particular activity or type of behaviour, especially an undesirable or unpleasant one. ❑ *the current wave of violence*

wave‧length /'weɪvleŋθ/ NOUN

NOUN [C] (**wavelengths**) **1** A **wavelength** is the distance between a part of a wave of energy such as light or sound and the next similar part. ❑ *Sunlight consists of different wavelengths of radiation.* **2** A **wavelength** is the size of radio wave that a particular radio station uses to broadcast its programmes. ❑ *She found the wavelength of their broadcasts, and left the radio tuned to their station.*

PHRASE **on the same wavelength** If two people are **on the same wavelength**, they find it easy to understand each other and they tend to agree, because they share similar interests or opinions. ❑ *We could complete each other's sentences because we were on the same wavelength.*

wa‧ver /'weɪvə/ VERB [I] (**wavers, wavering, wavered**) **1** If you **waver**, you cannot decide about something or you consider changing your mind about something. ❑ *Some military commanders wavered over whether to support the coup.* **2** If something **wavers**, it shakes with very slight movements or changes. ❑ *The shadows of the dancers wavered continually.*

wax /wæks/ NOUN, VERB

NOUN [C, U] (**waxes**) **1** [C, U] **Wax** is a solid, slightly shiny substance made of fat or oil that is used to make candles and polish. It melts when it is heated. ❑ *There were coloured candles which had spread pools of wax on the furniture.* **2** [U] **Wax** is the sticky yellow substance found in your ears. ❑ *Use a cotton bud to remove the wax from your ears.*

VERB [T] (**waxes, waxing, waxed**) **1** If you **wax** a surface, you put a thin layer of wax onto it, especially in order to polish it. ❑ *We'd have long talks while she helped me wax the floor.* **2** If you have a part of your body **waxed**, for example your legs, you have the hair removed from the area by having wax put on it and then pulled off quickly. ❑ *She has just had her legs waxed at the local beauty parlour.*

way ◆◆◆ /weɪ/ NOUN, ADV, COMB
`NOUN` [C, PL, SING] (**ways**) **1** [C] If you refer to a **way** of doing something, you are referring to how you can do it, for example, the action you can take or the method you can use to achieve it. ❑ *Freezing isn't a bad way of preserving food.* ❑ *I worked myself into a frenzy plotting ways to make him jealous.* ❑ *There just might be a way.* **2** [C] If you talk about the **way** someone does something, you are talking about the qualities their action has. ❑ *She smiled in a friendly way.* ❑ *He had a strange way of talking.* **3** [C] If a general statement or description is true **in** a particular **way**, this is the form of it that is true in a particular case. ❑ *Computerized reservation systems help airline profits in several ways.* ❑ *She was afraid in a way that was quite new to her.* **4** [C] You use **way** in expressions such as **in some ways**, **in many ways**, and **in every way** to indicate the degree or extent to which a statement is true. = respect ❑ *In some ways, the official opening is a formality.* **5** [PL] The **ways** of a particular person or group of people are their customs or their usual behaviour. ❑ *He denounces people who urge him to alter his ways.* ❑ *She began to study the ways of the Native Americans.* **6** [SING] If you refer to someone's **way**, you are referring to their usual or preferred type of behaviour. ❑ *She is now divorced and, in her usual resourceful way, has started her own business.* **7** [C] You use **way** to refer to one particular opinion or interpretation of something, when others are possible. ❑ *I suppose that's one way of looking at it.* ❑ *With most of Dylan's lyrics, however, there are other ways of interpreting the words.* **8** [C] You use **way** when mentioning one of a number of possible, alternative results or decisions. ❑ *There is no indication which way the vote could go.* **9** [SING] The **way** you feel about something is your attitude to it or your opinion about it. ❑ *I'm so sorry – I had no idea you felt that way.* **10** [SING] If you mention the **way** that something happens, you are mentioning the fact that it happens. ❑ *I hate the way he manipulates people.* **11** [SING] You use **way** in expressions such as **push your way**, **work your way**, or **eat your way**, followed by a prepositional phrase or adverb, in order to indicate movement, progress, or force as well as the action described by the verb. ❑ *She thrust her way into the crowd.* **12** [C] The **way** somewhere consists of the different places that you go through or the route that you take in order to get there. ❑ *Does anybody know the way to the bathroom?* ❑ *I'm afraid I can't remember the way.* **13** [SING] If you go or look a particular **way**, you go or look in that direction. ❑ *As he strode into the kitchen, he passed Pop coming the other way.* ❑ *They paused at the top of the stairs, doubtful as to which way to go next.* **14** [SING] (*spoken*) You can refer to the direction you are travelling in as your **way**. ❑ *She would say she was going my way and offer me a lift.* **15** [SING] If you lose your **way**, you take a wrong or unfamiliar route, so that you do not know how to get to the place that you want to go to. If you find your **way**, you manage to get to the place that you want to go to. ❑ *The men lost their way in a sandstorm and crossed the border by mistake.* **16** [C] You talk about people going their different **ways** in order to say that their lives develop differently and they have less contact with each other. ❑ *It wasn't until we each went our separate ways that I began to learn how to do things for myself.* **17** [SING] If something comes your **way**, you get it or receive it. ❑ *Take advantage of the opportunities coming your way in a couple of months.* **18** [SING] You use **way** in expressions such as **the right way up** and **the other way around** to refer to one of two or more possible positions or arrangements that something can have. ❑ *Books have a right and a wrong way up.* **19** [PL] If you split something a number of **ways**, you divide it into a number of different parts or quantities, usually fairly equal in size. ❑ *The region was split three ways, between Greece, Serbia and Bulgaria.* **20** [SING] **Way** is used in expressions such as **a long way**, **a little way**, and **quite a way**, to say how far away something is or how far you have travelled. ❑ *Some of them live in places quite a long way from here.* ❑ *A little way further down the lane we passed the driveway to a house.* **21** [SING] **Way** is used in expressions such as **a long way**, **a little way**, and **quite a way**, to say

how far away in time something is. ❑ *Success is still a long way off.* **22** [SING] You use **way** in expressions such as **all the way**, **most of the way** and **half the way** to refer to the extent to which an action has been completed. ❑ *He had unscrewed the caps most of the way.*

`PHRASES` **all the way** (*emphasis*) **1** You use **all the way** to emphasize how long a distance is. ❑ *He had to walk all the way home.* **2** You can use **all the way** to emphasize that your remark applies to every part of a situation, activity, or period of time. ❑ *Having started a revolution we must go all the way.*

you can't have it both ways If someone says that you **can't have it both ways**, they are telling you that you have to choose between two things and cannot do or have them both. ❑ *Countries cannot have it both ways: the cost of a cleaner environment may sometimes be fewer jobs in dirty industries.*

by the way (*spoken*) You say **by the way** when you add something to what you are saying, especially something that you have just thought of. = incidentally ❑ *The name Latifah, by the way, means 'delicate'.*

clear the way or **open the way** or **prepare the way** If you **clear the way**, **open the way**, or **prepare the way** for something, you create an opportunity for it to happen. ❑ *The talks are meant to clear the way for formal negotiations on a new constitution.*

the easy way out (*disapproval*) If you say that someone takes **the easy way out**, you disapprove of them because they do what is easiest for them in a difficult situation, rather than dealing with it properly. ❑ *As soon as things got difficult he took the easy way out.*

either way You use **either way** in order to introduce a statement that is true in each of the two possible or alternative cases that you have just mentioned. ❑ *The sea may rise or the land may fall; either way the sand dunes will be gone in a short time.*

the way forward (*approval*) If you say that a particular type of action or development is **the way forward**, you approve of it because it is likely to lead to success. ❑ *people who genuinely believe that anarchy is the way forward*

get one's way or **have one's way** or **get one's own way** or **have one's own way** If someone **gets** their way or **has** their **way**, nobody stops them from doing what they want to do. You can also say that someone **gets** their **own** way or **has** their **own way**. ❑ *She is very good at using her charm to get her way.*

give way to If one thing **gives way to** another, the first thing is replaced by the second. ❑ *First he had been numb. Then the numbness gave way to anger.*

give way If an object that is supporting something **gives way**, it breaks or collapses, so that it can no longer support that thing. ❑ *The hook in the ceiling had given way and the lamp had fallen blazing on to the table.*

in no way or **not in any way** (*emphasis*) You use **in no way** or **not in any way** to emphasize that a statement is not at all true. ❑ *In no way am I going to adopt any of his methods.*

in a way (*vagueness*) If you say that something is true **in a way**, you mean that although it is not completely true, it is true to a limited extent or in certain respects. You use **in a way** to reduce the force of a statement. ❑ *In a way, I suppose I'm frightened of failing.*

in the way If you say that someone **gets in the way** or **is in the way**, you are annoyed because their presence or their actions stop you from doing something properly. ❑ *'We wouldn't get in the way,' Suzanne promised. 'We'd just stand quietly in a corner.'*

get in the way To **get in the way of** something means to make it difficult for it to happen, continue, or be appreciated properly. ❑ *She had a job which never got in the way of her leisure interests.*

know one's way around something or **know one's way about something** If you **know your way around** a particular subject, system, or job, you know all the procedures and facts about it. ❑ *He knows his way around the intricate maze of patent law.*

lead the way 1 If you **lead the way** along a particular route, you go along it in front of someone in order to

W

show them where to go. □ *She grabbed his suitcase and led the way.* **2** If a person or group **leads the way in** a particular activity, they are the first person or group to do it or they make the most new developments in it. □ *Sony has also led the way in shrinking the size of compact-disc players.*

have come a long way If you say that someone or something **has come a long way**, you mean that they have developed, progressed, or become very successful. □ *He has come a long way since the days he could only afford one meal a day.*

a long way from or **some way from** (*emphasis*) If you say that something is **a long way from** being true, you are emphasizing that it is definitely not true. □ *She is a long way from being the richest person in Florida.*

go a long way If you say that something **goes a long way towards** doing a particular thing, you mean that it is an important factor in achieving that thing. □ *Being respectful and courteous goes a long way towards building a relationship.*

lose one's way (*disapproval*) If you say that someone has **lost** their **way**, you are criticizing them because they do not have any good ideas anymore, or seem to have become unsure about what to do. □ *Why has the White House lost its way on tax and budget policy?*

make one's way When you **make** your **way** somewhere, you walk or travel there. □ *He made his way to the marketplace.*

make way If one person or thing **makes way for** another, the first is replaced by the second. □ *He said he was prepared to make way for younger people in the party.*

there's no way (*emphasis*) If you say **there's no way** that something will happen, you are emphasizing that you think it will definitely not happen. □ *There was absolutely no way that we were going to be able to retrieve it.*

no way (*informal, emphasis*) You can say **no way** as an emphatic way of saying no. □ *Mike, no way am I playing cards with you for money.*

be on one's way If you **are on** your **way**, you have started your trip somewhere. □ *He has been allowed to leave the country and is on his way to Hawaii.*

on the way or **along the way** If something happens **on the way** or **along the way**, it happens during the course of a particular event or process. □ *You may have to learn a few new skills along the way.*

on one's way or **well on one's way** If you are **on** your **way** or **well on** your **way** to something, you have made so much progress that you are almost certain to achieve that thing. □ *I am now out of the hospital and well on the way to recovery.*

on the way or **on its way** If something is **on the way** or **on its way**, it will arrive soon. □ *The forecasters say more snow is on the way.*

one way or another or **one way or the other** **1** (*vagueness*) You can use **one way or another** or **one way or the other** when you want to say that something definitely happens, but without giving any details about how it happens. □ *You know pretty well everyone here, one way or the other.* **2** You use **one way or the other** or **one way or another** to refer to two possible decisions or conclusions that have previously been mentioned, without stating which one is reached or preferred. □ *We've got to make our decision one way or the other.*

the other way around You use **the other way around** to refer to the opposite of what you have just said. □ *You'd think you were the one who did me the favour, and not the other way around.*

on the way out If something or someone is **on the way out** or **on their way out**, they are likely to disappear or to be replaced very soon. □ *There are encouraging signs that cold war attitudes are on the way out.*

go out of one's way If you **go out of** your **way** to do something, for example, to help someone, you make a special effort to do it. □ *He was very kind to me and seemed to go out of his way to help me.*

keep out of someone's way or **stay out of someone's way** If you **keep out of** someone's **way** or **stay out of** their **way**, you avoid them or do not get involved with them. □ *I'd kept out of his way as much as I could.*

be out of the way When something is **out of the way**, it has finished or you have dealt with it, so that it is no longer a problem or needs no more time spent on it. □ *The plan has to remain confidential at least until the local elections are out of the way.*

go one's own way If you **go** your **own way**, you do what you want rather than what everyone else does or expects. □ *In school I was a loner. I went my own way.*

in the same way You use **in the same way** to introduce a situation that you are comparing with one that you have just mentioned, because there is a strong similarity between them. [= likewise] □ *There is no reason why an aircraft designer should also be a good pilot. In the same way, a good pilot can be a bad driver.*

that way or **this way** **1** You can use **that way** and **this way** to refer to a statement or comment that you have just made. □ *We have a beautiful city and we pray it stays that way.* **2** You can use **that way** or **this way** to refer to an action or situation that you have just mentioned, when you go on to mention the likely consequence or effect of it. □ *Keep the soil moist. That way, the seedling will flourish.* [ADV] [way + ADV/PREP] (*emphasis*) You can use **way** to emphasize, for example, that something is a great distance away or is very much below or above a particular level or amount. □ *Way down in the valley to the west is the town of Freiburg.* □ *You've waited way too long.* [COMB] [way + N] You use **way** with a number to indicate how many parts or quantities something is divided into. □ *a simple three-way division*
→ See also **underway**

⊙ **way of life** NOUN [C] (**ways of life**) **1** A **way of life** is the behaviour and habits that are typical of a particular person or group, or that are chosen by them. [= lifestyle] □ *Mining activities have totally disrupted the traditional way of life of the Yanomami Indians.* □ *Fighting among the boys was taken as a way of life.* **2** If you describe a particular activity as **a way of life** for someone, you mean that it has become a very important and regular thing in their life, rather than something they do or experience occasionally. □ *She likes travelling so much it's become a way of life for her.*

way·ward /ˈweɪwəd/ ADJ If you describe a person or their behaviour as **wayward**, you mean that they behave in a selfish, bad, or unpredictable way, and are difficult to control. □ *wayward children with a history of severe emotional problems*

we ♦♦♦ /wɪ, STRONG wiː/ PRON

> **We** is the first person plural pronoun. **We** is used as the subject of a verb.

1 A speaker or writer uses **we** to refer both to himself or herself and to one or more other people as a group. You can use **we** before a noun to make it clear which group of people you are referring to. □ *We both swore we'd be friends ever after.* □ *We ordered another bottle of champagne.* **2** **We** is sometimes used to refer to people in general. □ *We need to take care of our bodies.* **3** (*formal*) A speaker or writer may use **we** instead of 'I' in order to include the audience or reader in what they are saying, especially when discussing how a talk or book is organized. □ *We will now consider the raw materials from which the body derives energy.*

weak ♦♦◊ /wiːk/ ADJ, NOUN
[ADJ] (**weaker, weakest**) **1** If someone is **weak**, they are not healthy or do not have good muscles, so that they cannot move quickly or carry heavy things. □ *I was too weak to move or think or speak.* **2** If someone has an organ or sense that is **weak**, it is not very effective or powerful, or is likely to fail. □ *She tired easily and had a weak heart.* **3** If you describe someone as **weak**, you mean that they are not very confident or determined, so that they are often frightened or worried, or easily influenced by other people. □ *He was a nice doctor, but a weak man who wasn't going to stick his neck out.* **4** If you describe someone's voice or smile as **weak**, you mean that it is not very loud or big, suggesting that the person lacks confidence, enthusiasm, or physical strength. [= feeble] □ *His weak voice was almost inaudible.* **5** If an object or surface is **weak**, it breaks easily and cannot support a lot of weight or resist

a lot of strain. ◻ *The owner said the bird may have escaped through a weak spot in the aviary.* **6** If individuals or groups are **weak**, they do not have any power or influence. = powerless ◻ *The council was too weak to do anything about it.* **7** A **weak** government or leader does not have much control, and is not prepared or able to act firmly or severely. ◻ *The changes come after mounting criticism that the government is weak and indecisive.* **8** If you describe something such as a country's currency, economy, industry, or government as **weak**, you mean that it is not successful, and may be likely to fail or collapse. ◻ *The weak dollar means American goods are relative bargains for foreigners.* **9** If something such as an argument or case is **weak**, it is not convincing or there is little evidence to support it. ◻ *Do you think the prosecution made any particular errors, or did they just have a weak case?* **10** A **weak** drink, chemical, or drug contains very little of a particular substance, for example, because a lot of water has been added to it. ◻ *Grace poured a cup of weak tea.* **11** Your **weak** points are the qualities or talents you do not possess, or the things you are not very good at. ◻ *Geography was my weak subject.* **12** A **weak** physical force does not have much power or intensity. ◻ *The molecules in regular liquids are held together by relatively weak bonds.* ◻ *Strong winds can turn boats when the tide is weak.*

NOUN [PL] The **weak** are people who are weak. ◻ *He voiced his solidarity with the weak and defenceless.*

weak·ly /ˈwiːkli/ ADV **1** [weakly after V] ◻ *'I'm all right,' Max said weakly, but his breathing came in jagged gasps.* **2** *He smiled weakly at reporters.* **3** *the weakly-led movement for reform* **4** [weakly after V] ◻ *Bush listened to that statement and responded rather weakly.* **5** *The mineral is weakly magnetic.*

weak·en ♦◇◇ /ˈwiːkən/ VERB [I, T] (**weakens, weakening, weakened**) **1** [I, T] If you **weaken** something or if it **weakens**, it becomes less strong or less powerful. ◻ *The recession has weakened so many businesses that many can no longer survive.* ◻ *Family structures are weakening and breaking up.* **2** [I, T] If your resolve **weakens** or if something **weakens** it, you become less determined or less certain about taking a particular course of action that you had previously decided to take. ◻ *I looked at the list and felt my resolve weakening.* ◻ *Jennie weakened, and finally relented.* **3** [T] If something **weakens** you, it causes you to lose some of your physical strength. ◻ *Malnutrition obviously weakens the patient.* **4** [T] If something **weakens** an object, it does something to it that causes it to become less firm and more likely to break. ◻ *A bomb blast had weakened an area of brick on the back wall.*

weak·ness /ˈwiːknəs/ NOUN [U, C] (**weaknesses**) **1** [U] **Weakness** is the state of not being healthy or not having good muscles, so that you cannot move quickly or carry heavy things. ◻ *Symptoms of anaemia include weakness, fatigue, and iron deficiency.* **2** [U] **Weakness** is a state of not having any power or influence. ◻ *It made me feel patronized, in a position of weakness.* **3** [U] **Weakness** is a lack of confidence or determination, so that you are often frightened or worried, or easily influenced by other people. ◻ *Many people felt that admitting to stress was a sign of weakness.* **4** [U] If you talk about the **weakness** of a government or leader, you are referring to the fact that they do not have much control and are not prepared or able to act firmly or severely. ◻ *The weakness of his regime is showing more and more.* **5** [C, U] If you talk about the **weakness** of something such as an argument or case, you are referring to the fact that it is not convincing or there is little evidence to support it. ◻ *Critical thinking requires that you examine the weaknesses of any argument.* **6** [C, U] A **weakness** is a quality or talent you do not possess, or something you are not very good at. ◻ *His only weakness is his temperament.* **7** [C] If you have a **weakness for** something, you like it very much, although this is perhaps surprising or undesirable. ◻ *Stephen himself had a weakness for cats.*

wealth ♦◇◇ /welθ/ NOUN [U, SING] **1** [U] **Wealth** is the possession of a large amount of money, property, or other valuable things. You can also refer to a particular person's

money or property as their **wealth**. = affluence; ≠ poverty ◻ *Economic reform has brought relative wealth to peasant farmers.* ◻ *His own wealth grew.* **2** [SING] ['a' wealth 'of' N] (formal, emphasis) If you say that someone or something has **a wealth of** good qualities or things, you are emphasizing that they have a very large number or amount of them. = abundance ◻ *Their websites contain a wealth of information on the topic.* ◻ *The city boasts a wealth of beautiful churches.*

wealthy /ˈwelθi/ ADJ, NOUN

ADJ (**wealthier, wealthiest**) Someone who is **wealthy** has a large amount of money, property, or valuable possessions. = affluent, rich, well-off; ≠ poor ◻ *a wealthy international businessman*

NOUN [PL] The **wealthy** are people who are wealthy. ◻ *The best education should not be available only to the wealthy.*

weap·on ♦◇◇ /ˈwepən/ NOUN [C] (**weapons**) A **weapon** is an object such as a gun, a knife, or a missile, which is used to kill or hurt people in a fight or a war. ◻ *nuclear weapons*

wear ♦◇◇ /weə/ VERB, NOUN

VERB [T, I] (**wears, wearing, wore, worn**) **1** [T] When you **wear** something such as clothes, shoes, or jewellery, you have them on your body or on part of your body. ◻ *He was wearing a brown uniform.* ◻ *I sometimes wear contact lenses.* **2** [T] If you **wear** your hair or beard in a particular way, you have it cut or styled in that way. ◻ *She wore her hair in a long plait.* **3** [I] If something **wears**, it becomes thinner or weaker because it is constantly being used over a long period of time. ◻ *The stone steps, dating back to 1855, are beginning to wear.* **4** [I] You can use **wear** to talk about how well something lasts over a period of time. For example, if something **wears well**, it still seems quite new or useful after a long time or a lot of use. ◻ *Ten years on, the original concept was wearing well.*

PHRASAL VERBS **wear away** If you **wear** something **away** or if it **wears away**, it becomes thin and eventually disappears because it is used a lot or rubbed a lot. ◻ *It had a saddle with springs sticking out, which wore away the seat of my trousers.* **wear down 1** If you **wear** something **down** or if it **wears down**, it becomes flatter or smoother as a result of constantly rubbing against something else. ◻ *Pipe smokers sometimes wear down the tips of their teeth where they grip their pipes.* ◻ *The heels on his shoes had worn down.* **2** If you **wear** someone **down**, you make them gradually weaker or less determined until they eventually do what you want. ◻ *None can match your sheer will-power and persistence in wearing down the opposition.* ◻ *They hoped the waiting and the uncertainty would wear down my resistance.* **wear off** If a drug, sensation, or feeling **wears off**, it disappears slowly until it no longer exists or has any effect. ◻ *For many the philosophy was merely a fashion, and the novelty soon wore off.* **wear out 1** When something **wears out** or when you **wear** it **out**, it is used so much that it becomes thin or weak and unable to be used anymore. ◻ *Every time she consulted her watch, she wondered if the batteries were wearing out.* ◻ *Horses used for long-distance riding tend to wear their shoes out more quickly.* **2** (informal) If something **wears you out**, it makes you feel extremely tired. ◻ *The past few days had really worn him out.* ◻ *The young people run around kicking a ball, wearing themselves out.* **3** → See also **worn out**

NOUN [U] **1** You use **wear** to refer to clothes that are suitable for a certain time or place. For example, **evening wear** is clothes suitable for the evening. ◻ *The shop stocks an extensive range of beach wear.* **2** **Wear** is the amount or type of use that something has over a period of time. = use ◻ *You'll get more wear out of a hat if you choose one in a neutral colour.* **3** **Wear** is the damage or change that is caused by something being used a lot or for a long time. ◻ *a large, well-upholstered armchair which showed signs of wear*

wea·ry /ˈwɪəri/ ADJ (**wearier, weariest**) **1** If you are **weary**, you are very tired. = exhausted ◻ *Rachel looked pale and weary.* **2** [V-LINK + weary 'of' N/-ING] If you are **weary of** something, you have become tired of it and have lost your enthusiasm for it. = tired ◻ *They're getting awfully weary of this silly war.*

W

weath·er ♦♦◇ /ˈweðə/ NOUN, VERB

NOUN [U] The **weather** is the condition of the atmosphere in one area at a particular time, for example, if it is raining, hot, or windy. ❑ *The weather was bad.* ❑ *I like cold weather.*

PHRASE **under the weather** If you say that you are **under the weather**, you mean that you feel slightly ill. = unwell ❑ *I was still feeling a bit under the weather.*

VERB [I, T] (**weathers, weathering, weathered**) **1** [I, T] If something such as wood or rock **weathers** or **is weathered**, it changes colour or shape as a result of the wind, sun, rain, or cold. ❑ *Unpainted wooden furniture weathers to a grey colour.* **2** [T] If you **weather** a difficult time or a difficult situation, you survive it and are able to continue normally after it has passed or ended. ❑ *The company has weathered the recession.*

weave /wiːv/ VERB [I, T] (**weaves, weaving, wove, woven**) NOUN [U]

> The form **weaved** is used for the past tense and past participle for meaning 3.

1 [I, T] If you **weave** cloth or a carpet, you make it by crossing threads over and under each other using a frame or machine called a loom. ❑ *They would spin and weave cloth, cook, and attend to the domestic side of life.* ❑ *She sat at her loom and continued to weave.* **2** [T] If you **weave** something such as a basket, you make it by crossing long plant stems or fibres over and under each other. ❑ *Jenny weaves baskets from willow she grows herself.* **3** [I, T] If you **weave** your way somewhere, you move between and around things as you go there. ❑ *The cars then weaved in and out of traffic at top speed.* ❑ *He weaved around the tables to where she sat with Bob.*

weav·ing /ˈwiːvɪŋ/ ❑ *When I studied weaving, I became intrigued with natural dyes.*

web ♦♦♦ /web/ NOUN [SING, C] (**webs**) **1** [SING] [oft web + N] (*computing*) **The Web** is a computer system that links documents and pictures into a database that is stored in computers in many different parts of the world and that people everywhere can use. It is also referred to as the **World Wide Web**. ❑ *The handbook is available on the Web.* ❑ *She recommended the service on her Web journal after trying it out.* **2** [C] A **web** is a complicated pattern of connections or relationships, sometimes considered as an obstacle or a danger. ❑ *He's forced to untangle a complex web of financial dealings.* **3** [C] A **web** is the thin net made by a spider from a sticky substance that it produces in its body. = cobweb ❑ *the spider's web in the window*

web·site ♦♦◇ /ˈwebsaɪt/ also **Web site, web site** NOUN [C] (**websites**) (*computing*) A **website** is a set of data and information about a particular subject that is available on the Internet. ❑ *a website devoted to hip-hop music*

wed /wed/ VERB [RECIP] (**weds, wed, wed** or **wedded**) (*old-fashioned, journalism*) If one person **weds** another or if two people **wed** or **are wed**, they get married. = marry ❑ *In 1952 she wed film director Roger Vadim.*

wed·ding ♦◇◇ /ˈwedɪŋ/ NOUN [C] (**weddings**) A **wedding** is a marriage ceremony and the party or special meal that often takes place after the ceremony. ❑ *Most couples want a traditional wedding.* ❑ *the couple's 22nd wedding anniversary*

wedge /wedʒ/ VERB, NOUN

VERB [T] (**wedges, wedging, wedged**) **1** If you **wedge** something, you force it to remain in a particular position by holding it there tightly or by sticking something next to it to prevent it from moving. ❑ *I shut the shed door and wedged it with a log of wood.* **2** If you **wedge** something somewhere, you fit it there tightly. ❑ *Wedge the plug into the hole.*

NOUN [C] (**wedges**) A **wedge** of something such as fruit or cheese is a piece of it that has a thick, triangular shape. ❑ *Serve with a wedge of lime.*

weed /wiːd/ NOUN, VERB

NOUN [C] (**weeds**) A **weed** is a wild plant that grows in gardens or fields of crops and prevents the plants that you want from growing properly. ❑ *With repeated applications of weedkiller, the weeds were overcome.*

VERB [I, T] (**weeds, weeding, weeded**) If you **weed** an area, you remove the weeds from it. ❑ *Caspar was weeding the garden.* ❑ *Try not to walk on the flowerbeds while weeding.*

PHRASAL VERB **weed out** If you **weed out** things or people that are useless or unwanted in a group, you find them and get rid of them. = root out ❑ *He is eager to weed out the many applicants he believes may be frauds.*

week ♦♦♦ /wiːk/ NOUN [C, SING] (**weeks**) **1** [C] A **week** is a period of seven days. Some people consider that a week starts on Monday and ends on Sunday. ❑ *I had a letter from my mother last week.* ❑ *This has been on my mind all week.* **2** [C] A **week** is a period of about seven days. ❑ *Her mother stayed for another two weeks.* ❑ *Only 12 weeks ago he underwent major heart transplant surgery.* **3** [C] Your working **week** is the hours that you spend at work during a week. ❑ *It is not unusual for women to work a 40-hour week.* **4** [SING] **The week** is the part of the week that does not include Saturday and Sunday. ❑ *the hard work of looking after the children during the week* **5** [C] You use **week** in expressions such as 'a week last Monday', 'a week ago this Tuesday', and 'a week ago yesterday' to mean exactly one week before the day that you mention. ❑ *'That's the time you weren't well, wasn't it?'—'Yes, that's right, that was a week ago last Monday.'*

week·day /ˈwiːkdeɪ/ NOUN [C] (**weekdays**) A **weekday** is any of the days of the week except Saturday and Sunday. ❑ *If you want to avoid the crowds, it's best to come on a weekday.*

week·end ♦♦◇ /ˌwiːkˈend/ NOUN [C] (**weekends**) A **weekend** is Saturday and Sunday. ❑ *She had agreed to have dinner with him in town the following weekend.*

week·ly ♦◇◇ /ˈwiːkli/ ADJ, ADV, NOUN

ADJ **1** [weekly + N] A **weekly** event or publication happens or appears once a week or every week. ❑ *Each course comprises 10–12 informal weekly meetings.* ❑ *We go and do the weekly shopping every Thursday.* **2** [weekly + N] **Weekly** quantities or rates relate to a period of one week. ❑ *Of course, in addition to my weekly pay, I got a lot of tips.*

ADV [weekly after V] If something happens or appears **weekly**, it happens or appears once a week or every week. ❑ *The group meets weekly.*

NOUN [C] (**weeklies**) A **weekly** is a newspaper or magazine that is published once a week. ❑ *Two of the four national daily papers are to become weeklies.*

weep /wiːp/ VERB [I, T] (**weeps, weeping, wept**) (*literary*) If someone **weeps**, they cry. ❑ *She wanted to laugh and weep all at once.* ❑ *The weeping family hugged and comforted each other.* ❑ *She wept tears of joy.*

✪ **weigh** ♦◇◇ /weɪ/ VERB

VERB [T] (**weighs, weighing, weighed**) **1** If someone or something **weighs** a particular amount, this amount is how heavy they are. ❑ *It weighs nearly 27 kilos (about 65 pounds).* ❑ *This little ball of gold weighs a quarter of an ounce.* **2** If you **weigh** something or someone, you measure how heavy they are. = measure ❑ *The scales can be used to weigh other items such as parcels.* ❑ *Each sample was accurately weighed.* **3** If you **weigh** the facts about a situation, you consider them very carefully before you make a decision, especially by comparing the various facts involved. = consider ❑ *She weighed her options.* ❑ *He is weighing the possibility of filing criminal charges against the doctor.*

PHRASAL VERB **weigh down** If something that you are wearing or carrying **weighs** you **down**, it stops you moving easily by making you heavier. ❑ *He wrenched off his sneakers. If he had to swim, he didn't want anything weighing him down.*

✪ **weight** ♦♦◇ /weɪt/ NOUN, VERB

NOUN [C, U, SING] (**weights**) **1** [C, U] The **weight** of a person or thing is how heavy they are, measured in units such as kilograms, pounds, or tons. ❑ *What is your height and weight?* ❑ *This reduced the weight of the load.* ❑ *Turkeys can reach enormous weights of up to 50 pounds.* **2** [U] A person's or thing's **weight** is the fact that they are very heavy. ❑ *His weight was harming his health.* **3** [SING] If you move your **weight**, you change position so that most of the pressure of your body is on a particular part of your body. ❑ *He shifted his weight from one foot to the other.* **4** [C] **Weights**

W

are objects that weigh a known amount and that people lift as a form of exercise. ❑ *I was in the gym lifting weights.* **5** [c] **Weights** are metal objects that weigh a known amount and that are used on a set of scales to weigh other things. **6** [c] You can refer to a heavy object as a **weight**, especially when you have to lift it. ❑ *Straining to lift heavy weights can lead to a rise in blood pressure.* **7** [c, u] If something is given a particular **weight**, it is given a particular value according to how important or significant it is. = **weighting** ❑ *The scientists involved put different weight on the conclusions of different models.* **8** [u] If someone or something gives **weight** to what a person says, thinks, or does, they emphasize its significance. ❑ *The fact that he is gone has given more weight to fears that he may try to launch a civil war.* **9** [u] If you give something or someone **weight**, you consider them to be very important or influential in a particular situation. ❑ *Consumers generally place more weight on negative information than on the positive when deciding what to buy.*

PHRASES **lose weight** or **gain weight** or **put on weight** If someone **loses weight**, they become lighter. If they **gain weight** or **put on weight**, they become heavier. ❑ *I'm lucky really as I never put on weight.* ❑ *The boy appeared anxious, had lost weight and was not sleeping well.*

carry weight If a person or their opinion **carries weight**, they are respected and are able to influence people. ❑ *Senator Kerry carries considerable weight in Washington.*

worth your weight in gold *(emphasis)* If you say that someone or something is **worth their weight in gold**, you are emphasizing that they are so useful, helpful, or valuable that you feel you could not manage without them. ❑ *Any successful manager is worth his weight in gold.*

pull your weight If you **pull** your **weight**, you work as hard as everyone else who is involved in the same task or activity. ❑ *He accused the team of not pulling their weight.*

VERB [T] (**weights**, **weighting**, **weighted**) If you **weight** something, you make it heavier by adding something to it, for example, in order to stop it from moving easily. ❑ *It can be sewn into curtain hems to weight the curtain and so allow it to hang better.*

→ See also **weighting**
✦ **a weight off your mind** → see **mind**

weight·ing /ˈweɪtɪŋ/ NOUN [c] (**weightings**) A **weighting** is a value given to something according to how important or significant it is. ❑ *an index formed of equal weightings of three statistics*

weird /wɪəd/ ADJ (**weirder**, **weirdest**) *(informal)* If you describe something or someone as **weird**, you mean that they are strange. ❑ *That first day was weird.* ❑ *Drugs can make you do all kinds of weird things.*

wel·come ♦♦◇ /ˈwelkəm/ VERB, NOUN, CONVENTION, ADJ
VERB [T] (**welcomes**, **welcoming**, **welcomed**) **1** If you **welcome** someone, you greet them in a friendly way when they arrive somewhere. ❑ *Several people came by to welcome me.* ❑ *She was there to welcome him home from war.* ❑ *a welcoming speech* **2** If you **welcome** an action, decision, or situation, you approve of it and are pleased that it has occurred. ❑ *She welcomed this move but said that overall the changes didn't go far enough.* **3** If you say that you **welcome** certain people or actions, you are inviting and encouraging people to do something, for example, to come to a particular place. ❑ *We would welcome your views about the survey.*

NOUN [c] (**welcomes**) **1** A **welcome** is the act of greeting someone when they arrive somewhere. ❑ *There would be a fantastic welcome awaiting him back here.* **2** The **welcome** an action, decision, or situation is given is the way people react to it. ❑ *Environmental groups have given a guarded welcome to the prime minister's proposal.*

CONVENTION *(formulae)* **1** You use **welcome** in expressions such as **welcome home**, **welcome to Boston**, and **welcome back** when you are greeting someone who has just arrived somewhere. ❑ *Welcome to Washington.* **2** You say '**You're welcome**' to someone who has thanked you for something in order to acknowledge their thanks in a polite way. ❑ *'Thank you for the information.'—'You're welcome.'*

ADJ **1** If you describe something as **welcome**, you mean

that people wanted it and are happy that it has occurred. ❑ *Any progress in reducing chemical weapons is welcome.* **2** If you say that someone is **welcome** in a particular place, you are encouraging them to go there by telling them that they will be liked and accepted. ❑ *New members are always welcome.* **3** [V-LINK + welcome] If you tell someone that they are **welcome** to do something, you are encouraging them to do it by telling them that they are allowed to do it. ❑ *You are welcome to visit the hospital at any time.* **4** [V-LINK + welcome 'to' N] If you say that someone is **welcome to** something, you mean that you do not want it yourself because you do not like it and you are very willing for them to have it. ❑ *If women want to take on the business world they are welcome to it as far as I'm concerned.*

PHRASE **make someone welcome** If you **make** someone **welcome** or **make** them **feel welcome**, you make them feel happy and accepted in a new place. ❑ *Here are six Mexican hotels where children are made to feel welcome.*

✪ **wel·fare** ♦◇◇ /ˈwelfeə/ NOUN, ADJ *(academic word)*
NOUN [u] The **welfare** of a person or group is their health, comfort, and happiness. = **well-being** ❑ *I do not think he is considering Emma's welfare.* ❑ *For reasons of animal welfare, farmers can no longer keep pigs confined in stalls.* ❑ *He was the head of a charity for the welfare of children.*

ADJ **Welfare** services are provided to help with people's living conditions and financial problems. = **social** ❑ *Child welfare services are well established and comprehensive.* ❑ *He has urged complete reform of the welfare system.*

well ♦♦♦ /wel/ ADV, EXCLAM, CONVENTION, COMB, ADJ, NOUN, VERB
ADV (**better**, **best**) **1** [well + CL] You say **well** to indicate that you are about to say something. ❑ *Well, it's a pleasure to meet you.* **2** [well + CL] You say **well** just before or after you pause, especially to give yourself time to think about what you are going to say. ❑ *Look, I'm really sorry I woke you, and, well, I just wanted to tell you I was all right.* **3** [well + CL/GROUP] You say **well** when you are correcting something that you have just said. ❑ *The comet is going to come back in 2061 and we are all going to be able to see it. Well, our offspring are, anyway.* **4** [well + CL] You say **well** to express your doubt about something that someone has said. ❑ *'But finance is far more serious.'—'Well I don't know really.'* **5** [well after V] If you do something **well**, you do it to a high standard or to a great extent. ❑ *It's important that we play well at home.* ❑ *He speaks English better than I do.* **6** [well after V] If you do something **well**, you do it thoroughly and completely. = **thoroughly** ❑ *Mix all the ingredients well.* **7** [well after V] If you speak or think **well** of someone, you say or think favourable things about them. ❑ *'He speaks well of you.'—'I'm glad to hear that.'* **8** You use **well** to ask or talk about the extent or standard of something. ❑ *How well do you remember your mother, Franzi?* ❑ *He wasn't dressed any better than me.* **9** [well + PREP] You use **well** in front of a prepositional phrase to emphasize it. For example, if you say that one thing happened **well before** another, you mean that it happened a long time before it. ❑ *Franklin did not turn up until well after midnight.* ❑ *a war in which well over a million people died* **10** [well + ADJ] You use **well** before certain adjectives to emphasize them. ❑ *She has a close group of friends who are very well aware of what she has suffered.* **11** You use **well** after adverbs such as 'perfectly', 'jolly', or 'damn' in order to emphasize an opinion or the truth of what you are saying. ❑ *You know perfectly well I can't be blamed for the failure of that mission.* **12** [MODAL + well] You use **well** after verbs such as 'may' and 'could' when you are saying what you think is likely to happen. ❑ *Ours could well be the last generation for which filmgoing has a sense of magic.*

PHRASES **as well** You use **as well** when mentioning something that happens in the same way as something else already mentioned, or that should be considered at the same time as that thing. = **too** ❑ *It is most often diagnosed in women in their thirties and forties, although I've seen it in many younger women, as well.*

as well as You use **as well as** when you want to mention another item connected with the subject you are discussing. ❑ *The film will appeal to adults as well as children.*

be just as well If you say that something that has happened **is just as well**, you mean that it is fortunate that

W

it happened in the way it did. ◻ *Blue asbestos is far less common in buildings, which is just as well because it's more dangerous than white asbestos.*

might as well or **may as well** ◼ If you say that something, usually something bad, **might as well** be true or **may as well** be true, you mean that the situation is the same or almost the same as if it were true. ◻ *The couple might as well have been strangers.* ◼ If you say that you **might as well** do something, or that you **may as well** do it, you mean that you will do it although you do not have a strong desire to do it and may even feel slightly unwilling to do it. ◻ *If I've got to go somewhere I may as well go to Tulsa.* ◻ *Anyway, you're here; you might as well stay.*

well and truly (*mainly BrE, emphasis*) If you say that something is **well and truly** finished, gone, or done, you are emphasizing that it is completely finished or gone, or thoroughly done. ◻ *The war is well and truly over.*

EXCLAM (*feelings*) You say **well** to express your surprise or anger at something that someone has just said or done. ◻ *She beamed at Patty. 'Well! That was a bit of unexpected excitement.'*

CONVENTION (*feelings*) ◼ You say **well** to indicate that you are waiting for someone to say something and often to express your irritation with them. = **so** ◻ *'Well?' asked Barry, 'What does it tell us?'* ◻ *'Well, why don't you ask me?' he said finally.* ◼ You use **well** to indicate that you are amused by something you have heard or seen, and often to introduce a comment on it. ◻ *Well, well, well. How quickly things change.* ◼ You say **oh well** to indicate that you accept a situation or that someone else should accept it, even though you or they are not very happy about it, because it is not too bad and cannot be changed. ◻ *Oh well, it could be worse.* ◻ *'I called her and she said no.'—'Oh well.'*

COMB **Well** is used in front of past participles to indicate that something is done to a high standard or to a great extent. ◻ *Helen is a very well-known novelist in Australia.* ◻ *People live longer nowadays, and they are better educated.*

ADJ (**better, best**) If you are **well**, you are healthy and not ill. ◻ *I'm not very well today, I can't come in.*

NOUN [c] (**wells**) ◼ A **well** is a hole in the ground from which a supply of water is extracted. ◻ *I had to fetch water from the well.* ◼ A **well** is an oil well. ◻ *About 650 wells are on fire.*

VERB [i] (**wells, welling, welled**) If liquids **well**, they come to the surface and form a pool. ◻ *Tears welled in her eyes.*

PHRASAL VERB **well up** Well up means the same as **well** VERB. ◻ *Tears welled up in Anni's eyes.*

✦ **very well** → see **very**; **all very well** → see **all**; **know full well** → see **full**

well-balanced ADJ ◼ If you describe someone as **well-balanced**, you mean that they are sensible and do not have many emotional problems. = **stable** ◻ *a fun-loving, well-balanced individual* ◼ If you describe something that is made up of several parts as **well-balanced**, you mean that the way that the different parts are put together is good, because there is not too much or too little of any one part. ◻ *a well-balanced diet*

well-being NOUN [U] Someone's **well-being** is their health and happiness. ◻ *Singing can create a sense of well-being.*

well-established ADJ If you say that something is **well-established**, you mean that it has been in existence for a long time and is successful. ◻ *The university has a well-established tradition of welcoming postgraduate students from overseas.*

well-informed ADJ (**better-informed**) If you say that someone is **well-informed**, you mean that they know a lot about many different subjects or about one particular subject. ◻ *a lending library to encourage members to become as well-informed as possible*

well-known ♦◇◇ ADJ ◼ A **well-known** person or thing is known about by a lot of people and is therefore famous or familiar. If someone is **well-known** for a particular activity, a lot of people know about them because of their involvement with that activity. ◻ *Hubbard was well known for his work in the field of drug rehabilitation.* ◼ A **well-known**

fact is a fact that is known by people in general. ◻ *It is well-known that bamboo shoots are a panda's staple diet.*

went /went/ IRREG FORM **Went** is the past tense of **go**.

wept /wept/ IRREG FORM **Wept** is the past tense and past participle of **weep**.

we're /wɪə/ SHORT FORM **We're** is the usual spoken form of 'we are'. ◻ *I'm married, but we're separated.*

were /wə, STRONG wɜː/ IRREG FORM ◼ **Were** is the plural and the second person singular of the past tense of **be**. **be** ◼ (*formal*) **Were** is sometimes used instead of 'was' in certain structures, for example, in conditional clauses or after the verb 'wish'. ◻ *He told a diplomat that he might withdraw if he were allowed to keep part of a disputed oil field.*

✦ **as it were** → see **as**

◆ **west** ♦♦♦ /west/ also **West** NOUN, ADV, ADJ

NOUN [U, SING] ◼ [U] [also 'the' west] The **west** is the direction you look towards in the evening in order to see the sun set. ◻ *I pushed on towards Flagstaff, a hundred miles to the west.* ◻ *The sun crosses the sky from east to west.* ◼ [SING] The **west** of a place, country, or region is the part of it which is in the west. ◻ *Many of the buildings in the west of the city are on fire.* ◻ *physicists working at Bristol University in the west of England* ◼ [SING] The **West** is used to refer to the United States, Canada, and the countries of Western, Northern, and Southern Europe. ◻ *relations between Iran and the West* ◻ *the leaders of the industrialized West*

ADV ◼ [west after v] If you go **west**, you travel towards the west. ◻ *We are going west to California.* ◼ Something that is **west of** a place is positioned to the west of it. ◻ *Penryn is about 60 miles west of Philadelphia.*

ADJ ◼ [west + N] The **west** part of a place, country, or region is the part which is towards the west. ◻ *a small island off the west coast of South Korea* ◼ [west + N] **West** is used in the names of some countries, states, and regions in the west of a larger area. ◻ *Mark has been working in West Africa for about six months.* ◻ *his West Hollywood home* ◼ [west + N] A **west** wind blows from the west. ◻ *the warm west wind*

◆ **west·ern** ♦♦◇ /ˈwestən/ also **Western** ADJ, NOUN

ADJ ◼ [western + N] **Western** means in or from the west of a region, state, or country. ◻ *hand-made rugs from Western and Central Asia* ◻ *Moi University, in western Kenya* ◼ **Western** is used to describe things, people, ideas, or ways of life that come from or are associated with the United States, Canada, and the countries of Western, Northern, and Southern Europe. ◻ *Mexico had the support of the big western governments.* ◻ *Those statements have never been reported in the Western media.*

NOUN [c] (**westerns**) A **western** is a book or film about life in the western United States and territories in the nineteenth century, especially the lives of cowboys. ◻ *John Agar starred in westerns, war films and low-budget science fiction pictures.*

◆ **west·erni·za·tion** /ˌwestənaɪˈzeɪʃən/ also **westernisation** NOUN [U] The **westernization** of a country, place, or person is the process of them adopting ideas and behaviour that are typical of Europe and North America, rather than preserving the ideas and behaviour traditional in their culture. = **modernization** ◻ *fundamentalists unhappy with the westernization of Afghan culture* ◻ *The explosive growth in casinos is one of the most conspicuous signs of Westernisation.*

◆ **west·ern·ized** /ˈwestənaɪzd/ also **westernised** ADJ A **westernized** country, place, or person has adopted ideas and behaviour typical of Europe and North America, rather than preserving the ideas and behaviour that are traditional in their culture. = **modernized**; ≠ **traditional** ◻ *Rapid urbanization brings with it a more westernized and generally more sugary diet.* ◻ *Africans educated in Europe, and thoroughly Westernized in their thinking.* ◻ *But even in liberal, Westernized households, gender roles are strictly observed.*

west·ward /ˈwestwəd/ ADV, ADJ

The form **westwards** is also used for the adverb.

ADV **Westward** or **westwards** means towards the west. ◻ *He sailed westward from Palos de la Frontera.*

ADJ [westward + N] A **westward** direction or course is one that goes towards the west. ❑ *the one-hour westward flight over the Andes to Lima*

wet ◆◇◇ /wet/ ADJ, VERB, NOUN

ADJ (**wetter, wettest**) **1** If something is **wet**, it is covered in water, rain, sweat, tears, or another liquid. ❑ *He towelled his wet hair.* ❑ *I lowered myself to the water's edge, getting my feet wet.* **2** If the weather is **wet**, it is raining. = rainy ❑ *If the weather is wet or cold choose an indoor activity.* **3** If something such as paint, ink, or cement is **wet**, it is not yet dry or solid. ❑ *leaves dipped in wet paint then pressed on white paper*

VERB [T] (**wets, wetting, wet** or **wetted**) **1** To **wet** something means to get water or some other liquid over it. ❑ *When assembling the pie, wet the edges where the two crusts join.* **2** If people, especially children, **wet** their beds or clothes or **wet** themselves, they urinate in their beds or in their clothes because they cannot stop themselves. ❑ *A quarter of 4-year-olds frequently wet the bed.*

NOUN [SING] **The wet** is used to mean wet weather. ❑ *They had come in from the cold and the wet.*

whale /weɪl/ NOUN

NOUN [C] (**whales**) **Whales** are very large mammals that live in the sea.

PHRASE **have a whale of a time** (*informal*) If you say that someone **is having a whale of a time**, you mean that they are enjoying themselves very much. ❑ *I had a whale of a time in Fargo.*

what ◆◆◆ /wɒt/ QUEST, CONVENTION, CONJ, DET, PREDET, ADV

QUEST You use **what** in questions when you ask for specific information about something that you do not know. ❑ *What do you want?* ❑ *What did she tell you, anyway?* ❑ *'Has something happened?'—'It certainly has.'*

CONVENTION **1** (*spoken, formulae*) You say '**What?**' to tell someone who has indicated that they want to speak to you that you have heard them and are inviting them to continue. ❑ *'Dad?'—'What?'—'Can I have the car tonight?'* **2** (*spoken, formulae*) You say '**What?**' when you ask someone to repeat the thing that they have just said because you did not hear or understand it properly. 'What?' is more informal and less polite than expressions such as 'Pardon?' and 'Excuse me?' ❑ *'They could paint this place,' she said. 'What?' he asked.* **3** (*feelings*) You say '**What**' to express surprise. ❑ *'Adolphus Kelling, I arrest you on a charge of trafficking in narcotics.'—'What?'*

PHRASES **what about** **1** You use **what about** at the beginning of a question when you make a suggestion, offer, or request. ❑ *What about going out with me tomorrow?* **2** You say **what about** a particular person or thing when you ask someone to explain why they have asked you about that person or thing. ❑ *'This thing with the Corbett woman.'—'Oh, yeah. What about her?'*

what about or **what of** You use **what about** or **what of** when you introduce a new topic or a point that seems relevant to a previous remark. ❑ *Now you've talked about work on daffodils, what about other commercially important flowers, like roses?*

or what (*emphasis*) In conversation, you say **or what?** after a question as a way of stating an opinion forcefully and showing that you expect other people to agree. ❑ *Look at that moon. Is that beautiful or what?*

what if You say **what if** at the beginning of a question when you ask about the consequences of something happening, especially something undesirable. ❑ *What if this doesn't work out?*

tell you what You say '**Tell you what**' to introduce a suggestion or offer. ❑ *Tell you what, let's stay here another day.*

CONVENTIONS **guess what** or **do you know what** You say **guess what** or **do you know what** to introduce a piece of information that is surprising, that is not generally known, or that you want to emphasize. ❑ *Guess what? I'm going to dinner at Mrs Chang's tonight.*

so what or **what of it** You say **so what?** or **what of it?** to indicate that the previous remark seems unimportant, uninteresting, or irrelevant to you. = so ❑ *'What if there is no kerosene this winter?' said Al.—'So what?' she said. 'We still*

have electricity.' ❑ *'You're talking to yourself.'—'Well, what of it?'*

CONJ **1** You use **what** after certain words, especially verbs and adjectives, when you are referring to a situation that is unknown or has not been specified. ❑ *You can imagine what it would be like driving a car into a brick wall at 30 miles an hour.* ❑ *I want to know what happened to Norman.* **2** You use **what** at the beginning of a clause in structures where you are changing the order of the information to give special emphasis to something. ❑ *What precisely triggered off yesterday's riot is still unclear.* ❑ *What I wanted, more than anything, was a few days' rest.* **3** You use **what** in expressions such as **what is called** and **what amounts to** when you are giving a description of something. ❑ *She had been in what doctors described as an irreversible vegetative state for five years.* **4** You use **what** to indicate that you are talking about the whole of an amount that is available to you. ❑ *He drinks what is left in his glass as if it were water.*

DET **1** You use **what** in questions when you ask for specific information about something that you do not know. ❑ *What time is it?* ❑ *What crimes are the defendants being charged with?* ❑ *'The heater works.'—'What heater?'* **2** You use **what** after certain words, especially verbs and adjectives, when you are referring to a situation that is unknown or has not been specified. ❑ *I didn't know what college I wanted to go to.* ❑ *I didn't know what else to say.* **3** You use **what** to indicate that you are talking about the whole of an amount that is available to you. = whatever ❑ *They had used what money they had.* **4** You use **what** in exclamations to emphasize an opinion or reaction. ❑ *What pretty hair she has, nice and thick.*

PREDET (*emphasis*) You use **what** in exclamations to emphasize an opinion or reaction. ❑ *What a horrible thing to do.*

ADV [what + N] You use **what** to indicate that you are making a guess about something such as an amount or value. ❑ *It's, what, eleven years or more since he's seen her.*

✦ **what's more** → see **more**

what·ev·er ◆◆◇ /wɒt'evə/ CONJ, DET, ADV, QUEST, PRON

CONJ **1** You use **whatever** to refer to anything or everything of a particular type. ❑ *Franklin was free to do pretty much whatever he pleased.* ❑ *When you're older I think you're better equipped mentally to cope with whatever happens.* **2** You use **whatever** to say that something is the case in all circumstances. ❑ *We shall love you whatever happens, Diana.* ❑ *She runs on average about 15 miles a day every day, whatever the circumstances, whatever the weather.* **3** You use **whatever** when you are indicating that you do not know the precise identity, meaning, or value of the thing just mentioned. ❑ *I thought that my upbringing was 'normal', whatever that is.*

PHRASE **whatever someone does** (*emphasis*) You say **whatever** you **do** when giving advice or warning someone about something. ❑ *Whatever you do, don't ask for a pay increase.*

DET **Whatever** is used before a noun to refer to anything or everything of a particular type. = any ❑ *Whatever doubts he might have had about Ingrid were all over now.*

ADV [with BRD-NEG, N + whatever] (*emphasis*) You use **whatever** after a noun group in order to emphasize a negative statement. = whatsoever ❑ *There is no evidence whatever that competition in broadcasting has ever reduced costs.*

QUEST (*emphasis*) You use **whatever** to ask in an emphatic way about something which you are very surprised about. = what ❑ *Whatever can you mean?*

PRON

PHRASE **or whatever** (*informal*) You say **or whatever** to refer generally to something else of the same kind as the thing or things that you have just mentioned. ❑ *They're always protesting about something or saving the trees or whatever.*

what·so·ev·er /ˌwɒtsəʊ'evə/ ADV (*emphasis*) You use **whatsoever** after a noun group in order to emphasize a negative statement. ❑ *My school did nothing whatsoever in the way of athletics.*

wheat /wiːt/ NOUN [C, U] (**wheats**) **Wheat** is a cereal crop

W

grown for food. **Wheat** is also used to refer to the grain of this crop, which is usually ground into flour and used to make bread. ❑ *farmers growing wheat, corn, or other crops*

wheel ♦◇◇ /wiːl/ NOUN, VERB

NOUN [C, PL] (**wheels**) **1** [C] The **wheels** of a vehicle are the circular objects that are attached underneath it and that enable it to move along the ground. ❑ *The car wheels spun and slipped on some oil on the road.* **2** [C] A **wheel** is a circular object that forms a part of a machine, usually a moving part. ❑ *The wheels are usually fairly large.* **3** [C] The **wheel** of a car or other vehicle is the circular object that is used to steer it. The **wheel** is used in expressions to talk about who is driving a vehicle. For example, if someone is **at the wheel** or **behind the wheel** of a car, they are driving it. = steering wheel ❑ *My co-pilot suddenly grabbed the wheel.* ❑ *Curtis got behind the wheel and they started back towards the cottage.* **4** [PL] People talk about **the wheels of** an organization or system to mean the way in which it operates. ❑ *He knows the wheels of administration turn slowly.*

VERB [T] (**wheels, wheeling, wheeled**) If you **wheel** an object that has wheels somewhere, you push it along. ❑ *He wheeled his bike into the alley at the side of the house.*

→ See also **steering wheel**

wheel·chair /ˈwiːltʃeə/ NOUN [C] (**wheelchairs**) A **wheelchair** is a chair with wheels that you use in order to move around in if you cannot walk properly, for example, because you are disabled or sick.

when ♦♦♦ /wen/ QUEST, CONJ, PRON

QUEST You use **when** to ask questions about the time at which things happen. ❑ *When are you going home?* ❑ *When did you get married?*

CONJ **1** If something happens **when** something else is happening, the two things are happening at the same time. ❑ *When eating a whole cooked fish, you should never turn it over to get at the flesh on the other side.* **2** You use **when** to introduce a clause in which you mention something that happens at some point during an activity, event, or situation. ❑ *When I met the Gills, I had been gardening for nearly ten years.* **3** You use **when** to introduce a clause where you mention the circumstances under which the event in the main clause happened or will happen. ❑ *When he brought Imelda her drink she gave him a genuine, sweet smile of thanks.* **4** You use **when** after certain words, especially verbs and adjectives, to introduce a clause where you mention the time at which something happens. ❑ *I asked him when he'd be back to pick me up.* **5** You use **when** to introduce the reason for an opinion, comment, or question. ❑ *How can I love myself when I look like this?* **6** You use **when** in order to introduce a fact or comment which makes the other part of the sentence rather surprising or unlikely. = although ❑ *Our mothers sat us down to read and paint, when all we really wanted to do was to make a mess.*

PRON You use **when** to introduce a clause that specifies or refers to the time at which something happens. ❑ *He could remember a time when he had worked like that himself.*

when·ever ♦◇◇ /wenˈevə/ CONJ **1** You use **whenever** to refer to any time or every time that something happens or is true. ❑ *Whenever I talked to him, he seemed like a pretty regular guy.* ❑ *You can stay at my cottage in the country whenever you like.* **2** You use **whenever** to refer to a time that you do not know or are not sure about. ❑ *He married Miss Vancouver in 1963, or whenever it was.*

where ♦♦♦ /weə/ QUEST, CONJ, PRON

QUEST **1** You use **where** to ask questions about the place something is in, or is coming from or going to. ❑ *Where did you meet him?* ❑ *Where's Anna?* **2** You use **where** to ask questions about a situation, a stage in something, or an aspect of something. ❑ *If they get their way, where will it stop?*

CONJ **1** You use **where** after certain words, especially verbs and adjectives, to introduce a clause in which you mention the place in which something is situated or happens. ❑ *People began looking across to see where the noise was coming from.* ❑ *He knew where Henry Carter had gone.* **2** You use **where** after certain words, especially verbs and adjectives, to introduce a clause in which you mention a

situation, a stage in something, or an aspect of something. ❑ *It's not hard to see where she got her feelings about herself.* ❑ *She had a feeling she already knew where this conversation was going to lead.*

PRON **1** You use **where** at the beginning of a relative clause in which you mention the place in which something is situated or happens. ❑ *The area where the explosion occurred was closed off by police.* **2** You use **where** at the beginning of a relative clause in which you mention a situation, a stage in something, or an aspect of something. ❑ *The government is at a stage where it is willing to talk to almost anyone.*

where·abouts NOUN, QUEST

NOUN /ˈweərəbaʊts/ [SING] If you refer to the **whereabouts** of a particular person or thing, you mean the place where that person or thing may be found. ❑ *The police are anxious to hear from anyone who may know the whereabouts of the firearms.*

QUEST /ˌweərəˈbaʊts/ You use **whereabouts** in questions when you are asking precisely where something is. ❑ *'Whereabouts in France?'—'Normandy,' I said.* ❑ *Whereabouts are you living?*

✪**where·as** ♦◇◇ /weərˈæz/ CONJ (*academic word*) You use **whereas** to introduce a comment that contrasts with what is said in the main clause. = while ❑ *Benefits are linked to inflation, whereas they should be linked to the cost of living.* ❑ *Whereas the population of working age increased by 1 million between 1981 and 1986, today it is barely growing.*

✪**where·by** /weəˈbaɪ/ PRON (*academic word, formal*) A system or action **whereby** something happens is one that makes that thing happen. = by which ❑ *The company operates an arrangement whereby employees may select any 8-hour period between 6 am to 8 pm to go to work.* ❑ *the system whereby Britons choose their family doctors and the government pays those doctors* ❑ *a method of soil conservation whereby ploughing is undertaken along contours rather than with the slope*

where·upon /ˌweərəˈpɒn/ CONJ (*formal*) You use **whereupon** to say that one thing happens immediately after another thing, and usually as a result of it. ❑ *Mr Jones refused to talk to them except in the company of his legal colleagues, whereupon the police officers departed.*

wher·ever /weərˈevə/ CONJ, QUEST

CONJ **1** You use **wherever** to indicate that something happens or is true in any place or situation. ❑ *Some people enjoy themselves wherever they are.* **2** You use **wherever** when you indicate that you do not know where a person or place is. ❑ *I'd like to leave as soon as possible and join my children, wherever they are.*

QUEST (*emphasis*) You use **wherever** in questions as an emphatic form of 'where', usually when you are surprised about something. ❑ *Wherever did you get that idea?*

wheth·er ♦♦♦ /ˈweðə/ CONJ **1** You use **whether** when you are talking about a choice or doubt between two or more alternatives. ❑ *To this day, it's unclear whether he shot himself or was murdered.* ❑ *Whether it turns out to be a good idea or a bad idea, we'll find out.* **2** You use **whether** to say that something is true in any of the circumstances that you mention. ❑ *This happens whether the children are in two-parent or one-parent families.* ❑ *Whether they say it aloud or not, most men expect their wives to be faithful.*

which ♦♦♦ /wɪtʃ/ QUEST, DET, CONJ, PRON

QUEST You use **which** in questions when there are two or more possible answers or alternatives. ❑ *'You go down that passageway over there.'—'Which one?'* ❑ *Which vitamin supplements are good for you?*

DET **1** You use **which** to refer to a choice between two or more possible answers or alternatives. ❑ *I wanted to know which school it was you went to.* ❑ *I can't remember which teachers I had.* **2** You use **which** after a preposition to refer back to an idea or situation expressed in a previous sentence or sentences, especially when you want to give your opinion about it. ❑ *The chances are you haven't fully decided what you want from your career at the moment, in which case you're definitely not cut out to be a boss yet!*

CONJ You use **which** after certain words, especially verbs and adjectives, to introduce a clause in which there is a choice between two or more alternatives. ☐ *In her panic she couldn't remember which was Mr Grainger's cabin.*

PRON **1** You use **which** at the beginning of a relative clause when specifying the thing that you are talking about. In such clauses, which has the same meaning as **that.** ☐ *Soldiers opened fire on a car which failed to stop at an army checkpoint.* **2** You use **which** to refer back to an idea or situation expressed in a previous sentence or sentences, especially when you want to give your opinion about it. ☐ *They ran out of drink. Which actually didn't bother me because I wasn't drinking.*

PHRASE **which is which** If you cannot tell the difference between two things, you can say that you do not know **which is which.** ☐ *They all look so alike to me that I'm never sure which is which.*

which·ever /wɪtʃˈevə/ DET, CONJ
DET **1** You use **whichever** in order to indicate that it does not matter which of the possible alternatives happens or is chosen. = whatever ☐ *Whichever way you look at it, nuclear power is the energy of the future.* **2** You use **whichever** to specify which of a number of possibilities is the right one or the one you mean. ☐ *Learning to relax by whichever method suits you best is a positive way of contributing to your overall good health.*
CONJ **1** You use **whichever** to introduce a clause referring back to an idea or situation expressed in a previous clause, indicating that it does not matter which of the possible alternatives happens or is chosen. = whatever ☐ *If you are unhappy with anything you have bought from us, we will gladly exchange your purchase, or refund your money, whichever you prefer.* **2** You use **whichever** to introduce a clause referring back to an idea or situation expressed in a previous clause, specifying which of a number of possibilities is the right one or the one you mean. ☐ *He has been extraordinarily fortunate or clever, whichever is the right word.*

⊙**while** ♦♦♦ /waɪl/ CONJ, NOUN
CONJ (in BrE, also use **whilst**) **1** If something happens **while** something else is happening, the two things are happening at the same time. ☐ *They were grinning and watching while one man laughed and poured beer over the head of another.* ☐ *I sat on the chair to unwrap the package while he stood behind me.* **2** If something happens **while** something else happens, the first thing happens at some point during the time that the second thing is happening. ☐ *The two ministers have yet to meet, but may do so while in New York.* **3** You use **while** at the beginning of a clause to introduce information that contrasts with information in the main clause. = whereas ☐ *Most digital camera owners are male, while women prefer film.* ☐ *The first two services are free, while the third costs £35.00.* ☐ *While chronic anger increases the risk of heart disease in men, for women it is anxiety that poses this risk.* **4** You use **while** before making a statement, in order to introduce information that partly conflicts with your statement. = although ☐ *While the news, so far, has been good, there may be days ahead when it is bad.* ☐ *While the numbers of such developments are relatively small, the potential market is large.* ☐ *While details may vary, the essence remains the same.*
NOUN [SING] A **while** is a period of time. ☐ *They walked on in silence for a while.* ☐ *He was married a little while ago.*
PHRASE **all the while** You use **all the while** in order to say that something happens continually or that it happens throughout the time when something else is happening. ☐ *All the while the people at the next table watched me eat.*
PHRASAL VERB **while away** (whiles, whiling, whiled) If you **while away** the time in a particular way, you spend time in that way, because you are waiting for something else to happen, or because you have nothing else to do. ☐ *Craig had been whiling away his spare time in our basement.*
♦ once in a while → see once; worth your while → see worth

⊙**whilst** ♦◇◇ /waɪlst/ CONJ **Whilst** means the same as **while.** It is used mainly in British English in formal and literary contexts. **while** = whereas, although ☐ *Whilst droughts are not uncommon in many parts of the country, the coastal region remains humid throughout the year.* ☐ *Whilst*

every care has been taken to ensure accuracy, the publishers cannot accept legal responsibility for any problems that arise.

whim /wɪm/ NOUN [C, U] (**whims**) A **whim** is a wish to do or have something that seems to have no serious reason or purpose behind it, and often occurs suddenly. ☐ *We decided, more or less on a whim, to sail to Morocco.*

whip ♦◇◇ /wɪp/ NOUN, VERB
NOUN [C] (**whips**) A **whip** is a long, thin piece of material such as leather or rope, fastened to a stiff handle. It is used for hitting people or animals.
VERB [T] (**whips, whipping, whipped**) **1** If someone **whips** a person or animal, they beat them or hit them with a whip or something like a whip. ☐ *Eye-witnesses claimed Mr Melton whipped the horse up to 16 times.* **2** If someone **whips** something out or **whips** it off, they take it out or take it off very quickly and suddenly. ☐ *Bob whipped out his notebook.* ☐ *Players were whipping their shirts off.* **3** When you **whip** something liquid such as cream or an egg, you stir it very fast until it is thick or stiff. ☐ *Whip the cream until thick.* ☐ *Whip the eggs, oils, and honey together.* **4** If you **whip** people **into** an emotional state, you deliberately cause and encourage them to be in that state. ☐ *He could whip a crowd into hysteria.*
PHRASAL VERB **whip up** If someone **whips up** an emotion, especially a dangerous one such as hatred, or if they **whip** people **up** into an emotional state, they deliberately cause and encourage people to feel that emotion. = stir up ☐ *He accused politicians of whipping up anti-foreign sentiments in order to win right-wing votes.*

whip·ping /ˈwɪpɪŋ/ NOUN [C] (**whippings**) = beating ☐ *He threatened to give her a whipping.*

whirl·wind /ˈwɜːlwɪnd/ NOUN, ADJ
NOUN [C] (**whirlwinds**) **1** A **whirlwind** is a tall column of air that spins round and round very fast and moves across the land or sea. **2** You can describe a situation in which a lot of things happen very quickly and are very difficult for someone to control as a **whirlwind.** ☐ *I had been running around southern California in a whirlwind of activity.*
ADJ [whirlwind + N] A **whirlwind** event or action happens or is done much more quickly than normal. ☐ *He got married after a whirlwind romance.*

whis·ky /ˈwɪski/ NOUN [C, U] (**whiskies**) **1** [C, U] Whisky is a strong, alcoholic drink made, especially in Scotland and Canada, from grain such as barley or rye. **2** [C] A **whisky** is a glass of whisky.

whis·per ♦◇◇ /ˈwɪspə/ VERB, NOUN
VERB [I, T] (**whispers, whispering, whispered**) When you **whisper**, you say something very quietly, using your breath rather than your throat, so that only one person can hear you. ☐ *'Keep your voice down,' I whispered.* ☐ *She sat on Rossi's knee as he whispered in her ear.* ☐ *He whispered the message to David.*
NOUN [C] (**whispers**) A **whisper** is a very quiet tone of voice, using your breath rather than your throat, so that only one person can hear you. A **whisper** is also something uttered in such a voice. ☐ *Men were talking in whispers in every office.*

whis·tle /ˈwɪsəl/ VERB, NOUN
VERB [I, T] (**whistles, whistling, whistled**) **1** [I, T] When you **whistle** or when you **whistle** a tune, you make a series of musical notes by forcing your breath out between your lips, or your teeth. ☐ *He whistled and sang snatches of songs.* ☐ *He was whistling softly to himself.* **2** [I] When someone **whistles**, they make a sound by forcing their breath out between their lips or their teeth. People sometimes whistle when they are surprised, or to call a dog, to get someone's attention, or to show that they are impressed. ☐ *He whistled, surprised but not shocked.* ☐ *Jenkins whistled through his teeth, impressed at last.* **3** [I] If something such as a train or a kettle **whistles**, it makes a loud, high sound. ☐ *Somewhere a train whistled.* **4** [I] If something such as the wind or a bullet **whistles** somewhere, it moves there, making a loud, high sound. ☐ *The wind was whistling through the building.*
NOUN [C] (**whistles**) **1** A **whistle** is a sound or a series of musical notes you make by forcing your breath out between your lips or your teeth. ☐ *Jackson gave a low*

w

whistle. **2** A **whistle** is a loud sound produced by air or steam being forced through a small opening, or by something moving quickly through the air. ❏ *the whistle of the wind* ❏ *a shrill whistle from the boiling kettle* **3** A **whistle** is a small metal tube that you blow in order to produce a loud sound and attract someone's attention. ❏ *On the platform, the guard blew his whistle.*

PHRASES **blow the whistle** If you **blow the whistle on** someone, or on something secret or illegal, you tell another person, especially a person in authority, what is happening. = *inform* ❏ *Companies should protect employees who blow the whistle on dishonest workmates and work practices.*

clean as a whistle If you describe something as **clean as a whistle**, you mean that it is completely clean. ❏ *The kitchen was clean as a whistle.*

white ♦♦♦ /waɪt/ COLOUR, ADJ, NOUN

COLOUR Something that is **white** is the colour of snow or milk. ❏ *He had nice, square, white teeth.* ❏ *Issa's white beach hat gleamed in the harsh lights.*

ADJ (**whiter, whitest**) **1** A **white** person has a pale skin and belongs to a race of European origin. ❏ *Working with white people hasn't been a problem for me or for them.* **2** **White** wine is pale yellow in colour. ❏ *Gregory poured another glass of white wine and went back to his bedroom.* **3** [white + N] **White** blood cells are the cells in your blood your body uses to fight infection. ❏ *an AIDS drug that helps restore a patient's white blood cells*

NOUN [C, U] (**whites**) **1** [C] **Whites** are white people. ❏ *It's a school that's brought blacks and whites and Hispanics together.* **2** [C, U] The **white** of an egg is the transparent liquid that surrounds the yellow part called the yolk. ❏ *As soon as the whites of the eggs have set, remove the cover.* **3** [C] The **white** of someone's eye is the white part that surrounds the coloured part called the iris. ❏ *Susanne stared at me, the whites of her eyes gleaming in the streetlight.*

✪white-collar also **white collar** ADJ **1** [white-collar + N] **White-collar** workers work in offices rather than doing physical work such as making things in factories or building things. = *clerical* ❏ *White-collar workers now work longer hours.* ❏ *Low costs and high levels of efficiency are enticing firms to move white-collar jobs out of Britain.* **2** [white-collar + N] **White-collar** crime is committed by people who work in offices, and involves stealing money secretly from companies or the government, or getting money in an illegal way. ❏ *a New York lawyer who specializes in white-collar crime* ❏ *a notorious white-collar criminal who illegally took control of a Gold Coast company* ❏ *such white-collar crimes as price fixing and commercial bribery*

white·wash /ˈwaɪtwɒʃ/ NOUN, VERB

NOUN [U] **Whitewash** is a mixture of lime or chalk and water that is used for painting walls white.

VERB [T] (**whitewashes, whitewashing, whitewashed**) **1** If a wall or building **has been whitewashed**, it has been painted white with whitewash. ❏ *The walls had been whitewashed.* **2** If you say that people **whitewash** something, you are accusing them of hiding the unpleasant facts or truth about it in order to make it acceptable. = *cover up* ❏ *The administration is whitewashing the regime's actions.*

who ♦♦♦ /huː/ QUEST, CONJ, PRON

QUEST You use **who** in questions when you ask about the name or identity of a person or group of people. ❏ *Who's there?* ❏ *Who is the least popular man around here?* ❏ *'You reminded me of somebody.'—'Who?'*

CONJ You use **who** after certain words, especially verbs and adjectives, to introduce a clause where you talk about the identity of a person or a group of people. ❏ *Police have not been able to find out who was responsible for the forgeries.* ❏ *I went over to start up a conversation, asking her who she knew at the party.*

PRON You use **who** at the beginning of a relative clause when specifying the person or group of people you are talking about or when giving more information about them. ❏ *There are those who eat out for a special occasion, or treat themselves.*

who·ever /huːˈevə/ CONJ, QUEST

CONJ **1** You use **whoever** to refer to someone when their identity is not yet known. ❏ *Whoever did this will sooner or later be caught and will be punished.* ❏ *Whoever wins the election is going to have a tough job getting the economy back on its feet.* **2** You use **whoever** to indicate that the actual identity of the person who does something will not affect a situation. ❏ *You can have whoever you like to visit you.*

QUEST (emphasis) You use **whoever** in questions as an emphatic way of saying 'who', usually when you are surprised about something. = *who* ❏ *Whoever thought up that joke?*

✪whole ♦♦♦ /həʊl/ QUANT, ADJ, NOUN, ADV

QUANT ['the' whole 'of' DEF-N] If you refer to **the whole of** something, you mean all of it. = *entirety, all* ❏ *He has said he will make an apology to the whole of Asia for his country's past behaviour.* ❏ *I was cold throughout the whole of my body.* ❏ *the whole of August*

ADJ **1** [whole + N] You use **whole** before a noun to indicate that you are referring to all of something. = *entire* ❏ *We spent the whole summer in Italy that year.* **2** [V-LINK + whole, V N + whole] If something is **whole**, it is in one piece and is not broken or damaged. = *intact* ❏ *I struck the glass with my fist with all my might; yet it remained whole.* **3** [whole + N] You can say a **whole** something to emphasize what you are saying. ❏ *That saved me a whole bunch of money.*

NOUN [C] (**wholes**) A **whole** is a single thing that contains several different parts. ❏ *An atom itself is a complete whole, with its electrons, protons and neutrons and other elements.*

PHRASES **as a whole** If you refer to something **as a whole**, you are referring to it generally and as a single unit. = *in general, generally* ❏ *He described the move as a victory for the people of South Africa as a whole.* ❏ *As a whole we do not eat enough fibre in Britain.*

on the whole You use **on the whole** to indicate that what you are saying is true in general but may not be true in every case, or that you are giving a general opinion or summary of something. = *in general, generally, in the main* ❏ *On the whole, people miss the opportunity to enjoy leisure.* ❏ *On the whole, this strategy works.* ❏ *The wine towns encountered are, on the whole, quiet and modest.*

ADV [whole + ADJ] (informal, emphasis) You use **whole** to emphasize what you are saying. = *totally* ❏ *It was like seeing a whole different side of somebody.*

whole·hearted /ˌhəʊlˈhɑːtɪd/ ADJ (emphasis) If you support or agree to something in a **wholehearted** way, you support or agree to it enthusiastically and completely. ❏ *The governor deserves our wholehearted support for having taken a step in this direction.*

whole·heart·ed·ly /ˌhəʊlˈhɑːtɪdli/ ADV (emphasis) If you support something **wholeheartedly**, you support it enthusiastically and completely. ❏ *That's exactly right. I agree wholeheartedly with you.*

whole·sale /ˈhəʊlseɪl/ NOUN, ADV, ADJ

NOUN [U] (business) **Wholesale** is the activity of buying and selling goods in large quantities and therefore at cheaper prices, usually to shops who then sell them to the public. Compare **retail**. ❏ *Warehouse clubs allow members to buy goods at wholesale prices.*

ADV [wholesale after V] (business) If something is sold **wholesale**, it is sold in large quantities and at cheaper prices, usually to shops. ❏ *The fabrics are sold wholesale to retailers, fashion houses, and other manufacturers.*

ADJ [wholesale + N] (emphasis) You use **wholesale** to describe the destruction, removal, or changing of something when it affects a very large number of things or people. ❏ *They are only doing what is necessary to prevent wholesale destruction of vegetation.*

whole·some /ˈhəʊlsəm/ ADJ (approval) **1** If you describe something as **wholesome**, you approve of it because you think it is likely to have a positive influence on people's behaviour or mental state, especially because it does not involve anything sexually immoral. ❏ *The Dove Foundation aims to promote wholesome, family entertainment.* **2** If you describe food as **wholesome**, you approve of it because you think it is good for your health. = *nutritious* ❏ *fresh, wholesome ingredients*

whol·ly /ˈhəʊlli/ ADV (emphasis) You use **wholly** to

emphasize the extent or degree to which something is the case. = completely, entirely □ *While the two are only days apart in age they seem to belong to wholly different generations.*

whom ♦♦◇ /huːm/ QUEST, CONJ, PRON

> **Whom** is used in formal or written English instead of 'who' when it is the object of a verb or preposition.

QUEST You use **whom** in questions when you ask about the name or identity of a person or group of people. = who □ *'I want to send a telegram.'—'Fine, to whom?'* □ *Whom did he expect to answer his phone?*

CONJ You use **whom** after certain words, especially verbs and adjectives, to introduce a clause where you talk about the name or identity of a person or a group of people. = who □ *He asked whom I'd told about his having been away.*

PRON You use **whom** at the beginning of a relative clause when specifying the person or group of people you are talking about or when giving more information about them. □ *One writer in whom I had taken an interest was Immanuel Velikovsky.*

whose ♦♦♦ /huːz/ PRON, QUEST, DET, CONJ

PRON You use **whose** at the beginning of a relative clause where you mention something that belongs to or is associated with the person or thing mentioned in the previous clause. □ *I saw a man shouting at a driver whose car was blocking the street.* □ *a speedboat, whose fifteen-strong crew claimed to belong to China's navy*

QUEST You use **whose** in questions to ask about the person or thing that something belongs to or is associated with. □ *'Whose is this?'—'It's mine.'* □ *'It wasn't your fault, John.'—'Whose, then?'* □ *Whose car were they in?* □ *Whose daughter is she?*

DET You use **whose** to refer to the person or thing that something belongs to or is associated with. □ *I'm wondering whose mother she is then.* □ *I can't remember whose idea it was.*

CONJ You use **whose** after certain words, especially verbs and adjectives, to introduce a clause where you talk about the person or thing that something belongs to or is associated with. □ *I wondered whose the coat was.*

why ♦♦♦ /waɪ/ QUEST, CONJ, ADV, PRON, CONVENTION, EXCLAM

QUEST **1** You use **why** in questions when you ask about the reasons for something. □ *Why hasn't he brought the whisky?* □ *Why didn't he stop me?* **2** You use **why** with 'not' in questions in order to introduce a suggestion. □ *Why not give Charmaine a call?* **3** You use **why** with 'not' in questions in order to express your annoyance or anger. □ *Why don't you look where you're going?*

CONJ You use **why** at the beginning of a clause in which you talk about the reasons for something. □ *He still could not throw any further light on why the lift could have become jammed.* □ *Experts wonder why the US government is not taking similarly strong actions against AIDS in this country.*

ADV **1** **Why** is used after certain words, especially verbs and adjectives, when you talk about the reasons for something. □ *I don't know why.* □ *It's obvious why.* **2** [N + why] **Why** is used after the word 'reason' at the end of a clause to refer to the reasons for a situation mentioned in a previous clause. □ *He confirmed that the city had been closed to foreigners, but gave no reason why.*

PRON You use **why** to introduce a relative clause after the word 'reason'. □ *There's a reason why women don't read this stuff; it's not funny.*

CONVENTION (formulae) You say **why not** in order to agree with what someone has suggested. □ *'Want to spend the afternoon with me?'—'Why not?'*

EXCLAM (mainly AmE, feelings) People say '**Why**' at the beginning of a sentence when they are surprised, shocked, or angry. □ *Why hello, Tom.*

wick·ed /ˈwɪkɪd/ ADJ You use **wicked** to describe someone or something that is very bad and deliberately harmful to people. = evil □ *She described the shooting as a wicked attack.*

⚙**wide** ♦♦♦ /waɪd/ ADJ, ADV

ADJ (wider, widest) **1** Something that is **wide** measures a large distance from one side or edge to the other. = broad, large; ≠ narrow □ *All worktops should be wide enough to*

allow plenty of space for food preparation. **2** You use **wide** to talk or ask about how much something measures from one side or edge to the other. □ *a corridor of land four miles wide* □ *The road is only one lane wide.* □ *a desk that was almost as wide as the room* **3** You use **wide** to describe something that includes a large number of different things or people. = broad □ *The brochure offers a wide choice of hotels, apartments and holiday homes.* **4** You use **wide** to say that something is found, believed, known, or supported by many people or throughout a large area. = extensive □ *The case has attracted wide publicity.* **5** A **wide** difference or gap between two things, ideas, or qualities is a large difference or gap. □ *Research shows a wide difference in tastes around the country.* **6** [wider + N] **Wider** is used to describe something that relates to the most important or general parts of a situation, rather than to the smaller parts or to details. □ *He emphasized the wider issue of superpower co-operation.*

ADV (wider, widest) If you open or spread something **wide**, you open or spread it as far as possible or to the fullest extent. □ *'It was huge,' he announced, spreading his arms wide.*

wide·ly /ˈwaɪdli/ ADV **1** *He published widely in scientific journals.* **2** [widely with V] □ *At present, no widely approved vaccine exists for malaria.* **3** *The treatment regime may vary widely depending on the type of injury.*

♦ **wide of the mark** → see **mark**

wid·en /ˈwaɪdən/ VERB [I, T] (widens, widening, widened) **1** If you **widen** something or if it **widens**, it becomes greater in measurement from one side or edge to the other. □ *He had an operation last year to widen a heart artery.* **2** If you **widen** something or if it **widens**, it becomes greater in range or it affects a larger number of people or things. □ *US prosecutors have widened a securities-fraud investigation.* **3** If a difference or gap **widens** or if something **widens** it, it becomes greater. □ *Wage differences in the two areas are widening.*

wide-ranging ADJ If you describe something as **wide-ranging**, you mean it deals with or affects a great variety of different things. □ *a package of wide-ranging economic reforms*

⚙**wide·spread** ♦◇◇ /ˈwaɪdspred/ ADJ (academic word) Something that is **widespread** exists or happens over a large area, or to a great extent. = extensive; ≠ limited □ *There is widespread support for the new proposals.* □ *Food shortages are widespread.*

wid·ow /ˈwɪdəʊ/ NOUN [C] (widows) A **widow** is a woman whose husband has died and who has not married again. □ *She became a widow a year ago.*

wid·owed /ˈwɪdəʊd/ VERB [PASSIVE] If someone is **widowed**, their husband or wife dies. □ *More and more young men are widowed by cancer.*

⚙**width** ♦◇◇ /wɪdθ/ NOUN [C, u] (widths) The **width** of something is the distance it measures from one side or edge to the other. = span, breadth □ *Measure the full width of the window.* □ *The road was reduced to 18 ft in width by adding parking bays.* □ *Saddles are made in a wide range of different widths.*

wield /wiːld/ VERB [T] (wields, wielding, wielded) **1** If you **wield** a weapon, tool, or piece of equipment, you carry and use it. □ *He was attacked by a man wielding a knife.* **2** If someone **wields** power, they have it and are able to use it. □ *He remains chairman, but wields little power at the company.*

wife ♦♦♦ /waɪf/ NOUN [C] (wives) A man's **wife** is the woman he is married to. □ *He married his wife Jane 37 years ago.*

wig /wɪg/ NOUN [C] (wigs) A **wig** is a covering of false hair that you wear on your head, for example, because you have little hair of your own or because you want to cover up your own hair. □ *Jo wore a long wig that made her look very sexy.*

⚙**wild** ♦♦◇ /waɪld/ ADJ, NOUN

ADJ (wilder, wildest) **1** **Wild** animals or plants live or grow in natural surroundings and are not taken care of by people. = feral, untamed; ≠ tame, domestic □ *We saw two*

w

more wild cats creeping towards us in the darkness. ❑ The lane was lined with wild flowers. **2** Wild land is natural and is not used by people. ❑ a wild area of woods and lakes **3** Wild is used to describe the weather or the sea when it is stormy. = stormy ❑ The wild weather did not deter some people from taking an unseasonable dip in the sea. **4** Wild behaviour is uncontrolled, excited, or energetic. ❑ The children are wild with joy. ❑ As George himself came on stage they went wild. **5** If you describe someone or their behaviour as wild, you mean that they behave in a very uncontrolled way. ❑ The house is in a mess after a wild party. **6** [wild + N] A wild idea is unusual or extreme. A wild guess is one that you make without much thought. ❑ Browning's prediction is no better than a wild guess. NOUN [PL] (wilds) The wilds of a place are the natural areas that are far away from cities and towns. ❑ They went canoeing in the wilds of Canada. PHRASE in the wild Animals that live in the wild live in a free and natural state and are not taken care of by people. ❑ Fewer than a thousand giant pandas still live in the wild. ✦ beyond your wildest dreams → see dream; in your wildest dreams → see dream

wil·der·ness /ˈwɪldənəs/ NOUN [C] (wildernesses) A wilderness is a desert or other area of natural land which is not used by people. ❑ the icy Canadian wilderness

⊛ **wild·life** /ˈwaɪldlaɪf/ NOUN [U] You can use wildlife to refer to the animals and other living things that live in the wild. = animals, fauna ❑ People were concerned that pets or wildlife could be affected by the pesticides. ❑ Opponents say drilling could threaten the rich wildlife in the area.

wild·ly /ˈwaɪldli/ ADV **1** [wildly with V] If you do something wildly, you do it in an uncontrolled, excited, or energetic manner. ❑ As she finished each song, the crowd clapped wildly. **2** [wildly with V] If you behave wildly, you behave in a very uncontrolled way. ❑ Five people were injured as Reynolds slashed out wildly with a kitchen knife. **3** (emphasis) You use wildly to emphasize the degree, amount, or intensity of something. ❑ Here again, the community and police have wildly different stories of what happened. **4** If you guess wildly, you make a guess without much thought. ❑ 'Thirteen?' he guessed wildly.

will ◆◆◆ /wɪl/ VERB, NOUN

Will is a modal verb. It is used with the base form of a verb. In spoken English and informal written English, the form won't is often used in negative statements. The inflected forms wills, willing, and willed are used for meaning 14 of the verb.

VERB [MODAL, T] (wills, willing, willed) **1** [MODAL] You use will to indicate that you hope, think, or have evidence that something is going to happen or be the case in the future. ❑ I'm sure we will find a wide variety of choices available in school cafeterias. ❑ Will you ever feel at home here? ❑ The ship will not be ready for a month. **2** [MODAL] You use will in order to make statements about official arrangements in the future. ❑ The show will be open to the public at 2 pm; admission will be £5. **3** [MODAL] You use will in order to make promises and threats about what is going to happen or be the case in the future. ❑ I'll call you tonight. ❑ Price quotes on selected product categories will be sent on request. **4** [MODAL] You use will to indicate someone's intention to do something. ❑ I will say no more on these matters, important though they are. ❑ In this section we will describe common myths about cigarettes, alcohol, and marijuana. ❑ 'Dinner's ready.'—'Thanks, Carrie, but we'll have a drink first.' **5** [MODAL] ❑ Will you be remaining in the city? You use will in questions in order to make polite invitations or offers. ❑ Will you stay for supper? ❑ Will you join me for a drink? **6** [MODAL] You use will in questions in order to ask or tell someone to do something. = would ❑ Will you drive me home? ❑ Will you listen again, Andrew? **7** [MODAL] You use will to say that someone is willing to do something. You use will not or won't to indicate that someone refuses to do something. ❑ All right, I'll forgive you. **8** [MODAL] You use will to say that a person or thing is able to do something in the future. ❑ How the country will defend itself in the future has become increasingly important.

9 [MODAL] You use will to indicate that an action usually happens in the particular way mentioned. ❑ The thicker the material, the less susceptible the garment will be to wet conditions. **10** [MODAL] You use will in the main clause of some 'if' and 'unless' sentences to indicate something that you consider to be fairly likely to happen. ❑ If you overcook the meat it will be dry. **11** [MODAL] You use will to say that someone insists on behaving or doing something in a particular way and you cannot change them. You emphasize will when you use it in this way. ❑ He will leave his socks lying all over the place and it drives me crazy. **12** [MODAL] You use will have with a past participle when you are saying that you are fairly certain that something will be true by a particular time in the future. ❑ As many as ten million children will have been infected with the virus by the end of the decade. **13** [MODAL] You use will have with a past participle to indicate that something is the case. ❑ Jack will have been very upset by all this. **14** [T] If you will something to happen, you try to make it happen by using mental effort rather than physical effort. ❑ I looked at the telephone, willing it to ring. NOUN [C, U, SING] (wills) **1** [C, U] Will is the determination to do something. ❑ He was said to have lost his will to live. **2** [SING] If something is the will of a person or group of people with authority, they want it to happen. ❑ He has submitted himself to the will of God. **3** [C] A will is a document in which you declare what you want to happen to your money and property when you die. ❑ Attached to his will was a letter he had written to his wife just days before his death. PHRASE against someone's will If something is done against your will, it is done even though you do not want it to be done. ❑ No doubt he was forced to leave his family against his will. → See also willing

⊛ **will·ing** ◆◆◇ /ˈwɪlɪŋ/ ADJ **1** [V-LINK + willing + to-INF] If someone is willing to do something, they are fairly happy about doing it and will do it if they are asked or required to do it. = prepared; ≠ reluctant ❑ There are, of course, questions which she will not be willing to answer. ❑ The army now say they're willing to hold talks with the political parties. **2** Willing is used to describe someone who does something fairly enthusiastically and because they want to do it rather than because they are forced to do it. ❑ Have the party on a Saturday, when you can get your partner and other willing adults to help. **will·ing·ness** /ˈwɪlɪŋnəs/ NOUN [U] ❑ You should appeal to her loving nature and willingness to help. ✦ God willing → see god

will·power /ˈwɪlpaʊə/ also **will-power, will power** NOUN [U] Willpower is a very strong determination to do something. ❑ He came in for help after his attempts to stop smoking by willpower alone failed.

wilt /wɪlt/ VERB [I] (wilts, wilting, wilted) If a plant wilts, it gradually bends downwards and becomes weak because it needs more water or is dying. ❑ The roses wilted the next day.

win ◆◆◆ /wɪn/ VERB, NOUN VERB [I, T] (wins, winning, won) **1** [I, T] If you win something such as a competition, battle, or argument, you defeat those people you are competing or fighting against, or you do better than everyone else involved. ❑ He does not have any realistic chance of winning the election. ❑ The top four teams all won. **2** [T] If something wins you something such as an election, competition, battle, or argument, it causes you to defeat the people competing with you or fighting you, or to do better than everyone else involved. ❑ The Democrats had found a message that could win them the White House. **3** [T] If you win something such as a prize or medal, you get it because you have defeated everyone else in something such as an election, competition, battle, or argument, or have done very well in it. ❑ Trent Dimas won gold in the final men's gymnastic event. **4** [T] If you win something that you want or need, you succeed in getting it. = gain ❑ moves to win the support of the poor PHRASAL VERB win over (in BrE, also use win round) If you win someone over, you persuade them to support you or

W

agree with you. ❑ *He has won over a significant number of the left-wing deputies.*

NOUN [c] (**wins**) A **win** is the act of defeating those people you are competing or fighting against in a competition, election, battle or argument. = victory ❑ *The voters gave a narrow win to Vargas Llosa.*

→ See also **winning**

✦ **win hands down** → see **hand**

wind ♦♦◇ NOUN, VERB

> The form **winded** is used as the past tense and past participle for meaning 5 of the verb.

NOUN /wɪnd/ [c, u] (**winds**) **1** [c, u] A **wind** is a current of air that is moving across the earth's surface. ❑ *There was a strong wind blowing.* **2** [c] Journalists often refer to a trend or factor that influences events as a **wind of** a particular kind. ❑ *The winds of change are blowing across the country.*

PHRASES **break wind** If someone **breaks wind**, they release gas from their intestines through their anus. ❑ *If I break wind at dinner, should I say 'Pardon', or pretend nothing has happened?*

get wind of something (*informal*) If you **get wind of** something, you hear about it, especially when someone else did not want you to know about it. ❑ *I don't want the public, and especially not the press, to get wind of it at this stage.*

VERB /waɪnd/ [i, t] (**winds, winding, wound**) **1** [i, t] If a road, river, or line of people **winds** in a particular direction, it goes in that direction with a lot of bends or twists in it. ❑ *Quiet mountain roads wind through groves of bamboo and cedar.* ❑ *a narrow winding road* ❑ *We wound our way southeast.* **2** [t] When you **wind** something flexible around something else, you wrap it around it several times. ❑ *The horse jumped forward and around her, winding the rope around her waist.* **3** [t] When you **wind** a mechanical device, for example, a watch or a clock, you turn a knob, key, or handle on it several times in order to make it operate. ❑ *I still hadn't wound my watch so I didn't know the time.* **4** [t] To **wind** a tape or film **back** or **forward** means to make it move towards its starting or ending position. ❑ *The camcorder winds the tape back or forward at high speed.* **5** /wɪnd/ [t] If you **are winded** by something such as a blow, the air is suddenly knocked out of your lungs so that you have difficulty breathing for a short time. ❑ *He was winded and shaken.*

PHRASAL VERBS **wind down** **1** When you **wind down** something such as the window of a car, you make it move downwards by turning a handle. ❑ *Glass motioned to him to wind down the window.* **2** (*informal*) If you **wind down**, you relax after doing something that has made you feel tired or tense. = unwind ❑ *I regularly have a drink to wind down.* **3** If someone **winds down** a business or activity, they gradually reduce the amount of work that is done or the number of people that are involved, usually before closing or stopping it completely. ❑ *Aid workers have begun winding down their operation.*

wind up **1** Wind up means the same as wind VERB **3**. ❑ *I wound up the watch and listened to it tick.* **2** When you **wind up** an activity, you finish it or stop doing it. ❑ *The president is about to wind up his visit to Somalia.* **3** When you **wind up** something such as the window of a car, you make it move upwards by turning a handle. = roll up ❑ *He started winding the window up but I grabbed the door and opened it.*

win·dow ♦♦◇ /'wɪndəʊ/ NOUN

NOUN [c] (**windows**) **1** A **window** is a space in the wall of a building or in the side of a vehicle, which has glass in it so that light can come in and you can see out. ❑ *He stood at the window, moodily staring out.* ❑ *The room felt very hot and she wondered why someone did not open a window.* **2** A **window** is a glass-covered opening above a counter, for example, in a bank, post office, railway station, or museum, which the person serving you sits behind. ❑ *The woman at the ticket window told me that the admission fee was £12.* **3** (*computing*) On a computer screen, a **window** is one of the work areas into which the screen can be divided. ❑ *Yahoo! Pager puts a small window on your screen containing a list of your 'friends'.*

PHRASE **go out of the window** or **fly out of the window** or **be out the window** If you say that something such as a plan or a particular way of thinking or behaving **has gone out of the window** or **is out the window**, you mean that it has disappeared completely. ❑ *By now all logic had gone out of the window.*

wind·screen /'wɪndskriːn/ (*BrE*; in *AmE*, use **windshield**) NOUN [c] (**windscreens**) The **windscreen** of a car or other vehicle is the glass window at the front through which the driver looks.

windy /'wɪndi/ ADJ (**windier, windiest**) If it is **windy**, the wind is blowing a lot. ❑ *It was windy and Jake felt cold.*

wine ♦♦◇ /waɪn/ NOUN [c, u] (**wines**) **Wine** is an alcoholic drink made from grapes. You can also refer to alcoholic drinks made from other fruits or vegetables as **wine**. ❑ *a bottle of white wine*

✪wing ♦♦◇ /wɪŋ/ NOUN

NOUN [c, PL] (**wings**) **1** [c] The **wings** of a bird or insect are the two parts of its body that it uses for flying. ❑ *The bird flapped its wings furiously.* ❑ *the outstretched wings of an eagle* **2** [c] The **wings** of an aeroplane are the long flat parts sticking out of its side which support it while it is flying. ❑ *The plane made one pass, dipped its wings, then circled back.* **3** [c] A **wing** of a building is a part of it that sticks out from the main part. ❑ *We were given an office in the empty west wing.* **4** [c] A **wing** of an organization, especially a political organization, is a group within it which has a particular function or particular beliefs. ❑ *the military wing of the African National Congress* **5** [PL] In a theatre, **the wings** are the sides of the stage that are hidden from the audience by curtains or scenery. ❑ *On most nights I watched the start of the play from the wings.*

PHRASES **in the wings** If you say that someone is waiting **in the wings**, you mean that they are ready and waiting for an opportunity to take action. ❑ *There are now more than 20 big companies waiting in the wings to take over some of its business.*

spread your wings If you **spread** your **wings**, you do something new and somewhat difficult or move to a new place, because you feel more confident in your abilities than you used to and you want to gain wider experience. ❑ *I led a very confined life in my village so I suppose that I wanted to spread my wings.*

take someone under one's wing If you **take** someone **under** your **wing**, you look after them, help them, and protect them. ❑ *Her boss took her under his wing after fully realizing her potential.*

→ See also **left-wing, right-wing**

wink ♦◇◇ /wɪŋk/ VERB, NOUN

VERB [i] (**winks, winking, winked**) When you **wink at** someone, you look towards them and close one eye very briefly, usually as a signal that something is a joke or a secret. ❑ *Brian winked at his bride-to-be.*

NOUN [c] (**winks**) If you give someone a **wink**, you look towards them and close one eye very briefly, usually as a signal that something is a joke or a secret. ❑ *I gave her a wink.*

PHRASE **not sleep a wink** or **not get a wink of sleep** (*informal*) If you say that you **did not sleep a wink** or **did not get a wink of sleep**, you mean that you tried to go to sleep but could not. ❑ *I didn't get a wink of sleep on the flight.*

win·ner ♦♦◇ /'wɪnə/ NOUN [c] (**winners**) The **winner** of a prize, race, or competition is the person, animal, or thing that wins it. ❑ *She will present the trophies to the award winners.*

win·ning ♦◇◇ /'wɪnɪŋ/ ADJ **1** [winning + N] You can use **winning** to describe a person or thing that wins something such as a competition, game, or election. ❑ *the winning lottery ticket* **2** [winning + N] You can use **winning** to describe actions or qualities that please other people and make them feel friendly towards you. = engaging ❑ *She gave him another of her winning smiles.*

→ See also **win**

win·ter ♦◇◇ /'wɪntə/ NOUN [c, u] (**winters**) **Winter** is the season between autumn and spring. In the winter the weather is usually cold. ❑ *In winter the nights are long and cold.* ❑ *the late winter of 1941*

w

wipe ◆◇◇ /waɪp/ VERB, NOUN

VERB [T] (**wipes, wiping, wiped**) **1** If you **wipe** something, you rub its surface to remove dirt or liquid from it. ❑ *I'll just wipe the table.* ❑ *When he had finished washing he began to wipe the basin clean.* **2** If you **wipe** dirt or liquid from something, you remove it by using a cloth or your hand. ❑ *Gleb wiped the sweat from his face.*

PHRASAL VERB **wipe out** To **wipe out** something such as a place or a group of people or animals means to destroy them completely. ❑ *Experts say if the island is not protected, the spill could wipe out the gulf's turtle population.*

NOUN [C] (**wipes**) **1** If you give something a **wipe**, you rub its surface to remove dirt or liquid from it. ❑ *Tomorrow I'm going to give the toys a good wipe as some seem a bit greasy.* **2** A **wipe** is a small moist cloth for cleaning things and is designed to be used only once. ❑ *antiseptic wipes*

✪**wire** ◆◇◇ /waɪə/ NOUN, VERB

NOUN [C, U] (**wires**) **1** [C, U] A **wire** is a long thin piece of metal that is used to fasten things or to carry electric current. ❑ *fine copper wire* **2** [C] A **wire** is a cable that carries power or signals from one place to another. = cable ❑ *I ripped out the telephone wire that ran through to his office.*

PHRASE **to the wire** (*mainly journalism*) If something goes **to the wire**, it continues until the last possible moment. ❑ *Negotiators again worked right down to the wire to reach an agreement.*

VERB [T] (**wires, wiring, wired**) If you **wire** something such as a building or piece of equipment, you put wires inside it so that electricity or signals can pass into or through it. ❑ *learning to wire and plumb the house herself* ❑ *Each of the homes has a security system and is wired for cable television.*

PHRASAL VERB **wire up** Wire up means the same as **wire** VERB. ❑ *Wire the thermometers up to trigger off an alarm bell if the temperature drops.*

✪**wire·less** ◆◇◇ /'waɪələs/ ADJ Wireless technology uses radio waves rather than electricity and therefore does not require any wires. ❑ *the fast-growing wireless communication market* ❑ *transmitting data across a wireless network* ❑ *The company is going wireless.*

wis·dom /'wɪzdəm/ NOUN [U, SING] **1** [U] Wisdom is the ability to use your experience and knowledge in order to make sensible decisions or judgments. ❑ *the patience and wisdom that comes from old age* **2** [SING] If you talk about **the wisdom of** a particular decision or action, you are talking about how sensible it is. ❑ *Many Lithuanians have expressed doubts about the wisdom of the decision.*

wise ◆◇◇ /waɪz/ ADJ (**wiser, wisest**) **1** A **wise** person is able to use their experience and knowledge in order to make sensible decisions or judgments. ❑ *She has the air of a wise woman.* **2** A **wise** action or decision is sensible. = sensible ❑ *It's never wise to withhold evidence.* ❑ *She had made a very wise decision.*

wise·ly /'waɪzli/ ADV **1** [wisely with v] ❑ *The three of us stood around the machine nodding wisely.* **2** *They've invested their money wisely.*

wish ◆◇◇ /wɪʃ/ NOUN, VERB

NOUN [C, PL] (**wishes**) **1** [C] A **wish** is a desire or strong feeling that you want to have something or do something. ❑ *She was sincere and genuine in her wish to make amends for the past.* ❑ *The decision was made against the wishes of the party leader.* **2** [C] A **wish for** something is the act of expressing the desire for that thing silently to yourself. In fairy tales, wishes are often granted by magic. ❑ *The custom is for people to try and eat 12 grapes as the clock strikes midnight. Those who are successful can make a wish.* **3** [PL] If you express your good **wishes** towards someone, you are politely expressing your friendly feelings towards them and your hope that they will be successful or happy. ❑ *I found George's story very sad. Please give him my best wishes.*

VERB [I, T] (**wishes, wishing, wished**) **1** [I, T] (*formal*) If you **wish** to do something or to have it done for you, you want to do it or have it done. ❑ *If you wish to go away for the weekend, our office will be delighted to make hotel reservations.* ❑ *We can dress as we wish now.* **2** [T] If you **wish** something were true, you would like it to be true, even though you

know that it is impossible or unlikely. ❑ *I wish I could do that.* ❑ *Pa, I wish you wouldn't shout.* **3** [I] If you **wish for** something, you express the desire for that thing silently to yourself. In fairy tales, when a person wishes for something, the thing they wish for often happens by magic. ❑ *Be careful what you wish for. You might get it!* **4** [T] If you say that you would not **wish** a particular thing on someone, you mean that the thing is so unpleasant that you would not want them to be forced to experience it. ❑ *It's a horrid experience and I wouldn't wish it on my worst enemy.* **5** [T] If you **wish** someone something such as luck or happiness, you express the hope that they will be lucky or happy. ❑ *I wish you both a good trip.*

wit /wɪt/ NOUN [U, SING, PL] (**wits**) **1** [U] Wit is the ability to use words or ideas in an amusing, clever, and imaginative way. ❑ *Boulding was known for his biting wit.* **2** [SING] If you say that someone has **the wit to** do something, you mean that they have the intelligence and understanding to make the right decision or take the right action in a particular situation. = sense ❑ *The information is there and waiting to be accessed by anyone with the wit to use it.* **3** [PL] You can refer to your ability to think quickly and effectively in a difficult situation as your **wits**. ❑ *She has used her wits to progress to the position she holds today.* **4** [PL] You can use **wits** in expressions such as **frighten** someone **out of their wits** and **scare the wits out of** someone to emphasize that a person or thing worries or frightens someone very much. ❑ *You scared us out of our wits. We heard you had an accident.*

witch /wɪtʃ/ NOUN [C] (**witches**) **1** In fairy tales, a **witch** is a woman, usually an old woman, who has evil magic powers. Witches often wear a pointed black hat. **2** A **witch** is a man or woman who claims to have magic powers and to be able to use them for good or bad purposes.

with ◆◆◆ /wɪð, wɪθ/ PREP **1** If one person is **with** another, they are together in one place. ❑ *With her were her son and daughter-in-law.* **2** If something is put **with** or is **with** something else, they are used at the same time. ❑ *Serve hot, with pasta or rice and French beans.* **3** If you do something **with** someone else, you both do it together or are both involved in it. ❑ *Parents will be given reports on their child's progress and the right to discuss it with a teacher.* **4** If you fight, argue, or compete **with** someone, you oppose them. ❑ *About a thousand students fought with riot police in the capital.* **5** If you do something **with** a particular tool, object, or substance, you do it using that tool, object, or substance. ❑ *Remove the meat with a fork and divide it among four plates.* ❑ *Pack the fruits and nuts into the jars and cover with brandy.* **6** If someone stands or goes somewhere **with** something, they are carrying it. ❑ *A young woman came in with a cup of coffee.* **7** Someone or something **with** a particular feature or possession has that feature or possession. ❑ *He was in his early forties, tall and blond with bright blue eyes.* **8** Someone **with** an illness has that illness. ❑ *I spent a week in bed with flu.* **9** If something is filled or covered **with** a substance or **with** things, it has that substance or those things in it or on it. ❑ *His legs were caked with dried mud.* **10** [ADJ/N with + N] If you are, for example, pleased or annoyed **with** someone or something, you have that feeling towards them. ❑ *He was still a little angry with her.* **11** You use **with** to indicate what a state, quality, or action relates to, involves, or affects. ❑ *Our aim is to allow student teachers to become familiar with the classroom.* ❑ *He still has a serious problem with money.* **12** You use **with** when indicating the way that something is done or the feeling that a person has when they do something. ❑ *teaching her to read music with skill and sensitivity* **13** You use **with** when indicating a sound or gesture that is made when something is done, or an expression that a person has on their face when they do something. ❑ *With a sigh, she leant back and closed her eyes.* **14** You use **with** to indicate the feeling that makes someone have a particular appearance or type of behaviour. ❑ *Gil was white and trembling with anger.* **15** [with + N PREP/-ING] You use **with** when mentioning the position or appearance of a person or thing at the time that they do something, or what someone else is doing at that time. ☐ *Joanne stood with her hands on the sink, staring out the window.* **16** You use **with** to introduce a current situation that is a factor affecting another situation. ☐ *With all the night school courses available, there is no excuse for not getting some sort of training.* **17** You use **with** when making a comparison or contrast between the situations of different people or things. ☐ *We're not like them. It's different with us.* **18** [V + with + N] If something increases or decreases with a particular factor, it changes as that factor changes. ☐ *The risk of developing heart disease increases with the number of cigarettes smoked.* **19** If something moves **with** a wind or current, it moves in the same direction as the wind or current. ☐ *a piece of driftwood carried down with the current* **20** [V-LINK + with + N] (*informal*) If someone says that they are **with** you, they mean that they understand what you are saying. ☐ *Yes, I know who you mean. Yes, now I'm with you.* **21** [V-LINK + with + N] If someone says that they are **with** you, they mean that they support or approve of what you are doing. ☐ *'I'm with you all the way.'—'Thank you.'*

◐ **with·draw** ◆◆◇ /wɪðˈdrɔː/ VERB [T, I] (**withdraws, withdrawing, withdrew, withdrawn**) **1** [T] (*formal*) If you **withdraw** something, you remove it or take it away. = remove ☐ *He reached into his pocket and withdrew a sheet of notepaper.* ☐ *government plans to withdraw financial support* **2** [I, T] When groups of people such as troops **withdraw** or when someone **withdraws** them, they leave the place where they are fighting or where they are based and return nearer home. ☐ *He stated that all foreign forces would withdraw as soon as the crisis ended.* ☐ *The United States has announced it is to withdraw forty thousand troops from Western Europe in the next year.* **3** [T] If you **withdraw** money from a bank account, you take it out of that account. ☐ *Open a savings account that does not charge ridiculous fees to withdraw money.* **4** [I] If you **withdraw from** an activity or organization, you stop taking part in it. ☐ *The African National Congress threatened to withdraw from the talks.* ☐ *The team has withdrawn from the tournament due to high cost of travel.*

◐ **with·draw·al** ◆◇◇ /wɪðˈdrɔːəl/ NOUN [C, U] (**withdrawals**) **1** [C, U] (*formal*) The **withdrawal** of something is the act or process of removing it, or ending it. = removal ☐ *If you experience any unusual symptoms after withdrawal of the treatment then contact your doctor.* **2** [U] Someone's **withdrawal from** an activity or an organization is their decision to stop taking part in it. ☐ *his withdrawal from government in 1946* **3** [C] A **withdrawal** is an amount of money that you take from your bank account. ☐ *I went to the machine to make the withdrawal and it told me to see someone inside the bank.* **4** [U] **Withdrawal** is the period during which someone feels ill after they have stopped taking a drug they were addicted to. ☐ *Withdrawal from heroin is actually like a severe attack of gastric flu.*

with·drew /wɪðˈdruː/ IRREG FORM **Withdrew** is the past tense of **withdraw**.

with·er /ˈwɪðə/ VERB
VERB [I] (**withers, withering, withered**) **1** If someone or something **withers**, they become very weak. ☐ *When he went into retirement, he visibly withered.* **2** If a flower or plant **withers**, it dries up and dies. ☐ *The flowers in Isabel's room had withered.*
PHRASAL VERB **wither away** Wither away means the same as **wither** VERB **1**. ☐ *To see my body literally wither away before my eyes was exasperating.*

with·hold /wɪðˈhəʊld/ VERB [T] (**withholds, withholding, withheld**) (*formal*) If you **withhold** something that someone wants, you do not let them have it. ☐ *Police withheld the dead boy's name yesterday until relatives could be told.*

with·in ◆◆◆ /wɪˈðɪn/ PREP, ADV
PREP **1** (*formal*) If something is **within** a place, area, or object, it is inside it or surrounded by it. ☐ *Clients are entertained within private dining rooms.* **2** Something that happens or exists **within** a society, organization, or system, happens or exists inside it. = in ☐ *the spirit of self-sacrifice within an army* **3** If something is **within** a particular limit

or set of rules, it does not go beyond it or is not more than what is allowed. ☐ *Troops have agreed to stay within specific boundaries to avoid confrontations.* **4** If you are **within** a particular distance of a place, you are less than that distance from it. ☐ *The man was within a few feet of him.* **5** [within + AMOUNT] **Within** a particular length of time means before that length of time has passed. ☐ *About 40% of all students entering as freshmen graduate within 4 years.* **6** If something is **within sight**, **within earshot**, or **within reach**, you can see it, hear it, or reach it. ☐ *His twenty-five-foot boat was moored within sight of his house.*
ADV **1** If something comes from or happens **within**, it comes from or happens inside a place, area, or object. ☐ *A small voice called from within. 'Yes, just coming.'* **2** Something that happens or exists **within**, happens or exists inside a society, organization, or system. ☐ *The real dangers to these rebels came from within.*
✦ **within reason** → see **reason**

with·out ◆◆◆ /wɪˈðaʊt/ PREP

> In addition to the uses shown below, **without** is used in the phrasal verbs 'do without', 'go without', and 'reckon without'.

1 You use **without** to indicate that someone or something does not have or use the thing mentioned. ☐ *I don't like myself without a beard.* ☐ *She wore a brown shirt pressed without a wrinkle.* **2** [without + N/-ING] If one thing happens **without** another thing, or if you do something **without** doing something else, the second thing does not happen or occur. ☐ *He was offered a generous pension provided he left without a fuss.* ☐ *They worked without a break until about eight in the evening.* **3** If you do something **without** a particular feeling, you do not have that feeling when you do it. ☐ *Janet Magnusson watched his approach without enthusiasm.* **4** If you do something **without** someone else, they are not in the same place as you are or are not involved in the same action as you. ☐ *I told Franklin he would have to start dinner without me.*

◐ **with·stand** /wɪðˈstænd/ VERB [T] (**withstands, withstanding, withstood**) (*formal*) If something or someone **withstands** a force or action, they survive it or do not give in to it. = resist, stand up to; ≠ yield to ☐ *armoured vehicles designed to withstand chemical attack* ☐ *Such claims have failed to withstand scientific scrutiny.*

◐ **wit·ness** ◆◇◇ /ˈwɪtnəs/ NOUN, VERB
NOUN [C] (**witnesses**) **1** A **witness** to an event such as an accident or crime is a person who saw it. = eye-witness ☐ *Witnesses to the crash say they saw an explosion just before the disaster.* ☐ *No witnesses have come forward.* **2** A **witness** is someone who appears in a court of law to say what they know about a crime or other event. ☐ *In the next three or four days, eleven witnesses will be called to testify.* **3** A **witness** is someone who writes their name on a document to confirm that it really is your signature. ☐ *The codicil must first be signed and dated by you in the presence of two witnesses.*
VERB [T] (**witnesses, witnessing, witnessed**) **1** If you **witness** something, you see it happen. = see, experience ☐ *Anyone who witnessed the attack should call the police.* **2** If someone **witnesses** your signature on a document, they write their name after it, to confirm that it really is your signature. ☐ *Ask a friend (not your spouse) to witness your signature.* **3** If you say that a place, period of time, or person **witnessed** a particular event or change, you mean that it happened in that place, during that period of time, or while that person was alive. = see ☐ *India has witnessed many political changes in recent years.*

wit·ty /ˈwɪti/ ADJ (**wittier, wittiest**) Someone or something that is **witty** is amusing in a clever way. ☐ *His plays were very good, very witty.*

wives /waɪvz/ IRREG FORM **Wives** is the plural of **wife**.

woke /wəʊk/ IRREG FORM **Woke** is the past tense of **wake**.

wok·en /ˈwəʊkən/ IRREG FORM **Woken** is the past participle of **wake**.

wom·an ◆◆◆ /ˈwʊmən/ NOUN [C, U] (**women**) **1** [C] A **woman** is an adult, female, human being. ☐ *a young Lithuanian woman named Dayva* ☐ *men and women over 75*

years old **2** [U] You can refer to women in general as **woman**. ❑ *the oppression of woman*
→ See also **female**

wom·en /ˈwɪmɪn/ IRREG FORM **Women** is the plural of **woman**.

won /wʌn/ IRREG FORM **Won** is the past tense and past participle of **win**.

won·der ◆◆◇ /ˈwʌndə/ VERB, NOUN, ADJ

VERB [I, T] (**wonders, wondering, wondered**) **1** If you **wonder** about something, you think about it, either because it interests you and you want to know more about it, or because you are worried or suspicious about it. ❑ *I wondered what that noise was.* ❑ *'He claims to be her father,' said Max. 'We've been wondering about him.'* **2** If you **wonder at** something, you are very surprised about it or think about it in a very surprised way. ❑ *I could only wonder at how far this woman had come.* ❑ *I wonder you don't feel it too.*

PHRASE **I wonder** (*politeness*) You can say '**I wonder**' if you want to be very polite when you are asking someone to do something, or when you are asking them for their opinion or for information. ❑ *I was just wondering if you could help me.*

NOUN [SING, U, C] (**wonders**) **1** [SING] If you say that it is a **wonder that** something happened, you mean that it is very surprising and unexpected. ❑ *It's a wonder that it took almost ten years.* **2** [U] **Wonder** is a feeling of great surprise and pleasure that you have, for example, when you see something that is very beautiful, or when something happens that you thought was impossible. ❑ *'That's right!' Bobby exclaimed in wonder. 'How did you remember that?'* **3** [C] A **wonder** is something that causes people to feel great surprise or admiration. ❑ *a lecture on the wonders of space and space exploration*

PHRASES **no wonder** or **little wonder** or **small wonder** If you say '**no wonder**', '**little wonder**', or '**small wonder**', you mean that something is not surprising. ❑ *No wonder my brother wasn't feeling well.*

no wonder You can say '**No wonder**' when you find out the reason for something that has been puzzling you for some time. ❑ *Brad was Jane's brother! No wonder he reminded me so much of her!*

work wonders or **do wonders** If you say that a person or thing **works wonders** or **does wonders**, you mean that they have a very good effect on something. ❑ *A few moments of relaxation can work wonders.*

ADJ [wonder + N] If you refer, for example, to a young man as a **wonder** boy, or to a new product as a **wonder** drug, you mean that they are believed by many people to be very good or very effective. ❑ *Mickelson was hailed as the wonder boy of American golf.*

won·der·ful ◆◆◇ /ˈwʌndəfʊl/ ADJ If you describe something or someone as **wonderful**, you think they are extremely good. = fantastic ❑ *The cold, misty air felt wonderful on his face.* ❑ *It's wonderful to see you.*
won·der·ful·ly /ˈwʌndəfəli/ ADV ❑ *It's a system that works wonderfully well.*

won't /wəʊnt/ SHORT FORM **Won't** is the usual spoken form of 'will not'. ❑ *The space shuttle won't lift off the launch pad until Sunday at the earliest.*

woo /wuː/ VERB [T] (**woos, wooing, wooed**) If you **woo** people, you try to encourage them to help you, support you, or vote for you, for example, by promising them things which they would like. ❑ *They wooed customers by offering low interest rates.*

wood ◆◆◇ /wʊd/ NOUN

NOUN [C, U] (**woods**) **1** [C, U] **Wood** is the material that forms the trunks and branches of trees. ❑ *Their dishes were made of wood.* ❑ *There was a smell of damp wood and machine oil.* **2** [C] A **wood** or **woods** is a fairly large area of trees growing near each other. ❑ *After dinner Alice slipped away for a walk in the woods with Artie.*

PHRASE **not out of the woods** (*informal*) If something or someone is **not out of the woods** yet, they are still having difficulties or problems. ❑ *The nation's economy is not out of the woods yet.*

CONVENTION **touch wood** You can say '**touch wood**' to

indicate that you hope to have good luck in something you are doing, usually after saying that you have been lucky with it so far. ❑ *I got it all taken care of, touch wood.*

wood·en ◆◇◇ /ˈwʊdən/ ADJ [wooden + N] **Wooden** objects are made of wood. ❑ *the shop's bare, brick walls and faded, wooden floorboards*

wood·land /ˈwʊdlənd/ NOUN [C, U] (**woodlands**) **Woodland** is land with a lot of trees. ❑ *an area of dense woodland*

wool /wʊl/ NOUN [C, U] (**wools**) **1** **Wool** is the hair that grows on sheep and on some other animals. ❑ *A new invention means sheep do not have to be sheared – the wool just falls off.* **2** **Wool** is a material made from animal's wool that is used to make things such as clothes, blankets, and carpets. ❑ *a wool overcoat*

word ◆◆◆ /wɜːd/ NOUN, VERB

NOUN [C, PL, SING, U] (**words**) **1** [C] A **word** is a single unit of language that can be represented in writing or speech. In English, a word has a space on either side of it when it is written. ❑ *The words stood out clearly on the page.* ❑ *The word 'ginseng' comes from the Chinese word 'Shen-seng.'* **2** [PL] Someone's **words** are what they say or write. ❑ *I was devastated when her words came true.* **3** [PL] **The words** of a song consist of the text that is sung, in contrast to the music that is played. = lyric ❑ *Can you hear the words on the album?* **4** [SING] (*spoken*) If you have **a word** with someone, you have a short conversation with them. ❑ *I think it's time you had a word with him.* **5** [C] If you offer someone **a word of** something such as warning, advice, or praise, you warn, advise, or praise them. ❑ *A word of warning. Don't stick too precisely to what it says in the book.* **6** [SING] If you say that someone does **not** hear, understand, or say **a word**, you are emphasizing that they hear, understand, or say nothing at all. ❑ *I can't understand a word she says.* **7** [U] If there is **word** of something, people receive news or information about it. ❑ *There is no word from the authorities on the reported attack.* **8** [SING] If you give your **word**, you make a sincere promise to someone. ❑ *an adult who gave his word the boy would be supervised* **9** [SING] If someone gives **the word** to do something, they give an order to do it. ❑ *I want nothing said about this until I give the word.*

PHRASES **dirty word** If you say that people consider something to be a **dirty word**, you mean that they disapprove of it. ❑ *So many people think feminism is a dirty word.*

from the word go If you do it from the **word go**, you do it from the very beginning of a period of time or situation. ❑ *It's essential you make the right decisions from the word go.*

in someone's words or **in someone's own words** You can use in their **words** or in their **own words** to indicate that you are reporting what someone said using the exact words that they used. ❑ *Even the Assistant Secretary of State had to admit that previous policy did not, in his words, produce results.*

the last word or **the final word** If someone has **the last word** or **the final word** in a discussion, argument, or disagreement, they are the one who wins it or who makes the final decision. ❑ *She does like to have the last word in any discussion.*

word of mouth If news or information passes by **word of mouth**, people tell it to each other rather than it being printed in written form. ❑ *The story has been passed down by word of mouth.*

in other words You say **in other words** in order to introduce a different, and usually simpler, explanation or interpretation of something that has just been said. ❑ *coronary heart disease, in other words, heart attacks and strokes*

in one's own words If you say something **in your own words**, you express it in your own way, without copying or repeating someone else's description. ❑ *Now tell us in your own words about the events of Saturday.*

take my word for it If you say to someone '**take my word for it**', you mean that they should believe you because you are telling the truth. ❑ *You'll buy nothing but trouble if you buy that house, take my word for it.*

W

word for word If you repeat something **word for word**, you repeat it exactly as it was originally said or written. = verbatim ❑ *I don't try to memorize speeches word for word.* VERB [T] (**words, wording, worded**) To **word** something in a particular way means to choose or use particular words to express it. ❑ *If I had written the letter, I might have worded it differently.*
-worded /'wɜːdɪd/ COMB ❑ *a strongly-worded statement*
→ See also **wording**
✦ **the operative word** → see **operative**

word·ing /'wɜːdɪŋ/ NOUN [U] The **wording** of a piece of writing or a speech are the words used in it, especially when these are chosen to have a particular effect. ❑ *The two sides failed to agree on the wording of a final report.*

wore /wɔː/ IRREG FORM **Wore** is the past tense of **wear**.

✪ **work** ◆◆◆ /wɜːk/ VERB, NOUN
▪ VERB [I, T] (**works, working, worked**) **1** [I] People who **work** have a job, usually one which they are paid to do. ❑ *I started working in a recording studio.* ❑ *He worked as a teacher for 50 years.* ❑ *I want to work, I don't want to be on the dole.* **2** [I, T] When you **work**, you do the things that you are paid or required to do in your job. ❑ *I can't talk to you right now – I'm working.* ❑ *He was working at his desk.* ❑ *They work forty hours a week.* **3** [I] When you **work**, you spend time and effort doing a task that needs to be done or trying to achieve something. ❑ *Linda spends all her time working on the garden.* ❑ *The government expressed hope that all the sides will work towards a political solution.* **4** [I] If someone **is working on** a particular subject or question, they are studying or researching it. ❑ *Professor Bonnet has been working for many years on molecules of this type.* **5** [I] If you **work with** a person or a group of people, you spend time and effort trying to help them in some way. ❑ *She spent a period of time working with people dying of cancer.* **6** [I] If a machine or piece of equipment **works**, it operates and performs a particular function. ❑ *The pump doesn't work and we have no running water.* **7** [T] If an idea, system, or way of doing something **works**, it is successful, effective, or satisfactory. ❑ *95 per cent of these diets do not work.* **8** [I] If a drug or medicine **works**, it produces a particular physical effect. ❑ *I wake up at 6 a.m. as the sleeping pill doesn't work for more than nine hours.* **9** [I] If your mind or brain **is working**, you are thinking about something or trying to solve a problem. ❑ *My mind was working frantically, running over the events of the evening.* **10** [I] If you **work on** an assumption or idea, you act as if it were true or base other ideas on it, until you have more information. ❑ *We are working on the assumption that it was a gas explosion.* **11** [T] If you **work** someone, you make them spend time and effort doing a particular activity or job. ❑ *They're working me too hard. I'm too old for this.* **12** [T] When people **work** the land, they do all the tasks involved in growing crops. ❑ *Farmers worked the fertile valleys.* **13** [T] If you **work** a machine or piece of equipment, you use or control it. = operate ❑ *Many adults still depend on their children to work the video.* **14** [I] If something **works** into a particular state or condition, it gradually moves so that it is in that state or condition. ❑ *It's important to put a lock washer on that last nut, or it can work loose.*
▪ PHRASE **work your way somewhere** If you **work** your **way** somewhere, you move or progress there slowly, and with a lot of effort or work. ❑ *Rescuers were still working their way towards the trapped men.*
▪ PHRASAL VERBS **work off** If you **work off** energy, stress, or anger, you get rid of it by doing something that requires a lot of physical effort. ❑ *Cleaning my kitchen really works off frustration if I've had a fight with someone.*
work out **1** If you **work out** a solution to a problem or mystery, you manage to find the solution by thinking or talking about it. = figure out ❑ *Negotiators are due to meet later today to work out a compromise.* ❑ *It took me some time to work out what was causing this.* **2** If you **work out** the answer to a mathematical problem, you calculate it. = calculate ❑ *It is proving hard to work out the value of bankrupt companies' assets.* **3** If something **works out** at a particular amount, it is calculated to be that amount after all the facts and figures have been considered. ❑ *The price*

per pound **works out** at \$3.20. **4** If a situation **works out** well or **works out**, it happens or progresses in a satisfactory way. ❑ *Things just didn't work out as planned.* ❑ *The deal just isn't working out the way we were promised.* **5** If a process **works** itself **out**, it reaches a conclusion or satisfactory end. ❑ *People involved in it think it's a nightmare, but I'm sure it will work itself out.* **6** If you **work out**, you do physical exercises in order to make your body fit and strong. = exercise ❑ *Work out at a gym or swim twice a week.*
work up **1** If you **work** yourself **up**, you make yourself feel very upset or angry about something. ❑ *She worked herself up into a bit of a state.* **2** If you **work up** the enthusiasm or courage to do something, you succeed in making yourself feel it. ❑ *Your creative talents can also be put to good use, if you can work up the energy.* **3** If you **work up** a sweat or an appetite, you make yourself sweaty or hungry by doing exercise or hard work. ❑ *Even if you are not prepared to work up a sweat three times a week, any activity is better than none.*
▪ NOUN [U, C, PL] (**works**) **1** [U] People who have **work** or who are **in work** have a job, usually one which they are paid to do. ❑ *Fewer and fewer people are in work.* ❑ *I was out of work at the time.* **2** [U] Your **work** consists of the things you are paid or required to do in your job. ❑ *We're supposed to be running a business here. I've got work to do.* ❑ *I used to take work home, but I don't do it any more.* **3** [U] **Work** is tasks that need to be done or things that need to be achieved. ❑ *There was a lot of work to do on their house.* **4** [U] **Work** is the place where you do your job. ❑ *Many people travel to work by car.* **5** [U] **Work** is something that you produce as a result of an activity or as a result of doing your job. ❑ *It can help to have an impartial third party look over your work.* **6** [C] A **work** is something such as a painting, book, or piece of music produced by an artist, writer, or composer. = piece ❑ *In my opinion, this is Rembrandt's greatest work.* ❑ *the complete works of Shakespeare* ❑ *The church has several valuable works of art.* **7** [U] Someone's **work** is the study or research that they have done on a particular subject or question. ❑ *Their work shows that one-year-olds are much more likely to have allergies if either parent smokes.* **8** [U] **Work** with a particular person or a group of people is time and effort spent trying to help them in some way. ❑ *She became involved in social and relief work among the refugees.* **9** [C] A **works** is a place where something is manufactured or where an industrial process is carried out. **Works** is used to refer to one or to more than one of these places. ❑ *the steelworks in Gary, Indiana* **10** [PL] **Works** are activities such as digging the ground or building on a large scale. ❑ *six years of disruptive building works, road construction and urban development*
▪ PHRASES **at work** **1** If someone is **at work** they are doing their job or are busy doing a particular activity. ❑ *The salvage teams are already hard at work trying to deal with the spilled oil.* **2** If a force or process is **at work**, it is having a particular influence or effect. ❑ *It is important to understand the powerful economic and social forces at work behind our own actions.*
put someone to work or **set someone to work** If you **put** someone **to work** or **set** them **to work**, you give them a job or task to do. ❑ *By stimulating the economy, we're going to put people to work.*
get to work or **go to work** or **set to work** If you **get to work**, **go to work**, or **set to work** on a job, task, or problem, you start doing it or dealing with it. ❑ *He promised to get to work on the state's massive deficit.*
→ See also **working**

✪ **work·er** ◆◆◆ /'wɜːkə/ NOUN [C] (**workers**) **1** A particular kind of **worker** does the kind of work mentioned. ❑ *She ate her sandwich alongside several other office workers taking their break.* ❑ *The society was looking for a capable research worker.* **2** **Workers** are people who are employed in industry or business and who are not managers. = employee, member of staff; ≠ employer ❑ *Wages have been frozen and workers laid off.* ❑ *The agreement encourages worker participation in management decisions.* **3** You can use **worker** to say how well or badly someone works. ❑ *He is a hard worker and a skilled gardener.*
→ See also **social worker**

W

✪ **work·force** /ˈwɜːkfɔːs/ NOUN [c] (**workforces**) **1** The **workforce** is the total number of people in a country or region who are physically able to do a job and are available for work. ❑ *a country where half the workforce is unemployed* ❑ *large numbers of women entering the workforce* **2** The **workforce** is the total number of people who are employed by a particular company. = staff, personnel ❑ *an employer of a very large workforce* ❑ *44% of the workforce is female.*

work·ing ♦♦♦ /ˈwɜːkɪŋ/ ADJ, NOUN

ADJ **1** [working + N] **Working** people have jobs that they are paid to do. ❑ *Like working women anywhere, Asian women are buying convenience foods.* **2** [working + N] **Working** people are ordinary people who do not have professional or very highly paid jobs. = working class ❑ *The needs and opinions of ordinary working people were ignored.* **3** [working + N] Your **working** life is the period of your life in which you have a job or are of a suitable age to have a job. ❑ *He started his working life as a lorry driver.* **4** [working + N] The **working** population of an area consists of all the people in that area who have a job or who are of a suitable age to have a job. ❑ *Almost 13 per cent of the working population is already unemployed.* **5** [working + N] **Working** conditions or practices are ones that you have in your job. ❑ *The strikers are demanding higher pay and better working conditions.* **6** [working + N] A **working** farm or business exists to do normal work and make a profit, and not only for tourists or as someone's hobby. ❑ *a holiday spent on a working farm* **7** [working + N] The **working** parts of a machine are the parts that move and operate the machine, in contrast to the outer case or container in which they are enclosed. ❑ *The reel comes complete with a set of spares for all the working parts.* **8** [working + N] A **working** knowledge or majority is not very great, but is enough to be useful. ❑ *This book was designed in order to provide a working knowledge of finance and accounts.*

NOUN [PL] (**workings**) The **workings of** a piece of equipment, an organization, or a system are the ways in which it operates and the processes which are involved in it. ❑ *Neural networks are computer systems which mimic the workings of the brain.*

✦ in working order → see order

work·ing class NOUN, ADJ

> The adjective is usually spelled **working-class**.

NOUN [c] (**working classes**) The **working class** or the **working classes** are the group of people in a society who do not own much property, who have low social status, and who do jobs that involve using physical skills rather than intellectual skills. ❑ *A quarter of the working class voted for him.*

ADJ A **working-class** person is someone who is not middle class or upper class. People who do jobs that involve using physical skills rather than intellectual skills are usually regarded as working-class. ❑ *a self-educated man from a working-class background*

work·load /ˈwɜːkləʊd/ NOUN [c] (**workloads**) The **workload** of a person or organization is the amount of work that has to be done by them. ❑ *You need someone to bounce ideas off and share your workload.*

✪ **work·place** /ˈwɜːkpleɪs/ also **work place** NOUN [c] (**workplaces**) Your **workplace** is the place where you work. ❑ *the difficulties facing women in the workplace*

✪ **work·shop** /ˈwɜːkʃɒp/ NOUN [c] (**workshops**) **1** A **workshop** is a period of discussion or practical work on a particular subject in which a group of people share their knowledge or experience. = seminar, master class, tutorial ❑ *Trumpeter Marcus Belgrave ran a jazz workshop for young artists.* ❑ *Students attend a variety of workshops on topics ranging from public speaking to managing stress.* **2** A **workshop** is a building that contains tools or machinery for making or repairing things, especially using wood or metal. ❑ *a modestly equipped workshop*

world ♦♦♦ /wɜːld/ NOUN, ADJ

NOUN [SING, c] (**worlds**) **1** [SING] The **world** is the planet that we live on. ❑ *The satellite enables us to calculate their precise location anywhere in the world.* **2** [SING] The **world**

refers to all the people who live on this planet, and our societies, institutions, and ways of life. ❑ *The world was, and remains, shocked.* ❑ *He wants to show the world that anyone can learn to be an ambassador.* **3** [SING] You can use **world** in expressions such as **the Arab world**, **the Western world**, and **the ancient world** to refer to a particular group of countries or a particular period in history. ❑ *Athens had strong ties to the Arab world.* **4** [c] Someone's **world** is the life they lead, the people they have contact with, and the things they experience. ❑ *His world seemed so different from mine.* **5** [SING] You can use **world** to refer to a particular field of activity, and the people involved in it. ❑ *The publishing world had certainly never seen an event quite like this.* **6** [SING] You can use **world** to refer to a particular group of living things, for example, **the animal world**, **the plant world**, and **the insect world**. = kingdom ❑ *When it comes to dodging disaster, the champions of the insect world have to be cockroaches.*

PHRASES **the best of both worlds** If you say that someone has **the best of both worlds**, you mean that they have only the benefits of two things and none of the disadvantages. ❑ *Her living room provides the best of both worlds, with an office at one end and comfortable sofas at the other.*

do someone a world of good or **do something a world of good** (*informal*) If you say that something **has done** someone **a world of good**, you mean that it has made them feel better or improved their life. ❑ *Just sit for a while and relax. It will do you a world of good.*

what in the world or **who in the world** or **where in the world** (*emphasis*) You can use **in the world** in expressions such as **what in the world** and **who in the world** to emphasize a question, especially when expressing surprise or anger. ❑ *What in the world is he doing?*

in an ideal world or **in a perfect world** You can use **in an ideal world** or **in a perfect world** when you are talking about things that you would like to happen, although you realize that they are not likely to happen. = ideally ❑ *In an ideal world Karen Stevens says she would love to stay at home with her two-and-half-year-old son.*

the outside world You can use **the outside world** to refer to all the people who do not live in a particular place or who are not involved in a particular situation. ❑ *For many, the post office is the only link with the outside world.*

ADJ [world + N] You can use **world** to describe someone or something that is one of the most important or significant of its kind on earth. ❑ *China has once again emerged as a world power.*

→ See also **real world**, **Third World**

✦ not be the end of the world → see end; on top of the world → see top

world-class ADJ (*journalism*) A **world-class** athlete, performer, or organization is one of the best in the world. ❑ *He was determined to become a world-class player.*

world war ♦◇◇ NOUN [c, u] (**world wars**) A **world war** is a war that involves countries all over the world. ❑ *Many senior citizens have been through two world wars.*

✪ **world·wide** ♦◇◇ /ˈwɜːldwaɪd/ also **world-wide** ADV, ADJ

ADV If something exists or happens **worldwide**, it exists or happens throughout the world. = all over the world, around the world ❑ *His books have sold more than 20 million copies worldwide.* ❑ *Worldwide, an enormous amount of research effort goes into military technology.*

ADJ Something that is **worldwide** exists or happens throughout the world. ❑ *Today, doctors are fearing a worldwide epidemic.*

worm ♦◇◇ /wɜːm/ NOUN, VERB

NOUN [c] (**worms**) **1** A **worm** is a small animal with a long, thin body, no bones, and no legs. **2** (*computing*) A **worm** is a computer program that contains a virus which duplicates itself many times in a network. ❑ *a new computer worm that disables security software*

PHRASE **a can of worms** If you say that someone is opening **a can of worms**, you are warning them that they are planning to do or talk about something that is much more complicated, unpleasant, or difficult than they

W

realize and that might be better left alone. ❑ *Introducing this legislation would be like opening a can of worms.*

VERB [T] (**worms, worming, wormed**) *(disapproval)* If you say that someone **is worming** their **way** to success, or **is worming** their **way** into someone else's affection, you disapprove of the way that they are gradually making someone trust them or like them, often in order to deceive them or gain some advantage. ❑ *She never misses a chance to worm her way into the public's hearts.*

worn /wɔːn/ IRREG FORM, ADJ
IRREG FORM **Worn** is the past participle of **wear**.
ADJ **1** **Worn** is used to describe something that is damaged or thin because it is old and has been used a lot. ❑ *Worn rugs increase the danger of tripping.* **2** [V-LINK + worn] If someone looks **worn**, they look tired and old. ❑ *She was looking very haggard and worn.*

worn out also **worn-out** ADJ **1** Something that is **worn out** is so old, damaged, or thin from use that it cannot be used anymore. ❑ *Car buyers tend to replace worn-out tyres with the same brand.* **2** Someone who is **worn out** is extremely tired after hard work or a difficult or unpleasant experience. = exhausted ❑ *Before the race, he is fine. But afterwards he is worn out.*

wor·ried ◆◇◇ /'wʌrɪd, AmE 'wɜːrɪd/ ADJ When you are **worried**, you are unhappy because you keep thinking about problems that you have or about unpleasant things that might happen in the future. = anxious ❑ *He seemed very worried.*

wor·ry ◆◆◇ /'wʌri, AmE 'wɜːri/ VERB, NOUN
VERB [I, T] (**worries, worrying, worried**) **1** [I, T] If you **worry**, you keep thinking about problems that you have or about unpleasant things that might happen. ❑ *Don't worry, your luggage will come on afterwards by taxi.* ❑ *I worry about her constantly.* ❑ *They worry that high interest rates are keeping the dollar too high.* **2** [T] If someone or something **worries** you, they make you anxious because you keep thinking about problems or unpleasant things that might be connected with them. ❑ *I'm still in the early days of my recovery and that worries me.* **3** [T] *(spoken)* If someone or something does not **worry** you, you do not dislike them or you are not annoyed by them. = bother ❑ *The cold doesn't worry me.*
NOUN [U, C] (**worries**) **1** [U] **Worry** is the state or feeling of anxiety and unhappiness caused by the problems that you have or by thinking about unpleasant things that might happen. ❑ *Modern American life is full of worry: the job, the kids, money, the stock market.* **2** [C] A **worry** is a problem that you keep thinking about and that makes you unhappy. ❑ *My main worry was that Madeleine Johnson would still be there.*

wor·ry·ing /'wʌriɪŋ, AmE 'wɜːriɪŋ/ *(mainly BrE; in AmE, usually use worrisome)* ADJ If something is **worrying**, it causes people to worry.

worse /wɜːs/ IRREG FORM, NOUN
IRREG FORM **1** **Worse** is the comparative of **bad**. **2** **Worse** is the comparative of **badly**.
NOUN
PHRASE **change for the worse** If a situation changes **for the worse**, it becomes more unpleasant or more difficult. ❑ *The grandparents sigh and say how things have changed for the worse.*

✪ wors·en /'wɜːsən/ VERB [I, T] (**worsens, worsening, worsened**) If a bad situation **worsens** or if something **worsens** it, it becomes more difficult, unpleasant, or unacceptable. = deteriorate, get worse; ≠ improve ❑ *The security forces had to intervene to prevent the situation worsening.* ❑ *They remain in freezing weather and rapidly worsening conditions.*

wor·ship /'wɜːʃɪp/ VERB, NOUN
VERB [I, T] (**worships, worshipping, worshipped; in AmE, use worshiping, worshiped**) **1** [I, T] If you **worship** a god, you show your respect to the god, for example, by saying prayers. ❑ *disputes over ways of life and ways of worshipping God* ❑ *He prefers to worship in his own home.* **2** [T] If you **worship** someone or something, you love them or admire them very much. ❑ *She had worshipped him for years.*
NOUN [U] **Worship** is the expression of respect to a god, for

example, by saying prayers. ❑ *the worship of the ancient Roman gods*
wor·shipp·er /'wɜːʃɪpə/ NOUN [C] (**worshippers**) ❑ *She burst into tears and loud sobs that disturbed the other worshippers.*

worst /wɜːst/ IRREG FORM, NOUN
IRREG FORM **1** **Worst** is the superlative of **bad**. **2** **Worst** is the superlative of **badly**. **3** **Worst** is used to form the superlative of compound adjectives beginning with 'bad' and 'badly'. For example, the superlative of 'badly-affected' is 'worst-affected'. ❑ *The worst-affected areas were in Jefferson Parish.*
NOUN [SING] **The worst** is the most unpleasant or unfavourable thing that could happen or does happen. ❑ *Though mine safety has much improved, miners' families still fear the worst.*
PHRASES **worst of all** You say **worst of all** to indicate that what you are about to mention is the most unpleasant or has the most disadvantages out of all the things you are mentioning. ❑ *The people most closely affected are the passengers who were injured and, worst of all, those who lost relatives.*
at (the) worst You use **at worst** or **at the worst** to indicate that you are mentioning the worst thing that might happen in a situation. ❑ *At best Nella would be an invalid; at worst she would die.*
at one's worst When someone is **at their worst**, they are as unpleasant, bad, or unsuccessful as it is possible for them to be. ❑ *This was their mother at her worst. Her voice was strident, she was ready to be angry at anyone.*
if the worst comes to the worst You use **if the worst comes to the worst** or **if the worst comes to the worst** to say what you might do if a situation develops in the most unfavourable way possible. ❑ *If worst comes to worst, Europe could withstand a trade war.*

worth ◆◆◇ /wɜːθ/ VERB, COMB, PRON
VERB [T] **1** [V-LINK 'worth' + AMOUNT] If something is **worth** a particular amount of money, it can be sold for that amount or is considered to have that value. ❑ *A local jeweller says the pearl is worth at least £300.* ❑ *His mother inherited a business worth £15,000 a year.* **2** [V-LINK 'worth' -ING] If you say that something is **worth** having, you mean that it is pleasant or useful, and therefore a good thing to have. ❑ *He's decided to get a look at the house and see if it might be worth buying.* ❑ *Most things worth having never come easy.* **3** [V-LINK + worth + N/-ING] If something is **worth** a particular action, or if an action is **worth** doing, it is considered to be important enough for that action. ❑ *I am spending a lot of money and time on this boat, but it is worth it.* ❑ *This restaurant is well worth a visit.*
PHRASE **worth your while** If an action or activity is **worth** someone's **while**, it will be helpful, useful, or enjoyable for them if they do it, even though it requires some effort. = worthwhile ❑ *It might be worth your while to go to court and ask for the agreement to be changed.*
COMB **1** [worth 'of' N] **Worth** combines with amounts of money, so that when you talk about a particular amount of money's **worth of** something, you mean the quantity of it that you can buy for that amount of money. ❑ *I went and bought about three pounds' worth of crisps.* **2** [worth 'of' N] **Worth** combines with time expressions, so you can use **worth** when you are saying how long an amount of something will last. For example, a week's **worth** of food is the amount of food that will last you for a week. ❑ *You've got three years' worth of research money to do what you want with.*
PRON **1** **Worth** combines with amounts of money, so that when you talk about a particular amount of money's **worth**, you mean the quantity of it that you can buy for that amount of money. ❑ *Gold reserves had fallen to less than $3 billion worth.* **2** **Worth** combines with time expressions, so you can use **worth** when you are saying how long an amount of something will last. For example, a week's **worth** is the amount that will last you for a week. ❑ *There's really not very much food down there. About two weeks' worth.*
✦ **worth your weight in gold** → see **weight**

W

worth·less /'wɜːθləs/ ADJ **1** Something that is **worthless** is of no real value or use. = useless □ *The guarantee could be worthless if the store goes out of business.* □ *Training is worthless unless there is proof that it works.* **2** Someone who is described as **worthless** is considered to have no good qualities or skills. □ *You feel you really are completely worthless and unlovable.*

✪ worth·while /ˌwɜːθˈwaɪl/ ADJ If something is **worthwhile**, it is enjoyable or useful, and worth the time, money, or effort that is spent on it. = useful, helpful, valuable; ≠ useless, wasteful □ *The president's trip to Washington this week seems to have been worthwhile.* □ *an interesting and worthwhile project*

wor·thy /'wɜːði/ ADJ (**worthier, worthiest**) (*formal*) If a person or thing is **worthy** of something, they deserve it because they have the qualities or abilities required. □ *The bank might think you're worthy of a loan.*

would ◆◆◆ /wəd, STRONG wʊd/ VERB [MODAL] **1** You use **would** when you are saying what someone believed, hoped, or expected to happen or be the case. □ *No one believed the soldiers stationed at the border would actually open fire.* □ *Would he always be like this?* **2** You use **would** when saying what someone intended to do. □ *The statement added that although there were a number of differing views, these would be discussed by both sides.* **3** You use **would** when you are referring to the result or effect of a possible situation. □ *Ordinarily it would be fun to be taken to fabulous restaurants.* □ *It would be wrong to suggest that police officers were not annoyed by acts of indecency.* **4** You use **would**, or **would have** with a past participle, to indicate that you are assuming or guessing that something is true, because you have good reasons for thinking it. □ *You wouldn't know him.* □ *His fans would already be familiar with Caroline.* **5** You use **would** in the main clause of some 'if' and 'unless' sentences to indicate something you consider to be fairly unlikely to happen. □ *If only I could get some sleep, I would be able to cope.* **6** You use **would** to say that someone was willing to do something. You use **would not** to indicate that they refused to do something. □ *They said they would give the police their full cooperation.* □ *He wouldn't say where he had picked up the information.* **7** You use **would not** to indicate that something did not happen, often in spite of a lot of effort. □ *He kicked, pushed, and hurled his shoulder at the door. It wouldn't open.* **8** You use **would**, especially with 'like', 'love', and 'wish', when saying that someone wants to do or have a particular thing or wants a particular thing to happen. □ *She asked me what I would like to do and mentioned a particular job.* □ *Ideally, she would love to become pregnant again.* **9** You use **would** with 'if' clauses in questions when you are asking for permission to do something. □ *Do you think it would be all right if I smoked?* **10** You use **would**, usually in questions with 'like', when you are making a polite offer or invitation. □ *Would you like a drink?* □ *Would you like to stay?* **11** You use **would**, usually in questions, when you are politely asking someone to do something. = could □ *Would you do me a favour and get rid of this letter I've just received?* □ *Would you come in here a moment, please?* **12** You say that someone **would** do something when it is typical of them and you are critical of it. You emphasize the word **would** when you use it in this way. □ *Well, you would say that: you're a man.* **13** You use **would**, or sometimes **would have** with a past participle, when you are expressing your opinion about something or seeing if people agree with you, especially when you are uncertain about what you are saying. □ *I think you'd agree he's a very respected columnist.* □ *I would have thought he was too old to do that job.* **14** You use **I would** when you are giving someone advice in an informal way. □ *If I were you I would simply ring your friend's doorbell and ask for your bike back.* **15** You use **you would** in negative sentences with verbs such as 'guess' and 'know' when you want to say that something is not obvious, especially something surprising. □ *Chris is so full of artistic temperament you'd never think she was the daughter of a banker.* **16** You use **would have** with a past participle when you are saying what was likely to have happened by a particular time. □ *Within ten weeks of the introduction, 34*
million people would have been reached by our television commercials. **17** You use **would have** with a past participle when you are referring to the result or effect of a possible event in the past. □ *My daughter would have been 17 this week if she had lived.* **18** If you say that someone **would** liked or preferred something, you mean that they wanted to do it or have it but were unable to. □ *I would have liked a life in politics.*
✦ **would rather** → see **rather**

wound IRREG FORM, VERB, NOUN
 IRREG FORM /waʊnd/ **Wound** is the past tense and past participle of **wind**.
 VERB /wuːnd/ [T] (**wounds, wounding, wounded**) **1** If a weapon or something sharp **wounds** you, it damages your body. □ *A bomb exploded in a hotel, killing six people and wounding another five.* **2** If you **are wounded** by what someone says or does, your feelings are deeply hurt. = hurt □ *He was deeply wounded by his son's comments.*
 NOUN /wuːnd/ [C] (**wounds**) A **wound** is damage to part of your body, especially a cut or a hole in your flesh, which is caused by a gun, knife, or other weapon. □ *The wound is healing nicely and the patient is healthy.*
wounded /'wuːndɪd/ NOUN [PL] **The wounded** are people who are wounded. □ *Hospitals said they could not cope with the wounded.*

wove /wəʊv/ IRREG FORM **Wove** is the past tense of **weave**.

wo·ven /'wəʊvən/ IRREG FORM, ADJ
 IRREG FORM **Woven** is a past participle of **weave**.
 ADJ **1** A **woven** cloth or carpet has been made by crossing threads over and under each other using a frame or machine called a loom. □ *woven cotton fabrics* **2** A **woven** basket or mat has been made by crossing long plant stems or fibres over and under each other. □ *The floors are covered with woven straw mats.*

wrap ◆◇◇ /ræp/ VERB, NOUN
 VERB [T] (**wraps, wrapping, wrapped**) **1** When you **wrap** something, you fold paper or cloth tightly around it to cover it completely, for example, in order to protect it or so that you can give it to someone as a present. □ *Harry had carefully bought and wrapped presents for Mark to give the children.* **2** When you **wrap** something such as a piece of paper or cloth around another thing, you put it around it. □ *She wrapped a handkerchief around her bleeding palm in an effort to protect it.*
 PHRASAL VERB **wrap up** **1** **Wrap up** means the same as **wrap** VERB **1**. □ *Diana is taking the opportunity to wrap up the family presents.* **2** If you **wrap up**, you put warm clothes on. □ *She wrapped up in her mother's red shawl.* □ *Kids just love being able to romp around in the fresh air without having to wrap up warm.* **3** If you **wrap up** something such as a job or an agreement, you complete it in a satisfactory way. □ *NATO defence ministers wrap up their meeting in Brussels today.*
 NOUN
 PHRASE **under wraps** If you keep something **under wraps**, you keep it secret, often until you are ready to announce it at some time in the future. □ *The bids were submitted in May and were kept under wraps until October.*

wreck /rek/ VERB, NOUN
 VERB [T] (**wrecks, wrecking, wrecked**) To **wreck** something means to completely destroy or ruin it. □ *He wrecked the garden.* □ *His life has been wrecked by the tragedy.*
 NOUN [C] (**wrecks**) **1** A **wreck** is something such as a ship, car, plane, or building that has been destroyed, usually in an accident. □ *the wreck of a sailing ship* □ *The car was a total wreck.* **2** (*informal*) If you say that someone is a **wreck**, you mean that they are very exhausted or unhealthy. □ *You look a wreck.*

wreck·age /'rekɪdʒ/ NOUN [U] [also 'the' wreckage] When something such as a plane, car, or building has been destroyed, you can refer to what remains as **wreckage** or **the wreckage**. □ *Mark was dragged from the burning wreckage of his car just before it exploded.*

wretch·ed /'retʃɪd/ ADJ **1** [wretched + N] (*informal, feelings*) You use **wretched** to describe someone or something that you dislike or feel angry with. □ *Wretched woman, he thought, why the hell can't she wait?* **2** (*formal*)

Someone who feels **wretched** feels very unhappy.
= miserable ❑ *I feel really confused and wretched.*

wrig·gle /ˈrɪɡəl/ VERB

VERB [I, T] (**wriggles, wriggling, wriggled**) If you **wriggle** or **wriggle** part of your body, you twist and turn with quick movements, for example, because you are uncomfortable. ❑ *The babies are wriggling on their tummies.*

PHRASAL VERB **wriggle out of** (*disapproval*) If you say that someone has **wriggled out of** doing something, you disapprove of the fact that that they have managed to avoid doing it, although they should have done it. = get out of ❑ *He's wriggled out of doing the dishes again.*

wrin·kle /ˈrɪŋkəl/ NOUN, VERB

NOUN [C] (**wrinkles**) **1** Wrinkles are lines that form on someone's face as they grow old. ❑ *His face was covered with wrinkles.* **2** A **wrinkle** is a raised fold in a piece of cloth or paper that spoils its appearance. ❑ *Ben brushed smooth a wrinkle in his trousers.*

VERB [I, T] (**wrinkles, wrinkling, wrinkled**) **1** When someone's skin **wrinkles** or when something **wrinkles** it, lines start to form in it because the skin is getting old or damaged. ❑ *The skin on her cheeks and around her eyes was beginning to wrinkle.* **2** If cloth **wrinkles**, or if someone or something **wrinkles** it, it gets folds or lines in it. ❑ *Her stockings wrinkled at the ankles.* **3** When you **wrinkle** your nose or forehead, or when it **wrinkles**, you tighten the muscles in your face so that the skin folds. ❑ *Donna wrinkled her nose at her daughter.*

wrin·kled /ˈrɪŋkəld/ ADJ **1** *I did indeed look older and more wrinkled than ever.* **2** *His suit was wrinkled and he looked very tired.*

wrist /rɪst/ NOUN [C] (**wrists**) Your **wrist** is the part of your body between your hand and your arm that bends when you move your hand. ❑ *He broke his wrist climbing rocks for a cigarette advert.*

write ◆◆◆ /raɪt/ VERB

VERB [I, T] (**writes, writing, wrote, written**) **1** [I, T] When you **write**, you use something such as a pen or pencil to produce words, letters, or numbers. ❑ *Simply write your name and address on a postcard and send it to us.* ❑ *They were still trying to teach her to read and write.* **2** [T] If you **write** something such as a book, a poem, or a piece of music, you create it and record it on paper or perhaps on a computer. ❑ *I had written quite a lot of orchestral music in my student days.* ❑ *Thereafter she wrote articles for papers and magazines in Paris.* **3** [I] Someone who **writes** creates books, stories, or articles, usually for publication. ❑ *Jay wanted to write.* **4** [I, T] When you **write to** someone or **write** them a letter, you give them information, ask them something, or express your feelings in a letter.
❑ *Apparently she had written to her aunt in Holland asking for advice.* ❑ *She had written him a note a couple of weeks earlier.* ❑ *I wrote a letter to the car rental agency, explaining what had happened.* **5** [T] When someone **writes** something such as a cheque, receipt, or prescription, they put the necessary information on it and it usually sign it. ❑ *Snape wrote a receipt with a gold fountain pen.* **6** [I] (computing) If you **write** to a computer or a disk, you record data on it. ❑ *You should write-protect all disks that you do not usually need to write to.*

PHRASAL VERBS **write back** If you **write back** to someone who has sent you a letter, you write them a letter in reply. ❑ *Macmillan wrote back saying that he could certainly help.*

write down When you **write** something **down**, you record it on a piece of paper using a pen or pencil. ❑ *On the morning before starting a diet, write down your starting weight.*

write in If you **write in** to an organization, you send them a letter. ❑ *What's the point in writing in when you only print half the letter anyway?*

write into If a rule or detail **is written into** a contract, law, or agreement, it is included in it when the contract, law, or agreement is made. ❑ *They insisted that a guaranteed supply of Chinese food was written into their contracts.*

write off 1 (*business*) If someone **writes off** a debt or an amount of money that has been spent on a project, they accept that they are never going to get the money back.

❑ *It was the president who persuaded the West to write off Polish debts.* **2** If you **write** someone or something **off**, you decide that they are unimportant or useless and that they are not worth further serious attention. = dismiss ❑ *He is fed up with people writing him off because of his age.* ❑ *His critics write him off as too cautious to succeed.* **3** If you **write off** a plan or project, you accept that it is not going to be successful and do not continue with it. ❑ *We decided to write off the rest of the day and go shopping.* **4** If you **write off** something such as a living expense, you deduct it from your taxes. ❑ *Teachers are still entitled to write off business expenses.* **5** (BrE) If you **write off** to a company or organization, you send them a letter, usually asking for something. = write

write out 1 When you **write out** something fairly long such as a report or a list, you write it on paper. ❑ *We had to write out a list of ten jobs we'd like to do.* **2** If a character in a drama series **is written out**, he or she is taken out of the series. ❑ *Terry's character has been written out of the show.*

write up If you **write up** something that has been done or said, you record it on paper in a neat and complete form, usually using notes that you have made. ❑ *He wrote up his visit in a report of over 600 pages.*

→ See also **writing, written**

✦ nothing to write home about → see **home**

writ·er ◆◆◇ /ˈraɪtə/ NOUN [C] (**writers**) **1** A **writer** is a person who writes books, stories, or articles as a job. ❑ *Turner is a writer and critic.* ❑ *detective stories by American writers* **2** The **writer** of a particular article, report, letter, or story is the person who wrote it. ❑ *No one is to see the document without the permission of the writer of the report.*

writ·ing ◆◆◇ /ˈraɪtɪŋ/ NOUN [U] **1** Writing is something that has been written or printed. ❑ *If you have a complaint about your holiday, please inform us in writing.* **2** You can refer to any piece of written work as **writing**, especially when you are considering the style of language used in it. ❑ *The writing is brutally tough and savagely humorous.* **3** Writing is the activity of writing, especially of writing books for money. ❑ *She had begun to be a little bored with novel writing.* **4** Your **writing** is the way that you write with a pen or pencil, which can usually be recognized as belonging to you. = handwriting ❑ *It was a little difficult to read your writing.*

writ·ten ◆◇◇ /ˈrɪtən/ IRREG FORM, ADJ

IRREG FORM **Written** is the past participle of **write**.

ADJ **1** A **written** test or piece of work is one that involves writing rather than doing something practical or giving spoken answers. ❑ *knowledge that can be assessed in a short, written test* **2** [written + N] A **written** agreement, rule, or law has been officially written down. ❑ *The newspaper broke a written agreement not to sell certain photographs.*

wrong ◆◆◇ /rɒŋ, AmE rɔːŋ/ ADJ, ADV, NOUN

ADJ **1** [V-LINK + wrong] If you say there is something **wrong**, you mean there is something unsatisfactory about the situation, person, or thing you are talking about. ❑ *Pain is the body's way of telling us that something is wrong.* ❑ *Nobody seemed to notice anything wrong.* ❑ *What's wrong with him?* **2** If you choose the **wrong** thing, person, or method, you make a mistake and do not choose the one that you really want. ❑ *He went to the wrong house.* ❑ *The wrong man had been punished.* **3** [wrong + N] If something such as a decision, choice, or action is **the wrong** one, it is not the best or most suitable one. ❑ *I really made the wrong decision there.* ❑ *The wrong choice of job might limit your chances of success.* **4** If something is **wrong**, it is incorrect and not in accordance with the facts. ❑ *How do you know that this explanation is wrong?* ❑ *a clock which showed the wrong time* **5** [V-LINK + wrong] If something is **wrong** or goes **wrong** with a machine or piece of equipment, it stops working properly. ❑ *We think there's something wrong with the computer.* **6** [V-LINK + wrong] If you are **wrong** about something, what you say or think about it is not correct. ❑ *I was wrong about it being a casual meeting.* ❑ *I'm sure you've got it wrong. Kate isn't like that.* **7** [wrong + to-INF] If you think that someone was **wrong to** do something, you think that they should not have done it because it was bad or immoral. ❑ *She was wrong to leave her child alone.*

w

8 [V-LINK + wrong] **Wrong** is used to refer to activities or actions that are considered to be morally bad and unacceptable. ❑ *Is it wrong to try to save the life of someone you love?* ❑ *They thought slavery was morally wrong.*
9 [wrong + N] You use **wrong** to describe something that is not thought to be socially acceptable or desirable. ❑ *If you went to the wrong school, you won't get the job.*
PHRASE **go wrong** If a situation **goes wrong**, it stops progressing in the way that you expected or intended, and becomes much worse. ❑ *We should investigate what happened, what went wrong.*
ADV **1** [wrong after V] If you do something **wrong**, you make a mistake or do not do something in the best or most suitable way. ❑ *You've done it wrong.* **2** [wrong after V] If something is done **wrong**, it is incorrect and not in accordance with the facts. ❑ *I must have added it up wrong, then.* ❑ *It looks like it's spelled wrong.*
NOUN [U, C] (**wrongs**) **1** [U] **Wrong** is behaviour that is incorrect or inappropriate. ❑ *a man who believes that he has done no wrong.* **2** [U] **Wrong** is behaviour that is illegal, bad, or immoral. ❑ *Johnson didn't seem to be able to tell the difference between right and wrong.* **3** [C] A **wrong** is an

unfair or immoral action. ❑ *No matter how difficult it might be, she had to right the terrible wrong she'd done to him.*
PHRASE **in the wrong** If someone who is involved in an argument or dispute has behaved in a way which is morally or legally wrong, you can say that they are **in the wrong**. ❑ *He didn't press charges because he was in the wrong.*
wrong·ly /ˈrɒŋli, AmE ˈrɔːŋli/ ADV ❑ *A child was wrongly diagnosed as having a bone tumour.*
✦ **get off on the wrong foot** → see **foot**; **get hold of the wrong end of the stick** → see **stick**

wrong·doing /ˈrɒŋduːɪŋ, AmE ˈrɔːŋ-/ NOUN [C, U] (**wrongdoings**) **Wrongdoing** is behaviour that is illegal or immoral. ❑ *The city attorney's office hasn't found any evidence of criminal wrongdoing.*

wrong·ful /ˈrɒŋfʊl, AmE ˈrɔːŋ-/ ADJ A **wrongful** act is one that is illegal, immoral, or unjust. ❑ *He is on hunger strike in protest at what he claims is his wrongful conviction for murder.*
wrong·ful·ly /ˈrɒŋfəli, AmE ˈrɔːŋ-/ ADV [wrongfully with V] = **unjustly** ❑ *The criminal justice system is in need of urgent reform to prevent more people being wrongfully imprisoned.*

wrote /rəʊt/ IRREG FORM **Wrote** is the past tense of **write**.

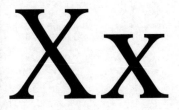

Xx

Yy

X also **x** /eks/ NOUN [C, U] (**X's, x's**) X is the twenty-fourth letter of the English alphabet.

✪**X-ray** also **x-ray** NOUN, VERB

NOUN [C] (**X-rays**) **1** X-rays are a type of radiation that can pass through most solid materials. X-rays are used by doctors to examine the bones or organs inside your body and are also used at airports to see inside people's luggage. ❑ *Checked baggage is passed through X-ray machines.* **2** An

X-ray is a picture made by sending X-rays through something, usually someone's body. = scan ❑ *She was advised to have an abdominal X-ray.* ❑ *The X-ray revealed minor head injuries.*

VERB [T] (**X-rays, X-raying, X-rayed**) If someone or something **is X-rayed**, an X-ray picture is taken of them. = scan ❑ *All hand baggage would be X-rayed.* ❑ *They took my pulse, took my blood pressure, and X-rayed my jaw.*

Yy

Y also **y** /waɪ/ NOUN [C, U] (**Y's, y's**) Y is the twenty-fifth letter of the English alphabet.

yacht ♦♢♢ /jɒt/ NOUN [C] (**yachts**) A **yacht** is a large boat with sails or a motor, used for racing or pleasure trips. ❑ *His 36-ft yacht sank suddenly last summer.*

✪ yard ♦♦♢ /jɑːd/ NOUN [C] (**yards**) **1** A **yard** is a unit of length equal to thirty-six inches or approximately 91.4 centimetres. ❑ *The incident took place about 500 yards from where he was standing.* ❑ *a long narrow strip of linen two or three yards long* ❑ *a yard of silk* **2** A **yard** is a flat area of concrete or stone that is next to a building and often has a wall around it. = courtyard ❑ *I saw him standing in the yard.* **3** You can refer to a large open area where a particular type of work is done as a **yard**. ❑ *a railway yard*

yard·stick /'jɑːdstɪk/ NOUN [C] (**yardsticks**) If you use someone or something as a **yardstick**, you use them as a standard for comparison when you are judging other people or things. ❑ *The book gives a yardstick for measuring assets.*

yawn /jɔːn/ VERB, NOUN
   VERB [I] (**yawns, yawning, yawned**) If you **yawn**, you open your mouth very wide and breathe in more air than usual, often when you are tired or when you are not interested in something. ❑ *She yawned, and stretched lazily.*
   NOUN [C] (**yawns**) A **yawn** is the act of opening your mouth very wide and breathing in more air than usual, often when you are tired or when you are not interested in something. ❑ *Rosanna stifled a huge yawn.*

year ♦♦♦ /jɪə/ NOUN
   NOUN [C, PL] (**years**) **1** [C] A **year** is a period of twelve months or 365 or 366 days, beginning on the first of January and ending on the thirty-first of December. ❑ *The year was 1840.* ❑ *We had an election last year.* **2** [C] A **year** is any period of twelve months. ❑ *The museums attract more than two and a half million visitors a year.* ❑ *She's done quite a bit of work this past year.* **3** [C] **Year** is used to refer to the age of a person. For example, if someone or something is twenty **years** old or twenty **years** of age, they have lived or existed for twenty years. ❑ *He's 58 years old.* ❑ *I've been in trouble since I was eleven years of age.* **4** [C] A school or academic **year** is the period of time in each twelve months when schools or colleges are open and students are studying there. The school year starts in September. ❑ *the 2015/16 academic year* **5** [C] (*business*) A financial or business **year** is an exact period of twelve months which businesses or institutions use as a basis for organizing their finances. ❑ *He announced big tax increases for the next two financial years.* **6** [PL] You can use **years** to emphasize that you are referring to a long time. = ages ❑ *I haven't laughed so much in years.*
   PHRASES **all year round** If you say something happens **all year round** or **all the year round**, it happens continually throughout the year. ❑ *Town gardens are ideal because they produce flowers nearly all year round.*
   year after year If something happens **year after year**, it happens regularly every year. ❑ *Regulars return year after year.*
   year by year If something changes **year by year**, it changes gradually each year. ❑ *This problem has increased year by year.*
   → See also **leap year**

year·ly /'jɪəli/ ADJ, ADV
   ADJ **1** [yearly + N] A **yearly** event happens once a year or every year. = annual ❑ *The two sisters looked forward to their yearly meetings.* **2** [yearly + N] You use **yearly** to describe something such as an amount that relates to a period of one year. = annual ❑ *In Holland, the government sets a yearly budget for health care.*
   ADV **1** [yearly after V] If something happens **yearly**, it happens once a year or every year. = annually ❑ *Clients normally pay fees in advance, monthly, quarterly, or yearly.* **2** [yearly after V] If a particular amount is spent **yearly**, it is spent over a period of one year. = annually ❑ *Novello says college students will spend $4.2 billion yearly on alcoholic beverages.*

yearn /jɜːn/ VERB [I, T] (**yearns, yearning, yearned**) If someone **yearns for** something that they are unlikely to get, they want it very much. = long ❑ *He yearned for freedom.* ❑ *I yearned to be an actor.*

yell /jel/ VERB, NOUN
   VERB [I, T] (**yells, yelling, yelled**) If you **yell**, you shout loudly, usually because you are excited, angry, or in pain. ❑ *'Eva!' he yelled.* ❑ *I'm sorry I yelled at you last night.*
   PHRASAL VERB **yell out** Yell out means the same as yell VERB. ❑ *'Are you coming or not?' they yelled out after him.*
   NOUN [C] (**yells**) A **yell** is a loud shout given by someone who is afraid or in pain. = cry ❑ *Something brushed past Bob's face and he let out a yell.*

yel·low ♦♦♦ /'jeləʊ/ COLOUR Something that is **yellow** is the colour of lemons, butter, or the middle part of an egg. ❑ *The walls have been painted bright yellow.*

yes ♦♦♦ /jes/
   CONVENTION

   In informal English, **yes** is often pronounced in a casual way that is usually written as **yeah**.

1 You use **yes** to give a positive response to a question. ❑ *'Are you a friend of Nick's?'—'Yes.'* ❑ *'You actually wrote it down, didn't you?'—'Yes.'* **2** You use **yes** to accept an offer or request, or to give permission. ❑ *'More wine?'—'Yes please.'* ❑ *'Will you take me there?'—'Yes, I will.'* **3** You use **yes** to tell someone that what they have said is correct. ❑ *'Well, I suppose it is based on the old lunar months, isn't it?'—'Yes, that's right.'* **4** You use **yes** to show that you are ready or willing to speak to the person who wants to speak to you, for example when you are answering a telephone or a knock at your door. ❑ *He pushed a button on the intercom. 'Yes?' came a voice.* **5** You use **yes** to indicate that you agree with, accept, or understand what the previous speaker has said. ❑ *'A lot of people find it very difficult indeed to give up smoking.'—'Oh yes. I used to smoke three packets a day.'* **6** You use **yes** to encourage someone to continue speaking. ❑ *'I remembered something funny today.'—'Yes?'* **7** You use **yes**, usually followed by 'but', as a polite way of introducing what you want to say when you disagree with something the previous speaker has just said. ❑ *'She is entitled to her personal allowance which is three thousand dollars of income.'—'Yes, but she doesn't earn any money.'* **8** You use **yes** to say that a negative statement or question that the previous speaker has made is wrong or untrue. ❑ *'That is not possible,' she said.—'Oh, yes, it is!' Mrs Gruen insisted.* **9** You can use **yes** to suggest that you do not believe or agree with what the previous speaker has said, especially when you want to express your annoyance about it. □ *'There was no way to stop it.'—'Oh yeah? Well, here's something else you won't be able to stop.'* **10** You use **yes** to indicate that you had forgotten something and have just remembered it. □ *What was I going to say. Oh yeah, we've finally got our second computer.* **11** You use **yes** to emphasize and confirm a statement that you are making. □ *He collected the $10,000 first prize. Yes, $10,000.* **12** You say **yes and no** in reply to a question when you cannot give a definite answer, because in some ways the answer is yes and in other ways the answer is no. □ *'Was it strange for you, going back after such a long absence?'—'Yes and no.'*

yes·ter·day ♦♦♦ /ˈjestədeɪ, -di/ ADV, NOUN
ADV [yesterday with CL] You use **yesterday** to refer to the day before today. □ *She left yesterday.*
NOUN [U] (**yesterdays**) **1** **Yesterday** is the day before today. □ *In yesterday's games, Switzerland beat the United States two to one.* **2** [also yesterdays] You can refer to the past, especially the recent past, as **yesterday**. □ *The worker of today is different from the worker of yesterday.*

yet ♦♦♦ /jet/ ADV, CONJ
ADV **1** You use **yet** in negative statements to indicate that something has not happened up to the present time, although it probably will happen. You can also use **yet** in questions to ask if something has happened up to the present time. □ *They haven't finished yet.* □ *No decision has yet been made.* □ *She hasn't yet set a date for her marriage.* **2** You use **yet** with a negative statement when you are talking about the past, to report something that was not the case then, although it became the case later. □ *There was so much that Sam didn't know yet.* **3** [with BRD-NEG, yet with V] If you say that something should not or cannot be done yet, you mean that it should not or cannot be done now, although it will have to be done at a later time. □ *Don't get up yet.* □ *The hostages cannot go home just yet.* **4** You use **yet** after a superlative to indicate, for example, that something is the worst or the best of its kind up to the present time. □ *This is the network's worst idea yet.* □ *Her latest novel is her best yet.* **5** [yet before V] You can use **yet** to say that there is still a possibility that something will happen. = still □ *Like the best stories, this one may yet have a happy ending.* **6** [N + yet] You can use **yet** after expressions that refer to a period of time, when you want to say how much longer a situation will continue for. □ *Unemployment will go on rising for some time yet.* □ *Nothing will happen for a few years yet.* **7** [yet + to-INF] If you say that you have **yet** to do something, you mean that you have never done it, especially when this is surprising or bad. □ *She has yet to spend a Christmas with her husband.* **8** You can use **yet** to emphasize a word, especially when you are saying that something is surprising because it is more extreme than previous things of its kind, or a further case of them. □ *I saw yet another doctor.* □ *They would criticize me, or worse yet, pay me no attention.*
PHRASE **as yet** (formal) You use **as yet** with negative statements to describe a situation that has existed up until the present time. □ *As yet it is not known whether the crash was the result of an accident.*
CONJ You can use **yet** to introduce a fact that is rather surprising after the previous fact you have just mentioned. = but □ *I don't eat much, yet I am a size 16.*

✪**yield** ♦◊◊ /jiːld/ VERB, NOUN
VERB [I, T] (**yields**, **yielding**, **yielded**) **1** [I] (formal) If you **yield to** someone or something, you stop resisting them. = give in □ *Carmen yielded to general pressure and grudgingly took the child to a specialist.* **2** [T] (formal) If you **yield** something that you have control of or responsibility for, you allow someone else to have control of or responsibility for it. = surrender □ *He may yield control.* **3** If something **yields**, it breaks or moves position because force or pressure has been put on it. □ *He reached the massive door of the barn and pushed. It yielded.* **4** [T] If an area of land **yields** a particular amount of a crop, this is the amount that is produced. You can also say that a number of animals **yield** a particular amount of meat. = produce □ *Last year 400,000 acres of land yielded a crop*

worth $1.75 billion. □ *The disappointing harvest yielded only 4.5 million tonnes of sugar.* **5** [T] (business) If a tax or investment **yields** an amount of money or profit, this money or profit is obtained from it. □ *It yielded a profit of at least $36 million.* **6** [T] If something **yields** a result or piece of information, it produces it. = produce, generate, allow □ *This research has been in progress since 1961 and has yielded a great number of positive results.* □ *Diagnostics could also yield scientific insights leading to new drugs.*
NOUN [C] (**yields**) **1** A **yield** is the amount of food produced on an area of land or by a number of animals. = harvest, produce □ *improving the yield of the crop* **2** (business) A **yield** is the amount of money or profit produced by an investment. □ *a yield of 4%* □ *The high yields available on the dividend shares made them attractive to private investors.*

yield VERB (formal)
If you **yield to** someone or something, you stop resisting them.
□ *The only way to get rid of temptation is to yield to it.*

give in VERB
If you **give in**, you admit that you are defeated or that you cannot do something.
□ *Officials say that they won't give in to the workers' demands.*

submit VERB (formal)
If you **submit** to something, you unwillingly allow something to be done to you, or you do what someone wants, for example because you are not powerful enough to resist.
□ *Mrs Jones submitted to an operation on her right knee to relieve the pain.*

succumb VERB (formal)
If you **succumb** to temptation or pressure, you do something that you want to do, or that other people want you to do, although you feel it might be wrong.
□ *The minister said his country would never succumb to that kind of pressure.*

surrender VERB (fairly formal)
If you **surrender**, you stop fighting or resisting someone and agree that you have been beaten.
□ *General Martin Bonnet called on the rebels to surrender.*

yoga /ˈjəʊɡə/ NOUN [U] **Yoga** is a type of exercise in which you move your body into various positions in order to become more fit or flexible, to improve your breathing, and to relax your mind. □ *I do yoga twice a week.*

you ♦♦♦ /juː/ PRON

You is the second person pronoun. You can refer to one or more people and is used as the subject of a verb or the object of a verb or preposition.

1 A speaker or writer uses **you** to refer to the person or people that they are talking or writing to. It is possible to use **you** before a noun to make it clear which group of people you are talking to. □ *When I saw you across the room I knew I'd met you before.* □ *You two seem very different to me.* **2** In spoken English and informal written English, **you** is sometimes used to refer to people in general. □ *Getting good results gives you confidence.* □ *In those days you did what you were told.*

✪**young** ♦♦♦ /jʌŋ/ ADJ, NOUN
ADJ (**younger**, **youngest** /ˈjʌŋɡɪst/) **1** A **young** person, animal, or plant has not lived or existed for very long and is not yet mature. □ *sex information written for young people* □ *I crossed the hill, and found myself in a field of young barley.* **2** [young + N] You use **young** to describe a time when a person or thing was young. □ *In her younger days my mother had been a successful saleswoman.* **3** Someone who is **young** in appearance or behaviour looks or behaves as if they are young. □ *I was twenty-three, I suppose, and young for my age.*

y

NOUN [PL] **1** **The young** are people who are young. ❑ *The association is advising pregnant women, the very young and the elderly to avoid such foods.* **2** **The young** of an animal are its babies. = babies, family, litter, offspring, brood ❑ *The hen may not be able to feed its young.* ❑ *Its young are vulnerable to a range of predators.*

young·ster ◆◇◇ /ˈjʌŋstə/ NOUN [C] (**youngsters**) Young people, especially children, are sometimes referred to as **youngsters**. ❑ *Other youngsters are not so lucky.*

your ◆◆◆ /jɔː, jʊə/ DET

> **Your** is the second person possessive determiner. **Your** can refer to one or more people.

1 A speaker or writer uses **your** to indicate that something belongs or relates to the person or people that they are talking or writing to. ❑ *Emma, I trust your opinion a great deal.* ❑ *I left all of your messages on your desk.* **2** In spoken English and informal written English, **your** is sometimes used to indicate that something belongs to or relates to people in general. ❑ *Painkillers are very useful in small amounts to bring your temperature down.* **3** In spoken English, a speaker sometimes uses **your** before an adjective such as 'typical' or 'normal' to indicate that the thing referred to is a typical example of its type. ❑ *This isn't your typical economics class.*

yours ◆◇◇ /jɔːz, jʊəz/ PRON, CONVENTION

> **Yours** is the second person possessive pronoun. **Yours** can refer to one or more people.

PRON A speaker or writer uses **yours** to refer to something that belongs or relates to the person or people that they are talking or writing to. ❑ *I'll take my coat upstairs. Shall I take yours, Roberta?* ❑ *I believe Paul was a friend of yours.* CONVENTION People write **yours**, **yours sincerely**, **sincerely yours**, or **yours truly** at the end of a letter before they sign their name. ❑ *With best regards, Yours, George.*

your·self ◆◆◇ /jɔːˈself, jʊə-/ PRON

> **Yourself** is the second person reflexive pronoun.

(**yourselves**) **1** [V + yourself, PREP + yourself] A speaker or writer uses **yourself** to refer to the person that they are talking or writing to. **Yourself** is used when the object of a verb or preposition refers to the same person as the subject of the verb. ❑ *Have the courage to be honest with yourself and about yourself.* ❑ *Your baby depends on you to look after yourself properly while you are pregnant.* **2** You use **yourself** to emphasize the person that you are referring to. ❑ *You can't convince others if you yourself aren't convinced.* **3** [V + yourself, PREP + yourself] You use **yourself** instead of 'you' for emphasis or in order to be more polite when 'you' is the object of a verb or preposition. ❑ *A wealthy man like yourself is bound to make an enemy or two along the way.*
✦ **by yourself** → see **by**

youth ◆◆◇ /juːθ/ NOUN [U, C, PL] (**youths**) **1** [U] Someone's **youth** is the period of their life during which they are a child, before they are a fully mature adult. ❑ *In my youth my ambition had been to be an inventor.* **2** [U] **Youth** is the quality or state of being young. ❑ *The team is now a good mixture of experience and youth.* **3** [C] Journalists often refer to young men as **youths**, especially when they are reporting that the young men have caused trouble. ❑ *A 17-year-old youth was arrested yesterday.* **4** [PL] **The youth** are young people considered as a group. ❑ *He represents the opinions of the youth of today.*

youth·ful /ˈjuːθfʊl/ ADJ Someone who is **youthful** behaves as if they are young or younger than they really are. ❑ *I'm a very youthful 50.* ❑ *youthful enthusiasm and high spirits*

USAGE NOTE

youth

Do not use **youths** to talk about young people in general. This word is mainly used by journalists to talk about young men who cause trouble. Use **young people** instead.

*A gang of **youths** was seen leaving the scene of the attack.*

*On leaving school, many **young people** take a year out for travel.*

Z also **z** /zed/ NOUN [C, U] (**Z's, z's**) Z is the twenty-sixth and last letter of the English alphabet.

zeal /ziːl/ NOUN [U] Zeal is great enthusiasm, especially in connection with work, religion, or politics. ❑ *his zeal for teaching*

✪**zero** /ˈzɪərəʊ/ NUM, NOUN, ADJ
 NUM (**zeros** or **zeroes**) Zero is the number 0. = nought
 ❑ *Visibility at the city's airport came down to zero, bringing air traffic to a standstill.* ❑ *a scale ranging from zero to seven*
 NOUN [U] Zero is a temperature of 0°. It is freezing point on the centigrade and Celsius scales, and 32° below freezing point on the Fahrenheit scale. ❑ *It's a sunny late winter day, just a few degrees above zero.* ❑ *That night the mercury fell to thirty degrees below zero.*
 ADJ You can use **zero** to say that there is none at all of the thing mentioned. ❑ *This new ministry was being created with zero assets and zero liabilities.*

zest /zest/ NOUN [U] **1** [also 'a' zest, oft zest 'for' N] Zest is a feeling of pleasure and enthusiasm. ❑ *He has a zest for life and a quick intellect.* **2** Zest is a quality in an activity or situation which you find exciting. ❑ *Live interviews add zest and a touch of the unexpected to any piece of research.*

zinc /zɪŋk/ NOUN [U] Zinc is a bluish-white metal which is used to make other metals such as brass, or to cover other metals such as iron to stop rust from forming.

zip /zɪp/ VERB, NOUN
 VERB [T] (**zips, zipping, zipped**) **1** When you **zip** something, you fasten it using a zip. ❑ *She zipped her jeans.* **2** (*computing*) To **zip** a computer file means to compress it so that it needs less space for storage on disk and can be transmitted more quickly. ❑ *If you zipped the files first, they did not become read-only when written to the CD.*
 PHRASAL VERB **zip up** **1** If you **zip up** something such as a piece of clothing or if it **zips up**, you are able to fasten it using its zip. ❑ *He zipped up his jeans.* **2** (*computing*) To **zip**

up a computer file means to compress it so that it needs less space for storage on disk and can be transmitted more quickly. ❑ *These files have been zipped up to take up less disk space so they take less time to download.*
 NOUN [C] (**zips**) (*mainly BrE*; in *AmE*, usually use **zipper**) A **zip** or **zip fastener** is a device used to open and close parts of clothes and bags. It consists of two rows of metal or plastic teeth which separate or fasten together as you pull a small handle along them. ❑ *He pulled the zip of his leather jacket down slightly.*

✪**zone** ♦◇◇ /zəʊn/ NOUN, VERB
 NOUN [C] (**zones**) A **zone** is an area that has particular features or characteristics. ❑ *Many people have stayed behind in the potential war zone.* ❑ *The area has been declared a disaster zone.* = area, region, section, territory
 VERB [T] (**zones, zoning, zoned**) If an area of land **is zoned**, it is formally set aside for a particular purpose. ❑ *The land was not zoned for commercial purposes.*
 zon•ing /ˈzəʊnɪŋ/ NOUN [U] ❑ *the use of zoning to preserve agricultural land*

zoo /zuː/ NOUN [C] (**zoos**) A **zoo** is a park where live animals are kept so that people can look at them. ❑ *He took his son Christopher to the zoo.*

zo•ol•o•gy /zuːˈɒlədʒi, zəʊ-/ NOUN [U] Zoology is the scientific study of animals.
 zoo•logi•cal /ˌzuːəˈlɒdʒɪkəl/ ADJ [zoological + N] ❑ *zoological specimens*

zoom /zuːm/ VERB
 VERB [I] (**zooms, zooming, zoomed**) (*informal*) If you **zoom** somewhere, you go there very quickly. = speed ❑ *We zoomed through the gallery.*
 PHRASAL VERB **zoom in** If a camera **zooms in** on something that is being filmed or photographed, it gives a close-up picture of it. ❑ *a tracking system which can follow a burglar around a building and zoom in on his face*

Writing for IELTS

Contents

Introduction to the writing section of the IELTS exam

The **writing** section of the IELTS exam can be intimidating, but it does not have to be. You can soon learn to plan your answers quickly, and use the opportunity to demonstrate your range of vocabulary and grammar as you write. *Writing for IELTS* will guide you through the writing part of the exam. Sample answers show how you can use appropriate phrases and expressions and grammatical structures, so that you will soon feel confident about your writing skills.

The following tips will help you use this writing guide more effectively.

When you are preparing for your exam, read as many sample answers and examples of model essays as you can, paying attention to the phrases and collocations used. Keep a notebook and make notes of useful phrases for future use.

- In the exam, plan your answer and write a short draft before you start writing the essay. Once you have a clear idea of what the content of your essay should be, you can more easily focus on the best language to express what you want to say. Remember to draw a line through your draft so that the examiner knows not to mark it.

- Organize your essay into paragraphs. Start with an introductory paragraph and end with an overall conclusion.

- Ensure that each paragraph in the body of the essay starts with a topic sentence. A topic sentence is a sentence that summarizes the key point of that paragraph.

- Learn to use discourse markers like 'however', 'because' or 'such as' to make your essay more cohesive.

- Avoid repeating the words in the exam questions, and avoid using the same vocabulary again and again. Think of other words and phrases that can express the same meaning.

- Avoid translating phrases and collocations from your language; such translations often make for incorrect or unnatural English.

Most importantly, keep practising! Good luck!

Section 1. Writing Task 1 (Academic)

In Writing Task 1 of the IELTS examination (Academic), candidates are required to look at a diagram or some data (graph, table or chart) and to present the information in their own words (150 words minimum).

In this section, we will focus on three aspects of language used for discussing data: describing trends, referring to groups and describing a process.

Describing trends

Sample task

> The pie charts below illustrate the different categories of expenditure in the average household in the UK at three different time periods.
>
> Summarize the information by selecting and reporting the most important information, and make comparisons where relevant.
>
> Write at least 150 words.

Average household expenditure in the UK

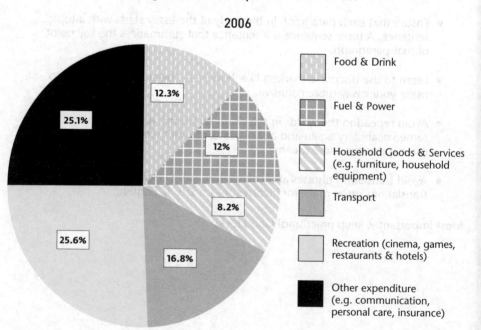

2006

Food & Drink

Fuel & Power

Household Goods & Services (e.g. furniture, household equipment)

Transport

Recreation (cinema, games, restaurants & hotels)

Other expenditure (e.g. communication, personal care, insurance)

12.3%

25.1%

12%

8.2%

25.6%

16.8%

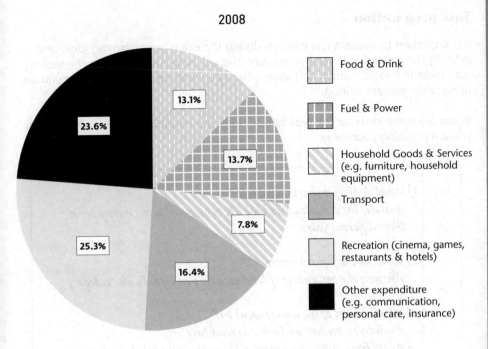

2008

- Food & Drink — 13.1%
- Fuel & Power — 13.7%
- Household Goods & Services (e.g. furniture, household equipment) — 7.8%
- Transport — 16.4%
- Recreation (cinema, games, restaurants & hotels) — 25.3%
- Other expenditure (e.g. communication, personal care, insurance) — 23.6%

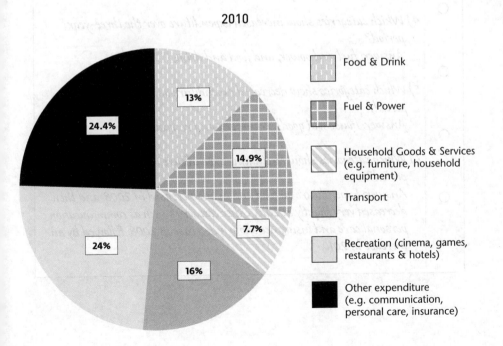

2010

- Food & Drink — 13%
- Fuel & Power — 14.9%
- Household Goods & Services (e.g. furniture, household equipment) — 7.7%
- Transport — 16%
- Recreation (cinema, games, restaurants & hotels) — 24%
- Other expenditure (e.g. communication, personal care, insurance) — 24.4%

Task preparation

It is important to spend a few minutes during the exam brainstorming ideas and drafting the general outline of your essay. This will help you to focus on presenting your ideas in a logical order, and allow you to concentrate on the language you are using while you are writing.

Below are some ideas for the type of questions you might like to ask yourself when you are planning your essay.

1) What do the pie charts illustrate?
Answer: the six categories that UK households spent money on in three different years

2) What do the figures represent?
Answer: the percentage of total spending on a particular category

3) What is most of the money spent on?
Answer: recreation and other expenditure
Apart from 2010, when most of the money was spent on other expenditure such as communication, personal care and insurance, in 2006 and 2008, most of the money was spent on recreation such as cinema, games, restaurants and hotels.

4) Which categories show increased expenditure over the three-year period?
Answer: fuel and power, and food and drink

5) Which categories show decreased expenditure over the three-year period?
Answer: household goods, transport, and recreation

6) Which categories show fluctuating expenditure over the three-year period?
Answer: Expenditure on food and drink increased in 2008, and then decreased very slightly in 2010. Other categories such as communication, personal care and insurance show a decrease in 2008, followed by an increase in 2010.

Sample answer

The charts show how much a typical UK household spent on the six different categories of expenditure in three different years: 2006, 2008 and 2010.

In all three years, the greatest expenditure was on both recreation and other expenses, such as personal care and insurance. Although expenditure on recreation, for instance cinema, games, restaurants and hotels, dominated in 2006 and 2008, it fell steadily from 25.6% in 2006 to 24% of total spending in 2010. Meanwhile, expenditure on other miscellaneous items saw a fluctuation, decreasing from 25.1% in 2006 to 23.6% in 2008, but bouncing back again to 24.4% of spending in 2010, overtaking the amount of money spent on recreation by 0.4%.

The biggest change was seen in the expenditure on fuel and power, the only category which showed an upward trend, increasing significantly from 12% in 2006 to 14.9% in 2010. Food and drink expenditure also grew from 12.3% to 13% in 2010. In contrast to the rise in expenditure on fuel and food, the money spent on transport decreased from 16.8% in 2006 to 16% in 2010. There was also a slight 0.5% drop in the money spent on household goods like furniture and household equipment, reaching 7.7% of total household expenditure in 2010.

On the whole, the average UK household tended to spend more on recreation and other expenditure like communication, personal care and insurance. Transport was also a significant expense, but, like expenditure on household goods and recreation, it declined over the given time period. On the other hand, expenditure on fuel and food and drink saw an overall increase.

In the text above, various expressions meaning *increase* and *decrease* are used to describe trends. Note the typical prepositions and adverbs that are used with the key words.

Below are some useful phrases for describing trends, taken from the sample answer above.

An upward trend ↗	
to increase/rise significantly (from ... to ...)	Life expectancy **rose significantly** during the twentieth century.
to show an upward trend	The number of female workers in the industry **showed an upward trend**.
to grow (from ... to ...)	The turnover **grew from** $9,000 **to** more than $100,000 within three years.
a rise/increase in	There was **a rise in** the demand for gas in 2012.

A downward trend ↘	
to fall (from ... to ...)	Africa's share of global trade **fell from** 5.9% in 1980 **to** under 2% at the end of the 1990s.
to decrease (from ... to ...)	Student numbers have **decreased from 685 to** fewer than 500.
a drop in something	Managers are concerned by a recent **drop in** sales.
to decline	The sales of DVD players **declined** over the five-year period.

Here are some more expressions for describing upward and downward trends.

Upward trends ↗	
to rise (from ... to ...) *to increase*	The number of complaints **rose** to record levels.
to be up *to be at a higher level than before:* *for talking about prices or levels*	Worldwide sales **were up** 15% last year.
to go up *to increase: for talking about prices or levels*	House prices **went up** a further 12% last year.
to push something up *to make something increase: for talking about prices or levels*	Recent bad weather **has pushed up** food prices.
to be on the increase *to be increasing steadily*	New cases of breast cancer seem **to be on the increase**.
to double *to increase to twice the original amount or level*	Oil prices have more than **doubled** since last year.
to treble *to increase to three times the original amount or level*	The last six months have seen the company's value **treble**.

Downward trends ↘	
to be down *to be less than before, especially in number, value or price*	Your cholesterol level **is down** on last month's figure.
to go/come down *to become less, especially in number, value or price*	The total build time **has come down** to under four weeks.
to drop/fall *to decrease in number or quality, especially by a large amount*	At night the temperature **drops** to below zero.

to decline	The party's membership **has declined** by 70% over the last ten years.
to decrease at a steady rate over a long period	

Focus on prepositions
to increase/rise/drop/fall + from ... to ... In the same period, the proportion of self-employed workers increased **from** 32% **to** 40%.
to increase/rise/drop/fall + by (size of change) The birth rate fell **by** 35% between 1970 and 1976.
a(n) increase/rise/drop/fall + from ... to ... The number of people speaking English showed a marked increase **from** 4.2% **to** 19.7%.
a(n) increase/rise/drop/fall + of (size of change) There was a temperature drop **of** 8°C overnight.
a(n) increase/rise/drop/fall + in ... There was a sharp rise **in** unemployment due to the economic recession.

Referring to groups

Sample task

The table and the graph below show the following data for five different countries:

(1) the percentage of men and women within the 16–20 age group who are married

(2) the average age of marriage for these men and women.

Summarize the information by selecting and reporting the main features. Make comparisons where relevant.

Write at least 150 words.

1.

	Percentage of married women in the 16–20 age group of the female population	Percentage of married men in the 16–20 age group of the male population
USA	5.9	4.3
Afghanistan	53.7	9.2
Australia	0.8	0.4
Thailand	11.2	3.4
China	1.2	0.3

2.

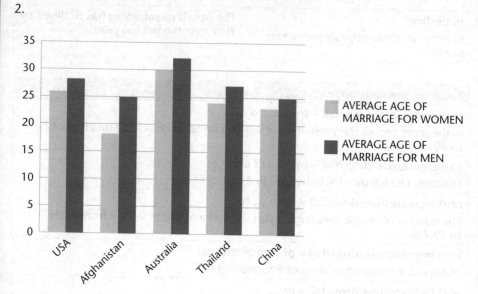

Task preparation

Below are some ideas for the type of questions you might like to ask yourself when you are planning your essay.

○	**1) What information is presented?** Answer: The table shows the percentages of 16- to 20-year-old women and men who are married in five different countries. The bar chart shows the average ages of marriage for women and men in the same five countries.
○	**2) What do the numbers represent?** Answer: In the table, the numbers represent percentages. In the bar graph, the numbers represent ages.
○	**3) Which country has the highest percentage of young married people and the lowest average age of marriage?** Answer: Afghanistan
○	**4) Which country has the lowest percentage of young married people and the highest average age of marriage?** Answer: Australia

Sample answer

The table illustrates the percentage of women and men aged between 16 and 20 who are married in the USA, Afghanistan, Australia, Thailand and China, while the bar graph shows the average age at which women and men in these five countries get married.

In Australia, only 0.8% of women and 0.4% of men in the 16–20 age group are married. The average Australian woman gets married at 30, while for Australian men, this happens at 32. Among the five countries, Australia has the highest average age of marriage and the lowest percentage of young married men and women.

In contrast, 53.7% of 16- to 20-year-old Afghan women are married, while only 9.2% of married men from Afghanistan are in that age group. On average, women from Afghanistan get married at 18, while the men get married at 26. Compared to the other four countries, this not only represents the highest percentage of young married men and women, but also the lowest average age of marriage.

The other three countries see their men and women getting married in their twenties, with the average age for men and women in Thailand standing at 27 and 24 respectively. This is not vastly different from the situation in China, where the average ages lie at 25 and 23. However, while the average ages for marriage in Thailand and China are quite similar, the percentage of 16- to 20-year-old women who are married in Thailand is 11.2% while that of women in the same age group in China is just 1.2%.

You might have to repeat certain phrases used in the question or in the graphs when writing Task 1, but you can avoid unnecessary repetition by using synonyms (= words that mean the same thing) or by rephrasing.

How can you rephrase the following?	Some ways to rephrase
married women	women who are married
16- to 20-year-old male population	males aged 16 to 20 men who are between 16 and 20 men from 16 to 20 years old 16- to 20-year-old men men in the 16–20 age group
the average age of marriage for women	the average age at which women get married how old the average women is when she gets married
Australian women	women from Australia women who are from Australia

Here are some other useful ways of rephrasing	
the graph/bar chart/table shows	the diagram illustrates
from 1999 to 2006	between 1999 and 2006
about 90%	approximately/roughly 90%
the population of a country	the people (who are) living in a country
20- to 29-year-old men	men (who are) in their twenties
married women	women who are married
unemployed workers	workers who are unemployed
home owners	people who own homes
frequent flyers	people who fly frequently
mobile phone users	people who use mobile phones

Another way of rephrasing is to use a relative clause to combine information. For example, consider the following two sentences:

The women are 16 to 20 years old.
The women are from Afghanistan.

They can be combined to become:

The women who are from Afghanistan are 16 to 20 years old.

Finally, try expanding noun phrases to describe categories in more detail.

Expanding a subject noun phrase	
The percentage	is 11%.
The percentage of women in Thailand	is 11%.
The percentage of 16- to 20-year-old women in Thailand	is 11%.
The percentage of 16- to 20-year-old women in Thailand who are married	is 11%.

Expanding an object noun phrase	
The table illustrates	the percentage.
The table illustrates	the percentage of women and men.
The table illustrates	the percentage of women and men aged between 16 and 20.
The table illustrates	the percentage of women and men aged between 16 and 20 in the USA, Afghanistan, Australia, Thailand and China.
The table illustrates	the percentage of women and men aged between 16 and 20 who are married in the USA, Afghanistan, Australia, Thailand and China.

Describing processes

Sample task

The diagrams below show how breakfast cornflakes are made.

Summarize the information by selecting and reporting the main features, and make comparisons where relevant.

Write at least 150 words.

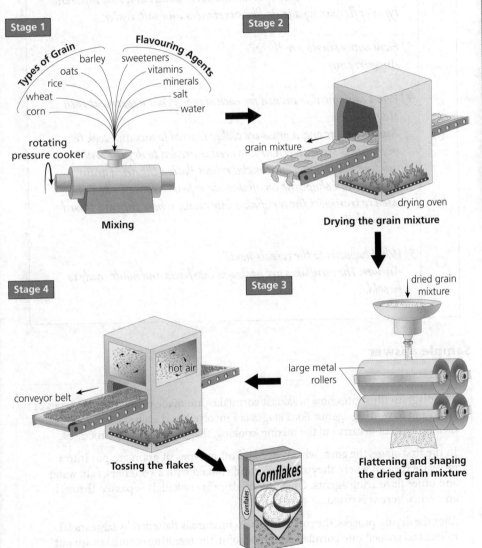

Stage 1

Types of Grain
barley
oats
rice
wheat
corn

Flavouring Agents
sweeteners
vitamins
minerals
salt
water

rotating
pressure cooker

Mixing

Stage 2

grain mixture

drying oven

Drying the grain mixture

Stage 3

dried grain
mixture

large metal
rollers

**Flattening and shaping
the dried grain mixture**

Stage 4

hot air

conveyor belt

Tossing the flakes

Cornflakes

Task preparation

Below are some ideas for the type of questions you might like to ask yourself when you are planning your essay.

○ 1) *What process is shown?*
   Answer: the making of breakfast cornflakes

○ 2) *What raw materials are needed?*
   Answer: different types of grain like corn, wheat and rice; different types of flavouring agents like sweeteners and salt; water

○ 3) *How many stages are there?*
   Answer: four

○ 4) *What equipment is needed for each stage? What happens at each stage?*
   Answer: stage one: a pressure cooker is used to mix and cook the ingredients stage two: a drying oven is needed to dry the grain mixture stage three: large metal rollers flatten the dried grain mixture and shape the cornflakes stage four: a conveyor belt is
○ *used to transport the cornflakes into ovens, where they are tossed in very hot air*

○ 5) *What happens to the cereals next?*
   Answer: The cornflakes are packaged into boxes and made ready to be sold.

Sample answer

The diagram illustrates how breakfast cornflakes are made using different types of grain and flavouring agents. Four stages are involved, and each stage requires its own equipment to carry out the mixing, cooking, shaping and drying processes.

In the first stage, the corn, wheat, rice and other types of grain are put into a pressure cooker, where they are mixed and cooked with sweeteners, salt, water and other flavouring agents. Once the mixture is cooked, it is passed through an oven, where it is dried.

After the drying process, the soft dried grain mixture is flattened by large metal rollers and shaped into cornflakes. At this point, the resulting cornflakes are put on a conveyor belt and brought to the ovens, where they are tossed in very hot air.

Next, the cornflakes are packaged into boxes and are finally ready to be sold.

Writing about a process often requires sequencing language.

Sequencing	
In the first/initial stage, + clause	**In the first stage**, the corn, wheat, rice and other types of grain are put into a pressure cooker.
Once + clause, + clause	**Once** the mixture is cooked, it is passed through an oven, where it is dried.
After/Before + noun/clause, + clause	**After** the drying process, the soft dried grain mixture is flattened.
At this point/stage, + clause	**At this point**, the resulting cornflakes are put on a conveyor belt.
Subject + (to be +) **then** + verb	The resulting cornflakes are **then** put on a conveyor belt.
Next/Then/Subsequently/After that, + clause	**Next**, the cornflakes are packaged into boxes.
Subject + **is/are finally ready** + to-infinitive	The cornflakes are **finally** ready to be sold.

Sometimes, you are required to describe the different parts of an object.

Describing parts of an object	
to involve + noun *for saying what the stages of the process are*	The process **involves** four stages.
Here are some other words you can use: **to consist of** + noun *for saying that it is formed from these parts*	The process **consists of** four stages. The machine **consists of** four parts.
to comprise + noun *for saying that it is made up of different parts*	The process **comprises** four stages. The machine **comprises** four parts.
to contain + noun *for saying what is inside it*	The machine **contains** four parts.

The passive is often used to write about processes.

Using the passive voice
Look at the passive verbs in the sample answer above.
1) Does the subject of the passive verb do the actions or receive the actions? **Answer:** It receives the actions.
2) Why do we often use the passive to describe a process? **Answer:** Because in a process, the action and the receiver of that action are more important than the performer of the action.
3) What is the structure of a verb in the passive voice? **Answer:** *to be* + past participle

Section 2. Writing Task 1 (General Training)

In Writing Task 1 of the IELTS Examination (General Training), candidates are required to write a short email or letter using an informal, semi-formal or formal style, depending on the situation and who the intended receiver of the letter is (150 words minimum).

In this section, we will look at how to write an email or letter at each of these three levels of language.

Informal email or letter

Sample task

> You are organizing a day out with some friends to celebrate your best friend's birthday.
>
> Write an email to confirm if one of your friends will be coming. Include the following points in your email:
>
> - Remind your friend why you are organizing this day out.
> - Describe what you have planned for the day.
> - Include information about anything that you would like your friend to bring.
> - Ask for confirmation that your friend will be coming.
>
> Write at least 150 words.
> You do not need to write any addresses.
> Begin your email as follows:
>
> Hi …

Sample answer

> Hi Sophie,
>
> This is just a quick email to remind you about Phil's birthday celebrations next weekend. We're planning to meet up at the café in the park for lunch on Saturday from 12.30. It's called Jack's Brasserie and it's near the entrance on the south side of the park. It's a great café and the food's really nice, but not too expensive. I need to book a table, so can you let me know whether you can come by the end of this week?
>
> If the weather's nice, we're planning to spend the afternoon in the park, maybe playing some games. It'd be fun if everyone could join in a game of softball or maybe volleyball. So wear comfortable shoes that you can run around in.
>
> I hope you can come. It's been ages since we met up. I'm sure Phil would be really pleased to see you. Let me know if you can make it.
>
> Love,
> Ana

Informal style

If the task requires you to write a short letter or email to a friend, as in the sample above, the style of language should be informal.

Informal openings
Start with **Dear** or **Hi** + the friend's name (first name only) + comma (,).
Hi is more informal than *Dear*.
Your first sentence often explains your reason for writing. This is just **a quick email/message/note** ... I'm **getting in touch/I'm just writing** ... <ul><li>to remind you about ...</li><li>to tell you about ...</li><li>to let you know about ...</li><li>to ask you about ...</li><li>to thank you for ...</li></ul>
Remember: You don't need to write your address at the start of your email or letter for this task. Do, however, give names to the people you are writing to.

Informal endings
If your message is about future plans or arrangements, you may end with a hope. **I hope** you can come/you have fun/you have a good trip.
If you have asked a question, you could remind your friend to reply. **Let me know** if you can come/if that's okay/when you can visit.
End your letter with a final greeting + your name (first name only). **Best wishes,** Ana (a polite ending to someone you do not know very well) **Thanks!** Ana (at the end of a letter of thanks) **With love,** Ana (very informal – to a close friend) **Love (from),** Ana (very informal – to a close friend)

Semi-formal email or letter

Sample task

Some of your colleagues have told you about a training course that is being organized by one of your managers. You would like to participate in the training course as it is relevant to your job.

Write an email to your manager. Include the following points in your email:

- Say why you are interested in the course.
- Ask the manager some questions to get information about the course.
- State what you would like the manager to do.

Write at least 150 words.
You do not need to write any addresses.
Begin your email as follows:

Dear ...

Sample answer

Dear Mr Pennant

I have recently heard about the management course that you are organizing for the staff of the company, and I'm getting in touch to express my interest in participating.

I currently work as a sales representative, and have just been promoted to the position of team leader, where I will be in charge of six sales representatives. I believe that the management training this course offers would enable me to better motivate my team and help them to produce more impressive results.

I would be grateful if you could provide me with information about the times and dates, and the location of the course. I would also like to know more about the details of the course content and the areas of management it would cover. Most importantly, could you let me know if I would be eligible for this course, and if so, how I could sign up for it?

I look forward to hearing from you soon.

Best wishes
David Wong

When making requests or asking for information, it is important to state why the information is needed. Here are some useful ways to express yourself.

Explaining the reason for your request	
to enable + somebody + to-infinitive	This course would **enable me to** better **motivate** my team.
to help + somebody + to-infinitive	… so I could **help them (to) produce** more impressive results.
to allow + somebody + to-infinitive	This course would **allow me to become** a better manager.
to support + somebody + in + -ing	This course could **support me in managing** my team.
to assist + somebody + in + -ing	This course could **assist me in taking** on bigger challenges at work.

When making requests or asking for a response to your email or letter, use the phrases below to be more polite.

Polite requests
I would be grateful if you could provide me with some information about …
I would be grateful if you could give me some information about …
I would like to know/learn more about …
Could you let me know if I would be eligible for the course?
I was wondering if you could tell me …

Formal email or letter

Sample task

> You and your family recently went to an expensive restaurant to celebrate a special occasion. However, you are not satisfied with your experience at the restaurant.
>
> Write a letter to the manager of the restaurant. Include the following points in your letter:
>
> - Explain why you were there.
> - Describe the problems that you had.
> - Say what action you would like the manager to take.
>
> Write at least 150 words.
> You do not need to write any addresses.
> Begin your letter as follows:
>
> Dear Sir/Madam

Sample answer

Dear Sir/Madam

I am writing to complain about my visit to your restaurant less than a week ago, and to ask for compensation.

As it was my husband's birthday, I had made a reservation in advance for a table next to the window, as the views from your restaurant are spectacular, especially at sunset. However, when we arrived, the waiter informed us that he had mistakenly given our table to another customer, and that the only way we could have a table with a view was if we waited for the customer to finish dining.

When we were finally seated after a one-hour wait, it took the waiter another 40 minutes to take our order, and another 60 minutes to bring us our food. All in all, we spent nearly three hours waiting in your restaurant. Furthermore, by the time our food was served, it had gone cold and was not particularly tasty since we had lost our appetite.

We were very disappointed by the standards of customer service at an award-winning restaurant like yours, and would therefore like to suggest a cash refund or a complimentary second visit to your restaurant as compensation for the time and money we wasted that day.

I look forward to hearing from you soon.

Yours faithfully

Rachel Green

Below are some useful phrases for making complaints, taken from the sample answer above.

Making complaints	
to complain (to somebody) about + noun *to say you are not satisfied with something*	I'm writing **to complain about** my visit to your restaurant.
to ask for compensation *to ask for money in return for the loss or suffering experienced*	I'm writing to complain and to **ask for some compensation.**
to spend (time) + -ing *to stay at a place for a period of time doing something*	We **spent** nearly three hours waiting.
to waste time/money + -ing *to use time or money doing something that is not important or necessary*	I would like compensation because we **wasted** a lot of **time and money** waiting around that day.
to be disappointed by/with + noun *to be sad because something is not as good as you had hoped*	I **was** very **disappointed by** the standards of customer service.
a cash refund *money returned to you*	I would like to suggest **a cash refund** as compensation.
(a) complimentary (visit) *(a) free (visit)*	I would like to suggest **a complimentary visit** as compensation.

It is important when reporting the sequence of events to use the correct verb forms.

In the sample answer above, the account of what happened at the restaurant is told in the past simple. However, when the story moves further back into the past, the past perfect is used.

Note that below the verbs **in bold** are in the past simple and describe the main events. The <u>underlined verbs</u> are in the past perfect. They give background information by describing things that happened before the main event.

The past perfect
The structure of the past perfect is: *had* + past participle   As it **was** my husband's birthday, I <u>had made</u> a reservation …   However, when we **arrived**, the waiter informed us that he <u>had</u> mistakenly <u>given</u> our table to another customer …   … it **took** the waiter another 60 minutes to bring us our food … the food <u>had gone</u> cold … since we <u>had lost</u> our appetite.

Section 3. Writing Task 2 (Academic and General Training)

In Writing Task 2 of the IELTS examination (both Academic and General Training), candidates are required to consider an argument or a problem and give their opinion on the issue (250 words minimum).

In this section, we will focus on two types of essay: the problem–solution essay and the agree/disagree essay.

Problem–solution essays

Sample task

> Shopping on the Internet might save us time and allow us to find the best products at the best prices, but it is not always a trouble-free experience. What are some of the problems faced by online shoppers today, and what solutions are there to these problems?

This is a problem–solution question. It is asking you to list the problems that online shoppers might experience, and to suggest possible solutions.

It is important to spend a few minutes during the exam brainstorming ideas and drafting the general outline of your essay. This will help you to focus on presenting your ideas in a logical order, and allow you to concentrate on the language you are using while you are writing.

Below are some ideas for the type of questions you might like to ask yourself when you are planning your essay.

Task preparation

- Why isn't shopping on the Internet always a good thing? What are some of the problems that people who shop online might face?

- What can businesses do on a shopping website that they can't do in a traditional store? Can they fool customers more easily on the Internet? How?

- Are there any items that you prefer not to buy online? What kinds of things are they? Why do you prefer not to buy them online?

- Do you know anyone who has had a bad experience buying something online? What happened? What can you learn from their experience? Is there anything you can do to avoid the same thing happening to you?

Now make a list of the different problems you might have when shopping online, and think of solutions for each of them. Here is example of a draft outline you might make before writing the actual essay.

Problems with shopping online	Solutions
Customers receive something which is completely different from what is advertised.	Be careful if you are buying things that you need to try on or test, e.g. an item of clothing or a bicycle. Check out such items in an actual shop before buying them online.
Identity fraud – personal details stolen	Buy only from reliable shops online. Make sure they have a secure website. If you have been a victim of identity fraud, make this known online using social media.

Sample answer

In the last few years, increasing numbers of people have been doing their shopping online. As a result, shopping has been made easy and convenient for consumers, allowing them to compare similar products and prices to get the best bargain. However, this has also brought about its own set of problems.

Although many companies make use of the Internet to offer their customers a wider range of products, some are taking advantage of the fact that we have to rely mainly on images when making our decisions to purchase. Therefore, customers sometimes end up not getting the items they expected to receive and wasting their money. In order to avoid such situations, customers should take extra care when buying products that they might prefer to test or try on beforehand, such as bicycles or clothes. Alternatively, they could check out the same products in the high street shops before buying them from online stores.

Another problem with internet shopping is that it can be dangerous to make payments online. Buyers often hand over personal bank details during a transaction, and this could result in identity fraud. For example, a friend of mine once received an enormous bill for a credit card she had never had. She realized much later that someone had stolen her details on the Internet and applied for a credit card in her name. Due to such widespread occurrences of identity fraud, consumers need to think about the security of the websites that will have access to their personal details. One way to deal with this issue is to shop online only from major retailers that are well-known and trustworthy. Shoppers who have been cheated of their money could also make this known by using social media to share their experiences. In this way, they might be able to reduce the probability of others having the same bad experience.

The Internet is now so important in our everyday lives that online shopping has become an unavoidable reality, bringing with it a new set of problems. Nevertheless, we can take measures to protect ourselves and tackle the problems associated with it so as to make internet shopping a safer experience.

Words and phrases

Verb + noun collocations

Problems and solutions	
to bring about problems *to cause problems*	However, this **has also brought about** its own set of **problems**.
to deal with the issue/problem *to give attention to a problem in order to try and solve it*	One way **to deal with this issue** is to shop online ...
to tackle the issue/problem *to try and solve a problem in a determined or efficient way*	Nevertheless, we can ... **tackle the problems** associated with it so as to make internet shopping a safer experience.
to take measures + to-infinitive *to carry out particular actions in order to achieve a particular result*	Nevertheless, we can **take measures to protect** ourselves ...
to reduce the probability of + -ing/noun *to make something less likely to happen*	In this way, we might be able **to reduce the probability of** others **having** the same bad experience.

Shopping and consumerism	
to get the best bargain *to find the item with the best value for money, usually because it is sold at a lower price than normal*	... allowing them to compare similar products and prices **to get the best bargain**.
to increase profitability *to make more money*	Although many companies are making use of this internet boom **to increase the profitability** of their business, ...
to make a decision *to choose to do something; to decide*	... we have to rely mainly on images when **making our decisions** to purchase.
to make a payment online *to give money for something you buy on the Internet; to pay for something using Internet*	Another problem with internet shopping is that it can be dangerous **to make payments online**.
to have access to personal details *to have the opportunity to see or use somebody's personal details*	... consumers need to think about the security of the websites that **will have access to their personal details**.
to cheat someone of their money *to get someone's money by behaving dishonestly, e.g. by lying*	Shoppers who **have been cheated of their money** could also make this known by using social media ...

Noun phrases

Internet shopping	
internet boom *an increase in internet activity; the success of the Internet*	... many companies are making use of this **internet boom** to increase the profitability of their business ...
online stores *shops on the Internet*	... check out the same products in the high street shops before buying them from **online stores**.
bank/personal details *facts or information about a person, such as their birth date, address and bank account numbers*	Hackers can steal the **bank details** that buyers hand over during a sale ... ... the security of the websites that will have access to their **personal details**.
identity fraud *a crime where someone gains money by lying and pretending to be someone else*	Buyers often hand over personal bank details during a transaction, and this could result in **identity fraud**.
widespread occurrence *something happening everywhere, over a large area or to a large extent*	Due to such **widespread occurrences** of identity fraud, ...
social media *internet-based applications where people meet, discuss and share content*	... using **social media** to share their experiences.

Grammar

(a) The present perfect (simple and continuous)

The present perfect is often used to describe a situation or a change that is connected to the present. It is also often used in the first sentence of an introductory paragraph in IELTS Writing Task 2.

Present perfect simple: has/have + past participle *for describing a result in the present*	As a result, shopping **has been** made easy and convenient for consumers, ... However, this **has** also **brought about** its own set of problems.
Present perfect continuous: has/have + been + -ing *for describing an ongoing action that began in the past and continues up to the present*	In the last few years, more and more people **have been doing** their shopping online.

(b) Modals

Modal verbs are commonly used in problem–solution essays to make suggestions or proposals.

could + bare infinitive *for suggesting possible solutions*	Alternatively, they **could check out** the same products in the high street shops before buying them from online stores. Shoppers who have been cheated of their money **could** also **make** this known by using social media to share their experiences.
might be able + to-infinitive *for suggesting possible solutions*	In this way, we **might be able to reduce** the probability of others having the same bad experience.
should + bare infinitive *for suggesting what is necessary*	In order to avoid such situations, customers **should take** extra care when buying products that they might prefer to test or try on beforehand, such as bicycles or clothes.

Getting your message across

(a) Stating the problem

It is important to state the problem clearly. You can use fixed expressions to do this.	
The problem with ... is + noun/-ing/ that + clause **Another problem with ... is** + noun/-ing/that + clause	**Another problem with** internet shopping **is that** it can be dangerous to make payments online.

(b) Purpose

When introducing a solution, it is sometimes important to give a reason for it.	
in order to + bare infinitive	**In order to avoid** such situations, customers should take extra care ...
so as to + bare infinitive	... we can take measures to protect ourselves and tackle the problems associated with it **so as to make** internet shopping a safer experience.

(c) Cause and effect

You might want to say what the cause of a problem is.	
clause + **as a result,** + clause *for showing effect*	In the last few years, more and more people have been doing their shopping online. **As a result**, shopping has been made easy and convenient for consumers, ...

clause + **resulting in** + noun *for showing effect*	Hackers can steal bank details that buyers hand over during a transaction, **resulting in** identity fraud.
clause + **therefore,** + clause *for showing effect*	… some are also taking advantage of the fact that we have to rely mainly on images when making our decisions to purchase. **Therefore,** customers sometimes end up not getting the items they expected to receive …
due to + noun *for showing cause*	**Due to** such widespread **occurrences** of identity fraud, consumers need to …
noun 1 + **bring about** + noun 2 *for showing cause (noun 1) and effect (noun 2)*	… this has also **brought about** its own **set of problems.**

(d) Showing contrast

You might want to show contrast and opposing ideas. Notice that the structure and position of 'However … ' and 'Nevertheless … ' are different from those with 'Although … '.	
clause + **however,** + clause	… shopping has been made easy and convenient … **However,** this has also brought about its own set of problems.
clause + **nevertheless,** + clause	… bringing with it a new set of problems. **Nevertheless,** we can take measures to protect ourselves …
although + clause, + clause	**Although** many companies are making use of this internet boom to increase the profitability of their business, some are also taking advantage …

Agree/disagree essays

Sample task

> *Schools spend too much time focusing on academic subjects like algebra, history and physics, which have no use in real life. Instead, students should be learning more practical skills like time management and banking.*
>
> *To what extent do you agree with the above statement?*

This is an agree/disagree question. It is asking you to consider both sides of the argument and to say why you agree or disagree with the statement.

It is important to spend a few minutes during the exam brainstorming ideas and drafting the general outline of your essay. This will help you to focus on presenting your ideas in a logical way and allow you to concentrate on the language you are using while you are writing.

Below are some ideas for the type of questions you might like to ask yourself when you are planning your essay.

Task preparation

○ • *Why are academic subjects taught? What are the advantages of learning algebra, history or physics?*

○ • *Why do some people think that academic subjects are a waste of time?*

○ • *Why should practical subjects be taught? What are the advantages of learning time management and banking?*

○ • *Why might some people think that academic subjects should take priority over practical subjects?*

○ • *What is your opinion on this subject?*

Now make a list of both sides of the argument. Here is an example of a draft outline you might make before writing the actual essay.

Teaching academic subjects	Teaching more practical subjects
Advantages	**Advantages**
Educating young people and expanding their minds. Building their knowledge of the world.	Developing skills that are useful and important in real life, and that can be put to immediate use.
Developing the brain – analytical and logical abilities, critical thinking skills, memorization skills.	Giving students experience of how to handle real life scenarios and problems.
Important skills and knowledge that are necessary for further education and specialization at university.	Can help develop problem-solving and creative-thinking skills.
What some people might argue:	**What some people might argue:**
It is more important to build independent thinking than memorization skills.	These are skills that can be picked up in a person's daily life.

Sample answer

Academic subjects like algebra, history and physics have been part of the national curriculum in most countries for a long time, and it is still widely believed that education should comprise the study of such theoretical subjects. However, others question the usefulness of these subjects, and propose that we replace them with the teaching of more practical skills such as time and money management.

Traditionally, subjects like algebra, history and physics are believed to form the basis of an education and to be essential because they help shape young minds. To begin with, such subjects can help expand a young student's knowledge of the world. For example, students learn about how things work through the study of physics, and through the study of history, they learn about how societies and countries were formed and how past events shaped them. Furthermore, mental capabilities such as memorization skills, logic and analytical skills could be developed when one tries to study historical facts or solve a mathematical problem. While some might argue that it is more important to build independent thinking than memorization skills, the basic skills that these subjects provide are also crucial when students decide to further their education in areas like engineering, business or the sciences.

Others who are against an emphasis on academic subjects claim that students need more training in practical skills; they support the introduction of subjects like time management and banking into the school curriculum. These skills are more likely to be put into immediate use in everyday life and students can therefore relate to them more easily and be more motivated to learn them. In addition, a focus on practical skills means that students are given the experience of handling real life problems. In this way, they develop creative-thinking and problem-solving abilities, which are thought to be vital life skills. Nevertheless, those who are less in favour of a change to the curriculum might perhaps maintain that these life skills can be picked up in daily life, and that precious school time should not be wasted teaching them.

Although there are good arguments supporting both points of view, in my opinion, the advantages of focusing on academic subjects far outweigh those of spending more classroom time on practical subjects that can be dealt with in real life.

Words and phrases

Agreeing/disagreeing

Agreeing	
to support + noun *to agree with an idea or aim*	Others … **support the introduction** of subjects like time management and banking into the school curriculum.
to be in favour of + noun *to support an idea and think it is a good thing*	Nevertheless, those who **are** less **in favour of a change** to the curriculum might perhaps maintain that these life skills can be picked up in daily life …
Disagreeing	
to be against + noun *to think that a plan, policy, system, etc. is wrong or ineffective*	Others who **are against an emphasis** on academic subjects …
to question + noun *to have or express doubts about whether something is true, reasonable or worthwhile*	… others **question the usefulness** of these subjects …

Showing both sides of an argument

advantage *a good or useful quality or condition that something has* **disadvantage** *a quality or condition that causes problems, or that makes someone or something less likely to be successful or effective*	The **advantage** of teaching academic subjects is that is builds analytical skills. The **disadvantage** is that these subjects can seem inapplicable to real life.
benefit *the help or advantage that you get from something* **drawback** *the disadvantage of something or aspect of it that makes it less acceptable*	The **benefit** to students is that they can immediately apply the skills they have learnt to their lives. The **drawback** is that they could pick these skills up themselves.
pros and cons *the advantages and disadvantages that you consider carefully before making a decision*	When weighing up the **pros and cons** of this argument, it is clear that it would be foolish to get rid of all academic subjects.

Reporting what people say

to claim (that) + clause *to say that something is true, even though it has not been proved*	Others ... **claim that** students need more training in practical skills.
to propose/suggest (that) + clause *to put forward a plan or idea for somebody to think about* Also: **propose/suggest + -ing**	... others ... **propose that** we replace them with the teaching of more practical skills ... They **proposed/suggested changing** the curriculum.
to argue (that) + clause *to state that you think something is true, giving reasons why you think so*	... some might **argue that** it is more important to build independent thinking than memorization skills ...
to believe (that) + clause *to think something is true*	... **it is** still widely **believed that** education should comprise the study of such theoretical subjects.
to maintain (that) + clause *to state your opinion strongly even though not everyone agrees with you or believes you*	... those who are less in favour ... **maintain that** these life skills can be picked up in daily life ...

Education

(a) Nouns

school curriculum *the different courses of study taught in a school, college or university*	Others ... support the introduction of subjects like time management and banking into the **school curriculum**.
national curriculum *the course of study that most school pupils in a particular country follow*	Academic subjects like algebra, history and physics have been part of the **national curriculum** in most countries for a long time.
skill *the knowledge or ability that enables you to do something well*	... the teaching of more practical **skills** such as time and money management ...
knowledge *the information and understanding of a subject that somebody has*	... such subjects can help expand a young student's **knowledge** of the world.
experience *the knowledge or skill you gain because you have done an activity for some time*	... students are given the **experience** of handling real life problems ...

(b) Verbs

to develop a skill/ability	... **memorization skills, logic and analytical skills could be developed** when one tries to study historical facts or solve a mathematical problem.
to become better or stronger at a skill/ ability	
to pick up a skill/ability	... these **life skills can be picked up** in daily life ...
to acquire a skill/ability without effort over a period of time	
to inform somebody	... **students are informed** how things work through the study of physics ...
to tell somebody about something	
to shape (young minds)	... subjects like algebra, history and physics ... are ... essential because they help **shape young minds**.
to have great influence on the way something develops (in young people's education)	

Adjectives

When you give reasons for an argument, you often state how important something is. Here are some alternatives to the adjective 'important'.

crucial	... the basic skills that these subjects provide are also **crucial** when students decide to further their education ...
vital	... creative-thinking and problem-solving abilities, which are thought to be **vital** life skills.
essential	... subjects like algebra, history and physics are ... **essential** because they help shape young minds.

Nouns and adjectives

When you are discussing education, you sometimes need to talk about school subjects and their corresponding adjectives. Can you spot any patterns?

Nouns	Adjectives
mathematics	mathematical
history	historical
geography	geographical
biology	biological
chemistry	chemical
sociology	sociological
psychology	psychological
science	scientific
language	linguistic

Grammar

(a) The passive

It is common to use a passive structure to show what most people believe or say.

it is believed that + clause	… **it is** still widely **believed that** education should comprise the study of such theoretical subjects.
subject + verb **to be** + **believed to** + infinitive	Traditionally, **subjects** like algebra, history and physics **are believed to form** the basis of an education …
You can replace 'believe' with the verbs 'say', 'claim', 'report', 'consider' or 'understand'.	**It is said that** academic subjects provide training for analytical skills. **Academic subjects are said to provide** training for analytical skills. **It is understood that** time management skills are more relevant to daily life. **Time management skills are understood to be** more relevant to daily life.

(b) Modals

It is common to use modal verbs in agree/disagree essays in order to 'soften' statements and to give them more credibility by lessening their certainty.

can + bare infinitive	… such subjects **can help** expand a young student's knowledge of the world.
could + bare infinitive	… memorization skills, logic and analytical skills **could be** developed when one tries to study historical facts or solve a mathematical problem.
might (perhaps) + bare infinitive	… those who are less in favour … **might perhaps maintain** that these life skills can be picked up in daily life …
to be (more) likely to + bare infinitive	These skills **are more likely to be** put into immediate use in everyday life …

Getting your message across

It is important to give your opinions and the opinions of others in an agree/disagree essay. You might choose to state your opinion from the beginning of the essay or state it after you have examined both sides of the argument.

(a) Stating your opinion

In my opinion, + clause You could also replace 'in my opinion' with 'I believe that' + clause, 'From my point of view,' + clause, and 'As far as I know,' + clause.	... **in my opinion**, the advantages of focusing on academic subjects far outweigh those of spending more classroom time on practical subjects ...

(b) Giving examples

When you are making a convincing argument, it is important to give examples to prove your point.

such as + noun/nouns	... the teaching of more practical skills **such as time and money management.**
like + noun/nouns	Academic subjects **like algebra, history and physics** have been part of the national curriculum ...
for example, + noun/nouns/clause	**For example**, students are informed how things work through the study of physics. Academic subjects, **for example**, algebra, history and physics, have been part of the national curriculum ...
for instance, + noun/nouns/clause	**For instance**, students are informed how things work through the study of physics.

(c) Adding reasons or facts

To support your arguments, you should add reasons or facts.

clause + **furthermore,** + clause	For example, students are informed how things work through the study of physics ... **Furthermore**, mental capabilities ... could be developed when one tries to study historical facts or solve a mathematical problem.
clause + **in addition,** + clause	These skills are more likely to be put into immediate use in everyday life, and students can ... be more motivated to learn them. **In addition**, a focus on practical skills means that students are given the experience of handling real life problems.
subject + verb **to be** + also	While some might argue that it is more important to build independent thinking than memorization skills, **the basic skills that these subjects provide are also** crucial when students decide to further their education in areas like engineering, business or the sciences.

Speaking for IELTS

Contents

Introduction to the speaking section of the IELTS exam

Preparing for the IELTS speaking exam can be an interesting and stimulating experience. Acquiring the ability to speak fluently and express yourself in English confidently will greatly increase your chances of getting a good score in your IELTS exam. Furthermore, it will prepare you for spoken interactions with teachers and fellow students as well as friends and colleagues with whom you may come into contact in the future.

This guide will give you an overview of the IELTS speaking exam and help you enhance your range of language so that you can express yourself more fluently and accurately. Whether you are asked to talk about topics familiar to you, to describe an experience or to discuss an abstract subject, this guide will give you all the help you need.

Each of the three parts starts with a list of useful tips. Next, you are introduced to the different types of questions that you might come across in the exam. Finally, you will find plenty of useful words and phrases that you can use in your answers.

The tips below relate to the speaking exam in general. Keep them in mind when using this speaking supplement.

In general:

Practise speaking in English whenever you can. Find opportunities to have conversations in English and don't worry about making mistakes. Practise using the phrases in this guide so that you become familiar with them.

During the exam:

- Speak clearly. Don't worry too much about your accent. The important thing is that the examiner can easily understand what you are saying.

- Speak as much as you can. Avoid one-word answers. Explain your ideas and opinions, and give details when you are describing something. The examiner needs to hear you talking.

- Speak up. Try to avoid mumbling. Be confident about what you are saying.

- Don't speak too quickly or too slowly. Maintain a steady pace.

- Make eye contact with the examiner when you are speaking. If you appear to believe in what you are saying, the examiner is likely to believe in it too. Use appropriate gestures and intonation to help you convey meaning.

- While it is generally a good idea to experiment using new words, avoid doing this during the exam. Use the words you know how to use, because you will be judged not just on your range of vocabulary, but also on your accuracy.

- Whenever possible and relevant, use collocations, phrases and expressions that you know. This will help your English sound more natural.

- Don't memorize prepared answers. You will lose marks if you do that.

Have fun, and good luck!

Section 1. Speaking Part 1

In Speaking Part 1 of the IELTS examination, you are often asked to talk about
a general topic that you might have talked about quite often before in English.
Therefore, Part 1 helps to build your confidence and gives the examiner some
idea of your ability to deal with familiar topics like your home, where you live,
your job or studies and your hobbies and interests. Part 1 often lasts between
four and five minutes.

Tips

- Greet the examiner with a smile and introduce yourself
  clearly.

- Be prepared to spell your name in case you are asked to
  do so.

- Avoid giving short answers like 'Yes' or 'No'. Elaborate on
  them and explain what you mean. Give examples to make
  what you are saying more vivid and interesting, and help
  the examiner understand what you mean.

- It is good to memorize words and phrases (like the ones
  in this guide) to help you speak, but avoid reciting long
  paragraphs that you have learnt by heart. The examiner
  will realize that you have memorized your answer and
  deduct marks.

- Speak naturally, as if you were talking to a colleague or
  a friend that you respect.

- The topics in Part 1 will be particularly familiar to you,
  so you can be confident about what you are going to say.

- Use appropriate gestures and facial expressions in addition
  to speech in order to communicate how you feel about what
  you are saying.

Talking about yourself

Sample questions

> *Where are you from? Let's talk about your home town:*
> - *What kind of place is it? What's it famous for?*
> - *I'm planning a visit to your city/town. What would you recommend I do?*
> - *Tell me what you like to do when you are in your home town.*
> - *Tell me about some of the popular dishes from your home town.*

Sample answers

Talking about your home

I was born in	a small/large town	
I come from	a coastal town	in the north/south of … .
My family are from	a small/tiny/remote village	near the sea/in the mountains.

I grew up in the city of Beijing/Berlin/Tokyo.

It's	a(n) industrial/mining/resort/port/market town.
	the capital city.
	a(n) ancient/old/modern/cosmopolitan city.

It's famous for its tall buildings/architecture/nightlife/natural scenery/good food.

I would recommend that visitors + *clause*
e.g. I would recommend that visitors go to the main shopping street.

I would suggest (that) you + *bare infinitive*
e.g. I would suggest you eat at a local restaurant.

noun + **is/are definitely worth** + *-ing*
e.g. The waterfall/museum/town square/market is definitely worth going to/seeing/visiting.

Our main staple is rice/noodles/potatoes.
Our local specialty is + *noun*.
You definitely must try the + *noun*.

Talking about where you live

Sample questions

> *I would like to know more about where you live.*
> - *What kind of accommodation do you live in?*
> - *What's the area/neighbourhood like?*
> - *Do you think it's a good place to live? Why?*
> - *What kind of place would you like to live in? Why?*

Sample answers

Talking about where you live

I / We	live in a	one-bedroom / two-bedroom / three-bedroom / four-bedroom	flat / semi-detached house / detached house / maisonette	in	the town centre. / an inner-city area. / the suburbs. / the shopping district.

My flat is in the south of the city.
Our house is on the outskirts of the city.

It's in a residential/financial/commercial area.
It's in a very quiet/noisy/convenient/rural area.

It's	close/near to / conveniently located close to /near / far away from	a wide variety of shops. / the best restaurants. / all the necessary amenities.

Most of the people living in my area are young couples/small families/old age pensioners.

Talking about what you do

Sample questions

Let's talk about what you do.
- *What's your job? What does it involve?*
- *Describe the company/organization you work for.*
- *What do you like about your job?*
- *What do you dislike about your job?*
- *If you're a student, what do you study? What do you like or dislike about it?*
- *What's your dream job? Why?*

Sample answers

Talking about your job/studies

I'm a(n) student/teacher/doctor/dentist/engineer/architect/secretary/marketing manager.

I work for a	small	local	company	specializing in	mobile phones.
	medium-sized	German	organization	that exports	children's toys.
	large	multinational	firm	that makes	clothes.

I'm in charge of	five other workers.
	marketing.
	international sales.
	the finance department.

I like my job because	it's fairly well-paid.
I like the fact that	I get to work with some very interesting colleagues.
The thing I like about my job is that	there's job security.

I'm studying	Business Administration	at	a business school.
	Economics		high school.
	Biology		university.

I would love to work in the field of education/entertainment/publishing/fashion.

I hope to become a musician/a fashion designer/the principal of a school/a politician.

My ideal job would:
- be well-paid.
- involve interesting tasks.
- have a lot of annual leave.
- allow me to travel around the world.
- give me opportunities to develop.
- have good career prospects.

Talking about your hobbies and interests

Sample questions

> *What do you do in your spare time?*
> - *What are your hobbies? What do you enjoy doing? Why?*
> - *Do you cook or do you prefer to eat out? What kind of food do you like?*
> - *How much time do you usually spend with your family? What kind of activities do you do with them?*
> - *What do you usually do with your friends?*
> - *What type of holidays do you like to go on? Why?*
> - *What is your favourite colour/season/sport/musical instrument/piece of clothing? Why?*

Sample answers

Talking about your hobbies and interests

In my spare time/free time	I enjoy/like/love	playing football/computer games.
At the weekends	I spend a lot of time	socializing with friends.
In the evening		walking in the countryside.

In the summer/winter I always/often/sometimes/occasionally + go + swimming/skiing/hiking/clubbing/bowling/shopping.

Table tennis/Diving		sport	
Yoga	is a popular	form of exercise	in my country/in Argentina.
Karaoke		activity	among young/older people.
Dancing/Kite flying		hobby	

| When I'm | in my home town, with my family, with my friends, | I tend to spend most of my time | eating out at restaurants. watching TV. shopping. |

I really enjoy beach/shopping/sightseeing/adventure/camping holidays.

I love being outdoors/active/surrounded by nature/immersed in a new culture/in a busy city/surrounded by shops.

There's nothing better than:
- relaxing at the beach with my favourite book.
- taking long leisurely walks in the countryside.
- exploring a new city.
- learning about the history of different places around the world.
- being pampered at the spa.
- being able to shop all day.

Talking about the weather

Sample questions

> *I would like to ask you about the weather.*
> - *What's the weather like in your city/town?*
> - *What's your favourite season of the year? Why?*
> - *Do you think the weather affects your mood? How?*
> - *What do you like to do when the weather is hot?*
> - *What do you like to do when the weather is cold?*

Sample answers

Talking about the weather

In my city/town, the weather is often cold/hot/rainy/sunny/cloudy.

The summer in my city/town is usually very pleasant.
It can also be extremely hot/dry/humid.

The winter in my city/town is often rather mild/bitter/cold.
It can also be quite dreary/windy/very wet.

I like	the summer the autumn the winter the spring	because it's/that's a time when	everyone seems happy. the leaves change colour. everything looks beautiful. new things replace the old.

I love the way the streets look when they are covered in snow/autumn leaves.

I hate it when it's rainy/cloudy/stormy/snowing.

Rainy/Cloudy/Hot/Sunny days make me feel	sad/down/depressed/irritable/positive/optimistic. like I'm full of hope/energy/life.

Summer	is a great time for	skiing/snowboarding/swimming/hill walking/sleeping.
Autumn	to me means	hot soups and stews/cold noodles/fresh fruit and vegetables.
Winter	is ideal for	winter sports/outdoor activities/indoor games/the sales!
Spring	is all about	taking holidays/staying at home/having parties.

Dealing with unfamiliar subjects

If you are asked to talk about a subject that you don't know much about, use the opportunity to show that you are able to use language effectively, even when the subject is unfamiliar.

Here are some expressions that you can use.

When you don't know much about a topic
That's interesting. It's not really something that I've thought about much before.
I have to admit, I don't really watch much TV/play a lot of sport/cook very often.
To be honest, I'm not particularly interested in films/computer games/shopping.
I don't really know much about architecture/reality TV/the education system in my country.
That's a tough question because I'm not an expert in that area.
Expanding on what you have just said: However, I know that some of my friends like to watch soap operas. Quite often at college, they talk about what happened on their favourite programme the night before.
When I was younger, I enjoyed playing football. But nowadays I'm usually busy with work and family, so I don't get so much free time.
As far as I know, there's a local festival to commemorate the dead, but I don't really know much about the traditions involved.

Asking for clarification or repetition

If you don't understand something the examiner has said, you can ask him/her to repeat it or to clarify what has just been said. However, try not to do this too many times. It is important to show that you have the ability to understand the overall meaning of what is said without needing to know every word.

Here are some expressions that you can use.

Asking for repetition
Sorry, I didn't catch that. Could you repeat it, please?
Sorry, I missed that. Could you say it again?
I'm sorry, but would you mind repeating that?
Asking for clarification
Sorry, but could you explain what you mean by 'reality TV'?
I'm sorry, but I've never heard that word/expression before. Would you mind explaining what you mean?
By 'reality TV', do you mean 'TV programmes showing ordinary people'?
When you say 'reality TV', are you talking about those TV competitions where the public can vote people out?

Section 2. Speaking Part 2

In Speaking Part 2 of the IELTS examination, you are given one minute to prepare a short talk lasting one to two minutes, based on a topic and some prompts. The topic usually requires you to describe an experience such as something you have seen, someone who is special to you or something you have done. After the talk, the examiner will ask one or two follow-up questions about the topic.

Tips

- Try to stick to the truth. Avoid inventing facts. Instead, put your efforts into using a wide range of vocabulary and grammar accurately.

- Quickly decide on the object/person/place/event that you are going to talk about. Try not to change your mind; this takes up time that could be better used preparing your talk.

- Use the one-minute preparation time wisely.

  1. Visualize the object/person/place/event you are going to describe. Seeing it/him/her in your mind will help you think of details to include in your talk.

  2. Use the rough paper provided to make notes of useful phrases and words to remind you of what you want to say.

  3. Make use of the prompts on the question card as well as the question words 'who', 'what', 'where', 'when, 'why' and 'how' to help you organize your talk.

- Avoid repeating the same words or facts too many times.

- Keep talking until the examiner tells you to stop.

- When the examiner tells you to stop, perhaps by saying 'Thank you', don't worry. He/She is only stopping you because your two minutes are up.

- Practise doing this task at home. Record yourself. Listen to the recording and think about how you can improve on it.

Introducing a topic

Before you start talking about a subject, it is a good idea to introduce the topic to your listener so that he/she is clear about your aim.

Here are some expressions you can use.

Introducing a topic
I'm going to describe the small coastal town where my grandparents live.
I'd like to tell you about my first job as a waitress in a local restaurant when I was fifteen.
I've chosen to talk about a trip I made to Australia last year.
The person I want to talk about is my history teacher from high school.

Describing an object

Sample task

> Describe a gift that you have received. You should say:
> - what kind of gift it was
> - what it looked like
> - who gave it to you and why
> - how it made you feel and why

Sample answers

Describing an object

Background information

I definitely/certainly wasn't expecting it.

I've never had one before.

My sister/partner/friend knew that I'd always wanted one of these.

It came wrapped in brown/pink/birthday wrapping paper with a red/blue/satin ribbon tied around it.

What it looks like

It's made of wood/plastic/glass/wool/cotton/silk/silver/gold.

It's made by a big/small/famous company in Japan/Italy/America.

It	consists of	a seat and armrests.
	's made up of	three parts.

It's square/round/oval/rectangular/triangular/cylindrical/diamond-shaped/almond-shaped.

It's shaped like a cat/rabbit/cone/cloud/banana/motorbike.

What it does

It/They + *present simple*

The hard drive stores information.

The ornament decorates the room and makes it look nice.

The perfume smells really nice.

It's/They're used to + *infinitive*

The tablet is used to play music and videos.

The slow cooker is used to make soups and stews.

It's/They're used for + *-ing*
The electronic reader is used for reading books and making notes.
The cream is used for reducing wrinkles and lines on the face.

It's/They're great for + *-ing*
The massage chair is great for relieving muscle aches and pains.
The silk robe is great for relaxing around the house in.

How you felt about it

It was	the most beautiful/useful/elegant	thing	on the market/in the world.
	the cutest/trendiest/shiniest	gadget	I'd ever seen/been given.
		piece of jewellery/ clothing	around.

It reminds me of + *noun*
It reminds me of my sister/my childhood/home/our holiday in London.

It reminds me of the time when + *clause*

It reminds me of the time when:

- I graduated from university.
- my parents took us on holiday to London.
- my sister won the singing competition.

I keep it handy in my bag/drawer/wardrobe and I take it out whenever I need to + *infinitive*.
I couldn't live without it.

Describing a person

Sample task

> Describe someone in your family who has had a great influence on you.
> You should say:
> - who this person is
> - what he/she looks like
> - what kind of person he/she is
> - what kind of influence he/she had on you

Sample answers

Describing a person

Age

He		around 35 years old.
She	is	in his/her early/mid/late teens/twenties/thirties.
		quite young/old.

Appearance

He/She is tall/short/attractive/average-looking/medium-built/slim.

He/She has:
- long hair.
- short hair.
- big brown eyes.
- a round face.
- a square jaw.

He/She looks + *adjective*

He/She looks gorgeous/intelligent/approachable, especially when he/she is ...

He/She looks like + *noun/clause*

He/She looks like a film star/my mother/an eccentric professor.

He/She always looks like he/she:
- is dressed up for a party.
- doesn't know what's happening.
- needs a shave.
- is in a rush.

Personality

He/She is generous/kind/loving/friendly/horrible/rude/mean to everyone.

He/She is the kind of person who always works hard/is never on time/lives life to the full/never forgets anything.

His/Her influence on me

He/She was the one who	showed me	what to do when + *clause*.
He/She	taught me	how to + *infinitive*.
It was my aunt/ father/sister who	gave me a lesson on	the importance of + *noun*.

| Without him/her, | I would/wouldn't have + *past participle*. |
| If it hadn't been for him/her, | |

Without him/her, I wouldn't have gone to university.

Without him/her, I would have dropped out of school.

If it hadn't been for him/her, I wouldn't have learnt the meaning of courage.

If it hadn't been for him/her, I would have given up.

Describing a place

Sample task

> Describe a memorable place that you have been to. You should say:
> - where this place is
> - why you went there
> - what it looked like
> - why it was memorable

Sample answers

Describing a place

Location and features

It's situated/located on the coast/in the middle of the city/opposite a market/near a forest.

It's known/famous for its hot springs/markets/national park/beautiful scenery/high cost of living/fast pace of life/historic monuments.

The park/lake/forest/nature reserve/river stretches … kilometres from north to south/east to west.

The building/museum/temple is a typical Ming Dynasty/1800s/1980s construction.

It's surrounded by forest/mountains/a large expanse of land/buildings/shopping centres.

What it looked/smelled/sounded like

The city centre/town/market square is/was really colourful/cosmopolitan/bustling with people/modern/historic/crowded/hectic/polluted/unfriendly.

The natural scenery/surrounding mountains/deep valleys/forest/lake/hot springs/waterfall/coast was/were truly stunning/breathtaking/peaceful/picturesque/gorgeous.

It's a place filled with magic/mystery/romance/peace/culture/history/beauty.

As I	went down	the street,	I could	hear the sound(s) of the birds/market/waves/band playing.
	walked along	the beach,		see the mountains/building in the background.
	strolled along	the trail,		smell the fragrance/aroma/sweetness from the + *noun*.

How it made me feel

What	I loved/liked/hated about it was	the atmosphere/the ambience.
The thing		the architecture/the noise/the liveliness.

The most unforgettable thing about it was that sense of calm/peace/history/being alive.

I felt alive/at one with nature/at peace/safe/moved/exhilarated/excited/amazed/calm/relaxed.

I had never seen/felt/experienced anything like this before.

Describing an event

Sample task

> Describe an event in your life that had a big impact on you. You should say:
> - when and where it happened
> - what happened
> - who was involved
> - why it had a big impact on you.

Sample answers

Describing an event

When and where it happened

It took place + *time reference*, + when + *clause*.

e.g. It took place five years ago, when I graduated from high school.

It took place when I was four years old, when I accidentally put chewing gum in my hair.

The event that	had a big impact on me		I got married.
The day that	changed my life	was when	I had stomach surgery.
	was most memorable		I decided what I wanted to study at university.

I remember it was on + *date*.

e.g. I remember it was on 8th August 2008.

I/We was/were in/on + place.

We were in the mountains.

The people involved

I was with people/friends/colleagues from my university/my school/workplace.

There were + *number* + of us.

There were five of us.

Setting the scene

Subject + past continuous / Subject + was/were *+ adjective*

It was raining.

It was dark.

The shops were closing.

The streets were empty.

I/We had just + *past participle* and we + *past continuous*

My colleagues and I had just finished work and we were heading to the nearest restaurant for dinner.

The outcome/result

We thought we were going to die **but it turned out that** the driver/pilot/captain had everything under control.

In the end, everything worked out.

After all that, the documents arrived in time and we were able to get married.

The significance

Because of this,	I've come to realize			nothing is more important than friendship.
As a result,	I've learnt		that	you shouldn't judge a book by its cover.
Consequently,	I now know/understand/believe			everyone has some goodness inside them.

I'll never forget this day/event/moment/experience.

Section 3. Speaking Part 3

In Speaking Part 3 of the IELTS examination, the examiner will ask you questions about topics linked to the themes in Part 2. You are often expected to give an opinion on the subject. Part 3 usually takes four to five minutes.

This section of the guide provides you with plenty of ideas for making your points more persuasively, expanding on your answers and organizing your arguments.

There are also lots of helpful ideas for dealing confidently with any tricky situations that you might find yourself in.

Tips

- The questions in Speaking Part 3 usually open with words like 'What', 'Why', and 'What do you think about ... '. You are expected to give longer answers than in Part 1.

- The topics in this part require discussion, so you should elaborate on your opinions by explaining what you mean and by giving examples.

- There are similarities between IELTS Writing Part 2 and Speaking Part 3, in that they both involve a discussion about a topic. You can practise for both parts together by brainstorming the key points and the pros and cons of different topics. However, you should remember that while a lot of the language can be used in both papers, you need to know the difference between language used in formal written essays and language used in spoken English.

- Part 3 is your chance to demonstrate to the examiner the wide range of vocabulary and grammatical structures you can use. Use conditional sentences to explore different possibilities in the discussion, and ensure that you use appropriate linking words like 'However' and 'On the other hand' to connect your ideas.

- Try not to stay silent for too long when you are thinking how to answer the examiner's question. Make use of time-buying strategies. (See below.)

- Avoid repeating the same words too many times. Use synonyms or pronouns like 'this', 'that', 'it' and 'she' instead.

- Avoid going off topic.

Organizing your answer

Whether the question asks you to agree or disagree with an issue, discuss the advantages and disadvantages of something or give the solutions to a problem, the answer is rarely simple. You will need to organize your answer into several parts and explain each part clearly.

Sample task

Let's consider the topic of health and nutrition:
- *How have the eating habits of young people changed in recent years?*
- *How might bad eating habits affect society in general?*
- *How do you think this problem should be solved?*

Sample answers

Organizing your answer
Bad eating habits can have several possible effects on society. **One is that** as people become overweight, their ability to work is affected. **Another is that** diseases related to obesity become more common, and so the government has to spend more on healthcare.
It really depends on whose point of view you're talking about. **If you're looking at things from the point of view of** the school, you might claim that it is the parents' responsibility to look after children's diet. But if you are a parent, you might say that your child spends most of his/her time at school, and so the school should take care of his or her dietary needs.
Basically, I think there are several ways to look at this. One way is to focus on the children who are currently overweight. **The alternative** is to look at the preventative measures we can take to stop kids from becoming overweight in the first place.
I believe there are two things that might happen. First of all, such a policy might cost the school a lot of money. **Secondly,** it could end up making students dislike healthy food even more.
There are three possible solutions to this problem. To begin with, we can make children more aware of the nutritional value of the food they eat through proper health education …
Overall, there are many advantages/disadvantages to banning the sale of unhealthy snacks at school. **One disadvantage would be that** students might start to bring in their own snacks.

Suggesting solutions and making recommendations
We can/could make children more aware of the nutritional value of the food they eat through proper health education.
The government **should** provide schools with more money to spend on healthy food.
It might be best if schools banned the sale of unhealthy snacks and fizzy drinks in school canteens.
I really think the best way to deal with this issue is to educate the nation.
One possible solution is to get children to keep a diary of what they eat every day.
I would suggest making use of the mass media to raise awareness of the issue.

Being persuasive

In order to be persuasive, you need to explain and justify the points you are making by expressing opinions, talking about your own experience, elaborating, giving examples or quoting others who agree with you. It is also important to show that you can understand a different point of view and present both sides of an argument when necessary.

Sample task

> Let's consider the role of sport:
> - Why is sport important?
> - What kinds of sports are popular in your country?
> - Do you think competitive sports bring people together or tear them apart?

Sample answers

Giving reasons and describing cause and effect
Sport is important **because** it encourages people to focus on their physical fitness.
When people lose at sport, they learn the valuable lesson of losing graciously and trying again. **That's why** it's important for children to participate in competitive sport.
The reason why some top professional athletes quit their sport is that there's a lack of job security, especially after they have reached a certain age.
Since sport is not usually tested in the national exams, many students get complacent about their athletic performance.
Participation in team sports can **lead to** better cooperation at work.
Some top professional athletes quit their sport **due to/because of** a lack of job security, especially after they have reached a certain age.
Thanks to/Owing to the recent Olympic Games, interest in sport has been on the increase.

Giving examples
Water sports **like/such as** swimming, wakeboarding and waterpolo are very popular in my city.
There are many benefits to competitive sports. **For example**, just look at people training for a competition and you can see that they're learning to persevere and work hard.
Conversely, there are also many drawbacks. **For instance**, in order to win, some people resort to illegal means like the use of performance-enhancing drugs.
A clear example of this was the famous case of Ben Johnson in the 1988 Seoul Olympics.
Take Ben Johnson **for example**. He won the gold medal but was stripped of the title when he tested positive for a performance-enhancing substance.
Cyclists are **a case in point**. Their trainers sometimes encourage them to take performance-enhancing drugs to succeed in competitions.
You hear of/see this happening quite often/all the time/every now and then/for the most part in international sporting events like the Tour de France and the Olympic Games.

Quoting and referring

According to an old Chinese saying, the greatest glory is not in never failing, but in getting up and trying again.

As we often say in Germany, one must be good at both mental and physical activities.

There is a saying in Chinese **that** we have to keep our body in good health; otherwise we won't be able to keep our mind strong and clear.

It's often said that the greatest wealth is health.

As I mentioned earlier, table tennis is a very popular sport in my town.

I know I might have said this before but I think it's really important to keep fit.

Giving two sides of an argument

On the one hand, sports can teach us a lot about being a good team player. **On the other (hand),** the competitive element can lead to arguments and fights.

Even though fair play and sportsmanship are often upheld as the core values of most sporting events, **in actual fact**, cheating and drug use are commonplace at many competitions.

While it's true that international sporting events bring people together, **they can also lead to** extreme expressions of nationalism.

There's no doubt that exposure to other cultures can be a great learning experience. **However, it can also result in** stereotyping, generalizations and racism.

Some people claim (that) nationalism is a good thing because it promotes a feeling of belonging to one's country. **Still,** nationalism is also the main cause of the hooliganism we see at football matches.

Talking about your own experience

From/In my experience, there's a lot of pressure on young people to be successful at team sports.

My own experience of playing team sports **has been** very unpleasant.

I can only speak/say from personal experience, but I've never had any problems with it.

For me, supporting a team **has been a very positive/valuable experience.**

I have to say, I haven't had much experience of rugby myself.

Participating in the national schools table tennis championships **has been my best experience so far.**

In my own life, I haven't had many opportunities to do winter sports.

I've known people who train for six hours a day.

Personally, I can't imagine life without sport.

Giving your opinion

In my opinion, it's unfair that some people use performance-enhancing drugs.

In my view, there should be more drug-testing.

From my point of view, a country's team manager should come from that country.

I have to say that footballers' salaries are far too high.

I (personally/strongly) believe (that) sport is important for people of all ages.

I think (that) children need more sporting role models.

I feel (that) parents should encourage their children to be more active.

I am convinced (that) football clubs should work more closely with the police to fight racism.

I suspect (that) most adults don't do any sport at all.

I guess most people can't afford to go to the gym every day.

If you ask me, there should be at least one hour of sport every day at school.

To be honest, I really don't understand why people get so passionate about snooker.

Talking about other people's opinion

Some people say/believe/feel (that) sporting competitions can damage the confidence of children who do not have good physical coordination.

There are others who say/believe/feel (that) learning to be a good loser is an important part of education.

Apparently, there are many athletes who get away with cheating at competitions.

Expanding on the subject

An important part of this section of the Speaking exam is showing that you are able to develop ideas relating to the subject you are discussing. In this section, we look at adding information while avoiding repeating the same words, considering negative aspects of a situation and talking about changes.

Sample task

Let's talk about tourism:
- *What are the benefits of travelling to other countries?*
- *Do you think there are any drawbacks to tourism?*
- *How has tourism changed in your country in the last few decades?*

Sample answers

Adding information
You can learn about the history of the country by visiting its famous sights. **Also/On top of that**, you can find out how other people live and learn to see the world from their point of view.
Travelling to a different place on holiday can help you to relieve stress. **What's more**, it can be a welcome change from your daily life.
One of the many advantages of travelling is that you get to taste the local dishes. **Besides**, you can meet the local people and learn to say things in a new language.
Not only do you learn about other cultures, but you also learn a lot of things about yourself. **Not only do you [+ verb], but you also [+ verb]**
Tourists benefit from travelling to a foreign country. **Likewise/Similarly**, the local tourism industry benefits from the money spent by tourists.

Using general terms to avoid repeating words
The price of hotels and guesthouses has really gone up. Some **holiday accommodation** is 50% more expensive than it was five years ago.
In China, we celebrate the Chinese New Year in January. It's a(n) **time/occasion/opportunity** for tourists to see some of our more spectacular customs.
There seem to have been more natural disasters like floods and landslides in recent years. And you have to wonder whether **these sorts of events** will affect tourism.
I'll never forget the first time I travelled by plane. It was an **experience** full of nerves and excitement.
One place I really enjoy visiting is Florence. It's a really beautiful **area** and a great **location** for a holiday.
People worry about the environmental damage caused by planes. They say that **air travel** should not be so cheap.
A lot more people go abroad now. It's a **trend/phenomenon** that's really grown in recent years.

Talking about problems and negative aspects
Although there are many benefits to travelling, **the downside/disadvantage is that** air travel causes a lot of pollution and therefore contributes to global warming.
The problem/trouble with tourism **is (that)** it often changes the culture of the local community and traditions can be lost.
One of the drawbacks of having a lot of tourists spending their money **is that** the cost of living goes up, making basic necessities unaffordable for locals.
The bad thing about tourism **is that** the locals who rely on it don't have job security.
Unfortunately/Sadly, tourism can destroy the local environment and cause damage to historical monuments.

Talking about changes
In the past, people went everywhere by horse or on foot, so they couldn't travel far. Nowadays, it's much easier to get around and see faraway places.
So much has changed in the last twenty years. Holidays are no longer the same.
People used to travel to a nearby town or city for their holiday. Nowadays, more people are going abroad.
I remember when it was a big deal to go to the Far East because flight tickets were so expensive. Things are different now. Flights are much more affordable.
Compared to the past, people travel much more these days.
People today can see the world on their TV and computer screens, whereas in the past, the only way to see the world was to travel to the different countries.

Identifying similarities, agreeing/disagreeing and making predictions

When you are discussing an area that is undergoing great changes, you may want to make predictions about how you see the situation developing in the future. It can also be useful to look at ways in which people's basic needs have *not* changed over the years.

Think about other people's ideas on the subject, too, and say whether you agree or disagree with their opinions.

Sample task

> I'd like to talk more about games and entertainment:
> * What are the similarities between how we entertain ourselves today and how people entertained themselves 50 years ago?
> * Young children are now playing some very violent video games. Do you think they should be banned?
> * What do you think entertainment will be like in the future?

Sample answers

Future predictions
The division between work and entertainment **will probably** continue to blur.
In the future, virtual reality technology **will be** more advanced and we'll be able to really feel as if we're in the game we're playing.
By the time I'm 70, **I don't think** TV as we know it **will exist**.
One day, we**'ll no longer need** laptops and smartphones because we'll have computer screens in our heads.
It might be possible to teleport ourselves into our friends' living rooms.
For all we know, there might be a return to playing games that don't require technology, like real chess.

Pointing out similarities		
Storylines in films today are	almost **identical to** still **similar to** **practically/almost the same as**	what they were 50 years ago. those of the 1960s. the ones in the films of the 1960s.
In the 1960s, many people developed their own photographs as a hobby. **Similarly/Likewise**, many people nowadays add effects to their own photos, but now they use photography applications to do it.		

Spectator sports are still popular these days, **as was the case** in the 1960s.
Adults **as well as** young people are fascinated by documentaries and reality programmes.
People still communicate by writing to each other, **much as** they did in the 1960s; however, today, the medium is email.

Agreeing and disagreeing

I **agree that** children should not have easy access to violent video games.
I (**totally/completely**) **agree** that there should be stricter age restrictions on the purchase of such games.
I'm **totally for** stricter age restrictions.

I really **disagree with**	
I'm **quite against**	banning video games.
I'm **not sure if** I would agree with	
I'm **not entirely comfortable with the idea of**	

It might be a better idea to make parents more aware of the games their children are playing.

Discussion strategies

You might find that you need to buy time to think about your answer before replying. One way of doing this is to repeat the question the examiner has just asked you in a slow and thoughtful tone of voice. Another way is to comment on how interesting or thought-provoking the question is.

Here are some expressions that you can use while thinking about your answer.

Buying time
That's a good question.
That's an interesting question.
Let me see.
Well, let me think.
This topic has never crossed my mind before, but if I think about it, …

If you think that what you have just said was unclear, try and clarify it further by explaining a bit more or giving more information.

Here are some expressions that you can use.

Clarifying
Not all kinds of music are the same. **What I mean is/What I'm trying to say is/ I'm just saying that** the kind of music that sounds lovely to you might sound horrible to me.
There's no such thing as luck. **Let me clarify that/Let me explain.** Luck relates to something that happens to us by chance. I believe we have to create our own opportunities.
You have to take responsibility for your own success. **In other words**, if you want to succeed, you must work hard for it and not just wait for it to happen.